Collins

COMPLETE
UK HIT
SINGLES
1952-2005

GRAHAM BETTS

First published in 2005 by Collins
an imprint of
HarperCollins*Publishers*
77–85 Fulham Palace Road
Hammersmith
London, W6 8JB

The Collins website address is www.colllins.co.uk

Collins is a registered trademark of
HarperCollins*Publishers* Ltd.

05
10 9 8 7 6 5 4 3 2 1

ISBN 0 00 720076 5

The Author – Graham Betts

UK writer (born 28/6/1957, London); he began his working career training to be an architect before switching to the music industry in 1978 as a Press Officer with Pye Records. He subsequently went on to work for CBS Records (where he was Head of Press) and a number of budget labels, including Tring, before becoming Artist & Repertoire Manager for the Hallmark label. He is currently A&R Manager for the Pickwick Group. He has written for numerous magazines and publications over the last twenty-five years, including *Blues & Soul*, *Record Buyer* and *The History Of Rock*. A contributor to numerous books on music and football, he has also had ten published under his own name, including *Read Without Prejudice* (a biography of George Michael) and *Spurs Day By Day* (a history of Tottenham Hotspur). He also won the 1978 *Melody Maker* essay contest. He currently lives in Aston Clinton with his wife Caroline and children Jo and Steven.

PRODUCED BY
Essential Works
168a Camden Street, London NW1 9PT

EDITORS Jo Lethaby, Nina Sharman, Mike Evans, and Fiona Screen
DESIGNER Mark Stevens and Kate Ward

INTRODUCTION

This will be the last edition of this book to incorporate chart data based entirely on record sales. After another year that saw sales of singles fall, a decision was taken during the year that at some point during 2005, the singles chart will be compiled based on sales of CD, cassette and vinyl (remember that?), as well as downloads.

There has been talk of doing something to re-invigorate the singles chart for a good few years. For a long time it looked as though radio airplay would be factored in, and the decision to go with downloads will at least go some way to appease those opposed to airplay, myself included. After all, in order to be truly representative, all airplay would have to be taken into account, with the possible result that *Bohemian Rhapsody* or some other classic track more than twenty years old would still be a feature on the chart! And besides, just because a radio producer likes a track enough to include it on his playlist, there is no guarantee the public will like it. The decision to ignore calls for airplay also ensures we do not have a situation where a track could top the singles chart without being commercially available, a fairly regular occurrence in America where, as noted in the first edition of this book, Aaliyah became the first artist to top the singles chart based entirely on airplay.

The popularity of downloads, both legal and illegal, has exploded in the last twelve months and, at the turn of 2005, downloads actually exceeded sales of singles – more of this in next year's edition, but it is indicative of how the market for singles has changed, even in the last twelve months. Only time will tell whether the introduction of the download factor revives the singles chart. Gone are the days when kids (and sometimes their parents) would gather around the radio to listen to the chart rundown. But, just as the draw for the FA Cup has restored some of its magic, maybe the singles chart can, too.

As was widely reported, Eric Prydz registered a new record with the lowest sales tally of any single to reach number one, selling barely 22,000 copies in the week he returned to the chart summit in October. The following week he beat his own record as he retained the position. Eric Prydz is not responsible for the quality of opposition, or lack of it. Similarly, those who claimed that having a UK number one hit no longer had the same kudos as it did five, ten, twenty or more years ago obviously never asked Eric, Eamon, Frankee, Shapeshifters or Natasha Bedingfield, all of whom topped the charts for the first time in their careers during 2004, whether they felt slighted.

Far more revealing is the fact that only eight records managed to sell sufficient quantities to qualify for a sales award, the lowest total since the awards were introduced in 1973. Of these eight records, only one, Band Aid 20's *Do They Know It's Christmas?*, managed to go beyond the silver mark, similarly the lowest total ever.

So much for the negative side of the singles chart during the last twelve months. The drop in sales needed to make the charts resulted in a lot more of the 'do it yourself' acts making a presence somewhere on the chart, and you will therefore find that the tally of buskers has increased since the first edition of this book! Similarly, actors, offspring of famous parents and other left-field acts have swelled their ranks.

The initial reaction to the first edition was hugely encouraging. While there was plenty of positive feedback from those of an older generation who wanted to know about the likes of John Leyton, Johnny Kidd and Louis Prima, the younger generation quickly turned to the likes of Blue and Westlife. I hope both ends of the age spectrum will be happy with this second edition; younger readers will find new additions in the likes of V, McFly and Keane, while older readers will find new information has been unearthed on John Paul Joans, The Lancastrians and Kulay, among countless others. Similarly, we have sadly lost the likes of Ray Charles, Johnny Bristol and Johnny Cash during the last twelve months, and these events have been noted throughout.

If 2005 promises to be something of a landmark year for singles, then there are still plenty of things that have occurred during the last 52 years to keep us interested, enthralled, enraged and occupied in equal measures. Hopefully, you can read all about it in this book. Football didn't start with the launch of the Premiership and the singles chart doesn't start with the incorporation of downloads. Yeovil Town may never make the Premiership, but they did hit the top 40 during 2004, and it is the quirkiness of the British Singles Chart that makes it so appealing.

You will recall in the first edition that I asked for any additional, verifiable information to be emailed to me. Unfortunately, technical gremlins ensured that none of these got through, but I am reliably assured that this has been rectified for this second edition. So, if you have any additional, verifiable information on any of the acts in this book, please email me! To those who wrote by snail mail (remember that?), my thanks because the additional information you provided has been incorporated into this new edition.

Graham Betts
Aston Clinton
January 2005

How to use this book

This book provides detailed information on each artist and their rise to chart success since the first chart was compiled in the UK in 1952 (by the *New Musical Express*) through to the present day. The book is organised alphabetically according to the surname of the artist/group.

COLUMNS – DATE/POS/WKS The date the single made its chart debut, the highest chart position it attained and the number of weeks it was in the chart, '+' denotes that it was still on the chart as of 25/12/2004

BPI AWARDS The first BPI (British Phonographic Industry) awards were made in 1973 and the respective sales figures required were 250,000 units for a silver disc, 500,000 for a gold disc and 1,000,000 units for a platinum disc. As of 1st January 1989, these figures were down rated to 200,000, 400,000 and 600,000 respectively. Sales of all formats (7-inch and 12-inch vinyl, cassette single and CD single, as appropriate) are added together for the purposes of certification

LABEL & NUMBER Record label and catalogue number. This number is that of the most popular format at the time of the hit

TOP 150 ARTISTS have a single sleeve beside their entry

BIOGRAPHY A brief background of the artist together with awards and honours received

TOP 10 SONGS in bold

UK No.1 HITS with weeks at number one

US No.1 HITS with weeks at number one

COLLABORATIONS The hit is credited to more than one artist

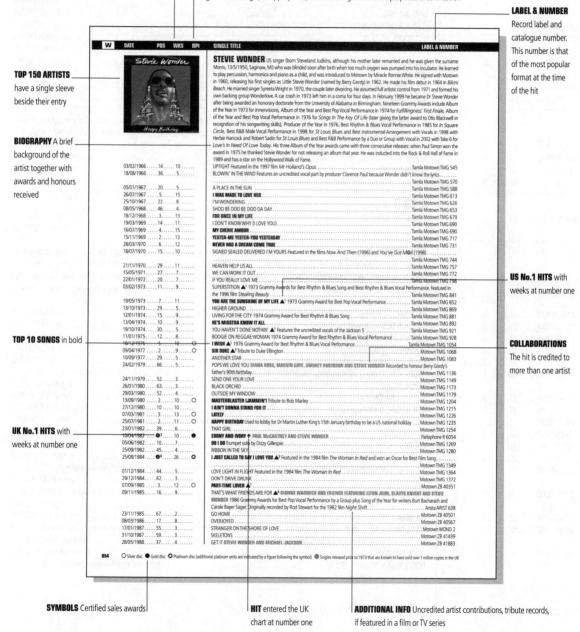

SYMBOLS Certified sales awards

HIT entered the UK chart at number one

ADDITIONAL INFO Uncredited artist contributions, tribute records, if featured in a film or TV series

A

A UK rock group with Jason Perry (vocals), Mark Chapman (guitar), Giles Perry (keyboards), Daniel Carter (bass) and Adam Perry (drums).

07/02/1998	63	1	FOGHORN . . . . Tycoon TYCD 5
11/04/1998	47	1	NUMBER ONE . . . . Tycoon TYCD 6
27/06/1998	57	1	SING-A-LONG . . . . Tycoon TYCD 7
24/10/1998	72	1	SUMMER ON THE UNDERGROUND . . . . Tycoon TYCD 8
05/06/1999	54	1	OLD FOLKS . . . . Tycoon TYCD 9
21/08/1999	59	1	I LOVE LAKE TAHOE . . . . Tycoon TYCD 10
02/03/2002	9	6	**NOTHING** . . . . London LONCD 463
01/06/2002	20	3	STARBUCKS . . . . London LONCD 467
30/11/2002	51	1	SOMETHING'S GOING ON . . . . London LONCD 471
13/09/2003	13	2	GOOD TIME . . . . London LONCD 480

A*TEENS Swedish vocal group formed by Dhani John Lennevald (born 24/7/1984, Stockholm), Marie Eleonor Serneholt (born 11/7/1983, Stockholm), Sara Helena Lumholdt (born 25/10/1984, Stockholm) and Amit Sebastian Paul (born 29/10/1983, Boden).

04/09/1999	12	5	MAMMA MIA . . . . Stockholm 5613432
11/12/1999	21	5	SUPER TROUPER . . . . Stockholm 5615002
26/05/2001	10	7	**UPSIDE DOWN** . . . . Stockholm 1588492
27/10/2001	30	2	HALFWAY AROUND THE WORLD . . . . Stockholm 0153612

A VS B UK production duo Daniel Thornton and Geoff Taylor.

09/05/1998	49	1	RIPPED IN 2 MINUTES Effectively two songs made into one: *Make My Body Work* by Jomanda and *Made In 2 Minutes* by Bug Kane . . . . Positiva CDTIV 89

AALIYAH US R&B singer (born Aaliyah Haughton, 16/1/1979, Brooklyn, NYC) whose name is Swahili for 'highest, most exulted one'. She appeared in the films *Romeo Must Die* (2000), *Sparkle* (2000), *Queen Of The Damned* (2002), and *The Matrix Reloaded* (2003). She is rumoured to have married fellow singer R Kelly in August 1994, though it may have been a publicity hoax. She was killed on 25/8/2001 when her plane crashed on take-off in the Bahamas. It was revealed that there were eight people on a plane designed for only five; excess weight was the most likely cause of the crash.

02/07/1994	16	5	BACK AND FORTH Features uncredited rap by writer and producer R Kelly . . . . Jive JIVECD 357
15/10/1994	27	2	(AT YOUR BEST) YOU ARE LOVE . . . . Jive JIVECD 359
11/03/1995	32	2	AGE AIN'T NOTHING BUT A NUMBER . . . . Jive JIVECD 369
13/05/1995	33	2	DOWN WITH THE CLIQUE . . . . Jive JIVECD 377
09/09/1995	33	2	THE THING I LIKE Featured in the 1994 film *A Low Down Dirty Shame* . . . . Jive JIVECD 382
03/02/1996	66	1	I NEED YOU TONIGHT **JUNIOR M.A.F.I.A. FEATURING AALIYAH** Contains a sample of Lisa Lisa & Cult Jam's *I Wonder If I Take You Home* . . . . Big Beat A 8130CD
24/08/1996	21	2	IF YOUR GIRL ONLY KNEW . . . . Atlantic A 5669CD
23/11/1996	37	2	GOT TO GIVE IT UP Features the uncredited contribution of Slick Rick . . . . Atlantic A 5632CD
24/05/1997	15	3	IF YOUR GIRL ONLY KNEW/ONE IN A MILLION A-side features the uncredited contribution of Timbaland . . . . Atlantic A 5610CD
30/08/1997	24	2	4 PAGE LETTER . . . . Atlantic AT 0010CD1
22/11/1997	30	2	THE ONE I GAVE MY HEART TO/HOT LIKE FIRE . . . . Atlantic AT 0017CD
18/04/1998	22	3	JOURNEY TO THE PAST Featured in the 1997 film *Anastasia* . . . . Atlantic AT 0026CD
12/09/1998	11	4	ARE YOU THAT SOMEBODY? Includes the uncredited contribution of Timbaland. Featured in the 1998 film *Dr Dolittle* . . . . Atlantic AT 0047CD
22/07/2000	5	12	**TRY AGAIN** ▲¹ Featured in the 2001 film *Romeo Must Die*. The track was the first album cut to top the *Billboard* Hot 100 (a track no longer has to be a single in order to qualify for inclusion on the US charts) . . . . Virgin VUSCD 167
21/07/2001	20	6	**WE NEED A RESOLUTION AALIYAH FEATURING TIMBALAND** . . . . Blackground VUSCD 206
19/01/2002	❶¹	12	**MORE THAN A WOMAN** ↑ A posthumous #1, the first female to achieve the feat. Replaced by George Harrison's re-issued *My Sweet Lord* the following week, also a posthumous #1 single. 2002 MOBO Award for Best Video . . . . Blackground VUSCD 230
18/05/2002	12	7	ROCK THE BOAT . . . . Blackground VUSCD 243
26/04/2003	22	3	DON'T KNOW WHAT TO TELL YA . . . . Independiente/Blackground/Unique ISOM 73MS

○ Silver disc ● Gold disc ✪ Platinum disc (additional platinum units are indicated by a figure following the symbol) ◉ Singles released prior to 1973 that are known to have sold over 1 million copies in the UK

ABBA

ABBA Swedish/Norwegian group formed by Anna-Frid (Frida) Lyngstad-Ruess (born 15/11/1945, Bjorkasen, Norway), Benny Andersson (born Goran Bror Benny Andersson, 16/12/1946, Stockholm), Bjorn Ulvaeus (born 25/4/1945, Gothenburg, Sweden) and Agnetha Ase Faltskog (born 5/4/1950, Jonkoping, Sweden), their name being their initials. After winning the 1974 Eurovision Song Contest they became one of the most popular groups of the decade. Bjorn and Agnetha married in 1971 and divorced in 1979; Benny and Frida married in 1978 and divorced in 1979. When the band split in the early 1980s, both female members went solo while Benny and Bjorn concentrated on songwriting, linking with Tim Rice to pen the stage musical *Chess*. At the height of their popularity in 1977, the Royal Albert Hall reported 3.5 million applications for 11,212 available tickets.

DATE	POS	WKS	BPI	SINGLE TITLE	LABEL & NUMBER
20/04/1974	❶²	9		**WATERLOO** 1974 Eurovision Song Contest winner	Epic EPC 2240
20/07/1974	32	5		RING RING Originally intended as Sweden's entry for the 1973 Eurovision Song Contest but not selected	Epic EPC 2452
02/08/1975	38	6		I DO I DO I DO I DO I DO Featured in the 1995 film *Muriel's Wedding*	Epic EPC 3229
27/09/1975	6	10		**S.O.S.** The only example of a palindrome group having a palindrome hit	Epic EPC 3576
13/12/1975	❶²	14	○	**MAMMA MIA** Owing to a Musicians Union ruling, they were forced to perform the song 'live' on *Top Of The Pops* when it hit #1, the only time the group performed live on the show. Featured in the films *Abba: The Movie* (1978) and *The Adventures Of Priscilla: Queen Of The Desert* (1994)	Epic EPC 3790
03/04/1976	❶⁴	15	●	**FERNANDO** Featured in the 1978 film *Abba: The Movie*	Epic EPC 4036
21/08/1976	❶⁶	15	●	**DANCING QUEEN** ▲¹ Featured in the films *Abba: The Movie* (1978), *Muriel's Wedding* (1995) and *Summer Of Sam* (1999)	Epic EPC 4499
20/11/1976	3	12	●	**MONEY MONEY MONEY**	Epic EPC 4713
05/03/1977	❶⁵	13	●	**KNOWING ME KNOWING YOU**	Epic EPC 4955
22/10/1977	❶⁴	12	●	**THE NAME OF THE GAME** Featured in the 1978 film *Abba: The Movie*	Epic EPC 5750
04/02/1978	❶³	10	●	**TAKE A CHANCE ON ME**	Epic EPC 5950
16/09/1978	5	9	○	**SUMMER NIGHT CITY**	Epic EPC 6395
03/02/1979	2	9	●	**CHIQUITITA**	Epic EPC 7030
05/05/1979	4	9	○	**DOES YOUR MOTHER KNOW** Featured in the 2003 film *Johnny English*	Epic EPC 7316
21/07/1979	3	11	○	**ANGEL EYES/VOULEZ-VOUS**	Epic EPC 7499
20/10/1979	3	12	○	**GIMME GIMME GIMME (A MAN AFTER MIDNIGHT)**	Epic EPC 7914
15/12/1979	2	10	●	**I HAVE A DREAM**	Epic EPC 8088
02/08/1980	❶²	10		**THE WINNER TAKES IT ALL**	Epic EPC 8835
15/11/1980	❶³	12	●	**SUPER TROUPER**	Epic EPC 9089
18/07/1981	7	7		**LAY ALL YOUR LOVE ON ME** Only available on 12-inch vinyl	Epic EPC A 1314
12/12/1981	3	10	●	**ONE OF US**	Epic EPC A 1740
27/02/1982	25	7		HEAD OVER HEELS	Epic EPC A 2037
30/10/1982	32	6		THE DAY BEFORE YOU CAME	Epic EPC A 2847
18/12/1982	26	8		UNDER ATTACK	Epic EPC A 2971
26/11/1983	33	6		THANK YOU FOR THE MUSIC Featured in the 1978 film *Abba: The Movie*	CBS A 3894
05/09/1992	16	5		DANCING QUEEN Re-issue of EPIC EPC 4499	Polydor PO231
29/05/2004	20	3		WATERLOO Re-issue of Epic EPC 2240	Polydor 9820539

ABBACADABRA

ABBACADABRA UK group assembled by Martyn Norris as a tribute group to Abba.

DATE	POS	WKS	BPI	SINGLE TITLE	LABEL & NUMBER
05/09/1992	57	1		DANCING QUEEN	PWL International PWL 246

RUSS ABBOT

RUSS ABBOT UK singer/comedian/actor (born Russell Roberts, 16/9/1947, Chester) who was a former member of the Black Abbotts and had his own network TV show.

DATE	POS	WKS	BPI	SINGLE TITLE	LABEL & NUMBER
06/02/1982	61	2		A DAY IN THE LIFE OF VINCE PRINCE Inspired by a character on his TV series	EMI 5249
12/01/1985	7	13	○	**ATMOSPHERE**	Spirit FIRE 4
13/07/1985	20	7		ALL NIGHT HOLIDAY	Spirit FIRE 6

GREGORY ABBOTT

GREGORY ABBOTT US R&B singer (born 2/4/1954, New York) of Antiguan and Venezuelan ancestry who was previously an English teacher at the University of Berkeley and married to fellow singer Freda Payne.

DATE	POS	WKS	BPI	SINGLE TITLE	LABEL & NUMBER
29/11/1986	6	13	○	**SHAKE YOU DOWN** ▲¹ Received 1 million US radio plays quicker than any other record in history	CBS A 7326

ABC

ABC UK group formed in Sheffield in 1980 by Martin Fry (born 9/3/1959, Manchester, vocals) and Mark White (born 1/4/1961, Sheffield, guitar), with Stephen Singleton (born 17/4/1959, Sheffield), Mark Lickley, David Robinson and David Palmer also contributing over the years. They launched the Neutron label to release their material in the UK. By 1997 the group was effectively just Martin Fry, who chose the name because 'the first three letters of the alphabet are known the world over'.

DATE	POS	WKS	BPI	SINGLE TITLE	LABEL & NUMBER
14/11/1981	19	8		TEARS ARE NOT ENOUGH	Neutron NT 101
06/03/1982	6	11	○	**POISON ARROW**	Neutron NT 102
15/05/1982	4	12	○	**THE LOOK OF LOVE**	Neutron NT 103
04/09/1982	5	8		**ALL OF MY HEART**	Neutron NT 104
05/11/1983	18	4		THAT WAS THEN BUT THIS IS NOW	Neutron NT 105
21/01/1984	39	5		S.O.S. Features the uncredited contribution of Frankie Goes to Hollywood on backing vocals	Neutron NT 106
10/11/1984	49	4		HOW TO BE A MILLIONAIRE	Neutron NT 107
06/04/1985	26	4		BE NEAR ME	Neutron NT 108
15/06/1985	70	1		VANITY KILLS	Neutron NT 109
18/01/1986	51	3		OCEAN BLUE	Neutron NT 110

❶⁹ Number of weeks single topped the UK chart ↑ Entered the UK chart at #1 ▲⁹ Number of weeks single topped the US chart

DATE	POS	WKS	BPI	SINGLE TITLE	LABEL & NUMBER
06/06/1987	11	10		WHEN SMOKEY SINGS Tribute to Smokey Robinson	Neutron NT 111
19/09/1987	31	8		THE NIGHT YOU MURDERED LOVE	Neutron NT 112
28/11/1987	44	3		KING WITHOUT A CROWN	Neutron NT 113
27/05/1989	32	4		ONE BETTER WORLD	Neutron NT 114
23/09/1989	68	1		THE REAL THING	Neutron NT 115
14/04/1990	68	1		THE LOOK OF LOVE (REMIX)	Neutron NT 116
27/07/1991	47	2		LOVE CONQUERS ALL	Parlophone R 6292
11/01/1992	42	3		SAY IT	Parlophone R 6298
22/03/1997	57	1		STRANGER THINGS	Blatant/Deconstruction 453632

PAULA ABDUL US singer (born 19/6/1963, Los Angeles, CA) and former cheerleader for the Los Angeles Lakers who began her career as a choreographer, notably for Janet Jackson. She married and later divorced actor Emilio Estevez. A marriage to record company executive Brad Beckerman also ended in divorce. She has a star on the Hollywood Walk of Fame and later became a judge on *American Idol*. The Wild Pair are duo Marv Gunn and Bruce Christian.

DATE	POS	WKS	BPI	SINGLE TITLE	LABEL & NUMBER
04/03/1989	3	13	○	STRAIGHT UP ▲³	Siren SRN 111
03/06/1989	24	6		FOREVER YOUR GIRL ▲²	Siren SRN 112
19/08/1989	45	3		KNOCKED OUT	Siren SRN 92
02/12/1989	74	1		(IT'S JUST) THE WAY THAT YOU LOVE ME	Siren SRN 101
07/04/1990	2	13	○	OPPOSITES ATTRACT ▲¹ PAULA ABDUL AND THE WILD PAIR Rap by Derrick Delite from Soul Purpose. 1990 Grammy Award for Best Music Video Short Form.	Siren SRN 124
21/07/1990	21	5		KNOCKED OUT Single originally released in 1988 and failed to chart	Virgin America VUS 23
29/09/1990	46	3		COLD HEARTED ▲¹	Virgin America VUS 27
22/06/1991	6	11		RUSH RUSH ▲⁵	Virgin America VUS 38
31/08/1991	52	2		THE PROMISE OF A NEW DAY ▲¹	Virgin America VUS 44
18/01/1992	19	6		VIBEOLOGY	Virgin America VUS 53
08/08/1992	73	1		WILL YOU MARRY ME Features the uncredited contribution of Stevie Wonder on harmonica	Virgin America VUS 58
17/06/1995	28	3		MY LOVE IS FOR REAL PAULA ABDUL FEATURING OFRA HAZA	Virgin VUSCD 91

ABERFELDY UK group formed in Edinburgh by Riley Briggs (guitar/vocals), Ruth Barrie (keyboards/glockenspiel), Sarah McFadyen (fiddle/glockenspiel), Ken McIntosh (bass) and Ian Stoddart (drums).

DATE	POS	WKS	BPI	SINGLE TITLE	LABEL & NUMBER
28/08/2004	66	1		HELIOPOLIS BY NIGHT	Rough Trade RTRADSCD192

ABI UK singer/drum and bass producer.

DATE	POS	WKS	BPI	SINGLE TITLE	LABEL & NUMBER
13/06/1998	44	2		COUNTING THE DAYS	Kuku CDKUKU 1

ABIGAIL UK dance singer Gayle Zeigmond who also recorded for All Around The World, Pulse 8, Inherit and Groovilicious Music.

DATE	POS	WKS	BPI	SINGLE TITLE	LABEL & NUMBER
16/07/1994	29	4		SMELLS LIKE TEEN SPIRIT	Klone CDKLONE 25

ABNEA – see JOHAN GIELEN PRESENTS ABNEA

COLONEL ABRAMS US R&B singer (born in Detroit, MI) who was lead singer with Conservative Manor, 94 East (a group with Prince on guitar) and Surprise Package before going solo. He later worked with Cameo's Larry Blackmon.

DATE	POS	WKS	BPI	SINGLE TITLE	LABEL & NUMBER
14/09/1985	3	23	●	TRAPPED	MCA 997
07/12/1985	53	3		THE TRUTH	MCA 1022
15/02/1986	24	7		I'M NOT GONNA LET YOU (GET THE BEST OF ME)	MCA 1031
15/08/1987	75	2		HOW SOON WE FORGET	MCA 1179

ABS UK singer (born Richard Abidin Breen, 29/6/1979, Enfield) who was a founder member of Five, going solo when they disbanded in September 2001.

DATE	POS	WKS	BPI	SINGLE TITLE	LABEL & NUMBER
31/08/2002	4	8		WHAT YOU GOT Contains a sample of Althia & Donna's *Uptown Top Ranking*	S 74321957192
07/06/2003	10	9		STOP SIGN Cover version of a Northern Soul hit from the 1960s by Mel Wynn & The Rhythm Aces	BMG 82876530392
06/09/2003	5	7		MISS PERFECT ABS FEATURING NODESHA	BMG 82876556742

ABSOLUTE US production duo Mark Picchiotti and Craig Snider, with singer Suzanne Palmer. Palmer later recorded with Club 69 while Picchiotti recorded under his own name and as Sandstorm and Basstoy.

DATE	POS	WKS	BPI	SINGLE TITLE	LABEL & NUMBER
18/01/1997	38	2		I BELIEVE ABSOLUTE FEATURING SUZANNE PALMER	AM:PM 5820752
14/03/1998	69	1		CATCH ME	AM:PM 5825032

ABSOLUTELY FABULOUS – see PET SHOP BOYS

AC/DC Australian hard-rock group formed in 1974 by brothers Angus (born 31/3/1959, Glasgow, Scotland, guitar) and Malcolm Young (born 6/1/1953, Glasgow, guitar), Bon Scott (born Ron Belford, 9/7/1946, Kirriemuir, Scotland, vocals), Phil Rudd (born 19/5/1954, Melbourne, drums) and Mark Evans (born 2/3/1956, bass). Scott died of alcohol poisoning on 19/2/1980, with former Geordie lead singer Brian Johnson (born 5/10/1947, Newcastle-upon-Tyne) his replacement. Simon Wright replaced Rudd in 1985, and when he left to join Dio in 1989 Chris Slade took his place. They were inducted into the Rock & Roll Hall of Fame in 2003.

DATE	POS	WKS	BPI	SINGLE TITLE	LABEL & NUMBER
24/06/1978	24	9		ROCK 'N' ROLL DAMNATION	Atlantic K 11142
01/09/1979	56	4		HIGHWAY TO HELL	Atlantic K 11321
16/02/1980	29	9		TOUCH TOO MUCH	Atlantic K 11435
28/06/1980	47	3		DIRTY DEEDS DONE DIRT CHEAP	Atlantic HM2

○ Silver disc ● Gold disc ✪ Platinum disc (additional platinum units are indicated by a figure following the symbol) ◎ Singles released prior to 1973 that are known to have sold over 1 million copies in the UK

DATE	POS	WKS	BPI	SINGLE TITLE	LABEL & NUMBER
28/06/1980	48	3		HIGH VOLTAGE (LIVE VERSION)	Atlantic HM1
28/06/1980	55	3		IT'S A LONG WAY TO THE TOP (IF YOU WANNA ROCK 'N' ROLL)	Atlantic HM3
28/06/1980	36	8		WHOLE LOTTA ROSIE	Atlantic HM4
13/09/1980	38	6		YOU SHOOK ME ALL NIGHT LONG Featured in the 1997 film *Private Parts*	Atlantic K 11600
29/11/1980	15	8		ROCK 'N' ROLL AIN'T NOISE POLLUTION	Atlantic K 11630
06/02/1982	13	6		LET'S GET IT UP	Atlantic K 11706
03/07/1982	15	6		FOR THOSE ABOUT TO ROCK (WE SALUTE YOU)	Atlantic K 11721
29/10/1983	37	4		GUNS FOR HIRE	Atlantic A 9774
04/08/1984	35	5		NERVOUS SHAKEDOWN	Atlantic A 9651
06/07/1985	48	4		DANGER	Atlantic A 9532
18/01/1986	24	5		SHAKE YOUR FOUNDATIONS	Atlantic A 9474
24/05/1986	16	5		WHO MADE WHO	Atlantic A 9425
30/08/1986	46	4		YOU SHOOK ME ALL NIGHT LONG	Atlantic A 9377
16/01/1988	12	6		HEATSEEKER	Atlantic A 9136
02/04/1988	22	5		THAT'S THE WAY I WANNA ROCK 'N' ROLL	Atlantic A 9098
22/09/1990	13	5		THUNDERSTRUCK	Atco B 8907
24/11/1990	36	3		MONEY TALKS	Atco B 8886
27/04/1991	34	3		ARE YOU READY	Atco B 8830
17/10/1992	14	4		HIGHWAY TO HELL (LIVE)	Atco B 8479
06/03/1993	68	1		DIRTY DEEDS DONE DIRT CHEAP (LIVE) This and above single recorded at Castle Donnington in 1991	Atco B 6073CD
10/07/1993	23	3		BIG GUN Featured in the 1993 film *The Last Action Hero*	Atco B 8396CD
30/09/1995	33	2		HARD AS A ROCK	Atlantic A 4368CD
11/05/1996	56	1		HAIL CAESAR	East West 7559660512
15/04/2000	65	1		STIFF UPPER LIP	EMI CDSTIFF 100

MARC ACARDIPANE – see SCOOTER

ACE
UK group formed in London in 1973 by Alan 'Bam' King (born 18/9/1946, London, guitar/vocals), Phil Harris (born 18/7/1948, London, guitar/vocals), Paul Carrack (born 22/4/1951, Sheffield, keyboards/vocals), Terry 'Tex' Comer (born 23/2/1949, Burnley, bass) and Steve Witherington (born 26/12/1953, Enfield, drums). Witherington was later replaced by Fran Byrne. They disbanded in 1977, Carrack joining Squeeze and then Mike + The Mechanics in 1985 and recording solo.

DATE	POS	WKS	BPI	SINGLE TITLE	LABEL & NUMBER
09/11/1974	20	10		HOW LONG	Anchor ANC 1002

RICHARD ACE
Jamaican singer/keyboard player who later formed Sons Of Ace with his sons Richard Jr, Franz, Ricardo and Craig.

DATE	POS	WKS	BPI	SINGLE TITLE	LABEL & NUMBER
02/12/1978	66	2		STAYIN' ALIVE	Blue Inc. INC 2

ACE OF BASE
Swedish group formed by sisters Jenny (born 19/5/1972, Gothenburg) and Malin Bergren (born 31/10/1970, Gothenburg) with brother Jonas (born 21/3/1967, Gothenburg) and family friend and programmer Ulf Ekberg (born 6/12/1970, Gothenburg) as Tech Noir, later changing their name to Ace Of Base. Initially signed to Danish record company Mega Records, their debut album *Happy Nation* sold over 21 million copies worldwide, making them the most successful debut act of all time.

DATE	POS	WKS	BPI	SINGLE TITLE	LABEL & NUMBER
08/05/1993	❶³	16	✪	ALL THAT SHE WANTS	London 8612702
28/08/1993	20	6		WHEEL OF FORTUNE Their debut release that failed in Sweden but hit #1 elsewhere in Europe	London 8615452
13/11/1993	42	3		HAPPY NATION	London 8619272
26/02/1994	2	16	●	THE SIGN ▲⁶	London ACECD 1
11/06/1994	5	11		DON'T TURN AROUND	London ACECD 2
15/10/1994	40	3		HAPPY NATION	London 8610972
14/01/1995	18	4		LIVING IN DANGER	Metronome ACECD 3
11/11/1995	20	5		LUCKY LOVE	London ACCDP 4
27/01/1996	15	6		BEAUTIFUL LIFE Featured in the 1998 film *A Night At The Roxbury*	Metronome ACECD 5
25/07/1998	5	11	○	LIFE IS A FLOWER	London ACECD 7
10/10/1998	8	5		CRUEL SUMMER	London ACECD 8
19/12/1998	12	10		ALWAYS HAVE, ALWAYS WILL	London ACECD 9
17/04/1999	22	4		EVERY TIME IT RAINS	London ACECD 10

ACEN
UK producer Acen Razvi who later recorded for Profile Records and also as Spacepimp for Clear Records.

DATE	POS	WKS	BPI	SINGLE TITLE	LABEL & NUMBER
08/08/1992	38	3		TRIP II THE MOON	Production House PNT 042
10/10/1992	71	1		TRIP II THE MOON (REMIX)	Production House PNT 042RX

ACES – see DESMOND DEKKER AND THE ACES

TRACY ACKERMAN – see Q

ACT
UK/German vocal/instrumental group formed by Claudia Brucken and Thomas Leer. Brucken was previously a member of Propaganda.

DATE	POS	WKS	BPI	SINGLE TITLE	LABEL & NUMBER
23/05/1987	60	2		SNOBBERY AND DECAY	ZTT ZTAS 28

ACT ONE
US studio group assembled and produced by Raeford Gerald (singer Ray Godfrey of The Determinations) with George Barker, Reginald Ross and Roger Terry.

DATE	POS	WKS	BPI	SINGLE TITLE	LABEL & NUMBER
18/05/1974	40	6		TOM THE PEEPER	Mercury 6008 005

❶⁹ Number of weeks single topped the UK chart ↑ Entered the UK chart at #1 ▲⁹ Number of weeks single topped the US chart

9

ACZESS UK producer Dave Bichard.

27/10/2001	65	1		DO WHAT WE WOULD .... INCredible 6719782

ADAM AND THE ANTS/ADAM ANT UK group formed in 1976 by Adam Ant (born Stuart Leslie Goddard, 3/11/1954, London, vocals). The original line-up was poached by Malcolm McLaren to form Bow Wow Wow, Adam putting together Marco Pirroni (born 27/4/1959, London), Kevin Mooney, Terry Lee Miall (born 8/11/1958, London) and Merrick (born Chris Hughes, 3/3/1954) as replacements. Ant disbanded them in 1982, retaining Pirroni as co-writer for his solo career. In 1985 Ant moved to the US to pursue acting, returning to the UK in 1990 to revive his musical career. *Kings Of The Wild Frontier* was named Best Album at the inaugural BRIT Awards of 1982. Hughes became a successful producer with Tears For Fears.

02/08/1980	48	5		KINGS OF THE WILD FRONTIER .... CBS 8877
11/10/1980	4	16	○	**DOG EAT DOG** .... CBS 9039
06/12/1980	2	18	●	**ANTMUSIC** .... CBS 9352
27/12/1980	9	13	○	**YOUNG PARISIANS** Originally released January 1979 .... Decca F 13803
24/01/1981	33	9		CARTROUBLE Originally released May 1980. .... Do It DUN 10
24/01/1981	45	9		ZEROX .... Do It DUN 8
21/02/1981	2	13		**KINGS OF THE WILD FRONTIER** .... CBS 8877
09/05/1981	❶⁵	15	●	**STAND AND DELIVER** ↑ .... CBS A 1065
12/09/1981	❶⁴	12	●	**PRINCE CHARMING** Promotional video included actress Diana Dors. ...... CBS A 1408
12/12/1981	3	10	●	**ANT RAP** .... CBS A 1738
27/02/1982	13	6		DEUTSCHER GIRLS Featured in the 1978 film *Jubilee*. .... Ego 5
13/03/1982	46	4		THE ANTMUSIC EP (THE B-SIDES) Tracks on EP: *Friends, Kick* and *Physical*. ...... Do It DUN 20
22/05/1982	❶²	11	○	**GOODY TWO SHOES** .... CBS A 2367
18/09/1982	9	8		**FRIEND OR FOE** .... CBS A 2736
27/11/1982	33	7		DESPERATE BUT NOT SERIOUS .... CBS A 2892
29/10/1983	5	11	○	**PUSS 'N' BOOTS** Produced by Phil Collins .... CBS A 3614
10/12/1983	41	6		STRIP .... CBS 3589
22/09/1984	13	8		APOLLO 9 .... CBS A 4719
13/07/1985	50	4		VIVE LE ROCK .... CBS A 6367
17/02/1990	13	7		ROOM AT THE TOP .... MCA 1387
28/04/1990	47	2		CAN'T SET THE RULES ABOUT LOVE .... MCA 1404
11/02/1995	32	3		WONDERFUL .... EMI CDEMS 366
03/06/1995	48	2		GOTTA BE A SIN This and the above ten hits credited to **ADAM ANT** .... EMI CDEMS 379

A.D.A.M. FEATURING AMY French dance duo Andrea Bellicapelli and singer Amy.

01/07/1995	16	11		ZOMBIE .... Eternal YZ 951CD

ARTHUR ADAMS US singer/guitarist (born in Medon, TN) who was a session player on projects including the *Bonnie And Clyde* soundtrack, during which he met Crusader Wayne Henderson, who got him a contract with Fantasy Records and produced his debut album in 1975.

24/10/1981	38	5		YOU GOT THE FLOOR. .... RCA 146

BRYAN ADAMS Canadian singer (born 5/11/1959, Kingston, Ontario) who was lead singer with local band Sweeney Todd in 1976 before forming a songwriting partnership with Jim Vallence in 1977 (for Bachman-Turner Overdrive, Loverboy, Bonnie Tyler and Joe Cocker, among others). He later worked with songwriter/producer Robert John 'Mutt' Lange. Adams won the 1994 MTV Europe Music Award for Best Male.

12/01/1985	11	12		RUN TO YOU .... A&M AM 224
16/03/1985	35	7		SOMEBODY .... A&M AM 236
25/05/1985	38	5		HEAVEN ▲² Featured in the 1985 film *A Night In Heaven* .... A&M AM 256
10/08/1985	42	7		SUMMER OF 69 .... A&M AM 267
02/11/1985	29	6		IT'S ONLY LOVE **BRYAN ADAMS AND TINA TURNER** .... A&M AM 285
21/12/1985	55	2		CHRISTMAS TIME .... A&M AM 297
22/02/1986	41	7		THIS TIME .... A&M AM 295
12/07/1986	51	3		STRAIGHT FROM THE HEART .... A&M AM 322
28/03/1987	50	2		HEAT OF THE NIGHT .... A&M ADAM 2
20/06/1987	57	3		HEARTS ON FIRE .... A&M ADAM 3
17/10/1987	68	2		VICTIM OF LOVE. .... A&M AM 407
29/06/1991	❶¹⁶	25	✪²	**(EVERYTHING I DO) I DO IT FOR YOU** ▲⁷ Featured in the 1991 film *Robin Hood: Prince Of Thieves*. Holds the record for the longest

				unbroken spell at #1 with sixteen weeks. Total worldwide sales exceed 8 million copies. 1991 Grammy Award for Best Song Written Specifically for a Motion Picture for Adams, Robert 'Mutt' Lange and Michael Kamen .... A&M AM 789
14/09/1991	12	6		CAN'T STOP THIS THING WE STARTED .... A&M AM 612
23/11/1991	32	3		THERE WILL NEVER BE ANOTHER TONIGHT .... A&M AM 838
22/02/1992	8	7		**THOUGHT I'D DIED AND GONE TO HEAVEN** .... A&M AM 848
18/07/1992	22	5		ALL I WANT IS YOU .... A&M AM 879
26/09/1992	30	3		DO I HAVE TO SAY THE WORDS .... A&M AM 0068
30/10/1993	2	16	●	**PLEASE FORGIVE ME** .... A&M 5804232
15/01/1994	2	13	○	**ALL FOR LOVE** ▲[3] **BRYAN ADAMS, ROD STEWART AND STING** Featured in the 1993 film *The Three Musketeers* ..... A&M 5804772
22/04/1995	4	9	○	**HAVE YOU EVER REALLY LOVED A WOMAN?** ▲[5] Featured in the 1995 film *Don Juan DeMarco* .... A&M 5810282
11/11/1995	50	2		ROCK STEADY .... Capitol CDCL 763
01/06/1996	6	7		**THE ONLY THING THAT LOOKS GOOD ON ME IS YOU** .... A&M 5813692
24/08/1996	10	8		**LET'S MAKE A NIGHT TO REMEMBER** .... A&M 5815672
23/11/1996	13	4		STAR Featured in the 1996 film *Jack* .... A&M 5820252
08/02/1997	10	7		**I FINALLY FOUND SOMEONE** BARBRA STREISAND AND BRYAN ADAMS Featured in the 1996 film *The Mirror Has Two Faces* ....
				.... A&M 5820832
19/04/1997	22	3		18 TIL I DIE .... A&M 5821852
20/12/1997	18	7		BACK TO YOU .... A&M 5824752
21/03/1998	20	4		I'M READY This and above single recorded live at New York's Hammerstein Ballroom in September 1997 for MTV.... A&M 5825352
10/10/1998	13	5		ON A DAY LIKE TODAY .... Mercury MERCD 516
12/12/1998	3	19	✪	**WHEN YOU'RE GONE** BRYAN ADAMS FEATURING MELANIE C .... A&M 5828212
15/05/1999	6	9		**CLOUD NUMBER 9** .... A&M 5828492
18/12/1999	47	3		THE BEST OF ME .... Mercury/A&M 4971952
18/03/2000	●[1]	14	○	**DON'T GIVE UP** ↑ CHICANE FEATURING BRYAN ADAMS .... Xtravaganza XTRAV 9CDS
20/07/2002	5	8		**HERE I AM** Featured in the 2002 film *Stallion Of The Cimarron* .... A&M 4977442
25/09/2004	21	3		OPEN ROAD .... Polydor 9868053
11/12/2004	39	2		FLYING .... Polydor 9869276

CLIFF ADAMS UK orchestra leader (born 21/8/1923, London), previously a member of the Stargazers. He devised the radio programme *Sing Something Simple* in 1959, which remains one of the longest-running in the country. He died on 22/10/2001.

| 28/04/1960 | 39 | 2 | | LONELY MAN THEME From the TV advertisement for Strand cigarettes .... Pye International 7N 25056 |

GAYLE ADAMS US R&B singer/songwriter (born in Washington DC).

| 26/07/1980 | 64 | 1 | | STRETCHIN' OUT .... Epic EPC 8791 |

MARK ADAMS – see JOHNNY OTIS SHOW

OLETA ADAMS US singer (born 4/5/1962, Yakima, WA) who was discovered singing in Kansas City by Tears For Fears. She subsequently became their backing singer for the *Seeds Of Love* album and tour, with Roland Orzabal producing her debut album. She later recorded gospel material for Harmony Records.

24/03/1990	52	2		RHYTHM OF LIFE .... Fontana OLETA 1
03/11/1990	56	3		RHYTHM OF LIFE .... Fontana OLETA 1
12/01/1991	4	12		**GET HERE** .... Fontana OLETA 3
13/04/1991	49	3		YOU'VE GOT TO GIVE ME ROOM/RHYTHM OF LIFE .... Fontana OLETA 4
29/06/1991	73	1		CIRCLE OF ONE .... Fontana OLETA 5
28/09/1991	33	5		DON'T LET THE SUN GO DOWN ON ME .... Fontana TRIBO 1
25/04/1992	57	1		WOMAN IN CHAINS TEARS FOR FEARS FEATURING OLETA ADAMS .... Fontana IDEA 16
10/07/1993	42	3		I JUST HAD TO HEAR YOUR VOICE .... Fontana OLETA 6
07/10/1995	22	3		NEVER KNEW LOVE .... Fontana OLECD 9
16/12/1995	38	2		RHYTHM OF LIFE (REMIX) .... Fontana OLECD 10
10/02/1996	51	1		WE WILL MEET AGAIN .... Mercury OLECD 11

RYAN ADAMS US singer/songwriter (born 5/11/1974) who was lead singer with Whiskeytown before going solo in 2000.

08/12/2001	53	1		NEW YORK NEW YORK.. Mercury 1722232
20/04/2002	39	2		ANSWERING BELL .... Lost Highway 1722402
28/09/2002	37	1		NUCLEAR .... Lost Highway 1722592
31/01/2004	21	2		SO ALIVE .... Lost Highway 9861611
10/07/2004	27	2		WONDERWALL .... Lost Highway 9863098

ADAMSKI UK singer (born Adam Tinley, 1966) who made his first record at the age of eleven as The Stupid Babies with *The Babysitters*. He signed with MCA in 1989 and initially recorded instrumentals before linking with the then-unknown Seal, later recording for ZTT. He was sued by Lucozade, who claimed his debut single had infringed their advertising, and forced to donate £5,000 to charity.

20/01/1990	12	6		N-R-G .... MCA 1386
07/04/1990	●[4]	18	●	**KILLER** Features the uncredited vocals of co-writer Seal. Featured in the 1992 film *Gladiator* .... MCA 1400
08/09/1990	7	8		**THE SPACE JUNGLE** .... MCA 1435
17/11/1990	46	2		FLASHBACK JACK .... MCA 1459
09/11/1991	51	2		NEVER GOIN' DOWN/BORN TO BE ALIVE ADAMSKI FEATURING JIMI POLO/ADAMSKI FEATURING SOHO .... MCA MCS 1578
04/04/1992	68	1		GET YOUR BODY ADAMSKI FEATURING NINA HAGEN .... MCA MCS 1613
04/07/1992	63	1		BACK TO FRONT .... MCA MCS 1644

❶[9] Number of weeks single topped the UK chart ↑ Entered the UK chart at #1 ▲[9] Number of weeks single topped the US chart

11

11/07/1998.....56......1....... ONE OF THE PEOPLE **ADAMSKI'S THING** .... ZTT 101CD

ADDAMS AND GEE UK instrumental duo Nick Addams and Mike Gee who later recorded with Gwen Dickey.
20/04/1991.....72......1....... CHUNG KUO (REVISITED).. Debut DEBT 3108

ADDIS BLACK WIDOW US rap duo Pigeon and Cream who later relocated to Sweden.
03/02/1996.....42......2....... INNOCENT Contains a sample of The Brothers Johnson's *Running For Your Love* .... Mercury Black Vinyl MBVCD 1

ADDRISI BROTHERS US vocal duo Dick (born 4/7/1941, Winthrop, MA) and Don Addrisi (born 14/12/1938, Winthrop).
Don died on 13/11/1984.
06/10/1979.....57......3....... GHOST DANCER .... Scotti Brothers K 11361

ADEMA US rock group formed in California by Mark Chavez (vocals), Mike Ransom (guitar), Tim Fluckey (guitar), Dave DeRoo (bass) and Kris Kohls (drums). Chavez is the half-brother of Korn's Jonathan Davis.
16/03/2002.....62......1....... GIVING IN .... Arista 74321924022
10/08/2002.....61......1....... THE WAY YOU LIKE IT.. Arista 74321954712
23/08/2003.....46......1....... UNSTABLE .... Arista 82876550862

ADEVA US R&B singer (born Patricia Daniels, Patterson, NJ), the youngest of six children, who started singing in her local church choir. She was a schoolteacher before becoming a professional singer against her parents' wishes, who insisted she sing gospel or nothing. Paul Simpson is a New York singer/producer.
14/01/1989.....17......9....... RESPECT .... Cooltempo COOL 179
25/03/1989.....22......8....... MUSICAL FREEDOM (MOVING ON UP) **PAUL SIMPSON FEATURING ADEVA** .... Cooltempo COOL 182
12/08/1989.....17......8....... WARNING.. Cooltempo COOL 185
21/10/1989.....17......7....... I THANK YOU .... Cooltempo COOL 192
16/12/1989.....57......5....... BEAUTIFUL LOVE .... Cooltempo COOL 195
28/04/1990.....62......2....... TREAT ME RIGHT .... Cooltempo COOL 200
06/04/1991.....20......5....... RING MY BELL **MONIE LOVE VS ADEVA** .... Cooltempo COOL 224
19/10/1991.....48......3....... IT SHOULD'VE BEEN ME .... Cooltempo COOL 236
29/02/1992.....34......4....... DON'T LET IT SHOW ON YOUR FACE .... Cooltempo COOL 248
06/06/1992.....45......3....... UNTIL YOU COME BACK TO ME .... Cooltempo COOL 254
17/10/1992.....51......2....... I'M THE ONE FOR YOU.. Cooltempo COOL 264
11/12/1993.....65......1....... RESPECT (REMIX) .... Network NWKCD 79
27/05/1995.....34......2....... TOO MANY FISH .... Virgin VUSCD 89
18/11/1995.....36......2....... WHADDA U WANT (FROM ME) This and above single credited to **FRANKIE KNUCKLES FEATURING ADEVA** .... Virgin VUSCD 98
06/04/1996.....54......1....... DO WATCHA DO **HYPER GO GO AND ADEVA** .... Avex UK AVEXCD 24
04/05/1996.....37......2....... I THANK YOU (REMIX).. Cooltempo CDCOOLS 318
12/04/1997.....60......1....... DO WATCHA DO (REMIX) .... Distinctive DISNCD 28
26/07/1997.....54......1....... WHERE IS THE LOVE/THE WAY THAT YOU FEEL .... Distinctive DISNCD 31

ADICTS UK punk group formed in Ipswich in 1980 by Monkey (born Keith Warren, vocals), Pete Davidson (guitar), Mel Ellis (bass) and Kid Dee (born Michael Davidson, drums), adopting black bowler hats and face make-up from Stanley Kubrick's *A Clockwork Orange*.
14/05/1983.....75......1....... BAD BOY .... Razor RZS 104

ADIEMUS UK instrumental duo Karl Jenkins and Mike Ratledge.
14/10/1995.....48......2....... ADIEMUS .... Venture VEND 4

LARRY ADLER – see **KATE BUSH**

ADONIS FEATURING 2 PUERTO RICANS, A BLACK MAN AND A DOMINICAN US production duo David Cole (born 3/6/1962, Johnson City, TN) and Robert Clivilles (born 30/8/1964, New York) began by remixing other people's work. They also recorded as S.O.U.L. System, Clivilles & Cole and C&C Music Factory. David Cole died from meningitis on 24/1/1995.
13/06/1987.....47......4....... DO IT PROPERLY ('NO WAY BACK')/NO WAY BACK.. London LON 136

ADRENALIN M.O.D. UK production group formed by Andy Shernoff.
08/10/1988.....49......5....... O-O-O .... MCA RAGAT 2

ADULT NET UK/US group formed in 1985 by Laura Elise Smith (aka Brix, vocals), Craig Gannon (guitar), Andy Rourke (bass) and Mick Joyce (drums). Later members included Clem Burke and James Eller. Brix was married to The Fall's Mark E Smith.
10/06/1989.....66......2....... WHERE WERE YOU .... Fontana BRX 2

ADVENTURES UK group formed in Belfast in 1984 by Terry Sharpe (vocals), Pat Gribben (guitar), Pat's wife Eileen (vocals), Gerard 'Spud' Murphy (guitar), Tony Ayre (bass) and Paul Crowder (drums), originally recording for Chrysalis. Eileen Gribben and Murphy left in 1989.
15/09/1984.....71......2...... ANOTHER SILENT DAY.. Chrysalis CHS 2000
01/12/1984.....62......4...... SEND MY HEART .... Chrysalis CHS 2001
13/07/1985.....58......3...... FEEL THE RAINDROPS.. Chrysalis AD 1
09/04/1988.....20......10...... BROKEN LAND .... Elektra EKR 69
02/07/1988.....44......4...... DROWNING IN THE THE SEA OF LOVE .... Elektra EKR 76

13/06/1992.....68......1....... RAINING ALL OVER THE WORLD .... Polydor PO 211

ADVENTURES OF STEVIE V
UK/US dance outfit formed by Stevie Vincent with singer Melodie Washington and multi-instrumentalist Mick Walsh.

21/04/1990.....2......13..... **DIRTY CASH** .... Mercury MER 311
29/09/1990.....29......5..... BODY LANGUAGE.. Mercury MER 331
02/03/1991.....58......3..... JEALOUSY .... Mercury MER 337
27/09/1997.....69......1..... DIRTY CASH (REMIX) .... Avex Trax AVEXCDX 57

ADVERTS
UK punk group formed in 1977 by Tim 'TV' Smith (guitar/vocals), Gaye Advert (bass), Howard Pickup (guitar) and Laurie Driver (drums). They later included John Towe, Rod Latter and Tim Cross. After disbanding in 1979, Smith formed TV Smith's Explorers. Pickup died from a brain tumour in July 1997.

27/08/1977.....18......7....... GARY GILMORE'S EYES Murderer Gilmore was executed by firing squad in the US and offered to donate his eyes to science ....
.... Anchor ANC 1043
04/02/1978.....34......4....... NO TIME TO BE 21 .... Bright BR1

AEROSMITH
US hard-rock band formed in 1970 by Steven Tyler (born Steven Tallarico, 26/3/1948, Yonkers, NY, vocals), Joe Perry (born 10/9/1950, Boston, MA, guitar), Brad Whitford (born 23/2/1952, Winchester, MA, guitar), Tom Hamilton (born 31/12/1951, Colorado Springs, CO, bass) and Joey Kramer (born 21/6/1950, The Bronx, NYC, drums). Their debut album was released in 1973. Perry left in 1979 to form the Joe Perry Project and was replaced by Jimmy Crespo. Whitford left in 1981 and was replaced by Rick Dulay. The original line-up re-formed in 1984. Four Grammy Awards include the non-charting Best Rock Performance by a Group with Vocal in 1990 for *Jane's Got A Gun*. They were named Best Rock Act at the 1994 and 1998 MTV Europe Music Awards and were inducted into the Rock & Roll Hall of Fame in 2001.

17/10/1987.....45......5..... DUDE (LOOKS LIKE A LADY) Featured in the film *Mrs Doubtfire* (1993) and *Wayne's World 2* (1993) .... Geffen GEF 29
16/04/1988.....69......2..... ANGEL .... Geffen GEF 34
09/09/1989.....13......8..... LOVE IN AN ELEVATOR .... Geffen GEF 63
24/02/1990.....20......5..... DUDE (LOOKS LIKE A LADY) Re-issue of Geffen GEF 29 .... Geffen GEF 72
14/04/1990.....42......4..... RAG DOLL .... Geffen GEF 76
01/09/1990.....46......2..... THE OTHER SIDE .... Geffen GEF 79
10/04/1993.....19......4..... LIVIN' ON THE EDGE 1993 Grammy Award for Best Rock Performance by a Group with Vocal .... Geffen GFSTD 35
03/07/1993.....34......3..... EAT THE RICH Featured in the 1993 film *Eat The Rich* .... Geffen GFSTD 46
30/10/1993.....17......6..... CRYIN' .... Geffen GFSTD 56
18/12/1993.....57......3..... AMAZING Features the uncredited contribution of Don Henley (of The Eagles) .... Geffen GFSTD 63
02/07/1994.....24......4..... SHUT UP AND DANCE Featured in the 1993 film *Wayne's World 2* .... Geffen GFSTD 75
20/08/1994.....74......1..... SWEET EMOTION .... Columbia 6604492
05/11/1994.....23......4..... CRAZY/BLIND MAN *Crazy* won the 1994 Grammy Award for Best Rock Performance by a Group with Vocal ..... Geffen GFSTD 80
08/03/1997.....22......4..... FALLING IN LOVE (IS HARD ON THE KNEES)................................... Columbia 6640752
21/06/1997.....29......2..... HOLE IN MY SOUL .... Columbia 6645012
27/12/1997.....38......2..... PINK 1998 Grammy Award for Best Rock Group Performance .... Columbia 6648722
12/09/1998.....4......20.....● **I DON'T WANT TO MISS A THING ▲4** Featured in the 1998 film *Armageddon* .... Columbia 6664082
26/06/1999.....13......6..... **PINK** Re-issue of Columbia 6648722 .... Columbia 6675342
17/03/2001.....13......7..... JADED .... Columbia 6709312

A.F.I.
US rock group formed in Ukiah, CA in 1991 by college students Davey Havok (vocals), Markus Stopholese (guitar), Vick (bass) and Adam Carson (drums). Vick left after a few months and was replaced by Geoff Kresge. By 1997 the line-up was Havok, Jade Puger (guitar), Hunter (bass) and Carson. Their name is short for A Fire Inside.

21/06/2003.....22......3..... GIRL'S NOT GREY .... DreamWorks 4504601
20/09/2003.....43......1..... THE LEAVING SONG PART 2.. DreamWorks 4504625

AFRICAN BUSINESS
Italian vocal/instrumental group formed by F Gatto, A Martinelli, M Catalano and C Ridolfi with rap by Space One.

17/11/1990.....73......1..... IN ZAIRE... Urban URB 64

AFRO CELT SOUND SYSTEM
UK/Irish/African group formed by Iarla O'Lionard (vocals), Davy Spillane (uillean pipes), Ronan Browne (uillean pipes), Jo Bruce (keyboards), James McNally (whistle), Ayub Ogada (nyatiti), Kauwding Cissakho and Massamba Diop.

29/04/2000.....71......1..... RELEASE .... Realworld RWSCD 10

AFRO MEDUSA
UK house group formed in London by Patrick Cole, Nick Bennett and Spanish singer Isabel Fructuoso. Cole is also a member of Afro Bloc and The Rebirth Brass Band.

28/10/2000.....31......2..... PASILDA .... Rulin 6CDS

AFROMAN
US rapper (born Joseph Foreman, Los Angeles, CA) who originally contemplated calling himself 'Heavenly Henry'.

06/10/2001.....45......3..... BECAUSE I GOT HIGH (IMPORT).. Universal 0152822
27/10/2001.....❶3.....19.....● **BECAUSE I GOT HIGH** Featured in the 2001 film *Jay And Silent Bob Strike Back* .... Universal MCSTD 40266
02/02/2002.....10......8..... **CRAZY RAP** .... Universal MCSTD 40273

AFTER 7
US R&B vocal group formed in Indianapolis by Keith Mitchell, and brothers Melvin and Kevon Edmonds. Mitchell is a cousin of LA Reid; the Edmondses are brothers to Kenneth 'Babyface' Edmonds. Mitchell left in 1997.

03/11/1990.....54......3..... CAN'T STOP .... Virgin America VUS 31

❶9 Number of weeks single topped the UK chart ↑ Entered the UK chart at #1 ▲9 Number of weeks single topped the US chart

13

AFTER THE FIRE
UK rock group formed in 1974 by Andy Piercy (vocals/bass), Peter Banks (keyboards), John Russell (guitar) and Pete King (drums), who later formed the Rapid label recording gospel music.

09/06/1979 . . . . . 40 . . . . . . 6	ONE RULE FOR YOU . . . . CBS 7025
08/09/1979 . . . . . 62 . . . . . . 2	LASER LOVE . . . . CBS 7769
09/04/1983 . . . . . 47 . . . . . . 4	DER KOMMISSAR . . . . CBS A 2399

AFTERNOON BOYS – see STEVE WRIGHT

AFTERSHOCK
US duo formed in 1985 in Staten Island, NYC by Guy Charles Routte and Jose 'The Frost' Rivera. They also worked with Family Stand.

21/08/1993 . . . . . 11 . . . . . . 8	SLAVE TO THE VIBE Featured in the 1993 film *Sliver* . . . . Virgin America VUSCD 75

AFX
UK producer Richard James who also records as Aphex Twin, Polygon Window and Powerpill.

11/08/2001 . . . . . 69 . . . . . . 1	2 REMIXES BY AFX . . . . MEN 1 MEN1CD

AGE OF CHANCE
UK group formed in Leeds by Steve Elvidge (vocals), Neil Howbs (guitar), Geoff Taylor (bass) and Jan Penny (drums). Elvidge left in 1990 and was replaced by Charles Hutchinson. The group disbanded in 1991.

17/01/1987 . . . . . 50 . . . . 6	KISS . . . . Fon AGE 5
30/05/1987 . . . . . 65 . . . . . . 2	WHO'S AFRAID OF THE BIG BAD NOISE? . . . . Fon VS 962
20/01/1990 . . . . . 53 . . . . . . 5	HIGHER THAN HEAVEN . . . . Virgin VS 1228

AGE OF LOVE
Belgian/Italian dance group comprising Roger Samya, Giuseppe Cherchia and Bruno Sanchioni, who is also a member of BBE.

05/07/1997 . . . . . 17 . . . . . . 4	AGE OF LOVE – THE REMIXES . . . . React CDREACT 100
19/09/1998 . . . . . 38 . . . . . . 2	AGE OF LOVE . . . . React CDREACT 135

AGENT BLUE
UK DJ and producer Richard Vine, who was a member of Creeping Jesus and Sweet Peace Three before going solo.

29/05/2004 . . . . . 71 . . . . . . 1	SEX DRUGS AND ROCKS THROUGH YOUR WINDOW . . . . Fierce Panda NING153CD
21/08/2004 . . . . . 59 . . . . . . 1	SOMETHING ELSE . . . . Island TEMPTCD011

AGENT 00
UK production duo.

07/03/1998 . . . . . 65 . . . . . . 1	THE MAGNIFICENT Contains a sample of Dave & Ansil Collins' *Double Barrel* . . . . Inferno CDFERN 002

AGENT PROVOCATEUR
UK production group formed by Danny Saber and John Gosling.

22/03/1997 . . . . . 49 . . . . . . 1	AGENT DAN . . . . Epic AGENT 3CD

AGENT SUMO
UK production/remixing duo Martin Cole and Steve Halliday.

09/06/2001 . . . . . 44 . . . . . . 2	24 HOURS Contains samples of Gladys Knight & The Pips' *The Way We Were – Try To Remember* and James' *Moses Theme* . . . . Virgin VSCDT 1806
20/04/2002 . . . . . 40 . . . . . . 2	WHY Contains a sample of BBCS And A's *Rock Shock* . . . . Virgin VSCDT 1819

AGNELLI AND NELSON
Irish DJ duo Chris James 'CJ' Agnelli and Robbie Nelson.

15/08/1998 . . . . . 21 . . . . . . 4	EL NINO . . . . Xtravaganza 0091575 EXT
11/09/1999 . . . . . 17 . . . . . . 4	EVERYDAY . . . . Xtravaganza XTRAV 2CDS
17/06/2000 . . . . . 35 . . . . . . 2	EMBRACE . . . . Xtravaganza XTRAV 11CDS
09/09/2000 . . . . . 29 . . . . . . 2	HUDSON STREET . . . . Xtravaganza XTRAV 13CDS
07/04/2001 . . . . . 48 . . . . . . 1	VEGAS . . . . Xtravaganza XTRAV 23CDS
15/06/2002 . . . . . 33 . . . . . . 2	EVERYDAY . . . . Xtravaganza XTRAV 31CDS
03/04/2004 . . . . . 41 . . . . . . 2	HOLDING ON TO NOTHING AGNELLI & NELSON FEATURING AUREUS . . . . Xtravaganza XTRAV 43CX

CHRISTINA AGUILERA
US singer (born 18/12/1980, Staten Island, NYC) who, at the age of twelve, landed a role on *The New Mickey Mouse Club* for Disney, the TV show that also gave a start to Britney Spears. Awards include a Grammy for Best New Artist in 1999 and the MTV Europe Music Award for Best Female Artist in 2003.

11/09/1999 . . . . . 50 . . . . . . 5	GENIE IN A BOTTLE (IMPORT) . . . . RCA 701062
16/10/1999 . . . . ❶² 19	GENIE IN A BOTTLE ↑ ▲⁵ . . . . RCA 74321705482
26/02/2000 . . . . . 3 . . . . . . 13	WHAT A GIRL WANTS Featured in the 2000 film *What Women Want* . . . . RCA 74321737522
22/07/2000 . . . . . 19 . . . . . . 6	I TURN TO YOU . . . . RCA 74321765472
11/11/2000 . . . . . 8 . . . . . . 8	COME ON OVER BABY (ALL I WANT IS YOU) ▲⁴ . . . . RCA 74321799912
10/03/2001 . . . . . 4 . . . . . . 12	NOBODY WANTS TO BE LONELY RICKY MARTIN WITH CHRISTINA AGUILERA . . . . Columbia 6709462
30/06/2001 . . . . ❶¹ . . . . . 16 . . . . . ●	LADY MARMALADE ↑ ▲⁵ CHRISTINA AGUILERA/LIL' KIM/MYA/PINK Featured in the 2001 film *Moulin Rouge*. 2001 Grammy Award for Best Pop Collaboration with Vocal . . . . Interscope 4975612
23/11/2002 . . . . ❶² . . . . . 9 . . . . . ✪	DIRRTY ↑ CHRISTINA AGUILERA FEATURING REDMAN 2003 MOBO Award for Best Video . . . . RCA 74321962722
22/02/2003 . . . . . 51 . . . . . . 2	BEAUTIFUL (IMPORT) . . . . RCA 74321983652
08/03/2003 . . . . ❶² 10	BEAUTIFUL ↑ 2003 Grammy Award for Best Female Pop Vocal Performance . . . . RCA 82876502462
21/06/2003 . . . . . 3 . . . . . . 13	FIGHTER . . . . RCA 82876524292
20/09/2003 . . . . . 6 . . . . . . 9	CAN'T HOLD US DOWN CHRISTINA AGUILERA FEATURING LIL' KIM . . . . RCA 82876556332
20/12/2003 . . . . . 9 . . . . . . 10	THE VOICE WITHIN . . . . RCA 82876584292
13/11/2004 . . . . . 4 . . . . . 7+	CAR WASH CHRISTINA AGUILERA AND MISSY ELLIOTT Featured in the 2004 film *Shark Tale* . . . . DreamWorks 9864630
04/12/2004 . . . . . 5 . . . . . 4+	TILT YA HEAD BACK NELLY AND CHRISTINA AGUILERA Contains a sample of Curtis Mayfield's *Superfly* . . . . . Universal MCSTD40396

○ Silver disc ● Gold disc ✪ Platinum disc (additional platinum units are indicated by a figure following the symbol) ◎ Singles released prior to 1973 that are known to have sold over 1 million copies in the UK

A-HA
Norwegian trio formed by Morten Harket (born 14/9/1959, Konigsberg, vocals), Pal Waaktaar (born 6/9/1961, Oslo, guitar) and Magne 'Mags' Furuholmen (born 1/11/1962, Oslo, keyboards). They moved to London in January 1983, and signed with Warners in late 1983. Furuholmen chose their name, a simple exclamation known the world over. The group went into semi-retirement in 1995 in order to undertake individual projects, Harket recording a solo album and Waaktaar forming Savoy, before re-forming in 1999.

DATE	POS	WKS	BPI	SINGLE TITLE	LABEL & NUMBER
28/09/1985	2	19	●	TAKE ON ME ▲¹ Released three times before it became a hit in the UK	Warner Brothers W 9006
28/12/1985	❶²	12	○	THE SUN ALWAYS SHINES ON TV	Warner Brothers W 8846
05/04/1986	8	8		TRAIN OF THOUGHT	Warner Brothers W 8736
14/06/1986	5	10		HUNTING HIGH AND LOW	Warner Brothers W 6663
04/10/1986	8	7		I'VE BEEN LOSING YOU	Warner Brothers W 8594
06/12/1986	5	9	○	CRY WOLF	Warner Brothers W 8500
28/02/1987	13	6		MANHATTAN SKYLINE	Warner Brothers W 8405
04/07/1987	5	9		THE LIVING DAYLIGHTS Featured in the 1987 James Bond film *The Living Daylights*	Warner Brothers W 8305
26/03/1988	5	6		STAY ON THESE ROADS	Warner Brothers W 7936
18/06/1988	25	4		THE BLOOD THAT MOVES THE BODY	Warner Brothers W 7840
27/08/1988	11	7		TOUCHY!	Warner Brothers W 7749
10/12/1988	13	10		YOU ARE THE ONE	Warner Brothers W 7636
13/10/1990	13	7		CRYING IN THE RAIN	Warner Brothers W 9547
15/12/1990	44	5		I CALL YOUR NAME	Warner Brothers W 9462
26/10/1991	47	2		MOVE TO MEMPHIS	Warner Brothers W 0070
05/06/1993	19	4		DARK IS THE NIGHT	Warner Brothers W 0175CD
18/09/1993	41	3		ANGEL	Warner Brothers W 0195CD
26/03/1994	27	3		SHAPES THAT GO TOGETHER	Warner Brothers W 0236CD
03/06/2000	33	2		SUMMER MOVED ON	WEA 275CD

AHMAD
US rapper (born Ahmad Ali Lewis, 12/12/1975, Los Angeles, CA).

DATE	POS	WKS	BPI	SINGLE TITLE	LABEL & NUMBER
09/07/1994	64	2		BACK IN THE DAY Contains a sample of The Staple Singers' *Let's Do It Again*	Giant 74321212942

AIDA
Dutch production duo.

DATE	POS	WKS	BPI	SINGLE TITLE	LABEL & NUMBER
19/02/2000	58	1		FAR AND AWAY	48K/Perfecto SPECT 03CDS

AIR
French instrumental/production duo formed in Paris in 1996 by Jean-Benoit Dunckel and Nicolas Godin who first met while at school in Versailles.

DATE	POS	WKS	BPI	SINGLE TITLE	LABEL & NUMBER
21/02/1998	13	4		SEXY BOY	Virgin VSCDT 1672
16/05/1998	18	3		KELLY WATCH THE STARS Tribute to Kelly from the TV series *Charlie's Angels*	Virgin VSCDT 1690
21/11/1998	29	3		ALL I NEED	Virgin VSCDT 1702
26/02/2000	25	2		PLAYGROUND LOVE Includes the uncredited contribution of Gordon Tracks. Featured in the 2000 film *The Virgin Suicides*	Virgin VSCDT 1764
02/06/2001	31	2		RADIO #1	Virgin VSCDT 1803
21/08/2004	44	2		ALPHA BETA GAGA	Source VSCDX 1880

AIR SUPPLY
Australian duo Russell Hitchcock (born 15/6/1949, Melbourne) and Graham Russell (born 1/6/1950, Nottingham, UK), joined later by Frank Esler-Smith (born 5/6/1948, London, UK, keyboards), Ralph Cooper (born 6/4/1951, Coffs Harbour, drums), David Green (born 30/10/1949, Melbourne, bass) and David Moyse (born 5/11/1957, Adelaide, lead guitar). Disbanding in 1988, they re-formed in 1991. Esler-Smith died from pneumonia on 1/3/1991.

DATE	POS	WKS	BPI	SINGLE TITLE	LABEL & NUMBER
27/09/1980	11	11		ALL OUT OF LOVE	Arista ARIST 362
02/10/1982	44	4		EVEN THE NIGHTS ARE BETTER	Arista ARIST 474
20/11/1993	66	2		GOODBYE	Giant 74321153462

AIRHEAD
UK group of Michael Wallis (vocals), Steve Marshall (keyboards), Ben Kesteven (bass) and Sam Kesteven (drums). They changed their name to Jefferson Airhead, inspired by Jefferson Airplane, but after objections from Airplane's record company reverted back to Airhead.

DATE	POS	WKS	BPI	SINGLE TITLE	LABEL & NUMBER
05/10/1991	57	3		FUNNY HOW	Korova KOW 47
28/12/1991	35	5		COUNTING SHEEP	Korova KOW 48
07/03/1992	50	2		RIGHT NOW	Korova KOW 49

AIRHEADZ
UK production duo Leigh Guest and Andrew Peach whose debut hit was originally a bootleg of Eminem's *Stan*, subsequently re-recorded as an answer record with vocals by Caroline Debatseleir. Guest is also a member of Double Trouble.

DATE	POS	WKS	BPI	SINGLE TITLE	LABEL & NUMBER
28/04/2001	36	2		STANLEY (HERE I AM)	AM:PM CDAMPM 145

AIRSCAPE
Belgian production group Johan Gielen, Peter Ramson and Sven Maes who also record as Balearic Bill and Cubic 22.

DATE	POS	WKS	BPI	SINGLE TITLE	LABEL & NUMBER
09/08/1997	27	2		PACIFIC MELODY	Xtravaganza 0091165
29/08/1998	46	1		AMAZON CHANT	Xtravaganza 0091605 EXT
04/12/1999	33	2		L'ESPERANZA	Xtravaganza XTRAV 7CD

LAUREL AITKEN AND THE UNITONE
Jamaican singer (born 1927) who first recorded during the 1950s, before coming to London in 1960. He was one of the pioneers of the blue beat reggae style.

DATE	POS	WKS	BPI	SINGLE TITLE	LABEL & NUMBER
17/05/1980	60	3		RUDI GOT MARRIED	I-Spy SEE 6

AKA
UK vocal group.

DATE	POS	WKS	BPI	SINGLE TITLE	LABEL & NUMBER
12/10/1996	43	2		WARNING	RCA 74321360662

❶⁹ Number of weeks single topped the UK chart ↑ Entered the UK chart at #1 ▲⁹ Number of weeks single topped the US chart

15

AKABU FEATURING LINDA CLIFFORD
UK producer Dave Lee with US singer Linda Clifford. Lee also records as Jakatta while Clifford recorded solo.

15/09/2001 . . . . . 69 . . . . . . 1 . . . . RIDE THE STORM . . . . NRK Sound Division NRKCD 053

JEWEL AKENS
US singer (born 12/9/1940, Houston, TX). One of ten children, he is called Jewel because his mother, who wanted a daughter, liked the name anyway. He subsequently became a producer.

25/03/1965 . . . . . 29 . . . . . . 8 . . . . THE BIRDS AND THE BEES . . . . London HLN 9954

AKIL – see DJ FORMAT FEATURING CHARLI 2NA AND AKIL

AKIN
UK vocal duo.

14/06/1997 . . . . . 60 . . . . . . 1 . . . . STAY RIGHT HERE . . . . WEA 117CD

AKON FEATURING STYLES P
US vocal duo Akon (born Aliaune Thiam, Senegal) and Styles P.

25/12/2004 . . . . . 74 . . . . . . 1+ . . . . . . LOCKED UP . . . . Universal E9864569

ALABAMA 3
UK group formed in London in 1989 by Robert Spragg (vocals), Jake Blake (vocals), Piers Marsh (programmer/engineer), Simon Edwards (percussion), Johnny Delofons (drums), Rob Bailey (guitar) and Orlando Harrison (keyboards), later adding Chris McKay, Madde Ross, Scott and Emma Lush and Stuart Green to the line-up. They are named after the Alabama Two, black American victims of racial violence in 1930s US.

22/11/1997 . . . . . 72 . . . . . . 1 . . . . SPEED AT THE SOUND OF LONELINESS . . . . Elemental ELM 42CDS
11/04/1998 . . . . . 40 . . . . . . 2 . . . . AIN'T GOIN' TO GOA . . . . Elemental ELM 45CDS1

ALANA – see MK

ALARM
UK group formed in Rhyl, North Wales in 1977 as The Toilets, comprising Mike Peters (born 25/2/1959, Prestatyn, guitar/vocals), Dave Sharp (born 28/1/1959, Salford, guitar), Eddie MacDonald (born 1/11/1959, St Asaph, bass) and Nigel Twist (born 18/7/1958, Manchester, drums). They changed their name to Alarm in 1981. They disbanded in 1991, with Peters going solo and Twist forming Fringe. The group re-formed in 2003 and initially recorded as The Poppyfields. The Morriston Orpheus Male Voice Choir is a Welsh choir.

24/09/1983 . . . . . 17 . . . . . . 7 . . . . 68 GUNS . . . . IRS PFP 1023
21/01/1984 . . . . . 22 . . . . . . 6 . . . . WHERE WERE YOU HIDING WHEN THE STORM BROKE . . . . IRS 101
31/03/1984 . . . . . 51 . . . . . . 4 . . . . THE DECEIVER . . . . IRS 103
03/11/1984 . . . . . 48 . . . . . . 4 . . . . THE CHANT HAS JUST BEGUN . . . . IRS 104
02/03/1985 . . . . . 35 . . . . . . 6 . . . . ABSOLUTE REALITY . . . . IRS ALARM 1
28/09/1985 . . . . . 40 . . . . . . 4 . . . . STRENGTH . . . . IRS IRM 104
18/01/1986 . . . . . 22 . . . . . . 5 . . . . SPIRIT OF '76 . . . . IRS IRM 109
26/04/1986 . . . . . 43 . . . . . . 3 . . . . KNIFE EDGE . . . . IRS IRM 112
17/10/1987 . . . . . 18 . . . . . . 5 . . . . RAIN IN THE SUMMERTIME . . . . IRS IRM 144
12/12/1987 . . . . . 48 . . . . . . 2 . . . . RESCUE ME . . . . IRS IRM 150
20/02/1988 . . . . . 44 . . . . . . 3 . . . . PRESENCE OF LOVE (LAUGHERNE) . . . . IRS IRM 155
16/09/1989 . . . . . 43 . . . . . . 3 . . . . SOLD ME DOWN THE RIVER . . . . IRS EIRS 123
11/11/1989 . . . . . 31 . . . . . . 5 . . . . A NEW SOUTH WALES/THE ROCK ALARM FEATURING THE MORRISTON ORPHEUS MALE VOICE CHOIR . . . . IRS EIRS 129
03/02/1990 . . . . . 48 . . . . . . 3 . . . . LOVE DON'T COME EASY . . . . IRS EIRS 134
27/10/1990 . . . . . 54 . . . . . . 2 . . . . UNSAFE BUILDING 1990 . . . . IRS ALARM 2
13/04/1991 . . . . . 51 . . . . . . 2 . . . . RAW . . . . IRS ALARM 3
03/07/2004 . . . . . 45 . . . . . . 1 . . . . NEW HOME NEW LIFE . . . . Snapper Music SMASCD062

MORRIS ALBERT
Brazilian singer/songwriter (born Morris Albert Kaisermann, 1951) originally in the Thunders. Ten years after *Feelings* was a worldwide hit, Albert lost a plagiarism suit brought by *Pour Toi* composer Louis Gaste, having to pay £250,000 in settlement.

27/09/1975 . . . . . 4 . . . . . . 10 . . . . . O **FEELINGS** . . . . Decca F 13591

ALBERTA
Sierra Leone singer.

26/12/1998 . . . . . 48 . . . . . . 3 . . . . YOYO BOY . . . . RCA 74321640602

ALBERTO Y LOS TRIOS PARANOIAS
UK comedy group formed in Manchester in 1973 by Les Prior (vocals), Chris 'C.P.' Lee (guitar/vocals), Jimmy Hibbert (bass), Bob Harding (guitar/bass/vocals), Simon White (steel guitar), Tony Bowers (guitar/bass), Bruce Mitchell (drums) and Ray 'Mighty Mongo' Hughes (drums). Prior died from leukaemia on 31/1/1980, the group disbanding soon after.

23/09/1978 . . . . . 47 . . . . . . 5 . . . . HEADS DOWN NO NONSENSE MINDLESS BOOGIE Lampoons the musical style of Status Quo . . . . Logo GO 323

AL ALBERTS – see FOUR ACES

ALBION
Dutch producer Ferry Corsten who also recorded as Gouryella, Starparty, Moonman, Veracocha and System F and under his own name.

03/06/2000 . . . . . 59 . . . . . . 1 . . . . AIR 2000 . . . . Platipus PLATCD 73

ALCATRAZZ
US production duo Victor Imbres and Jean-Philippe Aviance. Imbres later recorded as Lithium (with Sonya Madan) and Coco.

17/02/1996 . . . . . 12 . . . . . . 4 . . . . GIV ME LUV . . . . AM:PM 5814332

ALCAZAR
Swedish dance group formed by Andreas Lundstedt (born 1972, Uppsala), Tess Merkel (born 1970, Nykoping) and Annikafiore Johansson (born 1971, Hassleholm) whose name means 'bed of flowers'. Andreas came second in the Swedish Song for Europe Contest in 1996. Annikafiore portrayed Frida in the Abba tribute musical *Mamma Mia*, while Tess worked as a stage director and backing singer prior to joining Alcazar.

DATE	POS	WKS		SINGLE TITLE	LABEL & NUMBER
08/12/2001	13	12		CRYING AT THE DISCOTEQUE Contains a sample of Sheila B Devotion's *Spacer*	Arista 74321893432
16/03/2002	30	2		SEXUAL GUARANTEE Contains a sample of Chic's *My Forbidden Lover*	Arista 74321920252
02/10/2004	15	5		THIS IS THE WORLD WE LIVE IN Contains samples of Diana Ross' *Upside Down* and Genesis' *Land Of Confusion* .... RCA 82876652372

ALDA
Icelandic singer (born Alda Björk Ólafsdóttir, 1960) who made her UK debut performing at the FA Charity Shield between Arsenal and Manchester United at Wembley in 1998.

DATE	POS	WKS	SINGLE TITLE	LABEL & NUMBER
29/08/1998	7	7	**REAL GOOD TIME**	Wildstar CDWILD 7
26/12/1998	20	7	GIRLS NIGHT OUT	Wildstar CDWILD 10

CALI ALEMAN
— see TITO PUENTE JR AND THE LATIN RHYTHM FEATURING TITO PUENTE, INDIA AND CALI ALEMAN

ALENA
Jamaican singer (born Alena Lova).

DATE	POS	WKS	SINGLE TITLE	LABEL & NUMBER
13/11/1999	14	5	TURN IT AROUND	Wonderboy WBOYD 16

ALESSI
US vocal duo of twin brothers Billy and Bobby Alessi (born 12/7/1953, New York), previously members of Barnaby Bye.

DATE	POS	WKS	SINGLE TITLE	LABEL & NUMBER
11/06/1977	8	11	**OH LORI**	A&M AMS 7289

HANNAH ALETHIA
— see SODA CLUB FEATURING HANNAH ALETHIA

ALEX PARTY
Italian dance group assembled by brothers Venturi and Giovanni Visnadi who are also responsible for Livin' Joy.

DATE	POS	WKS	BPI	SINGLE TITLE	LABEL & NUMBER
18/12/1993	49	6		SATURDAY NIGHT PARTY (READ MY LIPS)	Cleveland City Imports CCICD 17000
28/05/1994	29	4		SATURDAY NIGHT PARTY (READ MY LIPS)	Cleveland City Imports CCICD 17000
18/02/1995	2	13	○	**DON'T GIVE ME YOUR LIFE**	Systematic SYSCD 7
18/11/1995	17	3		WRAP ME UP	Systematic SYSCD 22
19/10/1996	28	2		READ MY LIPS (REMIX)	Systematic SYSCD 30

ALEXIA
Italian dance singer (born Alessia Aquilani, 19/5/1967, La Spezia) who worked with Ragazzi Di Migliarina, Brother Machine and Ice MC before her first solo single in 1995.

DATE	POS	WKS	SINGLE TITLE	LABEL & NUMBER
21/03/1998	10	9	**UH LA LA LA**	Dance Pool ALEX 1CD
13/06/1998	17	4	GIMME LOVE	Dance Pool ALEX 2CDZ
10/10/1998	31	2	THE MUSIC I LIKE	Dance Pool ALEX 3CD
22/02/2003	48	1	RING	Virgin VSCDT 1836

ALFI AND HARRY
US singer David Seville (born Ross Bagdasarian, 27/1/1919, Fresno, CA) who was also responsible for the Chipmunks. He died on 16/1/1972.

DATE	POS	WKS	SINGLE TITLE	LABEL & NUMBER
23/03/1956	15	5	THE TROUBLE WITH HARRY Inspired by the 1955 Alfred Hitchcock film of the same name	London HLU 8242

ALFIE
UK group formed in Manchester by Lee Gorton (vocals), Ian Smith (guitar), Matt McGeever (cello), Sam Morris (bass) and Sean Kelly (drums).

DATE	POS	WKS	SINGLE TITLE	LABEL & NUMBER
08/09/2001	61	1	YOU MAKE NO BONES	Twisted Nerve TN 033CD
16/03/2002	66	1	A WORD IN YOUR EAR	Twisted Nerve TN 037CD
21/06/2003	53	1	PEOPLE	Regal Recordings REG 84CD
13/09/2003	51	1	STUNTMAN	Regal Recordings REG 87CDS
28/02/2004	66	1	NO NEED	Regal Recordings REG 99CD

JOHN ALFORD
UK actor/singer (born John Shannon, 30/10/1971, Glasgow) who appeared in TV's *Grange Hill* (as Robbie Wright) and *London's Burning* as Billy Ray – from which he was sacked (and jailed for nine months) after a newspaper revealed he was supplying drugs.

DATE	POS	WKS	SINGLE TITLE	LABEL & NUMBER
17/02/1996	13	5	SMOKE GETS IN YOUR EYES	Love This LUVTHISCD 7
25/05/1996	9	4	**BLUE MOON/ONLY YOU**	Love This LUVTHISCDX 9
23/11/1996	24	3	IF/KEEP ON RUNNING	Love This LUVTHISCD 15

ALI
UK singer (born Alistair Tennant, 1973, London).

DATE	POS	WKS	SINGLE TITLE	LABEL & NUMBER
23/05/1998	63	1	LOVE LETTERS	Wild Card 5698092
24/10/1998	63	1	FEELIN' YOU	Wild Card 5676992

TATYANA ALI
US singer (born Tatyana Marisol Ali, 24/1/1979, Brooklyn, NYC) who relocated to Los Angeles, CA with her family at the age of four. She appeared as an actress in TV's *Sesame Street* and (as Ashley Banks) with Will Smith in *The Fresh Prince Of Bel Air*, before launching a singing career.

DATE	POS	WKS	BPI	SINGLE TITLE	LABEL & NUMBER
14/11/1998	6	5		**DAYDREAMIN'** Features the uncredited contribution of Lord Tariq and Peter Gunz and contains a sample of Steely Dan's *Black Cow*	Epic 6669372
13/02/1999	3	9	○	**BOY YOU KNOCK ME OUT** TATYANA ALI FEATURING WILL SMITH Contains samples of Bobby Caldwell's *What You Won't Do For Love* and Kool & The Gang's *Summer Madness*	MJJ 6674742
19/06/1999	20	4		EVERYTIME	Epic 6665462

❶⁹ Number of weeks single topped the UK chart ↑ Entered the UK chart at #1 ▲⁹ Number of weeks single topped the US chart

17

ALI AND FRAZIER
UK vocal duo Kirsty Ali and Natasha Frazier. Both were seventeen at the time of their hit, sharing a flat in Streatham, London.

07/08/1993	33	4	UPTOWN TOP RANKING	Arista 74321158842

ALIBI
UK vocal duo.

15/02/1997	51	1	I'M NOT TO BLAME	Urgent 74321434762
07/02/1998	58	1	HOW MUCH I FEEL	Urgent 74321548472

ALICE BAND
UK/Irish/US group formed in London by Amy (born in Glasgow), Audrey (born in Dublin) and Charity (born in Plant City, FL).

23/06/2001	52	1	ONE DAY AT A TIME	Instant Karma KARMA 5CD
27/04/2002	44	1	NOW THAT YOU LOVE ME	Instant Karma KARMA 17CD

ALICE DEEJAY
Dutch dance group formed by producers Pronti (born Eelke Kalberg), Kalmani (born Sebastiaan Molijn) and DJ Jurgen, fronted by 23-year-old singer Judy with Gaby and Jane.

31/07/1999	2	16	✪ BETTER OFF ALONE DJ JURGEN PRESENTS ALICE DEEJAY	Positiva CDTIV 113
04/12/1999	4	15	● BACK IN MY LIFE	Positiva CDTIV 121
15/07/2000	7	10	WILL I EVER	Positiva CDTIV 134
21/10/2000	16	5	THE LONELY ONE	Positiva CDTIV 145
10/02/2001	17	4	CELEBRATE OUR LOVE	Positiva CDTIV 149

ALICE IN CHAINS
US group formed in Seattle, WA in 1987 by Jerry Cantrell (born 18/3/1966, Tacoma, WA, guitar), Layne Stanley (born 22/8/1967, Kirkland, WA, vocals), Mike Inez (born 14/5/1966, San Fernando, CA, bass) and Sean Kinney (born 27/6/1966, Seattle, drums). Signed by Columbia in 1989, their debut album appeared in 1990. Cantrell went solo in 1997. Stanley was found dead in his apartment on 19/4/2002, cause of death unknown, but the body may have lain undiscovered for up to two weeks.

23/01/1993	19	3	WOULD Featured in the 1992 film *Singles*	Columbia 6588882
20/03/1993	26	3	THEM BONES	Columbia 6590902
05/06/1993	33	2	ANGRY CHAIR	Columbia 6593652
23/10/1993	36	2	DOWN IN A HOLE	Columbia 6597512
11/11/1995	23	2	GRIND	Columbia 6626232
10/02/1996	35	2	HEAVEN BESIDE YOU	Columbia 6628935

ALIEN ANT FARM
US rock group formed in Los Angeles, CA in 1995 by Dryden Mitchell (vocals), Terry Corso (guitar), Tye Zamora (bass) and Mike Cosgrove (drums). They signed with Dreamworks imprint New Noize in 2000.

30/06/2001	53	1	MOVIES	DreamWorks 4508992
08/09/2001	74	2	SMOOTH CRIMINAL (IMPORT)	DreamWorks 4508852CD
29/09/2001	3	13	SMOOTH CRIMINAL Featured in the 2001 film *American Pie 2*	DreamWorks DRMDM 50887
16/02/2002	5	8	MOVIES Re-issue of DreamWorks 4508992	DreamWorks 4508492
25/05/2002	66	1	ATTITUDE	DreamWorks 4508292

ALIEN VOICES FEATURING THE THREE DEGREES
UK producer Andros Georgiou with US vocal trio The Three Degrees. Georgiou had recorded as Boogie Box High and Andy G's Starsky & Hutch All Stars, and also assembled Fierce.

26/12/1998	54	2	LAST CHRISTMAS	Wildstar CDWILD 15

ALISHA
US singer (born in Brooklyn, NYC) who was still a teenager at the time of her debut hit.

25/01/1986	67	2	BABY TALK	Total Control TOCO 6

ALISHA'S ATTIC
UK duo from Essex, sisters Karen (born 8/1/1971) and Shelley Poole (born 20/3/1972) who were daughters of former Tremeloes frontman Brian Poole. They were discovered after sending a demo to Dave Stewart, who produced their debut album.

03/08/1996	14	10	I AM, I FEEL	Mercury AATDD 1
02/11/1996	12	6	ALISHA RULES THE WORLD	Mercury AATCD 2
15/03/1997	12	6	INDESTRUCTIBLE	Mercury AATCD 3
12/07/1997	12	6	AIR WE BREATHE	Mercury AATCD 4
19/09/1998	13	7	THE INCIDENTALS	Mercury AATCD 5
09/01/1999	29	5	WISH I WERE YOU	Mercury AATDD 6
17/04/1999	34	2	BARBARELLA	Mercury AATCD 7
24/03/2001	24	4	PUSH IT ALL ASIDE	Mercury AATDD 8
28/07/2001	43	1	PRETENDER GOT MY HEART	Mercury AATDD 9

ALIVE FEATURING DD KLEIN
Italian production group fronted by singer DD Klein.

27/07/2002	49	1	ALIVE	Serious CDAMPM 153

ALIZEE
French singer (born Alizee Jacotet, 21/8/1984, Corsica) who took dancing lessons from the age of four and was chosen by songwriters Mylen Farmer and Laurent Boutonnat to record *Moi Lolita* in 2000, the single selling more than 1.5 million copies in France.

23/02/2002	9	9	MOI LOLITA	Polydor 5705952

ALKALINE TRIO
UK rock group formed in 1997 by Matt Skiba (guitar/vocals), Rob Doran (bass/vocals) and Glenn Porter (drums/vocals). Doran left the same year and was replaced by Dan Andriano. Porter left in 2000 and was replaced by Mike Felumlee.

○ Silver disc ● Gold disc ✪ Platinum disc (additional platinum units are indicated by a figure following the symbol) ◎ Singles released prior to 1973 that are known to have sold over 1 million copies in the UK

02/02/2002	51	1		PRIVATE EYE	B Unique/Vagrant BUN 013CDX
30/03/2002	53	1		STUPID KID	B Unique/Vagrant BUN 016CD
26/07/2003	50	1		WE'VE HAD ENOUGH	Vagrant 9809023
18/10/2003	60	1		ALL ON BLACK	Interscope 9811506

ALL ABOUT EVE
UK gothic-styled group formed in 1985 as The Swarm by Julianne Regan (vocals), Manuella Zwingman, James Jackson (bass) and Tim Bricheno (guitar). Re-forming as All About Eve, they comprised Regan, Bricheno, Andy Cousin (bass) and Mark Price (drums). They also set up the Eden label. Regan was previously a journalist for *Zig Zag* magazine, and a member of Gene Loves Jezabel. They disbanded in 1992, with Cousin joining The Mission and Regan going solo in 1995. The group re-formed in 2004.

31/10/1987	47	5		IN THE CLOUDS	Mercury EVEN 5
23/01/1988	33	4		WILD HEARTED WOMAN	Mercury EVEN 6
16/04/1988	30	5		EVERY ANGEL	Mercury EVEN 7
30/07/1988	10	8		**MARTHA'S HARBOUR**	Mercury EVEN 8
12/11/1988	29	4		WHAT KIND OF FOOL	Mercury EVEN 9
30/09/1989	37	4		ROAD TO YOUR SOUL	Mercury EVEN 10
23/12/1989	34	5		DECEMBER	Mercury EVEN 11
28/04/1990	34	2		SCARLET	Mercury EVEN 12
15/06/1991	36	2		FAREWELL MR SORROW	Mercury EVEN 14
10/08/1991	50	3		STRANGE WAY	Vertigo EVEN 15
19/10/1991	41	2		THE DREAMER	Vertigo EVEN 16
10/10/1992	38	2		PHASED (EP) Tracks on EP: *Phased, Mine, Infra Red* and *Ascent-Descent*	MCA MCS 1688
28/11/1992	57	1		SOME FINER DAY	MCA MCS 1706
05/06/2004	52	1		LET ME GO HOME	Voiceprint AAEVP 10CD2

ALL AMERICAN REJECTS
US rock group formed in Stillwater, OK in 2000 by Tyson Ritter (bass/vocals), Nick Wheeler (guitar/programming), Mike Kennerty (guitar) and Chris Gaylor (drums).

02/08/2003	13	5		SWING SWING Featured in the 2003 film *American Wedding*	DreamWorks 4504616
22/11/2003	69	1		THE LAST SONG	DreamWorks 4504641

ALL BLUE
UK vocal duo produced by Kerri Chandler and Jerome Sydenham.

21/08/1999	73	1		PRISONER	WEA 213CD1

ALL EYES
UK vocal group Dudley, Freddy, Nico and Owen who are managed by former Bros star Matt Goss. The four first met while recording an advertisement for Specsavers.

13/11/2004	65	1		SHE'S A VISION Released to raise funds for Guide Dogs	Specsavers CXSPECS1

ALL-4-ONE
US R&B vocal group formed in California by Jamie Jones, Tony Borowiak, Delious Kennedy and Alfred Nevarez.

02/04/1994	60	1		SO MUCH IN LOVE	Atlantic A 7261CD
18/06/1994	2	18	✪	I SWEAR ▲[11] 1994 Grammy Award for Best Pop Performance by a Group	Atlantic A 7255CD
19/11/1994	49	2		SO MUCH IN LOVE (REMIX)	Atlantic A 7216CD
15/07/1995	33	2		I CAN LOVE YOU LIKE THAT	Atlantic A 8193CD

ALL SAINTS
UK/Canadian vocal group formed by Melanie Blatt (born 25/3/1975, London), Shaznay Tricia Lewis (born 14/10/1975, London) and sisters Nicole (born 7/12/1974, Canada) and Natalie Appleton (born 14/5/1973, Canada). Originally formed as a trio in 1993 by Melanie, Shaznay and Simone Rainford, they recorded three singles for ZTT as All Saints 1.9.7.5. They won two MTV Europe Music Awards: Breakthrough Act in 1998 and Best Pop Act in 2000. Natalie, Nicole and Melanie appeared in the 2000 film *Honest*, directed by Dave Stewart. They disbanded in 2001.

06/09/1997	4	8		**I KNOW WHERE IT'S AT** Contains a sample of Steely Dan's *The Fez*	London LONCD 398
22/11/1997	❶[1]	24	✪[2]	**NEVER EVER** 1998 BRIT Awards for Best Single and Best Video	London LONCD 407
09/05/1998	❶[2]	14	●	**UNDER THE BRIDGE/LADY MARMALADE** ↑ Reclaimed the #1 position on 23/5/1998. B-side featured in the 1998 film *Dr Dolittle*. *Under The Bridge* won the 1998 MOBO Award for Best Video	London LONCD 408
12/09/1998	❶[1]	11		**BOOTIE CALL** ↑	London LONCD 415
05/12/1998	7	11	○	**WAR OF NERVES**	London LONCD 421
26/02/2000	❶[2]	16	✪	**PURE SHORES** ↑ Featured in the 2000 film *The Beach*	London LONCD 444
14/10/2000	❶[1]	18	○	**BLACK COFFEE** ↑	London LONCD 454
27/01/2001	7	7		**ALL HOOKED UP**	London LONCD 456

ALL SEEING I
UK production trio from Sheffield with Parrot, 'Rubber' Johnny Buckel and Dean Honer, and vocal contributions from Jarvis Cocker, Phil Oakey and Tony Christie. The group has its own studio, The Fractal Cabbage, and has launched its own website with a dedicated channel for net radio broadcasts. Honer later recorded with Jarrod Gosling of Add N To X as I Monster.

28/03/1998	11	7		BEAT GOES ON	ffrr FCD 334
23/01/1999	10	7		WALK LIKE A PANTHER '98 THE ALL SEEING I FEATURING TONY CHRISTIE	ffrr FCDP 351
18/09/1999	28	3		1ST MAN IN SPACE Features the uncredited vocals of Phil Oakey	Ffrr FCDP 370

ALL STAR CHOIR — see DONNA SUMMER

ALL SYSTEMS GO
UK group formed in 1988 by John Kastner (vocals), Mark Arnold (guitar), Peter Arsenault (bass) and Dean Bentley (drums).

18/06/1988	63	2		POP MUZIK	Unique NIQ 03

---

❶[9] Number of weeks single topped the UK chart ↑ Entered the UK chart at #1 ▲[9] Number of weeks single topped the US chart

RICHARD ALLAN US actor/singer (born 22/6/1923, Jacksonville, IL).

24/03/1960	43	1	AS TIME GOES BY .... Parlophone R 4634

STEVE ALLAN UK singer who was also a backing singer for the Biddu Orchestra, later producing and engineering for various acts.

27/01/1979	67	2	TOGETHER WE ARE BEAUTIFUL .... Creole CR 164

DONNA ALLEN US soul singer (born in Key West, FL, raised in Tampa) who became a cheerleader for the Tampa Bay Buccaneers. She fronted Hi-Octane and then Trama before going solo. Also a much-in-demand backing singer, she has appeared on tracks by Enrique Iglesias and Ricky Martin among others. East 57th Street are a UK production trio.

18/04/1987	8	12	**SERIOUS** .... Portrait PRT 6507447
03/06/1989	10	10	**JOY AND PAIN** .... BCM 257
21/01/1995	34	2	REAL Featured in the 1994 film *The Specialist* .... Epic 6610882
11/10/1997	29	3	SATURDAY **EAST 57TH STREET FEATURING DONNA ALLEN** .... AM:PM 5823752

KEITH ALLEN — see BLACK GRAPE AND JOE STRUMMER

DOT ALLISON UK singer/songwriter (born 17/8/1969, Edinburgh) who first became known as a member of One Dove.

17/08/2002	67	1	STRUNG OUT .... Mantra MNT 74CD

ALLISONS UK duo Brian Alford (born 31/12/1939, London) and Colin Day (born 21/2/1942, Trowbridge) who first sang together in a church choir. They were publicised as brothers (Brian being 'John Allison', Colin 'Bob Allison') before disbanding in 1963, with Brian later reviving the name with Mike King and then Tony Allen. Brian and Colin re-formed The Allisons in 1988.

23/02/1961	2	16	**ARE YOU SURE** UK entry for the 1961 Eurovision Song Contest, coming second behind Jean Claude Pascal of Luxembourg's *Nous Les Amoureux* .... Fontana H 294
18/05/1961	34	5	WORDS .... Fontana H 304
15/02/1962	30	6	LESSONS IN LOVE .... Fontana H 362

ALLNIGHT BAND UK instrumental group assembled by DJ Richard Searling for a cover version of a Northern Soul hit by The Milestones.

03/02/1979	50	3	THE JOKER (THE WIGAN JOKER) .... Casino Classics CC 6

ALL-STARS — see LOUIS ARMSTRONG

ALL-STARS — see JUNIOR WALKER AND THE ALL-STARS

ALLSTARS UK vocal group formed by Sandi Lee Hughes, Thaila Zucchi, Ashley Dawson, Rebecca Hunter and Sam Bloom, first seen in the TV series *Starstreet*.

23/06/2001	20	7	BEST FRIENDS Theme to the TV series *Starstreet* .... Island CID 775
22/09/2001	12	4	THINGS THAT GO BUMP IN THE NIGHT/IS THERE SOMETHING I SHOULD KNOW? .... Island CID 783
26/01/2002	9	8	**THE LAND OF MAKE BELIEVE** .... Island CID 791
11/05/2002	19	3	BACK WHEN/GOING ALL THE WAY .... Island CID 796

ALLURE US R&B vocal group formed in New York City by Alia Davis, Lalisha McLean, Linnie Belcher and Akissa Mendez. The first act signed to Mariah Carey's Crave label (Mariah wrote and co-produced their debut hit), they switched to MCA when Crave closed. By the time they joined Truwarier Records in 2004 they were a trio of Davis, McLean and Mendez.

14/06/1997	18	3	HEAD OVER HEELS **ALLURE FEATURING NAS** Contains samples of Frankie Beverly and Maze's *Before I Let Go* and MC Shan's *The Bridge* .... Epic 6645942
10/01/1998	12	5	ALL CRIED OUT **ALLURE FEATURING 112** .... Epic 6652715

ALMIGHTY UK heavy metal group formed in Scotland by Ricky Warwick (vocals), Tantrum (guitar), Floyd London (bass) and Stumpy Munroe (drums). Tantrum left in 1991 and was replaced by Peter Friesen (ex-Alice Cooper band).

30/06/1990	50	2	WILD AND WONDERFUL .... Polydor PO 75
02/03/1991	35	2	FREE 'N' EASY .... Polydor PO 127
11/05/1991	36	2	DEVIL'S TOY .... Polydor PO 144
29/06/1991	42	2	LITTLE LOST SOMETIMES .... Polydor PO 151
03/04/1993	38	2	ADDICTION .... Polydor PZCD 261
29/05/1993	41	2	OUT OF SEASON .... Polydor PZCD 266
30/10/1993	38	2	OVER THE EDGE .... Polydor PZCD 298
24/09/1994	26	2	WRENCH .... Chrysalis CDCHS 5014
14/01/1995	26	3	JONESTOWN MIND .... Chrysalis CDCHSS 5017
16/03/1996	28	2	ALL SUSSED OUT .... Chrysalis CDCHS 5030
25/05/1996	38	1	DO YOU UNDERSTAND .... Raw Power RAWX 1022

MARC ALMOND UK singer (born 9/7/1957, Southport) who featured in Soft Cell with David Ball before going solo in 1984. He also records as Marc And The Mambas and Marc Almond And The Willing Sinners.

02/07/1983	49	3	BLACK HEART **MARC AND THE MAMBAS** .... Some Bizzare BZS 19
02/06/1984	52	5	THE BOY WHO CAME BACK .... Some Bizzare BZS 23
01/09/1984	57	3	YOU HAVE .... Some Bizzare BZS 24

DATE	POS	WKS	BPI	SINGLE TITLE	LABEL & NUMBER
20/04/1985	3	12	O	**I FEEL LOVE (MEDLEY)** BRONSKI BEAT AND MARC ALMOND Medley of *I Feel Love, Love To Love You Baby* and *Johnny Remember Me*	Forbidden Fruit BITE 4
24/08/1985	23	5		STORIES OF JOHNNY	Some Bizzare BONK 1
26/10/1985	68	3		LOVE LETTER	Some Bizzare BONK 2
04/01/1986	55	3		THE HOUSE IS HAUNTED (BY THE ECHO OF YOUR LAST GOODBYE)	Some Bizzare GLOW 1
07/06/1986	41	5		A WOMAN'S STORY MARC AND THE WILLING SINNERS	Some Bizzare GLOW 2
18/10/1986	47	3		RUBY RED	Some Bizzare GLOW 3
14/02/1987	71	1		MELANCHOLY ROSE	Some Bizzare GLOW 4
03/09/1988	26	7		TEARS RUN RINGS	Parlophone R 6186
05/11/1988	40	3		BITTER SWEET	Some Bizzare R 6194
14/01/1989	❶⁴	12	O	**SOMETHING'S GOTTEN HOLD OF MY HEART** MARC ALMOND FEATURING SPECIAL GUEST STAR GENE PITNEY	Parlophone R 6201
08/04/1989	45	2		ONLY THE MOMENT	Parlophone R 6210
03/03/1990	29	4		A LOVER SPURNED	Some Bizzare R 6229
19/05/1990	45	2		THE DESPERATE HOURS	Some Bizzare R 6252
23/03/1991	38	3		SAY HELLO WAVE GOODBYE	Mercury SOFT 1
18/05/1991	5	8		**TAINTED LOVE** This and above single credited to SOFT CELL/MARC ALMOND	Mercury SOFT 2
28/09/1991	17	6		JACKY	Some Bizzare YZ 610
11/01/1992	33	5		MY HAND OVER MY HEART	Some Bizzare YZ 633
25/04/1992	4	7		**THE DAYS OF PEARLY SPENCER**	Some Bizzare YZ 638
27/03/1993	60	2		WHAT MAKES A MAN A MAN (LIVE)	Some Bizzare YZ 720CD
13/05/1995	25	3		ADORED AND EXPLORED	Some Bizzare MERCD 431
29/07/1995	44	2		THE IDOL	Some Bizzare MERCD 437
30/12/1995	41	1		CHILD STAR	Some Bizzare MERCD 450
28/12/1996	58	2		YESTERDAY HAS GONE PJ PROBY AND MARC ALMOND FEATURING THE MY LIFE STORY ORCHESTRA	EMI Premier CDPRESX 13

ALOOF UK dub-techno group formed by Dean Hatcher, Richard Thair, Ricky Barrow, Jagz Kooner and Gary Burns.

DATE	POS	WKS	BPI	SINGLE TITLE	LABEL & NUMBER
19/09/1992	64	1		ON A MISSION	Cowboy RODEO 5
18/05/1996	61	1		WISH YOU WERE HERE	East West EW 038CD
30/11/1996	30	2		ONE NIGHT STAND	East West EW 067CD
01/03/1997	43	1		WISH YOU WERE HERE (REMIX)	East West EW 083CD1
29/08/1998	70	1		WHAT I MISS THE MOST	East West EW 179CD1

HERB ALPERT US trumpeter (born 31/3/1935, Los Angeles, CA) who began playing at the age of eight. He was a staff writer for Keen Records in 1958, penning four consecutive hits for Sam Cooke before cutting his own records for Dore Records. He teamed up with Jerry Moss in 1962 and founded Carnival Records, which later became A&M (based on their initials) and was subsequently sold to Seagram for $500 million in 1989. He has won six Grammy Awards including Record of the Year, Best Instrumental Performance and Best Instrumental Arrangement in 1965 for *A Taste Of Honey,* and Best Instrumental Performance and Best Instrumental Arrangement in 1965 for *What Now My Love*. Tijuana Brass was a studio band until 1965 when a proper group was assembled. Along with Jerry Moss he has a star on the Hollywood Walk of Fame. The pair later formed Almo Records.

DATE	POS	WKS	BPI	SINGLE TITLE	LABEL & NUMBER
03/01/1963	22	9		THE LONELY BULL HERB ALPERT AND THE TIJUANA BRASS	Stateside SS 138
09/12/1965	3	20		**SPANISH FLEA** Theme to the US TV show *The Dating Game*	Pye International 7N 25335
24/03/1966	37	4		TIJUANA TAXI	Pye International 7N 25352
27/04/1967	27	14		CASINO ROYALE HERB ALPERT Featured in the 1967 James Bond spoof film *Casino Royale*. Alpert also recorded *Never Say Never Again,* another unofficial James Bond theme, that featured his wife Lani Hall on vocals	A&M AMS 700
03/07/1968	3	19		**THIS GUY'S IN LOVE WITH YOU** ▲⁵	A&M AMS 727
18/06/1969	36	5		WITHOUT HER	A&M AMS 755
12/12/1970	42	3		JERUSALEM	A&M AMS 810
13/10/1979	13	13		RISE ▲² 1979 Grammy Award for Best Pop Instrumental Performance	A&M AMS 7465
19/01/1980	46	3		ROTATION	A&M AMS 7500
28/03/1987	19	9		KEEP YOUR EYE ON ME	Breakout USA 602
13/06/1987	27	7		DIAMONDS Features the uncredited vocals of Janet Jackson and Lisa Keith	Breakout USA 605

ALPHA-BETA – see IZHAR COHEN AND THE ALPHA-BETA

ALPHAVILLE German rock group formed in Berlin in 1983 by Marian Gold (vocals), Frank Mertens (keyboards) and Bernhard Lloyd (drums).

DATE	POS	WKS	BPI	SINGLE TITLE	LABEL & NUMBER
18/08/1984	8	13		**BIG IN JAPAN**	WEA International X9505

ALPINESTARS FEATURING BRIAN MOLKO UK production duo from Manchester Richard Woolgar and Glyn Thomas, with singer Brian Molko.

DATE	POS	WKS	BPI	SINGLE TITLE	LABEL & NUMBER
22/06/2002	63	1		CARBON KID	Riverman RMR 11VS

ALSOU Russian singer (born Alsou Tenisheva, Siberia) whose debut hit when she was seventeen was Russia's entrant into the 2001 Eurovision Song Contest. She later relocated to London.

DATE	POS	WKS	BPI	SINGLE TITLE	LABEL & NUMBER
12/05/2001	27	3		BEFORE YOU LOVE ME	Mercury 1589142

GERALD ALSTON US singer (born 8/11/1942, North Carolina) who joined The Manhattans in 1970, eventually going solo in 1988.

DATE	POS	WKS	BPI	SINGLE TITLE	LABEL & NUMBER
15/04/1989	73	1		ACTIVATED	RCA ZB 42681

❶⁹ Number of weeks single topped the UK chart ↑ Entered the UK chart at #1 ▲⁹ Number of weeks single topped the US chart

ALTER EGO German production duo Roman Fluegel and Jorn Elling.

11/12/2004.....32.....3+......	ROCKER	Skint SKINT103CD

ALTERED IMAGES UK group formed in Scotland by Claire Grogan (born 17/3/1962, vocals), Tony McDaid (guitar), Jim McKinven (guitar/keyboards), Michael 'Tich' Anderson (drums) and John McElhone (bass). Grogan later became an actress, debuting in the 1981 film *Gregory's Girl* and later appearing in *Eastenders* as Ros Thorne. She formed Universal Love School in 1989; McElhone joined Hipsway and then Texas.

28/03/1981.....67......2......	DEAD POP STARS... Epic EPC A 1023
26/09/1981.....2.....17......O	**HAPPY BIRTHDAY**.. Epic EPC A 1522
12/12/1981.....7.....12......O	**I COULD BE HAPPY**.. Epic EPC A 1834
27/03/1982.....11......7......	SEE THOSE EYES... Epic EPC A 2198
22/05/1982.....35......6......	PINKY BLUE... Epic EPC A 2426
19/03/1983.....7......7......	**DON'T TALK TO ME ABOUT LOVE**.............................. Epic EPC A 3083
28/05/1983.....29......6......	BRING ME CLOSER.. Epic EPC A 3398
16/07/1983.....46......3......	LOVE TO STAY... Epic EPC A 3582

ALTERN 8 UK keyboard duo Chris Peat and Mark Archer, who claimed to have been deckchair attendants and met while working as studio engineers at Blue Chip Studios. Archer later joined Slo-Moshun.

13/07/1991.....28......7......	INFILTRATE 202... Network NWK 24
16/11/1991.....3......9......	**ACTIV 8 (COME WITH ME)**................................... Network NWK 34
08/02/1992.....41......1......	FREQUENCY.. Network NWK 37
11/04/1992.....6......6......	**EVAPOR 8** Features the uncredited contribution of PP Arnold...... Network NWK 38
04/07/1992.....16......4......	HYPNOTIC ST-8.. Network NWK 49
10/10/1992.....74......1......	SHAME.. Network NWKTEN 56
12/12/1992.....43......5......	BRUTAL-8-E... Network NWK 59
03/07/1993.....58......1......	EVERYBODY .... Network NWKCD 73

ALTHIA AND DONNA Jamaican vocal duo Althia Forest (born 1960) and Donna Reid (born 1959). Their debut hit was a rewrite of the reggae song *Three Piece Suit* by Trinity, with local slang words in the lyrics.

24/12/1977 ....●[1].....11......O	**UP TOWN TOP RANKING**..................................... Lightning LIG 506

ALVIN AND THE CHIPMUNKS – see CHIPMUNKS

ALY-US US vocal/instrumental group formed by Kyle Smith, Tony Humphries and Doc Martin.

21/11/1992.....43......2......	FOLLOW ME.. Cooltempo COOL 266
25/05/2002.....54......1......	FOLLOW ME (REMIX)... Strictly Rhythm SRUKCD 05

SHOLA AMA UK singer (born Mathurin Campbell) who was discovered at the age of fifteen by D'Influence, making her recording debut for Freak Street in 1995. She was named Best Rhythm & Blues Act and Best Newcomer at the 1997 MOBO Awards and Best UK Female Artist at the 1998 BRIT Awards.

19/04/1997 .....4.....14......O	**YOU MIGHT NEED SOMEBODY**................................. WEA 097CD
30/08/1997.....3......8......	**YOU'RE THE ONE I LOVE** Originally released the previous year without success.........Freakstreet WEA 121CD1
29/11/1997.....13......7......	WHO'S LOVING MY BABY..................................... Freakstreet WEA 145 CD1
21/02/1998.....17......3......	MUCH LOVE.. WEA 154CD1
11/04/1998.....28......3......	SOMEDAY I'LL FIND YOU **SHOLA AMA WITH CRAIG ARMSTRONG** Listed flip side was *I've Been To A Marvellous Party* **DIVINE COMEDY**. Both tracks were taken from the Noel Coward commemorative album *Twentieth Century Blues* .... EMI CDTCB 001
17/04/1999.....10......8......	**TABOO GLAMMA KID FEATURING SHOLA AMA** .... WEA 203CD
06/11/1999.....26......3......	STILL BELIEVE.. WEA 239CD1
29/04/2000.....24......4......	IMAGINE.. WEA 252CD
11/09/2004 .....8......8......	**YOU SHOULD REALLY KNOW** PIRATES, ENYA, SHOLA AMA, NAILA BOSS & ISHANI .... Relentless RELCD9

EDDIE AMADOR US DJ/producer (born in Phoenix, AZ) who moved to Los Angeles, CA in 1997 and later formed Saturated Soul with Ian Carey.

24/10/1998.....37......2......	HOUSE MUSIC.. Pukka CDPUKKA 18
22/01/2000.....19......3......	RISE... Defected DEFECT 9CDS

RUBY AMANFU Ghanaian singer (born 23/6/1979) who grew up in Nashville, TN.

15/03/2003.....32......2......	SUGAH.. Polydor 0658302

AMAR UK singer/instrumentalist (born Amar Nagi).

09/09/2000.....48......1......	SOMETIMES (IT SNOWS IN APRIL)............................. Blanco Y Negro NEG 129CD

AMAZULU UK group formed by Annie Ruddock (born 2/7/1961, vocals), Rose Minor (vocals), Sharon Bailey (born 22/11/1957, percussion), Lesley Beach (born 30/9/1954, saxophone), Margo Sagov (guitar), Claire Kenny (bass) and Debbie Evans (drums).

06/07/1985.....12.....13......	EXCITABLE... Island IS 201
23/11/1985.....15.....11......	DON'T YOU JUST KNOW IT.................................... Island IS 233
15/03/1986.....43......6......	THE THINGS THE LONELY DO................................. Island IS 267
31/05/1986 .....5.....13......O	**TOO GOOD TO BE FORGOTTEN**............................... Island IS 284
13/09/1986.....16......9......	MONTEGO BAY... Island IS 293

O Silver disc   ● Gold disc   ✪ Platinum disc (additional platinum units are indicated by a figure following the symbol)   ◉ Singles released prior to 1973 that are known to have sold over 1 million copies in the UK

10/10/1987.....38......5....... MONY MONY .... EMI EM 32

AMBASSADOR
Dutch producer Mischa Van Der Heiden who also records as DJ Misjah and is a member of Jonah.

12/02/2000.....67......1....... ONE OF THESE DAYS .... Platipus PLATCD 69

AMBASSADORS OF FUNK FEATURING MC MARIO
UK group formed by Simon Harris with MC Mario and rapper Einstein (Colin Case). Harris also recorded as World Warrior and under his own name.

31/10/1992.....8......8....... **SUPERMARIOLAND** .... Living Beat SMASH 23

AMBER
Dutch dance singer (born Marie-Claire Cremers) who also contributed to the soundtrack of the 1998 film *54*.

24/06/2000.....34......2....... SEXUAL.. Substance SUBS 2CDS

AMBUSH
– see **RMXCRAW FEATURING EBON-E PLUS AMBUSH**

AMEN
US group formed in Los Angeles, CA in 1994 by Casey Chaos (vocals), Paul Fig (guitar), Sonny Mayo (guitar) and Shannon Larkin (drums), adding bass player John 'Tumor' Fahnestock in 1998.

17/02/2001.....72......1....... TOO HARD TO BE FREE .... Virgin VUSCD 191
21/07/2001.....61......1....... THE WAITING 18 .... Virgin VUSCD 207
03/04/2004.....52......1....... CALIFORNIA'S BLEEDING.. Columbia 6746162

AMEN CORNER
UK group formed in Cardiff in 1966 by Andy Fairweather-Low (born 2/8/1950, Ystrad Mynach, Wales, guitar/vocals), Blue Weaver (born Derek Weaver, 3/3/1949, Cardiff, organ), Neil Jones (born 25/3/1949, Llanbradach, Wales, guitar), Clive Taylor (born 27/4/1949, Cardiff, bass), Mike Smith (born 4/11/1947, Neath, tenor sax), Alan Jones (born 6/2/1947, Swansea, baritone sax) and Dennis Bryon (born 14/4/1949, Cardiff, drums). Following their split in 1970, Fairweather-Low went solo. The group appeared in the 1969 horror film *Scream And Scream Again*.

26/07/1967.....12......10...... GIN HOUSE BLUES... Deram DM 136
11/10/1967.....24......6...... WORLD OF BROKEN HEARTS .... Deram DM 151
17/01/1968.....3......12...... **BEND ME SHAPE ME** Cover version of American Breed's US #5 hit .... Deram DM 172
31/07/1968.....6......13...... **HIGH IN THE SKY** .... Deram DM 197
29/01/1969....❶²......11...... **(IF PARADISE IS) HALF AS NICE** Originally written in Italy as *Il Paradiso Belavista*, with English lyrics added by Jack Fishman........ Immediate IM 073
25/06/1969.....4......10...... **HELLO SUZIE** .... Immediate IM 081
14/02/1976.....34......5...... (IF PARADISE IS) HALF AS NICE Re-issue of Immediate IM 073................ Immediate IMS 103

AMEN! UK
UK dance group formed by Panos Liassi, Luvian Maximen and Paul Masterson. Masterson is also in the Candy Girls, The Dope Smugglaz and Hi-Gate.

08/02/1997.....15......4....... PASSION .... Feverpitch CDFVR 1015
28/06/1997.....36......2....... PEOPLE OF LOVE .... Feverpitch CDFVR 18
06/09/2003.....40......2....... PASSION Remix of Feverpitch CDFVR 1015 .... Positiva CDTIV 195

AMERICA
US trio formed in the UK in 1969 by Dewey Bunnell (born 19/1/1951, Harrogate), Gerry Beckley (born 12/9/1952, Forth Worth, TX) and Dan Peek (born 1/11/1950, Panama City, FL), the sons of US Air Force servicemen stationed in the UK. They re-located to the US after the success of their debut single. Peek left in 1976 to become a contemporary Christian artist. The group was named Best New Artist at the 1972 Grammy Awards.

18/12/1971.....3......13...... **HORSE WITH NO NAME/EVERYONE I MEET IS FROM CALIFORNIA** ▲³ .... Warner Brothers K 16128
25/11/1972.....43......4....... VENTURA HIGHWAY .... Warner Brothers K 16219
06/11/1982.....59......3....... YOU CAN DO MAGIC.. Capitol CL 264

AMERICAN BREED
US rock group formed in Cicero, IL by Gary Loizzo (born 16/8/1945, guitar/vocals), Charles 'Chuck' Colbert (born 29/8/1944, bass), Alan Ciner (born 14/5/1947, guitar) and Lee Anthony Graziano (born 9/11/1943, drums) as Gary & The Nite Lights, signing to the Acta label in 1966. Later members Andre Fischer and Kevin Murphy formed Rufus.

07/02/1968.....24......6....... BEND ME SHAPE ME Biggest UK hit achieved by Amen Corner............................ Stateside SS 2078

AMERICAN HEAD CHARGE
US rock group formed in Minneapolis by David Rogers (guitar), Martin Cock (guitar/vocals), Christopher Emery (drums), Justin Fowler (keyboards), Chad Hanks (bass), Wayne Kile (guitar) and Aaron Zilch ('audio meat grinder').

08/06/2002.....52......1....... JUST SO YOU KNOW.. Mercury 5829622

AMERICAN HI-FI
US group formed in Boston, MA by Jaime Arentzen (guitar), Drew Parsons (bass), Brian Nolan (drums) and Stacy Jones (drums/vocals).

08/09/2001.....31......3....... FLAVOR OF THE WEAK Featured in the 2001 film *American Pie 2*........................... Mercury 5886722
26/04/2003.....75......1....... THE ART OF LOSING Featured in the films *American Wedding* (2003) and *Freaky Friday* (2003)............. Mercury 0779152

AMERICAN MUSIC CLUB
US group formed in San Francisco, CA by Mark Eitzel (born 1959, Walnut Creek, San Francisco, CA, guitar/vocals), Danny Pearson (bass), Vudi (guitar), Bruce Kaphan (steel guitar) and Tim Mooney (drums). Eitzel went solo in 1995.

24/04/1993.....58......2....... JOHNNY MATHIS' FEET .... Virgin VSCDG 1445
10/09/1994.....46......2....... WISH THE WORLD AWAY .... Virgin VSCDX 1512

AMERIE
US R&B singer (born Amerie Rogers, 1980, Brooklyn, NYC), with a Korean mother and US father, who was raised at various military camps before settling in Washington DC.

❶⁹ Number of weeks single topped the UK chart ↑ Entered the UK chart at #1 ▲⁹ Number of weeks single topped the US chart

23

| 09/11/2002.....40......2...... | WHY DON'T WE FALL IN LOVE **AMERIE FEATURING LUDACRIS**... Columbia 6732212 |
| 22/02/2003.....18......5...... | PARADISE **LL COOL J FEATURING AMERIE** Contains a sample of Keni Burke's *Risin' To The Top*............... Def Jam 0637242 |

AMES BROTHERS US family group formed in Malden, MA by Ed (born 9/7/1927), Gene (born 13/2/1925), Joe (born 3/5/1924) and Vic Ulrick (born 20/5/1926) who became the Ames Brothers. Ed Ames recorded solo after the group disbanded in 1960 and later acted in a number of stage productions in New York. Vic was killed in a car crash on 23/1/1978.

| 04/02/1955 .....6......6....... | **NAUGHTY LADY OF SHADY LANE**.. HMV 10800 |

AMIL – see **JAY-Z**

AMILLIONSONS UK production group formed by Robin Junga, Matt Shelton and Sam Toolan featuring US singer Taka Boom. Their debut hit was originally a white label sampling Dorothy Moore's version of *Misty Blue* but was released with Taka Boom having re-recorded the female vocal parts.

| 24/08/2002.....39......2...... | **MISTI BLU**.. London LONCD 468 |

AMIRA US singer (born Amira McNiel).

13/12/1997.....51......1.......	MY DESIRE.. VC Recordings VCRD 27
08/08/1998.....46......2.......	MY DESIRE (REMIX)... VC Recordings VCRD 36
10/02/2001.....20......4.......	MY DESIRE (2ND REMIX)... VC Recordings VCRD 71

CHERIE AMORE French singer.

| 15/04/2000.....33......2...... | I DON'T WANT NOBODY (TELLIN' ME WHAT TO DO) .... Eternal WEA 262CD |

VANESSA AMOROSI Australian vocalist (born 8/8/1981, Melbourne) discovered singing in a Russian restaurant in her hometown in 1997. She signed with management company MarJac Productions in 1998.

| 23/09/2000 .....7......10 ...... | **ABSOLUTELY EVERYBODY**.. Mercury 1582972 |

AMOS UK producer/remixer (born Amos Pizzey) who originally sang with Culture Club, later forming Dark City and Ice before going solo in 1993. He also recorded as Bleachin'.

03/09/1994.....48......2......	ONLY SAW TODAY – INSTANT KARMA .... Positiva CDTIV 16
25/03/1995.....31......2......	LET LOVE SHINE .... Positiva CDTIV 24
07/10/1995.....54......1......	CHURCH OF FREEDOM .... Positiva CDTIV 38
12/10/1996.....11......5......	STAMP! .... Positiva CDTIV 65
31/05/1997.....30......2......	ARGENTINA This and above single credited to **JEREMY HEALY AND AMOS** .... Positiva CDTIV 74

TORI AMOS US singer (born Myra Ellen Amos, 22/8/1963, Newton, NC) who first made demos with Narada Michael Walden in 1983, without success. She signed with US Atlantic in 1987 and fronted Y Kant Tori Read before going solo in 1991.

23/11/1991.....51......3......	SILENT ALL THESE YEARS... East West YZ 618
01/02/1992.....51......2......	CHINA... East West YZ 7531
21/03/1992.....25......4......	WINTER Tracks on EP: *Winter, Pool, Take To The Sky, Sweet Dreams, Angie, Smells Like Teen Spirit* and *Thank You*............
	.... East West A 7504
20/06/1992.....15......6......	CRUCIFY Tracks on EP: *Crucify (Remix), Here In My Head, Mary, Crucify, Little Earthquakes, Crucify (Live), Precious Things*
	and *Mother* .... East West A 7479
22/08/1992.....26......4......	SILENT ALL THESE YEARS... East West A 7433
22/01/1994.....4......6......	**CORNFLAKE GIRL**.. East West A 7281CD
19/03/1994.....7......4......	**PRETTY GOOD YEAR**... East West A 7263CD
28/05/1994.....31......3......	PAST THE MISSION Features the uncredited contribution of Trent Reznor of Nine Inch Nails .... East West YZ 7257CD
15/10/1994.....44......2......	GOD.. East West A 7251CD
13/01/1996.....20......3......	CAUGHT A LITE SNEEZE... East West A 5524CD2
23/03/1996.....22......2......	TALULA... East West A 8512CD
03/08/1996.....20......9......	HEY JUPITER/PROFESSIONAL WIDOW B-side featured in the 1996 film *Escape From L.A* .... East West A 5494CD
09/11/1996.....26......2......	BLUE SKIES.. Perfecto PERF 130CD1
11/01/1997 ....●[1].....10 .....○	**PROFESSIONAL WIDOW (IT'S GOT TO BE BIG) (REMIX)** .... East West A 5450CD
02/05/1998.....16......3......	SPARK .... East West AT 0031CD
13/11/1999.....46......1......	GLORY OF THE 80'S .... Atlantic AT 0077CD1
26/10/2002.....41......2......	A SORTA FAIRYTALE... Epic 6730432

AMOURE UK production duo Rod Edwards and Nick Magnus.

| 27/05/2000.....33......2...... | IS THAT YOUR FINAL ANSWER? (WHO WANTS TO BE A MILLIONAIRE – THE SINGLE)....................... Celador MILLION 2 |

AMP FIDDLER US keyboard player (born Joseph Fiddler in Detroit, MI) who was previously a member of P Funk and also recorded as Amp Dog Knight.

| 20/03/2004.....72......1...... | I BELIEVE IN YOU.. Genuine GEN022CD |
| 19/06/2004.....71......1...... | DREAMIN' .... Genuine GEN025CDM |

AMPS US group formed in 1994 by Kim Deal (guitar/vocals), Nathan Farley (guitar), Luis Lerma (bass) and Jim MacPherson (drums) as Tammy & The Amps. Deal and MacPherson had previously been in The Breeders.

| 21/10/1995.....61......1....... | TIPP CITY... 4AD BAD 5015CD |

ANDREA ANATOLA – see SODA CLUB

ANASTACIA
US singer (born Anastacia Newkirk, 17/9/1973, New York, raised in Chicago, IL) who, following her parents' divorce, graduated from the Professional Children's School in Manhattan. Diagnosed as suffering from Crohn's Disease at the age of thirteen, she overcame the symptoms to become a dancer, appearing on *Club MTV* and in the Salt-N-Pepa videos for *Everybody Get Up* and *Twist And Shout* (although in January 2003 she was diagnosed with breast cancer). After winning through to the final of the *Star Search* contest, she was signed by Daylight Records in March 1999. Named Best Pop Act at the 2001 MTV Europe Music Awards, she also performed at the 2002 FIFA World Cup draw in Japan.

30/09/2000	6	17	O	I'M OUTTA LOVE	Epic 6695782
03/02/2001	11	8		NOT THAT KIND	Epic 6707632
02/06/2001	28	5		COWBOYS & KISSES	Epic 6712622
25/08/2001	27	3		MADE FOR LOVIN' YOU	Epic 6717172
01/12/2001	14	9		PAID MY DUES	Epic 6721252
06/04/2002	11	9		ONE DAY IN YOUR LIFE	Epic 6724562
21/09/2002	25	5		WHY'D YOU LIE TO ME	Epic 6731112
07/12/2002	31	3		YOU'LL NEVER BE ALONE	Epic 6733802
03/04/2004	3	20	O	LEFT OUTSIDE ALONE	Epic 6746482
14/08/2004	4	11		SICK AND TIRED	Epic 6751092
27/11/2004	25	5+		WELCOME TO MY TRUTH	Epic 6754922

AND WHY NOT?
UK group formed by Wayne Gidden (guitar/vocals), Hylton Hayles (bass) and Michael Steer (drums).

14/10/1989	38	7		RESTLESS DAYS (SHE CRIES OUT LOUD)	Island IS 426
13/01/1990	13	8		THE FACE	Island IS 444
21/04/1990	39	3		SOMETHING YOU GOT	Island 452

...AND YOU WILL KNOW US BY THE TRAIL OF DEAD
US band formed in Austin, TX in 1994 by Jason Reece (guitar/drums/vocals), Conrad Keely (guitar/drums/vocals), Kevin Allen (guitar) and Neil Busch (bass/samples). Their debut album was for Trance Syndicate in 1998; following the label's collapse, the group joined Merge in 1999.

| 11/11/2000 | 69 | 1 | | MISTAKES AND REGRETS | Domino RUG 114CD |
| 11/05/2002 | 54 | 1 | | ANOTHER MORNING STONER | Interscope 4977162 |

ANGRY ANDERSON
Australian singer/actor (born Gary Stephen Anderson, 5/8/1948) who had previously been with Rose Tattoo before going solo.

| 19/11/1988 | 3 | 13 | O | SUDDENLY | Food For Thought YUM 113 |

CARL ANDERSON
US R&B singer (born 27/2/1945, Lynchburg, VA) who played Judas in the musical, film and Broadway version of *Jesus Christ Superstar* before recording with Gloria Loring and Weather Report. He died from leukaemia on 23/2/2004.

| 08/06/1985 | 49 | 4 | | BUTTERCUP | Streetwave KHAN 45 |

CARLEEN ANDERSON
US R&B singer (born 1957, Houston, TX), the daughter of former James Brown backing singer Vicki Anderson (her stepfather is Bobby Byrd, a member of Brown's Famous Flames). She trained as a music teacher in Los Angeles, CA before coming to London and guesting on The Young Disciples' hit *Apparently Nothing*. She became the Brand New Heavies' lead singer from 1999; their first hit was a cover version of *Apparently Nothing*.

12/02/1994	27	4		NERVOUS BREAKDOWN	Circa YRCDG 112
28/05/1994	26	4		MAMA SAID	Circa YRCD 114
13/08/1994	24	3		TRUE SPIRIT	Circa YRCD 118
14/01/1995	16	3		LET IT LAST	Circa YRCDG 119
07/02/1998	24	2		MAYBE I'M AMAZED	Circa YRCD 128
25/04/1998	74	1		WOMAN IN ME	Circa YRCD 129

GILLIAN ANDERSON – see HAL FEATURING GILLIAN ANDERSON

JOHN ANDERSON BIG BAND
UK orchestra leader (born in Derry City) who also formed the Forest City Jazz Band and John Anderson Trio.

| 21/12/1985 | 61 | 5 | | GLENN MILLER MEDLEY Medley of *In The Mood, American Patrol, Little Brown Jug* and *Pennsylvania 65000* | Modern GLEN 1 |

LAURIE ANDERSON
US singer/composer/violinist/sculptor/filmmaker (born 5/6/1947, Chicago, IL) who has made and scored films/multimedia productions including *United States I–IV* (1983; the soundtrack was originally released as a five-album box set), *Mister Heartbreak* (1984) and *Home Of The Brave* (1986).

| 17/10/1981 | 2 | 6 | | O SUPERMAN | Warner Brothers K 17870 |

LC ANDERSON VS PSYCHO RADIO
UK singer Leroy Charles Anderson with Italian production group Daniele Tignino and Pat Legoto.

| 26/07/2003 | 45 | 2 | | RIGHT STUFF | Faith & Hope FHCD039 |

LYNN ANDERSON
US country singer (born 26/9/1947, Grand Forks, ND, raised in Sacramento, CA) who won the California Horse Show Queen title in 1966.

| 20/02/1971 | 3 | 20 | | ROSE GARDEN 1970 Grammy Award for Best Country & Western Vocal Performance | CBS 5360 |

❶⁹ Number of weeks single topped the UK chart ↑ Entered the UK chart at #1 ▲⁹ Number of weeks single topped the US chart

25

LEROY ANDERSON AND HIS POPS CONCERT ORCHESTRA
US orchestra leader (born 29/6/1908, Cambridge, MA) and musical tutor at Radcliffe College. One of the best-known composers, conductors and arrangers in the US, he died on 18/5/1975.

28/06/1957	24	4		FORGOTTEN DREAMS	Brunswick 05485

MOIRA ANDERSON
UK singer (born 1938, Kirkintilloch, East Dunbartonshire) educated at Ayr Academy.

27/12/1969	43	2		THE HOLY CITY	Decca F 12989

SUNSHINE ANDERSON
US singer (born 26/10/1975, Charlotte, NC) who was discovered while queuing at a cafe at North Carolina Central University (where she earned a Bachelor of Science degree in criminal justice). She moved to Washington DC to work for the government, then relocated to Los Angeles and is managed by Macy Gray.

02/06/2001	9	7		**HEARD IT ALL BEFORE**	Atlantic AT 0100CD
22/09/2001	57	1		LUNCH OR DINNER	Atlantic AT 0109CD

ANDERSON BRUFORD WAKEMAN HOWE
UK group formed by Jon Anderson (born 25/10/1944, Accrington, vocals), Bill Bruford (born 17/5/1948, London, drums), Rick Wakeman (born 18/5/1949, London, keyboards) and Steve Howe (born 8/4/1947, London, guitar), all four ex-members of Yes.

24/06/1989	63	2		BROTHER OF MINE	Arista 112379

PETER ANDRE
UK singer (born Peter James Andrea, 27/2/1973, London, raised in Australia) who began his career as a model. He went into semi-retirement in 1998 but returned in 2004 after appearing in the TV series *I'm A Celebrity…Get Me Out Of Here*. Bubbler Ranx is a Jamaican toaster.

10/06/1995	64	1		TURN IT UP	Mushroom D 1000
16/09/1995	53	2		MYSTERIOUS GIRL	Mushroom D 1192
16/03/1996	16	4		ONLY ONE	Mushroom D 1307
01/06/1996	2	18	✪	**MYSTERIOUS GIRL** PETER ANDRE FEATURING BUBBLER RANX Re-issue of Mushroom D 1192	Mushroom DX 2000
14/09/1996	●[1]	9	○	**FLAVA** ↑	Mushroom DX 2003
07/12/1996	●[1]	11	○	**I FEEL YOU** ↑	Mushroom D 1521
08/03/1997	6	11		**NATURAL**	Mushroom DX 1577
09/08/1997	3	9		**ALL ABOUT US**	Mushroom MUSH 5CD
08/11/1997	6	9		**LONELY**	Mushroom MUSH 16CD
24/01/1998	16	4		ALL NIGHT ALL RIGHT PETER ANDRE FEATURING WARREN G Contains a sample of A Taste Of Honey's *Boogie Oogie Oogie*	Mushroom MUSH 21CD
25/07/1998	9	5		**KISS THE GIRL** Featured in the 1998 Walt Disney film *The Little Mermaid*	Mushroom MUSH 34CDSX
06/03/2004	●[1]	11		**MYSTERIOUS GIRL** PETER ANDRE FEATURING BUBBLER RANX Second re-issue of Mushroom D 1192, following Peter's appearance in *I'm A Celebrity…Get Me Out Of Here*. Proceeds from the single were donated to the NSPCC	Mushroom PA001CDX
12/06/2004	3	7		**INSANIA**	East West PA002CD
18/09/2004	14	5		THE RIGHT WAY	Atlantic ATUK001CD1

ANDRE 3000 – see KELIS

CHRIS ANDREWS
UK singer (born 15/10/1942, Romford) who first appeared professionally in 1957 and formed Chris Ravel And The Ravers. Signed by manager Eve Taylor as a songwriter, he penned numerous hits for Sandie Shaw and Adam Faith (also managed by Eve Taylor) before embarking on his singing career. He was immensely popular in Germany.

07/10/1965	3	15		**YESTERDAY MAN**	Decca F 12236
02/12/1965	13	10		TO WHOM IT CONCERNS	Decca F 22285
14/04/1966	41	3		SOMETHING ON MY MIND	Decca F 22365
02/06/1966	40	4		WHATCHA GONNA DO NOW	Decca F 22404
25/08/1966	36	4		STOP THAT GIRL	Decca F 22472

EAMONN ANDREWS WITH RON GOODWIN AND HIS ORCHESTRA
Irish TV/radio presenter (born 19/12/1922, Dublin) best known for *This Is Your Life* and early years of the children's TV show *Crackerjack*. He died from a heart attack on 5/11/1987.

20/01/1956	18	3		SHIFTING WHISPERING SANDS (PARTS 1 & 2)	Parlophone R 4106

MICHAEL ANDREWS FEATURING GARY JULES
US duo formed by composer Michael Andrews and singer Gary Jules. Andrews also scored the films *Orange County, Out Cold* and *Cypher*. Jules (born Gary Jules Aguirre in San Diego, CA) was previously a member of Origin (with Andrews) and launched a solo career with A&M.

27/12/2003	●[3]	15	✪	**MAD WORLD** ↑ Featured in the 2002 film *Donnie Darko*	Adventure/Sanctuary SANXD 250X

ANDROIDS
Australian group formed by Tim Henwood (guitar/vocals), Matt Tomlinson (guitar), Sam Grayson (bass) and Marty Grech (drums).

17/05/2003	15	5		DO IT WITH MADONNA	Universal MCSTD 40321

ANEKA
Scottish singer (born Mary Sandeman) usually associated with Gaelic folk material. The title *Japanese Boy* was rejected by Hansa's Japanese label for sounding 'too Chinese'.

08/08/1981	●[1]	12	○	**JAPANESE BOY**	Hansa 5
07/11/1981	50	4		LITTLE LADY	Hansa 8

○ Silver disc ● Gold disc ✪ Platinum disc (additional platinum units are indicated by a figure following the symbol) ◎ Singles released prior to 1973 that are known to have sold over 1 million copies in the UK

DAVE ANGEL UK producer (born Dave Gooden) who recorded for Black Market, Love, R&S, Apollo and his own Rotation label before linking with Fourth & Broadway.

02/08/1997 . . . . . 58 . . . . . . 1 . . . . TOKYO STEALTH FIGHTER . . . . Fourth & Broadway BRCD 355

SIMONE ANGEL Dutch singer (born 24/12/1971, Woerden).

13/11/1993 . . . . . 60 . . . . . . 1 . . . . LET THIS FEELING . . . . A&M 5803652

ANGEL CITY Dutch production duo Aldwin Oomen and Hugo Zentveld, with their debut hit fronted by Guildford model and singer Lara McAllen (born 1982).

08/11/2003 . . . . . 11 . . . . . . 8 . . . . LOVE ME RIGHT (OH SHEILA) ANGEL CITY FEATURING LARA McALLEN . . . . Data 59CDS
03/07/2004 . . . . . 18 . . . . . . 4 . . . . TOUCH ME . . . . Data 73CDX
16/10/2004 . . . . . 8 . . . . . . 4 . . . . DO YOU KNOW (I GO CRAZY) . . . . Data 76CDS

ANGELETTES UK vocal group 'invented, imagined, conceived, created, produced and directed by Jonathan King', later recording for his UK label as well as backing the likes of Bryan Ferry and Joe Henry.

13/05/1972 . . . . . 35 . . . . . . 5 . . . . DON'T LET HIM TOUCH YOU . . . . Decca F 13284

ANGELHEART UK producer.

06/04/1996 . . . . . 68 . . . . . . 1 . . . . COME BACK TO ME ANGELHEART FEATURING ROCHELLE HARRIS . . . . Hi-Life 5776312
22/03/1997 . . . . . 74 . . . . . . 1 . . . . I'M STILL WAITING ANGELHEART FEATURING ALETIA BOURNE . . . . Hi-Life 5735452

ANGELIC UK production group formed by Amanda O'Riordan (wife of Radio 1 DJ Judge Jules) and Darren Tate. Tate also records as Citizen Caned and Jurgen Vries and is a member of DT8.

17/06/2000 . . . . . 11 . . . . . 10 . . . . . IT'S MY TURN . . . . Serious MCSTD 40235
24/02/2001 . . . . . 12 . . . . . . 4 . . . . . CAN'T KEEP ME SILENT . . . . Serious SERR 023CD
10/11/2001 . . . . . 36 . . . . . . 2 . . . . . STAY WITH ME . . . . Serious SERR 35CD

ANGELIC UPSTARTS UK punk group formed in South Shields in 1977 by Mensi (born Thomas Mensforth, vocals), Mond (guitar), Ronnie Wooden (bass) and Decca (drums). They signed to Small Wonder indie label before joining Warner Brothers. They disbanded in 1986, re-forming in 1988 and 1992.

21/04/1979 . . . . . 31 . . . . . . 8 . . . . . I'M AN UPSTART . . . . Warner Brothers K 17354
11/08/1979 . . . . . 29 . . . . . . 6 . . . . . TEENAGE WARNING . . . . Warner Brothers K 17426
03/11/1979 . . . . . 52 . . . . . . 4 . . . . . NEVER 'AD NOTHIN' . . . . Warner Brothers K 17476
09/02/1980 . . . . . 58 . . . . . . 3 . . . . . OUT OF CONTROL . . . . Warner Brothers K 17558
22/03/1980 . . . . . 65 . . . . . . 2 . . . . . WE GOTTA GET OUT OF THIS PLACE . . . . Warner Brothers K 17576
02/08/1980 . . . . . 51 . . . . . . 4 . . . . . LAST NIGHT ANOTHER SOLDIER . . . . Zonophone Z 7
07/02/1981 . . . . . 57 . . . . . . 3 . . . . . KIDS ON THE STREET . . . . Zonophone Z 16

ANGELLE UK singer (born 1980, Birmingham) who began as a backing singer for the likes of Peter Andre and Louise. She is the first artist to have had an entire TV channel devoted to her, booking a satellite channel for two months and featuring live performances, video, interviews and a one-hour documentary.

17/08/2002 . . . . . 43 . . . . . . 1 . . . . JOY AND PAIN . . . . Innovation CXINNOV 1

STEVE ANGELLO – see ERIC PRYDZ AND STEVE ANGELLO

BOBBY ANGELO AND THE TUXEDOS UK rockabilly group. The Tuxedos included Roger Brown, Dave Brown and Colin Giffin, all of whom went on to become The Outlaws and then The Innocents.

10/08/1961 . . . . . 30 . . . . . . 6 . . . . BABY SITTIN' . . . . HMV POP 892

ANGELS US vocal group formed in Orange, NJ in 1961 by Phyllis 'Jiggs' Allbut, her sister Barbara and Linda Jansen as The Starlets. Jansen left in 1962 and was replaced by Peggy Santiglia. Barbara Allbut was replaced by Lana Shaw and Santiglia by Debbie Swisher.

03/10/1963 . . . . . 50 . . . . . . 1 . . . . MY BOYFRIEND'S BACK ▲[3] Featured in the 1979 film More American Graffiti . . . . Mercury AMT 1211

ANGELS OF LIGHT – see PSYCHIC TV

ANGELS REVERSE Dutch dance group formed by Samuel Skrbinsek (born 1972, Slovenia) who also records as DNS and DJ Sam-Pling.

31/08/2002 . . . . . 71 . . . . . . 1 . . . . DON'T CARE . . . . Inferno CDFERN 46

ANGELWITCH UK rock group formed by Kevin Heybourne (guitar), Kevin Riddles (bass) and Dave Dufort (drums). They disbanded after one album and Heybourne re-formed the group with Dave Tattum (vocals), Pete Gordelier (bass) and Dave Hogg (drums). A third line-up featured Heybourne, Grant Dennis (bass) and Spencer Holman (drums).

07/06/1980 . . . . . 75 . . . . . . 1 . . . . SWEET DANGER . . . . EMI 5064

ANIMAL US puppet and drummer who first came to prominence in TV's The Muppet Show.

23/07/1994 . . . . . 38 . . . . . . 3 . . . . WIPE OUT . . . . BMG Kidz 74321219532

ANIMAL NIGHTLIFE UK group formed by Andy Polaris (vocals), Billy Chapman (saxophone), Steve Shawley (bass), John Crichison (piano), Len Chignoli (percussion), Steve 'Flid' Brown (guitar), Declan John Barclay (trumpet) and Paul Waller (drums).

❶[9] Number of weeks single topped the UK chart ↑ Entered the UK chart at #1 ▲[9] Number of weeks single topped the US chart

27

DATE	POS	WKS	BPI	SINGLE TITLE	LABEL & NUMBER
13/08/1983	60	3		NATIVE BOY (UPTOWN)	Innervision A 3584
18/08/1984	25	12		MR. SOLITAIRE Backing vocals by David Joseph and Paul Weller	Island IS 193
06/07/1985	28	6		LOVE IS JUST THE GREAT PRETENDER	Island IS 200
05/10/1985	67	1		PREACHER PREACHER	Island IS 245

ANIMALHOUSE UK group formed in Oxford in 1997 by Hari T, Sam Williams, Mark Gardner and Laurence 'Loz' Colbert. Gardner and Colbert had previously been members of Ride.

DATE	POS	WKS	BPI	SINGLE TITLE	LABEL & NUMBER
15/07/2000	61	1		READY TO RECEIVE	Boilerhouse 74321771072

ANIMALS UK rock group formed in 1962 by Eric Burdon (born 11/5/1941, Newcastle-upon-Tyne, vocals), Alan Price (born 19/4/1941, Fatfield, keyboards), Hilton Valentine (born 21/5/1943, North Shields, guitar), Chas Chandler (born Bryan Chandler, 18/12/1938, Heaton, bass) and John Steel (born 4/2/1941, Gateshead, drums) who made their first recordings in 1964. Following early success they split in 1966 (mainly through internal divisions centred around Burdon), with Burdon re-forming the group and taking top billing, then recording with War. The Animals re-formed in 1983. Chandler died after a lengthy illness on 17/7/1996. The group was inducted into the Rock & Roll Hall of Fame in 1994.

DATE	POS	WKS	BPI	SINGLE TITLE	LABEL & NUMBER
16/04/1964	21	8		BABY LET ME TAKE YOU HOME	Columbia DB 7247
25/06/1964	**❶**[1]	12		**HOUSE OF THE RISING SUN** ▲[3] Featured in the films *Beloved Invaders* (1965) and *Casino* (1996)	Columbia DB 7301
17/09/1964	8	10		**I'M CRYING**	Columbia DB 7354
04/02/1965	3	9		**DON'T LET ME BE MISUNDERSTOOD**	Columbia DB 7445
08/04/1965	7	11		**BRING IT ON HOME TO ME**	Columbia DB 7539
15/07/1965	2	12		**WE GOTTA GET OUT OF THIS PLACE**	Columbia DB 7639
28/10/1965	7	11		**IT'S MY LIFE**	Columbia DB 7741
17/02/1966	12	8		INSIDE – LOOKING OUT	Decca F 12332
02/06/1966	6	8		**DON'T BRING ME DOWN**	Decca F 12407
27/10/1966	14	10		HELP ME GIRL	Decca F 12502
15/06/1967	45	3		WHEN I WAS YOUNG	MGM 1340
06/09/1967	20	11		GOOD TIMES	MGM 1344
18/10/1967	7	10		**SAN FRANCISCAN NIGHTS**	MGM 1359
14/02/1968	40	3		SKY PILOT	MGM 1373
15/01/1969	35	5		RING OF FIRE This and above five singles credited to **ERIC BURDON AND THE ANIMALS**	MGM 1461
07/10/1972	25	6		HOUSE OF THE RISING SUN Re-issue of Columbia DB 7301	RAK RR 1
18/09/1982	11	10		HOUSE OF THE RISING SUN Re-entry of re-issue	RAK RR 1

ANIMOTION US five-piece band fronted by Astrid Plane and Bill Wadhams. Later members included actress and dancer Cynthia Rhodes (born 1957, Nashville) and Paul Engemann (vocals).

DATE	POS	WKS	BPI	SINGLE TITLE	LABEL & NUMBER
11/05/1985	5	12		**OBSESSION**	Mercury PH 34

PAUL ANKA Canadian singer (born 30/7/1941, Ottawa, Ontario) who made his professional debut at the age of ten and recorded his self-penned first single *I Confess* at fifteen. A contract with ABC the following year was mainly on the strength of his songwriting, his biggest success later being the English lyrics to Frank Sinatra's *My Way*. He appeared in the films *Girls Town* (1959), *Look In Any Window* (1961) and *The Longest Day* (1962). He has a star on the Hollywood Walk of Fame. Odia Coates (born 1942, Mississippi) later became a member of the Edwin Hawkins Singers. She died from breast cancer on 19/5/1991.

DATE	POS	WKS	BPI	SINGLE TITLE	LABEL & NUMBER
09/08/1957	**❶**[9]	25	◉	**DIANA** ▲[1] Written about an infatuation with his babysitter, Diana Ayoub, and has sold over 9 million copies worldwide.	Columbia DB 3980
08/11/1957	3	15		**I LOVE YOU BABY**	Columbia DB 4022
08/11/1957	25	2		TELL ME THAT YOU LOVE ME B-side to *I Love You Baby*	Columbia DB 4022
31/01/1958	6	13		**YOU ARE MY DESTINY**	Columbia DB 4063
30/05/1958	26	1		CRAZY LOVE	Columbia DB 4110
26/09/1958	26	1		MIDNIGHT	Columbia DB 4172
30/01/1959	10	13		**(ALL OF A SUDDEN) MY HEART SINGS**	Columbia DB 4241
10/07/1959	3	17		**LONELY BOY** ▲[4] Featured in the 1959 film *Girls Town*	Columbia DB 4324
30/10/1959	7	12		**PUT YOUR HEAD ON MY SHOULDER**	Columbia DB 4355
26/02/1960	28	2		IT'S TIME TO CRY Featured in the 1959 film *Girls Town*	Columbia DB 4390
21/04/1960	33	7		PUPPY LOVE	Columbia DB 4434
15/09/1960	44	1		HELLO YOUNG LOVERS	Columbia DB 4504
15/03/1962	19	11		LOVE ME WARM AND TENDER	RCA 1276
26/07/1962	41	4		A STEEL GUITAR AND A GLASS OF WINE	RCA 1292
28/09/1974	6	10		**(YOU'RE) HAVING MY BABY** ▲[3] **PAUL ANKA FEATURING ODIA COATES**	United Artists UP 35713

ANA ANN UK singer (born Ana Petrovic) who was nineteen at the time of her debut hit. Previously classically trained, she pursued an R&B/jazz style and launched the LL Records label.

DATE	POS	WKS	BPI	SINGLE TITLE	LABEL & NUMBER
23/02/2002	24	2		RIDE	LL RIDELLR 100
06/03/2004	44	1		CHILDREN OF THE WORLD **ANA ANN AND THE LONDON COMMUNITY CHOIR**	Century Vista LLR104

ANNIA – see **XTM AND DJ CHUNKY PRESENTS ANNIA**

ANNIE Norwegian singer Anne Lila Berge-Strand who first came to prominence guesting on Richard X's album. He in turn produced her debut hit single.

DATE	POS	WKS	BPI	SINGLE TITLE	LABEL & NUMBER
25/09/2004	25	3		CHEWING GUM	679 679L075CD1

○ Silver disc ● Gold disc ✪ Platinum disc (additional platinum units are indicated by a figure following the symbol) ◉ Singles released prior to 1973 that are known to have sold over 1 million copies in the UK

ANOTHER LEVEL
UK vocal group formed in London by Bobak Kianoush (born 1/11/1978), Mark Baron (born 17/8/1974), Dane Bowers (born 28/11/1979) and Wayne Williams (born 20/1/1977). Williams quit in November 1999, Kianoush in December. Bowers later recorded with True Steppers. In June 2000 the remaining pair disbanded. Despite their nationality, they were named Best International Act at the 1997 MOBO Awards.

DATE	POS	WKS	BPI	SINGLE TITLE	LABEL & NUMBER
28/02/1998	6	9		**BE ALONE NO MORE**	Northwestside 74321551982
18/07/1998	❶[1]	12	●	**FREAK ME** ↑ 1998 MOBO Award for Best Single	Northwestside 74321582362
07/11/1998	5	13		**GUESS I WAS A FOOL**	Northwestside 74321621202
23/01/1999	2	8		**I WANT YOU FOR MYSELF** ANOTHER LEVEL/GHOSTFACE KILLAH	Northwestside 74321643632
10/04/1999	11	9		BE ALONE NO MORE (REMIX) ANOTHER LEVEL FEATURING JAY-Z A second CD issue had *Holding Back The Years* as the lead track and was released to help the Capital Radio charity Help A London Child	Northwestside 74321658482
12/06/1999	6	11		**FROM THE HEART** Featured in the 1999 film *Notting Hill*	Northwestside 74321673012
04/09/1999	7	7		**SUMMERTIME** ANOTHER LEVEL FEATURING TQ	Northwestside 74321694672
13/11/1999	6	12		**BOMB DIGGY** Subsequently used as the theme to Channel 4's *North Hollywood High*	Northwestside 74321712212

ANOTHERSIDE
UK vocal duo Alani Gibbon and Celena Cherry (born 26/4/1977, London) who had previously been with Kleshay and Honeyz respectively.

DATE	POS	WKS	BPI	SINGLE TITLE	LABEL & NUMBER
05/07/2003	41	1		THIS IS YOUR NIGHT	J-Did/V2 JAD 5023293

ANOUCHKA – see TERRY HALL

ADAM ANT – see ADAM AND THE ANTS

ANT AND DEC
UK duo Anthony McPartlin (born 18/11/1975, Newcastle-Upon-Tyne) and Declan Donnelly (born 25/9/1975, Newcastle-upon-Tyne) who both began as actors. They first recorded as PJ And Duncan (the names of their characters in the children's TV programme *Byker Grove*). Later they found greater acclaim presenting the TV shows *CD:UK* and *Pop Idol*. In 2002 they appeared in a remake of the TV comedy *The Likely Lads*.

DATE	POS	WKS	BPI	SINGLE TITLE	LABEL & NUMBER
18/12/1993	62	3		TONIGHT I'M FREE	Telstar CDSTAS 2706
23/04/1994	27	4		WHY ME	Telstar CDSTAS 2719
23/07/1994	9	11		**LET'S GET READY TO RHUMBLE**	Xsrhythm CDDEC 1
08/10/1994	15	7		IF I GIVE YOU MY NUMBER	Xsrhythm CDDEC 2
03/12/1994	12	9		ETERNAL LOVE	Xsrhythm CDDEC 3
25/02/1995	15	5		OUR RADIO ROCKS	Xsrhythm CDANT 4
29/07/1995	12	5		STUCK ON U	Telstar CDDEC 5
14/10/1995	15	4		U KRAZY KATZ	Xsrhythm CDDEC 6
02/12/1995	16	7		PERFECT	Telstar CDANT 7
30/03/1996	11	5		STEPPING STONE This and above nine singles credited to PJ AND DUNCAN	Telstar CDANT 8
24/08/1996	10	4		**BETTER WATCH OUT**	Telstar CDDEC 9
23/11/1996	12	8		WHEN I FALL IN LOVE	Telstar CDDEC 10
15/03/1997	10	5		**SHOUT** Features the uncredited contribution of Andy Bell of Erasure and contains a sample of Lou Reed's *Walk On The Wild Side*	Telstar CDDEC 11
10/05/1997	14	4		FALLING	Telstar CDDEC 12
08/06/2002	3	11		**WE'RE ON THE BALL** Official single of the England football team	Columbia 6727312

ANTARCTICA
Australian producer Steve Gibbs.

DATE	POS	WKS	BPI	SINGLE TITLE	LABEL & NUMBER
29/01/2000	53	1		RETURN TO REALITY	React CDREACT 173
08/07/2000	72	1		ADRIFT (CAST YOUR MIND)	React CDREACT 172

BILLIE ANTHONY WITH ERIC JUPP AND HIS ORCHESTRA
UK singer (born Philomena Brown, in the dressing room of a Glasgow theatre). Her cover version of Rosemary Clooney's chart topper so impressed the song's writer (Stuart Hamblen) that he wrote additional material for her, including the follow-up *Shake The Hand Of A Stranger*. She died in 1991.

DATE	POS	WKS	BPI	SINGLE TITLE	LABEL & NUMBER
15/10/1954	4	16		**THIS OLE HOUSE**	Columbia DB 3519

MARC ANTHONY
US salsa singer (born Marco Antonio Muniz, 16/9/1968, New York) who won the 1998 Grammy Award for Best Tropical Latin Recording for *Contra La Corriente*. He married fellow singer Jennifer Lopez in June 2004 (his second marriage, her third). Little Louie is US producer Louie Vega, a member of Masters At Work, who also record as Nuyorican Soul.

DATE	POS	WKS	BPI	SINGLE TITLE	LABEL & NUMBER
05/10/1991	71	1		RIDE ON THE RHYTHM LITTLE LOUIE VEGA AND MARC ANTHONY	Atlantic A 7602
31/01/1998	36	2		RIDE ON THE RHYTHM LITTLE LOUIE AND MARC ANTHONY	Perfecto PERF 151CD1
13/11/1999	28	3		I NEED TO KNOW	Columbia 6683612

MIKI ANTHONY
UK singer who had previously recorded for RCA and later became a producer for the likes of The Goodies and Pat McGlynn. His debut hit was originally recorded by The Hollies.

DATE	POS	WKS	BPI	SINGLE TITLE	LABEL & NUMBER
03/02/1973	27	7		IF IT WASN'T FOR THE REASON THAT I LOVE YOU	Bell 1275

RAY ANTHONY AND HIS ORCHESTRA
US bandleader/trumpeter (born Raymond Antonini, 20/1/1922, Bentleyville, PA). After working with Glenn Miller and Jimmy Dorsey, he formed his own band in 1946. He appeared in the 1959 film *The Five Pennies*.

DATE	POS	WKS	BPI	SINGLE TITLE	LABEL & NUMBER
04/12/1953	7	2		**DRAGNET** Theme to the TV series of the same name	Capitol CL 13983

RICHARD ANTHONY
French singer (born Richard Anthony Bush, 13/1/1938, Cairo, Egypt) who was one of the first French singers to make a rock 'n' roll record, *Peggy Sue*, in 1959.

❶[9] Number of weeks single topped the UK chart ↑ Entered the UK chart at #1 ▲[9] Number of weeks single topped the US chart

29

12/12/1963.....37......5......				WALKING ALONE .... Columbia DB 7133
23/04/1964.....18......10......				IF I LOVED YOU .... Columbia DB 7235

ANTHRAX US thrash group formed in New York by Scott 'Not' Ian (born 31/12/1963, New York, guitar), Neil Turbin (vocals), Dan Spitz (born 28/1/1963, Queens, NYC, guitar), Dan Lilker (born 18/10/1964, Queens, NYC, bass) and Charlie Benante (born 27/11/1962, New York, drums). Their first release was on their Megaforce label. Turbin and Lilker were replaced later by Frank Bello (born 9/7/1965, New York) and Joey Belladonna (born 30/10/1960, Oswego, NY) respectively, with John Bush (born 24/8/1963, Los Angeles, CA) in turn replacing Belladonna in 1992. Lilker went on to form Nuclear Assault, and Chuck D (born Carlton Douglas Ridenhour, 1/8/1960, Roosevelt, Long Island, NY) joined Public Enemy.

28/02/1987.....32......5......				I AM THE LAW .... Island IS LAW 1
27/06/1987.....44......4......				INDIANS .... Island IS 325
05/12/1987.....20......6......				I'M THE MAN .... Island IS 338
10/09/1988.....26......3......				MAKE ME LAUGH .... Island IS 379
18/03/1989.....44......3......				ANTI-SOCIAL .... Island IS 409
01/09/1990.....29......3......				IN MY WORLD .... Island IS 470
05/01/1991.....16......4......				GOT THE TIME .... Island IS 476
06/07/1991.....14......5......				BRING THE NOISE ANTHRAX FEATURING CHUCK D .... Island IS 490
08/05/1993.....36......3......				ONLY.. Elektra EKR 166CD
11/09/1993.....53......2......				BLACK LODGE .... Elektra EKR 171CD

ANTI-NOWHERE LEAGUE UK punk group formed in Tunbridge Wells and led by Animal (born Nick Karmer, vocals) and Magoo (guitar). The single *Streets Of London* (a thrash version of the Ralph McTell folk classic) was banned and copies seized by the police after the B-side *So What* was considered to be obscene. Disbanded in 1988, then briefly re-formed in 1989 for a one-off album.

23/01/1982.....48......5......				STREETS OF LONDON. .... WXYZ ABCD 1
20/03/1982.....46......3......				I HATE...PEOPLE.. WXYZ ABCD 2
03/07/1982.....72......2......				WOMAN .... WXYZ ABCD 4

ANTI-PASTI – see **EXPLOITED**

ANTICAPPELLA UK/Italian dance group formed by Gianfranco Bortolotti (previously responsible for Cappella, hence the group's name). MC Fixx It is an Italian singer.

16/11/1991.....24......4......				2√231 .... PWL Continental PWL 205
18/04/1992.....45......2......				EVERY DAY .... PWL Continental PWL 220
25/06/1994.....21......3......				MOVE YOUR BODY ANTICAPPELLA FEATURING MC FIXX IT .... Media MCSTD 1980
01/04/1995.....31......2......				EXPRESS YOUR FREEDOM .... Media MCSTD 2048
25/05/1996.....54......1......				2√2311/MOVE YOUR BODY (REMIX) .... Media MCSTD 40037

ANTONIA – see **BOMB THE BASS**

ANTS – see **ADAM AND THE ANTS**

ANUNA – see **BILL WHELAN FEATURING ANUNA AND THE RTE CONCERT ORCHESTRA**

A1 UK/Norwegian vocal group formed by Ben Adams (born 22/11/1981, Middlesex), Christian Ingebrigtsen (born 25/1/1977, Oslo), Paul Marrazi (born 24/1/1975, London) and Mark Read (born 7/11/1978, Kingston). They were named Best UK Newcomer at the 2001 BRIT Awards.

03/07/1999 .....6......9......				**BE THE FIRST TO BELIEVE** .... Columbia 6674222
11/09/1999 .....5......8......				**SUMMERTIME OF OUR LIVES**... Columbia 6678322
20/11/1999 .....3......11				**EVERYTIME/READY OR NOT** .... Columbia 6681872
04/03/2000 .....6......12				**LIKE A ROSE**... Columbia 6689032
09/09/2000 ....❶¹......11.....○				**TAKE ON ME** ↑ .... Columbia 6695902
18/11/2000 ....❶¹......10				**SAME OLD BRAND NEW YOU** ↑ .... Columbia 6705202
03/03/2001 .....6......13				**NO MORE.**... Columbia 6708742
02/02/2002 .....2......12				**CAUGHT IN THE MIDDLE**... Columbia 6722322
25/05/2002 .....11......5				MAKE IT GOOD.. Columbia 6726182

APACHE INDIAN UK reggae singer (born Steve Kapur, 11/5/1967, Birmingham) of Asian descent. He first recorded in 1990 (*Movie Over India* on the white label, which was subsequently distributed by Jet Star) and signed with Island in 1992. Tim Dog is a US rapper (born Timothy Blair, 1/1/1967, The Bronx, NYC). Frankie Paul is a Jamaican singer (born Paul Blake).

28/11/1992.....33......3......				JUST WANNA KNOW/FE' REAL MAXI PRIEST FEATURING APACHE INDIAN .... 10 TEN 416
02/01/1993.....16......6......				ARRANGED MARRIAGE... Island CID 544
27/03/1993.....30......4......				CHOK THERE .... Island CID 555
14/08/1993 .....5......10.....○				**NUFF VIBES EP** Tracks on EP: *Boom Shack A Lack, Fun, Caste System* and *Warning*. *Boom Shack A Lack* was featured in the films *Threesome* (1993) and *Dumb And Dumber* (1994)................................... Island CID 560
22/10/1993.....48......2......				MOVIN' ON .... Island CID 580
07/05/1994.....26......2......				WRECKX SHOP WRECKX-N-EFFECT FEATURING APACHE INDIAN .... MCA MCSTD 1969
11/02/1995.....29......2......				MAKE WAY FOR THE INDIAN APACHE INDIAN AND TIM DOG....................... Island CID 586
22/04/1995.....21......2......				RAGGAMUFFIN GIRL APACHE INDIAN FEATURING FRANKIE PAUL.................. Island CID 606
29/03/1997.....53......1......				LOVIN' (LET ME LOVE YOU) .... Coalition COLA 002CD
18/10/1997.....66......1.......				REAL PEOPLE .... Coalition COLA 019CD

APHEX TWIN
UK producer (born Richard James, 18/8/1971, Limerick, Ireland) who also records as AFX, Powerpill and Polygon Window. He allegedly used his royalties to buy an armoured tank.

09/05/1992	55	2		DIGERIDOO	R&S RSUK 12
27/11/1993	32	3		ON	Warp WAP 39CD
08/04/1995	49	1		VENTOLIN	Warp WAP 60CD
26/10/1996	64	1		GIRL/BOY (EP) Tracks on EP: *Girl/Boy Song, Milkman, Inkey $* and *Beatles Under My Carpet*. Wrongly listed on the singles chart, it should have qualified as an album.	Warp WAP 78CD
18/10/1997	36	2		COME TO DADDY	Warp WAP 94CD
03/04/1999	16	3		WINDOWLICKER	Warp WAP 105CD

APHRODITE FEATURING WILDFLOWER
UK drum and bass producer Gavin King. As a DJ he's known as DJ Aphro and he launched the Aphrodite Recordings label.

| 16/11/2002 | 68 | 1 | | SEE THRU IT | V2 VVR 5020983 |

APHRODITE'S CHILD
Greek group formed in 1963 by Demis Roussos (born 15/6/1947, Alexandria, Egypt), Lucas Sideras (born 5/12/1944, Athens) and Evangelos Papathanassiou (born 29/3/1943, Valos), better known as Vangelis. They split in the 1970s, with Roussos going solo and Vangelis joining Jon Anderson.

| 06/11/1968 | 29 | 7 | | RAIN AND TEARS | Mercury MF 1039 |

A+
US rapper (born Andre Levins, 29/8/1983, Hampstead, NY) whose debut hit also featured singer Keanne Henson.

| 13/02/1999 | 5 | 9 | | ENJOY YOURSELF | Universal UND 56230 |

APOLLO 440
UK production/instrumental group formed by Trevor Gray (keyboards/vocals), Howard Gray (backing vocals) and Noko (vocals/guitar/keyboards), who amended their name to Apollo Four Forty. They also remix as Stealthsonic.

22/01/1994	36	2		ASTRAL AMERICA	Stealth Sonic SSXCD 2
05/11/1994	35	2		LIQUID COOL	Stealth Sonic SSXCD 3
25/03/1995	35	2		(DON'T FEAR) THE REAPER	Stealth Sonic SSXCD 4
27/07/1996	23	4		KRUPA Tribute to jazz drummer Gene Krupa	Epic SSXCD 5
28/09/1996	24	4		KRUPA Single re-promoted	Epic SSXCD 5
15/02/1997	7	7		AIN'T TALKIN' 'BOUT DUB Contains a sample of Van Halen's *Ain't Talking About Love*	Stealth Sonic SSXCDX 6
05/07/1997	32	3		RAW POWER	Stealth Sonic SSXCD 7
11/07/1998	12	6		RENDEZ-VOUS 98 JEAN-MICHEL JARRE AND APOLLO 440 Used as the theme to ITV's coverage of the 1998 World Cup Finals	Epic 6661102
08/08/1998	4	9		LOST IN SPACE Featured in the 1998 film *Lost In Space*	Stealth Sonic SSX 9CD
28/08/1999	10	6		STOP THE ROCK Featured in the 2000 film *Gone In 60 Seconds*	Epic SSX 10CD
27/11/1999	57	1		HEART GO BOOM	Epic SSX 11CD
09/12/2000	29	6		CHARLIE'S ANGELS 2000 Featured in the 2000 film *Charlie's Angels*	Epic SSX 13CD
21/06/2003	58	1		DUDE DESCENDING A STAiRCASE APOLLO FOUR FORTY FEATURING THE BEATNUTS Contains a sample of Abiodun Oyewole's *When The Revolution Comes*	Sony Music SSX 14CDX

APOLLO PRESENTS HOUSE OF VIRGINISM
Swedish instrumentalist Apollo (born 1976) who had previously recorded as House Of Virginism.

| 17/02/1996 | 67 | 1 | | EXCLUSIVE | Logic 74321324102 |

FIONA APPLE
US singer/songwriter (born Fiona Apple Maggart, 13/9/1977, New York City) signed by Clean Slate Records in 1994. She won the 1997 Grammy Award for Best Female Rock Vocal Performance for *Criminal*.

| 26/02/2000 | 33 | 2 | | FAST AS YOU CAN | Columbia 6689962 |

KIM APPLEBY
UK singer (born 28/8/1961, London) who formed half of Mel And Kim with her sister until Mel's death in 1990.

03/11/1990	2	10	O	DON'T WORRY	Parlophone R 6272
09/02/1991	10	6		G.L.A.D.	Parlophone R 6281
29/06/1991	19	8		MAMA	Parlophone R 6291
19/10/1991	44	3		IF YOU CARED	Parlophone R 6297
31/07/1993	41	2		LIGHT OF THE WORLD	Parlophone CDR 6352
13/11/1993	56	1		BREAKAWAY	Parlophone CDR 6362
12/11/1994	51	1		FREE SPIRIT	Parlophone CDR 6397

APPLEJACKS
UK group from Solihull, Birmingham with Megan Davies (born 25/3/1944, Sheffield, bass), Martin Baggott (born 20/10/1947, Birmingham, guitar), Philip Cash (born 9/10/1947, guitar), Don Gould (born 23/3/1947, organ), Al Jackson (born 21/4/1945, vocals) and Gerry Freeman (born 24/5/1947, Birmingham, drums). They were first known as The Crestas and then The Jaguars before settling on The Applejacks. Megan is the sister of Ray and Dave Davies of The Kinks.

05/03/1964	7	13		TELL ME WHEN	Decca F 11833
11/06/1964	20	11		LIKE DREAMERS DO Written by Lennon and McCartney and performed by The Beatles at their audition for Decca Records	Decca F 11916
15/10/1964	23	5		THREE LITTLE WORDS	Decca F 11981

APPLES
UK vocal/instrumental group formed by Callum McNair, William Perry and Ian Stoddart.

| 23/03/1991 | 75 | 1 | | EYE WONDER | Epic 6566717 |

❶⁹ Number of weeks single topped the UK chart ↑ Entered the UK chart at #1 ▲⁹ Number of weeks single topped the US chart

31

APPLETON Canadian vocal duo formed by ex-All Saints sisters Nicole (born 7/12/1974, Canada) and Natalie Appleton (born 14/5/1973, Canada). Natalie married Prodigy's Liam Howlett in June 2002.

14/09/2002	2	10	**FANTASY**	Polydor 5709852
22/02/2003	5	10	**DON'T WORRY**	Polydor 0658192
26/07/2003	38	2	EVERYTHING EVENTUALLY	Polydor 9808278

CHARLIE APPLEWHITE US singer discovered by Milton Berle for his 1950s TV show. He later appeared on the All-Army Talent Show with Gary Crosby and Richard Hayes and worked with Jane Froman and Georgia Gibbs. He died on 27/4/2001.

23/09/1955	20	1	BLUE STAR (THE MEDIC THEME) **CHARLIE APPLEWHITE WITH VICTOR YOUNG AND HIS ORCHESTRA AND CHORUS** Theme to the TV series *The Medic*	Brunswick 05416

HELEN APRIL – see JOHN DUMMER AND HELEN APRIL

APRIL WINE Canadian group formed in Montreal, Quebec in 1969 by Myles Goodwyn (born 23/6/1948, Halifax, Nova Scotia, vocals), David Henman (guitar), Jim Clench (bass) and Richie Henman (drums). The best-known line-up featured Goodwyn, Brian Greenway (born 1/10/1951, guitar), Gary Moffet (born 22/6/1949, guitar), Steve Lang (born 24/3/1949, bass) and Jerry Mercer (born 27/4/1939, drums). They disbanded in 1985 and re-formed in 2000.

15/03/1980	41	5	I LIKE TO ROCK	Capitol CL 16121
11/04/1981	52	4	JUST BETWEEN YOU AND ME	Capitol CL 16184

AQUA Danish pop group formed by Rene Dif (born 17/10/1967, Fredriksberg), Lene Nystrom (born 2/10/1973, Tonsberg, Norway), Soren Rasted (born 13/6/1969, Blovstod) and Claus Norreen (born 5/6/1970, Charlottenlund).

25/10/1997	●⁴	26	✪²	**BARBIE GIRL** Mattel (makers of the Barbie doll) brought a lawsuit over the lyrics	Universal UMD 80413
07/02/1998	●²	14	●	**DOCTOR JONES** ↑	Universal UMD 80457
16/05/1998	●¹	10		**TURN BACK TIME** ↑ Featured in the 1998 film *Sliding Doors*	Universal UMD 80490
01/08/1998	6	11		MY OH MY	Universal UMD 85058
26/12/1998	18	7		GOOD MORNING SUNSHINE	Universal UMD 85086
26/02/2000	7	11		**CARTOON HEROES**	Universal MCSTD 40226
10/06/2000	26	6		AROUND THE WORLD	Universal MCSXD 40234

AQUA MARINA – see FAB

AQUAGEN German production duo Olaf Dieckmann and Gino Montesano.

09/12/2000	9	8	**PHATT BASS WARP BROTHERS VERSUS AQUAGEN** Featured in the 2000 film *The Blade*	NuLife 74321817102
01/03/2003	33	2	HARD TO SAY I'M SORRY	All Around The World CXGLOBE 265

AQUALUNG UK singer Matt Hayes whose debut hit was first used in a TV advertisement for Volkswagen.

28/09/2002	7	6	**STRANGE AND BEAUTIFUL**	B Unique BUN 032CDX
14/12/2002	71	1	GOOD TIMES GONNA COME	B Unique BUN 043CDX
25/10/2003	37	2	BRIGHTER THAN SUNSHINE	B Unique BUN 072CDX
27/03/2004	60	1	EASIER TO LIE	B Unique WEA 373CD2

AQUANUTS US/Argentinian production trio Luis Diaz, Ariel Baund and Martin Eyerer.

04/05/2002	75	1	DEEP SEA	Data 34T

AQUARIAN DREAM US R&B group formed by Sylvia Striplin (vocals), Patricia Shannon (vocals), Claude Bartee III (guitar), Winston Daley (keyboards), Ernie Adams (bass), Claude Bartee Jr (horns), David Worthy (percussion) and James Morrison (drums). They were discovered by producer Norman Connors. Sylvia later recorded solo.

24/02/1979	67	1	YOU'RE A STAR	Elektra LV 7

ARAB STRAP UK group formed in 1995 by long-time friends Aidan Moffett (vocals) and Malcolm Middleton (multi-instrumentalist). They released their debut record in 1996.

13/09/1997	74	1	THE GIRLS OF SUMMER (EP) Tracks on EP: *Hey! Fever, Girls Of Summer, The Beautiful Barmaids Of Dundee* and *One Day After School*	Chemikal Underground CHEM 017CD
04/04/1998	48	1	HERE WE GO/TRIPPY	Chemikal Underground CHEM 20CD
10/10/1998	74	1	(AFTERNOON) SOAPS	Chemikal Underground CHEM 27CD
10/02/2001	66	1	LOVE DETECTIVE	Chemikal Underground CHEM 049CD

ARCADIA UK group formed by Simon Le Bon (born 27/10/1958, Bushey), Nick Rhodes (born Nicholas Bates, 8/6/1962, Birmingham) and Roger Taylor (born 26/4/1960, Castle Bromwich). They were all previously in Duran Duran.

26/10/1985	7	7	**ELECTION DAY** Features the uncredited contribution of Grace Jones	Odeon NSR 1
25/01/1986	37	4	THE PROMISE	Odeon NSR 2
26/07/1986	58	2	THE FLAME	Odeon NSR 3

TASMIN ARCHER UK singer (born 1964, Bradford) who was a backing singer at Flexible Response studios when she formed a songwriting partnership with John Hughes and John Beck. She was named Best UK Newcomer at the 1993 BRIT Awards.

12/09/1992	●²	17	○	**SLEEPING SATELLITE**	EMI EM 233
20/02/1993	16	6		IN YOUR CARE	EMI CDEMS 260
29/05/1993	26	4		LORDS OF THE NEW CHURCH	EMI CDEM 266

21/08/1993.....30......4......	ARIENNE	EMI CDEM 275
08/01/1994.....40......4......	SHIPBUILDING	EMI CDEM 302
23/03/1996.....45......2......	ONE MORE GOOD NIGHT WITH THE BOYS	EMI CDEM 401

ARCHIES
US TV cartoon series about a rock group formed by Archie Andrews (vocals/guitar), Jughead Jones (bass), Veronica Lodge (organ), Betty Cooper (tambourine), Reggie (drums) and their mascot Hot Dog. Jeff Barry and Andy Kim mainly wrote the songs, with Ron Dante (born Carmine Granito, 22/8/1945, Staten Island, NY), Andy Kim and Tony Passalacqua on vocals. The series, created by Don Kirshner, ended in 1978 and was revived in 1987.

11/10/1969 ....❶⁸.....26	SUGAR SUGAR ▲⁴ Featured in the 1996 film *Now And Then*	RCA 1872

ARCHITECHS
UK garage duo Tre Lowe and City.

07/10/2000 .....3.....14....O	BODY GROOVE ARCHITECHS FEATURING NANA	Go Beat GOBCD 33
07/04/2001.....20......5......	SHOW ME THE MONEY Featured in the 2001 film *The Hole*	Go Beat GOBCD 38

JANN ARDEN
Canadian singer (born Jann Arden Richards, 27/3/1962, Calgary) who began performing at fourteen. A debut album for A&M in 1993 led to a Juno Award (the Canadian equivalent of a Grammy and BRIT).

13/07/1996.....40......2......	INSENSITIVE Featured in the 1996 film *Bed Of Roses*	A&M 5812652

A.R.E. WEAPONS
US group formed in New York City by Brain McPeck (vocals), Tom (keyboards) and Matt McAuley (bass), recommended to Rough Trade by Jarvis Cocker of Pulp. Tom left in 2001 and was replaced by Paul Sevigny. The A.R.E. in their name stands for Atomic Revenge Extreme.

04/08/2001.....72......1......	STREET GANG	Rough Trade RTRADESCD 022

TINA ARENA
Australian singer/songwriter (born Phillipa Arena, 1/11/1967, Melbourne) who began performing at eight and made her record debut in 1985. She married her manager Ralph Carr.

15/04/1995 .....6......11......	CHAINS	Columbia 6611255
12/08/1995.....25.....5......	HEAVEN HELP MY HEART	Columbia 6620975
02/12/1995.....29......3......	SHOW ME HEAVEN	Columbia 6626975
03/08/1996.....22......4......	SORRENTO MOON (I REMEMBER)	Columbia 6635435
27/06/1998.....24......5......	WHISTLE DOWN THE WIND From the musical *Whistle Down The Wind*.....	Really Useful 5672192
24/10/1998.....43......2......	IF I WAS A RIVER..	Columbia 6665605
13/03/1999.....47......1......	BURN..	Columbia 6667442
20/05/2000.....63......1......	LIVE FOR THE ONE I LOVE	Columbia 6691332
12/04/2003.....42......1......	NEVER (PAST TENSE) ROC PROJECT FEATURING TINA ARENA Contains a sample of Fused's *Twisted*	Illustrious CDILL 010

ARGENT
UK group formed in Hertfordshire in 1969 by Rod Argent (born 14/6/1945, St Albans, vocals/keyboards) with Jim Rodford (born 7/7/1941, St Albans, bass), Robert Henrit (born 2/5/1944, Broxbourne, drums) and Russ Ballard (born 31/10/1947, Waltham Cross, guitar). They disbanded in 1976, Argent later recording as Rodriguez Argentina and Ballard becoming a successful songwriter. Rodford and Henrit later joined The Kinks.

04/03/1972 .....5......12......	HOLD YOUR HEAD UP..	Epic EPC 7786
10/06/1972.....34......7......	TRAGEDY...	Epic EPC 8115
24/03/1973.....18......8......	GOD GAVE ROCK AND ROLL TO YOU	Epic EPC 1243

INDIA.ARIE
US singer (born India Arie Simpson, 1976, Denver, CO) who moved to Atlanta, GA when she was thirteen. She initially worked with Groovement and the EarthShare label. Groovement covered her songs on the EarthShare label and this led to a deal with Motown in 1998. She received the 2002 Grammy Award for the Best Rhythm & Blues Album for *Voyage To India*.

30/06/2001.....32......3......	VIDEO...	Motown TMGCD 1505
20/10/2001.....29......2......	BROWN SKIN...	Motown TMGCD 1507
12/04/2003.....62......1......	LITTLE THINGS 2002 Grammy Award for Best Urban/Alternative Performance.......................	Motown TMGCD 1509

ARIEL
UK production group.

27/03/1993.....57......2......	LET IT SLIDE...	Deconstruction 74321134512

ARIEL
Italian production group of Ariel Belloso and Ramon Zenker. Zenker was behind hits by Fragma and Bellini and masterminded Hardfloor.

21/06/1997.....47......1......	DEEP (I'M FALLING DEEPER)	Wonderboy WBOYD 005
17/06/2000.....28......3......	A9...	Essential Recordings ESCD 15

ARIZONA FEATURING ZEITIA
UK dance group formed by producers Mike Gray and Jon Pearn, who also recorded as Full Intention, Hustlers Convention, Ronaldo's Revenge, Disco Tex Presents Cloudburst and Sex-O-Sonique.

12/03/1994.....74......1......	I SPECIALIZE IN LOVE	Union City UCRCD 27

SHIP'S COMPANY & ROYAL MARINE BAND OF HMS ARK ROYAL
UK choir and marine band from HMS *Ark Royal*.

23/12/1978.....46......6......	THE LAST FAREWELL...	BBC RESL 61

ARKARNA
UK group formed by Ollie Jacobs (programming/vocals), James Barnett (guitar/backing vocals) and Lalo Crème (guitar), the son of former 10cc and Godley and Crème member Lol Crème.

25/01/1997.....33......2.....	HOUSE ON FIRE	WEA 088CD1

❶⁹ Number of weeks single topped the UK chart ↑ Entered the UK chart at #1 ▲⁹ Number of weeks single topped the US chart

33

02/08/1997	46	1		SO LITTLE TIME	WEA 108CD1

JOAN ARMATRADING UK singer/guitarist/pianist (born 9/12/1950, Basseterre, St Kitts, West Indies) whose family relocated to Birmingham in 1958. Linking with lyricist Pam Nestor in 1972, she made her first recordings for Cube Records in 1973. She also took part in the *Perfect Day* project for the BBC's Children In Need charity. She was awarded an MBE in the 2001 Queen's Birthday Honours List.

16/10/1976	10	9		LOVE AND AFFECTION	A&M AMS 7249
23/02/1980	49	5		ROSIE	A&M AMS 7506
14/06/1980	21	11		ME MYSELF I	A&M AMS 7527
06/09/1980	54	3		ALL THE WAY FROM AMERICA	A&M AMS 7552
12/09/1981	46	5		I'M LUCKY	A&M AMS 8163
16/01/1982	50	5		NO LOVE	A&M AMS 8179
19/02/1983	11	10		DROP THE PILOT	A&M AMS 8306
16/03/1985	65	2		TEMPTATION	A&M AM 238
26/05/1990	75	1		MORE THAN ONE KIND OF LOVE	A&M AM 561
23/05/1992	56	2		WRAPPED AROUND HER	A&M AM 877

ARMIN Dutch producer/remixer Armin Van Buuren who was 22 at the time of his debut hit. He is also a member of Moogwai and owns the Armind record label.

14/02/1998	45	1		BLUE FEAR	Xtravaganza 0091485 EXT
12/02/2000	18	3		COMMUNICATION	AM:PM CDAMPM 129
10/05/2003	70	1		YET ANOTHER DAY ARMIN VAN BUUREN FEATURING RAY WILSON	Nebula NEBCD 042
20/03/2004	45	2		BURNED WITH DESIRE ARMIN VAN BUUREN FEATURING JUSTINE SUISSA	Nebula NEBCDX 055
28/08/2004	52	2		BLUE FEAR 2004 ARMIN VAN BUUREN	Nebula NEBCD061

ARMOURY SHOW UK group formed in 1984 by Richard Jobson (born 6/10/1960, Dunfermline, guitar/vocals), Russell Webb (bass/vocals), John McGeoch (born 28/5/1955, Greenock, guitar) and John Doyle (drums). Jobson was previously in The Skids. Armoury Show disbanded in 1987.

25/08/1984	69	2		CASTLES IN SPAIN	Parlophone R 6079
26/01/1985	66	1		WE CAN BE BRAVE AGAIN	Parlophone R 6087
17/01/1987	63	3		LOVE IN ANGER	Parlophone R 6149

CRAIG ARMSTRONG – see SHOLA AMA

LOUIS ARMSTRONG US trumpeter/vocalist (born 4/8/1901, New Orleans, LA, although Armstrong claimed his birthday was 4/7/1900) who joined his first band in 1922. By 1930 he was the most successful black musician in the world, influencing just about every trumpeter around. Universally known as 'Satchmo', he made numerous appearances in films and on TV. He died on 6/7/1971 in New York and was inducted into the Rock & Roll Hall of Fame in 1990. His 1928 recording *West End Blues* was awarded a special Grammy in 1974. He has a star on the Hollywood Walk of Fame.

19/12/1952	6	10		TAKES TWO TO TANGO	Brunswick 04995
13/04/1956	8	11		THEME FROM THE THREEPENNY OPERA	Philips PB 574
15/06/1956	29	1		TAKE IT SATCH EP Tracks on EP: *Tiger Rag, Mack The Knife, The Faithful Hussar* and *Back O'Town Blues*. This was the first hit single to be issued in a picture sleeve	Philips BBE 12035
13/07/1956	27	2		THE FAITHFUL HUSSAR	Philips PB 604
06/11/1959	24	1		MACK THE KNIFE This and above three singles credited to LOUIS ARMSTRONG WITH HIS ALL-STARS This single is *Theme From The Threepenny Opera* under a different title	Philips PB 967
04/06/1964	4	14		HELLO DOLLY ▲[1] 1964 Grammy Award for Best Male Solo Vocal Performance. Featured in the 1969 film *Hello Dolly!*	London HLR 9878
07/02/1968	✪[4]	29		WHAT A WONDERFUL WORLD/CABARET A-side featured in the 1988 film *Good Morning Vietnam*. Armstrong is the oldest person to have topped both the UK and US charts	HMV POP 1615
26/06/1968	41	7		SUNSHINE OF LOVE	Stateside SS 2116
16/04/1988	53	5		WHAT A WONDERFUL WORLD	A&M AM 435
19/11/1994	3	13	●	WE HAVE ALL THE TIME IN THE WORLD Featured in the 1969 James Bond film *On Her Majesty's Secret Service* and revived following successful use in an advertisement for Guinness	EMI CDEM 357

ARMY OF LOVERS Swedish group formed in 1987 by Alexander Bard, Jean-Pierre Barda and Camilla Henemark (aka La Camilla). La Camilla left in 1992 and was replaced by Michaela Dornonville De La Cour. Dominika Peczynski joined in 1993. Michaela left in 1995 and was replaced by the returning La Camilla. Jean-Pierre Barda was previously hairdresser to the Swedish Royal Family.

17/08/1991	47	5		CRUCIFIED	Ton Son Ton WOK 2007
28/12/1991	67	1		OBSESSION	Ton Son Ton WOK 2009
15/02/1992	31	3		CRUCIFIED Re-issue of Ton Son Ton WOK 2007	Ton Son Ton WOK 2017
18/04/1992	67	1		RIDE THE BULLET	Ton Son Ton WOK 2018

ARNEE AND THE TERMINATORS UK group formed by Richard Easter and Mike Woolmans, both part of Steve Wright's Afternoon Posse on Radio 1.

24/08/1991	5	7		I'LL BE BACK	Epic 6574177

ARNIE'S LOVE US R&B group formed by Arnie Joseph, Debbie Allen and Arnelia Villanuea, who adopted their name because they only sing love songs.

26/11/1983	67	3		I'M OUT OF YOUR LIFE	Streetwave WAVE 9

DAVID ARNOLD
UK pianist/composer (born 1962, Luton). After failing auditions for The Waterboys and The Clash, he scored numerous low-budget films before bigger commissions such as *Stargate* (1994) and *Independence Day* (1996). In 1997 he put together *Shaken Not Stirred*, a collection of James Bond themes, featuring The Propellerheads, Chrissie Hynde, Pulp, David McAlmont and Iggy Pop among others. He won the 1996 Grammy Award for Best Instrumental for a Movie for *Independence Day*.

23/10/1993	12	6		PLAY DEAD **BJÖRK AND DAVID ARNOLD** Featured in the 1993 film *Young Americans*	Island CID 573
18/10/1997	7	5		**ON HER MAJESTY'S SECRET SERVICE** **PROPELLERHEADS AND DAVID ARNOLD**	East West EW 136CD
22/11/1997	39	2		DIAMONDS ARE FOREVER **DAVID McALMONT AND DAVID ARNOLD** This and above single are cover versions of the themes to the James Bond films of the same names and are taken from the *Shaken Not Stirred* album	East West EW 141CD
29/04/2000	49	1		THEME FROM 'RANDALL & HOPKIRK (DECEASED)' Theme to the TV revival of the same name	Island CID 762

EDDY ARNOLD
US country singer (born 15/5/1918, Henderson, TN) who had 145 country chart hits and worldwide sales estimated at 80 million. Known as The Tennessee Plowboy, he was elected to the Country Music Hall of Fame in 1966. He has a star on the Hollywood Walk of Fame.

17/02/1966	8	17		**MAKE THE WORLD GO AWAY**	RCA 1496
26/05/1966	46	3		I WANT TO GO WITH YOU	RCA 1519
28/07/1966	49	1		IF YOU WERE MINE MARY	RCA 1529

P.P. ARNOLD
US singer (born Patricia Arnold, 1946, Los Angeles, CA) who became a UK resident in 1966 after arriving as part of Ike and Tina Turner's backing group The Ikettes. Later she became a session singer and actress, and appeared in musicals.

04/05/1967	18	10		FIRST CUT IS THE DEEPEST	Immediate IM 047
02/08/1967	47	2		THE TIME HAS COME	Immediate IM 055
24/01/1968	41	4		(IF YOU THINK YOU'RE) GROOVY	Immediate IM 061
10/07/1968	29	11		ANGEL OF THE MORNING	Immediate IM 067
24/09/1988	14	10		BURN IT UP **BEATMASTERS WITH P.P. ARNOLD**	Rhythm King LEFT 27

ARPEGGIO
US studio group assembled by producer Simon Soussan.

31/03/1979	63	3		LOVE AND DESIRE (PART 1)	Polydor POSP 40

ARRESTED DEVELOPMENT
US hip hop group formed in Atlanta, GA in 1988 by Speech (born Todd Thomas, 25/10/1968, Milwaukee, WI), Aerie Taree (born 10/1/1973, Milwaukee), Monto Eshe (born 23/12/1974, Georgia), Nadriah, Rasa Don (born Donald Jones, 22/11/1968, New Jersey), DJ Headliner (born Tim Barnwell, 26/7/1967, New Jersey) and Baba Oje (born 15/5/1932, Laurie, MS). They disbanded in 1994, Speech going solo in 1996. Their two Grammy Awards include Best New Artist in 1992.

16/05/1992	46	7		TENNESSEE 1992 Grammy Award for Best Rap Performance by a Group	Cooltempo COOL 253
24/10/1992	2	14	○	**PEOPLE EVERYDAY** Contains a sample of Sly & The Family Stone's *Everyday People*	Cooltempo COOL 265
09/01/1993	4	9		**MR WENDAL/REVOLUTION** B-side featured in the 1992 film *Malcolm X*	Cooltempo CDCOOL 268
03/04/1993	18	6		TENNESSEE Re-issue of Cooltempo COOL 253	Cooltempo CDCOOL 270
28/05/1994	33	3		EASE MY MIND Contains a sample of George Clinton's *Open All Night Drums*	Cooltempo CDCOOL 293

STEVE ARRINGTON
US singer (born in Dayton, OH) who was lead singer with funk group Slave before going solo in 1982.

27/04/1985	5	10		**FEEL SO REAL**	Atlantic A 9576
06/07/1985	21	9		DANCIN' IN THE KEY OF LIFE	Atlantic A 9534

ARRIVAL
UK group formed in Liverpool by Dyan Birch (born 25/1/1949), Paddy McHugh (born 28/8/1946), Frank Collins (born 25/10/1947), Carroll Carter (born 10/6/1948), Don Hume (born 31/3/1950), Lloyd Courtney (born 20/12/1947) and Tom O'Malley (born 15/7/1948). They also recorded for CBS and Kaleidoscope. Birch, Collins, O'Malley and McHugh later formed Kokomo.

10/01/1970	8	9		**FRIENDS**	Decca F 12986
06/06/1970	16	11		I WILL SURVIVE	Decca F 13026

ARROLA – see **RUFF DRIVERZ**

ARROW
Montserrat singer (born Alphonsus Cassell) who made his first record in 1974 and later recorded for Mango, Island and his own Arrow label.

28/07/1984	59	5		HOT HOT HOT	Cooltempo ARROW 1
13/07/1985	30	7		LONG TIME	London LON 70
03/09/1994	38	3		HOT HOT HOT (REMIX)	The Hit Label HLC 7

ARROWS
US/UK group formed in 1973 by Alan Merrill (bass/vocals), Jake Hooker (guitar) and Paul Varley (drums). They are best known for having written and recorded the original version of *I Love Rock 'n' Roll*, a Joan Jett hit in 1982. Hooker, who later married Judy Garland's daughter Lorna Luft, went into music management. Merrill became part of Meatloaf's backing band.

25/05/1974	8	9		**A TOUCH TOO MUCH**	RAK 171
01/02/1975	25	7		MY LAST NIGHT WITH YOU	RAK 189

ARSENAL F.C. FIRST TEAM SQUAD
UK football club formed in London in 1886 as Dial Square FC, becoming Arsenal in 1914 (after spells as Woolwich Arsenal and Royal Arsenal).

08/05/1971	16	7		GOOD OLD ARSENAL Based on *Rule Britannia*	Pye 7N 45067
15/05/1993	34	3		SHOUTING FOR THE GUNNERS **ARSENAL FA CUP SQUAD FEATURING TIPPA IRIE AND PETER HUNNIGALE**	London LONCD 342
23/05/1998	9	5		**HOT STUFF** **ARSENAL FC**	Grapevine AFCCD 1
03/06/2000	46	1		ARSENAL NUMBER ONE/OUR GOAL	Grapevine CDGPS 280

❶⁹ Number of weeks single topped the UK chart ↑ Entered the UK chart at #1 ▲⁹ Number of weeks single topped the US chart

35

ART BRUT
UK rock group formed by Eddie Argos (vocals), Chris Chinchilla (guitar), Ian Catskilkin (guitar), Freddie Feedback (bass) and Mike (drums).

DATE	POS	WKS	BPI	SINGLE TITLE	LABEL & NUMBER
10/04/2004	52	1		FORMED A BAND	Rough Trade RTRADSCD174
18/12/2004	49	1		MODERN ART/MY LITTLE BROTHER	Fierce Panda NING164CD

ART COMPANY
Dutch pop group featuring Nol Havens on vocals. They later recorded for Polydor.

DATE	POS	WKS	BPI	SINGLE TITLE	LABEL & NUMBER
26/05/1984	12	11		SUSANNA	Epic A 4174

ART OF NOISE
UK studio group formed by Anne Dudley (born 7/5/1960, Chatham), Jonathan 'JJ' Jeczalik (born 11/5/1955) and Gary Langan, with Trevor Horn and Paul Morley of ZTT Records also contributing. They disbanded in 1990. Dudley was later a songwriter, winning an Oscar for her work on the 1997 film *The Full Monty*. The group was named by ZTT Records' Paul Morley after the 1909 avant garde Futurist Manifesto in Italy. Max Headroom is a TV animated character with Matt Frewer providing the voice.

DATE	POS	WKS	BPI	SINGLE TITLE	LABEL & NUMBER
24/11/1984	8	19		CLOSE (TO THE EDIT)	ZTT ZTPS 01
13/04/1985	51	4		MOMENTS IN LOVE/BEAT BOX	ZTT ZTPS 02
09/11/1985	69	1		LEGS	China WOK 5
22/03/1986	8	9		PETER GUNN ART OF NOISE FEATURING DUANE EDDY 1986 Grammy Award for Best Rock Instrumental Performance	China WOK 6
21/06/1986	12	9		PARANOIMIA ART OF NOISE FEATURING MAX HEADROOM	China WOK 9
18/07/1987	60	4		DRAGNET Featured in the 1987 film *Dragnet*	China WOK 14
29/10/1988	5	7		KISS ART OF NOISE FEATURING TOM JONES	China 11
12/08/1989	63	3		YEBO ART OF NOISE FEATURING MAHLATHINI AND THE MAHOTELLA QUEENS	China 18
16/06/1990	67	1		ART OF LOVE	China 23
11/01/1992	45	5		INSTRUMENTS OF DARKNESS (ALL OF US ARE ONE PEOPLE)	China WOK 2012
29/02/1992	53	2		SHADES OF PARANOIMIA	China WOK 2014
26/06/1999	53	1		METAFORCE	ZTT 129CD

ART OF TRANCE
UK instrumentalist/producer Simon Berry who founded the Platipus label in 1995.

DATE	POS	WKS	BPI	SINGLE TITLE	LABEL & NUMBER
31/10/1998	69	1		MADAGASCAR (2ND REMIX)	Platipus PLAT 43CD
07/08/1999	48	2		MADAGASCAR (REMIX)	Platipus PLAT 58CD
15/06/2002	41	2		MADAGASCAR	Platipus PLATCD 0102
10/08/2002	60	1		LOVE WASHES OVER	Platipus PLATCD 98

ARTEMESIA
Dutch producer Patrick Prinz who also records as Ethics, Movin' Melodies and Subliminal Cuts.

DATE	POS	WKS	BPI	SINGLE TITLE	LABEL & NUMBER
15/04/1995	46	2		BITS + PIECES	Hooj Choons HOOJ 31CD
23/09/1995	75	1		BITS + PIECES	Hooj Choons HOOJ 31CD
12/08/2000	51	1		BITS + PIECES (REMIX)	Tidy Trax TIDT 141CD

ARTFUL DODGER
UK production duo Mark Hill and Pete Devereux from Southampton. They split in July 2001, Devereux later joining Dave Low. The group also launched the Centric label.

DATE	POS	WKS	BPI	SINGLE TITLE	LABEL & NUMBER
11/12/1999	2	17	✪	RE-REWIND THE CROWD SAY BO SELECTA ARTFUL DODGER FEATURING CRAIG DAVID	Public Demand/Relentless RELENT 1CDS
04/03/2000	2	12	○	MOVIN' TOO FAST ARTFUL DODGER AND ROMINA JOHNSON	Locked On/XL Recordings LUX 117CD
15/07/2000	6	10		WOMAN TROUBLE ARTFUL DODGER FEATURING ROBBIE CRAIG AND CRAIG DAVID Featured in the 2001 film *Bridget Jones's Diary*	Public Demand/ffrr FCDP 380
25/11/2000	4	10		PLEASE DON'T TURN ME ON ARTFUL DODGER FEATURING LIFFORD	ffrr FCD 388
17/03/2001	11	8		THINK ABOUT ME ARTFUL DODGER FEATURING MICHELLE ESCOFFERY	ffrr FCD 394
15/09/2001	6	9		TWENTYFOURSEVEN ARTFUL DODGER FEATURING MELANIE BLATT	ffrr FCDP 400
15/12/2001	20	5		IT AIN'T ENOUGH DREEM TEEM VERSUS ARTFUL DODGER Featured in the 2001 film *Mike Bassett England Manager*	ffrr/Public Demand FCD 401

DAVEY ARTHUR – see FUREYS

NEIL ARTHUR
UK singer (born 15/6/1958, Darwen) who was previously a member of Blancmange.

DATE	POS	WKS	BPI	SINGLE TITLE	LABEL & NUMBER
05/02/1994	50	2		I LOVE I HATE	Chrysalis CDCHSS 5005

ARTIFICIAL FUNK FEATURING NELLIE ETTISON
Danish duo Rune 'RK' Kolsch and Nellie Ettison.

DATE	POS	WKS	BPI	SINGLE TITLE	LABEL & NUMBER
22/03/2003	40	2		TOGETHER	Skint 82CD

ARTIFICIAL INTELLIGENCE
German production duo Glenn Herweijer and Zula Warner.

DATE	POS	WKS	BPI	SINGLE TITLE	LABEL & NUMBER
21/08/2004	73	1		UPRISING/THROUGH THE GATE	V Recordings VRECS001UK

ARTIST – see PRINCE

ARTISTS AGAINST AIDS WORLDWIDE
Multinational charity ensemble with Bono (of U2), Nelly Furtado, Destiny's Child, Michael Stipe (of R.E.M.) and Fred Durst (of Limp Bizkit). Originally intended to raise funds for AIDS charities, after 11th September 2001 some of the funds raised were diverted to charities responding to the World Trade Center catastrophe in New York.

DATE	POS	WKS	BPI	SINGLE TITLE	LABEL & NUMBER
17/11/2001	6	12		WHAT'S GOING ON	Columbia 6721172

ARTISTS UNITED AGAINST APARTHEID
Multinational line-up of 49 superstars against the apartheid policy of the South African government, with proceeds donated to political prisoners. The project, conceived by Little Steven (aka Steve Van Zandt), features artists such as Pat Benatar, John Oates, Lou Reed, Bruce Springsteen, Ringo Starr, Pete Townsend and Bobby Womack.

23/11/1985 . . . . . 21 . . . . . . 8				SUN CITY . . . . Manhattan MT 7	

A.S.A.P. UK group that includes Adrian Smith (guitar/vocals), Andy Barnett (guitar/vocals), Dave Colwell (guitar/vocals), Richard Young (keyboards), Robin Clayton (bass) and Zak Starkey (drums). Smith had previously been with Iron Maiden; Starkey is the son of Beatles drummer Ringo Starr. Their name stands for Adrian Smith And Project.

14/10/1989 . . . . . 60 . . . . . . 2				SILVER AND GOLD . . . . EMI EM 107	
03/02/1990 . . . . . 67 . . . . . . 2				DOWN THE WIRE . . . . EMI EM 131	

ASCENSION UK production duo Ricky Simmons and Stephen Jones who also record as Chakra, Lustral, Oxygen and Space Brothers.

05/07/1997 . . . . . 55 . . . . . . 1				SOMEONE . . . . Perfecto PERF 141CD	
15/07/2000 . . . . . 43 . . . . . . 2				SOMEONE (REMIX) . . . . Code Blue BLU 011CD1	
23/03/2002 . . . . . 45 . . . . . . 1				FOR A LIFETIME ASCENSION FEATURING ERIN LORDAN . . . . Xtravaganza XTRAV 20CDS	

ASH UK group formed in Ulster by Tim Wheeler (born 4/1/1977, Downpatrick, vocals/guitar), Mark Hamilton (born 21/3/1977, Lisburn, bass) and Rick McMurray (born 11/7/1975, Larne, drums). They were still at school when they formed and signed with Infectious, adding Charlotte Hatherley (born 20/6/1979, London) for *A Life Less Ordinary*.

01/041995 . . . . . 57 . . . . . . 1				KUNG FU . . . . Infectious INFECT 21CD	
12/08/1995 . . . . . 11 . . . . . . 5				GIRL FROM MARS . . . . Infectious INFECT 24CD	
21/10/1995 . . . . . 14 . . . . . . 4				ANGEL INTERCEPTOR . . . . Infectious INFECT 27CD	
27/04/1996 . . . . . 5 . . . . . . 5				**GOLDFINGER** . . . . Infectious INFECT 39CD	
06/07/1996 . . . . . 6 . . . . . . 8				OH YEAH . . . . Infectious INFECT 41CD	
25/10/1997 . . . . . 10 . . . . . . 5				**A LIFE LESS ORDINARY** Featured in the 1998 film *A Life Less Ordinary* . . . . Infectious INFECT 50CD	
03/10/1998 . . . . . 15 . . . . . . 4				JESUS SAYS . . . . Infectious INFECT 59CD	
05/12/1998 . . . . . 31 . . . . . . 2				WILD SURF . . . . Infectious INFECT 61CDS	
10/02/2001 . . . . . 8 . . . . . . 4				**SHINING LIGHT** . . . . Infectious INFECT 98CDSX	
14/04/2001 . . . . . 13 . . . . . . 6				BURN BABY BURN . . . . Infectious INFECT 99CDS	
21/07/2001 . . . . . 21 . . . . . . 6				SOMETIMES . . . . Infectious INFEC 101CDS	
13/10/2001 . . . . . 20 . . . . . . 3				CANDY Contains a sample from The Walker Brothers' *Make It Easy On Yourself* . . . . Infectious INFEC 106CDSX	
12/01/2002 . . . . . 13 . . . . . . 3				THERE'S A STAR . . . . Infectious INFEC 112CDS	
07/09/2002 . . . . . 21 . . . . . . 2				ENVY . . . . Infectious INFECT 119CDSX	
15/05/2004 . . . . . 13 . . . . . . 4				ORPHEUS . . . . Infectious ASH01CD	
31/07/2004 . . . . . 22 . . . . . . 5				STARCROSSED . . . . Infectious ASH02CD	
18/12/2004 . . . . . 33 . . . . . . 2+				RENEGADE CAVALCADE . . . . Atlantic ASH03CD	

ASH – see QUENTIN AND ASH

ASHA Italian singer/keyboard player who later worked with Bob Andy, Boy Krazy and The Fantasy Band.

08/07/1995 . . . . . 38 . . . . . . 2				JJ TRIBUTE . . . . ffrreedom TABCD 228	

ASHANTI US singer (born Ashanti Douglas, 13/10/1980, Glen Cove, NY) first known as an actress. She appeared in *Malcolm X* (1992) and *Who's Da Man* and was guest singer on hits by Ja Rule and Fat Joe before going solo. On 20th April 2002 her debut album *Ashanti* entered the US charts at #1 (with a female debut record for first week sales of 503,000), the same week her first solo single *Foolish* topped the singles chart. Also, her single with Fat Joe (*What's Luv*) was at #2, making her the first female to hold the top two positions on the *Billboard* Hot 100. She won the 2002 Grammy Award for Best Contemporary Rhythm & Blues Album for *Ashanti* and the 2002 MOBO Award for Best Rhythm & Blues Act.

02/02/2002 . . . . . 6 . . . . . . 13				**ALWAYS ON TIME** ▲² JA RULE FEATURING ASHANTI . . . . Def Jam 5889462	
25/05/2002 . . . . . 4 . . . . . . 8				WHAT'S LUV FAT JOE FEATURING ASHANTI . . . . Atlantic AT 0128CD	
08/06/2002 . . . . . 69 . . . . . . 3				FOOLISH (IMPORT) ▲¹⁰ . . . . Mercury 5829372	
20/07/2002 . . . . . 3 . . . . . . 10				**FOOLISH** Contains a sample of El DeBarge's *Stay With Me* . . . . Murder Inc 0639942	
12/10/2002 . . . . . 4 . . . . . . 10				**DOWN 4 U** IRV GOTTI PRESENTS JA RULE, ASHANTI, CHARLI BALTIMORE AND VITA . . . . Murder Inc 0639002	
23/11/2002 . . . . . 13 . . . . . . 8				HAPPY . . . . Def Jam 0638242	
29/03/2003 . . . . . 12 . . . . . . 8				MESMERIZE JA RULE FEATURING ASHANTI Contains a sample of Diana Ross & Marvin Gaye's *Stop! Look, Listen (To Your Heart)* . . . . Murder Inc 0779582	
28/06/2003 . . . . . 7 . . . . . . 10				**ROCK WIT U (AWWW BABY)** . . . . Murder Inc 9808432	
01/11/2003 . . . . . 19 . . . . . . 4				RAIN ON ME . . . . Murder Inc 9813177	
06/11/2004 . . . . ❶¹ . . . 8+				**WONDERFUL** ↑ JA RULE FEATURING R KELLY AND ASHANTI . . . . Def Jam 9864606	

ASHAYE UK singer Trevor Ashaye.

15/10/1983 . . . . . 45 . . . . . . 3				MICHAEL JACKSON MEDLEY Medley of *Don't Stop 'Til You Get Enough*, *Wanna Be Startin' Something*, *Shake Your Body Down To The Ground* and *Blame It On The Boogie* . . . . Record Shack SOHO 10	

RICHARD ASHCROFT UK singer (born 11/9/1971, Wigan) who was lead vocalist with The Verve from their formation in 1989. He went solo when they disbanded in April 1999.

15/04/2000 . . . . . 3 . . . 11				**A SONG FOR LOVERS** . . . . Hut HUTCD 128	
24/06/2000 . . . . . 17 . . . . . . 4				MONEY TO BURN . . . . Hut HUTCD 136	
23/09/2000 . . . . . 21 . . . . . . 3				C'MON PEOPLE (WE'RE MAKING IT NOW) . . . . Hut HUTCD 138	
19/10/2002 . . . . . 11 . . . . . . 6				CHECK THE MEANING . . . . Hut HUTCD 161	
18/01/2003 . . . . . 14 . . . . . . 4				SCIENCE OF SILENCE . . . . Hut HUTCD 163	
19/04/2003 . . . . . 26 . . . . . . 2				BUY IT IN BOTTLES . . . . Hut HUTCD 167	

❶⁹ Number of weeks single topped the UK chart   ↑ Entered the UK chart at #1   ▲⁹ Number of weeks single topped the US chart

JOHN ASHER UK singer, previously compere of the ITV show *Tis Was* and member of the Black And White Minstrels.

15/11/1975.....14......6.......	LET'S TWIST AGAIN .... Creole CR 112

ASHFORD AND SIMPSON US husband and wife vocal duo Nicholas Ashford (born 4/5/1942, Fairfield, SC) and Valerie Simpson (born 26/8/1946, New York) who first recorded as Valerie & Nick in 1964. They became more successful as songwriters and producers at Motown Records. They resumed recording in 1973. Valerie made a number of singles with Marvin Gaye, uncredited, standing in for the ill Tammi Terrell. Ashford appeared in the 1991 film *New Jack City*.

18/11/1978.....48......4....... IT SEEMS TO HANG ON .... Warner Brothers K 17237
05/01/1985 .....3......15.....● **SOLID** .... Capitol CL 345
20/04/1985.....56......3....... BABIES .... Capitol CL 355

ASHTON, GARDNER AND DYKE UK trio Tony Ashton (born 1/3/1946, Blackburn, keyboards/vocals), Kim Gardner (born 27/1/1946, London, bass) and Roy Dyke (born 13/2/1946, drums). They were joined on their hit single by Dave Caswell (trumpet), Lyle Jenkins (saxophone) and Mick Lieber (guitar). Disbanded after three albums, Dyke went on to form Badger (Gardner joined later) and Ashton joined Family. Ashton died from cancer on 28/5/2001.

16/01/1971 .....3......14....... **RESURRECTION SHUFFLE** .... Capitol CL 15665

ASIA UK art rock group with John Wetton (born 12/7/1949, Derby, vocals, ex-King Crimson, Uriah Heep and Roxy Music), Steve Howe (born 8/4/1947, London, guitar, ex-Yes), Carl Palmer (born 20/3/1947, Birmingham, drums/percussion, ex-Emerson, Lake And Palmer) and Geoff Downes (keyboards, ex-Buggles and Yes). Later members included Mandy Meyer and Pat Thrall. Wetton was replaced by Greg Lake (born 10/11/1948, Bournemouth, ex-Emerson, Lake And Palmer) between 1983 and 1985.

03/07/1982.....46......5....... HEAT OF THE MOMENT .... Geffen GEF A 2494
18/09/1982.....54......3....... ONLY TIME WILL TELL .... Geffen GEF A 2228
13/08/1983.....33......5....... DON'T CRY .... Geffen A 3580

ASIA BLUE UK vocal group.

27/06/1992.....50......2....... ESCAPING .... Atomic WNR 882

ASIAN DUB FOUNDATION UK rock group formed in London in 1993 by Aniruddha Das (aka Doctor Das, bass), Deeder Zaman (aka Master D, raps), DJ John Pandit (aka Panfit G), Steve Chandra Savale (aka Chandrasonic, guitar) and Sanjay Tailor (aka Sun J).

21/02/1998.....56......1....... FREE SATPAL RAM Satpal Ram is an Asian man who was sentenced to life imprisonment in 1986 after killing a man who had attacked him in a Birmingham restaurant. Ram was freed on licence (but not cleared) in June 2002 .... ffrr FCD 326
02/05/1998.....31......2....... BUZZIN' .... ffrr FCDP 335
04/07/1998.....52......1....... BLACK WHITE .... ffrr FCD 337
18/03/2000.....41......2....... REAL GREAT BRITAIN .... ffrr FCD 376
03/06/2000.....49......1....... NEW WAY, NEW LIFE .... ffrr FCD 378
01/02/2003.....57......1....... FORTRESS EUROPE .... Virgin DINSDY 253

ASSEMBLY UK studio project of Vince Clarke (born 3/7/1960, South Woodford, ex-Depeche Mode, Yazoo and Erasure), singer Feargal Sharkey (born 13/8/1958, Londonderry) and Eric Radcliffe.

12/11/1983 .....4......10.....○ **NEVER NEVER** .... Mute TINY 1

ASSOCIATES UK new wave group formed in Dundee by Billy MacKenzie (born 27/3/1957, Dundee) and Alan Rankine who first met in 1976. Rankine later left and MacKenzie re-formed the group. MacKenzie was found dead in a garden shed on 22/1/1997, believed to have commited suicide following his mother's death, just after signing a six-album solo artist deal with Nude.

20/02/1982 .....9......10....... **PARTY FEARS TWO** .... Associates ASC 1
08/05/1982 .....13.....10....... CLUB COUNTRY .... Associates ASC 2
07/08/1982 .....21......8....... LOVE HANGOVER/18 CARAT LOVE AFFAIR .... Associates ASC 3
16/06/1984 .....43......6....... THOSE FIRST IMPRESSIONS .... WEA YZ 6
01/09/1984 .....53......4....... WAITING FOR THE LOVEBOAT .... WEA YZ 16
19/01/1985 .....49......6....... BREAKFAST .... WEA YX 28
17/09/1988 .....56......3....... HEART OF GLASS .... WEA YZ 310

ASSOCIATION US group formed in Los Angeles, CA in 1965 by Terry Kirkman (born 12/12/1941, Salina, KS, keyboards), Gary Alexander (born 25/9/1943, Chattanooga, TN, guitar), Brian Cole (born 8/9/1942, Tacoma, WA, bass), Jim Yester (born 24/11/1939, Birmingham, AL, guitar), Ted Bluechel (born 2/12/1942, San Pedro, CA, drums) and Russ Giguere (born 18/10/1943, Portsmouth, NH, guitar), with Larry Ramos (born 19/4/1942, Waimea, Hawaii) replacing Alexander in 1967. Cole died of a heroin overdose on 2/8/1972.

22/05/1968.....23......8....... TIME FOR LIVING .... Warner Brothers WB 7195

RICK ASTLEY UK singer (born 6/2/1966, Newton-le-Willows) who played drums with FBI before becoming their lead singer and subsequently being discovered by Stock, Aitken And Waterman.

08/08/1987 .....❶⁵.....18.....● **NEVER GONNA GIVE YOU UP** ▲² 1988 BRIT Award for Best Single. Featured in the 1995 film *Dead Presidents* ...... RCA PB 41447
31/10/1987 .....3......12....... **WHENEVER YOU NEED SOMEBODY** .... RCA PB 41567
12/12/1987 .....2......10.....○ **WHEN I FALL IN LOVE/MY ARMS KEEP MISSING YOU** .... RCA PB 41683
27/02/1988 .....2......9....... **TOGETHER FOREVER** ▲¹ .... RCA PB 41817
24/09/1988 .....6......10....... **SHE WANTS TO DANCE WITH ME** .... RCA PB 42189
26/11/1988 .....8......10....... **TAKE ME TO YOUR HEART** .... RCA PB 42573
11/02/1989 .....10......8....... **HOLD ME IN YOUR ARMS** .... RCA PB 42615
26/01/1991 .....7......7....... **CRY FOR HELP** .... RCA PB 44247

○ Silver disc ● Gold disc ✪ Platinum disc (additional platinum units are indicated by a figure following the symbol) ◎ Singles released prior to 1973 that are known to have sold over 1 million copies in the UK

DATE	POS	WKS	BPI	SINGLE TITLE	LABEL & NUMBER
30/03/1991	58	2		MOVE RIGHT OUT	RCA PB 44407
29/06/1991	70	1		NEVER KNEW LOVE	RCA PB 44737
04/09/1993	48	2		THE ONES YOU LOVE	RCA 74321160142
13/11/1993	33	2		HOPELESSLY	RCA 74321175642

ASTRO TRAX
UK production group Sonjay Prabhaker and Evren Omer with singers Shola Phillips and June Ham. They later launched the Astro Trax label.

24/10/1998	74	1		THE ENERGY (FEEL THE VIBE)	Satellite 74321622052

ASWAD
UK reggae group formed in 1975 by Brinsley Forde (born 1952, Guyana, guitar/vocals), Donald Benjamin (guitar), Courtney Hemmings (keyboards), Ras George (bass) and Angus 'Drummie' Zeb (drums), named from the Arabic word for 'black'. By 1986 they were the trio of Forde, Zeb and Tony Gad (guitar). Forde was previously a child actor in the TV series *Here Come The Double Deckers*. They received the Outstanding Contribution Award at the 2000 MOBO Awards.

03/03/1984	51	3		CHASING FOR THE BREEZE	Island IS 160
06/10/1984	70	3		54-66 (WAS MY NUMBER)	Island IS 170
27/02/1988	❶²	12	○	**DON'T TURN AROUND** Written by Albert Hammond and Diane Warren, and originally recorded by Tina Turner	Mango IS 341
21/05/1988	11	8		GIVE A LITTLE LOVE	Mango IS 358
24/09/1988	70	2		SET THEM FREE	Mango IS 383
01/04/1989	31	6		BEAUTY'S ONLY SKIN DEEP	Mango MNG 105
22/07/1989	25	8		ON AND ON	Mango MNG 708
18/08/1990	24	6		NEXT TO YOU	Mango MNG 753
17/11/1990	53	2		SMILE **ASWAD FEATURING SWEETIE IRIE**	Mango MNG 767
30/03/1991	61	2		TOO WICKED (EP) Tracks on EP: *Best Of My Love, Warrior Re-Charge, Fire* and *I Shot The Sheriff*	Mango MNG 771
31/07/1993	31	5		HOW LONG **YAZZ AND ASWAD**	Polydor PZCD 252
09/10/1993	48	2		DANCEHALL MOOD	Bubblin' CDBUBB 1
18/06/1994	5	14	○	**SHINE**	Bubblin' CDBUBB 3
17/09/1994	33	3		WARRIORS	Bubblin' CDBUBB 4
18/02/1995	35	3		YOU'RE NO GOOD	Bubblin' CDBUBB 5
05/08/1995	58	1		IF I WAS	Bubblin' CDBUBB 6
31/08/2002	62	1		SHY GUY **ASWAD FEATURING EASTHER BENNETT**	Universal Music TV 0192632

AT THE DRIVE-IN
US rock group from El Paso, TX with Cedric Bixler (vocals), Omar Rodriguez (guitar), Jim Ward (guitar), Paul Hinojos (bass) and Tony Hajjar (drums).

19/08/2000	64	1		ONE ARMED SCISSOR	Grand Royal GR 091CD
16/12/2000	54	1		ROLODEX PROPAGANDA	Grand Royal/Virgin VUSCD 189
24/03/2001	50	1		INVALID LITTER DEPT	Grand Royal/Virgin VUSCD 193

GALI ATARI – see MILK AND HONEY FEATURING GALI ATARI

ATARIS
US group with Kris Roe (vocals), Marco Pena (guitar), Mike Davenport (bass) and Derrick Plourde (drums). Plourde was subsequently replaced by Chris Knapp.

11/10/2003	49	1		THE BOYS OF SUMMER	Columbia 6743402

ATB
German DJ/producer Andre Tanneburger whose debut hit vocals were lifted from Spanish model Yolanda Riviera's TV appearance where she described her orgasms, hence the title.

13/03/1999	68	1		9PM (TILL I COME)	Ministry Of Sound DATA 1
22/05/1999	47	5		9PM (TILL I COME) (GERMAN IMPORT)	Club Tools CLU 66066
19/06/1999	63	1		9PM (TILL I COME) (AUSTRALIAN IMPORT)	Dancenet DNET 131
03/07/1999	❶²	15	✪	**9PM (TILL I COME)** ↑	Sound Of Ministry MOSCDS 132
09/10/1999	61	2		DON'T STOP (IMPORT)	Club Tools CLU 66406
23/10/1999	3	13	○	**DON'T STOP**	Sound Of Ministry MOSCDS 134
25/03/2000	4	9		**KILLER**	Sound Of Ministry MOSCDS 138
27/01/2001	16	4		**THE FIELDS OF LOVE ATB FEATURING YORK**	Club Tools 0124095 CLU
30/06/2001	34	2		**LET U GO** Features the uncredited contribution of Roberta Carter	Kontour 0117335 KTR

ATC
Multinational group formed by Joe (New Zealand), Sarah (Australia), Tracey (England) and Livio (Italy). They were all members of the German cast of the musical *Cats*. Their name stands for A Touch Of Class.

17/08/2002	15	4		AROUND THE WORLD (LA LA LA LA)	Liberty CDATC 001

ATEED
German singer (born 1981, Frankfurt), with an Iranian father and Greek-Turkish mother, who was the lead singer with Fusion before going solo.

04/10/2003	56	1		COME TO ME	Better The Devil BTD 4CD

A.T.F.C. PRESENTS ONEPHATDEEVA
UK producer Aydin Hasirci (A.T.F.C. stands for Aydin The Funki Chile) who is also a member of Weird Science.

30/10/1999	11	5		IN AND OUT OF MY LIFE Contains samples of Adeva's *In And Out Of My Life* and Fatboy Slim's *Right Here Right Now*	Defected DFECT 19CDX
16/09/2000	17	3		BAD HABIT **A.T.F.C. PRESENTS ONEPHATDEEVA FEATURING LISA MILLETT** Contains samples of Bad Habits' Bad Habits and Chaka Khan's I Know You – I Love You	Defected DFECT 8CDS

❶⁹ Number of weeks single topped the UK chart ↑ Entered the UK chart at #1 ▲⁹ Number of weeks single topped the US chart

09/02/2002 . . . . . 33 . . . . . . 2 . . . . SLEEP TALK **A.T.F.C. FEATURING LISA MILLETT** Contains a sample of Donna Summer's *Bad Girls* . . . . Defected DFECT 43CDS

ATGOC Italian instrumentalist/producer Andrea Mazzali.

21/11/1998 . . . . . 38 . . . . . . 2 . . . . REPEATED LOVE . . . . Wonderboy WBOYD 012

ATHLETE UK group formed in London in 2000 by Joel Pott (guitar/vocals), Carey Willetts (bass/vocals), Tim Wanstall (keyboards/vocals) and Steve Roberts (drums/vocals).

29/06/2002 . . . . . 37 . . . . . . 2 . . . . YOU GOT THE STYLE . . . . Parlophone CDATH 001
16/11/2002 . . . . . 41 . . . . . . 1 . . . . BEAUTIFUL . . . . Parlophone CDATH 002
05/04/2003 . . . . . 31 . . . . . . 2 . . . . EL SALVADOR . . . . Parlophone CDATHS 003
05/07/2003 . . . . . 42 . . . . . . 1 . . . . WESTSIDE . . . . Parlophone CDATHS 005
04/10/2003 . . . . . 42 . . . . . . 1 . . . . YOU GOT THE STYLE Re-issue of Parlophone CDATH 001 . . . . Parlophone CDATH 006

CHET ATKINS US guitarist (born Chester Burton Atkins, 20/6/1924 Luttrell, TN) who began as a fiddler with the Dixieland Swingers in Knoxville, TN in the 1940s. First recording in 1946, he joined RCA the following year, staying until the early 1980s. As well as being an artist in his own right (with over 100 albums to his name), Atkins worked with numerous RCA stars (as either a producer or session guitarist) including Elvis Presley, Jim Reeves and Don Gibson. He moved to Columbia in the early 1980s. He won thirteen Grammy Awards: Best Instrumental Performance (other than Jazz) in 1967 for *Chet Atkins Picks The Best*; Best Country Instrumental Performance in 1970 with Jerry Reed for *Me And Jerry*; Best Country Instrumental Performance in 1971 for *Snowbird*; Best Country Instrumental Performance in 1974 with Merle Travis for *The Atkins-Travis Traveling Show*; Best Country Instrumental Performance in 1975 for *The Entertainer*; Best Country Instrumental Performance in 1976 with Les Paul for *Chester And Lester*; Best Country Instrumental Performance in 1981 for *Country, After All These Years*; Best Country Instrumental Performance in 1985 with Mark Knoffler for *Cosmic Square Dance*; Best Country Vocal Collaboration in 1990 with Mark Knoffler for *Poor Boy Blues*; Best Country Instrumental Performance in 1990 with Mark Knoffler for *So Soft Your Goodbye*; Best Country Instrumental Performance in 1992 with Jerry Reed for *Sneakin' Around;* Best Country Instrumental Performance in 1994 for *Young Thing;* and Best Country Instrumental in 1996 for *Jam Man*. He died from cancer on 30/6/2001 and was inducted into the Rock and Roll Hall of Fame in 2002.

17/03/1960 . . . . . 46 . . . . . . 2 . . . . TEENSVILLE . . . . RCA 1174

ATL US vocal group formed in Atlanta, GA by Danger (aged eighteen at the time of their debut hit), Will (aged eighteen), L-Rock (aged sixteen) and Tre (aged eighteen) after winning a talent contest organised by Atlanta radio station V-103, which attracted 3,000 entrants.

29/05/2004 . . . . . 12 . . . . . . 5 . . . . CALLING ALL GIRLS . . . . Epic 6748272
28/08/2004 . . . . . 21 . . . . . . 4 . . . . MAKE IT UP WITH LOVE . . . . Epic 6751102

ATLANTIC OCEAN Dutch instrumental/production/remixing duo Rene Van Der Weyde and Lex Van Coeverden. Van Coeverden also recorded as Disco Anthem.

19/02/1994 . . . . . 22 . . . . . . 6 . . . . WATERFALL . . . . Eastern Bloc BLOCCD 001
02/07/1994 . . . . . 15 . . . . . . 4 . . . . BODY IN MOTION . . . . Eastern Bloc BLOCCD 009
26/11/1994 . . . . . 59 . . . . . . 1 . . . . MUSIC IS A PASSION . . . . Eastern Bloc BLOCCDX 017
30/11/1996 . . . . . 21 . . . . . . 3 . . . . WATERFALL (REMIX) . . . . Eastern Bloc BLOC 104CD

ATLANTIC RHYTHM SECTION US group formed in Doraville, GA in 1971 by Rodney Justo (vocals), Barry Bailey (born 12/6/1948, Decatur, GA, guitar), JR Cobb (born 5/2/1944, Birmingham, AL, guitar), Paul Goddard (born 23/6/1945, Rome, GA, bass), Dean Daughty (born 8/9/1946, Kingston, AL, keyboards) and Robert Nix (drums). They first met on a Roy Orbison session at Studio One in Doraville. Justo left after one album and was replaced by Ronnie Hammond. Nix left in 1978 and was replaced by Roy Yeager.

27/10/1979 . . . . . 48 . . . . . . 4 . . . . SPOOKY . . . . Polydor POSP 74

ATLANTIC STARR US soul group formed in White Plains, NY in 1976 by Sharon Bryant (vocals), David Lewis (vocals/keyboards/guitar), Jonathan Lewis (keyboards/trombone), Wayne Lewis (keyboards/vocals), Koran Daniels (saxophone), William Suddeeth (trumpet), Clifford Archer (bass), Joseph Phillips (percussion) and Porter Caroll Jr (drums). Bryant left in 1984 and was replaced by Barbara Weathers; Weathers left in 1989 and was replaced by Porscha Martin. Martin left in 1991 and was replaced by Rachel Oliver, who in turn left in 1993 and was replaced by Aisha Tanner.

09/09/1978 . . . . . 66 . . . . . . 3 . . . . GIMME YOUR LOVIN' . . . . A&M AMS 7380
29/06/1985 . . . . . 41 . . . . . . 6 . . . . SILVER SHADOW . . . . A&M AM 260
07/09/1985 . . . . . 58 . . . . . . 4 . . . . ONE LOVE . . . . A&M AM 273
15/03/1986 . . . . . 10 . . . . 12 . . . . . . SECRET LOVERS . . . . A&M AM 307
24/05/1986 . . . . . 48 . . . . . . 4 . . . . IF YOUR HEART ISN'T IN IT . . . . A&M AM 319
13/06/1987 . . . . . . 3 . . . . 14 . . . . . . ○ ALWAYS ▲[1] . . . . Warner Brothers W 8455
12/09/1987 . . . . . 57 . . . . . . 3 . . . . ONE LOVER AT A TIME . . . . Warner Brothers W 8327
27/08/1994 . . . . . 36 . . . . . . 2 . . . . EVERYBODY'S GOT SUMMER . . . . Arista 74321228072

ATLANTIS VS AVATAR UK production group of Seb Fontaine and Jules Vern with singer Miriam Stockley, who is also a member of Praise.

28/10/2000 . . . . . 52 . . . . . . 2 . . . . FIJI Contains a sample of Praise's *Only You* . . . . Inferno CDFERN 34

NATACHA ATLAS – see JEAN-MICHEL JARRE

ATMOSFEAR UK instrumental group with Andy Sojka (born 10/7/1951, guitar), Lester Batchelor (bass), Anthony Antoniou (guitar) and Stewart Cawthorne (saxophone). Sojka died from multiple myeloma in February 2000.

17/11/1979 . . . . . 46 . . . . . . 7 . . . . DANCING IN OUTER SPACE . . . . MCA 543

○ Silver disc ● Gold disc ✪ Platinum disc (additional platinum units are indicated by a figure following the symbol) ◎ Singles released prior to 1973 that are known to have sold over 1 million copies in the UK

ATOMIC KITTEN
UK vocal group formed in Liverpool by Natasha Hamilton (born 17/7/1982), Kerry Katona (born 6/9/1980) and Liz McClarnon (born 10/4/1981). Katona left the group in January 2001 and was replaced by Precious member Jenny Frost (born 22/2/1978). Early member Heidi Range later became a member of Sugababes. Katona presented the TV show *Elimidate*. Frost and McClarnon appeared in the 2001 film *Mike Bassett England Manager*. The group announced they were to temporarily disband in February 2004.

DATE	POS	WKS	BPI	SINGLE TITLE	LABEL & NUMBER
11/12/1999	10	9		**RIGHT NOW**	Innocent SINCD 15
08/04/2000	6	7		**SEE YA**	Innocent SINCD 17
15/07/2000	10	5		**I WANT YOUR LOVE** Contains samples of The City Of Prague Philharmonic's *The Big Country* and KLF's *Justified And Ancient*	Innocent SINDX 18
21/10/2000	20	5		FOLLOW ME	Innocent SINDX 22
10/02/2001	❶⁴	23	✪	**WHOLE AGAIN** ↑	Innocent SINDX 24
04/08/2001	❶²	19	●	**ETERNAL FLAME** ↑ Featured in the 2001 film *The Parole Officer*	Innocent SINCD 27
01/06/2002	3	13	○	**IT'S OK**	Innocent SINCD 36
07/09/2002	❶³	16	●	**THE TIDE IS HIGH (GET THE FEELING)** ↑	Innocent SINDX 38
07/12/2002	2	12		**THE LAST GOODBYE/BE WITH YOU** B-side features a sample from Electric Light Orchestra's *Last Train to London*	Innocent SINDX 42
12/04/2003	4	10		**LOVE DOESN'T HAVE TO HURT**	Innocent SINDX 45
08/11/2003	3	10		**IF YOU COME TO ME**	Innocent SINDX 50
27/12/2003	8	11		**LADIES NIGHT** ATOMIC KITTEN FEATURING KOOL AND THE GANG Featured in the 2004 film *Confessions Of A Teenage Drama Queen*	Innocent SINDX 53
10/04/2004	8	8		**SOMEONE LIKE ME/RIGHT NOW 2004**	Innocent SINDX 60

ATOMIC ROOSTER
UK rock band formed in 1969 by Vincent Crane (born Vincent Rodney Chessman, 21/5/1943, Reading, formerly organist with The Crazy World Of Arthur Brown), Nick Graham (bass) and Carl Palmer (born 20/3/1951, Birmingham, drums). The latter pair quit not long after the debut album (Palmer going on to Emerson, Lake And Palmer) and new recruits Paul Hammond (drums) and John Cann (guitar/vocals) were drafted in. The group disbanded in 1974, despite a change to blue-eyed soul with singer Chris Farlowe. Crane commited suicide by overdosing on sleeping pills on 4/2/1989. Cann later recorded solo as John Du Cann.

DATE	POS	WKS	BPI	SINGLE TITLE	LABEL & NUMBER
06/02/1971	11	12		TOMORROW NIGHT	B&C CB 131
10/07/1971	4	13		**THE DEVIL'S ANSWER**	B&C CB 157

ATTRACTIONS – see ELVIS COSTELLO

WINIFRED ATWELL
UK pianist (born 27/4/1914, Tunapuna, Trinidad) who began playing at the age of four and planned a career in classical music, but evolved a boogie style that was hugely popular in the 1950s. One of the best paid performers of the decade, she owed much of her success to the tinny sound of a piano that cost 50 shillings (£2.50). She died in Australia on 28/2/1983.

DATE	POS	WKS	BPI	SINGLE TITLE	LABEL & NUMBER
12/12/1952	5	6		**BRITANNIA RAG**	Decca F 10015
15/05/1953	5	6		**CORONATION RAG**	Decca F 10110
25/09/1953	10	3		**FLIRTATION WALTZ**	Decca F 10161
04/12/1953	2	15		**LET'S HAVE A PARTY** Medley of *Boomps A Daisy, Daisy Bell, If You Knew Suzie, Knees Up Mother Brown, The More We Are Together, She Was One Of The Early Birds, That's My Weakness* and *Three O'Clock In The Morning*	Philips PB 213
23/07/1954	9	9		**RACHMANINOFF'S 18TH VARIATION ON A THEME BY PAGANINI (THE STORY OF THREE LOVES)**	Philips PB 234
26/11/1954	❶⁵	8		**LET'S HAVE ANOTHER PARTY** Medley of *Another Little Drink, Broken Doll, Bye Bye Blackbird, Honeysuckle And The Bee, I Wonder Where My Baby Is Tonight, Lily Of Laguna, Nellie Dean, Sheik Of Araby, Somebody Stole My Gal* and *When The Red Red Robin*	Philips PB 268
04/11/1955	3	10		**LET'S HAVE A DING DONG** Medley of *Happy Days Are Here Again, Oh Johnny Oh Johnny Oh, Oh You Beautiful Doll, Ain't She Sweet, Yes We Have No Bananas, I'm Forever Blowing Bubbles, I'll Be Your Sweetheart, If These Lips Could Only Speak* and *Who's Taking You Home Tonight*	Decca F 10634
16/03/1956	❶³	16		**POOR PEOPLE OF PARIS** The original title was 'La Goulant Du Pauvre Jean' (The Ballad Of Poor John) but was either misread or wrongly translated, for it was listed as 'pauvre gens', meaning 'poor people', and released as *Poor People Of Paris*	Decca F 10681
18/05/1956	18	6		PORT AU PRINCE WINIFRED ATWELL AND FRANK CHACKSFIELD	Decca F 10727
20/07/1956	14	7		LEFT BANK	Decca F 10762
26/10/1956	7	12		**MAKE IT A PARTY** Medley of *Who Were You With Last Night, Hello Hello Who's Your Lady Friend, Yes Sir That's My Baby, Don't Dilly Dally On The Way, Beer Barrel Polka, After The Ball, Peggy O'Neil, Meet Me Tonight In Dreamland, I Belong To Glasgow* and *Down At The Old Bull And Bush*	Decca F 10796
22/02/1957	24	4		LET'S ROCK 'N' ROLL Medley of *Singin' The Blues, Green Door, See You Later Alligator, Shake Rattle And Roll, Rock Around The Clock* and *Razzle Dazzle*	Decca F 10852
06/12/1957	4	6		**LET'S HAVE A BALL** Medley of *Music Music Music, This Ole House, Heartbreaker, Woody Woodpecker, Last Train To San Fernando, Bring A Little Water Sylvie, Puttin' On The Style* and *Don't You Rock Me Daddy-O*	Decca F 10956
07/08/1959	24	2		SUMMER OF THE SEVENTEENTH DOLL	Decca F 11143
27/11/1959	10	7		**PIANO PARTY** Medley of *Baby Face, Comin' Thru' The Rye, Annie Laurie, Little Brown Jug, Let Him Go Let Him Tarry, Put Your Arms Around Me Honey, I'll Be With You In Apple Blossom Time, Shine On Harvest Moon, Blue Skies, I'll Never Say 'Never Again' Again* and *I'll See You In My Dreams*	Decca F 11183

AUDIO BULLYS
UK production duo formed in London by Tom Dinsdale and Simon Franks.

DATE	POS	WKS	BPI	SINGLE TITLE	LABEL & NUMBER
18/01/2003	15	3		WE DON'T CARE Contains samples from Miles Budd Wolf & Doug Braysfield's *Big Bad Wolf*	Source SOURCD 061
31/05/2003	22	3		THE THINGS/TURNED AWAY A-side features a sample of John Gregoery & His Orchestra's *Policewoman*	Source SOURCDX 084
26/06/2004	44	2		BREAK DOWN THE DOORS MORILLO FEATURING THE AUDIO BULLYS	Subliminal SUB124CD

AUDIOSLAVE
US group formed by Chris Cornell (born 20/7/1964, Seattle, WA, vocals), Tom Morello (guitar), Tim Commerford (bass) and Brad Wilk (drums). Cornell was previously in Soundgarden, Commerford in Rage Against The Machine.

DATE	POS	WKS	BPI	SINGLE TITLE	LABEL & NUMBER
01/02/2003	24	3		COCHISE	Epic/Interscope 6732762

❶⁹ Number of weeks single topped the UK chart ↑ Entered the UK chart at #1 ▲⁹ Number of weeks single topped the US chart

41

AUDIOWEB
UK group formed in Manchester by Martin 'Sugar' Merchant (vocals), Robin File (guitar), Sean McCann (bass) and Maxi (drums), evolving from Sugar Merchant. *Bankrobber* was a cover version of The Clash's hit. The publishers had originally refused to let the song be recorded until Joe Strummer of The Clash intervened.

DATE	POS	WKS	SINGLE TITLE	LABEL & NUMBER
14/10/1995	74	1	SLEEPER	Mother MUMCD 69
09/03/1996	73	1	YEAH.	Mother MUMCD 72
15/06/1996	42	1	INTO MY WORLD	Mother MUMCD 76
19/10/1996	50	2	SLEEPER (REMIX)	Mother MUMCD 78
15/02/1997	19	2	BANKROBBER	Mother MUMCD 85
24/05/1997	70	1	FAKER	Mother MUMCD 91
25/04/1998	21	2	POLICEMAN SKANK…(THE STORY OF MY LIFE)	Mother MUMCD 100
04/07/1998	65	1	PERSONAL FEELING	Mother MUMCD 104
20/02/1999	56	1	TEST THE THEORY	Mother MUMCD 110

AUF DER MAUR
Canadian singer/guitarist (born Melissa Auf Der Maur, 17/3/1972, Montreal) who was a member of Hole before going solo.

DATE	POS	WKS	SINGLE TITLE	LABEL & NUMBER
28/02/2004	35	2	FOLLOWED THE WAVES	EMI CDEM 635
15/05/2004	33	2	REAL A LIE	EMI CDEMS 642
09/10/2004	51	1	TASTE YOU	EMI CDEM 650

BRIAN AUGER – see JULIE DRISCOLL, BRIAN AUGER AND THE TRINITY

AURA – see POPPERS PRESENTS AURA

AURORA
UK production duo Sacha Collisson and Simon Greenaway who also recorded as Dive. Naimee Coleman is a Dublin-born singer.

DATE	POS	WKS	SINGLE TITLE	LABEL & NUMBER
05/06/1999	71	1	HEAR YOU CALLING	Addictive 12AD 040
05/02/2000	17	4	HEAR YOU CALLING	Positiva CDTIV 124
23/09/2000	5	7	ORDINARY WORLD AURORA FEATURING NAIMEE COLEMAN	Positiva CDTIV 139
13/04/2002	24	4	DREAMING	EMI CDEM 611
06/07/2002	29	3	THE DAY IT RAINED FOREVER	EMI CDEMS 613

AURRA
US soul group formed by Steve Washington, Tom Lockett, Curt Jones and Starleana Young, who worked together as Slave before forming Aurra in 1980 with the addition of Philip Fields. Washington later went solo and the group changed its name to Deja.

DATE	POS	WKS	SINGLE TITLE	LABEL & NUMBER
04/05/1985	51	5	LIKE I LIKE IT	10 TEN 45
19/04/1986	12	8	YOU AND ME TONIGHT	10 TEN 71
21/06/1986	43	5	LIKE I LIKE IT Re-issue of 10 TEN 45	10 TEN 126

ADAM AUSTIN
UK singer.

DATE	POS	WKS	SINGLE TITLE	LABEL & NUMBER
13/02/1999	41	1	CENTERFOLD	Media PSRCA 0107

DAVID AUSTIN
UK singer/keyboard player who later worked with George Michael, Andrew Ridgeley, Paul Goodyear and Nasty Savage.

DATE	POS	WKS	SINGLE TITLE	LABEL & NUMBER
21/07/1984	68	3	TURN TO GOLD	Parlophone R 6068

PATTI AUSTIN
US singer (born 10/8/1948, New York City) who is the goddaughter of Quincy Jones. She made her Apollo Theatre debut aged four and signed with RCA Records at five. She won the 1981 Grammy Award, with Quincy Jones, for Best Rhythm & Blues Vocal Performance by a Duo for *The Dude*.

DATE	POS	WKS	SINGLE TITLE	LABEL & NUMBER
20/06/1981	11	9	RAZZAMATAZZ QUINCY JONES FEATURING PATTI AUSTIN	A&M 8140
12/02/1983	11	10	BABY COME TO ME ▲² PATTI AUSTIN AND JAMES INGRAM Later the theme to the US TV series *General Hospital*	Qwest K 15005
05/09/1992	68	1	I'LL KEEP YOUR DREAMS ALIVE GEORGE BENSON AND PATTI AUSTIN	Ammi 101

AUTECHRE
UK instrumental duo formed in Sheffield in 1991 by Sean Booth and Rob Brown.

DATE	POS	WKS	SINGLE TITLE	LABEL & NUMBER
07/05/1994	56	1	BASSCAD	Warp WAP 44CD

AUTEURS
UK rock group formed in 1991 by Luke Haines (born 7/10/1967, Walton-on-Thames, guitar/vocals), Alice Readman (born 1967, Harrow, bass) and Glenn Collins (born 7/2/1968, Cheltenham, drums). Haines and Readman were previously in The Servants. James Banbury (cello) joined the line-up in 1993.

DATE	POS	WKS	SINGLE TITLE	LABEL & NUMBER
27/11/1993	41	2	LENNY VALENTINO	Hut HUTCD 36
23/04/1994	42	2	CHINESE BAKERY	Hut HUTDX 41
06/01/1996	45	3	BACK WITH THE KILLER AGAIN	Hut HUTCD 65
24/02/1996	58	1	LIGHT AIRCRAFT ON FIRE	Hut HUTCD 66
03/07/1999	66	1	THE RUBETTES	Hut HUTCD 113

AUTUMN
UK group with Ron Shaughnessy (guitar/vocals), Keith Parsons (guitar), John Court (guitar), Peter Cramer (bass) and Dave Charlwood (drums).

DATE	POS	WKS	SINGLE TITLE	LABEL & NUMBER
16/10/1971	37	6	MY LITTLE GIRL	Pye 7N 45090

PETER AUTY AND THE SINFONIA OF LONDON
UK boy soprano with orchestral backing conducted by Howard Blake. The single was remixed as a dance version in 1991 and released by Digital Dream Baby.

DATE	POS	WKS	SINGLE TITLE	LABEL & NUMBER
14/12/1985	42	5	WALKING IN THE AIR Featured in the 1985 animated film *The Snowman*	Stiff LAD 1

○ Silver disc ● Gold disc ✪ Platinum disc (additional platinum units are indicated by a figure following the symbol) ◉ Singles released prior to 1973 that are known to have sold over 1 million copies in the UK

19/12/1987	37	4		WALKING IN THE AIR Re-issue of Stiff LAD 1	CBS GA 3950

AVALANCHES Australian group of Robbie Chater, Darren Seltmann, Gordon McQuilten, Tony Diblasi, Dexter Fabay and James De La Cruz.

07/04/2001	16	7		SINCE I LEFT YOU 2001 MTV Europe Music Award for Best Video	XL Recordings XLS 128CD
21/07/2001	18	5		FRONTIER PSYCHIATRIST	XL Recordings XLS 134CD1

FRANKIE AVALON US singer (born Francis Avallone, 18/9/1939, Philadelphia, PA) who made his first record in 1957. He was awarded a star on the Hollywood Walk of Fame in 1991. His many films include *Jamboree* (1957), *Voyage To The Bottom Of The Sea* (1961), *The Stoned Age* (1994) and a series of 'beach/bikini' movies, plus a guest appearance in *Grease* (1978).

10/10/1958	30	1		GINGERBREAD Backing vocals by The Four Dates	HMV POP 517
24/04/1959	16	6		VENUS ▲5 Featured in the films *Born On The 4th Of July* (1989) and *She's Out Of Control* (1989).	HMV POP 603
22/01/1960	20	4		WHY ▲1	HMV POP 688
28/04/1960	37	4		DON'T THROW AWAY ALL THOSE TEARDROPS	HMV POP 727

AVALON BOYS – see **LAUREL AND HARDY WITH THE AVALON BOYS FEATURING CHILL WILLS**

AVERAGE WHITE BAND UK soul group formed by Hamish Stuart (born 8/10/1949, Glasgow, guitar/vocals), Alan Gorrie (born 19/7/1946, Perth, bass/vocals), Onnie McIntyre (born 25/9/1945, Lennoxtown, guitar/vocals), Malcolm 'Molly' Duncan (born 25/8/1945, Montrose, saxophone), Roger Ball (born 4/6/1944, Dundee, keyboards/saxophone) and Robbie McIntosh (born 6/5/1950, Dundee, drums). McIntosh died from drug poisoning on 23/9/1974 during the recording of their debut album and was replaced by Steve Ferrone (born 25/4/1950, Brighton), who was the only black member of the Average White Band. They later recorded with Ben E King. They were apparently named after a saying of a friend: any problem that was 'too much for the average white man to understand'; it's also been claimed that they were named by Bonnie Bramlett, who was surprised to see white soul musicians in Scotland.

22/02/1975	6	9		PICK UP THE PIECES ▲1 Featured in the films *The People Versus Larry Flynt* (1996) and *Swingers* (1996)	Atlantic K 10489
26/04/1975	31	4		CUT THE CAKE Featured in the 1997 film *Suicide Kings*	Atlantic K 10605
09/10/1976	23	7		QUEEN OF MY SOUL	Atlantic K 10825
28/04/1979	46	5		WALK ON BY	RCA XC 1087
25/08/1979	49	5		WHEN WILL YOU BE MINE	RCA XB 1096
26/04/1980	12	11		LET'S GO ROUND AGAIN PART 1	RCA AWB 1
26/07/1980	46	4		FOR YOU FOR LOVE	RCA AWB 2
26/03/1994	56	2		LET'S GO ROUND AGAIN (REMIX)	The Hit Label HLC 5

KEVIN AVIANCE US singer (born in New York) who first came to prominence on the city's gay scene.

13/06/1998	65	1		DIN DA DA	Distinctive DISNCD 42

AVONS UK vocal trio of sisters-in-law Valerie (born 1936, London) and Eileen Murtagh (born 1940, County Cork) and Ray Adams (born 1938, Jersey). Valerie later became a successful songwriter.

13/11/1959	3	13		SEVEN LITTLE GIRLS SITTING IN THE BACK SEAT	Columbia DB 4363
07/07/1960	45	2		WE'RE ONLY YOUNG ONCE	Columbia DB 4461
27/10/1960	45	3		FOUR LITTLE HEELS	Columbia DB 4522
26/01/1961	30	4		RUBBER BALL	Columbia DB 4569

AWESOME UK vocal group formed in London by Derek, Stevo, Alex and Steven.

08/11/1997	58	1		RUMOURS	Universal MCSTD 40145
21/03/1998	63	1		CRAZY	Universal MCSTD 40195

AWESOME 3 UK dance group fronted by singer Julie McDermott who also fronted the Third Dimension's *Don't Go*.

08/09/1990	55	3		HARD UP	A&M AM 591
03/10/1992	75	1		DON'T GO	Citybeat CBE 1271
04/06/1994	45	2		DON'T GO (REMIX)	Citybeat CBX 771CD
26/10/1996	27	2		DON'T GO (2ND REMIX) **AWESOME 3 FEATURING JULIE McDERMOTT**	XL Recordings XLS 78CD

HOYT AXTON US singer (born 25/3/1938, Duncan, OK), son of songwriter Mae Axton, who was initially a folk singer before including blues and country in his repertoire. He died from a heart attack on 26/10/1999.

07/06/1980	48	4		DELLA AND THE DEALER	Young Blood YB 82

AXUS UK producer Austin Bascomb who also records as Abacus.

26/09/1998	62	1		ABACUS (WHEN I FALL IN LOVE)	INCredible INCRL 8CD

ROY AYERS US vibraphonist/singer (born 10/9/1940, Los Angeles, CA) who played piano as a child, becoming interested in the vibes after meeting Lionel Hampton. His professional career began with Curtis Edward Amy, before recording for United Artists under his own name in 1964. Later with Atlantic, Polydor and CBS, he formed Ubiquity and recorded with former Crusader Wayne Henderson.

21/10/1978	41	4		GET ON UP, GET ON DOWN	Polydor AYERS 7
13/01/1979	43	5		HEAT OF THE BEAT **ROY AYERS AND WAYNE HENDERSON**	Polydor POSP 16
02/02/1980	56	3		DON'T STOP THE FEELING	Polydor STEP 6
16/05/1998	68	1		EXPANSIONS **SCOTT GROOVES FEATURING ROY AYERS**	Soma Recordings SOMA 65CDS

❶9 Number of weeks single topped the UK chart ⬆ Entered the UK chart at #1 ▲9 Number of weeks single topped the US chart

43

AYLA German trance DJ/producer Ingo Kunzi.

04/09/1999.....22......3.......	AYLA..	Positiva CDTIV 117

AZ US rapper (born Anthony Cruz, Brooklyn, NYC) who is also a member of The Firm.

30/03/1996.....67......1.......	SUGARHILL... Cooltempo CDCOOL 315

AZ YET US R&B vocal group formed in Philadelphia, PA by Mark Nelson, Shawn Rivera, Daryll Anthony, Dion Allen and Kenny Terry.

01/03/1997.....21......3.......	LAST NIGHT Featured in the 1996 film *The Nutty Professor*..LaFace 74321423202
21/06/1997 .....7 ......7.......	**HARD TO SAY I'M SORRY** AZ YET FEATURING PETER CETERA .... LaFace 74321481482

CHARLES AZNAVOUR French singer (born Shahnour Varenagh Aznavurjan, 22/5/1924, Paris) who was one of France's top performers of the 1950s, making his UK breakthrough when in his 50s. A prolific songwriter, his many film parts included *Candy* (1968), *The Blockhouse* (1973) and *The Heist* (1979).

22/09/1973.....38.....15	THE OLD FASHIONED WAY .... Barclay BAR 20
22/06/1974 ...❶⁴.....14 ..... ○	**SHE** Used as the theme to the TV series *Seven Faces Of Woman* .... Barclay BAR 26

AZTEC CAMERA UK group whose fluctuating line-up from 1980 to 1986 was a vehicle for singer/guitarist/songwriter Roddy Frame (born 29/1/1964, East Kilbride). Mick Jones (born 26/6/1955, London) was guitarist with The Clash and later formed Big Audio Dynamite.

19/02/1983.....47......6......	OBLIVIOUS .... Rough Trade RT 122
04/06/1983.....64......4......	WALK OUT TO WINTER .... Rough Trade RT 132
05/11/1983.....18.....11......	OBLIVIOUS .... WEA AZTEC 1
01/09/1984.....34......6......	ALL I NEED IS EVERYTHING/JUMP .... WEA AC 1
13/02/1988.....25......9......	HOW MEN ARE.. WEA YZ 168
23/04/1988 .....3.....14	**SOMEWHERE IN MY HEART** .... WEA YZ 181
06/08/1988.....31......5......	WORKING IN A GOLDMINE.. WEA YZ 199
08/10/1988.....55......3......	DEEP AND WIDE AND TALL .... WEA YZ 154
07/07/1990.....70......3......	THE CRYING SCENE .... WEA YZ 492
13/10/1990.....19......6......	GOOD MORNING BRITAIN AZTEC CAMERA AND MICK JONES.. WEA YZ 521
18/07/1992.....52......3......	SPANISH HORSES .... WEA YZ 688
01/05/1993.....67......2......	DREAM SWEET DREAMS .... WEA YZ 740CD1

AZTEC MYSTIC – see DJ ROLANDO AKA AZTEC MYSTIC

AZURE Italian/US vocal duo formed by Steve Schani.

25/04/1998.....56......1......	MAMA USED TO SAY .... Inferno CDFERN 005

AZYMUTH Brazilian jazz-funk group formed by Jose Roberto Bertrami (born 21/2/1946, Tatui, keyboards/vocals/percussion), Alex Malheiros (born 19/8/1946, Niteroi, bass/vocals), Ivan Conte (born 16/8/1946, Rio De Janeiro, drums/synthesisers) and Aleuda (percussion). Bertrami left in 1988 and was replaced by Jota Moraes, although he did return for some live performances in the 1990s.

12/01/1980.....19......8.......	JAZZ CARNIVAL .... Milestone MRC 101

BOB AZZAM AND HIS ORCHESTRA AND CHORUS Egyptian orchestra leader who later recorded *Amen Twist*.

26/05/1960.....23.....14	MUSTAPHA... Decca F 21235

B

DEREK B UK rapper (born Derek Bowland, 1966, East London) who began as a pirate radio DJ, later forming the Tuff Audio label.

27/02/1988	16	6	GOODGROOVE .... Music Of Life 7NOTE 12
07/05/1988	16	6	BAD YOUNG BROTHER .... Tuff Audio DRKB 1
02/07/1988	56	3	WE'VE GOT THE JUICE .... Tuff Audio DRKB 2

EMMA B – see NU CIRCLES FEATURING EMMA B

ERIC B AND RAKIM US hip hop duo Eric B (born Eric Barrier, Elmhurst, NY) and Rakim (born William Griffin, 28/1/1968, Long Island, NY) who later produced MCA acts including Jody Watley, and appeared in the 1994 film *Gunmen*. Rakim later went solo.

07/11/1987	15	6	PAID IN FULL .... Fourth & Broadway BRW 78
20/02/1988	53	2	MOVE THE CROWD .... Fourth & Broadway BRW 88
12/03/1988	13	6	I KNOW YOU GOT SOUL .... Cooltempo COOL 146
02/07/1988	21	5	FOLLOW THE LEADER .... MCA 1256
19/11/1988	74	1	THE MICROPHONE FIEND .... MCA 1300
12/08/1989	21	6	FRIENDS JODY WATLEY WITH ERIC B AND RAKIM .... MCA 1352

HOWIE B UK singer/musician/DJ (born Howard Bernstein, Glasgow) who was the producer for Everything But The Girl, U2's *Pop* album and engineer for Skylab before going solo. He later launched the Pussyfoot label.

19/07/1997	36	2	ANGELS GO BALD: TOO .... Polydor 5711672
18/10/1997	62	1	SWITCH .... Polydor 5717112
11/04/1998	74	1	TAKE YOUR PARTNER BY THE HAND HOWIE B FEATURING ROBBIE ROBERTSON .... Polydor 5693272

JAZZIE B – see MAXI PRIEST AND SOUL II SOUL

JOHN B UK jungle producer (born John B Williams, 1977, Maidenhead) who first recorded for the New Identity label.

22/06/2002	58	1	UP ALL NIGHT/TAKE CONTROL .... Metalheadz METH 041CD

JON B US singer/songwriter (born Jonathan Buck, 11/11/1974, Rhode Island, raised in California) who penned hits for Toni Braxton, Az Yet and After 7. He records for Yab Yum Records in the US, which is run by Babyface's wife Tracey.

17/10/1998	32	2	THEY DON'T KNOW .... Epic 6663975
26/05/2001	29	3	DON'T TALK .... Epic 6712792

KERRI B – see SYSTEM PRESENTS KERRI B

LISA B US singer (born Lisa Barbuscia, 18/6/1971, Brooklyn, NYC) who attended the New York School of Music and Performing Arts (as in the *Fame* film and TV series) before becoming a model. She switched to singing after winning a contract with ffrr and later turned to acting, appearing in the films *Serpent's Lair* (1995) and *Almost Heroes* (1998).

12/06/1993	49	2	GLAM .... ffrr FCD 210
25/09/1993	35	3	FASCINATED .... ffrr FCD 218
08/01/1994	39	4	YOU AND ME .... ffrr FCD 226

LORNA B UK singer Lorna Bannon who was previously with Shakatak.

28/01/1995	36	3	DO YOU WANNA PARTY .... Steppin' Out SPONCD 2
01/04/1995	37	2	SWEET DREAMS This and above single credited to DJ SCOTT FEATURING LORNA B .... Steppin' Out SPONCD 3
15/03/1997	69	1	FEELS SO GOOD ZERO VU FEATURING LORNA B .... Avex UK AVEXCD 53

MARK B AND BLADE UK rap/production duo Mark B (born Mark Barnes, Kingston) and Blade (born Vanik Torosian, Iraq, of Armenian parentage).

10/02/2001	49	1	THE UNKNOWN .... Wordplay WORDCDS 011
26/05/2001	23	3	YA DON'T SEE THE SIGNS .... Wordplay WORDCDSE 019
25/09/2004	61	1	MOVE NOW MARK B FEATURING TOMMY EVANS .... Genuine GEN033CD

MELANIE B UK singer (born Melanie Brown, 29/5/1973, Leeds) who was also a member of the Spice Girls (known as Mel B and/or Scary Spice). After marrying dancer Jimmy Gulzar she recorded as Melanie G, but reverted to Melanie B following their divorce in October 2000. She had an acting role in the TV series *Burn It*.

26/09/1998	❶¹	9	○	I WANT YOU BACK ↑ MELANIE B FEATURING MISSY 'MISDEMEANOR' ELLIOTT Featured in the 1998 film *Why Do Fools Fall In Love* .... Virgin VSCDT 1716

---

❶⁹ Number of weeks single topped the UK chart ↑ Entered the UK chart at #1 ▲⁹ Number of weeks single topped the US chart

45

DATE	POS	WKS	BPI	SINGLE TITLE	LABEL & NUMBER
10/07/1999	14	8		WORD UP **MELANIE G** Featured in the 1999 film *Austin Powers: The Spy Who Shagged Me*	Virgin VSCDT 1748
07/10/2000	4	7		**TELL ME**	Virgin VSCDX 1777
03/03/2001	5	8		**FEELS SO GOOD**	Virgin VSCDT 1787
16/06/2001	13	4		LULLABY	Virgin VSCDT 1798

SANDY B US singer Sandy Barber (born in Australia).

20/02/1993	60	1		FEEL LIKE SINGIN'	Nervous SANCD 1
18/05/1996	73	1		MAKE THE WORLD GO ROUND	Champion CHAMPCD 322
24/05/1997	35	2		MAKE THE WORLD GO ROUND (REMIX)	Champion CHAMPCD 327
08/11/1997	60	1		AIN'T NO NEED TO HIDE	Champion CHAMPCD 331
28/02/1998	20	3		MAKE THE WORLD GO ROUND (2ND REMIX)	Champion CHAMPCD 333
01/05/2004	51	3		MAKE THE WORLD GO ROUND 2004	Champion CHAMPCD 780

STEVIE B US singer Steven B Hill (born and based in Miami, FL).

23/02/1991	6	9		**BECAUSE I LOVE YOU (THE POSTMAN SONG)** ▲4	Polydor PO 126

TAIRRIE B US rapper Tairrie Beth who later joined Man Hole and My Ruin.

01/12/1990	71	2		MURDER SHE WROTE	MCA 1455

B B AND Q BAND US soul group formed by Jacques Fred Petrus (who previously created Change) and featuring singer Curtis Hairston and musicians Kevin Robinson, Tony Bridges, Cheili Minucci and Kevin Nance. The name stands for Brooklyn Bronx and Queens, the New York boroughs from which they originate.

18/07/1981	41	5		ON THE BEAT	Capitol CL 202
06/07/1985	40	4		GENIE **BROOKLYN BRONX AND QUEENS**	Cooltempo COOL 110
20/09/1986	35	5		(I'M A) DREAMER	Cooltempo COOL 132
17/10/1987	71	1		RICOCHET	Cooltempo COOL 154

B. BUMBLE AND THE STINGERS US session musicians Plas Johnson, Rene Hall, Earl Palmer, Al Hassan and pianist Lincoln Mayorga assumed the name and recorded *Nut Rocker*. Following its US success the line-up changed: pianist RC Gamble (born 1940, Spiro, OK) toured as B. Bumble, and the Stingers comprised Terry Anderson (born 1941, Harrison, AR, guitar), Jimmy King (born 1938, guitar) and Don Orr (drums).

19/04/1962	◎1	15		**NUT ROCKER** Adapted from Pyotr Tchaikovsky's *The Nutcracker* and arranged by Kim Fowley. Featured in the 1998 film *The Butcher Boy*	Top Rank JAR 611
03/06/1972	19	11		NUT ROCKER Re-issue of Top Rank JAR 611	Stateside SS 2203

B-CREW US vocal group assembled by Erick 'More' Morillo featuring Charlotte Small and Emey Polbert.

20/09/1997	45	1		PARTAY FEELING	Positiva CDTIV 78

B-15 PROJECT FEATURING CHRISSY D AND LADY G UK dance group formed in Birmingham by Ali Campbell, Angus Campbell, Brian Travers and Ian Wallman, with vocals by Jamaican DJs Chrissy D and Lady G, and named after the postcode of the studio where they first worked together.

17/06/2000	7	10		**GIRLS LIKE US**	Ministry Of Sound RELENT 3CDS

B-52S US group formed in Athens, GA in 1977 by Cindy Wilson (born 28/2/1957, Athens, guitar/vocals), Kate Pierson (born 27/4/1948, New Jersey, organ/vocals), Ricky Wilson (born 19/3/1953, Athens, guitar), Fred Schneider (born 1/7/1951, New Jersey, keyboards/vocals) and Keith Strickland (born 26/10/1953, Athens, drums). They were named after the slang term for the two female members' bouffant hairstyles. Ricky Wilson died from AIDS on 12/10/1985. The group appeared in the 1994 film *The Flintstones*.

11/08/1979	37	5		ROCK LOBSTER	Island WIP 6506
09/08/1980	61	3		GIVE ME BACK MY MAN	Island WIP 6579
07/05/1983	63	2		(SONG FOR A) FUTURE GENERATION	Island IS 107
10/05/1986	12	7		ROCK LOBSTER/PLANET CLAIRE Re-issue of Island WIP 6506	Island BFT 1
03/03/1990	2	13	○	**LOVE SHACK**	Reprise W 9917
19/05/1990	17	7		ROAM	Reprise W 9827
18/08/1990	61	2		CHANNEL Z	Reprise W 9737
20/06/1992	21	6		GOOD STUFF	Reprise W 0109
12/09/1992	61	3		TELL IT LIKE IT T-I-IS	Reprise W 0130
09/07/1994	3	12		**(MEET) THE FLINTSTONES** BC-52S Featured in the 1994 film *The Flintstones*	MCA MCSTD 1986
30/01/1999	66	1		LOVE SHACK 99	Reprise W 0461CD

B-MOVIE UK group formed in Mansfield by Paul Statham (guitar), Steve Hovington (bass/vocals) and Graham Boffey (drums) and known as Studio 10 before changing to B-Movie. They introduced Luciano Codemo on bass (Hovington concentrated on vocals) but Codemo was later replaced by Mike Pedham.

18/04/1981	61	3		REMEMBRANCE DAY	Deram DM 437
27/03/1982	67	4		NOWHERE GIRL	Some Bizzare BZZ 8

B REAL US rapper (born Louis Freeze, 2/6/1970, Los Angeles, CA) who was also a member of Cypress Hill.

05/04/1997	8	6		**HIT 'EM HIGH (THE MONSTARS' ANTHEM)** B REAL/BUSTA RHYMES/COOLIO/LL COOL J/METHOD MAN Featured in the 1996 film *Space Jam*	Atlantic A 5449CD

B-TRIBE German instrumentalist Claus Zundel.

| 25/09/1993 | 64 | 4 | | !FIESTA FATAL! | East West YZ 770CD |

B*WITCHED Irish vocal group formed in Dublin by Sinead O'Carroll (born 14/5/1973, Dublin, although she has sometimes claimed the year was 1978), Lindsay Armaou (born 18/12/1980, Athens, Greece) and twin sisters Edele and Keavy Lynch (born 15/12/1979, Dublin), who are also sisters of Shane Lynch of Boyzone. The first group to have their first four singles enter the chart at #1, they took part in the BRITS Trust *Thank Abba For The Music* project.

06/06/1998	❶²	19	✪	C'EST LA VIE ↑ Featured in the 2000 film *What Women Want*	Glow Worm 6660532
03/10/1998	❶²	15	●	ROLLERCOASTER ↑	Glow Worm 6664752
19/12/1998	❶¹	14	●	TO YOU I BELONG ↑	Glow Worm 6667712
27/03/1999	❶¹	9	○	BLAME IT ON THE WEATHERMAN ↑	Glow Worm 6670335
16/10/1999	4	12		JESSIE HOLD ON	Glow Worm 6679612
18/12/1999	13	9		I SHALL BE THERE B*WITCHED FEATURING LADYSMITH BLACK MAMBAZO	Glow Worm 6683332
08/04/2000	16	7		JUMP DOWN	Glow Worm 6691285

BABE INSTINCT UK duo Lindsay Humphries and Jo Wilner who were originally signed in Belgium.

| 16/01/1999 | 21 | 2 | | DISCO BABES FROM OUTER SPACE | Positiva CDTIV 103 |

BABE TEAM UK vocal group comprising Page 3 models Jessica, Nikki, Nicola, Ellie and Leilani from *The Sun* newspaper, plus Cathi Ogden and Catherine McQueen, star of the Wonderbra advertisements. Their debut hit capitalised on the 2002 World Cup finals.

| 08/06/2002 | 45 | 2 | | OVER THERE | Blacklist 0140695 ERE |

ALICE BABS Swedish singer (born Alice Nilsson, 26/1/1924, Kalmar) who began her career as an actress, appearing in a number of films from the late 1930s.

| 15/08/1963 | 43 | 1 | | AFTER YOU'VE GONE | Fontana TF 409 |

BABY BUMPS UK duo Sean Casey and Lisa Millett, Millett having also sung with Sheer Bronze, A.T.F.C. and Goodfellas.

| 08/08/1998 | 17 | 4 | | BURNING Contains a sample of The Trammps' *Disco Inferno* | Delirious DELICD 10 |
| 26/02/2000 | 22 | 2 | | I GOT THIS FEELING Contains a sample of Michael Jackson's *Don't Stop 'Til You Get Enough* | Ministry Of Sound MOSCDS 137 |

BABY D Maltese singer Dee Galdes who began as backing vocalist for a number of chart acts. Her first recording was with Jazz And The Brothers Grimm in 1989. The rest of her group comprise MC Nino, Claudio Galdez and Dice. They won Best Dance Act at the 1996 MOBO Awards.

18/12/1993	69	1		DESTINY	Production House PNC 057
23/07/1994	67	1		CASANOVA	Production House PNC 065
19/11/1994	❶²	14	●	LET ME BE YOUR FANTASY	Systematic SYSCD 4
03/06/1995	3	12	○	(EVERYBODY'S GOT TO LEARN SOMETIME) I NEED YOUR LOVING	Systematic SYSCD 11
13/01/1996	3	7		SO PURE	Systematic SYSCD 21
06/04/1996	15	5		TAKE ME TO HEAVEN	Systematic SYSCD 26
02/09/2000	16	5		LET ME BE YOUR FANTASY (REMIX)	Systematic SYSCD 35

BABY DC FEATURING IMAJIN US rapper Derrick Coleman Jr with R&B vocal group Imajin, comprising Olamide Asladejobi Patrick Alexander Faison (aka Olamide), John Anthony Finch (Jiz), Stanley Jamal Hampton (Jamal) and Talib Kareem.

| 24/04/1999 | 45 | 1 | | BOUNCE, ROCK, SKATE, ROLL | Jive 0522142 |

BABY FORD UK keyboardist Peter Ford (born in Bolton) who also recorded as Doucen for Brute Records.

10/09/1988	58	6		OOCHY KOOCHY (F. U. BABY YEAH YEAH)	Rhythm King 7BFORD 1
24/12/1988	54	4		CHIKKI CHIKKI AHH AHH	Rhythm King 7BFORD 2
17/06/1989	53	4		CHILDREN OF THE REVOLUTION	Rhythm King 7BFORD 4
17/02/1990	68	2		BEACH BUMP	Rhythm King 7BFORD 6

BABY JUNE UK singer Tim Hegarty.

| 15/08/1992 | 75 | 1 | | HEY! WHAT'S YOUR NAME | Arista 115271 |

BABY O US vocal/instrumental group assembled by Rafael Villafane and Greg Mathieson, named after a disco in Acapulco.

| 26/07/1980 | 46 | 5 | | IN THE FOREST | Calibre CAB 505 |

BABY ROOTS UK singer.

| 01/08/1992 | 71 | 1 | | ROCK ME BABY | ZYX 68027 |

BABYBIRD UK group formed in Telford in 1995 by Stephen Jones (vocals), Luke Scott (guitar), John Pedder (bass), Huw Chadbourn (keyboards) and Robert Gregory (drums), originally on Babybird Recordings before signing with Echo.

10/08/1996	28	2		GOODNIGHT	Echo ECSCD 24
12/10/1996	3	16	●	YOU'RE GORGEOUS	Echo ECSCD 26
01/02/1997	14	3		CANDY GIRL	Echo ECSCD 31
17/05/1997	37	2		CORNERSHOP	Echo ECSCD 33
09/05/1998	31	2		BAD OLD MAN	Echo ECSCD 60
22/08/1998	28	4		IF YOU'LL BE MINE	Echo ECSCX 65
27/02/1999	22	3		BACK TOGETHER	Echo ECSCD 73

❶⁹ Number of weeks single topped the UK chart ↑ Entered the UK chart at #1 ▲⁹ Number of weeks single topped the US chart

DATE	POS	WKS	BPI	SINGLE TITLE	LABEL & NUMBER
25/03/2000	35	2		THE F-WORD	Echo ECSCD 92
03/06/2000	58	1		OUT OF SIGHT	Echo ECSCD 97

BABYFACE US singer (born Kenneth Edmonds, 10/4/1959, Indianapolis, IN) who was a guitarist and backing singer for Manchild before meeting Antonio 'LA' Reid via the group Deele. The pair made their names as songwriters (usually with fellow Manchild member Daryl Simmons), forming the LaFace record label. Bootsy Collins coined Edmonds' nickname Babyface because of his youthful looks. Eight Grammy Awards include Best Rhythm & Blues Song in 1992 with LA Reid and Daryl Simmons for *The End Of The Road*, Best Rhythm & Blues Song in 1994 for *I'll Make Love To You*, Best Rhythm & Blues Song in 1996 for *Exhale (Shoop Shoop)* and Producer of the Year in 1992, 1995, 1996 and 1997.

DATE	POS	WKS	BPI	SINGLE TITLE	LABEL & NUMBER
09/07/1994	50	4		ROCK BOTTOM	Epic 6601832
01/10/1994	35	3		WHEN CAN I SEE YOU 1994 Grammy Award for Best Rhythm & Blues Vocal Performance	Epic 6606592
09/11/1996	12	5		THIS IS FOR THE LOVER IN YOU Features the uncredited contributions of LL Cool J, Howard Hewett, Jody Watley and Jeffrey Daniel (the last three ex-members of Shalamar)	Epic 6639352
08/03/1997	13	4		EVERYTIME I CLOSE MY EYES Features the uncredited contributions of Mariah Carey, Sheila E and Kenny G	Epic 6642492
19/07/1997	10	5		**HOW COME, HOW LONG BABYFACE FEATURING STEVIE WONDER**	Epic 6646202
25/10/1997	25	2		SUNSHINE **JAY-Z FEATURING BABYFACE AND FOXY BROWN**	Northwestside 74321528702

BABYLON ZOO UK group formed by Asian/native American Jas Mann (born Jaswinder Mann, 24/4/1971, Dudley). Signed by EMI's Parlophone in 1993 on the strength of a demo, they later followed their A&R director to WEA, and then back to EMI.

DATE	POS	WKS	BPI	SINGLE TITLE	LABEL & NUMBER
27/01/1996	❶⁵	14	✪	SPACEMAN ↑ First appeared as an advertisement for Levi Jeans	EMI CDEM 416
27/04/1996	17	3		ANIMAL ARMY	EMI CDEM 425
05/10/1996	32	2		THE BOY WITH X-RAY EYES	EMI CDEMS 440
06/02/1999	46	1		ALL THE MONEY'S GONE	EMI CDEM 519

BABYS UK rock group formed in 1976 by John Waite (born 4/7/1955, London, vocals), Walt Stocker (born 27/3/19554, London, guitar), Mike Corby (born 3/7/1955, London, guitar/keyboards) and Tony Brock (born 31/3/1954, Bournemouth, drums). Corby left in 1980 and was replaced by Jonathan Cain (later with Journey), with Ricky Phillips (bass) joining at the same time.

DATE	POS	WKS	BPI	SINGLE TITLE	LABEL & NUMBER
21/01/1978	45	3		ISN'T IT TIME	Chrysalis CHS 2173

BABYSHAMBLES UK rock group formed by ex-member of The Libertines Pete Doherty (vocals) with Patrick Walden (guitar), Drew McConnell (bass) and Gemma Clarke (drums).

DATE	POS	WKS	BPI	SINGLE TITLE	LABEL & NUMBER
11/12/2004	8	3+		**KILLAMANGIRO**	Rough Trade RTRADSCD201

BACCARA Spanish duo Maria Mendiola and Mayte Mateus.

DATE	POS	WKS	BPI	SINGLE TITLE	LABEL & NUMBER
17/09/1977	❶¹	16	●	**YES SIR I CAN BOOGIE**	RCA PB 5526
14/01/1978	8	9	○	**SORRY I'M A LADY** Featured in the 1978 film *The Stud*	RCA PB 5555

BURT BACHARACH US orchestra leader (born 12/5/1928, Kansas City, MO) and a hugely prolific and successful songwriter, often in conjunction with Hal David. He married singer Paula Stewart in 1953 (divorced 1958), actress Angie Dickinson in 1966 (divorced 1980) and fellow songwriter Carole Bayer Sager in 1982 (divorced 1992). Songwriting credits include *Magic Moments* (a hit for Perry Como), *Walk On By, Don't Make Me Over* and *Do You Know The Way To San Jose* (all Dionne Warwick) and *Arthur's Theme* (Christopher Cross). He has won five Grammy Awards: Best Instrumental Arrangement in 1967 for *Alfie*; Best Original Cast Show Album in 1969 for *Promises Promises*; Best Original Score in 1969 for *Butch Cassidy & The Sundance Kid*; Song of the Year in 1986 with Carole Bayer Sager for *That's What Friends Are For*; and Best Pop Collaboration with Vocals in 1998 with Elvis Costello for *I Still Have That Other Girl*.

DATE	POS	WKS	BPI	SINGLE TITLE	LABEL & NUMBER
20/05/1965	4	11		**TRAINS AND BOATS AND PLANES**	London HL 9968
01/05/1999	72	1		TOLEDO **ELVIS COSTELLO/BURT BACHARACH**	Mercury 8709652

BACHELORS Irish vocal group formed in Dublin in 1953 by brothers Declan (born 12/12/1942, Dublin) and Conleth Clusky (born 18/3/1941, Dublin) and John Stokes (born 13/8/1940, Dublin), originally known as The Harmonichords. They changed their name to The Bachelors despite the fact all were married. Stokes left in 1984 and was replaced by Peter Phipps.

DATE	POS	WKS	BPI	SINGLE TITLE	LABEL & NUMBER
24/01/1963	6	19		**CHARMAINE**	Decca F 11559
04/07/1963	36	3		FARAWAY PLACES	Decca F 11666
29/08/1963	18	10		WHISPERING	Decca F 11712
23/01/1964	❶¹	19		**DIANE**	Decca F 11799
19/03/1964	2	17		**I BELIEVE**	Decca F 11857
04/06/1964	4	13		**RAMONA**	Decca F 11910
13/08/1964	4	16		**I WOULDN'T TRADE YOU FOR THE WORLD**	Decca F 11949
03/12/1964	7	12		**NO ARMS CAN EVER HOLD YOU**	Decca F 12034
01/04/1965	34	6		TRUE LOVE FOR EVER MORE	Decca F 12108
20/05/1965	9	12		**MARIE**	Decca F 12156
28/10/1965	27	10		IN THE CHAPEL IN THE MOONLIGHT	Decca F 12256

DATE	POS	WKS	BPI	SINGLE TITLE	LABEL & NUMBER
06/01/1966	38	4		HELLO DOLLY	Decca F 12309
17/03/1966	3	13		**THE SOUND OF SILENCE**	Decca F 12351
07/07/1966	26	7		CAN I TRUST YOU	Decca F 12417
01/12/1966	22	9		WALK WITH FAITH IN YOUR HEART	Decca F 22523
06/04/1967	30	8		OH HOW I MISS YOU	Decca F 22592
05/07/1967	20	9		MARTA	Decca F 22634

RANDY BACHMAN – see BUS STOP

TAL BACHMAN
Canadian singer/guitarist (born 13/8/1969, Vancouver, British Columbia), son of Randy Bachman of Bachman-Turner Overdrive.

DATE	POS	WKS	BPI	SINGLE TITLE	LABEL & NUMBER
30/10/1999	30	2		SHE'S SO HIGH	Columbia 6679932

BACHMAN-TURNER OVERDRIVE
Canadian rock group formed in Winnipeg in 1972 by brothers Randy (born 27/9/1943, Winnipeg, guitar/vocals) and Robbie Bachman (born 18/2/1953, Winnipeg, drums) and C Fred Turner (born 16/10/1943, Winnipeg, bass/vocals). Chad Allen was a member briefly and was replaced by Tim Bachman (born 18/2/1953, Winnipeg). Tim left in 1973 and was replaced by Blair Thornton. Randy went solo in 1977.

DATE	POS	WKS	BPI	SINGLE TITLE	LABEL & NUMBER
16/11/1974	2	12	○	**YOU AIN'T SEEN NOTHIN' YET** ▲[1]	Mercury 6167 025
01/02/1975	22	6		ROLL ON DOWN THE HIGHWAY	Mercury 6167 071

BACK TO THE PLANET
UK group formed in London in 1989 by Fil 'The Girl' Walters (vocals), Fraggle (born David Fletcher, guitar), Guy McAffer (keyboards) and Henry Nicholas Cullen (drums). Cullen left in 1993 and was replaced by Amire Mojarad.

DATE	POS	WKS	BPI	SINGLE TITLE	LABEL & NUMBER
10/04/1993	52	1		TEENAGE TURTLES	Parallel LLLCD 3
04/09/1993	52	1		DAYDREAM	Parallel LLLCD 8

BACKBEAT BAND
US studio group assembled by producer Don Was for the soundtrack to the 1994 Beatles biopic film *Backbeat*, with Greg Dulli (of The Afghan Whigs), Dave Grohl (Nirvana), Mike Mills (R.E.M.), Thurston Moore (Sonic Youth) and Dave Pirner (Soul Asylum).

DATE	POS	WKS	BPI	SINGLE TITLE	LABEL & NUMBER
26/03/1994	48	4		MONEY	Virgin VSCDX 1489
14/05/1994	69	1		PLEASE MR POSTMAN This and above single featured in the 1994 film *Backbeat*	Virgin VSCDX 1502

BACKBEAT DISCIPLES – see ARTHUR BAKER

BACKROOM BOYS – see FRANK IFIELD

BACKSTREET BOYS
US vocal group formed in Orlando, FL in 1993 by Kevin Richardson (born 3/10/1972, Lexington, KY), Brian 'B-Rok' Littrell (born 20/2/1975, Lexington), Alexander James 'AJ' McLean (born 9/1/1978, Boynton Beach, FL), Nick Carter (born 28/1/1980, NYC) and Howard 'Howie D' Dorough (born 22/8/1973, Orlando). Carter's younger brother Aaron is a successful solo artist. Four MTV Europe Music Awards include Best Group in 1999 and 2000.

backstreet boys
show me the meaning of being lonely

DATE	POS	WKS	BPI	SINGLE TITLE	LABEL & NUMBER
28/10/1995	54	1		WE'VE GOT IT GOIN' ON	Jive JIVECD 386
16/12/1995	42	3		I'LL NEVER BREAK YOUR HEART	Jive JIVECD 389
01/06/1996	14	8		GET DOWN (YOU'RE THE ONE FOR ME) Video won the 1996 MTV Europe Music Select Award	Jive JIVECD 394
24/08/1996	3	7		**WE'VE GOT IT GOIN' ON** Re-issue of Jive JIVECD 386	Jive JIVECD 400
16/11/1996	8	8		**I'LL NEVER BREAK YOUR HEART** Re-issue of Jive JIVECD 389	Jive JIVECD 406
18/01/1997	2	10	○	**QUIT PLAYING GAMES (WITH MY HEART)**	Jive JIVECD 409
29/03/1997	4	8		**ANYWHERE FOR YOU**	Jive JIVECD 416
02/08/1997	3	11	○	**EVERYBODY (BACKSTREET'S BACK)**	Jive JIVECD 426
11/10/1997	3	19	●	**AS LONG AS YOU LOVE ME** Video won the 1997 MTV Europe Music Select Award	Jive JIVECD 434
14/02/1998	2	12	○	**ALL I HAVE TO GIVE**	Jive JIVECD 445
15/05/1999	❶[1]	14	●	**I WANT IT THAT WAY** ↑ Featured in the 2000 film *Drive Me Crazy*	Jive 0523392
30/10/1999	5	14		**LARGER THAN LIFE**	Jive 0550562
26/02/2000	66	1		SHOW ME THE MEANING OF BEING LONELY (IMPORT)	Jive 9250002
04/03/2000	3	11	○	**SHOW ME THE MEANING OF BEING LONELY**	Jive 9250002
24/06/2000	8	8		THE ONE	Jive 9250662
18/11/2000	4	9		SHAPE OF MY HEART	Jive 9251442
24/02/2001	8	5		THE CALL	Jive 9251702
07/07/2001	12	5		MORE THAN THAT	Jive 9252342
12/01/2002	4	7		**DROWNING**	Jive 9253082

BACKYARD DOG
UK production group with Anif Akinola and Lloyd Hanley. Akinola was an ex-member of Chapter & The Verse while Hanley later became a member of Lovebug.

DATE	POS	WKS	BPI	SINGLE TITLE	LABEL & NUMBER
07/07/2001	15	6		BADDEST RUFFEST Featured in the 2002 film *Bend It Like Beckham*	East West W 233CD

❶[9] Number of weeks single topped the UK chart ↑ Entered the UK chart at #1 ▲[9] Number of weeks single topped the US chart

BAD ANGEL – see BOOTH AND THE BD ANGEL

BAD BOYS INC UK vocal group formed by Matthew Pateman, David Ross, Tony Dowding and Ally Begg.

DATE	POS	WKS	BPI	SINGLE TITLE	LABEL & NUMBER
14/08/1993	19	5		DON'T TALK ABOUT LOVE	A&M 5803412
02/10/1993	26	3		WHENEVER YOU NEED SOMEONE	A&M 5804032
11/12/1993	24	6		WALKING ON AIR	A&M 5804692
21/05/1994	8	7		MORE TO THIS WORLD	A&M 5806072
23/07/1994	15	6		TAKE ME AWAY (I'LL FOLLOW YOU)	A&M 5806912
17/09/1994	26	4		LOVE HERE I COME	A&M 5807752

BAD COMPANY UK rock group formed in 1973 by Paul Rodgers (born 17/12/1949, Middlesbrough, vocals), Simon Kirke (born 28/7/1949, London, drums), Mick Ralphs (born 31/3/1948, Hereford, guitar) and Raymond 'Boz' Burrell (born 1/8/1946, Lincoln, bass). Rodgers and Kirke had previously been in Free, Ralphs in Mott The Hoople and Burrell in King Crimson. They disbanded in 1983 and re-formed in 1986. Burrell left in 1987 and by 1996 the line-up was Kirke, Ralphs, singer Robert Hart, guitarist Dave Colwell and bassist Rick Wills. Rodgers was later with Firm and The Law.

DATE	POS	WKS	BPI	SINGLE TITLE	LABEL & NUMBER
01/06/1974	15	8		CAN'T GET ENOUGH Featured in the 1993 film *Wayne's World 2*	Island WIP 6191
22/03/1975	31	6		GOOD LOVIN' GONE BAD	Island WIP 6223
30/08/1975	20	9		FEEL LIKE MAKIN' LOVE Featured in the 1997 film *G.I. Jane*	Island WIP 6242

BAD COMPANY UK drum and bass production group comprising Michael Wojicki, Darren White, Jason Maldini and Dan Stein, with their own BC Recordings label. Rawhill Cru is MC Navigator under an assumed name. Stein later recorded under the name Fresh.

DATE	POS	WKS	BPI	SINGLE TITLE	LABEL & NUMBER
09/03/2002	56	1		SPACEHOPPER/TONIGHT	Ram RAMM 37
04/05/2002	59	1		RUSH HOUR/BLIND	BC Recordings BCRUK 002CD
15/03/2003	24	3		MO' FIRE BAD COMPANY UK/RAWHILL CRU	BC Recordings BCRUK 003CD

BAD ENGLISH UK/US rock group formed in 1988 by John Waite (born 4/7/1955, London, vocals), Neal Schon (guitar), Jonathan Cain (keyboards), Ricky Phillips (bass) and Dene Castronovo (drums). Waite, Cain and Phillips were all previously in The Babys, Schon with Santana and Journey (that also included Cain), and Castronovo with Wild Dogs. They disbanded in 1991. Waite went solo, Phillips and Castronovo linked up with Jimmy Page and David Coverdale, and Schon and Cain re-formed Journey.

DATE	POS	WKS	BPI	SINGLE TITLE	LABEL & NUMBER
25/11/1989	61	3		WHEN I SEE YOU SMILE ▲²	Epic 6553471

BAD HABIT BOYS German production group formed by CJ Stone (Andreas Litterscheid), George Dee and Jurgen Dohr.

DATE	POS	WKS	BPI	SINGLE TITLE	LABEL & NUMBER
01/07/2000	41	1		WEEKEND	Inferno CDFERN 28

BAD MANNERS UK ska group formed in London in 1980 by Buster Bloodvessel (born Doug Trendle, 6/9/1958, London, vocals), Louis 'Alphonso' Cook (guitar), Winston Bazoomies (born Alan Sayag, harmonica), Brian 'Chew-It' Tuit (drums), David Farren (bass), Paul Hyman (trumpet), Gus 'Hot Lips' Herman (trumpet), Chris Kane (saxophone), Andrew 'Marcus Absent' Marson (saxophone) and Martin Stewart (keyboards).

DATE	POS	WKS	BPI	SINGLE TITLE	LABEL & NUMBER
01/03/1980	28	14		NE-NE-NA-NA-NA-NA-NU-NU	Magnet MAG 164
14/06/1980	15	14		LIP UP FATTY	Magnet MAG 175
27/09/1980	3	13	O	SPECIAL BREW	Magnet MAG 180
06/12/1980	21	12		LORRAINE	Magnet MAG 181
28/03/1981	13	9		JUST A FEELING	Magnet MAG 187
27/06/1981	3	13	O	CAN CAN	Magnet MAG 190
26/09/1981	10	9		WALKING IN THE SUNSHINE	Magnet MAG 197
21/11/1981	34	9		BUONA SERA	Magnet MAG 211
01/05/1982	44	5		GOT NO BRAINS	Magnet MAG 216
31/07/1982	9	7		MY GIRL LOLLIPOP (MY BOY LOLLIPOP)	Magnet MAG 232
30/10/1982	58	3		SAMSON AND DELILAH	Magnet MAG 236
14/05/1983	49	3		THAT'LL DO NICELY	Magnet MAG 243

BAD MEETS EVIL FEATURING EMINEM AND ROYCE DA 5' 9" US producer Dr Dre (born Andre Young, 18/2/1965, Compton, CA) with rappers Eminem (born Marshall Mathers, 17/10/1972, Kansas City, MO) and Royce Da 5' 9" (born Ryan Montgomery, 7/7/1977, Detroit), Eminem and Royce having first collaborated on *Bad Meets Evil* on Eminem's *Slim Shady* album.

DATE	POS	WKS	BPI	SINGLE TITLE	LABEL & NUMBER
01/09/2001	63	1		SCARY MOVIES Featured in the 2000 film *Scary Movie*	Mole UK MOLEUK 045

BAD NEWS UK group formed by Vim Fuego (guitar/vocals, played by Adrian Edmondson), Colin Grigson (bass, played by Rik Mayall), Den Dennis (guitar, played by Nigel Planer) and Spider Webb (drums, played by Peter Richardson) for *The Comic Strip Presents* TV show, a one-off parody of a London heavy metal band travelling to Grantham for a show. Its success prompted a second appearance, the group being required to play live at the Donington Festival.

DATE	POS	WKS	BPI	SINGLE TITLE	LABEL & NUMBER
12/09/1987	44	5		BOHEMIAN RHAPSODY	EMI EM 24

BAD RELIGION US punk group formed in Woodland Hills, CA in 1980 by Greg Graffin (vocals), Brett Gurewitz (guitar), Jay Bentley (bass) and Jay Lishrout (drums). Their early releases were on Gurewitz's Epitaph label. Line-up changes have included Pete Finestone and Bobby Schayer (both drums), Greg Hetson (guitar) and Tim Gallegos (bass). Gurewitz left in 1995 to concentrate on Epitaph and was replaced by Brian Baker.

DATE	POS	WKS	BPI	SINGLE TITLE	LABEL & NUMBER
11/02/1995	41	2		21ST CENTURY (DIGITAL BOY)	Columbia 6611435
21/08/2004	67	1		LOS ANGELES IS BURNING	Epitaph 11692

BAD SEEDS – see NICK CAVE AND THE BAD SEEDS

BAD YARD CLUB – see DAVID MORALES

ANGELO BADALAMENTI – see ORBITAL AND BOOTH AND THE BAD ANGEL

SHAHIN BADAR – see TIM DELUXE

WALLY BADAROU French keyboard player/producer (born 1955, Paris) who has worked with artists as diverse as Level 42, Robert Palmer, Melissa Etheridge, Talking Heads and Black Uhuru.

| 19/10/1985 | 46 | 6 | | CHIEF INSPECTOR | Fourth & Broadway BRW 37 |

BADDIEL AND SKINNER AND THE LIGHTNING SEEDS UK duo David Baddiel (born 28/5/1964) and Frank Skinner (born 28/1/1957, West Bromwich), hosts of the TV show *Fantasy Football*, who co-wrote *Three Lions* with The Lightning Seeds' Ian Broudie, whose football pedigree was established when *The Life Of Riley* was used for *Match Of The Day's* Goal of the Month slot. Effectively the anthem of the English football team, nevertheless the single was a huge European hit.

01/06/1996	❶²	15	✪	THREE LIONS (THE OFFICIAL SONG OF THE ENGLAND FOOTBALL TEAM) ↑ Reclaimed #1 position on 6/7/1996	Epic 6632732
20/06/1998	❶³	13	✪	THREE LIONS '98 ↑ Re-written version of their first hit	Epic 6660982
15/06/2002	16	6		THREE LIONS Second re-written version released to coincide with the 2002 FIFA World Cup	Epic 6728152

BADFELLAS FEATURING CK UK/Kenyan drum and bass duo.

| 15/02/2003 | 55 | 1 | | SOC IT TO ME | Serious SER 053CD |

BADFINGER UK group originally formed by Pete Ham (born 27/4/1947, Swansea guitar/piano/vocals), Mike Gibbins (born 12/3/1949, Swansea, drums), Ron Griffiths (bass), David Jenkins (rhythm guitar) and Terry Gleeson (drums), and known as The Iveys. When Paul McCartney signed the group to Apple Records, Tom Evans (born 5/6/1947, Liverpool) replaced Jenkins and Joey Molland (born 21/6/1948, Liverpool) replaced Griffits when they became Badfinger in 1969. McCartney wrote their debut hit, but Ham and Evans scored worldwide with *Without You*, a smash for both Nilsson and Mariah Carey. Both writers committed suicide, Ham on 23/4/1975 and Evans on 23/11/1983, by hanging themselves.

10/01/1970	4	11		COME AND GET IT Written by Paul McCartney. Featured in the 1970 film *The Magic Christian*	Apple 20
09/01/1971	5	12		NO MATTER WHAT Featured in the 1996 film *Now And Then*	Apple 31
29/01/1972	10	11		DAY AFTER DAY Produced by George Harrison and featuring Paul McCartney on piano	Apple 40

BADLY DRAWN BOY UK singer/songwriter (born Damon Gough, Manchester) named after a character in the adult cartoon magazine *Viz*.

04/09/1999	27	2		ONCE AROUND THE BLOCK	Twisted Nerve TNXL 003CD
17/06/2000	41	1		ANOTHER PEARL	Twisted Nerve TNXL 004CD
16/09/2000	26	2		DISILLUSION	Twisted Nerve TNXL 005CD
25/11/2000	27	2		ONCE AROUND THE BLOCK	Twisted Nerve TNXL 009CD
19/05/2001	22	2		PISSING IN THE WIND	Twisted Nerve TNXL 010CD
06/04/2002	16	7		SILENT SIGH	Twisted Nerve TNXL 012CD
22/06/2002	28	2		SOMETHING TO TALK ABOUT This and above single featured in the 2002 film *About A Boy*	Twisted Nerve TNXL 014CD
26/10/2002	9	3		YOU WERE RIGHT Featured in the 2003 film *American Wedding*	Twisted Nerve TNXL 015CD
18/01/2003	16	3		BORN AGAIN	Twisted Nerve TNXL 016CD
03/05/2003	24	2		ALL POSSIBILITIES	Twisted Nerve TNXL 017CD
31/07/2004	38	2		YEAR OF THE RAT	XL Recordings TNXL 018CD

BADMAN UK producer Julian Brettle.

| 02/02/1991 | 61 | 3 | | MAGIC STYLE | Citybeat CBE 759 |

ERYKAH BADU US singer (born Erica Wright, 26/2/1972, Dallas, TX) who began as rapper MC Apples and later relocated to New York. She appeared in the films *Blues Brothers 2000* (1998) and *The Cider House Rules* (1999). Three Grammy Awards include Best Rhythm & Blues Album in 1997 for *Baduizm*.

28/07/2001	63	1		SIGNS	Outcaste OUT 38CD1
19/04/1997	12	4		ON & ON 1997 Grammy Award for Best Female Rhythm & Blues Vocal Performance	Universal UND 56117
14/06/1997	30	3		NEXT LIFETIME	Universal UND 56132
29/11/1997	47	1		APPLE TREE	Universal UND 56150
11/07/1998	23	3		ONE BUSTA RHYMES FEATURING ERYKAH BADU Contains a sample of Stevie Wonder's *Love's In Need Of Love Today*	Elektra E 3833CD1
06/03/1999	31	2		YOU GOT ME THE ROOTS FEATURING ERYKAH BADU 1999 Grammy Award for Best Rap Group Performance	MCA MCSTD 48110
15/09/2001	23	4		SWEET BABY MACY GRAY FEATURING ERYKAH BADU	Epic 6718822

JOAN BAEZ US singer (born 9/1/1941, Staten Island, NYC) who first attracted attention at the 1959 Newport Folk Festival, later touring with Bob Dylan. Recording her debut in 1958, she signed with Vanguard in 1960. Initially with a broad-based repertoire, she became associated with the US civil rights movement, *We Shall Overcome*, becoming an anthem of the movement. Twice jailed for her part in anti-war protests, she is still involved in humanitarian work, founding Humanitas International in 1979.

06/05/1965	26	10		WE SHALL OVERCOME	Fontana TF 564
08/07/1965	8	12		THERE BUT FOR FORTUNE	Fontana TF 587
02/09/1965	22	8		IT'S ALL OVER NOW BABY BLUE	Fontana TF 604

❶⁹ Number of weeks single topped the UK chart　↑ Entered the UK chart at #1　▲⁹ Number of weeks single topped the US chart

23/12/1965	35	4		FAREWELL ANGELINA	Fontana TF 639
28/07/1966	50	1		PACK UP YOUR SORROWS	Fontana TF 727
09/10/1971	6	12		**THE NIGHT THEY DROVE OLD DIXIE DOWN**	Vanguard VS 35138

BAHA MEN Bahamian junkanoo group formed by Isiah Jackson (bass), Nehemiah Hield (vocals), Fred Ferguson (guitar/keyboards), Herschel Small (guitar/keyboards), Jeffrey Chea (keyboards) and Colyn 'Mo' Grant (drums). The group relocated to the US. By their debut hit Marvin Prosper (raps), Tony 'Monks' Flowers (percussion), Pat Carey (guitar) and his son Rick (vocals) had joined.

14/10/2000	2	23	✪	**WHO LET THE DOGS OUT** 2000 Grammy Award for Best Dance Recording	Edel 0115425 ERE
03/02/2001	14	5		YOU ALL DAT BAHA MEN:GUEST VOCAL IMANI COPPOLA Contains a sample of Tight Fit's *The Lion Sleeps Tonight*	
					Edel 0124855 ERE
13/07/2002	16	7		MOVE IT LIKE THIS	EMI CDEM 615

CAROL BAILEY UK singer who previously recorded for DFC.

| 25/02/1995 | 41 | 2 | | FEEL IT | Multiply CDMULTY 3 |

IMOGEN BAILEY – see MICHAEL WOODS FEATURING IMOGEN BAILEY

PHILIP BAILEY US singer (born 8/5/1951, Denver, CO) who joined Earth Wind & Fire as lead singer in 1971, going solo in 1983. He later recorded a number of gospel albums, winning the 1986 Grammy Award for Best Gospel Performance for *Triumph*.

| 09/03/1985 | ❶⁴ | 12 | ● | **EASY LOVER** PHILIP BAILEY (DUET WITH PHIL COLLINS) | CBS A 4915 |
| 18/05/1985 | 34 | 8 | | WALKING ON THE CHINESE WALL | CBS A 6202 |

MERRIL BAINBRIDGE Australian singer (born 2/6/1968, Melbourne).

| 07/12/1996 | 51 | 1 | | MOUTH | Gotham 74321431012 |

ADRIAN BAKER UK singer/multi-instrumentalist (born in Ilford) whose career began with Pebbles before joining the Beach Boys on tour after a successful Beach Boys medley he produced as Gidea Park. He also launched Polo Records.

| 19/07/1975 | 10 | 8 | | **SHERRY** | Magnet MAG 34 |

ANITA BAKER US singer (born 20/12/1957, Toledo, OH, raised in Detroit, MI) who was lead singer with soul group Chapter 8 from 1976 until 1980. She then worked in an office prior to a solo deal with Beverly Glen. Eight Grammy Awards include Best Rhythm & Blues Performance in 1986 for *Rapture*, Best Soul Gospel Performance by a Group in 1987 with The Winans for *Ain't No Need To Worry*, Best Rhythm & Blues Vocal Performance in 1990 for *Compositions* and Best Rhythm & Blues Singer in 1995 for *I Apologize*. She has a star on the Hollywood Walk of Fame and was given a Lifetime Achievement Award at the 2004 MOBO Awards.

15/11/1986	13	10		SWEET LOVE 1986 Grammy Award for Best Rhythm & Blues Song for writers Anita Baker, Louis Johnson and Gary Bias	
					Elektra EKR 44
31/01/1987	51	5		CAUGHT UP IN THE RAPTURE	Elektra EKR 49
08/10/1988	55	3		GIVING YOU THE BEST THAT I GOT Grammy Awards for Best Rhythm & Blues Song with writers Skip Scarborough and Randy Holland, and Best Rhythm & Blues Vocal Performance (both 1988), and Best Rhythm & Blues Vocal Performance in 1989	
					Elektra EKR 79
30/06/1990	68	2		TALK TO ME	Elektra EKR 111
17/09/1994	48	2		BODY & SOUL	Elektra EKR 190CD

ARTHUR BAKER US multi-instrumentalist (born 22/4/1955, Boston, MA) and legendary producer (with Rockers Revenge and Loleatta Holloway among others) who was originally a remixer, most notably with Bruce Springsteen's *Dancing In The Dark*. He also recorded as Wally Jump Jr And The Criminal Element Orchestra and Jack E Makossa.

20/05/1989	64	2		IT'S YOUR TIME ARTHUR BAKER FEATURING SHIRLEY LEWIS	Breakout USA 654
21/10/1989	38	5		THE MESSAGE IS LOVE ARTHUR BAKER AND THE BACKBEAT DISCIPLES FEATURING AL GREEN	Breakout USA 668
30/11/2002	64	1		CONFUSION ARTHUR BAKER VERSUS NEW ORDER	Whacked WACKT 002CD

GEORGE BAKER SELECTION Dutch group formed by George Baker (born Johannes Bouwens, 12/9/1944), Jan Hop, Jacobus Anthonius Greuter, George The, Jan Gerbrand and Nelleke Brzoskowsky.

| 06/09/1975 | 10 | 10 | | **PALOMA BLANCA** | Warner Brothers K 16541 |

HYLDA BAKER AND ARTHUR MULLARD UK duo formed by TV and film comedians Hylda Baker (born 1908, Farnsworth) and Arthur Mullard (born 11/11/1913). Their hit record was a parody of the John Travolta/Olivia Newton-John song from the 1978 film *Grease*. Baker died in May 1986 and Mullard in December 1995.

| 09/09/1978 | 22 | 6 | | YOU'RE THE ONE THAT I WANT | Pye 7N 46121 |

BAKSHELF DOG UK puppet dog Churchill, star of advertisements for the Churchill insurance group, whose debut hit raised funds for the National Canine Defence League. Despite this hit, Churchill won't even quote motor insurance rates for people who work in the record industry.

| 21/12/2002 | 51 | 2 | | NO LIMITS | WVC CDCHURCH 1 |

BALAAM AND THE ANGEL UK rock group formed in Motherwell, Scotland by brothers Mark Morris (born 15/1/1963, Motherwell, vocals/bass), Jim Morris (born 25/11/1960, Motherwell, guitar) and Des Morris (born 27/6/1964, Motherwell, drums). They set up Chapter 22 Records, later shortening their name to Balaam.

| 29/03/1986 | 70 | 2 | | SHE KNOWS | Virgin VS 842 |

○ Silver disc ● Gold disc ✪ Platinum disc (additional platinum units are indicated by a figure following the symbol) ⊚ Singles released prior to 1973 that are known to have sold over 1 million copies in the UK

LONG JOHN BALDRY
UK singer (born 12/1/1941, Haddon) nicknamed because of his 6' 7" height. He sang with numerous blues groups during the 1960s, including the Hoochie Coochie Men (with Rod Stewart), Steampacket (with Brian Auger and Rod Stewart) and Bluesology (whose pianist, Reg Dwight, adopted the surname John in his honour when going solo as Elton John).

Date	Pos	Wks		Title	Label & Number
08/11/1967	●²	13		**LET THE HEARTACHES BEGIN**	Pye 7N 17385
28/08/1968	29	7		WHEN THE SUN COMES SHINING THRU'	Pye 7N 17593
23/10/1968	15	8		MEXICO	Pye 7N 17563
29/01/1969	21	8		IT'S TOO LATE NOW	Pye 7N 17664

BALEARIC BILL
Belgian production group formed by Johan Gielen, Peter Ramson and Sven Maes who also recorded as Cubic 22 and Airscape. Gielen also records as Blue Bamboo.

02/10/1999	36	2		DESTINATION SUNSHINE	Xtravaganza XTRAV 3CDS

EDWARD BALL
UK singer (born in London) who was a member of Teenage Filmstars, The Missing Scientists, O-Level and Television Personalities before going solo.

20/07/1996	57	1		THE MILL HILL SELF HATE CLUB	Creation CRESCD 233
22/02/1997	59	1		LOVE IS BLUE	Creation CRESCD 244

KENNY BALL AND HIS JAZZMEN
UK trumpeter (born 22/5/1931, Ilford) originally with Charlie Galbraith's All Star Jazz Band from 1951. He formed the Jazzmen in 1958 and they made their TV debut on *New Faces*. Lonnie Donegan recommended him to Pye.

23/02/1961	13	15		SAMANTHA Originally appeared in the 1956 film *High Society*	Pye Jazz Today 7NJ 2040
11/05/1961	24	6		I STILL LOVE YOU ALL	Pye Jazz 7NJ 2042
31/08/1961	28	6		SOMEDAY (YOU'LL BE SORRY)	Pye Jazz 7NJ 2047
09/11/1961	2	21		**MIDNIGHT IN MOSCOW** Original Russian title *Padmeskoveeye Vietchera*	Pye Jazz 7NJ 2049
15/02/1962	4	13		**MARCH OF THE SIAMESE CHILDREN** Originally appeared in the 1956 film *The King And I*	Pye Jazz 7NJ 2051
17/05/1962	7	14		**THE GREEN LEAVES OF SUMMER** Originally appeared in the 1960 film *The Alamo*	Pye Jazz 7NJ 2054
23/08/1962	14	8		SO DO I	Pye Jazz 7NJ 2056
18/10/1962	23	6		THE PAY OFF	Pye Jazz 7NJ 2061
17/01/1963	10	13		**SUKIYAKI**	Pye Jazz 7NJ 2062
25/04/1963	21	11		CASABLANCA	Pye Jazz 7NJ 2064
13/06/1963	24	8		RONDO	Pye Jazz 7NJ 2065
22/08/1963	27	6		ACAPULCO 1922	Pye Jazz 7NJ 2067
11/06/1964	30	7		HELLO DOLLY	Pye Jazz 7NJ 2071
19/07/1967	43	2		WHEN I'M SIXTY FOUR	Pye 7N 17348

MICHAEL BALL
UK singer/actor (born 27/7/1962, Stratford-upon-Avon) who first made his mark in the Andrew Lloyd Webber musical *Aspects Of Love*.

28/01/1989	2	14	○	**LOVE CHANGES EVERYTHING** From the musical *Aspects Of Love*	Really Useful RUR 3
28/10/1989	68	2		THE FIRST MAN YOU REMEMBER **MICHAEL BALL AND DIANA MORRISON**	Really Useful RUR 6
10/08/1991	58	2		IT'S STILL YOU	Polydor PO 160
25/04/1992	20	7		ONE STEP OUT OF TIME UK entry for the 1992 Eurovision Song Contest, coming second to Ireland's Linda Martin with *Why Me?*	Polydor PO 206
12/12/1992	51	2		IF I CAN DREAM (EP) Tracks on EP: *If I Can Dream, You Don't Have To Say You Love Me, Always On My Mind* and *Tell Me There's A Heaven*	Polydor PO 248
11/09/1993	72	1		SUNSET BOULEVARD From the musical *Sunset Boulevard*	Polydor PZCD 293
30/07/1994	36	3		FROM HERE TO ETERNITY	Columbia 6606905
17/09/1994	63	2		THE LOVERS WE WERE	Columbia 6607972
09/12/1995	42	4		THE ROSE Theme to the TV series *The Ladykillers*	Columbia 6614535
17/02/1996	40	2		SOMETHING INSIDE SO STRONG	Columbia 6629005

STEVE BALSAMO
UK singer (born in Swansea) who was originally an actor, appearing in a local production of *Jesus Christ Superstar* and touring with *Les Miserables*. He made his London stage debut in *Jesus Christ Superstar*. He signed with Columbia Records in 2001.

16/03/2002	32	2		SUGAR FOR THE SOUL	Columbia 6718552

BALTIMORA
Irish singer (born Jimmy McShane, 23/5/1957, Londonderry) who later worked as a session singer and died from AIDS on 28/3/1995.

10/08/1985	3	12	○	**TARZAN BOY** Featured in the 1993 film *Teenage Mutant Ninja Turtles III*	Columbia DB 9102

CHARLI BALTIMORE
US rapper (born Tiffany Lane, 11/10/1973, Philadelphia, PA) who was a member of The Notorious B.I.G.'s group Commission before going solo. She is named after Geena Davis' character in the film *The Long Kiss Goodnight* (1996).

01/08/1998	12	4		MONEY Contains a sample of The O'Jays' *For The Love Of Money*. Featured in the 1998 film *Woo*	Epic 6662272
12/10/2002	4	10		**DOWN 4 U IRV GOTTI PRESENTS JA RULE, ASHANTI, CHARLI BALTIMORE AND VITA**	Murder Inc 0639002

BAM BAM
US singer/drummer Chris Westbrook.

19/03/1988	65	2		GIVE IT TO ME	Serious 7OUS 10

AFRIKA BAMBAATAA
US singer (born Kevin Donovan, aka Khayan Aasim, 10/4/1960, The Bronx, NYC) whose name means 'affectionate leader'.

28/08/1982	53	3		PLANET ROCK Contains a sample of Kraftwerk's *Trans Euro Express*	Polydor POSP 497

●⁹ Number of weeks single topped the UK chart   ↑ Entered the UK chart at #1   ▲⁹ Number of weeks single topped the US chart

53

DATE	POS	WKS	BPI	SINGLE TITLE	LABEL & NUMBER
10/03/1984	30	4		RENEGADES OF FUNK This and above single credited to **AFRIKA BAMBAATAA AND THE SONIC SOUL FORCE**	Tommy Boy AFR 1
01/09/1984	49	5		UNITY (PART 1 – THE THIRD COMING) **AFRIKA BAMBAATAA AND JAMES BROWN**	Tommy Boy AFR 2
27/02/1988	17	8		RECKLESS **AFRIKA BAMBAATAA FEATURING UB40 AND FAMILY**	EMI EM 41
12/10/1991	45	3		JUST GET UP AND DANCE	EMI USA MT 100
17/10/1998	22	4		GOT TO GET UP	Multiply CDMULTY 42
18/09/1999	7	5		**AFRIKA SHOX** LEFTFIELD/BAMBAATAA	Hard Hands HAND 057CD1
25/08/2001	47	1		PLANET ROCK **PAUL OAKENFOLD PRESENTS AFRIKA BAMBAATAA AND SOULSONIC FORCE** Contains a sample of Kraftwerk's *Trans Europe Express*	Tommy Boy TBCD 2266
13/03/2004	72	1		D-FUNKTIONAL **MEKON FEATURING AFRIKA BAMBAATAA**	Wall Of Sound WALLD092

BAMBOO UK producer Andrew 'Doc' Livingstone.

DATE	POS	WKS	BPI	SINGLE TITLE	LABEL & NUMBER
17/01/1998	2	10	O	**BAMBOOGIE** Contains a sample of KC & The Sunshine Band's *Get Down Tonight*. Featured in the 1998 film *A Night At The Roxbury*	VC Recordings VCRD 29
04/07/1998	36	2		THE STRUTT	VC Recordings VCRD 35

BANANARAMA UK vocal group formed by flatmates Sarah Dallin (born 17/12/1961, Bristol) and Keren Woodward (born 2/4/1961, Bristol) with Siobhan Fahey (born 10/9/1957, London). At one point they were the most successful girl group in the UK. Fahey left in 1988 to enjoy married life to Eurythmic Dave Stewart before forming Shakespears Sister, and was replaced by Jacqui Sullivan (born 7/8/1960, London). Sullivan left in 1991 and the group continued as a duo. La Na Nee Nee Noo Noo comprises TV comediennes Dawn French and Jennifer Saunders.

DATE	POS	WKS	BPI	SINGLE TITLE	LABEL & NUMBER
13/02/1982	4	10	O	**IT AIN'T WHAT YOU DO IT'S THE WAY THAT YOU DO IT** FUN BOY THREE AND BANANARAMA	Chrysalis CHS 2570
10/04/1982	5	10	O	**REALLY SAYING SOMETHING** BANANARAMA WITH FUN BOY THREE	Deram NANA 1
03/07/1982	4	11	O	**SHY BOY**	London NANA 2
04/12/1982	45	7		CHEERS THEN	London NANA 3
26/02/1983	5	10		**NA NA HEY HEY KISS HIM GOODBYE**	London NANA 4
09/07/1983	8	10		**CRUEL SUMMER** Featured in the 1983 film *The Karate Kid*	London NANA 5
03/03/1984	3	11	O	**ROBERT DE NIRO'S WAITING**	London NANA 6
26/05/1984	23	7		ROUGH JUSTICE	London NANA 7
24/11/1984	58	2		HOTLINE TO HEAVEN	London NANA 8
24/08/1985	31	6		DO NOT DISTURB	London NANA 9
31/05/1986	8	13		**VENUS ▲[1]** Featured in the films *Romy And Michele's High School Reunion* (1997) and *There's Only One Jimmy Grimble* (2000)	London NANA 10
16/08/1986	41	5		MORE THAN PHYSICAL	London NANA 11
14/02/1987	32	5		TRICK OF THE NIGHT Featured in the 1986 film *Jumpin' Jack Flash*	London NANA 12
11/07/1987	14	9		I HEARD A RUMOUR Featured in the 1987 film *Disorderlies*	London NANA 13
10/10/1987	3	12	O	**LOVE IN THE FIRST DEGREE** B-side *Mr Sleaze* credited to **STOCK AITKEN WATERMAN**	London NANA 14
09/01/1988	20	6		I CAN'T HELP IT	London NANA 15
09/04/1988	5	10		**I WANT YOU BACK**	London NANA 16
24/09/1988	23	8		LOVE, TRUTH AND HONESTY	London NANA 17
19/11/1988	15	9		NATHAN JONES Featured in the 1989 film *Rainman*	London NANA 18
25/02/1989	3	9	O	**HELP!** BANANARAMA/LA NA NEE NEE NOO NOO Released in aid of the Comic Relief charity	London LON 222
10/06/1989	19	6		CRUEL SUMMER (REMIX)	London NANA 19
28/07/1990	27	4		ONLY YOUR LOVE	London NANA 21
05/01/1991	20	6		PREACHER MAN	London NANA 23
20/04/1991	30	5		LONG TRAIN RUNNING	London NANA 24
29/08/1992	24	5		MOVIN' ON	London NANA 25
28/11/1992	71	2		LAST THING ON MY MIND	London NANA 26
20/03/1993	24	4		MORE MORE MORE	London NACPD 27

BAND Canadian group formed by Robbie Robertson (born 5/7/1944, Toronto, guitar/vocals), Richard Manuel (born 3/4/1945, Stratford, Ontario, piano/vocals), Garth Hudson (born 2/8/1937 London, Ontario, organ), Rick Danko (born 9/12/1943, Simcoe, bass/vocals) and Levon Helm (born 26/5/1942, Marvell, AR, drums/vocals). They recorded and toured extensively with Bob Dylan. Manuel committed suicide by hanging himself after a concert on 6/3/1986. Danko died in his sleep on 10/12/1999. They were inducted into the Rock & Roll Hall of Fame in 1994.

DATE	POS	WKS	BPI	SINGLE TITLE	LABEL & NUMBER
18/09/1968	21	9		THE WEIGHT Featured in the films *Easy Rider* (1969) and *Starsky & Hutch* (2004)	Capitol CL 15559
04/04/1970	16	9		RAG MAMA RAG	Capitol CL 15629

BAND AID Multinational supergroup assembled by Bob Geldof (of the Boomtown Rats) and Midge Ure (of Ultravox) to raise funds for Ethiopian famine. They took the name from a plaster, since the aim of the record was to heal famine in Africa. Their *Do They Know It's Christmas* is one of only five singles to have sold more than 2 million copies in the UK.

DATE	POS	WKS	BPI	SINGLE TITLE	LABEL & NUMBER
15/12/1984	●[5]	13	✪	**DO THEY KNOW IT'S CHRISTMAS?** ↑ Features Robert 'Kool' Bell (of Kool & The Gang); Bono (U2); Boy George (Culture Club); Adam Clayton (U2); Phil Collins (Genesis); Sarah Dallin (Bananarama); Siobhan Fahey (Bananarama); Bob Geldof (Boomtown Rats); Glenn Gregory (Heaven 17); Tony Hadley (Spandau Ballet); John Keeble (Spandau Ballet); Gary and Martin Kemp (Spandau Ballet); Simon Le	

Bon (Duran Duran); Marilyn; George Michael (Wham!); Jon Moss (Culture Club); Steve Norman (Spandau Ballet); Rick Parfitt (Status Quo); Nick Rhodes (Duran Duran); Francis Rossi (Status Quo); Sting (Police); Andy Taylor (Duran Duran); James Taylor (Kool & The Gang); John Taylor (Duran Duran); Roger Taylor (Duran Duran); Dennis Thomas (Kool & The Gang); Midge Ure (Ultravox); Martin Ware (Heaven 17); Paul Weller (Jam); Keren Woodward (Bananarama); and Paul Young. David Bowie and Paul McCartney contributed messages to the B-side. UK sales exceed 3.5 million copies and total worldwide sales 7 million copies . . . . Mercury FEED 1

07/12/1985 . . . . . 3 . . . . . . 7				**DO THEY KNOW IT'S CHRISTMAS?** Re-issued for the Christmas market with a new B-side . . . . Mercury FEED 1
23/12/1989 . . . . ❶³ . . . . 6 . . . . . . ✪				**DO THEY KNOW IT'S CHRISTMAS?** ↑ BAND AID II Remake assembled by producers Stock Aitken And Waterman, and featuring Sarah Dallin (Bananarama), Jason Donovan, Matt Goss (Bros), Kylie Minogue, Marti Pellow (Wet Wet Wet), Chris Rea, Cliff Richard, Sonia, Lisa Stansfield and Keren Woodward (Bananarama) . . . . PWL/Polydor FEED 2
11/12/2004 . . . . ❶³ . . . . 3+ . . . . ✪²				**DO THEY KNOW IT'S CHRISTMAS?** ↑ BAND AID 20 20th anniversary remake featuring Bono, Keane, Paul McCartney, The Sugababes, Skye (Morcheeba), Robbie Williams, Dido, Jamelia, Justin Hawkins (Darkness), Chris Martin (Coldplay), Fran Healy (Travis), Beverley Knight, Busted, Ms Dynamite, Danny Goffey (Supergrass), Katie Melua, Will Young, Natasha Bedingfield, Snow Patrol, Shaznay Lewis, Joss Stone, Rachel Stevens, The Thrills, Roisin Murphy (Moloko), Lemar, Estelle, Neil Hannon (Divine Comedy), Feeder and Dizzee Rascal . . . . Mercury 9869413

BAND AKA US soul group assembled by producer Joeson James Jarrett and featuring Kenny Allen, Michael Fitzhugh, Booker Hedlock, Philip Scott, Robin Holt, Stanley Hood, Jack Holmes and D'Arco Smith.

| 15/05/1982 . . . . . 41 . . . . . 5 . . . . . . | | | | GRACE . . . . Epic EPC A 2376 |
| 05/03/1983 . . . . 24 . . . . . . 7 . . . . . | | | | JOY . . . . Epic EPC A 3145 |

BAND OF GOLD Dutch studio group/session singers assembled by producer Paco Saval.

| 14/07/1984 . . . . 24 . . . . . 11 . . . . . . | | | | LOVE SONGS ARE BACK AGAIN (MEDLEY) Medley of *Let's Put It All Together*; *Betcha By Golly Wow*; *Side Show*; *Have You Seen Her*; *Reunited*; *You Make Me Feel Brand New*; and *Kiss And Say Goodbye* . . . . RCA 428 |

BAND OF THIEVES – see LUKE GOSS AND THE BAND OF THIEVES

BANDA SONARA UK producer Gerald Elms.

| 06/10/2001 . . . . 50 . . . . . . 2 . . . . . | | | | GUITARRA G. . . . . Defected DFECT 36CDS |
| 19/10/2002 . . . . . 46 . . . . . 1 . . . . . | | | | PRESSURE COOKER G CLUB PRESENTS BANDA SONARA . . . . Defected DFTD 060CDS |

BANDERAS UK duo Caroline Buckley (vocals) and Sally Herbert (violin/keyboards).

| 23/02/1991 . . . . . 16 . . . . . 10 . . . . . | | | | THIS IS YOUR LIFE . . . . London LON 290 |
| 15/06/1991 . . . . . 41 . . . . . 6 . . . . . | | | | SHE SELLS . . . . London LON 298 |

BANDITS – see BILLY COTTON AND HIS BAND

BANDITS UK group from Liverpool with John Robinson (vocals), Richie Bandit (guitar), Gary Murphy (guitar), Scott Bandit (bass), Tony Dunne (keyboards) and Swee Bandit (drums). They formed their own Centro Del Blanco label.

| 28/06/2003 . . . . . 32 . . . . . 1 . . . . . | | | | TAKE IT AND RUN . . . . B Unique BUN 055CDX |
| 20/09/2003 . . . . . 35 . . . . . 1 . . . . . | | | | 2 STEP ROCK . . . . B Unique BUN 065CDX |

BANDWAGON – see JOHNNY JOHNSON

HONEY BANE UK post-punk singer (born Donna Tracy Boylan) and previously lead singer with The Fatal Microbes before going solo. Later she became an actress, appearing as Molly in the 1983 film *Scrubbers*.

| 24/01/1981 . . . . 37 . . . . . 5 . . . . . | | | | TURN ME ON TURN ME OFF . . . . Zonophone Z 15 |
| 18/04/1981 . . . . 58 . . . . . 3 . . . . . | | | | BABY LOVE . . . . Zonophone Z 19 |

BANG UK duo Paul Calliris (vocals) and Billy Adams (keyboards).

| 06/05/1989 . . . . . 74 . . . . . . 2 . . . . . | | | | YOU'RE THE ONE . . . . RCA PB 42715 |

THOMAS BANGALTER AND DJ FALCON French duo Thomas Bangalter (born 1/1/1975) and DJ Falcon. Bangalter is also a member of Stardust and Daft Punk.

| 04/01/2003 . . . . . 71 . . . . . 1 . . . . . | | | | SO MUCH LOVE TO GIVE (IMPORT) . . . . Roule TOGETHER 2 |

BANGLES US rock group formed in Los Angeles, CA in 1981 and known as Supersonic Bangs, comprising Susanna Hoffs (born 17/1/1957, Los Angeles, guitar/vocals), Debbi Peterson (born 22/8/1961, Los Angeles, drums/vocals), Vicki Peterson (born 11/1/1958, Los Angeles, guitar/vocals) and Annette Zilinskas (born 6/11/1964, Van Nuys, CA, bass). Michael Steele (born 2/6/1954, Los Angeles) replaced Zilinskas in 1983 shortly after the group signed with CBS. They changed their name to Bangs but were forced to amend it to Bangles in 1982 as there was another group with the same name. They disbanded in 1989, with Hoffs, who had starred in films, going solo, although they re-formed in 2002. They won the Best International Group category of the 1987 BRIT Awards.

15/02/1986 . . . . . 2 . . . . . 12 . . . . . O				**MANIC MONDAY** Written by Prince under the name 'Christopher' . . . . CBS A 6796
26/04/1986 . . . . . 31 . . . . . 7				IF SHE KNEW WHAT SHE WANTS . . . . CBS A 7062
05/07/1986 . . . . . 56 . . . . . 3				GOING DOWN TO LIVERPOOL . . . . CBS A 7255
13/09/1986 . . . . . 3 . . . . . 19 . . . . . O				**WALK LIKE AN EGYPTIAN** ▲⁴ . . . . CBS 6500717
10/01/1987 . . . . . 16 . . . . . . 6				WALKING DOWN YOUR STREET . . . . CBS BANGS 1
18/04/1987 . . . . . 55 . . . . . 3				FOLLOWING . . . . CBS BANGS 2
06/02/1988 . . . . . 11 . . . . . 10				HAZY SHADE OF WINTER Featured in the 1988 film *Less Than Zero* . . . . CBS BANGS 8
05/11/1988 . . . . . 35 . . . . . 6				IN YOUR ROOM . . . . CBS BANGS 4

❶⁹ Number of weeks single topped the UK chart ↑ Entered the UK chart at #1 ▲⁹ Number of weeks single topped the US chart

55

DATE	POS	WKS	BPI	SINGLE TITLE	LABEL & NUMBER
18/02/1989	❶⁴	18	●	ETERNAL FLAME ▲¹	CBS BANGS 5
10/06/1989	23	8		BE WITH YOU	CBS BANGS 6
14/10/1989	74	1		I'LL SET YOU FREE	CBS BANGS 7
09/06/1990	73	1		WALK LIKE AN EGYPTIAN Re-issue of CBS 6500717	Def Jam BANGS 3
15/03/2003	38	2		SOMETHING THAT YOU SAID	Liberty BANGLES 003

LLOYD BANKS US rapper (born Christopher Lloyd, 30/4/1982, Jamaica, NY) who is also a member of G Unit.

21/08/2004	19	6		ON FIRE	Interscope 9863485

TONY BANKS – see FISH

BANNED UK rock group formed by Pete Fresh (guitar), Rick Mansworth (guitar/vocals) and John Thomas (bass).

17/12/1977	36	6		LITTLE GIRL	Harvest HAR 5145

BANSHEES – see SIOUXSIE AND THE BANSHEES

BUJU BANTON Jamaican singer (born Mark Myrie, 15/7/1973, Kingston) who made his first recordings in 1986.

07/08/1993	72	1		MAKE MY DAY	Mercury BUJCD 2

PATO BANTON UK reggae singer (born Patrick Murray, Birmingham) who first appeared with The Beat in 1982, making his debut single in 1984 (*Hello Tosh*). He also recorded for Fashion, Don Christie, Ariwa and Greensleeves. Ranking Roger (born Roger Charlery, 21/2/1961, Birmingham) is an ex-member of The Beat.

01/10/1994	❶⁴	18	✪	BABY COME BACK Ali and Robin Campbell are credited on the sleeve.	Virgin VSCDT 1522
11/02/1995	15	6		THIS COWBOY SONG STING FEATURING PATO BANTON Featured in the 1995 film *Terminal Velocity*. Originally written for Jimmy Nail's *Crocodile Shoes* TV series but submitted too late	A&M 5809652
08/04/1995	15	7		BUBBLING HOT PATO BANTON WITH RANKING ROGER	Virgin VSCDT 1530
20/01/1996	36	2		SPIRITS IN THE MATERIAL WORLD PATO BANTON WITH STING Featured in the 1995 film *Ace Ventura: When Nature Calls*	MCA MCSTD 2113
27/07/1996	14	4		GROOVIN' PATO BANTON AND THE REGGAE REVOLUTION Featured in the 1999 film *The Parent Trap*	IRS CDEIRS 195

BAR CODES FEATURING ALISON BROWN UK vocal group featuring Alison Brown and 'MC Dale'. Dale was presenter Dale Winton, host of the TV programme *Supermarket Sweep*. Later copies were credited to MC Dale & The Bar Codes.

17/12/1994	72	1		SUPERMARKET SWEEP (WILL YOU DANCE WITH ME)	Blanca Casa BC 101CD

BAR-KAYS US soul group formed by Al Jackson, drummer with Booker T & The MG's. The original line-up comprised James Alexander (bass), Ronnie Caldwell (organ), Ben Cauley (trumpet), Carl Cunningham (drums), Phalon Jones (saxophone) and Jimmy King (guitar). They also served as Otis Redding's backing band, and all but Alexander (who was not on the plane) and Cauley (who survived) perished with him in the December 1967 plane crash. Alexander later re-formed the band, with Charles Allen (trumpet), Michael Beard (drums), John Colbert (vocals), Sherman Gray (percussion), Harvey Henderson (saxophone), Winston Stewart (keyboards) and Frank Thompson (trombone).

23/08/1967	33	7		SOUL FINGER	Stax 601 014
22/01/1977	41	4		SHAKE YOUR RUMP TO THE FUNK	Mercury 6167 417
12/01/1985	51	4		SEXOMATIC	Club JAB 10

CHRIS BARBER'S JAZZ BAND UK trombonist (born 17/4/1930, Welwyn Garden City) who played with Cy Laurie's band after World War II before forming his own band in 1949, which included Lonnie Donegan and clarinettist Monty Sunshine (born 8/4/1928, London).

13/02/1959	3	24		PETITE FLEUR	Pye Nixa 2026
09/10/1959	27	2		LONESOME (SI TU VOIS MA MERE) CHRIS BARBER FEATURING MONTY SUNSHINE	Columbia DB 4333
04/01/1962	43	4		REVIVAL	Columbia SCD 2166

BARBRA AND NEIL – see BARBRA STREISAND AND NEIL DIAMOND

BARCLAY JAMES HARVEST UK group formed in Oldham by Stewart 'Wooly' Wolstenholme (born 15/4/1947, Oldham, keyboards/vocals), John Lees (born 13/1/1947, Oldham, guitar/vocals), Les Holroyd (born 12/3/1948, Bolton, bass/vocals) and Mel Pritchard (born 20/1/1948, Oldham, drums). Wolstenholme and Lees were previously with Heart And Soul; Holroyd and Pritchard were with The Wickeds. Pritchard died from a heart attack on 28/1/2004.

02/04/1977	49	2		LIVE (EP) Tracks on EP: *Rock N Roll Star* and *Medicine Man (Parts 1 & 2)*	Polydor 2229 198
26/01/1980	63	2		LOVE ON THE LINE	Polydor POSP 97
22/11/1980	61	3		LIFE IS FOR LIVING	Polydor POSP 195
21/05/1983	68	2		JUST A DAY AWAY	Polydor POSP 585

BARDO UK duo Stephen Fischer and Sally-Ann Triplett, assembled specifically for the Eurovision Song Contest in 1982. Triplett was previously in 1980 entrants Prima Donna, who finished third, four places better than Bardo. The competition was won by Nicole of Germany.

10/04/1982	2	8	○	ONE STEP FURTHER UK entry for the 1982 Eurovision Song Contest (came seventh).	Epic EPC A2265

BARDOT Australian vocal group formed by Belinda Chapple, Katie Underwood, Sally Polihronas, Sophie Monk and Chantelle Barrios, and the winners of the Australian version of *Popstars*. Barrios was replaced by Tiffany Wood before they recorded. Underwood left in June 2001, the rest disbanding in 2002 with Monk going solo.

14/04/2001 . . . . . 45 . . . . . . 1 . . . . POISON. . . . . East West EW 229CD

BAREFOOT MAN German singer George Nowak who relocated to the Cayman Islands.

05/12/1998 . . . . . 21 . . . . . . 7 . . . . BIG PANTY WOMAN . . . . Plaza PZACD 082

BARENAKED LADIES Canadian rock group formed in Scarborough, Toronto in Ontario in 1988 by Steven Page (born 22/6/1970, Scarborough, guitar/vocals) and Ed Robertson (born 25/10/1970, Scarborough, guitar) with brothers Jim (born 12/2/1970, double bass) and Andrew Creeggan (born 4/7/1971, keyboards) and Tyler Stewart (born 21/9/1967, drums). They signed with Warners subsidiary Sire in 1992. Keyboardist Kevin Hearn joined the live line-up in 1994, but was forced to take an eighteen-month sabbatical when leukaemia was diagnosed (Chris Brown was his temporary replacement); later he was given a clean bill of health.

20/02/1999 . . . . . 5 . . . . . . 8 . . . . **ONE WEEK ▲[1]** Featured in the 1999 film *American Pie* . . . . Reprise W 468CD
15/05/1999 . . . 28 . . . . . . 2 . . . . IT'S ALL BEEN DONE Featured in the 2000 film *Drive Me Crazy* . . . . Reprise W 476CD
24/07/1999 . . . . . 52 . . . . . . 1 . . . . CALL AND ANSWER Featured in the 1999 film *Edtv* . . . . Reprise W 498CD1
11/12/1999 . . . . . 73 . . . . . . 1 . . . . BRIAN WILSON Tribute to Brian Wilson of The Beach Boys . . . . Reprise W 511CD1

BARKIN BROTHERS FEATURING JOHNNIE FIORI UK production group formed by Tony Walker, Shaun Scott and Jonathon Colling with US singer Johnnie Fiori.

15/04/2000 . . . . . 51 . . . . . . 2 . . . . GONNA CATCH YOU Contains a sample of Lonnie Gordon's *Gonna Catch You* . . . . Brothers Organisation BRUVCD 15

GARY BARLOW UK singer (born 20/1/1971, Frodsham) and founding member of Take That in 1990 who quickly emerged as their chief songwriter. He went solo when the group disbanded in 1996.

20/07/1996 . . . . ❶[1] . . . . 16 . . . . . ● **FOREVER LOVE ↑** Featured in the 1996 film *The Leading Man* . . . . RCA 74321397922
10/05/1997 . . . . ❶[1] . . . . 9 . . . . . . ○ **LOVE WON'T WAIT ↑** Co-written by Madonna and Shep Pettibone, the only #1 penned by Madonna to hit the top of the charts for another artist . . . . RCA 74321470842
26/07/1997 . . . . 11 . . . . 11 . . . . . . SO HELP ME GIRL . . . . RCA 74321501202
15/11/1997 . . . . 7 . . . . . 5 . . . . . . **OPEN ROAD** . . . . RCA 74321518292
17/07/1999 . . . . 16 . . . . . 4 . . . . . . STRONGER . . . . RCA 74321682012
09/10/1999 . . . . . 24 . . . . . 2 . . . . . . FOR ALL THAT YOU WANT . . . . RCA 74321701012

GARY BARNACLE – see **BIG FUN AND SONIA**

BARNBRACK UK vocal/instrumental group formed by Paddy, Hufty and Mossey, and named after a traditional Irish Halloween cake.

16/03/1985 . . . . . 45 . . . . . . 7 . . . . . . BELFAST . . . . Homespun HS 092

BARNDANCE BOYS UK group formed by producers John Matthews and Darren 'Daz' Sampson and featuring Big Jeff, Waylan and Daisy.

13/09/2003 . . . . . 32 . . . . . . 2 . . . . . . YIPPIE I OH . . . . Concept CDCON 41

JIMMY BARNES AND INXS Australian singer (born 24/8/1956, Glasgow) with Cold Chisel until their demise in 1982. He then went solo with Geffen Records.

26/01/1991 . . . . . 18 . . . . . . 8 . . . . GOOD TIMES Originally released in 1987. Featured in the 1987 film *The Lost Boys* . . . . Atlantic A 7751

RICHARD BARNES UK singer/guitarist who originally recorded for Columbia and Bronze and later worked with Ben Harper, Dean Butterworth and Eric Sarafin.

23/05/1970 . . . . . 35 . . . . . 6 . . . . . . TAKE TO THE MOUNTAINS . . . . Philips BF 1840
24/10/1970 . . . . . 38 . . . . . 4 . . . . . . GO NORTH . . . . Philips 6006 039

BARON UK DJ Piers Bailey who was a member of Total Science before going solo. He is a cousin of Adam Clayton of U2.

07/02/2004 . . . . . 71 . . . . . . 1 . . . . . . THE WAY IT WAS/REDHEAD . . . . Virus VRS012

BARRACUDAS UK/US group formed in 1978 by Jeremy Gluck (vocals), David Buckley (bass), Robin Wills (guitar) and Nicky Turner (drums). Turner and Buckley departed after their hit and were replaced by Jim Dickson and Terry Smith, with Chris Wilson (guitar) joining at the same time. They disbanded in 1984 and re-formed in 1989.

16/08/1980 . . . . . 37 . . . . . . 6 . . . . . . SUMMER FUN . . . . EMI-Wipe Out Z 5

WILD WILLY BARRETT – see **JOHN OTWAY AND WILD WILLY BARRETT**

AMANDA BARRIE AND JOHNNIE BRIGGS UK actress Amanda Barrie (born Shirley Anne Broadbent, 14/9/1939, Ashton-under-Lyme) and actor Johnnie Briggs (born 5/9/1935, Battersea, London); best known for their roles as Mike and Alma Baldwin in the UK's longest-running soap opera, first aired in 1960, *Coronation Street*. The Alma Baldwin character was killed off in *Coronation Street* in June 2001, dying from cancer.

16/12/1995 . . . . . 35 . . . . . . 3 . . . . SOMETHING STUPID Listed flip side was *Always Look On The Bright Side Of Life* by **CORONATION STREET CAST FEATURING BILL WADDINGTON** . . . . EMI Premier CDEMS 411

J.J. BARRIE Canadian singer (born Barrie Authors, 7/7/1933, Ottawa, Ontario), former manager of Blue Mink and would-be songwriter who, along with Terry Britten, wrote *Where's The Reason* with Glen Campbell in mind. Campbell's producer convinced Barrie to record the song himself. His only hit was a cover version of a song written by Tammy Wynette.

24/04/1976 . . . . ❶[1] . . . . 11 . . . . . ○ **NO CHARGE** Uncredited singer is the late Vicki Brown, wife of Joe Brown. . . . . Power Exchange PX 209

❶[9] Number of weeks single topped the UK chart ↑ Entered the UK chart at #1 ▲[9] Number of weeks single topped the US chart

KEN BARRIE UK singer whose hit was the theme to the TV series of the same name, for which he also provided the voice-over.

10/07/1982	44	8		POSTMAN PAT	Post Music PP 001
25/12/1982	54	3		POSTMAN PAT	Post Music PP 001
24/12/1983	59	4		POSTMAN PAT	Post Music PP 001

BARRON KNIGHTS UK comedy/vocal group formed in Leighton Buzzard in 1960 by Barron Anthony Osmond (bass/vocals), Butch Baker (guitar/banjo/vocals), Dave Ballinger (drums), Duke D'Mond (born Richard Palmer, guitar/vocals) and Peter 'Peanuts' Langford (guitar/vocals).

09/07/1964	3	13		**CALL UP THE GROUPS** Medley of *Needles And Pins, You Were Made For Me, I Wanna Be Your Man, Diane, Bits And Pieces* and *Twist And Shout*	Columbia DB 7317
22/10/1964	42	2		COME TO THE DANCE	Columbia DB 7375
25/03/1965	5	13		**POP GO THE WORKERS** Medley of *Little Red Rooster, I Wouldn't Trade You For The World, Girl Don't Come, Walk Tall (Walk Straight)* and *Love Me Do*	Columbia DB 7525
16/12/1965	9	7		**MERRY GENTLE POPS** Medley of *Merry Gentle Pops, Catch The Wind, This Little Bird, (I Can't Get No) Satisfaction, Look Through Any Window, Tossing And Turning* and *Goodbye*	Columbia DB 7780
01/12/1966	15	9		UNDER NEW MANAGEMENT Medley of *With A Girl Like You, Mama, Lovers Of The World United, Daydream, God Only Knows* and *They're Coming To Take Me Away Ha-haa!*. This and above three singles credited to **BARRON KNIGHTS WITH DUKE D'MOND**	Columbia DB 8071
23/10/1968	35	4		AN OLYMPIC RECORD Medley of *Lazy Sunday, I Pretend, Delilah, Cinderella Rockafella, Dream A Little Dream Of Me* and *Here Comes The Judge*	Columbia DB 8485
29/10/1977	7	10	○	**LIVE IN TROUBLE**	Epic EPC 5752
02/12/1978	3	10	●	**A TASTE OF AGGRO**	Epic EPC 6829
08/12/1979	46	6		FOOD FOR THOUGHT	Epic EPC 8011
04/10/1980	44	4		THE SIT SONG	Epic EPC 8994
06/12/1980	17	8		NEVER MIND THE PRESENTS Medley of *Another Brick In The Wall Part 2, Day Trip To Bangor (Didn't We Have A Lovely Time)* and *The Sparrow*	Epic EPC 9070
05/12/1981	52	5		BLACKBOARD JUMBLE Medley of *Prince Charming, Wired For Sound, This Ole House* and *Mademoiselle From Armentiers*	CBS A 1795
19/03/1983	49	3		BUFFALO BILL'S LAST SCRATCH	Epic EPC A 3208

JOE BARRY US singer/guitarist (born Joe Barrios, 13/7/1939, Cut Off, LA).

24/08/1961	49	1		I'M A FOOL TO CARE	Mercury AMT 1149

JOHN BARRY ORCHESTRA UK bandleader (born John Barry Prendergast, 3/11/1933, York) who arranged Adam Faith's early hits and later became synonymous with film and TV scores, in particular James Bond, *Out Of Africa* (1985) and *Dances With Wolves* (1990) for which he won Oscars. Awarded the OBE in 1999, he has won three Grammy Awards: Best Instrumental Theme for *Midnight Cowboy* (1969), Best Jazz Performance by a Big Band with Bob Wilber for *The Cotton Club Soundtrack* (1985) and Best Instrumental Composition for *Out Of Africa Soundtrack* in 1986.

05/03/1960	10	14		**HIT AND MISS** JOHN BARRY SEVEN Signature tune to *Juke Box Jury*	Columbia DB 4414
28/04/1960	40	2		BEAT FOR BEATNIKS	Columbia DB 4446
14/07/1960	49	1		NEVER LET GO	Columbia DB 4480
18/08/1960	34	3		BLUEBERRY HILL JOHN BARRY SEVEN	Columbia DB 4480
08/09/1960	11	14		WALK DON'T RUN	Columbia DB 4505
08/12/1960	27	9		BLACK STOCKINGS	Columbia DB 4554
02/03/1961	45	5		THE MAGNIFICENT SEVEN Featured in the 1960 film *The Magnificent Seven*	Columbia DB 4598
26/04/1962	35	2		CUTTY SARK	Columbia DB 4806
01/11/1962	13	11		THE JAMES BOND THEME The first James Bond film in 1962 (*Dr No*) had no title song as such, but Barry later recorded the *James Bond Theme* (written by Monty Norman), with which the film series has become synonymous	Columbia DB 4898
21/11/1963	39	3		FROM RUSSIA WITH LOVE Featured in the 1963 James Bond film *From Russia With Love*, although the title theme was performed by Matt Monro	Ember S 181
11/12/1971	13	15		THEME FROM 'THE PERSUADERS' JOHN BARRY Theme to the TV series of the same name	CBS 7469

LEN BARRY US singer (born Leonard Borisoff, 6/12/1942, Philadelphia, PA) who was a member of The Dovells from 1957 to 1963. Later a successful songwriter, he penned hits for Booker Newbury and Fat Larry's Band.

04/11/1965	3	14		**1-2-3**	Brunswick 05942
13/01/1966	10	10		**LIKE A BABY**	Brunswick 05949

MICHAEL BARRYMORE UK comedian/entertainer (born Michael Kieran Parker, 4/5/1952, London) who hosted a number of prime time shows on UK TV.

16/12/1995	25	4		TOO MUCH FOR ONE HEART	EMI CDEM 412

LIONEL BART UK singer (born 1/8/1930, London) who was a member of The Cavemen with Tommy Steele before turning to songwriting, penning hits for Steele, Shirley Bassey, Max Bygraves and notably Anthony Newley. Successful musicals include *Oliver!* but drug and alcohol dependence led to virtual retirement in the 1970s and 1980s. Desperate for cash he sold the rights to *Oliver!* to Max Bygraves' company Lakeview Music for £350, only to see Lakeview sell them on to Essex Music for £250,000. He died on 3/4/1999.

25/11/1989	68	3		HAPPY ENDINGS (GIVE YOURSELF A PINCH) Originally written by Bart as a jingle for Abbey National building society	EMI EM 121

BART AND HOMER – see SIMPSONS

BARTHEZZ
Dutch DJ Bart Claessen who was a 21-year-old art student at the time of his debut hit after winning a competition organised by The Vengaboys to remix their single *Cheeka Bow Wow*.

22/09/2001	18	4		ON THE MOVE	Positiva CDTIV 158
20/04/2002	25	4		INFECTED	Positiva CDTIVS 168

BAS NOIR
US vocal duo Mary Ridley and Morie Bivins from Trenton, NJ.

11/02/1989	73	1		MY LOVE IS MAGIC	10 TEN 257

ROB BASE AND DJ E-Z ROCK
US rap duo formed in Harlem, NYC by Robert Ginyard and DJ Rodney 'Skip' Bryce, both members of high school group The Sureshot Seven. They split in 1989 and Rob Base (Ginyard) worked solo.

16/04/1988	24	6		IT TAKES TWO Contains a sample of Lyn Collins' *Think (About It)*. Featured in the 2000 film *Love And Basketball*.	Citybeat CBE 724
14/01/1989	14	7		GET ON THE DANCE FLOOR	Supreme SUPE 139
04/03/1989	49	3		IT TAKES TWO	Citybeat CBE 724
22/04/1989	47	3		JOY AND PAIN	Supreme SUPE 143

BASEMENT
UK group formed in Omagh by John Mullin (guitar/vocals), Mark McCausland (guitar), Graeme Hassall (bass) and Declan McManus (drums).

14/06/2003	48	1		SLAIN THE TRUTH (AT THE ROADHOUSE)	Deltasonic DLTCD 012

BASEMENT BOYS PRESENT ULTRA NATE
US production group formed in Baltimore, MD in 1986 by Jay Steinhour, Teddy Douglas and Thomas Davis with singer Ultra Nate. Nate later recorded solo; she was also a member of Stars On 54.

23/02/1991	71	1		IS IT LOVE	Eternal YZ 509

BASEMENT JAXX
UK dance/production duo formed in London by DJs Felix Buxton and Simon Ratcliffe who also ran the Atlantic Jaxx label. Previously recording as Summer Daze, they won Best Dance Act at the 2002 BRIT Awards and repeated the success in 2004. Lisa Kekaula is also lead singer with The Bellrays.

31/05/1997	19	3		FLY LIFE	Multiply CDMULTY 21
01/05/1999	5	10		RED ALERT Contains a sample of Locksmith's *Far Beyond*. Featured in the 2002 film *Bend It Like Beckham*	
					XL Recordings XLS 100CD
14/08/1999	4	8		RENDEZ-VU	XL Recordings XLS 110CD
06/11/1999	12	5		JUMP 'N' SHOUT Features the uncredited contributions of Slarta John and Madman Swyli	XL Recordings XLS 116CD
15/04/2000	13	4		BINGO BANGO Contains a sample of Boliva's *Merenque*	XL Recordings XLS 120CD
16/06/2001	6	10		ROMEO Features the uncredited contribution of Kele Le Roc	XL Recordings XLS 132CD
06/10/2001	23	4		JUS 1 KISS	XL Recordings XLS 136CD1
08/12/2001	9	8		WHERE'S YOUR HEAD AT Contains a sample of Gary Numan's *This Wreckage* and features the uncredited contribution of Damien Peachy. Featured in the 2001 film *Lara Croft: Tomb Raider*	XL Recordings XLS 140CD
29/06/2002	22	3		GET ME OFF	XL Recordings XLS 146CD
22/11/2003	23	4		LUCKY STAR BASEMENT JAXX FEATURING DIZZEE RASCAL	XL Recordings XLS 172CD
17/01/2004	12	8		GOOD LUCK BASEMENT JAXX FEATURING LISA KEKAULA	XL Recordings XLS 178CD
10/04/2004	22	4		PLUG IT IN BASEMENT JAXX FEATURING JC CHASEZ	XL Recordings XLS 180CD
10/07/2004	14	7		GOOD LUCK BASEMENT JAXX FEATURING LISA KEKAULA Remix of XL Recordings XLS 178CD and revived after the track was used by the BBC for its TV coverage of the 2004 European Championships	XL Recordings XLS 190CD

BASIA
Polish singer (born Basha Trzetrzelewska, 30/9/1954, Jaworzno, Poland) who was a member of Matt Bianco before she went solo.

23/01/1988	48	4		PROMISES	Epic BASH 4
28/05/1988	61	3		TIME AND TIDE	Epic BASH 5
14/01/1995	41	2		DRUNK ON LOVE	Epic 6611582

COUNT BASIE – see FRANK SINATRA

TONI BASIL
US singer (born Antonia Basilotta, 22/9/1948, Philadelphia, PA) who was originally an actress, then a dancer, choreographer (working on the 1973 film *American Graffiti*) and video producer before recording her debut album in 1981.

06/02/1982	2	12	●	MICKEY ▲¹ Originally released the year previously without success	Radialchoice TIC 4
01/05/1982	52	4		NOBODY	Radialchoice TIC 2

OLAV BASOSKI
Dutch producer (born 1968, Haarlem) who also recorded as Herbal 6.

26/08/2000	56	1		OPIUM SCUMBAGZ	Defected DFECT 20CDS

ALFIE BASS – see MICHAEL MEDWIN, BERNARD BRESSLAW, ALFIE BASS AND LESLIE FYSON

FONTELLA BASS
US singer (born 3/7/1940, St Louis, MO) who sang with gospel groups before being discovered by Ike Turner and recording for his labels Prann and Sonja.

02/12/1965	11	10		RESCUE ME Featured in the 1992 film *Sister Act*	Chess CRS 8023
20/01/1966	32	5		RECOVERY	Chess CRS 8027

NORMAN BASS German producer who had previously recorded under the name Object One.

21/04/2001	17	4	HOW U LIKE BASS	Substance SUBS 10CDS

BASS BOYZZ UK producer James Sammon who also records as Pianoman.

28/09/1996	74	1	GUNZ AND PIANOZ	Polydor 5753432

BASS BUMPERS UK/German group formed by Henning Reith, Caba Kroll and Nana. Rapper E-Mello (Ian Freeman) replaced Nana in 1991.

25/09/1993	68	1	RUNNIN'	Vertigo VERCD 78
05/02/1994	25	3	THE MUSIC'S GOT ME	Vertigo VERCD 84

BASS JUMPERS Dutch production duo Frank De Wulf and Phil Wilde.

13/02/1999	44	1	MAKE UP YOUR MIND	Pepper 0530112

BASS-O-MATIC UK multi-instrumentalist William Orbit (born William Wainwright).

12/05/1990	66	3	IN THE REALM OF THE SENSES	Virgin VS 1265
08/09/1990	9	11	**FASCINATING RHYTHM**	Virgin VS 1274
22/12/1990	61	4	EASE ON BY	Virgin VS 1295
03/08/1991	71	1	FUNKY LOVE VIBRATIONS	Virgin VS 1355

SHIRLEY BASSEY UK singer (born 8/1/1937, Cardiff) who turned professional at sixteen touring with the revue *Memories Of Al Jolson*. Discovered by Jack Hylton she became the most successful female performer in the UK for over a quarter of a century until eclipsed in the 1990s by Diana Ross and Madonna. She was named Best British Female Solo Artist at the 1977 BRIT Awards, awarded a CBE in 1993, named Show Business Personality of the Year in 1995 by the Variety Club, and was made a Dame in the 2000 New Year's Honours List. Bryn Terfel is a Welsh singer.

15/02/1957	8	10	BANANA BOAT SONG	Philips PB 668
23/08/1957	30	1	FIRE DOWN BELOW	Philips PB 723
06/09/1957	29	2	YOU YOU ROMEO B-side to *Fire Down Below*	Philips PB 723
19/12/1958	●4	19	**AS I LOVE YOU**	Philips PB 845
26/12/1958	3	17	KISS ME HONEY HONEY KISS ME	Philips PB 860
31/03/1960	38	6	WITH THESE HANDS	Columbia DB 4421
04/08/1960	2	30	**AS LONG AS HE NEEDS ME** Originally appeared in the musical *Oliver!*	Columbia DB 4490
11/05/1961	6	17	**YOU'LL NEVER KNOW**	Columbia DB 4643
27/07/1961	●1	18	**REACH FOR THE STARS/CLIMB EV'RY MOUNTAIN**	Columbia DB 4685
23/11/1961	10	8	**I'LL GET BY**	Columbia DB 4737
15/02/1962	21	8	TONIGHT Originally appeared in the 1961 film *West Side Story*	Columbia DB 4777
26/04/1962	31	4	AVE MARIA	Columbia DB 4816
31/05/1962	24	13	FAR AWAY Originally appeared in the musical *Blitz*	Columbia DB 4836
30/08/1962	5	17	**WHAT NOW MY LOVE**	Columbia DB 4882
28/02/1963	47	2	WHAT KIND OF FOOL AM I? Originally appeared in the musical *Stop The World I Want To Get Off*	Columbia DB 4974
26/09/1963	6	20	**I (WHO HAVE NOTHING)**	Columbia DB 7113
23/01/1964	32	7	MY SPECIAL DREAM	Columbia DB 7185
09/04/1964	36	5	GONE	Columbia DB 7248
15/10/1964	21	9	GOLDFINGER Featured in the 1965 James Bond film *Goldfinger*	Columbia DB 7360
20/05/1965	39	4	NO REGRETS (NON JE NE REGRETTE RIEN)	Columbia DB 7535
11/10/1967	21	15	BIG SPENDER Originally appeared in the musical *Sweet Charity*	United Artists UP 1192
20/06/1970	4	22	**SOMETHING**	United Artists UP 35125
02/01/1971	48	1	THE FOOL ON THE HILL	United Artists UP 35156
27/03/1971	34	9	(WHERE DO I BEGIN) LOVE STORY	United Artists UP 35194
07/08/1971	6	24	**FOR ALL WE KNOW**	United Artists UP 35267
15/01/1972	38	6	DIAMONDS ARE FOREVER Featured in the 1971 James Bond film *Diamonds Are Forever*. Bassey also recorded the theme to the 1979 Bond film *Moonraker* that did not chart	United Artists UP 35293
03/03/1973	8	19	**NEVER NEVER NEVER**	United Artists UP 35490
22/08/1987	54	2	THE RHYTHM DIVINE **YELLO FEATURING SHIRLEY BASSEY**	Mercury MER 253
16/11/1996	41	1	DISCO' LA PASSIONE **CHRIS REA AND SHIRLEY BASSEY** Featured in the 1996 film *La Passione*	East West EW 072CD
20/12/1997	19	7	HISTORY REPEATING **PROPELLERHEADS AND SHIRLEY BASSEY** Featured in the 1998 film *There's Something About Mary*	Wall Of Sound WALLD 036
23/10/1999	35	3	WORLD IN UNION **SHIRLEY BASSEY/BRYN TERFEL** Official theme to the 1999 Rugby World Cup	Universal TV 4669402

BASSHEADS UK dance group formed in Liverpool by Desa and Nick Murphy. Following their debut success they were sued by Afrika Bambaataa, The Osmonds, Pink Floyd and Talking Heads over samples they had used – there obviously was someone out there.

16/11/1991	5	8	**IS THERE ANYBODY OUT THERE**	Deconstruction R 6303
30/05/1992	12	4	BACK TO THE OLD SCHOOL	Deconstruction R 6310

○ Silver disc ● Gold disc ✪ Platinum disc (additional platinum units are indicated by a figure following the symbol) ◎ Singles released prior to 1973 that are known to have sold over 1 million copies in the UK

Date	Pos	Wks	BPI	Single Title	Label & Number
28/11/1992	38	2		WHO CAN MAKE ME FEEL GOOD	Deconstruction R 6326
28/08/1993	49	2		START A BRAND NEW LIFE (SAVE ME)	Deconstruction CDR 6353
15/07/1995	24	2		IS THERE ANYBODY OUT THERE (REMIX)	Deconstruction 74321293882

BASSTOY US DJ Mark Picchiotti who also records as Sandstorm and is a member of Ascension.

27/05/2000	62	1		RUNNIN	Neo NEOCD 029
19/01/2002	13	5		RUNNIN' **MARK PICCHIOTTI PRESENTS BASSTOY FEATURING DANA**	Black & Blue NEOCD 073

BATES German vocal/instrumental group formed in 1990 by Zimbl (bass/vocals), Reb (guitar), Dulli (guitar) and Klube (drums).

03/02/1996	67	1		BILLIE JEAN	Virgin International DINSD 151

MIKE BATT WITH THE NEW EDITION UK singer (born 6/2/1950) who began as an in-house songwriter for Liberty Records before becoming A&R manager. In 1974 he wrote the theme to the TV series *The Wombles*, enjoying a short-lived career with the creatures. When the novelty wore off, he returned to songwriting, penning *Bright Eyes* (about rabbits) for Art Garfunkel.

16/08/1975	4	8		SUMMERTIME CITY	Epic EPC 3460

BAUHAUS UK group formed in Northampton in 1978 by Peter Murphy (born 11/7/1957, Northampton, vocals), Daniel Ash (born 31/7/1957, Northampton, guitar/vocals), David Jay (born David Haskinsin, 24/4/1957, Northampton, bass/vocals) and Kevin Haskins (born 19/7/1960, Northampton, drums), originally known as Bauhaus 1919 (after the German art/design movement launched in 1919). They disbanded in 1983. Murphy linked up with Mick Karn (of Japan) to record one album as Dali's Car before going solo.

18/04/1981	59	3		KICK IN THE EYE	Beggars Banquet BEG 54
04/07/1981	56	2		THE PASSION OF LOVERS	Beggars Banquet BEG 59
06/03/1982	45	4		KICK IN THE EYE (EP) Tracks on EP: *Kick In The Eye (Searching For Satori)*, *Harry* and *Earwax*	Beggars Banquet BEG 74
19/06/1982	42	5		SPIRIT	Beggars Banquet BEG 79
09/10/1982	15	7		ZIGGY STARDUST	Beggars Banquet BEG 83
22/01/1983	44	4		LAGARTIJA NICK	Beggars Banquet BEG 88
09/04/1983	26	6		SHE'S IN PARTIES	Beggars Banquet BEG 91
29/10/1983	52	4		THE SINGLES 1981–83 Tracks on EP: *The Passion Of Lovers*, *Kick In The Eye*, *Spirit*, *Ziggy Stardust*, *Lagartija Nick* and *She's In Parties*	Beggars Banquet BEG 100E

LES BAXTER US singer (born 14/3/1922, Mexia, TX) who was an orchestra leader and noted arranger. He was also a member of Mel Torme's vocal group, the Mel-Tones, and scored over 100 films. He died from a heart attack on 15/1/1996 and has a star on the Hollywood Walk of Fame.

13/05/1955	10	9		UNCHAINED MELODY Featured in the 1955 film *Unchained*	Capitol CL 14257

TASHA BAXTER – see **ROGER GOODE FEATURING TASHA BAXTER**

TOM BAXTER UK singer/guitarist (born in Suffolk, raised in Cornwall) who was working as a painter and decorator before signing with Sony.

31/07/2004	65	1		THIS BOY	Sony Music 6751692

BAY CITY ROLLERS UK group formed in Edinburgh in 1967 by Leslie McKeown (born 12/11/1955, Edinburgh, vocals), Eric Faulkner (born 21/10/1955, Edinburgh, guitar), Stuart 'Woody' Wood (born 25/2/1957, Edinburgh, guitar), Alan Longmuir (born 20/6/1953, Edinburgh, bass) and his brother Derek (born 19/5/1955, Edinburgh, drums) as The Saxons. Bandleader Tom Paton discovered them, quit his job to become their manager and chose their name by sticking a pin in a map of the US. Although a group bearing their name still tours the nostalgia circuit to this day, the original line-up effectively dispersed in 1978.

18/09/1971	9	13		KEEP ON DANCING Revival of The Gentry's 1965 US #4 and produced by Jonathan King who was reportedly the lead singer	Bell 1164
09/02/1974	6	12	○	**REMEMBER (SHA-LA-LA)**	Bell 1338
27/04/1974	2	10	○	**SHANG-A-LANG**	Bell 1355
27/07/1974	3	10	○	**SUMMERLOVE SENSATION**	Bell 1369
12/10/1974	4	10	○	**ALL OF ME LOVES ALL OF YOU**	Bell 1382
08/03/1975	❶⁶	16	●	**BYE BYE BABY** Revival of The Four Seasons' 1965 US #12. Featured in the 2003 film *Love Actually*	Bell 1409
12/07/1975	❶³	9	●	**GIVE A LITTLE LOVE**	Bell 1425
22/11/1975	3	9	○	**MONEY HONEY**	Bell 1461
10/04/1976	4	9		**LOVE ME LIKE I LOVE YOU**	Bell 1477
11/09/1976	4	9	○	**I ONLY WANNA BE WITH YOU**	Bell 1493
07/05/1977	16	6		IT'S A GAME	Arista 108
30/07/1977	34	3		YOU MADE ME BELIEVE IN MAGIC	Arista 127

DUKE BAYSEE UK singer (born Baysee Kevin Rowe, London), previously a bus conductor on the Hackney to Victoria route.

03/09/1994	30	4		SUGAR SUGAR	Bell 74321228702
21/01/1995	46	2		DO YOU LOVE ME	Double Dekker CDDEK 1

BAZ UK soul singer (born Baz Gooden, London) from a musical family: her father was a jazz musician, her brother DJ Dave Angel and her sister the rapper Monie Love.

15/12/2001	36	2		BELIEVERS	One Little Indian 313 TP7CD
30/03/2002	58	1		SMILE TO SHINE	One Little Indian 316 TP7CD

❶⁹ Number of weeks single topped the UK chart ↑ Entered the UK chart at #1 ▲⁹ Number of weeks single topped the US chart

61

BBC CONCERT ORCHESTRA/BBC SYMPHONY CHORUS/STEPHEN JACKSON
UK orchestra and chorus. The BBC traditionally choose a piece of music from the host country as the theme tune for a major sporting tournament, so the choice of Beethoven's *Ode To Joy* with its German connections caused controversy when used for the 1996 European Football Championships that were held in England.

22/06/1996	36	3		ODE TO JOY (FROM BEETHOVEN'S SYMPHONY NO 9) 1996 European Football Championships theme tune	Virgin VSCDT 1591

BBE
Italian/French dance group formed by Bruno Sanchioni, Bruno Quartier and Emmanuel Top. Sanchioni is also responsible for Age Of Love.

28/09/1996	3	9	O	**SEVEN DAYS AND ONE WEEK** Title is a reference to how long the track took to record	Positiva CDTIV 67
29/03/1997	5	5		**FLASH**	Positiva CDTIV 73
14/02/1998	19	3		DESIRE	Positiva CDTIV 87
30/05/1998	19	3		DEEPER LOVE (SYMPHONIC PARADISE)	Positiva CDTIV 93

BBG
UK group formed by Ben Angwin, Phil Hope and Tony Newlan and featuring Dina Taylor on vocals.

28/04/1990	28	5		SNAPPINESS **BBG FEATURING DINA TAYLOR** Contains a sample of Soul II Soul's *Happiness*	Urban URB 54
11/08/1990	65	2		SOME KIND OF HEAVEN	Urban URB 59
23/03/1996	46	1		LET THE MUSIC PLAY **BBG FEATURING ERIN**	MCA MCSTD 40029
18/05/1996	50	1		SNAPPINESS (REMIX)	Hi-Life 5762972
05/07/1997	45	1		JUST BE TONIGHT	Hi-Life 5738972

BBM
UK rock group formed by Jack Bruce (born John Bruce, 14/5/1943, Lanarkshire, vocals/bass), Ginger Baker (born Peter Baker, 19/8/1939, London, drums) and Gary Moore (born 4/4/1952, Belfast, guitar). Bruce and Baker had previously been in Cream, Moore in Thin Lizzy.

06/08/1994	57	2		WHERE IN THE WORLD	Virgin VSCD 1495

BBMAK
UK vocal group formed in 1996 by Christian Burns (born 18/1/1974), Mark Barry (born 26/10/1978) and Stephen McNalty (born 4/7/1978).

28/08/1999	37	2		BACK HERE	Telstar CDSTAS 3053
24/02/2001	5	10		**BACK HERE** Re-issued following its success in the US	Telstar CDSTAS 3166
26/05/2001	8	4		**STILL ON YOUR SIDE**	Telstar CXSTAS 3185
16/11/2002	36	2		OUT OF MY HEART	Telstar CDSTAS 3281

BC-52'S – see B-52'S

BE BOP DELUXE
UK band formed in 1971 by Bill Nelson (born 18/12/1948, Wakefield, guitar/vocals), Nick Chatterton-Dew (drums), Robert Bryan (bass), Ian Parkin (guitar) and Richard Brown (keyboards). Re-formed by Nelson in 1974 with Charlie Tummahai (bass), Simon Fox (drums) and Andrew Clarke (keyboards). They disbanded in 1978 and Nelson formed Red Noise.

21/02/1976	23	8		SHIPS IN THE NIGHT	Harvest HAR 5104
13/11/1976	36	5		HOT VALVES EP Tracks on EP: *Maid In Heaven, Blaring Apostles, Jet Silver And The Dolls Of Venus* and *Bring Back The Spark*	Harvest HAR 5117

BEACH BOYS
US group formed in 1961 in Hawthorne, CA by brothers Brian (born 20/6/1942, Hawthorne, keyboards/bass), Carl (born 21/12/1946, Hawthorne, guitar) and Dennis Wilson (born 4/12/1944, Hawthorne, drums), cousin Mike Love (born 15/3/1941, Los Angeles, CA, lead vocals/saxophone) and Al Jardine (born 3/9/1942, Lima, OH, guitar). Originally called Carl And The Passions (later an album title), then The Pendeltones, they were eventually named The Beach Boys to reflect the Californian 'surfing' subject matter of their early singles. They quickly became one of the biggest US bands of the era, scoring worldwide hits. Dennis Wilson drowned on 28/12/1983 (his family's request that he should be buried at sea was only granted after personal intervention of President Ronald Reagan), while chief songwriter Brian Wilson stopped touring in 1964 (Glen Campbell was his replacement). His daughters, Carnie and Wendy Wilson, are members of Wilson Phillips. Carl Wilson, listed as a 'conscientious objector' during the Vietnam War (he was briefly jailed for refusing to undertake bedpan changing duties at the Los Angeles' Veterans Hospital in lieu of military service), died from cancer on 6/2/1998. The group was inducted into the Rock & Roll Hall of Fame in 1988 and has a star on the Hollywood Walk of Fame.

01/08/1963	34	7		SURFIN' USA Adaptation of Chuck Berry's *Sweet Little Sixteen*. Featured in the 1985 film *Teen Wolf*	Capitol CL 15305
09/07/1964	7	13		**I GET AROUND** ▲² Featured in the films *Good Morning Vietnam* (1988) and *Bean: The Ultimate Disaster Movie* (1997)	Capitol CL 15350
29/10/1964	27	7		WHEN I GROW UP TO BE A MAN	Capitol CL 15361
21/01/1965	24	6		DANCE DANCE DANCE	Capitol CL 15370
03/06/1965	27	10		HELP ME RHONDA ▲²	Capitol CL 15392
02/09/1965	26	8		CALIFORNIA GIRLS	Capitol CL 15409
17/02/1966	3	10		**BARBARA ANN** Cover of the Regents' 1961 hit and featuring the guest vocal of Dean Torrence (Jan & Dean). Featured in the 1973 film *American Graffiti*	Capitol CL 15432
21/04/1966	2	15		**SLOOP JOHN B** Featured in the 1994 film *Forrest Gump*	Capitol CL 15441
28/07/1966	2	14		**GOD ONLY KNOWS** Featured in the films *Boogie Nights* (1998) and *Love Actually* (2003)	Capitol CL 15459
03/11/1966	❶²	13		**GOOD VIBRATIONS** ▲¹	Capitol CL 15475
04/05/1967	4	11		**THEN I KISSED HER**	Capitol CL 15502
23/08/1967	8	9		**HEROES AND VILLAINS**	Capitol CL 15510
22/11/1967	29	6		WILD HONEY	Capitol CL 15521
17/01/1968	11	14		DARLIN'	Capitol CL 15527
08/05/1968	25	7		FRIENDS	Capitol CL 15545

DATE	POS	WKS	BPI	SINGLE TITLE	LABEL & NUMBER
24/07/1968	❶[1]	14		**DO IT AGAIN**	Capitol CL 15554
25/12/1968	33	5		BLUEBIRDS OVER THE MOUNTAIN	Capitol CL 15572
26/02/1969	10	13		**I CAN HEAR MUSIC**	Capitol CL 15584
11/06/1969	6	11		**BREAK AWAY**	Capitol CL 15598
16/05/1970	5	17		**COTTONFIELDS** Written by blues artist Huddie 'Leadbelly' Ledbetter	Capitol CL 15640
03/03/1973	37	5		CALIFORNIA SAGA-CALIFORNIA	Reprise K 14232
03/07/1976	18	7		GOOD VIBRATIONS Re-issue of Capitol CL 15475	Capitol CL 15875
10/07/1976	36	4		ROCK AND ROLL MUSIC	Reprise K 14440
31/03/1979	37	8		HERE COMES THE NIGHT Disco remake of a song originally recorded in 1967	Caribou CRB 7204
16/06/1979	6	11		**LADY LYNDA**	Caribou CRB 7427
29/09/1979	45	4		SUMAHAMA	Caribou CRB 7846
29/08/1981	47	4		BEACH BOYS MEDLEY Medley of Good Vibrations, Help Me Rhonda, I Get Around, Shut Down, Surfin' Safari, Barbara Ann, Surfin' USA and Fun Fun Fun	Capitol CL 213
22/08/1987	2	12	○	**WIPEOUT** FAT BOYS AND THE BEACH BOYS	Urban URB 5
19/11/1988	25	9		KOKOMO ▲[1] Featured in the 1988 film *Cocktail*	Elektra EKR 85
02/06/1990	58	1		WOULDN'T IT BE NICE	Capitol CL 579
29/06/1991	61	2		DO IT AGAIN Re-issue of Capitol CL 15554	Capitol EMCT 1
02/03/1996	24	4		FUN FUN FUN STATUS QUO WITH THE BEACH BOYS	Polygram TV 5762972

BEAR WHO – see DJ SNEAK FEATURING BEAR WHO

WALTER BEASLEY US singer/songwriter/saxophonist (born in Los Angeles, CA) who relocated to New York.

DATE	POS	WKS	BPI	SINGLE TITLE	LABEL & NUMBER
23/01/1988	70	3		I'M SO HAPPY	Urban URB 14

BEASTIE BOYS US rap trio formed in New York by King Ad-Rock (born Adam Horovitz, 31/10/1966, New York, son of playwright and screenwriter Israel Horovitz), MCA Adam (born Adam Yauch, 15/8/1967, New York, MCA stands for Master of Ceremonies) and Mike D (born Michael Diamond, 20/11/1965, New York). Their first DJ was DJ Double RR (record executive Rick Rubin) and later Dr Dre who went on to host MTV's *Yo! MTV Raps*. They started a craze for wearing logos from VW cars, which led to Volkswagen supplying them directly to fans to prevent them from stealing them. Two Grammies include Best Alternative Music Performance in 1998 for *Hello Nasty* and they were named Best Rap Act at the 1998 MTV Europe Music Awards. They launched the Grand Royal Records label in 1993 (acts included Bran Van 3000) that ceased business in August 2001.

DATE	POS	WKS	BPI	SINGLE TITLE	LABEL & NUMBER
28/02/1987	11	11		(YOU GOTTA) FIGHT FOR YOUR RIGHT TO PARTY	Def Jam 6504187
30/05/1987	14	7		NO SLEEP TO BROOKLYN	Def Jam BEAST 1
18/07/1987	10	8		**SHE'S ON IT** Featured in the 1985 film *Krush Groove*	Def Jam BEAST 2
03/10/1987	34	4		GIRLS/SHE'S CRAFTY	Def Jam BEAST 3
11/04/1992	47	2		PASS THE MIC	Capitol 12CL 653
04/07/1992	55	1		FROZEN METAL HEAD (EP) Tracks on EP: *Jimmy James, Jimmy James (Original), Drinkin' Wine* and *The Blue Nun* .... Capitol 12CL 665	
09/07/1994	19	4		GET IT TOGETHER/SABOTAGE A-side contains a sample of Eugene McDaniels' *Headless Heroes*	Capitol CDCL 716
26/11/1994	27	3		SURE SHOT	Capitol CDCLS 726
04/07/1998	5	7		INTERGALACTIC Contains samples of Les Baxter's *Prelude C# Minor* and various tracks from The Jazz Crusaders' album *Powerhouse*. 1998 Grammy Award for Best Rap Group Performance	Grand Royal CDCL 803
07/11/1998	15	5		BODY MOVIN'	Grand Royal CDCLS 809
29/05/1999	21	3		REMOTE CONTROL/3 MCS AND 1 DJ	Grand Royal CDCLS 812
18/12/1999	28	4		ALIVE Contains a sample of Boogie Down Productions' *I'm Still #1*	Grand Royal CDCL 818
12/06/2004	8	7		**CH-CHECK IT OUT**	Capitol CDCLS 857
25/09/2004	37	3		TRIPLE TROUBLE	Capitol CDCLS 859
18/12/2004	38	2+		AN OPEN LETTER TO NYC	Capitol CDCLS867

BEAT UK ska group formed in Birmingham in 1978 by Dave Wakeling (born 19/2/1956, Birmingham, guitar/vocals), Andy Cox (born 25/1/1956, Birmingham, guitar), David Steele (born 8/9/1960, Isle of Wight, bass) and Everett Morton (born 5/4/1951, St Kitts, drums), with 'toaster' Ranking Roger and saxophonist Saxa (who was 50 when they signed their record deal). The reggae/ska revival helped their debut single on 2 Tone hit the top ten, before they launched the Go Feet label. They split in 1983, Cox and Steele forming Fine Young Cannibals with Roland Gift. They were named The English Beat in the US as there was already a US group called The Beat.

DATE	POS	WKS	BPI	SINGLE TITLE	LABEL & NUMBER
08/12/1979	6	11	○	**TEARS OF A CLOWN/RANKING FULL STOP**	2 Tone CHSTT 6
23/02/1980	9	9		**HANDS OFF – SHE'S MINE**	Go Feet FEET 1
03/05/1980	4	9		**MIRROR IN THE BATHROOM** Featured in the 1997 film *Grosse Pointe Blank*	Go Feet FEET 2
16/08/1980	22	9		BEST FRIEND/STAND DOWN MARGARET (DUB)	Go Feet FEET 3
13/12/1980	7	11	○	**TOO NICE TO TALK TO**	Go Feet FEET 4
18/04/1981	22	8		DROWNING/ALL OUT TO GET YOU	Go Feet FEET 6
20/06/1981	33	6		DOORS OF YOUR HEART	Go Feet FEET 9
05/12/1981	70	2		HIT IT	Go Feet FEET 11
17/04/1982	47	4		SAVE IT FOR LATER Featured in the 1996 film *Kingpin*	Go Feet FEET 333
18/09/1982	45	3		JEANETTE	Go Feet FEET 15
04/12/1982	54	3		I CONFESS	Go Feet FEET 16
30/04/1983	3	11	○	**CAN'T GET USED TO LOSING YOU**	Go Feet FEET 17
02/07/1983	54	4		ACKEE 1-2-3	Go Feet FEET 18
27/01/1996	44	2		MIRROR IN THE BATHROOM (REMIX)	Go Feet 74321232062

❶[9] Number of weeks single topped the UK chart ↑ Entered the UK chart at #1 ▲[9] Number of weeks single topped the US chart

63

BEAT BOYS – see GENE VINCENT

BEAT RENEGADES
UK production duo Ian Bland and Paul Fitzpatrick. Bland had previously recorded as Dream Frequency, and the pair also record as Red and Dejure.

19/05/2001.....73......1....... AUTOMATIK .... Slinky Music SLINKY 014CD

BEAT SYSTEM
UK producer Derek Pierce.

03/03/1990.....63......2...... WALK ON THE WILD SIDE .... Fourth & Broadway BRW 163
18/09/1993.....70......1...... TO A BRIGHTER DAY (O' HAPPY DAY).. ffrr FCD 217

BEAT UP
UK rock group formed by Nick (guitar/vocals), Matt (guitar/vocals), Dino (bass) and Todd (drums) who previously recorded as The Beatings.

04/12/2004.....62......1...... MESSED UP .... Fantastic Plastic FPS043

BEATCHUGGERS FEATURING ERIC CLAPTON
Danish producer Michael Linde recording with Eric Clapton.

18/11/2000.....26......2...... FOREVER MAN (HOW MANY TIMES) Contains a sample of Eric Clapton's *Forever Man* .... ffrr FCD 386

BEATINGS
UK rock group formed by Nick (guitar/vocals), Matt (guitar/vocals), Dino (bass) and Todd (drums).

26/10/2002.....68......1....... BAD FEELINGS .... Fantastic Plastic FPS 034

BEATLES
UK group formed in Liverpool in 1957 as the Quarrymen, then Johnny & The Moondogs, The Silver Beetles and The Beatals, before settling on The Beatles in 1960 (in honour of The Crickets). The original line-up consisted of Paul McCartney (born 18/6/1942, Liverpool, guitar/vocals), John Lennon (born 9/10/1940, Liverpool, guitar/vocals), George Harrison (born 24/2/1943, Liverpool, guitar/vocals) and Stuart Sutcliffe (born 23/6/1940, Edinburgh, bass), with drummer Pete Best (born 24/11/1941, Madras, India) passing an audition in time for their first visit to Germany. Sutcliffe (who died from a brain haemorrhage on 10/4/1962) stayed in Hamburg with his fiancee Astrid Kirchher and McCartney switched to bass. An enquiry by Raymond Jones at Brian Epstein's NEMS record shop in Liverpool for a German recording of *My Bonnie* by Tony Sheridan & The Beat Brothers (the name Beatles was considered too risque by the German record company) led to Epstein managing the band in place of bar owner Alan Williams. They signed with Parlophone after being turned down by other companies including, most notably, Decca, for whom they auditioned. Two months later Ringo Starr (born Richard Starkey, 7/7/1940, Liverpool) replaced Best, although the original choice had been Johnny Hutchinson of The Big Three who turned it down. Parlophone's A&R manager George Martin produced all their singles. They formed the Apple label in 1968 (signing Mary Hopkin and Badfinger among others) but split in 1970, each going solo. They starred in the films *A Hard Day's Night* (1964), *Help!* (1965), *Let It Be* (1965; it won an Oscar for Best Original Song Score) and the TV special *Magical Mystery Tour*. The murder of John Lennon, shot in New York by fan Mark David Chapman on 8/12/1980, brought any reunion hopes to an end, although the remaining members have linked together. Having survived an attack by another crazed fan in December 1999, George Harrison died from cancer on 29/11/2001. The group was presented with the Outstanding Contribution Award at the 1983 BRIT Awards (in 1977 they were presented with the same award, named Best Group and saw *Sgt Pepper's Lonely Hearts Club Band* named Best Album). Total worldwide sales by 1999 were estimated at 1 billion records: the 1996 double album *Anthology* sold 10 million copies worldwide in just four weeks, while the 2000 album *1* was the fastest selling album in the world, with 13.5 million copies sold in its first month. They were inducted into the Rock & Roll Hall of Fame in 1988. Eight Grammy Awards include Best New Artist in 1964, Album of the Year and Best Contemporary Album in 1967 for *Sgt Pepper's Lonely Hearts Club Band*, Best Original Score Written for a Motion Picture or TV Show in 1970 for *Let It Be*, Best Pop Duo or Group and Best Music Video Short Form in 1996 for *Free As A Bird*, and Best Music Video Long Form in 1996 for *The Beatles Anthology*. Both *Revolver* and *Sgt Pepper's Lonely Hearts Club Band* won Grammy Awards for Best Album Cover, while *Michelle* was named Song of the Year in 1966 (despite the fact it was not released as a single, it received over 4 million radio plays in the US alone). Paul McCartney was given the Best Contemporary Rock & Roll Vocal Performance Grammy Award in 1966 for *Eleanor Rigby*, even though it was a group effort. The group has a star on the Hollywood Walk of Fame. On 7/12/1963 all four members made up the panel for *Juke Box Jury* and successfully predicted the success (or not) for seven of the ten titles. They were inducted into the UK Music Hall of Fame in 2004, one of its first inductees.

11/10/1962.....17.....18...... LOVE ME DO ▲[1] Features John Lennon on harmonica, which, legend has it, he shoplifted from a shop in Holland ....
.... Parlophone R 4949
17/01/1963.....2.....18...... **PLEASE PLEASE ME** .... Parlophone R 4983
18/04/1963....**O**[7].....21...... **FROM ME TO YOU** .... Parlophone R 5015
06/06/1963.....48......1...... MY BONNIE **TONY SHERIDAN AND THE BEATLES** Originally Tony Sheridan & The Beat Brothers (released 1962)... Polydor NH 66833
29/08/1963....**O**[6].....33.....◎ **SHE LOVES YOU** ▲[2] Reclaimed #1 position on 28/11/1963 .... Parlophone R 5055
05/12/1963....**O**[5].....22.....◎ **I WANT TO HOLD YOUR HAND** ▲[7] Replaced *She Loves You* at #1, the first instance of an artist replacing themselves at #1 (in the US, *I Want To Hold Your Hand* was replaced at the top by *She Loves You*, which in turn was replaced by *Can't Buy Me Love*, the only instance of an artist replacing themselves twice). Total worldwide sales exceeded 13 million copies .... Parlophone R 5084
26/03/1964....**O**[3].....15.....◎ **CAN'T BUY ME LOVE** ▲[5] Total worldwide sales exceeded 7 million copies. Featured in the films *A Hard Day's Night* (1964) and *Can't Buy Me Love* (1987). On 28/3/1964 it became the first record to be played on Radio Caroline.......... Parlophone R 5114
11/06/1964.....29......6...... AIN'T SHE SWEET Written in 1927, it was a hit for Ben Bernie & His Hotel Roosevelt Orchestra. This May 1961 version, with Pete Best on drums, was produced by Bert Kaempfert.. Polydor 52 317
16/07/1964....**O**[3].....13...... A HARD DAY'S NIGHT ▲[2] Featured in the films *A Hard Day's Night* (1964) and *Help!* (1965). 1964 Grammy Award for Best Performance by a Vocal Group .... Parlophone R 5160
03/12/1964....**O**[5].....13.....◎ **I FEEL FINE** ▲[3] .... Parlophone R 5200
15/04/1965....**O**[3].....12...... **TICKET TO RIDE** ▲[1] .... Parlophone R 5265
29/07/1965....**O**[3].....14...... **HELP!** ▲[3] This and above single featured in the 1965 film *Help!*. .... Parlophone R 5305
09/12/1965....**O**[5].....12.....◎ **DAY TRIPPER/WE CAN WORK IT OUT** ▲[3] Made The Beatles the first act to achieve three consecutive Christmas #1 hits, a record equalled by the Spice Girls in 1998 .... Parlophone R 5389
16/06/1966....**O**[2].....11...... **PAPERBACK WRITER** ▲[2] .... Parlophone R 5452

DATE	POS	WKS	BPI	SINGLE TITLE	LABEL & NUMBER
11/08/1966	❶⁴	13		**YELLOW SUBMARINE/ELEANOR RIGBY** A-side was the theme to the 1968 animated film *Yellow Submarine*	Parlophone R 5493
23/02/1967	2	11		**PENNY LANE/STRAWBERRY FIELDS FOREVER** ▲¹ A-side named after a Liverpool street, the B-side after a Salvation Army children's home in the city	Parlophone R 5570
12/07/1967	❶³	13		**ALL YOU NEED IS LOVE** ▲¹ Featured in the 1967 TV film *Magical Mystery Tour* and the 1968 animated film *Yellow Submarine*, which was first aired on 25/6/1967 on the BBC TV show *Our World* as part of a live global link-up	Parlophone R 5620
29/11/1967	❶⁷	12		**HELLO GOODBYE** ▲³	Parlophone R 5655
13/12/1967	2	12		**MAGICAL MYSTERY TOUR (DOUBLE EP)** Tracks on EP: *Magical Mystery Tour, Your Mother Should Know, I Am The Walrus, Fool On The Hill, Flying* and *Blue Jay Way.*	Parlophone SMMTIMMT 1
20/03/1968	❶²	8		**LADY MADONNA**	Parlophone R 5675
04/09/1968	❶²	16		**HEY JUDE** ▲⁹ Written by Paul to John's son Julian. Total worldwide sales exceed 8 million copies	Apple R 5722
23/04/1969	❶⁶ ↑	17		**GET BACK** ▲⁵ ↑ **BEATLES WITH BILLY PRESTON**	Apple R 5777
04/06/1969	❶³	14		**THE BALLAD OF JOHN AND YOKO**	Apple R 5786
08/11/1969	4	12		**SOMETHING/COME TOGETHER** ▲¹ A-side written by George Harrison, with over 4 million radio plays by 1990	Apple R 5814
14/03/1970	2	10		**LET IT BE** ▲² This and above single featured in the 1970 film *Let It Be*. 1970 Grammy Award for Best Original Score Written for a Motion Picture or TV Show.	Apple R 5833
13/03/1976	8	7		**YESTERDAY** ▲⁴ One of the most popular songs of all time, with over 3,000 known recorded versions and 8 million radio plays in the US alone (over 45 years of airplay!).	Apple R 6013
27/03/1976	12	7		HEY JUDE	Apple R 5722
27/03/1976	23	5		PAPERBACK WRITER	Parlophone R 5452
03/04/1976	32	3		STRAWBERRY FIELDS FOREVER	Parlophone R 5570
03/04/1976	28	5		GET BACK	Apple R 5777
10/04/1976	37	3		HELP! This and above four singles were all re-promoted, as was The Beatles' entire back catalogue	Parlophone R 5305
10/07/1976	19	6		BACK IN THE U.S.S.R.	Parlophone R 6016
07/10/1978	63	3		SGT PEPPER'S LONELY HEARTS CLUB BAND – WITH A LITTLE HELP FROM MY FRIENDS	Parlophone R 6022
05/06/1982	10	9		**BEATLES MOVIE MEDLEY** Medley of *Magical Mystery Tour, All You Need Is Love, You've Got To Hide Your Love Away, I Should Have Known Better, A Hard Day's Night, Ticket To Ride* and *Get Back*	Parlophone R 6055
16/10/1982	4	7		**LOVE ME DO**	Parlophone R 4949
22/01/1983	29	4		PLEASE PLEASE ME	Parlophone R 4983
23/04/1983	40	4		FROM ME TO YOU	Parlophone R 5015
03/09/1983	45	3		SHE LOVES YOU	Parlophone R 5055
26/11/1983	62	2		I WANT TO HOLD YOUR HAND	Parlophone R 5084
31/03/1984	53	2		CAN'T BUY ME LOVE	Parlophone R 5114
21/07/1984	52	2		A HARD DAY'S NIGHT	Parlophone R 5160
08/12/1984	65	1		I FEEL FINE	Parlophone R 5200
20/04/1985	70	2		TICKET TO RIDE	Parlophone R 5265
30/08/1986	63	1		YELLOW SUBMARINE/ELEANOR RIGBY	Parlophone R 5493
28/02/1987	65	2		PENNY LANE/STRAWBERRY FIELDS FOREVER	Parlophone R 5570
18/07/1987	47	3		ALL YOU NEED IS LOVE	Parlophone R 5620
05/12/1987	63	1		HELLO GOODBYE	Parlophone R 5655
26/03/1988	67	1		LADY MADONNA	Parlophone R 5675
10/09/1988	52	2		HEY JUDE	Apple R 5722
22/04/1989	74	1		GET BACK This and above fifteen singles were all re-promoted to coincide with the 20th anniversary of their original release	Apple R 5777
17/10/1992	53	1		LOVE ME DO Repromoted to coincide with the 30th anniversary of its original release	Parlophone R 4949
01/04/1995	7	7		**BABY IT'S YOU** Recorded as part of BBC Radio sessions on 1/5/1963	Apple CDR 6406
16/12/1995	2	8		**FREE AS A BIRD** Originally recorded as a demo by John Lennon in 1977. The surviving Beatles added new instrumentation and vocals in 1995 under the direction of Jeff Lynne	Apple CDR 6422
16/03/1996	4	7		**REAL LOVE** Originally recorded by John Lennon in 1979. The surviving Beatles added new instrumentation and vocals in 1995.	Apple CDR 6425

BEATMASTERS

UK group formed by Paul Carter, Amanda Glanfield and Richard Walmsley (born 28/9/1962) who had begun as jingle writers. They were also responsible for Yazz's hit *Stand Up For Your Love Rights*. Merlin, who fronted their third hit, was in youth custody at the time, having a police escort for appearances on *Top Of The Pops*. Walmsley was later in Goldbug.

DATE	POS	WKS	BPI	SINGLE TITLE	LABEL & NUMBER
09/01/1988	5	11		**ROK DA HOUSE BEATMASTERS FEATURING THE COOKIE CREW**	Rhythm King LEFT 11
24/09/1988	14	10		BURN IT UP **BEATMASTERS WITH PP ARNOLD**	Rhythm King LEFT 27
22/04/1989	8	9		**WHO'S IN THE HOUSE BEATMASTERS FEATURING MERLIN**	Rhythm King LEFT 31
12/08/1989	7	11		**HEY DJ I CAN'T DANCE TO THAT MUSIC YOU'RE PLAYING/SKA TRAIN BEATMASTERS FEATURING BETTY BOO**	Rhythm King LEFT 34
02/12/1989	51	2		WARM LOVE **BEATMASTERS FEATURING CLAUDIA FONTAINE**	Rhythm King LEFT 37
21/09/1991	62	1		BOULEVARD OF BROKEN DREAMS	Rhythm King 6573617
16/05/1992	43	3		DUNNO WHAT IT IS (ABOUT YOU) **BEATMASTERS FEATURING ELAINE VASSELL**	Rhythm King 6580017

BEATNUTS

US rap group formed in Queens, NYC in 1989 by Junkyard JuJu (born Jerry Tineo), Fashion (born Berntony Smalls) and Psycho Les (born Lester Fernandez). When Fashion went to prison they continued as a duo.

DATE	POS	WKS	BPI	SINGLE TITLE	LABEL & NUMBER
14/07/2001	47	1		NO ESCAPIN' THIS	Epic 6713412
21/06/2003	58	1		DUDE DESCENDING A STAiRCASE **APOLLO FOUR FORTY FEATURING THE BEATNUTS** Contains a sample of Abiodun Oyewole's *When The Revolution Comes*	Sony Music SSX 14CDX

BEATRICE – see MIKE KOGLIN

❶⁹ Number of weeks single topped the UK chart   ↑ Entered the UK chart at #1   ▲⁹ Number of weeks single topped the US chart

65

BEATS INTERNATIONAL
UK group formed by ex-Housemartin Norman Cook (born Quentin Cook, 31/7/1963, Brighton) after a stint as a record remixer, fronting the Urban All Stars and as a solo artist. The line-up comprised Andy Boucher (keyboards), Luke Cresswell (drums), Lester Noel (born 3/9/1962, London, vocals) and Lindy Layton (born Belinda Kimberley Layton, 7/12/1970 Chiswick, London, vocals). Layton was previously an actress, appearing in the children's TV series *Grange Hill*. She later recorded solo. Cook disbanded them in 1993 and went on to launch Freak Power.

DATE	POS	WKS	BPI	SINGLE TITLE	LABEL & NUMBER
10/02/1990	❶⁴	13	●	**DUB BE GOOD TO ME** BEATS INTERNATIONAL FEATURING LINDY LAYTON	Go Beat GOD 39
12/05/1990	9	7		**WON'T TALK ABOUT IT**	Go Beat GOD 43
15/09/1990	51	3		BURUNDI BLUES	Go Beat GOD 45
02/03/1991	60	2		ECHO CHAMBER	Go Beat GOD 51
21/09/1991	66	2		THE SUN DOESN'T SHINE	Go Beat GOD 59
23/11/1991	44	3		IN THE GHETTO	Go Beat GOD 64

BEAUTIFUL PEOPLE
UK production group comprising Du Kane, Luke Baldry, David Maskrey, Gavin George, Phyl D'Bass and Robin Goodridge, with Christell on spoken vocals.

DATE	POS	WKS	SINGLE TITLE	LABEL & NUMBER
28/05/1994	74	1	IF 60S WERE 90S Contains a sample of Jimi Hendrix' *If 6 Was 9*	Essential ESSX 2037

BEAUTIFUL SOUTH
UK group formed by Paul Heaton (born 9/5/1962, Birkenhead, vocals), Dave Hemingway (born 20/9/1960, Hull, vocals), Jacqueline Abbott (born 10/11/1973, Merseyside, vocals), Dave Rotheray (born 9/2/1963, Hull, guitar), Sean Welch (born 12/4/1965, Enfield, bass) and Dave Stead (born 15/10/1966, Huddersfield, drums). Heaton and Hemingway were previously in The Housemartins. Abbott left in 2000 and was replaced by Briana Corrigan.

THE BEAUTIFUL SOUTH
Old Red Eyes Is Back

DATE	POS	WKS	BPI	SINGLE TITLE	LABEL & NUMBER
03/06/1989	2	11	○	**SONG FOR WHOEVER**	Go Discs GOD 32
23/09/1989	8	8		**YOU KEEP IT ALL IN**	Go Discs GOD 35
02/12/1989	31	8		I'LL SAIL THIS SHIP ALONE	Go Discs GOD 38
06/10/1990	❶¹	14	●	**A LITTLE TIME** 1991 BRIT Award for Best Video	Go Discs GOD 47
08/12/1990	43	6		MY BOOK	Go Discs GOD 48
16/03/1991	51	2		LET LOVE SPEAK UP ITSELF	Go Discs GOD 53
11/01/1992	22	6		OLD RED EYES IS BACK	Go Discs GOD 66
14/03/1992	30	4		WE ARE EACH OTHER	Go Discs GOD 71
13/06/1992	16	5		BELL BOTTOMED TEAR	Go Discs GOD 78
26/09/1992	46	2		36D	Go Discs GOD 88
12/03/1994	23	5		GOOD AS GOLD	Go Discs GODCD 110
04/06/1994	12	8		EVERYBODY'S TALKIN'	Go Discs GODCD 113
03/09/1994	37	3		PRETTIEST EYES	Go Discs GODCD 119
12/11/1994	14	5		ONE LAST LOVE SONG	Go Discs GODCD 122
18/11/1995	18	4		PRETENDERS TO THE THRONE	Go Discs GODCD 134
12/10/1996	6	9		**ROTTERDAM**	Go Discs GODCD 155
14/12/1996	8	10		**DON'T MARRY HER** Re-recorded with slightly different lyrics in order to receive radio plays	Go Discs GOLCD 158
29/03/1997	23	5		BLACKBIRD ON THE WIRE	Go Discs 5821252
05/07/1997	43	1		LIARS' BAR	Go Discs 5822492
03/10/1998	2	14	○	**PERFECT 10**	Go Discs 5664832
19/12/1998	16	5		DUMB	Go Discs 5667532
20/03/1999	12	6		HOW LONG'S A TEAR TAKE TO DRY?	Go Discs 8708232
10/07/1999	47	2		THE TABLE	Go Discs 5621652
07/10/2000	22	4		CLOSER THAN MOST	Go Discs 5629682
23/12/2000	59	1		THE RIVER/JUST CHECKIN'	Go Discs 5727552
17/11/2001	50	1		THE ROOT OF ALL EVIL	Go Discs 5888712
25/10/2003	30	2		JUST A FEW THINGS THAT I AIN'T	Go Discs 9813039
13/12/2003	47	2		LET GO WITH THE FLOW	Go Discs 9815084
23/10/2004	24	2		LIVIN' THING	Sony Music 6753712
18/12/2004	43	2+		THIS OLD SKIN	Sony Music 6756842

BEAVIS AND BUTTHEAD – see CHER

GILBERT BECAUD
French singer (born François Silly, 24/10/1927, Toulon) and a major middle-of-the-road star in France, whose one hit was a rare excursion to recording in English. He was also a songwriter and penned numbers for Frank Sinatra, Edith Piaf, Bob Dylan, Nina Simone, James Brown and Cher. He died from lung cancer on 18/12/2001.

DATE	POS	WKS	SINGLE TITLE	LABEL & NUMBER
29/03/1975	10	12	**A LITTLE LOVE AND UNDERSTANDING**	Decca F 13537

BECK
US singer (born Beck David Campbell, 8/7/1970, Los Angeles, CA) who adopted the name Beck Hansen when his parents separated. He first recorded for the independent labels Bong Load, Sonic Enemy and Fingerpaint, before being snapped up by Geffen. He was named Best International Male at the BRIT Awards in 1997, 1999 and 2000. Three Grammy Awards include Best Alternative Music Performance in 1996 for *Odelay* and Best Alternative Music Performance in 1999 for *Mutations*.

05/03/1994	15	6		LOSER Contains a sample of Dr John's *I Walk On Gilded Splinters* . . . . Geffen GFSTD 67
29/06/1996	35	2		WHERE IT'S AT Contains a sample of *Get Up And Dance* by Mantronix. 1996 Grammy Award for Best Male Rock Vocal Performance . . . . Geffen GFSTD 22156
16/11/1996	22	2		DEVILS HAIRCUT Contains samples of Them's *Out Of Sight* and Pretty Purdie's *Soul Drums* . . . . Geffen GFSTD 22183
08/03/1997	14	5		THE NEW POLLUTION Contains a sample of Joe Thomas' *Venus* . . . . Geffen GFSTD 22205
24/05/1997	30	2		SISSYNECK Contains a sample of Dick Hyman's *The Moog And Me*. Featured in the 1997 film *Feather In Your Cap* . . . . Geffen GFSTD 22253
08/11/1997	23	3		DEADWEIGHT Featured in the 1997 film *A Life Less Ordinary* . . . . Geffen GFSTD 22293
19/12/1998	39	2		TROPICALIA . . . . Geffen GFSTD 22365
20/11/1999	27	3		SEXX LAWS . . . . Geffen 4971822
08/04/2000	34²	2		MIXED BIZNESS . . . . Geffen 4973012

JEFF BECK UK singer/guitarist (born 24/6/1944, Wallington) who played with Screaming Lord Sutch And The Nightshifts before replacing Eric Clapton in The Yardbirds. He formed the Jeff Beck Group in 1966 with Rod Stewart, Ron Wood and Aynsley Dunbar. He has won four Grammy Awards: Best Rock Instrumental Performance in 1985 for *Escape,* Best Rock Instrumental Performance in 1989 with Terry Bozzio and Tony Hyman for *Jeff Beck's Guitar Shop With Terry Bozzio And Tony Hyman*, Best Rock Instrumental Performance in 2001 for *Dirty Mind* and Best Rock Instrumental Performance in 2003 for *Plan B*.

23/03/1967	14	14		HI-HO SILVER LINING . . . . Columbia DB 8151
02/08/1967	30	3		TALLYMAN . . . . Columbia DB 8227
28/02/1968	23	7		LOVE IS BLUE . . . . Columbia DB 8359
09/07/1969	12	9		GOO GOO BARABAJAGAL (LOVE IS HOT) **DONOVAN WITH THE JEFF BECK GROUP** . . . . Pye 7N 17778
04/11/1972	17	11		HI-HO SILVER LINING Re-issue of Columbia DB 8151 . . . . RAK RR3
05/05/1973	27	6		I'VE BEEN DRINKING **JEFF BECK AND ROD STEWART** Originally the B-side to *Love Is Blue* . . . . RAK RR4
09/10/1982	62	4		HI-HO SILVER LINING . . . . RAK RR3
07/03/1992	49	3		PEOPLE GET READY **JEFF BECK AND ROD STEWART** . . . . Epic 6577567

ROBIN BECK Canadian singer who began her career as a backing singer for Patti Austin, Leo Sayer, David Bowie, Melissa Manchester, Eddie Money and George Benson before going solo.

22/10/1988	❶³	13	○	FIRST TIME Originally an advertisement for Coca-Cola . . . . Mercury MER 270

PETER BECKETT – see **BARRY GRAY ORCHESTRA**

VICTORIA BECKHAM UK singer (born Victoria Adams, 7/4/1974, Essex), a founding member of the Spice Girls, who launched a parallel solo career in 2000. Married to football star David Beckham, she was dropped by Virgin in June 2002 and subsequently signed to Telstar.

26/08/2000	2	20	●	OUT OF YOUR MIND **TRUE STEPPERS AND DANE BOWERS FEATURING VICTORIA BECKHAM** Features the uncredited contribution of husband David Beckham . . . . NuLife 74321782942
29/09/2001	6	14		NOT SUCH AN INNOCENT GIRL . . . . Virgin VSCDT 1816
23/02/2002	6	7		A MIND OF ITS OWN . . . . Virgin VSCDT 1824
10/01/2004	3	8		THIS GROOVE/LET YOUR HEAD GO . . . . 19 Recordings/Moody CXVB 1

BEDAZZLED UK instrumental group formed by Windo Carrington and Richard Goby.

04/07/1992	73	1		SUMMER SONG . . . . Columbia 6581627

DANIEL BEDINGFIELD UK singer/producer (born 1980, New Zealand, raised in London) whose debut hit was one of five songs he recorded at home for £1,000 on a Making Waves computer audio programme. He later wrote with Mariah Carey. On New Year's Day 2004 he was involved in a serious road accident in New Zealand when his car crashed, leaving him with a fractured skull. He was named Best British Male at the 2004 BRITS and his sister Natasha also launched a singing career.

08/12/2001	❶³	18	●	GOTTA GET THRU THIS ↑ Reclaimed #1 position on 12/01/2002 . . . . Relentless RELENT 27CD
24/08/2002	4	8		JAMES DEAN (I WANNA KNOW) . . . . Polydor 5709342
07/12/2002	❶¹	21	●	IF YOU'RE NOT THE ONE ↑ . . . . Polydor 0658632
19/04/2003	6	11		I CAN'T READ YOU . . . . Polydor 0657132
02/08/2003	❶¹	11		NEVER GONNA LEAVE YOUR SIDE ↑ . . . . Polydor 9809362
01/11/2003	28	2		FRIDAY . . . . Polydor 9812920
06/11/2004	3	1		NOTHING HURTS LIKE LOVE . . . . Polydor 9868820

NATASHA BEDINGFIELD UK singer (born 26/11/1981, London) who is the sister of fellow singer Daniel Bedingfield.

15/05/2004	3	10		SINGLE . . . . Phonogenic 82876615232
28/08/2004	❶²	11		THESE WORDS ↑ In hitting #1, Natasha and Daniel became the first siblings to have topped the chart with separate solo singles . . . . Phonogenic 82876639182
11/12/2004	6	3+		UNWRITTEN . . . . Phonogenic 82876663542

BEDLAM UK production and DJ duo Alan Thompson and Richard 'Diddy' Dearlove. Diddy had previously recorded solo.

06/02/1999	68	1		DA-FORCE Contains a sample of Real Thing's *Can You Feel The Force* . . . . Playola 0091695 PLA

BEDLAM AGO GO UK vocal/instrumental group formed in Leeds by Leigh Kenny, Phil Naylor, John Ludman and Scott Wilson.

04/04/1998	57	1		SEASON NO. 5 . . . . Sony S2 BDLM 2CD

❶⁹ Number of weeks single topped the UK chart ↑ Entered the UK chart at #1 ▲⁹ Number of weeks single topped the US chart

67

BEDROCK UK group formed by club DJ John Digweed, Nick Muir and Carol Leeming. Leeming also recorded with Staxx. Kyo is a UK singer.

01/06/1996	25	3		FOR WHAT YOU DREAM OF BEDROCK FEATURING KYO Featured in the 1996 film *Trainspotting*	Stress CDSTR 23
12/07/1997	71	1		SET IN STONE/FORBIDDEN ZONE	Stress CDSTR 80
06/11/1999	35	3		HEAVEN SCENT	Bedrock BEDRCDS 001
08/07/2000	44	2		VOICES	Bedrock BEDRCDS 005

BEDROCKS UK group formed in Leeds in 1967 by Trevor Wisdom (organ), Owen Wisdom (bass), Lenny Mills (trumpet), Reg Challenger (drums), William Hixon (guitar) and Paul Douglas (saxophone) who got their break with a cover of a song from The Beatles' 'White album', although Marmalade made #1 with their version. A belated US single release for The Beatles became their only record on Capitol not to make the US top 30. Bedrocks, meanwhile, were still releasing singles into 1970 for Columbia.

18/12/1968	20	7		OB-LA-DI OB-LA-DA	Columbia DB 8516

CELI BEE AND THE BUZZY BUNCH US dance group fronted by Puerto Rican singer Celinas Soto.

17/06/1978	72	1		HOLD YOUR HORSES BABE	TK TKR 6032

Bee Gees
YOU WIN AGAIN

BEE GEES UK group formed in Manchester in 1955 by brothers Barry (born 1/9/1947, Douglas, Isle of Man) and twins Robin and Maurice Gibb (born 22/12/1949, Douglas). The family emigrated to Australia soon after the birth of a fourth son Andy in 1958. At their first professional performance in 1955 they had intended miming to a Tommy Steele record that broke on the way to the concert so they had to sing live. Originally called The Gibbs and then The BG's (it's often thought this stands for 'Brothers Gibb' but they were named by early mentors Bill Good and Bill Gates), they finally settled on the Bee Gees. First successful as songwriters, penning Col Joye's Australian chart topper *Starlight Of Love,* they signed to Festival Records' Leedon subsidiary. A return to England in February 1967 saw two years of huge success before Barry and Maurice went solo in August 1969. The brothers reunited eight months later. The mid-1970s saw them embracing the disco scene, scoring the films *Saturday Night Fever* (1978), the soundtrack selling over 30 million copies worldwide, and *Staying Alive* (1983). They also appeared in the film *Sgt Pepper's Lonely Hearts Club Band* (1978). Younger brother Andy also embarked on a solo career. They received an Outstanding Achievement Award at the 1997 BRIT Awards and were inducted into the Rock & Roll Hall of Fame in 1997. Five Grammy Award include Album of the Year in 1978 for *Saturday Night Fever Soundtrack* and Producer of the Year in 1978. Barry Gibb also won the 1980 Grammy Award for Best Pop Vocal Performance by a Duo with Barbra Streisand for *Guilty.* Barry, Robin and Maurice were awarded CBEs in the 2002 New Year's Honours List. Maurice died from a heart attack on 12/1/2003.

27/04/1967	12	10		NEW YORK MINING DISASTER 1941	Polydor 56 161
12/07/1967	41	5		TO LOVE SOMEBODY	Polydor 56 178
20/09/1967	❶[4]	17		**MASSACHUSETTS**	Polydor 56 192
22/11/1967	9	16		**WORLD**	Polydor 56 220
31/01/1968	8	10		**WORDS**	Polydor 56 229
27/03/1968	25	7		JUMBO/THE SINGER SANG HIS SONG	Polydor 56 242
07/08/1968	❶[1]	15		**I'VE GOTTA GET A MESSAGE TO YOU**	Polydor 56 273
19/02/1969	6	11		**FIRST OF MAY** Featured in the 1971 film *Melody*	Polydor 56 304
04/06/1969	23	8		TOMORROW TOMORROW	Polydor 56 331
16/08/1969	2	15		**DON'T FORGET TO REMEMBER**	Polydor 56 343
28/03/1970	49	1		I.O.I.O.	Polydor 56 377
05/12/1970	33	9		LONELY DAYS	Polydor 2001 104
29/01/1972	16	9		MY WORLD	Polydor 2058 105
22/07/1972	9	10		**RUN TO ME**	Polydor 2058 255
28/06/1975	5	11	○	**JIVE TALKIN'** ▲[2]	RSO 2090 160
31/07/1976	5	10		**YOU SHOULD BE DANCING** ▲[1]	RSO 2090 195
13/11/1976	41	4		LOVE SO RIGHT	RSO 2090 207
29/10/1977	3	15	●	HOW DEEP IS YOUR LOVE ▲[3] 1977 Grammy Award for Best Pop Vocal Performance by a Group	RSO 2090 259
04/02/1978	4	18	○	STAYIN' ALIVE ▲[4] Featured in the 1983 film *Staying Alive.* 1978 Grammy Award for Best Arrangement for Vocals	RSO 2090 267
15/04/1978	❶[2]	20	●	NIGHT FEVER ▲[8] 1978 Grammy Award for Best Pop Vocal Performance by a Group. This and above four singles all featured in the 1978 film *Saturday Night Fever*	RSO 002
25/11/1978	3	13	●	TOO MUCH HEAVEN ▲[2]	RSO 25
17/02/1979	❶[2]	10	●	TRAGEDY ▲[2]	RSO 27
14/04/1979	13	9		LOVE YOU INSIDE OUT ▲[1]	RSO 31
05/01/1980	16	7		SPIRITS (HAVING FLOWN)	RSO 52
17/09/1983	49	4		SOMEONE BELONGING TO SOMEONE Featured in the 1983 film *Staying Alive*	RSO 96
26/09/1987	❶[4]	15	●	**YOU WIN AGAIN**	Warner Brothers W 8351
12/12/1987	51	5		E.S.P.	Warner Brothers W 8139
15/04/1989	54	3		ORDINARY LIVES	Warner Brothers W 7523
24/06/1989	71	1		ONE	Warner Brothers W 2916
02/03/1991	5	11		**SECRET LOVE**	Warner Brothers W 0014
21/08/1993	23	5		PAYING THE PRICE OF LOVE	Polydor PZCD 284
27/11/1993	4	14	○	**FOR WHOM THE BELL TOLLS**	Polydor PZCD 299
16/04/1994	30	4		HOW TO FALL IN LOVE PART 1	Polydor PZCD 311
01/03/1997	5	9	○	**ALONE**	Polydor 5735272
21/06/1997	14	3		I COULD NOT LOVE YOU MORE	Polydor 5712232
08/11/1997	18	3		STILL WATERS (RUN DEEP)	Polydor 5718892
18/07/1998	5	12	○	**IMMORTALITY** CELINE DION WITH THE BEE GEES	Epic 6661682
07/04/2001	18	5		THIS IS WHERE I CAME IN	Polydor 5879772

BEENIE MAN
Jamaican singer/toaster/rapper (born Anthony Moses David, 22/8/1972, Kingston) nicknamed Beenie Man because of his diminutive size. He guested on albums by Dennis Brown, Mad Cobra and Doug E Fresh before going solo, and appeared in the 1997 film *Dancehall Queen*. He won the 1997, 1998 and 2000 MOBO Awards for Best International Reggae Act and the 2000 Grammy Award for Best Reggae Album for *Art And Life*.

20/09/1997	70	1		DANCEHALL QUEEN CHEVELLE FRANKLYN FEATURING BEENIE MAN Featured in the 1997 film of the same name	
					Island Jamaica IJCD 2018
07/03/1998	10	5		WHO AM I . . . . Greensleeves GRECD 588	
08/08/1998	69	1		FOUNDATION BEENIE MAN AND THE TAXI GANG . . . . Shocking Vibes SVJCDS1	
04/03/2000	5	9		MONEY JAMELIA FEATURING BEENIE MAN . . . . Parlophone Rhythm CDRHYTHM 27	
24/03/2001	13	5		GIRLS DEM SUGAR BEENIE MAN FEATURING MYA . . . . Virgin VUSCD 173	
28/09/2002	9	7		FEEL IT BOY BEENIE MAN FEATURING JANET JACKSON Contains samples of Lloyd James' *Hold Me* and Clancey Eccles' *Say What You Say* . . . . Virgin VUSCD 258	
14/12/2002	50	2		DIRTY HARRY'S REVENGE ADAM F FEATURING BEENIE MAN . . . . Kaos 004P	
08/02/2003	13	5		STREET LIFE . . . . Virgin VUSDX 260	
13/03/2004	7	11		DUDE BEENIE MAN FEATURING MS THING . . . . Virgin VUSCDX 282	
21/08/2004	14	5		KING OF THE DANCEHALL . . . . Virgin VUSCD 293	

BEES
UK duo formed in the Isle of Wight by Paul Butler and Aaron Fletcher who are also known as The Band Of Bees but had to amend their name for US releases.

01/05/2004	31	3		WASH IN THE RAIN . . . . Virgin VSCDT 1868	
26/06/2004	41	2		HORSEMEN . . . . Virgin VSCDX 1869	

B.E.F. FEATURING LALAH HATHAWAY
UK group formed by Ian Craig Marsh (born 11/11/1956, Sheffield) and Martyn Ware (born 19/5/1956, Sheffield), both ex-Human League. The British Electric Foundation was a production umbrella for several projects, including Heaven 17, formed in 1980. Lalah is the daughter of soul legend Donny Hathaway.

27/07/1991	37	5		FAMILY AFFAIR . . . . 10 TEN 369	

LOU BEGA
German singer (born David Lubega, 13/4/1975, Munich) whose debut hit was based on a Perez Prado song with lyrics added by Bega. A further import single was too long for consideration for the chart, charting at #1 in the budget album list.

07/08/1999	31	4		MAMBO NO 5 (A LITTLE BIT OF…) (IMPORT) Popularised after being used for Channel 4's cricket coverage . . . Ariola 74321658012	
04/09/1999	❶²	15	✪	MAMBO NO 5 (A LITTLE BIT OF…) ↑ . . . . RCA 74321696722	
18/12/1999	55	2		I GOT A GIRL . . . . RCA 74321720642	

BEGGAR AND CO
UK group formed in 1981 by Canute 'Kenny' Wellington (trumpet), David 'Baps' Baptiste (trumpet) and Neville 'Breeze' McKreith (guitar) who were all ex-Light Of The World.

07/02/1981	15	10		(SOMEBODY) HELP ME OUT . . . . Ensign ENY 201	
12/09/1981	37	5		MULE (CHANT NO. 2) . . . . RCA 130	

BEGINERZ
UK vocal duo formed in London in 1999 by Def-e (born Euen MacNeil) and Ibi Tijani.

13/07/2002	28	3		RECKLESS GIRL Contains a sample of Irene Reid's *I Must Be Doing Something Right* . . . . Cheeky 74321942232	

BEGINNING OF THE END
Bahamian-based quartet formed by brothers Raphael 'Ray' (organ), Leroy 'Roy' (guitar) and Frank 'Bud' Munnings (drums), with Fred Henfield (bass). Ray Munnings later went solo. They took their name from the 1957 film of the same name.

23/02/1974	31	6		FUNKY NASSAU . . . . Atlantic K 10021	

BEIJING SPRING
UK vocal duo.

23/01/1993	43	3		I WANNA BE IN LOVE AGAIN . . . . MCA MCSTD 1709	
08/05/1993	53	2		SUMMERLANDS . . . . MCA MCSTD 1761	

BEL AMOUR
French production/vocal trio Edouard De Tricasse, Franck Keller and JC Sindress, with Sydney on lead vocals.

12/05/2001	23	3		BEL AMOUR . . . . Credence CDCRED 010	

BEL CANTO
Norwegian group formed in 1986 by Nils Johansen, Anneli Marian Drecker, Luc Van Lieshout, Geir Jenssen and Andreas Eriksen. Jenssen later recorded as Biosphere.

14/10/1995	65	1		WE'VE GOT TO WORK IT OUT . . . . Good Groove CDGG 2	

HARRY BELAFONTE
US singer (born 1/3/1927, Harlem, NYC) who began his career as an actor in the American Negro Theatre and Drama Workshop in the mid-1940s. Signing with Jubilee Records in 1949, he came to worldwide prominence via the late calypso craze in the 1950s. He starred in numerous films between 1954 and 1974, and in 1987 replaced Danny Kaye as UNICEF's goodwill ambassador. He won two Grammy Awards: Best Folk Performance in 1960 for *Swing Dat Hammer* and Best Folk Recording in 1965 with Miram Makeba for *An Evening With Belafonte/Makeba*, while his Belafonte Folk Singers won the Best Folk Recording in 1961 for *Belafonte Folk Singers At Home And Abroad*. He has a star on the Hollywood Walk of Fame. Odetta is a US singer/guitarist (born Odetta Holmes Feloius Gorden, 31/12/193, Birmingham, AL).

01/03/1957	2	18		BANANA BOAT SONG HARRY BELAFONTE WITH TONY SCOTT'S ORCHESTRA AND CHORUS AND MILLARD THOMAS, GUITAR Featured in the 1988 film *Beetlejuice* . . . . HMV POP 308	
14/06/1957	3	25		ISLAND IN THE SUN Featured in the 1957 film *Island In The Sun* starring Belafonte . . . . RCA 1007	
06/09/1957	18	6		SCARLET RIBBONS HARRY BELAFONTE AND MILLARD THOMAS . . . . HMV POP 360	
01/11/1957	❶⁷	12	◎	MARY'S BOY CHILD . . . . RCA 1022	

❶⁹ Number of weeks single topped the UK chart ↑ Entered the UK chart at #1 ▲⁹ Number of weeks single topped the US chart

22/08/1958.....16.......7......	LITTLE BERNADETTE **BELAFONTE**	RCA 1072
28/11/1958.....10.......6......	**MARY'S BOY CHILD** Re-promoted for the Christmas market	RCA 1022
12/12/1958.....18.......4......	SON OF MARY	RCA 1084
11/12/1959.....30.......1......	MARY'S BOY CHILD Re-promoted for a second time for Christmas	RCA 1022
28/09/1961.....32.......8......	HOLE IN THE BUCKET **HARRY BELAFONTE AND ODETTA**	RCA 1247

MAGGIE BELL
UK singer (born 12/1/1945, Glasgow) who originally sang with Alex Harvey and later his brother Les in a local band called The Power who then became Stone The Crows. Following Les Harvey's death in an on-stage electric accident, the band split and Bell went solo.

15/04/1978.....37.......4......	HAZELL Theme to the TV series of the same name	Swansong SSK 19412
17/10/1981.....11.......8......	HOLD ME **B A ROBERTSON AND MAGGIE BELL**	Swansong BAM 1

WILLIAM BELL
US singer (born William Yarborough, 16/7/1939, Memphis, TN) who was a mainstay with Stax Records in the early 1960s. He formed Peachtree Records in 1969 before signing for Mercury, scoring a US top ten hit with *Tryin' To Love Two* in 1977. Judy Clay is a US singer (born Judith Guion, 12/9/1938, St. Paul, NC) who died on 2/8/2001 in a car accident.

29/05/1968.....31.......7......	TRIBUTE TO A KING Tribute to Otis Redding	Stax 601 038
20/11/1968.....8.......14......	**PRIVATE NUMBER** JUDY CLAY AND WILLIAM BELL	Stax 101
26/04/1986.....70.......1......	HEADLINE NEWS	Absolute LUTE 1

BELL AND JAMES
US vocal duo Leroy Bell (nephew of songwriter/producer Thom Bell) and Casey James.

31/03/1979.....59.......3......	LIVIN' IT UP (FRIDAY NIGHT)	A&M AMS 7424

BELL AND SPURLING
UK duo formed by comics Martin Bellamy and Johnny Spurling. Their debut hit was a tribute to England football manager Sven Goran Ericksson and also featured commentary from radio DJ Jonathan Pearce.

13/10/2001.....7.......6......	**SVEN SVEN SVEN**	Eternal WEA 336CD
08/06/2002.....25.......4......	GOLDENBALLS (MR BECKHAM TO YOU)	Eternal WEA 350CD

BELL X1
Irish group formed in Kildare in 1994 by Damien Rice (vocals), Paul Noonan (vocals), Dave Geraghty (guitar/vocals), Brian Crosby (keyboards) and Dominic Phillips (bass) as Juniper. Rice left in 1999 and the remaining four members renamed the group Bell X1.

26/06/2004.....65.......1......	EVE THE APPLE OF MY EYE	Island CID 856

ARCHIE BELL AND THE DRELLS
US singer (born 1/9/1944, Henderson, TX) who formed a vocal group while at the Leo Smith Junior High School with James Wise (born 1/5/1948, Houston), Willie Parnell (born 12/4/1945, Houston), LC Watts and Cornelius Fuller. Their 1967 debut single for Ovid was picked up by Atlantic, the group making US #1 with *Tighten Up*, originally a B-side and released while Archie Bell was serving in the US Army. By his return it had sold 4 million copies. The follow-up, *I Can't Stop Dancing*, was written and produced by Gamble and Huff (who also penned the UK debut listed below), with whom they reunited in 1975, signing with Philadelphia International Records, by which time the group was Bell, Wise, Parnell and Lee Bell.

07/10/1972.....11.......10......	HERE I GO AGAIN	Atlantic K 10210
27/01/1973.....36.......5......	THERE'S GONNA BE A SHOWDOWN	Atlantic K 10263
08/05/1976.....13.......10......	SOUL CITY WALK	Philadelphia International PIR 4250
11/06/1977.....43.......4......	EVERYBODY HAVE A GOOD TIME	Philadelphia International PIR 5179
28/06/1986.....49.......4......	DON'T LET LOVE GET YOU DOWN	Portrait A 7254

FREDDIE BELL AND THE BELLBOYS
US group fronted by singer Freddie Bell. One of the earliest rock 'n' roll outfits, they included *Hound Dog* in their live show, which Elvis Presley saw them perform and of which he recorded a cover version. They were one of the first US rock groups to tour the UK, supporting Tommy Steele in 1956. Freddie Bell appeared in the films *Rock Around The Clock* (1956) and *Get Yourself A College Girl* (1964).

28/09/1956......4......10......	**GIDDY-UP-A-DING-DONG**	Mercury MT 122

BELL BIV DEVOE
US vocal group formed in Boston, MA in 1989 by Ricky Bell (born 18/9/1967, Boston), Michael Bivins (born 10/8/1968, Boston) and Ronnie DeVoe (born 17/11/1967, Boston), all ex-members of teen sensation group New Edition.

30/06/1990.....19.......11......	POISON	MCA 1414
22/09/1990.....56.......3......	DO ME	MCA 1440
15/08/1992.....2.......13.....○	**THE BEST THINGS IN LIFE ARE FREE** LUTHER VANDROSS AND JANET JACKSON WITH SPECIAL GUESTS BBD AND RALPH TRESVANT Featured in the 1992 film *Mo' Money*	Perspective PERSS 7400
09/10/1993.....60.......2......	SOMETHING IN YOUR EYES	MCA MCSTD 1934
16/12/1995.....7.......7......	**THE BEST THINGS IN LIFE ARE FREE (REMIX)** LUTHER VANDROSS AND JANET JACKSON WITH SPECIAL GUESTS BBD AND RALPH TRESVANT	A&M 5813092

BELL BOOK & CANDLE
German group formed by Jana Gross (vocals), Andy Birr (guitar and drums) and Hendrik Roder (bass).

17/10/1998.....63.......1......	RESCUE ME	Logic 74321616882

BELLAMY BROTHERS
US brothers Howard (born 2/2/1946, Darby, FL, guitar) and David Bellamy (born 16/9/1950, Darby, guitar/keyboards) who made their professional debut in 1958.

17/04/1976.....7.......12......	**LET YOUR LOVE FLOW** ▲[1]	Warner Brothers K 16690
21/08/1976.....43.......3......	SATIN SHEETS	Warner Brothers K 16775
11/08/1979.....3.......14.....○	**IF I SAID YOU HAD A BEAUTIFUL BODY WOULD YOU HOLD IT AGAINST ME**	Warner Brothers K 17405

BELLATRIX Icelandic vocal/instrumental group formed by Eliza, Kalli, Kidda, Anna Magga and Sigrun. Eliza later recorded solo.

16/09/2000 . . . . . 65 . . . . . . 1 . . . . JEDI WANNABE . . . . Fierce Panda NING 101CD

BELLBOYS – see FREDDIE BELL AND THE BELLBOYS

REGINA BELLE US singer (born 17/7/1963, Engelwood, NJ) who sang with The Manhattans for a year prior to signing a solo deal with CBS and releasing her debut album in 1987.

21/10/1989 . . . . . 73 . . . . . . 1 . . . . GOOD LOVIN' . . . . CBS 6552307

11/12/1993 . . . . . 12 . . . . . 12 . . . . . . A WHOLE NEW WORLD (ALADDIN'S THEME) ❶¹ PEABO BRYSON AND REGINA BELLE Featured in the 1992 Walt Disney film *Aladdin* and won an Oscar for Best Film Song. 1993 Grammy Award for Best Pop Performance by a Duo or Group with Vocal . . . . Columbia 6599002

BELLE AND SEBASTIAN UK group formed in Glasgow in 1996 by Chris Geddes (keyboards), Richard Colburn (drums), Mick Cooke (trumpet), Stuart Murdoch (guitar/vocals), Sarah Martin (violin), Stuart David (bass), Isobel Campbell (cello/vocals) and Stevie Jackson (guitar). They won the Best UK Newcomer award at the 1999 BRIT Awards.

24/05/1997 . . . . . 59 . . . . . . 1 . . . . DOG ON WHEELS . . . . Jeepster JPRCDS 001
09/08/1997 . . . . . 41 . . . . . . 2 . . . . LADY LINE PAINTER JANE . . . . Jeepster JPRCDS 002
25/10/1997 . . . . . 32 . . . . . . 2 . . . . 3 . . 6 . . 9 SECONDS OF LIGHT (EP) Tracks on EP: *A Century Of Fakers*, *Le Pastie De La Bourgeoisie*, *Beautiful* and *Put The Book Back On The Shelf* . . . . Jeepster JPRCDS 003
03/06/2000 . . . . . 15 . . . . . . 3 . . . . LEGAL MAN Features the uncredited contribution of The Maisonettes . . . . Jeepster JPRCDS 018
30/06/2001 . . . . . 31 . . . . . . 2 . . . . JONATHAN DAVID . . . . Jeepster JPRCDS 022
08/12/2001 . . . . . 39 . . . . . . 2 . . . . I'M WAKING UP TO US . . . . Jeepster JPRCDS 023
29/11/2003 . . . . . 32 . . . . . . 2 . . . . STEP INTO MY OFFICE BABY . . . . Rough Trade RTRADESCD 128
28/02/2004 . . . . . 14 . . . . . . 4 . . . . I'M A CUCKOO . . . . Rough Trade RTRADSCD 157
03/07/2004 . . . . . 20 . . . . . . 3 . . . . BOOKS . . . . Rough Trade RTRADSCD 180

BELLE AND THE DEVOTIONS UK vocal group formed by Kit Rolfe (as Belle), Linda Sofield and Laura James. Although their Eurovision entry was their only hit, they were not put together specifically for the competition (having released a couple of singles the previous year), although rumours abounded that they didn't actually sing on the record. Sofield and James were later in Toto Coelo.

21/04/1984 . . . . . 11 . . . . . . 8 . . . . LOVE GAMES UK entry for the 1984 Eurovision Song Contest (came seventh) . . . . CBS A 4332

BELLE STARS UK group formed by Jane Hirst (keyboards/saxophone), Jenni McKeown (vocals), Judy Parsons (drums), Lesley Shone (bass), Miranda Joyce (saxophone), Sarah Jane Owen (guitar) and Stella Barker (guitar). They all adopted the surname Belle Star. Judy, Miranda, Sarah Jane and Stella were previously in the Bodysnatchers, at the forefront of the ska revival. Sarah Jane later went solo.

05/06/1982 . . . . . 35 . . . . . . 6 . . . . IKO IKO Featured in the films *The Big Easy* (1986) and *Rain Man* (1989) . . . . Stiff BUY 150
17/07/1982 . . . . . 11 . . . . . . 9 . . . . THE CLAPPING SONG . . . . Stiff BUY 155
16/10/1982 . . . . . 51 . . . . . . 3 . . . . MOCKINGBIRD . . . . Stiff BUY 159
15/01/1983 . . . . . 3 . . . . . 11 . . . . . ○ SIGN OF THE TIMES . . . . Stiff BUY 167
16/04/1983 . . . . . 22 . . . . . . 9 . . . . SWEET MEMORY . . . . Stiff BUY 174
13/08/1983 . . . . . 52 . . . . . . 3 . . . . INDIAN SUMMER . . . . Stiff BUY 185
14/07/1984 . . . . . 71 . . . . . . 1 . . . . 80S ROMANCE . . . . Stiff BUY 200

BELLEFIRE Irish vocal group formed by Kelly Kilfeather (born 23/3/1979), Tara Lee (born 25/7/1982), Cathy Newell (born 14/7/1982) and Ciara Newell (born 7/7/1983) and discovered by Boyzone and Westlife manager Louis Walsh.

14/07/2001 . . . . . 18 . . . . . . 4 . . . . PERFECT BLISS . . . . Virgin VSCDT 1807
18/05/2002 . . . . . 18 . . . . . . 4 . . . . ALL I WANT IS YOU . . . . Virgin VSCDT 1820
24/04/2004 . . . . . 26 . . . . . . 3 . . . . SAY SOMETHING ANYWAY . . . . East West EW 287CD
16/10/2004 . . . . . 67 . . . . . . 1 . . . . SPIN THE WHEEL . . . . East West EW 293CD

BELLINI German production group formed by Gottfried Engels and Ramon Zenker. Zenker also making hits by Aria and Fragma.

27/09/1997 . . . . . 8 . . . . . . 7 . . . . SAMBA DE JANEIRO Melody based on Airto Moreira's *Celebration Suit* . . . . Virgin DINSD 165

BELLRAYS US R&B group formed in Los Angeles, CA in 1995 by Lisa Kekaula (vocals), Tony Fate (guitar), Bob Vennum (bass) and Todd Westover (drums). Kekaula later sang with Basement Jaxx.

20/07/2002 . . . . . 75 . . . . . . 1 . . . . THEY GLUED YOUR HEAD ON UPSIDE DOWN . . . . Poptones MC 5073SCD

LOUIS BELLSON – see DUKE ELLINGTON

BELLY US rock group formed in Newport, RI in 1991 by Tanya Donelly (born 14/7/1966, Newport, guitar/vocals), Thomas Gorman (born 20/5/1966, Buffalo, NY, guitar), Chris Gorman (born 29/7/1967, Buffalo, drums) and Fred Abong (bass). Abong left in 1993 and was replaced by Gail Greenwood (born 10/3/1960, Providence, RI). Donelly had been in Throwing Muses and The Breeders, and also recorded solo. They disbanded in 1997.

23/01/1993 . . . . . 32 . . . . . . 3 . . . . FEED THE TREE . . . . 4AD BAD 3001CD
10/04/1993 . . . . . 49 . . . . . . 2 . . . . GEPETTO . . . . 4AD BAD 2018CD
04/02/1995 . . . . . 28 . . . . . . 2 . . . . NOW THEY'LL SLEEP . . . . 4AD BAD 5003CD
22/07/1995 . . . . . 35 . . . . . . 2 . . . . SEAL MY FATE . . . . 4AD BADD 5007CD

BELMONTS – see DION

❶⁹ Number of weeks single topped the UK chart   ↑ Entered the UK chart at #1   ▲⁹ Number of weeks single topped the US chart

71

BELOVED
UK rock group formed in London in 1983 by Jon Marsh (guitar/vocals), Guy Gousden (drums) and Tim Harvard (bass) as the Journey Through. Steve Waddington (guitar/keyboards) joined in 1984, although by 1993 it was a duo of Marsh and his wife Helena. Marsh once reached the semi-final as a contestant on Channel 4's *Countdown*.

DATE	POS	WKS	BPI	SINGLE TITLE	LABEL & NUMBER
21/10/1989	26	2		THE SUN RISING	WEA YZ 414
27/01/1990	19	7		HELLO	WEA YZ 426
24/03/1990	39	3		YOUR LOVE TAKES ME HIGHER	East West YZ 463
09/06/1990	46	4		TIME AFTER TIME	East West YZ 482
10/11/1990	48	3		IT'S ALRIGHT NOW	East West YZ 541
23/01/1993	8	10		**SWEET HARMONY**	East West YZ 709CD
10/04/1993	23	4		YOU'VE GOT ME THINKING	East West YZ 738CD
14/08/1993	38	2		OUTERSPACE GIRL	East West YZ 726CD
30/03/1996	19	3		SATELLITE	East West EW 034CD
10/08/1996	43	2		EASE THE PRESSURE	East West EW 058CD
30/08/1997	31	2		THE SUN RISING Re-issue of WEA YZ 414	East West EW 122CD1

BELTRAM
US producer (born Joey Beltram, 1971, New York) also known as a remixer. He has a collection of over 70,000 dance records.

DATE	POS	WKS	BPI	SINGLE TITLE	LABEL & NUMBER
28/09/1991	52	2		ENERGY FLASH (EP)	R&S RSUK 3
07/12/1991	53	2		THE OMEN PROGRAM 2 BELTRAM	R&S RSUK 7

BENNY BENASSI PRESENTS THE BIZ
French producer (born Marco Benassi, 1968).

DATE	POS	WKS	BPI	SINGLE TITLE	LABEL & NUMBER
26/07/2003	2	11		**SATISFACTION**	Data 58CDS
14/02/2004	40	2		NO MATTER WHAT YOU DO	Data 66CDS

PAT BENATAR
US singer (born Patricia Andrzejewski, 10/1/1953, Long Island, NY) who trained as an opera singer before turning to rock music. She married her guitarist/producer Neil Giraldo in 1982 and later acted in the 1980 film *Union City*. Four Grammy Awards include Best Rock Vocal Performance in 1980 for *Crimes Of Passion*, Best Rock Vocal Performance in 1981 for *Fire And Ice* and Best Rock Vocal Performance in 1982 for *Shadows Of The Night*

DATE	POS	WKS	BPI	SINGLE TITLE	LABEL & NUMBER
21/01/1984	49	5		LOVE IS A BATTLEFIELD 1983 Grammy Award for Best Rock Vocal Performance. Featured in the films *Small Soldiers* (1998) and *13 Going On 30* (2004)	Chrysalis CHS 2747
12/01/1985	22	9		WE BELONG	Chrysalis CHS 2821
23/03/1985	17	10		LOVE IS A BATTLEFIELD Re-issue of Chrysalis CHS 2747	Chrysalis PAT 1
15/06/1985	50	4		SHADOWS OF THE NIGHT	Chrysalis PAT 2
19/10/1985	53	3		INVINCIBLE (THEME FROM 'THE LEGEND OF BILLIE JEAN') Featured in the 1985 film *The Legend Of Billie Jean*	Chrysalis PAT 3
15/02/1986	67	3		SEX AS A WEAPON	Chrysalis PAT 4
02/07/1988	19	10		ALL FIRED UP	Chrysalis PAT 5
01/10/1988	42	5		DON'T WALK AWAY	Chrysalis PAT 6
14/01/1989	59	3		ONE LOVE	Chrysalis PAT 7
30/10/1993	48	1		SOMEBODY'S BABY	Chrysalis CDCHS 5001

DAVID BENDETH
Canadian singer/multi-instrumentalist who was later a successful producer.

DATE	POS	WKS	BPI	SINGLE TITLE	LABEL & NUMBER
08/09/1979	44	5		FEEL THE REAL	Sidewalk SID 113

BENELUX AND NANCY DEE
Belgian/Dutch/Luxembourg vocal group (hence the name) fronted by Nancy Dee.

DATE	POS	WKS	BPI	SINGLE TITLE	LABEL & NUMBER
25/08/1979	52	4		SWITCH	Scope SC 4

ERIC BENET
US singer (born Eric Benet Jordan, 5/10/1969, Milwaukee, WI).

DATE	POS	WKS	BPI	SINGLE TITLE	LABEL & NUMBER
22/03/1997	62	1		SPIRITUAL THANG	Warner Brothers W 0390CD
01/05/1999	28	3		GEORGY PORGY ERIC BENET FEATURING FAITH EVANS	Warner Brothers W 478CD1
05/02/2000	48	1		WHY YOU FOLLOW ME	Warner Brothers W 491CD

NIGEL BENN – see PACK FEATURING NIGEL BENN

SIMONE BENN – see VOLATILE AGENTS FEATURING SIMONE BENN

BENNETT
UK group formed in 1993 by Jason Applin (guitar/vocals), Johnny Peer (guitar/vocals), Kevin Moorey (drums) and Andrew Bennett (bass).

DATE	POS	WKS	BPI	SINGLE TITLE	LABEL & NUMBER
22/02/1997	34	2		MUM'S GONE TO ICELAND	Roadrunner RR 22853
03/05/1997	69	1		SOMEONE ALWAYS GETS THERE FIRST	Roadrunner RR 22983

BOYD BENNETT AND HIS ROCKETS
US singer (born 7/12/1924, Muscle Shoals, AL) who formed his first band at high school. After his recording career he became a DJ in Kentucky, and also launched the Condom-Loc Rings company whose product was designed to keep condoms in place. He died on 2/6/2002.

DATE	POS	WKS	BPI	SINGLE TITLE	LABEL & NUMBER
23/12/1955	16	2		SEVENTEEN	Parlophone R 4063

CHRIS BENNETT – see MUNICH MACHINE

CLIFF BENNETT AND THE REBEL ROUSERS
UK singer (born 4/6/1940, Slough) who formed the Rebel Rousers in 1959 with Mick King (guitar), Frank Allen (born Francis McNeice, 14/12/1943, Hayes, bass), Ricky Winters (drums) and Sid Phillips

(saxophone/piano) covering US soul hits for the UK market. They split in 1969. Bennett attempted to move into the progressive rock market without success and Frank Allen joined The Searchers.

01/10/1964	9	9		**ONE WAY LOVE** Cover version of The Drifters' US #56 R&B hit	Parlophone R 5173
04/02/1965	42	3		I'LL TAKE YOU HOME	Parlophone R 5229
18/08/1966	6	11		**GOT TO GET YOU INTO MY LIFE** Written and produced by Paul McCartney. Bennett's cover appeared the same week as The Beatles' original version on the *Revolver* album	Parlophone R 5489

EASTHER BENNETT – see ASWAD

PETER E BENNETT WITH THE CO-OPERATION CHOIR UK singer with choir.

07/11/1970	45	1		THE SEAGULL'S NAME WAS NELSON	RCA 1991

TONY BENNETT US jazz-influenced singer (born Anthony Dominick Benedetto, 13/8/1925, Queens, NYC) popular on both sides of the Atlantic who enjoyed a renaissance in the 1990s. Eleven Grammy Awards include Best Traditional Pop Performance in 1992 for *Perfectly Frank*, Best Traditional Pop Performance in 1993 for *Steppin' Out*, Album of the Year and Best Traditional Pop Vocal Performance in 1994 for *MTV Unplugged*, Best Traditional Pop Vocal in 1996 for *Here's To The Ladies*, Best Traditional Pop Vocal Performance in 1997 for *Tony Bennett On Holiday*, Best Traditional Pop Vocal in 1999 for *Bennett Sings Ellington – Hot And Cool*, Best Traditional Pop Vocal Album in 2002 for *Playin' With My Friends: Bennett Sings The Blues* and Best Traditional Pop Vocal Album in 2003 with kd lang for *A Wonderful World*. He appeared in an episode of *The Simpsons*, busking on a street corner singing *Capital City*, and appeared as himself in the films *Analyze This* (1999) and *Bruce Almighty* (2003). He has a star on the Hollywood Walk of Fame.

15/04/1955	❶²	16		**STRANGER IN PARADISE** Originally written for the musical *Kismet*. Five other versions charted at the same time. Featured in the 1999 film *Liberty Heights*	Philips PB 420
16/09/1955	18	1		CLOSE YOUR EYES	Philips PB 445
13/04/1956	29	1		COME NEXT SPRING	Philips PB 537
05/01/1961	35	2		TILL	Philips PB 1079
18/07/1963	27	13		THE GOOD LIFE Featured in the films *The Seven Capital Sins* (1963) and *What Women Want* (2000)	CBS AAG 153
06/05/1965	40	5		IF I RULED THE WORLD From the musical *Pickwick*	CBS 201735
27/05/1965	46	2		I LEFT MY HEART IN SAN FRANCISCO 1962 Grammy Awards for Record of the Year and Best Male Solo Vocal Performance	CBS 201730
30/09/1965	25	12		I LEFT MY HEART IN SAN FRANCISCO	CBS 201730
23/12/1965	21	9		THE VERY THOUGHT OF YOU	CBS 202021

GARY BENSON UK singer/guitarist (born Harry Hyams, London) who appeared in the 1992 film *Honeymoon In Vegas* as an Elvis Presley impersonator. His single was originally released on B&C Records but subsequently leased to State following B&C's liquidation. He recorded three albums for State.

09/08/1975	20	8		DON'T THROW IT ALL AWAY	State STAT 10

GEORGE BENSON US singer/guitarist (born 22/3/1943, Pittsburgh, PA) who played guitar from the age of eight and joined Brother Jack McDuff's trio in 1963. House guitarist for Creed Taylor's CTI label in the early 1970s, ambitions as a vocalist led him to Warners. There, with producers including Tommy Lipuma and Quincy Jones, he became the biggest-selling jazz artist of the era, his style greatly influenced by Wes Montgomery. Ten Grammy Awards include Record of the Year in 1976 for *This Masquerade*, Best Pop Instrumental Performance in 1976 for *Breezin'*, Best Rhythm & Blues Instrumental Performance in 1976 for *Theme From 'Good King Bad'*, Best Rhythm & Blues Vocal Performance in 1978 for *On Broadway*, Best Rhythm & Blues Instrumental Performance in 1980 for *Off Broadway*, Best Jazz Vocal Performance in 1980 for *Moody's Mood*, Best Recording for Children in 1980 with various others for *In Harmony*, Best Pop Instrumental Performance in 1983 for *Being With You* and Best Jazz Performance by a Big Band in 1990 with the Count Basie Orchestra for *Basie's Bag*. He also won the 2003 MOBO Award for Lifetime Achievement. He has a star on the Hollywood Walk of Fame.

25/10/1975	30	6		SUPERSHIP **GEORGE 'BAD' BENSON**	CTI
04/06/1977	26	6		NATURE BOY	Warner Brothers K 16921
24/09/1977	27	7		THE GREATEST LOVE OF ALL Featured in the 1977 film *The Greatest*, a biopic of Muhammad Ali	Arista 133
31/03/1979	29	9		LOVE BALLAD	Warner Brothers K 17333
26/07/1980	7	10		**GIVE ME THE NIGHT** 1980 Grammy Award for Best Rhythm & Blues Vocal Performance	Warner Brothers K 17673
04/10/1980	10	8		**LOVE X LOVE**	Warner Brothers K 17699
07/02/1981	45	5		WHAT'S ON YOUR MIND	Warner Brothers K 17748
19/09/1981	49	3		LOVE ALL THE HURT AWAY **ARETHA FRANKLIN AND GEORGE BENSON**	Arista ARIST 428
14/11/1981	29	11		TURN YOUR LOVE AROUND	Warner Brothers K 17877
23/01/1982	14	10		NEVER GIVE UP ON A GOOD THING	Warner Brothers K 17902
21/05/1983	11	10		LADY LOVE ME (ONE MORE TIME)	Warner Brothers W 9614
16/07/1983	28	7		FEEL LIKE MAKIN' LOVE	Warner Brothers W 9551
24/09/1983	7	10		**IN YOUR EYES**	Warner Brothers W 9487
17/12/1983	57	5		INSIDE LOVE (SO PERSONAL)	Warner Brothers W 9427
19/01/1985	29	9		20/20	Warner Brothers W 9120
20/04/1985	60	3		BEYOND THE SEA (LA MER)	Warner Brothers W 9014
16/08/1986	60	4		KISSES IN THE MOONLIGHT	Warner Brothers W 8640
29/11/1986	19	9		SHIVER	Warner Brothers W 8523
14/02/1987	45	4		TEASER	Warner Brothers W 8437
27/08/1988	56	3		LET'S DO IT AGAIN	Warner Brothers W 7780
05/09/1992	68	1		I'LL KEEP YOUR DREAMS ALIVE **GEORGE BENSON AND PATTI AUSTIN**	Ammi 101
11/07/1998	22	3		SEVEN DAYS **MARY J. BLIGE FEATURING GEORGE BENSON**	MCA MCSTD 48083

❶⁹ Number of weeks single topped the UK chart ↑ Entered the UK chart at #1 ▲⁹ Number of weeks single topped the US chart

RHIAN BENSON
UK singer born in 1978 into the Ashanti tribe of Ghana to a Welsh mother and Ghanian father.

23/10/2004.....27......2......	SAY HOW I FEEL	DKG DKG710071002

BENT
UK duo from Nottingham, Simon Mills and Neil 'Nail' Halliday.

12/07/2003.....59......1......	STAY THE SAME Contains a sample of David Essex's *There's Something About You Baby*	Sport 9CDX

BENTLEY RHYTHM ACE
UK dance group formed by Richard March (aka Barry Island), Mike Stokes (aka Michael Barrywoosh), James and Fuzz, taking their name from a drum machine. March previously played bass for Pop Will Eat Itself.

06/09/1997.....17......4......	BENTLEY'S GONNA SORT YOU OUT!	Skint CDRS 6476
27/05/2000.....29......2......	THEME FROM GUTBUSTER Contains samples of Piero Umilani's *Open Face*, Kim Fowley's *Whittier Boulevard* and The Jimmy Castor Bunch's *E-Man Groove*	Parlophone CDRS 6537
02/09/2000.....57......1......	HOW'D I DO DAT	Parlophone CDRS 6543

BROOK BENTON
US singer/songwriter (born Benjamin Franklin Peay, 19/9/1931, Camden, SC) who first recorded under his own name for Okeh in 1953, making over twenty US hits. He died from bacterial meningitis on 9/4/1988.

10/07/1959.....28......2......	ENDLESSLY..	Mercury AMT 1043
06/10/1960.....41......6......	KIDDIO	Mercury AMT 1109
16/02/1961.....50......1......	FOOLS RUSH IN	Mercury AMT 1121
13/07/1961.....30......9......	BOLL WEEVIL SONG	Mercury AMT 1148

BENZ
UK group formed in London by Tim Shade, B.I.G. Ben and Dark Boy, Shade previously recording as Overlord X.

16/12/1995.....62......2......	BOOM ROCK SOUL...	Hacktown 74321329652
16/03/1996.....31......3......	URBAN CITY GIRL...	Hacktown 74321348732
25/05/1996.....35......2......	MISS PARKER	Hacktown 74321377292
29/03/1997.....59......1......	IF I REMEMBER...	Hendricks CDBENZ 1
09/08/1997.....73......1......	ON A SUN-DAY..	Hendricks CDBENZ 2

BERLIN
US electro-pop group formed in Los Angeles, CA in 1979 by John Crawford (born 17/1/1957, bass/keyboards), Terri Nunn (born 26/6/1961, vocals), Virginia McCalino (vocals), Jo Julian (keyboards), Chris Velasco (guitar) and Dan Van Patten (drums). They made one single before disbanding in 1981, Crawford and Nunn recruiting David Diamond (guitar), Rick Olsen (guitar), Matt Reid (keyboards) and Rod Learned (bass). By 1984 the group consisted of Crawford, Nunn and Rob Brill (born 21/1/1956, drums), Nunn leaving in 1987.

25/10/1986 ....❶⁴.....12.....●	**TAKE MY BREATH AWAY (LOVE THEME FROM 'TOP GUN')** ▲¹ Featured in the 1986 film *Top Gun*, winning an Oscar for Best Film Song, and in *Ocean's Eleven* (2001)	CBS A 7320
17/01/1987.....39......6......	YOU DON'T KNOW	Mercury MER 237
14/03/1987.....47......3......	LIKE FLAMES	Mercury MER 240
20/02/1988.....52......3......	TAKE MY BREATH AWAY (LOVE THEME FROM 'TOP GUN')............................	CBS A 7320
20/10/1990.....3......12......	**TAKE MY BREATH AWAY (LOVE THEME FROM 'TOP GUN')** Re-issue of CBS A 7320	CBS 6563617

ELMER BERNSTEIN
US orchestra leader (born 4/4/1922, New York City) who scored over 60 films, including the 1955 film *The Man With The Golden Arm*, his biggest US hit. He has a star on the Hollywood Walk of Fame. He died on 18/8/2004.

18/12/1959.....4......11......	**STACCATO'S THEME** Theme to the TV series *Johnny Staccato*	Capitol CL 15101

LEONARD BERNSTEIN
US conductor/composer/pianist (born 25/8/1918, Lawrence, MA) who studied at Harvard and the Curtis Institute, by 1944 having a reputation as a conductor. He was associated with the Israel Philharmonic Orchestra, the Boston Symphony Orchestra and the New York Philharmonic Orchestra, musical director with the latter from 1958 to 1969. He won fifteen Grammy Awards: Best Documentary or Spoken Word Recording for *Humor In Music* and Best Recording for Children for *Prokofiev: Peter And The Wolf* in 1961; Best Recording for Children in 1962 for *Saint-Saens: Carnival Of The Animals*; Best Recording for Children in 1963 conducting the New York Philharmonic with *Britten: Young Person's Guide To The Orchestra*; Album of the Year, Classical in 1964 conducting the New York Philharmonic for *Symphony No. 3 (Kaddish)*; Best Classical Performance, Choral (other than opera) in 1967 conducting the London Symphony Chorus and Orchestra for *Mahler: Symphony No. 8 In E Flat Major*; Best Opera Recording in 1973 conducting the Metropolitan Opera Orchestra and Manhattan Opera Chorus for *Bizet: Carmen*; Album of the Year, Classical in 1977 with Vladimir Horowitz, Isaac Stern, Mstislav Rostropovich, Dietrich Fischer-Dieskau, Yehudi Menuhin and Lyndon Woodside for *Concert Of The Century*; Best Classical Orchestral Recording (conductors award) in 1989 conducting the New York Philharmonic Orchestra for *Mahler: Symphony No. 3 In D Minor*; Best Classical Album in 1990 conducting the New York Philharmonic Orchestra for *Ives: Symphony No. 2: The Gong On The Hook And Ladder: Central Park In The Dark: The Unanswered Question*; Best Classical Orchestral Performance (conductors award) in 1990 conducting the Chicago Symphony Orchestra for *Shostakovich: Symphonies No. 1, Op. 10 And No. 7, Op. 60*; Best Contemporary Composition in 1990 for *Arias And Barcarolles*; Best Classical Album in 1991 conducting the London Symphony Orchestra for *Candide*; and Best Classical Album and Best Orchestral Performance in 1992 conducting the Berlin Philharmonic Orchestra for *Mahler: Symphonie No. 9*. He died in New York on 14/10/1990.

02/07/1994.....44......4......	AMERICA – WORLD CUP THEME 1994 Official theme to the 1994 FIFA World Cup	Deutsche Grammophon USACD 1

BERRI
UK singer Beverley Sleight.

26/11/1994.....26......6......	THE SUNSHINE AFTER THE RAIN NEW ATLANTIC/U4EA FEATURING BERRI	3 Beat TABCD 223
02/09/1995.....4......11......○	**THE SUNSHINE AFTER THE RAIN (REMIX)**...	ffrreedom TABCD 232
02/12/1995.....20......5......	SHINE LIKE A STAR	3 Beat TABCD 239

LAKIESHA BERRI
US R&B singer (born 1974, Cincinnati, Ohio).

05/07/1997.....54......1......	LIKE THIS AND LIKE THAT Featured in the 1987 Walt Disney film *Sixth Man*	Adept ADPTCD 7

○ Silver disc ● Gold disc ✪ Platinum disc (additional platinum units are indicated by a figure following the symbol) ◉ Singles released prior to 1973 that are known to have sold over 1 million copies in the UK

CHUCK BERRY

CHUCK BERRY US singer/guitarist (born Charles Edward Anderson Berry, 18/10/1926, San Jose, CA) who learned the guitar after leaving reform school in 1947. In 1952 he joined The Johnnie Johnson Trio, which became the Chuck Berry Trio. Introduced to Chess Records by Muddy Waters in 1955, he became a major force in music, winning Best New Rhythm & Blues Artist in *Billboard* in 1955. In 1959, after a show in El Paso, he was introduced to an Apache Indian, Janice Norine Escalanti, who was, unknown to Berry, only fourteen years old, working as a waitress and prostitute. Berry offered her a hat-check girl job at his club in St Louis, then fired her, suspecting she was working as a prostitute. She complained to the police, Berry being charged with violating the Mann Act, transporting a girl across state lines for immoral purposes. He was fined $2,000 and jailed for five years, the maximum punishment. When transcripts of the trial were made public, they revealed that the judge George H Moore Jr had made racist remarks against Berry, who was freed pending a retrial. In 1962 he was convicted again and sentenced to three years, of which he served two. He also served time on armed robbery charges and income tax evasion, (the latter one month after performing at the White House for President Jimmy Carter in 1979). He appeared in the 1956 film *Rock Rock Rock*, was inducted into the Rock & Roll Hall of Fame in 1986 and has a star on the Hollywood Walk of Fame.

DATE	POS	WKS	SINGLE TITLE	LABEL & NUMBER
21/06/1957	24	4	SCHOOL DAY Featured in the 1979 film *Rock 'N Roll High School*	Columbia DB 3951
25/04/1958	16	5	SWEET LITTLE SIXTEEN Featured in the 1978 film *American Hot Wax*	London HLM 8585
25/07/1963	38	6	GO GO GO	Pye International 7N 25209
10/10/1963	6	13	**LET IT ROCK/MEMPHIS TENNESSEE**	Pye International 7N 25218
19/12/1963	36	6	RUN RUDOLPH RUN	Pye International 7N 25228
13/02/1964	27	7	NADINE (IS IT YOU)	Pye International 7N 25236
07/05/1964	3	12	**NO PARTICULAR PLACE TO GO**	Pye International 7N 25242
20/08/1964	23	8	YOU NEVER CAN TELL Featured in the 1994 film *Pulp Fiction*	Pye International 7N 25257
14/01/1965	26	6	PROMISED LAND	Pye International 7N 25285
28/10/1972	❶4	17	**MY DING-A-LING** ▲2 Features backing by two members of the Average White Band. Originally recorded by Berry in 1966 as *My Tambourine*	Chess 6145 019
03/02/1973	18	7	REELIN' AND ROCKIN' This and above single recorded live in Manchester, England	Chess 6145 020

DAVE BERRY

DAVE BERRY UK singer (born Dave Holgate Grundy, 6/2/1941, Sheffield) who named himself after Chuck Berry, his debut hit a cover version of a Berry number (swiftly issued at the same time). The Cruisers comprised Frank Miles (guitar), Alan Taylor (rhythm guitar), John Fleet (bass) and Kenny Slade (drums).

DATE	POS	WKS	SINGLE TITLE	LABEL & NUMBER
19/09/1963	19	13	MEMPHIS TENNESSEE	Decca F 11734
09/01/1964	37	9	MY BABY LEFT ME This and above single credited to **DAVE BERRY AND THE CRUISERS**	Decca F 11803
30/04/1964	24	6	BABY IT'S YOU	Decca F 11876
06/08/1964	5	12	**THE CRYING GAME**	Decca F 11937
26/11/1964	41	2	ONE HEART BETWEEN TWO	Decca F 12020
25/03/1965	5	12	**LITTLE THINGS**	Decca F 12103
22/07/1965	37	6	THIS STRANGE EFFECT	Decca F 12188
30/06/1966	5	16	**MAMA**	Decca F 12435

MIKE BERRY

MIKE BERRY UK singer (born Michael Bourne, 24/9/1942, London) whose debut record was a cover of the Shirelles' *Will You Love Me Tomorrow*. The Outlaws backed his early hits, a group that included Ritchie Blackmore and Chas Hodges, Hodges producing his comeback hit in 1980. After his recording career he turned to acting, regular TV appearances including *Are You Being Served*.

DATE	POS	WKS	BPI	SINGLE TITLE	LABEL & NUMBER
12/10/1961	24	6		TRIBUTE TO BUDDY HOLLY	HMV POP 912
03/01/1963	6	12		**DON'T YOU THINK IT'S TIME**	HMV POP 1105
11/04/1963	34	7		MY LITTLE BABY This and above single credited to **MIKE BERRY WITH THE OUTLAWS**	HMV POP 1142
02/08/1980	9	12	○	**THE SUNSHINE OF YOUR SMILE**	Polydor 2059 261
29/11/1980	37	9		IF I COULD ONLY MAKE YOU CARE	Polydor POSP 202
05/09/1981	55	5		MEMORIES	Polydor POSP 287

NICK BERRY

NICK BERRY UK actor (born 16/5/1963, Woodford) who played Simon Wicks in the hit TV soap *Eastenders*, and later PC Nick Rowan in *Heartbeat*. He began his singing career in 1981 with *Diana*, which failed to chart.

DATE	POS	WKS	SINGLE TITLE	LABEL & NUMBER
04/10/1986	❶3	13	**EVERY LOSER WINS** Made the record leap within the charts by a single that eventually went on to make #1 – it rose 62 places from 66 to 4 on 11/10/1986, the following week hitting #1	BBC RESL 204
13/06/1992	2	8	**HEARTBEAT** Remake of Buddy Holly's 1959 hit and theme to the TV series of the same name	Columbia 6581517
31/10/1992	47	3	LONG LIVE LOVE	Columbia 6587597

ADELE BERTI – see JELLYBEAN

BEST COMPANY

BEST COMPANY UK vocal duo.

DATE	POS	WKS	SINGLE TITLE	LABEL & NUMBER
27/03/1993	65	1	DON'T YOU FORGET ABOUT ME	ZYX 69468

BEST SHOT

BEST SHOT UK rap group formed by Winston Riley, Terry Cooer, Jason Camilleri, Richard Vatsallo, Sanjua Chadhee and Martin Cole.

DATE	POS	WKS	SINGLE TITLE	LABEL & NUMBER
05/02/1994	64	2	UNITED COLOURS	East West YZ 795CD

BETA BAND

BETA BAND UK rock group formed by Stephen Mason (guitar/vocals), Richard Greentree (bass), Robin Jones (drums) and John McLean (decks/samples). The group disbanded in 2004.

DATE	POS	WKS	SINGLE TITLE	LABEL & NUMBER
14/07/2001	30	2	BROKE/WON	Regal Recordings REG 60CD
27/10/2001	57	1	HUMAN BEING Contains a sample of Carole King's *It's Too Late*	Regal Recordings REG 65CD
16/02/2002	42	1	SQUARES Contains a sample of Gunther Kallman Choir's *Daydream*	Regal Recordings REG 69CD
24/04/2004	31	2	ASSESSMENT	Regal Recordings REG 102CDS
24/07/2004	54	1	OUT-SIDE	Regal Recordings REG 110CDS

❶9 Number of weeks single topped the UK chart ↑ Entered the UK chart at #1 ▲9 Number of weeks single topped the US chart

75

MARTIN BETTINGHAUS – see TIMO MAAS

BEVERLEY SISTERS
UK family vocal group formed by Joy (born 1929) and twins Teddie and Babs Beverley (born 1932). They began their career in the early 1950s, touring the US in 1953. Joy was married to England football captain Billy Wright.

27/11/1953	6	5	**I SAW MOMMY KISSING SANTA CLAUS**	Philips PB 188
13/04/1956	23	4	WILLIE CAN	Decca F 10705
01/02/1957	24	2	I DREAMED	Decca F 10832
13/02/1959	6	13	**LITTLE DRUMMER BOY**	Decca F 11107
20/11/1959	14	7	LITTLE DONKEY	Decca F 11172
23/06/1960	29	3	GREEN FIELDS	Columbia DB 4444

FRANKIE BEVERLY – see MAZE FEATURING FRANKIE BEVERLY

BEYONCÉ – see BEYONCÉ KNOWLES

BEYOND
UK group formed in Derby in 1988 by John Whitby (vocals), Andy Gatford (guitar), Jim Kersey (bass) and Neil Cooper (drums).

21/09/1991	68	1	RAGING EP Tracks on EP: *Great Indifference, Nail* and *Eve Of My Release*	Harvest HARS 530

BG THE PRINCE OF RAP
US rapper (born Bernard Greene, Washington DC) who moved to Germany with the armed services, launching a rapping career in Frankfurt.

18/01/1992	71	2	TAKE CONTROL OF THE PARTY	Columbia 6576330

BHANGRA KNIGHTS VERSUS HUSAN
UK remixing duo Jules Spinner and Jack Berry (Bhangra Knights) with Dutch production duo Niels Zuiderhoek and Jeroen Den Hengst (Husan), and Indian singer Raja Mustaq. Their debut hit was originally recorded by Husan for a Peugeot cars advertisement, credited to Bald N Spikey, before being remixed by Bhangra Knights.

17/05/2003	7	7	**HUSAN** Featured in the 2002 film *Bend It Like Beckham*	Positiva CDTIV 188

BHOYS OF PARADISE
UK group formed by Simple Minds, Shane MacGowan and the Kick Horns, John McLaughlin and former Celtic footballer Jimmy 'Jinky' Johnstone.

03/07/2004	46	2	DIRTY OLD TOWN/THE ROAD TO PARADISE A-side performed by Simple Minds and Jimmy Johnstone, the B-side by Shane MacGowan and The Kick Horns. The single also featured a third track in *Lord Of The Wing* performed by John McLaughlin as a tribute to Jimmy Johnstone. The single was released to raise funds for the Motor Neurone Disease Tribute Fund, Radio Lollipop and the Children's Hospice Association	Lord Of The Wing LWSP7

BIBLE
UK rock group formed in Cambridge by Boo Hewerdine (guitar/vocals), Tony Shepherd (keyboards), Leroy Lendor (bass) and Dave Larcombe (drums) who released their debut single in 1986, Hewerdine later working with US singer/songwriter Darden Smith.

20/05/1989	51	4	GRACELAND	Chrysalis BIB 4
26/08/1989	54	4	HONEY BE GOOD	Chrysalis BIB 5

BIBLE OF DREAMS – see JOHNNY PANIC AND THE BIBLE OF DREAMS

BIDDU ORCHESTRA
Indian producer (born Biddu Appaiah, Bangalore) who moved to the UK and became a baker, eventually songwriting and producing at Beacon Records. Later freelance work included The Real Thing, Jimmy James And The Vagabonds and Tina Charles.

02/08/1975	14	8	SUMMER OF '42	Epic EPC 3318
17/04/1976	39	4	RAIN FOREST	Epic EPC 4084
11/02/1978	41	1	JOURNEY TO THE MOON	Epic EPC 5910

BIFFY CLYRO
UK group formed in Kilmarnock by Simon Neil (guitar/vocals), James Johnston (bass) and Ben Johnston (drums).

16/02/2002	61	1	57	Beggars Banquet BBQ 358CD
05/04/2003	46	1	THE IDEAL HEIGHT	Beggars Banquet BBQ 365CD
07/06/2003	26	2	QUESTIONS AND ANSWERS	Beggars Banquet BBQ 368CD
21/08/2004	21	3	GLITTER AND TRAUMA	Beggars Banquet BBQ 377CD
02/10/2004	24	2	MY RECOVERY INJECTION	Beggars Banquet BBQ 379CD

BIG APPLE BAND – see WALTER MURPHY AND THE BIG APPLE BAND

BIG AUDIO DYNAMITE
UK rock group formed by Mick Jones (born 26/6/1955, Brixton, London, guitar/vocals) after he left The Clash, featuring Don Letts (effects/vocals), Dan Donovan (keyboards), Leo Williams (bass) and Greg Roberts (drums). Jones reassembled the group in 1990 (as BAD II) with Nick Hawkins (born 3/2/1965, Luton, guitar), Gary Stonedage (born 24/11/1962, Southampton, bass) and Chris Kavanagh (born 4/6/1964, Woolwich, London, drums), later adding DJ Zonka (born Michael Custance, 4/7/1962 London).

22/03/1986	11	9	E = MC² Contains a sample of the Mick Jagger 1970 film *Performance*	CBS A 6963
07/06/1986	29	5	MEDICINE SHOW Contains samples of Clint Eastwood's dialogue from the 1964 film *A Fistful Of Dollars*	CBS 7181
18/10/1986	51	3	C'MON EVERY BEATBOX	CBS 6501477
21/02/1987	49	5	V THIRTEEN	CBS BAAD 2
28/05/1988	51	3	JUST PLAY MUSIC	CBS BAAD 4
12/11/1994	68	2	LOOKING FOR A SONG	Columbia 6610182

○ Silver disc ● Gold disc ✪ Platinum disc (additional platinum units are indicated by a figure following the symbol) ◉ Singles released prior to 1973 that are known to have sold over 1 million copies in the UK

BIG BAD HORNS – see LITTLE ANGELS

BIG BAM BOO UK/Canadian duo Simon Tedd and Shark who first met at a Nashville bus station, linking up a year later in London.

28/01/1989.....61......2...... SHOOTING FROM MY HEART .... MCA 1281

BIG BANG THEORY UK producer Seamus Haji.

02/03/2002.....51......1...... GOD'S CHILD .... Defected DFECT 45CDS

BIG BASS VS MICHELLE NARINE Canadian production group and singer.

02/09/2000.....67......1...... WHAT YOU DO .... Stonebridge/Edel 0110965 ERE

BIG BEN UK clock. 'Big Ben' is actually the fourteen-ton bell housed in the clock tower of the Palace of Westminster, named after Sir Benjamin Hall, the commissioner of the works when the clock was installed in 1829. The chimes were first broadcast in 1923.

01/01/2000.....53......2...... MILLENNIUM CHIMES .... London BIGONE 2000

BIG BEN BANJO BAND UK instrumental group assembled by producer Norrie Paramour, whose style borrowed heavily from that of Winifred Atwell: a collection of popular oldies put together in a medley, with the banjo substituting for Atwell's piano.

10/12/1954.....6......4...... **LET'S GET TOGETHER NO. 1** Medley of *I'm Just Wild About Harry, April Showers, Rock-A-Bye Your Baby, Swanee, Darktown Strutters Ball, For Me And My Girl, Oh You Beautiful Doll* and *Yes Sir That's My Baby* .... Columbia DB 3549

30/12/1955.....18......2...... LET'S GET TOGETHER AGAIN Medley of *I'm Looking Over A Four-Leafed Clover, By The Light Of The Silvery Moon, Oh Susannah, Baby Face, I'm Sitting On Top Of The World, My Mammy, Dixie's Land* and *Margie* .... Columbia DB 3676

BIG BOI – see KILLER MIKE

BIG BOPPER US singer (born Jiles Perry Richardson, 24/10/1930, Sabine Pass, TX) who called himself Big Bopper (reflecting his size) working as a DJ with KTRM Radio in Beaumont, TX. An amateur songwriter, he recorded some of his songs and went solo in 1958. Killed in the plane crash – later reported to be due to pilot error – that claimed the lives of Buddy Holly and Ritchie Valens on 2/2/1959, he'd swapped seats with Holly's bass guitarist Waylon Jennings.

26/12/1958.....12......8...... CHANTILLY LACE Originally the B-side to a novelty parody, *The Purple People Eater Meets The Witch Doctor*, based on hits by Sheb Wooley and David Seville. Featured in the films *American Graffiti* (1973), *The Buddy Holly Story* (1978) and *La Bamba* (1987) .... Mercury AMT 1002

BIG BOSS STYLUS PRESENTS RED VENOM UK production duo Martin Neary and Jason Barron with rapper Mike Neilson.

31/07/1999.....72......1...... LET'S GET IT ON .... All Around The World CDGLOBE 195

BIG BROVAZ UK vocal group formed in London by Cherise Roberts (born 29/12/1982, London), Dion Howell (21 at the time of their debut hit) and Nadia (born 28/1/1980, Reading) with members Flawless (born Tayo Aisida, 23/5/1981, Nigeria), J-Rock (born John Paul Horsley, 21/8/1979, Washington DC) and Skillz (born Abdul Bello, 23/11/1978, Kingston, Jamaica). They won the 2003 MOBO Awards for Best Newcomer and Best UK Act (won jointly with Lisa Maffia). Flawless was sacked in March 2004 after being caught carrying cannabis through customs at an American airport.

26/10/2002.....3......18......O **NU FLOW** Featured in the 2004 film *Scooby Doo 2: Monsters Unleashed* .... Epic 6730282
15/02/2003.....7......9...... **OK** .... Epic 6735212
17/05/2003.....2......11...... **FAVOURITE THINGS** Based on the Rodgers and Hammerstein song *My Favourite Things* .... Epic 6738075
13/09/2003.....4......12...... **BABY BOY** .... Epic 6743092
20/12/2003.....15......7...... AIN'T WHAT YOU DO .... Epic 6745105
17/04/2004.....17......4...... WE WANNA THANK YOU (THE THINGS YOU DO) Featured in the 2004 film *Scooby Doo 2: Monsters Unleashed* .... Epic 6748602
09/10/2004.....15......4...... YOURS FATALLY .... Epic 6753542

BIG C – see ALEX WHITCOMBE AND BIG C

BIG COUNTRY UK group formed in Dunfermline by ex-Skids Stuart Adamson (born 11/4/1958, Manchester, guitar/synthesiser/vocals), Bruce Watson (born 11/3/1961, Ontario, Canada, guitar), Tony Butler (born 3/2/1957, London, bass) and Mark Brzezicki (born 21/6/1957, Slough, drums). Brzezicki left in 1991, rejoining two years later. They disbanded in 2000, Adamson becoming a country singer/songwriter, but on 17/12/2001 he was found hanged in a hotel room in Honolulu, Hawaii, having been dead for a couple of days. Depressed after his second marriage collapsed, he had been declared missing from Nashville by his wife on 26/11/2001, failing to turn up after arranging to meet her.

26/02/1983.....10......12...... **FIELDS OF FIRE (400 MILES)** .... Mercury COUNT 2
28/05/1983.....17......7...... IN A BIG COUNTRY .... Mercury COUNT 3
03/09/1983.....9......9...... **CHANCE** .... Mercury COUNT 4
21/01/1984.....8......8...... **WONDERLAND** .... Mercury COUNT 5
29/09/1984.....17......6...... EAST OF EDEN .... Mercury MER 175
01/12/1984.....29......7...... WHERE THE ROSE IS SOWN .... Mercury MER 185
19/01/1985.....26......4...... JUST A SHADOW .... Mercury BCO 8
12/04/1986.....7......8...... **LOOK AWAY** .... Mercury BIGC 1
21/06/1986.....28......4...... THE TEACHER .... Mercury BIGC 2
20/09/1986.....19......6...... ONE GREAT THING .... Mercury BIGC 3
29/11/1986.....55......2...... HOLD THE HEART .... Mercury BIGC 4

❶⁹ Number of weeks single topped the UK chart ↑ Entered the UK chart at #1 ▲⁹ Number of weeks single topped the US chart

77

DATE	POS	WKS	BPI	SINGLE TITLE	LABEL & NUMBER
20/08/1988	16	6		KING OF EMOTION	Mercury BIGC 5
05/11/1988	47	4		BROKEN HEART (THIRTEEN VALLEYS)	Mercury BIGC 6
04/02/1989	39	3		PEACE IN OUR TIME	Mercury BIGC 7
12/05/1990	41	3		SAVE ME	Mercury BIGC 8
21/07/1990	50	2		HEART OF THE WORLD	Mercury BIGC 9
31/08/1991	37	2		REPUBLICAN PARTY REPTILE (EP) Tracks on EP: *Republican Party Reptile, Comes A Time* and *You And Me And The Truth*	Vertigo BIC 1
19/10/1991	72	1		BEAUTIFUL PEOPLE	Vertigo BIC 2
13/03/1993	24	3		ALONE	Compulsion CDPULSS 4
01/05/1993	29	3		SHIPS (WHERE WERE YOU)	Compulsion CDPULSS 6
10/06/1995	69	1		I'M NOT ASHAMED	Transatlantic TRAX 1009
09/09/1995	68	1		YOU DREAMER	Transatlantic TRAX 1012
21/08/1999	69	1		FRAGILE THING **BIG COUNTRY FEATURING EDDI READER**	Track 0004A

BIG DADDY US 1980s rock group, who claimed to be the last great unsigned band from the 1950s. According to Mark Kaniger (guitar/vocals), Tom Lee (guitar/vocals), Bob Wayne (keyboards/vocals), Don Raymond (guitar/vocals), John Hatton (bass), Norman A Norman (keyboards), Bob Sandman (reeds) and Damon DeGrignon (drums), their 24-year absence was due to having been kidnapped in Southeast Asia by Laotian guerrillas.

DATE	POS	WKS	BPI	SINGLE TITLE	LABEL & NUMBER
09/03/1985	21	8		DANCING IN THE DARK EP Tracks on EP: *Dancing In The Dark, I Write The Songs, Bette Davis Eyes* and *Eye Of The Tiger*	Making Waves SURF 1033

BIG DADDY KANE US rapper (born Antonio Hardy, 10/9/1969, Brooklyn, NYC). Kane is an acronym for King Asiatic Nobody's Equal.

DATE	POS	WKS	BPI	SINGLE TITLE	LABEL & NUMBER
13/05/1989	52	2		RAP SUMMARY/WRATH OF KANE	Cold Chillin' W 2973
26/08/1989	65	1		SMOOTHER OPERATOR	Cold Chillin' W 2804
13/01/1990	44	3		AIN'T NO STOPPIN' US NOW	Cold Chillin' W 2605

BIG DISH UK group formed in Airdrie in 1983 by Stephen Lindsay (vocals/guitar/keyboards), Brian McFie (guitar), Raymond Docherty (bass) and Ian Ritchie (saxophone); by 1991 the group was a duo of Lindsay and McFie.

DATE	POS	WKS	BPI	SINGLE TITLE	LABEL & NUMBER
12/01/1991	37	5		MISS AMERICA	East West YZ 529

BIG FAMILY – see **JT AND THE BIG FAMILY**

BIG FUN UK vocal group formed by Phil Cheswick (born 12/10/1965, Charlwood), Jason John (born 18/3/1967, Coventry) and Mark Gillespie (born 28/11/1966, Elgin, Scotland).

DATE	POS	WKS	BPI	SINGLE TITLE	LABEL & NUMBER
12/08/1989	4	11		**BLAME IT ON THE BOOGIE**	Jive 217
25/11/1989	8	9		**CAN'T SHAKE THE FEELING**	Jive 234
17/03/1990	21	6		HANDFUL OF PROMISES	Jive 243
23/06/1990	14	6		YOU'VE GOT A FRIEND **BIG FUN AND SONIA FEATURING GARY BARNACLE** Released for Childline charity	Jive CHILD 90
04/08/1990	62	1		HEY THERE LONELY GIRL	Jive 251

BIG MOUNTAIN US reggae group formed in San Diego, CA by Quino (vocals/percussion), Jerome Cruz (guitar/vocals), Manfred Reinke (vocals/keyboards), Gregory Blakney (percussion), Lynn Copeland (bass) and Lance Rhodes (drums).

DATE	POS	WKS	BPI	SINGLE TITLE	LABEL & NUMBER
04/06/1994	2	14	O	**BABY I LOVE YOUR WAY** Featured in the 1994 film *Reality Bites*	RCA 74321198062
24/09/1994	51	1		SWEET SENSUAL LOVE	Giant 74321234642

BIG PUN – see **JENNIFER LOPEZ**

BIG ROLL BAND – see **ZOOT MONEY AND THE BIG ROLL BAND**

BIG RON UK producer Aaron Gilbert. A member of Big Time Charlie, he also records as Jules Verne.

DATE	POS	WKS	BPI	SINGLE TITLE	LABEL & NUMBER
11/03/2000	57	1		LET THE FREAK Contains samples of Dan Hartman's *Relight My Fire* and Sinnamon's *I Need You Now*	48K SPECT 06CDS

BIG ROOM GIRL FEATURING DARRYL PANDY UK production duo formed Robert Chetcutti and Steve McGuinness with Chicago, IL-based singer Darryl Pandy. Pandy had previously worked with Farley 'Jackmaster' Funk, Big Room Girl also recording as the Rhythm Masters.

DATE	POS	WKS	BPI	SINGLE TITLE	LABEL & NUMBER
20/02/1999	40	2		RAISE YOUR HANDS	VC Recordings VCRD 44

BIG SOUND – see **SIMON DUPREE AND THE BIG SOUND**

BIG SOUND AUTHORITY UK group formed by Julie Hadwen (vocals), Tony Burke (guitar/vocals), Michael 'Mace' Garnochan (keyboards), Greg Brown (saxophone), Frank Seago (trombone), Kevin White (trumpet) and Steve Martinez (drums).

DATE	POS	WKS	BPI	SINGLE TITLE	LABEL & NUMBER
19/01/1985	21	9		THIS HOUSE (IS WHERE YOUR LOVE STANDS)	Source BSA 1
08/06/1985	54	3		A BAD TOWN	Source BSA 2

BIG SUPREME UK singer Barry Flynn, who also recorded as Bonk, The Chant Of Barry Flynn and Flynn.

DATE	POS	WKS	BPI	SINGLE TITLE	LABEL & NUMBER
20/09/1986	58	3		DON'T WALK	Polydor POSP 809
14/03/1987	64	2		PLEASE YOURSELF	Polydor POSP 840

O Silver disc ● Gold disc ✪ Platinum disc (additional platinum units are indicated by a figure following the symbol) ◉ Singles released prior to 1973 that are known to have sold over 1 million copies in the UK

BIG THREE
UK group formed in Liverpool by Casey Jones (guitar), Adrian Barber (guitar), John Gustavson (bass) and Johnny Hutchinson (drums) as Cass And The Casanovas. Jones was dropped in 1962 and they became The Big Three (so named because of their height), managed by Brian Epstein. Brian Griffiths replaced Barber the same year, but after brief success they were dropped by Epstein, the group unable to conform to his policy on image. They disbanded in late 1963, Gustavson later joining The Merseybeats and Roxy Music. Hutchinson turned down the chance to replace Pete Best in The Beatles in 1962.

11/04/1963	37	7		SOME OTHER GUY	Decca F 11614
11/07/1963	22	10		BY THE WAY	Decca F 11689

BIG TIGGER – see R KELLY

BIG TIME CHARLIE
UK DJ/production duo Aaron Gilbert and Les Sharma. Soozy Q is a UK singer. Gilbert also records as Jules Verne and Big Ron.

23/10/1999	22	2		ON THE RUN Contains samples of Diana Ross' *Ain't No Mountain High Enough* and Ecstasy, Passion And Pain's *Touch And Go*	Inferno CDFERN 18
18/03/2000	39	2		MR DEVIL BIG TIME CHARLIE FEATURING SOOZY Q Contains a sample of Chic's *My Forbidden Lover*	Inferno CDFERN 24

BIGFELLA FEATURING NOEL McCALLA
UK production duo Nick Woolfson and Dean Ross with singer Noel McCalla. Woolfson was previously a member of Sundance and Shimmon & Woolfson.

17/08/2002	52	1		BEAUTIFUL	NuLife 74321954381

BARRY BIGGS
Jamaican reggae singer (born 1953, St Andrews) who began his professional career in 1968.

28/08/1976	38	5		WORK ALL DAY	Dynamic DYN 101
04/12/1976	3	16	○	SIDESHOW	Dynamic DYN 118
23/04/1977	36	4		YOU'RE MY LIFE	Dynamic DYN 127
09/07/1977	22	8		THREE RING CIRCUS	Dynamic DYN 128
15/12/1979	55	7		WHAT'S YOUR SIGN GIRL	Dynamic DYN 150
20/06/1981	44	6		WIDE AWAKE IN A DREAM	Dynamic DYN 10

RONALD BIGGS – see SEX PISTOLS

IVOR BIGGUN AND THE RED NOSE BURGLARS
UK singer/comedian who appeared on TV's *That's Life* as Doc Cox and provided one of the voices on *Star Trek: Generations*. His debut hit was banned from the radio because of its content.

02/09/1978	22	12		WINKER'S SONG (MISPRINT)	Beggars Banquet BOP 1
12/09/1981	50	3		BRAS ON 45 (FAMILY VERSION)	Beggars Banquet BOP 6

BILBO
UK group formed in 1974 by Colin Chisholm (vocals), Brian Spence (guitar), Gordon McIntosh (guitar), Jimmy Devlin (bass) and Gordon Liddle (drums) as Bilbo Baggins, shortening their name in 1976.

26/08/1978	42	7		SHE'S GONNA WIN	Lightning LIG 548

MR ACKER BILK AND HIS PARAMOUNT JAZZ BAND
UK clarinettist/singer (born Bernard Stanley Bilk, 28/1/1929, Somerset) who took up the clarinet while jailed in an army guardhouse in Egypt in 1947. His band, formed in 1958, was one of the most popular bands of traditional jazz boom of the era. He received an MBE in the 2001 New Year's Honours List.

FOUR HITS and a MISTER ACKER BILK MONO
Stranger on the Shore / summer set / BUONA SERA / That's My Home

22/01/1960	5	20		SUMMER SET	Columbia DB 4382
09/06/1960	50	1		GOODNIGHT SWEET PRINCE	Melodisc MEL 1547
18/08/1960	30	9		WHITE CLIFFS OF DOVER	Columbia DB 4492
08/12/1960	7	18		BUONA SERA	Columbia DB 4544
13/07/1961	7	17		THAT'S MY HOME	Columbia DB 4673
02/11/1961	22	10		STARS AND STRIPES FOREVER/CREOLE JAZZ	Columbia SCD 2155
30/11/1961	2	55	◎	STRANGER ON THE SHORE ▲¹ MR ACKER BILK WITH THE LEON YOUNG STRING CHORALE Originally the title tune to the TV show *Stranger On The Shore*. Featured in the 1984 film *The Flamingo Kid*. One of only two records (Engelbert Humperdinck's *Release Me* is the other) to have spent more than a year on the singles chart in an unbroken run	Columbia DB 4750
15/03/1962	42	2		FRANKIE AND JOHNNY	Columbia DB 4795
26/07/1962	24	9		GOTTA SEE BABY TONIGHT	Columbia SCD 2176
27/09/1962	14	11		LONELY	Columbia DB 4897
24/01/1963	16	9		A TASTE OF HONEY This and above single credited to MR ACKER BILK WITH THE LEON YOUNG STRING CHORALE	Columbia DB 4949
21/08/1976	5	11		ARIA ACKER BILK, HIS CLARINET AND STRINGS	Pye 7N 45607

BILL
UK singer who was first featured on Steve Wright's Radio 1 show.

23/10/1993	73	1		CAR BOOT SALE	Mercury MINCD 1

❶⁹ Number of weeks single topped the UK chart   ↑ Entered the UK chart at #1   ▲⁹ Number of weeks single topped the US chart

79

BILL AND BEN
UK puppet duo that was originally aired on BBC TV during the 1950s and 1960s as part of *Watch With Mother*. It was revived in 2001 with John Thomson and Jimmy Hibbert providing the voices for the two Flowerpot Men.

13/07/2002.....23......4....... FLOBBADANCE .... BBC WMSS 60552

BILLIE – see H20

BILLIE – see BILLIE PIPER

BILLY TALENT
Canadian punk group formed in Streetsville, Ontario by Ben Kowalewicz (vocals), Ian D'Sa (guitar), Jon Gallant (bass) and Aaron Ess (drums) as Pezz, changing their name in 1999.

13/09/2003.....68......1...... TRY HONESTY... Atlantic AT 0160CD
10/04/2004.....61......1...... THE EX... Atlantic AT 0173CD
17/07/2004.....70......1...... RIVER BELOW.. Atlantic AT 0178CD

BIMBO JET
French studio group under songwriter Claude Morgan and singer Laurent Rossi, son of singer Tino Rossi.

26/07/1975.....12......10...... EL BIMBO .... EMI 2317

BINARY FINARY
UK production duo Matt Laws and Ricky Grant.

10/10/1998.....24......3...... 1998... Positiva CDTIV 98
28/08/1999.....11......6...... 1999.. Positiva CDTIV 118

UMBERTO BINDI
Italian singer (born 12/5/1936, Genoa) who died on 21/5/2002 after a long illness.

10/11/1960.....47......1...... IL NOSTRO CONCERTO.. Oriole CD 1577

BINI AND MARTINI
Italian production duo Gianni Bini and Martini. The pair also record as Goodfellas and House Of Glass, while Bini also records as Eclipse.

04/03/2000.....53......1...... HAPPINESS (MY VISION IS CLEAR)................................. Azuli AZNYCDX 113
10/03/2001.....65......1...... BURNING UP.. Azuli AZNY 137

BIOHAZARD
US rock group formed in Brooklyn, NYC in 1988 by Evan Seinfeld (bass/vocals), Billy Graziedi (guitar/vocals), Bobby Hambel (guitar) and Danny Swchuler (drums). Hambel was sacked in 1995 and replaced by Rob Echeverria.

09/07/1994.....47......2...... TALES FROM THE HARD SIDE....................................... Warner Brothers W 0254CD
20/08/1994.....62......2...... HOW IT IS .... Warner Brothers W 0259CD

BIOSPHERE
Norwegian keyboard player Geir Jenssen, previously in Bel Canto.

29/04/1995.....51......2...... NOVELTY WAVES... Apollo 20CDX

BIRDLAND
UK rock group formed by Robert Vincent (vocals), his brother Lee (guitar), Simon Rogers (bass) and Neil Hughes (drums).

01/04/1989.....70......1...... HOLLOW HEART.. Lazy 13
08/07/1989.....70......1...... PARADISE .... Lazy 14
03/02/1990.....32......3...... SLEEP WITH ME .... Lazy 17
22/09/1990.....47......1...... ROCK 'N' ROLL NIGGER.. Lazy 20
02/02/1991.....44......1...... EVERYBODY NEEDS SOMEBODY....................................... Lazy 24

BIRDS
UK group formed in West Drayton in 1964 by Ali McKenzie (vocals), Tony Munroe (guitar/vocals), Ron Wood (born 1/6/1947, Hillingdon, guitar), Kim Gardner (bass/vocals) and Pete McDaniels (drums) as The Thunderbirds, shortening their name to avoid confusion with Chris Farlowe's group. Their new name, however, brought them into confrontation with the US group The Byrds, with The Birds issuing writs in an attempt to get the Americans to change their name, without success. They disbanded in 1966, with Gardner later in Ashton, Gardner & Dyke, and Wood in The Jeff Beck Group, The Faces and The Rolling Stones.

27/05/1965.....45......1...... LEAVING HERE .... Decca F 12140

ZOE BIRKETT
UK singer (born 6/6/1985, Darlington) first known as one of the 10,000 entrants on *Pop Idol*.

25/01/2003.....12......6...... TREAT ME LIKE A LADY 10/Universal 0196832

JANE BIRKIN AND SERGE GAINSBOURG
UK/French vocal duo whose hit was one of the most notorious records ever released. It was written by French singer/songwriter/actor Serge Gainsbourg (born Lucien Ginsburg, 2/4/1928, Paris) who planned to record it with Brigitte Bardot. She thought it too erotic, so he used his actress girlfriend Jane Birkin (born 12/12/1947, London), who had appeared in the 1966 film *Blow Up*. Released on Fontana it was an instant hit, despite being banned by the BBC. With the record at #2, Fontana decided it was too risque for them and handed the licence over to Major Minor, who promptly hit #1. An instrumental version by Sounds Nice also hit the top twenty at the same time (ensuring the BBC had something to play), while a further version, by Judge Dread, was similarly banned. Birkin, previously married to John Barry, still pursues her acting career in France. Gainsbourg died from a heart attack on 2/3/1991.

30/07/1969.....2......11...... **JE T'AIME...MOI NON PLUS** Featured in the 1997 film *The Full Monty*................................. Fontana TF 1042
04/10/1969....●1.....14...... **JE T'AIME...MOI NON PLUS** Re-issue of Fontana TF 1042.................................... Major Minor MM 645
07/12/1974.....31......9...... JE T'AIME...MOI NON PLUS Re-issue of Major Minor MM 645 .... Antic K 11511

BIS
UK rock group formed in Glasgow in 1994 by Manda Rin (keyboards/vocals) and brothers Stephen (aka Sci-Fi Steve, guitar/vocals) and John Disko (guitar/vocals). In 1996 they were the first unsigned band to perform on *Top Of The Pops*.

○ Silver disc ● Gold disc ✪ Platinum disc (additional platinum units are indicated by a figure following the symbol) ◎ Singles released prior to 1973 that are known to have sold over 1 million copies in the UK

DATE	POS	WKS	BPI	SINGLE TITLE	LABEL & NUMBER
30/03/1996	25	2		THE SECRET VAMPIRE SOUNDTRACK EP Tracks on EP: *Kandy Pop, Secret Vampires, Teen-C Power* and *Diska. Kandy Pop* was featured in the 1997 film *Casper – A Spirited Beginning* .... Chemikal Underground CHEM 003CD	
22/06/1996	45	1		BIS VS THE DIY CORPS (EP) Tracks on EP: *This Is Fake DIY, Burn The Suit* and *Dance To The Disco Beat* .... Teen-C SKETCH 001CD	
09/11/1996	54	1		ATOM POWERED ACTION (EP) Tracks on EP: *Starbright Boy, Wee Love, Team Theme* and *Cliquesuck* .... Wiiija WIJ 55CD	
15/03/1997	46	1		SWEET SHOP AVENGERZ .... Wiiija WIJ 67CD	
10/05/1997	64	1		EVERYBODY THINKS THEY'RE GOING TO GET THEIRS .... Wiiija WIJ 69CD	
14/11/1998	37	2		EURODISCO .... Wiiija WIJ 86CD	
27/02/1999	50	1		ACTION AND DRAMA .... Wiiija WIJ 95CD	

BISCUIT BOY UK group formed by Paul Heaton, Martin Slattery, Scott Shields and Damon Butcher. Heaton is also a member of Beautiful South.

DATE	POS	WKS	BPI	SINGLE TITLE	LABEL & NUMBER
15/09/2001	75	1		MITCH .... Mercury 5887592	

ELVIN BISHOP US guitarist (born 21/10/1942, Tulsa, OK) who played lead with the Paul Butterfield Blues Band from 1965 until 1968.

DATE	POS	WKS	BPI	SINGLE TITLE	LABEL & NUMBER
15/05/1976	34	4		FOOLED AROUND AND FELL IN LOVE Features the uncredited lead vocal of Mickey Thomas of Starship. Featured in the films *Summer Of Sam* and *Big Daddy* (both 1999) .... Capricorn 2089 024	

BITI – see **DEGREES OF MOTION FEATURING BITI**

THE BIZ – see **BENNY BENASSI PRESENTS THE BIZ**

BIZARRE INC UK production/instrumental group formed in Stafford by Andrew Meecham (born 1968), Dean Meredith (born 1969) and Carl Turner (born 1969), with Angie Brown and Yvonne Yanni providing the vocals. Altern 8's Mark Archer was also briefly a member.

DATE	POS	WKS	BPI	SINGLE TITLE	LABEL & NUMBER
16/03/1991	43	5		PLAYING WITH KNIVES .... Vinyl Solution STORM 25R	
14/09/1991	13	9		SUCH A FEELING .... Vinyl Solution STORM 32S	
23/11/1991	4	8		**PLAYING WITH KNIVES** Re-issue of Vinyl Solution STORM 25R .... Vinyl Solution STORM 38S	
03/10/1992	3	13	○	**I'M GONNA GET YOU** .... Vinyl Solution STORM 46S	
27/02/1993	19	5		TOOK MY LOVE This and above single credited to **BIZARRE INC FEATURING ANGIE BROWN** .... Vinyl Solution STORM 60CD	
23/03/1996	33	2		KEEP THE MUSIC STRONG .... Some Bizzare MERCD 451	
06/07/1996	21	3		SURPRISE .... Some Bizzare MERCD 462	
14/09/1996	45	2		GET UP SUNSHINE SREET .... Some Bizzare MERCD 471	
13/03/1999	30	2		PLAYING WITH KNIVES (REMIX) .... Vinyl Solution VC 01CD1	

BIZZ NIZZ US/Belgian dance group assembled by producers Jean-Paul De Coster and Phil Wilde, who later masterminded 2 Unlimited.

DATE	POS	WKS	BPI	SINGLE TITLE	LABEL & NUMBER
31/03/1990	7	11		**DON'T MISS THE PARTY LINE** .... Cooltempo COOL 203	

BIZZI UK singer Basil Dixon.

DATE	POS	WKS	BPI	SINGLE TITLE	LABEL & NUMBER
06/12/1997	62	1		BIZZI'S PARTY .... Parlophone Rhythm CDRHYTHM 7	

BJORK Icelandic singer (born Bjork Gudmundsdottir, 21/10/1965, Reykjavik) who fronted the Sugarcubes before going solo in 1993, though she'd recorded her first solo album in 1977 aged eleven. Bjork has won four BRIT Awards: Best International Newcomer in 1994 and and Best International Female in 1994, 1996 and 1998. Also named Best Female at the 1995 MTV Europe Music Awards, she later acted in the film *The Dancer In The Dark* that won the Palme d'Or award at the 2000 Cannes Film Festival and collected a nomination for the Best Soundtrack at the 2001 BRIT Awards.

DATE	POS	WKS	BPI	SINGLE TITLE	LABEL & NUMBER
27/04/1991	42	3		OOOPS **808 STATE FEATURING BJORK** .... ZTT ZANG 19	
19/06/1993	36	2		HUMAN BEHAVIOUR .... One Little Indian 112 TP7CD	
04/09/1993	29	4		VENUS AS A BOY Featured in the 1994 film *Leon* .... One Little Indian 122 TP7CD	
23/10/1993	12	6		PLAY DEAD **BJORK AND DAVID ARNOLD** Featured in the 1993 film *Young Americans* .... Island CID 573	
04/12/1993	17	8		BIG TIME SENSUALITY .... One Little Indian 132 TP7CD	
19/03/1994	13	4		VIOLENTLY HAPPY .... One Little Indian 142 TP7CD	
06/05/1995	10	5		**ARMY OF ME** Featured in the 1995 film *Tank Girl* .... One Little Indian 162 TP7CD	
26/08/1995	23	3		ISOBEL .... One Little Indian 172 TP7CD	
25/11/1995	4	15	●	**IT'S OH SO QUIET** .... One Little Indian 182 TP7CD	
24/02/1996	8	4		**HYPERBALLAD** .... One Little Indian 192 TP7CD	
09/11/1996	13	3		POSSIBLY MAYBE .... One Little Indian 193 TP7CD	
01/03/1997	36	2		I MISS YOU .... One Little Indian 194 TP7CDL	
20/12/1997	21	5		BACHELORETTE .... One Little Indian 212 TP7CD	
17/10/1998	44	1		HUNTER Featured in the 1998 film *The X Files* .... One Little Indian 222 TP7CD	
12/12/1998	33	2		ALARM CALL .... One Little Indian 232 TP7CDL	
19/06/1999	24	2		ALL IS FULL OF LOVE .... One Little Indian 242 TP7CD	
18/08/2001	21	2		HIDDEN PLACE .... One Little Indian 332 TP7CD	
17/11/2001	38	2		PAGAN POETRY .... One Little Indian 352 TP7CD	
23/03/2002	35	1		COCOON .... One Little Indian 322 TP7CD	
07/12/2002	37	2		IT'S IN OUR HANDS .... One Little Indian 366 TP7CD	
30/10/2004	26	2		WHO IS IT .... One Little Indian 446 TP7CD	

❶⁹ Number of weeks single topped the UK chart ↑ Entered the UK chart at #1 ▲⁹ Number of weeks single topped the US chart

81

BJORN AGAIN Australian group formed in Melbourne in 1988 by Agnetha Falstart, Frida Longstokin, Benny Anderwear and Bjorn Volvo-us as a tribute band to Abba. More recently there have been claims of more than one Bjorn Again working the clubs.

24/10/1992	25	3		ERASURE-ISH (A LITTLE RESPECT/STOP!)	M&G MAGS 32
12/12/1992	55	4		SANTA CLAUS IS COMING TO TOWN	M&G MAGS 35
27/11/1993	65	1		FLASHDANCE…WHAT A FEELING	M&G MAGCD 50

BK UK producer Ben Keen. BK and Nick Sentience also recorded as Vinylgroover & The Red Hed.

25/11/2000	57	2		HOOVERS & HORNS FERGIE AND BK	Nukleuz NUKC 0185
08/12/2001	67	1		FLASH BK AND NICK SENTIENCE	Nukleuz NUKPA 0361
26/01/2002	48	1		ERECTION (TAKE IT TO THE TOP) CORTINA FEATURING BK AND MADAM FRICTION	Nukleuz NUKCD 0352
09/02/2002	61	1		FLASH (REMIX) BK AND NICK SENTIENCE	Nukleuz NUKC 0361
07/12/2002	42	2		REVOLUTION	Nukleuz NUKFB 0437
16/08/2003	43	2		KLUB KOLLABORATIONS	Nukleuz 0524 FNUK
17/01/2004	59	2		KLUB KOLLABORATIONS	Nukleuz 0524 FNUK

BLACK UK group that began as a trio of Dave Dickie (keyboards), Jimmy Sangster (bass) and Colin Vearncombe (vocals), but soon trimmed down to Vearncombe recording on his own under the group name.

27/09/1986	72	1		WONDERFUL LIFE	Ugly Man JACK 71
27/06/1987	8	10		SWEETEST SMILE	A&M AM 394
22/08/1987	8	9		WONDERFUL LIFE Re-issue of Ugly Man JACK 71.	A&M AM 402
16/01/1988	38	3		PARADISE	A&M AM 422
24/09/1988	54	4		THE BIG ONE	A&M AM 468
21/01/1989	66	2		NOW YOU'RE GONE	A&M AM 491
04/05/1991	56	2		FEEL LIKE CHANGE	A&M AM 780
15/06/1991	70	1		HERE IT COMES AGAIN	A&M AM 753
05/03/1994	42	3		WONDERFUL LIFE Re-issue of A&M AM 402	Polygram TV 5805552

CILLA BLACK UK singer (born Priscilla Marie Veronica White, 27/5/1943, Liverpool) who worked as a hat-check girl at The Cavern when discovered by Brian Epstein, who decided that as her voice sounded 'black' she should adopt that as her surname. Signed by Parlophone in 1963, and produced by George Martin, she became the most successful female singer of the Mersey boom. Later she became a leading TV presenter, hosting shows such as *Blind Date* and *Surprise Surprise*. She was awarded an OBE in the 1996 New Year's Honours List.

17/10/1963	35	6		LOVE OF THE LOVED Written by Paul McCartney and unrecorded by The Beatles.	Parlophone R 5065
06/02/1964	●³	17		ANYONE WHO HAD A HEART	Parlophone R 5101
07/05/1964	●⁴	17		YOU'RE MY WORLD	Parlophone R 5133
06/08/1964	7	10		IT'S FOR YOU Another previously unrecorded Paul McCartney song, on which he plays the piano.	Parlophone R 5162
14/01/1965	2	9		YOU'VE LOST THAT LOVIN' FEELIN'	Parlophone R 5225
22/04/1965	17	8		I'VE BEEN WRONG BEFORE	Parlophone R 5269
13/01/1966	5	11		LOVE'S JUST A BROKEN HEART	Parlophone R 5395
31/03/1966	9	12		ALFIE This was not the theme to the 1966 film of the same name, which was originally released with an instrumental soundtrack by jazz sax giant Sonny Rollins. Burt Bacharach wrote the song *Alfie* that was inspired by the film, recorded by Cher and added for the film's US release. Cilla Black's *Alfie* is a cover version of that, featuring Bacharach on piano.	Parlophone R 5427
09/06/1966	6	10		DON'T ANSWER ME	Parlophone R 5463
20/10/1966	13	9		A FOOL AM I	Parlophone R 5515
08/06/1967	24	7		WHAT GOOD AM I	Parlophone R 5608
29/11/1967	26	11		I ONLY LIVE TO LOVE YOU	Parlophone R 5652
13/03/1968	8	9		STEP INSIDE LOVE Theme song to Cilla Black's BBC TV series, again penned by Paul McCartney	Parlophone R 5674
12/06/1968	39	3		WHERE IS TOMORROW	Parlophone R 5706
19/02/1969	3	12		SURROUND YOURSELF WITH SORROW	Parlophone R 5759
09/07/1969	7	12		CONVERSATIONS	Parlophone R 5785
13/12/1969	20	9		IF I THOUGHT YOU'D EVER CHANGE YOUR MIND	Parlophone R 5820
20/11/1971	3	14		SOMETHING TELLS ME (SOMETHING IS GONNA HAPPEN TONIGHT) Theme song to her TV series, written by Roger Cook and Roger Greenaway.	Parlophone R 5924
09/02/1974	36	6		BABY WE CAN'T GO WRONG	EMI 2107
18/09/1993	54	1		THROUGH THE YEARS	Columbia 6596982
30/10/1993	75	1		HEART AND SOUL CILLA BLACK AND DUSTY SPRINGFIELD	Columbia 6598562

FRANK BLACK US singer (born Charles Francis Kitteridge III, 1965, Boston, MA) who was originally a singer/guitarist with The Pixies under the name Black Francis. He reverted to Frank Black for his solo career when The Pixies disbanded in 1993.

21/05/1994	53	1		HEADACHE	4AD BAD 4007CD
20/01/1996	37	2		MEN IN BLACK	Dragnet 6627862
27/07/1996	63	1		I DON'T WANT TO HURT YOU (EVERY SINGLE TIME)	Dragnet 6634635

○ Silver disc ● Gold disc ✪ Platinum disc (additional platinum units are indicated by a figure following the symbol) ◉ Singles released prior to 1973 that are known to have sold over 1 million copies in the UK

JEANNE BLACK US singer (born Gloria Jeanne Black, 25/10/1937, Pomona, CA).

23/06/1960.....41......4....... HE'LL HAVE TO STAY Song is an 'answer' record to Jim Reeves' hit *He'll Have To Go* .... Capitol CL 15131

BLACK AND WHITE ARMY UK vocal group comprising 250 fans of Newcastle United Football Club. The hit was released to coincide with an appearance in the FA Cup Final. It was written by Sting (formerly of the Police), who was born in Newcastle.

23/05/1998.....26......2....... BLACK & WHITE ARMY .... Toon 1CD

BLACK BOX Italian group who began life as a studio production, the creation of producer Daniel 'DJ Lelewel' Davoli, keyboard player Mirko Limoni and engineer Valerio Semplici, with the Loleatta Holloway song *Love Sensation*. For TV and video performances, model Katrine Quinol performed the role of lead singer, but an inability to mime the lyrics (she couldn't speak English) gave the game away and legal action was threatened. A session singer then re-recorded *Ride On Time* note for note, later releases invariably featuring ex-Weather Girl Martha Wash.

12/08/1989	❶⁶	22	✪	**RIDE ON TIME**	Deconstruction PB 43055
17/02/1990	4	8		**I DON'T KNOW ANYBODY ELSE**........................	Deconstruction PB 43479
02/06/1990	16	5		EVERYBODY EVERYBODY.....................................	Deconstruction PB 43715
03/11/1990	5	11	◯	**FANTASY**	Deconstruction PB 43895
15/12/1990	12	8		THE TOTAL MIX	Deconstruction PB 44235
06/04/1991	16	8		STRIKE IT UP	Deconstruction PB 44459
14/12/1991	48	4		OPEN YOUR EYES	Deconstruction PB 45053
14/08/1993	39	2		ROCKIN' TO THE MUSIC	Deconstruction 74321158122
24/06/1995	31	2		NOT ANYONE	Mercury MERCD 434
20/04/1996	21	3		I GOT THE VIBRATION/A POSITIVE VIBRATION Contains a sample of Diana Ross' *Love Hangover*	Manifesto MERCD 459
22/02/1997	46	1		NATIVE NEW YORKER This and above single credited to **BLACKBOX**...........	Manifesto FESCD 18

BLACK BOX RECORDER UK group formed by Luke Haines (born 7/10/1967, Walton-on-Thames), Sarah Nixey and John Moore. Haines was earlier in The Servants and The Auteurs, his spell in The Auteurs temporarily halted due to his breaking both ankles after a fall in Spain.

22/04/2000.....20......3....... THE FACTS OF LIFE .... Nude NUD 48CD1
15/07/2000.....53......1....... THE ART OF DRIVING .... Nude NUD 51CD1

BLACK CONNECTION Italian production group formed by Woody Bianchi, Corrado Rizza and Don Scuteri, Rizza previously being in Strings Of Love and Jam Machine.

14/03/1998.....32......2....... GIVE ME RHYTHM .... Xtravaganza 0091465 EXT
24/10/1998.....62......1....... I'M GONNA GET YA BABY .... Xtravaganza 0091615 EXT

BLACK CROWES US metal band formed in Atlanta, GA in 1984 by Chris Robinson (born 20/12/1966, Atlanta, vocals), Rich Robinson (born 24/5/1969, Atlanta, guitar), Jeff Cease (born 24/6/1967, Nashville, TN, guitar), Johnny Colt (born 1/5/1966, Cherry Point, NC, bass) and Steve Gorman (born 17/8/1965, Hopkinsville, KY, drums), and signed to the Def American label in 1989. Cease left in 1991 and was replaced by Marc Ford (born 13/4/1966, Los Angeles, CA). In 1995 they added Eddie Harsch (keyboards) and Chris Trujillo (percussion) to the line-up.

01/09/1990	45	5	HARD TO HANDLE	Def American DEFA 6
12/01/1991	47	3	TWICE AS HARD..	Def American DEFA 7
22/06/1991	70	1	JEALOUS AGAIN/SHE TALKS TO ANGELS	Def American DEFA 8
24/08/1991	39	4	HARD TO HANDLE Re-issue of Def American DEFA 6	Def American DEFA 10
26/10/1991	72	1	SEEING THINGS	Def American DEFA 13
02/05/1992	24	3	REMEDY	Def American DEFA 16
26/09/1992	42	2	STING ME	Def American DEFA 21
28/11/1992	47	3	HOTEL ILLNESS...	Def American DEFA 23
11/02/1995	25	2	HIGH HEAD BLUES/A CONSPIRACY	American Recordings 74321258492
22/07/1995	34	2	WISER TIME...	American Recordings 74321298272
27/07/1996	51	1	ONE MIRROR TO MANY.......................................	American Recordings 74321398572
07/11/1998	55	1	KICKING MY HEART AROUND	American Recordings 6666665

BLACK DIAMOND US singer Charles Diamond.

17/09/1994.....56......1....... LET ME BE .... Systematic SYSCD 1

BLACK DOG FEATURING OFRA HAZA UK instrumentalist/producer Ken Downie with Israeli singer Ofra Haza (born 19/11/1959, Hatikva). Ofra died from influenza and pneumonia brought on by AIDS on 23/2/2000.

03/04/1999.....65......1....... BABYLON .... warner.esp WESP 006 CD1

BLACK DUCK UK rapper Blair MacKichan (born 1970, London) who also recorded as Blair.

17/12/1994.....33......5....... WHIGGLE IN LINE Based on Whigfield's *Saturday Night* .... Flying South CDDUCK 1

BLACK EYED PEAS US hip hop trio formed in Los Angeles, CA by Will I Am (born William Adams, 15/3/1975), Apl de Ap (born Alan Ap Pineda, 28/11/1974) and Taboo (born Jamie Gomez, 14/7/1975). They later added singer Fergie (Stacey Ferguson) to the line-up. They were named Best Pop Act at the 2004 MTV Europe Music Awards.

10/10/1998.....53......1....... JOINTS & JAMS .... Interscope IND 95604
12/05/2001.....31......3....... REQUEST & LINE **BLACK EYED PEAS FEATURING MACY GRAY** Contains a sample of Paulinho Da Costa's *Love You Till The End Of Time* .... Interscope 4975032

13/09/2003	**❶**[6]	19	✪	WHERE IS THE LOVE ↑ Features the uncredited contribution of Justin Timberlake on vocals	A&M 9810996
13/12/2003	2	12	○	SHUT UP	A&M 9814501
20/03/2004	6	10		HEY MAMA Featured in the 2004 film *Garfield*	A&M 9861976
10/07/2004	11	10		LET'S GET IT STARTED	A&M 9863032

BLACK GORILLA UK pop group whose follow-up was *Bamboo Child*.

| 27/08/1977 | 29 | 6 | | GIMME DAT BANANA | Response SR 502 |

BLACK GRAPE UK group formed by ex-Happy Mondays Shaun Ryder (born 23/8/1962, Little Hulton, vocals), Mark 'Bez' Berry (born 18/4/1964, Manchester, vibes), Paul 'Kermit' Leveridge (born 10/11/1969, Manchester, vocals), Ged Lynch (born 19/7/1968, Oswaldtwistle, drums), Danny Saber (born 22/12/1966, New York, bass) and Paul 'Wags' Wagstaff (born 28/12/1964, Stockport, guitar). By the end of 1997 the group comprised Ryder and Saber. Joe Strummer (born John Mellors, 21/8/1952, Ankara, Turkey) was earlier in The Clash. Keith Allen is in Fat Les.

10/06/1995	9	5		REVEREND BLACK GRAPE	Radioactive RAXTD 16
05/08/1995	8	4		IN THE NAME OF THE FATHER	Radioactive RAXTD 19
02/12/1995	17	5		KELLY'S HEROES	Radioactive RAXDT 22
25/05/1996	10	3		FAT NECK	Radioactive RAXTD 24
29/06/1996	6	4		ENGLAND'S IRIE BLACK GRAPE FEATURING JOE STRUMMER AND KEITH ALLEN	Radioactive RAXTD 25
01/11/1997	24	3		GET HIGHER	Radioactive RAXTD 32
07/03/1998	46	1		MARBLES	Radioactive RAXTD 33

BLACK KEYS US duo formed in Akron, OH in 2001 by Dan Auerbach (guitar/vocals) and Patrick Carney (drums).

| 11/09/2004 | 66 | 1 | | 10AM AUTOMATIC | Epitah 11732 |
| 11/12/2004 | 62 | 1 | | TILL I GET MY WAY/GIRL IS ON MY MIND | Fat Possum 11832 |

BLACK LACE UK pop group formed in 1979 by Alan Barton (born 16/9/1953, Barnsley) and Colin Routh to represent the UK in the Eurovision Song Contest (their record *Mary Ann* finished seventh). They re-formed in 1983 with Dean Michael replacing Routh. Barton later joined Smokie and was killed in a car crash on 23/3/1995.

31/03/1979	42	4		MARY ANN	EMI 2919
24/09/1983	9	18	○	SUPERMAN (GIOCA JOUER)	Flair FLA 105
30/06/1984	2	30	●	AGADOO Originally a French record written seven years previously	Flair FLA 107
24/11/1984	10	9		DO THE CONGA	Flair FLA 108
01/06/1985	42	5		EL VINO COLLAPSO	Flair LACE 1
07/09/1985	49	4		I SPEAKA DA LINGO	Flair LACE 2
07/12/1985	31	6		HOKEY COKEY	Flair LACE 3
20/09/1986	63	3		WIG WAM BAM	Flair LACE 5
26/08/1989	52	3		I AM THE MUSIC MAN	Flair LACE 10
22/08/1998	64	1		AGADOO (RE-RECORDING)	Now CDWAG 260

BLACK LEGEND Italian dance group formed by J-Reverse and Ferrari, featuring the vocals of Elroy 'Spoon Face' Powell. Their debut single was re-recorded after permission for a sample by Barry White was refused. White's original version charted on import at #52.

20/05/2000	52	5		YOU SEE THE TROUBLE WITH ME (IMPORT)	Rise RISECD 072
24/06/2000	**❶**[1]	15	○	YOU SEE THE TROUBLE WITH ME ↑	Eternal WEA 282CD
04/08/2001	37	2		SOMEBODY SHORTIE VS BLACK LEGEND Contains a sample of First Choice's *Dr Love*	WEA 328CDX

BLACK MACHINE French/Nigerian vocal/instrumental duo Giuseppe 'Pippo' Landro and Mario Percali.

| 09/04/1994 | 17 | 5 | | HOW GEE | London LONCD 348 |

BLACK MAGIC US producer Louis Burns who also records as Lil' Louis.

| 01/06/1996 | 41 | 2 | | FREEDOM (MAKE IT FUNKY) | Positiva CDTIV 51 |

BLACK REBEL MOTORCYCLE CLUB US rock group formed in San Francisco, CA in 1998 by Robert Turner (guitar/bass/vocals), Peter Hayes (guitar/bass/vocals) and Nick Jago (drums) as The Elements, changing their name soon after.

02/02/2002	37	2		LOVE BURNS	Virgin VUSCD 234
01/06/2002	27	2		SPREAD YOUR LOVE	Virgin VUSCD 245
28/09/2002	46	2		WHATEVER HAPPENED TO MY ROCK AND ROLL	Virgin VUSCD 257
30/08/2003	19	3		STOP	Virgin VUSCD 273
29/11/2003	45	1		WE'RE ALL IN LOVE	Virgin VUSCDX 279

BLACK RIOT US remixer/producer Todd Terry (born 18/4/1967, Brooklyn, NYC) who mixed hits by Everything But The Girl, Brownstone, 3T and Jimmy Somerville among others, before going solo, also recording as Swan Lake, Royal House and Gypsymen.

| 03/12/1988 | 68 | 3 | | WARLOCK/A DAY IN THE LIFE | Champion CHAMP 75 |

BLACK ROB US rapper (born Robert Ross, 1970, Harlem, NYC).

| 12/08/2000 | 44 | 2 | | WHOA | Puff Daddy 74321782732 |
| 06/10/2001 | 13 | 6 | | BAD BOY FOR LIFE P DIDDY FEATURING BLACK ROB AND MARK CURRY | Arista 74321889982 |

BLACK SABBATH UK rock group formed in Birmingham in 1967 as Polka Tulk, soon changing their name to Earth. Named

○ Silver disc ● Gold disc ✪ Platinum disc (additional platinum units are indicated by a figure following the symbol) ◎ Singles released prior to 1973 that are known to have sold over 1 million copies in the UK

Black Sabbath after an early Polka Tulk song in 1969, they were John 'Ozzy' Osbourne (born 3/12/1948, Birmingham, vocals), Tony Iommi (born 19/2/1948, Birmingham, guitar), Terry 'Geezer' Butler (born 17/7/1949, Birmingham, bass) and Bill Ward (born 5/5/1948, Birmingham, drums). They were early pioneers of metal music, especially in the US, where they were extremely popular. Osbourne left in 1979 and was replaced by Ronnie James Dio (born 10/7/1949, New Hampshire); Ward left the following year and was replaced by Vincent Appice. The group disbanded in 1983. The original line-up re-formed in 1985 for Live Aid, and the group won the 1999 Grammy Award for Best Metal Performance for *Iron Man*.

29/08/1970	4	18		**PARANOID** Featured in the 1993 film *Dazed And Confused*	Vertigo 6059 010
03/06/1978	21	8		NEVER SAY DIE	Vertigo SAB 001
14/10/1978	33	4		HARD ROAD	Vertigo SAB 002
05/07/1980	22	9		NEON KNIGHTS	Vertigo SAB 3
16/08/1980	14	12		PARANOID Re-issue of Vertigo 6059 010	Nems BSS 101
06/12/1980	41	7		DIE YOUNG	Vertigo SAB 4
07/11/1981	46	4		MOB RULES	Vertigo SAB 5
13/02/1982	37	5		TURN UP THE NIGHT	Vertigo SAB 6
15/04/1989	62	1		HEADLESS CROSS	IRS EIRS 107
13/06/1992	33	2		TV CRIMES	IRS EIRSP 178

BLACK SHEEP US rap duo from The Bronx, NYC comprising Andre 'Dres' Titus and William 'Mista Lawnge' McLean.

| 19/11/1994 | 60 | 1 | | WITHOUT A DOUBT | Mercury MERCD 417 |

BLACK SLATE UK/Jamaican reggae group formed in London in 1974 by Keith Drummond (vocals), Cledwyn Rogers (guitar), Chris Hanson (guitar), Elroy Bailey (bass), Anthony Brightly (keyboards) and Desmond Mahoney (drums).

| 20/09/1980 | 9 | 9 | | **AMIGO** | Ensign ENY 42 |
| 06/12/1980 | 51 | 6 | | BOOM BOOM | Ensign ENY 47 |

BLACK UHURU Jamaican reggae group formed in 1974 by Garth Dennis, Derrick 'Ducky' Simpson and Don McCarlos. Dennis and McCarlos left soon after and were replaced by Michael Rose and Errol Nelson. Puma Jones replaced Nelson in 1977, Rose leaving in the mid-1980s and being replaced by Junior Reid. By the early 1990s the original line-up of Dennis, Simpson and Carlos re-formed (Don having dropped the Mc part of his name). Jones died from cancer on 28/1/1990. They won the 1984 Grammy Award for Best Reggae Recording for *Anthem*.

| 08/09/1984 | 56 | 6 | | WHAT IS LIFE? | Island IS 150 |
| 31/05/1986 | 62 | 3 | | THE GREAT TRAIN ROBBERY | Real Authentic Sound RAS 7018 |

BAND OF THE BLACK WATCH UK bagpipe band that later recorded *Highland Hustle* aimed at the disco market. John Carter, who also worked on more mainstream pop material by First Class and the Flowerpot Men, produced the 'group'. The band, officially formed in 1739 and consisting of 80 bagpipers, played at the funeral of US President John F Kennedy.

| 30/08/1975 | 8 | 14 | | **SCOTCH ON THE ROCKS** | Spark SRL 1128 |
| 13/12/1975 | 37 | 8 | | DANCE OF THE CUCKOOS (THE LAUREL AND HARDY THEME) | Spark SRL 1135 |

TONY BLACKBURN UK radio DJ (born Kenneth Blackburn, 29/1/1943, Guildford) who began his career with pirate stations and the fledgling Radio 1 (where he played the first record aired by the station in 1967). He made his first record in 1965 for Fontana.

| 24/01/1968 | 31 | 4 | | SO MUCH LOVE | MGM 1375 |
| 26/03/1969 | 42 | 3 | | IT'S ONLY LOVE **TONY BLACKBURN AND THE MAJORITY** | MGM 1467 |

BLACKBYRDS US jazz fusion group formed by Allan Barnes (saxophone), Kevin Toney (keyboards), Barney Perry (guitar), Joe Hall (bass), Keith Killgo (drums) and Perk Jacobs (percussion) under trumpet star Donald Byrd, whose most popular album at that time was called *Blackbyrd* and consisted of students of his at Howard University, Washington DC.

| 31/05/1975 | 23 | 6 | | WALKING IN RHYTHM | Fantasy FTC 114 |

BLACKFOOT US rock group formed in Jacksonville, FL in 1971 by ex-Lynyrd Skynyrd Rick Medlocke (guitar/vocals), Charlie Hargrett (guitar), Greg Walker (bass) and Jackson Spires (drums). They disbanded in 1984 following the release of *Vertical Smiles* but re-formed in 1989 with Medlocke, Neal Casal (guitar), Rikki Mayer (bass) and Gunner Ross (drums). By 1994 the line-up consisted of Medlocke, Mark Woerpel (guitar/vocals), Tim Stunson (bass) and Benny Rappa (drums); Rappa was replaced by Stet Howland during tours.

| 06/03/1982 | 43 | 4 | | DRY COUNTY | Atco K 11686 |
| 18/06/1983 | 66 | 1 | | SEND ME AN ANGEL | Atco B 9880 |

J BLACKFOOT US singer (born John Colbert, 20/11/1946, Greenville, MS) who was lead singer with The Soul Children before going solo.

| 17/03/1984 | 48 | 4 | | TAXI | Allegiance ALES 2 |

BLACKFOOT SUE UK rock band formed in 1966 by Dave Farmer (born 3/2/1952, drums), his twin brother Tom (bass/keyboards/vocals), Eddie Galga (born 9/4/1951, guitar/keyboards) and Alan Jones (born 1/5/1950, guitar/vocals).

| 12/08/1972 | 4 | 10 | | **STANDING IN THE ROAD** | Jam 13 |
| 16/12/1972 | 36 | 5 | | SING DON'T SPEAK | Jam 29 |

BLACKGIRL US vocal trio Nycolia 'Tye-V' Turman, Pamela Copeland and Rochelle Stuart who are often accompanied by singer Sam Salter.

| 16/07/1994 | 23 | 3 | | 90S GIRL Features the uncredited contribution of Menton 'Peanut' Smith | RCA 74321217882 |

●[9] Number of weeks single topped the UK chart ↑ Entered the UK chart at #1 ▲[9] Number of weeks single topped the US chart

85

BLACKHEARTS – see JOAN JETT AND THE BLACKHEARTS

HONOR BLACKMAN – see PATRICK MacNEE AND HONOR BLACKMAN

BLACKNUSS Swedish vocal/instrumental group formed by Christian Falk and Martin Jonsson, whose debut hit also featured Stephen Simmonds, ADL, Richie Pasta and Muladoe.

| 28/06/1997 | 56 | 1 | | DINAH | Arista 74321479762 |

BLACKOUT UK production duo Marc Dillon and Pat Dickins.

| 27/03/1999 | 46 | 1 | | GOTTA HAVE HOPE | Multiply CDMULTY 47 |

BLACKOUT UK rap group formed by Merlin and Vanya Raeburn.

| 31/03/2001 | 19 | 7 | | MR DJ | Independiente ISOM 48MS |
| 06/10/2001 | 67 | 1 | | GET UP | Independiente ISOM 52MS |

BILL BLACK'S COMBO US bass player (born 17/9/1926, Memphis, TN) who worked as a session musician in Memphis playing on Elvis Presley's earliest Sun releases, as well as touring and recording as part of Elvis' regular quartet in the mid-1950s, before forming his own band in 1959. He died of a brain tumour on 21/10/1965.

| 08/09/1960 | 50 | 1 | | WHITE SILVER SANDS | London HLU 9090 |
| 03/11/1960 | 32 | 7 | | DON'T BE CRUEL Black played bass on Elvis Presley's original version | London HLU 9212 |

BLACKSTREET US hip hop group formed by Teddy 'Street' Riley (born 8/10/1966, Harlem, NYC), Chauncey 'Black' Hannibal, Levi Little and David Hollister. By 1996 they were Riley, Hannibal, Mark L Middleton and Eric 'E' Williams. In August 1999 they split following bad publicity from Chauncey's revelation that he was bisexual, although they re-formed in 2001. They were named Best Rhythm & Blues Group at the 1997 MTV Europe Music Awards; Riley had earlier won the 1992 Grammy Award for Best Engineered Album with Bruce Swedien for Michael Jackson's *Dangerous*. Riley also won the 1996 MOBO Award for Best Producer. Blinky Blink is a US rapper.

19/06/1993	37	3		BABY BE MINE BLACKSTREET FEATURING TEDDY RILEY Featured in the 1993 film *CB4 – The Movie*	MCA MCSTD 1772
13/08/1994	56	1		BOOTI CALL Contains samples of George Clinton's *Atomic Dog* and Zapp's *Heartbreaker*	Interscope A 8250CD
11/02/1995	39	2		U BLOW MY MIND	Interscope A 8222CD
27/05/1995	56	2		JOY	Interscope A 8195CD
19/10/1996	9	7		NO DIGGITY ▲4 BLACKSTREET FEATURING DR DRE Contains a sample of Bill Withers' *Grandma's Hands*. 1997 Grammy Award for Best Rhythm and Blues Performance by a Group	Interscope IND 95003
08/03/1997	11	5		GET ME HOME FOXY BROWN FEATURING BLACKSTREET Contains a sample of Eugene Wilde's *Gotta Get You Home Tonight*	Def Jam DEFCD 32
26/04/1997	6	10		DON'T LEAVE ME Contains a sample of DeBarge's *A Dream*	Interscope IND 95534
27/09/1997	7	5		FIX Features Slash of Guns N' Roses on guitar and uncredited contributions of Fishbone and Ol' Dirty Bastard. Contains a sample of Grandmaster Flash's *The Message*	Interscope IND 97521
13/12/1997	18	6		(MONEY CAN'T) BUY ME LOVE Cover version of The Beatles' 1964 hit	Interscope IND 95563
27/06/1998	38	2		THE CITY IS MINE JAY-Z FEATURING BLACKSTREET Contains samples of Glenn Frey's *You Belong To The City* and The Jones Girls' *You Gonna Make Me Love Somebody Else*	Northwestside 74321588012
12/12/1998	7	9		TAKE ME THERE BLACKSTREET AND MYA FEATURING MA$E AND BLINKY BLINK Featured in the 1998 animated film *The Rugrats Movie*	Interscope IND 95620
17/04/1999	11	7		GIRLFRIEND/BOYFRIEND BLACKSTREET WITH JANET (Jackson)	Interscope IND 95640
10/07/1999	32	4		GET READY MA$E FEATURING BLACKSTREET Contains a sample of Shalamar's *A Night To Remember*	Puff Daddy 74321682612
08/02/2003	37	2		WIZZY WOW Features the uncredited contribution of rapper Mystikal	DreamWorks 4507902

BLACKWELLS US vocal group formed by DeWayne and Ronald Blackwell and produced by Phil Spector. Both Blackwells went on to be successful writers.

| 18/05/1961 | 46 | 2 | | LOVE OR MONEY | London HLW 9334 |

RICHARD BLACKWOOD UK singer/MTV presenter/comedian who is also the nephew of fellow singer Junior.

17/06/2000	3	7		MAMA – WHO DA MAN? Contains a sample of Junior's *Mama Used To Say*	East West MICKY 01CD1
16/09/2000	10	6		1-2-3-4 GET WITH THE WICKED RICHARD BLACKWOOD FEATURING DEETAH	East West MICKY 05CD1
25/11/2000	23	3		SOMEONE THERE FOR ME	Hopefield MICKY 06CD

BLADE – see MARK B AND BLADE

BLAGGERS I.T.A. UK vocal/instrumental group fronted by Matthew Roberts (aka Matt Vinyl and Matty Blag). He died from a drug overdose on 22/2/2000.

12/06/1993	56	2		STRESS	Parlophone CDITA 1
09/10/1993	51	2		OXYGEN	Parlophone CDITA 2
08/01/1994	48	3		ABANDON SHIP	Parlophone CDITA 3

BLAHZAY BLAHZAY US rap duo formed in Brooklyn, NYC by Out Loud and producer DJ PF Cuttin.

| 02/03/1996 | 56 | 1 | | DANGER Contains a sample of Gwen McCrae's *Rockin' Chair* | Mercury Black Vinyl MBVCD 2 |

VIVIAN BLAINE US singer (born Vivian Stapleton, 21/11/1921, New Jersey) who was first known as an actress in films such as *Thru Different Eyes* (1942), *Skirts Ahoy!* (1952) and *Guys And Dolls* (1955), making her Broadway debut in 1950. She died from

heart failure on 9/12/1995.

| 10/07/1953.....12......1...... | BUSHEL AND A PECK...Brunswick 05100 |

BLAIR – see **TERRY HALL**

BLAIR UK singer (born Blair MacKichan, 1970, London) who also recorded as Black Duck.

| 02/09/1995.....37......3...... | HAVE FUN, GO MAD! Featured in the 1998 film *Sliding Doors*...Mercury MERCD 443 |
| 06/01/1996.....44......2...... | LIFE Theme to the children's TV programme *Dear Dilemma*...Mercury MERCD 447 |

BLAK TWANG UK hip hop singer Tony Rotton who was named Best Hip Hop Act at the MOBO Awards in 1996.

| 29/06/2002.....54......1...... | TRIXSTAR BLAK TWANG FEATURING ESTELLE ....Bad Magic MAGIC24 |
| 26/10/2002.....48......1...... | SO ROTTEN BLAK TWANG FEATURING JAHMALI ....Bad Magic MAGICD 25 |

PETER BLAKE UK singer who also recorded for Acrobat, EMI and by 1995 White Cloud Records.

| 08/10/1977.....40......4...... | LIPSMACKIN' ROCK 'N' ROLLIN' ....Pepper UP 36295 |

BLAME UK production duo Conrad Shafie and Justice. Justice later left, Shafie continuing on his own.

| 11/04/1992.....48......2...... | MUSIC TAKES YOU...Moving Shadow SHADOW 11 |

BLAMELESS UK rock group formed in Sheffield by Jared Daley (vocals), Jason Legett (bass), Matthew Pirt (guitar) and Jon Dodd (drums) who made their first record for the Rough Trade Records singles club.

04/11/1995.....56......1......	TOWN CLOWNS ....China WOKCD 2046
23/03/1996.....27......3......	BREATHE (A LITTLE DEEPER) ....China WOKCD 2070
01/06/1996.....49......1......	SIGNS...China WOKCD 2077

BLANCMANGE UK synthesiser duo Neil Arthur (born 15/6/1958, Darwen) and Steven Luscombe (born 29/10/1954) who released their first record in 1980 and signed with London in 1981, disbanding in 1986 with Arthur going solo.

17/04/1982.....65......2......	GOD'S KITCHEN/I'VE SEEN THE WORD...London BLANC 1
31/07/1982.....46......5......	FEEL ME...London BLANC 2
30/10/1982 .....7......14 .....O	LIVING ON THE CEILING ....London BLANC 3
19/02/1983.....19......9......	WAVES ....London BLANC 4
07/05/1983.....10......8......	BLIND VISION ....London BLANC 5
26/11/1983.....33......8......	THAT'S LOVE, THAT IS...London BLANC 6
14/04/1984 ....8......10......	DON'T TELL ME ....London BLANC 7
21/07/1984.....22......8......	THE DAY BEFORE YOU CAME ....London BLANC 8
07/09/1985.....40......5......	WHAT'S YOUR PROBLEM?..London BLANC 9
10/05/1986.....71......2......	I CAN SEE IT ....London BLANC 11

BOBBY BLANCO AND MIKKI MOTO US duo formed by guitarist Bobby Blanco (born in El Paso, TX), ex-member of Height 611, and singer Mikki Moto.

| 29/05/2004.....70......1...... | 3AM ....Defected DFTD088 |

BILLY BLAND US singer (born 5/4/1932, Wilmington, NC), the youngest of nineteen children, who began his career with Lionel Hampton and Buddy Johnson. He formed The Four Bees in 1954 before going solo with Old Town in 1955.

| 19/05/1960.....15......10...... | LET THE LITTLE GIRL DANCE ....London HL 9096 |

BLANK AND JONES German DJs Piet Blank and Jaspa Jones whose debut hit was inspired by a visit to the legendary Liverpool club Cream.

26/06/1999.....24......3......	CREAM...Deviant DVNT 31CDS
27/05/2000.....57......1......	AFTER LOVE ....Nebula NEBCDS 3
30/09/2000.....55......1......	THE NIGHTFLY...Nebula NEBCDS 010
03/03/2001.....53......2......	BEYOND TIME...Gang Go/Edel 01245115 GAG
29/06/2002.....45......2......	DJS FANS AND FREAKS ....Incentive CENT 42CDS

BLAQUE IVORY US vocal group formed by Natina Reed, Shamari Fears and Brandi Williams, discovered by Lisa 'Left Eye' Lopes of TLC. The 'Blaque' stands for Believing In Life And Achieving A Quest For Unity In Everything.

| 03/07/1999.....31......3...... | 808 ....Columbia 6674962 |

BLAST FEATURING VDC Italian dance group formed by Roberto Masi and Fabio Fiorentino, featuring Luigi Puma 'Tuma' on vocals and Red Jerry on keyboards.

| 18/06/1994.....22......3...... | CRAZY MAN..UMM MCSTD 1982 |
| 12/11/1994.....40......2...... | PRINCES OF THE NIGHT ....UMM MCSTD 2011 |

MELANIE BLATT UK singer (born 25/3/1975, London) who was a member of All Saints before going solo. She also appeared in the 2000 film *Honest*.

15/09/2001 .....6......9......	TWENTYFOURSEVEN ARTFUL DODGER FEATURING MELANIE BLATT ....ffrr FCDP 400
02/03/2002.....41......2......	I'M LEAVIN' OUTSIDAZ FEATURING RAH DIGGA AND MELANIE BLATT ....Rufflife RLCDM 03
06/09/2003.....18......3......	DO ME WRONG ....London LONCD 479

❶⁹ Number of weeks single topped the UK chart ↑ Entered the UK chart at #1 ▲⁹ Number of weeks single topped the US chart

87

BLAZE FEATURING PALMER BROWN US production duo Josh Milan and Kevin Hedge with singer Palmer Brown.

10/03/2001	53	2	MY BEAT . . . . Black & Blue/Kickin NEOCD 053
21/09/2002	55	1	DO YOU REMEMBER HOUSE . . . . Slip N Slide SLIPCD 151

BLAZIN' SQUAD UK vocal group formed in London by MC Freek, Melo-D, Strider, Reepa, Krazy, Spike-E, Flava, Rockie B, Kenzie and DJ Tommy B. The ten members, most of whom were sixteen years old at the time of their debut hit, met at Highams Park School.

31/08/2002	❶¹	13	CROSSROADS ↑ . . . . East West SQUAD 01CD
23/11/2002	6	13	LOVE ON THE LINE . . . . East West SQUAD 02CD
22/02/2003	8	8	REMINISCE/WHERE THE STORY ENDS . . . . East West SQUAD 03CD
05/07/2003	3	9	WE JUST BE DREAMIN' . . . . East West SQUAD 04CD
15/11/2003	2	10	FLIP REVERSE . . . . East West SQUAD 05CD
14/02/2004	6	5	HERE 4 ONE . . . . East West SQUAD 06CD

BLEACHIN' UK dance group formed by Amos Pizzey and Richard Berg, Pizzey having previously worked with Jeremy Healy.

22/07/2000	32	4	PEAKIN' . . . . Boiler House! 74321774822

BLESSID UNION OF SOULS US group formed in Cincinnati, OH by Eliot Sloan (vocals), Jeff Pence (guitar), Charley 'CP' Roth (keyboards) and Eddie Hedges (drums).

27/05/1995	29	5	I BELIEVE . . . . EMI CDEM 374
23/03/1996	74	1	LET ME BE THE ONE . . . . EMI CDEM 387

BLESSING UK group formed by William Topley (vocals), Kevin Hime-Knowles (bass), Luke Brighty (bass) and Mike Westergaard (keyboards) as Just William, who finally got a recording contract in the US after four years touring the UK.

11/05/1991	42	6	HIGHWAY 5 . . . . MCA MCS 1509
18/01/1992	30	6	HIGHWAY 5 (REMIX) . . . . MCA MCS 1603
19/02/1994	73	1	SOUL LOVE . . . . MCA MCSTD 1940

MARY J. BLIGE US R&B singer (born 11/1/1971, Atlanta, GA, raised in The Bronx, NYC) who signed with Uptown in 1991 on the strength of a demo of the Anita Baker song *Caught Up In The Rapture* made in a shopping mall karaoke studio. She took part in the *It's Only Rock 'N' Roll* project for the Children's Promise charity, and won the 2002 Grammy Award for Best Female Rhythm & Blues Vocal Performance for *He Think I Don't Know*.

28/11/1992	68	2	REAL LOVE . . . . Uptown MCSTD 1721
27/02/1993	31	4	REMINISCE . . . . Uptown MCSTD 1731
12/06/1993	48	3	YOU REMIND ME . . . . Uptown MCSTD 1770
28/08/1993	26	4	REAL LOVE (REMIX) . . . . Uptown MCSTD 1922
04/12/1993	36	2	YOU DON'T HAVE TO WORRY Contains samples of James Brown's *Papa Don't Take No Mess* and Lou Donaldson's *Ode To Billie Joe*. Featured in the 1992 film *Who's The Man* . . . . Uptown MCSTD 1948
14/05/1994	29	3	MY LOVE . . . . Uptown MCSTD 1972
10/12/1994	30	4	BE HAPPY Contains a sample of Curtis Mayfield's *You're Too Good To Me*. . . . . Uptown MCSTD 2033
15/04/1995	12	4	I'M GOIN' DOWN . . . . Uptown MCSTD 2053
29/07/1995	10	5	I'LL BE THERE FOR YOU/YOU'RE ALL I NEED TO GET BY METHOD MAN FEATURING MARY J. BLIGE Both songs written by Ashford & Simpson. Method Man raps over *I'll Be There For You* while Blige sings the chorus of *You're All I Need To Get By*. It won the 1995 Grammy Award for Best Rap Performance by a Duo . . . . Def Jam DEFDX11
30/09/1995	17	4	MARY JANE (ALL NIGHT LONG) . . . . Uptown MCSTD 2088
16/12/1995	23	3	(YOU MAKE ME FEEL LIKE A) NATURAL WOMAN . . . . Uptown MCSTD 2108
30/03/1996	39	2	NOT GON' CRY Featured in the 1995 film *Waiting To Exhale* . . . . Arista 74321358252
01/03/1997	30	2	CAN'T KNOCK THE HUSTLE JAY-Z FEATURING MARY J. BLIGE . . . . Northwestside 74321447192
17/05/1997	15	4	LOVE IS ALL WE NEED Contains a sample of Rick James' *Moonchild* . . . . Uptown MCSTD 48053
16/08/1997	6	9	EVERYTHING Contains samples of The Stylistics' *You Are Everything*, James Brown's *The Payback* and A Taste Of Honey's *Sukiyaki* . . . . MCA MCSTD 48059
29/11/1997	19	5	MISSING YOU . . . . MCA MCSTD 48071
11/07/1998	22	3	SEVEN DAYS MARY J. BLIGE FEATURING GEORGE BENSON . . . . MCA MCSTD 48083
13/03/1999	4	10	◯	AS GEORGE MICHAEL AND MARY J. BLIGE . . . . Epic 6670122
21/08/1999	29	3	ALL THAT I CAN SAY . . . . MCA MCSTD 40215
11/12/1999	42	2	DEEP INSIDE Contains a sample of Elton John's *Bennie And The Jets* and features the additional uncredited contribution of Elton John on acoustic piano . . . . MCA MCSTD 40224
29/04/2000	19	4	GIVE ME YOU Features the uncredited contribution of Eric Clapton . . . . MCA MCSTD 40230
16/12/2000	9	10	911 WYCLEF FEATURING MARY J. BLIGE Contains samples of James Brown's *The Payback* and Edie Brickell & The New Bohemians' *What I Am* . . . . Columbia 6706122
06/10/2001	8	16	FAMILY AFFAIR ▲⁶ . . . . MCA MCSTD 40267
09/02/2002	13	7	DANCE FOR ME MARY J. BLIGE FEATURING COMMON Contains a sample of The Police's *The Bed's Too Big Without You*. . . . . MCA MCSXD 40274
11/05/2002	9	7	NO MORE DRAMA Contains an interpolation of Barry Devorzan and Perry Borkin Jr's *The Young And The Restless Theme* . . . . MCA MCSXD 40281
24/08/2002	17	5	RAINY DAYZ MARY J. BLIGE FEATURING JA RULE . . . . MCA MCSXD 40288
27/09/2003	18	5	LOVE @ 1ST SIGHT MARY J. BLIGE FEATURING METHOD MAN Contains a sample of a A Tribe Called Quest's *Hot Sex* . . . . MCA MCSTD 40338
06/12/2003	40	2	NOT TODAY MARY J. BLIGE FEATURING EVE. . . . . Geffen MCSTD 40349

◯ Silver disc ● Gold disc ✪ Platinum disc (additional platinum units are indicated by a figure following the symbol) ◎ Singles released prior to 1973 that are known to have sold over 1 million copies in the UK

| 20/12/2003 | 60 | 1 | | WHENEVER I SAY YOUR NAME **STING AND MARY J. BLIGE** 2003 Grammy Award for Best Pop Collaboration with Vocals . . . . A & M 9815304 |
| 18/12/2004 | 59 | 1 | | I TRY **TALIB KWELI FEATURING MARY J. BLIGE** . . . . Island MCSTD40390 |

BLIND MELON US pop-rock group formed in Los Angeles, CA in 1990 by Glen Graham (born Columbus, MS, drums), Shannon Hoon (born 26/9/1967, Lafayette, IN, vocals), Roger Stevens (born West Point, MS, guitar), Christopher Thorn (born Dover, PA, guitar) and Brad Smith (born West Point, bass). Hoon died from a drug overdose on 21/10/1995.

12/06/1993	62	2		TONES OF HOME . . . . Capitol CDCL 687
11/12/1993	17	6		NO RAIN . . . . Capitol CDCL 699
09/07/1994	35	3		CHANGE . . . . Capitol CDCL 717
05/08/1995	37	2		GALAXIE . . . . Capitol CDCLS 755

BLINK Irish group formed by Dermot Lambert (guitar/vocals), John O'Neill (guitar), Ellen Leahy (strings/vocals), Robbie Sexton (keyboards), Brian McLoughlin (bass), Mick The Brick (whistles) and Barry Campbell (drums).

| 16/07/1994 | 57 | 1 | | HAPPY DAY . . . . Lime CDR 6385 |

BLINK 182 US group formed in San Diego, CA in 1993 by Tom Delonge (born 13/12/1975, guitar), Markus Hoppus (born 15/3/1972, bass/vocals) and Travis Barker (born 14/11/1975, drums) as Blink, then Blink 182 in 1995 after a similarly titled group threatened legal action. They were named Best New Act at the 2000 MTV Europe Music Awards and Best Rock Act in 2001. Delonge and Barker later formed Box Car Racer.

02/10/1999	38	2		WHAT'S MY AGE AGAIN? . . . . MCA MCSTD 40219
25/03/2000	2	10		**ALL THE SMALL THINGS** . . . . MCA MCSTD 40223
08/07/2000	17	6		WHAT'S MY AGE AGAIN? Despite the slightly different catalogue number, this a re-release of MCSTD 40219. . . MCA MCSZD 40219
14/07/2001	14	7		THE ROCK SHOW . . . . MCA MCSTD 40259
06/10/2001	31	4		FIRST DATE . . . . MCA MCSTD 40264
06/12/2003	15	5		FEELING THIS . . . . Geffen MCSTD 40347
13/03/2004	8	10		**I MISS YOU** . . . . Geffen MCSTD 40359
03/07/2004	24	3		DOWN . . . . Geffen MCSTD 40366
25/12/2004	36	1+		ALWAYS . . . . Geffen MCSTD 40400

BLINKY BLINK – see **BLACKSTREET**

BLOC PARTY UK rock group, originally called Union, formed in London by Kele Okereke (guitar/vocals), Russell Lissack (guitar), Gordon Moakes (bass) and Matt Tong (drums).

15/05/2004	51	1		BANQUET/STAYING FAT . . . . Moshi Moshi MOSHI10CD
24/07/2004	38	2		LITTLE THOUGHT/TULIPS . . . . Wichita WEBB067SCD
06/11/2004	26	1		HELICOPTER . . . . Wichita WEBB070SCD

BLOCKHEADS – see **IAN DURY AND THE BLOCKHEADS**

BLOCKSTER UK record producer/singer (born Brandon Block, 8/3/1967, Hackney, London) with Ricky Morrison and Frank Sidoli. Block is also in Mystic 3 and Grifters.

| 16/01/1999 | 3 | 9 | | **YOU SHOULD BE...** Based on the Bee Gees' *You Should Be Dancin'* . . . . Sound Of Ministry MOSCDS 128 |
| 24/07/1999 | 18 | 2 | | GROOVELINE Cover version of Heatwave's 1978 hit. . . . . Sound Of Ministry MOSCDS 131 |

BLOKES – see **BILLY BRAGG**

KRISTINE BLOND Danish singer who signed with EMI Denmark in 1995 but was dropped before she released anything, although *Love Shy* from a planned album got picked up by Reverb Records.

11/04/1998	22	3		LOVE SHY . . . . Reverb BNOISE 1CD
11/11/2000	28	2		LOVE SHY (REMIX) . . . . Relentless RELENT 4CDS
04/05/2002	35	2		YOU MAKE ME GO OOH . . . . WEA 343CD1

Blondie Sunday Girl

BLONDIE US new wave group formed in New York in 1975 by Debbie Harry (born 1/7/1945, Miami, FL, lead vocals), Chris Stein (born 5/1/1950, New York, guitar), Jimmy Destri (born 13/4/1954, New York, keyboards), Gary Valentine (bass) and Clem Burke (born 24/11/1955, New York, drums). Valentine left in 1977 and was replaced by New Yorker Frank Infante. Originally signed to Private Stock, Chrysalis bought their contract in 1977. They disbanded in 1983, Harry going solo, and re-formed in 1998.

18/02/1978	2	14	●	**DENIS** Remake of Randy & The Rainbows' US #10 *Denise* . . . . Chrysalis CHS 2204
06/05/1978	10	9	●	**(I'M ALWAYS TOUCHED BY YOUR) PRESENCE DEAR** . . . . Chrysalis CHS 2217
26/08/1978	12	11	○	PICTURE THIS . . . . Chrysalis CHS 2242
11/11/1978	5	12	○	**HANGING ON THE TELEPHONE** . . . . Chrysalis CHS 2266
27/01/1979	●4	12	✪	**HEART OF GLASS** ▲1 Featured in the films *Donnie Brasco* (1997) and *54* (1998) . . . . Chrysalis CHS 2275

●9 Number of weeks single topped the UK chart ⬆ Entered the UK chart at #1 ▲9 Number of weeks single topped the US chart

89

DATE	POS	WKS	BPI	SINGLE TITLE	LABEL & NUMBER
19/05/1979	❶³	13	●	SUNDAY GIRL	Chrysalis CHS 2320
29/09/1979	2	8	○	DREAMING	Chrysalis CHS 2350
24/11/1979	13	10	○	UNION CITY BLUE Featured in the 1979 film *Union City*	Chrysalis CHS 2400
23/02/1980	❶²	9	○	ATOMIC Featured in the 2002 film *Bend It Like Beckham*	Chrysalis CHS 2410
12/04/1980	❶¹	9	○	CALL ME ▲⁶ Featured in the films *American Gigolo* (1980), *Partners* (1982) and *Deuce Bigalow: Male Gigolo* (1999)	
					Chrysalis CHS 2414
08/11/1980	❶²	12	●	THE TIDE IS HIGH ▲¹ Featured in the films *Muriel's Wedding* (1995) and *Striptease* (1996)	Chrysalis CHS 2465
24/01/1981	5	8	○	RAPTURE ▲² Featured in the 1999 film *200 Cigarettes*	Chrysalis CHS 2485
08/05/1982	11	9		ISLAND OF LOST SOULS	Chrysalis CHS 2608
24/07/1982	39	4		WAR CHILD	Chrysalis CHS 2624
03/12/1988	50	3		DENIS (REMIX)	Chrysalis CHS 3328
11/02/1989	61	2		CALL ME (REMIX)	Chrysalis CHS 3342
10/09/1994	19	4		ATOMIC (REMIX)	Chrysalis CDCHS 5013
08/07/1995	15	3		HEART OF GLASS (REMIX)	Chrysalis CDCHS 5023
28/10/1995	31	2		UNION CITY BLUES	Chrysalis CDCHSS 5027
13/02/1999	❶¹	12	●	MARIA ↑ Featured in the 1999 film *200 Cigarettes*	Beyond 74321645632
12/06/1999	26	3		NOTHING IS REAL BUT THE GIRL	Beyond 74321669472
18/10/2003	12	3		GOOD BOYS	Epic 6743995

BLOOD SWEAT AND TEARS
US rock group formed by Al Kooper (born 5/2/1944, NYC) as a jazz-rock group in 1968 with David Clayton-Thomas (born David Thompsett, 13/9/1941, Walton-on-Thames, UK, lead vocals), Steve Katz (born 9/5/1945, NYC, guitar/harmonica/vocals), Jim Fielder (born 4/10/1947, Denton, TX, bass), Bobby Colomby (born 20/12/1944, NYC, drums/vocals), Fred Lipsius (born 19/11/1943, NYC, saxophone), Dick Halligan (born 29/8/1943, NYC, trombone), Chuck Wingfield (born 5/2/1943, Monessen, PA, trumpet/flugelhorn), Lew Soloff (born 20/2/1944, NYC, trumpet/flugelhorn) and Jerry Hyman (born 19/5/1947, NYC, trombone/recorder). The group won two Grammy Awards: Album of the Year in 1969 for *Blood, Sweat And Tears* and Best Contemporary Instrumental Performance that same year for *Variations On A Theme By Erik Satie*.

30/04/1969	35	6		YOU'VE MADE ME SO VERY HAPPY Revival of a Motown ballad	CBS 4116

BLOODHOUND GANG
US rock group formed in Philadelphia, PA by Jimmy Pop Ali (vocals), Lupus Thunder (guitar), Evil Jared Hasselhoff (bass), DJ Q-Ball (DJ) and Spanky G (drums), although Spanky G was subsequently replaced by Willie The New Guy.

23/08/1997	56	1		WHY'S EVERYBODY ALWAYS PICKIN' ON ME?	Geffen GFSTD 22252
15/04/2000	4	14	●	THE BAD TOUCH	Geffen 4972682
02/09/2000	15	6		THE BALLAD OF CHASEY LAIN	Geffen 4973822

BLOODSTONE
US soul group formed in Kansas City, MO by Charles Love (guitar/vocals), Roger Durham (percussion), Henry Williams (drums), Melvin Webb and Charles McCormick (vocals/bass) as The Sinceres. Later members included Willis Draften (guitar), Eddie Summers, Ronald Wilson and Steve Ferrone (later drummer for the Average White Band). Webb died from diabetes in 1973, Durham died from a heart attack after falling off a horse in 1973 and Draften died on 8/2/2002. They appeared in the 1975 film *Train Ride To Hollywood*.

18/08/1973	40	4		NATURAL HIGH Featured in the 1997 film *Jackie Brown*	Decca F 13382

BOBBY BLOOM
US session singer (born 1946, New York City) who was initially a songwriter, penning hits for Tommy James And The Shondells (*Mony Mony*) and The Monkees. He shot himself in the head in a Hollywood hotel on 28/2/1974, although it was believed to have been an accident.

05/09/1970	3	19		MONTEGO BAY	Polydor 2058 051
09/01/1971	31	5		HEAVY MAKES YOU HAPPY	Polydor 2001 122

BLOOMSBURY SET
UK vocal/instrumental group with future Magnum member Jim Simpson.

25/06/1983	56	3		HANGING AROUND WITH THE BIG BOYS	Stiletto STL 13

TANYA BLOUNT
US singer (born 25/9/1977, Washington DC) who was first known via a TV talent show hosted by Natalie Cole.

11/06/1994	69	1		I'M GONNA MAKE YOU MINE	Polydor OZCD 315

KURTIS BLOW
US rapper (born Kurt Walker, 9/8/1959, New York) who was one of the pioneers of rap as an early member of Grandmaster Flash And The Furious Five. Later a producer, he also appeared in films, including *Krush Groove* in 1985.

15/12/1979	30	6		CHRISTMAS RAPPIN'	Mercury BLOW 7
11/10/1980	47	4		THE BREAKS	Mercury BLOW 8
16/03/1985	67	1		PARTY TIME (THE GO-GO EDIT)	Club JAB 12
15/06/1985	66	1		SAVE YOUR LOVE (FOR NUMBER 1) RENE AND ANGELA FEATURING KURTIS BLOW	Club JAB 14
18/01/1986	24	8		IF I RULED THE WORLD Featured in the 1985 film *Krush Groove* starring Kurtis Blow	Club JAB 26
08/11/1986	64	2		I'M CHILLIN'	Club JAB 42

BLOW MONKEYS
UK group formed by Dr Robert (born Bruce Robert Howard, 2/5/1961, Norfolk, guitar/vocals), Mick Anker (born 2/7/1957, bass), Neville Henry (saxophone) and Tony Kiley (born 16/2/1962, drums), taking their name from jazz slang for saxophone players. They first signed with RCA in 1984. Robert Howard later recorded solo, worked with Kym Mazelle and became a successful songwriter.

01/03/1986	12	10		DIGGING YOUR SCENE	RCA PB 40599
17/05/1986	60	2		WICKED WAYS	RCA MONK 2
31/01/1987	5	8		IT DOESN'T HAVE TO BE THIS WAY	RCA MONK 4

○ Silver disc ● Gold disc ✪ Platinum disc (additional platinum units are indicated by a figure following the symbol) ⓜ Singles released prior to 1973 that are known to have sold over 1 million copies in the UK

28/03/1987	30	6		OUT WITH HER	RCA MONK 5
30/05/1987	52	2		(CELEBRATE) THE DAY AFTER YOU **BLOW MONKEYS WITH CURTIS MAYFIELD** The anti-Margaret Thatcher (then UK Prime Minister) single was banned from radio until after the General Election.	RCA MONK 6
15/08/1987	67	1		SOME KIND OF WONDERFUL	RCA MONK 7
06/08/1988	70	2		THIS IS YOUR LIFE	RCA PB 42149
08/04/1989	32	5		THIS IS YOUR LIFE (REMIX)	RCA PB 42695
15/07/1989	22	6		CHOICE? **BLOW MONKEYS FEATURING SYLVIA TELLA**	RCA PB 42885
14/10/1989	73	2		SLAVES NO MORE	RCA PB 43201
26/05/1990	69	2		SPRINGTIME FOR THE WORLD	RCA PB 43623

ANGEL BLU – see JAMIESON FEATURING ANGEL BLU

BLU PETER UK producer Peter Harris who began as a DJ before turning to production.

21/03/1998	70	1		TELL ME WHAT YOU WANT/JAMES HAS KITTENS	React CDREACT 285

BLUE UK pop group formed in Glasgow in 1973 by Timmy Donald (vocals), Hugh Nicholson (guitar) and Ian MacMillan (bass). Robert Smith joined in 1974. By the time of their hit Charlie Smith (drums) and David Nicholson (keyboards) had replaced Donald and Smith. In 2003 this Blue sued the group below over their name but subsequently lost.

30/04/1977	18	8		GONNA CAPTURE YOUR HEART	Rocket ROKN 522

BLUE UK vocal group formed in London by Antony 'Ant' Costa (born 23/6/1981, Edgeware), Lee Ryan (born 17/6/1983, Chatham), Simon 'Shaft' Webbe (born 30/3/1978, Manchester) and Duncan 'Dunk' James (born 7/4/1979, Salisbury). They were named Best UK Newcomer at the 2002 BRIT Awards, and Best Pop Act the following year.

02/06/2001	4	13	○	ALL RISE	Innocent SINCD 28
08/09/2001	❶¹	13	○	TOO CLOSE ↑	Innocent SINCD 30
24/11/2001	❶¹	13	○	IF YOU COME BACK ↑	Innocent SINCD 32
30/03/2002	6	12		FLY BY II Contains a sample of Herb Alpert's *Rise*	Innocent SINCD 33
02/11/2002	3	12	○	ONE LOVE	Innocent SINCD 41
21/12/2002	❶¹	17	○	SORRY SEEMS TO BE THE HARDEST WORD ↑ **BLUE FEATURING ELTON JOHN**	Innocent SINCD 43
29/03/2003	4	10		U MAKE ME WANNA	Innocent SINCD 44
01/11/2003	2	11		GUILTY	Innocent SINCD 51
27/12/2003	11	10		SIGNED SEALED DELIVERED I'M YOURS **BLUE FEATURING STEVIE WONDER AND ANGIE STONE**	Innocent SINCD 54
03/04/2004	4	12		BREATHE EASY	Innocent SINDX 58
10/07/2004	9	8		BUBBLIN'	Innocent SINDX 64
20/11/2004	4	6+		CURTAIN FALLS Contains a sample of Stevie Wonder's *Pastime Paradise*	Innocent SINDX 67

BABBITY BLUE UK singer whose debut hit featured instrumental backing from The Tremeloes. Her follow-up was *Don't Hurt Me*.

11/02/1965	48	2		DON'T MAKE ME (FALL IN LOVE WITH YOU)	Decca F 12053

BARRY BLUE UK singer (born Barry Green) who began as a songwriter and producer, co-writing *Sugar Me* with Lynsey De Paul (a massive hit for her in 1972, the same pair penning Blue's debut hit). When his hits dried up his backing group became The Rubettes and Blue became a producer, notably with Heatwave. At the end of the 1980s he recorded as Cry Sisco!

28/07/1973	2	15	○	(DANCING) ON A SATURDAY NIGHT	Bell 1295
03/11/1973	7	12		DO YOU WANNA DANCE	Bell 1336
02/03/1974	11	9		SCHOOL LOVE	Bell 1345
03/08/1974	26	7		MISS HIT AND RUN	Bell 1364
26/10/1974	23	5		HOT SHOT	Bell 1379

BLUE ADONIS FEATURING LIL' MISS MAX Belgian production group formed by Wim Perdean, Joachin Helder and Christian Hellburg with singer Lil' Miss Max.

17/10/1998	27	3		DISCO COP	Serious SERR 002CD

BLUE AEROPLANES UK group formed in Bristol by Gerard Langley (vocals), Nick Jacobs (guitar), Dave Chapman (various instruments), Wojtek Dmochowski (dancer) and John Langley (drums).

17/02/1990	72	1		JACKET HANGS	Ensign ENY 628
26/05/1990	63	2		…AND STONES	Ensign ENY 632

BLUE AMAZON UK production duo James Reid and Lee Softley with singer Vicky Webb.

17/05/1997	53	1		AND THEN THE RAIN FALLS	Sony S2 BAS 301 CD
01/07/2000	73	1		BREATHE	Subversive SUB 61D

BLUE BAMBOO Belgian producer Johan Gielen. He is also a member of Airscape, Balearic Bill, Svenson & Gielen and Cubic 22 as well as recording under his own name.

03/12/1994	23	4		ABC AND D	Escapade CDJAPE 6

BLUE BOY UK DJ Lex Blackmore.

01/02/1997	8	13	○	REMEMBER ME Contains a sample of Marlena Shaw's 1976 Montreux Jazz Festival performance	Pharm CDPHARM 1
23/08/1997	25	3		SANDMAN Contains a sample of Undisputed Truth's *Sandman*	Sidewalk CDSWALK 001

❶⁹ Number of weeks single topped the UK chart ↑ Entered the UK chart at #1 ▲⁹ Number of weeks single topped the US chart

91

BLUE CAPS – see GENE VINCENT

BLUE FEATHERS Dutch vocal/instrumental group formed by JW Weeda, E Brouwer and R Brouwer.
03/07/1982 . . . . . 50 . . . . . 4 . . . .   LET'S FUNK TONIGHT . . . . Mercury MER 109

BLUE FLAMES – see GEORGIE FAME

BLUE GRASS BOYS – see JOHNNY DUNCAN AND THE BLUE GRASS BOYS

BLUE HAZE UK pop group with a reggae cover version of The Platters' #1, the song originally written in 1933 for the musical *Roberta*.
18/03/1972 . . . . . 32 . . . . . 6 . . . .   SMOKE GETS IN YOUR EYES . . . . A&M AMS 891

BLUE JEANS – see BOB B SOXX AND THE BLUE JEANS

BLUE MELONS UK vocal/instrumental group.
08/06/1996 . . . . . 70 . . . . . 1 . . . .   DO WAH DIDDY DIDDY . . . . Fundamental FUNDCD 1

BLUE MERCEDES UK duo David Titlow (vocals) and Duncan Miller (guitar/keyboards). Miller also records as Esoterix, Monica De Luxe, As One and Feelgood Factor, and has produced a number of acts including Robert Owens.
10/10/1987 . . . . . 23 . . . . . 11 . . . . . .   I WANT TO BE YOUR PROPERTY . . . . RCA BONA 1
13/02/1988 . . . . . 57 . . . . . 2 . . . .   SEE WANT MUST HAVE . . . . RCA BONA 2
23/07/1988 . . . . . 46 . . . . . 5 . . . .   LOVE IS THE GUN . . . . RCA BONA 3

BLUE MINK UK group formed by songwriter and session singer Roger Cook (born 19/8/1940, Bristol, vocals) featuring Madeline Bell (born 23/7/1942, Newark, NJ, vocals), Roger Coulam (keyboards), Herbie Flowers (bass), Barry Morgan (drums) and Alan Parker (guitar), specifically to record a song by Cook and his songwriting partner Roger Greenaway, *Melting Pot*. After its success they stayed together for six years, Flowers later becoming a founding member of Sky and Bell fronting disco group Space.
15/11/1969 . . . . . 3 . . . . . 15 . . . . . .   **MELTING POT** . . . . Philips BF 1818
28/03/1970 . . . . . 10 . . . . . 10 . . . . . .   GOOD MORNING FREEDOM . . . . Philips BF 1838
19/09/1970 . . . . . 17 . . . . . 9 . . . .   OUR WORLD . . . . Philips 6006 042
29/05/1971 . . . . . 3 . . . . . 14 . . . . . .   **THE BANNER MAN** . . . . Regal Zonophone RZ 3034
11/11/1972 . . . . . 11 . . . . . 15 . . . . . .   STAY WITH ME . . . . Regal Zonophone RZ 3064
03/03/1973 . . . . . 26 . . . . . 9 . . . .   BY THE DEVIL (I WAS TEMPTED) . . . . EMI 2007
30/06/1973 . . . . . 9 . . . . . 11 . . . . . .   **RANDY** . . . . EMI 2028

BLUE NILE UK rock group formed in Glasgow in 1981 by Paul Buchanan (vocals/guitar/synthesiser), Robert Bell (keyboards) and Paul Joseph Moore (keyboards). They were originally signed by RSO, but the label folded after the group's first single. They added Nigel Thomas to the line-up in 1996.
30/09/1989 . . . . . 67 . . . . . 1 . . . .   THE DOWNTOWN LIGHTS . . . . Linn LKS 3
29/09/1990 . . . . . 72 . . . . . 1 . . . .   HEADLIGHTS ON PARADE . . . . Linn LKS 4
19/01/1991 . . . . . 50 . . . . . 2 . . . .   SATURDAY NIGHT . . . . Linn LKS 5
04/09/2004 . . . . . 52 . . . . . 1 . . . .   I WOULD NEVER . . . . Sanctuary SANXD305

BLUE OYSTER CULT US heavy rock group formed in New York in 1969 by Eric Bloom (born 1/12/1944, vocals/guitar/keyboards), Donald 'Buck Dharma' Roeser (born 12/11/1947, guitar/vocals), Albert Bouchard (born 24/5/1947, Watertown, NY, drums/vocals), Allen Lanier (born 25/6/1946, rhythm guitar/keyboards) and Joe Bouchard (born 9/11/1948, Watertown, bass/vocals) as Soft White Underbelly (a name they retain for low-key concerts). They became Blue Oyster Cult the following year.
20/05/1978 . . . . . 16 . . . . . 14 . . . . . .   (DON'T FEAR) THE REAPER Featured in the 1978 film *Halloween* . . . . CBS 6333

BLUE PEARL UK/US group formed by Pig Youth (Martin 'Pig Youth' Glover, born 27/12/1960, Africa) and Brilliant, with vocals by Pamela Carol 'Durga' McBroom.
07/07/1990 . . . . . 4 . . . . . 13 . . . . . .   **NAKED IN THE RAIN** . . . . Big Life BLR 23
03/11/1990 . . . . . 31 . . . . . 5 . . . .   LITTLE BROTHER . . . . Big Life BLR 32
11/01/1992 . . . . . 14 . . . . . 6 . . . .   (CAN YOU) FEEL THE PASSION . . . . Big Life BLR 67
25/07/1992 . . . . . 50 . . . . . 2 . . . .   MOTHER DAWN . . . . Big Life BLR 73
27/11/1993 . . . . . 71 . . . . . 1 . . . .   FIRE OF LOVE JUNGLE HIGH WITH BLUE PEARL . . . . Logic 74321170292
04/07/1998 . . . . . 22 . . . . . 2 . . . .   NAKED IN THE RAIN (REMIX) . . . . Malarky MLKD 7

BLUE RONDO A LA TURK UK group formed in London in 1981 by Moses Mount Bassie, Lloyd Bynoe, Art Collins, Geraldo D'Arbilly, Kito Poccioni, Mark Reilly (born 20/2/1960, High Wycombe), Chris Sullivan, Chris Tolera, Tholo Peter Tsegona and Daniel White (born 26/8/1959, High Wycombe), taking their name from a song title by jazz musician Dave Brubeck. Reilly and White went on to form Matt Bianco.
14/11/1981 . . . . . 40 . . . . . 4 . . . .   ME AND MR SANCHEZ . . . . Virgin VS 463
13/03/1982 . . . . . 50 . . . . . 5 . . . .   KLACTOVEESEDSTEIN . . . . Diable Noir VS 476

BLUE ZOO UK group formed in 1980 by Mike Ansell (bass), Andy O (vocals), Tim Parry (guitar) and Micky Sparrow (drums). Parry had been a member of The Crooks, later forming Big Life Records with Jazz Summers.
12/06/1982 . . . . . 55 . . . . . 3 . . . .   I'M YOUR MAN . . . . Magnet MAG 224

○ Silver disc ● Gold disc ✪ Platinum disc (additional platinum units are indicated by a figure following the symbol) ◉ Singles released prior to 1973 that are known to have sold over 1 million copies in the UK

| 16/10/1982 | 13 | 10 | | CRY BOY CRY | Magnet MAG 234 |
| 28/05/1983 | 60 | 4 | | I JUST CAN'T (FORGIVE AND FORGET) | Magnet MAG 241 |

BLUEBELLS UK rock group formed in 1982 by Ken McCluskey (born 8/2/1962, vocals), David McCluskey (born 13/1/1964, drums), Robert 'Bobby Bluebell' Hodgens (born 6/6/1959, guitar) and Craig Gannon (born 30/7/1966, guitar). They were sued, unsuccessfully, in 1982 by a French dance troupe called the Blubells, who felt the Scottish group's scruffy image tarnished their own. They disbanded before the re-issue of *Young At Heart* topped the charts, but did reunite to do *Top Of The Pops*.

12/03/1983	62	2		CATH/WILL SHE ALWAYS BE WAITING	London LON 20
09/07/1983	72	1		SUGAR BRIDGE (IT WILL STAND)	London LON 27
24/03/1984	11	12		I'M FALLING	London LON 45
23/06/1984	8	12		**YOUNG AT HEART**	London LON 49
01/09/1984	38	7		CATH Re-issue of London LON 20	London LON 54
09/02/1985	58	3		ALL I AM (IS LOVING YOU)	London LON 58
27/03/1993	❶⁴	12	●	**YOUNG AT HEART** Re-issue of London LON 49 following the song's use in an advertisement for Volkswagen. In 2002 violinist Bobby Valentino persuaded a judge he had co-written the song (with Siobhan Fahey and Robert Hodgens). Having been paid £75 when it was originally recorded, he stood to collect £100,000 in back royalties.	London LONCD 338

BLUENOTES – see **HAROLD MELVIN AND THE BLUENOTES**

BLUES BAND UK group formed in 1979 by ex-Manfred Mann vocalist Paul Jones (born Paul Pond, 24/2/1942, Portsmouth).

| 12/07/1980 | 68 | 2 | | BLUES BAND (EP) Tracks on EP: *Maggie's Farm, Ain't It Tuff, Diddy Wah Diddy* and *Back Door Man* | Arista BOOT 2 |

BLUES BROTHERS US group formed in Chicago, IL in 1976 by Joliet 'Jake' Blues (played by John Belushi, born 24/1/1949, Wheaton, IL) and Elwood Blues (played by Dan Aykroyd, born 1/7/1952, Ottawa, Canada), who originally came together for the TV series *Saturday Night Live* before making the 1980 film *The Blues Brothers* directed by John Landis. The film's subsequent cult status prompted a touring band featuring Steve Cropper, Donald 'Duck' Dunn and Matt Murphy, the current singer being Eddie Floyd. Belushi died from a drug overdose in Los Angeles, CA on 5/3/1982. (The cocaine and heroin 'cocktail' was supplied by girlfriend Cathy Evelyn Smith, who fled to Canada to evade prosecution. Surrendering to the Canadian authorities, she was extradited back to the US where she was convicted of involuntary manslaughter and sentenced to three years in prison, serving eighteen months.)

| 07/04/1990 | 12 | 8 | | EVERYBODY NEEDS SOMEBODY TO LOVE Featured in the 1980 film *The Blues Brothers*. B-side is *Think* by **ARETHA FRANKLIN** and is also from the soundtrack to *The Blues Brothers* | East West A 7591 |

BLUESKINS UK group formed in Wakefield by Ryan Spendlove (born 1/1/1979, guitar/keyboards/vocals), Ritchie Townsend (born 27/5/1985, guitar/vocals), Maff Smith (born 8/6/1980, bass) and Paul Brown (born 11/10/1980, drums).

| 21/02/2004 | 56 | 1 | | CHANGE MY MIND/I WANNA KNOW | Domino RUG174CD |
| 05/06/2004 | 61 | 1 | | THE STUPID ONES | Domino RUG175CD |

BLUETONES UK rock group formed in London in 1990 by Adam Devlin (born 17/9/1969, Hounslow, Middlesex, lead guitar), Mark Morriss (born 18/10/1971, Hounslow, lead vocals), Ed Chesters (born 24/10/1971, Darlington, drums) and Scott Morriss (born 10/10/1973, Hounslow, drums).

17/06/1995	31	2		ARE YOU BLUE OR ARE YOU BLIND?	Superior Quality BLUE 001CD
14/10/1995	19	3		BLUETONIC	Superior Quality BLUE 002CD
03/02/1996	2	8		**SLIGHT RETURN** Originally released in 1994 and failed to chart	Superior Quality BLUE 003CD
11/05/1996	7	6		**CUT SOME RUG/CASTLE ROCK**	Superior Quality BLUE 005CD
28/09/1996	7	6		**MARBLEHEAD JOHNSON**	Superior Quality BLUE 006CD
21/02/1998	10	3		**SOLOMON BITES THE WORM**	Superior Quality BLUE 007CD
09/05/1998	13	5		IF...	Superior Quality BLUED 009
08/08/1998	35	2		SLEAZY BED TRACK	Superior Quality BLUED 010
04/03/2000	13	3		KEEP THE HOME FIRES BURNING	Superior Quality BLUED 012
20/05/2000	18	3		AUTOPHILIA	Superior Quality BLUEDD 013
06/04/2002	26	2		AFTER HOURS	Mercury BLUED 016
03/05/2003	25	2		FAST BOY/LIQUID LIPS	Superior Quality BLUE 18CDS
23/08/2003	40	1		NEVER GOING NOWHERE	Superior Quality BLUE 020CDS2

COLIN BLUNSTONE UK singer (born 24/6/1945, Hatfield) who was lead singer with The Zombies until they disbanded in 1967. After a year working in an insurance office he went solo, his first hit (under the name Neil McArthur) a cover version of The Zombies' *She's Not There*, prompting calls for the group to re-form. Blunstone, however, stayed solo.

12/02/1972	15	9		SAY YOU DON'T MIND	Epic EPC 7765
11/11/1972	31	6		I DON'T BELIEVE IN MIRACLES	Epic EPC 8434
17/02/1973	45	2		HOW COULD WE DARE TO BE WRONG	Epic EPC 1197
14/03/1981	13	10		WHAT BECOMES OF THE BROKEN HEARTED **DAVE STEWART. GUEST VOCALS: COLIN BLUNSTONE**	Stiff BROKEN 1
29/05/1982	60	2		TRACKS OF MY TEARS	PRT 7P 236

BLUR UK rock group formed in London in 1988 by Damon Albarn (born 23/3/1968, London, guitar/keyboards/vocals), Alex James (born 21/11/1968, Boscombe, bass) and Graham Coxon (born 12/3/1969, Rintein, Germany, guitar), later adding Dave Rowntree (born 8/5/1964, Colchester, drums). Originally named Seymour, they changed to Blur upon signing with Food in 1991. They were the major winners at the 1995 BRIT Awards, heading the Best UK Group, Best Album (for *Parklife*), Best Single and Best Video categories (their four awards is the most won by a group or artist in a single year). Albarn later formed Gorillaz with Jamie Elliott, Coxon recording solo.

| 27/10/1990 | 48 | 3 | | SHE'S SO HIGH/I KNOW | Food 26 |

❶⁹ Number of weeks single topped the UK chart   ↑ Entered the UK chart at #1   ▲⁹ Number of weeks single topped the US chart

27/04/1991	8	8		THERE'S NO OTHER WAY		Food 29
10/08/1991	24	4		BANG		Food 31
11/04/1992	32	2		POPSCENE		Food 37
01/05/1993	28	4		FOR TOMORROW		Food CDFOODS 40
10/07/1993	28	4		CHEMICAL WORLD		Food CDFOODS 45
16/10/1993	26	3		SUNDAY SUNDAY		Food CDFOODS 46
19/03/1994	5	7		GIRLS AND BOYS		Food CDFOODS 47
11/06/1994	16	5		TO THE END		Food CDFOODS 50
03/09/1994	10	7		PARKLIFE 1995 BRIT Awards for Best Single and Best Video		Food CDFOODS 53
19/11/1994	19	3		END OF A CENTURY		Food CDFOODS 56
26/08/1995	❶²	11	●	COUNTRY HOUSE ↑		Food CDFOODS 63
09/09/1995	57	1		COUNTRY HOUSE 7-inch vinyl version of the above single. As chart rules allow for only three versions of a single, the two CDs and cassette contributed to the above placing and the 7-inch version was listed separately		Food 63
25/11/1995	5	9	○	THE UNIVERSAL		Food CDFOODS 69
24/02/1996	7	5		STEREOTYPES		Food CDFOOD 73
11/05/1996	5	5		CHARMLESS MAN		Food CDFOOD 77
01/02/1997	❶¹	7		BEETLEBUM ↑		Food CDFOODS 89
19/04/1997	2	5		SONG 2		Food CDFOODS 93
28/06/1997	5	5		ON YOUR OWN		Food CDFOOD 98
27/09/1997	15	3		MOR		Food CDFOOD 107
06/03/1999	2	10	○	TENDER		Food CDFOODS 117
10/07/1999	11	7		COFFEE + TV Featured in the 1999 film *Cruel Intentions*. 1999 MTV Europe Music Award for Best Video		Food CDFOODS 122
27/11/1999	14	4		NO DISTANCE LEFT TO RUN		Food CDFOOD 123
28/10/2000	10	9		MUSIC IS MY RADAR		Food CDFOODS 135
26/04/2003	5	9		OUT OF TIME		Parlophone CDR 6606
19/07/2003	18	3		CRAZY BEAT		Parlophone CDR 6610
18/10/2003	22	2		GOOD SONG		Parlophone CDR 6619

BM DUBS PRESENT MR RUMBLE FEATURING BRASSTOOTH AND KEE
UK production group formed by Cecil Glenn, Steve Gibson and Ralph Sall. They are also members of Sniper Cru with MC Terrorist, MC Stama and singer Laverne Shirfield.

17/03/2001	32	2		WHOOMP THERE IT IS		Incentive CENT 16CDS

BMR FEATURING FELICIA
German producer Michi Lange recording with singer Felicia.

01/05/1999	29	2		CHECK IT OUT (EVERYBODY) Contains a sample of MFSB Featuring The Three Degrees' *TSOP (The Sound Of Philadelphia)*		AM:PM CDAMPM 120

BMU
US/UK ensemble of the top R&B stars of the era: R Kelly, Tevin Campbell, Aaron Hall, Brian McKnight, Boyz II Men (Wanya 'Squirt' Morris, Michael 'Bass' McCrary, Shawn 'Slim' Stockman and Nathan 'Alex Vanderpool' Morris), Tony Toni Tone (Dwayne and Raphael Wiggins and cousin Timothy Christian), Silk (Timothy Cameron, Jimmy Gates Jr, Johnathen Rasboro, Gary Jenkins and Gary Glenn), Keith Sweat, Stokley (from Mint Condition), H-Town (Shazam and John 'Dino' Conner and Darryl 'GI' Jackson), Christopher Williams, Portrait (Eric Kirkland, Michael Angelo Saulsberry, Irving Washington III and Phillip Johnson), Gerald Levert, Al B Sure!, Damian Hall, Lil' Joe (of the Rude Boys), Intro (Kenny Greene, Clinton Wike and Jeff Sanders), DRS (Endo, Pic, Jail Bait, Deuce Deuce and Blunt), El DeBarge, After 7 (Keith Mitchell, Kevon and Melvin Edmonds), Usher, Sovory, Joe, D'Angelo and Lenny Kravitz. The name stands for Black Men United.

18/02/1995	23	2		U WILL KNOW Featured in the 1994 film *Jason's Lyric*		Mercury MERCD 420

BO SELECTA
UK TV character created by comic Leigh Francis (born 30/5/1973) and featuring celebrity stalker Avid Merrion.

27/12/2003	4	9		PROPER CRIMBO		BMG 82876581412

BOB AND EARL
US duo formed in 1957 by Bobby Byrd (born 1/7/1932, Fort Worth, TX), who later recorded as Bobby Day, and Earl Nelson. Bobby Relf replaced Byrd in 1959, and it was this duo that recorded their hit single in 1963, produced and arranged by Barry White, although it didn't become a hit until six years later when re-released. Day died from cancer on 15/7/1990.

12/03/1969	7	13		HARLEM SHUFFLE		Island WIP 6053

BOB AND MARCIA
Jamaican vocal duo Bob Andy (born Keith Anderson, 1944, Kingston) and Marcia Griffiths (born 1954, Kingston) put successful solo careers on hold to record a cover version of Nina Simone's *Young Gifted And Black*. After further success they resumed their solo careers, Griffiths later joining the I-Threes.

14/03/1970	5	12		YOUNG GIFTED AND BLACK		Harry J HJ 6605
05/06/1971	11	13		PIED PIPER		Trojan TR 7818

BOB THE BUILDER
UK animated TV character whose voice is supplied by actor Neil Morrissey. As the name implies, Bob The Builder is a building contractor. The debut hit was the best-selling single of 2000 with sales of 853,000 copies. it went on to become the most successful single in BBC history, topping 1 million in sales by June 2001.

16/12/2000	❶³	22	✪	CAN WE FIX IT		BBC Music WMSS 60372
15/09/2001	❶¹	19	●	MAMBO NO 5 ↑		BBC Music WMSS 60442

BOBBYSOCKS
Norwegian/Swedish vocal duo Hanne Krogh and Elisabeth Andreasson.

25/05/1985	44	4		LET IT SWING 1985 Eurovision Song Contest winner, beating the UK entry by Vikki, *Love Is,* into fourth place. Original Norwegian		

○ Silver disc   ● Gold disc   ✪ Platinum disc (additional platinum units are indicated by a figure following the symbol)   ◎ Singles released prior to 1973 that are known to have sold over 1 million copies in the UK

title *La Det Swinge* . . . . RCA PB 40127

ANDREA BOCELLI
Italian singer (born 22/9/1958, Laiatico, near Pisa) who studied law at the University of Pisa and was briefly a lawyer before his singing career. Visually impaired from birth, he lost his eyesight completely at twelve following an accident playing football. He won the 2003 Classical BRIT Awards for Album of the Year and Best Selling Album for *Sentimento*.

24/05/1997 . . . . . 2 . . . . . . 14 . . . . . ●	TIME TO SAY GOODBYE (CON TE PARTIRO) SARAH BRIGHTMAN AND ANDREA BOCELLI . . . . Coalition COLA 003CD
25/09/1999 . . . . . 25 . . . . . . 5	CANTO DELLA TERRA . . . . Sugar 5613192
18/12/1999 . . . . . 65 . . . . . . 1	AVE MARIA . . . . Philips 4644852
01/07/2000 . . . . . 24 . . . . . . 2	CANTO DELLA TERRA Re-issued following its use by the BBC for its European Championship 2000 coverage . . . . Sugar 5613192

KAREN BODDINGTON AND MARK WILLIAMS
Australian vocal duo who later worked as backing singers for Margaret Urlich. Boddington later toured with Beverley Craven.

| 02/09/1989 . . . . . 73 . . . . . . 1 . . . . | HOME AND AWAY Theme to the TV series of the same name . . . . First Night SCORE 19 |

BODY COUNT
US rap/heavy metal group assembled by Ice-T (born Tracy Morrow, 16/2/1958, Los Angeles, CA) and featuring Ernie-C (guitar), D-Roc (guitar), Mooseman (bass) and Beatmaster V (drums). Their *Cop Killer* got them thrown off Sire Records after protests led by actor Charlton Heston (a major shareholder in Time Warner, owners of Sire), Oliver North and President George Bush, with death threats being made to record company employees. D-Roc died from mycosis fungoides on 17/8/2004.

| 08/10/1994 . . . . . 28 . . . . . . 2 . . . . . . | BORN DEAD . . . . Rhyme Syndicate SYNDG 4 |
| 17/12/1994 . . . . . 45 . . . . . . 2 . . . . . . | NECESSARY EVIL . . . . Virgin VSCDX 1529 |

BODYSNATCHERS
UK group formed in 1979 by Miranda Joyce (saxophone), Sara Jane Owen (guitar), Stella Barker (guitar), Judy Parsons (drums) and Penny Leyton (keyboards). They broke up less than a year later, all but Leyton joining The Belle Stars.

| 15/03/1980 . . . . . 22 . . . . . . 9 . . . . . . | LET'S DO ROCK STEADY . . . . 2 Tone CHSTT 9 |
| 19/07/1980 . . . . . 50 . . . . . . 3 . . . . . . | EASY LIFE . . . . 2 Tone CHSTT 12 |

HAMILTON BOHANNON
US singer/songwriter/producer/drummer (born 7/3/1942, Newnam, GA) who was a session musician and musical director at Motown Records (after being introduced by Stevie Wonder) before going solo in 1972 with Dakar.

15/02/1975 . . . . . 22 . . . . . . 8	SOUTH AFRICAN MAN . . . . Brunswick BR 16
24/05/1975 . . . . . 6 . . . . . . 12	DISCO STOMP . . . . Brunswick BR 19
05/07/1975 . . . . . 23 . . . . . . 6	FOOT STOMPIN' MUSIC . . . . Brunswick BR 21
06/09/1975 . . . . . 49 . . . . . . 3	HAPPY FEELING . . . . Brunswick BR 24
26/08/1978 . . . . . 56 . . . . . . 4	LET'S START THE DANCE Featured in the 1998 film *54* . . . . Mercury 6167 700
13/02/1982 . . . . . 49 . . . . . . 5	LET'S START TO DANCE AGAIN . . . . London HL 10582

BOILING POINT
US funk group formed in Atlanta, GA by Arcelious Daniels, Willie Harnell and Clyde Howard.

| 27/05/1978 . . . . . 41 . . . . . . 6 . . . . . . | LET'S GET FUNKTIFIED . . . . Bang 1312 |

MARC BOLAN — see T REX

CJ BOLLAND
UK producer (born Christian Jay Bolland, 18/6/1971, Stockton-on-Tees, raised in Antwerp, Belgium) who has also recorded as Sonic Solution, Ravesignal III, Pulse, The Project and Space Opera.

05/10/1996 . . . . . 11 . . . . . . 5	SUGAR IS SWEETER Features the uncredited vocals of Jade 4 U . . . . Internal LIECD 35
17/05/1997 . . . . . 19 . . . . . . 3	THE PROPHET . . . . ffrr FCD 300
03/07/1999 . . . . . 35 . . . . . . 2	IT AIN'T GONNA BE ME Contains samples of Samuel L Jackson's dialogue from the 1997 film *Jackie Brown*. Featured in the 1999 film *Human Traffic* . . . . Essential Recordings ESCDP 5

MICHAEL BOLTON
US singer (born Michael Bolotin, 26/2/1953, New Haven, CT) who was lead singer with Blackjack in the late 1970s. He went solo as Michael Bolton in 1983. He released an album of operatic pieces in 1998 as *Secret Passion – The Arias*. He has a star on the Hollywood Walk of Fame.

17/02/1990 . . . . . 3 . . . . . . 10	HOW AM I SUPPOSED TO LIVE WITHOUT YOU ▲3 1990 Grammy Award for Best Pop Vocal Performance . . . . CBS 6553977
28/04/1990 . . . . . 10 . . . . . 10	HOW CAN WE BE LOVERS . . . . CBS 6559187
21/07/1990 . . . . . 44 . . . . . . 5	WHEN I'M BACK ON MY FEET AGAIN . . . . CBS 6560777
20/04/1991 . . . . . 23 . . . . . . 8	LOVE IS A WONDERFUL THING The Isley Brothers later sued Bolton for $3.3 million over the similarities between this and another song. . . . . Columbia 6567717
27/07/1991 . . . . . 28 . . . . . . 7	TIME LOVE AND TENDERNESS. . . . . Columbia 6569897
09/11/1991 . . . . . 8 . . . . . . 9	WHEN A MAN LOVES A WOMAN ▲1 1991 Grammy Award for Best Pop Vocal Performance . . . . Columbia 6574887
08/02/1992 . . . . . 17 . . . . . . 6	STEEL BARS . . . . Columbia 6577257
09/05/1992 . . . . . 28 . . . . . . 4	MISSING YOU NOW MICHAEL BOLTON FEATURING KENNY G . . . . Columbia 6579917
31/10/1992 . . . . . 16 . . . . . . 6	TO LOVE SOMEBODY . . . . Columbia 6584557
26/12/1992 . . . . . 18 . . . . . . 5	DRIFT AWAY . . . . Columbia 6588657
13/03/1993 . . . . . 37 . . . . . . 4	REACH OUT I'LL BE THERE . . . . Columbia 6588972
13/11/1993 . . . . . 15 . . . . . . 8	SAID I LOVED YOU BUT I LIED . . . . Columbia 6598762
26/02/1994 . . . . . 32 . . . . . . 3	SOUL OF MY SOUL . . . . Columbia 6601772
14/05/1994 . . . . . 14 . . . . . . 7	LEAN ON ME. . . . . Columbia 6604132
09/09/1995 . . . . . 6 . . . . . . 9	CAN I TOUCH YOU…THERE? . . . . Columbia 6624385
02/12/1995 . . . . . 27 . . . . . . 5	A LOVE SO BEAUTIFUL. . . . . Columbia 6627092
16/03/1996 . . . . . 35 . . . . . . 3	SOUL PROVIDER . . . . Columbia 6629812
08/11/1997 . . . . . 14 . . . . . . 4	THE BEST OF LOVE/GO THE DISTANCE B-side featured in the 1997 Walt Disney film *Hercules* . . . . Columbia 6652802

❶9 Number of weeks single topped the UK chart ↑ Entered the UK chart at #1 ▲9 Number of weeks single topped the US chart

95

BOMB THE BASS
UK studio group (hence so many guest singers), the brainchild of writer/producer Tim Simenon (born 1968, London). He recorded under his own name (sensing Gulf War sensitivity over the group name), returning as Bomb The Bass in 1994 with his Stoned Heights label.

20/02/1988	2	9	○	**BEAT DIS**	Mister-ron DOOD 1
27/08/1988	6	9		**MEGABLAST/DON'T MAKE ME WAIT** BOMB THE BASS FEATURING MERLIN AND ANTONIA/BOMB THE BASS FEATURING LORRAINE Mister-ron DOOD 2	
26/11/1988	10	10		**SAY A LITTLE PRAYER** BOMB THE BASS FEATURING MAUREEN	Rhythm King DOOD 3
27/07/1991	7	9		**WINTER IN JULY**	Rhythm King 6572757
09/11/1991	52	3		THE AIR YOU BREATHE	Rhythm King 6575387
02/05/1992	62	2		KEEP GIVING ME LOVE	Rhythm King 6579887
01/10/1994	24	3		BUG POWDER DUST BOMB THE BASS FEATURING JUSTIN WARFIELD	Stoned Heights BRCD 300
17/12/1994	35	3		DARKHEART BOMB THE BASS FEATURING SPIKEY TEE	Stoned Heights BRCD 305
01/04/1995	53	1		1 TO 1 RELIGION BOMB THE BASS FEATURING CARLTON	Stoned Heights BRCD 313
16/09/1995	54	1		SANDCASTLES BOMB THE BASS FEATURING BERNARD FOWLER	Fourth & Broadway BRCD 324

BOMBALURINA
UK studio group assembled by Andrew Lloyd-Webber and produced by Nigel Wright. The record and name of the group (after a character in Lloyd-Webber's musical *Cats*) were selected before the actual performer. Timmy Mallett is a children's TV presenter.

28/07/1990	❶[3]	13	○	**ITSY BITSY TEENY WEENY YELLOW POLKA DOT BIKINI** BOMBALURINA FEATURING TIMMY MALLETT	Carpet CRPT 1
24/11/1990	18	7		SEVEN LITTLE GIRLS SITTING IN THE BACKSEAT	Carpet CRPT 2

BOMBERS
Canadian disco aggregation assembled by producer Pat De Sario.

05/05/1979	37	7		(EVERYBODY) GET DANCIN'	Flamingo FM 1
18/08/1979	58	3		LET'S DANCE	Flamingo FM 4

BOMFUNK MC'S
UK/Finnish dance group formed by Raymond Ebanks and Jaakko Salovaara, aka B.O.W. and DJ Gismo. Salovaara also produces as JS 16. They were named Best Nordic Act at the 2000 MTV Europe Music Awards.

05/08/2000	2	12		**FREESTYLER** First single to be awarded an IFPI Platinum Award, recognising sales of 2.5 million in Europe in 2000 Dancepool DPS 2CD	
02/12/2000	11	9		UP ROCKING BEATS	INCredible 6706132

BON
German vocal duo formed by Guy Gross and Claus Capek.

03/02/2001	15	5		BOYS	Epic 6707092

BON JOVI
US hard rock quintet formed in New Jersey in 1982 by Jon Bon Jovi (born Jon Bongiovi, 2/3/1962, Perth Amboy, NJ, lead vocals), Richie Sambora (born 11/7/1959, Perth Amboy, guitar), Dave Bryan (born David Rashbaum, 7/2/1962, Edison, NJ, keyboards), Alec John Such (born 14/11/1956, Yonkers, NY, bass) and Tico Torres (born 7/10/1953, Colonia, NJ, drums). Sambora is married to actress Heather Locklear, who was previously married to ex-Motley Crue drummer Tommy Lee, Torres is married to supermodel Eva Herzigova. They were named Best International Group at the 1996 BRIT Awards and Best Rock Act at the 1995 MTV Europe Music Awards.

31/08/1985	68	1		HARDEST PART IS THE NIGHT	Vertigo VER 22
09/08/1986	14	10		YOU GIVE LOVE A BAD NAME ▲[1]	Vertigo VER 26
25/10/1986	4	15		**LIVIN' ON A PRAYER** ▲[4] Featured in the 2003 film *Charlie's Angels: Full Throttle*	Vertigo VER 28
11/04/1987	13	7		WANTED DEAD OR ALIVE Featured in the 2004 film *Scooby Doo 2: Monsters Unleashed*	Vertigo JOV 2
15/08/1987	21	5		NEVER SAY GOODBYE	Vertigo JOV 3
24/09/1988	17	7		BAD MEDICINE ▲[2]	Vertigo JOV 3
10/12/1988	22	7		BORN TO BE MY BABY	Vertigo JOV 4
29/04/1989	18	7		I'LL BE THERE FOR YOU ▲[1]	Vertigo JOV 5
26/08/1989	18	6		LAY YOUR HANDS ON ME	Vertigo JOV 6
09/12/1989	35	6		LIVING IN SIN	Vertigo JOV 7
24/10/1992	5	6		**KEEP THE FAITH**	Jambco JOV 8
23/01/1993	13	6		BED OF ROSES	Jambco JOVCD 9
15/05/1993	9	7		**IN THESE ARMS**	Jambco JOVCD 10
07/08/1993	17	5		I'LL SLEEP WHEN I'M DEAD	Jambco JOVCD 11
02/10/1993	11	6		I BELIEVE	Jambco JOVCD 12
26/03/1994	9	6		**DRY COUNTY**	Jambco JOVCD 13
24/09/1994	2	18		**ALWAYS**	Jambco JOVCD 14
17/12/1994	7	10		PLEASE COME HOME FOR CHRISTMAS	Jambco JOVCD 16
25/02/1995	7	7		**SOMEDAY I'LL BE SATURDAY NIGHT**	Jambco JOVDD 15
10/06/1995	6	9		**THIS AIN'T A LOVE SONG**	Mercury JOVCX 17
30/09/1995	8	7		**SOMETHING FOR THE PAIN**	Mercury JOVCX 18
25/11/1995	10	8		LIE TO ME	Mercury JOVCD 19
09/03/1996	7	6		**THESE DAYS**	Mercury JOVCD 20
06/07/1996	13	5		HEY GOD	Mercury JOVCX 21

○ Silver disc   ● Gold disc   ✪ Platinum disc (additional platinum units are indicated by a figure following the symbol)   ◉ Singles released prior to 1973 that are known to have sold over 1 million copies in the UK

DATE	POS	WKS	BPI	SINGLE TITLE	LABEL & NUMBER
10/04/1999	21	5		REAL LIFE Featured in the 1999 film *Edtv*	Reprise W 479CD
03/06/2000	3	13		**IT'S MY LIFE**	Mercury 5627682
09/09/2000	10	7		**SAY IT ISN'T SO**	Mercury 5688982
09/12/2000	12	6		THANK YOU FOR LOVING ME	Mercury 5727312
19/05/2001	10	7		**ONE WILD NIGHT**	Mercury 5729502
28/09/2002	5	6		**EVERYDAY**	Mercury 0639372
21/12/2002	21	5		MISUNDERSTOOD	Mercury 0638162
24/05/2003	9	6		**ALL ABOUT LOVIN' YOU**	Mercury 9800242

JON BON JOVI US singer (born John Bongiovi, 2/3/1962, Perth Amboy, NJ) who is lead singer with Bon Jovi. He wrote the soundtrack to the 1990 film *Young Guns II* (*Blaze Of Glory* is the title track), making a cameo appearance in the film. He also appeared in the films *The Leading Man* (1997) and *U-571* (2000). Named Best International Male Artist at the 1998 BRIT Awards and Best Male Artist at the 1995 and 1997 MTV Europe Music Awards, he took part in the *It's Only Rock 'N' Roll* project for the Children's Promise charity.

DATE	POS	WKS	BPI	SINGLE TITLE	LABEL & NUMBER
04/08/1990	13	8		BLAZE OF GLORY ▲[1] Features Jeff Beck and Aldo Nova on guitars and Randy Jackson on bass	Vertigo JBJ 1
10/11/1990	29	5		MIRACLE This and above single featured in the 1990 film *Young Guns II*	Vertigo JBJ 2
14/06/1997	4	7		**MIDNIGHT IN CHELSEA**	Mercury MERCD 488
30/08/1997	10	4		**QUEEN OF NEW ORLEANS**	Mercury MERCD 493
15/11/1997	13	3		JANIE, DON'T TAKE YOUR LOVE TO TOWN	Mercury 5749872

RONNIE BOND UK singer/drummer (born Ronald Bullis, 4/5/1943, Andover) who was a founding member of The Troggs in 1964. He died on 13/11/1992.

DATE	POS	WKS	BPI	SINGLE TITLE	LABEL & NUMBER
31/05/1980	52	5		IT'S WRITTEN ON YOUR BODY	Mercury MER 13

GARY U.S. BONDS US singer (born Gary Anderson, 6/6/1939, Jacksonville, FL) christened US Bonds by record boss Frank Guida, with 'buy US Bonds' the marketing slogan. He made modest chart entries twenty years later with titles produced by Bruce Springsteen and Miami Steve Van Zandt.

DATE	POS	WKS	BPI	SINGLE TITLE	LABEL & NUMBER
19/01/1961	16	11		NEW ORLEANS	Top Rank JAR 527
20/07/1961	7	13		**QUARTER TO THREE** ▲[2]	Top Rank JAR 575
30/05/1981	43	6		THIS LITTLE GIRL	EMI America EA 122
22/08/1981	51	3		JOLE BLON	EMI America EA 127
31/10/1981	43	3		IT'S ONLY LOVE	EMI America EA 128
17/07/1982	59	3		SOUL DEEP	EMI America EA 140

BONE UK duo James Ormandy and Sam Mollison. Mollison also recorded with Sasha.

DATE	POS	WKS	BPI	SINGLE TITLE	LABEL & NUMBER
02/04/1994	55	1		WINGS OF LOVE	Deconstruction 74321176282

BONE THUGS-N-HARMONY US rap group from Cleveland, OH formed by Krayzie Bone (born Anthony Henderson), Layzie Bone (Steven Howse), Bizzy Bone (Byron McCane), Wish Bone (Curtis Scruggs) and Flesh-N-Bone (Stanley Howse), discovered by Eazy-E of NWA.

DATE	POS	WKS	BPI	SINGLE TITLE	LABEL & NUMBER
04/11/1995	32	2		1ST OF THA MONTH	Epic 6625172
10/08/1996	8	11		**THA CROSSROADS** Contains an interpolation of The Isley Brothers' *Make Me Say It Again Girl*. 1996 Grammy Award for Best Rap Group Performance	Epic 6635502
09/11/1996	15	4		1ST OF THA MONTH Re-issue of Epic 6625172	Epic 6638505
15/02/1997	37	2		DAYS OF OUR LIVEZ Featured in the 1996 film *Set It Off*	East West A 3982CD
26/07/1997	16	3		LOOK INTO MY EYES Featured in the 1997 film *Batman And Robin*	Epic 6647862
24/05/2003	19	4		HOME **BONE THUGS-N-HARMONY FEATURING PHIL COLLINS**	Epic 6738305

ELBOW BONES AND THE RACKETEERS US group formed by Ginchy Dan and Stephanie Fuller, proteges of August Darnell (aka Kid Creole).

DATE	POS	WKS	BPI	SINGLE TITLE	LABEL & NUMBER
14/01/1984	33	9		A NIGHT IN NEW YORK	EMI America EA 165

BONEY M Jamaican/Antilles/Montserrat brainchild of German record producer Frank Farian who recorded the first single (*Baby Do You Wanna Bump*) and then advertised for four singers to become Boney M. Marcia Barrett (born 14/10/1948, St Catherines, Jamaica), Bobby Farrell (born 6/10/1949, Aruba, West Indies), Liz Mitchell (born 12/7/1952, Clarendon, Jamaica) and Masie Williams (born 25/3/1951, Montserrat, West Indies) became one of Eurodisco's most successful acts, Farian repeating the formula with Milli Vanilli and Far Corporation. *Rivers Of Babylon/Brown Girl In The Ring* is one of only five singles to have sold over 2 million copies in the UK.

DATE	POS	WKS	BPI	SINGLE TITLE	LABEL & NUMBER
18/12/1976	6	13	O	**DADDY COOL**	Atlantic K 10827
12/03/1977	3	10		**SUNNY**	Atlantic K 10892
25/06/1977	2	13		**MA BAKER** Features the uncredited contributions of Lorraine Pollack (as Ma Baker) and Bill Swisher (radio announcer)	Atlantic K 10965
29/10/1977	8	13		**BELFAST**	Atlantic K 11020
29/04/1978	❶[5]	40	✪	**RIVERS OF BABYLON/BROWN GIRL IN THE RING** A-side was a cover of The Melodians' 1970 hit. B-side was based on a Jamaican nursery rhyme	Atlantic/Hansa K 11120

❶[9] Number of weeks single topped the UK chart ↑ Entered the UK chart at #1 ▲[9] Number of weeks single topped the US chart

97

07/10/1978 .....2.....10.....●	**RASPUTIN** Banned in Russia..	Atlantic/Hansa K 11192
02/12/1978 ....❶⁴.....8.....✪	**MARY'S BOY CHILD – OH MY LORD**	Atlantic/Hansa K 11221
03/03/1979.....10.....6.....○	**PAINTER MAN**	Atlantic/Hansa K 11255
28/04/1979 ....3.....9.....○	**HOORAY HOORAY IT'S A HOLI-HOLIDAY**...................	Atlantic/Hansa K 11279
11/08/1979.....12.....11.....○	GOTTA GO HOME/EL LUTE......................................	Atlantic/Hansa K 11351
15/12/1979.....35.....7......	I'M BORN AGAIN...	Atlantic/Hansa K 11410
26/04/1980.....57.....5......	MY FRIEND JACK...	Atlantic/Hansa K 11463
14/02/1981.....66.....2......	CHILDREN OF PARADISE..	Atlantic/Hansa K 11637
21/11/1981.....39.....5......	WE KILL THE WORLD (DON'T KILL THE WORLD)	Atlantic/Hansa K 11689
24/12/1988.....52.....3......	MEGAMIX/MARY'S BOY CHILD (REMIX).......................	Ariola 111947
05/12/1992.....7.....9......	**BONEY M MEGAMIX**	Arista 74321125127
17/04/1993.....38.....3......	BROWN GIRL IN THE RING (REMIX)...........................	Arista 74321137052
08/05/1999.....22.....2......	MA BAKER...SOMEBODY SCREAM **BONEY ME VS HORNY UNITED**	Logic 74321653872
29/12/2001.....47.....2......	DADDY COOL 2001..	BMG 74321913512

BONIFACE UK singer (born Bruce Boniface, 1983).

31/08/2002.....25.....3......	CHEEKY...	Columbia 6729902

GRAHAM BONNET UK singer (born 12/12/1947, Skegness) who was formerly a member of Marbles before joining heavy rock group Rainbow in 1979 as lead singer, leaving after eighteen months to go solo.

21/03/1981 .....6.....11.....○	**NIGHT GAMES**..	Vertigo VER 1
13/06/1981.....51.....4......	LIAR..	Vertigo VER 2

GRAHAM BONNEY UK singer (born 2/6/1945, Stratford, London) with the Riot Squad and a session singer before going solo in 1965. He was later a regular on German TV.

24/03/1966.....19.....8......	SUPERGIRL..	Columbia DB 7843

BONNIE PRINCE BILLY US singer Will Oldham who also records as the Palace Brothers and Palace Music.

04/09/2004.....69.....1......	AGNES QUEEN OF SORROW.......................................	Domino RUG185CD

BONO Irish singer (born Paul Hewson, 10/5/1960, Dublin) and lead singer with U2. He took part in the *Perfect Day* project for the BBC's Children In Need charity, and was awarded the Free Your Mind Award at the 1999 MTV Europe Music Awards in recognition of charitable work.

25/01/1986.....20.....5......	IN A LIFETIME	RCA PB 40535
10/06/1989.....17.....7......	IN A LIFETIME Re-issue of RCA PB 40535 This and above single credited to **CLANNAD FEATURING BONO**	RCA PB 42873
04/12/1993 ....4.....9......	**I'VE GOT YOU UNDER MY SKIN** FRANK SINATRA WITH BONO Listed flip side was *Stay (Faraway, So Close)* by U2	Island CID 578
09/04/1994.....46.....2......	IN THE NAME OF THE FATHER **BONO AND GAVIN FRIDAY** Featured in the 1994 film *In The Name Of The Father*.....	Island CID 593
23/10/1999.....23.....2......	NEW DAY **WYCLEF JEAN FEATURING BONO** Featured in the 1999 film *Life*	Columbia 6682122

BONZO DOG DOO-DAH BAND UK group formed in 1966 by London art students Vivian Stanshall (born 21/3/1943, Shillingford, vocals), Neil Innes (born 9/12/1944, Danbury, guitar), 'Legs' Larry Smith (born 18/1/1944, Oxford, drums), Dennis Cowan (born 6/5/1947, London, bass), Roger Ruskin Spear (born 29/6/1943, London, saxophone/robots), Rodney Slater (born 8/11/1941, Crowland, saxophone) and Sam Spoons (born Martin Stafford Ashon, 8/2/1942, Bridgewater, percussion). Their act, a mix of traditional jazz and comedy, included mechanical robots. They appeared in The Beatles TV film *Magical Mystery Tour* (1967) and Monty Python's TV series *Do Not Adjust Your Set*. They disbanded in 1969, Innes forming the Beatles parody The Rutles with Eric Idle. Stanshall died in a house fire on 5/3/1995.

06/11/1968 .....5.....14......	**I'M THE URBAN SPACEMAN** Produced by Paul McCartney as Apollo C Vermouth	Liberty LBF 15144

BETTY BOO UK singer (born Alison Moira Clarkson, 6/3/1970, Kensington, London) with rap trio She-Rockers. She became Betty Boo (after the 1930s cartoon Betty Boop, being forced to amend it by lawyers representing the character) and signed with Rhythm King Records, guesting with label mates The Beatmasters on a top ten record. She went solo in 1990 and was named Best UK Newcomer at the 1991 BRIT Awards. Forced to cancel a 1991 Australian tour after it was discovered she was miming to backing tracks, she later co-wrote Hear'Say's debut hit *Pure & Simple*.

12/08/1989 .....7.....11......	HEY DJ I CAN'T DANCE TO THAT MUSIC YOU'RE PLAYING/SKA TRAIN **BEATMASTERS FEATURING BETTY BOO** ...	Rhythm King LEFT 34
19/05/1990.....7.....12......	**DOIN' THE DO** Contains a sample of Reparata & The Delrons' *Captain Of Your Ship*	Rhythm King LEFT 39
11/08/1990.....3.....10.....○	**WHERE ARE YOU BABY**..	Rhythm King LEFT 43
01/12/1990.....25.....8......	24 HOURS..	Rhythm King LEFT 45
08/08/1992.....12.....8......	LET ME TAKE YOU THERE Contains a sample of The Four Tops' *It's All In The Game*	WEA YZ 677
03/10/1992.....44.....3......	I'M ON MY WAY..	WEA YZ 693
10/04/1993.....50.....3......	HANGOVER..	WEA YZ 719CD

BOO RADLEYS UK rock group formed in Liverpool in 1988 by Sice (born Simon Rowbottom, 18/6/1969, Wallasey, guitar/vocals), Martin Carr (born 29/11/1968, Turso, Highlands, guitar), Timothy Brown (born 26/2/1969, Wallasey, bass) and Steve Drewitt (drums), named after a character in the novel *To Kill A Mockingbird*. Drewitt left in 1990 and was replaced by Robert Cieka (born 4/8/1968, Birmingham).

20/06/1992.....67.....1......	DOES THIS HURT/BOO! FOREVER	Creation CRE 128
23/10/1993.....75.....1......	WISH I WAS SKINNY...	Creation CRESCD 169
12/02/1994.....48.....2......	BARNEY (...& ME)...	Creation CRESCD 178
11/06/1994.....50.....2......	LAZARUS..	Creation CRESCD 187
11/03/1995 .....9.....8......	**WAKE UP BOO!**	Creation CRESCD 191

13/05/1995	37	3		FIND THE ANSWER WITHIN	Creation CRESCD 202
29/07/1995	25	2		IT'S LULU	Creation CRESCD 211
07/10/1995	24	2		FROM THE BENCH AT BELVIDERE	Creation CRESCD 214
17/08/1996	25	2		WHAT'S IN THE BOX? (SEE WHATCHA GOT)	Creation CRESCD 220
19/10/1996	18	2		C'MON KIDS	Creation CRESCD 236
01/02/1997	38	1		RIDE THE TIGER	Creation CRESCD 248X
17/10/1998	54	1		FREE HUEY	Creation CRESCD 299X

BOO-YAA T.R.I.B.E. US rap group formed in Los Angeles, CA by Ganxsta Ridd (born Paul Devoux), EKA (Danny Devoux), Rosco Devoux, Ganxsta OMB (David Devoux), The Godfather (Ted Devoux) and Don-L (Donald Devoux). The Devoux brothers got into music when another brother, Robert 'Youngman' Devoux, was shot dead in a gangland feud.

04/07/1987	7	11		JIVE TALKIN'	Hardback 7BOSS 4
30/06/1990	43	3		PSYKO FUNK	Fourth & Broadway BRW 179
06/11/1993	26	3		ANOTHER BODY MURDERED FAITH NO MORE AND BOO-YAA T.R.I.B.E.	Epic 6597942

BOOGIE DOWN PRODUCTIONS US rap duo formed in The Bronx, NYC by DJ Scott LaRock (born 2/3/1962) and KRS-One (born Lawrence 'Kris' Parker, 1966), having first met at a homeless person's shelter. LaRock was shot to death sitting in his pick-up truck on 27/8/1987, KRS-One (Knowledge Reigns Supreme Over Nearly Everyone) going solo.

04/06/1988	69	2		MY PHILOSOPHY/STOP THE VIOLENCE	Jive JIVEX 170

BOOGIE PIMPS German production duo formed in Erfurt by Mark J Klak and Mirco Jakobs.

17/01/2004	3	15		SOMEBODY TO LOVE	Data 61CDS
08/05/2004	10	6		SUNNY	Data 67CDX

BOOKER T AND THE MG'S US group formed in 1962 by Booker T Jones (born 12/11/1944, Memphis, TN, keyboards), Steve Cropper (born 21/10/1941, Ozark Mountains, MO, guitar), Lewis Steinberg (born 13/9/1933, Memphis, bass) and Al Jackson Jr (born 27/11/1935, Memphis, drums). Steinberg was replaced in 1964 by Donald 'Duck' Dunn (born 24/11/1941, Memphis). Al Jackson was murdered by two intruders at his Memphis home on 1/10/1975; his wife, who was tied up and unable to warn him as he entered the house, was first suspected as she had shot him the previous July. No one has ever been charged with the crime. Cropper and Dunn later appeared in the 1980 film *The Blues Brothers*. MG stands for Memphis Group. They were inducted into the Rock & Roll Hall of Fame in 1992, and won the 1994 Grammy Award for Best Pop Instrumental Performance for *Cruisin'*.

11/12/1968	30	9		SOUL LIMBO	Stax 102
07/05/1969	4	18		TIME IS TIGHT Featured in the films *Up Tight* (1968) and *Fear And Loathing In Las Vegas* (1998).	Stax 119
30/08/1969	35	4		SOUL CLAP '69	Stax 127
15/12/1979	7	12	○	GREEN ONIONS Originally released in the US in 1962. Featured in the films *American Graffiti* (1973), *American Hot Wax* (1978), *Quadrophenia* (1979), *Andre* (1995), *Get Shorty* (1996) and *Striptease* (1996).	Atlantic K 10109

BOOM! UK vocal group formed by Rachael Carr, Shakti Edwards, Vickey Palmer, Shaun Angel, Nick Donaghy and Johnny Shentall. Shentall later replaced Kym Marsh in Hear'Say.

27/01/2001	11	5		FALLING	London LONCD 458

TAKA BOOM US singer (born Yvonne Stevens, 1954, Chicago, IL) who was a member of Undisputed Truth and Glass Family before going solo. She is the sister of Chaka Khan and Mark Stevens (of The Jamaica Boys).

19/02/2000	8	5		MUST BE THE MUSIC	Incentive CENT 4CDS
16/09/2000	41	1		SATURDAY This and above single credited to JOEY NEGRO FEATURING TAKA BOOM	Yola CDX03
09/06/2001	36	2		JUST CAN'T GET ENOUGH (NO NO NO NO) EYE TO EYE FEATURING TAKA BOOM	Xtravaganza XTRAV 25CD

BOOM BOOM ROOM UK vocal/instrumental group formed by Andy Makanza, Jeremy Thornton Jones and Simon Etchell.

08/03/1986	74	1		HERE COMES THE MAN	Fun After All FUN 101

BOOMKAT US duo, brother and sister Kellin and Taryn Manning. Taryn was previously an actress, appearing in the films *8 Mile* (2002) and *Crossroads* (2002).

31/05/2003	37	2		THE WRECKONING	DreamWorks 4504580

BOOMTOWN RATS Irish group formed in Dublin in 1975 by former music journalist Bob Geldof (born 5/10/1954, Dublin), Johnnie Fingers (born John Moylett, 10/9/1956, keyboards), Pete Briquette (born Patrick Cusack, 2/7/1954, bass), Gerry Roberts (born 16/6/1954, guitar) and Simon Crowe (drums). Originally The Nightlife Thugs, they signed to Ensign in 1976 as The Boomtown Rats. Their chart career ended in 1984 (with one re-issue entry in 1994). Geldof founded Band Aid and Live Aid, devoting much of his time to famine relief.

27/08/1977	11	9		LOOKING AFTER NO. 1	Ensign ENY 4
19/11/1977	15	9		MARY OF THE FOURTH FORM	Ensign ENY 9
15/04/1978	12	11		SHE'S SO MODERN	Ensign ENY 13
17/06/1978	6	13	○	LIKE CLOCKWORK	Ensign ENY 14
14/10/1978	❶²	15	●	RAT TRAP	Ensign ENY 16
21/07/1979	❶⁴	12	●	I DON'T LIKE MONDAYS Inspired by San Diego incident when schoolgirl Brenda Spencer ran amok on 29/1/1979, shooting dead two schoolmates, her reason being 'I don't like Mondays'. Her parents tried to have the single banned in the US, without success .... Ensign ENY 30
17/11/1979	13	10		DIAMOND SMILES	Ensign ENY 33
26/01/1980	4	9		SOMEONE'S LOOKING AT YOU	Ensign ENY 34
22/11/1980	3	11	○	BANANA REPUBLIC	Ensign BONGO 1

❶⁹ Number of weeks single topped the UK chart ↑ Entered the UK chart at #1 ▲⁹ Number of weeks single topped the US chart

99

DATE	POS	WKS	BPI	SINGLE TITLE	LABEL & NUMBER
31/01/1981	26	6		THE ELEPHANT'S GRAVEYARD (GUILTY)	Ensign BONGO 2
12/12/1981	62	4		NEVER IN A MILLION YEARS	Mercury MER 87
20/03/1982	24	8		HOUSE ON FIRE	Mercury MER 91
18/02/1984	73	1		TONIGHT	Mercury MER 154
19/05/1984	50	3		DRAG ME DOWN	Mercury MER 163
02/07/1994	38	2		I DON'T LIKE MONDAYS Re-issue of Ensign ENY 30	Vertigo VERCD 87

CLINT BOON EXPERIENCE UK group formed by ex-Inspiral Carpets Clint Boon (born 28/6/1959, Oldham), Matt Hayden (guitar), Richard Stubbs (bass/trumpet), Kathryn Stubbs (keyboards) and Tony Thompson (drums).

DATE	POS	WKS	BPI	SINGLE TITLE	LABEL & NUMBER
06/11/1999	61	1		WHITE NO SUGAR	Artful CDARTFUL 32
05/02/2000	70	1		BIGGEST HORIZON	Artful CDARTFUL 33
05/08/2000	63	1		DO WHAT YOU DO (EARWORM SONG)	Artful CDARTFUL 34

DANIEL BOON UK singer (born Peter Lee Stirling, 31/7/1942, Birmingham) who worked in jewellery, then sang with the Beachcombers for five years before going solo.

DATE	POS	WKS	BPI	SINGLE TITLE	LABEL & NUMBER
14/08/1971	17	15		DADDY DON'T YOU WALK SO FAST	Penny Farthing PEN 764
01/04/1972	21	10		BEAUTIFUL SUNDAY	Penny Farthing PEN 781

DEBBY BOONE US singer (born 22/9/1956, Leonia, NJ) and daughter of vocalist Pat Boone. After working with the family act in the 1960s she went solo in 1977. She won three Grammy Awards: Best New Artist in 1977, Best Inspirational Recording in 1980 for *With My Song I Will Praise Him* and Best Gospel Performance by a Duo or Group in 1984 with Phil Driscoll for *Keep The Flame Burning*.

DATE	POS	WKS	BPI	SINGLE TITLE	LABEL & NUMBER
24/12/1977	48	2		YOU LIGHT UP MY LIFE Featured in the 1977 film *You Light Up My Life*	Warner Brothers K 17043

PAT BOONE US singer (born Charles Eugene Boone, 1/6/1934, Jacksonville, FL) who was a direct descendant of US pioneer Daniel Boone. Two talent contest wins led to a contract with Republic Records in 1954, Boone continuing studies alongside recording, graduating from Columbia University, NY in 1958. His third daughter Debby later launched a singing career. After his chart career finished, he recorded sporadically for ABC, MCA, Hitsville, Motown and Lamb & Lion. He hosts a weekly TV show *Gospel America*. He has two stars on the Hollywood Walk of Fame, one for his contribution to the recording arts and one for TV.

DATE	POS	WKS	BPI	SINGLE TITLE	LABEL & NUMBER
18/11/1955	7	9		AIN'T THAT A SHAME ▲2	London HLD 8172
27/04/1956	❶5	22		I'LL BE HOME	London HLD 8253
27/07/1956	18	7		LONG TALL SALLY	London HLD 8291
17/08/1956	14	7		I ALMOST LOST MY MIND ▲4	London HLD 8303
07/12/1956	3	21		FRIENDLY PERSUASION Featured in the 1956 film *Friendly Persuasion*	London HLD 8346
11/01/1957	22	2		AIN'T THAT A SHAME	London HLD 8172
11/01/1957	19	2		I'LL BE HOME	London HLD 8253
01/02/1957	2	16		DON'T FORBID ME ▲1	London HLD 8370
26/04/1957	17	7		WHY BABY WHY	London HLD 8404
05/07/1957	2	21		LOVE LETTERS IN THE SAND ▲7 Featured in the 1957 film *Bernadine*	London HLD 8445
27/09/1957	5	18		REMEMBER YOU'RE MINE/THERE'S A GOLDMINE IN THE SKY	London HLD 8479
06/12/1957	7	23		APRIL LOVE ▲6 Featured in the 1957 film *April Love*	London HLD 8512
13/12/1957	29	1		WHITE CHRISTMAS	London HLD 8520
04/04/1958	2	17		A WONDERFUL TIME UP THERE	London HLD 8574
11/04/1958	7	12		IT'S TOO SOON TO KNOW B-side to *A Wonderful Time Up There*	London HLD 8574
27/06/1958	6	12		SUGAR MOON	London HLD 8640
29/08/1958	16	11		IF DREAMS CAME TRUE	London HLD 8675
05/12/1958	30	1		GEE BUT IT'S LONELY	London HLD 8739
06/02/1959	18	9		I'LL REMEMBER TONIGHT Featured in the 1959 film *Mardi Gras*	London HLD 8775
10/04/1959	21	3		WITH THE WIND AND THE RAIN IN YOUR HAIR	London HLD 8824
22/05/1959	19	9		FOR A PENNY	London HLD 8855
31/07/1959	18	7		'TWIXT TWELVE AND TWENTY	London HLD 8910
23/06/1960	39	5		WALKING THE FLOOR OVER YOU	London HLD 9138
06/07/1961	18	10		MOODY RIVER ▲1	London HLD 9350
07/12/1961	4	13		JOHNNY WILL	London HLD 9461
15/02/1962	27	9		I'LL SEE YOU IN MY DREAMS	London HLD 9504
24/05/1962	41	4		QUANDO QUANDO QUANDO	London HLD 9543
12/07/1962	2	19		SPEEDY GONZALES Features uncredited vocals by Mel Blanc, the voice of Bugs Bunny and Daffy Duck, as 'Speedy Gonzales'. Featured in the 1969 film *Baby Love*	London HLD 9573
15/11/1962	12	11		THE MAIN ATTRACTION Featured in the 1962 film *The Main Attraction* starring Boone	London HLD 9620

BOOOM – see **BORIS DUGLOSCH**

BOOT ROOM BOYZ – see **LIVERPOOL FC**

DUKE BOOTEE – see GRANDMASTER FLASH, MELLE MEL AND THE FURIOUS FIVE

BOOTH AND THE BAD ANGEL UK/US duo formed by Tim Booth (lead singer with James) and Angelo Badalamenti, the Italian composer of film and TV themes, including *Twin Peaks* for which he won the 1990 Grammy Award for Best Pop Instrumental Performance.

22/06/1996	25	3		I BELIEVE	Fontana BBDD 1
11/07/1998	57	1		FALL IN LOVE WITH ME Featured in the 1998 film *Martha Meet Frank, Daniel And Lawrence*	Mercury MERCD 503

TIM BOOTH UK singer (born 4/2/1960, Manchester) who was previously lead singer with James and recorded with Angelo Badalamenti before going solo.

10/07/2004	68	1		DOWN TO THE SEA	Sanctuary SANXS279

KEN BOOTHE Jamaican singer (born 22/3/1946, Denham Town) first known in his homeland in the late 1960s rock steady boom. An unsuccessful cover of Sandie Shaw's *Puppet On A String* in 1967 was followed by a hit version of a Bread original seven years later, in which he amended the lyrics: despite the title he sang 'anything I own'.

21/09/1974	❶³	12	○	EVERYTHING I OWN	Trojan TR 7920
14/12/1974	11	10		CRYING OVER YOU	Trojan TR 7944

BOOTHILL FOOT-TAPPERS UK group formed in 1982 by Wendy May (vocals), Merrill Heatley (vocals), Chris Thompson (born 19/3/1957, Ashford, banjo/vocals), Kevin Walsh (guitar/vocals), Slim (born Clive Pain, piano), Marnie Stephenson (washboard/vocals) and Danny Heatley (drums). They disbanded in 1985.

14/07/1984	64	3		GET YOUR FEET OUT OF MY SHOES	Go Discs TAP 1

BOOTSY'S RUBBER BAND US funk group formed by William 'Bootsy' Collins (born 26/10/1951, Cincinnati, OH, guitar/bass/drums/vocals), Phelps Collins (guitar), Garry Shider (guitar), Joel Johnson (keyboards), Bernie Worrell (keyboards), Frankie Waddy (drums), Gary Cooper (drums), Rick Gardner (trumpet), Richard Griffith (trumpet), Fred Wesley (trombone), Maceo Parker (saxophone), Eli Fontaine (saxophone) and Robert Johnson (vocals), all also in Parliament/Funkadelic. Bootsy won the 1997 MOBO Award for Lifetime Achievement.

08/07/1978	43	3		BOOTZILLA	Warner Brothers K 17196

BOOTZILLA ORCHESTRA – see MALCOLM McLAREN

BOSS US producer (born David Morales, 21/8/1961, New York) with Puerto Rico parents. He was a DJ and remixer before recording as Pulse, Bad Yard Club and under his own name. He won the 1998 Grammy Award for Best Remixer.

27/08/1994	54	1		CONGO	Cooltempo CDCOOL 296

NAILA BOSS UK singer (born 1985, Hackney, London), one of eight children.

22/05/2004	8	1		IT CAN'T BE RIGHT 2PLAY FEATURING RAGHAV AND NAILA BOSS	2PSL/Inferno 2PSLCD04
10/07/2004	65	1		LA LA LA	La Boss NBCD1
11/09/2004	8	8		YOU SHOULD REALLY KNOW PIRATES, ENYA, SHOLA AMA, NAILA BOSS & ISHANI	Relentless RELCD9

BOSTON US rock group featuring songwriter Tom Scholz (born 10/3/1947, Toledo, OH) with Brad Delp (born 12/6/1951, Boston, MA, guitar), Fran Sheehan (born 26/3/1949, Boston, bass), Barry Goudreau (born 29/11/1951, Boston, guitar) and Sib Hashian (born 17/8/1949, Boston, drums). Scholz's apparent perfectionism did not please his record labels, the band being absent from the US charts for eight years after their peak.

29/01/1977	22	8		MORE THAN A FEELING Featured in the 1978 film *F.M.*	Epic EPC 4658
07/10/1978	43	5		DON'T LOOK BACK	Epic EPC 6653

EVE BOSWELL Hungarian singer (born Eva Keiti, 11/5/1924, Budapest) who began touring in a circus, settling in South Africa where she married the son of Boswell's Circus. Moved to the UK in 1949, she appeared in theatre before going into semi-retirement. She died in South Africa on 14/8/1998.

30/12/1955	9	13		PICKIN' A CHICKEN EVE BOSWELL WITH GLEN SOMERS AND HIS ORCHESTRA	Parlophone R 4082

JUDY BOUCHER UK reggae singer (born in St Vincent) who moved to the UK at the age of fifteen.

04/04/1987	2	14	○	CAN'T BE WITH YOU TONIGHT Originally released in 1986 and re-issued when used on Breakfast TV's Mad Lizzie Aerobics spot	Orbitone OR 721
04/07/1987	18	9		YOU CAUGHT MY EYE	Orbitone OR 722

PETER BOUNCER – see SHUT UP AND DANCE

BOUNCING CZECKS UK vocal/instrumental group fronted by Paul Gadsby who later relocated to Australia.

29/12/1984	72	1		I'M A LITTLE CHRISTMAS CRACKER	RCA 463

BOUNTY KILLER Jamaican rapper (born Rodney Price, 26/6/1972, Riverton City).

27/02/1999	65	1		IT'S A PARTY	Edel 0066135 BLA

BOURGEOIS TAGG US rock group formed in Los Angeles, CA by Brent Bourgeois (keyboards/vocals), Larry Tagg (bass/vocals), Lyle Workman (guitar), Scott Moon (keyboards) and Michael Urbano (drums) and produced by Todd Rundgren. Bourgeois later recorded solo.

06/02/1988	35	6		I DON'T MIND AT ALL	Island IS 353

❶⁹ Number of weeks single topped the UK chart ⬆ Entered the UK chart at #1 ▲⁹ Number of weeks single topped the US chart

101

BOURGIE BOURGIE UK vocal/instrumental group fronted by Paul Quinn.

03/03/1984.....48......4....... BREAKING POINT ....MCA BOU 1

TOBY BOURKE WITH GEORGE MICHAEL UK vocal duo. Bourke (born 7/2/1965, London) was discovered by George Michael who signed him to his Aegean label.

07/06/1997.....10......4....... **WALTZ AWAY DREAMING** ....Aegean AECD 01

ALETIA BOURNE – see ANGELHEART

BOW WOW – see LIL' BOW WOW

BOW WOW WOW UK group formed by Malcolm McLaren, who lured Dave Barbarossa (born 1961, Mauritius, drums), Matthew Ashman (born 1962, London, guitar) and Leigh Gorman (born 1961, London, bass) away from Adam and the Ants, teaming them with fourteen-year-old Burmese-born Annabella Lwin (born Myant Myant Aye, 1966, Rangoon, vocals). McLaren created extensive news exposure, including having Lwin controversially pose naked for an album sleeve, her mother claiming to have not been consulted. They split after recording with producer Mike Chapman in 1983, a new line-up playing US live dates in 1997. Barbarossa was later in Republica. Ashman died from diabetes on 21/11/1995.

26/07/1980.....34......7......	C30, C60, C90, GO First single to be released on cassette.. EMI 5088
06/12/1980.....58......6......	YOUR CASSETTE PET Cassette-only EP featuring the following tracks: *Louis Quatorze, Gold He Said, Umo-Sex-Al Apache, I Want My Baby On Mars, Sexy Eiffel Towers, Giant Sized Baby Thing, Fools Rush In* and *Radio G String* .... EMI WOW 1
28/03/1981.....62......3......	W.O.R.K. (N.O. NAH NO NO MY DADDY DON'T) .... EMI 5153
15/08/1981.....58......4......	PRINCE OF DARKNESS .... RCA 100
07/11/1981.....51......4......	CHIHUAHUA... RCA 144
30/01/1982 .....7......13 .....O	**GO WILD IN THE COUNTRY** ....RCA 175
01/05/1982.....45......3......	SEE JUNGLE (JUNGLE BOY)/TV SAVAGE... RCA 220
05/06/1982 .....9......8......	**I WANT CANDY** Featured in the films *Romy And Michele's High School Reunion* (1997) and *200 Cigarettes* (1999)..... RCA 238
31/07/1982.....66......2......	LOUIS QUATORZE... RCA 263
12/03/1983.....47......4......	DO YOU WANNA HOLD ME?.. RCA 314

BOWA FEATURING MALA US vocal/instrumental duo.

07/12/1991.....64......1...... DIFFERENT STORY ....Dead Dead Good 8

DANE BOWERS UK singer (born 28/11/1979) who was a member of Another Level before going solo. It was rumoured that *Shut Up And Forget About It* was aimed at his former girlfriend, the model Jordan.

29/04/2000 .....6......8......	**BUGGIN'** TRUE STEPPERS AND DANE BOWERS ....NuLife 74321753342
26/08/2000 .....2......20.....●	**OUT OF YOUR MIND** TRUE STEPPERS AND DANE BOWERS FEATURING VICTORIA BECKHAM Features the uncredited contribution of Victoria's husband, footballer David Beckham ....NuLife 74321782942
03/03/2001 .....9......5......	**SHUT UP AND FORGET ABOUT IT** ....Arista 74321835342
07/07/2001 .....9......5......	**ANOTHER LOVER** This and above single credited to DANE ....Arista 74321863412

DAVID BOWIE UK singer (born David Robert Jones, 8/1/1947, Brixton, London) who debuted in 1964 as Davy Jones With The King Bees with *Liza Jane* on the Vocation Pop label. Parlophone and Pye (with three singles produced by Tony Hatch) followed without success. To avoid confusion with The Monkees' Davy Jones, he chose the name David Bowie 'after the knife, to cut through the bullshit'. He signed with Deram in 1966 (his second single there, a novelty item *The Laughing Gnome,* finally charting in 1973), was rejected by Apple and finally appeared on Philips in 1969. His debut hit was originally released in July 1969, making the top ten after use on a BBC astronomy programme. Signed by RCA on the strength of demos for *Hunky Dory* and his songwriting (he penned *Oh You Pretty Thing,* a hit for Peter Noone) in 1971, he was successful throughout the decade. He switched to EMI in 1983 and also made a mark as an actor, with *The Elephant Man* (1980) and *Merry Christmas, Mr Lawrence* (1983). He won the 1984 award for Best UK Male, and Outstanding Contribution at the 1996 BRIT Awards. In 1997 he raised £33 million ($55 million) by issuing bonds against his catalogue and publishing royalties that were bought by Prudential Insurance. Inducted into the Rock & Roll Hall of Fame in 1996, he also took part in the *Perfect Day* project for the BBC's Children In Need charity. He won the 1984 Grammy Award for Best Video Short Form for *David Bowie.* Bowie has a star on the Hollywood Walk of Fame. Pat Metheny is a jazz-rock guitarist (born 12/8/1954, Kansas City, MO). Al B. Sure! is a US singer (born Al Brown, 1969, Boston, MA).

06/09/1969 .....5......14	**SPACE ODDITY** Featured in the films *Ziggy Stardust The Movie* (1973) and *Love You Till Tuesday* (1984) .... Philips BF 1801
24/06/1972.....10......11	**STARMAN**... RCA 2199
16/09/1972.....12......10	JOHN I'M ONLY DANCING .... RCA 2263
09/12/1972 .....2......13	**THE JEAN GENIE**.. RCA 2302
14/04/1973 .....3......10	**DRIVE-IN SATURDAY** .... RCA 2352
30/06/1973 .....3......13	**LIFE ON MARS** .... RCA 2316
15/09/1973 .....6......12 .....O	**THE LAUGHING GNOME** Originally released in 1967 but failed to chart .... Deram DM 123
20/10/1973 .....3......15 .....O	**SORROW**... RCA 2424
23/02/1974 .....5......7......	**REBEL REBEL** Featured in the films *Detroit Rock City* (1999) and *Charlie's Angels: Full Throttle* (2003) .... RCA LPBO 5009
20/04/1974.....22......6......	ROCK 'N' ROLL SUICIDE .... RCA LPBO 5021
22/06/1974.....21......6......	DIAMOND DOGS.. RCA APBO 0293
28/09/1974.....10......6......	**KNOCK ON WOOD**... RCA 2466
01/03/1975.....18......7......	YOUNG AMERICANS Features Luther Vandross on backing vocals and David Sanborn on alto saxophone .... RCA 2523
02/08/1975.....17......8......	FAME ▲² Features backing vocals by John Lennon.. RCA 2579
11/10/1975.....❶²......10	**SPACE ODDITY** Re-issue of Philips BF 1801... RCA 2593
29/11/1975 .....8......10	**GOLDEN YEARS** Featured in the 2001 film *A Knight's Tale*...................................... RCA 2640

○ Silver disc ● Gold disc ✪ Platinum disc (additional platinum units are indicated by a figure following the symbol) ⊚ Singles released prior to 1973 that are known to have sold over 1 million copies in the UK

DATE	POS	WKS	BPI	SINGLE TITLE	LABEL & NUMBER
22/05/1976	33	4		TVC 15	RCA 2682
19/02/1977	3	11		**SOUND AND VISION**	RCA PB 0905
15/10/1977	24	8		HEROES Featured in the films *Christiane F* (1981) and *The Parole Officer* (2001)	RCA PB 1121
21/01/1978	39	3		BEAUTY AND THE BEAST	RCA PB 1190
02/12/1978	54	7		BREAKING GLASS (EP) Tracks on EP: *Breaking Glass, Art Decade* and *Ziggy Stardust*	RCA BOW 1
05/05/1979	7	10		**BOYS KEEP SWINGIN'**	RCA BOW 2
21/07/1979	29	5		D.J	RCA BOW 3
15/12/1979	12	8		JOHN I'M ONLY DANCING (AGAIN) (1975)/JOHN I'M ONLY DANCING (1972)	RCA BOW 4
01/03/1980	23	5		ALABAMA SONG	RCA BOW 5
16/08/1980	❶²	10	○	**ASHES TO ASHES**	RCA BOW 6
01/11/1980	5	12	○	**FASHION**	RCA BOW 7
10/01/1981	20	6		SCARY MONSTERS (AND SUPER CREEPS)	RCA BOW 8
28/03/1981	32	6		UP THE HILL BACKWARDS	RCA BOW 9
14/11/1981	❶²	11	○	**UNDER PRESSURE** QUEEN AND DAVID BOWIE Featured in the 1997 film *Grosse Pointe Blank*	EMI 5250
28/11/1981	24	10		WILD IS THE WIND	RCA BOW 10
06/03/1982	29	5		BAAL'S HYMN (EP) Tracks on EP: *Baal's Hymn, The Drowned Girl, Remembering Marie, The Dirty Song* and *Ballad Of The Adventurers*	RCA BOW 11
10/04/1982	26	6		CAT PEOPLE (PUTTING OUT THE FIRE) Featured in the 1982 film *Cat People*	MCA 770
27/11/1982	3	8	○	**PEACE ON EARTH – LITTLE DRUMMER BOY** DAVID BOWIE AND BING CROSBY Recorded on the 1977 TV special *Bing Crosby's Merrie Olde Christmas*	RCA BOW 12
26/03/1983	❶³	14	●	**LET'S DANCE** ▲¹ Features Stevie Ray Vaughan on guitar. Featured in the 1996 film *Private Parts*	EMI America EA 152
11/06/1983	2	8	○	**CHINA GIRL** Featured in the 1998 film *The Wedding Singer*	EMI America EA 157
24/09/1983	2	8	○	**MODERN LOVE**	EMI America EA 158
05/11/1983	46	3		WHITE LIGHT, WHITE HEAT	RCA 372
22/09/1984	6	8		**BLUE JEAN**	EMI America EA 181
08/12/1984	53	4		TONIGHT	EMI America EA 187
09/02/1985	14	7		THIS IS NOT AMERICA DAVID BOWIE AND THE PAT METHENY GROUP Featured in the 1984 film *The Falcon And The Snowman*	EMI America EA 190
08/06/1985	19	7		LOVING THE ALIEN	EMI America EA 195
07/09/1985	❶⁴	12	●	**DANCING IN THE STREET** ↑ DAVID BOWIE AND MICK JAGGER Fundraiser for Ethiopian famine relief	EMI America EA 204
15/03/1986	2	9	○	**ABSOLUTE BEGINNERS** Featured in the 1985 film *Absolute Beginners*	Virgin VS 838
21/06/1986	21	6		UNDERGROUND Featured in the 1988 film *Labyrinth*	EMI America EA 216
08/11/1986	44	4		WHEN THE WIND BLOWS Featured in the 1987 animated film *When The Wind Blows*	Virgin VS 906
04/04/1987	17	6		DAY-IN DAY-OUT	EMI America EA 230
27/06/1987	33	4		TIME WILL CRAWL	EMI America EA 237
29/08/1987	34	6		NEVER LET ME DOWN	EMI America EA 239
07/04/1990	28	4		FAME (REMIX) Featured in the 1990 film *Pretty Woman*	EMI-USA FAME 90
22/08/1992	53	1		REAL COOL WORLD Featured in the 1992 film *Cool World*	Warner Brothers W 0127
27/03/1993	9	6		**JUMP THEY SAY**	Arista 74321139422
12/06/1993	36	2		BLACK TIE WHITE NOISE DAVID BOWIE FEATURING AL B. SURE!	Arista 74321148682
23/10/1993	40	2		MIRACLE GOODNIGHT	Arista 74321162262
04/12/1993	35	3		BUDDHA OF SUBURBIA DAVID BOWIE FEATURING LENNY KRAVITZ Theme to the TV series of the same name	Arista 74321177052
23/09/1995	35	2		THE HEART'S FILTHY LESSON	RCA 74321307032
02/12/1995	39	2		STRANGERS WHEN WE MEET/THE MAN WHO SOLD THE WORLD (LIVE)	RCA 74321329402
02/03/1996	12	4		HALLO SPACEBOY Features the uncredited vocals of the Pet Shop Boys	RCA 74321353842
08/02/1997	14	3		LITTLE WONDER	RCA 74321452072
26/04/1997	32	2		DEAD MAN WALKING Featured in the 1997 film *The Saint*	RCA 74321475852
30/08/1997	61	1		SEVEN YEARS IN TIBET	RCA 74321512542
21/02/1998	73	1		I CAN'T READ	Velvet ZYX 87578
02/10/1999	16	3		THURSDAY'S CHILD	Virgin VSCDT 1753
18/12/1999	14	7		UNDER PRESSURE QUEEN AND DAVID BOWIE Re-issue of EMI 5250	Parlophone CDQUEEN 28
05/02/2000	28	2		SURVIVE	Virgin VSCDT 1767
29/07/2000	32	2		SEVEN	Virgin VSCDT 1776
11/05/2002	41	1		LOVING THE ALIEN SCUMFROG VS DAVID BOWIE	Positiva CDTIV 172
28/09/2002	20	3		EVERYONE SAYS 'HI'	Columbia 6731342
12/07/2003	73	1		JUST FOR ONE DAY (HEROES) DAVID GUETTA VS DAVID BOWIE	Virgin DINST 263
26/06/2004	47	2		REBEL NEVER GETS OLD	Columbia 6750406

BOWLING FOR SOUP
US rock group formed in Wichita Falls, TX in 1994 by Jaret Reddick (guitar/vocals), Chris Burney (guitar/vocals), Erik Chandler (bass) and Gary Wiseman (drums).

DATE	POS	WKS	BPI	SINGLE TITLE	LABEL & NUMBER
17/08/2002	8	7		**GIRL ALL THE BAD GUYS WANT**	Music For Nations CDXKUT 194
16/11/2002	67	1		EMILY	Music For Nations CDXKUT 198
06/09/2003	43	1		PUNK ROCK 101	Music For Nations CDKUT 203
16/10/2004	35	2		1985	Jive 82876647652

GEORGE BOWYER
UK singer whose debut hit – in defence of fox hunting – also featured William McClintock Bunbury and fiddle and banjo playing by The Pedigrees.

DATE	POS	WKS	BPI	SINGLE TITLE	LABEL & NUMBER
22/08/1998	33	2		GUARDIANS OF THE LAND	Boys BYSCD 01

❶⁹ Number of weeks single topped the UK chart ↑ Entered the UK chart at #1 ▲⁹ Number of weeks single topped the US chart

BOX CAR RACER US group formed by ex-Blink 182 Tom Delonge (guitar) and Travis Landon Barker (drums), plus David Kennedy (guitar) and Anthony Celestino (bass).

06/07/2002	41	1		I FEEL SO .... MCA MCSTD 40290

BOX TOPS US pop-rock group formed in Memphis, TN in 1967 by Alex Chilton (born 28/12/1950, Memphis, guitar/vocals), Gary Talley (born 17/8/1947, Memphis, guitar), John Evans (born 18/6/1948, Memphis, organ), Bill Cunningham (born 23/1/1950, Memphis, bass/piano) and Danny Smythe (born 25/8/1948, Memphis, drums). Evans and Smythe left in 1967 and were replaced by Tom Boggs (born 16/7/1947, Wynn, AZ, drums) and Rick Allen (born 28/1/1946, Little Rock, AR, organ). They disbanded in 1970.

13/09/1967	5	12		THE LETTER ▲4 .... Stateside SS 2044
20/03/1968	15	12		CRY LIKE A BABY .... Bell 1001
23/08/1969	22	9		SOUL DEEP .... Bell 1068

BOXER REBELLION UK rock group formed by Nathan Nicholson (guitar/vocals), Todd Howe (guitar), Adam Harrison (bass) and Piers Hewitt (drums).

10/04/2004	57	1		IN PURSUIT .... Poptones MC5088SCD
09/10/2004	61	1		CODE RED .... Vertigo 9867001

BOY GEORGE UK singer (born George O'Dowd, 14/6/1961, Eltham), formerly lead singer with Culture Club, who began his career as Lieutenant Lush, a backing singer for Bow Wow Wow, Malcolm McLaren planning that he replace Annabella Lwin as lead singer. He went solo in 1987 after receiving treatment for drug abuse, later recording as Jesus Loves You.

07/03/1987	❶2	9	○	EVERYTHING I OWN .... Virgin BOY 100
06/06/1987	29	4		KEEP ME IN MIND .... Virgin BOY 101
18/07/1987	24	5		SOLD .... Virgin BOY 102
21/11/1987	13	7		TO BE REBORN .... Virgin BOY 103
05/03/1988	62	2		LIVE MY LIFE .... Virgin BOY 105
18/06/1988	57	3		NO CLAUSE 28 .... Virgin BOY 106
08/10/1988	60	2		DON'T CRY .... Virgin BOY 107
04/03/1989	68	2		DON'T TAKE MY MIND ON A TRIP .... Virgin BOY 108
19/09/1992	22	4		THE CRYING GAME Cover version of Dave Berry's 1964 hit. Featured in the films *The Crying Game* (1993) and *Ace Ventura: Pet Detective* (1994) .... Spaghetti CIAO 6
12/06/1993	40	3		MORE THAN LIKELY PM DAWN FEATURING BOY GEORGE .... Gee Street GESCD 49
01/04/1995	45	2		FUNTIME .... Virgin VSCDG 1538
01/07/1995	50	2		IL ADORE .... Virgin VSCDX 1543
21/10/1995	56	1		SAME THING IN REVERSE .... Virgin VSCDT 1561

BOY MEETS GIRL US songwriting/recording duo from Seattle, WA, husband and wife (married in 1988) George Merrill and Shannon Rubicam.

03/12/1988	9	13		WAITING FOR A STAR TO FALL Featured in the 1998 film *Three Men And A Baby* .... RCA PB 49519

BOY WUNDA – see **PROGRESS PRESENTS THE BOY WUNDA**

JIMMY BOYD US singer (born 9/1/1939, McComb, MS) who sang at local fairs from the age of seven. He was signed by Columbia after being spotted on a Frank Sinatra TV show. He later hosted his own radio show, and has a star on the Hollywood Walk of Fame.

04/09/1953	5	16		TELL ME A STORY FRANKIE LAINE AND JIMMY BOYD .... Philips PB 126
27/11/1953	3	6		I SAW MOMMY KISSING SANTA CLAUS ▲2 .... Columbia DB 3365

JACQUELINE BOYER French singer who won the 1960 Eurovision Song Contest, beating the UK's Bryan Johnson into second place, and the first winner to reach the UK charts, five years after the competition was introduced. She appeared in the 1945 film *Caravan* (starring Stewart Granger) and two German 1960 films, *Das Ratsel Der Grunnen Spinne* and *Gauner-Serenade*.

28/04/1960	33	2		TOM PILLIBI 1960 Eurovision Song Contest winner .... Columbia DB 4452

BOYS US vocal group formed by brothers Khiry (born 8/11/1973, Carson City, CA), Hakim (born 27/3/1975, Carson City), Tajh (born 10/12/1976, Carson City) and Bilal Abdulsamad (born 17/4/1979, Carson City).

12/11/1988	61	2		DIAL MY HEART .... Motown ZB 42245
29/09/1990	57	3		CRAZY .... Motown ZB 44037

BOYSTEROUS UK vocal group formed by Chris Broadhurst, Gary Goulding, Mike Parkinson and Mitch Powell.

22/11/2003	53	1		UP AND DOWN .... Square Biz SBR4

BOYSTOWN GANG US Hi-NRG vocal group with Jackson Moore, Tom Morley, Bruce Carlton, Margaret Reynolds and Cynthia Manley.

22/08/1981	46	6		AIN'T NO MOUNTAIN HIGH ENOUGH – REMEMBER ME (MEDLEY) .... WEA DICK 1
31/07/1982	4	11	○	CAN'T TAKE MY EYES OFF YOU .... ERC 101
09/10/1982	50	3		SIGNED SEALED DELIVERED (I'M YOURS) .... ERC 102

BOYZ – see **HEAVY D AND THE BOYZ**

BOYZ II MEN US R&B quartet formed by Wanya 'Squirt' Morris (born 29/7/1973, Philadelphia, PA), Michael 'Bass' McCrary

○ Silver disc ● Gold disc ✪ Platinum disc (additional platinum units are indicated by a figure following the symbol) ◎ Singles released prior to 1973 that are known to have sold over 1 million copies in the UK

(born 16/12/1972, Philadelphia), Shawn 'Slim' Stockman (born 26/9/1972, Philadelphia) and Nathan 'Alex Vanderpool' Morris (born 18/6/1971, Philadelphia) at Philadelphia's High School of Creative and Performing Arts. Michael Bivins (of Bell Biv DeVoe) helped get them a contract with Motown. They appeared in the 1992 TV mini-series *The Jacksons: An American Dream*. Their debut hit single (*End Of The Road*) spent most consecutive weeks at #1 in the US, racking up 13 weeks, surpassing Elvis Presley's record, then beating their own record with first *I'll Make Love To You* (14 weeks) and then *One Sweet Day* (16 weeks) with Mariah Carey. Four Grammy Awards include Best Rhythm & Blues Performance by a Group with Vocal in 1991 for *Cooleyhighharmony*, and Best Rhythm & Blues Album in 1994 for *Boyz II Men II*. Wanya Morris later wrote and produced Uncle Sam. McCrary left the group in 2004 owing to illness.

05/09/1992	❶³	21	●	**END OF THE ROAD** ▲¹³ Featured in the 1992 film *Boomerang*. 1992 Grammy Awards for Best Rhythm & Blues Performance by a Group with Vocal, plus Best Rhythm & Blues Song for writers LA Reid, Babyface and Daryl Simmons	Motown TMG 1411
19/12/1992	23	6		MOTOWNPHILLY	Motown TMG 1402
27/02/1993	27	4		IN THE STILL OF THE NITE (I'LL REMEMBER) Featured in the TV mini-series *The Jacksons: An American Dream*	Motown TMGCD 1415
03/09/1994	5	15		**I'LL MAKE LOVE TO YOU** ▲¹⁴ 1994 Grammy Award for Best Rhythm & Blues Performance by a Group with Vocal	Motown TMGCD 1431
26/11/1994	20	3		ON BENDED KNEE ▲⁶	Motown TMGCD 1433
22/04/1995	26	3		THANK YOU Contains a sample of Doug E Fresh' *La-Di-Da-Di*	Motown TMGCD 1438
08/07/1995	24	3		WATER RUNS DRY	Motown TMGCD 1443
09/12/1995	6	11	○	**ONE SWEET DAY** ▲¹⁶ **MARIAH CAREY AND BOYZ II MEN**	Columbia 6626035
20/01/1996	17	4		HEY LOVER **LL COOL J FEATURING BOYZ II MEN** Contains a sample of Michael Jackson's *The Lady In My Life*. 1996 Grammy Award for Best Rap Solo Performance	Def Jam DEFCD 14
20/09/1997	10	6		**4 SEASONS OF LONELINESS** ▲¹	Motown 8606992
06/12/1997	34	2		A SONG FOR MAMA Featured in the 1997 film *Soul Food*	Motown 8607372
25/07/1998	23	3		CAN'T LET HER GO Contains a sample of Cameo's *I Just Want To Be*	Motown 8607952

BOYZONE Irish vocal group with Ronan Keating (born 3/3/1977, Dublin), Stephen Gately (born 17/3/1976, Dublin), Keith Duffy (born 1/10/1974, Dublin), Shane Lynch (born 3/7/1976, Dublin) and Mikey Graham (born 15/8/1972, Dublin), put together by manager Louis Walsh. Mark Walton, whose idea it was to form the band, left before they made their breakthrough. Shane Lynch married Eternal singer Easther Bennett in March 1998, and his two sisters, Edele and Keavy, are members of B*Witched. Thus the Lynch family offshoots have enjoyed eleven #1 hits (six for Boyzone, four for B*Witched and one for Eternal). Part of the *Perfect Day* project for the BBC's Children In Need charity, they won the Select UK & Ireland Award at the 1999 MTV Europe Music Awards, the same year that *By Request* was named Best Album. They disbanded in 2000, Keating, Graham and Gately going solo and Duffy and Lynch recording as a duo. Duffy then became an actor, appearing in the TV series *Coronation Street* as Ciaran McCarthy.

10/12/1994	2	13	●	**LOVE ME FOR A REASON**	Polydor 8512802
29/04/1995	3	8	○	**KEY TO MY LIFE**	Polydor PZCD 342
12/08/1995	3	6		**SO GOOD**	Polydor 5797732
25/11/1995	2	16	✪	**FATHER AND SON**	Polydor 5775762
09/03/1996	4	9	○	**COMING HOME NOW**	Polydor 5775722
19/10/1996	❶¹	14	●	**WORDS** ↑	Polydor 5755372
14/12/1996	❶¹	15		**A DIFFERENT BEAT** ↑	Polydor 5732072
22/03/1997	2	14		**ISN'T IT A WONDER**	Polydor 5735472
02/08/1997	2	18		**PICTURE OF YOU** Featured in the films *Bean: The Ultimate Disaster Movie* (1997) and *Snow Day* (2000)	Polydor 5713112
06/12/1997	2	14	●	**BABY CAN I HOLD YOU/SHOOTING STAR** B-side featured in the 1997 Walt Disney film *Hercules* and is a solo track by Stephen Gately	Polydor 5691652
02/05/1998	❶¹	14	✪	**ALL THAT I NEED** ↑	Polydor 5698732
15/08/1998	❶³	15	✪	**NO MATTER WHAT** ↑ Polydor reduced the dealer price to below that stipulated by the charts' compilers CIN in order to remove competition from the next Boyzone single *I Love The Way You Love Me*. The action prompted songwriters Andrew Lloyd-Webber and Tim Rice to write a letter of protest to the national press	Polydor 5675672
05/12/1998	2	13	●	**I LOVE THE WAY YOU LOVE ME**	Polydor 5631992
13/03/1999	❶²	16	✪	**WHEN THE GOING GETS TOUGH** ↑ Released in aid of the Comic Relief charity. The uncredited B-side was Alison Moyet's *What A Wonderful World*	Polydor 5699132
22/05/1999	❶¹	15	○	**YOU NEEDED ME** ↑	Polydor 5639332
04/12/1999	3	13	○	**EVERY DAY I LOVE YOU**	Polydor 5615802

BRAD US rock group formed by Stone Gossard of Pearl Jam as a one-off project, also featuring Shawn Smith (keyboards/vocals), Jeremy Toback (bass) and Regan Hagar (drums). They were originally to be called Shame, but Los Angeles musician Brad Wilson held the copyright to that name so they became known as Brad and the album was called *Shame*, something of a tongue-in-cheek retort.

26/06/1993	64	1		20TH CENTURY	Epic 6592482

SCOTT BRADLEY UK singer.

15/10/1994	61	1		ZOOM	Hidden Agenda HIDDCD 1

PAUL BRADY Irish singer/guitarist (born 19/5/1947, Strabane, County Tyrone) who was briefly in R&B outfit Kult while studying in Dublin, then the folk group The Johnstons. After a spell with Planxty and as a duo with Andy Irvine, he went solo in 1978. His songs have been covered by Santana, Dave Edmunds and Roger Chapman, and he has worked with Mark Knopfler (they shared the same management for a time).

13/01/1996	67	1		THE WORLD IS WHAT YOU MAKE IT Theme to the TV series *Faith In The Future*	Mercury PBCD 1

❶⁹ Number of weeks single topped the UK chart ↑ Entered the UK chart at #1 ▲⁹ Number of weeks single topped the US chart

105

BILLY BRAGG
UK singer (born Steven William Bragg, 20/12/1957, Barking) who formed Riff Raff in 1977, which recorded for Chiswick and Geezer before disbanding. He then spent 90 days in the army before going solo in 1982. Cara Tivey is a UK pianist.

DATE	POS	WKS	BPI	SINGLE TITLE	LABEL & NUMBER
16/03/1985	15	6		BETWEEN THE WARS (EP) Tracks on EP: *Between The Wars, Which Side Are You On, World Turned Upside Down* and *It Says Here*	Go Discs AGOEP 1
28/12/1985	43	5		DAYS LIKE THESE	Go Discs GOD 8
28/06/1986	29	6		LEVI STUBBS TEARS	Go Discs GOD 12
15/11/1986	58	2		GREETINGS TO THE NEW BRUNETTE	Go Discs GOD 15
14/05/1988	❶⁴	11	○	SHE'S LEAVING HOME BILLY BRAGG WITH CARA TIVEY Flip side *With A Little Help From My Friends* credited to WET WET WET	Childline CHILD 1
10/09/1988	52	3		WAITING FOR THE GREAT LEAP FORWARDS	Go Discs GOD 23
08/07/1989	29	6		WON'T TALK ABOUT IT NORMAN COOK FEATURING BILLY BRAGG	Go Beat GOD 33
06/07/1991	27	5		SEXUALITY	Go Discs GOD 56
07/09/1991	54	2		YOU WOKE UP MY NEIGHBOURHOOD	Go Discs GOD 60
29/02/1992	33	3		ACCIDENT WAITING TO HAPPEN (EP) Tracks on EP: *Accident Waiting To Happen, Revolution, Sulk* and *The Warmest Home*	Go Discs GOD 67
31/08/1996	46	1		UPFIELD	Cooking Vinyl FRYCD 051
17/05/1997	55	1		THE BOY DONE GOOD	Cooking Vinyl FRYCD 064
01/06/2002	22	2		TAKE DOWN THE UNION JACK	Cooking Vinyl FRYCD 131XX

BRAIDS
US R&B vocal duo formed in Oakland, CA by Caitlin Cornwell and Zoe Ellis.

DATE	POS	WKS	BPI	SINGLE TITLE	LABEL & NUMBER
02/11/1996	21	3		BOHEMIAN RHAPSODY Featured in the 1996 film *High School High*	Atlantic A 5640CD

BRAIN BASHERS
UK production duo Rachel Shock and Graham Eden.

DATE	POS	WKS	BPI	SINGLE TITLE	LABEL & NUMBER
01/07/2000	64	1		DO IT NOW	Tidy Trax TIDY 137CD

BRAINBUG
Italian producer Alberto Bertapelle.

DATE	POS	WKS	BPI	SINGLE TITLE	LABEL & NUMBER
03/05/1997	11	5		NIGHTMARE	Positiva CDTIV 76
22/11/1997	24	2		BENEDICTUS/NIGHTMARE	Positiva CDTIV 86
04/09/2004	63	1		NIGHTMARE	Positiva 12TIV 200

BRAINCHILD
German producer Matthias Hoffmann.

DATE	POS	WKS	BPI	SINGLE TITLE	LABEL & NUMBER
30/10/1999	31	2		SYMMETRY C	Multiply CDMULTY 55

WILFRID BRAMBELL AND HARRY H CORBETT
UK actors from the TV comedy series *Steptoe And Son*. Wilfred Brambell (born 22/3/1912, Dublin) died on 18/1/1985, Harry H Corbett (born 28/2/1925, Rangoon, Burma) died on 21/3/1982.

DATE	POS	WKS	BPI	SINGLE TITLE	LABEL & NUMBER
28/11/1963	25	12		AT THE PALACE (PARTS 1 & 2) Live recording from the 1963 Royal Variety Performance	Pye 7N 15588

BEKKA BRAMLETT – see JOE COCKER

BRAN VAN 3000
Canadian vocal/instrumental group formed in 1996 in Montreal by DJ/remixer James DiSalvio and 'Electronic-Pierre' Bergen, with twenty musicians and singers including Sara Johnston, Jayne Hill, Shine Like Stars, Stephane Moraille, Doughboy John Kastner and Jean Leloup.

DATE	POS	WKS	BPI	SINGLE TITLE	LABEL & NUMBER
06/06/1998	34	2		DRINKING IN LA	Capitol CDCL 802
21/08/1999	3	11	○	DRINKING IN LA Re-issued after being featured in a TV advertisement for Rolling Rock lager	Capitol CDCL 811
16/06/2001	40	2		ASTOUNDED BRAN VAN 3000 FEATURING CURTIS MAYFIELD Contains a sample of Curtis Mayfield's *Move On Up*	Virgin VUSCD 194

BRANCACCIO AND AISHER
UK production duo Luke Brancaccio and Bruce Aisher.

DATE	POS	WKS	BPI	SINGLE TITLE	LABEL & NUMBER
16/03/2002	40	2		IT'S GONNA BE (A LOVELY DAY) Contains a sample of Soul System's *Lovely Day*	Credence CDCRED 017

MICHELLE BRANCH
US singer (born 2/7/1983, Sedona, AZ) who learned to play guitar at fourteen, signing with Maverick Records three years later and later appearing in the TV series *Buffy The Vampire Slayer*.

DATE	POS	WKS	BPI	SINGLE TITLE	LABEL & NUMBER
13/04/2002	18	6		EVERYWHERE Featured in the 2001 film *American Pie 2*	Maverick W 577CD
03/08/2002	33	2		ALL YOU WANTED	Maverick W 585CDX
23/11/2002	16	8		THE GAME OF LOVE SANTANA FEATURING MICHELLE BRANCH 2002 Grammy Award for Best Pop Collaboration with Vocals	Arista 74321959442
12/07/2003	31	2		ARE YOU HAPPY NOW?	Maverick W 613CD

BRAND NEW
US group formed in Long Island, NY by Jesse Lacey (guitar/vocals), Vinnie Accardi (guitar), Garrett Tierney (bass) and Brian Lane (drums).

DATE	POS	WKS	BPI	SINGLE TITLE	LABEL & NUMBER
14/02/2004	37	2		SIC TRANSIT GLORIA GLORY FADES	Sore Point SORE011CDS
29/05/2004	39	2		THE QUIET THINGS THAT NO ONE EVER KNOWS	Sore Point SORE014CDS

BRAND NEW HEAVIES
UK/US jazz-funk group comprising Simon Bartholomew (born 16/10/1965, London, guitar), Andy Levy (born 20/7/1966, London, bass), Jan Kincaid (born 17/5/1966, London, drums) and Ceri Evans (keyboards). First recording for Acid Jazz, their breakthrough came via former George Clinton backing singer N'Dea Davenport. Evans left in 1992, and Davenport left in 1996, being replaced by Seidah Garrett. Garrett left in 1999 and was replaced by Carleen Anderson, who covered *Apparently Nothing* with The Brand New Heavies, having been the singer on the original by The Young Disciples.

DATE	POS	WKS	BPI	SINGLE TITLE	LABEL & NUMBER
05/10/1991	43	3		NEVER STOP	ffrr F 165
15/02/1992	24	4		DREAM COME TRUE	ffrr F 180
18/04/1992	19	6		ULTIMATE TRUNK FUNK EP Tracks on EP: *Never Stop, Stay This Way, Mr Tanaka* and *Never Stop (Remix)*	ffrr F 185
01/08/1992	24	4		DON'T LET IT GO TO YOUR HEAD	ffrr BNH 1
19/12/1992	40	5		STAY THIS WAY	ffrr BNH 2
26/03/1994	15	4		DREAM ON DREAMER	ffrr BNHCD 3
11/06/1994	23	4		BACK TO LOVE	ffrr BNHCD 4
13/08/1994	13	6		MIDNIGHT AT THE OASIS	ffrr BNHCDP 5
05/11/1994	26	4		SPEND SOME TIME	ffrr BNHCD 6
11/03/1995	38	3		CLOSE TO YOU Featured in the 1994 film *Ready To Wear (Pret-A-Porter)*. This and all the above singles credited to **BRAND NEW HEAVIES FEATURING N'DEA DAVENPORT**	ffrr BNCDP 7
12/04/1997	11	5	O	SOMETIMES	ffrr BNHCD 8
28/06/1997	21	4		YOU ARE THE UNIVERSE	ffrr BNHCD 9
18/10/1997	9	8		**YOU'VE GOT A FRIEND**	ffrr BNHCD 10
10/01/1998	31	4		SHELTER	London BNHCD 11
11/09/1999	35	2		SATURDAY NITE Contains a sample of Marvin Gaye's *Got To Give It Up*	ffrr BNHCD 12
29/01/2000	32	2		APPARENTLY NOTHING	ffrr BNHCD 13
23/10/2004	66	1		BOOGIE **BRAND NEW HEAVIES FEATURING NICOLE**	Onetwo TBNHCDS001

JOHNNY BRANDON UK singer who also recorded for Decca, Parlophone, Philips and Top Rank, appearing in the 1956 film *Fun At St Fanny's*.

DATE	POS	WKS	BPI	SINGLE TITLE	LABEL & NUMBER
11/03/1955	8	8		**TOMORROW JOHNNY BRANDON AND THE PHANTOMS AND THE NORMAN WARREN MUSIC**	Polygon P 1131
01/07/1955	18	4		DON'T WORRY	Polygon P 1163

BRANDY US singer (born Brandy Norwood, 11/2/1979, McComb, MS, raised in California) who appeared on the TV show *Thea*. Signed by Atlantic at thirteen years of age, she appeared in the 1997 film *I Know What You Did Last Summer* and the 1999 film *Double Platinum* (alongside Diana Ross). Her brother Ray J is also a professional singer.

DATE	POS	WKS	BPI	SINGLE TITLE	LABEL & NUMBER
10/12/1994	44	3		I WANNA BE DOWN	Atlantic A 7217CD
03/06/1995	36	3		I WANNA BE DOWN (REMIX)	Atlantic A 7186CD
03/02/1996	30	4		SITTIN' UP IN MY ROOM Featured in the 1995 film *Waiting To Exhale*	Arista 74321344012
06/06/1998	2	20	O	**THE BOY IS MINE ▲13 BRANDY AND MONICA** 1998 Grammy Award for Best Rhythm & Blues Performance by a Duo	Atlantic AT 0036CD
10/10/1998	2	9	O	**TOP OF THE WORLD BRANDY FEATURING MA$E**	Atlantic AT 0046CD
12/12/1998	13	8		HAVE YOU EVER? ▲2	Atlantic AT 0058CD
19/06/1999	15	5		ALMOST DOESN'T COUNT Featured in the 1999 film *Double Platinum*	Atlantic AT 0068CD1
16/06/2001	5	10		**ANOTHER DAY IN PARADISE BRANDY & RAY J**	WEA 327CD1
23/02/2002	4	11		**WHAT ABOUT US**	Atlantic AT 0125CD
15/06/2002	72	1		FULL MOON (IMPORT)	Atlantic 7567853092
29/06/2002	15	9		FULL MOON Contains a sample of Freeez' *I.O.U.*	Atlantic AT 0130CD
26/06/2004	6	10		**TALK ABOUT OUR LOVE BRANDY FEATURING KANYE WEST**	Atlantic AT 0177CD
16/10/2004	11	4		AFRODISIAC	Atlantic AT 0183CD

LAURA BRANIGAN US singer (born 3/7/1957, Brewster, NY) who was a former backing singer with Leonard Cohen and also appeared in the TV show *CHIPS* and the 1984 film *Mugsy's Girl*. She died from a brain aneurysm on 26/8/2004.

DATE	POS	WKS	BPI	SINGLE TITLE	LABEL & NUMBER
18/12/1982	6	13		**GLORIA**	Atlantic K 11759
07/07/1984	5	17	O	**SELF CONTROL**	Atlantic A 9676
06/10/1984	56	3		THE LUCKY ONE	Atlantic A 9636

BRASS CONSTRUCTION Multinational funk outfit formed in 1968 by Randy Muller (keyboards/flute/percussion), American Larry Payton (drums), Jamaican Wayne Parris (trumpet), Trinidadian Joseph Arthur Wong (guitar), American Sandy Billups (congas), Jamaican Michael 'Mickey' Grudge (saxophone), American Morris Price (trumpet/percussion), American Jesse Ward (saxophone) and Wade Williamston (bass) as Dynamic Soul. They disbanded in 1986, Muller producing the likes of New York Skyy and Tamiko Jones.

DATE	POS	WKS	BPI	SINGLE TITLE	LABEL & NUMBER
03/04/1976	23	6		MOVIN'	United Artists UP 36090
05/02/1977	37	5		HA CHA CHA (FUNKTION)	United Artists UP 36205
26/01/1980	39	6		MUSIC MAKES YOU FEEL LIKE DANCING	United Artists UP 615
28/05/1983	47	3		WALKIN' THE LINE	Capitol CL 292
16/07/1983	70	2		WE CAN WORK IT OUT	Capitol CL 299
07/07/1984	56	4		PARTYLINE	Capitol CL 335
27/10/1984	70	2		INTERNATIONAL	Capitol CL 341
09/11/1985	62	3		GIVE AND TAKE	Capitol CL 377
28/05/1988	24	4		MOVIN' 1988 (REMIX)	Syncopate SY 11

BRASSTOOTH – see **BM DUBS PRESENTS MR RUMBLE FEATURING BRASSTOOTH AND KEE**

BRAT UK singer Roger Kitter, lampooning US tennis star John McEnroe. He later became an actor, his best-known role that of Captain Alberto Bertorelli in *'Allo 'Allo*.

DATE	POS	WKS	BPI	SINGLE TITLE	LABEL & NUMBER
10/07/1982	19	8		CHALK DUST – THE UMPIRE STRIKES BACK	Hansa SMASH 1

❶9 Number of weeks single topped the UK chart ↑ Entered the UK chart at #1 ▲9 Number of weeks single topped the US chart

107

BRAVADO UK vocal/instrumental group with Paul Riordan, DJ Marie and Gary Watson, featuring world harmonica champion Paul Lamb on their debut hit.

18/06/1994.....37.....3....... HARMONICA MAN .... Peach PEACHCD 5

BRAVEHEARTS – see QB FINEST FEATURING NAS AND BRAVEHEARTS

BRAVO ALL STARS UK/German/US vocal/instrumental group with members of the Backstreet Boys, Aaron Carter, Scooter, N Sync, Caught In The Act, The Boyz, Blumchen, Gil, Squeezer, Mr President, Touche, R 'N' G and the Moffatts, the single in aid of Nordoff Robbins Music Therapy Trust.

29/08/1998.....36.....2....... LET THE MUSIC HEAL YOUR SOUL .... Edel 0039335 ERE

ALAN BRAXE AND FRED FALKE French production duo.

25/11/2000.....35.....3....... INTRO Contains a sample of The Jets' *Crush On You*... Vulture/Credence CDCRED 006

DHAR BRAXTON US vocalist from Pleasantville, NJ.

31/05/1986.....32.....8....... JUMP BACK (SET ME FREE) .... Fourth & Broadway BRW 47

TONI BRAXTON US singer (born 7/10/1968, Severn, MD) who originally recorded with her sisters as The Braxtons for Arista, going solo in 1992 with LaFace Records. A 1997 lawsuit against Arista and LaFace was an attempt to dissolve her contract with the companies, though she did record a third album for them in 2000. In January 1998 she filed for Chapter 7 bankruptcy protection for her companies Madame Ashlee, Princess Ashlee and Lady Ashlee. She married keyboard player Keri Lewis (of Mint Condition) in April 2001. Six Grammy Awards include Best New Artist in 1993.

18/09/1993.....51.....2.......	ANOTHER SAD LOVE SONG 1993 Grammy Award for Best Female Rhythm & Blues Vocal Performance.......	LaFace 74321163502
15/01/1994 .....2.....12.....O	**BREATHE AGAIN** 1994 Grammy Award for Best Female Rhythm & Blues Vocal Performance	LaFace 74321163502
02/04/1994.....15.....8.......	ANOTHER SAD LOVE SONG Re-issue of LaFace 74321163502	LaFace 74321196682
09/07/1994.....30.....5.......	YOU MEAN THE WORLD TO ME...	LaFace 74321214702
03/12/1994.....33.....3.......	LOVE SHOULDA BROUGHT YOU HOME Featured in the 1992 film *Boomerang*.........	LaFace 74321249412
13/07/1996.....7.....11.......	**YOU'RE MAKIN' ME HIGH** ▲[1] 1996 Grammy Award for Best Female Rhythm & Blues Vocal Performance.....	LaFace 74321395402
02/11/1996 .....2.....19.....✪	**UN-BREAK MY HEART** ▲[11] 1996 Grammy Award for Best Female Pop Vocal Performance..........	LaFace 74321410632
24/05/1997 .....9.....8.......	**I DON'T WANT TO**	LaFace 74321468612
08/11/1997.....22.....4.......	HOW COULD AN ANGEL BREAK MY HEART TONI BRAXTON WITH KENNY G	LaFace 74321531982
29/04/2000 .....5.....11.......	**HE WASN'T MAN ENOUGH** 2000 Grammy Award for Best Female Rhythm & Blues Vocal Performance........	LaFace 74321757852
08/03/2003.....29.....3.......	HIT THE FREEWAY TONI BRAXTON FEATURING LOON	Arista 82876506372

BRAXTONS US vocal group formed in 1990 by sisters Toni (age 22 at the time), Tamar (12), Towanda (15) and Traci (18) Braxton from Maryland. Toni and Traci later went solo, Toni in 1992 and Traci in 1995, with Trina Braxton joining the family group.

01/02/1997.....32.....2.......	SO MANY WAYS Featured in the 1996 film *High School High*............................	Atlantic A 5469CD
29/03/1997.....31.....3.......	THE BOSS	Atlantic A 5441CD
19/07/1997.....26.....2.......	SLOW FLOW	Atlantic AT 0001CD

BREAD US singer/guitarist/keyboard player/songwriter David Gates (born 11/12/1940, Tulsa, OK), who was a successful session musician (with Chuck Berry, Duane Eddy, Glen Campbell and Merle Haggard among others) before forming Bread in 1969 with James Griffin (born 10/8/1943, Cincinnati, guitar), Robb Royer (guitar) and Jim Gordon (drums), with Larry Knetchtel (born 4/8/1940, Bell, CA) and Mike Botts (born 8/12/1944, Sacramento, CA) later replacing them. They disbanded in 1973 but briefly reunited in 1976. Gates enjoyed a brief solo career before going into retirement.

01/08/1970 .....5.....14......	**MAKE IT WITH YOU** ▲[1]	Elektra 2101 010
15/01/1972.....14.....10......	BABY I'M A-WANT YOU..	Elektra K 12033
29/04/1972.....32.....6.......	EVERYTHING I OWN Taken to #1 by both Ken Boothe and Boy George	Elektra K 12041
30/09/1972.....16.....9.......	THE GUITAR MAN Featured in the 2002 film *Maid In Manhattan*	Elektra K 12066
25/12/1976.....27.....7.......	LOST WITHOUT YOUR LOVE	Elektra K 12241

BREAK MACHINE US dance trio from New York comprising brothers Lindsay and Lindell Blake, and Cortez Jordan.

04/02/1984 .....3.....14......	**STREET DANCE**	Record Shack SOHO 13
12/05/1984 .....9.....10......	**BREAKDANCE PARTY**	Record Shack SOHO 20
11/08/1984.....27.....8.......	ARE YOU READY?..	Record Shack SOHO 24

BREAKBEAT ERA UK drum and bass trio Roni Size, DJ Die and singer/songwriter Leonie Laws.

18/07/1998.....38.....2.......	BREAKBEAT ERA	XL Recordings XLS 95CD
21/08/1999.....48.....2.......	ULTRA-OBSCENE..	XL Recordings XLS 107CD
11/03/2000.....65.....1.......	BULLITPROOF...	XL Recordings XLS 115CD

BREAKFAST CLUB US group comprising Dan Gilroy (vocals), Ed Gilroy (guitar), Gary Burke (bass) and Steven Bray (drums) whose main claim to fame was that Madonna was once a member. They refused her the lead singer role, prompting her to go solo.

27/06/1987.....54.....3....... RIGHT ON TRACK .... MCA 1146

BREATHE UK group formed in London by David Glasper (born 4/1/1965, vocals), Ian 'Spike' Spice (born 18/9/1966, drums), Marcus Lillington (guitar) and Michael Delahunty (bass), who left in 1988.

30/07/1988 .....4.....12.......	**HANDS TO HEAVEN**	Siren SRN 68
22/10/1988.....60.....3.......	JONAH	Siren SRN 95

O Silver disc   ● Gold disc   ✪ Platinum disc (additional platinum units are indicated by a figure following the symbol)   ◉ Singles released prior to 1973 that are known to have sold over 1 million copies in the UK

03/12/1988.....48......7........			HOW CAN I FALL..	Siren SRN 102
11/03/1989.....45......5........			DON'T TELL ME LIES...	Siren SRN 109

FREDDY BRECK German singer (born 21/1/1942, Sonneberg).

13/04/1974.....44......4........	SO IN LOVE WITH YOU..	Decca F 13481

BRECKER BROTHERS US duo Michael (born 29/3/1949, Philadelphia, PA, saxophone) and Randy Brecker (born 27/11/1945, Philadelphia, trumpet/flugelhorn). The brothers won the 1994 Grammy Award for Best Contemporary Jazz Performance for *Out Of The Loop*, Michael also winning a further ten Grammy Awards: Best Jazz Instrumental Performance by a Soloist in 1988 for *Don't Try This At Home*, Best Instrumental Composition in 1994 for *African Skies*, Best Jazz Instrumental Solo in 1995 for *Impressions*, Best Jazz Instrumental Performance in 1995 with the McCoy Tyner Trio for *Infinity*, Best Jazz Instrumental Solo in 1996 for *Cabin Fever*, Best Jazz Instrumental Individual or Group in 1996 for *Tales From The Hudson*, Best Jazz Instrumental Solo in 2001 for *Chan's Song*, Best Large Jazz Instrumental Album Individual or Group in 2002 with Herbie Hancock and Roy Hargrove for *Directions In Music*, Best Large Jazz Ensemble Album in 2003 for *Wide Angles* and Best Instrumental Arrangement with Gil Goldstein in 2003 for *Timbuktu*. Randy Brecker won the 1997 Grammy Award for Best Contemporary Jazz Performance for *Into The Sun* and the 2003 award for Best Contemporary Jazz Album for *34th N Lex*.

04/11/1978.....34......5........	EAST RIVER..	Arista ARIST 211

BREED 77 Gibraltan group formed by Paul Isola (vocals), Danny Felice (guitar), Pedro Caparros (guitar), Stuart Cavilla (bass) and Pete Chichone (drums) who relocated to London in 1997.

01/05/2004.....39......2........	THE RIVER...	Albert Productions JASCDUKL007
07/08/2004.....43......2........	WORLD'S ON FIRE..	Albert Productions JASCDUK011

BREEDERS US/UK rock group formed by Kim Deal (guitar/synthesiser/vocals), previously with The Puxies and Amps, and Tayna Donelly (guitar), later adding Josephine Wiggs (bass) and Britt Walford (drums). By the time of their hit the group consisted of Deal, her sister Kelley (guitar), Wiggs and Jim MacPherson (drums), Donelly later joining Belly.

18/04/1992.....69......1........	SAFARI (EP) Tracks on EP: *Do You Love Me Now, Don't Call Home, Safari* and *So Sad About Us*...............	4AD BAD 2003
21/08/1993.....40......3........	CANNONBALL (EP) Tracks on EP: *Cannonball, Cro-Aloha, Lord Of The Thighs* and *900*....................	4AD BAD 3011CD
06/11/1993.....59......1........	DIVINE HAMMER...	4AD BAD 3017CD
23/07/1994.....68......1........	HEAD TO TOE (EP) Tracks on EP: *Head To Toe, Shocker In Gloom Town* and *Freed Pig*. 10-inch vinyl-only release	
	....	4AD BAD 4012CD
14/09/2002.....72......1........	SON OF THREE..	4AD BAD 2213CD

BREEKOUT KREW US vocal duo.

24/11/1984.....51......3........	MATT'S MOOD..	London LON 59

ANN BREEN Irish singer (born in Downpatrick, County Down).

19/03/1983.....69......1........	PAL OF MY CRADLE DAYS..	Homespun HS 052
07/01/1984.....74......1........	PAL OF MY CRADLE DAYS..	Homespun HS 052

MARK BREEZE – see DARREN STYLES/MARK BREEZE

JO BREEZER UK singer (born 18/5/1983, London) who was first known as an actress, appearing in TV's *Grange Hill*.

13/10/2001.....27......2........	VENUS AND MARS...	Columbia 6717612

BRENDON UK singer (born Brendon Dunning, 1954, Andover) whose debut hit was originally released in 1976 on Jonathan King's UK label.

19/03/1977.....14......9........	GIMME SOME..	Magnet MAG 80

MAIRE BRENNAN Irish singer (born Maire Ni Bhraonain, 4/8/1952, Dublin), also lead singer with family group Clannad.

16/05/1992.....64......2........	AGAINST THE WIND...	RCA PB 45399
05/06/1999.....6......10......	SALTWATER CHICANE FEATURING MAIRE BRENNAN OF CLANNAD Effectively two songs made into one: Chicane's *Saltwater* and Clannad's *Theme From Harry's Game*...	Xtravaganza XTRAV 1CDS

ROSE BRENNAN Irish singer (born 1/1/1931, Dublin) who also recorded for HMV and Top Rank.

07/12/1961.....31......9........	TALL DARK STRANGER..	Philips PB 1193

WALTER BRENNAN US singer (born 25/7/1894, Swampscott, MA) who was a well-known character actor, making his Hollywood debut in 1927. He was the first actor to win three Oscars, all for Best Supporting Actor, beginning with *Come And Get It* in 1936. On TV he was in *The Real McCoys* and a couple of episodes of *Alias Smith And Jones*. He died from emphysema in 21/9/1974.

28/06/1962.....38......3........	OLD RIVERS...	Liberty LIB 55436

TONY BRENT UK singer (born Reginald Bretagne, 26/8/1927, Bombay, India) who moved to the US in the 1940s and then to the UK in 1950. After winning a talent contest he worked regularly with the BBC Showband, later relocating to Australia.

19/12/1952.....7......7........	WALKIN' TO MISSOURI..	Columbia DB 3147
02/01/1953.....9......7........	MAKE IT SOON..	Columbia DB 3187
23/01/1953.....12......1........	GOT YOU ON MY MIND..	Columbia DB 3226
30/11/1956.....16......7........	CINDY OH CINDY..	Columbia DB 3844
28/06/1957.....17......14......	DARK MOON...	Columbia DB 3950
28/02/1958.....20......5........	THE CLOUDS WILL SOON ROLL BY..	Columbia DB 4066

●[9] Number of weeks single topped the UK chart   ↑ Entered the UK chart at #1   ▲[9] Number of weeks single topped the US chart

109

DATE	POS	WKS	BPI	SINGLE TITLE	LABEL & NUMBER
05/09/1958	16	7		GIRL OF MY DREAMS	Columbia DB 4177
24/07/1959	24	4		WHY SHOULD I BE LONELY	Columbia DB 4304

BERNARD BRESSLAW UK singer (born 25/2/1934, London) who was better known as an actor, appearing in fourteen of the *Carry On* films. Named Most Promising Newcomer in 1958 by the Variety Club of Great Britain, he died in Manchester on 11/6/1993.

DATE	POS	WKS	BPI	SINGLE TITLE	LABEL & NUMBER
30/05/1958	5	9		THE SIGNATURE TUNE OF 'THE ARMY GAME' MICHAEL MEDWIN, BERNARD BRESSLAW, ALFIE BASS AND LESLIE FYSON Theme to the TV series *The Army Game*	HMV POP 490
05/09/1958	6	11		MAD PASSIONATE LOVE	HMV POP 522

TERESA BREWER US singer (born 7/5/1931, Toledo, OH), a child prodigy at the age of five, who toured with the Major Bowes Amateur Show until she was twelve. With a record debut in 1949, she also appeared in films, including *Those Redheads From Seattle* in 1953. She has a star on the Hollywood Walk of Fame.

DATE	POS	WKS	BPI	SINGLE TITLE	LABEL & NUMBER
11/02/1955	9	10		LET ME GO LOVER TERESA BREWER WITH THE LANCERS	Vogue Coral Q 72043
13/04/1956	2	15		A TEAR FELL	Vogue Coral Q 72146
13/07/1956	3	15		SWEET OLD-FASHIONED GIRL	Vogue Coral Q 72172
10/05/1957	26	2		NORA MALONE	Vogue Coral Q 72224
23/06/1960	21	11		HOW DO YOU KNOW IT'S LOVE	Coral Q 72396

BRIAN AND MICHAEL UK vocal duo Michael Coleman and Brian Burke. They were touring Northern workingmen's clubs when they came up with the idea for a tribute single to the painter LS Lowry. Burke left before the release date, producer Kevin Parrott (who later produced The Ramblers, another chart act) taking his place for TV appearances.

DATE	POS	WKS	BPI	SINGLE TITLE	LABEL & NUMBER
25/02/1978	❶³	19	●	MATCHSTALK MEN AND MATCHSTALK CATS AND DOGS Features backing vocals by the St Winifred's School Choir	Pye 7N 46035

BRICK US disco/jazz act formed in Atlanta, GA by Jimmy Brown (saxophone), Ray Ransom (bass), Donald Nevis (keyboards), Reggie Hargis (guitar) and Eddie Irons (drums), Ransom later recording solo.

DATE	POS	WKS	BPI	SINGLE TITLE	LABEL & NUMBER
05/02/1977	36	4		DAZZ Title is an amalgamation of disco and jazz. Featured in the films *10 Things I Hate About You* (1999) and *Starsky & Hutch* (2004)	Bang 004

EDIE BRICKELL AND THE NEW BOHEMIANS US singer Brickell (born 10/3/1966 Oak Cliff, TX) who joined the Dallas-based band as lead singer in 1985. The rest of the group comprised Brad Hauser (bass), Kenny Withrow (guitar), John Bush (percussion) and Brandon Ally (drums). Ally left and was replaced by Matt Chamberlain, with Wes Martin (guitar) joining at the same time. The New Bohemians disbanded in 1991. Brickell married singer Paul Simon in May 1992.

DATE	POS	WKS	BPI	SINGLE TITLE	LABEL & NUMBER
04/02/1989	31	7		WHAT I AM	Geffen GEF 49
27/05/1989	74	1		CIRCLE	Geffen GEF 51
01/10/1994	40	2		GOOD TIMES EDIE BRICKELL Features the uncredited contribution of Barry White	Geffen GFSTD 78

ALICIA BRIDGES US singer (born 15/7/1953, Lawndale, NC).

DATE	POS	WKS	BPI	SINGLE TITLE	LABEL & NUMBER
11/11/1978	32	10		I LOVE THE NIGHTLIFE (DISCO ROUND) Featured in the films *The Adventures Of Priscilla: Queen Of The Desert* (1994), *Breast Men* (1997) and *The Last Days Of Disco* (1998)	Polydor 2066 936
08/10/1994	61	1		I LOVE THE NIGHTLIFE (DISCO ROUND) (REMIX)	Mother MUMCD 57

JOHNNY BRIGGS – see AMANDA BARRIE AND JOHNNY BRIGGS

BRIGHOUSE AND RASTRICK BRASS BAND UK brass band from the West Yorkshire towns of Brighouse and Rastrick (situated between Bradford and Huddersfield). They appeared in the 2000 film *Brassed Off*.

DATE	POS	WKS	BPI	SINGLE TITLE	LABEL & NUMBER
12/11/1977	2	13	●	THE FLORAL DANCE	Transatlantic BIG 548

BETTE BRIGHT UK singer (born Anne Martin, Whitstable) who was previously with Deaf School before going solo in 1979. She retired from the music business after her marriage to Graham 'Suggs' McPherson of Madness.

DATE	POS	WKS	BPI	SINGLE TITLE	LABEL & NUMBER
08/03/1980	50	5		HELLO I AM YOUR HEART	Korova KOW 3

SARAH BRIGHTMAN UK singer (born 14/8/1961) and a member of the dance troupe Hot Gossip. She fronted their first single, a top ten hit, and its less successful follow-up (the rest of the group comprised Debbie Ash, Floyd, Roy Gayle, Virginia Hartley, Alison Hierlehy, Richard Lloyd King, Kim Leeson, Perry Lister, Jane Newman, Julia Redburn and Chrissie Wickham). She re-emerged in 1981 in the hit musical *Phantom Of The Opera,* since becoming highly successful in the MOR market. She was married to songwriter Andrew Lloyd-Webber between 1984 and 1990. Paul Miles-Kingston was aged twelve at the time of their hit.

DATE	POS	WKS	BPI	SINGLE TITLE	LABEL & NUMBER
11/11/1978	6	14	●	I LOST MY HEART TO A STARSHIP TROOPER SARAH BRIGHTMAN AND HOT GOSSIP	Ariola/Hansa AHA 527
07/04/1979	53	5		THE ADVENTURES OF THE LOVE CRUSADER SARAH BRIGHTMAN AND THE STARSHIP TROOPERS	Ariola/Hansa AHA 538
30/07/1983	55	4		HIM SARAH BRIGHTMAN AND THE LONDON PHILHARMONIC	Polydor POSP 625
23/03/1985	3	8	O	PIE JESU SARAH BRIGHTMAN AND PAUL MILES-KINGSTON Featured in the musical *Requiem*	HMV WEBBER 1
11/01/1986	7	10		THE PHANTOM OF THE OPERA SARAH BRIGHTMAN AND STEVE HARLEY	Polydor POSP 800
04/10/1986	3	16	O	ALL I ASK OF YOU CLIFF RICHARD AND SARAH BRIGHTMAN	Polydor POSP 802
10/01/1987	7	11		WISHING YOU WERE SOMEHOW HERE AGAIN Flip side *Music Of The Night* listed as MICHAEL CRAWFORD This and above two singles featured in the musical *Phantom Of The Opera*	Polydor POSP 803
11/07/1992	11	11		AMIGOS PARA SIEMPRE (FRIENDS FOR LIFE) JOSE CARRERAS AND SARAH BRIGHTMAN Theme to the 1992 Barcelona Olympics	Really Useful RUR 10
24/05/1997	2	14	●	TIME TO SAY GOODBYE (CON TE PARTIRO) SARAH BRIGHTMAN AND ANDREA BOCELLI	Coalition COLA 003CD
23/08/1997	45	1		WHO WANTS TO LIVE FOREVER	Coalition COLA 014CD
06/12/1997	54	2		JUST SHOW ME HOW TO LOVE YOU SARAH BRIGHTMAN AND THE LSO FEATURING JOSE CURA	Coalition COLA 035CD

O Silver disc ● Gold disc ✪ Platinum disc (additional platinum units are indicated by a figure following the symbol) ⓜ Singles released prior to 1973 that are known to have sold over 1 million copies in the UK

14/02/1998	58	1		STARSHIP TROOPERS Dance remix of Ariola/Hansa AHA 527	Coalition COLA 040CD
13/02/1999	68	1		EDEN	Coalition COLA 065CD

BRIGHTON AND HOVE ALBION FC UK professional football club formed in 1901. Their single was released to tie in with their FA Cup Final appearance.

28/05/1983	65	2		THE BOYS IN THE OLD BRIGHTON BLUE	Energy NRG 2

BRILLIANT UK group with Jimmy Cauty of KLF, and Youth of Killing Joke, also featuring June Montana on vocals. Their debut album was produced by Stock Aitken Waterman.

19/10/1985	58	5		IT'S A MAN'S MAN'S MAN'S WORLD	Food 5
22/03/1986	64	4		LOVE IS WAR	Food 6
02/08/1986	67	4		SOMEBODY	Food 7

DANIELLE BRISEBOIS US singer who was first known as an actress playing Stephanie Mills in the US TV comedies *All In The Family* and *Archie Bunker's Place*. Later in The New Radicals, after Gregg Alexander disbanded the group to concentrate on production she resumed her solo career.

09/09/1995	75	1		GIMME LITTLE SIGN	Epic 6610782

JOHNNY BRISTOL US singer (born 3/2/1939, Morgantown, NC) who began his career with Jackie Beaver, billed as Johnny & Jackie and signed by Tri-Phi. He was a successful songwriter and producer at Motown Records, usually with his mentor Harvey Fuqua. When Motown relocated to California he started producing for Columbia, although the label rejected him as a singer and he signed with MGM. Writing credits include *Someday We'll Be Together* (Diana Ross & The Supremes) and *Love Me For A Reason* (Osmonds and Boyzone). He died on 21/3/2004.

24/08/1974	3	11		**HANG ON IN THERE BABY**	MGM 2006 443
19/07/1980	39	5		MY GUY – MY GIRL (MEDLEY) AMII STEWART AND JOHNNY BRISTOL	Atlantic/Hansa K 11550

BRIT PACK UK/Irish vocal group formed by Damien Flood, Tom Ashton, Stepps, Kevin Andrew and Richard Taylor Woods.

12/02/2000	41	2		SET ME FREE	When! WENX 2000

BRITISH SEA POWER UK rock group (with trademark military uniforms) formed in Brighton in 2000 by Yan (vocals), Noble (guitar), Hamilton (bass) and Wood (drums).

12/07/2003	36	1		CARRION/APOLOGIES TO INSECT LIFE	Rough Trade RTRADESCD 92X
01/11/2003	30	2		REMEMBER ME	Rough Trade RTRADESCD 126

BRITS – see VARIOUS ARTISTS (MONTAGES)

ANDREA BRITTON UK singer (born 1975, London) who also recorded with Reflektive and Slovo.

11/01/2003	30	3		AM I ON YOUR MIND OXYGEN FEATURING ANDREA BRITTON	Innocent SINCD 40
19/06/2004	23	1		TAKE MY HAND JURGEN VRIES FEATURING ANDREA BRITTON	Direction 6749932

BROCK LANDARS UK production duo, DJs David Seaman and Paul Oakenfold. Brock Landars was supposed to be a pornographic film star.

11/07/1998	49	2		S.M.D.U. Contains samples of Blur's *Song 2* and Prodigy's *Smack My Bitch Up*. Title stands for 'Smack My Dick Up' .... Parlophone CDBLUE 001	

BROCKIE/ED SOLO UK production duo DJ Brockie (founder of Undiluted Records) and Ed Solo (born Ed Hicks).

24/04/2004	68	1		SYSTEM CHECK	Undiluted UD010

BROKEN ENGLISH UK vocal/instrumental group formed by Steve Elson (guitar/vocals), Jamie Moses (guitar) and Chris Brookes (guitar).

30/05/1987	18	10		COMIN' ON STRONG	EMI EM 5
03/10/1987	69	3		LOVE ON THE SIDE	EMI EM 55

BRONSKI BEAT UK trio formed by Jimmy Somerville (born 22/6/1961, Glasgow), Larry Steinbachek (born 6/5/1960, London) and Steve Bronski (born 7/2/1960, Glasgow), a strong gay following reflecting their musical stance on gay issues. Despite quitting through 'pop star pressure', Somerville later successfully fronted The Communards before going solo.

02/06/1984	3	13	○	**SMALLTOWN BOY**	Forbidden Fruit BITE 1
22/09/1984	6	10	○	**WHY?**	Forbidden Fruit BITE 2
01/12/1984	16	11		IT AIN'T NECESSARILY SO	Forbidden Fruit BITE 3
20/04/1985	3	12	○	**I FEEL LOVE (MEDLEY)** BRONSKI BEAT AND MARC ALMOND Medley of *I Feel Love, Love To Love You Baby* and *Johnny Remember Me*	Forbidden Fruit BITE 4
30/11/1985	3	14	○	**HIT THAT PERFECT BEAT** Featured in the 1985 film *A Letter To Brezhnev*	Forbidden Fruit BITE 6
29/03/1986	20	7		COME ON, COME ON	Forbidden Fruit BITE 7
01/07/1989	32	7		CHA CHA HEELS EARTHA KITT AND BRONSKI BEAT	Arista 112331
02/02/1991	32	4		SMALLTOWN BOY (REMIX) JIMMY SOMERVILLE WITH BRONSKI BEAT	London LON 287

BRONX US punk rock group formed in Los Angeles, CA in 2002 by Matt Caughthran (vocals), Joby J Ford (guitar), James Tweedy (bass) and Jorma Vik (drums).

24/04/2004	65	1		THEY WILL KILL US ALL (WITHOUT MERCY)	Wichita WEBB060SCD

❶⁹ Number of weeks single topped the UK chart ↑ Entered the UK chart at #1 ▲⁹ Number of weeks single topped the US chart

111

17/07/2004 . . . . . 73 . . . . . . 1 . . . . . .   FALSE ALARM . . . . Wichita WEBB062SCD

JET BRONX AND THE FORBIDDEN
UK instrumental group fronted by *Through The Keyhole* TV presenter Lloyd Grossman, who was awarded an OBE in the Queen's 2003 Birthday Honours List.

17/12/1977 . . . . . 49 . . . . . . 1 . . . . . .   AIN'T DOIN' NOTHIN' . . . . Lightning LIG 50

BROOK BROTHERS
UK vocal duo Geoffrey (born 12/4/1943) and Ricky Brook (born 24/10/1940) from Winchester who debuted in 1956 and released their first record in 1960. They appeared in the 1961 film *It's Trad, Dad* and later recorded as The Brooks.

30/03/1961 . . . . . 5 . . . . . . 14 . . . . . .   **WARPAINT** . . . . Pye 7N 15333
24/08/1961 . . . . . 13 . . . . . 10 . . . . . .   AIN'T GONNA WASH FOR A WEEK . . . . Pye 7N 15369
25/01/1962 . . . . . 37 . . . . . . 1 . . . . . .   HE'S OLD ENOUGH TO KNOW BETTER . . . . Pye 7N 15409
16/08/1962 . . . . . 33 . . . . . . 6 . . . . . .   WELCOME HOME BABY . . . . Pye 7N 15453
21/02/1963 . . . . . 38 . . . . . . 4 . . . . . .   TROUBLE IS MY MIDDLE NAME . . . . Pye 7N 15498

BRUNO BROOKES
– see **LIZ KERSHAW AND BRUNO BROOKES**

BROOKLYN BOUNCE
German production group formed by Matthias 'Double M' Menck and Dennis Bohn with vocalists Alex, Ulrika and Diablo.

30/05/1998 . . . . . 67 . . . . . . 1 . . . . . .   THE MUSIC'S GOT ME . . . . Club Tools 0064795 CLU

BROOKLYN BRONX AND QUEENS
– see **B B AND Q BAND**

ELKIE BROOKS
UK singer (born Elaine Bookbinder, 25/2/1945, Manchester) whose career began in the 1960s with a dance band, touring with jazz musician Humphrey Lyttelton and session work. She was in Vinegar Joe with Robert Palmer, both of them going solo when the group folded in 1973.

02/04/1977 . . . . . 8 . . . . . 9 . . . . . .   **PEARL'S A SINGER** . . . . A&M AMS 7275
20/08/1977 . . . . . 10 . . . . . 9 . . . . . .   **SUNSHINE AFTER THE RAIN** . . . . A&M AMS 7306
25/02/1978 . . . . . 16 . . . . . 7 . . . . . .   LILAC WINE . . . . A&M AMS 7333
03/06/1978 . . . . . 43 . . . . . 5 . . . . . .   ONLY LOVE CAN BREAK YOUR HEART . . . . A&M AMS 7353
11/11/1978 . . . . . 12 . . . . . 11 . . . . . .   DON'T CRY OUT LOUD . . . . A&M AMS 7395
05/05/1979 . . . . . 50 . . . . . 5 . . . . . .   THE RUNAWAY . . . . A&M AMS 7428
16/01/1982 . . . . . 17 . . . . . 10 . . . . . .   FOOL IF YOU THINK IT'S OVER . . . . A&M AMS 8187
01/05/1982 . . . . . 43 . . . . . 5 . . . . . .   OUR LOVE . . . . A&M AMS 8214
17/07/1982 . . . . . 33 . . . . . 5 . . . . . .   NIGHTS IN WHITE SATIN . . . . A&M AMS 8235
22/01/1983 . . . . . 52 . . . . . 5 . . . . . .   GASOLINE ALLEY . . . . A&M AMS 8305
22/11/1986 . . . . . 5 . . . . . 16 . . . . . .   **NO MORE THE FOOL** . . . . Legend LM 4
04/04/1987 . . . . . 55 . . . . . 3 . . . . . .   BREAK THE CHAIN . . . . Legend LM 8
11/07/1987 . . . . . 69 . . . . . 1 . . . . . .   WE'VE GOT TONIGHT . . . . Legend LM 9

GARTH BROOKS
US singer (born Troyal Garth Brooks, 7/2/1962, Yukon, OK) who performed in Nashville for four years before signing with Capitol after a gig at the Bluebird Cafe filling in for a no-show artist. The biggest selling country artist of all time, he appeared in the 1999 film *The Lamb* as Chris Gaines. He won two Grammy Awards: Best Male Country Vocal Performance in 1991 for *Ropin' The Wind* and Best Country Collaboration with Vocals in 1997 with Trisha Yearwood for *In Another's Eyes*. He has a star on the Hollywood Walk of Fame.

01/02/1992 . . . . . 71 . . . . . . 1 . . . . . .   SHAMELESS . . . . Capitol CL 646
22/01/1994 . . . . . 13 . . . . . 5 . . . . . .   THE RED STROKES/AIN'T GOING DOWN (TILL THE SUN COMES UP) . . . . Liberty CDCLS 704
16/04/1994 . . . . . 28 . . . . . 4 . . . . . .   STANDING OUTSIDE THE FIRE . . . . Liberty CDCL 712
18/02/1995 . . . . . 36 . . . . . 3 . . . . . .   THE DANCE/FRIENDS IN LOW PLACES . . . . Capitol CDCL 735
17/02/1996 . . . . . 55 . . . . . 1 . . . . . .   SHE'S EVERY WOMAN . . . . Capitol CDCL 767
13/11/1999 . . . . . 70 . . . . . 1 . . . . . .   LOST IN YOU Featured in the 1999 film *The Lamb* starring Garth Brooks. Capitol CDCL 814

HARRY BROOKS
– see **STUDIO B/ROMEO AND HARRY BROOKS**

MEL BROOKS
US film director (born Melvin Kaminsky, 28/6/1926, Brooklyn, NYC) and cult figure who has been married to actress Anne Bancroft since 1964.

18/02/1984 . . . . . 12 . . . . . 10 . . . . . .   TO BE OR NOT TO BE (THE HITLER RAP) Based on Brooks' 1984 film *To Be Or Not To Be,* but not actually featured in it . . . .
. . . . Island IS 158

MEREDITH BROOKS
US singer (born 12 June – she refuses to reveal year, probably 1958 – in Oregon City, OR) who was a member of Lips and The Graces before going solo.

02/08/1997 . . . . . 6 . . . . . 10 . . . . . O   **BITCH** Featured in the 2000 film *What Women Want* . . . . Capitol CDCL 790
06/12/1997 . . . . . 28 . . . . . 2 . . . . . .   I NEED . . . . Capitol CDCLS 794
07/03/1998 . . . . . 49 . . . . . 1 . . . . . .   WHAT WOULD HAPPEN . . . . Capitol CDCL 798

NORMAN BROOKS
Canadian singer (born Norman Joseph Arie) with backing group The Go Boys. He portrayed Al Jolson in the 1956 film *The Best Things In Life Are Free*.

12/11/1954 . . . . . 17 . . . . . . 1 . . . . . .   A SKY BLUE SHIRT AND A RAINBOW TIE . . . . London L 1228

BROS
UK group who were originally the trio Caviar, and then Gloss with twin brothers Matt and Luke Goss (born 29/9/1968, London) and Craig Logan (born 22/4/1969, Fife, Scotland). Songwriter/producer Nicky Graham spotted them, changed the name to Bros

   ◯ Silver disc   ⬤ Gold disc   ✪ Platinum disc (additional platinum units are indicated by a figure following the symbol)   ◎ Singles released prior to 1973 that are known to have sold over 1 million copies in the UK

and signed them to CBS. Logan was sacked in 1989, winning a court settlement of £1 million, the two brothers continuing as a duo. Financial and management problems – and declining popularity – heralded their splitting in 1991, both brothers trying solo and group projects. Logan later worked in the record business and band management. Named Best British Newcomers at the 1989 BRIT Awards.

Date	POS	WKS	BPI	Single Title	Label & Number
05/12/1987	2	15		**WHEN WILL I BE FAMOUS**	CBS ATOM 2
19/03/1988	2	10	○	**DROP THE BOY**	CBS ATOM 3
18/06/1988	❶²	11		**I OWE YOU NOTHING** Originally released in 1987 but failed to chart.	CBS ATOM 4
17/09/1988	4	8		**I QUIT**	CBS ATOM 5
03/12/1988	2	8	○	**CAT AMONG THE PIGEONS/SILENT NIGHT**	CBS ATOM 6
29/07/1989	2	7	○	**TOO MUCH**	CBS ATOM 7
07/10/1989	9	6		**CHOCOLATE BOX**	CBS ATOM 8
16/12/1989	10	6		**SISTER**	CBS ATOM 9
10/03/1990	14	4		MADLY IN LOVE	CBS ATOM 10
13/07/1991	12	5		ARE YOU MINE	Columbia 6568707
21/09/1991	27	4		TRY	Columbia 6574047

BROTHER BEYOND
UK pop group formed by Nathan Moore (vocals), David White (guitar), Carl Fysh (keyboards) and Steve Alexander (drums).

Date	POS	WKS	BPI	Single Title	Label & Number
04/04/1987	62	3		HOW MANY TIMES	EMI 5591
08/08/1987	57	3		CHAIN-GANG SMILE	Parlophone R 6160
23/01/1988	56	4		CAN YOU KEEP A SECRET	Parlophone R 6174
30/07/1988	2	14	○	**THE HARDER I TRY**	Parlophone R 6184
05/11/1988	6	10		**HE AIN'T NO COMPETITION**	Parlophone R 6193
21/01/1989	14	6		BE MY TWIN	Parlophone R 6195
01/04/1989	22	5		CAN YOU KEEP A SECRET (REMIX)	Parlophone R 6197
28/10/1989	39	4		DRIVE ON	Parlophone R 6233
09/12/1989	43	5		WHEN WILL I SEE YOU AGAIN	Parlophone R 6239
10/03/1990	53	2		TRUST	Parlophone R 6245
19/01/1991	48	2		THE GIRL I USED TO KNOW	Parlophone R 6265

BROTHER BROWN PRESENTS FRANK'EE
Danish DJ/production duo Henrik Olsen and Atle Thorberg, with vocals by Marie Frank.

Date	POS	WKS	BPI	Single Title	Label & Number
02/10/1999	18	4		UNDER THE WATER	ffrr FCD 367
24/11/2001	51	1		STAR CATCHING GIRL	Rulin 21CDS

BROTHERHOOD
UK hip hop group formed in London by Spice, Dexter and Shylock, evolving out of Jewish Public Enemy.

Date	POS	WKS	BPI	Single Title	Label & Number
27/01/1996	55	1		ONE SHOT/NOTHING IN PARTICULAR	Bite It BHOODD 3

BROTHERHOOD OF MAN
UK group with two incarnations. The first was in 1970 when ex- Edison Lighthouse and Pipkins session singer Tony Burrows (born 14/4/1942, Exeter) was asked to sing *United We Stand*. A group was formed to promote the record, with Johnny Goodison, singers Sue and Sunny and UK songwriter Roger Greenaway. The group was re-formed in 1976 when songwriter/producer Tony Hiller (responsible for *United We Stand*) penned the UK's entry for the Eurovision Song Contest, this time with Nicky Stevens, Sandra Stevens, Lee Sheridan and Martin Lee. Success in the competition and a UK #1 heralded more hit singles.

Date	POS	WKS	BPI	Single Title	Label & Number
14/02/1970	10	9		**UNITED WE STAND** Adopted by the US gay community as an anthem	Deram DM 284
04/07/1970	22	10		WHERE ARE YOU GOING TO MY LOVE	Deram DM 298
13/03/1976	❶⁶	16	✪	**SAVE YOUR KISSES FOR ME** 1976 Eurovision Song Contest winner	Pye 7N 45569
19/06/1976	30	7		MY SWEET ROSALIE	Pye 7N 45602
26/02/1977	8	12		**OH BOY (THE MOOD I'M IN)**	Pye 7N 45656
09/07/1977	❶¹	12	●	**ANGELO**	Pye 7N 45699
14/01/1978	❶¹	11	●	**FIGARO**	Pye 7N 46037
27/05/1978	15	12		BEAUTIFUL LOVER	Pye 7N 46071
30/09/1978	41	6		MIDDLE OF THE NIGHT	Pye 7N 46117
03/07/1982	67	2		LIGHTNING FLASH	EMI 5309

BROTHERS
UK group of five brothers from Mauritius, based in London. Featuring Clarel (lead vocals), Lindsay (guitar), Gervais (keyboards/guitar), Daniel (bass) and Clarey Bayou (drums), they won TV's *Opportunity Knocks* and the 1976 Variety Club Award before teaming with producers Mitch Murray and Pete Callander.

Date	POS	WKS	BPI	Single Title	Label & Number
29/01/1977	8	9		**SING ME**	Bus Stop Bus 1054

BROTHERS FOUR
US folk-pop quartet formed at the University of Washington by Dick Foley (bongos/cymbals), Bob Flick (bass fiddle), John Paine (guitar) and Mike Kirkland (banjo).

Date	POS	WKS	BPI	Single Title	Label & Number
23/06/1960	40	2		GREENFIELDS	Philips PB 1009

BROTHERS IN RHYTHM
UK instrumental/production duo Steve Anderson and David Seaman. As well as their own success they have remixed for Frankie Goes To Hollywood, Heaven 17, Kylie Minogue, Ce Ce Peniston, Pet Shop Boys and Judy Cheeks. The first UK remixing team to work with Michael Jackson (on *Who Is It*) and later his sister Janet, they also record as Brothers Love Dub and The Creative Thieves

Date	POS	WKS	BPI	Single Title	Label & Number
16/03/1991	64	2		SUCH A GOOD FEELING Contains a sample of Ronnie Laws' *Always There*	Fourth & Broadway BRW 228
14/09/1991	14	8		SUCH A GOOD FEELING	Fourth & Broadway BRW 228
30/04/1994	51	2		FOREVER AND A DAY **BROTHERS IN RHYTHM PRESENT CHARVONI**	Stress CDSTR 36

❶⁹ Number of weeks single topped the UK chart   ↑ Entered the UK chart at #1   ▲⁹ Number of weeks single topped the US chart

BROTHERS JOHNSON
US duo George (born 17/5/1953, Los Angeles, CA) and Louis Johnson (born 13/4/1955, Los Angeles), originally in Billy Preston's band before being discovered by producer Quincy Jones, who took guitarist George (aka Lightning Licks) and bass player Louis (Thunder Thumbs) on tour to Japan. Recording a number of their songs for his *Mellow Madness* album, Jones fixed a contract with A&M, the duo becoming mainstays of the jazz-funk circuit. They won the 1977 Grammy Award for Best Rhythm & Blues Instrumental Performance for *Q*. Louis Johnson also won the 1986 Grammy Award for Best Rhythm & Blues Song with Anita Baker and Gary Bias for *Sweet Love*.

DATE	POS	WKS		SINGLE TITLE	LABEL & NUMBER
09/07/1977	35	5		STRAWBERRY LETTER 23 Featured in the 1997 film *Jackie Brown*	A&M AMS 7297
02/09/1978	43	6		AIN'T WE FUNKIN' NOW	A&M AMS 7379
04/11/1978	50	4		RIDE-O-ROCKET	A&M AMS 7400
23/02/1980	6	12		**STOMP**	A&M AMS 7509
31/05/1980	47	4		LIGHT UP THE NIGHT	A&M AMS 7526
25/07/1981	50	3		THE REAL THING	A&M AMS 8149

BROTHERS LIKE OUTLAW FEATURING ALISON EVELYN
UK vocal group (previously Outlaw Posse) with Bello B, Jacko Martin Virgo, Cyril McCammon, Junior Nelson, DJ K-Gee, Femi Femm and Alison Evelyn.

DATE	POS	WKS		SINGLE TITLE	LABEL & NUMBER
23/01/1993	74	1		GOOD VIBRATIONS	Gee Street GESCD 44

EDGAR BROUGHTON BAND
UK rock band formed in 1969 by Edgar Broughton (guitar/vocals), Steve Broughton (drums), Arthur Grant (bass) and Victor Unitt (guitar).

DATE	POS	WKS		SINGLE TITLE	LABEL & NUMBER
18/04/1970	39	5		OUT DEMONS OUT	Harvest HAR 5015
23/01/1971	33	5		APACHE DROPOUT Adaptation of the Shadows hit	Harvest HAR 5032

ALISON BROWN – see BAR CODES FEATURING ALISON BROWN

ANDREA BROWN – see GOLDTRIX PRESENTS ANDREA BROWN

ANGIE BROWN
UK singer who also worked with Culture Club and Sarah Cracknell.

DATE	POS	WKS		SINGLE TITLE	LABEL & NUMBER
03/10/1992	3	13	○	**I'M GONNA GET YOU**	Vinyl Solution STORM 46S
27/02/1993	19	5		TOOK MY LOVE This and above single credited to **BIZARRE INC FEATURING ANGIE BROWN**	Vinyl Solution STORM 60CD
17/07/1993	67	1		ROCKIN' FOR MYSELF **MOTIV 8 FEATURING ANGIE BROWN**	Nuff Respect NUFF 002CD

CRAZY WORLD OF ARTHUR BROWN
UK singer (born Arthur Wilton, 24/6/1944, Whitby) and former philosophy student who was in R&B bands before forming The Crazy World Of Arthur Brown with Vincent Crane (born Vincent Rodney Chessman, 21/5/1943, Reading, keyboards) and Drachen Theaker (drums), who was replaced by Carl Palmer (born 20/3/1947, Birmingham). Songwriters Crane and Brown were later successfully sued by Peter Kerr and Michael Finesilver over similarities with an identically titled song. Crane and Palmer later formed Atomic Rooster, before Palmer was one third of Emerson Lake & Palmer. Crane committed suicide on 14/2/1989.

DATE	POS	WKS		SINGLE TITLE	LABEL & NUMBER
26/06/1968	●[1]	14		**FIRE** Featured in the 1995 film *Backfire*	Track 604 022

BOBBY BROWN
US singer (born 5/2/1969, Roxbury, MA) who was a member of teen group New Edition, formed in 1983. He left in 1986 to go solo (replaced by Johnny Gill), becoming the most successful of the ex-members. He married Whitney Houston in 1992 and their first child was born the following year. Imprisoned in January 1998 for driving under the influence of alcohol and drugs, in May 2000 (having tested positive for cocaine) he was refused bail and incarcerated while waiting sentence the following month.

DATE	POS	WKS		SINGLE TITLE	LABEL & NUMBER
06/08/1988	42	7		DON'T BE CRUEL	MCA 1268
17/12/1988	6	17		**MY PREROGATIVE** ▲[1]	MCA 1299
25/03/1989	13	8		DON'T BE CRUEL Re-issue of MCA 1268	MCA 1310
20/05/1989	6	9		**EVERY LITTLE STEP** 1989 Grammy Award for Best Rhythm & Blues Vocal Performance	MCA 1338
15/07/1989	4	9	○	**ON OUR OWN (FROM GHOSTBUSTERS II)** Featured in the 1989 film *Ghostbusters II*	MCA 1350
23/09/1989	33	6		ROCK WIT'CHA	MCA 1367
25/11/1989	21	7		RONI	MCA 1384
09/06/1990	14	7		THE FREE STYLE MEGA-MIX	MCA 1421
30/06/1990	12	9		SHE AIN'T WORTH IT ▲[2] **GLENN MEDEIROS FEATURING BOBBY BROWN**	London LON 265
22/08/1992	19	6		HUMPIN' AROUND	MCA MCS 1680
17/10/1992	41	4		GOOD ENOUGH	MCA MCS 1704
19/06/1993	56	2		THAT'S THE WAY LOVE IS	MCA MCSTD 2073
22/01/1994	16	5		SOMETHING IN COMMON **BOBBY BROWN AND WHITNEY HOUSTON**	MCA MCSTD 1957
25/06/1994	38	3		TWO CAN PLAY THAT GAME	MCA MCSTD 1973
01/04/1995	3	12	○	**TWO CAN PLAY THAT GAME** Re-promoted	MCA MCSTD 1973
08/07/1995	8	6		**HUMPIN' AROUND (REMIX)**	MCA MCSTD 1783
14/10/1995	17	3		MY PREROGATIVE (REMIX)	MCA MCSTD 2094
03/02/1996	25	2		EVERY LITTLE STEP (REMIX)	MCA MCSTD 48004
22/11/1997	40	1		FEELIN' INSIDE	MCA MCSTD 48067
21/12/2002	15	8		THUG LOVIN' **JA RULE FEATURING BOBBY BROWN** Contains a sample of Stevie Wonder's *Knocks Me Off My Feet*. Def Jam 637872

CARL BROWN – see DOUBLE TROUBLE

DENNIS BROWN
Jamaican singer (born Clarence Brown, 1/2/1956, Kingston) who took up professional music as a child and later joined the Falcons. He was admitted to hospital with respiratory problems and died from pneumonia on 1/7/1999, leaving a wife and thirteen children.

○ Silver disc ● Gold disc ✪ Platinum disc (additional platinum units are indicated by a figure following the symbol) ◉ Singles released prior to 1973 that are known to have sold over 1 million copies in the UK

DATE	POS	WKS	BPI	SINGLE TITLE	LABEL & NUMBER
03/03/1979	14	9		MONEY IN MY POCKET	Lightning LV 5
03/07/1982	47	6		LOVE HAS FOUND ITS WAY	A&M AMS 8226
11/09/1982	56	3		HALFWAY UP HALFWAY DOWN	A&M AMS 8250

DIANA BROWN AND BARRIE K. SHARPE UK vocal duo, Diana an ex-member of the Brand New Heavies.

DATE	POS	WKS	BPI	SINGLE TITLE	LABEL & NUMBER
02/06/1990	39	6		THE MASTERPLAN	ffrr F 133
01/09/1990	61	2		SUN WORSHIPPERS (POSITIVE THINKING)	ffrr F 144
23/03/1991	71	1		LOVE OR NOTHING	ffrr F 152
27/06/1992	53	2		EATING ME ALIVE	ffrr F 190

ERROL BROWN UK singer (born 12/11/1948, Kingston, Jamaica) who formed Hot Chocolate in 1970. The group disbanded in 1987 and Brown went solo, with production by Tony Swain and Steve Jolley. He was awarded an MBE in the Queen's 2003 Birthday Honours List.

DATE	POS	WKS	BPI	SINGLE TITLE	LABEL & NUMBER
04/07/1987	25	8		PERSONAL TOUCH	WEA YZ 130
28/11/1987	51	2		BODY ROCKIN'	WEA YZ 162
14/02/1998	18	3		IT STARTED WITH A KISS HOT CHOCOLATE FEATURING ERROL BROWN Re-issue of Hot Chocolate's RAK 344.	EMI CDHOT 101

FOXY BROWN US singer (born Inga Marchand, 6/9/1979, Brooklyn, NYC) who first appeared guesting on other artists' records before going solo with Def Jam.

DATE	POS	WKS	BPI	SINGLE TITLE	LABEL & NUMBER
21/09/1996	26	3		TOUCH ME TEASE ME CASE FEATURING FOXY BROWN Contains a sample of Schooly D's *PSK What Does It Mean*. Featured in the 1996 film *The Nutty Professor*.	Def Jam DEFCD 18
08/03/1997	11	5		GET ME HOME FOXY BROWN FEATURING BLACKSTREET Contains a sample of Eugene Wilde's *Gotta Get You Home Tonight*	Def Jam DEFCD 32
10/05/1997	31	2		AIN'T NO PLAYA JAY-Z FEATURING FOXY BROWN	Northwestside 74321474842
21/06/1997	9	5		I'LL BE FOXY BROWN FEATURING JAY-Z Contains samples of Rene & Angela's *I'll Be Good* and Blondie's *Rapture* .	Def Jam 5710432
11/10/1997	12	3		BIG BAD MAMA FOXY BROWN FEATURING DRU HILL Contains a sample of Carl Carlton's *She's A Bad Mama Jama*. Featured in the 1997 film *Def Jam's How To Be A Player*.	Def Jam 5749792
25/10/1997	25	2		SUNSHINE JAY-Z FEATURING BABYFACE AND FOXY BROWN	Northwestside 74321528702
13/03/1999	31	2		HOT SPOT	Def Jam 8708352
08/09/2001	27	3		OH YEAH FOXY BROWN FEATURING SPRAGGA BENZ Contains samples of Bob Marley's *Africa Unite* and *Lively Up Yourself* and Byron Lee's *54-56 (That's My Number)*	Def Jam 5887312

GLORIA D BROWN US singer (born 1959, Montgomery, AL).

DATE	POS	WKS	BPI	SINGLE TITLE	LABEL & NUMBER
08/06/1985	57	3		THE MORE THEY KNOCK, THE MORE I LOVE YOU	10 TEN 52

HORACE BROWN US R&B singer (born in Charlotte, NC) who also recorded with Case and Faith Evans, and previously supplied backing vocals for the likes of Father MC and Christopher Williams.

DATE	POS	WKS	BPI	SINGLE TITLE	LABEL & NUMBER
25/02/1995	58	1		TASTE YOUR LOVE Contains a sample of The Cookie Crew's *Word To The Conscious*	Uptown MCSTD 2026
18/05/1996	12	4		ONE FOR THE MONEY Contains a sample of Craig Mack's *Flava In Ya Ear*	Motown 8605232
12/10/1996	27	2		THINGS WE DO FOR LOVE Contains a sample of James Brown's *Blues And Pants*	Motown 8605712

IAN BROWN UK singer (born Ian George Brown, 20/2/1963, Ancoats) who formed The Stone Roses in 1984. He went solo in 1997. In 1998 he was jailed after being found guilty of air rage.

DATE	POS	WKS	BPI	SINGLE TITLE	LABEL & NUMBER
24/01/1998	5	4		MY STAR	Polydor 5719872
04/04/1998	14	4		CORPSES Features the uncredited contribution of Noel Gallagher of Oasis	Polydor 5696552
20/06/1998	21	3		CAN'T SEE ME	Polydor 5440452
20/02/1999	8	6		BE THERE UNKLE FEATURING IAN BROWN	Mo Wax MW 108CD1
06/11/1999	23	3		LOVE LIKE A FOUNTAIN	Polydor 5615162
19/02/2000	5	4		DOLPHINS WERE MONKEYS	Polydor 5616372
17/06/2000	29	2		GOLDEN GAZE	Polydor 5618452
29/09/2001	13	4		F.E.A.R.	Polydor 5872842
23/02/2002	33	2		WHISPERS	Polydor 5705382
02/10/2004	18	3		KEEP WHAT YA GOT	Fiction 9868284
27/11/2004	40	2		REIGN UNKLE FEATURING IAN BROWN	Mo Wax GUSIN007CDS

JAMES BROWN US singer (born 3/5/1928, Macon, GA, his birthdate often given as 3/5/1933 due to Brown's frequent use of fake ID) who was abandoned by his mother at the age of four and raised by his aunt Handsome 'Honey' Washington in Augusta, GA. Frequently in trouble as a teenager, once sentenced to serve 8–16 years hard labour for petty theft, then released on parole after three years and one day, he recorded a demo version of *Please Please Please* with pianist Bobby Byrd. Radio plays led to a contract with King's Federal subsidiary and a re-recorded version of the single, as James Brown And The Famous Flames, hit #6 on the R&B charts, selling over 1 million copies, but never making the pop top 100. His US top 40 debut with *Think* in 1960 heralded fourteen years as a chart regular. His groups have included the JB's (spotlighting Bootsy Collins, Maceo Parker and Fred Wesley for the first time) and the Famous Flames, and he has been known as 'The Godfather of Soul', 'Soul Brother #1' and 'The New Minister of Super Heavy Heavy Funk', all self-bestowed. He made a cameo appearance in the 1980 film *The Blues Brothers*. In 1988 he was sentenced to six years for firearms and evading arrest charges, serving three. Inducted into the Rock & Roll Hall of Fame in 1986, he also took part in the *It's Only Rock 'N' Roll* project for the Children's Promise charity. His *Star Time* compilation album won a 1991 Grammy for the Best Album Notes, the same year Brown collected the NARAS' Lifetime Achievement Award. He has a star on the Hollywood Walk of Fame.

DATE	POS	WKS	BPI	SINGLE TITLE	LABEL & NUMBER
23/09/1965	25	7		PAPA'S GOT A BRAND NEW BAG 1965 Grammy Award for Best Rhythm & Blues Recording. Featured in the films *Mrs Doubtfire* (1993) and *Face/Off* (1997).	London HL 9990

❶⁹ Number of weeks single topped the UK chart ⬆ Entered the UK chart at #1 ▲⁹ Number of weeks single topped the US chart

115

	DATE	POS	WKS	BPI	SINGLE TITLE	LABEL & NUMBER
	24/02/1966	29	6		I GOT YOU (I FEEL GOOD) Featured in the films *Good Morning Vietnam* (1988), *Who's Harry Crumb* (1989), *K9* (1989) and *The Nutty Professor* (1996)	Pye International 7N 25350
	16/06/1966	13	9		IT'S A MAN'S MAN'S MAN'S WORLD This and above singles credited to JAMES BROWN AND THE FAMOUS FLAMES Featured in the films *A Bronx Tale* (1994), *The Associate* (1997) and *Payback* (1999)	Pye International 7N 25371
	10/10/1970	32	7		GET UP I FEEL LIKE BEING A SEX MACHINE	Polydor 2001 071
	27/11/1971	47	3		HEY AMERICA	Mojo 2093 006
	18/09/1976	22	6		GET UP OFFA THAT THING	Polydor 2066 687
	29/01/1977	36	4		BODY HEAT	Polydor 2066 763
	10/01/1981	39	5		RAPP PAYBACK (WHERE IZ MOSES?)	RCA 28
	02/07/1983	45	4		BRING IT ON…BRING IT ON	Sonet SON 2258
	01/09/1984	49	5		UNITY (PART 1 – THE THIRD COMING) AFRIKA BAMBAATA AND JAMES BROWN	Tommy Boy AFR 2
	27/04/1985	50	3		FROGGY MIX	Boiling Point FROG 1
	01/06/1985	47	5		GET UP I FEEL LIKE BEING A SEX MACHINE Re-issue of Polydor 2001 071	Boiling Point POSP 751
	25/01/1986	5	10		LIVING IN AMERICA Featured in the 1985 film *Rocky IV*. 1986 Grammy Award for Best Rhythm & Blues Vocal Performance	Scotti Brothers A 6701
	01/03/1986	46	4		GET UP I FEEL LIKE BEING A SEX MACHINE	Boiling Point POSP 751
	18/10/1986	65	2		GRAVITY	Scotti Brothers 6500597
	30/01/1988	45	3		SHE'S THE ONE	Urban URB 13
	23/04/1988	12	6		THE PAYBACK MIX	Urban URB 17
	04/06/1988	31	4		I'M REAL JAMES BROWN FEATURING FULL FORCE	Scotti Brothers JSB 1
	23/07/1988	52	3		I GOT YOU (I FEEL GOOD) Listed flip side was *Nowhere To Run* by MARTHA REEVES & THE VANDELLAS Released following the use of both songs in the 1988 film *Good Morning Vietnam*	A&M AM 444
	16/11/1991	69	2		GET UP I FEEL LIKE BEING A SEX MACHINE Second re-issue of Polydor 2001 071	Polydor PO 185
	24/10/1992	72	1		I GOT YOU (I FEEL GOOD) (REMIX) JAMES BROWN VS DAKEYNE	FBI 9
	17/04/1993	59	2		CAN'T GET ANY HARDER	Polydor PZCD 262
	17/04/1999	40	2		FUNK ON AH ROLL	Inferno/Eagle EAGXA 073
	22/04/2000	63	1		FUNK ON AH ROLL (REMIX) Contains a sample of James Brown's *Hot Pants*	Eagle EAGXS 127

JENNIFER BROWN Swedish singer (born 1972).

	DATE	POS	WKS	BPI	SINGLE TITLE	LABEL & NUMBER
	01/05/1999	57	1		TUESDAY AFTERNOON	RCA 74321604092

JOANNE BROWN – see TONY OSBORNE SOUND

JOCELYN BROWN US singer (born 25/11/1950, Kingston, NC) who began as a session singer with Bruce Springsteen, Bob Dylan and Bette Midler among many. She went solo in 1984 with the self-penned *Somebody Else's Guy*, as well as frequently charting as a guest on other acts' records.

	DATE	POS	WKS	BPI	SINGLE TITLE	LABEL & NUMBER
	21/04/1984	13	9		SOMEBODY ELSE'S GUY	Fourth & Broadway BRW 5
	22/09/1984	51	3		I WISH YOU WOULD	Fourth & Broadway BRW 14
	15/03/1986	70	1		LOVE'S GONNA GET YOU	Warner Brothers W 8889
	29/06/1991	6	9		ALWAYS THERE INCOGNITO FEATURING JOCELYN BROWN	Talkin Loud TLK 10
	14/09/1991	57	3		SHE'S GOT SOUL JAMESTOWN FEATURING JOCELYN BROWN	A&M AM 819
	07/12/1991	3	11		DON'T TALK JUST KISS RIGHT SAID FRED. GUEST VOCALS: JOCELYN BROWN	Tug SNOG 2
	20/03/1993	61	1		TAKE ME UP	A&M AMCD 210
	11/06/1994	13	7		NO MORE TEARS (ENOUGH IS ENOUGH)	Ding Dong 74321209032
	08/10/1994	22	3		GIMME ALL YOUR LOVIN' This and above single credited to KYM MAZELLE AND JOCELYN BROWN	Ding Dong 74321231322
	13/07/1996	8	6		KEEP ON JUMPIN' TODD TERRY FEATURING MARTHA WASH AND JOCELYN BROWN	Manifesto FESCD 11
	10/05/1997	26	2		IT'S ALRIGHT, I FEEL IT! NUYORICAN SOUL FEATURING JOCELYN BROWN	Talkin Loud TLCD 22
	12/07/1997	5	10		SOMETHING GOIN' ON TODD TERRY FEATURING MARTHA WASH AND JOCELYN BROWN	Manifesto FESCD 25
	25/10/1997	31	2		I AM THE BLACK GOLD OF THE SUN NUYORICAN SOUL FEATURING JOCELYN BROWN	Talkin Loud TLCD 26
	22/11/1997	45	2		HAPPINESS KAMASUTRA FEATURING JOCELYN BROWN	Sony S3 KAMCD 2
	02/05/1998	33	2		FUN DA MOB FEATURING JOCELYN BROWN	INCredible INCRL 2CD
	29/08/1998	35	2		AIN'T NO MOUNTAIN HIGH ENOUGH	INCredible INCRL 7CD
	27/03/1999	62	1		I BELIEVE JAMESTOWN FEATURING JOCELYN BROWN	Playola 0091705 PLA
	03/07/1999	54	1		IT'S ALL GOOD DA MOB FEATURING JOCELYN BROWN	INCredible INCRL 14CD
	11/03/2000	45	2		BELIEVE MINISTERS DE LA FUNK FEATURING JOCELYN BROWN	Defected DFECT 14CDS
	27/01/2001	42	2		BELIEVE (REMIX) MINISTERS DE LA FUNK FEATURING JOCELYN BROWN	Defected DFECT 26CDS
	07/09/2002	54	1		THAT'S HOW GOOD YOUR LOVE IS IL PADRINOS FEATURING JOCELYN BROWN	Defected DFTD 057CDS

JOE BROWN AND THE BRUVVERS UK singer (born 13/5/1941, Lincolnshire) who began as guitarist with Clay Nicholls & The Blue Flames, then was discovered by Larry Parnes when appearing on ITV's *Boy Meets Girl*. He graduated from solo guitar spots to singing, with a string of hit singles, then films and West End musicals. His wife, the late Vicki Brown, appeared (uncredited) on the #1 hit by JJ Barrie, and daughter Sam has also hit the charts. Bruvvers' member and songwriter Peter Oakman (he penned *A Picture Of You*) later fronted Harley Quinne.

	DATE	POS	WKS	BPI	SINGLE TITLE	LABEL & NUMBER
	17/03/1960	34	6		DARKTOWN STRUTTERS BALL	Decca F 11207
	26/01/1961	33	6		SHINE JOE BROWN	Pye 7N 15322
	11/01/1962	37	2		WHAT A CRAZY WORLD WE'RE LIVING IN	Piccadilly 7N 35024
	17/05/1962	2	19		A PICTURE OF YOU	Piccadilly 7N 35047
	13/09/1962	31	6		YOUR TENDER LOOK	Piccadilly 7N 35058
	15/11/1962	6	14		IT ONLY TOOK A MINUTE	Piccadilly 7N 35082

○ Silver disc ● Gold disc ✪ Platinum disc (additional platinum units are indicated by a figure following the symbol) ◉ Singles released prior to 1973 that are known to have sold over 1 million copies in the UK

07/02/1963	3	14		THAT'S WHAT LOVE WILL DO	Piccadilly 7N 35106
27/06/1963	26	6		NATURE'S TIME FOR LOVE	Piccadilly 7N 35129
26/09/1963	28	9		SALLY ANN	Piccadilly 7N 35138
29/06/1967	32	4		WITH A LITTLE HELP FROM MY FRIENDS	Pye 7N 17339
14/04/1973	33	6		HEY MAMA This and above single credited to JOE BROWN	Ammo AMO 101

KAREN BROWN – see DJ'S RULE

KATHY BROWN US singer (born in South Carolina) who sang gospel before joining Sweet Cinnamon and then going solo.

25/11/1995	44	2		TURN ME OUT	Stress CDSTR 40
20/09/1997	35	3		TURN ME OUT (TURN TO SUGAR) PRAXIS FEATURING KATHY BROWN	ffrr FCD 314
10/04/1999	63	1		JOY	Azuli AZNYCDX 094
05/05/2001	34	2		LOVE IS NOT A GAME J MAJIK FEATURING KATHY BROWN	Defected DFECT 31CDS
02/06/2001	42	1		OVER YOU WARREN CLARKE FEATURING KATHY BROWN	Defected DFECT 28CDS

MIQUEL BROWN US singer (born in Detroit, MI) who began as an actress appearing in the films *Rollerball* (1975) and *Superman* (1978). Her daughter Sinitta was also a successful vocalist.

18/02/1984	68	4		HE'S A SAINT, HE'S A SINNER	Record Shack SOHO 15
24/08/1985	63	3		CLOSE TO PERFECTION	Record Shack SOHO 48

PALMER BROWN – see BLAZE FEATURING PALMER BROWN

PETER BROWN US singer/songwriter (born 11/7/1953, Blue Island, IL) who penned hits for the likes of Madonna.

11/02/1978	43	4		DO YA WANNA GET FUNKY WITH ME	TK TKR 6009
17/06/1978	57	5		DANCE WITH ME	TK TKR 6027

POLLY BROWN UK singer (born 18/4/1947, Birmingham) who was previously with Pickettywitch and Sweet Dreams.

14/09/1974	43	5		UP IN A PUFF OF SMOKE	GTO GT 2

ROY CHUBBY BROWN UK comedian (born Royston Vasey, 5/2/1945, Middlesbrough) whose real name was adopted for the fictional village in the TV comedy series *League Of Gentlemen*.

13/05/1995	64	2		LIVING NEXT DOOR TO ALICE (WHO THE F**K IS ALICE)	NOW CDWAG 245
12/08/1995	3	17	O	LIVING NEXT DOOR TO ALICE (WHO THE F**K IS ALICE) This and above single credited to SMOKIE FEATURING ROY 'CHUBBY' BROWN	NOW CDWAG 245
21/12/1996	51	3		ROCKIN' GOOD CHRISTMAS	Polystar 5732612

SAM BROWN UK singer (born 7/10/1964, London) who is the daughter of singer Joe Brown and his late wife Vicki. With a recording debut at twelve, she appeared in numerous TV shows including Jack Good's *Let's Rock* as well as performing with Adam & The Ants and Spandau Ballet.

11/06/1988	52	3		STOP	A&M AM 440
04/02/1989	4	12	O	STOP	A&M AM 440
13/05/1989	15	7		CAN I GET A WITNESS	A&M AM 509
03/03/1990	44	4		WITH A LITTLE LOVE	A&M AM 539
05/05/1990	23	8		KISSING GATE	A&M AM 549
26/08/1995	63	1		JUST GOOD FRIENDS FISH FEATURING SAM BROWN	Dick Bros. DDICK 014CD1

SHARON BROWN US singer (born in Boston, MA) working as a New York-based club and session singer.

17/04/1982	38	9		I SPECIALIZE IN LOVE	Virgin VS 494
26/02/1994	62	2		I SPECIALIZE IN LOVE (REMIX)	Deep Distraxion OILYCD 025

SLEEPY BROWN – see OUTKAST

BROWN SAUCE UK trio Noel Edmonds, Keith Chegwin and Maggie Philbin who at the time of their hit were presenters of the TV show *Multicoloured Swap Shop*. BA Robertson wrote the single. Chegwin and Philbin later married, then divorced.

12/12/1981	15	12		I WANNA BE A WINNER	BBC RESL 101

BROWN SUGAR – see SEX CLUB FEATURING BROWN SUGAR

DUNCAN BROWNE UK singer/guitarist (born 1946) who first recorded for the Immediate label in the late 1960s and was later a member of Metro. He died from cancer on 28/5/1993.

19/08/1972	23	6		JOURNEY	RAK 135
22/12/1984	68	2		THEME FROM 'THE TRAVELLING MAN' Theme to the TV series *The Travelling Man*	Towerbell TOW 54

JACKSON BROWNE US singer (born 9/10/1948, Heidelberg, West Germany) whose family settled in Los Angeles, CA in 1951. He was a successful songwriter for Linda Ronstadt, Joe Cocker, The Byrds, Bonnie Raitt and others before launching his own career in 1972. His US top ten hit *Doctor My Eyes* was a UK hit for the Jackson Five. His wife Phyllis committed suicide on 25/3/1976. He took part in the *It's Only Rock 'N' Roll* project for the Children's Promise charity. He was inducted into the Rock & Roll Hall of Fame in 2004.

01/07/1978	12	11		STAY	Asylum K 13128
18/10/1986	66	2		IN THE SHAPE OF A HEART	Elektra EKR 42

❶⁹ Number of weeks single topped the UK chart   ↑ Entered the UK chart at #1   ▲⁹ Number of weeks single topped the US chart

117

25/06/1994....67.....1......	EVERYWHERE I GO	Elektra EKR 184CD1

RONNIE BROWNE – see SCOTTISH RUGBY TEAM WITH RONNIE BROWNE

TOM BROWNE US trumpeter (born 1959, Queens, NYC) who switched from piano after being inspired by his father's collection of jazz albums. His first professional job was in 1975, four years later recording his debut solo album.

19/07/1980.....10.....11......	**FUNKIN' FOR JAMAICA (N.Y.)** Lead vocals by session singer Toni Smith .... Arista ARIST 357
25/10/1980....45.....5......	THIGHS HIGH (GRIP YOUR HIPS AND MOVE) .... Arista ARIST 367
30/01/1982....58.....4......	FUNGI MAMA (BEBOPAFUNKADISCOLYPSO).. Arista ARIST 450
11/01/1992.....45.....4......	FUNKIN' FOR JAMAICA (REMIX) .... Arista 114998

BROWNS US family group consisting of Jim Ed Brown (born 1/4/1934, Arkansas) and his sisters Maxine (born 27/4/1932, Louisiana) and Bonnie (born 31/7/1937, Arkansas). Maxine and Jim Ed later recorded solo.

18/09/1959 .....6.....13......	**THE THREE BELLS** ▲⁴ .... RCA 1140

BROWNSTONE US R&B vocal group based in Los Angeles, CA featuring Monica 'Mimi' Dolby, Nichole 'Nicci' Gilbert and Charmayne 'Maxee' Maxwell. Doby left in 1995 due to ill health and was replaced by Kina Cosper.

01/04/1995 .....8.....12......	**IF YOU LOVE ME** Contains a sample of K-Solo's *Spellbound*. Featured in the 1998 film *Living Out Loud* .... MJJ 6614135
15/07/1995.....16.....4......	GRAPEVYNE... MJJ 6620942
23/09/1995....27.....2......	I CAN'T TELL YOU WHY .... MJJ 6623775
17/05/1997.....12.....4......	5 MILES TO EMPTY .... MJJ 6640962
27/09/1997.....21.....2......	KISS AND TELL .... Epic 6649852

BROWNSVILLE STATION US rock trio formed in Michigan by Cub Koda (born 1/10/1948, Detroit, MI, guitar), Michael Lutz (vocals) and Henry Weck (drums). Koda was famous as an avid record collector and author (he co-wrote *Blues For Dummies*). He died from kidney disease on 30/6/2000.

02/03/1974.....27.....6.......	SMOKIN' IN THE BOYS' ROOM Featured in the 1979 film *Rock 'N' Roll High School* .... Philips 6073 834

DAVE BRUBECK QUARTET US pianist (born David Warren, 6/12/1920, Concord, CA) with Paul Desmond (alto saxophone), Joe Morello (drums) and Eugene Wright (bass). They were initially popular on the US college circuit. Brubeck founded Fantasy Records in 1949 with Sol and Max Weiss. He has a star on the Hollywood Walk of Fame. Desmond died on 30/5/1977.

26/10/1961 .....6.....15......	**TAKE FIVE** Featured in the 1995 film *Mighty Aphrodite* .... Fontana H 339
08/02/1962....36.....3......	IT'S A RAGGY WALTZ .... Fontana H 352
17/05/1962.....14.....12......	UNSQUARE DANCE .... CBS AAG 102

TOMMY BRUCE AND THE BRUISERS UK singer (born 1939, London) who worked as a driver's mate at Covent Garden when he recorded a demo, resulting in a contract with legendary producer Norrie Paramour at Columbia Records. His style likened to The Big Bopper (which Bruce denied), he and the group were TV regulars. The Bruisers later recorded separately, Bruce recording with Polydor, RCA and CBS.

26/05/1960 .....3.....16......	**AIN'T MISBEHAVIN'** .... Columbia DB 4453
08/09/1960....36.....4......	BROKEN DOLL.. Columbia DB 4498
22/02/1962.....50.....1.......	BABETTE TOMMY BRUCE .... Columbia DB 4776

CLAUDIA BRUCKEN German singer previously with Propaganda, going solo after her marriage to ZTT label boss Paul Morley caused friction within the group. She reunited with Propaganda in 2000.

11/08/1990.....71......1.......	ABSOLUT(E) .... Island IS 471
16/02/1991.....63......1.......	KISS LIKE ETHER.. Island IS 479

BRUISERS UK group originally backing Tommy Bruce. Their hit featured Peter Lee Stirling on lead vocals.

08/08/1963.....31.....7.......	BLUE GIRL .... Parlophone R 5042

BRUNO AND LIZ – see LIZ KERSHAW AND BRUNO BROOKES

FRANK BRUNO UK boxer (born 16/11/1961, London) who started singing after winning the World Heavyweight Championship, his only hit a cover of Survivor's smash – itself the theme to the 1982 film *Rocky III,* the third of Sylvester Stallone's popular boxing films.

23/12/1995.....28.....4......	EYE OF THE TIGER .... RCA 74321336282

TYRONE BRUNSON US singer/bass player (born in Washington DC) who was later a backing singer for Levert.

25/12/1982.....52......5.......	THE SMURF .... Epic EPC A 3024

BASIL BRUSH FEATURING INDIA BEAU UK puppet character created in 1963 by Peter Frimin for the children's TV show *The Three Scampys*. Originally featuring the voice of Ivan Owen he later had his own show.

27/12/2003.....44......3......	BOOM BOOM/CHRISTMAS SLIDE .... Right RRBB001

BRUVVERS – see JOE BROWN AND THE BRUVVERS

DORA BRYAN UK actress (born Dora Broadbent, 7/2/1926, Southport) whose only hit reflected the Beatlemania sweeping the country at the time, although she did record other material. Her 1947 film debut was in *Once Upon A Dream,* and she is still a regular on TV, having appeared in *Casualty, Absolutely Fabulous* and *Dinner Ladies.*

○ Silver disc ● Gold disc ✪ Platinum disc (additional platinum units are indicated by a figure following the symbol) ◎ Singles released prior to 1973 that are known to have sold over 1 million copies in the UK

05/12/1963	20	6		ALL I WANT FOR CHRISTMAS IS A BEATLE	Fontana TF 427

KELLE BRYAN UK singer (born 12/3/1975, London) who was previously in Eternal before going solo. She attended the Italia Conti stage school with Louise Nurding before joining Eternal. She also took part in the *It's Only Rock 'N' Roll* project for the Children's Promise charity.

02/10/1999	14	4		HIGHER THAN HEAVEN	1st Avenue MERCD 522

ANITA BRYANT US singer (born 25/3/1940, Barnsdale, OK) who was Miss Oklahoma and runner-up in the Miss America competition of 1958.

26/05/1960	24	4		PAPER ROSES	London HLL 9144
06/10/1960	48	2		MY LITTLE CORNER OF THE WORLD	London HLL 9171

PEABO BRYSON US singer (born Robert Peabo Bryson, 13/4/1951, Greenville, SC) who recorded his debut single for Bang in 1975, but has proved more successful with duets. Regina Belle is a US singer (born 15/7/1963, Englewood, NJ).

20/08/1983	2	13	O	**TONIGHT I CELEBRATE MY LOVE** PEABO BRYSON AND ROBERTA FLACK	Capitol CL 302
16/05/1992	9	7		**BEAUTY AND THE BEAST** CELINE DION AND PEABO BRYSON Featured in the 1992 Walt Disney film *Beauty And The Beast* and won an Oscar for Best Film Song. 1992 Grammy Award for Best Pop Performance by a Duo	Epic 6576607
17/07/1993	56	3		BY THE TIME THIS NIGHT IS OVER KENNY G WITH PEABO BRYSON	Arista 74321157142
11/12/1993	12	12		A WHOLE NEW WORLD (ALADDIN'S THEME) ▲¹ PEABO BRYSON AND REGINA BELLE Featured in the 1992 Walt Disney film *Aladdin* and won an Oscar for Best Film Song. 1993 Grammy Award for Best Pop Performance by a Duo	Columbia 6599002

BT US producer (born Brian Transeau, 1973, Maryland) and a major name on the UK dance scene who also worked with Echobelly singer Sonya Madden.

18/03/1995	34	2		EMBRACING THE SUNSHINE	Perfecto YZ 895CD
16/09/1995	28	2		LOVING YOU MORE	Perfecto PERF 110CD
10/02/1996	14	3		LOVING YOU MORE (REMIX) This and above single credited to BT FEATURING VINCENT COVELLO	Perfecto PERF 117CD
09/11/1996	26	2		BLUE SKIES BT FEATURING TORI AMOS . , ...	Perfecto PERF 130CD1
19/07/1997	19	4		FLAMING JUNE	Perfecto PERF 145CD1
29/11/1997	41	1		LOVE, PEACE & GREASE	Perfecto PERF 153CD1
10/01/1998	28	4		FLAMING JUNE (REMIX)	Perfecto PERF 157CD1
18/04/1998	27	2		REMEMBER	Perfecto PERF 160CD1
21/11/1998	54	1		GODSPEED	Renaissance RENCD 002
09/10/1999	38	2		MERCURY AND SOLACE	Headspace HEDSCD 001
24/06/2000	38	2		DREAMING BT FEATURING KIRSTY HAWKSHAW	Headscape HEDSCD 002
23/06/2001	51	1		NEVER GONNA COME BACK DOWN	Ministry Of Sound MOSBT CDS1
15/05/2004	30	3		LOVE COMES AGAIN TIESTO FEATURING BT	Nebula NEBCD 058

B.T. EXPRESS US group formed by Bill Risbrook (saxophone), Louis Risbrook (bass/organ/vocals), Dennis Rowe (percussion), Richie Thompson (guitar/vocals), Carlos Ward (saxophone), Terrell Woods (drums) and Barbara Joyce Lomas (vocals) as the King Davis House Rockers, Madison Street Express, Brothers Trucking and Brooklyn Transit Express before settling on B.T. Express. Keyboard player Michael Jones, a member of the group from 1975 until 1979, was later a successful singer, songwriter and producer operating as Kashif.

29/03/1975	34	6		EXPRESS	Pye International 7N 25674
26/07/1980	52	4		DOES IT FEEL GOOD/GIVE UP THE FUNK (LET'S DANCE)	Calibre CAB 503
23/04/1994	67	1		EXPRESS (REMIX).	PWL International PWCD 285

B2K US vocal group formed in Los Angeles, CA by Omarion (born Omarion Grandberry, 12/11/1985), Raz-B (born De-Maio Thornton, 13/6/1985), Lil Fizz (born Druex Fredericks, 26/11/1985) and J-Boog (born Jarrell Houston, 11/8/1985). The group disbanded in 2004 to pursue solo careers.

24/08/2002	35	2		UH HUH	Epic 6729512
29/03/2003	11	8		BUMP BUMP BUMP ▲¹ B2K FEATURING P DIDDY	Epic 6736452
21/06/2003	10	8		**GIRLFRIEND**	Epic 6739335
18/10/2003	31	2		UH HUH 2003 Remix of Epic 6729512.	Epic 6744012
20/03/2004	26	5		BADABOOM B2K FEATURING FABOLOUS	Epic 6747512

BUBBLEROCK UK singer Jonathan King (born Kenneth King, 6/12/1944, London).

26/01/1974	29	5		(I CAN'T GET NO) SATISFACTION	UK 53

CATHERINE BUCHANAN – see JELLYBEAN

ROY BUCHANAN US singer (born 23/9/1939, Ozark, TN, raised in California) who toured with Dale Hawkins before becoming a session guitarist. Acclaimed as a guitarist, seemingly he was offered Brian Jones' position in the Rolling Stones, and also declined a place with Eric Clapton in Derek And The Dominoes in favour of a solo career. He committed suicide by hanging himself in a police cell on 14/8/1988.

31/03/1973	40	3		SWEET DREAMS	Polydor 2066 307

BUCKETHEADS US producer/guitarist Kenny 'Dope' Gonzalez who was also a member of Masters At Work and the mastermind behind Nuyorican Soul.

04/03/1995	5	13	O	**THE BOMB! (THESE SOUNDS FALL INTO MY MIND)** Contains a sample of Chicago's *Street Player*	Positiva CDTIV 33
20/01/1996	12	3		GOT MYSELF TOGETHER Contains a sample of Brass Construction's *Movin'*	Positiva CDTIV 48

❶⁹ Number of weeks single topped the UK chart ↑ Entered the UK chart at #1 ▲⁹ Number of weeks single topped the US chart

119

LINDSEY BUCKINGHAM US singer (born 3/10/1947, Palo Alto, CA) who was a member of Fritz before joining Fleetwood Mac in 1975 with girlfriend Stevie Nicks. He made his first solo album during a lull in group activities and left the band in 1987.

16/01/1982.....31......7....... TROUBLE .... Mercury MER 85

JEFF BUCKLEY US singer/guitarist (born 1/8/1966, Orange County, CA) and the son of musician Tim Buckley, whom he met only once at the age of eight, some two months before his father died from a heroin overdose. Raised by his mother and stepfather, after training at the Los Angeles Musicians' Institute he moved to Manhattan where after a brief spell with Gods & Monsters he went solo. On the night of 29/5/1997 he jumped fully clothed into the Mississippi River at Memphis Harbour after saying he fancied a late night swim. Drowned when the waves from two passing boats swept him under, his body was not washed ashore for several days.

27/05/1995.....54......2....... LAST GOODBYE .... Columbia 6620422
06/06/1998.....43......1....... EVERYBODY HERE WANTS YOU .... Columbia 6657912

BUCKS FIZZ UK vocal group formed by Cheryl Baker (born Rita Crudgington, 8/3/1954, London), Jay Aston (born 4/5/1961, London), Mike Nolan (born 7/12/1954, Dublin) and Bobby G (born Robert Gubby, 23/8/1953, Epsom) to represent the UK in the 1981 Eurovision Song Contest, Baker being previously in 1978 entrants Co-Co. The success in Dublin owed as much to the dance routine (in which the girls' skirts were ripped off) as to the song. Aston left in 1985 after an alleged affair with songwriter Andy Hill (who was married to the group's manager) and was replaced by Shelley Preston (born 14/5/1960, Salisbury). They dissolved in 1989, regrouping for occasional live projects. Baker became a TV presenter.

28/03/1981	❶³	12	●	**MAKING YOUR MIND UP** 1981 Eurovision Song Contest winner	RCA 56
06/06/1981	12	9	○	PIECE OF THE ACTION	RCA 88
15/08/1981	20	10		ONE OF THOSE NIGHTS	RCA 114
28/11/1981	❶²	16		**THE LAND OF MAKE BELIEVE**	RCA 163
27/03/1982	❶¹	8	○	**MY CAMERA NEVER LIES**	RCA 202
19/06/1982	8	9	○	**NOW THOSE DAYS ARE GONE**	RCA 241
27/11/1982	10	11	○	**IF YOU CAN'T STAND THE HEAT**	RCA 300
12/03/1983	14	7		RUN FOR YOUR LIFE	RCA FIZ 1
18/06/1983	10	8		WHEN WE WERE YOUNG	RCA 342
01/10/1983	34	6		LONDON TOWN	RCA 363
17/12/1983	57	6		RULES OF THE GAME	RCA 380
25/08/1984	15	9		TALKING IN YOUR SLEEP	RCA FIZ 2
27/10/1984	42	4		GOLDEN DAYS	RCA FIZ 3
29/12/1984	34	8		I HEAR TALK	RCA FIZ 4
22/06/1985	43	4		YOU AND YOUR HEART SO BLUE	RCA PB 40233
14/09/1985	57	3		MAGICAL	RCA PB 40367
07/06/1986	8	10		**NEW BEGINNING (MAMBA SEYRA)**	Polydor POSP 794
30/08/1986	47	3		LOVE THE ONE YOU'RE WITH	Polydor POSP 813
15/11/1986	45	4		KEEP EACH OTHER WARM	Polydor POSP 835
05/11/1988	50	3		HEART OF STONE	RCA PB 42035

BUCKSHOT LEFONQUE US group formed by Branford Marsalis (saxophone/keyboards), DJ Apollo (mixing), Carl Burnett (guitar), Russell Gunn (trumpet), Reginald Veal (bass), Rocky Bryant (drums) and 50 Styles: The Unknown Soldier (raps).

06/12/1997.....65......1....... ANOTHER DAY .... Columbia 6653762

ROY BUDD UK composer/jazz pianist (born 14/3/1947, London) who made his name writing various movie themes, including the films *Soldier Blue* (1970), *Pulp* (1972), *Paper Tiger* (1975), *Sinbad And The Eye Of The Tiger* (1977) and *The Wild Geese* (1978). *Get Carter*, his first chart album, was originally released in 1971. Married to French singer Caterina Valente between 1972 and 1979, he died from a brain haemorrhage on 7/8/1993.

10/07/1999.....68......1....... GET CARTER .... Cinephile CINX 1003

JOE BUDDEN US rapper (born 1981, Harlem, NYC, raised in Queens, NYC and Jersey City, NJ).

19/07/2003.....13......7....... PUMP IT UP Contains a sample of Kool & The Gang's *Soul Vibration*. Featured in the 2003 film *2 Fast 2 Furious*. . Def Jam 9808879
16/10/2004.....9......4....... **WHATEVER U WANT** CHRSTINA MILIAN FEATURING JOE BUDDEN Contains a sample of The Bar-Kays' *Spellbound*. Def Jam 9864266

BUDGIE UK hard rock group formed in Cardiff in 1968 by John Shelley (born 10/4/1947, Cardiff, bass guitar/vocals), Tony Bourge (born 23/11/1948, Cardiff, guitar/vocals) and Ray Phillips (drums). Phillips left in 1974 and was replaced by Pete Boot (born 30/9/1950, West Bromwich), who left later the same year and was replaced by Steve Williams. Bourge left in 1978 (to join Phillips in a venture called Tredegar) and was replaced by John Thomas. Shelley disbanded the group in 1987.

03/10/1981.....71......2....... KEEPING A RENDEZVOUS .... RCA BUDGIE 3

BUFFALO G Irish rapping duo formed in Dublin by Olive Tucker and Naomi Lynch, both sixteen years old on their debut hit. Naomi is the sister of Boyzone member Shane Lynch and B*Witched members Keavy and Edele.

10/06/2000.....17......4....... WE'RE REALLY SAYING SOMETHING .... Epic 6694182

BUFFALO TOM: LIAM GALLAGHER AND STEVE CRADDOCK US group formed in Boston in 1986 by Chris Colbourn (vocals/bass), Bill Janovitz (guitar/vocals) and Tom Maginnis (drums), their debut hit a tribute to The Jam. The EP also featured Oasis' Liam Gallagher and Ocean Colour Scene's Steve Craddock performing *Carnation*, attracting more radio plays.

23/10/1999 .....6......5....... **GOING UNDERGROUND** .... Ignition IGNSCD 16

BUG KHAN AND THE PLASTIC JAM UK vocal/instrumental group with Jimmy Low, Paul Gregory, Grant Bowden and singer Patti Low.

31/08/1991.....70......1...... MADE IN TWO MINUTES BUG KHAN AND PLASTIC JAM FEATURING PATTI LOW AND DOOGIE ....Optimum Dance BKPJ 1S
26/02/1994.....64......1...... MADE IN TWO MINUTES (REMIX) ....PWL International PWCD 286

BUGGLES UK duo Geoff Downes and Trevor Horn who were previously together in Tina Charles' backing group. They began writing songs with friend Bruce Woolley in 1978, releasing Video a year later. Both went on to join Yes, with Downes later joining Asia and Horn becoming a major producer.

22/09/1979 ....❶[1].....11.....● VIDEO KILLED THE RADIO STAR First video shown on MTV on 1/8/1981 ....Island WIP 6524
26/01/1980.....16......8...... THE PLASTIC AGE..Island WIP 6540
05/04/1980.....38......5...... CLEAN CLEAN ....Island WIP 6584
08/11/1980.....55......4...... ELSTREE ....Island WIP 6624

JAMES BULLER UK singer/actor who appeared in the TV series Casualty, Babes In The Wood and Sunburn.

06/03/1999.....51......1...... CAN'T SMILE WITHOUT YOU Featured in the TV series Sunburn.....................................BBC Music WMSS 60092

SILVAH BULLET – see JOHNNY L

BULLETPROOF UK producer Paul Chambers.

10/03/2001.....62......1...... SAY YEAH/DANCE TO THE RHYTHM ....Tidy Trax TIDY 148CD

BUMP UK instrumental/production duo DJ Mark Auerbach and Steve Travell, who also launched the Good Boy label.

04/07/1992.....40......4...... I'M RUSHING...Good Boy EDGE7 1
11/11/1995.....45......1...... I'M RUSHING (REMIX) ....Deconstruction 74321320692

BUMP AND FLEX UK production duo formed by Alan Nelson and KC Ross.

23/05/1998.....73......1...... LONG TIME COMING ....Heat Recordings HEATCD 014

BUNKER KRU – see HARLEQUIN 4S/BUNKER KRU

BUNNYMEN – see ECHO AND THE BUNNYMEN

EMMA BUNTON UK singer (born 21/1/1976, London) who was also a member of the Spice Girls and known as Baby Spice. She began her career acting in the TV soap Eastenders.

13/11/1999 .....2......12.....○ WHAT I AM TIN TIN OUT FEATURING EMMA BUNTON ....VC Recordings VCRD 53
14/04/2001 ....❶[2].....12.....○ WHAT TOOK YOU SO LONG ↑ ....Virgin VSCDT 1796
08/09/2001.....5......9...... TAKE MY BREATH AWAY ....Virgin VSCDT 1814
22/12/2001.....20......5...... WE'RE NOT GONNA SLEEP TONIGHT..Virgin VSCDT 1821
07/06/2003.....5......9...... FREE ME 19/Universal 9807473
25/10/2003.....6......9...... MAYBE 19/Universal 9812785
07/02/2004.....7......8...... I'LL BE THERE 19/Universal 9816268
1/06/2004.....15......4...... CRICKETS SING FOR ANAMARIA 19 9866856

ERIC BURDON – see ANIMALS

TIM BURGESS UK singer (born 30/5/1968, Salford) who was a founder member of The Charlatans.

18/12/1993.....37......5...... I WAS BORN ON CHRISTMAS DAY SAINT ETIENNE CO-STARRING TIM BURGESS.........................Heavenly HVN 36CD
06/09/2003.....44......1...... I BELIEVE IN THE SPIRIT ....PIAS PIASB109CD
15/11/2003.....54......1...... ONLY A BOY ....PIAS PIASB119CD

GEOFFREY BURGON UK orchestra leader (born 16/7/1941).

26/12/1981.....48......4...... BRIDESHEAD THEME Theme to the TV series Brideshead Revisited.................................Chrysalis CHS 2562

KENI BURKE US R&B singer (born 28/9/1953, Chicago, IL) who was previously bass player with the family group The Five Stairsteps, doing session work after they disbanded. He was later a successful songwriter/producer for other acts.

27/06/1981.....59......3...... LET SOMEBODY LOVE YOU ....RCA 93
18/04/1992.....70......1...... RISIN' TO THE TOP...RCA PB 49103

SOLOMON BURKE – see JUNKIE XL

BURN UK rock group formed in Blackburn by Daniel Davidson, Graham Rodgerson, Michael Spencer, Jason Place and Lee Walsh.

08/06/2002.....72......1...... THE SMILING FACE...Hut HUTCD 155
29/03/2003.....54......1...... DRUNKEN FOOL...Hut HUTCD 166

HANK C. BURNETTE Swedish multi-instrumentalist particularly noted on the guitar.

30/10/1976.....21......8...... SPINNING ROCK BOOGIE...Sonet SON 2094

JOHNNY BURNETTE US singer (born 25/3/1934, Memphis, TN) who formed The Rock'n'Roll Trio with his brother Dorsey and friend Paul Burlison, making their first record for Von in 1956. They disbanded in 1957, Johnny and Dorsey songwriting, penning hits

❶[9] Number of weeks single topped the UK chart ↑ Entered the UK chart at #1 ▲[9] Number of weeks single topped the US chart

for Ricky Nelson before Johnny went solo, appearing in the film *Rock Rock Rock* (1956). He drowned in a fishing trip accident on Clear Lake, CA on 1/8/1964, after his unlit boat was rammed by a larger vessel. His son Rocky also enjoyed a recording career.

DATE	POS	WKS	SINGLE TITLE	LABEL & NUMBER
29/09/1960	5	16	DREAMIN'	London HLG 9172
12/01/1961	3	12	YOU'RE SIXTEEN	London HLG 9254
13/04/1961	12	12	LITTLE BOY SAD	London HLG 9315
10/08/1961	37	5	GIRLS	London HLG 9388
17/05/1962	35	3	CLOWN SHOES	Liberty LIB 55416

ROCKY BURNETTE US singer (born Jonathan Burnette, 12/6/1953 Memphis, TN), son of Johnny Burnette. He began as a songwriter, penning songs for Donny Osmond and David Cassidy, before his singing career. Legend has it that he did not attend his father's funeral, going fishing in order to pay his respects.

17/11/1979	58	7	TIRED OF TOEIN' THE LINE	EMI 2992

JERRY BURNS UK singer (born in Glasgow) who later contributed to the soundtrack to the 1996 film *Walking And Talking*. She also worked with Craig Armstrong.

25/04/1992	64	1	PALE RED	Columbia 6579467

PETE BURNS UK singer (born 5/8/1959, Liverpool) who was lead singer with Dead Or Alive before going solo.

19/06/2004	75	1	JACK AND JILL PARTY	Olde English LKCD02

RAY BURNS UK singer who began professionally after leaving the RAF in 1945. He made his first recordings with the Ambrose Orchestra in 1949.

11/02/1955	4	13	MOBILE	Columbia DB 3563
26/08/1955	14	6	THAT'S HOW A LOVE SONG WAS BORN	Columbia DB 3640

BURRELLS – see **RESONANCE FEATURING THE BURRELLS**

MALANDRA BURROWS UK singer (born 4/11/1965, Liverpool) who is better known as an actress for her role of Kathy Bates/Tate/Glover in the TV soap *Emmerdale*, although her career began with a win on the talent contest *Opportunity Knocks*.

01/12/1990	11	8	JUST THIS SIDE OF LOVE Featured in the TV series *Emmerdale*	Yorkshire Television DALE 1
18/01/1997	49	1	CARNIVAL IN HEAVEN	warner.esp WESP 001CD
29/08/1998	54	1	DON'T LEAVE ME	warner.esp WESP 004CD

JENNY BURTON US singer (born 18/11/1957, New York City).

30/03/1985	68	2	BAD HABITS	Atlantic A 9583

BURUNDI STEIPHENSON BLACK Burundi tribal drummers and chanting with orchestral additions added by Frenchman Mike Steiphenson (on one side only). Although not high in the chart, their hit was a steady seller and an influence some ten years later, when Adam Ant, among others, borrowed heavily on its style.

13/11/1971	31	14	BURUNDI BLACK	Barclay BAR 3

BUS 75 – see **WHALE**

BUS STOP UK/Canadian production group formed by Mark Hall and Graham Turner with various guest singers. Hall was previously in 2 For Joy, and the pair later recorded as Flip & Fill.

23/05/1998	8	11	KUNG FU FIGHTING BUS STOP FEATURING CARL DOUGLAS Contains a sample of Carl Douglas' *Kung Fu Fighting* ... All Around The World CDGLOBE 173
24/10/1998	22	4	YOU AIN'T SEEN NOTHIN' YET BUS STOP FEATURING RANDY BACHMAN	All Around The World CDGLOBE 187
10/04/1999	23	3	JUMP	All Around The World CXGLOBE 186
07/10/2000	59	1	GET IT ON BUS STOP FEATURING T REX Contains a sample of T Rex' *Get It On*	All Around The World CDGLOBE 225

LOU BUSCH US orchestra leader/pianist (born 18/7/1910, Louisville, KY) who also recorded as Joe 'Fingers' Carr and began playing with George Olsen and Hal Kemp before becoming an in-house producer for Capitol Records. With his own orchestra in the 1950s, he backed the likes of Margaret Whiting (his future wife) and Kay Starr, also composing the themes for TV shows, including *What's My Line* in 1950. He was killed in a car crash on 19/9/1979.

27/01/1956	2	17	ZAMBESI	Capitol CL 14504

BUSH UK rock group from London formed by Gavin Rossdale (born 30/10/1967, London, guitar/vocals), Nigel Pulsford (born 11/4/1965, Newport, guitar), ex-Transvision Vamp Dave Parsons (born 2/7/1966, Uxbridge, bass) and Robin Goodridge (born 10/9/1966, Crawley, drums), taking their name from Shepherd's Bush, the London area where they grew up.

08/06/1996	48	2	MACHINEHEAD	Interscope IND 95505
01/03/1997	7	5	SWALLOWED	Interscope IND 95528
07/06/1997	22	2	GREEDY FLY	Interscope IND 95536
01/11/1997	49	1	BONE DRIVEN	Interscope IND 95553
04/12/1999	46	1	THE CHEMICALS BETWEEN US	Trauma/Polydor 4972222
18/03/2000	45	1	WARM MACHINE	Trauma/Polydor 4972752
03/06/2000	51	1	LETTING THE CABLES SLEEP	Trauma/Polydor 4973352

KATE BUSH UK singer (born 30/7/1958, Bexleyheath) who signed with EMI while still at convent school and spent the next two years writing material for her first album. Her first single, the lyrics inspired by Emily Bronte's novel (Bronte and Bush shared the same birthday), was a UK smash with subsequent albums selling well. She won the Best UK Female Award at the 1987 BRIT Awards. Larry Adler is a US mouth organist (born 10/2/1914, Baltimore, MD).

DATE	POS	WKS	BPI	SINGLE TITLE	LABEL & NUMBER
11/02/1978	❶⁴	13	●	**WUTHERING HEIGHTS**	EMI 2719
10/06/1978	6	11		**MAN WITH THE CHILD IN HIS EYES** Lyrics written when Bush was fourteen years of age. Won the Outstanding UK Lyric category at the Ivor Novello Awards	EMI 2806
11/11/1978	44	6		HAMMER HORROR	EMI 2887
17/03/1979	14	10		WOW	EMI 2911
15/09/1979	10	9		**KATE BUSH ON STAGE EP** Tracks on EP: *Them Heavy People, Don't Push Your Foot On The Heartbrake, James And The Cold Gun* and *L'Amour Looks Something Like You*	EMI MIEP 2991
26/04/1980	16	7		BREATHING	EMI 5058
05/07/1980	5	10	○	**BABOOSHKA**	EMI 5085
04/10/1980	16	9		ARMY DREAMERS	EMI 5106
06/12/1980	29	7		DECEMBER WILL BE MAGIC AGAIN	EMI 5121
11/07/1981	11	7		SAT IN YOUR LAP	EMI 5201
07/08/1982	48	3		THE DREAMING	EMI 5296
17/08/1985	3	11	○	**RUNNING UP THAT HILL**	EMI KB 1
26/10/1985	20	6		CLOUDBURSTING	EMI KB 2
01/03/1986	18	5		HOUNDS OF LOVE	EMI KB 3
10/05/1986	37	3		THE BIG SKY	EMI KB 4
01/11/1986	9	11		**DON'T GIVE UP** PETER GABRIEL AND KATE BUSH Featured in the 1999 film *The Bone Collector*	Virgin PGS 2
08/11/1986	23	4		EXPERIMENT IV	EMI KB 5
30/09/1989	12	5		THE SENSUAL WORLD	EMI EM 102
02/12/1989	25	5		THIS WOMAN'S WORK	EMI EM 119
10/03/1990	38	3		LOVE AND ANGER	EMI EM 134
07/12/1991	12	8		ROCKET MAN (I THINK IT'S GOING TO BE A LONG LONG TIME) Recorded as part of a tribute to the songwriting of Elton John and Bernie Taupin	Mercury TRIBO 2
18/09/1993	12	5		RUBBERBAND GIRL	EMI CDEM 280
27/11/1993	26	3		MOMENTS OF PLEASURE	EMI CDEM 297
16/04/1994	21	3		THE RED SHOES	EMI CDEMS 316
30/07/1994	27	2		THE MAN I LOVE **KATE BUSH AND LARRY ADLER**	Mercury MERCD 408
19/11/1994	26	2		AND SO IS LOVE	EMI CDEMS 355

BUSTED UK group formed by James Bourne (born 13/9/1983, Southend-on-Sea, guitar/piano), Charlie Simpson (born 7/6/1985, Ipswich, guitar/bass/drums/piano) and Mattie Jay Willis (born 8/5/1983, Kingston, bass guitar/drums). They were named British Breakthrough Act and Best Pop Act at the 2004 BRIT Awards. They disbanded in January 2005 with Simpson forming Fightstar.

DATE	POS	WKS	BPI	SINGLE TITLE	LABEL & NUMBER
28/09/2002	3	12		**WHAT I GO TO SCHOOL FOR**	Universal MCSXD 40294
25/01/2003	2	15		**YEAR 3000**	Universal MCSXD 40306
03/05/2003	❶¹	10		**YOU SAID NO** ↑	Universal MCSXD 40318
23/08/2003	3	10		**SLEEPING WITH THE LIGHT ON**	Universal MCSXD 40327
22/11/2003	❶¹	12		**CRASHED THE WEDDING** ↑	Universal MCSXD 40345
28/02/2004	❶¹	10		**WHO'S DAVID?** ↑	Universal MCSXD 40355
08/05/2004	2	10		**AIR HOSTESS**	Universal MCSXD 40361
07/08/2004	❶²	13		**THUNDERBIRDS/3 AM** ↑ A-side featured in the 2004 film *Thunderbirds*. The single was voted Record of the Year.	Universal MCSXD 40375

BUSTER UK group formed in Liverpool by Rob Fennah (guitar/vocals), Peter Leahy (guitar), Kevin Roberts (bass) and Leslie Brians (drums).

DATE	POS	WKS	BPI	SINGLE TITLE	LABEL & NUMBER
19/06/1976	49	1		SUNDAY	RCA 2678

BERNARD BUTLER UK guitarist (born 1/5/1970) who joined Suede in 1990, later recording with David McAlmont before going solo.

DATE	POS	WKS	BPI	SINGLE TITLE	LABEL & NUMBER
27/05/1995	8	8		**YES**	Hut HUTCD 53
04/11/1995	17	4		YOU DO This and above single credited to **McALMONT AND BUTLER**	Hut HUTDG 57
17/01/1998	12	4		STAY	Creation CRESCD 281
28/03/1998	27	3		NOT ALONE	Creation CRESCD 289
27/06/1998	45	1		A CHANGE OF HEART	Creation CRESCD 297
23/10/1999	44	1		YOU MUST GO ON	Creation CRESCD 324
10/08/2002	23	3		FALLING	Chrysalis CDCHS 5141
09/11/2002	36	2		BRING IT BACK This and above single credited to **McALMONT AND BUTLER**	Chrysalis CDCHSS 5145

❶⁹ Number of weeks single topped the UK chart ↑ Entered the UK chart at #1 ▲⁹ Number of weeks single topped the US chart

123

JONATHAN BUTLER South African singer (born 1/10/1961, Athlone, Cape Town) who was the youngest of seventeen children. He began professionally as a child and was established by the age of thirteen. He emigrated to London in 1985 (following disillusionment with the apartheid regime) at the invitation of Jive Records founders Clive Calder and Ralph Simon.

| 25/01/1986 | 30 | 7 | | IF YOU'RE READY (COME GO WITH ME) RUBY TURNER FEATURING JONATHAN BUTLER | Jive 109 |
| 08/08/1987 | 18 | 11 | | LIES | Jive 141 |

BUTTERSCOTCH UK vocal group featuring David Martin on lead vocals, Chris Arnold and Geoff Morrow who later recorded for Jam, Ammo and Bell.

| 02/05/1970 | 17 | 11 | | DON'T YOU KNOW | RCA 1937 |

BUTTHOLE SURFERS US rock group originally known as Ashtray Baby Heads, formed in Austin, TX by Gibson 'Gibby' Haynes (vocals), Paul Leary (guitar) and King Koffey (drums), with Jeff Pinker later joining on bass. Leary subsequently recorded solo and Haynes became a DJ at KROX Radio in Austin.

| 05/10/1996 | 59 | 1 | | PEPPER | Capitol CDCL 778 |

BUZZCOCKS UK rock group formed in Manchester by philosophy student Howard Devoto (born Howard Trafford, vocals), Pete Shelley (born Peter McNeish, 17/4/1955, guitar/vocals), Steve Garvey (bass), Steve Diggle (guitar) and John Maher (drums). Devoto left after their debut release to form Magazine, Shelley taking over as lead singer and chief songwriter. They launched the New Hormones label in 1979.

18/02/1978	37	3		WHAT DO I GET	United Artists UP 36348
13/05/1978	55	2		I DON'T MIND	United Artists UP 36386
15/07/1978	34	6		LOVE YOU MORE	United Artists UP 36433
23/09/1978	12	11		EVER FALLEN IN LOVE (WITH SOMEONE YOU SHOULDN'T'VE) Featured in the films _Shrek 2_ (2004) and _The Football Factory_ (2004)	United Artists UP 36455
25/11/1978	20	10		PROMISES	United Artists UP 36471
10/03/1979	29	6		EVERYBODY'S HAPPY NOWADAYS	United Artists UP 36499
21/07/1979	32	6		HARMONY IN MY HEAD	United Artists UP 36541
25/08/1979	31	6		SPIRAL SCRATCH EP Tracks on EP: _Breakdown, Time's Up, Boredom_ and _Friends Of Mine_	New Hormones ORG 1
06/09/1980	61	3		ARE EVERYTHING/WHY SHE'S A GIRL FROM THE CHAINSTORE	United Artists BP 365

BUZZY BUNCH – see CELI BEE AND THE BUZZY BUNCH

B.V.S.M.P. US vocal trio Calvin Williams, Percy Rodgers and Frederick Byrd.

| 23/07/1988 | 3 | 12 | | I NEED YOU Originally released in March 1988 and failed to chart | Debut DEBT 3044 |

BY ALL MEANS US group formed in Los Angeles, CA by Lynn Roderick (vocals), James Varner (piano/vocals) and Billy Sheppard (guitar), with various session musicians helping out.

| 18/06/1988 | 65 | 2 | | I SURRENDER TO YOUR LOVE | Fourth & Broadway BRW 102 |

MAX BYGRAVES UK singer (born Walter Bygraves, 16/10/1922, London) who named himself after comic Max Miller. After successful singles in the 1950s he became an all-round entertainer, but scored biggest with a series of 'sing-a-long' albums, medleys of well-known numbers appealing to a middle-of-the-road market. An astute businessman, he set up Lakeview Music, which paid £350 for the rights to Lionel Bart's _Oliver!_ show and later sold them to Essex Music for £250,000. He was awarded an OBE in 1982 and later hosted the TV show _Family Fortunes_.

14/11/1952	6	8		COWPUNCHER'S CANTATA Medley of _Cry Of The Wild Goose, Riders In The Sky, Mule Train_ and _Jezebel_	HMV B 10250
14/05/1954	7	8		HEART OF MY HEART	HMV B 10654
10/09/1954	7	8		GILLY GILLY OSSENFEFFER KATZENELLEN BOGEN BY THE SEA	HMV B 10734
21/01/1955	16	1		MR SANDMAN	HMV B 10801
18/11/1955	2	11		MEET ME ON THE CORNER	HMV POP 116
17/02/1956	20	1		BALLAD OF DAVY CROCKETT	HMV POP 153
25/05/1956	18	7		OUT OF TOWN	HMV POP 164
05/04/1957	14	8		HEART MAX BYGRAVES WITH MALCOLM LOCKYER AND HIS ORCHESTRA	Decca F 10862
02/05/1958	3	25		YOU NEED HANDS/TULIPS FROM AMSTERDAM MAX BYGRAVES WITH THE CLARK BROTHERS AND ERIC RODGERS AND HIS ORCHESTRA	Decca F 11004
22/08/1958	28	2		LITTLE TRAIN/GOTTA HAVE RAIN _Little Train_ featured in the 1958 film _A Cry From The Streets_ starring Max Bygraves	Decca F 11046
02/01/1959	19	4		MY UKELELE	Decca F 11077
18/12/1959	7	4		JINGLE BELL ROCK	Decca F 11176
10/03/1960	5	15		FINGS AIN'T WOT THEY USED T'BE	Decca F 11214
28/07/1960	50	1		CONSIDER YOURSELF	Decca F 11251
01/06/1961	36	5		BELLS OF AVIGNON	Decca F 11350
19/02/1969	34	4		YOU'RE MY EVERYTHING Featured in the 1969 film _The Laugh Parade_	Pye 7N 17705
06/10/1973	13	15		DECK OF CARDS	Pye 7N 45276
09/12/1989	71	4		WHITE CHRISTMAS	Parkfield PMS 5012

BYKER GROOOVE! UK vocal group with Donna Air and Jayni Hoy, who went on to form Crush.

| 24/12/1994 | 48 | 3 | | LOVE YOUR SEXY...!! | Groove GROVD 01 |

CHARLIE BYRD – see STAN GETZ

○ Silver disc ● Gold disc ✪ Platinum disc (additional platinum units are indicated by a figure following the symbol) ◎ Singles released prior to 1973 that are known to have sold over 1 million copies in the UK

DEBRA BYRD – see BARRY MANILOW

DONALD BYRD US trumpeter (born 9/12/1932, Detroit, MI) who began his jazz career performing with the likes of John Coltrane, Art Blakey, Sonny Rollins and Jackie McLean before linking with Pepper Adams. At the turn of the 1960s he began tutoring at Rutgers and Howard Universities, encountering the Mizell brothers, Fonce and Larry, who made him one of the pioneers of jazz-funk, or fusion music. He in turn assembled The Blackbyrds from students of his at university.

26/09/1983 ..... 41 ...... 6 ...... LOVING YOU/LOVE HAS COME AROUND .... Elektra K 12559

GARY BYRD AND THE GB EXPERIENCE US rapper/DJ Gary Byrd (born Gary De Wit) met Stevie Wonder and subsequently wrote the lyrics to *Black Man* and *Village Ghetto Land* on the album *Songs In The Key Of Life*. He worked extensively on US radio before co-writing (with Wonder) the first release, *The Crown*, on Wonder's Wondirection label. The single was only available on 12-inch vinyl or cassette single. In the 1980s Byrd hosted a gospel show for BBC Radio.

23/06/1983 ..... 6 ...... 9 .... **THE CROWN** Features the uncredited vocal of Stevie Wonder .... Motown TMGT 1312

BYRDS US folk-pop group formed in 1964 by Roger McGuinn (born 13/7/1942, Chicago, IL, guitar/vocals), Gene Clark (born 17/11/1944, Tipton, OH, percussion), David Crosby (born David Van Cortland, 14/8/1941, Los Angeles, CA, guitar/vocals), Chris Hillman (born 4/12/1942, Los Angeles, bass/vocals) and Michael Clarke (born 3/6/1944, Spokane, WA, drums). Gene Clark left in 1966, Crosby the following year, with McGuinn, Hillman, Kevin Kelly (drums) and Gram Parsons re-forming under the name. Parsons and Hillman left the same year, McGuinn then recruiting Clarence White (guitar), John York (bass) and Gene Parsons (drums). The original members reunited in 1973 and 1979. White was killed by a drunk driver while loading equipment on 14/7/1973, Gram Parsons died from a heroin overdose on 19/9/1973 (his body was stolen by manager Phil Kaufmann and burned), Gene Clark died on 24/5/1991 of natural causes (although a heavy drug and alcohol user) and Michael Clarke died from liver failure caused by alcohol abuse on 19/12/1993. The group was inducted into the Rock & Roll Hall of Fame in 1991.

17/06/1965 .... ❶² ..... 14 ...... **MR TAMBOURINE MAN** ▲¹ Featured in the films *Big T.N.T. Show* (1966) and *More American Graffiti* (1979) .... CBS 201765
12/08/1965 ..... 4 ...... 10 ..... **ALL I REALLY WANT TO DO** This and above single written by Bob Dylan .... CBS 201796
11/11/1965 ..... 26 ...... 8 ...... TURN! TURN! TURN! ▲³ Lyrics adapted by Pete Seeger from a passage in the Bible's Book of Ecclesiastes. Featured in the films *Homer* (1973) and *Forrest Gump* (1994) .... CBS 202008
05/05/1966 ..... 24 ...... 9 .... EIGHT MILES HIGH Banned by many radio stations that feared it contained drug connotations. David Crosby later said 'Of course it was about drugs, I was stoned when I wrote it' .... CBS 202067
05/06/1968 ..... 45 ...... 3 .... YOU AIN'T GOIN' NOWHERE .... CBS 3411
13/02/1971 ..... 19 ...... 8 .... CHESTNUT MARE .... CBS 5322

DAVID BYRNE – see X-PRESS 2

EDWARD BYRNES AND CONNIE STEVENS US actor Edd Byrnes (born Edward Breitenber, 30/7/1933, New York City) was a regular on the TV series *77 Sunset Strip* when it began in 1958, playing Kookie. Fellow US actor Connie Stevens was in a parallel series, *Hawaiian Eye,* in which she played Cricket Blake. They teamed up for a one-off novelty featured in an episode of *77 Sunset Strip*, released as a single, and becoming a success on both sides of the Atlantic (Warner Brothers Records' first hit). Byrnes later appeared in the films *Stardust* (1974) and *Grease* (1978).

05/05/1960 ..... 27 ...... 8 .... KOOKIE KOOKIE (LEND ME YOUR COMB) Originally featured in the TV series *77 Sunset Strip* .... Warner Brothers WB 5

BYSTANDERS UK rock group formed by Micky Jones (born 7/6/1946, Merthyr Tydfil, guitar/vocals), Vic Oakley (guitar), Clive John (guitar/keyboards), Ray Williams (bass) and Jeff Jones (drums), which later evolved into Man.

09/02/1967 ..... 45 ...... 1 .... 98.6. .... Piccadilly 7N 35363

❶⁹ Number of weeks single topped the UK chart ↑ Entered the UK chart at #1 ▲⁹ Number of weeks single topped the US chart

125

C

ANDY C – see SHIMON AND ANDY C

MELANIE C UK singer (born 12/1/1974, Liverpool), aka Mel C and Sporty Spice, who was a member of The Spice Girls. She went solo in 1998.

12/12/1998	3	19	✪	WHEN YOU'RE GONE BRYAN ADAMS FEATURING MELANIE C . . . . A&M 5828212
09/10/1999	4	6		GOIN' DOWN . . . . Virgin VSCDT 1744
04/12/1999	4	11		NORTHERN STAR . . . . Virgin VSCDT 1762
01/04/2000	❶¹	16	●	NEVER BE THE SAME AGAIN ↑ MELANIE C AND LISA LEFT EYE LOPES . . . . Virgin VSCDT 1786
19/08/2000	❶¹	12	○	I TURN TO YOU ↑ Featured in the 2002 film *Bend It Like Beckham* . . . . Virgin VSCDT 1772
09/12/2000	18	10		IF THAT WERE ME Single raised funds for Kandu Arts For Sustainable Development, a charity for the homeless . . . Virgin VSCDT 1786
08/03/2003	7	8		HERE IT COMES AGAIN . . . . Virgin VSCDT 1842
14/06/2003	14	7		ON THE HORIZON . . . . Virgin VSCDT 1851
22/11/2003	27	2		MELT/YEH YEH YEH . . . . Virgin VSCDY 1858

ROY C US singer (born Roy Charles Hammond, 1943, New York City) who was a member of the Genies prior to going solo in 1965. He recorded for Alaga (his own label), Shout, Black Hawk and Mercury, and joined Ichiban in 1989.

21/04/1966	6	11	SHOTGUN WEDDING . . . . Island WI 273
25/11/1972	8	13	SHOTGUN WEDDING Re-issue of Island WI 273. . . . . UK 19

C & C MUSIC FACTORY/CLIVILLES & COLE US production duo David Cole (born 3/6/1962, Johnson City, TN) and Robert Clivilles (born 30/8/1964, New York City) who began by remixing other people's work. Their first own production was as Adonis Featuring Two Puerto Ricans, A Black Man And A Dominican, with a minor hit before the first C & C Music Factory record in 1990. Thereafter releases were as C & C Music Factory or Clivilles & Cole. They also recorded as S.O.U.L. System. David Cole died from meningitis on 24/1/1995. Freedom Williams (born 1966, New York) is a rapper. Zelma Davis is a Liberian singer (born 1967). Q Unique is a US singer, as is Deborah Cooper, who also sang with The Fatback Band and Change.

15/12/1990	3	12	GONNA MAKE YOU SWEAT (EVERYBODY DANCE NOW) ▲² Featured in the 2000 film *The Replacements* . . . . CBS 6564540
30/03/1991	20	7	HERE WE GO. . . . . Columbia 6567557
06/07/1991	4	11	THINGS THAT MAKE YOU GO HMMM This and above two singles credited to C & C MUSIC FACTORY (FEATURING FREEDOM WILLIAMS) . . . . Columbia 6566907
23/11/1991	31	3	JUST A TOUCH OF LOVE EVERYDAY C & C MUSIC FACTORY FEATURING ZELMA DAVIS Featured in the 1992 film *Sister Act* . . . . Columbia 6575247
18/01/1992	15	5	PRIDE (IN THE NAME OF LOVE). . . . . Columbia 6577017
14/03/1992	15	5	A DEEPER LOVE This and above single credited to CLIVILLES AND COLE. . . . . Columbia 6578497
03/10/1992	34	3	KEEP IT COMIN' (DANCE TILL YOU CAN'T DANCE NO MORE) C & C MUSIC FACTORY FEATURING Q UNIQUE AND DEBORAH COOPER Featured in the 1992 film *Buffy The Vampire Slayer* . . . . Columbia 6584307
27/08/1994	27	3	DO YOU WANNA GET FUNKY C & C MUSIC FACTORY . . . . Columbia 6607622
18/02/1995	26	2	I FOUND LOVE/TAKE A TOKE C & C MUSIC FACTORY FEATURING ZELMA DAVIS/C & C MUSIC FACTORY FEATURING MARTHA WASH A-side featured in the 1992 film *Gladiator*. . . . . Columbia 6612112
11/11/1995	42	2	I'LL ALWAYS BE AROUND C & C MUSIC FACTORY . . . . MCA MCSTD 40001

CA VA CA VA UK group with Steven Parris (vocals), Richard Hixson (guitar), Jon Hallett (bass/keyboards) and Derek Ritchie (drums).

18/09/1982	49	5	WHERE'S ROMEO . . . . Regard RG 103
19/02/1983	65	3	BROTHER BRIGHT . . . . Regard RG 105

MONTSERRAT CABALLE Spanish operatic singer (born 12/4/1933, Barcelona) who studied at the Barcelona Liceo, making her concert debut in 1954. Famous as a Verdi and Donizetti soprano, she debuted at Covent Garden in 1972. She won the 1968 Grammy Award for Best Classical Solo Vocal Performance for *Rossini Rarities*.

07/11/1987	8	9	BARCELONA. . . . . Polydor POSP 887
08/08/1992	2	8	BARCELONA Re-issue of Polydor POSP 887. Both singles credited to FREDDIE MERCURY AND MONTSERRAT CABALLE . . Polydor PO 221

CABANA Brazilian duo Gaetan Schurrer (programming/tequila worms) and Krzysztof Pietkiewicz (percussion).

15/07/1995	65	1	BAILANDO CON LOBOS . . . . Hi-Life 5792512

CABARET VOLTAIRE UK group formed in Sheffield in 1974 by Stephen Mallinder (bass/vocals), Richard Kirk (guitar) and Chris Watson (electronics/tapes). Watson left in 1981 and was eventually replaced by Eric Random (guitar); until such time Mallinder and Kirk continued as a duo.

18/07/1987	69	2	DON'T ARGUE . . . . Parlophone R 6157

○ Silver disc ● Gold disc ✪ Platinum disc (additional platinum units are indicated by a figure following the symbol) ⓜ Singles released prior to 1973 that are known to have sold over 1 million copies in the UK

04/11/1989.....66......2...... HYPNOTISED .... Parlophone R 6227
12/05/1990.....55......2...... KEEP ON .... Parlophone R 6250
18/08/1990.....61......2...... EASY LIFE .... Parlophone R 6261

CABLE US rock group formed in Rockville, CT in 1994 by Randy Larsen (bass/vocals), Matt Becker (guitar), Jeff Caxide (guitar) and Vic Szalaj (drums). Bernie Roanowski later replaced Caxide.

14/06/1997.....44......2...... FREEZE THE ATLANTIC .... Infectious INFECT 38CD

CACIQUE UK vocal/instrumental group formed by Junior Alphonso, Chris Buckley and Eddie Lewison.

01/06/1985.....69......1....... DEVOTED TO YOU .... Diamond Duel DISC 1

CACTUS WORLD NEWS Irish group formed in Dublin in 1985 by Eoin Moody (vocals), Frank Kearns (guitar), Fergal MacAindris (bass) and Wayne Sheehy (drums). A demo tape sent to Bono of U2 led to his recording their debut album. They were signed by MCA in 1986, who deleted their second album, *No Shelter*, in 1989 before it was distributed. They disbanded in 1990.

08/02/1986.....59......3...... YEARS LATER .... MCA 1024
26/04/1986.....58......3...... WORLDS APART .... MCA 1040
20/09/1986.....74......1...... THE BRIDGE .... MCA 1080

CADILLAC TAH – see JENNIFER LOPEZ

CADETS WITH EILEEN REID Irish showband with Eileen Reid (vocals), Brendan O'Connell (guitar), Patrick Murphy (harmonica), Jas Fagan (trombone), Paddy Burns (trumpet/vocals), Gerry Hayes (piano), Jimmy Day (saxophone/guitar) and Willie Devey (drums). They disbanded in 1970.

03/06/1965.....42......1....... JEALOUS HEART .... Pye 7N 15852

SUSAN CADOGAN UK reggae singer (born Alison Susan Cadogan, 1959, Kingston, Jamaica) who was working as a librarian when discovered by Lee Perry. She later recorded for Trojan, Hawkeye, C&E and Solid Gold.

05/04/1975 .....4......12.....O **HURT SO GOOD** .... Magnet MAG 23
19/07/1975.....22......7...... LOVE ME BABY .... Magnet MAG 36

CAESARS Swedish rock group formed in Stockholm by Caesar Vidal (vocals), Jocke Ahlund (guitar), David Lindquist (bass) and Nino Kellar (drums). Their full name Caesar's Palace was amended for UK release because of an entertainment chain of the same name.

19/04/2003.....60......1...... JERK IT OUT .... Virgin DINSD 244

AL CAIOLA US orchestra leader/guitarist (born Alexander Emil Caiola, 7/9/1920, Jersey City, NJ) who began as an arranger and conductor for United Artists before making debut records for Savoy in 1955.

15/06/1961.....34......6....... THE MAGNIFICENT SEVEN Featured in the 1961 film *The Magnificent Seven* .... HMV POP 889

CAKE US rock group formed in Sacramento, CA in 1991 by John McCrea (guitar/vocals), Vince di Fiore (trumpet), Victor Damien (bass), Todd Roper (drums) and Greg Brown (guitar). Their debut album was with Capricorn in 1994.

22/03/1997.....22......3...... THE DISTANCE .... Capricorn 5742212
31/05/1997.....29......2...... I WILL SURVIVE .... Capricorn 5744712
01/05/1999.....66......1...... NEVER THERE .... Capricorn 8708112
03/11/2001.....63......1...... SHORT SKIRT LONG JACKET .... Columbia 6720402

CALIBRE CUTS – see VARIOUS ARTISTS (MONTAGES)

CALIFORNIA SUNSHINE Israeli and Italian production group formed by P Har-Ell and DJ Miko.

16/08/1997.....56......1...... SUMMER '89 .... Perfecto PERF 143CD

CALL US group formed in San Francisco, CA in 1980 by Michael Breen (guitar/vocals), Tom Ferrier (guitar), Greg Freeman (bass) and Scott Musick (drums). Freeman left in 1984 and was replaced by Jim Goodwin (keyboards). They disbanded in 1990, re-forming in 1997.

30/09/1989.....42......6....... LET THE DAY BEGIN .... MCA 1362

TERRY CALLIER US singer/guitarist (born 24/5/1945, Chicago, IL).

13/12/1997.....36......3....... BEST BIT EP BETH ORTON FEATURING TERRY CALLIER Tracks on EP: *Best Bit, Skimming Stone, Dolphins* and *Lean On Me* ....
.... Heavenly HVN 72CD
23/05/1998.....57......1....... LOVE THEME FROM SPARTACUS .... Talkin Loud TLCD 32

CALLING US rock group formed in Los Angeles, CA by Alex Band (vocals), Aaron Kamin (guitar), Sean Woolstenhulme (guitar), Billy Mohler (bass) and Nate Wood (drums). They debuted for RCA in 2001 and were named Best New Act at the 2002 MTV Europe Music Awards.

29/06/2002.....64......1....... WHEREVER YOU WILL GO (IMPORT) .... RCA 74321912242
06/07/2002 .....3......11...... **WHEREVER YOU WILL GO** Featured in the 2003 film *Love Actually* .... RCA 74321947652
02/11/2002.....18......3....... ADRIENNE .... RCA 74321968352
29/05/2004.....13......4....... OUR LIVES .... RCA 82876618652
28/08/2004.....34......2....... THINGS WILL GO MY WAY .... RCA 82876637372

❶[9] Number of weeks single topped the UK chart ↑ Entered the UK chart at #1 ▲[9] Number of weeks single topped the US chart

EDDIE CALVERT UK trumpeter (born 1922, Preston) who became known as 'the man with the golden trumpet'. Popular throughout the 1950s, he moved to South Africa in 1968, where he died on 7/8/1978 from a heart attack.

18/12/1953	❶⁹	21	**OH MEIN PAPA** Recorded at Abbey Road Studios and produced by Norrie Paramour, the first #1 for either	Columbia DB 3337
08/04/1955	❶⁴	21	**CHERRY PINK AND APPLE BLOSSOM WHITE**	Columbia DB 3581
13/05/1955	14	4	STRANGER IN PARADISE	Columbia DB 3594
29/07/1955	6	11	**JOHN AND JULIE** Featured in the 1955 film *John And Julie*	Columbia DB 3624
09/03/1956	13	7	ZAMBESI	Columbia DB 3747
07/02/1958	9	14	**MANDY (LA PANSE)**	Columbia DB 3956
20/06/1958	28	2	LITTLE SERENADE	Columbia DB 4105

CALVIN – see I DREAM FEATURING FRANKIE AND CALVIN

DONNIE CALVIN – see ROCKER'S REVENGE FEATURING DONNIE CALVIN

CAMEO US R&B group formed in 1976 as a thirteen-piece band, the New York City Players, becoming Cameo a year later. By the 1980s they were a three-piece under leader Larry Blackmon (born 29/5/1956, New York, vocals/drums), Tomi Jenkins (vocals) and Nathan Leftenant (trumpet). Blackmon moved the group to Atlanta, GA, founding the Atlanta Artists label with acts including Cashflow. In 1992 he was made R&B A&R Vice President for Warner Brothers Records, a position he held for three years.

31/03/1984	37	8	SHE'S STRANGE	Club JAB 2
13/07/1985	65	2	ATTACK ME WITH YOUR LOVE	Club JAB 16
14/09/1985	15	10	SINGLE LIFE	Club JAB 21
07/12/1985	22	8	SHE'S STRANGE Re-issue of Club JAB 2	Club JAB 25
22/03/1986	65	2	A GOODBYE	Club JAB 28
30/08/1986	3	13	○ **WORD UP**	Club JAB 38
29/11/1986	27	9	CANDY	Club JAB 43
25/04/1987	11	9	BACK AND FORTH	Club JAB 49
17/10/1987	35	4	SHE'S MINE	Club JAB 57
29/10/1988	74	1	YOU MAKE ME WORK	Club JAB 70
28/07/2001	12	5	LOVERBOY **MARIAH CAREY FEATURING CAMEO** Contains a sample of Cameo's *Candy* and features the uncredited contributions of Da Brat, Ludacris, Twenty II and Shawnna	Virgin VUSCD 211

ANDY CAMERON UK singer and Scottish football fanatic, as his hit single and follow-up four years later (*We're On The March Again*) confirm.

04/03/1978	6	8	**ALLY'S TARTAN ARMY**	Klub 03

CAMILLA – see MOJOLATORS FEATURING CAMILLA

TONY CAMILLO'S BAZUKA US producer Tony Camillo fronting an instrumental studio aggregation. Previously with Cecil Holmes' Soulful Sounds, he was in-house arranger for Invictus before producing the likes of Gladys Knight and Dionne Warwick.

31/05/1975	28	5	DYNOMITE (PART 1)	A&M AMS 7168

CAMISRA UK dance group formed by DJ 'Tall Paul' Newman and singer Sara Hearnden. Newman also recorded as Partizan and Escrima, and with Brandon Block in Grifters.

21/02/1998	5	8	**LET ME SHOW YOU**	VC Recordings VCRD 31
11/07/1998	32	2	FEEL THE BEAT	VC Recordings VCRD 39
22/05/1999	34	2	CLAP YOUR HANDS	VC Recordings VCRD 49

CAMOUFLAGE FEATURING MYSTI US studio group assembled by producers Meco Monardo, Tony Bongiovi, Harold Wheeler and Jay Ellis.

24/09/1977	48	3	BEE STING	State STAT 58

A CAMP Swedish vocal/instrumental group formed by Cardigans singer Nina Persson (born 1975), Niclas Frisk and Nathan Larson.

01/09/2001	46	1	I CAN BUY YOU	Stockholm 0152162

CAMP LO US rap duo from New York City comprising Salahadeen 'Geechie Suede' Wallace and Saladine 'Sonny Cheeba' Wilds.

16/08/1997	74	1	LUCHINI AKA (THIS IS IT) Contains a sample of Dynasty's *Adventures In The Land Of Music*	ffrr FCD 305

CAMPAG VELOCET UK group formed by Pete Voss (vocals), Ian Cater (guitar), Barnaby Slater (bass) and Lascelles Gordon (drums).

19/02/2000	75	1	VITO SATAN	Pias Recordings PIASX 010CD

ALI CAMPBELL UK singer (born 15/2/1959, Birmingham), son of Scottish folk singer Ian Campbell and lead singer with UB40. He set up the Kuff label through Virgin Records. Kibibi is his daughter.

20/05/1995	5	10	**THAT LOOK IN YOUR EYE**	Kuff KUFFDG 1
26/08/1995	25	4	LET YOUR YEAH BE YEAH	Kuff KUFFD 2
09/12/1995	30	4	SOMETHIN' STUPID **ALI AND KIBIBI CAMPBELL**	Kuff KUFFDG 5

DANNY CAMPBELL AND SASHA UK singer Danny Campbell and producer Sasha (born Alexander Coe, 4/9/1969, Bangor, Wales).

31/07/1993	57	1	TOGETHER	ffrr FCD 212

○ Silver disc ● Gold disc ✪ Platinum disc (additional platinum units are indicated by a figure following the symbol) ◎ Singles released prior to 1973 that are known to have sold over 1 million copies in the UK

DON CAMPBELL – see GENERAL SAINT

ELLIE CAMPBELL UK singer (born in Huddersfield), one of ten children, discovered when working as a chambermaid at a hotel.

03/04/1999	42	1	SWEET LIES	Eastern Bloc 0519222
14/08/1999	26	3	SO MANY WAYS	Eastern Bloc 0519362
09/06/2001	50	1	DON'T WANT YOU BACK	Jive 9201302

ETHNA CAMPBELL UK singer who previously recorded for Mercury (debut single in 1964), Polydor and Pye.

| 27/12/1975 | 33 | 11 | THE OLD RUGGED CROSS | Philips 6006 475 |

GLEN CAMPBELL US singer (born 22/4/1936, Billstown, AR) who joined his uncle Dick Bills' band in 1954. After four years he moved to Los Angeles, CA and recorded with The Champs. An in-demand studio guitarist for the next five years, he briefly replaced Brian Wilson in The Beach Boys in 1965. After going solo he appeared in films including *True Grit* (1969) and *Strange Homecoming* (1974) and hosted his own TV show. He has won six Grammy Awards: Best Male Solo Vocal Performance and Best Contemporary Solo Vocal Performance in 1967 for *By The Time I Get To Phoenix*, Best Country & Western Recording and Best Country & Western Vocal Performance in 1967 for *Gentle On My Mind*, Album of the Year in 1968 for *By The Time I Get To Phoenix*, and Best Recording for Children in 1981 with Crystal Gayle, Loretta Lynn, Tanya Tucker and the Muppets for *Sesame Country*. He has a star on the Hollywood Walk of Fame.

29/01/1969	7	13	WICHITA LINEMAN	Ember EMBS 261
07/05/1969	14	10	GALVESTON	Ember EMBS 263
06/12/1969	3	14	ALL I HAVE TO DO IS DREAM BOBBIE GENTRY AND GLEN CAMPBELL	Capitol CL 15619
07/02/1970	45	2	TRY A LITTLE KINDNESS	Capitol CL 15622
09/05/1970	4	19	HONEY COME BACK	Capitol CL 15638
26/09/1970	32	5	EVERYTHING A MAN COULD EVER NEED	Capitol CL 15653
21/11/1970	4	14	IT'S ONLY MAKE BELIEVE	Capitol CL 15663
27/03/1971	39	3	DREAM BABY	Capitol CL 15674
04/10/1975	4	12	○ RHINESTONE COWBOY ▲²	Capitol CL 15824
26/03/1977	28	6	SOUTHERN NIGHTS ▲¹ Featured in the 1978 film *Convoy*	Capitol CL 15907
30/11/2002	12	8	RHINESTONE COWBOY (GIDDY UP GIDDY UP) RIKKI AND DAZ FEATURING GLEN CAMPBELL	Serious SER 059CD

IAN CAMPBELL FOLK GROUP UK group formed in Birmingham in 1956 by Ian Campbell (born 10/6/1933, Aberdeen, guitar/vocals), his sister Lorna (born 1939, Aberdeen, vocals), Dave Phillips (guitar) and Goron McCulloch (banjo). McCulloch left in 1959 and was replaced by John Dunkerly (guitar/banjo/accordion). They later added Dave Swarbrick (born 5/4/1941, London, fiddle/mandola) to the line-up. Phillips left in 1963 and was replaced by Brian Clark. After other changes (including Dave Pegg, later in Fairport Convention) they disbanded in 1978. Dunkerly died from Hodgkinson's Disease in 1977.

| 11/03/1965 | 42 | 5 | THE TIMES THEY ARE A-CHANGIN' | Transatlantic SP 5 |

JO ANN CAMPBELL US singer (born 20/7/1938, Jacksonville, FL) first known through TV talent shoes the *Colgate Comedy Hour* and the *Milton Berle Show*, signing with Elderado in 1956. Later recording with her husband Troy Seals as Jo Ann & Troy, she appeared in films including *Go Johnny Go* (1958) and *Let's Twist* (1961).

| 08/06/1961 | 41 | 3 | MOTORCYCLE MICHAEL | HMV POP 873 |

JUNIOR CAMPBELL UK singer (born Wullie Campbell, 31/5/1947, Glasgow) who was a founding member of Marmalade playing guitar and piano. He left in 1971 and signed a solo deal with Deram in 1972.

| 14/10/1972 | 10 | 9 | HALLELUJAH FREEDOM | Deram DM 364 |
| 02/06/1973 | 15 | 9 | SWEET ILLUSION | Deram DM 387 |

KIBIBI CAMPBELL – see ALI CAMPBELL

NAOMI CAMPBELL UK singer (born 22/5/1970) famous as a 'supermodel' before recording and later writing novels. She appeared in the video for Michael Jackson's hit *In The Closet*.

| 24/09/1994 | 40 | 3 | LOVE AND TEARS | Epic 6608352 |

PAT CAMPBELL Irish singer who continued making records into the 1970s.

| 15/11/1969 | 31 | 5 | THE DEAL | Major Minor MM 648 |

STAN CAMPBELL UK singer (born 1962, Coventry) who was briefly in The Specials AKA before going solo.

| 06/06/1987 | 65 | 3 | YEARS GO BY | WEA YZ 127 |

TEVIN CAMPBELL US singer (born 12/11/1978, Waxahachie, TX) discovered by producer Quincy Jones. He later appeared in the 1990 film *Graffiti Bridge*.

| 18/04/1992 | 63 | 2 | TELL ME WHAT YOU WANT ME TO DO | Qwest W 0102 |

CAM'RON US rapper (born Cameron Giles, 4/2/1976, Harlem, NYC). As a basketball player he received scholarship offers from various universities but dropped out to become a drug dealer in New York and signed with Untertainment in 1988. Juelz Santana (born LaRon James, 1984, Manhattan) is a US rapper.

19/09/1998	12	4	HORSE AND CARRIAGE CAM'RON FEATURING MA$E	Epic 6662612
17/08/2002	13	7	OH BOY CAM'RON FEATURING JUELZ SANTANA	Roc-A-Fella 0639642
08/02/2003	8	10	HEY MA CAM'RON FEATURING JUELZ SANTANA Contains a sample of the Commodores' *Easy*	Roc-A-Fella 0637242
05/04/2003	17	6	BOY (I NEED YOU) MARIAH CAREY FEATURING CAM'RON Has an interpolation of Rose Royce's *I'm Going Down*	Def Jam 0779282

❶⁹ Number of weeks single topped the UK chart   ↑ Entered the UK chart at #1   ▲⁹ Number of weeks single topped the US chart

129

CAN German electronic rock group formed in Cologne in 1968 as Inner Space by Holger Czukay (born 24/3/1938, Gdansk, Poland, bass), Damo Suzuki (born 16/1/1950, Japan, vocals), Peter Gilmore, Michael Karoli (born 29/4/1948, Straubing, bass), Jaki Liebezeit (born 26/5/1938, Dresden, drums), Irmin Schmidt (born 29/5/1937, Berlin, keyboards) and Rene Tinner. They changed their name at the suggestion of US singer Malcolm Mooney. Despite limited chart success, they were extremely influential; Human League, New Order *et al* followed in their footsteps. Karoli died from unknown causes on 17/11/2001.

28/08/1976	26	10		I WANT MORE	Virgin VS 153

CANDIDO Cuban percussionist (born 22/4/1921, Havana); he first recorded in Cuba in the early 1950s, moving to New York at the invitation of Dizzy Gillespie in 1954.

18/07/1981	55	3		JINGO	Excalibur EXC 102

CANDLEWICK GREEN UK group formed in Liverpool by Tony Webb (vocals), Lennie Coswell (guitar), Jimmy Nunnen (bass/vocals), Andy Bell (keyboards) and Alan Leyland (drums).

23/02/1974	21	8		WHO DO YOU THINK YOU ARE	Decca F 13480

CANDY FLIP UK vocal/instrumental duo Rick Peet (born Richard Anderson-Peet, 1970, Liverpool) and Daniel 'Dizzy' Dee (born Daniel Spencer, 1970, Stoke-on-Trent). Both were previously in house band This Ain't Chicago and later recorded as Sound 5.

17/03/1990	3	10		**STRAWBERRY FIELDS FOREVER**	Debut DEBT 3092
14/07/1990	60	4		THIS CAN BE REAL	Debut DEBT 3099

CANDY GIRLS UK dance group formed by Rachel Auburn and Paul Masterson, with singer Valerie Malcolm. Masterson is also with Amen! UK, The Dope Smugglaz and Hi-Gate, and records as Sleazesister.

30/09/1995	23	4		FEE FI FO FUM	VC Recordings VCRD 1
24/02/1996	20	4		WHAM BAM This and above single credited to CANDY GIRLS FEATURING SWEET PUSSY PAULINE	VC Recordings VCRD 6
07/12/1996	30	2		I WANT CANDY CANDY GIRLS FEATURING VALERIE MALCOLM	Feverpitch CDFVR 1013

CANDYLAND UK group formed by Felix Todd (vocals), David Wesley Ayers Jr (guitar), Kenedid Osman (bass) and Derrick McKenzie (drums).

09/03/1991	72	1		FOUNTAIN O' YOUTH	Non Fiction YES 4

CANDYSKINS UK rock group from Oxford formed by Mark Cope (guitar), Nick Cope (guitar/vocals), Nick Burton (guitar), Karl Shule (bass) and John Halliday (drums).

19/10/1996	65	1		MRS HOOVER	Ultimate TOPP 051CD
08/02/1997	34	2		MONDAY MORNING	Ultimate TOPP 055CD
03/05/1997	65	1		HANG MYSELF ON YOU	Ultimate TOPP 059CD

CANIBUS US rapper (born Germaine Williams, 12/9/1976, Jamaica, raised in UK and US) who was discovered and managed by Wyclef Jean of The Fugees. His debut single was an attack on LL Cool J and was prompted by his guest appearance on LL Cool J's *4,3,2,1* single, which began a feud between the two rappers.

27/06/1998	35	2		SECOND ROUND KO Features guest vocal by boxer Mike Tyson and is directed at fellow rapper LL Cool J	Universal UND 56198
10/10/1998	52	1		HOW COME YOUSSOU N'DOUR AND CANIBUS Featured in the 1998 film *Bulworth*	Interscope IND 95598

CANNED HEAT US blues-rock band formed in Los Angeles, CA in 1966 by Bob 'The Bear' Hite (born 26/2/1945, Torrance, CA, vocals/harmonica), Alan 'Blind Owl' Wilson (born 4/7/1943, Boston, MA, guitar/harmonica/vocals), Henry Vestine (born 25/12/1944, Washington DC, guitar), Larry Taylor (born 26/6/1942, New York, bass) and Frank Cook (drums). Cook was replaced by Fito De La Parra (born 8/2/1946, Mexico City) in 1968, Vestine by Harvey Mandel in 1969. Wilson died from a drug overdose on 3/9/1970, Hite died on 5/4/1981 from a drug-related heart attack and Vestine died from respiratory failure on 21/10/1997. They took their name from a song by Tommy Johnson.

24/07/1968	8	15		**ON THE ROAD AGAIN**	Liberty LBS 15090
01/01/1969	19	10		GOING UP THE COUNTRY Featured in the 1988 film *1969*	Liberty LBF 15169
17/01/1970	2	15		**LET'S WORK TOGETHER** Featured in the 1994 film *Forrest Gump*	Liberty LBF 15302
11/07/1970	49	1		SUGAR BEE	Liberty LBF 15350

FREDDY CANNON US singer (born Frederick Picariello, 4/12/1939, Lynn, MA) whose first band was Freddy Kamon & The Hurricanes. He changed his name to Freddy Cannon, the surname being a derivative of Kamon and reflecting his nickname 'Boom Boom' (after the big bass drum sound on his records).

14/08/1959	17	8		TALLAHASSEE LASSIE Written by Cannon's mother	Top Rank JAR 135
01/01/1960	3	18		**WAY DOWN YONDER IN NEW ORLEANS**	Top Rank JAR 247
05/03/1960	25	3		CALIFORNIA HERE I COME	Top Rank JAR 309
17/03/1960	42	1		INDIANA B-side to *California Here I Come*	Top Rank JAR 309
19/05/1960	18	10		THE URGE	Top Rank JAR 369
20/04/1961	32	5		MUSKRAT RAMBLE	Top Rank JAR 548
28/06/1962	20	9		PALISADES PARK	Stateside SS 101

BLU CANTRELL US R&B singer (born Tiffany Cantrell, 13/12/1976, Providence, RI) who began as a backing singer for Gerald Levert, Faith Evans and Puff Daddy before going solo, it later being revealed that she was previously a nude model.

24/11/2001	12	9		HIT 'EM UP STYLE (OOPS)	Arista 74321891632
19/07/2003	59	3		BREATHE (IMPORT) Contains a sample of Dr Dre's *What's The Difference*	Arista 82876534002
09/08/2003	●④ 4	18	○	BREATHE ↑ This and above single credited to BLU CANTRELL FEATURING SEAN PAUL	Arista 82876545722

13/12/2003.....24......2....... MAKE ME WANNA SCREAM Features the uncredited contribution of Ian Lewis of Inner Circle ....Arista 82876583432

JIM CAPALDI UK singer/drummer (born 24/8/1944, Evesham), notably with Traffic, the group founded by Steve Winwood when he left the Spencer Davis Group. He first recorded solo in 1972 while Traffic was inactive.

27/07/1974.....27......6....... IT'S ALL UP TO YOU ....Island WIP 6198

25/10/1975 .....4.....11 .....O **LOVE HURTS** ....Island WIP 6246

CAPERCAILLIE UK/Canadian/Irish group formed in Oban in 1984 by Karen Matheson (born 11/2/1963, Oban, vocals), Marc Duff (born 8/9/1963, Ontario, Canada, bodhran/whistles), Manus Lunny (born 8/2/1962, Dublin, bouzouki/vocals), Charlie McKerron (born 14/6/1960, London, fiddle), John Saich (born 22/5/1960, Irvine, bass/vocals) and Donald Shaw (born 6/5/1967, Ketton, keyboards/accordion/vocals).

23/05/1992.....39......2....... A PRINCE AMONG ISLANDS EP Tracks on EP: *Coisich A Ruin (Walk Me Beloved), Fagail Bhearnaraid (Leaving Bernaray), The Lorn Theme* and *Gun Teann Mi Ris Na Ruinn Tha Seo (Remembrance)* ....Survival ZB 45393

17/06/1995.....65......1....... DARK ALAN (AILEIN DUNN) ....Survival SURCD 55

CAPPADONNA – see **WU-TANG CLAN**

CAPPELLA Italian producer Gianfranco Bortolotti who also produced The 49ers. In 1993 he assembled a vocal duo comprising Rodney Bishop (who later became a member of Perpetual Motion) and Kelly Overett. Bortolotti later formed Anticappella.

09/04/1988.....60......2....... PUSH THE BEAT/BAUHAUS..Fast Globe FGL 1

13/05/1989.....11......9....... HELYOM HALIB ....Music Man MMPS 7004

23/09/1989.....73......1....... HOUSE ENERGY REVENGE ....Music Man MMPS 7009

27/04/1991.....66......1....... EVERYBODY ....ffrr F 158

18/01/1992.....25......5....... TAKE ME AWAY **CAPPELLA FEATURING LOLEATTA HOLLOWAY** ....PWL Continental PWL 210

03/04/1993 .....6.....11....... **U GOT 2 KNOW** ....Internal Dance IDC 1

14/08/1993.....43......3....... U GOT 2 KNOW (REMIX) ....Internal Dance IDCR 2

23/10/1993 .....2.....12.....O **U GOT 2 LET THE MUSIC** ....Internal Dance IDC 3

19/02/1994 .....7......7....... **MOVE ON BABY** ....Internal Dance IDC 4

18/06/1994.....10......7....... **U & ME**...Internal Dance IDCC 6

15/10/1994.....16......6....... MOVE IT UP/BIG BEAT ....Internal Dance IDC 7

16/09/1995.....17......3....... TELL ME THE WAY ....Systematic SYSCD 17

06/09/1997.....53......1....... BE MY BABY ....Nukleuz PSNC 0072

CAPRICCIO UK production duo Matt Jackson and Matt Dunning.

27/03/1999.....44......2....... EVERYBODY GET UP Contains a sample of Jazzy Dee's *Get On Up* ....Defected DFECT 2CDS

CAPRICE US singer (born Caprice Bourett, 24/10/1971, Whittier, CA); she won the Miss California Beauty Pageant aged 16, appearing on the covers of *Vogue* and *Cosmopolitan* and famously modelling for Wonderbra. She launched a singing career in 1999.

04/09/1999.....24......3....... OH YEAH ....Virgin VSCDT 1745

10/03/2001.....24......2....... ONCE AROUND THE SUN ....Virgin VSCDT 1750

CAPRICORN Belgian producer Hans Weekout.

29/11/1997.....73......1....... 20 HZ (NEW FREQUENCIES) ....R&S RS 97126CD

TONY CAPSTICK AND THE CARLTON MAIN/FRICKLEY COLLIERY BAND UK radio DJ/folk singer/comedian (born 4//4/1944, Rotherham), backed on record by a local brass band. *Capstick Comes Home* received most airplay, thus boosting sales. Later an actor, appearing in *Coronation Street* as Harvey Nuttall, he died on 23/10/2003.

21/03/1981 .....3......8.....O **THE SHEFFIELD GRINDER/CAPSTICK COMES HOME** ....Dingles SID 27

CAPTAIN BEAKY – see **KEITH MICHELL**

CAPTAIN HOLLYWOOD PROJECT US group led by Captain Hollywood (born Tony Harrison, New Jersey, raised in Detroit, MI). Twenty 4 Seven are German duo Stay-C and Stella.

22/09/1990 .....7.....10....... **I CAN'T STAND IT** ....BCM BCMR 395

24/11/1990.....17.....10....... ARE YOU DREAMING This and above single credited to **TWENTY 4 SEVEN FEATURING CAPTAIN HOLLYWOOD** ....BCM 07504

27/03/1993.....67......1....... ONLY WITH YOU ....Pulse 8 CDLOSE 40

06/11/1993.....23......5....... MORE AND MORE..Pulse 8 CDLOSE 50

05/02/1994.....29......3....... IMPOSSIBLE...Pulse 8 CDLOSE 54

11/06/1994.....61......1....... ONLY WITH YOU Re-issue of Pulse 8 CDLOSE 40 ....Pulse 8 CDLOSE 62

01/04/1995.....58......1....... FLYING HIGH ....Pulse 8 CDLOSE 82

CAPTAIN AND TENNILLE US husband and wife duo Captain (born Daryl Dragon, 27/8/1942, Los Angeles, CA) and Toni Tennille (born 27/8/1942, Montgomery, AL). Dragon, the son of noted conductor Carmen Dragon, met Toni when both were performing in a musical in San Francisco. They toured with The Beach Boys, Dragon as keyboard player and Tennille a backing singer, after which they made their debut single (*The Way I Want To Touch You*), paying for the initial pressings themselves – costs were later met by A&M. Toni eventually went solo.

02/08/1975.....32......5....... LOVE WILL KEEP US TOGETHER ▲⁴ 1975 Grammy Award for Record of the Year. Featured in the 1997 film *Picture Perfect* ....
....A&M AMS 7165

❶⁹ Number of weeks single topped the UK chart ⬆ Entered the UK chart at #1 ▲⁹ Number of weeks single topped the US chart

131

24/01/1976	28	6		THE WAY I WANT TO TOUCH YOU...A&M AMS 7203
04/11/1978	63	3		YOU NEVER DONE IT LIKE THAT...A&M AMS 7384
16/02/1980	7	10		**DO THAT TO ME ONE MORE TIME** ▲[1]...Casablanca CAN 175

CAPTAIN SENSIBLE UK singer (born Raymond Burns, 23/4/1955, London) who was bass player in early punk band The Damned. Going solo in 1982, he didn't actually leave The Damned until 1984.

HAPPY TALK Originally written for the musical *South Pacific*, Sensible's single held the record for the biggest leap within the charts to #1 – from 33 to 1 – until beaten by DJ Otzi in 2001.

26/06/1982	❶[2]	8	○	...A&M CAP 1
14/08/1982	26	7		WOT...A&M CAP 2
24/03/1984	6	10		**GLAD IT'S ALL OVER/DAMNED ON 45**...A&M CAP 6
28/07/1984	57	5		THERE ARE MORE SNAKES THAN LADDERS...A&M CAP 7
10/12/1994	71	1		THE HOKEY COKEY...Have A Nice Day CDHOKEY 1

IRENE CARA US singer (born 18/3/1959, New York) who made her debut at the age of seven, was in a Broadway musical at eight and Madison Square Garden at ten, before appearing in *Roots* and other TV shows. Performing the title track to *Fame,* she played the role of Coco Hernandez in the film.

03/07/1982	❶[3]	16	●	**FAME** Featured in the 1980 film *Fame* and won an Oscar for Best Film Song...RSO 90
04/09/1982	58	3		OUT HERE ON MY OWN Featured in the 1980 film *Fame*...RSO 66
04/06/1983	2	14	○	**FLASHDANCE...WHAT A FEELING** ▲[6] 1983 Grammy Award for Best Pop Vocal Performance. Featured in the 1983 film *Flashdance* and won an Oscar for Best Film Song. Later featured in the 1997 film *The Full Monty*...Casablanca CAN 1016

CARAMBA Swedish singer/multi-instrumentalist Michael Tretow. His debut hit features him impersonating a dog.

12/11/1983	56	6		FEDORA (I'LL BE YOUR DAWG)...Billco BILL 101

CARAVELLES UK duo Andrea Simpson (born 12/9/1946) and Lois Wilkinson (born 3/41944, Sleaford). Wilkinson later recorded solo as Lois Lane.

08/08/1963	6	13		**YOU DON'T HAVE TO BE A BABY TO CRY**...Decca F 11697

CARDIGANS Swedish rock group formed in Jonkoping in 1992 by Peter Svensson (born 1974, guitar), Magnus Sveningsson (born 1972, bass), Nina Persson (born 1975, vocals), Bengt Lagerberg (born 1973, drums) and Olaf-Lasse Johansson (born 1973, guitar/keyboards). Debut single *Emmerdale* was a tribute to the UK TV series. Persson later formed A Camp.

17/06/1995	72	1		CARNIVAL Featured in the 1997 film *Austin Powers – International Man Of Mystery*...Trampolene PZCD 345
30/09/1995	34	3		SICK & TIRED...Stockholm 5773112
02/12/1995	35	2		CARNIVAL...Trampolene PZCD 345
17/02/1996	29	2		RISE & SHINE...Trampolene 5778252
21/09/1996	21	4		LOVEFOOL Featured in the 1996 film *Romeo And Juliet*...Stockholm 5752952
07/12/1996	56	1		BEEN IT...Stockholm 5759672
03/05/1997	2	13	●	**LOVEFOOL** Re-issue of Stockholm 5752952...Stockholm 5710502
06/09/1997	35	2		YOUR NEW CUCKOO...Stockholm 5716632
17/10/1998	14	18		MY FAVOURITE GAME...Stockholm 5679912
06/03/1999	7	9		**ERASE/REWIND**...Stockholm 5635352
24/07/1999	17	4		HANGING AROUND...Stockholm 5612692
25/09/1999	7	7		**BURNING DOWN THE HOUSE** TOM JONES AND THE CARDIGANS...Gut CDGUT 26
22/03/2003	31	2		FOR WHAT IT'S WORTH...Stockholm 0657232
26/07/2003	74	1		YOU'RE THE STORM...Stockholm 9809673

CARE UK duo, ex-Teardrop Explodes Paul Simpson (keyboards) and ex-Big In Japan Ian Broudie (born 4/8/1958, Liverpool, guitar). Disbanding after one album, Broudie then formed The Lightning Seeds.

12/11/1983	48	4		FLAMING SWORD...Arista KBIRD 2

MARIAH CAREY US singer (born 22/3/1970, New York City) with Irish and black/Venezuelan parents, who began as a backing singer for Brenda K Starr while songwriting with Ben Margulies. In 1990 she was signed by Columbia president Tommy Mottola after he heard her demo tape. Mariah and Tommy were married on 5/6/1993, separated in 1997 and divorced on 4/3/1998. She launched Crave in 1997; Allure was the first act signed and the label later closed down. Her acting debut was in the 1999 film *The Bachelor*; she later wrote the soundtrack for and starred in the 2001 film *Glitter*. Two Grammy Awards include Best New Artist in 1990, and she won the 1994 MTV Europe Music Award for Best Female. Her deal with Virgin is the largest in recording history, netting $25 million per album; she left after just one album with a $30 million 'golden handshake' and subsequently signed with Island. She also formed another label, Monarc.

04/08/1990	9	12		**VISION OF LOVE** ▲[4] 1990 Grammy Award for Best Pop Vocal Performance...CBS 6559320
10/11/1990	37	8		LOVE TAKES TIME ▲[3]...CBS 6563647
26/01/1991	38	5		SOMEDAY ▲[2] Featured in the 1991 film *The Hunchback Of Notre Dame*...Columbia 6565837
01/06/1991	54	3		THERE'S GOT TO BE A WAY...Columbia 6569317
05/10/1991	17	9		EMOTIONS ▲[3]...Columbia 6574037
11/01/1992	20	7		CAN'T LET GO...Columbia 6576627
18/04/1992	17	5		MAKE IT HAPPEN...Columbia 6579417
27/06/1992	2	9		**I'LL BE THERE** ▲[2] Recorded live on MTV's *Unplugged* featuring the uncredited vocal of Trey Lorenz...Columbia 6581377

DATE	POS	WKS	BPI	SINGLE TITLE	LABEL & NUMBER
21/08/1993	9	10		**DREAMLOVER** ▲8 Contains a sample of The Emotions' *Blind Alley*	Columbia 6594445
06/11/1993	7	15		**HERO** ▲4	Columbia 6598122
19/02/1994	❶4	14	●	**WITHOUT YOU** ↑ The first time a female solo artist has debuted at #1	Columbia 6599192
18/06/1994	8	10		**ANYTIME YOU NEED A FRIEND**	Columbia 6603542
17/09/1994	3	16		**ENDLESS LOVE** LUTHER VANDROSS AND MARIAH CAREY	Epic 6608062
10/12/1994	2	8	●	**ALL I WANT FOR CHRISTMAS IS YOU**	Columbia 6610702
23/09/1995	4	11	○	**FANTASY** ▲8 Contains a sample of Tom Tom Club's *Genius Of Love*, the first single by a female artist to enter the US charts at #1	Columbia 6624952
09/12/1995	6	11	○	**ONE SWEET DAY** ▲16 MARIAH CAREY AND BOYZ II MEN	Columbia 6626035
17/02/1996	4	6		**OPEN ARMS**	Columbia 6629772
22/06/1996	3	10		**ALWAYS BE MY BABY** ▲2	Columbia 6633345
06/09/1997	3	8		**HONEY** ▲3 Contains a sample of the Treacherous 3's *Body Rock*	Columbia 6650192
13/12/1997	22	6		**BUTTERFLY**	Columbia 6653365
13/06/1998	4	8		**MY ALL** ▲1	Columbia 6660592
19/12/1998	4	13		**WHEN YOU BELIEVE** MARIAH CAREY AND WHITNEY HOUSTON Featured in the 1998 film *The Prince Of Egypt* and won the 1998 Oscar for Best Film Song for writers Stephen Schwartz and Kenneth Edmonds	Columbia 6667522
10/04/1999	16	7		**I STILL BELIEVE**	Columbia 6670735
06/11/1999	5	13		**HEARTBREAKER** ▲2 MARIAH CAREY FEATURING JAY-Z Contains a sample of Stacy Lattishaw's *Attack Of The Name Game*	Columbia 6683012
11/03/2000	10	10		**THANK GOD I FOUND YOU** ▲1 MARIAH CAREY FEATURING JOE & 98 DEGREES Features the uncredited contribution of Trey Lorenz. In September 2000, Seth Swirsky and Warryn Campbell filed a suit against James Harris III, Terry Lewis and Mariah, the song's writers, claiming they had infringed their copyright on a song called *One Of Those Love Songs* that had been recorded in 1998 by Xscape	Columbia 6690582
30/09/2000	❶2	12	○	**AGAINST ALL ODDS** ↑ MARIAH CAREY FEATURING WESTLIFE	Columbia 6698872
28/07/2001	12	5		**LOVERBOY** MARIAH CAREY FEATURING CAMEO Contains a sample of Cameo's *Candy* and features the uncredited contributions of Da Brat, Ludacris, Twenty II and Shawnna	Virgin VUSCD 211
29/12/2001	32	4		**NEVER TOO FAR/DON'T STOP (FUNKIN' 4 JAMAICA)** MARIAH CAREY/MARIAH CAREY FEATURING MYSTIKAL *Don't Stop (Funkin' 4 Jamaica)* contains a sample of Tom Browne's *Funkin' for Jamaica*	Virgin VUSCD 228
30/11/2002	8	8		**THROUGH THE RAIN**	Mercury 0638072
05/04/2003	17	6		BOY (I NEED YOU) MARIAH CAREY FEATURING CAM'RON Contains an interpolation of Rose Royce's *I'm Going Down*	Def Jam 0779282
07/06/2003	3	13		**I KNOW WHAT YOU WANT** BUSTA RHYMES AND MARIAH CAREY	J Records 82876528292

CARL – see CLUBHOUSE

BELINDA CARLISLE US singer (born 17/8/1958, Hollywood, CA) named after her mother's favourite film, *Johnny Belinda* (1948). Lead singer with the all-girl group The Go-Go's from 1978 until their split in 1985, she went solo while still signed to the Go-Go's label (IRS), having a US top three single before signing with MCA for the US, and Virgin for the UK, in 1987.

DATE	POS	WKS	BPI	SINGLE TITLE	LABEL & NUMBER
12/12/1987	❶2	14	○	**HEAVEN IS A PLACE ON EARTH** ▲1 Featured in the films *Romy And Michele's High School Reunion* (1997) and *American Wedding* (2003)	Virgin VS 1036
27/02/1988	10	9		**I GET WEAK**	Virgin VS 1046
07/05/1988	4	11		**CIRCLE IN THE SAND**	Virgin VS 1074
06/08/1988	67	3		MAD ABOUT YOU Featured in the 2004 film *13 Going On 30*	IRS IRM 118
10/09/1988	34	6		WORLD WITHOUT YOU	Virgin VS 1114
10/12/1988	54	5		LOVE NEVER DIES	Virgin VS 1150
07/10/1989	4	10	○	**LEAVE A LIGHT ON** Features the uncredited contribution of George Harrison	Virgin VS 1210
09/12/1989	38	6		LA LUNA	Virgin VS 1230
24/02/1990	40	5		RUNAWAY HORSES	Virgin VS 1244
26/05/1990	41	4		VISION OF YOU	Virgin VS 1264
13/10/1990	6	10		**(WE WANT) THE SAME THING**	Virgin VS 1219
22/12/1990	23	10		SUMMER RAIN	Virgin VS 1323
20/04/1991	71	1		VISION OF YOU	Virgin VS 1264
28/09/1991	12	7		LIVE YOUR LIFE BE FREE	Virgin VS 1370
16/11/1991	29	4		DO YOU FEEL LIKE I FEEL	Virgin VS 1383
11/01/1992	35	2		HALF THE WORLD	Virgin VS 1388
29/08/1992	28	5		LITTLE BLACK BOOK	Virgin VS 1428
25/09/1993	12	6		BIG SCARY ANIMAL	Virgin VSCDT 1472
27/11/1993	27	6		LAY DOWN YOUR ARMS	Virgin VSDG 1476
13/07/1996	6	7		**IN TOO DEEP**	Chrysalis CDCHS 5033
21/09/1996	8	6		**ALWAYS BREAKING MY HEART**	Chrysalis CDCHS 5037
30/11/1996	20	3		LOVE IN THE KEY OF C	Chrysalis CDCHS 5044
01/03/1997	31	2		CALIFORNIA	Chrysalis CDCHSS 5047
27/11/1999	66	1		ALL GOD'S CHILDREN	Virgin VSCDT 1756

BOB CARLISLE US singer (born 29/9/1956, Santa Anna, CA) who began as a backing singer, going solo in 1993, mainly recording Christian material.

DATE	POS	WKS	BPI	SINGLE TITLE	LABEL & NUMBER
30/08/1997	56	2		BUTTERFLY KISSES A remix of a single originally released in the US and available from Christian bookstores only	Jive JIVECD 249

DON CARLOS – see SINGING DOGS

❶9 Number of weeks single topped the UK chart   ↑ Entered the UK chart at #1   ▲9 Number of weeks single topped the US chart

133

SARA CARLSON – see MANIC MCS FEATURING SARA CARLSON

CARLTON UK singer Carlton McCarthy.
| 16/02/1991.....56......2....... | LOVE AND PAIN..Smith & Mighty SNM 4 |
| 01/04/1995.....53......1....... | 1 TO 1 RELIGION BOMB THE BASS FEATURING CARLTON ....Stoned Heights BRCD 313 |

CARL CARLTON US singer (born 22/10/1952, Detroit, MI) signed at twelve by Golden World (having already recorded for Lando Records), who hoped for a teen star to rival Little Stevie Wonder. He had a few minor hits, and was 22 when he had the US top ten pop hit *Everlasting Love* in 1974.
| 18/07/1981.....34......8....... | SHE'S A BAD MAMA JAMA (SHE'S BUILT, SHE'S STACKED)................................20th Century TC 2488 |

LARRY CARLTON – see MIKE POST

VANESSA CARLTON US singer/keyboardist/songwriter (born 16/8/1980, Milford, PA) who first signed with Universal in 1999.
03/08/2002.....6......13......	A THOUSAND MILES Featured in the 2001 film *Legally Blonde*.............................A&M 4977542
30/11/2002.....53......1......	ORDINARY DAY..A&M 4978132
15/02/2003.....16......9.......	BIG YELLOW TAXI COUNTING CROWS WITH VANESSA CARLTON Featured in the 2003 film *Two Weeks Notice* ....Geffen 4978492

CARLTON MAIN/FRICKLEY COLLIERY BAND – see TONY CAPSTICK AND THE CARLTON MAIN/FRICKLEY COLLIERY BAND

CARMEL UK group formed by Carmel McCourt (born 24/11/1958, Scunthorpe, vocals), Jim Paris (born 13/1/1957, London, bass) and Gerry Darby (born 13/10/1959, London, drums). Carmel left in 1991 for a solo deal with Warner Brothers.
06/08/1983.....15......9.......	BAD DAY..London LON 29
11/02/1984.....23......7.......	MORE, MORE, MORE...London LON 44
14/06/1986.....60......3.......	SALLY..London LON 90

ERIC CARMEN US singer (born 11/8/1949, Cleveland, OH), classically trained, who sang lead with the Raspberries 1970–1974, before going solo in 1975.
| 10/04/1976.....12......7....... | ALL BY MYSELF Based on Rachmaninov's *Piano Concerto No 2*.............................Arista 42 |

TRACEY CARMEN – see RUTHLESS RAP ASSASSINS

JEAN CARN – see BOBBY M FEATURING JEAN CARN

KIM CARNEGIE UK female singer.
| 19/01/1991.....73......1...... | JAZZ RAP...Best ZB 44085 |

KIM CARNES US singer (born 20/7/1946, Los Angeles, CA) with the New Christy Minstrels with her husband/co-writer Dave Ellington and Kenny Rogers. She also wrote and performed in commercials, making her US chart debut as one of the Sugar Bears. After a debut solo album in 1976, she later recorded with Kenny Rogers, Gene Cotton and James Ingram.
09/05/1981.....10......9.......	BETTE DAVIS EYES ▲9 1981 Grammy Awards for Record of the Year and Song of the Year (for writers Donna Weiss and Jackie DeShannon)...EMI America EA 121
08/08/1981.....49......4.......	DRAW OF THE CARDS...EMI America EA 125
09/10/1982.....68......2.......	VOYEUR..EMI America EA 143

CARNIVAL FEATURING RIP VS RED RAT UK production group formed by Tim 'Deluxe' Liken.
| 12/09/1998.....51......1....... | ALL OF THE GIRLS (ALL AI-DI-GIRL DEM)...Pepper 0530072 |

RENATO CAROSONE AND HIS SEXTET Italian singer (born 2/1/1920, Naples) who later acted and composed for films, doing both in *Toto, Peppino E Le Fanatiche* in 1958, and appearing in *Caravan Patrol* in 1960. He died on 27/4/2001.
| 04/07/1958.....25......1....... | TORERO – CHA CHA CHA...Parlophone R 4433 |

MARY CHAPIN CARPENTER US singer (born 21/2/1958, Princeton, NJ) who began as a folk singer in clubs and bars around Washington. Five local music awards led to debut album for Columbia in 1987. Scoring in both the pop and country charts, her five Grammy Awards include Best Female Country Vocal Performance in 1991 for *Down At The Twist And Shout*, Best Female Country Vocal Performance in 1992 for *I Feel Lucky*, Best Female Country Vocal Performance in 1993 for *Passionate Kisses* and Best Country Album in 1994 for *Stones In The Road*.
20/11/1993.....71......1.......	HE THINKS HE'LL KEEP HER...Columbia 6598632
07/01/1995.....40......3.......	ONE COOL REMOVE SHAWN COLVIN WITH MARY CHAPIN CARPENTER............................Columbia 6611342
03/06/1995.....35......2.......	SHUT UP AND KISS ME 1994 Grammy Award for Best Female Country Vocal Performance ....Columbia 6613675

○ Silver disc ● Gold disc ✪ Platinum disc (additional platinum units are indicated by a figure following the symbol) ◉ Singles released prior to 1973 that are known to have sold over 1 million copies in the UK

CARPENTERS US brother and sister duo Richard (born 15/10/1946, New Haven, CT) and Karen Carpenter (born 2/3/1950, New Haven) whose family relocated to Downey, CA in 1963. Richard played piano from nine, while Karen began learning bass from thirteen. By 1965 both were in the same group, along with Wes Jacobs. After their 1966 debut single *Looking For Love* for the Magic Lamp label, they signed as the Richard Carpenter Trio to RCA in 1966, but were dropped before releasing anything. Signed by A&M in 1969 (minus Jacobs, but using other outside musicians), they later hosted their own TV show. Karen died on 4/2/1983 from heart failure due to the slimming disease anorexia. Three Grammy Awards included Best New Artist in 1970, and Best Pop Vocal Performance in 1971 for *Carpenters*. They have a star on the Hollywood Walk of Fame.

05/09/1970	6	18		**(THEY LONG TO BE) CLOSE TO YOU** ▲4 Written by Bacharach and David and originally recorded by Dionne Warwick. It won the 1970 Grammy Award for Best Contemporary Pop Vocal Performance	A&M AMS 800
09/01/1971	28	7		WE'VE ONLY JUST BEGUN Originally written as an advertisement jingle for US bank Crocker Bank. Featured in the 1995 film *Muriel's Wedding*	A&M AMS 813
18/09/1971	18	13		SUPERSTAR/FOR ALL WE KNOW B-side featured in the 1970 film *Lovers And Other Strangers* and won an Oscar for Best Film Song	A&M AMS 864
01/01/1972	45	1		MERRY CHRISTMAS DARLING	A&M AME 601
23/09/1972	9	16		**I WON'T LAST A DAY WITHOUT YOU/GOODBYE TO LOVE**	A&M AMS 7023
07/07/1973	2	17	○	**YESTERDAY ONCE MORE**	A&M AMS 7073
20/10/1973	5	18	○	**TOP OF THE WORLD** ▲2	A&M AMS 7086
02/03/1974	12	11		JAMBALAYA (ON THE BAYOU)/MR. GUDER.	A&M AMS 7098
08/06/1974	32	5		I WON'T LAST A DAY WITHOUT YOU Re-issue of A&M AMS 7023	A&M AMS 7111
18/01/1975	2	12	○	**PLEASE MR. POSTMAN** ▲1 Cover version of The Marvelettes' US #1	A&M AMS 7141
19/04/1975	7	10		**ONLY YESTERDAY**	A&M AMS 7159
30/08/1975	32	5		SOLITAIRE	A&M AMS 7187
20/12/1975	37	4		SANTA CLAUS IS COMIN' TO TOWN	A&M AMS 7144
27/12/1976	22	6		THERE'S A KIND OF HUSH (ALL OVER THE WORLD)	A&M AMS 7219
03/07/1976	36	5		I NEED TO BE IN LOVE	A&M AMS 7238
08/10/1977	9	9		**CALLING OCCUPANTS OF INTERPLANETARY CRAFT (THE RECOGNISED ANTHEM OF WORLD CONTACT DAY)**	A&M AMS 7318
11/02/1978	40	4		SWEET SWEET SMILE	A&M AMS 7327
22/10/1983	60	3		MAKE BELIEVE IT'S YOUR FIRST TIME	A&M AM 147
08/12/1990	25	5		MERRY CHRISTMAS DARLING/(THEY LONG TO BE) CLOSE TO YOU Both titles re-issued	A&M AM 716
13/02/1993	63	2		RAINY DAYS AND MONDAYS Released to coincide with the 10th anniversary of Karen Carpenter's death	A&M AMCD 0180
24/12/1994	44	2		TRYIN' TO GET THE FEELING AGAIN	A&M 5807612

CARPET BOMBERS FOR PEACE Multinational group fronted by former Dead Kennedys leader Jello Biafra (as The Cowboy President From Hell) and also featuring members of Chumbawamba, Change and Conflict. Their debut single was in protest at the Allied forces' invasion of Iraq.

| 05/04/2003 | 67 | 1 | | SALT IN THE WOUND | Jungle JUNG 066CD |

DICK CARR – see SLIM DUSTY

JOE 'FINGERS' CARR US orchestra leader/pianist (born Lou Busch, 18/7/1910, Louisville, LA) who began playing with George Olsen and Hal Kemp before becoming an in-house producer for Capitol Records. With his own orchestra in the 1950s he backed the likes of Margaret Whiting (his future wife) and Kay Starr. He also composed themes for TV shows, including *What's My Line* in 1950. He was killed in a car crash on 19/9/1979.

| 29/06/1956 | 20 | 5 | | PORTUGUESE WASHERWOMAN | Capitol CL 14587 |

LINDA CARR US singer who began backing James Brown (replacing Tammi Terrell), before going solo with Stax and then Stateside, without success, although a couple of Stateside singles were popular on the Northern Soul scene.

| 12/07/1975 | 15 | 8 | | HIGHWIRE LINDA CARR AND THE LOVE SQUAD | Chelsea 2005 025 |
| 05/06/1976 | 36 | 4 | | SOLD MY ROCK 'N' ROLL (GAVE IT FOR FUNKY SOUL) LINDA AND THE FUNKY BOYS | Spark SRL 1139 |

LUCY CARR UK singer (born in Flint, North Wales) who began as a dancer. Her then boyfriend, nightclub owner Peter Stringfellow, launched Lickin' Records to assist her career.

| 25/01/2003 | 28 | 2 | | MISSING YOU | Lickin LICKINCD 001 |
| 09/08/2003 | 41 | 1 | | THIS IS GOODBYE | Lickin LICKINCX 002 |

PEARL CARR AND TEDDY JOHNSON UK husband and wife duo Pearl Carr (born 2/11/1923, Exmouth) and Teddy Johnson (born 4/9/1920, Surbiton) who married in 1955. Selected to represent the UK in the 1959 Eurovision Song Contest, they came second behind Teddy Scholten of Holland's entry *Een Beetje*. Teddy Johnson appeared in the 1958 film *Girls At Sea*.

| 20/03/1959 | 12 | 8 | | SING LITTLE BIRDIE UK's entry for the 1959 Eurovision Song Contest | Columbia DB 4275 |
| 06/04/1961 | 23 | 11 | | HOW WONDERFUL TO KNOW TEDDY JOHNSON AND PEARL CARR | Columbia DB 4603 |

SUZI CARR US singer who sang with Will To Power before going solo.

| 08/10/1994 | 45 | 1 | | ALL OVER ME | Cowboy RODEO 947CD |

VALERIE CARR US R&B singer (born 1936, New York City) who recorded for King and then Roulette.

❶9 Number of weeks single topped the UK chart ↑ Entered the UK chart at #1 ▲9 Number of weeks single topped the US chart

135

04/07/1958 . . . . . 29 . . . . . . 2 . . . . WHEN THE BOYS TALK ABOUT THE GIRLS . . . . Columbia DB 4131

VIKKI CARR US singer (born Florencia Bisenta de Casillas Martinez Cardona, 19/7/1941, El Paso, TX). After successful English versions of her Spanish hits she performed many hospital benefits, set up a scholarship foundation for Chicano children and resumed her Spanish singing career in Mexico. She has won three Grammy Awards: Best Mexican-American Performance in 1985 for *Simplemente Mujer*, Best Latin Pop Album in 1991 for *Cosas Del Amor* and Best Mexican-American Album in 1994 for *Recuerdo A Javier Solis*. She has a star on the Hollywood Walk of Fame.

01/06/1967 . . . . . 2 . . . . . . 20 . . . . . . **IT MUST BE HIM (SEUL SUR SON ETOILE)** . . . . Liberty LIB 55917
30/08/1967 . . . . . 50 . . . . . . 1 . . . . THERE I GO . . . . Liberty LBF 15022
12/03/1969 . . . . . 39 . . . . . . 5 . . . . WITH PEN IN HAND . . . . Liberty LBF 15166

RAFFAELLA CARRA Italian singer (born Raffaella Pelloni, 18/6/1943, Bologna) who was a media star in her own country before her singing career. Her hit single was originally the B-side when released in Italy. She has also appeared in numerous films, including *Von Ryan's Express* in 1965.

15/04/1978 . . . . . 9 . . . . . . 12 . . . . . . **DO IT DO IT AGAIN** . . . . Epic EPC 6094

PAUL CARRACK UK singer (born 22/4/1951, Sheffield) who was lead vocalist with Ace 1973–76 and later played with Squeeze, Roxy Music and Mike + The Mechanics, going solo in 1982.

16/05/1987 . . . . . 48 . . . . . . 5 . . . . WHEN YOU WALK IN THE ROOM . . . . Chrysalis CHS 3109
18/03/1989 . . . . . 60 . . . . . . 3 . . . . DON'T SHED A TEAR . . . . Chrysalis CHS 3166
06/01/1996 . . . . . 40 . . . . . . 4 . . . . EYES OF BLUE . . . . IRS CDEIRS 192
06/04/1996 . . . . . 32 . . . . . . 5 . . . . HOW LONG? . . . . IRS CDEIRS 193
24/08/1996 . . . . . 45 . . . . . . 1 . . . . EYES OF BLUE (REMIX) . . . . IRS CDEIRS 194

CARRAPICHO – see CHILLI FEATURING CARRAPICHO

JOSE CARRERAS Spanish singer (born 5/12/1946, Barcelona). Surviving leukaemia in the late 1980s, he set up the Jose Carreras International Leukaemia Foundation. Musical director of the opening and closing ceremonies at the 1992 Olympic Games in Barcelona, he won the 1990 Grammy Award for Best Classical Solo Vocal Performance with Placido Domingo and Luciano Pavarotti for *Carreras, Domingo, Pavarotti In Concert*. Mehta is Indian conductor Zubin Mehta (born 29/4/1936, Bombay).

11/07/1992 . . . . . 11 . . . . . . 11 . . . . . . AMIGOS PARA SIEMPRE (FRIENDS FOR LIFE) JOSE CARRERAS AND SARAH BRIGHTMAN Theme to the 1992 Barcelona Olympics . . .
. . . . Really Useful RUR 10
30/07/1994 . . . . . 21 . . . . . . 4 . . . . LIBIAMO/LA DONNA E MOBILE JOSE CARRERAS, PLACIDO DOMINGO AND LUCIANO PAVAROTTI . . . . Teldec YZ 843CD
25/07/1998 . . . . . 35 . . . . . . 4 . . . . YOU'LL NEVER WALK ALONE CARRERAS/DOMINGO/PAVAROTTI WITH MEHTA . . . . Decca 4607982

TIA CARRERE US singer (born Althea Rae Duhinio Janairo, 2/1/1967, Honolulu, HI) first known as an actress, appearing in TV's *General Hospital* and the films *Wayne's World* (1992; she turned down a part in *Baywatch* to audition for it) and *Wayne's World 2* (1993). She later worked with producers Ted Templeman and Andres Levin, before returning to acting, playing the lead role of Sydney in the TV series *Relic Hunter*.

30/05/1992 . . . . . 26 . . . . . . 6 . . . . BALLROOM BLITZ Featured in the 1992 film *Wayne's World* . . . . Reprise W 0105

JIM CARREY Canadian actor/singer (born 17/1/1962, Newmarket, Ontario) who found fame as a comic actor in lead roles in *Ace Ventura – Pet Detective*, *Mask*, *Dumb And Dumber*, *Liar Liar*, *The Grinch*, *The Truman Show*, *Man On The Moon* and *The Cable Guy*.

21/01/1995 . . . . . 31 . . . . . . 3 . . . . CUBAN PETE Featured in the 1994 film *Mask* . . . . Columbia 6606625

CARRIE UK/US group formed by Steven Ludwin (vocals), Dennis Dicker (guitar), Zak Foley (bass) and Bruce Pawsey (drums).

14/03/1998 . . . . . 56 . . . . . . 1 . . . . MOLLY . . . . Island CID 687
09/05/1998 . . . . . 55 . . . . . . 1 . . . . CALIFORNIA SCREAMIN' . . . . Island CID 694

DINA CARROLL UK singer (born 21/8/1968, Newmarket) with a British mother and US serviceman father. Dina spent a few years in Philadelphia, PA but was mainly brought up in England. She began doing session work for Streetsounds, and as a member of Masquerade, releasing her first record for Jive in 1989 (as Deana Carroll). Named Best British Female at the 1994 BRIT Awards, she also took part in the *It's Only Rock 'N' Roll* project for the Children's Promise charity.

02/02/1991 . . . . . 8 . . . . . . 14 . . . . . . **IT'S TOO LATE** QUARTZ INTRODUCING DINA CARROLL . . . . Mercury ITM 3
15/06/1991 . . . . . 39 . . . . . . 3 . . . . NAKED LOVE (JUST SAY YOU WANT ME) QUARTZ AND DINA CARROLL . . . . Mercury ITM 4
11/07/1992 . . . . . 16 . . . . . . 8 . . . . AIN'T NO MAN . . . . A&M AM 0001
10/10/1992 . . . . . 16 . . . . . . 5 . . . . SPECIAL KIND OF LOVE . . . . A&M AM 0088
05/12/1992 . . . . . 20 . . . . . . 8 . . . . SO CLOSE . . . . A&M AM 0101
27/02/1993 . . . . . 23 . . . . . . 6 . . . . THIS TIME . . . . A&M AMCD 0184
15/05/1993 . . . . . 12 . . . . . . 6 . . . . EXPRESS . . . . A&M 5802632
16/10/1993 . . . . . 3 . . . . . . 13 . . . . O **DON'T BE A STRANGER** . . . . A&M 5803892
11/12/1993 . . . . . 5 . . . . . . 11 . . . . O **THE PERFECT YEAR** . . . . A&M 5804812
28/09/1996 . . . . . 3 . . . . . . 8 . . . . **ESCAPING** . . . . Mercury DCCD 1
21/12/1996 . . . . . 33 . . . . . . 4 . . . . ONLY HUMAN . . . . Mercury DCCD 2
24/10/1998 . . . . . 16 . . . . . . 4 . . . . ONE, TWO, THREE . . . . 1st Avenue MERCD 514
24/07/1999 . . . . . 13 . . . . . . 7 . . . . WITHOUT LOVE . . . . 1st Avenue FESCDD 57
16/06/2001 . . . . . 38 . . . . . . 2 . . . . SOMEONE LIKE YOU Featured in the 2001 film *Bridget Jones's Diary* . . . . 1st Avenue 5689072

O Silver disc ● Gold disc ✪ Platinum disc (additional platinum units are indicated by a figure following the symbol) ◉ Singles released prior to 1973 that are known to have sold over 1 million copies in the UK

RON CARROLL
US singer/DJ (born 1968, Chicago, IL) who first worked with Little Louis Vega, penning songs for Barbara Tucker.

04/03/2000.....42......1......	LUCKY STAR **SUPERFUNK FEATURING RON CARROLL** Contains a sample of Chris Rea's *Josephine* .... Virgin DINSD 198
28/04/2001.....73......1......	MY LOVE **KLUSTER FEATURING RON CARROLL** Contains a sample of Odyssey's *Native New Yorker* .... Scorpio Music 1928112

RONNIE CARROLL
UK singer (born Ronald Cleghorn, 18/8/1934, Belfast) who began as an impersonator on the *Hollywood Doubles* show. He married singer Millicent Martin in 1959. Twice representing the UK in the Eurovision Song Contest, in 1962 he came fourth with *Ring A Ding Girl* behind Isabelle Aubret of France's *Un Premier Amour*. The following year he came fourth with *Say Wonderful Things* behind the Danish entry by Grethe and Jorgen Ingmann, *Dansevise*.

27/07/1956.....13......8......	WALK HAND IN HAND .... Philips PB 605
29/03/1957.....20......2......	THE WISDOM OF A FOOL .... Philips PB 667
31/03/1960.....36......3......	FOOTSTEPS .... Philips PB 1004
22/02/1962.....46......3......	RING A DING GIRL .... Philips PB 1222
02/08/1962 .....3......16......	**ROSES ARE RED** .... Philips 326532 BF
15/11/1962.....33......4......	IF ONLY TOMORROW .... Philips 326550 BF
07/03/1963 .....6......14......	**SAY WONDERFUL THINGS** .... Philips 326574 BF

JASPER CARROTT
UK singer/comedian (born Bob Davies, 14/3/1945, Birmingham), a popular figure on UK TV with his own show and numerous spin-offs, including *The Detectives* and *Carrott Commercial*. The hit single sold mainly on the strength of the non-broadcastable B-side, a parody of the children's TV programme of the same name. He was awarded an MBE in the 2003 New Year's Honours List.

16/08/1975 .....5......15.....○	**FUNKY MOPED/MAGIC ROUNDABOUT** .... DJM DJS 388

CARS
US rock group formed in Boston, MA in 1976 by Ric Ocasek (born Richard Otcasek, 23/3/1949, Baltimore, MD, lead guitar/vocals), Benjamin Orr (born Benjamin Orzechowski, 9/8/1955, Cleveland, OH, bass/vocals), Elliot Easton (born Elliot Shapiro, 18/12/1953, Brooklyn, NYC, guitar), Greg Hawkes (born in Baltimore, keyboards) and David Robinson (born 2/1/1953, Boston, drums). Robinson chose the name Cars, Ocasek wrote all of the songs. Although they didn't appear, The Cars produced one of the most memorable moments of 1985's Live Aid, a video of Ethiopian famine footage, accompanied by *Drive*. Ocasek donated all royalties from the single to the Band Aid Trust. The group disbanded in 1988, and Benjamin Orr died from pancreatic cancer on 3/10/2000.

11/11/1978 .....3......10......	**MY BEST FRIEND'S GIRL** This is believed to have been the first single to be released as a picture disc............. Elektra K 12301
17/02/1979.....17......10......	JUST WHAT I NEEDED Featured in the 1999 film *200 Cigarettes*..................................... Elektra K 12312
28/07/1979.....51......4......	LET'S GO .... Elektra K 12371
05/06/1982.....37......4......	SINCE YOU'RE GONE .... Elektra K 13177
29/09/1984 .....5......11.....○	**DRIVE** .... Elektra E 9706
03/08/1985 .....4......12.....●	**DRIVE** Re-promoted following exposure at Live Aid .... Elektra E 9706

ALEX CARTANA
UK singer (born 1981, Brighton) who was raised in Majorca and later relocated to London.

06/09/2003.....16......6......	SHAKE IT (MOVE A LITTLE CLOSER) **LEE CABRERA FEATURING ALEX CARTANA** .... Credence CDCRED 039
08/05/2004.....34......2......	HEY PAPI. .... EMI PAP1CDS

AARON CARTER
US singer (born 7/12/1987, Tampa, FL), younger brother of Nick Carter of The Backstreet Boys. The fourth youngest ever UK chart entrant, having not reached ten at the time of his debut hit.

29/11/1997 .....9......8......	**CRUSH ON YOU** .... Ultra Pop 6099605 ULT
07/02/1998 .....7......6......	**CRAZY LITTLE PARTY GIRL** .... Ultra Pop 0099645 ULT
28/03/1998.....24......5......	I'M GONNA MISS YOU FOREVER .... Ultra Pop 0099725 ULT
04/07/1998.....18......5......	SURFIN' USA. .... Ultra Pop 0099805 ULT
16/09/2000.....31......3......	I WANT CANDY... Jive 9250892
28/10/2000.....51......2......	AARON'S PARTY (COME GET IT) .... Jive 9251272
13/04/2002.....22......4......	LEAVE IT UP TO ME.. Jive 9253262

BRAD CARTER
UK producer who is also a member of Ruff Driverz.

23/10/2004.....48......1......	MORNING ALWAYS COMES TOO SOON .... Positiva CDTIVS210

CLARENCE CARTER
US singer (born 14/1/1936, Montgomery, AL) who lost his sight at the age of one. Undeterred, he learned to play the guitar at eleven, gained a music degree and formed a duo with Calvin Scott that lasted until 1966, when Calvin was injured in a car accident. Signing with Fame records in 1967, he discovered and later married Candi Staton. General Johnson of Chairmen Of The Board wrote his debut hit.

10/10/1970 .....2......13......	**PATCHES** 1970 Grammy Award for Best Rhythm & Blues Song for Ronald Dunbar and General Johnson .... Atlantic 2091 030

NICK CARTER
US singer (born 28/1/1980, New York), also a member of The Backstreet Boys, whose younger brother Aaron also enjoyed a successful solo career.

19/10/2002.....17......3......	HELP ME .... Jive 9254332

CARTER – THE UNSTOPPABLE SEX MACHINE
UK rock group formed in London in 1986 by Fruitbat (born Leslie Carter, 12/12/1958, London, guitar/programming) and Jimbob (born Jim Morrison, 22/11/1960, London, vocals). In 1995 they recruited full-time drummer Wez, and split in January 1998.

26/01/1991.....48......2......	BLOODSPORTS FOR ALL.. Rough Trade R 20112687
22/06/1991.....23......7......	SHERIFF FATMAN .... Big Cat USM 1
26/10/1991.....11......5......	AFTER THE WATERSHED The Rolling Stones launched a lawsuit as the song featured a snippet of *Ruby Tuesday* ..... Big Cat USM 2
11/01/1992.....14......5......	RUBBISH .... Big Cat USM 3

25/04/1992	7	5		THE ONLY LIVING BOY IN NEW CROSS	Big Cat USM 4
04/07/1992	22	3		DO RE ME SO FAR SO GOOD	Chrysalis USM 5
28/11/1992	21	3		THE IMPOSSIBLE DREAM	Chrysalis USM 6
04/09/1993	16	3		LEAN ON ME I WON'T FALL OVER	Chrysalis CDUSM 7
16/10/1993	40	2		LENNY AND TERENCE	Chrysalis CDUSM 8
12/03/1994	24	3		GLAM ROCK COPS	Chrysalis CDUSMS 10
19/11/1994	30	3		LET'S GET TATTOOS	Chrysalis CDUSMS 30
04/02/1995	34	3		THE YOUNG OFFENDER'S MUM	Chrysalis CDUSMS 12
30/09/1995	35	2		BORN ON THE 5TH OF NOVEMBER	Chrysalis CDUSM 13

CARTER TWINS Irish vocal duo Stephen and Tony Carter.

| 08/03/1997 | 61 | 1 | | THE TWELFTH OF NEVER/TOO RIGHT TO BE WRONG | RCA 74321453082 |

JUNIOR CARTIER UK producer Jon Carter, who previously recorded as Artery, is a member of Monkey Mafia, and is married to Radio 1 DJ Sara Cox.

| 06/11/1999 | 70 | 1 | | WOMEN BEAT THEIR MEN Contains a sample of Dominatrix's *The Dominatrix Sleeps Tonight* | Nucamp CAMPD 3X |

CARTOONS Danish pop group formed by Toonie, Sponge, Shooter, Buzz, Puddy and Boop.

03/04/1999	2	13	●	WITCH DOCTOR	Flex TOONCD 1
19/06/1999	7	12		DOODAH Originally written in 1850 by Stephen Foster as *The Camptown Races*, which was subsequently adapted as a campaign song for Abraham Lincoln in 1860. Foster, who also wrote the best-selling sheet music song of all time, *The Old Folks At Home* (which has sold more than 20 million copies), died virtually penniless in 1864	Flex CDTOON 002
04/09/1999	16	5		AISY WAISY	Flex CDTOONS 003

RICHARD CARTRIDGE UK singer who is also a DJ for BBC Radio Solent and a member of Mike Williams' Shadowlands, a Shadows tribute group.

| 25/09/2004 | 50 | 1 | | I'VE FOUND LOVE AGAIN Released for BBC's Children In Need appeal | Springboard Media SMCDSRC001 |

SAM CARTWRIGHT – see VOLCANO

CARVELLS UK singer/multi-instrumentalist Alan Carvell.

| 26/11/1977 | 31 | 4 | | THE L.A. RUN | Creole CR 143 |

CASCADES US group formed in San Diego, CA by John Gummoe (guitar/vocals), Eddie Snyder (piano), David Stevens (bass), David Wilson (saxophone) and David Zabo (drums). They later recorded for RCA, Charter, Liberty, Arwin, Smash, Probe, UNI, London and Can Base, all without success, before disbanding in 1970.

| 28/02/1963 | 5 | 16 | | RHYTHM OF THE RAIN | Warner Brothers WB 88 |

CASE US singer (born Case Woodward, 10/1/1973, New York City) who has appeared on the soundtracks to the films *Rush Hour* (1998), *The Best Man* (1999) and *Nutty Professor II* (2000), releasing his debut album in 1996.

21/09/1996	26	3		TOUCH ME TEASE ME CASE FEATURING FOXY BROWN Contains a sample of Schooly D's *PSK What Does It Mean*. Featured in the 1996 film *The Nutty Professor*	Def Jam DEFCD 18
10/11/2001	27	4		LIVIN' IT UP JA RULE FEATURING CASE Contains a sample of Stevie Wonder's *Do I Do*	Def Jam 5888142
03/08/2002	5	8		LIVIN' IT UP (REMIX) JA RULE FEATURING CASE	Def Jam 0639782

ED CASE UK producer Edward Makromallies.

21/10/2000	38	2		SOMETHING IN YOUR EYES	Red Rose CDROSE 003
15/09/2001	29	2		WHO? ED CASE FEATURING SWEETIE IRIE	Columbia 6718302
20/07/2002	49	1		GOOD TIMES ED CASE AND SKIN	Columbia 6727672

BRIAN AND BRANDON CASEY – see NIVEA

NATALIE CASEY UK singer/actress (born 15/4/1980), just three at the time of her debut hit (although not the youngest person to have had a hit record, being slightly older than Ian Doody recording as Microbe). She later played Carol Groves in TV's *Hollyoaks* and became an MTV presenter.

| 07/01/1984 | 72 | 1 | | CHICK CHICK CHICKEN | Polydor CHICK 1 |

JOHNNY CASH US country singer (born 26/2/1932, Kingsland, AR) who moved with his family to Dyees, AR aged three. After serving in the US Air Force (1950–54) he formed a trio with Luther Perkins and Marshall Grant in 1955, later the same year making debut recordings for Sun. He worked with June Carter from 1961 and married her in 1968. His daughter Rosanne Cash and stepdaughter Carlene Carter are also successful vocalists. Famous for his concerts recorded in prisons, the album *Johnny Cash At San Quentin* topped the US charts in 1969. He announced in 1997 that he had Parkinson's Disease after falling on stage while picking up a guitar pick. Perkins died on 5/8/1968 after falling asleep smoking and setting fire to his house. Cash has suffered similar tragedies and mishaps: a brother died when he fell on an electric saw, a drunken doctor removed a cyst from Cash's cheek and left a visible scar, and a German girl stuck a pencil down his ear, leaving him partially deaf. He was inducted into the Rock & Roll Hall of Fame in 1992, and his twelve Grammy Awards include: Best Country & Western Performance by a Duo in 1967 with June Carter for *Jackson*; Best Country & Western Vocal Performance and Best Album Notes in 1968 for *Folsom Prison Blues*; Best Album Notes in 1969 for Bob Dylan's *Nashville Skyline*; Best Country & Western Performance by a Duo in 1970 with June Carter for *If I Were A Carpenter*; Best Spoken Word Documentary in 1986 with various others for *Interviews From The Class of '55*; Best Contemporary Folk Album in 1994 for *American*

Recordings; Best Country Album in 1997 for *Unchained*; Best Male Country Vocal Performance in 2000 for *Solitary Man*; Best Male Country Vocal Performance in 2002 for *Give My Love To Rose*; and Best Short Form Music Video in 2003 for *Hurt*. He has a star on the Hollywood Walk of Fame. Johnny died on 12/9/2003. The Tennessee Three were formed by Luther Perkins (lead guitar), Marshall Grant (bass) and W S Holland (drums).

03/06/1965	28	8	IT AIN'T ME, BABE	CBS 201760
06/09/1969	4	19	**A BOY NAMED SUE** Recorded live in San Quentin prison. 1969 Grammy Award for Best Country & Western Performance	CBS 4460
23/05/1970	21	11	WHAT IS TRUTH	CBS 4934
15/04/1972	4	14	**A THING CALLED LOVE** JOHNNY CASH WITH THE EVANGEL TEMPLE CHOIR	CBS 7797
03/07/1976	32	7	ONE PIECE AT A TIME JOHNNY CASH WITH THE TENNESSEE THREE	CBS 4087
10/05/2003	42	1	HURT/PERSONAL JESUS	American/Lost Highway 0779982
15/11/2003	39	2	HURT/PERSONAL JESUS	American/Lost Highway 0779982

PAT CASH – see JOHN McENROE AND PAT CASH WITH THE FULL METAL RACKETS

CA$HFLOW US soul group formed in Atlanta, GA by Gaylord Parsons (drums/vocals/raps), Kary Hubbert (lead vocals), James Duffie (keyboards/vocals) and Regis Ferguson (keyboards), discovered by Cameo leader Larry Blackmon, who signed them to his Atlanta Artists label.

| 24/05/1986 | 15 | 8 | MINE ALL MINE/PARTY FREAK Coupled two separate US R&B hits | Club JAB 30 |

CASHMERE US group formed in 1982 by two top session musicians, Daryl Burgess and Dwight Ronnell Dukes, later adding pianist/songwriter McKinley Horton (co-writer of Eugene Wilde's *Got To Get You Home Tonight*) in 1984.

| 19/01/1985 | 29 | 8 | CAN I | Fourth & Broadway BRW 19 |
| 23/03/1985 | 52 | 3 | WE NEED LOVE | Fourth & Broadway BRW 22 |

CASINO UK production group Paul Gotel, Jonathan Edwards and Aron Friedman, with singer Melanie Lewis.

| 17/05/1997 | 52 | 1 | SOUND OF EDEN | Worx WORXCD 006 |
| 10/07/1999 | 72 | 1 | ONLY YOU | Pow! CDPOW 006 |

CASINOS US vocal group formed in Cincinnati, OH in 1958 by Gene Hughes, his brother Glen Hughes, Pete Bolton, Joe Patterson and Ray White. First recording for the local labels Terry and Fraternity, they later added Bob Armstrong, Tom Matthews, Bill Hawkins and Mickey Denton to the line-up.

| 23/02/1967 | 28 | 7 | THEN YOU CAN TELL ME GOODBYE | President PT 123 |

CASSANDRA – see RUI DA SILVA FEATURING CASSANDRA

CASSIDY US singer (born Barry Reese, 1983, Philadelphia, PA). Mashonda is singer Mashonda Tifrere.

| 29/05/2004 | 3 | 14 | **HOTEL** CASSIDY FEATURING R KELLY Contains a sample of Sugarhill Gang's *Rapper's Delight* | J Records 82876618612 |
| 25/09/2004 | 24 | 4 | GET NO BETTER CASSIDY FEATURING MASHONDA | J Records 82876649282 |

DAVID CASSIDY US singer/actor (born 12/4/1950, New York), son of actor Jack Cassidy and Evelyn Ward, who appeared in various TV shows before being cast as Keith Partridge in *The Partridge Family* in 1970 (with his stepmother Shirley Jones playing his mother Shirley). The 'Family' were subsequently signed by Bell Records. After considerable success with the group, Cassidy concentrated on his solo career from 1973, especially in the UK where his fan base was strongest.

08/04/1972	2	17	**COULD IT BE FOREVER/CHERISH**	Bell 1224
16/09/1972	❶²	11	**HOW CAN I BE SURE**	Bell 1258
25/11/1972	11	9	ROCK ME BABY	Bell 1268
24/03/1973	3	12	I'M A CLOWN/SOME KIND OF A SUMMER	Bell MABEL 4
13/10/1973	❶³	15	**DAYDREAMER/THE PUPPY SONG**	Bell 1334
11/05/1974	9	9	IF I DIDN'T CARE	Bell 1350
27/07/1974	16	6	PLEASE PLEASE ME	Bell 1371
05/07/1975	11	8	I WRITE THE SONGS/GET IT UP FOR LOVE A-side won the 1976 Grammy Award for Song of the Year for writer Bruce Johnston	RCA 2571
25/10/1975	16	8	DARLIN'	RCA 2622
23/02/1985	6	9	**THE LAST KISS** Features the uncredited contribution of George Michael	Arista ARIST 589
11/05/1985	54	6	ROMANCE (LET YOUR HEART GO)	Arista ARIST 620

EVA CASSIDY US singer (born 2/2/1963, Oxon Hill, MD) who began her career as a backing singer before teaming up with soul singer Chuck Brown. She first recorded in her own right in 1994 for Blue Note Records, touring with Pieces Of A Dream, but was experiencing increasing pain owing to a hip problem. Tests revealed she had advanced melanoma, and she died on 2/11/1996. Five years later a Radio 2 airing of two albums she had recorded for Blix Street led to a resurgence of interest in her career.

| 21/04/2001 | 42 | 9 | OVER THE RAINBOW | Blix Street/Hot HIT 16 |
| 11/10/2003 | 54 | 1 | YOU TAKE MY BREATH AWAY | Blix Street/Hot HIT 27 |

CASSIUS French production duo Phillipe Zdar and Hubert Blanc-Francart (also known as Boombass) who also record as Motorbass and La Funk Mob.

23/01/1999	7	7	**CASSIUS 1999** Contains a sample of Donna Summer's *Love Is Just A Breath Away*	Virgin DINSD 177
15/05/1999	16	4	FEELING FOR YOU Contains a sample of Gwen McCrae's *All This Love That I'm Giving*	Virgin DINSD 181
20/11/1999	53	1	LA MOUCHE	Virgin DINSD 188
05/10/2002	49	1	THE SOUND OF VIOLENCE	Virgin DINSD 241

CAST
CAST UK rock group formed in Liverpool in 1994 by John Power (born 14/9/1967, Liverpool, guitar/vocals), Skin (born Liam Tyson, 7/9/1969, Liverpool, guitar), Peter Wilkinson (born 9/5/1969, Liverpool, bass) and Keith O'Neill (born 18/2/1969, Liverpool, drums). Power had previously been in The La's, naming Cast after a line from The La's *Looking Glass*. They disbanded in August 2001 after Power walked out following disagreements with the others.

DATE	POS	WKS	SINGLE TITLE	LABEL & NUMBER
15/07/1995	17	4	FINETIME	Polydor 5795072
30/09/1995	13	4	ALRIGHT	Polydor 5799272
20/01/1996	8	5	**SANDSTORM**	Polydor 5778732
30/03/1996	9	7	**WALKAWAY** Featured in the 1998 film *Up 'N' Under*	Polydor 5762852
26/10/1996	4	5	**FLYING**	Polydor 5754772
05/04/1997	7	7	**FREE ME**	Polydor 5736512
28/06/1997	9	6	**GUIDING STAR**	Polydor 5711732
13/09/1997	7	5	**LIVE THE DREAM**	Polydor 5716852
15/11/1997	14	3	I'M SO LONELY	Polydor 5690592
08/05/1999	9	5	**BEAT MAMA**	Polydor 5635952
07/08/1999	28	3	MAGIC HOUR	Polydor 5612272
28/07/2001	45	1	DESERT DROUGHT	Polydor 5871762

CAST OF CASUALTY
CAST OF CASUALTY UK vocal group formed by actors from the TV drama *Casualty*. The series began in 1986 with Derek Thompson (as Charge Nurse Charlie Fairhead), the longest-serving actor. Rebecca Wheatley, who plays Amy Howard in the show, also enjoyed a hit record.

DATE	POS	WKS	SINGLE TITLE	LABEL & NUMBER
14/03/1998	5	6	**EVERLASTING LOVE**	warner.esp WESP 003CD

CAST OF THE NEW ROCKY HORROR SHOW
CAST OF THE NEW ROCKY HORROR SHOW UK vocal group with a song from the Richard O'Brien-written stage show.

DATE	POS	WKS	SINGLE TITLE	LABEL & NUMBER
12/12/1998	57	1	THE TIMEWARP	Damn It Janet DAMJAN 1CD

ROY CASTLE
ROY CASTLE UK singer/multi-instrumentalist (born 31/8/1932, Huddersfield), better known as a TV personality presenting *Record Breakers* based on the Guinness Book of Records. He died on 2/9/1994 from lung cancer.

DATE	POS	WKS	SINGLE TITLE	LABEL & NUMBER
22/12/1960	40	3	LITTLE WHITE BERRY	Philips PB 1087

CASUALS
CASUALS UK four-piece pop group formed by Howard Newcomb, Bob O'Brien, Alan Taylor and John Tebb who won TV's *Opportunity Knocks* three times, also being voted most promising UK group in 1968.

DATE	POS	WKS	SINGLE TITLE	LABEL & NUMBER
14/08/1968	2	18	**JESAMINE**	Decca F 22784
04/12/1968	30	8	TOY	Decca F 22852

CAT
CAT UK singer Danny John-Jules (born 16/9/1960, London) who appeared as The Cat in the TV comedy *Red Dwarf*.

DATE	POS	WKS	SINGLE TITLE	LABEL & NUMBER
23/10/1993	17	4	TONGUE TIED	EMI CDEM 286

CATATONIA
CATATONIA UK rock group formed in Cardiff in 1992 by Cerys Matthews (born 11/4/1969, Cardiff, vocals), Mark Roberts (born 3/11/1969, Colwyn Bay, guitar), Owen Powell (born 9/7/1969, Cambridge, guitar), Paul Jones (born 5/2/1960, Colwyn Bay, bass) and Aled Richards (born 5/7/1969, Carmarthen, drums). Former member Dafydd Ieuan went on to join Super Furry Animals. In September 2001 Cerys returned from rehab and announced she was going solo.

DATE	POS	WKS	BPI	SINGLE TITLE	LABEL & NUMBER
03/02/1996	61	1		SWEET CATATONIA	Blanco Y Negro NEG 85CD
04/05/1996	41	1		LOST CAT	Blanco Y Negro NEG 88CD1
07/09/1996	35	2		YOU'VE GOT A LOT TO ANSWER FOR	Blanco Y Negro NEG 93CD1
30/11/1996	46	1		BLEED	Blanco Y Negro NEG 97CD1
18/10/1997	40	2		I AM THE MOB	Blanco Y Negro NEG 107CD
31/01/1998	3	10		**MULDER AND SCULLY**	Blanco Y Negro NEG 109CD
07/03/1998	4	8	○	**THE BALLAD OF TOM JONES** SPACE WITH CERYS OF CATATONIA	Gut CDGUT 18
02/05/1998	5	8		**ROAD RAGE**	Blanco Y Negro NEG 112CD
01/08/1998	11	6		STRANGE GLUE	Blanco Y Negro NEG 113CD
07/11/1998	33	2		GAME ON	WEA NEG 114CD
10/04/1999	7	8		**DEAD FROM THE WAIST DOWN**	Blanco Y Negro NEG 115CD
24/07/1999	20	3		LONDINIUM	Blanco Y Negro NEG 117CD
13/11/1999	36	2		KARAOKE QUEEN	Blanco Y Negro NEG 119CD
04/08/2001	19	4		STONE BY STONE	Blanco Y Negro NEG 134CD

CATCH
CATCH UK vocal/instrumental group fronted by Stu Allen, who later joined Clock.

DATE	POS	WKS	SINGLE TITLE	LABEL & NUMBER
17/11/1990	70	1	FREE (C'MON)	ffrr F 147

CATCH
CATCH UK group formed by Toby Slater (keyboards/vocals), Ben Etchells (guitar) and Wayne Murray (bass). Slater is the son of Stephanie De Sykes.

DATE	POS	WKS	SINGLE TITLE	LABEL & NUMBER
11/10/1997	23	4	BINGO	Virgin VSCDT 1656
21/02/1998	44	2	DIVE IN	Virgin VSCDT 1665

CATHERINE WHEEL
CATHERINE WHEEL UK rock group formed in Great Yarmouth in 1990 by Rob Dickinson (guitar/vocals), Brian Futter (guitar), Neil Sims (drums) and David Hawes (bass). They recorded for local Norwich label Wilde Club before signing with Fontana.

DATE	POS	WKS	SINGLE TITLE	LABEL & NUMBER
23/11/1991	68	1	BLACK METALLIC (EP) Tracks on EP: *Black Metallic, Crawling Over Me, Let Me Down Again* and *Saccharine*	Fontana CW 1
08/02/1992	59	1	BALLOON	Fontana CW 2

18/04/1992	35	2		I WANT TO TOUCH YOU	Fontana CW 3
09/01/1993	47	2		30TH CENTURY MAN	Fontana CWCD 4
16/01/1993	62	1		SHOW ME MARY	Fontana CWCDA 6
10/07/1993	66	1		CRANK	Fontana CWCD 5
05/08/1995	67	1		WAYDOWN	Fontana CWCD 7
13/12/1997	53	1		DELICIOUS	Chrysalis CDCHS 5071
28/02/1998	53	1		MA SOLITUDA	Chrysalis CDCHS 5077
02/05/1998	48	1		BROKEN NOSE	Chrysalis CDCHS 5086

LORRAINE CATO UK singer who later worked with Fyrus.

06/02/1993	46	2		HOW CAN YOU TELL ME IT'S OVER	Columbia 6587662
03/08/1996	41	1		I WAS MADE TO LOVE YOU	MCA MCSTD 40055

CATS UK instrumental group with a reggae version of Tchaikovsky's first theme from *Swan Lake*.

09/04/1969	48	2		SWAN LAKE	BAF 1

CATS U.K. UK studio group assembled by Paul Curtis and John Worseley. Their one hit single referred to a TV advert featuring Lorraine Chase promoting a well-known drink with the catch line 'truly were you wafted here from paradise – No, Luton Airport!'

06/10/1979	22	8		LUTON AIRPORT	WEA K 18075

NICK CAVE AND THE BAD SEEDS Australian singer (born 22/9/1957, Wangarrata), a member of Birthday Party until 1983 when he went solo. Appeared in the film *Wings Of Desire* in 1987. The Bad Seeds comprised Mick Harvey (born 29/9/1958, Rochester, Australia, multi-instrumentalist), Blixa Bargeld (born 12/1/1959, Berlin, Germany, guitar/vocals), Conway Savage (born 27/7/1960, Foster, Australia, bass), Thomas Wydler (born 9/10/1959, Zurich, Switzerland, drums) and Martyn Casey (born 10/7/1960, Chesterfield, England, keyboards).

11/04/1992	68	1		STRAIGHT TO YOU/JACK THE RIPPER	Mute 140
12/12/1992	72	1		WHAT A WONDERFUL WORLD **NICK CAVE AND SHANE MacGOWAN**	Mute 151
09/04/1994	68	1		DO YOU LOVE ME	Mute CDMUTE 160
14/10/1995	11	4		WHERE THE WILD ROSES GROW **NICK CAVE + KYLIE MINOGUE**	Mute CDMUTE 185
09/03/1996	36	1		HENRY LEE **NICK CAVE AND THE BAD SEEDS AND PJ HARVEY**	Mute CDMUTE 189
22/02/1997	53	1		INTO MY ARMS	Mute CDMUTE 192
31/05/1997	67	1		(ARE YOU) THE ONE THAT I'VE BEEN	Mute CDMUTE 206
31/03/2001	42	1		AS I SAT SADLY BY HER SIDE	Mute CDMUTE 249
02/06/2001	52	1		FIFTEEN FEET OF PURE WHITE SNOW	Mute CDMUTE 262
08/03/2003	58	1		BRING IT ON	Mute CDMUTE 265
18/09/2004	37	2		NATURE BOY	Mute CDMUTE 324
27/11/2004	45	1		BREATHLESS/THERE SHE GOES MY BEAUTIFUL WORLD	Mute CDMUTE 329

CAVE IN US alternative metal group formed in Methuen, MA in 1995 by Jay Frechette (vocals), Stephen Brodsky (guitar), Adam McGrath (guitar), Justin Matthes (bass) and John-Robert Conners (drums). Matthes left after their debut release and was replaced by Andy Kyte; Frechette was replaced by Dave Scrod in 1997. Scrod left in 1998 and was replaced by Caleb Scofield.

31/05/2003	53	1		ANCHOR	RCA 82876522992

CAVEMAN UK rap duo MCM and Diamond J.

09/03/1991	65	2		I'M READY	Profile PROF 330

C.C.S. UK blues/pop group assembled by guitarist/singer Alexis Korner (born 19/4/1928, Paris), Peter Thorup and arranger John Cameron, featuring a flexible line-up. The name stood for Collective Consciousness Society. Korner died from cancer on 1/1/1984.

31/10/1970	13	13		WHOLE LOTTA LOVE Cover of the Led Zeppelin song used as the theme to *Top Of The Pops* 1970–76	RAK 104
27/02/1971	7	16		**WALKIN'**	RAK 109
04/09/1971	5	13		**TAP TURNS ON THE WATER**	RAK 119
04/03/1972	25	8		BROTHER	RAK 126
04/08/1973	36	5		THE BAND PLAYED THE BOOGIE	RAK 154

CECIL UK group formed in Liverpool by Steve Williams (guitar/vocals), Patrick Harrison (guitar), Anthony Hughes (guitar), Jason Bennett (bass) and Allan Lambert (drums).

25/01/1997	68	1		HOSTAGE IN A FROCK	Parlophone CDRS 6471
28/03/1998	69	1		THE MOST TIRING DAY	Parlophone CDRS 6490

CELEDA US singer (born Victoria Sharpe, Chicago, IL).

05/09/1998	36	3		MUSIC IS THE ANSWER (DANCING' & PRANCIN') **DANNY TENAGLIA AND CELEDA**	Twisted UK TWCD 10038
12/06/1999	61	1		BE YOURSELF	Twisted UK TWCD 10049
23/10/1999	50	1		MUSIC IS THE ANSWER (DANCING' & PRANCIN') **CELEDA WITH DANNY TENAGLIA**	Twisted UK TWCD 10052

CELETIA UK singer/songwriter (born Celetia Martin, London), daughter of singer Mary Martin. Her uncle is DJ Eric.

11/04/1998	29	2		REWIND	Big Life BLRD 142
08/08/1998	66	1		RUNAWAY SKIES	Big Life BLRD 144

CELTIC CHORUS – see **LISBON LIONS FEATURING MARTIN O'NEILL AND CELTIC CHORUS**

❶⁹ Number of weeks single topped the UK chart ↑ Entered the UK chart at #1 ▲⁹ Number of weeks single topped the US chart

CENOGINERZ Dutch producer Michael Pollen.

02/02/2002	75	1		GIT DOWN .... Tripoli Trax TTRAX 081CD

CENTORY US rap group formed by Alex Trime, Sven 'Delgado' Jordan and Gary Carrolla.

17/12/1994	67	1		POINT OF NO RETURN .... EMI CDEM 354

CENTRAL LINE UK funk group formed in London by Linton Breckles (vocals/percussion), Camelle Hinds (bass/vocals), Lipson Francis (keyboards) and Henry Defoe (guitar).

31/01/1981	67	3		(YOU KNOW) YOU CAN DO IT .... Mercury LINE 7
15/08/1981	42	10		WALKING INTO SUNSHINE .... Mercury MER 78
30/01/1982	55	3		DON'T TELL ME .... Mercury MER 90
20/11/1982	58	3		YOU'VE SAID ENOUGH .... Mercury MER 117
22/01/1983	21	8		NATURE BOY .... Mercury MER 131
11/06/1983	48	3		SURPRISE SURPRISE .... Mercury MER 133

CERRONE French producer/multi-instrumentalist (born Jean-Marc Cerrone, 1952, Paris) who recorded in the US and returned to France in 1983, becoming a best-selling author. He composed the music for the 1990 film *Dancing Machine*.

05/03/1977	31	4		LOVE IN C MINOR .... Atlantic K 10895
29/07/1978	8	12	O	**SUPERNATURE** Features the uncredited contributions of Stephanie De Sykes and Madeline Bell .... Atlantic K 11089
13/01/1979	39	4		JE SUIS MUSIC .... CBS 6918
10/08/1996	66	1		SUPERNATURE (REMIX) .... Encore CDCOR 013

A CERTAIN RATIO UK punk group formed in Manchester by Simon Topping (vocals/trumpet), Martin Moscrop (guitar/trumpet), Martha Tilson (vocals), Jeremy Kerr (bass), Peter Terrell (electronics) and Donald Johnson (drums). Tilson left in 1982; Topping and Terrell left in 1983 and were replaced by Andy Connell. The group signed with Factory in 1979, then A&M in 1987, though with no new material until 1989 they left the label soon after.

16/06/1990	55	3		WON'T STOP LOVING YOU .... A&M ACR 540

PETER CETERA US singer (born 13/9/1944, Chicago, IL) who was the lead singer and bass guitarist with The Exceptions before joining Chicago in 1967, with whom he stayed until 1985. He recorded his debut solo album in 1981.

02/08/1986	3	13	O	**GLORY OF LOVE** ▲² Featured in the 1986 film *Karate Kid Part II* .... Full Moon W 8662
21/06/1997	7	7		**HARD TO SAY I'M SORRY** AZ YET FEATURING PETER CETERA .... LaFace 74321481482

FRANK CHACKSFIELD UK orchestra leader (born 9/5/1914, Battle) who worked in a solicitor's office and played church organ before starting his musical career in the mid-1930s. He died on 9/6/1995. Claviolinist Jack Jordan was also a composer – he penned *Little Red Monkey*.

03/04/1953	10	3		**LITTLE RED MONKEY** FRANK CHACKSFIELD'S TUNESMITHS, FEATURING JACK JORDAN – CLAVIOLINE .... Parlophone R 3658
22/05/1953	2	24		**TERRY'S THEME FROM 'LIMELIGHT'** Written by Charlie Chaplin for his 1952 film *Limelight* .... Decca F 10106
12/02/1954	9	2		**EBB TIDE** .... Decca F 10122
24/02/1956	15	4		IN OLD LISBON .... Decca F 10689
18/05/1956	18	6		PORT AU PRINCE WINIFRED ATWELL AND FRANK CHACKSFIELD .... Decca F 10727
31/08/1956	26	2		DONKEY CART .... Decca F 10743

CHAIRMEN OF THE BOARD US R&B group formed in Detroit, MI in 1968 by ex-Showmen lead singer General Johnson (born Norman Johnson, 23/5/1944, Norfolk, VA), ex-Showmen Danny Woods (born 10/4/1944, Atlanta, GA), Eddie Curtis (born in Philadelphia, PA) and Harrison Kennedy (born in Canada, ex-Stone Soul Children) as The Gentlemen, signed to Invictus in 1969 as Chairmen Of The Board. They stopped recording in 1971, disbanding for twelve months before re-forming for live dates. Johnson went solo in 1976 but still tours with Danny Woods as The Chairmen. Johnson and Ronald Dunbar won the 1970 Grammy Award for Best Rhythm & Blues Song with Clarence Carter's hit *Patches*.

22/08/1970	3	13		**GIVE ME JUST A LITTLE MORE TIME** .... Invictus INV 501
14/11/1970	5	13		**YOU'VE GOT ME DANGLING ON A STRING** .... Invictus INV 504
20/02/1971	12	9		EVERYTHING'S TUESDAY .... Invictus INV 507
15/05/1971	34	7		PAY TO THE PIPER .... Invictus INV 511
04/09/1971	48	2		CHAIRMAN OF THE BOARD .... Invictus INV 516
15/07/1972	20	8		WORKING ON A BUILDING OF LOVE .... Invictus INV 519
07/10/1972	21	7		ELMO JAMES .... Invictus INV 524
16/12/1972	30	6		I'M ON MY WAY TO A BETTER PLACE .... Invictus INV 527
23/06/1973	21	9		FINDERS KEEPERS .... Invictus INV 530
13/09/1986	56	3		LOVERBOY CHAIRMEN OF THE BOARD FEATURING GENERAL JOHNSON .... EMI EM 5585

CHAKACHAS Belgian group supposedly formed in the late 1950s by Gaston Boogaerts, though Boogaerts didn't exist as the group were a studio creation. A New York Latino group called Barrio capitalised on the US success of *Jungle Fever*, touring as The Chakachas.

11/01/1962	48	1		TWIST TWIST .... RCA 1264
27/05/1972	29	7		JUNGLE FEVER Featured in the 1998 film *Boogie Nights* .... Polydor 2121 064

GEORGE CHAKIRIS US singer/actor (born 16/9/1934, Norwood, OH) who played Bernardo in the 1961 film version of *West Side Story*.

02/06/1960	49	1		HEART OF A SINGLE GIRL .... Triumph ROM 1010

CHAKKA BOOM BANG Dutch instrumental/production group formed by Koen Groeneveld, Addy Van Der Zwan and Jan Voermans. They also record as Klubheads, Da Techno Bohemian, Drunkenmunky, Cooper, and Itty Bitty Boozy Woozy.

20/01/1996 . . . . . 57 . . . . . . 1 . . . . . . TOSSING AND TURNING. . . . . Hooj Choons HOOJCD 39

CHAKRA UK production duo Ricky Simmons and Stephen Jones who also record as Ascension, Lustral, Oxygen and Space Brothers.

18/01/1997	24	2		I AM	WEA 091CD
23/08/1997	46	1		HOME	WEA 116CD2
23/10/1999	67	1		LOVE SHINES THROUGH	WEA 227CD
26/08/2000	47	1		HOME (REMIX)	WEA 266CD

SUE CHALONER UK singer (born 1953, London) who relocated to Holland in 1971.

22/05/1993 . . . . . 64 . . . . . . 1 . . . . . . MOVE ON UP. . . . . Pulse 8 CDLOSE 41

RICHARD CHAMBERLAIN US singer/actor (born 31/3/1935, Los Angeles, CA) who played the lead in Dr Kildare 1961–66, later starring in The Thorn Birds. He has a star on the Hollywood Walk of Fame.

07/06/1962	12	10		THEME FROM 'DR. KILDARE' (THREE STARS WILL SHINE TONIGHT) Theme to the TV series Dr Kildare	MGM 1160
01/11/1962	15	11		LOVE ME TENDER	MGM 1173
21/02/1963	20	9		HI-LILI HI-LO	MGM 1189
18/07/1963	30	6		TRUE LOVE	MGM 1205

BRYAN CHAMBERS – see CLEPTOMANIACS FEATURING BRYAN CHAMBERS

CHAMELEON UK duo Tom Middleton and Mark Pritchard.

18/05/1996 . . . . . 34 . . . . . . 2 . . . . . . THE WAY IT IS . . . . Stress CDSTR 65

CHAMELEONS – see LORI AND THE CHAMELEONS

CHAMONIX – see KURTIS MANTRONIK

CHAMPAIGN US soul group formed in Champaign, IL by Michael Day (lead vocals), Pauli Carmen (lead vocals), Rena Jones (lead vocals), Howard Reeder (guitar), Dana Walden (keyboards), Michael Reed (bass) and Rocky Maffitt (percussion), with Marshall Titus joining later.

09/05/1981 . . . . . 5 . . . . . . 13 . . . . . O **HOW 'BOUT US** . . . . CBS A 1046

CHAMPIONSHIP LEGEN – see RAZE

CHAMPS US instrumental group formed in Los Angeles, CA by Chuck Rio (born Danny Flores, saxophone), Dave Burgess (rhythm guitar), Buddy Bruce (lead guitar), Cliff Hills (bass) and Gene Alden (drums). Following a successful debut single, a new group was assembled by Rio, Burgess, Alden, Dale Norris (guitar) and Joe Burnas (bass). Flores and Alden left at the end of 1958, replaced by Jim Seals (born 17/10/1941, Sidney, TX, saxophone), Dash Crofts (born 14/8/1940, Cisco, TX, drums) and Dean Beard (piano). Burgess was later replaced by Glen Campbell (born 22/4/1936, Billstown, AR, guitar). Named after record company boss Gene Autry's horse Champion. They disbanded in 1964, with Seals and Crofts finding fame as a duo and as songwriters.

04/04/1958	5	9		**TEQUILA** ▲5 1958 Grammy Award for Best Rhythm & Blues Performance. Featured in the 1979 film The Wanderers	London HLU 8580
17/03/1960	49	1		TOO MUCH TEQUILA	London HLH 9052

CHAMPS BOYS French instrumental group assembled by Patrick Boceno.

19/06/1976 . . . . . 41 . . . . . . 6 . . . . . . TUBULAR BELLS . . . . Philips 6006 519

CHANCE – see SUNKIDS FEATURING CHANCE

GENE CHANDLER US singer (born Eugene Dixon, 6/7/1937, Chicago, IL) who was in various doo-wop groups including the Dukays before going solo in 1961 (taking the name of his favourite actor Johnny Chandler). After a US #1 with Duke Of Earl in 1962 (revived in the UK by Darts in 1979), he later launched the labels Bamboo and Mr Chand. His UK career flourished in the late 1970s disco-boom, and he subsequently recorded for Salsoul and FastFire Records.

05/06/1968	41	4		NOTHING CAN STOP ME	Soul City SC 102
03/02/1979	11	11	O	GET DOWN	20th Century BTC 1040
01/09/1979	43	5		WHEN YOU'RE NUMBER 1	20th Century TC 2411
19/07/1980	28	9		DOES SHE HAVE A FRIEND	20th Century TC 2451

CHANELLE US R&B singer (born Charlene Munford, Virginia) who later relocated to New Jersey.

11/03/1989	16	8		ONE MAN	Cooltempo COOL 183
10/12/1994	50	1		ONE MAN (REMIX)	Deep Distraxion OILYCD 031

CHANGE US group originally conceived as a studio group by French producers Jacques Fred Petrus and Mauro Malavasi, featuring Paolo Granolio (guitar) and David Romani (bass). After their first two hit singles, a group was formed with James Robinson on lead vocals. When Robinson went solo, a new group was assembled, featuring Debra Cooper (vocals), Rick Brenna (vocals), Timmy Allen (bass), Vince Henry (saxophone) and Michael Campbell (guitar). Jam and Lewis handled later production work.

28/06/1980 . . . . . 14 . . . . . . 8 . . . . . . A LOVER'S HOLIDAY/GLOW OF LOVE . . . . WEA K 79141

❶9 Number of weeks single topped the UK chart ↑ Entered the UK chart at #1 ▲9 Number of weeks single topped the US chart

143

06/09/1980	11	10		SEARCHING Features the uncredited lead vocal of Luther Vandross	WEA K 79156
02/06/1984	17	10		CHANGE OF HEART	WEA YZ 7
11/08/1984	48	4		YOU ARE MY MELODY	WEA YZ 14
16/03/1985	37	7		LET'S GO TOGETHER	Cooltempo COOL 107
25/05/1985	56	2		OH WHAT A FEELING	Cooltempo COOL 109
13/07/1985	60	2		MUTUAL ATTRACTION	Cooltempo COOL 111

CHANGING FACES
US vocal duo formed in New York by Charisse Rose and Cassandra Lucas.

24/09/1994	43	3		STROKE YOU UP	Big Beat A 8251CD
26/07/1997	10	5		G.H.E.T.T.O.U.T.	Atlantic AT 0003CD
01/11/1997	42	1		I GOT SOMEBODY ELSE Contains a sample of Average White Band's *Person To Person*. Featured in the 1996 film *High School High*	Atlantic AT 0014CD
04/04/1998	35	2		TIME AFTER TIME	Atlantic AT 0027CD
01/08/1998	53	1		SAME TEMPO Featured in the 1998 film *The Players Club*	Atlantic 5826952

BRUCE CHANNEL
US singer (born 28/11/1940, Jacksonville, TX) whose debut hit featured a distinctive harmonica part by Delbert McClinton. When Channel toured the UK in 1962, support band The Beatles were inspired to use a harmonica on their first hit *Love Me Do,* although John Lennon later denied the song's influence. Channel first recorded with the Smash label, then later with Le Cam, Mel-O-Dy and Mala.

22/03/1962	2	12		HEY! BABY ▲³	Mercury AMT 1171
26/06/1968	12	16		KEEP ON	Bell 1010

CHANNEL X
Belgian dance group formed by Olivier Adams, Corneli Van Lierop and Maurice Engelen at the Boccaccio club, Brussels.

14/12/1991	67	1		GROOVE TO MOVE	PWL Continental 209

CHANSON
US R&B group formed by James Jamerson Jr (son of the legendary Motown session musician) and David Williams plus studio musicians and session singers, named after the French for 'song'.

13/01/1979	33	7		DON'T HOLD BACK	Ariola ARO 140

CHANTAL – see MOONMAN

CHANTAYS
US group formed in high school in Santa Ana, CA in 1962 by Brian Carman (rhythm guitar), Bob Marshall (piano), Bob Spickard (lead guitar), Warren Waters (bass) and Bob Welsh (drums). Welsh was later replaced by Steve Khan (born 28/4/1947, Los Angeles, CA), who left the group in 1963 to become a session guitarist. He worked with the likes of George Benson, Maynard Ferguson, Billy Joel, Hubert Laws, Players Association and Steely Dan as well as making solo albums.

18/04/1963	16	14		PIPELINE Featured in the 1979 film *More American Graffiti*	London HLD 9696

CHANTER SISTERS
UK vocal group formed by Doreen and Irene Chanter with musical accompaniment from their five brothers. The duo later sang backing for the likes of UB40.

17/07/1976	43	5		SIDE SHOW	Polydor 2058 735

CHAOS
UK vocal group assembled by producer Nigel Wright.

03/10/1992	55	2		FAREWELL MY SUMMER LOVE	Arista 74321116397

HARRY CHAPIN
US singer (born 7/12/1942, New York) who made his first album in 1971 and had a number of US hits. He also wrote a Broadway musical and won an Emmy (US TV award) for his work on the children's series *Make A Wish*. Driving to a business meeting on 16/7/1981 he was killed on the Long Island Expressway near New York when a tractor-trailer hit the back of his car, rupturing the fuel tank and exploding. An autopsy revealed he had suffered a heart attack either immediately before or after the incident. It was also revealed that his driving licence had been suspended.

11/05/1974	34	5		W.O.L.D.	Elektra K 12133

SIMONE CHAPMAN – see ILLEGAL MOTION FEATURING SIMONE CHAPMAN

TRACY CHAPMAN
US singer (born 30/3/1964, Cleveland, OH) who graduated from Tufts University with degrees in anthropology and African studies. Her UK break came at the 1988 Nelson Mandela Birthday Show at Wembley when her set was extended owing to Stevie Wonder's enforced curtailment after his synthesiser programmes were stolen. Named Best International Female and Best International Newcomer at the 1989 BRIT Awards, her four Grammy Awards include Best New Artist in 1988, Best Contemporary Folk Recording in 1988 for *Tracy Chapman* and Best Rock Song in 1996 for *Give Me One Reason*.

11/06/1988	5	12		FAST CAR 1988 Grammy Award for Best Pop Vocal Performance	Elektra EKR 73
30/09/1989	61	3		CROSSROADS	Elektra EKR 95

CHAPTERHOUSE
UK rock group formed in Reading in 1987 by Andrew Sherriff (born 5/5/1969, Wokingham, guitar/vocals), Stephen Patman (born 8/11/1968, Windsor, guitar), Simon Rowe (born 23/6/1969, Reading, guitar), Jon Curtis (bass) and Ashley Bates (born 2/11/1971, Reading, drums). Curtis left soon after, replaced by Russell Barrett (born 7/11/1968, Vermont, US).

30/03/1991	67	1		PEARL	Dedicated STONE 003
12/10/1991	60	2		MESMERISE	Dedicated HOUSE 001

CHAQUITO ORCHESTRA
UK orchestra arranged and produced by Johnny Gregory.

27/10/1960	50	1		NEVER ON SUNDAY	Fontana H 265

○ Silver disc ● Gold disc ✪ Platinum disc (additional platinum units are indicated by a figure following the symbol) ◎ Singles released prior to 1973 that are known to have sold over 1 million copies in the UK

CHARLATANS
UK rock group formed in Manchester by Tim Burgess (born 30/5/1968, Salford, vocals), Martin Blunt (born 21/5/1964, bass), Jon Baker (born 1969, guitar), Jon Brookes (born 21/9/1968, drums) and Rob Collins (born 23/2/1963, Sedgeley, keyboards). Blunt suffered a nervous breakdown in 1991, while Baker left the group, replaced by Mark Collins (born 14/8/1965, guitar), the same year. Rob Collins was involved in an armed robbery and jailed for eight months in 1993, and killed in a road accident (while over twice the legal alcohol limit) on 22/7/1996. He was replaced by Tony Rodgers.

DATE	POS	WKS	SINGLE TITLE	LABEL & NUMBER
02/06/1990	9	9	**THE ONLY ONE I KNOW**	Situation Two SIT 70T
22/09/1990	12	5	THEN	Situation Two SIT 74T
09/03/1991	15	5	OVER RISING	Situation Two SIT 76
17/08/1991	57	1	INDIAN ROPE	Dead Dead Good GOOD 1T
09/11/1991	28	3	ME. IN TIME	Situation Two SIT 84
07/03/1992	19	4	WEIRDO	Situation Two SIT 88
18/07/1992	44	2	TREMELO SONG (EP) Tracks on EP: *Tremelo Song, Happen To Die* and *Normality Swing*	Situation Two SIT 97T
05/02/1994	24	3	CAN'T GET OUT OF BED	Beggars Banquet BBQ 27CD
19/03/1994	38	1	I NEVER WANT AN EASY LIFE IF ME AND HE WERE EVER TO GET THERE	Beggars Banquet BBQ 31CD
02/07/1994	48	2	JESUS HAIRDO	Beggars Banquet BBQ 32CD
07/01/1995	31	2	CRASHIN' IN.	Beggars Banquet BBQ 44CD
27/05/1995	32	3	JUST LOOKIN'/BULLET COMES	Beggars Banquet BBQ 55CD
26/08/1995	12	3	JUST WHEN YOU'RE THINKING THINGS OVER.	Beggars Banquet BBQ 60CD
07/09/1996	3	6	**ONE TO ANOTHER.**	Beggars Banquet BBQ 301CD
05/04/1997	4	6	**NORTH COUNTRY BOY**	Beggars Banquet BBQ 309CD
21/06/1997	6	5	**HOW HIGH**	Beggars Banquet BBQ 312CD
01/11/1997	16	3	TELLIN' STORIES.	Beggars Banquet BBQ 318CD
16/10/1999	12	3	FOREVER.	Universal MCSTD 40220
18/12/1999	31	3	MY BEAUTIFUL FRIEND	Universal MCSTD 40225
27/05/2000	15	3	IMPOSSIBLE	Universal MCSTXD 40231
08/09/2001	16	3	LOVE IS THE KEY	Universal MCSTD 40262
01/12/2001	31	2	A MAN NEEDS TO BE TOLD	Universal MCSTD 40271
22/05/2004	23	3	UP AT THE LAKE	Universal MCSTD 40363
07/08/2004	24	3	TRY AGAIN TODAY	Universal MCSTD 40370

CHARLENE
US singer (born Charlene D'Angelo, later Duncan, 1/6/1950, Hollywood, CA) whose debut hit had originally been released in 1977 on the Motown subsidiary Prodigal and was revived in the US following extensive plays on a Tampa, FL radio station. She later recorded with Stevie Wonder.

DATE	POS	WKS	SINGLE TITLE	LABEL & NUMBER
15/05/1982	❶¹	12	○	**I'VE NEVER BEEN TO ME** Featured in the 1994 film *The Adventures Of Priscilla: Queen Of The Desert*	Motown TMG 1260

ALEX CHARLES — see DJ INNOCENCE FEATURING ALEX CHARLES

DON CHARLES
UK singer who made his first record for Parlophone. His backing group later became The Tornados, and he later wrote with producer Joe Meek.

DATE	POS	WKS	SINGLE TITLE	LABEL & NUMBER
22/02/1962	39	5	WALK WITH ME MY ANGEL	Decca F 11424

RAY CHARLES
US singer (born Ray Charles Robinson, 23/9/1930, Albany, GA) who moved to Greenville, FL while still a child. Partially blinded at five and totally blind at seven due to glaucoma, after the death of both parents in 1948 he became a full-time musician and moved to Seattle, WA and then on to Los Angeles, CA. After debut records in 1949 for Swingtime, he switched to Atlantic in 1952 and had many US soul and pop hits over the next eight years. He signed for ABC in 1960, founding the Tangerine label (through ABC) in 1968 and changing its name to Crossover in 1973. He toured relentlessly with his own band and backing singers The Raelettes. Thirteen Grammy Awards include: Best Male Vocal Performance Album in 1960 for *The Genius Of Ray Charles;* Best Rhythm & Blues Performance in 1960 for *Let The Good Times Roll;* Best Vocal Performance Album in 1961 for *The Genius Of Ray Charles;* Best Rhythm & Blues Vocal Performance in 1975 for *Living For The City;* and Best Rhythm & Blues Male Vocal Performance in 1993 for *A Song For You.* He was inducted into the Rock & Roll Hall of Fame in 1986. Ray was the only artist to appear in advertisements for both Coca-Cola and Pepsi Cola, in 1969 and 1992 respectively. He has a star on the Hollywood Walk of Fame and died from liver disease on 9/6/2004.

DATE	POS	WKS	SINGLE TITLE	LABEL & NUMBER
01/12/1960	24	8	GEORGIA ON MY MIND ▲¹ 1960 Grammy Awards for Best Male Vocal Performance Single or Track and Best Performance by a Pop Single Artist	HMV POP 792
19/10/1961	6	12	**HIT THE ROAD JACK** ▲² 1961 Grammy Award for Best Rhythm & Blues Recording	HMV POP 935
14/06/1962	❶²	17	**I CAN'T STOP LOVING YOU** ▲⁵ 1962 Grammy Award for Best Rhythm & Blues Recording	HMV POP 1034
13/09/1962	9	13	**YOU DON'T KNOW ME**	HMV POP 1064
13/12/1962	13	8	YOUR CHEATING HEART	HMV POP 1099
28/03/1963	37	3	DON'T SET ME FREE	HMV POP 1133
16/05/1963	5	20	**TAKE THESE CHAINS FROM MY HEART**	HMV POP 1161
12/09/1963	35	7	NO ONE	HMV POP 1202
31/10/1963	21	10	BUSTED 1963 Grammy Award for Best Rhythm & Blues Recording	HMV POP 1221
24/09/1964	38	3	NO ONE TO CRY TO	HMV POP 1333
21/01/1965	42	4	MAKIN' WHOOPEE	HMV POP 1383
10/02/1966	50	1	CRYIN' TIME 1966 Grammy Awards for Best Rhythm & Blues Recording and Best Rhythm & Blues Solo Vocal Performance	HMV POP 1502
21/04/1966	48	1	TOGETHER AGAIN	HMV POP 1519
05/07/1966	38	3	HERE WE GO AGAIN.	HMV POP 1595
20/12/1967	44	4	YESTERDAY	Stateside SS 2071
31/07/1968	36	9	ELEANOR RIGBY	Stateside SS 2170

❶⁹ Number of weeks single topped the UK chart ↑ Entered the UK chart at #1 ▲⁹ Number of weeks single topped the US chart

13/01/1990.....21......7....... I'LL BE GOOD TO YOU QUINCY JONES FEATURING RAY CHARLES AND CHAKA KHAN 1990 Grammy Award for Best Rhythm & Blues
Vocal Performance by a Duo .... Qwest W 2697

SUZETTE CHARLES US singer first known as a beauty queen who was crowned Miss Jersey and then Miss America in 1984 (after Vanessa Williams was forced to resign following the publication of nude photographs).
21/08/1993.....58......2....... FREE TO LOVE AGAIN .... RCA 74321158372

TINA CHARLES UK singer (born Tina Hoskins, 10/3/1954, London) who was working as a session musician in 1975 when she sang lead on a track called *I'm On Fire*, later released under the group name 5000 Volts. A different person was chosen for their TV performances, so Tina went solo, with production handled by Biddu. Her touring band included Trevor Horn and Geoff Downes, who later formed Buggles.
07/02/1976 .... ●³... 12 ..... ● **I LOVE TO LOVE (BUT MY BABY LOVES TO DANCE)** .... CBS 3937
01/05/1976...31......7...... LOVE ME LIKE A LOVER .... CBS 4237
21/08/1976.....6......13.....○ **DANCE LITTLE LADY DANCE** .... CBS 4480
04/12/1976.....4......10.....○ **DR LOVE** .... CBS 4779
14/05/1977...27......6...... RENDEZVOUS .... CBS 5174
29/10/1977...26......4...... LOVE BUG – SWEETS FOR MY SWEET (MEDLEY) .... CBS 5680
11/03/1978...27......8...... I'LL GO WHERE YOUR MUSIC TAKES ME .... CBS 6062
30/08/1986...67......3...... I LOVE TO LOVE (REMIX) .... DMC DECK 1

CHARLES AND EDDIE US duo Charles Pettigrew (from Philadelphia, PA) and Eddie Chacon (from Oakland, CA) who discovered a mutual interest in soul music after meeting on the New York subway. Chacon had been with The Dust Brothers and Daddy-O, Pettigrew with Down Avenue. Pettigrew died from cancer on 6/4/2001 at the age of 37.
31/10/1992 .... ●²... 17 ..... ✪ **WOULD I LIE TO YOU** .... Capitol CL 673
20/02/1993.....33......5...... N.Y.C. (CAN YOU BELIEVE THIS CITY) .... Capitol CDCL 681
22/05/1993.....29......4...... HOUSE IS NOT A HOME .... Capitol CDCLS 688
13/05/1995.....38......4...... 24-7-365 .... Capitol CDCLS 747

DICK CHARLESWORTH AND HIS CITY GENTS UK jazz group formed by Dick Charlesworth (clarinet/vocals), Robert Henry Masters (trumpet), Cyril Preston trombone/vocals), Bill Dixon (banjo), Graham Beazley (bass) and Ron Darby (drums).
04/05/1961.....43......1....... BILLY BOY .... Top Rank JAR 558

CHARLI 2NA – see DJ FORMAT FEATURING CHARLI 2NA AND AKIL

CHARLISE – see KID CRÈME

CHARLOTTE UK singer Charlotte Kelly.
12/03/1994.....54......1....... QUEEN OF HEARTS .... Big Life BLRD 106
02/05/1998.....59......1....... BE MINE .... Parlophone Rhythm CDRHYTHM 10
29/05/1999.....56......1....... SKIN .... Parlophone Rhythm CDRHYTHM 20
04/09/1999.....74......1....... SOMEDAY .... Parlophone Rhythm CDRHYTHM 23

CHARME US vocal group assembled by Jorge Alberto Pino and featuring Luther Vandross on lead vocals.
17/11/1984.....68......2....... GEORGY PORGY .... RCA 464

CHARO AND THE SALSOUL ORCHESTRA US singer (born Maria Rosario Pilar Martinez, 15/1/1942, Murcia, Spain).
29/04/1978.....44......4....... DANCE A LITTLE BIT CLOSER.. Salsoul SSOL 101

CHARVONI – see BROTHERS IN RHYTHM

CHAS AND DAVE UK duo Charles Hodges (born 28/12/1943, London, piano) and Dave Peacock (born 25/5/1945, London, guitar); their mix of rock and Cockney humour was dubbed Rockney (also the nickname of their drummer Mickey Burt). First known through TV commercials, they also made the Tottenham Hotspur hit singles. The Matchroom Mob are snooker players Steve Davis, Tony Griffiths, Tony Meo, Dennis Taylor and Willie Thorne.
11/11/1978.....52......3....... STRUMMIN' CHAS AND DAVE WITH ROCKNEY .... EMI 2874
26/05/1979.....20......8....... GERTCHA .... EMI 2947
01/09/1979.....55......3....... THE SIDEBOARD SONG (GOT MY BEER IN THE SIDEBOARD HERE) .... EMI 2986
29/11/1980 .....8......11.....○ **RABBIT** .... Rockney 9
12/12/1981.....21......8....... STARS OVER 45 .... Rockney KOR 12
13/03/1982 .....2......11.....○ **AIN'T NO PLEASING YOU** .... Rockney KOR 14
17/07/1982.....46......4....... MARGATE .... Rockney KOR 15
19/03/1983.....63......3....... LONDON GIRLS .... Rockney KOR 17
03/12/1983.....51......6....... MY MELANCHOLY BABY .... Rockney KOR 21
10/05/1986 .....6......9....... **SNOOKER LOOPY** MATCHROOM MOB WITH CHAS AND DAVE .... Rockney POT 147

JC CHASEZ US singer (born Joshua Scott Chasez, 8/8/1976, Washington DC) who was a founder member of N Sync and went solo in 2004.
10/04/2004.....22......4....... PLUG IT IN BASEMENT JAXX FEATURING JC CHASEZ .... XL Recordings XLS 180CD
24/04/2004.....13......6....... SOME GIRLS/BLOWIN' ME UP .... Jive 82876605442

CHEAP TRICK US rock group formed in Rockford, IL by Bun E Carlos (born Brad Carlson, 12/6/1951, Rockford, drums), Rick

○ Silver disc ● Gold disc ✪ Platinum disc (additional platinum units are indicated by a figure following the symbol) ◉ Singles released prior to 1973 that are known to have sold over 1 million copies in the UK

Nielsen (born 22/12/1946, Rockford, guitar), Tom Petersson (born 9/5/1950, Rockford, bass) and Robin Zender (born 23/1/1953, Loves Park, IL, vocals). Petersson was replaced by Jon Brant in 1980, returning in 1988.

05/05/1979	29	9		I WANT YOU TO WANT ME	Epic EPC 7258
02/02/1980	73	2		WAY OF THE WORLD	Epic EPC 8114
31/07/1982	57	3		IF YOU WANT MY LOVE	Epic EPC A 2406

OLIVER CHEATHAM
US singer (born 1948, Detroit, MI) who was lead singer with Sins Of Satan who subsequently recorded as Round Trip. Later recording for Critique and Warlock Records, and with Jocelyn Brown, his hit with Room 5 originally featured a sample of *Get Down Saturday Tonight* but Cheatham subsequently re-recorded his vocal parts.

02/07/1983	38	5		GET DOWN SATURDAY NIGHT	MCA 828
05/04/2003	❶4	15	○	**MAKE LUV** ↑ Used in a TV advertisement for Lynx deodorant	Positiva CDTIV 187
06/12/2003	38	2		MUSIC AND YOU This and above single credited to **ROOM 5 FEATURING OLIVER CHEATHAM**	Positiva CDTIVS 197

CHECK 1-2 – see CRAIG McLACHLAN

CHUBBY CHECKER
US singer (born Ernest Evans, 3/10/1941, Andrews, SC) raised in Philadelphia, PA where he was working at a chicken market when he signed with the Cameo Parkway label. His debut single *The Class* featured impersonations of Fats Domino, the Coasters, Elvis Presley, Cozy Cole and the Chipmunks, before Dick Clark, host of top TV show *American Bandstand*, suggested he cover Hank Ballard's *The Twist*. Checker's version swept to #1 in the US, while his most popular UK hit, *Let's Twist Again*, was originally released in the US on the first anniversary of *The Twist*.

22/09/1960	44	2		THE TWIST ▲3 Featured in the 1988 film *Scandal*	Columbia DB 4503
30/03/1961	27	6		PONY TIME ▲3	Columbia DB 4591
17/08/1961	37	3		LET'S TWIST AGAIN 1961 Grammy Award for Best Rock & Roll Recording	Columbia DB 4691
28/12/1961	2	31		**LET'S TWIST AGAIN**	Columbia DB 4691
11/01/1962	14	10		THE TWIST	Columbia DB 4503
05/04/1962	23	8		SLOW TWISTIN' Features the uncredited vocals of Dee Dee Sharp	Columbia DB 4808
19/04/1962	45	1		TEACH ME TO TWIST	Columbia DB 4802
09/08/1962	19	13		DANCIN' PARTY Gary 'US' Bonds sued for plagiarism for $100,000 over the similarities between this and his hit *Quarter To Three*; the matter eventually settled out of court	Columbia DB 4876
01/11/1962	32	10		LIMBO ROCK	Cameo Parkway P 849
20/12/1962	40	3		JINGLE BELL ROCK CHUBBY CHECKER AND BOBBY RYDELL	Cameo Parkway C 205
31/10/1963	37	4		WHAT DO YA SAY	Cameo Parkway P 806
29/11/1975	5	10	○	**LET'S TWIST AGAIN/THE TWIST**	London HL 10512
18/06/1988	2	11		**THE TWIST (YO, TWIST)** FAT BOYS AND CHUBBY CHECKER	Urban URB 20

CHECKMATES – see EMILE FORD AND THE CHECKMATES

CHECKMATES LTD.
US vocal group formed in Fort Wayne, IN by Sonny Charles, Bobby Stevens, Harvey Trees, Bill Van Buskirk and Marvin Smith. Charles later recorded solo.

15/11/1969	30	8		PROUD MARY	A&M AMS 769

JUDY CHEEKS
US singer (born in Miami, FL), daughter of gospel singer and preacher Reverend Julius Cheeks, who had a US R&B hit in 1978 but only made the UK charts fifteen years later. She appeared in the 1980 film *La Playa Del Amor*.

13/11/1993	27	3		SO IN LOVE (THE REAL DEAL)	Positiva CDTIV 6
07/05/1994	17	4		REACH	Positiva CDTIV 12
04/03/1995	23	2		THIS TIME/RESPECT	Positiva CDTIV 28
17/06/1995	30	3		YOU'RE THE STORY OF MY LIFE/AS LONG AS YOU'RE GOOD TO ME	Positiva CDTIV 34
13/01/1996	22	3		REACH (REMIX)	Positiva CDTIV 42

CHEEKY GIRLS
Romanian duo, twin sisters Monica and Gabriela Irimia (born 31/10/1982, Transylvania), Gabriela being older by ten minutes. They attracted attention after auditioning for *Popstars* where Pete Waterman rated them the worst act ever.

14/12/2002	2	14	○	**CHEEKY SONG (TOUCH MY BUM)**	Multiply CDMULTY 97
17/05/2003	3	10		**TAKE YOUR SHOES OFF**	Multiply CXMULTY 101
16/08/2003	3	7		**HOORAY HOORAY (IT'S A CHEEKY HOLIDAY)**	Multiply CXMULTY 106
20/12/2003	10	5		**HAVE A CHEEKY CHRISTMAS**	Multiply CXMULTY 110
09/10/2004	29	2		CHEEKY FLAMENCO	XBN XBNCD1
18/12/2004	50	2+		BOYS AND GIRLS	XBN XBNCDS3

CHEETAHS
UK group formed by Ray Bridger (guitar/vocals), Nigel Wright (guitar), Rodney Wright (bass) and Evan Rose (drums).

01/10/1964	36	3		MECCA	Philips BF 1362
21/01/1965	39	3		SOLDIER BOY	Philips BF 1383

CHEF
US cartoon character Jerome 'Chef' McElroy from the TV series *South Park*. The actual singer on the record is Isaac Hayes (born 20/8/1942, Covington, TN).

26/12/1998	❶1	13	✪	**CHOCOLATE SALTY BALLS (PS I LOVE YOU)**	Columbia 6667985

CHELSEA F.C.
UK professional football club formed in London in 1905. The records were released to coincide with appearances in League and FA Cup finals.

26/02/1972	5	12		**BLUE IS THE COLOUR**	Penny Farthing PEN 782

❶9 Number of weeks single topped the UK chart ↑ Entered the UK chart at #1 ▲9 Number of weeks single topped the US chart

14/05/1994	23	3		NO ONE CAN STOP US NOW	RCA 74321210452
17/05/1997	22	5		BLUE DAY SUGGS AND CO FEATURING CHELSEA TEAM	WEA 112CD
27/05/2000	22	2		BLUE TOMORROW	Telstar TV CFCCD 2000

CHEMICAL BROTHERS
UK acid house/hip hop duo Ed Simons (born 9/6/1970, Oxford) and Tom Rowlands (born 11/1/1971, Kingston) who formed as The Dust Brothers in 1994 and became the Chemical Brothers in 1995. Named Best UK Dance Act at the 2000 BRIT Awards.

17/06/1995	17	4		LEAVE HOME Featured in the 2000 film *Gone In 60 Seconds*	Junior Boy's Own CHEMSD 1
09/09/1995	25	3		LIFE IS SWEET Features the uncredited lead vocal of Tim Burgess of The Charlatans	Junior Boy's Own CHEMSDX 2
27/01/1996	13	1		LOOPS OF FURY EP Tracks on EP: *Loops Of Fury, Breaking Up, Get Up On It Like This* and *Chemical Beats*	Freestyle Dust CHEMSD 3
12/10/1996	❶[1]	7	○	SETTING SUN ↑ Includes the uncredited lead vocal of Noel Gallagher (Oasis). Featured in the 1997 film *The Saint*	Virgin CHEMSD 4
05/04/1997	❶[1]	7		BLOCK ROCKIN' BEATS ↑ Contains a sample of Schoolly D's *Gucci Again*. 1997 Grammy Award for Best Rock Instrumental Performance	Virgin CHEMSD 5
20/09/1997	17	4		ELEKTROBANK	Virgin CHEMSD 6
12/06/1999	3	10	○	HEY BOY HEY GIRL Contains a sample of Rockmaster Scott and the Brothers' *The Roof Is On Fire (Scratchin')*.	Virgin CHEMSD 8
14/08/1999	9	7		LET FOREVER BE Includes the uncredited lead vocal of Noel Gallagher (Oasis) and was featured in the 2000 film *There's Only One Jimmy Grimble*	Virgin CHEMSD 9
23/10/1999	21	4		OUT OF CONTROL	Virgin CHEMSD 10
22/09/2001	8	6		IT BEGAN IN AFRIKA	Virgin CHEMSD 12
26/01/2002	8	8		STAR GUITAR	Virgin CHEMSD 14
04/05/2002	14	3		COME WITH US/THE TEST	Virgin CHEMSD 15
27/09/2003	17	4		THE GOLDEN PATH CHEMICAL BROTHERS FEATURING THE FLAMING LIPS	Virgin CHEMSD 18

CHEQUERS
UK disco group formed in Aylesbury by John Mathias (producer/bass), Richard Mathias (guitar), Paul War (keyboards), George Young (drums), Jackie Robins (vocals) – who was not on their debut hit – and Andy (flute).

18/10/1975	21	5		ROCK ON BROTHER	Creole CR 111
28/02/1976	32	5		HEY MISS PAYNE	Creole CR 116

CHER
US singer (born Cherilyn Sarkasian LaPierre, 20/5/1946, El Centro, CA) who began as a backing singer for Phil Spector. She later worked solo as Bonnie Jo Mason (her first single was *Ringo I Love You*, a Beatlemania cash-in) and Cherilyn, teaming up with Sonny Bono in 1963 as Caesar & Cleo. The duo (who later married) recorded as Sonny And Cher from 1963 to 1974, both also pursuing solo projects from 1965 onwards, Cher with most success. Divorcing Sonny in 1974, her marriage to Greg Allman in 1975 lasted just 10 days. They were divorced in 1979. Film parts included *Mask* (1974), *The Witches Of Eastwick* (1987) and *Moonstruck* (1987), for which she won an Oscar as Best Actress. Beavis and Butt-Head are MTV cartoon heroes who also feature in the 1996 film *Beavis And Butt-Head Do America*.

19/08/1965	9	10		ALL I REALLY WANT TO DO	Liberty LIB 66114
31/03/1966	3	12		BANG BANG (MY BABY SHOT ME DOWN)	Liberty LIB 66160
04/08/1966	43	2		I FEEL SOMETHING IN THE AIR	Liberty LIB 12034
22/09/1966	32	5		SUNNY	Liberty LIB 12083
06/11/1971	4	13		GYPSYS TRAMPS AND THIEVES ▲[2]	MCA MU 1142
16/02/1974	36	4		DARK LADY ▲[1]	MCA 101
19/12/1987	5	10		I FOUND SOMEONE	Geffen GEF 31
02/04/1988	47	5		WE ALL SLEEP ALONE	Geffen GEF 35
02/09/1989	6	14		IF I COULD TURN BACK TIME	Geffen GEF 59
13/01/1990	11	11		JUST LIKE JESSE JAMES	Geffen GEF 69
07/04/1990	43	5		HEART OF STONE	Geffen GEF 75
11/08/1990	55	3		YOU WOULDN'T KNOW LOVE	Geffen GEF 77
13/04/1991	❶[5]	15	●	THE SHOOP SHOOP SONG (IT'S IN HIS KISS) Featured in the 1990 film *Mermaids*	Epic 6566737
13/07/1991	10	8		LOVE AND UNDERSTANDING	Geffen GFS 5
12/10/1991	37	5		SAVE UP ALL YOUR TEARS	Geffen GFS 11
07/12/1991	43	5		LOVE HURTS	Geffen GFS 16
18/04/1992	31	4		COULD'VE BEEN YOU	Geffen GFS 19
14/11/1992	33	4		OH NO NOT MY BABY	Geffen GFS 29
16/01/1993	37	3		MANY RIVERS TO CROSS	Geffen GFSTD 31
06/03/1993	72	1		WHENEVER YOU'RE NEAR	Geffen GFSTD 32
15/01/1994	35	3		I GOT YOU BABE CHER WITH BEAVIS AND BUTT-HEAD	Geffen GFSTD 64
18/03/1995	❶[1]	8	○	LOVE CAN BUILD A BRIDGE CHER, CHRISSIE HYNDE AND NENEH CHERRY WITH ERIC CLAPTON Released in aid of the Comic Relief charity	London COCD 1
28/10/1995	11	7		WALKING IN MEMPHIS	WEA 021CD1
20/01/1996	7	9		ONE BY ONE	WEA 032CD
27/04/1996	31	2		NOT ENOUGH LOVE IN THE WORLD	WEA 052CD
17/08/1996	26	3		THE SUN AIN'T GONNA SHINE ANYMORE	WEA 071CD
31/10/1998	❶[7]	28	✪[2]	BELIEVE ↑ ▲[4] 1999 Grammy Award for Best Pop Dance Performance. Sold over 1.5 million copies in the UK and is the biggest-selling single by a female solo artist	WEA 175CD

DATE	POS	WKS	BPI	SINGLE TITLE	LABEL & NUMBER
06/03/1999	5	10	O	STRONG ENOUGH	WEA 201CD
19/06/1999	12	7		ALL OR NOTHING	WEA 212CD1
06/11/1999	21	3		DOV'E L'AMORE	WEA 230CD1
17/11/2001	8	10		THE MUSIC'S NO GOOD WITHOUT YOU	WEA 337CD

CHERI Canadian vocal duo formed in Montreal by Rosalind Milligan Hunt and Amy Roslyn, although Hunt and Lyn Cullerier recorded the single.

19/06/1982	13	9		MURPHY'S LAW	Polydor POSP 459

CHEROKEES UK group formed in Worcester by John Kirby (vocals), David Dower (guitar), Terry Stokes (guitar), Mike Sweeney (bass) and Jim Green (drums).

03/09/1964	33	5		SEVEN DAFFODILS	Columbia DB 7341

CHERRELLE US singer (born Cheryl Norton, 13/10/1958, Los Angeles, CA) who, after moving to Detroit, MI with her family, was invited by next-door neighbour Michael Henderson to sing on his *Night Time* album and spent the next four years touring. Back in Los Angeles she was signed by Tabu and was teamed with the Jam and Lewis hit production team. Also a capable drummer, she is the cousin of singer Pebbles.

28/12/1985	6	11		SATURDAY LOVE CHERRELLE WITH ALEXANDER O'NEAL	Tabu A 6829
01/03/1986	57	3		WILL YOU SATISFY?	Tabu A 6927
06/02/1988	26	7		NEVER KNEW LOVE LIKE THIS ALEXANDER O'NEAL FEATURING CHERRELLE	Tabu 6513827
06/05/1989	67	2		AFFAIR	Tabu 6546737
24/03/1990	55	2		SATURDAY LOVE (REMIX) CHERRELLE WITH ALEXANDER O'NEAL	Tabu 6558007
02/08/1997	56	1		BABY COME TO ME ALEXANDER O'NEAL FEATURING CHERRELLE	One World Entertainment OWECD 1

DON CHERRY US singer (born 11/1/1924, Wichita Falls, TX) who was with Jan Garber's band in the 1940s and also a professional golfer. He died on 19/10/1995.

10/02/1956	6	11		BAND OF GOLD	Philips PB 549

EAGLE-EYE CHERRY US singer (born 7/5/1969, Stockholm, Sweden), son of jazz musician Don Cherry (not the singer listed above) and stepbrother of Neneh Cherry. After auditioning with MTV as a DJ, he made his debut album in 1997 for Swedish label Superstudio/Diesel, winning the Select North award at the 1998 MTV Europe Music Awards.

04/07/1998	6	13	O	SAVE TONIGHT	Polydor 5695952
14/11/1998	8	8		FALLING IN LOVE AGAIN	Polydor 5630252
20/03/1999	43	1		PERMANENT YEARS	Polydor 5636752
29/04/2000	21	4		ARE YOU STILL HAVING FUN?	Polydor 5618032
11/11/2000	48	2		LONG WAY AROUND EAGLE-EYE CHERRY FEATURING NENEH CHERRY	Polydor 5677812

NENEH CHERRY US singer (born 10/8/1964, Stockholm, Sweden) of Swedish and West African parents, raised in New York City. The stepdaughter of jazz trumpeter (not the singer) Don Cherry, she was previously in the jazz trio Rip Rig And Panic. She was named Best International Female and Best International Newcomer at the 1990 BRIT Awards and is married to producer Cameron McVey.

10/12/1988	3	13	O	BUFFALO STANCE Featured in the 1989 film *Slaves Of New York*	Circa YR 21
20/05/1989	5	10		MANCHILD	Circa YR 30
12/08/1989	20	6		KISSES ON THE WIND	Circa YR 33
23/12/1989	31	7		INNA CITY MAMMA	Circa YR 42
29/09/1990	25	5		I'VE GOT YOU UNDER MY SKIN	Circa YR 53
03/10/1992	23	4		MONEY LOVE	Circa YR 83
19/06/1993	35	3		BUDDY X Contains a sample of Juicy's *Sugar Free*	Circa YRCD 98
25/06/1994	3	25	O	7 SECONDS YOUSSOU N'DOUR (FEATURING NENEH CHERRY) 1994 MTV Europe Music Award for Best Song for writers Youssou N'Dour, Neneh Cherry and Cameron McVey	Columbia 6605082
18/03/1995	❶[1]	8	O	LOVE CAN BUILD A BRIDGE CHER, CHRISSIE HYNDE AND NENEH CHERRY WITH ERIC CLAPTON Released in aid of the Comic Relief Charity	London COCD 1
03/08/1996	9	7		WOMAN	Hut HUTD 70
14/12/1996	38	2		KOOTCHI	Hut HUTCD 75
22/02/1997	68	1		FEEL IT	Hut HUTCD 79
06/11/1999	15	5		BUDDY X 99 DREEM TEEM VS NENEH CHERRY	4 Liberty LIBTCD33
11/11/2000	48	2		LONG WAY AROUND EAGLE-EYE CHERRY FEATURING NENEH CHERRY	Polydor 5677812

CHERRYFALLS UK rock group formed by Joe McAdam (guitar/vocals), Adrian Woodward (guitar), Jim Lewis (bass) and Reuben Humphries (drums).

14/08/2004	64	1		STANDING WATCHING	Island CID 868

CORY CHESTNUTT – see ROOTS

CHIC US R&B group formed by Bernard Edwards (born 31/10/1952, Greensville, NC) and Nile Rodgers (born 19/9/1952, New York), who teamed with Tony Thompson (born 15/11/1954) in 1972 and formed The Big Apple Band, a rock-fusion group that backed the likes of New York City and Carol Douglas. Singer Norma Jean Wright joined in 1976 but was soon replaced by Luci Martin (born 10/1/1955). Known as Allah And The Knife-Wielding Punks, they then added another singer, Alfa Anderson (born 7/9/1946), to the line-up and became Chic. As top production team of the era, Rodgers and Edwards produced albums for Diana Ross, Sister Sledge, Norma Jean Wright, Sheila B Devotion and later David Bowie and Madonna. The group disbanded in 1983, re-forming in 1992 with singers Sylvester

❶[9] Number of weeks single topped the UK chart ↑ Entered the UK chart at #1 ▲[9] Number of weeks single topped the US chart

149

Logan Sharp and Jenn Thomas. Bernard Edwards was found dead in a hotel room on 18/4/1996, during a Japanese tour, the cause of death given as pneumonia. Tony Thompson died from renal cell cancer 12/11/2003.

26/11/1977	6	12	O	**DANCE DANCE DANCE (YOWSAH YOWSAH YOWSAH)** Featured in the 1998 film *54*	Atlantic K 11038
01/04/1978	9	11		**EVERYBODY DANCE** Featured in the 1999 film *Summer Of Sam*. This and above single feature Luther Vandross on backing vocals . . .	Atlantic K 11097
18/11/1978	7	16	●	**LE FREAK** ▲6 Featured in the 2004 film *Shrek 2*	Atlantic K 11209
24/02/1979	4	11		**I WANT YOUR LOVE** Featured in the 1982 film *Soup For One*	Atlantic LV 16
30/06/1979	5	11		**GOOD TIMES** ▲1 Featured in the 1998 film *The Last Days Of Disco*	Atlantic K 11310
13/10/1979	15	8		MY FORBIDDEN LOVER	Atlantic K 11385
08/12/1979	21	9		MY FEET KEEP DANCING	Atlantic K 11415
12/03/1983	64	1		HANGIN'	Atlantic A 9898
19/09/1987	19	6		JACK LE FREAK	Atlantic A 9198
14/07/1990	58	2		MEGACHIC – CHIC MEDLEY	East West A 7949
15/02/1992	48	3		CHIC MYSTIQUE	Warner Brothers W 0083

CHICAGO US rock group formed in Chicago, IL in 1966 by Peter Cetera (born 13/9/1944, Chicago, bass/vocals), Robert Lamm (born 13/10/1944, Brooklyn, NY, keyboards), Terry Kath (born 31/1/1946, Chicago, guitar), Danny Seraphine (born 28/8/1948, Chicago, drums), James Pankow (born 20/8/1947, Chicago, trombone), Lee Loughnane (born 21/10/1946, Chicago, trumpet), Walter Parazaider (born 14/3/1945, Chicago, reeds) and Laudir de Oliveira (percussion) as Big Thing. After legal threats from the Chicago transport department, their 1967 name-change to Chicago Transit Authority was amended to Chicago a few months later. Kath shot himself to death, cleaning a gun he thought was unloaded, on 23/1/1978; he was replaced by Donnie Dacus. Bill Champlin (keyboards) joined in 1982. Cetera went solo in 1985 and was replaced by Jason Scheff; DaWayne Bailey joined in 1989 as replacement for Seraphine. They have a star on the Hollywood Walk of Fame.

10/01/1970	8	11		**I'M A MAN CHICAGO TRANSIT AUTHORITY**	CBS 4715
18/07/1970	7	13		**25 OR 6 TO 4**	CBS 5076
09/10/1976	❶3	16	●	**IF YOU LEAVE ME NOW** ▲2 1976 Grammy Award for Best Pop Vocal Performance by a Group	CBS 4603
05/11/1977	41	3		BABY WHAT A BIG SURPRISE	CBS 5672
21/08/1982	4	15	O	**HARD TO SAY I'M SORRY** ▲2 Featured in the 1982 film *Summer Lovers*	Full Moon K 79301
27/10/1984	8	13		**HARD HABIT TO BREAK**	Full Moon W 9214
26/01/1985	14	10		YOU'RE THE INSPIRATION	Warner Brothers W 9126

CHICANE UK production artist Nick Bracegirdle who also records as the Disco Citizens and later launched the Modena Records and Cyanide Music labels.

21/12/1996	14	7		OFFSHORE	Xtravaganza 0091005 EXT
14/06/1997	21	3		SUNSTROKE	Xtravaganza 0091125 EXT
13/09/1997	17	4		OFFSHORE '97 **CHICANE WITH THE POWER CIRCLE** Effectively two songs made into one: *Offshore* by Chicane and *A Little Love* by Power Circle	Xtravaganza 0091255 EXT
20/12/1997	35	3		LOST YOU SOMEWHERE	Xtravaganza 0091415 EXT
10/10/1998	32	2		STRONG IN LOVE **CHICANE FEATURING MASON**	Xtravaganza 0091675 EXT
05/06/1999	6	10		**SALTWATER CHICANE FEATURING MAIRE BRENNAN OF CLANNAD** Effectively two songs made into one: *Saltwater* by Chicane and *Theme From Harry's Game* by Clannad	Xtravaganza XTRAV 1CDS
18/03/2000	❶1	14	O	**DON'T GIVE UP** ↑ **CHICANE FEATURING BRYAN ADAMS**	Xtravaganza XTRAV 9CDS
22/07/2000	28	3		NO ORDINARY MORNING/HALCYON Features the uncredited contribution of Tracy Ackerman	Xtravaganza XTRAV 12CDS
28/10/2000	44	2		AUTUMN TACTICS	Xtravaganza XTRAV 17CDS
08/02/2003	43	2		SALTWATER	Xtravaganza XTRAV 35CDS
08/03/2003	33	2		LOVE ON THE RUN **CHICANE FEATURING PETER CUNNAH**	WEA 361CD1
14/02/2004	43	1		DON'T GIVE UP 2004	Xtravaganza XTRAV 44CDS

CHICKEN SHACK UK group formed in Birmingham in 1965 by Stan Webb (guitar/vocals) and Andy Sylvester (bass). Christine Perfect (born 12/7/1943, Birmingham, piano/vocals) and Dave Bidwell (drums) joined later. After their brief success Perfect left to join her husband John McVie in Fleetwood Mac. Chicken Shack, who later recruited Tony Ashton (piano), Bob Daisley (bass), John Glascock (bass), Paul Hancox (drums/percussion), Chris Mercer (saxophone) and Paul Raymond (guitar/keyboards/vocals), continued until 1974.

07/05/1969	14	13		I'D RATHER GO BLIND	Blue Horizon 57-3153
06/09/1969	29	6		TEARS IN THE WIND	Blue Horizon 57-3160

CHICKEN SHED THEATRE UK vocal group formed by a children's charity workshop that enjoyed the patronage of Diana, Princess of Wales. The lead vocals were by Lissa Hermans.

27/12/1997	15	6		I AM IN LOVE WITH THE WORLD Proceeds were donated to the Diana, Princess of Wales Memorial Fund	Columbia 6654172

CHICKS ON SPEED Multinational group formed in Munich in 1997 by Melissa Logan (from the US), Alex Murray-Leslie (from Australia) and Kiki Moorse (from Germany). The group run the Go Records, Stop Records and Chicks On Speed Records labels.

21/02/2004	50	1		WHAT WAS HER NAME **DAVE CLARKE FEATURING CHICKS ON SPEED**	Skint 94CD
13/03/2004	66	1		WORDY RAPPINGHOOD	Labels 5478360

CHICORY TIP UK group formed in Maidstone by Peter Hewson (born 1/9/1950, Gillingham, vocals), Rick Foster (guitar) and Barry Magyer (born 1/6/1950, Maidstone, bass). Drummer Brian Shearer (born 4/5/1951, London) joined eighteen months before their chart breakthrough. Foster left in October 1972 and was replaced by Rod Cloutt (born 26/1/1949, Gillingham). Their debut hit was the first UK #1 to feature a synthesiser.

29/01/1972	❶3	13		**SON OF MY FATHER** Written by Giorgio Moroder and Pete Bellotte	CBS 7737

| 20/05/1972 | 13 | 8 | | WHAT'S YOUR NAME | CBS 8021 |
| 31/03/1973 | 17 | 13 | | GOOD GRIEF CHRISTINA | CBS 1258 |

CHIEFTAINS Irish folk group originally formed by Paddy Moloney (uillean pipes/tin whistle), Michael Tubridy (flute/concertina/tin whistle), Sean Potts (tin whistle), Martin Fay (fiddle) and David Fallon (bodhran). By 1973 the line-up was Moloney, Fay, Potts, Tubridy, Pendar Mercier (bodhran/bones) and Derek Bell (harp/oboe/tiompan). Over the years collaborating with artists as diverse as The Corrs, James Galway, Art Garfunkel, Gary Moore, Van Morrison and Nanci Griffith, they have won six Grammy Awards including: Best Traditional Folk Album in 1992 for *An Irish Evening Live At The Grand Opera House, Belfast, With Roger Daltry And Nanci Griffith*; Best Contemporary Folk Album in 1992 for *Another Country*; Best Traditional Folk Album in 1993 for *The Celtic Harp*; Best World Music Album in 1996 for *Santiago*; and Best Traditional Folk Album in 1998 for *Long Journey Home*.

| 18/03/1995 | 71 | 1 | | HAVE I TOLD YOU LATELY THAT I LOVE YOU CHIEFTAINS WITH VAN MORRISON 1995 Grammy Award for Best Pop Collaboration with Vocal | RCA 74321271702 |
| 12/06/1999 | 37 | 3 | | I KNOW MY LOVE CHIEFTAINS FEATURING THE CORRS | RCA Victor 74321670622 |

CHIFFONS US vocal group formed by Bronx high school classmates Judy Craig (born 1946, The Bronx, NYC), Barbara Lee (born 16/5/1947, The Bronx), Patricia Bennett (born 7/4/1947, The Bronx) and Sylvia Peterson (born 30/9/1946, The Bronx). Lee died from a heart attack on 15/5/1992, although the group (minus Craig, who left in 1969) were still working. *He's So Fine* was the subject of a plagiarism suit. The estate of writer Ronnie Mack successfully sued George Harrison over similarities in his song *My Sweet Lord*. The group also recorded as The Four Pennies – not be confused with a UK group of the same name.

11/04/1963	16	12		HE'S SO FINE ▲4 Featured in the films *Quadrophenia* (1979) and *The Flamingo Kid* (1984)	Stateside SS 172
18/07/1963	29	6		ONE FINE DAY Featured in the films *The Flamingo Kid* (1984) and *One Fine Day* (1997)	Stateside SS 202
26/05/1966	31	8		SWEET TALKIN' GUY	Stateside SS 512
18/03/1972	4	14		SWEET TALKIN' GUY Re-issue of Stateside SS 512	London HL 10271

CHIKINKI UK rock group formed in Bristol by Rupert Brown (vocals), Ed East (guitar), Trevor Wensley (keyboards), Boris Ecton (keyboards) and Steve Bond (drums).

29/11/2003	72	1		ASSASSINATOR 13	Island CID 834
27/03/2004	65	1		LIKE IT OR LEAVE IT	Island CID 848
19/06/2004	50	1		ETHER RADIO	Island CID 860
06/11/2004	74	1		ALL EYES	Island CIDX 875

CHILD UK group formed by Graham Billbrough (born 23/3/1958, Fairburn, guitar/vocals), Mike McKenzie (born 20/8/1955, Edinburgh, bass) and twins Keith (born 5/4/1959, Wakefield, guitar) and Tim Attack (drums).

29/04/1978	38	5		WHEN YOU WALK IN THE ROOM	Ariola Hansa AHA 511
22/07/1978	10	12	○	IT'S ONLY MAKE BELIEVE	Ariola Hansa AHA 522
28/04/1979	33	5		ONLY YOU (AND YOU ALONE)	Ariola Hansa AHA 536

JANE CHILD Canadian singer (born 15/2/1969, Toronto) who became a member of the Children's Chorus of the Canadian Opera Company at the age of twelve.

| 12/05/1990 | 22 | 8 | | DON'T WANNA FALL IN LOVE | Warner Brothers W 9817 |

CHILDLINERS Multinational charity ensemble comprising members of East 17, Boyzone, Gemini, Dannii Minogue and Sean Maguire.

| 16/12/1995 | 9 | 6 | | THE GIFT OF CHRISTMAS | London LONCD 376 |

CHILDREN FOR RWANDA UK choir.

| 10/09/1994 | 57 | 2 | | LOVE CAN BUILD A BRIDGE Proceeds were donated to various Rwandan aid charities | East West YZ 849CD |

CHILDREN OF THE NIGHT UK singer/producer.

| 26/11/1988 | 52 | 2 | | IT'S A TRIP (TUNE IN, TURN ON, DROP OUT) | Jive 189 |

CHILDREN OF THE REVOLUTION – see KLF

TONI CHILDS US singer (born 1958, Orange County, CA) who grew up in various parts of the US and Europe, spending four years in the UK. After a first contract with Island Records in London, she enjoyed greater success with Warner Brothers USA.

| 25/03/1989 | 53 | 4 | | DON'T WALK AWAY | A&M AM 462 |

CHILI HI FLY Australian group formed by twelve producers, remixers, DJs and dance music artists from Sydney's Dog House studios (previously a brothel). The group's leaders are Simon Lewicki and Noel Burgess.

| 18/03/2000 | 37 | 2 | | IS IT LOVE? Contains a sample of Kool & The Gang's *Be My Lady* | Ministry Of Sound MOSCDS 141 |

CHI-LITES US R&B group formed in Chicago, IL in 1960 by Eugene Record (born 23/12/1940, Chicago, IL), Marshall Thompson (born April 1941, Chicago), Robert 'Squirrel' Lester (born 1942, McComb, MS), Creadel Jones (born 1939, St Louis, MO) and Clarence Johnson (who left before they signed with Dakar in 1967) as The Hi-Lites, the name change reflecting their Chicago roots. Main songwriter Record went solo in 1976, returning in 1980, by which time they were a trio (with Thompson and Lester). In October 2001 Thompson was sentenced to a year and a day in a federal minimum security camp and fined $5,000 for his part in a scheme to sell police badges to businessmen, the badges authorising the holders to carry guns.

| 28/08/1971 | 32 | 6 | | (FOR GOD'S SAKE) GIVE MORE POWER TO THE PEOPLE | MCA MU 1138 |
| 15/01/1972 | 3 | 12 | | HAVE YOU SEEN HER | MCA MU 1146 |

❶⁹ Number of weeks single topped the UK chart ↑ Entered the UK chart at #1 ▲⁹ Number of weeks single topped the US chart

151

DATE	POS	WKS	BPI	SINGLE TITLE	LABEL & NUMBER
27/05/1972	14	9		OH GIRL ▲[1]	MCA MU 1156
23/03/1974	5	13		HOMELY GIRL	Brunswick BR 9
20/07/1974	35	5		I FOUND SUNSHINE	Brunswick BR 12
02/11/1974	10	11		TOO GOOD TO BE FORGOTTEN	Brunswick BR 13
21/06/1975	5	9		HAVE YOU SEEN HER/OH GIRL Re-issue of MCA MU 1146 and MCA MU 1156	Brunswick BR 20
13/09/1975	5	10		IT'S TIME FOR LOVE	Brunswick BR 25
31/07/1976	3	11		YOU DON'T HAVE TO GO	Brunswick BR 34
13/08/1983	61	3		CHANGING FOR YOU	R&B RBS 215

CHILL FAC-TORR US group formed in Philadelphia, PA by Lark Lowry (vocals/percussion), Lennie Sampson (vocals/keyboards), Nate Clory (bass), Tyrone Lewison (keyboards), Tony Fountain (guitar/vocals) and Gus Wallace (vocals/drums).

DATE	POS	WKS	BPI	SINGLE TITLE	LABEL & NUMBER
02/04/1983	37	8		TWIST (ROUND 'N' ROUND)	Phillyworld PWS 109

CHILLI FEATURING CARRAPICHO US/Ghanaian/Brazilian group.

DATE	POS	WKS	BPI	SINGLE TITLE	LABEL & NUMBER
20/09/1997	59	1		TIC, TIC TAC	Arista 74321511332

CHIMES UK group formed in the late 1980s by Edinburgh-born musicians Mike Peden (keyboards/bass) and James Locke (keyboards/drums), with singer Pauline Henry from London who later recorded solo.

DATE	POS	WKS	BPI	SINGLE TITLE	LABEL & NUMBER
19/08/1989	60	3		1-2-3	CBS 6551667
02/12/1989	66	5		HEAVEN	CBS 6554327
19/05/1990	6	9		STILL HAVEN'T FOUND WHAT I'M LOOKING FOR	CBS CHIM 1
28/07/1990	48	3		TRUE LOVE	CBS CHIM 2
29/09/1990	24	6		HEAVEN Re-issue of CBS 6554327	CBS CHIM 3
01/12/1990	49	2		LOVE COMES TO MIND	CBS CHIM 4

CHIMIRA South African singer.

DATE	POS	WKS	BPI	SINGLE TITLE	LABEL & NUMBER
06/12/1997	70	1		SHOW ME HEAVEN	Neoteric NRDCD 11

CHINA BLACK UK vocal/instrumental duo Errol Reid and Simon Fung.

DATE	POS	WKS	BPI	SINGLE TITLE	LABEL & NUMBER
16/07/1994	4	20	○	SEARCHING	Wild Card CARDD 7
29/10/1994	19	7		STARS	Wild Card CARDD 9
11/02/1995	31	2		ALMOST SEE YOU (SOMEWHERE)	Wild Card CARDW 15
03/06/1995	15	6		SWING LOW SWEET CHARIOT LADYSMITH BLACK MAMBAZO FEATURING CHINA BLACK	Polygram TV SWLDW 2

CHINA CRISIS UK group formed in Kirkby in 1979 by Gary Daly (born 5/5/1962, Kirkby, vocals), Eddie Lundon (born 9/6/1962, Kirkby, guitar), Brian McNeil (keyboards), Gazza Johnson (bass) and Kevin Wilkinson (drums). Wilkinson committed suicide in July 1999.

DATE	POS	WKS	BPI	SINGLE TITLE	LABEL & NUMBER
07/08/1982	45	5		AFRICAN AND WHITE	Inevitable INEV 011
22/01/1983	12	9		CHRISTIAN	Virgin VS 562
21/05/1983	46	6		TRAGEDY AND MYSTERY	Virgin VS 587
15/10/1983	48	5		WORKING WITH FIRE AND STEEL	Virgin VS 620
14/01/1984	9	8		WISHFUL THINKING	Virgin VS 647
10/03/1984	44	3		HANNA HANNA	Virgin VS 665
30/03/1985	14	9		BLACK MAN RAY	Virgin VS 752
01/06/1985	19	9		KING IN A CATHOLIC STYLE (WAKE UP)	Virgin VS 765
07/09/1985	54	3		YOU DID CUT ME	Virgin VS 799
08/11/1986	47	4		ARIZONA SKY	Virgin VS 898
24/01/1987	36	5		BEST KEPT SECRET	Virgin VS 926

CHINA DRUM UK group formed in 1989 by Bill McQueen (guitar/vocals), Dave McQueen (bass/vocals) and Adam Lee (drums/vocals), later adding Jan Alkema and shortening their name to The Drum.

DATE	POS	WKS	BPI	SINGLE TITLE	LABEL & NUMBER
02/03/1996	65	1		CAN'T STOP THESE THINGS	Mantra MNT 8CD
20/04/1996	60	1		LAST CHANCE	Mantra MNT 10CD
09/08/1997	65	1		FICTION OF LIFE	Mantra MNT 21CD
27/09/1997	74	1		SOMEWHERE ELSE	Mantra MNT022CD1

JONNY CHINGAS US keyboard player whose debut hit used the catchphrase from the 1982 film *E.T.*

DATE	POS	WKS	BPI	SINGLE TITLE	LABEL & NUMBER
19/02/1983	43	6		PHONE HOME	CBS A 3121

CHINGY US rapper (born Howard Bailey Jr, 9/3/1980, St Louis, MO) discovered by Ludacris. J Weav is US singer Jason Weaver.

DATE	POS	WKS	BPI	SINGLE TITLE	LABEL & NUMBER
25/10/2003	17	5		RIGHT THURR	Capitol CDCLS 849
21/02/2004	35	3		HOLIDAE INN	Capitol CDCLS 852
29/05/2004	26	4		ONE CALL AWAY CHINGY FEATURING J WEAV	Capitol CDCL 856
13/11/2004	34	3		BALLA BABY	Parlophone CDCLS865

CHIPMUNKS US group, the creation of David Seville (born Ross Bagdasarian, 27/1/1919, Fresno, CA of Armenian extraction), comprising Alvin, Simon and Theodore, all named after executives of Seville's US record company Liberty. The Chipmunks had their own animated TV show in the early 1960s and were later revived as a cartoon series in the 1980s. Seville won three Grammy Awards: Best Comedy Performance and Best Recording for Children in 1958 for *The Chipmunk Song* and Best Recording for Children in 1960 for *Let's All Sing With The Chipmunks*. Seville died from a heart attack on 16/1/1972. His son Ross Jr revived the act in 1980.

○ Silver disc ● Gold disc ✪ Platinum disc (additional platinum units are indicated by a figure following the symbol) ◎ Singles released prior to 1973 that are known to have sold over 1 million copies in the UK

24/07/1959	11	8		RAGTIME COWBOY JOE DAVID SEVILLE AND THE CHIPMUNKS	London HLU 8916
19/12/1992	53	3		ACHY BREAKY HEART ALVIN AND THE CHIPMUNKS FEATURING BILLY RAY CYRUS	Epic 6588837
14/12/1996	65	1		MACARENA LOS DEL CHIPMUNKS	Sony Wonder 6639981

CHIPPENDALES US/UK dance group whose act was aimed specifically at women.

31/10/1992	28	4		GIVE ME YOUR BODY	Xsrhythm XSR 3

GEORGE CHISHOLM – see JOHNSTON BROTHERS

CHOCOLATE PUMA Dutch house group formed by DJ Ziki (Rene Terhost) and DJ Dobre (Gaston Steenkist) with singer Evo. Ziki and Dobre also recorded as Tomba Vira, DJ Manta, Jark Prongo, Goodmen, Rhythmkillaz and Riva.

24/03/2001	6	9		I WANNA BE U	Cream 13CD

CHOO CHOO PROJECT US duo Harry Romero and Octahvia Lambert. DJ/producer Romero, based in New York, worked with Erick 'More' Morillo and his Subliminal Records label, also recording under his own name.

15/01/2000	21	3		HAZIN' & PHAZIN'	Defected DEFECT 10CDS

CHOPS-EMC + EXTENSIVE UK drum and bass group formed by Ricky Chopp, Colin Grainge, Frank McFarlane and Elvis McFarlane.

08/08/1992	60	1		THE ISRAELITES	Faze 2 FAZE 6

CHORDETTES US group formed in Sheboygan, WI in 1946 by Janet Ertel, Carol Buschman, Dorothy Schwartz and Jinny Lockard, the latter two members being replaced by Lynn Evans and Margie Needham in 1953. They disbanded in 1961, re-forming in 1988. Janet married Cadence label boss Archie Bleyer in 1954, and died from cancer on 22/11/1988.

17/12/1954	11	8		MR. SANDMAN ▲[7] Uncredited singer is Archie Bleyer	Columbia DB 3553
31/08/1956	8	9		BORN TO BE WITH YOU	London HLA 8302
18/04/1958	6	8		LOLLIPOP Featured in the 1986 film Stand By Me	London HLD 8584

CHORDS UK group formed during the late 1970s Mod-revival by Brett 'Buddy' Ascott (drums), Billy Hassett (guitar), Chris Pope (guitar/vocals) and Mick Talbot (born 11/9/1958, London, keyboards) who was later in Style Council.

06/10/1979	63	2		NOW IT'S GONE	Polydor 2059 141
02/02/1980	40	5		MAYBE TOMORROW	Polydor POSP 101
26/04/1980	55	3		SOMETHING'S MISSING	Polydor POSP 146
12/07/1980	54	3		THE UK WAY OF LIFE	Polydor 2059 258
18/10/1980	50	4		IN MY STREET	Polydor POSP 185

CHRIS AND JAMES UK instrumental/production group formed by Chris Day, James Bradley and James Wiltshire.

17/09/1994	74	1		CALM DOWN (BASS KEEPS PUMPIN')	Stress 12STR 38
04/11/1995	71	1		FOX FORCE FIVE	Stress CDSTR 61
07/11/1998	66	1		CLUB FOR LIFE '98	Stress CDSTR 85

NEIL CHRISTIAN UK singer (born Christopher Tidmarsh, 14/2/1943, London) whose backing group The Crusaders variously included Jimmy Page, Albert Lee and Mick Abrahams, and at the time of the hit comprised Richie Blackmore (guitar), Eimer Twitch (piano), Bibi Blange (bass) and Tornado Evans (drums).

07/04/1966	14	10		THAT'S NICE	Strike JH 301

ROGER CHRISTIAN UK singer (born 1950).

30/09/1989	63	3		TAKE IT FROM ME	Island IS 427

CHRISTIANS UK group formed in 1984 by ex-It's Immaterial Henry Priestman (born 21/6/1955, Hull) after meeting three of the eleven Christian brothers – Garry (born Garrison Christian, 27/2/1955, Liverpool), Russell (born 8/7/1956, Liverpool) and Roger (born 13/2/1950, Liverpool). Previously called Equal Temperament, The Gems and Natural High, the latter name was used when they appeared on Opportunity Knocks in 1974.

31/01/1987	22	11		FORGOTTEN TOWN	Island IS 291
13/06/1987	21	10		HOOVERVILLE (THEY PROMISED US THE WORLD)	Island IS 326
26/09/1987	34	7		WHEN THE FINGERS POINT	Island IS 335
05/12/1987	14	13		IDEAL WORLD	Island IS 347
23/04/1988	25	7		BORN AGAIN	Island IS 365
15/10/1988	8	7		HARVEST FOR THE WORLD	Island IS 395
20/05/1989	❶[3]	7		FERRY 'CROSS THE MERSEY ↑ CHRISTIANS, HOLLY JOHNSON, PAUL McCARTNEY, GERRY MARSDEN AND STOCK AITKEN WATERMAN Charity record to aid relatives of the Hillsborough football disaster victims	PWL 41
23/12/1989	18	8		WORDS	Island IS 450
07/04/1990	56	2		I FOUND OUT	Island IS 453
15/09/1990	63	2		GREENBANK DRIVE	Island IS 466
05/09/1992	33	5		WHAT'S IN A WORD	Island IS 536
14/11/1992	55	2		FATHER	Island IS 543
06/03/1993	39	3		THE BOTTLE	Island CID 549

❶[9] Number of weeks single topped the UK chart ↑ Entered the UK chart at #1 ▲[9] Number of weeks single topped the US chart

153

CHRISTIE UK group hastily put together by songwriter Jeff Christie after *Yellow River* had been turned down by The Tremeloes, with Mike Blakely (brother of The Tremeloes' Alan Blakely) and Chris Elms. Drummer Paul Fenton joined after the #1 success.

02/05/1970 ....❶¹....22.....	**YELLOW RIVER** .... CBS 4911
10/10/1970 .....7.....14.....	**SAN BERNADINO** .... CBS 5169
25/03/1972.....47......1......	IRON HORSE .... CBS 7747

DAVID CHRISTIE French singer/songwriter whose one hit single took three months to peak. He later recorded for Record Shack and Ocean.

14/08/1982 .....9......12......   **SADDLE UP** .... KR 9

JOHN CHRISTIE Australian singer/pianist who later recorded for Polydor.

25/12/1976.....24......6.......   HERE'S TO LOVE (AULD LANG SYNE) .... EMI 2554

LOU CHRISTIE US singer (born Lugee Sacco, 19/2/1943, Glen Willard, PA) who first recorded for Star Records in 1960 and sang briefly as Lugee and the Lions, adopting the name Lou Christie in 1963.

24/02/1966.....11......8......	LIGHTNIN' STRIKES ▲¹ .... MGM 1297
28/04/1966.....37......2......	RHAPSODY IN THE RAIN The song had to be re-recorded to remove lyrics that were deemed to be sexually offensive .... MGM 1308
13/09/1969 .....2.....17......	**I'M GONNA MAKE YOU MINE**.. Buddah 201 057
27/12/1969.....25......8......	SHE SOLD ME MAGIC .... Buddah 201 073

TONY CHRISTIE UK singer (born Anthony Fitzgerald, 25/4/1944, Conisborough), professional from the age of twenty, produced by Mitch Murray and Pete Callander.

09/01/1971.....21......9.....	LAS VEGAS .... MCA MK 5058
08/05/1971.....2.....17......	**I DID WHAT I DID FOR MARIA** .... MCA MK 5064
20/11/1971.....18.....13.....	IS THIS THE WAY TO AMARILLO.. MCA MKS 5073
10/02/1973.....37......4.....	AVENUES AND ALLEYWAYS .... MCA MKS 5101
17/01/1976.....35......4.....	DRIVE SAFELY DARLIN' Theme to the TV series *The Protectors*................. MCA 219
23/01/1999.....10......7.....	**WALK LIKE A PANTHER '98 THE ALL SEEING I FEATURING TONY CHRISTIE** .... ffrr FCDP 351

SHAWN CHRISTOPHER US singer (born in Chicago, IL) whose brother Gavin also made records. She also sang backing vocals for Chaka Khan.

22/09/1990.....74......1.....	ANOTHER SLEEPLESS NIGHT MIKE 'HITMAN' WILSON FEATURING SHAWN CHRISTOPHER ..... Arista 113506
04/05/1991.....50......4.....	ANOTHER SLEEPLESS NIGHT Re-issue of Arista 113506, even though the artist credit is just to Shawn Christopher ... Arista 114186
21/03/1992.....30......5.....	DON'T LOSE THE MAGIC .... Arista 115097
02/07/1994.....57......1.....	MAKE MY LOVE .... BTB BTBCD 502

CHUCKS UK studio vocal group assembled by producer Ivor Raymonde.

24/01/1963.....22......7......   LOO-BE-LOO.. Decca F 11569

CHUMBAWAMBA UK rock group formed in Leeds in 1983 by Alice Nutter (vocals), Harry Hamer, Boff (guitar), Mavis Dillon (horns), Louise Mary Watts (keyboards), Danbert Nobacon, Paul Greco and Dunstan Bruce. They had previously recorded for Agit Prop and One Little Indian, where they recorded with Credit To The Nation.

18/09/1993.....56......2.....	ENOUGH IS ENOUGH CHUMBAWAMBA AND CREDIT TO THE NATION........................ One Little Indian 79 TP7CD
04/12/1993.....59......1.....	TIMEBOMB .... One Little Indian 89 TP7CD
23/08/1997 .....2.....20 .....✪	**TUBTHUMPING** .... EMI CDEM 486
31/01/1998.....10......5.....	**AMNESIA** .... EMI CDEM 498
13/06/1998.....21......3.....	TOP OF THE WORLD (OLÉ OLÉ OLÉ) .... EMI CDEM 511

CHUBBY CHUNKS UK singer/producer Scott Tinsley.

04/06/1994.....52......1.....	TESTAMENT 4 CHUBBY CHUNKS VOLUME II .... Cleveland City CLECD 13017
29/05/1999.....61......1.....	I'M TELLIN' YOU CHUBBY CHUNKS FEATURING KIM RUFFIN .... Cleveland City CLECD 13052

CHUPITO Spanish singer.

23/09/1995.....54......2.....   AMERICAN PIE.. Eternal WEA 018CD

CHARLOTTE CHURCH UK singer (born 211/2/1986, Cardiff) who, with her debut album *Voice Of An Angel*, is the youngest female to appear in the US top 30, while her *Dream A Dream* Christmas album made her the youngest female to make the top ten. In January 2000 she sacked her manager Jonathan Shalit who received a £2.3 million out-of-court settlement in November 2000. She appeared in the 2003 film *I'll Be There*.

25/12/1999.....34......4.....	JUST WAVE HELLO... Sony Classical 6685312
01/02/2003 .....3......10.....	**THE OPERA SONG (BRAVE NEW WORLD) JURGEN VRIES FEATURING CMC** .... Direction 6734642

CHYNA – see INCOGNITO

CICA – see PQM FEATURING CICA

CICERO UK singer Dave Cicero.

18/01/1992.....19......8.....	LOVE IS EVERYWHERE .... Spaghetti CIAO 3
18/04/1992.....46......3.....	THAT LOVING FEELING .... Spaghetti CIAO 4

  ○ Silver disc ● Gold disc ✪ Platinum disc (additional platinum units are indicated by a figure following the symbol) ◎ Singles released prior to 1973 that are known to have sold over 1 million copies in the UK

01/08/1992.....70......1....... HEAVEN MUST HAVE SENT YOU BACK..Spaghetti CIAO 5

CINDERELLA US rock group formed in Philadelphia, PA in 1983 by Tom Keifer (guitar/vocals), Eric Brittingham (bass), Michael Kelly Smith (guitar) and Tony Destra (drums). Smith and Destra left soon after and were replaced by Jeff LaBar and Jody Cortez. Cortez left in 1986, replaced by Fred Coury. Coury also left a few years later and was initially replaced by Kevin Valentine before Keifer's health problems put the group on hold. They returned in 1994 with the album *Still Climbing* and with Kevin Conway as the new drummer.

06/08/1988.....54......2....... GYPSY ROAD ....Vertigo VER 40
04/03/1989.....54......2....... DON'T KNOW WHAT YOU GOT ....Vertigo VER 43
17/11/1990.....55......2....... SHELTER ME ....Vertigo VER 51
27/04/1991.....63......1....... HEARTBREAK STATION ....Vertigo VER 53

CINDY AND THE SAFFRONS UK vocal group formed by Joanne Whalley (born 25/8/1964, Manchester), Lindsay Neil and Sally Stairs. Whalley became better known as an actress, appearing in such films as *Scandal* and the TV series *The Singing Detective*. She was briefly married to actor Val Killmer. The group's debut hit (a cover of the Shangri-Las' classic) was based on Beethoven's *Piano Sonata No.14 in C minor, Op.27 No.2*, aka the *Moonlight Sonata*.

15/01/1983.....56......3....... PAST, PRESENT AND FUTURE ....Stiletto STL 9

CINERAMA UK vocal/instrumental duo David Gedge (formerly of Wedding Present) and Sally Murrell.
18/07/1998.....71......1....... KERRY KERRY ....Cooking Vinyl FRYCD 072

GIGLIOLA CINQUETTI Italian singer (born 20/12/1947, Verona) who won the 1964 Eurovision Song Contest in her late teens (the English title of her winning entry was *I'm Not Old Enough To Love You*), only the second Eurovision winner to reach the UK charts in the eight years of the competition (and it would be another three before another winner charted, Sandie Shaw's *Puppet On A String*, which reached #1 in 1967). Ten years later she was second to Abba's *Waterloo*, her song becoming a UK top ten hit. 1974 was a vintage year for Eurovision, producing no fewer than four hits: Abba, Cinquetti, UK entry Olivia Newton-John's *Long Live Love* and Mouth And Macneal all hitting the top twenty.

23/04/1964.....17.....17...... NON HO L'ETA PER AMARTI 1964 Eurovision Song Contest winner for Italy ....Decca F 21882
04/05/1974.....8......10...... **GO (BEFORE YOU BREAK MY HEART)** Italy's entry for the 1974 Eurovision Song Contest (came second) ....CBS 2294

CIRCA FEATURING DESTRY UK production group comprising Dan Bewick, Mat Frost, Tommy Jones, Simon Thorne and US singer Destry. Jones and Thorne also record as Staxx.
27/11/1999.....70......1....... SUN SHINING DOWN Contains a sample of *Back Stabbers* by The O'Jays................................Inferno CDFERN 22

CIRCUIT UK group formed by Mark Jolley (guitar), his sister Anna (vocals) and Brian Harris (percussion) who also recorded as Innocence.
20/07/1991.....44......2....... SHELTER ME ....Cooltempo COOL 237
01/04/1995.....50......1....... SHELTER ME Re-issue of Cooltempo COOL 237................................Pukka CDPUKA 2

CIRCULATION UK production duo Matt Jackson and Paul Davis.
01/09/2001.....64......1....... TURQUOISE ....Hooj Choons HOOJ 109CCD

CIRRUS UK vocal group.
30/09/1978.....62......1....... ROLLIN' ON ....Jet 123

CITIZEN CANED UK producer Darren Tate, also a member of Angelic and DT8, and who recorded as Jurgen Vries.
07/04/2001.....41......2....... THE JOURNEY ....Serious SERR 029CD

CITY BOY UK rock group formed by Lol Mason (percussion/vocals), Mike 'Max' Slamer (guitar), Max Thomas (keyboards), Steve Broughton (guitar/mandolin/vocals), Chris Dunn (bass) and Roger Kent (drums/percussion). Kent left in 1978 and was replaced by Roy Ward. They disbanded in 1982 with Mason forming The Maisonettes.

08/07/1978.....8......12.....O **5-7-0-5** ....Vertigo 6059 207
28/10/1978.....39......5....... WHAT A NIGHT ....Vertigo 6059 211
15/09/1979.....67......3....... THE DAY THE EARTH CAUGHT FIRE ....Vertigo 6059 238

CITY HIGH US rap group formed in Willingboro, NJ by Toby Ryan, Robby Pardlo and rapper and singer Claudette Ortiz. Ryan and Pardlo had worked as a duo until persuaded to recruit Ortiz by mentor Wyclef Jean. Ortiz later recorded with Wyclef Jean.
06/10/2001.....3......17...... **WHAT WOULD YOU DO** Contains a sample of Notorious B.I.G.'s *Things Done Changed*. Featured in the 1999 film *Life*.............
....Interscope IND 97617
16/03/2002.....9......10...... **CARAMEL CITY HIGH FEATURING EVE**...Interscope 4976742

CITY SPUD – see NELLY

CJ & CO US disco group assembled by Dennis Coffey and Mike Theodore featuring Cornelius Brown Jr, Charles Clark, Connie Durden, Curtis Durden and Joni Tolbert.
30/07/1977.....43......2....... DEVIL'S GUN ....Atlantic K 10956

CK – see BADFELLAS FEATURING CK

●[9] Number of weeks single topped the UK chart ↑ Entered the UK chart at #1 ▲[9] Number of weeks single topped the US chart

155

CK AND SUPREME DREAM TEAM Dutch production group formed by Remy 'Martinez' De Groot, Danny 'Decoy' Van Wauve and Serge Ramaekers.

11/01/2003	23	3	DREAMER .... Multiply CDMULTY 96

GARY CLAIL ON-U SOUND SYSTEM UK singer/producer with musical backing provided by musicians from Tackhead, Roots Radics, Akabu and Dub Syndicate. Clail, of Irish descent, grew up in Bristol.

14/07/1990	64	2	BEEF GARY CLAIL ON-U SOUND SYSTEM FEATURING BIM SHERMAN .... RCA PB 49265
30/03/1991	10	9	HUMAN NATURE .... Perfecto PB 44401
08/06/1991	44	3	ESCAPE .... Perfecto PB 44563
14/11/1992	31	3	WHO PAYS THE PIPER .... Perfecto 74321117017
22/05/1993	45	2	THESE THINGS ARE WORTH FIGHTING FOR .... Perfecto 74321147222

CLAIRE AND FRIENDS UK singer aged eight and a half with similarly youthful backing group, making her debut hit via the children's TV programme *Saturday Superstore*.

21/06/1986	13	11	IT'S 'ORRIBLE BEING IN LOVE (WHEN YOU'RE 8½) .... BBC RESL 189

CLANNAD Irish folk band formed in Dublin in 1970 by Maire Ni Bhraonain (born 4/8/1952, Dublin), Pol O'Bhraonain, Calran O'Bhraonain and their uncles Noel O'Dugain and Padraig O'Dugain: Clannad is Gaelic for 'family'. They were joined by sister Enya Ni Bhraonain (born 17/5/1961) in 1980 who left in 1982 and emerged in 1988 as Enya. They won the 1998 Grammy Award for Best New Age Recording for *Landmarks*.

06/11/1982	5	10	O	THEME FROM HARRY'S GAME From the TV drama *Harry's Game* and winner of the Best Theme From a Television or Radio Production at the Ivor Novello Awards. The song was later featured in the 1992 film *Patriot Games* .... RCA 292
02/07/1983	65	1		NEW GRANGE .... RCA 340
12/05/1984	42	5		ROBIN (THE HOODED MAN) .... RCA HOOD 1
25/01/1986	20	5		IN A LIFETIME .... RCA PB 40535
10/06/1989	17	7		IN A LIFETIME Re-issue of RCA PB 40535. This and above single credited to CLANNAD FEATURING BONO .... RCA PB 42873
10/08/1991	74	1		BOTH SIDES NOW CLANNAD AND PAUL YOUNG .... MCA MCS 1546
05/06/1999	6	10		SALTWATER CHICANE FEATURING MAIRE BRENNAN OF CLANNAD Effectively two songs made into one: *Saltwater* by Chicane and *Theme From Harry's Game* by Clannad. .... Xtravaganza XTRAV 1CDS

JIMMY CLANTON US singer (born 2/9/1940, Baton Rouge, LA) who appeared in the 1958 film *Go Johnny Go,* later becoming a radio DJ.

21/07/1960	50	1	ANOTHER SLEEPLESS NIGHT .... Top Rank JAR 382

ERIC CLAPTON UK singer/guitarist (born Eric Clapp, 30/3/1945, Ripley) who joined the Yardbirds in 1963 and left in 1965 for John Mayall's Bluesbreakers. He then formed Cream with Ginger Baker and Jack Bruce. Blind Faith and tours with Delaney and Bonnie preceded his first solo record in 1970. One of the best guitarists of his era, he has had to overcome personal tragedies and drug addiction. He received the Outstanding Contribution to British Music Award at the 1987 BRIT Awards and was awarded an OBE in the 1995 New Year's Honours List. He also recorded as Derek And The Dominos. Fifteen Grammy Awards include Album of the Year and Best Male Rock Vocal Performance in 1992 for *Unplugged*; Best Traditional Blues Album in 1994 for *From The Cradle*; Best Rock Instrumental Performance in 1996 with Jimmie Vaughan, Bonnie Raitt, Robert Cray, BB King, Buddy Guy, Dr John and Art Neville for *SRV Shuffle*; Best Rock Instrumental in 1999 with Santana for *The Calling*; Best Traditional Blues Album in 2000 with BB King for *Riding With The King*; and Best Pop Instrumental Performance in 2001 for *Reptile*. He was inducted into the Rock & Roll Hall of Fame in 2000 and awarded a CBE in the 2004 New Year's Honours List.

20/12/1969	16	9	COMIN' HOME DELANEY AND BONNIE AND FRIENDS FEATURING ERIC CLAPTON .... Atlantic 584 308
12/08/1972	7	11	LAYLA DEREK AND THE DOMINOES .... Polydor 2058 130
27/07/1974	9	9	I SHOT THE SHERIFF ▲[1] Written by Bob Marley and featuring Yvonne Elliman on backing vocals .... RSO 2090 132
10/05/1975	19	9	SWING LOW SWEET CHARIOT .... RSO 2090 158
16/08/1975	38	4	KNOCKIN' ON HEAVEN'S DOOR .... RSO 2090 166
24/12/1977	39	6	LAY DOWN SALLY Features Yvonne Elliman and Marcy Levy on backing vocals. .... RSO 2090 264
21/10/1978	37	7	PROMISES .... RSO 21
06/03/1982	4	10	LAYLA Re-issue of Polydor 2058 130, which was originally credited to Derek And The Dominoes. Written in 1972, it won the 1992 Grammy Award for Best Rock Song for writers Eric Clapton and Jim Gordon .... RSO 87
05/06/1982	64	2	I SHOT THE SHERIFF .... RSO 88
23/04/1983	75	1	THE SHAPE YOU'RE IN .... Duck W 9701
16/03/1985	51	4	FOREVER MAN. .... Warner Brothers W 9069
04/01/1986	65	3	EDGE OF DARKNESS ERIC CLAPTON FEATURING MICHAEL KAMEN Theme to the TV series of the same name .... BBC RESL 178
17/01/1987	15	11	BEHIND THE MASK. .... Duck W 8461
20/06/1987	56	3	TEARING US APART ERIC CLAPTON AND TINA TURNER. .... Duck W 8299
27/01/1990	25	7	BAD LOVE 1990 Grammy Award for Best Rock Vocal Performance. .... Duck W 2644
14/04/1990	53	3	NO ALIBIS .... Duck W 3644
16/11/1991	30	7	WONDERFUL TONIGHT (LIVE) Recorded at the Royal Albert Hall, London .... Duck W 0069
08/02/1992	5	12	TEARS IN HEAVEN Inspired by the death of four-year old son Conor, who fell from the 53rd floor of the East 57th Street, NYC apartment where he lived with his mother. Featured in the 1991 film *Rush*. 1992 Grammy Awards for Record of the Year and Best Male Pop Vocal Performance, and Song of the Year for writers Clapton and Will Jennings. .... Reprise W 0081
01/08/1992	31	4	RUNAWAY TRAIN ELTON JOHN AND ERIC CLAPTON .... Rocket EJS 29
29/08/1992	30	5	IT'S PROBABLY ME STING WITH ERIC CLAPTON This and above single featured in the 1992 film *Lethal Weapon 3*. .... A&M AM 883
03/10/1992	45	3	LAYLA (ACOUSTIC). .... Duck W 0134
15/10/1994	63	1	MOTHERLESS CHILD .... Duck W 0271CD

○ Silver disc ● Gold disc ✪ Platinum disc (additional platinum units are indicated by a figure following the symbol) ⊚ Singles released prior to 1973 that are known to have sold over 1 million copies in the UK

18/03/1995 .... ❶¹ .... 8 ...... ○ **LOVE CAN BUILD A BRIDGE** CHER, CHRISSIE HYNDE AND NENEH CHERRY WITH ERIC CLAPTON Released in aid of the Comic Relief charity .... London COCD 1

20/07/1996 ..... 18 ...... 5 .... CHANGE THE WORLD Featured in the 1996 film *Phenomenon*. 1996 Grammy Awards for Record of the Year and Best Male Pop Vocal Performance .... Reprise W 0358CD

04/04/1998 ..... 33 ...... 2 .... MY FATHER'S EYES 1998 Grammy Award for Best Male Pop Vocal Performance .... Duck W 0443CD

04/07/1998 ..... 39 ...... 2 .... CIRCUS .... Duck W 0447CD

18/11/2000 ..... 26 ...... 2 .... FOREVER MAN (HOW MANY TIMES) **BEATCHUGGERS FEATURING ERIC CLAPTON** Contains a sample of Eric Clapton's *Forever Man* . ... ffrr FCD 386

CLARISSA – see DJ VISAGE FEATURING CLARISSA

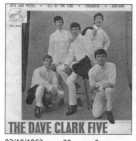

THE DAVE CLARK FIVE

DAVE CLARK FIVE
UK group formed in London in 1958 by film stuntman Dave Clark (born 15/12/1942, Tottenham, London, drums) and Chris Walls (bass), who advertised for musicians, enrolling Rick Huxley (born 5/8/1942, Dartford, guitar), Stan Saxon (saxophone/vocals) and Mick Ryan (guitar). By 1961 they had a long-term residency on the Mecca ballroom circuit with a line-up of Clark, Huxley, Lenny Davidson (born 30/5/1944, Enfield, guitar/vocals), Denis Payton (born 11/8/1943, Walthamstow, saxophone) and Mike Smith (born 12/12/1943, Edmonton, keyboards/vocals). According to one US source, they were formed to raise funds for 'Tottenham Hotspurs' (sic). After two singles on Piccadilly they signed with Columbia in 1963, turning professional the following year. They made their first film (*Catch Us If You Can*) in 1965 and disbanded in 1970. Clark later wrote the musical *Time*.

03/10/1963 ..... 30 ...... 6 ...... DO YOU LOVE ME Cover version of the Contours' US hit .... Columbia DB 7112

21/11/1963 .... ❶² ...... 19 ...... **GLAD ALL OVER** .... Columbia DB 7154

20/02/1964 ..... 2 ...... 11 ...... **BITS AND PIECES** .... Columbia DB 7210

28/05/1964 ..... 10 ...... 11 ...... **CAN'T YOU SEE THAT SHE'S MINE** .... Columbia DB 7291

13/08/1964 ..... 26 ...... 4 ...... THINKING OF YOU BABY .... Columbia DB 7335

22/10/1964 ..... 25 ...... 5 ...... ANYWAY YOU WANT IT .... Columbia DB 7377

14/01/1965 ..... 37 ...... 4 ...... EVERYBODY KNOWS .... Columbia DB 7453

11/03/1965 ..... 24 ...... 8 ...... REELIN' AND ROCKIN' .... Columbia DB 7503

27/05/1965 ..... 16 ...... 8 ...... COME HOME .... Columbia DB 7580

15/07/1965 ..... 5 ...... 11 ...... **CATCH US IF YOU CAN** Featured in the films *Catch Us If You Can* (1965; US title *Having A Wild Weekend*) and *Look Who's Talking Too* (1990) .... Columbia DB 7625

11/11/1965 ..... 45 ...... 4 ...... OVER AND OVER .... Columbia DB 7744

19/05/1966 ..... 50 ...... 1 ...... LOOK BEFORE YOU LEAP .... Columbia DB 7909

16/03/1967 ..... 28 ...... 8 ...... YOU GOT WHAT IT TAKES .... Columbia DB 8152

01/11/1967 ..... 2 ...... 14 ...... **EVERYBODY KNOWS** This is a different song from the *Everybody Knows* that appeared on Columbia DB 7377... Columbia DB 8286

28/02/1968 ..... 28 ...... 7 ...... NO ONE CAN BREAK A HEART LIKE YOU .... Columbia DB 8342

18/09/1968 ..... 7 ...... 11 ...... **RED BALLOON** .... Columbia DB 8465

27/11/1968 ..... 39 ...... 6 ...... LIVE IN THE SKY .... Columbia DB 8505

25/10/1969 ..... 31 ...... 4 ...... PUT A LITTLE LOVE IN YOUR HEART .... Columbia DB 8624

06/12/1969 ..... 7 ...... 12 ...... **GOOD OLD ROCK 'N' ROLL** Medley of *Good Old Rock 'N' Roll, Sweet Little Sixteen, Long Tall Sally, Whole Lotta Shakin' Goin' On, Blue Suede Shoes, Lucille, Reelin' And Rockin'* and *Memphis Tennessee* .... Columbia DB 8638

07/03/1970 ..... 8 ...... 8 ...... **EVERYBODY GET TOGETHER** .... Columbia DB 8660

04/07/1970 ..... 44 ...... 3 ...... HERE COMES SUMMER .... Columbia DB 8689

07/11/1970 ..... 34 ...... 6 ...... MORE GOOD OLD ROCK 'N ROLL Medley of *Rock And Roll Music, Blueberry Hill, Good Golly Miss Molly, My Blue Heaven, Keep A Knockin', Loving You, One Night* and *Lawdy Miss Clawdy* .... Columbia DB 8724

01/05/1993 ..... 37 ...... 3 ...... GLAD ALL OVER Re-issue of Columbia DB 7154 .... EMI CDEMCT 8

DEE CLARK
US singer (born Delecta Clark, 7/11/1938, Blytheville, AR, raised in Chicago) who sang in local R&B groups including The Kool Gents and The Delegates before recording solo in 1957. After a heart attack in 1987 he began performing again, against his doctors' advice, and died from a second attack on 7/12/1990.

02/10/1959 ..... 26 ...... 1 .... JUST KEEP IT UP .... London HL 8915

11/10/1975 ..... 16 ...... 8 .... RIDE A WILD HORSE .... Chelsea 2005 037

GARY CLARK
UK singer/drummer/guitarist/keyboard player, previously with Danny Wilson and King L.90. His backing group featured his brother Kit, Karlos Edwards, Ged Grimes and Gary Thompson.

30/01/1993 ..... 34 ...... 4 .... WE SAIL ON THE STORMY WATERS .... Circa YRCDX 93

03/04/1993 ..... 50 ...... 3 .... FREEFLOATING .... Circa YRCDX 94

19/06/1993 ..... 70 ...... 1 .... MAKE A FAMILY .... Circa YRCDX 105

LONI CLARK
US singer (born in New York City) who sang with Harlem church choirs before joining Luther Vandross and then going solo in 1981 with West End Records.

05/06/1993 ..... 37 ...... 2 .... RUSHING .... A&M 5802862

22/01/1994 ..... 28 ...... 3 .... U .... A&M 5804752

17/12/1994 ..... 59 ...... 1 .... LOVE'S GOT ME ON A TRIP SO HIGH .... A&M 5808872

❶⁹ Number of weeks single topped the UK chart ↑ Entered the UK chart at #1 ▲⁹ Number of weeks single topped the US chart

157

PETULA CLARK
UK singer (born 15/11/1932, Epsom) who was a child performer on radio during World War II and in over 150 shows between 1942 and 1944. With her first (*Murder In Reverse*) in 1943, she made more than twenty films over the next decade, including *Vice Versa* (1948), *The Happiness Of Three Women* (1954) and *The Runaway Bus* (1954). Her record debut was in 1949 for EMI's Columbia label (*Put Your Shoes On Lucy*), switching to the newly formed Polygon in 1950 and remaining with them through label name changes of Nixa and Pye until 1971. Numerous US hits include two #1s (*Downtown* and *My Love*). She was popular in Europe (frequently singing in French) and was still recording in the 1990s. She was awarded a CBE in the 1998 New Year's Honours List.

DATE	POS	WKS	BPI	SINGLE TITLE	LABEL & NUMBER
11/06/1954	7	10		**THE LITTLE SHOEMAKER**	Polygon P 1117
18/02/1955	12	5		MAJORCA	Polygon P 1146
25/11/1955	7	10		**SUDDENLY THERE'S A VALLEY**	Pye Nixa N 15013
26/07/1957	4	18		**WITH ALL MY HEART**	Pye Nixa N 15096
15/11/1957	8	12		**ALONE**	Pye Nixa N 15112
28/02/1958	12	7		BABY LOVER	Pye Nixa N 15126
26/01/1961	❶¹	15		**SAILOR**	Pye 7N 15324
13/04/1961	44	1		SOMETHING MISSING Song originally featured in the 1935 film *Top Hat*	Pye 7N 15337
13/07/1961	3	15		**ROMEO**	Pye 7N 15361
16/11/1961	7	13		**MY FRIEND THE SEA**	Pye 7N 15389
08/02/1962	41	2		I'M COUNTING ON YOU	Pye 7N 15407
28/06/1962	14	13		YA YA TWIST	Pye 7N 15448
02/05/1963	39	7		CASANOVA/CHARIOT	Pye 7N 15522
12/11/1964	2	15		**DOWNTOWN** ▲² Originally intended for The Drifters, it topped the charts in the US, the first UK female to hit #1 since Vera Lynn in 1952. 1964 Grammy Award for Best Rock & Roll Recording. Featured in the films *Big T.N.T. Show* (1966) and *Girl, Interrupted* (1999)	Pye 7N 15722
11/03/1965	17	8		I KNOW A PLACE 1965 Grammy Award for Best Female Contemporary Rock & Roll Performance	Pye 7N 15772
12/08/1965	44	3		YOU BETTER COME HOME	Pye 7N 15864
14/10/1965	43	3		ROUND EVERY CORNER	Pye 7N 15945
04/11/1965	23	9		YOU'RE THE ONE	Pye 7N 15991
10/02/1966	4	9		**MY LOVE** ▲²	Pye 7N 17038
21/04/1966	49	1		A SIGN OF THE TIMES	Pye 7N 17071
30/06/1966	6	11		**I COULDN'T LIVE WITHOUT YOUR LOVE**	Pye 7N 17133
02/02/1967	❶²	14		**THIS IS MY SONG** This and above single featured in the 1967 film *A Countess From Hong Kong*. It was written by Charlie Chaplin, who directed and had a cameo role in the film	Pye 7N 17258
25/05/1967	12	11		DON'T SLEEP IN THE SUBWAY	Pye 7N 17325
13/12/1967	20	9		THE OTHER MAN'S GRASS (IS ALWAYS GREENER)	Pye 7N 17416
06/03/1968	50	1		KISS ME GOODBYE	Pye 7N 17466
30/01/1971	32	12		THE SONG OF MY LIFE	Pye 7N 45026
15/01/1972	47	2		I DON'T KNOW HOW TO LOVE HIM	Pye 7N 45112
19/11/1988	10	11		**DOWNTOWN '88 (REMIX)**	PRT PYS 19

ROLAND CLARK
US singer.

DATE	POS	WKS	BPI	SINGLE TITLE	LABEL & NUMBER
01/05/1999	18	6		FLOWERZ **ARMAND VAN HELDEN FEATURING ROLAND CLARK**	ffrr FCD 361
23/03/2002	68	1		SPEED (CAN YOU FEEL IT?) **AZZIDO DA BASS FEATURING ROLAND CLARK**	Club Tools 0135815 CLU

DAVE CLARKE
UK DJ/producer who had previously recorded for XL and also set up the Magnetic North label.

DATE	POS	WKS	BPI	SINGLE TITLE	LABEL & NUMBER
30/09/1995	45	2		RED THREE, THUNDER/STORM	Deconstruction 74321306992
03/02/1996	34	2		SOUTHSIDE	Bush 74321335382
15/06/1996	37	2		NO ONE'S DRIVING	Bush 74321380162
08/12/2001	46	1		THE COMPASS	Skint 73CD
28/12/2002	66	1		THE WOLF	Skint 78
25/10/2003	59	1		WAY OF LIFE	Skint 93CD
21/02/2004	50	1		WHAT WAS HER NAME **DAVE CLARKE FEATURING CHICKS ON SPEED**	Skint 94CD

JOHN COOPER CLARKE
UK singer (born 25/1/1949, Manchester), known as the UK's only punk poet, who reads his poems to music invariably produced by Martin Hannett and featuring the Invisible Girls. For many years he provided the voice for the Sugar Puff's Honey Monster.

DATE	POS	WKS	BPI	SINGLE TITLE	LABEL & NUMBER
10/03/1979	39	3		GIMMIX! PLAY LOUD	Epic EPC 7009

RICK CLARKE
UK singer (born in London) who also recorded as a duo with Emma Haywoode.

DATE	POS	WKS	BPI	SINGLE TITLE	LABEL & NUMBER
30/04/1988	63	2		I'LL SEE YOU ALONG THE WAY	WA 1

SHARON DEE CLARKE
– see **SERIOUS ROPE**

WARREN CLARKE FEATURING KATHY BROWN
UK producer and US singer.

DATE	POS	WKS	BPI	SINGLE TITLE	LABEL & NUMBER
02/06/2001	42	1		OVER YOU	Defected DFECT 28CDS

○ Silver disc ● Gold disc ✪ Platinum disc (additional platinum units are indicated by a figure following the symbol) ◎ Singles released prior to 1973 that are known to have sold over 1 million copies in the UK

KELLY CLARKSON
US singer (born 24/4/1982, Burleson, TX) who won *American Idol* in September 2002, with her debut single *A Moment Like This* rising from #52 to #1, the biggest ever leap to #1 in US chart history.

06/09/2003	6	10		MISS INDEPENDENT	S 82876553642
29/11/2003	25	3		LOW/THE TROUBLE WITH LOVE IS B-side featured in the 2003 film *Love Actually*	S 82876570702

CLARKSVILLE
UK singer (born Michael Clarke, Birmingham).

07/02/2004	72	1		SPINNIN'	Wildstar CDWILD 53

CLASH
UK rock group formed in London in 1976 by Mick Jones (born 26/6/1955, London, guitar), Paul Simonon (born 15/12/1955, London, bass), Keith Levene (guitar) and Terry Chimes (later calling himself Tory Crimes, drums), with Joe Strummer (born John Mellors, 21/8/1952, Ankara, Turkey, singer/guitarist) being persuaded to leave the 101ers to join them. Chimes left in 1977 as the group recorded their debut album and was replaced by Nicky 'Topper' Headon (born 30/5/1955, Bromley). With four top ten albums they were a massive draw live. Debut album *The Clash* was deemed unsuitable for US release, but still sold over 100,000 import copies. Headon left in 1983 and was replaced by Pete Howard; Strummer and Simonon announced Mick Jones' departure in September 1983. Jones formed Big Audio Dynamite, while after one more album (*Cut The Crap*) The Clash disbanded in 1986. In November 1987 Headon was jailed for fifteen months for supplying heroin to an addict who subsequently died. Strummer died from a heart attack on 22/12/2002. The group's *Westway To The World* video, directed by Don Letts, won the 2002 Grammy Award for Best Long Form Music Video. The group was inducted into the Rock & Roll Hall of Fame in 2003.

02/04/1977	38	3		WHITE RIOT	CBS 5058
08/10/1977	28	2		COMPLETE CONTROL	CBS 5664
04/03/1978	35	4		CLASH CITY ROCKERS	CBS 5834
24/06/1978	32	7		(WHITE MAN) IN HAMMERSMITH PALAIS	CBS 6383
02/12/1978	19	10		TOMMY GUN	CBS 6788
03/03/1979	25	6		ENGLISH CIVIL WAR (JOHNNY COMES MARCHING HOME)	CBS 7082
19/05/1979	22	8		THE COST OF LIVING EP Tracks on EP: *I Fought The Law, Groovy Times, Gates Of The West* and *Capital Radio*	CBS 7324
15/12/1979	11	10		LONDON CALLING Featured in the film *Billy Elliott* (2000) and the James Bond film *Die Another Day* (2003)	CBS 8087
09/08/1980	12	10		BANKROBBER	CBS 8323
06/12/1980	40	6		THE CALL UP	CBS 9339
24/01/1981	56	4		HITSVILLE UK	CBS 9480
25/04/1981	34	5		THE MAGNIFICENT SEVEN	CBS 1133
28/11/1981	47	6		THIS IS RADIO CLASH	CBS A 1797
01/05/1982	43	3		KNOW YOUR RIGHTS	CBS A 2309
26/06/1982	30	10		ROCK THE CASBAH	CBS A 2429
25/09/1982	17	9		SHOULD I STAY OR SHOULD I GO/STRAIGHT TO HELL	CBS A 2646
12/10/1985	24	5		THIS IS ENGLAND	CBS A 6122
12/03/1988	29	5		I FOUGHT THE LAW	CBS CLASH 1
07/05/1988	46	3		LONDON CALLING Re-issue of CBS 8087	CBS CLASH 2
21/07/1990	57	2		RETURN TO BRIXTON	CBS 6560727
02/03/1991	❶²	9		SHOULD I STAY OR SHOULD I GO Re-issue of CBS A 2646 following use in a Levi Jeans advertisement	Columbia 6566677
13/04/1991	15	6		ROCK THE CASBAH Re-issue of CBS A 2429	Columbia 6568147
08/06/1991	64	2		LONDON CALLING Second re-issue of CBS 8087	Columbia 6569467

CLASS ACTION FEATURING CHRIS WILTSHIRE
US vocal group assembled by producer Leroy Burgess in New York, fronted by Christine Wiltshire, who later sang with Major Harris and Luther Vandross, and fronted Musique.

07/05/1983	49	3		WEEKEND	Jive 35

CLASSICS IV
US rock group formed in Jacksonville, FL by Dennis Yost (vocals), James Cobb (guitar), Wally Eaton (guitar), Joe Wilson (bass) and Kim Venable (drums). Dean Daughtry (bass) joined later. Cobb and Daughtry then formed the Atlanta Rhythm Section.

28/02/1968	46	1		SPOOKY	Liberty LBS 15051

CLASSIX NOUVEAUX
UK group formed in London in 1979 by singer/songwriter Sal Solo (born 5/9/1954, Hatfield) with Gary Steadman (guitar), Mik Sweeney (bass/vocals) and BP Hurding (drums). Steadman left in 1982 to be replaced by Jimi Sumen. BP Hurding and Sumen left in 1984, replaced by Rick Driscoll and Paul Turley. They disbanded in 1985; Solo (living up to his name) went solo.

28/02/1981	43	7		GUILTY	Liberty BP 388
16/05/1981	67	3		TOKYO	Liberty BP 397
08/08/1981	45	5		INSIDE OUTSIDE	Liberty BP 403
07/11/1981	44	4		NEVER AGAIN (THE DAYS TIME ERASED)	Liberty BP 406
13/03/1982	11	9		IS IT A DREAM	Liberty BP 409
29/05/1982	43	4		BECAUSE YOU'RE YOUNG	Liberty BP 411
30/10/1982	60	2		THE END…OR THE BEGINNING	Liberty BP 414

CLAWFINGER
Swedish/Norwegian rock group formed in 1990 by Zak Tell (vocals), Erland Ottem (guitar), Bard Tortensen (guitar) and Jocke Skog (keyboards/vocals).

19/03/1994	54	1		WARFAIR	East West YZ 804CD1

JUDY CLAY – see WILLIAM BELL

ADAM CLAYTON AND LARRY MULLEN
Irish duo Adam Clayton (born 13/3/1960, Chinnor, Oxfordshire, bass) and Larry Mullen (born 31/10/1961, Dublin, drums), both in top Irish group U2.

15/06/1996	7	12		THEME FROM MISSION: IMPOSSIBLE Featured in the 1996 film *Mission Impossible*	Mother MUMCD 75

❶⁹ Number of weeks single topped the UK chart ↑ Entered the UK chart at #1 ▲⁹ Number of weeks single topped the US chart

159

MERRY CLAYTON US singer (born Mary Clayton, 25/12/1948, New Orleans, LA), ex-member of Ray Charles' Raelettes, who formed Sisters Love before signing solo with A&M in 1975.

21/05/1988.....70......1....... YES Featured in the 1987 film *Dirty Dancing* .... RCA PB 49563

CLAYTOWN TROUPE UK group formed by Christian Riou (vocals), Adrian Bennett (guitar), Paul Waterson (bass), Rick Williams (keyboards) and Andy Holt (drums).

16/06/1990.....57......2....... WAYS OF LOVE .... Island IS 464
14/03/1992.....74......1....... WANTED IT ALL .... EMI USA MT 102

CLEA UK vocal group formed by Chloe Staines (born 24/1/1984, Havering), Lynsey Brown (born 29/11/1982, Manchester), Emma Beard (born 18/10/1983, Northampton) and Aimee Kearsley (born 26/10/1985, Southport), competitors on *Popstars: The Rivals*. Although not selected to form the winning female group (Girls Aloud), they formed their own group.

04/10/2003.....21......3....... DOWNLOAD IT 1967 CLEA01CD
28/02/2004.....23......2....... STUCK IN THE MIDDLE 1967 CLEA02CD

JOHNNY CLEGG AND SAVUKA UK singer (born 13/7/1953, Rochdale) who moved to South Africa in 1959 and formed Juluka (Zulu for 'sweat') with Sipho Mchunu in 1976. He formed Savuka in 1986.

16/05/1987.....75......1....... SCATTERLINGS OF AFRICA .... EMI 5605

CLEOPATRA UK vocal trio formed by sisters Yonah (born 27/4/1984, Birmingham), Cleopatra (born 29/4/1982, Birmingham) and Zainam Higgins (born 5/12/1980, Birmingham), and signed by Madonna's Maverick label for the US. They also took part in the BRITS Trust *Thank Abba For The Music* project.

14/02/1998 .....3......10 ..... CLEOPATRA'S THEME .... WEA 133CD
16/05/1998 .....4......7....... LIFE AIN'T EASY .... WEA 159CD1
22/08/1998 .....4......7....... I WANT YOU BACK .... WEA 172CD1
06/03/1999.....24......4....... A TOUCH OF LOVE .... WEA 199CD
29/07/2000.....29......3....... COME AND GET ME .... WEA 261CD1

CLEPTOMANIACS FEATURING BRYAN CHAMBERS UK production group formed by Bryan Tappert, Mark Pomeroy and John Julius Knight with lead vocals by Bryan Chambers.

03/02/2001.....23......3....... ALL I DO .... Defected DFECT 27CDS

CLERGY UK production duo Judge Jules (born Julius O'Riordan) and Paul Masterton, who also collaborated as Yomanda and Hi-Gate. Masterton is also in Amen! UK, The Candy Girls and The Dope Smugglaz.

20/07/2002.....50......1....... THE OBOE SONG .... ffrr DFCD 005

CLICK US rap group formed by E-40 (born Earl Stevens), his brother D-Shot, sister Suga-T and cousin B-Legit.

29/06/1996.....54......1....... SCANDALOUS Contains a sample of Zapp's *Computer Love*.................................. Jive JIVECD 393

CLIENT UK duo Client A and Client B. The pair refused to divulge their names, stating 'We wish to be judged on our artistic merit, as opposed to our personalities.' They were subsequently revealed as Sarah Blackwood (born 6/5/1971, Halifax), formerly of Dubstar, and Kate Holmes, formerly with Frazier Chorus, who first came to prominence supporting Depeche Mode and subsequently signed with Depeche Mode member Andy Fletcher's Toast Hawaii label.

26/06/2004.....51......1....... IN IT FOR THE MONEY .... Toast Hawaii CDTH005
02/10/2004.....68......1....... RADIO .... Toast Hawaii CDTH006

JIMMY CLIFF Jamaican singer (born James Chambers, 1/4/1948, St Catherine) who, after scoring a local hit with *Hurricane Hattie* in 1962, was persuaded to come to the UK in 1965 by Island Records, initially as a backing singer before going solo. After five unsuccessful singles on Island he signed with Trojan and scored immediately. He also wrote hits for Desmond Dekker (*You Can Get It If You Really Want*) and the Pioneers (*Let Your Yeah Be Yeah*). He starred in the films *The Harder They Come* (1973) and *Club Paradise* (1986) and later recorded with Kool & The Gang. He won the 1985 Grammy Award for Best Reggae Recording for *Cliff Hanger* and was given a Contribution to Urban Music Award at the 2002 MOBO Awards.

25/10/1969 .....6......13 ..... WONDERFUL WORLD BEAUTIFUL PEOPLE .... Trojan TR 690
14/02/1970.....46......3....... VIETNAM .... Trojan TR 7722
08/08/1970 .....8......12 ..... WILD WORLD .... Island WIP 6087
19/03/1994.....23......5....... I CAN SEE CLEARLY NOW Featured in the 1993 film *Cool Runnings*..................... Columbia 6601982

BUZZ CLIFFORD US singer (born Reese Francis Clifford III, 8/10/1942, Berwyn, IL) signed by Columbia Records after winning a New Jersey talent contest, later recording folk rock and country rock.

02/03/1961.....17.....13 ..... BABY SITTIN' BOOGIE Baby voices supplied by the children of the producer .... Fontana H 297

LINDA CLIFFORD US singer (born 1944, Brooklyn, NYC) who first recorded for Paramount in 1973. The former beauty queen (Miss New York State, 1965) is also an actress, appearing in the 1968 film *Rosemary's Baby*.

10/06/1978.....50......5....... IF MY FRIENDS COULD SEE ME NOW .... Curtom K 17163
05/05/1979.....28......7....... BRIDGE OVER TROUBLED WATER .... RSO 30
19/09/2001.....69......1....... RIDE THE STORM **AKABU FEATURING LINDA CLIFFORD** .... NRK Sound Division NRKCD 053

CLIMAX BLUES BAND UK group formed in Stafford in 1968 by Colin Cooper (born 7/10/1939, Stafford, saxophone/vocals), Peter Haycock (born 4/4/1952, Stafford, guitar/vocals), Derek Holt (born 26/1/1949, Stafford, bass) and George Newsome (born

○ Silver disc ● Gold disc ✪ Platinum disc (additional platinum units are indicated by a figure following the symbol) ◉ Singles released prior to 1973 that are known to have sold over 1 million copies in the UK

14/8/1947, Stafford, drums) as Climax Chicago Blues Band, with Richard Jones (bass) also a member at the time of their hit.

09/10/1976	10	9		COULDN'T GET IT RIGHT	BTM SBT 105

SIMON CLIMIE
UK singer/songwriter (born 7/4/1960) who penned the George Michael/Aretha Franklin hit *I Knew You Were Waiting Waiting (For Me)* and was one half of the duo Climie Fisher.

19/09/1992	60	2		SOUL INSPIRATION	Epic 6582837

CLIMIE FISHER
UK duo Simon Climie (born 7/4/1960, vocals/keyboards) and ex-Naked Eyes' Rob Fisher (born 5/11/1959, keyboards). Climie is also a songwriter – *I Knew You Were Waiting (For Me)* for George Michael and Aretha Franklin – and producer (Eric Clapton's *The Pilgrim* album). Fisher died after stomach surgery on 25/8/1999.

05/09/1987	67	2		LOVE CHANGES (EVERYTHING)	EMI EM 15
12/12/1987	10	11		RISE TO THE OCCASION	EMI EM 33
12/03/1988	2	12		LOVE CHANGES EVERYTHING (REMIX)	EMI EM 47
21/05/1988	22	5		THIS IS ME	EMI EM 58
20/08/1988	35	4		I WON'T BLEED FOR YOU	EMI EM 66
24/12/1988	22	7		LOVE LIKE A RIVER	EMI EM 81
23/09/1989	50	3		FACTS OF LOVE	EMI EM 103

PATSY CLINE
US singer (born Virginia Patterson Hensley, 8/9/1932, Gore, VA) who made her first record in 1955 and debuted at the Grand Old Opry the same year. She was killed in a plane crash, with Cowboy Copas and Hawkshaw Hawkins, on 5/3/1963 near Camden, TN. A film of her life, *Sweet Dreams* starring Jessica Lange, was made in 1985. She has a star on the Hollywood Walk of Fame.

26/04/1962	43	1		SHE'S GOT YOU	Brunswick 05866
29/11/1962	31	5		HEARTACHES	Brunswick 05878
08/12/1990	14	11		CRAZY Written by Willie Nelson and originally a US hit in 1961	MCA 1465

CLINIC
UK vocal/instrumental group formed in Liverpool in 1997 by Ade Blackburn, Hartley, Brian Campbell and Carl Turney, their debut release appearing on their own Aladdin's Cave Of Golf label.

22/04/2000	70	1		THE RETURN OF EVIL BILL	Domino RUG 093CD
04/11/2000	56	1		THE SECOND LINE Featured in a Levi Jeans advertisement	Domino RUG 116CD
02/03/2002	65	1		WALKING WITH THEE	Domino RUG 134CD

GEORGE CLINTON
US singer (born 22/7/1941, Kannapolis, NC) first known as the leader of Parliament/Funkadelic, going solo in 1982.

04/12/1982	57	5		LOOPZILLA	Capitol CL 271
26/04/1986	57	2		DO FRIES GO WITH THAT SHAKE	Capitol CL 402
27/08/1994	22	3		BOP GUN (ONE NATION) ICE CUBE FEATURING GEORGE CLINTON	Fourth & Broadway BRCD 308

CLIPSE
US rap duo formed in Virginia in 1992 by brothers Malice (Gene Thornton) and Pusha T (Terence Thornton).

22/02/2003	41	2		WHEN THE LAST TIME	Arista 82876502212
24/05/2003	38	3		MA I DON'T LOVE HER CLIPSE FEATURING FAITH EVANS	Arista 82876526482

CLIPZ
UK DJ and producer (born Hugh Pescod, London).

06/03/2004	71	1		COCOA/JIGGY	Full Cycle FCY064

CLOCK
UK dance group formed by DJ and songwriter Stu Allen and Pete Pritchard. They later added O.D.C., M.C. and Tinka before Lorna Saunders and Che-Gun Peters became permanent members.

30/10/1993	66	1		HOLDING ON Contains a sample of The 49ers' *Move Your Feet*	Media MRLCD 007
21/05/1994	28	2		THE RHYTHM	Media MCSTD 1971
10/09/1994	36	3		KEEP THE FIRES BURNING	Media MCSTD 1998
04/03/1995	7	9		AXEL F/KEEP PUSHIN'	Media MCSXD 2041
01/07/1995	4	9		WHOOMPH! (THERE IT IS)	Media MCSTD 2059
26/08/1995	6	5		EVERYBODY	Media MCSTD 2077
18/11/1995	23	3		IN THE HOUSE	Media MCSTD 40005
24/02/1996	27	2		HOLDING ON 4 U	Media MCSTD 40019
07/09/1996	13	10		OH WHAT A NIGHT Cover version of the Four Seasons' *December '63*	Power Station MCSTD 40057
22/03/1997	10	5		IT'S OVER	Media MCSTD 40100
18/10/1997	11	9		U SEXY THING Cover version of Hot Chocolate's 1975 hit	Media MCSTD 40138
17/01/1998	11	4		THAT'S THE WAY (I LIKE IT)	Media MCSTD 40148
11/07/1998	30	3		ROCK YOUR BODY	Media MCSTD 40160
28/11/1998	16	4		BLAME IT ON THE BOOGIE	Media MCSTD 40191
31/07/1999	58	1		SUNSHINE DAY	Media MCSTD 40208

ROSEMARY CLOONEY
US singer (born 23/5/1928, Maysville, KY) who first sang, with her sister Betty, in the late 1940s in the Tony Pastor Band, before going solo. Married for a time to the actor Jose Ferrer, their son Gabriel married Debby Boone. Her biggest UK hit, *Mambo Italiano*, was banned by all ABC radio stations in the US as 'it did not reach standards of good taste', but it still made #9 on the *Billboard* charts. Her nephew is the actor George Clooney. She died from lung cancer on 29/6/2002. She has a star on the Hollywood Walk of Fame.

14/11/1952	3	9		HALF AS MUCH ▲3	Columbia DB 3129

❶9 Number of weeks single topped the UK chart ↑ Entered the UK chart at #1 ▲9 Number of weeks single topped the US chart

161

DATE	POS	WKS	BPI	SINGLE TITLE	LABEL & NUMBER
05/02/1954	7	5		**MAN (UH-HUH)** Listed flip side was *Woman (Uuh-Huh)* by **JOSE FERRER** and both tracks featured in the 1954 film *Deep In My Heart*	Philips PB 220
08/10/1954	❶1	18		**THIS OLE HOUSE** ▲3	Philips PB 336
17/12/1954	❶3	16		**MAMBO ITALIANO** Reclaimed #1 position on 4/2/1955. Featured in the 1996 film *Big Night*	Philips PB 382
20/05/1955	6	13		**WHERE WILL THE BABY'S DIMPLE BE** This and above single credited to **ROSEMARY CLOONEY AND THE MELLOMEN**	Philips PB 428
30/09/1955	4	11		**HEY THERE** ▲6	Philips PB 494
29/03/1957	17	9		MANGOS Featured in the musical revue *Ziegfeld Follies 1957*	Philips PB 671

CLOUD UK instrumental funk group formed in Brighton.

| 31/01/1981 | 72 | 1 | | ALL NIGHT LONG/TAKE IT TO THE TOP | UK Champagne FUNK 1 |

CLOUDBURST – see **DISCO TEX PRESENTS CLOUDBURST**

CLOUT South African group formed in Johannesburg by Cindi Alter (vocals), Bones Brettell (drums), Jennie Garson (keyboards), Inge Herbst (guitar), Sandie Robbie (guitar) and Lee Tomlinson (bass). Popular in their homeland, their only UK hit was a cover of a Righteous Brothers album track. They disbanded in the early 1980s.

| 17/06/1978 | 2 | 15 | ● | **SUBSTITUTE** | Carrere EMI 2788 |

CLS US production duo.

| 30/05/1998 | 46 | 1 | | CAN YOU FEEL IT | Satellite 74321580162 |

CLUB NOUVEAU US group formed in Sacramento, CA by Jay King (producer/owner of the record label), Valerie Watson and Samuelle Prater (vocals) plus instrumentalists Denzil Foster and Thomas McElroy. Prater, Foster and McElroy left in 1988, the latter two producing En Vogue, with their replacements being David Agent and Kevin Irving. Agent left in 1989.

| 21/03/1987 | 3 | 12 | ○ | **LEAN ON ME** ▲2 | King Jay W 8430 |

CLUB 69 Austrian/US duo Suzanne Palmer and Kim Cooper, created by producer Peter Rauhofer. Their debut hit included *Hot Pants Underground Club*, *Slicker Nicker Disco* and *Boxer Short Piano Dub* mixes. Rauhofer won the 1999 Grammy Award for Best Remixer.

| 05/12/1992 | 33 | 5 | | LET ME BE YOUR UNDERWEAR | ffrr F 204 |
| 14/11/1998 | 70 | 1 | | ALRIGHT **CLUB 69 FEATURING SUZANNE PALMER** | Twisted UK TWCD 10039 |

CLUBHOUSE Italian studio group assembled by session singer Silvio Pozzoli and featuring Stephano Scalero and Mauro Interlandi.

23/07/1983	11	6		DO IT AGAIN – BILLIE JEAN (MEDLEY) Mixes/remakes of Steely Dan's *Do It Again* and Michael Jackson's *Billie Jean*	Island IS 132
03/12/1983	59	3		SUPERSTITION – GOOD TIMES (MEDLEY) Mixes/remakes of Stevie Wonder's *Superstition* and Chic's *Good Times*	Island IS 147
01/07/1989	69	3		I'M A MAN – YE KE YE KE (MEDLEY) Mixes/remakes of Spencer Davis Group's *I'm A Man* and Mory Kante's *Yeke Yeke*	Music Man MMPS 7003
20/04/1991	55	4		DEEP IN MY HEART	ffrr F 157
04/09/1993	45	12		LIGHT MY FIRE	PWL Continental PWCD 272
30/04/1994	7	8		**LIGHT MY FIRE (REMIX)**	PWL Continental PWCD 288
23/07/1994	21	3		LIVING IN THE SUNSHINE	PWL Continental PWCD 309
11/03/1995	56	1		NOWHERE LAND This and above three singles credited to **CLUBHOUSE FEATURING CARL**	PWL International PWCD 318

CLUBZONE UK/German group formed by Mike Koglin and Ricky Lyte.

| 19/11/1994 | 50 | 1 | | HANDS UP | Logic 74321236982 |

CLUELESS US vocal/production group fronted by singer Gina Pincosy.

| 05/04/1997 | 61 | 1 | | DON'T SPEAK | ZYX 660738 |

JEREMY CLYDE – see **CHAD STUART AND JEREMY CLYDE**

CLYDE VALLEY STOMPERS UK band formed in the early 1950s by Ian Menzies, later part of the 'trad jazz' boom. They had previously recorded for Decca.

| 09/08/1962 | 25 | 8 | | PETER AND THE WOLF | Parlophone R 4928 |

CMC – see **CHARLOTTE CHURCH**

CM2 FEATURING LISA LAW UK dance group fronted by singer Lisa Law.

| 18/01/2003 | 66 | 1 | | FALL AT YOUR FEET | INCredible 6732532 |

COAST TO COAST UK group fronted by singer Sandy Fontaine, featuring Pattie Hem (vocals), Donna Page (vocals), Sonnie Torlot (saxophone), Jamie Ling (guitar), Budd Smith (bass) and Earl Barton (drums). Their debut hit features vocalist Alan Mills, who left just before the record charted.

| 31/01/1981 | 5 | 15 | ○ | **(DO) THE HUCKLEBUCK** | Polydor POSP 214 |
| 23/05/1981 | 28 | 7 | | LET'S JUMP THE BROOMSTICK | Polydor POSP 249 |

COAST 2 COAST FEATURING DISCOVERY Irish production duo with singer Discovery.

| 16/06/2001 | 44 | 1 | | HOME | Religion 0126955 RLG |

COASTERS

US R&B vocal group formed in Los Angeles, CA in 1955 by Carl Gardner (born 29/4/1928, Tyler, TX), Leon Hughes (born 1938, Los Angeles), Billy Guy (born 20/6/1936, Attasca, TX), Bobby Nunn (born 25/6/1925, Birmingham, AL) and Adolph Jacobs, who left shortly afterwards. Many personnel changes have included Young Jessie replacing Hughes in 1957, then Nunn and Jessie leaving in 1958 when the group relocated to New York. They were replaced by Cornelius Gunter (born 14/11/1938, Los Angeles) and Will 'Dub' Jones. Gunter left in 1961 and was replaced by Earl 'Speedo' Carroll (born 2/11/1937, New York). Among several acts touring as the Coasters, Carl Gardner heads the only genuine group. They have suffered several tragedies: saxophonist King Curtis, known as the fifth Coaster (and who won the 1969 Grammy Award for Best Rhythm & Blues Group Performance [Instrumental] for *Games People Play*), was stabbed to death in a bar brawl on 13/8/1971; Nate Wilson, a member in 1980, was shot and his body dismembered in April 1980 (with former Coasters' manager Patrick Cavanaugh convicted of his murder in 1984); Nunn died of a heart attack on 5/11/1986, and Gunter was shot to death sitting in a Las Vegas car park on 26/1/1990. Will 'Dub' Jones died from diabetes on 16/1/2000. Billy Guy died in November 2002. The group, named after their West Coast roots, were inducted into the Rock & Roll Hall of Fame in 1987.

27/09/1957	30	1		SEARCHIN'	London HLE 8450
15/08/1958	12	8		YAKETY YAK ▲1 Featured in the films *Stand By Me* (1986) and *Andre* (1995)	London HLE 8665
27/03/1959	6	12		**CHARLIE BROWN**	London HLE 8819
30/10/1959	15	7		POISON IVY	London HLE 8938
09/04/1994	41	4		SORRY BUT I'M GONNA HAVE TO PASS Originally released in 1958 and revived following its use in an advertisement for Volkswagen cars	Rhino A 4519CD

ODIA COATES – see PAUL ANKA

LUIS COBOS FEATURING PLACIDO DOMINGO

Spanish orchestra leader and Spanish operatic singer.

16/06/1990	59	2		NESSUN DORMA FROM 'TURANDOT'	Epic 6560057

EDDIE COCHRAN

US singer (born Edward Ray Cochrane, 3/10/1938, Oklahoma City, OK, raised in Minnesota). After moving to Bell Gardens in California in 1953 he teamed up with Hank Cochran (no relation) as the Cochran Brothers, who recorded for Ekko Records in 1954 as a country act. They parted in 1956, Eddie making a single for Crest before landing roles in a number of films. A popular live act, he was on a UK tour in 1960 when the car carrying him and Gene Vincent (on the London-bound A4) skidded into a lamppost. Vincent suffered numerous fractures but Cochran was thrown head first through the windscreen, dying sixteen hours later on 17/4/1960 without regaining consciousness. He was inducted into the Rock & Roll Hall of Fame in 1987.

07/11/1958	18	6		SUMMERTIME BLUES Featured in the 1987 film *La Bamba*	London HLU 8702
13/03/1959	6	13		**C'MON EVERYBODY**	London HLU 8792
16/10/1959	22	3		SOMETHIN' ELSE	London HLU 8944
22/01/1960	22	4		HALLELUJAH I LOVE HER SO	London HLW 9022
12/05/1960	❶2	15		**THREE STEPS TO HEAVEN** Posthumous #1. Featured in the 1988 film *Scandal*	London HLG 9115
06/10/1960	38	3		SWEETIE PIE	London HLG 9196
03/11/1960	41	1		LONELY	London HLG 9196
15/06/1961	15	16		WEEKEND	London HLG 9362
30/11/1961	31	4		JEANNIE, JEANNIE, JEANNIE	London HLG 9460
25/04/1963	23	10		MY WAY	Liberty LIB 10088
24/04/1968	34	8		SUMMERTIME BLUES Re-issue of London HLU 8702	Liberty LBF 15071
13/02/1988	14	7		C'MON EVERYBODY Re-issue of London HLU 8792 following use in a Levi Jeans advertisement	Liberty EDDIE 501

TOM COCHRANE

Canadian singer (born 13/5/1955, Lynn Lake, Manitoba) who formed Red Rider in 1976 before going solo in 1992.

27/06/1992	62	2		LIFE IS A HIGHWAY	Capitol CL 660

COCK ROBIN

US group formed in Los Angeles, CA in 1984 by Peter Kingsbery (vocals/bass), Anna LaCazio (vocals/keyboards), Clive Wright (guitar) and Louis Molino III (drums). They disbanded in 1990.

31/05/1986	28	12		THE PROMISE YOU MADE	CBS A 6764

JOE COCKER

UK singer (born John Robert Cocker, 20/5/1944, Sheffield) who formed skiffle group the Cavaliers in 1960 and signed his first contract with Decca in 1964 while working for the Gas Board. After little success he returned to the Gas Board, forming the Grease Band in 1965, and two years later signed with Regal Zonophone in 1968. He hit #1 in the UK with a cover of The Beatles' *With A Little Help From My Friends* (who were so impressed they sent him a telegram of congratulations). Subsequent appearances at Woodstock, Filmore and the Isle of Wight broadened his appeal. He took part in the *It's Only Rock 'N' Roll* project for the Children's Promise charity.

22/05/1968	48	1		MARJORINE	Regal Zonophone RZ 3006
02/10/1968	❶1	13		**WITH A LITTLE HELP FROM MY FRIENDS**	Regal Zonophone RZ 3013
27/09/1969	10	11		**DELTA LADY** Written by Leon Russell as a tribute to Rita Coolidge	Regal Zonophone RZ 3024
04/07/1970	39	6		THE LETTER	Regal Zonophone RZ 3027
26/09/1981	61	3		I'M SO GLAD I'M STANDING HERE TODAY CRUSADERS, FEATURED VOCALIST JOE COCKER	MCA 741
15/01/1983	7	13	O	UP WHERE WE BELONG ▲3 JOE COCKER AND JENNIFER WARNES Featured in the 1982 film *An Officer And A Gentleman*. It is referred to as the 'love theme', although it appears over the end titles. 1982 Grammy Award for Best Vocal Performance by a Duo and Oscar for Best Film Song	Island WIP 6830
14/11/1987	46	4		UNCHAIN MY HEART	Capitol CL 465
13/01/1990	65	2		WHEN THE NIGHT COMES	Capitol CL 535
07/03/1992	25	5		(ALL I KNOW) FEELS LIKE FOREVER	Capitol CL 645
09/05/1992	28	6		NOW THAT THE MAGIC HAS GONE	Capitol CL 657
04/07/1992	17	6		UNCHAIN MY HEART	Capitol CL 664

❶9 Number of weeks single topped the UK chart   ↑ Entered the UK chart at #1   ▲9 Number of weeks single topped the US chart

DATE	POS	WKS	BPI	SINGLE TITLE	LABEL & NUMBER
21/11/1992	61	3		WHEN THE NIGHT COMES	Capitol CL 674
13/08/1994	17	5		THE SIMPLE THINGS	Capitol CDCLS 722
22/10/1994	41	3		TAKE ME HOME JOE COCKER FEATURING BEKKA BRAMLETT	Capitol CDCLS 729
17/12/1994	32	5		LET THE HEALING BEGIN	Capitol CDCLS 727
23/09/1995	67	2		HAVE A LITTLE FAITH	Capitol CDCLS 744
12/10/1996	53	1		DON'T LET ME BE MISUNDERSTOOD	Parlophone CDCLS 779

COCKEREL CHORUS UK group of Tottenham Hotspur football supporters adopting a catchphrase from a TV advert for bread, turning it into a tribute to full back Cyril Knowles (who died from a brain tumour in 1991).

DATE	POS	WKS	BPI	SINGLE TITLE	LABEL & NUMBER
24/02/1973	14	12		NICE ONE CYRIL	Young Blood YB 1017

COCKNEY REBEL – see STEVE HARLEY AND COCKNEY REBEL

COCKNEY REJECTS UK punk group formed in London in 1978 by Jefferson 'Stinky' Turner (vocals), Vince Riordan (bass), Micky Geggus (guitar) and Keith Warrington (drums). They disbanded in 1985, re-forming in 1990.

DATE	POS	WKS	BPI	SINGLE TITLE	LABEL & NUMBER
01/12/1979	65	2		I'M NOT A FOOL	EMI 5008
16/02/1980	65	3		BADMAN	EMI 5035
26/04/1980	21	7		THE GREATEST COCKNEY RIPOFF	Zonophone Z 2
17/05/1980	35	5		I'M FOREVER BLOWING BUBBLES	Zonophone Z 4
12/07/1980	65	2		WE CAN DO ANYTHING	Zonophone Z 6
25/10/1980	54	3		WE ARE THE FIRM	Zonophone Z 10

COCO UK dance group formed by Victor Imbres and Rob Davies, fronted by singer Coco. Their debut hit was later part of the #1 *Toca's Miracle* by Fragma: the record utilised the instrumental *Toca Me* by Fragma with the vocals from *I Need A Miracle*.

DATE	POS	WKS	BPI	SINGLE TITLE	LABEL & NUMBER
08/11/1997	39	2		I NEED A MIRACLE	Positiva CDTIV 81

CO-CO UK vocal group specifically formed by Terry Bradford, Keith Hasler, Paul Rogers, Josie Andrews and Cheryl Baker to represent the UK in the Eurovision Song Contest. They came eleventh behind Israel's entry *A Ba Ni Bi* by Izhar Cohen & Alphabeta. Baker was later in Bucks Fizz, another specially formed UK Eurovision entrant.

DATE	POS	WKS	BPI	SINGLE TITLE	LABEL & NUMBER
22/04/1978	13	7		BAD OLD DAYS UK entry for the 1978 Eurovision Song Contest	Ariola Hansa AHA 513

COCONUTS US vocal group formed by Fonda Rae, Lordes Cotto and Brooksi Wells, who were assembled by Kid Creole and sang backing on his hits.

DATE	POS	WKS	BPI	SINGLE TITLE	LABEL & NUMBER
11/06/1983	60	3		DID YOU HAVE TO LOVE ME LIKE YOU DID	EMI America EA 156

COCTEAU TWINS UK group formed in Grangemouth in 1981 by Elizabeth Fraser (born 29/8/1958, Grangemouth, vocals), Robin Guthrie (born 4/1/1962, Grangemouth, bass/drum programming/keyboards) and Will Heggie. Heggie left in 1984 and was replaced by Simon Raymonde (born 3/4/1962, London, bass/piano/keyboards). Guthrie and Raymonde launched the Bella Union label in 1997. Fraser has also recorded with the Future Sound Of London, Massive Attack and Ian McCulloch.

DATE	POS	WKS	BPI	SINGLE TITLE	LABEL & NUMBER
28/04/1984	29	5		PEARLY-DEWDROPS' DROPS	4AD 405
30/03/1985	41	3		AIKEA-GUINEA	4AD AD 501
23/11/1985	52	2		TINY DYNAMITE (EP) Tracks on EP: *Pink Orange Red, Ribbed And Veined, Plain Tiger* and *Sultitan Itan*	4AD BAD 510
07/12/1985	65	1		ECHOES IN A SHALLOW BAY (EP) Tracks on EP: *Great Spangled Fritillary, Melonella, Pale Clouded White* and *Eggs And Their Shells*	4AD BAD 511
25/10/1986	53	1		LOVE'S EASY TEARS	4AD BAD 610
08/09/1990	38	3		ICEBLINK LUCK	4AD AD 0011
02/10/1993	34	2		EVANGELINE	Fontana CTCD 1
18/12/1993	58	1		WINTER WONDERLAND/FROSTY THE SNOWMAN	Fontana COCCD 1
26/02/1994	33	2		BLUEBEARD	Fontana CTCD 2
07/10/1995	59	1		TWINLIGHTS (EP) Tracks on EP: *Golden-Vein, Half-Gifts, Pink Orange Red* and *Rilkean Heart*	Fontana CTCD 3
04/11/1995	59	1		OTHERNESS (EP) Tracks on EP: *Cherry Coloured Funk, Feet Like Fins, Seekers Who Are Lovers* and *Violaine*	Fontana CTCD 4
30/03/1996	34	2		TISHBITE	Fontana CTCD 5
20/07/1996	56	1		VIOLAINE	Fontana CTCD 6

C.O.D. US R&B group produced by Raul A Rodriguez.

DATE	POS	WKS	BPI	SINGLE TITLE	LABEL & NUMBER
14/05/1983	54	2		IN THE BOTTLE	Streetwave WAVE 2

CODE RED UK vocal group formed by Roger Ratajczak (born 15/3/1976, London), Lee Missen (born 21/3/1977, London), Neil Watts (born 7/1/1974, Bedfordshire) and Phil Rodell (born 15/8/175, St Albans).

DATE	POS	WKS	BPI	SINGLE TITLE	LABEL & NUMBER
06/07/1996	50	1		I GAVE YOU EVERYTHING	Polydor 5763992
16/11/1996	59	1		THIS IS OUR SONG	Polydor 5766332
14/06/1997	29	2		CAN WE TALK	Polydor 5710992
09/08/1997	34	2		IS THERE SOMEONE OUT THERE?	Polydor 5714652
04/07/1998	55	1		WHAT WOULD YOU DO IF...?	Polydor 5673312

COFFEE US R&B vocal group formed in New York by Lenora Dee Bryant, Glenda Hester and Elaine Sims, their debut hit a cover of a song recorded by Ruby Andrews and Loleatta Holloway.

DATE	POS	WKS	BPI	SINGLE TITLE	LABEL & NUMBER
27/09/1980	13	10		CASANOVA	De-Lite MER 38
06/12/1980	57	3		SLIP AND DIP/I WANNA BE WITH YOU	De-Lite DE 1

○ Silver disc ● Gold disc ✪ Platinum disc (additional platinum units are indicated by a figure following the symbol) ◎ Singles released prior to 1973 that are known to have sold over 1 million copies in the UK

ALMA COGAN UK singer (born 19/5/1932, London) who was popular in the the 1950s with her trademark 'chuckle' and extravagant dresses. She also recorded duets with Frankie Vaughan, Ronnie Hilton and Ocher Nebbish (a pseudonym for songwriter Lionel Bart, who intended marrying Alma, though they never wed). As a songwriter she wrote *Wait For Me* for Ronnie Carroll and *I Only Dream Of You* for Joe Dolan under the pseudonym of Al Western. Shortly before her death from cancer on 26/10/1966 she had completed tracks with Rolling Stones producer Andrew Loog Oldham, which were later scrapped.

19/03/1954	4	9		**BELL BOTTOM BLUES**	HMV B 10653
27/08/1954	11	5		LITTLE THINGS MEAN A LOT	HMV B 10717
03/12/1954	6	11		**I CAN'T TELL A WALTZ FROM A TANGO**	HMV B 10786
27/05/1955	❶²	16		**DREAMBOAT**	HMV B 10872
23/09/1955	17	1		BANJO'S BACK IN TOWN	HMV B 10917
14/10/1955	16	4		GO ON BY B-side to *Banjo's Back In Town*	HMV B 10917
16/12/1955	17	1		TWENTY TINY FINGERS	HMV POP 129
23/12/1955	6	5		**NEVER DO A TANGO WITH AN ESKIMO** B-side to *Twenty Tiny Fingers*	HMV POP 129
30/03/1956	13	8		WILLIE CAN **ALMA COGAN WITH DESMOND LANE – PENNY WHISTLE**	HMV POP 187
13/07/1956	25	4		THE BIRDS AND THE BEES	HMV POP 223
10/08/1956	22	3		WHY DO FOOLS FALL IN LOVE	HMV POP 223
02/11/1956	20	4		IN THE MIDDLE OF THE HOUSE	HMV POP 261
18/01/1957	18	6		YOU ME AND US	HMV POP 284
29/03/1957	26	2		WHATEVER LOLA WANTS	HMV POP 317
31/01/1958	25	2		THE STORY OF MY LIFE	HMV POP 433
14/02/1958	16	11		SUGARTIME	HMV POP 450
23/01/1959	27	2		LAST NIGHT ON THE BACK PORCH	HMV POP 573
18/12/1959	26	4		WE GOT LOVE	HMV POP 670
12/05/1960	48	1		DREAM TALK	HMV POP 728
11/08/1960	27	5		TRAIN OF LOVE	HMV POP 760
20/04/1961	37	6		COWBOY JIMMY JOE	Columbia DB 4607

SHAYE COGAN US singer who had previously recorded for Roulette. She was also an actress, appearing in the 1950 TV series *The Vaughan Monroe Show* and films such as *Jack And The Beanstalk* (1952) and *Mister Rock And Roll* (1957).

| 24/03/1960 | 40 | 1 | | MEAN TO ME | MGM 1063 |

COHEN VS DELUXE Brazilian and UK duo Renato Cohen (born 1974, Sao Paulo) and Tim 'Deluxe' Liken.

| 13/03/2004 | 70 | 1 | | JUST KICK | Intec INTEC024 |

IZHAR COHEN AND ALPHABETA Israeli singer whose winning entry in the 1978 Eurovision Song Contest beat Co-Co into eleventh place. The winning song was written by Ehud Manor and Nurit Hirsh.

| 13/05/1978 | 20 | 7 | | A BA NI BI 1978 Eurovision Song Contest winner | Polydor 2001 781 |

MARC COHN US singer/pianist/songwriter (born 5/7/1959, Cleveland, OH) with a fourteen-piece band called the Supreme Court. Discovered by Carly Simon at the wedding of Caroline Kennedy and won the 1991 Grammy Award for Best New Artist.

25/05/1991	66	4		WALKING IN MEMPHIS	Atlantic A 7747
10/08/1991	54	3		SILVER THUNDERBIRD	Atlantic A 7657
12/10/1991	22	5		WALKING IN MEMPHIS Re-issue of Atlantic A 7747	Atlantic A 7585
29/05/1993	37	3		WALK THROUGH THE WORLD	Atlantic A 7340CD

COLA BOY UK duo Andrew Midgely and Janey Lee Grace. The hit credited Jesse Chin, a Hong Kong teenager who sold his collection of rare Coca-Cola bottles to finance the single, hence the Cola Boy artist credit, but the story was completely fictitious.

| 06/07/1991 | 8 | 7 | | **7 WAYS TO LOVE** | Arista 114526 |

COLD JAM FEATURING GRACE US vocal/instrumental group.

| 28/07/1990 | 64 | 2 | | LAST NIGHT A DJ SAVED MY LIFE | Big Wave BWR 39 |

COLDCUT UK duo Matt Black and Jonathan Moore who also remix other people's hits. They launched their own Ahead Of Our Time and Ninjas Tune labels.

20/02/1988	6	9		**DOCTORIN' THE HOUSE COLDCUT FEATURING YAZZ AND THE PLASTIC POPULATION**	Ahead Of Our Time CCUT 2
10/09/1988	21	7		STOP THIS CRAZY THING COLDCUT FEATURING JUNIOR REID AND THE AHEAD OF OUR TIME ORCHESTRA	Ahead Of Our Time CCUT 4
25/03/1989	11	9		PEOPLE HOLD ON **COLDCUT FEATURING LISA STANSFIELD**	Ahead Of Our Time CCUT 5
03/06/1989	52	2		MY TELEPHONE	Ahead Of Our Time CCUT 6
16/12/1989	67	3		COLDCUT'S CHRISTMAS BREAK	Ahead Of Our Time CCUT 7
26/05/1990	52	2		FIND A WAY **COLDCUT FEATURING QUEEN LATIFAH**	Ahead Of Our Time CCUT 8
04/09/1993	54	2		DREAMER	Arista 74321156642
22/01/1994	50	2		AUTUMN LEAVES	Arista 74321171052
16/08/1997	37	2		MORE BEATS & PIECES The first enhanced CD (featuring additional text and video) to chart	Ninja Tune ZENCDS 58
16/06/2001	67	1		REVOLUTION **COLDCUT AND THE GUILTY PARTY**	Ninja Tune ZENCDS 88

COLDPLAY UK rock group formed in London in January 1998 by Chris Martin (born 2/3/1977, Exeter, guitar/keyboards/vocals), Jonny Buckland (born 11/9/1977, Mold, guitar), Guy Berryman (born 12/4/1978, Kirkcaldy, bass) and Will Champion (born 31/7/1978, Southampton, drums) as Starfish, then changing their name to Coldplay. Financing their first release, they also recorded for Fierce Panda before linking with Parlophone in 1999. They won two BRIT Awards in 2001: Best UK Group and Best UK Album for *Parachutes*,

❶⁹ Number of weeks single topped the UK chart ↑ Entered the UK chart at #1 ▲⁹ Number of weeks single topped the US chart

165

repeating the success in 2003, collecting Best UK Group and Best UK Album for *A Rush Of Blood To The Head*. They have also won four Grammy Awards including Best Alternative Music Album in 2001 for *Parachutes*, and Best Alternative Music Album in 2002 for *A Rush Of Blood To The Head*. They also won the 2002 MTV Europe Music Award for Select UK & Ireland Act and the 2003 award for Best Group. Martin married actress Gwyneth Paltrow in December 2003.

DATE	POS	WKS	BPI	SINGLE TITLE	LABEL & NUMBER
18/03/2000	35	3		SHIVER	Parlophone CDR 6536
08/07/2000	4	11		**YELLOW**	Parlophone CDR 6538
04/11/2000	10	9		**TROUBLE**	Parlophone CDRS 6549
17/08/2002	2	10		**IN MY PLACE** 2002 Grammy Award for Best Rock Performance by a Duo or Group with Vocal	Parlophone CDR 6579
23/11/2002	10	9		**THE SCIENTIST**	Parlophone CDR 6588
05/04/2003	9	8		**CLOCKS** 2003 Grammy Award for Record of the Year	Parlophone CDR 6594

ANDY COLE
UK singer (born 15/10/1971, Nottingham), better known as a footballer, having played for Arsenal, Fulham, Bristol City, Newcastle United, Manchester United and Blackburn Rovers as well as England.

DATE	POS	WKS	BPI	SINGLE TITLE	LABEL & NUMBER
18/09/1999	68	1		OUTSTANDING	WEA 224CD

COZY COLE
US drummer (born William Randolph Cole, 17/10/1909, East Orange, NJ) who played with the likes of Benny Carter, Cab Calloway and Louis Armstrong during the swing era. He also appeared in films, including *Make Mine Music* (1946) and *The Glenn Miller Story* (1954). He died from cancer on 29/1/1981.

DATE	POS	WKS	BPI	SINGLE TITLE	LABEL & NUMBER
05/12/1958	29	1		TOPSY (PARTS 1 AND 2)	London HL 8750

GEORGE COLE – see DENNIS WATERMAN

LLOYD COLE AND THE COMMOTIONS
UK singer (born 31/1/1961, Buxton, guitar/vocals) who formed the Commotions in 1983 with Blair Cowan (keyboards), Neil Clark (born 3/7/1955, guitar), Steven Irvine (born 16/12/1959, drums) and Lawrence Donegan (born 13/7/1961, bass). They signed with Polydor on the strength of demo tapes and local gigs. The group disbanded in 1989 and Cole went solo.

DATE	POS	WKS	BPI	SINGLE TITLE	LABEL & NUMBER
26/05/1984	26	9		PERFECT SKIN	Polydor COLE 1
25/08/1984	41	6		FOREST FIRE	Polydor COLE 2
17/11/1984	65	2		RATTLESNAKES	Polydor COLE 3
14/09/1985	19	8		BRAND NEW FRIEND	Polydor COLE 4
09/11/1985	17	7		LOST WEEKEND	Polydor COLE 5
18/01/1986	38	4		CUT ME DOWN	Polydor COLE 6
03/10/1987	46	4		MY BAG	Polydor COLE 7
09/01/1988	31	5		JENNIFER SHE SAID	Polydor COLE 8
23/04/1988	59	2		FROM THE HIP (EP) **LLOYD COLE** Tracks on EP: *From The Hip, From The Hip (Remix), Lonely Mile, Love Your Wife* and *Please*	Polydor COLE 9
03/02/1990	42	4		NO BLUE SKIES	Polydor COLE 11
07/04/1990	59	3		DON'T LOOK BACK	Polydor COLE 12
31/08/1991	55	2		SHE'S A GIRL AND I'M A MAN	Polydor COLE 14
25/09/1993	72	2		SO YOU'D LIKE TO SAVE THE WORLD	Fontana VIBE D1
16/09/1995	24	3		LIKE LOVERS DO	Fontana LCDD 1
02/12/1995	73	1		SENTIMENTAL FOOL	Fontana LCDD 2

MJ COLE
UK producer Matt Coleman (born 1973, London) who won the 2000 MOBO Award for Best Producer.

DATE	POS	WKS	BPI	SINGLE TITLE	LABEL & NUMBER
23/05/1998	38	2		SINCERE	AM:PM 5826912
06/05/2000	10	7		**CRAZY LOVE**	Talkin Loud TLCD 59
12/08/2000	13	5		SINCERE Re-issue of AM:PM 5826912	Talkin Loud TLCD 60
02/12/2000	35	2		**HOLD ON TO ME MJ COLE FEATURING ELISABETH TROY**	Talkin Loud TLCD 62
29/03/2003	30	3		**WONDERING WHY**	Talkin Loud 0779522

NAT 'KING' COLE
US singer/pianist (born Nathaniel Adams Coles, 17/3/1917, Montgomery, AL, raised in Chicago, IL) who formed the Royal Dukes in 1934 and recorded two years later with his brother Eddie. In 1939 he formed a trio with Oscar Moore (guitar) and Wesley Prince (bass), who was later replaced by Johnny Miller. The trio's success led to his going solo in 1950. He later moved into films, which included *St Louis Blues* (1958), an inaccurate biopic of WC Handy, and *Cat Ballou* (1965). He stopped performing in 1964 due to ill health and died from lung cancer on 15/2/1965. His 1946 recording *The Christmas Song* was honoured with a Grammy Hall of Fame award in 1974, and daughter Natalie won three awards in 1991 for her use of his vocal on *Unforgettable* and a further award in 1996 for *When I Fall In Love*. Inducted into the Rock & Roll Hall of Fame in 2000, he has a star on the Hollywood Walk of Fame for his contribution to recording, and a second star for TV.

DATE	POS	WKS	BPI	SINGLE TITLE	LABEL & NUMBER
14/11/1952	3	7		**SOMEWHERE ALONG THE WAY**	Capitol CL 13774
19/12/1952	6	4		**BECAUSE YOU'RE MINE**	Capitol CL 13811
02/01/1953	10	4		**FAITH CAN MOVE MOUNTAINS** B-side to *Because You're Mine*	Capitol CL 13811
24/04/1953	2	18		**PRETEND**	Capitol CL 13878
14/08/1953	6	8		**CAN'T I?**	Capitol CL 13937
18/09/1953	7	7		**MOTHER NATURE AND FATHER TIME**	Capitol CL 13912
16/04/1954	10	1		**TENDERLY**	Capitol CL 14061
10/09/1954	2	14		**SMILE**	Capitol CL 14149

DATE	POS	WKS	BPI	SINGLE TITLE	LABEL & NUMBER
08/10/1954	11	2		MAKE HER MINE B-side to *Smile*	Capitol CL 14149
25/02/1955	3	10		**A BLOSSOM FELL**	Capitol CL 14235
26/08/1955	17	2		MY ONE SIN	Capitol CL 14327
27/01/1956	10	9		**DREAMS CAN TELL A LIE**	Capitol CL 14513
11/05/1956	8	14		**TOO YOUNG TO GO STEADY** From the musical *Strip For Action*	Capitol CL 14573
14/09/1956	11	15		LOVE ME AS IF THERE WERE NO TOMORROW	Capitol CL 14621
19/04/1957	2	20		**WHEN I FALL IN LOVE** Tune originally the main theme to the 1952 film *One Minute To Zero*	Capitol CL 14709
05/07/1957	28	1		WHEN ROCK 'N ROLL CAME TO TRINIDAD	Capitol CL 14733
18/10/1957	21	2		MY PERSONAL POSSESSION **NAT 'KING' COLE AND THE FOUR KNIGHTS**	Capitol CL 14765
25/10/1957	24	2		STARDUST Featured in the 1993 film *Sleepless In Seattle*	Capitol CL 14787
29/05/1959	22	3		YOU MADE ME LOVE YOU	Capitol CL 15017
04/09/1959	23	4		MIDNIGHT FLYER 1959 Grammy Award for Best Performance by a Top 40 Artist	Capitol CL 15056
12/02/1960	23	5		TIME AND THE RIVER	Capitol CL 15111
26/05/1960	10	8		**THAT'S YOU**	Capitol CL 15129
10/11/1960	18	10		JUST AS MUCH AS EVER	Capitol CL 15163
02/02/1961	36	10		THE WORLD IN MY ARMS	Capitol CL 15178
16/11/1961	29	10		LET TRUE LOVE BEGIN	Capitol CL 15224
22/03/1962	34	4		BRAZILIAN LOVE SONG	Capitol CL 15241
31/05/1962	42	4		THE RIGHT THING TO SAY	Capitol CL 15250
19/07/1962	11	14		LET THERE BE LOVE **NAT 'KING' COLE WITH GEORGE SHEARING**	Capitol CL 15257
27/09/1962	5	14		**RAMBLIN' ROSE**	Capitol CL 15270
20/12/1962	37	3		DEAR LONELY HEARTS	Capitol CL 15280
12/12/1987	4	7		**WHEN I FALL IN LOVE** Re-issue of Capitol CL 14709	Capitol CL 15975
22/06/1991	19	8		UNFORGETTABLE **NATALIE COLE WITH NAT 'KING' COLE** Features the vocals of Nat 'King' Cole dubbed from his 1952 original. 1991 Grammy Award for Song of the Year for writer Irving Gordon, even though the song had originally been written in 1951	Elektra EKR 128
14/12/1991	69	2		THE CHRISTMAS SONG	Capitol CL 641
19/03/1994	30	3		LET'S FACE THE MUSIC AND DANCE Featured in a TV advertisement for Allied Dunbar	EMI CDEM 312

NATALIE COLE US singer (born 6/2/1950, Los Angeles, CA) and daughter of Nat 'King' Cole. Debuting at eleven, she met producers Charles Jackson and Marvin Yancy in 1973 and landed a deal with Capitol in 1975. She married Yancey, later divorced him and married ex-Rufus drummer Andre Fischer. Eight Grammy Awards include: Best New Artist in 1975; Best Rhythm & Blues Vocal Performance in 1976 for *Sophisticated Lady*; Record of the Year, Album of the Year and Best Traditional Pop Vocal Performance in 1991 for *Unforgettable*; Best Jazz Vocal Performance in 1993 for *Take A Look*; and Best Pop Collaboration with Vocals in 1996 for *When I Fall In Love*. She has a star on the Hollywood Walk of Fame.

DATE	POS	WKS	BPI	SINGLE TITLE	LABEL & NUMBER
11/10/1975	32	5		THIS WILL BE Featured in the films *The Parent Trap* (1999) and *Charlie's Angels: Full Throttle* (2003). 1975 Grammy Award for Best Rhythm & Blues Vocal Performance	Capitol CL 15834
08/08/1987	44	8		JUMP START	Manhattan MT 22
26/03/1988	5	12		**PINK CADILLAC**	Manhattan MT 35
25/06/1988	28	6		EVERLASTING	Manhattan MT 46
20/08/1988	36	5		JUMP START	Manhattan MT 50
26/11/1988	23	14		I LIVE FOR YOUR LOVE	Manhattan MT 57
15/04/1989	2	15	○	**MISS YOU LIKE CRAZY**	EMI-USA MT 63
22/07/1989	56	2		REST OF THE NIGHT	EMI-USA MT 69
16/12/1989	56	4		STARTING OVER AGAIN	EMI-USA MT 77
21/04/1990	16	7		WILD WOMEN DO Featured in the 1990 film *Pretty Woman*	EMI-USA MT 81
22/06/1991	19	8		UNFORGETTABLE **NATALIE COLE WITH NAT 'KING' COLE** Features the vocals of Nat 'King' Cole dubbed from his 1952 original. 1991 Grammy Award for Song of the Year for writer Irving Gordon, even though the song had originally been written in 1951	Elektra EKR 128
16/05/1992	71	1		THE VERY THOUGHT OF YOU	Elektra EKR 147

PAULA COLE US singer/songwriter/producer (born 5/4/1968, Rockport, MA) who was previously in Peter Gabriel's backing band. She won the Best New Artist award at the 1997 Grammy Awards and appeared in the 1998 film *Don't Explain*.

DATE	POS	WKS	BPI	SINGLE TITLE	LABEL & NUMBER
28/06/1997	15	8		WHERE HAVE ALL THE COWBOYS GONE?	Warner Brothers W 0406CD
01/08/1998	43	1		I DON'T WANT TO WAIT	Warner Brothers W 0422CD

NAIMEE COLEMAN – see **AURORA**

COLETTE – see **SISTER BLISS**

JOHN FORD COLEY – see **ENGLAND DAN AND JOHN FORD COLEY**

COLLAGE US dance group formed in Los Angeles, CA by Richard Aguon (drums/vocals), Dean Boysen (trumpet), Emilio Conesa (guitar/vocals), Kirk Crumpler (bass), Albert DeGracia (keyboards), Ruben Laxamana (saxophone), Melecioi Magdaluyo (saxophone), Lee Peters (vocals), Larry White (guitar) and Ross Wilson (trumpet).

DATE	POS	WKS	BPI	SINGLE TITLE	LABEL & NUMBER
21/09/1985	46	5		ROMEO WHERE'S JULIET	MCA 1006

COLLAPSED LUNG UK rock group formed in 1993 by Jim Burke (vocals), Anthony Chapman (vocals), Jonny Douve (bass), Steve Harcourt (guitar) and Jerry Hawkins (drums).

❶⁹ Number of weeks single topped the UK chart ↑ Entered the UK chart at #1 ▲⁹ Number of weeks single topped the US chart

167

DATE	POS	WKS	BPI	SINGLE TITLE	LABEL & NUMBER
22/06/1996	31	3		LONDON TONIGHT/EAT MY GOAL	Deceptive BLUFF 029CD
30/05/1998	18	5		EAT MY GOAL Re-issue of Deceptive BLUFF 029CD	Deceptive BLUFF 060CD

DAVE AND ANSIL COLLINS Jamaican duo session singer Dave Barker and keyboard player Ansell Collins who linked in 1971. Ansell's forename has caused confusion ever since – he was billed Ansil on the hit single but records as Ansell solo.

DATE	POS	WKS	BPI	SINGLE TITLE	LABEL & NUMBER
27/03/1971	❶²	15		**DOUBLE BARREL**	Technique TE 901
26/06/1971	7	12		**MONKEY SPANNER**	Technique TE 914

EDWYN COLLINS UK singer (born 23/8/1959, Edinburgh) and a member of the Nu-Sonics before singing lead with Orange Juice in 1979.

DATE	POS	WKS	BPI	SINGLE TITLE	LABEL & NUMBER
11/08/1984	72	2		PALE BLUE EYES PAUL QUINN AND EDWYN COLLINS	Swamplands SWP 1
12/11/1994	42	3		EXPRESSLY (EP) Track on EP: *A Girl Like You*	Setanta ZOP 001CD1
17/06/1995	4	14	O	A GIRL LIKE YOU Featured in the films *Empire Records* (1995), *Never Talk To Strangers* (1995) and *Charlie's Angels: Full Throttle* (2003)	Setanta ZOP 003CD
02/03/1996	45	2		KEEP ON BURNING	Setanta ZOP 004CD1
02/08/1997	32	3		THE MAGIC PIPER (OF LOVE) Featured in the 1997 film *Austin Powers – International Man Of Mystery*	Setanta SETCDA 041
18/10/1997	71	1		ADIDAS WORLD	Setanta SETCDA 045

FELICIA COLLINS – see LUKK FEATURING FELICIA COLLINS

JEFF COLLINS UK singer who had previously recorded for RCA.

DATE	POS	WKS	BPI	SINGLE TITLE	LABEL & NUMBER
18/11/1972	40	8		ONLY YOU	Polydor 2058 287

JUDY COLLINS US singer (born 1/5/1939, Seattle, WA, raised in Denver) who originally trained as a classical pianist but became involved in folk music from the mid-1950s. She turned professional in 1959 and signed with Elektra in 1961, initially recording traditional folk before more contemporary material. Still recording, by the 1990s she had also become an author.

DATE	POS	WKS	BPI	SINGLE TITLE	LABEL & NUMBER
17/01/1970	14	11		BOTH SIDES NOW 1968 Grammy Award for Best Folk Recording	Elektra EKSN 45043
05/12/1970	5	67		**AMAZING GRACE** Recorded at St Paul's Chapel, Columbia University	Elektra 2101 020
10/05/1975	6	8		**SEND IN THE CLOWNS** From the musical *A Little Night Music*	Elektra K 12177

MICHELLE COLLINS UK singer (born 28/5/1963) best known as an actress, appearing in TV's *Eastenders* as Cindy Beale and subsequently starring in *Sunburn* and *Real Women*.

DATE	POS	WKS	BPI	SINGLE TITLE	LABEL & NUMBER
27/02/1999	28	3		SUNBURN Theme to the TV series of the same name	BBC Music WMSS 60082

PHIL COLLINS UK singer/drummer (born 31/1/1951, London), a former child actor, he joined Genesis as drummer in 1970, assuming the dual role of lead singer when Peter Gabriel left in 1975. In 1981 he went solo, was in demand as a producer (Adam Ant and Philip Bailey) and played with the progressive jazz-rock outfit Brand X. He appeared in the 1988 film *Buster* (Best Soundtrack at the 1989 BRIT Awards) and later *Frauds,* and was named Best British Male at the 1986, 1989 and 1990 BRIT Awards. His album *No Jacket Required* was Best Album at the 1986 BRIT Awards. Six Grammy Awards include Album of the Year and Best Pop Vocal Performance in 1985 for *No Jacket Required,* and Producer of the Year in 1985 with Hugh Padgham. In 2000 he won an Oscar for Best Film Song with *You'll Be In My Heart* from the Walt Disney film *Tarzan* (1999). He has a star on the Hollywood Walk of Fame. Marilyn Martin is a US singer raised in Louisville, initially a backing singer for the likes of Kenny Loggins, Stevie Nicks, Tom Petty and Joe Walsh.

DATE	POS	WKS	BPI	SINGLE TITLE	LABEL & NUMBER
17/01/1981	2	10	●	IN THE AIR TONIGHT Featured in the 1984 film *Risky Business*	Virgin VSK 102
07/03/1981	14	8		I MISSED AGAIN	Virgin VS 402
30/05/1981	17	8		IF LEAVING ME IS EASY	Virgin VS 423
23/10/1982	56	2		THRU' THESE WALLS	Virgin VS 524
04/12/1982	❶²	16	●	**YOU CAN'T HURRY LOVE**	Virgin VS 531
19/03/1983	45	5		DON'T LET HIM STEAL YOUR HEART AWAY ▲³	Virgin VS 572
07/04/1984	2	14	●	**AGAINST ALL ODDS (TAKE A LOOK AT ME NOW)** ▲³ 1984 Grammy Award for Best Pop Vocal Performance. Featured in the 1984 film *Against All Odds*	Virgin VS 674
26/01/1985	12	9		SUSSUDIO ▲¹	Virgin VS 736
09/03/1985	❶⁴	12	●	**EASY LOVER** PHILIP BAILEY (DUET WITH PHIL COLLINS)	CBS A 4915
13/04/1985	4	9		**ONE MORE NIGHT** ▲²	Virgin VS 755
27/07/1985	19	9		TAKE ME HOME	Virgin VS 777
23/11/1985	4	13	O	**SEPARATE LIVES** ▲¹ PHIL COLLINS AND MARILYN MARTIN Featured in the 1985 film *White Nights*	Virgin VS 818
18/06/1988	4	9		**IN THE AIR TONIGHT (REMIX)**	Virgin VS 102
03/09/1988	❶²	13	O	**A GROOVY KIND OF LOVE** ▲²	Virgin VS 1117
26/11/1988	6	11	O	**TWO HEARTS** ▲² This and above single featured in the 1988 film *Buster*. It won the 1988 Grammy Award for Best Song Written Specifically for a Motion Picture for Phil Collins and Lamont Dozier	Virgin VS 1141
04/11/1989	2	11	O	**ANOTHER DAY IN PARADISE** ▲⁴ 1990 Best Single BRIT Award and Grammy Award for Record of the Year	Virgin VS 1234
27/01/1990	7	9		**I WISH IT WOULD RAIN DOWN**	Virgin VS 1240
28/04/1990	15	7		SOMETHING HAPPENED ON THE WAY TO HEAVEN	Virgin VS 1251
28/07/1990	26	5		THAT'S JUST THE WAY IT IS	Virgin VS 1277
06/10/1990	34	3		HANG IN LONG ENOUGH	Virgin VS 1300
08/12/1990	57	5		DO YOU REMEMBER (LIVE)	Virgin VS 1305
15/05/1993	56	3		HERO	Atlantic A 7360

30/10/1993	7	6	**BOTH SIDES OF THE STORY**	Virgin VSCDT 1500
15/01/1994	15	5	EVERYDAY	Virgin VSCDT 1505
07/05/1994	45	2	WE WAIT AND WE WONDER	Virgin VSCDT 1510
05/10/1996	9	6	**DANCE INTO THE LIGHT**	Face Value EW 066CD
14/12/1996	30	4	IT'S IN YOUR EYES	Face Value EW 076CD1
12/07/1997	43	2	WEAR MY HAT	Face Value EW 113CD
07/11/1998	26	4	TRUE COLOURS	Virgin VSCDT 1715
06/11/1999	17	6	YOU'LL BE IN MY HEART Used in the 1999 Walt Disney film *Tarzan*, for which it won an Oscar for Best Film Song in 2000 .... Walt Disney 0100735 DNY
22/09/2001	26	2	IN THE AIR TONITE **LIL' KIM FEATURING PHIL COLLINS**	WEA 331CD
16/11/2002	28	2	CAN'T STOP LOVING YOU	Face Value EW 254CD
24/05/2003	19	4	HOME **BONE THUGS-N-HARMONY FEATURING PHIL COLLINS**	Epic 6738305
29/11/2003	61	1	LOOK THROUGH MY EYES Used in the 2003 Walt Disney film *Brother Bear*	Walt Disney DISNEY001

RODGER COLLINS US singer (born 1940, Texas, raised in Oakland, CA) whose first R&B hit was in 1967 on the Galaxy label.

03/04/1976	22	6	YOU SEXY SUGAR PLUM (BUT I LIKE IT)	Fantasy FTC 132

WILLIE COLLINS US singer (born in New York) who was working as a postman before being discovered as a singer and signing with Capitol Records.

28/06/1986	46	4	WHERE YOU GONNA BE TONIGHT?	Capitol CL 410

WILLIE COLON US singer/trombonist who also recorded with Celia Cruz, Tito Puente, Hector Lavo and Ruben Blades.

28/06/1986	41	7	SET FIRE TO ME	A&M AM 330

COLOR ME BADD US vocal group formed in high school in Oklahoma City, OK by Bryan Abrams (born 16/11/1969), Sam Watters (born 23/7/1970), Mark Calderon (born 27/9/1970) and Kevin Thomton (born 17/6/1969). Spotted by Robert Bell (of Kool & The Gang), the dance-orientated group relocated to New York.

18/05/1991	❶³	14	○	**I WANNA SEX YOU UP** Featured in the 1991 film *New Jack City*	Giant W 0036
03/08/1991	5	10	ALL 4 LOVE ▲¹	Giant W 0053
12/10/1991	44	4	I ADORE MI AMOR ▲²	Giant W 0067
22/02/1992	58	1	HEARTBREAKER	Giant W 0078
20/11/1993	62	1	TIME AND CHANCE	Giant 74321168992
16/04/1994	65	1	CHOOSE	Giant 74321199432

COLORADO UK vocal group fronted by Geordie Jack, who later changed their name to Caledonia.

21/10/1978	45	3	CALIFORNIA DREAMIN'	Pinnacle PIN 67

COLOUR FIELD UK group formed in Coventry in 1983 by ex-Specials and Fun Boy Three member Terry Hall (born 19/3/1959, Coventry, vocals) with Karl Sharle (bass), Paul Burgess (drums) and Toby Lyons (guitar/keyboards). Burgess left in 1985 and was replaced by Gary Dwyer. They dissolved in 1987, Hall recording solo.

21/01/1984	43	4	THE COLOUR FIELD	Chrysalis COLF 1
28/07/1984	70	1	TAKE	Chrysalis COLF 2
26/01/1985	12	10	THINKING OF YOU	Chrysalis COLF 3
13/04/1985	51	3	CASTLES IN THE AIR	Chrysalis COLF 4

COLOUR GIRL UK singer/songwriter Rebecca Skingley, signed by 4 Liberty Records after being spotted performing at the Notting Hill Carnival in 1997.

11/03/2000	31	3	CAN'T GET USED TO LOSING YOU	4 Liberty LIBTCD 037
09/09/2000	51	1	JOYRIDER (YOU'RE PLAYING WITH FIRE)	4 Liberty LIBTCD 039
03/02/2001	57	1	MAS QUE NADA **COLOUR GIRL FEATURING PSG**	4 Liberty LIBTCD 040

COLOURS FEATURING EMMANUEL AND ESKA UK producer Stephen Emmanuel with singer Eska. Emmanuel also records as En-Core.

27/02/1999	51	1	WHAT U DO	Inferno CDFERN 12

COLOURSOUND UK rock group formed by ex-Alarm Mike Peters (guitar/vocals), ex-Cult Billy Duffy (guitar), ex-Mission Craig Adams (bass), ex-Saw Doctors Johnny Donnelly (drums) and ex-Stiff Little Fingers Steve Grantley (drums).

28/09/2002	49	2	FLY WITH ME	City Rockers ROCKERS 20CD

COLUMBO FEATURING OOE UK production duo formed by Jules Bromley, who is also a member of The Trailermen.

15/05/1999	59	1	ROCKABILLY BOB	V2/Milkgems VVR 5006903

SHAWN COLVIN US singer/guitarist (born 10/1/1958, Vermillion, SD) who taught herself to play guitar at ten. Formerly a member of Suzanne Vega's backing group, her three Grammy Awards include Best Contemporary Folk Recording in 1990 for *Steady On*.

27/11/1993	62	1	I DON'T KNOW WHY Featured in the 1993 film *Clockwork Mice*	Columbia 6598272
12/02/1994	73	1	ROUND OF BLUES	Columbia 6594282
03/09/1994	65	2	EVERY LITTLE THING HE DOES IS MAGIC	Columbia 6607742
07/01/1995	40	3	ONE COOL REMOVE **SHAWN COLVIN WITH MARY CHAPIN CARPENTER**	Columbia 6611342

❶⁹ Number of weeks single topped the UK chart ↑ Entered the UK chart at #1 ▲⁹ Number of weeks single topped the US chart

DATE	POS	WKS	BPI	SINGLE TITLE	LABEL & NUMBER
12/08/1995	52	1		I DON'T KNOW WHY	Columbia 6622725
15/03/1997	70	1		GET OUT OF THIS HOUSE	Columbia 6638522
30/05/1998	29	3		SUNNY CAME HOME 1997 Grammy Awards for Record of the Year and Song of the Year (for writers Shawn Colvin and John Leventhal)	Columbia 6648022

COMETS – see BILL HALEY AND HIS COMETS

COMING OUT CREW US vocal duo Coco and Raphael Pabon.

DATE	POS	WKS	BPI	SINGLE TITLE	LABEL & NUMBER
18/03/1995	50	1		FREE, GAY AND HAPPY	Out On Vinyl CDOOV 002

COMMANDER TOM German producer Tom Weyer.

DATE	POS	WKS	BPI	SINGLE TITLE	LABEL & NUMBER
23/12/2000	75	1		EYE BEE M	Tripoli Trax TTRAX 069CD

COMMENTATORS UK impersonator Rory Bremner (born 6/4/1961, Edinburgh) who has his own TV programme on Channel 4, with a parody record inspired by Paul Hardcastle's *19*.

DATE	POS	WKS	BPI	SINGLE TITLE	LABEL & NUMBER
22/06/1985	13	7		N-N-NINETEEN NOT OUT	Oval 100

COMMITMENTS Irish group assembled by film director Alan Parker for the film *The Commitments* (1991). The storyline concerned a Dublin soul group and featured Andrew Strong on lead vocals with Robert Arkins, Michael Aherne, Angeline Ball, Maria Doyle, Dave Finnegan, Bronagh Gallagher, Felim Gormley, Glen Hansard, Dick Massey, Johnny Murphy and Kenneth McCluskey also appearing in the film. They won the 1992 BRIT Award for Best Soundtrack Album for *The Commitments*.

DATE	POS	WKS	BPI	SINGLE TITLE	LABEL & NUMBER
30/11/1991	63	1		MUSTANG SALLY	MCA MCS 1598

COMMODORES US R&B group formed in Tuskegee, AL in 1967 by Lionel Richie (born 20/6/1949, Tuskegee, vocals/piano/saxophone), William King (born 30/1/1949, Alabama, trumpet), Thomas McClary (born 6/10/1950, guitar) and Milan Williams (born 28/3/1948, Mississippi, keyboards) as the Mighty Mystics, with Ronald LaPread (born 4/9/1946, Alabama, bass) and Walter 'Clyde' Orange (born 10/12/1947, Florida, drums) joining in 1969, by which time they were the Commodores, having picked the name at random from a dictionary. After one single for Atlantic they were signed by Motown in 1972. They formed their own backing band the Mean Machine and appeared in the 1978 film *Thank God It's Friday*. Richie left to go solo in 1982. McClary also recorded solo in 1983. By 1993 the group was down to a trio of Orange, King and ex-Heatwave singer J D Nicholas (born 12/4/1952, Watford).

DATE	POS	WKS	BPI	SINGLE TITLE	LABEL & NUMBER
24/08/1974	20	11		MACHINE GUN Featured in the films *Looking For Mr Goodbar* (1977) and *Boogie Nights* (1998)	Tamla Motown TMG 902
23/11/1974	44	2		THE ZOO (THE HUMAN ZOO)	Tamla Motown TMG 924
02/07/1977	9	10		EASY	Motown TMG 1073
08/10/1977	32	6		SWEET LOVE/BRICK HOUSE In 1991 the group was inducted into the National Association of Brick Distributors' Brick Hall of Fame in recognition of the publicity generated by their hit record. *Brick House* featured in the 1995 film *To Wong Foo, Thanks For Everything! Julie Newmar*	Motown TMG 1086
11/03/1978	38	4		TOO HOT TO TROT/ZOOM A-side featured in the 1978 film *Thank God It's Friday*	Motown TMG 1096
24/06/1978	37	7		FLYING HIGH	Motown TMG 1111
05/08/1978	❶⁵	14	●	**THREE TIMES A LADY** ▲²	Motown TMG 1113
25/11/1978	62	4		JUST TO BE CLOSE TO YOU	Motown TMG 1127
25/08/1979	8	10		**SAIL ON**	Motown TMG 1155
03/11/1979	4	11	○	**STILL** ▲¹	Motown TMG 1166
19/01/1980	40	4		WONDERLAND	Motown TMG 1172
19/01/1980	56	5		LADY (YOU BRING ME UP)	Motown TMG 1238
01/08/1981	44	3		OH NO	Motown TMG 1245
26/01/1985	3	14	○	**NIGHTSHIFT** Tribute to Marvin Gaye and Jackie Wilson. 1985 Grammy Award for Best Rhythm & Blues Vocal Performance	Motown TMG 1371
11/05/1985	74	1		ANIMAL INSTINCT	Motown ZB 40097
25/10/1986	43	4		GOIN' TO THE BANK	Polydor POSPA 826
13/08/1988	15	11		EASY Revived after use in an advertisement for the Halifax Building Society	Motown ZB 41793

COMMON US rapper (born Lonnie Lynn, aka Rasheed Lynn, 1971, Chicago, IL) who was originally billed as Common Sense.

DATE	POS	WKS	BPI	SINGLE TITLE	LABEL & NUMBER
08/11/1997	59	1		REMINDING ME (OF SEF) **COMMON FEATURING CHANTAY SAVAGE**	Relativity 6560762
14/10/2000	56	1		THE LIGHT/THE 6TH SENSE A-side contains a sample of Bobby Caldwell's *Open Your Eyes*	MCA MCSTD 40237
28/04/2001	48	1		GETO HEAVEN **COMMON FEATURING MACY GRAY**	MCA MCSTD 40246
09/02/2002	13	7		DANCE FOR ME **MARY J. BLIGE FEATURING COMMON** Contains a sample of The Police's *The Bed's Too Big Without You*	MCA MCSXD 40274

COMMOTIONS – see LLOYD COLE AND THE COMMOTIONS

COMMUNARDS UK duo formed in 1985 by ex-Bronski Beat singer Jimmy Somerville (born 22/6/1961, Glasgow) and keyboard player Richard Coles (born 23/6/1962, Northampton). They were going to be called The Committee but the name was already in use. They disbanded in 1988 and Somerville went solo the following year. Sarah-Jane Morris is a UK singer.

DATE	POS	WKS	BPI	SINGLE TITLE	LABEL & NUMBER
12/10/1985	30	8		YOU ARE MY WORLD	London LON 77
24/05/1986	29	5		DISENCHANTED	London LON 89
23/08/1986	❶⁴	14	●	**DON'T LEAVE ME THIS WAY COMMUNARDS WITH SARAH-JANE MORRIS**	London LON 103
29/11/1986	8	10		**SO COLD THE NIGHT**	London LON 110
21/02/1987	21	6		YOU ARE MY WORLD	London LON 123
12/09/1987	23	7		TOMORROW	London LON 143

○ Silver disc　● Gold disc　✪ Platinum disc (additional platinum units are indicated by a figure following the symbol)　◉ Singles released prior to 1973 that are known to have sold over 1 million copies in the UK

07/11/1987 ..... 4 ...... 11 ..... O NEVER CAN SAY GOODBYE .... London LON 158
20/02/1988 ..... 28 ...... 7 ...... FOR A FRIEND .... London LON 166
11/06/1988 ..... 20 ...... 8 ...... THERE'S MORE TO LOVE .... London LON 173

PERRY COMO US singer (born Pierino Como, 18/5/1912, Canonsburg, PA) initially dubbed the 'singing barber' (he owned a barbershop in his hometown). He began in 1933 with the Freddy Carlone band, moving to Ted Weems in 1936. After six years he went solo, scoring hits into the 1970s. He also made a number of films, including *Something For The Boys* (1944), *Doll Face* (1945) and *Words And Music* (1948). His TV show ran from 1948 until 1963. Como received the very first US gold disc for *Catch A Falling Star*, presented on 14/3/1958. He died in his sleep on 12/5/2001. He has a star on the Hollywood Walk of Fame for his contribution to radio, and another for TV.

16/01/1953 .... ❶5 ... 15 ..... **DON'T LET THE STARS GET IN YOUR EYES** ▲5 PERRY COMO WITH THE RAMBLERS .... HMV B 10400
04/06/1954 ..... 4 ...... 15 ..... **WANTED** ▲8 .... HMV B 10667
25/06/1954 ..... 3 ...... 15 ..... **IDLE GOSSIP** .... HMV B 10710
10/12/1954 ... 16 ...... 1 ...... PAPA LOVES MAMBO Featured in the 2001 film *Ocean's Eleven* .... HMV B 10776
30/12/1955 ... 24 ...... 1 ...... TINA MARIE .... HMV POP 103
27/04/1956 ... 22 ...... 6 ...... JUKE BOX BABY .... HMV POP 191
25/05/1956 ..... 4 ...... 13 ..... **HOT DIGGITY (DOG ZIGGITY BOOM)** ▲1 .... HMV POP 212
21/09/1956 ... 10 ...... 12 ..... **MORE** .... HMV POP 240
28/09/1956 ... 18 ...... 6 ...... GLENDORA B-side of *More* .... HMV POP 240
07/02/1958 .... ❶8 ... 17 ..... **MAGIC MOMENTS** Featured in the 1998 film *Fear And Loathing In Las Vegas* .... RCA 1036
07/03/1958 ..... 9 ...... 10 ..... **CATCH A FALLING STAR** ▲1 B-side of *Magic Moments*. Featured in the 1993 film *A Perfect World*. 1958 Grammy Award for Best Male Vocal Performance .... RCA 1036
09/05/1958 ..... 9 ...... 7 ...... **KEWPIE DOLL** .... RCA 1055
30/05/1958 ... 15 ...... 8 ...... I MAY NEVER PASS THIS WAY AGAIN .... RCA 1062
05/09/1958 ... 17 ...... 11 ..... MOON TALK .... RCA 1071
07/11/1958 ..... 6 ...... 14 ..... **LOVE MAKES THE WORLD GO ROUND** .... RCA 1086
21/11/1958 ... 13 ...... 12 ..... MANDOLINS IN THE MOONLIGHT B-side of *Love Makes The World Go Round* .... RCA 1086
27/02/1959 ... 10 ...... 12 ..... **TOMBOY** .... RCA 1111
10/07/1959 ... 13 ...... 16 ..... I KNOW .... RCA 1126
26/02/1960 ..... 3 ...... 14 ..... **DELAWARE** .... RCA 1170
10/05/1962 ... 37 ...... 6 ...... CATERINA .... RCA 1283
30/01/1971 ..... 4 ...... 23 ..... **IT'S IMPOSSIBLE** .... RCA 2043
15/05/1971 ... 14 ...... 11 ..... I THINK OF YOU .... RCA 2075
21/04/1973 ..... 3 ...... 35 ..... **AND I LOVE YOU SO** .... RCA 2346
25/08/1973 ..... 7 ...... 27 ..... O FOR THE GOOD TIMES .... RCA 2402
08/12/1973 ... 33 ...... 10 ..... WALK RIGHT BACK .... RCA 2432
25/05/1974 ... 31 ...... 6 ...... I WANT TO GIVE .... RCA LPBO 7518

LES COMPAGNONS DE LA CHANSON French vocal group formed by Jean-Louis Jaubert who backed Edith Piaf. Their debut hit was a US #14 in 1952, revived in the UK following the US success of cover versions by The Browns and Dick Flood. The song was originally a French hit for Edith Piaf in 1946.
09/10/1959 ..... 21 ...... 3 ...... THE THREE BELLS (THE JIMMY BROWN SONG) .... Columbia DB 4358

COMSAT ANGELS UK rock group formed in Sheffield by Stephen Fellows (guitar/vocals), Kevin Bacon (bass), Andy Peake (keyboards) and Mik Gaisher (drums) as Radio Earth, changing to Comsat Angels soon after. In the US they changed their name again, to CS Angels, after the Comsat communications company threatened legal action. Recording for Polydor, CBS, Island and RPM Records, they briefly changed name a third time to Headhunters.
21/01/1984 ..... 71 ...... 2 ...... INDEPENDENCE DAY .... Jive 54

CON FUNK SHUN US R&B group formed in Vallejo, CA in 1968 by Mike Cooper (guitar vocals) and Louis McCall (drums) as Project Soul. They relocated to Memphis, TN in 1972, changing their name to Con Funk Shun, augmented by Karl Fuller (trumpet/vocals), Paul Harrell (saxophone/vocals), Cendric Martin (bass/vocals), Felton Pilate (keyboards/vocals) and Danny Thomas (keyboards/vocals). Pilate later became a successful producer.
19/07/1986 ..... 68 ...... 2 ...... BURNIN' LOVE .... Club JAB 32

CONCEPT US singer/keyboard player Eric Reed from Los Angeles, CA who recorded for the Tuckwood label.
14/12/1985 ..... 27 ...... 6 ...... MR DJ .... Fourth & Broadway BRW 40

CONCRETES Swedish group formed in Stockholm in 1995 by Victoria Bergsman (vocals), Maria Eriksson (guitar) and Lisa Milberg (drums), subsequently adding Daniel Varjo (guitar), Martin Hansson (bass), Per Nystrom (keyboards) Ludvig Rylander (horns) and Ulrik Karlsson (horns). They launched their own Licking Fingers label.
26/06/2004 ..... 55 ...... 1 ...... YOU CAN'T HURRY LOVE .... EMI LFS011
02/10/2004 ..... 52 ...... 1 ...... SEEMS FINE .... EMI LFSX013

❶9 Number of weeks single topped the UK chart   ↑ Entered the UK chart at #1   ▲9 Number of weeks single topped the US chart

171

CONDUCTOR AND THE COWBOY
UK production/instrumental duo Adam Pracy and Lee Hallett who first came to prominence as remixers.

20/05/2000 . . . . . 35 . . . . . . 2 . . . . FEELING THIS WAY . . . . Serious SERR 016CD

CONFEDERATES – see ELVIS COSTELLO

CONGREGATION
UK vocal group formed specifically to record the hit single written by Roger Cook and Roger Greenaway, with Brian Keith (ex-Plastic Penny) on lead vocals.

27/11/1971 . . . . . 4 . . . . . . 14 . . . . . . **SOFTLY WHISPERING I LOVE YOU** . . . . Columbia DB 8830

CONGRESS
UK production duo Danny Harrison and Julian Jonah (Danny Matlock) who also recorded as Congress, Nush, Nu-Birth, M Factor, Reflex, Stella Browne and 187 Lockdown.

26/10/1991 . . . . . 26 . . . . . . 4 . . . . 40 MILES . . . . Inner Rhythm 7HEART 01

CONJURE ONE
Canadian producer Rhys Fulber (born in Vancouver, British Columbia) who recorded his debut album in 2001.

15/02/2003 . . . . . 42 . . . . . . 1 . . . . SLEEP/TEARS FROM THE MOON A-side features the uncredited contribution of Marie-Calire D'Ubaido, the B-side Sinead O'Connor .
. . . . Nettwerk 331792

ARTHUR CONLEY
US singer (born 4/1/1946, Atlanta, GA) discovered by Otis Redding who signed him to his Jotis label in 1965. He was later in The Soul Clan with Solomon Burke, Don Covay, Ben E King and Joe Tex. He died from intestinal cancer on 17/11/2003.

27/04/1967 . . . . . 7 . . . . . . 14 . . . . . . **SWEET SOUL MUSIC** Originally written by Sam Cooke as *Yeah Man* . . . . Atlantic 584 083
10/04/1968 . . . . . 46 . . . . . . 1 . . . . . . FUNKY STREET . . . . Atlantic 583 175

CONNELLS
US rock group formed in Raleigh, NC in 1984 by David Connell (bass), Mike Connell (guitar), John Schultz (drums) and Doug MacMillan (vocals). Peele Wimberley replaced Schultz on drums, and Steve Potak (keyboards) joined in 1990.

12/08/1995 . . . . . 14 . . . . . . 8 . . . . '74–'75 Featured in the 1996 film *Heavy* . . . . TNT LONCD 369
16/03/1996 . . . . . 21 . . . . . . 3 . . . . '74–'75 . . . . TNT LONCD 369

HARRY CONNICK JR.
US singer (born 11/9/1967, New Orleans, LA) who later became an actor, appearing in the films *Memphis Belle* (1990), *Copycat* (1995) and *Independence Day* (1996). He has won three Grammy Awards: Best Male Jazz Vocal Performance in 1989 for *When Harry Met Sally,* Best Male Jazz Vocal Performance in 1990 for *We Are In Love* and Best Traditional Pop Vocal Album in 2001 for *Songs I Heard*.

25/05/1991 . . . . . 32 . . . . . . 6 . . . . RECIPE FOR LOVE/IT HAD TO BE YOU B-side written by and a hit for Isham Jones in 1924. Connick's version featured in the 1989 film *When Harry Met Sally* . . . . Columbia 6568907
03/08/1991 . . . . . 62 . . . . . . 2 . . . . WE ARE IN LOVE . . . . Columbia 6572847
23/11/1991 . . . . . 54 . . . . . . 3 . . . . BLUE LIGHT RED LIGHT (SOMEONE'S THERE) . . . . Columbia 6575367

BILLY CONNOLLY
UK singer/comedian (born 24/11/1942, Glasgow) whose career began with the Humblebums (which included Gerry Rafferty), before going solo. As the jokes between the songs got longer he moved from music to comedy, becoming a big hit with ex-patriate audiences in the US and Australia as well as in the UK. His hit singles were usually parodies of other well-known songs. He later appeared in the film *Still Crazy* and was awarded a CBE in the Queen's 2003 Birthday Honours List.

01/11/1975 . . . . ●¹ . . . 10 . . . . ○ **D.I.V.O.R.C.E.** Recorded live at the Apollo Theatre in Glasgow, a parody of Tammy Wynette's hit . . . . Polydor 2058 652
17/07/1976 . . . . . 24 . . . . . . 5 . . . . . . NO CHANCE (NO CHARGE) Parody of JJ Barrie's hit *No Charge* . . . . Polydor 2058 748
25/08/1979 . . . . . 38 . . . . . . 7 . . . . . . IN THE BROWNIES Parody of Village People's *In The Navy* . . . . Polydor 2059 160
09/03/1985 . . . . . 32 . . . . . . 9 . . . . SUPER GRAN Theme to the children's TV programme of the same name . . . . Stiff BUY 218

SARAH CONNOR
German singer/multi-instrumentalist who was twenty years old at the time of her debut hit.

13/10/2001 . . . . . 16 . . . . . . 5 . . . . . . LET'S GET BACK TO BED…BOY SARAH CONNOR FEATURING TQ . . . . Epic 6718662
05/06/2004 . . . . . 14 . . . . . . 5 . . . . . . BOUNCE . . . . Epic 6749001

CONQUERING LION
UK rapper/singer (born Mike West, 27/8/1965, London) who had previously been a member of Double Trouble And The Rebel MC and later set up the Tribal Bass label.

08/10/1994 . . . . . 53 . . . . . . 1 . . . . . . CODE RED . . . . Mango CIDM 821

LEENA CONQUEST AND HIP HOP FINGER
US singer who later worked with the William Parker Quartet.

18/06/1994 . . . . . 67 . . . . . . 1 . . . . . . BOUNDARIES Contains a sample of Average White Band's *Stop The Rain* . . . . Naturalresponse 74321208522

JESS CONRAD
UK singer (born Jesse James, 24/2/1936, London) who began his career as an actor and film extra before playing a pop singer in a TV drama. Although his voice was initially overdubbed (by Gary Mills), he became a bona fide pop star after Jack Good championed his cause.

30/06/1960 . . . . . 39 . . . . . . 1 . . . . . . CHERRY PIE . . . . Decca F 11236
26/01/1961 . . . . . 18 . . . . 10 . . . . . . MYSTERY GIRL . . . . Decca F 11315
11/10/1962 . . . . . 50 . . . . . . 2 . . . . PRETTY JENNY . . . . Decca F 11511

CONSORTIUM
UK group formed by Rubbie Fair (vocals), Brian Bronson (guitar), Geoffrey Simpson (guitar/keyboards), John Barker (bass/trombone) and John Podbury (drums).

12/02/1969 . . . . . 22 . . . . . . 9 . . . . ALL THE LOVE IN THE WORLD . . . . Pye 7N 17635

○ Silver disc   ● Gold disc   ✪ Platinum disc (additional platinum units are indicated by a figure following the symbol)   ◉ Singles released prior to 1973 that are known to have sold over 1 million copies in the UK

ANN CONSUELO – see SUBTERRANIA FEATURING ANN CONSUELO

CONTOURS US R&B vocal group formed in Detroit, MI by Joe Billingslea, Huey Davis, Billy Gordon, Billy Hoggs, Hubert Johnson (born 14/1/1941, Detroit) and Sylvester Potts in 1958. Auditioned by Motown boss Berry Gordy via Johnson's cousin Jackie Wilson, they were offered a contract, scoring a US top three hit in 1962 with *Do You Love Me* (covered in the UK by the Dave Clark Five and Brian Poole And The Tremeloes). Johnson left in 1964. Dennis Edwards became a member in 1967, but left for the Temptations the following year. They group disbanded in 1968, re-forming in 1987 after *Do You Love Me* featured that year in the film *Dirty Dancing*. Johnson committed suicide by shooting himself on 11/7/1981. Davis died on 23/2/2002.

24/01/1970	31	6		JUST A LITTLE MISUNDERSTANDING	Tamla Motown TMG 723

CONTRABAND German/US rock group formed by Richard Black (vocals), Michael Schenker (guitar), Tracii Guns (guitar), Share Pederson (bass) and Bobby Blotzer (drums) as a one-off project, Schenker having fronted his own group while Guns had been in Guns N' Roses and L.A. Guns.

20/07/1991	65	2		ALL THE WAY FROM MEMPHIS	Impact American EM 195

CONTROL UK vocal/instrumental group with Simon Riley, Mark Cooper, Kevin Barry and Jo Ramsey.

02/11/1991	17	5		DANCE WITH ME (I'M YOUR ECSTASY)	All Around The World GLOBE 105

CONVERT Belgian instrumental/production duo Peter Ramson and Danny Van Wauwe who also record as Transformer 2.

11/01/1992	39	4		NIGHTBIRD	A&M AM 845
29/05/1993	42	2		ROCKIN' TO THE RHYTHM	A&M 5802532
31/01/1998	45	1		NIGHTBIRD Re-issue of A&M AM 845	Wonderboy WBOYD 008

CONWAY BROTHERS US family group from Chicago, IL comprising Huston (lead vocals/bass), James L (guitar/vocals), Hiawatha (drums) and Frederick Conway (keyboards/vocals).

22/06/1985	11	10		TURN IT UP	10 TEN 57

RAZ CONWAY – see MORJAC FEATURING RAZ CONWAY

RUSS CONWAY UK pianist (born Trevor Stanford, 2/9/1927, Bristol) who left the Royal Navy in 1955 to become a pianist (despite having lost part of a finger in an accident with a bread slicer), accompanying the likes of Gracie Fields, Lita Rosa and Dorothy Squires. Signed by EMI in 1957, his run of hits was curtailed by the early 1960s' beat boom, but he continued to perform live until ill-health forced retirement. He died from cancer on 16/11/2000.

29/11/1957	24	5		PARTY POPS Medley of *When You're Smiling, I'm Looking Over A Four-Leafed Clover, When You Wore A Tulip, Row Row Row, For Me And My Girl, Shine On Harvest Moon, By The Light Of The Silvery Moon* and *Side By Side*	Columbia DB 4031
29/08/1958	30	1		GOT A MATCH	Columbia DB 4166
28/11/1958	10	7		**MORE PARTY POPS** Medley of *Music Music Music, If You Were The Only Girl In The World, Nobody's Sweetheart, Yes Sir That's My Baby, Some Of These Days, Honeysuckle And The Bee, Hello Hello Who's Your Lady Friend* and *Shanty In Old Shanty Town*	Columbia DB 4204
23/01/1959	24	1		THE WORLD OUTSIDE	Columbia DB 4234
20/02/1959	❶⁴	30		**SIDE SADDLE**	Columbia DB 4256
06/03/1959	24	3		THE WORLD OUTSIDE	Columbia DB 4234
15/05/1959	❶²	19		**ROULETTE**	Columbia DB 4298
21/08/1959	5	13		**CHINA TEA**	Columbia DB 4337
13/11/1959	7	9		**SNOW COACH**	Columbia DB 4368
20/11/1959	5	8		**MORE AND MORE PARTY POPS** Medley of *Sheik Of Araby, Who Were You With Last Night, Any Old Iron, Tiptoe Through The Tulips, If You Were The Only Girl In The World* and *When I Leave The World Behind*	Columbia DB 4373
05/03/1960	15	8		ROYAL EVENT Song was written to celebrate the birth of HRH Prince Andrew on 19/2/1960	Columbia DB 4418
21/04/1960	47	1		FINGS AIN'T WOT THEY USED TO BE	Columbia DB 4422
19/05/1960	14	9		LUCKY FIVE	Columbia DB 4457
29/09/1960	16	10		PASSING BREEZE	Columbia DB 4508
24/11/1960	27	9		EVEN MORE PARTY POPS Medley of *Ain't She Sweet, I Can't Give You Anything But Love, Yes We Have No Bananas, I May Be Wrong, Happy Days And Lonely Nights* and *Glad Rag Doll*	Columbia DB 4535
19/01/1961	19	9		PEPE	Columbia DB 4564
25/05/1961	45	2		PABLO	Columbia DB 4649
24/08/1961	23	10		SAY IT WITH FLOWERS **DOROTHY SQUIRES AND RUSS CONWAY**	Columbia DB 4665
30/11/1961	7	11		**TOY BALLOONS**	Columbia DB 4738
22/02/1962	21	7		LESSON ONE	Columbia DB 4784
29/11/1962	33	7		ALWAYS YOU AND ME	Columbia DB 4934

MARTIN COOK – see RICHARD DENTON AND MARTIN COOK

❶⁹ Number of weeks single topped the UK chart ↑ Entered the UK chart at #1 ▲⁹ Number of weeks single topped the US chart

173

NORMAN COOK UK producer/instrumentalist (born Quentin Cook, 31/7/1963, Brighton), formerly the lead singer with The Housemartins before recording under his own name and then forming Beats International. He later recorded as Freak Power, Mighty Dub Katz, Pizzaman and Fatboy Slim. He is married to DJ/TV presenter Zoe Ball. MC Wildski was later in Beats International.

| 08/07/1989 | 29 | 6 | | WON'T TALK ABOUT IT/BLAME IT ON THE BASSLINE NORMAN COOK FEATURING BILLY BRAGG/NORMAN COOK FEATURING MC WILDSKI | Go Beat GOD 33 |
| 21/10/1989 | 48 | 4 | | FOR SPACIOUS LIES NORMAN COOK FEATURING LESTER | Go Beat GOD 37 |

PETER COOK UK comedian/writer/performer/entrepreneur (born 17/11/1937, Torquay) whose influential TV series with Dudley Moore, *Not Only…But Also* included as closing song the chart hit *Goodbye-ee*. Dudley Moore (born 19/4/1935, Dagenham) became a Hollywood star in the films *10* (1979) and *Arthur* (1981), briefly returning with Peter Cook for the *Derek And Clive* albums that were successful despite no radio play. Cook died from cancer in January 1995. The pair won the 1974 Grammy Award for Best Spoken Word Recording for *Good Evening*. Dudley Moore was awarded a CBE in the 2001 Queen's Birthday Honours List and died from brain disease on 27/3/2002.

| 17/06/1965 | 18 | 10 | | GOODBYE-EE PETER COOK AND DUDLEY MOORE | Decca F 12158 |
| 15/07/1965 | 34 | 5 | | THE BALLAD OF SPOTTY MULDOON | Decca F 12182 |

BRANDON COOKE FEATURING ROXANNE SHANTE US producer and US rapper.

| 29/10/1988 | 45 | 3 | | SHARP AS A KNIFE | Club JAB 73 |

SAM COOKE US singer (born 22/1/1931, Clarksdale, MS, raised in Chicago, IL) who sang with the gospel group the Highway QC's before joining the Soul Stirrers as lead singer in 1950, leaving in 1956 to go solo. He was replaced by Johnnie Taylor. His first official release *You Send Me* was a US #1 and began a string of hits over the next seven years. His son Vincent drowned in the family's swimming pool in 1963. Sam was shot to death in a Los Angeles, CA motel on 11/12/1964 by the owner Bertha Franklin amid rumours of rape and assault on 22-year-old Elisa Boyer (who had accompanied Cooke to the motel), although Franklin was later cleared on the grounds of justifiable homicide. It was later claimed that Boyer, a known prostitute, had been robbing Cooke as she ran out of his room carrying his clothes, although this was not followed up by the police, who did not make public the details surrounding his death for almost two years in order to protect his family. Over 200,000 people tried to attend his funeral (the bronze marker at Forest Lawn in Los Angeles, under which lies his body, has the year of Sam's birth wrongly engraved as 1930). He was inducted into the Rock & Roll Hall of Fame in 1986. He has a star on the Hollywood Walk of Fame. Elisa Boyer (aka Crystal Chan Young, Jasmine Jay and Elsie Nakama) was convicted of the second-degree murder of her lover Louis Reynolds in 1979.

17/01/1958	29	1		YOU SEND ME ▲³ Credits Charles Cooke, Sam's brother, as the songwriter since Sam was signed to another label as a writer	London HLU 8506
14/08/1959	23	4		ONLY SIXTEEN Credits Barbara Campbell (a pseudonym for Herb Alpert and Lou Adler) as the songwriter	HMV POP 642
07/07/1960	27	8		WONDERFUL WORLD Featured in the films *Baby Love* (1969), *Animal House* (1978) and *Witness* (1985)	HMV POP 754
29/09/1960	9	11		CHAIN GANG	RCA 1202
27/07/1961	7	14		CUPID	RCA 1242
08/03/1962	6	14		TWISTIN' THE NIGHT AWAY	RCA 1277
16/05/1963	23	12		ANOTHER SATURDAY NIGHT	RCA 1341
05/09/1963	30	6		FRANKIE AND JOHNNY	RCA 1361
22/03/1986	2	11	○	WONDERFUL WORLD Revived after use in a Levi Jeans advertisement	RCA PB 49871
10/05/1986	75	1		ANOTHER SATURDAY NIGHT Re-issue of RCA 1341	RCA PB 49849

COOKIE CREW UK rap group with Susie Q (Susie Banfield, sister of The Pasadenas' Andrew Banfield), MC Remedee (Debbie Prince) and DJ Max (Maxine).

09/01/1988	5	11		ROK DA HOUSE BEATMASTERS FEATURING THE COOKIE CREW	Rhythm King LEFT 11
07/01/1989	23	5		BORN THIS WAY (LET'S DANCE)	ffrr FFR 19
01/04/1989	17	9		GOT TO KEEP ON	ffrr FFR 25
15/07/1989	42	3		COME AND GET SOME	ffrr F 110
27/07/1991	53	3		SECRETS (OF SUCCESS) COKKIE CREW FEATURING DANNY D	ffrr F 159

COOKIES US R&B vocal group formed in New York City by Dorothy Jones, Pat Lyles, Ethel McCrae and Margorie Hendricks. They were better known as backing singers for other acts, with Hendricks subsequently forming Ray Charles' vocal group The Raelettes.

| 10/01/1963 | 50 | 1 | | CHAINS | London HLU 9634 |

COOL DOWN ZONE UK group formed in Manchester in 1983 by Diane Charmelagne (vocals), John Dennison (keyboards), Tony Henry (guitar/bass) and Tony Bowry (bass/vocals) and known as 52nd Street, changing to Cool Down Zone in 1989.

| 30/06/1990 | 52 | 4 | | HEAVEN KNOWS | 10 TEN 309 |

COOL JACK Italian production duo Angelino Albanese and Giovanni Visnadi. Visnadi is also in Alex Party and Livin' Joy.

| 09/11/1996 | 44 | 1 | | JUS' COME | AM:PM 5819892 |

COOL NOTES UK group formed in London by Steve McIntosh (keyboards/vocals), Lorraine McIntosh (lead vocals), Heather Austin (lead vocals), Joseph 'JC' Charles (guitar), Ian Dunstan (bass), Peter 'Lee' Gordon (guitar) and Peter 'Rattie' Rolands (drums). By 1988 they were the trio of Steve and Lorraine McIntosh and JC.

18/08/1984	42	5		YOU'RE NEVER TOO YOUNG	Abstract Dance AD 1
17/11/1984	63	2		I FORGOT	Abstract Dance AD 2
23/03/1985	11	9		SPEND THE NIGHT	Abstract Dance AD 3
13/07/1985	13	9		IN YOUR CAR	Abstract Dance AD 4
19/10/1985	73	1		HAVE A GOOD FOREVER	Abstract Dance AD 5

○ Silver disc ● Gold disc ✪ Platinum disc (additional platinum units are indicated by a figure following the symbol) ◎ Singles released prior to 1973 that are known to have sold over 1 million copies in the UK

17/05/1986 . . . . . 66 . . . . . . 2	INTO THE MOTION . . . . Abstract Dance AD 8		

COOL, THE FAB, AND THE GROOVY PRESENT QUINCY JONES UK production duo Jamie Ford and Jamie White (who also recorded as Mirrorball) with singer Zoe O'Shaugnessy and US orchestra leader Quincy Jones.

01/08/1998 . . . . . 47 . . . . . . 1	SOUL BOSSA NOVA . . . . Manifesto FESCD 48

RITA COOLIDGE US singer (born 1/5/1944, Nashville, TN) who toured with Delaney & Bonnie, Joe Cocker and Leon Russell before going solo. Married to Kris Kristofferson from 1973 to 1980, she was known as the Delta Lady, the title of a US hit for Leon Russell written in her honour. Her two Grammy Awards were both with Kris Kristofferson: Best Country & Western Performance by a Duo in 1973 for *From The Bottle To The Bottom* and Best Country Performance by a Duo in 1975 for *Lover Please*.

25/06/1977 . . . . . 6 . . . . . . 13	WE'RE ALL ALONE. . . . . A&M AMS 7295
15/10/1977 . . . . . 48 . . . . . . 2	(YOUR LOVE HAS LIFTED ME) HIGHER AND HIGHER . . . . A&M AMS 7315
04/02/1978 . . . . . 25 . . . . . . 8	WORDS. . . . . A&M AMS 7330
25/06/1983 . . . . . 75 . . . . . . 1	ALL TIME HIGH Featured in the 1983 James Bond film *Octopussy* . . . . A&M AM 007

COOLIO US rapper (born Artis Ivey Jr, 1/8/1963, Compton, CA) and a member of WC and the MAAD Circle. His DJ partner is Bryan 'Wino' Dobbs. His first US hit was in June 1994 with *Fantastic Voyage*. In 1999 he was jailed for ten days for illegal possession of a firearm, his second such conviction. He won the 1997 MOBO Award for Best International Hip Hop Act. Yo-Yo is US rapper Yolanda Whittaler (born 4/8/1971, Los Angeles, CA).

23/07/1994 . . . . . 41 . . . . . . 2	FANTASTIC VOYAGE. . . . . Tommy Boy TB 0617CD
15/10/1994 . . . . . 73 . . . . . . 1	I REMEMBER Contains a sample of Al Green's *Tomorrow's Dream* . . . . Tommy Boy TBXCD 635
28/10/1995 . . ❶² . . . . . 20 . . . . . ✪	GANGSTA'S PARADISE ↑ ▲³ COOLIO FEATURING LV Contains a sample of Stevie Wonder's *Pastime Paradise*. Featured in the 1995 film *Dangerous Minds*. 1995 Grammy Award for Best Rap Solo Performance . . . . Tommy Boy MCSTD 2104
20/01/1996 . . . . . 9 . . . . . . 6	TOO HOT Contains a sample of Kool & The Gang's *Too Hot*. . . . . Tommy Boy TBCD 718
06/04/1996 . . . . . 13 . . . . . . 7	1,2,3,4 (SUMPIN' NEW) Contains a sample of The Evasions' *Wikka Wrap*. . . . . Tommy Boy TBCD 7721
17/08/1996 . . . . . 34 . . . . . . 2	IT'S ALL THE WAY LIVE (NOW) Features the uncredited contribution of Lakeside and was used in the 1996 film *Eddie*. . . . . Tommy Boy TBCD 7731
14/09/1996 . . . . . 28 . . . . . . 2	STOMP – THE REMIXES QUINCY JONES FEATURING MELLE MEL, COOLIO, YO-YO, SHAQUILLE O'NEAL & THE LUNIZ . Qwest W 0372CD
05/04/1997 . . . . . 8 . . . . . . 6	HIT 'EM HIGH (THE MONSTARS' ANTHEM) B REAL/BUSTA RHYMES/COOLIO/LL COOL J/METHOD MAN Featured in the 1996 film *Space Jam* . . . . Atlantic A 5449CD
07/06/1997 . . . . . 53 . . . . . . 1	THE WINNER. . . . . Atlantic A 5433CD
19/07/1997 . . . . . 3 . . . . . 12 . . . . . ○	C U WHEN U GET THERE COOLIO FEATURING 40 THEVZ Featured in the 1997 film *Nothing To Lose*. . . . . Tommy Boy TBCD 785
11/10/1997 . . . . . 14 . . . . . . 5	OOH LA LA Contains a sample of Grace Jones' *Pull Up To The Bumper* . . . . Tommy Boy TBCD 799

COOLY'S HOT BOX – see ROGER SANCHEZ

COOPER Dutch instrumental/production group formed by Koen Groeneveld, Addy Van Der Zwan and Jan Voermans. They also recorded as Klubheads, Drunkenmunky, Itty Bitty Boozy Woozy and Da Techno Bohemian.

11/01/2003 . . . . . 50 . . . . . . 2	I BELIEVE IN LOVE . . . . Incentive PDT 05CDS

ALICE COOPER US singer (born Vincent Furnier, 4/2/1948, Detroit, MI) who formed his first band in 1965 and moved to Los Angeles, CA in 1968. The band became known as Alice Cooper (after a ouija board had spelled out the name) and so did Furnier. They debuted on Frank Zappa's Straight label in 1969, before signing with Warner Brothers in 1971. The line-up for these hits featured Cooper (vocals), Glen Buxton (guitar), Michael Bruce (guitar/keyboards), Dennis Dunaway (bass) and Neal Smith (drums). Cooper re-emerged in the late 1980s as a solo artist, also making film appearances, including the role of Freddy Krueger's father in *A Nightmare On Elm Street* (1984), *Prince Of Darkness* (1987) and *Wayne's World* (1992). In April 1988 he nearly strangled himself when a safety rope snapped during a concert, leaving him dangling off the ground before a roadie saved him. Buxton died from drug and alcohol abuse on 19/10/1997. Cooper has a star on the Hollywood Walk of Fame.

15/07/1972 . . . . ❶³ 12	SCHOOL'S OUT Featured in the films *Rock 'N' Roll High School* (1979) and *Dazed And Confused* (1993) . Warner Brothers K 16188
07/10/1972 . . . . . 4 . . . . . . 10	ELECTED . . . . Warner Brothers K 16214
10/02/1973 . . . . . 6 . . . . . . 12	HELLO HURRAY . . . . Warner Brothers K 16248
21/04/1973 . . . . . 10 . . . . . . 10	NO MORE MR. NICE GUY Featured in the 1989 film *Shocker* . . . . Warner Brothers K 16262
19/01/1974 . . . . . 12 . . . . . . 7	TEENAGE LAMENT '74 . . . . Warner Brothers K 16345
21/05/1977 . . . . . 44 . . . . . . 2	(NO MORE) LOVE AT YOUR CONVENIENCE . . . . Warner Brothers K 16935
23/12/1978 . . . . . 61 . . . . . . 6	HOW YOU GONNA SEE ME NOW . . . . Warner Brothers K 17270
06/03/1982 . . . . . 62 . . . . . . 3	SEVEN AND SEVEN IS (LIVE). . . . . Warner Brothers K 17924
08/05/1982 . . . . . 66 . . . . . . 2	FOR BRITAIN ONLY/UNDER MY WHEELS . . . . Warner Brothers K 17940
18/10/1986 . . . . . 61 . . . . . . 2	HE'S BACK (THE MAN BEHIND THE MASK) . . . . MCA 1090
09/04/1988 . . . . . 50 . . . . . . 3	FREEDOM . . . . MCA 1241
29/07/1989 . . . . . 2 . . . . . . 11	POISON. . . . . Epic 6550617
07/10/1989 . . . . . 38 . . . . . . 5	BED OF NAILS . . . . Epic ALICE 3
02/12/1989 . . . . . 65 . . . . . . 2	HOUSE OF FIRE . . . . Epic ALICE 4
22/06/1991 . . . . . 21 . . . . . . 6	HEY STOOPID . . . . Epic 6569837
05/10/1991 . . . . . 38 . . . . . . 3	LOVE'S A LOADED GUN . . . . Epic 6574387
06/06/1992 . . . . . 27 . . . . . . 3	FEED MY FRANKENSTEIN Featured in the 1992 film *Wayne's World*. . . . . Epic 6580927
28/05/1994 . . . . . 22 . . . . . . 3	LOST IN AMERICA . . . . Epic 6603472
23/07/1994 . . . . . 34 . . . . . . 2	IT'S ME . . . . Epic 6605632

DEBORAH COOPER – see C & C MUSIC FACTORY

❶⁹ Number of weeks single topped the UK chart ↑ Entered the UK chart at #1 ▲⁹ Number of weeks single topped the US chart

TOMMY COOPER UK comedian (born 19/3/1923, Caerphilly, Wales) who first became known in the 1950s with an anarchic act mixing conjuring with comedy. TV enhanced his reputation and at the time of his death he had his own show. He died on stage after suffering a heart attack on 15/4/1984, most of the audience assuming it was part of his act.

29/06/1961.....40.....3....... DON'T JUMP OFF THE ROOF DAD .... Palette PG 9019

CO-OPERATION CHOIR – see PETER E BENNETT WITH THE CO-OPERATION CHOIR

COOPER TEMPLE CAUSE UK rock group formed in Reading by Ben Gautrey (vocals), Tom Bellamy (guitar), Dan Fisher (bass), Didz (bass), Kieran Mayhem (keyboards) and Jon Harpener (drums).

29/09/2001.....41......1.......	LET'S KILL MUSIC.. Morning 9
09/02/2002.....20......3.......	FILM MAKER/BEEN TRAINING DOGS.. Morning 16
18/05/2002.....22......2.......	WHO NEEDS ENEMIES .... Morning 25
13/09/2003.....19......2.......	PROMISES PROMISES .... Morning 30
22/11/2003.....37......2.......	BLIND PILOTS.. Morning 38

CO-ORDINATE – see PESHAY

JULIAN COPE UK singer (born 21/10/1957, Bargoed, Wales) and a member of The Crucial Three with Ian McCulloch and Pete Wylie before forming Teardrop Explodes in 1978. He went solo in 1984.

19/11/1983.....64......1.......	SUNSHINE PLAYROOM .... Mercury COPE 1
31/03/1984.....52......5.......	THE GREATNESS AND PERFECTION OF LOVE .... Mercury MER 155
27/09/1986.....19......8.......	WORLD SHUT YOUR MOUTH .... Island IS 290
17/01/1987.....31......6.......	TRAMPOLENE .... Island IS 305
11/04/1987.....41......5.......	EVE'S VOLCANO (COVERED IN SIN)... Island IS 318
24/09/1988.....35......6.......	CHARLOTTE ANNE.. Island IS 380
21/01/1989.....42......4.......	5 O'CLOCK WORLD .... Island IS 399
24/06/1989.....53......2.......	CHINA DOLL .... Island IS 406
09/02/1991.....32......6.......	BEAUTIFUL LOVE .... Island IS 483
20/04/1991.....51......3.......	EAST EASY RIDER .... Island IS 492
03/08/1991.....57......2.......	HEAD .... Island IS 497
08/08/1992.....44......3.......	WORLD SHUT YOUR MOUTH Re-issue of Island IS 290 .... Island IS 534
17/10/1992.....42......2.......	FEAR LOVES THIS PLACE .... Island IS 545
12/08/1995.....24......3.......	TRY TRY TRY .... Echo ECSCD 11
27/07/1996.....34......2.......	I COME FROM ANOTHER PLANET, BABY... Echo ECSCD 22
05/10/1996.....34......1.......	PLANETARY SIT-IN (EVERY GIRL HAS YOUR NAME) .... Echo ECSCD 25

IMANI COPPOLA US singer/rapper/violinist who was still studying at New York State University when she launched her solo career.

28/02/1998.....32......3.......	LEGEND OF A COWGIRL Contains a sample of Donovan's *Sunshine Superman* .... Columbia 6656015
03/02/2001.....14......5.......	YOU ALL DAT BAHA MEN: GUEST VOCAL IMANI COPPOLA Contains a sample of Tight Fit's *The Lion Sleeps Tonight* .... Edel 0124855 ERE

CORAL UK group formed in Liverpool in 1996 by James Skelly (lead vocals), Lee Southall (guitar/vocals), Paul Duffy (bass/saxophone), Nick Power (keyboards/vocals), Bill Ryder-Jones (guitar/trumpet) and Ian Skelly (drums).

27/07/2002.....21......2.......	GOODBYE... Deltasonic DLTCD 2005
19/10/2002.....13......5.......	DREAMING OF YOU.. Deltasonic DLTCD 2008
15/03/2003.....10......4.......	DON'T THINK YOU'RE THE FIRST .... Deltasonic DLTCDC 2010
26/07/2003.....5......7.......	PASS IT ON .... Deltasonic DLTCD 2013
18/10/2003.....25......2.......	SECRET KISS.. Deltasonic DLTCD 2015
06/12/2003.....23......2.......	BILL MCCAI .... Deltasonic DLTCD 2017

HARRY H CORBETT – see WILFRED BRAMBELL AND HARRY H CORBETT

FRANK CORDELL UK orchestra leader (born 1918) who composed the music to many films, including *Murder Will Out* (1952) and *God Told Me To* (1977). He died on 6/7/1980.

24/08/1956.....29......2.......	SADIE'S SHAWL... HMV POP 229
16/02/1961.....44......2.......	BLACK BEAR .... HMV POP 824

LOUISE CORDET French singer (born Louise Boisot, 1946), daughter of actress Helene Cordet and goddaughter of HRH Prince Philip. She appeared in the 1963 film *Just For Fun* and recorded the original version of *Don't Let The Sun Catch You Crying*, written specifically for her by Gerry Marsden.

05/07/1962.....13.....13...... I'M JUST A BABY .... Decca F 11476

COREE – see ICEBERG SLIMM

CHRIS CORNELL US singer (born 20/7/1964, Seattle, WA), guitarist and lead singer with Soundgarden from their formation in 1984, going solo after they disbanded in 1997.

23/10/1999.....62......1....... CAN'T CHANGE ME... A&M 4971732

○ Silver disc ● Gold disc ✪ Platinum disc (additional platinum units are indicated by a figure following the symbol) ◉ Singles released prior to 1973 that are known to have sold over 1 million copies in the UK

DON CORNELL US singer (born 21/4/1919, New York City) who worked as a singer and guitarist from the late 1930s before finding fame with Sammy Kaye's band from 1947 until 1950, subsequently going solo. He has a star on the Hollywood Walk of Fame. He died from emphysema and diabetes on 23/2/2004.

| 03/09/1954 | ❶5 | 21 | | **HOLD MY HAND** Featured in the 1954 film *Susan Slept Here*. Reclaimed #1 position on 19/11/1954. | Vogue Q 2013 |
| 22/04/1955 | 19 | 2 | | STRANGER IN PARADISE | Vogue Q 72073 |

LYNN CORNELL UK singer (born in Liverpool) who later became a member of the Vernon Girls and the Pearls.

| 20/10/1960 | 30 | 9 | | NEVER ON SUNDAY | Decca F 11277 |

CORNERSHOP UK group formed in Leicester in 1991 by Tjinder Singh (guitar/vocals), Avtar Singh (bass), Ben Ayres (guitar/vocals), Anthony Saffrey (sitar) and David Chambers (drums). By the time of their debut hit, they were the duo of Singh and Ayres.

30/08/1997	60	1		BRIMFUL OF ASHA	Wiiija WIJ 75CD
28/02/1998	❶1	12	●	**BRIMFUL OF ASHA (REMIX)** ↑	Wiiija WIJ 81CD
16/05/1998	23	3		SLEEP ON THE LEFT SIDE	Wiiija WIJ 80CD
16/03/2002	37	2		LESSONS LEARNED FROM ROCKY I TO ROCKY III	Wiiija WIJ 129CD
07/08/2004	53	1		TOPKNOT	Rough Trade RTRADSCD168

CHARLOTTE CORNWELL – see JULIE COVINGTON, RULA LENSKA, CHARLOTTE CORNWELL AND SUE JONES-DAVIES

HUGH CORNWELL UK guitarist/singer (born 28/8/1949, London) who was a founder of The Stranglers in 1974 until he left in 1990, having already begun a parallel solo career. In 1980 he was sentenced to three months imprisonment on drugs charges.

| 24/01/1987 | 61 | 2 | | FACTS + FIGURES | Virgin VS 922 |
| 07/05/1988 | 71 | 1 | | ANOTHER KIND OF LOVE | Virgin VS 945 |

CO-RO FEATURING TARLISA German vocal/production group formed by Paps Cozzi and Maurizio Rossi with singer Tarlisa.

| 12/12/1992 | 61 | 1 | | BECAUSE THE NIGHT | ZYX 68227 |

CORONA Italian studio creation of producers Checco and Soul Train with vocals by Ice MC and Brazilian singer Olga DeSouza. The name is Spanish for 'crown'.

10/09/1994	2	18	O	**THE RHYTHM OF THE NIGHT**	WEA YZ 837CD1
08/04/1995	5	8		**BABY BABY**	Eternal YZ 919CD
22/07/1995	6	10	O	**TRY ME OUT**	Eternal YZ 955CD
23/12/1995	22	6		I DON'T WANNA BE A STAR	Eternal 029CD
22/02/1997	36	2		MEGAMIX Megamix of *The Rhythm Of The Night, Baby Baby, Try Me* Out and *I Don't Wanna Be A Star*	Eternal 092CD

CORONATION STREET CAST FEATURING BILL WADDINGTON The UK's longest-running soap opera, first aired in 1960, with Bill Waddington (born 10/6/1916, Oldham) playing Percy Sugden. He died on 9/9/2000.

| 16/12/1995 | 35 | 3 | | ALWAYS LOOK ON THE BRIGHT SIDE OF LIFE Listed flip side was *Something Stupid* by AMANDA BARRIE AND JOHNNY BRIGGS | |
| | | | | | EMI Premier CDEMS 411 |

CORONETS UK vocal group, initially backing Ray Burns before recording on their own.

| 26/08/1955 | 14 | 6 | | THAT'S HOW A LOVE SONG WAS BORN RAY BURNS WITH THE CORONETS | Columbia DB 3640 |
| 25/11/1955 | 20 | 1 | | TWENTY TINY FINGERS | Columbia DB 3671 |

BRIANA CORRIGAN UK singer who replaced Jacqueline Abbott in The Beautiful South in 2000.

| 11/05/1996 | 48 | 2 | | LOVE ME NOW | East West EW 041CD1 |

CORRS Irish family group formed in Dundalk (where they were all born) in 1990 by Andrea (born 17/5/1974, whistle/lead vocals), Caroline (born 17/3/1973, drums), Sharon (born 24/3/1970, violin) and Jim Corr (born 31/7/1968, guitar/keyboards). Named Best International Group at the 1999 BRIT Awards, they also took part in the *It's Only Rock 'N' Roll* project for the Children's Promise charity.

17/02/1996	49	2		RUNAWAY	Atlantic A 5727CD
07/12/1996	60	1		RUNAWAY	Atlantic A 5727CD
01/02/1997	62	1		LOVE TO LOVE YOU/RUNAWAY	Atlantic A 5621CD
25/10/1997	58	1		ONLY WHEN I SLEEP	Atlantic AT 0015CD
20/12/1997	43	2		I NEVER LOVED YOU ANYWAY	Atlantic AT 0018CD
28/03/1998	53	1		WHAT CAN I DO	Atlantic AT 0029CD
16/05/1998	6	10	O	**DREAMS** Recorded live at the Royal Albert Hall on 17/3/1998 and features the uncredited contribution of Mick Fleetwood	
					Atlantic AT 0032CD
29/08/1998	3	11	O	**WHAT CAN I DO (REMIX)**	Atlantic AT 0044CD
28/11/1998	6	13		**SO YOUNG**	Atlantic AT 0057CD1
27/02/1999	2	11	●	**RUNAWAY (REMIX)**	Atlantic AT 0062CD
12/06/1999	37	3		I KNOW MY LOVE CHIEFTAINS FEATURING THE CORRS	RCA Victor 74321670622
11/12/1999	18	9		RADIO	Atlantic AT 0079CD
15/07/2000	❶1	13	O	**BREATHLESS** ↑	Atlantic AT 0084CD
11/11/2000	20	7		IRRESISTIBLE	Atlantic AT 0089CD
28/04/2001	27	2		GIVE ME A REASON	Atlantic AT 0097CD
10/11/2001	14	5		WOULD YOU BE HAPPIER	Atlantic AT 0115CD

❶9 Number of weeks single topped the UK chart   ↑ Entered the UK chart at #1   ▲9 Number of weeks single topped the US chart

177

29/05/2004	6	8		SUMMER SUNSHINE	Atlantic AT 0179CD
25/09/2004	16	4		ANGEL	Atlantic AT 0182CD
18/12/2004	31	2+		LONG NIGHT	Atlantic AT 0190CD1

CORRUPTED CRU FEATURING MC NEAT UK garage group formed by Scott Garcia and Mike Kenny with MC Neat (Michael Rose).

| 02/03/2002 | 59 | 1 | | GARAGE | Red Rose CDRROSE 011 |

FERRY CORSTEN Dutch DJ/singer who had previously recorded as Albion, Gouryella, Starparty, Moonman, Veracocha and System F.

08/06/2002	29	3		PUNK	Positiva CDTIV 173
21/02/2004	11	6		ROCK YOUR BODY ROCK	Positiva CDTIVS 202
10/07/2004	51	2		IT'S TIME	Positiva CDTIVS 206

CORTINA UK producer Ben Keen who also records as BK.

| 24/03/2001 | 42 | 2 | | MUSIC IS MOVING | Nukleuz NUKC 0159 |
| 26/01/2002 | 48 | 1 | | ERECTION (TAKE IT TO THE TOP) CORTINA FEATURING BK & MADAM FRICTION | Nukleuz NUKCD 0352 |

VLADIMIR COSMA Hungarian orchestra leader who later recorded the music to the TV soundtrack *Mistral's Daughter* with Nana Mouskouri.

| 14/07/1979 | 64 | 1 | | DAVID'S SONG (MAIN THEME FROM 'KIDNAPPED') Theme to the TV series *Kidnapped* | Decca FR 13841 |

COSMIC BABY German producer (born Harald Bluechel, 19/2/1966, Nuremberg) who studied at the Nuremberg Conservatory at the age of seven, first coming to the attention of UK audiences with his collaboration with Paul Van Dyk as Visions of Shiva.

| 26/02/1994 | 70 | 1 | | LOOPS OF INFINITY | Logic 74321191432 |

COSMIC GATE German production/remix duo DJ Delicious (born Nicolas Chagall, 10/11/1972, Duisberg) and DJ Bossi (born Stefan Bossems, 27/2/1967, Munchengladbach), whose debut hit was named after the data port used for transferring digital video onto a PC.

04/08/2001	9	7		FIREWIRE	Data 24CDS
11/05/2002	29	3		EXPLORATION OF SPACE	Data 30CDS
25/01/2003	48	2		THE WAVE/RAGING	Nebula NEBCD 036

COSMIC ROUGH RIDERS UK rock group with Daniel Wylie (vocals), Gary Cuthbert (guitar), Stephen Flemming (guitar), James Clifford (bass) and Mark Brown (drums).

04/08/2001	35	1		REVOLUTION (IN THE SUMMERTIME)	Poptones MC 5047SCX
29/09/2001	36	1		THE PAIN INSIDE	Poptones MC 5052SCX
05/07/2003	34	1		BECAUSE YOU	Measured MRCOSMIC 002SCX
20/09/2003	39	1		JUSTIFY THE RAIN	Measured MRCOSMIC 3SC

COSMOS US producer Tom Middleton who is also a member of Global Communication.

| 18/09/1999 | 49 | 1 | | SUMMER IN SPACE | Island Blue PFACD 3 |
| 05/10/2002 | 32 | 2 | | TAKE ME WITH YOU | Polydor 0659952 |

DON COSTA US orchestra leader (born 10/6/1925, Boston, MA) and arranger for Vaughn Monroe, Frank Sinatra, Vic Damone and the Ames Brothers among others. Later A&R director for ABC and United Artists, he discovered Paul Anka. His daughter Nikka also enjoyed a successful recording career. He died on 19/1/1983.

| 13/10/1960 | 27 | 10 | | NEVER ON SUNDAY Featured in the 1959 film *Never On Sunday* | London HLT 9195 |

NIKKA COSTA US singer (born 4/6/1972, Los Angeles, CA), daughter of Don Costa.

| 11/08/2001 | 53 | 1 | | LIKE A FEATHER | Virgin VUSCD 199 |

ELVIS COSTELLO UK singer (born Declan McManus, 25/8/1954, Liverpool), son of bandleader Ross McManus. Renamed himself Elvis Costello (Costello is his grandmother's maiden name) in 1976 and formed the Attractions in 1977, shortly after signing with Radar Records. He also recorded infrequently as the Imposter for his Imp label. He married Pogues bass player Cait O'Riordan in 1986 and has made a number of film appearances. He won the 1998 Grammy Award for Best Pop Collaboration with Vocals with Burt Bacharach for *I Still Have That Other Girl*. He was inducted into the Rock & Roll Hall of Fame in 2003.

05/11/1977	15	11		WATCHING THE DETECTIVES	Stiff BUY 20
11/03/1978	16	10		(I DON'T WANNA GO TO) CHELSEA	Radar ADA 3
13/05/1978	24	10		PUMP IT UP	Radar ADA 10
28/10/1978	29	7		RADIO RADIO	Radar ADA 24
10/02/1979	2	12	●	OLIVER'S ARMY	Radar ADA 31
12/05/1979	28	8		ACCIDENTS WILL HAPPEN This and above four singles credited to ELVIS COSTELLO AND THE ATTRACTIONS	Radar ADA 35

DATE	POS	WKS	BPI	SINGLE TITLE	LABEL & NUMBER
16/02/1980	4	8		I CAN'T STAND UP FOR FALLING DOWN	F. Beat XX 1
12/04/1980	30	5		HI FIDELITY	F. Beat XX 3
07/06/1980	36	6		NEW AMSTERDAM	F. Beat XX 5
20/12/1980	60	4		CLUBLAND **ELVIS COSTELLO AND THE ATTRACTIONS**	F. Beat XX 12
03/10/1981	6	11		**A GOOD YEAR FOR THE ROSES**	F. Beat XX 17
12/12/1981	42	8		SWEET DREAMS	F. Beat XX 19
10/04/1982	51	3		I'M YOUR TOY **ELVIS COSTELLO AND THE ATTRACTIONS WITH THE ROYAL PHILHARMONIC ORCHESTRA**	F. Beat XX 21
19/06/1982	52	3		YOU LITTLE FOOL	F. Beat XX 26
31/07/1982	58	2		MAN OUT OF TIME	F. Beat XX 28
25/09/1982	43	4		FROM HEAD TO TOE	F. Beat XX 30
11/12/1982	48	6		PARTY PARTY **ELVIS COSTELLO AND THE ATTRACTIONS WITH THE ROYAL HORN GUARDS** Featured in the 1982 film *Party Party*	A&M AMS 8267
11/06/1983	16	4		PILLS AND SOAP **IMPOSTER**	Imp 001
09/07/1983	28	8		EVERYDAY I WRITE THE BOOK Featured in the 1998 film *The Wedding Singer*	F. Beat XX 32
17/09/1983	59	2		LET THEM ALL TALK	F. Beat XX 33
28/04/1984	48	3		PEACE IN OUR TIME **IMPOSTER**	Imposter TRUCE 1
16/06/1984	25	6		I WANNA BE LOVED/TURNING THE TOWN RED *Turning The Town Red* featured in the TV series *Scully*	F. Beat XX 35
25/08/1984	71	2		THE ONLY FLAME IN TOWN	F. Beat XX 37
04/05/1985	68	2		GREEN SHIRT	F. Beat ZB 40085
01/02/1986	33	4		DON'T LET ME BE MISUNDERSTOOD **COSTELLO SHOW FEATURING THE CONFEDERATES**	F. Beat ZB 40555
30/08/1986	73	1		TOKYO STORM WARNING	Imp 007
04/03/1989	31	6		VERONICA	Warner Brothers W 7558
20/05/1989	65	1		BABY PLAYS AROUND (EP) Tracks on EP: *Baby Plays Around, Poisoned Rose, Almost Blue* and *My Funny Valentine*	Warner Brothers W 2949
04/05/1991	43	4		THE OTHER SIDE OF SUMMER	Warner Brothers W 0025
05/03/1994	22	3		SULKY GIRL	Warner Brothers W 0234CD
30/04/1994	59	1		13 STEPS LEAD DOWN	Warner Brothers W 0245CD
26/11/1994	48	2		LONDON'S BRILLIANT PARADE	Warner Brothers W 0270CD1
11/05/1996	58	1		IT'S TIME This and above three singles credited to **ELVIS COSTELLO AND THE ATTRACTIONS**	Warner Brothers W 0348CD
01/05/1999	72	1		TOLEDO **ELVIS COSTELLO/BURT BACHARACH**	Mercury 8709652
31/07/1999	19	10		SHE Featured in the 1998 film *Notting Hill*	Mercury MERDD 521
20/04/2002	58	1		TEAR OFF YOUR OWN HEAD	Mercury 5828872

COTTAGERS – see TONY REES AND THE COTTAGERS

BILLY COTTON AND HIS BAND
UK orchestra leader (born 6/5/1899, London). The youngest of ten children, he joined the army as a bugler in 1914 and saw action in the Dardanelles Campaign before spending the rest of World War I in the Flying Corps. He later drove a London bus, played amateur football for Brentford and Wimbledon, and raced cars and motorcycles. In the 1920s he played drums with Laurie Johnson's Band, then formed the London Savannah Band, initially just as drummer and then in 1925 fronting the outfit. With over 40 years as one of the longest-running UK bandleaders, he was best known for his catchphrase of 'wakey, wakey' from his radio series *The Billy Cotton Band Show*. The show later transferred to TV, with the BBC connection continued by his son, Bill Cotton Jr, as controller of BBC 1. Billy Cotton was awarded the Ivor Novello Outstanding Personal Services to Popular Music Award in 1958, and died watching a boxing match at Wembley on 25/3/1969.

DATE	POS	WKS	BPI	SINGLE TITLE	LABEL & NUMBER
01/05/1953	3	10		IN A GOLDEN COACH **BILLY COTTON AND HIS BAND, VOCALS BY DOREEN STEPHENS** Song written to celebrate the coronation of Queen Elizabeth II	Decca F 10058
18/12/1953	11	3		I SAW MOMMY KISSING SANTA CLAUS **BILLY COTTON AND HIS BAND, VOCALS BY THE MILL GIRLS AND THE BANDITS**	Decca F 10206
30/04/1954	3	12		**FRIENDS AND NEIGHBOURS** BILLY COTTON AND HIS BAND, VOCALS BY THE BANDITS	Decca F 10299

MIKE COTTON'S JAZZMEN
UK trumpeter (born 12/8/1939, London) who later recorded as the Mike Cotton Band and the Mike Cotton Sound. His group featured, at various times, Dave Rowberry (keyboards), Jim Rodford (bass), Johnny Crocker (trombone), Derek Tearle (bass) and Jim Garforth (drums).

DATE	POS	WKS	BPI	SINGLE TITLE	LABEL & NUMBER
20/06/1963	36	4		SWING THAT HAMMER	Columbia DB 7029

JOHN COUGAR – see JOHN COUGAR MELLENCAMP

COUGARS
UK instrumental group formed in Bristol in 1961 by Keith 'Rod' Owen (guitar), Dave Tanner (guitar), Adrian Morgan (bass) and Dave Hack (drums). Their hit was banned by the BBC as it 'defaced a classical melody' – the song was based on Tchaikovsky's *Swan Lake*.

DATE	POS	WKS	BPI	SINGLE TITLE	LABEL & NUMBER
28/02/1963	33	8		SATURDAY NITE AT THE DUCK POND	Parlophone R 4989

COUNCIL COLLECTIVE
UK/US charity ensemble formed by The Style Council (Paul Weller, born John Weller, 25/5/1958, Woking, and Mick Talbot, born 11/9/1958, London) with guests Jimmy Ruffin (born 7/5/1939, Collinsville, MS) and Junior (born Norman Giscombe, 10/11/1961, London). The record was inspired by the miners' strike and the royalties went to the organisation Women Against Pit Closures, and the family of taxi driver David Wilkie, killed during the dispute.

DATE	POS	WKS	BPI	SINGLE TITLE	LABEL & NUMBER
22/12/1984	24	6		SOUL DEEP (PART 1)	Polydor MINE 1

COUNT INDIGO
UK singer Bruce Marcus.

DATE	POS	WKS	BPI	SINGLE TITLE	LABEL & NUMBER
09/03/1996	59	1		MY UNKNOWN LOVE	Cowboy RODEO 952CD

❶⁹ Number of weeks single topped the UK chart ↑ Entered the UK chart at #1 ▲⁹ Number of weeks single topped the US chart

179

COUNTING CROWS
US folk-rock group formed in San Francisco, CA by Adam Duritz (born 1/8/1964, Baltimore, MD, vocals), David Byron (born 5/10/1961, San Francisco, guitar), Matt Malley (born 4/7/1963, bass), Steve Bowman (born 14/1/1967, drums), Charlie Gillingham (born 12/1/1960, Torrance, CA, keyboards) and Dan Vickrey (born 26/8/1966, Walnut Creek, CA, guitar). Bowman joined Third Eye Blind in 1994 and was replaced by Ben Mize (born 2/2/1971).

30/04/1994.....28......2.......	MR JONES..	Geffen GFSTD 69
09/07/1994....70.....1.......	ROUND HERE..	Geffen GFSTD 74
15/10/1994....49......3.......	RAIN KING...	Geffen GFSTD 82
19/10/1996....41......1.......	ANGELS OF THE SILENCES....................................	Geffen GFSTD 22182
14/12/1996....62......1.......	A LONG DECEMBER...	Geffen GFSTD 22190
31/05/1997....54......1.......	DAYLIGHT FADING...	Geffen GFSTD 22247
20/12/1997....68......1.......	A LONG DECEMBER...	Geffen GFSTD 22190
30/10/1999....46......1.......	HANGING AROUND..	Geffen 4971842
29/06/2002....33......2.......	AMERICAN GIRLS..	Geffen 4977452
15/02/2003....16......9.......	BIG YELLOW TAXI COUNTING CROWS FEATURING VANESSA CARLTON Featured in the 2003 film Two Weeks Notice....	Geffen 4978492
21/06/2003....50......1.......	IF I COULD GIVE YOU ALL MY LOVE...........................	Geffen GED 9806831
27/03/2004....68......1.......	HANGINAROUND..	Geffen 9861994
24/07/2004....28......5.......	ACCIDENTLY IN LOVE..	DreamWorks 9862881

COUNTRYMEN
UK vocal group.

03/05/1962.....45......2.......	I KNOW WHERE I'M GOING....................................	Piccadilly 7N 35029

COURSE
Dutch DJ/production group fronted by Keepon with vocalist Dewi Lopulalan.

19/04/1997 .....5......7.......	READY OR NOT..	The Brothers Organisation CDBRUV 2
05/07/1997 .....8......6.......	AIN'T NOBODY..	The Brothers Organisation CDBRUV 3
20/12/1997.....51......2.......	BEST LOVE...	The Brothers Organisation CDBRUV 6

MICHAEL COURTNEY
UK singer from Blackpool who launched the Nap Music label and whose debut hit raised funds for Lincoln City Football Club.

04/05/2002......64......1.......	CHIRPY CHIRPY CHEEP CHEEP/JAGGED EDGE.....................	Nap Music SLCPCD 001

TINA COUSINS
UK singer (born 1975) who began as a model, appearing in a Rolling Stones video before going solo. She also took part in the BRITS Trust Thank Abba For The Music project.

15/08/1998 .....2......12......O	MYSTERIOUS TIMES SASH! FEATURING TINA COUSINS.............	Multiply CDMULTY 40
21/11/1998....20......3.......	PRAY..	Jive 0519162
27/03/1999....15......4.......	KILLIN' TIME..	Jive/Eastern Bloc 0519232
10/07/1999....45......2.......	FOREVER...	Jive 0519332
09/10/1999....46......1.......	ANGEL...	Ebul/Jive 0519432
22/04/2000 .....8......7.......	JUST AROUND THE HILL SASH! FEATURING TINA COUSINS.........	Multiply CDMULTY 62

DON COVAY
US singer (born March 1938, Orangeburg, SC) who grew up in Washington and joined the Rainbows, including Marvin Gaye and Billy Stewart, in 1955. First recording in 1957 as Pretty Boy, he formed his own group the Goodtimers in 1960, signing solo with Atlantic in 1964. He was also a songwriter for Aretha Franklin and Gene Chandler. He was later in The Soul Clan with Solomon Burke, Arthur Conley, Ben E King and Joe Tex.

07/09/1974.....29......6.......	IT'S BETTER TO HAVE (AND DON'T NEED)......................	Mercury 6052 634

VINCENT COVELLO – see BT

COVENTRY CITY FC
UK football club formed in 1883 as Singer FC, changing their name to Coventry in 1898. They won the FA Cup at the time of the single in 1987.

23/05/1987.....61......2.......	GO FOR IT!..	Sky Blue SKB 1

COVER GIRLS
US group formed in 1986 by Louis 'Angel' Sabater, Caroline Jackson and Sunshine Wright, who left in 1989 and was replaced by Margo Urban. By 1992 the line-up consisted of Jackson, Evelyn Escalera and Michelle Valentine.

01/08/1992.....38......4.......	WISHING ON A STAR...	Epic 6581437

DAVID COVERDALE AND WHITESNAKE
UK heavy rock group formed in 1978 by David Coverdale (born 22/9/1949, Saltburn-By-The-Sea, Cleveland, vocals), Mickey Moody (guitar), Bernie Marsden (guitar), Brian Johnston (keyboards), Neil Murray (bass) and John Dowie (drums). Ex-Deep Purple Coverdale had released two solo albums under the name Whitesnake after he left Deep Purple in 1976. Marsden later recorded solo.

07/06/1997.....46......1.......	TOO MANY TEARS..	EMI CDEM 471

COVERDALE PAGE
UK duo of ex-Deep Purple and Whitesnake David Coverdale (born 22/9/1949, Saltburn-By-The-Sea, Cleveland) and ex-Led Zeppelin Jimmy Page (born 9/1/1944, Heston, Middlesex).

03/07/1993.....29......2.......	TAKE ME FOR A LITTLE WHILE................................	EMI CDEM 270
23/10/1993.....43......1.......	TAKE A LOOK AT YOURSELF...................................	EMI CDEM 279

JULIE COVINGTON
UK singer (born 1947, London) who recorded her first album in 1971 but had to wait until 1975 and the success of the TV series Rock Follies to break through. She was on the Evita album (including her debut hit single) but refused to appear in the stage show.

DATE	POS	WKS	BPI	SINGLE TITLE	LABEL & NUMBER
25/12/1976	❶¹	15	●	**DON'T CRY FOR ME ARGENTINA** Written by Tim Rice and Andrew Lloyd Webber for the show *Evita*	MCA 260
03/12/1977	12	11		ONLY WOMEN BLEED	Virgin VS 196
15/07/1978	63	3		DON'T CRY FOR ME ARGENTINA	MCA 260

JULIE COVINGTON, RULA LENSKA, CHARLOTTE CORNWELL AND SUE JONES-DAVIES
UK group from the TV series *Rock Follies* with music mainly written by Andy Mackay of Roxy Music. Rula Lenska (born Rosa-Marie Leopoldnya Lubienska, 30/9/1947, St Neots) was married to Dennis Waterman. Julie Covington was born in London in 1947. Charlotte Cornwell is the sister of author John Le Carré.

DATE	POS	WKS	BPI	SINGLE TITLE	LABEL & NUMBER
21/05/1977	10	6		**O.K.?** Featured in the TV series *Rock Follies*	Polydor 2001 714

WARREN COVINGTON – see TOMMY DORSEY ORCHESTRA STARRING WARREN COVINGTON

PATRICK COWLEY – see SYLVESTER

CARL COX
UK producer (born 29/7/1962, Oldham) who worked as a painter and decorator, hod carrier, plasterer and scaffolder before turning to music.

DATE	POS	WKS	BPI	SINGLE TITLE	LABEL & NUMBER
28/09/1991	23	7		I WANT YOU (FOREVER)	Perfecto PB 44885
08/08/1992	35	3		DOES IT FEEL GOOD TO YOU This and above single credited to **DJ CARL COX**	Perfecto 74321102877
06/11/1993	44	2		THE PLANET OF LOVE	Perfecto 74321161772
09/03/1996	24	2		TWO PAINTINGS AND A DRUM EP Tracks on EP: *Phoebus Apollo, Yum Yum* and *Siberian Snow Storm*	Edel 0090715 COX
08/06/1996	25	2		SENSUAL SOPHIS-TI-CAT/THE PLAYER	Ultimatum 0090875 COX
12/12/1998	52	1		THE LATIN THEME	Edel 0091685 COX
22/05/1999	40	2		PHUTURE 2000	Worldwide Ultimatum 0091715 COX

DEBORAH COX
Canadian R&B singer (born 13/7/1974, Toronto) who started singing professionally at the age of twelve.

DATE	POS	WKS	BPI	SINGLE TITLE	LABEL & NUMBER
11/11/1995	34	3		SENTIMENTAL	Arista 74321324962
24/02/1996	31	3		WHO DO U LOVE	Arista 74321337942
31/07/1999	49	1		IT'S OVER NOW Contains a sample of Harold Melvin & The Bluenotes' *Bad Luck*	Arista 74321686942
09/10/1999	55	1		NOBODY'S SUPPOSED TO BE HERE	Arista 74321702102

MICHAEL COX
UK singer (born Michael James Cox, Liverpool) whose sisters wrote to TV producer Jack Good demanding he be given an audition. His debut hit was on producer Joe Meek's Triumph label, and he later recorded for HMV and Parlophone. Following a ouija board experience he dropped the surname Cox, performing as Michael James.

DATE	POS	WKS	BPI	SINGLE TITLE	LABEL & NUMBER
09/06/1960	7	13		**ANGELA JONES**	Triumph RGM 1011
20/10/1960	41	2		ALONG CAME CAROLINE	HMV POP 789

PETER COX
UK singer (born 17/11/1955) who was previously a songwriter and member of Go West before going solo.

DATE	POS	WKS	BPI	SINGLE TITLE	LABEL & NUMBER
02/08/1997	37	2		AIN'T GONNA CRY AGAIN	Chrysalis CDCHS 5056
15/11/1997	24	2		IF YOU WALK AWAY	Chrysalis CDCHSS 5069
20/06/1998	39	2		WHAT A FOOL BELIEVES	Chrysalis CDCHS 5089

GRAHAM COXON
UK guitarist (born 12/3/1969, Rintein, Germany) who was a founder member of Seymour in 1988. The group later changed its name to Blur in 1991 when they signed with Food Records. Coxon subsequently launched the Transcopic label in 1997 with his own album as its debut release.

DATE	POS	WKS	BPI	SINGLE TITLE	LABEL & NUMBER
20/03/2004	37	1		FREAKIN' OUT	Transcopic R 6632
15/05/2004	22	3		BITTERSWEET BUNDLE OF MAN	Transcopic CDRS 6637
07/08/2004	32	2		SPECTACULAR	Transcopic CDRS 6643
06/11/2004	19	3		FREAKIN' OUT/ALL OVER ME	Transcopic CDRS 6652

CRACKER
US rock group formed in 1991 by David Lowery (guitar/vocals) and Johnny Hickman (guitar) with an ever-changing rhythm section. Lowery had previously been with Camper Van Beethoven.

DATE	POS	WKS	BPI	SINGLE TITLE	LABEL & NUMBER
28/05/1994	43	4		LOW	Virgin America VUSDG 80
23/07/1994	41	3		GET OFF THIS	Virgin America VUSCD 83
03/12/1994	54	2		LOW	Virgin America VUSDG 80

SARAH CRACKNELL
UK singer (born 12/4/1967, Chelmsford) who was lead singer with St Etienne before going solo.

DATE	POS	WKS	BPI	SINGLE TITLE	LABEL & NUMBER
14/09/1996	39	1		ANYMORE	Gut CDGUT 3

CRACKOUT
UK group formed by Steven Eagles (born 20/7/1981, guitar/vocals), Jack Dunkley (born 28/4/1979, bass) and Nicholas Millard (born 22/5/1981, drums).

DATE	POS	WKS	BPI	SINGLE TITLE	LABEL & NUMBER
22/06/2002	72	1		I AM THE ONE	Hut HUTCD 156
09/08/2003	63	1		OUT OF OUR MINDS	Hut HUTCD 170
13/03/2004	65	1		THIS IS WHAT WE DO	Hut HUTCD 174

STEVE CRADDOCK – see BUFFALO TOM: LIAM GALLAGHER AND STEVE CRADDOCK

CRADLE OF FILTH
UK group formed in 1991 by Dani Davey (vocals), Paul Ryan (guitar), his brother Benjamin (keyboards), John Richard (bass) and Darren (drums). Robin Eaglestone (guitar) was added to the line-up the following year, switching to bass on the departure of Richard. Paul Allender (guitar) joined at the same time and Nicholas Barker (drums) shortly after. The Ryan brothers and

❶⁹ Number of weeks single topped the UK chart ↑ Entered the UK chart at #1 ▲⁹ Number of weeks single topped the US chart

181

Allender left in 1995 and were replaced by Stuart Antsis (guitar), Jared Demeter (guitar) and Damien Gregori (keyboards). Demeter and Gregori left later the same year and were replaced by Gian Pyres and Les Smith. By 2000 Adrian Erlandson had joined on drums, Allender had returned and Martin Powell was on keyboards in place of Smith.

15/03/2003 . . . . . 35 . . . . . . 2 . . . . BABYLON A.D. (SO GLAD FOR THE MADNESS) . . . . Epic 6735549

CRAIG UK singer Craig Phillips who was a winner of the TV series *Big Brother*. He donated all of the £70,000 first prize to the Downs Syndrome Association and then gave them the proceeds from his hit record as well.

23/12/2000 . . . . . 14 . . . . . . 6 . . . . . . O AT THIS TIME OF YEAR . . . . WEA 321CD

ROBBIE CRAIG – see ARTFUL DODGER

FLOYD CRAMER US pianist (born 27/10/1933, Samti, LA) who began playing at the age of five and moved to Nashville in 1955, becoming a top session musician. He also toured with Elvis Presley, Johnny Cash, Perry Como and Chet Atkins. He died from lung cancer on 31/12/1997.

13/04/1961 . . . . ⦿[1] . . . 14 . . . . . . ON THE REBOUND . . . . RCA 1231
20/07/1961 . . . . . 36 . . . . . . 8 . . . . . . SAN ANTONIO ROSE . . . . RCA 1241
23/08/1962 . . . . . 46 . . . . . . 2 . . . . . . HOT PEPPER . . . . RCA 1301

CRAMPS US group formed in New York by Lux Interior (Erick Lee Purkhiser, vocals), Poison Ivy Rorschach (Kirsty Marlana Wallace, guitar), Bryan Gregory (guitar) and Mariam Linna (drums). Linna left in 1977 and was replaced by Nick Knox; Gregory left in 1980 and was replaced by Kid Congo Powers. By 1991 the group were Interior, Rorschach, Slim Chance (bass) and Jim Sclavunos (drums). Gregory died on 7/1/2001 at 46 from unknown causes, although he had recently suffered a heart attack.

09/11/1985 . . . . . 68 . . . . . . 1 . . . . . . CAN YOUR PUSSY DO THE DOG? . . . . Big Beat NS 110
10/02/1990 . . . . . 35 . . . . . 3 . . . . . . BIKINI GIRLS WITH MACHINE GUNS . . . . Enigma ENV 17

CRANBERRIES Irish rock group formed in Limerick in 1990 by Noel Hogan (born 25/12/1971, Woycross, guitar), Mike Hogan (born 29/4/1973, Woycross, bass) and Fergal Lawler (born 4/3/1971, Limerick, drums) as The Cranberry Saw Us. Joined by Delores O'Riordan (born 6/9/1971, Limerick, lead vocals) in 1991, they shortened their name to The Cranberries.

27/02/1993 . . . . . 74 . . . . . . 1 . . . . . . LINGER . . . . Island CID 556
12/02/1994 . . . . . 14 . . . . . 11 . . . . . . LINGER Re-issue of Island CID 556 . . . . Island CID 559
07/05/1994 . . . . . 27 . . . . . . 5 . . . . . . DREAMS Featured in the films *Boys On The Side* (1995), *Back Of Beyond* (1995) and *You've Got Mail* (1998) . . . Island CIDX 594
01/10/1994 . . . . . 14 . . . . . . 6 . . . . . . ZOMBIE MTV 1995 Europe Music Award for Best Song. . . . . Island CID 600
03/12/1994 . . . . . 38 . . . . . . 6 . . . . . . ODE TO MY FAMILY . . . . Island CIDX 601
11/03/1995 . . . . . 23 . . . . . . 5 . . . . . . I CAN'T BE WITH YOU . . . . Island CIDX 605
12/08/1995 . . . . . 20 . . . . . . 3 . . . . . . RIDICULOUS THOUGHTS Featured in the 1995 film *Butterfly Kiss* . . . . Island CID 616
20/04/1996 . . . . . 13 . . . . . . 5 . . . . . . SALVATION . . . . Island CID 633
13/07/1996 . . . . . 33 . . . . . . 3 . . . . . . FREE TO DECIDE . . . . Instant CIDX 637
17/04/1999 . . . . . 13 . . . . . . 4 . . . . . . PROMISES . . . . Island US 5725912
17/07/1999 . . . . . 54 . . . . . . 1 . . . . . . ANIMAL INSTINCT . . . . Island US 5621972

LES CRANE US singer (born 1935, San Francisco, CA) who first came to prominence as a TV talk-show host in San Francisco, before appearing in the films *An American Dream* (1966) and *I Love A Mystery* (1973).

19/02/1972 . . . . . 7 . . . . . . 14 . . . . . . DESIDERATA 1971 Grammy Award for Best Spoken Word Recording . . . . Warner Brothers K 16119

WHITFIELD CRANE – see ICE T AND MOTORHEAD

CRANES UK rock group formed in Portsmouth in 1988 by Alison Shaw (bass/vocals), Jim Shaw (drums), Mark Francombe (guitar) and Matt Cope (bass).

25/09/1993 . . . . . 29 . . . . . . 1 . . . . . . JEWEL . . . . Dedicated CRANE 007CD
03/09/1994 . . . . . 57 . . . . . . 1 . . . . . . SHINING ROAD . . . . Dedicated CRANE 008CD1

CRASH TEST DUMMIES Canadian rock group formed by Brad Roberts (born 10/1/1964, Winnipeg, vocals), Dan Roberts (born 22/5/1967, Winnipeg, bass), Ellen Reid (born 14/7/1966, Selkirk, keyboards) and Benjamin Darvill (born 4/1/1967, Winnipeg, harmonica), adding drummer Mitch Dorge (born 15/9/1960, Winnipeg) after their first album. They won the 1994 MTV Europe Music Award for Breakthrough Artist.

23/04/1994 . . . . . 2 . . . . . . 11 . . . . . O MMM MMM MMM MMM Featured in the 1994 film *Dumb And Dumber* . . . . RCA 74321201512
16/07/1994 . . . . . 23 . . . . . . 5 . . . . . . AFTERNOONS & COFFEESPOONS. . . . . RCA 74321219622
15/04/1995 . . . . . 30 . . . . . . 4 . . . . . . THE BALLAD OF PETER PUMPKINHEAD CRASH TEST DUMMIES FEATURING ELLEN REID Cover of an XTC song. Featured in the 1994 film *Dumb And Dumber* . . . . RCA 74321276772

BEVERLEY CRAVEN UK singer/pianist (born 28/6/1963, Sri Lanka) who grew up in England and moved to London at the age of nineteen. Named Best British Newcomer at the 1992 BRIT Awards.

20/04/1991 . . . . . 3 . . . . . . 13 . . . . . O PROMISE ME . . . . Epic 6559437
20/07/1991 . . . . . 32 . . . . . . 7 . . . . . . HOLDING ON . . . . Epic 6565507
05/10/1991 . . . . . 40 . . . . . . 5 . . . . . . WOMAN TO WOMAN . . . . Epic 6574647
07/12/1991 . . . . . 68 . . . . . . 2 . . . . . . MEMORIES. . . . . Epic 6576617
25/09/1993 . . . . . 34 . . . . . . 4 . . . . . . LOVE SCENES. . . . . Epic 6595952
20/11/1993 . . . . . 61 . . . . . . 2 . . . . . . MOLLIE'S SONG . . . . Epic 6598132

O Silver disc ● Gold disc ✪ Platinum disc (additional platinum units are indicated by a figure following the symbol) ◉ Singles released prior to 1973 that are known to have sold over 1 million copies in the UK

BILLY CRAWFORD US singer (born 16/5/1982, Philippines) who relocated to Texas in 1994.

10/10/1998	48	2		URGENTLY IN LOVE	V2 VVR 5003063
03/05/2003	35	2		YOU DIDN'T EXPECT THAT	V2 VVR 5022083
30/08/2003	32	2		TRACKIN'	V2 VVR 5023108

JIMMY CRAWFORD UK singer (born Ronald Lindsey).

08/06/1961	49	1		LOVE OR MONEY	Columbia DB 4633
16/11/1961	18	10		I LOVE HOW YOU LOVE ME	Columbia DB 4717

MICHAEL CRAWFORD UK actor (born Michael Patrick Dumble-Smith, 19/1/1942, Salisbury) best known as Frank Spencer, the hero in the TV comedy *Some Mothers Do 'Ave 'Em*. Also a musical actor, appearing in *Barnum* and *Phantom Of The Opera*, he was awarded an OBE in 1987.

10/01/1987	7	11		MUSIC OF THE NIGHT Flip side listed as SARAH BRIGHTMAN *Wishing You Were Somehow Here Again*. Both sides featured in the musical *Phantom Of The Opera*	Polydor POSP 803
15/01/1994	54	3		THE MUSIC OF THE NIGHT BARBRA STREISAND (DUET WITH MICHAEL CRAWFORD)	Columbia 6597382

RANDY CRAWFORD US singer (born 18/2/1952, Macon, GA) whose career began in 1967 but did not release a debut album until 1976. The success of the Crusaders' *Street Life* in 1979, on which she was lead vocalist, led to the group producing her *Now We May Begin*, her solo chart breakthrough. She won the 1982 BRIT Award for Best Female (even though the award was actually for the Best *British* Female).

21/06/1980	61	2		LAST NIGHT AT DANCELAND	Warner Brothers K 17631
30/08/1980	2	11	O	ONE DAY I'LL FLY AWAY	Warner Brothers K 17680
30/05/1981	11	13		YOU MIGHT NEED SOMEBODY	Warner Brothers K 17803
08/08/1981	18	9		RAINY NIGHT IN GEORGIA	Warner Brothers K 17840
31/10/1981	48	3		SECRET COMBINATION	Warner Brothers K 17872
30/01/1982	60	2		IMAGINE	Warner Brothers K 17906
05/06/1982	48	4		ONE HELLO	Warner Brothers K 17948
19/02/1983	65	1		HE REMINDS ME	Warner Brothers K 17970
08/10/1983	51	4		NIGHT LINE	Warner Brothers W 9530
29/11/1986	4	17		ALMAZ	Warner Brothers W 8583
18/01/1992	44	7		DIAMANTE ZUCCHERO WITH RANDY CRAWFORD	London LON 313
15/11/1997	60	1		GIVE ME THE NIGHT	WEA 142CD

ROBERT CRAY BAND US blues guitarist (born 1/8/1953, Columbus, GA) who formed his first band in 1974 with the best-known line-up featuring Jim Pugh (keyboards), Karl Sevareid (bass) and Kevin Haves (drums). He also recorded with Eric Clapton. He has won five Grammy Awards: Best Traditional Blues Recording in 1986 with Albert Collins and Johnny Copeland for *Showdown*, Best Contemporary Blues Recording in 1987 for *Strong Persuader*, Best Contemporary Blues Recording in 1988 for *Don't Be Afraid Of The Dark*, Best Rock Instrumental in 1996 with Jimmie Vaughan, Eric Clapton, Bonnie Raitt, BB King, Buddy Guy, Dr John and Art Neville for *SRV Shuffle* and Best Contemporary Blues Recording in 1999 for *Take Your Shoes Off*.

20/06/1987	50	4		RIGHT NEXT DOOR (BECAUSE OF ME)	Mercury CRAY 3
20/04/1996	65	1		BABY LEE JOHN LEE HOOKER WITH ROBERT CRAY	Silvertone ORECD 81

CRAZY ELEPHANT US studio group assembled by producers Jerry Kasenetz and Jeff Katz, with ex-Cadillac member Robert Spencer singing lead. A touring group was subsequently put together with Hal King (vocals), Larry Laufer (keyboards/vocals), Ronnie Bretone (bass), Bob Avery (drums) and Jethro.

21/05/1969	12	13		GIMME GIMME GOOD LOVIN'	Major Minor MM 609

CRAZY TOWN US rock/rap group formed in Los Angeles, CA by lyricists/singers/producers Seth 'Shifty Shellshock' Binzer and Bret 'Epic' Mazur, Doug 'Faydoedeelay' Miller (bass), Kraig 'Squirrel' Tyler (guitar), Rust Epique (guitar), Anthony 'Trouble' Valli (guitar), DJ AM (turntables) and James 'JBJ' Bradley Junior (drums). Epique died from a heart attack on 9/3/2004.

07/04/2001	3	13	O	BUTTERFLY ▲[2] Contains a sample of Red Hot Chili Peppers' *Pretty Little Ditty*	Columbia 6710012
11/08/2001	23	5		REVOLVING DOOR	Columbia 6714942
30/11/2002	50	1		DROWNING	Columbia 6733262

CRAZYHEAD UK group formed in Leicester in 1986 by Ian 'Anderson Pork Beast' (vocals), Vom, Superfast Blind Dick and Kevin.

16/07/1988	65	2		TIME HAS TAKEN ITS TOLL ON YOU	Food 12
25/02/1989	68	2		HAVE LOVE WILL TRAVEL (EP) Tracks on EP: *Have Love Will Travel*, *Out On A Limb (Live)*, *Baby Turpentine (Live)* and *Snake Eyes (Live)*	Food SGE 2025

CREAM UK group formed in 1966 by Eric Clapton (born Eric Clapp, 30/3/1945, Ripley, guitar/vocals), Jack Bruce (born John Bruce, 14/5/1943, Lanarkshire, vocals/bass) and Ginger Baker (born Peter Baker, 19/8/1939, London, drums). All three were famous with other outfits: Clapton with the Yardbirds, Bruce with Manfred Mann, and Baker with Alexis Korner and Graham Bond. They announced their disbandment in 1968, finally splitting in August 1969, and were inducted into the Rock & Roll Hall of Fame in 1993.

20/10/1966	34	6		WRAPPING PAPER	Reaction 591 007
15/12/1966	11	12		I FEEL FREE	Reaction 591 011
08/06/1967	17	9		STRANGE BREW Featured in the films *More American Graffiti* (1979) and *Blow* (2001)	Reaction 591 015
05/06/1968	40	3		ANYONE FOR TENNIS (THE SAVAGE SEVEN THEME)	Polydor 56 258
09/10/1968	25	7		SUNSHINE OF YOUR LOVE	Polydor 56 286
15/01/1969	28	8		WHITE ROOM Featured in the 1988 film *1969*	Polydor 56 300

O[9] Number of weeks single topped the UK chart ↑ Entered the UK chart at #1 ▲[9] Number of weeks single topped the US chart

	DATE	POS	WKS	BPI	SINGLE TITLE	LABEL & NUMBER

09/04/1969 . . . . . 18 . . . . . . 10 . . . . . . BADGE Written by George Harrison . . . . Polydor 56 315

28/10/1972 . . . . . 42 . . . . . . 4 . . . . BADGE Re-issue of Polydor 56 315 . . . . Polydor 2058 285

CREATION UK group formed in 1966 by Bob Garner (bass), Jack Jones (drums), Eddie Phillips (guitar) and Kenny Pickett (born 3/9/1942, Middlesex, lead vocals). They disbanded in 1968, Phillips and Pickett reuniting as Creation in the early 1990s and signing with Creation Records. Pickett collapsed and died on 10/1/1997.

07/07/1966 . . . . . 49 . . . . . . 1 . . . . . . MAKING TIME Featured in the 1998 film *Rushmore* . . . . Planet PLF 116

03/11/1966 . . . . . 36 . . . . . . 2 . . . . . . PAINTER MAN . . . . Planet PLF 119

CREATURES UK spin-off group formed by ex-Siouxsie And The Banshees Siouxsie (born Susan Dillon, 27/5/1957) and her husband drummer Budgie (born Peter Clark, 21/8/1957).

03/10/1981 . . . . . 24 . . . . . . 7 . . . . . . MAD EYED SCREAMER . . . . Polydor POSPD 354

23/04/1983 . . . . . 21 . . . . . . 7 . . . . . . MISS THE GIRL . . . . Wonderland SHE 1

16/07/1983 . . . . . 14 . . . . . . 10 . . . . . . RIGHT NOW . . . . Wonderland SHE 2

14/10/1989 . . . . . 53 . . . . . . 2 . . . . . . STANDING HERE . . . . Wonderland SHE 17

27/03/1999 . . . . . 72 . . . . . . 1 . . . . . . SAY . . . . Sioux 6CD

25/10/2003 . . . . . 53 . . . . . . 1 . . . . . . GODZILLA . . . . Sioux 14CD3

CREDIT TO THE NATION UK rap group with Matty Hanson (aka MC Fusion) and dancers Tyrone (aka T-Swing) and Kelvin (aka Mista G).

22/05/1993 . . . . . 57 . . . . . . 3 . . . . . . CALL IT WHAT YOU WANT . . . . One Little Indian 94 TP7CD

18/09/1993 . . . . . 56 . . . . . . 2 . . . . . . ENOUGH IS ENOUGH CHUMBAWAMBA AND CREDIT TO THE NATION . . . . One Little Indian 79 TP7CD

12/03/1994 . . . . . 24 . . . . . . 3 . . . . . . TEENAGE SENSATION . . . . One Little Indian 124 TP7DC

14/05/1994 . . . . . 72 . . . . . . 1 . . . . . . SOWING THE SEEDS OF HATRED . . . . One Little Indian 134 TP7DC

22/07/1995 . . . . . 60 . . . . . . 1 . . . . . . LIAR LIAR . . . . One Little Indian 144 TP7DC

12/09/1998 . . . . . 60 . . . . . . 1 . . . . . . TACKY LOVE SONG . . . . Chrysalis CDCHS 5097

CREED US rock group formed in Tallahassee, FL in 1995 by Scott Stapp (vocals), Mark Tremonti (guitar), Brian Marshall (bass) and Scott Phillips (drums). Marshall left in 2000 and was replaced by Brett Hestla.

15/01/2000 . . . . . 47 . . . . . . 1 . . . . . . HIGHER . . . . Epic 6683152

20/01/2001 . . . . . 13 . . . . . . 5 . . . . . . WITH ARMS WIDE OPEN ▲¹ 2000 Grammy Award for Best Rock Song for writers Scott Stapp and Mark Tremonti . . . . . Epic 6706952

29/09/2001 . . . . . 64 . . . . . . 1 . . . . . . HIGHER Re-issue of Epic 6683152 . . . . Epic 6710642

16/03/2002 . . . . . 18 . . . . . . 5 . . . . . . MY SACRIFICE . . . . Epic 6723162

03/08/2002 . . . . . 47 . . . . . . 1 . . . . . . ONE LAST BREATH/BULLETS . . . . Epic 6728262

CREEDENCE CLEARWATER REVIVAL US rock group formed at high school at El Cerrito, CA by John Fogerty (born 28/5/1945, Berkeley, CA, guitar/vocals), Tom Fogerty (born 9/11/1941, Berkeley, guitar), Stuart Cook (born 25/4/1945, Oakland, CA, keyboards/bass) and Doug 'Cosmo' Clifford (born 24/4/1945, Palo Alto, CA, drums). Their first dates were as Tommy Fogerty And The Blue Velvets, and they first recorded as the Golliwogs For Fantasy in 1964. Their name changed again in 1967; 'Creedence' was the name of a friend, 'Clearwater' was from a beer advertisement and 'Revival' reflected their music. Tom Fogerty went solo in 1971 and the group disbanded in 1972. Tom Fogerty died from tuberculosis on 6/9/1990. They were inducted into the Rock & Roll Hall of Fame in 1993. John Fogerty won the 1997 Grammy Award for Best Rock Album for *Blue Moon Swamp* and has a star on the Hollywood Walk of Fame.

28/05/1969 . . . . . 8 . . . . . . 13 . . . . . . **PROUD MARY** . . . . Liberty LBF 15223

16/08/1969 . . . ◉³ . . . . . 15 . . . . . . **BAD MOON RISING** Featured in the films *An American Werewolf In London* (1981), *The Big Chill* (1984) and *My Girl* (1991) . . . .
. . . . Liberty LBF 15230

15/11/1969 . . . . . 19 . . . . . . 11 . . . . . . GREEN RIVER Featured in the 1988 film *1969* . . . . Liberty LBF 15250

14/02/1970 . . . . . 31 . . . . . . 6 . . . . . . DOWN ON THE CORNER . . . . Liberty LBF 15283

04/04/1970 . . . . . 8 . . . . . . 13 . . . . . . **TRAVELLIN' BAND** . . . . Liberty LBF 15310

20/06/1970 . . . . . 3 . . . . . . 12 . . . . . . **UP AROUND THE BEND** Featured in the 2000 Walt Disney film *Remember The Titans* . . . . Liberty LBF 15354

05/09/1970 . . . . . 20 . . . . . . 9 . . . . . . LONG AS I CAN SEE THE LIGHT . . . . Liberty LBF 15384

20/03/1971 . . . . . 36 . . . . . . 6 . . . . . . HAVE YOU EVER SEEN THE RAIN . . . . Liberty LBF 15440

24/07/1971 . . . . . 36 . . . . . . 8 . . . . . . SWEET HITCH-HIKER . . . . United Artists UP 35261

02/05/1992 . . . . . 71 . . . . . . 1 . . . . . . BAD MOON RISING Re-issue of Liberty LBF 15230 . . . . Epic 6580047

KID CREOLE AND THE COCONUTS US singer Kid Creole (born Thomas Darnell August Browder, 1951, Haiti) who moved to New York with his family. He spent time songwriting with Chappell before forming Dr Buzzard's Original Savannah Band with his brother Stony. Despite success in the UK during the mid-1970s swing revival, litigation ended Dr Buzzard. Darnell joined Coati Mundi (born Andy Hernandez) to form the Coconuts, with Fonda Rae, Lordes Cotto, Brooksi Wells, Franz Krauns, Andrew Lloyd, Winston Grennan and Peter Schott, signing with the Ze label. Both the Coconuts and Coati Mundi later recorded on their own. Kid Creole appeared in the 1984 film *Against All Odds*.

13/06/1981 . . . . . 32 . . . . . . 7 . . . . . . ME NO POP I KID CREOLE AND THE COCONUTS PRESENTS COATI MUNDI . . . . Ze WIP 6711

15/05/1982 . . . . . 4 . . . . . . 11 . . . . . . **I'M A WONDERFUL THING, BABY** . . . . Ze WIP 6756

24/07/1982 . . . . . 7 . . . . . . 9 . . . . . . **STOOL PIGEON** . . . . Ze WIP 6793

09/10/1982 . . . . . 2 . . . . . . 8 . . . . . . **ANNIE I'M NOT YOUR DADDY** . . . . Ze WIP 6801

11/12/1982 . . . . . 29 . . . . . . 7 . . . . . . DEAR ADDY . . . . Ze WIP 6840

10/09/1983 . . . . . 35 . . . . . . 5 . . . . . . THERE'S SOMETHING WRONG IN PARADISE . . . . Island IS 130

19/11/1983 . . . . . 49 . . . . . . 4 . . . . . . THE LIFEBOAT PARTY . . . . Island IS 142

14/04/1990 . . . . . 29 . . . . . . 5 . . . . . . THE SEX OF IT . . . . CBS 6556987

10/04/1993 . . . . . 60 . . . . . . 2 . . . . . . I'M A WONDERFUL THING, BABY (REMIX) . . . . Island CID 551

○ Silver disc   ● Gold disc   ✪ Platinum disc (additional platinum units are indicated by a figure following the symbol)   ◎ Singles released prior to 1973 that are known to have sold over 1 million copies in the UK

CRESCENDO UK/US duo Steve and Serena Hitchcock. Steve worked in his home-based studio for three years before forming Crescendo, while New Yorker Serena had been busking for four years across Europe.

23/12/1995 . . . . . 20 . . . . . . 5 . . . . . .   ARE YOU OUT THERE . . . . ffrr FCD 270

CRESCENT UK group formed in Liverpool by Wayne Whitfield (guitar/vocals), Karl Rowlands (guitar), Sean Longworth (bass) and Joey Harrison (drums), taking their name from the street where they used to hang out as youngsters.

18/05/2002 . . . . . 49 . . . . . . 1	ON THE RUN . . . . Hut HUTCD 153
27/07/2002 . . . . . 60 . . . . . . 1	TEST OF TIME . . . . Hut HUTCD 157
28/09/2002 . . . . . 61 . . . . . . 1	SPINNIN' WHEELS . . . . Hut HUTDX 160

CREW CUTS Canadian vocal group formed in 1952 by John Perkins (born 28/8/1931, Toronto), Ray Perkins (born 28/11/1932, Toronto), Pat Barrett (born 15/9/1931, Toronto) and Rudi Maugeri (born 21/1/1931, Toronto) as the Canadaires, changing their name to the Crew Cuts in 1954. They disbanded in 1963.

01/10/1954 . . . . . 12 . . . . . . 9 . . . . . .   SH-BOOM ▲[9] . . . . Mercury MB 3140

15/04/1955 . . . . . 4 . . . . . 20 . . . . . .   **EARTH ANGEL** Song written by Jesse Belvin who was killed in a car crash on 6/2/1960, four hours after he gave the first concert to an integrated audience in Little Rock, AR. Later evidence revealed that in addition to six serious death threats during the day, the rear tyres on Belvin's car had been tampered with . . . . Mercury MB 3202

BERNARD CRIBBINS UK comedian/TV personality (born 29/12/1928) who was the narrator of children's TV programmes such as the *Wombles* and *Paddington Bear*. He began his recording career with Parlophone in 1960. A much-remembered TV role was as spoon salesman Mr Hutchinson in 'The Hotel Inspectors' episode of *Fawlty Towers,* and more recently he appeared in *Coronation Street* as Wally Bannister.

15/02/1962 . . . . . 9 . . . . . 13	**HOLE IN THE GROUND** . . . . Parlophone R 4869
05/07/1962 . . . . . 10 . . . . . 10	**RIGHT SAID FRED** . . . . Parlophone R 4923
13/12/1962 . . . . . 25 . . . . . . 6	GOSSIP CALYPSO . . . . Parlophone R 4961

CRIBS UK group formed in Wakefield by brothers Gary (bass/vocals), Ryan (guitar) and Ross Jarman (drums).

06/03/2004 . . . . . 66 . . . . . . 1	YOU WERE ALWAYS THE ONE . . . . Wichita WEBB059SCD
29/05/2004 . . . . . 75 . . . . . . 1	WHAT ABOUT ME . . . . Wichita WEBB061SCD

CRICKETS US group formed by Buddy Holly who had signed with Decca Records in 1956. The Crickets included long-term drummer Jerry Allison (born 31/8/1939, Hillsboro, TX), Niki Sullivan (rhythm guitar) and Joe Maudlin (bass). They re-recorded *That'll Be The Day*, which was released by Brunswick in the US. Its success enabled Holly to operate as a soloist with Coral and as a member of The Crickets for Brunswick, although both labels were from the same stable. Holly split with The Crickets in 1958 and the group underwent numerous personnel changes based around the nucleus of Allison and singer/guitarist Sonny Curtis (born 9/5/1937, Meadow, TX). The Crickets also provided backing on Holly's early hits. Sullivan died on 6/4/2004.

27/09/1957 . . . . ❶[3] . . . . . 15 . . . . . .   **THAT'LL BE THE DAY** ▲[1] Featured in the films *That'll Be The Day* (1973), *American Graffiti* (1973) and *The Buddy Holly Story* (1978) . . . . Vogue Coral Q 72279

27/12/1957 . . . . . 3 . . . . . 15	**OH BOY** Featured in the 1978 film *The Buddy Holly Story* . . . . Coral Q 72298
14/03/1958 . . . . . 4 . . . . . 10	**MAYBE BABY** Featured in the 1973 film *American Graffiti*. . . . . Coral Q 72307
25/07/1958 . . . . . 11 . . . . . . 7	THINK IT OVER This and above three singles all feature the uncredited vocals of Buddy Holly . . . . Coral Q 72329
24/04/1959 . . . . . 26 . . . . . . 2	LOVE'S MADE A FOOL OF YOU . . . . Coral Q 72365
15/01/1960 . . . . . 27 . . . . . . 1	WHEN YOU ASK ABOUT LOVE . . . . Coral Q 72382
12/05/1960 . . . . . 42 . . . . . . 1	MORE THAN I CAN SAY . . . . Coral Q 72395
26/05/1960 . . . . . 33 . . . . . . 4	BABY MY HEART . . . . Coral Q 72395
21/06/1962 . . . . . 5 . . . . . 13	**DON'T EVER CHANGE** . . . . Liberty LIB 55441
24/01/1963 . . . . . 17 . . . . . . 9	MY LITTLE GIRL . . . . Liberty LIB 10067
06/06/1963 . . . . . 37 . . . . . . 4	DON'T TRY TO CHANGE ME . . . . Liberty LIB 10092
14/05/1964 . . . . . 40 . . . . . . 6	YOU'VE GOT LOVE BUDDY HOLLY AND THE CRICKETS . . . . Coral Q 72472
02/07/1964 . . . . . 21 . . . . . 10	(THEY CALL HER) LA BAMBA . . . . Liberty LIB 55696

CRIMINAL ELEMENT ORCHESTRA – see WALLY JUMP JR AND THE CRIMINAL ELEMENT ORCHESTRA

CRISPY AND COMPANY US disco aggregation formed in Paris to record a cover version of *Brazil*, then breaking in the US charts and UK club circuit by Ritchie Family.

16/08/1975 . . . . . 26 . . . . . . 5	BRAZIL. . . . . Creole CR 109
27/12/1975 . . . . . 21 . . . . . . 6	GET IT TOGETHER . . . . Creole CR 114

CRITTERS US pop group formed in New Jersey in 1964 by Don Ciccone (guitar/vocals), Jim Ryan (guitar), Chris Darway (keyboards), Kenny Gorka (bass) and Jack Decker (drums) as The Vibratones. Ciccone was later in the Four Seasons. Jeff Pelosi (drums) and Bob Spinella (keyboards) joined in 1967. They disbanded in 1969.

30/06/1966 . . . . . 38 . . . . . . 5 . . . . . .   YOUNGER GIRL . . . . London HL 10047

TONY CROMBIE AND HIS ROCKETS UK drummer (born 27/8/1925, London) who made his first recordings in 1949 and played with Duke Ellington, Ronnie Scott and other jazz names. He formed the Rockets in 1956 to cash in on the rock 'n' roll craze sweeping the UK. In response to being banned from many hotels when they were on tour, they booked under assumed names, Professor Cromberg and a party of students being their usual alias. Tony Crombie died on 18/10/1999.

19/10/1956 . . . . . 25 . . . . . . 2 . . . . . .   TEACH YOU TO ROCK/SHORT'NIN' BREAD . . . . Columbia DB 3822

---

❶[9] Number of weeks single topped the UK chart ↑ Entered the UK chart at #1 ▲[9] Number of weeks single topped the US chart

CROOKLYN CLAN – see **FATMAN SCOOP FEATURING CROOKLYN CLAN**

BING CROSBY US singer/actor (born Harry Lills Crosby, 2/5/1901, Tacoma, WA, though his year of birth is sometimes given as 1904). He first teamed with Al Rinker in 1926 in Paul Whiteman's band, later adding Harry Barris to the line-up to become the Rhythm Boys. The trio split with Whiteman in 1930; the following year Crosby won a CBS radio contract and went solo. He sold more than 300 million records and starred in more than 50 films, earning an Oscar for *Going My Way* in 1944. His 1942 recording of *White Christmas* was honoured with a Grammy Hall of Fame Award in 1974. He died from a heart attack while playing golf near Madrid on 14/10/1977. He has a star on the Hollywood Walk of Fame for his contribution to recording, a second for motion pictures and a third star for radio. Jane Wyman (born 4/1/1914, St Joseph, MO) is perhaps best known for having married future US President Ronald Reagan (she has two stars on the Hollywood Walk of Fame). Actress Grace Kelly (born 1928) made her debut in the 1951 film *Fourteen Hours* before marrying Prince Rainier of Monaco in 1956. She was killed in a car crash on 14/9/1982 and has a star on the Hollywood Walk of Fame.

14/11/1952	3	12			**ISLE OF INNISFREE**	Brunswick 04900
05/12/1952	10	2			**ZING A LITTLE ZONG** BING CROSBY AND JANE WYMAN Featured in the 1952 film *Just For You*	Brunswick 04981
19/12/1952	8	2			**SILENT NIGHT** Originally recorded in 1942. Total worldwide sales exceed 30 million copies	Brunswick 03929
19/03/1954	9	3			**CHANGING PARTNERS**	Brunswick 05244
07/01/1955	11	3			COUNT YOUR BLESSINGS	Brunswick 05339
29/04/1955	17	2			STRANGER IN PARADISE	Brunswick 05410
27/04/1956	22	3			IN A LITTLE SPANISH TOWN	Brunswick 05543
23/11/1956	4	27			**TRUE LOVE** BING CROSBY AND GRACE KELLY Featured in the 1956 film *High Society* starring Crosby and Kelly	Capitol CL 14645
24/05/1957	5	15			**AROUND THE WORLD** Featured in the 1956 film *Around The World In Eighty Days*	Brunswick 05674
09/08/1975	41	4			THAT'S WHAT LIFE IS ALL ABOUT	United Artists UP 35852
03/12/1977	5	7	○		**WHITE CHRISTMAS** Featured in the 1942 film *Holiday Inn*. Total worldwide sales exceed 30 million copies, which comes from the combined sales of two versions: the original recording of 1942 and the re-recorded version of 1947	MCA 111
27/11/1982	3	8	○		**PEACE ON EARTH – LITTLE DRUMMER BOY** DAVID BOWIE AND BING CROSBY Recorded on the 1977 TV special *Bing Crosby's Merrie Olde Christmas*	RCA BOW 12
17/12/1983	70	3			TRUE LOVE Re-issue of Capitol CL 14645	Capitol CL 315
21/12/1985	69	2	◎		WHITE CHRISTMAS Re-issue of MCA 111	MCA BING 1
19/12/1998	29	4			WHITE CHRISTMAS Re-issue of MCA 111	MCA MCSTD 48105

DAVID CROSBY FEATURING PHIL COLLINS US singer/guitarist (born 14/8/1941, Los Angeles, CA) with UK drummer and singer Phil Collins (born 31/1/1951, London). Crosby was previously in Crosby Stills Nash And Young, Collins in Genesis.

15/05/1993	56	3			HERO	Atlantic A 7360

CROSBY STILLS NASH AND YOUNG US/UK rock trio formed in 1968 by David Crosby (born David Van Cortland, 14/8/1941, Los Angeles, CA, guitar), Stephen Stills (born 3/1/1945, Dallas, TX, guitar/keyboards/bass) and Graham Nash (born 2/2/1942, Blackpool, guitar), all famous via other groups: Crosby with Byrds, Stills with Buffalo Springfield and Nash with the Hollies. Canadian guitarist Neil Young (born 12/11/1945, Toronto) joined in 1969 and left in 1974; the group reunited in 1988. David Crosby spent periods in prison for drug-related offences but was allowed out to join with Stills and Nash at Live Aid in 1984. The group was named Best New Artist at the 1969 Grammy Awards and inducted into the Rock & Roll Hall of Fame in 1997. They have a star on the Hollywood Walk of Fame.

16/08/1969	17	9			MARRAKESH EXPRESS CROSBY STILLS AND NASH	Atlantic 584 283
21/01/1989	55	3			AMERICAN DREAM	Atlantic A 9003

CROSS UK group formed in 1987 by Roger Taylor (born Roger Meddows-Taylor, 26/1/1949, King's Lynn, Norfolk, guitar/vocals), Clayton Moss (guitar), Spike Edney (keyboards), Peter Noone (bass) and Josh Macrae (drums). Taylor was also in Queen and had made two solo albums prior to forming Cross.

17/10/1987	74	1			COWBOYS AND INDIANS	Virgin VS 1007

CHRISTOPHER CROSS US singer (born Christopher Geppert, 3/5/1951, San Antonio, TX) who formed his own group in 1973 with Rob Meurer, Andy Salmon and Tommy Taylor. He went solo in 1980 and won four Grammy Awards that year: Album of the Year for *Christopher Cross*, Record of the Year and Song of the Year for *Sailing* and Best New Artist. He also won the 1982 Oscar for Best Film Song for *Arthur's Theme (Best That You Can Do)* from the 1981 film *Arthur* with Burt Bacharach, Carole Bayer Sager and Peter Allen.

19/04/1980	69	1			RIDE LIKE THE WIND	Warner Brothers K 17582
14/02/1981	48	6			SAILING ▲[1]	Warner Brothers K 17695
17/10/1981	56	4			ARTHUR'S THEME (BEST THAT YOU CAN DO) ▲[3]	Warner Brothers K 17847
09/01/1982	7	11			**ARTHUR'S THEME (BEST THAT YOU CAN DO)**	Warner Brothers K 17847
05/02/1983	51	5			ALL RIGHT	Warner Brothers W 9843

CROW German production duo David Rzenno and David Nothroff.

19/05/2001	60	1			WHAT YA LOOKIN' AT	Tidy Trax TIDY 153CD

SHERYL CROW US singer (born 11/2/1963, Kennett, MO) who began as a backing singer for Michael Jackson, Don Henley and George Harrison among others, before signing with A&M in 1991. Named Best International Female at the 1997 BRIT Awards, her ten Grammy Awards include: Best New Artist in 1994, Best Rock Album in 1996 for *Sheryl Crow*, Best Rock Album in 1998 for *The Globe Sessions* and Best Female Rock Vocal Performance in 2000 for *There Goes The Neighborhood*.

18/06/1994	66	1			LEAVING LAS VEGAS	A&M 5806472
05/11/1994	4	13	○		**ALL I WANNA DO** 1994 Grammy Awards for Record of the Year and Best Female Pop Vocal Performance	A&M 5808452
11/02/1995	33	4			STRONG ENOUGH Featured in the 1993 film *Kalifornia*	A&M 5809212
27/05/1995	33	3			CAN'T CRY ANYMORE	A&M 5810552
29/07/1995	24	4			RUN, BABY, RUN Originally released in 1993 without success	A&M 5811492

○ Silver disc ● Gold disc ✪ Platinum disc (additional platinum units are indicated by a figure following the symbol) ◎ Singles released prior to 1973 that are known to have sold over 1 million copies in the UK

11/11/1995	43	1		WHAT I CAN DO FOR YOU	A&M 5812292
21/09/1996	9	6		**IF IT MAKES YOU HAPPY** 1996 Grammy Award for Best Female Rock Vocal Performance	A&M 5819032
30/11/1996	12	6		EVERYDAY IS A WINDING ROAD	A&M 5820232
29/03/1997	22	3		HARD TO MAKE A STAND	A&M 5821492
12/07/1997	8	5		**A CHANGE WOULD DO YOU GOOD**	A&M 5822092
18/10/1997	25	2		HOME	A&M 5823992
13/12/1997	12	9		TOMORROW NEVER DIES Featured in the 1997 James Bond film *Tomorrow Never Dies*	A&M 5824572
12/09/1998	9	6		**MY FAVORITE MISTAKE**	A&M 5827632
05/12/1998	19	7		THERE GOES THE NEIGHBORHOOD	A&M 5828092
06/03/1999	19	4		ANYTHING BUT DOWN	A&M 5828292
11/09/1999	30	3		SWEET CHILD O' MINE Featured in the 1999 film *Big Daddy*. 1999 Grammy Award for Best Female Rock Vocal Performance	Columbia 6678882
13/04/2002	16	8		SOAK UP THE SUN	A&M 4977052
13/07/2002	44	1		STEVE McQUEEN 2002 Grammy Award for Best Female Rock Vocal Performance	A&M 4977422
01/11/2003	37	3		FIRST CUT IS THE DEEPEST	A&M 9813556
03/07/2004	73	1		LIGHT IN YOUR EYES	A&M 9862700

CROWD Multinational charity group assembled by Graham Gouldman of 10cc to raise funds in aid of victims of the Bradford City football fire of 11/5/1985 in which 56 people were killed. The record, one of the best-known football songs, had originally been a hit for Gerry & The Pacemakers, and it was the same Gerry Marsden who provided the lead vocals on The Crowd's version. The sleeve credited the following personalities as having helped (although not all of them actually perform on the record): Gerry Marsden, Tony Christie, Denny Laine, Tim Healy, Gary Holton, Ed Stewart, Tony Hicks, Kenny Lynch, Colin Blunstone, Chris Robinson, A Curtis, Phil Lynott, Bernie Winters, Girlschool, Black Lace, John Otway, Rick Wakeman, Barron Knights, Tim Hinkley, Brendan Shine, Tim Verity, Rolf Harris, Rob Heaton, Patrick McDonald, Smokie, Bruce Forsyth, Johnny Logan, Colbert Hamilton, Dave Lee Travis, Rose Marie, Frank Allen, Jim Diamond, Graham Gouldman, Pete Spencer, Chris Norman, Gerard Kenny, the Nolans, Graham Dene, Suzy Grant, Peter Cook, The Foxes, Jess Conrad, Kim Kelly, Motorhead, John Entwistle, Jimmy Henney, Joe Fagin, David Shilling, Karen Clark, Gary Hughes, Zak Starkey, Eddie Hardin, Paul McCartney, Kiki Dee and Keith Chegwin.

01/06/1985	❶²	11	●	**YOU'LL NEVER WALK ALONE**	Spartan BRAD 1

CROWDED HOUSE Australian/New Zealand group formed in 1985 by Neil Finn (born 27/5/1958, Te Awamutu, NZ, guitar/vocals), Paul Hester (born 8/1/1959, Melbourne, Australia, drums) and Nick Seymour (born 9/12/1958, Benalla, Australia, bass) following the demise of Split Enz. Neil's brother and another former Split Enz member Tim (born 25/6/1952, Te Awamutu) briefly joined the group in 1991 before going solo. Named Best International Group at the 1994 BRIT Awards, they disbanded in 1996.

06/06/1987	27	8		DON'T DREAM IT'S OVER	Capitol CL 438
22/06/1991	69	2		CHOCOLATE CAKE	Capitol CL 618
02/11/1991	17	7		FALL AT YOUR FEET	Capitol CL 626
29/02/1992	7	9		**WEATHER WITH YOU**	Capitol CL 643
20/06/1992	26	5		FOUR SEASONS IN ONE DAY	Capitol CL 655
26/09/1992	24	4		IT'S ONLY NATURAL	Capitol CL 661
02/10/1993	19	6		DISTANT SUN	Capitol CDCLS 697
20/11/1993	22	4		NAILS IN MY FEET	Capitol CDCLS 701
19/02/1994	12	4		LOCKED OUT	Capitol CDCLS 707
11/06/1994	25	3		FINGERS OF LOVE	Capitol CDCL 715
24/09/1994	27	3		PINEAPPLE HEAD	Capitol CDCL 723
22/06/1996	12	4		INSTINCT	Capitol CDCLS 774
17/08/1996	20	3		NOT THE GIRL YOU THINK YOU ARE	Capitol CDCLS 776
09/11/1996	25	2		DON'T DREAM IT'S OVER Re-issue of Capitol CL 438	Capitol CDCL 780

CROWN HEIGHTS AFFAIR US R&B group formed in New York by Philip Thomas (vocals), Bert Reid (saxophone), Raymond Reid (guitar), William Anderson (guitar), James 'Ajax' Baynard (trumpet), Raymond Rock (drums/percussion), Howie Young (keyboards) and Muki Wilson (bass) in the early 1970s as Neu Day Express. They made one album for RCA before switching to De-Lite in 1975.

19/08/1978	24	10		GALAXY OF LOVE	Mercury 6168 801
11/11/1978	47	4		I'M GONNA LOVE YOU FOREVER	Mercury 6168 803
14/04/1979	44	4		DANCE LADY DANCE	Mercury 6168 804
03/05/1980	10	12		**YOU GAVE ME LOVE**	De-Lite MER 9
09/08/1980	44	4		YOU'VE BEEN GONE	De-Lite MER 28

JULEE CRUISE US singer (born 1/12/1956, Creston, IA) whose debut hit was featured in the TV series *Twin Peaks* and the subsequent 1992 film. Cruise also appeared in both as a roadhouse singer.

10/11/1990	7	11		**FALLING** Featured in the 1992 film *Twin Peaks*	Warner Brothers W 9544
02/03/1991	66	2		ROCKIN' BACK INSIDE MY HEART	Warner Brothers W 0004
11/09/1999	52	1		IF I SURVIVE **HYBRID FEATURING JULEE CRUISE**	Distinctive DISNCD 55

CRUISERS – see **DAVE BERRY**

CRUSADERS US group formed in Houston, TX by Joe Sample (born 1/2/1939, Houston, keyboards), Wilton Felder (born 31/8/1940, Houston, saxophone), Nesbert 'Stix' Hooper (born 15/8/1938, Houston, drums), Wayne Henderson (born 24/9/1938, Houston, trombone) and Robert 'Pops' Popwell (bass) as the Swingsters in the early 1950s. Relocating to Los Angeles, CA in the 1960s, they became session regulars and made their own jazz recordings for Pacific. They switched to Blue Thumb/ABC and scored numerous

club hits as pioneers of jazz-funk, then in 1979 made the pop charts with *Street Life*. By then they were a trio of Sample, Felder and Hooper. The group split in the 1990s, all the members undertaking solo projects, before Sample, Hooper and Felder reunited in 2002.

18/08/1979	5	11		**STREET LIFE** Features the uncredited lead vocal of Randy Crawford. Featured in the films *Sharky's Machine* (1982) and *Jackie Brown* (1997) .... MCA 513
26/09/1981	61	3		I'M SO GLAD I'M STANDING HERE TODAY **CRUSADERS, FEATURED SINGER JOE COCKER** .... MCA 741
07/04/1984	55	2		NIGHT LADIES .... MCA 853

CRUSH
UK vocal duo Donna Air (born 2/8/1979, Newcastle-Upon-Tyne) and Jayni Hoy, both previously in Byker Grooove! Hoy was subsequently replaced by Luciana Caporaso. Air later became a TV presenter while Caporaso fronted Shooter and then Portobella.

| 24/02/1996 | 50 | 2 | | JELLYHEAD .... Telstar CDSTAS 2809 |
| 03/08/1996 | 45 | 1 | | LUV'D UP .... Telstar CDSTAS 2833 |

BOBBY CRUSH
UK pianist (born 1955) who charted briefly when he won TV's *Opportunity Knocks* in 1972 and was named Best New Artist by the Variety Club the same year. In the 1980s he wrote the music for the hit single *Orville's Song* by Keith Harris.

| 04/11/1972 | 37 | 4 | | BORSALINO .... Philips 6006 248 |

CRW
Italian dance group assembled by producer Mauro Picotto, who also recorded under his own name and RAF.

26/02/2000	15	4		I FEEL LOVE Featured in the 2000 film *Kevin And Perry Go Large* .... VC Recordings VRCD 63
25/11/2000	49	2		LOVIN' .... VC Recordings VRCD 77
27/04/2002	57	1		LIKE A CAT .... BXR BXRC 0397
26/10/2002	57	1		PRECIOUS LIFE This and above single credited to **CRW PRESENTS VERONIKA** .... BXR BXRC 0395

CRY BEFORE DAWN
Irish group formed in Wexford by Brendan Wade (guitar/vocals), Tony Hall (guitar), Vince Doyle (bass) and Pat Hayes (drums).

| 17/06/1989 | 67 | 2 | | WITNESS FOR THE WORLD .... Epic GONE 3 |

CRY OF LOVE
US group formed in North Carolina in 1989 by Kelly Holland (guitar/vocals), Audley Freed (guitar), Robert Kearns (bass) and Jason Patterson (drums). Holland left in 1994 and was replaced by Robert Mason.

| 15/01/1994 | 60 | 1 | | BAD THING .... Columbia 6600462 |

CRY SISCO!
UK singer/producer Barry Blue (born Barry Green).

| 02/09/1989 | 42 | 9 | | AFRO DIZZI ACT .... Escape AWOL 1 |

CRYIN' SHAMES
UK group with Paul Crane (vocals), Joey Keen (vocals), Richard 'Ritchie' Routledge (guitar), George Robinson (bass), Phil Roberts (keyboards) and Charlie Gallagher (drums).

| 31/03/1966 | 26 | 7 | | PLEASE STAY .... Decca F 12340 |

CRYPT-KICKERS – see BOBBY 'BORIS' PICKETT AND THE CRYPT-KICKERS

CRYSTAL METHOD
US instrumental duo formed in Los Angeles, CA in 1993 by Ken Jordan and Scott Kirkland.

11/10/1997	39	2		(CAN'T YOU) TRIP LIKE I DO **FILTER AND THE CRYSTAL METHOD** Featured in the 1997 film *Spawn* .... Epic 6650862
07/03/1998	71	1		KEEP HOPE ALIVE .... Sony S2 CM 3CD
08/08/1998	73	1		COMIN' BACK .... Sony S2 CM 4CD

CRYSTAL PALACE WITH THE FAB FOUR
UK football club formed in 1905. The Fab Four is a UK group not to be confused with The Beatles, who were also known as The Fab Four.

| 12/05/1990 | 50 | 2 | | GLAD ALL OVER/WHERE EAGLES FLY .... Parkfield PMS 5019 |

CRYSTALS
US vocal group from Brooklyn, NYC discovered by producer/songwriter Phil Spector. The line-up was Barbara Alston, Merna Girard, Delores 'Dee Dee' Kennibrew (born 1945, Brooklyn), Mary Thomas (born 1946, Brooklyn) and Patricia Wright (born 1945, Brooklyn), with Delores 'La La' Brooks (born 1946, Brooklyn) replacing Girard in 1962, Thomas leaving the same year and Frances Collins replacing Wright in 1964. They bought themselves out of Spector's Philles label in 1965, signed with United Artists and disbanded after two singles, re-forming in 1971. They took their name from the daughter of songwriter Leroy Bates.

22/11/1962	19	13		HE'S A REBEL ▲² The actual performers on the record are Darlene Love & The Blossoms .... London HLU 9611
20/06/1963	5	16		**DA DOO RON RON** Featured in the 1979 film *Quadrophenia* .... London HLU 9732
19/09/1963	2	14		**THEN HE KISSED ME** Featured in the 1988 film *A Night On The Town* .... London HLU 9773
05/03/1964	36	3		I WONDER .... London HLU 9852
19/10/1974	15	8		DA DOO RON RON Re-issue of London HLU 9732 .... Warner Brothers K 19010

CSILLA
Hungarian singer discovered by producer Joe T Vanelli.

| 13/07/1996 | 69 | 1 | | MAN IN THE MOON .... Worx WORXCD 001 |

ALEX CUBA BAND FEATURING RON SEXSMITH
Cuban band fronted by Alexis Puentes which features the sons of the Buena Vista Social Club and Canadian singer Ron Sexsmith.

| 06/11/2004 | 52 | 1 | | LO MISMO QUE YO (IF ONLY) .... Shell GET2CD |

CUBAN BOYS
UK group formed by Jenny McLaren, her brother Ricardo Autobahn, Skreen and Blu. Their debut hit was inspired by the Hamster Dance website.

| 25/12/1999 | 4 | 9 | O | **COGNOSCENTI VERSUS THE INTELLIGENTSIA** .... EMI CDCUBAN 001 |

CUBIC 22 Belgian production group formed by Johan Gielen, Peter Ramson and Sven Maes. They later recorded as Airscape and Balearic Bill, Gielen also recording as Blue Bamboo.

22/06/1991.....15......7......	NIGHT IN MOTION	XL Recordings XLS 20

CUD UK rock group formed in Leeds by Carl Puttnam (born 1967, Ilford, vocals), Mike Dunphy (born 1967, Northumberland, guitar), William Porter (born 1968, Derby, bass) and Steve 'The Drummer From Cud' Goodwin (born 1967, Croydon, drums). They first recorded for Reception.

19/10/1991.....49......2......	OH NO WON'T DO (EP) Tracks on EP: *Oh No Won't Do, Profession, Ariel* and *Price Of Love* .... A&M AMB 829
28/03/1992.....44......2......	THROUGH THE ROOF .... A&M AM 857
30/05/1992.....24......3......	RICH AND STRANGE .... A&M AM 871
15/08/1992.....27......3......	PURPLE LOVE BALLOON .... A&M AM 0024
10/10/1992.....45......1......	ONCE AGAIN .... A&M AM 0081
12/02/1994.....37......2......	NEUROTICA .... A&M 5805172
02/04/1994.....68......1......	STICKS AND STONES .... A&M 5805472
03/09/1994.....52......2......	ONE GIANT LOVE .... A&M 5807292

CUFF LINKS US vocal group. Following the worldwide success of *Tracy* featuring the overdubbed voice of Ron Dante (also singer on the Archies' *Sugar Sugar* at the same time), a group was hastily assembled with Rupert Holmes, Joe Chord, Andrew Denno, Rich Dimino, Bob Gill, Dave Lavender, Pat Rizzo and Danny Valentine. After Cuff Links had ran their course, all but Holmes and Rizzo slipped into obscurity: Holmes recorded solo and Rizzo later played horns for Sly & The Family Stone, Ry Cooder and Greg Allman.

29/11/1969 .....4......16......	**TRACY** .... MCA MU 1101
14/03/1970.....10......14......	**WHEN JULIE COMES AROUND** .... MCA MU 1112

JAMIE CULLUM UK singer/pianist (born 20/8/1979, Malmesbury, Wilts) who formed the Jamie Cullum Trio with Geoff Gascoyne and Sebastian De Krom, and was named Best Jazz Act at the 2004 MOBO Awards.

20/03/2004.....12......5......	THESE ARE THE DAYS/FRONTIN' .... UCJ 9866211
20/11/2004.....20......6+......	EVERLASTING LOVE Featured in the 2004 film *Bridget Jones Diary 2: Edge Of Reason* .... UCJ 9868834

CULT UK rock group formed in Bradford in 1982 by singer Ian Astbury (born Ian Lindsey, 14/5/1962, Heswell) as Southern Death Cult. The group lasted one year before disbanding. Astbury joined guitarist Billy Duffy (born 12/5/1962, Manchester), the two remaining the nucleus ever since, and shortened the name to Cult in 1984. They achieved a US breakthrough with Def Jam label chief Rick Rubin in 1987 and moved to Los Angeles, CA in 1988.

22/12/1984.....74......2......	RESURRECTION JOE .... Beggars Banquet BEG 122
25/05/1985.....15......19......	SHE SELLS SANCTUARY Featured in the 1994 film *With Honors* .... Beggars Banquet BEG 135
05/10/1985.....17......8......	RAIN .... Beggars Banquet BEG 147
30/11/1985.....30......7......	REVOLUTION .... Beggars Banquet BEG 152
28/02/1987.....18......7......	LOVE REMOVAL MACHINE Featured in the 1998 film *Small Soldiers* .... Beggars Banquet BEG 182
02/05/1987.....11......7......	LIL' DEVIL .... Beggars Banquet BEG 188
22/08/1987.....24......2......	WILD FLOWER (DOUBLE SINGLE) Tracks: *Wild Flower, Love Trouper, Outlaw* and *Horse Nation* ...... Beggars Banquet BEG 195D
29/08/1987.....30......4......	WILD FLOWER .... Beggars Banquet BEG 195
01/04/1989.....15......4......	FIRE WOMAN .... Beggars Banquet BEG 228
08/07/1989.....32......5......	EDIE (CIAO BABY) .... Beggars Banquet BEG 230
18/11/1989.....39......2......	SUN KING/EDIE (CIAO BABY) Re-issue of Beggars Banquet BEG 230 .... Beggars Banquet BEG 235
10/03/1990.....42......4......	SWEET SOUL SISTER .... Beggars Banquet BEG 241
14/09/1991.....40......2......	WILD HEARTED SON .... Beggars Banquet BEG 255
29/02/1992.....51......1......	HEART OF SOUL .... Beggars Banquet BEG 260
30/01/1993.....15......4......	SHE SELLS SANCTUARY (REMIX) .... Beggars Banquet BEG 253CD
08/10/1994.....50......1......	COMING DOWN .... Beggars Banquet BBQ 40CD
07/01/1995.....65......1......	STAR .... Beggars Banquet BBQ 45CD

CULT JAM – see LISA LISA

SMILEY CULTURE UK reggae singer (born David Emanuel, 1960, London). He appeared in the 1986 film *Absolute Beginners*.

15/12/1984.....12......10......	POLICE OFFICER .... Fashion FAD 7012
06/04/1985.....71......1......	COCKNEY TRANSLATION .... Fashion FAD 7028
13/09/1986.....59......2......	SCHOOLTIME CHRONICLE .... Polydor POSP 815

CULTURE BEAT Multinational dance group formed by German producer Torsten Fenslau, Juergen Katzmann and Peter Zweier with stage performances handled by Tania Evans and rapper Jay Supreme. Fenslau was killed in a car crash on 6/11/1993 aged 29.

03/02/1990.....55......3......	CHERRY LIPS (DER ERDBEERMUND) .... Epic 6556337
07/08/1993.....❶⁴......15......●	**MR. VAIN** The first UK #1 *not* to be made available on 7-inch vinyl. It was only available as a CD or cassette single .... Epic 6594682
06/11/1993 .....4......11......	**GOT TO GET IT** .... Epic 6597212
15/01/1994 .....5......8......	**ANYTHING** .... Epic 6600252
02/04/1994.....20......4......	WORLD IN YOUR HANDS .... Epic 6602292
27/01/1996.....32......2......	INSIDE OUT .... Epic 6626562
15/06/1996.....29......2......	CRYING IN THE RAIN .... Epic 6633582
28/09/1996.....52......1......	TAKE ME AWAY .... Epic 6637552
20/09/2003.....51......1......	MR VAIN RECALL .... East West EW 270CD

❶⁹ Number of weeks single topped the UK chart ↑ Entered the UK chart at #1 ▲⁹ Number of weeks single topped the US chart

189

CULTURE CLUB
UK group formed in London in 1981 by Boy George (born George O'Dowd, 14/6/1961, Bexley, vocals), Roy Hay (born 12/8/1961, Southend-on-Sea, guitar/keyboards), Michael Craig (born 15/2/1960, London, bass) and Jon Moss (born 11/9/1957, London, drums). Signed to Virgin six months after their debut gig, they were one of the top groups of the early 1980s, the media focusing on the gender of the lead singer. They disbanded in 1987, Boy George having already gone solo, and they re-formed in 1997. They were named Best British Group at the 1984 BRIT Awards and also won the 1983 Grammy Award for Best New Artist.

DATE	POS	WKS	BPI	SINGLE TITLE	LABEL & NUMBER
18/09/1982	**❶³**	18	●	**DO YOU REALLY WANT TO HURT ME** Featured in the films *The Wedding Singer* (1998) and *The Day After Tomorrow* (2004)	Virgin VS 518
27/11/1982	3	12	●	**TIME (CLOCK OF THE HEART)**	Virgin VS 558
09/04/1983	2	9	○	**CHURCH OF THE POISON MIND**	Virgin VS 571
17/09/1983	**❶⁶**	20	✪	**KARMA CHAMELEON** ▲³ 1984 BRIT Award for Best Single. Featured in the 1997 film *Romy And Michele's High School Reunion*. Songwriter Phil Pickett was later sued for alleged plagiarism by the writers of *Handy Man*, a 1960 hit for Jimmy Jones	Virgin VS 612
10/12/1983	3	10	●	**VICTIMS**	Virgin VS 641
24/03/1984	4	9		**IT'S A MIRACLE**	Virgin VS 662
06/10/1984	2	8	○	**THE WAR SONG**	Virgin VS 694
01/12/1984	32	5		THE MEDAL SONG	Virgin VS 730
15/03/1986	7	7		**MOVE AWAY**	Virgin VS 845
07/06/1986	31	5		GOD THANK YOU WOMAN	Virgin VS 861
31/10/1998	4	10		**I JUST WANNA BE LOVED**	Virgin VSCDT 1710
07/08/1999	25	4		YOUR KISSES ARE CHARITY	Virgin VSCDT 1736
27/11/1999	43	2		COLD SHOULDER/STARMAN	Virgin VSCDT 1758

PETER CUNNAH – see CHICANE

LARRY CUNNINGHAM AND THE MIGHTY AVONS
Irish country singer with one hit single in a lengthy career. He describes his mix of traditional Irish folk music and country & western as 'country and Irish'.

DATE	POS	WKS	BPI	SINGLE TITLE	LABEL & NUMBER
10/12/1964	40	11		TRIBUTE TO JIM REEVES	King KG 1016

CUPID'S INSPIRATION
UK group formed by Terry Rice-Milton (born 5/6/1946, vocals), Wyndham George (born 20/2/1947, guitar), Laughton James (born 21/12/1946, bass) and Roger Gray (born 29/4/1949, drums), later adding Garfield Tonkin (born 28/9/1946, keyboards). They disbanded at the end of 1968, Rice-Milton forming a new group with Gordon Haskell (bass) and Bernie Lee (guitar), they too disbanding in 1969. Rice-Milton later recorded solo for Pye Records.

DATE	POS	WKS	BPI	SINGLE TITLE	LABEL & NUMBER
19/06/1968	4	11		**YESTERDAY HAS GONE**	Nems 56 3500
02/10/1968	33	8		MY WORLD	Nems 56 3702

JOSE CURA – see SARAH BRIGHTMAN

MIKE CURB CONGREGATION – see LITTLE JIMMY OSMOND

CURE
UK rock group initially formed in 1977 answering a record company advertisement offering a contract. Known as Easy Cure, they were dropped before releasing anything because they wanted to record their own material. They subsequently signed with Fiction in 1978. With various changes over the years, the chief line-up was Robert Smith (born 21/4/1959, Blackpool, guitar/vocals), Lol Tolhurst (born 3/2/1959, keyboards), Simon Gallup (born 1/6/1960, Duxhurst, bass), Porl Thompson (born 8/11/1957, London, guitar) and Boris Williams (born 24/4/1958, Versailles, France, drums). Smith later joined Siouxsie & The Banshees' Steve Severin in the one-off project The Glove. They were named Best British Group at the 1991 BRIT Awards.

DATE	POS	WKS	BPI	SINGLE TITLE	LABEL & NUMBER
12/04/1980	31	8		A FOREST	Fiction FICS 10
04/04/1981	43	6		PRIMARY	Fiction FICS 12
17/10/1981	44	4		CHARLOTTE SOMETIMES	Fiction FICS 14
24/07/1982	34	4		HANGING GARDEN	Fiction FICS 15
27/11/1982	44	5		LET'S GO TO BED	Fiction FICS 17
09/07/1983	12	8		THE WALK	Fiction FICS 18
29/10/1983	7	11		**THE LOVE CATS**	Fiction FICS 19
07/04/1984	14	7		THE CATERPILLAR	Fiction FICS 20
27/07/1985	15	10		IN BETWEEN DAYS	Fiction FICS 22
21/09/1985	24	8		CLOSE TO ME	Fiction FICS 23
03/05/1986	22	6		BOYS DON'T CRY	Fiction FICS 24
18/04/1987	21	5		WHY CAN'T I BE YOU	Fiction FICS 25
04/07/1987	27	6		CATCH	Fiction FICS 26
17/10/1987	29	5		JUST LIKE HEAVEN	Fiction FICS 27
20/02/1988	45	3		HOT HOT HOT!!!	Fiction FICSX 28
22/04/1989	5	6		**LULLABY**	Fiction FICS 29
02/09/1989	18	7		LOVESONG 1990 BRIT Award for Best Video	Fiction FICS 30
31/03/1990	24	6		PICTURES OF YOU	Fiction FICS 34
29/09/1990	13	5		NEVER ENOUGH	Fiction FICS 35
03/11/1990	13	5		CLOSE TO ME (REMIX)	Fiction FICS 36
28/03/1992	8	3		**HIGH**	Fiction FICS 39
11/04/1992	44	1		HIGH (REMIX)	Fiction FICSX 41
23/05/1992	6	7		**FRIDAY I'M IN LOVE**	Fiction FICS 42
17/10/1992	28	2		A LETTER TO ELSIE	Fiction FICS 46

04/05/1996	15	2		THE 13TH	Fiction 5764692
29/06/1996	31	2		MINT CAR	Fiction FICSD 52
14/12/1996	60	1		GONE	Fiction FICD 53
29/11/1997	62	1		WRONG NUMBER	Fiction FICD 54
10/11/2001	54	1		CUT HERE	Fiction 5873892
31/07/2004	25	3		THE END OF THE WORLD	Geffen 9862976
30/10/2004	39	1		TAKING OFF	Geffen 9864491

CURIOSITY KILLED THE CAT
UK four-piece group formed by Ben Volpeliere-Pierrot (born 19/5/1964, London, vocals), Julian Godfrey Brookhouse (born 13/5/1963, London, guitar), Nicholas Bernard Throp (born 25/10/1964, London, bass) and Michael Drummond (born 27/1/1964, Middlesex, drums) as The Twilight Children. Adding keyboard player Toby Anderson in 1984, they changed their name to Curiosity Killed The Cat, later shortening it to Curiosity.

13/12/1986	3	18		DOWN TO EARTH	Mercury CAT 2
04/04/1987	11	7		ORDINARY DAY	Mercury CAT 3
20/06/1987	7	9		MISFIT CURIOSITY Accompanying video was directed by Andy Warhol, his last such assignment	Mercury CAT 4
19/09/1987	56	2		FREE	Mercury CAT 5
16/09/1989	14	9		NAME AND NUMBER	Mercury CAT 6
25/04/1992	3	10		HANG ON IN THERE BABY	RCA PB 45377
29/08/1992	47	2		I NEED YOUR LOVIN'	RCA 74321111377
30/10/1993	73	1		GIMME THE SUNSHINE	RCA 74321168602

CHANTAL CURTIS
French disco singer whose debut single was first a hit on the New York club scene.

| 14/07/1979 | 51 | 3 | | GET ANOTHER LOVE | Pye 7P 5003 |

TC CURTIS
Jamaican singer.

| 23/02/1985 | 50 | 4 | | YOU SHOULD HAVE KNOWN BETTER | Holt Melt VS 754 |

CURVE
UK rock group formed by Toni Halliday (vocals), Dean Garcia (guitar), Debbie Smith (guitar), Alex Mitchell (guitar) and Monti (drums). They disbanded in 1994 and re-formed in 1997.

16/03/1991	68	1		THE BLINDFOLD (EP) Tracks on EP: Ten Little Girls, I Speak Your Every Word, Blindfold and No Escape From Heaven	AnXious ANX 27
25/05/1991	34	3		COAST IS CLEAR	AnXious ANX 30
09/11/1991	36	2		CLIPPED	AnXious ANX 35
07/03/1992	22	3		FAIT ACCOMPLI	AnXious ANX 36
18/07/1992	31	2		HORROR HEAD (EP) Tracks on EP: Horror Head, Falling Free, Mission From God and Today Is Not The Day	AnXious ANXT 38
04/09/1993	39	2		BLACKERTHREETRACKER EP Track on EP: Missing Link was the only track available on all formats	AnXious ANXCD 42
16/05/1998	51	1		COMING UP ROSES	Universal UND 80489

CURVED AIR
UK rock group formed by Ian Eyre (born 11/9/1949, Knaresborough, bass), Sonia Kristina (born 14/4/1949, Brentwood, vocals), Francis Monkman (born 9/6/1949, London, guitar/keyboards), Florian Pilkington-Miska (born 3/6/1950, London, drums) and Darryl Way (born 17/12/1948, Taunton, violin). After a 1970 debut album they were college circuit regulars for the rest of the decade. When Pilkington-Miska left, he was replaced by Stewart Copeland (born 16/7/1952, Alexandria, Egypt), later in Police. Monkman later became a founding member of Sky.

| 07/08/1971 | 4 | 12 | | BACK STREET LUV | Warner Brothers K 16092 |

MALACHI CUSH
Irish singer (born 1980, Donaghmore, County Tyrone), first known as one of the competitors on *Fame Academy*. He worked as a gas fitter before turning to singing.

| 19/04/2003 | 49 | 1 | | JUST SAY YOU LOVE ME | Mercury 0779072 |

FRANKIE CUTLASS
US rapper (born Francis Parker, Puerto Rico).

| 05/04/1997 | 59 | 1 | | THE CYPHER: PART 3 | Epic 6641445 |

ADGE CUTLER – see WURZELS

JON CUTLER FEATURING E-MAN
US DJ (born in New York) who runs his own Distant Music label. E-Man is US singer Eric Clark.

| 19/01/2002 | 38 | 2 | | IT'S YOURS | Direction 6720532 |

CUT 'N' MOVE
Danish vocal/instrumental group formed by Per Holm, Jorn Kristensen, Jens 'MC Zipp' Larsen and Theras Hoeymans.

| 02/10/1993 | 61 | 2 | | GIVE IT UP | EMI CDEM 273 |
| 09/09/1995 | 49 | 2 | | I'M ALIVE | EMI CDEM 375 |

CUTTING CREW
UK rock group formed by Nick Van Eede (born 14/6/1958, East Grinstead, vocals), Kevin Scott MacMichael (born 7/11/1951, Halifax, Canada, guitar), Colin Farley (born 24/2/1959, bass) and Martin Beedle (born 18/9/1961, Hull, drums). MacMichael died from cancer on 31/12/2002.

16/08/1986	4	12	O	(I JUST) DIED IN YOUR ARMS ▲2	Siren 21
25/10/1986	31	10		I'VE BEEN IN LOVE BEFORE	Siren 29
07/03/1987	52	5		ONE FOR THE MOCKINGBIRD	Siren 40

❶9 Number of weeks single topped the UK chart ↑ Entered the UK chart at #1 ▲9 Number of weeks single topped the US chart

191

DATE	POS	WKS	BPI	SINGLE TITLE	LABEL & NUMBER
21/11/1987	24	8		I'VE BEEN IN LOVE BEFORE (REMIX)	Siren SRN 29
22/07/1989	66	2		(BETWEEN A) ROCK AND A HARD PLACE	Siren SRN 108

CYBERSONIK US production group formed by Dan Bell, John Acquaviva and Richie Hawtin.

| 10/11/1990 | 73 | 1 | | TECHNARCHY | Champion CHAMP 264 |

CYCLEFLY Irish rock group formed in Dublin by Declan O'Shea (vocals), his brother Ciaran (voals), Nono Presta (guitar), Christian Montagne (bass) and Jean Michel Cavallo (drums).

| 06/04/2002 | 68 | 1 | | NO STRESS | Radioactive RAXTD 41 |

CYGNUS X German producer AC Bousten.

| 11/03/2000 | 43 | 2 | | THE ORANGE THEME | Hooj Choons HOOJ 88CD |
| 18/08/2001 | 33 | 3 | | SUPERSTRING | Xtravaganza XTRAV 28CDS |

JOHNNY CYMBAL UK singer/songwriter/producer (born 3/2/1945, Ochitree, Scotland) whose family moved to Goderich in Ontario in 1952; Cymbal relocated to Cleveland in 1960. He also recorded as Derek, scoring two US hits under that name. His UK hit was a tribute to the previously unsung heroes of rock 'n' roll: bass singers. He died from a heart attack on 16/3/1993.

| 14/03/1963 | 24 | 10 | | MR. BASS MAN Bass voice provided by Ronnie Bright, a member of the Valentines and Cadillacs | London HLR 9682 |

CYPRESS HILL US rap group formed in Los Angeles, CA by Sennen 'Sen Dog' Reyes (born 20/11/1965, Cuba), Louis 'B Real' Freeze (born 2/6/1970, Los Angeles, CA) and Lawrence 'Mixmaster Muggs' Muggerud (born 28/1/1968, New York). B Real later recorded solo. They appeared in the 1993 film *The Meteor Man*.

31/07/1993	32	4		INSANE IN THE BRAIN	Ruffhouse 6595332
02/10/1993	19	4		WHEN THE SH.. GOES DOWN	Ruffhouse 6596702
11/12/1993	15	7		I AIN'T GOIN' OUT LIKE THAT Contains a sample of Black Sabbath's *The Wizard*	Ruffhouse 6596902
26/02/1994	21	4		INSANE IN THE BRAIN Re-issue of Ruff House 6595332	Ruffhouse 6601762
07/05/1994	20	3		LICK A SHOT	Ruffhouse 6603192
07/10/1995	15	3		THROW YOUR SET IN THE AIR	Ruffhouse 6623542
17/02/1996	23	2		ILLUSIONS	Columbia 6629052
10/10/1998	23	2		TEQUILA SUNRISE	Columbia 6664935
10/04/1999	34	2		DR GREENTHUMB	Columbia 6671202
26/06/1999	19	3		INSANE IN THE BRAIN JASON NEVINS VERSUS CYPRESS HILL	INCredible INCRL 17CD
29/04/2000	13	5		RAP SUPERSTAR/ROCK SUPERSTAR Featured in the 2000 film *Little Nicky*	Columbia 6692645
16/09/2000	35	2		HIGHLIFE/CAN'T GET THE BEST OF ME	Columbia 6697895
08/12/2001	33	2		LOWRIDER/TROUBLE	Columbia 6721662
27/03/2004	44	2		WHAT'S YOUR NUMBER?	Columbia 6746172

BILLY RAY CYRUS US singer (born 25/8/1961, Flatwood, KY) who initially made his name backing country star Reba McEntire. Signed by Mercury as a solo artist in 1992, he scored a US #1 with his debut single and album. He later recorded a parody of his debut with The Chipmunks and became an actor, appearing on the TV series *Doc*.

25/07/1992	3	10	O	ACHY BREAKY HEART	Mercury MER 373
10/10/1992	24	4		COULD'VE BEEN ME	Mercury MER 378
28/11/1992	63	1		THESE BOOTS ARE MADE FOR WALKIN'	Mercury MER 384
19/12/1992	53	3		ACHY BREAKY HEART ALVIN AND THE CHIPMUNKS FEATURING BILLY RAY CYRUS	Epic 6588837

CZR FEATURING DELANO US production group formed by C Hernandez and G Hernandez with singer Delano.

| 30/09/2000 | 57 | 1 | | I WANT YOU | Credence CDCRED 002 |

D

ASHER D
UK singer Ashley Walters, also a member of So Solid Crew. In March 2002 he was sentenced to eighteen months in prison for possession of a loaded revolver.

04/08/2001	75	1	BABY, CAN I GET YOUR NUMBER **OBI PROJECT FEATURING HARRY, ASHER D & DJ WHAT?** .... East West EW 235CD
08/06/2002	43	1	BACK IN THE DAY/WHY ME .... Independiente ISOM 57MS

CHUCK D
US rapper (born Carlton Douglas Ridenhour, 1/8/1960, Long Island, NY) who was later a member of Public Enemy.

06/07/1991	14	5	BRING THE NOISE **ANTHRAX FEATURING CHUCK D** .... Island IS 490
26/10/1996	55	1	NO .... Mercury MERCD 476
23/06/2001	19	3	ROCK DA FUNKY BEATS **PUBLIC DOMAIN FEATURING CHUCK D** .... Xtrahard X2H3 CDS

CRISSY D
– see **B-15 PROJECT FEATURING CRISSY D AND LADY G**

DANNY D
– see **COOKIE CREW**

DIMPLES D
US rapper Crystal Smith.

17/11/1990	17	10	SUCKER DJ Contains a sample of the theme to the TV series *I Dream Of Jeannie* .... FBI 11

LONGSY D'S HOUSE SOUND
UK instrumentalist/producer.

04/03/1989	56	7	THIS IS SKA .... Big One VBIG 13

MAXWELL D
UK DJ Maxwell Donaldson who formed The Ladies Hit Squad in 1998 with Carl, Target and Wiley. He was later a member of Pay As U Go.

15/09/2001	38	2	SERIOUS .... 4 Liberty LIBTCD 046

NIKKI D
US rapper (born Nichelle Strong, 10/9/1968, Los Angeles, CA).

06/05/1989	34	5	MY LOVE IS SO RAW **ALYSON WILLIAMS FEATURING NIKKI D** .... Def Jam 6548987
30/03/1991	75	1	DADDY'S LITTLE GIRL .... Def Jam 6567347

VICKY D
US dance singer.

13/03/1982	42	6	THIS BEAT IS MINE .... Virgin VS 486

D BO GENERAL
– see **URBAN SHAKEDOWN**

D-INFLUENCE
UK vocal/instrumental/production group formed by Kwame Amankwa Kwaten, Edward James Baden-Powell, Steven Marston and Sarah-Ann Webb.

20/06/1992	46	2	GOOD LOVER Contains a sample of Eleanore Mills' *Mr Right* .... East West A 8573
27/03/1993	61	1	GOOD LOVER (REMIX) .... East West America A 8439CD
24/06/1995	58	1	MIDNITE .... East West A 4418CD
16/08/1997	33	2	HYPNOTIZE .... Echo ECSCD 41
11/10/1997	45	1	MAGIC .... Echo ECSCD 45
05/09/1998	30	3	ROCK WITH YOU .... Echo ECSCD 56

D KAY AND EPSILON FEATURING STAMINA MC
Austrian drum and bass duo David Kulenkamff and Dragoljub Drobnjakovic with UK rapper Linden Reeves.

30/08/2003	14	5	BARCELONA .... Alphamagic/BC/BMG BCAU001CD

D MOB
UK dance/disco aggregation led by producer/writer Dancin' Danny D (born Daniel Kojo Poku) who first recorded as The Taurus Boys. Their debut hit was banned by the BBC's *Top Of The Pops* because of the title. Poku stated that he didn't even take an aspirin for a headache. Gary Haisman is a UK singer. LRS are the London Rhyme Syndica.

15/10/1988	3	12	**WE CALL IT ACIEED D MOB FEATURING GARY HAISMAN** .... ffrr FFR 13
03/06/1989	9	10	**IT'S TIME TO GET FUNKY D MOB FEATURING LRS** .... ffrr F 107
21/10/1989	15	10	C'MON AND GET MY LOVE **D MOB WITH CATHY DENNIS** Featured in the 1989 film *She-Devil* .... ffrr F 117
06/01/1990	7	8	**PUT YOUR HANDS TOGETHER D MOB FEATURING NUFF JUICE** .... ffrr F 124
07/04/1990	48	3	THAT'S THE WAY OF THE WORLD .... ffrr F 132
12/02/1994	23	3	WHY This and above single credited to **D MOB WITH CATHY DENNIS** .... ffrr FCD 227
03/09/1994	41	2	ONE DAY .... ffrr FCDP 239

🔴[9] Number of weeks single topped the UK chart ↑ Entered the UK chart at #1 ▲[9] Number of weeks single topped the US chart

D NOTE UK musician/filmmaker Matt Winn.

12/07/1997 . . . . . 46 . . . . . . 1	WAITING HOPEFULLY . . . . VC Recordings VCRD 21
15/11/1997 . . . . . 59 . . . . . . 1	LOST AND FOUND . . . . VC Recordings VCRD 25
27/04/2002 . . . . . 73 . . . . . . 1	SHED MY SKIN . . . . Channel 4 Music C4M 00182

D:REAM UK duo Peter Cunnah (born 30/8/1966, Derry, Northern Ireland, vocals) and Al McKenzie (born 31/10/1968, Edinburgh, keyboards). Cunnah began his career with Ciderboy before moving to London where he met McKenzie, a successful DJ, at the Gardening Club, and the two formed D:Ream. Cunnah was later a successful songwriter.

04/07/1992 . . . . . 72 . . . . . . 1	U R THE BEST THING Featured in the 1994 film *Naked In New York* . . . . FXU 3
30/01/1993 . . . . . 24 . . . . . . 5	THINGS CAN ONLY GET BETTER . . . . Magnet MAG 1010CD
24/04/1993 . . . . . 19 . . . . . . 8	U R THE BEST THING Re-issue of FXU 3 . . . . Magnet MAG 1011CD
31/07/1993 . . . . . 29 . . . . . . 3	UNFORGIVEN . . . . Magnet MAG 1016CD
02/10/1993 . . . . . 26 . . . . . . 4	STAR/I LIKE IT . . . . Magnet MAG 1019CD
08/01/1994 . . . . . ❶⁴ . . . . . . 16 . . . . . . ●	**THINGS CAN ONLY GET BETTER** Re-issue of Magnet Mag 1010CD . . . . Magnet MAG 1020CD
26/03/1994 . . . . . 4 . . . . . . 10	**U R THE BEST THING (REMIX)** . . . . Magnet MAG 1021CD
18/06/1994 . . . . . 18 . . . . . . 5	TAKE ME AWAY . . . . Magnet MAG 1025CD
10/09/1994 . . . . . 25 . . . . . . 5	BLAME IT ON ME . . . . Magnet MAG 1027CD
08/07/1995 . . . . . 7 . . . . . . 7	**SHOOT ME WITH YOUR LOVE** . . . . Magnet MAG 1034CD
09/09/1995 . . . . . 20 . . . . . . 6	PARTY UP THE WORLD . . . . Magnet MAG 1037CD
11/11/1995 . . . . . 40 . . . . . . 1	THE POWER (OF ALL THE LOVE IN THE WORLD) . . . . Magnet MAG 1039CD
03/05/1997 . . . . . 19 . . . . . . 3	THINGS CAN ONLY GET BETTER Re-issue of Magnet MAG 1020CD, re-released after being used by the Labour Party prior to the 1997 General Election . . . . Magnet MAG 1050CD

D-SHAKE Dutch producer Adrianus De Mooy.

02/06/1990 . . . . . 20 . . . . . . 6	YAAH/TECHNO TRANCE . . . . Cooltempo COOL 213
02/02/1991 . . . . . 42 . . . . . . 2	MY HEART THE BEAT . . . . Cooltempo COOL 228

D-SIDE Irish vocal group formed in Dublin by Derek Moran (born 15/12/1983, Dublin), Dane Guiden (born in Dublin), Damien Bowe (born 5/5/1981, Laois), Shane Creevey (born 13/12/1982, Dublin) and Derek Ryan (born in Carlow).

26/04/2003 . . . . . 9 . . . . . . 8	**SPEECHLESS** . . . . WEA 366CD
26/07/2003 . . . . . 7 . . . . . . 6	**INVISIBLE** . . . . WEA 369CD
13/12/2003 . . . . . 9 . . . . . . 8	**REAL WORLD** . . . . Blacklist/edel 9814017
12/06/2004 . . . . . 21 . . . . . . 3	PUSHIN' ME OUT . . . . Blacklist/Edel 0155826ERE

D-TEK UK production group comprising John Gilpin, Raza Shamshad, Richard Brown and Nicholas Simpson.

06/11/1993 . . . . . 70 . . . . . . 1	DROP THE ROCK (EP) Tracks on EP: *Drop The Rock, Chunkafunk, Drop The Rock (Remix)* and *Don't Breathe* . . . . Positiva 12TIV 5

D TRAIN US singer/songwriter James Williams (born in Brooklyn, NYC) with Hubert Eaves III (keyboards). They split in 1985, and Williams went solo. He also recorded with Bob Sinclair.

06/02/1982 . . . . . 30 . . . . . . 8	YOU'RE THE ONE FOR ME Featured in the 2004 film *The Football Factory* . . . . Epic EPC A 2016
08/05/1982 . . . . . 44 . . . . . . 6	WALK ON BY . . . . Epic EPC A 2298
07/05/1983 . . . . . 23 . . . . . . 7	MUSIC PART 1 . . . . Prelude A 3332
16/07/1983 . . . . . 65 . . . . . . 2	KEEP GIVING ME LOVE . . . . Prelude A 3497
27/07/1985 . . . . . 15 . . . . . . 11	YOU'RE THE ONE FOR ME (REMIX) . . . . Prelude ZB 40302
12/10/1985 . . . . . 62 . . . . . . 2	MUSIC (REMIX) . . . . Prelude ZB 40431

AZZIDO DA BASS German DJ Ingo Martens.

04/03/2000 . . . . . 58 . . . . . . 1	DOOMS NIGHT . . . . Club Tools 0067285 CLU
24/06/2000 . . . . . 46 . . . . . . 2	DOOMS NIGHT . . . . Club Tools 0067285 CLU
21/10/2000 . . . . . 8 . . . . . . 9	**DOOMS NIGHT (REMIX)** AZZIDO DA BASS FEATURING ROLAND CLARK . . . . Club Tools 0120285 CLU
23/03/2002 . . . . . 68 . . . . . . 1	SPEED (CAN YOU FEEL IT?) AZZIDO DA BASS FEATURING ROLAND CLARK . . . . Club Tools 0135815 CLU

DA BRAT US rapper (born Shawntae Harris, 14/4/1974, Chicago, IL) who came to prominence after winning a rap contest at a Kriss Kross concert.

22/10/1994 . . . . . 65 . . . . . . 1	FUNKDAFIED Contains a sample of The Isley Brothers' *Between The Sheets* . . . . Columbia 6609212

DA CLICK UK rap group formed by Ronnie Nwaha, Eugene Nwaha, Christopher Reid and Paul Gabriel.

16/01/1999 . . . . . 14 . . . . . . 6	GOOD RHYMES Contains a sample of Chic's *Good Times* . . . . ffrr FCD 353
29/05/1999 . . . . . 38 . . . . . . 2	WE ARE DA CLICK Contains a sample of Tom Browne's *Funkin' For Jamaica* . . . . ffrr FCD 363

DA FOOL US DJ/producer Mike Stewart whose debut hit was previously known as *Meet Him At The Blue Oyster Bar*.

16/01/1999 . . . . . 38 . . . . . . 2	NO GOOD Contains a sample of SIL's *Blue Oyster* . . . . ffrr FCD 352

RICARDO DA FORCE UK rapper Ricardo Lyte.

18/03/1995 . . . . . 51 . . . . . . 2	PUMP UP THE VOLUME GREED FEATURING RICARDO DA FORCE . . . . Stress CDSTR 49
16/09/1995 . . . . . 2 . . . . . . 11 . . . . . ○	**STAYIN' ALIVE** N-TRANCE FEATURING RICARDO DA FORCE . . . . All Around The World CDGLOBE 131
31/08/1996 . . . . . 58 . . . . . . 1	WHY . . . . ffrr FCD 280

○ Silver disc ● Gold disc ✪ Platinum disc (additional platinum units are indicated by a figure following the symbol) ◉ Singles released prior to 1973 that are known to have sold over 1 million copies in the UK

DA HOOL German rapper/DJ (born Frank Tomiczek, Bottrop) who first recorded as DJ Hooligan in 1990 before a disagreement with his record label resulted in the name change.

14/02/1998.....15......4.......	MEET HER AT THE LOVE PARADE..	Manifesto FESCD 39
22/08/1998.....35......3.......	BORA BORA	Manifesto FESCD 47
28/07/2001.....11......6.......	MEET HER AT THE LOVE PARADE 2001...	Manifesto FESCD 85

DA LENCH MOB US rap group formed in Los Angeles, CA by Terry Gray, DeSean Cooper and Jerome Washington. Cooper left in 1993 and was replaced by Maulkie.

20/03/1993.....51......2....... FREEDOM GOT AN A.K. .... East West America A 8431CD

DA MOB FEATURING JOCELYN BROWN US vocal/instrumental group comprising Erick 'More' Morillo, DJ Sneak and Jose Nunez and session singer Jocelyn Brown. DJ Sneak later went solo.

02/05/1998.....33......2....... FUN... INCredible INCRL 2CD
03/07/1999.....54......1....... IT'S ALL GOOD .... INCredible INCRL 14CD

DA MUTTZ UK production duo Alex Rizzo and Elliott Ireland. Their hit was inspired by a catchphrase from a Budweiser beer commercial. They also record as Shaft.

09/12/2000.....11....10...... WASSUUP .... Eternal WEA 319CD

RUI DA SILVA FEATURING CASSANDRA Portuguese producer/DJ (born in Lisbon) who now lives in London, where he set up the Kismet label and discovered singer Cassandra Fox busking in Piccadilly Circus.

13/01/2001 ....❶[1]....14.....○ **TOUCH ME ↑** .... Kismet 74321823992

DA SLAMMIN' PHROGZ French production duo DJs Sami and Bibi. Both work at the Les Bains-Douches club in Paris.

29/04/2000.....53......1....... SOMETHING ABOUT THE MUSIC Contains samples of Brat Pack's *Can You Feel It* and Love Committee's *Just As Long As I Have You* .... WEA 251CD

DA TECHNO BOHEMIAN Dutch instrumental/production group with Koen Groeneveld, Addy Van Der Zwan and Jan Voermans. They also recorded as Klubheads, Drunkenmunky, Cooper and Itty Bitty Boozy Woozy.

25/01/1997.....63......1....... BANGIN' BASS Contains a sample of Tyree's *Turn Up The Bass* .... Hi-Life 5731772

PAUL DA VINCI UK singer Paul Prewer who was formerly the lead singer with The Rubettes before going solo.

20/07/1974.....20......8....... YOUR BABY AIN'T YOUR BABY ANYMORE............................... Penny Farthing PEN 843

TERRY DACTYL AND THE DINOSAURS UK group led by John Lewis (born 1943) who usually recorded as Brett Marvin & The Thunderbirds. Lewis later recorded as Jona Lewie.

15/07/1972.....2......12...... **SEASIDE SHUFFLE** .... UK 5
13/01/1973.....45......4...... ON A SATURDAY NIGHT .... UK 21

DADA US group formed by Joie Calio (bass/vocals), Michael Gurley (guitar) and Phil Leavitt (drums).

04/12/1993.....71......1....... DOG .... IRS CDEIRSS 185

DADDY FREDDY – see SIMON HARRIS

DADDY'S FAVOURITE UK producer James Harrigan (born in Glasgow) who also records as DJ Harri and is resident DJ at Glasgow's The Sub Club.

21/11/1998.....44......2....... I FEEL GOOD THINGS FOR YOU Contains a sample of Patrice Rushen's *Haven't You Heard*................. Go Beat GONCD 12
09/10/1999.....50......1....... I FEEL GOOD THINGS FOR YOU Re-issue of Go Beat GONCD 12 .... Go Beat GONCD 22

DAFFY DUCK FEATURING GROOVE GANG German instrumental/production group.

06/07/1991.....58......3....... PARTY ZONE .... East West YZ 592

DAFT PUNK French production duo Thomas Bangalter (born 1/1/1975) and Guy Manuel De Homem Christo (born 8/2/1974). Bangalter also produces Stardust and recorded with DJ Falcon.

22/02/1997 .....7......5...... **DA FUNK/MUSIQUE** A-side featured in the 1997 film *The Saint*.......................... Soma VSCDT 1625
26/04/1997 .....5......5...... **AROUND THE WORLD**.. Virgin VSCDT 1633
04/10/1997.....30......2...... BURNIN'.. Virgin VSCDT 1649
28/02/1998.....47......1...... REVOLUTION 909 .... Virgin VSCDT 1682
25/11/2000 .....2......12...... **ONE MORE TIME** Features the uncredited contribution of Romanthony.............. Virgin VSCDT 1791
23/06/2001.....14......7...... DIGITAL LOVE Contains a sample of George Duke's *Love You More* .... Virgin VSCDT 1810
17/11/2001.....25......3...... HARDER BETTER FASTER STRONGER Contains a sample of Edwin Birdsong's *Cola Bottle Baby* .... Virgin VSCDT 1822

ETIENNE DAHO – see SAINT ETIENNE

DAINTEES – see MARTIN STEPHENSON AND THE DAINTEES

DAISY CHAINSAW UK group with Katie Jane Garside (vocals), Richard Adams (drums), Vince Johnson (drums) and Crispin Grey (guitar). Garside left after their album debut in 1992.

18/01/1992.....26......5....... LOVE YOUR MONEY .... Deva 001

❶[9] Number of weeks single topped the UK chart   ↑ Entered the UK chart at #1   ▲[9] Number of weeks single topped the US chart

195

	DATE	POS	WKS	BPI	SINGLE TITLE	LABEL & NUMBER

D

28/03/1992......65......1....... PINK FLOWER/ROOM ELEVEN .... Deva 82 TP7

DAJAE – see JUNIOR SANCHEZ FEATURING DAJAE

DAKAYNE – see JAMES BROWN

DAKOTAS UK group formed in 1962 by Mike Maxfield (born 23/2/1944, Manchester, guitar), Robin MacDonald (born 18/7/1943, Nairn, Scotland, rhythm guitar), Ray Jones (born 22/10/1939, Oldham, bass) and Tony Mansfield (born Anthony Bookbinder, 28/5/1943, Salford, drums). They were chosen by Brian Epstein to provide backing for Billy J Kramer. Their hit instrumental, written eighteen months earlier by Maxfield and named after a Nicholas Monserrat novel, followed on from Kramer's debut success. They disbanded in 1968.

11/07/1963.....18.....13...... THE CRUEL SEA.. Parlophone R 5044

JIM DALE UK singer (born Jim Smith, 15/8/1935, Rothwell, Northants) who became better known as an actor, appearing in thirteen of the *Carry On* films. As a songwriter, he co-wrote *Georgy Girl*, a hit for The Seekers, with Tom Springfield (the pair were nominated for an Academy Award for the song, which used in the film of the same name). He also won a 1980 Tony Award for his performance in the stage show *Barnum* and a 2000 Grammy Award for Best Spoken Word Album for Children for his narration of JK Rowling's *Harry Potter And The Goblet Of Fire*.

11/10/1957.....2.....16...... BE MY GIRL .... Parlophone R 4343
10/01/1958.....27.....1...... JUST BORN .... Parlophone R 4376
17/01/1958.....24.....2...... CRAZY DREAM B-side to *Just Born* .... Parlophone R 4376
07/03/1958.....25.....3...... SUGARTIME.. Parlophone R 4402

DALE AND GRACE US vocal duo Dale Houston (born in Ferriday, LA) and Grace Broussard (born in Prairieville, LA).

09/01/1964.....42.....2...... I'M LEAVING IT UP TO YOU ▲[2] .... London HL 9807

DALE SISTERS US family vocal group with Julie, Hazel and Betty Dunderdale who also recorded as The England Sisters.

17/03/1960.....33.....1...... HEARTBEAT ENGLAND SISTERS... HMV POP 710
23/11/1961.....36.....6...... MY SUNDAY BABY .... Ember S 140

DALI'S CAR UK group formed in 1984 by Peter Murphy (born 11/7/195, Northampton, vocals) and Mick Karn (born Anthony Michaelides, 24/7/1958, London, bass). They recorded one album before both went solo.

03/11/1984.....66.....2...... THE JUDGEMENT IS THE MIRROR .... Paradox DOX 1

DALLAS SUPERSTARS Finnish production duo Heikki Liimatainen and Jaakko Salovaara.

27/09/2003.....64.....1...... HELIUM .... All Around The World CDGLOBE 289

ROGER DALTREY UK singer (born 1/3/1944, Hammersmith, London) and lead singer with The Who. By 1972 the members of the band were involved in various solo projects, Daltrey opening his own barn studio to work on an album with songwriters Dave Courtney and Leo Sayer. He later appeared in films, including the lead in *McVicar* (1980). Also a fish breeder, he got a settlement of £155,000 from Home Farm after 500,000 fish were found dead at his Iwerne Springs trout farm in Dorset. He featured on The Chieftains' *An Irish Evening Live*, which won the 1992 Grammy Award for Best Traditional Folk Album.

14/04/1973.....5.....11...... GIVING IT ALL AWAY .... Track 2094 110
04/08/1973.....13.....10...... I'M FREE .... Ode ODS 66302
14/05/1977.....46.....2...... WRITTEN ON THE WIND .... Polydor 2121 319
02/08/1980.....39.....6...... FREE ME .... Polydor 2001 980
11/10/1980.....55.....4...... WITHOUT YOUR LOVE This and above single featured in the 1980 film *McVicar*.... Polydor POSP 181
03/03/1984.....56.....3...... WALKING IN MY SLEEP .... WEA U 9686
05/10/1985.....50.....5...... AFTER THE FIRE .... 10 TEN 69
08/03/1986.....43.....5...... UNDER A RAGING MOON .... 10 TEN 81

DAMAGE UK R&B vocal group formed in London by Andrez Harriott (born 11/8/1978), Coree Richards (born 29/3/1978), Jayde Jones (born 12/2/1979), Noel Simpson (born 1/1/1976) and Rahsaan 'Ras' Bromfield (born 3/11/1976).

20/07/1996.....68.....1...... ANYTHING... Big Life BLRD 129
12/10/1996.....12.....6...... LOVE II LOVE .... Big Life BLRD 131
14/12/1996.....6.....9.....○ FOREVER... Big Life BLRDB 132
22/03/1997.....7.....7...... LOVE GUARANTEED .... Big Life BLRDA 133
17/05/1997.....3.....8...... WONDERFUL TONIGHT .... Big Life BLRDA 134
09/08/1997.....33.....2...... LOVE LADY .... Big Life BLRDB 137
01/07/2000.....7.....7...... GHETTO ROMANCE .... Cooltempo CDCOOL 347
28/10/2000.....22.....4...... RUMOURS .... Cooltempo CDCOOLS 352
31/03/2001.....11.....7...... STILL BE LOVIN' YOU Features Coree Richards' then girlfriend Emma Bunton on backing vocals .... Cooltempo CDCOOLS 355
14/07/2001.....12.....6...... SO WHAT IF I .... Cooltempo CDCOOLS 357
15/12/2001.....42.....2...... AFTER THE LOVE HAS GONE .... Cooltempo CDCOOLS 360

CAROLINA DAMAS – see SUENO LATINO

BOBBY D'AMBROSIO FEATURING MICHELLE WEEKS US producer/remixer with singer Michelle Weeks.

02/08/1997.....23.....3....... MOMENT OF MY LIFE .... Ministry Of Sound MOSCDS 1

DAMIAN UK singer/actor (born Damian Davey, 30/9/1964, Manchester) who first recorded his hit for Sedition in 1986.

26/12/1987.....51......6......	THE TIME WARP 2	Jive 160
27/08/1988.....64......3......	THE TIME WARP 2 Re-issue of Jive 160	Jive 182
26/08/1989 .....7......13	**THE TIME WARP (REMIX)**	Jive 209
16/12/1989.....49......4.......	WIG WAM BAM	Jive 236

DAMNED UK punk group formed in 1976 by Captain Sensible (born Raymond Burns, 23/4/1955, London, bass), Brian James (born Brian Robertson, 18/2/1955, Brighton, guitar) and Rat Scabies (born Chris Miller, 30/7/1957, Kingston-upon-Thames, drums), with Dave Vanian (born David Letts, 12/10/1956, Hemel Hempstead, lead vocals) joining later. Debuting as support to the Sex Pistols, two months later they signed with Stiff Records, releasing *New Rose* the following month. It failed to chart, but is regarded as the first UK punk record (and was also Stiff's first release). The first UK punk group to tour the US, they also released the first UK punk album, *Damned Damned Damned*. They split in 1978, later re-forming (after a legal wrangle over the name the Damned) with Alistair Ward replacing James. Ward left in 1980 and was replaced by ex-Eddie & The Hot Rods Paul Gray. Sensible had a simultaneous solo career in 1982, before leaving the group in 1984. The others split in 1989, re-forming in 1991.

05/05/1979.....20......8......	LOVE SONG .... Chiswick CHIS 112
20/10/1979.....35......5......	SMASH IT UP .... Chiswick CHIS 116
01/12/1979.....46......5......	I JUST CAN'T BE HAPPY TODAY .... Chiswick CHIS 120
04/10/1980.....51......4......	HISTORY OF THE WORLD (PART 1) .... Chiswick CHIS 135
28/11/1981.....50......4......	FRIDAY 13TH (EP) Tracks on EP: *Disco Man, Limit Club, Billy Bad Breaks* and *Citadel* .... Stale One TRY 1
10/07/1982.....42......4......	LOVELY MONEY .... Bronze BRO 149
09/06/1984.....43......4......	THANKS FOR THE NIGHT .... Damned 1
30/03/1985.....21......7......	GRIMLY FIENDISH .... MCA GRIM 1
22/06/1985.....25......8......	THE SHADOW OF LOVE (EDITION PREMIERE) .... MCA GRIM 2
21/09/1985.....34......4......	IS IT A DREAM .... MCA GRIM 3
08/02/1986 .....3......10.....○	**ELOISE** .... MCA GRIM 4
22/11/1986.....32......4......	ANYTHING .... MCA GRIM 5
07/02/1987.....29......3......	GIGOLO .... MCA GRIM 6
25/04/1987.....27......6......	ALONE AGAIN OR .... MCA GRIM 7
28/11/1987.....72......1......	IN DULCE DECORUM .... MCA GRIM 8

KENNY DAMON US singer who had an acting role in the 1969 film *The Adding Machine*.

19/05/1966.....48......1.......	WHILE I LIVE .... Mercury MF 907

VIC DAMONE US singer (born Vito Farinola, 12/6/1928, Brooklyn, NYC) who was a popular ballad singer in the 1950s. He also appeared in films including *Rich Young And Pretty* (1951), *Deep In My Heart* (1954) and *Kismet* (1955), and had his own TV series for two years. He has a star on the Hollywood Walk of Fame, as does his wife Diahann Carroll, whom he married in 1987.

06/12/1957.....29......2......	AN AFFAIR TO REMEMBER Featured in the 1957 film *An Affair To Remember* .... Philips PB 745
09/05/1958 ....❶².....17......	**ON THE STREET WHERE YOU LIVE** From the musical *My Fair Lady* .... Philips PB 819
01/08/1958.....24......3......	THE ONLY MAN ON THE ISLAND .... Philips PB 837

RICHIE DAN UK producer Richard Gittens.

12/08/2000.....34......3......	CALL IT FATE .... Pure Silk CDPSR 1

DANA UK singer (born Rosemary Brown, 30/8/1951, Belfast) whose family moved to the Irish Republic when she was two. Starting singing professionally at sixteen, she won the Eurovision Song Contest while still at school, and became the first Irish winner and the first Eurovision entry from a foreign country to make the UK top ten. A regular TV performer, in 1997 she came third in the election for President of Eire.

04/04/1970 ....❶².....16	**ALL KINDS OF EVERYTHING** 1970 Eurovision Song Contest winner .... Rex R 11054
13/02/1971.....14......11	WHO PUT THE LIGHTS OUT. .... Rex R 11062
25/01/1975.....8......14	**PLEASE TELL HIM I SAID HELLO** .... GTO GT 6
13/12/1975.....4......6......	**IT'S GONNA BE A COLD COLD CHRISTMAS** .... GTO GT 45
06/03/1976.....31......4......	NEVER GONNA FALL IN LOVE AGAIN .... GTO GT 55
16/10/1976.....13......16	FAIRYTALE .... GTO GT 66
31/03/1979.....44......5......	SOMETHING'S COOKIN' IN THE KITCHEN .... GTO GT 243
15/05/1982.....66......3......	I FEEL LOVE COMIN' ON .... Creole CR 32

DANA – see **BASSTOY**

DANA INTERNATIONAL Israeli singer (born Yaron Cohen, later Sharon Cohen) who had previously been a man before undergoing a sex change. She won the 1998 Eurovision Song Contest, beating the UK's entry by Imaani into second place.

27/06/1998.....11......4.......	DIVA 1998 Eurovision Song Contest winner .... Dance Pool DANA 1CD

DANCE CONSPIRACY UK production duo Ashley Brown and Neil Vass.

03/10/1992.....72......1......	DUB WAR .... XL Recordings XLT 34

DANCE FLOOR VIRUS Italian vocal/instrumental group formed by Alex Caracas and Eddie 'Cosmic Debris'.

21/10/1995.....49......2.......	MESSAGE IN A BOTTLE .... Epic 6623742

DANCE TO TIPPERARY Irish traditional/fusion group formed in 1998 by Danielle Piffner (vocals), Trisha Kelly (accordion), Sharon Keane (fiddle), Brian Kelly (banjo), Joe Moran (flute), Jason Swindle (guitar) and backing vocalists Sharmine Barett and Ashling

❶⁹ Number of weeks single topped the UK chart   ↑ Entered the UK chart at #1   ▲⁹ Number of weeks single topped the US chart

197

Maloney. When they charted they were Katy Godfrey (vocals), Trisha Kelly (accordion), Kieran MacManus (keyboards), Ruairi MacManus (guitar) and Liam MacManus (drums), with backing vocals by Mick Loftus, Michael Loftus, Geoff Mitchell and Richie Twomey. Their debut hit was a tribute to Celtic FC.

24/05/2003	44	2		THE BHOYS ARE BACK IN TOWN	Nede NRCD 2105

DANCE 2 TRANCE
German trance/techno project formed in Frankfurt by Jam El Mar (Rolf Ellmer) and DJ Dag Lerner. They split in 1995, Jam El Mar later recording as Jam And Spoon.

24/04/1993	25	4		POWER OF A.MERICAN N.ATIVES	Logic 74321139582
24/07/1993	36	3		TAKE A FREE FALL	Logic 74321153602
04/02/1995	56	1		WARRIOR	Logic 74321257722

EVAN DANDO
US guitarist/singer (born 4/3/1967, Boston) and ex-leader of The Lemonheads.

24/06/1995	75	1		PERFECT DAY KIRSTY MacCOLL AND EVAN DANDO	Virgin VSCDT 1552
31/05/2003	38	1		STOP MY HEAD	Setanta SETCDB 127
13/12/2003	68	1		IT LOOKS LIKE YOU	Setanta SETCDA 130

DANDY WARHOLS
US group formed in Portland, OR in 1994 by Courtney Taylor (vocals/guitar/keyboards), Peter Holmstrom (guitar), Zia McCabe (keyboards/bass) and Eric Hedford (drums). Hedford left in 1998 and was replaced by Brent De Boer.

28/02/1998	29	2		EVERY DAY SHOULD BE A HOLIDAY Featured in the 1998 film *There's Something About Mary*	Capitol CDCL 797
02/05/1998	13	4		NOT IF YOU WERE THE LAST JUNKIE ON EARTH	Capitol CDCL 800
08/08/1998	36	2		BOYS BETTER	Capitol CDCLS 805
10/06/2000	38	2		GET OFF	Capitol CDCLS 821
09/09/2000	42	1		BOHEMIAN LIKE YOU Featured in the 2000 film *The Replacements*	Capitol CDCLS 823
07/07/2001	66	1		GODLESS	Capitol CDCL 829
10/11/2001	5	10		**BOHEMIAN LIKE YOU**	Capitol CDCLX 823
16/03/2002	34	2		GET OFF Re-issue of Capitol CDCLS 821	Capitol CDCL 835
17/05/2003	18	3		WE USED TO BE FRIENDS	Capitol CDCL 843
09/08/2003	34	2		YOU WERE THE LAST HIGH	Parlophone CDCLX 845
06/12/2003	66	1		PLAN A	Parlophone CDCLS 851

DANDYS
UK group formed in 1996 by Andrew Firth (born 22/9/1975, vocals), Ben Davies (born 30/1/1978, guitar), Tony Beasley (bass), Mike Brooke (born 25/11/1973, keyboards) and Bryan Munslow (drums). Munslow was later replaced by Paul Blant.

14/03/1998	71	1		YOU MAKE ME WANT TO SCREAM	Artificial ATFCD 3
30/05/1998	57	1		ENGLISH COUNTRY GARDEN	Artificial ATFCD 4

D'ANGELO
US singer (born Michael D'Angelo Archer, 11/2/1974, Richmond, VA), the son of a preacher, who began singing in church and with the Boys Choir of Harlem before signing with EMI in 1993. His partner Angie Stone is also a successful singer. He won two 2000 Grammy Awards: Best Rhythm & Blues Album for *Voodoo* and Best Male Rhythm & Blues Vocal Performance for *How Does It Feel*.

28/10/1995	24	3		BROWN SUGAR	Cooltempo CDCOOL 307
02/03/1996	40	2		COLD WORLD GENIUS/GZA FEATURING D'ANGELO Based on Stevie Wonder's *Rocket Love*	Geffen GFSTD 22114
02/03/1996	31	2		CRUISIN'	Cooltempo CDCOOL 316
15/06/1996	21	2		LADY	Cooltempo CDCOOLS 323
22/05/1999	33	2		BREAK UPS 2 MAKE UPS METHOD MAN FEATURING D'ANGELO	Def Jam 8709272

DANGER DANGER
US rock group formed in Queens, NYC by Ted Poley (vocals), Andy Timmons (guitar), Kasey Smith (keyboards), Bruno Ravel (bass) and Steve West (drums).

08/02/1992	42	2		MONKEY BUSINESS	Epic 6577517
28/03/1992	46	2		I STILL THINK ABOUT YOU	Epic 6578387
13/06/1992	75	1		COMIN' HOME	Epic 6581337

DAN-I
UK reggae singer Selmore Lewinson.

10/11/1979	30	9		MONKEY CHOP	Island WIP 6520

CHARLIE DANIELS BAND
US singer/guitarist/fiddle player (born 28/10/1937, Wilmington, NC) whose band, formed in 1971, included Tom Crain (guitar), Joe 'Taz' DiGregorio (keyboards), Charles Hayward (bass) and James W Marshall (drums). Later playing sessions in Nashville, he appeared in the 1980 film *Urban Cowboy*.

22/09/1979	14	10		THE DEVIL WENT DOWN TO GEORGIA 1979 Grammy Award for Best Country Performance by a Group. Featured in the films *Urban Cowboy* (1980) and *Coyote Ugly* (2000)	Epic EPC 7737

JOHNNY DANKWORTH
UK bandleader/saxophonist (born 20/9/1927, London) who studied at the Royal Academy of Music from 1944 to 1946, then played on transatlantic liners before forming his own band, the Johnny Dankworth Seven, in 1950. In 1953 he formed a big band that included singer Cleo Laine (whom he married in 1958) and top players like Kenny Wheeler, Danny Moss, Peter King, Dudley Moore and Kenny Clare. He founded the Wavendon Allmusic Plan in 1969, and was made a Companion of the British Empire in 1974.

22/06/1956	7	12		**EXPERIMENTS WITH MICE**	Parlophone R 4185
23/02/1961	9	21		**AFRICAN WALTZ**	Columbia DB 4590

DANNII – see DANNII MINOGUE

○ Silver disc ● Gold disc ✪ Platinum disc (additional platinum units are indicated by a figure following the symbol) ◎ Singles released prior to 1973 that are known to have sold over 1 million copies in the UK

DANNY AND THE JUNIORS
US vocal group formed in Philadelphia, PA in 1955 by Danny Rapp (born 10/5/1941, Philadelphia), David White (born September 1940, Philadelphia), Frank Maffei and Joe Terranova (born 30/1/1941, Philadelphia) as the Juvenairs. Their debut hit was originally titled *Do The Bop* and changed at the suggestion of Dick Clark. They later signed for Clark's Swan Records and appeared in the 1958 film *Let's Rock*. Rapp committed suicide on 5/4/1983.

| 17/01/1958 | 3 | 14 | | AT THE HOP ▲7 Featured in the 1973 film *American Graffiti* | HMV POP 436 |
| 10/07/1976 | 39 | 5 | | AT THE HOP Re-issue of HMV POP 436 | ABC 4123 |

DANNY WILSON
UK group formed by Gary Clark (lead guitar/vocals), his brother Kit (keyboards/percussion) and Ged Grimes (bass). Originally called Spencer Tracy, their name came from the 1952 Frank Sinatra film *Meet Danny Wilson*. They disbanded in 1990, Clark going solo and releasing a debut album in 1993.

22/08/1987	42	7		MARY'S PRAYER Featured in the 1998 film *There's Something About Mary*	Virgin VS 934
02/04/1988	3	11		**MARY'S PRAYER**	Virgin VS 934
17/06/1989	23	9		THE SECOND SUMMER OF LOVE	Virgin VS 1186
16/09/1989	69	1		NEVER GONNA BE THE SAME	Virgin VS 1203

DANSE SOCIETY
UK group formed in Sheffield by Steve Rawlings (vocals), Dave Patrick (guitar), Bubble (bass), Paul Hampshire (keyboards) and Paul Gilmartin (drums) and known as Y?. Paul Nash (guitar) and Lyndon Scarfe (guitar) were added to the line-up and the name changed to Danse Crazy. Hampshire and Patrick left at the end of 1980 and the name changed again to Danse Society. Tim Wright (bass) joined in 1981. After early releases on IKF and Pax, they signed with Arista in 1983.

| 27/08/1983 | 61 | 3 | | WAKE UP | Society SOC 5 |
| 05/11/1983 | 60 | 2 | | HEAVEN IS WAITING | Society SOC 6 |

STEVEN DANTE
UK R&B singer (born Steven Dennis, London) who was taken to the US in search of a recording contract. While there he worked with Marcus Miller and Ray Bardini (Luther Vandross' producers) and sang with Jellybean.

| 26/09/1987 | 13 | 10 | | THE REAL THING JELLYBEAN FEATURING STEVEN DANTE | Chrysalis CHS 3167 |
| 09/07/1988 | 34 | 6 | | I'M TOO SCARED | Cooltempo DANTE 1 |

TONJA DANTZLER
US singer who later became a teacher at the Institute of Creativity in New London, CT.

| 17/12/1994 | 66 | 1 | | IN AND OUT OF MY LIFE | ffrr FCD 246 |

DANY – see DOUBLE DEE FEATURING DANY

DANZEL
Belgian singer (born Johan Waem) who took his name in honour of actor Denzel Washington. He was one of the 20 finalists in the 2003 Belgian *Pop Idol* competition.

| 06/11/2004 | 11 | 5 | | PUMP IT UP Contains a sample of Mixmaster's *In The Mix* | Data 75CDS |

DANZIG
US rock group formed by Glenn Danzig (born 23/6/1959, New Jersey, vocals), John Christ (guitar), Eerie Von (bass) and Chuck Biscuits (drums). Biscuits left in 1994 and was replaced by Joey Castillo; Von left in 1996 and was replaced by John Lazie.

| 14/05/1994 | 62 | 1 | | MOTHER | American Recordings MOMDD 1 |

DAPHNE
US singer who worked with Danny Tenaglia, Doc Martin and Quazar.

| 09/12/1995 | 71 | 1 | | CHANGE | Stress CDSTR 54 |

DAPHNE AND CELESTE
US vocal duo formed in New Jersey by Daphne DiConcetto and Celeste Cruz.

05/02/2000	8	12		**OOH STICK YOU!**	Universal MCSTD 40209
17/06/2000	18	12		UGLY	Universal MCSTD 40232
02/09/2000	12	4		SCHOOL'S OUT	Universal MCSTD 40238

TERENCE TRENT D'ARBY
US singer (born 15/3/1962, New York) who enlisted in the US Army in 1980 and was discharged in 1983. He moved to London in 1984, making demos for two years before signing with CBS/Columbia. A former regional Golden Gloves boxing champion, he was named Best International Newcomer at the 1988 BRIT Awards. He also won the 1988 Grammy Award for Best Rhythm & Blues Vocal Performance for *Introducing The Hardline According To Terence Trent D'Arby*.

14/03/1987	7	13		**IF YOU LET ME STAY**	CBS TRENT 1
20/06/1987	4	11		**WISHING WELL ▲1**	CBS TRENT 2
10/10/1987	20	7		DANCE LITTLE SISTER (PART ONE)	CBS TRENT 3
09/01/1988	2	10		**SIGN YOUR NAME**	CBS TRENT 4
20/01/1990	55	3		TO KNOW SOMEONE DEEPLY IS TO KNOW SOMEONE SOFTLY	CBS TRENT 6
17/04/1993	14	6		DO YOU LOVE ME LIKE YOU SAY	Columbia 6590732
19/06/1993	14	6		DELICATE TERENCE TRENT D'ARBY FEATURING DES'REE	Columbia 6593312
28/08/1993	16	7		SHE KISSED ME	Columbia 6595922
20/11/1993	18	7		LET HER DOWN EASY	Columbia 6598642
08/04/1995	20	6		HOLDING ON TO YOU	Columbia 6614235
05/08/1995	57	1		VIBRATOR	Columbia 6622585

RICHARD DARBYSHIRE
UK singer (born 8/3/1960, Stockport) who was lead singer with Living In A Box before going solo.

20/08/1988	41	3		COMING BACK FOR MORE JELLYBEAN FEATURING RICHARD DARBYSHIRE	Chrysalis JEL 4
24/07/1993	50	3		THIS I SWEAR	Dome CDDOME 1003
12/02/1994	54	1		WHEN ONLY LOVE WILL DO	Dome CDDOME 1008

❶9 Number of weeks single topped the UK chart ↑ Entered the UK chart at #1 ▲9 Number of weeks single topped the US chart

199

DARE UK rock group formed in 1978 by Darren Wharton (keyboards/vocals), Vinny Burns (guitar), Shelley (bass), Brian Cox (keyboards) and James Ross (drums).

29/04/1989	62	2	THE RAINDANCE .... A&M AM 483
29/07/1989	71	2	ABANDON .... A&M AM 519
10/08/1991	52	2	WE DON'T NEED A REASON .... A&M AM 775
05/10/1991	67	1	REAL LOVE .... A&M AM 824

DARE Dutch vocal group comprising Kelly Keet, Tatiana Linck and Chelina Manahutu. Sponsored by Coca Cola in Holland, their debut began as a commercial for the company.

13/09/2003	45	1	CHIHUAHUA .... All Around The World CDGLOBE 311

MATT DAREY UK dance producer/instrumentalist who has also remixed for the likes of ATB, Moloko and Gabrielle. Darey also recorded as Sunburst and Space Baby, as a member of Lost Tribe, and with Marcella Woods and Michael Woods as M3 for Inferno.

09/10/1999	19	3	LIBERATION (TEMPTATION – FLY LIKE AN EAGLE) MATT DAREY PRESENTS MASH UP .... Incentive CENT 1CDS
22/04/2000	40	2	FROM RUSSIA WITH LOVE MATT DAREY PRESENTS DSP .... Liquid Asset ASSETCD 003
15/07/2000	21	4	BEAUTIFUL MATT DAREY'S MASH UP FEATURING MARCELLA WOODS. .... Incentive CENT 7CDS
20/04/2002	10	6	BEAUTIFUL (REMIX) .... Incentive CENT 38CDS
14/12/2002	34	2	U SHINE ON This and above single credited to MATT DAREY FEATURING MARCELLA WOODS .... Incentive CENT 50CDS

BOBBY DARIN US singer/pianist/guitarist/drummer (born Walden Robert Cassotto, 14/5/1936, The Bronx, NYC) who first recorded with the Jaybirds in 1956, also having US success under the pseudonym the Rinky Dinks. Two Grammy Awards include a Special Trustees Awards for Artists & Repertoire Contribution with Ahmet Ertegun for *Mack The Knife*, and he was nominated for an Oscar for Best Supporting Actor for his performance in the 1963 film *Captain Newman, MD*. He formed the Direction record company and later signed for Motown. He died following surgery to repair a heart valve on 20/12/1973. He was inducted into the Rock & Roll Hall of Fame in 1990 and has a star on the Hollywood Walk of Fame.

01/08/1958	18	7	SPLISH SPLASH Featured in the films *American Hot Wax* (1978) and *You've Got Mail* (1998) .... London HLE 8666
09/01/1959	24	2	QUEEN OF THE HOP .... London HLE 8737
29/05/1959	❶⁴	19	DREAM LOVER .... London HLE 8867
25/09/1959	❶²	18	MACK THE KNIFE ▲⁹ 1959 Grammy Award for Record of the Year. Featured in the 2000 film *What Women Want* ....
			.... London HLK 8939
29/01/1960	8	13	LA MER (BEYOND THE SEA) Featured in the films *Tequila Sunrise* (1988) and *A Life Less Ordinary* (1998) .... London HLK 9034
31/03/1960	8	12	CLEMENTINE .... London HLK 9086
30/06/1960	34	2	BILL BAILEY .... London HLK 9142
16/03/1961	2	13	LAZY RIVER .... London HLK 9303
06/07/1961	24	7	NATURE BOY .... London HLK 9375
12/10/1961	10	11	YOU MUST HAVE BEEN A BEAUTIFUL BABY .... London HLK 9429
26/10/1961	50	1	THEME FROM 'COME SEPTEMBER' BOBBY DARIN ORCHESTRA .... London HLK 9407
21/12/1961	5	13	MULTIPLICATION Featured in the 1961 film *Come September* .... London HLK 9474
19/07/1962	2	17	THINGS .... London HLK 9575
04/10/1962	24	6	IF A MAN ANSWERS Featured in the 1962 film *If A Man Answers* .... Capitol CL 15272
29/11/1962	40	4	BABY FACE .... London HLK 9624
25/07/1963	37	4	EIGHTEEN YELLOW ROSES .... Capitol CL 15306
13/10/1966	9	12	IF I WERE A CARPENTER .... Atlantic 584 051
14/04/1979	64	1	DREAM LOVER/MACK THE KNIFE .... Lightning LIG 9017

DARIO G UK dance trio formed in Crewe by Scott Rosser, Paul Spencer and Stephen Spencer and named after Crewe Alexandra's manager Dario Gradi. Their debut single was personally selected by Nelson Mandela as the anthem of the South African Red Cross.

27/09/1997	2	18	●	SUNCHYME Contains a sample of Dream Academy's *Life In A Northern Town* .... Eternal 130CD
20/06/1998	5	9	○	CARNAVAL DE PARIS Official song of the 1998 FIFA World Cup. Featured in the 2001 film *Mean Machine* .... Eternal 162CD
12/09/1998	17	4		SUNMACHINE. .... Eternal 173CD
25/03/2000	37	2		VOICES Featured in the 2000 film *The Beach* .... Eternal 256CD1
03/02/2001	9	6		DREAM TO ME Features the uncredited vocals of Ingrid Straumstoyl .... Manifesto FESCD 79
08/06/2002	34	3		CARNAVAL 2002 .... Eternal WEA 349CD
25/01/2003	39	2		HEAVEN IS CLOSER (FEELS LIKE HEAVEN). .... Serious SER 61CD

DARIUS UK singer (born Darius Danesh, 19/8/1980, Glasgow) who first became known as a contestant on *Popstars*. He then competed in *Pop Idol* and made the final 50, although he was later eliminated. When illness struck Rik Waller, Darius was reinstated and finished third behind Will Young and Gareth Gates.

10/08/2002	❶²	16	○	COLOURBLIND ↑ .... Mercury 639662
07/12/2002	5	12		RUSHES .... Mercury 0638052
15/03/2003	9	8		INCREDIBLE (WHAT I MEANT TO SAY) .... Mercury 0779782
21/06/2003	21	3		GIRL IN THE MOON. .... Mercury 9808234
30/10/2004	8	7		KINDA LOVE .... Mercury 9868350

○ Silver disc ● Gold disc ✪ Platinum disc (additional platinum units are indicated by a figure following the symbol) ◉ Singles released prior to 1973 that are known to have sold over 1 million copies in the UK

DARK GLOBE FEATURING AMANDA GHOST UK production duo Matt Frost and Pete Diggens, with singer Amanda Ghost.

01/05/2004.....52......1....... BREAK MY WORLD...Island CID 853

DARK MONKS UK production duo Jan Carbon and James Reynolds.

14/09/2002.....62......1....... INSANE Contains an interpolation of Moby's *Let's Go*..Incentive CENT 45CDS

DARK STAR UK rock group formed by Bic Hayes (born 10/6/1964, guitar/vocals), Laurence O'Keefe (born 2/1/1965, Newcastle-upon-Tyne) and Dave Francolini (born 13/9/1969, Hamilton, Bermuda).

26/06/1999.....50......1......	ABOUT 3AM...Harvest CDEM 545
15/01/2000.....25......3......	GRACEADELICA..Harvest CDEMS 556
13/05/2000.....31......2......	I AM THE SUN...Harvest CDEMS 566

DARKMAN UK rapper (born Brian Mitchell, 1970) of West Indian descent who grew up in London. Founding the Powercut label at the age of seventeen, after the success of *This Is How It Should Be Done* (the first hybrid of reggae and hip hop) he switched to Slam Jam. He later set up the Vinyl Lab label.

14/05/1994.....49......2......	YABBA DABBA DOO..Wild Card CARDD 6
20/08/1994.....46......2......	WHO'S THE DARKMAN..Wild Card CARDD 8
03/12/1994.....37......2......	YABBA DABBA DOO Re-issue of Wild Card CARDD 6..........Wild Card CARDD 11
21/10/1995.....74......1......	BRAND NEW DAY..Wild Card 5771892

DARKNESS UK rock group formed in London by Justin Hawkins (guitar/vocals), Dan Hawkins (guitar), Frankie Poullain (bass) and Ed Graham (drums). They won Best UK and Ireland Act at the 2003 MTV Europe Music Awards, and three awards at the 2004 BRITS: Best British Group, Best Rock Act and Best British Album for *Permission To Land*.

08/03/2003.....43......2......	GET YOUR HANDS OFF MY WOMAN............................Must Destory DUSTY 006CD
28/06/2003.....11......5......	GROWING ON ME..Must Destory DUSTY 010CD
04/10/2003 .....2......11......	I BELIEVE IN A THING CALLED LOVE Originally released in 2002 but failed to chart. Featured in the 2004 film *Bridget Jones Diary 2: Edge Of Reason*...Must Destroy DARK 01CD
27/12/2003 .....2......7......●	**CHRISTMAS TIME (DON'T LET THE BELLS END)**.................Must Destroy DARK 02CD
03/04/2004 .....5......8......	**LOVE IS ONLY A FEELING**.................................Must Destroy DARK 03CD

DARLING BUDS UK rock group formed in Wales in 1987 by Andrea Lewis (born 25/3/1967, Newport, vocals), Harley Farr (born 4/7/1964, Singapore, guitar), Bloss (drums) and Chris McDonagh (born 6/3/1962, Newport, bass). The group was named after the novel *The Darling Buds of May* by HE Bates. They first recorded for the Native label before signing with CBS in 1988. Bloss was later replaced by Liverpool-born Jimmy Hughes.

08/10/1988.....50......5......	BURST..Epic BLOND 1
07/01/1989.....27......5......	HIT THE GROUND...CBS BLOND 2
25/03/1989.....49......4......	LET'S GO ROUND THERE..CBS BLOND 3
22/07/1989.....45......3......	YOU'VE GOT TO CHOOSE..CBS BLOND 4
02/06/1990.....60......2......	TINY MACHINE...CBS BLOND 5
12/09/1992.....71......1......	SURE THING...Epic 6582157

GUY DARRELL UK singer, formerly a waiter at Butlins, who also recorded for Pye, Warwick, Page One, Oriole, Columbia, Piccadilly and Route.

18/08/1973.....12.....13...... I'VE BEEN HURT..Santa Ponsa PNS 4

JAMES DARREN US singer/actor (born James William Ercolani, 3/10/1936, Philadelphia, PA) who studied acting in New York, moved to Hollywood in 1955 and then signed with Columbia Pictures. His many films include *Rumble In The Docks* (his debut in 1956), *Operation Mad Ball* (1957) and *The Guns Of Navarone* (1961) and the TV series *The Time Tunnel* and *TJ Hooker*. He later recorded for Warner Brothers, Kirshner, Buddah, MGM, Private Stock and RCA.

11/08/1960.....29......7.......	BECAUSE THEY'RE YOUNG Featured in the 1960 film *Because They're Young*.....Pye International 7N 25059
14/12/1961.....28......9.......	GOODBYE CRUEL WORLD....................................Pye International 7N 25116
29/03/1962.....36......3.......	HER ROYAL MAJESTY......................................Pye International 7N 25125
21/06/1962.....30......6.......	CONSCIENCE...Pye International 7N 25138

DARTS UK doo wop revival group formed in the mid-1970s by George Currie (vocals), John Drummer (drums), Griff Fender (born Ian Collier, vocals), Bob Fish (vocals), Den Hegarty (vocals), Horatio Hornblower (born Nigel Trubridge, saxophone), Hammy Howell (keyboards), Ian 'Thump' Thompson (bass) and Rita Ray (vocals). Hegarty left in 1979 to form Rocky Sharpe And The Replays and was replaced by Kenny Andrews. Howell left in 1980 and was replaced by Mike Deacon; Howell returned later.

05/11/1977 .....6......13.....O	**DADDY COOL/THE GIRL CAN'T HELP IT**.......................Magnet MAG 100
28/01/1978 .....2......12.....●	**COME BACK MY LOVE**.....................................Magnet MAG 110
06/05/1978 .....2......13.....O	**BOY FROM NEW YORK CITY** Originally a US hit for the Ad-Libs in 1965.......Magnet MAG 116
05/08/1978 .....2......11.....●	**IT'S RAINING**...Magnet MAG 126
11/11/1978.....18......11......	DON'T LET IT FADE AWAY.................................Magnet MAG 134
10/02/1979.....10......9.......	**GET IT**...Magnet MAG 140
21/07/1979 .....6......11.....O	**DUKE OF EARL** Originally a US hit for Gene Chandler in 1962................Magnet MAG 147
20/10/1979.....43......6......	CAN'T GET ENOUGH OF YOUR LOVE..........................Magnet MAG 156
01/12/1979.....51......7......	REET PETITE..Magnet MAG 160
31/05/1980.....11.....14......	LET'S HANG ON..Magnet MAG 174

❶⁹ Number of weeks single topped the UK chart ↑ Entered the UK chart at #1 ▲⁹ Number of weeks single topped the US chart

201

	DATE	POS	WKS	BPI	SINGLE TITLE	LABEL & NUMBER
	06/09/1980	66	3		PEACHES	Magnet MAG 179
	29/11/1980	48	7		WHITE CHRISTMAS/SH-BOOM (LIFE COULD BE A DREAM)	Magnet MAG 184

DARUDE Finnish dance artist Ville Virtanen who was discovered by Bomfunk's Jaako Salovaara.

	DATE	POS	WKS	BPI	SINGLE TITLE	LABEL & NUMBER
	24/06/2000	3	15	○	**SANDSTORM**	Neo NEOCD 033
	25/11/2000	5	10		**FEEL THE BEAT**	Neo NEOCD 045
	15/09/2001	13	4		OUT OF CONTROL (BACK FOR MORE)	Neo NEOCD 067

DAS EFX US rap duo Drayz (born Andre Weston, 9/9/1970, New Jersey) and Skoob (born Willie Hines, 27/11/1970, Brooklyn, NYC).

	DATE	POS	WKS	BPI	SINGLE TITLE	LABEL & NUMBER
	07/08/1993	36	4		CHECK YO SELF ICE CUBE FEATURING DAS EFX Contains a sample of Grandmaster Flash & The Furious Five's *The Message* .... Fourth & Broadway BRCD 283
	25/04/1998	42	1		RAP SCHOLAR DAS EFX FEATURING REDMAN	East West E 3853CD

DASHBOARD CONFESSIONAL US rock group formed in Boca Raton, FL by Chris Carrabba (guitar/vocals), John Lefler (guitar), Scott Shoenback (bass) and Mike Marsh (drums).

	DATE	POS	WKS	BPI	SINGLE TITLE	LABEL & NUMBER
	22/11/2003	60	1		HANDS DOWN	Interscope 9813790
	27/03/2004	75	1		RAPID HOPE LOSS	Vagrant 9861991

DATSUNS New Zealand rock group formed in Cambridge by Wolf De Datsun (bass/vocals), Christian Livingstone Datsun (guitar), Phil Buscke Datsun (guitar) and Matt Osment Datsun (drums), all four adopting the surname Datsun.

	DATE	POS	WKS	BPI	SINGLE TITLE	LABEL & NUMBER
	05/10/2002	25	2		IN LOVE	V2 VVR 5020953
	22/02/2003	33	2		HARMONIC GENERATOR	V2 VVR 5021228
	06/09/2003	55	1		MF FROM HELL	V2 VVR 5021753
	12/06/2004	48	1		BLACKEN MY THUMB	V2 VVR 5026953
	23/10/2004	71	1		GIRLS BEST FRIEND	V2 VVR 5028893

N'DEA DAVENPORT US singer (born in Atlanta, GA) who began as a backing singer for George Clinton and Bruce Willis. She appeared in a number of videos for Young MC and the Breakfast Club before joining The Brand New Heavies and later going solo.

	DATE	POS	WKS	BPI	SINGLE TITLE	LABEL & NUMBER
	05/10/1991	43	3		NEVER STOP	ffrr F 165
	15/02/1992	24	4		DREAM COME TRUE	ffrr F 180
	18/04/1992	19	6		ULTIMATE TRUNK FUNK EP Tracks on EP: *Never Stop, Stay This Way, Mr Tanaka* and *Never Stop (Remix)*	ffrr F 185
	01/08/1992	24	4		DON'T LET IT GO TO YOUR HEAD	ffrr BNH 1
	19/12/1992	40	5		STAY THIS WAY This and all the above singles credited to BRAND NEW HEAVIES FEATURING N'DEA DAVENPORT	ffrr BNH 2
	11/09/1993	34	2		TRUST ME GURU FEATURING N'DEA DAVENPORT	Cooltempo CDCOOL 278
	26/03/1994	15	4		DREAM ON DREAMER	ffrr BNHCD 3
	11/06/1994	23	4		BACK TO LOVE	ffrr BNHCD 4
	13/08/1994	13	6		MIDNIGHT AT THE OASIS	ffrr BNHCDP 5
	05/11/1994	26	4		SPEND SOME TIME	ffrr BNHCD 6
	11/03/1995	38	3		CLOSE TO YOU This and above four singles credited to BRAND NEW HEAVIES FEATURING N'DEA DAVENPORT	ffrr BNCDP 7
	20/06/1998	52	1		BRING IT ON	Gee Street VVR 5002033
	15/12/2001	25	4		YOU CAN'T CHANGE ME ROGER SANCHEZ FEATURING ARMAND VAN HELDEN AND N'DEA DAVENPORT	Defected DFECT 41CDS

ANNE-MARIE DAVID Luxembourg singer who won the 1973 Eurovision Song Contest with *Tu Te Reconnaitras*, beating Cliff Richard into third place. The single was later re-recorded in English. Her follow-up was *Sing For Your Supper*.

	DATE	POS	WKS	BPI	SINGLE TITLE	LABEL & NUMBER
	28/04/1973	13	9		WONDERFUL DREAM 1973 Eurovision Song Contest winner	Epic EPC 1446

CRAIG DAVID UK singer (born 5/5/1981, Southampton) discovered by production duo Artful Dodger. Four MOBO Awards include Best British Act in 2000 and 2001, and Best Newcomer in 2000, although it was the 2001 BRIT Awards that attracted attention: nominated in six categories, he won nothing. After a major US breakthrough he won two MTV Europe Music Awards: Best Rhythm & Blues Act and Select UK & Ireland Act.

	DATE	POS	WKS	BPI	SINGLE TITLE	LABEL & NUMBER
	11/12/1999	2	17	✪	**RE-REWIND THE CROWD SAY BO SELECTA** ARTFUL DODGER FEATURING CRAIG DAVID	Public Demand/Relentless RELENT 1CDS
	15/04/2000	❶[1]	14	●	**FILL ME IN ↑** 2000 MOBO Award for Best Single	Wildstar CDWILD 28
	15/07/2000	6	10		**WOMAN TROUBLE** ARTFUL DODGER FEATURING ROBBIE CRAIG AND CRAIG DAVID Featured in the 2001 film *Bridget Jones's Diary* .... Public Demand/ffrr FCDP 380
	05/08/2000	❶[1]	15		**7 DAYS ↑**	Wildstar CDWILD 30
	02/12/2000	3	13	○	**WALKING AWAY**	Wildstar CDWILD 35
	31/03/2001	8	10		**RENDEZVOUS**	Wildstar CDWILD 36
	09/11/2002	8	10		**WHAT'S YOUR FLAVA?**	Wildstar CDWILD 43
	01/02/2003	10	6		**HIDDEN AGENDA**	Wildstar CDWILD 44
	10/05/2003	2	10		**RISE & FALL** CRAIG DAVID AND STING	Wildstar CDWILD 45
	09/08/2003	8	6		**SPANISH**	Wildstar CXWILD 49
	25/10/2003	15	4		WORLD FILLED WITH LOVE	Wildstar CDWILD 51
	10/01/2004	43	2		YOU DON'T MISS YOUR WATER	Wildstar CDWILD 52

F.R. DAVID French singer (born Elli Robert Fitoussi, 1/1/1947, Tunis) who moved to Paris in 1964. He also recorded with Vangelis' group Les Variations.

	DATE	POS	WKS	BPI	SINGLE TITLE	LABEL & NUMBER
	02/04/1983	2	12		**WORDS**	Carrere CAR 248
	18/06/1983	71	1		MUSIC	Carrere CAR 282

○ Silver disc ● Gold disc ✪ Platinum disc (additional platinum units are indicated by a figure following the symbol) ◎ Singles released prior to 1973 that are known to have sold over 1 million copies in the UK

DAVID AND JONATHAN
UK songwriting/production duo Roger Greenaway (aka David, born 23/8/1938, Bristol) and Roger Cook (aka Jonathan, born 19/8/1940, Bristol). First together in the Kestrels, their songwriting partnership began in 1965 with *You've Got Your Troubles* for the Fortunes, although their first hit as performers was a Lennon & McCartney song. They penned hits for the Hollies (*Gasoline Alley Bred*), Andy Williams (*Home Lovin' Man*), New Seekers (*I'd Like To Teach The World To Sing*), Congregation (*Softly Whispering I Love You,* which was first recorded by 'David And Jonathan'), White Plains (*My Baby Loves Lovin'*) and Cilla Black (*Something Tells Me Something's Gonna Happen Tonight*). Cook later formed Blue Mink, both having solo hits as songwriters (Greenaway had a US country #1 with Crystal Gayle's *It's Like We Never Said Goodbye*, Cook penning *Talking In Your Sleep* for Gayle). Greenaway was awarded an OBE in the 2001 New Year's Honours List.

| 13/01/1966 | 11 | 6 | | MICHELLE Written by Lennon & McCartney, produced by George Martin; the Overlanders had the bigger hit | Columbia DB 7800 |
| 07/07/1966 | 7 | 16 | | **LOVERS OF THE WORLD UNITE** | Columbia DB 7950 |

DAVID DEVANT AND HIS SPIRIT WIFE
UK group formed by Vessel (vocals/various instruments), Colonel (bass), Professor G Rimschott (drums), Pope (guitar), Bryn (keyboards), Foz (guitar), Iceman, Cocky Young 'Un, Lantern, Jet Boy and The Spectrettes.

| 05/04/1997 | 54 | 1 | | GINGER | Rhythm King KIND 4CD |
| 21/06/1997 | 61 | 1 | | THIS IS FOR REAL | Rhythm King KIND 5CD |

JIM DAVIDSON
UK singer (born 12/12/1953 Bexleyheath, Kent) mainly known as a comic after winning the TV talent contest *Opportunity Knocks*. Later a host of TV shows including *The Generation Game*, he was awarded an OBE in 2001.

| 27/12/1980 | 52 | 4 | | WHITE CHRISTMAS/TOO RISKY | Scratch SCR 001 |

PAUL DAVIDSON
Jamaican singer (born in Kingston) who was a studio engineer before scoring with a reggae version of the Allman Brothers song.

| 27/12/1975 | 10 | 10 | | **MIDNIGHT RIDER** | Tropical ALO 56 |

DAVE DAVIES
UK singer/guitarist (born 3/2/1947, Muswell Hill, London). The younger brother of Kinks lead singer Ray (who encouraged him to play the guitar), Dave was also in the Kinks.

| 19/07/1967 | 3 | 10 | | **DEATH OF A CLOWN** | Pye 7N 17356 |
| 06/12/1967 | 20 | 7 | | SUSANNAH'S STILL ALIVE | Pye 7N 17429 |

WINDSOR DAVIES AND DON ESTELLE
UK actors, both in the TV comedy *It Ain't Half Hot Mum*. Davies (born 28/8/1930, London) played Battery Sgt Major Williams, Estelle (born 1933, Manchester) Gunner 'Lofty' Sugden. Estelle died on 2/8/2003.

| 17/05/1975 | ●³ | 12 | ● | **WHISPERING GRASS** Originally recorded by the Inkspots | EMI 2290 |
| 25/10/1975 | 41 | 4 | | PAPER DOLL | EMI 2361 |

BILLIE DAVIS
UK singer (born Carol Hedges, 1945, Woking, Surrey) who was a teenager when she featured on Mike Sarne's follow-up to his #1 *Come Outside*. Her solo hit debut was a cover of the Exciters' US smash.

30/08/1962	18	10		WILL I WHAT MIKE SARNE WITH BILLIE DAVIS	Parlophone R 4932
07/02/1963	10	12		**TELL HIM**	Decca F 11572
30/05/1963	40	3		HE'S THE ONE	Decca F 11658
09/10/1968	33	8		I WANT YOU TO BE MY BABY	Decca F 12823

BILLY DAVIS JR – see MARILYN McCOO AND BILLY DAVIS JR

DARLENE DAVIS
US singer/actress who appeared in the 1987 film *Jaws 4*.

| 07/02/1987 | 55 | 5 | | I FOUND LOVE | Serious 7OUS 1 |

JOHN DAVIS AND THE MONSTER ORCHESTRA
US singer/songwriter/producer/arranger (born 31/8/1952, Philadelphia, PA).

| 10/02/1979 | 70 | 2 | | AIN'T THAT ENOUGH FOR YOU | Miracle M 2 |

MAC DAVIS
US singer (born Mac Scott Davis, 21/1/1942, Lubbock, TX) who began as a sales rep for the Vee-Jay and Liberty labels, later writing *In The Ghetto* and *Don't Cry Daddy* for Elvis Presley, *Something's Burning* for Kenny Rogers and *You're Good For Me* for Lou Rawls. He also hosted his own TV show in the 1970s and appeared in a number of films, including *North Dallas Forty* (1979), *Cheaper To Keep Her* (1980) and *The Sting II* (1983). He has a star on the Hollywood Walk of Fame.

| 04/11/1972 | 29 | 6 | | BABY DON'T GET HOOKED ON ME ▲³ | CBS 8250 |
| 15/11/1980 | 27 | 16 | | IT'S HARD TO BE HUMBLE | Casablanca CAN 210 |

RICHIE DAVIS – see SHUT UP AND DANCE

ROY DAVIS JR FEATURING PEVEN EVERETT
US dance group fronted by producers Roy Davis Jr and Peven Everett, who sang lead on their debut hit. Earlier, Davis produced The Believers and the Radical Nomads, first recording solo in 1993.

| 01/11/1997 | 22 | 4 | | GABRIEL | XL Recordings XLS 88CD |
| 31/01/2004 | 70 | 1 | | ABOUT LOVE ROY DAVIS JR | Classic CMC21 |

RUTH DAVIS – see BO KIRKLAND AND RUTH DAVIS

SAMMY DAVIS JR
US singer/actor/dancer (born 8/12/1925, Harlem, NYC) who debuted at the age of three as 'Silent Sam, The Dancing Midget'. After World War II army service he appeared in countless Broadway, film and TV shows. A member of the infamous

---

●⁹ Number of weeks single topped the UK chart ⬆ Entered the UK chart at #1 ▲⁹ Number of weeks single topped the US chart

203

Rat Pack with Frank Sinatra and Dean Martin, he lost his left eye and broke his nose in a car crash in 1954 but was performing two months later. His films include *Anna Lucasta* (1949), *Porgy And Bess* (1959) and *Sweet Charity* (1969). He died from throat cancer on 16/5/1990. He has a star on the Hollywood Walk of Fame.

DATE	POS	WKS	BPI	SINGLE TITLE	LABEL & NUMBER
29/07/1955	11	7		SOMETHING'S GOTTA GIVE Featured in the films *Daddy Long Legs* (1955) and *What Women Want* (2000)	Brunswick 05428
09/09/1955	8	8		**LOVE ME OR LEAVE ME** B-side of *Something's Gotta Give* and featured in the 1955 film *Love Me Or Leave Me*	Brunswick 05428
30/09/1955	16	1		THAT OLD BLACK MAGIC	Brunswick 05450
07/10/1955	19	1		HEY THERE	Brunswick 05469
20/04/1956	28	1		IN A PERSIAN MARKET	Brunswick 05518
28/12/1956	28	1		ALL OF YOU	Brunswick 05629
16/06/1960	46	1		HAPPY TO MAKE YOUR ACQUAINTANCE SAMMY DAVIS JR AND CARMEN McRAE	Brunswick 05830
22/03/1962	26	8		WHAT KIND OF FOOL AM I?/GONNA BUILD A MOUNTAIN A-side from the musical *Stop The World I Want To Get Off*	Reprise R 20048
13/12/1962	20	9		ME AND MY SHADOW FRANK SINATRA AND SAMMY DAVIS JR	Reprise R 20128

SKEETER DAVIS US singer (born Mary Frances Penick, 30/12/1931, Dry Ridge, KY) who originally sang with Betty Jack Davis (born 3/3/1932, Corbin, TX). They were known as The Davis Sisters. Betty was killed in a car accident in August 1953. Seriously injured in the crash, Skeeter retired for several years. She was persuaded back to perform with Betty Jack's sister Georgia Davis before going solo in 1955. Barred from the Grand Ole Opry in 1974 after an on-stage tirade against Nashville's police (the ban was later lifted), she was one of the first black country performers to have crossed over to white audiences.). She died from breast cancer on 19/9/2004.

DATE	POS	WKS	BPI	SINGLE TITLE	LABEL & NUMBER
14/03/1963	18	13		END OF THE WORLD	RCA 1328

SPENCER DAVIS GROUP UK rock group formed in 1963 by Spencer Davis (born 14/7/1941, Swansea, guitar), Steve Winwood (born 12/5/1948, Birmingham, guitar/keyboards/vocals), his brother Mervin (known as 'Muff', after TV puppet Muffin The Mule, born 15/6/1943, Birmingham, bass) and Pete York (born 15/8/1942, Redcar, Cleveland, drums). Initially called The Muff-Woody Jazz Band, then Rhythm & Blues Quartet, they were signed by Island Records' Chris Blackwell, although the label was still developing and licensing its product to Fontana. Covers of US hits preceded their #1 charter *Keep On Running*, written by Blackwell protege, Jamaican Jackie Edwards. The group appeared in the 1966 film *The Ghost Goes Gear*. Steve Winwood left in 1967 to form Traffic, before going solo. Muff left the same year for band management, went on to produce (including Dire Straits' first album) and then became an A&R director with Island and CBS/Columbia. The group disbanded in 1969; Davis re-formed a Spencer Davis Group in 1990.

DATE	POS	WKS	BPI	SINGLE TITLE	LABEL & NUMBER
05/11/1964	47	3		I CAN'T STAND IT	Fontana TF 499
25/02/1965	41	3		EVERY LITTLE BIT HURTS	Fontana TF 530
10/06/1965	44	4		STRONG LOVE	Fontana TF 571
02/12/1965	●[1]	14		**KEEP ON RUNNING** Featured in the films *Buster* (1988) and *Mr Holland's Opus* (1997)	Fontana TF 632
24/03/1966	●[2]	10		**SOMEBODY HELP ME**	Fontana TF 679
01/09/1966	12	9		WHEN I COME HOME Featured in the 1966 film *The Ghost Goes Gear*	Fontana TF 739
03/11/1966	2	12		**GIMME SOME LOVING** Featured in the films *Striptease* (1996) and *Notting Hill* (1999)	Fontana TF 762
26/01/1967	9	7		**I'M A MAN**	Fontana TF 785
09/08/1967	30	5		TIME SELLER	Fontana TF 854
10/01/1968	35	4		MR SECOND CLASS	United Artists UP 1203

TJ DAVIS UK singer who also sang with Nylon, Sash! and Bjorn Again.

DATE	POS	WKS	BPI	SINGLE TITLE	LABEL & NUMBER
27/07/1996	72	1		BRILLIANT FEELING FULL MONTY ALLSTARS FEATURING TJ DAVIS	Arista 74321380902
29/12/2001	42	3		WONDERFUL LIFE	Melting Pot MPRCD 20

ZELMA DAVIS – see C&C MUSIC FACTORY

DAVIS PINCKNEY PROJECT – see GO GO LORENZO AND THE DAVIS PINCKNEY PROJECT

DAWN US vocal trio formed in New York City by Tony Orlando (born 3/4/1944, NYC). A solo singer between 1961 and 1963, Orlando was working at music publishers April-Blackwood when he formed Dawn with backing singers Telma Hopkins and Joyce Vincent. The group had their own TV show from 1974 to 1976, after which Orlando played the cabaret circuit while Hopkins appeared in various TV series.

DATE	POS	WKS	BPI	SINGLE TITLE	LABEL & NUMBER
16/01/1971	9	11		**CANDIDA**	Bell 1118
10/04/1971	●[5]	27		**KNOCK THREE TIMES** ▲[3] Featured in the 1996 film *Now And Then*	Bell 1146
31/07/1971	3	12		**WHAT ARE YOU DOING SUNDAY**	Bell 1169
10/03/1973	●[4]	40		**TIE A YELLOW RIBBON ROUND THE OLD OAK TREE** ▲[4] Symbolic with yellow ribbons being tied on trees across the US when the hostages returned from the US Embassy in Tehran in 1980. Featured in the 1994 film *Forrest Gump*	Bell 1287
04/08/1973	12	15		SAY, HAS ANYBODY SEEN MY SWEET GYPSY ROSE This and above two singles credited to DAWN FEATURING TONY ORLANDO	Bell 1322
09/03/1974	37	4		WHO'S IN THE STRAWBERRY PATCH WITH SALLY TONY ORLANDO AND DAWN	Bell 1343

JULIE DAWN – see CYRIL STAPLETON AND HIS ORCHESTRA

LIZ DAWN – see JOE LONGTHORNE

DAWN OF THE REPLICANTS UK group with Paul Vickers (vocals), Roger Simian (guitar), Donald Kyle (bass), Grant Pringle (drums) and Mike Small (various instruments).

DATE	POS	WKS	BPI	SINGLE TITLE	LABEL & NUMBER
07/02/1998	52	1		CANDLEFIRE	EastWest EW 147CD1
04/04/1998	65	1		HOGWASH FARM (THE DIESEL HANDS EP) Tracks on EP: *Hogwash Farm (Re-built)*, *Night Train To Lichtenstein*, *The Duchess Of Surin* and *Crow Valley*	EastWest EW 157CD

○ Silver disc ● Gold disc ✪ Platinum disc (additional platinum units are indicated by a figure following the symbol) ◎ Singles released prior to 1973 that are known to have sold over 1 million copies in the UK

DANA DAWSON US singer (born 7/8/1976, New York) who appeared in the Broadway production of *Annie* at eight, making her recording debut at fifteen. She also appeared in *Starlight: A Musical Movie* in 1988.

15/07/1995	9	8		3 IS FAMILY	EMI CDEM 378
28/10/1995	27	2		GOT TO GIVE ME LOVE	EMI CDEM 392
04/05/1996	28	3		SHOW ME	EMI CDEMS 423
20/07/1996	42	1		HOW I WANNA BE LOVED	EMI CDEMS 432

BOBBY DAY US singer (born Robert Byrd, 1/7/1930, Fort Worth, TX) who moved to Los Angeles, CA in 1948, forming the Hollywood Flames in 1950. He later teamed with fellow-Flame Earl Nelson as Bob & Earl, although Day had left before *Harlem Shuffle* was recorded. He died from cancer on 15/7/1990.

07/11/1958	29	2		ROCKIN' ROBIN Featured in the 1998 film *You've Got Mail*	London HL 8726

DARREN DAY UK singer (born 17/7/1968, Colchester, Essex) who is best known as the TV presenter of *You Bet*. He was also in the revival of the musical *Summer Holiday*.

08/10/1994	42	2		YOUNG GIRL	Bell 74321231082
08/06/1996	17	4		SUMMER HOLIDAY MEDLEY	RCA 74321384472
09/05/1998	71	1		HOW CAN I BE SURE?	Eastcoast DDCD 001

DORIS DAY US singer (born Doris Kappelhoff, 3/4/1922, Cincinnati, OH) who was initially a dancer but turned to singing after she broke her leg in a car crash at fourteen. First working with Bob Crosby, she became a star with the Les Brown band before going solo. Movies followed pop success, with her debut in the 1948 film *Romance On The High Sea* being the first of many, making her the #1 box office star of the 1950s and early 1960s. Her son Terry Melcher was a musician, producing The Beach Boys and The Byrds, and Day's last UK hit *Move Over Darling*. She has a star on the Hollywood Walk of Fame for her contribution to recording, and a second one for motion pictures.

14/11/1952	8	8		SUGARBUSH DORIS DAY AND FRANKIE LAINE	Columbia DB 3123
21/11/1952	10	2		MY LOVE AND DEVOTION	Columbia DB 3157
03/04/1953	12	1		MA SAYS PA SAYS	Columbia DB 3242
17/04/1953	11	1		FULL TIME JOB B-side to *Ma Says Pa Says*	Columbia DB 3242
24/07/1953	4	14		LET'S WALK THATA-WAY This and above two singles credited to DORIS DAY AND JOHNNIE RAY	Philips PB 157
02/04/1954	❶⁹	29		SECRET LOVE ▲⁴ Reclaimed #1 position on 7/5/1954	Philips PB 230
27/08/1954	7	8		BLACK HILLS OF DAKOTA Featured in the 1953 film *Calamity Jane*, starring Doris Day	Philips PB 287
01/10/1954	4	11		IF I GIVE MY HEART TO YOU DORIS DAY WITH THE MELLOMEN	Philips PB 325
08/04/1955	7	9		READY WILLING AND ABLE Featured in the 1954 film *Young At Heart*, starring Doris Day	Philips PB 402
09/09/1955	20	1		LOVE ME OR LEAVE ME Featured in the 1955 film *Love Me Or Leave Me*, starring Doris Day	Philips PB 479
21/10/1955	17	3		I'LL NEVER STOP LOVING YOU Featured in the 1955 film *Love Me Or Leave Me*, starring Doris Day	Philips PB 497
29/06/1956	❶⁶	22		WHATEVER WILL BE WILL BE Featured in the 1956 film *The Man Who Knew Too Much*, starring Doris Day	Philips PB 586
13/06/1958	16	11		A VERY PRECIOUS LOVE	Philips PB 799
15/08/1958	25	4		EVERYBODY LOVES A LOVER	Philips PB 843
12/03/1964	8	16		MOVE OVER DARLING Featured in the 1964 film *Move Over Darling*, starring Doris Day	CBS AAG 183
18/04/1987	45	6		MOVE OVER DARLING Re-issue of CBS AAG 183 and revived after being used in a TV advertisement for Pretty Polly tights	CBS LEGS 1

INAYA DAY US singer (born Inya Davis, New York City) who graduated from the University of Bridgeport in musical theatre.

22/05/1999	39	2		JUST CAN'T GET ENOUGH HARRY 'CHOO CHOO' ROMERO PRESENTS INAYA DAY	AM:PM CDAMPM 121
07/10/2000	51	1		FEEL IT	Positiva CDTIV 141

PATTI DAY US singer (born in Washington DC).

09/12/1989	69	1		RIGHT BEFORE MY EYES	Debut DEBT 3080

DAY ONE UK electronic duo formed in Bristol, Avon by Phelim Byrne (vocals) and Donni Hardwidge (all instruments). They were signed by Massive Attack's Melankolic label via a three-song demo sent to 3D.

13/11/1999	68	1		I'M DOIN' FINE	Melankolic/Virgin SADD6

DAYEENE Swedish vocal duo, sisters Diane and Jeanette Soderholm.

17/07/1999	63	1		AND IT HURTS	Pukka CDPUKKA 20

TAYLOR DAYNE US singer (born Leslie Wunderman, 7/3/1963, Baldwin, NY). Debuting at the age of six, she was in rock groups Felony and Next before signing solo with Arista in 1987.

23/01/1988	3	13		TELL IT TO MY HEART	Arista 109616
19/03/1988	8	10		PROVE YOUR LOVE	Arista 109830
11/06/1988	41	7		I'LL ALWAYS LOVE YOU	Arista 111536
18/11/1989	53	2		WITH EVERY BEAT OF MY HEART	Arista 112760
14/04/1990	43	5		I'LL BE YOUR SHELTER	Arista 112996
04/08/1990	69	1		LOVE WILL LEAD YOU BACK ▲¹	Arista 113277
03/07/1993	14	8		CAN'T GET ENOUGH OF YOUR LOVE	Arista 74321147852
16/04/1994	29	3		I'LL WAIT	Arista 74321203472
04/02/1995	63	1		ORIGINAL SIN (THEME FROM 'THE SHADOW')	Arista 74321223462
18/11/1995	58	1		SAY A PRAYER	Arista 74321324292
13/01/1996	23	3		TELL IT TO MY HEART Re-issue of Arista 109616	Arista 74321335962

❶⁹ Number of weeks single topped the UK chart ↑ Entered the UK chart at #1 ▲⁹ Number of weeks single topped the US chart

205

DAYTON US funk group formed in Ohio by Jenny Douglas (vocals), Rachel Beavers (vocals), David Shawn Sandridge (guitar/vocals), Chris Jones (guitar/vocals), Derrick Armstrong (bass), Dean Hummons (keyboards) and Kevin Hurt (drums). They later added Rahni Harris (keyboards/vocals) to the line-up.

10/12/1983.....75......1....... THE SOUND OF MUSIC .... Capitol CL 318

DAZZ BAND US group formed by Bobby Harris (saxophone/vocals), Pierre Demudd (trumpet/vocals), Keith Harrison (keyboards/vocals), Sennie 'Skip' Martin II (trumpet/vocals), Eric Fearman (guitar), Marlon McClain (guitar), Kevin Kendrick (keyboards), Kenny Pettus (percussion/vocals), Isaac Wiley Jr (drums), Michael Wiley (bass) and Juan Lively (lead vocals) as jazz band Bell Telephunk. They signed with 20th Century as Kingsman Dazz, becoming the Dazz Band upon signing for Motown. They later recorded for Geffen and RCA. They won the 1982 Grammy Award for Best Rhythm & Blues Vocal Performance by a Group for *Let It Whip*.

03/11/1984.....12.....12...... LET IT ALL BLOW .... Motown TMG 1361

DB BOULEVARD Italian production group formed by Roxy, Azzetto and Broggio with singer Moony. Their debut hit was recorded almost a year before release but, with large portions of *Heatwave* by French group Phoenix, it was only released after lengthy negotiations.

23/02/2002 .....3......12 ...... **POINT OF VIEW** .... Illustrious CDILL 002

DBM German studio group.

12/11/1977.....45......3....... DISCO BEATLEMANIA .... Atlantic K 11027

D, B, M AND T UK group formed by Dozy (born Trevor Davies, 27/11/1944, Enford, bass), Beaky (born John Dymond, 10/7/1944, Salisbury, guitar), Mick (born Michael Wilson, 4/3/1944, Amesbury, drums) and Tich (born Ian Amey, 15/5/1944, Salisbury, lead guitar), recording without their lead singer Dave Dee.

01/08/1970.....33......8....... MR PRESIDENT... Fontana 6007 022

D'BORA US singer (born Deborah Walker) based in Brooklyn, NYC who was with the Freestyle Orchestra before signing solo with the Vibe label in 1991.

14/09/1991.....75......1....... DREAM ABOUT YOU .... Polydor PO 161
01/07/1995.....40......2...... GOING ROUND. .... Vibe MCSTD 2055
30/03/1996.....58......1....... GOOD LOVE REAL LOVE .... Music Plant MCSTD 40023

NINO DE ANGELO German singer (born Namen Domenico Gerhard Gorgoglione, 18/12/1963).

21/07/1984.....57......5....... GUARDIAN ANGEL... Carrere CAR 335

DE BOS Dutch DJ/producer (born Andre Van Den Bosch, 4/1/1973).

25/10/1997.....51......1....... ON THE RUN .... Jive JIVECD 433

CHRIS DE BURGH UK singer (born Christopher Davidson, 15/10/1948, Buenos Aires, Argentina) who graduated from Trinity College in Dublin and toured Eire with Horslips, before developing as a singer/songwriter while helping run his family's 12th-century hotel in Ireland. Signing with A&M in 1974, he released his debut album the following year. His daughter, Rosanna Davison, was named Miss World in 2003.

23/10/1982.....48......5...... DON'T PAY THE FERRYMAN .... A&M AMS 8256
12/05/1984.....44......5...... HIGH ON EMOTION .... A&M AM 190
12/07/1986 ... ❶³ ... 15 ... ● **THE LADY IN RED** Featured in the 1988 film *Working Girl* .... A&M AM 331
20/09/1986.....44......4...... FATAL HESITATION. .... A&M AM 346
13/12/1986.....40......5...... A SPACEMAN CAME TRAVELLING/THE BALLROOM OF ROMANCE .... A&M AM 365
12/12/1987.....55......3...... THE SIMPLE TRUTH (A CHILD IS BORN) .... A&M AM 427
29/10/1988.....3......12...... **MISSING YOU** .... A&M AM 474
07/01/1989.....43......6...... TENDER HANDS .... A&M AM 486
14/10/1989.....59......3...... THIS WAITING HEART .... A&M AM 528
25/05/1991.....36......2...... THE SIMPLE TRUTH (A CHILD IS BORN) Re-issue of A&M AM 427 for the Red Cross campaign for Kurdish refugees..... A&M RELF 1
11/04/1992.....30......4...... SEPARATE TABLES .... A&M AM 863
21/05/1994.....51......1...... BLONDE HAIR BLUE JEANS.. A&M 5805932
09/12/1995.....60......1...... THE SNOWS OF NEW YORK .... A&M 5813132
27/09/1997.....29......4...... SO BEAUTIFUL .... A&M 5823932
18/09/1999.....59......1...... WHEN I THINK OF YOU .... A&M 4971302

DE CASTRO SISTERS WITH SKIP MARTIN AND HIS ORCHESTRA US family trio Peggy, Babette and Cherie DeCastro, all raised on the family sugar plantation in Cuba.

11/02/1955.....20......1...... TEACH ME TONIGHT .... London HL 8104

DE-CODE FEATURING BEVERLI SKEETE UK vocal/instrumental group. Skeete was previously a member of Gat Decor.

18/05/1996.....69......1....... WONDERWALL/SOME MIGHT SAY .... Neoteric NRCD 2

ETIENNE DE CRECY French DJ/producer (born in Lyon) who also recorded as Super Discount.

28/03/1998.....60......1....... PRIX CHOC REMIXES .... Different DIF 007CD
20/01/2001.....44......2....... AM I WRONG Contains a sample of Millie Jackson's *If Loving You Is Wrong (I Don't Want To Be Right)* . XL Recordings XLS 127CD

○ Silver disc ● Gold disc ✪ Platinum disc (additional platinum units are indicated by a figure following the symbol) ◉ Singles released prior to 1973 that are known to have sold over 1 million copies in the UK

DE FUNK FEATURING F45 UK/Italian production group formed by Marc Williams, Andrew Tumi, Panos Liassi and Mr Jones.

| 25/09/1999 | 49 | 1 | | PLEASURE LOVE Contains a sample of Earth, Wind & Fire's *September* | INCredible INCS 3CD |

LENNIE DE ICE UK drum and bass producer.

| 17/04/1999 | 61 | 1 | | WE ARE I. E. | Distinctive DISNCD 50 |

DE LA SOUL US rap trio from Amityville, Long Island, NY formed by Kelvin Mercer (born 17/8/1969, Brooklyn, NYC), Vincent Mason Jr (born 24/3/1970, Brooklyn) and David Jolicoeur (born 21/9/1968, Brooklyn) as The Monkeys Of Hip Hop. They adopted stage names Posdnous (Mercer), PA Pacemaker Mase (Mason) and Trugoy The Dove (Jolicoeur).

08/04/1989	22	8		ME MYSELF AND I Contains a sample of Funkadelic's *(Not Just) Knee Deep*	Big Life BLR 7
08/07/1989	18	7		SAY NO GO	Big Life BLR 10
21/10/1989	14	7		EYE KNOW Contains a sample of Otis Redding's *(Sittin' On) The Dock Of The Bay*	Big Life BLR 13
23/12/1989	7	8		**THE MAGIC NUMBER/BUDDY**	Big Life BLR 14
24/03/1990	14	7		MAMA GAVE BIRTH TO THE SOUL CHILDREN QUEEN LATIFAH + DE LA SOUL	Gee Street GEE 26
27/04/1991	10	7		**RING RING RING (HA HA HEY)** Contains samples of The Whatnauts' *Help Is On The Way* and The JB's *Pass The Peas*	Big Life BLR 42
03/08/1991	22	5		A ROLLER SKATING JAM NAMED 'SATURDAYS' Contains a sample of Frankie Valli's *Grease*	Big Life BLR 55
23/11/1991	50	2		KEEPIN' THE FAITH	Big Life BLR 64
18/09/1993	39	3		BREAKADAWN Contains samples of Michael Jackson's *I Can't Help*, The Bar-Kays' *Song And Dance* and Smokey Robinson's *Quiet Storm*	Big Life BLRD 103
02/04/1994	59	1		FALLIN' TEENAGE FANCLUB AND DE LA SOUL Contains a sample of Tom Petty's *Free Fallin'*. Featured in the 1994 film *Judgement Night*	Epic 6602622
29/06/1996	55	1		STAKES IS HIGH	Tommy Boy TBCD 7730
08/03/1997	52	1		4 MORE	Tommy Boy TBCD 7779A
22/07/2000	29	2		OOOH DE LA SOUL FEATURING REDMAN Contains an interpolation of Run DMC's *Together Forever*	Tommy Boy TBCD 2102B
11/11/2000	33	3		ALL GOOD DE LA SOUL FEATURING CHAKA KHAN	Tommy Boy TBCD 2154B
02/03/2002	55	1		BABY PHAT	Tommy Boy TBCD 2359B

DONNA DE LORY US singer (born in Los Angeles, CA) who moved to Nashville when she was fifteen. Returning to LA, she joined Madonna's touring group as a backing singer and dancer.

| 24/07/1993 | 71 | 1 | | JUST A DREAM | MCA MCSTD 1750 |

WALDO DE LOS RIOS Argentinian orchestra leader (born Osvaldo Ferraro Guiterrez) who composed *South American Suite* and the music to many films, including *Murders In The Rue Morgue* (1971), *Bad Man's River* (1972) and *La Espada Negra* (1976). He committed suicide on 28/3/1977.

| 10/04/1971 | 5 | 16 | | **MOZART SYMPHONY NO. 40 IN G MINOR K550 1ST MOVEMENT (ALLEGRO MOLTO)** | A&M AMS 836 |

VINCENT DE MOOR Dutch producer (born 1973, Delft) who began recording as Fix To Fax and is also in Veracocha with Ferry Corsten.

| 16/08/1997 | 54 | 1 | | FLOWTATION | XL Recordings XLS 89CD |
| 07/04/2001 | 30 | 3 | | FLY AWAY | VC Recordings VCRD 87 |

DE NADA UK dance group from Southampton comprising Justin, Alistair and singer Nadia.

| 25/08/2001 | 15 | 4 | | LOVE YOU ANYWAY | Wildstar CDWILD 37 |
| 09/02/2002 | 24 | 3 | | BRING IT ON TO MY LOVE | Wildstar CDWILD 39 |

DE NUIT Italian production duo Francesco De Leo and Fabio Seveso.

| 23/11/2002 | 38 | 2 | | ALL THAT MATTERED (LOVE YOU DOWN) | Credence CDCRED 029 |

LYNSEY DE PAUL UK singer/songwriter (born Lynsey Rubin, 11/6/1950, London) whose chart debut was as co-writer, with Barry Blue, of the Fortunes' *Storm In A Teacup*; the two also penned hits for each other. Later teamed with producer Mike Moran, she co-wrote the 1977 Eurovision Song Contest entry *Rock Bottom*.

19/08/1972	5	11		**SUGAR ME**	MAM 81
02/12/1972	18	8		GETTING A DRAG	MAM 88
27/10/1973	14	7		WON'T SOMEBODY DANCE WITH ME	MAM 109
08/06/1974	25	6		OOH I DO	Warner Brothers K 16401
02/11/1974	7	11		**NO HONESTLY** Theme to the TV series of the same name	Jet 747
22/03/1975	40	4		MY MAN AND ME	Jet 750
26/03/1977	19	7		ROCK BOTTOM LYNSEY DE PAUL AND MIKE MORAN UK entry for the 1977 Eurovision Song Contest, coming second to the French entry *L'Oiseau Et L'Enfant* by Marie Myriam	Polydor 2058 859

TULLIO DE PISCOPO Italian singer/drummer who later formed the Nuova Accademia Music Media giving percussion courses.

| 28/02/1987 | 58 | 4 | | STOP BAJON...PRIMAVERA | Greyhound GREY 9 |

REBECCA DE RUVO Swedish singer who had previously been a DJ on MTV.

| 01/10/1994 | 72 | 1 | | I CAUGHT YOU OUT | Arista 74321230782 |

TERI DE SARIO US singer (born in Miami, FL) who later worked with KC of KC & The Sunshine Band.

| 02/09/1978 | 52 | 5 | | AIN'T NOTHING GONNA KEEP ME FROM YOU | Casablanca CAN 128 |

❶⁹ Number of weeks single topped the UK chart ↑ Entered the UK chart at #1 ▲⁹ Number of weeks single topped the US chart

207

STEPHANIE DE SYKES
UK singer (born Stephanie Ryton) who was first seen widely on TV's *Opportunity Knocks*. She also recorded as Debbie Stanford. Later a top session singer and writer, she penned the UK's entry for the 1978 Eurovision Song Contest by Co-Co. Her son Toby Slater fronts Catch.

20/07/1974	2	10	O	**BORN WITH A SMILE ON MY FACE** STEPHANIE DE SYKES WITH RAIN .... Bradley's BRAD 7409
19/04/1975	17	7		WE'LL FIND OUR DAY .... Bradley's BRAD 7509

WILLIAM DE VAUGHN
US R&B singer/songwriter/guitarist (born 1948, Washington DC) who worked for the federal government and was a Jehovah's Witness. He recorded the self-penned *Be Thankful For What You've Got* in Philadelphia, PA in 1974, accompanied by core members of MFSB. It was released on Roxbury in the US and he later recorded for TEC and Excalibur.

06/07/1974	31	5	BE THANKFUL FOR WHAT YOU'VE GOT Featured in the 2004 film *Scooby Doo 2: Monsters Unleashed* .... Chelsea 2005 002
20/09/1980	44	5	BE THANKFUL FOR WHAT YOU'VE GOT Re-recording of Chelsea 2005 002 .... EMI 5101

TONY DE VIT
UK singer (born 12/9/1957, Kidderminster) who began as a DJ before remixing and producing. He launched the Jump Wax label and died from an AIDs-related disease on 2/7/1998.

04/03/1995	25	3	BURNING UP .... Icon ICONCD 001
12/08/1995	28	2	HOOKED 99TH FLOOR ELEVATORS FEATURING TONY DE VIT .... Labello Dance LAD 18CD
09/09/1995	44	2	TO THE LIMIT .... X:Plode BANG 1CD
30/03/1996	37	2	I'LL BE THERE 99TH FLOOR ELEVATORS FEATURING TONY DE VIT .... Labello Dance LAD 25CD2
28/10/2000	56	2	DAWN .... Tidy Trax TIDY 140CD
21/12/2002	65	1	I DON'T CARE .... Tidy Trax TIDY 181T
12/07/2003	53	1	GIVE ME A REASON TONY DE VIT FEATURING NIKI MAK .... Tidy Two 123C

DEACON BLUE
UK rock group formed in Scotland in 1985 by Ricky Ross (born 22/12/1957, Dundee, vocals), James Prime (born 3/11/1960, Kilmarnock, keyboards), Douglas Vipond (born 15/10/1966, Johnstone, drums/percussion), Graeme Kelling (born 4/4/1957, Paisley, guitar) and Ewan Vernal (born 27/2/1964, Glasgow, bass/keyboards/bass), with Ross' girlfriend and future wife Lorraine McIntosh (born 13/5/1964, Glasgow) joining in 1987. The group took their name from a song by Steely Dan. Ricky Ross later went solo; Kelling died after a lengthy illness on 10/6/2004.

23/01/1988	31	8	DIGNITY Originally released in March 1987 and failed to chart. Charted version is a remix .... CBS DEAC 4
09/04/1988	34	7	WHEN WILL YOU MAKE MY TELEPHONE RING .... CBS DEAC 5
16/07/1988	43	7	CHOCOLATE GIRL .... CBS DEAC 6
15/10/1988	8	13	**REAL GONE KID** .... CBS DEAC 7
04/03/1989	18	6	WAGES DAY .... CBS DEAC 8
20/05/1989	14	6	FERGUS SINGS THE BLUES .... CBS DEAC 9
16/09/1989	28	5	LOVE AND REGRET .... CBS DEAC 10
06/01/1990	21	5	QUEEN OF THE NEW YEAR .... CBS DEAC 11
25/08/1990	2	9	**FOUR BACHARACH AND DAVID SONGS EP**: Tracks on EP: *I'll Never Fall In Love Again, The Look Of Love, Message To Michael* and *Are You There (With Another Girl)* .... CBS DEAC 12
25/05/1991	23	4	YOUR SWAYING ARMS .... Columbia 6568937
27/07/1991	10	9	**TWIST AND SHOUT** .... Columbia 6573027
12/10/1991	42	3	CLOSING TIME .... Columbia 6575027
14/12/1991	31	4	COVER FROM THE SKY .... Columbia 6576737
28/11/1992	14	8	YOUR TOWN .... Columbia 6587867
13/02/1993	31	4	WILL WE BE LOVERS .... Columbia 6589732
24/04/1993	22	4	ONLY TENDER LOVE .... Columbia 6591842
17/07/1993	21	3	HANG YOUR HEAD .... Columbia 6594602
02/04/1994	32	3	I WAS RIGHT AND YOU WERE WRONG .... Columbia 6602222
28/05/1994	20	3	DIGNITY Original version of CBS DEAC 4, first released in 1987 .... Columbia 6604485
28/04/2001	64	1	EVERYTIME YOU SLEEP .... Papillon BTFLY 0011

DEAD DRED
UK production duo Lee Smith and Warren Smith.

05/11/1994	60	2	DRED BASS .... Moving Shadow SHADOW 50CD

DEAD END KIDS
UK pop group formed in Glasgow by Alistair Kerr, Colin Ivory, Davey Johnston, Ricky Squires and Robbie Gray, produced by Barry Blue.

26/03/1977	6	10	**HAVE I THE RIGHT** .... CBS 4972

DEAD KENNEDYS
US punk group formed in San Francisco, CA in 1977 by Jello Biafra (born Eric Boujet, 17/6/1958, Boulder, CO, vocals), East Bay Ray (born Ray Glasser, Castro Valley, CA, guitar), Klaus Flurodie (born in Detroit, MI, bass) and Bruce 'Ted' Slesinger (drums). Darren Peligro (born in East St Louis, IL) replaced Slesinger in 1982. Their debut single *California Uber Alles*, an attack on California Governor Jerry Brown, was banned by many stores, equally offended by the group's name. Many US and UK shops refused to stock their *Frankenchrist* album because of the cover. Biafra, who was charged under obscenity laws, stood for election as San Francisco mayor, finishing fourth out of ten. Later recording solo, in 1994 he had both legs broken by members of the audience, who accused him of 'selling out'.

01/11/1980	49	3	KILL THE POOR .... Cherry Red CHERRY 16
30/05/1981	36	6	TOO DRUNK TO FUCK .... Cherry Red CHERRY 24

DEAD OR ALIVE
UK group formed in Liverpool in 1979 by Pete Burns (born 5/8/1959, Liverpool, lead singer) as Nightmares In Wax, the name changing to Dead Or Alive in 1980. When they charted the remaining three members comprised Timothy Lever (born 21/5/1960, keyboards), Michael Percy (born 11/3/1961, bass) and Stephen McCoy (born 15/3/1962, drums), Burns having gone through over 30 musicians, including Wayne Hussey, later of Sisters Of Mercy and Mission.

24/03/1984	22	9		THAT'S THE WAY (I LIKE IT)	Epic A 4271
01/12/1984	❶²	23	●	**YOU SPIN ME ROUND (LIKE A RECORD)** Featured in the 1998 film *The Wedding Singer*	Epic A 4861
20/04/1985	11	8		LOVER COME BACK TO ME	Epic A 6086
29/06/1985	14	8		IN TOO DEEP	Epic A 6360
21/09/1985	23	6		MY HEART GOES BANG (GET ME TO THE DOCTOR)	Epic A 6571
20/09/1986	31	4		BRAND NEW LOVER	Epic 6500757
10/01/1987	12	7		SOMETHING IN MY HOUSE	Epic BURNS 1
04/04/1987	69	2		HOOKED ON LOVE	Epic BURNS 2
03/09/1988	70	1		TURN AROUND AND COUNT 2 TEN	Epic BURNS 4
22/07/1989	62	2		COME HOME WITH ME BABY	Epic BURNS 5
17/05/2003	23	3		YOU SPIN ME ROUND Remix of Epic A 4861	Epic 6735785

DEAD PREZ US rap duo Lavon Alford and Clayton Gavin from Brooklyn, NYC.

| 11/03/2000 | 41 | 2 | | HIP HOP | Epic 6689862 |

DEAD 60'S UK group formed in Liverpool by Matt McManamon (guitar/vocals), Charlie Turner (bass), Ben Gordon (keyboards) and Bryan Johnson (drums).

| 16/10/2004 | 30 | 2 | | RIOT RADIO | Deltasonic DLTCD025 |

DEADLY SINS UK/Italian duo Michele Comis and Walter Cremonini.

| 30/04/1994 | 45 | 2 | | WE ARE GOING ON DOWN | ffrreedom TABCD 220 |

HAZELL DEAN UK singer (born 27/10/1958, Chelmsford, Essex) who began her career by fronting various groups. In the early 1980s she attempted to represent the UK in the Eurovision Song Contest and first recorded for Proto in 1983.

18/02/1984	63	3		EVERGREEN/JEALOUS LOVE	Proto ENA 114
21/04/1984	6	15		**SEARCHIN' (I GOTTA FIND A MAN)** Originally released in June 1983 and failed to chart	Proto ENA 109
28/07/1984	4	11		**WHATEVER I DO (WHEREVER I GO)**	Proto ENA 119
03/11/1984	41	4		BACK IN MY ARMS (ONCE AGAIN)	Proto ENA 122
02/03/1985	41	5		NO FOOL (FOR LOVE)	Proto ENA 123
12/10/1985	58	4		THEY SAY IT'S GONNA RAIN	Parlophone R 6107
02/04/1988	4	11		**WHO'S LEAVING WHO**	EMI EM 45
25/06/1988	15	6		MAYBE (WE SHOULD CALL IT A DAY)	EMI EM 62
24/09/1988	21	7		TURN IT INTO LOVE	EMI EM 71
26/08/1989	48	4		LOVE PAINS	Lisson DOLE 12
23/03/1991	72	1		BETTER OFF WITHOUT YOU	Lisson DOLE 19

JIMMY DEAN US country singer (born Seth Ward, 10/8/1928, Plainview, TX) who made his US chart debut with the Wildcats, and also recorded with the Tennessee Haymakers. He had his own TV series from 1957 to 1958, and also from 1963 to 1966. He retired from music in the mid-1970s; his business interests included a line of pork sausages.

| 26/10/1961 | 2 | 13 | | **BIG BAD JOHN** ▲⁵ 1961 Grammy Award for Best Country & Western Recording, the first song Dean ever wrote | Philips PB 1187 |
| 08/11/1962 | 33 | 4 | | LITTLE BLACK BOOK | CBS AAG 122 |

LETITIA DEAN AND PAUL MEDFORD UK actors from the hit soap *Eastenders*, playing the roles of Sharon Watts/Mitchell and Kelvin Carpenter. Dean (born 14/11/1967, Potters Bar) and Medford (born 1967, London) performed their hit as 'The Banned' in the TV series.

| 25/10/1986 | 12 | 7 | | SOMETHING OUTA NOTHING | BBC RESL 203 |

SHERYL DEANE – see **THRILLSEEKERS**

DEANNA – see **DAVID MORALES**

DEAR JON UK vocal/instrumental group whose debut hit – written by leukaemia sufferer Graeme Watson – was first aired in the UK 'Song For Europe' competition, coming second to Gina G.

| 22/04/1995 | 68 | 1 | | ONE GIFT OF LOVE | MDMC DEVCS 2 |

DEARS Canadian group formed in Montreal in 1995 by Murray Lightburn.

| 20/11/2004 | 49 | 1 | | LOST IN THE PLOT | Bella Union BELLACD86 |

DEATH FROM ABOVE 1979 Canadian duo formed in Toronto by Sebastien Grainger (drums/vocals) and Jesse F Keeler (bass/keyboards).

| 13/11/2004 | 57 | 1 | | ROMANTIC RIGHTS | 679 679L090CD |

DEATH IN VEGAS UK production duo formed in 1995 by Richard Fearless and Steve Hellier as Dead Elvis. Hellier left in 1997 and was replaced by Tim Holmes.

02/08/1997	61	1		DIRT	Concrete HARD 27CD
01/11/1997	51	1		ROCCO	Concrete HARD 29CD
12/02/2000	9	4		**AISHA** Features the uncredited contribution of Iggy Pop	Concrete HARD 43CD
06/05/2000	24	2		DIRGE	Concrete HARD 44CD
21/09/2002	36	1		HANDS AROUND MY THROAT	Concrete HARD 48CD

❶⁹ Number of weeks single topped the UK chart ↑ Entered the UK chart at #1 ▲⁹ Number of weeks single topped the US chart

209

DATE	POS	WKS	BPI	SINGLE TITLE	LABEL & NUMBER
28/12/2002	14	8		SCORPIO RISING **DEATH IN VEGAS FEATURING LIAM GALLAGHER** Contains a sample of Status Quo's *Pictures Of Matchstick Men* . .	Concrete HARD 54CD

DeBARGE US family group formed in Los Angeles, CA by brothers Eldra (born 4/6/1961, Grand Rapids, MI, keyboards/vocals), James (keyboards/vocals), Randy (bass/vocals), Mark (trumpet/saxophone/vocals) and sister Bunny DeBarge (vocals). They formed as Switch with elder brothers Bobby and Tommy as members, signing with Motown as DeBarge in 1982. Eldra (El) and Bunny and a further brother Chico (born Jonathan DeBarge, 1966, Grand Rapids) later recorded solo albums for Motown, while James eloped with the youngest member of the family DeBarge were hoping to emulate: Janet Jackson. Bobby died from AIDS on 16/8/1995.

DATE	POS	WKS	BPI	SINGLE TITLE	LABEL & NUMBER
06/04/1985	4	14		**RHYTHM OF THE NIGHT** Featured in the 1984 film *The Last Dragon*	Gordy TMG 1376
21/09/1985	54	3		YOU WEAR IT WELL **EL DEBARGE WITH DEBARGE**	Gordy ZB 40345

CHICO DeBARGE US singer (born Jonathan DeBarge, 1966, Grand Rapids, MI) who was a member of the DeBarge family, who also enjoyed singing success.

DATE	POS	WKS	BPI	SINGLE TITLE	LABEL & NUMBER
14/03/1998	50	1		IGGIN' ME	Universal UND 56170

EL DeBARGE US singer (born Eldra DeBarge, 4/6/1961, Grand Rapids, MI) who was a member of the family group DeBarge before going solo.

DATE	POS	WKS	BPI	SINGLE TITLE	LABEL & NUMBER
21/09/1985	54	3		YOU WEAR IT WELL **EL DEBARGE WITH DEBARGE**	Gordy ZB 40345
28/06/1986	60	2		WHO'S JOHNNY ('SHORT CIRCUIT' THEME) Featured in the 1986 film *Short Circuit*	Gordy ELD 1
31/03/1990	67	1		SECRET GARDEN **QUINCY JONES FEATURING AL B SURE!, JAMES INGRAM, EL DEBARGE AND BARRY WHITE** Featured in the 1997 film *Sprung*	Qwest W 9992

DIANA DECKER US singer (born 1926) was was primarily an actress. Her films include *San Demetrio, London* (1943), *Is Your Honeymoon Really Necessary* (1952), *The Barefoot Contessa* (1954) and the UK TV series *Mark Saber*.

DATE	POS	WKS	BPI	SINGLE TITLE	LABEL & NUMBER
23/10/1953	2	10		**POPPA PICCOLINO**	Columbia DB 3325

DECLAN FEATURING THE YOUNG VOICES CHOIR UK singer Declan Galbraith, who was ten years old at the time of his debut hit.

DATE	POS	WKS	BPI	SINGLE TITLE	LABEL & NUMBER
21/12/2002	29	4		TELL ME WHY	Liberty CDDECS 004

DECOY AND ROY Belgian dance group formed by DJs Decoy (born Danny Van Wauwe) and Roy (Roy Van Luffelen) with producer Tim Janssens.

DATE	POS	WKS	BPI	SINGLE TITLE	LABEL & NUMBER
01/02/2003	45	1		INNER LIFE	Data/Ministry Of Sound/Heat DATA 43CDS

DAVE DEE UK singer (born David Harman, 17/12/1943, Salisbury) who was lead singer with Dave Dee, Dozy, Beaky, Mick & Tich before he left to go solo in 1969, subsequently becoming A&R director at WEA.

DATE	POS	WKS	BPI	SINGLE TITLE	LABEL & NUMBER
14/03/1970	42	4		MY WOMAN'S MAN	Fontana TF 1074

DAVE DEE, DOZY, BEAKY, MICK AND TICH UK group formed in Salisbury in 1961 by Dave Dee (born David Harman, 17/12/1943, Salisbury, lead vocals), Dozy (born Trevor Davies, 27/11/1944, Enford, bass), Beaky (born John Dymond, 10/7/1944, Salisbury, guitar) and Tich (born Ian Amey, 15/5/1944, Salisbury, lead guitar) as Dave Dee And The Bostons, with Mick (born Michael Wilson, 4/3/1944, Amesbury) joining at the end of the year. The name change in 1964 was suggested by managers Ken Howard and Alan Blaikley (who also managed the Honeycombs). Their debut single was released in 1965. Dee went solo 1969 and was later A&R director at WEA. After one hit single as D,B,M & T, the remaining group disbanded in 1970. Briefly reunited in 1974 and 1982, D,B,M & T still play the nostalgia circuit.

DATE	POS	WKS	BPI	SINGLE TITLE	LABEL & NUMBER
23/12/1965	26	8		YOU MAKE IT MOVE	Fontana TF 630
03/03/1966	4	17		**HOLD TIGHT**	Fontana TF 671
09/06/1966	10	11		**HIDEAWAY**	Fontana TF 711
15/09/1966	2	12		**BEND IT**	Fontana TF 746
08/12/1966	3	10		**SAVE ME**	Fontana TF 775
09/03/1967	13	9		TOUCH ME TOUCH ME	Fontana TF 798
18/05/1967	4	11		**OKAY!**	Fontana TF 830
11/10/1967	3	14		**ZABADAK!**	Fontana TF 873
14/02/1968	❶[1]	12		**THE LEGEND OF XANADU**	Fontana TF 903
03/07/1968	8	11		**LAST NIGHT IN SOHO**	Fontana TF 953
02/10/1968	14	9		WRECK OF THE ANTOINETTE	Fontana TF 971
05/03/1969	23	9		DON JUAN	Fontana TF 1000
14/05/1969	23	8		SNAKE IN THE GRASS	Fontana TF 1020

NANCY DEE – see **BENELUX FEATURING NANCY DEE**

DEE DEE Belgian singer Diana Trippaers, produced by Christophe Chantiz and Erik Vanspauwen, the team behind Ian Van Dahl.

DATE	POS	WKS	BPI	SINGLE TITLE	LABEL & NUMBER
20/07/2002	12	7		FOREVER	Incentive CENT 43CDS
01/03/2003	28	2		THE ONE	Incentive CENT 52CDX

JAZZY DEE US rapper Darren Williams.

DATE	POS	WKS	BPI	SINGLE TITLE	LABEL & NUMBER
05/03/1983	53	5		GET ON UP	Laurie LRS 101

JOEY DEE AND THE STARLITERS US singer (born Joseph DiNicola, 11/6/1940, Passaic, NJ) who became the leader of the Starliters (Carlton Latimer on keyboards, Willie Davis on drums, Larry Vernierl and David Brigati on backing vocals) in 1960. They

secured a residency at New York's Peppermint Lounge, which was the centre of the twist craze, hence the title of their only UK hit. Later members of the Starliters included three future Young Rascals and Jimi Hendrix.

08/02/1962.....33......8...... PEPPERMINT TWIST ▲³ Featured in the films *American Graffiti* (1973) and *Andre* (1995) .... Columbia DB 4758

KIKI DEE
UK singer (born Pauline Matthews, 6/3/1947, Yorkshire) who recorded soul covers from 1963 and was the first white UK artist to sign for the Motown label. She signed with Elton John's Rocket Records in 1973, where Anne Orson and Carte Blanche provided most of her material (pseudonyms of John and co-writer Bernie Taupin). Originally intended for a cover version of the Four Tops' *Loving You Is Sweeter Than Ever,* her collaboration with Elton John on a John/Taupin original became a UK and US #1. She later appeared in stage in musicals, such as *Pump Boys And Dinettes,* and was nominated for a Laurence Olivier Award for her role in the stage musical *Blood Brothers.*

10/11/1973.....13.....13......	AMOUREUSE .... Rocket PIG 4
07/09/1974.....19.....8......	I GOT THE MUSIC IN ME .... Rocket PIG 12
12/04/1975.....33.....4......	(YOU DON'T KNOW) HOW GLAD I AM This and above single credited to KIKI DEE BAND .... Rocket PIG 16
03/07/1976 ...❶⁶.....14.....●	**DON'T GO BREAKING MY HEART** ▲⁴ **ELTON JOHN AND KIKI DEE** .... Rocket ROKN 512
11/09/1976.....13.....8......	LOVING AND FREE/AMOUREUSE .... Rocket ROKN 515
19/02/1977.....32.....5......	FIRST THING IN THE MORNING .... Rocket ROKN 520
11/06/1977.....28.....4......	CHICAGO Flip side was *Bite Your Lip (Get Up And Dance)* by **ELTON JOHN** .... Rocket ROKN 526
21/02/1981.....13.....10......	STAR... Ariola ARO 251
23/05/1981.....66.....3......	PERFECT TIMING .... Ariola ARO 257
20/11/1993 .....2......10.....○	**TRUE LOVE ELTON JOHN AND KIKI DEE** .... Rocket EJSCX 32

SUZANNA DEE – see SAINT FEATURING SUZANNA DEE

DEEE-LITE
Multinational New York-based dance trio formed in 1982 by Super DJ Dmitry (born Dmitry Brill, Kiev, Russia), Jungle DJ Towa Towa (born Doug Wa-Chung, Tokyo, Japan) and lead singer Lady Miss Kirby (born Kierin Kirby, Youngstown, OH). Towa left in 1994, renaming himself Towa Tei; he was replaced by Ani. Brill and Kirby were later married.

18/08/1990 .....2......13......	**GROOVE IS IN THE HEART/WHAT IS LOVE** *Groove Is In The Heart* contains backing vocals by Bootsy Collins and rap by Q-Tip of A Tribe Called Quest, a sample of Vernon Burch's *Get Up,* and is featured in the 2000 film *Charlie's Angels* .... Elektra EKR 114
24/11/1990.....25.....7......	POWER OF LOVE/DEEE-LITE THEME .... Elektra EKR 117
23/02/1991.....52.....2......	HOW DO YOU SAY...LOVE/GROOVE IS IN THE HEART (REMIX) .... Elektra EKR 118
27/04/1991.....53.....3......	GOOD BEAT .... Elektra EKR 122
13/06/1992.....45.....3......	RUNAWAY .... Elektra EKR 148
30/07/1994.....43.....2......	PICNIC IN THE SUMMERTIME .... Elektra EKR 186CD1

DEEJAY PUNK-ROC
US DJ (born 1971, Brooklyn, NYC) who was in the US Army from the age of sixteen. He was stationed in Japan, Germany and England, where he first recorded *My Beatbox* for the Airdog Recordings label.

21/03/1998.....71.....1......	DEAD HUSBAND .... Independiente ISOM 9MS
09/05/1998.....43.....1......	MY BEATBOX .... Independiente ISOM 12MS
08/08/1998.....43.....2......	FAR OUT .... Independiente ISOM 17MS
20/02/1999.....59.....1......	ROC-IN-IT **DEEJAY PUNK-ROC VS ONYX** .... Independiente ISOM 21MS

DEEJAY SVEN – see MC MIKER 'G' AND DEEJAY SVEN

CAROL DEENE
UK singer (born 1944, Yorkshire) who made her debut on the Joan Regan TV show in 1961, signing with HMV immediately after. Later a DJ on Radio Luxembourg, she also appeared in the film *Band Of Thieves* (1962) with Acker Bilk.

26/10/1961.....44.....3......	SAD MOVIES (MAKE ME CRY) .... HMV POP 922
25/01/1962.....24.....8......	NORMAN... HMV POP 973
05/07/1962.....32.....4......	JOHNNY GET ANGRY .... HMV POP 1027
23/08/1962.....25.....10......	SOME PEOPLE Featured in the 1962 film *Some People* .... HMV POP 1058

SCOTTI DEEP
US producer Scott Kinchen.

| 15/03/1997.....67.....1...... | BROOKLYN BEATS .... Xtravaganza 0090095 |

DEEP BLUE
UK producer Sean O'Keefe.

| 16/04/1994.....68.....2...... | HELICOPTER TUNE .... Moving Shadow SHADOW 41CD |

DEEP BLUE SOMETHING
US rock group formed in Denton, Dallas in 1992 by Todd Pipes (born 9/11/1967, bass/vocals), Toby Pipes (born 28/6/1971, guitar), Kirk Tatom (guitar) and John Kirkland (born 16/7/1969, drums) as Leper Mesiah, changing their name the following year. Tatom was later replaced by Clay Bergus (born 29/4/1971).

06/07/1996.....55.....2......	BREAKFAST AT TIFFANY'S .... Interscope IND 80032
21/09/1996.....❶¹.....12......	**BREAKFAST AT TIFFANY'S** .... Interscope IND 80032
07/12/1996.....27.....3......	JOSEY .... Interscope IND 95518

DEEP C
UK vocal/instrumental group formed by Chris Clark and Alex Whittle. They later worked with Wamdue Project.

| 19/01/1991.....75.....1...... | AFRICAN REIGN .... M&G MAGS 4 |
| 08/06/1991.....73.....2...... | CHILL TO THE PANIC .... M&G MAGS 10 |

DEEP COVER
UK DJ/production duo Scott 'Angry' Anderson and Leon McCormack who also record under their own names.

| 11/05/2002.....63.....1...... | SOUNDS OF EDEN (EVERYTIME I SEE THE GIRL) .... Attitude 0158392 |

❶⁹ Number of weeks single topped the UK chart ↑ Entered the UK chart at #1 ▲⁹ Number of weeks single topped the US chart

211

DEEP CREED '94 US producer Armand Van Helden.

07/05/1994	59	1	CAN U FEEL IT	Eastern Bloc BLOCCD 005

DEEP DISH US production/instrumental duo formed in 1992 by Ali 'Dubfire' Shirizania and Sharam Tayebi, both originally from Iran. They won the 2001 Grammy Award for Best Remix for Dido's *Thank You*.

26/10/1996	41	1	STAY GOLD	Deconstruction 74321418222
01/11/1997	60	1	STRANDED	Deconstruction 74321512232
03/10/1998	31	2	THE FUTURE OF THE FUTURE (STAY GOLD) DEEP DISH WITH EVERYTHING BUT THE GIRL	Deconstruction 74321616252
09/10/2004	3	12+	FLASHDANCE	Positiva CDTIVS211

DEEP FEELING UK group originally formed by Dave Mason, Jim Capaldi, Luther Grosvenor and John Palmer as The Hellions, changing their name in 1967, with David Meredith joining later. Mason and Capaldi left to join Traffic, and then Mason joined Family. Deep Feeling reorganised with John Swail (vocals), Derek Elson (keyboards), Martin Jenner (guitar) and Dave Green (bass/flute).

25/04/1970	34	5	DO YOU LOVE ME	Page One POF 165

DEEP FOREST French instrumental duo formed in Paris in 1993 by Eric Mouquet and film music composer Michael Sanchez. They won the 1995 Grammy Award for Best World Music Album for *Boheme*.

05/02/1994	10	6	SWEET LULLABY	Columbia 6599242
21/05/1994	20	4	DEEP FOREST	Columbia 6604115
23/07/1994	28	2	SAVANNA DANCE	Columbia 6606355
24/06/1995	26	2	MARTA'S SONG Featured in the 1994 film *Ready To Wear (Pret-A-Porter)*	Columbia 6621402

DEEP PURPLE UK heavy rock group formed by Ritchie Blackmore (born 14/4/1945, Weston-super-Mare, guitar), Jon Lord (born 9/6/1941, Leicester, keyboards), Chris Curtis (born 26/8/1941, Oldham, vocals), Dave Curtis (bass) and Bobby Woodman (drums) as Roundabout in 1968. After a month of rehearsals, both Curtises and Woodman left and were replaced by Ian Paice (born 29/6/1948, Nottingham, drums), Rod Evans (born 19/1/1945, Edinburgh, vocals) and Nick Simper (born 3/11/1946, Southall, bass). Debuting in Denmark, they changed their name to Deep Purple in April 1968, signing to EMI the following month. Evans and Simper left in 1969, with Roger Glover (born 30/11/1945, Brecon, bass) and Ian Gillan (born 18/8/1945, Hounslow, vocals) replacing them. Gillan and Glover left in 1973 and were replaced by David Coverdale (born 22/9/1949, Saltburn-by-the-Sea) and Glenn Hughes (born 21/8/1952, Penkridge). Blackmore quit after two further albums to form Rainbow; Tommy Bolin (born 1/8/1951, Sioux City, IN) was recruited, but they disbanded in 1976. They re-formed in 1984 with Blackmore, Gillan, Lord and Paice, with Gillan leaving in 1989. Bolin died from a drug overdose on 4/12/1976, reportedly wearing the same ring Jimi Hendrix had been wearing when he died.

15/08/1970	2	21	BLACK NIGHT	Harvest HAR 5020
27/02/1971	8	12	STRANGE KIND OF WOMAN	Harvest HAR 5033
13/11/1971	15	13	FIREBALL	Harvest HAR 5045
01/04/1972	35	6	NEVER BEFORE	Purple PUR 102
16/04/1977	21	7	SMOKE ON THE WATER Featured in the films *Made In America* (1993) and *Private Parts* (1997)	Purple PUR 132
15/10/1977	31	4	NEW LIVE AND RARE EP Tracks on EP: *Black Night (Live), Painted Horse,* and *When A Blind Man Cries*	Purple PUR 135
07/10/1978	45	3	NEW LIVE AND RARE II (EP) Tracks on EP: *Burn (Edited Version), Coronarias Redig* and *Mistreated (Interpolating Rock Me Baby)*	Purple PUR 137
02/08/1980	43	6	BLACK NIGHT	Harvest PUR 5210
01/11/1980	48	3	NEW LIVE AND RARE VOLUME 3 EP Tracks on EP: *Smoke On The Water, Bird Has Flown* and *Grabsplatter*	Harvest SHEP 101
26/01/1985	48	3	PERFECT STRANGERS	Polydor POSP 719
15/06/1985	68	1	KNOCKING AT YOUR BACK DOOR/PERFECT STRANGERS	Polydor POSP 749
18/06/1988	62	2	HUSH	Polydor PO 4
20/10/1990	70	1	KING OF DREAMS	RCA PB 49247
02/03/1991	57	2	LOVE CONQUERS ALL	RCA PB 49225
24/06/1995	66	1	BLACK NIGHT (REMIX)	EMI CDEM 382

DEEP RIVER BOYS US R&B vocal group formed at the Hampton Institute in Virginia by George Lawson, Vernon Gardner, Harry Douglass, Edward Ware and Ray Duran. Ware died in 1956.

07/12/1956	29	1	THAT'S RIGHT	HMV POP 263

DEEP SENSATION UK duo Paul Hunter (aka Brother Of Soul, Red Hook Project, Second Crusade and Small World, who is a member of Stunts Blunts And Beats) and Colin Gate (also in Move A Head).

04/09/2004	74	1	SOMEHOW SOMEWHERE	In The House ITHS07

DEEPEST BLUE Israeli producer Matti Schwartz with vocals by Joel Edwards. Schwartz is also in 4 Tune 500.

02/08/2003	7	8	DEEPEST BLUE	Data 55CDS
28/02/2004	9	8	GIVE IT AWAY	Data 65CDS
05/06/2004	24	2	IS IT A SIN?	Open OPEN3CDX
04/09/2004	57	1	SHOOTING STAR	Open OPEN05CDS

RICK DEES AND HIS CAST OF IDIOTS US singer (born Rigdon Osmond Dees III, 1950, Memphis, TN) who was working as a DJ for WMPS in Memphis when he thought up *Disco Duck,* a US #1. Currently a top US DJ, he also hosted the TV show *Solid Gold*. He has a star on the Hollywood Walk of Fame.

18/09/1976	6	9	DISCO DUCK (PART ONE) ▲[1]	RSO 2090 204

DEETAH Chilean singer/rapper (born Claudia Ogalde, 1976) who was raised in Sweden by a family of performing musicians and developed her own musical style, which mixes blues, jazz, samba, salsa and boss nova.

26/09/1998	11	8		RELAX Contains a sample of Dire Straits' *Why Worry*	ffrr FCDP 345
01/05/1999	39	2		EL PARAISO RICO	ffrr FCD 356

DEF LEPPARD UK heavy rock group formed in Sheffield in 1977 by Joe Elliott (born 1/8/1959, Sheffield, vocals), Rick Savage (born 2/12/1960, Sheffield, bass), Steve Clark (born 23/4/1960, Sheffield, guitar), Frank Noon (drums) and Pete Willis (guitar). Drummer Rick Allen (born 1/11/1963, Sheffield) was recruited in 1978 shortly after they recorded their first EP, *Getcha Rocks Off*, Noon having left to rejoin the Next Band. Local sales and national radio plays led to a deal with Phonogram (although all releases are on their own Bludgeon Riffola label). In 1982 Willis was fired and replaced by Phil Collen (born 8/12/1957, London). Allen lost an arm in a road crash midway through recording a new album in 1984, but with the aid of modern technology has remained the group's drummer (and managed to play 'acoustic' drums on the 1996 album *Slang*). Clark died on 8/1/1991 from excessive alcohol mixed with anti-depressants and painkillers, and was replaced the following year by Vivian Campbell (born 25/8/1962, Belfast).

17/11/1979	61	3		WASTES	Vertigo 6059 247
23/02/1980	45	4		HELLO AMERICA	Vertigo LEPP 1
05/02/1983	66	3		PHOTOGRAPH	Vertigo VER 5
27/08/1983	41	4		ROCK OF AGES	Vertigo VER 6
01/08/1987	6	9		**ANIMAL**	Bludgeon Riffola LEP 1
19/09/1987	18	6		POUR SOME SUGAR ON ME	Bludgeon Riffola LEP 2
28/11/1987	26	6		HYSTERIA	Bludgeon Riffola LEP 3
09/04/1988	20	5		ARMAGEDDON IT	Bludgeon Riffola LEP 4
16/07/1988	11	8		LOVE BITES ▲¹	Bludgeon Riffola LEP 5
11/02/1989	15	7		ROCKET	Bludgeon Riffola LEP 6
28/03/1992	2	7		**LET'S GET ROCKED**	Bludgeon Riffola DEF 7
27/06/1992	12	5		MAKE LOVE LIKE A MAN	Bludgeon Riffola LEP 7
12/09/1992	16	5		HAVE YOU EVER NEEDED SOMEONE SO BAD	Bludgeon Riffola LEP 8
30/01/1993	13	5		HEAVEN IS	Bludgeon Riffola LEPCD 9
01/05/1993	34	3		TONIGHT	Bludgeon Riffola LEPCD 10
18/09/1993	32	4		TWO STEPS BEHIND Featured in the 1993 film *The Last Action Hero*	Bludgeon Riffola LEPCD 12
15/01/1994	14	5		ACTION	Bludgeon Riffola LEPCD 13
14/10/1995	2	10	○	**WHEN LOVE & HATE COLLIDE**	Bludgeon Riffola LEPCD 14
04/05/1996	17	5		SLANG	Bludgeon Riffola LEPDD 15
13/07/1996	22	3		WORK IT OUT	Bludgeon Riffola LEPCD 16
28/09/1996	38	2		ALL I WANT IS EVERYTHING	Bludgeon Riffola LEPDD 17
30/11/1996	43	1		BREATHE A SIGH	Bludgeon Riffola LEPCD 18
24/07/1999	41	1		PROMISES	Bludgeon Riffola 5621362
09/10/1999	54	1		GOODBYE	Bludgeon Riffola 5622892
17/08/2002	23	2		NOW	Bludgeon Riffola 0639692
26/04/2003	40	2		LONG LONG WAY TO GO	Bludgeon Riffola 9800024

DEFAULT Canadian group formed in Vancouver in 1999 by Dallas Smith (vocals), Jeremy Hora (guitar), Dave Benedict (bass) and Danny Craig (drums) as The Fallout, changing their name in 2000.

08/02/2003	73	1		WASTING MY TIME	Island CID 809

DEFINITION OF SOUND UK rap duo Kevwon (born Kevin Anthony Clark, 1971) and The Don (born Desmond Raymond Weekes, 1969). Kevwon first became known guesting on Krush's *House Arrest* before teaming with The Don in 1988 as Top Billin'. They changed their name after their record label Dance Yard closed.

09/03/1991	17	9		WEAR YOUR LOVE LIKE HEAVEN	Circa YR 61
01/06/1991	46	4		NOW IS TOMORROW	Circa YR 66
08/02/1992	34	4		MOIRA JANE'S I	Circa YR 80
19/09/1992	68	1		WHAT ARE YOU UNDER	Circa YR 95
14/11/1992	61	2		CAN I GET OVER	Circa YR 97
20/05/1995	59	1		BOOM BOOM	Fontana DOSCD 1
02/12/1995	23	3		PASS THE VIBES	Fontana DOSCD 2
24/02/1996	48	1		CHILD	Fontana DOSCD 3

DEFTONES US rock group formed in Los Angeles, CA in 1988 by Chino Moreno (vocals), Stephen Carpenter (guitar), Chi Cheng (bass/vocals) and Abe Cunningham (drums). They recorded their debut album for Maverick in 1995 and won the 2000 Grammy Award for Best Metal Performance for *Elite*.

21/03/1998	29	2		MY OWN SUMMER (SHOVE IT)	Maverick W 0432CD
11/07/1998	50	1		BE QUIET AND DRIVE (FAR AWAY)	Maverick W 0445CD
26/08/2000	53	1		CHANGE (IN THE HOUSE OF FLIES)	Maverick W 531CD
24/05/2003	15	3		MINERVA	Maverick W 605CD
04/10/2003	68	2		HEXAGRAM	Maverick W 623CD

DEGREES OF MOTION FEATURING BITI US vocal group comprising Biti, Kit West, Balle Legend and Mariposa. Their debut hit (first recorded by Taylor Dayne) was originally released on the Esquire label.

25/04/1992	31	5		DO YOU WANT IT RIGHT NOW	ffrr F 184
18/07/1992	43	3		SHINE ON **DEGREES OF MOTION FEATURING BITI WITH KIT WEST**	ffrr F 192

●⁹ Number of weeks single topped the UK chart ↑ Entered the UK chart at #1 ▲⁹ Number of weeks single topped the US chart

213

07/11/1992.....64......1......	SOUL FREEDOM – FREE YOUR SOUL .... ffrr FX 201
19/03/1994.....8......8......	**SHINE ON (REMIX)** .... ffrr FCD 229
25/06/1994.....26......4......	DO YOU WANT IT RIGHT NOW (REMIX) .... ffrr FCD 236

DEJA US duo Curt Jones (all instruments) and Starleana Young (vocals) also known as Symphonic Express. They first teamed up in Slave and Aurra. Young left in 1991 and was replaced by Mysti Day.

29/08/1987.....75......1......	SERIOUS .... 10 TEN 132

DEJA VU UK dance group fronted by singer Tasmin.

05/02/1994.....57......1......	WHY WHY WHY.. Cowboy CDRODEO 941

DEJURE UK production duo Ian Bland and Paul Fitzpatrick with singer Laura Rigg. Bland and Fitzpatrick also record as Beat Renegades and Red.

23/08/2003.....62......1......	SANCTUARY .... Nebula NEBT 032

DESMOND DEKKER AND THE ACES
Jamaican singer (born Desmond Dacres, 16/7/1941, Kingston) who made his first single in 1963. He formed the Aces and teamed up with hit producer Leslie Kong in 1966 (with whom he worked until Kong's death in 1971). With over twenty domestic #1s, he was the first Jamaican to top the UK charts and also hit the US top ten.

12/07/1967.....14.....11......	007 .... Pyramid PYR 6004
19/03/1969.....❶[1].....15......	THE ISRAELITES Featured in the films *The Harder They Come* (1972) and *Drugstore Cowboy* (1990) .... Pyramid PYR 6058
25/06/1969.....7.....11......	**IT MEK**. .... Pyramid PYR 6068
10/01/1970.....42......3......	PICKNEY GAL .... Pyramid PYR 6078
22/08/1970.....2.....15......	**YOU CAN GET IT IF YOU REALLY WANT**. .... Trojan TR 7777
10/05/1975.....10......9......	**ISRAELITES** Re-issue of Pyramid PYR 6058 .... Cactus CT 57
30/08/1975.....16......7......	SING A LITTLE SONG This and above two singles credited to **DESMOND DEKKER**. .... Cactus CT 73

DEL AMITRI
UK rock group formed in Glasgow in 1982 by Justin Currie (born 11/12/1964, Glasgow, vocals/bass), Bryan Tolland (guitar), Iain Harvie (born 19/5/1962, Glasgow, guitar) and Paul Tyagi (drums). Brian McDermott (drums) and David Cummings (guitar) replaced Tolland and Tyagi. McDermott left in 1995, and later members included Mark Price (drums) and Kris Dollimore (guitar). They first recorded for the No Strings label before signing with Chrysalis for their Big Star imprint. Leaving after one album, they signed with A&M in 1987.

19/08/1989.....59......2......	KISS THIS THING GOODBYE. .... A&M AM 515
13/01/1990.....11......9......	NOTHING EVER HAPPENS .... A&M AM 536
24/03/1990.....43......4......	KISS THIS THING GOODBYE Re-issue of A&M AM515. .... A&M AM 551
16/06/1990.....36......6......	MOVE AWAY JIMMY BLUE .... A&M AM 555
03/11/1990.....21......6......	SPIT IN THE RAIN .... A&M AM 589
09/05/1992.....13......7......	ALWAYS THE LAST TO KNOW .... A&M AM 870
11/07/1992.....30......4......	BE MY DOWNFALL. .... A&M AM 884
12/09/1992.....25......4......	JUST LIKE A MAN .... A&M AM 0057
23/01/1993.....20......3......	WHEN YOU WERE YOUNG .... A&M AMCD 0132
18/02/1995.....21......4......	HERE AND NOW .... A&M 5809692
29/04/1995.....18......4......	DRIVING WITH THE BRAKES ON .... A&M 5810072
08/07/1995.....22......4......	ROLL TO ME .... A&M 5811312
28/10/1995.....32......2......	TELL HER THIS .... A&M 5812172
21/06/1997.....21......3......	NOT WHERE IT'S AT .... A&M 5822532
06/12/1997.....46......1......	SOME OTHER SUCKER'S PARADE. .... A&M 5824352
13/06/1998.....15......4......	DON'T COME HOME TOO SOON Official song of the 1998 Scottish FIFA World Cup Squad. .... A&M 5827052
05/09/1998.....40......2......	CRY TO BE FOUND .... A&M MERCD 513
13/04/2002.....37......2......	JUST BEFORE YOU LEAVE .... Mercury 4976972

DE'LACY US R&B group formed by De Lacy Davis (percussion), Glen Branch (drums/vocals), Gary Griffin (bass/keyboards) and Raine Lassiter, all ex-members of Spectrum.

02/09/1995.....9.....10......	**HIDEAWAY** .... Slip 'N' Slide 74321310472
31/08/1996.....19......4......	THAT LOOK .... Slip 'N' Slide 74321398322
14/02/1998.....21......2......	HIDEAWAY 1998 (REMIX) .... Slip 'N' Slide 74321561052

DELAGE UK vocal group formed by Karena, Judy, Rhonda and Charlotte.

15/12/1990.....63......2......	ROCK THE BOAT .... PWL/Polydor PO 113

DELAKOTA UK vocal/instrumental duo formed in 1997 by Des Murphy and ex-Smashing Things Cass Browne.

18/07/1998.....60......1......	THE ROCK .... Go Beat GOBCD 10
19/09/1998.....55......1......	C'MON CINCINNATI **DELAKOTA FEATURING ROSE SMITH** .... Go Beat GOBCD 11
13/02/1999.....42......1......	555 .... Go Beat GOBCD 14

DELANEY AND BONNIE AND FRIENDS FEATURING ERIC CLAPTON
US husband and wife duo Delaney Bramlett (born 1/7/1939, Pontotoc County, MS) and Bonnie Lynn Bramlett (born 8/11/1944, Acton, IL) whose friends included, at various times, Leon Russell, Rita Coolidge, Dave Mason, Duane Allman and Eric Clapton, who toured with them following his departure from Blind Faith. They split in 1973, both recording solo – Delaney for MGM and Prodigal, Bonnie (who later recorded gospel material) for Capricorn.

20/12/1969.....16......9......	COMIN' HOME .... Atlantic 584 308

DELANO – see CZR FEATURING DELAND

DELAYS UK rock group formed in Southampton by Greg Gilbert (guitar/vocals), Aaron Gilbert (keyboards), Colin Fox (bass) and Rowdy (drums).

02/08/2003.....40......1......	HEY GIRL..	Rough Trade RTRADESCD103
31/01/2004.....16......4......	LONG TIME COMING...	Rough Trade RTRADESCD136
03/04/2004.....21......3......	NEARER THAN HEAVEN...	Rough Trade RTRADSCD175
04/12/2004.....28......2......	LOST IN A MELODY/WANDERLUST.....................................	Rough Trade RTRADSCD197

DELEGATION UK soul group formed in Birmingham in 1976 by Ricky Bailey, Ray Patterson and Len Coley. Later members included Bruce Dunbar (replacing Coley) and Texan-born singer Kathy Bryant.

23/04/1977.....22......6......	WHERE IS THE LOVE (WE USED TO KNOW) .... State STAT 40
20/08/1977.....49......1......	YOU'VE BEEN DOING ME WRONG.................................... State STAT 55

DELERIUM Canadian production duo Bill Leeb and Rhys Fulber, both also members of Front Line Assembly, initially fronted by singer Sarah McLachlan. Leigh Nash is a member of Sixpence None The Richer. Rani is singer/poet Rani Kamal who wrote the lyrics to their hit *Underwater*.

12/06/1999.....73......1......	SILENCE .... Nettwerk 398152
05/02/2000.....44......1......	HEAVEN'S EARTH.. Nettwerk 331032
14/10/2000 .....3....16 ....○	**SILENCE (REMIXES)** DELERIUM FEATURING SARAH McLACHLAN .... Nettwerk 331082
07/07/2001.....32......3......	INNOCENTE (FALLING IN LOVE) DELERIUM FEATURING LEIGH NASH...... Nettwerk 331182
24/11/2001.....33......1......	UNDERWATER DELERIUM FEATURING RANI .... Nettwerk 331432
12/07/2003.....46......1......	AFTER ALL DELERIUM FEATURING JAEL .... Nettwerk 332012
28/02/2004.....54......2......	TRULY .... Nettwerk 332202
27/11/2004.....38......4......	SILENCE 2004 DELERIUM FEATURING SARAH McLACHLAN................ Nettwerk 332422

DELFONICS US group formed in Washington, DC in 1965 by William Hart (born 17/1/1945, Washington), Wilbert Hart (born 19/10/1947, Philadelphia, PA), Randy Cain (born 2/5/1945, Philadelphia) and Ritchie Daniels as the Four Gents. Daniels left in 1968 to do his national service. Cain left in 1971 and was replaced by ex-Jarmels singer Major Harris (born 9/2/1947, Richmond, VA). Their debut release *He Don't Really Love You* was Thom Bell's production debut, and after their Moonshot label closed their manager Stan Watson founded Philly Groove, outlet for all their US hits. Harris went solo in 1974. By 2000 the group comprised Major Harris, William Hart and Frank Washington.

10/04/1971.....22......9.......	DIDN'T I (BLOW YOUR MIND THIS TIME) Featured in the 1991 film *Queen's Logic*. 1970 Grammy Award for Best Rhythm & Blues Performance.. Bell 1099
10/07/1971.....19......10	LA-LA MEANS I LOVE YOU Originally a US hit in 1968 .... Bell 1165
16/10/1971.....41......4.......	READY OR NOT HERE I COME Originally a US hit in 1968. This and above two singles featured in the 1997 film *Jackie Brown* ...... Bell 1175

DELGADOS UK group formed by Emma Pollock (guitar/vocals), Alun Woodward (guitar/vocals), Stewart Henderson (bass) and Paul Savage (drums). Woodward, Henderson and Savage were all ex-Bubblegum. They also formed the Chemikal Underground label.

23/05/1998.....69......1......	PULL THE WIRES FROM THE WALL .... Chemikal Underground CHEM 0233CD
03/06/2000.....61......1......	AMERICAN TRILOGY .... Chemikal Underground CHEM 0339CD
01/03/2003.....72......1......	ALL YOU NEED IS HATE .... Mantra MNT 79CD
18/09/2004.....67......1......	EVERYBODY COME DOWN .... Chemikal Underground CHEM073CD

DELIRIOUS? UK gospel/rock group formed in Littlehampton by Martin Smith (guitar/vocals), Stewart Smith (drums), Tim Jupp (keyboards), Stuart Garrad (guitar) and Jon Thatcher (bass).

01/03/1997.....41......2......	WHITE RIBBON DAY .... Furious? CDFURY 1
17/05/1997.....20......3......	DEEPER .... Furious? CDFURY 2
26/07/1997.....20......2......	PROMISE .... Furious? CDFURY 3
15/11/1997.....36......2......	DEEPER (EP) Tracks on EP: *Deeper, Summer Of Love, Touch* and *Sanctify* .... Furious? CXFURY 4
27/03/1999.....16......2......	SEE THE STAR .... Furious? CDFURY 5
04/03/2000.....18......2......	IT'S OK.. Furious? CDFURY 6
16/06/2001.....26......2......	WAITING FOR THE SUMMER .... Furious? CDFURY 7
22/12/2001.....40......2......	I COULD SING OF YOUR LOVE FOREVER............................... Furious? CDFURY 9

'DELIVERANCE' SOUNDTRACK US session musicians Eric Weissberg (banjo) and Steve Mandell (guitar) who, having worked with the likes of Judy Collins and John Denver, teamed up for the *Deliverance* soundtrack. The hit single had originally been written in 1955.

31/03/1973.....17......7.......	DUELLING BANJOS Featured in the 1972 film *Deliverance*. 1973 Grammy Award for Best Country Instrumental Performance .... Warner Brothers K 16223

DELLS US R&B vocal group formed at the Thornton Township High School in Harvey, IL by Johnny Funches (born 13/7/1935, Chicago, IL), Marvin Junior (born 31/1/1936, Harrell, AR), Laverne Allison (born 22/6/1936, Chicago), Mickey McGill (born 17/2/1937, Chicago), Lucius McGill (born 1935, Chicago) and Chuck Barksdale (born 11/1/1935, Chicago) as The El-Rays in 1953, changing their name in 1962. Lucius McGill left while they were still The El-Rays, and John Carter (born 2/6/1934, Chicago) replaced Funches in 1960. Funches died from emphysema on 23/1/1998. They were inducted into the Rock & Roll Hall of Fame in 2004.

16/07/1969.....15......9.......	I CAN SING A RAINBOW – LOVE IS BLUE (MEDLEY)...................... Chess CRS 8099

❶⁹ Number of weeks single topped the UK chart ↑ Entered the UK chart at #1 ▲⁹ Number of weeks single topped the US chart

215

DELORES – see MONOBOY FEATURING DELORES

DELRONS – see REPARATA AND THE DELRONS

DELSENA – see ORIN JAY PRESENTS DELSENA

DELTA – see DAVID MORALES AND CRYSTAL WATERS

DELUXE US singer Dolores 'Deluxe' Springer.

18/03/1989	74	1		JUST A LITTLE MORE	Unyque UNQ 5

TIM DELUXE UK producer Tim Liken, previously a member of RIP Productions and then Double 99.

20/07/2002	14	7		IT JUST WON'T DO TIM DELUXE FEATURING SAM OBERNIK	Underwater H2O 016CD
04/10/2003	45	2		LESS TALK MORE ACTION	Underwater H2O 028CD
07/02/2004	61	1		MUNDAYA (THE BOY) TIM DELUXE FEATURING SHAHIN BADAR	Underwater H2O 040CD
13/03/2004	70	1		JUST KICK COHEN VS DELUXE	Intec INTEC024

DEM 2 UK production duo Spencer Edwards and Dean Boylan.

24/10/1998	58	2		DESTINY	Locked On LOX 101CD

DEMETREUS – see CHRISTIAN FALK FEATURING DEMETREUS

DEMOLITION MAN – see PRIZNA FEATURING DEMOLITION MAN

DEMON VS HEARTBREAKER French production group formed by Jeremie Mondon and based in Paris.

19/05/2001	70	1		YOU ARE MY HIGH Contains a sample of The Gap Band's *You Are My High*	Source SOURCDSE 1032

D'EMPRESS – see 187 LOCKDOWN

CHAKA DEMUS AND PLIERS Jamaican singer (born John Taylor, 1964) who was a DJ when he teamed up with reggae singer Pliers (born Everton Bonner, 1963, Jamaica) and producer Sly Dunbar.

12/06/1993	3	15	●	TEASE ME	Mango CIDM 806
18/09/1993	4	10	○	SHE DON'T LET NOBODY	Mango CIDM 810
18/12/1993	❶²	14	●	TWIST AND SHOUT CHAKA DEMUS AND PLIERS FEATURING JACK RADICS AND TAXI GANG	Mango CIDM 814
12/03/1994	27	4		MURDER SHE WROTE Featured in the 2001 film *Save The Last Dance*	Mango CIDM 812
18/06/1994	19	6		I WANNA BE YOUR MAN Featured in the 1993 film *Poetic Justice*	Mango CIDM 817
27/08/1994	20	4		GAL WINE	Mango CIDM 818
31/08/1996	47	1		EVERY KINDA PEOPLE	Island Jamaica IJCD 2005
30/08/1997	51	1		EVERY LITTLE THING SHE DOES IS MAGIC	Virgin VSCDT 1654

TERRY DENE UK singer (born Terry Williams, 20/12/1938, London), an early star on the *6.5 Special* TV show, who even made a film at the height of his success. Conscripted in 1959 he was discharged on medical grounds two weeks later. By the early 1960s religious material dominated his act. He is married to singer Edna Savage. In 1978 Decca released a compilation album *I Thought Terry Dene Was Dead* – he isn't.

07/06/1957	18	7		A WHITE SPORT COAT	Decca F 10895
19/07/1957	15	8		START MOVIN'	Decca F 10914
16/05/1958	16	5		STAIRWAY OF LOVE	Decca F 11016

DENISE AND JOHNNY – see DENISE VAN OUTEN

CATHY DENNIS UK singer (born 25/3/1970, Norwich) who debuted with her father's Alan Dennis Band at holiday camps, before singing lead with D Mob in 1989. She went solo, with success on both sides of the Atlantic, working with Shep Pettibone and later Mark Saunders. She is also a successful songwriter, penning #1 hits for S Club 7 (*Never Had A Dream Come True*) and Kylie Minogue (*Can't Get You Out Of My Head*).

21/10/1989	15	10		C'MON AND GET MY LOVE Featured in the 1989 film *She-Devil*	ffrr F 117
07/04/1990	48	3		THAT'S THE WAY OF THE WORLD This and above single credited to D MOB WITH CATHY DENNIS	ffrr F 132
04/05/1991	5	10		TOUCH ME (ALL NIGHT LONG)	Polydor CATH 3
20/07/1991	13	7		JUST ANOTHER DREAM	Polydor CATH 2
05/10/1991	17	7		TOO MANY WALLS	Polydor CATH 4
07/12/1991	25	8		EVERYBODY MOVE	Polydor CATH 5
29/08/1992	34	4		YOU LIED TO ME	Polydor CATH 6
21/11/1992	24	6		IRRESISTIBLE	Polydor CATH 7
06/02/1993	32	2		FALLING	Polydor CATHD 8
12/02/1994	23	3		WHY D MOB WITH CATHY DENNIS	ffrr FCD 227
10/08/1996	25	2		WEST END PAD	Polydor 5752812
01/03/1997	11	5		WATERLOO SUNSET	Polydor 5759612
21/06/1997	43	1		WHEN DREAMS TURN TO DUST Featured in the 1997 film *Picture Perfect*	Polydor 5711852

JACKIE DENNIS UK singer (born 1942, Edinburgh) who, having been recommended to agent Eve Taylor by comedians Mike

○ Silver disc ● Gold disc ✪ Platinum disc (additional platinum units are indicated by a figure following the symbol) ◉ Singles released prior to 1973 that are known to have sold over 1 million copies in the UK

and Bernie Winters, immediately hit the charts. A film biography was announced, and he was invited to appear on US TV, yet he faded from the scene as quickly as he had arrived.

| 14/03/1958 | 4 | 9 | | LA DEE DAH | Decca F 10992 |
| 27/06/1958 | 29 | 1 | | PURPLE PEOPLE EATER | Decca F 11033 |

STEFAN DENNIS Australian actor (born 30/10/1958) best known as Paul Robinson in the soap series *Neighbours*.

| 06/05/1989 | 16 | 7 | | DON'T IT MAKE YOU FEEL GOOD | Sublime LIME 105 |
| 07/10/1989 | 67 | 1 | | THIS LOVE AFFAIR | Sublime LIME 113 |

DENNISONS UK group formed in Liverpool by Eddie Parry (vocals), Steve McLaren (guitar), Clive Hornsby (drums), Alan Willis and Ray Scragge. Willis was later replaced by Terry Carson, the group disbanding in 1965.

| 15/08/1963 | 46 | 6 | | BE MY GIRL | Decca F 11691 |
| 07/05/1964 | 36 | 7 | | WALKIN' THE DOG | Decca F 11880 |

RICHARD DENTON AND MARTIN COOK UK instrumental duo Richard Denton (guitar) and Martin Cook (keyboards) who later recorded the theme to the TV programme *Tomorrow's World*.

| 15/04/1978 | 25 | 7 | | THEME FROM 'THE HONG KONG BEAT' Theme to the TV series *The Hong Kong Beat* | BBC RESL 52 |

JOHN DENVER US singer (born John Henry Deutschendorf, 31/12/1943, Roswell, NM) who moved to Los Angeles, CA in 1964 and was a member of the Chad Mitchell Trio from 1965 until 1968. His 1969 debut album included his composition *Leaving On A Jet Plane*, successfully covered by Peter, Paul & Mary. He appeared in the 1977 film *Oh, God!* and numerous TV specials. He had a life-long love of flying and in 1988 he asked the Russians if he could go to the Mir Space Station, a request the Russians were considering for a fee of $10 million. He was killed in a plane crash at Monterey Bay, CA on 12/10/1997. It was later revealed that he was flying illegally as the Federal Aviation Authority had suspended his medical certificate. He won the 1997 Grammy Award for Best Musical Album for Children for *All Aboard!* He was awarded a star on the Hollywood Walk of Fame in 1982 but at the time of his death it had not been installed as Denver had been unable to schedule the investiture.

| 17/08/1974 | ❶[1] | 13 | ○ | ANNIE'S SONG ▲[2] Inspired by and written for Denver's then wife Ann Martell | RCA APBO 0295 |
| 12/12/1981 | 46 | 9 | | PERHAPS LOVE PLACIDO DOMINGO WITH JOHN DENVER | CBS A 1905 |

KARL DENVER UK singer/guitarist (born Angus McKenzie, 16/12/1934, Glasgow) with a trio featuring Kevin Neill and Gerry Cottrell. He died from a brain tumour on 21/12/1998.

22/06/1961	8	20		MARCHETA	Decca F 11360
19/10/1961	8	11		MEXICALI ROSE	Decca F 11395
25/01/1962	4	17		WIMOWEH	Decca F 11420
22/02/1962	9	18		NEVER GOODBYE	Decca F 11431
07/06/1962	19	10		A LITTLE LOVE A LITTLE KISS	Decca F 11470
20/09/1962	33	5		BLUE WEEKEND	Decca F 11505
21/03/1963	32	8		CAN YOU FORGIVE ME	Decca F 11608
13/06/1963	32	8		INDIAN LOVE CALL	Decca F 11674
22/08/1963	13	15		STILL	Decca F 11720
05/03/1964	29	6		MY WORLD OF BLUE	Decca F 11828
04/06/1964	37	6		LOVE ME WITH ALL YOUR HEART	Decca F 11905
09/06/1990	46	3		LAZYITIS – ONE ARMED BOXER HAPPY MONDAYS AND KARL DENVER	Factory FAC 2227

DENZIE – see MONSTA BOY FEATURING DENZIE

DEODATO Brazilian keyboard player (born Eumir Deodato Almeida, 21/6/1942, Rio de Janeiro) who was initially an arranger and producer, working on Roberta Flack's *Chapter Two* album, before signing a solo deal with CTI Records. His hit single was a jazz-funk take on Richard Strauss' tune originally intended for label-mate Bob James. As a producer from the late 1970s he returned Kool & The Gang to the charts, also producing Con Funk Shun, Juicy and One Way.

| 05/05/1973 | 7 | 9 | | ALSO SPRACH ZARATHUSTRA (2001) 1973 Grammy Award for Best Pop Instrumental Performance | CTI 4000 |

DEPARTMENT S UK rock quintet formed by Vaughan Toulouse (born Vaughan Cotillard, 30/7/1959, St Helier, Jersey, lead vocals), Mike Herbage (guitar), Tony Lordan (bass), Eddie Roxy (keyboards) and Stuart Mizan (drums, later replaced by Mike Haslar) as Guns For Hire, changing their name in 1980 after one single (*I'm Gonna Rough My Girlfriend's Boyfriend Up Tonight*). Roxy left in 1981 and was replaced by Mark Taylor. Toulouse died from AIDS in August 1991.

| 04/04/1981 | 22 | 10 | | IS VIC THERE? | Demon D 1003 |
| 11/07/1981 | 55 | 3 | | GOING LEFT RIGHT | Stiff BUY 118 |

DEPARTURE UK rock group formed in Londion in 2004 by David Jones (vocals), Sam Harvey (guitar), Lee Irons (guitar), Ben Winton (bass) and Andy Hobson (drums).

| 14/08/2004 | 30 | 2 | | ALL MAPPED OUT | Parlophone CDR 6642 |
| 30/10/2004 | 41 | 1 | | BE MY ENEMY | Parlophone CDRS 6653 |

❶[9] Number of weeks single topped the UK chart   ↑ Entered the UK chart at #1   ▲[9] Number of weeks single topped the US chart

217

DEPECHE MODE UK synthesiser group formed in Basildon, Essex in 1980 by Vince Clarke (born 3/7/1960, South Woodford), Martin Gore (born 23/7/1961, Dagenham), Andy Fletcher (born 9/7/1960, Nottingham) and David Gahan (born 9/5/1962, Epping, lead vocals), taking their name from a French fashion magazine ('fast fashion'). Clarke left in 1981 and was replaced by Alan Wilder (born 1/6/1959, London); Gahan has provided much of the group's material since.

DATE	POS	WKS	BPI	SINGLE TITLE	LABEL & NUMBER
04/04/1981	57	4		DREAMING OF ME	Mute 013
13/06/1981	11	15		NEW LIFE	Mute 014
19/09/1981	8	10	○	**JUST CAN'T GET ENOUGH** Featured in the films *Summer Lovers* (1982) and *The Wedding Singer* (1998)	Mute 016
13/02/1982	6	10		**SEE YOU**	Mute 018
08/05/1982	12	8		THE MEANING OF LOVE	Mute 022
28/08/1982	18	10		LEAVE IN SILENCE	Mute BONG 1
12/02/1983	13	8		GET THE BALANCE RIGHT	Mute 7BONG 2
23/07/1983	6	11	○	**EVERYTHING COUNTS**	Mute 7BONG 3
01/10/1983	21	7		LOVE IN ITSELF	Mute 7BONG 4
24/03/1984	4	10	○	**PEOPLE ARE PEOPLE**	Mute 7BONG 5
01/09/1984	9	9		**MASTER AND SERVANT**	Mute 7BONG 6
10/11/1984	16	6		SOMEBODY/BLASPHEMOUS RUMOURS	Mute 7BONG 7
11/05/1985	18	9		SHAKE THE DISEASE	Mute BONG 8
28/09/1985	18	4		IT'S CALLED A HEART	Mute BONG 9
22/02/1986	15	5		STRIPPED Featured in the 1989 film *Say Anything*	Mute BONG 10
26/04/1986	28	5		A QUESTION OF LUST	Mute BONG 11
23/08/1986	17	6		A QUESTION OF TIME	Mute BONG 12
09/05/1987	16	5		STRANGELOVE	Mute BONG 13
05/09/1987	22	4		NEVER LET ME DOWN AGAIN	Mute BONG 14
09/01/1988	21	5		BEHIND THE WHEEL	Mute BONG 15
28/05/1988	60	2		LITTLE 15 (IMPORT)	Mute LITTLE 15
25/02/1989	22	7		EVERYTHING COUNTS Live version of Mute 7BONG 3	Mute BONG 16
09/09/1989	13	8		PERSONAL JESUS	Mute BONG 17
17/02/1990	6	9		**ENJOY THE SILENCE** 1991 BRIT Award for Best Single	Mute BONG 18
19/05/1990	16	6		POLICY OF TRUTH Featured in the 1996 film *Confessional*	Mute BONG 19
29/09/1990	17	6		WORLD IN MY EYES	Mute BONG 20
27/02/1993	8	7		**I FEEL YOU**	Mute CDBONG 21
08/05/1993	14	4		WALKING IN MY SHOES	Mute CDBONG 22
25/09/1993	9	4		**CONDEMNATION**	Mute CDBONG 23
22/01/1994	8	4		**IN YOUR ROOM**	Mute CDBONG 24
15/02/1997	4	4		**BARREL OF A GUN**	Mute CDBONG 25
12/04/1997	5	5		**IT'S NO GOOD**	Mute CDBONG 26
28/06/1997	23	4		HOME	Mute CDBONG 27
01/11/1997	28	2		USELESS	Mute CDBONG 28
19/09/1998	17	3		ONLY WHEN I LOSE MYSELF	Mute CDBONG 29
05/05/2001	6	5		**DREAM ON**	Mute LCDBONG 30
11/08/2001	12	6		I FEEL LOVED	Mute LCDBONG 31
17/11/2001	19	3		FREELOVE	Mute LCDBONG 32
30/10/2004	7	5		**ENJOY THE SILENCE 04**	Mute LCDBONG 34
04/12/2004	75	1		SOMETHING TO DO	Mute L12BONG34

DEPTH CHARGE UK producer Jonathan Kane.

DATE	POS	WKS	BPI	SINGLE TITLE	LABEL & NUMBER
29/07/1995	75	1		LEGEND OF THE GOLDEN SNAKE	DC 01CD

DER DRITTE RAUM German producer Andreas Kruger (the name means 'the third room').

DATE	POS	WKS	BPI	SINGLE TITLE	LABEL & NUMBER
04/09/1999	75	1		HALE BOPP	Addictive 12AD 042

DEREK AND THE DOMINOES – see ERIC CLAPTON

YVES DERUYTER Belgian producer who later worked with Jon The Dentist, John Digweed and M.I.K.E.

DATE	POS	WKS	BPI	SINGLE TITLE	LABEL & NUMBER
14/04/2001	63	1		BACK TO EARTH	UK Bonzai UKBONZAICD 01
19/01/2002	56	2		BACK TO EARTH (REMIX)	UK Bonzai UKBONZA 109CD

DESERT UK production duo Paul Kane and Paul Pringle. Pringle also records as Pascal Vegas.

DATE	POS	WKS	BPI	SINGLE TITLE	LABEL & NUMBER
20/10/2001	74	1		LETTIN' YA MIND GO	Future Groove CDFGR 017

DESERT EAGLE DISCS FEATURING KEISHA UK production/vocal duo Desert Eagle Discs and Keisha White. Desert Eagle Discs also works as a DJ under the name DJ Syze-up.

01/03/2003 . . . . . 67 . . . . . . 1 . . . . BIGGER BETTER DEAL . . . . Echo ECSCD 129

DESERT SESSIONS
US rock group formed by Josh Homme with an assortment of guest musicians. Homme is also a member of Queens Of The Stone Age.

15/11/2003 . . . . . 41 . . . . . . 2 . . . . CRAWL HOME . . . . Island CID 835

DESIDERIO
UK/Dutch production duo Phil Radford and Michiel Van Der Kuy.

03/06/2000 . . . . . 57 . . . . . . 1 . . . . STARLIGHT . . . . Code Blue BLU 010CD

KEVIN DESIMONE – see BARRY MANILOW

DESIRELESS
French singer (born Claudie Fritsch, 25/12/1952, Paris).

31/10/1987 . . . . . 53 . . . . . . 6 . . . . . . VOYAGE VOYAGE . . . . CBS DESI 1
28/05/1988 . . . . . 5 . . . . . . 13 . . . . . . VOYAGE VOYAGE (REMIX) . . . . CBS DESI 2

DESIYA FEATURING MELISSA YIANNAKOU
UK vocal/instrumental duo Matthew Parkhouse and Melissa Yiannakou.

01/02/1992 . . . . . 74 . . . . . . 1 . . . . COMIN' ON STRONG . . . . Black Market 12MKT 2

DESKEE
UK instrumentalist Derrick Crumpley.

03/02/1990 . . . . . 52 . . . . . . 2 . . . . . . LET THERE BE HOUSE . . . . Big One VBIG 19
08/09/1990 . . . . . 74 . . . . . . 1 . . . . . . DANCE DANCE . . . . Big One VBIG 22

DES'REE
UK singer (born Des'ree Weeks, 30/11/1968, London) with West Indian parents; she spent three years in Barbados before returning to London. Writing her first song at thirteen, she signed with Dusted Sound in 1991. She was named Best British Female Artist at the 1999 BRIT Awards.

31/08/1991 . . . . . 51 . . . . . . 5 . . . . . . FEEL SO HIGH . . . . Dusted Sound 6573667
11/01/1992 . . . . . 13 . . . . . . 7 . . . . . . FEEL SO HIGH Re-issue of Dusted Sound 6573667. . . . . Dusted Sound 6576897
21/03/1992 . . . . . 43 . . . . . . 3 . . . . . . MIND ADVENTURES . . . . Dusted Sound 6578637
27/06/1992 . . . . . 44 . . . . . . 3 . . . . . . WHY SHOULD I LOVE YOU . . . . Dusted Sound 6580917
19/06/1993 . . . . . 14 . . . . . . 6 . . . . . . DELICATE TERENCE TRENT D'ARBY FEATURING DES'REE . . . . Columbia 6593312
09/04/1994 . . . . . 20 . . . . . . 7 . . . . . . YOU GOTTA BE . . . . Dusted Sound 6601342
18/06/1994 . . . . . 44 . . . . . . 3 . . . . . . I AN'T MOVIN' . . . . Dusted Sound 6604672
03/09/1994 . . . . . 69 . . . . . . 1 . . . . . . LITTLE CHILD . . . . Dusted Sound 6604515
11/03/1995 . . . . . 14 . . . . . . 8 . . . . . . YOU GOTTA BE (REMIX) . . . . Dusted Sound 6613215
20/06/1998 . . . . . 8 . . . . . . 15 . . . . . . LIFE . . . . Sony S2 6659302
07/11/1998 . . . . . 19 . . . . . . 4 . . . . . . WHAT'S YOUR SIGN . . . . Sony S2 6665165
03/04/1999 . . . . . 10 . . . . . . 8 . . . . . . YOU GOTTA BE (2ND REMIX) . . . . Dusted Sound S2 6668935
16/10/1999 . . . . . 42 . . . . . . 2 . . . . . . AIN'T NO SUNSHINE . . . . Universal Music TV 1564332
05/04/2003 . . . . . 69 . . . . . . 1 . . . . . . IT'S OKAY . . . . Sony Music 6736495

DESTINY'S CHILD
US vocal group formed in Houston, TX by Beyoncé Knowles (born 18/9/1981, Houston), Kelendria 'Kelly' Rowland (born 11/2/1981, Houston), LaTavia Roberson (born 1/11/1981, Houston) and LeToya Luckett (born 11/3/1981, Houston). Roberson and Luckett left early in 2000 and were replaced by Farrah Franklin (born 3/5/1981) and Michelle Williams (born 23/7/1980). Franklin left five months later and the group continued as a trio of Knowles, Rowland and Williams. Awards include the 1999 MOBO Award for Best International Act and Best International Group at the 2002 BRIT Awards. When *Survivor* reached #1 in April 2001, Destiny's Child became the first US female group to have two UK #1 hits. Beyoncé also began acting, appearing in *Carmen – A Hip Hopera* (2001) and *Austin Powers – Goldmember* (2002), for which she recorded the theme song. Her father Matthew (with whom she wrote a number of Destiny's Child hits) launched the Music World Music label that released the *Carmen – A Hip Hopera* soundtrack. Rowland later recorded with Nelly and solo, while Williams recorded gospel material.

28/03/1998 . . . . . 5 . . . . . . 8 . . . . . . NO NO NO DESTINY'S CHILD FEATURING WYCLEF JEAN Contains a sample of Barry White's *Strange Games & Things*. . . . .
. . . . Columbia 6656592
11/07/1998 . . . . . 19 . . . . . . 3 . . . . . . WITH ME Features the uncredited contribution of Jermaine Dupri . . . . Columbia 6661472
07/11/1998 . . . . . 24 . . . . . . 3 . . . . . . SHE'S GONE MATTHEW MARSDEN FEATURING DESTINY'S CHILD . . . . Columbia 6664915
23/01/1999 . . . . . 15 . . . . . . 5 . . . . . . GET ON THE BUS DESTINY'S CHILD FEATURING TIMBALAND Featured in the 1998 film *Why Do Fools Fall In Love*
. . . . East West E 3780CD
24/07/1999 . . . . . 6 . . . . . . 9 . . . . . . BILLS, BILLS, BILLS ▲¹ . . . . Columbia 6676902
30/10/1999 . . . . . 9 . . . . . . 7 . . . . . . BUG A BOO . . . . Columbia 6681882
08/04/2000 . . . . . 3 . . . . . . 11 . . . . . . SAY MY NAME ▲² Features the uncredited contribution of Kobe Bryant. 2000 Grammy Awards for Best Rhythm & Blues Performance by a Duo or Group with Vocal plus Best Rhythm & Blues Song for writers LaShawn Daniels, Fred Jerkins III, Rodney Jerkins, Beyoncé Knowles, LeToya Luckett, LaTavia Roberson and Kelendria Rowland. . . . . Columbia 6691882
29/07/2000 . . . . . 5 . . . . . . 11 . . . . . . JUMPIN' JUMPIN' . . . . Columbia 6696292
02/12/2000 . . . ❶¹ . . . . . 15 . . . . . ● INDEPENDENT WOMEN PART 1 ↑ ▲¹¹ Featured in the 2000 film *Charlie's Angels*. 2001 MOBO Award for Best Single . . . .
. . . . Columbia 6705932
28/04/2001 . . . . ❶¹ . . . . . 13 . . . . . ○ SURVIVOR ↑ 2001 Grammy Award for Best Rhythm & Blues Performance by a Duo or Group with Vocal . . . . Columbia 6711732
04/08/2001 . . . . . 2 . . . . . . 11 . . . . . . BOOTYLICIOUS ▲² Contains a sample of Stevie Nicks' *Edge Of Seventeen* . . . . Columbia 6717382
24/11/2001 . . . . . 3 . . . . . . 14 . . . . . . EMOTION . . . . Columbia 6721112
13/11/2004 . . . . . 2 . . . . . 7+ . . . . . . LOSE MY BREATH . . . . Columbia 6754912

❶⁹ Number of weeks single topped the UK chart ↑ Entered the UK chart at #1 ▲⁹ Number of weeks single topped the US chart

219

DESTRY US singer who also worked with Aretha Franklin, Van McCoy and Stacy Lattishaw.

22/08/1992	66	1	LOVE'S GOTTA HOLD ON ME ZOO EXPERIENCE FEATURING DESTRY .... Cooltempo COOL 261
27/11/1999	70	1	SUN SHINING DOWN CIRCA FEATURING DESTRY... Inferno CDFERN 22

MARCELLA DETROIT US singer (born Marcella Levy, 21/6/1959, Detroit, MI) who was first known as a songwriter, co-writing Eric Clapton's hit *Lay Down Sally*, before joining ex-Bananarama Siobhan Fahey in Shakespears Sister in 1989. The duo had a two-year break (both having babies), resuming in 1991. They disbanded in 1993, Marcella going solo.

12/03/1994	11	8	I BELIEVE .... London LONCD 347
14/05/1994	24	4	AIN'T NOTHING LIKE THE REAL THING MARCELLA DETROIT AND ELTON JOHN .... London LONCD 350
16/07/1994	33	4	I'M NO ANGEL .... London LOCDP 351

DETROIT COBRAS US rock group formed in Detroit, MI in 1995 by Rachel Nagy (vocals), Steve Shaw (guitar), Maribel Restrepo (guitar), Jeff Meyer (bass) and Damian Lang (drums). By the time of their debut hit the group comprised Nagy, Restrepo, Steve Nawara (guitar), Joey Mazzola (bass) and Kenny Tudrick (drums).

25/09/2004	59	1	CHA CHA TWIST .... Rough Trade RTRADSCD189

DETROIT EMERALDS US group formed in Little Rock, AR by the four Tilmon brothers: Abrim (born 1943, Little Rock), Ivory (born 1941, Little Rock), Cleophus and Raymond. They relocated to Detroit, MI and signed with Ric Tic, by which time the line-up was Abrim and Ivory and friend James Mitchell (born 1941, Perry, FL, lead vocals). They later added Marvin Willis in place of Abrim, who didn't want to tour. In 1977 James and Marvin formed the offshoot The Floaters and their backing band became Chapter 8. Towards the end of the 1970s there were two groups called Detroit Emeralds on the cabaret circuit. Abrim died of a heart attack in July 1982.

10/02/1973	4	15	FEEL THE NEED IN ME... Janus 6146 020
05/05/1973	12	9	YOU WANT IT YOU GOT IT .... Westbound 6146 103
11/08/1973	27	9	I THINK OF YOU.. Westbound 6146 104
18/06/1977	12	11	FEEL THE NEED IN ME Re-recording of Janus 6146 020.. Atlantic K 10945

DETROIT GRAND PU BAHS US electro group formed in Detroit, MI by Paris The Black FU (born Mack Gouy Jr) and Andy 'Dr Toefinger' Toth.

08/07/2000	29	3	SANDWICHES .... Jive Electro 9230252

DETROIT SPINNERS US R&B vocal group formed in Detroit, MI in 1955 by Henry Famborough (born 10/5/1935, Detroit), Billy Henderson (born 9/8/1939, Detroit), Pervis Jackson, CP Spencer and Bobby Smith (born 10/4/1937, Detroit) as the Domingos. They changed their name in 1957 to avoid confusion with the Flamingos and the Dominoes. Spinners are the hubcaps on Cadillacs. They signed with ex-Moonglows Harvey Fuqua's Tri-Phi label, which was acquired by Motown in 1964. Leaving Motown for Atlantic and producer Thom Bell in 1972, they became a major R&B group of the era. Line-up changes have included the departure of CP Spencer; a later addition GC Cameron leaving to go solo with Motown and being replaced by Philippe Wynne (born Philip Walker, 3/4/1941, Detroit), who also recorded solo and toured with Parliament/Funkadelic; and John Edwards, who joined in 1977. Wynne died from a heart attack on 14/7/1984, performing in San Francisco, CA. The group has a star on the Hollywood Walk of Fame.

14/11/1970	20	11	IT'S A SHAME MOTOWN SPINNERS .... Tamla Motown TMG 755
21/04/1973	11	11	COULD IT BE I'M FALLING IN LOVE Featured in the 1996 film *Beautiful Girls*........................... Atlantic K 10283
29/09/1973	7	10	GHETTO CHILD .... Atlantic K 10359
19/10/1974	29	6	THEN CAME YOU ▲¹ DIONNE WARWICK AND THE DETROIT SPINNERS .... Atlantic K 10495
11/09/1976	16	11	THE RUBBERBAND MAN Featured in the 2004 film *Scooby Doo 2: Monsters Unleashed*.................. Atlantic K 10807
29/01/1977	29	6	WAKE UP SUSAN .... Atlantic K 10799
07/05/1977	32	3	COULD IT BE I'M FALLING IN LOVE EP Tracks on EP: *Could It Be I'm Falling In Love, You're Throwing A Good Love Away, Games People Play* and *Lazy Susan* .... Atlantic K 10935
23/02/1980	●²	14	○	WORKING MY WAY BACK TO YOU – FORGIVE ME GIRL (MEDLEY) .... Atlantic K 11432
10/05/1980	40	7	BODY LANGUAGE .... Atlantic K 11392
28/06/1980	4	10	CUPID – I'VE LOVED YOU FOR A LONG TIME (MEDLEY) Featured in the 1987 film *Innerspace*.......... Atlantic K 11498
24/06/1995	30	4	I'LL BE AROUND RAPPIN' 4-TAY FEATURING THE SPINNERS Rappin' 4-Tay raps a new verse over the Detroit Spinners 1972 US hit, with the original music and chorus... Cooltempo CDCOOL 306

DETROIT WHEELS – see MITCH RYDER AND THE DETROIT WHEELS

DEUCE UK vocal group formed in 1994 by Kelly O-Keefe, Lisa Armstrong, Paul Holmes and Craig Young. Kelly left in 1995 and was replaced by Mandy Perkins.

21/01/1995	11	10	CALL IT LOVE .... London LONCD 355
22/04/1995	10	5	I NEED YOU Originally entered in the UK 'Song for Europe' competition; it came third behind Gina G and Dear Jon .... London LONCD 365
12/08/1995	13	6	ON THE BIBLE.. London LONCD 368
29/06/1996	29	2	NO SURRENDER .... Love This LUVTHISCD 10

DEUS Belgian rock group formed in Antwerp by Tom Barman (guitar/vocals), Rudy Toruve (guitar), Steff Kamil Carlens (bass), Klaas Janzoons (violin) and Julle De Borgher (drums).

11/02/1995	55	1	HOTEL LOUNGE (BE THE DEATH OF ME)... Island CID 603
13/07/1996	68	1	THEME FROM TURNPIKE (EP) Tracks on EP: *Theme From Turnpike, Worried About Satan, Overflow* and *My Little Contessa* .... Island CID 630
19/10/1996	44	2	LITTLE ARITHMETICS .... Island CID 643
15/03/1997	56	1	ROSES .... Island CID 645

○ Silver disc ● Gold disc ✪ Platinum disc (additional platinum units are indicated by a figure following the symbol) ◉ Singles released prior to 1973 that are known to have sold over 1 million copies in the UK

24/04/1999	49	1		INSTANT STREET	Island CID 742
03/07/1999	62	1		SISTER DEW	Island CID 750

SYDNEY DEVINE
UK singer who began his career in 1957, still touring with his band The Legend at the turn of the century.

01/04/1978	48	1		SCOTLAND FOREVER	Philips SCOT 1

DEVO
US rock group formed in Akron, OH in 1972 by Mark Mothersbaugh (keyboards/guitar/vocals), his brother Bob (guitar/vocals), Bob Casle (guitar/vocals), his brother Gerald (bass/vocals) and Alan Myers (drums). Myers was later replaced by David Kendrick.

22/04/1978	41	8		(I CAN'T GET ME NO) SATISFACTION	Stiff BOY 1
13/05/1978	62	3		JOCKO HOMO	Stiff DEV 1
12/08/1978	71	1		BE STIFF	Stiff BOY 2
02/09/1978	60	4		COME BACK JONEE	Virgin VS 223
22/11/1980	51	7		WHIP IT	Virgin VS 383

SHEILA B. DEVOTION
French singer (born Anny Chancel, 1946, Paris) who later worked with Bernard Edwards and Nile Rodgers. In the US her records were credited Sheila & B. Devotion, B. Devotion being her backing group.

11/03/1978	11	13		SINGIN' IN THE RAIN PART 1	Carrere EMI 2751
22/07/1978	44	6		YOU LIGHT MY FIRE	Carrere EMI 2828
24/11/1979	18	14		SPACER SHEILA AND B. DEVOTION	Carrere CAR 128

DEVOTIONS – see BELLE AND THE DEVOTIONS

DEXY'S MIDNIGHT RUNNERS
UK group formed in 1978 by Kevin Rowland (born 17/8/1953, Wolverhampton, guitar/vocals), Al Archer (guitar), Pete Saunders (organ), Steve 'Babyface' Spooner (alto saxophone), 'Big' Jimmy Patterson (trombone), Pete Williams (bass), Jeff 'J.B.' Blythe (tenor saxophone) and Bobby Junior (drums). Their name is taken from the drug Dexedrine (despite their strict 'no drink and no drugs' policy). Signing with EMI in 1979, their brief success was followed by the group splitting up after Rowland insisted on releasing *Keep It* against the instinct of both the record company and the rest of the band. Most of them re-formed as Bureau, while Rowland moved to Phomogram with the remaining members. By 1986 it was basically a vehicle for Rowland as a soloist, despite a 1991 comeback with Creation Records. Ex-member Nick Gatfield became an A&R manager (responsible for signing Radiohead) and later MD of Polydor.

19/01/1980	40	6		DANCE STANCE	Oddball Productions R 6028
22/03/1980	❶²	14	◯	GENO Tribute to Geno Washington	Late Night Feelings R 6033
12/07/1980	7	9		THERE THERE MY DEAR	Late Night Feelings R 6038
21/03/1981	58	2		PLAN B	Parlophone R 6046
11/07/1981	16	9		SHOW ME	Mercury DEXYS 6
20/03/1982	45	4		THE CELTIC SOUL BROTHERS	Mercury DEXYS 8
03/07/1982	❶⁴	17	✪	COME ON EILEEN ▲¹ DEXY'S MIDNIGHT RUNNERS WITH THE EMERALD EXPRESS 1983 BRIT Award for Best Single	Mercury DEXYS 9
02/10/1982	5	7		JACKIE WILSON SAID Cover version of Van Morrison's 1972 US hit. When the group performed the single on *Top Of The Pops*, the BBC put up a picture of darts player Jackie Wilson!	Mercury DEXYS 10
04/12/1982	17	9		LET'S GET THIS STRAIGHT (FROM THE START)/OLD	Mercury DEXYS 11
02/04/1983	20	6		THE CELTIC SOUL BROTHERS This and above two singles credited to KEVIN ROWLAND AND DEXY'S MIDNIGHT RUNNERS	Mercury DEXYS 12
22/11/1986	13	10		BECAUSE OF YOU Theme to the TV comedy *Brush Strokes*	Mercury BRUSH 1

D4
New Zealand rock group formed by Dangerous Dion (guitar/vocals) and Jimmy Christmas (guitar/vocals), both previously in Nothing At All. Debuting as D4 in 1999, they also feature English Jake (bass) and Rich Mixture (drums).

28/09/2002	64	1		GET LOOSE	Infectious INFEC 117CDSX
07/12/2002	50	1		COME ON	Infectious INFEC 121CDSX
29/03/2003	41	1		LADIES MAN	Infectious INFEC 122CDSX

DHANY – see KMC FEATURING DHANY

DHS
UK producer Ben Stokes.

09/02/2002	72	1		HOUSE OF GOD	Club Tools 0135825 CLU

DI – see SHY FX AND T-POWER

TONY DI BART
UK singer (born Tony Di Bartholomew, Slough) who began singing in gospel choirs at sixteen, and despite being white graduated to lead singer. A session singer, he was signed by Wolverhampton-based Cleveland City.

09/04/1994	❶¹	12	◯	THE REAL THING	Cleveland City Blues CCBCD 15001
20/08/1994	21	4		DO IT	Cleveland City Blues CCBCD 15003
20/05/1995	46	1		WHY DID YA	Cleveland City Blues CCBCD 15004
02/03/1996	66	1		TURN YOUR LOVE AROUND	Cleveland City Blues CCBCD 15006
17/10/1998	51	1		THE REAL THING (REMIX)	Cleveland City CLECD 13050

GREGG DIAMOND BIONIC BOOGIE
US instrumentalist (born 4/4/1949, Bryn Mawr, PA) who was first known as a producer for the likes of Andrea True Connection. He died on 14/3/1999.

20/01/1979	61	3		CREAM (ALWAYS RISES TO THE TOP)	Polydor POSP 18

❶⁹ Number of weeks single topped the UK chart   ↑ Entered the UK chart at #1   ▲⁹ Number of weeks single topped the US chart

221

JIM DIAMOND UK singer (born 28/9/1953, Scotland) who was a member of PhD before going solo.

03/11/1984 .... ❶[1].. 13	**I SHOULD HAVE KNOWN BETTER**	A&M AM 220
02/02/1985..... 72...... 1......	I SLEEP ALONE AT NIGHT...	A&M AM 229
18/05/1985..... 42...... 5.......	REMEMBER I LOVE YOU	A&M AM 247
22/02/1986 ..... 5.... 11 ....O	**HI HO SILVER** Theme to the TV series *Boon*	A&M AM 296

NEIL DIAMOND US singer (born Noah Kaminsky, 24/1/1941, Brooklyn, NYC), initially a songwriter, who made the big time in 1966 with several top twenty hits in both the UK and US (although his first royalty cheque was for just 73 cents). Simultaneously performing, he made his debut single in 1965. Initially signed to Bang, he linked with MCA (through its Uni imprint) in 1968, then CBS/Columbia in 1973. His films included a 1980 remake of *The Jazz Singer*. He won the 1973 Grammy Award for Best Album of Original Score Written for a Motion Picture for *Jonathan Livingston Seagull*.

07/11/1970 ..... 3.... 17	**CRACKLIN' ROSIE** ▲[1]	Uni UN 529
20/02/1971..... 8.... 11......	**SWEET CAROLINE** Featured in the 1996 film *Beautiful Girls*	Uni UN 531
08/05/1971..... 4.... 12......	**I AM...I SAID** Featured in the 1999 film *Holy Smoke*	Uni UN 532
13/05/1972..... 14.... 13......	SONG SUNG BLUE ▲[1]	Uni UN 538
14/08/1976..... 35...... 4......	IF YOU KNOW WHAT I MEAN	CBS 4398
23/10/1976..... 13...... 9......	BEAUTIFUL NOISE	CBS 4601
24/12/1977..... 39...... 6......	DESIREE...	CBS 5869
25/11/1978 ..... 5.... 12 ...... ●	**YOU DON'T BRING ME FLOWERS** ▲[2] **BARBRA** (STREISAND) **AND NEIL**	CBS 6803
03/03/1979..... 16.... 12......	FOREVER IN BLUE JEANS	CBS 7047
15/11/1980..... 17.... 12......	LOVE ON THE ROCKS	Capitol CL 16173
14/02/1981..... 51...... 4......	HELLO AGAIN This and above single featured in the 1980 film *The Jazz Singer*...........	Capitol CL 16176
20/11/1982..... 47...... 7......	HEARTLIGHT Inspired by the 1982 film *E.T.*	CBS A 2814
21/11/1992..... 36...... 2......	MORNING HAS BROKEN	Columbia 6588267

DIAMOND HEAD UK group formed in Stourbridge in 1979 by Sean Harris (vocals), Brian Tatler (guitar), Colin Kimberley (bass) and Duncan Scott (drums). Kimberley and Scott left in 1983 and were replaced by Merv Goldsworthy and Robbie France. They disbanded in 1985, re-forming in 1991 with Sean Harris, Brian Tatler, Eddie Nooham (bass) and Karl Wilcox (drums).

11/09/1982..... 67...... 2......	IN THE HEAT OF THE NIGHT	MCA DHM 102

DIAMONDS Canadian vocal group formed in Toronto, Ontario in 1953 by Dave Somerville (lead), Ted Kowalski (tenor), Phil Leavitt (baritone) and Bill Reed (bass). They debuted on Coral in 1955. Leavitt retired in 1958 and was replaced by Michael Douglas; the same year Reed and Kowalski were replaced by John Felton and Evan Fisher. Somerville went solo and they disbanded in 1967. Felton re-formed the group in 1973 (having to obtain permission to use the name), enjoying a number of country hits before he was killed in a plane crash on 18/5/1982.

31/05/1957 ..... 3...... 17	**LITTLE DARLIN'** Featured in the films *American Graffiti* (1973) and *Ishtar* (1987)	Mercury MT 148

DICK AND DEEDEE US duo Dick St John Gosting (born 1944, Santa Monica, CA) and Dee Sperling (born 1945, Santa Monica) who formed at high school in Santa Monica. Their debut hit was originally on the Lama label before being picked up by Liberty in the US. Dick St John fell off a ladder and died on 27/12/2003.

26/10/1961..... 37...... 3.......	THE MOUNTAIN'S HIGH...	London HLG 9408

CHARLES DICKENS UK singer (born David Anthony) who began as a fashion photographer. He later toured with The Rolling Stones and recorded briefly for the Immediate label, covering the Jagger/Richards song *So Much In Love* before retiring from music.

08/07/1965..... 37...... 8.......	THAT'S THE WAY LOVE GOES...	Pye 7N 15887

GWEN DICKEY US singer, lead voice with Total Concept Unlimited, who backed Edwin Starr at Motown. The group later became Rose Royce, joining Norman Whitfield's eponymous label.

27/01/1990..... 72...... 2......	CAR WASH	Swanyard SYR 7
02/07/1994..... 21...... 4......	AIN'T NOBODY (LOVES ME BETTER) **KWS AND GWEN DICKEY**	X-clusive XCLU 010CD
14/02/1998..... 13...... 4......	WISHING ON A STAR **JAY-Z FEATURING GWEN DICKEY**..........................	Northwestside 74321554632
31/10/1998..... 18...... 3......	CAR WASH **ROSE ROYCE FEATURING GWEN DICKEY**..........................	MCA MCSTD 48096

NEVILLE DICKIE UK jazz pianist (born 1/1/1937, County Durham).

25/10/1969..... 33..... 10	ROBIN'S RETURN	Major Minor MM 644

DICKIES US punk group formed in Los Angeles, CA in 1977 by Chuck Wagon (keyboards), Stan Lee (guitar), Billy Club (bass), Leonard Graves Phillips (vocals) and Karlos Kaballero (drums). Wagon committed suicide in 1981.

16/12/1978..... 47...... 4......	SILENT NIGHT...	A&M AMS 7403
21/04/1979 ..... 7 ...... 8......	**BANANA SPLITS (TRA LA LA SONG)**	A&M AMS 7431
21/07/1979..... 45...... 6......	PARANOID	A&M AMS 7368
15/09/1979..... 39...... 5......	NIGHTS IN WHITE SATIN	A&M AMS 7469
16/02/1980..... 57...... 3......	FAN MAIL	A&M AMS 7504
19/07/1980..... 72...... 2......	GIGANTOR	A&M AMS 7544

BRUCE DICKINSON UK singer (born Paul Bruce Dickinson, 7/8/1958, Worksop, raised in Sheffield) who was a member of Samson before replacing Paul Di'anno as lead singer with Iron Maiden in 1981. In 1990 he launched a parallel solo career. He represented Great Britain in fencing, at one stage being ranked seventh in the country. Mr Bean is the creation of UK comedian Rowan Atkinson.

28/04/1990..... 18...... 5......	TATTOOED MILLIONAIRE	EMI EM 138
23/06/1990..... 23...... 5......	ALL THE YOUNG DUDES...	EMI EM 142

25/08/1990	45	2		DIVE! DIVE! DIVE!	EMI EM 151
04/04/1992	9	5		**(I WANT TO BE) ELECTED** MR BEAN AND SMEAR CAMPAIGN FEATURING BRUCE DICKINSON	London LON 319
28/05/1994	28	2		TEARS OF THE DRAGON	EMI CDEM 322
08/10/1994	37	2		SHOOT ALL THE CLOWNS	EMI CDEMS 341
13/04/1996	68	1		BACK FROM THE EDGE	Raw Power RAWX 1012
03/05/1997	54	1		ACCIDENT OF BIRTH	Raw Power RAWX 1042

BARBARA DICKSON
UK singer (born 27/9/1947, Dunfermline) who started in folk music, making her first albums in the early 1970s. She appeared in the show *John Paul George Ringo And Bert* and signed with RSO in 1975. Later a TV presenter, she also acted, winning a Laurence Olivier Award for her role in the stage musical *Blood Brothers*. She was awarded an OBE in the 2002 New Year's Honours List.

17/01/1976	9	7		**ANSWER ME**	RSO 2090 174
26/02/1977	18	7		ANOTHER SUITCASE IN ANOTHER HALL From the musical *Evita*	MCA 266
19/01/1980	41	7		CARAVAN SONG	Epic EPC 8103
15/03/1980	11	10		JANUARY FEBRUARY	Epic EPC 8115
14/06/1980	48	2		IN THE NIGHT	Epic EPC 8593
05/01/1985	❶4	16	●	**I KNOW HIM SO WELL** ELAINE PAIGE AND BARBARA DICKSON From the musical *Chess*	RCA CHESS 3

DICTATORS
US rock group formed in New York City in 1974 by Scott 'Top Ten' Kempner (guitar), Ross 'The Boss' Funicello (guitar), Andy Shernoff (bass) and Stu 'Boy' King (drums), with singer 'Handsome' Dick Manitoba joining for their debut album. King left before the album's release and was replaced by Ritchie Teeter, with Mark Mendoza (bass) joining at the same time and Shernoff switching to keyboards. Mendoza left in 1978 and the group disbanded soon after.

17/09/1977	49	2		SEARCH AND DESTROY	Asylum K 13091

BO DIDDLEY
US singer/guitarist (born Otha Elias Bates McDaniel, 30/12/1928, McComb, MS) who debuted with Checker/Chess in 1955. Named after a one-stringed African guitar, he was first called the name as a youth when he trained as a boxer. He appeared in the 1984 film *Trading Places* and was inducted into the Rock & Roll Hall of Fame in 1987. He was also a successful songwriter.

10/10/1963	34	6		PRETTY THING	Pye International 7N 25217
18/03/1965	39	4		HEY GOOD LOOKIN'	Chess 8000

DIDDY
UK producer Richard Dearlove who was later in Bedlam with Alan Thompson.

19/02/1994	52	1		GIVE ME LOVE	Positiva CDTIV 8
12/07/1997	23	2		GIVE ME LOVE (REMIX)	Feverpitch CDFVR 19

P DIDDY – see PUFF DADDY

DIDO
UK singer (born Dido Florian Cluod de Bounevialle Armstrong, 25/12/1971, London) and sister of Rollo Armstrong of Faithless. Initially taking off in the US, she achieved her UK break after a sample of *Thank You* was included on Eminem's #1 hit single *Stan*. Awards include Best New Act at the 2001 MTV Europe Music Awards and three BRIT Awards: Best British Female and Best British Album for *No Angel* in 2002 and Best British Female in 2004.

24/02/2001	4	12	O	**HERE WITH ME** Later used as the theme to the TV series *Roswell High* and featured in the 2003 film *Love Actually*.	Cheeky 74321832732
02/06/2001	3	10		**THANK YOU** Featured in the 1997 film *Sliding Doors*. The remixed version by Deep Dish won the 2001 Grammy Award for Remix of the Year, Non-Classical	Cheeky 74321853042
22/09/2001	17	8		HUNTER Effectively a double A-side with *Take My Hand*.	Cheeky 74321885722
20/04/2002	6	3		**ONE STEP TOO FAR** Would have charted higher but for a decision by the record company (BMG) to delete it midway through its first week on sale	Cheeky 74321926412
04/05/2002	68	1		ONE STEP TOO FAR 12-inch remix of above track. Both singles credited to FAITHLESS FEATURING DIDO	Cheeky 74321936742
13/09/2003	2	13		**WHITE FLAG** 2004 BRIT Award for Best British Single	Cheeky 82876546022
13/12/2003	8	9		**LIFE FOR RENT**	Cheeky 82876579472
24/04/2004	25	6		DON'T LEAVE HOME	Cheeky 82876611722
25/09/2004	29	3		SAND IN MY SHOE	Cheeky 82876626922

DIESEL PARK WEST
UK group formed by Richie Barton (guitar/vocals), Geoff Beavan (bass/vocals), John Butler (guitar/vocals), Rick Willson (guitar/vocals) and Dave Anderson (drums).

04/02/1989	66	2		ALL THE MYTHS ON SUNDAY	Food 17
01/04/1989	58	3		LIKE PRINCES DO	Food 19
05/08/1989	62	2		WHEN THE HOODOO COMES	Food 20
18/01/1992	48	3		FALL TO LOVE	Food 35
21/03/1992	58	2		BOY ON TOP OF THE NEWS	Food 36
05/09/1992	57	3		GOD ONLY KNOWS	Food 39

DIFFERENT GEAR VS POLICE
UK/Italian production group with Nigel Gray and Luigi Scaetti.

05/08/2000	28	3		WHEN THE WORLD IS RUNNING DOWN Featured in the 2000 film *Red Planet*. The single was an illegal bootleg before being released by Pagan	Pagan 039CDS

DIFFORD AND TILBROOK
UK duo Chris Difford (born 4/11/1954, London, guitar/vocals) and Glenn Tilbrook (born 31/8/1957, London, guitar/vocals), both ex-Squeeze, who disbanded in 1982. The eponymous group also featured Keith Wilkinson (bass), Guy Fletcher (keyboards) and Andy Duncan (drums). Difford and Tilbrook rejoined a revived Squeeze in 1985.

30/06/1984	57	2		LOVE'S CRASHING WAVES	A&M AM 193

❶9 Number of weeks single topped the UK chart ↑ Entered the UK chart at #1 ▲9 Number of weeks single topped the US chart

223

DIFF'RENT DARKNESS UK tribute group to The Darkness formed by Guided Missile Records. The label refuses to disclose the group members, but previous tribute groups to The Strokes (Diff'rent Strokes) and White Stripes (Diff'rent Stripes) featured members of Blur, Pulp, The Strokes and Bill Drummond.

27/12/2003.....66......1....... ORCHESTRAL MANOEUVRES IN THE DARKNESS EP Tracks on EP: *I Believe In A Thing Called Love*, *Get Your Hands Off My Woman* and *Love On The Rocks With No Ice* .... Guided Missile GUIDE49CD

DIGABLE PLANETS US rap group formed in Washington DC by Ishmael 'Butterfly' Butler, Mary Ann 'Ladybug' Vierra and Craig 'Doodle Bug' Irving.

13/02/1993.....67......2....... REBIRTH OF SLICK (COOL LIKE DAT)... Pendulum EKR 159CD

RAH DIGGA US rapper (born Raisha Fisher, 1975, New Jersey) who was a member of Twice The Flavor and Outsidaz before joining the Flipmode Squad and then going solo in 2000.

02/03/2002.....41......2....... I'M LEAVIN' OUTSIDAZ FEATURING RAH DIGGA AND MELANIE BLATT .... Rufflife RLCDM 03
21/06/2003.....37......2....... BOUT JAMELIA FEATURING RAH DIGGA .... Parlophone CDRS 6597

DIGITAL DREAM BABY UK producer Steven Teear whose debut hit was a dance remix of Peter Auty's *Walking In The Air*.

14/12/1991.....49......4....... WALKING IN THE AIR .... Columbia 6576067

DIGITAL EXCITATION Belgian producer Frank De Wulf.

29/02/1992.....37......2....... PURE PLEASURE .... R&S RSUK 10

DIGITAL ORGASM Belgian dance group formed by Praga Khan and Jade, featuring Maurice Engelen and Nikki Van Lierop. They also recorded as MNO.

07/12/1991.....16......9....... RUNNING OUT OF TIME .... Dead Dead Good GOOD 009
18/04/1992.....31......3....... STARTOUCHERS.. DDG International GOOD 13
25/07/1992.....62......2....... MOOG ERUPTION .... DDG International GOOD 17

DIGITAL UNDERGROUND US rap group formed in Oakland, CA by Shock-G (born Gregory Jacobs, keyboards/vocals), Chopmaster J (samples/percussion) and DJ Fuze (born David Elliott) with various floating members including Tupac Shakur, DJ Jay-Z and Saafir The Saucy Nomad.

16/03/1991.....52......4....... SAME SONG .... Big Life BLR 40

DILATED PEOPLES US rap group formed in Los Angeles, CA by Michael 'Evidence' Perretta, Rakaa 'Iriscience' Taylor and Christopher 'DJ Babu' Orec.

23/02/2002.....29......3....... WORST COMES TO THE WORST Contains samples of William Bell's *I Forgot How To Be Your Lover* and Mobb Deep's *Survival Of The Fittest* .... Capitol CDCL 834
10/04/2004.....35......3..... THIS WAY .... Capitol CDCL 854

DILEMMA Italian instrumental/production group formed by Davide Sabadin, Elvio Moratto and Claudio Collina.

06/04/1996.....42......1....... IN SPIRIT .... ffrr FCDE 274

RICKY DILLARD – see FARLEY 'JACKMASTER' FUNK

DILLINJA UK drum and bass producer Karl Francis.

09/11/2002.....50......1..... TWIST 'EM OUT... Renegade Hardware RH40
21/12/2002.....53......1..... LIVE OR DIE/SOUTH MANZ .... Valve VLV007
10/05/2003.....47......1..... THIS IS A WARNING/SUPER DJ .... Valve VLV 008
28/06/2003.....35......3..... TWIST 'EM OUT DILLINJA FEATURING SKIBADEE.................................. Trouble On Vinyl TOV 56CD
27/09/2003.....56......2..... FAST CAR .... Valve VLV011
12/06/2004.....71......1..... ALL THE THINGS/FORSAKEN DREAMS .... Valve VLV012
10/07/2004.....71......1..... IN THE GRIND/ACID TRAK .... Valve VLV013

DIMESTARS UK vocal/instrumental group with Roxanne Wilde (vocals), Morgan Quaintance (guitar), Tom Hanna (bass) and Joe Holweger (drums). Wilde is the daughter of Marty Wilde and sister of Kim Wilde. She later went solo and sang with DT8.

16/06/2001.....72......1....... MY SUPERSTAR .... Polydor 5870912

PAOLO DINI – see FPI PROJECT

MARK DINNING US singer (born 17/8/1933, Drury, OK) who learned to play the guitar at seventeen, auditioning for Wesley Nash who got him a contract with MGM. Brother of the vocal trio The Dinning Sisters, his sister Jean wrote his debut hit *Teen Angel*, a US #1 in 1960. Its UK performance was marred by its being banned by radio stations as a 'death disc'. Dinning died of a heart attack on 22/3/1986.

10/03/1960.....37......4....... TEEN ANGEL ▲[1] Featured in the 1973 film *American Graffiti* .... MGM 1053

DINOSAUR JR. US rock group formed in Amherst, MA in 1984 by Joseph Mascis (born 10/12/1965, Amherst, guitar/vocals), Lou Barlow (born 17/7/1966, Northampton, MA, bass), both ex-Deep Wound, and ex-All White Jury Emmett Murphy (born 21/12/1964, drums). Later members included Mike Johnson, Don Fleming, Jay Spiegel and Van Connor. Mascis went solo in 1995 and the group split in 1997.

02/02/1991.....49......2....... THE WAGON .... Blanco Y Negro NEG 48

○ Silver disc ● Gold disc ✪ Platinum disc (additional platinum units are indicated by a figure following the symbol) ◉ Singles released prior to 1973 that are known to have sold over 1 million copies in the UK

14/11/1992.....44......1......	GET ME..Blanco Y Negro NEG 60
30/01/1993.....20......3......	START CHOPPIN...Blanco Y Negro NEG 61CD
12/06/1993.....44......2......	OUT THERE Featured in the 1993 film *Wayne's World 2* ....Blanco Y Negro NEG 63CD
27/08/1994.....25......3......	FEEL THE PAIN...Blanco Y Negro NEG 74CD
11/02/1995.....67......1......	I DON'T THINK SO...Blanco Y Negro NEG 77CD
05/04/1997.....53......1......	TAKE A RUN AT THE SUN...Blanco Y Negro NEG 103CD

DINOSAURS – see TERRY DACTYL AND THE DINOSAURS

DIO US heavy rock group named after lead singer Ronnie James Dio (born Ronald Padavona, 10/7/1949, New Hampshire). Dio had previously been with Rainbow and Black Sabbath (replacing Ozzy Osbourne). The group also included Vinny Appice (drums), Jimmy Bain (bass), Vivian Campbell (guitar) and Claude Schnell (keyboards). Campbell left in 1987 and was replaced by Craig Goldie.

20/08/1983.....72......2......	HOLY DIVER..Vertigo DIO 1
29/10/1983.....46......3......	RAINBOW IN THE DARK...Vertigo DIO 2
11/08/1984.....42......3......	WE ROCK...Vertigo DIO 3
29/09/1984.....34......4......	MYSTERY...Vertigo DIO 4
10/08/1985.....26......6......	ROCK 'N' ROLL CHILDREN...Vertigo DIO 5
02/11/1985.....72......1......	HUNGRY FOR HEAVEN Featured in the 1985 film *Vision Quest*.........Vertigo DIO 6
17/05/1986.....56......2......	HUNGRY FOR HEAVEN Re-issue of Vertigo DIO 6.....................Vertigo DIO 7
01/08/1987.....69......1......	I COULD HAVE BEEN A DREAMER...................................Vertigo DIO 8

DION US singer (born Dion DiMucci, 18/7/1939, The Bronx, NYC) who debuted in 1957. The following year he formed the Belmonts (named after Belmont Avenue in The Bronx) with Angelo D'Aleo (born 3/2/1940), Fred Milano (born 22/8/1939) and Carlo Mastrangelo (born 5/10/1938), all from The Bronx. Dion went solo in 1960, occasionally reviving the Belmonts since, and has also recorded contemporary Christian material. He was inducted into the Rock & Roll Hall of Fame in 1989.

26/06/1959.....28......2......	A TEENAGER IN LOVE DION AND THE BELMONTS Originally called *Great To Be In Love*. Featured in the 1982 film *Diner* ....
	....London HLU 8874
19/01/1961.....47......1......	LONELY TEENAGER..Top Rank JAR 521
02/11/1961.....11......9......	RUNAROUND SUE ▲² Featured in the films *That'll Be The Day* (1973), *The Flamingo Kid* (1984) and *Picture Perfect* (1997) .....
	....Top Rank JAR 586
15/02/1962.....10.....12......	THE WANDERER Featured in the films *The Wanderers* (1979) and *Behind Enemy Lines* (2001)..................HMV POP 971
22/05/1976.....16......9......	THE WANDERER Re-issue of HMV POP 971 ....Philips 6146 700
19/08/1989.....74......2......	KING OF THE NEW YORK STREET..................................Arista 112556

CELINE DION Canadian singer (born 30/3/1968, Charlemagne, Quebec) who won the Eurovision Song Contest for Switzerland in 1988 singing *Ne Partez Sans Moi*. Married to Rene Angelil, her manager since 1981, she had a son in January 2001. Five Grammy Awards include Album of the Year and Best Pop Album in 1996 for *Falling Into You*. She has a star on the Hollywood Walk of Fame.

16/05/1992 .....9......7......	BEAUTY AND THE BEAST CELINE DION AND PEABO BRYSON Featured in the 1992 Walt Disney film *Beauty And The Beast* and won an Oscar for Best Film Song. 1992 Grammy Award for Best Pop Performance by a Duo ....Epic 6576607
04/07/1992.....60......2......	IF YOU ASKED ME TO..Epic 6581927
14/11/1992.....46......2......	LOVE CAN MOVE MOUNTAINS ....Epic 6587787
26/12/1992.....57......3......	IF YOU ASKED ME TO..Epic 6581927
03/04/1993.....72......1......	WHERE DOES MY HEART BEAT NOW ....Epic 6563265
29/01/1994 .....4.....10......	THE POWER OF LOVE ▲⁴ ....Epic 6597992
23/04/1994.....40......3......	MISLED..Epic 6602922
22/10/1994 .....❶⁶.....31.....✪	THINK TWICE ....Epic 6606422
20/05/1995 .....8......8......	ONLY ONE ROAD ....Epic 6613535
09/09/1995 .....7......9......	TU M'AIMES ENCORE (TO LOVE ME AGAIN).........................Epic 6624255
02/12/1995.....15......6......	MISLED Re-issue of Epic 6602922 ....Epic 6626495
02/03/1996.....10.....10......	FALLING INTO YOU ....Epic 6629795
01/06/1996 .....5.....16.....○	BECAUSE YOU LOVED ME (THEME FROM UP CLOSE AND PERSONAL) ▲⁶ Featured in the 1996 film *Up Close And Personal* ....
	....Epic 6632382
05/10/1996 .....3.....14.....○	IT'S ALL COMING BACK TO ME NOW ....Epic 6637112
21/12/1996 .....6.....13.....○	ALL BY MYSELF..Epic 6640622
28/06/1997.....11......6......	CALL THE MAN ....Epic 6646922
15/11/1997 .....3.....15.....●	TELL HIM BARBRA STREISAND AND CELINE DION ....Epic 6653052
20/12/1997.....11......8......	THE REASON ....Epic 6653812
21/02/1998 .....❶².....20.....✪²	MY HEART WILL GO ON ↑ ▲² Featured in the 1997 film *Titanic* and won an Oscar for Best Film Song. 1998 Grammy Awards for Record of the Year and Best Female Pop Vocal Performance; also Song of the Year and Best Song for a Motion Picture for writers James Horner and Will Jennings. The video is the most requested on *The Box*, receiving over 60,000 requests between January 1998 and July 1999. Reclaimed #1 position on 14/3/1998 ....Epic 6655472

❶⁹ Number of weeks single topped the UK chart   ↑ Entered the UK chart at #1   ▲⁹ Number of weeks single topped the US chart

225

18/07/1998	5	12	O	IMMORTALITY CELINE DION WITH THE BEE GEES	Epic 6661682
28/11/1998	3	13	O	I'M YOUR ANGEL ▲6 CELINE DION AND R KELLY	Epic 6666282
10/07/1999	29	3		TREAT HER LIKE A LADY	Epic 6675525
11/12/1999	12	11		THAT'S THE WAY IT IS	Epic 6684622
08/04/2000	19	7		THE FIRST TIME EVER I SAW YOUR FACE	Epic 6691942
23/03/2002	7	10		A NEW DAY HAS COME.	Epic 6725032
31/08/2002	17	6		I'M ALIVE	Epic 6730652
07/12/2002	38	2		GOODBYE'S (THE SADDEST WORD).	Epic 6733732
20/09/2003	27	2		ONE HEART	Epic 6743482

KATHRYN DION – see 2 FUNKY 2 STARRING KATHRYN DION

DIONNE Canadian singer Dionne Warren.

| 23/09/1989 | 69 | 2 | | COME GET MY LOVIN' | Citybeat CBC 745 |

WASIS DIOP FEATURING LENA FIAGBE Senegalese producer/guitarist based in Paris, France with UK singer Lena Fiagbe.

| 10/02/1996 | 44 | 2 | | AFRICAN DREAM | Mercury MERCD 453 |

DIRE STRAITS UK rock group formed in 1977 by Mark Knopfler (born 12/8/1949, Glasgow, guitar/vocals), his brother David (born 27/12/1952, Glasgow, guitar), John Illsley (born 24/6/1949, Leicester, bass) and Pick Withers (born 4/4/1948, Leicester, drums). After radio plays of their self-funded debut record they signed with Phonogram's Vertigo label. David left in 1980 and was replaced by Hal Lindes (born 30/6/1953, Monterey, CA), who left in 1985. Withers left in 1983; Terry Williams was his replacement. Alan Clark (born 5/3/1955, Durham, keyboards) was added in 1980 and Guy Fletcher in 1984. Knopfler has recorded solo, and with Fletcher was in The Notting Hillbillies. Named Best British Group at the 1983 and 1986 BRIT Awards, they won the Best Album Award in 1987 for *Brothers In Arms* (the first CD to sell over 1 million copies in the UK). Their name reflected their financial state when they formed. Knopfler was awarded an OBE in the 2000 New Year's Honours List.

10/03/1979	8	11	O	SULTANS OF SWING	Vertigo 6059 206
28/07/1979	51	6		LADY WRITER	Vertigo 6059 230
17/01/1981	8	11		ROMEO AND JULIET Featured in the 1999 film *200 Cigarettes*	Vertigo MOVIE 1
04/04/1981	37	5		SKATEAWAY	Vertigo MOVIE 2
10/10/1981	54	3		TUNNEL OF LOVE	Vertigo MUSIC 3
04/09/1982	2	8	O	PRIVATE INVESTIGATIONS	Vertigo DSTR 2
22/01/1983	14	7		TWISTING BY THE POOL	Vertigo DSTR 2
18/02/1984	50	3		LOVE OVER GOLD (LIVE)/SOLID ROCK (LIVE)	Vertigo DSTR 6
20/04/1985	20	6		SO FAR AWAY	Vertigo DSTR 9
06/07/1985	4	16	O	MONEY FOR NOTHING ▲3 1985 Grammy Award for Best Rock Vocal Performance by a Group	Vertigo DSTR 10
26/10/1985	16	13		BROTHERS IN ARMS 1986 Grammy Award for Best Video Short Form	Vertigo DSTR 11
11/01/1986	2	11		WALK OF LIFE	Vertigo DSTR 12
03/05/1986	26	6		YOUR LATEST TRICK Proceeds donated to Great Ormond Street Hospital	Vertigo DSTR 13
05/11/1988	62	1		SULTANS OF SWING Re-issue of Vertigo 6059 206	Vertigo DSTR 15
31/08/1991	21	4		CALLING ELVIS	Vertigo DSTR 16
02/11/1991	55	2		HEAVY FUEL	Vertigo DSTR 17
29/02/1992	42	2		ON EVERY STREET	Vertigo DSTR 18
27/06/1992	67	1		THE BUG	Vertigo DSTR 19
22/05/1993	31	3		ENCORES EP Tracks on EP: *Your Latest Trick, The Bug, Solid Rock* and *Local Hero – Wild Theme*	Vertigo DSCD 20

DIRECKT UK production/instrumental duo Mike 'E-Bloc' Kirwin and Danny 'Hybrid' Bennett, who also record as E-Lustrious.

| 13/08/1994 | 36 | 2 | | TWO FATT GUITARS (REVISITED) | UFG 7CD |

DIRECT DRIVE UK vocal/instrumental group formed by Bones (congas/percussion/vocals), Derek Green (vocals), Paul Hardcastle (keyboards/vocals), Mick Ward (bass/vocals), Bob Williams (guitar) and Pete Quinton (drums). Green and Hardcastle left to form First Light in 1982.

| 26/01/1985 | 67 | 2 | | ANYTHING | Polydor POSP 728 |
| 04/05/1985 | 75 | 1 | | A.B.C. (FALLING IN LOVE'S NOT EASY) | Boiling Point POSP 742 |

DIRT DEVILS UK/Finnish production/instrumental duo Jono Grant and Paavo Siljamaki, first known as remixers for the likes of Dario G and Madonna. They are also in Oceanlab.

| 02/02/2002 | 15 | 6 | | THE DRILL | NuLife 74321915262 |
| 06/12/2003 | 53 | 2 | | MUSIC IS LIFE | NuLife 82876571412 |

DIRTY ROTTEN SCOUNDRELS – see LISA STANSFIELD

DIRTY VEGAS UK production group with Paul Harris, Steve Smith and Ben Harris.

19/05/2001	27	4		DAYS GO BY	Credence CDCRED 011
03/08/2002	31	3		GHOSTS	Credence CDCRED 028
12/10/2002	16	4		DAYS GO BY (REMIX) 2002 Grammy Award for Best Dance Recording	Credence CDCREDS 030
23/10/2004	54	1		WALK INTO THE SUN	Parlophone CDRS6647

DISCHARGE
UK rock group formed in 1977 by Terry 'Tezz' Roberts (vocals), his brother Tony 'Bones' (guitar), Roy 'Rainy' Wainwright (bass) and Hacko (drums). Hacko left in 1979, at which point Terry Roberts switched to drums, with Cal joining as lead singer. Terry Roberts left in 1981; Bambi was the temporary drummer until Garry Maloney joined. Tony Roberts left in 1982 and was replaced by Peter 'Pooch' Pyrtle, who left after a year along with Maloney. Their replacements were Les 'The Mole' Hunt (guitar) and Nick Haymaker (drums). These two proved short-lived too, Maloney returning in 1986 and Stephen Brooks joining on guitar. By 1997 the early line-up of Cal, Bones, Rainy and Tezz had re-formed.

24/10/1981 . . . . . 64 . . . . . . 3 . . . . NEVER AGAIN . . . . Clay 6

DISCO ANTHEM
Dutch producer Lex Van Coeverden who is also a member of Atlantic Ocean.

18/06/1994 . . . . . 47 . . . . . . 2 . . . . SCREAM Contains a sample of Farley 'Jackmaster' Funk's *Love Can't Turn Around* . . . . Sweat MCSTD 1977

DISCO CITIZENS
UK production artist Nick Bracegirdle. He also records as Chicane and later launched the Modena Records and Cyanide Music labels.

22/07/1995 . . . . . 40 . . . . . . 2	RIGHT HERE RIGHT NOW . . . . Deconstruction 74321293872
12/04/1997 . . . . . 34 . . . . . . 2	FOOTPRINT . . . . Xtravaganza 0091115
04/07/1998 . . . . . 56 . . . . . . 1	NAGASAKI BADGER . . . . Xtravaganza 0091595 EXT

DISCO EVANGELISTS
UK instrumental/production group formed by David Holmes, Ashley 'Daddy Ash' Beedle and Lindsay Edwards. Beedle also records as Black Science Orchestra and was later a member of X-Press 2.

08/05/1993 . . . . . 59 . . . . . . 2 . . . . DE NIRO . . . . Positiva CDTIV 2

DISCO TEX AND THE SEX-O-LETTES
US studio group assembled by noted producer Bob Crewe, with Sir Monti Rock III (born Joseph Montanez Jr), a former hairdresser, providing lead vocals.

23/11/1974 . . . . . 8 . . . . . . 12 . . . . . O	**GET DANCING** . . . . Chelsea 2005 013
26/04/1975 . . . . . 6 . . . . . . 10	**I WANNA DANCE WIT CHOO** DISCO TEX AND THE SEX-O-LETTES FEATURING SIR MONTI ROCK III . . . . Chelsea 2005 024

DISCO TEX PRESENTS CLOUDBURST
UK dance group formed by producers Mike Gray and Jon Pearn who also recorded as Arizona, Hustlers Convention, Ronaldo's Revenge, Full Intention and Sex-O-Sonique.

24/03/2001 . . . . . 35 . . . . . . 2 . . . . I CAN CAST A SPELL . . . . Absolution CDABSOL 1

DISCOVERY – see COAST 2 COAST FEATURING DISCOVERY

DISPOSABLE HEROES OF HIPHOPRISY
US hip hop duo formed in San Francisco, CA by Michael Franti (vocals) and Rono Tse (percussion), both previously in The Beatnigs.

04/04/1992 . . . . . 57 . . . . . . 2	TELEVISION THE DRUG OF THE NATION . . . . Fourth & Broadway BRW 241
30/05/1992 . . . . . 68 . . . . . . 1	LANGUAGE OF VIOLENCE . . . . Fourth & Broadway 12BRW 248
19/12/1992 . . . . . 44 . . . . . . 4	TELEVISION THE DRUG OF THE NATION . . . . Fourth & Broadway BRW 241

DISTANT SOUNDZ
UK garage group formed in Essex by Mark Shrimpton with Robby Beaumont and Jack Berry.

09/03/2002 . . . . . 20 . . . . . . 4 . . . . TIME AFTER TIME . . . . W10/Incentive CENT 36CDS

SACHA DISTEL
French singer/guitarist (born 29/1/1933, Paris) who was especially popular during the 1970s. He made countless TV, cabaret, variety and concert appearances and appeared in films, his first being the 1953 film *Femmes De Paris*. He died on 21/7/2004.

10/01/1970 . . . . . 10 . . . . . 27 . . . . . . **RAINDROPS KEEP FALLING ON MY HEAD** . . . . Warner Brothers WB 7345

DISTILLERS
US and Australian rock group formed in 1998 by Brody Armstrong (guitar and vocals), Rose Casper (guitar), Kim Chi (bass) and Matt (drums). By 2002 the group consisted of Brody, Tony (guitar), Ryan (bass) and Andy (drums).

15/11/2003 . . . . . 51 . . . . . . 1	DRAIN THE BLOOD . . . . Sire W 628CD
10/04/2004 . . . . . 48 . . . . . . 1	THE HUNGER . . . . Sire W 636CD
19/06/2004 . . . . . 74 . . . . . . 1	BEAT YOUR HEART OUT . . . . Sire W 644CD

DISTORTED MINDS
UK drum and bass production duo formed in Bristol by Jon Midwinter and Alistair Vickery.

29/03/2003 . . . . . 43 . . . . . . 2	T-10/THE TENTH PLANET . . . . Kaos 006P
24/01/2004 . . . . . 45 . . . . . . 2	T-10/THE TENTH PLANET . . . . Kaos 006P

DISTURBED
US rock group formed in Chicago, IL by David Craiman (vocals), Dan Donegan (guitar), Fuzz Kmak (bass) and Mike Wengren (drums).

07/04/2001 . . . . . 52 . . . . . . 1	VOICES . . . . Giant 74321848962
28/09/2002 . . . . . 31 . . . . . . 2	PRAYER . . . . Reprise W 591CD
14/12/2002 . . . . . 56 . . . . . . 1	REMEMBER . . . . Reprise W 596CD

DIVA
Norwegian vocal duo Helene Sommer and Elene Nyborg.

07/10/1995 . . . . . 53 . . . . . . 1	THE SUN ALWAYS SHINES ON TV . . . . East West YZ 947CD
20/07/1996 . . . . . 44 . . . . . . 1	EVERYBODY (MOVE YOUR BODY) . . . . East West YZ 035CD

DIVA SURPRISE FEATURING GEORGIA JONES
US/Spanish production duo Walter Taieb and Giuseppe 'DJ Pippi' Nuzzo with singer Georgia Jones. Taieb had previously produced Original.

14/11/1998 . . . . . 29 . . . . . . 2 . . . . ON THE TOP OF THE WORLD . . . . Positiva CDTIV 100

❶⁹ Number of weeks single topped the UK chart ↑ Entered the UK chart at #1 ▲⁹ Number of weeks single topped the US chart

227

DIVE UK production duo Sacha Collison and Simon Greenaway who also recorded as Aurora. Their debut hit featured singer Nasreeb Shah.

21/02/1998	35	1		BOOGIE		WEA 147CD1

DIVERSIONS UK reggae group with Glen Cartlidge (guitar), Les Chappell (guitar), Lene Lovich (saxophone/vocals), Dave Quinn (bass), Steve Saxon (saxophone), Gregg Sheehan (drums) and Jeffrey Ray Smith (keyboards). Lovich later recorded solo.

20/09/1975	34	3		FATTIE BUM BUM		Gull GULS 18

DIVINE US singer/actor (born Harris Glenn Milstead, 1946) named by film director John Walters. He appeared in films, many aimed at the gay and transvestite market, including the 1988 film *Hairspray*. He died from a heart attack on 7/3/1988.

15/10/1983	65	2	LOVE REACTION	Design Communication DES 4
14/07/1984	16	10	YOU THINK YOU'RE A MAN	Proto ENA 118
20/10/1984	52	2	I'M SO BEAUTIFUL	Proto ENA 121
27/04/1985	23	7	WALK LIKE A MAN	Proto ENA 125
20/07/1985	47	3	TWISTIN' THE NIGHT AWAY	Proto ENA 127

DIVINE US vocal group formed in New Jersey by Nikki Bratcher, Tonia Tash and Kia Thornton

16/10/1999	52	1	LATELY ▲[1]	Mushroom/Red Ant RA 002CDS

DIVINE COMEDY UK group formed in Enniskillen, Northern Ireland in 1989 as a five-piece band, reducing to just Neil Hannon (born 7/11/1970, Londonderry) after one album.

29/06/1996	14	5	SOMETHING FOR THE WEEKEND	Setanta SETCD 26
24/08/1996	27	2	BECOMING MORE LIKE ALFIE	Setanta SETCD 27
16/11/1996	15	2	THE FROG PRINCESS	Setanta SETCD 32
22/03/1997	14	4	EVERYBODY KNOWS (EXCEPT YOU)	Setanta SETCDA 038
11/04/1998	28	3	I'VE BEEN TO A MARVELLOUS PARTY Listed flip side was *Someday I'll Find You* by **SHOLA AMA AND CRAIG ARMSTRONG**	
				EMI CDTCB 001
26/09/1998	19	3	GENERATION SEX	Setanta SETCDA 050
28/11/1998	49	1	THE CERTAINTY OF CHANCE	Setanta SETCDA 067
06/02/1999	8	7	**NATIONAL EXPRESS**	Setanta SETCDB 069
21/08/1999	17	4	THE POP SINGER'S FEAR OF THE POLLEN COUNT	Setanta SETCDB 070
13/11/1999	38	2	GIN SOAKED BOY	Setanta SETCD 071
10/03/2001	26	2	LOVE WHAT YOU DO	Parlophone CDRS 6554
26/05/2001	34	2	BAD AMBASSADOR	Parlophone CDRS 6558
10/11/2001	42	1	PERFECT LOVESONG	Parlophone CDRS 6561
03/04/2004	25	2	COME HOME BILLY BIRD	Parlophone CDRS 6630
26/06/2004	38	2	ABSENT FRIENDS	Parlophone CDRS 6641

DIVINE INSPIRATION UK production group Paul Crawley, Lee Robinson and Dave Levin, with singer Sarah-Jane Scott.

18/01/2003	5	7	**THE WAY (PUT YOUR HAND IN MY HAND)**	Data/Ministry Of Sound/Heat DATA 42CDS
15/11/2003	55	1	WHAT WILL BE WILL BE (DESTINY)	Heat Recordings HEATCD036

DIVINYLS Australian rock group formed in Sydney in 1981 by Christina Amphlett (vocals), Mark McEntee (guitar), Bjorn Olin (keyboards), JJ Harris (drums) and Rick Grossman (bass). By 1991 the group was a duo of Amphlett and McEntee.

18/05/1991	10	12	**I TOUCH MYSELF** Featured in the 1997 film *Austin Powers – International Man Of Mystery*	Virgin America VUS 36

DIXIE CHICKS US country group formed by Martha Seide (born 12/10/1969, fiddle/mandolin), her sister Emily Robinson (born 16/8/1972, guitar/banjo) and Natalie Maines (born 14/10/1974, lead vocals). Seven Grammy Awards include: Best Country Album in 1998 for *Wide Open Spaces*; Best Country Album in 1999 for *Fly*; Best Country Performance by a Duo or Group with Vocal in 2002 for *Long Time Gone*; Best Country Instrumental Performance in 2002 for *Lil' Jack Slade*; and Best Country Album in 2002 for *Home*. In July 2001 they filed a suit against Sony Music seeking to break their recording contract, even though they were still required to deliver a further five albums (their first two for the label had sold over 14 million copies in the US alone). Sony claimed non-delivery of the five albums could cost them as much as $100 million. A compromise was reached a year later when the group were given their own label, Open Wide Records, via Sony.

03/07/1999	26	5	THERE'S YOUR TROUBLE 1998 Grammy Award for Best Country Group Performance	Epic 6675165
06/11/1999	53	1	READY TO RUN Featured in the 1999 film *Runaway Bride*. 1999 Grammy Award for Best Country Group Performance	
				Epic 6682472
19/04/2003	55	1	LANDSLIDE	Epic 6737392

DIXIE CUPS US group formed in New Orleans, LA in 1963 by Barbara Ann Hawkins (born 23/10/1943, New Orleans), Rosa Lee Hawkins (born 24/9/1944, New Orleans) and their cousin Joan Marie Johnson (born 15/1/1945, New Orleans) as The Meltones. They were discovered by Joe Jones at a high school talent show and recorded their debut hit with Jerry Leiber and Mike Stoller's Red Bird label (the Ronettes and Crystals having failed to score with the song). The girls claimed they never saw more than a couple of hundred dollars from the #1 smash hit, and disbanded in 1966 after a brief spell with ABC-Paramount. All three became models, the Hawkins sisters later re-forming with Dale Mickie on the nostalgia circuit.

18/06/1964	22	8	CHAPEL OF LOVE ▲[3] Featured in the 1987 film *Full Metal Jacket*	Pye International 7N 25245
13/05/1965	23	8	IKO IKO Featured in the 1987 film *The Big Easy*	Red Bird RB 10024

DIZZY HEIGHTS UK rapper.

18/12/1982	49	4	CHRISTMAS RAPPING	Polydor WRAP 1

○ Silver disc ● Gold disc ✪ Platinum disc (additional platinum units are indicated by a figure following the symbol) ◎ Singles released prior to 1973 that are known to have sold over 1 million copies in the UK

DJ ALIGATOR PROJECT Danish producer Aliasghar Movasat.

07/10/2000.....57......1......	THE WHISTLE SONG..EMI CDBLOW 001		
19/01/2002.....5......10......	THE WHISTLE SONG (BLOW MY WHISTLE BITCH)..................................All Around The World CDGLOBE 247		

DJ ARABESQUE – see MARIO PIU

DJ BADMARSH AND SHRI FEATURING UK APACHE Yemeni/Indian instrumental/production duo formed in 1997 by Mohammed Aktar Ali and Shrikanth Sriram with UK rapper Andre Williams. Badmarsh (Hindi for 'rascal' or 'black sheep') had previously recorded as Easy Mo.

28/07/2001.....63......1.......	SIGNS...Outcaste OUT 38CD1

DJ BOBO Swiss producer Rene Baumann.

24/09/1994.....47......2......	EVERYBODY...PWL Continental PWCD 312
17/06/1995.....49......2......	LOVE IS ALL AROUND..Avex UK AVEXCD 7
25/10/2003.....36......3......	CHIHUAHUA..Fuelin 82876559422

DJ CASPER US DJ (born William Perry Jr in Brooklyn, NY) whose debut hit was originally recorded in 1996 and first charted in the US in 2001 under the moniker Mr C The Slide Man.

13/03/2004.....1......18......	CHA CHA SLIDE..All Around The World CDGLOBE329
16/10/2004.....16......6......	OOPS UPSIDE YOUR HEAD DJ CASPER FEATURING THE GAP BAND.........................All Around The World CDGLOBE376

DJ CHUNKY – see XTM AND DJ CHUNKY PRESENTS ANNIA

DJ CHUS PRESENTS GROOVE FOUNDATION Spanish DJ (born Chus L Esteban, 1971, Madrid) who began 'DJing' at the age of sixteen at Alien.

02/11/2002.....65......1.......	THAT FEELING...Defected DFTD 055R2

DJ DADO Italian producer Roberto Gallo. He was previously a remixer and worked with Alexia, Moella, Imperio and Irene Cara.

06/04/1996.....8......6......	X-FILES..ZYX 8065R8
14/03/1998.....63......1......	COMING BACK..ffrr TABCD 247
11/07/1998.....59......1......	GIVE ME LOVE DJ DADO VS MICHELLE WEEKS..VC Recordings VCRD 37
08/05/1999.....51......1......	READY OR NOT DJ DADO AND SIMONE JAY...Chemistry CDKEM 006

DJ DAN PRESENTS NEEDLE DAMAGE US DJ (born Dan Wherrett in Seattle, WA, raised in California) who also records as Electroliners.

05/05/2001.....53......1......	THAT ZIPPER TRACK..Duty Free DF 213CD

DJ DEE KLINE UK DJ/producer Nick Annand, 21 years of age at the time of his debut hit.

03/06/2000.....11......6......	I DON'T SMOKE Contains a sample of Harry Hill's Barking dialogue from his Channel 4 TV programme.......East West EW 213CD

DJ DISCIPLE US DJ/producer David Banks, based in New York, who launched the Catch 22 Recordings label.

12/11/1994.....67......1......	ON THE DANCEFLOOR..Mother MUMCD 55

DJ DOC SCOTT UK producer Scott McIlroy from Coventry who launched the Metalheads label with Goldie.

01/02/1992.....64......2......	NHS (EP) Tracks on EP: Surgery and Night Nurse...............................Absolute 2 ABS 001DJ

DJ DUKE US producer/DJ Ken Larson from New York who made his first record in 1990 and set up Power Music Records, Power Music Trax, Sex Mania and DJ Exlusive. He also records as Club People, Inner Soul, The Music Choir, The Pleasure Dome and Tribal Liberation.

08/01/1994.....15......5......	BLOW YOUR WHISTLE...ffrr FCD 228
16/07/1994.....31......2......	TURN IT UP (SAY YEAH)...ffrr FCD 235

DJ EMPIRE PRESENTS GIORGIO MORODER German producers Alexander Wilkie and Giorgio Moroder.

12/02/2000.....46......1......	THE CHASE (RE-RECORDING)..Logic 74321732112

DJ ERIC UK production duo Andy Ford and Neil Stedman with singer Jeanette Olsson.

13/02/1999.....37......2......	WE ARE LOVE Contains samples of Hall & Oates' I Can't Go For That and Alexander Hope's Brothers & Sisters...Distinctive DISNCD 49
10/06/2000.....67......1......	DESIRE Contains a sample of Ian Dury & The Blockheads' Hit Me With Your Rhythm Stick...............Distinctive DISNCD 56

DJ E-Z ROCK – see ROB BASE AND DJ E-Z ROCK

DJ 'FAST' EDDIE US DJ Eddie Smith.

11/04/1987.....71......2......	CAN U DANCE..Champion CHAMP 41
14/11/1987.....67......2......	CAN U DANCE This and above single credited to KENNY 'JAMMIN' JASON AND 'FAST' EDDIE SMITH.......Champion CHAMP 41
21/01/1989.....47......4......	HIP HOUSE/I CAN DANCE...DJ International DJIN 5
11/03/1989.....54......3......	YO YO GET FUNKY..DJ International DJIN 7
28/10/1989.....49......4......	GIT ON UP DJ 'FAST' EDDIE FEATURING SUNDANCE...............................DJ International 6553667

DJ FALCON – see THOMAS BANGALTER AND DJ FALCON

❶⁹ Number of weeks single topped the UK chart ↑ Entered the UK chart at #1 ▲⁹ Number of weeks single topped the US chart

DJ FLAVOURS UK DJ Neil Rumney whose debut hit was fronted by singer Savanna, who had previously worked with Solid HarmoniE and the Porn Kings.

11/10/1997.....19......4....... YOUR CARESS (ALL I NEED) Contains a sample of Pacha's *One Kiss* .... All Around The World CDGLOBE 160

DJ FORMAT FEATURING CHARLI 2NA AND AKIL UK DJ Matt Ford. Charli 2na and Akil are both in J5. Charli 2na was previously with Ozomatli.

22/03/2003.....73......1....... WE KNOW SOMETHING YOU DON'T KNOW .... Genuine GEN 004CDX

DJ FRESH UK producer/DJ who launched the Breakbeat Kaos label with Adam F.

01/11/2003.....60......1....... DA LICKS/TEMPLE OF DOOM .... Breakbeat Kaos BBK001P
31/07/2004.....73......1....... SUBMARINES .... Breakbeat Kaos BBK004
30/10/2004.....68......1....... WHEN THE SUN GOES DOWN **DJ FRESH FEATURING ADAM F** .... Breakbeat Kaos BBK005SCD

DJ GARRY Belgian producer Marino Stephano.

19/01/2002.....36......2....... DREAM UNIVERSE... Xtravaganza XTRAV 32CDS

DJ GERT Belgian producer Gert Rossenbacker.

26/05/2001.....50......1....... GIVE ME SOME MORE Contains a sample of Exodus' *Together Forever* .... Mostika 23200253

DJ GREGORY French DJ Gregory Darsa, based in Paris, who runs his own Faya label.

09/11/2002.....59......1....... TROPICAL SOUNDCLASH .... Defected DFTD 061CDS
11/10/2003.....73......1....... ELLE/TROPICAL SOUNDCLASH .... Defected DFTD 077CDX

DJ HYPE UK DJ Kevin Ford began producing in 1990 and later launched Ganja Records. He was named Best Male DJ 1994 and Best Radio DJ 1995 at the UK Hardcore Awards.

20/03/1993.....63......1....... SHOT IN THE DARK... Suburban Base SUBBASE 20CD
02/06/2001.....58......1....... CASINO ROYALE/DEAD A'S **DJ ZINC/DJ HYPE** .... True Playaz TPRCD 004

DJ INNOCENCE FEATURING ALEX CHARLES UK DJ Gary Booker with singer Alex Charles.

06/04/2002.....51......1....... SO BEAUTIFUL.. Echo ECSCD 119

DJ JAZZY JEFF AND THE FRESH PRINCE – see JAZZY JEFF AND THE FRESH PRINCE

DJ JEAN Dutch DJ Jan Engelaar, resident at the Amsterdam club It, who was 28 at the time of his debut hit.

11/09/1999 .....2......11.....O **THE LAUNCH** .... AM:PM CDAMPM 123

DJ JURGEN PRESENTS ALICE DEEJAY – see ALICE DEEJAY

DJ KOOL US rapper/DJ/producer John Bowman from Washington DC, whose hit was originally a 1995 US release on the CLR label.

22/02/1997 .....8......7....... **LET ME CLEAR MY THROAT** Contains a sample of Kool & The Gang's *Hollywood Swingin'* ..... American Recordings 74321452092

DJ KRUSH US producer/DJ Hideaki Ishii from New York who first recorded in 1990. He set up the Power Music Records, Power Music Trax, Sex Mania and DJ Exclusive labels and also records as Club People, Inner Soul, The Music Choir, The Pleasure Dome and Tribal Liberation.

16/03/1996.....52......1....... MEISO .... Mo Wax MW 042CD
12/10/1996.....71......1....... ONLY THE STRONG SURVIVE .... Mo Wax MW 060CD

DJ LUCK AND MC NEAT UK garage duo DJ Luck (Joel Samuels) and MC Neat (Michael Rose). Neat also recorded with N+G and Kallaghan. Winners of the 2000 MOBO Award for Best British Garage Act, they later dropped their 'DJ' and 'MC' prefixes.

25/12/1999 .....9......15....... **A LITTLE BIT OF LUCK**.. Red Rose CDRROSE 1
27/05/2000 .....5......8....... **MASTERBLASTER 2000** .... Red Rose RROSE 002CD
07/10/2000 .....8......6....... **AIN'T NO STOPPIN' US** This and above single credited to **DJ LUCK AND MC NEAT FEATURING JJ**........... Red Rose CDRROSE 004
17/03/2001.....12......8....... PIANO LOCO... Island CID 773
08/09/2001.....18......5....... I'M ALL ABOUT YOU **DJ LUCK AND MC NEAT FEATURING ARI GOLD** .... Island CID 781
25/05/2002.....31......2....... IRIE **LUCK AND NEAT** .... Island CID 795

DJ MANTA Dutch instrumental/production duo DJ Ziki (Rene Terhorst) and DJ Dobre (Gaston Steenkist) who also recorded as Chocolate Puma, Tomba Vira, Jark Prongo, Goodmen, Rhythmkillaz and Riva.

09/10/1999 .....47......1....... HOLDING ON Contains a sample of Orchestral Manoeuvres In The Dark's *Maid Of Orleans (The Waltz Of Joan Of Arc)* ....
.... AM:PM CDAMPM 125

DJ MARKY AND XRS FEATURING STAMINA MC Brazilian drum and bass production duo Marco Antonio Silva and Michael Nicassio with UK DJ/producer Stamina MC (Linden Reeves).

20/07/2002.....17......6....... LK (CAROLINA CAROL BELA)... V Recordings V 035
16/11/2002.....45......1....... LK (REMIX) .... V Recordings V 038

DJ MIKO Italian producer Monier Quartramo who began working as a DJ in Milan at the age of fourteen.

13/08/1994 .....6......10....... **WHAT'S UP** .... Systematic SYSCD 2

DJ MILANO FEATURING SAMANTHA FOX Italian DJ/producer Mirko Milano with UK singer Samantha Fox.

28/03/1998.....31......2...... SANTA MARIA..All Around The World CDGLOBE 163

DJ MISJAH AND DJ TIM Dutch instrumental/production duo Mischa Van Der Heiden (later in Jonah, and recording as AMBassador) and DJ Tim Hoogestegger.

23/03/1996.....16......3...... ACCESS...ffrreedom TABCD 240
27/05/2000.....45......1...... ACCESS (REMIX) ....Tripoli Trax TTRAXCD 063

DJ NATION – see NUKLEUZ DJS

DJ OTZI Austrian producer/DJ Gerry Friedle who turned to music during chemotherapy for testicular cancer. He previously recorded as Anton Of Tirol, and was twenty when he had his debut hit.

18/08/2001.....41......5...... HEY BABY (IMPORT) ....EMI 8892462
22/09/2001 ....❶¹.....24......✪ **HEY BABY** Going straight to #1 in the top 40, it was at #45 the week before on import, therefore making the biggest leap within the chart to #1 ....EMI CDOTZI 001
01/12/2001.....9......9...... **DO WAH DIDDY**...EMI CDOTZI 002
29/12/2001.....51......2...... X-MAS TIME. ....EMI CDOTZI 003
08/06/2002.....10......7...... **HEY BABY (UNOFFICIAL WORLD CUP REMIX)** ....EMI CDOTZI 004
28/12/2002.....50......1...... LIVE IS LIFE HERMES HOUSE BAND AND DJ OTZI ....Liberty CDLIVE001

DJ PIED PIPER AND THE MASTERS OF CEREMONIES UK production group comprising DJ Pied Piper, Unknown MC, DT (Deetei Thompson), Sharkie P and Melody. Brothers Pied Piper and Unknown MC were previously in Hijack.

02/06/2001 ....❶¹.....14......● **DO YOU REALLY LIKE IT** ↑ ....Relentless RELMOS 1

DJ POWER Italian producer Steve Gambaroli.

07/03/1992.....46......2...... EVERYBODY PUMP ....Cooltempo COOL 252

DJ PROFESSOR Italian producer (born Luca Lauri, 20/1/1969, Bucharest, Romania).

10/08/1991.....57......2...... WE GOTTA DO IT DJ PROFESSOR FEATURING FRANCESCO ZAPPALA ....Fourth & Broadway BRW 225
28/03/1992.....49......2...... ROCK ME STEADY...PWL Continental PWL 219
08/10/1994.....56......1...... ROCKIN' ME PROFESSOR ....Citra 1CD
01/03/1997.....64......1...... WALKIN' ON UP DJ PROF-X-OR ....Nukleuz MCSTD 40098

DJ QUICKSILVER Belgian/Turkish production duo Tomasso De Donatis and Ohran Terzi who also record as Watergate.

05/04/1997 .....4......17......● **BELLISSIMA** ....Positiva CDTIV 72
06/09/1997 .....7......7...... **FREE** ....Positiva CDTIVS 77
21/02/1998.....12......5...... PLANET LOVE ....Positiva CDTIV 88

DJ QUIK – see TONY TONI TONE

DJ RAP UK DJ/singer Charissa Saverio, born to an Italian father and an Irish-Malaysian mother in Singapore, the family moving to Southampton when she was a teenager.

04/07/1998.....32......2...... BAD GIRL ....Higher Ground HIGHS 8CD
17/10/1998.....36......2...... GOOD TO BE ALIVE Featured in the 1999 film Go ....Higher Ground HIGHS 14CD
03/04/1999.....47......1...... EVERYDAY GIRL ....Higher Ground HIGHS 19CD

DJ ROLANDO AKA AZTEC MYSTIC US DJ/producer Roland Rocha.

21/10/2000.....43......2...... JAGUAR ....430 West 430 WUKTCD1

DJ SAKIN AND FRIENDS German DJ/producer Sakin Botzkurt whose debut hit was a dance version of the theme to Braveheart (1995), complete with bagpipes, and vocals by Janet Taylor.

20/02/1999 .....4......11......○ **PROTECT YOUR MIND (FOR THE LOVE OF A PRINCESS)** Contains a sample of James Horner's For The Love Of A Princess ....
....Positiva CDTIV 107
05/06/1999.....14......7...... NOMANSLAND (DAVID'S SONG) Contains a sample of the theme to the TV show The Adventures Of David Belfour.............
....Positiva CDTIV 112

DJ SAMMY AND YANOU FEATURING DO Spanish DJ/producer Samuel Bouriah (born 29/10/1969, Majorca) who also recorded as DJ Porno. Do is Dutch singer Dominique Van Hulst.

09/11/2002 ....❶¹.....19......○ **HEAVEN** ↑ ....Data 45CDS
08/03/2003 .....2......13...... **THE BOYS OF SUMMER**...................................Data 49CDS
21/06/2003 .....8......9...... **SUNLIGHT**...Data 54CDS

DJ SANDY VS HOUSETRAP German DJ/producer DJ Sandy De Sutter with Housetrap, aka Plexic (ex-Montini Experience), earlier with Nitric Records and Kosmo Records.

01/07/2000.....32......2...... OVERDRIVE ....Positiva CDTIV 133

DJ SCOT PROJECT German DJ/producer Frank Zenker.

27/07/1996.....66......1...... U (I GOT THE FEELING) ....Positiva CDTIV 55
14/02/1998.....57......1...... Y (HOW DEEP IS YOUR LOVE)................................Perfecto PERF 158CD1

❶⁹ Number of weeks single topped the UK chart ↑ Entered the UK chart at #1 ▲⁹ Number of weeks single topped the US chart

231

DJ SCOTT FEATURING LORNA B Scottish producer/remixer Scott Robertson. Lorna B previously sang with Shakatak.

| 28/01/1995 | 36 | 3 | | DO YOU WANNA PARTY | Steppin' Out SPONCD 2 |
| 01/04/1995 | 37 | 2 | | SWEET DREAMS | Steppin' Out SPONCD 3 |

DJ SEDUCTION UK producer John Kallum.

| 22/02/1992 | 26 | 5 | | HARDCORE HEAVEN/YOU AND ME | ffrreedom TAB 103 |
| 11/07/1992 | 37 | 3 | | COME ON | ffrreedom TAB 111 |

DJ SHADOW US producer (born Josh Davis, 1973, Los Angeles, CA) who worked with Depeche Mode and Massive Attack.

25/03/1995	59	1		WHAT DOES YOUR SOUL LOOK LIKE	Mo Wax MW 027CD
14/09/1996	54	1		MIDNIGHT IN A PERFECT WORLD	Mo Wax MW 057CD
09/11/1996	74	1		STEM	Mo Wax MW 058CD
11/10/1997	22	2		HIGH NOON	Mo Wax MW 063CD
20/12/1997	62	1		CAMEL BOBSLED RACE	Mo Wax MW 084CD
24/01/1998	54	1		WHAT DOES YOUR SOUL LOOK LIKE (PART 1)	Mo Wax MW 087
01/06/2002	30	2		YOU CAN'T GO HOME AGAIN	Island CID 797
02/11/2002	28	2		SIX DAYS	Island CID 807

DJ SHOG German DJ/producer Sven Greiner.

| 20/07/2002 | 40 | 2 | | THIS IS MY SOUND | NuLife 74321942272 |

DJ SHORTY – see LENNY FONTANA AND DJ SHORTY

DJ SKRIBBLE – see MR REDZ VS DJ SKRIBBLE

DJ SNEAK FEATURING BEAR WHO US DJ (born Carlos Sosa, 1969, Puerto Rico) who moved to Chicago, IL and was a member of Da Mob.

| 01/02/2003 | 26 | 3 | | FIX MY SINK | Credence CDCREDS 033 |

DJ SS UK DJ/producer (born Leroy Small, 27/8/1970, Leicester) who formed the New Identity label with Goldie.

| 20/04/2002 | 63 | 1 | | THE LIGHTER | Formation FORM 12093 |

DJ SUPREME UK producer Nick Destri who also records as Space Cowboy and Loop Da Loop.

05/10/1996	39	2		THA WILD STYLE Contains a sample of Hijack's *The Badman Is Robbin'*	Distinctive DISNCD 19
03/05/1997	24	2		THA WILD STYLE (REMIX)	Distinctive DISNCD 29
06/12/1997	49	1		ENTER THE SCENE DJ SUPREME VS THE RHYTHM MASTERS	Distinctive DISNCD 40
21/02/1998	29	2		THA HORNS OF JERICHO	All Around The World CDGLOBE 164
16/01/1999	10	4		UP TO THE WILDSTYLE PORN KINGS VERSUS DJ SUPREME	All Around The World CDGLOBE 170

DJ TAUCHER German producer Ralf Armand Beck.

| 08/05/1999 | 74 | 1 | | CHILD OF THE UNIVERSE | Addictive 12AD 037 |

DJ TIESTO Dutch DJ Tijs Verwest (born 17/1/1969) who is also a member of Gouryella with Ferry Corsten.

12/05/2001	56	1		FLIGHT 643	Nebula NEBCD 016
29/09/2001	22	3		URBAN TRAIN DJ TIESTO FEATURING KIRSTY HAWKSHAW	VC Recordings/Nebula VCRD 95
13/04/2002	25	3		LETHAL INDUSTRY	Nebula VCRD 103
29/06/2002	36	2		643 (LOVE'S ON FIRE) DJ TIESTO FEATURING SUZANNE PALMER	Nebula VCRD 106
30/11/2002	56	1		OBSESSION TIESTO AND JUNKIE XL	Nebula NEBCD 029
11/10/2003	48	2		TRAFFIC TIESTO	Nebula NEBCD 052
15/05/2004	30	3		LOVE COMES AGAIN TIESTO FEATURING BT	Nebula NEBCD 058
23/10/2004	43	2		JUST BE TIESTO FEATURING KIRSTY HAWKSHAW	Nebula NEBCD062

DJ TIM – see DJ MISJAH AND DJ TIM

DJ TOUCHE UK producer and DJ Theo Keating who also records as Wiseguys.

| 31/01/2004 | 65 | 1 | | THE PADDLE/THE GIRL'S A FREAK | Southern Fried ECB60 |

DJ VISAGE FEATURING CLARISSA Danish DJ Martin Vig (born 13/6/1973, Copenhagen) with Danish singer Clarissa, who lives in Munich, Germany.

| 10/06/2000 | 58 | 1 | | THE RETURN (TIME TO SAY GOODBYE) | One Step Music OSMCDS 13 |

DJ WHAT? – see OBI PROJECT FEATURING HARRY, ASHER D AND DJ WHAT?

DJ ZINC UK drum and bass artist Benjamin Pettit whose debut hit started off as a B-side.

18/11/2000	27	3		138 TREK	Phaze One CDX033
02/06/2001	58	1		CASINO ROYALE/DEAD A'S DJ ZINC/DJ HYPE	True Playaz TPRCD 004
13/04/2002	73	1		REACHOUT	True Playaz TPR 12039
21/09/2002	72	1		FAIR FIGHT/AS WE DO	Bingo Beats BINGO 008
13/03/2004	54	1		SKA	True Playaz TPR 12051

○ Silver disc ● Gold disc ✪ Platinum disc (additional platinum units are indicated by a figure following the symbol) ⦿ Singles released prior to 1973 that are known to have sold over 1 million copies in the UK

15/05/2004.....62......1...... STEPPIN STONES/SOUTH PACIFIC .... Bingo Beats BINGO 012

DJAIMIN Swiss producer Dario Mancini who has an Italian father and English mother. He later formed The Black And White Brothers with Mr Mike.

19/09/1992.....45......2...... GIVE YOU .... Cooltempo COOL 262

DJD PRESENTS HYDRAULIC DOGS UK DJ/producer Dominic Dawson.

08/06/2002.....56......1...... SHAKE IT BABY Contains a sample of 2Pac's *California Love* .... Direction 6721812

DJH FEATURING STEFY Italian production group Marco Bongiovanni and Fabio Carniel with singer Stefy.

16/02/1991.....22......6...... THINK ABOUT… Contains a sample of Aretha Franklin's *Rock-A-Lott* .... RCA PB 44385
13/07/1991.....16......7...... I LIKE IT .... RCA PB 44741
19/10/1991.....73......1...... MOVE YOUR LOVE Also contains a sample of Aretha Franklin's *Rock-A-Lott* .... RCA PB 44965

DJPC Belgian producer Patrick Cools.

26/10/1991.....62......4...... INSSOMNIAK .... Hype 7PUM 005
29/02/1992.....64......1...... INSSOMNIAK Re-issue of Hype 7PUM 005 .... Hype PUMR 005

DJ'S RULE Canadian instrumental/production duo Nick Fiorucci and Michael Ova.

02/03/1996.....72......1...... GET INTO THE MUSIC .... Distinctive DISNCD 9
05/04/1997.....65......1...... GET INTO THE MUSIC (REMIX) **DJ'S RULE FEATURING KAREN BROWN** .... Distinctive DISNCDD 27

DJUM DJUM – see **LEFTFIELD**

BORIS DLUGOSCH German/US instrumental/vocal duo of producers Boris Dlugosch and Mousse T. Roisin Murphy is a member of the UK dance group Moloko.

07/12/1996.....41......2...... KEEP PUSHIN' .... Manifesto FESCD 17
13/09/1997.....23......2...... HOLD YOUR HEAD UP HIGH This and above single credited to **BORIS DLUGOSCH PRESENTS BOOOM! VOCALS BY INAYA DAVIS (AKA INAYA DAY)** .... Positiva CDTIV 79
16/06/2001.....16......4...... NEVER ENOUGH **BORIS DLUGOSCH FEATURING ROISIN MURPHY** .... Positiva CDTIV 156

D'LUX UK vocal/instrumental group with James Diplock and singer Claire Board.

22/06/1996.....58......1...... LOVE RESURRECTION .... Logic 74321371012

DMAC UK singer Derek McDonald (born in Glasgow) who was previously a member of Mero.

27/07/2002.....33......2...... THE WORLD SHE KNOWS .... Chrysalis CDCHS 5140

D'MENACE UK production duo Sandy Rivera and John Alverez.

08/08/1998.....20......3...... DEEP MENACE (SPANK) .... Inferno CDFERN 8

DMX US rapper/producer (born Earl Simmons, 18/12/1973, Yonkers, NY) whose name stands for Dark Man X (aka Divine Master Of The Unknown). He later launched Bloodline Records through Def Jam and became an actor, appearing in *Never Die Alone*.

15/05/1999.....30......2...... SLIPPIN' Contains a sample of Grover Washington Jr's *Moonstream* .... Def Jam 8707552
15/12/2001.....34......3...... WHO WE BE.. Def Jam 5888512
03/05/2003.....6......12...... **X GON GIVE IT TO YA** Featured in the 2003 film *Cradle 2 The Grave*................ Def Jam 0779042
11/10/2003.....16......5...... WHERE THE HOOD AT?... Def Jam 9811251
10/01/2004.....34......4...... GET IT ON THE FLOOR **DMX FEATURING SWIZZ BEATZ** .... Def Jam 9815206

DNA UK production duo formed in Bristol by Neal Slateford and Nick Bett. They also recorded with the Urban Dance Squad.

28/07/1990.....2......10.....O **TOM'S DINER DNA FEATURING SUZANNE VEGA**................................ A&M AM 592
08/09/1990.....34......8...... LA SERENISSIMA .... Raw Bass RBASS 006
03/08/1991.....42......4...... REBEL WOMAN **DNA FEATURING JAZZI P** Contains a sample of David Bowie's *Rebel Rebel* .... DNA 7DNA 001
01/02/1992.....17......5...... CAN YOU HANDLE IT **DNA FEATURING SHARON REDD** .... EMI EM 219
09/05/1992.....66......2...... BLUE LOVE (CALL MY NAME) **DNA FEATURING JOE NYE** .... EMI EM 226

DO – see **DJ SAMMY AND YANOU FEATURING DO**

DO ME BAD THINGS UK group formed in London in 2003 by Clara Mac, Chantal Dellusional, Kimberley Dimonde, Lewi Lewis, Nicolai Prowse, Rich Man, The Woods and Hurricane Tommy.

06/11/2004.....57......1...... TIME FOR DELIVERANCE... Must Destroy MDA002CD

CARL DOBKINS JR US singer (born 13/1/1941, Cincinnati, OH) who first recorded for Fraternity Records in 1958.

31/03/1960.....44......1...... LUCKY DEVIL .... Brunswick 05817

ANITA DOBSON UK actress (born 29/4/1949, London) best known as Angie Watts in the TV soap *Eastenders*.

09/08/1986.....4......9.....O **ANYONE CAN FALL IN LOVE ANITA DOBSON FEATURING THE SIMON MAY ORCHESTRA** Theme to *Eastenders* with lyrics added .... BBC RESL 191
18/07/1987.....43......4...... TALKING OF LOVE.. Parlophone R 6159

❶⁹ Number of weeks single topped the UK chart   **↑** Entered the UK chart at #1   **▲⁹** Number of weeks single topped the US chart

233

FEFE DOBSON Canadian singer (born Felicia Dobson, 28/2/1985, Scarborough).

08/05/2004	42	2		EVERYTHING	Mercury 9862501

DR ALBAN Nigerian producer Alban Nwapa who later relocated to Sweden. A qualified dentist (so the 'Dr', for once, is genuine), he later launched the Dr label with artists such as Amadin. His songwriting partner Denniz Pop (Dag Volle) died from cancer on 30/8/1998.

05/09/1992	2	12	**IT'S MY LIFE**	Logic 74321153307
14/11/1992	45	2	ONE LOVE	Logic 74321108727
10/04/1993	16	8	SING HALLELUJAH!	Logic 74321136202
26/03/1994	55	3	LOOK WHO'S TALKING	Logic 74321195342
13/08/1994	42	2	AWAY FROM HOME	Logic 74321222682
29/04/1995	59	1	SWEET DREAMS SWING FEATURING DR ALBAN	Logic 74321251552

DOCTOR AND THE MEDICS UK group with Clive Jackson (Doctor), sisters Collette and Wendi (aka the Anadin Brothers), Steve (guitar), Steve 'Vom' Ritchie (drums) and Richard Searle (bass; he was later a TV presenter).

10/05/1986	❶³	15	○ SPIRIT IN THE SKY	IRS IRM 113
09/08/1986	29	6	BURN	IRS IRM 119
22/11/1986	45	4	WATERLOO DOCTOR AND THE MEDICS FEATURING ROY WOOD	IRS IRM 125

DR DRE US rapper (born Andre Young, 18/2/1965 Compton, CA) and founder member of NWA (Niggaz With Attitude) and World Class Wreckin' Cru. He also founded Death Row Records, selling his stake in 1996. Warren G's half-brother, he won the 1993 Grammy Award for Best Rap Solo Performance for *Let Me Ride,* and Best Producer Award in 2000. Named Best Producer at the 2001 MOBO Awards, he has worked with 2Pac, BLACKstreet, LL Cool J, Eminem and Snoop Doggy Dogg.

22/01/1994	31	3	NUTHIN' BUT A 'G' THANG/LET ME RIDE A-side contains a sample of Leon Haywood's *I Wanta Do Something Freaky To You*. B-side contains a sample of Parliament's *Mothership Connection (Star Child)* and features uncredited vocals by George Clinton (leader of Parliament)	Death Row A 8328CD
03/09/1994	59	2	DRE DAY Features the uncredited contribution of Snoop Doggy Dogg	Death Row A 8292CD
15/04/1995	45	2	NATURAL BORN KILLAZ Featured in the 1995 film *Murder Was The Case*	Death Row A 8197CD
10/06/1995	25	4	KEEP THEIR HEADS RINGIN' Featured in the 1995 film *Friday*	Priority PTYCD 103
13/04/1996	6	8	**CALIFORNIA LOVE 2PAC FEATURING DR DRE** Features the uncredited contribution of Roger Troutman and contains samples of Roger's *So Ruff So Tuff* and Joe Cocker's *Woman To Woman*	Death Row DRWCD 3
19/10/1996	9	7	**NO DIGGITY ▲⁴ BLACKSTREET FEATURING DR DRE** Contains a sample of Bill Withers' *Grandma's Hands*	Interscope IND 95003
11/07/1998	15	3	ZOOM DR DRE AND LL COOL J Featured in the 1998 film *Bulworth*	Interscope IND 95594
14/08/1999	5	8	**GUILTY CONSCIENCE EMINEM FEATURING DR DRE** Featured in the 1999 film *Getting Straight*	Interscope IND 4971282
25/03/2000	6	10	**STILL DRE DR DRE FEATURING SNOOP DOGGY DOGG**	Interscope 4972862
10/06/2000	7	9	**FORGET ABOUT DRE DR DRE FEATURING EMINEM** 2000 Grammy Award for Best Rap Performance by a Duo	Interscope 4973422
03/02/2001	3	10	**THE NEXT EPISODE DR DRE FEATURING SNOOP DOGGY DOGG**	Interscope 4974762
19/01/2002	4	10	**BAD INTENTIONS DR DRE FEATURING KNOC-TURN'AL**	Interscope 4973932
14/02/2004	58	2	THE NEXT EPISODE DR DRE FEATURING SNOOP DOGGY DOGG	Interscope 4974762
14/02/2004	67	1	BAD INTENTIONS DR DRE FEATURING KNOC-TURN'AL	Interscope 4973932

DR. FEELGOOD UK group formed on Canvey Island in 1971 by Lee Brilleaux (born Lee Collinson, 10/5/1952, Durban, South Africa, guitar/vocals), Wilko Johnson (born John Wilkinson, 12/7/1947, guitar), John B Sparks (born 22/2/1953, bass) and The Big Figure (born Johnny Martin, 8/11/1946, drums). They backed 1960s star Heinz for three years before signing with United Artists, and took their name from a record by US bluesman Piano Red. Brilleaux died from throat cancer on 7/4/1994.

11/06/1977	47	3	SNEAKIN' SUSPICION	United Artists UP 36255
24/09/1977	34	5	SHE'S A WIND UP	United Artists UP 36304
30/09/1978	48	5	DOWN AT THE DOCTOR'S	United Artists UP 36444
20/01/1979	9	9	○ **MILK AND ALCOHOL**	United Artists UP 36468
05/05/1979	40	6	AS LONG AS THE PRICE IS RIGHT	United Artists YUP 36506
08/12/1979	73	1	PUT HIM OUT OF YOUR MIND	United Artists BP 306

DR. HOOK US group formed in Union City, NJ in 1968 by Dennis Locorriere (born 13/6/1949, Union City, NJ, guitar), Ray Sawyer (born 1/2/1937, Chicksaw, AL, lead guitar/vocals), who became known as Dr. Hook because of his eye patch, George Cummings (born 1938, steel and lead guitar), Jance Garfat (born 3/3/1944, California, bass), Rik Elswit (born 6/7/1945, New York, guitar) and John Wolters (born 28/4/1945, drums), calling themselves Dr. Hook & The Medicine Show the following year. They shortened their name in 1974. They disbanded in 1982; Sawyer formed a new group in 1988. Wolters died from liver cancer on 16/6/1997.

24/06/1972	2	13		**SYLVIA'S MOTHER DR. HOOK AND THE MEDICINE SHOW**	CBS 7929
26/06/1976	2	14	●	**A LITTLE BIT MORE**	Capitol CL 15871
30/10/1976	5	10		**IF NOT YOU**	Capitol CL 15885
25/03/1978	14	10		MORE LIKE THE MOVIES	Capitol CL 15967
22/09/1979	❶³	17	●	**WHEN YOU'RE IN LOVE WITH A BEAUTIFUL WOMAN**	Capitol CL 16039
05/01/1980	8	8		**BETTER LOVE NEXT TIME**	Capitol CL 16112
29/03/1980	4	9		**SEXY EYES**	Capitol CL 16127
23/08/1980	47	6		YEARS FROM NOW	Capitol CL 16154
08/11/1980	43	4		SHARING THE NIGHT TOGETHER	Capitol CL 16171
22/11/1980	40	5		GIRLS CAN GET IT	Mercury MER 51
01/02/1992	44	4		WHEN YOU'RE IN LOVE WITH A BEAUTIFUL WOMAN Re-issue of Capitol CL 16039	Capitol EMCT 4
06/06/1992	47	4		A LITTLE BIT MORE Re-issue of Capitol CL 15871	EMI EMCT 6

○ Silver disc ● Gold disc ✪ Platinum disc (additional platinum units are indicated by a figure following the symbol) ◉ Singles released prior to 1973 that are known to have sold over 1 million copies in the UK

DR MOUTHQUAKE – see E-ZEE POSSEE

DR OCTAGON US producer Keith Thornton.

07/09/1996	66	1		BLUE FLOWERS	Mo Wax MW 055CD

DOCTOR SPIN UK instrumental/production duo comprising ex-Shakatak Nigel Wright and Andrew Lloyd Webber, who is better known for his stage musicals.

03/10/1992	6	8		TETRIS	Carpet CRPT 4

KEN DODD UK singer/comedian (born 8/11/1927, Liverpool) who started professionally in 1954, becoming a household name in the 1960s and 1970s via TV and his 'Diddymen' characters. Surprisingly, most of his hit singles were romantic ballads. He was awarded an OBE in 1982.

07/07/1960	8	18		LOVE IS LIKE A VIOLIN	Decca F 11248
15/06/1961	28	18		ONCE IN EVERY LIFETIME	Decca F 11355
01/02/1962	21	15		PIANISSIMO	Decca F 11422
29/08/1963	35	10		STILL	Columbia DB 7094
06/02/1964	22	11		EIGHT BY TEN	Columbia DB 7191
23/07/1964	31	13		HAPPINESS	Columbia DB 7325
26/11/1964	31	7		SO DEEP IS THE NIGHT	Columbia DB 7398
02/09/1965	❶⁵	24	◎	TEARS	Columbia DB 7659
18/11/1965	3	14		THE RIVER (LE COLLINE SONO IN FIORO)	Columbia DB 7750
12/05/1966	6	14		PROMISES	Columbia DB 7914
04/08/1966	14	11		MORE THAN LOVE	Columbia DB 7976
27/10/1966	36	7		IT'S LOVE	Columbia DB 8031
19/01/1967	11	10		LET ME CRY ON YOUR SHOULDER	Columbia DB 8101
30/07/1969	22	11		TEARS WON'T WASH AWAY THESE HEARTACHES	Columbia DB 8600
05/12/1970	15	10		BROKEN HEARTED	Columbia DB 8725
10/07/1971	19	16		WHEN LOVE COMES ROUND AGAIN (L'ARCA DI NOE)	Columbia DB 8796
18/11/1972	29	11		JUST OUT OF REACH (OF MY TWO EMPTY ARMS)	Columbia DB 8947
29/11/1975	21	8		(THINK OF ME) WHEREVER YOU ARE	EMI 2342
26/12/1981	44	5		HOLD MY HAND	Images IMGS 0002

RORY DODD – see JIM STEINMAN

DODGY UK group formed in Birmingham in 1986 by Nigel Clarke (born 18/9/1966, Redditch, vocals/bass), Andy Miller (born 18/12/1968, London, guitar) and Matthew Priest (born 2/4/1970, Birmingham, drums). They disbanded in 1998, re-forming soon after with Miller, Priest, David Bassey (vocals), Nick Abnett (bass) and Chris Hallam (keyboards).

08/05/1993	65	2		LOVEBIRDS	A&M AMCD 0177
03/07/1993	67	2		I NEED ANOTHER (EP) Tracks on EP: *I Need Another, If I Fall* and *Hendre DDU*	A&M 5803172
06/08/1994	53	1		THE MELOD-EP Tracks on EP: *Melodies Haunt You, The Snake, Don't Go* and *Summer Fayre*	Bostin 5806772
01/10/1994	38	2		STAYING OUT FOR THE SUMMER	Bostin 5807972
07/01/1995	30	3		SO LET ME GO FAR	Bostin 5809032
11/03/1995	22	3		MAKING THE MOST OF DODGY WITH THE KICK HORNS	Bostin 5809892
10/06/1995	19	5		STAYING OUT FOR THE SUMMER (REMIX)	Bostin 5810952
08/06/1996	12	6		IN A ROOM	A&M 5816252
10/08/1996	4	8		GOOD ENOUGH Featured in the 1998 film *Sliding Doors*	A&M 5818152
16/11/1996	11	4		IF YOU'RE THINKING OF ME	A&M 5819992
15/03/1997	19	3		FOUND YOU	A&M 5821332
26/09/1998	32	2		EVERY SINGLE DAY	A&M MERCD 512

TIM DOG US rapper (born Timothy Blair, 12/1/1967 The Bronx, NYC) who was briefly in Ultramagnetic MCs.

29/10/1994	49	1		BITCH WITH A PERM	Dis-stress DISCD 1
11/02/1995	29	2		MAKE WAY FOR THE INDIAN APACHE INDIAN AND TIM DOG	Island CID 586

DOG EAT DOG US rock/rap six-piece group formed in New York by John Connor (vocals), Dan Nastasi (guitar/vocals), Marc DeBacker (guitar), Dave Neabore (bass), Sean Kilkenny (guitar), Brandon Finley (drums) and Scott Mueller (saxophone/keyboards). Their 1994 debut album contained the original version of *No Fronts*, having issued an EP the year before. They were named Breakthrough Act at the 1995 MTV Europe Music Awards.

19/08/1995	64	1		NO FRONTS	Roadrunner RR 23312
03/02/1996	9	5		NO FRONTS – THE REMIXES	Roadrunner RR 23313
13/07/1996	43	1		ISMS	Roadrunner RR 23083

❶⁹ Number of weeks single topped the UK chart   ↑ Entered the UK chart at #1   ▲⁹ Number of weeks single topped the US chart

235

NATE DOGG
US rapper (born Nathan Hale, Los Angeles) who is the cousin of rapper Snoop Doggy Dogg. He later formed rap supergroup 213 with Snoop Dogg and Warren G. Kurupt is US rapper Ricardo Brown, who is also a member of Tha Dogg Pound (with Delmar 'Daz Dillinger' Arnaud). Shade Sheist is a West Coast singer, previously with Ja Rule and Bone Thugs N Harmony.

23/07/1994	5	14	○	**REGULATE** WARREN G AND NATE DOGG Contains a sample of Michael McDonald's *I Keep Forgettin'*. Featured in the 1994 film *Above The Rim*	Death Row A 8290CD
03/03/2001	24	4		OH NO MOS DEF AND NATE DOGG FEATURING PHAROAHE MONCH	Rawkus RWK 302
25/08/2001	14	7		WHERE I WANNA BE SHADE SHEIST FEATURING NATE DOGG AND KURUPT Contains a sample of Toto's *Waiting For Your Love*	London LONCD 461
29/09/2001	25	3		AREA CODES LUDACRIS FEATURING NATE DOGG	Def Jam 5887722
01/03/2003	48	2		THE STREETS WC FEATURING SNOOP DOGG AND NATE DOGG	Def Jam 0779852
12/07/2003	6	8		**21 QUESTIONS** 50 CENT FEATURING NATE DOGG	Interscope 9807195
14/02/2004	32	3		THE SET UP (YOU DON'T KNOW) OBIE TRICE FEATURING NATE DOGG	Interscope 9815333

DOGS D'AMOUR
UK heavy rock group formed in Birmingham in 1983 by Tyla (guitar), Ned Christie (vocals), Nick Halls (guitar), Carl (bass) and Bam Bam (drums). Halls, Bam Bam and Christie soon left and were replaced by Dave Kusworth (guitar) and Paul Hornby (drums). They were based in Finland in 1983–85, where they became popular. Later members included Mark Duncan and Steve James. The group disbanded in 1991 and a 1993 reunion was short-lived, Tyla going solo and James and Bam Bam forming Mary Jane.

04/02/1989	44	3	HOW COME IT NEVER RAINS	China 13
05/08/1989	26	3	SATELLITE KID	China 17
14/10/1989	47	3	TRAIL OF TEARS	China 20
23/06/1990	36	3	VICTIMS OF SUCCESS	China 24
15/09/1990	61	2	EMPTY WORLD	China 27
19/06/1993	53	1	ALL OR NOTHING	China WOKCD 2033

DOGS DIE IN HOT CARS
UK rock group formed in Glasgow by Craig MacIntosh (guitar/vocals), Gary Smith (guitar), Lee Worrall (bass), Ruth Quigley (keyboards) and Laurence Davey (drums).

08/05/2004	24	2	GODHOPPING	V2 VVR 5025868
17/07/2004	32	2	I LOVE YOU 'CAUSE I HAVE TO	V2 VVR 5025878
16/10/2004	43	1	LOUNGER	V2 VVR 5028213

KEN DOH
UK DJ Michael Devlin from Newcastle.

30/03/1996	7	7	**NAKASAKI EP (I NEED A LOVER TONIGHT)** Tracks on EP: *I Need A Lover Tonight (2 Mixes)* and *Kaki Traki*	ffrr FCD 272

PETE DOHERTY
UK singer, ex-member of The Libertines who was asked to leave the group in June 2003 because of a drug habit. He was later sentenced to six months in prison (reduced to two on appeal) for committing a burglary at fellow Libertine Carl Barat's flat.

24/04/2004	7	6	**FOR LOVERS** WOLFMAN FEATURING PETE DOHERTY	Rough Trade RTRADSCD177
22/05/2004	32	1	BABYSHAMBLES	High Society HSCDS003

JOE DOLAN
Irish singer (born 16/10/1943, Mullingar) who was lead singer with the Irish group The Drifters (also on Pye) before going solo.

25/06/1969	3	19	**MAKE ME AN ISLAND**	Pye 7N 17738
01/11/1969	20	7	TERESA	Pye 7N 17833
28/02/1970	17	13	YOU'RE SUCH A GOOD LOOKING WOMAN	Pye 7N 17891
17/09/1977	43	1	I NEED YOU	Pye 7N 45702

THOMAS DOLBY
UK singer (born Thomas Morgan Robertson, 14/10/1958, Cairo, Egypt) who was a session musician for the likes of Foreigner, Joan Armatrading and Lene Lovich before going solo. He named himself after the sound engineer (Dolby Laboratories sued him for copyright infringement and he had to license the name). He later worked with George Clinton and Joni Mitchell.

03/10/1981	48	3	EUROPA AND THE PIRATE TWINS	Parlophone R 6051
14/08/1982	31	8	WINDPOWER	Venice In Peril VIPS 103
06/11/1982	49	4	SHE BLINDED ME WITH SCIENCE Single and video feature the uncredited contribution of scientist Magnus Pike	Venice In Peril VIPS 104
16/07/1983	56	4	SHE BLINDED ME WITH SCIENCE Re-issue of Venice In Peril VIPS 104	Venice In Peril VIPS 105
21/01/1984	17	9	HYPERACTIVE	Parlophone Odeon R 6065
31/03/1984	46	5	I SCARE MYSELF	Parlophone Odeon R 6067
16/04/1988	53	3	AIRHEAD	Manhattan MT 38
09/05/1992	22	5	CLOSE BUT NO CIGAR	Virgin VS 1410
11/07/1992	36	4	I LOVE YOU GOODBYE	Virgin VS 1417
26/09/1992	62	2	SILK PYJAMAS	Virgin VS 1430
22/01/1994	23	4	HYPERACTIVE (REMIX)	Parlophone CDEMCTS 10

JOE DOLCE MUSIC THEATRE
US singer (born 1947, Painesville, OH) who formed his first group Sugarcreek in 1966 and made his first record in 1974. He moved to Australia in 1978, formed the Joe Dolce Music Theatre, created the character Giuseppi and had a huge novelty hit in Australia and the UK.

07/02/1981	❶[3]	10	●	**SHADDAP YOU FACE**	Epic EPC 9518

DOLL
UK new wave group formed in 1977 by Marion Valentine (guitar/vocals), Christos Yianni (bass), Adonis Yianni (keyboards) and Mario Watts (drums).

13/01/1979	28	8	DESIRE ME	Beggars Banquet BEG 11

○ Silver disc ● Gold disc ✪ Platinum disc (additional platinum units are indicated by a figure following the symbol) ◎ Singles released prior to 1973 that are known to have sold over 1 million copies in the UK

DOLLAR
UK duo David Van Day (born 28/11/1957) and Thereze Bazar, both ex-Guys And Dolls. Produced by Trevor Horn, they both later went solo,although by 2000 Van Day was operating a burger van in Brighton.

DATE	POS	WKS	BPI	SINGLE TITLE	LABEL & NUMBER
11/11/1978	14	12	O	SHOOTING STAR	Carrere 2871
19/05/1979	14	12		WHO WERE YOU WITH IN THE MOONLIGHT	Carrere CAR 110
18/08/1979	4	13	O	LOVE'S GOTTA HOLD ON ME	Carrere CAR 122
24/11/1979	9	14		I WANNA HOLD YOUR HAND	Carrere CAR 131
25/10/1980	62	3		TAKIN' A CHANCE ON YOU	WEA K 18353
15/08/1981	19	12		HAND HELD IN BLACK AND WHITE	WEA BUCK 1
14/11/1981	4	17	O	MIRROR MIRROR (MON AMOUR)	WEA BUCK 2
20/03/1982	61	2		RING RING	Carrere CAR 225
27/03/1982	4	9	O	GIVE ME BACK MY HEART	WEA BUCK 3
19/06/1982	17	10		VIDEOTHEQUE	WEA BUCK 4
18/09/1982	34	6		GIVE ME SOME KINDA MAGIC	WEA BUCK 5
16/08/1986	61	4		WE WALKED IN LOVE	Arista DIME 1
26/12/1987	7	11		O L'AMOUR	London LON 146
16/07/1988	58	3		IT'S NATURE'S WAY (NO PROBLEM)	London LON 179

PLACIDO DOMINGO
Spanish opera singer (born 21/1/1941, Madrid) whose first venture into pop territory was an album with John Denver. He has won three Grammy Awards: Best Latin Pop Recording in 1984 for *Always In My Heart (Siempre En Mi Corazon)*, Best Classical Performance Vocal Soloist in 1990 with Jose Carreras and Luciano Pavarotti for *Carreras, Domingo, Pavarotti In Concert* and Best Mexican-US Performance in 1999 for *100 Anos De Mariachi*. Mehta is Indian conductor Zubin Mehta (born 29/4/1936, Bombay).

DATE	POS	WKS	BPI	SINGLE TITLE	LABEL & NUMBER
12/12/1981	46	9		PERHAPS LOVE PLACIDO DOMINGO WITH JOHN DENVER	CBS A 1905
27/05/1989	24	9		TILL I LOVED YOU PLACIDO DOMINGO AND JENNIFER RUSH	CBS 6548437
16/06/1990	59	2		NESSUN DORMA FROM 'TURANDOT' LUIS COBOS FEATURING PLACIDO DOMINGO	Epic 6560057
30/07/1994	21	4		LIBIAMO/LA DONNA E MOBILE JOSE CARRERAS, PLACIDO DOMINGO AND LUCIANO PAVAROTTI	Teldec YZ 843CD
25/07/1998	35	4		YOU'LL NEVER WALK ALONE CARRERAS/DOMINGO/PAVAROTTI WITH MEHTA	Decca 4607982

DOMINO
US rapper (born Shawn Ivy, 1972, St Louis, MO, raised in California) who first recorded for Outburst.

DATE	POS	WKS	BPI	SINGLE TITLE	LABEL & NUMBER
22/01/1994	33	4		GETTO JAM	Chaos 6600402
14/05/1994	42	2		SWEET POTATO PIE	Chaos 6603292

FATS DOMINO
US singer (born Antoine Domino, 26/2/1928, New Orleans, LA) who joined the Dave Bartholomew Band in the 1940s, signing solo with Imperial Records in 1949. His 1949 debut single *The Fat Man* had sold over 1 million by 1953. Through the 1950s and early 1960s he had over 60 pop hits. A pioneer of rock 'n' roll, he was inducted into the Rock & Roll Hall of Fame in 1986. He has a star on the Hollywood Walk of Fame.

DATE	POS	WKS	BPI	SINGLE TITLE	LABEL & NUMBER
27/07/1956	12	14		I'M IN LOVE AGAIN	London HLU 8280
30/11/1956	6	15		BLUEBERRY HILL	London HLU 8330
25/01/1957	23	2		AIN'T THAT A SHAME Featured in the 1973 film *American Graffiti*	London HLU 8173
01/02/1957	29	1		HONEY CHILE	London HLU 8356
29/03/1957	23	2		BLUE MONDAY Featured in the 1957 film *The Girl Can't Help It*	London HLP 8377
19/04/1957	19	7		I'M WALKIN'	London HLP 8407
19/07/1957	25	1		VALLEY OF TEARS	London HLP 8449
28/03/1958	20	4		THE BIG BEAT Featured in the 1957 film *The Big Beat*	London HLP 8575
04/07/1958	26	1		SICK AND TIRED	London HLP 8628
22/05/1959	18	5		MARGIE	London HLP 8865
16/10/1959	14	5		I WANT TO WALK YOU HOME	London HLP 8942
18/12/1959	11	12		BE MY GUEST	London HLP 9005
17/03/1960	19	11		COUNTRY BOY	London HLP 9073
21/07/1960	19	10		WALKING TO NEW ORLEANS	London HLP 9163
10/11/1960	45	2		THREE NIGHTS A WEEK	London HLP 9198
05/01/1961	32	4		MY GIRL JOSEPHINE	London HLP 9244
27/07/1961	49	1		IT KEEPS RAININ'	London HLP 9374
30/11/1961	43	1		WHAT A PARTY	London HLP 9456
29/03/1962	41	1		JAMBALAYA	London HLP 9520
31/10/1963	34	6		RED SAILS IN THE SUNSET	HMV POP 1219
24/04/1976	41	5		BLUEBERRY HILL Re-issue of London HLU 8330	United Artists UP 35797

SIOBHAN DONAGHY
UK singer (born 19/6/1984, London) who was a founder member of the Sugababes. She left in August 2001 to go solo.

DATE	POS	WKS	BPI	SINGLE TITLE	LABEL & NUMBER
05/07/2003	19	4		OVERRATED	London LONCD 476
27/09/2003	52	1		TWIST OF FATE	London LONCD 481

DON-E
UK singer/producer (born Donald McLean, London) who later produced Cat's hit *Tongue Tied*.

DATE	POS	WKS	BPI	SINGLE TITLE	LABEL & NUMBER
09/05/1992	18	6		LOVE MAKES THE WORLD GO ROUND	Fourth & Broadway BRW 242
25/07/1992	41	1		PEACE IN THE WORLD	Fourth & Broadway BRW 256
28/02/1998	52	1		DELICIOUS DENI HINES FEATURING DON-E	Mushroom MUSH 20CD

DON PABLO'S ANIMALS
Italian instrumental dance group formed by Christian Hornbostel.

DATE	POS	WKS	BPI	SINGLE TITLE	LABEL & NUMBER
19/05/1990	4	10		VENUS	Rumour RUMA 18

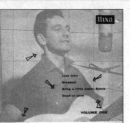

Lonnie Donegan HIT PARADE

LONNIE DONEGAN
UK singer (born Anthony Donegan, 29/4/1931, Glasgow) who named himself after US blues singer Lonnie Johnson. He joined Ken Colyer's Jazzmen on guitar and banjo in 1952, leaving for Chris Barber's Jazz Band in 1954, newly signed to Decca. His debut hit was originally a track on a Barber album credited to Lonnie Donegan's Skiffle Group. It made the US top ten and sold over 1 million copies, but Donegan received no royalties, having been paid a flat £50 session fee. He was hugely successful in his own right with Pye Nixa through the mid- to late 1950s. He appeared as a panellist on the TV talent show *New Faces* in the 1970s and still played the cabaret circuit until 1976, when a heart attack forced him into semi-retirement. After various come-back tours, he was awarded an MBE in the 2000 Queen's Birthday Honours List. He collapsed and died on 4/11/2002.

06/01/1956	8	22		**ROCK ISLAND LINE** Featured in the 1999 film *Liberty Heights*	Decca F 10647
20/04/1956	27	1		STEWBALL	Pye Nixa N 15036
27/04/1956	2	17		**LOST JOHN** B-side to *Stewball*	Pye Nixa N 15036
06/07/1956	20	2		SKIFFLE SESSION EP Tracks on EP: *Railroad Bill, Stackalee, Ballad Of Jesse James* and *Ol' Riley*	Pye Nixa NJE 1017
07/09/1956	7	13		**BRING A LITTLE WATER SYLVIE/DEAD OR ALIVE**	Pye Nixa N 15071
21/12/1956	26	3		LONNIE DONEGAN SHOWCASE (LP) Tracks on LP: *Wabash Cannonball, How Long, How Long Blues, Nobody's Child, I Shall Not Be Moved, I'm Alabamy Bound, I'm A Rambling Man, Wreck Of The Old '97* and *Frankie And Johnny*. It was the first LP to enter the singles chart	Pye Nixa NPT 19012
18/01/1957	4	17		**DON'T YOU ROCK ME DADDY-O**	Pye Nixa N 15080
05/04/1957	●[5]	12		**CUMBERLAND GAP**	Pye Nixa N 15087
07/06/1957	●[2]	19		**GAMBLIN' MAN/PUTTING ON THE STYLE** Recorded live at the London Palladium on 9/5/1957	Pye Nixa N 15093
11/10/1957	10	15		**MY DIXIE DARLING**	Pye Nixa N 15108
20/12/1957	14	7		JACK O' DIAMONDS	Pye Nixa 7N 15116
11/04/1958	6	15		**GRAND COOLIE DAM**	Pye Nixa 7N 15129
11/07/1958	11	7		SALLY DON'T YOU GRIEVE/BETTY BETTY BETTY	Pye Nixa 7N 15148
26/09/1958	28	1		LONESOME TRAVELLER	Pye Nixa 7N 15158
14/11/1958	23	5		LONNIE'S SKIFFLE PARTY	Pye Nixa 7N 15165
21/11/1958	3	14		**TOM DOOLEY**	Pye Nixa 7N 15172
06/02/1959	3	12		**DOES YOUR CHEWING GUM LOSE ITS FLAVOUR** Recorded by Ernest Hare & Billy Jones in 1924 as *Does The Spearmint Lose Its Flavor On The Bedpost Overnight*. Donegan's version was recorded live at the New Theatre, Oxford on 13/12/1958 . Pye 7N 15181
08/05/1959	14	5		FORT WORTH JAIL	Pye Nixa 7N 15196
26/06/1959	2	16		**THE BATTLE OF NEW ORLEANS** Recorded live at the Bristol Hippodrome	Pye 7N 15206
11/09/1959	13	4		SAL'S GOT A SUGAR LIP Recorded live at the Royal Aquarium, Great Yarmouth	Pye 7N 15223
04/12/1959	19	4		SAN MIGUEL	Pye 7N 15237
24/03/1960	●[4]	13		**MY OLD MAN'S A DUSTMAN** Recorded live at the Gaumont Cinema, Doncaster	Pye 7N 15256
26/05/1960	5	17		**I WANNA GO HOME**	Pye 7N 15267
25/08/1960	10	8		**LORELEI**	Pye 7N 15275
24/11/1960	13	9		LIVELY	Pye 7N 15312
08/12/1960	27	5		VIRGIN MARY	Pye 7N 15315
11/05/1961	8	15		**HAVE A DRINK ON ME**	Pye 7N 15354
31/08/1961	6	11		**MICHAEL ROW THE BOAT/LUMBERED** Recorded live at the Winter Gardens Pavilion Theatre, Blackpool	Pye 7N 15371
18/01/1962	14	10		THE COMANCHEROS	Pye 7N 15410
05/04/1962	9	12		**THE PARTY'S OVER**	Pye 7N 15424
16/08/1962	11	10		PICK A BALE OF COTTON	Pye 7N 15455

TANYA DONELLY
US guitarist/singer (born 14/7/1966, Newport, RI) and founder member of Throwing Muses. She was later with The Breeders and Belly before going solo when Belly disbanded in 1997. She is the sister of Kristine Hersh, also ex-Throwing Muses.

| 30/08/1997 | 55 | 1 | | PRETTY DEEP | 4AD BAD 7007CD |
| 06/12/1997 | 64 | 1 | | THE BRIGHT LIGHT | 4AD BAD 7012CD |

DONNAS
US rock group formed by Donna A (born Brett, 30/5/1979, vocals), Donna R (born Allison, 26/8/1979, guitar), Donna F (born Maya, 8/1/1979, bass) and Donna C (born Torry, 8/1/1979, drums).

12/04/2003	38	2		TAKE IT OFF	Atlantic AT 0148CD
05/07/2003	61	1		WHO INVITED YOU	Atlantic AT 0156CD
23/10/2004	55	1		FALL BEHIND ME	Atlantic AT 0186CD

RAL DONNER
US singer (born Ralph Stuart Emanuel Donner, 10/2/1943, Chicago, IL) in the mould of Elvis Presley, and performing passable imitations from the age of fifteen. Discovered by Sammy Davis Jr, his first US hit was a song (*Girl Of My Best Friend*) Elvis had recorded but not yet released in 1961. He narrated the 1981 film *This Is Elvis* and died from cancer on 6/4/1984.

| 21/09/1961 | 25 | 10 | | YOU DON'T KNOW WHAT YOU'VE GOT | Parlophone R 4820 |

DONOVAN
UK singer (born Donovan Leitch, 10/5/1946, Maryhill, Glasgow) who was a part-time waiter and performer at folk clubs when discovered in 1964. Demos got him a three-week spot on TV's *Ready Steady Go* and a contract with Pye Records. Likened to Bob Dylan (they met in 1965, and both their chart debuts were in the same week), he moved from folk material, with production handled by Mickie Most. He later scored and appeared in films, including 1973's *Brother Sun, Sister Moon*, and was still touring in the 1990s.

| 25/03/1965 | 4 | 13 | | **CATCH THE WIND** | Pye 7N 15801 |
| 03/06/1965 | 4 | 12 | | **COLOURS** | Pye 7N 15866 |

DATE	POS	WKS	BPI	SINGLE TITLE	LABEL & NUMBER
11/11/1965	30	6		TURQUOISE	Pye 7N 15984
08/12/1966	2	11		**SUNSHINE SUPERMAN** ▲[1]	Pye 7N 17241
09/02/1967	8	8		**MELLOW YELLOW** Features uncredited vocals by Paul McCartney	Pye 7N 17267
25/10/1967	8	11		**THERE IS A MOUNTAIN**	Pye 7N 17403
21/02/1968	5	11		**JENNIFER JUNIPER** Written about Jenny Boyd (sister of Patti Boyd, later the wife of George Harrison and then Eric Clapton and the subject of Clapton's song *Layla*)	Pye 7N 17457
29/05/1968	4	10		**HURDY GURDY MAN** Co-written by George Harrison.	Pye 7N 17537
04/12/1968	23	8		ATLANTIS	Pye 7N 17660
09/07/1969	12	9		GOO GOO BARABAJAGAL (LOVE IS HOT) **DONOVAN WITH THE JEFF BECK GROUP**	Pye 7N 17778
01/12/1990	68	1		JENNIFER JUNIPER Re-issue of Pye 7N 17457	Fontana SYP 1

JASON DONOVAN Australian singer (born 1/6/1968, Malvern, Melbourne), son of TV actor Terry and presenter Sue McIntosh, who began as an actor. He appeared in the TV series *Skyways* (opposite actress Kylie Minogue), *Home* and *Marshland*, and then took the role of Scott Robinson in *Neighbours* (also with Minogue) in 1986. Travelling to London in 1986 to record two numbers for Mushroom Records written by Noiseworks, he met Pete Waterman, who had guided Minogue's early recording career, and agreed to record a Stock Aitken Waterman song. Record success prompted him to leave *Neighbours* in 1989, although he later appeared in films and the stage musical *Joseph And The Amazing Technicolour Dreamcoat*. Linzi Hately, David Easter and Johnny Amobi were all members of the cast of *Joseph And The Amazing Technicolour Dreamcoat*.

DATE	POS	WKS	BPI	SINGLE TITLE	LABEL & NUMBER
10/09/1988	5	12	○	**NOTHING CAN DIVIDE US**	PWL 17
10/12/1988	❶[3]	14	●	**ESPECIALLY FOR YOU** KYLIE MINOGUE AND JASON DONOVAN	PWL 24
04/03/1989	❶[2]	13	●	**TOO MANY BROKEN HEARTS**	PWL 32
10/06/1989	❶[2]	10		**SEALED WITH A KISS** ↑	PWL 39
09/09/1989	2	9		**EVERY DAY (I LOVE YOU MORE)**	PWL 43
09/12/1989	2	11	●	**WHEN YOU COME BACK TO ME**	PWL 46
07/04/1990	8	7		**HANG ON TO YOUR LOVE**	PWL 51
30/06/1990	18	5		ANOTHER NIGHT	PWL 58
01/09/1990	9	6		**RHYTHM OF THE RAIN**	PWL 60
27/10/1990	22	6		I'M DOING FINE	PWL 69
18/05/1991	17	5		RSVP	PWL 80
22/06/1991	❶[2]	12	●	**ANY DREAM WILL DO** From the musical *Joseph And The Amazing Technicolour Dreamcoat*	Really Useful RUR 7
24/08/1991	10	6		**HAPPY TOGETHER**	PWL 203
07/12/1991	13	8		JOSEPH MEGA REMIX **JASON DONOVAN AND ORIGINAL LONDON CAST FEATURING LINZI HATELY, DAVID EASTER AND JOHNNY AMOBI** From the musical *Joseph And The Amazing Technicolour Dreamcoat*	Really Useful RUR 9
18/07/1992	26	4		MISSION OF LOVE	Polydor PO 222
28/11/1992	26	6		AS TIME GOES BY	Polydor PO 245
07/08/1993	41	3		ALL AROUND THE WORLD	Polydor PZCD 278

DOOBIE BROTHERS US rock group formed in San Jose, CA by Tom Johnston (born in Visalia, CA, guitar/vocals), John Hartman (born 18/3/1950, Falls Church, VA, drums) and Greg Murph (bass) and known as Pud In March. Patrick Simmons (born 23/1/1950, Aberdeen, WA, guitar/vocals) joined in September 1970, and they changed their name to Doobie Brothers ('doobie' is California slang for a marijuana joint), signing with Warner's on the strength of their demo. Numerous changes have included Michael McDonald (born 2/12/1952, St Louis, MO, keyboards/vocals), Jeff 'Skunk' Baxter (born 13/12/1948, Washington DC, guitars), Tiran Porter (born in Los Angeles, CA, bass), Mike Hossack (born 17/10/1946, Paterson, NJ, drums), Keith Knudsen (born 18/2/1948, LeMars, IN, drums/vocals), Cornelius Bumpus (born 13/1/1946, saxophone) and Dave Shogren (bass). Both Baxter and McDonald were ex-Steely Dan. They disbanded in 1982 and re-formed in 1988. Three Grammy Awards include the Best Record for Children in 1980 with various others for *In Harmony*. One-time percussionist Bobby LaKind died from cancer on 24/12/1992. Bumpus died from a heart attack on 3/2/2004.

DATE	POS	WKS	BPI	SINGLE TITLE	LABEL & NUMBER
09/03/1974	29	7		LISTEN TO THE MUSIC	Warner Brothers K 16208
07/06/1975	29	5		TAKE ME IN YOUR ARMS	Warner Brothers K 16559
17/02/1979	31	11		WHAT A FOOL BELIEVES ▲[1] Featured in the 1991 film *Frankie And Johnny*. 1979 Grammy Awards for Record of the Year; Best Arrangement Accompanying a Singer for Michael McDonald, and Song of the Year for Michael McDonald and Kenny Loggins	Warner Brothers K 17314
14/07/1979	47	4		MINUTE BY MINUTE 1979 Grammy Award for Best Pop Vocal Performance by a Group.	Warner Brothers K 17411
24/01/1987	57	3		WHAT A FOOL BELIEVES **DOOBIE BROTHERS FEATURING MICHAEL McDONALD** Re-issue of Warner Brothers K 17314	Warner Brothers W 8451
29/07/1989	73	2		THE DOCTOR	Capitol CL 536
27/11/1993	7	10		**LONG TRAIN RUNNIN'**	Warner Brothers W 0217CD
14/05/1994	37	3		LISTEN TO THE MUSIC (REMIX)	Warner Brothers W 0228CD

DOOGIE – see BUG KANN AND THE PLASTIC JAM

DOOLALLY UK production duo Stephen Mead and Daniel Langsman. Trained as a barrister, Mead was also a magazine sub-editor before producing. They also recorded as Shanks and Bigfoot.

DATE	POS	WKS	BPI	SINGLE TITLE	LABEL & NUMBER
14/11/1998	20	10		STRAIGHT FROM THE HEART	Locked On LOX 104CD
07/08/1999	9	6		**STRAIGHT FROM THE HEART** Remix of Locked On LOX 104CD. Features the uncredited vocals of Sharon Woolf	Chocolate Boy LOX 112CD

DOOLEYS UK family vocal group comprising Jim, John, Frank, Kathy, Anne and Helen Dooley, with Bob Walsh (Anne's husband) and Alan Bogan.

DATE	POS	WKS	BPI	SINGLE TITLE	LABEL & NUMBER
13/08/1977	13	10		THINK I'M GONNA FALL IN LOVE WITH YOU	GTO GT 95

❶[9] Number of weeks single topped the UK chart ↑ Entered the UK chart at #1 ▲[9] Number of weeks single topped the US chart

DATE	POS	WKS	BPI	SINGLE TITLE	LABEL & NUMBER
12/11/1977	9	11	O	**LOVE OF MY LIFE**	GTO GT 110
13/05/1978	60	3		DON'T TAKE IT LYIN' DOWN	GTO GT 220
02/09/1978	11	11		A ROSE HAS TO DIE	GTO GT 229
10/02/1979	24	9		HONEY I'M LOST	GTO GT 242
16/06/1979	3	14	O	**WANTED**	GTO GT 249
22/09/1979	7	11	O	**THE CHOSEN FEW**	GTO GT 258
08/03/1980	29	7		LOVE PATROL	GTO GT 260
06/09/1980	46	4		BODY LANGUAGE	GTO GT 276
10/10/1981	52	3		AND I WISH	GTO GT 300

VAL DOONICAN Irish singer (born Michael Valentine Doonican, 3/2/1928, Waterford) who played mandolin and guitar as a young boy and toured Ireland with various bands. He came to England in 1951, joining Irish vocal quartet the Four Ramblers, who had a BBC radio show. Going solo in the late 1950s, he was the first Irish act to top the UK albums chart with *Val Doonican Rocks But Gently* in 1967 (a reference to the trademark rocking chair ever-present in his act). With his own TV series in the late 1970s and early 1980s, he was voted Television Personality of the Year on three occasions.

DATE	POS	WKS	BPI	SINGLE TITLE	LABEL & NUMBER
15/10/1964	3	21		**WALK TALL**	Decca F 11982
21/01/1965	7	13		**THE SPECIAL YEARS**	Decca F 12049
08/04/1965	25	5		I'M GONNA GET THERE SOMEHOW	Decca F 12118
17/03/1966	5	12		**ELUSIVE BUTTERFLY**	Decca F 12358
03/11/1966	2	17		**WHAT WOULD I BE**	Decca F 12505
23/02/1967	11	12		MEMORIES ARE MADE OF THIS	Decca F 12566
25/05/1967	39	4		TWO STREETS	Decca F 12608
18/10/1967	3	19		**IF THE WHOLE WORLD STOPPED LOVING**	Pye 7N 17396
21/02/1968	37	4		YOU'RE THE ONLY ONE	Pye 7N 17465
12/06/1968	43	2		NOW	Pye 7N 17534
23/10/1968	14	13		IF I KNEW THEN WHAT I KNOW NOW	Pye 7N 17616
23/04/1969	48	1		RING OF BRIGHT WATER	Pye 7N 17713
04/12/1971	12	13		MORNING	Philips 6006 177
10/03/1973	34	7		HEAVEN IS MY WOMAN'S LOVE	Philips 6028 031

DOOP Dutch production duo Frederick Ridderhof and Peter Garnefski based in The Hague. Ridderhof, who wrote the hit, claimed that the song reflected similarities between 1920s jazz and 1990s house music.

DATE	POS	WKS	BPI	SINGLE TITLE	LABEL & NUMBER
12/03/1994	❶³	12	●	**DOOP**	Citybeat CBE 774CD

DOORS US rock group formed in Los Angeles, CA in 1965 by Jim Morrison (born 9/12/1943, Melbourne, FL, lead singer), Ray Manzarek (born 12/2/1935, Chicago, IL, keyboards), John Densmore (born 1/12/1944, Los Angeles, drums) and Robbie Krieger (born 8/1/1946, Los Angeles, guitar). Initially signed by CBS/Columbia in 1965, they were released without producing any records and promptly signed with Elektra. Morrison's controversial stage shows involved several brushes with the law: he was arrested in New Haven, CT in December 1967 for breach of the peace and resisting arrest; in Las Vegas in 1968 for public drunkenness; in Miami in March 1969 for lewd and lascivious behaviour, indecent exposure, open profanity and public drunkenness; in Phoenix in November 1969 for drunk and disorderly conduct and interfering with airline staff while on board the plane; and finally in Los Angeles in August 1970 for public drunkenness. After being given eight months hard labour and a $500 fine for the Miami offences, he appealed, announced he was leaving The Doors and moved to Paris to write poetry, with the rest of the group staying in the US, hoping he might change his mind. On 3/7/1971 he was found dead in his bath in his Paris apartment. Despite rumours of a drug overdose, the cause of death was given as heart failure caused by acute respiratory distress; he had twice called doctors out to treat his asthma, but not on the night he died. With the only witnesses his wife Pam and the doctor who signed the death certificate, there has been speculation that he is still alive and that his pet Alsatian dog is buried in his grave. His grave in Paris has been an attraction for many ever since. In 1991 a film of their career, *The Doors* starring Val Kilmer as Morrison, was released. The group took their name from a section of text by Aldous Huxley: 'all the other Doors in the Wall are labelled Dope.' They were inducted into the Rock & Roll Hall of Fame in 1993.

DATE	POS	WKS	BPI	SINGLE TITLE	LABEL & NUMBER
28/08/1968	49	1		LIGHT MY FIRE ▲³	Elektra EKSN 45014
28/08/1968	15	12		HELLO I LOVE YOU ▲² Featured in the films *Platoon* (1987), *The Doors* (1991) and *Forrest Gump* (1994)	Elektra EKSN 45037
16/10/1971	22	11		RIDERS ON THE STORM Featured in the 1995 film *The Basketball Diaries*	Elektra K 12021
20/03/1976	33	5		RIDERS ON THE STORM Re-issue of Elektra K 12021	Elektra K 12203
03/02/1979	71	2		HELLO I LOVE YOU Re-issue of Elektra EKSN 45037	Elektra K 12215
27/04/1991	64	2		BREAK ON THROUGH	Elektra EKR 121
01/06/1991	7	8		**LIGHT MY FIRE** Re-issue of Elektra EKSN 45014; revived following the release of the 1991 film *The Doors*	Elektra EKR 125
10/08/1991	68	1		RIDERS ON THE STORM Second re-issue of Elektra K 12021; revived following the release of the 1991 film *The Doors* .... Elektra EKR 131	

D.O.P. UK instrumental/production duo Kevin Hurry and Kevin Swain. Their name is an acronym for Dance Only Productions.

DATE	POS	WKS	BPI	SINGLE TITLE	LABEL & NUMBER
03/02/1996	58	1		STOP STARTING TO START STOPPING (EP) Tracks on EP: *Gusta, Dance To The House, Can You Feel It* and *How Do Y'All Feel* .... Hi-Life 5779472	
13/07/1996	54	1		GROOVY BEAT	Hi-Life 5750652

DOPE SMUGGLAZ UK production duo formed in Leeds by Tim Sheridan (aka Timmy Christmas) and Keith Binner (aka Beef Dinners), who work from their own studio The Gimp Box.

DATE	POS	WKS	BPI	SINGLE TITLE	LABEL & NUMBER
05/12/1998	62	1		THE WORD Contains a sample of Frankie Valli's *Grease*	Mushroom PERFCDS 1
07/08/1999	15	4		DOUBLE DOUBLE DUTCH	Perfecto PERF 2CDS

O Silver disc   ● Gold disc   ✪ Platinum disc (additional platinum units are indicated by a figure following the symbol)   ◉ Singles released prior to 1973 that are known to have sold over 1 million copies in the UK

CHARLIE DORE
UK singer (born 1956, London) who attended drama school before forming Charlie Dore's Prairie Oyster in 1977. She was later a successful songwriter for Sheena Easton and Jimmy Nail.

17/11/1979.....66......2...... PILOT OF THE AIRWAVES.. Island WIP 6526

ANDREA DORIA
Italian engineer who worked with producer Dino Lanni.

26/04/2003.....57......1....... BUCCI BAG .... Southern Fried ECB 38CDS

DOROTHY
UK instrumental duo formed by Paul Masterson, also in Amen! UK, The Candy Girls and Hi-Gate. His debut hit was a dance version of the theme to the TV show *Blind Date*.

09/12/1995.....31......5...... WHAT'S THAT TUNE (DOO-DOO-DOO-DOO-DOO-DOO-DOO-DOO-DOO-DOO) .... RCA 74321330912

LEE DORSEY
US singer (born Irving Lee Dorsey, 24/12/1924, New Orleans, LA) who was a boxer (Kid Chocolate) in the early 1950s before he began singing under the guidance of Allen Toussaint and Marshall Sehorn. He went into semi-retirement, concentrating on his panel-beating workshop, before returning and supporting The Clash on their 1980 US tour. He died from emphysema on 1/12/1986.

03/02/1966.....22......7......	GET OUT OF MY LIFE WOMAN.. Stateside SS 485
05/05/1966.....38......6......	CONFUSION... Stateside SS 506
11/08/1966.....8......11......	**WORKING IN THE COALMINE** Featured in the 1996 film *Casino* .... Stateside SS 528
27/10/1966.....6......12......	**HOLY COW**.. Stateside SS 552

MARC DORSEY
US R&B singer (born in Washington DC).

19/06/1999.....58......1....... IF YOU REALLY WANNA KNOW .... Jive 0522592

TOMMY DORSEY ORCHESTRA STARRING WARREN COVINGTON
US bandleader/trombonist (born 19/11/1905, Mahanoy Plane, PA) whose career started in the 1920s when he began recording with his brother Jimmy as the Dorsey Brothers Orchestra (from 1928 to 1935). They reunited in 1953. Tommy Dorsey choked to death on 26/11/1956 and Warren Covington took over as bandleader. Tommy Dorsey has a star on the Hollywood Walk of Fame, as does his brother.

17/10/1958.....3......19...... **TEA FOR TWO CHA CHA** .... Brunswick 05757

D.O.S.E. FEATURING MARK E SMITH
UK production group formed by Bassburger and Johnny Jay, and featuring Mark E Smith of The Fall.

23/03/1996.....50......1....... PLUG MYSELF IN .... Coliseum TOGA 001CD1

DOUBLE
Swiss vocal/instrumental duo Kurt Maloo and Felix Haug who previously recorded with jazz trio Ping Pong.

| 25/01/1986.....8......9...... | **THE CAPTAIN OF HER HEART** .... Polydor POSP 779 |
| 05/12/1987.....71......1...... | DEVIL'S BALL .... Polydor POSP 888 |

DOUBLE DEE FEATURING DANY
Italian vocal/instrumental duo Davide Domenella and Donato 'Dany' Losito.

01/12/1990.....63......2......	FOUND LOVE .... Epic 6563766
25/11/1995.....33......2......	FOUND LOVE (REMIX) .... Sony S2 DANUCD 1
27/09/2003.....58......1......	SHINING **DOUBLE DEE** .... Positiva CDTIV 194

DOUBLE 99
UK production team of Tim 'Deluxe' Liken and DJ Omar Adimora. They also record as RIP Productions and Carnival Featuring RIP Vs Red Rat.

| 31/05/1997.....31......3...... | RIPGROOVE .... Satellite 74321485132 |
| 01/11/1997.....14......6...... | RIPGROOVE (REMIX) .... Satellite 74321529322 |

DOUBLE SIX
UK vocal/instrumental group formed by Mike Rowe, Phil Hope and Ben Angwin.

| 19/09/1998.....66......1...... | REAL GOOD .... Multiply CDMULTY 39 |
| 12/06/1999.....59......1...... | BREAKDOWN .... Multiply CDMULTY 50 |

DOUBLE TROUBLE AND THE REBEL MC
UK instrumental/production duo Leigh Guest and Michael Menson who paired with Rebel MC (born Mike West, 27/8/1965, London) for their initial hits. Rebel MC went his own way in 1990 and Guest joined Airheadz. Menson died in January 1997 after being soaked in petrol and set alight, surviving long enough to tell the police that it wasn't a suicide attempt as they first believed.

27/05/1989.....11......12......	JUST KEEP ROCKIN' .... Desire WANT 9
07/10/1989.....3......14......	**STREET TUFF** .... Desire WANT 18
12/05/1990.....71......1......	TALK BACK **WITH VOCALS BY JANETTE SEWELL** .... Desire WANT 27
30/06/1990.....21......6......	LOVE DON'T LIVE HERE ANYMORE **DOUBLE TROUBLE FEATURING JANETTE SEWELL AND CARL BROWN**........... Desire WANT 32
15/06/1991.....66......2......	RUB-A-DUB .... Desire WANT 41

DOUBLE YOU?
Italian singer Willie Morales.

02/05/1992.....41......3...... PLEASE DON'T GO ZYX later sued KWS and their record label Network over the similarities between the arrangements of the two versions of the song .... ZYX 67488

ROB DOUGAN
UK singer/instrumentalist/producer (born in Australia) who formed Cheeky Records with Rollo Armstrong.

04/04/1998.....42......1......	FURIOUS ANGELS.. Cheeky CHEKCD 025
06/07/2002.....24......3......	CLUBBED TO DEATH Contains a sample of Skull Snaps' *It's A New Day*. Featured in the 2003 film *The Matrix Reloaded* ....
	.... Cheeky 74321941702

❶[9] Number of weeks single topped the UK chart ↑ Entered the UK chart at #1 ▲[9] Number of weeks single topped the US chart

241

CARL DOUGLAS
Jamaican singer (born 1942, raised in California) who began as a backing singer in London in the early 1970s. His debut hit, originally intended as a B-side to Douglas' single *I Want To Give You My Everything*, was flipped due to the popularity of Bruce Lee-inspired kung fu.

17/08/1974	❶³	13	●	**KUNG FU FIGHTING** ▲² Featured in the 1994 film *Wayne's World 2* .... Pye 7N 45377
30/11/1974	35	5		DANCE THE KUNG FU .... Pye 7N 45418
03/12/1977	25	10		RUN BACK .... Pye 7N 46018
23/05/1998	8	11		**KUNG FU FIGHTING** BUS STOP FEATURING CARL DOUGLAS .... All Around The World CDGLOBE 173

CAROL DOUGLAS
US singer (born Carol Strickland, 7/4/1948, Brooklyn, NYC) who was a member of The Chantels before going solo.

22/07/1978	66	4	NIGHT FEVER .... Gull GULS 61

CRAIG DOUGLAS
UK singer (born Terence Perkins, 13/8/1941, Isle of Wight) who was a milkman when he won a local talent contest and appeared on the *6.5 Special* TV show. He also appeared in the film *It's Trad Dad* (1961) and later played the international cabaret circuit.

12/06/1959	13	11	A TEENAGER IN LOVE Originally called *Great To Be In Love*. .... Top Rank JAR 133
07/08/1959	❶⁴	15	**ONLY SIXTEEN** .... Top Rank JAR 159
22/01/1960	4	14	**PRETTY BLUE EYES** .... Top Rank JAR 268
28/04/1960	10	9	**THE HEART OF A TEENAGE GIRL** .... Top Rank JAR 340
11/08/1960	43	1	OH! WHAT A DAY .... Top Rank JAR 406
20/04/1961	9	9	**A HUNDRED POUNDS OF CLAY** .... Top Rank JAR 555
29/06/1961	9	14	**TIME** .... Top Rank JAR 569
22/03/1962	9	13	**WHEN MY LITTLE GIRL IS SMILING** .... Top Rank JAR 610
28/06/1962	9	10	**OUR FAVOURITE MELODIES** .... Columbia DB 4854
18/10/1962	15	12	OH LONESOME ME .... Decca F 11523
28/02/1963	36	4	TOWN CRIER .... Decca F 11575

DOVE
Irish group formed in Dublin by Hazel Kaneswaran, Graham Cruz and Don Ade. Their debut hit was a cover of *Don't Dream It's Over* by Crowded House.

11/09/1999	37	2	DON'T DREAM .... ZTT 135CD

DOVES
UK group formed in Manchester by Jez and Andy Williams and Jimi Goodwin, who previously recorded as Sub Sub.

14/08/1999	73	1	HERE IT COMES .... Casino CHIP 003CD
01/04/2000	33	2	THE CEDAR ROOM .... Heavenly HVN 95CD
10/06/2000	32	2	CATCH THE SUN Featured in the 2000 film *On The Edge* .... Heavenly HVN 96CDS
11/11/2000	32	2	THE MAN WHO TOLD EVERYTHING .... Heavenly HVN 98CDS
27/04/2002	3	3	**THERE GOES THE FEAR** Deleted on the day of release, hence its high chart entry and rapid fall (in its second week it tumbled 31 places to #34). .... Heavenly HVN 111CD
03/08/2002	21	3	POUNDING .... Heavenly HVN 116CD
26/10/2002	29	2	CAUGHT BY THE RIVER .... Heavenly HVN 126CDS

DOWLANDS
UK vocal duo, brothers Gordon and David Dowland, who both became graphic designers after their recording career was over.

09/01/1964	33	7	ALL MY LOVING .... Oriole CB 1897

ROBERT DOWNEY JR
US singer (born 4/4/1965, New York City) best known as an actor; he played the lead in the 1992 Charles Chaplin biopic, *Chaplin*. Earlier films included *Baby, It's You* (1983), *Firstborn* (1984) and *Air America* (1990) and he later featured in *Natural Born Killers* (1994). An ongoing drug problem saw him jailed on more than one occasion.

30/01/1993	68	1	SMILE Featured in the 1992 film *Chaplin* .... Epic 6589052

DON DOWNING
US singer (born in Texas) and brother of R&B singer Al Downing. He began his career with the Roadshow label.

10/11/1973	32	10	LONELY DAYS, LONELY NIGHTS .... People PEO 102

WILL DOWNING
US singer (born in New York) who was a session vocalist before joining producer Arthur Baker's group Wally Jump Jr. He went solo in 1988, his biggest succeess so far being in the UK.

02/04/1988	14	10	A LOVE SUPREME By sax giant John Coltrane with lyrics added by Will Downing .... Fourth & Broadway BRW 90
25/06/1988	34	6	IN MY DREAMS .... Fourth & Broadway BRW 104
01/10/1988	58	5	FREE .... Fourth & Broadway BRW 112
21/01/1989	19	7	WHERE IS THE LOVE MICA PARIS AND WILL DOWNING .... Fourth & Broadway BRW 122
28/10/1989	67	2	TEST OF TIME .... Fourth & Broadway BRW 146
24/02/1990	48	4	COME TOGETHER AS ONE .... Fourth & Broadway BRW 159
18/09/1993	67	1	THERE'S NO LIVING WITHOUT YOU .... Fourth & Broadway BRCD 278

JASON DOWNS FEATURING MILK
US singer (born in Arkansas) and New York University drama graduate, whose musical style is a mixture of country and hip hop.

12/05/2001	19	5	WHITE BOY WITH A FEATHER .... Pepper 9230412
14/07/2001	65	1	CAT'S IN THE CRADLE .... Pepper 9230442

LAMONT DOZIER – see HOLLAND-DOZIER FEATURING LAMONT DOZIER

DRAGONHEART UK vocal group formed by Casey Jay Wilcox-Simmonds (born 3/1/1987), Vicci Leigh Lewis (born 19/5/1988), Tara Panayi (born 5/12/1987) and Niki Fitzgerald (born 6/2/1988).

27/11/2004......74......1....... VIDEO KILLED THE RADIO STAR .... Lipstick 6150304

CHARLIE DRAKE UK singer/comedian (born Charles Sprigall, 19/6/1925, London) who was popular via his own TV series in the 1960s.

08/08/1958.....7......11...... **SPLISH SPLASH** .... Parlophone R 4461
24/10/1958.....28......2...... VOLARE .... Parlophone R 4478
27/10/1960.....12......12...... MR CUSTER... Parlophone R 4701
05/10/1961.....14......11...... MY BOOMERANG WON'T COME BACK .... Parlophone R 4824
01/01/1972.....47......1....... PUCKWUDGIE .... Columbia DB 8829

NICK DRAKE UK singer (born 19/6/1948, Rangoon, Burma) who made his debut album in 1969 and made two further albums before his death from an overdose of antidepressant tablets on 25/11/1974, although this was not believed to have been a suicide.

29/05/2004.....31......2...... MAGIC... Island CID 854
25/09/2004.....48......1....... RIVER MAN .... Island CID 871

DRAMATIS UK group formed by Denis Haines (keyboards/vocals), Chris Payne (viola/keyboards), Russell Bell (guitar) and Cedric Sharpley (drums).

05/12/1981.....33......7...... LOVE NEEDS NO DISGUISE GARY NUMAN AND DRAMATIS.............. Beggars Banquet BEG 33
13/11/1982.....57......1....... I CAN SEE HER NOW .... Rocket XPRES 83

RUSTY DRAPER US country singer (born Farrell H Draper, 25/1/1923, Kirksville, MO) who began playing guitar and singing on the radio in Tulsa, OK at the age of twelve. He died from pneumonia on 28/3/2003.

11/08/1960.....39......4...... MULE SKINNER BLUES .... Mercury AMT 1101

DREAD FLIMSTONE AND THE MODERN TONE AGE FAMILY US group formed by Dread Flimstone (born Ron Morgan), Antonio 'Jah-T' Surjue, Hillroy 'Yaie' Distin, Kenyatta, Jeff Shelprock and DJ Rob One.

30/11/1991.....66......1....... FROM THE GHETTO .... Urban URB 87

DREAD ZEPPELIN US rock group formed in 1989 by Greg 'Tortelvis' Tortell (vocals), Carl 'Jah' Hassis (guitar), Joe 'Jah Paul Jo' Ramsey (guitar), Gary 'Put-Mon' Putman (bass), Bryant 'Ed Zeppelin' Fernandez (percussion) and Paul 'Fresh Cheese' Masselli (drums). Tortelvis left in 1992.

01/12/1990.....59......1....... YOUR TIME IS GONNA COME.................................... IRS DREAD 1
13/07/1991.....62......2...... STAIRWAY TO HEAVEN .... IRS DREAD 2

DREADZONE UK group formed by Greg Roberts ('Dread creator and sample scanner'), Tim Bran ('Computer roots and sound navigator') and Leo Williams ('Earth to bass transmitter'). Roberts and Williams were in Big Audio Dynamite before forming Screaming Target with Don Letts.

06/05/1995.....49......2...... ZION YOUTH .... Virgin VSCDG 1537
29/07/1995.....49......2...... CAPTAIN DREAD Featured in the 2001 film *Mean Machine* .... Virgin VSCDG 1541
23/09/1995.....56......2...... MAXIMUM (EP) Tracks on EP: *Maximum, Fight The Power 95* and *One Way*.......... Virgin VSCDT 1555
06/01/1996.....20......6...... LITTLE BRITAIN Features the uncredited contribution of Earl Sixteen .... Virgin VSCDG 1565
30/03/1996.....56......1....... LIFE LOVE AND UNITY.. Virgin VSCDT 1583
10/05/1997.....51......1....... EARTH ANGEL .... Virgin VSCDT 1593
26/07/1997.....58......1....... MOVING ON .... Virgin VSCDT 1635

DREAM US group formed in California by Diana Ortiz (born 23/9/1985, San Fernando Valley, CA), Holly Arnstein (born 3/8/1985, Los Angeles, CA), Melissa Schuman (born 21/8/1984, San Clemente, CA) and Ashley Poole (born 10/5/1985, Blythe, CA). They auditioned for a Los Angeles production company before signing with Puff Daddy's Bad Boy label in 2000. Schuman left in 2002 to pursue an acting career and was replaced by Kasey Sheridan (born 28/12/1986, Santa Monica, CA).

17/03/2001.....17......7...... HE LOVES U NOT .... Bad Boy 74321823542

DREAM ACADEMY UK trio Nick Laird-Clowes (guitar/vocals), Gilbert Gabriel (keyboards) and Kate St John (vocals).

30/03/1985.....15......8...... LIFE IN A NORTHERN TOWN .... Blanco Y Negro NEG 10
14/09/1985.....68......2...... THE LOVE PARADE... Blanco Y Negro NEG 16

DREAM FREQUENCY UK producer Ian Bland, later in Beat Renegades.

12/01/1991.....71......2...... LOVE PEACE AND UNDERSTANDING............................. Citybeat CBE 756
25/01/1992.....23......5...... FEEL SO REAL DREAM FREQUENCY FEATURING DEBBIE SHARP .... Citybeat CBE 763
25/04/1992.....39......3...... TAKE ME .... Citybeat CBE 768
21/05/1994.....67......1....... GOOD TIMES/THE DREAM .... Citybeat CBE 773CD
10/09/1994.....65......1....... YOU MAKE ME FEEL MIGHTY REAL .... Citybeat CBE 775CD

DREAM WARRIORS Canadian rap group formed by King Lou (born Louis Robinson, Jamaica) and Capital Q (born Frank Lennon Alert, 10/8/1969, Port of Spain, Trinidad).

14/07/1990.....16......8...... WASH YOUR FACE IN MY SINK .... Fourth & Broadway BRW 183
24/11/1990.....13......8...... MY DEFINITION OF A BOOMBASTIC JAZZ STYLE Based on Quincy Jones' *Soul Bossanova*.......... Fourth & Broadway BRW 197
02/03/1991.....39......3...... LUDI... Fourth & Broadway BRW 206

❶⁹ Number of weeks single topped the UK chart ↑ Entered the UK chart at #1 ▲⁹ Number of weeks single topped the US chart

243

DREAMCATCHER UK dance group with producers Paul Castle and Simon Langford (of Phreaq) and singer Emma Finch-Turner.

12/01/2002 ..... 14 ...... 4 .... I DON'T WANT TO LOSE MY WAY .... Positiva CDTIVS 157

DREAMERS – see FREDDIE AND THE DREAMERS

DREAMHOUSE UK vocal/instrumental group with Paul Barry, David Riley and Jules Tulley.

03/06/1995 ..... 62 ...... 2 ...... STAY .... Chase CDPALACE 1

DREAMWEAVERS US studio group (Mary Carr, Eddie Newton, Mary Rude, Sally Sanborn and Lee Turner) assembled by writers Gene Adkinson and Wade Buff to record a song that had been turned down by others.

10/02/1956 .... ❶³ ..... 18 ...... **IT'S ALMOST TOMORROW** .... Brunswick 05515

DREEM TEEM UK instrumental/production trio from London with Timmi 'Timmi Magic' Eugene, Michael 'Mikee B' Bennett and Jonathan 'DJ Spoony' Joseph. Spoony was named Best British Club DJ at the 2001 MOBO Awards.

13/12/1997 ..... 34 ...... 4 .... THE THEME .... 4 Liberty 74321542032
06/11/1999 ..... 15 ...... 5 .... BUDDY X 99 DREEM TEEM VERSUS NENEH CHERRY .... 4 Liberty LIBTCD33
15/12/2001 ..... 20 ...... 5 .... IT AIN'T ENOUGH DREEM TEEM VERSUS ARTFUL DODGER .... ffrr/Public Demand FCD 401

DRELLS – see ARCHIE BELL AND THE DRELLS

EDDIE DRENNON AND B.B.S. UNLIMITED US songwriter/producer/arranger/violinist from New York City and ex-member of Bo Diddley's backing group. B.B.S. Unlimited comprised Esther Williams (vocals), Dorothy Pritchett (vocals), Norris Berry (keyboards), Raymond Gassaway (drums), Thomas Newman (guitar), Eugene Spruill (bass), Audrey Maxwell (viola), Theresa Fay (cello), Lincoln Ross (trombone), John Latum (French horn), Arthur Dawkins (flute) and Paul Hawkins (percussion).

28/02/1976 ..... 20 ...... 6 .... LET'S DO THE LATIN HUSTLE .... Pye International 7N 25702

ALAN DREW UK singer.

26/09/1963 ..... 48 ...... 2 ...... ALWAYS THE LONELY ONE .... Columbia DB 7090

DRIFTERS US R&B group formed by ex-Domino Clyde McPhatter (born 15/11/1931, Durham, NC) and his manager George Treadwell, and comprising Gerhard Thrasher, David Baughan, Andrew Thrasher and Willie Ferbee. The original line-up signed with Atlantic in 1953. McPhatter went solo in 1955 and the group continued with various lead singers until Treadwell disbanded them in 1958. He brought in the Five Crowns and re-christened them The Drifters. The various lead singers were Ben E King (born 23/9/1938, Henderson, NC) 1959–60, Rudy Lewis (born 27/5/1935, Chicago, IL) 1961–63 and Johnny Moore (born 1934, Selina, AL) 1955–57 and again in 1964–66. Their later success in the 1970s (all their Bell and Arista hits were UK-made and didn't chart in the US) featured Bill Fredericks and then Johnny Moore on lead. Their 1959 US hit *There Goes My Baby* was the first song of the rock era to use a string section. There have been several groups, all with the Drifters name, appearing at more than one venue at the same time. Lewis died from a heart attack on 20/5/1964, Baughan died in 1970, McPhatter died from heart, kidney and liver disease on 13/6/1972 and Moore died from respiratory failure on 30/12/1998. McPhatter was inducted into the Rock & Roll Hall of Fame in 1987 while the group were inducted in 1988.

08/01/1960 ..... 17 ...... 5 ...... DANCE WITH ME .... London HLE 8988
03/11/1960 ..... 2 ...... 18 ...... **SAVE THE LAST DANCE FOR ME** ▲³ .... London HLK 9201
16/03/1961 ..... 28 ...... 6 ...... I COUNT THE TEARS .... London HLK 9287
05/04/1962 ..... 31 ...... 3 ...... WHEN MY LITTLE GIRL IS SMILING .... London HLK 9522
10/10/1963 ..... 37 ...... 5 ...... I'LL TAKE YOU HOME .... London HLK 9785
24/09/1964 ..... 45 ...... 4 ...... UNDER THE BOARDWALK .... Atlantic AT 9785
08/04/1965 ..... 35 ...... 7 ...... AT THE CLUB .... Atlantic AT 4019
29/04/1965 ..... 40 ...... 5 ...... COME ON OVER TO MY PLACE .... Atlantic AT 4023
02/02/1967 ..... 49 ...... 1 ...... BABY WHAT I MEAN .... Atlantic 584 065
25/03/1972 ..... 3 ...... 20 ..... **AT THE CLUB/SATURDAY NIGHT AT THE MOVIES** .... Atlantic K 10148
26/08/1972 ..... 9 ...... 11 ..... **COME ON OVER TO MY PLACE** .... Atlantic K 10216
04/08/1973 ..... 7 ...... 12 ..... **LIKE SISTER AND BROTHER** .... Bell 1313
15/06/1974 ..... 2 ...... 13 ..... O **KISSIN' IN THE BACK ROW OF THE MOVIES** .... Bell 1358
12/10/1974 ..... 7 ...... 9 ...... **DOWN ON THE BEACH TONIGHT** .... Bell 1381
08/02/1975 ..... 33 ...... 6 ...... LOVE GAMES .... Bell 1396
06/09/1975 ..... 3 ...... 12 ..... O **THERE GOES MY FIRST LOVE** .... Bell 1433
29/11/1975 ..... 10 ...... 10 ..... **CAN I TAKE YOU HOME LITTLE GIRL** .... Bell 1462
13/03/1976 ..... 12 ...... 8 ...... HELLO HAPPINESS .... Bell 1469
11/09/1976 ..... 29 ...... 7 ...... EVERY NITE'S A SATURDAY NIGHT WITH YOU .... Bell 1491
18/12/1976 ..... 5 ...... 12 ..... O **YOU'RE MORE THAN A NUMBER IN MY LITTLE RED BOOK** ..... Arista 78
14/04/1979 ..... 69 ...... 2 ...... SAVE THE LAST DANCE FOR ME/WHEN MY LITTLE GIRL IS SMILING Re-issue of London HLK 9201 .... Lightning LIG 9014

DRIFTERS – see SHADOWS

DRIFTWOOD Dutch production group formed by Thijs Ploegmaker, Ron Van Kroonenburg and Dirk Jans.

01/02/2003 ..... 32 ...... 2 .... FREELOADER .... Positiva CDTIV 185

JULIE DRISCOLL, BRIAN AUGER AND THE TRINITY UK singer (born 8/6/1947, London) who first starred in the R&B group Steampacket, then briefly went solo when they folded in 1968. She joined Steampacket's backing band Brian Auger

(born 18/7/1939, London, keyboards) and The Trinity, which also featured Rick Laird (bass), John McLaughlin (guitar), Glen Hughes (saxophone) and Phil Kinnora (drums). Driscoll quit in 1968 following their hit and married jazz pianist/composer Ken Tippett.

17/04/1968 . . . . . 5 . . . . . . 16 . . . . . . **THIS WHEEL'S ON FIRE** . . . . Marmalade 598 006

DRIVER 67 UK singer Paul Phillips.

23/12/1978 . . . . . 7 . . . . . . 12 . . . . . O **CAR 67** . . . . Logo GO 336

MINNIE DRIVER UK singer (born Amelia Driver, 31/1/1970, London) who began as an actress, appearing in *Good Will Hunting* (for which she was nominated for an Oscar as Best Supporting Actress) and *Grosse Pointe Blank,* before launching a singing career.

09/10/2004 . . . . . 34 . . . . . . 2 . . . . . . EVERYTHING I'VE GOT IN MY POCKET . . . . Liberty 8674202

DRIZABONE UK production/instrumental group with Vincent Garcia, Billy Jones and singer Sophie Jones, who left after one single and was replaced by Dee Heron. She too left after one single and was replaced by Kymberly Peer. They later shortened their name to Driza.

22/06/1991 . . . . . 16 . . . . . . 8	REAL LOVE . . . . Fourth & Broadway BRW 223
26/10/1991 . . . . . 54 . . . . . . 2	CATCH THE FIRE . . . . Fourth & Broadway BRW 232
23/04/1994 . . . . . 33 . . . . . . 2	PRESSURE . . . . Fourth & Broadway BRCD 264
15/10/1994 . . . . . 45 . . . . . . 2	BRIGHTEST STAR . . . . Fourth & Broadway BRCD 293
04/03/1995 . . . . . 24 . . . . . . 4	REAL LOVE (RE-RECORDING) . . . . Fourth & Broadway BRCD 311

FRANK D'RONE US singer who by the end of the decade was recording for Cadet.

22/12/1960 . . . . . 24 . . . . . . 6 . . . . . . STRAWBERRY BLONDE (THE BAND PLAYED ON) . . . . Mercury AMT 1123

DROWNING POOL US rock group formed in Dallas, TX by Dave Williams (vocals), CJ Pierce (guitar), Stevie Benton (bass) and Mike Luce (drums), taking their name from the 1975 film of the same name. Williams was found dead on 19/8/2002 with the cause of death later being given as cardiomyopathy, a disease of the heart muscle.

| 27/04/2002 . . . . . 34 . . . . . . 2 . . . . . . | BODIES . . . . Epic 6723172 |
| 10/08/2002 . . . . . 65 . . . . . . 1 . . . . . . | TEAR AWAY . . . . Epic 6729832 |

DRU HILL US R&B vocal group formed by Sisqo (born Mark Andrews, 9/11/1977, Baltimore, MD), Woody (born James Green), Nokio (born Tamir Ruffin, 21/1/1979) and Jazz (born Larry Anthony Jr). They were named after their Baltimore neighbourhood Druid Hill Park. Woody left in 1999 for a gospel career as Woody Rock. Sisqo started a parallel solo career in 2000.

15/02/1997 . . . . . 30 . . . . . . 3	TELL ME Featured in the 1996 film *Eddie* . . . . Fourth & Broadway BRCD 342
10/05/1997 . . . . . 16 . . . . . . 3	IN MY BED . . . . Fourth & Broadway BRCD 353
11/10/1997 . . . . . 12 . . . . . . 3	BIG BAD MAMA **FOXY BROWN FEATURING DRU HILL** Contains a sample of Carl Carlton's *She's A Bad Mama Jama*. Featured in the 1997 film *Def Jam's How To Be A Player* . . . . Def Jam 5749792
06/12/1997 . . . . . 22 . . . . . . 3	5 STEPS . . . . Island Black Music CID 675
24/10/1998 . . . . . 9 . . . . . . 8	HOW DEEP IS YOUR LOVE **DRU HILL FEATURING REDMAN** Featured in the 1998 film *Rush Hour* . . . . Island Black Music CID 725
06/02/1999 . . . . . 4 . . . . . . 6	THESE ARE THE TIMES . . . . Island Black Music CID 733
10/07/1999 . . . . . 2 . . . . . . 16 . . . . . ●	WILD WILD WEST ▲[1] **WILL SMITH FEATURING DRU HILL** Based on Stevie Wonder's *I Wish*. Featured in the 1999 film *Wild Wild West* . . . . Columbia 6675962

DRUGSTORE UK/US/Brazilian rock group formed by Brazilian Isabel Monteiro (bass/vocals), American Mike Chylinski (drums) and Briton Daron Robinson (guitar).

10/06/1995 . . . . . 72 . . . . . . 1	FADER . . . . Honey HONCD 7
02/05/1998 . . . . . 20 . . . . . . 3	EL PRESIDENT **ADDITIONAL VOCALS BY THOM YORKE** . . . . Roadrunner RR 22369
04/07/1998 . . . . . 68 . . . . . . 1	SOBER . . . . Roadrunner RR 22303

DRUM CLUB UK duo Lol Hammond (born 7/1/1960, Stoke Newington, London) and Charlie Hall (born 25/10/1959, Whitstable, Kent). Named after a club in Sunderland, they made their debut single in 1992.

06/11/1993 . . . . . 62 . . . . . . 1 . . . . . . SOUND SYSTEM . . . . Butterfly BFLD 10

DRUM THEATRE UK group comprising Gari Tarn (vocals/drums), Simon Moore (guitar/drums), Kent B (keyboards/drums), Paul Snook (bass/drums), Patrick Gallagher (keyboards/drums) and Myles Benedict (drums).

| 15/02/1986 . . . . . 67 . . . . . . 2 . . . . . . | LIVING IN THE PAST . . . . Epic A 6798 |
| 17/01/1987 . . . . . 44 . . . . . . 6 . . . . . . | ELDORADO . . . . Epic EMU 1 |

DRUMSOUND/SIMON BASSLINE SMITH UK production duo Andy Drumsound and Simon Smith from Derby.

| 26/07/2003 . . . . . 67 . . . . . . 1 . . . . . . | JUNGLIST . . . . Technique TECH021 |
| 12/06/2004 . . . . . 66 . . . . . . 1 . . . . . . | THE ODYSSEY/BODY MOVIN . . . . Prototype PROUK004 |

DRUNKENMUNKY Dutch instrumental/production group comprising Koen Groeneveld, Addy Van Der Zwan and Jan Voermans. They also recorded as Klubheads, Cooper, Itty Bitty Boozy Woozy and Da Techno Bohemian.

04/10/2003 . . . . . 41 . . . . . . 2 . . . . . . E . . . . All Around The World CDGLOBE 285

DRUPI Italian singer (born Gian Piero Anelli, 1949, Pavia).

01/12/1973 . . . . . 17 . . . . . 12 . . . . . VADO VIA . . . . A&M AMS 7083

❶[9] Number of weeks single topped the UK chart ↑ Entered the UK chart at #1 ▲[9] Number of weeks single topped the US chart

245

DSK UK vocal/instrumental/production group comprising Joe Stone, Lawrence Julian and Paul Klein.

31/08/1991	46	3		WHAT WOULD WE DO/READ MY LIPS	Boys Own BOI 6
22/11/1997	55	1		WHAT WOULD WE DO (REMIX)	Fresh FRSHD 63

DSM US rap group.

07/12/1985	68	4		WARRIOR GROOVE	10 DAZZ 45-7

DSP – see **MATT DAREY**

DT8 FEATURING ROXANNE WILDE UK duo Darren Tate and Roxanne Wilde. Tate, also a member of Angelic, was previously with Citizen Caned and Jurgen Vries. Ex-Dimestars Wilde (born 1979) is the daughter of Marty and sister of Kim Wilde.

03/05/2003	23	3		DESTINATION	ffrr DFCD 007
14/08/2004	17	3		THE SUN IS SHINING (DOWN ON ME) **DT8 PROJECT**	Mondo MND019CD

DTI US vocal/instrumental group fronted by Paul Lewis III.

16/04/1988	73	1		KEEP THIS FREQUENCY CLEAR	Premiere UK ERE 501

DTOX UK vocal/instrumental group fronted by Mark Stagg.

21/11/1992	75	1		SHATTERED GLASS	Vitality VITal 1

D12 US rap group formed in Detroit, MI in 1990 by Bizarre (Rufus Johnson aka Peter S Bizarre) and Proof (DeShaun Holton aka Dirty Harry), later adding Eminem (born Marshall Bruce Mathers III, 17/10/1972, Kansas City, MO), Kon Artis (Denine Porter), Bugz and Kuniva (aka Von Carlisle and Hannz G) to the line-up. Eminem later went solo and Bugz was shot dead at a picnic party in 1998; he was replaced by Swift (aka O'Moore and Swifty McVay). The group's name stands for Dirty Dozen. They were named Best Hip Hop Act at the 2004 MTV Europe Music Awards.

17/03/2001	10	7		SHIT ON YOU	Interscope 4974962
21/07/2001	2	12	O	PURPLE PILLS Contains a sample of Curtis Mayfield's *(Don't Worry) If There's A Hell Below We're All Going To Go*. It fell foul of chart rules, an ineligible sticker being included on one format, sales of which were excluded from the first week's sales .... Interscope 4975692
17/11/2001	11	5		FIGHT MUSIC	Shady/Interscope 4976522
14/02/2004	71	1		SHIT ON YOU	Interscope 4974962
24/04/2004	2	13		**MY BAND**	Interscope 9862352
07/08/2004	4	8		**HOW COME**	Interscope 9863318

JOHN DU CANN UK singer who was previously in Atomic Rooster before going solo.

22/09/1979	33	6		DON'T BE A DUMMY	Vertigo 6059 241

JOHN DU PREZ – see **MODERN ROMANCE**

DUALERS UK brothers Si Cristone and Tyber O'Neil, previously buskers in Croydon, who funded their debut release.

30/10/2004	21	2		KISS ON THE LIPS	Galley Music GALLEY10003

DUB CONSPIRACY – see **TRU FAITH AND DUB CONSPIRACY**

DUB PISTOLS UK group formed in 1996 by Barry Ashworth, Planet Asia, Sight Beyond Light and TK Lawrence.

10/10/1998	63	1		CYCLONE	Concrete HARD 36CD
18/10/2003	66	1		PROBLEM IS **DUB PISTOLS FEATURING TERRY HALL**	Distinctive DISNCD 107

DUB WAR UK group comprising Benji Webbe (vocals), Jeff Rose (guitar), Richie Glover (bass) and Martin 'Ginger' Ford (drums).

03/06/1995	70	1		STRIKE IT	Earache MOSH 138CD
27/01/1996	41	2		ENEMY MAKER	Earache MOSH 147CD
24/08/1996	59	1		CRY DIGNITY	Earache MOSH 163CD
29/03/1997	73	1		MILLION DOLLAR LOVE	Earache MOSH 170CD1

DUBLINERS Irish folk group formed in Dublin in 1962 by Ciaran Bourke (born 18/2/1936, Dublin), Ronnie Drew (born 18/9/1935, Dun Laoghaire, Dublin), Luke Kelly (born 16/11/1940, Dublin) and Barny McKenna (born 16/12/1939, Dublin). Kelly left in 1964 and two new members were recruited, Bob Lynch and John Shehan (born 19/5/1939, Dublin). Lynch left in 1965 and was replaced by a returning Kelly. Bourke was forced into retirement following a brain haemorrhage in 1974 and was replaced by Jim McCann (born 26/10/1944, Dublin).

30/03/1967	7	17		**SEVEN DRUNKEN NIGHTS**	Major Minor MM 506
30/08/1967	15	15		BLACK VELVET BAND	Major Minor MM 530
20/12/1967	43	3		MAIDS WHEN YOU'RE YOUNG NEVER WED AN OLD MAN	Major Minor MM 551
28/03/1987	8	8		**THE IRISH ROVER**	Stiff BUY 258
16/06/1990	63	2		JACK'S HEROES/WHISKEY IN THE JAR This and above single credited to **POGUES AND THE DUBLINERS**	Pogue Mahone YZ 500

DUBSTAR UK group formed in Gateshead in 1994 by Sarah Blackwood (born 6/5/1971, Halifax, vocals), Steve Hillier (born 14/5/1969, Kent, keyboards) and Chris Wilkie (born 25/1/1973, Gateshead, guitar). The group disbanded in 2000 and Blackwood later formed Client with Kate Holmes (formerly of Frazier Chorus).

08/07/1995	40	3		STARS	Food CDFOOD 61
30/09/1995	37	3		ANYWHERE	Food CDFOOD 67

○ Silver disc ● Gold disc ✪ Platinum disc (additional platinum units are indicated by a figure following the symbol) ◎ Singles released prior to 1973 that are known to have sold over 1 million copies in the UK

DATE	POS	WKS	BPI	SINGLE TITLE	LABEL & NUMBER
06/01/1996	18	5		NOT SO MANIC NOW	Food CDFOODS 71
30/03/1996	15	6		STARS Re-issue of Food CDFOOD 61	Food CDFOODS 75
03/08/1996	25	2		ELEVATOR SONG	Food CDFOOD 80
19/07/1997	20	3		NO MORE TALK	Food CDFOOD 96
20/09/1997	41	1		CATHEDRAL PARK	Food CDFOOD 104
07/02/1998	28	2		I WILL BE YOUR GIRLFRIEND	Food CDFOODS 108
27/05/2000	37	1		I (FRIDAY NIGHT)	Food CDFOODS 128

RICARDO 'RIKROK' DUCENT – see SHAGGY

HILARY DUFF
US singer (born 28/9/1987, Houston, TX) who was first known as an actress in the TV shows *True Women* and *Caspar Meets Wendy* before playing the lead in *Lizzie McGuire*, a role that required her to sing and prompted a recording career.

DATE	POS	WKS	BPI	SINGLE TITLE	LABEL & NUMBER
01/11/2003	9	8		SO YESTERDAY	Hollywood HOL003CD1
24/04/2004	18	4		COME CLEAN	Hollywood HOL005CD1

MARY DUFF – see DANIEL O'DONNELL

DUFFO
Australian singer Jeff Duff.

DATE	POS	WKS	BPI	SINGLE TITLE	LABEL & NUMBER
24/03/1979	60	2		GIVE ME BACK ME BRAIN	Beggars Banquet BEG 15

STEPHEN 'TIN TIN' DUFFY
UK singer (born 30/5/1960, Birmingham) and an original member of Duran Duran. He left in 1979 to go solo.

DATE	POS	WKS	BPI	SINGLE TITLE	LABEL & NUMBER
09/07/1983	55	4		HOLD IT TIN TIN	Curve X 9763
02/03/1985	4	11	○	KISS ME	10 TIN 2
18/05/1985	14	9		ICING ON THE CAKE	10 TIN 3

DUKE
UK singer/producer Mark Adams whose debut hit became a pan-European smash.

DATE	POS	WKS	BPI	SINGLE TITLE	LABEL & NUMBER
25/05/1996	66	1		SO IN LOVE WITH YOU	Encore CDCOR 009
26/10/1996	22	4		SO IN LOVE WITH YOU Re-issue of Encore CDCOR 009	Pukka CDPUKKA 11
11/11/2000	65	1		SO IN LOVE WITH YOU (REMIX)	48k/Perfecto SPECT 08CDS

GEORGE DUKE
US singer/keyboard player (born 12/1/1946, San Raphael, CA) who began as a jazz pianist, backing Al Jarreau and working with Jean Luc-Ponty. Later a member of Frank Zappa's Mothers Of Invention, he also formed the Cobham/Duke Band (with drummer Billy Cobham), the Clarke-Duke Project (with bass player Stanley Clarke) and recorded solo. As a producer he has worked with Sister Sledge, The Blackbyrds, Deniece Williams and Smokey Robinson.

DATE	POS	WKS	BPI	SINGLE TITLE	LABEL & NUMBER
12/07/1980	36	6		BRAZILIAN LOVE AFFAIR	Epic EPC 8751

DUKE SPIRIT
UK group formed in London by Leila Moss (vocals/harmonica), Luke Ford (guitar/vocals), Toby Butler (bass), Dan Higgins (guitar/keyboards) and Olly 'The Kid' Betts (drums).

DATE	POS	WKS	BPI	SINGLE TITLE	LABEL & NUMBER
12/06/2004	55	1		DARK IS LIGHT ENOUGH	Loog 9866673
16/10/2004	45	1		CUTS ACROSS THE LAND	Loog 9868119

DUKES
UK vocal duo formed by Dominic Busker and Frank Musker.

DATE	POS	WKS	BPI	SINGLE TITLE	LABEL & NUMBER
17/10/1981	47	7		MYSTERY GIRL	WEA K 18867
01/05/1982	53	6		THANK YOU FOR THE PARTY	WEA K 19136

CANDY DULFER
Dutch saxophonist (born 19/9/1970, Amsterdam) who first became known via Prince and then David A Stewart. She later recorded with Dave Gilmour and Van Morrison as well as maintaining a solo career.

DATE	POS	WKS	BPI	SINGLE TITLE	LABEL & NUMBER
24/02/1990	6	12		LILY WAS HERE DAVID A STEWART FEATURING CANDY DULFER	RCA ZB 43045
04/08/1990	60	2		SAXUALITY	RCA PB 43769

DUM DUMS
UK group formed by Josh Doyle (guitar/vocals), Steve Clark (bass/vocals) and Stuart 'Baxter' Wilkinson (drums/vocals).

DATE	POS	WKS	BPI	SINGLE TITLE	LABEL & NUMBER
11/03/2000	21	5		EVERYTHING	Good Behaviour CDGOOD1
08/07/2000	18	5		CAN'T GET YOU OUT OF MY THOUGHTS	Good Behaviour CDGOOD2
23/09/2000	27	3		YOU DO SOMETHING TO ME	Good Behaviour CXGOOD3
17/02/2001	27	2		ARMY OF TWO	Good Behaviour CXGOOD5

THULI DUMAKUDE
South African singer who later relocated to the US and appeared in the Broadway musical *The Lion King* as Rafiki. Her later theatrical appearances were directed by her husband Welcome Msomi.

DATE	POS	WKS	BPI	SINGLE TITLE	LABEL & NUMBER
02/01/1988	75	1		THE FUNERAL (SEPTEMBER 25TH, 1977) Listed flip side was *Cry Freedom* by GEORGE FENTON AND JONAS GWANGWA	MCA 1228

JOHN DUMMER AND HELEN APRIL
UK vocal duo. Dummer had been leader of The John Dummer Blues Band, and a member of Darts.

DATE	POS	WKS	BPI	SINGLE TITLE	LABEL & NUMBER
28/08/1982	54	3		BLUE SKIES	Speed 8

DUMONDE
German production duo Jurgen Mutschall (JamX) and Dominik De Leon who also record as JamX & DeLeon.

DATE	POS	WKS	BPI	SINGLE TITLE	LABEL & NUMBER
27/01/2001	60	1		TOMORROW	Variation VART 6
19/05/2001	36	2		NEVER LOOK BACK	Manifesto FESCD 83

❶[9] Number of weeks single topped the UK chart   ↑ Entered the UK chart at #1   ▲[9] Number of weeks single topped the US chart

247

DUNBLANE
UK charity group comprising fourteen child singers, all relatives of the victims of the Dunblane, Scotland massacre in which Thomas Hamilton shot sixteen children and their teacher before killing himself on 13/3/1996. Bob Dylan (who charted with the original version of the A-side) gave his permission for an extra verse to be written. Although the record spent only four weeks in the top 40, it spent fifteen weeks in the top 75, so was still in the charts on the first anniversary of the tragedy. The success of the single and its message led to hand guns being banned in the UK.

| 21/12/1996 | ●¹ | 15 | ● | KNOCKIN' ON HEAVEN'S DOOR/THROW THESE GUNS AWAY ↑ | BMG 74321442182 |

JOHNNY DUNCAN AND THE BLUE GRASS BOYS
US singer (born 7/9/1931, Oliver Springs, TN) who was posted to the UK in 1952 while in the US Army. After marrying a local woman he settled in the UK and formed the Blue Grass Boys in 1957 with Denny Wright, Jack Fallon, Danny Levan and Leslie Hastings. He later emigrated to Australia, working as a country singer. He died on 17/7/2000.

26/07/1957	2	17		LAST TRAIN TO SAN FERNANDO	Columbia DB 3959
25/10/1957	27	1		BLUE BLUE HEARTACHES	Columbia DB 3996
29/11/1957	27	2		FOOTPRINTS IN THE SNOW	Columbia DB 4029

DAVID DUNDAS
UK singer/keyboard player/songwriter (born 1945, Oxford) who was an advertising jingle writer when *Jeans On*, a tune he had written for Brutus, began to gain attention. Made into a single with the help of Roger Greenaway, after its brief success Dundas went back to jingles. A member of the aristocracy, his full title is Lord David Paul Nicholas Dundas, the second son of the Earl of Zetland.

| 24/07/1976 | 3 | 9 | ○ | JEANS ON Began as an advertising jingle for Brutus Jeans | Air CHS 2094 |
| 09/04/1977 | 29 | 5 | | ANOTHER FUNNY HONEYMOON | Air CHS 2136 |

ERROLL DUNKLEY
Jamaican reggae singer (born 1951, Kingston) who made his first record at fourteen (*Gypsy,* a duet with Roy Shirley for the Gaydisc label). He lived in the UK following the success of *O.K. Fred*, a cover of a song previously recorded by John Holt

| 22/09/1979 | 11 | 11 | | O.K. FRED | Scope SC 6 |
| 02/02/1980 | 52 | 3 | | SIT DOWN AND CRY | Scope SC 11 |

CLIVE DUNN
UK actor (born 1919) who was first known via the TV series *Bootsie And Snudge* before becoming a household name in the comedy series *Dad's Army*, in which he played Lance-Corporal Jones. Although the role was that of an old man, Dunn was still in his forties when the show began, and had actually fought in World War II, having been captured by the Germans in Greece while serving in the 4th Hussars. The success of the single (written by Herbie Flowers and Kenny Pickett) prompted the BBC to give him his own TV show, also called *Grandad*. He was awarded an OBE in 1978.

| 28/11/1970 | ●³ | 28 | | GRANDAD | Columbia DB 8726 |

SIMON DUPREE AND THE BIG SOUND
UK group formed by Derek Shulman (born 11/2/19147, Glasgow, vocals), Ray Shulman (born 3/12/1949, Portsmouth, guitar), Phil Shulman (born 27/8/1937, Glasgow, saxophone/trumpet), Eric Hine (keyboards), Pete O'Flaherty (bass) and Tony Ransley (drums). They became Gentle Giant in the 1970s.

| 22/11/1967 | 9 | 13 | | KITES | Parlophone R 5646 |
| 03/04/1968 | 43 | 3 | | FOR WHOM THE BELL TOLLS | Parlophone R 5670 |

DURAN DURAN
UK pop group formed in Birmingham in 1978 by Nick Rhodes (born Nicholas Bates, 8/6/1962, Birmingham, keyboards), John Taylor (born Nigel John Taylor, 20/6/1960, Birmingham, guitar, later bass), Simon Colley (bass/clarinet), Stephen Duffy (born 30/5/1960, Birmingham, vocals) and a drum machine. Colley and Duffy left in 1979 and were replaced by Andy Wickett (vocals) and Roger Taylor (born 26/4/1960, Birmingham, drums), with Andy Taylor (born 16/2/1961, Wolverhampton, guitar) joining later in the year after responding to an advertisement. Eventually Simon Le Bon (born 27/10/1958, Bushey) joined as singer after finishing university. Andy and Roger left in 1984; Andy and John later joined Power Station. Simon, Nick and Roger recorded as Arcadia. In 1986 Duran Duran was the trio of Simon, Nick and John, with Warren Cuccurullo and Sterling Campbell joining later. They were named after Milo O'Shea's character in the Jane Fonda film *Barbarella*, which was also the name of the club where they first played. None of the Taylors are related. Two Grammy Awards include Best Video Album in 1983 for *Duran Duran*. They have a star on the Hollywood Walk of Fame and were presented with the Outstanding Achievement Award at the 2004 BRIT Awards.

21/02/1981	12	11		PLANET EARTH	EMI 5137
09/05/1981	37	7		CARELESS MEMORIES	EMI 5168
25/07/1981	5	11		GIRLS ON FILM 1983 Grammy Award for Best Video Short Form, jointly with *Hungry Like The Wolf*	EMI 5206
28/11/1981	14	11		MY OWN WAY	EMI 5254
15/05/1982	5	12	○	HUNGRY LIKE THE WOLF 1983 Grammy Award for Best Video Short Form, jointly with *Girls On Film*	EMI 5295
21/08/1982	2	9	○	SAVE A PRAYER	EMI 5327
13/11/1982	9	11	○	RIO	EMI 5346
26/03/1983	●²	9	●	IS THERE SOMETHING I SHOULD KNOW ↑	EMI 5371
29/10/1983	3	11	○	UNION OF THE SNAKE	EMI 5429
04/02/1984	9	7		NEW MOON ON MONDAY	EMI DURAN 1
28/04/1984	●⁴	14	○	THE REFLEX ▲²	EMI DURAN 2
03/11/1984	2	14	○	WILD BOYS 1985 BRIT Award for Best Video	EMI DURAN 3
18/05/1985	2	16	○	A VIEW TO A KILL ▲² Featured in the 1985 James Bond film *A View To A Kill*	EMI DURAN 007
01/11/1986	7	7		NOTORIOUS	EMI DDN 45
21/02/1987	22	6		SKIN TRADE	EMI TRADE 1
25/04/1987	24	5		MEET EL PRESIDENTE	EMI TOUR 1

○ Silver disc ● Gold disc ✪ Platinum disc (additional platinum units are indicated by a figure following the symbol) ◉ Singles released prior to 1973 that are known to have sold over 1 million copies in the UK

01/10/1988	14	5		I DON'T WANT YOUR LOVE	EMI YOUR 1
07/01/1989	9	5		**ALL SHE WANTS IS**	EMI DD 11
22/04/1989	30	4		DO YOU BELIEVE IN SHAME Featured in the 1988 film *Tequila Sunrise*	EMI DD 12
16/12/1989	31	5		BURNING THE GROUND	EMI DD 13
04/08/1990	20	4		VIOLENCE OF SUMMER (LOVE'S TAKING OVER)	Parlophone DD 14
17/11/1990	48	3		SERIOUS	Parlophone DD 15
30/01/1993	6	9		**ORDINARY WORLD**	Parlophone CDDDS 16
10/04/1993	13	8		COME UNDONE	Parlophone CDDDS 17
04/09/1993	35	3		TOO MUCH INFORMATION	Parlophone CDDDS 18
25/03/1995	28	4		PERFECT DAY	Parlophone CDDDS 20
17/06/1995	17	5		WHITE LINES (DON'T DO IT) **DURAN DURAN FEATURING MELLE MEL & GRANDMASTER FLASH & THE FURIOUS FIVE**	
					Parlophone CDDD 19
24/05/1997	21	2		OUT OF MY MIND Featured in the 1997 film *The Saint*	Virgin VSCDT 1639
30/01/1999	23	3		ELECTRIC BARBARELLA	EMI CDELEC 2000
10/06/2000	53	1		SOMEONE ELSE NOT ME	Hollywood 0108845 HWR
16/10/2004	5	4		**(REACH UP FOR THE) SUNRISE**	Epic 6753532

JIMMY DURANTE
US singer (born 10/2/1893, New York City) who was best known as a comedian and actor, with his own TV series between 1954 and 1956. He died from pneumonia on 29/1/1980. He has a star on the Hollywood Walk of Fame.

14/12/1996	69	1		MAKE SOMEONE HAPPY	Warner Brothers W 0385CD

JUDITH DURHAM
Australian singer (born 3/7/1943, Melbourne) and lead singer with The Seekers. She went solo shortly before the group disbanded.

15/06/1967	33	5		OLIVE TREE	Columbia DB 8207

IAN DURY AND THE BLOCKHEADS
UK singer (born 12/5/1942, Upminster, Essex) who contracted polio at the age of seven, leaving him partially disabled. He formed Kilburn & The High Roads in 1970, signing with Raft (who closed down before releasing anything), then Dawn. The High Roads disbanded in 1975 and Dury formed a new group with Chaz Jankel, signing with Stiff in 1977. At their peak the Blockheads comprised Dury, Jankel, Davey Payne, John Turnball, Norman Watt-Roy, Mickey Gallagher and Charley Charles (born 1945). Charles died from cancer on 5/9/1990. Dury died from cancer on 27/3/2000.

29/04/1978	9	12		**WHAT A WASTE**	Stiff BUY 27
09/12/1978	❶¹	15	●	**HIT ME WITH YOUR RHYTHM STICK** **IAN AND THE BLOCKHEADS**	Stiff BUY 38
11/08/1979	3	8	○	**REASONS TO BE CHEERFUL (PART 3)**	Stiff BUY 50
30/08/1980	22	7		I WANT TO BE STRAIGHT	Stiff BUY 90
15/11/1980	51	3		SUPERMAN'S BIG SISTER	Stiff BUY 100
25/05/1985	55	4		HIT ME WITH YOUR RHYTHM STICK (REMIX)	Stiff BUY 214
26/10/1985	45	5		PROFOUNDLY IN LOVE WITH PANDORA **IAN DURY** Theme to the TV series *The Secret Diary Of Adrian Mole*	EMI EM 5534
27/07/1991	73	1		HIT ME WITH YOUR RHYTHM STICK (REMIX)	Flying FLYR 1
11/03/2000	55	1		DRIP FED FRED **MADNESS FEATURING IAN DURY**	Virgin VSCDT 1768

DUST BROTHERS
US production duo Mike Simpson and John King. Their debut hit featured vocals from actor Brad Pitt.

11/12/1999	60	1		THIS IS YOUR LIFE Featured in the 1999 Brad Pitt film *The Fight Club*	Restless 74321713962

DUST JUNKYS
UK group with Nicky Lockett (vocals), Steve Oliver Jones (bass), Mykey Wilson (drums), Sam Brox (guitar) and Ganiyu Pierre Gasper (DJ). Lockett previously recorded as MC Tunes.

15/11/1997	47	2		(NONSTOPOPERATION)	Polydor 5719732
28/02/1998	39	2		WHAT TIME IS IT?	Polydor 5694912
16/05/1998	62	1		NOTHIN' PERSONAL Contains a sample of Fleetwood Mac's *Oh Well*	Polydor 5699092

DUSTED
UK dance group assembled by Faithless member Rollo Armstrong and Mark Bates. The lead vocals are by twelve-year-old choirboy Alan Young.

20/01/2001	31	2		ALWAYS REMEMBER TO RESPECT AND HONOUR YOUR MOTHER	Go Beat GOLCD 36

SLIM DUSTY
Australian singer/guitarist (born David Gordon Kirkpatrick, 1927). He died in September 2003.

30/01/1959	3	15		**A PUB WITH NO BEER** **SLIM DUSTY WITH DICK CARR AND HIS BUSHLANDERS**	Columbia DB 4212

DUTCH FEATURING CRYSTAL WATERS
Dutch producer Jesse Houk who also records as Scumfrog.

20/09/2003	22	4		MY TIME	Illustrious/Epic CDILL 018

DUTCH FORCE
Dutch producer Benno De Goeij.

06/05/2000	35	2		DEADLINE	Inferno CDFERN 27

ONDREA DUVERN – see HUSTLERS CONVENTION FEATURING LAUDAT AND ONDREA DUVERN

DWEEB
UK vocal/instrumental trio Kris 'Dweeb' Beltrami, Lara Dweeb and John Stanley.

22/02/1997	63	1		SCOOBY DOO	Blanco Y Negro NEG 100CD
07/06/1997	70	1		OH YEAH, BABY	Blanco Y Negro NEG 102CD

SARAH DWYER – see LANGE

❶⁹ Number of weeks single topped the UK chart   ↑ Entered the UK chart at #1   ▲⁹ Number of weeks single topped the US chart

249

BOB DYLAN

BOB DYLAN US singer/guitarist (born Robert Allen Zimmerman, 24/5/1941, Duluth, MN) who was named after the poet Dylan Thomas. He moved to New York in 1960 and worked in Greenwich Village folk clubs. He signed with CBS/Columbia in 1961 after appearing on a Carolyn Hester recording session. A folk-rock pioneer, he briefly retired after a 1966 motorcycle accident before returning to the studio (with The Band) in 1967. He later appeared in films including *Don't Look Back* (1967) and *Pat Garrett And Billy The Kid* (1973). He formed Accomplice Records in 1979, and was in the Traveling Wilburys supergroup in 1988. He was the only music artist (apart from The Beatles) on the cover of *Sgt Pepper's Lonely Hearts Club Band*. Inducted into the Rock & Roll Hall of Fame in 1988, he has won six Grammy Awards: Best Rock Vocal Performance in 1979 for *Gotta Serve Somebody*; Best Traditional Folk Album in 1994 for *World Gone Wrong*; Album of the Year and Best Contemporary Folk album in 1997 for *Time Out Of Mind*; Best Male Rock Vocal Performance in 1997 for *Cold Irons Bound*; and Best Contemporary Folk Album in 2001 for *Love And Theft*. He also collected the 1989 Grammy Award for Best Rock Performance by a Group with Vocals as a member of the Traveling Wilburys for *Traveling Wilburys Volume One* (the album was known as *Handle With Care* in the UK). He won the 2000 Oscar for Best Original Song for *Things Have Changed* from the film *Wonder Boys*. His son Jakob is lead singer with rock group The Wallflowers.

DATE	POS	WKS	SINGLE TITLE	LABEL & NUMBER
25/03/1965	9	11	**TIMES THEY ARE A-CHANGIN'**	CBS 201751
29/04/1965	9	9	**SUBTERRANEAN HOMESICK BLUES**	CBS 201753
17/06/1965	22	8	MAGGIE'S FARM	CBS 201781
19/08/1965	4	12	**LIKE A ROLLING STONE** Featured in the 1979 film *More American Graffiti*	CBS 201811
28/10/1965	8	12	**POSITIVELY FOURTH STREET**	CBS 201824
27/01/1966	17	5	CAN YOU PLEASE CRAWL OUT YOUR WINDOW	CBS 201900
14/04/1966	33	5	ONE OF US MUST KNOW (SOONER OR LATER)	CBS 202053
12/05/1966	7	8	**RAINY DAY WOMEN NOS. 12 & 35** Featured in the 1994 film *Forrest Gump*	CBS 202307
21/07/1966	16	9	I WANT YOU	CBS 202258
14/05/1969	30	6	I THREW IT ALL AWAY	CBS 4219
13/09/1969	5	12	**LAY LADY LAY** Originally written for the film *Midnight Cowboy* but subsequently rejected	CBS 4434
10/07/1971	24	9	WATCHING THE RIVER FLOW	CBS 7329
06/10/1973	14	9	KNOCKIN' ON HEAVEN'S DOOR Featured in the 1973 film *Pat Garrett And Billy The Kid*	CBS 1762
07/02/1976	43	4	HURRICANE Dedicated to boxer Rubin 'Hurricane' Carter, twice convicted of a triple murder in 1966.	CBS 3878
20/05/1978	56	3	IS YOUR LOVE IN VAIN	CBS 6718
29/07/1978	13	11	BABY STOP CRYING	CBS 6499
20/05/1995	33	2	DIGNITY	Columbia 6620762
11/07/1998	64	1	LOVE SICK	Columbia 6659972
14/10/2000	58	1	THINGS HAVE CHANGED Featured in the 2000 film *Wonder Boys* and won an Oscar for Best Original Song	Columbia 6693792

DYNAMITE MC AND ORIGIN UNKNOWN

DYNAMITE MC AND ORIGIN UNKNOWN UK producer/DJ Dominic Smith with production duo Andy Clarke and Ant Miles.

DATE	POS	WKS	SINGLE TITLE	LABEL & NUMBER
20/09/2003	66	1	HOTNESS	Ram RAMM 45
05/06/2004	54	1	RIDE **DYNAMITE MC**	Utlimate Dilemma EW 288CD

DYNAMIX II FEATURING TOO TOUGH TEE

DYNAMIX II FEATURING TOO TOUGH TEE US duo formed in Miami, FL in 1985 by David Noller and Scott Weiser with rapper Too Tough Tee.

DATE	POS	WKS	SINGLE TITLE	LABEL & NUMBER
08/08/1987	50	4	JUST GIVE THE DJ A BREAK	Cooltempo COOL 151

DYNASTY

DYNASTY US soul group assembled by producer Leon Sylvers in 1978 with Kevin Spencer, Nidra Beard and Linda Carriere. Sylvers and brother Foster joined the group in 1981 and William Shelby joined later. By 1988 the group was back to a trio of Spencer, Shelby and Beard (who had by this time married Leon Sylvers).

DATE	POS	WKS	SINGLE TITLE	LABEL & NUMBER
13/10/1979	20	13	I DON'T WANT TO BE A FREAK (BUT I CAN'T HELP MYSELF)	Solar FB 1694
09/08/1980	51	4	I'VE JUST BEGUN TO LOVE YOU	Solar SO 10
21/05/1983	53	3	DOES THAT RING A BELL	Solar E 9911

DYSFUNCTIONAL PSYCHEDELIC WALTONS – see PSYCHEDELIC WALTONS

RONNIE DYSON

RONNIE DYSON US singer (born 5/6/1950, Washington DC, raised in Brooklyn, NYC) who was a gospel singer before landing a part in the Broadway show *Hair*. Subsequently signing with CBS, his first hit was *(If You Let Me Make Love To You Then) Why Can't I Touch You?* He died from heart failure on 10/11/1990.

DATE	POS	WKS	SINGLE TITLE	LABEL & NUMBER
04/12/1971	34	6	WHEN YOU GET RIGHT DOWN TO IT	CBS 7449

DYVERSE

DYVERSE UK vocal group formed in Liverpool by Chantel Coleman, Sarah Shields, Jo Wharton, Joanne Christie and Kellie Birchall.

DATE	POS	WKS	SINGLE TITLE	LABEL & NUMBER
31/01/2004	71	1	MISGUIDED	Chilli Discs CCHIL 002

E

KATHERINE E US singer Katherine Ellis.

06/04/1991.....41......5.......	I'M ALRIGHT...Dead Dead Good GOOD 2
18/01/1992.....56......2.......	THEN I FEEL GOOD...PWL Continental PWL 13

LIZZ E – see FRESH 4 FEATURING LIZZ E

SHEILA E US singer/percussionist (born Sheila Escovedo, 12/12/1959, San Francisco, CA) who began with father Pete's group Azteca in the 1970s. She did sessions for Herbie Hancock, The Crusaders, Diana Ross, George Duke and Prince, Prince helping her to gain a solo contract.

23/02/1985.....18......9....... THE BELLE OF ST MARK...Warner Brothers W 9180

E-LUSTRIOUS UK production/instrumental duo Mike 'E-Bloc' Kirwin and Danny 'Hybrid' Bennett. They also record as Direckt.

15/02/1992.....58......1.......	DANCE NO MORE E-LUSTRIOUS FEATURING DEBORAH FRENCH...MOS 001T
02/07/1994.....69......1.......	IN YOUR DANCE...UFG 6CD

E-MALE UK vocal/instrumental group formed by Mike Olton, Mervyn Africa, T-Money and C-Pone.

31/01/1998.....44......1....... WE ARE E-MALE...East West EW 137CD

E-MAN – see JON CUTLER

E-MOTION UK duo Alan Angus and Justin Oliver.

03/02/1996.....20......3.......	THE NAUGHTY NORTH & THE SEXY SOUTH...Soundproof MCSTD 40017
17/08/1996.....60......1.......	I STAND ALONE...Soundproof MCSTD 40061
26/10/1996.....17......3.......	THE NAUGHTY NORTH & THE SEXY SOUTH (REMIX)...Soundproof MCSTD 40076

E-ROTIC German/US vocal/instrumental group comprising David Brandes, John O'Flynn and Felix Gauder. Gauder later recorded as Novaspace.

03/06/1995.....45......2....... MAX DON'T HAVE SEX WITH YOUR EX...Stip CDSTIP 2

E-SMOOVE FEATURING LATANZA WATERS US producer Eric Miller with singer Latanza Waters who also record as Thick D.

15/08/1998.....63......1....... DEJA VU...AM:PM 5827671

E-TRAX German production duo Ramon Zenker and Jens Lissat. Zenker is also responsible for Fragma, Ariel and Hardfloor. Lissat and Zenker are also members of Interactive.

09/06/2001.....60......1....... LET'S ROCK...Tidy Trax TIDY 155CD

E-TYPE Swedish singer Martin Eriksson (born 1965).

23/09/1995.....53......1.......	THIS IS THE WAY...ffrreedom TABCD 237
24/06/2000.....58......1.......	CAMPIONE 2000 Official theme of the Euro 2000 football championships...Polydor 1580822

E-Z ROLLERS UK dance group formed by Jay Hurren, Alex Banks and singer Kelly Richards.

24/04/1999.....18......3.......	WALK THIS LAND Featured in the 1998 film *Lock Stock And Two Smoking Barrels*.................Moving Shadow 130CD1
08/02/2003.....61......1.......	BACK TO LOVE...Moving Shadow 159CD

E-ZEE POSSEE UK vocal/instrumental group formed by MC Kinky (born Caron Geary), ex-Culture Club Boy George (born George O'Dowd), ex-Haysi Fantayzee Jeremy Healy and Simon Rogers. Healy later joined Amos and MC Kinky later recorded as Kinky.

26/08/1989.....69......1.......	EVERYTHING STARTS WITH AN 'E'...More Protein PROT 1
20/01/1990.....59......3.......	LOVE ON LOVE WITH DR MOUTHQUAKE...More Protein PROT 3
17/03/1990.....15......8.......	EVERYTHING STARTS WITH AN 'E'...More Protein PROT 1
30/06/1990.....62......3.......	THE SUN MACHINE...More Protein PROT 4
21/09/1991.....72......1.......	BREATHING IS E-ZEE E-ZEE POSSEE FEATURING TARA NEWLEY...More Protein PROT 12

EAGLES US rock group formed in Los Angeles, CA in 1971 by Glenn Frey (born 6/11/1948, Detroit, MI, guitar/vocals), Bernie Leadon (born 19/7/1947, Minneapolis, MN, guitar), Randy Meisner (born 8/3/1946, Scottsbluff, NE, bass) and Don Henley (born 22/7/1947, Gilmer, TX, drums). Signed by David Geffen to Asylum, they recorded their 1972 debut LP in England with Glyn Johns. Don Felder (born 21/9/1947, Topanga, CA, guitars) was added in 1975. Leadon left in same year and was replaced by Joe Walsh (born 20/11/1947,

❶⁹ Number of weeks single topped the UK chart ↑ Entered the UK chart at #1 ▲⁹ Number of weeks single topped the US chart

251

Wichita, KS). Meisner was replaced by Timothy Schmidt (born 30/10/1947, Sacramento, CA) in 1977. They disbanded in 1982, all launching solo ventures, Frey and Henley with greatest success. Walsh tried for nomination as Vice President of the United States in two presidential campaigns. They were inducted into the Rock & Roll Hall of Fame in 1998.

09/08/1975.....23......7......	ONE OF THESE NIGHTS ▲¹ .... Asylum AYM 543
01/11/1975.....23......7......	LYIN' EYES Featured in the 1980 film *Urban Cowboy*. 1975 Grammy Award for Best Pop Vocal Performance by a Group ....
	.... Asylum AYM 548
06/03/1976.....12......7......	TAKE IT TO THE LIMIT... Asylum K 13029
15/01/1977.....20......7......	NEW KID IN TOWN ▲¹ 1977 Grammy Award for Best Arrangement for Vocals .... Asylum K 13069
16/04/1977.....8.....10......	**HOTEL CALIFORNIA** ▲¹ 1977 Grammy Award for Record of the Year................... Asylum K 13079
16/12/1978.....30......5......	PLEASE COME HOME FOR CHRISTMAS.. Asylum K 13145
13/10/1979.....40......5......	HEARTACHE TONIGHT ▲¹ 1979 Grammy Award for Best Rock Performance by a Group .... Asylum K 12394
01/12/1979.....66......2......	THE LONG RUN .... Elektra K 12404
13/07/1996.....52......1......	LOVE WILL KEEP US ALIVE.. Geffen GFSTD 21980
25/10/2003.....69......1......	HOLE IN THE WORLD .... Eagles 8122745472

EAMON
US singer Eamon Doyle (born 1984, Staten Island) whose debut hit inspired an 'answer' record by Frankee, who claimed to be the ex-girlfriend referred to in Eamon's hit. Despite her claims that the couple had gone out with each other when they were fifteen, the whole story was concocted for publicity purposes.

03/04/2004.....46......3......	F**K IT (I DON'T WANT YOU BACK) (IMPORT) .... Jive 82876604852
24/04/2004 ↑ ❶⁴.....19.....○	F**K IT (I DON'T WANT YOU BACK) ↑ On 5/6/2004 the single became the first #1 on the MEF Official Ringtones Chart........ Jive 82876608522
16/10/2004.....27......4......	LOVE THEM EAMON FEATURING GHOSTFACE .... Jive 82876639212

ROBERT EARL
UK singer (born Brian Budge, 17/11/1926) who turned professional in 1950, and was a regular on radio and TV. His son, also named Robert, is co-owner of the Hard Rock Cafe and Planet Hollywood chain of restaurants.

25/04/1958.....14.....13......	I MAY NEVER PASS THIS WAY AGAIN .... Philips PB 805
24/10/1958.....26......4......	MORE THAN EVER (COME PRIMA) .... Philips PB 867
13/02/1959.....17.....10......	WONDERFUL SECRET LOVE .... Philips PB 891

CHARLES EARLAND
US keyboard player (born 24/5/1941, Philadelphia, PA) who began playing alto saxophone with Jimmy McGriff before switching to keyboards in 1963. He died from a heart attack on 11/12/1999.

19/08/1978.....46......5......	LET THE MUSIC PLAY Featured in the 1991 film *Young Soul Rebels*, even though the film is set around the Queen's Silver Jubilee in 1977, before the track was recorded. .... Mercury 6167 703

STEVE EARLE
US guitarist/singer (born 17/1/1955, Fort Monroe, VA) who formed the Dukes in Texas, signing with Columbia then MCA. Married six times (to five women), he has served time in prison for offences including assaulting a police officer. A heroin user at thirteen, he kicked the habit in the mid-1990s, claiming his 1997 album *El Corazon* 'the first I've ever done 100 per cent clean'.

15/10/1988.....45......6......	COPPERHEAD ROAD .... MCA 1280
31/12/1988.....75......1......	JOHNNY COME LATELY .... MCA 1301

EARLIES
UK/US group formed by Brandon Carr (guitar/vocals), John Mark Lapham (keyboards/samples), Giles Hatton (keyboards) and Christian Madden (keyboards). Live the group are augmented by Alex Berry (bass), Rich Young (drums), Gareth Maybury (percussion/trombone), Tom Knott (guitar/trumpet), Nicky Madden (various instruments), Semay Wu (cello/keyboards) and Sara Lowes (keyboards).

06/11/2004.....67......1......	MORNING WONDER.. WEA IAMNAMES07

EARLY MUSIC CONSORT DIRECTED BY DAVID MUNROW
UK instrumental group conducted by David Munrow.

03/04/1971.....49......1......	HENRY VIII SUITE (EP) Tracks on EP: *Fanfare Passomezo Du Roy Gaillarde D'Escosse, Pavane Mille Ducates, Larocque Gaillarde, Allemande, Wedding March La Mourisque, If Loce Now Reigned* and *Rone Pouquoi* .... BBC RESL 1

EARTH, WIND AND FIRE
US soul group formed by Maurice White (born 19/12/1942, Memphis, TN), a session musician and drummer with the Ramsey Lewis Trio. The ten-strong band signed with Warner's, releasing two albums before White dismantled the group, re-assembling with his brother Verdine (born 25/7/1951, vocals/bass), Philip Bailey (born 8/5/1951, Denver, CO, vocals), Larry Dunn (born 19/6/1953, Colorado, keyboards), Al McKay (guitars), Fred White (drums), Ralph Johnson (born 4/7/1951, drums), Johnny Graham (guitar) and Andrew Woolfolk (saxophone). White produced after the death of Charles Stepney, later founding the American Record Company (ARC) with acts like Deniece Williams and the Emotions. Dunn and Verdine also produced the Pockets and Level 42. The group appeared in the films *That's The Way Of The World* (1975) and *Sgt Pepper's Lonely Hearts Club Band* (1978). Saxophonist Donald Myrick, in the band between 1975 and 1982, was shot dead by police searching his home for drugs on 30/7/1993 after they mistook a butane lighter he was holding for a gun. In 2000 it was announced that Maurice White was suffering from Parkinson's Disease, which had first been diagnosed in 1992. Five Grammy Awards include Best Rhythm & Blues Vocal Performance by a Group in 1975 for *Shining Star*, Best Rhythm & Blues Vocal Performance by a Group in 1978 for *All 'N' All* and Best Rhythm & Blues Instrumental Performance in 1978 for *Runnin'*. Inducted into the Rock & Roll Hall of Fame in 2000, they also have a star on the Hollywood Walk of Fame.

12/02/1977.....17......9......	SATURDAY NITE .... CBS 4835
11/02/1978.....14.....10......	FANTASY .... CBS 6056
13/05/1978.....41......5......	JUPITER .... CBS 6267
29/07/1978.....54......5......	MAGIC MIND .... CBS 6490
07/10/1978.....33......7......	GOT TO GET YOU INTO MY LIFE Featured in the 1978 film *Sgt Pepper's Lonely Hearts Club Band*. 1979 Grammy Award for Best Arrangement Accompanying Singers for Maurice White .... CBS 6553

○ Silver disc ● Gold disc ✪ Platinum disc (additional platinum units are indicated by a figure following the symbol) ◉ Singles released prior to 1973 that are known to have sold over 1 million copies in the UK

09/12/1978	3	13	O	**SEPTEMBER** Featured in the 1997 film *Soul Food*	CBS 6922
12/05/1979	4	13	●	**BOOGIE WONDERLAND** EARTH WIND AND FIRE WITH THE EMOTIONS 1979 Grammy Award for Best Rhythm & Blues Instrumental Performance	CBS 7292
28/07/1979	4	10	O	**AFTER THE LOVE HAS GONE** 1979 Grammy Awards for Best Rhythm & Blues Vocal Performance by a Group plus Best Rhythm & Blues Song for writers David Foster, Jay Graydon and Bill Champlin the same year	CBS 7721
06/10/1979	16	8		STAR	CBS 7092
15/12/1979	46	7		CAN'T LET GO	CBS 8077
08/03/1980	53	3		IN THE STONE	CBS 8252
11/10/1980	29	5		LET ME TALK	CBS 8982
20/12/1980	63	4		BACK ON THE ROAD	CBS 9377
07/11/1981	3	13	O	**LET'S GROOVE** Featured in the 1999 film *The Waterboy*	CBS A 1679
06/02/1982	29	6		I'VE HAD ENOUGH	CBS A 1959
05/02/1983	47	4		FALL IN LOVE WITH ME	CBS A 2927
07/11/1987	54	3		SYSTEM OF SURVIVAL	CBS EWF 1
31/07/1999	25	3		SEPTEMBER 99 (REMIX)	INCredible INCR 24CD

EARTHLING UK production duo formed in Bristol by Andy Edison and Tim Saul with vocals by Mau.

14/10/1995	61	1		ECHO ON MY MIND PART II	Cooltempo CDCOOL 312
01/06/1996	69	1		BLOOD MUSIC (EP) Tracks on EP: *First Transmission, Because The Night, Soup Or No Soup* and *Infinite M.*	Cooltempo CDCOOL 319

EAST 57TH STREET FEATURING DONNA ALLEN US dance group formed by Brian Tappert and Marc Pomeroy with singer Donna Allen.

11/10/1997	29	3		SATURDAY	AM:PM 5823752

EAST OF EDEN UK group formed in 1968 by Dave Arbus (violin), Ron Gaines (saxophone), Geoff Nicholson (guitar), Andy Sneddon (bass) and Geoff Britton (drums). By 1972 the group comprised Joe O'Donnell (violin), Garth Watt-Roy (guitar), Martin Fisher (bass) and Jeff Allen (drums).

17/04/1971	7	12		**JIG A JIG**	Deram DM 297

EAST 17 UK group formed by Tony Mortimer (born 21/10/1970, London), John Hendy (born 26/3/1971, Barking), Brian Harvey (born 8/8/1974, London) and Terry Coldwell (born 21/7/1974, London), named after their local postcode for Walthamstow. They were named Best Dance Act at the 1995 MTV Europe Music Awards. Harvey was sacked in January 1997 but later reinstated. When Mortimer left to pursue songwriting, the group re-formed as E-17, finally disbanding at the end of 1999. Brian Harvey later went solo on Edel Records.

29/08/1992	10	9		**HOUSE OF LOVE**	London LON 325
14/11/1992	28	8		GOLD	London LON 331
30/01/1993	5	10	O	**DEEP** Featured in the 1994 film *Kalifornia*	London LOCDP 334
10/04/1993	13	7		SLOW IT DOWN	London LONCD 339
26/06/1993	11	7		WEST END GIRLS	London LONCD 344
04/12/1993	3	14	O	**IT'S ALRIGHT**	London LONCD 345
14/05/1994	3	13	O	**AROUND THE WORLD**	London LONCD 349
01/10/1994	7	8		**STEAM** Featured in the 1998 film *Up 'N Under*	London LONCD 353
03/12/1994	❶⁵	16	✪	**STAY ANOTHER DAY**	London LONCD 354
25/03/1995	10	7		**LET IT RAIN**	London LOCDP 363
17/06/1995	12	7		HOLD MY BODY TIGHT	London LOCDP 367
04/11/1995	4	14	O	**THUNDER**	London LOCDP 373
10/02/1996	7	7		**DO U STILL?**	London LOCDP 379
10/08/1996	16	8		SOMEONE TO LOVE	London LONCD 385
02/11/1996	2	15	●	**IF YOU EVER** EAST 17 FEATURING GABRIELLE	London LONCD 388
18/01/1997	3	5		**HEY CHILD**	London LONCD 390
14/11/1998	2	10		**EACH TIME**	Telstar CDSTAS 3017
13/03/1999	12	5		BETCHA CAN'T WAIT This and above single credited to E-17	Telstar CDSTAS 3031

EAST SIDE BEAT Italian instrumental/production duo Carl Fanini and Francesco Petrocchi. According to their publicity, East Side was a solo artist, abandoned as a baby and found by the Orphanage for Babies Abandoned by Highly Strung Mothers and named East Side after the New York area where he was found.

30/11/1991	3	11		**RIDE LIKE THE WIND**	ffrr F 176
19/12/1992	26	6		ALIVE AND KICKING	ffrr F 206
29/05/1993	65	1		YOU'RE MY EVERYTHING	ffrr FCD 207

EASTERN LANE UK rock group from Berwick-upon-Tweed formed in 2000 with Derek Meins (guitar/vocals), Andy Lawton (guitar), Stuart Newland (bass) and Danny Ferguson (drums).

15/11/2003	72	1		FEED YOUR ADDICTION	Rough Trade RTRADESCD132

❶⁹ Number of weeks single topped the UK chart ↑ Entered the UK chart at #1 ▲⁹ Number of weeks single topped the US chart

253

13/03/2004.....55......1.......	SAFFRON	Rough Trade RTRADSCD156
06/11/2004.....65......1.......	I SAID PIG ON FRIDAY	Rough Trade RTRADSCD199

SHEENA EASTON UK singer (born Sheena Orr, 27/4/1959, Glasgow) whose debut EMI single *Modern Girl* was a minor hit. When she was the subject of the TV documentary *Big Time* as an up-and-coming singer, however, her second single exploded onto the charts, followed by a re-entry for her debut. After moving to the US, she was also an actress (in the TV show *Miami Vice* as Sonny Crockett's wife) and property speculator. She also worked extensively with Prince. She has won two Grammy Awards: Best New Artist in 1981 and Best Mexican-American Performance in 1984 with Luis Miguel for *Me Gustas Tal Como Eres*.

05/04/1980.....56......3.......	MODERN GIRL	EMI 5042
19/07/1980 .....3......15.....●	9 TO 5 ▲²	EMI 5066
09/08/1980 .....8......12.....○	MODERN GIRL Re-promoted following exposure in the TV show *Big Time*	EMI 5042
25/10/1980.....14......6.......	ONE MAN WOMAN	EMI 5114
14/02/1981.....44......5.......	TAKE MY TIME	EMI 5135
02/05/1981.....12......8.......	WHEN HE SHINES	EMI 5166
27/06/1981 .....8......13.......	FOR YOUR EYES ONLY Featured in the 1981 James Bond film *For Your Eyes Only*. Easton was on screen singing the theme.	EMI 5195
12/09/1981.....33......8.......	JUST ANOTHER BROKEN HEART	EMI 5232
05/12/1981.....54......3.......	YOU COULD HAVE BEEN WITH ME	EMI 5252
31/07/1982.....38......5.......	MACHINERY	EMI 5326
12/02/1983.....28......7.......	WE'VE GOT TONIGHT KENNY ROGERS AND SHEENA EASTON	Liberty UP 658
21/01/1989.....15......8.......	THE LOVER IN ME	MCA 1289
18/03/1989.....43......3.......	DAYS LIKE THIS	MCA 1325
15/07/1989.....54......2.......	101	MCA 1348
18/11/1989.....27......5.......	THE ARMS OF ORION PRINCE WITH SHEENA EASTON Featured in the 1989 film *Batman*	Warner Brothers W 2757
09/12/2000.....54......1.......	GIVING UP GIVING IN	Universal MCSTD 40244

EASTSIDE CONNECTION US disco aggregation assembled by Harry Scorzo Jr.

08/04/1978.....44......3.......	YOU'RE SO RIGHT FOR ME...	Creole CR 149

CLINT EASTWOOD US actor (born31/5/1930, San Francisco, CA). His half of the hit single with Lee Marvin only charted for two weeks while Marvin made it all the way to the top. Clint later entered politics, becoming Mayor of Carmel.

07/02/1970.....18......2.......	I TALK TO THE TREES Listed flip side was *Wand'rin' Star* by LEE MARVIN Both sides featured in the 1969 film *Paint Your Wagon*..	Paramount PARA 3004

CLINT EASTWOOD AND GENERAL SAINT UK vocal duo formed in the early 1980s. Clint Eastwood (Robert Brammer) was already known in reggae circles for earlier Jamaican hits, General Saint (Winston Hislop) being known as a dancehall DJ. Eastwood's brother Trinity has also enjoyed a successful recording career.

29/09/1984.....51......3.......	LAST PLANE (ONE WAY TICKET)	MCA 910
02/04/1994.....54......5.......	OH CAROL!	Copasetic COPCD 0009

EASY RIDERS – see FRANKIE LAINE

EASYBEATS Australian group originally formed in Sydney in 1963 by George Young (born 6/11/1947, Glasgow, rhythm guitar), Gordon 'Snowy' Fleet (born 16/8/1946, Bootle, drums), Harry Vanda (born Harold Wandon 22/3/1947, The Hague, Holland, lead guitar) and Dick Diamonde (born 28/12/1947, Hilversum, Holland, bass). Moving to England in 1966, they added singer Steven Wright (born 20/12/1948, Leeds). Fleet left before they toured the US and was replaced by Tony Cahill. They split in 1970, Vanda and Young (elder brother of AC/DC's Angus and Malcolm Young) forming Flash And The Pan. The group were named after the TV programme *Easybeat*.

27/10/1966 .....6......15......	FRIDAY ON MY MIND	United Artists UP 1157
10/04/1968.....20......9.......	HELLO, HOW ARE YOU	United Artists UP 2209

EASYWORLD UK group formed by Glenn Hooper (born 18/4/1979, Eastbourne), David James Ford (born 16/5/1978, Dartford) and Jo Taylor (born 29/10/1977, Eastbourne).

01/06/2002.....67......1.......	BLEACH..	Jive 9253552
21/09/2002.....57......1.......	YOU AND ME	Jive 9254102
08/02/2003.....40......1.......	JUNKIES..	Jive 9254522
18/10/2003.....42......1.......	2ND AMENDMENT	Jive 82876554692
31/01/2004.....27......2.......	'TIL THE DAY	Jive 82876585372
11/09/2004.....50......1.......	HOW DID IT EVER COME TO THIS?..	Jive 82876632102

EAT UK/US group with Ange Little (vocals), Jem Moorshead (guitar), Max Lavilla (guitar) Tim Sewell (bass) and Pete Howard (drums).

12/06/1993.....73......1.......	BLEED ME WHITE	Fiction FICCD 48

EAT STATIC UK instrumental duo formed in Somerset by Merv Peopler (drums) and Joe Hinton (keyboards), both previously in Ozric Tentacles. Eat Static are primarily concerned with UFOs, the inspiration for all their hit albums.

22/02/1997.....41......1.......	HYBRID...	Planet Dog BARK 024CD
27/09/1997.....44......1.......	INTERCEPTOR	Planet Dog BARK 030CD
27/06/1998.....67......1.......	CONTACT...	Planet Dog BARK 033CD

CLEVELAND EATON US singer/bass player from Chicago, IL who replaced Eldee Young on bass in the Ramsey Lewis Trio in 1965, with drummer Maurice White (who later formed EWF). As a solo artist, he recorded jazz-funk albums and worked with George Benson.

23/09/1978.....35......6.......	BAMA BOOGIE WOOGIE...	Gull GULS 63

EAV Austrian vocal/instrumental group formed by Eik Breit, Gunter Heinemann, Reinhard Brummer, Thomas Rabitsch and Anders Stenmo. Their name is short for Erste Allgemeine Verunsicherung.

| 27/09/1986.....63......4....... | BA-BA-BANKROBBERY (ENGLISH VERSION)..................................... | Columbia DB 9139 |

EAZY-E US rapper (born Eric Wright, 7/9/1964, Compton, CA) who was also a member of NWA (Niggaz With Attitude) and founded Ruthless Records (supposedly using money that was raised from drug dealing). He died from AIDS on 26/3/1995.

| 06/01/1996.....30......3....... | JUST TAH LET U KNOW... | Ruthless 6628162 |

EBON-E – see RMXCRAW FEATURING EBON-E PLUS AMBUSH

EBONY DUBSTERS UK production duo Shy FX (Andre Williams) and T-Power (Mark Royal).

| 24/01/2004.....59......2....... | MURDERATION.. | Ebony EBR029 |
| 22/05/2004.....58......1....... | NUMBER 1/THE RITUAL... | Ebony EBR030 |

ECHELON UK rock group formed by Paul Usher (guitar/keyboards/vocals), Mark Brandon (guitar), Owain North (bass) and Andy Grant (drums).

| 20/11/2004.....57......1....... | PLUS.. | Poptones MC5095SCD |

ECHO AND THE BUNNYMEN UK rock group formed in Liverpool in 1978 by Ian McCulloch (born 5/5/1959, Liverpool, vocals, formerly of the Crucial Three with Pete Wylie and Julian Cope), Will Sergeant (born 12/4/1958, Liverpool, guitar) and Les Pattinson (born 18/4/1958, Liverpool, bass), plus a drum machine called 'Echo'. They signed with Korova in 1979, adding Pete De Freitas (born 2/8/1961, Port of Spain, Trinidad, drums) and making Echo redundant. They split in 1988, McCulloch going solo before forming Electrafixion, then re-formed in 1996. De Freitas was killed in a motorcycle crash on 15/6/1989. They were in the England United recording for the 1998 World Cup finals.

17/05/1980.....62......1.......	RESCUE..	Korova KOW 1
18/04/1981.....37......4.......	SHINE SO HARD (EP) Tracks on EP: *Crocodiles, All That Jazz, Zimbo* and *Over The Wall*.....................	Korova ECHO 1
18/07/1981.....49......4.......	A PROMISE...	Korova KOW 15
29/05/1982.....19......7.......	THE BACK OF LOVE..	Korova KOW 24
22/01/1983....8......8.......	**THE CUTTER**...	Korova KOW 26
16/07/1983.....15......7.......	NEVER STOP..	Korova KOW 28
28/01/1984.....9......6.......	**THE KILLING MOON**..	Korova KOW 32
21/04/1984.....30......5.......	SILVER...	Korova KOW 34
14/07/1984.....16......7.......	SEVEN SEAS..	Korova KOW 35
19/10/1985.....21......7.......	BRING ON THE DANCING HORSES Featured in the 1986 film *Pretty In Pink*.........	Korova KOW 43
13/06/1987.....28......4.......	THE GAME..	WEA YZ 134
01/08/1987.....36......4.......	LIPS LIKE SUGAR...	WEA YZ 144
20/02/1988.....29......5.......	PEOPLE ARE STRANGE Featured in the 1987 film *The Lost Boys*....................	WEA YZ 175
02/03/1991.....34......4.......	PEOPLE ARE STRANGE Re-issue of WEA YZ 175..	East West YZ 567
28/06/1997....8......6.......	**NOTHING LASTS FOREVER**..	London LOCDP 396
13/09/1997.....30......2.......	I WANT TO BE THERE WHEN YOU COME..	London LONCD 399
08/11/1997.....50......1.......	DON'T LET IT GET YOU DOWN..	London LOCDP 406
27/03/1999.....22......3.......	RUST..	London LONCD 424
05/05/2001.....41......1.......	IT'S ALRIGHT...	Cooking Vinyl FRY CD104

ECHOBASS UK producer Simon Woodgate.

| 14/07/2001.....53......1....... | YOU ARE THE WEAKEST LINK Contains a sample of Anne Robinson's catchphrase from TV quiz *The Weakest Link*.............. |
| | .... | House Of Bush CDANNE 001 |

ECHOBEATZ UK DJ/production duo Dave De Braie and Paul Moody. Their debut hit was a drum and bass version of a song originally recorded by Sergio Mendes, revived by Nike for a TV advertisement to coincide with the World Cup.

| 25/07/1998.....10......5....... | **MAS QUE NADA**.. | Eternal WEA 176CD |

ECHOBELLY UK rock group formed in London in 1993 by Sonya Aurora Madan (vocals), Glenn Johannson (guitar), Debbie Smith (guitar), Andy Henderson (drums) and Alex Keyser (bass). Madan later recorded with Victor Imbres as Lithium, and Smith left in 1997.

02/04/1994.....47......1.......	INSOMNIAC..	Fauve FAUV 1CS
02/07/1994.....39......2.......	I CAN'T IMAGINE THE WORLD WITHOUT ME...	Fauve FAUV 2CD
05/11/1994.....59......1.......	CLOSE...BUT..	Fauve FAUV 4CD
02/09/1995.....13......3.......	GREAT THINGS...	Fauve FAUV 5CD
04/11/1995.....25......3.......	KING OF THE KERB...	Fauve FAUV 7CD
02/03/1996.....20......3.......	DARK THERAPY...	Fauve FAUV 8CD
23/08/1997.....31......2.......	THE WORLD IS FLAT...	Epic 6648152
08/11/1997.....56......1.......	HERE COMES THE BIG RUSH...	Epic 6652452

BILLY ECKSTINE US singer (born 8/7/1913, Pittsburgh, PA), nicknamed 'Mr B' during the 1940s and 1950s. Sarah Vaughan had been a member of his band from 1944 to 1945. He died from a stroke on 8/3/1993. He has a star on the Hollywood Walk of Fame.

| 12/11/1954.....3......17...... | **NO ONE BUT YOU** Featured in the 1954 film *The Flame And The Flesh*........... | MGM 763 |
| 27/09/1957.....22......2....... | PASSING STRANGERS BILLY ECKSTINE AND SARAH VAUGHAN........................... | Mercury MT 164 |

❶[9] Number of weeks single topped the UK chart ↑ Entered the UK chart at #1 ▲[9] Number of weeks single topped the US chart

DATE	POS	WKS	BPI	SINGLE TITLE	LABEL & NUMBER
13/02/1959	8	14		**GIGI** Featured in the 1958 film *Gigi*	Mercury AMT 1018
12/03/1969	20	15		PASSING STRANGERS BILLY ECKSTINE AND SARAH VAUGHAN Re-issue of Mercury MT 164	Mercury MF 1082

ECLIPSE Italian producer/instrumentalist Gianni Bini. He was in Goodfellas with Martini, who also record as House Of Glass.

14/08/1999	25	4		MAKES ME LOVE YOU Contains a sample of Sister Sledge's *Thinking Of You*	Azuli AZNYCDX 100

SILVIO ECOMO Dutch producer (born 18/4/1970, The Hague).

15/07/2000	70	1		STANDING	Hooj Choons HOOJ 098CD

EDDIE AND THE HOT RODS UK rock group formed in Southend in 1975 by Barrie Masters (vocals), Dave Higgs (guitar), Paul Gray (bass) and Steve Nicol (drums). Graeme Douglas was added on guitar in 1977. They disbanded 1978, Masters forming a new Eddie And The Hot Rods for one album in 1985.

11/09/1976	43	5		LIVE AT THE MARQUEE (EP) Tracks on EP: *96 Tears, Get Out Of Denver* and *Medley: Gloria/Satisfaction*	Island IEP 2
13/11/1976	35	4		TEENAGE DEPRESSION	Island WIP 6354
23/04/1977	44	3		I MIGHT BE LYING	Island WIP 6388
13/08/1977	9	10		**DO ANYTHING YOU WANT TO DO** RODS	Island WIP 6401
21/01/1978	36	4		QUIT THIS TOWN	Island WIP 6411

EDDY UK singer Edith Emenike.

09/07/1994	49	2		SOMEDAY	Positiva CDTIV 14

DUANE EDDY AND THE REBELS US singer/guitarist (born 26/4/1938, New York) who played guitar from the age of five. In his teens he formed the Rebels, recording a debut single in 1958 with producer Lee Hazlewood. They included top session players Larry Knechtel (piano, later in Bread), Jim Horn and Steve Douglas (saxophone). Eddy appeared in films, including *The Savage Seven* (1968) and *Because They're Young* (1960). Douglas died from heart failure on 19/4/1993. Eddy was inducted into the Rock & Roll Hall of Fame in 1994.

05/09/1958	19	10		REBEL ROUSER Featured in the 1994 film *Forrest Gump*	London HL 8669
02/01/1959	22	4		CANNONBALL	London HL 8764
19/06/1959	6	11		**PETER GUNN THEME**	London HLW 8879
24/07/1959	17	5		YEP	London HLW 8879
04/09/1959	11	9		FORTY MILES OF BAD ROAD	London HLW 8929
18/12/1959	12	5		SOME KINDA EARTHQUAKE At 77 seconds this is the shortest single to have hit the top 40	London HLW 9007
19/02/1960	12	11		BONNIE CAME BACK	London HLW 9050
28/04/1960	4	13		**SHAZAM!**	London HLW 9104
21/07/1960	2	18		**BECAUSE THEY'RE YOUNG** This and above single featured in the 1960 film *Because They're Young*	London HLW 9162
10/11/1960	13	10		KOMMOTION	London HLW 9225
12/01/1961	2	14		**PEPE** Featured in the 1960 film *Pepe*	London HLW 9257
20/04/1961	7	10		**THEME FROM DIXIE**	London HLW 9324
22/06/1961	17	10		RING OF FIRE	London HLW 9370
14/09/1961	30	4		DRIVIN' HOME	London HLW 9406
05/10/1961	42	3		CARAVAN	Parlophone R 4826
24/05/1962	19	8		DEEP IN THE HEART OF TEXAS	RCA 1288
23/08/1962	10	10		**BALLAD OF PALADIN** This and above two singles credited to **DUANE EDDY**	RCA 1300
08/11/1962	4	16		**DANCE WITH THE GUITAR MAN**	RCA 1316
14/02/1963	27	8		BOSS GUITAR	RCA 1329
30/05/1963	35	4		LONELY BOY LONELY GUITAR	RCA 1344
29/08/1963	49	1		YOUR BABY'S GONE SURFIN'	RCA 1357
08/03/1975	9	9		**PLAY ME LIKE YOU PLAY YOUR GUITAR** This and above four singles credited to **DUANE EDDY AND THE REBELETTES**	GTO GT 11
22/03/1986	8	9		**PETER GUNN** ART OF NOISE FEATURING DUANE EDDY 1986 Grammy Award for Best Rock Instrumental Performance	China WOK 6

EDDY AND THE SOUL BAND US percussionist Eddy Conrad who formed the Soul Band in Holland.

23/02/1985	13	7		THE THEME FROM 'SHAFT'	Club JAB 11

RANDY EDELMAN US singer/songwriter/pianist (born 10/6/1947, Patterson, NJ) who made his debut album in 1972. He worked mainly as a songwriter, penning *Weekend In New England* for Barry Manilow, and scoring the films *Ghostbusters II* (1989), *Twins* (1988), *Parenthood* (1989) and *Anaconda* (1997).

06/03/1976	11	7		CONCRETE AND CLAY	20th Century BTC 2261
18/09/1976	25	7		UPTOWN UPTEMPO WOMAN	20th Century BTC 2225
15/01/1977	49	2		YOU	20th Century BTC 2253
17/07/1982	60	2		NOBODY MADE ME	Rocket XPRES 81

EDELWEISS Austrian group formed by Martin Gletschermayer featuring the yodelling of Maria Mathis. They claimed to be the first group to combine authentic Austrian folk music with rap, hip hop and house.

○ Silver disc ● Gold disc ✪ Platinum disc (additional platinum units are indicated by a figure following the symbol) ◎ Singles released prior to 1973 that are known to have sold over 1 million copies in the UK

29/04/1989 . . . . . 5 . . . . . 10	**BRING ME EDELWEISS** . . . . WEA YZ 353

EDEN UK/Australian group formed by Andrew Skeoch, Paula Coster and Ross Healy.

06/03/1993 . . . . . 51 . . . . . . 2	DO U FEEL 4 ME . . . . Logic 74321135422

LYN EDEN – see SMOKIN BEATS FEATURING LYN EDEN

EDISON LIGHTHOUSE UK studio group assembled by songwriters Barry Mason and Tony Macaulay with session singer Tony Burrows (born 14/4/1942, Exeter). Success prompted the creation of a group, which floundered after the hit single. Burrows went on to front Brotherhood Of Man.

24/01/1970 . . . . ❶⁵ 12	**LOVE GROWS (WHERE MY ROSEMARY GOES)** Featured in the films *The Most Fertile Man In Ireland* (2000) and *Shallow Hal* (2001) . . . . Bell 1091
30/01/1971 . . . . . 49 . . . . . . 1	IT'S UP TO YOU PETULA . . . . Bell 1136

DAVE EDMUNDS UK singer/guitarist (born 15/4/1944, Cardiff). Learning guitar while at school, he was in the Raiders in the mid-1960s before joining Love Sculpture. They split in 1969, Edmunds seting up Rockfield Recording Studios in Wales and embarking on a solo career and as a producer, working with Shakin' Stevens, Brinsley Schwarz and the Stray Cats.

21/11/1970 . . . . ❶⁶ 14	**I HEAR YOU KNOCKIN'** DAVE EDMUNDS' ROCKPILE . . . . MAM 1
20/01/1973 . . . . . 8 . . . . . 13	**BABY I LOVE YOU** . . . . Rockfield ROC 1
09/06/1973 . . . . . 5 . . . . . 12	**BORN TO BE WITH YOU** . . . . Rockfield ROC 2
02/07/1977 . . . . . 26 . . . . . . 8	I KNEW THE BRIDE . . . . Swansong SSK 19411
30/06/1979 . . . . 4 . . . . 11 . . . . ○	**GIRLS TALK** . . . . Swansong SSK 19418
22/09/1979 . . . . . 11 . . . . . . 9	QUEEN OF HEARTS . . . . Swansong SSK 19419
24/11/1979 . . . . . 59 . . . . . . 4	CRAWLING FROM THE WRECKAGE . . . . Swansong SSK 19420
09/02/1980 . . . . . 28 . . . . . . 8	SINGING THE BLUES . . . . Swansong SSK 19422
28/03/1981 . . . . . 58 . . . . . . 3	ALMOST SATURDAY NIGHT . . . . Swansong SSK 19424
20/06/1981 . . . . . 34 . . . . . . 6	THE RACE IS ON DAVE EDMUNDS AND THE STRAY CATS . . . . Swansong SSK 19425
26/03/1983 . . . . . 60 . . . . . . 4	SLIPPING AWAY . . . . Arista ARIST 522
07/04/1990 . . . . . 68 . . . . . . 1	KING OF LOVE . . . . Capitol CL 568

ALTON EDWARDS Zimbabwean singer who moved to Zurich in 1978 and London in 1981, was formerly in the South African groups Sabu and Unity.

09/01/1982 . . . . . 20 . . . . . . 9	I JUST WANNA (SPEND SOME TIME WITH YOU) . . . . Streetwave STRA 1897

DENNIS EDWARDS FEATURING SIEDAH GARRETT US singer (born 3/2/1943, Birmingham, AL) who was in The Fireworks before joining The Contours, signing to Motown Records in 1965. When the Contours disbanded in 1967 he joined The Temptations, replacing David Ruffin as lead singer in 1968. He stayed with Motown as a solo act when the group moved to Atlantic, rejoining them when they returned two albums later. He went solo again in 1984, with more success, returning to the group a third time in 1987, leaving for good a few years later. He later toured as Dennis Edwards' Temptations, until blocked by The Temptations. Garrett (born in Los Angeles, CA) toured with Sergio Mendes and Quincy Jones before songwriting, penning *Man In The Mirror* for Michael Jackson.

24/03/1984 . . . . . 45 . . . . . . 5	DON'T LOOK ANY FURTHER . . . . Gordy TMG 1334
20/06/1987 . . . . . 55 . . . . . . 5	DON'T LOOK ANY FURTHER . . . . Gordy TMG 1334

RUPIE EDWARDS Jamaican singer (born Robert Edwards, March 1942, St Andrews) who was first known as a producer in his homeland. His debut hit was banned by Radio 1.

23/11/1974 . . . . . 9 . . . . . 10	**IRE FEELINGS (SKANGA)** . . . . Cactus CT 38
08/02/1975 . . . . . 32 . . . . . . 6	LEGO SKANGA . . . . Cactus CT 51

TOMMY EDWARDS US singer (born 17/2/1922, Richmond, VA). After minor hits in the early 1950s MGM got him to re-record them in stereo, all of which re-charted. He died from a brain aneurysm on 23/10/1969.

03/10/1958 . . . . ❶³ 17	**IT'S ALL IN THE GAME** ▲⁶ Written in 1912 by US Vice President Charles Dawes. Featured in the 1982 film *Diner* . . . . MGM 989
07/08/1959 . . . . . 29 . . . . . . 1	MY MELANCHOLY BABY . . . . MGM 1020

EELS US rock group formed in Los Angeles, CA in 1995 by E (born Mark Everett, guitar/vocals), Butch Norton (drums) and Tommy Walter (bass). They were named Best International Newcomer at the 1998 BRIT Awards.

15/02/1997 . . . . . 10 . . . . . . 5	**NOVOCAINE FOR THE SOUL** . . . . DreamWorks DRMCD 22174
17/05/1997 . . . . . 9 . . . . . 5	**SUSAN'S HOUSE** . . . . DreamWorks DRMCD 22238
13/09/1997 . . . . . 35 . . . . . . 2	YOUR LUCKY DAY IN HELL . . . . DreamWorks DRMCD 22277
26/09/1998 . . . . . 23 . . . . . . 3	LAST STOP THIS TOWN . . . . DreamWorks DRMCD 22346
12/12/1998 . . . . . 60 . . . . . . 1	CANCER FOR THE CURE . . . . DreamWorks DRMCD 22373
26/02/2000 . . . . . 11 . . . . . . 4	MR E'S BEAUTIFUL BLUES . . . . DreamWorks DRMCD 4509772
24/06/2000 . . . . . 55 . . . . . . 1	FLYSWATER . . . . DreamWorks DRMCD 4509462
22/09/2001 . . . . . 30 . . . . . . 2	SOULJACKER PART 1 . . . . DreamWorks 4508932

EFUA UK singer Efua Baker, the wife of Soul II Soul member Jazzy B.

03/07/1993 . . . . . 42 . . . . . . 5	SOMEWHERE . . . . Virgin VSCDT 1463

EGG UK vocal/instrumental group formed by Tim Holmes, Paul Herman and Pauline Taylor.

30/01/1999 . . . . . 58 . . . . . . 1	GETTING AWAY WITH IT . . . . Indochina ID 079CD

❶⁹ Number of weeks single topped the UK chart   ↑ Entered the UK chart at #1   ▲⁹ Number of weeks single topped the US chart

257

EGGS ON LEGS UK singer Richard Orford whose debut hit was the theme to Channel 4's *The Big Breakfast Eggs On Legs* tour.

23/09/1995.....42......1....... COCK A DOODLE DO IT..Avex UKAVEXCD 18

EGYPTIAN EMPIRE UK producer Tim Taylor.

24/10/1992.....61......2....... THE HORN TRACK..ffrreedom TAB 115

EIFFEL 65 Italian dance group formed by Maurizio Lobina, Gianfrancco Radone and Gabrielle Ponte. Their debut hit charted on import sales alone. Only three records have made the top 40 just on import sales: The Jam's *That's Entertainment* in 1981, then Lou Bega's *Mambo No 5* and Eiffel 65 in 1999. Randone is also a member of Minimal Funk 2.

21/08/1999.....39......5...... BLUE (DA BA DEE) (IMPORT)...Logic 74321688212
25/09/1999.....❶³.....21......● **BLUE (DA BA DEE)** ↑..Eternal WEA 226CD1
19/02/2000.....3....10...... **MOVE YOUR BODY**...Eternal WEA 255CD1

808 STATE UK group formed in Manchester in 1988 by Graham Massey (born 4/8/1960, Manchester), Martin Price (born 26/3/1955, Manchester) and DJ Gerald Simpson, naming themselves after a drum machine. Simpson left and recorded as A Guy Called Gerald, with DJs Andrew Barker (born 9/3/1968, Manchester) and Darren Partington (born1/11/1969, Manchester) joining 808 State. Price left in 1990.

18/11/1989.....10......9...... **PACIFIC**..ZTT ZANG 1
31/03/1990.....56......1...... THE EXTENDED PLEASURE OF DANCE (EP) Tracks on EP: *Cobra Bora, Ancodia* and *Cubik*. Available only on 12-inch vinyl ....
....ZTT ZANG 2T
02/06/1990.....10.....10..... **THE ONLY RHYME THAT BITES**..ZTT ZANG 3
15/09/1990.....18......7..... TUNES SPLITS THE ATOM This and above single credited to **MC TUNES VERSUS 808 STATE**.............ZTT ZANG 6
10/11/1990.....10.....10..... **CUBIK/OLYMPIC**..ZTT ZANG 5
16/02/1991.....9......6..... **IN YER FACE**...ZTT ZANG 14
27/04/1991.....42......3..... OOOPS...ZTT ZANG 19
17/08/1991.....38......4..... LIFT/OPEN YOUR MIND..ZTT ZANG 20
29/08/1992.....59......1..... TIME BOMB/NIMBUS...ZTT ZANG 33
12/12/1992.....17......8..... ONE IN TEN **808 STATE VS UB40**...ZTT ZANG 39
30/01/1993.....50......2..... PLAN 9...ZTT ZANG 38CD
26/06/1993.....67......1..... 10 X 10..ZTT ZANG 42CD
13/08/1991.....67......1..... BOMBADIN...ZTT ZANG 54CD
29/06/1996.....57......1..... BOND...ZTT ZANG 80CD
08/02/1997.....20......2..... LOPEZ..ZTT ZANG 87CD
16/05/1998.....21......3..... PACIFIC/CUBIK Re-issue of ZTT Zang 1 and Zang 5..ZTT ZANG 98CD1
06/03/1999.....53......1..... THE ONLY RHYME THAT BITES 99...ZTT 125CD

18 WHEELER UK vocal/instrumental group with Sean Jackson (guitar/vocals), David Keenan (guitar/vocals), Alan Hake (bass) and Neil Halliday (drums). Keenan left in 1994 and was replaced by Steven Haddow. They split in 1997, Haddow forming Astro Naughty.

15/03/1997.....59......1...... STAY..Creation CRESCD 249

EIGHTH WONDER UK group originally formed as Spice by Jamie Kensit (guitar), later featuring his sister Patsy (born 4/3/1968, London, lead singer), Geoff Beauchamp (guitar) and Alex Godson (keyboards). Patsy began as a child actress, appearing as the 'pea pod' girl for Birds Eye. She subsequently resumed acting (appearing in the 1989 film *Lethal Weapon 2*) and has been married to Dan Donovan (Big Audio Dynamite), Jim Kerr (Simple Minds) and Liam Gallagher (Oasis), all three marriages ending in divorce.

02/11/1985.....65......2...... STAY WITH ME...CBS A 6594
20/02/1988.....7.....13...... **I'M NOT SCARED** Written and produced by The Pet Shop Boys. Featured in the 1989 film *Lethal Weapon 2*..........CBS SCARE 1
25/06/1988.....13......8...... CROSS MY HEART...CBS 6515527
01/10/1988.....65......2...... BABY BABY..CBS BABE 1

EIGHTIES MATCHBOX B-LINE DISASTER UK rock group formed in Brighton by Guy McKnight (vocals), Andy Huxley (guitar), Marc Norris (guitar), Sym Gharial (bass) and Tom Diamantepoulo (drums).

28/09/2002.....66......1...... CELEBRATE YOUR MOTHER..Universal MCSTD 40296
18/01/2003.....26......2...... PSYCHOSIS SAFARI...Universal MCSTD 40308
24/05/2003.....30......2...... CHICKEN..Island MCSXD 40317
24/01/2004.....25......2...... MISTER MENTAL Featured in the 2004 film *Shaun Of The Dead*..................................Universal MCSXD 40353
10/07/2004.....35......2...... I COULD BE AN ANGLE..Island MCSTD 40368
23/10/2004.....40......2...... RISE OF THE EAGLES...Universal MCSTD 40382

88.3 – see LISA MAY

EINSTEIN UK rapper Colin Case. He was also a member of Ambassadors Of Funk with Simon Harris.

18/11/1989.....65......1...... ANOTHER MONSTERJAM **SIMON HARRIS FEATURING EINSTEIN**.......................................ffrr F 116
15/12/1990.....42......4...... TURN IT UP **TECHNOTRONIC FEATURING MELISSA AND EINSTEIN**..................................Swanyard SYD 9
24/08/1996.....42......1...... THE POWER 96 **SNAP FEATURING EINSTEIN**..Arista 74321398672

EL COCO US disco group of producers, songwriters and multi-instrumentalists W Michael Lewis (born in San Diego, CA) and Laurin Rinder (born 3/4/1943, Los Angeles, CA) with Doug Richardson (tenor saxophone), Harry Kim (trumpet) and Merria Ross (lead vocals).

14/01/1978.....31......4...... COCOMOTION...Pye International 7N 25761

○ Silver disc ● Gold disc ✪ Platinum disc (additional platinum units are indicated by a figure following the symbol) ⓜ Singles released prior to 1973 that are known to have sold over 1 million copies in the UK

EL MARIACHI US producer Roger Sanchez (born 1/6/1967, New York City) who also records as Funk Junkeez and under his own name.

09/11/1996	38	2		CUBA	ffrr FCD 286

ELASTICA UK rock group formed in London in 1993 by Justine Frischmann (born 16/9/1969, Twickenham, guitar/vocals), Donna Matthews (born 2/12/1971, Newport, Wales, guitar), Justin Welch (born 4/12/1972, Nuneaton, drums) and Annie Holland (born 26/8/1965, Brighton, bass). They added Dave Bush (keyboards) in 1995. Holland left in 1995 and was replaced by Abby Travis. Travis later left and was replaced by Sheila Chipperfield (born 17/6/1976). Frischmann had been rhythm guitarist with Suede. They split in 2001.

12/02/1994	20	3		LINE UP Featured in the 1995 film *Mallrats*	Deceptive BLUFF 004CD
22/10/1994	17	4		CONNECTION	Deceptive BLUFF 010CD
25/02/1995	13	4		WAKING UP	Deceptive BLUFF 011CD
24/06/2000	44	1		MAD DOG	Deceptive BLUFF 077CD

ELATE UK voca/instrumental trio formed by Andrew Stevenson, Danny Hibrid and Nigel Ipinson.

26/07/1997	38	2		SOMEBODY LIKE YOU Contains a sample of Clannad's *Theme From Harry's Game*	VC Recordings VCRD 22

DONNIE ELBERT US singer (born 25/5/1936, New Orleans, LA) who first recorded with De Luxe in 1957 and later Vee-Jay. He also recorded as Val Martin for All Platinum. He moved to England in the 1960s, returned to the US in 1970 and then went on to Canada, where he was A&R director for Polygram in the mid-1980s. He died from a stroke on 26/1/1989.

08/01/1972	8	10		WHERE DID OUR LOVE GO	London HL 10352
26/02/1972	11	10		I CAN'T HELP MYSELF	Avco 6105 009
29/04/1972	27	9		LITTLE PIECE OF LEATHER	London HL 10370

ELBOW UK group formed by Guy Garvey (vocals), Craig Potter (keyboards), brother Mark (guitar), Pete Turner (bass) and Richard Jupp (drums), known as General Public, RPM and Miscellaneous Sales before Elbow. They were signed by Island but dropped after a year.

05/05/2001	36	1		RED	V2 VVR 5016158
21/07/2001	41	1		POWDER BLUE	V2 VVR 5016163
20/10/2001	42	1		NEWBORN	V2 VVR 5016173
16/02/2002	19	3		ASLEEP IN THE BACK	V2 VVR 5018703
16/08/2003	19	3		FALLEN ANGEL	V2 VVR 5021808
08/11/2003	44	1		FUGITIVE MOTEL	V2 VVR 5021828
06/03/2004	26	2		NOT A JOB	V2 VVR 5024678

ELECTRA UK voca/instrumental group formed by Velez Marin, Rob Dais and Paul Oakenfold.

06/08/1988	54	3		JIBARO	ffrr F 9
30/12/1989	51	4		IT'S YOUR DESTINY/AUTUMN LOVE	London F 121

ELECTRAFIXION UK group formed in 1994 by Ian McCulloch (born 5/5/195, Liverpool, vocals) and Will Sergeant (born 12/4/1958, Liverpool, guitar), both ex-Echo & The Bunnymen, with Leon De Sylva (bass) and Tony McGuigan (drums). McCulloch and Sergeant re-formed Echo & The Bunnymen at the end of 1996.

19/11/1994	47	2		ZEPHYR	WEA YZ 865CD
09/09/1995	54	2		LOWDOWN	WEA YZ 977CD
04/11/1995	58	1		NEVER	Spacejunk 022CD
16/03/1996	27	1		SISTER PAIN	Spacejunk 037CD

ELECTRASY UK vocal/instrumental group formed by Ali McKinnel (vocals), Nigel Nisbet (guitar), Steve Atkins (guitar), Alex Meadows (bass), Jim Hayden (keyboards) and Paul Pridmore (drums). According to the *Guinness Book Of Records* the video for *Best Friend's Girl* features the group and members of the Official Laurel And Hardy Fan Club throwing 4,400 custard pies in three minutes.

13/06/1998	60	1		LOST IN SPACE	MCA MCSTD 40171
05/09/1998	19	4		MORNING AFTERGLOW	MCA MCSTD 40184
28/11/1998	41	2		BEST FRIEND'S GIRL	MCA MCSXD 40195

ELECTRIBE 101 UK group formed in 1987 by Joe Stevens, Les Fleming, Rob Cimarosti, Brian Nordhoff and singer Billie Ray Martin. They split in 1990, with Martin going solo and Stevens, Fleming, Cimarosti and Nordhoff forming Groove Corporation.

28/10/1989	32	5		TELL ME WHEN THE FEVER ENDED	Mercury MER 310
24/02/1990	23	5		TALKING WITH MYSELF	Mercury MER 316
22/09/1990	50	3		YOU'RE WALKING	Mercury MER 328
10/10/1998	39	2		TALKING WITH MYSELF '98 (REMIX)	Manifesto FESDD 49

❶[9] Number of weeks single topped the UK chart ↑ Entered the UK chart at #1 ▲[9] Number of weeks single topped the US chart

259

THE ELECTRIC LIGHT ORCHESTRA
CONFUSION
LAST TRAIN TO LONDON

ELECTRIC LIGHT ORCHESTRA
UK rock group formed in Birmingham in 1971 by Jeff Lynne (born 20/12/1947, Birmingham, guitar/vocals), Roy Wood (born Ulysses Wood, 8/11/1946, Birmingham, guitar/vocals), Bev Bevan (born Beverley Bevan, 24/11/1946, Birmingham, drums), Hugh McDowell (born 31/7/1953, London, cello), Richard Tandy (born 26/3/1948, Birmingham, keyboards/vocals) and Andy Craig, Wilf Gibson and Bill Hunt. Wood, Lynne and Bevan had previously been in The Move. Wood left after one album to form Wizzard, Lynne taking over as leader. By 1986 ELO were the trio of Lynne, Bevan and Tandy. Lynne later became a member of The Traveling Wilburys.

DATE	POS	WKS	BPI	SINGLE TITLE	LABEL & NUMBER
29/07/1972	9	8		**10538 OVERTURE**	Harvest HAR 5053
27/01/1973	6	10		**ROLL OVER BEETHOVEN**	Harvest HAR 5063
06/10/1973	12	10		SHOWDOWN Featured in the 1996 film *Kingpin*	Harvest HAR 5077
09/03/1974	22	8		MA-MA-MA-BELLE	Warner Brothers K 16349
10/01/1976	10	8		**EVIL WOMAN**	Jet 764
03/07/1976	38	3		STRANGE MAGIC	Jet 779
13/11/1976	4	12	◯	**LIVIN' THING** Featured in the 1998 film *Boogie Nights*	Jet UP 36184
19/02/1977	9	9		**ROCKARIA!**	Jet UP 36209
21/05/1977	8	10		**TELEPHONE LINE**	Jet UP 36254
29/10/1977	18	12		TURN TO STONE	Jet UP 36313
28/01/1978	6	11	◯	**MR BLUE SKY**	Jet UP 36342
10/06/1978	6	14	◯	**WILD WEST HERO**	Jet 109
07/10/1978	6	9	◯	**SWEET TALKIN' WOMAN**	Jet 121
09/12/1978	34	8		ELO EP Tracks on EP: *Out Of My Head, Strange Magic, Ma-Ma-Ma-Belle* and *Evil Woman*	Jet ELO 1
19/05/1979	6	10	◯	**SHINE A LITTLE LOVE**	Jet 144
21/07/1979	8	9	◯	**THE DIARY OF HORACE WIMP**	Jet 150
01/09/1979	3	9	◯	**DON'T BRING ME DOWN** Featured in the 1997 film *Donnie Brasco*	Jet 153
17/11/1979	8	10	◯	**CONFUSION/LAST TRAIN TO LONDON**	Jet 166
24/05/1980	20	9		I'M ALIVE	Jet 179
21/06/1980	❶²	11	◯	**XANADU** OLIVIA NEWTON-JOHN AND ELECTRIC LIGHT ORCHESTRA	Jet 185
02/08/1980	11	8		ALL OVER THE WORLD	Jet 195
22/11/1980	21	10		DON'T WALK AWAY This and above three singles featured in the 1980 film *Xanadu*	Jet 7004
01/08/1981	4	12	◯	**HOLD ON TIGHT**	Jet 7011
24/10/1981	30	7		TWILIGHT	Jet 7015
09/01/1982	24	8		TICKET TO THE MOON/HERE IS THE NEWS	Jet 7018
18/06/1983	13	9		ROCK 'N' ROLL IS KING	Jet A 3500
03/09/1983	48	3		SECRET MESSAGES	Jet A 3720
01/03/1986	28	7		CALLING AMERICA	Epic A 6844
11/05/1991	60	1		HONEST MEN ELECTRIC LIGHT ORCHESTRA PART 2	Telstar ELO 100

ELECTRIC PRUNES
US group formed in Los Angeles, CA in 1965 by Jim Lowe (guitar/vocals), Ken Williams (guitar), James 'Weasel' Spagnola (guitar), Mark Tulin (bass) and Michael 'Quint' Weakley (drums). Weakley left soon after and was replaced by Preston Ritter.

DATE	POS	WKS	BPI	SINGLE TITLE	LABEL & NUMBER
09/02/1967	49	1		I HAD TOO MUCH TO DREAM LAST NIGHT	Reprise RS 20532
11/05/1967	42	4		GET ME TO THE WORLD ON TIME	Reprise RS 20564

ELECTRIC SIX
US rock group formed in Detroit, MI in 1997 by Dick Valentine (vocals), Surge Joebot (guitar), Rock 'N' Roll Indian (guitar), Disco (bass), Tait Nucleus (keyboards) and M (drums) as The Wildbunch. Rock 'N' Roll Indian, Surge Joebot and Disco left in June 2003 and were replaced by Johnny Nashinal, The Colonel and Frank Lloyd Bonaventure.

DATE	POS	WKS	BPI	SINGLE TITLE	LABEL & NUMBER
18/01/2003	2	11		**DANGER HIGH VOLTAGE** Featured in the 2003 film *Charlie's Angels: Full Throttle*	XL Recordings XLS 151CD
14/06/2003	5	10		**GAY BAR**	XL Recordings XLS 158CD
25/10/2003	40	1		DANCE COMMANDER	XL Recordings XLS 170CD
25/12/2004	21	1		RADIO GAGA	WEA WEA381CD1

ELECTRIC SOFT PARADE
UK rock group formed by brothers Alex (guitar/vocals) and Tom White (drums), who were nineteen and seventeen respectively at the time of their debut hit. Originally Feltro Media, they changed their name in 2001 to Soft Parade, a Doors tribute band of the same name prompting a further change to Electric Soft Parade. They were later augmented by Matt (bass) and Steve (keyboards).

DATE	POS	WKS	BPI	SINGLE TITLE	LABEL & NUMBER
04/08/2001	65	1		EMPTY AT THE END/SUMATRAN SOFT PARADE	DB 0067JC
10/11/2001	52	1		THERE'S A SILENCE	DB 007CD7JC
16/03/2002	23	2		SILENT TO THE DARK II	DB DB008 CDE7
01/06/2002	39	1		EMPTY AT THE END	DB DB009 ECD7

ELECTRIQUE BOUTIQUE
UK/French production group formed by Simon Grainger, Paul Woods and Jerry Boutheir.

DATE	POS	WKS	BPI	SINGLE TITLE	LABEL & NUMBER
26/08/2000	37	2		REVELATION!	Data 14CDS

ELECTRONIC
UK group originally formed as an ad hoc combination of Johnny Marr (born John Maher, 31/10/1963, Ardwick, Manchester) of The Smiths, Pet Shop Boys singer Neil Tennant (born 19/7/1954, Gosforth, Tyne & Wear) and New Order's Barney Sumner,

◯ Silver disc ● Gold disc ✪ Platinum disc (additional platinum units are indicated by a figure following the symbol) ◎ Singles released prior to 1973 that are known to have sold over 1 million copies in the UK

(born Bernard Dicken, 4/1/1956, Salford). By the 1990s they were down to a duo of Marr and Sumner, both having left their respective groups. Marr had been a much-in-demand session guitarist since the demise of The Smiths.

16/12/1989	12	9		GETTING AWAY WITH IT	Factory FAC 2577
27/04/1991	8	7		**GET THE MESSAGE**	Factory FAC 2877
28/09/1991	39	4		FEEL EVERY BEAT	Factory FAC 3287
04/07/1992	6	5		**DISAPPOINTED** Featured in the 1992 film *Cool World*	Parlophone R 6311
06/07/1996	14	4		FORBIDDEN CITY	Parlophone CDR 6436
28/09/1996	16	2		FOR YOU	Parlophone CDR 6445
15/02/1997	35	2		SECOND NATURE	Parlophone CDR 6455
24/04/1999	17	3		VIVID	Parlophone CDR 6514

ELECTRONICAS Dutch instrumental group who may have recorded the original but saw The Tweets score the bigger hit.

| 19/09/1981 | 22 | 8 | | ORIGINAL BIRD DANCE | Polydor POSP 360 |

ELECTROSET UK instrumental/production group comprising Kirk, Fox, Deckard and Ralf.

| 21/11/1992 | 27 | 3 | | HOW DOES IT FEEL Based on New Order's *Blue Monday* | ffrr F 203 |
| 15/07/1995 | 69 | 1 | | SENSATION Based on INXS' *New Sensation* | ffrreedom TABCD 231 |

ELEGANTS US vocal group formed in Staten Island, NYC in 1957 by Vito Picone (born 17/3/1940, Staten Island), Arthur Venosa (born 3/9/1939, Staten Island), Frank Tardogna (born 18/9/1941, Staten Island), Carmen Romano (born 17/8/1939, Staten Island) and James Moschella (born 10/5/1938, Staten Island). Their hit was based on Mozart's *Twinkle Twinkle Little Star*.

| 26/09/1958 | 25 | 2 | | LITTLE STAR ▲[1] Featured in the 1978 film *American Hot Wax* | HMV POP 520 |

ELEMENT FOUR UK group formed by Andy Gray and Paul Oakenfold. The TV programme followed the antics of ten people locked in a house and voting one out a week in order to win a prize of £70,000, with Craig Phillips of Liverpool emerging victorious.

| 09/09/2000 | 4 | 9 | | **BIG BROTHER UK TV THEME** Theme to the TV series *Big Brother* | Channel 4 Music C4M 00072 |
| 04/08/2001 | 63 | 2 | | BIG BROTHER UK TV THEME Re-entered the charts during the screening of *Big Brother 2* | Channel 4 Music C4M 00072 |

ELEPHANT MAN Jamaican singer (born O'Neil Bryan, 1974, Kingston) also known as Energy God, nicknamed Elephant because he had extremely large ears as a child.

| 22/11/2003 | 29 | 3 | | PON DE RIVER, PON DE BANK | Atlantic AT 0168CD |
| 04/09/2004 | 41 | 2 | | JOOK GAL | VP VPCD6416 |

ELEVATION UK instrumental/production duo Shaun Imrei and John O'Halloran.

| 23/05/1992 | 62 | 1 | | CAN YOU FEEL IT | Nova Mute 12NOMU 3 |

ELEVATOR SUITE UK instrumental/production trio formed by Andy Childs, Steve Grainger and Paul Roberts.

| 12/08/2000 | 71 | 1 | | BACK AROUND | Infectious INFECT 85CDS |

ELEVATORMAN UK instrumental/production group.

| 14/01/1995 | 37 | 3 | | FUNK AND DRIVE | Wired 211 |
| 01/07/1995 | 44 | 1 | | FIRED UP | Wired 216 |

ELGINS US R&B vocal group formed in Detroit, MI by Johnny Dawson, Norman McLean, Jimmy Charles and Saundra Edwards, later replaced by Yvonne Allen. Originally The Sensations, they changed to The Elgins on signing with Motown, the first name having been used by The Temptations.

| 01/05/1971 | 3 | 13 | | **HEAVEN MUST HAVE SENT YOU** | Tamla Motown TMG 771 |
| 09/10/1971 | 28 | 7 | | PUT YOURSELF IN MY PLACE | Tamla Motown TMG 787 |

ELIAS AND HIS ZIGZAG JIVE FLUTES South African instrumental group fronted by Elias Lerole whose brother Aaron wrote their debut hit. The song was revived by The Piranhas, who added lyrics to it in 1980.

| 25/04/1958 | 2 | 14 | | **TOM HARK** | Columbia DB 4109 |

YVONNE ELLIMAN US singer (born 29/12/1951, Honolulu, HI) who portrayed Mary Magdalene in the 1973 film *Jesus Christ Superstar* (and charted in the US with a song from the film) and later toured with Eric Clapton.

29/01/1972	47	1		I DON'T KNOW HOW TO LOVE HIM Part of a four-track single from the musical show *Jesus Christ Superstar*, with Murray Head's *Superstar* also charting during the single's chart run	MCA MMKS 5077
06/11/1976	6	13		**LOVE ME**	RSO 2090 205
07/05/1977	26	5		HELLO STRANGER	RSO 2090 236
13/08/1977	17	13		I CAN'T GET YOU OUT OF MY MIND	RSO 2090 251
06/05/1978	4	12	○	**IF I CAN'T HAVE YOU** ▲[1] Featured in the films *Saturday Night Fever* (1978) and *Big Daddy* (1999)	RSO 2090 266

DUKE ELLINGTON US orchestra leader (born Edward Kennedy Ellington, 29/4/1899, Washington DC) who led a number of bands in Washington before moving to New York and establishing his band, the core of which remained unchanged for the next 30 years, making frequent concert tours in Europe. He won eleven Grammies: Best Performance by a Dance Band, Best Musical Composition and Best Soundtrack Album of Background Score in 1959 for *Anatomy Of A Murder*, Best Jazz Performance, Large Group in 1965 for *Ellington 66*, Best Original Jazz Composition in 1966 for *In The Beginning*, Best Instrumental Jazz Performance in 1967 for *Far East Suite*, Best Instrumental Jazz Performance in 1968 for *And His Mother Called Him Bill*, Best Jazz Performance by a Big Band in 1971 for *New Orleans Suite*, Best Jazz Performance by a Big Band in 1972 for *Togo Brava Suite*, Best Jazz Performance by a Big Band in

1976 for *The Ellington Suites* and Best Jazz Performance by a Big Band in 1979 for *At Fargo, 1940 Live* (the Duke Ellington Orchestra also won the Best Jazz Performance by a Big Band in 1987 for *Digital Duke*). Three of his recordings have gained Grammy Hall of Fame Awards: 1928's *Black and Tan Fantasy,* 1931's *Mood Indigo* and 1941's *Take The A Train*. He died on 24/5/1974. He has a star on the Hollywood Walk of Fame.

05/03/1954 . . . . . 7 . . . . . . 4	**SKIN DEEP DUKE ELLINGTON WITH LOUIS BELLSON (DRUMS)** . . . . Philips PB 243

LANCE ELLINGTON UK singer, backing the likes of Sting, Pet Shop Boys, Deniece Williams and Mike Oldfield before going solo.

21/08/1993 . . . . . 57 . . . . . . 1	LONELY (HAVE WE LOST OUR LOVE) . . . . RCA 74321158332

RAY ELLINGTON UK band leader best known in the 1950s via *The Goon Show* radio programme, providing musical interludes with harmonica player Max Geldray. The hit single was based on a dance craze in the US in 1960. He died on 27/2/1985.

15/11/1962 . . . . . 36 . . . . . . 4	THE MADISON . . . . Ember S 102

BERN ELLIOTT AND THE FENMEN UK group formed in Kent in 1961 by Bern Elliott with Alan Judge (guitar), Wally Allen (guitar), Eric Willmer (bass) and Jon Povey (drums). Elliott and the group parted company after their second hit, Elliott forming the Klan. Allen and Povey were later members of the Pretty Things.

21/11/1963 . . . . . 14 . . . . . 13	MONEY . . . . Decca F 11770
19/03/1964 . . . . . 24 . . . . . . 9	NEW ORLEANS . . . . Decca F 11852

JOE ELLIOTT – see MICK RONSON WITH JOE ELLIOTT

MISSY 'MISDEMEANOR' ELLIOTT US rapper (born Melissa Elliott, 1/7/1971, Portsmouth, VA) who was originally in Sista, where she was known as Misdemeanor Of Sista. After they split she concentrated on songwriting, penning hits for SWV, Aaliyah, MC Lyte and Jodeci before going solo. Her awards include a MOBO for Best Hip Hop Act in 2001 and a Grammy in 2002 for Best Female Rap Solo Performance for *Scream A.K.A. Itchin'*.

30/08/1997 . . . . . 16 . . . . . . 3	THE RAIN (SUPA DUPA FLY) Contains a sample of Ann Peebles' *I Can't Stand The Rain* . . . . East West E 3919CD
29/11/1997 . . . . . 33 . . . . . . 2	SOCK IT 2 ME Features the uncredited contribution of Da Brat and containing a sample of The Delfonics' *Ready Or Not Here I Come* . . . . East West E 3890CD
25/04/1998 . . . . . 14 . . . . . . 3	BEEP ME 911 . . . . East West E 3859CD
22/08/1998 . . . . . 25 . . . . . . 3	MAKE IT HOT **NICOLE FEATURING MISSY 'MISDEMEANOR' ELLIOTT** . . . . East West E 3824CD1
22/08/1998 . . . . . 22 . . . . . . 4	HIT 'EM WIT DA HEE **MISSY 'MISDEMEANOR' ELLIOTT FEATURING LIL' KIM** Featured in the 1998 film *Can't Hardly Wait* . . . . East West E 3821CD
26/09/1998 . . . ●[1] . . . 9 . . . . . . ○	**I WANT YOU BACK ↑** **MELANIE B FEATURING MISSY 'MISDEMEANOR' ELLIOTT** . . . . Virgin VSCDT 1716
21/11/1998 . . . . . 72 . . . . . . 1	5 MINUTES **LIL' MO FEATURING MISSY 'MISDEMEANOR' ELLIOTT** This and above single featured in the 1998 film *Why Do Fools Fall In Love* . . . . Elektra E 3803CD
13/03/1999 . . . . . 43 . . . . . . 1	HERE WE COME **TIMBALAND/MISSY ELLIOTT AND MAGOO** Contains a sample from the cartoon series *Spiderman* . . . . Virgin DINSD 179
25/09/1999 . . . . . 20 . . . . . . 4	ALL N MY GRILL **MISSY 'MISDEMEANOR' ELLIOTT FEATURING MC SOLAAR** . . . . Elektra E 3742CD
22/01/2000 . . . . . 18 . . . . . 3	HOT BOYZ **MISSY 'MISDEMEANOR' ELLIOTT FEATURING NAS, EVE & Q TIP** . . . . Elektra E 7002CD
28/04/2001 . . . . . 4 . . . . . 11	**GET UR FREAK ON MISSY ELLIOTT** Featured in the 2001 film *Lara Croft: Tomb Raider.* 2001 Grammy Award for Best Rap Solo Performance . . . . Elektra E 7206CD
18/08/2001 . . . . . 10 . . . . . . 8	**ONE MINUTE MAN MISSY ELLIOTT FEATURING LUDACRIS** . . . . The Gold Mind/Elektra E 7245CD
13/10/2001 . . . . . 72 . . . . . . 1	SUPERFREAKON . . . . Elektra 7559672550
22/12/2001 . . . . . 13 . . . . . 10	SON OF A GUN (BETCHA THINK THIS SONG) **JANET JACKSON WITH CARLY SIMON FEATURING MISSY ELLIOTT** Contains a sample of Carly Simon's *You're So Vain* . . . . Virgin VUSCDX 232
06/04/2002 . . . . . 5 . . . . . 13	**4 MY PEOPLE** . . . . Elektra E 7286CD
16/11/2002 . . . . . 6 . . . . . . 9	**WORK IT** 2003 Grammy Award for Best Female Rap Solo Performance . . . . Elektra E 7344CD
22/03/2003 . . . . . 9 . . . . . . 9	**GOSSIP FOLKS MISSY ELLIOTT FEATURING LUDACRIS** Featured in the 2003 film *Hollywood Homicide* . . . . Elektra E 7380CD
22/11/2003 . . . . . 10 . . . . . 11	**PASS THAT DUTCH** Contains samples of War's *Magic Mountain* and De La Soul's *Potholes In My Lawn*. Featured in the 2004 film *Mean Girls* . . . . Elektra E 7509CD
13/03/2004 . . . . . 22 . . . . . . 3	COP THAT SHIT **TIMBALAND/MAGOO/MISSY ELLIOTT** . . . . Unique Corp TIMBACD001
03/04/2004 . . . . . 22 . . . . . . 4	I'M REALLY HOT . . . . Elektra E 7552CD
17/07/2004 . . . . . 34 . . . . . . 3	PUSH **GHOSTFACE FEATURING MISSY ELLIOTT** . . . . Def Jam 9862837
13/11/2004 . . . . . 4 . . . 7+	**CAR WASH CHRISTINA AGUILERA AND MISSY ELLIOTT** Featured in the 2004 film *Shark Tale* . . . . DreamWorks 9864630

GREG ELLIS – see REVA RICE AND GREG ELLIS

JOEY B. ELLIS US rapper (born in Philadelphia, PA). Tynetta Hare (born in Charlotte, NC) is a member of Soft Touch.

16/02/1991 . . . . . 20 . . . . . . 8	GO FOR IT (HEART AND SOUL) **ROCKY V FEATURING JOEY B ELLIS AND TYNETTA HARE** Featured in the 1990 film *Rocky V* . . . . Capitol CL 601
18/05/1991 . . . . . 58 . . . . . . 2	THOUGHT U WERE THE ONE FOR ME . . . . Capitol CL 614

SHIRLEY ELLIS US singer (born 1941, The Bronx, NYC) who wrote and sang with the Metronomes before going solo.

06/05/1965 . . . . . 6 . . . . . 13	**THE CLAPPING SONG** . . . . London HLR 9961
08/07/1978 . . . . . 59 . . . . . . 4	THE CLAPPING SONG (EP) Tracks on EP: *The Clapping Song, Ever See A Diver Kiss His Wife While The Bubbles Bounce Above The Water, The Name Game* and *The Nitty Gritty* . . . . MCA MCEP 1

SOPHIE ELLIS BEXTOR UK singer (born 1980), daughter of former *Blue Peter* presenter Janet Ellis, who was lead singer with Theaudience and then fronted Spiller's hit Groovejet before signing solo in October 2000 with Polydor. Her debut hit was originally

recorded by Cher in 1979 and slightly re-written for Sophie, Cher subsequently complaining that the new lyrics were 'too raunchy'.

25/08/2001	2	12	O	TAKE ME HOME (A GIRL LIKE ME)	Polydor 5872312
15/12/2001	2	16		MURDER ON THE DANCEFLOOR	Polydor 5704942
22/06/2002	3	13		GET OVER YOU/MOVE THIS MOUNTAIN	Polydor 5708342
16/11/2002	14	10		MUSIC GETS THE BEST OF ME	Polydor 0659232
25/10/2003	7	6		MIXED UP WORLD	Polydor 9812108
10/01/2004	9	6		I WON'T CHANGE YOU	Polydor 9815124

ELLIS, BEGGS AND HOWARD
UK vocal/instrumental group formed by Simon Ellis, Nick Beggs and Austin Howard. Beggs had previously been a member of Kajagoogoo.

| 02/07/1988 | 59 | 3 | | BIG BUBBLES, NO TROUBLES | RCA PB 42089 |
| 11/03/1989 | 41 | 5 | | BIG BUBBLES, NO TROUBLES | RCA PB 42089 |

JENNIFER ELLISON
UK singer/actress (born 1/5/1983, Liverpool) who played Emily Shadwick O'Leary in the TV series *Brookside*. She won ITV's *Hell's Kitchen* in 2004.

| 28/06/2003 | 6 | 10 | | BABY I DON'T CARE | East West EW 268CD |
| 07/08/2004 | 13 | 4 | | BYE BYE BOY | Sky-rocket CDSKYCON1 |

ELWOOD
US rapper/singer Elwood Strickland.

| 26/08/2000 | 72 | 1 | | SUNDOWN | Palm Pictures PPCD 70342 |

EMBRACE
UK rock group formed in Huddersfield in 1991 by Danny McNamara (guitar/vocals), Richard McNamara (guitar/vocals), Steven Firth (bass) and Mike Heaton (drums). They previously recorded for Dischord Records, releasing their debut in 1992.

17/05/1997	34	2		FIREWORKS EP Tracks on EP: *The Last Gas, Now You're Nobody, Blind* and *Fireworks*	Hut HUTCD 84
19/07/1997	21	3		ONE BIG FAMILY EP Tracks on EP: *One Big Family, Dry Kids, You've Only Got To Stop To Get Better* and *Butter Wouldn't Melt*	Hut HUTCD 86
08/11/1997	8	4		ALL YOU GOOD GOOD PEOPLE EP Tracks on EP: *All You Good People (Radio Edit), One Big Family (Perfecto Mix), All You Good People (Fierce Panda Version)* and *All You Good People (Orchestral Mix)*. Originally released on the group's Fierce Panda label	Hut HUTCD 90
06/06/1998	6	8		COME BACK TO WHAT YOU KNOW	Hut HUTCD 93
29/08/1998	9	4		MY WEAKNESS IS NONE OF YOUR BUSINESS	Hut HUTCD 103
13/11/1999	18	3		HOOLIGAN	Hut HUTCD 123
25/03/2000	14	3		YOU'RE NOT ALONE	Hut HUTCD 126
10/06/2000	29	3		SAVE ME	Hut HUTCD 133
19/08/2000	23	2		I WOULDN'T WANNA HAPPEN TO YOU	Hut HUTDX 137
01/09/2001	14	4		WONDER	Hut HUTDX 142
17/11/2001	35	2		MAKE IT LAST	Hut HUTCD 144
11/09/2004	7	7		GRAVITY Co-written by Chris Martin of Coldplay	Independiente ISOM87SMS
27/11/2004	11	5+		ASHES	Independiente ISOM89SMS

EMERSON – see SASHA

KEITH EMERSON
UK keyboard player (born 2/11/1944, Todmorden) who was a founding member of Emerson, Lake & Palmer in 1970, recording his hit single during a lull in the group's activities.

| 10/04/1976 | 21 | 5 | | HONKY TONK TRAIN BLUES | Manticore K 13513 |

EMERSON, LAKE AND PALMER
UK rock group formed in 1970 by Keith Emerson (born 2/11/1944, Todmorden, keyboards), Greg Lake (born 10/11/1948, Bournemouth, bass/vocals) and Carl Palmer (born 20/3/1947, Birmingham, drums). Lake had previously been with King Crimson, Palmer with Crazy World Of Arthur Brown, Atomic Rooster and Chris Farlowe. They split in 1979, Emerson and Lake reuniting (with Cozy Powell, born 29/12/1947) in 1986, Palmer himself returning the following year and Powell joining Black Sabbath in 1990. Powell was killed in a road crash on 5/4/1998.

| 04/06/1977 | 2 | 13 | O | FANFARE FOR THE COMMON MAN | Atlantic K 10946 |

DICK EMERY
UK comedian (born 7/2/1917, London) who found fame via his own TV series (his catchphrase of 'you are awful' later became a minor hit on record). He died on 2/1/1983.

| 26/02/1969 | 32 | 4 | | IF YOU LOVE HER | Pye 7N 17644 |
| 13/01/1973 | 43 | 4 | | YOU ARE AWFUL | Pye 7N 45202 |

EMF
UK rock group formed in a sports shop in Cinderford, Forest of Dean in 1989 by Zak Foley (born 9/12/1970, Gloucester, bass), Ian Dench (born 7/8/1964, Cheltenham, guitar), Derry Brownson (born Derry Brownstone, 10/11/1970, Gloucester, keyboards/percussion), James Atkin (born 28/3/1969, Cinderford, vocals) and Mark Decloedt (born 26/6/1969, Gloucester, drums) as a dance-punk outfit. Their name stands for either Ecstasy Mother Fuckers or Epsom Mad Funkers depending on sources. The group disbanded in 1996. Foley collapsed and died on 3/1/2002.

03/11/1990	3	13	O	UNBELIEVABLE ▲[1] Featured in the 2000 films *There's Only One Jimmy Grimble* and *The Replacements*	Parlophone R 6273
02/02/1991	6	7		I BELIEVE	Parlophone R 6279
27/04/1991	19	5		CHILDREN	Parlophone R 6288
31/08/1991	28	3		LIES Recut after Yoko Ono objected to the sample of the voice of Mark Chapman (John Lennon's killer)	Parlophone R 6295
02/05/1992	18	4		UNEXPLAINED EP Tracks on EP: *Getting Through, Far From Me, The Same* and *Search And Destroy*	Parlophone SGE 2026
19/09/1992	29	3		THEY'RE HERE	Parlophone R 6321

❶[9] Number of weeks single topped the UK chart ↑ Entered the UK chart at #1 ▲[9] Number of weeks single topped the US chart

263

21/11/1992.....23......3......				IT'S YOU..	Parlophone R 6327
25/02/1995.....27......3......				PERFECT DAY...	Parlophone CDRS 6401
08/07/1995.....3......8......				**I'M A BELIEVER** EMF AND REEVES AND MORTIMER	Parlophone CDR 6412
28/10/1995.....51......1......				AFRO KING...	Parlophone CDRS 6416

EMILIA Swedish singer/songwriter (born Emilia Rydberg, 5/1/1978).

12/12/1998 .....5......13.....○	**BIG BIG WORLD**...Universal UMD 87190
01/05/1999.....54......1......	GOOD SIGN ....Universal UMD 87206

EMINEM US rapper (born Marshall Bruce Mathers III, 17/10/1972, Kansas City, MO) who began performing at fourteen and made his debut album in 1996. He is also known as Slim Shady, the title of his 1999 album. Eight Grammy Awards include Best Rap Album in 1999 for *Slim Shady*, Best Rap Album in 2000 for *The Marshall Mathers LP* and Best Rap Album in 2002 for *The Eminem Show*. Named Best International Male at the 2001 and 2003 BRIT Awards, he also won the Best International Album award in 2003 for *The Eminem Show*. He has also won eight MTV Europe Music Awards: Best Album in 2000 for *The Marshall Mathers LP* and in 2002 for *The Eminem Show*, Best Male in 2002 and Best Hip Hop Act in 1999, 2000, 2001 2002 and 2003 (each of the five years it has been awarded). Eminem has also collected two MOBO Awards: Best International Single in 1999 for *My Name Is* and Best Hip Hop Act in 2000. He made his film debut on 2002 in *8 Mile*. In July 2001 the following message appeared on the internet: 'Eminem's tour of Australia is to go ahead despite a sickening attitude to women, appallingly obscene language, an irresponsible attitude to sex and violence and, of course, the dungarees. But Eminem said despite these shocking traits he was willing to judge Australians for himself.'

10/04/1999 .....2......12......	**MY NAME IS** Contains a sample of Labi Siffre's *I Got The*. 1999 Grammy Award for Best Rap Solo Performance and 1999 MOBO Award for Best International Single..Interscope IND 95639
14/08/1999 .....5......8......	**GUILTY CONSCIENCE** EMINEM FEATURING DR DRE ....Interscope IND 4971282
10/06/2000 .....7......9......	**FORGET ABOUT DRE** DR DRE FEATURING EMINEM 2000 Grammy Award for Best Rap Performance by a Duo .... Interscope 4973422
08/07/2000 .....❶¹......15.....○	**THE REAL SLIM SHADY** ↑ 2000 Grammy Award for Best Rap Solo Performance .... Interscope 4973792
14/10/2000 .....8......9......	**THE WAY I AM** ....Interscope 4974252
16/12/2000 .....❶¹......17.....✪	**STAN** ↑ Contains a sample of Dido's *Thank You*...Interscope 4974702
01/09/2001 .....63......1......	SCARY MOVIES BAD MEETS EVIL FEATURING EMINEM AND ROYCE DA 5' 9".......................Mole UK MOLEUK 045
01/06/2002 .....❶¹......16.....●	**WITHOUT ME** ↑ 2002 Grammy Award for Best Short Form Music Video..........................Interscope 4977282
28/09/2002 .....4......13......	**CLEANIN' OUT MY CLOSET** ....Interscope 4973942
14/12/2002 .....❶¹......21.....○	**LOSE YOURSELF** ↑ ▲¹² Featured in the 2002 film *8 Mile*. 2003 Grammy Awards for Best Male Rap Solo Performance and Best Rap Song. It also won the Oscar for Best Film Song for writers Eminem, Jeff Bass and Luis Resto in 2002...........Interscope 4978282
15/03/2003 .....6......10......	**SING FOR THE MOMENT** Contains a sample of Aerosmith's *Dream On* ....Interscope 4978612
19/07/2003 .....6......9......	BUSINESS ....Interscope 9809382
14/02/2004 .....72......1......	THE REAL SLIM SHADY ....Interscope 4973792
13/11/2004 .....❶¹......7+......	**DON'T LOSE IT** ↑ ....Interscope 2103242

EMMA UK singer Emma Booth who represented the UK in the 1990 Eurovision Song Contest, finishing sixth. The competition was won by Italy's *Insieme: 1992* performed by Toto Cotugno.

28/04/1990.....33......6.......	GIVE A LITTLE LOVE BACK TO THE WORLD UK entry for the 1990 Eurovision Song Contest (came sixth).........Big Wave BWR 33

BRANDI EMMA – see STELLAR PROJECT FEATURING BRANDI EMMA

EMMANUEL AND ESKA – see COLOURS FEATURING EMMANUEL AND ESKA and EN-CORE FEATURING STEPHEN EMMANUEL AND ESKA

EMMIE UK dance singer Emmie Norton-Smith who later became a member of Lovebug.

23/01/1999 .....5......8.......	**MORE THAN THIS** ....Indirect FESCD 52
16/02/2002.....53......1......	I WON'T LET YOU DOWN W.I.P. FEATURING EMMIE ....Decode/Telstar CDSTAS 3210

AN EMOTIONAL FISH Irish group formed in Dublin by Gerard Whelan (vocals), Dave Frew (guitar), Enda Wyatt (bass) and Martin Murphy (drums), first signed by U2's Mother label. They had domestic success with *Celebrate*, subsequently issued in the UK.

23/06/1990.....46......5.......	CELEBRATE ....East West YZ 489

EMOTIONS US vocal group formed in Chicago, IL by sisters Wanda (born 17/12/1951), Sheila, Pamela and Jeanette Hutchinson, though there are never more than three family members in the group at the same time. The group also briefly included cousin Theresa Davis. Initially formed as gospel group the Heavenly Sunbeams, they became the Emotions in 1968, signing with Stax' Volt subsidiary. They switched to CBS/Columbia in 1976, worked with Maurice White of EWF and later recorded for Motown.

10/09/1977 .....4......10.....○	**BEST OF MY LOVE** ▲⁵ Featured in the films *Boogie Nights* (1998) and *Summer Of Sam* (1999). 1977 Grammy Award for Best Rhythm & Blues Vocal Performance by a Group ....CBS 5555
24/12/1977.....40......5......	I DON'T WANNA LOSE YOUR LOVE ....CBS 5819
12/05/1979 .....4......13.....●	**BOOGIE WONDERLAND** EARTH WIND AND FIRE WITH THE EMOTIONS 1979 Grammy Award for Best Rhythm & Blues Instrumental Performance ....CBS 7292

ALEC EMPIRE German producer who is also a member of Atari Teenage Riot and formed the Digital Hardcore label.

13/04/2002.....64......1.......	ADDICTED TO YOU ....Digital Empire DHRMCD 38CD1

EMPIRION UK instrumental/production group formed by Jamie Smart, Bob Glennie and Oz.

06/07/1996.....64......1......	NARCOTIC INFLUENCE ....XL Recordings XLS 72CD
21/06/1997.....75......1......	BETA ....XL Recordings XLS 77CD

○ Silver disc ● Gold disc ✪ Platinum disc (additional platinum units are indicated by a figure following the symbol) ◎ Singles released prior to 1973 that are known to have sold over 1 million copies in the UK

EN VOGUE
US vocal group formed in San Francisco, CA in 1988 by Terry Ellis (born 5/9/1966, Houston, TX), Cindy Herron (born 26/9/1965, San Francisco, CA), Dawn Robinson (born 28/11/1968, New London, CT) and Maxine Jones (born 16/1/1965, Paterson, NJ), and produced by Thomas McElroy and Denzil Foster. Robinson went solo in 1996 and Ellis recorded solo in 1995. Robinson later became a member of Lucy Pearl with Raphael Saadiq (of Tony Toni Tone) and Ali Shaheed Muhammad (of A Tribe Called Quest) before going solo again in 2001.

05/05/1990	5	11		**HOLD ON** Contains a sample of James Brown's *The Payback*	East West America 7908
21/07/1990	44	4		LIES	East West America 7893
04/04/1992	4	12		**MY LOVIN'**	East West America A 8578
15/08/1992	44	3		GIVING HIM SOMETHING HE CAN FEEL	East West America A 8524
07/11/1992	16	8		FREE YOUR MIND/GIVING HIM SOMETHING HE CAN FEEL A-side featured in the 1994 film *The Cowboy Way*	
					East West America A 8524
16/01/1993	22	4		GIVE IT UP TURN IT LOOSE	East West America A 8445CD
10/04/1993	64	1		LOVE DON'T LOVE YOU	East West America A 8424CD
09/10/1993	36	3		RUNAWAY LOVE	East West America A 8359CD
19/03/1994	7	10		**WHATTA MAN** SALT-N-PEPA WITH EN VOGUE Contains a sample of Linda Lyndell's *What A Man*	ffrr FCD 222
11/01/1997	5	16	○	**DON'T LET GO (LOVE)** Featured in the 1996 film *Set It Off*	East West A 3976CD
14/06/1997	14	5		WHATEVER	East West E 3642CD
06/09/1997	20	3		TOO GONE, TOO LONG	East West E 3908CD
28/11/1998	53	1		HOLD ON (REMIX)	East West E 3796CD
01/07/2000	33	2		RIDDLE	Elektra E7053CD

EN-CORE FEATURING STEPHEN EMMANUEL AND ESKA
UK producer (born Stephen Boreland) who also records as Colours with singer Eska Mtungwazi.

| 09/09/2000 | 32 | 2 | | COOCHY COO | VC Recordings VCRD 72 |

ENCORE
French singer Sabine Ohmes.

| 14/02/1998 | 12 | 4 | | LE DISC JOCKEY | Sum CDSUM 2 |

ENERGISE
UK vocal/instrumental group formed by Dave Lee who later recorded as Jakatta, Joey Negro, Li Kwan, Z Factor, Raven Maize and Akabu. Lee was also a member of Hed Boys and Il Padrinos.

| 16/02/1991 | 69 | 1 | | REPORT TO THE DANCEFLOOR | Network NWKT 16 |

ENERGY 52
German DJ/producer Paul Schmitz-Moormann.

08/03/1997	51	1		CAFE DEL MAR	Hooj Choons HOOJCD 51
25/07/1998	12	6		I DEL MAR '98 (REMIX)	Hooj Choons HOOJ 64CD
12/10/2002	24	4		CAFE DEL MAR (2ND REMIX)	Lost Language LOST 019CD

ENERGY ORCHARD
Irish group formed in Belfast by Martin 'Bap' Kennedy (born 17/6/1962, vocals) and Paul Toner (guitar).

| 27/01/1990 | 52 | 4 | | BELFAST | MCA 1392 |
| 07/04/1990 | 73 | 2 | | SAILORTOWN | MCA 1402 |

HARRY ENFIELD
UK comedian (born 30/5/1961) who first became well known via the TV comedy show *Friday Night Live*. He later hosted his own BBC series and recorded as Precocious Brats Featuring Kevin & Perry.

| 07/05/1988 | 4 | 7 | | **LOADSAMONEY (DOIN' UP THE HOUSE)** Loadsamoney was one of Enfield's characters on *Friday Night Live* | Mercury DOSH 1 |

ENGLAND BOYS
UK singer Darryl Denham. He is also a DJ on Virgin Radio.

| 08/06/2002 | 26 | 3 | | GO ENGLAND Re-written version of The Jam's *Going Underground* | Mercury 5829592 |

ENGLAND DAN AND JOHN FORD COLEY
US duo Dan Seals (born 8/2/1948, Austin, TX) and John Ford Coley (born 13/10/1948, Austin). Seals is the brother of Jim Seals of Seals And Croft.

| 25/09/1976 | 26 | 7 | | I'D REALLY LOVE TO SEE YOU TONIGHT | Atlantic K 10810 |
| 23/06/1979 | 45 | 5 | | LOVE IS THE ANSWER | Big Tree K 11296 |

ENGLAND RUBY WORLD CUP SQUAD – see UNION FEATURING THE ENGLAND RUGBY WORLD CUP SQUAD

ENGLAND SISTERS – see DALE SISTERS

ENGLAND SUPPORTERS BAND
UK soccer supporters band formed in Sheffield by John Hemmingham (trumpet), Chris Hancock (euphonium), Stephen Holmes (tenor drum), Laurence Garratty (trumpet), Bram Denton (saxophone), Ian Bamforth (trombone), Steve Wood (euphonium) and Max Patrick (snare drum). They first appeared at Sheffield Wednesday games and were adopted by the national side at the request of manager Glenn Hoddle. Their debut hit was originally the theme to the 1963 film *The Great Escape* and was first recorded by the band for the 1998 World Cup in France. It was re-recorded in 2000 for the European Championships in Holland and Belgium and is usually chanted whenever England play Germany.

| 27/06/1998 | 46 | 2 | | THE GREAT ESCAPE | V2 VVR 5002163 |
| 24/06/2000 | 26 | 2 | | THE GREAT ESCAPE 2000 | V2 VVR 5014293 |

ENGLAND UNITED
Amalgamation of UK stars including the Spice Girls and Echo And The Bunnymen with the official England theme to the 1998 World Cup Finals held in France.

| 13/06/1998 | 9 | 11 | | **(HOW DOES IT FEEL TO BE) ON TOP OF THE WORLD** Official England song for the 1998 FIFA World Cup | London LONCD 414 |

❶⁹ Number of weeks single topped the UK chart ↑ Entered the UK chart at #1 ▲⁹ Number of weeks single topped the US chart

265

ENGLAND WORLD CUP SQUAD The England football team (the Football Association was formed in 1863 and the team played their first match in 1872). Needless to say, the 'group' line-up differs on each hit.

18/04/1970	❶³	17		**BACK HOME**	Pye 7N 17920
10/04/1982	2	13		**THIS TIME (WE'LL GET IT RIGHT)/ENGLAND WE'LL FLY THE FLAG**	England ER 1
19/04/1986	66	2		WE'VE GOT THE WHOLE WORLD AT OUR FEET/WHEN WE ARE FAR FROM HOME	Columbia DB 9128
21/05/1988	64	2		ALL THE WAY **ENGLAND FOOTBALL TEAM AND THE 'SOUND' OF STOCK, AITKEN AND WATERMAN**	MCA GOAL 1
02/06/1990	❶²	12	●	**WORLD IN MOTION** Rap is by footballer John Barnes	Factory/MCA FAC 2937
15/06/2002	43	2		WORLD IN MOTION Re-issue of Factory/MCA FAC 2937. This and above single credited to **ENGLANDNEWORDER**	
					London NUDOCD 12

ENGLAND'S BARMY ARMY UK vocal group formed by 5,000 supporters of the England cricket team.

12/06/1999	45	1		COME ON ENGLAND!	Wildstar CDWILD 20

KIM ENGLISH US singer based in Chicago, IL who first worked with Byron Burke and Byron Stingily.

23/07/1994	35	2		NITE LIFE	Hi-Life PZCD 323
04/03/1995	48	1		TIME FOR LOVE	Hi-Life HICD 8
09/09/1995	52	1		I KNOW A PLACE	Hi-Life 5798072
30/11/1996	35	2		NITE LIFE (REMIX)	Hi-Life 5755332
26/04/1997	50	1		SUPERNATURAL	Hi-Life 5736972

SCOTT ENGLISH US singer/songwriter whose hit was revived and christened *Mandy* by Barry Manilow and taken to US #1.

09/10/1971	12	10		BRANDY	Horse HOSS 7

ENIAC – see **TOM NOVY**

ENIGMA UK studio group put together to record cover versions of hits made famous by others in a similar style to Star Sound.

23/05/1981	11	8		AIN'T NO STOPPING	Creole CR 9
08/08/1981	25	7		I LOVE MUSIC	Creole CR 14

ENIGMA Romanian/German group of husband and wife duo Michael and Sandra Cretu. Michael (born 18/5/1957, Bucharest, Romania) moved to Germany in 1975, working as a studio musician with the likes of Vangelis before working on his own material. His German-born wife provided the vocals, which were released under the group name Enigma. In 1999 EMI Records settled out of court a claim by Kuo Ying-nan, a Taiwanese tribesman, that he sang on the chorus of the hit *Return To Innocence*. Accordingly, Kuo and his wife Kuo Hsiu-chu were presented with platinum discs for worldwide sales in excess of 1 million copies.

15/12/1990	❶¹	12	○	**SADNESS PART 1**	Virgin International DINS 101
30/03/1991	55	3		MEA CULPA PART II	Virgin International DINS 104
10/08/1991	59	2		PRINCIPLES OF LUST	Virgin International DINS 110
11/01/1992	68	2		THE RIVERS OF BELIEF	Virgin International DINS 112
29/01/1994	3	14	○	**RETURN TO INNOCENCE**	Virgin International DINSD 123
14/05/1994	21	4		THE EYES OF TRUTH	Virgin International DINSD 126
20/08/1994	21	5		AGE OF LONELINESS Featured in the 1993 film *Sliver*	Virgin International DINSD 135
25/01/1997	26	2		BEYOND THE INVISIBLE	Virgin International DINSD 155
19/04/1997	60	1		TNT FOR THE BRAIN	Virgin International DINSD 161

ENYA Irish singer (born Eithne Ni Bhraonain, 17/5/1961, Gweedore, County Donegal) who joined the family group Clannad in 1979 as singer/keyboard player before going solo after two albums. After a 1987 debut album for the BBC her career took off with *Watermark*. Plays on Radio 1 for *Orinoco Flow* ensured its chart success. She has won three Grammy Awards for Best New Age Album: in 1992 for *Shepherd Moons*, 1996 for *The Memory Of Trees* and 2001 for *A Day Without Rain*.

15/10/1988	❶³	13	○	**ORINOCO FLOW**	WEA YZ 312
24/12/1988	20	4		EVENING FALLS	WEA YZ 356
10/06/1989	41	4		STORMS IN AFRICA (PART II)	WEA YZ 368
19/10/1991	13	7		CARIBBEAN BLUE	WEA YZ 604
07/12/1991	32	5		HOW CAN I KEEP FROM SINGING	WEA YZ 365
01/08/1992	10	6		**BOOK OF DAYS** Featured in the 1992 film *Far And Away*	WEA YZ 640
14/11/1992	29	4		THE CELTS	WEA YZ 705
18/11/1995	7	12		**ANYWHERE IS**	WEA 023CD
07/12/1996	26	2		ON MY WAY HOME	WEA 047CD
13/12/1997	43	2		ONLY IF	WEA 143CD
25/11/2000	32	3		ONLY TIME Featured in the 2000 film *Sweet November*	WEA 316CD
31/03/2001	72	1		WILD CHILD	WEA 324CD
02/02/2002	50	2		MAY IT BE Featured in the 2002 film *Lord Of The Rings – The Fellowship Of The Rings*	WEA W 578CD
05/06/2004	71	1		I DON'T WANNA KNOW (IMPORT) Contains a sample of Enya's *Boadicea*	Universal 9862372PMI
12/06/2004	❶²	14	○	**I DON'T WANNA KNOW ↑** This and above single credited to **MARIO WINANS FEATURING ENYA AND P DIDDY**	Bad Boy MCSTD 40369
11/09/2004	8	8		**YOU SHOULD REALLY KNOW** PIRATES, ENYA, SHOLA AMA, NAILA BOSS & ISHANI	Relentless RELCD9

EON UK producer Ian Bela.

17/08/1991	63	1		FEAR, THE MINDKILLER	Vinyl Solution STORM 33

EPMD US rap duo formed in Brentwood, Long Island, NY by Erick 'E' Sermon (born 25/11/1968, Brentwood) and Parrish 'P' Smith

○ Silver disc ● Gold disc ✪ Platinum disc (additional platinum units are indicated by a figure following the symbol) ◎ Singles released prior to 1973 that are known to have sold over 1 million copies in the UK

(born 13/5/1968, Brentwood), their name standing for Erick and Parrish Making Dollars. The pair split in 1993 with Sermon recording solo and Smith recording as PMD.

15/08/1998	43	1		STRICTLY BUSINESS **MANTRONIK VS EPMD** Contains a sample of Eric Clapton's *I Shot The Sheriff*	Parlophone CDR 6502

EPSILON – see D KAY AND EPSILON FEATURING STAMINA MC

EQUALS
Multinational pop group formed in England in 1965 by Derv Gordon (born 29/6/1948, Jamaica, vocals), his twin brother Lincoln (guitar), Eddie Grant (born 5/3/1948, Guyana, guitar), John Hall (born 25/10/1947, London, drums) and Pat Lloyd (born 17/3/1948, London, guitar). Legal problems with the record company stopped them recording, but Grant later emerged as a solo artist.

DATE	POS	WKS		SINGLE TITLE	LABEL & NUMBER
21/02/1968	44	4		I GET SO EXCITED	President PT 180
01/05/1968	❶3	18		**BABY COME BACK**	President PT 135
21/08/1968	35	5		LAUREL AND HARDY	President PT 200
27/11/1968	48	3		SOFTLY SOFTLY	President PT 222
02/04/1969	24	7		MICHAEL AND THE SLIPPER TREE	President PT 240
30/07/1969	6	14		**VIVA BOBBY JOE**	President PT 260
27/12/1969	34	7		RUB A DUB DUB	President PT 275
19/12/1970	9	11		**BLACK SKIN BLUE EYED BOYS**	President PT 325

ERASURE
UK group formed in London in 1985 by ex-Depeche Mode, Yazoo and Assembly keyboard wizard Vince Clarke (born 3/7/1960, South Woodford) who advertised for a singer in *Melody Maker* and picked Andy Bell (born 25/4/1964, Peterborough) from the 42 he auditioned. They were named Best UK Group at the 1989 BRIT Awards.

DATE	POS	WKS	BPI	SINGLE TITLE	LABEL & NUMBER
05/10/1985	55	2		WHO NEEDS LOVE LIKE THAT	Mute 40
25/10/1986	2	17	○	**SOMETIMES**	Mute 51
28/02/1987	12	9		IT DOESN'T HAVE TO BE	Mute 56
30/05/1987	7	9		**VICTIM OF LOVE**	Mute 61
03/10/1987	6	10		**THE CIRCUS**	Mute 66
05/03/1988	6	8		**SHIP OF FOOLS**	Mute 74
11/06/1988	11	7		CHAINS OF LOVE	Mute 83
01/10/1988	4	10		**A LITTLE RESPECT**	Mute 85
10/12/1988	2	13		**CRACKERS INTERNATIONAL EP** Tracks on EP: *Stop, The Hardest Part, Knocking On Your Door* and *She Won't Be Home*	Mute 93
30/09/1989	4	8		**DRAMA!**	Mute 89
09/12/1989	15	9		YOU SURROUND ME	Mute 99
10/03/1990	3	10		**BLUE SAVANNAH**	Mute 109
02/06/1990	11	7		STAR	Mute 111
29/06/1991	3	9		**CHORUS**	Mute 125
21/09/1991	4	9		**LOVE TO HATE YOU**	Mute 131
07/12/1991	15	6		AM I RIGHT (EP) Tracks on EP: *Am I Right, Carry On Clangers, Let It Flow* and *Waiting For Sex*	Mute 134
11/01/1992	22	3		AM I RIGHT (EP) (REMIX) Tracks on EP: *Am I Right, Chorus, Love To Hate You* and *Perfect Stranger*	Mute L12MUTE 134
28/03/1992	8	6		BREATH OF LIFE	Mute 142
13/06/1992	❶5	12	●	**ABBA-ESQUE EP** ↑ Tracks on EP: *Lay All Your Love On Me, SOS, Take A Chance On Me* and *Voulez-Vous. Take A Chance On Me* also features the uncredited contribution of MC Kinky	Mute 144
07/11/1992	10	4		**WHO NEEDS LOVE LIKE THAT**	Mute 150
23/04/1994	4	9		**ALWAYS**	Mute CDMUTE 152
30/07/1994	6	5		**RUN TO THE SUN**	Mute CDMUTE 153
03/12/1994	20	6		I LOVE SATURDAY	Mute CDMUTE 166
23/09/1995	15	4		STAY WITH ME	Mute LDMUTE 174
09/12/1995	20	3		FINGERS AND THUMBS (COLD SUMMER'S DAY)	Mute CDMUTE 178
18/01/1997	13	4		IN MY ARMS	Mute CDMUTE 190
08/03/1997	23	2		DON'T SAY YOUR LOVE IS KILLING ME	Mute CDMUTE 195
21/10/2000	27	2		FREEDOM	Mute LCDMUTE 244
18/01/2003	10	3		**SOLSBURY HILL**	Mute LCDMUTE 275
19/04/2003	14	3		MAKE ME SMILE (COME UP AND SEE ME)	Mute LCDMUTE 292
25/10/2003	13	3		OH L'AMOUR	Mute LCDMUTE 213

ERIC AND THE GOOD GOOD FEELING
UK vocal/instrumental group formed by Eric Gooden, Reis Etan and Eric Robinson.

03/06/1989	73	1		GOOD GOOD FEELING	Equinox EQN 1

ERIK
UK singer Erik De Vries (born 1967) discovered by Pete Waterman.

10/04/1993	44	2		LOOKS LIKE I'M IN LOVE AGAIN **KEY WEST FEATURING ERIK**	PWL Sanctuary PWCD 252
29/01/1994	42	2		GOT TO BE REAL	PWL International PWCD 278
01/10/1994	55	1		WE GOT THE LOVE	PWL International PWCD 305

❶9 Number of weeks single topped the UK chart ↑ Entered the UK chart at #1 ▲9 Number of weeks single topped the US chart

267

ERIN UK singer Erin Lordan.

15/08/1992	69	1		THE ART OF MOVING BUTTS **SHUT UP AND DANCE FEATURING ERIN**	Shut And Dance SUAD 34S
23/03/1996	46	1		LET THE MUSIC PLAY **BBG FEATURING ERIN**	MCA MCSTD 40029
23/03/2002	45	1		FOR A LIFETIME **ASCENSION FEATURING ERIN LORDAN**	Xtravaganza XTRAV 20CDS

ERIRE – see SCIENCE DEPARTMENT FEATURING ERIRE

EROTIC DRUM BAND Canadian disco group assembled by producers Peter DiMilo and George Cucuzzella.

09/06/1979	47	3		LOVE DISCO STYLE	Scope SC 1

ERUPTION US group, British-based, originally from Jamaica, formed in 1974 by Precious Wilson (vocals), Greg Perrineau (guitar), Morgan Perrineau (bass), Gerry Williams (keyboards) and Eric Kingsley (drums). They signed with RCA after winning a talent contest.

18/02/1978	5	11	O	I CAN'T STAND THE RAIN **ERUPTION FEATURING PRECIOUS WILSON**	Atlantic K 11068
21/04/1979	9	10	O	ONE WAY TICKET	Atlantic/Hansa K 11266

MICHELLE ESCOFFERY – see ARTFUL DODGER

SHAUN ESCOFFERY UK singer (born in London) who was 26 years of age at the time of his debut hit.

10/03/2001	52	1		SPACE RIDER	Oyster Music OYSCD 4
20/07/2002	53	1		DAYS LIKE THIS	Oyster Music OYSCDS 8

ESCORTS UK vocal/instrumental group formed by Terry Sylvester (guitar/vocals), John Kinrade (guitar), Mick Gregory (bass) and Pete Clarke (drums). Clarke was replaced by Johnny Sticks after one single and he in turn was replaced by Tom Kelly. Paddy Chambers (guitar) also joined the group after their hit single.

02/07/1964	49	2		THE ONE TO CRY	Fontana TF 474

ESCRIMA UK dance group fronted by DJ 'Tall Paul' Newman. Newman also remixed for the Stone Roses, East 17 and the Renegade Masters and later recorded as Tall Paul and with Brandon Block in Grifters.

11/02/1995	36	2		TRAIN OF THOUGHT Contains a sample of King Bee's *Back By Dope Demand*	ffrreedom TABCD 225
07/10/1995	27	2		DEEPER	Hooj Choons TABCD 236

ESKA UK singer Eska Mtungwazi.

27/02/1999	51	1		WHAT U DO **COLOURS FEATURING EMMANUEL AND ESKA**	Inferno CDFERN 12
09/09/2000	32	2		COOCHY COO **EN-CORE FEATURING STEPHEN EMMANUEL AND ESKA**	VC Recordings VCRD 72
28/07/2001	65	1		SUNSET **NITIN SAWHNEY FEATURING ESKA**	V2 VVR 5016768

ESKIMOS & EGYPT UK vocal/instrumental group formed by Christopher O'Hare, David Cameron-Pryde, John Cundall and Graham Compton.

13/02/1993	51	2		FALL FROM GRACE	One Little Indian EEF 96CD
29/05/1993	52	2		UK-USA	One Little Indian 99 TP7CD

ESPIRITU UK/French duo Chris Chaplin and Vanessa Quinones.

06/03/1993	47	2		CONQUISTADOR	Heavenly HVN 28CD
07/08/1993	45	2		LOS AMERICANOS	Heavenly HVN 33CD
20/08/1994	50	1		BONITA MANANA	Columbia 6606925
25/03/1995	14	5		ALWAYS SOMETHING THERE TO REMIND ME **TIN TIN OUT FEATURING ESPIRITU**	WEA YZ 911CD

ESSENCE UK production group formed by Stephen Jones and Ricky Simmonds. They also record as Ascension, Chakra, Lustral and Space Brothers

21/03/1998	27	2		THE PROMISE	Innocent SINCD 1

ESSEX US R&B vocal group formed in 1962 by Anita Humes, Billy Hill, Rudolph Johnson, Rodney Taylor and Walter Vickers. All five were serving in the US Marine Corps at Camp LeJeune, NC when they formed.

08/08/1963	41	5		EASIER SAID THAN DONE ▲²	Columbia DB 7077

DAVID ESSEX UK singer (born David Albert Cook, 23/7/1947, Plaistow, London) who began his career as drummer with the Everons before going solo in 1964. Singles with Fontana, Uni, Pye and Decca led to the role of Jesus in the West End musical *Godspell* and the lead role in the 1973 film *That'll Be The Day*. He was awarded an OBE in the 1999 New Year's Honours List.

18/08/1973	3	11	O	ROCK ON	CBS 1693
10/11/1973	7	15		LAMPLIGHT	CBS 1902
11/05/1974	32	5		AMERICA	CBS 2176

DATE	POS	WKS	BPI	SINGLE TITLE	LABEL & NUMBER
12/10/1974	❶³	17	●	**GONNA MAKE YOU A STAR**	CBS 2492
14/12/1974	7	10		**STARDUST** Featured in the 1974 film *Stardust*	CBS 2828
05/07/1975	5	7		**ROLLIN' STONE**	CBS 3425
13/09/1975	❶³	10	●	**HOLD ME CLOSE**	CBS 3572
06/12/1975	13	8		IF I COULD	CBS 3776
20/03/1976	24	4		CITY LIGHTS	CBS 4050
16/10/1976	24	6		COMING HOME	CBS 4486
17/09/1977	23	6		COOL OUT TONIGHT	CBS 5495
11/03/1978	45	5		STAY WITH ME BABY	CBS 6063
19/08/1978	3	11	●	**OH WHAT A CIRCUS**	Mercury 6007 185
21/10/1978	55	3		BRAVE NEW WORLD Featured in Jeff Wayne's *War Of The Worlds*	CBS 6705
03/03/1979	32	8		IMPERIAL WIZARD	Mercury 6007 202
05/04/1980	4	11	○	**SILVER DREAM MACHINE (PART 1)** Featured in the 1980 film *Silver Dream Racer*	Mercury BIKE 1
14/06/1980	57	4		HOT LOVE	Mercury HOT 11
26/06/1982	13	10		ME AND MY GIRL (NIGHT-CLUBBING)	Mercury MER 107
11/12/1982	2	10	○	**A WINTER'S TALE**	Mercury MER 127
04/06/1983	52	4		THE SMILE	Mercury ESSEX 1
27/08/1983	8	11		**TAHITI** Featured in the musical *Mutiny On The Bounty*	Mercury BOUNT 1
26/11/1983	59	6		YOU'RE IN MY HEART	Mercury ESSEX 2
23/02/1985	29	7		FALLING ANGELS RIDING (MUTINY) Featured in the musical *Mutiny On The Bounty*	Mercury ESSEX 5
18/04/1987	41	7		MYFANWY	Arista RIS 11
26/11/1994	38	3		TRUE LOVE WAYS **DAVID ESSEX AND CATHERINE ZETA JONES**	Polygram TV TLWCD 2

GLORIA ESTEFAN US singer (born Gloria Maria Fajardo, 1/9/1957, Havana, Cuba) whose family moved to Miami when she was two (her father had been President Batista's bodyguard). She joined future husband Emilio Estefan's Miami Latin Boys in 1974, suggesting a name change to Miami Sound Machine. They recorded in English for the first time in 1984 and by 1987 Gloria was getting top billing. In 1989 the name was shortened further. Both were injured (Gloria seriously) in a crash involving their tour bus in 1990. She has won three Grammy Awards: Best Tropical Latin Album in 1993 for *Mi Tierra*, Best Tropical Latin Performance in 1995 for *Abriendo Puertas* and Best Traditional Tropical Latin Album in 2000 for *Alma Caribe*. She has a star on the Hollywood Walk of Fame.

DATE	POS	WKS	BPI	SINGLE TITLE	LABEL & NUMBER
16/07/1988	10	16		**ANYTHING FOR YOU**	Epic 6516737
22/10/1988	9	10		**1-2-3**	Epic 6529587
17/12/1988	16	9		RHYTHM IS GONNA GET YOU	Epic 6545147
11/02/1989	7	12		**CAN'T STAY AWAY FROM YOU** This and above singles credited to **GLORIA ESTEFAN AND MIAMI SOUND MACHINE**	Epic 6514447
15/07/1989	6	10		**DON'T WANNA LOSE YOU** ▲¹	Epic 6550540
16/09/1989	16	8		OYE MI CANTO (HEAR MY VOICE)	Epic 6552877
25/11/1989	23	7		GET ON YOUR FEET	Epic 6554507
03/03/1990	23	6		HERE WE ARE	Epic 6554737
26/05/1990	49	5		CUTS BOTH WAYS	Epic 6559827
26/01/1991	25	5		COMING OUT OF THE DARK ▲²	Epic 6565747
06/04/1991	24	7		SEAL OUR FATE	Epic 6567737
08/06/1991	22	6		REMEMBER ME WITH LOVE	Epic 6569687
21/09/1991	33	5		LIVE FOR LOVING YOU	Epic 6573837
24/10/1992	24	4		ALWAYS TOMORROW	Epic 6583977
12/12/1992	8	9		**MIAMI HIT MIX/CHRISTMAS THROUGH YOUR EYES**	Epic 6588377
13/02/1993	48	2		I SEE YOUR SMILE	Epic 6589612
03/04/1993	13	6		GO AWAY Featured in the 1993 film *Made In America*	Epic 6590952
03/07/1993	36	3		MI TIERRA	Epic 6593512
14/08/1993	40	3		IF WE WERE LOVERS/CON LOS ANOS QUE ME QUEDAN	Epic 6595702
18/12/1993	55	2		MONTUNO	Epic 6599972
15/10/1994	21	6		TURN THE BEAT AROUND Featured in the 1994 film *The Specialist*	Epic 6606822
03/12/1994	11	11	○	HOLD ME THRILL ME KISS ME	Epic 6610802
18/02/1995	19	5		EVERLASTING LOVE	Epic 6611595
25/05/1996	15	8		REACH Official theme of the 1996 Olympic Games in Atlanta, GA	Epic 6632642
24/08/1996	18	3		YOU'LL BE MINE (PARTY TIME)	Epic 6636505
14/12/1996	28	3		I'M NOT GIVING YOU UP	Epic 6640225
06/06/1998	17	4		HEAVEN'S WHAT I FEEL Featured in the 1998 film *Dance With Me*	Epic 6660042
10/10/1998	33	2		OYE	Epic 6664645
16/01/1999	28	2		DON'T LET THIS MOMENT END	Epic 6667472
08/01/2000	34	3		MUSIC OF MY HEART **'N SYNC AND GLORIA ESTEFAN** Featured in the 1999 film *Music Of The Heart*	Epic 6678052

ESTELLE UK singer (born Estelle Swaray, 18/1/1985, London) who also sang with 57th Dynasty, Social Misfits, Source and Against The Grain before going solo. She was named Best Newcomer at the 2004 MOBO Awards.

DATE	POS	WKS	BPI	SINGLE TITLE	LABEL & NUMBER
29/06/2002	54	1		TRIXSTAR **BLAK TWANG FEATURING ESTELLE**	Bad Magic MAGIC24
31/07/2004	14	7		1980 Contains a sample of Tony Orlando's *Lazy Susan*	V2/J-Did JAD5027813

❶⁹ Number of weeks single topped the UK chart   ↑ Entered the UK chart at #1   ▲⁹ Number of weeks single topped the US chart

269

DATE	POS	WKS	BPI	SINGLE TITLE	LABEL & NUMBER
16/10/2004	15	6		FREE	V2/J-Did JAD5027848

DON ESTELLE – see WINDSOR DAVIES AND DON ESTELLE

ESTHERO – see IAN POOLEY

DEON ESTUS US singer/bass player (born in Detroit, MI) who previously toured with George Michael, Wham!, Brainstorm and Marvin Gaye.

DATE	POS	WKS	BPI	SINGLE TITLE	LABEL & NUMBER
25/01/1986	63	3		MY GUY – MY GIRL (MEDLEY) AMII STEWART AND DEON ESTUS	Sedition EDIT 3310
29/04/1989	41	4		HEAVEN HELP ME	Mika 2

ETA Danish instrumental group formed by Thy, Henry Gargarin and Martin Aston.

DATE	POS	WKS	BPI	SINGLE TITLE	LABEL & NUMBER
28/06/1997	28	3		CASUAL SUB (BURNING SPEAR)	East West EW 110CD
31/01/1998	28	2		CASUAL SUB (BURNING SPEAR) (REMIX)	East West Dance EW 145CD

ETERNAL UK R&B vocal group formed by Kelle Bryan (born 12/3/1975, London), sisters Easther (born 11/12/1972, Croydon) and Vernie Bennett (born 17/5/1971, Croydon) and Louise Nurding (born 4/11/1974, Lewisham, London). Nurding went solo in 1995. Easther married Boyzone singer Shane Lynch in 1998. Kelle went solo in 1999 and was replaced by TJ, but Easther and Vernie later decided to continue as a duo. BeBe Winans is Benjamin Winans, the seventh of ten children and also a member of the family group.

DATE	POS	WKS	BPI	SINGLE TITLE	LABEL & NUMBER
02/10/1993	4	9		STAY	EMI CDEM 284
15/01/1994	8	7		SAVE OUR LOVE	EMI CDEM 296
30/04/1994	8	10		JUST A STEP FROM HEAVEN	EMI CDEM 311
20/08/1994	13	7		SO GOOD	EMI CDEMS 339
05/11/1994	4	13	○	OH BABY I...	EMI CDEM 353
24/12/1994	15	7		CRAZY	EMI CDEMX 364
21/10/1995	5	8		POWER OF A WOMAN	EMI CDEM 396
09/12/1995	7	12		I AM BLESSED	EMI CDEMS 408
09/03/1996	8	6		GOOD THING	EMI CDEM 419
17/08/1996	4	9		SOMEDAY Featured in the 1996 film *The Hunchback Of Notre Dame*	EMI CDEMS 439
07/12/1996	9	7		SECRETS	EMI CDEM 459
08/03/1997	3	7		DON'T YOU LOVE ME	EMI CDEMS 465
31/05/1997	●¹	15	●	I WANNA BE THE ONLY ONE ↑ ETERNAL FEATURING BEBE WINANS 1997 MOBO Award for Best Single	EMI CDEM 472
11/10/1997	4	13	○	ANGEL OF MINE	EMI CDEM 493
30/10/1999	16	4		WHAT'CHA GONNA DO	EMI CDEM 552

ETHER UK vocal/instrumental group formed by Rory Meredith (guitar/vocals), Gareth Driscoll (bass) and Brett Sawmy (drums).

DATE	POS	WKS	BPI	SINGLE TITLE	LABEL & NUMBER
28/03/1998	74	1		WATCHING YOU	Parlophone CDR 6491

ETHICS Dutch producer Patrick Prinz who has also recorded as Artemesia, Movin' Melodies and Subliminal Cuts.

DATE	POS	WKS	BPI	SINGLE TITLE	LABEL & NUMBER
25/11/1995	13	5		TO THE BEAT OF THE DRUM (LA LUNA)	VC Recordings VCRD 5

ETHIOPIANS Jamaican reggae group formed in 1966 by Leonard 'Jack Sparrow' Dillon, Stephen Taylor and Aston Morris. Morris left later the same year, with Dillon and Taylor recording as a duo. Taylor was killed in a car crash in 1975, with Dillon carrying on solo until recruiting Harold Bishop and Neville Duncan.

DATE	POS	WKS	BPI	SINGLE TITLE	LABEL & NUMBER
13/09/1967	40	6		TRAIN TO SKAVILLE	Rio 130

TONY ETORIA UK singer who later recorded for Cobra.

DATE	POS	WKS	BPI	SINGLE TITLE	LABEL & NUMBER
04/06/1977	21	8		I CAN PROVE IT	GTO GT 89

NELLIE ETTISON – see ARTIFICIAL FUNK FEATURING NELLIE ETTISON

E.U. – see SALT-N-PEPA

EUROGROOVE UK vocal group fronted by Tetsuya Komuro.

DATE	POS	WKS	BPI	SINGLE TITLE	LABEL & NUMBER
20/05/1995	29	2		MOVE YOUR BODY	Avex UK AVEXCD 4
05/08/1995	31	2		DIVE TO PARADISE	Avex UK AVEXCD 10
21/10/1995	25	2		IT'S ON YOU (SCAN ME)	Avex UK AVEXCD 17
03/02/1996	44	1		MOVE YOUR BODY (REMIX)	Avex UK AVEXCD 22

EUROPE Swedish rock group formed in 1983 by Joey Tempest (born 19/8/1963, Stockholm, vocals), John Norum (guitar), John Leven (bass), Mic Michael (keyboards) and Ian Haugland (drums) as Force. The group won a national talent contest and recorded two albums before signing with Epic in 1986, the line-up being Tempest, Haughland, Michael and Kee Marcello (who had replaced Norum).

DATE	POS	WKS	BPI	SINGLE TITLE	LABEL & NUMBER
01/11/1986	●²	15	●	THE FINAL COUNTDOWN Featured in the 1985 film *Rock IV*	Epic A 7127
31/01/1987	12	9		ROCK THE NIGHT	Epic EUR 1
18/04/1987	22	8		CARRIE	Epic EUR 2
20/08/1988	34	5		SUPERSTITIOUS	Epic EUR 3
01/02/1992	28	5		I'LL CRY FOR YOU	Epic 6576977
21/03/1992	42	4		HALFWAY TO HEAVEN	Epic 6578517
25/12/1999	36	4		THE FINAL COUNTDOWN 2000 Re-recording of Epic A 7127	Epic 6685042

○ Silver disc ● Gold disc ✪ Platinum disc (additional platinum units are indicated by a figure following the symbol) ⊚ Singles released prior to 1973 that are known to have sold over 1 million copies in the UK

EURYTHMICS
WHO'S THAT GIRL?

EURYTHMICS UK group formed in 1980 by ex-Tourists Annie Lennox (born 25/12/1954, Aberdeen, vocals) and Dave Stewart (born 9/9/1952, Sunderland, Tyne & Wear, keyboards/guitar). Their album debut was in Germany with former members of Can and DAF. They were signed to RCA Records (after legal wrangles with the Tourists' former label, Logo) and named after the 1900s music-through-movement dance mime of Emile Jacques-Dalcrose. Stewart married ex-Bananarama and future Shakespears Sister Siobhan Fahey in 1987 (she appeared in the video to *Who's That Girl*). Lennox left in 1990 but the pair reunited in 1999. BRIT Awards for Lennox include Best British Female in 1984, 1986, 1989, 1990 (all of which relate to her time with the group), 1993 and 1996 and the Best Album Award (for *Diva*) in 1993. Stewart won the Best Producer category on three occasions: 1986, 1987 and 1990. The Eurythmics finally received the Outstanding Contribution to UK Music Award at the 1999 BRIT Awards.

04/07/1981	63	3		NEVER GONNA CRY AGAIN	RCA 68
20/11/1982	54	5		LOVE IS A STRANGER	RCA DA 1
12/02/1983	2	14	○	**SWEET DREAMS (ARE MADE OF THIS)** ▲¹ Featured in the films *Striptease* (1996) and *Big Daddy* (1999)	RCA DA 2
09/04/1983	6	8		**LOVE IS A STRANGER**	RCA DA 1
09/07/1983	3	10		**WHO'S THAT GIRL?**	RCA DA 3
05/11/1983	10	11		**RIGHT BY YOUR SIDE** Featured in the 1989 film *True Love*	RCA DA 4
21/01/1984	8	8	○	**HERE COMES THE RAIN AGAIN**	RCA DA 5
03/11/1984	4	13	○	**SEXCRIME (NINETEEN EIGHTY FOUR)** Featured in the 1984 film *1984*	Virgin VS 728
19/01/1985	44	4		JULIA	Virgin VS 734
20/04/1985	17	8		WOULD I LIE TO YOU?	RCA PB 40101
06/07/1985	❶¹	13		**THERE MUST BE AN ANGEL (PLAYING WITH MY HEART)** Features the uncredited contribution of Stevie Wonder on harmonica	RCA PB 40247
02/11/1985	9	11		**SISTERS ARE DOING IT FOR THEMSELVES** EURYTHMICS AND ARETHA FRANKLIN Featured in the 1996 film *The First Wives Club*	RCA PB 40339
11/01/1986	12	8		IT'S ALRIGHT (BABY'S COMING BACK)	RCA PB 40375
14/06/1986	30	6		WHEN TOMORROW COMES	RCA DA 7
06/09/1986	5	11		**THORN IN MY SIDE**	RCA DA 8
29/11/1986	23	9		THE MIRACLE OF LOVE	RCA DA 9
28/02/1987	31	4		MISSIONARY MAN 1986 Grammy Award for Best Rock Vocal Performance by a Duo	RCA DA 10
24/10/1987	25	5		BEETHOVEN (I LOVE TO LISTEN TO)	RCA DA 11
26/12/1987	41	6		SHAME	RCA DA 12
09/04/1988	26	5		I NEED A MAN	RCA DA 15
11/06/1988	16	8		YOU HAVE PLACED A CHILL IN MY HEART	RCA DA 16
26/08/1989	26	6		REVIVAL	RCA DA 17
04/11/1989	25	6		DON'T ASK ME WHY	RCA DA 19
03/02/1990	29	5		THE KING AND QUEEN OF AMERICA	RCA DA 20
12/05/1990	23	6		ANGEL	RCA DA 21
09/03/1991	46	3		LOVE IS A STRANGER	RCA PB 44265
16/11/1991	48	2		SWEET DREAMS (ARE MADE OF THIS)	RCA PB 45031
16/10/1999	11	6		I SAVED THE WORLD TODAY	RCA 74321695632
05/02/2000	27	4		17 AGAIN	RCA 74321726262

EUSEBE UK hip hop group formed by rapper Steven 'Fatcat' Eusebe, sister Sharon 'Saybe' Eusebe and cousin Allison 'Noddy' Ettienn.

| 26/08/1995 | 32 | 3 | | SUMMERTIME HEALING | Mama's Yard CDMAMA 4 |

EVANESCENCE US rock group formed in Little Rock, AR by Amy Lee (vocals), Ben Moody (guitar), John LeCompt (guitar) and Rocky Gray (drums). They have two Grammy Awards including the 2003 award for Best New Artist.

31/05/2003	60	2		BRING ME TO LIFE (IMPORT) Features the uncredited contribution of Paul McCoy and used in the 2003 film *Daredevil*	Epic 8734881CD
14/06/2003	❶⁴	17		**BRING ME TO LIFE** ↑ 2003 Grammy Award for Best Hard Rock Performance	Epic 6739762
04/10/2003	8	6		**GOING UNDER**	Epic 6743522
20/12/2003	7	9		**MY IMMORTAL**	Epic 6745422
12/06/2004	24	3		EVERYBODY'S FOOL	Epic 6747992

EVANGEL TEMPLE CHOIR – see JOHNNY CASH

FAITH EVANS US rapper (born 10/6/1973, New York City) married to fellow rapper The Notorious B.I.G. She began her career providing backing vocals for the likes of Usher, Mary J. Blige and Hi-Five. Eric Benet (born Eric Benet Jordan, 5/10/1969, Milwuakee) is a singer.

14/10/1995	42	2		YOU USED TO LOVE ME	Puff Daddy 74321299812
23/11/1995	33	2		STRESSED OUT A TRIBE CALLED QUEST FEATURING FAITH EVANS AND RAPHAEL SAADIQ	Jive JIVECD 404
28/06/1997	❶⁶	21	❂²	**I'LL BE MISSING YOU** ↑ ▲¹¹ PUFF DADDY AND FAITH EVANS AND 112 Contains a sample of Police's *Every Breath You Take*. It is a tribute to The Notorious B.I.G. and was the first record to have entered both the UK and US charts at #1. It reclaimed #1 position on 24/7/1997. 1997 Grammy Award for Best Rap Performance by a Group	Puff Daddy 74321499102
14/11/1998	24	4		LOVE LIKE THIS Contains a sample of Chic's *Chic Cheer*	Puff Daddy 74321665692
01/05/1999	23	3		ALL NIGHT LONG FAITH EVANS FEATURING PUFF DADDY Contains a sample of Unlimited Touch's *I Hear Music In The Streets*	Puff Daddy 74321625592
01/05/1999	28	3		GEORGY PORGY ERIC BENET FEATURING FAITH EVANS	Warner Brothers W 478CD1

❶⁹ Number of weeks single topped the UK chart　↑ Entered the UK chart at #1　▲⁹ Number of weeks single topped the US chart

30/12/2000 . . . . . 26 . . . . . 5	HEARTBREAK HOTEL **WHITNEY HOUSTON FEATURING FAITH EVANS AND KELLY PRICE**	Arista 74321820572
24/05/2003 . . . . 38 . . . . . 3	MA I DON'T LOVE HER **CLIPSE FEATURING FAITH EVANS**	Arista 82876526482

MAUREEN EVANS UK singer (born 1940, Cardiff) who was a local star in Wales during the late 1950s before her debut hit.

22/01/1960 . . . . . 26 . . . . . 2	THE BIG HURT	Oriole CB 1533
17/03/1960 . . . . . 44 . . . . . 1	LOVE KISSES AND HEARTACHES	Oriole CB 1540
02/06/1960 . . . . . 40 . . . . . 5	PAPER ROSES	Oriole CB 1550
29/11/1962 . . . . . 3 . . . . 18	**LIKE I DO** Based on the song *Dance Of The Hours*.	Oriole CB 1763
27/02/1964 . . . . . 34 . . . . . 11	I LOVE HOW YOU LOVE ME	Oriole CB 1906

PAUL EVANS US singer (born 5/3/1938, New York) who first recorded for RCA in 1957 but later became known as a songwriter, penning hits such as *When* for the Kalin Twins, *Roses Are Red (My Love)* for Bobby Vinton and *I Gotta Know* for Elvis Presley. The Curls were backing duo Sue Singleton and Sue Terry.

27/11/1959 . . . . . 25 . . . . . 1	SEVEN LITTLE GIRLS SITTING IN THE BACK SEAT **PAUL EVANS AND THE CURLS**	London HLL 8968
31/03/1960 . . . . . 41 . . . . . 1	MIDNITE SPECIAL	London HLL 9045
16/12/1978 . . . . . 6 . . . . . 12 . . . . O	**HELLO THIS IS JOANNIE (THE TELEPHONE ANSWERING MACHINE SONG)**	Spring 2066 932

TOMMY EVANS – see MARK B

EVASIONS UK studio group led by Adrian Sear and featuring Graham De Wilde with a tribute to TV presenter Alan Whicker. They later recorded *Jocks Rap*.

13/06/1981 . . . . . 20 . . . . . 8	WIKKA WRAP	Groove GP 107

E.V.E. UK/US R&B vocal group formed by Edie May Grant, Jenisa Garland, Mia Ambrester and Gina 'Go-Go' Gomez. Their name stands for Ebony Vibe Everlasting.

01/10/1994 . . . . . 30 . . . . . 3	GROOVE OF LOVE . . . . Gasoline Alley MCSTD 2007
28/01/1995 . . . . . 39 . . . . . 2	GOOD LIFE . . . . Gasoline Alley MCSTD 2038

EVE US rapper (born Eve Jeffers, 10/11/1978, Philadelphia, PA) who is also a member of Ruff Ryders. Gwen Stefani (born 3/10/1969, Anaheim, CA) is lead singer with No Doubt.

22/01/2000 . . . . . 18 . . . . . 3	HOT BOYZ **MISSY 'MISDEMEANOR' ELLIOTT FEATURING NAS, EVE & Q TIP**.	Elektra E 7002CD
19/05/2001 . . . . . 6 . . . . . 8	**WHO'S THAT GIRL**	Interscope 4975572
25/08/2001 . . . . . 4 . . . . . 12	**LET ME BLOW YA MIND** **EVE FEATURING GWEN STEFANI** 2001 Grammy Award for Best Rap/Sung Performance.	Interscope 4976052
09/03/2002 . . . . . 37 . . . . . 2	BROTHA PART II **ANGIE STONE FEATURING ALICIA KEYS AND EVE** Contains a sample of Albert King's *I'll Play The Blues For You*	J Records 74321922142
16/03/2002 . . . . . 9 . . . . . 10	**CARAMEL** **CITY HIGH FEATURING EVE**	Interscope 4976742
05/10/2002 . . . . . 6 . . . . . 8	**GANGSTA LOVIN'** **EVE FEATURING ALICIA KEYS** Contains a sample of Yarbrough & Peoples' *Don't Stop The Music*	Interscope 4978042
12/04/2003 . . . . . 20 . . . . . 4	SATISFACTION	Interscope 4978262
06/12/2003 . . . . . 40 . . . . . 2	NOT TODAY **MARY J. BLIGE FEATURING EVE**	Geffen MCSTD 40349

JESSICA EVE – see WHO DA FUNK FEATURING JESSICA EVE

ALISON EVELYN – see BROTHERS LIKE OUTLAW FEATURING ALISON EVELYN

EVERCLEAR US rock group formed in Portland, OR in 1993 by Art Alexakis (guitar/vocals), Craig Montoya (bass/vocals) and Greg Eklund (drums). They originally recorded for Fire Records.

01/06/1996 . . . . . 48 . . . . . 2	HEARTSPARK DOLLARSIGN	Capitol CDCLS 773
31/08/1996 . . . . . 40 . . . . . 2	SANTA MONICA (WATCH THE WORLD DIE)	Capitol CDCL 775
09/05/1998 . . . . . 41 . . . . . 1	EVERYTHING TO EVERYONE	Capitol CDCL 799
14/10/2000 . . . . . 36 . . . . . 2	WONDERFUL	Capitol CDCLS 824

BETTY EVERETT US singer (born 23/11/1939, Greenwood, MS) who began by singing in gospel choirs before moving to Chicago, IL. She made her first recordings for Cobra in 1958. She died on 22/8/2001.

14/01/1965 . . . . . 29 . . . . . 7	GETTING MIGHTY CROWDED	Fontana TF 520
30/10/1968 . . . . . 34 . . . . . 7	IT'S IN HIS KISS Later revived by Cher as *The Shoop Shoop Song (It's In His Kiss)*.	President PT 215

KENNY EVERETT UK singer/comedian/radio DJ/TV personality (born Maurice James Christopher Cole, 25/12/1948, Liverpool) who was first known as a radio DJ before moving to TV. Both hit singles related to characters he created (Captain Kremmen and Sid Snot respectively). He died from an AIDS-related illness on 4/4/1995.

12/11/1977 . . . . . 32 . . . . . 4	CAPTAIN KREMMEN (RETRIBUTION) **KENNY EVERETT AND MIKE VICKERS**	DJM DJS 10810
26/03/1983 . . . . . 9 . . . . . 8	**SNOT RAP**	RCA KEN 1

PEVEN EVERETT – see ROY DAVIS JR FEATURING PEVEN EVERETT

EVERLAST US rapper (born Erik Schrody, 18/8/1969, New York) who was previously a member of House Of Pain.

27/02/1999 . . . . . 34 . . . . . 2	WHAT IT'S LIKE.	Tommy Boy TBCD 7470
03/07/1999 . . . . . 47 . . . . . 1	ENDS Contains a sample of Wu Tang Clan's *C.R.E.A.M.*	Tommy Boy TBCD 346

20/01/2001	37	2		BLACK JESUS	Tommy Boy TBCD 2180B

PHIL EVERLY US singer (born 19/1/1939, Chicago, IL) and one of The Everly Brothers until 1973. The brothers reunited in 1983.

06/11/1982	47	6		LOUISE	Capitol CL 266
19/02/1983	9	9		**SHE MEANS NOTHING TO ME** PHIL EVERLY AND CLIFF RICHARD	Capitol CL 276
10/12/1994	14	9		ALL I HAVE TO DO IS DREAM CLIFF RICHARD AND PHIL EVERLY	EMI CDEMS 359

EVERLY BROTHERS US family duo Donald (born Isaac Donald, 1/2/1937, Brownie, KY) and Philip Everly (born 19/1/1939, Chicago, IL) who debuted at the age of eight and six as Little Donnie & Baby Boy Phil on their parents' radio show. Their first recordings with Chet Atkins in 1957 were unsuccessful. They subsequently signed to Cadence in the same year. In 1973 they split but reunited in 1983. They were inducted into the Rock & Roll Hall of Fame in 1986 and have a star on the Hollywood Walk of Fame.

12/07/1957	6	16		**BYE BYE LOVE**	London HLA 8440
08/11/1957	2	13		**WAKE UP LITTLE SUSIE** ▲4	London HLA 8498
23/05/1958	❶7	21		**ALL I HAVE TO DO IS DREAM/CLAUDETTE** ▲5	London HLA 8618
12/09/1958	2	16		**BIRD DOG** ▲1	London HLA 8685
23/01/1959	6	12		**PROBLEMS**	London HLA 8781
22/05/1959	20	10		TAKE A MESSAGE TO MARY	London HLA 8863
29/05/1959	14	11		POOR JENNY	London HLA 8863
11/09/1959	2	15		**('TIL) I KISSED YOU**	London HLA 8934
12/02/1960	13	10		LET IT BE ME	London HLA 9039
14/04/1960	❶7	18		**CATHY'S CLOWN** ▲5 First UK release on the Warner Brothers label	Warner Brothers WB 1
14/07/1960	4	16		**WHEN WILL I BE LOVED**	London HLA 9157
22/09/1960	4	15		**LUCILLE/SO SAD (TO WATCH GOOD LOVE GO BAD)**	Warner Brothers WB 19
15/12/1960	11	10		LIKE STRANGERS	London HLA 9250
09/02/1961	❶3	16		**WALK RIGHT BACK/EBONY EYES**	Warner Brothers WB 33
15/06/1961	❶2	15		**TEMPTATION**	Warner Brothers WB 42
05/10/1961	20	6		MUSKRAT/DON'T BLAME ME	Warner Brothers WB 50
18/01/1962	6	15		**CRYIN' IN THE RAIN**	Warner Brothers WB 56
17/05/1962	12	10		HOW CAN I MEET HER	Warner Brothers WB 67
25/10/1962	11	11		NO ONE CAN MAKE MY SUNSHINE SMILE	Warner Brothers WB 79
21/03/1963	23	11		SO IT WILL ALWAYS BE	Warner Brothers WB 94
13/06/1963	26	5		IT'S BEEN NICE	Warner Brothers WB 99
17/10/1963	25	9		THE GIRL SANG THE BLUES	Warner Brothers WB 109
16/07/1964	22	10		FERRIS WHEEL	Warner Brothers WB 135
03/12/1964	36	7		GONE GONE GONE	Warner Brothers WB 146
06/05/1965	30	4		THAT'LL BE THE DAY	Warner Brothers WB 158
20/05/1965	2	14		**THE PRICE OF LOVE**	Warner Brothers WB 161
26/08/1965	35	5		I'LL NEVER GET OVER YOU	Warner Brothers WB 5639
21/10/1965	11	9		LOVE IS STRANGE	Warner Brothers WB 5649
08/05/1968	39	6		IT'S MY TIME	Warner Brothers WB 7192
22/09/1984	41	9		ON THE WINGS OF A NIGHTINGALE	Mercury MER 170

EVERTON FC UK football club formed in Liverpool in 1878 with records released to coincide with appearances in FA Cup finals.

11/05/1985	14	5		HERE WE GO	Columbia DB 9106
20/05/1995	24	3		ALL TOGETHER NOW EVERTON 1985	MDMC DEVCS 3

EVERYTHING BUT THE GIRL UK duo Tracey Thorn (born 26/9/1962, Brookman's Park, vocals) and Ben Watt (born 6/12/1962, London, guitars/keyboards/vocals) who were introduced in 1982 and debuted in 1983. Their name came from a second-hand furniture store in Hull (where both attended university). Thorn was also in Marine Girls. Soul Vision are a UK production group.

12/05/1984	28	7		EACH AND EVERYONE	Blanco Y Negro NEG 1
21/07/1984	58	2		MINE	Blanco Y Negro NEG 3
06/10/1984	73	2		NATIVE LAND	Blanco Y Negro NEG 6
02/08/1986	44	7		COME ON HOME	Blanco Y Negro NEG 21
11/10/1986	72	2		DON'T LEAVE ME BEHIND	Blanco Y Negro NEG 23
13/02/1988	75	1		THESE EARLY DAYS	Blanco Y Negro NEG 30
09/07/1988	3	9		**I DON'T WANT TO TALK ABOUT IT** Originally recorded by Neil Young and Crazy Horse in 1971	Blanco Y Negro NEG 34
27/01/1990	54	2		DRIVING	Blanco Y Negro NEG 40
22/02/1992	13	6		COVERS EP Tracks on EP: *Love Is Strange, Tougher Than The Rest, Time After Time* and *Alison*	Blanco Y Negro NEG 54
24/04/1993	42	5		THE ONLY LIVING BOY IN NEW YORK (EP) Tracks on EP: *The Only Living boy In New York, Birds, Gabriel* and *Horses In The Room*	Blanco Y Negro NEG 62CD
19/06/1993	72	1		I DIDN'T KNOW I WAS LOOKING FOR LOVE (EP) Tracks on EP: *I Didn't Know I Was Looking For Love, My Head Is My Only House Unless It Rains, Political Science* and *A Piece Of My Mind*	Blanco Y Negro NEG 64CD

❶9 Number of weeks single topped the UK chart　↑ Entered the UK chart at #1　▲9 Number of weeks single topped the US chart

DATE	POS	WKS	BPI	SINGLE TITLE	LABEL & NUMBER
04/06/1994	65	1		ROLLERCOASTER (EP) Tracks on EP: *Rollercoaster, Straight Back To You, Lights Of Te Touan* and *I Didn't Know I Was Looking For Love (Demo)*	Blanco Y Negro NEG 69CD
20/08/1994	69	1		MISSING	Blanco Y Negro NEG 71CD
28/10/1995	3	22	✪	**MISSING** Remix by Todd Terry of a single that originally charted in August 1994. It was the first record to spend an entire year on the US charts (it finally registered 55 weeks on the chart). Featured in the 1996 film *Set It Off*	Blanco Y Negro NEG 84CD
20/04/1996	6	6		**WALKING WOUNDED**	Virgin VSCDT 1577
29/06/1996	8	7		**WRONG**	Virgin VSCDT 1589
05/10/1996	20	3		SINGLE Contains samples of Tim Buckley's *Song To The Siren* and Stan Tracey's *Starless And Bible Black*	Virgin VSCDT 1600
07/12/1996	36	2		DRIVING (REMIX)	Blanco Y Negro NEG 99CD1
01/03/1997	25	2		BEFORE TODAY Featured in the 1997 film *The Saint*	Virgin VSCDT 1624
03/10/1998	31	2		THE FUTURE OF THE FUTURE (STAY GOLD) **DEEP DISH WITH EBTG**	Deconstruction 74321616252
25/09/1999	27	3		FIVE FATHOMS	Virgin VSCDT 1742
04/03/2000	72	1		TEMPERAMENTAL	Virgin VSCDT 1761
27/01/2001	34	2		TRACEY IN MY ROOM **EBTG VERSUS SOUL VISION** Effectively two songs made into one: Everything But The Girl's *Wrong* and Sandy Rivera's *Come Into My Room*	VC Recordings VCRD 78

E'VOKE UK vocal duo Marlaine Gordon and Kerry Potter. Both girls were previously actresses; Marlaine appeared in *Eastenders* and later with Kerry in *Us Girls Together*.

DATE	POS	WKS	BPI	SINGLE TITLE	LABEL & NUMBER
25/11/1995	30	3		RUNAWAY	ffrreedom TABCD 238
24/08/1996	25	3		ARMS OF LOREN	Manifesto FESCD 10
02/02/2002	31	3		ARMS OF LOREN 2001	Inferno CDFERN 001

EVOLUTION UK production duo Jon Sutton and Barry Jamieson. They later worked with Jayn Hanna.

DATE	POS	WKS	BPI	SINGLE TITLE	LABEL & NUMBER
20/03/1993	32	2		LOVE THING	Deconstruction 74321134272
03/07/1993	19	5		EVERYBODY DANCE	Deconstruction 74321152012
08/01/1994	52	3		EVOLUTIONDANCE PART ONE (EP) Tracks on EP: *Escape 2 Alcatraz (Remix), Everybody* and *Don't Stop The Rain*	Deconstruction 74321171912
04/11/1995	55	1		LOOK UP TO THE LIGHT	Deconstruction 74321318042
19/10/1996	60	1		YOUR LOVE IS CALLING	Deconstruction 74321422872

EX PISTOLS UK punk rock group formed by Johnny Rotten (born John Lydon, 31/1/1956, London, vocals), Steve Jones (born 3/5/1955, London, guitar), Glen Matlock (born 27/8/1956, London, bass) and Paul Cook (born 20/7/1956, London, drums).

DATE	POS	WKS	BPI	SINGLE TITLE	LABEL & NUMBER
02/02/1985	69	2		LAND OF HOPE AND GLORY	Virginia PISTOL 76

EXCITERS US R&B vocal group formed in Jamaica, NY by Herb Rooney, his wife Brenda Reid, Carol Johnson and Lillian Walker in the early 1960s.

DATE	POS	WKS	BPI	SINGLE TITLE	LABEL & NUMBER
21/02/1963	46	1		TELL HIM Featured in the 1997 film *My Best Friend's Wedding*	United Artists UP 1011
04/10/1975	31	6		REACHING FOR THE BEST	20th Century BTC 1005

!!! US group formed in Sacramento, CA in 1995 by Nic Offer (vocals), Mario Andreoni (guitar), Tyler Pope (guitar/keyboards), Justin Van Dervolgen (bass/sound engineering), Allan Wilson (horns/percussion), Dan Gorman (horns/percussion), Jason Racine (percussion) and John Pugh (drums). According to the group, their name can be pronounced as 'any three repetitive sounds such as chicchicchic, powpowpow or uhuhuh. It is listed here as Exclamation Mark (x three).

DATE	POS	WKS	BPI	SINGLE TITLE	LABEL & NUMBER
21/08/2004	74	1		HELLO? IS THIS ON?	Warp WAP176CD

EXETER BRAMDEAN BOYS' CHOIR UK vocal choir.

DATE	POS	WKS	BPI	SINGLE TITLE	LABEL & NUMBER
18/12/1993	46	3		REMEMBERING CHRISTMAS	Golden Sounds DSCC 1

EXILE US country group formed in Lexington, KY in 1963 by JP Pennington (guitar/vocals), Jimmy Stokley (vocals), Buzz Cornelison (keyboards), Sonny Lemaire (bass) and Steve Goetzman (drums) as The Exiles, changing to Exile in 1973. Pennington left the group in 1989 and was replaced by Paul Martin.

DATE	POS	WKS	BPI	SINGLE TITLE	LABEL & NUMBER
19/08/1978	6	12	○	**KISS YOU ALL OVER** ▲⁴ Featured in the 1999 film *Man On The Moon*	RAK 279
12/05/1979	67	2		HOW COULD THIS GO WRONG	RAK 293
12/09/1981	54	4		HEART AND SOUL	RAK 333

EXOTERIX UK producer Duncan Miller.

DATE	POS	WKS	BPI	SINGLE TITLE	LABEL & NUMBER
24/04/1993	58	1		VOID	Positiva CDTIV 1
05/02/1994	62	1		SATISFY MY LOVE	Union City UCRCD 26

EXOTICA FEATURING ITSY FOSTER UK/Italian vocal/instrumental group formed by the Rapino Brothers with singer Itsy Foster.

DATE	POS	WKS	BPI	SINGLE TITLE	LABEL & NUMBER
16/09/1995	68	1		THE SUMMER IS MAGIC	Polydor 5798392

EXPLOITED UK punk-rock group formed in East Kilbride in 1979 by Wattie Buchan (vocals), Gary McCormick (bass), Big John Duncan (guitar) and Dru Stix Campbell (drums).

DATE	POS	WKS	BPI	SINGLE TITLE	LABEL & NUMBER
18/04/1981	63	4		DOGS OF WAR	Secret SHH 110
17/10/1981	31	5		DEAD CITIES	Secret SHH 120
05/12/1981	70	1		DON'T LET 'EM GRIND YOU DOWN **EXPLOITED AND ANTI-PASTI**	Superville EXP 1003
08/05/1982	50	3		ATTACK	Secret SHH 130

○ Silver disc ● Gold disc ✪ Platinum disc (additional platinum units are indicated by a figure following the symbol) ◉ Singles released prior to 1973 that are known to have sold over 1 million copies in the UK

EXPOSE US vocal group formed in Miami, FL by Ann Curless, Jeanette Jurado and Giola Bruno. Bruno left in 1992 and was replaced by Kelly Moneymaker.

28/08/1993.....75......1....... I'LL NEVER GET OVER YOU (GETTING OVER ME) .... Arista 74321158962

EXPRESS OF SOUND Italian instrumental/production group formed by Stefano Mango and Gianni Coleti.

02/11/1996.....45......1....... REAL VIBRATION .... Positiva CDTIV 66

EXPRESSOS UK vocal/instrumental group featuring Rayner, Toldi, Christo and Zekavica with Dimthings (drums).

21/06/1980.....60......3...... HEY GIRL .... WEA K 18246
14/03/1981.....70......2...... TANGO IN MONO .... WEA K 18431

EXTENSIVE – see CHOPS-EMC + EXTENSIVE

EXTREME US metal/funk quartet formed in Boston, MA in 1985 by Gary Cherone (born 24/7/1961, Malden, MA, vocals) and Paul Geary (born 2/7/1961, Medford, MA, drums), both ex-Dream, and Sinful member Nuno Bettencourt (born 20/9/1966, Azores, Portugal). Pat Badger (born 22/7/1967, Boston, bass) joined in 1986. They were signed by A&M on the strength of winning an MTV video contest. Cherone later joined Van Halen as lead singer.

08/06/1991.....19......7....... GET THE FUNK OUT .... A&M AM 737
27/07/1991.....2......11.....○ **MORE THAN WORDS** ▲[1] .... A&M AM 792
12/10/1991.....36......3...... DECADENCE DANCE .... A&M AM 773
23/11/1991.....12......7...... HOLE HEARTED .... A&M AM 839
02/05/1992.....12......6...... SONG FOR LOVE .... A&M AM 698
05/09/1992.....13......5...... REST IN PEACE... A&M AM 0055
14/11/1992.....22......2...... STOP THE WORLD .... A&M AM 0096
06/02/1993.....15......4...... TRAGIC COMIC... A&M AMCD 0156
11/03/1995.....44......1....... HIP TODAY .... A&M 5809932

E.Y.C. US vocal group formed by Damon Butler, David Loeffler, Trey Parker, Marlen Landin and rapper Gangsta Ridd. The name stands for Express Yourself Clearly.

11/12/1993.....16......8...... FEELIN' ALRIGHT .... MCA MCSTD 1952
05/03/1994.....14......7...... THE WAY YOU WORK IT .... MCA MCSTD 1963
14/05/1994.....27......5...... NUMBER ONE .... MCA MCSTD 1976
30/07/1994.....13......6...... BLACK BOOK .... MCA MCSTD 1987
10/12/1994.....25......6...... ONE MORE CHANCE .... MCA MCSTD 2025
23/09/1995.....33......2...... OOH-AH-AA (I FEEL IT)... Gasoline Alley MCSTD 2096
02/12/1995.....41......2...... IN THE BEGINNING... Gasoline Alley MCSTD 2107

EYE TO EYE FEATURING TAKA BOOM UK production duo Stuart Crichton and Andy Morris with US singer Taka Boom who began her career as a member of Undisputed Truth and is the sister of Chaka Khan.

09/06/2001.....36......2....... JUST CAN'T GET ENOUGH (NO NO NO NO) .... Xtravaganza XTRAV 25CD

EYEOPENER UK group formed by Lee Monteverde and Rachel Macfarlane (of LMC) with Graham Turner and Mark Hall (of Flip & Fill).

20/11/2004.....16.....6+...... HUNGRY EYES .... All Around The World CDGLOBE362

EYES CREAM Italian producer Agostino Carollo with Stephanie Haley. Carollo later recorded as Spankox.

16/10/1999.....53......1....... FLY AWAY (BYE BYE)... Accolade CDAC 001

F

ADAM F
UK drum and bass producer (born Adam Fenton, 8/2/1972, Liverpool), son of singer Shane Fenton (aka Alvin Stardust), who launched the F-Jam label. He won the 1998 MOBO Award for Best Album for *Colours*.

27/09/1997	20	3	CIRCLES .... Positiva CDFJ 002
07/03/1998	27	3	MUSIC IN MY MIND .... Positiva CDFJ 003
15/09/2001	11	7	SMASH SUMTHIN' REDMAN FEATURING ADAM F. .... Def Jam 5886932
01/12/2001	43	1	STAND CLEAR ADAM F FEATURING M.O.P. .... Chrysalis CDEM 597
06/04/2002	37	2	WHERE'S MY ADAM F FEATURING LIL' MO .... EMI CDEMS 598
27/04/2002	54	1	METROSOUND ADAM F AND J MAJIK. .... Kaos 001P
08/06/2002	50	1	STAND CLEAR (REMIX) ADAM F FEATURING M.O.P. .... Kaos KAOSCD 002
31/08/2002	47	2	SMASH SUMTHIN (REMIX) ADAM F FEATURING REDMAN .... Kaos KOASCD 003
14/12/2002	50	2	DIRTY HARRY'S REVENGE ADAM F FEATURING BEENIE MAN .... Kaos 004P
30/10/2004	68	1	WHEN THE SUN GOES DOWN DJ FRESH FEATURING ADAM F .... Breakbeat Kaos BBK005SCD

FAB FEATURING MC PARKER
UK production group formed by Rod Anderson and Jason Mayo.

07/07/1990	5	8	THUNDERBIRDS ARE GO. .... Brothers Organisation FAB 1
20/10/1990	56	2	THE PRISONER FAB FEATURING MC NUMBER 6. .... Brothers Organisation FAB 6
01/12/1990	66	1	THE STINGRAY MEGAMIX FAB FEATURING AQUA MARINA .... Brothers Organisation FAB 2

FAB!
Irish vocal group assembled by producer Ben 'Jammin' Robbins.

01/08/1998	59	1	TURN AROUND .... Break Records BRCX 107

FAB FOR FEATURING ROBERT OWENS
German/US group formed by producer King Brain, DJs Micha K and Pippi, and singer Robert Owens. Their debut hit, based on Indeep's 1983 hit *Last Night A DJ Saved My Life*, was recorded after a phrase created by King Brain: *Last Night A DJ Screwed My Wife*.

15/02/2003	34	1	LAST NIGHT A DJ BLEW MY MIND. .... Illustrious CDILL 013

SHELLEY FABARES
US singer (born 19/1/1944, Santa Monica, CA) whose film appearances include three with Elvis Presley.

26/04/1962	41	4	JOHNNY ANGEL ▲2 .... Pye International 7N 25132

FABIAN
US singer (born Fabiano Fortem, 6/2/1943, Philadelphia, PA) who appeared in the 1960 film *Hound Dog Man*. He has a star on the Hollywood Walk of Fame.

10/03/1960	46	1	HOUND DOG MAN Featured in the 1960 film *Hound Dog Man* .... HMV POP 695

LARA FABIAN
Belgian singer (born in Brussels) who began singing in French, later performing on the soundtrack to the French-Canadian version of the 1996 Walt Disney film *The Hunchback Of Notre Dame*.

28/10/2000	63	1	I WILL LOVE AGAIN. .... Columbia 6694062

FABOLOUS
US rapper (born John Jackson, 18/11/1979, Brooklyn, NYC).

16/08/2003	14	5	CAN'T LET YOU GO FABOLOUS FEATURING MIKE SHOREY AND LIL' MO .... Elektra E 7408CD
01/11/2003	18	6	INTO YOU FABOLOUS FEATURING TAMIA .... Elektra E 7470CD
20/03/2004	26	5	BADABOOM B2K FEATURING FABOLOUS .... Epic 6747512
27/11/2004	28	5+	BREATHE .... Atlantic AT0189CD

FABULOUS BAKER BOYS
UK production/DJ duo Paul Jay Kay and Olly M.

15/11/1997	34	2	OH BOY .... Multiply CDMULTY 28

FACE
— see DAVID MORALES

FACES
UK rock group formed in 1969 by members of the Small Faces and Jeff Beck Group, with Rod Stewart (born 10/1/1945, Highgate, London, lead vocals), Ronnie Lane (born 1/4/1946, Plaistow, London, guitar), Kenny Jones (born 16/9/1948, Stepney, London, drums), Ron Wood (born 1/6/1947, Hillingdon, Middlesex, guitar) and Ian McLagan (born 12/5/1945, Hounslow, Middlesex, keyboards), with Art Wood (Ron's elder brother), Long John Baldry and Jimmy Horowitz augmenting the line-up. Initially Quiet Melon, they changed their name in 1971. Lane left in 1973 and was replaced by Tetsu Yamauchi (ex-Free bass player). Jones joined The Who in 1978. Stewart signed a solo contract as the Faces were formed, subsequently often being billed as Rod Stewart & The Faces, the group eventually disbanding in 1975. Wood joined The Rolling Stones in 1976. Lane died from multiple sclerosis on 4/6/1997.

18/12/1971	6	14	STAY WITH ME .... Warner Brothers K 16136
17/02/1973	2	9	CINDY INCIDENTALLY .... Warner Brothers K 16247

○ Silver disc ● Gold disc ✪ Platinum disc (additional platinum units are indicated by a figure following the symbol) ◎ Singles released prior to 1973 that are known to have sold over 1 million copies in the UK

08/12/1973	8	11		**POOL HALL RICHARD/I WISH IT WOULD RAIN**	Warner Brothers K 16341
07/12/1974	12	9		YOU CAN MAKE ME DANCE SING OR ANYTHING (EVEN TAKE THE DOG FOR A WALK, MEND A FUSE, FOLD AWAY THE IRONING BOARD OR ANY OTHER DOMESTIC SHORTCOMINGS) **ROD STEWART AND THE FACES**	Warner Brothers K 16494
04/06/1977	41	3		THE FACES (EP) Tracks on EP: *Memphis, You Can Make Me Dance Sing Or Anything, Stay With Me* and *Cindy Incidentally*.	Riva 8

FACTORY OF UNLIMITED RHYTHM Jamaican vocal/instrumental group.

01/06/1996	59	1		THE SWEETEST SURRENDER	Kuff KUFFD 6

DONALD FAGEN US singer/keyboard player (born 10/1/1948, Passiac, NJ) who first teamed with long-time musical partner Walker Becker while they were still students, both backing Jay & The Americans before launching Steely Dan in the early 1970s, basically a vehicle for the songwriting and production of Becker and Fagen. They split in 1981, Fagen going solo. Steely Dan was revived in the late 1980s and went on to win three Grammy Awards in 2000.

03/07/1993	46	2		TOMORROW'S GIRLS	Reprise W 0180CDX

JOE FAGIN UK singer (born in Liverpool) who had a hit with the theme to the TV series *Auf Weidersehen Pet* and appeared in such shows as *Blott On The Landscape* and *To Be The Best*.

07/01/1984	3	11	O	**THAT'S LIVIN' ALRIGHT** Theme to TV series *Auf Weidersehen Pet*	Towerbell TOW 46
05/04/1986	53	9		BACK WITH THE BOYS AGAIN/GET IT RIGHT Theme to TV series *Auf Weidersehen Pet II*	Towerbell TOW 84

JAD FAIR – see TEENAGE FANCLUB

YVONNE FAIR US singer (born 1942, Virginia, raised in New York) who first sang with the Chantels and then James Brown. Norman Whitfield produced her debut album for Motown. Her hit was originally recorded by Kim Weston in 1963 and was a 1968 smash for Gladys Knight. She was later personal manager for Dionne Warwick, and appeared in the 1972 film *Lady Sings The Blues*. She died on 5/3/1994.

24/01/1976	5	11		**IT SHOULD HAVE BEEN ME**	Tamla Motown TMG 1013

FAIR WEATHER UK group formed in 1970 by ex-Amen Corner Andy Fairweather-Low (born 2/8/1950, Ystrad Mynach, Wales, guitar/vocals), Blue Weaver (born Derek Weaver, 3/3/1949, Cardiff, organ), Dennis Bryon (born 14/4/1949, Cardiff, drums), Clive Taylor (born 27/4/1949, Cardiff, bass) and Neil Jones (born 25/3/1949, Llanbradach, Wales, guitar). They disbanded the same year.

18/07/1970	6	12		**NATURAL SINNER**	RCA 1977

FAIRGROUND ATTRACTION UK skiffle-style group formed in Scotland by Eddi Reader (born 28/8/1959, Glasgow, vocals), Mark Nevin (guitar), Simon Edwards (bass) and Roy Dodds (drums). 1989 BRIT Awards included Best Album for *First Of A Million Kisses*. Reader later recorded solo.

16/04/1988	❶[1]	13	O	**PERFECT** 1989 BRIT Award for Best Single	RCA PB 41845
30/07/1988	7	10		**FIND MY LOVE**	RCA PB 42079
19/11/1988	75	1		A SMILE IN A WHISPER	RCA PB 42249
28/01/1989	49	3		CLARE	RCA PB 42607

FAIRPORT CONVENTION UK group formed in London in 1966 by Ashley Hutchings (born 26/1/1945, London, bass), Simon Nicol (born 13/10/1950, London, guitar), Richard Thompson (born 3/4/1949, London, bass), Judy Dyble (born 13/2/1949, London, vocals), Ian Matthews (born 16/6/1946, Scunthorpe, vocals) and Shaun Frater (drums) as the Ethnic Shuffle Orchestra. Frater left after one concert and was replaced by Martin Lamble (born 28/8/1949, London). Dyble left in 1968 and was replaced by Sandy Denny (born 6/1/1947, London). Lamble was killed on 14/5/1969 in a group van accident; Dave Mattacks (born March 1948, London) was his replacement. Numerous additional changes before they split in 1979 have been followed by many reunions since. Denny died of a brain haemorrhage on 21/4/1978.

23/07/1969	21	9		SI TU DOIS PARTIR French translation of the Bob Dylan song *If You Gotta Go, Go Now*	Island WIP 6064

ANDY FAIRWEATHER-LOW UK singer (born 2/8/1950, Ystrad Mynach, Wales) and founding member of Amen Corner. He formed Fair Weather in 1970 after Corner's demise. Also a session guitarist, he joined Eric Clapton's band in 1991.

21/09/1974	10	8		**REGGAE TUNE**	A&M AMS 7129
06/12/1975	6	10		**WIDE EYED AND LEGLESS**	A&M AMS 7202

ADAM FAITH UK singer (born Terence Nelhams, 23/6/1940, Acton, London) who first worked as assistant film editor for Rank Screen Service. His skiffle group made up of fellow workmates appeared on TV's *6.5 Special*; Faith went solo and signed with EMI in 1957. He acted in films (including 1960's *Beat Girl*) and TV shows (including *Budgie* and *Love Hurts*), produced Roger Daltrey's first solo album and managed Leo Sayer. He died from a heart attack on 8/3/2003.

20/11/1959	❶[3]	19		**WHAT DO YOU WANT**	Parlophone R 4591
22/01/1960	❶[1]	17		**POOR ME**	Parlophone R 4623
14/04/1960	2	13		**SOMEONE ELSE'S BABY**	Parlophone R 4643
30/06/1960	5	13		**WHEN JOHNNY COMES MARCHING HOME/MADE YOU** A-side featured in the 1960 film *Never Let Go*, B-side featured in the 1960 film *Beat Girl*, both of which starred Adam Faith	Parlophone R 4665

❶[9] Number of weeks single topped the UK chart ↑ Entered the UK chart at #1 ▲[9] Number of weeks single topped the US chart

	DATE	POS	WKS	BPI	SINGLE TITLE	LABEL & NUMBER
	15/09/1960	4	14		**HOW ABOUT THAT**	Parlophone R 4689
	17/11/1960	4	11		**LONELY PUP (IN A CHRISTMAS SHOP)**	Parlophone R 4708
	09/02/1961	5	14		**WHO AM I/THIS IS IT!**	Parlophone R 4735
	27/04/1961	12	10		EASY GOING ME	Parlophone R 4766
	20/07/1961	12	10		DON'T YOU KNOW IT	Parlophone R 4807
	26/10/1961	4	14		**THE TIME HAS COME**	Parlophone R 4837
	18/01/1962	12	9		LONESOME	Parlophone R 4864
	03/05/1962	5	15		**AS YOU LIKE IT**	Parlophone R 4896
	30/08/1962	8	11		**DON'T THAT BEAT ALL** ADAM FAITH WITH JOHNNY KEATING AND HIS ORCHESTRA	Parlophone R 4930
	13/12/1962	22	6		BABY TAKE A BOW	Parlophone R 4964
	31/01/1963	31	5		WHAT NOW ADAM FAITH WITH JOHNNY KEATING AND HIS ORCHESTRA	Parlophone R 4990
	11/07/1963	23	6		WALKIN' TALL	Parlophone R 5039
	19/09/1963	5	13		**THE FIRST TIME**	Parlophone R 5061
	12/12/1963	11	12		WE ARE IN LOVE	Parlophone R 5091
	12/03/1964	25	9		IF HE TELLS YOU	Parlophone R 5109
	28/05/1964	33	6		I LOVE BEING IN LOVE WITH YOU This and above three singles credited to **ADAM FAITH AND THE ROULETTES**	Parlophone R 5138
	26/11/1964	12	11		MESSAGE TO MARTHA (KENTUCKY BLUEBIRD)	Parlophone R 5201
	11/02/1965	23	6		STOP FEELING SORRY FOR YOURSELF	Parlophone R 5235
	17/06/1965	34	5		SOMEONE'S TAKEN MARIA AWAY	Parlophone R 5289
	20/10/1966	46	2		CHERYL'S GOIN' HOME	Parlophone R 5516

HORACE FAITH
Jamaican reggae singer who later recorded for DJM.

	DATE	POS	WKS	BPI	SINGLE TITLE	LABEL & NUMBER
	12/09/1970	13	10		BLACK PEARL	Trojan TR 7790

PERCY FAITH
Canadian orchestra leader (born 7/4/1908, Toronto) who moved to the US in 1940. From 1950 onwards he became a conductor and arranger at Columbia Records, producing three million-selling singles with Tony Bennett. He wrote music for films including *Love Me Or Leave Me* (1955), *Tammy Tell Me True* (1961), *I'd Rather Be Rich* (1964) and *The Oscar* (1966), which despite the title did not win one. He did, however, win two Grammy Awards, including Best Contemporary Pop Performance in 1969 for *Love Theme From Romeo And Juliet*. He died from cancer on 9/2/1976. He has a star on the Hollywood Walk of Fame.

	DATE	POS	WKS	BPI	SINGLE TITLE	LABEL & NUMBER
	05/03/1960	2	31		**THEME FROM 'A SUMMER PLACE'** ▲⁹ 1960 Grammy Award for Record of the Year. Featured in the films *A Summer Place* (1959), *Con Air* (1997) and *Ocean's Eleven* (2001).	Philips PB 989

FAITH BROTHERS
UK group formed by Billy Franks (guitar/vocals), Lee Hirons (bass), Mark Hirons (guitar), Steve Howlett (drums), Will Tipper (trumpet), Henry Trezise (keyboards) and Mark Waterman (saxophone).

	DATE	POS	WKS	BPI	SINGLE TITLE	LABEL & NUMBER
	13/04/1985	63	3		THE COUNTRY OF THE BLIND	Siren 2
	06/07/1985	69	3		A STRANGER ON HOME GROUND	Siren 4

FAITH, HOPE AND CHARITY
US R&B vocal trio formed in Tampa, FL by Brenda Hilliard, Albert Bailey and Zulema Cusseaux, discovered by Van McCoy. Zulema went solo in 1971. Hilliard and Bailey continued as a duo until joined by Diane Destry in 1974.

	DATE	POS	WKS	BPI	SINGLE TITLE	LABEL & NUMBER
	31/01/1976	38	4		JUST ONE LOOK	RCA 2632

FAITH, HOPE AND CHARITY
UK vocal group that featured TV presenter and model Dani Behr.

	DATE	POS	WKS	BPI	SINGLE TITLE	LABEL & NUMBER
	23/06/1990	53	3		BATTLE OF THE SEXES	WEA YZ 4801

FAITH NO MORE
US rock group formed in San Francisco, CA in 1980 by Billy Gould (born 24/4/1963, Los Angeles, CA, bass), Roddy Bottum (born 1/7/1963, Los Angeles, keyboards), Mike 'Puffy' Bordin (born 27/11/1962, San Francisco, drums) and Jim Martin (born 21/7/1961, Oakland, CA, guitar), named after a greyhound on which they had placed a bet. Singer Chuck Mosely joined in 1983 but was replaced by Mike Patton (born 27/1/1968, Eureka, CA) in 1988. Signed to Mordam in 1984, then Warners subsidiary Slash in 1986, they split in 1998. Boo-Yaa T.R.I.B.E. are a US rap group with Ganxsta Ridd, EKA, Rosco, Ganxsta OMB, The Godfather and Don-L.

	DATE	POS	WKS	BPI	SINGLE TITLE	LABEL & NUMBER
	06/02/1988	53	3		WE CARE A LOT	Slash LASH 17
	10/02/1990	37	4		EPIC	Slash LASH 21
	14/04/1990	23	6		FROM OUT OF NOWHERE	Slash LASH 24
	14/07/1990	41	3		FALLING TO PIECES	Slash LASH 25
	08/09/1990	25	5		EPIC	Slash LASH 26
	06/06/1992	10	5		**MIDLIFE CRISIS**	Slash LASH 37
	15/08/1992	29	5		A SMALL VICTORY	Slash LASH 39
	12/09/1992	55	1		A SMALL VICTORY (REMIX)	Slash LASHX 40
	21/11/1992	28	3		EVERYTHING'S RUINED	Slash LASH 43
	16/01/1993	3	8		**I'M EASY/BE AGGRESSIVE**	Slash LACDP 44
	06/11/1993	26	3		ANOTHER BODY MURDERED **FAITH NO MORE AND BOO-YAA T.R.I.B.E.** Featured in the 1993 film *Judgment Night*	Epic 6597942
	11/03/1995	16	4		DIGGING THE GRAVE	Slash LACDP 51
	27/05/1995	27	2		RICOCHET	Slash LASCD 53
	29/07/1995	32	3		EVIDENCE	Slash LACDP 54
	31/05/1997	15	3		ASHES TO ASHES	Slash LASCD 61
	16/08/1997	51	1		LAST CUP OF SORROW	Slash LASCD 62
	13/12/1997	40	2		THIS TOWN AIN'T BIG ENOUGH FOR THE BOTH OF US **SPARKS VERSUS FAITH NO MORE**	Roadrunner RR 22513
	17/01/1998	29	3		ASHES TO ASHES	Slash LASCD 63
	07/11/1998	49	1		I STARTED A JOKE	Slash LASCD 65

○ Silver disc ● Gold disc ✪ Platinum disc (additional platinum units are indicated by a figure following the symbol) ◎ Singles released prior to 1973 that are known to have sold over 1 million copies in the UK

MARIANNE FAITHFULL
UK singer (born 29/12/1946, Hampstead, London) discovered by Rolling Stones manager Andrew Loog Oldham. Her debut hit was a Jagger/Richard song. She married artist John Dunbar in 1965, then later Vibrators bass player Ben Brierly and writer Giorgio Della Terza, and also had a long relationship with Mick Jagger. She appeared in a number of films.

DATE	POS	WKS	BPI	SINGLE TITLE	LABEL & NUMBER
13/08/1964	9	13		**AS TEARS GO BY**	Decca F 11923
18/02/1965	4	13		**COME AND STAY WITH ME**	Decca F 12075
06/05/1965	6	11		**THIS LITTLE BIRD**	Decca F 12162
22/07/1965	10	10		**SUMMER NIGHTS**	Decca F 12193
04/11/1965	36	4		YESTERDAY	Decca F 12268
09/03/1967	43	1		IS THIS WHAT I GET FOR LOVING YOU	Decca F 22524
24/11/1979	48	6		THE BALLAD OF LUCY JORDAN	Island WIP 6491

FAITHLESS
UK group formed in 1995 by producer Rollo (born Roland Armstrong), DJ Sister Bliss (born Ayalah Ben-Tovim), singer Jamie Catto and rapper Maxi Jazz (born Max Fraser). Ex-Dusted Rollo had also previously recorded as Rollo Goes Mystic and Rollo Goes Camping, and written with his sister Dido.

DATE	POS	WKS	BPI	SINGLE TITLE	LABEL & NUMBER
05/08/1995	30	2		SALVA MEA (SAVE ME)	Cheeky CHEKCD 008
09/12/1995	27	2		INSOMNIA Featured in the 1998 film *A Night At The Roxbury*	Cheeky CHEKCD 010
23/03/1996	34	2		DON'T LEAVE Featured in the 1998 film *A Life Less Ordinary*	Cheeky CHEKCD 012
26/10/1996	3	13	○	**INSOMNIA (REMIX)**	Cheeky CHEKCD 017
21/12/1996	9	7		**SALVA MEA (SAVE ME) (REMIX)**	Cheeky CHEKXCD 018
26/04/1997	10	3		**REVERENCE**	Cheeky CHEKCD 019
15/11/1997	21	2		DON'T LEAVE (REMIX)	Cheeky CHEKXCD 024
05/09/1998	6	8		**GOD IS A DJ**	Cheeky CHEKCD 028
05/12/1998	15	6		TAKE THE LONG WAY HOME	Cheeky CHEKCD 031
01/05/1999	14	5		BRING MY FAMILY BACK Featured in the 1999 film *Forces Of Nature*	Cheeky CHEKCD 035
16/06/2001	3	10		**WE COME 1**	Cheeky 74321858352
29/09/2001	29	4		MUHAMMAD ALI	Cheeky 74321886452
29/12/2001	29	5		TARANTULA	Cheeky 74321903592
20/04/2002	6	3		**ONE STEP TOO FAR** Would have charted higher but for a decision by the record company (BMG) to delete it midway through its first week on sale	Cheeky 74321926412
04/05/2002	68	1		ONE STEP TOO FAR 12-inch remix of above track. Both singles credited to **FAITHLESS FEATURING DIDO**	Cheeky 74321936742
12/06/2004	7	8		**MASS DESTRUCTION**	Cheeky 82876614922
04/09/2004	22	3		I WANT MORE	BMG 82876641902

FALCO
Austrian singer (born Johann Holzel, 19/2/1957, Vienna) who was killed in a car crash in the Dominican Republic on 6/2/1998.

DATE	POS	WKS	BPI	SINGLE TITLE	LABEL & NUMBER
22/03/1986	❶[1]	15	●	**ROCK ME AMADEUS** ▲[3]	A&M AM 278
31/05/1986	10	8		**VIENNA CALLING**	A&M AM 318
02/08/1986	68	1		JEANNY	A&M AM 333
27/09/1986	61	2		THE SOUND OF MUSIK	WEA U 8591

CHRISTIAN FALK FEATURING DEMETREUS
Swedish producer Christian Falk and singer Demetreus.

DATE	POS	WKS	BPI	SINGLE TITLE	LABEL & NUMBER
26/08/2000	22	3		MAKE IT RIGHT	London LONCD 452

FRED FALKE – see ALAN BRAXE AND FRED FALKE

FALL
UK group formed in Manchester in 1977 by Mark E Smith (born 5/3/1957, Manchester, vocals), Martin Bramah (guitar), Una Baines (keyboards), Tony Friel (bass) and Karl Burns (drums). Smith's wife Brix joined in 1983 and left in 1989. Smith is the only original member left in the group.

DATE	POS	WKS	BPI	SINGLE TITLE	LABEL & NUMBER
13/09/1986	75	1		MR PHARMACIST	Beggars Banquet BEG 168
20/12/1986	59	1		HEY! LUCIANI	Beggars Banquet BEG 176
09/05/1987	30	4		THERE'S A GHOST IN MY HOUSE	Beggars Banquet BEG 187
31/10/1987	57	5		HIT THE NORTH	Beggars Banquet BEG 200
30/01/1988	35	3		VICTORIA	Beggars Banquet BEG 206
26/11/1988	59	2		BIG NEW PRINZ/JERUSALEM Tracks on single: *Big New Prinz, Wrong Place Right Time Number Two, Jerusalem* and *Acid Priest 2088*	Beggars Banquet FALL 2/3
27/01/1990	58	1		TELEPHONE THING	Cog Sinister SIN 4
08/09/1990	56	2		WHITE LIGHTNING	Cog Sinister SIN 6
14/03/1992	40	1		FREE RANGE	Cog Sinister SINS 8
17/04/1993	43	1		WHY ARE PEOPLE GRUDGEFUL	Permanent CDSPERM 9
25/12/1993	75	1		BEHIND THE COUNTER	Permanent CDSPERM 13
30/04/1994	65	1		15 WAYS	Permanent CDSPERM 14
17/02/1996	60	1		THE CHISELERS	Jet JETSCD 500
21/02/1998	69	1		MASQUERADE	Artful CDARTFUYL 1
14/12/2002	64	1		THE FALL VS 2003 Tracks on single: *Susan Vs Youthclub, Remix* and *Janey Vs Johnny*	Action TAKE 020CD
10/07/2004	66	1		THEME FROM SPARTA FC	Action TAKE23CD

FALLACY AND FUSION
UK production/rap duo formed in London by Fallacy (aka Fat Danny Vicious) and Fusion, who later left.

DATE	POS	WKS	BPI	SINGLE TITLE	LABEL & NUMBER
22/06/2002	47	2		THE GROUNDBREAKER	Wordplay WORCD 036
24/05/2003	45	2		BIG N BASHY **FALLACY FEATURING TUBBY T** Contains a sample of W Levine's *I Stand Accused*	Virgin VSCDT 1847

HAROLD FALTERMEYER
German keyboard player/songwriter/producer/arranger (born 5/10/1952, Hamburg) who played on the scores to the films *Midnight Express* (1978) and *American Gigolo* (1980), both scores being written by Giorgio Moroder. He won the 1986 Grammy Award for Best Pop Instrumental Performance with Steve Stevens for *Top Gun Anthem*.

23/03/1985	2	22	O	**AXEL F**	MCA 949
24/08/1985	74	1		FLETCH THEME This and above single featured in the 1985 film *Beverly Hills Cop*	MCA 991

AGNETHA FALTSKOG
Swedish singer (born 5/4/1950, Jonkoping) who signed with CBS at seventeen and had a Swedish #1 with *I Was So In Love*. She appeared in the Swedish production of *Jesus Christ Superstar* before meeting Bjorn Ulvaeus in 1969 and marrying him in 1971. They formed ABBA in 1972 with Benny Andersson and Frida Lyngstad. The group disbanded in 1982; Faltskog went solo. Agnetha divorced Bjorn in 1979, married surgeon Tomas Sonnenfield in 1990 and retired for a while from the record industry, returning in 2004.

28/05/1983	35	6		THE HEAT IS ON	Epic A 3436
13/08/1983	44	5		WRAP YOUR ARMS AROUND ME	Epic A 3622
22/10/1983	63	1		CAN'T SHAKE LOOSE	Epic A 3812
24/04/2004	11	5		IF I THOUGHT YOU'D EVER CHANGE YOUR MIND	WEA 375CD
26/06/2004	34	2		WHEN YOU WALK IN THE ROOM	WEA 378CD

GEORGIE FAME
UK singer/pianist (born Clive Powell, 26/9/1943, Leigh) who was signed and given his stage name by manager Larry Parnes after doing holiday camp gigs in 1959. His first recording was backing Gene Vincent on *Pistol Packin' Mama* in 1960. In 1961 he joined Billy Fury's group the Blue Flames. He went on to lead the Blue Flames until 1966, thereafter fronting various ensembles. By 2001 he was a member of Bill Wyman's Rhythm Kings.

17/12/1964	●²	12		**YEH YEH**	Columbia DB 7428
04/03/1965	22	8		IN THE MEANTIME	Columbia DB 7494
29/07/1965	33	7		LIKE WE USED TO BE	Columbia DB 7633
28/10/1965	23	7		SOMETHING	Columbia DB 7727
23/06/1966	●¹	11		**GET AWAY** This and above four singles credited to GEORGIE FAME AND THE BLUE FLAMES	Columbia DB 7946
22/09/1966	13	8		SUNNY	Columbia DB 8015
22/12/1966	12	10		SITTING IN THE PARK GEORGIE FAME AND THE BLUE FLAMES	Columbia DB 8096
23/03/1967	15	8		BECAUSE I LOVE YOU	CBS 202587
13/09/1967	37	5		TRY MY WORLD	CBS 2945
13/12/1967	●¹	13		**BALLAD OF BONNIE AND CLYDE**	CBS 3124
09/07/1969	16	9		PEACEFUL	CBS 4295
13/12/1969	25	7		SEVENTH SON	CBS 4659
10/04/1971	11	10		ROSETTA FAME AND PRICE TOGETHER (Alan Price)	CBS 7108

FAMILY
UK rock group formed in Leicester as the Farinas in 1966, evolving into Family in 1967 with Roger Chapman (born 8/4/1942, Leicester, vocals), Charlie Whitney (born 24/6/1944, Skipton, guitar), Ron Townsend (born 7/7/1947, Leicester, drums), Rick Grech (born 1/11/1946, Bordeaux, France, violin/bass) and John 'Poli' Palmer (born 25/5/1942, keyboards). Grech left in 1969 and was replaced by John Weider (born 21/4/1947). Weider left in 1971 and was replaced by John Wetton. Palmer and Wetton left in 1972 and were replaced by Tony Ashton (born 1/3/1946, Blackburn) and Jim Cregan. They disbanded in 1973. Grech died from kidney and liver failure on 16/3/1990 and Ashton died from cancer on 28/5/2001.

01/11/1969	29	7		NO MULE'S FOOL	Reprise RS 27001
22/08/1970	11	12		STRANGE BAND	Reprise RS 27009
17/07/1971	4	13		**IN MY OWN TIME**	Reprise K 14090
23/09/1972	13	12		BURLESQUE	Reprise K 14196

FAMILY CAT
UK group formed in Yeovil in 1988 by Paul Frederick (guitar/vocals), Steven Jelbert (guitar), Tim McVey (guitar), John Graves (bass) and Kevin Downing (drums).

28/08/1993	69	1		AIRPLANE GARDENS/ATMOSPHERIC ROAD	Dedicated FCUK 00CD
21/05/1994	48	1		WONDERFUL EXCUSE	Dedicated 74321208432
30/07/1994	42	2		GOLDENBOOK	Dedicated 74321220072

FAMILY COOKIN' – see LIMMIE AND THE FAMILY COOKIN'

FAMILY DOGG
UK group formed by Steve Rowland, Albert Hammond, Mike Hazlewood, Doreen De Veuve and Zooey, backed on the hit by Led Zeppelin. De Veuve was later replaced by Christine Holmes, Zooey by Ireen Scheer. They disbanded in the 1970s.

28/05/1969	6	14		**A WAY OF LIFE**	Bell 1055

FAMILY FOUNDATION
UK vocal/instrumental group formed by producer Johnny Jay.

13/06/1992	42	4		XPRESS YOURSELF	380 PEW 1

FAMILY STAND
US group formed in 1986 by Peter Lord (vocals/keyboards), V Jeffrey Smith (guitar/bass/flute/saxophone/vocals/drum programmes) and Sandra St Victor (vocals) as The Stand. Lord and Smith later produced Goodfellaz, among others.

31/03/1990	10	11		**GHETTO HEAVEN**	East West A 7997
17/01/1998	30	2		GHETTO HEAVEN (REMIX)	Perfecto PERD 156CD1

FAMILY STONE – see SLY AND THE FAMILY STONE

FAMOUS FLAMES – see JAMES BROWN

O Silver disc ● Gold disc ✪ Platinum disc (additional platinum units are indicated by a figure following the symbol) ◎ Singles released prior to 1973 that are known to have sold over 1 million copies in the UK

FANTASTIC FOUR US R&B group formed in Detroit, MI in 1965 by 'Sweet' James Epps, Robert Pruitt, Joseph Pruitt and Toby Childs. Robert Pruitt and Childs were later replaced by Paul Scott and Cleveland Horne. Horne died from a heart attack on 13/4/2000, Epps (also from a heart attack) on 11/9/2000.

24/02/1979	62	4		B.Y.O.F. (BRING YOUR OWN FUNK)	Atlantic LV 14

FANTASTICS US group formed in New York in the 1960s as the Velours by John Cheatdom, Richard Pitts, Jerome Ramos and Donald Haywoode. They toured the UK in 1970 as the Temptations. They remained in the country, renaming themselves the Fantastics.

27/03/1971	9	12		SOMETHING OLD, SOMETHING NEW	Bell 1141

FANTASY UFO UK instrumental group formed by Mark Ryder who later recorded as M-D-Emm and under his own name.

29/09/1990	56	3		FANTASY	XL XLT 15
10/08/1991	50	3		MIND BODY SOUL FANTASY UFO FEATURING JAY GROOVE	Strictly Underground YZ 591

FAR CORPORATION Multinational studio group assembled by producer Frank Farian with Pitt Low, Johan Daansen, Steve Lukather, Bernd Berwanger, Mats Bjorklund, Bobby Kimball and Robin McCauley.

26/10/1985	8	11		STAIRWAY TO HEAVEN	Arista ARIST 639

DON FARDON UK singer (born Don Maughn, 19/8/1943, Coventry) who fronted The Sorrows, then Don Fardon & The Soul Machine, before going solo.

18/04/1970	32	5		BELFAST BOY Tribute to footballer George Best	Young Blood YB 1010
10/10/1970	3	17		INDIAN RESERVATION Originally released in 1968 and failed to chart, although it made the US top twenty	Young Blood YB 1015

FARGETTA Italian DJ Mario Fargetta (born in Milan).

23/01/1993	34	2		MUSIC FARGETTA AND ANNE-MARIE SMITH	Synthetic CDR 6334
10/08/1996	74	1		THE MUSIC IS MOVING	Arista 74321381572

CHRIS FARLOWE UK singer (born John Henry Deighton, 13/10/1940, London) and talent contest winner in 1957 with the John Henry Skiffle Group. Fronting the Thunderbirds from 1962, he later signed solo with Andrew Loog Oldham's Immediate label. Also ex-lead singer with Colosseum and Atomic Rooster, when not singing he runs a shop in Islington, London.

27/01/1966	37	3		THINK	Immediate IM 023
23/06/1966	❶1	13		OUT OF TIME Written by Mick Jagger and Keith Richard, their only #1 composition with another act.	Immediate IM 035
27/10/1966	31	7		RIDE ON BABY	Immediate IM 038
16/02/1967	48	1		MY WAY OF GIVING IN	Immediate IM 041
29/06/1967	46	2		MOANIN'	Immediate IM 056
13/12/1967	33	6		HANDBAGS AND GLADRAGS	Immediate IM 065
27/09/1975	44	4		OUT OF TIME Re-Issue of Immediate IM 035	Immediate IMS 101

FARM UK group formed in Liverpool in 1983 by Peter Hooton (born 28/9/1962, Liverpool, lead vocals) and Steve Grimes (born 4/6/1962, Liverpool, guitar) as the Excitements, with Roy Boulter (born 2/7/1964, Liverpool, drums), Carl Hunter (born 14/4/1965, Bootle, bass), Ben Leach (born 2/5/1969, Liverpool, keyboards) and Keith Mullen (guitar). Renamed The Farm in 1984, they founded the Produce label in 1989 with £20,000 from Littlewoods pools heir Barney Moore.

05/05/1990	58	4		STEPPING STONE/FAMILY OF MAN	Produce MILK 101
01/09/1990	6	10		GROOVY TRAIN	Produce MILK 102
08/12/1990	4	12	O	ALL TOGETHER NOW Based on Pachelbel's Canon	Produce MILK 103
13/04/1991	28	5		SINFUL! (SCARY JIGGIN' WITH DOCTOR LOVE) PETE WYLIE WITH THE FARM	Siren SRN 138
04/05/1991	36	3		DON'T LET ME DOWN	Produce MILK 104
24/08/1991	31	4		MIND	Produce MILK 105
14/12/1991	58	4		LOVE SEE NO COLOUR	Produce MILK 106
04/07/1992	48	3		RISING SUN	End Product 6581737
17/10/1992	18	5		DON'T YOU WANT ME	End Product 6584687
02/01/1993	35	4		LOVE SEE NO COLOUR (REMIX)	End Product 6588682
12/06/2004	5	5		ALL TOGETHERNOW 2004 FARM FEATURING SFX BOYS CHOIR Official theme of the England side for the 2004 European Championships	DMG ENGLCD2004

FARMERS BOYS UK group formed in Norwich by Baz, Frog, Mark and Stan (only using their forenames). They debuted in 1983 and disbanded in 1985.

09/04/1983	48	6		MUCK IT OUT	EMI 5380
30/07/1983	66	3		FOR YOU	EMI 5401
04/08/1984	44	5		IN THE COUNTRY	EMI FAB 2
03/11/1984	59	3		PHEW WOW	EMI FAB 3

JOHN FARNHAM UK singer/actor (born 1/7/1949, Dagenham) who emigrated to Australia, having a hit there in 1968 with *Sadie The Cleaning Lady* and later joining the Little River Band. His UK hit made the US chart in 1990.

25/04/1987	6	17		YOU'RE THE VOICE	Wheatley PB 41093

JOANNE FARRELL UK singer who later appeared in stage shows *Stop The World I Want To Get Off* and *The Rocky Horror Picture Show*.

24/06/1995	40	2		ALL I WANNA DO	Big Beat A 8194CD

---

❶9 Number of weeks single topped the UK chart ↑ Entered the UK chart at #1 ▲9 Number of weeks single topped the US chart

JOE FARRELL US saxophonist (born Joseph Firrantello, 16/12/1937, Chicago, IL) who worked with Maynard Ferguson, George Benson and Elvin Jones, and was also in Return To Forever. He died from bone cancer on 10/1/1986.

16/12/1978.....57......4....... NIGHT DANCING .... Warner Brothers LV 2

DIONNE FARRIS US singer (born in Bordentown, NJ) who worked with TLC and Arrested Development before going solo.

18/03/1995.....47......2....... I KNOW .... Columbia 6613542
27/05/1995.....41......3....... I KNOW .... Columbia 6613542
07/06/1997.....42......1....... HOPELESS Featured in the 1997 film *Love Jones* .... Columbia 6645165

GENE FARRIS US DJ and producer who first recorded for Cajual/Relief and Force Inc.

20/12/2003.....74......1....... WELCOME TO CHICAGO EP Tracks on EP: *Sanctified Love (Club Mix)*, *Sanctified Love (Club Dub)*, *Voice ID* and *Alien Instruction*
.... Defected DFTD081R

GENE FARROW AND G.F. BAND UK production group formed by Gene Farrow, Chris Warren and John Hudson.

01/04/1978.....33......6....... MOVE YOUR BODY .... Magnet MAG 109
05/08/1978.....71......2....... DON'T STOP NOW .... Magnet MAG 125

FASCINATIONS US R&B vocal group formed in Detroit, MI in 1960 by Shirley Walker, Joanne Levell, Bernadine Boswell Smith and Fern Bledsie, discovered by Curtis Mayfield. Splitting in 1969, they re-formed to tour the UK in 1971 after their single's success, which had previously been a US hit in 1967.

03/07/1971.....32......6....... GIRLS ARE OUT TO GET YOU .... Mojo 2092 004

FASHION UK group formed in Birmingham by John Mulligan (bass), Luke (guitar) and Dix (drums), later adding Tony (vocals), De Harris (vocals) and Martin Stoker (drums) to the line-up.

03/04/1982.....46......5....... STREETPLAYER (MECHANIK) .... Arista ARIST 456
21/08/1982.....51......5....... LOVE SHADOW .... Arista ARIST 483
18/02/1984.....69......2....... EYE TALK .... De Stijl A 4106

SUSAN FASSBENDER UK singer from Sheffield. After her hit she retired from music to raise a family.

17/01/1981.....21......8....... TWILIGHT CAFÉ .... CBS 9468

FAST FOOD ROCKERS UK vocal group formed by Ria Scott (aged 20 at the time of their debut hit), Martin Rycroft (19) and Lucy Meggitt (21), with their mascot Hot Dog (3).

28/06/2003 .....2......14...... FAST FOOD SONG .... Better The Devil BTD1CD
18/10/2003.....10......7....... SAY CHEESE (SMILE PLEASE) .... Better The Devil BTD5CD
27/12/2003.....25......3....... I LOVE CHRISTMAS .... Better The Devil BTD6CDX

FASTBALL US group formed in Austin, TX by Tony Scalzo (bass/vocals), Miles Zuniga (guitar/vocals) and Joey Shuffield (drums).

03/10/1998.....21......5....... THE WAY .... Polydor 5689472

FASTWAY UK rock group formed in 1982 by ex-Motorhead 'Fast' Eddie Clarke (guitar) and Pete Way (bass), with Dave King (vocals) and Jerry Shirley (drums). Way left and was replaced by Charlie McCracken. Shirley and McCracken left after their second album, Clarke re-forming in 1988 with Paul Gray (bass), Lea Hart (guitar/vocals) and Steve Clarke (drums). After one album this line-up was replaced by Eddie Clarke, Lea Hart, KB Bren (bass) and Riff Raff (drums), who disbanded after a further LP; Eddie Clarke went solo.

02/04/1983.....74......1....... EASY LIVIN' .... CBS A 3196

FAT BOYS US rap group formed in Brooklyn, NYC by Darren 'The Human Beat Box' Robinson (born 10/6/1967, New York), Mark 'Prince Markie Dee' Morales and Damon 'Kolo Rock-ski' Wimbley, named after their combined weight of over 750 pounds. They appeared in the 1987 film *Disorderlies*. Robinson died from a heart attack on 10/12/1995.

04/05/1985.....63......2.......○ JAIL HOUSE RAP .... Sultra U 9123
22/08/1987 .....2......12.....○ WIPEOUT FAT BOYS AND THE BEACH BOYS .... Urban URB 5
18/06/1988 .....2......11...... THE TWIST (YO, TWIST) FAT BOYS AND CHUBBY CHECKER .... Urban URB 20
05/11/1988.....46......4....... LOUIE LOUIE .... Urban URB 26

FAT JOE US rapper (born Joseph Cartagena, 19/8/1970, The Bronx, NYC) with Puerto Rican and Cuban parents. Rapper Big Pun (born Christopher Rios, 9/11/1971, New York City), who also recorded as Big Punisher, died from a heart attack on 7/2/2000 as a result of being overweight – he was 698 pounds.

01/04/2000.....15......6....... FEELIN' SO GOOD JENNIFER LOPEZ FEATURING BIG PUN AND FAT JOE Contains a sample of Strafe's *Set It Off* .. Columbia 6691972
30/03/2002.....48......1....... WE THUGGIN' .... Atlantic AT 0124CD
25/05/2002 .....4......8....... WHAT'S LUV FAT JOE FEATURING ASHANTI .... Atlantic AT 0128CD
14/12/2002.....42......2....... CRUSH TONIGHT FAT JOE FEATURING GINUWINE .... Atlantic AT 0142CD
16/10/2004.....24......5....... LEAN BACK TERROR SQUAD FEATURING FAT JOE AND REMY .... Universal MCSTD 40385

FAT LADY SINGS Irish vocal/instrumental group formed in Dublin in 1986 by Robert Hamilton (vocals), Nick Kelly (guitar/vocals), Tim Bradhsaw (keyboards), Dermot Lynch (bass) and Nic France (drums). Hamilton left in 1991.

17/07/1993.....56......2....... DRUNKARD LOGIC .... East West YZ 756CD

○ Silver disc ● Gold disc ✪ Platinum disc (additional platinum units are indicated by a figure following the symbol) ◎ Singles released prior to 1973 that are known to have sold over 1 million copies in the UK

FAT LARRY'S BAND
US group formed in Philadelphia, PA in 1977 by drummer/singer/producer Larry James (born 2/8/1949, Philadelphia) with Theodore Cohen (guitar), Larry La Bes (bass/percussion), Terry Price (keyboards/vocals), Frederick Campbell (vocals), Alfonzo Smith (percussion/vocals) and Douglas Jones (saxophone/vocals). James died from a heart attack on 5/12/1987.

02/07/1977	31	5		CENTRE CITY	Atlantic K 10951
10/03/1979	46	4		BOOGIE TOWN F.L.B.	Fantasy FTC 168
18/08/1979	46	6		LOOKING FOR LOVE TONIGHT	Fantasy FTC 179
18/09/1982	2	11	○	ZOOM	Virgin VS 546

FAT LES
UK comedian Keith Allen and artist Damien Hirst. Their debut hit was a football anthem during the 1998 World Cup, their third hit being the official fan song for the 2000 European Championships. Allen was previously with Black Grape on another football hit, during the 1996 European Championships.

20/06/1998	2	12	●	VINDALOO	Telstar CDSTAS 2982
19/12/1998	21	5		NAUGHTY CHRISTMAS (GOBLIN IN THE OFFICE)	Turtleneck NECKCD 001
17/06/2000	10	5		JERUSALEM FAT LES Official England football song for the 2000 European Championships	Parlophone CDRS 6540

FATBACK BAND
US funk group formed in the late 1960s by Bill Curtis (born 1932, Fayetteville, NC, drums/percussion) as a house band for his Fatback Records. Closing the label in 1972, he signed the group to New York-based Perception Records, then with Event (via Spring) in 1973. Initially they featured Curtis, Johnny King (guitar), Johnny Flippin (bass), George Adams (trumpet), Earl Shelton (saxophone), Wayne Woolford (congas), Artie Simmons (trombone), Gerry Thomas (keyboards) and two backing singers. Shortening their name to Fatback in 1982, they added Michael Walker (vocals) and also recorded with Evelyn Thomas. Fatback is a style of drumming.

06/09/1975	40	6		YUM YUM (GIMME SOME)	Polydor 2066 590
06/12/1975	18	10		(ARE YOU READY) DO THE BUS STOP	Polydor 2066 637
21/02/1976	10	7		(DO THE) SPANISH HUSTLE	Polydor 2066 656
29/05/1976	41	4		PARTY TIME	Polydor 2066 682
14/08/1976	38	4		NIGHT FEVER Features the uncredited vocal contribution of Phyllis Hyman	Spring 2066 706
12/03/1977	31	4		DOUBLE DUTCH	Spring 2066 777
09/08/1980	41	9		BACKSTROKIN' FATBACK	Spring POSP 149
23/06/1984	49	4		I FOUND LOVIN'	Master Mix CHE 8401
04/05/1985	69	2		GIRLS ON MY MIND FATBACK	Atlantic/Cotillion FBACK 1
06/09/1986	55	5		I FOUND LOVIN' Re-issue of Master Mix CHE 8401	Important TAN 10
05/09/1987	7	12		I FOUND LOVIN'	Master Mix CHE 8401

FATBOY SLIM
UK singer Norman Cook (born Quentin Cook, 31/7/1963, Brighton). Ex-Housemartins, he recorded solo and formed Beats International and Freakpower. He also records as Pizzaman and The Mighty Dub Katz. He married DJ Zoe Ball in August 1999. Named Best Dance Act at the 1999 and 2001 BRIT Awards, he was also cited as the Best Dance Act at the 1999 MTV Europe Music Awards, and won the 2001 Grammy for Best Short Form Music Video with Bootsy Collins for *Weapon Of Choice*. Freddy Fresh is US producer Frederick Schmid.

03/05/1997	57	1		GOING OUT OF MY HEAD	Skint 19CD
01/11/1997	34	2		EVERYBODY NEEDS A 303 Featured in the 199 film *Lost In Space*	Skint 31CD
20/06/1998	6	10		THE ROCKAFELLER SKANK Contains samples of The Just Brothers' *Sliced Tomatoes* and The John Barry Seven's *Beat Girl*. Featured in the films *She's All That* (2000) and *Bruce Almighty* (2003)	Skint 35CD
17/10/1998	3	8		GANGSTER TRIPPIN Contains samples of The Dust Junkys' *Beatbox Wish* and DJ Shadows' *Entropy*. Featured in the 1999 film *Go*.	Skint 39CD
16/01/1999	❶[1]	12	○	PRAISE YOU ↑ Contains a sample of Camille Yarborough's *Take Yo Praise*. Featured in the 1999 film *Cruel Intentions*	Skint 42CD
01/05/1999	34	2		BADDER BADDER SCHWING FREDDY FRESH FEATURING FATBOY SLIM	Eye-Q EYEUK 040CD
01/05/1999	2	10		RIGHT HERE RIGHT NOW Contains a sample of The James Gang's *The Ashes The Rain And I*. Featured in the 2000 film *There's Only One Jimmy Grimble*	Skint 46CD
28/10/2000	9	13		SUNSET (BIRD OF PREY) Contains a sample of The Doors' *Bird Of Prey*	Skint 58CD
20/01/2001	16	5		DEMONS FATBOY SLIM FEATURING MACY GRAY Contains a sample of Bill Withers' *I Can't Write Left Handed*	Skint 60CD
05/05/2001	10	7		STAR 69	Skint 64XCD
15/09/2001	30	2		A SONG FOR SHELTER/YA MAMA	Skint 71CD
26/01/2002	73	1		RETOX	Skint FAT 18
02/10/2004	12	3		SLASH DOT DASH	Skint SKINT100CDX
11/12/2004	51	2		WONDERFUL NIGHT	Skint SKINT104CD

FATHER ABRAHAM – see SMURFS

FATHER ABRAPHART AND THE SMURPS
UK singer Jonathan King (born Kenneth King, 6/12/1944, London).

| 16/12/1978 | 58 | 4 | | LICK A SMURP FOR CHRISTMAS (ALL FALL DOWN) | Petrol GAS 1/Magnet MAG 139 |

FATIMA MANSIONS
Irish rock group formed by ex-Microdisney Cathal Coughlan (vocals) with Andreas O'Gruama (guitar), first recording for Kitchenware and named after a housing estate in Dublin.

23/05/1992	59	1		EVIL MAN	Radioactive SKX 56
01/08/1992	61	3		1000%	Radioactive SKX 59
19/09/1992	7	6		(EVERYTHING I DO) I DO IT FOR YOU Listed B-side was *Theme From M*A*S*H (Suicide Is Painless)* by MANIC STREET PREACHERS.	Columbia 6583827
06/08/1994	58	1		THE LOYALISER	Kitchenware SKCD 67

❶[9] Number of weeks single topped the UK chart ↑ Entered the UK chart at #1 ▲[9] Number of weeks single topped the US chart

FATMAN SCOOP FEATURING THE CROOKLYN CLAN
US rapper/DJ (born Isaac Freeman III in New York City) who has his own show on Hot97.com. His debut hit was originally released in the US in 1998 and barely made the R&B charts (position #92).

01/11/2003	❶²	16	○	**BE FAITHFUL** ↑ Features samples of Faith Evans' *Love Like This* and Chic's *Chic Cheer* .... Def Jam 9812716
21/02/2004	9	6		**IT TAKES SCOOP** Contains samples of Lyn Collins' *Think (About It)*, Rob Base & DJ E-Z Rock's *It Takes Two*, Chubb Rock's *Treat Em Right*, Chubb Rock's *Caught Up* and Grandmaster Flash & Melle Mel's *White Lines (Don't Do It)*. .... Def Jam 9816983

FBI – see REDHEAD KINGPIN AND THE FBI

FC KAHUNA
UK group formed by brothers Jon and Dan Kahuna.

Date	Pos	Wks	Title
06/04/2002	64	1	GLITTERBALL .... City Rockers ROCKERS 11CD
20/07/2002	58	1	MACHINE SAYS YES .... City Rockers ROCKERS 18CD
22/03/2003	49	1	HAYLING .... Skint 84CD

FEAR FACTORY
US rock group formed in Los Angeles, CA in 1991 by Burton Bell (vocals), Dino Cazares (guitar), Andrew Shives (bass) and Raymond Herrera (drums).

09/10/1999	57	1	CARS Features the uncredited contribution of Gary Numan .... Roadrunner RR 21893

PHIL FEARON
UK singer (born 30/7/1950, Jamaica) who was lead vocalist with Kandidate before launching Galaxy in the early 1980s, then going solo in 1986.

Date	Pos	Wks	BPI	Title
23/04/1983	4	11		**DANCING TIGHT** .... Ensign ENY 501
30/07/1983	20	8		WAIT UNTIL TONIGHT (MY LOVE) This and above single credited to **GALAXY FEATURING PHIL FEARON** .... Ensign ENY 503
22/10/1983	41	6		FANTASY REAL .... Ensign ENY 507
10/03/1984	5	10	○	**WHAT DO I DO** .... Ensign ENY 510
14/07/1984	10	10		**EVERYBODY'S LAUGHING** .... Ensign ENY 514
15/06/1985	42	4		YOU DON'T NEED A REASON This and above three singles credited to **PHIL FEARON AND GALAXY** .... Ensign ENY 517
27/07/1985	70	3		THIS KIND OF LOVE **PHIL FEARON AND GALAXY FEATURING DEE GALDES** .... Ensign ENY 521
02/08/1986	8	9		**I CAN PROVE IT** .... Ensign PF 1
15/11/1986	60	2		AIN'T NOTHING BUT A HOUSEPARTY .... Ensign PF 2

FEEDER
UK group formed in Newport, Wales in 1992 by Grant Nicholas (guitar/vocals) and Jon Lee (drums), with Japanese bassist Taka Hirose joining later. Lee committed suicide on 7/1/2002, hanging himself in Miami, allegedly taking revenge on his wife after she refused to move to Wales.

Date	Pos	Wks	Title
08/03/1997	60	1	TANGERINE .... Echo ECSCD 32
10/05/1997	53	1	CEMENT .... Echo ECSCX 36
23/08/1997	48	1	CRASH .... Echo ECSCD 42
18/10/1997	24	2	HIGH Featured in the 1998 film *Can't Hardly Wait* .... Echo ECSCD 44
28/02/1998	37	1	SUFFOCATE .... Echo ECSCX 52
03/04/1999	31	2	DAY IN DAY OUT .... Echo ECSCD 75
12/06/1999	22	3	INSOMNIA .... Echo ECSCD 77
21/08/1999	20	3	YESTERDAY WENT TOO SOON .... Echo ECSCD 79
20/11/1999	41	2	PAPERFACES .... Echo ECSCD 85
20/01/2001	5	6	**BUCK ROGERS** Featured in the 2001 film *Behind Enemy Lines* .... Echo ECSCX 106
14/04/2001	14	6	SEVEN DAYS IN THE SUN .... Echo ECSCD 107
14/07/2001	27	2	TURN .... Echo ECSCD 116
22/12/2001	12	7	JUST A DAY EP Tracks on EP: *Just A Day, Can't Stop Losing You* and *Piece By Piece*. The latter was a video-only track .... Echo ECSCX 121
12/10/2002	14	5	COME BACK AROUND .... Echo ECSCX 130
25/01/2003	10	8	**JUST THE WAY I'M FEELING** .... Echo ECSCX 133
17/05/2003	12	4	FORGET ABOUT TOMORROW .... Echo ECSCX 135
04/10/2003	24	2	FIND THE COLOUR .... Echo ECSCD 145

WILTON FELDER
US saxophonist/bass player (born 31/8/1940, Houston, TX) and a member of The Crusaders from their inception in 1953.

Date	Pos	Wks	Title
01/11/1980	39	5	INHERIT THE WIND Features the uncredited vocal of Bobby Womack .... MCA 646
16/02/1985	63	2	(NO MATTER HOW HIGH I GET) I'LL STILL BE LOOKIN' UP TO YOU **FEATURING BOBBY WOMACK AND INTRODUCING ALLTRINA GRAYSON** .... MCA 919

FELICIA – see B.M.R. FEATURING FELICIA

JOSE FELICIANO
US singer/guitarist (born 10/9/1945, Lares, Puerto Rico, raised in New York). Blind from birth, he left home at eighteen for a musical career, making his debut album in 1964. Many TV appearances included *Kung Fu* and *McMillan & Wife*. Six Grammy Awards include Best New Artist in 1968, Best Latin Pop Recording in 1983 for *Me Enamore*, Best Latin Pop Recording in 1986 for *Lelolai*, Best Latin Pop Recording in 1989 for *Cielito Lindo* and Best Latin Pop Recording in 1990 for *Por Que Te Tengo Que Olvidar?* He has a star on the Hollywood Walk of Fame.

Date	Pos	Wks	Title
18/09/1968	6	16	**LIGHT MY FIRE** 1968 Grammy Award for Best Solo Vocal Performance .... RCA 1715
18/10/1969	25	7	AND THE SUN WILL SHINE .... RCA 1871

FELIX
UK producer/house artist (born Francis Wright, 1972, Essex). Maintaining complete anonymity, at one awards ceremony he turned up in a lion's outfit.

08/08/1992	6	11		**DON'T YOU WANT ME**	Deconstruction 74321110507
24/10/1992	11	6		IT WILL MAKE ME CRAZY	Deconstruction 74321118137
22/05/1993	29	3		STARS	Deconstruction 74321147102
12/08/1995	10	5		**DON'T YOU WANT ME (REMIX)**	Deconstruction 74321293972
19/10/1996	17	4		DON'T YOU WANT ME (2ND REMIX)	Deconstruction 74321418142

JULIE FELIX US folk singer/guitarist (born 14/6/1938, Santa Barbara, CA) who moved to the UK in the mid-1960s, getting her break on TV's *The Frost Report*. She appeared in the 1980 film *Fabian*.

| 18/04/1970 | 19 | 11 | | IF I COULD (EL CONDOR PASA) | RAK 101 |
| 17/10/1970 | 22 | 8 | | HEAVEN IS HERE | RAK 105 |

FELIX DA HOUSECAT US producer Felix Stallings Jr who formed the Radikal Fear record label.

06/09/1997	66	1		DIRTY MOTHA **QWILO AND FELIX DA HOUSECAT**	Manifesto FESCD 29
14/07/2001	55	1		SILVER SCREEN SHOWER SCENE	City Rockers ROCKERS 1CD
02/03/2002	66	1		WHAT DOES IT FEEL LIKE?	City Rockers ROCKERS 8CD
05/10/2002	39	2		SILVER SCREEN SHOWER SCENE	City Rockers ROCKERS 19CD
14/08/2004	55	1		ROCKET RIDE	Rykodisc ENR522
27/11/2004	49	2		WATCHING CARS GO BY	Emperor Norton ENR532

FELLY – see **TECHNOTRONIC**

FELON UK singer Simone Locker whose name came from her time spent in prison for robbery. Her debut hit was recorded while she was on day release from prison.

| 23/03/2002 | 31 | 2 | | GET OUT | Serious SERR 32CD |

FE-M@IL UK vocal group formed by Oyana (aged 19 at the time of their hit), Ans (18), Nicci (18), Lauz (17) and her sister Sally (15).

| 05/08/2000 | 46 | 2 | | FLEE FLY FLO | Jive 9250592 |

FEMME FATALE US rock group with Lorraine Lewis (vocals), Bill D'Angelo (guitar), Mazzi Rawd (guitar), Rick Rael (bass) and Bobby Murray (drums).

| 11/02/1989 | 69 | 2 | | FALLING IN AND OUT OF LOVE | MCA 1309 |

FENDERMEN US duo Phil Humphrey (born 26/11/1937, Stoughton, WI) and Jim Sundquist (born 26/11/1937, Niagra, WI) who met at university. Their debut hit also featured John Howard (drums).

| 18/08/1960 | 32 | 9 | | MULE SKINNER BLUES | Top Rank JAR 395 |

FENIX TX US rock group formed in Houston, TX by Willie Salazar (guitar/vocals), Damon De La Paz (guitar), Adam Lewis (bass) and Donnie Vomit (drums). Vomit left after one album and was replaced by De La Paz, with James Love joining as guitarist.

| 11/05/2002 | 66 | 1 | | THREESOME | MCA MCSTD 40279 |

FENMEN – see **BERN ELLIOTT AND THE FENMEN**

GEORGE FENTON AND JONAS GWANGWA UK/South African instrumental/production duo. Fenton (born 19/10/1949) has scored numerous films, including *Gandhi* (1982), which was nominated for an Oscar and a Grammy, *Dangerous Liaisons* (1988) and *The Jewel In The Crown* (1984).

| 02/01/1988 | 75 | 1 | | CRY FREEDOM Featured in the 1988 film *Cry Freedom*. Listed flip side was *The Funeral* by **THULI DUMAKUDE** | MCA 1228 |

PETER FENTON UK singer whose debut was a cover version of Drafi Deutscher's German hit *Marmor Stein Und Eisen Bricht*.

| 10/11/1966 | 46 | 3 | | MARBLE BREAKS IRON BENDS | Fontana TF 748 |

SHANE FENTON AND THE FENTONES UK singer (born Bernard Jewry, 27/9/1942, Muswell Hill, London). He was a road manager for Johnny Theakston, who sent a tape of his group Shane Fenton & The Fentones to the BBC. Theakston died soon after and Jewry assumed the role of Shane Fenton. He stopped recording in 1964, going into management, but returned in 1973 as leather-clad Alvin Stardust. The Fentones comprised Jerry Wilcox (guitar), Mickey Eyre (guitar), William 'Bonney' Oliver (bass) and Tony Hinchcliffe (drums).

26/10/1961	22	8		I'M A MOODY GUY	Parlophone R 4827
01/02/1962	38	5		WALK AWAY	Parlophone R 4866
05/04/1962	29	7		IT'S ALL OVER NOW	Parlophone R 4883
12/07/1962	19	8		CINDY'S BIRTHDAY	Parlophone R 4921

FENTONES UK group formed by Jerry Wilcox (guitar), Mickey Eyre (guitar), William 'Bonney' Oliver (bass) and Tony Hinchcliffe (drums) who also backed Shane Fenton.

| 19/04/1962 | 41 | 3 | | THE MEXICAN | Parlophone R 4899 |
| 27/09/1962 | 48 | 1 | | THE BREEZE AND I | Parlophone R 4937 |

FERGIE Irish DJ/producer Robert Ferguson.

09/09/2000	47	1		DECEPTION	Duty Free DF 020CD
25/11/2000	57	2		HOOVERS & HORNS **FERGIE AND BK**	Nukleuz NUKC 0185
10/08/2002	47	2		THE BASS EP Tracks on EP: *Bass Generator* and *Bass Has Got Me On*	Duty Free DFTELCDX 004

❶[9] Number of weeks single topped the UK chart ↑ Entered the UK chart at #1 ▲[9] Number of weeks single topped the US chart

285

SHEILA FERGUSON
US singer (born 8/10/1947, Philadelphia, PA) who joined The Three Degrees as lead singer in 1966. Her debut hit was a remake of The Three Degrees' 1974 #1.

05/02/1994.....60......1.......	WHEN WILL I SEE YOU AGAIN .... Xsrhythm CDSTAS 2711

FERKO STRING BAND
US string band from Philadelphia, PA directed by William Connors.

| 12/08/1955.....20......2....... | ALABAMA JUBILEE .... London HL 8140 |

LUISA FERNANDEZ
Spanish singer whose follow-up was *Give Love A Second Chance*.

| 11/11/1978.....31......8....... | LAY LOVE ON YOU .... Warner Brothers K 17061 |

PAMELA FERNANDEZ
US singer from Chicago, IL who was later a member of Rhythm City.

| 17/09/1994.....43......2....... | KICKIN' IN THE BEAT. .... Ore AG 5CD |
| 03/06/1995.....59......1....... | LET'S START OVER/KICKIN' IN THE BEAT (REMIX) .... Ore AG 9CD |

FERRANTE AND TEICHER
US pianist duo Arthur Ferrante (born 7/9/1921, New York) and Louis Teicher (born 24/8/1924, Wilke-Barre, PA).

| 18/08/1960.....44......1....... | THEME FROM 'THE APARTMENT' Written in 1949 as *Jealous Love*. Featured in the 1960 film *The Apartment*.... London HLT 9164 |
| 09/03/1961 .....6.....17...... | **THEME FROM 'EXODUS'** Featured in the 1960 film *Exodus*. United Artists changed its UK outlet from London to HMV midway through its chart run, hence its appearance on two labels .... London HLT 9298/HMV POP 881 |

JOSE FERRER
US singer (born Jose Vicente Ferrer Y Centron, 8/1/1912, Puerto Rico) better known as an actor. His only UK hit was with his wife Rosemary Clooney, with whom he made the 1954 film *Deep In My Heart*. He won an Oscar for the title role in the 1950 film *Cyrano De Bergerac*. He died on 21/1/1992.

| 19/02/1954 .....7 .....3....... | **WOMAN (UH-HUH)** Listed flip side was *Man (Uh-Huh)* by **ROSEMARY CLOONEY** Both tracks featured in the 1954 film *Deep In My Heart* .... Philips PB 220 |

TONY FERRINO
UK singer/comedian Steve Coogan (born 14/10/1965, Manchester) who also recorded as Alan Partridge.

| 23/11/1996.....42......2....... | HELP YOURSELF/BIGAMY AT CHRISTMAS .... RCA 74321430302 |

FERRY AID
Multinational charity ensemble. On 6/3/1987 the ferry *Herald Of Free Enterprise* sank after leaving Zeebrugge in Belgium, killing nearly 200 people. *The Sun* newspaper organised a charity record, produced by Stock Aitken Waterman and featuring Paul McCartney, Mel And Kim, Kate Bush, Boy George, Suzi Quatro, Alvin Stardust, Bonnie Tyler, Bucks Fizz, Dr And The Medics, Frankie Goes To Hollywood, New Seekers, Edwin Starr, Kim Wilde and Mark Knopfler, among others. It raised over £700,000 for the victims' relatives.

| 04/04/1987 .....❶³ .....7......● | LET IT BE ↑ .... The Sun AID 1 |

BRYAN FERRY
UK singer (born 26/9/1945, Washington, Tyne & Wear) who formed the Banshees in 1964 but by 1970 was a full-time teacher. Sacked for making his lessons musical ones, he formed Roxy Music in 1971 and went solo in parallel in 1973.

29/09/1973.....10......9......	**A HARD RAIN'S GONNA FALL**. .... Island WIP 6170
25/05/1974.....13......6......	THE IN CROWD Featured in the 1992 film *A Prelude To A Kiss*. .... Island WIP 6196
31/08/1974.....17......8......	SMOKE GETS IN YOUR EYES . ... Island WIP 6205
05/07/1975.....33......3......	YOU GO TO MY HEAD . ... Island WIP 6234
12/06/1976 .....4 .....10.....○	**LET'S STICK TOGETHER** Video features Ferry's then girlfriend Jerry Hall, who later married Rolling Stone Mick Jagger... Island WIP 6307
07/08/1976.....7......9......	**EXTENDED PLAY EP** Tracks on EP: *Price Of Love, Shame Shame Shame, Heart On My Sleeve* and *It's Only Love* ...... Island IEP 1
05/02/1977 .....9 .....9......	**THIS IS TOMORROW** . ... Polydor 2001 704
14/05/1977.....15......7......	TOKYO JOE. .... Polydor 2001 711
13/05/1978.....67......2......	WHAT GOES ON . ... Polydor POSP 3
05/08/1978.....37......8......	SIGN OF THE TIMES . ... Polydor 2001 798
11/05/1985.....10......9......	**SLAVE TO LOVE** . ... EG FERRY 1
31/08/1985.....21......7......	DON'T STOP THE DANCE . ... EG FERRY 2
07/12/1985.....46......3......	WINDSWEPT . ... EG FERRY 3
29/03/1986.....22......7......	IS YOUR LOVE STRONG ENOUGH Featured in the 1993 film *Threesome*. .... EG FERRY 4
10/10/1987.....37......6......	THE RIGHT STUFF . ... Virgin VS 940
13/02/1988.....41......5......	KISS AND TELL Featured in the 1988 film *Bright Lights Big City*. .... Virgin VS 1034
29/10/1988.....12......9......	LET'S STICK TOGETHER (REMIX) . ... EG EGO 44
11/02/1989.....49......3......	THE PRICE OF LOVE (REMIX) . ... EG EGO 46
22/04/1989.....63......1......	HE'LL HAVE TO GO . ... EG EGO 48
06/03/1993.....18......5......	I PUT A SPELL ON YOU . ... Virgin VSCDG 1400
29/05/1993.....23......5......	WILL YOU LOVE ME TOMORROW . ... Virgin VSCDG 1455
04/09/1993.....57......2......	GIRL OF MY BEST FRIEND . ... Virgin VSCDG 1468
29/10/1994.....52......1......	YOUR PAINTED SMILE . ... Virgin VSCDG 1508
11/02/1995.....57......1......	MAMOUNA. .... Virgin VSCDG 1528

FEVER FEATURING TIPPA IRIE
UK instrumental/production group with reggae singer Tippa Irie.

| 08/07/1995.....48......1....... | STAYING ALIVE 95 . ... Telstar CDSTAS 2776 |

F45 – see DE FUNK FEATURING F45

LENA FIAGBE
UK singer (born Lena Fiagbe Joan Ayavowi, 1969, London) named after jazz singer Lena Horne.

| 24/07/1993.....69......1....... | YOU COME FROM EARTH LENA .... Mother MUMCD 42 |

○ Silver disc ● Gold disc ✪ Platinum disc (additional platinum units are indicated by a figure following the symbol) ◉ Singles released prior to 1973 that are known to have sold over 1 million copies in the UK

23/10/1993.....20......5......	GOTTA GET IT RIGHT...	Mother MUMCD 44
16/04/1994.....52......3......	WHAT'S IT LIKE TO BE BEAUTIFUL..	Mother MUMCD 49
25/06/1994.....48......2......	VISIONS...	Mother MUMCD 53
10/02/1996.....44......2......	AFRICAN DREAM WASIS DIOP FEATURING LENA FIAGBE..............................	Mercury MERCD 453

KAREL FIALKA UK keyboard player (born in Bengal, Czechoslovakia) who first recorded for his own Red Shift label. The 'Matthew' of his hit single is his stepson.

17/05/1980.....52......4......	THE EYES HAVE IT.. Blueprint BLU 2005
05/09/1987.....9......8......	HEY MATTHEW... IRS IRM 140

FIAT LUX UK vocal/instrumental group formed in Wakefield in 1982 by Dave Crickmore, Ian Nelson and Steve Wright. They disbanded in 1985.

28/01/1984.....65......3......	SECRETS.. Polydor FIAT 2
17/03/1984.....59......1......	BLUE EMOTION.. Polydor FIAT 3

FICTION FACTORY UK group formed by Kevin Patterson (vocals), Eddie Jordan (keyboards), Charley 'Chic' Medley (guitar), Graham McGregor (bass) and Mike Ogletree (drums).

14/01/1984.....6......9......	(FEELS LIKE) HEAVEN... CBS A 3996
17/03/1984.....64......2......	GHOST OF LOVE.. CBS A 3819

FIDDLER'S DRAM UK folk group formed in Kent in 1975 by Cathy Lesurf, Ian Telfer, Chris Taylor, Alan Prosser and Will Ward. Debbie Cook was a Kent housewife when she wrote their debut hit.

15/12/1979.....3......9......	DAY TRIP TO BANGOR (DIDN'T WE HAVE A LOVELY TIME)............................... Dingles SID 211

FIDELFATTI FEATURING RONNETTE Italian producer Piero Fidelfatti with singer Ronnette.

27/01/1990.....65......1......	JUST WANNA TOUCH ME.. Urban URB 46

BILLY FIELD Australian singer/pianist who worked on a Riverina station before moving to Sydney in his early twenties.

12/06/1982.....67......3......	YOU WEREN'T IN LOVE WITH ME.. CBS A 2344

ERNIE FIELD'S ORCHESTRA US bandleader (born 26/8/1905, Nacogdoches, TX) who played trombone and piano. He died on 11/5/1997.

25/12/1959.....13......8......	IN THE MOOD.. London HL 8985

GRACIE FIELDS UK singer (born Grace Stansfield, 9/1/1898, Rochdale) who first recorded in 1928, making her film debut in 1931. By 1939 she was the most popular and highest paid performer in the UK, but her marriage to Italian Monty Banks in 1940 (having divorced comedian Archie Pitt) and move to the US (Banks being threatened with World War II internment in the UK) meant a brief slump in her popularity. She returned in triumph to the Palladium theatre in 1946. Semi-retiring to Capri in 1960 with third husband Boris Alperovic, she made her last London appearance in 1978. Awarded a CBE in 1938, she was made a Dame shortly before her death on 27/9/1979. She has a star on the Hollywood Walk of Fame.

31/05/1957.....8......9......	AROUND THE WORLD.. Columbia DB 3953
06/11/1959.....20......6......	LITTLE DONKEY... Columbia DB 4360

RICHARD 'DIMPLES' FIELDS US R&B singer (born 1942, San Francisco) nicknamed Dimples because he was always smiling. He died from a stroke on 12/1/2000.

20/02/1982.....56......4......	I'VE GOT TO LEARN TO SAY NO.. Epic EPC A 1918

FIELDS OF THE NEPHILIM UK rock group formed in Stevenage in 1983 by Carl McCoy (vocals), Tony Pettitt (bass), Peter Yates (guitar) and brothers Alexander 'Nod' (drums) and Paul Wright (guitar). McCoy left in 1991, retaining rights to the name. The other members regrouping (with singer Alan Delaney) as Rubicon.

24/10/1987.....75......1......	BLUE WATER... Situation Two SIT 48
04/06/1988.....28......3......	MOONCHILD.. Situation Two SIT 52
27/05/1989.....35......3......	PSYCHONAUT.. Situation Two ST 57
04/08/1990.....54......1......	FOR HER LIGHT.. Beggars Banquet BEG 244T
24/11/1990.....37......1......	SUMERLAND (DREAMED).. Beggars Banquet BEG 250
28/09/2002.....62......1......	FROM THE FIRE.. Jungle JUNG 65CD

FIERCE US R&B vocal group formed by Aisha, Chantal and Sabrina, masterminded by ex-Boogie Box High leader Andreas Georgiou.

09/01/1999.....25......5......	RIGHT HERE RIGHT NOW.. Wildstar CXWILD 13
15/05/1999.....11......5......	DAYZ LIKE THAT... Wildstar CDWILD 19
14/08/1999.....15......5......	SO LONG... Wildstar CDWILD 27
12/02/2000.....3......8......	SWEET LOVE 2K... Wildstar CDWILD 34

FIERCE GIRL UK production duo Greg Oliver and Scott Pilford.

11/09/2004.....74......1......	DOUBLE DROP.. Red Flag RF012CDS

FIERY FURNACES US brother and sister duo Matthew (guitar) and Eleanor Friedberger (guitar/vocals) who were born in Chicago, IL and raised in Brooklyn.

06/03/2004.....52......1......	TROPICAL ICE-LAND.. Rough Trade RTRADESCD152

❶⁹ Number of weeks single topped the UK chart ↑ Entered the UK chart at #1 ▲⁹ Number of weeks single topped the US chart

287

17/07/2004 . . . . . 49 . . . . . . 1 . . . .   SINGLE AGAIN . . . . Rough Trade RTRADSCD 190

FIFTH DIMENSION US R&B vocal group formed in Los Angeles, CA in 1966 by Lamonte McLemore (born 17/9/1939, St Louis, MO), Marilyn McCoo (born 30/9/1943, New Jersey), Billy Davis Jr (born 26/6/1940, St Louis), Florence LaRue (born 4/2/1944, Philadelphia, PA) and Ron Townson (born 20/1/1933, St Louis) as The Versatiles. The name changed the following year. McCoo and Davis married at the end of 1969, with LaRue marrying manager Marc Gordon. McCoo and Davis left to work as a duo in 1976, with Daniel Beard replacing Davis. Six Grammy Awards included Record of the Year, Best Performance by a Vocal Group, Best Contemporary Single and Best Contemporary Performance by a Group in 1967 for *Up Up And Away*. They have a star on the Hollywood Walk of Fame. Beard died in a fire deliberately started at his Manhattan apartment block on 27/7/1982. Townson died from kidney failure on 2/8/2001.

16/04/1969 . . . . . 11 . . . . . . 12 . . . . . .   AQUARIUS/LET THE SUNSHINE IN (MEDLEY) ▲6 Originally featured in the musical *Hair*. 1969 Grammy Awards for Record of the Year and Best Contemporary Performance by a Group. Featured in the 1994 film *Forrest Gump*. . . . . Liberty LBF 15193

17/01/1970 . . . . . 16 . . . . . . 9 . . . .   WEDDING BELL BLUES ▲3 Featured in the 1991 film *My Girl* . . . . Liberty LBF 15288

50 CENT US rapper (born Curtis Jackson, 6/7/1976 Queens, NYC) whose debut album on Columbia, *Power Of The Dollar*, was planned for 2000, but after he was shot nine times on 24/5/2000, the label dropped him and he signed with Eminem and Dr Dre's Shady/Aftermath labels. Three MOBO Awards include Best Hip Hop Act and Best Album for *Get Rich Or Die Tryin'* in 2003, and he was named Best International Breakthrough Act at the 2004 BRIT Awards.

22/03/2003 . . . . . 3 . . . . . 24 . . . . . . ○   IN DA CLUB ▲9 2003 MOBO Award for Best Single . . . . Interscope 4978742

12/07/2003 . . . . . 6 . . . . . . 8 . . . . . .   21 QUESTIONS 50 CENT FEATURING NATE DOGG Contains a sample of Barry White's *It's Only Love Doing Its' Thing* . . . . Interscope 9807195

18/10/2003 . . . . . 74 . . . . . . 1 . . . . . .   PIMP (IMPORT) . . . . Interscope 9811812CD

25/10/2003 . . . . . 5 . . . . . . 11 . . . . . .   PIMP . . . . Interscope 9812333

06/03/2004 . . . . . 10 . . . . . . 8 . . . . . .   IF I CAN'T/THEM THANGS 50 CENT FEATURING G-UNIT . . . . Interscope 9815279

5050 UK production duo Jason Powell and Andy Lysandrou, who is also in True Steppers.

13/10/2001 . . . . . 54 . . . . . . 1 . . . . . .   WHO'S COMING ROUND . . . . Obsessive FIFTYCD 01

23/03/2002 . . . . . 73 . . . . . . 1 . . . . . .   BAD BOYS HOLLER BOO . . . . Logic 74321910202

50 GRIND FEATURING POKEMON ALLSTARS UK nu-metal group formed in London by Nick Atkinson (vocals), James Goldigay (guitar), Harry Callow (bass), John Hendicott (DJ), and David Scales (drums).

22/12/2001 . . . . . 57 . . . . . . 1 . . . . . .   GOTTA CATCH 'EM ALL Distributors Recognition collapsed two weeks prior to release, so only 3,000 copies were distributed to stores . . . . Recognition CDREC 21

56K FEATURING BEJAY German dance group.

19/04/2003 . . . . . 46 . . . . . . 1 . . . . . .   SAVE A PRAYER . . . . Kontor 0146495 KON

53RD AND 3RD FEATURING THE SOUND OF SHAG UK singer Jonathan King (born Kenneth King, 6/12/1944, London).

20/09/1975 . . . . . 36 . . . . . . 4 . . . . . .   CHICK-A-BOOM (DON'T YA JES LOVE IT) . . . . UK 2012 002

52ND STREET UK group formed in Manchester with Diane Charlemagne (vocals), Tony Henry (guitar/vocals), John Dennison (keyboards/bass) and Tony Bowry (bass/synthesiser/vocals), later known as Cool Down Zone.

02/11/1985 . . . . . 54 . . . . . . 5 . . . . . .   TELL ME (HOW IT FEELS) . . . . 10 TEN 74

11/01/1986 . . . . . 49 . . . . . . 4 . . . . . .   YOU'RE MY LAST CHANCE . . . . 10 TEN 89

08/03/1986 . . . . . 57 . . . . . . 4 . . . . . .   I CAN'T LET YOU GO . . . . 10 TEN 114

FIGHT CLUB FEATURING LAURENT KONRAD French DJ born in Paris.

07/02/2004 . . . . . 70 . . . . . . 1 . . . . . .   SPREAD LOVE . . . . Nebula NEBCD054

FILTER US rock group formed in Chicago, IL by Richard Patrick (born 10/5/1968, Chicago, guitar), Brian Liesegang (programming), Frank Cavanagh (bass), Geno Lenardo (guitar) and Matt Walker (drums), who was later replaced by Steven Gillis. The Crystal Method are US duo Ken Jordan and Scott Kirkland who linked in Los Angeles, CA in 1993.

11/10/1997 . . . . . 39 . . . . . . 2 . . . .   (CAN'T YOU) TRIP LIKE I DO FILTER AND THE CRYSTAL METHOD Featured in the 1997 film *Spawn* . . . . Epic 6650862

18/03/2000 . . . . . 25 . . . . . . 3 . . . .   TAKE A PICTURE Featured in the films *Little Nicky* (2000) and *Valentine* (2001) . . . . Reprise W 515CD

FINCH US rock group formed in Temecula, CA by Nate Barcalow (vocals), Randy Strohmeyer (guitar), Alex Linares (guitar), Derek Doherty (bass) and Alex Pappas (drums) as Numb, changing their name in 2000.

05/04/2003 . . . . . 39 . . . . . . 2 . . . .   LETTERS TO YOU . . . . MCA MCSXD 40310

FINAL CUT – see TRUE FAITH AND BRIDGETTE GRACE WITH FINAL CUT

FINE YOUNG CANNIBALS UK group formed in 1984 by ex-Beat members Andy Cox (born 25/1/1960, Birmingham, guitar) and David Steele (born 8/9/1960, Isle of Wight, keyboards/bass) with singer Roland Gift (born 28/5/1962, Birmingham). Named after a 1960 Natalie Wood and Robert Wagner film (*All The Fine Young Cannibals*), they signed with London Records after a home video appeared on the TV music show *The Tube*. They were named Best British Group at the 1990 BRIT Awards, where *The Raw And The Cooked* won the Best Album category. They returned both trophies stating 'it is wrong and inappropriate for us to be associated with what amounts to a photo opportunity for Margaret Thatcher and the Conservative Party'. Gift signed solo with MCA in 2001.

08/06/1985 . . . . . 8 . . . . . 13 . . . . . .   JOHNNY COME HOME . . . . London LON 68

09/11/1985 . . . . . 41 . . . . . . 6 . . . . . .   BLUE . . . . London LON 79

11/01/1986	8	9		**SUSPICIOUS MINDS**	London LON 82
12/04/1986	58	4		FUNNY HOW LOVE IS	London LON 88
21/03/1987	9	10		**EVER FALLEN IN LOVE** Featured in the 1987 film *Something Wild*	London LON 121
07/01/1989	5	11		**SHE DRIVES ME CRAZY** ▲[1] Featured in the 1999 film *The Other Sister*	London LON 199
15/04/1989	7	8		**GOOD THING** ▲[1] Featured in the 1987 film *Tin Men*	London LON 218
19/08/1989	34	4		DON'T LOOK BACK	London LON 220
18/11/1989	20	8		I'M NOT THE MAN I USED TO BE	London LON 244
24/02/1990	46	3		I'M NOT SATISFIED	London LON 252
16/11/1996	17	3		THE FLAME	ffrr LONCD 389
11/01/1997	36	2		SHE DRIVES ME CRAZY (REMIX)	ffrr LONCD 391

FINITRIBE UK instrumental/production group comprising David Miller, Chris Connelly, Philip Pinsky, Simon McGlynn, Thomas McGregor and John Vick. By 1988 they were down to Miller, Vick and Pinsky, later adding vocalist Katy Morrison and recording film music.

| 11/07/1992 | 51 | 1 | | FOREVERGREEN | One Little Indian 74 TP12F |
| 19/11/1994 | 69 | 1 | | BRAND NEW | ffrr FCD 247 |

FINK BROTHERS UK vocal/instrumental duo Suggs (born Graham McPherson, 13/1/1961, Hastings) and Chas Smash (born Cathal Smyth 14/1/1959, London), both also in Madness.

| 09/02/1985 | 50 | 4 | | MUTANTS IN MEGA CITY ONE | Zarjazz JAZZ 2 |

FINN New Zealand vocal/instrumental duo of brothers Tim (born 25/6/1952, Te Awamutu) and Neil Finn (born 27/5/1958, Te Awamutu), both ex-Split Enz and Crowded House.

| 14/10/1995 | 29 | 3 | | SUFFER NEVER | Parlophone CDRS 6417 |
| 09/12/1995 | 41 | 2 | | ANGEL'S HEAP | Parlophone CDRS 6421 |

MICKY FINN – see URBAN SHAKEDOWN

NEIL FINN New Zealand guitarist/singer (born 27/5/1958, Te Awamutu) previously with Split Enz, Finn and Crowded House (all with brother Tim) before going solo.

13/06/1998	26	2		SHE WILL HAVE HER WAY	Parlophone CDR 6495
17/10/1998	39	1		SINNER	Parlophone CDR 6505
07/04/2001	32	2		WHEREVER YOU ARE	Parlophone CDRS 6557
22/09/2001	43	1		HOLE IN THE ICE	Parlophone CDRS 6563

TIM FINN New Zealand singer (born 25/6/1952, Te Awamutu) previously with Split Enz, Crowded House and Finn (all with brother Neil) before going solo.

| 26/06/1993 | 43 | 3 | | PERSUASION | Capitol CDCLS 692 |
| 18/09/1993 | 50 | 3 | | HIT THE GROUND RUNNING | Capitol CDCLS 694 |

FINN BROTHERS New Zealand family duo Neil (born 27/5/1958, Te Awamutu) and Tim Finn (born 25/6/1952, Te Awamutu).

| 21/08/2004 | 26 | 2 | | WON'T GIVE IN | Parlophone CDRS 6644 |
| 20/11/2004 | 31 | 1 | | NOTHING WRONG WITH YOU | Parlophone CDRS 6655 |

JOHNNIE FIORI – see BARKIN BROTHERS FEATURING JOHNNIE FIORI

ELISA FIORILLO US singer (born 1970, Philadelphia, PA).

| 28/11/1987 | 10 | 10 | | **WHO FOUND WHO** JELLYBEAN FEATURING ELISA FIORILLO | Chrysalis CHS JEL 1 |
| 13/02/1988 | 50 | 4 | | HOW CAN I FORGET YOU | Chrysalis ELISA 1 |

FIRE INC – see JIM STEINMAN

FIRE ISLAND UK instrumental/production group fronted by Pete Heller and Tony Farley.

08/08/1992	66	1		IN YOUR BONES/FIRE ISLAND	Boy's Own BOIX 11
12/03/1994	32	3		THERE BUT FOR THE GRACE OF GOD FIRE ISLAND FEATURING LOVE NELSON	Junior Boy's Own JBO 1BCD
04/03/1995	51	1		IF YOU SHOULD NEED A FRIEND FIRE ISLAND FEATURING MARK ANTHONI	Junior Boy's Own JBO 26CDS
11/04/1998	23	2		SHOUT TO THE TOP FIRE ISLAND FEATURING LOLEATTA HOLLOWAY	JBO JNR 5001573

FIREBALLS US rock group formed in Raton, NM by George Tomso (born 24/4/1940, Raton, lead guitar), Dan Trammell (born 14/07/40, rhythm guitar), Eric Budd (born 23/10/1938, drums), Stan Lark (born 27/7/1940, bass) and Chuck Tharp (born 3/2/1941, vocals). Trammell left in 1959. Budd left in 1962 and was replaced by Doug Roberts. Tharp left in 1960 and was replaced by Jimmy Gilmer. Roberts died on 18/11/1981.

| 27/07/1961 | 29 | 9 | | QUITE A PARTY | Pye International 7N 25092 |
| 14/11/1963 | 45 | 8 | | SUGAR SHACK ▲[5] JIMMY GILMER AND THE FIREBALLS | London HLD 9789 |

FIREHOUSE US rock group formed in North Carolina by CJ Snare (vocals), Bill Leverty (guitar), Perry Richardson (bass) and Michael Foster (drums).

| 13/07/1991 | 71 | 1 | | DON'T TREAT ME BAD | Epic 6567807 |
| 19/12/1992 | 65 | 1 | | WHEN I LOOK INTO YOUR EYES | Epic 6588347 |

❶[9] Number of weeks single topped the UK chart ↑ Entered the UK chart at #1 ▲[9] Number of weeks single topped the US chart

289

FIRM UK comedy/pop group fronted by Graham Lister and John O'Connor. Their two hits relate to the TV programmes *Minder* and *Star Trek*. They also included ex-Rubette Alan Williams.

17/07/1982.....14......9.......	ARTHUR DALEY ('E'S ALRIGHT)	Bark HID 1
06/06/1987 ...❶²....12.....○	**STAR TREKKIN'**	Bark TREK 1

FIRM FEATURING DAWN ROBINSON US rap group formed by Nas (born Nasir Jones, 1974, Long Island, NY), AZ (born Anthony Cruz, Brooklyn, NYC), Foxy Brown (born Inga Marchand, 6/9/1979, Brooklyn) and Dawn Robinson (born 28/11/1968, New London, CT). Robinson was also in En Vogue and Lucy Pearl before going solo in 2001.

29/11/1997.....18......3.......	FIRM BIZZ	Columbia 6651612

FIRST CHOICE US vocal group formed in Philadelphia, PA by Rochelle Fleming (born 11/2/1950, Philadelphia), Annette Guest (born 19/11/1954, Chester, PA) and Joyce Jones (born 30/7/1949, Philadelphia) as the Debronettes in the late 1960s. Jones left in 1977 and was replaced by Debbie Martin. They disbanded in 1984. Rochelle revived the group in 1987 with cousin Laconya Fleming and Lawrence Cottel, recording for Prelude.

19/05/1973.....16.....10......	ARMED AND EXTREMELY DANGEROUS	Bell 1297
04/08/1973 .....9......11......	**SMARTY PANTS**..	Bell 1324

FIRST CLASS UK studio group formed by Tony Burrows (born 14/4/1942, Exeter), John Carter, Del John and Chas Mills, backed by Spencer James (guitar), Clive Barrett (keyboards), Robin Straw (bass) and Eddie Richards (drums). Carter was also involved in the Flowerpot Men.

15/06/1974.....13.....10......	BEACH BABY	UK 66

FIRST EDITION – see KENNY ROGERS

FIRST LIGHT UK vocal/instrumental duo formed in 1982 by Paul Hardcatle and Derek Green, both ex-Direct Drive. Hardcastle later went solo.

21/05/1983.....65......3.......	EXPLAIN THE REASONS	London LON 26
28/01/1984.....71......2.......	WISH YOU WERE HERE	London LON 43

FIRSTBORN Irish producer Oisin Lunny.

19/06/1999.....69......1.......	THE MOOD CLUB Featured in the 1999 film *Human Traffic*..............................	Independiente ISOM 28MS

FISCHER-Z UK group formed by multi-instrumentalist/songwriter John Watts. By 1982 Watts recorded solo under his own name.

26/05/1979.....53......5.......	THE WORKER...	United Artists UP 36509
03/05/1980.....72......2.......	SO LONG	United Artists BP 342

FISCHERSPOONER US instrumental duo formed in New York by Warren Fischer and Casey Spooner.

20/07/2002.....25......3.......	EMERGE	Ministry Of Sound FSMOS 1CDS

FISH UK singer (born Derek William Dick, 25/5/1958, Dalkeith, Edinburgh) who was with Nottingham band the Stone Dome before successfully auditioning with Marillion in 1981. Fish left to go solo in September 1989.

18/10/1986.....75......1.......	SHORT CUT TO SOMEWHERE **FISH AND TONY BANKS**	Charisma CB 426
28/10/1989.....32......3.......	STATE OF MIND	EMI EM 109
06/01/1990.....25......4.......	BIG WEDGE...	EMI EM 125
17/03/1990.....30......3.......	A GENTLEMAN'S EXCUSE ME..	EMI EM 135
28/09/1991.....37......2.......	INTERNAL EXILE	Polydor FISHY 1
11/01/1992.....38......2.......	CREDO	Polydor FISHY 2
04/07/1992.....51......2.......	SOMETHING IN THE AIR	Polydor FISHY 3
16/04/1994.....46......1.......	LADY LET IT LIE	Dick Bros. DDICK 3CD1
01/10/1994.....67......1.......	FORTUNES OF WAR	Dick Bros. DDICK 008CD1
26/08/1995.....63......1.......	JUST GOOD FRIENDS **FISH FEATURING SAM BROWN**	Dick Bros. DDICK 014CD1

FISHBONE US group formed in Los Angeles, CA by 'Big' John Bigham (born 3/3/1969, Lidsville), Chris 'Maverick Meat' Dowd (born 20/9/1965, Las Vegas, NV), John Fisher (born 9/12/1965, El Camino, CA), Philip 'Fish' Fisher (born 16/7/1967, El Camino), Kendall Jones, 'Dirty' Walter Kibby (born 13/11/1964, Columbus, OH) and Angelo Moore (born 5/11/1965). Jones left in 1993 to join a religious sect, the rest being accused of kidnap when they tried to 'rescue' him.

01/08/1992.....60......2.......	EVERYDAY SUNSHINE/FIGHT THE YOUTH..	Columbia 6581937
28/08/1993.....54......1.......	SWIM...	Columbia 6596252

CEVIN FISHER US DJ/producer/singer based in New York.

03/10/1998.....34......2.......	THE FREAKS COME OUT **CEVIN FISHER'S BIG BREAK**................................	Sound Of Ministry MOSCDS 127
20/02/1999.....14......4.......	(YOU GOT ME) BURNING UP **CEVIN FISHER FEATURING LOLEATTA HOLLOWAY** Contains a sample of Loleatta Holloway's *Love Sensation*..	Wonderboy BOYD 013
07/08/1999.....67......1.......	MUSIC SAVED MY LIFE	Sm:☺e Communications SM 90982
20/01/2001.....54......1.......	IT'S A GOOD LIFE **CEVIN FISHER FEATURING RAMONA KELLY**	Wonderboy BOYD 022
24/02/2001.....60......1.......	LOVE YOU SOME MORE **CEVIN FISHER FEATURING SHELIA SMITH**	Subversive SUB 68D

EDDIE FISHER US singer (born Edwin Jack Fisher, 10/1/1928, Philadelphia, PA) who began on radio while still at school, playing New York's Copacabana at the age of seventeen. After stints with Buddy Morrow, Charlie Ventura and Eddie Cantor, and service in the

US Armed Forces Special Services, he was a major star in the 1950s. Marrying Debbie Reynolds in 1955 (their daughter is actress Carrie Fisher), he later wed Elizabeth Taylor and Connie Stevens. Films included *All About Eve* in 1950. He has two stars on the Hollywood Walk of Fame, for his contribution to recording and to TV.

02/01/1953	❶[1]	17		**OUTSIDE OF HEAVEN**	HMV B 10362
23/01/1953	8	5		**EVERYTHING I HAVE IS YOURS**	HMV B 10398
01/05/1953	3	15		**DOWNHEARTED**	HMV B 10450
22/05/1953	❶[1]	18		**I'M WALKING BEHIND YOU** ▲[7] EDDIE FISHER WITH SALLY SWEETLAND (SOPRANO)	HMV B 10489
06/11/1953	8	9		**WISH YOU WERE HERE** ▲[1]	HMV B 10564
22/01/1954	9	4		**OH MY PAPA** ▲[8]	HMV B 10614
29/10/1954	13	10		I NEED YOU NOW ▲[3]	HMV B 10755
18/03/1955	5	11		**WEDDING BELLS**	HMV B 10839
23/11/1956	5	16		**CINDY OH CINDY**	HMV POP 273

MARK FISHER FEATURING DOTTY GREEN
UK keyboard player who was discovered by Paul Hardcastle, with singer Dotty Green.

29/06/1985	59	2		LOVE SITUATION	Total Control TOCO 3

TONI FISHER
US singer (born 1931, Los Angeles, CA) known as Miss Toni Fisher on her US releases. She also had a US hit with *West Of The Wall*, inspired by the Berlin Wall. She died from a heart attack on 12/2/1999.

12/02/1960	30	1		THE BIG HURT	Top Rank JAR 261

FITS OF GLOOM
UK/Italian vocal/production duo Lizzy Mack and Gianfranco Bortolotti.

04/06/1994	47	2		HEAVEN	Media MCSTD 1981
05/11/1994	49	2		THE POWER OF LOVE FITS OF GLOOM FEATURING LIZZY MACK	Media MCSTD 2016

ELLA FITZGERALD
US singer (born 25/4/1917, Newport News, VA) who was discovered after winning the Harlem Amateur Hour in 1934 and hired by Chick Webb. After his death in 1939 she fronted Webb's band for the next three years. Known as 'The First Lady Of Jazz', her films included *St Louis Blues* (1939) and *Pete Kelly's Blues* (1955). Thirteen Grammy Awards included Best Female Vocal Performance and Best Individual Jazz Performance in 1958 for *Ella Fitzgerald Sings The Irving Berlin Song Book*, Best Individual Jazz Performance in 1959 for *Ella Swings Lightly*, Best Female Vocal Performance (Album) in 1960 for *Mack The Knife*, Best Female Solo Vocal Performance in 1962 for *Ella Swings Brightly With Nelson Riddle*, Best Jazz Vocal Performance in 1976 for *Fitzgerald And Pass...Again*, Best Jazz Vocal Performance in 1979 for *Fine And Mellow*, Best Female Jazz Vocal Performance in 1980 for *A Perfect Match*, Best Female Jazz Vocal Performance in 1981 for *Digital III At Montreaux*, Best Female Jazz Vocal Performance in 1983 for *The Best Is Yet To Come* and Best Female Jazz Vocal Performance in 1990 for *All That Jazz*. She was awarded a Lifetime Achievement Grammy in 1967. After complications from diabetes she had both legs amputated below the knee in 1993, and died from a stroke on 15/6/1996. She has a star on the Hollywood Walk of Fame.

23/05/1958	15	5		SWINGIN' SHEPHERD BLUES	HMV POP 486
16/10/1959	25	3		BUT NOT FOR ME 1959 Grammy Award for Best Female Vocal Performance. Featured in the 1959 film *But Not For Me*	HMV POP 657
21/04/1960	19	9		MACK THE KNIFE 1960 Grammy Award for Best Female Vocal Performance, Single or Track	HMV POP 736
06/10/1960	46	1		HOW HIGH THE MOON	HMV POP 782
22/11/1962	38	6		DESAFINADO	Verve VS 502
30/04/1964	34	5		CAN'T BUY ME LOVE	Verve VS 519

SCOTT FITZGERALD
UK singer (born William McPhail) and a top session singer. Yvonne Keeley had recorded unsuccessfully when they teamed up. His 1988 Eurovision entry came second to Celine Dion singing *Ne Partez Sans Moi* for Switzerland.

14/01/1978	3	10	O	**IF I HAD WORDS** SCOTT FITZGERALD AND YVONNE KEELEY AND THE ST. THOMAS MORE SCHOOL CHOIR Featured in the 1995 film *Babe*	Pepper UP 36333
07/05/1988	52	2		GO UK entry for the 1988 Eurovision Song Contest (came second)	PRT PYS 10

FIVE
UK vocal group formed by James 'J' Brown (born 13/6/1976, Aldershot), Scott Robinson (born 22/11/1979, Basildon), Sean Conlon (born 20/5/1981, Leeds), Abs (born Richard Abidin Breen, 29/6/1979, Enfield) and Richard Neville (born Richard Dobson, 23/8/1979, Birmingham). They began as 5IVE, changing after the first three singles. Named Best Pop Act at the 2000 BRIT Awards, they had previously won the Select UK & Ireland Award at the 1998 MTV Europe Music Awards. They disbanded in September 2001.

13/12/1997	10	9		**SLAM DUNK (DA FUNK)** Contains a sample of Herbie's *Clap Your Hands*	RCA 74321537352
14/03/1998	4	9		**WHEN THE LIGHTS GO OUT**	RCA 74321562312
20/06/1998	3	13	O	**GOT THE FEELIN'**	RCA 74321584892
12/09/1998	2	12		**EVERYBODY GET UP** Contains a sample of Joan Jett's *I Love Rock 'N' Roll*	RCA 74321613752
28/11/1998	2	12	O	**UNTIL THE TIME IS THROUGH**	RCA 74321632602
31/07/1999	2	12	O	**IF YA GETTING' DOWN** Contains a sample of Indeep's *Last Night A DJ Saved My Life*	RCA 74321689692
06/11/1999	❶[1]	17	●	**KEEP ON MOVIN'** ↑	RCA 74321709862
18/03/2000	9	12		**DON'T WANNA LET YOU GO**	RCA 74321745302
29/07/2000	❶[1]	13		**WE WILL ROCK YOU** ↑ FIVE AND QUEEN	RCA 74321774022
25/08/2001	❶[2]	12		**LET'S DANCE** ↑	RCA 74321875962
03/11/2001	4	12		**CLOSER TO ME**	RCA 74321900742

FIVE FOR FIGHTING
US guitarist/singer John Ondrasik (born in Los Angeles, CA) who made his first album in 1997.

01/06/2002	48	1		SUPERMAN (IT'S NOT EASY)	Columbia 6727202

5,6,7,8'S Japanese group formed in Osaka by Sachiko Fujii, Yoshiko Yamaguchi and Ronnie Yoshiko who appeared in the film *Kill Bill*. Their debut hit was originally released in 1996.

17/07/2004.....28......2.......	WOO HOO Featured in the 2003 film *Kill Bill*. The track was revived after featuring in an advertisement for Carlsberg............. ....Sweet Nothing CSSN028
18/09/2004.....71......1.......	I'M BLUE...Sweet Nothing CSSN029

FIVE SMITH BROTHERS UK family vocal group who were first widely heard on the Tony Hancock radio show *Forces All Star Bill* in 1952 and later became popular in Scotland and Ireland. Their albums were billed *Mr & Mrs Smith's Five Little Boys*.

22/07/1955.....20......1.......	I'M IN FAVOUR OF FRIENDSHIP ....Decca F 10527

FIVE STAR UK family group formed as a trio in Romford in 1983 by Doris (born 8/6/1966, Romford), Lorraine (born 10/8/1967, Romford) and Deniece Pearson (born 13/6/1968, Romford). A successful demo prompted father Buster to launch the Tent label, adding his two sons Stedman (born 29/6/1964, Romford) and Delroy (born 11/4/1970, Romford) to the line-up, although they were still studying. As Five Star on BBC's *Pebble Mill At One* they attracted RCA, Buster informing the company that the group was already signed but that Tent as a label was available. They were named Best British Group at the 1987 BRIT Awards.

04/05/1985.....15......12......	ALL FALL DOWN ....Tent PB 40039
20/07/1985.....18......9......	LET ME BE THE ONE ....Tent PB 40193
14/09/1985.....25......9......	LOVE TAKE OVER ....Tent PB 40353
16/11/1985.....45......5......	RSVP ....Tent PB 40445
11/01/1986 .....3......11......O	**SYSTEM ADDICT** ....Tent PB 40515
12/04/1986 .....7......10......	**CAN'T WAIT ANOTHER MINUTE** ....Tent PB 40697
26/07/1986 .....7......10......	**FIND THE TIME** ....Tent PB 40799
13/09/1986 .....2......11......O	**RAIN OR SHINE**...Tent PB 40901
22/11/1986.....15......9......	IF I SAY YES ....Tent PB 40981
07/02/1987 .....9......8......	**STAY OUT OF MY LIFE**...Tent PB 41131
18/04/1987 .....4......9......	**THE SLIGHTEST TOUCH** ....Tent PB 41265
22/08/1987.....11......6......	WHENEVER YOU'RE READY..Tent PB 41477
10/10/1987.....16......7......	STRONG AS STEEL ....Tent PB 41565
05/12/1987.....23......6......	SOMEWHERE SOMEBODY...Tent PB 41661
04/06/1988.....18......4......	ANOTHER WEEKEND ....Tent PB 42081
06/08/1988.....28......4......	ROCK MY WORLD ....Tent PB 42145
17/09/1988.....61......2......	THERE'S A BRAND NEW WORLD ....Tent PB 42235
19/11/1988.....51......3......	LET ME BE YOURS...Tent PB 42343
08/04/1989.....49......2......	WITH EVERY HEARTBEAT ....Tent PB 42693
10/03/1990.....54......2......	TREAT ME LIKE A LADY ....Tent FIVE 1
07/07/1990.....68......1......	HOT LOVE ....Tent FIVE 2

FIVE THIRTY UK group formed in London by Tara Milton (bass/vocals), Paul Bassett (guitar/vocals) and Phil Hooper (drums).

04/08/1990.....75......1......	ABSTAIN ....East West YZ 530
25/05/1991.....67......1......	13TH DISCIPLE ....East West YZ 577
03/08/1991.....75......1......	SUPERNOVA ....East West YZ 594
02/11/1991.....72......1......	YOU (EP) Tracks on EP: *You, Cuddly Drug* and *Slow Train Into The Ocean*....................East West YZ 624

5000 VOLTS UK studio group featuring Tina Charles, Martin Jay, Roger O'Dell and Tony Eyers. For publicity purposes Luan Peters (an actress who played Australian guest Raylene Miles in *Fawlty Towers*) was shown as the female singer. After the single's success via TV appearances with Peters, Tina Charles went solo so Linda Kelly recorded the vocals for the second hit.

06/09/1975 .....4......9......	**I'M ON FIRE** ....Philips 6006 464
24/07/1976 .....8......9......	**DR KISS KISS**..Philips 6006 533

FIXATE UK vocal group formed by Paul Middleton (born 2/12/1979, London), Christian Fry (born 14/12/1976, London), Justin Osuji (born 17/10/1983, Glasgow), Jamie and John, the latter two later replaced by Rich.

14/07/2001.....42......1......	24/7 ....Epark EPKFIX CD1

FIXX UK group formed in London by Cy Curnin (guitar/vocals), Jamie West-Oram (guitar), Rupert Greenall (keyboards), Charlie Barrett (bass) and Adam Woods (drums). Barrett left in 1983 and was replaced by Alfred Agies, who left in 1985 and was replaced by Dan K Brown.

24/04/1982.....54......4......	STAND OR FALL...MCA FIXX 2
17/07/1982.....57......4......	RED SKIES ....MCA FIXX 3

FKW UK vocal/instrumental group fronted by Steve Lee.

02/10/1993.....48......2......	NEVER GONNA (GIVE YOU UP) ....PWL International PWCD 273
11/12/1993.....45......2......	SEIZE THE DAY ....PWL International PWCD 279
05/03/1994.....30......3......	JINGO ....PWL International PWCD 283
04/06/1994.....63......1......	THIS IS THE WAY ....PWL International PWCD 307

ROBERTA FLACK US singer (born 10/2/1937, Black Mountain, NC). After graduating in music (she was a university classmate of Donny Hathaway), she taught music at high school, singing in clubs in her spare time. She was spotted by Atlantic artist Les McCann and released her first album in 1970.

27/05/1972.....14......14......	THE FIRST TIME EVER I SAW YOUR FACE ▲[6] Featured in the 1971 film *Play Misty For Me*. 1972 Grammy Award for Record of the Year ....Atlantic K 10161

05/08/1972.....29......7......	WHERE IS THE LOVE **ROBERTA FLACK AND DONNY HATHAWAY** 1972 Grammy Award for Best Pop Vocal Performance by a Duo......
	.... Atlantic K 10202
17/02/1973 .....6......14......	**KILLING ME SOFTLY WITH HIS SONG** ▲5 1973 Grammy Awards for Record of the Year, Best Pop Vocal Performance plus Song of the Year for writers Norman Gimbel and Charles Fox. Originally written for Lori Lieberman about singer Don McLean .... Atlantic K 10282
24/08/1974.....34......7......	FEEL LIKE MAKING LOVE ▲1 .... Atlantic K 10467
06/05/1978.....42......4......	THE CLOSER I GET TO YOU .... Atlantic K 11099
17/05/1980.....3......11......	**BACK TOGETHER AGAIN** This and above single credited to **ROBERTA FLACK AND DONNY HATHAWAY**............ Atlantic K 11481
30/08/1980.....44......7......	DON'T MAKE ME WAIT TOO LONG .... Atlantic K 11555
20/08/1983 .....2......13.....O	**TONIGHT I CELEBRATE MY LOVE PEABO BRYSON AND ROBERTA FLACK** .... Capitol CL 302
29/07/1989.....72......2......	UH-UH OOH OOH LOOK OUT (HERE IT COMES).. Atlantic A 8491

FLAJ – see **GETO BOYS FEATURING FLAJ**

FLAMING LIPS US rock group formed in Oklahoma City in 1983 by Michael Ivins (born 17/3/1965, Omaha, NE, bass/vocals), Ron Jones (born 26/11/1970, Angeles, Philippines, guitar), Mark Coyne and Wayne Coyne (born 17/3/1965, Pittsburgh, PA, guitar/vocals). By 1999 the group comprised Ivins, Wayne Coyne and Steven Drozd (born 6/12/1969, Houston, TX, drums). They won the 2002 Grammy Award for Best Rock Instrumental Performance for *Approaching Pavonis Mons By Balloon (Utopia Planitia)*.

09/03/1996.....72......1......	THIS HERE GIRAFFE .... Warner Brothers W 0335CD
26/06/1999.....39......2......	RACE FOR THE PRIZE .... Warner Brothers W 494CD
20/11/1999.....73......1......	WAITIN' FOR A SUPERMAN .... Warner Brothers W 505CD
31/08/2002.....32......2......	DO YOU REALIZE.. Warner Brothers W 586CD
25/01/2003.....18......3......	YOSHIMI BATTLES THE PINK ROBOTS PART 1 .... Warner Brothers W 595CD
05/07/2003.....28......2......	FIGHT TEST Shared royalties with Cat Stevens because of the similarities between this song and Steven's *Father And Son* ....
	.... Warner Brothers W 611CD
27/09/2003.....17......4......	THE GOLDEN PATH **CHEMICAL BROTHERS FEATURING THE FLAMING LIPS**................................... Virgin CHEMSD 18

FLAMINGOS US R&B vocal group formed in Chicago, IL in 1951 by Zeke Carey (born 24/1/1933), Jake Carey (born 9/9/1926), Paul Wilson (born 6/1/1935) and Johnny Carter (born 2/6/1934) with lead singer Sollie McElroy (born 16/7/1933). They debuted for Chess in 1953. McElroy left in 1954 and was replaced by Nate Nelson (born 10/4/1932). Later members included Tommy Hunt and Terry Johnson. Nelson died from a heart attack on 1/6/1984, Wilson on 15/5/1988, McElroy from cancer on 16/1/1995 and Jake Carey from a heart attack on 10/12/1997. They were inducted into the Rock & Roll Hall of Fame in 2001.

04/06/1969.....26......5.......	BOOGALOO PARTY Originally a US hit in 1966 reaching #93 .... Philips BF 1786

MICHAEL FLANDERS UK singer (born 1/3/1922, London), better known as half of the Flanders And Swann duo with Donald Swann (born 30/9/1923, Llanelli, died 23/3/1994). First teaming up in 1940, they were still working together into the 1960s. Flanders was awarded an OBE in 1964 and died on 14/4/1975.

27/02/1959.....20......3.......	LITTLE DRUMMER BOY **MICHAEL FLANDERS WITH THE MICHAEL SAMMES SINGERS** .... Parlophone R 4528

FLASH AND THE PAN Australian group built around George Young (born 6/11/1947, Glasgow), elder brother of AC/DC's Angus and Malcolm, and Harry Vanda (born Harold Wandon, 22/3/1947, The Hague, Holland), both of whom were ex-Easybeats and later responsible for John Paul Young's hit *Love Is In The Air*.

23/09/1978.....54......4.......	AND THE BAND PLAYED ON (DOWN AMONG THE DEAD MEN)... Ensign ENY 15
21/05/1983 .....7......11.......	**WAITING FOR A TRAIN** .... Easybeat EASY 1

FLASH BROTHERS Israeli trio formed in Nazareth by brothers Ruven, Ilan and Shmuel Flaishler.

06/11/2004.....75......1.......	AMEN (DON'T BE AFRAID) .... Direction 6754362

LESTER FLATT AND EARL SCRUGGS US banjo duo Lester Flatt (born 28/6/1914, Overton County, TN) and Earl Scruggs (born 6/1/1924, Cleveland County, NC) who teamed up in 1948. Two versions of their hit were available, the 1949 Mercury original and a 1965 re-recording on CBS, sales being totalled to calculate the chart position. The UK success prompted similar US releases, which combined reached #55 in April 1966. They also recorded the theme to the TV series *The Beverly Hillbillies*. Lester Flatt died in Nashville on 11/5/1979; Earl Scruggs has a star on the Hollywood Walk of Fame.

15/11/1967.....39......6.......	FOGGY MOUNTAIN BREAKDOWN Featured in the 1967 film *Bonnie And Clyde*. 1968 Grammy Award for Best Country & Western Performance by a Duo .... CBS 3038/Mercury MF 1007

FOGWELL FLAX AND THE ANKLEBITERS FROM FREEHOLD JUNIOR SCHOOL UK singer/comedian/impressionist (born in Liverpool) who became known via the TV series *Search For A Star*.

26/12/1981.....68......2.......	ONE NINE FOR SANTA .... EMI 5255

FLB – see **FAT LARRY'S BAND**

FLEE-REKKERS UK instrumental group formed by Peter Fleerackers (saxophone), Elmy Durrant (saxophone), Dave 'Tex' Cameron (guitar), Ronald Marion (guitar), Derek Skinner (bass) and Phil Curtis (drums). They were originally called the Ramblers, then Statesiders, before Flee-Rekkers.

19/05/1960.....23 .....13	GREEN JEANS Based on the traditional folk song *Greensleeves* .... Triumph RGM 1008

❶9 Number of weeks single topped the UK chart ↑ Entered the UK chart at #1 ▲9 Number of weeks single topped the US chart

293

FLEETWOOD MAC
UK/US rock group formed in 1967 by Mick Fleetwood (born 24/6/1942, Redruth, Cornwall, drums), Peter Green (born Peter Greenbaum, 29/10/1946, London, guitar), Jeremy Spencer (born 4/7/1948, West Hartlepool, guitar) and Bob Brunning (bass). John McVie (born 26/11/1945, London), who had been in John Mayall's Bluesbreakers with Fleetwood and Green, replaced Brunning a month later. Among numerous changes, Danny Kirwan (guitar) was added in 1968, Green and Spencer left in 1970, McVie's wife Christine (born Christine Perfect, 12/7/1943, Birmingham, keyboards) joined in 1970, Bob Welch (guitar) joined in 1971 and left in 1974 when they moved to California. There they recruited Lindsey Buckingham (born 3/10/1947, Palo Alto, CA) and girlfriend Stevie Nicks (born 26/5/1948, Pheonix, AZ) in December 1974. Buckingham went solo in 1987. Christine McVie and Nicks stopped touring in 1990, both going solo. They were presented with the Outstanding Contribution to British Music at the 1998 BRIT Awards and were inducted into the Rock & Roll Hall of Fame in 1998. They won the 1977 Grammy Award for Album of the Year for *Rumours* and have a star on the Hollywood Walk of Fame.

DATE	POS	WKS	BPI	SINGLE TITLE	LABEL & NUMBER
10/04/1968	37	7		BLACK MAGIC WOMAN	Blue Horizon 57 3138
17/07/1968	31	13		NEED YOUR LOVE SO BAD	Blue Horizon 57 3139
04/12/1968	◉¹	20		**ALBATROSS**	Blue Horizon 57 3145
16/04/1969	2	14		**MAN OF THE WORLD**	Immediate IM 080
23/07/1969	32	9		NEED YOUR LOVE SO BAD	Blue Horizon 57 3157
04/10/1969	2	16		**OH WELL**	Reprise RS 27000
23/05/1970	10	12		**THE GREEN MANALISHI (WITH THE TWO-PRONG CROWN)**	Reprise RS 27007
12/05/1973	2	15	○	**ALBATROSS** Re-issue of Blue Horizon 57 3145	CBS 8306
13/11/1976	40	4		SAY YOU LOVE ME	Reprise K 14447
19/02/1977	38	4		GO YOUR OWN WAY Featured in the films *Forrest Gump* (1994) and *Casino* (1996)	Warner Brothers K 16872
30/04/1977	32	5		DON'T STOP Subsequently adopted by Bill Clinton for his presidential campaign. The group performed the song at his inauguration at the Capitol Centre, Landover, MD in January 1993	Warner Brothers K 16930
09/07/1977	24	9		DREAMS ▲¹	Warner Brothers K 16969
22/10/1977	45	2		YOU MAKE LOVING FUN	Warner Brothers K 17013
11/03/1978	46	3		RHIANNON	Warner Brothers K 14430
06/10/1979	6	10	○	TUSK Features the uncredited contribution of the USC Trojan Marching Band (the 260-piece band was too large to fit into a studio, so their contribution was recorded live at the Dodger Stadium in Los Angeles)	Warner Brothers K 17468
22/12/1979	37	8		SARA	Warner Brothers K 17533
25/09/1982	46	3		GYPSY	Warner Brothers K 17997
18/12/1982	9	15		**OH DIANE**	Warner Brothers FLEET 1
04/04/1987	9	12		**BIG LOVE**	Warner Brothers W 8398
11/07/1987	56	4		SEVEN WONDERS	Warner Brothers W 8317
26/09/1987	5	12		**LITTLE LIES**	Warner Brothers W 8291
26/12/1987	54	5		FAMILY MAN	Warner Brothers W 8114
02/04/1988	4	10		**EVERYWHERE**	Warner Brothers W 8143
18/06/1988	60	2		ISN'T IT MIDNIGHT	Warner Brothers W 7860
17/12/1988	66	3		AS LONG AS YOU FOLLOW	Warner Brothers W 7644
05/05/1990	53	3		SAVE ME	Warner Brothers W 9866
25/08/1990	58	3		IN THE BACK OF MY MIND	Warner Brothers W 9739

FLEETWOODS
US trio formed in high school in Olympia, WA by Gary Troxell (born 28/11/1939, Centralia, WA), Gretchen Christopher (born 29/2/1940, Olympia) and Barbara Ellis (born 20/2/1940, Olympia) as Two Girls And A Guy. They were renamed The Fleetwoods by Bob Reisdorff, who founded Dolphin Records for their debut. Troxell, drafted into the navy, was replaced by Vic Dana.

DATE	POS	WKS	BPI	SINGLE TITLE	LABEL & NUMBER
24/04/1959	6	8		**COME SOFTLY TO ME** ▲⁴	London HLU 8841

JOHN 'OO' FLEMING
UK DJ/producer born in Worthing.

DATE	POS	WKS	BPI	SINGLE TITLE	LABEL & NUMBER
25/12/1999	74	1		LOST IN EMOTION	React CDREACT 170
12/08/2000	61	1		FREE	React CDREACT 186
02/02/2002	74	1		BELFAST TRANCE JOHN 'OO' FLEMING AND SIMPLE MINDS	Nebula BELFCD 001

FLESH AND BONES
Belgian production duo Regi Penxten and DJ Wout Van Dessel with singer Birgit Casteleyn. Van Dessel had previously recorded as Sylver.

DATE	POS	WKS	BPI	SINGLE TITLE	LABEL & NUMBER
10/08/2002	70	1		I LOVE YOU	Multiply CDMULTY 86

FLICKMAN
Italian dance group formed by Andrea Mazzali and Giuliano Orlandi.

DATE	POS	WKS	BPI	SINGLE TITLE	LABEL & NUMBER
04/03/2000	11	5		THE SOUND OF BAMBOO Contains a sample of Eddy Grant's *The House Of Bamboo*	Inferno CDFERN 25
28/04/2001	69	1		HEY! PARADISE	Inferno CDFERN 37

KC FLIGHTT
US rapper Franklin Toson. Funky Junction is Italian producer Constantino 'Mixmaster' Padovano.

DATE	POS	WKS	BPI	SINGLE TITLE	LABEL & NUMBER
01/04/1989	48	4		PLANET E Contains a sample of Talking Head's *Once In A Lifetime*	RCA PT 49404
12/05/2001	59	1		VOICES KC FLIGHTT VS FUNKY JUNCTION Contains a sample of Police's *Voices In My Head*	Hooj Choons HOOJ 106CD

BERNIE FLINT
UK singer (born 1952, Southport) who won various TV talent contests, including *Opportunity Knocks* twelve times. When the singles charted he was working as a delivery man for a laundry company.

DATE	POS	WKS	BPI	SINGLE TITLE	LABEL & NUMBER
19/03/1977	3	10	○	**I DON'T WANT TO PUT A HOLD ON YOU**	EMI 2599
23/07/1977	48	1		SOUTHERN COMFORT	EMI 2621

FLINTLOCK UK group fronted by singer/songwriter Mike Holloway. Their follow-up was *Sea Of Flames*. Later TV presenter Keith Chegwin was briefly a member.

29/05/1976.....30......5...... DAWN...Pinnacle P 8419

FLIP AND FILL UK production duo Graham Turner and Mark Hall. They also record as Bus Stop.

24/03/2001.....34......3...... TRUE LOVE NEVER DIES....................................All Around The World CDGLOBE 240
02/02/2002......7......10...... **TRUE LOVE NEVER DIES (REMIX)** This and above single credited to **FLIP AND FILL FEATURING KELLY LLORENNA**..................
....All Around The World CDGLOBE 248
27/07/2002......3......10...... **SHOOTING STAR** Features the uncredited contribution of Karen Parry....................All Around The World CDGLOBE 258
18/01/2003.....13......7...... I WANNA DANCE WITH SOMEBODY Features the uncredited contribution of Jo James........All Around The World CDGLOBE 275
22/03/2003.....28......2...... SHAKE YA SHIMMY **PORN KINGS VERSUS FLIP & FILL FEATURING 740 BOYZ**.....All Around The World CXGLOBE 213
28/06/2003.....28......2...... FIELD OF DREAMS **FLIP & FILL FEATURING JO JAMES**...........................All Around The World CDGLOBE 273
17/01/2004.....20......4...... IRISH BLUE **FLIP & FILL FEATURING JUNIOR VAN-BROWN**..................All Around The World CXGLOBE 309
24/07/2004.....11......7...... DISCOLAND **FLIP & FILL FEATURING KAREN PARRY**.........................All Around The World CDGLOBE 346

FLIPMODE SQUAD US rap group formed in New York by Busta Rhymes (born Trevor Smith, 20/5/1972, Brooklyn, NYC), Rampage, Rah Digga (born Rashia Fisher, 1975, Newark, NJ), Serious and Spliff Star.

31/10/1998.....54......1....... CHA CHA CHA...Elektra E 3810CD

F.L.O. – see **RAHNI HARRIS AND F.L.O.**

FLOATERS US R&B vocal group assembled in Detroit, MI by ex-Detroit Emeralds James Mitchell and Marvin Willis, with Charles Clark (Libra), Larry Cunningham (Cancer), Paul Mitchell (Leo) and Ralph Mitchell (Aquarius), their hit single being based around their star signs and the type of girls they liked.

23/07/1977.....❶[1].....11.....○ **FLOAT ON**...ABC 4187

A FLOCK OF SEAGULLS UK techno-rock group formed in Liverpool in 1979 by Mike Score (born 5/11/1957, keyboards/vocals), Frank Maudsley (born 10/11/1959, bass), Paul Reynolds (born 4/8/1962, guitar) and Ali Score (drums). They won the 1982 Grammy Award for Best Rock Instrumental Performance for *D.N.A.*, disbanding in 1986.

27/03/1982.....43......6..... I RAN...Jive 14
12/06/1982.....34......6....... SPACE AGE LOVE SONG Featured in the 1998 film *The Wedding Singer*...........................Jive 17
06/11/1982.....10.....12.....○ **WISHING (IF I HAD A PHOTOGRAPH OF YOU)**...............................Jive 25
23/04/1983.....53......3..... NIGHTMARES..Jive 33
25/06/1983.....38......5..... TRANSFER AFFECTION...Jive 41
14/07/1984.....26.....11..... THE MORE YOU LIVE, THE MORE YOU LOVE..Jive 62
19/10/1985.....66......3..... WHO'S THAT GIRL (SHE'S GOT IT)..Jive 106

FLOETRY UK duo formed in London by Marsha Ambrosius and Natalie Stewart, later relocating to the US.

26/04/2003.....73......1....... FLOETIC..DreamWorks 4507752

FLOORPLAY UK production duo A Fresco and S Gali.

27/01/1996.....50......1....... AUTOMATIC...Perfecto PERF 115CD

FLOWER POWER – see **DANNII MINOGUE**

FLOWERED UP UK group formed in London in 1989 by Liam Maher (vocals), Joe Maher (guitar), Andy Jackson (bass), Tim Dorney (keyboards) and John Tovey (drums), their act often 'supplemented' by Barry Mooncult dancing on stage wearing a giant flower.

28/07/1990.....54......4....... IT'S ON..Heavenly HVN 3
24/11/1990.....75......1....... PHOBIA...Heavenly HVN 7
11/05/1991.....34......4....... TAKE IT..London FUP 1
17/08/1991.....38......3....... IT'S ON/EGG RUSH (RE-RECORDING)..London FUP 2
02/05/1992.....20......5....... WEEKENDER..Heavenly HVN 16

FLOWERPOT MEN UK vocal group formed by Tony Burrows (born 14/4/1942, Exeter), Robin Shaw, Perry Ford and Neil Landon, assembled by writers and producers John Carter and Ken Lewis. All four were earlier in the Ivy League; the production team were responsible for First Class. For live dates they were backed by Jon Lord (keyboards), Nick Simper (bass), Ged Peck (guitar) and Carlo Little (drums).

23/08/1967......4......12...... **LET'S GO TO SAN FRANCISCO**..Deram DM 142

MIKE FLOWERS POPS UK group fronted by Mike Flowers. With a 1960s feel, and Flowers wearing a blond wig and flares, their hits were basically parodies of the originals.

30/12/1995......2......9.....○ **WONDERWALL**...London LONCD 378
08/06/1996.....39......2...... LIGHT MY FIRE/PLEASE RELEASE ME...London LONCD 384
28/12/1996.....30......3...... DON'T CRY FOR ME ARGENTINA..Love This LUVTHISCD 16

EDDIE FLOYD US singer (born 25/6/1935, Montgomery, AL, raised in Detroit, MI) who was a founder member of the Falcons. He recorded solo for Lupine and Safice before moving to Memphis in 1965 and signing with Stax.

02/02/1967.....19.....18...... KNOCK ON WOOD..Atlantic 584 041
16/03/1967.....42......3...... RAISE YOUR HAND..Stax 601 001
09/08/1967.....31......8...... THINGS GET BETTER...Stax 601 016

❶[9] Number of weeks single topped the UK chart ↑ Entered the UK chart at #1 ▲[9] Number of weeks single topped the US chart

295

FLUFFY
UK group formed by Amanda Rootes (vocals), Bridget Jones (guitar), Helen Storer (bass) and Angie Adams (drums).

| 17/02/1996 | 58 | 1 | | HUSBAND | Parkway PARK 006CD |
| 05/10/1996 | 52 | 1 | | NOTHING | Virgin VSCDT 1614 |

FLUKE
UK instrumental/production group formed in 1989 by Mike Bryant (born 1/5/1960, High Wycombe), Michael Tournier (born 24/5/1963, High Wycombe) and Jonathan Fugler (born 13/10/1962, St Austell, Cornwall). They also record as Lucky Monkeys. Tournier and Fugler were both earlier in Skin, Tournier later recording as Syntax.

20/03/1993	59	1		SLID	Circa YRCD 103
19/06/1993	58	2		ELECTRIC GUITAR Contains a sample of Jimi Hendrix' *Crosstown Traffic*	Circa YRCD 104
11/09/1993	45	3		GROOVY FEELING	Circa YRCD 106
23/04/1994	37	2		BUBBLE	Circa YRCD 110
29/07/1995	23	3		BULLET	Circa YRCD 121
16/12/1995	32	3		TOSH	Circa YRCD 122
16/11/1996	20	3		ATOM BOMB Featured in the films *The Saint* (1997) and *Behind Enemy Lines* (2001)	Virgin YRCD 125
31/05/1997	25	2		ABSURD Used as the theme to Sky TV's Monday night football coverage. Featured in the 2001 film *Lara Croft: Tomb Raider*	Virgin YRCD 126
27/09/1997	46	1		SQUIRT	Circa YRCD 127

FLUSH – see SLADE

FLYING LIZARDS
UK group formed by David Cunningham, featuring the half-spoken vocals of Deborah Evans. Their debut was a cover of Barrett Strong's 1960 US hit and cost £10 to record. Later members included Patti Paladin, Peter Gordan, Steve Beresford and David Toop.

| 04/08/1979 | 5 | 10 | O | MONEY Featured in the films *The Wedding Singer* (1998) and *Charlies Angels* (2000) | Virgin VS 276 |
| 09/02/1980 | 43 | 6 | | TV | Virgin VS 325 |

FLYING PICKETS
UK a cappella group formed in 1980 by Rick Lloyd, Ken Gregson, Gareth Williams, David Brett, Brian Hibbard (born 25/11/1946, Wales) and Red Stripe. Hibbard was later an actor, playing garage mechanic Doug Murray in *Coronation Street*.

26/11/1983	❶⁵	11	●	ONLY YOU	10 TEN 14
21/04/1984	7	8		WHEN YOU'RE YOUNG AND IN LOVE	10 TEN 20
08/12/1984	71	1		WHO'S THAT GIRL	10 GIRL 1

FM
UK rock group formed in 1985 by Steve Overland (guitar/vocals), Chris Overland (guitar), Didge Digital (keyboards), Merv Goldsworthy (bass) and Pete Jupp (drums). They disbanded in 1990, re-forming in 1991 with Andy Barnett replacing Chris Overland, and Digital leaving after one more album.

31/01/1987	64	2		FROZEN HEART	Portrait DIDGE 1
20/06/1987	71	2		LET LOVE BE THE LEADER	Portrait MERV 1
05/08/1989	54	4		BAD LUCK	Epic 6550317
07/10/1989	64	2		SOMEDAY (YOU'LL COME RUNNING)	CBS DINK 1
10/02/1990	73	1		EVERYTIME I THINK OF YOU	Epic DINK 2

FOCUS
Dutch rock group formed in Amsterdam in 1969 by Jan Akkerman (born 24/12/1946, Amsterdam, guitar), Thijs Van Leer (born 31/3/1948, Amsterdam, flute/keyboards), Martin Dresden (bass) and Hans Cleuver (drums). They disbanded in 1978.

| 20/01/1973 | 20 | 10 | | HOCUS POCUS | Polydor 2001 211 |
| 27/01/1973 | 4 | 11 | | SYLVIA | Polydor 2001 422 |

FOG
US DJ/producer Ralph Falcon.

| 19/02/1994 | 44 | 2 | | BEEN A LONG TIME | Columbia 6601212 |
| 06/06/1998 | 27 | 2 | | BEEN A LONG TIME (REMIX) | Pukka CDPUKKA 16 |

DAN FOGELBERG
US guitarist/songwriter (born 13/8/1951, Peoria, IL) who began as a folk singer in Los Angeles. He toured with Van Morrison before relocating to Nashville and signing solo with Columbia. He later switched to Full Moon.

| 15/03/1980 | 59 | 4 | | LONGER | Epic EPC 8230 |

BEN FOLDS FIVE
US rock group formed in North Carolina in 1993 by Ben Folds (born 12/9/1966, Winston-Salem, NC, keyboards/vocals), Darren Jessee (born 8/4/1971, drums) and Robert Sledge (born 9/3/1968, bass). They disbanded in 2001, Folds going solo.

14/09/1996	37	2		UNDERGROUND	Caroline CDCAR 008
01/03/1997	26	3		BATTLE OF WHO COULD CARE LESS	Epic 6642302
07/06/1997	39	2		KATE	Epic 6645365
18/04/1998	26	3		BRICK	Epic 6656612
24/04/1999	28	2		ARMY	Epic 6672182
29/09/2001	53	1		ROCKIN' THE SUBURBS BEN FOLDS	Epic 6718492

FOLK IMPLOSION
US duo Lou Barlow (bass/vocals) and John Davis (guitar/drums).

| 15/06/1996 | 45 | 1 | | NATURAL ONE Featured in the 1995 film *Kids* | London LONCD 382 |

CLAUDIA FONTAINE – see BEATMASTERS

O Silver disc ● Gold disc ✪ Platinum disc (additional platinum units are indicated by a figure following the symbol) ◎ Singles released prior to 1973 that are known to have sold over 1 million copies in the UK

FONTANA FEATURING DARRYL D'BONNEAU
US duo with producer Fontana and singer Darryl D'Bonneau.

24/03/2001	62	1	POW WOW WOW .... Strictly Rhythm SRUKCD 01

LENNY FONTANA AND DJ SHORTY
US dance group assembled by producers Lenny Fontana and Dominik 'DJ Shorty' Huebler. Fontana formed Down Under Productions and is also responsible for Powerhouse.

04/03/2000	39	2	CHOCOLATE SENSATION Contains samples of Johnny Hammond's *Los Conquistadores Chocolates* and Salsoul Orchestra's *Love Sensation* .... ffrr FCD 375

WAYNE FONTANA
UK group formed in Manchester in 1963 by Wayne Fontana (born Glyn Geoffrey Ellis, 28/10/1945, Manchester). The Mindbenders comprised Eric Stewart (born 20/1/1946, Manchester, lead guitar/vocals), Bob Lang (born 10/1/1946, Manchester, bass) and Ric Rothwell (born Eric Rothwell, 11/3/1944, Stockport, drums). Fontana left acrimoniously in 1965 to go solo, the group enjoying a few more hits. He named the group after a psychological thriller starring Dirk Bogarde that was playing at his local cinema in Manchester.

11/07/1963	46	2	HELLO JOSEPHINE .... Fontana TF 404
28/05/1964	37	4	STOP LOOK AND LISTEN .... Fontana TF 451
08/10/1964	5	15	**UM UM UM UM UM UM** .... Fontana TF 497
04/02/1965	2	11	**GAME OF LOVE** ▲[1] Featured in the 1988 film *Good Morning Vietnam* .... Fontana TF 535
17/06/1965	20	7	JUST A LITTLE BIT TOO LATE .... Fontana TF 579
30/09/1965	32	6	SHE NEEDS LOVE This and above five singles credited to **WAYNE FONTANA AND THE MINDBENDERS** .... Fontana TF 611
09/12/1965	36	6	IT WAS EASIER TO HURT HER .... Fontana TF 642
21/04/1966	16	12	COME ON HOME .... Fontana TF 684
25/08/1966	49	1	GOODBYE BLUEBIRD .... Fontana TF 737
08/12/1966	11	12	PAMELA PAMELA .... Fontana TF 770

FOO FIGHTERS
US rock group formed in 1994 by Dave Grohl (born 14/1/1969, Warren, OH, guitar/vocals), Nate Mendel (bass), William Goldsmith (drums), Pat Smear (guitar) and Greg Dulli (drums). Grohl had been drummer with Nirvana, and considered joining Tom Petty And The Heartbreakers when Nirvana disbanded following Kurt Cobain's death. Smear left in 1997, and by 1999 the group consisted of Grohl, Mendel, Franz Stahl (guitar, left in 1999), Taylor Hawkins (drums) and Chris Shiflett (guitar, only plays on tour). The group took their name from a term used by World War II pilots for UFOs. Ween are US duo Gene (born Aaron Freeman) and Dean Ween (born Micky Melchiondo) from New Hope, PA. Four Grammy Awards include Best Rock Album for *There Is Nothing Left To Lose* and Best Rock Album for *One By One*.

01/07/1995	5	4	**THIS IS A CALL** .... Roswell CDCL 753
16/09/1995	18	3	I'LL STICK AROUND .... Roswell CDCL 757
02/12/1995	28	2	FOR ALL THE COWS .... Roswell CDCL 762
06/04/1996	19	3	BIG ME .... Roswell CDCL 768
10/05/1997	12	4	MONKEY WRENCH .... Roswell CDCLS 788
30/08/1997	18	3	EVERLONG .... Roswell CDCL 792
31/01/1998	21	2	MY HERO Featured in the 1999 film *Varsity Blues* .... Roswell CDCL 796
29/08/1998	20	3	WALKING AFTER YOU:BEACON LIGHT **FOO FIGHTERS:WEEN** Featured in the 1998 film *The X Files* .... Elektra E 4100CD
30/10/1999	21	3	LEARN TO FLY 2000 Grammy Award for Best Short Form Video .... RCA 74321706622
30/09/2000	29	2	BREAKOUT Featured in the 2000 film *Me, Myself & Irene* .... RCA 74321790112
16/12/2000	42	2	NEXT YEAR .... RCA 74321809262
19/10/2002	5	9	**ALL MY LIFE** 2002 Grammy Award for Best Hard Rock Performance .... RCA 74321973152
18/01/2003	12	5	TIMES LIKE THESE .... RCA 74321989562
05/07/2003	21	2	LOW .... RCA 82876522572
04/10/2003	37	2	HAVE IT ALL .... RCA 82876563702

FOOL BOONA
UK DJ/producer Colin Tevendale.

10/04/1999	52	1	POPPED! Contains an interpolation of Iggy Pop's *The Passenger* .... Virgin/VC Recordings/Uber Disko VCRD 46

FOOL'S GARDEN
German group formed by Peter Freudenthaler (vocals), Volker Hinkel (guitar), Roland Rohl (keyboards), Thomas Mangold (bass) and Ralf Wochele (drums).

25/05/1996	61	1	LEMON TREE .... Encore CDCOR 014
03/08/1996	26	3	LEMON TREE (REMIX) .... Encore CDCOR 018

FOOLPROOF
US rock group formed in Orange County, CA by Jake (vocals), Scott (guitar), Joel (guitar), George (bass) and Ben (drums).

26/06/2004	53	1	PAPER HOUSE .... Island CID 863

FOR REAL
US R&B vocal group formed in Los Angeles, CA by LaTanyia Baldwin, Necia Bray, Josina Elder and Wendi Williams.

01/07/1995	54	1	YOU DON'T KNOW NOTHIN' .... A&M 5811232
12/07/1997	45	1	LIKE I DO .... Rowdy 74321486582

BILL FORBES
UK singer (born in London) whose follow-up was *You're Sixteen*.

15/01/1960	29	1	TOO YOUNG .... Columbia DB 4386

DAVID FORBES
UK producer (born in Singapore) who relocated to Glasgow, starting his club career at the Mayfair Club. He made his first record in 1994.

25/08/2001	57	1	QUESTIONS (MUST BE ASKED) .... Serious SERR 031CD

---

❶[9] Number of weeks single topped the UK chart ↑ Entered the UK chart at #1 ▲[9] Number of weeks single topped the US chart

FORBIDDEN – see JET BRONX AND THE FORBIDDEN

FORCE AND STYLES FEATURING KELLY LLORENNA
UK production duo Paul Force and Darren Styles with singer Kelly Llorenna, who also sang with Flip & Full and solo.

25/07/1998.....55......1.......	HEART OF GOLD .... Diverse VERSE 2CD

FORCE MD'S
US rap group formed on Staten Island, NYC by Antoine Maurice 'TCD' Lundy, Stevie Lundy, Jesse Lee Daniels, Trisco Pearson and Charles 'Mercury' Richard Nelson (born 19/12/1964, Staten Island) as Dr Rock & The MC's, changing their name to the Force MC's and finally Force MD's. They began entertaining passengers on the Staten Island Ferry before signing with Tommy Boy. Nelson died from a heart attack on 10/3/1995.

12/04/1986.....23......9....... TENDER LOVE Featured in the 1985 film *Krush Groove* .... Tommy Boy IS 269

CLINTON FORD
UK singer (born Ian George Stopford-Harrison) who also recorded for Pye, Channel, Columbia and Warwick.

23/10/1959.....27......1.......	OLD SHEP .... Oriole CB 1500
17/08/1961.....48......1.......	TOO MANY BEAUTIFUL GIRLS .... Oriole CB 1623
08/03/1962.....22.....10......	FANLIGHT FANNY .... Oriole CB 1706
05/01/1967.....25.....13......	RUN TO THE DOOR.. Piccadilly 7N 35361

EMILE FORD AND THE CHECKMATES
UK singer (born Emile Sweetman, 16/10/1937, Nassau, Bahamas) who moved to the UK with his family as a young boy. The Checkmates consisted of George Sweetman (bass), Dave Sweetman (saxophone), Ken Street (guitar), Les Hart (saxophone), Peter Carter (guitar), Alan Hawkshaw (piano) and John Cuffley (drums). Ford moved to Sweden after his hit career ended. Hawkshaw later scored a hit as The Mohawks.

30/10/1959 .....❶[6].....26.....	**WHAT DO YOU WANT TO MAKE THOSE EYES AT ME FOR** Revival of a song written in 1917 .... Pye 7N 15225
05/02/1960 .....3.....15.....	**ON A SLOW BOAT TO CHINA** .... Pye 7N 15245
26/05/1960.....12......9.....	YOU'LL NEVER KNOW WHAT YOU'RE MISSING ('TIL YOU TRY)................................ Pye 7N 15268
01/09/1960.....18.....16.....	THEM THERE EYES **EMILE FORD** .... Pye 7N 15282
08/12/1960.....4.....12.....	**COUNTING TEARDROPS**... Pye 7N 15314
02/03/1961.....33......6.....	WHAT AM I GONNA DO .... Pye 7N 15331
18/05/1961.....42......4.....	HALF OF MY HEART... Piccadilly 7N 35003
08/03/1962.....43......1.......	I WONDER WHO'S KISSING HER NOW This and above single credited to **EMILE FORD** .... Piccadilly 7N 35033

LITA FORD
UK singer/guitarist (born 23/9/1959, London) who was a member of The Runaways (that also included Joan Jett and future Bangles Micki Steele), joining the group in 1975 at fifteen. She left in 1979, initially combining her solo career with working as a beautician. She was briefly married to W.A.S.P. guitarist Chris Holmes.

17/12/1988.....75......1.......	KISS ME DEADLY .... RCA PB 49575
20/05/1989.....47......3.......	CLOSE MY EYES FOREVER **LITA FORD DUET WITH OZZY OSBOURNE** .... Dreamland PB 49409
11/01/1992.....63......3.......	SHOT OF POISON .... RCA PB 49145

MARTYN FORD ORCHESTRA
UK orchestra leader who began as an arranger for the likes of Shawn Phillips and the Spencer Davis Group. The follow-up was *Going To A Disco*.

14/05/1977.....38......3....... LET YOUR BODY GO DOWNTOWN .... Mountain TOP 26

MARY FORD – see LES PAUL AND MARY FORD

PENNY FORD
US singer who also backed for the likes of Soul II Soul, Truth Inc, Jack Wagner, Wailing Souls and Tashan.

04/05/1985.....43......5.......	DANGEROUS **PENNYE FORD** .... Experience FB 49975
29/05/1993.....43......2.......	DAYDREAMING .... Columbia 6590592

TENNESSEE ERNIE FORD
US singer (born Ernest Jennings Ford, 13/2/1919, Bristol, TN). Initially a radio DJ, he began singing after leaving the US Air Force, recording country music in the late 1940s and broadening to pop in the 1950s with great success. He hosted TV shows and recorded religious material, winning the 1964 Grammy Award for Best Gospel or Other Religious Recording for *Great Gospel Songs*. He also recorded with Kay Starr and Betty Hutton. Elected into the Country Music Hall of Fame in 1990, he died on 17/10/1991 from liver complications. He has three stars on the Hollywood Walk of Fame, for his contribution to recording, radio and TV.

21/01/1955 .....❶[7].....24.....	GIVE ME YOUR WORD... Capitol CL 14005
06/01/1956 .....❶[4].....11.....	SIXTEEN TONS ▲[8].. Capitol CL 14500
13/01/1956.....3......7.......	THE BALLAD OF DAVY CROCKETT .... Capitol CL 14506

JULIA FORDHAM
UK singer (born 10/8/1962, Portsmouth) who was in Mari Wilson's backing group The Wilsations before going solo in 1986.

02/07/1988.....27......9.......	HAPPY EVER AFTER... Circa YR 15
25/02/1989.....41......5.......	WHERE DOES TIME GO .... Circa YR 23
31/08/1991.....64......2.......	I THOUGHT IT WAS YOU .... Circa YR 69
18/01/1992.....19......9.......	LOVE MOVES IN MYSTERIOUS WAYS Featured in the 1991 film *The Butcher's Wife* .... Circa YR 73
30/05/1992.....45......3.......	I THOUGHT IT WAS YOU (REMIX) .... Circa YR 90
30/04/1994.....41......3.......	DIFFERENT TIME DIFFERENT PLACE .... Circa YRCD 111
23/07/1994.....62......1.......	I CAN'T HELP MYSELF .... Circa YRCD 116

FOREIGNER
UK/US rock group formed by Londoners Mick Jones (born 27/12/1944, guitar), Dennis Elliott (born 18/8/1950, drums), Ian McDonald (born 25/6/1946, guitar/keyboards) and Americans Ed Gagliardi (born 13/2/1952, New York, bass), Al Greenwood

(born 20/10/1951, New York, keyboards) and Lou Gramm (born Lou Grammatico, 2/5/1950, Rochester, NY, vocals). Gagliardi left in 1979 and was replaced by Rick Wills. Greenwood and McDonald left in 1980. Gramm left in 1991 and was replaced by Johnny Edwards. They were so named because of multinational line-up.

DATE	POS	WKS	BPI	SINGLE TITLE	LABEL & NUMBER
06/05/1978	39	6		FEELS LIKE THE FIRST TIME	Atlantic K 11086
15/07/1978	24	10		COLD AS ICE Featured in the 1978 film *F.M.*	Atlantic K 10986
28/10/1978	42	3		HOT BLOODED Featured in the 1985 film *Vision Quest*	Atlantic K 11167
24/02/1979	45	4		BLUE MORNING BLUE DAY	Atlantic K 11236
29/08/1981	54	4		URGENT Features the uncredited contribution of saxophonist Junior Walker	Atlantic K 11664
10/10/1981	48	4		JUKE BOX HERO	Atlantic K 11678
12/12/1981	8	13		**WAITING FOR A GIRL LIKE YOU** Featured in the 2000 film *Snow Day*	Atlantic K 11696
08/05/1982	45	5		URGENT Re-issue of Atlantic K 11664	Atlantic K 11728
08/12/1984	❶³	16	●	**I WANT TO KNOW WHAT LOVE IS** ▲² Features the uncredited contributions of Tom Bailey of The Thompson Twins and Jennifer Holliday	Atlantic A 9596
06/04/1985	28	6		THAT WAS YESTERDAY	Atlantic A 9571
22/06/1985	64	2		COLD AS ICE (REMIX)	Atlantic A 9539
19/12/1987	71	4		SAY YOU WILL	Atlantic A 9169
22/10/1994	58	1		WHITE LIE	Arista 74321232862

FORMATIONS
US vocal group formed in Philadelphia, PA by Jerry Akines, Johnny Bellmon, Reginald Turner and Victor Drayton as The Extremes. Their chart debut was originally a US hit on MGM in 1968, previously released unsuccessfully a year earlier on Bank.

31/07/1971	28	11		AT THE TOP OF THE STAIRS	Mojo 2027 001

GEORGE FORMBY
UK singer/ukulele player (born George Hoy Booth, 26/5/1904, Wigan) who was an apprentice jockey before turning to entertainment after the death of his singer/comedian father in 1921. His wife Beryl Ingham masterminded his career, introducing the ukulele into his act. The UK's most popular performer during World War II, he was also successful in films. His best known song *When I'm Cleaning Windows* was banned by the BBC; they claimed it was voyeuristic. He was awarded an OBE in 1946. His wife died on 26/12/1960 and two weeks later he was controversially engaged to schoolteacher Pat Hewson. The marriage was planned for May 1961 but he died from a heart attack on 6/3/1961. He left the bulk of his fortune to Pat Hewson; his family contested the will.

21/07/1960	40	3		HAPPY GO LUCKY ME/BANJO BOY	Pye 7N 15269

FORREST
US singer Forrest M Thomas Jr (born 1953) who assembled the studio group Forrest in Holland in 1982.

26/02/1983	4	10	○	**ROCK THE BOAT**	CBS A 3163
14/05/1983	17	8		FEEL THE NEED IN ME	CBS A 3411
17/09/1983	67	2		ONE LOVER (DON'T STOP THE SHOW)	CBS A 3734

SHARON FORRESTER
Jamaican singer (born 1956, Kingston) who began her recording career in 1973.

11/02/1995	50	1		LOVE INSIDE	ffrr FCD 253

LANCE FORTUNE
UK singer (born Chris Morris, Birkenhead) who joined manager Larry Parnes' roster of acts at nineteen.

19/02/1960	4	13		**BE MINE**	Pye 7N 15240
05/05/1960	26	5		THIS LOVE I HAVE FOR YOU	Pye 7N 15260

FORTUNES
UK group formed in Birmingham in 1963 by Rod Allen (born Rodney Bainbridge, 31/3/1944, Leicester, bass/vocals), Andy Brown (born 7/1/1946, Birmingham, drums), David Carr (born 4/8/1943, Leyton, keyboards), Glen Dale (born Richard Garforth, 2/4/1943, Deal, guitar/vocals) and Barry Pritchard (born 3/4/1944, Birmingham, guitar/vocals). Dale left in 1966 and was replaced by Shel MacRae (born Andrew Semple, 8/3/1943). When Carr left in 1968 they continued as a quartet until George McAllister joined in 1971.

08/07/1965	2	14		**YOU'VE GOT YOUR TROUBLES**	Decca F 12173
07/10/1965	4	14		**HERE IT COMES AGAIN**	Decca F 12243
03/02/1966	15	9		THIS GOLDEN RING	Decca F 12321
11/09/1971	6	17		**FREEDOM COME FREEDOM GO**	Capitol CL 15693
29/01/1972	7	11		**STORM IN A TEACUP**	Capitol CL 15707

45 KING (DJ MARK THE 45 KING)
UK DJ/producer Mark James.

28/10/1989	60	5		THE KING IS HERE/THE 900 NUMBER	Dance Trax DRX 9
11/08/1990	73	1		THE KING IS HERE/THE 900 NUMBER	Dance Trax DRX 9

49ERS
Italian studio project assembled by producers Gianfranco Bortolotti and Paolo Rossini with singer Dawn Mitchell (later replaced by Ann-Marie Smith), the 49th person they auditioned. Bortolotti also produces Cappella.

16/12/1989	3	13		**TOUCH ME** Contains a sample of Alisha Warren's *Touch Me*. Featured in the 1992 film *Aces: Iron Eagle III*	Fourth & Broadway BRW 157
17/03/1990	12	6		DON'T YOU LOVE ME	Fourth & Broadway BRW 167
09/06/1990	31	3		GIRL TO GIRL	Fourth & Broadway BRW 174
06/06/1992	46	2		GIRL TO GIRL	Fourth & Broadway BRW 255
29/08/1992	68	1		THE MESSAGE	Fourth & Broadway BRW 257
18/03/1995	31	2		ROCKIN' MY BODY **49ERS FEATURING ANN-MARIE SMITH**	Media MCSTD 2021

ITSY FOSTER
— see **EXOTICA FEATURING ITSY FOSTER**

❶⁹ Number of weeks single topped the UK chart ↑ Entered the UK chart at #1 ▲⁹ Number of weeks single topped the US chart

PENNY FOSTER – see STAGECOACH FEATURING PENNY FOSTER

FOSTER AND ALLEN Irish duo formed in 1975 by Mick Foster (born in County Kildare) and Tony Allen (born in Mount Temple).

DATE	POS	WKS	SINGLE TITLE	LABEL & NUMBER
27/02/1982	18	11	A BUNCH OF THYME	Ritz 5
30/10/1982	51	8	OLD FLAMES	Ritz 028
19/02/1983	27	9	MAGGIE	Ritz 025
29/10/1983	49	6	I WILL LOVE YOU ALL MY LIFE	Ritz 056
30/06/1984	47	6	JUST FOR OLD TIME'S SAKE	Ritz 066
29/03/1986	43	7	AFTER ALL THESE YEARS	Ritz 106

FOUNDATION FEATURING NATALIE ROSSI US duo Rob Huddleston and Natalie Rossi. Huddleston (born in Richmond, VA) was previously in punk group Ann Beretta.

12/07/2003	40	2	ALL OUT OF LOVE	Arista 82876513292

FOUNDATIONS UK group formed by Clem Curtis (born 28/11/1940, Trinidad, vocals), Eric Allandale (born 4/3/1936, Dominica, trombone), Pat Burke (born 9/10/1937, Jamaica, flute), Mike Elliott (born 6/8/1929, Jamaica, tenor saxophone), Tony Gomez (born 13/12/1948, Colombo, Sri Lanka, organ), Tim 'Sticks' Harris (born 14/1/1948, London, drums), Peter Macbeth (born 2/2/1943, London, bass) and Alan Warner (born 21/4/1941, London, lead guitar). Curtis went solo in 1968 and was replaced by Colin Young (born 12/9/1944, Barbados). They disbanded in 1970.

27/09/1967	❶²	16	**BABY NOW THAT I'VE FOUND YOU** Featured in the 2001 film *Shallow Hal*	Pye 7N 17366
24/01/1968	18	10	BACK ON MY FEET AGAIN	Pye 7N 17417
01/05/1968	48	2	ANY OLD TIME	Pye 7N 17503
20/11/1968	2	15	**BUILD ME UP BUTTERCUP** Featured in the 1998 film *There's Something About Mary*	Pye 7N 17636
12/03/1969	8	10	**IN THE BAD BAD OLD DAYS**	Pye 7N 17702
13/09/1969	46	3	BORN TO LIVE AND BORN TO DIE	Pye 7N 17809
12/12/1998	71	1	BUILD ME UP BUTTERCUP Re-issue of Pye 7N 17636 following its use in the 1998 film *There's Something About Mary*	Castle NEEX 1001

FOUNTAINS OF WAYNE US duo Chris Collingwood and Adam Schlesinger, both from New York. Schlesinger wrote The Wonders' hit *That Thing You Do!* in the 1996 Tom Hanks film of the same name.

22/03/1997	32	2	RADIATION VIBE	Atlantic 7567956262
10/05/1997	42	1	SINK TO THE BOTTOM	Atlantic A 5612CD
26/07/1997	53	1	SURVIVAL CAR	Atlantic AT 0004CD
27/12/1997	36	2	I WANT AN ALIEN FOR CHRISTMAS	Atlantic AT 0020CD
20/03/1999	57	1	DENISE	Atlantic AT 0053CD
20/03/2004	11	7	STACY'S MUM	Virgin VSCDX 1860
18/09/2004	57	1	HEY JULIE	Virgin VSCDX 1881

FOUR ACES FEATURING AL ALBERTS US vocal group formed in Chester, PA in 1949 by Al Alberts, Dave Mahoney, Sol Vaccaro and Lou Silvestri. They funded their debut *Sin [Not A Sin]* for the Victoria label in 1951. Picked up by Decca later, it sold over 1 million copies. Alberts went solo in 1955. They appeared in the 1958 film *The Big Beat*, and had sold 22 million records by 1970.

30/07/1954	5	6	**THREE COINS IN THE FOUNTAIN** ▲¹ Featured in the 1954 film *Three Coins In A Fountain* and won an Oscar for Best Film Song	Brunswick 05308
07/01/1955	9	5	**MR SANDMAN**	Brunswick 05355
20/05/1955	6	6	**STRANGER IN PARADISE** FOUR ACES	Brunswick 05418
18/11/1955	2	13	**LOVE IS A MANY SPLENDOURED THING** ▲⁶ Featured in the 1955 film *Love Is A Many Splendoured Thing* and won an Oscar for Best Film Song	Brunswick 05480
19/10/1956	19	3	WOMAN IN LOVE Featured in the 1955 film *Guys And Dolls*	Brunswick 05589
04/01/1957	29	1	FRIENDLY PERSUASION Featured in the 1956 film *Friendly Persuasion*	Brunswick 05623
23/01/1959	18	6	THE WORLD OUTSIDE FOUR ACES	Brunswick 05773

FOUR BUCKETEERS UK group featuring the presenters of the children's TV show *Tis Was*: Chris Tarrant, ex-Scaffold John Gorman, Sally James and Bob Carolgees. Tarrant went on to Capital Radio and the TV programmes *Tarrant On TV* and *Who Wants To Be A Millionaire?* and was awarded an OBE in 2004.

03/05/1980	26	6	THE BUCKET OF WATER SONG	CBS 8393

4 CLUBBERS German production group formed by Jens, Bernd, Markus Boehme and Martin Hensing. Jens and Bernd are also in Junkfood Junkies; Markus and Martin record as Future Breeze.

14/09/2002	45	1	CHILDREN	Code Blue BLU 026CD

FOUR ESQUIRES US vocal group formed in Boston, MA by Boston University students Bill Courtney, Frank Mahoney, Bob Golden and Wally Gold. Gold (born 28/5/1928) was later a successful songwriter, penning *It's My Party* (for Lesley Gore), *Because They're Young* (Duane Eddy) and *It's Now Or Never* and *Good Luck Charm* for Elvis Presley. He died from colitis on 7/6/1998.

31/01/1958	23	2	LOVE ME FOREVER	London HLO 8533

4-4-2 UK group formed by Steve Fox, Mark Knight, Jimi McCafferty, Neil Murray, Marky Millin, Nick Lacey, Dan Warwick, Lucy Wills, Phil Doleman and Barry Ratcliffe. Their debut hit single was organised by BURBS, British Underground Rock Bands.

19/06/2004	2	5	**COME ON ENGLAND**	Gut CDGUT58

4 HERO
UK group formed in 1986 by Dego McFarlane, Mark 'Mac' Clair, Iain Bardouille and Gus Lawrence. By 1989 Dego and Mark Mac were performing as a duo, while Bardouille and Lawrence ran the quartet's label Reinforced Records. Dego later recorded as Tek9, Mark Mac as Nu Era. Both also linked up as Jacob's Optical Stairway. They signed with Talkin Loud in 1998. Mark Mac and Bardouille also recorded as Manix. They won the 1998 MOBO Award for Best Drum & Bass Act.

Date	Pos	Wks	Title	Label
24/11/1990	73	2	MR KIRK'S NIGHTMARE	Reinforced RIVET 1203
09/05/1992	59	2	COOKIN' UP YAH BRAIN	Reinforced RIVET 1216
15/08/1998	41	1	STAR CHASERS	Talkin Loud TLCD 36
03/11/2001	53	1	LES FLEUR	Talkin Loud TLCD 66

400 BLOWS
UK vocal/instrumental group formed by Alexander Fraser, Robert Taylor and Edward Beer. Their hit line-up featured Beer and Anothony Thorpe.

Date	Pos	Wks	Title	Label
29/06/1985	54	4	MOVIN'	Illuminated ILL 61

411
UK vocal group, formed in London by Carolyn Owlett (born 8/3/1984), Suzie Furlonger (born 30/9/1981), Tanya Boniface (born 25/10/1981) and Tisha Martin (born 20/11/1984), who took their name from an album by Mary J. Blige. Ghostface Killah is US rapper (born Dennis Coles, 9/5/1970, Staten Island, NY).

Date	Pos	Wks	Title	Label
29/05/2004	4	11	ON MY KNEES 411 FEATURING GHOSTFACE KILLAH	Sony Music 6749382
04/09/2004	3	10	DUMB	Sony/Streetside 6752622
27/11/2004	23	5+	TEARDROPS	Sony/Streetside 6754812

FOUR JAYS – see BILLY FURY

FOUR KESTRELS – see BILLY FURY

FOUR KNIGHTS
US vocal group formed in Charlotte, NC in 1943 by Gene Alford, Oscar Broadway, Clarence Dixon and John Wallace as the Southland Jubilee Singers. Moving to New York in 1945 they changed their name to The Four Knights, often backing Nat 'King' Cole. Alford died in 1960, Wallace in 1976.

Date	Pos	Wks	Title	Label
04/06/1954	5	11	(OH BABY MINE) I GET SO LONELY	Capitol CL 14076
18/10/1957	21	2	MY PERSONAL POSSESSION NAT 'KING' COLE AND THE FOUR KNIGHTS	Capitol CL 14765

FOUR LADS
Canadian vocal group formed in Toronto by Bernie Toorish, Jimmie Arnold, Frankie Busseri and Connie Codarini, all from the St Michael's cathedral choir in Toronto. On moving to the US, they worked hotels and clubs before signing with Columbia in 1950 as session singers, backing Johnnie Ray on his hit *Cry*.

Date	Pos	Wks	Title	Label
19/12/1952	7	3	FAITH CAN MOVE MOUNTAINS JOHNNIE RAY AND THE FOUR LADS	Columbia DB 3154
22/10/1954	8	16	RAIN RAIN RAIN FRANKIE LAINE AND THE FOUR LADS	Philips PB 311
28/04/1960	34	4	STANDING ON THE CORNER	Philips PB 1000

4 NON BLONDES
US rock group formed in San Francisco, CA in 1989 by Linda Perry (guitar/vocals), Christa Hillhouse (bass), Roger Rocha (guitar) and Dawn Richardson (drums). They disbanded in 1996, Perry becoming a successful songwriter.

Date	Pos	Wks	BPI	Title	Label
19/06/1993	2	17	O	WHAT'S UP	Interscope A 8412CD
16/10/1993	53	2		SPACEMAN	Interscope A 8349CD

4 OF US
Irish group formed in Newry, County Down by Brendan Murphy (vocals), Declan Murphy (guitar), Paul Murphy (piano), Peter McKinney (drums) and John McCandless (bass).

Date	Pos	Wks	Title	Label
27/02/1993	35	4	SHE HITS ME	Columbia 6589192
01/05/1993	62	2	I MISS YOU	Columbia 6591722

FOUR PENNIES
UK pop group formed in Blackburn by Lionel Morton (born 14/8/1942, Blackburn, lead vocals/rhythm guitar), Fritz Fryer (born 6/12/1944, Oldham, guitar), Mike Wilsh (born 21/7/1945, Stoke-on-Trent, piano) and Alan Buck (born 7/4/1943, Brierfield, drums) as the Lionel Morton Four before name-changing to the Four Pennies.

Date	Pos	Wks	Title	Label
16/01/1964	47	2	DO YOU WANT ME TO	Philips BF 1296
02/04/1964	❶¹	15	JULIET	Philips BF 1322
16/07/1964	14	11	I FOUND OUT THE HARD WAY	Philips BF 1349
29/10/1964	20	12	BLACK GIRL	Philips BF 1366
07/10/1965	19	11	UNTIL IT'S TIME FOR YOU TO GO	Philips BF 1435
17/02/1966	32	5	TROUBLE IS MY MIDDLE NAME	Philips BF 1469

FOUR PREPS
US vocal group formed at Hollywood High School, CA by Bruce Belland, Glen Larson, Ed Cobb and Marvin Ingraham. Cobb later wrote *Tainted Love*, a UK #1 for Soft Cell, while Larson produced TV programmes including *Battlestar Galactica* and *McCloud*.

Date	Pos	Wks	Title	Label
13/06/1958	2	14	BIG MAN	Capitol CL 14873
26/05/1960	28	7	GOT A GIRL	Capitol CL 15128
09/11/1961	39	2	MORE MONEY FOR YOU AND ME (MEDLEY) Medley of *Mr Blue, Alley Oop, Smoke Gets In Your Eyes, In The Whole Wide World, Worried Man, Tom Dooley* and *A Teenager In Love*	Capitol CL 15217

FOUR SEASONS
US vocal group formed in 1954 by Frankie Valli (born Francis Castelluccio, 3/5/1937, Newark, NJ), Tommy DeVito (born 19/6/1936, Montclair, NJ), Nick DeVito and Hank Majewski as the Variatones. Signing to RCA in 1956 as the Four Lovers, in 1959 they became Frank Valle & the Romans on Cindy. Nick Massi (born Nicholas Macioco, 19/9/1935, Newark) replaced Majewski in 1960. Nick DeVito quit in 1961 and was replaced by Bob Gaudio (born 17/11/1942, The Bronx, NYC). They became

❶⁹ Number of weeks single topped the UK chart ↑ Entered the UK chart at #1 ▲⁹ Number of weeks single topped the US chart

301

the Four Seasons in 1962, after a New Jersey bowling alley. Producer Bob Crewe leased *Sherry* (written by Gaudio) to Vee-Jay, making US #1 in four weeks. Massi left in 1965 and was replaced by their arranger Charlie Callelo, and later Joe Long (born 5/9/1941). Tommy DeVito retired in 1971, Gaudio left in 1972 and various changes since have included Valli recording solo. They also recorded as the Wonder Who? The group was inducted into the Rock & Roll Hall of Fame in 1990. Nick Massi died of cancer on 24/12/2000.

DATE	POS	WKS	BPI	SINGLE TITLE	LABEL & NUMBER
04/10/1962	8	16		**SHERRY** ▲⁵	Stateside SS 122
17/01/1963	13	10		BIG GIRLS DON'T CRY ▲⁵ Featured in the films *Main Event* (1979), *Dirty Dancing* (1987) and *Mermaids* (1990)	Stateside SS 145
28/03/1963	12	12		WALK LIKE A MAN ▲³ Featured in the films *A Fine Mess* (1986) and *Mrs Doubtfire* (1993)	Stateside SS 169
27/06/1963	38	3		AIN'T THAT A SHAME	Stateside SS 194
27/08/1964	2	13		**RAG DOLL** ▲²	Philips BF 1347
18/11/1965	4	16		**LET'S HANG ON** This and above single credited to **FOUR SEASONS WITH THE SOUND OF FRANKIE VALLI**	Philips BF 1439
31/03/1966	50	3		WORKING MY WAY BACK TO YOU	Philips BF 1474
02/06/1966	20	9		OPUS 17 (DON'T YOU WORRY 'BOUT ME)	Philips BF 1493
29/09/1966	12	11		I'VE GOT YOU UNDER MY SKIN	Philips BF 1511
12/01/1967	37	5		TELL IT TO THE RAIN This and above three singles credited to **FOUR SEASONS WITH FRANKIE VALLI**	Philips BF 1538
19/04/1975	7	9		**THE NIGHT** FRANKIE VALLI AND THE FOUR SEASONS	Mowest MW 3024
20/09/1975	6	9		**WHO LOVES YOU**	Warner Brothers K 16602
31/01/1976	❶²	10	●	**DECEMBER '63 (OH WHAT A NIGHT)** ▲³	Warner Brothers K 16688
24/04/1976	3	9		**SILVER STAR**	Warner Brothers K 16742
27/11/1976	34	4		WE CAN WORK IT OUT	Warner Brothers K 16845
18/06/1977	37	3		RHAPSODY	Warner Brothers K 16932
20/08/1977	34	5		DOWN THE HALL	Warner Brothers K 16982
29/10/1988	49	4		DECEMBER '63 (OH WHAT A NIGHT) (REMIX) FRANKIE VALLI AND THE FOUR SEASONS	BR 45277

4 STRINGS Dutch producer Carlos Resoort, previously in Rank 1 and also recording as Madelyne.

DATE	POS	WKS	BPI	SINGLE TITLE	LABEL & NUMBER
23/12/2000	48	3		DAY TIME	A&M CDAMPM 139
11/05/2002	15	7		TAKE ME AWAY INTO THE NIGHT	Nebula VCRD 107
14/09/2002	38	2		DIVING	Nebula VCRD 108
13/09/2003	49	1		LET IT RAIN	Nebula NEBTCD 049
31/07/2004	50	2		TURN IT AROUND	Nebula NEBCD059

4 THE CAUSE US vocal group formed in Chicago, IL by Ms Lady, her brother J-Man and cousins Shorty and Bennie. They were 16, 15, 13 and 15 respectively at the time of their debut hit.

DATE	POS	WKS	BPI	SINGLE TITLE	LABEL & NUMBER
10/10/1998	12	9		STAND BY ME	RCA 74321622442

FOUR TOPS US vocal group formed in Detroit, MI in 1953 by Levi Stubbs (born Levi Stubbles, 6/6/1936, Detroit), Renaldo 'Obie' Benson (born 1937, Detroit), Lawrence Payton (born 2/3/1938, Detroit) and Abdul 'Duke' Fakir (born 26/12/1935, Detroit) as the Four Aims, changing their name in 1956 to avoid confusion with the Ames Brothers. Debuting for Chess, they also recorded for Red Top and Columbia before signing with Tamla Motown in 1963. They were initially jazz-orientated until they worked with the songwriting/production team Holland/Dozier/Holland. They stayed in Detroit when Motown switched to LA, signing with Dunhill. The first personnel change came with the death of Payton from liver cancer on 20/6/1997; ex-Temptation Theo Peoples his replacement. Levi Stubbs provided the voice of Audrey II (the voracious vegetation) in the 1986 film *The Little Shop Of Horrors*. They were inducted into the Rock & Roll Hall of Fame in 1990 and have a star on the Hollywood Walk of Fame.

DATE	POS	WKS	BPI	SINGLE TITLE	LABEL & NUMBER
01/07/1965	23	9		I CAN'T HELP MYSELF ▲² Featured in the films *Into The Night* (1985) and *Forrest Gump* (1994)	Tamla Motown TMG 515
02/09/1965	34	8		IT'S THE SAME OLD SONG Featured in the 1984 film *The Big Chill*	Tamla Motown TMG 528
21/07/1966	21	12		LOVING YOU IS SWEETER THAN EVER	Tamla Motown TMG 568
13/10/1966	❶³	16		**REACH OUT I'LL BE THERE** ▲²	Tamla Motown TMG 579
12/01/1967	6	8		**STANDING IN THE SHADOWS OF LOVE**	Tamla Motown TMG 589
30/03/1967	8	10		**BERNADETTE**	Tamla Motown TMG 601
15/06/1967	12	9		SEVEN ROOMS OF GLOOM	Tamla Motown TMG 612
11/10/1967	26	7		YOU KEEP RUNNING AWAY	Tamla Motown TMG 623
13/12/1967	3	11		**WALK AWAY RENEE**	Tamla Motown TMG 634
13/03/1968	7	11		**IF I WERE A CARPENTER**	Tamla Motown TMG 647
21/08/1968	23	15		YESTERDAY'S DREAMS	Tamla Motown TMG 665
13/11/1968	27	13		I'M IN A DIFFERENT WORLD	Tamla Motown TMG 675
28/05/1969	16	11		WHAT IS A MAN	Tamla Motown TMG 698
27/09/1969	11	11		DO WHAT YOU GOTTA DO	Tamla Motown TMG 710
21/03/1970	10	11		**I CAN'T HELP MYSELF** Re-issue of Tamla Motown TMG 515	Tamla Motown TMG 732
30/05/1970	5	16		**IT'S ALL IN THE GAME**	Tamla Motown TMG 736
03/10/1970	10	12		**STILL WATER (LOVE)**	Tamla Motown TMG 752
01/05/1971	36	5		JUST SEVEN NUMBERS (CAN STRAIGHTEN OUT MY LIFE)	Tamla Motown TMG 770
26/06/1971	11	10		RIVER DEEP MOUNTAIN HIGH SUPREMES AND THE FOUR TOPS	Tamla Motown TMG 777
25/09/1971	3	11		**SIMPLE GAME**	Tamla Motown TMG 785
20/11/1971	25	10		YOU GOTTA HAVE LOVE IN YOUR HEART SUPREMES AND THE FOUR TOPS	Tamla Motown TMG 793
11/03/1972	23	7		BERNADETTE Re-issue of Tamla Motown TMG 601	Tamla Motown TMG 803
05/08/1972	32	6		WALK WITH ME TALK WITH ME DARLING	Tamla Motown TMG 823

○ Silver disc ● Gold disc ✪ Platinum disc (additional platinum units are indicated by a figure following the symbol) ◉ Singles released prior to 1973 that are known to have sold over 1 million copies in the UK

18/11/1972.....18.....9.....	KEEPER OF THE CASTLE	Probe PRO 575
10/11/1973.....29.....10.....	SWEET UNDERSTANDING LOVE...	Probe PRO 604
17/10/1981.....3.....10.....○	**WHEN SHE WAS MY GIRL**	Casablanca CAN 1005
19/12/1981.....16.....11......	DON'T WALK AWAY	Casablanca CAN 1006
06/03/1982.....43.....4......	TONIGHT I'M GONNA LOVE YOU ALL OVER	Casablanca CAN 1008
26/06/1982.....62.....2......	BACK TO SCHOOL AGAIN Featured in the 1982 film *Grease 2*	RSO 89
23/07/1988.....11.....9......	REACH OUT I'LL BE THERE	Motown ZB 41943
17/09/1988.....55.....4......	INDESTRUCTIBLE **FOUR TOPS FEATURING SMOKEY ROBINSON**	Arista 111717
03/12/1988.....7.....13......	**LOCO IN ACAPULCO** Featured in the 1988 film *Buster*	Arista 111850
25/02/1989.....30.....7......	INDESTRUCTIBLE **FOUR TOPS FEATURING SMOKEY ROBINSON**	Arista 112074

4 TUNE 500
UK/Israeli production duo DJ Jo Mills and Matt Schwartz with vocalist Tricky Leigh. Schwartz is also in Deepest Blue.

16/08/2003.....75.....1......	DANCING IN THE DARK.	Black Gold BLGD04CSC 01

4 VINI FEATURING ELISABETH TROY
UK nu-skool breakbeat group, a tribute to record label boss Vini Medley who died from a brain tumour in November 2000, fronted by singer Elisabeth Troy.

18/05/2002.....75.....1.......	FOREVER YOUNG	Botchit & Scarper BOS2CD 033

4MANDU
UK vocal group.

29/07/1995.....45.....3......	THIS IS IT	Final Vinyl 74321291222
17/02/1996.....45.....2......	DO IT FOR LOVE	Final Vinyl 74321343902
15/06/1996.....47.....1......	BABY DON'T GO	Final Vinyl 74321375912

FOURMOST
UK pop group formed in Liverpool in 1958 by Brian O'Hara (born 12/3/1942, Liverpool, guitar/vocals) and Billy Hatton (born 9/6/1941, Liverpool, bass) with two friends and known as the Four Jays. Mike Millward (born 9/5/1942, Bromborough, guitar/vocals) joined in 1961, Dave Lovelady (born 16/10/1942, Liverpool, drums) in 1962, and the group turned professional calling themselves the Four Mosts. Brian Epstein signed them as manager in 1963, shortening their name to the Fourmost. Millward died from leukaemia on 7/3/1966 and was replaced by Joey Bowers.

12/09/1963.....9.....17......	**HELLO LITTLE GIRL**.	Parlophone R 5056
26/12/1963.....17.....12......	I'M IN LOVE This and above single written by John Lennon and Paul McCartney	Parlophone R 5078
23/04/1964.....6.....13......	**A LITTLE LOVING**	Parlophone R 5128
13/08/1964.....33.....4......	HOW CAN I TELL HER	Parlophone R 5157
26/11/1964.....24.....12......	BABY I NEED YOUR LOVIN'	Parlophone R 5194
09/12/1965.....33.....6......	GIRLS GIRLS GIRLS	Parlophone R 5379

14–18
UK singer/producer Peter Waterman (born 15/1/1947), then A&R manager for Magnet, reviving a song from World War I. The single features session musicians, and 'singers' drafted in from the local pub. Waterman later married Denise Gyngell of Tight Fit.

01/11/1975.....33.....4.......	GOODBYE-EE	Magnet MAG 48

40 THEVZ – see COOLIO

BERNARD FOWLER – see BOMB THE BASS

FOX
UK group formed by Noosha Fox (vocals), Herbie Armstrong (guitar/vocals), Kenny Young (guitar/vocals) and Jim Gannon (guitar/vocals), with session musicians Pete Solley (keyboards), Jim Frank (drums) and Gary Taylor (bass) in the line-up. Fox later went solo, Young and Armstrong forming Yellow Dog.

15/02/1975.....3.....11.....○	**ONLY YOU CAN**	GTO GT 8
10/05/1975.....15.....8......	IMAGINE ME IMAGINE YOU	GTO GT 21
10/04/1976.....4.....10......	**S-S-S-SINGLE BED**	GTO GT 57

GEMMA FOX FEATURING MC LYTE
UK singer (born 1980, London) with US rapper MC Lyte (born Lana Moorer).

08/05/2004.....38.....3.......	GIRLFRIEND'S STORY	Polydor 9866362

JAMES FOX
UK singer who first came to prominence as a contestant on *Fame Academy* in 2003. His debut hit was the UK's entry in the 2004 Eurovision Song Contest and came sixteenth in a competition won by the Ukraine's entry *Wild Dances* by Ruslana.

01/05/2004.....13.....7.......	HOLD ON TO OUR LOVE	Sony Music 6748732

NOOSHA FOX
UK singer, former lead singer with Fox.

12/11/1977.....31.....6......	GEORGINA BAILEY	GTO GT 106

SAMANTHA FOX
UK singer/model (born 15/4/1966, London) best known as a topless Page 3 model with *The Sun*. Later a successful actress in Bollywood films, she also appeared in the 1999 film *The Match*.

22/03/1986.....3.....10.....○	**TOUCH ME (I WANT YOUR BODY)**	Jive FOXY 1
28/06/1986.....10.....7......	**DO YA DO YA (WANNA PLEASE ME)**	Jive FOXY 2
06/09/1986.....26.....5......	HOLD ON TIGHT	Jive FOXY 3
13/12/1986.....41.....6......	I'M ALL YOU NEED	Jive FOXY 4

❶⁹ Number of weeks single topped the UK chart   ↑ Entered the UK chart at #1   ▲⁹ Number of weeks single topped the US chart

303

DATE	POS	WKS	BPI	SINGLE TITLE	LABEL & NUMBER
30/05/1987	8	9		NOTHING'S GONNA STOP ME NOW	Jive FOXY 5
25/07/1987	25	7		I SURRENDER (TO THE SPIRIT OF THE NIGHT)	Jive FOXY 6
17/10/1987	58	3		I PROMISE YOU (GET READY)	Jive FOXY 7
19/12/1987	62	3		TRUE DEVOTION	Jive FOXY 8
21/05/1988	31	5		NAUGHTY GIRLS SAMANTHA FOX FEATURING FULL FORCE	Jive FOXY 9
19/11/1988	32	6		LOVE HOUSE	Jive FOXY 10
28/01/1989	16	8		I ONLY WANNA BE WITH YOU	Jive FOXY 11
17/06/1989	63	2		I WANNA HAVE SOME FUN	Jive FOXY 12
28/03/1998	31	2		SANTA MARIA DJ MILANO FEATURING SAMANTHA FOX	All Around The World CDGLOBE 163

BRUCE FOXTON UK singer/bass player (born 1/9/1955, Woking, Surrey) who was a founder member of The Jam in 1976 and with them until their disbandment in 1982.

DATE	POS	WKS	BPI	SINGLE TITLE	LABEL & NUMBER
30/07/1983	23	5		FREAK	Arista BFOX 1
29/10/1983	56	3		THIS IS THE WAY	Arista BFOX 2
21/04/1984	74	1		IT MAKES ME WONDER	Arista BFOX 3

INEZ FOXX US singer (born 9/9/1942, Greensboro, NC) who, with her brother Charlie (born 23/10/1939, Greensboro, died from leukaemia 18/9/1998), recorded for Sue subsidiary Symbol, Musicor (part of the Scepter/Wand family) and Dynamo Records. She later recorded solo for the Stax subsidiary Volt.

DATE	POS	WKS	BPI	SINGLE TITLE	LABEL & NUMBER
23/07/1964	40	3		HURT BY LOVE	Sue WI 323
19/02/1969	33	5		MOCKINGBIRD INEZ AND CHARLIE FOXX Originally a US hit in 1963 (reached #7)	United Artists UP 2269

JOHN FOXX UK singer (born Dennis Leigh, Chorley) who was a founder member of Tiger Lily in 1973. Tiger Lily became Ultravox in 1976. Foxx went solo in 1979.

DATE	POS	WKS	BPI	SINGLE TITLE	LABEL & NUMBER
26/01/1980	31	8		UNDERPASS	Virgin VS 318
29/03/1980	32	4		NO-ONE DRIVING (DOUBLE SINGLE) Tracks on single: *No-One Driving, Glimmer, Mr No* and *This City*	Virgin VS 338
19/07/1980	35	7		BURNING CAR	Virgin VS 360
08/11/1980	51	3		MILES AWAY	Virgin VS 382
29/08/1981	40	5		EUROPE (AFTER THE RAIN)	Virgin VS 393
02/07/1983	66	3		ENDLESSLY	Virgin VS 543
17/09/1983	61	1		YOUR DRESS	Virgin VS 615

FPI PROJECT Italian production group formed by Marco Fratty, Roberto Intrallazz and Corrado Presti.

DATE	POS	WKS	BPI	SINGLE TITLE	LABEL & NUMBER
09/12/1989	9	12		GOING BACK TO MY ROOTS/RICH IN PARADISE *Going Back To My Roots* was available in two formats featuring either Paolo Dini or Sharon Dee Clarke performing the vocals	Rumour RUMAT 9
09/03/1991	65	3		EVERYBODY (ALL OVER THE WORLD)	Rumour RUMA 29
07/08/1993	59	1		COME ON (AND DO IT)	Synthetic SYNTH 006CD
13/03/1999	67	1		EVERYBODY (ALL OVER) (REMIX)	99 North CDNTH 14

FRAGGLES UK/US puppet group created by Jim Henson (*The Muppets* and *Sesame Street*) with Gobo, Red, Travelling Matt, Mokey, Boober and Wembley.

DATE	POS	WKS	BPI	SINGLE TITLE	LABEL & NUMBER
18/02/1984	33	8		'FRAGGLE ROCK' THEME Theme to the children's TV series *Fraggle Rock*	RCA 389

FRAGMA German production team formed by DJs Dirk and Murko Duderstadt and Ramon Zenker, with singer Eva Martinez on their debut hit. Zenker had also produced Ariel and Hardfloor. By 2001 they were joined by singer Damae.

DATE	POS	WKS	BPI	SINGLE TITLE	LABEL & NUMBER
25/09/1999	11	6		TOCA ME	Positiva CDTIV 120
22/04/2000	●²	17	●	TOCA'S MIRACLE ↑ Effectively two songs made into one: Fragma's *Toca Me* and Coco's *I Need A Miracle*	Positiva CDTIV 128
13/01/2001	3	11	○	EVERYTIME YOU NEED ME FRAGMA FEATURING MARIA RUBIA	Positiva CDTIVS 147
19/05/2001	4	9		YOU ARE ALIVE	Positiva CDTIVS 153
08/12/2001	25	2		SAY THAT YOU'RE HERE	Illustrious CD1LL

RODDY FRAME UK singer/guitarist (born 29/1/1964, East Kilbride), a founder of Aztec Camera who later went solo.

DATE	POS	WKS	BPI	SINGLE TITLE	LABEL & NUMBER
19/09/1998	45	2		REASON FOR LIVING	Independiente ISOM 18MS

PETER FRAMPTON UK singer/guitarist (born 22/4/1950, Beckenham) who learned guitar as a child, joining the Herd in 1966. He formed Humble Pie in 1969, leaving in 1971 to form Frampton's Camel, then went solo in 1974. He has a star on the Hollywood Walk of Fame.

DATE	POS	WKS	BPI	SINGLE TITLE	LABEL & NUMBER
01/05/1976	10	12		SHOW ME THE WAY	A&M AMS 7218
11/09/1976	43	5		BABY I LOVE YOUR WAY	A&M AMS 7246
06/11/1976	39	4		DO YOU FEEL LIKE WE DO	A&M AMS 7260
23/07/1977	41	3		I'M IN YOU	A&M AMS 7298

○ Silver disc ● Gold disc ✪ Platinum disc (additional platinum units are indicated by a figure following the symbol) ◉ Singles released prior to 1973 that are known to have sold over 1 million copies in the UK

CONNIE FRANCIS US singer (born Concetta Rosa Maria Franconero, 12/12/1938, Newark, NJ) who debuted for MGM at sixteen, hitting the US charts for the first time in 1957. She made her first film *Where The Boys Are* in 1961, but stopped performing after being raped following a show at Howard Johnson's Motel on 8/11/1974 (for which she was awarded $3 million). She made a showbiz comeback in 1981.

04/04/1958	❶⁶	25		WHO'S SORRY NOW	MGM 975
27/06/1958	11	10		I'M SORRY I MADE YOU CRY	MGM 982
22/08/1958	❶⁶	19		CAROLINA MOON/STUPID CUPID	MGM 985
31/10/1958	19	6		I'LL GET BY	MGM 993
21/11/1958	20	5		FALLIN' B-side of *I'll Get By*	MGM 993
26/12/1958	13	7		YOU ALWAYS HURT THE ONE YOU LOVE	MGM 998
13/02/1959	4	15		MY HAPPINESS	MGM 1001
03/07/1959	3	16		LIPSTICK ON YOUR COLLAR	MGM 1018
11/09/1959	18	6		PLENTY GOOD LOVIN'	MGM 1036
04/12/1959	11	10		AMONG MY SOUVENIRS Originally written in 1927, a hit for Paul Whiteman & His Concert Orchestra	MGM 1046
17/03/1960	27	8		VALENTINO	MGM 1060
19/05/1960	2	19		MAMA/ROBOT MAN	MGM 1076
18/08/1960	5	13		EVERYBODY'S SOMEBODY'S FOOL ▲²	MGM 1086
03/11/1960	3	15		MY HEART HAS A MIND OF ITS OWN ▲²	MGM 1100
12/01/1961	12	9		MANY TEARS AGO	MGM 1111
16/03/1961	5	14		WHERE THE BOYS ARE/BABY ROO A-side featured in the 1960 film *Where The Boys Are*	MGM 1121
15/06/1961	12	11		BREAKIN' IN A BRAND NEW BROKEN HEART	MGM 1136
14/09/1961	6	11		TOGETHER Originally written in 1927, a hit for Paul Whiteman & His Concert Orchestra	MGM 1138
14/12/1961	30	4		BABY'S FIRST CHRISTMAS	MGM 1145
26/04/1962	39	3		DON'T BREAK THE HEART THAT LOVES YOU ▲¹	MGM 1157
02/08/1962	10	9		VACATION	MGM 1165
20/12/1962	48	1		I'M GONNA BE WARM THIS WINTER	MGM 1185
10/06/1965	26	6		MY CHILD	MGM 1271
20/01/1966	44	2		JEALOUS HEART	MGM 1293

JILL FRANCIS UK singer.

| 03/07/1993 | 70 | 1 | | MAKE LOVE TO ME | Glady Wax GW 003CD |

CLAUDE FRANCOIS French singer (born 4/2/1942, Egypt) who recorded the original of the song that ultimately became *My Way*. The female vocal on his debut hit was by Kathy Barnet. He was electrocuted on 11/3/1978 trying to change a lightbulb while having a bath.

| 10/01/1976 | 35 | 4 | | TEARS ON THE TELEPHONE | Bradley's BRAD 7528 |

FRANK AND WALTERS Irish trio formed in Cork by Paul Linehan (vocals/bass), Niall Linehan (guitar) and Ashley Keating (drums), naming themselves after two tramps from a nearby village.

21/03/1992	49	2		HAPPY BUSMAN	Setanta HOO 2
12/09/1992	46	3		THIS IS NOT A SONG	Setanta HOO 3
09/01/1993	11	5		AFTER ALL	Setanta HOOCD 4
17/04/1993	42	3		FASHION CRISIS HITS NEW YORK	Setanta HOOCD 5

FRANKE UK singer Franke Pharoah.

| 07/11/1992 | 60 | 2 | | UNDERSTAND THIS GROOVE | China WOK 2028 |
| 21/05/1994 | 73 | 1 | | LOVE COME HOME OUR TRIBE WITH FRANKE PHARDAH AND KRISTINE W | Triangle BLUESCD 001 |

FRANK'EE – see BROTHER BROWN FEATURING FRANK'EE

FRANKEE US singer (born Frankee Nicole Aiello, 9/6/1983, Staten Island) whose debut hit was an 'answer' record to Eamon's hit. It was initially claimed that Frankee was the ex-girlfriend of Eamon and the subject of his hit, then that Eamon had selected Frankee to record an answer record, but both these stories were publicity stunts.

| 01/05/2004 | 43 | 3 | | F.U.R.B. – F U RIGHT BACK (IMPORT) | All Around The World 5603242CD |
| 22/05/2004 | ❶³ | 16 | | F.U.R.B. (F U RIGHT BACK) ↑ Replaced Eamon's hit *F**k It (I Don't Want You Back)* at #1, the first time an 'answer' record has topped the chart and replaced its inspiration. The song also replaced Eamon's hit on the Ringtones chart on 19/6/2004. | All Around The World CDGLOBE 355 |

FRANKIE – see I DREAM FEATURING FRANKIE AND CALVIN

FRANKIE GOES TO HOLLYWOOD UK group formed in Liverpool in 1980 by William 'Holly' Johnson (born 19/2/1960, Khartoum, Sudan, vocals), Paul Rutherford (born 8/12/1959, Liverpool, vocals), Brian 'Nasher' Nash (born 20/5/1963, Liverpool, guitar), Mark O'Toole (born 6/1/1964, Liverpool, bass) and Peter 'Ged' Gill (born 8/3/1964, Liverpool, drums). Signed by ZTT (Zang Tumb Tumm)

❶⁹ Number of weeks single topped the UK chart ↑ Entered the UK chart at #1 ▲⁹ Number of weeks single topped the US chart

in 1982, their 1983 debut reached #1 after a ban by the BBC, orchestrated by DJ Mike Read. Johnson went solo in 1987, Rutherford in 1988. Cited Best British Newcomers at the 1985 BRIT Awards, their name has been alternatively explained as being from an old newspaper headline covering either Frank Sinatra's or Frankie Vaughan's move to Hollywood.

DATE	POS	WKS	BPI	SINGLE TITLE	LABEL & NUMBER
26/11/1983	❶⁵	52	✪	**RELAX** Featured in the films *Police Academy* (1984) and *Body Double* (1984). 1985 BRIT Award for Best Single	ZTT ZTAS 1
16/06/1984	❶⁹	21	✪	**TWO TRIBES** ↑ *Two Tribes* was at #1 and *Relax* at #2 for two weeks from 7/7/1984. Featured in the films *The Supergrass* (1985) and *There's Only One Jimmy Grimble* (2000)	ZTT ZTAS 3
01/12/1984	❶¹	12	●	**THE POWER OF LOVE**	ZTT ZTAS 5
30/03/1985	2	11	○	**WELCOME TO THE PLEASURE DOME**	ZTT ZTAS 7
06/09/1986	4	7	○	**RAGE HARD**	ZTT ZTAS 22
22/11/1986	19	8		**WARRIORS (OF THE WASTELAND)**	ZTT ZTAS 25
07/03/1987	28	6		**WATCHING THE WILDLIFE**	ZTT ZTAS 26
02/10/1993	5	7		**RELAX** Re-issue of ZTT ZTAS 1	ZTT FGTH 1CD
20/11/1993	18	3		**WELCOME TO THE PLEASURE DOME (REMIX)**	ZTT FGTH 2CD
18/12/1993	10	7		**THE POWER OF LOVE** Re-issue of ZTT ZTAS 5	ZTT FGTH 3CD
26/02/1994	16	3		**TWO TRIBES (REMIX)** Remix of ZTT ZTAS 3 by Fluke	ZTT FGTH 4CD
01/07/2000	6	6		**THE POWER OF LOVE** Remix of ZTT ZTAS 5 by Rob Searle	ZTT ZTT150CD
09/09/2000	17	3		**TWO TRIBES** Second remix of ZTT ZTAS 3 by Rob Searle	ZTT 154CD
18/11/2000	45	1		**WELCOME TO THE PLEASURE DOME (REMIX)**	ZTT 166CD

ARETHA FRANKLIN US singer (born 25/3/1942, Memphis, TN). After recording religious material for Wand from 1956, she switched to secular music at the suggestion of Sam Cooke in 1960, signing to Columbia. Hits on Atlantic from 1966 earned her the nickname First Lady Of Soul. She appeared in the 1980 film *The Blues Brothers,* performing *Think*. In 1984 she was sued for failing to appear in the Broadway musical *Mahalia,* due to her fear of flying. Inducted into the Rock & Roll Hall of Fame in 1987, her sixteen Grammy Awards include Best Rhythm & Blues Vocal Performance in 1969 for *Share Your Love With Me*, Best Rhythm & Blues Vocal Performance in 1971 for *Bridge Over Troubled Water*, Best Rhythm & Blues Vocal Performance in 1972 for *Young Gifted And Black*, Best Soul Gospel Performance in 1972 for *Amazing Grace*, Best Rhythm & Blues Vocal Performance in 1973 for *Master Of Eyes*, Best Rhythm & Blues Vocal Performance in 1974 for *Ain't Nothing Like The Real Thing*, Best Rhythm & Blues Vocal Performance in 1981 for *Hold On I'm Comin'*, Best Rhythm & Blues Vocal Performance in 1985 for *Freeway Of Love*, Best Rhythm & Blues Vocal Performance in 1987 for *Aretha*, Best Soul Gospel Performance in 1988 for *One Lord, One Faith, One Baptism* and Best Traditional Rhythm & Blues Vocal Performance in 2003 for *Wonderful*. She has a star on the Hollywood Walk of Fame.

DATE	POS	WKS	BPI	SINGLE TITLE	LABEL & NUMBER
08/06/1967	10	14		**RESPECT** ▲² Featured in the films *More American Graffiti* (1979), *Back To School* (1986), *Platoon* (1987), *Forrest Gump* (1994), *Bicentennial Man* (1999) and *Bridget Jones's Diary* (2001). 1967 Grammy Awards for Best Rhythm & Blues Recording and Best Rhythm & Blues Vocal Performance	Atlantic 584 115
23/08/1967	39	4		**BABY I LOVE YOU**	Atlantic 584 127
20/12/1967	43	2		**CHAIN OF FOOLS/SATISFACTION** A-side featured in the 1996 film *Michael*. 1968 Grammy Award for Best Rhythm & Blues Vocal Performance	Atlantic 584 157
10/01/1968	37	5		**SATISFACTION**	Atlantic 584 157
13/03/1968	47	1		**SINCE YOU'VE BEEN GONE**	Atlantic 584 172
22/05/1968	26	9		**THINK** Featured in the films *The Blues Brothers* (1980), *War* (1994), *The First Wives Club* (1996) and *Bridget Jones Diary 2: Edge Of Reason* (2004)	Atlantic 584 186
07/08/1968	4	14		**I SAY A LITTLE PRAYER FOR YOU**	Atlantic 584 206
22/08/1970	13	11		**DON'T PLAY THAT SONG** 1970 Grammy Award for Best Rhythm & Blues Vocal Performance	Atlantic 2091 027
02/10/1971	14	9		**SPANISH HARLEM**	Atlantic 2091 138
08/09/1973	37	5		**ANGEL**	Atlantic K 10346
16/02/1974	26	8		**UNTIL YOU COME BACK TO ME (THAT'S WHAT I'M GONNA DO)**	Atlantic K 10399
06/12/1980	46	7		**WHAT A FOOL BELIEVES**	Arista ARIST 377
19/09/1981	49	3		**LOVE ALL THE HURT AWAY** ARETHA FRANKLIN AND GEORGE BENSON	Arista ARIST 428
04/09/1982	42	5		**JUMP TO IT**	Arista ARIST 479
23/07/1983	74	2		**GET IT RIGHT**	Arista ARIST 537
13/07/1985	68	3		**FREEWAY OF LOVE**	Arista ARIST 624
02/11/1985	9	11		**SISTERS ARE DOIN' IT FOR THEMSELVES** EURYTHMICS AND ARETHA FRANKLIN Featured in the 1996 film *The First Wives Club*	RCA PB 40339
23/11/1985	11	14		**WHO'S ZOOMIN' WHO**	Arista ARIST 633
22/02/1986	54	6		**ANOTHER NIGHT**	Arista ARIST 657
10/05/1986	51	3		**FREEWAY OF LOVE**	Arista ARIST 624
25/10/1986	58	3		**JUMPIN' JACK FLASH** Featured in the 1986 film *Jumpin' Jack Flash*	Arista ARIST 678
31/01/1987	❶²	9	●	**I KNEW YOU WERE WAITING (FOR ME)** ▲² ARETHA FRANKLIN AND GEORGE MICHAEL 1987 Grammy Award for Best Rhythm & Blues Vocal Performance by a Duo	Epic DUET 2
14/03/1987	46	4		**JIMMY LEE**	Arista RIS 6
06/05/1989	41	3		**THROUGH THE STORM** ARETHA FRANKLIN AND ELTON JOHN	Arista 112185
09/09/1989	29	5		**IT ISN'T, IT WASN'T, IT AIN'T NEVER GONNA BE** ARETHA FRANKLIN AND WHITNEY HOUSTON	Arista 112545
07/04/1990	31	2		**THINK** Re-recording of Atlantic 584 186 and the B-side to *Everybody Needs Somebody To Love* by the BLUES BROTHERS. Listed for only the first week of that record's run in the top 40	East West A 7951
27/07/1991	69	1		**EVERYDAY PEOPLE**	Arista 114420
12/02/1994	5	7		**A DEEPER LOVE** Featured in the 1993 film *Sister Act 2: Back In The Habit*	Arista 74321187022
25/06/1994	17	7		**WILLING TO FORGIVE**	Arista 74321213342
09/05/1998	22	4		**A ROSE IS STILL A ROSE** Contains a sample of Edie Brickell & The New Bohemians' *What I Am*	Arista 74321569742
26/09/1998	68	1		**HERE WE GO AGAIN**	Arista 74321612742

ERMA FRANKLIN US singer (born 1943, Memphis, TN) and younger sister of Aretha Franklin (a third sister, Carolyn, wrote *Ain't No Way*, a #16 US hit for Aretha). Erma died from cancer on 7/9/2002.

10/10/1992 . . . . . 9 . . . . . . 10 . . . . . . **(TAKE A LITTLE) PIECE OF MY HEART** Originally recorded in 1967 and revived following use in a Levi Jeans advertisement . . . .
. . . . Epic 6583847

RODNEY FRANKLIN US pianist (born 16/9/1958, Berkeley, CA). Learning jazz piano from the age of six, he signed with CBS in 1978.

19/04/1980 . . . . . 7 . . . . . 9 . . . . . . **THE GROOVE** . . . . CBS 8529

CHEVELLE FRANKLYN FEATURING BEENIE MAN Jamaican vocal duo Chevelle Franklyn (born 1974, St Catherine) and Beenie Man (born Anthony Moses David, 22/8/1972, Kingston).

20/09/1997 . . . . . 70 . . . . . . 1 . . . . **DANCEHALL QUEEN** Featured in the 1997 film *Dancehall Queen* . . . . Island Jamaica IJCD 2018

FRANTIC FIVE – see **DON LANG**

FRANTIQUE US disco group assembled by Philadelphia International Records in 1979 with lead vocals by Vivienne Savoie. When they played *Top Of The Pops*, the line-up was Tricia Lynne Cheyenne, Florence Raynor and Denise Russelle.

11/08/1979 . . . . . 10 . . . . . 12 . . . . . . **STRUT YOUR FUNKY STUFF** . . . . Philadelphia International PIR 7728

FRANZ FERDINAND UK rock group formed in Glasgow by Alexander Kapranos (guitar/vocals), Nicholas McCarthy (guitar), Robert Hardy (bass) and Paul Thomson (drums).

20/09/2003 . . . . . 44 . . . . . . 1 . . . . . . DARTS OF PLEASURE . . . . Domino RUG 164CD
24/01/2004 . . . . . 3 . . . . . 9 . . . . . . **TAKE ME OUT** . . . . Domino RUG 172CD
01/05/2004 . . . . . 8 . . . . . 6 . . . . . . **MATINEE** . . . . Domino RUG 176CD
28/08/2004 . . . . . 17 . . . . . . 4 . . . . . . MICHAEL . . . . Domino RUG 184CD

ELIZABETH FRASER UK singer (born 29/8/1958, Grangemouth) who was also in the Cocteau Twins.

12/05/1990 . . . . . 75 . . . . . . 1 . . . . . . CANDLELAND (THE SECOND COMING) **IAN McCULLOCH FEATURING ELIZABETH FRASER** . . . . East West YZ 452
13/08/1994 . . . . . 14 . . . . . . 3 . . . . . . LIFEFORMS **FUTURE SOUND OF LONDON VOCALS BY ELIZABETH FRASER** . . . . Virgin VSCD 1484

WENDY FRASER – see **PATRICK SWAYZE FEATURING WENDY FRASER**

FRASH UK vocal/instrumental group.

18/02/1995 . . . . . 69 . . . . . . 1 . . . . . . HERE I GO AGAIN . . . . PWL International FLIPCD 1

FRAZIER CHORUS UK group formed in Brighton by Tim Freeman (keyboards/vocals), Kate Holmes (flute), Chris Taplin (clarinet) and Michele Allardyce (percussion) as Plop! (the name a parody of Wham!), becoming Frazier Chorus (seen on the back of a 1950s baseball jacket) upon signing with 4AD in 1987. Holmes later formed Client with Sarah Blackwood (formerly of Dubstar).

04/02/1989 . . . . . 57 . . . . . . 3 . . . . . . DREAM KITCHEN . . . . Virgin VS 1145
15/04/1989 . . . . . 53 . . . . . . 2 . . . . . . TYPICAL! . . . . Virgin VS 1174
15/07/1989 . . . . . 73 . . . . . . 1 . . . . . . SLOPPY HEART . . . . Virgin VS 1192
09/06/1990 . . . . . 52 . . . . . . 3 . . . . . . CLOUD 8 . . . . Virgin VS 1252
25/08/1990 . . . . . 51 . . . . . . 3 . . . . . . NOTHING . . . . Virgin VS 1284
16/02/1991 . . . . . 60 . . . . . . 2 . . . . . . WALKING ON AIR . . . . Virgin VS 1330

FREAKPOWER UK group formed by ex-Housemartin and Beats International Norman Cook (born Quentin Cook, 31/7/1963, Brighton) who also records as Pizzaman and The Mighty Dub Katz.

16/10/1993 . . . . . 29 . . . . . . 5 . . . . . . TURN ON, TUNE IN, COP OUT . . . . Fourth & Broadway BRCD 284
26/02/1994 . . . . . 62 . . . . . . 2 . . . . . . RUSH . . . . Fourth & Broadway BRCD 291
18/03/1995 . . . . . 3 . . . . . 9 . . . . . . O **TURN ON, TUNE IN, COP OUT** Revived following use in a Levi Jeans advertisement. Featured in the 1998 film *Up 'N Under* . . . .
. . . . Fourth & Broadway BRCD 317
08/06/1996 . . . . . 60 . . . . . . 1 . . . . . . NEW DIRECTION . . . . Fourth & Broadway BRCD 331
09/05/1998 . . . . . 29 . . . . . . 3 . . . . . . NO WAY . . . . Deconstruction 74321578572

FREAKY REALISTIC UK/Japanese vocal/instrumental group formed in Peckham, London by Justin 'Liquid' Anderson, Aki Omori and rapper MPL. Omori was later in The Orb.

03/04/1993 . . . . . 52 . . . . . . 2 . . . . . . KOOCHIE RYDER . . . . Frealism FRESCD 2
03/07/1993 . . . . . 71 . . . . . . 1 . . . . . . LEONARD NIMOY . . . . Frealism FRESCD 3

FREAKYMAN Dutch producer Andre Van Den Bosch.

27/09/1997 . . . . . 68 . . . . . . 1 . . . . . . DISCOBUG '97 . . . . Xtravaganza 0091285 EXT

STAN FREBERG US singer (born 7/8/1926, Pasadena, CA) who did impersonations on radio and voices for cartoon films. After his hits dried up he did radio and TV jingles, collecting 21 Clio awards for the genre. He won a Grammy Award for Best Documentary or Spoken Word Recording in 1958 for *The Best Of The Stan Freberg Show*. He has a star on the Hollywood Walk of Fame.

19/11/1954 . . . . . 15 . . . . . . 2 . . . . . . SH-BOOM **STAN FREBERG WITH THE TOADS** . . . . Capitol CL 14187
27/07/1956 . . . . . 24 . . . . . . 2 . . . . . . ROCK ISLAND LINE/HEARTBREAK HOTEL **STAN FREBERG AND HIS SNIFFLE GROUP** . . . . Capitol CL 14608
12/05/1960 . . . . . 40 . . . . . . 1 . . . . . . THE OLD PAYOLA ROLL BLUES **STAN FREBERG WITH JESSE WHITE** . . . . Capitol CL 15122

❶⁹ Number of weeks single topped the UK chart ↑ Entered the UK chart at #1 ▲⁹ Number of weeks single topped the US chart

307

FRED AND ROXY
UK vocal duo, sisters Phaedra 'Fred' (born in London) and Roxanna 'Roxy' Aslami (born in Santa Monica, CA).

| 05/02/2000 | 36 | 2 | | SOMETHING FOR THE WEEKEND | Echo ECSCD 81 |

JOHN FRED AND THE PLAYBOY BAND
US singer (born John Fred Gourrier, 8/5/1941, Baton Rouge, LA) who formed the Playboy Band in 1956. Their hit was a parody of The Beatles' *Lucy In The Sky With Diamonds*. They comprised Andrew Bernard (saxophone), Howard Cowart (bass), Tommy de Geweres (organ), Ronnie Goodson (trumpet), John Micely (drums), Jimmy O'Rourke (guitar) and Charlie Spin (trumpet).

| 03/01/1968 | 3 | 12 | | JUDY IN DISGUISE (WITH GLASSES) ▲² Featured in the 1990 film *Drugstore Cowboy* | Pye International 7N 25442 |

FREDDIE AND THE DREAMERS
UK group formed in Manchester in 1961 by Freddie Garrity (born 14/11/1936, Manchester, vocals), Roy Crewdson (born 29/5/1941, rhythm guitar), Derek Quinn (born 24/5/1942, lead guitar), Pete Birrell (born 9/5/1941, bass) and Bernie Dwyer (born 11/9/1940, drums). They disbanded in 1968, Garrity continuing on the cabaret circuit with a new line-up. They appeared in the 1965 film *Cuckoo Patrol* and Garrity was in the TV series *Heartbeat* in the 1990s.

09/05/1963	3	14		IF YOU GOTTA MAKE A FOOL OF SOMEBODY	Columbia DB 7032
08/08/1963	2	11		I'M TELLING YOU NOW ▲²	Columbia DB 7086
07/11/1963	3	15		YOU WERE MADE FOR ME	Columbia DB 7147
20/02/1964	13	11		OVER YOU	Columbia DB 7214
14/05/1964	16	8		I LOVE YOU BABY	Columbia DB 7286
16/07/1964	41	3		JUST FOR YOU	Columbia DB 7322
05/11/1964	5	15		I UNDERSTAND	Columbia DB 7381
22/04/1965	26	5		A LITTLE YOU	Columbia DB 7526
04/11/1965	44	3		THOU SHALT NOT STEAL	Columbia DB 7720

FREDERICK – see NINA AND FREDERICK

DEE FREDRIX
UK singer.

| 27/02/1993 | 56 | 4 | | AND SO I WILL WAIT FOR YOU | East West YZ 725CD |
| 03/07/1993 | 74 | 1 | | DIRTY MONEY | East West YZ 750CD |

FREE
UK rock group formed in London in 1968 by Paul Kossoff (born 14/9/1950, London, guitar), Simon Kirke (born 28/7/1949, London, drums), Paul Rodgers (born 12/12/1949, Middlesbrough, lead vocals) and Andy Fraser (born 7/8/1952, London, bass). Disbanding in 1971, Kossoff and Kirke joined bass player Tetsu Yamauchi (born 21/10/1947, Japan) and keyboard player John 'Rabbit' Bundrick for *Kossoff, Kirke, Tetsu And Rabbit*. This four re-formed Free with Rodgers in 1972 but Kossoff was often too ill to tour or record. Splitting again in 1973, Rodgers and Kirke formed Bad Company. Kossoff died from a heart attack on 19/3/1976 on a Los Angeles to New York flight. Rodgers was later in The Firm and The Law.

06/06/1970	2	16		ALL RIGHT NOW Featured in the films *Now And Then* (1996) and *American Beauty* (1999)	Island WIP 6082
01/05/1971	4	11		MY BROTHER JAKE	Island WIP 6100
27/05/1972	13	10		LITTLE BIT OF LOVE	Island WIP 6129
13/01/1973	7	10		WISHING WELL	Island WIP 6146
21/07/1973	15	9		ALL RIGHT NOW	Island WIP 6082
18/02/1978	11	7		FREE EP Tracks on EP: *All Right Now, My Brother Jake* and *Wishing Well*	Island IEP 6
23/10/1982	57	3		FREE EP Tracks as above	Island IEP 6
09/02/1991	8	9		ALL RIGHT NOW (REMIX)	Island IS 486

FREE
US vocal group.

| 12/04/1997 | 31 | 2 | | MR BIG STUFF QUEEN LATIFAH, SHADES AND FREE | Motown 5736572 |
| 14/11/1998 | 5 | 6 | | ANOTHER ONE BITES THE DUST QUEEN WITH WYCLEF JEAN FEATURING PRAS MICHEL/FREE Featured in the 1998 film *Small Soldiers* | DreamWorks DRMCD 22364 |

FREE ASSOCIATION
UK group formed by Petra Jean Philipson, MC Sean Reveron, David Holmes and Steve Hilton.

| 12/04/2003 | 74 | 1 | | EVERYBODY KNOWS | Ramp 001CDS |
| 13/09/2003 | 53 | 1 | | SUGARMAN | 13 Amp 9809471 |

FREE SPIRIT
UK vocal duo fronted by Elaine Vassel.

| 13/05/1995 | 68 | 1 | | NO MORE RAINY DAYS | Columbia 6612822 |

FREEEZ
UK funk group formed by John Rocca (born 23/9/1960, London, vocals), Peter Maas (bass), Andy Stenner (keyboards) and Paul Morgan (drums). Their self-funded debut *Keep In Touch* for their own Pink I label was subsequently picked up by Pye's Calibre Records. Rocca went solo in 1984.

07/06/1980	49	3		KEEP IN TOUCH	Calibre CAB 103
07/02/1981	8	11	○	SOUTHERN FREEEZ FREEEZ FEATURING INGRID MANSFIELD ALLMAN	Beggars Banquet BEG 51
18/04/1981	35	5		FLYING HIGH	Beggars Banquet BEG 55
18/06/1983	2	15	●	I.O.U.	Beggars Banquet BEG 96
01/10/1983	26	6		POP GOES MY LOVE	Beggars Banquet BEG 98
17/01/1987	23	6		I.O.U. (REMIX) FREEEZ FEATURING JOHN ROCCA	Citybeat CBE 709
30/05/1987	63	2		SOUTHERN FREEEZ (REMIX) FREEEZ FEATURING INGRID MANSFIELD ALLMAN	Total Control TOCO 14

FREEFALL FEATURING JAN JOHNSTON
UK/Australian production duo Alan Bremner and Anthony Pappa (born Anthony Pappalardo) with singer Jan Johnston.

○ Silver disc   ● Gold disc   ✪ Platinum disc (additional platinum units are indicated by a figure following the symbol)   ◎ Singles released prior to 1973 that are known to have sold over 1 million copies in the UK

28/11/1998	75	1		SKYDIVE	Stress CDSTR 89
22/07/2000	43	2		SKYDIVE (REMIX)	Renaissance Recordings RENCDS 002
08/09/2001	35	2		SKYDIVE (I FEEL WONDERFUL) (2ND REMIX)	Incentive CENT 22CDS

FREEFALL FEATURING PSYCHOTROPIC
UK/US instrumental/production group formed by Nick Nicely and Gavin Mills.

| 27/07/1991 | 63 | 1 | | FEEL SURREAL | ffrr FX 160 |

FREEHOLD JUNIOR SCHOOL – see FOGWELL FLAX AND THE ANKLEBITERS FROM FREEHOLD JUNIOR SCHOOL

FREELAND
UK DJ/producer (born Adam Freeland, 7/8/1973, Welwyn Garden City).

| 13/09/2003 | 35 | 2 | | WE WANT YOUR SOUL | Maximise Profit FREECDS01 |
| 07/02/2004 | 65 | 1 | | SUPERNATURAL THING | Marine Parade MAPACDS024 |

CLAIRE FREELAND
UK singer (born 1977, Glasgow) who first appeared in the TV contest *Popstars*. She launched the Statuesque label after being rejected from *Popstars* because she was overweight.

| 21/07/2001 | 44 | 1 | | FREE | Statuesque CDSTATU 1 |

FREESTYLERS
UK group formed by Matt Cantor, Aston Harvey and Andrew Galea. Galea was later in Giresse.

07/02/1998	23	3		B-BOY STANCE FREESTYLERS FEATURING TENOR FLY	Freskanova FND 7
14/11/1998	68	1		WARNING FREESTYLERS FEATURING NAVIGATOR	Freskanova FND 14
24/07/1999	45	1		HERE WE GO	Freskanova FND 19
20/03/2004	66	1		GET A LIFE	Against The Grain ATG008
26/06/2004	22	4		PUSH UP	Against The Grain ATG009CD

FREEWAY – see CASSIUS HENRY

FREIHEIT
German group with Stefan Zaumer (vocals), Aron Strober (guitar), Michael Kunzi (bass), Alix Grunberg (keyboards) and Rennie Hatzke (drums).

| 17/12/1988 | 14 | 9 | | KEEPING THE DREAM ALIVE | CBS 6529897 |

DEBORAH FRENCH – see E-LUSTRIOUS

NICKI FRENCH
UK singer from Carlisle who represented the UK in the 2000 Eurovision Song Contest, which was won by Jorgen and Niels Olsen of Denmark's *Beautiful Like A Shooting Star* (original Danish title *Smuk Som Et Stjerneskud*).

15/10/1994	54	1		TOTAL ECLIPSE OF THE HEART	Bags Of Fun BAGSCD 1
14/01/1995	5	12	O	TOTAL ECLIPSE OF THE HEART	Bags Of Fun BAGSCD 1
22/04/1995	42	2		FOR ALL WE KNOW	Bags Of Fun BAGSCD 4
15/07/1995	55	1		DID YOU EVER REALLY LOVE ME	Love This LUVTHISCD 2
27/05/2000	34	2		DON'T PLAY THAT SONG AGAIN UK entry for the 2000 Eurovision Song Contest (came sixteenth).	RCA 74321764572

FRENCH AFFAIR
French production duo the Dreyer brothers with singer Barbara Alcindor.

| 16/09/2000 | 44 | 3 | | MY HEART GOES BOOM | Arista 74321780562 |

FRESH BC
UK producer Dan Stein who is also in Bad Company.

25/10/2003	58	1		SIGNAL/BIG LOVE	Ram RAMM 46
18/09/2004	74	1		COLOSSUS/HOODED	Ram RAMM 51
25/12/2004	70	1+		CAPTURE THE FLAG	Ram RAMM 53

FREDDY FRESH
US producer Frederick Schmid.

| 01/05/1999 | 34 | 2 | | BADDER BADDER SCHWING FREDDY FRESH FEATURING FATBOY SLIM | Eye-Q EYEUK 040CD |
| 31/07/1999 | 63 | 1 | | WHAT IT IS | Eye-Q EYEUK 043CD |

DOUG E FRESH AND THE GET FRESH CREW
US rap group formed in 1985 by Doug E Fresh (born Douglas E Davies, St Thomas, Virgin Islands), Barry Bee, Chill Will and Slick Rick (aka MC Ricky D, born Ricky Walters, 14/1/1965, London).

| 09/11/1985 | 7 | 11 | O | THE SHOW | Cooltempo COOL 116 |

FRESH 4 FEATURING LIZZ E
UK group formed in Bristol by DJs Judge, Krust, Suv D, rapper Flynn and singer Lizz E.

| 07/10/1989 | 10 | 9 | | WISHING ON A STAR | 10 TEN 287 |

FRESH PRINCE – see JAZZY JEFF AND THE FRESH PRINCE

FRESHIES
UK vocal/instrumental group formed by Chris Sievey, Barry Spencer, Rick Sarke and Mike Dohertey.

| 14/02/1981 | 54 | 3 | | I'M IN LOVE WITH THE GIRL ON A CERTAIN MANCHESTER VIRGIN MEGASTORE CHECKOUT DESK Originally released on the Razz label in 1980, the reference to Virgin was removed from later MCA issues | MCA 670 |

MATT FRETTON
UK singer (born 15/3/1965, Hillingdon, Middlesex) who later went into artist management.

| 11/06/1983 | 50 | 5 | | IT'S SO HIGH | Chrysalis MATT 1 |

❶⁹ Number of weeks single topped the UK chart ↑ Entered the UK chart at #1 ▲⁹ Number of weeks single topped the US chart

309

FREUR UK group formed in Cardiff in 1981 by Karl Hyde, Rick Smith, Jake Bowie and Alfie Thomas with Bryn Burrows on drums. Smith and Hyde later formed Underworld.

23/04/1983.....59......4....... DOOT DOOT...CBS A 3141

GLENN FREY US singer (born 6/11/1948, Detroit, MI) who was a founding member of the Eagles, going solo when they disbanded in 1981.

02/03/1985.....12.....12...... THE HEAT IS ON Featured in the 1985 film *Beverley Hills Cop* ....MCA 941
22/06/1985.....22......8...... SMUGGLER'S BLUES Featured in the TV series *Miami Vice* ....BBC RESL 170

FRIDA Norwegian singer (born Anna-Frid Lyngstad-Ruess, 15/11/1945, Bjorkasen) who was a founder member of Abba. When they disbanded in 1982, she was the first to make a solo album, with Phil Collins producing. Married to Abba's Benny Andersson in 1978, they divorced in 1979.

21/08/1982.....43......7...... I KNOW THERE'S SOMETHING GOING ON ....Epic EPC A 2603
17/12/1983.....45......5...... TIME **FRIDA AND BA ROBERTSON**...Epic A 3983

GAVIN FRIDAY – see **BONO**

RALPH FRIDGE German producer Ralf Fritsch.

24/04/1999.....68......1....... PARADISE..Addictive 12AD 036
08/04/2000.....20......3...... ANGEL Contains a sample of Spectrasonics' *Symphony Of Voices*.................................Incentive CENT 6CDS

DEAN FRIEDMAN US singer/songwriter/guitarist/keyboard player (born 1955, New Jersey). Legal problems prevented him from recording for two years.

03/06/1978.....52......5...... WOMAN OF MINE ....Lifesong LS 401
23/09/1978 .....3.....10.....O **LUCKY STARS** Features the uncredited vocal of Denise Marsa ....Lifesong LS 402
18/11/1978.....31......7...... LYDIA ....Lifesong LS 403

FRIENDS AGAIN UK group formed in Glasgow in 1982 by Chris Thompson (guitar/vocals), James Grant (guitar/vocals), Neil Cunningham (bass), Paul McGeechan (keyboards) and Stuart Kerr (drums). They disbanded in 1985. Grant, McGeechan and Kerr later formed Love And Money.

04/08/1984.....59......3....... THE FRIENDS AGAIN EP Tracks on EP: *Lullaby On Board, Wand You Wave* and *Thank You For Being An Angel*.....Mercury FA 1

FRIENDS OF MATTHEW UK vocal/instrumental group formed by Mike Gray, Jon Pearn and Nick Ratcliffe with singer Sally Kemp.

10/07/1999.....61......1....... OUT THERE ....Serious SERR 007CD

FRIGID VINEGAR UK rap/production duo Marvin and Alex Lusty from Milton Keynes.

21/08/1999.....53......1....... DOGMONAUT 2000 (IS THERE ANYONE OUT THERE) Contains a sample of Tom Jones' *It's Not Unusual*...........Gut CDGUT 27

FRIJID PINK US rock group formed in Detroit, MI by Kelly Green (vocals), Gary Thomson (guitar), Tom Beaudry (bass) and Rich Stevens (drums).

28/03/1970 .....4......16...... **HOUSE OF THE RISING SUN**...Deram DM 288

ROBERT FRIPP – see **DAVID SYLVIAN**

JANE FROMAN US singer (born Ellen Jane Froman, 10/11/1907, St Louis, MO) who began on radio in the 1930s, later appearing on Broadway and in the films *Stars Over Broadway* (1935) and *Radio City Revels* (1938). She survived a plane crash in Portugal in 1943 en route to entertain US troops, and was the subject of the 1952 biopic *With A Song In My Heart* starring Susan Hayward (nominated for a Best Actress Oscar). She died on 22/4/1980 and has three stars on the Hollywood Walk of Fame for her contributions to recording, radio and TV.

17/06/1955.....14......4....... I WONDER ....Capitol CL 14254

FRONT 242 Belgian duo Patrick Codenys (born 16/11/1958, Brussels) and Daniel Bressanutti (born 27/8/1954, Brussels). They have also been a trio with Jean-Luc De Meyer and a quartet with Geoff Bellingham (later replaced by ex-Revolting Cocks Richard 23).

01/05/1993.....46......1....... RELIGION ....RRE 106CD

FROU FROU UK duo Imogen Heap and Guy Sigsworth who got together in 1998.

06/07/2002.....44......1....... BREATHE IN...Island CID 799

CHRISTIAN FRY UK singer.

14/11/1998.....45......2...... YOU GOT ME...Mushroom MUSH 33CDS
03/04/1999.....48......1...... WON'T YOU SAY ....Mushroom MUSH 46CDS

FUGAZI US rock group formed by ex-Minor Threat Ian Mackaye (guitar/vocals), ex-Rites Of Spring Guy Picciotto (guitar/vocals), Joe Lally (bass) and Brendan Canty (drums).

20/10/2001.....61......1....... FURNITURE ....Dischord DIS 129CD

FUGEES US rap band formed in New York in 1994 by Wyclef 'Clef' Jean (born 17/10/1972, Haiti), Lauryn 'L-Boogie' Hill (born 25/5/1975, East Orange, NJ) and Prakazrel 'Pras' Michel (born 19/10/1972, Haiti). Their name, short for 'refugees', was chosen because

their parents were refugees from Haiti. They later recorded as The Refugee Allstars. Named Best International Group at the 1997 BRIT Awards, their two Grammy Awards included Best Rap Album in 1996 for *The Score*. They also won the MTV Amour Award at the MTV Europe Music Awards in 1996 and the MOBO Award for Best International Act the same year.

06/04/1996	21	5		FU-GEE-LA Contains a sample of Teena Marie's *Ooh La La La*	Columbia 6630662
08/06/1996	❶⁵	20	✪²	**KILLING ME SOFTLY** ↑ Reclaimed #1 position on 13/7/1996. 1996 Grammy Award for Best Rhythm & Blues Performance by a Group and 1996 MOBO Award for Best International Single	Columbia 6633435
14/09/1996	❶²	12	●	**READY OR NOT** Contains samples of Enya's *Song For Bodecia* and The Delfonics' *Ready Or Not*	Columbia 6637215
30/11/1996	2	9		**NO WOMAN NO CRY**	Columbia 6639925
15/03/1997	3	8		**RUMBLE IN THE JUNGLE** Contains a sample of Abba's *The Name Of The Game* and features the uncredited vocals of A Tribe Called Quest, Busta Rymes and Rappin' 4-Tay. Featured in the 1997 film *When We Were Kings*	Mercury 5740692
28/06/1997	13	5		WE TRYING TO STAY ALIVE WYCLEF JEAN AND THE REFUGEE ALLSTARS	Columbia 6646815
06/09/1997	18	4		THE SWEETEST THING REFUGEE CAMP ALLSTARS FEATURING LAURYN HILL	Columbia 6649785
27/09/1997	25	2		GUANTANAMERA WYCLEF JEAN AND THE REFUGEE ALLSTARS	Columbia 6650852
27/10/2001	20	3		LOVING YOU (OLE OLE OLE) BRIAN HARVEY AND THE REFUGEE CREW	Blacklist 0133045 ERE

FULL CIRCLE US vocal group formed by Albert Lee, Larry Marsden, Glenn 'Chango' Everett, Anthony McEwan and Richard Sinclair.

07/03/1987	41	5		WORKIN' UP A SWEAT	EMI America EA 229

FULL FORCE US rap/hip hop group formed in New York by brothers Lucien 'Lou', Paul Anthony and Brian 'B-Fine' George and cousins Curtis Bedeau, Gerald Charles and Junior 'Shy-Shy' Clark. Originally the Amplifiers, they name-changed in 1978. They were first known for producing Lisa Lisa & Cult Jam, later working with artists as diverse as James Brown and Samantha Fox.

10/08/1985	12	17		I WONDER IF I TAKE YOU HOME LISA LISA AND CULT JAM WITH FULL FORCE	CBS A 6057
28/12/1985	9	11		**ALICE I WANT YOU JUST FOR ME**	CBS A 6640
21/05/1988	31	5		NAUGHTY GIRLS SAMANTHA FOX FEATURING FULL FORCE	Jive FOXY 9
04/06/1988	31	4		I'M REAL JAMES BROWN FEATURING FULL FORCE	Scotti Brothers JSB 1

FULL INTENTION UK dance group formed by producers Mike Gray and Jon Pearn who also recorded as Arizona, Hustlers Convention, Ronaldo's Revenge, Disco Tex Presents Cloudburst and Sex-O-Sonique.

06/04/1996	32	2		AMERICA (I LOVE AMERICA)	Stress CDSTR 56
10/08/1996	61	1		UPTOWN DOWNTOWN	Stress CDSTR 67
26/07/1997	34	2		SHAKE YOUR BODY (DOWN TO THE GROUND)	Sugar Daddy CDSTR 82
22/11/1997	56	1		AMERICA (I LOVE AMERICA) (REMIX)	Sugar Daddy CDSTR 56
06/06/1998	75	1		YOU ARE SOMEBODY	Sugar Daddy CDSD 001
01/09/2001	44	1		I'LL BE WAITING FULL INTENTION PRESENTS SHENA	Rulin 17CDS

FULL METAL RACKETS – see JOHN McENROE AND PAT CASH WITH THE FULL METAL RACKETS

FULL MONTY ALLSTARS FEATURING TJ DAVIS UK vocal/instrumental group with singer TJ Davis.

27/07/1996	72	1		BRILLIANT FEELING	Arista 74321380902

BOBBY FULLER FOUR US singer (born 22/10/1943, Baytown, TX), in the Four with brother Randy (bass), DeWayne Quirico (drums) and Jim Reese (born 7/12/1941, El Paso, TX, guitar). He died in mysterious circumstances, found on 18/7/1966 in his car, his body beaten and soaked in petrol. It was revealed that petrol had been forced down his throat, though the Los Angeles coroner ruled it was suicide. Rumour had it he was having an affair with the wife of a local gangster. Reese died from a heart attack on 26/10/1991.

14/04/1966	33	4		I FOUGHT THE LAW	London HL 10030

FUN BOY THREE UK group formed in 1981 by three ex-Specials, Terry Hall (born 19/3/1959, Coventry), Lynval Golding (born 7/7/1952, St Catherine's, Jamaica) and Neville Staples (born 11/4/1956, Christiana, Jamaica). They split after two years, Hall forming Colour Field.

07/11/1981	20	12		THE LUNATICS (HAVE TAKEN OVER THE ASYLUM)	Chrysalis CHS 2563
13/02/1982	4	10	○	**IT AIN'T WHAT YOU DO IT'S THE WAY THAT YOU DO IT** FUN BOY THREE AND BANANARAMA	Chrysalis CHS 2570
10/04/1982	5	10	○	**REALLY SAYING SOMETHING** BANANARAMA WITH FUN BOY THREE	Deram NANA 1
08/05/1982	17	9		THE TELEPHONE ALWAYS RINGS	Chrysalis CHS 2609
31/07/1982	18	8		SUMMERTIME	Chrysalis CHS 2629
15/01/1983	68	1		THE MORE I SEE (THE LESS I BELIEVE)	Chrysalis CHS 2664
05/02/1983	10	10		**TUNNEL OF LOVE**	Chrysalis CHS 2678
30/04/1983	7	10		**OUR LIPS ARE SEALED** Featured in the 1997 film *Romy And Michele's High School Reunion*	Chrysalis FUNB 1

FUN LOVIN' CRIMINALS US rock group formed in Syracuse, NY in 1993 by New Yorkers Hugh 'Huey' Morgan (guitar/vocals), Steve Borovini (drums) and Brian 'Fast' Leiser (bass/trumpet). Huey was in the *Perfect Day* project for the BBC's Children In Need charity, and the group was in *It's Only Rock 'N' Roll* for the Children's Promise charity.

08/06/1996	72	1		THE GRAVE AND THE CONSTANT	Chrysalis CDCHS 5031
17/08/1996	22	3		SCOOBY SNACKS Contains a sample of Tones On Tail's *Movements Of Fear*	Chrysalis CDCHSS 5034
16/11/1996	26	3		THE FUN LOVIN' CRIMINAL	Chrysalis CDCHS 5040
29/03/1997	28	3		KING OF NEW YORK	Chrysalis CDCHS 5049
05/07/1997	12	5		I'M NOT IN LOVE/SCOOBY SNACKS	Chrysalis CDCHS 5060
15/08/1998	18	4		LOVE UNLIMITED	Chrysalis CDCHS 5096
17/10/1998	29	2		BIG NIGHT OUT Contains samples of Tom Petty's *American Girl* and The Marshall Tucker Band's *Can't You See* .... Chrysalis CDCHSS 5101

❶⁹ Number of weeks single topped the UK chart ↑ Entered the UK chart at #1 ▲⁹ Number of weeks single topped the US chart

311

08/05/1999	15	3		KOREAN BODEGA .... Chrysalis CDCHSS 5108
17/02/2001	5	6		**LOCO** Contains a sample of Little River Band's *Happy Anniversary* .... Chrysalis CDCHSS 5121
01/09/2001	50	1		BUMP/RUN DADDY RUN .... Chrysalis CDHSS 5128
13/09/2003	61	1		TOO HOT .... Sanctuary SANXD 205X

FUNERAL FOR A FRIEND UK group formed in Wales by Matt Davies (vocals), Kris Roberts (guitar), Darren Smith (guitar), Gareth Davies (bass) and Ryan Richards (drums/vocals).

09/08/2003	19	3		JUNEAU .... Infectious EW 269CD1
18/10/2003	20	2		SHE DROVE ME TO DAYTIME TELEVISION .... Infectious EW 274CD2
14/02/2004	19	3		ESCAPE ARTISTS NEVER DIE .... Infectious EW 283CD

FARLEY 'JACKMASTER' FUNK US singer/DJ (born Farley Keith Williams, 25/1/1962, Chicago, IL) with Darryl Pandy (vocals), both based in Chicago. This was the first house record to hit the pop charts.

23/08/1986	10	12		**LOVE CAN'T TURN AROUND** .... DJ International LON 105
11/02/1989	49	2		AS ALWAYS **FARLEY 'JACKMASTER' FUNK FEATURING RICKY DILLARD** .... Champion CHAMP 90
14/12/1996	40	2		LOVE CAN'T TURN AROUND **FARLEY JACKMASTER FUNK FEATURING DARRYL PANDY** .... 4 Liberty LIBTCD 27R

FUNK D'VOID Swedish producer Lara Sandberg.

20/10/2001	70	1		DIABLA .... Soma 112
31/01/2004	74	1		EMOTIONAL CONTENT .... Soma 139R

FUNK JUNKEEZ US producer/remixer (born Roger Sanchez, 1/6/1967, New York City) who earlier recorded as El Mariachi and Transatlantic Soul, records as Roger S or the S Man in the US, and runs the R-Senal label.

21/02/1998	57	1		GOT FUNK .... Evocative EVOKE 1CDS

FUNK MASTERS UK group with Bo Kool, Tony Williams and Juliet Roberts.

18/06/1983	8	12		**IT'S OVER** .... Master Funk Records 7MP 004

FUNKADELIC US funk group formed by George Clinton (born 22/7/1941, Kannapolis, NC), Gary Shider, Mike 'Kidd Funkadelic' Hampton, Bobby Lewis, Bernie Worrell (born 19/4/1944, New Jersey), Junie Morrison, Tyrone Lampkin, Jerome Brailey, Eddie Hazel (born 10/4/1950, New York), Larry Fratangelo, Cordell 'Boogie' Mosson, Rodney 'Skeet' Curtis, Glen Goins and William 'Bootsy' Collins (born 26/10/1951, Cincinnati, OH) and seven more singers. The group also recorded as Parliament. Goins died from Parkinson's Disease on 30/7/1978, Hazel from stomach cancer on 23/12/1992. The group (as Parliament/Funkadelic) was inducted into the Rock & Roll Hall of Fame in 1997.

09/12/1978	9	12		**ONE NATION UNDER A GROOVE (PART 1)** Featured in the 1991 film *Young Soul Rebels*, even though the film is set around the Queen's Silver Jubilee in 1977, eighteen months before the track was recorded .... Warner Brothers K 17246
21/08/1999	55	1		MOTHERSHIP RECONNECTION **SCOTT GROOVES FEATURING PARLIAMENT/FUNKADELIC** .... Virgin DINSD 185

FUNKAPOLITAN UK eight-piece funk group formed by Nicholas Jones, Toby Anderson, Kadir Guirey, Guy Pratt and Simon Ollivierre and produced by August Darnell (aka Kid Creole).

22/08/1981	41	7		AS THE TIME GOES BY .... London LON 001

FUNKDOOBIEST US rap group with Jason 'Son Doobie' Vasquez, Ralph 'DJ Ralph M The Mexican' Medrano and Tyrone 'Tomahawk Funk (T-Bone)' Pachenco.

11/12/1993	37	4		WOPBABALUBOP .... Immortal 6597112
05/03/1994	34	2		BOW WOW WOW .... Immortal 6594052

FUNKSTAR DE LUXE Danish producer/remixer Martin Ottesen (born 1973, Odense).

25/09/1999	3	10	O	**SUN IS SHINING** .... Club Tools 0066895 CLU
22/01/2000	11	6		RAINBOW COUNTRY This and above single credited to **BOB MARLEY VS FUNKSTAR DE LUXE** .... Club Tools 0067225 CLU
13/05/2000	42	1		WALKING IN THE NAME **FUNKSTAR DE LUXE VS TERRY MAXX** .... Club Tools 0067375 CLU
25/11/2000	60	1		PULL UP TO THE BUMPER **GRACE JONES VS FUNKSTAR DE LUXE** .... Club Tools 0120375 CLU

FUNKY BOYS – see **LINDA CARR**

FUNKY BUNCH – see **MARKY MARK AND THE FUNKY BUNCH**

FUNKY CHOAD FEATURING NICK SKITZ Australian/Italian production duo with singer Nick Skitz.

29/08/1998	51	1		THE ULTIMATE .... ffrr FCD 341

FUNKY GREEN DOGS US group formed in 1991 by Oscar Gaetan and Ralph Falcon as Funky Green Dogs From Outer Space, later adding Pamela Williams as lead singer.

12/04/1997	17	3		FIRED UP! .... Twisted UK TWCD 10016
28/06/1997	43	1		THE WAY .... Twisted UK TWCD 10026
20/06/1998	75	1		UNTIL THE DAY .... Twisted UK TWCD 10034
27/02/1999	46	1		BODY .... Twisted UK TWCD 110041

FUNKY JUNCTION – see **KC FLIGHTT**

FUNKY POETS
US rap group formed by Paul Frazier, brother Ray and cousins Christian Jordon and Gene Johnson.

| 07/05/1994 | 72 | 1 | | BORN IN THE GHETTO | Epic 6603522 |

FUNKY WORM
UK group formed by Julie Stewart (vocals), Richard Barrett (brass/keyboards) and Carl Munson (keyboards/brass).

30/07/1988	13	8		HUSTLE! (TO THE MUSIC…)	Fon 15
26/11/1988	61	3		THE SPELL!	Fon 16
20/05/1989	46	3		U + ME = LOVE	Fon 19

FUREYS
Irish family group from Ballyfermont formed by brothers Eddie (born 23/12/1944, Dublin, guitar/mandola/mandolin/harmonica/fiddle/bodhran/vocals), Finbar (born 28/9/1946, Dublin, pipes/banjo/whistles/flute/vocals), George (born 11/6/1951, Dublin, guitar/accordion/mandola/autoharp/whistles/vocals) and Paul Furey (born 6/5/1948, Dublin, accordion/melodeon/concertina/whistles/bones/spoons/vocals), and their friend Davey Arthur (born 24/9/1954, Edinburgh, assorted instruments) who left in 1993 to form Davey Arthur And Co.

| 10/10/1981 | 14 | 11 | | WHEN YOU WERE SWEET SIXTEEN FUREYS WITH DAVEY ARTHUR | Ritz 003 |
| 03/04/1982 | 54 | 3 | | I WILL LOVE YOU (EV'RY TIME WHEN WE ARE GONE) | Ritz 012 |

FURIOUS FIVE
– see GRANDMASTER FLASH, MELLE MEL AND THE FURIOUS FIVE

FURNITURE
UK indie group formed in London in 1981 by James Irwin (born 20/7/1959, London, vocals), Timothy Whelan (born 15/9/1958, London, guitar/piano/vocals) and Hamilton Lee (born 7/9/1958, London, drums), later adding Sally Still (born 5/2/1964, London, bass) and Maya Gilder (born 25/4/1964, Poonak, India, keyboards). Their debut single was on their own The Guy From Paraguay label. Stiff Records folded after the group released one further single, and they spent two years trying to cancel their contract with ZTT, who had acquired Stiff. Later signing with Arista, they disbanded in 1990.

| 14/06/1986 | 21 | 10 | | BRILLIANT MIND Featured in the 1987 film Some Kind Of Wonderful | Stiff BUY 251 |

NELLY FURTADO
Canadian singer (born 2/12/1978, Victoria, British Columbia) with Portuguese parents who plays guitar, ukulele and trombone and sings in English, Portuguese and Hindi. She won four Juno Awards (Canadian equivalent of Grammies and BRITs) at the 2001 ceremony.

10/03/2001	5	16	○	I'M LIKE A BIRD 2001 Grammy Award for Best Pop Vocal Performance	DreamWorks 4509192
01/09/2001	4	10		TURN OFF THE LIGHT	DreamWorks DRMDM 50891
19/01/2002	18	6		…ON THE RADIO (REMEMBER THE DAYS)	DreamWorks DRMDM 50856
20/12/2003	13	10		POWERLESS (SAY WHAT YOU WANT)	DreamWorks 4504645
27/03/2004	15	7		TRY	DreamWorks 4505113
24/07/2004	40	3		FORCA Official theme to the 2004 European football championships	DreamWorks 9862823

BILLY FURY
UK singer (born Ronald Wycherley, 17/4/1941, Liverpool) who had rheumatic fever as a child, leaving him with a weak heart. Talking his way into Marty Wilde's dressing room in 1958, manager Larry Parnes signed him, changing his name. Health problems plagued his later career and he was attempting a comeback when he died from heart failure on 28/1/1983.

27/02/1959	18	9		MAYBE TOMORROW	Decca F 11102
26/06/1959	28	1		MARGO	Decca F 11128
10/03/1960	9	10		COLETTE	Decca F 11200
26/05/1960	19	11		THAT'S LOVE BILLY FURY WITH THE FOUR JAYS	Decca F 11237
22/09/1960	25	9		WONDROUS PLACE	Decca F 11267
19/01/1961	14	10		A THOUSAND STARS	Decca F 11311
27/04/1961	40	2		DON'T WORRY BILLY FURY WITH THE FOUR KESTRELS	Decca F 11334
11/05/1961	3	23		HALFWAY TO PARADISE	Decca F 11349
07/09/1961	2	12		JEALOUSY	Decca F 11384
14/12/1961	5	15		I'D NEVER FIND ANOTHER YOU	Decca F 11409
15/03/1962	32	6		LETTER FULL OF TEARS	Decca F 11437
03/05/1962	4	16		LAST NIGHT WAS MADE FOR LOVE	Decca F 11458
19/07/1962	7	13		ONCE UPON A DREAM Featured in the 1962 film Play It Cool starring Billy Fury	Decca F 11485
25/10/1962	18	14		BECAUSE OF LOVE	Decca F 11508
14/02/1963	3	15		LIKE I'VE NEVER BEEN GONE	Decca F 11582
16/05/1963	3	12		WHEN WILL YOU SAY I LOVE YOU	Decca F 11655
25/07/1963	5	11		IN SUMMER	Decca F 11701
03/10/1963	18	7		SOMEBODY ELSE'S GIRL	Decca F 11744
02/01/1964	13	10		DO YOU REALLY LOVE ME TOO	Decca F 11792
30/04/1964	14	12		I WILL	Decca F 11888
23/07/1964	10	10		IT'S ONLY MAKE BELIEVE	Decca F 11939
14/01/1965	16	10		I'M LOST WITHOUT YOU	Decca F 12048
22/07/1965	9	11		IN THOUGHTS OF YOU	Decca F 12178

❶⁹ Number of weeks single topped the UK chart ↑ Entered the UK chart at #1 ▲⁹ Number of weeks single topped the US chart

313

				SINGLE TITLE	LABEL & NUMBER
16/09/1965	25	7		RUN TO MY LOVIN' ARMS	Decca F 12230
10/02/1966	35	5		I'LL NEVER QUITE GET OVER YOU	Decca F 12325
04/08/1966	27	7		GIVE ME YOUR WORD	Decca F 12459
04/09/1982	57	5		LOVE OR MONEY	Polydor POSP 488
13/11/1982	58	4		DEVIL OR ANGEL	Polydor POSP 528
04/06/1983	59	4		FORGET HIM	Polydor POSP 558

FUSED Swedish instrumental/production duo Samuel Onervas and Brian Harris with singer Petra Hallberg.

20/03/1999	64	1		THIS PARTY SUCKS!	Columbia 6669302

FUTURE BREEZE German production duo Markus Boehme and Martin Hensing, both later in 4 Clubbers.

06/09/1997	50	1		WHY DON'T YOU DANCE WITH ME	AM:PM 5823312
20/01/2001	67	1		SMILE	Nebula NEBCD 014
13/04/2002	21	6		TEMPLE OF DREAMS	Data 31CDS
21/12/2002	46	3		OCEAN OF ETERNITY	Data 44CD

FUTURE FORCE UK/US duo.

17/08/1996	47	1		WHAT YOU WANT	AM:PM 5816592

FUTURE SOUND OF LONDON UK instrumental/production duo Garry Cobain and Brian Dougan who later launched the Electronic Brain Violence label, recording as Amorphous Androgynous. Cobain had mercury poisoning (from teeth fillings) in 1998, halting their career. They resumed in late 2000 when Cobain had recovered.

23/05/1992	22	6		PAPUA NEW GUINEA	Jumpin' & Pumpin' TOT 17
06/11/1993	27	3		CASCADE	Virgin VSCDT 1478
30/07/1994	72	1		EXPANDER	Jumpin' & Pumpin' CDSTOR 37
13/08/1994	14	3		LIFEFORMS FUTURE SOUND OF LONDON VOCALS BY ELIZABETH FRASER	Virgin VSCD 1484
27/05/1995	22	3		FAR-OUT SON OF LUNG & THE RAMBLINGS OF A MADMAN	Virgin VSCDT 1540
26/10/1996	13	3		MY KINGDOM Contains a sample of Vangelis' Rachel's Song	Virgin VSCDT 1605
12/04/1997	12	3		WE HAVE EXPLOSIVE	Virgin VSCDX 1616
29/09/2001	28	3		PAPUA NEW GUINEA 2001 (REMIX)	Jumpin' & Pumpin' CDSTOT 44

FUTUREHEADS UK rock group formed in Sunderland by Barry Hyde (guitar/vocals), Ross Millard (guitar/vocals), David Craig (bass/vocals) and Peter Brewis (drums/vocals).

09/08/2003	58	1		FIRST DAY	Fantastic Plastic FPS 036
07/08/2004	23	2		DECENT DAYS AND NIGHTS	679 Recordings 679L080CD
30/10/2004	49	1		MEANTIME	679 Recordings 679L088CD

FUTURESHOCK UK production duo Alex Tepper and Phil Dockerty.

15/03/2003	51	1		ON MY MIND FUTURESHOCK FEATURING BEN ONONO	Junior/Parlophone CDR 6595
16/08/2003	60	1		PRIDE'S PARANOIA	Parlophone CDR 6616
01/11/2003	73	1		LATE AT NIGHT	Parlophone CDR 6617

FUZZBOX – see WE'VE GOT A FUZZBOX AND WE'RE GONNA USE IT

FYA UK vocal group formed in Slough by Kizzi Bennett, Tenza Foster and Emma Nhamburo.

13/03/2004	13	7		MUST BE LOVE FYA FEATURING SMUJJI	Def Jam UK 9817508
24/07/2004	49	2		TOO HOT	Def Jam 9867145

LESLIE FYSON – see MICHAEL MEDWIN, BERNARD BRESSLAW, ALFIE BASS AND LESLIE FYSON

○ Silver disc   ● Gold disc   ✪ Platinum disc (additional platinum units are indicated by a figure following the symbol)   ◉ Singles released prior to 1973 that are known to have sold over 1 million copies in the UK

G

G TOM MAC – see LOST BROTHERS FEATURING G TOM MAC

ALI G AND SHAGGY UK TV comedian (born Saccha Baron-Cohen, 1970, London) with Jamaican singer Shaggy.

23/03/2002	2	14	O

ME JULIE Featured in the 2002 film *Ali G Indahouse* .... Island CID 793

ANDY G'S STARSKY & HUTCH ALL STARS UK producer Andros Georgiou who also recorded as Alien Voices and Boogie Box High.

03/10/1998	51	1	

STARSKY & HUTCH – THE THEME .... Virgin VSCDT 1708

BOBBY G UK singer (born Robert Gubby, 23/8/1953, Epsom) who was in Bucks Fizz from 1981 until their disbandment in 1989.

01/12/1984	65	6	
19/10/1985	46	6	

BIG DEAL Theme to the BBC TV series of the same name .... BBC RESL 151
BIG DEAL .... BBC RESL 151

GINA G Australian singer (born Gina Gardiner, 3/8/1970, Queensland) who began as a DJ and singer before emigrating to the UK in 1994. She recorded her debut after hearing it in a studio and was offered a contract by Warner's on its strength. It was heard by Jonathan King who suggested entering it into Song For Europe. It won, Gina G being the first overseas singer to represent the UK in the Eurovision competition. It failed to win but became a worldwide smash. Reaching the US top 20, it was the most successful UK Eurovision entry on the US charts. Her career was delayed for two years in 1998 with the collapse of record company FX Music, boss Steve Rodway (who previously recorded as Motiv8) being made bankrupt for 'having acted improperly and dishonestly in knowingly swearing false evidence'.

06/04/1996	❶[1]	25	✪
09/11/1996	6	11	
22/03/1997	6	7	
07/06/1997	11	5	
06/09/1997	25	2	
15/11/1997	52	1	

OOH AAH...JUST A LITTLE BIT UK entry for the 1996 Eurovision Song Contest (came seventh) .... Eternal 041CD
I BELONG TO YOU .... Eternal 081CD
FRESH! .... Eternal 095CD
TI AMO .... Eternal 107CD1
GIMME SOME LOVE .... Eternal 101CD1
EVERY TIME I FALL .... Eternal 134CD

HURRICANE G – see PUFF DADDY

KENNY G US saxophonist (born Kenny Gorelick, 6/7/1956, Seattle, WA) who was in the Love Unlimited Orchestra at seventeen, later auditioning for Jeff Lorber who got him a contract with Arista. He recorded his debut album in 1982 and won the 1993 Grammy Award for Best Instrumental Composition for *Forever In Love*. He has a star on the Hollywood Walk of Fame.

21/04/1984	70	3	
30/08/1986	64	2	
04/07/1987	22	7	
09/05/1992	28	4	
24/04/1993	47	3	
17/07/1993	56	3	
08/11/1997	22	4	

HI! HOW YA DOIN'? .... Arista ARIST 561
WHAT DOES IT TAKE (TO WIN YOUR LOVE) .... Arista ARIST 672
SONGBIRD .... Arista RIS 18
MISSING YOU NOW MICHAEL BOLTON FEATURING KENNY G .... Columbia 6579917
FOREVER IN LOVE .... Arista 74321145552
BY THE TIME THIS NIGHT IS OVER KENNY G WITH PEABO BRYSON .... Arista 74321157142
HOW COULD AN ANGEL BREAK MY HEART TONI BRAXTON WITH KENNY G .... LaFace 74321531982

WARREN G US rapper (born Warren Griffin III, 1971, Long Beach, CA) who later set up the G-Funk label. He is Dr Dre's half-brother. Both Warren G and Nate Dogg had been part of Dr Dre's Dogg Pound Collective. Warren later formed rap supergroup 213 with Nate Dogg and Snoop Dogg.

23/07/1994	5	14	O
12/11/1994	12	7	
25/03/1995	29	2	
23/11/1996	2	12	
22/02/1997	2	8	
31/05/1997	14	5	
10/01/1998	15	7	
24/01/1998	16	4	
16/03/2002	60	1	

REGULATE WARREN G AND NATE DOGG Contains a sample of Michael McDonald's *I Keep Forgettin'*. Featured in the 1994 film *Above The Rim* .... Death Row A 8290CD
THIS DJ .... RAL RALCD 1
DO YOU SEE Contains a sample of Junior's *Mama Used To Say* .... RAL RALCD 3
WHAT'S LOVE GOT TO DO WITH IT WARREN G FEATURING ADINA HOWARD Featured in the 1996 film *Supercop* ... Interscope IND 97008
I SHOT THE SHERIFF Contains a sample of Boogie Down Productions' *Love's Gonna Get Cha* .... Def Jam DEFCD 31
SMOKIN' ME OUT WARREN G FEATURING RON ISLEY Contains an interpolation of The Isley Brothers' *Coolin' Me Out* .... Def Jam 5744432
PRINCE IGOR THE RHAPSODY FEATURING WARREN G AND SISSEL .... Def Jam 5749652
ALL NIGHT ALL RIGHT PETER ANDRE FEATURING WARREN G Contains a sample of A Taste Of Honey's *Boogie Oogie Oogie* .... Mushroom MUSH 21CD
LOOKIN' AT YOU WARREN G FEATURING TOI .... Universal MCSTD 40275

G NATION FEATURING ROSIE UK production duo Jake Moses and Mark Smith with singer Rosie.

09/08/1997	58	1	

FEEL THE NEED .... Cooltempo CDCOOL 327

---

❶[9] Number of weeks single topped the UK chart ↑ Entered the UK chart at #1 ▲[9] Number of weeks single topped the US chart

G-CLEFS
US R&B vocal group formed in Roxbury, MA by brothers Teddy, Chris, Timmy and Arnold Scott with Ray Gibson. They scored their first US hit in 1956, disbanding while the members finished their schooling. They re-formed in 1960.

DATE	POS	WKS	BPI	SINGLE TITLE	LABEL & NUMBER
30/11/1961	17	12		I UNDERSTAND Adaptation of *Auld Lang Syne*	London HLU 9433

G-UNIT
US rap group formed by 50 Cent (born Curtis Jackson, 6/7/1976, Queens, NY), Lloyd Banks (born Christopher Lloyd, 30/4/1982, Jamaica, NY) and Tony Yayo with DJs Whookid and Cutmaster C. Yayo left the group after being sent to prison for gun possession and was replaced by Young Buck (born David Brown, 15/3/1981).

DATE	POS	WKS	BPI	SINGLE TITLE	LABEL & NUMBER
27/12/2003	25	7		STUNT 101	Interscope 9815335
06/03/2004	10	8		**IF I CAN'T/THEM THANGS** 50 CENT FEATURING G-UNIT	Interscope 9815279
17/04/2004	27	5		WANNA GET TO KNOW YA	Interscope 9862268
24/04/2004	12	7		RIDE WIT U/MORE & MORE JOE FEATURING G-UNIT	Jive 82876609392

G.O.S.H.
UK charity ensemble raising funds for Great Ormond Street Hospital.

DATE	POS	WKS	BPI	SINGLE TITLE	LABEL & NUMBER
28/11/1987	22	11		THE WISHING WELL	MBS GOSH 1

ERIC GABLE
US R&B singer (born in New Orleans, LA).

DATE	POS	WKS	BPI	SINGLE TITLE	LABEL & NUMBER
19/03/1994	63	1		PROCESS OF ELMINATION	Epic 6602282

PETER GABRIEL
UK singer (born 13/2/1950, London) who was lead singer with Genesis from 1966 to 1975 when he went solo. His debut album took two years to materialise. He won Best British Male at the 1987 BRIT Awards and Best Producer at the 1993 awards. His four Grammy Awards included Best New Age Recording in 1989 for *Passion – Music For 'The Last Temptation Of Christ'* and Best Music Video Long Form in 1995 for *Secret World Live*.

DATE	POS	WKS	BPI	SINGLE TITLE	LABEL & NUMBER
09/04/1977	13	9		SOLSBURY HILL	Charisma CB 301
09/02/1980	4	11	○	**GAMES WITHOUT FRONTIERS**	Charisma CB 354
10/05/1980	33	6		NO SELF CONTROL	Charisma CB 360
23/08/1980	38	3		BIKO	Charisma CB 370
25/09/1982	58	5		SHOCK THE MONKEY	Charisma SHOCK 1
09/07/1983	62	3		I DON'T REMEMBER	Charisma GAB 1
02/06/1984	69	3		WALK THROUGH THE FIRE	Virgin VS 689
26/04/1986	4	16	○	**SLEDGEHAMMER** ▲[1] 1987 BRIT Award for Best Video	Virgin PGS 1
01/11/1986	9	11		**DON'T GIVE UP** PETER GABRIEL AND KATE BUSH Featured in the 1999 film *The Bone Collector*	Virgin PGS 2
28/03/1987	13	7		BIG TIME	Virgin PGS 3
11/07/1987	46	3		RED RAIN	Virgin PGS 4
21/11/1987	49	6		BIKO (LIVE)	Virgin PGS 6
03/06/1989	61	3		SHAKING THE TREE YOUSSOU N'DOUR AND PETER GABRIEL	Virgin VS 1167
22/12/1990	57	4		SOLSBURY HILL/SHAKING THE TREE PETER GABRIEL/YOUSSOU N'DOUR AND PETER GABRIEL	Virgin VS 1322
19/09/1992	24	4		DIGGING THE DIRT 1992 Grammy Award for Best Music Video Short Form	Realworld PGS 7
16/01/1993	10	7		**STEAM** 1993 Grammy Award for Best Music Video Short Form	Realworld PGSDG 8
03/04/1993	43	4		BLOOD OF EDEN	Realworld PGSDG 9
25/09/1993	46	3		KISS THAT FROG	Realworld PGSDG 10
25/06/1994	49	2		LOVETOWN Featured in the 1994 film *Philadelphia*	Epic 6604802
03/09/1994	39	2		SW LIVE EP Tracks on EP: *Red Rain* and *San Jacinto*	Realworld PGSCD 11
11/01/2003	47	2		MORE THAN THIS	Realworld PGSCD 14

GABRIELLE
UK singer (born Louise Gabrielle Bobb, 16/4/1970, London) whose debut hit was initially a white-label release on the Victim label before being picked up by Jetstar. It was deleted after objections by Tracy Chapman to the sample of *Fast Car*. Signed by Go Beat, the song was re-recorded without the sample. She was named Best British Newcomer at the 1994 BRIT Awards and Best British Female at the 1997 Awards. She also won the 2000 MOBO award for Best Album for *Rise* and took part in the *Perfect Day* project for the BBC's Children In Need charity. In December 1995 former boyfriend Tony Antoniou, with whom she had a son, was charged with the murder of his father after beheading him with a samurai sword. Gabrielle was taken in for questioning and had to give evidence at his trial.

DATE	POS	WKS	BPI	SINGLE TITLE	LABEL & NUMBER
19/06/1993	❶[3]	15	●	**DREAMS**	Go Beat GODCD 99
02/10/1993	9	7		**GOING NOWHERE**	Go Beat GODCD 106
11/12/1993	26	5		I WISH	Go Beat GODCD 108
26/02/1994	24	5		BECAUSE OF YOU	Go Beat GOLCD 109
24/02/1996	5	18	○	**GIVE ME A LITTLE MORE TIME** 1996 MOBO Award for Best Single	Go Beat GOLCD 139
22/06/1996	23	5		FORGET ABOUT THE WORLD	Go Beat GOLCD 146
05/10/1996	15	5		IF YOU REALLY CARED	Go Beat GODCD 153
02/11/1996	2	15	●	**IF YOU EVER** EAST 17 FEATURING GABRIELLE	London LONCD 388
01/02/1997	7	8		**WALK ON BY**	Go Beat GODCD 159
09/10/1999	9	8		SUNSHINE	Go Beat GOBCD 23
05/02/2000	❶[2]	15	●	**RISE** ↑ Contains a sample of Bob Dylan's *Knockin' On Heaven's Door*	Go Beat GOLCD 25
17/06/2000	6	8		WHEN A WOMAN	Go Beat GOLCD 27
04/11/2000	13	7		SHOULD I STAY	Go Beat GOLCD 32
21/04/2001	4	16	○	**OUT OF REACH** Featured in the 2001 film *Bridget Jones's Diary*	Go Beat GOLCD 39
03/11/2001	9	7		**DON'T NEED THE SUN TO SHINE (TO MAKE ME SMILE)**	Go Beat GOLCD 47
15/05/2004	20	3		STAY THE SAME	Go! Beat 9866529
14/08/2004	43	1		TEN YEARS TIME	Go! Beat 9867550

YVONNE GAGE
US R&B singer (born 20/12/1959, Chicago, IL).

○ Silver disc ● Gold disc ✪ Platinum disc (additional platinum units are indicated by a figure following the symbol) ◎ Singles released prior to 1973 that are known to have sold over 1 million copies in the UK

DATE	POS	WKS	BPI	SINGLE TITLE	LABEL & NUMBER
16/06/1984	45	4		DOIN' IT IN A HAUNTED HOUSE	Epic A 4519

DANNI'ELLE GAHA Australian singer who had previously recorded with John Farnham before going solo.

DATE	POS	WKS	BPI	SINGLE TITLE	LABEL & NUMBER
01/08/1992	68	2		STUCK IN THE MIDDLE	Epic 6581247
27/02/1993	52	2		DO IT FOR LOVE	Epic 6584612
12/06/1993	41	3		SECRET LOVE	Epic 6592212

DAVE GAHAN UK singer (born 9/5/1962, Epping, Essex) who is also lead singer with Depeche Mode.

DATE	POS	WKS	BPI	SINGLE TITLE	LABEL & NUMBER
07/06/2003	18	2		DIRTY STICKY FLOORS	Mute LCDMUTE 294
30/08/2003	27	2		I NEED YOU	Mute LCDMUTE 301
08/11/2003	36	2		BOTTLE LIVING	Mute LCDMUTE 310

BILLY AND SARAH GAINES US husband and wife vocalists who were in the gospel group Living Sacrifice before embarking on their duo career in 1981.

DATE	POS	WKS	BPI	SINGLE TITLE	LABEL & NUMBER
14/06/1997	48	1		I FOUND SOMEONE	Expansion CDEXP 27

ROSIE GAINES US singer (born in Oakland, CA) who worked with Flash before her first solo deal with Epic in 1985. After a time in Prince's backing group New Power Generation, she re-launched her solo career. She has a six-octave range singing voice.

DATE	POS	WKS	BPI	SINGLE TITLE	LABEL & NUMBER
11/11/1995	70	1		I WANT U	Motown 8604852
31/05/1997	4	12	O	CLOSER THAN CLOSE 1997 MOBO Award for Best International Single	Big Bang CDBBANG 1
29/11/1997	39	2		I SURRENDER	Big Bang CDBBANG 2

SERGE GAINSBOURG – see JANE BIRKIN AND SERGE GAINSBOURG

GALA Italian singer (born Gala Rizzatto, 1973) who was named after Salvador Dali's wife.

DATE	POS	WKS	BPI	SINGLE TITLE	LABEL & NUMBER
19/07/1997	2	14	●	FREED FROM DESIRE	Big Life BLRD 135
06/12/1997	11	8		LET A BOY CRY	Big Life BLRD 140
22/08/1998	38	2		COME INTO MY LIFE	Big Life BLRD 147

GALAXY – see PHIL FEARON

DEE GALDES – see PHIL FEARON

EVE GALLAGHER UK singer (born in Sunderland, raised in West Africa) who studied languages in Switzerland and Italy. She was discovered by Boy George, who produced her debut album.

DATE	POS	WKS	BPI	SINGLE TITLE	LABEL & NUMBER
01/12/1990	61	4		LOVE COME DOWN	More Protein PROT 6
15/04/1995	43	2		YOU CAN HAVE IT ALL	Cleveland City CLECD 13023
28/10/1995	57	1		LOVE COME DOWN	Cleveland City CLECD 13028
06/07/1996	44	1		HEARTBREAK MRS WOOD FEATURING EVE GALLAGHER	React CDREACT 78

LIAM GALLAGHER UK singer (born 21/9/1972, Manchester), lead singer with Oasis and involved in various outside projects.

DATE	POS	WKS	BPI	SINGLE TITLE	LABEL & NUMBER
23/10/1999	6	3		GOING UNDERGROUND:CARNATION BUFFALO TOM:LIAM GALLAGHER AND STEVE CRADDOCK	Ignition IGNSCD 16
28/12/2002	14	8		SCORPIO RISING DEATH IN VEGAS FEATURING LIAM GALLAGHER	Concrete HARD 54CD

GALLAGHER AND LYLE UK duo Benny Gallagher and Graham Lyle (both born in Largs, Scotland) originally teamed up in Scotland before moving to London to join McGuinness Flint and then Slim Chance. Debuting together in 1974, their final album was in 1979. Lyle's songwriting included Grammy Award winner What's Love Got To Do With It, a smash for Tina Turner and Warren G.

DATE	POS	WKS	BPI	SINGLE TITLE	LABEL & NUMBER
28/02/1976	6	9		I WANNA STAY WITH YOU	A&M AMS 7211
22/05/1976	6	10		HEART ON MY SLEEVE	A&M AMS 7227
11/09/1976	35	4		BREAKAWAY	A&M AMS 7245
29/01/1977	32	4		EVERY LITTLE TEARDROP	A&M AMS 7274

PATSY GALLANT Canadian singer/pianist (born 1950, New Brunswick) who first performed with her sisters as The Gallant Sisters. She left in 1967 to go solo and later recorded in French and English.

DATE	POS	WKS	BPI	SINGLE TITLE	LABEL & NUMBER
10/09/1977	6	9		FROM NEW YORK TO L.A.	EMI 2620

GALLEON French house group formed by Marseille natives Phil and Michel. Multi-instrumentalist Phil was 24 at the time of their debut hit, producer and DJ Michel 28.

DATE	POS	WKS	BPI	SINGLE TITLE	LABEL & NUMBER
20/04/2002	36	2		SO I BEGIN	Epic 6724102

LUKE GALLIANA UK singer (born 1980) whose debut hit first featured in the UK's Song For Europe competition.

DATE	POS	WKS	BPI	SINGLE TITLE	LABEL & NUMBER
12/05/2001	42	1		TO DIE FOR	Jive 9201272

GALLIANO UK jazz funk group with Rob Gallagher, Constantine Weir, Crispin Robinson and Michael Snaith. Gallagher also adopted the name Galliano.

DATE	POS	WKS	BPI	SINGLE TITLE	LABEL & NUMBER
30/05/1992	41	2		SKUNK FUNK	Talkin Loud TLK 23
01/08/1992	47	3		PRINCE OF PEACE	Talkin Loud TLK 24
10/10/1992	66	2		JUS' REACH (RECYCLED)	Talkin Loud TLK 29
28/05/1994	15	3		LONG TIME GONE	Talkin Loud TLKCD 48

●[9] Number of weeks single topped the UK chart ↑ Entered the UK chart at #1 ▲[9] Number of weeks single topped the US chart

317

	30/07/1994	37	2		TWYFORD DOWN	Talkin Loud TLKDD 49
	27/07/1996	45	2		EASE YOUR MIND	Talkin Loud TLKDD 10

JAMES GALWAY UK flautist (born 8/12/1939, Belfast) who is considered one of the world's top flautists. His interpretation of Elton John's song *Basque* was named Best Instrumental Composition at the 1991 Grammy Awards.

	27/05/1978	3	13		**ANNIE'S SONG**	RCA Red Seal RB 5085

GAMBAFREAKS Italian production duo Stefano Gambarelli and Davide Riva with singer Paco Rivaz.

	12/09/1998	57	1		INSTANT REPLAY GAMBAFREAKS FEATURING PACO RIVAZ	Evocative EVOKE 7CDS
	13/05/2000	57	1		DOWN DOWN DOWN	Azuli AZNYCDX 116

GANG OF FOUR UK rock group formed in Leeds in 1977 by Jon King (melodica/vocals), Andy Gill (guitar), Dave Allen (drums) and Hugo Barnham (drums). Allen left in 1981 and was replaced by bassist Sara Lee. Barnham was sacked in 1983, the group using session drummers before disbanding soon after. They were revived in 1990 by Jon King and Andy Gill, adding drummer Steve Monti to the line-up the following year.

	16/06/1979	58	3		AT HOME HE'S A TOURIST	EMI 2956
	22/05/1982	65	2		I LOVE A MAN IN UNIFORM	EMI 5299

GANG STARR US hip hop duo Guru Keith (born Keith Elam, 18/7/1966, Boston, MA) and DJ Premier (born Christopher Martin, Brooklyn, NYC). Guru later recorded solo.

	13/10/1990	66	2		JAZZ THING	CBS 6563777
	23/02/1991	63	1		TAKE A REST	Cooltempo COOL 230
	25/05/1991	50	3		LOVESICK	Cooltempo COOL 234
	13/06/1992	67	2		2 DEEP	Cooltempo COOL 256

GANT UK production duo Danny Harrison and Julian Jonah (born Danny Matlock). They also recorded as Congress, Nush, Nu-Birth, M Factor, Reflex, Stella Browne and 187 Lockdown.

	27/12/1997	67	1		SOUND BWOY BURIAL/ALL NIGHT LONG	Positiva CDTIV 85

GAP BAND US R&B group with brothers Charles, Ronnie and Robert Wilson. They took their name from three streets in their hometown of Tulsa in Oklahoma: Greenwood, Archer and Pine. They are cousins of William 'Bootsy' Collins.

	12/07/1980	6	14	○	**OOPS UP SIDE YOUR HEAD** Owed much of its success to a 'rowing boat' dance craze	Mercury MER 22
	27/09/1980	30	8		PARTY LIGHTS	Mercury MER 37
	27/12/1980	22	11		BURN RUBBER ON ME (WHY YOU WANNA HURT ME)	Mercury MER 52
	11/04/1981	36	6		HUMPIN'	Mercury MER 63
	27/06/1981	47	4		YEARNING FOR YOUR LOVE	Mercury MER 73
	05/06/1982	55	3		EARLY IN THE MORNING	Mercury MER 97
	19/02/1983	68	2		OUTSTANDING	Total Experience TE 001
	07/04/1984	17	8		SOMEDAY Features the uncredited vocal contribution of Stevie Wonder	Total Experience TE 5
	23/06/1984	64	2		JAMMIN' IN AMERICA	Total Experience TE 6
	13/12/1986	4	12		**BIG FUN**	Total Experience FB 49779
	14/03/1987	61	2		HOW MUSIC CAME ABOUT (BOP B DA B DA DA)	Total Experience FB 49755
	18/07/1987	20	8		OOPS UPSIDE YOUR HEAD (REMIX)	Club JAB 54
	18/02/1989	63	2		I'M GONNA GIT YOU SUCKA Featured in the 1989 film *I'm Gonna Git You Sucka*	Arista 112016
	16/10/2004	16	6		OOPS UPSIDE YOUR HEAD DJ CASPER FEATURING THE GAP BAND	All Around The World CDGLOBE376

GARBAGE US/UK group formed by Butch Vig (born Brian Vig, Viroqua, US), Steve Markes, Duke Erikson and lead singer Shirley Manson (born in Edinburgh). Manson had been singer with Goodbye Mr McKenzie. Vig is also an independent producer, having produced albums by The Smashing Pumpkins, U2 and Nirvana. They were named Breakthrough Act at the 1996 MTV Europe Music Awards.

	19/08/1995	50	1		SUBHUMAN	Mushroom D 1138
	30/09/1995	29	3		ONLY HAPPY WHEN IT RAINS	Mushroom D 1199
	02/12/1995	13	4		QUEER	Mushroom D 1237
	23/03/1996	4	7		**STUPID GIRL** Contains a sample of The Clash's *Train In Vain*	Mushroom D 1271
	23/11/1996	10	8		**MILK** GARBAGE FEATURING TRICKY	Mushroom D 1494
	09/05/1998	9	5		**PUSH IT** Contains samples of Salt-N-Pepa's *Push It* and The Beach Boys' *Don't Worry Baby*	Mushroom MUSH 28CDS
	18/07/1998	9	5		**I THINK I'M PARANOID**	Mushroom MUSH 35CDS
	17/10/1998	15	4		SPECIAL Contains a sample of The Pretenders' *The Talk Of The Town*	Mushroom MUSH 39CDS
	06/02/1999	9	7		**WHEN I GROW UP** Featured in the 1999 film *Big Daddy*	Mushroom MUSH 43CDS
	05/06/1999	19	4		YOU LOOK SO FINE	Mushroom MUSH 49CDS
	27/11/1999	11	9		THE WORLD IS NOT ENOUGH Featured in the 1999 James Bond film *The World Is Not Enough*	Radioactive RAXTD 40
	06/02/2001	24	2		ANDROGYNY	Mushroom MUSH 94CDSX
	02/02/2002	22	4		CHERRY LIPS	Mushroom MUSH 98CDS
	20/04/2002	27	2		BREAKING UP THE GIRL	Mushroom MUSH 101CDS
	05/10/2002	20	1		SHUT YOUR MOUTH	Mushroom MUSH 106CDSXX

ADAM GARCIA Australian singer (born 1/6/1973) who appeared in the London stage musical *Saturday Night Fever*.

	16/05/1998	15	5		NIGHT FEVER	Polydor 5697972

SCOTT GARCIA FEATURING MC STYLES UK singer/producer Scott Garcia with UK rapper Daryl Turner.

○ Silver disc ● Gold disc ✪ Platinum disc (additional platinum units are indicated by a figure following the symbol) ◎ Singles released prior to 1973 that are known to have sold over 1 million copies in the UK

01/11/1997 . . . . . 29 . . . . . 3 . . . . A LONDON THING . . . . Connected CDCONNECT 1

BORIS GARDINER
Jamaican singer (born 1954, Kingston) whose debut hit was credited to Byron Lee. It was amended after six weeks in the chart.

17/01/1970 . . . . . 14 . . . . . 14 . . . . . . ELIZABETHAN REGGAE . . . . Duke DU 39

26/07/1986 . . . . ❶³ . . . . 15 . . . . ● **I WANT TO WAKE UP WITH YOU** . . . . Revue REV 733

04/10/1986 . . . . . 11 . . . . . 8 . . . . . . YOU'RE EVERYTHING TO ME . . . . Revue REV 735

27/12/1986 . . . . . 69 . . . . . 1 . . . . . . THE MEANING OF CHRISTMAS . . . . Revue REV 740

PAUL GARDINER
UK bass player with Robert Palmer and Gary Numan (in Tubeway Army) before going solo. He died from a heroin overdose in 1984.

25/07/1981 . . . . . 49 . . . . . 4 . . . . . . STORMTROOPER IN DRAG Features the uncredited contribution of Gary Numan . . . . Beggars Banquet BEG 61

ART GARFUNKEL
US singer (born 13/10/1942, Forest Hills, NYC) who teamed up with Queens schoolmate Paul Simon when aged eleven, becoming the most successful duo since the Everly Brothers. They split in 1970 after completing *Bridge Over Troubled Water*, Garfunkel appearing in the film *Catch 22* the same year. He returned to music in 1973 and has since reunited with Simon on numerous occasions. He was inducted into the Rock & Roll Hall of Fame in 1990 (as part of Simon & Garfunkel).

13/09/1975 . . . . ❶² . . . . 11 . . . . ○ **I ONLY HAVE EYES FOR YOU** . . . . CBS 3575

03/03/1979 . . . . ❶⁶ . . . . 19 . . . . ✪ **BRIGHT EYES** Featured in the 1978 film *Watership Down* . . . . CBS 6947

07/07/1979 . . . . . 38 . . . . . 7 . . . . . . SINCE I DON'T HAVE YOU . . . . CBS 7371

JUDY GARLAND
US singer/actress (born Frances Ethel Gumm, 10/6/1922, Grand Rapids, MN) who made her stage debut at three and then worked with her siblings as The Gumm Sisters. Signed by Louis B Mayer to MGM Pictures at twelve, she made her first film in 1936 (a short, *Every Sunday*, followed by her debut feature film *Pigskin Parade*), her most famous role being Dorothy in *The Wizard Of Oz* in 1939 (gaining a Special Academy Award 'for her outstanding performance as a screen juvenile'). She won two Grammy Awards: Album of the Year and Best Female Solo Vocal Performance in 1961 for *Judy At Carnegie Hall* (the album sold over 2 million copies). She died from an accidental drug overdose in London on 22/6/1969. She has a star on the Hollywood Walk of Fame. Liza Minnelli is her daughter by film director Vincent Minnelli.

10/06/1955 . . . . . 18 . . . . . 2 . . . . . . THE MAN THAT GOT AWAY Featured in the 1954 film remake of *A Star Is Born* . . . . Philips PB 366

JESSICA GARLICK
UK singer (born 1982, Kidwelly, Wales) who first became known as one of the 10,000 entrants in *Pop Idol*, making the final ten. Although she didn't win, she was chosen to represent the UK in the 2002 Eurovision Song Contest, which was won by Marie N with *I Wanna* for Latvia.

25/05/2002 . . . . . 13 . . . . . 6 . . . . . . COME BACK Britain's representative in the 2002 Eurovision Song Contest (came third) . . . . Columbia 6725662

LAURENT GARNIER
French DJ/producer (born 1/2/1966, Boulogne Sur Seine), he worked at the French Embassy in London before beginning his career as a DJ in Manchester.

15/02/1997 . . . . . 60 . . . . . 1 . . . . . . CRISPY BACON . . . . F Communications F 055CD

22/04/2000 . . . . . 65 . . . . . 1 . . . . . . MAN WITH THE RED FACE . . . . F Communications F 119CD

11/11/2000 . . . . . 36 . . . . . 2 . . . . . . GREED/THE MAN WITH THE RED FACE Features the uncredited contribution of Philippe Nadaud on saxophone . . . .
. . . . F Communications F127 CDUK

LEE GARRETT
US singer (born in Mississippi) who formed a friendship with Stevie Wonder that led to songwriting collaborations (including *Signed Sealed Delivered*). Garrett signed as a solo performer with Chrysalis in 1975. Like Stevie Wonder, he was blind at birth.

29/05/1976 . . . . . 15 . . . . . 7 . . . . . . YOU'RE MY EVERYTHING . . . . Chrysalis CHS 2087

LEIF GARRETT
US singer (born 8/11/1961, Hollywood) who began as a child actor in 1969, appearing in films such as *Walking Tall* (1973) and its two sequels. He has been credited with helping to popularise skateboarding in the UK.

20/01/1979 . . . . . 4 . . . . . 10 . . . . ○ **I WAS MADE FOR DANCIN'** . . . . Scotti Brothers K 11202

21/04/1979 . . . . . 38 . . . . . 4 . . . . . . FEEL THE NEED . . . . Scotti Brothers K 11274

LESLEY GARRETT AND AMANDA THOMPSON
UK duo of operatic singer Lesley Garrett (born 10/4/1955) and Amanda Thompson, the latter a leukaemia sufferer. Their duet was first broadcast on the BBC TV programme *Hearts Of Gold*. Garrett was also in the *Perfect Day* project for the BBC's Children In Need charity and received a CBE in the 2002 New Year's Honours List.

06/11/1993 . . . . . 16 . . . . . 10 . . . . . AVE MARIA . . . . Internal Affairs KGBD 012

SIEDAH GARRETT — see DENNIS EDWARDS FEATURING SIEDAH GARRETT

DAVID GARRICK
UK singer (born Phillip Darryl Core, 1946, Liverpool) who began his career at the Cavern Club as a member of the Dions before moving to London and signing with Piccadilly. His debut hit had previously been recorded by the Rolling Stones.

09/06/1966 . . . . . 28 . . . . . 7 . . . . . . LADY JANE . . . . Piccadilly 7N 35317

22/09/1966 . . . . . 22 . . . . . 9 . . . . . . DEAR MRS APPLEBEE . . . . Piccadilly 7N 35335

GARY'S GANG
US disco group formed in Queens, NYC by Eric Matthews (guitar/vocals), Al Lauricella (keyboards), Rino Minetti (keyboards), Bill Castalano (percussion), Bob Forman (saxophone), Jay Leon (trombone) and Gary Turnier (drums). Their debut hit was recorded live in a garage and funded by the group.

24/02/1979 . . . . . 8 . . . . . 10 . . . . . **KEEP ON DANCIN'** Featured in the 1998 film *54* . . . . CBS 7109

02/06/1979 . . . . . 49 . . . . . 4 . . . . . . LET'S LOVE DANCE TONIGHT . . . . CBS 7328

06/11/1982 . . . . . 45 . . . . . 4 . . . . . . KNOCK ME OUT . . . . Arista ARIST 499

❶⁹ Number of weeks single topped the UK chart ↑ Entered the UK chart at #1 ▲⁹ Number of weeks single topped the US chart

319

BARBARA GASKIN – see DAVE STEWART

GAT DECOR UK instrumental group formed by Simon Slater and featuring Beverli Skeete on vocals.

16/05/1992	29	4		PASSION	Effective EFFS 1
09/03/1996	6	6		PASSION (REMIX) Theme to the TV series *Ski Sunday*	Way Of Life WAYDA 1

STEPHEN GATELY Irish singer (born 17/3/1976, Dublin) who was with Boyzone from 1993 to 2000.

10/06/2000	3	11	○	NEW BEGINNING/BRIGHT EYES B-side was the theme to the TV series *Watership Down*	A&M 5618202
14/10/2000	11	4		I BELIEVE Featured in the 2000 film *Billy Elliott*	Polydor 5877482
12/05/2001	13	4		STAY	A&M 5870672

DAVID GATES US singer/guitarist/producer/songwriter (born 11/12/1940, Tulsa, OK) who began as a session musician for Chuck Berry, Duane Eddy, Glen Campbell, Merle Haggard and others. He formed Bread in 1969 with James Griffin (guitar), Robb Rover (guitar) and Jim Gordon (drums), Larry Knetchtel and Mike Botts later replacing the latter two. They disbanded in 1973, briefly reuniting in 1976, with Gates enjoying a brief solo career before going into retirement.

22/07/1978	50	2		TOOK THE LAST TRAIN	Elektra K 12307

GARETH GATES UK singer (born 12/7/1984, Bradford) who became famous in the TV series *Pop Idol*, overcoming a chronic stammer during the course of the competition and finishing second to Will Young. He was seventeen at the time of his debut hit and duly became the youngest UK male to top the UK singles chart. The Kumars are the cast of the TV programme *The Kumars At No 42*.

30/03/2002	●4	30	✪2	UNCHAINED MELODY ↑ Voted Record of the Year in the BBC poll	S 74321930882
20/07/2002	●3	15	●	ANYONE OF US (STUPID MISTAKE) ↑	S 74321950602
05/10/2002	●2	18	●	THE LONG AND WINDING ROAD/SUSPICIOUS MINDS ↑ WILL YOUNG AND GARETH GATES B-side credited to Gareth and featured in the 2002 Walt Disney film *Lilo & Stitch*	S 74321965972
21/12/2002	5	13		WHAT MY HEART WANTS TO SAY	S 74321985602
22/03/2003	●2	15	✪	SPIRIT IN THE SKY GARETH GATES FEATURING THE KUMARS Recorded for the Comic Relief charity	S 82876511202
20/09/2003	3	10		SUNSHINE	S 82876560042
13/12/2003	4	8		SAY IT ISN'T SO	S 82876583422

GAY DAD UK rock group formed in 1996 by ex-*Mojo* and *The Face* journalist Cliff Jones (guitar/vocals), Nigel Hoyle (bass/guitar), Nicholas 'Baz' Crowe (drums) and James Risebero (keyboards). They are augmented by singer/guitarist Charley Stone for live dates.

30/01/1999	10	4		TO EARTH WITH LOVE	London LONCD 413
05/06/1999	22	3		JOY!	London LONCD 428
14/08/1999	47	1		OH JIM	London LONCD 437
31/03/2001	41	1		NOW ALWAYS AND FOREVER	B Unique BUN 004CD
22/09/2001	58	1		TRANSMISSION	B Unique BUN 009CDX

GAY GORDON AND THE MINCE PIES UK studio group.

06/12/1986	60	5		THE ESSENTIAL WALLY PARTY MEDLEY Medley of *Let's Twist Again, The Birdie Song, I Came I Saw I Conga'd* and *Knees Up Mother Brown*	Lifestyle XY 2

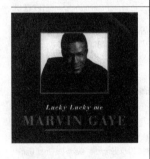
Lucky Lucky me
MARVIN GAYE

MARVIN GAYE US singer (born Marvin Pentz Gay Jr, 2/4/1939, Washington DC) who sang in his father's church before joining local groups the Rainbows and Marquees. Invited by Harvey Fuqua to join the re-formed Moonglows for two singles for Chess, he followed Fuqua to Detroit, MI and joined Motown as a session drummer. First recording for the label in 1961, he established himself as a solo performer, also recording highly successful duets. He married Berry Gordy's sister Anna in 1961; they divorced in 1975 (part of the alimony settlement called for Anna to receive all royalties from a forthcoming album: he recorded *Here My Dear* detailing almost every aspect of their relationship together). His second marriage to Jan also ended in divorce. The death of Tammi Terrell in 1970 sent him into seclusion, but his brother Frankie's accounts of the horrors of Vietnam prompted him to record *What's Going On*. He also appeared in the 1971 film *Chrome And Hot Leather*. After various problems he left Motown and lived in Europe for three years. He returned to the US following the success of *(Sexual) Healing* and was shot to death by his father the day before his birthday on 1/4/1984. He was inducted into the Rock & Roll Hall of Fame in 1987 and has a star on the Hollywood Walk of Fame. Kim Weston is a US singer (born Agatha Weston, 30/12/1939, Detroit, M).

30/07/1964	50	1		ONCE UPON A TIME MARVIN GAYE AND MARY WELLS	Stateside SS 316
10/12/1964	49	1		HOW SWEET IT IS	Stateside SS 360
29/09/1966	50	1		LITTLE DARLIN'	Tamla Motown TMG 574
26/01/1967	16	11		IT TAKES TWO MARVIN GAYE AND KIM WESTON	Tamla Motown TMG 590
17/01/1968	41	7		IF I COULD BUILD MY WHOLE WORLD AROUND YOU	Tamla Motown TMG 635
12/06/1968	34	7		AIN'T NOTHING LIKE THE REAL THING	Tamla Motown TMG 655
02/10/1968	19	19		YOU'RE ALL I NEED TO GET BY	Tamla Motown TMG 668
22/01/1969	21	8		YOU AIN'T LIVIN' TILL YOU'RE LOVIN' This and above three singles credited to MARVIN GAYE AND TAMMI TERRELL	Tamla Motown TMG 681
12/02/1969	●3	15		I HEARD IT THROUGH THE GRAPEVINE ▲7 Featured in the films *The Big Chill* (1984), *Friday* (1995) and *The Walking Dead* (1995)	Tamla Motown TMG 686
04/06/1969	26	8		GOOD LOVIN' AIN'T EASY TO COME BY MARVIN GAYE AND TAMMI TERRELL Female singer is actually Valerie Ashford as Terrell was too ill to record the song	Tamla Motown TMG 697
23/07/1969	5	16		TOO BUSY THINKING ABOUT MY BABY Featured in the 1997 film *A Smile Like Yours*	Tamla Motown TMG 705
15/11/1969	9	12		ONION SONG MARVIN GAYE AND TAMMI TERRELL Female singer is actually Valerie Ashford as Terrell was too ill to record the song	Tamla Motown TMG 715

09/05/1970 . . . . . 9 . . . . . . 14			**ABRAHAM MARTIN AND JOHN** Tribute to Abraham Lincoln, Martin Luther King and John F Kennedy . . . . . . Tamla Motown TMG 734
11/12/1971. . . . . 41. . . . . . 6.			SAVE THE CHILDREN . . . . Tamla Motown TMG 796
22/09/1973. . . . . 31. . . . . . 7.			LET'S GET IT ON ▲² Featured in the films *Into The Night* (1985), *Deuce Bigalow: Male Gigolo* (1999), *Foolish* (1999), *Austin Powers: The Spy Who Shagged Me* (1999) and *The Parole Officer* (2001) . . . . Tamla Motown TMG 868
23/03/1974 . . . . . 5. . . . . . 12 . . . . . O			**YOU ARE EVERYTHING** . . . . Tamla Motown TMG 890
20/07/1974. . . . . 25. . . . . . 8.			STOP LOOK LISTEN (TO YOUR HEART) Featured in the 2001 film *Bridget Jones's Diary*. This and above single credited to **DIANA ROSS AND MARVIN GAYE** . . . . Tamla Motown TMG 906
07/05/1977 . . . . . 7. . . . . . 10			**GOT TO GIVE IT UP** ▲¹ Featured in the films *Boogie Nights* (1998), *Practical Magic* (1999), *Summer Of Sam* (1999) and *Charlie's Angels* (2000) . . . . Motown TMG 1069
24/02/1979. . . . . 66. . . . . . 5.			POPS WE LOVE YOU **DIANA ROSS, MARVIN GAYE, SMOKEY ROBINSON AND STEVIE WONDER** Recorded to honour Berry Gordy's father's 90th birthday. . . . . Motown TMG 1136
30/10/1982 . . . . . 4. . . . . . 14 . . . . . O			**(SEXUAL) HEALING** Marvin Gaye was sued by David Ritz over his songwriting contribution and his name was later added to the credits. 1982 Grammy Awards for Best Rhythm & Blues Vocal Performance and Best Rhythm & Blues Instrumental Performance. . . . CBS A 2855
08/01/1983. . . . . 34. . . . . . 5.			MY LOVE IS WAITING . . . . CBS A 3048
18/05/1985. . . . . 51. . . . . . 4.			SANCTIFIED LADY . . . . CBS A 4894
26/04/1986 . . . . . 8 . . . . . . 8			**I HEARD IT THROUGH THE GRAPEVINE** Re-issue of Tamla Motown TMG 686 after use in a Levi Jeans advertisement . . . . Tamla Motown ZB 40701
14/05/1994. . . . . 67. . . . . . 1.			LUCKY LUCKY ME . . . . Motown TMGCD 1426
06/10/2001. . . . . 36. . . . . . 2.			MUSIC **ERICK SERMON FEATURING MARVIN GAYE** Featured in the 2001 film *What's The Worst That Could Happen?* . . . . Polydor 4976222

GAYE BYKERS ON ACID UK group formed by Mary Millington (aka Mary Mary, born Ian Hoxley, vocals), Robber (born Ian Reynolds, bass), Tony (born Richard Anthony Horsfall, guitar) and Kevin Hyde (drums). The group set up their own Naked Brain label.

31/10/1987. . . . . 54. . . . . . 2.			GIT DOWN (SHAKE YOUR THANG) . . . . Purple Fluid VS 1008

CRYSTAL GAYLE US country singer (born Brenda Gail Web, 9/1/1951, Paintsville, KY, raised in Wabash, IN) who began in sister Loretta Lynn's road show at sixteen, scoring her first country hit in 1970. Three Grammy Awards include Best Recording for Children in 1981 with The Muppets, Glen Campbell, Loretta Lynn and Tanya Tucker for *Sesame Country* and Best Recording for Children in 1982 with various others for *In Harmony 2*.

12/11/1977 . . . . . 5. . . . . . 14 . . . . . O			**DON'T IT MAKE MY BROWN EYES BLUE** Featured in the 1978 film *Convoy*. 1977 Grammy Awards for Best Country Vocal Performance plus Best Country Song for writer Richard Leigh . . . . United Artists UP 36307
26/08/1978. . . . . 11. . . . . 14 . . . . . O			TALKING IN YOUR SLEEP . . . . United Artists UP 36422

MICHELLE GAYLE UK singer (born 2/2/1971, London) who was first known as an actress in the TV series *Grange Hill* and as Hattie Tavernier in *Eastenders* before launching a singing career. She married footballer Mark Bright in 1997.

07/08/1993. . . . . 11. . . . . . 6.			LOOKING UP. . . . . RCA 74321154532
24/09/1994 . . . . . 4. . . . . 16 . . . . . O			**SWEETNESS** . . . . RCA 74321230192
17/12/1994. . . . . 26. . . . . . 7.			I'LL FIND YOU . . . . RCA 74321247762
27/05/1995. . . . . 16. . . . . . 6.			FREEDOM . . . . RCA 74321284692
26/08/1995. . . . . 11. . . . . . 3.			HAPPY JUST TO BE WITH YOU . . . . RCA 74321302692
08/02/1997 . . . . . 6. . . . . . 6.			**DO YOU KNOW** . . . . RCA 74321419282
26/04/1997. . . . . 14. . . . . . 4.			SENSATIONAL Contains an interpolation of The Isley Brothers' *For The Love Of You* . . . . RCA 74321419302

ROY GAYLE – see **MIRAGE**

GAYLE AND GILLIAN Australian vocal duo of twin sisters Gayle and Gillian Blakely (born 9/7/1966, Brisbane, Queensland). They first appeared as actresses in the TV series *Neighbours* as Christina Robinson and Caroline Alessi respectively.

03/07/1993. . . . . 75. . . . . . 1.			MAD IF YA DON'T . . . . Mushroom CDMUSH 1
19/03/1994. . . . . 62. . . . . . 1.			WANNA BE YOUR LOVER . . . . Mushroom D 11598

GLORIA GAYNOR US singer (born 7/9/1949, Newark, NJ) who began with the Soul Satisfiers before signing solo with CBS in the early 1970s. She switched to MGM in 1974 and quickly became established as one of the top disco singers of the era.

07/12/1974 . . . . . 2. . . . . . 13 . . . . . O			**NEVER CAN SAY GOODBYE** . . . . MGM 2006 463
08/03/1975. . . . . 14. . . . . . 8.			REACH OUT I'LL BE THERE . . . . MGM 2006 499
09/08/1975. . . . . 44. . . . . . 3.			ALL I NEED IS YOUR SWEET LOVIN' . . . . MGM 2006 531
17/01/1976. . . . . 33. . . . . . 4.			HOW HIGH THE MOON . . . . MGM 2006 558
03/02/1979 . . . ❶⁴. . . . . 15 . . . . . ●			**I WILL SURVIVE** ▲³ Featured in the films *The Adventures Of Priscilla: Queen Of The Desert* (1994), *Jenseits Der Stille* (1996), *The First Wives Club* (1996) and *The Replacements* (2000). 1979 Grammy Award for Best Disco Recording . . . . Polydor 2095 017
06/10/1979. . . . . 32. . . . . . 7.			LET ME KNOW (I HAVE THE RIGHT). . . . . Polydor STEP 5
14/01/1984. . . . . 13. . . . . . 12			I AM WHAT I AM (FROM 'LA CAGE AUX FOLLES') Featured in the 1983 film *La Cage Aux Folles* . . . . Chrysalis CHS 2765
26/06/1993 . . . . . 5. . . . . . 10			**I WILL SURVIVE (REMIX)** . . . . Polydor PZCD 270
03/06/2000. . . . . 67. . . . . . 1.			LAST NIGHT . . . . Logic 74321738082

GAZ US studio group assembled by Salsoul Records.

24/02/1979. . . . . 60. . . . . . 4.			SING SING. . . . . Salsoul SSOL 116

GAZZA UK singer/footballer Paul Gascoigne (born 27/5/1967, Gateshead) who was with Tottenham Hotspur and enjoyed a successful World Cup in 1990 with England, with a brief record career as a result, aided by Newcastle (his first club) band Lindisfarne.

10/11/1990 . . . . . 2. . . . . . 9.			**FOG ON THE TYNE (REVISITED)** **GAZZA AND LINDISFARNE**. . . . . Best ZB 44083

❶⁹ Number of weeks single topped the UK chart   ↑ Entered the UK chart at #1   ▲⁹ Number of weeks single topped the US chart

22/12/1990	31	5		GEORDIE BOYS (GAZZA RAP)	Best ZB 44229

GBH UK group formed in 1980 by Colin Abrahall (vocals), Jock Blyth (guitar), Ross (bass) and Wilf (drums) as Charged GBH ('grievous bodily harm'). They became GBH in 1986. Kai replaced Wilf on drums in 1989. Anthony Morgan later took over on bass.

06/02/1982	63	2		NO SURVIVORS	Clay 8
20/11/1982	69	3		GIVE ME FIRE	Clay 16

NIGEL GEE UK producer.

27/01/2001	57	1		HOOTIN'	Neo NEOCD 040

J. GEILS BAND US group formed in Boston, MA in 1967 by Jerome Geils (born 20/2/1946, New York, guitar), Danny Klein (born 13/5/1946, New York, bass), Magic Dick (born Richard Salwitz, 13/5/1945, New London, CT, harmonica), Peter Wolf (born Peter Blankfield, 7/3/1946, The Bronx, NYC, vocals) and Stephen Jo Bladd (born 13/7/1942, Boston, drums/vocals) as the J Geils Blues Band. Seth Justman (born 27/1/1951, Washington DC, keyboards) joined in 1969 and 'Blues' was dropped from their name. Wolf went solo in 1983; the group split in 1987.

09/06/1979	74	1		ONE LAST KISS	EMI America AM 507
13/02/1982	3	9	○	CENTERFOLD ▲6	EMI America EA 135
10/04/1982	27	7		FREEZE-FRAME	EMI America EA 134
26/06/1982	55	3		ANGEL IN BLUE	EMI America EA 138

BOB GELDOF Irish singer (born 5/10/1954, Dublin), formerly a journalist with the *NME*, who formed the Boomtown Rats in 1975. In 1984, moved by TV coverage of the famine in Ethiopia, he organised Band Aid with Midge Ure. The single's success prompted the 1985 'global concert' Live Aid, taking up much of Geldof's time over the next five years. He appeared in the 1982 film *The Wall* and went solo in 1986. With Band Aid raising over $100 million, he was awarded an honorary knighthood in 1986 and nominated for a Nobel Peace Prize.

01/11/1986	25	5		THIS IS THE WORLD CALLING	Mercury BOB 101
21/02/1987	61	3		LOVE LIKE A ROCKET	Mercury BOB 102
23/06/1990	15	6		THE GREAT SONG OF INDIFFERENCE	Mercury BOB 104
07/05/1994	65	1		CRAZY	Vertigo VERCX 85

GEM – see OUR TRIBE/ONE TRIBE

GEMINI UK duo of identical twins Michael and David Smallwood from Shropshire.

30/09/1995	40	3		EVEN THOUGH YOU BROKE MY HEART	EMI CDEMS 391
10/02/1996	37	2		STEAL YOUR LOVE AWAY	EMI CDEMS 407
29/06/1996	38	2		COULD IT BE FOREVER	EMI CDEM 426

GEMS FOR JEM UK instrumental/production duo Darren Pearce and Steve Mac (Steve McCutcheon). McCutcheon later linked with Wayne Hector to form a successful songwriting partnership.

06/05/1995	28	2		LIFTING ME HIGHER Contains a sample of Evelyn Thomas' *High Energy*	Box 21 CDSBOK 3

GENE UK group formed in 1993 by Steve Mason (born 1971, guitar), Martin Rossiter (born 1971, vocals), Kevin Miles (born 1967, bass) and Matt James (born 1966, drums). The Costermonger label was formed for Gene.

13/08/1994	54	1		BE MY LIGHT BE MY GUIDE	Costermonger COST 002CD
12/11/1994	36	2		SLEEP WELL TONIGHT	Costermonger COST 003CD
04/03/1995	32	2		HAUNTED BY YOU	Costermonger COST 004CD
22/07/1995	18	2		OLYMPIAN	Costermonger COST 005CD
13/01/1996	14	3		FOR THE DEAD	Costermonger COST 006CD
02/11/1996	22	2		FIGHTING FIT	Polydor COST 9CD
01/02/1997	17	2		WE COULD BE KINGS	Polydor COSCD 10
10/05/1997	22	2		WHERE ARE THEY NOW?	Polydor COSCD 11
09/08/1997	30	2		SPEAK TO ME SOMEONE	Polydor COSCD 12
27/02/1999	23	2		AS GOOD AS IT GETS	Polydor COSCD 14
24/04/1999	36	2		FILL HER UP	Polydor COSCD 15
25/12/2004	69	1+		LET ME MOVE ON	Costermonger COST 10CD1

GENE AND JIM ARE INTO SHAKES UK vocal/instrumental duo Neil Cunningham (aka Johnny Lovemuscle) and Martin Noakes.

19/03/1988	68	2		SHAKE! (HOW ABOUT A SAMPLING GENE?)	Rough Trade RT 216

GENE LOVES JEZEBEL UK group formed in 1981 by twin brothers Jay (vocals) and Mike Aston (vocals) with Ian Hudson (guitar), Julianne Regan (bass) and Dick Hawkins (drums). Hawkins left soon after their debut and was replaced by John Murphy and then Steve Goulding. Regan left to join All About Eve. Subsequent changes included Pete Rizzo (bass), Chris Bell (drums) and James Stevenson (guitar) joining in 1984. Mike Aston left in 1989. By 1993 they were Jay Aston, Rizzo, Stevenson and Robert Adam (drums).

29/03/1986	75	1		SWEETEST THING	Beggars Banquet BEG 156
14/06/1986	71	2		HEARTACHE	Beggars Banquet BEG 161
05/09/1987	56	3		THE MOTION OF LOVE	Beggars Banquet BEG 192
05/12/1987	68	1		GORGEOUS	Beggars Banquet BEG 202

GENERAL DEGREE – see RICHIE STEPHENS

○ Silver disc ● Gold disc ✪ Platinum disc (additional platinum units are indicated by a figure following the symbol) ◉ Singles released prior to 1973 that are known to have sold over 1 million copies in the UK

GENERAL LEVY UK singer/rapper Paul Levy who began his recording career in 1987.

04/09/1993	75	1		MONKEY MAN	ffrr FCD 214
18/06/1994	39	3		INCREDIBLE	Renk 42CD
10/09/1994	8	9		**INCREDIBLE (REMIX)** This and above single credited to **M-BEAT FEATURING GENERAL LEVY**	Renk CDRENK 44
13/03/2004	21	1		SHAKE (WHAT YA MAMA GAVE YA) **GENERAL LEVY VS ZEUS**	East West EW281CD

GENERAL PUBLIC UK group formed by Dave Wakeling (vocals), Ranking Roger (vocals), Kevin White (guitar), Micky Billingham (keyboards), Horace Panter (bass), Saxa (saxophone) and Stoker (drums). Wakeling and Ranking Roger had previously been with The Beat, Panter with The Specials. By 1994 the line-up was Wakeling, Ranking Roger, Michael Railton (keyboards/vocals), Norman Jones (percussion/vocals), Wayne Lothian (bass) and Dan Chase (drums).

10/03/1984	60	3		GENERAL PUBLIC	Virgin VS 659
02/07/1994	73	1		I'LL TAKE YOU THERE Featured in the 1994 film *Threesome*	Epic 6605532

GENERAL SAINT UK reggae singer (born Winston Hislo, Jamaica).

29/09/1984	51	3		LAST PLANE (ONE WAY TICKET)	MCA 910
02/04/1994	54	5		OH CAROL! This and above single credited to **CLINT EASTWOOD AND GENERAL SAINT**	Copasetic COPCD 0009
06/08/1994	75	1		SAVE THE LAST DANCE FOR ME **GENERAL SAINT FEATURING DON CAMPBELL**	Copasetic COPCD 12

GENERATION X UK punk group comprising Billy Idol (born William Broad, 30/11/1955, Stanmore, vocals), Tony James (bass), John Trowe (drums), Bob Andrews (guitar) in 1976. Idol later went solo while James was a founding member of Sigue Sigue Sputnik.

17/09/1977	36	4		YOUR GENERATION	Chrysalis CHS 2165
11/03/1978	47	3		READY STEADY GO	Chrysalis CHS 2207
20/01/1979	11	9		KING ROCKER	Chrysalis CHS 2261
07/04/1979	23	7		VALLEY OF THE DOLLS	Chrysalis CHS 2310
30/06/1979	62	2		FRIDAY'S ANGELS	Chrysalis CHS 2330
18/10/1980	62	2		DANCING WITH MYSELF	Chrysalis CHS 2444
24/01/1981	60	4		DANCING WITH MYSELF (EP) Tracks on EP: *Dancing With Myself, Untouchables, Rock On* and *King Rocker*. This and above single credited to **GEN X**	Chrysalis CHS 2488

GENERATOR Dutch producer Robert Smit.

23/10/1999	60	1		WHERE ARE YOU NOW?	Tidy Trax TIDY 130CD

GENESIS UK rock group formed at Charterhouse School in Godalming by Peter Gabriel (born 13/5/1950, Cobham, vocals), Tony Banks (born 27/3/1950, East Heathley, keyboards), Chas Stewart (drums), Mike Rutherford (born 2/10/1950, Guildford, guitars) and Anthony Phillips (guitar) from the remnants of Garden Wall and Anon. They adopted the name (New) Anon, sending a demo to Jonathan King at Decca, who renamed them Genesis. Stewart left in 1968 after their debut single and was replaced by John Silver. Their first album, *From Genesis To Revelation,* sold 650 copies, the group temporarily going under the name Revelation (there was a US group Genesis: when they disbanded, the English group reverted back). Silver left in 1969 and was replaced by John Mayhew. They signed with Charisma in 1970, and shortly after their first album there Phillips and Mayhew left. Steve Hackett (born 12/2/1950, London) joined from 1971 to 1977. Phil Collins (born 31/1/1951, Chiswick, London) was brought in on drums. Gabriel went solo in 1975, Collins becoming lead singer. Banks, Collins and Rutherford all launched parallel careers: Banks and Collins solo, Rutherford with Mike + The Mechanics. By 1997 the group comprised Banks, Rutherford and new singer Ray Wilson (formerly of Stiltskin).

06/04/1974	21	7		I KNOW WHAT I LIKE (IN YOUR WARDROBE)	Charisma CB 224
26/02/1977	43	3		YOUR OWN SPECIAL WAY	Charisma CB 300
28/05/1977	14	7		SPOT THE PIGEON EP Tracks on EP: *Match Of The Day, Pigeons* and *Inside And Out*	Charisma GEN 001
11/03/1978	7	13	○	**FOLLOW YOU FOLLOW ME**	Charisma CB 309
08/07/1978	43	5		MANY TOO MANY	Charisma CB 315
15/03/1980	8	10		**TURN IT ON AGAIN**	Charisma CB 356
17/05/1980	46	5		DUCHESS	Charisma CB 363
13/09/1980	42	5		MISUNDERSTANDING	Charisma CB 369
22/08/1981	9	8		**ABACAB**	Charisma CB 388
31/10/1981	33	4		KEEP IT DARK	Charisma CB 391
13/03/1982	41	5		MAN ON THE CORNER	Charisma CB 393
22/05/1982	10	8		3 X 3 EP Tracks on EP: *Paperlate, You Might Recall* and *Me And Virgil*	Charisma GEN 1
03/09/1983	4	10	○	**MAMA**	Virgin/Charisma MAMA 1
12/11/1983	16	11		THAT'S ALL	Charisma/Virgin TATA 1
11/02/1984	46	4		ILLEGAL ALIEN	Charisma/Virgin AL 1
31/05/1986	15	8		INVISIBLE TOUCH ▲[1]	Virgin GENS 1
30/08/1986	19	9		IN TOO DEEP Featured in the 1986 film *Mona Lisa*	Virgin GENS 2
22/11/1986	14	12		LAND OF CONFUSION 1987 Grammy Award for Best Concept Music Video	Virgin GENS 3
14/03/1987	18	6		TONIGHT TONIGHT TONIGHT	Virgin GENS 4
20/06/1987	22	8		THROWING IT ALL AWAY	Virgin GENS 5
02/11/1991	6	7		**NO SON OF MINE**	Virgin GENS 6
11/01/1992	7	9		**I CAN'T DANCE**	Virgin GENS 7
18/04/1992	16	5		HOLD ON MY HEART	Virgin GENS 8
25/07/1992	20	7		JESUS HE KNOWS ME	Virgin GENS 9
21/11/1992	7	4		**INVISIBLE TOUCH**	Virgin GENS 10
20/02/1993	40	3		TELL ME WHY	Virgin GENDG 11

❶[9] Number of weeks single topped the UK chart ↑ Entered the UK chart at #1 ▲[9] Number of weeks single topped the US chart

323

27/09/1997 . . . . . 29 . . . . . . 2	CONGO . . . . Virgin GENSD 12
13/12/1997 . . . . . 54 . . . . . . 1	SHIPWRECKED . . . . Virgin GENDX 14
07/03/1998 . . . . . 66 . . . . . . 1	NOT ABOUT US . . . . Virgin GENSD 15

LEE A GENESIS – see **BOB SINCLAIR**

GENEVA UK rock group formed in Aberdeen in 1992 by Andrew Montgomery (vocals), Steven Dara (guitar), Stuart Evans (guitar), Keith Graham (bass) and Douglas Caskie (drums) as Sunfish, changing their name upon signing with Nude.

26/10/1996 . . . . . 32 . . . . . . 2	NO ONE SPEAKS . . . . Nude NUD 22CD
08/02/1997 . . . . . 26 . . . . . . 2	INTO THE BLUE . . . . Nude NUD 25CD
31/05/1997 . . . . . 24 . . . . . . 2	TRANQUILLIZER . . . . Nude NUD 28CD1
16/08/1997 . . . . . 38 . . . . . . 1	BEST REGRETS . . . . Nude NUD 31CD1
27/11/1999 . . . . . 59 . . . . . . 1	DOLLARS IN THE HEAVENS . . . . Nude NUD 46CD1
11/03/2000 . . . . . 69 . . . . . . 1	IF YOU HAVE TO GO . . . . Nude NUD 49CD1

GENEVIEVE UK singer (born Susan Hunt, Sedddlescombe) whose publicity at the time of the hit claimed she was a French teenager.

05/05/1966 . . . . . 43 . . . . . . 1	ONCE . . . . CBS 202061

GENIUS CRU UK dance group formed in 1998 by Trimmer, Sean T, Capone, Keflon and Fizzy.

03/02/2001 . . . . . 12 . . . . . . 5	BOOM SELECTION . . . . Incentive CENT 17CDS
27/10/2001 . . . . . 39 . . . . . . 2	COURSE BRUV . . . . Incentive CENT 28CDS

GENIUS/GZA FEATURING D'ANGELO US rapper (born Gary Grice, 22/8/1966, Brooklyn, NYC) whose debut album in 1989 was for Cold Chillin' Records, while D'Angelo has enjoyed solo success. Genius/GZA is also in the rap supergroup Wu-Tang Clan.

02/03/1996 . . . . . 40 . . . . . . 2	COLD WORLD Contains samples of Stevie Wonder's *Rocket Love* and DeBarge's *Love Me In A Special Way* . . Geffen GFSTD 22114

BOBBIE GENTRY US singer (born Roberta Lee Streeter, 27/7/1944, Chickasaw County, MS, raised in Greenwood) who launched her solo career in 1967. Her three Grammy Awards included Best New Artist for 1967. She married singer Jim Stafford in 1978.

13/09/1967 . . . . . 13 . . . . . 11	ODE TO BILLY JOE ▲4 Featured in the 1976 film *Ode To Billy Joe*. 1967 Grammy Awards for Best Female Solo Vocal Performance and Best Contemporary Solo Vocal Performance . . . . Capitol CL 15511
30/08/1969 . . . . ❶1 . . . . . 19	**I'LL NEVER FALL IN LOVE AGAIN** . . . . Capitol CL 15606
06/12/1969 . . . . . 3 . . . . . 14	**ALL I HAVE TO DO IS DREAM BOBBIE GENTRY AND GLEN CAMPBELL** . . . . Capitol CL 15619
21/02/1970 . . . . . 40 . . . . . . 4	RAINDROPS KEEP FALLIN' ON MY HEAD . . . . Capitol CL 15626

GEORDIE UK rock group formed by Brian Johnson (born 5/10/1947, Newcastle-upon-Tyne, vocals), Vic Malcolm (guitar), Tom Hill (bass) and Brian Gibson (drums), with Malcolm providing most of the material. Johnson was later lead singer with AC/DC following Bon Scott's death.

02/12/1972 . . . . . 32 . . . . . . 7	DON'T DO THAT . . . . Regal Zonophone RZ 3067
17/03/1973 . . . . . 6 . . . . . 13	**ALL BECAUSE OF YOU** . . . . EMI 2008
16/06/1973 . . . . . 13 . . . . . . 9	CAN YOU DO IT . . . . EMI 2031
25/08/1973 . . . . . 32 . . . . . . 6	ELECTRIC LADY . . . . EMI 2048

ROBIN GEORGE UK guitarist/producer (born in Wolverhampton) who began in the Byron Band, including playing on their debut album in 1981. A year later he went solo, signed with Arista in 1983, was dropped in 1984 and then signed with Bronze. He was more successful as a producer.

27/04/1985 . . . . . 68 . . . . . . 2	HEARTLINE . . . . Bronze BRO 191

SOPHIE GEORGE Jamaican singer from Kingston who was working as a teacher of deaf children at the time of her hit.

07/12/1985 . . . . . . 7 . . . . . 11	**GIRLIE GIRLIE** . . . . Winner WIN 01

GEORGIA SATELLITES US rock group formed in Atlanta, GA in 1980 by Dan Baird (vocals), Rick Richards (guitar), Rick Price (bass) and Mauro Magellan (drums). The group disbanded in 1991 with Richards going on to join Izzy Stradlin & The Ju Ju Hounds.

07/02/1987 . . . . . 69 . . . . . . 1	KEEP YOUR HANDS TO YOURSELF . . . . Elektra EKR 50
16/05/1987 . . . . . 44 . . . . . . 4	BATTLESHIP CHAINS . . . . Elektra EKR 58
21/01/1989 . . . . . 63 . . . . . . 3	HIPPY HIPPY SHAKE . . . . Elektra EKR 86

GEORGIE PORGIE US producer (born George Andros, Chicago, IL) who launched the Music Plant and Vinyl Soul labels.

12/08/1995 . . . . . 61 . . . . . . 1	EVERYBODY MUST PARTY . . . . Vibe MCSTD 2068
04/05/1996 . . . . . 61 . . . . . . 1	TAKE ME HIGHER . . . . Music Plant MCSTD 40031
26/08/2000 . . . . . 54 . . . . . . 1	LIFE GOES ON . . . . Neo NEOCD 039

GEORGIO US singer (born Giorgio Allentin, Los Angeles, CA).

20/02/1988 . . . . . 54 . . . . . . 3	LOVER'S LANE . . . . Motown ZB 41611

DANYEL GERARD French pop and folk singer (born Gerard Daniel Kherlakian, 7/3/1939, Paris).

18/09/1971 . . . . . 11 . . . . . 12	BUTTERFLY . . . . CBS 7454

GERIDEAU US singer Theo Gerideau.

27/08/1994 . . . . . 65 . . . . . . 1	BRING IT BACK 2 LUV **PROJECT FEATURING GERIDEAU** . . . . Fruittree FTREE 10CD
04/07/1998 . . . . . 63 . . . . . . 1	MASQUERADE . . . . Inferno CDFERN 7

GERRY AND THE PACEMAKERS
UK group formed in Liverpool in 1959 by Gerry Marsden (born 24/9/1942, Liverpool, vocals/lead guitar), brother Freddie (born 23/11/1940, Liverpool, drums), Les Chadwick (born John Leslie Chadwick, 11/5/1943, Liverpool, bass) and Anthony McMahon (piano) as the Mars Bars. The name was intended to get sponsorship from the confectionery company, who instead insisted that they change it: they settled on the Pacemakers. McMahon left in 1961 and was replaced by Les Maguire (born 27/12/1941, Wallasey, piano/saxophone). They signed with Brian Epstein in 1962, securing a contract with Parlophone. They split in 1967. They were the first act to get their first three singles at #1, a record broken by the Spice Girls in 1997. Marsden was awarded an MBE in the Queen's 2003 Birthday Honours List.

14/03/1963	❶³	18		HOW DO YOU DO IT? Originally recorded by The Beatles but never released. Featured in the 1988 film *Buster*	Columbia DB 4987
30/05/1963	❶⁴	15		I LIKE IT	Columbia DB 7041
10/10/1963	❶⁴	19		YOU'LL NEVER WALK ALONE Originally written for the 1956 film *Carousel* and first recorded by Frank Sinatra	Columbia DB 7126
16/01/1964	2	15		I'M THE ONE	Columbia DB 7189
16/04/1964	6	11		DON'T LET THE SUN CATCH YOU CRYING Later sued by Ray Charles over a similar song of the same title	Columbia DB 7268
03/09/1964	24	7		IT'S GONNA BE ALL RIGHT	Columbia DB 7353
17/12/1964	8	13		FERRY ACROSS THE MERSEY This and above single featured in the 1965 film *Ferry Cross The Mersey*	Columbia DB 7437
25/03/1965	15	9		I'LL BE THERE	Columbia DB 7504
18/11/1965	29	7		WALK HAND IN HAND	Columbia DB 7738

GET FRESH CREW – see DOUG E FRESH AND THE GET FRESH CREW

GET READY
UK vocal group formed by Matthew Biddle.

| 03/06/1995 | 65 | 1 | | WILD WILD WEST | Mega GACXCD 2698 |

GETO BOYS FEATURING FLAJ
US rap group formed in Houston, TX by Bushwick Bill (Richard Shaw), Brad 'Scarface' Jordan, Willie 'D' Dennis and DJ Ready Red (Collins Lyaseth). Bushwick Bill lost an eye after forcing his girlfriend to shoot him in 1991.

| 11/05/1996 | 49 | 1 | | THE WORLD IS A GHETTO Featured in the 1996 film *Original Gangstas* | Virgin America VUSCD 104 |

STAN GETZ
US saxophonist (born Stan Gayetzsky, 2/2/1927, Philadelphia, PA) who played with Stan Kenton, Jimmy Dorsey, Benny Goodman and Woody Herman's bands, one of the the top tenor saxophonists in the world. Five Grammy Awards included Album of the Year and Best Jazz Performance in 1964 with Astrud Gilberto for *Getz/Gilberto* and Best Jazz Instrumental Solo in 1991 for *I Remember You*. Getz died from liver cancer on 6/6/1991. Charlie Byrd is a US guitarist (born 16/9/1925, Chuckatuck, VA). Guitarist Joao Gilberto is married to Astrud Gilberto. The 1964 UK release of *The Girl From Ipanema* was credited to Joao rather than Astrud.

08/11/1962	11	13		DESAFINADO STAN GETZ AND CHARLIE BYRD 1962 Grammy Award for Best Jazz Performance	HMV POP 1061
23/07/1964	29	10		THE GIRL FROM IPANEMA (GAROTA DE IPANEMA) STAN GETZ AND JOAO GILBERTO 1964 Grammy Award for Record of the Year. Featured in the films *The Color Of Money* (1964) and *Girl, Interupted* (1999)	Verve VS 520
25/08/1984	55	6		THE GIRL FROM IPANEMA ASTRUD GILBERTO Although the re-issue was credited to Astrud Gilberto alone as singer, the single is exactly the same as above	Verve IPA 1

AMANDA GHOST
UK singer Amanda Gosein (born in London), with Indian and Spanish parents, who studied at the London College of Fashion before launching a singing career.

| 08/04/2000 | 63 | 1 | | IDOL | Warner Brothers W 518CD |
| 01/05/2004 | 52 | 1 | | BREAK MY WORLD DARK GLOBE FEATURING AMANDA GHOST | Island CID 853 |

GHOST DANCE
UK group formed in 1985 by ex-Sisters Of Mercy Gary Marx (guitar), Anne-Marie Hurst (vocals), Etch, (guitar), Richard Steel (guitar) and John Grant (drums).

| 17/06/1989 | 66 | 2 | | DOWN TO THE WIRE | Chrysalis CHS 3376 |

GHOSTFACE KILLAH
US rapper (born Dennis Coles, 9/5/1970, Staten Island, NYC) who also records under the names Tony Starks and Ironman. He is also a member of the rap supergroup Wu-Tang Clan.

12/07/1997	11	4		ALL THAT I GOT IS YOU Contains a sample of the Jackson 5's *Maybe Tomorrow*	Epic 6646842
23/01/1999	2	8		I WANT YOU FOR MYSELF ANOTHER LEVEL/GHOSTFACE KILLAH	Northwestside 74321643632
04/11/2000	64	1		MISS FAT BOOTY – PART II MOS DEF FEATURING GHOSTFACE KILLAH Contains a sample of Aretha Franklin's *One Step*	
					Rawkus RWK 282CD
29/05/2004	4	11		ON MY KNEES 411 FEATURING GHOSTFACE KILLAH	Sony Music 6749382
17/07/2004	34	3		PUSH GHOSTFACE FEATURING MISSY ELLIOTT	Def Jam 9862837
16/10/2004	27	4		LOVE THEM EAMON FEATURING GHOSTFACE	Jive 82876639212

ANDY GIBB
UK singer (born 5/3/1958, Manchester) whose family emigrated to Australia when he was six months old, returning nine years later. Encouraged by his brothers (Barry, Robin and Maurice – the Bee Gees) to pursue a musical career, his debut single penned by Barry hit #1 in the US. He later hosted the TV programme *Solid Gold* in the US. He died from a heart virus on 10/3/1988.

25/06/1977	26	7		I JUST WANNA BE YOUR EVERYTHING ▲⁴ Featured in the 2003 film *Charlie's Angels: Full Throttle*	RSO 2090 237
13/05/1978	42	6		SHADOW DANCING ▲⁷	RSO 001
12/08/1978	10	10		AN EVERLASTING LOVE	RSO 015
27/01/1979	32	7		(OUR LOVE) DON'T THROW IT ALL AWAY	RSO 26

BARRY GIBB – see BARBRA STREISAND

ROBIN GIBB
UK singer (born 22/12/1949, Douglas, Isle of Man), one third of the Bee Gees with brothers Barry and Maurice (Robin is Maurice's twin brother). He left to go solo in 1969, prompting manager Robert Stigwood to issue legal proceedings against him. The Bee Gees reunited in 1970.

❶⁹ Number of weeks single topped the UK chart ↑ Entered the UK chart at #1 ▲⁹ Number of weeks single topped the US chart

325

DATE	POS	WKS	BPI	SINGLE TITLE	LABEL & NUMBER
09/07/1969	2	17		**SAVED BY THE BELL**	Polydor 56 337
07/02/1970	45	3		AUGUST OCTOBER	Polydor 56 371
11/02/1984	71	1		ANOTHER LONELY NIGHT IN NEW YORK	Polydor POSP 668
01/02/2003	23	4		PLEASE	SPV Recordings 05571463

BETH GIBBONS AND RUSTIN MAN UK vocal duo Beth Gibbons (born 4/1/1965, Devon) and Rustin Man (born Paul Webb). Gibbons was previously lead singer with Portishead.

DATE	POS	WKS	BPI	SINGLE TITLE	LABEL & NUMBER
15/03/2003	70	1		TOM THE MODEL	Go Beat GOBCD 55

STEVE GIBBONS BAND UK group formed in Birmingham by Steve Gibbons (guitar/vocals), Bob Wilson (guitar), Trevor Burton (bass) and Bob Lamb (drums).

DATE	POS	WKS	BPI	SINGLE TITLE	LABEL & NUMBER
06/08/1977	12	10		TULANE	Polydor 2058 889
13/05/1978	56	4		EDDY VORTEX	Polydor 2059 017

GEORGIA GIBBS US singer (born Fredda Gibbons, 17/8/1920, Worcester, MA) who began her career on the *Lucky Strike* radio show in 1937. She was later dubbed 'Her Nibs, Miss Gibbs' by Garry Moore who worked with her on a late 1940s radio show with Jimmy Durante. She has a star on the Hollywood Walk of Fame.

DATE	POS	WKS	BPI	SINGLE TITLE	LABEL & NUMBER
22/04/1955	20	1		TWEEDLE DEE	Mercury MB 3196
13/07/1956	24	1		KISS ME ANOTHER	Mercury MT 110

DEBBIE GIBSON US singer (born 31/8/1970, Long Island, NY) who learned piano from five, wrote her first song at six and signed with Atlantic while still at school. In 1993 she took on the role of Sandy in the 20th anniversary production of *Grease*, having previously been Eponine in the Broadway version of *Les Miserables*.

DATE	POS	WKS	BPI	SINGLE TITLE	LABEL & NUMBER
26/09/1987	54	5		ONLY IN MY DREAMS	Atlantic A 9322
23/01/1988	7	8		**SHAKE YOUR LOVE**	Atlantic A 9187
19/03/1988	11	7		ONLY IN MY DREAMS	Atlantic A 9322
07/05/1988	19	7		OUT OF THE BLUE	Atlantic A 9091
09/07/1988	9	9		**FOOLISH BEAT** ▲[1]	Atlantic A 9059
15/10/1988	53	2		STAYING TOGETHER	Atlantic A 9020
28/01/1989	34	7		LOST IN YOUR EYES ▲[3]	Atlantic A 8970
29/04/1989	14	8		ELECTRIC YOUTH	Atlantic A 8919
19/08/1989	22	8		WE COULD BE TOGETHER	Atlantic A 8896
09/03/1991	51	2		ANYTHING IS POSSIBLE	Atlantic A 7735
03/04/1993	74	1		SHOCK YOUR MAMA	Atlantic A 7386CD
24/07/1993	13	6		YOU'RE THE ONE THAT I WANT **CRAIG McLACHLAN AND DEBBIE GIBSON**	Epic 6595222

DON GIBSON US singer (born 3/4/1928, Shelby, NC) who began singing professionally in 1942 and joined the Grand Ole Opry in 1958. He died from natural causes on 17/11/2003.

DATE	POS	WKS	BPI	SINGLE TITLE	LABEL & NUMBER
31/08/1961	14	13		SEA OF HEARTBREAK	RCA 1243
01/02/1962	47	3		LONESOME NUMBER ONE	RCA 1272

WAYNE GIBSON UK singer who formed The Dynamic Sounds with Shel Talmy in 1963. The group disbanded after four singles, Gibson going solo. His biggest hit was with a cover version of a Rolling Stones track, while his version of The Beatles' *For No One* was the first record by a UK male singer to be released on Motown.

DATE	POS	WKS	BPI	SINGLE TITLE	LABEL & NUMBER
03/09/1964	48	2		KELLY	Pye 7N 15680
23/11/1974	17	11		UNDER MY THUMB	Pye Disco Demand DDS 2001

GIBSON BROTHERS Martinique family group formed by Chris (percussion/vocals), Patrick (drum/vocals) and Alex Gibson (piano/vocals). The family relocated to Paris while the brothers were still children.

DATE	POS	WKS	BPI	SINGLE TITLE	LABEL & NUMBER
10/03/1979	41	9		CUBA	Island WIP 6483
21/07/1979	10	12		**OOH! WHAT A LIFE**	Island WIP 6503
17/11/1979	5	11	○	**QUE SERA MI VIDA (IF YOU SHOULD GO)** Featured in the 1998 film *54*.	Island WIP 6525
23/02/1980	12	9		CUBA/BETTER DO IT SALSA Re-issue of Island WIP 6483	Island WIP 6561
12/07/1980	11	10		MARIANA	Island WIP 6617
09/07/1983	56	3		MY HEART'S BEATING WILD (TIC TAC TIC TAC)	Stiff BUY 184

GIDEA PARK UK group project of Adrian Baker who arranged, produced, sang harmony and played most of the instruments on the releases, a concept inspired by Star Sound. After the success of *Beach Boy Gold*, the Beach Boys invited Baker to join the group.

DATE	POS	WKS	BPI	SINGLE TITLE	LABEL & NUMBER
04/07/1981	11	13		BEACH BOY GOLD	Stone SON 2162
12/09/1981	28	6		SEASONS OF GOLD	Polo 14

JOHAN GIELEN Belgian producer who is also a member of Airscape, Balearic Bill and Cubic 22, and records as Blue Bamboo.

DATE	POS	WKS	BPI	SINGLE TITLE	LABEL & NUMBER
18/08/2001	74	1		VELVET MOODS **JOHAN GIELEN PRESENTS ABNEA**	Data 17T
22/09/2001	41	2		THE BEAUTY OF SILENCE **SVENSON AND GIELEN**	Xtrahard/Xtravaganza X2H 5CDS

GIFTED UK instrumentalist Carl Turner with singer Denise Gordon.

DATE	POS	WKS	BPI	SINGLE TITLE	LABEL & NUMBER
23/08/1997	60	1		DO I	Perfecto PERF 140CD

○ Silver disc ● Gold disc ✪ Platinum disc (additional platinum units are indicated by a figure following the symbol) ◉ Singles released prior to 1973 that are known to have sold over 1 million copies in the UK

GIGOLO AUNTS US rock group formed in Boston, MA by Dave Gibbs (guitar/vocals), Steve Hurley (bass/vocals), Phil Hurley (guitar/vocals) and Paul Brouwer (drums).

23/04/1994	74	1		MRS WASHINGTON	Fire BLAZE 68CD
13/05/1995	29	3		WHERE I FIND MY HEAVEN Featured in the 1994 film *Dumb And Dumber*	Fire BLAZE 87CD

ASTRUD GILBERTO – see STAN GETZ

JOAO GILBERTO – see STAN GETZ

DONNA GILES US singer who later appeared on the album *God Shave The Queen*, an album by ten drag queens.

13/08/1994	43	2		AND I'M TELLING YOU I'M NOT GOING	Ore AG 4CD
10/02/1996	27	2		AND I'M TELLING YOU I'M NOT GOING (REMIX)	Ore/XL Recordings AGR 4CD

JOHNNY GILL US singer (born 22/5/1966, Washington DC) who sang with family gospel group Wings Of Faith with his three brothers before recording with Stacy Lattishaw, who passed on his demo tape to Atlantic Records. He signed with them in 1983, though with little initial success. He replaced Bobby Brown in New Edition and when they disbanded relaunched his solo career, with Jimmy Jam, Terry Lewis, LA Reid and Babyface handling production, and with greater success second time around.

23/02/1991	57	2		WRAP MY BODY TIGHT	Motown ZB 44271
28/11/1992	17	7		SLOW AND SEXY SHABBA RANKS FEATURING JOHNNY GILL	Epic 6587727
17/07/1993	53	1		THE FLOOR	Motown TMGCD 1416
29/01/1994	46	2		A CUTE SWEET LOVE ADDICTION	Motown TMGCD 1420

VINCE GILL US country singer (born 12/4/1957, Norman, OK) in Bluegrass Alliance and Pure Prairie League, going solo in 1984.

14/10/1995	46	2		HOUSE OF LOVE AMY GRANT WITH VINCE GILL	A&M 5812332
30/10/1999	26	3		IF YOU EVER LEAVE ME BARBRA STREISAND/VINCE GILL	Columbia 6681242

GILLAN UK singer (born Ian Gillan, 19/8/1945, Hounslow) who was in Episode Six when invited to join Deep Purple as lead singer in 1969, leaving to go solo in 1973. In 1983 he joined Black Sabbath as lead, then left the following year to rejoin Deep Purple, whom he left again in 1989. He played the role of Jesus on the album version of *Jesus Christ Superstar*.

14/06/1980	55	3		SLEEPIN' ON THE JOB	Virgin VS 355
04/10/1980	14	6		TROUBLE	Virgin VS 377
14/02/1981	32	5		MUTUALLY ASSURED DESTRUCTION	Virgin VS 103
21/03/1981	17	10		NEW ORLEANS	Virgin VS 406
20/06/1981	31	6		NO LAUGHING IN HEAVEN	Virgin VS 425
10/10/1981	36	6		NIGHTMARE	Virgin VS 441
23/01/1982	25	7		RESTLESS	Virgin VS 465
04/09/1982	50	3		LIVING FOR THE CITY	Virgin VS 519

GILLETTE – see 20 FINGERS

STUART GILLIES UK singer, a winner on TV's *Opportunity Knocks,* whose only hit was produced by industry veteran Norman Newell.

31/03/1973	13	10		AMANDA	Philips 6006 293

JIMMY GILMER – see FIREBALLS

THEA GILMORE UK singer (born 1979, Oxfordshire).

16/08/2003	35	1		JULIET (KEEP THAT IN MIND)	Hungry Dog YRGNUHS 2
08/11/2003	50	1		MAINSTREAM	Hungry Dog YRGNUHS 4

JAMES GILREATH US singer/songwriter/guitarist (born 14/11/1939, Prairie, MS).

02/05/1963	29	10		LITTLE BAND OF GOLD	Pye International 7N 25190

JIM GILSTRAP US session singer (born in Pittsburgh, TX, based in LA) whose hit was written and produced by Kenny Nolan.

15/03/1975	4	11		SWING YOUR DADDY	Chelsea 2005 021

GORDON GILTRAP UK guitarist/session musician (born 6/4/1948, Tonbridge) who began his solo career in 1971.

14/01/1978	21	7		HEARTSONG Subsequently used as the theme to the BBC TV series *Holiday*	Electric WOT 19
28/04/1979	58	3		FEAR OF THE DARK GORDON GILTRAP BAND	Electric WOT 29

GIN BLOSSOMS US rock group formed in Tempe, AZ in 1989 by Robin Wilson (guitar/vocals), Jesse Valenzuela (guitar/vocals), Scott Johnson (guitar), Bill Leen (bass) and Philip Rhodes (drums). They financed their own debut release, attracting interest from A&M, who signed them in 1992. Original member and songwriter Doug Hopkins was sacked in 1992 and committed suicide by shooting himself on 4/12/1993, two weeks after an earlier suicide attempt from a drugs overdose. They split in 1997, re-forming in 2001.

05/02/1994	24	5		HEY JEALOUSY	Fontana GINCD 3
16/04/1994	40	3		FOUND OUT ABOUT YOU	Fontana GINCD 4
10/02/1996	39	2		TIL I HEAR IT FROM YOU Featured in the 1995 film *Empire Records*	A&M 5812272
27/04/1996	30	2		FOLLOW YOU DOWN	A&M 5815512

⓿⁹ Number of weeks single topped the UK chart ↑ Entered the UK chart at #1 ▲⁹ Number of weeks single topped the US chart

327

GINGERBREADS – see GOLDIE AND THE GINGERBREADS

GINUWINE US singer (Elgin Baylor Lumpkin, named after a basketball player, 15/10/1975, Washington DC).

25/01/1997	16	6	PONY	Epic 6641282
24/05/1997	16	3	TELL ME DO U WANNA	Epic 6645272
06/09/1997	10	5	**WHEN DOVES CRY**	Epic 6649245
14/03/1998	13	4	HOLLER	Epic 6653372
13/03/1999	10	4	**WHAT'S SO DIFFERENT?** Contains an interpolation of The Monkees' *Valleri*	Epic 6670522
14/12/2002	42	2	CRUSH TONIGHT FAT JOE FEATURING GINUWINE	Atlantic AT 0142CD
07/06/2003	27	3	HELL YEAH	Epic 6739245

GIPSY KINGS French flamenco group formed from the family group Los Reyes and led by Jose Reyes. They changed their name to the Gipsy Kings in 1983. The many musicians who have been members of the Gipsy Kings include Nicolas Reyes, Andre Reyes, Canut Reyes, Paul Reyes, Patchai Reyes, Francois Reyes, Chico Bouchiki, Tonino Baliardo, Diego Baliardo, Paco Baliardo, Claude Maissoneuve, Walter De Auraujo, Guillermo Fellove, Christian Martinez, Philippe Slominiski, Dominique Perrier, Dominique Droin, Jean Musy, Gerard Prevost, Claude Salmieri, Negrito Trasante-Crocco, Marc Chantereau and Charles Benarroch.

03/09/1994	53	2	HITS MEDLEY	Columbia 6606022

MARTINE GIRAULT UK singer who started her career with Rumour Records.

29/08/1992	53	2	REVIVAL	ffrr FX 195
30/01/1993	37	3	REVIVAL Re-Issue of ffrr FX 195	Ffrr FCD 205
28/10/1995	63	1	BEEN THINKING ABOUT YOU	RCA 74321316142
01/02/1997	61	1	REVIVAL (REMIX)	RCA 74321432162

GIRESSE UK DJ/production duo Andy Galea and Justin Scharvona. Galea had previously been a member of Freestylers.

14/04/2001	61	1	MON AMI Contains an interpolation of Tubeway Army's *Are Friends Electric*	Inferno CDFERN 36

GIRL UK rock group formed in London in 1979 by Philip Lewis (vocals), Phil Collen (guitar), Gerry Laffy (guitar), his brother Simon (bass) and Dave Gaynor (drums). Gaynor left after their debut album and was replaced by Pete Barnacle. The group disbanded after their second album. Collen later joined Def Leppard, while Lewis joined LA Guns.

12/04/1980	50	3	HOLLYWOOD TEASE	Jet 176

GIRL NEXT DOOR – see M & S PRESENTS GIRL NEXT DOOR

GIRL THING UK/Dutch vocal group formed by Anika Bostelaar (born 5/6/1981, Etten-Leur, near Rotterdam), Michelle Claire Barber (born 5/1/1979, Blackpool), Linsey Sarah Martin (born 2/4/1981, Manchester), Nicola Jane Stuart (born 4/7/1979, Bradford) and Jodi Albert (born 22/7/1983, Chingford). They recorded the original version of *Pure And Simple,* which was released in Japan but later withdrawn after the song's writers decided to give it to the winners of the *Popstars* TV series Hear'Say. While Hear'Say's version went on to sell over 1 million copies, Girl Thing were dropped by their record company in March 2001.

01/07/2000	8	10	**LAST ONE STANDING**	RCA 74321762422
18/11/2000	25	3	GIRLS ON TOP	RCA 74321801172

GIRLFRIEND Australian vocal group formed by Jackie Sewell, Siobban Hiedenreick, Robyn Loau, Lorinda Noble and Melanie Alexander. Robyn Loau later recorded solo.

30/01/1993	47	4	TAKE IT FROM ME	Arista 74321142252
15/05/1993	68	2	GIRL'S LIFE	Arista 74321138452

GIRLS ALOUD UK vocal group formed by Cheryl Tweedy (born 30/6/1983, Newcastle-upon-Tyne), Nadine Coyle (born 15/6/1985, Derry, Ireland), Sarah Harding (born 17/11/1981, Ascot), Nicola Roberts (born 5/10/1985, Stanford) and Kimberly Walsh (born 20/11/1981, Bradford). They were the winners of the TV programme *Popstars: The Rivals*. It was later revealed that their debut hit was originally recorded by another girl group, Orchid, the Girls Aloud vocals merely added over the top.

21/12/2002	●4	21	✪	**SOUND OF THE UNDERGROUND** ↑	Polydor 0658272
24/05/2003	2	14	**NO GOOD ADVICE**	Polydor 9800051
30/08/2003	3	9	**LIFE GOT COLD**	Polydor 9810656
29/11/2003	2	14	**JUMP** Featured in the 2003 film *Love Actually*	Polydor 9814104
10/07/2004	2	10	**THE SHOW**	Polydor 9867041
25/09/2004	2	10	**LOVE MACHINE**	Polydor 9867984
27/11/2004	●2	5+	**I'LL STAND BY YOU** ↑ Released to raise funds for the BBC Children In Need Fund	Polydor 9869130

GIRLS @ PLAY UK vocal group formed by Shelley Nash (born 13/1/1978), Lynsey Shaw (born 15/6/1976), Rita Simons (born 10/3/1977), Vicky Dowdall (born 23/1/1979) and Lisa-Jay White (born 23/5/1979). They disbanded after two singles.

24/02/2001	18	5	AIRHEAD	GSM GSMCDR 1
13/10/2001	29	2	RESPECTABLE	Redbus Music RBMCD 101

GIRLS OF FHM UK vocal group assembled by men's magazine *FHM* to celebrate 10 years of *FHM*'s 100 Sexiest Women and raise funds for the Breakthrough Breast Cancer fund. Among the more than 100 women featured were Naomi Campbell (model), Myleene Klass (formerly of Hear'Say), Keli Young (Liberty X), Jessica Taylor (Liberty X), Michelle Heaton (Liberty X), Liz McClarnon (Atomic Kitten), Tina Barrett (S Club), Jakki Degg (model), Jodie Marsh (model), Michelle Marsh (model), Nush (*Big Brother* contestant), Lady Isabelle Hervey (socialite), Sophie Anderton (model), Nikki Sanderson (actress) and Samia Ghadie (actress).

○ Silver disc ● Gold disc ✪ Platinum disc (additional platinum units are indicated by a figure following the symbol) ◉ Singles released prior to 1973 that are known to have sold over 1 million copies in the UK

03/07/2004 . . . . . 10 . . . . . . 5 . . . . DA YA THINK I'M SEXY? 2PSL 2PSLCD5

GIRLSCHOOL
UK heavy metal group formed in 1978 by Kim McAuliffe (born 13/4/1959, rhythm guitar/vocals), Kelly Johnson (lead guitar), Enid Williams (bass) and Denise Dufort (drums) as Painted Lady. They changed their name the same year and signed with Bronze in 1980. They disbanded in 1988 but re-formed in 1992.

02/08/1980 . . . . . 49 . . . . . . 6	RACE WITH THE DEVIL. . . . . Bronze BRO 100
21/02/1981 . . . . . 5 . . . . . . 8 . . . . . . O	ST VALENTINE'S DAY MASSACRE EP MOTORHEAD AND GIRLSCHOOL (ALSO KNOWN AS HEADGIRL) Tracks on EP: *Please Don't Touch, Emergency* and *Bomber*. . . . . Bronze BRO 116
11/04/1981 . . . . . 32 . . . . . . 6	HIT AND RUN. . . . . Bronze BRO 118
11/07/1981 . . . . . 42 . . . . . . 3	C'MON LET'S GO . . . . Bronze BRO 126
03/04/1982 . . . . . 58 . . . . . . 2	WILDLIFE (EP) Tracks on EP: *Don't Call It Love, Wildlife* and *Don't Stop*. . . . . Bronze BRO 144

JUNIOR GISCOMBE – see JUNIOR

GITTA Danish/Italian vocal/instrumental group.
19/08/2000 . . . . . 54 . . . . . . 1 . . . . NO MORE TURNING BACK. . . . . Pepper 9230302

GLADIATOR FEATURING IZZY UK production duo Bobak Rembrandt and Dave Lambert with classical singer Izzy.
29/05/2004 . . . . . 19 . . . . . . 4 . . . . NOW WE ARE FREE . . . . Universal TV 9866813

GLADIATORS – see NERO AND THE GLADIATORS

GLADIATORS UK vocal group formed by the house contestants on the TV series *Gladiator,* including Hunter, Wolf and Shadow.
30/11/1996 . . . . . 70 . . . . . . 1 . . . . THE BOYS ARE BACK IN TOWN Theme to the TV series *Gladiators*. . . . . RCA 74321417002

GLAM Italian instrumental/production group formed by Ricardo Persi, Davide Rizzardi and Elvio Moratto.
01/05/1993 . . . . . 42 . . . . . . 2 . . . . HELL'S PARTY . . . . Six6 SIXCD 001

GLAM METAL DETECTIVES UK vocal/instrumental group formed by *Comic Strip* actor Peter Richardson for a 1995 TV series. Produced by Trevor Horn, it featured Gary Beadle, Mark Caven, Phil Vornwell, Doon Mackichan, Sara Stockbridge and George Yiascumi.
11/03/1995 . . . . . 29 . . . . . . 2 . . . . EVERYBODY UP! Theme to the TV series *Glam Metal Detectives*. . . . . ZTT ZANG 62CD

GLAMMA KID UK singer/rapper (born Iyael Iyasus Tafari Constable) who won the 1998 MOBO Award for Best Reggae Act.
21/11/1998 . . . . . 49 . . . . . . 1	FASHION '98 . . . . WEA 179CD
17/04/1999 . . . . . 10 . . . . . . 8	TABOO GLAMMA KID FEATURING SHOLA AMA . . . . WEA 203CD
27/11/1999 . . . . . 10 . . . . . . 10	WHY . . . . WEA 229CD1
02/09/2000 . . . . . 17 . . . . . . 6	BILLS 2 PAY Contains samples of Blondie's *Rapture* and Visage's *Fade To Grey* . . . . WEA 268CD1

GLASS TIGER Canadian rock group formed in Newmarket, Ontario in 1984 by Alan Frew (vocals), Sam Reid (keyboards), Al Connelly (guitar), Wayne Parker (bass) and Michael Hanson (drums). The group disbanded in 1991.
18/10/1986 . . . . . 29 . . . . . . 9	DON'T FORGET ME (WHEN I'M GONE) Features the uncredited vocal of Bryan Adams . . . . Manhattan MT 13
31/01/1987 . . . . . 66 . . . . . . 2	SOMEDAY . . . . Manhattan MT 17
26/10/1991 . . . . . 33 . . . . . . 7	MY TOWN Features the uncredited vocal of Rod Stewart. . . . . EMI EM 212

MAYSON GLEN ORCHESTRA – see PAUL HENRY AND THE MAYSON GLEN ORCHESTRA

GLENN AND CHRIS UK professional footballers at Tottenham Hotspur, Glenn Hoddle (born 27/10/1957, Hayes) and Chris Waddle (born 14/12/1960, Hepworth). Though they were household names, the hit single was initially promoted without reference to the identity of the singers.
18/04/1987 . . . . . 12 . . . . . . 8 . . . . DIAMOND LIGHTS . . . . Record Shack Records KICK 1

GARY GLITTER UK singer (born Paul Gadd, 8/5/1940, Banbury, Oxon) who adopted his stepfather's surname to front Paul Russell & His Rebels in 1958 and made his first record with Decca as Paul Raven. Unsuccessful, he dropped out of recording in 1961 and linked with the Mike Leander Orchestra, before forming Paul Raven & Boston International, a popular live draw in West Germany. After one single as Rubber Bucket in 1969, he adopted the name Gary Glitter in 1971. The early hits were all written by Glitter and Leander (born 30/6/1941, died 18/4/1996). In November 1999 Glitter was jailed for four months after admitting 54 offences of downloading indecent photographs of children. He served two months before being released.

10/06/1972 . . . . . 2 . . . . . . 15	ROCK AND ROLL (PARTS 1 & 2) Featured in the films *D2: The Mighty Ducks* (1994), *Eddie* (1996), *Kingpin* (1996), *The Full Monty* (1997), *Small Soldiers* (1998) and *The Replacements* (2000). . . . . Bell 1216
23/09/1972 . . . . . 4 . . . . . . 11	I DIDN'T KNOW I LOVED YOU (TILL I SAW YOU ROCK 'N' ROLL) . . . . Bell 1259
20/01/1973 . . . . . 2 . . . . . . 11 . . . . . . O	DO YOU WANNA TOUCH ME (OH YEAH!). . . . . Bell 1280
07/04/1973 . . . . . 2 . . . . . . 14 . . . . . . O	HELLO! HELLO! I'M BACK AGAIN. . . . . Bell 1299
21/07/1973 . . . ❶⁴ . . . 12 . . . . . ●	I'M THE LEADER OF THE GANG (I AM) . . . . Bell 1321
17/11/1973 . . . ❶⁴ . . . 14 . . . . . ✪	I LOVE YOU LOVE ME LOVE ↑ First single to be certified platinum (indicating domestic sales in excess of 1 million copies) . . . Bell 1337

DATE	POS	WKS	BPI	SINGLE TITLE	LABEL & NUMBER
30/03/1974	3	8	○	**REMEMBER ME THIS WAY**	Bell 1349
15/06/1974	❶¹	9	○	**ALWAYS YOURS**	Bell 1359
23/11/1974	2	10	○	**OH YES! YOU'RE BEAUTIFUL**	Bell 1391
03/05/1975	10	6		**LOVE LIKE YOU AND ME**	Bell 1423
21/06/1975	6	7		**DOING ALRIGHT WITH THE BOYS**	Bell 1429
08/11/1975	38	5		PAPA OOM MOW MOW	Bell 1451
13/03/1976	40	5		YOU BELONG TO ME	Bell 1473
22/01/1977	25	6		IT TAKES ALL NIGHT LONG	Arista 85
16/07/1977	31	5		A LITTLE BOOGIE WOOGIE IN THE BACK OF MY MIND	Arista 112
20/09/1980	57	3		GARY GLITTER (EP) Tracks on EP: *I'm The Leader Of The Gang (I Am)*, *Rock And Roll (Part 2)*, *Hello Hello I'm Back Again* and *Do You Wanna Touch Me? (Oh Yeah!)*	GTO GT 282
10/10/1981	39	5		AND THEN SHE KISSED ME	Bell 1497
05/12/1981	48	5		ALL THAT GLITTERS	Bell 1498
23/06/1984	25	5		DANCE ME UP	Arista ARIST 570
01/12/1984	7	7	○	**ANOTHER ROCK AND ROLL CHRISTMAS**	Arista ARIST 592
10/10/1992	58	2		AND THE LEADER ROCKS ON	EMI EM 252
21/11/1992	49	3		THROUGH THE YEARS	EMI EM 256
16/12/1995	50	2		HELLO! HELLO! I'M BACK AGAIN (AGAIN) Re-recording of Bell 1299	Carlton Sounds 3036000192

GLITTER BAND

UK backing band for Gary Glitter on tour (producer Mike Leander reportedly played all instruments in the studio), given a parallel recording career while their frontman was at the peak of his popularity. The band featured John Springate, Tony Leonard, Pete Phipps, Harvey Ellison and Gerry Shephard. Shephard died from cancer in May 2003.

DATE	POS	WKS	BPI	SINGLE TITLE	LABEL & NUMBER
23/03/1974	4	10	○	**ANGEL FACE**	Bell 1348
03/08/1974	10	8		**JUST FOR YOU**	Bell 1368
19/10/1974	8	8		**LET'S GET TOGETHER AGAIN**	Bell 1383
18/01/1975	2	9		**GOODBYE MY LOVE**	Bell 1395
12/04/1975	8	8		**THE TEARS I CRIED**	Bell 1416
09/08/1975	15	8		LOVE IN THE SUN	Bell 1437
28/02/1976	5	9		**PEOPLE LIKE YOU AND PEOPLE LIKE ME** Although not credited, the single also sold because of the B-side *Makes You Blind*, which attracted considerable club play and became a US R&B hit, peaking at #91	Bell 1471

GLOBAL COMMUNICATION

UK instrumental/production duo formed in 1991 by Mark Pritchard and Tom Middleton. They also record as Link, Reload, Jedi Knights, The Chameleon and Pulusha while Middleton also records as Cosmos.

DATE	POS	WKS	BPI	SINGLE TITLE	LABEL & NUMBER
11/01/1997	51	1		THE WAY/THE DEEP	Dedicated GLOBA 002CD

GLOVE

UK group formed by The Cure's Robert Smith (born 21/4/1959, Blackpool, guitar/vocals), The Banshees' Steve 'Havoc' Severin (born Steven Bailey, 25/9/1955, London, bass) and Jeanette Landray (vocals/dancing), a one-off project for Smith and Severin.

DATE	POS	WKS	BPI	SINGLE TITLE	LABEL & NUMBER
20/08/1983	52	3		LIKE AN ANIMAL	Wonderland SHE 3

DANA GLOVER

US singer (born in Rocky Mount, NC, raised in Nashville, Los Angeles and New York) who was a model before launching a singing career.

DATE	POS	WKS	BPI	SINGLE TITLE	LABEL & NUMBER
10/05/2003	38	1		THINKING OVER	DreamWorks 4507762

GLOWORM

UK/US group formed by Sedric Johnson, Pauline Taylor, Will Mount and Rollo.

DATE	POS	WKS	BPI	SINGLE TITLE	LABEL & NUMBER
06/02/1993	20	4		I LIFT MY CUP	Pulse 8 CDLOSE 37
14/05/1994	9	11		**CARRY ME HOME**	Go Beat GODCD 112
06/08/1994	46	2		I LIFT MY CUP Re-issue of Pulse 8 CDLOSE 37	Pulse 8 CDLOSE 67

GO GO LORENZO AND THE DAVIS PINCKNEY PROJECT

US vocal/instrumental group formed by Lorenzo Queen, Kenny Davis and Larry Pinckney.

DATE	POS	WKS	BPI	SINGLE TITLE	LABEL & NUMBER
06/12/1986	46	8		YOU CAN DANCE (IF YOU WANT TO)	Boiling Point POSP 836

GO-GO'S

US rock group formed in Los Angeles, CA in 1978 by Belinda Carlisle (born 17/8/1958, Hollywood, vocals), Jane Wiedlin (born 20/5/1958, Oconomowoc, WI, guitar), Charlotte Caffey (born 21/10/1953, Santa Monica, CA, guitar), Kathy Valentine (born 7/1/1959, Austin, TX, bass) and Gina Schock (born 31/8/1957, Baltimore, MD, drums). They disbanded in 1984 (Carlisle and Wiedlin pursued successful solo careers) and held a reunion tour in 1990.

DATE	POS	WKS	BPI	SINGLE TITLE	LABEL & NUMBER
15/05/1982	47	6		OUR LIPS ARE SEALED Featured in the films *Romy And Michele's High School Reunion* (1997) and *200 Cigarettes* (1999)	IRS GDN 102
26/01/1991	60	1		COOL JERK	IRS AM 712
18/02/1995	29	3		THE WHOLE WORLD LOST ITS HEAD	IRS CDEIRS 190

THE GO! TEAM

UK group formed in Brighton by Ian Parton (guitar/vocals), MC Ninja (vocals), Sam Dook (guitar), Silkie (multi-instrumentalist), Jamie Bell (bass) and Chi (drums).

DATE	POS	WKS	BPI	SINGLE TITLE	LABEL & NUMBER
04/12/2004	68	1		LADYFLASH	Memphis Industries MI041CDS

GO WEST

UK duo Peter Cox (born 17/11/1955, vocals) and Richard Drummie (guitar/vocals). They wrote songs for Peter Frampton and David Grant among others before launching Go West in 1982. They were named Best British Newcomer at the 1986 BRIT Awards. Cox later went solo.

DATE	POS	WKS	BPI	SINGLE TITLE	LABEL & NUMBER
23/02/1985	5	14	○	**WE CLOSE OUR EYES**	Chrysalis CHS 2850

○ Silver disc ● Gold disc ✪ Platinum disc (additional platinum units are indicated by a figure following the symbol) ◎ Singles released prior to 1973 that are known to have sold over 1 million copies in the UK

11/05/1985.....12.....10......				CALL ME	Chrysalis GOW 1
03/08/1985.....25.....7......				GOODBYE GIRL...	Chrysalis GOW 2
23/11/1985.....13.....10......				DON'T LOOK DOWN – THE SEQUEL	Chrysalis GOW 3
29/11/1986.....48.....7......				TRUE COLOURS...	Chrysalis GOW 4
09/05/1987.....43.....3......				I WANT TO HEAR IT FROM YOU	Chrysalis GOW 5
12/09/1987.....67.....2......				THE KING IS DEAD	Chrysalis GOW 6
28/07/1990.....18.....10......				THE KING OF WISHFUL THINKING Featured in the 1990 film *Pretty Woman*	Chrysalis GOW 8
17/10/1992.....13.....6......				FAITHFUL	Chrysalis GOW 9
16/01/1993.....15.....5......				WHAT YOU WON'T DO FOR LOVE	Chrysalis CDGOWS 10
27/03/1993.....43.....3......				STILL IN LOVE	Chrysalis CDGOWS 11
02/10/1993.....16.....5......				TRACKS OF MY TEARS..	Chrysalis CDGOWS 12
04/12/1993.....40.....3......				WE CLOSE OUR EYES (REMIX)	Chrysalis CDGOWS 13

GOATS US rap trio formed in Philadelphia, PA by Oatie Kato, Madd and Swayzack. Oatie left in 1993, Madd and Swayzack continuing as a duo.

29/05/1993.....53......2.......	AAAH D YAAA/TYPICAL AMERICAN	Ruffhouse 6593032

GOD MACHINE US group comprising San Diego, CA school friends Robyn Proper-Sheppard (guitar/vocals), Jimmy Fernandez (bass) and Ronald Austin (drums), forming the group in London in 1990. They disbanded after Fernandez died from a brain tumour on 23/5/1994.

30/01/1993.....65......2.......	HOME	Fiction FICCD 47

GODIEGO Japanese/US vocal/instrumental group who released the English version of the theme to the TV series *Monkey*. The record shared its chart credit with Pete Mac Jr's Japanese version.

15/10/1977.....37......4.......	THE WATER MARGIN	BBC RESL 50
16/02/1980.....56......7.......	GHANDARA Theme to the TV series *Monkey*	BBC RESL 66

GODLEY AND CREME UK duo Kevin Godley (born 7/10/1945, Manchester) and Lol Creme (born19/9/1947, Manchester). Both had been in Hotlegs, which became 10cc. They left 10cc in 1976 to work as a duo, later moving into video production.

12/09/1981 .....3......11.....O	**UNDER YOUR THUMB**	Polydor POSP 322
21/11/1981 .....7......11.....O	**WEDDING BELLS**	Polydor POSP 369
30/03/1985.....19.....14......	CRY..	Polydor POSP 732

GOD'S PROPERTY US rap, funk and gospel group assembled in Dallas, TX by Linda Searight. The 50-plus singers, all aged between 16 and 26, are members of Kirk Franklin's Nu Nation.

22/11/1997.....60......1.......	STOMP Contains an interpolation of Funkadelic's *One Nation Under A Groove*	B-rite Music IND 95559

ALEX GOLD FEATURING PHILIP OAKEY UK duo formed by producer Alex Gold and singer Philip Oakey (born 2/10/1955, Leicester). Oakey had previously been a member of Human League, and Gold was the founder of the Xtravaganza label.

26/04/2003.....68......1.......	LA TODAY...	Xtravaganza XTRAV 37CDS

ANDREW GOLD US singer/pianist (born 2/8/1951 Burbank, CA) who was a session singer and Linda Ronstadt arranger from the early 1970s. He later formed Wax with former 10cc member Graham Gouldman.

02/04/1977.....11......9.......	LONELY BOY Features the uncredited contribution of Linda Ronstadt	Asylum K 13076
25/03/1978 .....5.....13.....O	**NEVER LET HER SLIP AWAY**	Asylum K 13112
24/06/1978.....19.....10......	HOW CAN THIS BE LOVE..................................	Asylum K 13126
14/10/1978.....42......4.......	THANK YOU FOR BEING A FRIEND Later adapted as the theme tune to the US TV comedy *Golden Girls*	Asylum K 13135

ARI GOLD – see DJ LUCK AND MC NEAT

BRIAN AND TONY GOLD Jamaican vocal duo Brian Thompson and Anthony Johnson.

30/07/1994 .....2.....15.....O	**COMPLIMENTS ON YOUR KISS** RED DRAGON WITH BRIAN AND TONY GOLD	Mango CIDM 820
09/11/2002.....10......7.......	**HEY SEXY LADY** SHAGGY FEATURING BRIAN AND TONY GOLD	MCA MCSTD 40304

GOLD BLADE UK vocal/instrumental group formed by John Robb (vocals). By 2003 the line-up consisted of Robb, Brother Johnny Skullknuckles (guitar), Brother Pete G.O.R.G.E.O.U.S. (guitar), Brother Keith (bass), Brother Rob (drums) and Brother Martin (percussion).

22/03/1997.....64......1.......	STRICTLY HARDCORE.....................................	Ultimate TOPP 056CD

GOLDBUG UK group formed by ex-Beatmasters Richard Walmsley (born 28/9/1962) and Adil. They took their name from a computer virus. Their debut hit was a cover of Led Zeppelin's song.

27/01/1996 .....3......5.......	**WHOLE LOTTA LOVE** Contains a sample of *Asteroid*, the tune used by cinema advertising company Pearl and Dean. .... Make Dust JAZID 125CD

GOLDEN BOY WITH MISS KITTIN Swiss producer Stefan Altenburger with singer Miss Kittin (born Caroline Herve).

07/09/2002.....67......1.......	RIPPIN KITTIN	Illustrious CDILL 007

GOLDEN EARRING Dutch group formed in 1964 by Barry Hay (born 16/8/1948, Faizabad, India, vocals), George Kooymans (born 11/3/1948, The Hague, guitar/vocals), Cesar Zuiderwijk (born 18/7/1950, The Hague, drums) and Rinus Gerritsen (born Marinus Gerritsen, 9/8/1946, The Hague, bass/keyboards). An early member was Jaap Eggermont, who scored success in the 1980s as Starsound.

08/12/1973 .....7......13.....O	**RADAR LOVE** Featured in the 1993 film *Wayne's World 2*.................................	Track 2094 116

❶⁹ Number of weeks single topped the UK chart ↑ Entered the UK chart at #1 ▲⁹ Number of weeks single topped the US chart

331

08/10/1977.....44......3.......				RADAR LOVE Re-issue of Track 2094 116	Polydor 2121 335

GOLDEN GIRLS UK producer/instrumentalist Mike Hazell.

03/10/1998.....38......2......	KINETIC	Distinctive DISNCD 46
04/12/1999.....56......1......	KINETIC '99.	Distinctive DISNCD 59

GOLDENSCAN UK DJ/production duo Ed Goring and Mark McCormick.

11/11/2000.....52......1......	SUNRISE.	VC Recordings VCRD 79

GOLDFINGER UK group formed in 1996 by John Feldmann (guitar/vocals), Brian Arthur (guitar), Kelly LeMieux (bass) and Darrin Pfeiffer (drums).

22/06/2002.....75......1.......	OPEN YOUR EYES	Jive 9270052

GOLDFRAPP UK duo Allison Goldfrapp (born in Bath, keyboards/vocals) and Will Gregory. Allison began as a solo artist and backing singer, appearing on Tricky's album *Maxinquaye* and Orbital's *Snivilisation*. She linked with Gregory in 1999.

23/06/2001.....62......1......	UTOPIA	Mute CDMUTE 264
17/11/2001.....68......1......	PILOTS	Mute LCDMUTE 267
26/04/2003.....23......3......	TRAIN	Mute LCDMUTE 291
02/08/2003.....25......3......	STRICT MACHINE	Mute LCDMUTE 295
15/11/2003.....31......2......	TWIST	Mute LCDMUTE 311
13/03/2004.....28......2......	BLACK CHERRY	Mute LCDMUTE 320
22/05/2004.....20......3......	STRICT MACHINE Re-issue of Mute LCDMUTE 295	Mute LCDMUTE 335

GOLDIE UK group produced by Tab Martin. Follow-ups, including *We'll Make The Same Mistake Again* and *How Many Times*, all failed.

27/05/1978 .....7......11	**MAKING UP AGAIN**	Bronze BRO 50

GOLDIE UK dance artist (born Clifford Price, 1966, Walsall) who was earlier a graffiti artist, working with Afrika Bambaata and appearing with him in the 1986 film *Bombing*. Goldie later worked with Soul II Soul before launching Metalheads. Also an actor, he had roles in the TV series *Eastenders* and the 1999 James Bond film *The World Is Not Enough*. He won two MOBO Awards in 1996: Best Jungle Artist and Best Album for *Timeless*.

03/12/1994.....49......2......	INNER CITY LIFE **GOLDIE PRESENTS METALHEADZ**	ffrr FCD 251
09/09/1995.....41......3......	ANGEL	ffrr FCD 266
11/11/1995.....39......3......	INNER CITY LIFE (REMIX)	ffrr FCD 267
01/11/1997.....13......3......	DIGITAL	ffrr FCD 316
24/01/1998.....13......4......	TEMPERTEMPER This and above single credited to **GOLDIE FEATURING KRS ONE**	ffrr FCD 325
18/04/1998.....36......2......	BELIEVE	ffrr FCD 332

GOLDIE AND THE GINGERBREADS US group formed in Brooklyn, NYC in 1963 by Goldie Zelkowitz (born 1943, Brooklyn), Carol McDonald (born 1944, Wilmington, DE), Margo Crocitto (born 1943, Brooklyn) and Ginger Panebianco (born 1945, Long Island, NY). Goldie later went solo.

25/02/1965.....25......5.......	CAN'T YOU HEAR MY HEART BEAT?	Decca F 12070

GOLDIE LOOKIN CHAIN UK rap group formed in Newport by P Xain (aka Dwayne Xain Xedong aka Ganja Bizniz), Mr Love-Eggs (aka Eggsy aka Rene La Loux aka Chon Benwa Balls), Adam Hussain (aka Benny Blanco), One-Step Down Media Assassin, 2-Hats (aka 2000AD), Mystikal (aka Dr Boris Gobshite aka The Druid), The Maggot (aka The Hip Hop Vampire), Billy Webb (aka DVS aka Tim Westcountry), DCI Burnside (aka Lastman Standing), Mike Balls Hardest Man In Soccer Violence, Stress Armstrong (aka The Walsh aka Mr Compact), Eugene the Genius (aka Don Conlioni), Cannesy T (aka The T-Spot), C.Live (aka Clifford T Justice) and Will from Dionysus. The group sometimes expands to 34 members.

01/05/2004.....32......3......	HALF MAN HALF MACHINE/SELF SUICIDE	Must Destroy DUSTY 019CD
28/08/2004 .....3......9......	**GUNS DON'T KILL PEOPLE RAPPERS DO**.	Atlantic GLC01CD
06/11/2004.....14......3......	YOUR MOTHER'S GOT A PENIS.	East West GLC02CD
25/12/2004.....22......1+......	YOU KNOWS I LOVES YOU	Atlantic GLC03CD

GOLDRUSH UK group formed by Joe Bennett, his brother Robin, Jef Clayton, Garo and G.

22/06/2002.....64......1......	SAME PICTURE	Virgin VSCDT 1833
07/09/2002.....70......1......	WIDE OPEN SKY	Virgin VSCDT 1834

BOBBY GOLDSBORO US singer (born 18/1/1941, Marianna, FL) who joined Roy Orbison's band in 1962 as guitarist, making his first solo records for Laurie the same year. He left Orbison in 1964 and later hosted his own TV show.

17/04/1968 .....2......15	**HONEY** ▲[5]	United Artists UP 2215
04/08/1973 .....9......10	**SUMMER (THE FIRST TIME)**	United Artists UP 35558
03/08/1974.....14......10	HELLO SUMMERTIME	United Artists UP 35705
29/03/1975 .....2......12	**HONEY** Re-issue of United Artists UP2215.	United Artists UP 35633

GLEN GOLDSMITH UK pop/soul singer (born Glenford Norman Goldsmith, Slough) who later did sessions, providing backing vocals for the likes of Juliet Rogers.

07/11/1987.....34......7......	I WON'T CRY	Reproduction PB 41493
12/03/1988.....12......11	DREAMING	Reproduction PB 41711

| 11/06/1988 | 33 | 5 | | WHAT YOU SEE IS WHAT YOU GET | Reproduction PB 42075 |
| 03/09/1988 | 73 | 1 | | SAVE A LITTLE BIT | Reproduction PB 42147 |

GOLDTRIX PRESENTS ANDREA BROWN
UK production duo of producer Matrix and keyboard player Danny Goldstein with US singer Andrea Brown (sister of singer Kathy Brown).

| 19/01/2002 | 6 | 9 | | **IT'S LOVE (TRIPPIN')** | AM:PM/Serious/Evolve CDAMPM 152 |

GOMEZ
UK group formed in Liverpool in 1996 by Tom Gray (vocal/guitar/keyboards), Ian Ball (guitar/vocals), Ben Ottewell (guitar), Paul Blackburn (bass) and Olly Peacock (drums).

11/04/1998	44	1		78 STONE WOBBLE	Hut HUTCD 95
13/06/1998	45	1		GET MYSELF ARRESTED	Hut HUTCD 97
12/09/1998	35	3		WHIPPIN' PICCADILLY	Hut HUTCD 105
10/07/1999	21	3		BRING IT ON	Hut HUTCD 112
11/09/1999	18	3		RHYTHM & BLUES ALIBI	Hut HUTCD 114
27/11/1999	38	2		WE HAVEN'T TURNED AROUND Featured in the 1997 film *Grosse Pointe Blank*	Hut HUTCD 117
16/03/2002	28	2		SHOT SHOT	Hut HUTCDX 149
15/06/2002	48	1		SOUND OF SOUNDS/PING ONE DOWN	Hut HUTDX 154
20/03/2004	36	2		CATCH ME UP	Hut HUTDX 175
22/05/2004	41	1		SILENCE	Hut HUTDX 178

LEROY GOMEZ – see SANTA ESMERALDA AND LEROY GOMEZ

GOMPIE
Dutch vocal/instrumental group formed by Rob Perters and Peter Koelewijn whose hit was one of three versions vying for chart honours at the same time (the other two being by Smokie, who had the biggest hit, and The Steppers, which failed to chart).

| 20/05/1995 | 34 | 5 | | ALICE (WHO THE X IS ALICE?) (LIVING NEXT DOOR TO ALICE) | Habana HABSCD 5 |
| 02/09/1995 | 17 | 7 | | ALICE (WHO THE X IS ALICE?) (LIVING NEXT DOOR TO ALICE) Re-promoted after the successful Smokie version | Habana HABSCD 5 |

GONZALES – see FUNK MASTERS

GONZALEZ
UK disco group formed in London by Richard 'Big Dipper' Jones with Linda Taylor (vocals), Alan Marshall (vocals), Roy Davies (keyboards), Hugh Bullen (bass), Mick Eve (horns), Chris Mercer (horns), Bud Beadle (horns), Colin Jacas (horns), Ron McCarthy (horns), Martin Drover (horns), Bobby Stignac (percussion) and Sergio Castillo (drums).

| 31/03/1979 | 15 | 11 | | HAVEN'T STOPPED DANCING YET Featured in the 1998 film *54* | Sidewalk SID 102 |

GOO GOO DOLLS
US group formed in New York in 1985 by Johnny Rzenzik (born 5/12/1965, Buffalo, NY, guitar/vocals), Robby Takac (born 30/9/1964, Buffalo, bass/vocals) and George Tutuska (drums) as the Sex Maggots, changing their name soon after. Mike Mallini (born 10/10/1967, Washington DC) replaced George Tutuska in 1995.

01/08/1998	50	1		IRIS Featured in the 1998 film *City Of Angels*	Reprise W 0449CD
27/03/1999	43	1		SLIDE	Edel/Hollywood/Third Rail 0102035 HWR
17/07/1999	26	2		IRIS Re-issue of Reprise W 0449CD	Hollywood 0102485 HWR

GOOD CHARLOTTE
US rock group formed in Waldorf, MD in 1996 by Joel Madden (born 3/11/1979, Waldorf, vocals), his twin brother Benji (guitar), Billy Martin (born 15/6/1981, Naptown, MD, guitar), Paul Thomas (born 5/10/1980, Waldorf, bass) and Aaron (drums). Aaron left in 2002 and was replaced by Chris Wilson.

15/02/2003	8	10		**LIFESTYLES OF THE RICH AND FAMOUS**	Epic 6735562
17/05/2003	6	9		**GIRLS AND BOYS**	Epic 6738775
30/08/2003	10	4		**THE ANTHEM** Featured in the 2003 film *American Wedding*	Epic 6742552
20/12/2003	34	4		THE YOUNG AND THE HOPELESS/HOLD ON	Epic 6745435
16/10/2004	12	4		PREDICTABLE	Epic 6753882

GOOD GIRLS
US vocal group formed in Westchester, CA by Shireen Crutchfield, DeMonica Santiago and Joyce Tolbert.

| 24/07/1993 | 75 | 1 | | JUST CALL ME | Motown TMGCD 1417 |

GOODBYE MR MACKENZIE
UK group formed in 1981 by Martin Metcalfe (guitar/vocals), Rona Scobie (keyboards/vocals), Shirley Manson (keyboards/vocals), Chuck Parker (bass) and Derek Kelly (drums). They made their first record for Wet Wet Wet's Precious Organisation. They disbanded in 1995, with Manson later fronting Garbage.

20/08/1988	62	2		GOODBYE MR MACKENZIE	Capitol CL 501
11/03/1989	37	6		THE RATTLER	Capitol CL 522
29/07/1989	49	2		GOODWILL CITY/I'M SICK OF YOU	Capitol CL 538
21/04/1990	52	2		LOVE CHILD	Parlophone R 6247
23/06/1990	61	1		BLACKER THAN BLACK	Parlophone R 6257

ROGER GOODE FEATURING TASHA BAXTER
South African producer with singer Tasha Baxter.

| 13/04/2002 | 33 | 2 | | IN THE BEGINNING | ffrr DFCDP 004 |

GOODFELLAS FEATURING LISA MILLETT
Italian production duo Gianni Bini and Martini with singer Lisa Millett. Bini is also responsible for Eclipse. Lisa Millet was previously on A.T.F.C. Presents Onephatdeeva's *Bad Habit*. Bini and Martini also record under their own names and as House Of Glass.

| 21/07/2001 | 27 | 2 | | SOUL HEAVEN | Direction 6713852 |

❶[9] Number of weeks single topped the UK chart   ↑ Entered the UK chart at #1   ▲[9] Number of weeks single topped the US chart

333

GOODFELLAZ
US R&B vocal group formed in New York in 1995 by DeLouie Avant Jr, Ray Vencier and Angel Vasquez. Their debut hit also features rapper Kahron.

10/05/1997 . . . . . 25 . . . . . . 2 . . . . SUGAR HONEY ICE TEA. . . . . Wild Card 5736132

GOODIES
UK TV comedy trio formed by Tim Brooke-Taylor (born 17/7/1940, Buxton), Graeme Garden (born 18/2/1943, Aberdeen) and Bill Oddie (born 7/7/1941, Rochdale). Oddie was awarded an OBE in the Queen's 2003 Birthday Honours List.

07/12/1974 . . . . . 7 . . . . . . 9 . . . . . . O	**THE IN BETWEENIES/FATHER CHRISTMAS DO NOT TOUCH ME** . . . . Bradley's BRAD 7421
15/03/1975 . . . . . 4 . . . . . . 10	**FUNKY GIBBON/SICK MAN BLUES** . . . . Bradley's BRAD 7504
21/06/1975 . . . . . 19 . . . . . 7	BLACK PUDDING BERTHA (THE QUEEN OF NORTHERN SOUL) . . . . Bradley's BRAD 7517
27/09/1975 . . . . . 21 . . . . . 6	NAPPY LOVE/WILD THING . . . . Bradley's BRAD 7524
13/12/1975 . . . . . 20 . . . . . 6	MAKE A DAFT NOISE FOR CHRISTMAS . . . . Bradley's BRAD 7533

CUBA GOODING
US R&B singer (born 27/4/1944, New York) who replaced Donald McPherson in The Main Ingredient in 1971 and went solo in 1978. His son Cuba Gooding Jr later became an Oscar-winning actor.

19/11/1983 . . . . . 72 . . . . . . 2 . . . . HAPPINESS IS JUST AROUND THE BEND . . . . London LON 41

GOODMEN
Dutch instrumental/production duo DJ Ziki (Rene Terhorst) and DJ Dobre (Gaston Steenkist) who also recorded as Chocolate Puma, Tomba Vira, DJ Manta, Jark Prongo, Rhythmkillaz and Riva.

07/08/1993 . . . . . 5 . . . . . . 19 . . . . O GIVE IT UP . . . . Fresh Fruit TABCD 118

DELTA GOODREM
Australian singer (born 9/11/1984, Sydney,) who first became famous as an actress, playing Nina Tucker on the TV series *Neighbours*. She was diagnosed as having Hodgkin's disease in July 2003.

22/03/2003 . . . . . 3 . . . . . 13	**BORN TO TRY** . . . . Epic 6736342
28/06/2003 . . . . . 4 . . . . . 11	**LOST WITHOUT YOU** . . . . Epic 6739555
04/10/2003 . . . . . 9 . . . . . 9	**INNOCENT EYES** . . . . Epic 6743155
13/12/2003 . . . . . 18 . . . . . 6	**NOT ME NOT I** . . . . Epic 6745372
20/11/2004 . . . . . 9 . . . . . 6+	**OUT OF THE BLUE** . . . . Epic 6754732

RON GOODWIN
UK orchestra leader (born 17/2/1925, Plymouth) who began as an arranger and bandleader, later becoming a conductor and composer. He scored his first film in 1958 (*Whirlpool*) and wrote the music to over 60 others. He died on 8/1/2003.

15/05/1953 . . . . . 3 . . . . . 23	**TERRY'S THEME FROM 'LIMELIGHT'** Written by Charlie Chaplin. . . . . Parlophone R 3686
28/10/1955 . . . . . 20 . . . . . 1	BLUE STAR (THE MEDIC THEME) . . . . Parlophone R 4074
20/01/1956 . . . . . 18 . . . . . 3	SHIFTING WHISPERING SANDS (PARTS 1 & 2) EAMONN ANDREWS WITH RON GOODWIN AND HIS ORCHESTRA . . . . Parlophone R 4106

GOODY GOODY
US studio group assembled by producer Vince Montana. Lead vocals were by Denise Montana.

02/12/1978 . . . . . 55 . . . . . . 5 . . . . . . NUMBER ONE DEE JAY . . . . Atlantic LV 3

GOOMBAY DANCE BAND
Multinational dance band comprising Oliver Bendt, his wife Alicia, Dorothy Hellings, Wendy Dorseen and Mario Slijngaard. The Bendt's two children, Danny and Yasmin, also appeared as backing singers.

27/02/1982 . . . . . ❶³ . . . . . 12 . . . . ●	**SEVEN TEARS** . . . . Epic EPC A 1242
15/05/1982 . . . . . 50 . . . . . 4	SUN OF JAMAICA . . . . Epic EPC A 2345

GOONS
UK radio comedy trio formed by Spike Milligan (born Terence Alan Milligan, 16/4/1918, Ahmed Nagar, India), Peter Sellers (born 8/9/1925, Southsea) and Harry Secombe (born 8/9/1921, Swansea). Michael Bentine (born 26/1/1922, Watford) was also an early member. Peter Sellers died from a heart attack on 24/7/1980, Michael Bentine died from prostate cancer on 26/11/1996 and Harry Secombe died from cancer on 11/4/2001. Spike Milligan was knighted in the 2001 New Year's Honours List and died on 27/2/2002.

29/06/1956 . . . . . 4 . . . . . 10	**I'M WALKING BACKWARDS FOR CHRISTMAS/BLUEBOTTLE BLUES** . . . . Decca F 10756
14/09/1956 . . . . . 3 . . . . . 10	**BLOODNOK'S ROCK 'N' ROLL CALL/YING TONG SONG** . . . . Decca E 10780
21/07/1973 . . . . . 9 . . . . . 10	YING TONG SONG Re-issue of Decca E 10780 . . . . Decca F 13414

LONNIE GORDON
US singer (born in The Bronx, NYC) whose career first took off in the UK.

24/06/1989 . . . . . 60 . . . . . 3	(I'VE GOT YOUR) PLEASURE CONTROL SIMON HARRIS FEATURING LONNIE GORDON . . . . ffrr F 106
27/01/1990 . . . . . 4 . . . . . 10	**HAPPENIN' ALL OVER AGAIN** . . . . Supreme SUPE 159
11/08/1990 . . . . . 48 . . . . . 2	BEYOND YOUR WILDEST DREAMS. . . . . Supreme SUPE 167
17/11/1990 . . . . . 68 . . . . . 1	IF I HAVE TO STAND ALONE . . . . Supreme SUPE 181
04/05/1991 . . . . . 32 . . . . . 5	GONNA CATCH YOU. . . . . Supreme SUPE 185
07/10/1995 . . . . . 32 . . . . . 2	LOVE EVICTION QUARTZ LOCK FEATURING LONNIE GORDON . . . . X:Plode BANG 2CD

LESLEY GORE
US singer (born 2/5/1946, New York). Fronting a seven-piece jazz group, she sent demos to Mercury Records who signed her (without the group) to a singles-only deal in 1962, with producer Quincy Jones. Her debut single was rush-released because Phil Spector intended recording the song with the Crystals. She made her film debut in 1964 and appeared in TV shows such as *Batman*.

20/06/1963 . . . . . 9 . . . . . 12	**IT'S MY PARTY** ▲² Featured in the 1990 film *Mermaids*. . . . . Mercury AMT 1205
24/09/1964 . . . . . 20 . . . . . 8	MAYBE I KNOW . . . . Mercury MF 829

MARTIN L GORE
UK multi-instrumentalist/producer (born 23/7/1961, Dagenham, Essex) who was a founding member of Depeche Mode. He launched a parallel solo career in 1989.

26/04/2003 . . . . . 44 . . . . . . 1 . . . . . . STARDUST . . . . Mute CDMUTE 296

GORILLAZ
UK animated group formed by Murdoc, 2-D, Noodle and Russel. The ad hoc group was assembled by Damon Albarn

O Silver disc ● Gold disc ✪ Platinum disc (additional platinum units are indicated by a figure following the symbol) ◉ Singles released prior to 1973 that are known to have sold over 1 million copies in the UK

of Blur (born 23/3/1968, London) and Jamie Hewlett, the illustrator of *Tank Girl*. Their self-titled debut album was nominated for a Mercury Music Prize, although the group refused to accept the nomination. They did, however, accept two awards at the 2001 MTV Europe Music Awards, for Best Song and Best Dance Act.

Date	Pos	Wks	BPI	Title	Label
17/03/2001	4	17	●	**CLINT EASTWOOD** The actor isn't mentioned in the lyrics. 2001 MTV Europe Music Award for Best Song	Parlophone CDR 6552
07/07/2001	6	10		**19/2000**	Parlophone CDR 6559
03/11/2001	18	8		ROCK THE HOUSE	Parlophone CDRS 6565
09/03/2002	33	3		TOMORROW COMES TODAY	Parlophone CDR 6573
03/08/2002	73	1		LIL' DUB CHEFIN' SPACE MONKEY VS GORILLAZ	Parlophone CDR 6584

GORKY'S ZYGOTIC MYNCI
UK group formed in Carmarthen, Wales in 1990 by Euros Childs (keyboards/vocals), John Lawrence (guitar), Richard James (bass), Megan Childs (violin) and Euros Rowlands (drums). They were signed with Ankst before joining Mercury Records in 1996.

Date	Pos	Wks	Title	Label
09/11/1996	41	1	PATIO SONG	Fontana GZMCD 1
29/03/1997	42	1	DIAMOND DEW	Fontana GZMCD 2
21/06/1997	49	1	YOUNG GIRLS & HAPPY ENDINGS/DARK NIGHT	Fontana GZMCD 3
06/06/1998	60	1	SWEET JOHNNY	Fontana GZMCD 4
29/08/1998	43	1	LET'S GET TOGETHER (IN OUR MINDS)	Fontana GZMCD 5
02/10/1999	47	1	SPANISH DANCE TROUPE	Mantra/Beggars Banquet MNT 47CD
04/03/2000	52	1	POODLE ROCKIN'	Mantra/Beggars Banquet MNT 52CD
15/09/2001	65	1	STOOD ON GOLD	Mantra MNT 64CD

EYDIE GORME
US singer (born 16/8/1931, New York) who sang with Tommy Tucker and Tex Beneke bands in the late 1940s. She married Steve Lawrence in 1957. They won the 1960 Grammy Award for Best Performance by a Vocal Group for *We Got Us*, and she won the Best Female Solo Vocal Performance in 1966 for *If He Walked Into My Life*. The couple have a star on the Hollywood Walk of Fame.

Date	Pos	Wks	Title	Label
24/01/1958	21	5	LOVE ME FOREVER	HMV POP 432
21/06/1962	10	9	**YES MY DARLING DAUGHTER**	CBS AAG 105
31/01/1963	32	6	BLAME IT ON THE BOSSA NOVA	CBS AAG 131
22/08/1963	3	13	**I WANT TO STAY HERE** STEVE AND EYDIE (Steve Lawrence)	CBS AAG 163

LUKE GOSS AND THE BAND OF THIEVES
UK group fronted by Luke Goss (born 29/9/1968, London). Previously a member of Bros with his twin brother Matt and Craig Logan, he later became an actor, appearing in the 2002 film *Queen Of The Damned*.

Date	Pos	Wks	Title	Label
12/06/1993	52	2	SWEETER THAN THE MIDNIGHT RAIN	Sabre CDSAB 1
21/08/1993	68	1	GIVE ME ONE MORE CHANCE	Sabre CDSAB 2

MATT GOSS
UK singer (born 29/9/1968, London) who, with twin brother Luke and Craig Logan, were late 1980s teen idols Bros. By the early 1990s Logan had left, financial and management problems seeing the demise of the group. Both brothers have gone solo, with Matt being the first to hit the top 40.

Date	Pos	Wks	Title	Label
26/08/1995	40	2	THE KEY	Atlas 5811532
27/04/1996	23	3	IF YOU WERE HERE TONIGHT	Atlas 5762932
15/11/2003	22	2	I'M COMING WITH YA	Concept CDCON 49
31/07/2004	31	2	FLY	Concept CDCON 57
02/10/2004	54	1	I NEED THE KEY MINIMAL CHIC FEATURING MATT GOSS	Inferno CDFERN63

IRV GOTTI PRESENTS JA RULE, ASHANTI, CHARLI BALTIMORE AND VITA
US producer/record company executive (born Irving Lorenzo, 1971, New York) who first became prominent producing the likes of Ja Rule, Ashanti and Jennifer Lopez. He launched the Murder Inc label in 1997.

Date	Pos	Wks	Title	Label
12/10/2002	4	10	**DOWN 4 U**	Murder Inc 0639002

NIGEL GOULDING
— see ABIGAIL MEAD AND NIGEL GOULDING

GRAHAM GOULDMAN
UK singer/guitarist (born 10/5/1946, Manchester) who was previously in 10cc, later forming Wax with US singer Andrew Gold.

Date	Pos	Wks	Title	Label
23/06/1979	52	4	SUNBURN Featured in the 1979 film *Sunburn*	Mercury SUNNY 1

GOURYELLA
Dutch dance group formed by DJ Tiesto (born Tijs Verswest) and Ferry Corsten. Corsten also records as Veracocha, Moonman, Albion, Starparty and System F. Verwest also records as DJ Tiesto.

Date	Pos	Wks	Title	Label
10/07/1999	15	7	GOURYELLA	Code Blue BLU 001CD
04/12/1999	27	2	WALHALLA	Code Blue BLU 006CD
23/12/2000	45	2	TENSHI	Code Blue BLU 017CD

GQ
US soul group formed in New York in 1968 by Emmanuel Rahiem LeBlanc (guitar/vocals), Keith 'Sabu' Crier (bass/vocals), Herb Lane (keyboards/vocals) and Paul Service (drums/vocals) as Sabu & The Survivors and then The Rhythm Makers, changing to GQ when they signed with Arista. Crier subsequently recorded as Keith Sweat.

Date	Pos	Wks	Title	Label
10/03/1979	42	6	DISCO NIGHTS (ROCK FREAK) Featured in the 1998 film *54*	Arista ARIST 245

GRACE
UK singer Dominique Atkins.

Date	Pos	Wks	Title	Label
08/04/1995	6	8	**NOT OVER YET**	Perfecto PERF 104CD
23/09/1995	30	2	I WANT TO LIVE	Perfecto PERF 109CD

❶⁹ Number of weeks single topped the UK chart ↑ Entered the UK chart at #1 ▲⁹ Number of weeks single topped the US chart

335

	DATE	POS	WKS	BPI	SINGLE TITLE	LABEL & NUMBER
	24/02/1996	21	3		SKIN ON SKIN	Perfecto PERF 116CD
	01/06/1996	20	2		DOWN TO EARTH	Perfecto PERF 120CD
	28/09/1996	29	2		IF I COULD FLY	Perfecto PERF 127CD
	03/05/1997	38	1		HAND IN HAND	Perfecto PERF 129CD
	26/07/1997	29	2		DOWN TO EARTH	Perfecto PERF 142CD1
	14/08/1999	16	4		NOT OVER YET 99 PLANET PERFECTO FEATURING GRACE	Code Blue BLU 004CD

BRIDGETTE GRACE – see TRUE FAITH AND BRIDGETTE GRACE WITH FINAL CUT

GRACE BROTHERS UK instrumental duo.

	20/04/1996	51	1		ARE YOU BEING SERVED	EMI Premier PRESCD 1

CHARLIE GRACIE US singer (born Charles Graci, 14/5/1936, Philadelphia, PA) who made his recording debut in 1951 for Cadillac and then became a regular on *American Grandstand*.

	19/04/1957	12	8		BUTTERFLY ▲²	Parlophone R 4290
	14/06/1957	8	16		FABULOUS	Parlophone R 4313
	23/08/1957	14	4		I LOVE YOU SO MUCH IT HURTS	London HLU 8467
	23/08/1957	6	14		WANDERIN' EYES B-side to *I Love You So Much It Hurts*. The two records were listed together for the first two weeks of their respective chart runs	London HLU 8467
	10/01/1958	26	1		COOL BABY	London HLU 8521

GRAFITI UK DJ Mike Skinner (born in Birmingham, later moved to London) who also records as The Streets.

	30/08/2003	37	2		WHAT IS THE PROBLEM?	679 Recordings 679L 021CD

EVE GRAHAM – see NEW SEEKERS

JAKI GRAHAM UK singer (born 15/9/1956, Birmingham) who sang with the Medium Wave Band before linking with Derek Bramble and signing with EMI as a solo artist, recording her debut in 1984. She later formed Kiss The Sky with Paul Hardcastle.

	23/03/1985	5	11		COULD IT BE I'M FALLING IN LOVE DAVID GRANT AND JAKI GRAHAM	Chrysalis GRAN 6
	29/06/1985	9	11		ROUND AND ROUND	EMI JAKI 4
	31/08/1985	59	3		HEAVEN KNOWS	EMI JAKI 5
	16/11/1985	20	10		MATED DAVID GRANT AND JAKI GRAHAM	EMI JAKI 6
	03/05/1986	7	12		SET ME FREE	EMI JAKI 7
	09/08/1986	16	8		BREAKING AWAY	EMI JAKI 8
	15/11/1986	15	12		STEP RIGHT UP	EMI JAKI 9
	09/07/1988	60	2		NO MORE TEARS	EMI JAKI 12
	24/06/1989	73	2		FROM NOW ON	EMI JAKI 15
	16/07/1994	44	2		AIN'T NOBODY	Pulse 8 CDLOSE 64
	04/02/1995	62	1		YOU CAN COUNT ON ME	Avex UK AVEXCD 1
	08/07/1995	69	1		ABSOLUTE E-SENSUAL	Avex UK AVEXCD 5

LARRY GRAHAM US singer/bass player (born 14/8/1946, Beaumont, TX) who was a member of Sly & The Family Stone from 1967 until 1972, when he left to form Graham Central Station. He went solo in 1980.

	03/07/1982	54	4		SOONER OR LATER	Warner Brothers K 17925

MIKEY GRAHAM Irish singer (born 15/8/1972, Dublin), a founder member of Boyzone, who went solo at their split in 2000.

	10/06/2000	13	5		YOU'RE MY ANGEL	Public PR 001CDS
	14/04/2001	62	1		YOU COULD BE MY EVERYTHING	Public PR 003CDS

RON GRAINER ORCHESTRA UK orchestra leader. He died on 21/2/1981.

	09/12/1978	60	7		A TOUCH OF VELVET A STING OF BRASS	Casino Classics CC 5

GRAM'MA FUNK US singer (born in New York) who was also an MC at Manumission.

	27/11/1999	17	6		I SEE YOU BABY GROOVE ARMADA FEATURING GRAM'MA FUNK	Pepper 9230002
	02/09/2000	72	1		CHEEKY ARMADA ILLICIT FEATURING GRAM'MA FUNK	Yola YOLACDX 01

GRAND FUNK RAILROAD US heavy rock group formed in Flint, MI in 1968 by Mark Farner (born 29/9/1948, Flint, guitar), Don Brewer (born 3/9/1948, Schwartz Creek, MI, drums) and Mel Schacher (born 3/4/1951, Owosso, MI, bass), signing with Capitol in July 1969. Craig Frost (born 20/4/1948, Flint, keyboards) was added in 1972. They disbanded in 1976, re-formed in 1981 and disbanded for good in 1983. Farner later recorded religious material. Their name was inspired by the Grand Trunk Railroad in the US.

	06/02/1971	40	1		INSIDE LOOKING OUT This is a 33⅓ RPM single that clocked in at 9 minutes 27 seconds	Capitol CL 15668

GRAND PLAZ UK instrumental/production group. Despite production credit to DJ Crazyhouse, this was actually Mike Stock, Matt Aitken and Pete Waterman.

	08/09/1990	41	4		WOW WOW – NA NA Contains an interpolation of Steam's *Na Na Hey Hey Kiss Him Goodbye*	Urban URB 60

GRAND PRIX UK rock group formed by Bernard Shaw (vocals), Michael O'Donahue (guitar/vocals), Ralph Hood (bass), Phil Lanzon (keyboards/vocals) and Andy Beirne (drums). Shaw was later replaced by Robin McAuley.

	27/02/1982	75	1		KEEP ON BELIEVING	RCA 162

○ Silver disc ● Gold disc ✪ Platinum disc (additional platinum units are indicated by a figure following the symbol) ◉ Singles released prior to 1973 that are known to have sold over 1 million copies in the UK

GRAND PUBA
US rapper Maxwell Dixon (born 4/3/1966, The Bronx, NYC).

| 13/01/1996 | 11 | 5 | WHY YOU TREAT ME SO BAD SHAGGY FEATURING GRAND PUBA Contains a sample of Bob Marley's *Mr Brown*.. Virgin VSCDT 1566 |
| 30/03/1996 | 53 | 1 | WILL YOU BE MY BABY INFINITI FEATURING GRAND PUBA...GHQ 74321339092 |

GRAND THEFT AUDIO
UK group formed by Jay Butler (vocals), Chris McCormack (guitar), Ralph Jezzard (bass) and Ritch Battersby (drums). McCormack had previously been a member of 3 Colours Red.

| 24/03/2001 | 70 | 1 | WE LUV U Featured in the 2001 film *Dude Where's My Car*...Sci-Fi SCIFI 1CD |

GRANDAD ROBERTS AND HIS SON ELVIS
UK vocal duo. The hit was originally a terrace chant at Oldham Athletic FC. The project was assembled by Andy Wilkinson and Arthur Kelly.

| 20/06/1998 | 67 | 1 | MEAT PIE SAUSAGE ROLL...WEA 160CD |

GRANDADDY
US rock group formed in Modesto, CA in 1992 by Jason Lytle (guitar/vocals), Kevin Garcia (bass) and Aaron Burtch (drums). They added Jim Fairchild (guitar) and Tim Dryden (keyboards) in 1995.

02/09/2000	71	1	HEWLETT'S DAUGHTER..V2 VVR 5014333
10/02/2001	38	2	THE CRYSTAL LAKE..V2 VVR 5015158
14/06/2003	23	2	NOW IT'S ON..V2 VVR 5022248
06/09/2003	48	1	EL CAMINOS IN THE WEST..V2 VVR 5023663

GRANDMASTER FLASH AND THE FURIOUS FIVE
US rapper (born Joseph Saddler, 1/1/1958, Barbados) who was a mobile DJ when he formed the Furious Five, adding rappers Cowboy (born Keith Wiggins, 20/9/1960), Kidd Creole (Nathaniel Glover), Melle Mel (Melvin Glover), Duke Bootee (Ed Fletcher) and Kurtis Blow. Blow was later replaced by Raheim (Guy Todd Williams). They made their record debut for Enjoy in 1979. Melle Mel won the 1990 Grammy Award for Best Rap Performance by a Group with Ice-T, Daddy Kane and Kool Moe Dee for *Back On The Block* by Quincy Jones. Yo-Yo is US rapper Yolanda Whittaler (born 4/8/1971, Los Angeles, CA).

28/08/1982	8	9		THE MESSAGE..Sugarhill SHL 117
22/01/1983	74	2		MESSAGE II (SURVIVAL) MELLE MEL AND DUKE BOOTEE......................................Sugarhill SHL 119
19/11/1983	7	43	O	WHITE LINES (DON'T DON'T DO IT) GRANDMASTER FLASH AND MELLE MEL Featured in the 2004 film *Shaun Of The Dead*........ Sugarhill SHL 130
30/06/1984	42	7		BEAT STREET BREAKDOWN...Atlantic A 9659
22/09/1984	45	4		WE DON'T WORK FOR FREE..Sugarhill SH 136
15/12/1984	8	12		STEP OFF (PART 1) This and above two singles credited to GRANDMASTER MELLE MEL AND THE FURIOUS FIVE.... Sugarhill SHL 139
16/02/1985	72	1		SIGN OF THE TIMES GRANDMASTER FLASH...Elektra E 9677
16/03/1985	45	6		PUMP ME UP GRANDMASTER MELLE MEL AND THE FURIOUS FIVE.....................................Sugarhill SH 141
08/01/1994	59	3		WHITE LINES (DON'T DON'T DO IT) (REMIX) GRANDMASTER AND MELLE MEL......................WGAF WGAFCD 103
14/09/1996	28	2		STOMP–THE REMIXES QUINCY JONES FEATURING MELLE MEL, COOLIO, YO-YO, SHAQUILLE O'NEAL & THE LUNIZ.... Qwest W 0372CD

GRANDMIXER D.ST
US DJ/producer Derek Howells.

| 24/12/1983 | 71 | 3 | CRAZY CUTS..Island IS 146 |

GRANGE HILL CAST
UK cast of BBC TV children's series *Grange Hill* with an anti-drug message. They followed it up with *You Know The Teacher*.

| 19/04/1986 | 5 | 6 | JUST SAY NO...BBC RESL 183 |

GERRI GRANGER
US singer who recorded for Bell, United Artists and 20th Century, and began her career touring with Sammy Davis Jr. She later became an English teacher in New Jersey working with prison inmates.

| 30/09/1978 | 50 | 3 | I GO TO PIECES (EVERYTIME)..Casino Classics CC 3 |

AMY GRANT
US singer (born 25/11/1960, Augusta, GA) who made her debut album in 1976 and is regarded as the first lady of contemporary Christian music, selling more than 15 million albums in her career. She has won five Grammies: Best Contemporary Gospel Performance in 1982 for *Age To Age*, Best Gospel Performance in 1983 for *Ageless Melody*, Best Gospel Performance in 1984 for *Angels*, Best Gospel Performance in 1985 for *Unguarded* and Best Gospel Performance in 1988 for *Lead Me On*.

11/05/1991	2	13	O	BABY BABY ▲[2]...A&M AM 727
03/08/1991	25	7		EVERY HEARTBEAT...A&M AM 783
02/11/1991	60	3		THAT'S WHAT LOVE IS FOR...A&M AM 666
15/02/1992	60	1		GOOD FOR ME...A&M AM 810
13/08/1994	60	1		LUCKY ONE..A&M 5807322
22/10/1994	41	2		SAY YOU'LL BE MINE...A&M 5808292
24/06/1995	20	10		BIG YELLOW TAXI...A&M 5809972
14/10/1995	46	2		HOUSE OF LOVE AMY GRANT WITH VINCE GILL..A&M 5812332

ANDREA GRANT
UK singer.

| 14/11/1998 | 75 | 1 | REPUTATIONS (JUST BE GOOD TO ME)..WEA 192CD |

BOYSIE GRANT
– see EZZ RECO AND THE LAUNCHERS WITH BOYSIE GRANT

DAVID GRANT
UK singer (born 8/8/1956, Hackney, London) who was a founding member of Linx in the early 1980s before launching a solo career masterminded by Derek Bramble. He won the 1998 MOBO Award for Best Gospel Act with Carrie.

| 30/04/1983 | 19 | 9 | STOP AND GO..Chrysalis GRAN 1 |
| 16/07/1983 | 10 | 13 | WATCHING YOU WATCHING ME..Chrysalis GRAN 2 |

❶[9] Number of weeks single topped the UK chart   ↑ Entered the UK chart at #1   ▲[9] Number of weeks single topped the US chart

337

08/10/1983.....24......6......	LOVE WILL FIND A WAY	Chrysalis GRAN 3
26/11/1983.....46......4......	ROCK THE MIDNIGHT	Chrysalis GRAN 4
23/03/1985 .....5......11......	**COULD IT BE I'M FALLING IN LOVE**	Chrysalis GRAN 6
16/11/1985.....20......10	MATED This and above single credited to **DAVID GRANT AND JAKI GRAHAM**	EMI JAKI 6
01/08/1987.....55......4......	CHANGE	Polydor POSP 871
12/05/1990.....56......2......	KEEP IT TOGETHER	Fourth & Broadway BRW 169

EDDY GRANT Guyanan singer/multi-instrumentalist (born Edmond Montague Grant, 5/3/1948, Plaisance) who moved to London in 1960 and formed The Equals in 1967. When legal problems prevented the group from recording in the early 1970s, Grant quit to concentrate on production, in 1977 going solo. A shrewd businessman, his earnings set up Ice Records in Guyana and then in the UK.

02/06/1979.....11......11......	LIVING ON THE FRONT LINE	Ensign ENY 26
15/11/1980 .....8......11......O	**DO YOU FEEL MY LOVE**	Ensign ENY 45
04/04/1981.....13......10......	CAN'T GET ENOUGH OF YOU	Ensign ENY 207
25/07/1981.....37......6......	I LOVE YOU, YES I LOVE YOU	Ensign ENY 216
16/10/1982.....$\mathbf{0}^3$......15......●	**I DON'T WANNA DANCE**	Ice 56
15/01/1983.....2......9......O	**ELECTRIC AVENUE**	Ice 57
19/03/1983.....47......4......	LIVING ON THE FRONT LINE/DO YOU FEEL MY LOVE Re-issue of Ensign ENY 26	Mercury MER 135
23/04/1983.....42......4......	WAR PARTY	Ice 58
29/10/1983.....42......7......	TILL I CAN'T TAKE LOVE NO MORE	Ice 60
19/05/1984.....52......3......	ROMANCING THE STONE	Ice 61
23/01/1988.....7......12......	**GIMME HOPE JO'ANNA**	Ice 78701
27/05/1989.....63......2......	WALKING ON SUNSHINE	Blue Wave R 6217
09/06/2001 .....5......12......O	**ELECTRIC AVENUE**	Ice EW 232CD
24/11/2001.....57......1......	WALKING ON SUNSHINE	Ice EW 242CD

GOGI GRANT US singer (born Audrey Arinsberg, 20/9/1924, Philadelphia, PA) who moved to Los Angeles, CA at twelve and later provided the vocals for the film *The Helen Morgan Story* (1957).

29/06/1956 .....9......11......	**WAYWARD WIND** ▲[8]	London HLB 8282

JULIE GRANT UK singer (born 12/7/1946, Blackpool) who initially shared her manager Eric Easton with The Rolling Stones, touring with them on their first major UK tour.

03/01/1963.....33......3......	UP ON THE ROOF	Pye 7N 15483
28/03/1963.....24......9......	COUNT ON ME	Pye 7N 15508
24/09/1964.....31......5......	COME TO ME	Pye 7N 15684

RUDY GRANT Guyanan singer and brother of singer Eddy Grant.

14/02/1981.....58......3......	LATELY	Ensign ENY 202

GRAPEFRUIT UK group formed in 1967 by John Perry (born16/7/1949, London, vocals), Pete Sweetenham (born 24/4/1949, London, guitar), his brother Geoff (born 8/3/1948, London, drums) and George Alexander (born 28/12/1948, Glasgow, bass). The group were given their name by John Lennon (after a book by Yoko Ono) and was the first act signed to The Beatles' Apple publishing group. Pete Sweetenham left in 1969 and was replaced by Bobby Ware and Mike Fowler. They disbanded in 1970.

14/02/1968.....21......9......	DEAR DELILAH	RCA 1656
14/08/1968.....31......10......	C'MON MARIANNE	RCA 1716

GRASS-SHOW Swedish group formed in 1994 by Peter Agren (keyboards/vocals), Erik Kinell (guitar/vocals), Roberg Gehring (guitar), Andrew Dry (bass) and Mattias Moberg (drums).

22/03/1997.....53......1......	1962	Food CDFOOD 90
23/08/1997.....75......1......	OUT OF THE VOID	Food CDFOOD 103

GRAVEDIGGAZ US rap group formed by Prince Paul (born Paul Huston, also a member of Stetsasonic), RZA (born Robert Diggs, member of Wu-Tang Clan) and Fruitkwan (born Arnold Hamilton). Prince Paul and Fruitkwan also adopted additional stage names in the Undertaker and the Gatekeeper respectively. The group also featured Poetic The Grym Reaper and re-christened RZA the Ressurector. Poetic The Grym Reaper died from colon cancer in July 2001.

11/03/1995.....64......1......	SIX FEET DEEP (EP) Tracks on EP: *Bang Your Head, Mommy* and *Suicide*.	Gee Street GESCD 62
05/08/1995.....12......3......	THE HELL EP Tracks on EP: *Hell Is Round The Corner, Hell Is Round The Corner (Remix), Psychosis* and *Tonite Is A Special Nite* .... Fourth & Broadway BRCD 326
24/01/1998.....44......1......	THE NIGHT THE EARTH CRIED	Gee Street GEE 5001013
25/04/1998.....48......1......	UNEXPLAINED	Gee Street GEE 5001623

DAVID GRAY UK singer (born 1968, some sources give 1970, Manchester) who made his debut album in 1993 for Hut Records, later recording for EMI and forming the IHT label. His *White Ladder* album finally hit the #1 spot two years and five months after it was released, the second longest run to #1 by any album (only Tyrannosaurus Rex's *My People Were Fair And Had Sky In Their Hair* took longer, at nearly four years).

04/12/1999.....72......1......	PLEASE FORGIVE ME	IHT IHTCDS 003
01/07/2000 .....5......12......	**BABYLON**	IHT/East West EW 215CD1
28/10/2000.....18......6......	PLEASE FORGIVE ME Re-issue of IHT IHTCDS 003 and featured in the 2000 film *On The Edge*	IHT/East West EW 219CD
17/03/2001.....20......5......	THIS YEAR'S LOVE Featured in the 2001 film *This Year's Love*	IHT/East West EW 228CD1
28/07/2001.....26......6......	SAIL AWAY	IHT/East West EW 234CD

DATE	POS	WKS	BPI	SINGLE TITLE	LABEL & NUMBER
29/12/2001	26	4		SAY HELLO WAVE GOODBYE	IHT/East West EW 243CD
21/12/2002	35	3		THE OTHER SIDE	IHT/East West EW 259CD
19/04/2003	23	3		BE MINE	IHT/East West EW 264CD

DOBIE GRAY
US singer (born Lawrence Darrow Brown, 26/7/1942, Brookshire, TX) who moved to Los Angeles, CA in 1960 to make records but had more success in Nashville. He also recorded as Leonard Victor Ainsworth, Larry Curtis and Larry Dennis. He is best known for 1973's *Drift Away*, a UK hit for Michael Bolton in 1992. He had an acting role in the musical *Hair* and later sang lead in rock group Pollution.

DATE	POS	WKS	BPI	SINGLE TITLE	LABEL & NUMBER
25/02/1965	25	7		THE IN CROWD	London HL 9953
27/09/1975	42	4		OUT ON THE FLOOR	Black Magic BM 107

DORIAN GRAY
UK singer (born Tony Ellingham, Gravesend), named after the Oscar Wilde book *The Picture Of Dorian Gray*.

DATE	POS	WKS	BPI	SINGLE TITLE	LABEL & NUMBER
27/03/1968	36	7		I'VE GOT YOU ON MY MIND	Parlophone R 5667

LES GRAY
UK singer (born 9/4/1946, Carshalton) who was a founding member of Mud in 1966 before going solo. He died from cancer on 21/2/2004.

DATE	POS	WKS	BPI	SINGLE TITLE	LABEL & NUMBER
26/02/1977	32	5		A GROOVY KIND OF LOVE	Warner Brothers K 16883

MACY GRAY
US singer (born Natalie McIntyre, 9/9/1969, Canton, OH) who moved to Los Angeles, CA to enrol in a screenwriting programme before beginning a singing career. Her backing group comprises Dawn Beckman (vocals), Musiic Galloway (vocals), DJ Kiilu (DJ), Dion Murdock (drums), Jeremy Ruzumna (keyboards), Dave Wilder (bass), Arik Marshall (guitar), Matt DeMerritt, Tracy Wannomae and Todd Simon (all horns). She was named Best International Newcomer and Best International Female Artist at the 2000 BRIT Awards.

DATE	POS	WKS	BPI	SINGLE TITLE	LABEL & NUMBER
03/07/1999	51	1		DO SOMETHING	Epic 6675932
09/10/1999	6	22	●	I TRY Featured in the 1997 film *Picture Perfect*. 2000 Grammy Award for Best Female Pop Vocal Performance	Epic 6681832
25/03/2000	18	9		STILL	Epic 6689622
05/08/2000	38	3		WHY DIDN'T YOU CALL ME	Epic 6696682
20/01/2001	16	5		DEMONS FATBOY SLIM FEATURING MACY GRAY Contains a sample of Bill Withers' *I Can't Write Left Handed*	Skint 60CD
28/04/2001	48	1		GETO HEAVEN COMMON FEATURING MACY GRAY	MCA MCSTD 40246
12/05/2001	31	3		REQUEST & LINE BLACK EYED PEAS FEATURING MACY GRAY Contains a sample of Paulinho Da Costa's *Love You Till The End Of Time*	Interscope 4975032
15/09/2001	23	4		SWEET BABY MACY GRAY FEATURING ERYKAH BADU	Epic 6718822
08/12/2001	45	1		SEXUAL REVOLUTION Featured in the 2002 film *The Sweetest Thing*	Epic 6721462
03/05/2003	26	3		WHEN I SEE YOU	Epic 6738405

MICHAEL GRAY
UK producer who is also a member of Full Intention with Jon Pearn. They also record as Arizona, Hustlers Convention, Ronaldo's Revenge, Disco Tex Presents Cloudburst and Sex-O-Sonique.

DATE	POS	WKS	BPI	SINGLE TITLE	LABEL & NUMBER
13/11/2004	7	7+		THE WEEKEND	Eye Industries/UMTV 9868865

BARRY GRAY ORCHESTRA
UK orchestra leader.

DATE	POS	WKS	BPI	SINGLE TITLE	LABEL & NUMBER
11/07/1981	61	2		THUNDERBIRDS	PRT 7P 216
14/06/1986	53	6		JOE 90 (THEME)/CAPTAIN SCARLET THEME BARRY GRAY ORCHESTRA WITH PETER BECKETT – KEYBOARDS	PRT 7PX 354

ALLTRINNA GRAYSON – see WILTON FELDER

GREAT WHITE
US rock group formed in Los Angeles, CA in 1981 by Jack Russell (vocals), Mark Kendall (guitar), Lorne Black (bass) and Gary Holland (drums). Holland left in 1986 and was replaced by Audie Desbrow; Black left in 1987 and was replaced by Tony Montana. Michael Lardie was added on keyboards in 1987. Montana left in 1993 and was replaced by Teddy Cook. On 21/2/2003 a fire in a Rhode Island club, sparked by the group's pyrotechnics, left 97 people dead, including the group's bass player Ty Longley.

DATE	POS	WKS	BPI	SINGLE TITLE	LABEL & NUMBER
24/02/1990	44	2		HOUSE OF BROKEN LOVE	Capitol CL 562
16/02/1991	62	1		CONGO SQUARE	Capitol CL 605
07/09/1991	67	2		CALL IT ROCK 'N' ROLL	Capitol CL 625

MARTIN GRECH
UK guitarist/singer (born 1982, Aylesbury) whose band features Peter Miles (keyboards/guitar), Tim Elsenburg (guitar), Bish (bass) and Al Hamer (drums).

DATE	POS	WKS	BPI	SINGLE TITLE	LABEL & NUMBER
12/10/2002	68	1		OPEN HEART ZOO	Island CID 811

BUDDY GRECO
US singer/pianist (born 14/8/1926, Philadelphia, PA) who made his radio debut at the age of four and led his own trio between 1944 and 1949 as well as working with Benny Goodman's band. His piano style was influenced by Art Tatum.

DATE	POS	WKS	BPI	SINGLE TITLE	LABEL & NUMBER
07/07/1960	26	8		LADY IS A TRAMP	Fontana H 225

GREED FEATURING RICARDO DA FORCE
UK instrumental duo with rapper Ricardo Da Force, who also recorded with N-Trance.

DATE	POS	WKS	BPI	SINGLE TITLE	LABEL & NUMBER
18/03/1995	51	2		PUMP UP THE VOLUME	Stress CDSTR 49

GREEDIES
Multinational seasonal offering from Phil Lynott and Sex Pistols members Steve Jones and Paul Cook.

DATE	POS	WKS	BPI	SINGLE TITLE	LABEL & NUMBER
15/12/1979	28	5		A MERRY JINGLE Song is actually *We Wish You A Merry Christmas*	Vertigo GREED 1

ADAM GREEN
US singer who is also a member of Moldy Peaches with Kimya Dawson.

DATE	POS	WKS	BPI	SINGLE TITLE	LABEL & NUMBER
03/04/2004	63	1		JESSICA/KOKOMO	Rough Trade RTRADESCD112

❶⁹ Number of weeks single topped the UK chart ↑ Entered the UK chart at #1 ▲⁹ Number of weeks single topped the US chart

339

AL GREEN

US singer (born Al Greene, 13/4/1946, Forrest City, AR) who joined the family gospel group and was fired by his father for listening to Jackie Wilson records. He formed the Creations in 1964, going solo when they disbanded in 1968. He returned to gospel music in 1980, although apparently his spiritual rebirth occurred in 1973 (as Green claims) or 1974 when ex-girlfriend Mary Woodson attacked him with boiling hot grits and shot herself with Green's own gun. He was inducted into the Rock & Roll Hall of Fame in 1995. He has won nine Grammy Awards: Best Traditional Soul Gospel Performance in 1981 for *The Lord Will Make A Way*, Best Traditional Soul Gospel Performance in 1982 for *Precious Lord*, Best Contemporary Soul Gospel Performance in 1982 for *Higher Plane*, Best Soul Gospel Performance in 1983 for *I'll Rise Again*, Best Soul Gospel Performance by a Duo in 1984 with Shirley Caesar for *Sailin' On The Sea Of Your Love*, Best Soul Gospel Performance in 1986 for *Going Away*, Best Soul Gospel Performance in 1987 for *Everything's Gonna Be Alright*, Best Soul Gospel Performance in 1989 for *As Long As We're Together* and Best Pop Vocal Collaboration in 1994 with Lyle Lovett for *Funny How Time Slips Away*.

DATE	POS	WKS	BPI	SINGLE TITLE	LABEL & NUMBER
09/10/1971	4	13		TIRED OF BEING ALONE Featured in the 1995 film *Dead Presidents*	London HL 10337
08/01/1972	7	12		LET'S STAY TOGETHER ▲¹ Featured in the films *Pulp Fiction* (1994), *Blue Chips* (1994) and *Hellboy* (2004)	London HL 10348
20/05/1972	44	4		LOOK WHAT YOU DONE FOR ME	London HL 10369
02/09/1972	35	5		I'M STILL IN LOVE WITH YOU	London HL 10382
16/11/1974	20	11		SHA-LA-LA (MAKES ME HAPPY) Featured in the 2004 film *Scooby Doo 2: Monsters Unleashed*	London HL 10470
15/03/1975	24	8		L.O.V.E.	London HL 10482
03/12/1988	28	8		PUT A LITTLE LOVE IN YOUR HEART ANNIE LENNOX AND AL GREEN Featured in the 1988 film *Scrooged*	A&M AM 484
21/10/1989	38	5		THE MESSAGE IS LOVE ARTHUR BAKER AND THE BACKBEAT DISCIPLES FEATURING AL GREEN	Breakout USA 668
02/10/1993	56	2		LOVE IS A BEAUTIFUL THING	Arista 74321162692

DOTTY GREEN – see MARK FISHER FEATURING DOTTY GREEN

JESSE GREEN

Jamaican singer (born 1948, St James) who moved to the UK in 1965. He toured the UK with numerous reggae acts for the next decade before going solo.

DATE	POS	WKS	BPI	SINGLE TITLE	LABEL & NUMBER
07/08/1976	17	12		NICE AND SLOW	EMI 2492
18/12/1976	26	8		FLIP	EMI 2564
11/06/1977	29	6		COME WITH ME	EMI 2615

ROBSON GREEN AND JEROME FLYNN

UK vocal duo Robson Golightly Green (born 18/12/1964, Hexham, Northumberland) and Jerome Flynn (born 16/3/1963), first known as Paddy and Dave in the TV series *Soldier Soldier*.

DATE	POS	WKS	BPI	SINGLE TITLE	LABEL & NUMBER
20/05/1995	●⁷	17	✪²	UNCHAINED MELODY/(THERE'LL BE BLUEBIRDS OVER) THE WHITE CLIFFS OF DOVER ↑	RCA 74321284362
11/11/1995	●⁴	14	✪	I BELIEVE/UP ON THE ROOF ↑	RCA 74321326882
09/11/1996	●²	14	●	WHAT BECOMES OF THE BROKEN HEARTED/SATURDAY NIGHT AT THE MOVIES/YOU'LL NEVER WALK ALONE ↑	RCA 74321424732

GREEN DAY

US rock group formed in Berkeley, CA in 1989 by Billy Joe Armstrong (born 17/2/1972, San Pablo, CA, guitar/vocals), Mike Dirnt (born Michael Pritchard, 4/5/1972, Berkeley, bass/vocals) and Tre Cool (born Frank Edwin Wright III, 9/12/1972, Willis, CA, drums). Successful touring led to a bidding war that was finally won by Reprise in 1993. The group won the 1994 Grammy Award for Best Alternative Music Performance for *Dookie*.

DATE	POS	WKS	BPI	SINGLE TITLE	LABEL & NUMBER
20/08/1994	55	2		BASKET CASE	Reprise W 0257CD
29/10/1994	20	3		WELCOME TO PARADISE	Reprise W 0269CDX
28/01/1995	7	6		BASKET CASE Re-issue of Reprise W 0257CD	Reprise W 0279CDX
18/03/1995	30	3		LONGVIEW	Reprise W 0287CDX
20/05/1995	27	4		WHEN I COME AROUND	Reprise W 0294CD
07/10/1995	16	3		GEEK STINK BREATH	Reprise W 0320CD
06/01/1996	24	3		STUCK WITH ME	Reprise W 0327CD1
06/07/1996	28	2		BRAIN STEW/JADED A-side featured in the 1998 film *Godzilla*	Reprise W 0339CD
11/10/1997	25	2		HITCHIN' A RIDE	Reprise W 0424CD
31/01/1998	11	5		TIME OF YOUR LIFE (GOOD RIDDANCE)	Reprise W 0430CD1
09/05/1998	27	2		REDUNDANT	Reprise W 0438CD1
30/09/2000	18	3		MINORITY	Reprise W 532CD
23/12/2000	27	4		WARNING	Reprise W 548CD1
10/11/2001	34	2		WAITING	Reprise W 570CD
25/09/2004	3	7		AMERICAN IDIOT	Reprise W 652CD
11/12/2004	5	3+		BOULEVARD OF BROKEN DREAMS	Reprise W659CD1

GREEN JELLY

US comedy act with twelve members led by Bill Manspeaker (aka Marshall 'Duh' Staxx and Moronic Dicktator). The group formed in 1981 as Green Jello, and has since got through 74 members. Up until 1993 their US releases were only available on video. Hulk Hogan is a US wrestler.

DATE	POS	WKS	BPI	SINGLE TITLE	LABEL & NUMBER
05/06/1993	5	8		THREE LITTLE PIGS	Zoo 74321151422
14/08/1993	27	3		ANARCHY IN THE UK Featured in the 1994 film *The Flintstones*	Zoo 74321174892
25/12/1993	25	4		I'M THE LEADER OF THE GANG HULK HOGAN WITH GREEN JELLY	Arista 74321174892

GREEN VELVET

US DJ Curtis A Jones (aka Cajmere). He first recorded for Cajual Records in 1992.

DATE	POS	WKS	BPI	SINGLE TITLE	LABEL & NUMBER
25/05/2002	29	2		LA LA LAND	Credence CDCRED 025

NORMAN GREENBAUM

US singer (born 20/11/1942, Malden, MA) who formed psychedelic group Dr West's Medicine Show & Junk Band in 1965. He was lead singer until 1967 when they split. After a final album in 1972, he retired from music to breed goats.

DATE	POS	WKS	BPI	SINGLE TITLE	LABEL & NUMBER
21/03/1970	●²	20		SPIRIT IN THE SKY Featured in the films *Wayne's World 2* (1993), *War* (1994), *Michael* (1996), *Apollo 13* (1997), Walt Disney's *Remember The Titans* (2000) and *Ocean's Eleven* (2001)	Reprise RS 20885

LORNE GREENE Canadian singer (born 12/2/1914, Ottawa) who began his career reading the news for CBS radio. As an actor he appeared in the TV series *Bonanza* and *Battlestar Galactica*. He died on 11/9/1987 from pneumonia after an operation for a perforated ulcer. His hit single was derived from *Bonanza*: he recorded a tie-in album entitled *Welcome To The Ponderosa*, with *Ringo* being a track about gunslinger Johnny Ringo.

17/12/1964.....22......8....... RINGO ▲[1] .... RCA 1428

LEE GREENWOOD US country singer (born 27/10/1942, Los Angeles, CA) who began his career playing in a Dixie-land jazz band at Disneyland but went on to become a country star after being discovered by Larry McFadden of Mel Tillis' band.

19/05/1984.....49......6....... THE WIND BENEATH MY WINGS .... MCA 877

IAIN GREGORY UK singer who later recorded for Columbia. He appeared in the 1965 film *Gonks Go Beat* with Lulu and Long And The Short.

04/01/1962.....39......2....... CAN'T YOU HEAR THE BEAT OF A BROKEN HEART .... Pye 7N 15397

JOHNNY GREGORY – see RUSS HAMILTON

BAND OF THE GRENADIER GUARDS – see ST JOHN'S COLLEGE SCHOOL CHOIR AND THE BAND OF THE GRENADIER GUARDS

GREYHOUND Jamaican reggae group formed by Danny Smith and Freddie Notes as Freddie Notes & The Rudies. They initially backed Dandy Livingstone. Notes left in the early 1970s and was replaced by Glenroy Oakley. Members of Greyhound and The Pioneers later recorded as The Uniques.

26/06/1971 .....6......13...... **BLACK AND WHITE** .... Trojan TR 7820
08/01/1972.....12......11...... MOON RIVER .... Trojan TR 7848
25/03/1972.....20......9....... I AM WHAT I AM... Trojan TR 7853

GRID UK duo ex-Soft Cell David Ball (born 3/5/1959, Blackpool) and Richard Norris (born 23/6/1965, London), who teamed up in 1990 for East-West Records. Norris had been with East Of Eden, Innocent Vicars and The Fruitbats, and later set up Candy Records.

07/07/1990.....60......2....... FLOATATION .... East West YZ 475
29/09/1990.....64......4....... A BEAT CALLED LOVE .... East West YZ 498
25/07/1992.....50......3....... FIGURE OF 8 .... Virgin VSCDT 1421
03/10/1992.....72......2....... HEARTBEAT .... Virgin VSCDT 1427
13/03/1993.....27......4....... CRYSTAL CLEAR.. Virgin VSCDT 1442
30/10/1993.....21......3....... TEXAS COWBOYS .... Deconstruction 74321167762
04/06/1994 .....3......17....○ **SWAMP THING** .... Deconstruction 74321205842
17/09/1994.....19......4....... ROLLERCOASTER .... Deconstruction 74321230772
03/12/1994.....17......6....... TEXAS COWBOYS Re-issue of Deconstruction 74321167762.............. Deconstruction 74321244032
23/09/1995.....32......2....... DIABLO .... Deconstruction 74321308402

ZAINE GRIFF New Zealand singer (born 4/10/1957, Auckland) who was in The Misfits and Screemer before going solo.
16/02/1980.....54......3....... TONIGHT .... Automatic K 17547
31/05/1980.....68......3....... ASHES AND DIAMONDS .... Automatic K 17619

ALISTAIR GRIFFIN UK singer (born 1/11/1977, Castleton) who first came to prominence as one of the contestants on *Fame Academy*.
10/01/2004 .....5......6....... **BRING IT ON/MY LOVER'S PRAYER** .... Pro TV 9814926
27/03/2004.....18......3....... YOU AND ME (TONIGHT)... Universal TV 9817777

BILLY GRIFFIN US singer (born 15/8/1950, Detroit, MI) who was with Last Dynasty when chosen for the Miracles when Smokey Robinson went solo. He remained with the group until they split in 1982 and then launched his own career. He later became a noted producer and songwriter and helped Take That with their initial hits.
08/01/1983.....17......9....... HOLD ME TIGHTER IN THE RAIN .... CBS A 2935
14/01/1984.....64......3....... SERIOUS.. CBS A 4053

CLIVE GRIFFIN UK singer (born in London) who backed Take That, Tears For Fears and Bobby Womack as well as dueting with Celine Dion.
24/06/1989.....60......2....... HEAD ABOVE WATER .... Mercury STEP 4
11/05/1991.....56......3....... I'LL BE WAITING .... Mercury STEP 6

RONI GRIFFITH US singer discovered by producer Bobby Orlando.
30/06/1984.....63......4....... (THE BEST PART OF) BREAKING UP .... Making Waves SURF 101

GRIFTERS UK production duo 'Tall' Paul Newman and Brandon Block. Block is also a member of Blockster and Mystic 3 while Paul Newman had been a member of Camisra, Escrima and Partizan.
20/02/1999.....63......1....... FLASH Contains a sample of Liason D's *Future FJP*.................................. Duty Free DF 004CD

GRIM NORTHERN SOCIAL UK rock group formed in Scotland by Ewan McFarlane (guitar/vocals), Tommy Regan (guitar/vocals), Pete Cowan (bass), Andy Wee Man (keyboards) and Liam McAteer (drums).
06/09/2003.....60......1....... URBAN PRESSURE .... One Little Indian 353 TP7CD

❶[9] Number of weeks single topped the UK chart ↑ Entered the UK chart at #1 ▲[9] Number of weeks single topped the US chart

GRIMETHORPE COLLIERY BAND – see PETER SKELLERN

JAY GROOVE – see FANTASY UFO

GROOVE ARMADA UK production/instrumental duo Tom Findlay and Andy Cato.

08/05/1999	25	2	IF EVERYBODY LOOKED THE SAME Contains samples of The Chi-Lites' *We Are Neighbors* and A Tribe Called Quest's *1nce Again*. Featured in the 2000 film *The Replacements* .... Pepper 0530292
07/08/1999	19	5	AT THE RIVER Contains a sample of Patti Page's *Old Cape Cod*. Featured in the 1999 film *The Big Tease* .... Pepper 0530062
27/11/1999	17	6	I SEE YOU BABY GROOVE ARMADA FEATURING GRAM'MA FUNK Featured in the films *What Women Want* (2000) and *American Wedding* (2003).. Pepper 9230002
25/08/2001	12	7	SUPERSTYLIN' Features the uncredited contribution of MAD (aka Mike Daniel)............................. Pepper 9230472
17/11/2001	36	2	MY FRIEND Contains a sample of The Fatback Band's *Gotta Learn How To Dance*............................. Pepper 9230532
02/11/2002	36	2	PURPLE HAZE Contains a sample of Status Quo's *(April) Spring, Summer And Wednesdays* .... Pepper 9230652
17/05/2003	31	2	EASY Contains a sample of Cerrone's *Standing In The Rain*.. Pepper 9230712
06/09/2003	50	1	BUT I FEEL GOOD .... Pepper 82876556812
02/10/2004	11	4	I SEE YOU BABY Remixed by Fatboy Slim .... Jive 82876649982

GROOVE CONNEKTION 2 UK producer/instrumentalist.

11/04/1998	54	1	CLUB LONELY .... XL Recordings XLT 94CD

GROOVE CORPORATION UK group comprising ex-Electribe 101 Joe Stevens, Les Fleming, Robert Cimarosti and Brian Nordhoff.

16/04/1994	71	1	RAIN... Six6 SIXCD 109

GROOVE FOUNDATION – see DJ CHUS PRESENTS GROOVE FOUNDATION

GROOVE GANG – see DAFFY DUCK FEATURING THE GROOVE GANG

GROOVE GENERATION FEATURING LEO SAYER UK production group with a UK singer who re-recorded the vocals from his 1976 hit.

08/08/1998	32	3	YOU MAKE ME FEEL LIKE DANCING .... Brothers Organisation CDBRUV 8

GROOVE THEORY US duo Bryce Wilson and Amel Larrieux. Wilson had previously been with Mantronix under the name Bryce Luvah. Their debut hit features Trey Lorenz on backing vocals.

18/11/1995	31	3	TELL ME .... Epic 6623882

GROOVERIDER UK singer/DJ (born 16/4/1967, London) who doesn't reveal his real name, but admits to being also known as Ray B. He made his name as a radio presenter with Fabio, first with Kiss FM and then later Radio 1. He previously recorded as Codename John and won the 1999 MOBO Award for Best Drum & Bass Act.

26/09/1998	40	2	RAINBOWS OF COLOUR .... Higher Ground HIGHS 13CD
19/06/1999	61	1	WHERE'S JACK THE RIPPER .... Higher Ground HIGHS 20CD

SCOTT GROOVES US DJ/producer born in Detroit, MI. Discovered by Kevin Saunderson, he was in Inner City before going solo.

16/05/1998	68	1	EXPANSIONS SCOTT GROOVES FEATURING ROY AYERS .... Soma Recordings SOMA 65CDS
28/11/1998	55	1	MOTHERSHIP RECONNECTION Contains a sample of Parliament/Funkadelic's *Mothership Connection Live*..................... .... Soma Recordings SOMA 71CDS
21/08/1999	55	1	MOTHERSHIP RECONNECTION (REMIX) SCOTT GROOVES FEATURING PARLIAMENT/FUNKADELIC............. Virgin DINSD 185

HENRY GROSS US singer/guitarist (born 1951, Brooklyn, NYC) who had previously been lead guitarist with Sha-Na-Na. His debut hit was a tribute to his pet dog that died.

28/08/1976	32	4	SHANNON .... Life Song ELS 45002

GROUND LEVEL Australian instrumental/production group whose follow-up was *Journey Through The Night*.

30/01/1993	54	2	DREAMS OF HEAVEN .... Faze 2 CDFAZE 14

GROUP THERAPY US rap group assembled by Dr Dre and featuring Nicole Johnson, B Real, KRS-1, Nas and RBX.

30/11/1996	51	1	EAST COAST/WEST COAST KILLAS .... Interscope IND 95516

BORING BOB GROVER – see PIRANHAS

GSP UK instrumental/production duo from Cardiff, Ian Gallivan and Justin Stride.

03/10/1992	37	3	THE BANANA SONG .... Yoyo 1

GTO UK duo Lee Newman and Michael Wells whose name stands for Greater Than One, after an early album. They also record as Tricky Disco and Technohead.

04/08/1990	57	3	PURE .... Cooltempo COOL 218
07/09/1991	72	2	LISTEN TO THE RHYTHM FLOW/BULLFROG .... React 7001
02/05/1992	59	2	ELEVATION .... React 4

○ Silver disc ● Gold disc ✪ Platinum disc (additional platinum units are indicated by a figure following the symbol) ◎ Singles released prior to 1973 that are known to have sold over 1 million copies in the UK

GUESS WHO

Canadian rock group formed in Winnipeg, Canada in 1962 by Allan 'Chad Allen' Kobel (guitar/vocals), Bob Ashley (piano), Jim Kale (bass), Randy Bachman (guitar) and Garry Peterson (drums) as Chad Allan & The Reflections. Burton Cummings replaced Ashley in 1966, taking over as lead singer when Allan left shortly after. They took the name Guess Who after a record company promotion intended to make potential buyers believe this was a UK 'supergroup'.

| 16/02/1967 | 45 | 1 | | HIS GIRL | King KG 1044 |
| 09/05/1970 | 19 | 13 | | AMERICAN WOMAN ▲³ Featured in the 1999 film *American Beauty* | RCA 1943 |

DAVID GUETTA French DJ (born 1969, Paris).

31/08/2002	46	1		LOVE WON'T LET ME GO DAVID GUETTA FEATURING CHRIS WILLIS	Virgin DINSD 243
12/07/2003	73	1		JUST FOR ONE DAY (HEROES) DAVID GUETTA VS DAVID BOWIE	Virgin DINST 263
25/10/2003	19	4		JUST A LITTLE MORE LOVE DAVID GUETTA FEATURING CHRIS WILLIS	Virgin DINSD 250

GUN

UK rock group formed by brothers Adrian (born Adrian Curtis, 26/6/1949, London, guitar/vocals) and Paul Gurvitz (born Paul Curtis, 6/7/1947, bass) and Louie Farrell (born Brian Farrell, 12/12/1947, drums). The brothers were later in the Baker-Gurvitz Army and Adrian subsequently recorded solo.

| 20/11/1968 | 8 | 11 | | RACE WITH THE DEVIL | CBS 3734 |

GUN

UK heavy rock group formed in Glasgow in 1986 by Mark Rankin (vocals), Baby Stafford (guitar), Giuliano 'Joolz' Gizzi (guitar), Dante Gizzi and Scott Shields (drums). By 1995 they were a four-piece comprising Rankin, both Gizzis and drummer Mark Kerr.

01/07/1989	33	9		BETTER DAYS	A&M AM 505
16/09/1989	73	2		MONEY (EVERYBODY LOVES HER)	A&M AM 520
11/11/1989	57	2		INSIDE OUT	A&M AM 531
10/02/1990	50	3		TAKING ON THE WORLD	A&M AM 541
14/07/1990	33	4		SHAME ON YOU	A&M AM 573
14/03/1992	24	4		STEAL YOUR FIRE	A&M AM 851
02/05/1992	48	2		HIGHER GROUND	A&M AM 869
04/07/1992	43	2		WELCOME TO THE REAL WORLD	A&M AM 885
09/07/1994	8	7		WORD UP 1994 MTV Europe Music Award for Best Cover	A&M 5806672
24/09/1994	19	3		DON'T SAY IT'S OVER	A&M 5807572
25/02/1995	29	3		THE ONLY ONE	A&M 5809552
15/04/1995	39	2		SOMETHING WORTHWHILE	A&M 5810452
26/04/1997	21	2		CRAZY YOU	A&M 5821932
12/07/1997	51	1		MY SWEET JANE This and above single credited to G.U.N.	A&M 5822792

GUNS N' ROSES

US heavy rock group formed in Los Angeles, CA in 1985 by Axl Rose (born William Bailey, 6/2/1962, Lafayette, lead vocals) who allegedly adopted the name because it is an anagram of oral sex, Izzy Stradlin (born Jeffrey Isbell, 8/4/1962, Lafayette, guitar), Steven Adler (born 22/1/1965, Cleveland, drums), Michael 'Duff' McKagan (born 5/2/1964, Seattle, bass) and Slash (born Saul Hudson, 23/7/1965, Stoke-on-Trent, guitar). Adler left in 1990 and was replaced by ex-Cult drummer Matt Sorum (born 19/11/1960), with keyboard player Dizzy Reed supplementing the group the same year. Stradlin left in 1991 and was replaced by Gilby Clarke. Clarke later became a member of Colonel Parker with ex-Stray Cats Slim Jim Phantom, ex-LA Guns Muddy Stardust and Teddy Andreadis (formerly of Slash's Snakepit), the first contemporary act signed to actor Mel Gibson's Icon Records label.

03/10/1987	67	2		WELCOME TO THE JUNGLE	Geffen GEF 30
20/08/1988	24	8		SWEET CHILD O' MINE ▲² Featured in films *Bad Dreams* (1988) and *Big Daddy* (1999)	Geffen GEF 43
29/10/1988	24	5		WELCOME TO THE JUNGLE/NIGHTRAIN A-side featured in the 1988 film *The Dead Pool*	Geffen GEF 47
18/03/1989	6	9		PARADISE CITY Featured in the 1998 film *Can't Hardly Wait*	Geffen GEF 50
03/06/1989	6	9		SWEET CHILD O' MINE Re-issue of Geffen GEF 43	Geffen GEF 55
01/07/1989	10	7		PATIENCE	Geffen GEF 56
02/09/1989	17	5		NIGHTRAIN Re-issue of Geffen GEF 47	Geffen GEF 60
13/07/1991	3	10		YOU COULD BE MINE Featured in the 1991 film *Terminator 2 – Judgment Day*	Geffen GFS 6
21/09/1991	8	4		DON'T CRY	Geffen GFS 9
21/12/1991	5	7		LIVE AND LET DIE Featured in the 1997 film *Grosse Pointe Blank*	Geffen GFS 17
07/03/1992	4	5		NOVEMBER RAIN At 8 minutes 40 seconds this is the longest single to have made the US top twenty	Geffen GFS 18
23/05/1992	2	9		KNOCKIN' ON HEAVEN'S DOOR Featured in the 1990 film *Days Of Thunder*	Geffen GFS 21
21/11/1992	8	9		YESTERDAYS/NOVEMBER RAIN	Geffen GFS 27
29/05/1993	11	3		THE CIVIL WAR EP Tracks on EP: *Civil War, Garden Of Eden, Dead Horse* and *Interview*	Geffen GEFSTD 43
20/11/1993	9	3		AIN'T IT FUN	Geffen GFSTD 62
04/06/1994	10	6		SINCE I DON'T HAVE YOU	Geffen GFSTD 70
14/01/1995	9	6		SYMPATHY FOR THE DEVIL Featured in the 1994 film *Interview With The Vampire*	Geffen GFSTD 86

GUNTHER AND THE SUNSHINE GIRLS Swedish singer Gunther Levi.

| 15/05/2004 | 14 | 4 | | DING DONG SONG | WEA 376CD |

PETER GUNZ – see LORD TARIQ

GURU

US instrumentalist/rapper (born Keith Elam, 18/7/1966, Boston, MA) who is also a member of Gang Starr with Chris Martin and has recorded as Guru's Jazzamatazz. His debut solo album featured Donald Byrd and Roy Ayers.

11/09/1993	34	2		TRUST ME GURU FEATURING N'DEA DAVENPORT	Cooltempo CDCOOL 278
13/11/1993	25	3		NO TIME TO PLAY GURU FEATURING DEE C LEE	Cooltempo CDCOOL 282
19/08/1995	28	3		WATCH WHAT YOU SAY GURU FEATURING CHAKA KHAN	Cooltempo CDCOOL 308

❶⁹ Number of weeks single topped the UK chart ↑ Entered the UK chart at #1 ▲⁹ Number of weeks single topped the US chart

18/11/1995.....34......2....... FEEL THE MUSIC Contains a sample of Martine Girault's *Revival*........................... Cooltempo CDCOOLS 313
13/07/1996.....61......1....... LIVIN' IN THIS WORLD/LIFESAVER Features the uncredited contributions of Donald Byrd (trumpet) and N'Dea Davenport (vocals)....
.... Cooltempo CDCOOL 320
16/12/2000.....57......1....... KEEP YOUR WORRIES **GURU'S JAZZMATAZZ FEATURING ANGIE STONE**........................ Virgin VUSCD 177

GURU JOSH UK producer Paul Walden (born 1964) who had previously been with Joshua Cries Wolf.
24/02/1990 .....5......10 ..... **INFINITY**.. Deconstruction PB 43475
16/06/1990.....26......4....... WHOSE LAW (IS IT ANYWAY) .... Deconstruction PB 43647

ADRIAN GURVITZ UK singer (born Adrian Curtis, 26/6/1949) who was formerly in Gun, and also the Baker-Gurvitz Army with
Ginger Baker.
30/01/1982 .....8......13 .....○ **CLASSIC** .... RAK 339
12/06/1982.....61......3....... YOUR DREAM... RAK 343

GUS GUS Icelandic vocal/instrumental group formed in 1995 by Siggi Agust, Daniel Agust, Biggi Veira, Johann Asmundsson and
Herb Legowitz.
21/02/1998.....55......1....... POLYESTERDAY.. 4AD BAD 8002CD
13/03/1999.....64......1....... LADYSHAVE .... 4AD BAD 9001CD
24/04/1999.....62......1....... STARLOVERS .... 4AD BADD 9004CD
08/02/2003.....52......1....... DAVID .... Underwater H2O 022CD
28/06/2003.....75......1....... CALL OF THE WILD .... Underwater H2O 032CD
10/04/2004.....72......1....... DAVID (REMIX) .... Underwater H2O 042P

GUSTO UK producer Edward Green.
02/03/1996 .....9......5....... **DISCO'S REVENGE** Contains a sample of Harvey Mason's *Groovin' You*.................... Manifesto FESCD 6
07/09/1996.....21......3....... LET'S ALL CHANT .... Manifesto FESCD 13

GWEN GUTHRIE US singer (born 9/7/1950, Newark, NJ) who began as a backing singer for the likes of Billy Preston and
Aretha Franklin as well as songwriting before going solo in 1982. She also provided the lead vocals to the Limit hit single. She died from
cancer on 4/2/1999.
19/07/1986 .....5......12 .....○ **AIN'T NOTHING GOIN' ON BUT THE RENT** .... Boiling Point POSP 807
11/10/1986.....25......7....... (THEY LONG TO BE) CLOSE TO YOU..................................... Boiling Point POSP 822
14/02/1987.....37......4....... GOOD TO GO LOVER/OUTSIDE IN THE RAIN .... Boiling Point POSP 841
04/09/1993.....42......2....... AIN'T NOTHING GOIN' ON BUT THE RENT (REMIX)........................ Polydor PZCD 276

GUY US R&B group formed in New York in 1988 by Teddy Riley (born 8/10/1966, Harlem, NYC) and brothers Damion (born 6/6/1968,
Brooklyn, NYC) and Aaron Hall (born 10/8/1964, Brooklyn). They disbanded in 1991, with Riley forming BLACKstreet and working
extensively as a producer, while Aaron Hall recorded solo. Guy re-formed in 1999 after Riley had dissolved BLACKstreet.
04/05/1991.....58......4....... HER .... MCA MCS 1575

A GUY CALLED GERALD UK producer Gerald Simpson who had previously been a member of 808 State.
08/04/1989.....12......18 ..... VOODOO RAY .... Rham! RS 804
16/12/1989.....52......5....... FX/EYES OF SORROW.. Subscape AGCG 1

GUYS AND DOLLS UK vocal group formed in 1969 by Vicky Marcelle and two other singers. The group was re-formed in
1973 with Paul Griggs, Dominic Grant, David Van Day, Thereze Bazar, Martine Howard and Julie Forsythe. Van Day and Bazar left to form
Dollar, with the remaining members continuing as a quartet until the early 1980s.
01/03/1975 .....2......11 .....○ **THERE'S A WHOLE LOT OF LOVING** .... Magnet MAG 20
17/05/1975.....33......5....... HERE I GO AGAIN .... Magnet MAG 30
21/02/1976 .....5......8....... **YOU DON'T HAVE TO SAY YOU LOVE ME**................................. Magnet MAG 50
06/11/1976.....38......4....... STONEY GROUND... Magnet MAG 76
13/05/1978.....42......5....... ONLY LOVING DOES IT .... Magnet MAG 115

GUYVER UK DJ/remixer Guy Mearns.
29/03/2003.....72......1....... TRAPPED/DIFFERENCES .... Tidy Two 118

JONAS GWANGWA – see GEORGE FENTON AND JONAS GWANGWA

GYPSYMEN US remixer/producer Todd Terry (born 18/4/1967, Brooklyn, NYC) who mixed hits by Everything But The Girl,
Brownstone, 3T and Jimmy Somerville among others, before going solo. He has also recorded as Swan Lake, Royal House and Black Riot.
11/08/2001.....32......2....... BABARABATIN Contains a sample of Benny Moore and Perez Prado's *Babarabatiri* .... Sound Design SDES 09CDS

GYRES UK vocal/instrumental group formed in Scotland and fronted by Andy McLinden.
13/04/1996.....71......1....... POP COP .... Sugar SUGA 9CD
06/07/1996.....71......1....... ARE YOU READY... Sugar SUGA 11CD

H

H AND CLAIRE UK vocal duo formed by ex-Steps members Ian Watkins (born 8/5/1976) and Claire Richards (born 17/8/1977).

18/05/2002	3	11	DJ .... WEA 347CD
24/08/2002	8	6	HALF A HEART .... WEA 359CDX
16/11/2002	10	8	ALL OUT OF LOVE .... WEA 360CDX

HABIT UK vocal/instrumental group formed by Michael Martin, Nicholas Amour and Andrew Carroll.

30/04/1988	56	2	LUCY .... Virgin VS 1063

STEVE HACKETT UK singer/guitarist (born 12/2/1950, London) who played with numerous groups, including Canterbury Glass, Heel Pier, Quiet World and Sarabande, before joining Genesis in 1971. Remained with them until 1977 when he went solo, his debut album having been released in 1975. In 1985 he was a founding member of GTR with Steve Howe and Max Bacon; they enjoyed two minor US hits before disbanding. Hackett then resumed his solo career.

02/04/1983	66	2	CELL 151 .... Charisma CELL 1

HADDAWAY Trinidadian singer/dancer (born Nestor Alexander Haddaway, 1966) who moved with his family to Chicago, IL at the age of nine. He was a professional American footballer with the Cologne Crocodiles before launching a singing career.

05/06/1993	2	15	●	**WHAT IS LOVE** Featured in the 1998 film *A Night At The Roxbury* .... Logic 74321148502
25/09/1993	6	9		**LIFE** .... Logic 74321164212
18/12/1993	9	14		**I MISS YOU** .... Logic 74321181522
02/04/1994	9	9		**ROCK MY HEART** .... Logic 74321194122
24/06/1995	20	3		FLY AWAY .... Logic 74321286942
23/09/1995	39	2		CATCH A FIRE .... Logic 74321306652

TONY HADLEY UK singer (born 2/6/1960, London) and founding member of New Romantic group Spandau Ballet in 1979; later went solo. In 2003 he won ITV's *Reborn In The USA* competition.

07/03/1992	42	4	LOST IN YOUR LOVE .... EMI EM 222
29/08/1992	67	2	FOR YOUR BLUE EYES ONLY .... EMI EM 234
16/01/1993	72	1	GAME OF LOVE .... EMI CDEM 254
10/05/1997	35	2	DANCE WITH ME TIN TIN OUT FEATURING TONY HADLEY .... VC Recordings VCRD 17

SAMMY HAGAR US singer/guitarist (born 13/10/1947, Monterey, CA) who played with the Fabulous Castillas, Skinny, Justice Brothers and Dust Cloud before becoming lead singer of Montrose in 1973. He went solo in 1975, with his own band comprising Bill Church (bass), Alan Fitzgerald (keyboards) and Denny Carmassi (drums). He replaced David Lee Roth as lead singer with Van Halen in 1986.

15/12/1979	52	5	THIS PLANET'S ON FIRE/SPACE STATION NO. 5 .... Capitol CL 16114
16/02/1980	36	5	I'VE DONE EVERYTHING FOR YOU .... Capitol CL 16120
24/05/1980	67	2	HEARTBEAT/LOVE OR MONEY .... Capitol RED 1
16/01/1982	67	3	PIECE OF MY HEART .... Geffen GEF A 1884

PAUL HAIG UK lead singer with Josef K until they disbanded in the early 1980s; he then went solo. His debut hit album featured contributions from Bernie Worrell (of Parliament/Funkadelic), Tom Bailey (The Thompson Twins) and Anton Fier (Pere Ubu). He then recorded with Cabaret Voltaire and Bernard Sumner before linking with Alan Rankine. He recorded for Crepuscule and Circa Haig and launched his own Rhythm Of Life label.

28/05/1983	74	3	HEAVEN SENT .... Island IS 111

HAIRCUT 100 UK pop group formed in Beckenham in 1980 by Nick Heyward (born 20/5/1961, Beckenham, guitar/vocals), Les Nemes (born 5/12/1960, Croydon, bass) and Graham Jones (born 8/7/1961, Bridlington, Humberside, guitar), with Phil Smith (born 1/5/1959, Redbridge, saxophone), Mark Fox (born 13/2/1958, percussion/congas) and Blair Cunningham (born 11/10/1957, Harlem, NY, drums) joining the following year. Heyward went solo in 1982, with Fox taking over as lead singer when the group switched to Polydor. They disbanded in 1984 and Cunningham later resurfaced as drummer with The Pretenders.

24/10/1981	4	14	○	**FAVOURITE SHIRTS (BOY MEETS GIRL)** .... Arista CLIP 1
30/01/1982	3	12	●	**LOVE PLUS ONE** .... Arista CLIP 2
10/04/1982	9	9		**FANTASTIC DAY** .... Arista CLIP 3
21/08/1982	9	7		**NOBODY'S FOOL** .... Arista CLIP 4
06/08/1983	46	5		PRIME TIME .... Polydor HC 1

❶⁹ Number of weeks single topped the UK chart ↑ Entered the UK chart at #1 ▲⁹ Number of weeks single topped the US chart

345

CURTIS HAIRSTON
US singer (born 10/10/1961, Winston-Salem, NC) who later became lead singer with B.B.&Q. He died from diabetes on 18/1/1996.

15/10/1983	44	5		I WANT YOU (ALL TONIGHT)	RCA 368
27/04/1985	13	7		I WANT YOUR LOVIN' (JUST A LITTLE BIT)	London LON 66
06/12/1986	57	4		CHILLIN' OUT	Atlantic A 9335

GARY HAISMAN – see D MOB

SEAMUS HAJI
UK producer who also worked for Slip N Slide and Defected Records as an A&R manager.

| 18/12/2004 | 69 | 1 | | LAST NIGHT A DJ SAVED MY LIFE (BIG LOVE) | Big Love BL013 |

HAL
Irish rock group formed in Dublin in 2001 by Dave Allen (guitar/vocals), his brother Paul (bass), Stephen O'Brien (keyboards) and Brian Murphy (drums).

| 08/05/2004 | 53 | 1 | | WORRY ABOUT THE WIND | Rough Trade RTRADESCD172 |

HAL FEATURING GILLIAN ANDERSON
UK/French production group formed by Duncan Lomax, Paul Gallagher and Pascal Derycke with US singer/actress Gillian Anderson (born 9/8/1968, Chicago, IL), better known as Agent Scully in TV series *The X-Files*.

| 24/05/1997 | 23 | 3 | | EXTREMIS | Virgin VSCDT 1636 |

HALE AND PACE AND THE STONKERS
UK comedy duo Gareth Hale (born 15/1/1953, London) and Norman Pace (born 17/2/1953, Dudley) who rose to popularity with their own national TV series and teamed up with Queen's Brian May to produce a single to raise money in aid of Comic Relief. Fellow comedienne Victoria Wood performed the unlisted flip side.

| 09/03/1991 | ●1 | 7 | | **THE STONK** Single released in aid of the Comic Relief Charity | London LON 296 |

BILL HALEY AND HIS COMETS
US singer/guitarist (born William John Clifton Haley Jr, 6/7/1925, Highland Park, Detroit, MI) who joined the Downhomers in 1944 replacing Kenny Roberts (who had been drafted: Haley was exempt as he was blind in one eye). He formed the Four Aces Of Western Swing in 1948, disbanded them in 1950, formed the Saddlemen and recorded for a number of labels before discarding the cowboy image and becoming Bill Haley & His Comets in 1953. The line-up at this time comprised Danny Cedrone (lead guitar), Joey D'Ambrose (saxophone), Billy Williamson (steel guitar), Johnny Grande (piano), Marshall Lytle (bass) and Dick Richards (drums). They introduced *Shake Rattle And Roll* to their stage act in 1953 (the song had first been recorded in 1952 by Sunny Dae & His Knights) and made their first recordings for Decca in 1954. Cedrone died after falling down a flight of stairs on 18/6/1954. Haley died of a heart attack on 9/2/1981. He was inducted into the Rock & Roll Hall of Fame in 1987 and has a star on the Hollywood Walk of Fame.

17/12/1954	4	14		**SHAKE RATTLE AND ROLL** Featured in the 1987 film *The Big Town*	Brunswick 05338
07/01/1955	17	2		ROCK AROUND THE CLOCK ▲8 Featured in the films *Blackboard Jungle* (1955), *Rock Around The Clock* (1956) and *American Graffiti* (1973)	Brunswick 05317
15/04/1955	14	2		MAMBO ROCK	Brunswick 05405
14/10/1955	●5	17	◎	**ROCK AROUND THE CLOCK** Reclaimed #1 position on 6/1/1956. Total worldwide sales exceed 25 million	Brunswick 05317
30/12/1955	4	9		**ROCK-A-BEATIN' BOOGIE**	Brunswick 05509
09/03/1956	7	13		**SEE YOU LATER ALLIGATOR** Featured in the 1956 film *Rock Around The Clock*	Brunswick 05530
25/05/1956	5	24		**THE SAINTS ROCK 'N' ROLL**	Brunswick 05565
17/08/1956	3	23		**ROCKIN' THROUGH THE RYE**	Brunswick 05582
14/09/1956	13	8		RAZZLE DAZZLE	Brunswick 05453
21/09/1956	5	17		**ROCK AROUND THE CLOCK**	Brunswick 05317
21/09/1956	12	8		SEE YOU LATER ALLIGATOR	Brunswick 05530
09/11/1956	4	18		**RIP IT UP**	Brunswick 05615
09/11/1956	30	1		ROCK 'N' ROLL STAGE SHOW (LP) Tracks on LP: *Calling All Comets, Rockin' Through The Rye, A Rockin' Little Tune, Hide And Seek, Hey There Now, Goofin' Around, Hook Line And Sinker, Rudy's Rock, Choo Choo Ch'Boogie, Blue Comets Rock, Hot Dog Buddy Buddy* and *Tonight's The Night*	Brunswick LAT 8139
23/11/1956	26	5		RUDY'S ROCK	Brunswick 05616
01/02/1957	20	4		ROCK THE JOINT	London HLF 8371
08/02/1957	7	8		**DON'T KNOCK THE ROCK**	Brunswick 05640
03/04/1968	20	11		ROCK AROUND THE CLOCK Re-issue of Brunswick 05317	MCA MU 1013
16/03/1974	12	10		ROCK AROUND THE CLOCK Re-issue of MCA MU 1013	MCA 128
25/04/1981	50	5		HALEY'S GOLDEN MEDLEY	MCA 694

AARON HALL
US singer (born 10/8/1964, Brooklyn, NY) who was a member of Guy from their formation in 1988 and went solo (as did his younger brother Damion) when they disbanded in 1991.

| 13/06/1992 | 56 | 2 | | DON'T BE AFRAID Featured in the 1992 film *Juice* | MCA MCS 1632 |
| 23/10/1993 | 66 | 1 | | GET A LITTLE FREAKY WITH ME | MCA MCSTD 1936 |

AUDREY HALL
Jamaican singer (born 1948); she first recorded with Dandy Livingstone. Her sister Pam also recorded.

| 25/01/1986 | 20 | 11 | | ONE DANCE WON'T DO | Germain DG7-1985 |
| 05/07/1986 | 14 | 9 | | SMILE | Germain DG 15 |

DARYL HALL
US singer (born Daryl Franklin Hohl, 11/10/1948, Philadelphia, PA) who began his career as a backing singer for

○ Silver disc ● Gold disc ✪ Platinum disc (additional platinum units are indicated by a figure following the symbol) ◎ Singles released prior to 1973 that are known to have sold over 1 million copies in the UK

the likes of The Delfonics and The Stylistics before he teamed with John Oates in 1969 and launched a parallel solo career in 1986. He also recorded one single as part of Kenny Gamble & The Romeos with Kenny Gamble and Leon Huff.

DATE	POS	WKS	BPI	SINGLE TITLE	LABEL & NUMBER
02/08/1986	28	8		DREAMTIME	RCA HALL 1
25/09/1993	59	2		I'M IN A PHILLY MOOD	Epic 6595555
08/01/1994	30	6		STOP LOVING ME LOVING YOU	Epic 6599982
26/03/1994	52	2		I'M IN A PHILLY MOOD	Epic 6595555
14/05/1994	70	1		HELP ME FIND A WAY TO YOUR HEART	Epic 6604102
02/07/1994	36	4		GLORYLAND DARYL HALL AND THE SOUNDS OF BLACKNESS The official song of the 1994 FIFA World Cup	Mercury MERCD 404
10/06/1995	44	3		WHEREVER WOULD I BE DUSTY SPRINGFIELD AND DARYL HALL	Columbia 6620592

DARYL HALL AND JOHN OATES
US duo Daryl Hall (born Daryl Franklin Hohl, 11/10/1948, Philadelphia, PA) and John Oates (born 7/4/1949, New York) who first met in 1967 and recorded a number of demos in 1969. Their official pairing came in 1972 when they signed with Atlantic. They made their US chart breakthrough in 1974. Daryl Hall later went solo.

DATE	POS	WKS	BPI	SINGLE TITLE	LABEL & NUMBER
16/10/1976	42	4		SHE'S GONE	Atlantic K 10828
14/06/1980	41	6		RUNNING FROM PARADISE	RCA RUN 1
20/09/1980	55	3		YOU'VE LOST THAT LOVIN' FEELIN'	RCA 1
15/11/1980	33	8		KISS ON MY LIST ▲³	RCA 15
23/01/1982	8	10	O	I CAN'T GO FOR THAT (NO CAN DO) ▲¹	RCA 172
10/04/1982	32	7		PRIVATE EYES ▲²	RCA 134
30/10/1982	6	11		MANEATER ▲⁴ Featured in the 1999 film *Runaway Bride*	RCA 290
22/01/1983	63	3		ONE ON ONE	RCA 305
30/04/1983	15	7		FAMILY MAN	RCA 323
12/11/1983	69	3		SAY IT ISN'T SO	RCA 375
10/03/1984	63	2		ADULT EDUCATION	RCA 396
20/10/1984	48	5		OUT OF TOUCH ▲²	RCA 449
09/02/1985	21	8		METHOD OF MODERN LOVE	RCA 472
22/06/1985	62	2		OUT OF TOUCH (REMIX)	RCA PB 49967
21/09/1985	58	2		A NIGHT AT THE APOLLO LIVE! DARYL HALL AND JOHN OATES FEATURING DAVID RUFFIN AND EDDIE KENDRICK	RCA PB 49935
29/09/1990	69	1		SO CLOSE HALL AND OATES	Arista 113600
26/01/1991	74	1		EVERYWHERE I LOOK	Arista 113980

LYNDEN DAVID HALL
UK singer/multi-instrumentalist (born 1974, London) who played guitar, bass guitar, keyboards and drums on every track of his debut album. He won the 1998 MOBO Award for Best Newcomer.

DATE	POS	WKS	BPI	SINGLE TITLE	LABEL & NUMBER
25/10/1997	45	2		SEXY CINDERELLA	Cooltempo CDCOOL 328
14/03/1998	26	2		DO I QUALIFY?	Cooltempo CDCOOLS 331
04/07/1998	45	1		CRESCENT MOON	Cooltempo CDCOOL 333
31/10/1998	17	3		SEXY CINDERELLA	Cooltempo CDCOOLS 340
11/03/2000	30	2		FORGIVE ME	Cooltempo CDCOOLS 346
27/05/2000	49	1		SLEEPING WITH VICTOR	Cooltempo CDCOOL 348
23/09/2000	69	1		LET'S DO IT AGAIN	Cooltempo CDCOOL 351

PAM HALL
Jamaican singer and sister of fellow recording artist Audrey Hall.

DATE	POS	WKS	BPI	SINGLE TITLE	LABEL & NUMBER
16/08/1986	54	4		DEAR BOOPSIE	Bluemountain BM 027

TERRY HALL
UK singer (born 19/3/1959, Coventry) who sang with The Specials, Fun Boy Three, Colour Field, Terry Blair & Anouchka and Vegas, as well as launching a solo career in 1994.

DATE	POS	WKS	BPI	SINGLE TITLE	LABEL & NUMBER
11/11/1989	75	1		MISSING The sleeve to the single credits Terry, Blair & Anouchka	Chrysalis CHS 3381
27/08/1994	67	1		FOREVER J	AnXious ANX 1024CDX
12/11/1994	54	2		SENSE	AnXious ANX 1027CD
28/10/1995	62	1		RAINBOWS (EP) Tracks on EP: *Chasing A Rainbow, Mistakes, See No Evil* and *Ghost Train*	AnXious ANX 1033CD1
14/06/1997	50	1		BALLAD OF A LANDLORD	Southsea Bubble CDBUBBLE 1
18/10/2003	66	1		PROBLEM IS DUB PISTOLS FEATURING TERRY HALL	Distinctive DISNCD 107

TONI HALLIDAY
UK female singer who is also a member of Curve.

DATE	POS	WKS	BPI	SINGLE TITLE	LABEL & NUMBER
25/03/1995	18	3		ORIGINAL LEFTFIELD FEATURING TONI HALLIDAY	Hard Hands HAND 18CD
15/11/1997	54	1		WORDS PAUL VAN DYK FEATURING TONI HALLIDAY	Deviant DVNT 26CDS

GERI HALLIWELL
UK singer (born 6/8/1972: year of birth variously listed as 1970, 1972 and 1975, Watford) who was a founding member of all-girl group The Spice Girls (as Ginger Spice) before leaving to go solo. The Union Jack dress she wore at the 1997 BRIT Awards was auctioned in 1998 for £41,320. She also served the United Nations as a Goodwill Ambassador.

DATE	POS	WKS	BPI	SINGLE TITLE	LABEL & NUMBER
22/05/1999	2	14	●	LOOK AT ME	EMI CDEM 542
28/08/1999	❶¹	13	O	MI CHICO LATINO ↑	EMI CDEMS 548
13/11/1999	❶¹	17	O	LIFT ME UP ↑	EMI CDEM 554
25/03/2000	❶¹	13	O	BAG IT UP ↑	EMI CDEMS 560
12/05/2001	❶²	15	●	IT'S RAINING MEN ↑ Featured in the 2001 film *Bridget Jones' Diary*	EMI CDEM 584
11/08/2001	8	11		SCREAM IF YOU WANNA GO FASTER	EMI CDEM 595
08/12/2001	7	10		CALLING	EMI CDEMS 606
04/12/2004	4	4+		RIDE IT	Innocent SINDX69

❶⁹ Number of weeks single topped the UK chart   ↑ Entered the UK chart at #1   ▲⁹ Number of weeks single topped the US chart

HALO UK group formed by Graeme Moncrieff (guitar/vocals), his brother Ian (guitar/vocals), Steve Yoemans (bass/keyboards) and Jim Davey (drums).

16/02/2002.....49......1......	COLD LIGHT OF DAY...	Sony S2 6723072
01/06/2002.....44......1......	SANCTIMONIOUS..	Sony S2 6725965
07/09/2002.....56......1......	NEVER ENDING...	Sony S2 6730125

HALO JAMES UK group formed by Christian James (vocals), Ray St John (guitar) and Neil Palmer (keyboards).

07/10/1989.....45......5......	WANTED..	Epic HALO 1
13/01/1990.....6......12......	COULD HAVE TOLD YOU SO..	Epic HALO 2
17/03/1990.....43......4......	BABY..	Epic HALO 3
19/05/1990.....59......3......	MAGIC HOUR..	Epic HALO 4

ASHLEY HAMILTON US singer (born 30/9/1974, Los Angeles, CA), son of George Hamilton IV and Alana Stewart (Rod Stewart was his step-father). Initially known as an actor, he is also an accomplished songwriter, having co-written with Robbie Williams.

14/06/2003.....27......4......	WIMMIN'...	Columbia 6739305

GEORGE HAMILTON IV US singer (born 19/7/1937, Winston-Salem, NC) who toured with Buddy Holly, Gene Vincent and the Everly Brothers, before moving to Nashville and joining the Grand Ole Opry. He later had his own TV series; and his son Ashley launched a successful solo career.

07/03/1958.....22......9......	WHY DON'T THEY UNDERSTAND.....................................	HMV POP 429
18/07/1958.....23......4......	I KNOW WHERE I'M GOING..	HMV POP 505

LYNNE HAMILTON UK singer who was a member of The Caravelles before emigrating to Australia.

29/04/1989.....3......11......	ON THE INSIDE (THEME FROM 'PRISONER CELL BLOCK H') Theme to the TV series, originally released in Australia in 1979....	A1 311

RUSS HAMILTON UK singer (born Ronald Hulme, 1934, Liverpool); he was working as a Butlin's redcoat when he wrote his debut hit single. The B-side (*Rainbow*) made the US top ten. UK orchestra leader Johnny Gregory also recorded as Chaquito.

24/05/1957.....2......20......	WE WILL MAKE LOVE...	Oriole CB 1359
27/09/1957.....20......6......	WEDDING RING RUSS HAMILTON WITH JOHNNY GREGORY AND HIS ORCHESTRA WITH THE TONETTES............	Oriole CB 1388

HAMILTON, JOE FRANK AND REYNOLDS US vocal trio formed by Dan Hamilton (born 1/6/1946, Spokane, WA), Joe Frank Carollo and Tommy Reynolds. Reynolds left in 1972 and was replaced by Alan Dennison, but the name was retained for recording purposes until 1976. Hamilton died while undergoing abdominal surgery on 23/12/1994.

13/09/1975.....33......6......	FALLIN' IN LOVE ▲[1]...	Pye International 7N 25690

MARVIN HAMLISCH US pianist (born 2/6/1944, New York City) who became one of the top composers of film scores, including *The Way We Were*, which won him an Oscar and a Grammy. He also collaborated with Carole Bayer Sager. He won four Grammy Awards in 1974 including Song of the Year with Marilyn and Alan Bergman for *The Way We Were*, Best Album of Original Score Written for a Motion Picture for *The Way We Were* and Best New Artist.

30/03/1974.....25......13......	THE ENTERTAINER Written by Scott Joplin in 1902. Featured in the 1974 film *The Sting*. It won the 1974 Grammy Award for Best Pop Instrumental Performance..	MCA 121

HAMMER US rapper (born Stanley Burrell, 30/3/1962, Oakland, CA) who began his musical career after baseball players Mike Davis and Dwayne Murphy invested $40,000 for him to make his first record in 1987, copies of which he sold from the boot of his car. In 1990 he won three Grammy Awards including Best Music Video Long Form for *Please Hammer Don't Hurt 'Em The Movie*. He was named Best International Newcomer at the 1991 BRIT Awards.

09/06/1990.....3......16.....O	U CAN'T TOUCH THIS Based on Rick James' *Super Freak*. It won two 1990 Grammy Awards: Best Rap Solo Performance, and Best Rhythm & Blues Song for writers MC Hammer, Rick James and Alonzo Miller. Featured in the 2003 film *Charlie's Angels: Full Throttle*..	Capitol CL 578
06/10/1990.....8......7......	HAVE YOU SEEN HER...	Capitol CL 590
08/12/1990.....8......10......	PRAY Based on Prince's *When Doves Cry*. Featured in the 1990 film *Teenage Mutant Ninja Turtles*............	Capitol CL 599
23/02/1991.....15......5......	HERE COMES THE HAMMER Contains a sample of James Brown's *Super Bad*...	Capitol CL 610
01/06/1991.....16......5......	YO! SWEETNESS...	Capitol CL 616
20/07/1991.....20......4......	(HAMMER HAMMER) THEY PUT ME IN THE MIX This and above five singles credited to MC HAMMER............	Capitol CL 607
26/10/1991.....60......2......	2 LEGIT 2 QUIT..	Capitol CL 636
21/12/1991.....4......9......	ADDAMS GROOVE Featured in the 1991 film *The Addams Family*..............	Capitol CL 642
21/03/1992.....14......6......	DO NOT PASS ME BY...	Capitol CL 650
12/03/1994.....52......2......	IT'S ALL GOOD Contains a sample of Brick's *Dusic*.............	RCA 74321188612
13/08/1994.....72......1......	DON'T STOP..	RCA 74321220012
03/06/1995.....57......1......	STRAIGHT TO MY FEET HAMMER FEATURING DEION SAUNDERS Featured in the 1995 film *Street Fighter 2*.....	Priority PTYCD 102

JAN HAMMER Czechoslovakian keyboard player (born 17/4/1948, Prague) who won a scholarship to Berkley in Boston, MA and subsequently played with jazz-rock artists Billy Cobham, Stanley Clarke and the Mahavishnu Orchestra.

12/10/1985.....5......8.....O	MIAMI VICE THEME ▲[1] 1985 Grammy Awards for Best Pop Instrumental Performance and Best Instrumental Composition for Jan Hammer...	MCA 1000
19/09/1987.....2......12.....O	CROCKETT'S THEME This and above single from the TV series *Miami Vice*...............	MCA 1193
01/06/1991.....47......6......	CROCKETT'S THEME Re-issue of MCA 1193.........................	MCA MCS 1541

ALBERT HAMMOND UK singer (born 18/5/1942, London) who was raised in Gibraltar. He teamed up with Mike Hazelwood

in 1966 and returned to Britain, penning *Little Arrows* for Leapy Lee. He moved to America in 1972 to launch a solo career, but also continued writing (Hollies' *The Air I Breathe* and Leo Sayer's *When I Need You*).

30/06/1973.....19.....11...... FREE ELECTRIC BAND .... Mums 1494

BERES HAMMOND – see MAXI PRIEST

HAMPENBERG Danish producer (born 14/1/1977, Stenbuk).

21/09/2002.....30......2....... DUCK TOY .... Serious SERR 49CD

HERBIE HANCOCK US pianist/keyboard player (born 12/4/1940, Chicago, IL) who joined Donald Byrd's band in 1960 and recorded solo for Blue Note in 1963. He joined Miles Davis in 1963 and left in 1968 to form his own sextet. In 1978 he began recording with a vocoder and introduced 'scratching' to the UK. He won an Oscar in 1986 for the music to the film *Round Midnight* (in which he appeared) and also took part in the *It's Only Rock 'N' Roll* project for the Children's Promise charity. He has nine Grammy Awards including Best Rhythm & Blues Instrumental Performance in 1984 for *Sound System*, Best Instrumental Composition in 1987 with Dexter Gordon, Wayne Shorter, Ron Carter and Billy Higgins for *Call Street Blues*, Best Jazz Instrumental Performance in 1994 with Ron Carter, Wallace Ronay, Wayne Shorter and Tony Williams for *A Tribute To Miles*, Best Instrumental Composition in 1996 with Jean Hancock for *Manhattan*, Best Jazz Instrumental Performance in 1998 for *Gershwin's World*, Best Instrumental Arrangement with Vocals in 1998 with Stevie Wonder and Robert Sadin for *St Louis Blues*, Best Jazz Instrumental Solo in 2002 for *My Ship* and Best Jazz Instrumental Album, Individual or Group in 2002 with Michael Brecker and Roy Hargrove for *Directions In Music*. He has a star on the Hollywood Walk of Fame.

26/08/1978.....15......9......				I THOUGHT IT WAS YOU..	CBS 6530
03/02/1979.....18.....10......				YOU BET YOUR LOVE..	CBS 7010
30/07/1983.....8.....12......				**ROCKIT** 1983 Grammy Award for Best Rhythm & Blues Instrumental Performance	CBS A 3577
08/10/1983.....33......4.......				AUTO DRIVE..	CBS A 3802
21/01/1984.....54......3.......				FUTURE SHOCK..	CBS A 4075
04/08/1984.....65......3.......				HARDROCK...	CBS A 4616

HANDBAGGERS UK vocal/instrumental group formed by producer Andy Pickles.

15/06/1996.....55......1....... U FOUND OUT Contains a sample of Depeche Mode's *Just Can't Get Enough*........................... Tidy Trax TIDY 104CD

HANDLEY FAMILY UK family vocal group initially known for winning TV's *Opportunity Knocks*.

07/04/1973.....30......7....... WAM BAM .... GL 100

HANI US DJ/producer who also worked with Todd Terry, Frankie Knuckles and Sasha, among others.

11/03/2000.....70......1....... BABY WANTS TO RIDE.. Neo CD025

JAYN HANNA UK singer who sang with Evolution before going solo.

13/04/1996.....42......1.......				LOVELIGHT (RIDE ON A LOVE TRAIN)	VC Recordings VCRD 10
01/02/1997.....44......1.......				LOST WITHOUT YOU	VC Recordings VCRD 16

HANNAH UK singer Hannah Waddingham, who first appeared in the musical *The Beautiful Game*.

21/10/2000.....41......2....... OUR KIND OF LOVE .... Telstar CDSTAS 3149

HANNAH AND HER SISTERS – see HANNAH JONES

HANOI ROCKS Finnish rock group formed in 1980 by Michael Monroe (born Matti Fagerholm, vocals), Nasty Suicide (born Jan Stenfors, guitar), Andy McCoy (born Antti Hulkko, guitar), Sam Yaffa (born Sami Takamaki, bass) and Gyp Casino (born Jesper Sporre, drums). Casino was sacked after two albums and replaced by Razzle (born Nicholas Dingley) as the group relocated to London. Signed by CBS in 1983. they released their major label debut in 1984. Razzle was killed on 7/12/1984 when a car driven by Motley Crue's Vince Neil was involved in a head-on crash (Neil was charged with drunken driving and vehicular manslaughter and sentenced to five years probation, 30 days in jail, 200 hours of community service and ordered to pay $2.6 million in damages, although only $200,000 went to the family of the only dead victim, Razzle). Razzle was replaced by Terry Chimes (ex-The Clash), Yaffa left and was replaced by Rene Berg; group leader Monroe never fully accepted the loss of Razzle and announced his departure soon after. The group disbanded in 1985.

07/07/1984.....61......2...... UP AROUND THE BEND .... CBS A 4513

HANSON US family group from Tulsa, OK formed by brothers Isaac (born Clark Isaac Hanson, 17/11/1980), Taylor (born Jordan Taylor Hanson, 14/3/1983) and Zachary (born Zachary Taylor Hanson, 22/10/1985). In 1997 they won two MTV Europe Music Awards: Breakthrough Act and Best Song for *Mmm-Bop*.

07/06/1997 ....❶³....13.....✪				**MMMBOP ↑ ▲³**..	Mercury 5745012
13/09/1997 .....4......9......○				**WHERE'S THE LOVE**..	Mercury 5749032
22/11/1997 .....5......9......				I WILL COME TO YOU	Mercury 5680072
28/03/1998.....19......5......				WEIRD	Mercury 5685412
04/07/1998.....23......7......				THINKING OF YOU	Mercury 5688132
29/04/2000.....15......4.......				IF ONLY	Mercury 5627502

HAPPENINGS US vocal group formed in New Jersey by Bob Miranda, Tom Giuliano, Ralph DiVito and Dave Libert. DiVito left in 1968 and was replaced by Bernie LaPorta. Pye Records gave the BT Puppy label its own identity midway through *My Mammy's* chart run, hence its appearance on two labels. Miranda later recorded solo.

18/05/1967.....28......9......				I GOT RHYTHM	Stateside SS 2013
16/08/1967.....34......5......				MY MAMMY Song was originally Al Jolson's theme tune and written in 1920........	Pye International 25501/BT Puppy BTS 45530

❶⁹ Number of weeks single topped the UK chart   ↑ Entered the UK chart at #1   ▲⁹ Number of weeks single topped the US chart

349

HAPPY CLAPPERS
UK group formed by Chris Scott from Newcastle and Sandra Edwards from London. The group originally included Graeme Ripley and Martin Knotts.

03/06/1995	21	3	I BELIEVE .... Shindig SHIN 4CD
26/08/1995	27	2	HOLD ON .... Shindig SHIN 7CD
18/11/1995	7	8	**I BELIEVE** Re-issue of Shindig SHIN 4CD .... Shindig SHIN 9CD
15/06/1996	18	3	CAN'T HELP IT .... Coliseum TOGA 004CD
21/12/1996	49	1	NEVER AGAIN .... Coliseum TOGA 012CD
22/11/1997	28	2	I BELIEVE 97 Remix of Shindig SHIN 4CD .... Coliseum COLA 027CD

HAPPY MONDAYS
UK group formed in Manchester in 1984 by Shaun Ryder (born 23/8/1962, Little Hulton, vocals), brother Paul Ryder (born 24/4/1964, Manchester, bass), Mark 'Cow' Day (born 29/12/1961, Manchester, guitar), Gary 'Gaz' Whelan (born 12/2/1966, Manchester, drums) and Paul Davis (born 7/3/1966, Manchester, keyboards), adding Mark 'Bez' Berry (born 18/4/1964, Manchester, percussion) in 1985. First record for Factory in 1985 but after Factory's demise in 1992 the group split. Ryder went on to form Black Grape and re-formed the Happy Mondays in 1998. Their name was inspired by the New Order hit *Blue Monday*.

30/09/1989	68	2	WFL .... Factory FAC 2327
25/11/1989	19	14	MADCHESTER RAVE ON EP Tracks on EP: *Hallelujah, Holy Ghost, Clap Your Hands* and *Rave On* .... Factory FAC 2427
07/04/1990	5	11	**STEP ON** Cover version of John Kongos' *Tokoloshe Man* .... Factory FAC 2727
09/06/1990	46	3	LAZYITIS – ONE ARMED BOXER **HAPPY MONDAYS AND KARL DENVER** .... Factory FAC 2227
20/10/1990	5	7	**KINKY AFRO** .... Factory FAC 3027
16/03/1991	17	7	LOOSE FIT .... Factory FAC 3127
30/11/1991	24	3	JUDGE FUDGE .... Factory FAC 3327
19/09/1992	31	3	STINKIN THINKIN .... Factory FAC 3627
21/11/1992	62	1	SUNSHINE AND LOVE .... Factory FAC 3727
22/05/1999	24	2	THE BOYS ARE BACK IN TOWN .... London LONCD 432

HAPPYLIFE
UK rock group formed in 2001 by Kevin Brown (guitar/vocals), Ian Pellman (guitar), Chris Drinkwater (bass) and Rupert Mann (drums).

09/10/2004	73	1	SILENCE WHEN YOU'RE BURNING .... Albert Productions JASCDUK012

HAR MAR SUPERSTAR
US singer (born Sean Tillman, St Paul, MN), with Calvin Krime before going solo.

05/07/2003	59	1	EZ PASS .... B Unique BUN 054CDS
04/09/2004	46	2	DUI .... Record Collection W651CD

ED HARCOURT
UK multi-instrumentalist and singer (born 14/8/1977), with Snug before going solo.

02/02/2002	61	1	APPLE OF MY EYE .... Heavenly HVN 107CDS
15/02/2003	35	1	ALL OF YOUR DAYS WILL BE BLESSED .... Heavenly HVN 127CDS
11/09/2004	41	1	THIS ONE'S FOR YOU .... Heavenly HVN 140CD
13/11/2004	61	1	BORN IN THE 70S .... Heavenly HVN 146CD

PAUL HARDCASTLE
UK producer (born 10/12/1957, London) who played with Direct Drive and First Light, and formed the Total Control record company in 1984. Also recorded as Silent Underdog, the Def Boys, Beeps International, Jazzmasters and Kiss The Sky, the latter with singer Jaki Graham. Carol Kenyon is a UK singer who was with Heaven 17, appearing on their hit *Temptation*.

07/04/1984	41	4	YOU'RE THE ONE FOR ME – DAYBREAK – AM .... Total Control TOCO 1
28/07/1984	55	3	GUILTY .... Total Control TOCO 2
22/09/1984	41	5	RAIN FOREST .... Bluebird BR 8
17/11/1984	59	4	EAT YOUR HEART OUT .... Cooltempo COOL 102
04/05/1985	●5 16	●	**19** Mike Oldfield later sued Paul Hardcastle over the similarities between *19* and *Tubular Bells* (and thus collected an Ivor Novello Award for International Hit of the Year by default) .... Chrysalis CHS 2860
15/06/1985	53	4	RAIN FOREST .... Bluebird/10 BR 15
09/11/1985	19	5	JUST FOR MONEY Features the uncredited vocals of Laurence Olivier, Bob Hoskins, Ed O'Ross and Alan Talbot ..... Chrysalis CASH 1
01/02/1986	8	11	**DON'T WASTE MY TIME PAUL HARDCASTLE FEATURING CAROL KENYON** .... Chrysalis PAUL 1
21/06/1986	51	3	FOOLIN' YOURSELF .... Chrysalis PAUL 2
11/10/1986	15	6	THE WIZARD Theme to TV series *Top Of The Pops* from 1986 until 1991 .... Chrysalis PAUL 3
09/04/1988	54	3	WALK IN THE NIGHT .... Chrysalis PAUL 4
04/06/1988	53	2	40 YEARS .... Chrysalis PAUL 5

HARDCORE RHYTHM TEAM
UK vocal and production team.

14/03/1992	69	1	HARDCORE – THE FINAL CONFLICT .... Furious FRUT 001

DUANE HARDEN
US singer/songwriter who first met Armand Van Helden while studying at Boston University. He later moved to New York to work for UPS and then turned to singing and songwriting.

06/02/1999	●1 11	○	**YOU DON'T KNOW ME** ↑ **ARMAND VAN HELDEN FEATURING DUANE HARDEN** .... ffrr FCD 357
22/05/1999	13	5	WHAT YOU NEED **POWERHOUSE FEATURING DUANE HARDEN** .... Defected DEFECT 3CDS

HARDFLOOR
German group formed by Oliver Bandzio and Ramon Zenker; record debut in 1992 for the Harthouse label. Zenker was later responsible for Ariel and Fragma.

26/12/1992	56	4	HARDTRANCE ACPERIENCE .... Harthouse UK HARTUK 1
10/04/1993	72	1	TRANCESCRIPT .... Harthouse UK HARTUK 5CD
25/10/1997	60	1	ACPERIENCE (REMIX) .... Eye-Q EYEUK 018CD1

○ Silver disc ● Gold disc ✪ Platinum disc (additional platinum units are indicated by a figure following the symbol) ◎ Singles released prior to 1973 that are known to have sold over 1 million copies in the UK

TIM HARDIN US singer/guitarist (born 23/12/1941, Eugene, OR) and a descendant of the notorious outlaw John Wesley Hardin. He first recorded in 1964 and later began songwriting, penning *If I Were A Carpenter*. He died from a heroin overdose on 29/12/1980.

05/01/1967.....50......1....... HANG ON TO A DREAM .... Verve VS 1504

CAROLYN HARDING – see **PROSPECT PARK/CAROLYN HARDING**

MIKE HARDING UK singer/comedian (born 1944, Crumpsall).

02/08/1975.....22......8....... ROCHDALE COWBOY.. Rubber ADUB 3

HARDSOUL FEATURING RON CARROLL Dutch production duo Greg and Roog Van Bueren with singer Ron Carroll.

12/06/2004.....60......1....... BACK TOGETHER .... In The House ITH02CDS

FRANCOISE HARDY French singer/actress/model (born 17/1/1944, Paris) who made her recording debut in 1960 after graduating from La Bruyere College.

25/06/1964.....36......7...... TOUS LES GARCONS ET LES FILLES .... Pye 7N 15653
07/01/1965.....31......4...... HOWEVER MUCH (ET MEME) .... Pye 7N 15740
25/03/1965.....16.....15...... ALL OVER THE WORLD .... Pye 7N 15802

TYNETTA HARE – see **JOEY B ELLIS**

NIKI HARIS – see **SNAP!**

MORTEN HARKET Norwegian singer (born 14/9/1959, Konigsberg) and a founder member of A-Ha. He went solo in 1995 when the group went into semi-retirement.

19/08/1995.....53......1....... A KIND OF CHRISTMAS CARD .... Warner Brothers 0304CD

HARLEM COMMUNITY CHOIR – see **JOHN LENNON**

HARLEQUIN 4S/BUNKER KRU US vocal/instrumental group with UK production duo.

19/03/1988.....55......4....... SET IT OFF .... Champion CHAMP 64

STEVE HARLEY AND COCKNEY REBEL UK singer (born Steven Nice, 27/2/1951, London); he was a local journalist before forming his first band Cockney Rebel in 1973; the band comprised Milton Reame (keyboards), Jean Paul Crocker (violin/guitars), Paul Jeffreys (born 13/2/1952, bass) and Stuart Elliott (drums). The original line-up survived one album before disbanding. They re-formed with Harley and Elliott being joined by Jim Cregan (born 9/3/1946, guitar), Duncan Mackay (born 2/7/1950, keyboards) and George Ford (bass) as the new Cockney Rebel. Harley disbanded the group for good in 1977, by which time he was already recording solo. Paul Jeffreys was killed in the Lockerbie air disaster on 21/12/1988 while flying out for his honeymoon with his wife Rachel.

11/05/1974.....5......11...... **JUDY TEEN**.. EMI 2128
10/08/1974.....8......9...... **MR. SOFT** This and above single credited to **COCKNEY REBEL**........ EMI 2191
08/02/1975....❶²......9......○ **MAKE ME SMILE (COME UP AND SEE ME)** Featured in the 1997 film *The Full Monty* .... EMI 2263
07/06/1975.....13......6...... MR RAFFLES (MAN IT WAS MEAN) .... EMI 2299
31/07/1976.....10......7...... **HERE COMES THE SUN** .... EMI 2505
06/11/1976.....41......4...... LOVE'S A PRIMA DONNA.. EMI 2539
20/10/1979.....58......3...... FREEDOM'S PRISONER.. EMI 2994
13/08/1983.....51......5...... BALLERINA (PRIMA DONNA) This and above three singles credited to **STEVE HARLEY**........ Stiletto STL 14
11/01/1986.....7......10..... **THE PHANTOM OF THE OPERA** SARAH BRIGHTMAN AND STEVE HARLEY .... Polydor POSP 800
25/04/1992.....46......2...... MAKE ME SMILE (COME UP AND SEE ME) **STEVE HARLEY** .... EMI EMCT 5
30/12/1995.....33......3...... MAKE ME SMILE (COME UP AND SEE ME) This and above single re-issues of EMI 2263. .... EMI CDHARLEY 1

HARLEY QUINNE UK vocal group assembled by Roger Cook and Roger Greenaway and fronted by lead singer Peter Oakman, ex-The Bruvvers.

14/10/1972.....19......8....... NEW ORLEANS .... Bell 1255

HARMONIX UK producer Hamish Brown.

30/03/1996.....28......2....... LANDSLIDE Contains a sample of U2's *Where The Streets Have No Name*. .... Deconstruction 74321330762

HARMONY GRASS UK group formed in Essex in 1968 by Tony Rivers (vocals), Tony Ferguson (guitar), Tom Marshall (guitar/piano), Ray Brown (bass), Kenny Rowe (bass) and Bill Castle (drums). Rivers later contributed to many *Top Of The Pops* cover albums.

29/01/1969.....24......7...... MOVE IN A LITTLE CLOSER .... RCA 1772

BEN HARPER US singer/guitarist (born 28/10/1969, Pomona, CA); he made his first record in 1994 and later formed his own backing group, The Innocent Criminals, with Juan Nelson (bass) and Dean Butterworth (drums).

04/04/1998.....54......1....... FADED .... Virgin VUSCD 134

CHARLIE HARPER UK singer (born David Charles Perez, 25/4/1944, London) who was a founder member of UK Subs and launched a parallel solo career in 1980.

19/07/1980.....68......1....... BARMY LONDON ARMY .... Gem GEMS 35

❶⁹ Number of weeks single topped the UK chart ↑ Entered the UK chart at #1 ▲⁹ Number of weeks single topped the US chart

351

HARPERS BIZARRE US vocal group formed in 1963 by Eddie James, John Peterson, Dick Scoppettone, Ted Templeman (born 24/10/1944) and Dick Young as the Tikis. Templeman later became a successful producer.

30/03/1967	34	7	59TH STREET BRIDGE SONG (FEELING GROOVY)	Warner Brothers WB 5890
04/10/1967	33	6	ANYTHING GOES	Warner Brothers WB 7063

HARPO Swedish singer (born Jan Svensson) who followed up his hit single with a cover version of Charlie Chaplin's *Smile*.

17/04/1976	24	6	MOVIE STAR	DJM DJS 400

T HARRINGTON – see **RAHNI HARRIS AND F.L.O.**

ANITA HARRIS UK singer/actress (born 8/6/1944, Midsomer Norton, Somerset) who began her career as a cabaret singer at the age of 17. She later joined the Cliff Adams Singers and made her first solo record in 1961 for Parlophone. She also appeared in two of the *Carry On* films and is married to writer-director Mike Margolis.

29/06/1967	6	30	JUST LOVING YOU	CBS 2724
11/10/1967	46	3	PLAYGROUND	CBS 2991
24/01/1968	21	9	ANNIVERSARY WALTZ	CBS 3211
14/08/1968	33	8	DREAM A LITTLE DREAM OF ME	CBS 3637

EMMYLOU HARRIS US singer (born 2/4/1947, Birmingham, AL) who released her debut album in 1970 before linking up with Gram Parsons. Following his death in 1973 she resumed her solo career. She also took part in the *Perfect Day* project for the BBC's Children In Need charity. She has won ten Grammy Awards: Best Country Vocal Performance in 1976 for *Elite Hotel*, Best Country Vocal Performance in 1979 for *Blue Kentucky Girl*, Best Country Vocal Performance by a Duo in 1980 with Roy Orbison for *That Lovin' You Feelin' Again*, Best Country Vocal Performance in 1984 for *In My Dreams*, Best Country Performance by a Group in 1987 with Dolly Parton and Linda Ronstadt for *Trio*, Best Country Performance by a Group in 1992 with the Nash Ramblers for *Emmylou Harris And The Nash Ramblers At The Ryman*, Best Contemporary Folk Album in 1995 for *Wrecking Ball*, Best Country Vocal Collaboration in 1998 with various others for *Same Old Train*, Best Country Vocal Collaboration in 1999 with Dolly Parton and Linda Ronstadt for *After The Gold Rush* and Best Contemporary Folk Album in 2000 for *Red Dirt Girl*.

06/03/1976	30	6	HERE THERE AND EVERYWHERE	Reprise K 14415

JET HARRIS UK bass player (born Terence Harris, 6/7/1939, Kingsbury, London) who joined The Shadows in 1958, remaining with them until 1962 when he went solo. He later linked with Tony Meehan.

24/05/1962	22	7	BESAME MUCHO	Decca F 11466
16/08/1962	12	11	MAIN TITLE THEME FROM 'MAN WITH THE GOLDEN ARM'	Decca F 11488

JET HARRIS AND TONY MEEHAN UK duo of ex-Shadows' Jet Harris (born Terence Harris, 6/7/1939, Kingsbury, London, bass) and Tony Meehan (born Daniel Joseph Anthony Meehan 2/3/1943, Hampstead, London, drums). Meehan had played drums on Harris' debut solo hit. Their pairing came to an end in September 1963 when Harris was involved in a serious car crash.

10/01/1963	●³	13	DIAMONDS	Decca F 11563
25/04/1963	2	13	SCARLETT O'HARA	Decca F 11644
05/09/1963	4	13	APPLEJACK	Decca F 11710

KEITH HARRIS AND ORVILLE UK singer/ventriloquist (born 21/9/1947, Lyndhurst) with dummy duck (Orville) and ape (Cuddles) whose act was extremely popular on TV. Pianist Bobby Crush supplied the music.

18/12/1982	4	11	○ ORVILLE'S SONG	BBC RESL 124
24/12/1983	44	4	COME TO MY PARTY KEITH HARRIS AND ORVILLE WITH DIPPY	BBC RESL 138
14/12/1985	40	5	WHITE CHRISTMAS	Columbia DB 9121

MAJOR HARRIS US singer (born 9/2/1947, Richmond, VA) who sang with the Jarmels, Impacts and Rebellion before joining The Delfonics in 1971. He went solo in 1974.

09/08/1975	37	7	LOVE WON'T LET ME WAIT	Atlantic K 10585
05/11/1983	61	2	ALL MY LIFE	London LON 37

MAX HARRIS UK orchestra leader who had been in the bands of Ambrose, Ronnie Munro, Maurice Winnick, George Chisholm and Jack Parnell. As well as his one hit single, he also composed the theme to TV comedy *On The Buses*. He died on 13/3/2004.

01/12/1960	11	10	GURNEY SLADE Theme to the TV series *The World Of Gurney Slade* starring Anthony Newley	Fontana H 282

RAHNI HARRIS AND F.L.O. US keyboard player whose debut hit was in support of a charity run by Andy West; he ran 2,500 miles from Caribou, ME to Marathon, FL to raise funds for the Muscular Dystrophy Association. It featured vocals by T Harrington (born Anthony C Harrington) and O Rasbury (Ollie Rasbury). Harris later joined Dayton and changed his name to Yasha Barjona.

16/12/1978	43	7	SIX MILLION STEPS (WEST RUNS SOUTH)	Mercury 6007 198

RICHARD HARRIS Irish singer/actor (born 1/10/1930, Limerick) who began acting in 1958. He appeared in *Camelot, A Man Called Horse, The Terrorists, Robin And Marian, Patriot Games* and *Gladiator* during an illustrious career. He received Oscar nominations for *This Sporting Life* and *The Field*. He won the 1973 Grammy Award for Best Spoken Word Recording for *Jonathan Livingston Seagull*. He died from cancer on 25/10/2002.

26/06/1968	4	12	MACARTHUR PARK	RCA 1699
08/07/1972	38	6	MACARTHUR PARK Re-issue of RCA 1699	Probe GFF 101

○ Silver disc ● Gold disc ✪ Platinum disc (additional platinum units are indicated by a figure following the symbol) ◎ Singles released prior to 1973 that are known to have sold over 1 million copies in the UK

ROCHELLE HARRIS – see ANGELHEART

ROLF HARRIS Australian singer/TV personality/painter (born 30/3/1930, Perth, Australia); he moved to Britain in the mid-1950s, eventually becoming a kids' TV presenter with his own series from 1970 and later presenting *Animal Hospital*. His biggest hit, *Two Little Boys*, was originally written in 1903 and his version went on to become the biggest selling single of 1969.

21/07/1960	9	13		TIE ME KANGAROO DOWN SPORT ROLF HARRIS WITH HIS WOBBLE BOARD AND THE RHYTHM SPINNERS	Columbia DB 4483
25/10/1962	3	16		SUN ARISE	Columbia DB 4888
28/02/1963	44	2		JOHNNY DAY	Columbia DB 8553
16/04/1969	30	8		BLUER THAN BLUE	Columbia DB 8553
22/11/1969	❶6	25		TWO LITTLE BOYS	Columbia DB 8630
13/02/1993	7	6		STAIRWAY TO HEAVEN	Vertigo VERCD 73
01/06/1996	50	1		BOHEMIAN RHAPSODY	Living Beat LBECD 41
25/10/1997	26	3		SUN ARISE Re-issue of Columbia DB 4888	EMI CDROO 001
14/10/2000	24	3		FINE DAY	Tommy Boy TBCD 2155

RONNIE HARRIS UK male singer.

24/09/1954	12	3		STORY OF TINA	Columbia DB 3499

SAM HARRIS US singer/actor (born 4/6/1961, Cushing, OK) who appeared in the 1994 Broadway production of *Grease*.

09/02/1985	67	2		HEARTS ON FIRE/OVER THE RAINBOW	Motown TMG 1370

SIMON HARRIS UK singer/producer (born 10/9/1962, London) who subsequently became an in-demand remixer. He also recorded as Ambassadors Of Funk and World Warrior.

19/03/1988	12	6		BASS (HOW LOW CAN YOU GO) Contains a sample of Public Enemy's *Bring The Noise*	ffrr FFR 4
29/10/1988	38	4		HERE COMES THAT SOUND	ffrr FFR 12
24/06/1989	60	3		(I'VE GOT YOUR) PLEASURE CONTROL SIMON HARRIS FEATURING LONNIE GORDON	ffrr F 106
18/11/1989	65	1		ANOTHER MONSTERJAM SIMON HARRIS FEATURING EINSTEIN	ffrr F 116
10/03/1990	56	3		RAGGA HOUSE (ALL NIGHT LONG) SIMON HARRIS FEATURING DADDY FREDDY	Living Beat 7SMASH 9

GEORGE HARRISON UK singer/guitarist (born 24/2/1943, Liverpool, although George believed it to be the 25th until learning in his 40s that he had been born at 11.42pm on the 24th); he formed his first group, The Rebels, when he was 13 and linked with Paul McCartney and John Lennon in the Quarrymen in 1958; the group subsequently became the Beatles. After the Beatles split he achieved his first #1 with his debut solo single, although legal wrangles with the estate of Ronnie Mack and the song *He's So Fine* blighted its success. He launched the Dark Horse record label and in 1988 became a member of the Traveling Wilburys (as Nelson). He was attacked by a crazed fan in December 1999 and received multiple stab wounds but survived the attempted murder. Having won eight Grammy Awards while a member of the Beatles, George won the 1972 Album of the Year award for *The Concert For Bangla Desh* and the 2003 award for Best Pop Instrumental Performance for *Marwa Blues*. He also collected the 1989 Grammy Award for Best Rock Performance by a Group with Vocals as a member of the Traveling Wilburys for *Traveling Wilburys Volume One* (the album was known as *Handle With Care* in the UK). He 'appeared' in an episode of *The Simpsons* chatting to Homer Simpson backstage at the Grammy Awards ceremony. In 1999 it was reported that he was battling with throat cancer and, despite frequent announcements that the treatment he was receiving was working, he died in Los Angeles on 29/11/2001. A family statement issued after his death said, 'He left this world as he lived in it, conscious of God, fearless of death, and at peace, surrounded by family and friends. He often said, "Everything else can wait but the search for God cannot wait, and love one another."' He was inducted into the Rock & Roll Hall of Fame in 2004.

23/01/1971	❶5	17		MY SWEET LORD ▲4 Ronnie Mack's estate sued George Harrison over similarities between this and *He's So Fine*	Apple R 5884
14/08/1971	10	9		BANGLA DESH	Apple R 5912
02/06/1973	8	10		GIVE ME LOVE (GIVE ME PEACE ON EARTH) ▲1	Apple R 5988
21/12/1974	38	5		DING DONG	Apple R 6002
11/10/1975	38	5		YOU	Apple R 6007
10/03/1979	51	5		BLOW AWAY	Dark Horse K 17327
23/05/1981	13	7		ALL THOSE YEARS AGO Tribute to John Lennon and featuring Ringo Starr and Paul and Linda McCartney	Dark Horse K 17807
24/10/1987	2	14	O	GOT MY MIND SET ON YOU ▲1 Cover version of James Ray's 1962 US R&B hit	Dark Horse W 8178
06/02/1988	25	7		WHEN WE WAS FAB	Dark Horse W 8131
25/06/1988	55	3		THIS IS LOVE	Dark Horse W 7913
26/01/2002	❶1	10		MY SWEET LORD ↑ A posthumous #1 (the previous week's #1 had been by Aaliyah, also a posthumous #1 and therefore the first time in the chart's history that one posthumous act has been replaced by another at #1)	Parlophone CDR 6571
24/05/2003	37	2		ANY ROAD	Parlophone CDRS 6601

NOEL HARRISON UK singer (born 29/1/1934, London), son of late actor Rex Harrison, who made his acting debut in 1962 and first scored on the US charts in 1966.

26/02/1969	8	14		WINDMILLS OF YOUR MIND Featured in the 1968 film *The Thomas Crown Affair* and won an Oscar for Best Film Song	Reprise RS20758

HARRY – see OBI PROJECT FEATURING HARRY, ASHER D AND DJ WHAT?

HARRY UK trio formed by singer Harry (born Victoria Harrison), Eden (bass) and Oly (drums). They are also known as Dirty Harry.

02/11/2002	53	1		SO REAL	Dirty World DWRCD 003
19/04/2003	43	1		UNDER THE COVERS EP Tracks on EP: *Imagination, Push It (Real Good), She's In Parties* and *Imagination (Video)*	Dirty World DWRCD 005

❶9 Number of weeks single topped the UK chart   ↑ Entered the UK chart at #1   ▲9 Number of weeks single topped the US chart

353

DEBORAH HARRY US singer (born 1/7/1945, Miami, FL) who was a Playboy bunny waitress before launching Wind In The Willows, the Stilettos and finally Blondie in 1974. When Blondie dissolved in 1982 she concentrated on a film career and then went solo. Blondie re-formed in 1998 with Harry once again lead singer.

01/08/1981	32	6		BACKFIRED	Chrysalis CHS 2526
15/11/1986	8	10		**FRENCH KISSIN' IN THE USA**	Chrysalis CHS 3066
28/02/1987	46	4		FREE TO FALL	Chrysalis CHS 3093
09/05/1987	45	5		IN LOVE WITH LOVE This and above three singles credited to **DEBBY HARRY**	Chrysalis CHS 3128
07/10/1989	13	10		I WANT THAT MAN	Chrysalis CHS 3369
02/12/1989	59	4		BRITE SIDE	Chrysalis CHS 3452
31/03/1990	57	3		SWEET AND LOW	Chrysalis CHS 3491
05/01/1991	42	4		WELL DID YOU EVAH! **DEBORAH HARRY AND IGGY POP**	Chrysalis CHS 3646
03/07/1993	23	4		I CAN SEE CLEARLY NOW	Chrysalis CDCHSS 4900
18/09/1993	46	2		STRIKE ME PINK	Chrysalis CDCHSS 5000

RICHARD HARTLEY/MICHAEL REED ORCHESTRA UK synthesiser player and UK-based orchestra. Jane Torvill and Christopher Dean are ice-skaters who won gold medals for Britain at the Winter Olympics with a celebrated routine accompanied by Ravel's *Bolero*. This was the second time *Bolero* had become popular: its earlier inclusion in the film *10* starring Dudley Moore and Bo Derek had resulted in a surge of album sales.

25/02/1984	9	10	O	**THE MUSIC OF TORVILL AND DEAN EP** Tracks on EP: *Bolero* and *Capriccio Espagnole Opus 34 (Nos 4 and 5)* by Richard Hartley: *Barnum On Ice* and *Discoskate* by the Michael Reed Orchestra	Safari SKATE 1

DAN HARTMAN US singer/multi-instrumentalist (born 8/12/1950, Harrisburg, PA) who was bass player with the Edgar Winter Group from 1972–76 when he went solo. He gained his initial success with disco music and later produced and wrote for acts such as James Brown, The Average White Band, Diana Ross and Chaka Khan. He died from AIDS-related complications on 22/3/1994.

21/10/1978	8	15	O	**INSTANT REPLAY**	Blue Sky 6706
13/01/1979	17	8		THIS IS IT	Blue Sky 6999
18/05/1985	66	2		SECOND NATURE	MCA 957
24/08/1985	12	8		I CAN DREAM ABOUT YOU Featured in the 1984 film *Streets Of Fire*	MCA 988
01/04/1995	49	1		KEEP THE FIRE BURNIN' **DAN HARTMAN STARRING LOLEATTA HOLLOWAY**	Columbia 6611552

HARVEY UK rapper Michael Harvey who first came to prominence as a member of So Solid Crew.

07/09/2002	24	2		GET UP AND MOVE	Go Beat GOBCD 52

SENSATIONAL ALEX HARVEY BAND UK rock group formed in 1972 by Alex Harvey (born 5/2/1935, Glasgow, vocals), Hugh McKenna (keyboards), Chris Glen (bass), Zal Cleminson (guitar) and Ted McKenna (drums). Harvey died from a heart attack on 4/2/1982.

26/07/1975	7	7		**DELILAH**	Vertigo ALEX 001
22/11/1975	38	8		GAMBLIN' BAR ROOM BLUES	Vertigo ALEX 002
19/06/1976	13	10		THE BOSTON TEA PARTY	Mountain TOP 12

BRIAN HARVEY UK singer (born 8/8/1974, London) and member of East 17/E-17 until they disbanded in 2000 when he went solo.

02/12/2000	25	3		TRUE STEP TONIGHT **TRUE STEPPERS FEATURING BRIAN HARVEY AND DONELL JONES**	Nulife 74321811312
28/04/2001	26	2		STRAIGHT UP NO BENDS	Edel 0126605ERE
27/10/2001	20	3		LOVING YOU (OLE OLE OLE) **BRIAN HARVEY FEATURING THE REFUGEE CREW**	Blacklist 0133045 ERE

LEE HARVEY – see **N*E*R*D**

PJ HARVEY UK band formed in Yeovil, Somerset in 1991 by Polly Jean Harvey (born 9/10/1969, Yeovil, Somerset), Ian Olliver (bass) and Rob Ellis (born 13/2/1962, Bristol, drums). Olliver left in 1991 and was replaced by Stephen Vaughan (born 22/6/1962, Wolverhampton), although by 1995 the group consisted of Harvey, John Parish (guitar), Jean-Marc Butty (drums), Nick Bagnoll (bass), Joe Gore (guitar) and Eric Drew Feldman (keyboards).

29/02/1992	69	1		SHEELA-NA-GIG	Too Pure PURE 008
01/05/1993	27	2		50FT QUEENIE	Island CID 538
17/07/1993	42	2		MAN-SIZE	Island CID 569
18/02/1995	38	2		DOWN BY THE WATER	Island CID 607
22/07/1995	29	2		C'MON BILLY	Island CIDX 614
28/10/1995	34	2		SEND HIS LOVE TO ME	Island CID 610
09/03/1996	36	1		HENRY LEE **NICK CAVE AND THE BAD SEEDS AND PJ HARVEY**	Mute CDMUTE 189
23/11/1996	75	1		THAT WAS MY VEIL **JOHN PARISH AND POLLY JEAN HARVEY**	Island CID 648
26/09/1998	25	2		A PERFECT DAY ELISE	Island CID 718
23/01/1999	29	2		THE WIND	Island CID 730
25/11/2000	41	2		GOOD FORTUNE	Island CID 769
10/03/2001	43	2		A PLACE CALLED HOME	Island CID 771
20/10/2001	41	1		THIS IS LOVE	Island CID 785
29/05/2004	28	2		THE LETTER	Island CIDX 861
31/07/2004	41	2		YOU COME THROUGH	Island CIDX 869
02/10/2004	45	1		SHAME	Island CID 873

STEVE HARVEY UK singer (born Aberdeen) and member of Private Lives before going solo. He later worked with Total Contrast.

O Silver disc ● Gold disc ✪ Platinum disc (additional platinum units are indicated by a figure following the symbol) ◉ Singles released prior to 1973 that are known to have sold over 1 million copies in the UK

DATE	POS	WKS	BPI	SINGLE TITLE	LABEL & NUMBER
28/05/1983	46	4		SOMETHING SPECIAL	London LON 25
29/10/1983	63	2		TONIGHT	London LON 36

HARVEY DANGER US rock group formed in Seattle, WA by Sean Nelson (vocals), Jeff Lin (guitar), Aaron Huffman (bass) and Evan Sult (drums).

01/08/1998	57	1		FLAGPOLE SITTA	Slash LASCD 64

GORDON HASKELL UK singer/guitarist who was a member of King Crimson before going solo. After missing out with the single *Boat Trip* in 1969 he did not release another single until 2001.

29/12/2001	2	6	O	HOW WONDERFUL YOU ARE	Flying Sparks TDBCDS 04

LEE HASLAM UK DJ (born Aylesbury) who became label manager for Tidy Trax. He is also a member of Sinphony and Tomorrow People.

14/08/2004	71	1		LIBERATE/HERE COMES THE PAIN	Tidy Trax TIDYTWO135

DAVID HASSELHOFF US actor (born 17/7/1952, Baltimore, MD), best known for the TV series *Baywatch,* a series he later produced and directed. He has a star on the Hollywood Walk of Fame.

13/11/1993	35	2		IF I COULD ONLY SAY GOODBYE	Arista 74321172262

TONY HATCH UK orchestra leader (born 30/6/1940, Pinner), initially known as a songwriter and producer (he worked freelance for Top Rank and Pye and while on National Service he was allowed to supervise recording sessions). He later became staff producer at Pye and was responsible for hits by The Searchers, Petula Clark (*Downtown*, which he wrote, was originally intended for The Drifters) and Sweet Sensation, among others. He was the resident expert opinion on the TV talent show *New Faces* and wrote the themes to the TV series *Mr And Mrs, Neighbours* and *Crossroads*. He is married to singer Jackie Trent.

04/10/1962	50	1		OUT OF THIS WORLD	Pye 7N 15460

JULIANA HATFIELD US singer/guitarist (born 2/7/1967, Wiscasset, ME) who attended the Berklee College of Music and became a member of Blake Babies before going solo. She formed the Juliana Hatfield Three with Dean Fisher (bass) and Todd Phillips (drums) and has also played with the Lemonheads (she has had an on-off relationship with Evan Dando of that group).

11/09/1993	71	1		MY SISTER JULIANA HATFIELD THREE	Mammoth YZ 767CD
18/03/1995	65	1		UNIVERSAL HEART-BEAT	East West YZ 916CD

DONNY HATHAWAY US R&B singer (born 1/10/1945, Chicago, IL) raised in St Louis. Began as a producer for Curtis Mayfield's Curtom label before going solo with Atlantic in 1970 with *The Ghetto*. Major chart successes both sides of the Atlantic came with Roberta Flack (whom he first met at school). He plunged from the 15th floor of the Essex House hotel in New York on 13/1/1979: he is widely believed to have committed suicide but a number of friends remain sceptical. His daughter Lalah began recording in 1990.

05/08/1972	29	7		WHERE IS THE LOVE 1972 Grammy Award for Best Pop Vocal Performance by a Duo	Atlantic K 10202
06/05/1978	42	4		THE CLOSER I GET TO YOU	Atlantic K 11099
17/05/1980	3	11		BACK TOGETHER AGAIN This and above two singles credited to ROBERTA FLACK AND DONNY HATHAWAY	Atlantic K 11481

LALAH HATHAWAY US singer (born 1969, Chicago, IL), daughter of Donny Hathaway and classical singer Eulalah Hathaway.

01/09/1990	66	2		HEAVEN KNOWS	Virgin America VUS 28
02/02/1991	54	3		BABY DON'T CRY	Virgin America VUS 35
27/07/1991	37	5		FAMILY AFFAIR B.E.F. FEATURING LALAH HATHAWAY	10 TEN 369

CHARLOTTE HATHERLEY UK singer/guitarist (born 20/6/1979, London) who is also a member of Ash.

21/08/2004	31	2		SUMMER	Double Dragon DD2014CD

HATIRAS FEATURING SLARTA JOHN Canadian producer (born George Hatiras, 1975, Toronto) with UK rapper Slarta John (born Mark James), ex-singer with Basement Jaxx.

27/01/2001	14	5		SPACED INVADER	Defected DFECT 25CDS

HAVANA UK instrumental and production group formed by Tony Scott, Archie Miller and Gypsy.

06/03/1993	71	1		ETHNIC PRAYER	Limbo 007CD

HAVEN UK rock group formed in Cornwall by Gary Briggs (guitar/vocals), Nat Wason (guitar), Iwan Gronow (bass) and Jack Mitchell (drums). The four relocated to Manchester in 1999.

22/09/2001	72	1		LET IT LIVE	Radiate RDT 3
02/02/2002	24	3		SAY SOMETHING	Radiate RDTX 4
04/05/2002	28	2		TIL THE END	Radiate RDTX 6
27/03/2004	57	1		WOULDN'T CHANGE A THING	Radiate RDTCD 14

NIC HAVERSON UK male singer.

30/01/1993	48	3		HEAD OVER HEELS Theme to the TV series of the same name	Telstar CDHOH 1

CHESNEY HAWKES UK singer (born 12/9/1971) who is the son of the Tremeloes' lead singer Chip Hawkes. He starred in the film *Buddy's Song* as Roger Daltrey's son Buddy.

23/02/1991	❶5	16	●	THE ONE AND ONLY Featured in the 1991 films *Buddy's Song* and *Doc Hollywood*	Chrysalis CHS 3627
22/06/1991	27	5		I'M A MAN NOT A BOY Featured in the 1991 film *Buddy's Song*	Chrysalis CHS 3708

❶9 Number of weeks single topped the UK chart ↑ Entered the UK chart at #1 ▲9 Number of weeks single topped the US chart

28/09/1991.....57......3.......	SECRETS OF THE HEART Featured in the 1991 film *Buddy's Song*	Chrysalis CHS 3681
29/05/1993......63......1.......	WHAT'S WRONG WITH THIS PICTURE	Chrysalis CDCHS 3969
12/01/2002.....74......1.......	STAY AWAY BABY JANE	ARC DSART 13

EDWIN HAWKINS SINGERS FEATURING DOROTHY COMBS MORRISON US singer Edwin

Hawkins (born August 1943, Oakland, CA) was a gospel choir leader; the single was a track lifted from an album recorded privately by the North California State Youth Choir to raise funds. Dorothy Combs Morrison (born 1945, Longview, TX) later recorded solo while the choir recorded with Melanie. The group has won four Grammy Awards including Best Soul Gospel Performance in 1970 for *Every Man Wants To Be Free*, Best Soul Gospel Performance, Contemporary in 1977 for *Wonderful* and Best Gospel Album by a Choir in 1992 for *Edwin Hawkins Music And Arts Seminar Mass Choir*.

21/05/1969 .....2......13......	**OH HAPPY DAY** 1969 Grammy Award for Best Soul Gospel Performance... Buddah 201 048

SCREAMING JAY HAWKINS US singer (born Jalacy Hawkins, 18/7/1929, Cleveland, OH), he was supposedly raised by

a tribe of Blackfoot Indians. He began his career as a boxer and was Middleweight Champion of Alaska in 1949, but switched to music soon after, making his first record in 1952 (although it was withdrawn after three weeks). He later appeared in films, including *American Hot Wax* and *Mystery Train*. He died on 12/2/2000.

03/04/1993.....42......3.......	HEART ATTACK AND VINE .... Columbia 6591092

SOPHIE B HAWKINS US singer (born Sophie Ballantine Hawkins, 1967, Manhattan, NY) who was percussionist with Bryan

Ferry's backing group in the early 1980s before going solo. She launched Trumpet Swan Records in 2000 as a joint venture with Rykodisc.

04/07/1992.....14......9......	DAMN I WISH I WAS YOUR LOVER	Columbia 6581077
12/09/1992....53......3......	CALIFORNIA HERE I COME	Columbia 6583177
06/02/1993....49......2......	I WANT YOU	Columbia 6587772
13/08/1994.....13....12	RIGHT BESIDE YOU	Columbia 6606915
26/11/1994....36......5......	DON'T DON'T TELL ME NO	Columbia 6610152
11/03/1995.....24......6......	AS I LAY ME DOWN	Columbia 6612125

KIRSTY HAWKSHAW UK singer who was a member of Opus III and sang with Orbital and Way Out West before going solo.

24/06/2000.....38......2......	DREAMING BT FEATURING KIRSTY HAWKSHAW	Headscape HEDSCD 002
29/09/2001....22......3......	URBAN TRAIN DJ TIESTO FEATURING KIRSTY HAWKSHAW	VC Recordings/Nebula VCRD 95
21/09/2002....67......1......	STEALTH WAY OUT WEST FEATURING KIRSTY HAWKSHAW	Distinctive Breaks DISNCD 90
23/11/2002....62......1......	FINE DAY	Mainline CDMAIN002
23/10/2004.....43......2......	JUST BE TIESTO FEATURING KIRSTY HAWKSHAW	Nebula NEBCD062

HAWKWIND UK rock group formed in London in 1969 by Dave Brock (born 20/8/1941, Isleworth, guitar/vocals), Mick Slattery

(guitar) and Nick Turner (born 26/8/1940, Oxford, saxophone/flute/vocals) as Group X, changing the name shortly after to Hawkwind Zoo and subsequently Hawkwind. Numerous personnel changes have included Lemmy (born Ian Kilmister, 24/12/1945, Stoke-on-Trent, who later formed Motorhead), Dik Mik and Robert Calvert (born 9/3/1945, Pretoria, South Africa, died from a heart attack 14/8/1988). Legal problems in 1978 prevented them from using the name Hawkwind and they recorded one album as Hawklords.

01/07/1972 .....3......15	**SILVER MACHINE**	United Artists UP 35381
11/08/1973....39......3......	URBAN GUERRILLA	United Artists UP 35566
21/10/1978....34......5......	SILVER MACHINE	United Artists UP 35381
19/07/1980....59......3......	SHOT DOWN IN THE NIGHT	Bronze BRO 98
15/01/1983....67......2......	SILVER MACHINE	United Artists UP 35381

BILL HAYES WITH ARCHIE BLEYER'S ORCHESTRA US singer Bill Hayes (born 5/6/1926, Harvey, IL) was a

regular on Sid Caesar's TV series and later appeared in *Days Of Our Lives*.

06/01/1956 .....2......9......	**BALLAD OF DAVY CROCKETT** ▲[5] .... London HLA 8220

DARREN HAYES Australian singer (born 1973, Brisbane) who was lead singer with Savage Garden before going solo.

30/03/2002 .....8......14......	**INSATIABLE**	Columbia 6723992
20/07/2002....15......8......	STRANGE RELATIONSHIP	Columbia 6728685
16/11/2002....20......5......	I MISS YOU	Columbia 6733315
01/02/2003....19......3......	CRUSH	Columbia 6734905
11/09/2004....12......5......	POP!ULAR	Columbia 6751112

GEMMA HAYES Irish singer (born 1978, County Tipperary) signed by French label Source after submitting a demo in 2001.

25/05/2002....62......1......	HANGING AROUND	Source SOURCD 046
10/08/2002....54......1......	LET A GOOD THING GO	Source SOURCDX 051

ISAAC HAYES US singer (born 20/8/1942, Covington, TN) who formed numerous groups in Memphis before being taken on by

Stax as an in-house musician and producer. He scored the films *Shaft* and *Truck Turner*, appeared in the film *Escape From New York* and launched the Hot Buttered Soul label. He was jailed in 1989 for owing over $346,000 in child support and alimony. In 1994 he was crowned a King in Ghana and given the title Nene Katey Ocansey in return for having brought investors into the country. He also recorded as Chef, a character from the cartoon series *South Park* in 1998. He has won three Grammy Awards including Best Pop Instrumental Performance with Vocal Coloring in 1972 for *Black Moses*. Isaac was inducted into the Rock & Roll Hall of Fame in 2002.

04/12/1971 .....4......12......	**THEME FROM 'SHAFT'** ▲[2] Featured in the films *Shaft* (1971) and *The Commitments* (1991). 1971 Grammy Award for Best Instrumental Arrangement for arrangers Isaac Hayes and Johnny Allen. It also won the Grammy Award for Best Original Score Written for a Motion Picture and then went on to win an Oscar for Best Film Song .... Stax 2025 069

03/04/1976	10	9	⊘	**DISCO CONNECTION** ISAAC HAYES MOVEMENT	ABC 4100
26/12/1998	❶¹	13	✪	**CHOCOLATE SALTY BALLS (PS I LOVE YOU)** CHEF	Columbia 6667985
30/09/2000	53	1		THEME FROM 'SHAFT' (RE-RECORDING) Featured in the 2000 film *Shaft* (itself a remake of the 1971 film, with Samuel L Jackson in the lead role instead of Richard Roundtree)	LaFace 74321792582

HAYSI FANTAYZEE UK trio formed by Kate Garner (born 9/7/1953, Wigan), Paul Caplin and Jeremiah Healy (born 18/1/1962), with both male members recording solo after their group success. Healy is also a much in-demand remixer.

24/07/1982	11	10		JOHN WAYNE IS BIG LEGGY	Regard RG 100
13/11/1982	51	3		HOLY JOE	Regard RG 104
22/01/1983	16	10		SHINY SHINY	Regard RG 106
25/06/1983	62	2		SISTER FRICTION	Regard RG 108

JUSTIN HAYWARD UK singer/guitarist (born David Justin Hayward, 14/10/1946, Swindon) who worked briefly with Marty Wilde before launching an unsuccessful solo career and then joined the Moody Blues as guitarist in 1966. The group took a break in 1974, with Hayward linking with fellow Moody Blue John Lodge (born 20/7/1945, Birmingham) for his initial hit.

25/10/1975	8	7		**BLUE GUITAR** JUSTIN HAYWARD AND JOHN LODGE	Threshold TH 21
08/07/1978	5	13	○	**FOREVER AUTUMN** From Jeff Wayne's concept album *War Of The Worlds*	CBS 6368

LEON HAYWOOD US singer (born 11/2/1942, Houston, TX) who was a session keyboard player for the likes of Sam Cooke before going solo, scoring his first US success in 1965.

15/03/1980	12	11		DON'T PUSH IT, DON'T FORCE IT	20th Century TC 2443

HAYWOODE UK singer, Sharon Haywoode, who began her career as an actress and had a non-speaking part in *Superman*.

17/09/1983	48	7		A TIME LIKE THIS	CBS A 3651
29/09/1984	63	4		I CAN'T LET YOU GO	CBS A 4664
13/04/1985	65	3		ROSES	CBS A 6069
05/10/1985	67	2		GETTING CLOSER	CBS A 6582
21/06/1986	11	11		ROSES Re-issue of CBS A 6069	CBS A 7224
13/09/1986	50	4		I CAN'T LET YOU GO Re-issue of CBS A 4664	CBS 6500767

OFRA HAZA Israeli singer (born 19/11/1959, Hatikva) who joined the Hatikva Theatre Group at the age of thirteen and seven years later launched a solo career. She represented Israel in the 1983 Eurovision Song Contest and came second. She later worked with Sisters of Mercy. Ofra died from influenza and pneumonia brought on by AIDS on 23/2/2000.

30/04/1988	15	8		IM NIN'ALU	WEA YZ 190
17/06/1995	28	3		MY LOVE IS FOR REAL PAULA ABDUL FEATURING OFRA HAZA	Virgin VUSCD 91
03/04/1999	65	1		BABYLON BLACK DOG FEATURING OFRA HAZA	warner.esp WESP 006 CD1

HAZE US producer Harikrish Menon.

18/01/2003	48	2		CHANGES SANDY RIVERA FEATURING HAZE	Defected DFTD 059R
31/07/2004	69	1		DREAMS KINGS OF TOMORROW FEATURING HAZE	Defected DFTD 090CDS

HAZIZA Swedish production duo fronted by Daniel Ellenson. He also records as Spacehorn.

28/04/2001	75	1		ONE MORE	Tidy Trax TIDY 152T

LEE HAZLEWOOD US singer/songwriter/producer (born Barton Lee Hazlewood, 9/7/1929, Mannford, OK) who produced Sanford Clark before devising the distinctive 'twangy' guitar sound for Duane Eddy. He formed the Dot and LHI labels, then joined Reprise as staff producer in 1965 and worked with Dean Martin, Dino Desi and Billy before enjoying major success with Nancy Sinatra.

05/07/1967	11	19		YOU ONLY LIVE TWICE/JACKSON NANCY SINATRA/NANCY SINATRA AND LEE HAZLEWOOD A-side featured in the 1967 James Bond film *You Only Live Twice*	Reprise RS 20595
08/11/1967	47	1		LADYBIRD NANCY SINATRA AND LEE HAZLEWOOD	Reprise RS 20629
21/08/1971	2	19		**DID YOU EVER** NANCY AND LEE	Reprise K 14093

HAZZARDS US vocal and ukele duo formed in New York by Sydney Maresca and Anne Harris. They were originally known as The Ukes of Hazzard but shortened their name for legal reasons.

22/11/2003	67	1		GAY BOYFRIEND	Better The Devil BTD3CD

MURRAY HEAD UK singer/actor (born 5/3/1946, London) who played the role of Judas Iscariot in the rock opera *Jesus Christ Superstar* and scored a US top twenty hit with a track from the album in 1971.

29/01/1972	47	1		SUPERSTAR This was part of a four track single from the musical show *Jesus Christ Superstar*, with Yvonne Elliman's *I Don't Know How to Love Him* also charting during the single's chart run	MCA MMKS 5077
10/11/1984	12	14		ONE NIGHT IN BANGKOK From the musical *Chess*	RCA CHESS 1

ROY HEAD US singer (born 9/1/1943, Three Rivers, TX) well known as a rock and country singer/guitarist. His backing group, The Traits (uncredited on the single) featured Johnny Winter, Francis Zambone, John Clark, Dick Martin, Gary Bowen and Joe Charles.

04/11/1965	30	5		TREAT HER RIGHT	Vocalion V-P 928

HEADBANGERS UK studio group assembled by Biddu with a tribute to Status Quo.

10/10/1981	60	3		STATUS ROCK	Magnet MAG 206

❶⁹ Number of weeks single topped the UK chart ↑ Entered the UK chart at #1 ▲⁹ Number of weeks single topped the US chart

HEADBOYS UK group formed in Edinburgh by Lou Lewis (guitar/vocals), George Boyter (bass/vocals), Calum Malcolm (keyboards/vocals) and Davy Ross (drums/vocals). They disbanded soon after the release of their debut album.

22/09/1979.....45......8....... THE SHAPE OF THINGS TO COME .... RSO 40

HEADGIRL – see MOTORHEAD AND GIRLSCHOOL

MAX HEADROOM – see ART OF NOISE

HEADS UK studio group.

21/06/1986.....45......4....... AZTEC LIGHTNING (THEME FROM BBC WORLD CUP GRANDSTAND) .... BBC RESL 184

HEADS WITH SHAUN RYDER US/UK group formed by Tina Weymouth (born 22/11/1950, Coronado, CA, bass), Chris Frantz (born 8/5/1951, Fort Campbell, KY, drums), Jerry Harrison (born 21/2/1949, Milwaukee, WI, keyboards) and Shaun Ryder (born 23/8/1962, Little Hulton, Manchester, vocals) – effectively Talking Heads without David Byrne, with Happy Mondays' Shaun Ryder.

09/11/1996.....60......1....... DON'T TAKE MY KINDNESS FOR WEAKNESS .... Radioactive MCSTD 48024

HEADSWIM UK rock group formed by Dan Glendining (vocals), Tom Glendining (drums), Nick Watts (keyboards) and Clovis Taylor (bass).

25/02/1995.....64......1.......	CRAWL .... Epic 6612252
14/02/1998.....30......3.......	TOURNIQUET .... Epic 6656442
16/05/1998.....42......1.......	BETTER MADE .... Epic 6658402

JEREMY HEALY AND AMOS UK singer (born 18/1/1962, Woolwich, London); Healy was an ex-member of Haysi Fantayzee and then became a DJ. Amos Pizzey began his career singing with Culture Club.

| 12/10/1996.....11......5..... | STAMP! .... Positiva CDTIV 65 |
| 31/05/1997.....30......2..... | ARGENTINA .... Positiva CDTIV 74 |

IMOGEN HEAP – see URBAN SPECIES

HEAR 'N' AID All-star charity ensemble including members of Judas Priest, Dio, Iron Maiden and Motorhead.

19/04/1986.....26......6....... STARS .... Vertigo HEAR 1

HEAR'SAY UK group comprising Myleene Klass (born 6/4/1978, Norfolk), Kym Marsh (born 13/6/1976, Wiston), Suzanne Shaw (born 29/9/1981, Bury), Noel Sullivan (born 28/7/1980, Cardiff) and Danny Foster (born 3/5/1979, London). They were the winners of the TV series *Popstars*, which had auditioned over 2,000 hopefuls. Their debut single *Pure And Simple* was the biggest selling UK chart debut ever, shifting more than 500,000 copies in its first week. They became only the fourth act (after The Monkees in 1967, Tubeway Army in 1979 and Hanson in 1997) to simultaneously top the single and album charts with their debut releases. In January 2002 Kym Marsh left to go solo. After auditioning some 5,000 entrants, Johnny Shentall was announced as her replacement. It was later claimed to have been a 'fix' as he had performed with the group as a dancer at the Top of the Pops Awards. They disbanded in September 2002.

24/02/2001 ....❶³....25...❷²	PURE AND SIMPLE ↑ .... Polydor 5870069
07/07/2001 ....❶¹....17.....	THE WAY TO YOUR LOVE ↑ .... Polydor 5871492
08/12/2001 ....4......11.....	EVERYBODY .... Polydor 5705122
24/08/2002 ....6......7.....	LOVIN' IS EASY .... Polydor 5708552

HEART US rock group formed in 1970 by Ann Wilson (born 19/6/1951, San Diego, CA, lead vocals), Steve Fossen (born 15/11/1949, bass) and brothers Mike and Roger Fisher (born 14/2/1950, guitar) as the Army. Renamed White Heart in 1972, they shortened it to Heart in 1974. Ann's sister Nancy (born 16/3/1954, San Francisco, CA) joined in 1974 with Mike Fisher becoming manager. The group relocated to Vancouver, Canada in 1975 so Mike Fisher could avoid being drafted. Roger Fisher left in 1980, being replaced by Howard Leese (born 13/6/1951, Los Angeles, CA, keyboards/guitar). Since 1982 the line-up has consisted of the Wilson sisters, Leese, bass player Mark Andes (born 19/2/1948) and drummer Denny Carmassi.

29/03/1986.....62......4.......	THESE DREAMS ▲¹ .... Capitol CL 394
13/06/1987 .....3......16.....○	ALONE ▲³ .... Capitol CL 448
19/09/1987.....30......7.......	WHO WILL YOU RUN TO .... Capitol CL 457
12/12/1987.....34......7.......	THERE'S THE GIRL .... Capitol CL 473
05/03/1988 .....8......9.......	NEVER/THESE DREAMS B-side re-issue of Capitol CL 394 ...... Capitol CL 482
14/05/1988.....14......6.......	WHAT ABOUT LOVE .... Capitol CL 487
22/10/1988.....38......3.......	NOTHIN' AT ALL .... Capitol CL 507
24/03/1990 .....8......13.....	ALL I WANNA DO IS MAKE LOVE TO YOU .... Capitol CL 569
28/07/1990.....47......3.......	I DIDN'T WANT TO NEED YOU .... Capitol CL 580
17/11/1990.....60......2.......	STRANDED .... Capitol CL 595
14/09/1991.....56......2.......	YOU'RE THE VOICE .... Capitol CL 624
20/11/1993.....19......4.......	WILL YOU BE THERE (IN THE MORNING) .... Capitol CDCLS 700

HEARTBEAT UK vocal/instrumental group formed in Malmsbury.

| 24/10/1987.....32......4....... | TEARS FROM HEAVEN .... Priority P 17 |
| 23/04/1988.....70......1....... | THE WINNER .... Priority P 19 |

HEARTBEAT COUNTRY UK singer Bill Maynard (born 8/10/1928, Farnham) who is better known as an actor. He appeared in the TV series *Heartbeat* but retired through ill-health in 2000.

31/12/1994.....75......1....... HEARTBEAT .... MMM 01CD

○ Silver disc ● Gold disc ❂ Platinum disc (additional platinum units are indicated by a figure following the symbol) ◉ Singles released prior to 1973 that are known to have sold over 1 million copies in the UK

HEARTBREAKER – see **DEMON VS HEARTBREAKER**

HEARTBREAKERS – see **TOM PETTY AND THE HEARTBREAKERS**

HEARTISTS Italian DJ/production trio formed by Claudio Coccoluto, Savino Martinez and Alberto Moreira.

09/08/1997	42	3		BELO HORIZONTI	VC Recordings VCRD 23
31/01/1998	40	2		BELO HORIZONTI (REMIX)	VC Recordings VCRD 28

HEARTLESS CREW UK garage group formed by MC Bushkin, MC Mighty Moe and DJ Fonti.

25/05/2002	21	3		THE HEARTLESS CREW THEME	East West HEART 02CD
28/06/2003	50	1		WHY (LOOKING BACK)	East West HEART 03CD

TED HEATH UK orchestra leader/trombonist (born 30/3/1900, Wandsworth, London) who formed his own band in 1944 and led it until ill-health forced him to leave in 1964, although the band carried on with the same name for a further five years. In 1957 he was awarded the Ivor Novello Oustanding Personal Services to Popular Music Award. Heath died on 18/11/1969.

16/01/1953	11	1		VANESSA	Decca F 9983
03/07/1953	6	11		**HOT TODDY**	Decca F 10093
23/10/1953	9	5		**DRAGNET**	Decca F 10176
12/02/1954	9	3		**SKIN DEEP**	Decca F 10246
06/07/1956	18	9		THE FAITHFUL HUSSAR	Decca F 10746
14/03/1958	3	14		**SWINGIN' SHEPHERD BLUES**	Decca F 11000
11/04/1958	21	6		TEQUILA	Decca F 11003
04/07/1958	24	2		TOM HARK	Decca F 11025
05/10/1961	36	5		SUCU SUCU	Decca F 11392

HEATWAVE US/UK soul group formed in Germany by American GI Johnnie Wilder (born 3/7/1949, Dayton, OH, vocals) and his brother Keith (born Dayton, OH, vocals). The best-known line-up featured Rod Temperton (who retired from live work to concentrate on writing), Eric Johns, Mario Mantese and Ernest 'Bilbo' Berger. Other group members included Jessie Whitten (stabbed to death in 1977), his replacement Roy Carter and Derek Bramble. Mantese was paralysed in a car crash in July 1978 and forced to retire, while Johnnie Wilder was left paralysed from a car accident on 24/2/1979 but returned to the group. Rod Temperton went on to win the 1990 Grammy Award for Best Arrangement on an Instrumental with Quincy Jones and Jerry Hey for *Birdland* by Quincy Jones.

22/01/1977	2	14	O	**BOOGIE NIGHTS**	GTO GT 77
07/05/1977	15	11		TOO HOT TO HANDLE/SLIP YOUR DISC TO THIS	GTO GT 91
14/01/1978	12	8		THE GROOVE LINE Featured in the 1978 film *The Stud*	GTO GT 115
03/06/1978	12	11		MIND BLOWING DECISIONS	GTO GT 226
04/11/1978	9	14	O	**ALWAYS AND FOREVER/MIND BLOWING DECISIONS**	GTO GT 236
26/05/1979	43	5		RAZZLE DAZZLE	GTO GT 248
17/01/1981	19	8		GANGSTER OF THE GROOVE	GTO GT 285
21/03/1981	34	7		JITTERBUGGIN'	GTO GT 290
01/09/1990	65	2		MIND BLOWING DECISIONS Re-recording	Brothers Organisation HW 1

HEAVEN 17 UK electronic dance group formed in Sheffield by ex-Human League members Ian Craig Marsh (born 11/11/1956, Sheffield) and Martyn Ware (born 19/5/1956, Sheffield) with Glenn Gregory (born 16/5/1958, Sheffield). Also responsible for BEF (British Electric Foundation). Heaven 17 was named after the group in Anthony Burgess' novel and Stanley Kubrick's film *A Clockwork Orange*.

21/03/1981	45	5		(WE DON'T NEED THIS) FASCIST GROOVE THANG The single was banned by the BBC for its derogatory lyrics aimed at US President Ronald Reagan	Virgin VS 400
05/09/1981	46	7		PLAY TO WIN Featured in the 1982 film *Summer Lovers*	Virgin VS 433
14/11/1981	57	3		PENTHOUSE AND PAVEMENT Featured in the 1993 film *Sliver*	Virgin VS 455
30/10/1982	41	6		LET ME GO	Virgin VS 532
16/04/1983	2	13	O	**TEMPTATION** Features the uncredited vocals of Carol Kenyon	Virgin VS 570
25/06/1983	5	11		**COME LIVE WITH ME**	Virgin VS 607
10/09/1983	17	7		CRUSHED BY THE WHEELS OF INDUSTRY	Virgin VS 628
01/09/1984	24	6		SUNSET NOW	Virgin VS 708
27/10/1984	23	7		THIS IS MINE	Virgin VS 722
19/01/1985	52	5		...(AND THAT'S NO LIE)	Virgin VS 740
17/01/1987	51	3		TROUBLE	Virgin VS 920
21/11/1992	4	11	O	**TEMPTATION (REMIX)**	Virgin VS 1446
27/02/1993	40	2		(WE DON'T NEED THIS) FASCIST GROOVE THANG (REMIX)	Virgin VSCDT 1451
10/04/1993	54	1		PENTHOUSE AND PAVEMENT (REMIX)	Virgin VSCDT 1457

HEAVENS CRY Dutch production duo.

06/10/2001	68	1		TILL TEARS DO US PART	Tidy Trax TIDY 158CD
19/01/2002	71	1		TILL TEARS DO US PART	Tidy Trax TIDY 158CD

HEAVY D AND THE BOYZ US rap group formed in Mount Vernon, NY by Heavy D (born Dwight Meyers, 24/5/1957), G Whiz (born Glen Parrish), Trouble T-Roy (born Troy Dixon) and DJ Eddie F (born Edward Ferrell). Dixon was killed after falling off a balcony on 15/7/1990. Heavy D made his film debut in the 1993 film *Who's The Man?*

06/12/1986	61	8		MR BIG STUFF	MCA 1106
15/07/1989	69	2		WE GOT OUR OWN THANG (IMPORT)	MCA 23942

❶[9] Number of weeks single topped the UK chart ↑ Entered the UK chart at #1 ▲[9] Number of weeks single topped the US chart

359

					SINGLE TITLE	LABEL & NUMBER
06/07/1991	2	12			NOW THAT WE FOUND LOVE	MCA 1550
28/09/1991	46	3			IS IT GOOD TO YOU Contains a sample of Junior's *Mama Used To Say*	MCA MCS 1564
08/10/1994	30	3			THIS IS YOUR NIGHT Contains samples of Kool & The Gang's *Ladies Night* and George Benson's *Give Me The Night* .... MCA MCSTD 2010	

HEAVY PETTIN' UK group formed in Glasgow by Steve Hayman (vocals), Gordon Bonnar (guitar), Punky Mendoza (guitar), Brian Waugh (bass) and Gary Moat (drums).

17/03/1984	69	2			LOVE TIMES LOVE	Polydor HEP 3

HEAVY STEREO UK group formed by Colin 'Gem' Murray Archer (guitar/piano/vocals), Pete Downing (guitar), Nez (bass) and Nick Jones (drums). They disbanded in 1999 with Archer going on to join Oasis.

22/07/1995	46	1			SLEEP FREAK	Creation CRESCD 203
28/10/1995	46	1			SMILER	Creation CRESCD 213
10/02/1996	45	1			CHINESE BURN	Creation CRESCD 218
24/08/1996	53	1			MOUSE IN A HOLE	Creation CRESCD 230

HEAVY WEATHER US singer Peter Lee.

29/06/1996	56	1			LOVE CAN'T TURN AROUND	Pukka CDPUKKA 6

BOBBY HEBB US singer (born 26/7/1941, Nashville, TN); he featured on the Grand Ole Opry at the age of 12, the first black performer to appear at the venue.

08/09/1966	12	9			SUNNY Tribute to Bobby's brother Hal who was killed in a mugging on 23/11/1963 (the day after President John Kennedy was assassinated). Featured in the 1994 film *War*	Philips BF 1503
19/08/1972	32	6			LOVE LOVE LOVE	Philips 6051 023

SHARLENE HECTOR UK singer who sang with the London Community Gospel Choir and Basement Jaxx before going solo.

17/04/2004	28	4			I WISH I KNEW HOW IT WOULD FEEL Song originally an advertisement for Coca Cola	Radar RAD0006CD

HED BOYS UK production duo Dave Lee and Andrew Livingstone (also known as The Doc). Lee also records as Joey Negro, Jakatta, Li Kwan, Akabu, Z Factor and Raven Maize.

06/08/1994	21	4			GIRLS & BOYS Contains a sample of Jessie Velez' *Girls Out On The Floor*	Deconstruction 74321223322
04/11/1995	36	2			GIRLS & BOYS (REMIX)	Deconstruction 74321322032

HEDGEHOPPERS ANONYMOUS UK group formed in 1963 by Leslie Dash, Ray Honeyball, John Stewart and Mick Tinsley, all of whom were RAF ground staff at Leighton Buzzard, as the Trendsetters. Producer Jonathan King changed their name in 1965. Mick Tinsley later went solo.

30/09/1965	5	12			IT'S GOOD NEWS WEEK	Decca F 12241

HEFNER UK group formed in 1994 by Darren Hayman (guitar/vocals), John Morrison (bass) and Anthony Harding (drums).

26/08/2000	50	1			GOOD FRUIT	Too Pure PURE 108CDS
14/10/2000	64	1			THE GREEDY UGLY PEOPLE	Too Pure PURE 111CDS
08/09/2001	58	1			ALAN BEAN	Too Pure PURE 118CDS

NEAL HEFTI US orchestra leader (born 29/10/1922, Hastings, NE) who was an arranger for Woody Herman, Harry James and Count Basie before becoming the composer of various TV themes.

09/04/1988	55	4			BATMAN THEME The original theme to the *Batman* TV series that previously charted in the US in 1966 (position #35) and was re-released when the first of the films starring Michael Keaton was made	RCA PB 49571

DAN HEGARTY UK singer and member of Darts before going solo in 1979. He then formed Rocky Sharpe & The Replays.

31/03/1979	73	2			VOODOO VOODOO	Magnet MAG 143

ANITA HEGERLAND – see **MIKE OLDFIELD**

HEINZ German singer and bass player (born Heinz Burt, 24/7/1942, Hargin, Germany) who was bass player with the Tornadoes from their formation in 1961 until he went solo in 1963. His backing group were The Wild Boys and featured future Deep Purple guitarist Richie Blackmore. Heinz died from motor neurone disease on 7/4/2000.

08/08/1963	5	15			JUST LIKE EDDIE Tribute to Eddie Cochran	Decca F 11693
28/11/1963	26	9			COUNTRY BOY	Decca F 11768
27/02/1964	26	8			YOU WERE THERE	Decca F 11831
15/10/1964	39	2			QUESTIONS I CAN'T ANSWER	Columbia DB 7374
18/03/1965	49	1			DIGGIN' MY POTATOES HEINZ AND THE WILD BOYS	Columbia DB 7482

HELICOPTER UK instrumental/production duo Rob Davy and Dylan Barnes who also record as Mutiny UK.

27/08/1994	32	2			ON YA WAY	Helicopter TIG 007CD
22/06/1996	37	2			ON YA WAY (REMIX)	Systematic SYSCD 27

HELIOCENTRIC WORLD UK vocal/instrumental group.

14/01/1995	71	2			WHERE'S YOUR LOVE BEEN	Talkin Loud TLKCD 51

○ Silver disc ● Gold disc ✪ Platinum disc (additional platinum units are indicated by a figure following the symbol) ◉ Singles released prior to 1973 that are known to have sold over 1 million copies in the UK

HELIOTROPIC FEATURING VERNA V UK dance group fronted by producers Nick Hale and Gez Dewar.

16/10/1999.....33......2....... ALIVE..Multiply CDMULTY 52

HELL IS FOR HEROES UK rock group formed in London in 2000 by Justin Schlossberg (vocals), Will McGonagle (guitar), Tom O'Donoghue (guitar), James 'Fin' Findlay (bass) and Joe Birch (drums).

09/02/2002.....63......1....... YOU DROVE ME TO IT ....Wishakismo CDWISH 003
17/08/2002.....41......2....... I CAN CLIMB MOUNTAINS ....Chrysalis CDCHS 5143
02/11/2002.....38......1....... NIGHT VISION ....Chrysalis CDCHSS 5147
01/02/2003.....28......2....... YOU DROVE ME TO IT Re-issue of Wishakismo CDWISH 003 ....EMI CDCHSS 5149
17/05/2003.....39......1....... RETREAT...EMI CDEMS 619
28/08/2004.....71......1....... ONE OF US ....Captains Of Industry CAPT008
27/11/2004.....72......1....... KAMICHI ....Factotum TUM001CD

HELLER AND FARLEY PROJECT UK duo formed by Pete Heller and Terry Farley, ex-Boy's Own collective. They also recorded as Fire Island and Roach Motel.

24/02/1996.....22......3....... ULTRA FLAVA ....AM:PM 5814372
28/12/1996.....32......4....... ULTRA FLAVA (REMIX)...AM:PM 5820551
15/05/1999.....12......7....... BIG LOVE PETE HELLER'S BIG LOVE Contains a sample of Stargard's *Wear It Out*...................Essential Recordings ESCD 4

HELLO UK rock group formed in London in 1971 by Bob Bradbury (lead guitar/vocals), Keith Marshall (lead guitar/vocals), Vic Faulkner (bass guitar/vocals) and Jeff Allen (drums/vocals) as The Age. After considerable European success, particularly in Germany, they disbanded in 1979, and Marshall went solo. Bradbury re-formed the group in 1996.

09/11/1974 .....6......12 .....O TELL HIM ....Bell 1377
18/10/1975 .....9......9....... NEW YORK GROOVE..Bell 1438

HELLOWEEN German rock group formed in Hamburg in 1984 by Kai Hansen (guitar/vocals), Michael Weikath (guitar), Markus Grosskopf (bass) and Ingo Schwichenburg (drums), later adding Michael Kiske (vocals). Hansen left in 1989 and was briefly replaced by Roland Grapow. Kiske and Schwichenburg were sacked in 1990 and replaced by Andri Deris and Ulli Kusch respectively.

27/08/1988.....57......3....... DR STEIN ....Noise International 7HELLO 1
12/11/1988.....69......2....... I WANT OUT ....Noise International 7HELLO 2
02/03/1991.....56......2....... KIDS OF THE CENTURY ....EMI EM 178

BOBBY HELMS US singer (born 15/8/1933, Bloomington, IN) who was a regular on the US country charts. He died from emphysema and asthma on 19/6/1997.

29/11/1957.....22......3....... MY SPECIAL ANGEL BOBBY HELMS WITH THE ANITA KERR SINGERS ....Brunswick 05271
21/02/1958.....30......1....... NO OTHER BABY ....Brunswick 05730
01/08/1958.....20......3....... JACQUELINE BOBBY HELMS WITH THE ANITA KERR SINGERS Featured in the 1958 film *The Case Against Brooklyn* ....
....Brunswick 05748

JIMMY HELMS US singer (born 1944, Florida) who made his first recordings in 1959 for Scottie, but spent more time as a session singer than as a solo performer. He became a member of Londonbeat in 1989.

24/02/1973 .....8......10 ..... GONNA MAKE YOU AN OFFER YOU CAN'T REFUSE ....Cube BUG 27

HELTAH SKELTAH AND ORIGINOO GUNN CLAPPAZ AS THE FABULOUS FIVE US rap group formed by Tawl Sean (aka Ruck or Sparky) and Da Rockness Monsta (aka Rock or Dutch). Also members of Boot Camp Clik.

01/06/1996.....60......1....... BLAH ....Priority PTYCD 117

HEMSTOCK – see PAUL van DYK

AINSLIE HENDERSON UK singer (born 28/1/1979), best known as one of the contestants on TV's *Fame Academy*, finishing fourth behind David Sneddon and Sinead Quinn.

08/03/2003 .....5......7....... KEEP ME A SECRET ....Mercury 0779812

EDDIE HENDERSON US trumpet player (born 26/10/1940, New York) who played with John Handy, Herbie Hancock and Art Blakey's Jazz Messengers before going solo. He also has a Bachelor of Science degree in zoology.

28/10/1978.....44......6....... PRANCE ON ....Capitol CL 16015

JOE 'MR PIANO' HENDERSON UK pianist (born 2/5/1920, Glasgow); he formed his own band while still at school and was effectively a professional pianist from the age of 13. He later backed Petula Clark on her hits. He died in 1980.

03/06/1955.....14......4....... SING IT WITH JOE Medley of *Margie*, *I'm Nobody's Sweetheart*, *Somebody Stole My Gal*, *Moonlight Bay*, *By The Light Of The Silvery Moon* and *Cuddle Up A Little Closer* ....Polygon P 1167
02/09/1955.....18......3....... SING IT AGAIN WITH JOE Medley of *Put Your Arms Around Me Honey*, *Ain't She Sweet*, *When You're Smiling*, *Shine On Harvest Moon*, *My Blue Heaven* and *Show Me The Way To Go Home* ....Polygon P 1184
25/07/1958.....14......14....... TRUDIE..Pye Nixa N 15147
23/10/1959.....28......1....... TREBLE CHANCE ....Pye 7N 15224
24/03/1960.....44......1....... OOH! LA! LA! ....Pye 7N 15257

WAYNE HENDERSON – see ROY AYERS

●⁹ Number of weeks single topped the UK chart ↑ Entered the UK chart at #1 ▲⁹ Number of weeks single topped the US chart

361

BILLY HENDRIX
German producer, born Sharam 'Jey' Khososi. He was later a member of Three 'N One.

12/09/1998.....55......2.......	THE BODY SHINE (EP) Tracks on EP: *The Body Shine, Funky Shine, Colour Systems Inc's Amber Dub* and *Timewriter (remix)*	
	.... Hooj Choons HOOJ 65CD	

JIMI HENDRIX
US singer/guitarist (born Johnny Allen Hendrix 27/11/1942, Seattle, WA and renamed James Marshall Hendrix four years later by his father) who taught himself to play the guitar at the age of 12. After serving a year in the army (he was discharged after breaking his ankle in a parachute jump) he toured with Curtis Mayfield, The Marvelettes, Sam Cooke, Jackie Wilson and a host of others as well as appearing on numerous sessions. Briefly a member of the Isley Brothers, he formed his own group in 1966, Jimmy James & the Blue Flames, and was spotted by Chas Chandler of The Animals. Chandler brought him to London and formed a new group with Mitch Mitchell (born John Mitchell, 9/6/1947, Ealing, London) and Noel Redding (born David Redding, 25/12/1945, Folkestone), the Jimi Hendrix Experience. Hendrix formed the Band of Gypsies in 1969 with Buddy Miles (drums) and Billy Cox (bass). He died from a drug overdose in London on 18/9/1970. One of the most influential guitarists of all time, his back catalogue sells an estimated 3 million units a year. He was inducted into the Rock & Roll Hall of Fame in 1992 and won the 1999 Grammy Award for Best Video Long Form for *Jimi Hendrix's Band Of Gypsys – Live At Fillmore East*. He has a star on the Hollywood Walk of Fame. Redding died on 12/5/2003.

05/01/1967 .....6......11	HEY JOE Featured in the 1994 film *Forrest Gump*... Polydor 56 139	
23/03/1967 .....3......14	PURPLE HAZE Featured in the 1997 film *Apollo 13* .... Track 604 001	
11/05/1967 .....6......11	THE WIND CRIES MARY .... Track 604 004	
30/08/1967.....18......9.......	BURNING OF THE MIDNIGHT LAMP .... Track 604 007	
30/10/1968 .....5......11	ALL ALONG THE WATCHTOWER Featured in the films *196 9* (1988), *Forrest Gump* (1994) and *Private Parts* (1996)... Track 604 025	
16/04/1969.....37......3.......	CROSSTOWN TRAFFIC .... Track 604 029	
07/11/1970 ....❶¹......13 ...	VOODOO CHILE Posthumous #1. Featured in the films *In The Name Of The Father* (1993) and *Payback* (1999) ..... Track 2095 001	
30/10/1971.....35......5.......	GYPSY EYES/REMEMBER This and above six singles credited to JIMI HENDRIX EXPERIENCE....................... Track 2094 010	
12/02/1972.....35......5.......	JOHNNY B. GOODE .... Track 2001 277	
21/04/1990.....61......3.......	CROSSTOWN TRAFFIC... Polydor PO 71	
20/10/1990.....52......3.......	ALL ALONG THE WATCHTOWER (EP) Tracks on EP: *All Along The Watchtower, Voodoo Chile* and *Hey Joe* .... Polydor PO 100	

NONA HENDRYX
US singer (born 18/8/1945, Trenton, NJ) who was a member of The Del Capris before becoming a founder member of Labelle. The group disbanded in 1976 and Nona went solo.

16/05/1987.....60......2.......	WHY SHOULD I CRY .... EMI America EA 234	

DON HENLEY
US singer (born 22/7/1947, Gilmer, TX); he was a member of the Four Speeds in the mid-1960s, moving to Los Angeles, CA in 1970 to record an album with Shiloh. He formed the Eagles with Glenn Frey in 1971 and when they ceased recording in 1980 he went solo. Having won four Grammy Awards with The Eagles Don has collected a further two awards as a solo artist including Best Rock Vocal Performance in 1989 for *The End Of Innocence*.

12/02/1983.....59......3.......	DIRTY LAUNDRY... Asylum E 9894	
09/02/1985.....12......10	THE BOYS OF SUMMER 1985 Grammy Award for Best Rock Vocal Performance .... Geffen A 4945	
03/10/1992.....48......5.......	THE END OF THE INNOCENCE .... Geffen GEF 57	
03/10/1992.....22......6.......	SOMETIMES LOVE JUST AIN'T ENOUGH PATTY SMYTH WITH DON HENLEY .... MCA MCS 1692	
18/07/1998.....12......6.......	BOYS OF SUMMER Re-issue of Geffen A 4945 .... Geffen GFSTD 22350	

CASSIUS HENRY
UK singer (born 1982, London).

30/03/2002.....31......2.......	BROKE .... Blacklist 0130265 ERE	
03/07/2004.....56......1.......	THE ONE CASSIUS HENRY FEATURING FREEWAY .... Universal MCSTD 40334	

CLARENCE 'FROGMAN' HENRY
US singer (born 19/3/1937, Algiers, LA) who, aged 17, scored his first US hit *Ain't Got No Home* that featured his impressions of frog noises and gave him his nickname. He later worked in clubs in New Orleans, LA.

04/05/1961 .....3......19	(I DON'T KNOW WHY) BUT I DO Featured in the 1994 film *Forrest Gump* .... Pye International 7N 25078	
13/07/1961 .....6......12	YOU ALWAYS HURT THE ONE YOU LOVE .... Pye International 7N 25089	
21/09/1961.....42......2.......	LONELY STREET/WHY CAN'T YOU .... Pye International 7N 25108	
17/07/1993.....65......2.......	(I DON'T KNOW WHY) BUT I DO Re-issue of Pye International 7N 25078 .... MCA MCSTD 1797	

KEVIN HENRY – see LA MIX

PAUL HENRY AND THE MAYSON GLEN ORCHESTRA
UK actor (born 1947, Birmingham); he became a household name thanks to his portrayal of Benny Hawkins in the TV series *Crossroads*.

14/01/1978.....39......2.......	BENNY'S THEME .... Pye 7N 46027	

PAULINE HENRY
UK singer (born London) who was lead singer with The Chimes before going solo.

18/09/1993.....38......2.......	TOO MANY PEOPLE .... Sony S2 6595942	
06/11/1993.....12......7.......	FEEL LIKE MAKING LOVE .... Sony S2 6597972	
29/01/1994.....30......3.......	CAN'T TAKE YOUR LOVE .... Sony S2 6599902	
21/05/1994.....54......1.......	WATCH THE MIRACLE START .... Sony S2 6602772	
30/09/1995.....57......2.......	SUGAR FREE .... Sony S2 6624362	
23/12/1995.....37......3.......	LOVE HANGOVER .... Sony S2 6626132	
24/02/1996.....40......2.......	NEVER KNEW LOVE LIKE THIS PAULINE HENRY FEATURING WAYNE MARSHALL .... Sony S2 6629382	
01/06/1996.....46......1.......	HAPPY .... Sony S2 6630692	

○ Silver disc ● Gold disc ✪ Platinum disc (additional platinum units are indicated by a figure following the symbol) ◎ Singles released prior to 1973 that are known to have sold over 1 million copies in the UK

PIERRE HENRY
French instrumentalist (born 9/12/1927, Paris) whose debut hit was originally recorded in 1967 and remixed by Fatboy Slim and William Orbit.

04/10/1997 . . . . . 58 . . . . . . 1	**PSYCHE ROCK** . . . . Hi-Life 4620312

HEPBURN
UK group formed by Jamie Benson (vocals), Lisa Lister (guitar), Sara Davies (bass) and Beverley Fullen (drums).

29/05/1999 . . . . . 8 . . . . . 7	**I QUIT** . . . . Columbia 6674012
28/08/1999 . . . . . 14 . . . . 5	BUGS . . . . Columbia 6677385
19/02/2000 . . . . . 16 . . . . 3	DEEP DEEP DOWN . . . . Columbia 6683382

HERD
UK group formed in 1965 by Andy Bown (bass, keyboards/vocals), Peter Frampton (born 22/4/1950, Beckenham, guitar), Andrew Steele (drums) and Gary Taylor (guitar). Frampton quit in 1969 to form Humble Pie and subsequently went solo.

13/09/1967 . . . . . 6 . . . . . . 13	**FROM THE UNDERWORLD** . . . . Fontana TF 856
20/12/1967 . . . . . 15 . . . . 9	PARADISE LOST . . . . Fontana TF 887
10/04/1968 . . . . 5 . . . . . . 13	**I DON'T WANT OUR LOVING TO DIE** . . . . Fontana TF 925

HERMAN'S HERMITS
UK pop group formed in Manchester in 1963 by Peter Noone (born 5/11/1947, Davyhulme, Manchester, vocals), Karl Green (born 31/7/1947, Salford, bass), Keith Hopwood (born 26/10/1946, Manchester, rhythm guitar), Derek 'Lek' Leckenby (born 14/5/1946, Leeds, lead guitar) and Barry 'Bean' Whitwam (born 21/7/1946, Manchester, drums) as the Heartbeats. They changed their name in 1963 to Herman's Hermits, which was derived from the character Sherman in *The Rocky And Bullwinkle Show* cartoon series. Noone left in 1972 to go solo. The Hermits didn't actually play on their hits, producer Mickie Most used session musicians. Leckenby died from non-Hodgkins lymphoma on 4/6/1996.

20/08/1964 . . . . ❶² 15	**I'M INTO SOMETHING GOOD** . . . . Columbia DB 7338
19/11/1964 . . . . . 19 . . . . 9	SHOW ME GIRL . . . . Columbia DB 7408
18/02/1965 . . . . . 3 . . . . . . 12	**SILHOUETTES** . . . . Columbia DB 7475
29/04/1965 . . . . . 7 . . . . . . 9	**WONDERFUL WORLD** . . . . Columbia DB 7546
02/09/1965 . . . . . 15 . . . . 9	JUST A LITTLE BIT BETTER . . . . Columbia DB 7670
23/12/1965 . . . . . 6 . . . . . . 11	**A MUST TO AVOID** . . . . Columbia DB 7791
24/03/1966 . . . . . 20 . . . 7	YOU WON'T BE LEAVING . . . . Columbia DB 7861
23/06/1966 . . . . . 18 . . . 7	THIS DOOR SWINGS BOTH WAYS . . . . Columbia DB 7947
06/10/1966 . . . . . 7 . . . . . . 11	**NO MILK TODAY** . . . . Columbia DB 8012
01/12/1966 . . . . . 37 . . . 7	EAST WEST . . . . Columbia DB 8076
09/02/1967 . . . . . 7 . . . . . . 11	**THERE'S A KIND OF HUSH** . . . . Columbia DB 8123
17/01/1968 . . . . . 11 . . . . 9	I CAN TAKE OR LEAVE YOUR LOVING . . . . Columbia DB 8327
01/05/1968 . . . . . 12 . . . . 10	SLEEPY JOE . . . . Columbia DB 8404
17/07/1968 . . . . . 8 . . . . . . 14	**SUNSHINE GIRL** . . . . Columbia DB 8446
18/12/1968 . . . . . 6 . . . . . . 15	**SOMETHING'S HAPPENING** . . . . Columbia DB 8504
23/04/1969 . . . . . 2 . . . . . . 12	**MY SENTIMENTAL FRIEND** . . . . Columbia DB 8563
08/11/1969 . . . . . 33 . . . 9	HERE COMES THE STAR . . . . Columbia DB 8626
07/02/1970 . . . . . 7 . . . . . . 12	**YEARS MAY COME, YEARS MAY GO** . . . . Columbia DB 8556
23/05/1970 . . . . . 22 . . . . 10	BET YER LIFE I DO . . . . RAK 102
14/11/1970 . . . . . 13 . . . . 12	LADY BARBARA PETER NOONE AND HERMAN'S HERMITS . . . . RAK 106

HERMES HOUSE BAND
Dutch dance group formed in Rotterdam in 1984 by Robin, Judith and Jop, taking their name from their student fraternity.

15/12/2001 . . . . . 7 . . . . . . 12	**COUNTRY ROADS** . . . . Liberty CDHHB 001
13/04/2002 . . . . . 53 . . . . . 1	QUE SERA SERA . . . . EMI CDHHB 002
28/12/2002 . . . . . 50 . . . . . 1	LIVE IS LIFE HERMES HOUSE BAND AND DJ OTZI . . . . Liberty CDLIVE001

HERNANDEZ
UK singer.

15/04/1989 . . . . . 58 . . . . 3	ALL MY LOVE . . . . Epic HER 1

PATRICK HERNANDEZ
Guadeloupe singer (born 6/4/1949, Paris, to a Spanish father and Austrian/Italian mother and raised in Guadeloupe).

16/06/1979 . . . . . 10 . . . . 14 . . . . O	**BORN TO BE ALIVE** . . . . Gem 4

HERREYS
Swedish vocal group.

26/05/1984 . . . . . 46 . . . . 3	DIGGI LOO-DIGGI LEY The song won the 1984 Eurovision Song Contest . . . . Panther PAN 5

KRISTIN HERSH
US guitarist/singer (born 1966, Atlanta, GA); she was a founding member of Throwing Muses with her step-sister Tanya Donelly. The group effectively disbanded in 1993, and Hersh went solo the following year, although she re-formed Throwing Muses after the success of *Hips And Makers*.

22/01/1994 . . . . . 45 . . . . . 2	YOUR GHOST . . . . 4AD BAD 4001CD
16/04/1994 . . . . . 60 . . . . . 1	STRINGS . . . . 4AD BAD 4006CD

NICK HEYWARD UK singer (born 20/5/1961, Beckenham) who formed Haircut 100 in 1980 and was responsible for penning all their hits. Following a series of personality clashes with other members, in 1982 he left the group and went solo.

19/03/1983	13	8	WHISTLE DOWN THE WIND	Arista HEY 1
04/06/1983	11	10	TAKE THAT SITUATION	Arista HEY 2
24/09/1983	14	8	BLUE HAT FOR A BLUE DAY	Arista HEY 3
03/12/1983	52	5	ON A SUNDAY	Arista HEY 4
02/06/1984	31	6	LOVE ALL DAY	Arista HEY 5
03/11/1984	25	9	WARNING SIGN	Arista HEY 6
08/06/1985	45	4	LAURA	Arista HEY 8
10/05/1986	43	5	OVER THE WEEKEND	Arista HEY 9
10/09/1988	67	2	YOU'RE MY WORLD	Warner Brothers W 7758
21/08/1993	44	2	KITE	Epic 6594882
16/10/1993	58	2	HE DOESN'T LOVE YOU LIKE I DO	Epic 6597282
30/09/1995	47	2	THE WORLD	Epic 6623845
13/01/1996	37	2	ROLLERBLADE	Epic 6627915

HHC UK DJ/production duo.

19/04/1997	44	1	WE'RE NOT ALONE	Perfecto PERF 138CD

HI-FIVE US vocal group formed in Waco, TX by Rod Clark, Toriano Easley, Russell Neal, Marcus Saunders and Tony Thompson. Easley left the group midway through recording their debut album and was replaced by Preston Irby; Thompson later recorded solo.

01/06/1991	43	6	I LIKE THE WAY (THE KISSING GAME) ▲¹	Jive 271
24/10/1992	55	2	SHE'S PLAYING HARD TO GET	Jive 316

HI-GATE UK dance group formed by Paul Masterson and Judge Jules (born Julius O'Riordan). The pair also collaborated as Yomanda and Clergy. Masterson is also a member of Amen! UK, The Candy Girls and The Dope Smugglaz.

29/01/2000	6	6	**PITCHIN' (IN EVERY DIRECTION)**	Incentive CENT 3CD
26/08/2000	12	5	I CAN HEAR VOICES/CANED AND UNABLE	Incentive CENT 9CDS
07/04/2001	25	3	GONNA WORK IT OUT	Incentive CENT 20CDS

HI-GLOSS US studio disco group assembled by producer Giuliana Salerni and featuring Timmy Allen (bass), Kae Williams (keyboards) and the lead vocal of Phillip Ballou. Luther Vandross appeared as one of the background singers.

08/08/1981	12	13	YOU'LL NEVER KNOW	Epic EPC A 1387

HI-LUX UK instrumental/production duo.

18/02/1995	41	2	FEEL IT	Cheeky CHEKCD 006
02/09/1995	58	1	NEVER FELT THIS WAY/FEEL IT B-side re-issue of Cheeky CHEKCD 006	Champion CHAMPCD 319

HI POWER German rap group.

01/09/1990	73	1	CULT OF SNAP/SIMBA GROOVE	Rumour RUMAT 34

HI-TEK FEATURING JONELL US producer Tony Cottrell recording under an assumed name.

20/10/2001	73	1	ROUND & ROUND	Rawkus RWK 3432

HI-TEK 3 FEATURING YA KID K Belgian dance group assembled by producer/DJ Jo 'Thomas DeQuincy' Bogaert and rapper Manuella 'Ya Kid K' Komosi with MC Eric. Their videos feature model Felly. They also recorded as Hi-Tek 3 Featuring Technotronic.

03/02/1990	69	3	SPIN THAT WHEEL Featured in the 1990 film *Teenage Mutant Ninja Turtles*	Brothers Organisation BORG 1
29/09/1990	15	7	SPIN THAT WHEEL (TURTLES GET REAL) Re-issue of Brothers Organisation BORG 1	Brothers Organisation BORG 16

HI TENSION UK funk group formed as Hot Waxx by David Joseph (keyboards/vocals), Ken Joseph (bass/vocals), Paul Phillips (guitar/vocals), Leroy Williams (percussion), Jeff Guishard (percussion/lead vocals), Paul McLean (saxophone), David Reid (drums), Paapa Mensah (drums), Guy Barker (trumpet), Peter Thomas (trombone), Bob Sydor (saxophone) and Ray Alan Eko (saxophone). They changed their name to Hi Tension in 1977.

06/05/1978	13	12	HI TENSION	Island WIP 6422
12/08/1978	8	11	**BRITISH HUSTLE/PEACE ON EARTH**	Island WIP 6446

AL HIBBLER US singer (born 16/8/1915, Little Rock, AR) blind since birth. He made his first recordings in 1942 and was a one-time singer for the Duke Ellington Orchestra. He died on 24/4/2001. He has a star on the Hollywood Walk of Fame.

13/05/1955	2	17	**UNCHAINED MELODY** Song featured in the 1955 film *Unchained*	Brunswick 05420

HINDA HICKS UK singer (born Tunisia, raised West Sussex) discovered by producer Jazz Black who became her manager.

07/03/1998	25	3	IF YOU WANT ME Contains a sample of Kool & The Gang's *Too Hot*	Island CID 689
16/05/1998	19	4	YOU THINK YOU OWN ME	Island CID 700
15/08/1998	14	5	I WANNA BE YOUR LADY	Island CID 709
24/10/1998	31	2	TRULY	Island CID 721
14/10/2000	61	1	MY REMEDY	Island CID 765

HIDDEN CAMERAS Canadian rock group formed in Toronto by Joel Gibb (guitar/vocals), featuring up to 30 musicians, dancers and strippers. The usual line-up includes Gibb, Justin Stayshyn, Matias Rozenberg, Magali Meagher, Paul P and Alex McClelland.

14/03/2003 . . . . . 70 . . . . . . 1 . . . . A MIRACLE . . . . Rough Trade RTRADESCD 105

BERTIE HIGGINS US singer (born 8/12/1944, Tarpon Springs, FL) who worked as a drummer with Tommy Roe's backing group, The Roemans, between 1964 and 1968 and first recorded for ABC in 1964.

05/06/1982 . . . . . 60 . . . . . . 4 . . . . KEY LARGO . . . . Epic EPC A 2168

HIGH UK group formed in Manchester in 1987 by Andy Couzens (guitar), John Matthews (vocals), Simon Davies (bass) and Chris Goodwin (drums).

25/08/1990 . . . . . 53 . . . . . . 4				UP AND DOWN	London LON 272
27/10/1990 . . . . . 56 . . . . . . 2				TAKE YOUR TIME.	London LON 280

25/08/1990 . . . . . 53 . . . . . . 4 . . . . UP AND DOWN. . . . . London LON 272
27/10/1990 . . . . . 56 . . . . . . 2 . . . . TAKE YOUR TIME. . . . . London LON 280
12/01/1991 . . . . . 28 . . . . . . 3 . . . . BOX SET GO . . . . London LONG 286
06/04/1991 . . . . . 67 . . . . . . 2 . . . . MORE. . . . . London LON 297

HIGH CONTRAST UK drum and bass producer (born Lincoln Barrett, Cardiff).

01/06/2002 . . . . . 68 . . . . . . 1 . . . . GLOBAL LOVE Contains a sample of Antonio Carlos Jobim's *Agua De Beber* . . . . Hospital NHS 44CD
09/08/2003 . . . . . 65 . . . . . . 1 . . . . BASEMENT TRACK. . . . . Hospital NHS 60
26/06/2004 . . . . . 74 . . . . . . 1 . . . . TWILIGHTS LAST GLEAMING/MADE IT LAST . . . . Hospital NHS 73
18/09/2004 . . . . . 73 . . . . . . 1 . . . . RACING GREEN . . . . Hospital NHS 76

HIGH FIDELITY UK group formed by Sean Dickson (vocals), Paul Dallaway (guitar), Adrian Barry (bass) and Ross McFarlane (drums).

25/07/1998 . . . . . 70 . . . . . . 1 . . . . LUV DUP . . . . Plastique FAKE 03CDS

HIGH NUMBERS UK rock group formed in London in 1962 by Roger Daltrey (born 1/3/1944, London, vocals), Pete Townshend (born 19/5/1945, London, guitar), John Entwistle (born 9/10/1944, London, bass) and Doug Sandom (drums) as the Detours, changing their name to the High Numbers in 1964 and recruiting Keith Moon (born 23/8/1947, London) as drummer. In 1964 they changed their name to The Who – manager Kit Lambert thought that 'High Numbers' on a billboard would make people think it was a bingo session!

05/04/1980 . . . . . 49 . . . . . . 4 . . . . I'M THE FACE Originally released in 1964 . . . . Back Door DOOR 4

HIGH SOCIETY UK vocal/instrumental group.

15/11/1980 . . . . . 53 . . . . . . 4 . . . . I NEVER GO OUT IN THE RAIN . . . . Eagle ERS 002

HIGHLY LIKELY UK studio group.

21/04/1973 . . . . . 35 . . . . . . 4 . . . . WHATEVER HAPPENED TO YOU ('LIKELY LADS' THEME) Theme to the TV series *The Likely Lads* starring Rodney Bewes and James Bolan . . . . BBC RESL 10

HIGHWAYMEN US folk group formed in 1959 at the Wesleyan University in Connecticut by Dave Fisher, Bob Burnett, Steve Trott, Steve Butts and Chan Daniels. Daniels died on 2/8/1975.

07/09/1961 . . . ❶¹ . . . 14 . . . . . . **MICHAEL ▲²** . . . . HMV POP 910
07/12/1961 . . . . . 41 . . . . . . 4 . . . . . . GYPSY ROVER . . . . HMV POP 948

HIJACK UK rap group formed by Kamanchi Sly, DJ Supreme, DJ Undercover, Agent Cleuso, Agent Fritz and Ulysses.

06/01/1990 . . . . . 56 . . . . . . 3 . . . . . . THE BADMAN IS ROBBIN' . . . . Rhyme Syndicate 6555177

BENNY HILL UK singer/comedian (born Alfred Hawthorne Hill, 25/1/1924, Southampton); he made his name after World War II and had his own TV comedy show in the 1960s for the BBC. Switched to ITV in 1969. He died from a heart attack on 18/4/1992.

16/02/1961 . . . . . 12 . . . . . . 8 . . . . . . GATHER IN THE MUSHROOMS. . . . . Pye 7N 15327
01/06/1961 . . . . . 24 . . . . . . 6 . . . . . . TRANSISTOR RADIO . . . . Pye 7N 15359
16/05/1963 . . . . . 20 . . . . . . 8 . . . . . . HARVEST OF LOVE . . . . Pye 7N 15520
13/11/1971 . . . ❶⁴ . . . . 17 . . . . . . **ERNIE (THE FASTEST MILKMAN IN THE WEST)** . . . . Columbia DB 8833
30/05/1992 . . . . . 29 . . . . . . 4 . . . . . . ERNIE (THE FASTEST MILKMAN IN THE WEST) Re-issue of Columbia DB 8833 . . . . EMI ERN 1

CHRIS HILL UK DJ who later handled A&R for Ensign Records. His hits contain snippets of other hits of the era.

06/12/1975 . . . . . 10 . . . . . . 7 . . . . . . **RENTA SANTA** . . . . Philips 6006 491
04/12/1976 . . . . . 10 . . . . . . 7 . . . . . . **BIONIC SANTA** . . . . Philips 6006 551

DAN HILL Canadian singer (born 3/6/1954, Toronto), he released his first album in 1975. His hit was co-written with Barry Mann.

18/02/1978 . . . . . 13 . . . . . 13 . . . . . . SOMETIMES WHEN WE TOUCH Featured in the 1979 film *Moment By Moment* . . . . 20th Century BTC 2355

FAITH HILL US country singer (born Audrey Faith Perry Hill, 21/9/1967, Jackson, MS) who made her debut album in 1993, the same year she made her debut at the Grand Ol' Opry. She later launched the Faith Hill Family Literacy Project. Her touring group features Steve Hornbeak (keyboards), Anthony Joyner (bass), Tom Rutledge (guitar and fiddle), Karen Staley (guitar/vocals), Lou Toomey (guitar), Gary Carter (guitar) and Trey Grey (drums). Faith has won four Grammy Awards including Best Country Album for *Breathe* and Best Country Collaboration with Vocals with Tim McGraw for *Let's Make Love*.

14/11/1998 . . . . . 13 . . . . . 11 . . . . . . THIS KISS Featured in the 1999 film *Practical Magic* . . . . Warner Brothers W 463CD
17/04/1999 . . . . . 72 . . . . . . 1 . . . . . . LET ME LET GO Featured in the 1999 film *Message In A Bottle* . . . . Warner Brothers W 473CD
20/05/2000 . . . . . 33 . . . . . . 2 . . . . . . BREATHE 2000 Grammy Award for Best Female Country Vocal Performance . . . . WEA W 520CDX
21/04/2001 . . . . . 15 . . . . . . 5 . . . . . . THE WAY YOU LOVE ME . . . . WEA W 541CD1
30/06/2001 . . . . . . 3 . . . . . . 11 . . . . . . **THERE YOU'LL BE** Featured in the 2001 film *Pearl Harbor* . . . . Warner Brothers W 563CD

❶⁹ Number of weeks single topped the UK chart ↑ Entered the UK chart at #1 ▲⁹ Number of weeks single topped the US chart

365

13/10/2001	36	2		BREATHE (REMIX)	Warner Brothers W 572CD
26/10/2002	25	2		CRY 2002 Grammy Award for Best Female Country Vocal Performance	Warner Brothers W 593CD

LAURYN HILL
US rapper (born 25/5/1975, East Orange, NJ) who was a member of both The Fugees and the Refugee All Stars before going solo. Having won two Grammy Awards as a member of The Fugees, Lauryn has collected a further five awards as a solo artist including Album of the Year and Best Rhythm & Blues Album in 1998 for *The Miseducation Of Lauryn Hill* and Best New Artist in 1998. She also won the 1999 MOBO Award for Best International Act. She is married to Bob Marley's son Ziggy.

06/09/1997	18	4		THE SWEETEST THING REFUGEE ALLSTARS FEATURING LAURYN HILL Featured in the 1997 film *Love Jones*	Columbia 6649785
27/12/1997	57	1		ALL MY TIME PAID & LIVE FEATURING LAURYN HILL	One World Entertainment OWECD 2
03/10/1998	3	7	O	DOO WOP (THAT THING) ▲² 1998 Grammy Award for Best Female Rhythm & Blues Vocal Performance. The song won the Grammy Award for Best Rhythm & Blues Song for writer Lauryn Hill the same year	Ruffhouse 6665152
27/02/1999	4	10		EX-FACTOR Contains a sample of Wu-Tang Clan's *Can It All Be So Simple*	Columbia/Ruffhouse 6669452
10/07/1999	19	6		EVERYTHING IS EVERYTHING Featured in the 2001 film *Down To Earth*	Columbia/Ruffhouse 6675745
11/12/1999	15	7		TURN YOUR LIGHTS DOWN LOW BOB MARLEY FEATURING LAURYN HILL Featured in the 1999 film *The Best Man*	Columbia 6684362

LONNIE HILL
US singer (born Austin, TX) who first made his name as a gospel singer in The Gospel Keynotes before going solo.

22/03/1986	51	4		GALVESTON BAY	10 TEN 111

RONI HILL
US singer (born 1952, Baltimore, MD); she began singing with her mother in a gospel group. She later joined the All Maryland State Choir and then moved to Germany following her marriage to a GI.

07/05/1977	36	4		YOU KEEP ME HANGIN' ON – STOP IN THE NAME OF LOVE (MEDLEY)	Creole CR 138

VINCE HILL
UK singer (born 16/4/1937, Coventry) who trained as a baker and then became a soft drinks salesman while singing part-time. Formed The Raindrops in 1958 before going solo in 1962.

07/06/1962	41	2		THE RIVER'S RUN DRY	Piccadilly 7N 35043
06/01/1966	13	11		TAKE ME TO YOUR HEART AGAIN	Columbia DB 7781
17/03/1966	28	5		HEARTACHES	Columbia DB 7852
02/06/1966	36	6		MERCI CHERI	Columbia DB 7924
09/02/1967	2	17		EDELWEISS	Columbia DB 8127
11/05/1967	13	11		ROSES OF PICARDY	Columbia DB 8185
27/09/1967	23	9		LOVE LETTERS IN THE SAND	Columbia DB 8268
26/06/1968	32	12		IMPORTANCE OF YOUR LOVE	Columbia DB 8414
12/02/1969	50	1		DOESN'T ANYBODY KNOW MY NAME?	Columbia DB 8515
25/10/1969	42	1		LITTLE BLUE BIRD	Columbia DB 8616
25/09/1971	12	16		LOOK AROUND (AND YOU'LL FIND ME THERE)	Columbia DB 8804

HILLMAN MINX
UK/French vocal/instrumental group.

05/09/1998	72	1		I'VE HAD ENOUGH	Mercury MERCD 509

HILLTOPPERS
US vocal group formed in 1952 at the Western Kentucky College in Bowling Green by Jimmy Sacca, Don McGuire, Seymour Spiegelman and Billy Vaughn, taking their name from the school's nickname. Vaughn left in 1955 and was replaced by Chuck Schrouder. Spiegelman died in 1987, Vaughn on 26/9/1991.

27/01/1956	3	23		ONLY YOU	London HLD 8221
14/09/1956	30	1		TRYIN'	London HLD 8298
05/04/1957	20	6		MARIANNE	London HLD 8381

RONNIE HILTON
UK singer (born Adrian Hill, 26/1/1926, Hull) spotted by an A&R scout from HMV in 1950. After hair lip surgery and a name change to Ronnie Hilton in 1954 he became very popular. When his recording career ended he became a DJ at Radio Two, presenting the *Sounds of the Fifties*. But he suffered from depression and received several convictions for shoplifting. He died on 21/2/2001.

26/11/1954	3	14		I STILL BELIEVE	HMV B 10785
10/12/1954	12	8		VENI VIDI VICI B-side to *I Still Believe*	HMV B 10785
11/03/1955	10	5		A BLOSSOM FELL	HMV B 10808
26/08/1955	13	7		STARS SHINE IN YOUR EYES	HMV B 10901
11/11/1955	15	2		YELLOW ROSE OF TEXAS	HMV B 10924
10/02/1956	17	3		YOUNG AND FOOLISH	HMV POP 154
20/04/1956	❶⁶	14		NO OTHER LOVE	HMV POP 198
29/06/1956	6	12		WHO ARE WE	HMV POP 221
21/09/1956	30	1		WOMAN IN LOVE	HMV POP 248
09/11/1956	13	13		TWO DIFFERENT WORLDS	HMV POP 274
24/05/1957	4	18		AROUND THE WORLD	HMV POP 338
02/08/1957	27	2		WONDERFUL WONDERFUL	HMV POP 364
21/02/1958	22	2		MAGIC MOMENTS	HMV POP 446
18/04/1958	27	3		I MAY NEVER PASS THIS WAY AGAIN	HMV POP 468
09/01/1959	18	6		THE WORLD OUTSIDE This and above single credited to RONNIE HILTON WITH THE MICHAEL SAMMES SINGERS	HMV POP 559
21/08/1959	22	3		THE WONDER OF YOU	HMV POP 638
21/05/1964	21	10		DON'T LET THE RAIN COME DOWN	HMV POP 1291
11/02/1965	23	13		A WINDMILL IN OLD AMSTERDAM	HMV POP 1378

H.I.M. Finnish rock group formed in 1995 by Ville Valo (born Ville Hermanni Valo, 22/11/1976, vocals), Linde Lazer (born Mikko Lindstrom, 12/8/1976, guitar), Mige Amour (born Mikko Pannanen, 19/12/1974, bass), Zoltan Pluto (born Juska Salminen, 26/9/1976, keyboards) and Gas Lipstick (born Mikko Karppinen, 8/2/1971, drums). Pluto left in 2000 and was replaced by Emerson Burton (born Jani Purttinen, 17/10/1974). Their name stands for His Infernal Majesty.

17/05/2003	30	2		BURIED ALIVE BY LOVE	RCA 82876523182
20/09/2003	23	2		THE SACREMENT	RCA 82876558892
24/01/2004	15	4		THE FUNERAL OF HEARTS	RCA 82876585792
08/05/2004	9	4		**SOLITARY MAN**	RCA 82876610652

HINDSIGHT UK vocal/instrumental group formed by Camelle Hinds, Henri Defoe and Paul 'Groucho' Smykle.

| 05/09/1987 | 62 | 3 | | LOWDOWN | Circa YR 5 |

DENI HINES Australian R&B singer who began her career as singer with The Rock Melons before going solo in 1996.

14/06/1997	35	2		IT'S ALRIGHT	Mushroom D 1593
20/09/1997	37	2		I LIKE THE WAY	Mushroom MUSH 7CDX
28/02/1998	52	1		DELICIOUS **DENI HINES FEATURING DON-E**	Mushroom MUSH 20CD
23/05/1998	47	1		JOY	Mushroom MUSH 30CDS

GREGORY HINES – see **LUTHER VANDROSS**

HIPSWAY UK group formed by Graham Skinner (vocals), John McElhone (bass), Pim Jones (guitar) and Harry Travers (drums). McElhone was an ex-member of Altered Images and later joined Texas.

13/07/1985	72	3		THE BROKEN YEARS	Mercury MER 193
14/09/1985	72	1		ASK THE LORD	Mercury MER 195
22/02/1986	17	9		THE HONEYTHIEF	Mercury MER 212
10/05/1986	50	5		ASK THE LORD Re-recording	Mercury LORD 1
20/09/1986	55	2		LONG WHITE CAR	Mercury MER 230
01/04/1989	66	1		YOUR LOVE	Mercury MER 279

HISS US rock group formed in Atlanta, GA by Adrian Barrera (guitar/vocals), Ian Franco (guitar), Mahjula Bah-Kamara (bass) and Todd Galpin (drums).

01/03/2003	53	1		TRIUMPH	Polydor 0657782
09/08/2003	49	1		CLEVER KICKS	Polydor 9809462
15/11/2003	65	1		BACK ON THE RADIO	Polydor 9813415

HISTORY FEATURING Q-TEE UK production duo with female rapper Q-Tee.

| 21/04/1990 | 42 | 5 | | AFRIKA | SBK 7008 |

CAROL HITCHCOCK Australian singer (born in Melbourne) who also made her name as a model and actress.

| 30/05/1987 | 56 | 5 | | GET READY | A&M AM 391 |

HITHOUSE Dutch producer Peter Slaghuis recording under an assumed group name.

| 05/11/1988 | 14 | 12 | | JACK TO THE SOUND OF THE UNDERGROUND | Supreme SUPE 137 |
| 19/08/1989 | 69 | 1 | | MOVE YOUR FEET TO THE RHYTHM OF THE BEAT | Supreme SUPE 149 |

HITMAN HOWIE TEE – see **REAL ROXANNE**

HIVES Swedish rock group formed in Fagersta in 1993 by Vigilante Carlstroem, Dr Matt Destruction, Howlin' Pelle Almqvist, Chris Dangerous and Nicholaus Arson, originally signing with Burning Heart in 1995.

23/02/2002	23	3		HATE TO SAY I TOLD YOU SO	Burning Heart BHR 1059
18/05/2002	24	2		MAIN OFFENDER	Poptones MC 5076SCD
17/07/2004	13	9		WALK IDIOT WALK	Polydor 9867038
30/10/2004	44	1		TWO TIMING TOUCH AND BROKEN BONES	Polydor 9868351

HELEN HOBSON – see **CLIFF RICHARD**

EDMUND HOCKRIDGE Canadian singer (born 9/8/1923, Vancouver, Canada) who first visited the UK while serving in the Canadian Air Force in 1941. He returned in 1951 as a singer and made regular appearances on stage and TV.

17/02/1956	10	9		**YOUNG AND FOOLISH**	Nixa N 15039
11/05/1956	24	4		NO OTHER LOVE	Nixa N 15048
31/08/1956	17	5		BY THE FOUNTAINS OF ROME	Pye Nixa N 15063

EDDIE HODGES US singer (born 5/3/1947, Hattiesburg, MS) and noted actor, appearing in *A Hole In Your Head*, *Johnny Shiloh* and *The Happiest Millionaire*.

| 28/09/1961 | 37 | 6 | | I'M GONNA KNOCK ON YOUR DOOR | London HLA 9369 |
| 09/08/1962 | 37 | 4 | | MADE TO LOVE (GIRLS GIRLS GIRLS) | London HLA 9576 |

ROGER HODGSON – see **SUPERTRAMP**

❶[9] Number of weeks single topped the UK chart   ↑ Entered the UK chart at #1   ▲[9] Number of weeks single topped the US chart

367

MANI HOFFMAN – see SUPERMEN LOVERS FEATURING MANI HOFFMAN

SUSANNA HOFFS US singer (born 17/1/1957, Newport Beach, CA); she was lead singer with Bangles from 1981 until they disbanded in 1989. She appeared in the films *The Allnighter* and *Austin Powers: International Man Of Mystery* (her husband M Jay Roach was the film's director).

02/03/1991	44	4	MY SIDE OF THE BED	Columbia 6565547
11/05/1991	65	2	UNCONDITIONAL LOVE	Columbia 6567827
19/10/1996	32	2	ALL I WANT	London LONCD 387

HULK HOGAN WITH GREEN JELLY US wrestler/singer (born Terry Bollea) with US comedy group Green Jelly.

25/12/1993	25	4	I'M THE LEADER OF THE GANG	Arista 74321174892

HOGGBOY UK group formed in Sheffield in 2000 by Hogg (guitar/vocals), Hugh (guitar), Bailey (bass) and Richy (drums).

27/04/2002	74	1	SHOULDN'T LET THE SIDE DOWN	Sobriety SOB 4CDA

DEMI HOLBORN UK singer from Pontypool, South Wales, discovered after a talent contest organised by GMTV, *Totstars*. Demi is a Junior Associate of the Royal Ballet and at ten-years-and-one-month-old at the time of the hit she became the youngest female to have had a UK top 40 hit single, beating Lena Zavaroni by three months.

27/07/2002	27	2	I'D LIKE TO TEACH THE WORLD TO SING	Universal Classics & Jazz 0190982

HOLDEN AND THOMPSON UK duo James Holden and Julie Thompson.

17/05/2003	51	1	NOTHING	Loaded LOAD 98CD

HOLE US rock group formed by Courtney Love (born Love Michelle Harrison, 9/7/1965, San Francisco, CA, guitar/vocals), Caroline Rue (drums), Jill Emery (bass) and Eric Erlandson (born 9/1/1963, Los Angeles, CA, guitar). Emery and Rue left in 1992 and were replaced by Kristen Pfaff (bass) and Patty Schemel (born 24/4/1967, Seattle, WA, drums); Pfaff died from a heroin overdose shortly after and was replaced by Melissa Auf Der Maur (born 17/3/1972, Montreal, Canada). Schemel left and was replaced by Samantha Maloney. Auf Der Maur left to join the Smashing Pumpkins. Courtney Love, widow of Nirvana's Kurt Cobain, became an actress, appearing in *Man On The Moon* and *The People Versus Larry Flint*. In September 2001 she sued Universal Music Group and the surviving members of Nirvana (Dave Grohl and Krist Novoselic) seeking to get all rights to their recordings. In June that year she had sued Grohl and Novoselic seeking the dissolution of Nirvana LLC, a company that had split the group's rights among the three parties. She had been successful in getting the release of *You Know You're Right* on a box set blocked, claiming the track was not crucial to the set's success. These suits were in conjunction with her own action against UMG in which she claimed her contract with Geffen Records was terminated once the label was sold to UMG. She also claimed UMG had withheld $3.1 million in royalties relating to Nirvana. Hole disbanded in May 2002.

17/04/1993	54	1	BEAUTIFUL SON	City Slang EFA 0491603
09/04/1994	64	1	MISS WORLD	City Slang EFA 049362
15/04/1995	16	3	DOLL PARTS	Geffen GFSXD 91
29/07/1995	17	2	VIOLET	Geffen GFSTD 94
12/09/1998	19	4	CELEBRITY SKIN Featured in the 1999 film *American Pie*	Geffen GFSTD 22345
30/01/1999	22	2	MALIBU	Geffen GFSTD 22369
10/07/1999	42	2	AWFUL	Geffen INTDE 97098

HOLE IN ONE Dutch DJ and producer Marcel Hol.

15/02/1997	36	2	LIFE'S TOO SHORT	Manifesto FESCD 21

HOLIDAY PLAN UK rock group formed in London by Matt Rider (vocals), Blue Quinn (guitar/vocals), Gary Jenkins (guitar) and Daniel Bodie (drums).

26/06/2004	58	1	STORIES/SUNSHINE	Island CID 858

JOOLS HOLLAND AND JAMIROQUAI UK singer/pianist (born Julian Holland, 24/1/1958, London); he was a founder member of Squeeze in 1974 and left in 1980 to form the Millionaires with Mike Paice (saxophone), Pino Palladino (bass) and Martin Deegan (drums). He went solo in 1983 and combined this with TV work, becoming one of the presenters of *The Tube*. He rejoined Squeeze in 1985 and remained until 1990. He hosted his own TV series *Later* and formed the Rhythm & Blues Orchestra in 1994 as well as recording with Jamiroquai later. He was awarded an OBE in the Queen's 2003 Birthday Honours List.

24/02/2001	29	3	I'M IN THE MOOD FOR LOVE	warner.esp WSMS 001CD

HOLLAND-DOZIER FEATURING LAMONT DOZIER US songwriting/production trio formed by Eddie Holland (born 30/10/1939, Detroit, MI), his brother Brian (born 15/2/1941, Detroit) and Lamont Dozier (born 16/6/1941, Detroit), Tamla Motown's most successful songwriting partnership, penning *Baby Love* and *Reach Out I'll Be There* among countless hits for the Four Tops and Supremes. They left the label in 1968 amid a welter of lawsuits, but established the Invictus and Hot Wax labels. It is believed they wrote under pseudonyms at Invictus, including Edith Wayne and Ronald Dunbar, while their legal battle with Motown was going on. Dozier later recorded solo. They were inducted into the Rock & Roll Hall of Fame in 1990. Dozier, with Phil Collins, won the 1988 Grammy Award for Best Song Written Specifically for a Motion Picture, for *Two Hearts* from the film *Buster*.

28/10/1972	29	5	WHY CAN'T WE BE LOVERS	Invtictus INV 525

JENNIFER HOLLIDAY US singer (born 19/10/1960, Riverside, TX) who appeared in the Broadway musical *Dreamgirls* (loosely based on the Supremes story). She has two Grammy Awards including Best Inspirational Performance in 1985 for *Come Sunday*.

04/09/1982	32	6	AND I'M TELLING YOU I'M NOT GOING From the musical *Dreamgirls*. 1982 Grammy Award for Best Rhythm & Blues Vocal Performance	Geffen GEF A 2644

○ Silver disc ● Gold disc ✪ Platinum disc (additional platinum units are indicated by a figure following the symbol) ⊚ Singles released prior to 1973 that are known to have sold over 1 million copies in the UK

MICHAEL HOLLIDAY
UK singer (born Norman Michael Milne, 26/11/1925, Liverpool) who began singing in the Royal Navy. He won a talent contest in New York and returned to Liverpool to launch a professional career, adopting his mother's maiden name as his stage name. He had his own TV show in 1956, *Relax With Mike*, and later appeared in the film *Life Is A Circus*. Dubbed 'The British Bing Crosby', he was unable to cope once the hits dried up and committed suicide by overdosing on drugs on 29/10/1963.

30/03/1956	20	3		NOTHIN' TO DO	Columbia DB 3746
15/06/1956	13	6		GAL WITH THE YALLER SHOES	Columbia DB 3783
22/06/1956	14	8		HOT DIGGITY (DOG DIGGITY BOOM) B-side to *Gal With The Yaller Shoes*	Columbia DB 3783
05/10/1956	24	3		TEN THOUSAND MILES	Columbia DB 3813
17/01/1958	❶²	15		**THE STORY OF MY LIFE**	Columbia DB 4058
14/03/1958	26	3		IN LOVE	Columbia DB 4087
16/05/1958	3	13		**STAIRWAY OF LOVE**	Columbia DB 4121
11/07/1958	27	1		I'LL ALWAYS BE IN LOVE WITH YOU	Columbia DB 4155
01/01/1960	❶¹	13		**STARRY EYED** MICHAEL HOLLIDAY WITH THE MICHAEL SAMMES SINGERS	Columbia DB 4378
14/04/1960	39	3		SKYLARK	Columbia DB 4437
01/09/1960	50	1		LITTLE BOY LOST	Columbia DB 4475

HOLLIES
UK group formed in Manchester in 1961 by Allan Clarke (born Harold Allan Clarke, 5/4/1942, Salford, vocals), Graham Nash (born 2/2/1942, Blackpool, guitar), Eric Haydock (born 3/2/1943, Stockport, bass) and Don Rathbone (drums) as the Fourtones. They added another guitarist and changed their name to the Deltas, then settled on the Hollies in 1962. As the second guitarist did not want to turn professional he was replaced by Tony Hicks (born 16/12/1943, Nelson) in 1963; Rathbone moved to management and was replaced by Bobby Elliott (born 8/12/1942, Burnley). Made their first record in 1963 for Parlophone. Haydock left in 1966 and was replaced by Bernie Calvert (born 16/9/1942, Brierfield). Nash left in 1968 to link up with David Crosby and Stephen Stills, and Terry Sylvester (born 8/1/1945, Liverpool) replaced him. Nash, Hicks, Clarke, Elliott and Haydock reunited in 1982, with all but Haydock recording together in 1983.

30/05/1963	25	10		(AIN'T THAT) JUST LIKE ME	Parlophone R 5030
29/08/1963	12	14		SEARCHIN'	Parlophone R 5052
21/11/1963	8	16		**STAY**	Parlophone R 5077
27/02/1964	2	13		**JUST ONE LOOK** Featured in the 1988 film *Buster*	Parlophone R 5104
21/05/1964	4	12		**HERE I GO AGAIN**	Parlophone R 5137
17/09/1964	7	11		**WE'RE THROUGH**	Parlophone R 5178
28/01/1965	9	13		**YES I WILL**	Parlophone R 5232
27/05/1965	❶³	14		**I'M ALIVE** Reclaimed #1 position on 8/7/1965	Parlophone R 5287
02/09/1965	4	11		**LOOK THROUGH ANY WINDOW**	Parlophone R 5322
09/12/1965	20	9		IF I NEEDED SOMEONE	Parlophone R 5392
24/02/1966	2	10		**I CAN'T LET GO**	Parlophone R 5409
23/06/1966	5	9		**BUS STOP**	Parlophone R 5469
13/10/1966	2	12		**STOP STOP STOP**	Parlophone R 5508
16/02/1967	4	11		**ON A CAROUSEL**	Parlophone R 5562
01/06/1967	3	11		**CARRIE-ANNE**	Parlophone R 5602
27/09/1967	18	8		KING MIDAS IN REVERSE	Parlophone R 5637
27/03/1968	7	11		**JENNIFER ECCLES**	Parlophone R 5680
02/10/1968	11	11		LISTEN TO ME	Parlophone R 5733
05/03/1969	3	12		**SORRY SUZANNE**	Parlophone R 5765
04/10/1969	3	15		**HE AIN'T HEAVY, HE'S MY BROTHER**	Parlophone R 5806
18/04/1970	7	10		**I CAN'T TELL THE BOTTOM FROM THE TOP**	Parlophone R 5837
03/10/1970	14	7		GASOLINE ALLEY BRED	Parlophone R 5862
22/05/1971	22	7		HEY WILLY	Parlophone R 5905
26/02/1972	26	6		THE BABY	Polydor 2058 199
02/09/1972	32	8		LONG COOL WOMAN IN A BLACK DRESS Featured in the 2000 Walt Disney film *Remember The Titans*	Parlophone R 5939
13/10/1973	24	6		THE DAY THAT CURLY BILLY SHOT DOWN CRAZY SAM MCGHEE	Polydor 2058 403
09/02/1974	2	13	○	**THE AIR THAT I BREATHE**	Polydor 2058 435
14/06/1980	58	3		SOLDIER'S SONG	Polydor 2059 246
29/08/1981	28	7		HOLLIEDAZE (MEDLEY)	EMI 5229
03/09/1988	❶²	11	○	**HE AIN'T HEAVY, HE'S MY BROTHER** Re-issue of Parlophone R 5806, revived after use in a Miller Lite Beer advertisement	EMI EM 74
03/12/1988	60	5		THE AIR THAT I BREATHE Re-issue of Polydor 2058 435	EMI EM 80
20/03/1993	42	2		THE WOMAN I LOVE	EMI CDEM 264

LOLEATTA HOLLOWAY
US singer (born 5/11/1946, Chicago, IL) who made her first solo recording in 1971 and signed with Salsoul in 1976. She worked with producers Norman Harris and Dan Hartman, with her track *Love Sensation* (1983) being utilised by Black Box for their #1 hit *Ride On Time*.

31/08/1991	14	7		GOOD VIBRATIONS ▲¹ MARKY MARK AND THE FUNKY BUNCH FEATURING LOLEATTA HOLLOWAY	Interscope A 8764
18/01/1992	25	5		TAKE ME AWAY CAPPELLA FEATURING LOLEATTA HOLLOWAY	PWL Continental PWL 210
26/03/1994	68	1		STAND UP	Six6 SIXCD 111
01/04/1995	49	1		KEEP THE FIRE BURNIN' DAN HARTMAN STARRING LOLEATTA HOLLOWAY	Columbia 6611552

❶⁹ Number of weeks single topped the UK chart ↑ Entered the UK chart at #1 ▲⁹ Number of weeks single topped the US chart

	11/04/1998	23	2		SHOUT TO THE TOP FIRE ISLAND FEATURING LOLEATTA HOLLOWAY	JBO JNR 5001573
	20/02/1999	14	4		(YOU GOT ME) BURNING UP CEVIN FISHER FEATURING LOLEATTA HOLLOWAY	Wonderboy BOYD 013
	25/11/2000	59	1		DREAMIN'	Defected DFECT 22CDS

HOLLOWAY & CO UK producer Nicky Holloway.

	21/08/1999	58	1		I'LL DO ANYTHING – TO MAKE YOU MINE	INCredible INCS 2CD

BUDDY HOLLY US singer (born Charles Hardin Holley, 7/9/1936, Lubbock, TX) who began his career recording country music until the success of Elvis Presley dictated a musical change. He formed a duo with Bob Montgomery and recorded a number of demos as Buddy and Bob (with Larry Welborn on bass), with Decca expressing interest in signing Holly as a solo artist. Holly formed a new band with Sonny Curtis and Don Guess, touring as Buddy Holly & The Two-Tunes (recordings of this time later appeared as Buddy Holly & The Three-Tunes: drummer Jerry Allison having joined the line-up). In February 1957 Buddy gathered The Crickets (Allison, Niki Sullivan and Joe B Maudlin) to re-record *That'll Be The Day*, the success of which landed Holly a solo deal with Coral, a subsidiary of the Brunswick label the Crickets recorded for. He split with the Crickets in 1958 and thereafter recorded solo. On 3/2/1959 he, Ritchie Valens and the Big Bopper were killed when their plane crashed near Mason City, IA. It was later reported that the crash was due to pilot error: after a successful take-off, pilot Roger Peterson experienced vertigo and flew straight into the ground. Buddy Holly was inducted into the Rock & Roll Hall of Fame in 1986.

	06/12/1957	6	17		PEGGY SUE Featured in the 1978 film *The Buddy Holly Story*	Coral Q 72293
	14/03/1958	16	2		LISTEN TO ME	Coral Q 72288
	20/06/1958	5	14		RAVE ON Featured in the 1978 films *The Buddy Holly Story* and *American Hot Wax*	Coral Q 72325
	29/08/1958	17	4		EARLY IN THE MORNING Originally written and recorded by Bobby Darin under the pseudonym Rinky Dinks	Coral Q 72333
	16/01/1959	30	1		HEARTBEAT	Coral Q 72346
	27/02/1959	❶³	21		IT DOESN'T MATTER ANYMORE Posthumous #1	Coral Q 72360
	31/07/1959	26	3		MIDNIGHT SHIFT	Brunswick 05800
	11/09/1959	13	10		PEGGY SUE GOT MARRIED	Coral Q 72376
	28/04/1960	30	3		HEARTBEAT Re-issue of Coral Q 72346	Coral Q 72392
	26/05/1960	25	7		TRUE LOVE WAYS Featured in the 1978 film *The Buddy Holly Story*	Coral Q 72397
	20/10/1960	36	3		LEARNIN' THE GAME	Coral Q 72411
	09/02/1961	34	6		WHAT TO DO	Coral Q 72419
	06/07/1961	12	14		BABY I DON'T CARE/VALLEY OF TEARS	Coral Q 72432
	15/03/1962	48	1		LISTEN TO ME	Coral Q 72449
	13/09/1962	17	11		REMINISCING	Coral Q 72455
	14/03/1963	3	17		BROWN-EYED HANDSOME MAN	Coral Q 72459
	06/06/1963	4	12		BO DIDDLEY	Coral Q 72463
	05/09/1963	10	11		WISHING	Coral Q 72466
	19/12/1963	27	8		WHAT TO DO	Coral Q 72469
	14/05/1964	40	6		YOU'VE GOT LOVE BUDDY HOLLY AND THE CRICKETS	Coral Q 72472
	10/09/1964	39	6		LOVE'S MADE A FOOL OF YOU	Coral Q 72475
	03/04/1968	32	9		PEGGY SUE/RAVE ON	MCA MU 1012
	10/12/1988	65	4		TRUE LOVE WAYS Re-issue of Coral Q 72397	MCA 1302

HOLLY AND THE IVYS UK studio group who made a medley record similar in style to Star Sound, with a Christmas theme.

	19/12/1981	40	4		CHRISTMAS ON 45	Decca SANTA 1

HOLLYWOOD ARGYLES US singer Gary Paxton; signed to Brent Records, he recorded the chart hit solo and made up the name Hollywood Argyles (the studio was based on Hollywood Boulevard and Argyle Street) for the single released by Lute Records. This led to the creation of a group featuring Paxton, Bobby Rey, Ted Marsh, Gary Webb, Deary Weaver and Ted Winters.

	21/07/1960	24	10		ALLEY OOP ▲¹	London HLU 9146

HOLLYWOOD BEYOND UK group formed in Birmingham by Mark Rogers and Jamie B Rose. Rogers later recorded solo.

	12/07/1986	7	10		WHAT'S THE COLOUR OF MONEY?	WEA YZ 76
	20/09/1986	47	4		NO MORE TEARS	WEA YZ 81

EDDIE HOLMAN US singer (born 3/6/1946, Norfolk, VA) who recorded for Leopard in the early 1960s and later for Salsoul. He recorded gospel material in 1985.

	19/10/1974	4	13	O	(HEY THERE) LONELY GIRL Originally recorded by Ruby & The Romantics in 1963 as *Hey There Lonely Boy*. Holman's version became a US hit in 1970	ABC 4012

DAVE HOLMES UK producer (born Mustepha Alici) who also records as Alici, Clubbers Delight, DJ Alici, Steve Morley and Underground Nation of Rotterdam.

	16/05/2001	66	1		DEVOTION	Tidy Trax TIDY 154CD

DAVID HOLMES UK singer (born 14/2/1969, Belfast) who also recorded as The Disco Evangelists and Death Before Disco and is a member of Free Association. He runs the clubs Sugar Sweet and Exploding Plastic Inevitable.

	06/04/1996	75	1		GONE	Go Discs GODCD 140
	23/08/1997	53	1		GRITTY SHAKER	Go Beat GOBCD 2
	10/01/1998	33	3		DON'T DIE JUST YET	Go Beat GOLCD 6
	04/04/1998	39	2		MY MATE PAUL	Go Beat GOBCD 8

O Silver disc ● Gold disc ✪ Platinum disc (additional platinum units are indicated by a figure following the symbol) ◎ Singles released prior to 1973 that are known to have sold over 1 million copies in the UK

19/08/2000 . . . . . 53 . . . . . . 1 . . . . 69 POLICE . . . . Go Beat GOBCD 30

RUPERT HOLMES US singer (born 24/2/1947, Cheshire, to Anglo-American parents; moved to New York at the age of six) who began his career as a songwriter (penning numbers for the Drifters, Platters and Gene Pitney) and session singer with Street People and Cufflinks before launching his own career in 1974.

12/01/1980 . . . . . 23 . . . . . . 7 . . . . ESCAPE (THE PINA COLADA SONG) ▲³ Featured in the films *The Sweetest Thing* (2002) and *American Splendor* (2003). . . . .
. . . . Infinity INF 120

22/03/1980 . . . . . 31 . . . . . . 7 . . . . HIM . . . . MCA 565

ADELE HOLNESS – see BEN SHAW FEATURING ADELE HOLNESS

JOHN HOLT Jamaican reggae singer (born 1947, Kingston); he originally recorded with the Paragons, leaving them in the late 1960s to go solo (although he had first recorded solo in 1963 with *I Cried A Tear* for the Beverley label).

14/12/1974 . . . . . . 6 . . . . . . 14 . . . . . . **HELP ME MAKE IT THROUGH THE NIGHT** . . . . Trojan TR 7909

NICHOLA HOLT UK singer (born 1971, Bolton) who first came to prominence as a contestant on TV's *Big Brother*, the series won by fellow hitmaker Craig Phillips.

21/10/2000 . . . . . 72 . . . . . . 1 . . . . THE GAME . . . . RCA 74321798992

PAUL HOLT UK singer based in Manchester who first came to prominence on the TV show *The X-Factor*. Panelist Simon Cowell told him 'You get a record deal, get a No1 single and I'll give you £50,000 myself.'

18/12/2004 . . . . . 35 . . . . . . 2+ . . . . . . FIFTY GRAND FOR CHRISTMAS . . . . Sanctuary SANXS348

A HOMEBOY, A HIPPIE AND A FUNKI DREDD UK vocal/instrumental group that featured Caspar Pound, the founder of Rising High Records as The Hippie and who also recorded as Hypnotist.

13/10/1990 . . . . . 56 . . . . . . 3 . . . . . . TOTAL CONFUSION . . . . Tam Tam 7TTT 031

29/12/1990 . . . . . 68 . . . . . . 4 . . . . . . FREEDOM . . . . Tam Tam 7TTT 039

08/01/1994 . . . . . 57 . . . . . . 2 . . . . . . HERE WE GO AGAIN . . . . Polydor PZCD 302

HONDY Italian dance group featuring Gabriello Rinaldi (vocals), Sergio Della Monica (keyboards), Dada Canu (keyboards) and Andro Sommella (keyboards).

12/04/1997 . . . . . 26 . . . . . . 2 . . . . HONDY (NO ACCESS) . . . . Manifesto FESCD 20

HONEYBUS UK pop group comprising Pete Dello (born Peter Blumson), Ray Cane, Colin Hare and Pete Kircher. Dello recorded the single solo with the group put together following its success. Dello later returned to teaching and is currently a music teacher in Wembley.

20/03/1968 . . . . . . 8 . . . . . . 12 . . . . . . **I CAN'T LET MAGGIE GO** Track subsequently used as an advertisement for Nimble bread . . . . Deram DM 182

HONEYCOMBS UK pop group formed in 1963 by Martin Murray (born 7/10/1941, lead guitar), Alan Ward (born 12/12/1945, rhythm guitar), John Lantree (born 20/8/1940, bass), Dennis D'Ell (born 10/10/1943, vocals) and Ann Lantree (born 28/8/1940, drums). Their name was derived from Ann's nickname (Honey) and her profession (hairdresser).

23/07/1964 . . . . ❶² . . . . . 15 . . . . . . **HAVE I THE RIGHT** . . . . Pye 7N 15664

22/10/1964 . . . . . 38 . . . . . . 6 . . . . IS IT BECAUSE . . . . Pye 7N 15705

29/04/1965 . . . . . 39 . . . . . . 4 . . . . SOMETHING BETTER BEGINNING . . . . Pye 7N 15827

05/08/1965 . . . . . 12 . . . . . 14 . . . . . . THAT'S THE WAY . . . . Pye 7N 15890

HONEYCRACK UK rock group formed in August 1994 by CJ (born Chris Jagdhar, guitar/vocals), Mark McRae (guitar), Pete Clark (bass), Willie Dowling (keyboards) and Hugh Degenhardt (drums). They disbanded in 1997.

04/11/1995 . . . . . 42 . . . . . . 2 . . . . . . SITTING AT HOME . . . . Epic 6625382

24/02/1996 . . . . . 41 . . . . . . 2 . . . . . . GO AWAY . . . . Epic 6628642

11/05/1996 . . . . . 32 . . . . . . 2 . . . . . . KING OF MISERY . . . . Epic 6631475

20/07/1996 . . . . . 32 . . . . . . 2 . . . . . . SITTING AT HOME . . . . Epic 6635032

16/11/1996 . . . . . 67 . . . . . . 1 . . . . . . ANYWAY . . . . EG EGO 52A

HONEYDRIPPERS UK/US group formed in 1984 by Robert Plant (born 20/8/1948, West Bromwich, lead vocals), Jimmy Page (born 9/1/1944, Heston, guitar), Nile Rodgers (born 19/9/1952, New York, bass) and Jeff Beck (born 24/6/1944, Wallington, guitar), with Tony Thompson on drums. Page and Plant were ex-members of Led Zeppelin, Rodgers and Thompson were ex-Chic and Beck was with The Yardbirds, having also enjoyed a solo career. The project was abandoned after one album.

02/02/1985 . . . . . 56 . . . . . . 3 . . . . SEA OF LOVE . . . . Es Paranza YZ 33

HONEYZ UK vocal group formed by Heavenli Abdi, Celena Cherry (born 26/4/1977, London) and Naima Belkhaiti (born 4/12/1973, Avignon, France). Heavenli left in early 1999 and was replaced by ex-Solid HarmoniE singer Mariama Goodman (born 25/12/1977, London). By August 2000 Heavenli returned. Celena later linked with ex-Kleshay member Alani Gibbon to form Anotherside.

05/09/1998 . . . . . . 4 . . . . . . 12 . . . . . O **FINALLY FOUND** . . . . 1ˢᵗ Avenue HNZCD 1

19/12/1998 . . . . . . 5 . . . . . . 14 . . . . . O **END OF THE LINE** . . . . 1ˢᵗ Avenue HNZCD 2

24/04/1999 . . . . . . 9 . . . . . . 9 . . . . . . **LOVE OF A LIFETIME** . . . . 1ˢᵗ Avenue HNZCD 3

23/10/1999 . . . . . . 7 . . . . . . 6 . . . . . . **NEVER LET YOU DOWN** . . . . 1ˢᵗ Avenue HNZCD 4

11/03/2000 . . . . . . 7 . . . . . . 8 . . . . . . **WON'T TAKE IT LYING DOWN** . . . . 1ˢᵗ Avenue HNZCD 5

28/10/2000 . . . . . 24 . . . . . . 5 . . . . . . NOT EVEN GONNA TRIP Featured in the 2000 film *The Nutty Professor II: The Klumps*. . . . . 1ˢᵗ Avenue HNZDD 7

18/08/2001 . . . . . 28 . . . . . . 3 . . . . . . I DON'T KNOW . . . . 1ˢᵗ Avenue HNZDD 8

❶⁹ Number of weeks single topped the UK chart ↑ Entered the UK chart at #1 ▲⁹ Number of weeks single topped the US chart

371

HONKY
UK disco group formed by Cliff Barks, Malcolm Baggott, Trevor Cummins, Clark Newton, Ray Othen, Ron Taylor and Bob White.

04/06/1977.....28......5.......	JOIN THE PARTY .... Creole CR 137

HONKY
UK vocal/instrumental group.

30/10/1993.....61......1.......	THE HONKY DOODLE DAY EP Tracks on EP: *KKK (Boom Boom Tra La La La)*, *Honky Doodle Dub* and *Chains* .... ZTT ZANG 45CD
19/02/1994.....41......2.......	THE WHISTLER .... ZTT ZANG 48CD
20/04/1996.....70......1.......	HIP HOP DON'T YA DROP .... Higher Ground HIGHS 1CD
10/08/1996.....49......1.......	WHAT'S GOIN' DOWN Contains a sample of Ian Dury's *Sex And Drugs And Rock And Roll* .... Higher Ground HIGHS 2CD

HOOBASTANK
US rock group formed in Agoura Hills, CA in 1994 by Douglas Robb (vocals), Dan Estrin (guitar), Markku Lappalainen (bass) and Chris Hesse (drums).

13/04/2002.....47......2.......	CRAWLING IN THE DARK .... Mercury 5828622
12/06/2004.....12......7.......	THE REASON .... Mercury 9862567

PETER HOOK – see HYBRID

FRANKIE HOOKER AND POSITIVE PEOPLE
US vocal/instrumental group formed in Washington DC and discovered by label executive Cory Robbins. Frankie Hooker was born in Brooklyn, NY.

05/07/1980.....48......4.......	THIS FEELIN' .... DJM DJS 10947

JOHN LEE HOOKER
US singer/guitarist (born 22/8/1917, Clarksdale, MS) who was taught to play the guitar by his grandfather. Made his debut recording in 1948 and was still recording in the 1990s with his *Mr Lucky* album making him the oldest artist to have reached the top three of the charts (he was 74 at the time). He was inducted into the Rock & Roll Hall of Fame in 1991. He won four Grammy Awards: Best Traditional Blues Recording in 1989 with Bonnie Raitt for *I'm In The Mood*, Best Traditional Blues Album in 1995 for *Chill Out*, Best Pop Collaboration with Vocals in 1997 with Van Morrison for *Don't Look Back* and Best Traditional Blues Album in 1997 for *Don't Look Back*. John Lee Hooker died on 21/6/2001. He has a star on the Hollywood Walk of Fame.

11/06/1964.....23.....10......	DIMPLES.. Stateside SS 297
24/10/1992.....16......5......	BOOM BOOM Originally a US hit in 1962 (position #60). Featured in the 1999 film *Play It To The Bone* .... Pointblank POB 3
16/01/1993.....53......2......	BOOGIE AT RUSSIAN HILL .... Pointblank POBDX 4
15/05/1993.....31......3......	GLORIA VAN MORRISON AND JOHN LEE HOOKER .... Exile VANCD 11
11/02/1995.....45......2......	CHILL OUT (THINGS GONNA CHANGE) .... Pointblank POBD 10
20/04/1996.....65......1......	BABY LEE JOHN LEE HOOKER WITH ROBERT CRAY.. Silvertone ORECD 81

HOOTERS
US rock group formed in Philadelphia, PA by Rob Hyman (keyboards/vocals), Eric Bazilian (guitar/vocals), John Lilley (guitar), Andy King (bass) and David Uosikkinen (drums). King left in 1989 and was replaced by Fran Smith Jr.

21/11/1987.....22......9.......	SATELLITE .... CBS 6511687

HOOTIE AND THE BLOWFISH
US rock group formed at the University of South Carolina by Darius Rycker (vocals), Mark Bryan (guitar), Dean Felber (bass) and Jim 'Son' Sonefield (drums). Two Grammies include Best New Artist in 1995.

25/02/1995.....50......3.......	HOLD MY HAND .... Atlantic A 7230CD
27/05/1995.....75......1.......	LET HER CRY 1995 Grammy Award for Best Pop Performance by a Duo or Group with Vocal .... Atlantic A 7188CD
04/05/1996.....57......1.......	OLD MAN AND ME (WHEN I GET TO HEAVEN) .... Atlantic A 5513CD
07/11/1998.....57......1.......	I WILL WAIT .... Atlantic AT 0048CD

HOPE A.D.
UK producer David Hope who also recorded as Mind Of Kane.

04/06/1994.....73......1.......	TREE FROG .... Sun-Up SUN 003CD

HOPE OF THE STATES
UK rock group formed in Chichester by Sam Herlihy (guitar/vocals), Jimi Lawrence (guitar), Ant Theaker (guitar/keyboards), Paul Wilson (bass), Mike Sidell (violin) and Simon Jones (drums). Lawrence was found hanging in a recording studio on 15/1/2004.

11/10/2003.....25......2.......	ENEMIES FRIENDS .... Sony Music 6742572
05/06/2004.....15......3.......	THE RED, THE WHITE, THE BLUE .... Sony Music 6749922
28/08/2004.....30......2.......	NEHEMIAH .... Sony Music 6752472

MARY HOPKIN
UK singer (born 3/5/1950, Pontardawe, Wales) who won *Opportunity Knocks* in 1968, an event spotted by model Twiggy who recommended her to Paul McCartney and the Apple label. Her debut single launched the label, along with the Beatles' own *Hey Jude* (her single replaced the Beatles at #1). Married producer Tony Visconti in 1971, the relationship ending in 1981. In 1983 joined with Julian Lloyd Webber, Bill Lovelady and Peter Skellern to form Oasis, a group that scored one hit album.

04/09/1968.....●6....21......	THOSE WERE THE DAYS Based on the Russian folk song *Darogoi Dlimmoyo* .... Apple 2
02/04/1969.....2.....14......	GOODBYE This and above single produced by Paul McCartney, who also wrote *Goodbye* .... Apple 10
31/01/1970.....6.....11......	TEMMA HARBOUR .... Apple 22
28/03/1970.....2.....14......	KNOCK KNOCK WHO'S THERE Britain's entry for the 1970 Eurovision Song Contest (came second) ...... Apple 26
31/10/1970.....19......9......	THINK ABOUT YOUR CHILDREN .... Apple 30
31/07/1971.....46......1......	LET MY NAME BE SORROW .... Apple 34
20/03/1976.....32......4......	IF YOU LOVE ME .... Good Earth GD 2

ANTHONY HOPKINS
UK actor/singer (born 1937, Port Talbot, Wales) who made his acting debut in *The Lion In Winter* in

○ Silver disc ● Gold disc ✪ Platinum disc (additional platinum units are indicated by a figure following the symbol) ⓜ Singles released prior to 1973 that are known to have sold over 1 million copies in the UK

1968. His best-known role is that of Hannibal Lecter in *Silence Of The Lambs* (for which he won the Oscar for Best Actor in 1991) and *Hannibal Lecter*. He was knighted in the 1993 New Years Honours List.

27/12/1986	75	1		DISTANT STAR	Juice AA 5

NICK HORNBY – see PRETENDERS

BRUCE HORNSBY AND THE RANGE US pianist/singer (born 23/11/1954, Williamsburg, VA); he moved to Los Angeles, CA in 1980 at the suggestion of Michael McDonald. He joined Sheena Easton's backing band in 1983 and formed the Range in 1984 with David Mansfield (guitar), Joe Puerta (bass), John Molo (drums) and George Marinelli (guitar). Mansfield was later replaced by Peter Harris who left in 1990. Hornsby filled in for Brent Mydland of the Grateful Dead when Mydland died. The group was named Best New Artist at the 1986 Grammy Awards. Bruce has gone on to collect a further two Grammies: Best Bluegrass Recording in 1989 with the Nitty Gritty Dirt Band for *The Valley Road* and Best Pop Instrumental Performance in 1993 with Branford Marsalis for *Barcelona Mona*.

02/08/1986	15	10		THE WAY IT IS ▲1	RCA PB 49805
25/04/1987	70	1		MANDOLIN RAIN	RCA PB 49769
28/05/1988	44	4		THE VALLEY ROAD	RCA PB 49561

HORNY UNITED – see BONEY M

HORSE UK group formed by Horse McDonald (vocals), George Hutchison (guitar), Angela McAlinden (guitar), Graham Brierton (bass), Steve Vantsis (bass), Steve Cooke (keyboards) and and Steve Cochrane (drums).

24/11/1990	52	3		CAREFUL	Capitol CL 587
21/08/1993	52	2		SHAKE THIS MOUNTAIN	Oxygen GASPD 7
23/10/1993	56	1		GOD'S HOME MOVIE	Oxygen GASXD 10
15/01/1994	49	2		CELEBRATE	Oxygen GASPD 11
05/04/1997	44	2		CAREFUL (STRESS) (REMIX)	Stress CDSTRX 79

JOHNNY HORTON US singer (born 30/4/1925, Los Angeles, CA and raised in Tyler, TX). He married Hank Williams' widow Billie Jean Jones. He was killed in a car crash on 5/11/1960.

26/06/1959	16	4		THE BATTLE OF NEW ORLEANS ▲6 1959 Grammy Award for Best Country & Western Performance	Philips PB 932
19/01/1961	23	11		NORTH TO ALASKA Featured in the 1960 film *North To Alaska*	Philips PB 1062

HOT ACTION COP US rock group formed by Rob Werthner (guitar/vocals), Tim Flaherty (guitar), Luis Espaillat (bass) and Kory Knipp (drums).

14/06/2003	41	1		FEVER FOR THE FLAVA	Lava AT 0152CD

HOT BLOOD French instrumental disco group.

09/10/1976	32	5		SOUL DRACULA	Creole CR 132

HOT BUTTER US moog synthesiser player and member of The Boston Pops Stan Free. The single was masterminded by producers Steve and Bill Jerome and Danny Jordan.

22/07/1972	5	19		**POPCORN**	Pye International 7N 25583

HOT CHOCOLATE UK group formed in London in 1969 by Patrick Olive (born 22/3/1947, Grenada, percussion), Ian King (drums) and Franklyn De Allie (guitar), subsequently adding Errol Brown (born 12/11/1948, Kingston, Jamaica, vocals), Tony Wilson (born 8/10/1947, Trinidad, bass) and Larry Ferguson (born 14/4/1948, Nassau, Bahamas, piano). They recorded their first single for Apple (a version of *Give Peace A Chance*) in 1969 before signing with RAK in 1970 and enjoying their first hit as songwriters, penning *Bet Yer Life I Do* for labelmates Herman's Hermits. De Allie was replaced by Harvey Hinsley (born 19/1/1948, Northampton) in 1970, Tony Connor (born 6/4/1947, Romford) replaced King on drums in 1973. Co-songwriter Wilson left in 1976, with Brown assuming full writing control. In 1987 the group announced they had split, and Brown went solo. Brown was awarded an MBE in the Queen's 2003 Birthday Honours List.

15/08/1970	6	12		LOVE IS LIFE	RAK 103
06/03/1971	22	9		YOU COULD HAVE BEEN A LADY	RAK 110
28/08/1971	8	11		**I BELIEVE (IN LOVE)**	RAK 118
28/10/1972	23	8		YOU'LL ALWAYS BE A FRIEND	RAK 139
14/04/1973	7	10		**BROTHER LOUIE**	RAK 149
18/08/1973	44	3		RUMOURS	RAK 157
16/03/1974	3	10	O	**EMMA**	RAK 168
30/11/1974	31	9		CHERI BABE	RAK 188
24/05/1975	11	7		DISCO QUEEN	RAK 202
09/08/1975	7	10		**A CHILD'S PRAYER**	RAK 212
08/11/1975	2	12	O	**YOU SEXY THING** Featured in the films *The Full Monty* (1997), *Boogie Nights* (1998) and *Deuce Bigalow: Male Gigolo* (1999) .... RAK 221	
20/03/1976	11	8		DON'T STOP IT NOW	RAK 230
26/06/1976	14	8		MAN TO MAN	RAK 238
21/08/1976	25	8		HEAVEN IS IN THE BACK SEAT OF MY CADILLAC	RAK 240

❶9 Number of weeks single topped the UK chart ↑ Entered the UK chart at #1 ▲9 Number of weeks single topped the US chart

373

DATE	POS	WKS	BPI	SINGLE TITLE	LABEL & NUMBER
18/06/1977	●³	11	○	**SO YOU WIN AGAIN**	RAK 259
26/11/1977	10	9	○	**PUT YOUR LOVE IN ME**	RAK 266
04/03/1978	12	11		EVERY 1'S A WINNER	RAK 270
02/12/1978	13	11	○	I'LL PUT YOU TOGETHER AGAIN	RAK 286
19/05/1979	46	5		MINDLESS BOOGIE	RAK 292
28/07/1979	53	4		GOING THROUGH THE MOTIONS	RAK 296
03/05/1980	2	11	○	**NO DOUBT ABOUT IT**	RAK 310
19/07/1980	17	7		ARE YOU GETTING ENOUGH OF WHAT MAKES YOU HAPPY	RAK 318
13/12/1980	50	5		LOVE ME TO SLEEP	RAK 324
30/05/1981	52	4		YOU'LL NEVER BE SO WRONG	RAK 331
17/04/1982	7	11		**GIRL CRAZY**	RAK 341
10/07/1982	5	12	○	**IT STARTED WITH A KISS**	RAK 344
25/09/1982	32	5		CHANCES	RAK 350
07/05/1983	10	9		**WHAT KINDA BOY YOU LOOKING FOR (GIRL)**	RAK 357
17/09/1983	37	5		TEARS ON THE TELEPHONE	RAK 363
04/02/1984	13	10		I GAVE YOU MY HEART (DIDN'T I)	RAK 369
17/01/1987	10	10		**YOU SEXY THING (REMIX)**	EMI 5592
04/04/1987	69	2		EVERY 1'S A WINNER (REMIX)	EMI 5607
06/03/1993	31	5		IT STARTED WITH A KISS Re-issue of RAK 344	EMI CDEMCTS 7
22/11/1997	6	8		**YOU SEXY THING** Re-issue of RAK 221 and re-released owing to inclusion in the film *The Full Monty*	EMI CDHOT 100
14/02/1998	18	3		IT STARTED WITH A KISS **HOT CHOCOLATE FEATURING ERROL BROWN** Second re-issue of RAK 344	EMI CDHOT 101

HOT GOSSIP – see SARAH BRIGHTMAN

HOT HOT HEAT Canadian rock group formed in Vancouver, British Columbia in 1999; they were re-formed in 2001 by Steve Bays (keyboards/vocals), Dante DeCaro (guitar), Dustin Hawthorne (bass) and Paul Hawley (drums).

DATE	POS	WKS	BPI	SINGLE TITLE	LABEL & NUMBER
05/04/2003	25	3		BANDAGES	B Unique BUN 045CDS
09/08/2003	38	1		NO, NOT NOW	Sub Pop W 615CD

HOT HOUSE UK vocal/instrumental group.

DATE	POS	WKS	BPI	SINGLE TITLE	LABEL & NUMBER
14/02/1987	74	1		DON'T COME TO STAY	Deconstruction CHEZ 1
24/09/1988	70	2		DON'T COME TO STAY Re-issue of Deconstruction CHEZ 1	Deconstruction PB 42233

HOT 'N' JUICY – see MOUSSE T

HOT PANTZ UK vocal duo from Southampton, Kelly Robinson (aged 23) and Shelley Mintrim (22), discovered by songwriter/producer Barry Upton.

DATE	POS	WKS	BPI	SINGLE TITLE	LABEL & NUMBER
25/12/2004	64	1+		GIVE U ONE 4 CHRISTMAS	Tug CDSNOG13

HOT RODS – see EDDIE AND THE HOT RODS

HOT STREAK US group formed in New York by Derrick Dupree (vocals), Al Tanner Jr (guitar), Jacob Dixon (bass) and Ricci Burgess (drums) as A Different Flavor.

DATE	POS	WKS	BPI	SINGLE TITLE	LABEL & NUMBER
10/09/1983	19	8		BODY WORK	Polydor POSP 642

HOTHOUSE FLOWERS Irish folk-rock group formed in Dublin in 1986 by Liam O'Maonlai (born 7/11/1964, Dublin, vocals/keyboards), Fiachna O'Braonain (born 27/11/1965, Dublin, guitar), Peter O'Toole (born 1/4/1965, Dublin, bass), Jerry Fehily (born 29/8/1963, Bishops Town, drums) and Leo Barnes (born 5/10/1965, Dublin, saxophone). Name taken from an album title by Wynton Marsalis.

DATE	POS	WKS	BPI	SINGLE TITLE	LABEL & NUMBER
14/05/1988	11	8		DON'T GO	London LON 174
23/07/1988	53	3		I'M SORRY	London LON 187
12/05/1990	30	5		GIVE IT UP	London LON 258
28/07/1990	23	7		I CAN SEE CLEARLY NOW	London LON 269
20/10/1990	68	2		MOVIES	London LON 276
13/02/1993	38	4		EMOTIONAL TIME	London LONCD 335
08/05/1993	45	3		ONE TONGUE	London LOCDP 340
19/06/1993	46	2		ISN'T IT AMAZING	London LOCDP 343
27/11/1993	67	1		THIS IS IT (YOUR SOUL)	London LONCD 346
16/05/1998	65	1		YOU CAN LEAVE ME NOW	London LONCD 410

HOTLEGS UK group put together by Eric Stewart (born 20/1/1945, Manchester), Lol Crème (born Lawrence Crème, 19/9/1947, Manchester) and Kevin Godley (born 7/10/1945, Manchester) in order to test equipment installed at their own Strawberry Studios. A demo of *Neanderthal Man* was heard by Philips' Dick Leahy and released on the label, selling over 2 million copies worldwide. Graham Gouldman (born 10/5/1946, Manchester) joined later to tour with the group. They split after one album but re-emerged as 10CC.

DATE	POS	WKS	BPI	SINGLE TITLE	LABEL & NUMBER
04/07/1970	2	14		**NEANDERTHAL MAN**	Fontana 6007 019

HOTSHOTS UK reggae group formed by Clive Crawley and Tony King whose one hit was a revival of the Royal Guardsmen's hit.

DATE	POS	WKS	BPI	SINGLE TITLE	LABEL & NUMBER
02/06/1973	4	15		**SNOOPY VS. THE RED BARON**	Mooncrest MOON 5

STEVEN HOUGHTON
UK actor/singer (born 1972, Sheffield), best known as Gregg Blake in TV's *London's Burning*. He has also appeared in *Bugs* and *Indian Summer* and has used both spellings (Steven and Stephen) of his first name as an actor.

29/11/1997	3	15		**WIND BENEATH MY WINGS**	RCA 74321529272
07/03/1998	23	7		TRULY This and above single featured in the TV series *London's Burning*	RCA 74321558552

A HOUSE
Irish group formed by Dave Couse (vocals), Fergal Bunbury (guitar) and Martin Healy (bass). They originally recorded for Blanco Y Negro in 1987.

13/06/1992	46	3		ENDLESS ART	Setanta AHOU 1
08/08/1992	55	2		TAKE IT EASY ON ME	Setanta AHOU 2
25/06/1994	52	1		WHY ME	Setanta CDAHOU 4
01/10/1994	37	2		HERE COME THE GOOD TIMES	Setanta CDAHOUS 5

HOUSE ENGINEERS
UK vocal/instrumental group; initially known as the remixers of *House Nation* by Housemaster Boyz and the Rude Boy of House.

05/12/1987	69	2		GHOST HOUSE	Syncopate SY 8

HOUSE OF GLASS
Italian production duo Gianni Bini and Paolo Martini. Bini is also responsible for Eclipse. Bini and Martini also record under their own names, Goodfellas and House of Glass.

14/04/2001	72	1		DISCO DOWN	Azuli AZNY 138

HOUSE OF LOVE
UK rock group formed in London by Guy Chadwick (guitar/vocals), Terry Bickers (guitar), Chris Groothuizen (bass) and Pete Evans (drums). Bickers left in 1989 and was replaced by Simon Walker. Walker left in 1992.

22/04/1989	41	2		NEVER	Fontana HOL 1
18/11/1989	41	3		I DON'T KNOW WHY	Fontana HOL 2
03/02/1990	20	4		SHINE ON	Fontana HOL 3
07/04/1990	36	4		BEATLES AND THE STONES	Fontana HOL 4
26/10/1991	58	1		THE GIRL WITH THE LONELIEST EYES	Fontana HOL 5
02/05/1992	45	3		FEEL	Fontana HOL 6
27/06/1992	46	3		YOU DON'T UNDERSTAND	Fontana HOL 7
05/12/1992	67	1		CRUSH ME	Fontana HOL 810

HOUSE OF PAIN
US rap group formed in Los Angeles, CA by Erik 'Everlast' Schrody, 'Danny Boy' O'Connor and Leor 'DJ Lethal' DiMant. Everlast subsequently recorded solo for Tommy Boy.

10/10/1992	32	4		JUMP AROUND	Ruffness XLS 32
22/05/1993	8	7		**JUMP AROUND/TOP O' THE MORNING TO YA** Re-issue of Ruffness XLS 32. A-side contains samples of Bob & Earl's *Harlem Shuffle* and Kriss Kross' *Jump*. Featured in the 1993 film *Mrs Doubtfire*. B-side featured in the 2003 film *Daredevil*	Ruffness XLS 43CD
23/10/1993	23	4		SHAMROCKS AND SHENIGANS/WHO'S THE MAN A-side contains a sample of John Lee Hooker's *Come To You Baby*. B-side contains a sample of The Kay Gees' *The Masterplan*	Ruffness XLS 46CD
16/07/1994	19	3		ON POINT Contains samples of Cannonball Adderly's *Inside Straight,* Freddy Robinson's *Rivers Invitation* and Pete Rock & C.L. Smooth's *Death Becomes You*	Ruffness XLS 52CD
12/11/1994	37	2		IT AIN'T A CRIME Contains a sample of Red Hot Chili Peppers' *Under The Bridge*	Ruffness XLS 55CD1
01/07/1995	20	3		OVER THERE (I DON'T CARE)	Ruffness XLS 61CD2
05/10/1996	68	1		FED UP Contains a sample of Mitch Ryder's *Blessing In Disguise*	Tommy Boy TBCD 7744
20/11/2004	65	4		JUMP AROUND Remix of Ruffness XLS 43CD	Tommy Boy 5046760110

HOUSE OF VIRGINISM
Swedish singer/dancer Apollo (born 1976); he later recorded as Apollo Presents House Of Virginism.

20/11/1993	29	3		I'LL BE THERE FOR YOU (DOYA DODODO DOYA)	ffrr FCD 221
30/07/1994	35	2		REACHIN	ffrr FCD 238
17/02/1996	67	1		EXCLUSIVE APOLLO PRESENTS HOUSE OF VIRGINISM	Logic 74321324102

HOUSE OF ZEKKARIVAS – see WOMACK AND WOMACK

HOUSE TRAFFIC
Italian/UK vocal/production group formed by Pietro Rossini, C Aiello, P Peroni and M Giorgi.

04/10/1997	24	3		EVERYDAY OF MY LIFE	Logic 74321249442

HOUSEMARTINS
UK group formed in Hull, Humberside in 1984 by Paul Heaton (born 9/5/1962, Birkenhead, guitar/vocals), Stan Cullimore (born 6/4/1962, Hull, bass), Hugh Whitaker (drums) and Ted Key (vocals). Norman Cook (born Quentin Cook, 31/7/1963, Brighton) replaced Key in 1985. Whitaker left in 1987 and was replaced by Dave Hemingway (born 20/9/1960, Hull). The group was named Best British Newcomers at the 1987 BRIT Awards. They dissolved in 1989; Heaton formed the Beautiful South, and Cook recorded solo, subsequently forming Beats International and Freakpower and recording as Fatboy Slim. In 1993 Hugh Whitaker was sent to prison for six years for assaulting James Hewitt with an axe and setting fire to his house on three occasions.

08/03/1986	54	4		SHEEP	Go Discs GOD 9
14/06/1986	3	13	O	**HAPPY HOUR**	Go Discs GOD 11
04/10/1986	18	8		THINK FOR A MINUTE	Go Discs GOD 13
06/12/1986	❶[1]	11	●	**CARAVAN OF LOVE**	Go Discs GOD 16
23/05/1987	11	6		FIVE GET OVER EXCITED	Go Discs GOD 18
05/09/1987	15	5		ME AND THE FARMER	Go Discs GOD 19
21/11/1987	15	8		BUILD	Go Discs GOD 21
23/04/1988	35	4		THERE IS ALWAYS SOMETHING THERE TO REMIND ME	Go Discs GOD 22

❶[9] Number of weeks single topped the UK chart ↑ Entered the UK chart at #1 ▲[9] Number of weeks single topped the US chart

DATE	POS	WKS	BPI	SINGLE TITLE	LABEL & NUMBER
10/05/2003	51	1		CHANGE THE WORLD DINO LENNY VS THE HOUSEMARTINS	Free 2 Air 0146685 F2A

HOUSEMASTER BOYZ AND THE RUDE BOY OF HOUSE US singer Farley 'Jackmaster' Funk (who previously recorded as Rude Boy Farley Keith) recorded the single that was subsequently remixed by a UK duo known as House Engineers. By the time the record was released, an unconnected UK trio were put together to promote it.

DATE	POS	WKS	BPI	SINGLE TITLE	LABEL & NUMBER
09/05/1987	48	6		HOUSE NATION	Magnetic Dance MAGD 1
12/09/1987	8	8		**HOUSE NATION**	Magnetic Dance MAGD 1

HOUSETRAP – see DJ SANDY VS HOUSETRAP

HOUSTON US singer (born Houston Summers, 1982, Belize) who attended the Hamilton High School and Accdemy of Music before going solo.

DATE	POS	WKS	BPI	SINGLE TITLE	LABEL & NUMBER
18/09/2004	11	6		I LIKE THAT	Capitol CDCL 861

MARQUES HOUSTON US singer (born 4/8/1981, Los Angeles, CA), ex-member of Immature, who went solo in 2003.

DATE	POS	WKS	BPI	SINGLE TITLE	LABEL & NUMBER
20/03/2004	15	6		CLUBBIN'	Elektra E 7544CD
31/07/2004	23	5		POP THAT BOOTY MARQUES HOUSTON FEATURING JERMAINE	East West E7609CD
27/11/2004	51	1		BECAUSE OF YOU	Atlantic AT0188CD

THELMA HOUSTON US singer (born 7/5/1946, Leland, MS and raised in California), she has combined singing with acting, with appearances in the films *Norman…Is That You* and *Death Scream*.

DATE	POS	WKS	BPI	SINGLE TITLE	LABEL & NUMBER
05/02/1977	13	8		DON'T LEAVE ME THIS WAY ▲[1] Featured in the films *Looking For Mr Goodbar* (1977), *54* (1998) and *Summer Of Sam* (1999). 1977 Grammy Award for Best Rhythm & Blues Vocal Performance	Motown TMG 1060
27/06/1981	48	4		IF YOU FEEL IT	RCA 77
01/12/1984	49	8		YOU USED TO HOLD ME SO TIGHT	MCA 932
21/01/1995	35	2		DON'T LEAVE ME THIS WAY (RE-RECORDING)	Dynamo DYND 001

WHITNEY HOUSTON US singer (born 9/8/1963, Newark, NJ) who is the daughter of soul singer Cissy Houston and a cousin of Dionne Warwick. She began her career singing gospel and modelling for the likes of *Vogue* before moving into session work for Chaka Khan and Lou Rawls, among others. Signed by Arista in 1983, she released her debut album in 1985 and continued her career as a model, having appeared on numerous front covers. She married singer Bobby Brown on 18/7/1992 and gave birth to their daughter Bobbi in March 1993. She has won six Grammy Awards including Album of the Year in 1993 for *The Bodyguard* (which in the UK is listed as a various artists album). She was also named Best Rhythm & Blues Artist at the 1999 MTV Europe Music Awards.

DATE	POS	WKS	BPI	SINGLE TITLE	LABEL & NUMBER
16/11/1985	●[2]	16	●	**SAVING ALL MY LOVE FOR YOU** ▲[1] 1985 Grammy Award for Best Pop Vocal Performance	Arista ARIST 640
25/01/1986	44	5		HOLD ME TEDDY PENDERGRASS WITH WHITNEY HOUSTON	Asylum EKR 32
25/01/1986	5	12	○	**HOW WILL I KNOW** ▲[2]	Arista ARIST 656
12/04/1986	8	11		**GREATEST LOVE OF ALL** ▲[3]	Arista ARIST 658
23/05/1987	●[2]	16	●	**I WANNA DANCE WITH SOMEBODY (WHO LOVES ME)** ▲[2] 1987 Grammy Award for Best Pop Vocal Performance. Featured in the 2004 film *13 Going On 30*.	Arista RIS 1
22/08/1987	14	8		DIDN'T WE ALMOST HAVE IT ALL ▲[2]	Arista RIS 31
14/11/1987	5	11		**SO EMOTIONAL** ▲[1]	Arista RIS 43
12/03/1988	14	8		WHERE DO BROKEN HEARTS GO ▲[2]	Arista 109793
28/05/1988	10	7		LOVE WILL SAVE THE DAY	Arista 111516
24/09/1988	●[2]	12	○	**ONE MOMENT IN TIME** Song used by NBC TV for their 1988 Olympic Games coverage	Arista 111613
09/09/1989	29	5		IT ISN'T, IT WASN'T, IT AIN'T NEVER GONNA BE ARETHA FRANKLIN AND WHITNEY HOUSTON	Arista 112545
20/10/1990	5	10		**I'M YOUR BABY TONIGHT** ▲[1]	Arista 113594
22/12/1990	13	10		ALL THE MAN THAT I NEED ▲[2]	Arista 114000
06/07/1991	29	5		MY NAME IS NOT SUSAN	Arista 114510
28/09/1991	54	2		I BELONG TO YOU	Arista 114727
14/11/1992	●[10]	23	●[2]	**I WILL ALWAYS LOVE YOU** ▲[14] Cover version of Dolly Parton's song that was featured in the 1982 film *The Best Little Whorehouse In Texas*. 1993 Grammy Awards for Record of the Year and Best Pop Vocal Performance	Arista 74321120657
20/02/1993	4	11		**I'M EVERY WOMAN**	Arista 74321131502
24/04/1993	3	10		**I HAVE NOTHING**	Arista 74321146142
31/07/1993	15	6		RUN TO YOU	Arista 74321153332
06/11/1993	14	5		QUEEN OF THE NIGHT This and above four titles featured in the 1992 film *The Bodyguard*	Arista 74321169302
25/12/1993	25	6		I WILL ALWAYS LOVE YOU	Arista 74321120657
22/01/1994	16	5		SOMETHING IN COMMON BOBBY BROWN AND WHITNEY HOUSTON	MCA MCSTD 1957
18/11/1995	11	9		EXHALE (SHOOP SHOOP) ▲[1] Featured in the 1995 film *Waiting To Exhale*	Arista 74321332472
24/02/1996	12	6		COUNT ON ME WHITNEY HOUSTON AND CECE WINNANS	Arista 74321345842
21/12/1996	13	13		STEP BY STEP	Arista 74321449332
29/03/1997	16	5		I BELIEVE IN YOU AND ME This and above title featured in the 1996 film *The Preacher's Wife*	Arista 74321468602
19/12/1998	4	13		**WHEN YOU BELIEVE** MARIAH CAREY AND WHITNEY HOUSTON Featured in the 1998 film *The Prince Of Egypt* and won the 1998 Oscar for Best Song for writers Stephen Schwartz and Kenneth Edmonds	Columbia 6667522
06/03/1999	3	15	●	**IT'S NOT RIGHT BUT IT'S OKAY** 1999 Grammy Award for Best Rhythm & Blues Vocal Performance	Arista 74321652412

○ Silver disc ● Gold disc ✪ Platinum disc (additional platinum units are indicated by a figure following the symbol) ◎ Singles released prior to 1973 that are known to have sold over 1 million copies in the UK

03/07/1999 . . . . . 2 . . . . . . 12	MY LOVE IS YOUR LOVE . . . . Arista 74321672872
11/12/1999 . . . . . 19 . . . . . 11	I LEARNED FROM THE BEST . . . . Arista 74321723992
17/06/2000 . . . . . 9 . . . . . . 11	IF I TOLD YOU THAT WHITNEY HOUSTON AND GEORGE MICHAEL . . . . Arista 74321766282
14/10/2000 . . . . . 7 . . . . . . 8	COULD I HAVE THIS KISS FOREVER WHITNEY HOUSTON AND ENRIQUE IGLESIAS . . . . Arista 74321795992
30/12/2000 . . . . . 25 . . . . . 5	HEARTBREAK HOTEL WHITNEY HOUSTON FEATURING FAITH EVANS AND KELLY PRICE . . . . Arista 74321820572
09/11/2002 . . . . . 13 . . . . . 3	WHATCHULOOKINAT . . . . Arista 74321975732

ADINA HOWARD US R&B singer (born 14/11/1974, Grand Rapids, MI).

04/03/1995 . . . . . 33 . . . . . . 4	FREAK LIKE ME Contains a sample of Bootsy Collins *I'd Rather Be With You* . . . . East West A 4473CD
23/11/1996 . . . . . 2 . . . . . . 12	WHAT'S LOVE GOT TO DO WITH IT WARREN G FEATURING ADINA HOWARD Featured in the 1996 film *Supercop* . . . .
	. . . . Interscope IND 97008

BILLY HOWARD UK comedian/impersonator (born London) whose hit featured him impersonating numerous TV policemen. He later appeared on the TV series *Who Do You Do?*

13/12/1975 . . . . . 6 . . . . . . 12	KING OF THE COPS Based on Roger Miller's hit *King Of The Road* . . . . Penny Farthing PEN 892

MIKI HOWARD US singer (born 1962, Chicago, IL) who was lead singer with Side Effect before going solo. She also made her name as an actress, portraying Billie Holiday in the film *Malcolm X* (and subsequently released an album of Billie Holiday songs).

26/05/1990 . . . . . 67 . . . . . . 2	UNTIL YOU COME BACK (THAT'S WHAT I'M GONNA DO) . . . . East West 7935

NICK HOWARD Australian singer.

21/01/1995 . . . . . 64 . . . . . . 1	EVERYBODY NEEDS SOMEBODY . . . . Bell 74321220942

ROBERT HOWARD – see KYM MAZELLE

DANNY HOWELLS AND DICK TREVOR UK production duo. Howells (born in Hastings) began as a DJ at Bedrock before working with Dick Trevor and vocalist Erire.

09/10/2004 . . . . . 37 . . . . . . 2	DUSK TIL DAWN C2 CDC2004

HOWLIN' WOLF US singer/guitarist (born Chester Burnett, 10/6/1910, West Point, MS); he initially mixed working on various farms with performing, sometimes under the name Big Foot and Bull Cow before settling on Howlin' Wolf. He died from cancer on 10/1/1976 and was inducted into the Rock & Roll Hall of Fame in 1991.

04/06/1964 . . . . . 42 . . . . . . 5	SMOKESTACK LIGHTNIN' . . . . Pye International 7N 25244

H2O UK group formed by Ian Donaldson (vocals), Pete Kean (guitar), Colin Ferguson (bass), Russ Alcock (keyboards), Colin Gavigan (saxophone) and Kenny Dorman (drums).

21/05/1983 . . . . . 17 . . . . . 10	DREAM TO SLEEP . . . . RCA 330
13/08/1983 . . . . . 38 . . . . . . 6	JUST OUTSIDE OF HEAVEN . . . . RCA 349

H2O US and Swiss vocal/instrumental dance group.

14/09/1996 . . . . . 19 . . . . . . 3	NOBODY'S BUSINESS H2O FEATURING BILLIE . . . . AM:PM 5818832
30/08/1997 . . . . . 66 . . . . . . 1	SATISFIED (TAKE ME HIGHER) . . . . AM:PM 5853252

AL HUDSON US singer (born Detroit, MI) who worked as a solo artist in the late 1960s until taking on the Soul Partners as his backing band. The name changed to One Way in 1982 with a line-up of Dave Robertson (guitar), Kevin McCord (bass), Cortez Harris (guitar), Candyce Edwards (vocals), Gregory Green (drums) and Jonathan Meadows (drums). Solo artist Alicia Myers was a former member.

09/09/1978 . . . . . 57 . . . . . . 4	DANCE, GET DOWN (FEEL THE GROOVE)/HOW DO YOU DO . . . . ABC 4229
15/09/1979 . . . . . 15 . . . . . 10	YOU CAN DO IT AL HUDSON AND THE PARTNERS . . . . MCA 511
08/12/1979 . . . . . 56 . . . . . . 6	MUSIC ONE WAY FEATURING AL HUDSON . . . . MCA 542

LAVINE HUDSON UK singer (born in Brixton), trained at the Berklee School of Music in Boston, MA.

21/05/1988 . . . . . 57 . . . . . . 3	INTERVENTION . . . . Virgin VS 1067

HUDSON-FORD UK duo formed by Richard Hudson (born 9/5/1948, London, guitar/vocals) and John Ford (born 1/7/1948, London, bass/vocals), ex-members of the Velvet Opera and The Strawbs. They left in 1973. Their backing group also consisted of Micky Keene (guitar), Chris Parren (keyboards) and Ken Laws (drums). They later recorded as The Monks.

18/08/1973 . . . . . 8 . . . . . . 9	PICK UP THE PIECES . . . . A&M AMS 7078
16/02/1974 . . . . . 15 . . . . . . 9	BURN BABY BURN . . . . A&M AMS 7096
29/06/1974 . . . . . 35 . . . . . . 2	FLOATING IN THE WIND . . . . A&M AMS 7116

HUE AND CRY UK duo formed by Glasgow-born brothers Pat (born 10/3/1964) and Greg Kane (11/9/1966) who first recorded for Stampede in 1986.

13/06/1987 . . . . . 6 . . . . . . 16	LABOUR OF LOVE . . . . Circa YR 4
19/09/1987 . . . . . 46 . . . . . . 5	STRENGTH TO STRENGTH . . . . Circa YR 6
30/01/1988 . . . . . 47 . . . . . . 3	I REFUSE . . . . Circa YR 8
22/10/1988 . . . . . 42 . . . . . . 6	ORDINARY ANGEL . . . . Circa YR 18
28/01/1989 . . . . . 15 . . . . . . 9	LOOKING FOR LINDA . . . . Circa YR 24
06/05/1989 . . . . . 21 . . . . . . 6	VIOLENTLY (EP) Tracks on EP: *Violently, The Man With The Child In His Eyes* and *Calamity John* . . . . Circa YR 29

❶⁹ Number of weeks single topped the UK chart ↑ Entered the UK chart at #1 ▲⁹ Number of weeks single topped the US chart

377

30/09/1989 . . . . . 55 . . . . . . 3	SWEET INVISIBILITY . . . . Circa YR 37
25/05/1991 . . . . . 47 . . . . . . 3	MY SALT HEART . . . . Circa YR 64
03/08/1991 . . . . . 48 . . . . . 3	LONG TERM LOVERS OF PAIN (EP) Tracks on EP: *Long Term Lovers Of Pain, Heart Of Saturday Night, Remembrance And Gold*
	and *Stars Crash Down* . . . . Circa YR 71
11/07/1992 . . . . . 74 . . . . . . 1	PROFOUNDLY YOURS . . . . Fidelity FIDEL 1
13/03/1993 . . . . . 25 . . . . . . 4	LABOUR OF LOVE (REMIX) . . . . Circa HUESCD 1

HUES CORPORATION
US R&B vocal trio formed by Hubert Ann Kelly (born 24/4/1947, Fairchild, AL), St Clair Lee (born Bernard St Clair Lee Calhoun Henderson 24/4/1944, San Francisco, CA) and Fleming Williams (born Flint, MI). Williams was replaced by Tommy Brown (born Birmingham, AL) after their first hit. Their name was a pun on billionaire Howard Hughes' corporation.

27/07/1974 . . . . . 6 . . . . . . 10 . . . . . O	**ROCK THE BOAT** ▲[1] Featured in the 1999 film *Man On The Moon* . . . . RCA APBO 0232
19/10/1974 . . . . . 24 . . . . . . 6	ROCKIN' SOUL . . . . RCA PB 10066

HUFF AND HERB
UK production duo Ben Langmaid (Huff) and Jeff Patterson (Herb).

06/12/1997 . . . . . 31 . . . . . . 3	FEELING GOOD Contains a sample of Nina Simone's *Feeling Good* . . . . Planet 3 GXY 2018CD
07/11/1998 . . . . . 69 . . . . . . 1	FEELING GOOD '98 (REMIX) . . . . Planet 3 GXY 2020CD

HUFF AND PUFF
UK instrumental/production duo Ben Langmaid (Huff) and Faithless member Rollo Armstrong (Puff).

02/11/1996 . . . . . 31 . . . . . . 2	HELP ME MAKE IT Contains a sample of Gladys Knight & The Pips' *Help Me Make It Through The Night* . . . . . . Skyway SKYWCD 4
21/06/1997 . . . . . 37 . . . . . . 2	HELP ME MAKE IT (REMIX) . . . . Skyway SKYWCD 8

DAVID HUGHES
UK singer (born Geoffrey Paddison, 11/10/1929, Birmingham); he became a star of TV, theatre and opera despite limited chart appeal. His hit won an Ivor Novello Award for the 'most outstanding song of the year.' He died on 19/10/1972.

21/09/1956 . . . . . 27 . . . . . . 1	BY THE FOUNTAINS OF ROME . . . . Philips PB 606

HUGO AND LUIGI
US producers/songwriters Hugo Peretti (born 6/12/1916) and Luigi Creatore (born 21/12/1920). They owned the Roulette, Avco/Embassy and H&L labels, with The Stylistics among their greatest successes. They also worked with Sam Cooke (and bought half his publishing company from his widow Barbara in 1966, although less than a year later they sold their shares to Cooke's ex-manager Allen Klein), The Isley Brothers and Van McCoy. They also wrote under the pseudonym of Mark Markwell and scored a million seller with Jimmy Rodgers *Oh Oh I'm Falling In Love Again*. Peretti died on 1/5/1986.

24/07/1959 . . . . . 29 . . . . . . 2	LA PLUME DE MA TANTE . . . . RCA 1127

HUMAN LEAGUE

UK group formed in 1977 by Martyn Ware (born 19/5/1956, Sheffield, keyboards), Ian Craig Marsh (born 11/11/1956, Sheffield, keyboards), Addy Newton and Phil Oakey (born 2/10/1955, Leicester, vocals/synthesiser) as the Future, changing to Human League later the same year (the name was taken from a science-fiction computer game). Newton left soon after, with Adrian Wright (born 30/6/1956) his replacement, although his initial role within the group was to look after visuals. Signed to Fast Product Records in 1978, the group was switched to Virgin in 1979. Ware and Marsh left in 1980 to form Heaven 17. Oakley recruited Ian Burden (born 24/12/1957, bass), Joanne Catherall (born 18/9/1962, Sheffield, vocals) and Susanne Sulley (born 22/3/1963, Sheffield, vocals), later adding Jo Callis (born 2/5/1955) on synthesiser. Oakey also launched a solo career. The group was named Best British Newcomer at the inaugural BRIT Awards in 1982.

03/05/1980 . . . . . 56 . . . . . . 5	HOLIDAY 80 (DOUBLE SINGLE) Tracks on double single: *Being Boiled, Marianne, Rock And Roll – Nightclubbing* and
	Dancevision . . . . Virgin SV 105
21/06/1980 . . . . . 52 . . . . . . 2	EMPIRE STATE HUMAN . . . . Virgin VS 351
28/02/1981 . . . . . 48 . . . . . . 4	BOYS AND GIRLS . . . . Virgin VS 395
02/05/1981 . . . . . 12 . . . . . . 10	THE SOUND OF THE CROWD . . . . Virgin VS 416
08/08/1981 . . . . . 3 . . . . . . 13 . . . . . O	**LOVE ACTION (I BELIEVE IN LOVE)** . . . . Virgin VS 435
10/10/1981 . . . . 6 . . . . . . 9 . . . . . O	**OPEN YOUR HEART** . . . . Virgin VS 453
05/12/1981 . . . . . ❶[5] . . . . . . 13 . . . . . ✪	**DON'T YOU WANT ME** ▲[3] . . . . Virgin VS 466
09/01/1982 . . . . . 6 . . . . . . 9	**BEING BOILED** Originally released in June 1978 and failed to chart . . . . EMI FAST 4
06/02/1982 . . . . . 46 . . . . . . 5	HOLIDAY 80 (DOUBLE SINGLE) . . . . Virgin SV 105
20/11/1982 . . . . . 2 . . . . . . 10 . . . . . O	**MIRROR MAN** . . . . Virgin VS 522
23/04/1983 . . . . . 2 . . . . . . 9 . . . . . O	**(KEEP FEELING) FASCINATION** . . . . Virgin VS 569
05/05/1984 . . . . . 11 . . . . . . 7	THE LEBANON . . . . Virgin VS 672
30/06/1984 . . . . . 16 . . . . . . 6	LIFE ON YOUR OWN . . . . Virgin VS 688
17/11/1984 . . . . . 13 . . . . . . 10	LOUISE . . . . Virgin VS 723
23/08/1986 . . . . . 8 . . . . . . 8	**HUMAN** ▲[1] . . . . Virgin VS 880
22/11/1986 . . . . . 72 . . . . . . 1	I NEED YOUR LOVING . . . . Virgin VS 900
15/10/1988 . . . . . 41 . . . . . . 5	LOVE IS ALL THAT MATTERS . . . . Virgin VS 1025
18/08/1990 . . . . . 29 . . . . . . 5	HEART LIKE A WHEEL . . . . Virgin VS 1262
07/01/1995 . . . . . 6 . . . . . . 9	**TELL ME WHEN** . . . . East West YZ 882CD1
18/03/1995 . . . . . 13 . . . . . . 8	ONE MAN IN MY HEART . . . . East West YZ 904CD1
17/06/1995 . . . . . 36 . . . . . . 2	FILLING UP WITH HEAVEN . . . . East West YZ 944CD
28/10/1995 . . . . . 16 . . . . . . 3	DON'T YOU WANT ME (REMIX) . . . . Virgin VSCDT 1557
20/01/1996 . . . . . 40 . . . . . . 2	STAY WITH ME TONIGHT . . . . East West EW 020CD
11/08/2001 . . . . . 47 . . . . . . 1	ALL I EVER WANTED . . . . Papillpn BTFLYS 0012

HUMAN MOVEMENT FEATURING SOPHIE MOLETA
UK production duo Marc Mitchell and Paul MacDonald with Australian singer Sophie Moleta.

03/02/2001.....53......1....... LOVE HAS COME AGAIN .... Renaissance Recordings RENCDS 005

HUMAN NATURE
Australian pop group formed in 1997 by brothers Andrew and Michael Tierney, Phil Burton and Toby Allen. Although the group's debut hit was written and produced by the UK songwriting team of Steve Mac and Wayne Hector, the Tierney brothers are accomplished songwriters in their own right and have penned songs with ex-Take That singer Gary Barlow.

10/05/1997.....44......1....... WISHES.. Epic 6644485
30/08/1997.....53......1....... WHISPER YOUR NAME .... Epic 6649465
10/03/2001.....18......4....... HE DON'T LOVE YOU .... Epic 6708922
30/06/2001.....43......1....... WHEN WE WERE YOUNG .... Epic 6713792

HUMAN RESOURCE
Dutch instrumental/production group formed by Robert Mahu and Guido Pernet.

14/09/1991.....36......7....... DOMINATOR .... R&S RSUK 4
21/12/1991.....18......7....... THE COMPLETE DOMINATOR (REMIX) .... R&S RSUK 4X

HUMANOID
UK producer Brian Dougan who later became a member of Future Sound of London.

26/11/1988.....17......8....... STAKKER HUMANOID .... Westside WSR 12
22/04/1989.....54......2....... SLAM.. Westside WSR 14
08/08/1992.....40......3....... STAKKER HUMANOID Re-issue of Westside WSR 12 .... Jumpin' & Pumpin' TOT 27
03/03/2001.....65......1....... STAKKER HUMANOID (REMIX) .... Jumpin' & Pumpin' CDSTOT 43

HUMATE
German dance group fronted by Paul Van Dyk and Gerret Frerichs. Van Dyk later recorded under his own name.

30/01/1999.....18......4....... LOVE STIMULATION .... Deviant DVNT 22CDS

HUMBLE PIE
UK rock group formed in London in 1969 by Peter Frampton (born 22/4/1950, Beckenham, guitar/vocals), Steve Marriott (born 30/1/1947, London, guitar/vocals), Greg Ridley (born 23/10/1947, Carlisle, Cumbria, bass) and Jerry Shirley (born 4/2/1952, drums), all of whom had been with other groups – the three principal members having been with The Herd, Small Faces and Spooky Tooth respectively. Frampton left in 1971 to go solo and was replaced by Dave 'Clem' Clempson (born 5/9/1949). The group split in 1975, briefly re-forming in 1980. Marriott was killed in a house fire on 20/4/1991.

23/08/1969.....4......10...... **NATURAL BORN BUGIE** .... Immediate IM 082

ENGELBERT HUMPERDINCK
UK singer (born Arnold George Dorsey, 2/5/1936, Madras, India) who made his first recordings for Decca in 1958 as Gerry Dorsey. In 1965 he met Tom Jones' manager Gordon Mills, who suggested he change his name to Engelbert Humperdinck (a 19th-century German composer), which considerably improved his fortune. He also broke in America to where he relocated and went on the cabaret circuit. Hosted his own TV variety show. He has a star on the Hollywood Walk of Fame.

26/01/1967 ....❶6.....56.....◎ RELEASE ME One of only two records (Acker Bilk's *Stranger On The Shore* is the other) to have spent more than a year on the singles chart in an unbroken run .... Decca F 12541
25/05/1967 ....2.....29...... **THERE GOES MY EVERYTHING** .... Decca F 12610
23/08/1967 ....❶5....27.....◎ **THE LAST WALTZ** .... Decca F 12655
10/01/1968 ....3.....13...... **AM I THAT EASY TO FORGET** .... Decca F 12722
24/04/1968 ....2.....15...... **A MAN WITHOUT LOVE** .... Decca F 12770
25/09/1968 ....5.....15...... **LES BICYCLETTES DE BELSIZE** .... Decca F 12834
05/02/1969 ....3.....14...... **THE WAY IT USED TO BE** .... Decca F 12879
09/08/1969 ....15.....13...... I'M A BETTER MAN (FOR HAVING LOVED YOU). .... Decca F 12957
15/11/1969 ....7.....13...... WINTER WORLD OF LOVE .... Decca F 12980
30/05/1970.....31.....7...... MY MARIE .... Decca F 13032
12/09/1970.....22.....7...... SWEETHEART .... Decca F 13068
11/09/1971.....13.....12...... ANOTHER TIME ANOTHER PLACE .... Decca F 13212
04/03/1972.....14.....10...... TOO BEAUTIFUL TO LAST Featured in the 1971 film *Nicholas And Alexandra* .... Decca F 13281
20/10/1973.....44.....4...... LOVE IS ALL .... Decca F 13443
30/01/1999.....40.....3...... QUANDO QUANDO QUANDO .... The Hit Label HLC 15
06/05/2000.....59.....1...... HOW TO WIN YOUR LOVE .... Universal TV 8822682
12/06/2004.....51.....1...... RELEASE ME Re-issue of Decca F 12541 and revived after use in an advertisement for John Smith's Bitter .... Universal TV 9819567

HUNDRED REASONS
UK five-piece rock group formed in Surrey by Colin Doran (vocals), Larry Hibbitt (guitar), Paul Townsend (guitar), Andy Gilmour (bass) and Andy Bews (drums). They were named Best New British Band at the 2000 Kerrang! Awards.

18/08/2001.....47......1...... EP TWO Tracks on EP: *Remmus*, *Soapbox* and *Shine* .... Columbia 6713922
15/12/2001.....37......2...... EP THREE Tracks on EP: *I'll Find You*, *Sunny* and *Slow Motion* .... Columbia 6720782
16/03/2002.....19......3...... IF I COULD. .... Columbia 6724402
18/05/2002.....15......3...... SILVER .... Columbia 6726642
28/09/2002.....38......1...... FALTER. .... Columbia 6731455

❶9 Number of weeks single topped the UK chart   ↑ Entered the UK chart at #1   ▲9 Number of weeks single topped the US chart

379

15/11/2003.....29......2......	THE GREAT TEST...Columbia 6743762
28/02/2004.....30......2......	WHAT YOU GET..Columbia 6745495
16/10/2004.....47......1......	HOW SOON IS NOW...Sore Point SORE029CDS

PETER HUNNIGALE – see **ARSENAL FC**

GERALDINE HUNT US singer (born Chicago, IL and later based in New York), she previously recorded for Bombay and Roulette. Her daughter Rosalind Hunt was later a member of Cheri.

25/10/1980.....44......5......	CAN'T FAKE THE FEELING ....Champagne FIZZ 501

LISA HUNT – see **LOVESTATION**

MARSHA HUNT US singer who utilised the services of Trash as her backing group.

21/05/1969.....46......2......	WALK ON GILDED SPLINTERS ....Track 604 030
02/05/1970.....41......1......	KEEP THE CUSTOMER SATISFIED ....Track 604 037

TOMMY HUNT US singer (born Charles Hunt, 18/6/1933, Pittsburgh, PA); he settled in Chicago, IL and joined the Five Echoes (who included Johnnie Taylor) before joining the Flamingos. He went solo in 1960 with the Scepter and Wand labels (he recorded the original version of Burt Bacharach and Hal David's *Walk On By,* later a huge hit for Dionne Warwick) and recorded for Atlantic, Capitol, Dynamo, Polydor and Pye. Highly regarded on the Northern Soul circuit, hence his revival in the 1970s. He is a nephew of Billy Eckstine.

11/10/1975.....39......5......	CRACKIN' UP ....Spark SRL 1132
21/08/1976.....28......9......	LOVING ON THE LOSING SIDE ....Spark SRL 1146
04/12/1976.....44......3......	ONE FINE MORNING ....Spark SRL 1148

ALFONZO HUNTER US saxophonist (born 1973, Chicago, IL); he began his professional career playing with local jazz bands.

22/02/1997.....38......2......	JUST THE WAY ....Cooltempo CDCOOL 326

HUNTER FEATURING RUBY TURNER UK vocal duo. Hunter was first known as one of the regular gladiators on the TV series *Gladiators*.

09/12/1995.....64......1.......	SHAKABOOM! ....Telstar HUNTCD 1

IAN HUNTER UK singer (born 3/6/1946, Shrewsbury), he auditioned for Mott The Hoople in 1969 and was taken on as lead singer. He collapsed suffering from exhaustion in 1974, prompting the group to disband. He had recovered by 1975 and went solo.

03/05/1975.....14....10......	ONCE BITTEN TWICE SHY ....CBS 3194

TAB HUNTER US singer (born Arthur Andrew Kelm, 11/7/1931, New York City), initially known as an actor appearing in such films as *Damn Yankees, Lust In The Dust* and *The Lawless*. He has a star on the Hollywood Walk of Fame.

08/02/1957....❶⁷...18......	**YOUNG LOVE ▲⁶** Song later revived by Donny Osmond and again taken to #1 ....London HLD 8380
12/04/1957.....5......12......	**NINETY-NINE WAYS** ....London HLD 8410

TERRY HUNTER US DJ/producer.

26/07/1997.....48......1......	HARVEST FOR THE WORLD ....Delirious DELICD 4

STEVE 'SILK' HURLEY US singer (born 9/11/1962, Chicago, IL) who had been a member of J.M. Silk (which stands for Jack Master Silk) with Keith Nunnally. They scored two minor UK hits as 'house' music began to gain a foothold. Hurley then recorded solo and hit #1, house music's first such success, and later recorded for Atlantic. He also made his name as a producer and songwriter, working with the likes of Kym Sims. He was later a member of Voices Of Life.

10/01/1987....❶²......9......O	**JACK YOUR BODY**...DJ International LON 117

HURLEY AND TODD UK dance/production duo Russell Hurley and Drew Todd.

29/04/2000.....38......2.......	SUNSTORM Contains a sample of Elton John's *Song For Guy* ....Multiply CDMULTY 58

HURRICANE #1 UK group formed by Andy Bell (born 11/8/1970, Cardiff, guitar) following the demise of Ride and featuring Gaz Farmer (drums), Will Pepper (bass) and Alex Lowe (vocals). In November 1999 Bell joined Gay Dad, but a few days later joined Oasis.

10/05/1997.....29......2......	STEP INTO MY WORLD...Creation CRESCD 253
05/07/1997.....35......2......	JUST ANOTHER ILLUSION ....Creation CRESCD 264
06/09/1997.....30......2......	CHAIN REACTION ....Creation CRESCD 271
01/11/1997.....19......3......	STEP INTO MY WORLD (REMIX) ....Creation CRESCD 276
21/02/1998.....19......6......	ONLY THE STRONGEST WILL SURVIVE ....Creation CRESCD 285
24/10/1998.....47......1......	RISING SIGN ....Creation CRESCD 303
03/04/1999.....43......1......	THE GREATEST HIGH ....Creation CRESCD 309

HURRICANES – see **JOHNNY AND THE HURRICANES**

PHIL HURTT US singer (born Philadelphia, PA) who first made a name for himself as a songwriting partner of Thom Bell (they penned *I'll Be Around* for the Detroit Spinners) and then working with Bunny Sigler. He later co-wrote Hi-Gloss' hit.

11/11/1978.....36......5......	GIVING IT BACK..Fantasy FTC 161

O Silver disc ● Gold disc ✪ Platinum disc (additional platinum units are indicated by a figure following the symbol) ◉ Singles released prior to 1973 that are known to have sold over 1 million copies in the UK

HUSAN – see **BHANGRA KNIGHTS VS HUSAN**

HUSTLERS CONVENTION FEATURING DAVE LAUDAT AND ONDREA DUVERNEY UK dance group formed by producers Mike Gray and Jon Pearn. They also recorded as Arizona, Sex-O-Sonique, Full Intention, Disco Tex Presents Cloudburst and Ronaldo's Revenge.

20/05/1995.....71......1....... DANCE TO THE MUSIC.. Stress CDSTR 53

WILLIE HUTCH US singer/songwriter (born Willie Hutchinson, 1946, Los Angeles, CA) who was a staff producer at Motown before going solo.

04/12/1982.....51......7....... IN AND OUT... Motown TMG 1285
06/07/1985.....73......1....... KEEP ON JAMMIN'... Motown ZB 40173

JUNE HUTTON AND AXEL STORDAHL AND THE BOYS NEXT DOOR US singer June Hutton was formerly a member of the Pied Pipers while her husband Axel Stordahl was a noted arranger who worked extensively with Frank Sinatra. Hutton died on 2/5/1973.

07/08/1953 .....6......7....... **SAY YOU'RE MINE AGAIN**.. Capitol CL 13918

HWA FEATURING SONIC THE HEDGEHOG UK producer Jeremy Healy recording under an assumed group name. Healy was an ex-member of Haysi Fantayzee and also recorded solo.

05/12/1992.....33......6....... SUPERSONIC.. Internal Affairs KGB 008

HYBRID UK trio of producers formed in Swansea by Mike Truman, Chris Healings and Lee Mullin. They have worked extensively with Julee Cruise and later toured with Moby as the opening act on his US tour.

10/07/1999.....58......1....... FINISHED SYMPHONY... Distinctive DISNCD 52
11/09/1999.....52......1....... IF I SURVIVE **HYBRID FEATURING JULEE CRUISE**.. Distinctive DISNCD 55
03/06/2000.....32......2....... KID 2000 **HYBRID FEATURING CHRISSIE HYNDE**.. Virgin VTS CD2
20/09/2003.....59......1....... TRUE TO FORM **HYBRID FEATURING PETER HOOK**... Distinctive DISNCD 111

HYDRAULIC DOGS – see **DJD PRESENTS HYDRAULIC DOGS**

BRIAN HYLAND US singer (born 12/11/1943, Queens, NY) who formed the Delphis when he was 12 and was only 16 when his debut single topped the US charts and made the UK top ten.

07/07/1960 .....8......13..... **ITSY BITSY TEENY WEENY YELLOW POLKA DOT BIKINI** ▲[1] Features the uncredited contribution of Trudy Packer ... London HLR 9161
20/10/1960.....29......6..... FOUR LITTLE HEELS.. London HLR 9203
10/05/1962 ....5......15..... **GINNY COME LATELY**... HMV POP 1013
02/08/1962 ....3......15..... **SEALED WITH A KISS**.. HMV POP 1051
08/11/1962.....28......6..... WARMED OVER KISSES.. HMV POP 1079
27/03/1971.....42......6..... GYPSY WOMAN.. Uni UN 530
28/06/1975 ....7......11..... **SEALED WITH A KISS** Re-issue of HMV POP 1051... ABC 4059

SHEILA HYLTON Jamaican singer who began her career as an air hostess before becoming a singer. Her biggest hit was produced by Harry Johnson of Harry J All Stars.

15/09/1979.....57......5...... BREAKFAST IN BED.. United Artists BP 304
17/01/1981.....35......7...... THE BED'S TOO BIG WITHOUT YOU... Island WIP 6671

PHYLLIS HYMAN US singer (born 1949, Pittsburgh, PA) who began her career as a fashion model before being discovered singing by Norman Connors. After appearing as a guest singer on his album with Michael Henderson, she landed a solo contract with Buddah Records and was initially placed with veteran producer Thom Bell. She later recorded for Philadelphia International, Arista, EMI and Zoo and appeared on Broadway in a number of musicals. She committed suicide on 30/6/1995.

16/02/1980.....47......6...... YOU KNOW HOW TO LOVE ME.. Arista ARIST 323
12/09/1981.....56......3...... YOU SURE LOOK GOOD TO ME... Arista ARIST 424

DICK HYMAN TRIO US pianist (born 8/3/1927, New York City); he toured with Benny Goodman in 1950 and later became resident pianist at two New York radio stations.

16/03/1956 .....9......10 ..... **THEME FROM 'THE THREEPENNY OPERA'**... MGM 890

CHRISSIE HYNDE US singer (born 7/9/1951, Akron, OH) who moved to London in 1970 and spent time in Paris and Cleveland before returning to the UK to form The Pretenders. Due to marry Ray Davies (of the Kinks) in 1982, but the couple were turned away by the registrar for arguing too much! She married Simple Minds leader Jim Kerr in 1984, but divorced in 1991. She appeared as Stephanie Schiffer in the TV comedy *Friends*. She also took part in the *It's Only Rock 'N' Roll* project for the Children's Promise charity.

03/08/1985 ....●[1].....13 .....● **I GOT YOU BABE**... DEP International DEP 20
18/06/1988 .....6......11 ..... **BREAKFAST IN BED** This and above single credited to **UB40 FEATURING CHRISSIE HYNDE** .... DEP International DEP 29
12/10/1991.....66......2...... SPIRITUAL HIGH (STATE OF INDEPENDENCE)... Arista 114528
23/01/1993.....47......2...... SPIRITUAL HIGH (STATE OF INDEPENDENCE) (REMIX) This and above single credited to **MOODSWINGS FEATURING CHRISSIE HYNDE**
                                                                                             Arista 74321127712
18/03/1995 ....●[1] .....8......○ **LOVE CAN BUILD A BRIDGE** CHER, CHRISSIE HYNDE AND NENEH CHERRY WITH ERIC CLAPTON Single released in aid of the Comic Relief Charity .... London COCD 1
03/06/2000.....32......2....... KID 2000 **HYBRID FEATURING CHRISSIE HYNDE** Featured in the 2000 film *Kevin And Perry Go Large*............. Virgin VTS CD2

●[9] Number of weeks single topped the UK chart ↑ Entered the UK chart at #1 ▲[9] Number of weeks single topped the US chart

381

	07/02/2004	29	3		STRAIGHT AHEAD TUBE AND BERGER FEATURING CHRISSIE HYNDE	Direction 6746222

HYPER GO GO UK instrumental/production duo James Diplock and Alex Ball.

22/08/1992	30	5	HIGH	Deconstruction 74321110497
31/07/1993	45	3	NEVER LET GO	Positiva CDTIV 3
05/02/1994	36	2	RAISE	Positiva CDTIV 9
26/11/1994	49	1	IT'S ALRIGHT	Positiva CDTIV 20
06/04/1996	54	1	DO WATCHA DO HYPER GO GO AND ADEVA	Avex UK AVEXCD 24
12/10/1996	32	2	HIGH (REMIX)	Distinctive DISNCD 24
12/04/1997	60	1	DO WATCHA DO (REMIX) HYPER GO GO AND ADEVA	Distinctive DISNCD 28

HYPERLOGIC UK instrumental/production duo.

29/07/1995	35	2	ONLY ME Contains samples of U2's *New Year's Day* and Alyson Williams' *Sleep Talk*	Systematic SYSCD 15
09/05/1998	48	1	ONLY ME (REMIX)	Tidy Trax TIDY 113CD1

HYPERSTATE UK vocal/instrumental duo with singer Janey Lee Grace.

06/02/1993	71	1	TIME AFTER TIME	M&G MAGCD 34

HYPNOTIST UK producer Caspar Pound recording under an assumed name. He was an ex-member of A Homeboy, A Hippie And A Funki Dredd (as A Hippie) and was also the founder of Rising High Records.

28/09/1991	65	2	THE HOUSE IS MINE	Rising High RSN 4
21/12/1991	68	3	THE HARDCORE EP Tracks on EP: *Hardcore U Know The Score, The Ride, Night Of The Livin' E Heads* and *God Of The Universe*	Rising High RSN 13

HYPO PSYCHO UK-based group formed by Mikey Koltes (vocals), Millsy (guitar), Gary 'Kill' Kilminster (bass) and Jonny South (drums).

24/07/2004	53	1	PUBLIC ENEMY NO 1	Believe Music SMASCD059

HYSTERIC EGO UK producer Rob White recording under an assumed name.

31/08/1996	28	4	WANT LOVE	WEA 070CD
21/06/1997	39	2	MINISTRY OF LOVE	WEA 094CD
28/02/1998	46	1	WANT LOVE – THE REMIXES	WEA 150CD
13/02/1999	50	1	TIME TO GET BACK Contains a sample of N-Joi's *Adrenalin*	WEA 198CD

HYSTERICS UK vocal/instrumental group formed by Larry Robins and Danny O'Keefe.

12/12/1981	44	5	JINGLE BELLS LAUGHING ALL THE WAY/GESUNDHEIT	Record Delivery KA 5

HYSTERIX UK vocal/instrumental group formed by 'Tokyo' Tony Quinn, Darren Black and Richard Belgrave, with the addition of numerous female singers over the years. These have included Maxine, Marie Harper and Sally Anne Marsh.

07/05/1994	40	3	MUST BE THE MUSIC	Deconstruction 74321207362
18/02/1995	65	1	EVERYTHING IS EVERYTHING	Deconstruction 74321236882

○ Silver disc ● Gold disc ✪ Platinum disc (additional platinum units are indicated by a figure following the symbol) ◎ Singles released prior to 1973 that are known to have sold over 1 million copies in the UK

I

I AM KLOOT UK group from Manchester with John Bramwell (guitar/vocals), Pete Jobson (guitar/bass) and Andy Hargreaves (drums).

21/06/2003	43	1	LIFE IN A DAY .... Echo ECSCX 140
20/09/2003	46	1	3 FEET TALL .... Echo ECSCX 143

I DREAM FEATURING FRANKIE AND CALVIN UK vocal duo Frankie Sandford (born 14/1/1989, Havering) and Calvin Goldspink (born 24/1/1989, Great Yarmouth), both members of S Club Juniors/S Club 8. Their debut single came from the TV series *I Dream*.

27/11/2004	19	5+	DREAMING 19/UMTV 9868872

I KAMANCHI UK drum/bass duo DJ Krust (Keith Thompson) and DJ Die (Daniel Cawsman), both members of Roni Size Reprazent.

14/06/2003	69	1	NEVER CAN TELL/SOUL BEAT CALLING .... Full Cycle FCY 052

I-LEVEL UK funk group formed by Sam Jones, Joe Dworniak and Duncan Bridgeman.

16/04/1983	52	6	MINEFIELD .... Virgin VS 563
18/06/1983	56	3	TEACHER .... Virgin VS 595

I MONSTER UK production duo Dean Honer and Jarrod Gosling. Honer is also a member of All Seeing I; Gosling is also with Add N To X.

16/06/2001	20	6	DAYDREAM IN BLUE .... Instant Karma KARMA 7CD

JANIS IAN US singer (born Janis Eddy Fink, 7/4/1951, New York City) who began recording in 1967, later relocating to California to write for other artists.

17/11/1979	44	7	FLY TOO HIGH .... CBS 7936
28/06/1980	44	3	THE OTHER SIDE OF THE SUN .... CBS 8611

IAN VAN DAHL Belgian producer/songwriter AnneMie Coene who was given the nickname 'Ian' when she was a child. The vocals on her debut hit were not by an 'Ian' but by a female singer, Marsha. By the second single it was revealed that the 'group' was the brainchild of producers Christophe Chantiz and Erik Vanspauwen.

21/07/2001	3	16	O	CASTLES IN THE SKY .... NuLife 74321867142
22/12/2001	5	13		WILL I? .... NuLife 74321903402
01/06/2002	8	8		REASON .... NuLife 74321938722
12/10/2002	15	5		TRY .... NuLife 74321967942
1/11/2003	20	4		I CAN'T LET YOU GO .... NuLife 82876570712
17/07/2004	27	3		BELIEVE .... NuLife 82876626542

ICE CUBE US rapper (born O'Shea Jackson, 15/6/1969, Los Angeles, CA) and founder member of NWA (Niggaz With Attitude), which he left in 1990 to form his own 'posse', Lench Mob. He also began acting, appearing in the 1991 film *Boyz N The Hood*. Das EFX are US rap duo Drayz (born Andre Weston, 9/9/1970, New Jersey) and Skoob (born Willie Hines, 27/11/1970, Brooklyn, NYC). George Clinton (born 22/7/1941, Kannapolis, NC) is the leader of Parliament/Funkadelic. Mack 10 is US rapper D'Mon Rolison (born 9/8/1971, Inglewood, CA). Ms Toi is US rapper Toikeon Parham (born in Chicago, IL).

27/03/1993	27	4	IT WAS A GOOD DAY Contains samples of The Moments' *Sexy Mama* and The Isley Brothers' *Footsteps In The Dark* .... Fourth & Broadway BRCD 270
07/08/1993	36	4	CHECK YO SELF **ICE CUBE FEATURING DAS EFX** Contains a sample of Grandmaster Flash & The Furious Five's *The Message* .... Fourth & Broadway BRCD 283
11/09/1993	62	1	WICKED Contains samples of The Ohio Players' *Funky Worm,* Public Enemy's *Welcome To The Terrordome* and *Can't Truss It* and DAS EFX's *Loosey's*.. Fourth & Broadway BRCD 282
18/12/1993	66	1	REALLY DOE... Fourth & Broadway BRCD 302
26/03/1994	41	3	YOU KNOW HOW WE DO IT Contains a sample of Evelyn King's *The Show Is Over*.......... Fourth & Broadway BRCD 303
27/08/1994	22	3	BOP GUN (ONE NATION) **ICE CUBE FEATURING GEORGE CLINTON** Contains a sample of Funkadelic's *One Nation Under A Groove* . ... Fourth & Broadway BRCD 308
24/12/1994	46	2	YOU KNOW HOW WE DO IT.. Fourth & Broadway BRCD 303
11/03/1995	41	2	HAND OF THE DEAD BODY **SCARFACE FEATURING ICE CUBE**................. Virgin America VUSCD 88
15/04/1995	45	2	NATURAL BORN KILLAZ **DR DRE AND ICE CUBE** Featured in the 1995 film *Murder Was The Case*.......... Death Row A 8197CD
22/03/1997	60	1	THE WORLD IS MINE Featured in the 1997 film *Dangerous Ground*................................ Jive JIVECD 419
11/12/2004	2	3+	**YOU CAN DO IT** ICE CUBE FEATURING MACK 10 AND MS TOI .... All Around The World CDGLOBE396

❶⁹ Number of weeks single topped the UK chart ↑ Entered the UK chart at #1 ▲⁹ Number of weeks single topped the US chart

383

ICE MC UK rapper Ian Campbell.

06/08/1994.....42.....2......	THINK ABOUT THE WAY (BOM DIGI DIGI BOM…)..	WEA YZ 829CD
08/04/1995.....73.....1......	IT'S A RAINY DAY..	Eternal YZ 902CD
14/09/1996.....38.....2......	BOM DIGI BOM (THINK ABOUT THE WAY) Re-issue of WEA YZ 829CD	Eternal 073CD

ICE-T US rapper (born Tracy Morrow, 16/2/1958, Newark, NJ) who took his name from black exploitation writer Iceberg Slim. He also began a career as an actor, appearing in the films *New Jack City* (1991) and *Looters* (1992) with Ice Cube. He previously recorded for Sire Records but was thrown off the label following the outcry (led by shareholder Charlton Heston) over the single *Cop Killer* by Body Count, which Ice-T wrote and produced. He won the 1990 Grammy Award for Best Rap Performance by a Group with Melle Mel, Daddy Kane and Kool Moe Dee for *Back On The Block* by Quincy Jones.

18/03/1989.....63.....2......	HIGH ROLLERS	Sire W 7574
17/02/1990.....64.....2......	YOU PLAYED YOURSELF	Sire W 9994
29/09/1990.....48.....3......	SUPERFLY 1990 CURTIS MAYFIELD AND ICE-T	Capitol CL 586
08/05/1993.....62.....2......	I AIN'T NEW TA THIS	Rhyme Syndicate SYNDD 1
18/12/1993.....21.....6......	THAT'S HOW I'M LIVIN'	Rhyme Syndicate SYNDD 2
09/04/1994.....24.....4......	GOTTA LOTTA LOVE Contains a sample of Mike Oldfield's *Tubular Bells*	Rhyme Syndicate SYNDD 3
10/12/1994.....47.....2......	BORN TO RAISE HELL MOTORHEAD/ICE-T/WHITFIELD CRANE Featured in the 1994 film *Airheads*	Fox 74321230152
01/06/1996.....23.....3......	I MUST STAND Contains a sample of Portishead's *Numb*	Rhyme Syndicate SYNDD 5
07/12/1996.....18.....5......	THE LANE Contains a sample of Jaques Perry's *Era*..	Virgin SYNDD 6

ICEBERG SLIMM UK rapper (born Duane Dyer, Hackney, London) named after black exploitation writer Iceberg Slim.

07/10/2000.....37.....2......	NURSERY RHYMES Contains a sample of Normand Roger's *Mystery*	Polydor 5877632
06/11/2004.....73.....1......	STARSHIP ICEBERG SLIMM FEATURING COREE..	V2 ARV5029063

ICEHOUSE Australian rock group formed in 1980 by Iva Davies (born 22/5/1955, multi-instrumentalist/vocals), Bob Kretshmer (guitar), Guy Pratt (guitar), Andy Qunta (keyboards), Michael Hoste (keyboards) and John Lloyd (drums) as Flowers. Icehouse was the Flowers' first album title, derived from Australian slang for a mental hospital.

05/02/1983.....17.....10......	HEY LITTLE GIRL	Chrysalis CHS 2670
23/04/1983.....62.....4......	STREET CAFE	Chrysalis COOL 1
03/05/1986.....72.....1......	NO PROMISES..	Chrysalis CHS 2978
29/08/1987.....74.....1......	CRAZY	Chrysalis CHS 3156
13/02/1988.....38.....8......	CRAZY	Chrysalis CHS 3156
14/05/1988.....53.....4......	ELECTRIC BLUE	Chrysalis CHS 3239

ICICLE WORKS UK rock group formed in Liverpool in 1980 by Ian McNabb (born 3/11/1960, Liverpool, guitar/vocals), Chris Layhe (bass) and Chris Sharrock (drums). The group took their name from a sci-fi book. McNabb later recorded solo.

24/12/1983.....15.....8......	LOVE IS A WONDERFUL COLOUR	Beggars Banquet BEG 99
10/03/1984.....53.....4......	BIRDS FLY (WHISPER TO A SCREAM)/IN THE CAULDRON OF LOVE................................	Beggars Banquet BEG 108
26/07/1986.....52.....3......	UNDERSTANDING JANE	Beggars Banquet BEG 160
04/10/1986.....54.....4......	WHO DO YOU WANT FOR YOUR LOVE	Beggars Banquet BEG 172
14/02/1987.....53.....4......	EVANGELINE	Beggars Banquet BEG 181
30/04/1988.....59.....4......	LITTLE GIRL LOST	Beggars Banquet BEG 215
17/03/1990.....73.....1......	MOTORCYCLE RIDER	Epic WORKS 100

ICON UK vocal/instrumental duo with singer Juliette Jaimes.

15/06/1996.....51.....1......	TAINTED LOVE	Eternal WEA 057CD

IDEAL UK producer Jon Da Silva.

06/08/1994.....49.....2......	HOT	Cleveland City CLECD 13019

IDEAL U.S. FEATURING LIL' MO US group formed by J-Dante, Maverick, PZ and Swab with singer Lil' Mo.

23/09/2000.....31.....3......	WHATEVER	Virgin VUSCD 172

IDES OF MARCH US rock group formed in Chicago in 1964 by James Peterik (lead vocals), Ray Herr (guitar/bass), Larry Milas (guitar/organ), Bob Bergland (bass), John Larson (trumpet), Chuck Somar (horn) and Michael Borch (drums). Peterik later joined Survivor.

06/06/1970.....31.....9......	VEHICLE	Warner Brothers WB 7378

ERIC IDLE FEATURING RICHARD WILSON UK duo Eric Idle (born 29/3/1943, South Shields) and Richard Wilson (born 9/7/1936, Greenock, Scotland). Idle was previously with the Monty Python comedy team and also The Rutles; Wilson is better known from the TV comedy series *One Foot In The Grave,* playing Victor Meldrew.

17/12/1994.....50.....3......	ONE FOOT IN THE GRAVE Theme to the TV series of the same name...........................	Victa CDVICTA 1

IDLEWILD UK group formed in Edinburgh, Scotland by Roddy Woomble (vocals), Rod Jones (guitar), Bob Fairfoull (bass) and Colin Newton (drums).

09/05/1998.....53.....1......	A FILM FOR THE FUTURE	Food CDFOOD 111
25/07/1998.....47.....1......	EVERYONE SAYS YOU'RE SO FRAGILE	Food CDFOOD 113
24/10/1998.....41.....1......	I'M A MESSAGE	Food CDFOOD 114
13/02/1999.....19.....2......	WHEN I ARGUE I SEE SHAPES	Food CDFOODS 116
02/10/1999.....24.....2......	LITTLE DISCOURAGE	Food CDFOODS 124

○ Silver disc ● Gold disc ✪ Platinum disc (additional platinum units are indicated by a figure following the symbol) ◎ Singles released prior to 1973 that are known to have sold over 1 million copies in the UK

08/04/2000	23	3		ACTUALLY IT'S DARKNESS	Food CDFOODS 127
24/06/2000	32	3		THESE WOODEN IDEAS	Food CDFOODS 132
28/10/2000	38	2		ROSEABILITY	Food CDFOODS 134
04/05/2002	9	4		**YOU HELD THE WORLD IN YOUR ARMS**	Parlophone CDRS 6575
13/07/2002	15	7		AMERICAN ENGLISH	Parlophone CDRS 6582
02/11/2002	26	2		LIVE IN A HIDING PLACE	Parlophone CDRS 6587
22/02/2003	28	2		A MODERN WAY OF LETTING GO	Parlophone CDR 6598

BILLY IDOL UK singer (born William Broad, 30/11/1955, Stanmore, Middlesex) and an early follower of punk rock and in the TV audience when the Sex Pistols had their notorious interview with Bill Grundy. He formed Generation X with Tony James, John Towe and Bob Andrews in 1976, quitting in 1981 for a solo career masterminded by Kiss manager Bill Aucoin. A February 1990 motorcycle smash in LA broke his right leg and left wrist.

11/09/1982	58	4		HOT IN THE CITY	Chrysalis CHS 2625
24/03/1984	62	2		REBEL YELL Featured in the 1990 film *Look Who's Talking Too*	Chrysalis IDOL 2
30/06/1984	18	11		EYES WITHOUT A FACE	Chrysalis IDOL 3
29/09/1984	54	3		FLESH FOR FANTASY	Chrysalis IDOL 4
13/07/1985	6	15	O	**WHITE WEDDING** Featured in the 1998 film *The Wedding Singer*	Chrysalis IDOL 5
14/09/1985	6	12		**REBEL YELL** Re-issue of Chrysalis IDOL 2	Chrysalis IDOL 6
04/10/1986	22	8		TO BE A LOVER	Chrysalis IDOL 8
07/03/1987	26	5		DON'T NEED A GUN	Chrysalis IDOL 9
13/06/1987	17	9		SWEET SIXTEEN	Chrysalis IDOL 10
03/10/1987	7	10		**MONY MONY** ▲[1] Featured in the films *Car Trouble* (1987), *Vice Versa* (1988) and *Striptease* (1996)	Chrysalis IDOL 11
16/01/1988	13	9		HOT IN THE CITY (REMIX)	Chrysalis IDOL 12
13/08/1988	63	3		CATCH MY FALL	Chrysalis IDOL 13
28/04/1990	34	4		CRADLE OF LOVE Featured in the 1990 film *The Adventures Of Ford Fairlane*	Chrysalis IDOL 14
11/08/1990	70	2		L.A. WOMAN	Chrysalis IDOL 15
22/12/1990	47	4		PRODIGAL BLUES	Chrysalis IDOL 16
26/06/1993	30	3		SHOCK TO THE SYSTEM	Chrysalis CDCHS 3994
10/09/1994	47	2		SPEED Featured in the 1994 film *Speed*	Fox 74321223472

IDOLS UK vocal group formed by ten of the finalists in TV's 2003 Pop Idols competition – Roxanne Cooper, Kirsty Crawford, Kim Gee, Chris Hide, Susanne Manning, Leon McPherson, Sam Nixon, Brian Ormond, Mark Rhodes and Andy Scott-Lee.

27/12/2003	5	5		**HAPPY XMAS (WAR IS OVER)**	S 82876583822

FRANK IFIELD UK singer (born 30/11/1937, Coventry, raised in Australia) who began his career at fifteen on Australian radio and TV before trying his luck in the UK. He signed to the UK Columbia label in 1959, working with producer Norrie Paramour.

19/02/1960	22	8		LUCKY DEVIL	Columbia DB 4399
29/09/1960	49	1		GOTTA GET A DATE	Columbia DB 4496
05/07/1962	●[7]	28	◎	**I REMEMBER YOU** Originally recorded by Jimmy Dorsey and featured in 1942 film *The Fleet's In*	Columbia DB 4856
25/10/1962	●[5]	17		**LOVESICK BLUES**	Columbia DB 4913
24/01/1963	●[3]	13		**WAYWARD WIND**	Columbia DB 4960
11/04/1963	4	16		**NOBODY'S DARLIN' BUT MINE**	Columbia DB 7007
27/06/1963	●[2]	16		**CONFESSIN'**	Columbia DB 7062
17/10/1963	22	6		MULE TRAIN	Columbia DB 7131
09/01/1964	8	13		**DON'T BLAME ME**	Columbia DB 7184
23/04/1964	25	8		ANGRY AT THE BIG OAK TREE	Columbia DB 7263
23/07/1964	33	3		I SHOULD CARE	Columbia DB 7319
01/10/1964	25	6		SUMMER IS OVER	Columbia DB 7355
19/08/1965	26	9		PARADISE	Columbia DB 7655
23/06/1966	25	4		NO ONE WILL EVER KNOW	Columbia DB 7940
08/12/1966	24	11		CALL HER YOUR SWEETHEART	Columbia DB 8078
07/12/1991	40	4		THE YODELLING SONG FRANK IFIELD FEATURING THE BACKROOM BOYS	EMI 7YODEL 1

ENRIQUE IGLESIAS Spanish singer (born 8/5/1975, Madrid), son of fellow singer Julio Iglesias. He began his professional career in 1995 and won the 1996 Grammy Award for Best Latin Pop Recording for *Enrique Iglesias*. When *Hero* hit #1, Julio and Enrique became the first father and son to top the UK singles chart.

11/09/1999	4	9	O	**BAILAMOS** ▲[2] Featured in the 1999 film *Wild Wild West*	Interscope IND 97131
18/12/1999	45	2		RHYTHM DIVINE	Interscope 4972242
14/10/2000	7	8		**COULD I HAVE THIS KISS FOREVER** WHITNEY HOUSTON AND ENRIQUE IGLESIAS	Arista 74321795992
02/02/2002	●[4]	19	●	**HERO** ↑	Interscope IND 97671

●[9] Number of weeks single topped the UK chart ↑ Entered the UK chart at #1 ▲[9] Number of weeks single topped the US chart

DATE	POS	WKS	BPI	SINGLE TITLE	LABEL & NUMBER
27/04/2002	71	2		ESCAPE (IMPORT)	Interscope 4976922
25/05/2002	3	14	O	**ESCAPE** The accompanying video features tennis star Anna Kournikova	Interscope 4977232
07/09/2002	12	7		LOVE TO SEE YOU CRY	Interscope IND 97760
07/12/2002	12	9		MAYBE	Interscope 4978232
26/04/2003	19	4		TO LOVE A WOMAN LIONEL RICHIE FEATURING ENRIQUE IGLESIAS	Mercury 0779082
29/11/2003	11	6		ADDICTED	Interscope 9814328
20/03/2004	5	8		NOT IN LOVE ENRIQUE FEATURING KELIS	Interscope 9862023

JULIO IGLESIAS Spanish singer (born 23/9/1943, Madrid) who planned a career as a goalkeeper with football team Real Madrid until a car accident left him temporarily paralysed. He learned to play the guitar in hospital. Initially popular within the Spanish-speaking world, he subsequently recorded in seven languages and became a worldwide star. He won the 1987 Grammy Award for Best Latin Pop Recording for *Un Hombre Solo*, and has a star on the Hollywood Walk of Fame. Both Julio's sons, Enrique (see entry) and Julio Jr, have successful recording careers.

DATE	POS	WKS	BPI	SINGLE TITLE	LABEL & NUMBER
24/10/1981	●[1]	14	O	**BEGIN THE BEGUINE (VOLVER A EMPEZAR)** Originally written in 1935 for the musical *Jubilee*	CBS A 1612
06/03/1982	3	9	O	**QUIEREME MUCHO (YOURS)**	CBS A 1939
09/10/1982	32	7		AMOR	CBS A 2801
09/04/1983	31	7		HEY!	CBS JULIO 1
07/04/1984	17	10		TO ALL THE GIRLS I'VE LOVED BEFORE JULIO IGLESIAS AND WILLIE NELSON	CBS A 4252
07/07/1984	43	8		ALL OF YOU JULIO IGLESIAS AND DIANA ROSS	CBS A 4522
06/08/1988	5	11		MY LOVE JULIO IGLESIAS FEATURING STEVIE WONDER	CBS JULIO 2
04/06/1994	43	5		CRAZY	Columbia 6603695
26/11/1994	53	4		FRAGILE	Columbia 6610192

IGNORANTS UK vocal duo Trevor Henry and Anthony Marshall.

DATE	POS	WKS	BPI	SINGLE TITLE	LABEL & NUMBER
25/12/1993	59	3		PHAT GIRLS	Spaghetti CIOCD 8

IIO US producer Marcus Moser with vocals by Nadia Li. The original name of Vaiio was changed to avoid association with a laptop computer.

DATE	POS	WKS	BPI	SINGLE TITLE	LABEL & NUMBER
10/11/2001	2	12	O	**RAPTURE**	Made/Data/MoS 27CDS
14/06/2003	20	3		AT THE END	Free 2 Air 0148065 F2A

IKARA COLT UK rock group formed in London in 1999 by Paul Resende (vocals), Claire Ingram (guitar), Jon Ball (bass) and Dominic Young (drums), taking their name from two types of gun.

DATE	POS	WKS	BPI	SINGLE TITLE	LABEL & NUMBER
02/03/2002	72	1		RUDD	Fantastic Plastic FPS 029
28/02/2004	49	1		WANNA BE THAT WAY	Fantastic Plastic FPS 038X
05/06/2004	55	1		WAKE IN THE CITY	Fantastic Plastic FPS 040X
23/10/2004	61	1		MODERN FEELING	Fantastic Plastic FPS 042

IL PADRINOS FEATURING JOCELYN BROWN UK production group formed by Dave Lee and Danny Rampling with US singer Jocelyn Brown. Lee has also recorded as Joey Negro, Jakatta, Akubu, Hed Boys (with Andrew Livingstone), Z Factor, Li Kwan and Raven Maize.

DATE	POS	WKS	BPI	SINGLE TITLE	LABEL & NUMBER
07/09/2002	54	1		THAT'S HOW GOOD YOUR LOVE IS	Defected DFTD 057CDS

ILLEGAL MOTION FEATURING SIMONE CHAPMAN UK vocal/instrumental duo Jekyll and Simone Chapman.

DATE	POS	WKS	BPI	SINGLE TITLE	LABEL & NUMBER
09/10/1993	67	1		SATURDAY LOVE	Arista 74321163032

ILLICIT FEATURING GRAM'MA FUNK UK producer with singer Gram'ma Funk.

DATE	POS	WKS	BPI	SINGLE TITLE	LABEL & NUMBER
02/09/2000	72	1		CHEEKY ARMADA Contains a sample of Teddy Pendergrass' *You Can't Hide From Yourself*	Yola YOLACDX 01

ILS UK DJ and producer Adam Freeland.

DATE	POS	WKS	BPI	SINGLE TITLE	LABEL & NUMBER
23/02/2002	75	1		NEXT LEVEL	Marine Parade MAPA 012

IMAANI UK singer Imaani Saleem (born Melanie Crosdale) whose debut hit was the UK entry in the 1998 Eurovision Song Contest, which came second to Israel's entry by Dana International, *Diva*.

DATE	POS	WKS	BPI	SINGLE TITLE	LABEL & NUMBER
16/05/1998	15	7		WHERE ARE YOU	EMI CDEM 510

IMAGINATION UK group formed in London in 1980 by Leee John (born John Lesley McGregor, 23/6/1957, London, vocals/keyboards), Ashley Ingram (born 27/11/1960, Northampton, bass/vocals) and Errol Kennedy (born in Montego Bay, Jamaica, drummer).

DATE	POS	WKS	BPI	SINGLE TITLE	LABEL & NUMBER
16/05/1981	4	18	O	**BODY TALK**	R&B RBS 201
05/09/1981	16	9		IN AND OUT OF LOVE	R&B RBS 202
14/11/1981	16	13		FLASHBACK	R&B RBS 206
06/03/1982	2	11	O	**JUST AN ILLUSION** Featured in the 1986 film *Prospects*	R&B RBS 208
26/06/1982	5	9	●	**MUSIC AND LIGHTS**	R&B RBS 210
25/09/1982	22	8		IN THE HEAT OF THE NIGHT	R&B RBS 211
11/12/1982	31	8		CHANGES	R&B RBS 213
04/06/1983	29	7		LOOKING AT MIDNIGHT	R&B RBS 214
05/11/1983	56	3		NEW DIMENSIONS	R&B RBS 216
26/05/1984	67	2		STATE OF LOVE	R&B RBS 218

24/11/1984 . . . . . 22 . . . . . 15 . . . . . . THANK YOU MY LOVE . . . . R&B RBS 219
16/01/1988 . . . . . 62 . . . . . 2 . . . . INSTINCTUAL . . . . RCA PB 41697

IMAJIN US vocal group formed by Olamide Asladejobi Patrick Alexander Faison (stage name Olamide), John Anthony Finch (Jiz), Stanley Jamal Hampton (Jamal) and Talib Kareem.

27/06/1998 . . . . . 22 . . . . . . 3 . . . . . . SHORTY (YOU KEEP PLAYIN' WITH MY MIND) **IMAJIN FEATURING KEITH MURRAY** Contains a sample of Peter Brown's *Dance With Me* . . . . Jive 0521212
20/02/1999 . . . . . 42 . . . . . . 2 . . . . . . NO DOUBT Contains a sample of The Detroit Spinners' *It's A Natural Affair*. . . . . Jive 0521772
24/04/1999 . . . . . 45 . . . . . . 1 . . . . . . BOUNCE, ROCK, SKATE, ROLL **BABY DC FEATURING IMAJIN** . . . . Jive 0522142
12/02/2000 . . . . . 64 . . . . . . 1 . . . . . . FLAVA . . . . Jive 9250012

NATALIE IMBRUGLIA Australian singer (born 4/2/1975, Sydney) who was initially famous for playing Beth in TV's *Neighbours,* before launching a singing career. Her debut single *Torn* was a cover version of a Norwegian hit by Trine Rein of two years earlier. She won Best International Female and Best International Newcomer at the 1999 BRIT Awards, took part in the *It's Only Rock 'N' Roll* project for the Children's Promise charity and starred in the 2003 film *Johnny English*.

08/11/1997 . . . . . 2 . . . . . 17 . . . . ✪ **TORN** 1998 MTV Europe Music Award for Best Song . . . . RCA 74321527982
14/03/1998 . . . . . 2 . . . . . 10 . . . . . . **BIG MISTAKE** . . . . RCA 74321566782
06/06/1998 . . . . . 19 . . . . . 5 . . . . . . WISHING I WAS HERE . . . . RCA 74321585062
17/10/1998 . . . . . 5 . . . . . 7 . . . . . . **SMOKE** . . . . RCA 74321621942
10/11/2001 . . . . . 11 . . . . . 5 . . . . . . THAT DAY . . . . RCA 74321896792
23/03/2002 . . . . . 10 . . . . . 7 . . . . . . **WRONG IMPRESSION** . . . . RCA 74321928352
03/08/2002 . . . . . 26 . . . . . 2 . . . . . . BEAUTY ON THE FIRE . . . . RCA 74321950362

IMMACULATE FOOLS UK pop group formed by Kevin Weatherall, brother Paul, Andy Ross and brother Peter, plus Barry Wickens.

26/01/1985 . . . . . 51 . . . . . . 4 . . . . . . IMMACULATE FOOLS . . . . A&M AM 227

IMMATURE FEATURING SMOOTH US R&B vocal trio from Los Angeles, with 'Bat Man' Houston, Jerome 'Romeo' Jones, Kelton 'LDB' Kessee and singer Smooth – all aged fourteen at the time of their debut hit.

16/03/1996 . . . . . 26 . . . . . . 2 . . . . . . WE GOT IT Contains a sample of Chocolate Milk's *Girl Callin'* . . . . MCA MCSTD 48009

IMPALAS US vocal group from Brooklyn, NYC with Joe 'Speedo' Frazier, Richard Wagner, Lenny Renda and Tony Carlucci. Frazier became singer with Love's Own in 1973.

21/08/1959 . . . . . 28 . . . . . . 1 . . . . . . SORRY (I RAN ALL THE WAY HOME) . . . . MGM 1015

IMPEDANCE UK producer Daniel Haydon.

11/11/1989 . . . . . 54 . . . . . . 4 . . . . . . TAINTED LOVE . . . . Jumpin' & Pumpin' TOT 4

IMPERIAL DRAG UK group with Eric Dover (guitar/vocals), Joseph Karnes (bass/vocals), Roger Joseph Manning Jr (keyboards/vocals) and Eric Skodis (drums/vocals).

12/10/1996 . . . . . 54 . . . . . . 1 . . . . . . BOY OR A GIRL . . . . Columbia 6632992

IMPERIAL TEEN US group formed by Will Schwartz (vocals), Roddy Bottum (keyboards), Jone Stebbings (bass) and Lynn Perko (drums). Bottum had previously been a member of Faith No More.

07/09/1996 . . . . . 69 . . . . . . 1 . . . . . . YOU'RE ONE . . . . Slash LASCD 57

IMPERIALS US vocal group formed by Little Anthony (born Anthony Gourdine, 8/1/1940, Brooklyn, NYC) in 1958 with Clarence Collins (born 17/3/1941, Brooklyn), Tracy Lord, Ernest Wright (born 24/8/1941, Brooklyn) and Nat Rogers (born 1940, Brooklyn). Anthony went solo in 1960, re-forming the group in 1964 with Wright, Collins and Sammy Strain (born 9/12/1941, Brooklyn), who was later a member of the O'Jays. The R&B group had a UK hit in 1977 with a third line-up under Clarence Collins.

24/12/1977 . . . . . 17 . . . . . . 9 . . . . . . WHO'S GONNA LOVE ME . . . . Power Exchange PX 266

IMPERIALS QUARTET – see **ELVIS PRESLEY**

IMPOSTER – see **ELVIS COSTELLO**

IMPRESSIONS US R&B group formed in Chattanooga, TN in 1957 by Arthur Brooks, Richard Brooks, Sam Gooden (born 2/9/1939, Chattanooga), Fred Cash (born 8/10/1940, Chattanooga) and Emanuel Thomas as the Roosters. Gooden and the Brook brothers relocated to Chicago, IL in 1958 and linked up with Jerry Butler (born 8/12/1939, Sunflower, MS) and Curtis Mayfield (born 3/6/1942, Chicago), renaming the group the Impressions. After their first hit (*For Your Precious Love*) Butler went solo in 1958, with Fred Cash his replacement. Mayfield re-formed the group with Cash and Gooden in Chicago, with the Brooks brothers remaining in New York. Mayfield left in 1972 and was replaced by Leroy Hutson, who left in 1973 and was replaced by Reggie Torian and Ralph Johnson (who joined Mystique in 1976). Mayfield, paralysed when a lighting gantry fell on him in 1990, died on 26/12/1999. The group was inducted into the Rock & Roll Hall of Fame in 1991.

22/11/1975 . . . . . 16 . . . . . 10 . . . . . . FIRST IMPRESSIONS . . . . Curtom K 16638

IN CROWD UK group with Keith West (vocals), Les Jones (guitar), John 'Junior' Wood (guitar), Simon 'Boots' Alcot (bass) and Ken Lawrence (drums). After one single Jones was replaced by Steve Howe, West later going solo.

20/05/1965 . . . . . 48 . . . . . . 1 . . . . . . THAT'S HOW STRONG MY LOVE IS . . . . Parlophone R 5276

❶⁹ Number of weeks single topped the UK chart ↑ Entered the UK chart at #1 ▲⁹ Number of weeks single topped the US chart

387

IN TUA NUA Irish group formed by Leslie Dowdall, Brian O'Briaian, Martin Colncy, Vinnie Kilduf and Steve Wickham. They first recorded for Island in 1984. Wickham joined The Waterboys in 1986 and was replaced by Angela De Burca.

14/05/1988 . . . . . 69 . . . . . . 2 . . . . ALL I WANTED . . . . Virgin VS 1072

INAURA UK vocal/instrumental group fronted by Matt Carey and originally called Polaroid until forced to change by the camera manufacturer.

18/05/1996 . . . . . 57 . . . . . . 1 . . . . COMA AROMA . . . . EMI CDEM 421

INCANTATION UK group formed by Forbes Henderson (guitar), Tony Hinnigan (quenas/sikus/tarka/percussion/guitar/guitarron/pinkillo), Simon Rogers (charango/guitar/tiple/percussion), Chris Swithinbank (sikus/voice guitar/guitar/guitarron) and Mike Taylor (quenas/sikus/anata/bombo). They later contributed to the soundtracks to the films *The Mission* (1986) and *Patriot Games* (1992).

04/12/1982 . . . . . 12 . . . . . 12 . . . . . . CACHARPAYA (ANDES PUMPSA DAESI) Theme to BBC TV's *The Flight Of The Condor* . . . . Beggars Banquet BEG 84

INCOGNITO UK jazz-funk group formed in 1981 by ex-Light Of The World bass player Paul 'Tubbs' Williams with Peter Hinds (keyboards), Jean Paul Maunick (guitar) and Jeff Dunn (drums). Their later line-up featured Maunick, Hinds, Thomas Dyani-Akuru (percussion), Randy Hope-Taylor (bass), Graham Harvey (keyboards), Patrick Clahar (saxophone), Kevin Robinson (trumpet), Fayyaz Virgi (trombone), Andy Gangadeen (drums) and Maysa Leak (vocals). They won the 2001 MOBO Award for Best Jazz Act.

15/11/1980 . . . . . 73 . . . . . . 2 . . . . PARISIENNE GIRL . . . . Ensign ENY 44
29/06/1991 . . . . . 6 . . . . . . 9 . . . . **ALWAYS THERE** INCOGNITO FEATURING JOCELYN BROWN . . . . Talkin Loud TLK 10
14/09/1991 . . . . . 59 . . . . . . 2 . . . . CRAZY FOR YOU **INCOGNITO FEATURING CHYNA** . . . . Talkin Loud TLK 14
06/06/1992 . . . . . 19 . . . . . . 6 . . . . DON'T YOU WORRY 'BOUT A THING . . . . Talkin Loud TLK 21
15/08/1992 . . . . . 52 . . . . . . 2 . . . . CHANGE . . . . Talkin Loud TLK 26
21/08/1993 . . . . . 47 . . . . . . 2 . . . . STILL A FRIEND OF MINE . . . . Talkin Loud TLKCD 42
20/11/1993 . . . . . 43 . . . . . . 2 . . . . GIVIN' IT UP . . . . Talkin Loud TLKCD 44
12/03/1994 . . . . . 35 . . . . . . 2 . . . . PIECES OF A DREAM . . . . Talkin Loud TLKCD 46
27/05/1995 . . . . . 23 . . . . . . 3 . . . . EVERYDAY . . . . Talkin Loud TLKCD 55
05/08/1995 . . . . . 42 . . . . . . 2 . . . . I HEAR YOUR NAME . . . . Talkin Loud TLKCD 56
11/05/1996 . . . . . 29 . . . . . . 3 . . . . JUMP TO MY LOVE/ALWAYS THERE B-side is a re-recording . . . . Talkin Loud TLCD 7
26/10/1996 . . . . . 57 . . . . . . 1 . . . . OUT OF THE STORM . . . . Talkin Loud TLCD 14
10/04/1999 . . . . . 56 . . . . . . 1 . . . . NIGHTS OVER EGYPT . . . . Talkin Loud TLCD 40

INCUBUS US group formed in Calabasas, CA in 1991 by Brandon Boyd (vocals/percussion), Mike Einziger (guitar), Dirk Lance (bass), Jose Pasillas (drums) and DJ Chris Kilmore (turntables).

20/05/2000 . . . . . 61 . . . . . . 1 . . . . PARDON ME . . . . Epic 6693462
23/06/2001 . . . . . 40 . . . . . . 2 . . . . DRIVE . . . . Epic 6713782
02/02/2002 . . . . . 27 . . . . . . 3 . . . . WISH YOU WERE HERE . . . . Epic 6722552
14/09/2002 . . . . . 34 . . . . . . 2 . . . . ARE YOU IN . . . . Epic 6728485
07/02/2004 . . . . . 23 . . . . . . 3 . . . . MEGLOMANIAC . . . . Epic 6746465
19/06/2004 . . . . . 43 . . . . . . 1 . . . . TALK SHOWS ON MUTE . . . . Epic 6749022

INDEEP US group from New York consisting of Michael Cleveland, Reggie Megliore and Rose Marie Ramsey.

22/01/1983 . . . . . 13 . . . . . . 9 . . . . LAST NIGHT A DJ SAVED MY LIFE . . . . Sound Of New York SNY 1
14/05/1983 . . . . . 67 . . . . . . 2 . . . . WHEN BOYS TALK . . . . Sound Of New York SNY 3

INDIA US vocalist Linda Caballero.

05/08/1995 . . . . . 44 . . . . . . 2 . . . . I CAN'T GET NO SLEEP **MASTERS AT WORK PRESENTS INDIA** . . . . A&M 5811412
26/02/1996 . . . . . 50 . . . . . . 2 . . . . LOVE AND HAPPINESS (YEMAYA Y OCHUN) **RIVER OCEAN FEATURING INDIA** . . . . Cooltempo CDCOOL 287
16/03/1996 . . . . . 36 . . . . . . 2 . . . . OYE COMO VA **TITO PUENTE JR AND THE LATIN RHYTHM FEATURING TITO PUENTE, INDIA AND CALI ALEMAN** . . . . Media MCSTD 40013
08/02/1997 . . . . . 24 . . . . . . 6 . . . . RUNAWAY **NUYORICAN SOUL FEATURING INDIA** . . . . Talkin Loud TLCD 20
19/07/1997 . . . . . 56 . . . . . . 1 . . . . OYE COMO VA **TITO PUENTE JR AND THE LATIN RHYTHM FEATURING TITO PUENTE, INDIA AND CALI ALEMAN** Re-issue of Media MCSTD 40013 . . . . Nukleuz MCSTD 40120
31/07/1999 . . . . . 23 . . . . . . 3 . . . . TO BE IN LOVE **MAW PRESENTS INDIA** . . . . Defected DEFECT 5CD
06/07/2002 . . . . . 62 . . . . . . 1 . . . . BACKFIRED **MASTERS AT WORK FEATURING INDIA** . . . . Susu CDSUSU 4

INDIAN VIBES UK group formed by ex-Jam/Syle Council Paul Weller (guitar) with Gerrard Farrell (sitar), Marco Nelson (bass) and Crispin Taylor (drums).

24/09/1994 . . . . . 68 . . . . . . 1 . . . . MATHAR . . . . Virgin International DINSD 136
02/05/1998 . . . . . 52 . . . . . . 1 . . . . MATHAR (REMIX) . . . . VC Recordings VCRD 32

INDIEN UK production/vocal duo Mark Hadfield and Emmie Norton-Smith. The pair were later members of Lovebug.

09/08/2003 . . . . . 69 . . . . . . 1 . . . . SHOW ME LOVE . . . . Concept CDCON 40

INDO US rapper/producer who later worked with Dead Prez and Minority Militia.

18/04/1998 . . . . . 31 . . . . . . 3 . . . . R U SLEEPING . . . . Satellite 74321568212

INDUSTRY STANDARD UK DJ/production duo Dave Deller and Clayton Mitchell.

10/01/1998 . . . . . 34 . . . . . . 3 . . . . VOLUME 1 (WHAT YOU WANT WHAT YOU NEED) . . . . Satellite 74321543742

○ Silver disc ● Gold disc ✪ Platinum disc (additional platinum units are indicated by a figure following the symbol) ◎ Singles released prior to 1973 that are known to have sold over 1 million copies in the UK

INFARED VS GIL FELIX
US production group Jamie Spratling (who also records as J Majik), Gil Felix, Tim B and Wickerman.

04/10/2003	67	1	CAPOIERA	Infrared INFRA 24CD

INFINITI – see GRAND PUBA

INGRAM
US vocal/instrumental family group formed in Camden, NJ by Norman 'Butch', James, Barbara, Billy, John, Timmy, Frances, Edith and Virginia Ingram. (NB: Not the same James Ingram referred to below.)

11/06/1983	56	2	SMOOTHIN' GROOVIN'	Streetwave WAVE 3

JAMES INGRAM
US singer (born 1956, Akron, OH) who moved to Los Angeles in 1973, became the keyboard player for Leon Haywood and then formed Revelation Funk. He was signed by Quincy Jones after the latter heard a demo, and appeared on *The Dude* album. Two Grammy Awards include Best Rhythm & Blues Vocal Performance in 1981 for *One Hundred Ways*.

12/02/1983	11	10	BABY COME TO ME ▲² PATTI AUSTIN AND JAMES INGRAM	Qwest K 15005
18/02/1984	44	8	YAH MO B THERE JAMES INGRAM WITH MICHAEL McDONALD	Qwest W 9394
19/01/1985	12	8	YAH MO B THERE 1984 Grammy Award for Best Rhythm & Blues Vocal Performance by a Duo	Qwest W 9394
11/07/1987	8	13	SOMEWHERE OUT THERE LINDA RONSTADT AND JAMES INGRAM Featured in the 1987 film *An American Tail*	MCA 1132
31/03/1990	67	1	SECRET GARDEN QUINCY JONES FEATURING AL B SURE!, JAMES INGRAM, EL DEBARGE AND BARRY WHITE Featured in the 1997 film *Sprung*	Qwest W 9992
16/04/1994	64	2	THE DAY I FALL IN LOVE DOLLY PARTON AND JAMES INGRAM Featured in the 1994 film *Beethoven's 2nd*	Columbia 6600282

INK SPOTS
US R&B vocal group formed in 1931 by four porters from New York's Paramount Theatre – Jerry Daniels, Charles Fuqua, Ivory 'Deek' Watson and Orville 'Hoppy' Jones (born 17/2/1905, Chicago, IL) – as the King, Jack & Jesters. They changed their name to the Ink Spots in 1932 and first recorded for Victor in 1935. There have been numerous personnel changes over the years and, although a group of the name still works today, no original members remained after 1952. Film appearances included *The Great American Broadcast* (1941) and *Pardon My Sarong* (1942). Their debut US hit *If I Didn't Care* (1939) was awarded a Grammy in 1988 and the group was inducted into the Rock & Roll Hall of Fame in 1989.

29/04/1955	10	4	MELODY OF LOVE	Parlophone R 3977

JOHN INMAN
UK actor (born 28/6/1935, Preston) famous as Mr Humphries in the TV comedy *Are You Being Served*.

25/10/1975	39	6	ARE YOU BEING SERVED SIR	DJM DJS 602

INMATES
UK group formed by Bill Hurley (vocals), Peter Gunn (guitar/vocals), Tony Oliver (guitar), Ben Donnelly (bass) and Jim Russell (drums/vocals).

08/12/1979	36	9	THE WALK	Radar ADA 47

INME
UK rock group with Dave McPherson (guitar/vocals), Joe Morgan (bass/vocals) and Simon Taylor (drums).

27/07/2002	66	1	UNDERDOSE	Music For Nations CDKUT 195
28/08/2002	43	1	FIREFLY	Music For Nations CDKUT 197
18/01/2003	25	2	CRUSHED LIKE FRUIT	Music For Nations CDKUT 200
26/04/2003	46	1	NEPTUNE	Music For Nations CDXKUT 201
05/06/2004	31	2	FASTER THE CHASE	Music For Nations CDXKUT 210

INNER CIRCLE
Jamaican group originally formed in 1968 by brothers Roger 'Fat Man' (lead guitar) and Ian 'Munty' Lewis (bass). They re-formed in 1972 with Calvin McKensie (drums), Bernard 'Touter' Harvey and Charles Farquharson (keyboards) being added to the line-up. Singer Jacob Miller joined in 1974 and they signed with Capitol in 1977, then Island in 1978. Miller was killed in a car crash on 21/2/1980. The group won the 1993 Grammy Award for Best Reggae Album for *Bad Boys*.

24/02/1979	37	8	EVERYTHING IS GREAT	Island WIP 6472
12/05/1979	50	3	STOP BREAKING MY HEART	Island WIP 6488
31/10/1992	43	5	SWEAT (A LA LA LA LONG)	Magnet 9031776802
01/05/1993	3	14	○	SWEAT (A LA LA LA LA LONG)	Magnet 9031776802
31/07/1993	52	3	BAD BOYS	Magnet MAG 1017CD
10/09/1994	67	2	GAMES PEOPLE PLAY	Magnet MAG 1026CD

INNER CITY
US dance duo Kevin Saunderson (born 9/5/1964, New York, keyboards) and Paris Grey (from Glencove, IL, vocals). Dennis White, who later enjoyed a chart career as Static Revenger, joined in 1989. Saunderson later recorded as Reese Project.

03/09/1988	8	14	BIG FUN INNER CITY FEATURING KEVIN SAUNDERSON	10 TEN 240
10/12/1988	4	12	○	GOOD LIFE Featured in the 1989 film *Slaves Of New York*	10 TEN 249
22/04/1989	10	7	AIN'T NOBODY BETTER	10 TEN 252
29/07/1989	16	7	DO YOU LOVE WHAT YOU FEEL	10 TEN 237
18/11/1989	12	9	WATCHA GONNA DO WITH MY LOVIN'	10 TEN 290
13/10/1990	42	4	THAT MAN (HE'S ALL MINE)	10 TEN 334
23/02/1991	47	2	TILL WE MEET AGAIN	10 TEN 337
07/12/1991	51	2	LET IT REIGN	10 TEN 392
04/04/1992	22	4	HALLELUJAH '92	10 TEN 398
13/06/1992	24	4	PENNIES FROM HEAVEN	10 TEN 405
12/09/1992	59	2	PRAISE	10 TENX 408
27/02/1993	55	1	TILL WE MEET AGAIN (REMIX)	10 TENCD 414
14/08/1993	49	1	BACK TOGETHER AGAIN	Six6 SIXCD 104
05/02/1994	44	2	DO YA	Six6 SIXCD 107

❶⁹ Number of weeks single topped the UK chart **↑** Entered the UK chart at #1 **▲**⁹ Number of weeks single topped the US chart

389

DATE	POS	WKS	BPI	SINGLE TITLE	LABEL & NUMBER
09/07/1994	62	1		SHARE MY LIFE	Six6 SIXCD 114
10/02/1996	28	2		YOUR LOVE	Six6 SIXCD 127
05/10/1996	47	1		DO ME RIGHT	Six6 SIXXCD 2
06/02/1999	10	6		**GOOD LIFE (BUENA VIDA)** This is a re-recording of 10 Ten 249	Pias Recordings PIASX 002CD

INNER SANCTUM Canadian producer Steve Bolton.

DATE	POS	WKS	BPI	SINGLE TITLE	LABEL & NUMBER
23/05/1998	75	1		HOW SOON IS NOW	Malarky MLKD 6

INNERZONE ORCHESTRA US producer Carl Craig.

DATE	POS	WKS	BPI	SINGLE TITLE	LABEL & NUMBER
28/09/1996	68	1		BUG IN THE BASSBIN	Mo Wax MW 049CD

INNOCENCE UK group Mark Jolley (guitar), his sister Anna (vocals) and Brian Harris (percussion) who also recorded as Circuit, Gee Morris also being a member briefly.

DATE	POS	WKS	BPI	SINGLE TITLE	LABEL & NUMBER
03/03/1990	16	7		NATURAL THING	Cooltempo COOL 201
21/07/1990	37	5		SILENT VOICE	Cooltempo COOL 212
13/10/1990	25	6		LET'S PUSH IT	Cooltempo COOL 220
08/12/1990	37	7		A MATTER OF FACT	Cooltempo COOL 223
30/03/1991	56	2		REMEMBER THE DAY	Cooltempo COOL 226
20/06/1992	26	3		I'LL BE THERE	Cooltempo COOL 255
03/10/1992	40	2		ONE LOVE IN MY LIFETIME	Cooltempo COOL 263
21/11/1992	72	1		BUILD	Cooltempo COOL 267

INSANE CLOWN POSSE US rap duo with Joe 'Violent J' Bruce and Joe 'Shaggy 2 Dope' Utsler.

DATE	POS	WKS	BPI	SINGLE TITLE	LABEL & NUMBER
17/01/1998	56	1		HALLS OF ILLUSION	Island CID 685
06/06/1998	53	1		HOKUS POKUS	Island CIDX 705

INSPIRAL CARPETS UK dance-rock group formed in Oldham, Manchester in 1987 by Clint Boon (born 28/6/1959, Oldham, organ), Stephen Holt (vocals), David Swift (bass), Graham Lambert (born 10/7/1964, Oldham, guitar) and Craig Gill (born 5/12/1971, Manchester, drums). Holt and Swift were replaced by Tom Hingley (born 9/7/1965, Oxford) and Martyn 'Bungle' Walsh (born 8/7/1968, Manchester) respectively.

DATE	POS	WKS	BPI	SINGLE TITLE	LABEL & NUMBER
18/11/1989	49	2		MOVE	Cow DUNG 6
17/03/1990	14	8		THIS IS HOW IT FEELS	Cow DUNG 7
30/06/1990	27	6		SHE COMES IN THE FALL	Cow DUNG 10
17/11/1990	21	4		ISLAND HEAD EP Tracks on EP: *Biggest Mountain, Gold Top, Weakness* and *I'll Keep It In Mind*	Cow DUNG 11
30/03/1991	30	5		CARAVAN	Cow DUNG 13
22/06/1991	50	2		PLEASE BE CRUEL	Cow DUNG 15
29/02/1992	12	5		DRAGGING ME DOWN	Cow DUNG 16
30/05/1992	32	2		TWO WORLDS COLLIDE	Cow DUNG 17
19/09/1992	28	3		GENERATIONS	Cow DUNG 18T
14/11/1992	36	2		BITCHES BREW	Cow DUNG 20T
05/06/1993	49	1		HOW IT SHOULD BE	Cow DUNG 22CD
22/01/1994	20	4		SATURN 5	Cow DUNG 23CD
05/03/1994	18	3		I WANT YOU **INSPIRAL CARPETS FEATURING MARK E SMITH**	Cow DUNG 24CD
07/05/1994	51	1		UNIFORM	Cow DUNG 26CD
16/09/1995	37	2		JOE	Cow DUNG 27CD
26/07/2003	43	1		COME BACK TOMORROW Contains a sample of Tyron Brunson's *The Smurf*	Mute DUNG 13CD

INSPIRATIONAL CHOIR US gospel choir whose full name is The Inspirational Choir Of The Pentecostal First Born Church Of The Living God, with the label also crediting the Royal Choral Society. The choir, fronted by John Francis, also performed with Madness on their hit *Wings Of A Dove*.

DATE	POS	WKS	BPI	SINGLE TITLE	LABEL & NUMBER
22/12/1984	44	5		ABIDE WITH ME	Epic A 4997
14/12/1985	36	6		ABIDE WITH ME Re-issue of Epic A 4997	Portrait A 4997

INSTANT FUNK US funk group formed in Philadelphia, PA by James Carmichael (vocals), Kim Miller (guitar), George Bell (guitar), Raymond Earl (bass), Dennis Richardson (keyboards), Larry Davis (trumpet), Johnny Onderlinde (saxophone), Eric Huff (trombone) and Scotty Miller (drums).

DATE	POS	WKS	BPI	SINGLE TITLE	LABEL & NUMBER
20/01/1979	46	5		GOT MY MIND MADE UP Featured in the 1998 film *54*	Salsoul SSOL 114

INTASTELLA UK group formed in Manchester by Stella Grundy (vocals), Anthony Green (guitar) plus ex-Laugh members Martin Wright (guitar/vocals), Martin Mittler (bass) and Spencer Birtwhistle (drums).

DATE	POS	WKS	BPI	SINGLE TITLE	LABEL & NUMBER
25/05/1991	69	1		DREAM SOME PARADISE	MCA MCS 1520
24/08/1991	74	2		PEOPLE	MCA MCS 1559
16/11/1991	70	2		CENTURY	MCA MCS 1585
23/09/1995	60	1		THE NIGHT	Planet 3 GXY 2005CD

INTELLIGENT HOODLUM US rapper (born Percy Chapman, Long Island, NY).

DATE	POS	WKS	BPI	SINGLE TITLE	LABEL & NUMBER
06/10/1990	55	3		BACK TO REALITY	A&M AM 598

INTENSO PROJECT UK duo DJ Rods (Rodney Williams) and Leigh Guest.

○ Silver disc ● Gold disc ✪ Platinum disc (additional platinum units are indicated by a figure following the symbol) ◎ Singles released prior to 1973 that are known to have sold over 1 million copies in the UK

17/08/2002.....22......2...... LUV DA SUNSHINE Contains a sample of 10 CC's *Dreadlock Holiday*.....................................Inferno CDFERN 47
26/07/2003.....32......2...... YOUR MUSIC **INTENSO PROJECT FEATURING LAURA JAYE**...Concept CDCON 43
04/12/2004.....23......3...... GET IT ON **INTENSO PROJECT FEATURING LISA SCOTT-LEE**..Inspired INSPMOS1CDS

INTERACTIVE German technopop group formed by Christoph 'Doom' Schneider (born 5/11/1966), Ramon Zenker and Jens Lissat. Schneider is also a member of Rammstein, while Zenker and Lissat record as E-Trax.

13/04/1996.....28......4...... FOREVER YOUNG...ffrreedom TABCD 235
08/03/2003.....37......2...... FOREVER YOUNG Remix of ffrreedom TABCD 235.....................................All Around The World CDGLOBE 253

INTERNATIONAL AIRPORT – see TEENAGE FANCLUB

INTERPOL US rock group formed in New York in 1998 by UK-born Paul Banks (guitar/vocals), fellow-Brit Daniel Kessler (guitar/vocals), plus Carlos Dengler (bass) and Sam Fogarino (drums).

23/11/2002.....72......1...... OBSTACLE 1..Matador OLE 5702
26/04/2003.....65......1...... SAY HELLO TO THE ANGELS..Matador OLE 5822
27/09/2003.....41......1...... OBSTACLE 1 Re-issue of Matador OLE 5702...Matador OLE 5942
25/09/2004.....36......2...... SLOW HANDS...Matador OLE 6362

INTRUDERS US R&B vocal group formed in Philadelphia, PA in 1960 by Sam 'Little Sonny' Brown, Eugene 'Bird' Daughtrey (born 29/10/1939, Kinston, NC), Phil Terry (born 1/11/1943, Philadelphia) and Robert 'Big Sonny' Edwards (born 22/2/1942, Philadelphia). After recording with local label Gowen in 1961, they linked up with Leon Huff and Kenny Gamble in 1964, and signed the following year with Excel (where they had their first hits), which changed its name to Gamble shortly after. The group followed Gamble and Huff when they set up Philadelphia International. The original members split in 1975. Daughtrey died from liver and kidney disease on 25/12/1994. Brown committed suicide the following year.

13/04/1974.....32......7...... I'LL ALWAYS LOVE MY MAMA ....Philadelphia International PIR 2149
06/07/1974.....14......9...... (WIN PLACE OR SHOW) SHE'S A WINNER ....Philadelphia International PIR 2212
22/12/1984.....65......5...... WHO DO YOU LOVE?...Streetwave KHAN 34

INVADERS OF THE HEART – see JAH WOBBLE'S INVADERS OF THE HEART

INVISIBLE GIRLS – see PAULINE MURRAY AND THE INVISIBLE GIRLS

INVISIBLE MAN UK producer Graham Mew.

17/04/1999.....48......1...... GIVE A LITTLE LOVE ....Serious SERR 006CD

INXS Australian rock group formed in 1977 by Tim Farris (born 16/8/1957, Perth, guitar), Andrew Farris (born 27/3/1959, Perth, keyboards), Jon Farris (born 10/8/1961, Perth, drums/vocals), Michael Hutchence (born 22/1/1962, Sydney, vocals), Kirk Pengilly (born 4/7/1958, Sydney, guitar/saxophone/vocals) and Garry Beers (born 22/6/1957, Sydney, bass/vocals) as the Farris Brothers. The name INXS came at the suggestion of Midnight Oil manager Garry Morris in 1979. After their debut recording on Deluxe, from 1983 they concentrated on the international market, signing with Atlantic for the US with a top 30 hit in 1983, and making their UK breakthrough in 1985. Hutchence was named Best International Male at the 1991 BRIT Awards, when the band was also named Best International Group. Hutchence – who appeared in the 1987 film *Dogs In Space* – was found hanged in a Sydney hotel room on 22/11/1997. Despite a suicide verdict there is considerable speculation that he died after an autoerotic sex act went wrong. At the time he had been working on a solo album with producer Andy Gill. In June 2004 the group announced they were to hold a worldwide reality TV competition to find a new lead singer.

19/04/1986.....51......6...... WHAT YOU NEED ....Mercury INXS 5
28/06/1986.....46......7...... LISTEN LIKE THIEVES...Mercury INXS 6
30/08/1986.....54......3...... KISS THE DIRT (FALLING DOWN THE MOUNTAIN) ....Mercury INXS 7
24/10/1987.....58......3...... NEED YOU TONIGHT...Mercury INXS 8
09/01/1988.....25......6...... NEW SENSATION..Mercury INXS 9
12/03/1988.....47......5...... DEVIL INSIDE..Mercury INXS 10
25/06/1988.....24......7...... NEVER TEAR US APART...Mercury INXS 11
12/11/1988 ......2.....11...... **NEED YOU TONIGHT** ▲¹ Featured in the 2000 film *Coyote Ugly*...........................Mercury INXS 12
08/04/1989.....14......7...... MYSTIFY...Mercury INXS 13
15/09/1990.....11......6...... SUICIDE BLONDE...Mercury INXS 14
08/12/1990.....21......8...... DISAPPEAR...Mercury INXS 15
26/01/1991.....18......8...... GOOD TIMES **JIMMY BARNES AND INXS** Originally released in 1987. Featured in the 1987 film *The Lost Boys* .....Atlantic A 7751
30/03/1991.....42......4...... BY MY SIDE...Mercury INXS 16
13/07/1991.....30......3...... BITTER TEARS...Mercury INXS 17
02/11/1991.....27......3...... SHINING STAR (EP) Tracks on EP: *Shining Star, Send A Message (Live), Faith In Each Other (Live)* and *Bitter Tears (Live)*........
....Mercury INXS 18
18/07/1992.....31......3...... HEAVEN SENT..Mercury INXS 19
05/09/1992.....20......5...... BABY DON'T CRY...Mercury INXS 20
14/11/1992.....21......4...... TASTE IT...Mercury INXS 23
13/02/1993.....23......5...... BEAUTIFUL GIRL...Mercury INXCD 24
23/10/1993.....11......4...... THE GIFT...Mercury INXCD 25
11/12/1993.....50......3...... PLEASE (YOU GOT THAT...) Features the uncredited contribution of Ray Charles.............Mercury INXCD 26
22/10/1994.....15......5...... THE STRANGEST PARTY (THESE ARE THE TIMES)..Mercury INXCD 27
22/03/1997.....20......4...... ELEGANTLY WASTED...Mercury INXCD 28

❶⁹ Number of weeks single topped the UK chart ↑ Entered the UK chart at #1 ▲⁹ Number of weeks single topped the US chart

391

	DATE	POS	WKS	BPI	SINGLE TITLE	LABEL & NUMBER
	07/06/1997	71	1		EVERYTHING	Mercury INXDD 29
	18/08/2001	14	5		PRECIOUS HEART TALL PAUL VS INXS	Duty Freee/Decode DFTELCD 001
	03/11/2001	19	6		I'M SO CRAZY PAR-T-ONE VS INXS Contains a sample of INXS' *Just Keep Walking*	Credence CDCRED 016

SWEETIE IRIE Jamaican reggae singer.

	17/11/1990	53	2		SMILE ASWAD FEATURING SWEETIE IRIE	Mango MNG 767
	03/08/1991	47	3		TAKE ME IN YOUR ARMS AND LOVE ME SCRITTI POLITTI AND SWEETIE IRIE	Virgin VS 1346
	15/09/2001	29	2		WHO? ED CASE FEATURING SWEETIE IRIE	Columbia 6718302

TIPPA IRIE UK reggae singer (born Anthony Garfield Henry) who has also recorded for Greensleeves, IRS and Ariwa.

	22/03/1986	22	7		HELLO DARLING	UK Bubblers TIPPA 4
	19/07/1986	59	3		HEARTBEAT	UK Bubblers TIPPA 5
	15/05/1993	34	3		SHOUTING FOR THE GUNNERS ARSENAL FA CUP SQUAD FEATURING TIPPA IRIE AND PETER HUNNIGALE	London LONCD 342
	08/07/1995	48	1		STAYING ALIVE 95 FEVER FEATURING TIPPA IRIE	Telstar CDSTAS 2776

IRON MAIDEN UK heavy metal group (named after a medieval instrument of torture) formed in 1976 by Steve Harris (born 12/3/1957, Leytonstone, London, bass), Dave Murray (born 23/12/1958, London, guitar), Paul Di'anno (vocals) and Doug Sampson (drums). Tony Parsons joined in November 1979 but was replaced in January 1980 by Dennis Stratton (born 9/11/1954, London), at the same time as the drummer's stool was vacated by Sampson and taken by Clive Burr (born 8/3/1958). Before the year was out Stratton had left, being replaced by Adrian Smith (born 27/2/1957, London). Di'anno left in 1981 and was replaced by Bruce Dickinson (born 7/8/1958, Worksop, Nottinghamshire), after which they broke big on both sides of the Atlantic. Gurr left in 1983 and was replaced by Nicko McBrain (born 5/6/1954, London); Smith left in 1990 and was replaced by Janick Gers (born 27/1/1957, Hartlepool, Cleveland).

	23/02/1980	34	5		RUNNING FREE Refusing to mime to the record on TV chart show *Top Of The Pops*, they became the first band to play live on the programme since The Who in 1973	EMI 5032
	07/06/1980	29	5		SANCTUARY	EMI 5065
	08/11/1980	35	4		WOMEN IN UNIFORM	EMI 5105
	14/03/1981	31	5		TWILIGHT ZONE/WRATH CHILD	EMI 5145
	27/06/1981	52	3		PURGATORY	EMI 5184
	26/09/1981	43	4		MAIDEN JAPAN	EMI 5219
	20/02/1982	7	10		RUN TO THE HILLS	EMI 5263
	15/05/1982	18	8		THE NUMBER OF THE BEAST	EMI 5287
	23/04/1983	11	6		FLIGHT OF ICARUS	EMI 5378
	02/07/1983	12	7		THE TROOPER	EMI 5397
	18/08/1984	11	6		2 MINUTES TO MIDNIGHT	EMI 5849
	03/11/1984	20	5		ACES HIGH	EMI 5502
	05/10/1985	19	5		RUNNING FREE (LIVE)	EMI 5532
	14/12/1985	26	6		RUN TO THE HILLS (LIVE)	EMI 5542
	06/09/1986	18	4		WASTED YEARS	EMI 5583
	22/11/1986	22	5		STRANGER IN A STRANGE LAND	EMI 5589
	26/03/1988	3	6		CAN I PLAY WITH MADNESS	EMI EM 49
	13/08/1988	5	6		THE EVIL THAT MEN DO	EMI EM 64
	19/11/1988	6	8		THE CLAIRVOYANT	EMI EM 79
	18/11/1989	6	6		INFINITE DREAMS	EMI EM 117
	22/09/1990	3	4		HOLY SMOKE	EMI EM 153
	05/01/1991	●²	5		BRING YOUR DAUGHTER...TO THE SLAUGHTER ↑ Featured in the 1990 film *A Nightmare On Elm Street 5 – The Dream Child*	EMI EMPD 171
	25/04/1992	2	4		BE QUICK OR BE DEAD	EMI EM 229
	11/07/1992	21	4		FROM HERE TO ETERNITY	EMI EMS 240
	13/03/1993	8	3		FEAR OF THE DARK (LIVE)	EMI CDEMS 263
	16/10/1993	9	3		HALLOWED BE THY NAME (LIVE)	EMI CDEM 288
	07/10/1995	10	3		MAN ON THE EDGE	EMI CDEMS 398
	21/09/1996	16	3		VIRUS	EMI CDEM 443
	21/03/1998	18	3		THE ANGEL AND THE GAMBLER	EMI CDEM 507
	20/05/2000	9	4		THE WICKER MAN	EMI CDEMS 568
	04/11/2000	20	3		OUT OF THE SILENT PLANET	EMI CDEM 576
	23/03/2002	9	4		RUN TO THE HILLS	EMI CDEMS 612
	13/09/2003	6	6		WILDEST DREAMS	EMI CDEM 627
	06/12/2003	13	5		RAINMAKER	EMI CDEM 633

IRONHORSE Canadian band formed by Randy Bachman (born 27/9/1943, Winnipeg, guitar/vocals), Tom Sparks (guitar), John Pierce (bass) and Mike Baird (drums). Bachman had previously been in Guess Who and Bachman Turner Overdrive.

| | 05/05/1979 | 60 | 3 | | SWEET LUI-LOUISE | Scotti Brothers K 11271 |

BIG DEE IRWIN US singer (born Defosca Ervin, 4/8/1939, New York). He was lead singer with The Pastels who formed in 1954, recorded as Dee Ervin for Signpost and then became a songwriter. He died from heart failure on 27/8/1995.

○ Silver disc ● Gold disc ✪ Platinum disc (additional platinum units are indicated by a figure following the symbol) ◉ Singles released prior to 1973 that are known to have sold over 1 million copies in the UK

21/11/1963 . . . . . 7 . . . . . . 17 . . . . . | **SWINGING ON A STAR** 1944 Oscar for Best Film Song as featured in *Going My Way*. Irwin's single was a duet with Little Eva, who was uncredited on the UK release . . . . Colpix PX 11010

CHRIS ISAAK US singer (born 26/6/1956, Stockton, CA) who went to college in Japan and made cameo appearances in the films *Married To The Mob* (1988) and *Silence Of The Lambs* (1991).

24/11/1990 . . . . . 10 . . . . . 10	**WICKED GAME** Featured in the 1990 film *Wild At Heart* . . . . London LON 279
02/02/1991 . . . . . 17 . . . . . . 7	BLUE HOTEL . . . . Reprise W 0005
03/04/1993 . . . . . 36 . . . . . . 3	CAN'T DO A THING (TO STOP ME) . . . . Reprise W 0161CD
10/07/1993 . . . . . 62 . . . . . . 1	SAN FRANCISCO DAYS . . . . Reprise W 0182CD
02/10/1999 . . . . . 44 . . . . . . 1	BABY DID A BAD BAD THING Featured in the 1999 film *Eyes Wide Shut* . . . . Reprise W 503CD

ISHA-D UK vocal/instrumental duo Phil Coxon and Beverley Reppion.

22/07/1995 . . . . . 28 . . . . . . 3	STAY (TONIGHT) . . . . Cleveland City Blues CCBCD 15005
05/07/1997 . . . . . 58 . . . . . . 1	STAY Re-issue of Cleveland City Blues CCBCD 15005 . . . . Satellite 74321498212

ISHANI — see PIRATES, ENYA, SHOLA AMA, NAILA BOSS & ISHANI

YUSUF ISLAM — see CAT STEVENS

RONALD ISLEY US singer (born 21/5/1941, Cincinnati, OH) and a member of The Isley Brothers from their formation in 1955. He married singer Angela Winbush in 1993.

11/11/1989 . . . . . 51 . . . . . . 3	THIS OLD HEART OF MINE **ROD STEWART FEATURING RONALD ISLEY** . . . . Warner Brothers W 2686
02/03/1996 . . . . . 23 . . . . . . 3	DOWN LOW (NOBODY HAS TO KNOW) **R KELLY FEATURING RONALD ISLEY** Ronald Isley plays the part of Mr Biggs in the accompanying video . . . . Jive JIVERCD 392
31/05/1997 . . . . . 14 . . . . . . 5	SMOKIN' ME OUT **WARREN G FEATURING RON ISLEY** Contains an interpolation of The Isley Brothers' *Coolin' Me Out* . . . . Def Jam 5744432

ISLEY BROTHERS US R&B vocal group formed as a quartet in Cincinnati, OH in 1955 by brothers Rudolph (born 1/4/1939, Cincinnati), Ronald (born 21/5/1941, Cincinnati), O'Kelly (born 25/12/1937, Cincinnati) and Vernon Isley. Vernon was killed in a bicycle accident but they re-formed as a trio. The group moved to New York and recorded for Teenage Records and other labels before signing to RCA in 1959 and working with Hugo & Luigi on *Shout*, a million seller. After recording for Atlantic, Bang and United Artists they set up the T-Neck label (named after Teaneck, the area where they lived) and recorded *Testify* with Jimi Hendrix. They joined Motown in 1965, enjoying considerable success, especially in the UK, before leaving the label in 1969 and reviving T-Neck. The group was extended by younger brothers Marvin (born 18/8/1953, bass/percussion) and Ernie (born 7/3/1952, guitar/drums), and cousin Chris Jasper (keyboards). In 1984 the younger brothers and Jasper left to form Isley Jasper Isley (signed to Epic), the older brothers retaining the Isley Brothers moniker. Jasper recorded solo in 1988. O'Kelly died from a heart attack on 31/3/1986. Ernie, Marvin and Ronald recorded together again in 1992, the year the group were inducted into the Rock & Roll Hall of Fame.

25/07/1963 . . . . . 42 . . . . . . 1	TWIST AND SHOUT . . . . Stateside SS 112
28/04/1966 . . . . . 47 . . . . . . 1	THIS OLD HEART OF MINE . . . . Tamla Motown TMG 555
01/09/1966 . . . . . 45 . . . . . . 2	I GUESS I'LL ALWAYS LOVE YOU . . . . Tamla Motown TMG 572
23/10/1968 . . . . . 3 . . . . . . 16	**THIS OLD HEART OF MINE** . . . . Tamla Motown TMG 555
15/01/1969 . . . . . 11 . . . . . . 9	I GUESS I'LL ALWAYS LOVE YOU Re-issue of Tamla Motown TMG 572 . . . . Tamla Motown TMG 683
16/04/1969 . . . . . 5 . . . . . . 12	**BEHIND A PAINTED SMILE** . . . . Tamla Motown TMG 693
25/06/1969 . . . . . 30 . . . . . . 5	IT'S YOUR THING 1969 Grammy Award for Best Rhythm & Blues Vocal Performance by a Group . . . . Major Minor MM 621
30/08/1969 . . . . . 13 . . . . . . 11	PUT YOURSELF IN MY PLACE . . . . Tamla Motown TMG 708
22/09/1973 . . . . . 14 . . . . . . 9	THAT LADY Featured in the films *Breast Men* (1997), *Boys Don't Cry* (1999) and *Scooby Doo 2: Monsters Unleashed* (2004) . . . . Epic EPC 1704
19/01/1974 . . . . . 25 . . . . . . 8	HIGHWAYS OF MY LIFE . . . . Epic EPC 1980
25/05/1974 . . . . . 16 . . . . . . 8	SUMMER BREEZE Originally a US hit for Seals And Crofts . . . . Epic EPC 2244
10/07/1976 . . . . . 10 . . . . . . 8	**HARVEST FOR THE WORLD** . . . . Epic EPC 4369
13/05/1978 . . . . . 50 . . . . . . 4	TAKE ME TO THE NEXT PHASE . . . . Epic EPC 6292
03/11/1979 . . . . . 14 . . . . . . 11	IT'S A DISCO NIGHT (ROCK DON'T STOP) . . . . Epic EPC 7911
16/07/1983 . . . . . 52 . . . . . . 3	BETWEEN THE SHEETS . . . . Epic A 3513

ISLEY JASPER ISLEY US group formed by brothers Marvin (born 18/8/1953, bass/percussion) and Ernie Isley (born 7/3/1952, guitar/drums) and cousin Chris Jasper, previously members of The Isley Brothers.

23/11/1985 . . . . . 52 . . . . . . 5	CARAVAN OF LOVE . . . . Epic A 6612

ISOTONIK UK producer Chris Paul.

11/01/1992 . . . . . 12 . . . . . . 5	DIFFERENT STROKES . . . . ffrreedom TAB 101
02/05/1992 . . . . . 25 . . . . . . 4	EVERYWHERE I GO/LET'S GET DOWN . . . . ffrreedom TAB 108

IT BITES UK rock group formed in Cumbria by Francis Dunnery (guitar/vocals), John Beck (keyboards), Dick Nolan (bass) and Bob Dalton (drums).

12/07/1986 . . . . . 6 . . . . . . 12	**CALLING ALL THE HEROES** . . . . Virgin VS 872
18/10/1986 . . . . . 54 . . . . . . 3	WHOLE NEW WORLD . . . . Virgin VS 896
23/05/1987 . . . . . 72 . . . . . . 1	THE OLD MAN AND THE ANGEL . . . . Virgin VS 941
13/05/1989 . . . . . 66 . . . . . . 3	STILL TOO YOUNG TO REMEMBER . . . . Virgin VS 1184
24/02/1990 . . . . . 60 . . . . . . 2	STILL TOO YOUNG TO REMEMBER Re-issue of Virgin VS 1184 . . . . Virgin VS 1238

❶⁹ Number of weeks single topped the UK chart ↑ Entered the UK chart at #1 ▲⁹ Number of weeks single topped the US chart

393

IT'S IMMATERIAL UK duo formed in Liverpool by John Campbell and Jarvis Whitehead.

12/04/1986.....18......7.......	DRIVING AWAY FROM HOME (JIM'S TUNE)	Siren 15
02/08/1986.....65......3.......	ED'S FUNKY DINER (FRIDAY NIGHT, SATURDAY MORNING)	Siren 24

ITTY BITTY BOOZY WOOZY Dutch instrumental/production group of Koen Groeneveld, Addy Van Der Zwan and Jan Voermans. They also recorded as Klubheads, Drunkenmunky, Cooper and Da Techno Bohemian.

25/11/1995.....34......2.......	TEMPO FIESTA (PARTY TIME) .... Systematic SYSCD 23

BURL IVES US folk singer (born 14/6/1909, Huntington Township, IL) who played semi-pro football before beginning a Broadway career in the late 1930s. He had his own radio show during the 1940s and his films included *East Of Eden* (1955), *The Big Country* (1958) and *Our Man In Havana* (1960). He also worked on the 1949 Disney film *So Dear To My Heart,* singing *Lavender Blue (Dilly Dilly).* He died on 14/4/1995.

25/01/1962 .....9......15......	**A LITTLE BITTY TEAR**. .... Brunswick 05863
17/05/1962.....29.....10......	FUNNY WAY OF LAUGHIN'1962 Grammy Award for Best Country & Western Recording .... Brunswick 05868

IVY LEAGUE UK vocal group initially formed in 1965 by John Carter (born John Shakespeare, 20/10/1942, Birmingham), Perry Ford (born Bryan Pugh, 1940, Lincoln) and Ken Lewis (born Kenneth Hawker, 3/12/1942, Birminham). Carter quit in 1966 and was replaced by Tony Burrows; Lewis was replaced by Neil Landon. They became the Flowerpot Men, Burrows going on to sing the lead on studio projects for Edison Lighthouse, Brotherhood of Man, First Class, White Plains and the Pipkins.

04/02/1965 .....8......9.......	**FUNNY HOW LOVE CAN BE**. .... Piccadilly 7N 35222
06/05/1965.....22......8.......	THAT'S WHY I'M CRYING .... Piccadilly 7N 35228
24/06/1965 .....3......13	**TOSSING AND TURNING** .... Piccadilly 7N 35251
14/07/1966.....50......1.......	WILLOW TREE. .... Piccadilly 7N 35326

IZIT UK group formed by Tony Colman (guitar/keyboards), Peter Shrubshall (flute/saxophone), his sister Catherine (saxophone) and Andrew Messingham (drums). They later added singer Sam Edwards.

02/12/1989.....52......3.......	STORIES .... ffrr F 122

IZZY – see GLADIATOR FEATURING IZZY

J

HARRY J. ALL STARS Jamaican reggae group led by keyboard player Harry Johnson. Formerly an insurance salesman, after his success he opened a recording studio and record label. As producer had hits with Bob and Marcia (*Young Gifted And Black*, which appeared on Harry J Records) and Sheila Hylton (*The Bed's Too Big Without You*).

25/10/1969	9	20	LIQUIDATOR	Trojan TR 675
29/03/1980	42	5	LIQUIDATOR Re-issue of Trojan TR 675 and coupled with The Pioneers' *Long Shot Kick De Bucket*	Trojan TRO 9063

GEMMA J – see ONYX FEATURING GEMMA J

RAY J US singer (born Willie Ray Norwood, 17/1/1981, McComb, MS), brother of fellow singer Brandy. He appeared in the film *Steel*.

17/10/1998	71	1	THAT'S WHY I LIE Featured in the 1998 film *Dr Dolittle*	Atlantic AT 0049CD
16/06/2001	5	10	ANOTHER DAY IN PARADISE BRANDY & RAY J	WEA 327CD1
11/08/2001	54	1	WAIT A MINUTE RAY J FEATURING LIL' KIM	Atlantic AT 0106CD

J-KWON US rapper (born Jerrell Jones, 1986, St Louis, MO).

24/07/2004	4	11	TIPSY	LaFace 82876634162

J MAGIK – see IAN POOLEY

J PAC UK vocal/instrumental duo.

22/07/1995	51	2	ROCK 'N' ROLL (DOLE)	East West YZ 953CD

JA RULE US rapper Jeffrey Atkins (born 29/2/1976, New York City). Also in The Murderers with Black Child, Tah Murdah and Vita, he won the 2002 MOBO Award for Best Hip Hop Act. US female rapper Amil (Amil Whitehead) is in rap group Major Coinz.

13/03/1999	24	3	CAN I GET A... JAY-Z FEATURING AMIL AND JA RULE Featured in the 1998 film *Rush Hour*	Def Jam 5668472
03/03/2001	26	3	BETWEEN ME AND YOU JA RULE FEATURING CHRISTINA MILIAN	Def Jam 5727402
18/08/2001	3	9	AIN'T IT FUNNY JENNIFER LOPEZ FEATURING JA RULE AND CADILLAC TAH	Epic 6717592
10/11/2001	4	15	I'M REAL ▲5 JENNIFER LOPEZ FEATURING JA RULE	Epic 6720322
10/11/2001	27	4	LIVIN' IT UP JA RULE FEATURING CASE Contains a sample of Stevie Wonder's *Do I Do*	Def Jam 5888142
02/02/2002	6	13	ALWAYS ON TIME ▲2 JA RULE FEATURING ASHANTI	Def Jam 5889462
03/08/2002	5	8	LIVIN' IT UP (REMIX) JA RULE FEATURING CASE	Def Jam 0639782
24/08/2002	17	5	RAINY DAYZ MARY J. BLIGE FEATURING JA RULE	MCA MCSXD 40288
12/10/2002	4	10	DOWN 4 U IRV GOTTI PRESENTS JA RULE, ASHANTI, CHARLI BALTIMORE AND VITA	Murder Inc 0639002
21/12/2002	15	8	THUG LOVIN' JA RULE FEATURING BOBBY BROWN Contains a sample of Stevie Wonder's *Knocks Me Off My Feet*	Def Jam 637872
29/03/2003	12	8	MESMERIZE JA RULE FEATURING ASHANTI Contains a sample of Diana Ross & Marvin Gaye's *Stop! Look, Listen (To Your Heart)*	Murder Inc 0779582
06/12/2003	9	9	CLAP BACK/REIGNS A-side contains a sample of Toto's *Africa*	Def Jam 9861552
06/11/2004	❶1	8+	WONDERFUL ↑ JA RULE FEATURING R KELLY AND ASHANTI	Def Jam 9864606

JACK 'N' CHILL UK group with Ed Stratton, Vlad Naslas and Rodney. Their debut hit was the first UK instrumental house hit.

06/06/1987	48	5	THE JACK THAT HOUSE BUILT	Oval TEN 174
09/01/1988	6	11	THE JACK THAT HOUSE BUILT	Oval TEN 174
09/07/1988	42	5	BEATIN' THE HEAT	10 TEN 234

JACKNIFE LEE – see RUN DMC

TERRY JACKS Canadian singer (born 29/3/1944, Winnipeg), lead singer with the Chessmen in the 1960s. He married Susan Pesklevits in 1973 (who later recorded as Susan Jacks) and together they formed the Poppy Family. The marriage and the group ended in 1973, both going solo. A TV film entitled *Seasons In The Sun* was made in 1986, with Jacks starring as Terry Brandon.

23/03/1974	❶4	12	○	SEASONS IN THE SUN ▲3	Bell 1344
29/06/1974	8	9	IF YOU GO AWAY	Bell 1362

CHAD JACKSON UK producer from Manchester (born Mark Chadwick), also a member of Beatnik.

02/06/1990	3	10	HEAR THE DRUMMER (GET WICKED)	Big Wave BWR 36

DEE D. JACKSON UK singer from Oxford (born Deidre Cozier), popular in Europe, especially Germany.

22/04/1978	4	9	○	AUTOMATIC LOVER	Mercury 6007 171
02/09/1978	48	5	METEOR MAN	Mercury 6007 182

❶9 Number of weeks single topped the UK chart ↑ Entered the UK chart at #1 ▲9 Number of weeks single topped the US chart

FREDDIE JACKSON
US singer (born 2/10/1956, Harlem, NYC); began as a backing singer for Melba Moore, Evelyn King and Angela Bofill before singing lead with Mystic Merlin. After one album he went solo, later appearing in the film *Def By Temptation*.

23/11/1985	49	4		YOU ARE MY LADY	Capitol CL 379
22/02/1986	18	9		ROCK ME TONIGHT (FOR OLD TIME'S SAKE)	Capitol CL 358
11/10/1986	73	1		TASTY LOVE	Capitol CL 428
07/02/1987	33	6		HAVE YOU EVER LOVED SOMEBODY	Capitol CL 437
09/07/1988	56	2		NICE 'N' SLOW	Capitol CL 502
15/10/1988	41	3		CRAZY (FOR ME)	Capitol CL 510
05/09/1992	32	5		ME AND MRS JONES	Capitol CL 668
15/01/1994	70	1		MAKE LOVE EASY	RCA 74321179162

GISELE JACKSON
US singer who recorded for Waako in America and also as Miz Gisele.

| 30/08/1997 | 54 | 1 | | LOVE COMMANDMENTS | Manifesto FESCD 28 |

JANET JACKSON
US singer (born 16/5/1966, Gary, IN), youngest of the nine Jackson children. Appeared with her brothers at seven, but started TV career as an actress, appearing in *Good Times*, *Diff'rent Strokes* and *Fame*. She signed with A&M in 1982. Briefly married to James DeBarge in 1984. With her *Rhythm Nation 1814* album in 1991, she became the first artist to have seven top five singles from one album in the US. Five Grammies include Best Music Video Long Form in 1989 for *Rhythm Nation*. Named Best Female at the 1997 MTV Europe Music Awards, she was in the 2000 film *Nutty Professor II: The Klumps* and has a star on the Hollywood Walk of Fame. She was given a Hall of Fame Award at the 2004 MOBO Awards.

22/03/1986	3	14	○	**WHAT HAVE YOU DONE FOR ME LATELY**	A&M AM 308
31/05/1986	19	9		NASTY	A&M AM 316
09/08/1986	10	10		**WHEN I THINK OF YOU** ▲[2]	A&M AM 337
01/11/1986	42	5		CONTROL	A&M AM 359
21/03/1987	3	10	○	**LET'S WAIT AWHILE**	Breakout USA 601
13/06/1987	24	5		PLEASURE PRINCIPLE	Breakout USA 604
14/11/1987	59	2		FUNNY HOW TIME FLIES (WHEN YOU'RE HAVING FUN)	Breakout USA 613
02/09/1989	22	7		MISS YOU MUCH ▲[4]	Breakout USA 663
04/11/1989	23	5		RHYTHM NATION	Breakout USA 673
27/01/1990	20	7		COME BACK TO ME	Breakout USA 681
31/03/1990	17	7		ESCAPADE ▲[3]	Breakout USA 684
07/07/1990	20	5		ALRIGHT	A&M USA 693
08/09/1990	15	6		BLACK CAT ▲[1] Features Vernon Reid of Living Colour on guitar	A&M EM 587
27/10/1990	34	4		LOVE WILL NEVER DO (WITHOUT YOU) ▲[1]	A&M EM 700
15/08/1992	2	13	○	**THE BEST THINGS IN LIFE ARE FREE** LUTHER VANDROSS AND JANET JACKSON WITH SPECIAL GUESTS BBD AND RALPH TRESVANT Featured in the 1992 film *Mo' Money*	Perspective PERSS 7400
08/05/1993	2	10	○	**THAT'S THE WAY LOVE GOES** ▲[8] Contains a sample of James Brown's *Papa Don't Take No Mess*. 1993 Grammy Award for Best Rhythm & Blues Song for writers Janet Jackson, James Harris III and Terry Lewis	Virgin VSCDG 1460
31/07/1993	14	7		IF Contains a sample of Diana Ross & The Supremes' *Someday We'll Be Together*	Virgin VSCDT 1474
20/11/1993	6	11		AGAIN ▲[2] Featured in the 1993 film *Poetic Justice* which also starred Jackson	Virgin VSCDG 1481
12/03/1994	19	4		BECAUSE OF LOVE	Virgin VSCDG 1488
18/06/1994	13	5		ANY TIME ANY PLACE	Virgin VSCDT 1501
26/11/1994	14	3		YOU WANT THIS Contains a sample of Diana Ross & The Supremes' *Love Child*	Virgin VSCDT 1519
18/03/1995	9	8		**WHOOPS NOW/WHAT'LL I DO**	Virgin VSCDT 1533
10/06/1995	3	13		**SCREAM** MICHAEL JACKSON AND JANET JACKSON The accompanying video is the most expensive ever produced at $7 million (£4.4 million). 1995 Grammy Award for Best Music Video Short Form	Epic 6620222
24/06/1995	43	2		SCREAM (REMIX) MICHAEL JACKSON AND JANET JACKSON	Epic 6621277
23/09/1995	6	7		**RUNAWAY**	A&M 5811972
16/12/1995	7	7		**THE BEST THINGS IN LIFE ARE FREE (REMIX)** LUTHER VANDROSS AND JANET JACKSON WITH SPECIAL GUESTS BBD AND RALPH TRESVANT	A&M 5813092
06/04/1996	22	4		TWENTY FOREPLAY	A&M 5815112
04/10/1997	6	9	○	**GOT 'TIL IT'S GONE** JANET FEATURING Q-TIP AND JONI MITCHELL Contains a sample of Joni Mitchell's *Big Yellow Taxi*. 1997 Grammy Award for Best Music Video Short Form	Virgin VSCDG 1666
13/12/1997	4	19	✪	**TOGETHER AGAIN** ▲[2]	Virgin VSCDG 1670
04/04/1998	5	7		**I GET LONELY** Features the uncredited contribution of BLACKstreet	Virgin VSCDT 1683
27/06/1998	13	5		GO DEEP	Virgin VSCDT 1680
19/12/1998	46	1		EVERY TIME	Virgin VSCDT 1720
17/04/1999	11	7		GIRLFRIEND/BOYFRIEND BLACKSTREET WITH JANET	Interscope IND 95640
01/05/1999	6	7		**WHAT'S IT GONNA BE?!** BUSTA RHYMES FEATURING JANET	Elektra E 3762CD1
19/08/2000	6	11	○	**DOESN'T REALLY MATTER** ▲[3] Featured in the 2000 film *The Nutty Professor II: The Klumps*	Def Soul 5629152
21/04/2001	3	11		**ALL FOR YOU** ▲[7] Contains a sample of Change's *The Glow Of Love*. 2001 Grammy Award for Best Dance Recording	Virgin VSCDT 1801
11/08/2001	11	5		SOMEONE TO CALL MY LOVER	Virgin VSCDT 1813

22/12/2001	13	10		SON OF A GUN (BETCHA THINK THIS SONG) JANET JACKSON WITH CARLY SIMON FEATURING MISSY ELLIOTT Contains a sample of Carly Simon's *You're So Vain*	Virgin VUSCDX 232
28/09/2002	9	7		**FEEL IT BOY** BEENIE MAN FEATURING JANET JACKSON Contains samples of Lloyd James' *Hold Me* and Clancey Eccles' *Say What You Say*	Virgin VUSCD 258
24/04/2004	15	5		JUST A LITTLE WHILE	Virgin VUSDX 285
19/06/2004	19	4		ALL NITE (DON'T STOP)/I WANT YOU	Virgin VUSDX 292

JERMAINE JACKSON

US singer (born 11/12/1954, Gary, IN), the fourth of nine children, a member of the Jackson 5 from their formation in 1963 until they left Motown for Epic in 1975 (replaced by Randy). Married to Motown founder Berry Gordy's daughter Hazel in 1973 (divorced 1987), he stayed with the company, going solo. Moving to Arista in 1984, production credits included a track on Whitney Houston's debut album. Rejoining brothers in 1984 for *Victory*, he also made their biographical TV mini series.

10/05/1980	8	11		**LET'S GET SERIOUS** Features the uncredited vocal of Stevie Wonder	Motown TMG 1183
26/07/1980	32	6		BURNIN' HOT	Motown TMG 1194
30/05/1981	41	5		YOU LIKE ME DON'T YOU	Motown TMG 1222
12/05/1984	52	4		SWEETEST SWEETEST	Arista JJK 1
27/10/1984	68	2		WHEN THE RAIN BEGINS TO FALL JERMAINE JACKSON AND PIA ZADORA Featured in the 1984 film *Voyage Of The Rock Aliens*	Arista ARIST 584
16/02/1985	6	13	O	**DO WHAT YOU DO**	Arista ARIST 609
21/10/1989	69	2		DON'T TAKE IT PERSONAL	Arista 112634

JOE JACKSON

UK singer (born 11/8/1954, Burton-on-Trent) who played with Johnny Dankworth and the National Youth Jazz Orchestra before joining Arms & Legs. He left in 1977 to become Musical Director to Coffee & Cream, recording his solo debut in 1978. He relocated to New York in 1982 and won the 2000 Grammy Award for Best Pop Instrumental Album for *Symphony No.1*.

04/08/1979	13	9		IS SHE REALLY GOING OUT WITH HIM? Featured in the 1998 film *There's Something About Mary*	A&M AMS 7459
12/01/1980	5	9	O	**IT'S DIFFERENT FOR GIRLS** Featured in the 1999 film *200 Cigarettes*	A&M AMS 7493
04/07/1981	43	5		JUMPIN' JIVE JOE JACKSON'S JUMPIN' JIVE	A&M AMS 8145
08/01/1983	6	8		**STEPPIN' OUT**	A&M AMS 8262
12/03/1983	59	4		BREAKING US IN TWO	A&M AM 101
28/04/1984	58	3		HAPPY ENDING	A&M AM 186
07/07/1984	70	2		BE MY NUMBER TWO	A&M AM 200
07/06/1986	32	9		LEFT OF CENTER SUZANNE VEGA FEATURING JOE JACKSON Featured in the 1986 film *Pretty In Pink*	A&M AM 320

MICHAEL JACKSON

US singer (born 29/8/1958, Gary, IN), the seventh of nine children; lead singer with the Jackson 5 at the age of five. A parallel solo career began at Motown in 1971, and he later appeared as the Scarecrow in *The Wiz*. Relaunching himself in 1979, he became one of the biggest acts in the world – 1982's *Thriller* album sold over 47 million worldwide. Filming a Pepsi advertisement in January 1984, his hair was set alight by a spark from a pyrotechnic leading to second degree burns of the skull; he donated the $1.5 million compensation to the Brotman Memorial Hospital where he had been treated. In 1985 he bought ATV publishing, controlling more than 250 Lennon and McCartney songs. He married Elvis Presley's daughter Lisa Marie in 1994, divorced in 1996, and married Debbie Rowe in November 1996, with whom he had two children (Prince Michael Jr and Paris Michael Katherine) – they filed for divorce in October 1999. He also had a second son by an un-named woman. Michael has won six BRIT Awards: Best International Male in 1984, 1988 and 1989, Best Album (for *Thriller*) in 1984 and an Artist of a Generation Award in 1996, the year he performed at the ceremony. Launched the MJJ record label with acts such as Brownstone and 3T. In 1984 he won eight Grammy Awards, the most by one artist in a single year until equalled by Carlos Santana in 2000. He signed the biggest ever recording deal, worth a reported $1 billion, with Sony in 1991. Accused of child molestation, settling out of court in 1994. Thirteen Grammies include Album of the Year in 1983 for *Thriller*, Best Pop Vocal Performance in 1983 for *Thriller*, Best Recording for Children in 1983 for *E.T. The Extra-Terrestrial*, Producer of the Year in 1983, Best Video Album in 1984 for *Making Michael Jackson's 'Thriller'*, and Song of the Year in 1985 with Lionel Richie for *We Are The World*. He was inducted into the Rock & Roll Hall of Fame in 2001. He has two stars on the Hollywood Walk of Fame, for his contribution to recording and radio. In 2003 there were further child molestation charges and he was subsequently charged. He was inducted into the UK Music Hall of Fame in 2004, one of its first inductees.

12/02/1972	5	11		**GOT TO BE THERE**	Tamla Motown TMG 797
20/05/1972	3	14		**ROCKIN' ROBIN**	Tamla Motown TMG 816
19/08/1972	8	11		AIN'T NO SUNSHINE 1971 Grammy Award for Best Rhythm & Blues Song for writer Bill Withers	Tamla Motown TMG 826
25/11/1972	7	14		BEN ▲[1] Featured in the 1972 film *Ben*	Tamla Motown TMG 834
18/11/1978	45	4		EASE ON DOWN THE ROAD DIANA ROSS AND MICHAEL JACKSON Featured in the 1978 film *The Wiz*	MCA 396
15/09/1979	3	12	O	**DON'T STOP 'TIL YOU GET ENOUGH** ▲[1] 1979 Grammy Award for Best Rhythm & Blues Vocal Performance	Epic EPC 7763
24/11/1979	7	10		**OFF THE WALL**	Epic EPC 8045
09/02/1980	7	9		**ROCK WITH YOU** ▲[4]	Epic EPC 8206
03/05/1980	3	9		**SHE'S OUT OF MY LIFE**	Epic EPC 8384
26/07/1980	41	5		GIRLFRIEND	Epic EPC 8782
23/05/1981	●[2]	14	●	**ONE DAY IN YOUR LIFE** Originally recorded in 1975	Motown TMG 976
01/08/1981	46	4		WE'RE ALMOST THERE Originally recorded in 1975	Motown TMG 977
06/11/1982	8	10		**THE GIRL IS MINE** MICHAEL JACKSON AND PAUL McCARTNEY	Epic A 2729
29/01/1983	●[1]	15	●	**BILLIE JEAN** ▲[7] 1983 Grammy Award for Best Rhythm & Blues Vocal Performance. The song won the Grammy Award for Best Rhythm & Blues Song for writer Michael Jackson the same year. Featured in the 2000 film *Charlies Angels*	Epic EPC A 3084
09/04/1983	3	12	O	**BEAT IT** ▲[3] Lead guitar by Eddie Van Halen. Featured in the 1989 film *Back To The Future II*. 1983 Grammy Awards for Record of the Year and Best Rock Vocal Performance	Epic EPC A 3258
11/06/1983	8	9		**WANNA BE STARTIN' SOMETHING**	Epic A 3427
23/07/1983	52	3		HAPPY (LOVE THEME FROM 'LADY SINGS THE BLUES')	Tamla Motown TMG 986
15/10/1983	2	15	O	**SAY SAY SAY** ▲[6] PAUL McCARTNEY AND MICHAEL JACKSON	Parlophone R 6062

●[9] Number of weeks single topped the UK chart   ↑ Entered the UK chart at #1   ▲[9] Number of weeks single topped the US chart

DATE	POS	WKS	BPI	SINGLE TITLE	LABEL & NUMBER
19/11/1983	10	18	O	**THRILLER** Features the uncredited vocal of actor Vincent Price. 1983 Grammy Award for Best Pop Vocal Performance. Featured in the 2004 film *13 Going On 30*	Epic A 3643
31/03/1984	11	8		**P.Y.T. (PRETTY YOUNG THING)**	Epic A 4136
02/06/1984	7	12		**FAREWELL MY SUMMER LOVE** Originally recorded in 1973	Motown TMG 1342
07/07/1984	14	8		**STATE OF SHOCK** JACKSONS, LEAD VOCALS MICK JAGGER AND MICHAEL JACKSON	Epic A 4431
11/08/1984	33	8		**GIRL YOU'RE SO TOGETHER** Originally recorded in 1973	Motown TMG 1355
08/08/1987	●²	9		**I JUST CAN'T STOP LOVING YOU ▲¹** Features the uncredited vocal of Siedah Garrett.	Epic 6502027
26/09/1987	3	11		**BAD ▲²**	Epic 6511557
05/12/1987	3	10		**THE WAY YOU MAKE ME FEEL ▲¹** Featured in the 2000 film *Center Stage*	Epic 6512757
20/02/1988	21	5		**MAN IN THE MIRROR ▲²**	Epic 6513887
16/04/1988	8	9		**I WANT YOU BACK (REMIX)** MICHAEL JACKSON WITH THE JACKSON FIVE	Motown ZB 41913
28/05/1988	37	4		**GET IT** STEVIE WONDER AND MICHAEL JACKSON	Motown ZB 41883
16/07/1988	4	8		**DIRTY DIANA ▲¹**	Epic 6515467
10/09/1988	15	6		**ANOTHER PART OF ME**	Epic 6528447
26/11/1988	8	10		**SMOOTH CRIMINAL** 1989 BRIT Award for Best Video	Epic 6530267
25/02/1989	2	9		**LEAVE ME ALONE** 1989 Grammy Award for Best Music Video Short Form	Epic 6546727
15/07/1989	13	6		**LIBERIAN GIRL**	Epic 6549470
23/11/1991	●²	10	O	**BLACK OR WHITE ↑ ▲⁷** Guitar intro by Slash of Guns N' Roses.	Epic 6575987
18/01/1992	14	4		**BLACK OR WHITE (REMIX)** Remix by Clivilles and Cole	Epic 6577316
15/02/1992	3	8		**REMEMBER THE TIME/COME TOGETHER**	Epic 6577747
02/05/1992	8	6		**IN THE CLOSET** Mystery Girl vocal is by Princess Stephanie of Monaco, the original choice was Madonna. The accompanying video featured supermodel Naomi Campbell and was considered so raunchy it was banned in South Africa	Epic 6580187
25/07/1992	10	7		**WHO IS IT**	Epic 6581797
12/09/1992	13	5		**JAM**	Epic 6583607
05/12/1992	2	15	●	**HEAL THE WORLD**	Epic 6584887
27/02/1993	2	9		**GIVE IN TO ME**	Epic 6590692
10/07/1993	9	8		**WILL YOU BE THERE** Featured in the 1993 film *Free Willy*	Epic 6592222
18/12/1993	33	5		**GONE TOO SOON**	Epic 6599762
10/06/1995	3	13		**SCREAM** MICHAEL JACKSON AND JANET JACKSON The accompanying video is the most expensive ever produced at $7 million (£4.4 million). 1995 Grammy Award for Best Music Video Short Form	Epic 6620222
24/06/1995	43	2		**SCREAM (REMIX)** MICHAEL JACKSON AND JANET JACKSON	Epic 6621277
02/09/1995	●²	15	●	**YOU ARE NOT ALONE ▲¹** The single was the first to enter the US chart at #1	Epic 6623102
09/12/1995	●⁶	17	✪	**EARTH SONG ↑**	Epic 6626955
20/04/1996	4	14	O	**THEY DON'T CARE ABOUT US**	Epic 6629502
24/08/1996	2	9		**WHY** 3T FEATURING MICHAEL JACKSON	Epic 6636482
16/11/1996	4	11		**STRANGER IN MOSCOW**	Epic 6637872
03/05/1997	●¹	9		**BLOOD ON THE DANCE FLOOR ↑**	Epic 6644625
19/07/1997	5	8		**HISTORY/GHOSTS**	Epic 6647962
20/10/2001	2	15		**YOU ROCK MY WORLD**	Epic 6720292
29/03/2003	12	8		**MESMERIZE** JA RULE FEATURING ASHANTI	Murder Inc 0779582
06/12/2003	5	7		**ONE MORE CHANCE**	Epic 6744805

MICK JACKSON UK singer/songwriter based in Germany, whose debut hit (which he co-wrote) competed with the Jacksons in the chart. He had previously been bass player with Love Affair.

DATE	POS	WKS	BPI	SINGLE TITLE	LABEL & NUMBER
30/09/1978	15	8		BLAME IT ON THE BOOGIE	Atlantic K 11102
03/02/1979	38	8		WEEKEND	Atlantic K 11224

MILLIE JACKSON US R&B singer (born 15/7/1944, Thompson, GA), a model in New Jersey before turning to singing in 1964. Her 1970 debut disc was for Spring, with whom she had over 30 R&B hits, eight also making the pop charts. Best known for her *Caught Up* and *Still Caught Up* albums that explored extra-marital affairs, she later recorded country songs, and with Isaac Hayes.

DATE	POS	WKS	BPI	SINGLE TITLE	LABEL & NUMBER
18/11/1972	50	1		MY MAN A SWEET MAN	Mojo 2093 022
10/03/1984	55	2		I FEEL LIKE WALKIN' IN THE RAIN	Sire W 9348
15/06/1985	32	5		ACT OF WAR ELTON JOHN AND MILLIE JACKSON	Rocket EJS 8

PAUL JACKSON AND STEVE SMITH UK duo producer Paul Jackson and singer Steve Smith who is also a member of Dirty Vegas.

DATE	POS	WKS	BPI	SINGLE TITLE	LABEL & NUMBER
24/01/2004	51	2		THE PUSH (FAR FROM HERE)	Underwater H2O041CD

STONEWALL JACKSON US singer (born 6/11/1932, Tabor City, NC), a direct descendant of Confederate General Thomas Jonathan 'Stonewall' Jackson, his name being his real one. He appeared in the 1985 film *Sweet Dreams*.

DATE	POS	WKS	BPI	SINGLE TITLE	LABEL & NUMBER
17/07/1959	24	2		WATERLOO	Philips PB 941

TONY JACKSON – see Q

TONY JACKSON AND THE VIBRATIONS UK singer/bass player (born 16/7/1940, Liverpool), a founding member of the Searchers until leaving in 1964 to go solo. After his recording career ended he opened a golf and leisure club, then toured the nostalgia circuit in the 1990s. He died on 20/8/2003.

DATE	POS	WKS	BPI	SINGLE TITLE	LABEL & NUMBER
08/10/1964	38	3		BYE BYE BABY	Pye 7N 15685

O Silver disc ● Gold disc ✪ Platinum disc (additional platinum units are indicated by a figure following the symbol) ◎ Singles released prior to 1973 that are known to have sold over 1 million copies in the UK

WANDA JACKSON US singer (born 20/10/1937, Maud, OK); she started with Decca in 1954 recording country music switching to rock 'n' roll at the end of the decade, one of the first women to do so. She toured with Elvis Presley in 1955 and 1956.

01/09/1960	32	8		LET'S HAVE A PARTY	Capitol CL 15147
26/01/1961	40	3		MEAN MEAN MAN	Capitol CL 15176

JACKSON SISTERS US vocal group of sisters Gennie, Jackie, Lyn, Pat and Rae Jackson, raised in Compton, Los Angeles, CA.

20/06/1987	72	2		I BELIEVE IN MIRACLES	Urban URB 4

JACKSON 5/JACKSONS US group formed in Gary, IN as a trio in 1963 by Jackie (born Sigmund, 4/5/1951, Gary), Tito (born Toriano, 15/10/1953, Gary) and Jermaine Jackson (born 11/12/1954, Gary) as the Jackson Family. Younger brothers Marlon (born 12/3/1957, Gary) and Michael (born 29/8/1958, Gary) joined soon after and they began working as the Jackson 5. They supported Gladys Knight & The Pips in 1967, who recommended them to Motown's Berry Gordy, although their debut record was on Steeltown in 1968. They signed with Motown in 1968, initially a one-year deal. They left for Epic in 1975, Motown retaining both the name Jackson 5 and Jermaine (replaced by youngest brother Randy, born 29/10/1961, Gary). Three sisters (Janet, LaToya and Rebbie) also backed the group, and all recorded solo. Jermaine returned in 1984 for the *Victory* album and tour. Marlon left in 1987 to go solo, with Jackie, Tito, Jermaine and Randy the line-up since 1989. They were inducted into the Rock & Roll Hall of Fame in 1997 and have a star on the Hollywood Walk of Fame.

31/01/1970	2	13		I WANT YOU BACK ▲[1] Featured in the 1996 film *Now And Then*	Tamla Motown TMG 724
16/05/1970	8	11		ABC ▲[2] Featured in the 1994 film *Crooklyn*	Tamla Motown TMG 738
01/08/1970	7	9		THE LOVE YOU SAVE ▲[2]	Tamla Motown TMG 746
21/11/1970	4	16		I'LL BE THERE ▲[5] Featured in the 1996 film *Now And Then*	Tamla Motown TMG 758
10/04/1971	25	7		MAMA'S PEARL	Tamla Motown TMG 769
17/07/1971	33	7		NEVER CAN SAY GOODBYE	Tamla Motown TMG 778
11/11/1972	9	11		LOOKIN' THROUGH THE WINDOWS	Tamla Motown TMG 833
23/12/1972	43	3		SANTA CLAUS IS COMING TO TOWN	Tamla Motown TMG 837
17/02/1973	9	10		DOCTOR MY EYES	Tamla Motown TMG 842
09/06/1973	20	9		HALLELUJAH DAY	Tamla Motown TMG 856
08/09/1973	25	8		SKYWRITER This and above ten singles credited to THE JACKSON 5	Tamla Motown TMG 865
09/04/1977	42	4		ENJOY YOURSELF	Epic EPC 5063
04/06/1977	❶[1]	10	○	SHOW YOU THE WAY TO GO	Epic EPC 5266
13/08/1977	22	9		DREAMER	Epic EPC 5458
05/11/1977	26	7		GOIN' PLACES	Epic EPC 5732
11/02/1978	31	4		EVEN THOUGH YOU'VE GONE	Epic EPC 5919
23/09/1978	8	12	○	BLAME IT ON THE BOOGIE	Epic EPC 6683
03/02/1979	39	6		DESTINY	Epic EPC 6983
24/03/1979	4	12	○	SHAKE YOUR BODY (DOWN TO THE GROUND) Featured in the 1996 film *Robocop 3*	Epic EPC 7181
25/10/1980	29	6		LOVELY ONE	Epic EPC 9302
13/12/1980	44	6		HEARTBREAK HOTEL	Epic EPC 9391
28/02/1981	6	15	○	CAN YOU FEEL IT	Epic EPC 9554
04/07/1981	7	11		WALK RIGHT NOW	Epic EPC A 1294
07/07/1984	14	8		STATE OF SHOCK JACKSONS, LEAD VOCALS MICK JAGGER AND MICHAEL JACKSON	Epic A 4431
08/09/1984	26	6		TORTURE Lead vocals by Jermaine and Michael Jackson	Epic A 4675
16/04/1988	8	9		I WANT YOU BACK (REMIX) MICHAEL JACKSON WITH THE JACKSON FIVE	Motown ZB 41913
13/05/1989	33	6		NOTHIN' (THAT COMPARES 2 U)	Epic 6548087

JACKY – see JACKIE LEE

JACQUELINE – see MACK VIBE FEATURING JACQUELINE

JADA – see SKIP RAIDERS FEATURING JADA

JADE US vocal trio formed in Los Angeles, CA by Joi Marshall, Tonya Kelly and Di Reed. P.O.V. are a New Jersey-based vocal group formed by Hakim Bell (son of Kool & The Gang's Robert Bell), Lincoln DeVlught, Mark Sherman and Ewarner Mills.

20/03/1993	7	8		DON'T WALK AWAY	Giant W 0160CD
03/07/1993	13	7		I WANNA LOVE YOU Featured in the 1993 film *Class Act*	Giant 74321151662
18/09/1993	22	5		ONE WOMAN	Giant 74321165122
05/02/1994	32	3		ALL THRU THE NITE P.O.V. FEATURING JADE	Giant 74321187552
11/02/1995	19	5		EVERY DAY OF THE WEEK	Giant 74321260242

ASHLEY JADE – see SODA CLUB

JADE 4 U – see PRAGA KHAN

JAEL – see DELERIUM

JAGGED EDGE UK group formed by Matti Alfonzetti (vocals), Myke Gray (guitar), Andy Robbins (bass) and Fabio Del Rio (drums).

15/09/1990	66	2		YOU DON'T LOVE ME	Polydor PO 97

❶[9] Number of weeks single topped the UK chart ↑ Entered the UK chart at #1 ▲[9] Number of weeks single topped the US chart

399

JAGGED EDGE US R&B vocal group from Atlanta, GA with identical brothers Brian 'Case Dinero' and Brandon 'Brasco' Casey, Richard 'Wingo Dollar' Wingo, Kyle 'Quick' Norman. They signed with So So Def in 1997.

27/10/2001.....25......3......	WHERE'S THE PARTY AT JAGGED EDGE FEATURING NELLY .... Columbia 6719012
21/02/2004.....21......5......	WALKED OUTTA HEAVEN .... Columbia 6745452

MICK JAGGER UK singer (born 26/7/1943, Dartford), lead singer with The Rolling Stones since they began in 1962. He appeared in the film *Ned Kelly* in 1970 (during which he was accidentally shot!) and married Bianca Rose Perez Moreno de Macias in 1971 and model Jerry Hall in 1990 (although in 1999 they were in divorce talks, Jagger claiming their Hindu ceremony was not a recognised marriage). Featured on the cover of *Rolling Stone* sixteen times, more than any other artist, he was knighted in the 2002 Queen's Birthday Honours List.

14/11/1970.....32......5......	MEMO FROM TURNER Featured in the 1970 film *Performance* which also starred Mick Jagger .... Decca F 13067
07/07/1984.....14......8......	STATE OF SHOCK JACKSONS, LEAD VOCALS MICK JAGGER AND MICHAEL JACKSON........................... Epic A 4431
16/02/1985.....32......6......	JUST ANOTHER NIGHT .... CBS A 4722
07/09/1985 ● ❶⁴.....12.....●	DANCING IN THE STREET ↑ DAVID BOWIE AND MICK JAGGER Released in aid of Ethiopian famine relief....... EMI America EA 204
12/09/1987.....31......7......	LET'S WORK .... CBS 6510287
06/02/1993.....24......4......	SWEET THING... Atlantic A 7410CD
23/03/2002.....43......1......	VISIONS OF PARADISE .... Virgin VUSCD 240
06/11/2004.....45......2......	OLD HABITS DIE HARD MICK JAGGER AND DAVE STEWART Featured in the 2004 film *Alfie* .... Virgin VSCDX1887

JAGS UK group from Scarborough with John Alder (guitar), Alex Baird (drums), Steve Prudence (bass) and Nick Watkinson (guitar /vocals).

08/09/1979.....17......10......	BACK OF MY HAND.. Island WIP 6501
02/02/1980.....75......1......	WOMAN'S WORLD .... Island WIP 6531

JAHAZIEL – see RAGHAV

JAHEIM US hip hop artist/rapper (born Jaheim Hoagland, 28/5/1978, New Brunswick, NJ). His grandfather Victor Hoagland was once in The Drifters. Jaheim won the Apollo Theater Talent Contest three times when he was just fifteen.

24/03/2001.....33......3......	COULD IT BE .... Warner Brothers W 551CDX
11/08/2001.....34......2......	JUST IN CASE .... Warner Brothers W 564CDX
29/06/2002.....38......3......	JUST IN CASE (REMIX) .... Warner Brothers W 581CD
08/03/2003.....41......2......	FABULOUS... Warner Brothers W 598CD

JAHMALI – see BLAK TWANG

JAIMESON UK keyboard player(born Jamie Williams, 1975, London) who also records as Jameson, Kinetic, Rock Steady, DJ Infinity and 2Deep.

25/01/2003 .....4......10......	TRUE JAIMESON FEATURING ANGEL BLU .... V2/J-Did JAD 5021363
23/08/2003 .....4......8......	COMPLETE .... V2/J-Did JAD 5021713
07/02/2004 .....16......5......	TAKE CONTROL JAIMESON FEATURING ANGEL BLU AND CK... V2/J-Did JAD 5021738

JAKATTA UK producer Dave Lee. He also records as Joey Negro, Li Kwan, Akubu, Hed Boys (with Andrew Livingstone), Z Factor and Raven Maize, with the *American Dream* single originally released on his Z Records. His debut hit, with vocals by Swati Natekar, originally titled *American Booty*, after the film *American Beauty* (including a soundtrack sample) but changed after the film company objected.

24/02/2001 .....3......14.....O	AMERICAN DREAM .... Rulin 15CDS
11/08/2001.....63......1......	AMERICAN DREAM (REMIX)... Rulin 20CDS
16/02/2002 .....8......5......	SO LONELY .... Rulin 25CDS
12/10/2002 .....6......8......	MY VISION JAKATTA FEATURING SEAL .... Rulin 26CDS
01/03/2003.....39......2......	ONE FINE DAY .... Rulin 29CDX

JALN BAND UK disco group formed by lead singer Roy Gee Hemmings from two others, Tenderness and Superbad. They added Alan Holmes (saxophone), Laurie Brown (trumpet) and Rob Goodale (trombone). Their name stands for Just Another Lonely Night.

11/09/1976.....21......9......	DISCO MUSIC (I LIKE IT) .... Magnet MAG 73
27/08/1977.....40......4......	I GOT TO SING .... Magnet MAG 97
01/07/1978....53......4.......	GET UP.. Magnet MAG 118

JAM UK group formed in Woking in 1976 by Paul Weller (born John Weller, 25/5/1958, Woking, guitar/vocals), Steve Brookes (guitar), Bruce Foxton (born 1/9/1955, Woking, bass) and Rick Buckler (born Paul Richard Buckler, 6/12/1955, Woking, drums). Brookes left before the year's end, the group signing with Polydor in 1977 for a £6,000 advance. At the forefront of the UK mod revival, they were unable to break in America. Disbanded in 1982, Weller launching Style Council and then going solo, Foxton recording solo and joining the re-formed Stiff Little Fingers, and Buckler joining Time UK.

07/05/1977.....40......6......	IN THE CITY .... Polydor 2058 866
23/07/1977.....13......8......	ALL AROUND THE WORLD .... Polydor 2058 903
05/11/1977.....36......4......	THE MODERN WORLD .... Polydor 2058 945

DATE	POS	WKS	BPI	SINGLE TITLE	LABEL & NUMBER
11/03/1978	27	5		NEWS OF THE WORLD.	Polydor 2058 995
26/08/1978	25	8		DAVID WATTS/'A' BOMB IN WARDOUR STREET	Polydor 2059 054
21/10/1978	15	7		DOWN IN THE TUBE STATION AT MIDNIGHT	Polydor POSP 8
17/03/1979	15	9	O	STRANGE TOWN	Polydor POSP 34
25/08/1979	17	7		WHEN YOU'RE YOUNG	Polydor POSP 69
03/11/1979	3	12	O	**THE ETON RIFLES**	Polydor POSP 83
22/03/1980	**❶³**	9	●	**GOING UNDERGROUND/DREAMS OF CHILDREN** ↑ *Going Underground* featured in the 2004 film *The Football Factory.*	
					Polydor POSP 113
26/04/1980	43	3		ALL AROUND THE WORLD	Polydor 2058 903
26/04/1980	54	3		'A' BOMB IN WARDOUR STREET	Polydor 2059 054
26/04/1980	54	3		DAVID WATTS	Polydor 2059 054
26/04/1980	40	4		IN THE CITY	Polydor 2058 866
26/04/1980	53	3		NEWS OF THE WORLD.	Polydor 2058 995
26/04/1980	44	4		STRANGE TOWN	Polydor POSP 34
26/04/1980	52	3		THE MODERN WORLD	Polydor 2058 945
23/08/1980	**❶¹**	8	O	**START** Featured in the 2000 film *On The Edge.*	Polydor 2059 266
07/02/1981	21	7		THAT'S ENTERTAINMENT Only available as a German import	Metronome 0030 364
06/06/1981	4	6	O	**FUNERAL PYRE**	Polydor POSP 257
24/10/1981	4	6		**ABSOLUTE BEGINNERS** Featured in the 1997 film *Grosse Pointe Blank.*	Polydor POSP 350
13/02/1982	**❶³**	8	●	**A TOWN CALLED MALICE/PRECIOUS** ↑ A-side featured in the films *Billy Elliott* and *On The Edge* (both 2000)	Polydor POSP 400
03/07/1982	8	5		**JUST WHO IS THE FIVE O'CLOCK HERO**	Polydor 2059 504
18/09/1982	2	7	O	**THE BITTEREST PILL (I EVER HAD TO SWALLOW)**	Polydor POSP 505
04/12/1982	**❶²**	9	O	**BEAT SURRENDER** ↑	Polydor POSP 540
22/01/1983	38	4		ALL AROUND THE WORLD	Polydor 2058 903
22/01/1983	50	4		'A' BOMB IN WARDOUR STREET	Polydor 2059 054
22/01/1983	50	4		DAVID WATTS	Polydor 2059 054
22/01/1983	30	6		DOWN IN THE TUBE STATION AT MIDNIGHT	Polydor POSP 8
22/01/1983	21	4		GOING UNDERGROUND/DREAMS OF CHILDREN	Polydor POSP 113
22/01/1983	47	4		IN THE CITY	Polydor 2058 866
22/01/1983	39	4		NEWS OF THE WORLD.	Polydor 2058 995
22/01/1983	51	4		THE MODERN WORLD	Polydor 2058 945
22/01/1983	53	4		WHEN YOU'RE YOUNG	Polydor POSP 69
29/01/1983	60	3		THAT'S ENTERTAINMENT	Polydor POSP 482
05/02/1983	62	2		START	Polydor 2059 266
05/02/1983	54	3		THE ETON RIFLES	Polydor POSP 83
05/02/1983	73	1		PRECIOUS	Polydor POSP 400
05/02/1983	73	1		A TOWN CALLED MALICE This and above thirteen singles were re-promoted to coincide with the group disbanding.	Polydor POSP 400
29/06/1991	57	2		THAT'S ENTERTAINMENT	Polydor PO 155
11/10/1997	30	2		THE BITTEREST PILL (I EVER HAD TO SWALLOW) Re-issue of Polydor POSP 505	Polydor 5715992
11/05/2002	36	1		IN THE CITY Re-issue of Polydor 2058 866 to commemorate the 25th anniversary of its first release	Polydor 5876117

JAM AND SPOON FEATURING PLAVKA German instrumental/production duo Jam El Mar (Rolf Ellmer) and DJ Mark Spoon (Markus Loeffel) with Plavka singing lead. Jam and Spoon also recorded as Tokyo Ghetto Pussy and later as Storm.

DATE	POS	WKS	BPI	SINGLE TITLE	LABEL & NUMBER
02/05/1992	49	1		TALES FROM A DANCEOGRAPHIC OCEAN (EP) Tracks on EP: *Stella, Keep On Movin'* and *My First Fantastic FF*	R&S RSUK 14
06/06/1992	66	2		THE COMPLETE STELLA (REMIX)	R&S RSUK 14X
26/02/1994	31	4		RIGHT IN THE NIGHT (FALL IN LOVE WITH MUSIC)	Epic 6600822
24/09/1994	37	3		FIND ME (ODYSSEY TO ANYOONA)	Epic 6608082
10/06/1995	10	8		**RIGHT IN THE NIGHT (FALL IN LOVE WITH MUSIC)** Re-issue of Epic 6600822	Epic 6620182
16/09/1995	22	3		FIND ME (ODYSSEY TO ANYOONA) Re-issue of Epic 6608082	Epic 6623242
25/11/1995	26	2		ANGEL (LADADI O-HEYO)	Epic 6626382
30/08/1997	48	1		KALEIDOSCOPE SKIES	Epic 6647612
02/03/2002	31	2		BE ANGLED JAM AND SPOON FEATURING REA	NuLife 74321878992

JAM MACHINE Italian vocal/instrumental group formed by Max and Frank Minoia and Corrado Rizza.

DATE	POS	WKS	BPI	SINGLE TITLE	LABEL & NUMBER
23/12/1989	68	1		EVERYDAY	Deconstruction PB 43299

JAM ON THE MUTHA UK vocal/ instrumental group.

DATE	POS	WKS	BPI	SINGLE TITLE	LABEL & NUMBER
11/08/1990	62	2		HOTEL CALIFORNIA	M&G MAGS 3

JAM TRONIK German vocal/ instrumental group fronted by Charlie Glass (born 30/1/1967, Munich).

DATE	POS	WKS	BPI	SINGLE TITLE	LABEL & NUMBER
24/03/1990	19	7		ANOTHER DAY IN PARADISE	Debut DEBT 3093

JAMAICA UNITED Jamaican vocal group with Ziggy Marley, Buju Banton, Diana King, Shaggy, Maxi Priest, Ini Kamoze and Toots Hibber.

DATE	POS	WKS	BPI	SINGLE TITLE	LABEL & NUMBER
04/07/1998	54	1		RISE UP	Columbia 6660522

JAMELIA UK singer from Birmingham (born Jamelia Davis, 1/10/1981) who was signed by Parlophone at the age of fifteen. She won three MOBO Awards in 2004 including UK Act of the Year (jointly with Dizzee Rascal).

DATE	POS	WKS	BPI	SINGLE TITLE	LABEL & NUMBER
31/07/1999	36	2		I DO	Parlophone Rhythm CDRHYTHM 21
04/03/2000	5	9		**MONEY** JAMELIA FEATURING BEENIE MAN	Parlophone Rhythm CDRHYTHM 27

❶⁹ Number of weeks single topped the UK chart ↑ Entered the UK chart at #1 ▲⁹ Number of weeks single topped the US chart

401

24/06/2000	11	5		CALL ME	Parlophone Rhythm CDRHYTHS 28
21/10/2000	42	2		BOY NEXT DOOR	Parlophone Rhythm CDRHYTHS 29
21/06/2003	37	2		BOUT JAMELIA FEATURING RAH DIGGA	Parlophone CDRS 6597
27/09/2003	3	20	O	**SUPERSTAR**	Parlophone CDRS 6615
06/03/2004	2	14		**THANK YOU** 2004 MOBO Award for Best Single	Parlophone CDRS 6621
24/07/2004	5	11		**SEE IT IN A BOY'S EYES** 2004 MOBO Award for Best Video	Parlophone CDRS 6635
13/11/2004	9	7+		**DJ/STOP** Stop featured in the 2004 film *Bridget Jones Diary 2: Edge Of Reason*	Parlophone CDR 6646

JAMES UK group formed in Manchester in 1983 by Tim Booth (born 4/2/1960, lead vocals), Jim Glennie (born 10/10/1963, guitar), Danny Ryan (vocals), James Gott (guitar) and Gavin Whelan (drums). Initially signed with Factory, they joined Sire in 1986. Whelan left in 1990, replaced by Dave Boynton-Power (born 29/1/1961) and added Saul Davies (born 28/6/1965, guitar/violin), Andy Diagram (trumpet) and Mark Hunter (born 5/11/1968, keyboards) shortly before joining Fontana. Larry Gott (born 24/7/1957) joined in 1991.

12/05/1990	32	3		HOW WAS IT FOR YOU	Fontana JIM 5
07/07/1990	32	4		COME HOME	Fontana JIM 6
08/12/1990	38	5		LOSE CONTROL	Fontana JIM 7
30/03/1991	2	10	O	**SIT DOWN**	Fontana JIM 8
30/11/1991	9	7		**SOUND**	Fontana JIM 9
01/02/1992	13	6		BORN OF FRUSTRATION	Fontana JIM 10
04/04/1992	37	2		RING THE BELLS	Fontana JIM 11
18/07/1992	46	2		SEVEN (EP) Tracks on EP: *Seven, Goalie's Ball, William Burroughs* and *Still Alive*	Fontana JIM 12
11/09/1993	18	4		SOMETIMES	Fontana JIMCD 13
13/11/1993	25	4		LAID	Fontana JIMCD 14
02/04/1994	24	4		JAM J/SAY SOMETHING	Fontana JIMCD 152
22/02/1997	9	5		**SHE'S A STAR**	Fontana JIMCD 16
03/05/1997	12	3		TOMORROW Featured in the 1998 film *Up 'N Under*	Fontana JIMCD 17
05/07/1997	23	4		WALTZING ALONG	Fontana JIMCD 18
21/03/1998	17	4		DESTINY CALLING	Fontana JIMCD 19
06/06/1998	29	2		RUNAGROUND	Fontana JIMCD 20
21/11/1998	7	7		**SIT DOWN**	Fontana JIMCD 21
31/07/1999	22	5		I KNOW WHAT I'M HERE FOR	Fontana JIMDD 22
16/10/1999	17	3		JUST LIKE FRED ASTAIRE	Mercury JIMCD 23
25/12/1999	48	2		WE'RE GOING TO MISS YOU	Mercury JIMCD 24
07/07/2001	22	3		GETTING AWAY WITH IT (ALL MESSED UP)	Mercury JIMDD 25

JAMES – see **CHRIS AND JAMES**

DAVID JAMES UK DJ/producer who is also a member of Audio Drive with Martijn Ten Velden.

11/08/2001	60	1		ALWAYS A PERMANENT STATE	Hooj Choons HOOJ 108CD

DICK JAMES UK singer (born Isaac Vapnick, 1919, London) who started as Lee Sheridan before becoming Dick James and joining The Stargazers, later going solo. He launched publishing company Dick James Music, and later the DJM record label. His best deal came with Northern Songs, publishing company for The Beatles' songs. He died from a heart attack on 1/2/1986.

20/01/1956	14	8		ROBIN HOOD Features Stephen James and His Chums, theme to the TV series *The Adventures Of Robin Hood*	Parlophone R 4117
18/05/1956	29	1		ROBIN HOOD/BALLAD OF DAVY CROCKETT	Parlophone R 4117
11/01/1957	18	4		GARDEN OF EDEN	Parlophone R 4255

DUNCAN JAMES AND KEEDIE UK vocal duo Duncan James (born 7/4/1979, Salisbury) and Keedie Babb (born 1983, Torquay) whose debut hit comes from the Andrew Lloyd Webber musical *The Woman In White*. James is a member of Blue.

23/10/2004	2	7		**I BELIEVE MY HEART**	Innocent 8677122

ETTA JAMES US singer (born Jamesetta Hawkins, 25/1/1938, Los Angeles, CA), first recording in 1954 for Modern after being discovered by Johnny Otis. Signed to Chess subsidiary Argo in 1959, she also recorded duets with Harvey Fuqua (leader of the Moonglows and Marvin Gaye mentor) as Etta & Harvey. Inducted into the Rock & Roll Hall of Fame in 1993, she won the 1994 Grammy Award for Best Jazz Vocal Performance for *Mystery Lady (The Songs Of Billie Holiday)* and the 2003 award for Best Contemporary Blues Album for *Let's Roll*. She has a star on the Hollywood Walk of Fame.

10/02/1996	5	7		**I JUST WANT TO MAKE LOVE TO YOU** Originally released in 1961 and revived after use in an advertisement for Diet Coke Chess MCSTD 48003

FREDDIE JAMES US singer (born 1964, Chicago, IL), son of singer Geraldine Hunt and brother of Rosalind Hunt of Cheri; he later recorded for Arista.

24/11/1979	54	3		GET UP AND BOOGIE	Warner Brothers K 17478

HOLLY JAMES – see **JASON NEVINS**

JO JAMES – see **FLIP & FILL**

JONI JAMES US singer (born Joan Carmello Babbo, 22/9/1930, Chicago, IL). A dancer at the age of 12 and later a model before recording for Sharp Records in 1952. She has a star on the Hollywood Walk of Fame.

06/03/1953	11	1		WHY DON'T YOU BELIEVE ME ▲6	MGM 582

30/01/1959	24	1		THERE MUST BE A WAY	MGM 1002

RICK JAMES US R&B singer (born James Ambrose Johnson, 1/2/1948, Buffalo, NY); he formed the Mynah Birds in 1965 with Neil Young, Bruce Palmer and Goldie McJohn and signed with Motown, although nothing was released, partly due to his arrest for draft evasion! Moving to London in 1970 he formed Main Line, before returning to the US and signing with Motown a second time, this time solo. He also formed The Stony City Band and the Mary Jane Girls, and produced such acts as Teena Marie and Eddie Murphy. He died on 6/8/2004.

08/07/1978	46	7		YOU AND I	Motown TMG 1110
07/07/1979	43	8		I'M A SUCKER FOR YOUR LOVE TEENA MARIE, CO-LEAD VOCALS RICK JAMES	Motown TMG 1146
06/09/1980	41	6		BIG TIME	Motown TMG 1198
04/07/1981	47	3		GIVE IT TO ME BABY	Motown TMG 1229
12/06/1982	53	3		STANDING ON THE TOP (PART 1) TEMPTATIONS FEATURING RICK JAMES	Motown TMG 1263
03/07/1982	53	3		DANCE WIT' ME	Motown TMG 1266

SONNY JAMES US singer (born James Loden, 1/5/1929, Hackleburg, AL) who was taken to Nashville by Chet Atkins. He later appeared in films including *Las Vegas Hillbillies* before retiring in 1983 to raise cattle in Alabama.

30/11/1956	30	1		THE CAT CAME BACK	Capitol CL 14635
08/02/1957	11	7		YOUNG LOVE ▲¹	Capitol CL 14683

TYLER JAMES UK singer (born 1982, London).

13/11/2004	25	4		WHY DO I DO	Island CID872

WENDY JAMES UK singer (born 21/6/1966, London), formerly lead vocalist with Transvision Vamp.

20/02/1993	34	3		THE NAMELESS ONE	MCA MCSTD 1732
17/04/1993	62	1		LONDON'S BRILLIANT	MCA MCSTD 1763

JIMMY JAMES AND THE VAGABONDS UK singer (born September 1940, Jamaica); successful in Jamaica before settling in the UK in 1964. Joined the Vagabonds with Wallace Wilson (lead guitar), Carl Noel (organ), Matt Fredericks (saxophone), Milton James (saxophone), Philip Chen (bass), Rupert Balgobin (drums) and Count Prince Miller (vocals), touring the UK extensively performing US soul hits. He re-formed the Vagabonds in 1975.

11/09/1968	36	8		RED RED WINE	Pye 7N 17579
24/04/1976	23	8		I'LL GO WHERE YOUR MUSIC TAKES ME	Pye 7N 45585
17/07/1976	5	9		NOW IS THE TIME	Pye 7N 45606

TOMMY JAMES AND THE SHONDELLS US singer (born Thomas Jackson, 29/4/1947, Dayton, OH); he formed the Shondells when he was twelve. He recorded *Hanky Panky* in 1963 for Snap after hearing the Raindrops (the song's writers, Jeff Barry and Ellie Greenwich) perform it at a club. Two years later a hit on Roulette (although a bootleg version also appeared on Red Fox), James re-formed the Shondells with Ronnie Rosman (organ), Mike Vale (bass), Vince Pietropaoli (drums) and George Magura (saxophone), the latter two soon replaced by Eddie Gray (guitar) and Peter Lucia (drums). James recorded solo from 1970.

21/07/1966	38	7		HANKY PANKY ▲² Featured in the 1994 film *Forrest Gump*	Roulette RK 7000
05/06/1968	❶³	18		MONY MONY Originally released in America on Snap in 1963 and reclaimed #1 position on 21/8/1968	Major Minor MM 567

JAMES BOYS UK vocal duo Bradley Palmer and Stewart Palmer.

19/05/1973	39	6		OVER AND OVER	Penny Farthing PEN 806

JAMESON AND VIPER UK duo producer/singer Jameson (born Jamie Williams, 1975, London) and MC Viper. Jameson has also worked under the names Jaimeson, Kinetic, Rock Steady, DJ Infinity and 2Deep.

14/09/2002	51	1		SELECTA (URBAN HEROES)	Soundproof SPR 1CD

JAMESTOWN FEATURING JOCELYN BROWN US producer Kent Brainerd with US singer Jocelyn Brown.

14/09/1991	57	3		SHE'S GOT SOUL	A&M AM 819
27/03/1999	62	1		I BELIEVE	Playola 0091705 PLA

JAMIROQUAI UK jazz-funk group formed in London in 1992 by Jason 'Jay' Kay (born 30/12/1969, Manchester, vocals), Simon Katz (born 16/5/1971, Nottingham, guitar), Toby Smith (born 29/10/1970, London, keyboards), Stuart Zender (born 18/3/1974, Philadelphia, PA, bass), Derrick McKenzie (born 27/3/1962, London, drums) and Wallace Buchanan (born 27/11/1965, London, didgeridoo). After one single for Acid Jazz they signed with Sony. Zender left in 1998. Kay was engaged for a time to TV presenter Denise Van Outen, and was in the *It's Only Rock 'N' Roll* project for the Children's Promise charity. They won the 1997 MOBO Award for Best Album for *Travelling Without Moving*.

31/10/1992	52	2		WHEN YOU GONNA LEARN	Acid Jazz JAZID 46
20/02/1993	69	1		WHEN YOU GONNA LEARN	Acid Jazz JAZID 46
13/03/1993	10	7		TOO YOUNG TO DIE	Sony S2 6590112
05/06/1993	12	6		BLOW YOUR MIND	Sony S2 6592972
14/08/1993	32	3		EMERGENCY ON PLANET EARTH	Sony S2 6595782
25/09/1993	28	3		WHEN YOU GONNA LEARN	Sony S2 6596952
08/10/1994	17	5		SPACE COWBOY	Sony S2 6608512
19/11/1994	15	8		HALF THE MAN	Sony S2 6610032
01/07/1995	9	5		STILLNESS IN TIME	Sony S2 6620255
01/06/1996	12	5		DO U KNOW WHERE YOU'RE COMING FROM M-BEAT FEATURING JAMIROQUAI	Renk CDRENK 63

❶⁹ Number of weeks single topped the UK chart ↑ Entered the UK chart at #1 ▲⁹ Number of weeks single topped the US chart

403

VIRTUAL INSANITY 1997 Grammy Award for Best Pop Performance by a Group . . . . Sony S2 6636132 — 31/08/1996 . . . . . 3 . . . . . . 11 . . . . . .

COSMIC GIRL Featured in the 2000 film *Center Stage* . . . . Sony S2 6638292 — 07/12/1996 . . . . . 6 . . . . . . 10 . . . . . .

ALRIGHT Contains a sample of Eddie Harris' *It's Alright Now* . . . . Sony S2 6642352 — 10/05/1997 . . . . 6 . . . . . 5 . . . .

HIGH TIMES Contains a sample of Esther Williams' *Last Night Changed It All* . . . . Sony S2 6653702 — 13/12/1997 . . . . . 20 . . . . . . 6 . . . .

DEEPER UNDERGROUND ↑ Featured in the 1998 film *Godzilla* . . . . Sony S2 6662182 — 25/07/1998 . . . . ●1 . . . . 11 . . . . . .

CANNED HEAT Featured in the 2000 film *Center Stage* . . . . Sony S2 6673022 — 05/06/1999 . . . . . 4 . . . . . . 10 . . . . . .

SUPERSONIC . . . . Sony S2 6678392 — 25/09/1999 . . . . . 22 . . . . . 4 . . . . . .

KING FOR A DAY . . . . Sony S2 6679732 — 11/12/1999 . . . . . 20 . . . . . 7 . . . . . .

I'M IN THE MOOD FOR LOVE JOOLS HOLLAND JAMIROQUAI . . . . warner.esp WSMS 001CD — 24/02/2001 . . . . . 29 . . . . . 3 . . . . . .

LITTLE L Featured in the 2002 film *The Sweetest Thing* . . . . Sony S2 6717182 — 25/08/2001 . . . . 5 . . . . . 11 . . . . . .

YOU GIVE ME SOMETHING . . . . Sony S2 6720072 — 01/12/2001 . . . . . 16 . . . . . 9 . . . . . .

LOVE FOOLOSOPHY . . . . Sony S2 6723255 — 09/03/2002 . . . . . 14 . . . . . 6 . . . . . .

CORNER OF THE EARTH . . . . Sony S2 6727885 — 20/07/2002 . . . . . 31 . . . . . 3 . . . . . .

JAMMERS US dance group formed in New York City by producer and songwriter Ritchie Weeks and fronted by Debby Blackwell.
BE MINE TONIGHT . . . . Salsoul SAL 101 — 29/01/1983 . . . . . 65 . . . . . . 2 . . . . . .

JAMX AND DELEON German production duo Jurgen Mutschall (JamX) and Dominik De Leon. They also record as Dumonde.
CAN U DIG IT Contains a sample of Laura Branigan's *Self Control* . . . . Serious SERR 052CD — 07/09/2002 . . . . . 40 . . . . . . 2 . . . . . .

JAN AND DEAN US duo Jan Berry (born 3/4/1941, Los Angeles, CA) and Dean Torrence (born 10/3/1940, Los Angeles), who formed the Barons in 1957 with four school friends. When they left school Berry, Torrence and Arnie Ginsburg continued, recording *Jennie Lee* in Berry's garage, which was released by Arwin Records as Jan & Arnie (Torrence was away in the army reserve at the time) and hit #8 on the US charts. As Torrence returned, Ginsburg joined the navy, Torrence taking his role in the duo. Berry ended up in a coma after a car smash on 12/4/1966, winding up the partnership, although they reunited in 1973, 1975 and 1978. Berry died on 27/3/2004.
HEART AND SOUL . . . . London HLH 9395 — 24/08/1961 . . . . . 24 . . . . . 8 . . . . . .

SURF CITY ▲2 . . . . London LIB 55580 — 15/08/1963 . . . . . 26 . . . . 10 . . . . . .

JAN AND KJELD Danish vocal duo from Copenhagen, brothers Jan and Kjeld Wennick who were aged twelve and fourteen at the time of their hit. The English lyrics were written by Buddy Kaye..
BANJO BOY . . . . Ember S 101 — 21/07/1960 . . . . . 36 . . . . . . 4 . . . . . .

JANE'S ADDICTION US rock group formed in Los Angeles, CA in 1986 by Perry Farrell (born Perry Bernstein, 29/3/1959, New York, vocals), Dave Navarro (born 6/6/1967, Santa Monica, CA, guitar), Eric Avery (born 6/6/1967, Los Angeles, bass) and Stephen Perkins (born 13/9/1967, Los Angeles, drums). Debut album for Triple X in 1987, signing with Warner's in 1988. They split in 1992, Farrell and Perkins forming Porno For Pyros, but re-formed (minus Avery, replaced by Red Hot Chili Peppers' Michael 'Flea' Balzary) in 1997. Navarro joined Red Hot Chilli Peppers in 1993. Named after a prostitute who introduced Farrell to Navarro and Avery.
BEEN CAUGHT STEALING . . . . Warner Brothers W 0011 — 23/03/1991 . . . . . 34 . . . . . 3 . . . . . .

CLASSIC GIRL . . . . Warner Brothers W 0031 — 01/06/1991 . . . . . 60 . . . . . 1 . . . . . .

JUST BECAUSE . . . . Capitol CDCL 847 — 26/07/2003 . . . . . 14 . . . . . 4 . . . . . .

TRUE NATURE . . . . Parlophone CDCLS 850 — 08/11/2003 . . . . . 41 . . . . . 2 . . . . . .

HORST JANKOWSKI German pianist (born 30/1/1936, Berlin) strongly influenced by Ray Conniff; he later worked with Ella Fitzgerald and Miles Davis. He began his professional career in 1952 with Caterina Valente.
A WALK IN THE BLACK FOREST . . . . Mercury MF 861 — 29/07/1965 . . . . 3 . . . . . . 18 . . . . . .

SAMANTHA JANUS UK singer (born 2/11/1972) more successful as an actress, most notably in the TV comedy *Game On* and the film *Up 'N Under*. The winning entry was Sweden's *Fangad Av En Stormvind*, performed by Carola.
A MESSAGE TO YOUR HEART Britain's entry for the 1991 Eurovision Song Contest (came tenth) . . . . Hollywood HWD 104 — 11/05/1991 . . . . . 30 . . . . . 3 . . . . . .

PHILIP JAP UK singer who first recorded for Blueprint and later joined Department Of Sound.
SAVE US . . . . A&M AMS 8217 — 31/07/1982 . . . . . 53 . . . . . . 4 . . . . . .

TOTAL ERASURE . . . . A&M JAP 1 — 25/09/1982 . . . . . 41 . . . . . . 4 . . . . . .

JAPAN UK group formed in London in 1977 by David Sylvian (born David Batt, 23/2/1958, London, guitar/vocals), Steve Jansen (born Stephen Batt, 1/12/1959, London, drums), Richard Barbieri (born 30/11/1957, keyboards) and Mick Karn (born Anthony Michaelides, 24/7/1958, London, bass), later adding Rob Dean on guitar. Winning a talent contest, they signed with Ariola-Hansa, debuting in 1978. Switching to Virgin in 1980, Dean left the following year. They disbanded in 1982, Sylvian and Karn going solo. Karn also joined ex-Bauhaus Peter Murphy for one album as Dali's Car. Sylvian, Karn, Jansen and Barbieri reunited in 1991 as Rain Tree Crow.
GENTLEMEN TAKE POLAROIDS . . . . Virgin VS 379 — 18/10/1980 . . . . . 60 . . . . . . 2 . . . . . .

THE ART OF PARTIES . . . . Virgin VS 409 — 09/05/1981 . . . . . 48 . . . . . . 5 . . . . . .

QUIET LIFE . . . . Hansa 6 — 19/09/1981 . . . . . 19 . . . . . 9 . . . . . .

VISIONS OF CHINA . . . . Virgin VS 436 — 07/11/1981 . . . . . 32 . . . . 12 . . . . . .

EUROPEAN SON . . . . Hansa 10 — 23/01/1982 . . . . . 31 . . . . . . 6 . . . . . .

GHOSTS . . . . Virgin VS 472 — 20/03/1982 . . . . 5 . . . . . . 8 . . . . . .

CANTONESE BOY . . . . Virgin VS 502 — 22/05/1982 . . . . . 24 . . . . . . 6 . . . . . .

I SECOND THAT EMOTION . . . . Hansa 12 — 03/07/1982 . . . . . 9 . . . . . 11 . . . . . .

LIFE IN TOKYO . . . . Hansa 17 — 09/10/1982 . . . . . 28 . . . . . . 6 . . . . . .

NIGHT PORTER . . . . Virgin VS 554 — 20/11/1982 . . . . . 29 . . . . . 9 . . . . . .

○ Silver disc ● Gold disc ✪ Platinum disc (additional platinum units are indicated by a figure following the symbol) ◉ Singles released prior to 1973 that are known to have sold over 1 million copies in the UK

| 12/03/1983 | 38 | 4 | | ALL TOMORROW'S PARTIES | Hansa 18 |
| 21/05/1983 | 42 | 3 | | CANTON (LIVE) | Virgin VS 581 |

JARK PRONGO Dutch instrumental/production duo DJ Ziki (Rene Terhorst) and DJ Dobre (Gaston Steenkist) who also recorded as Chocolate Puma, DJ Manta, Tomba Vira, Goodmen, Rhythmkillaz and Riva.

| 03/04/1999 | 58 | 1 | | MOVIN' THRU YOUR SYSTEM | Hooj Choons HOOJ 72CD |

JEAN-MICHEL JARRE French synthesiser player (born 24/8/1948, Lyon); he abandoned musical studies in 1967 to experiment with synthesisers. He married actress Charlotte Rampling in 1976. In 1981 was the first Western artist to perform in China.

27/08/1977	4	9	O	OXYGENE PART IV	Polydor 2001 721
20/01/1979	45	5		EQUINOXE PART 5.	Polydor POSP 20
23/08/1986	65	4		FOURTH RENDEZ-VOUS	Polydor POSP 788
05/11/1988	52	2		REVOLUTIONS	Polydor PO 25
07/01/1989	52	3		LONDON KID JEAN-MICHEL JARRE FEATURING HANK MARVIN	Polydor 32
07/10/1989	65	2		OXYGENE PART IV (REMIX)	Polydor PO 55
26/06/1993	55	2		CHRONOLOGIE PART 4.	Polydor PZCD 274
30/10/1993	56	1		CHRONOLOGIE PART 4 (REMIX)	Polydor PZ 274
22/03/1997	17	3		OXYGENE 8	Epic 6643232
05/07/1997	21	2		OXYGENE 10	Epic 6647152
11/07/1998	12	6		RENDEZ-VOUS 98 JEAN-MICHEL JARRE AND APOLLO 440 The single was used as the theme to ITV's coverage of the 1998 World Cup Finals.	Epic 6661102
26/02/2000	40	1		C'EST LA VIE JEAN-MICHEL JARRE FEATURING NATACHA ATLAS	Epic 6689302

AL JARREAU US singer (born 12/3/1940, Milwaukee, WI); a resident singer at San Francisco, CA nightclub in the 1960s with George Duke, his pianist. Signed to Reprise in 1975, he has won six Grammy Awards: Best Jazz Vocal Performance in 1977 for *Look To The Rainbow,* Best Jazz Vocal Performance in 1978 for *All Fly Home,* Best Recording for Children in 1980 with various others for *In Harmony,* Best Pop Vocal Performance in 1981 for *Breaking Away,* Best Jazz Vocal Performance in 1981 for *Blue Rondo A La Turk* and Best Rhythm & Blues Vocal Performance in 1992 for *Heaven And Earth.* He has a star on the Hollywood Walk of Fame.

26/09/1981	55	4		WE'RE IN THIS LOVE TOGETHER	Warner Brothers K 17849
14/05/1983	28	6		MORNIN'	WEA U9929
16/07/1983	36	5		TROUBLE IN PARADISE	WEA International U9871
24/09/1983	63	3		BOOGIE DOWN	WEA U9814
16/11/1985	53	3		DAY BY DAY SHAKATAK FEATURING AL JARREAU	Polydor POSP 770
05/04/1986	75	1		THE MUSIC OF GOODBYE (LOVE THEME FROM 'OUT OF AFRICA') MELISSA MANCHESTER AND AL JARREAU	MCA 1038
07/03/1987	8	8		'MOONLIGHTING' THEME Theme to the TV series *Moonlighting*	WEA U8407

KENNY 'JAMMIN' JASON AND 'FAST' EDDIE SMITH US DJ/production duo.

| 11/04/1987 | 71 | 2 | | CAN U DANCE | Champion CHAMP 41 |
| 14/11/1987 | 67 | 2 | | CAN U DANCE | Champion CHAMP 41 |

JAVELLS FEATURING NOSMO KING UK vocal group formed by Stephen Jameson (born 1949, London). He was a member of Truth and recorded solo before recording as Nosmo King.

| 09/11/1974 | 26 | 8 | | GOODBYE NOTHING TO SAY | Pye Disco Demand DDS 2003 |

JAVINE UK singer (born Javine Hylton, 27/12/1981, London) who first came to prominence on the TV programme *Popstars: The Rivals.* Although generally considered to be one of the best singers on the series, she was voted out before the final.

19/07/2003	4	9		REAL THINGS Contains an interpolation of MOP's *Ante Up.*	Innocent SINCD 46
22/11/2003	15	5		SURRENDER (YOUR LOVE) Contains an interpolation of Diana Ross' *Surrender*	Innocent SINDX 52
26/06/2004	18	4		BEST OF MY LOVE	Innocent SINDX 63
21/08/2004	16	4		DON'T WALK AWAY	Innocent SINDX 65

CANDEE JAY Dutch singer (born 1/9/1981, Rotterdam), previously a member of Alice Deejay before going solo.

| 19/06/2004 | 14 | 6 | | IF I WERE YOU | Incentive CENT 58CDX |
| 13/11/2004 | 23 | 2 | | BACK FOR ME | Incentive CENT 67CDS |

SIMONE JAY – see DJ DADO

ORIS JAY PRESENTS DELSENA Dutch DJ (born Peran Van Dijk, 1974) who also records as Darqwan. Delsena is a UK female singer.

| 23/03/2002 | 42 | 2 | | TRIPPIN' | Gusto CDGUS 3 |

PETER JAY AND THE JAYWALKERS UK instrumental group: Peter Jay (drums), Peter Miller (guitar), Tony Webster (guitar), Mac McIntyre (saxophone/flute), Lloyd Baker (piano/saxophone), Geoff Moss (bass) and Johnny Larke (bass). They split in 1966.

| 08/11/1962 | 31 | 11 | | CAN CAN 62 | Decca F 11531 |

JAYDEE Dutch producer/remixer (born Robin Albers, 1958) whose debut hit was originally released in Holland in 1993.

| 20/09/1997 | 18 | 3 | | PLASTIC DREAMS | R&S RS 97117CD |
| 10/01/2004 | 35 | 4 | | PLASTIC DREAMS (REMIX) | Positiva CDTIVS 198 |

❶⁹ Number of weeks single topped the UK chart ↑ Entered the UK chart at #1 ▲⁹ Number of weeks single topped the US chart

405

LAURA JAYE – see INTENSO PROJECT

OLLIE JAYE – see JON THE DENTIST VS OLLIE JAYE

JAYHAWKS US group formed in Minneapolis, MN by Marc Olson (guitar/vocals), Gary Louris (guitar/vocals), Marc Perlman (bass) and Ken Callaghan (drums), later adding Benmont Tench on keyboards.

15/07/1995	70	1	BAD TIME .... American Recordings 74321291632

JAY-Z US rapper (born Jason Shawn Carter, Brooklyn, NYC); he later formed Payroll Records with Fanatic and Ski and appeared in the film *Streets Is Watching*. He won the 1998 Grammy Award for Best Rap Album for *Volume 2 – Hard Knock Life* and the 1999 MOBO Award for Best International Hip Hop Act. US female rapper Amil (Amil Whitehead) is a member of rap group Major Coinz.

01/03/1997	30	2		CAN'T KNOCK THE HUSTLE **JAY-Z FEATURING MARY J. BLIGE** Contains a sample of Marcus Miller's *Much Too Much* .... Northwestside 74321447192
10/05/1997	31	2		AIN'T NO PLAYA **JAY-Z FEATURING FOXY BROWN** .... Northwestside 74321474842
21/06/1997	9	5		**I'LL BE FOXY BROWN FEATURING JAY-Z** Contains a sample of Rene & Angela's *I'll Be Good*................... Def Jam 5710432
23/08/1997	65	1		WHO YOU WIT Featured in the 1997 film *Sprung* .... Qwest W 0411CD
25/10/1997	25	2		SUNSHINE **JAY-Z FEATURING BABYFACE AND FOXY BROWN**.................... Northwestside 74321528702
14/02/1998	13	4		WISHING ON A STAR **JAY-Z FEATURING GWEN DICKEY** .... Northwestside 74321554632
28/02/1998	38	2		THE CITY IS MINE **JAY-Z FEATURING BLACKSTREET** Contains samples of Glenn Frey's *You Belong To The City* and The Jones Girls' *You Gonna Make Me Love Somebody Else*................................... Northwestside 74321588012
27/06/1998	2	11	O	**HARD KNOCK LIFE (GHETTO ANTHEM)** Contains a sample of the Original Broadway Cast of Annie's *Hard Knock Life*.............. .... Northwestside 74321635332
13/03/1999	24	3		CAN I GET A... **JAY-Z FEATURING AMIL AND JA RULE** Featured in the 1998 film *Rush Hour* .... Def Jam 5668472
10/04/1999	11	9		BE ALONE NO MORE (REMIX) **ANOTHER LEVEL FEATURING JAY-Z** A second CD issue had *Holding Back The Years* as the lead track and was released to help the Capital Radio charity Help A London Child .... Northwestside 74321658482
19/06/1999	48	1		LOBSTER & SCRIMP **TIMBALAND FEATURING JAY-Z** .... Virgin DINSD 186
06/11/1999	5	13		**HEARTBREAKER ▲² MARIAH CAREY FEATURING JAY-Z** Contains a sample of Stacy Lattishaw's *Attack Of The Name Game*....... .... Columbia 6683012
04/12/1999	58	1		WHAT YOU THINK OF THAT **MEMPHIS BLEEK FEATURING JAY-Z** Contains a sample of Keith Mansfield's *High Velocity*............ .... Def Jam 8708292
26/02/2000	18	4		ANYTHING Contains a sample of the Original Broadway Cast of Oliver's *I'll Do Anything* .... Def Jam 5626502
24/06/2000	29	3		BIG PIMPIN' Features the uncredited contribution of UGK .... Def Jam 5627742
16/12/2000	17	8		I JUST WANNA LOVE U (GIVE IT TO ME) Contains samples of Rick James' *Give It To Me Baby* and The Notorious B.I.G.'s *The World Is Filled* .... Def Jam 5727462
23/06/2001	23	3		FIESTA **R KELLY FEATURING JAY-Z**... Jive 9252142
27/10/2001	21	4		IZZO (H.O.V.A.) .... Roc-A-Fella 5888152
19/01/2002	11	7		GIRLS GIRLS GIRLS Contains a sample of Tom Brock's *I Love You More And More Everytime*........ Roc-A-Fella/Def Jam 5889062
25/05/2002	35	2		HONEY **R KELLY AND JAY-Z** Contains a sample of The Bee Gees' *Love You Inside Out*............................. Jive 9253662
01/02/2003	2	12		03 BONNIE AND CLYDE **JAY-Z FEATURING BEYONCÉ KNOWLES** Contains samples of Prince's *If I Was Your Girlfriend* and Tupac's *Me And My Girlfriend* .... Roc-A-Fella 0770102
26/04/2003	17	7		EXCUSE ME MISS .... Roc-A-Fella 0779122
05/07/2003	25	3		JOGI/BEWARE OF THE BOYS **PANJABI MC FEATURING JAY-Z**.................... Showbiz/Dharma DHARMA 1CDS
16/08/2003	6	10		**FRONTIN' PHARRELL WILLIAMS FEATURING JAY-Z** Contains a sample of Michael Jackson's *Human Nature* ... Arista 82876553332
20/12/2003	32	7		CHANGE CLOTHES .... Roc-A-Fella 9815226
22/05/2004	12	8		99 PROBLEMS/DIRT OFF YOUR SHOULDER .... Roc-A-Fella 9862392
04/12/2004	14	4+		NUMB/ENCORE **JAY-Z VS LINKIN PARK** .... WEA W660CD

JAZZ AND THE BROTHERS GRIMM UK vocal/ instrumental group formed in 1986 by Paul Owen (vocals), Keith Dyce (keyboards) and David Santos (samples).

09/07/1988	57	2	(LET'S ALL GO BACK) DISCO NIGHTS .... Ensign ENY 616

JAZZY JEFF AND THE FRESH PRINCE US rap duo from Philadelphia, PA, DJ Jeff Townes (born 22/1/1965) and Will Smith (born 25/9/1968, Philadelphia). Actor Smith appeared in the comedy *Fresh Prince Of Bel Air* and the films *Independence Day* and *Men In Black*. Smith later recorded solo. Two Grammies include Best Rap Performance in 1988 for *Parents Just Don't Understand*.

04/10/1986	21	8		GIRLS AIN'T NOTHING BUT TROUBLE .... Champion CHAMP 18
03/08/1991	8	8		**SUMMERTIME** Based on Kool & The Gang's *Summer Madness*. 1991 Grammy Award for Best Rap Performance by a Duo . . Jive 279
09/11/1991	53	2		RING MY BELL This and above two singles credited to **DJ JAZZY JEFF AND THE FRESH PRINCE** .... Jive JIVECD 288
11/09/1993	●²	13	O	**BOOM! SHAKE THE ROOM** Contains a sample of The Ohio Players' *Funky Worm* .... Jive JIVECD 335
20/11/1993	24	4		I'M LOOKING FOR THE ONE (TO BE WITH ME) .... Jive JIVECD 345
19/02/1994	29	4		CAN'T WAIT TO BE WITH YOU Contains a sample of Luther Vandross' *Never Too Much* .... Jive JIVECD 348
04/06/1994	62	4		TWINKLE TWINKLE (I'M NOT A STAR) .... Jive JIVECD 354
06/08/1994	29	4		SUMMERTIME Re-issue of Jive 279 .... Jive JIVECD 279
02/12/1995	40	2		BOOM! SHAKE THE ROOM Re-issue of Jive JIVECD 335 .... Jive JIVECD 387
11/07/1998	37	2		LOVELY DAZE Cover version of the Bill Withers' hit *Lovely Day*.............................. Jive 0518902

JAZZY M UK producer Michael Connelly.

21/10/2000	47	2	JAZZIN' THE WAY YOU KNOW .... Perfecto PERF 08CDS

NORMA JEAN – see ROMINA JOHNSON

JB'S ALL STARS UK vocal/instrumental group formed by ex-Specials member John Bradbury with lead vocals by Drew Barfield.

11/02/1984 . . . . . 48 . . . . . . 4 . . . . BACKFIELD IN MOTION . . . . RCA Victor 384

JC UK male producer.

07/02/1998 . . . . . 74 . . . . . . 1 . . . . SO HOT . . . . East West EW 146CD

JC 001 UK rapper (born 16/6/1966) who first recorded in 1987. He came second to Daddy Freddy in a speed rapping contest organised by the Guinness Book of Records.

24/04/1993 . . . . . 67 . . . . . . 2 . . . . NEVER AGAIN . . . . AnXious ANX 1012CD

26/06/1993 . . . . . 56 . . . . . . 2 . . . . CUPID . . . . AnXious ANX 1014CD

JD AKA DREADY UK rapper/remixer (born Karl Jairzhino Daniel, Birmingham) who worked with Lisa Maffia before going solo.

02/08/2003 . . . . . 64 . . . . . . 1 . . . . SIGNAL . . . . Independiente SSB2MS

JDS UK DJ/production duo Darren Pearce and Julian Napolitano. Napolitano also produces as Quo Vadis and Perpetual Motion.

27/09/1997 . . . . . 61 . . . . . . 1 . . . . NINE WAYS . . . . ffrr FCD 310

23/05/1998 . . . . . 49 . . . . . . 1 . . . . LONDON TOWN . . . . Jive 0530042

03/03/2001 . . . . . 47 . . . . . . 1 . . . . NINE WAYS (REMIX) . . . . ffrr FCD 391

WYCLEF JEAN US rapper (born 17/10/1972, Haiti); also a member of The Fugees and the Refugee Allstars. He launched Clef Records in 2000. The Rock is US wrestler Dwayne Johnson (born 2/5/1972, Hayward, CA) and part of the WWF (World Wrestling Federation, though only representing Americans!). Melky Sedeck are a US vocal/instrumental duo. Claudette Ortiz is in City High.

28/06/1997 . . . . . 13 . . . . . . 5 . . . . WE TRYING TO STAY ALIVE **WYCLEF JEAN AND THE REFUGEE ALLSTARS** Contains samples of The Bee Gees' *Stayin' Alive* and Audio Two's *Top Billin'* . . . . Columbia 6646815

27/09/1997 . . . . . 25 . . . . . . 2 . . . . GUANTANAMERA **WYCLEF JEAN AND THE REFUGEE ALLSTARS** . . . . Columbia 6650852

16/05/1998 . . . . . 3 . . . . . 9 . . . . . . O **GONE TILL NOVEMBER** The lyrics contain parts of Bob Dylan's *Knockin' On Heaven's Door,* while Dylan appears in the video . . . . Columbia 6658712

14/11/1998 . . . . . 5 . . . . . . 6 . . . . **ANOTHER ONE BITES THE DUST QUEEN WITH WYCLEF JEAN FEATURING PRAS MICHEL/FREE** Featured in the 1998 film *Small Soldiers* . . . . DreamWorks DRMCD 22364

23/10/1999 . . . . . 23 . . . . . . 2 . . . . NEW DAY **WYCLEF JEAN FEATURING BONO** Featured in the 1999 film *Life* . . . . Columbia 6682122

16/09/2000 . . . . . 3 . . . . . 8 . . . . **IT DOESN'T MATTER WYCLEF JEAN FEATURING THE ROCK AND MELKY SEDECK** Contains samples of Ricky Martin's *Livin' La Vida Loca* and John Denver's *Take Me Home Country Roads*. . . . . Columbia 6697782

16/12/2000 . . . . . 9 . . . . . 10 . . . . **911 WYCLEF FEATURING MARY J. BLIGE** Contains samples of James Brown's *The Payback* and Edie Brickell & The New Bohemians' *What I Am* . . . . Columbia 6706122

21/07/2001 . . . . . 4 . . . . 14 . . . . . O **PERFECT GENTLEMAN** . . . . Columbia 6710522

08/12/2001 . . . . . 28 . . . . . . 6 . . . . WISH YOU WERE HERE . . . . Columbia 6721562

06/07/2002 . . . . . 14 . . . . . . 6 . . . . TWO WRONGS (DON'T MAKE A RIGHT) **WYCLEF JEAN FEATURING CLAUDETTE ORTIZ** . . . . Columbia 6728902

JEEVAS UK group with ex-Kula Shaker Crispian Mills (born 18/1/1973, London, guitar/vocals), Dan McKinna (bass) and ex-Straw Andy Nixon (drums).

22/03/2003 . . . . . 61 . . . . . . 1 . . . . ONCE UPON A TIME IN AMERICA . . . . Cowboy Music COWCDB 005

28/02/2004 . . . . . 70 . . . . . . 1 . . . . HAVE YOU EVER SEEN THE RAIN? . . . . Cowboy Music COWCDB 008

JEFFERSON UK singer (born Geoff Turton, 11/3/1944, Birmingham); previously lead singer with the Rockin' Berries.

09/04/1969 . . . . . 22 . . . . . . 8 . . . . COLOUR OF MY LOVE. . . . . Pye 7N 17706

JEFFERSON STARSHIP – see **STARSHIP**

GARLAND JEFFREYS US singer (born 1944, Brooklyn, NYC) who started in the mid-1960s, making his debut album in 1973.

08/02/1992 . . . . . 72 . . . . . . 1 . . . . HAIL HAIL ROCK 'N' ROLL . . . . RCA PB 49171

JELLYBEAN US producer (born John Benitez, 7/11/1957, South Bronx, NYC) who began as a DJ, then remixing. In the early 1980s he began producing and recording, signing with Liberty in 1984. He also appeared as a DJ in the film *Nighthawks*.

01/02/1986 . . . . . 47 . . . . . . 4 . . . . SIDEWALK TALK . . . . EMI America EA 210

26/09/1987 . . . . . 13 . . . . . 10 . . . . . . THE REAL THING **JELLYBEAN FEATURING STEVEN DANTE** . . . . Chrysalis CHS 3167

28/11/1987 . . . . . 10 . . . . . 10 . . . . . . **WHO FOUND WHO JELLYBEAN FEATURING ELISA FIORILLO** . . . . Chrysalis CHS JEL 1

12/12/1987 . . . . . 12 . . . . . 10 . . . . . . JINGO. . . . . Chrysalis JEL 2

12/03/1988 . . . . . 13 . . . . . 10 . . . . . . JUST A MIRAGE **JELLYBEAN FEATURING ADELE BERTEI**. . . . . Chrysalis JEL 3

20/08/1988 . . . . . 41 . . . . . . 3 . . . . COMING BACK FOR MORE **JELLYBEAN FEATURING RICHARD DARBYSHIRE** . . . . Chrysalis JEL 4

JELLYFISH US rock group formed in San Francisco, CA by Andy Sturmer (drums/vocals), Jason Faulkner (guitar), Chris Manning (bass) and Roger Manning (keyboards).

26/01/1991 . . . . . 39 . . . . . . 6 . . . . THE KING IS HALF UNDRESSED . . . . Charisma CUSS 1

27/04/1991 . . . . . 51 . . . . . . 4 . . . . BABY'S COMING BACK. . . . . Charisma CUSS 2

03/08/1991 . . . . . 49 . . . . . . 3 . . . . THE SCARY-GO-ROUND EP Tracks on EP: *Now She Knows She's Wrong, Bedspring Kiss, She Still Loves Him (Live)* and *Baby's Coming Back (Live)*. . . . . Charisma CUSS 3

26/10/1991 . . . . . 59 . . . . . . 2 . . . . I WANNA STAY HOME . . . . Charisma CUSS 4

01/05/1993 . . . . . 43 . . . . . . 3 . . . . THE GHOST AT NUMBER ONE . . . . Charisma CUSDG 10

17/07/1993 . . . . . 55 . . . . . . 2 . . . . NEW MISTAKE . . . . Charisma CUSDG 11

❶⁹ Number of weeks single topped the UK chart ↑ Entered the UK chart at #1 ▲⁹ Number of weeks single topped the US chart

407

JEMINI UK vocal duo formed in Liverpool by Gemma Abbey and Chris Crosbey as Tricity, name-changing to Jemini shortly before winning the Song For Europe competition (they name-changed again to Jemani after objections from US rapper Jemini). Their hit was Britain's entry in the 2003 Eurovision Song Contest, coming last with no points, the UK's worst ever showing in the competition.

07/06/2003.....15......3....... CRY BABY .... Integral INTEG 001CD

JENTINA UK singer (born 1985, Woking, in a caravan to a Romany mother).

03/07/2004.....22......3....... BAD ASS STRIPPA Contains a sample of The O'Jays' *For The Love Of Money* .... Virgin VSCDX 1873
09/10/2004.....20......3....... FRENCH KISSES .... Virgin VSCDX 1877

JERMAINE – see **MARQUES HOUSTON**

JERU THE DAMAJA US rapper (born Kendrick Jeru Davis, 1971, Brooklyn, NYC) whose full stage name is Jeru The Damaja: D Original Dirty Rotten Scoundrel.

07/12/1996.....67......1....... YA PLAYIN YASELF .... ffrr FCD 289

JESSICA Swedish singer (born Jessica Folcker, 9/7/1975, Stockholm) who was a backing singer for Ace Of Base before going solo.

20/03/1999.....47......1....... HOW WILL I KNOW (WHO YOU ARE) .... Jive 0522412

JESSY Belgian singer (born Jessy De Smet, 8/7/1976, Zottegem).

12/04/2003.....29......3....... LOOK AT ME NOW .... Data 46CDS

JESUS AND MARY CHAIN UK group formed in Scotland in 1983 by William Reid (born 28/10/1958, Glasgow, guitar/vocals), Jim Reid (born 29/12/1961, Glasgow, guitar/vocals), Douglas Hart (bass) and Murray Dalglish (drums) as the Poppy Seeds. They moved to London in 1984, recruiting Bobby Gillespie (ex-Primal Scream) in place of Dalglish. Debuted on Creation in 1984 and signed with Blanco Y Negro the following year. By 1992 line-up was the Reid brothers, Ben Laurie (guitar), Mathew Parkin (bass) and Barry Blacker (drums).

02/03/1985.....47......4....... NEVER UNDERSTAND .... Blanco Y Negro NEG 8
08/06/1985.....55......3....... YOU TRIP ME UP .... Blanco Y Negro NEG 13
12/10/1985.....45......3....... JUST LIKE HONEY... Blanco Y Negro NEG 17
26/07/1986.....13......5....... SOME CANDY TALKING.. Blanco Y Negro NEG 19
02/05/1987 .....8 ......6....... **APRIL SKIES**... Blanco Y Negro NEG 24
15/08/1987.....25......5....... HAPPY WHEN IT RAINS... Blanco Y Negro NEG 25
07/11/1987.....33......1....... DARKLANDS .... Blanco Y Negro NEG 29
09/04/1988.....30......3....... SIDEWALKING .... Blanco Y Negro NEG 32
23/09/1989.....32......2....... BLUES FROM A GUN .... Blanco Y Negro NEG 41
18/11/1989.....57......2....... HEAD ON .... Blanco Y Negro NEG 42
08/09/1990.....46......2....... ROLLERCOASTER (EP) Tracks on EP: *Rollercoaster, Silverblade, Lowlife* and *Tower Of Song* .... Blanco Y Negro NEG 45
15/02/1992.....10......4....... **REVERENCE** .... Blanco Y Negro NEG 55
14/03/1992.....23......3....... FAR GONE AND OUT .... Blanco Y Negro NEG 56
04/07/1992.....41......2....... ALMOST GOLD.. Blanco Y Negro NEG 57
10/07/1993.....30......2....... SOUND OF SPEED (EP) Tracks on EP: *Snakedriver, Something I Can't Have, Write Record Release Blues* and *Little Red Rooster* ..
.... Blanco Y Negro NEG 66CD
30/07/1994.....22......3....... SOMETIMES ALWAYS .... Blanco Y Negro NEG 70CD
22/10/1994.....52......2....... COME ON .... Blanco Y Negro NEG 73CD1
17/06/1995.....61......1....... I HATE ROCK 'N' ROLL .... Blanco Y Negro NEG 81CD
18/04/1998.....35......2....... CRACKING UP .... Creation CRESCD 292
30/05/1998.....38......1....... ILOVEROCKNROLL .... Creation CRESCD 296

JESUS JONES UK group formed in 1986 by Mike Edwards (born 22/6/1964, London, guitar/vocals), Gen (born Simon Matthews, 23/4/1964, Devizes, drums) and Al Jaworski (born 31/1/1966, Plymouth) as Big Colour, becoming Jesus Jones in 1988. Added Jerry De Borg (born 30/10/1963, London, guitar/vocals) and Iain 'Barry D' Baker (born 29/9/1965, Carshalton, keyboards/samples) in 1988, and signed with the Food label.

25/02/1989.....42......3....... INFO-FREAKO .... Food 18
08/07/1989.....42......3....... NEVER ENOUGH .... Food 21
23/09/1989.....46......3....... BRING IT ON DOWN .... Food 22
07/04/1990.....19......8....... REAL REAL REAL .... Food 24
06/10/1990.....31......4....... RIGHT HERE RIGHT NOW .... Food 25
12/01/1991 .....7 ......7....... **INTERNATIONAL BRIGHT YOUNG THING** .... Food 27
02/03/1991.....21......7....... WHO WHERE WHY .... Food 28
20/07/1991.....31......4....... RIGHT HERE RIGHT NOW Re-issue of Food 25 .... Food 30
09/01/1993.....10......5....... **THE DEVIL YOU KNOW** .... Food CDPERV 1
10/04/1993.....36......3....... THE RIGHT DECISION .... Food CDPERV 2
10/07/1993.....30......3....... ZEROES AND ONES .... Food CDFOODS 44
14/06/1997.....49......1....... THE NEXT BIG THING .... Food CDFOOD 95
16/08/1997.....71......1....... CHEMICAL #1 .... Food CDFOOD 102

JESUS LIZARD US rock group formed in 1989 by David Yow (vocals), David Sims (bass) and Duane Denison (guitar) with a drum machine, though later joined by Mac McNeilly (drums). Yow and Sims had previously been with Scratch Acid.

06/03/1993.....12......2....... PUSS Listed flip side was *Oh, The Guilt* by **NIRVANA** .... Touch And Go TG 83CD

○ Silver disc ● Gold disc ✪ Platinum disc (additional platinum units are indicated by a figure following the symbol) ◎ Singles released prior to 1973 that are known to have sold over 1 million copies in the UK

JESUS LOVES YOU
UK group with Boy George (born George O'Dowd, 14/6/1961, Bexley) on his More Protein label in 1989.

11/11/1989	68	1		AFTER THE LOVE	More Protein PROT 2
23/02/1991	27	8		BOW DOWN MISTER	More Protein PROT 8
08/06/1991	35	8		GENERATIONS OF LOVE	More Protein PROT 10
12/12/1992	65	1		SWEET TOXIC LOVE	Virgin VS 1449

JET
Australian group from Melbourne with Nic Cester (guitar/vocals), Cameron Muncy (guitar/vocals), Mark Wilson (bass) and Chris Cester (drums/vocals).

06/09/2003	23	2		ARE YOU GONNA BE MY GIRL?	Elektra E 7456CD1
15/11/2003	34	2		ROLLOVER DJ	Elektra E 7486CD1
20/03/2004	28	3		LOOK WHAT YOU'VE DONE	Elektra E 7527CD
05/06/2004	16	5		ARE YOU GONNA BE MY GIRL? Re-issue of Elektra E 7456CD1 and revived after the song was used in an advertisement for Vodaphone	Elektra E 7599CD
18/09/2004	34	2		COLD HARD BITCH	Elektra E7607CD

JETHRO TULL
UK group formed in Luton in 1967 by Ian Anderson (born 10/8/1947, Edinburgh, vocals/flute), Glenn Cornick (born 24/4/1947, Barrow-in-Furness, bass), Mick Abrahams (born 7/4/1943, guitar) and Clive Bunker (born 12/12/1946, Blackpool, drums) and named after the 18th-century agriculturist. Debut single in 1968 on MGM, by the end of the year Abrahams left (to form Blodwyn Pig), replaced by Martin Barre (born 17/11/1946, Birmingham). John Evans (in Anderson's first band, the Blades, in 1963) joined on keyboards in 1970, with another ex-Blade, Jeffrey Hammond-Hammond, replacing Cornick later that year. Bunker left in 1971, replaced by Barriemore Barlow. Hammond-Hammond left in 1976, replaced by John Glascock, who died after open-heart surgery on 17/11/1979, his replacement being Dave Pegg (born 2/11/1947, Birmingham). The line-up on their 20th anniversary tour was Anderson, Barre, Pegg, Doane Perry and Martin Allcock. They won the 1988 Grammy Award for Best Hard Rock/Metal Performance for *Crest Of A Knave*.

01/01/1969	29	8		LOVE STORY	Island WIP 6048
14/05/1969	3	14		**LIVING IN THE PAST**	Island WIP 6056
01/11/1969	7	11		**SWEET DREAM**	Chrysalis WIP 6070
24/01/1970	4	9		**TEACHER/THE WITCH'S PROMISE**	Chrysalis WIP 6077
18/09/1971	11	8		LIFE IS A LONG SONG/UP THE POOL	Chrysalis WIP 6106
11/12/1976	28	6		RING OUT SOLSTICE BELLS (EP) Tracks on EP: *Ring Out Solstice Bells, March The Mad Scientist, The Christmas Song* and *Pan Dance*	Chrysalis CXP 2
15/09/1984	70	2		LAP OF LUXURY	Chrysalis TULL 1
16/01/1988	55	4		SAID SHE WAS A DANCER	Chrysalis TULL 4
21/03/1992	47	3		ROCKS ON THE ROAD	Chrysalis TULLX 7
29/05/1993	32	3		LIVING IN THE (SLIGHTLY MORE RECENT) PAST Live version of Island WIP 6056	Chrysalis CDCHSS 3970

JETS
UK group formed by brothers Bobby, Ray and Tony Cotton.

22/08/1981	55	3		SUGAR DOLL	EMI 5211
31/10/1981	25	11		YES TONIGHT JOSEPHINE	EMI 5247
06/02/1982	21	9		LOVE MAKES THE WORLD GO ROUND	EMI 5262
24/04/1982	58	3		THE HONEYDRIPPER	EMI 5289
09/10/1982	56	3		SOMEBODY TO LOVE	EMI 5342
06/08/1983	53	3		BLUE SKIES	EMI 5405
17/12/1983	62	4		ROCKIN' AROUND THE CHRISTMAS TREE	PRT 7P 297
13/10/1984	72	2		PARTY DOLL	PRT JETS 2

JETS
US group formed in Minneapolis, MN by eight brothers and one sister – Leroy, Eddie, Eugene, Haini, Rudy, Kathi, Elizabeth and Moana Wolfgramm. Eugene left in 1988, forming Boys Club with Joe Pasquale, although he went under the name Gene Hunt in this venture. The Wolfgramm's parents are from Tonga.

31/01/1987	5	13		**CRUSH ON YOU**	MCA 1048
25/04/1987	41	4		CURIOSITY	MCA 1119
28/05/1988	69	2		ROCKET 2 U	MCA 1226

JOAN JETT AND THE BLACKHEARTS
US singer (born Joan Larkin, 22/9/1960, Philadelphia, PA); guitarist with the all-girl Runaways from 1975 until 1978, forming the Blackhearts with Ricky Bird (guitar), Gary Ryan (bass) and Lee Crystal (drums) in 1980. She appeared in the 1987 film *Light Of Day* as leader of the band The Barbusters.

24/04/1982	4	10	O	**I LOVE ROCK 'N' ROLL** ▲7 Featured in the films *Wayne's World 2* (1993) and *Charlie's Angels* (2000)	Epic EPC A 2152
10/07/1982	60	3		CRIMSON AND CLOVER	Epic EPC A 2485
20/08/1988	46	6		I HATE MYSELF FOR LOVING YOU	London LON 195
31/03/1990	69	1		DIRTY DEEDS JOAN JETT	Chrysalis CHS 3518
19/02/1994	75	1		I LOVE ROCK 'N' ROLL Re-issue of Epic EPC A 2152	Reprise W 0232CD

JEWEL
US singer/guitarist (born Jewel Kilcher, 23/5/1974, Payson, UT, raised in Homer, Alaska). She studied opera in Illinois before moving to California and going solo. Her 1995 debut album sold over 8 million copies in America alone.

14/06/1997	52	1		WHO WILL SAVE YOUR SOUL	Atlantic A 8514CD
09/08/1997	53	1		YOU WERE MEANT FOR ME	Atlantic A 5463CD
22/11/1997	32	2		YOU WERE MEANT FOR ME	Atlantic A 5463CD
21/11/1998	41	2		HANDS	Atlantic AT 0055CD
26/06/1999	38	2		DOWN SO LONG	Atlantic AT 0069CD
30/08/2003	52	1		INTUITION	Atlantic W 619CD

❶9 Number of weeks single topped the UK chart ↑ Entered the UK chart at #1 ▲9 Number of weeks single topped the US chart

409

JEZ AND CHOOPIE UK/Israeli DJ/production duo Jeremy Ansell and David Geyra.

21/03/1998.....36......2.......	YIM	Multiply CDMULTY 31

JFK UK producer JF Kinch who is also the resident DJ at Passion And Peach.

15/09/2001.....71......1.......	GOOD GOD	Y2K 025CD
26/01/2002.....47......1.......	WHIPLASH	Y2K 027CD
04/05/2002.....55......1.......	THE SOUND OF BLUE	Y2K 030CD

JHELISA US singer Jhelisa Anderson (raised in Kentucky) who began as a backing singer for the likes of Bryan Ferry before going solo.

01/07/1995.....75......1.......	FRIENDLY PRESSURE	Dorado DOR 040CD

JIGSAW UK group formed by ex-Pinkerton's Assorted Colours Barrie Bernard (born 27/11/1944, Coventry, bass), ex-Mighty Avengers Tony Campbell (born 24/6/1944, Rugby, guitar), Des Dyer (born 22/5/1948, Rugby, percussion/vocals) and Clive Scott (born 24/2/1945, Coventry, keyboards/vocals), who started the Splash label at the same time.

01/11/1975 .....9......11......	**SKY HIGH** Featured in the 1975 film *The Man From Hong Kong* (US title *The Dragon Flies*)......................	Splash CPI 1
06/08/1977.....36......5......	IF I HAVE TO GO AWAY	Splash CP 11

JILTED JOHN UK singer (born Graham Fellows, 1959, Sheffield) whose hit inspired answer records from Gordon The Moron and Julie and Gordon. Fellows later appeared in *Coronation Street* as an un-named young man in 1981 and the following year as Les Charlton. He later created the characters John Shuttleworth and Brian Appleton.

12/08/1978 .....4......12.....O	**JILTED JOHN**	EMI International INT 567

JIMMY EAT WORLD US group from Mesa, AZ with Jim Adkins (guitar/vocals), Tom Linton (guitar/vocals), Rick Burch (bass) and Zach Lind (drums). First recorded for Wooden Blue in 1994, then Christie Front Drive, Emery and Blueprint before Capitol in 1996.

17/11/2001.....60......1.......	SALT SWEAT SUGAR..	DreamWorks 4508782
09/02/2002.....26......3.......	THE MIDDLE	DreamWorks 4508482
15/06/2002.....38......2.......	SWEETNESS..	DreamWorks 4508342
16/10/2004.....38......2.......	PAIN	Interscope 9864179

JIMMY THE HOOVER UK pop group formed in 1982 by Simon Barker, Derek Dunbar, Carla Duplantier, Flinto and Mark Rutherford. They were given their name by Malcolm McLaren.

25/06/1983.....18......8.......	TANTALISE (WO WO EE YEH YEH)..	Innervision A 3406

JINGLE BELLES UK studio group assembled by producer Nigel Wright to record seasonal tracks made popular by the Crystals, the Ronettes and Darlene Love, all of whom had originally recorded with Phil Spector, hence the single's title.

17/12/1983.....37......4.......	CHRISTMAS SPECTRE	Passion PASH 14

JINNY Italian singer (born Janine Brown, 1975, France).

29/06/1991.....68......3.......	KEEP WARM	Virgin VS 1356
22/05/1993.....74......1.......	FEEL THE RHYTHM	Logic 1633001022
15/07/1995.....11......8.......	KEEP WARM (REMIX)..	Multiply CDMULTY 5
16/12/1995.....30......4.......	WANNA BE WITH YOU	Multiply CDMULTY 8

JIVE BUNNY AND THE MASTERMIXERS UK production/mixing group with Andy Pickles, Les Hemstock, John Pickles and Ian Morgan.

15/07/1989 ...●⁵...19.....✪	**SWING THE MOOD**	Music Factory Dance MFD 001
14/10/1989 ...●³...12.....●	**THAT'S WHAT I LIKE**	Music Factory Dance MFD 002
02/12/1989.....53......2......	IT TAKES TWO BABY **LIZ KERSHAW, BRUNO BROOKES, JIVE BUNNY AND LONDONBEAT**........................	Spartan CIN 101
16/12/1989 ...●¹...6.....●	**LET'S PARTY** ↑	Music Factory Dance MFD 003
17/03/1990 .....4......6......	THAT SOUNDS GOOD TO ME	Music Factory Dance MFD 004
25/08/1990 .....8......6......	**CAN CAN YOU PARTY**	Music Factory Dance MFD 007
17/11/1990.....19......5......	LET'S SWING AGAIN..	Music Factory Dance MFD 009
22/12/1990.....13......5......	THE CRAZY PARTY MIXES	Music Factory Dance MFD 010
23/03/1991.....28......5......	OVER TO YOU JOHN (HERE WE GO AGAIN)	Music Factory Dance MFD 012
20/07/1991.....43......2......	HOT SUMMER SALSA	Music Factory Dance MFD 013
23/11/1991.....48......2......	ROCK 'N' ROLL DANCE PARTY	Music Factory Dance MFD 015

JJ UK vocal/ instrumental duo Terry Jones and Jonathan James.

09/02/1991.....55......3.......	IF THIS IS LOVE	Columbia 6566097
27/05/2000 .....5......8.......	**MASTERBLASTER 2000**	Red Rose RROSE 002CD
07/10/2000 .....8......6.......	**AIN'T NO STOPPIN US** This and above single credited to **DJ LUCK AND MC NEAT FEATURING JJ**	Red Rose CDRROSE 004

JJ72 Irish rock group formed by Mark Greaney (guitar/vocals), Hillary Woods (bass) and Fergal Matthews (drums). Despite much speculation, their name doesn't represent anything at all!

03/06/2000.....68......1.......	LONG WAY SOUTH	Lakota LAK 0015CD
26/08/2000.....23......3.......	OXYGEN...	Lakota LAK 0016CD
04/11/2000.....29......3.......	OCTOBER SWIMMER	Lakota LAK 0018CD
10/02/2001.....21......3.......	SNOW	Lakota LAK 0019CD
12/10/2002.....28......2.......	FORMULAE	Columbia 6731595

22/02/2003 . . . . . 43 . . . . . . 1 . . . . ALWAYS AND FOREVER . . . . Columbia 6734325

JKD BAND UK studio group assembled by Henry Hadaway, Paul Jenkins and David Katz.
01/07/1978 . . . . . 58 . . . . . . 4 . . . . DRAGON POWER. . . . . Satril SAT 132

JM SILK US vocal/instrumental duo Steve 'Silk' Hurley and Keith Nunnally.
25/10/1986 . . . . . 62 . . . . . 3 . . . . . . I CAN'T TURN AROUND Re-recorded by Farley Jackmaster Funk and Darryl Pandy as *Love Can't turn Around* . . . . . . RCA PB 49793
07/03/1987 . . . . . 47 . . . . . 3 . . . . . . LET THE MUSIC TAKE CONTROL . . . . RCA PB 49767

JMD – see **TYREE**

JO JINGLES UK vocal group/music, singing and movement class for children aged six months to five years, formed by Gill Thomas in 1991. The single was made by the Paddock Wood branch.
13/11/2004 . . . . . 21 . . . . . . 3 . . . . WIND THE BOBBIN UP Released in aid of the BBC's Children In Need charity . . . . Jo Jingles JJ21CD

JO JO GUNNE US group with Mark Andes (born 19/2/1948, Philadelphia, PA, bass/vocals), Matt Andes (guitar/vocals), Jay Ferguson (born John Ferguson, 10/5/1947, Burbank, CA, keyboards/vocals) and Curly Smith (drums/vocals), plus Jimmie Randall (bass) and John Staehely (guitar). Mark and Jay had formerly been members of Spirit, and upon Jo Jo Gunne's demise revived the group.
25/03/1972 . . . . . 6 . . . . . . 12 . . . . . . **RUN RUN RUN** . . . . Asylum AYM 501

JOAN COLLINS FAN CLUB UK singer Julian Clary (born 25/5/1959, Teddington), he dropped the name after objections from the real Joan Collins.
18/06/1988 . . . . . 60 . . . . . . 3 . . . . LEADER OF THE PACK . . . . 10 TEN 227

JOHN PAUL JOANS UK singer/comedian (John Davidge) whose name was deliberately chosen in order to create confusion with Led Zeppelin member John Paul Jones
19/12/1970 . . . . . 25 . . . . . . 7 . . . . MAN FROM NAZARETH . . . . RAK 107

JOBABE – see **REAL AND RICHARDSON FEATURING JOBABE**

JOBOXERS UK group formed by Dig Wayne (born 20/7/1958, vocals), Rob Marche (born 13/10/1962, Bristol, guitar), Dave Collard (born 17/1/1961, Bristol, keyboards), Chris Bostock (born 23/11/1962, Bristol, bass) and Sean McLusky (born 5/5/1961, Bristol, drums) evolving from Subway Sect. They disbanded in 1986.
19/02/1983 . . . . . 3 . . . . . 15 . . . . . . **BOXER BEAT** . . . . RCA BOXX 1
21/05/1983 . . . . . 7 . . . . . 9 . . . . . . **JUST GOT LUCKY** . . . . RCA BOXX 2
13/08/1983 . . . . . 31 . . . . . . 8 . . . . . . JOHNNY FRIENDLY . . . . RCA BOXX 3
12/11/1983 . . . . . 72 . . . . . . 1 . . . . . . JEALOUS LOVE . . . . RCA BOXX 4

JOCASTA UK group with Tim Arnold (guitar/vocals), Jack Reynolds (guitar), Andy Lewis (bass) and Adrian Meehan (drums).
15/02/1997 . . . . . 50 . . . . . . 1 . . . . . . GO. . . . . Epic 6641415
03/05/1997 . . . . . 60 . . . . . . 1 . . . . . . CHANGE ME . . . . Epic 6643902

JOCKMASTER B.A. – see **MAD JOCKS FEATURING JOCKMASTER B.A.**

JOCKO US DJ and rapper Douglas Henderson, who began his career on radio in Baltimore in 1950. He died on 15/7/2000.
23/02/1980 . . . . . 56 . . . . . . 3 . . . . . . RHYTHM TALK Contains an interpolation of McFadden & Whitehead's *Ain't No Stoppin' Us Now* . . . . Philadelphia International PIR 8222

JODE FEATURING YO-HANS UK duo Anthony Clark and Ben 'Jammin' Robbins' with singer Yo-Hans.
19/12/1998 . . . . . 48 . . . . . . 2 . . . . . . WALK...(THE DOG) LIKE AN EGYPTIAN . . . . Logic 74321640332

JODECI US R&B vocal group formed by two sets of brothers: Joel 'JoJo' (born 10/6/1971, Charlotte, NC) and Gedric 'K-Ci' Hailey (born 2/9/1969, Charlotte) and Dalvin (born 23/7/1971, Newport News, VA) and Donald 'DeVante Swing' DeGrate. The Hailey brothers later recorded as K-Ci and Jojo while Dalvin DeGrate recorded solo.
16/01/1993 . . . . . 56 . . . . . . 2 . . . . . . CHERISH Featured in the 1992 film *Fried Green Tomatoes* . . . . Uptown MCSTD 1726
11/12/1993 . . . . . 56 . . . . . . 1 . . . . . . CRY FOR YOU . . . . Uptown MCSTD 1951
16/07/1994 . . . . . 18 . . . . . . 3 . . . . . . FEENIN' Contains a sample of EPMD's *Get Off My Bandwagon* . . . . MCA MCSTD 1984
28/01/1995 . . . . . 20 . . . . . . 3 . . . . . . CRY FOR YOU Re-issue of Uptown MCSTD 1951 . . . . Uptown MCSTD 2039
24/06/1995 . . . . . 17 . . . . . . 5 . . . . . . FREEK 'N YOU . . . . Uptown MCSTD 2072
09/12/1995 . . . . . 23 . . . . . . 3 . . . . . . LOVE U 4 LIFE . . . . Uptown MCSTD 2105
25/05/1996 . . . . . 20 . . . . . . 2 . . . . . . GET ON UP Contains a sample of Quincy Jones' *Velas*. . . . . MCA MCSTD 48010

JODIE Australian singer.
25/02/1995 . . . . . 47 . . . . . . 1 . . . . . . ANYTHING YOU WANT . . . . Mercury MERCD 423

JOE US singer (born Joseph Lewis Thomas, 1972, Cuthbert, GA), discovered singing in church by producer Vincent Henry.
22/01/1994 . . . . . 22 . . . . . . 4 . . . . . . I'M IN LUV . . . . Mercury JOECD 1
25/06/1994 . . . . . 34 . . . . . . 2 . . . . . . THE ONE FOR ME. . . . . Mercury JOECD 2
22/10/1994 . . . . . 56 . . . . . . 1 . . . . . . ALL OR NOTHING. . . . . Mercury JOECD 3

❶⁹ Number of weeks single topped the UK chart ↑ Entered the UK chart at #1 ▲⁹ Number of weeks single topped the US chart

411

DATE	POS	WKS	BPI	SINGLE TITLE	LABEL & NUMBER
27/04/1996	34	3		ALL THE THINGS (YOUR MAN WON'T DO) Featured in the 1996 film *Don't Be A Menace To South Central While Drinking Your Juice In The Hood*	Island CID 634
14/06/1997	16	3		DON'T WANNA BE A PLAYER Featured in the 1997 film *Booty Call*	Jive JIVECD 410
27/09/1997	22	2		THE LOVE SCENE	Jive JIVECD 430
10/01/1998	29	3		GOOD GIRLS	Jive JIVECD 442
22/08/1998	41	2		NO ONE ELSE COMES CLOSE	Jive 0521682
31/10/1998	52	1		ALL THAT I AM	Jive 0518532
11/03/2000	10	10		**THANK GOD I FOUND YOU** ▲[1] **MARIAH CAREY FEATURING JOE & 98 DEGREES** Features the uncredited contribution of Trey Lorenz. In September 2000 Seth Swirsky and Warryn Campbell filed a suit against James Harris III, Terry Lewis and Mariah, the song's writers, claiming they had infringed their copyright on a song called *One Of Those Love Songs* that had been recorded in 1998 by Xscape.	Columbia 6690582
15/07/2000	60	1		TREAT HER LIKE A LADY	Jive 9250772
17/02/2001	7	8		**STUTTER** ▲[4] **JOE FEATURING MYSTIKAL** Contains a sample of The Pharcyde's *Passin' Me By*. Featured in the 2000 film *Double Take*	Jive 9251632
05/05/2001	37	2		I WANNA KNOW Featured in the 2000 film *The Wood*	Jive 9252102
16/02/2002	29	2		LET'S STAY HOME TONIGHT	Jive 9253222
14/09/2002	53	1		WHAT IF A WOMAN Contains a sample of War's *Slippin' Into Darkness*	Jive 9253962
24/04/2004	12	7		RIDE WIT U/MORE & MORE **JOE FEATURING G-UNIT**	Jive 82876609392

JOE PUBLIC US R&B group formed in Buffalo, NY by Joe Carter, Joe Sayles, Kevin Scott and Dwight Wyatt.

DATE	POS	WKS	BPI	SINGLE TITLE	LABEL & NUMBER
11/07/1992	43	4		LIVE AND LEARN	Columbia 6575267
28/11/1992	75	1		I'VE BEEN WATCHIN'	Columbia 6587657

BILLY JOEL US singer (born 9/5/1949, Hicksville, NY); he formed the Echoes in 1964, who became the Emeralds then the Lost Souls. He joined the Hassles in 1967 and when they split in 1969 he formed Attila with drummer Jon Small. One album for Epic before going solo, his debut album on Family Productions in 1971. When the album failed (mainly through badmastering and mixing) he played piano at a lounge club, was spotted by Columbia and signed with them in 1973. He married Elizabeth Weber (who became his manager) in 1973 and supermodel Christie Brinkley in 1985, both ending in divorce. He was inducted into the Rock & Roll Hall of Fame in 1999. Six Grammy Awards include Album of the Year and Best Pop Vocal Performance in 1979 for *52nd Street*, Best Rock Vocal Performance in 1980 for *Glass Houses* and Best Recording for Children in 1982 with various others for *In Harmony 2*. He has a star on the Hollywood Walf of Fame.

DATE	POS	WKS	BPI	SINGLE TITLE	LABEL & NUMBER
11/02/1978	19	9		JUST THE WAY YOU ARE Featured in the 1978 film *F.M.* 1978 Grammy Award for Record of the Year. The song won the Grammy Award for Song of the Year for writer Billy Joel the same year	CBS 5872
24/06/1978	35	6		MOVIN' OUT (ANTHONY'S SONG)	CBS 6412
02/12/1978	12	15	○	MY LIFE	CBS 6821
28/04/1979	50	3		UNTIL THE NIGHT	CBS 7242
12/04/1980	40	4		ALL FOR LEYNA	CBS 8325
09/08/1980	14	11		IT'S STILL ROCK AND ROLL TO ME ▲[2]	CBS 8753
15/10/1983	❶[5]	17	●	**UPTOWN GIRL** Accompanying video features Christie Brinkley, later Joel's wife	CBS A 3775
10/12/1983	4	10	○	**TELL HER ABOUT IT** ▲[1]	CBS A 3655
18/02/1984	8	10	○	**AN INNOCENT MAN**	CBS A 4142
28/04/1984	25	8		THE LONGEST TIME	CBS A 4280
23/06/1984	29	7		LEAVE A TENDER MOMENT ALONE/GOODNIGHT SAIGON	CBS A 4521
22/02/1986	53	1		SHE'S ALWAYS A WOMAN/JUST THE WAY YOU ARE	CBS A 6862
20/09/1986	52	4		A MATTER OF TRUST	CBS 6500577
30/09/1989	7	10		**WE DIDN'T START THE FIRE** ▲[2]	CBS JOEL 1
16/12/1989	53	4		LENINGRAD	CBS JOEL 3
10/03/1990	70	2		I GO TO EXTREMES	CBS JOEL 2
29/08/1992	27	4		ALL SHOOK UP Featured in the 1992 film *Honeymoon In Vegas*	Columbia 6583437
31/07/1993	3	14		**THE RIVER OF DREAMS**	Columbia 6595432
23/10/1993	32	4		ALL ABOUT SOUL Features Color Me Badd on backing vocals	Columbia 6597362
26/02/1994	50	3		NO MAN'S LAND	Columbia 6599202

JOHAN German producer Johan Bley. He is also a member of Juno Reactor and Jungle High.

DATE	POS	WKS	BPI	SINGLE TITLE	LABEL & NUMBER
16/03/1996	54	1		NEW KICKS	Perfecto PERF 118CD

ANGELA JOHN – see **JOSE PADILLA FEATURING ANGELA JOHN**

ELTON JOHN UK singer/pianist (born Reginald Kenneth Dwight, 25/3/1947, Pinner); he joined Bluesology in 1961. They turned professional in 1965, supporting visiting US R&B acts before becoming Long John Baldry's backing band. Left in 1967 (adopting his name from group members Elton Dean and John Baldry) to go solo and met up with lyricist Bernie Taupin. Recorded first single (via Philips) in 1968 and signed with DJM in 1969. Launched the Rocket label in 1973 and publishing company Big Pig in 1974. Later Chairman of Watford FC. Married recording engineer Renate Blauer in 1984 (ended in divorce). He sang a re-written version of *Candle In The Wind* at the funeral of Diana, Princess of Wales, the only time he performed the song live. The single, with advance orders of 8.7 million, entered the US chart at #1 and sold over 11 million copies, only the seventh time a record had entered at pole position, Elton being the first artist to enter the US album charts at #1 (the single also topped the Canadian charts for 45 weeks, spent eighteen months in the top three and 30 months in the top ten, earning nineteen platinum awards). He won the Best Male Award at the 1991 BRIT Awards and Outstanding Contribution Award in 1986 (jointly with Wham!) and 1995, and The Freddie Mercury Award (in recognition of his charity work) at the 1998 BRIT Awards. He was awarded a CBE in 1996 and a knighthood in the 1998 New Year's Honours List. He was

inducted into the Rock & Roll Hall of Fame in 1994. He took part in the Perfect Day project for the BBC's Children In Need charity. In 2000 the *Original Broadway Cast Album Of Aida*, written by Elton and Tim Rice, won the Grammy Award for Best Musical Show Album. His *Candle In The Wind 1997/Something About The Way You Look Tonight* is one of only five singles to have sold over 2 million copies in the UK. He has a star on the Hollywood Walk of Fame.

DATE	POS	WKS	BPI	SINGLE TITLE	LABEL & NUMBER
23/01/1971	7	12		**YOUR SONG**	DJM DJS 233
22/04/1972	2	13		**ROCKET MAN** Featured in the 1997 film of the same name	DJM DJX 501
09/09/1972	31	6		HONKY CAT Featured in the 1998 film *Sliding Doors*	DJM DJS 269
04/11/1972	5	14		**CROCODILE ROCK** ▲[3]	DJM DJS 271
20/01/1973	4	10		**DANIEL** Featured in the films *Alice Doesn't Live Here Anymore* (1973) and *Sliding Doors* (1997)	DJM DJS 275
07/07/1973	7	9		**SATURDAY NIGHT'S ALRIGHT FOR FIGHTING**	DJM DJX 502
29/09/1973	6	16		**GOODBYE YELLOW BRICK ROAD**	DJM DJS 285
08/12/1973	24	7		STEP INTO CHRISTMAS	DJM DJS 290
02/03/1974	11	9		CANDLE IN THE WIND Tribute to Marilyn Monroe. Featured in the 1980 film *Marilyn: The Untold Story*	DJM DJS 297
01/06/1974	16	8		DON'T LET THE SUN GO DOWN ON ME	DJM DJS 302
14/09/1974	15	7		THE BITCH IS BACK	DJM DJS 322
23/11/1974	10	10		**LUCY IN THE SKY WITH DIAMONDS** ▲[2] Featured in the 1976 film *All This And World War II*	DJM DJS 340
08/03/1975	12	9		PHILADELPHIA FREEDOM ▲[2] **ELTON JOHN BAND** Written for Billie Jean King's tennis team Philadelphia Freedom	DJM DJS 354
28/06/1975	22	5		SOMEONE SAVED MY LIFE TONIGHT	DJM DJS 385
04/10/1975	14	8		ISLAND GIRL ▲[3]	DJM DJS 610
20/03/1976	7	7		PINBALL WIZARD Featured in the 1976 film *Tommy*	DJM DJS 652
03/07/1976	❶[6]	14	●	**DON'T GO BREAKING MY HEART** ▲[4] **ELTON JOHN AND KIKI DEE** Featured in the 1999 film *Summer Of Sam*	Rocket ROKN 512
25/09/1976	37	5		BENNIE AND THE JETS ▲[1] Featured in the 1997 film *Sliding Doors*	DJM DJS 10705
13/11/1976	11	10		SORRY SEEMS TO BE THE HARDEST WORD Featured in the 1977 film *Slap Shot*	Rocket ROKN 517
26/02/1977	27	6		CRAZY WATER	Rocket ROKN 521
11/06/1977	28	4		BITE YOUR LIP (GET UP AND DANCE) Flip side was *Chicago* by **KIKI DEE**	Rocket ROKN 526
15/04/1978	34	6		EGO	Rocket ROKN 538
21/10/1978	15	13	○	PART TIME LOVE	Rocket XPRES 1
16/12/1978	4	10		**SONG FOR GUY** Tribute to Guy Burchett, aged seventeen, Rocket's motorcycle messenger boy killed in a road accident	Rocket XPRES 5
12/05/1979	42	6		ARE YOU READY FOR LOVE	Rocket XPRES 13
24/05/1980	33	7		LITTLE JEANNIE	Rocket XPRES 32
23/08/1980	44	5		SARTORIAL ELOQUENCE	Rocket XPRES 41
21/03/1981	40	4		I SAW HER STANDING THERE **ELTON JOHN BAND FEATURING JOHN LENNON AND THE MUSCLE SHOALS HORNS**	DJM DJS 10965
23/05/1981	42	5		NOBODY WINS	Rocket XPRES 54
27/03/1982	8	10		BLUE EYES	Rocket XPRES 71
12/06/1982	51	4		EMPTY GARDEN	Rocket XPRES 77
30/04/1983	5	15		**I GUESS THAT'S WHY THEY CALL IT THE BLUES**	Rocket XPRES 91
30/07/1983	4	11	○	**I'M STILL STANDING**	Rocket EJS 1
15/10/1983	20	7		KISS THE BRIDE	Rocket EJS 2
10/12/1983	33	6		COLD AS CHRISTMAS	Rocket EJS 3
26/05/1984	7	12		**SAD SONGS (SAY SO MUCH)**	Rocket PH 7
11/08/1984	5	11	○	**PASSENGERS**	Rocket EJS 5
20/10/1984	50	3		WHO WEARS THESE SHOES	Rocket EJS 6
02/03/1985	59	3		BREAKING HEARTS (AIN'T WHAT IT USED TO BE)	Rocket EJS 7
15/06/1985	32	5		ACT OF WAR **ELTON JOHN AND MILLIE JACKSON**	Rocket EJS 8
12/10/1985	3	13	○	**NIKITA** Features the uncredited vocal of George Michael and Nik Kershaw on keyboards	Rocket EJS 9
09/11/1985	16	9		THAT'S WHAT FRIENDS ARE FOR ▲[4] **DIONNE WARWICK AND FRIENDS FEATURING ELTON JOHN, STEVIE WONDER AND GLADYS KNIGHT** Originally recorded by Rod Stewart in 1982 for the film *Night Shift*. 1986 Grammy Award for Best Pop Vocal Performance by a Group, and 1986 Grammy Award for Song of the Year for writers Burt Bacharach and Carole Bayer Sager	Arista ARIST 638
07/12/1985	12	10		WRAP HER UP Features the uncredited vocal of George Michael	Rocket EJS 10
01/03/1986	47	4		CRY TO HEAVEN	Rocket EJS 11
04/10/1986	45	4		HEARTACHE ALL OVER THE WORLD	Rocket EJS 12
29/11/1986	44	8		SLOW RIVERS	Rocket EJS 13
20/06/1987	59	3		FLAMES OF PARADISE **JENNIFER RUSH AND ELTON JOHN**	Columbia 6508657
16/01/1988	5	11		**CANDLE IN THE WIND** Live version of his 1974 hit recorded with the Melbourne Symphony Orchestra	Rocket EJS 15
04/06/1988	30	8		I DON'T WANNA GO ON WITH YOU LIKE THAT	Rocket EJS 16
03/09/1988	74	1		TOWN OF PLENTY	Rocket EJS 17
06/05/1989	41	3		THROUGH THE STORM **ARETHA FRANKLIN AND ELTON JOHN**	Arista 112185
26/08/1989	45	5		HEALING HANDS	Rocket EJS 19
04/11/1989	55	3		SACRIFICE	Rocket EJS 20
09/06/1990	❶[5]	15	✪	**SACRIFICE/HEALING HANDS** Both tracks are re-issues	Rocket EJS 22
18/08/1990	47	3		CLUB AT THE END OF THE STREET/WHISPERS	Rocket EJS 23
20/10/1990	33	4		YOU GOTTA LOVE SOMEONE Featured in the 1990 film *Days Of Thunder*	Rocket EJS 24
15/12/1990	63	2		EASIER TO WALK AWAY	Rocket EJS 25
07/12/1991	❶[2]	10	○	**DON'T LET THE SUN GO DOWN ON ME** ↑ ▲[1] **GEORGE MICHAEL AND ELTON JOHN** Live version of Elton John's 1974 hit.	Epic 6576467
06/06/1992	10	8		**THE ONE**	Rocket EJS 28
01/08/1992	31	4		RUNAWAY TRAIN **ELTON JOHN AND ERIC CLAPTON** Featured in the 1992 film *Lethal Weapon 3*	Rocket EJS 29
07/11/1992	21	4		THE LAST SONG	Rocket EJS 30
22/05/1993	44	2		SIMPLE LIFE	Rocket EJSCD 31
20/11/1993	2	10	○	**TRUE LOVE ELTON JOHN AND KIKI DEE**	Rocket EJSCX 32

26/02/1994 ..... 7 ...... 7	**DON'T GO BREAKING MY HEART** ELTON JOHN AND RUPAUL .... Rocket EJCD 33
14/05/1994 .... 24 ...... 4	AIN'T NOTHING LIKE THE REAL THING MARCELLA DETROIT AND ELTON JOHN .... London LONCD 350
09/07/1994 .... 14 ...... 9	CAN YOU FEEL THE LOVE TONIGHT Featured in the 1994 film *The Lion King* and won an Oscar for Best Film Song. 1994 Grammy Award for Best Male Pop Vocal Performance .... Mercury EJCD 34
08/10/1994 ..... 11 ..... 12	CIRCLE OF LIFE Featured in the 1994 film *The Lion King* .... Rocket EJSCD 35
04/03/1995 ..... 15 ...... 7	BELIEVE .... Rocket EJSDD 36
20/05/1995 ..... 18 ...... 5	MADE IN ENGLAND .... Rocket EJSDD 37
03/02/1996 ..... 33 ...... 3	PLEASE .... Rocket EJSCD 40
14/12/1996 ..... 9 ...... 6	**LIVE LIKE HORSES** ELTON JOHN AND LUCIANO PAVAROTTI ↑ .... Rocket LLHDD 1
20/09/1997 .... ●⁵ .... 24 ..... ✪⁹	**CANDLE IN THE WIND 1997/SOMETHING ABOUT THE WAY YOU LOOK TONIGHT** ↑ ▲¹⁴ ◆¹¹ A-side is a re-recorded version of his 1974 hit as a tribute to Diana, Princess of Wales, killed in a car crash on 31/8/1997. It was first performed at her funeral on 6/9/1997 and released a week later in aid of the Princess Diana Memorial Fund. Entered the chart at #1 after only one day's sales – a total of 658,000 copies making it the fastest selling single of all time. It sold a million copies within four days, with UK sales of five million after six weeks. Total worldwide sales exceed 33 million, the biggest selling single ever. Produced by Sir George Martin, his 28th #1. The best selling single of 1997 in the UK, accounting for 6.7% of all singles sold. The re-written lyrics, autographed by both John and Taupin, were sold at auction for $442,500 (£240,963) in Los Angeles in February 1998. John won the 1997 Grammy Award for Best Male Pop Vocal Performance, it also received a RIAA Diamond Disc for US sales over 10 million (the only single to get such an award) .... Rocket PTCD 1
14/02/1998 ..... 16 ...... 3	RECOVER YOUR SOUL .... Rocket EJSCD 42
13/06/1998 ..... 32 ...... 2	IF THE RIVER CAN BEND .... Rocket EJSDD 43
06/03/1999 ..... 10 ...... 8	**WRITTEN IN THE STARS** ELTON JOHN AND LEANN RIMES Featured in the 1999 Walt Disney film *Aida* .... Mercury EJSDD 45
06/10/2001 ..... 9 ...... 10	I WANT LOVE .... Rocket 5887072
26/01/2002 .... 24 ...... 4	THIS TRAIN DON'T STOP THERE ANYMORE .... Rocket 5888972
13/04/2002 .... 39 ...... 2	ORIGINAL SIN .... Rocket 5889992
27/07/2002 ..... 4 ...... 10	**YOUR SONG** ELTON JOHN AND ALESSANDRO SAFINA .... Mercury 639972
21/12/2002 .... ●¹ ..... 17 ..... ○	**SORRY SEEMS TO BE THE HARDEST WORD** ↑ BLUE FEATURING ELTON JOHN .... Innocent SINCD 43
19/07/2003 ..... 66 ...... 1	ARE YOU READY FOR LOVE Remix of Rocket XPRES 13 and only available on 12-inch vinyl. The single was revived after being featured in advertisements for Sky TV's football coverage .... Southern Fried ECB 50LOVE
06/09/2003 .... ●¹ 13	**ARE YOU READY FOR LOVE** ↑ Remix of Rocket XPRES 13 .... Southern Fried ECB 50CDS
13/11/2004 ..... 20 ...... 5	ALL THAT I'M ALLOWED (I'M THANKFUL) .... Rocket/Mercury 9868258

JENNIFER JOHN – see 100% FEATURING JENNIFER JOHN

ROBERT JOHN US singer (born Robert John Pedrick Jr, 1946, Brooklyn, NYC); he made his first recording for Big Top in 1958.

17/07/1968 ..... 42 ...... 5	IF YOU DON'T WANT MY LOVE .... CBS 3436
20/10/1979 ..... 31 ...... 8	SAD EYES ▲¹ .... EMI US EA 101

JOHNNA US female singer Johnna Lee Cummings.

10/02/1996 ..... 43 ...... 2	DO WHAT YOU FEEL .... PWL International PWL 323CD
11/05/1996 ..... 66 ...... 1	IN MY DREAMS .... PWL International PWL 325CD

JOHNNY AND CHARLEY Spanish vocal duo.

14/10/1965 ..... 49 ...... 1	LA YENKA .... Pye International 7N 25326

JOHNNY AND THE HURRICANES US group formed in Toledo, OH in 1958 by John Pocisk 'Paris' (sax), Paul Tesluk (organ), Dave Yorko (guitar), Lionel 'Butch' Mattice (bass) and Tony Kaye (drums) as the Orbits. Kaye left in 1959, replaced by Bo Savich.

09/10/1959 ..... 3 ...... 16	**RED RIVER ROCK** .... London HL 8948
25/12/1959 ..... 14 ...... 5	REVEILLE ROCK .... London HL 9017
17/03/1960 ..... 8 ...... 19	BEATNIK FLY .... London HLI 9072
16/06/1960 ..... 8 ...... 11	**DOWN YONDER** .... London HLX 9134
29/09/1960 ..... 3 ...... 20	**ROCKING GOOSE** .... London HLX 9190
02/03/1961 ..... 14 ...... 9	JA-DA .... London HLX 9289
06/07/1961 ..... 24 ...... 8	OLD SMOKEY/HIGH VOLTAGE .... London HLX 9378

JOHNNY BOY UK rock duo Lolly Hayes (Lorraine Howard) and Davo.

14/08/2004 ..... 50 ...... 2	YOU ARE THE GENERATION THAT BOUGHT MORE SHOES .... Mercury 9866935

JOHNNY CORPORATE US production duo Tommy Musto and Dave Walters with singer Yolanda Wyns.

28/10/2000 ..... 45 ...... 2	SUNDAY SHOUTIN' .... Defected DFECT 21CDS

JOHNNY HATES JAZZ UK group formed by Clark Datchler (keyboards/vocals), Calvin Hayes (keyboards/drums) and Mike Nocito (guitar/bass). Hayes, son of producer Mickie Most, was briefly engaged to Kim Wilde. Datchler left in 1988, replaced by Phil Thornalley (born 5/1/1964, Worlington, Suffolk).

11/04/1987 ..... 5 ...... 14	**SHATTERED DREAMS** .... Virgin VS 948
29/08/1987 ..... 11 ...... 10	I DON'T WANT TO BE A HERO .... Virgin VS 1000
21/11/1987 ..... 12 ...... 11	TURN BACK THE CLOCK .... Virgin VS 1017
27/02/1988 ..... 19 ...... 7	HEART OF GOLD .... Virgin VS 1045
09/07/1988 ..... 48 ...... 3	DON'T SAY IT'S LOVE .... Virgin VS 1081

JOHNSON UK vocal/instrumental duo.
27/03/1999 . . . . . 56 . . . . . 1 . . . . . . | | | | SAY YOU LOVE ME . . . . Higher Ground HIGHS 18CD

ANDREAS JOHNSON Swedish singer (born Lund) of jazz musician parents, he was lead singer with Planet Waves, going solo when the group disbanded after one album.
05/02/2000 . . . . . 4 . . . . . 11 . . . . . | | | | **GLORIOUS** . . . . WEA 254CD
27/05/2000 . . . . 41 . . . . . 1 . . . . . . | | | | THE GAMES WE PLAY . . . . WEA 264CD

BRYAN JOHNSON UK singer/actor (born 18/7/1926, London) and the brother of Teddy Johnson. He represented Britain in the 1960 Eurovision Song Contest, finishing second behind Jacqueline Boyer of France's *Tom Pillibi*. He died on 18/10/1995.
10/03/1960 . . . . . 20 . . . . . 11 . . . . . . | | | | LOOKING HIGH HIGH HIGH Britain's entry for the 1960 Eurovision Song Contest (came second) . . . . Decca F 11213

CAREY JOHNSON Australian singer Reginald Carey Johnson.
25/04/1987 . . . . . 19 . . . . . 8 . . . . . . | | | | REAL FASHION REGGAE STYLE . . . . Oval TEN 170

DENISE JOHNSON UK singer (born 31/8/1966, Manchester), backed Primal Scream, A Certain Ratio and Electronic and then worked with Maze.
24/08/1991 . . . . 41 . . . . . 2 . . . . . . | | | | DON'T FIGHT IT FEEL IT **PRIMAL SCREAM FEATURING DENISE JOHNSON** . . . . Creation CRE 110
14/05/1994 . . . . 45 . . . . . 2 . . . . . . | | | | RAYS OF THE RISING SUN . . . . Magnet MAG 1022CD

DON JOHNSON US singer and actor (born 15/12/1949, Flatt Creek, MO), best known for his role in *Miami Vice*.
18/10/1986 . . . . . 46 . . . . . 5 . . . . . . | | | | HEARTBEAT . . . . Epic 6500647
05/11/1988 . . . . . 16 . . . . . 7 . . . . . . | | | | TILL I LOVED YOU (LOVE THEME FROM 'GOYA') **BARBRA STREISAND AND DON JOHNSON** . . . . CBS BARB 2

GENERAL JOHNSON – see CHAIRMEN OF THE BOARD

HOLLY JOHNSON UK singer (born William Johnson, 19/2/1960, Khartoum, Sudan); he was with Big In Japan before leaving for an unsuccessful solo career. Formed the Hollycaust, and then Frankie Goes To Hollywood in 1980 where he was lead singer. He left the group in 1987 to resume his solo career, this time with more success. In 1993 it was revealed he was HIV positive.
14/01/1989 . . . . . 4 . . . . . 11 . . . . O | | | | **LOVE TRAIN** . . . . MCA 1306
01/04/1989 . . . . . 4 . . . . . 11 . . . . O | | | | **AMERICANOS** . . . . MCA 1323
20/05/1989 . . . . ❶³ . . . . . 7 . . . . . . | | | | FERRY 'CROSS THE MERSEY ↑ **CHRISTIANS, HOLLY JOHNSON, PAUL McCARTNEY, GERRY MARSDEN AND STOCK AITKEN WATERMAN** Charity record to aid relatives of the Hillsborough football disaster victims . . . . PWL 41
24/06/1989 . . . . . 18 . . . . . 4 . . . . . . | | | | ATOMIC CITY . . . . MCA 1342
30/09/1989 . . . . 62 . . . . . 2 . . . . . . | | | | HEAVEN'S HERE . . . . MCA 1365
01/12/1990 . . . . 73 . . . . . 1 . . . . . . | | | | WHERE HAS LOVE GONE? . . . . MCA 1460
25/12/1999 . . . . 56 . . . . . 2 . . . . . . | | | | THE POWER OF LOVE . . . . Pleasure Dome PLDCD 2005

HOWARD JOHNSON US singer from Miami, FL. In Niteflyte in 1977, solo in 1981. Joined Regis Branson as Johnson & Branson.
04/09/1982 . . . . 45 . . . . . 6 . . . . . . | | | | KEEPIN' LOVE NEW/SO FINE . . . . A&M USA 1221

JOHNNY JOHNSON AND THE BANDWAGON US singer (born 1945, Florida); he formed Bandwagon in Rochester, NY in 1967 with Terry Lewis (born 1946, Baltimore, MD), Arthur Fullilove (born 1947, New York) and Billy Bradley (born 1945, New York). Moved to UK where singles sold better. Sole US hit *Baby Make Your Own Sweet Music* just made top 50 R&B.
16/10/1968 . . . . . 4 . . . . . 15 . . . . . | | | | **BREAKIN' DOWN THE WALLS OF HEARTACHE** . . . . Direction 58 3670
05/02/1969 . . . . 34 . . . . . 4 . . . . . . | | | | YOU . . . . Direction 58 3923
28/05/1969 . . . . 36 . . . . . 6 . . . . . . | | | | LET'S HANG ON This and above two singles credited to **BANDWAGON** . . . . Direction 58 4180
25/07/1970 . . . . . 10 . . . . . 13 . . . . . | | | | **SWEET INSPIRATION** . . . . Bell 1111
28/11/1970 . . . . . 7 . . . . . 12 . . . . . | | | | (BLAME IT) ON THE PONY EXPRESS . . . . Bell 1128

KEVIN JOHNSON Australian singer (born in Rockhampton) whose hit, originally released in Australia in 1973 by Mainstream, was a US hit for Mac Davis.
11/01/1975 . . . . 23 . . . . . 6 . . . . . . | | | | ROCK 'N ROLL (I GAVE YOU THE BEST YEARS OF MY LIFE) . . . . UK UKR 84

LAURIE JOHNSON ORCHESTRA UK composer/orchestra leader (born Lawrence Reginald Ward Johnson); he wrote music for the TV series *The New Avengers* and *The Professionals* and films such as *Moonraker*, *Dr Strangelove* and *Hedda*.
28/09/1961 . . . . . 9 . . . . . 12				**SUCU SUCU** Theme to the TV series *Top Secret* . . . . Pye 7N 15383
17/05/1997 . . . . 36 . . . . . 2				THEME FROM THE PROFESSIONALS **LAURIE JOHNSON'S LONDON BIG BAND** Theme to the TV series *The Professionals* . . . .
				. . . . Virgin VSCDT 1643

L.J. JOHNSON US soul singer (born Louis Maurice Johnson, 10/12/1950, Chicago, IL); discovered by UK producer Ian Levine while with Mood Mixers, a group that also included Evelyn Thomas.
07/02/1976 . . . . . 27 . . . . . 6 . . . . . . | | | | YOUR MAGIC PUT A SPELL ON ME . . . . Philips 6006 492

LOU JOHNSON US singer (born 1941); a former member of The Zionettes. He recorded with Burt Bacharach in 1963 and later recorded for Stax. His debut hit was also recorded by Dionne Warwick as *Message To Michael* and reached the top ten in America.
26/11/1964 . . . . 36 . . . . . 2 . . . . . . | | | | MESSAGE TO MARTHA (KENTUCKY BLUEBIRD) . . . . London HL 9929

MARV JOHNSON US singer (born15/10/1938, Detroit, MI); with the Serenaders when discovered by Berry Gordy. Debut

❶⁹ Number of weeks single topped the UK chart ↑ Entered the UK chart at #1 ▲⁹ Number of weeks single topped the US chart

415

(*Come To Me*) was Tamla Motown's first single, its US success prompting Gordy to license the track to United Artists. Johnson signed with Motown in 1965, moving into promotion and retiring from performing in 1968. The success of the re-released *I'll Pick A Rose For My Rose*, originally issued in 1966, prompted a brief comeback, returning to his sales executive post at Motown. He returned to performing in 1987 for Ian Levine's Nightmare/Motor City labels. He died from a stroke on 16/5/1993.

12/02/1960 ..... 7 ...... 17	**YOU GOT WHAT IT TAKES**	London HLT 9013
05/05/1960 ..... 35 ...... 3	I LOVE THE WAY YOU LOVE	London HLT 9109
11/08/1960 ..... 50 ...... 1	AIN'T GONNA BE THAT WAY	London HLT 9165
22/01/1969 ..... 10 ...... 11	**I'LL PICK A ROSE FOR MY ROSE**	Tamla Motown TMG 680
25/10/1969 ..... 25 ...... 8	I MISS YOU BABY	Tamla Motown TMG 713

ORLANDO JOHNSON – see SECCHI FEATURING ORLANDO JOHNSON

PAUL JOHNSON UK singer (born 1960, London), a member of Paradise before going solo. He later recorded with Mica Paris.

21/02/1987 ..... 52 ...... 5	WHEN LOVE COME CALLING	CBS PJOHN 1
25/02/1989 ..... 67 ...... 2	NO MORE TOMORROWS	CBS PJOHN 7

PAUL JOHNSON US producer/singer based in Chicago, IL; he made his debut album in 1994.

25/09/1999 ..... 5 ...... 8	**GET GET DOWN**	Defected DEFECT 7CDS

PUFF JOHNSON US R&B singer (born 1973, Detroit, MI). She began singing at two, taking formal singing lessons at seven. Offered her first recording contract at thirteen, she opted to continue her education at the High School for the Arts in Los Angeles, CA.

18/01/1997 ..... 20 ...... 4	OVER AND OVER Featured in the 1996 film *First Wives Club*	Columbia 6640345
12/04/1997 ..... 29 ...... 2	FOREVER MORE	Work 6644075

ROMINA JOHNSON UK singer (born in Rome to an American father and Italian mother), now based in London.

04/03/2000 ..... 2 ...... 12 ..... O	**MOVIN TOO FAST** ARTFUL DODGER AND ROMINA JOHNSON	Locked On/XL Recordings LUX 117CD
17/06/2000 ..... 59 ...... 1	MY FORBIDDEN LOVER ROMINA JOHNSON FEATURING LUCI MARTIN AND NORMA JEAN	51 Lexington CDLEX 1

SYLEENA JOHNSON US R&B singer (born 1976, Chicago, IL). Her debut hit also features Busta Rhymes, Rampage, Sham and Spliff Star (of Flipmode Squad).

26/10/2002 ..... 38 ...... 2	TONIGHT I'M GONNA LET GO Contains samples of Busta Rhymes' *Put Your Hands Where My Eyes Can See* and Seals & Crofts' *Sweet Green Fields*	Jive 9254252
19/06/2004 ..... 10 ...... 8	**ALL FALLS DOWN** KANYE WEST FEATURING SYLEENA JOHNSON	Roc-A-Fella 9862670

TEDDY JOHNSON – see PEARL CARR AND TEDDY JOHNSON

ANA JOHNSSON Swedish singer (born 1977).

14/08/2004 ..... 8 ...... 6	**WE ARE** Featured in the 2004 film *Spider Man 2*	Epic 6751622

JOHNSTON BROTHERS UK vocal group (who were not related) with Johnny Johnston (Johnny Reine), Miff King, Eddie Lester and Frank Holmes, with Jean Campbell also a frequent member.

03/04/1953 ..... 4 ...... 8	**OH HAPPY DAY**	Decca F 10071
05/11/1954 ..... 18 ...... 1	WAIT FOR ME DARLING JOAN REGAN AND THE JOHNSTON BROTHERS	Decca F 10362
21/01/1955 ..... 14 ...... 2	HAPPY DAYS AND LONELY NIGHTS SUZI MILLER AND THE JOHNSTON BROTHERS	Decca F 10389
07/10/1955 ..... ❶² 13	**HERNANDO'S HIDEAWAY**	Decca F 10608
30/12/1955 ..... 9 ...... 1	**JOIN IN AND SING AGAIN** JOHNSTON BROTHERS & THE GEORGE CHISHOLM SOUR-NOTE SIX Medley of *Sheik Of Araby, Yes Sir That's My Baby, CA Here I Come, Some Of These Days, Charleston* and *Margie*	Decca F 10636
13/04/1956 ..... 22 ...... 1	NO OTHER LOVE	Decca F 10721
30/11/1956 ..... 27 ...... 1	IN THE MIDDLE OF THE HOUSE	Decca F 10781
07/12/1956 ..... 24 ...... 2	JOIN IN AND SING (NO. 3) Medley of *Coal Black Morning, When You're Smiling, Alexander's Ragtime Band, Sweet Sue Just You, When You Wore A Tulip* and *If You Were The Only Girl In The World*	Decca F 10814
08/02/1957 ..... 27 ...... 1	GIVE HER MY LOVE	Decca F 10828
19/04/1957 ..... 23 ...... 3	HEART	Decca F 10860

BRUCE JOHNSTON US keyboard player, formerly in the Beach Boys. Aside from his hit disco version of a 1960s surf hit, he also penned *I Write The Songs*, a major hit for David Cassidy, for which he won the 1976 Grammy Award for Song of the Year.

27/08/1977 ..... 33 ...... 4	PIPELINE	CBS 5514

JAN JOHNSTON UK singer (born Salford).

08/02/1997 ..... 28 ...... 2	TAKE ME BY THE HAND SUB MERGE FEATURING JAN JOHNSTON	AM:PM 5821012
22/07/1998 ..... 43 ...... 2	SKYDIVE	Renaissance Recordings RENCDS 002
28/11/1998 ..... 75 ...... 1	SKYDIVE (REMIX) This and above single credited to FREEFALL FEATURING JAN JOHNSTON	Stress CDSTR 89
12/02/2000 ..... 31 ...... 2	LOVE WILL COME TOMSKI FEATURING JAN JOHNSTON	Xtravaganza XTRAV 6CDS
21/04/2001 ..... 36 ...... 2	FLESH	Perfecto PERF 05CDS
28/07/2001 ..... 57 ...... 1	SILENT WORDS	Perfecto PERF 16CDS
08/09/2001 ..... 35 ...... 2	SKYDIVE (I FEEL WONDERFUL) (2ND REMIX) FREEFALL FEATURING JAN JOHNSTON	Incentive CENT 22CDS

SABRINA JOHNSTON US singer (born in Rosell, NJ) who worked with Alexander O'Neal and as lead singer with Unknown Society and Key To Life.

07/09/1991 . . . . . 8 . . . . . . 10	**PEACE** . . . . East West YZ 616
07/12/1991 . . . . . 58 . . . . . . 4	FRIENDSHIP . . . . East West YZ 637
11/07/1992 . . . . . 46 . . . . . . 2	I WANNA SING . . . . East West YZ 661
03/10/1992 . . . . . 35 . . . . . . 2	PEACE (REMIX) Listed flip side was *Gypsy Woman* by **CRYSTAL WATERS** . . . . Epic 6584377
13/08/1994 . . . . . 62 . . . . . . 1	SATISFY MY LOVE . . . . Champion CHAMPCD 311

JOJO – see 2PAC AND K-CI AND JOJO

JOJO US singer (born Joanna Levesque, 20/12/1990, Boston, MA) discovered singing on the TV shows *Kids Say The Darndest Things: On The Road In Boston* and *America's Most Talented Kids*. At thirteen years and eight months, she is the youngest female to have made the UK top three.

11/09/2004 . . . . . 2 . . . . . . 8	**LEAVE (GET OUT)** . . . . Mercury 9867841
27/11/2004 . . . . . 8 . . . . . . 5+	**BABY IT'S YOU** JOJO FEATURING BOW WOW . . . . Mercury 9869056

JAMES JOLIS – see BARRY MANILOW

JOLLY BROTHERS Jamaican vocal/ instrumental group with Joseph Bennett, Moses Dean, Noel Howard and Allan Swymmer. They later recorded as The Jolly Boys.

28/07/1979 . . . . . 46 . . . . . . 7	CONSCIOUS MAN . . . . United Artists UP 36415

JOLLY ROGER UK singer from Milton Keynes (born Eddie Richards).

10/09/1988 . . . . . 23 . . . . . 12	ACID MAN . . . . 10 TEN 236

JOMALSKI – see WILDCHILD

JOMANDA US R&B vocal group formed in New Jersey by Joanne Thomas, Renee Washington and Cheri Williams.

22/04/1989 . . . . . 44 . . . . . . 3	MAKE MY BODY ROCK . . . . RCA PB 42749
29/06/1991 . . . . . 43 . . . . . . 4	GOT A LOVE FOR YOU . . . . Giant W 0040
11/09/1993 . . . . . 67 . . . . . . 1	I LIKE IT . . . . Big Beat A 8377CD
13/11/1993 . . . . . 40 . . . . . . 2	NEVER . . . . Big Beat A 8347CD

JON AND VANGELIS UK /Greek duo of ex-Yes Jon Anderson (born 25/10/1944, Accrington) and Vangelis (born Evangelos Papathanassiou, 29/3/1943, Valos, Greece). Anderson had also recorded solo, Vangelis was a founder member of Aphrodite's Child.

05/01/1980 . . . . . 8 . . . . . 11	**I HEAR YOU NOW** . . . . Polydor POSP 96
12/12/1981 . . . . . 6 . . . . . 13 . . . . . O	**I'LL FIND MY WAY HOME** . . . . Polydor JV 1
30/07/1983 . . . . . 61 . . . . . . 2	HE IS SAILING . . . . Polydor JV 4
18/08/1984 . . . . . 67 . . . . . . 2	STATE OF INDEPENDENCE . . . . Polydor JV 5

JON OF THE PLEASED WIMMIN UK transvestite DJ (born Jonathan Cooper, 1969, Africa); he was DJ at Glam, Kinky Gerlinky and Camp before launching his own club, Pleased.

18/02/1995 . . . . . 27 . . . . . . 3	PASSION . . . . Perfecto YZ 884CD
06/04/1996 . . . . . 30 . . . . . . 2	GIVE ME STRENGTH . . . . Perfecto PERF 119CD

JON THE DENTIST VS OLLIE JAYE UK DJ/production duo who also recorded as High School Drop Outs and Madely. Jon The Dentist took his name after briefly studying at a dental college.

24/07/1999 . . . . . 72 . . . . . . 1	IMAGINATION . . . . Tidy Trax TIDY 126CD
10/06/2000 . . . . . 72 . . . . . . 1	FEEL SO GOOD . . . . Tidy Trax TIDY 135CD

JONAH Dutch dance group assembled by producers Piet Bervoets, Benno De Goeij and Mischa Van Der Heiden. They had previously been responsible for the debut hit by Rank 1 while Van Der Heiden also recorded as DJ Misjah.

22/07/2000 . . . . . 25 . . . . . . 4	SSSST (LISTEN) . . . . VC Recordings VCRD 69

JONELL – see HI-TEK FEATURING JONELL

ALED JONES UK choirboy (born 1971, Llandegfan, Wales); he made a duet with himself. The first half of the song, *What Can You Tell Me?*, was recorded while he was still a child star and shelved until his voice had broken, then he added his baritone half. He later became a regular on the Chris Moyles show on Radio 1.

20/07/1985 . . . . . 42 . . . . . . 4	MEMORY: THEME FROM THE MUSICAL 'CATS' . . . . BBC RESL 175
30/11/1985 . . . . . 5 . . . . . 11 . . . . . O	**WALKING IN THE AIR** Featured in the 1985 film *The Snowman* . . . . HMV ALED 1
14/12/1985 . . . . . 50 . . . . . . 6	PICTURES IN THE DARK MIKE OLDFIELD FEATURING ALED JONES AND BARRY PALMER . . . . Virgin VS 836
20/12/1986 . . . . . 51 . . . . . . 3	A WINTER STORY . . . . HMV ALED 2

BARBARA JONES Jamaican reggae singer (born Barbara Nation).

31/01/1981 . . . . . 31 . . . . . . 7	JUST WHEN I NEEDED YOU MOST . . . . Sonet SON 2221

CATHERINE ZETA JONES UK actress/singer (born 25/9/1969, Swansea), first known as Mariette Larkin in the TV series *The Darling Buds Of May*, later moving to Los Angeles, CA and appearing in *The Mask Of Zorro* and *The Haunting*, among other films. She is married to fellow actor Michael Douglas.

19/09/1992 . . . . . 36 . . . . . . 5	FOR ALL TIME . . . . Columbia 6583547

❶⁹ Number of weeks single topped the UK chart ↑ Entered the UK chart at #1 ▲⁹ Number of weeks single topped the US chart

417

26/11/1994	38	3		TRUE LOVE WAYS DAVID ESSEX AND CATHERINE ZETA JONES	Polygram TV TLWCD 2
01/04/1995	72	1		IN THE ARMS OF LOVE	Wow! WOWCD 7101

DONELL JONES US singer (born Detroit, MI), first known as a songwriter with hits for Usher, Madonna, Brownstone and 702. He signed with LaFace in 1996.

15/02/1997	58	1		KNOCKS ME OFF MY FEET	LaFace 74321458502
22/01/2000	2	11	O	U KNOW WHAT'S UP Features the uncredited contribution of Lisa 'Left Eye' Lopes of TLC. Featured in the 2001 film *Save The Last Dance*	LaFace 74321722762
20/05/2000	19	3		SHORTY (GOT HER EYES ON ME)	LaFace 74321748902
02/12/2000	25	3		TRUE STEP TONIGHT TRUE STEPPERS FEATURING BRIAN HARVEY AND DONELL JONES	NuLife 74321811312
24/08/2002	41³	2		YOU KNOW THAT I LOVE YOU	Arista 74321956962

GEORGIA JONES US singer who started by backing the likes of Cyndi Lauper, Junior Vasquez and John Mellencamp.

04/05/1996	33	2		OVER & OVER PLUX FEATURING GEORGIA JONES	ffrr FCD 277
14/11/1998	29	2		ON THE TOP OF THE WORLD DIVA SURPRISE FEATURING GEORGIA JONES	Positiva CDTIV 100

GRACE JONES US singer (born 15/5/1952, Spanishtown, Jamaica) who moved to Syracuse at the age of 12. First a model and actress, appearing in the film *Gordon's War*. Returned to acting in the 1990s; films include *McGinsey's Island* and *View To A Kill*.

26/07/1980	17	8		PRIVATE LIFE	Island WIP 6629
20/06/1981	53	4		PULL UP TO THE BUMPER	Island WIP 6696
30/10/1982	50	4		THE APPLE STRETCHING/NIPPLE TO THE BOTTLE	Island WIP 6779
09/04/1983	56	3		MY JAMAICAN GUY	Island IS 103
12/10/1985	12	8		SLAVE TO THE RHYTHM Featured in the 1985 film *The Supergrass*	ZTT IS 206
18/01/1986	12	9		PULL UP TO THE BUMPER/LA VIE EN ROSE B-side featured in the 1999 film *Summer Of Sam*	Island IS 240
01/03/1986	35	4		LOVE IS THE DRUG	Island IS 266
15/11/1986	56	3		I'M NOT PERFECT (BUT I'M PERFECT FOR YOU)	Manhattan MT 15
07/05/1994	28	2		SLAVE TO THE RHYTHM (REMIX)	Zance ZANG 50CD1
25/11/2000	60	1		PULL UP TO THE BUMPER GRACE JONES VS FUNKSTAR DE LUXE	Club Tools 0120375 CLU

HANNAH JONES US singer who later worked with former Human League member Martyn Ware.

14/09/1991	21	8		BRIDGE OVER TROUBLED WATER PJB FEATURING HANNAH AND HER SISTERS	Dance Pool 6565467
30/01/1993	67	1		KEEP IT ON	TMRC CDTMRC 7

HOWARD JONES UK singer (born John Howard Jones, 23/2/1955, Southampton); he played with Warrior, the Bicycle Thieves and Skin Tight before signing to WEA in 1983 as a solo artist. He opened a vegetarian restaurant in New York in 1987.

17/09/1983	3	15	O	NEW SONG	WEA HOW 1
26/11/1983	2	15	O	WHAT IS LOVE	WEA HOW 2
18/02/1984	12	9		HIDE AND SEEK	WEA HOW 3
26/05/1984	7	10		PEARL IN THE SHELL	WEA HOW 4
11/08/1984	4	12	O	LIKE TO GET TO KNOW YOU WELL	WEA HOW 5
09/02/1985	6	8	O	THINGS CAN ONLY GET BETTER	WEA HOW 6
20/04/1985	10	6		LOOK MAMA	WEA HOW 7
29/06/1985	14	7		LIFE IN ONE DAY	WEA HOW 8
15/03/1986	16	7		NO ONE IS TO BLAME	WEA HOW 9
04/10/1986	35	4		ALL I WANT	WEA HOW 10
29/11/1986	43	3		YOU KNOW I LOVE YOU...DON'T YOU	WEA HOW 11
21/03/1987	70	1		A LITTLE BIT OF SNOW	WEA HOW 12
04/03/1989	62	3		EVERLASTING LOVE	WEA HOW 13
11/04/1992	52	3		LIFT ME UP	WEA HOW 15

JANIE JONES UK singer (born Marion Mitchell, Seaham, County Durham), first known in cabaret but later achieved notoriety by appearing at a 1964 London film premiere in a topless gown. After a brief recording career she next made news in 1973, jailed for seven years (serving four) for controlling prostitutes. Immortalised in song by The Clash, she recorded with them as Janie Jones And The Lash. She published her memoirs in 1993.

27/01/1966	46	3		WITCHES' BREW	HMV POP.1495

JIMMY JONES US singer (born 2/6/1937, Birmingham, AL); in Sparks Of Rhythm in 1955 and own group the Savoys in 1956.

17/03/1960	3	24		HANDY MAN	MGM 1051
16/06/1960	◎³	15		GOOD TIMIN'	MGM 1078
08/09/1960	35	4		I JUST GO FOR YOU	MGM 1091
17/11/1960	46	1		READY FOR LOVE	MGM 1103
06/04/1961	33	3		I TOLD YOU SO	MGM 1123

JUGGY JONES US soul musician (born Henry Jones) who first came to prominence as the founder and producer of Sue Records, a label that was home to the likes of Inez and Charlie Foxx, Ike and Tina Turner, Don Covay and Jimmy Helms.

07/02/1976	39	4		INSIDE AMERICA	Contempo CS 2080

KELLY JONES – see MANCHILD

LAVINIA JONES South African singer.

18/02/1995 . . . . 45 . . . . . 2 . . . . . . SING IT TO YOU (DEE-DOOB-DEE-DOO) . . . . Virgin International DINDG 142

MICK JONES – see AZTEC CAMERA

NORAH JONES US singer/pianist (born 30/3/1979, New York City), daughter of Ravi Shankar. She worked with the Wax Poetic then formed her own band with Jesse Harris (guitar), Lee Alexander (bass) and Dan Rieser (drums). Named International Breakthrough Artist at the 2003 BRIT Awards, five days later she collected five Grammy Awards including Album of the Year and Best Pop Vocal Album for *Come Away With Me*, and Best New Artist. *Come Away With Me* also collected awards for Best Engineered Album for S Husky Hoskulds and Jay Newland and Producer of the Year for Arif Mardin. Norah also won the 2002 MOBO Award for Best Jazz Act.

25/05/2002 . . . . . 59 . . . . . . 1 . . . . . . DON'T KNOW WHY 2002 Grammy Awards for Best Female Vocal Performance, Record of the Year, and Song of the Year for writer Jesse Harris the same year. Featured in the 2002 film *Maid In Manhattan* . . . . Parlophone CDCL 836

17/08/2002 . . . . . 72 . . . . . . 1 . . . . . . FEELIN' THE SAME WAY . . . . Parlophone CDCL 838

13/09/2003 . . . . . 67 . . . . . . 1 . . . . . . DON'T KNOW WHY/I'LL BE YOUR BABY TONIGHT . . . . Parlophone CDCL 848

10/04/2004 . . . . . 30 . . . . . . 3 . . . . . . SUNRISE . . . . Blue Note CDCL 853

ORAN 'JUICE' JONES US singer (born 1959, Houston, TX, raised in Harlem); he was signed by Def Jam in 1985. He later recorded with Alyson Williams.

15/11/1986 . . . . . 4 . . . . . . 14 . . . . . O THE RAIN . . . . Def Jam A 7303

PAUL JONES UK singer (born Paul Pond, 24/2/1942, Portsmouth); lead singer with Manfred Mann from their formation in 1962 until 1965, when he gave notice of quitting in a year's time to go solo. He left earlier, being laid up following a road accident.

06/10/1966 . . . . . 4 . . . . . . 15 . . . . . . HIGH TIME . . . . HMV POP 1554

19/01/1967 . . . . . 5 . . . . . . 9 . . . . . . I'VE BEEN A BAD BAD BOY Featured in the 1967 film *Privilege* . . . . HMV POP 1576

23/08/1967 . . . . . 32 . . . . . . 8 . . . . . . THINKIN' AIN'T FOR ME . . . . HMV POP 1602

05/02/1969 . . . . . 45 . . . . . . 2 . . . . . . AQUARIUS . . . . Columbia DB 8514

QUINCY JONES US producer/keyboard player (born Quincy Delight Jones Jr, 14/3/1933, Chicago, IL, raised in Seattle). A trumpeter with Lionel Hampton from 1950, in 1961 became musical director of Mercury Records, later promoted to Vice President. Produced Lesley Gore's *It's My Party* (his first US #1) and later Michael Jackson's albums, including *Thriller*. He nearly died from a cerebral aneurysm in 1974 but recovered and set up the Qwest label in 1981. Numerous film and TV themes included *Ironside*. Previously married to Jeri Caldwell, Ulla Anderson and Peggy Lipton, he had a child by Natassja Kinski. Nineteen Grammy Awards include Best Instrumental Arrangement in 1963 for Count Basie's *I Can't Stop Lovin' You*, Best Instrumental Jazz Performance in 1969 for *Walking In Space*, Best Contemporary Instrumental Performance in 1971 for *Smackwater Jack*, Best Instrumental Arrangement in 1973 for *Summer In The City*, Best Instrumental Arrangement in 1976 with Robert Freedman for *The Wiz*, Best Instrumental Arrangement in 1980 with Jerry Hay for George Benson's *Dinorah, Dinorah*, Best Rhythm & Blues Vocal Performance by a Duo in 1981 for *The Dude*, Best Instrumental Arrangement in 1981 for *Velas*, Best Instrumental Arrangement in 1984 for *Grace (Gymnastics Theme)*, Album of the Year in 1990 for *Back On The Block*, Best Jazz Fusion Performance in 1990 for *Birdland*, Best Arrangement on an Instrumental in 1990 with Ian Prince, Rod Temperton and Jerry Hey for *Birdland*, Best Instrumental Arrangement Accompanying Vocals in 1990 with Jerry Hey, Glen Ballard and Cliff Magness for *The Places You Find Love*, Best Large Jazz Ensemble Performance in 1993 with Miles Davis for *Miles And Quincy Live At Montreux*, Best Spoken Word Album in 2001 for *Q: The Autobiography of Quincy Jones* and Producer of the Year in 1981, 1983 and 1990. He has a star on the Hollywood Walk of Fame.

29/07/1978 . . . . . 34 . . . . . . 9 . . . . . . STUFF LIKE THAT Features the uncredited vocals of Ashford and Simpson . . . . A&M AMS 7367

11/04/1981 . . . . . 14 . . . . . . 10 . . . . . . AI NO CORRIDA (I-NO-KO-REE-DA) QUINCY JONES FEATURING DUNE 1981 Grammy Award for Best Arrangement Accompanying Singers for arrangers Quincy Jones and Jerry Hey . . . . A&M AMS 8109

20/06/1981 . . . . . 11 . . . . . . 9 . . . . . . RAZZAMATAZZ QUINCY JONES FEATURING PATTI AUSTIN . . . . A&M 8140

05/09/1981 . . . . . 52 . . . . . . 3 . . . . . . BETCHA' WOULDN'T HURT ME . . . . A&M AMS 8157

13/01/1990 . . . . . 21 . . . . . . 7 . . . . . . I'LL BE GOOD TO YOU QUINCY JONES FEATURING RAY CHARLES AND CHAKA KHAN 1990 Grammy Award for Best Rhythm & Blues Vocal Performance by a Duo . . . . Qwest W 2697

31/03/1990 . . . . . 67 . . . . . . 1 . . . . . . SECRET GARDEN QUINCY JONES FEATURING AL B SURE! JAMES INGRAM, EL DEBARGE AND BARRY WHITE Featured in the 1997 film *Sprung* . . . . Qwest W 9992

14/09/1996 . . . . . 28 . . . . . . 2 . . . . . . STOMP – THE REMIXES QUINCY JONES FEATURING MELLE MEL, COOLIO, YO-YO, SHAQUILLE O'NEAL & THE LUNIZ . Qwest W 0372CD

01/08/1998 . . . . . 47 . . . . . . 1 . . . . . . SOUL BOSSA NOVA COOL, THE FAB AND THE GROOVY PRESENT QUINCY JONES Featured in the films *Austin Powers – International Man Of Mystery* (1997) and *Austin Powers – The Spy Who Shagged Me* (1999) . . . . Manifesto FESCD 48

RICKIE LEE JONES US singer (born 8/11/1954, Chicago, IL); she moved to Los Angeles, CA in 1977. She has won two Grammy Awards: Best New Artist in 1979 and Best Jazz Vocal Performance by a Duo in 1989 with Dr John for *Makin' Whoopee*.

23/06/1979 . . . . . 18 . . . . . . 9 . . . . . . CHUCK E'S IN LOVE Chuck E is Rickie Lee Jones' friend Chuck E Weiss . . . . Warner Brothers K 17390

SHIRLEY JONES – see PARTRIDGE FAMILY

SONNY JONES FEATURING TARA CHASE German singer with a Canadian rapper.

07/10/2000 . . . . . 42 . . . . . . 2 . . . . . . FOLLOW YOU FOLLOW ME . . . . Logic 74321772892

TAMMY JONES UK country singer (born in Bangor), first seen widely on a TV talent show. She later recorded for Monarch and Blue Waters and moved to New Zealand.

26/04/1975 . . . . . 5 . . . . . . 10 . . . . . . LET ME TRY AGAIN . . . . Epic EPC 3211

❶⁹ Number of weeks single topped the UK chart ↑ Entered the UK chart at #1 ▲⁹ Number of weeks single topped the US chart

419

Tom Jones and Mousse T.
Sex Bomb

TOM JONES UK singer (born Thomas Jones Woodward, 7/6/1940, Pontypridd, Wales); he formed his own group Tommy Scott & The Senators in 1963, recording tracks for EMI. Spotted supporting Mandy Rice-Davies by manager Gordon Mills in 1964, who suggested the name Tom Jones and secured a deal with Decca. With his own US TV series, he moved to California in 1969, performing regularly in Las Vegas. He was awarded the OBE in the 1999 New Year's Honours List. Named Best New Artist at the 1965 Grammy Awards and Best UK Male Solo Artist at the 2000 BRIT Awards. He was in the *Perfect Day* project for the BBC's Children In Need charity and has a star on the Hollywood Walk of Fame.

DATE	POS	WKS	BPI	SINGLE TITLE	LABEL & NUMBER
11/02/1965	❶¹	14		IT'S NOT UNUSUAL Featured in the films *Lost Flight* (1969), *Flipper* and *Home For The Holidays* (1996) and *Lake Placid* (1996).	Decca F 12062
06/05/1965	32	4		ONCE UPON A TIME.	Decca F 12121
08/07/1965	13	11		WITH THESE HANDS.	Decca F 12191
12/08/1965	11	10		WHAT'S NEW PUSSYCAT Featured in the films *What's New Pussycat* (1965) and *Cats And Dogs* (2001).	Decca F 12203
13/01/1966	35	4		THUNDERBALL Featured in the 1965 James Bond film *Thunderball*	Decca F 12292
19/05/1966	18	9		ONCE THERE WAS A TIME/NOT RESPONSIBLE	Decca F 12390
18/08/1966	44	3		THIS AND THAT.	Decca F 12461
10/11/1966	❶⁷	22	◎	**GREEN GREEN GRASS OF HOME** First Decca single by a UK artist to sell more than a million (over 1,220,000) copies	Decca F 22511
16/02/1967	8	10		**DETROIT CITY**	Decca F 22555
13/04/1967	7	15		**FUNNY FAMILIAR FORGOTTEN FEELINGS**	Decca F 12599
26/07/1967	2	25		**I'LL NEVER FALL IN LOVE AGAIN**	Decca F 12639
22/11/1967	2	16		**I'M COMING HOME**	Decca F 12693
28/02/1968	2	17		**DELILAH**.	Decca F 12747
17/07/1968	5	26		**HELP YOURSELF**.	Decca F 12812
27/11/1968	14	15		A MINUTE OF YOUR TIME	Decca F 12854
14/05/1969	9	12		**LOVE ME TONIGHT**	Decca F 12924
13/12/1969	10	12		**WITHOUT LOVE**	Decca F 12990
18/04/1970	5	15		**DAUGHTER OF DARKNESS**	Decca F 13013
15/08/1970	16	11		I (WHO HAVE NOTHING)	Decca F 13061
16/01/1971	13	10		SHE'S A LADY Featured in the films *To Wong Foo, Thanks For Everything! Julie Newmar* (1995) and *Fear And Loathing In Las Vegas* (1998).	Decca F 13113
05/06/1971	49	2		PUPPET MAN	Decca F 13183
23/10/1971	2	15		**TILL**	Decca F 13236
01/04/1972	6	12		**THE YOUNG NEW MEXICAN PUPPETEER**	Decca F 13298
14/04/1973	31	8		LETTER TO LUCILLE.	Decca F 13393
07/09/1974	36	5		SOMETHING 'BOUT YOU BABY I LIKE.	Decca F 13550
16/04/1977	40	3		SAY YOU'LL STAY UNTIL TOMORROW.	EMI 2583
18/04/1987	2	12	○	**A BOY FROM NOWHERE** Featured in the musical *Matador* .	Epic OLE 1
30/05/1987	17	8		IT'S NOT UNUSUAL Re-issue of Decca F 12062	Decca F 103
02/01/1988	61	1		I WAS BORN TO BE ME Featured in the musical *Matador*	Epic OLE 4
29/10/1988	5	7		**KISS ART OF NOISE FEATURING TOM JONES**	China 11
29/04/1989	49	3		MOVE CLOSER.	Jive 203
26/01/1991	51	2		COULDN'T SAY GOODBYE.	Dover ROJ 10
16/03/1991	57	2		CARRYING A TORCH.	Dover ROJ 12
04/07/1992	68	2		DELILAH.	The Hit Label TOM 10
06/02/1993	19	4		ALL YOU NEED IS LOVE Recorded with Dave Stewart and is a charity record in aid of Childline	Childline CHILDCD 93
05/11/1994	11	9		IF I ONLY KNEW.	ZTT ZANG 59CD
25/09/1999	7	7		**BURNING DOWN THE HOUSE TOM JONES AND THE CARDIGANS**	Gut CDGUT 26
18/12/1999	17	7		BABY, IT'S COLD OUTSIDE TOM JONES AND CERYS MATTHEWS	Gut CDGUT 29
18/03/2000	4	7		**MAMA TOLD ME NOT TO COME TOM JONES AND STEREOPHONICS**.	Gut CXGUT 031
20/05/2000	3	10		**SEX BOMB TOM JONES AND MOUSSE T**.	Gut CXGUT 33
18/11/2000	24	3		YOU NEED LOVE LIKE I DO TOM JONES AND HEATHER SMALL.	Gut CXGUT 36
09/11/2002	31	2		TOM JONES INTERNATIONAL	V2 VVR 5021083
08/03/2003	50	2		BLACK BETTY/I WHO HAVE NOTHING	V2 VVR 5021763

SUE JONES-DAVIES – see JULIE COVINGTON, RULA LENSKA, CHARLOTTE CORNWELL AND SUE JONES-DAVIES

JONESTOWN US vocal duo Aris Bulent and Tony Cottura.

13/06/1998	49	1		SWEET THANG Contains a sample of Sister Sledge's *He's The Greatest Dancer* .	Universal UMD 70376

ALISON JORDAN UK singer; her hit a cover of Darts' 1978 hit (itself a cover of the Ad Libs US hit). Later a member of Cappella.

09/05/1992	23	4		BOY FROM NEW YORK CITY .	Arista 74321100427

DICK JORDAN UK singer.

17/03/1960	47	1		HALLELUJAH I LOVE HER SO.	Oriole CB 1534
09/06/1960	39	3		LITTLE CHRISTINE .	Oriole CB 1548

JACK JORDAN – see FRANK CHACKSFIELD AND HIS ORCHESTRA

MONTELL JORDAN
US R&B singer (born 3/12/1968, Los Angeles, CA). Graduating from Pepperdine University, he spent the next seven years trying to get a record deal. Six-foot-eight-inches tall, he appeared in the film *The Nutty Professor*. Master P and Silkk The Shocker are rapping brothers Percy Miller and Zyshone Miller. Master P (born 29/4/1970, New Orleans) is the founder of No Limit records and leader of rap group Tru, which also features Silkk The Shocker.

13/05/1995	11	8		THIS IS HOW WE DO IT ▲7 Contains a sample of Slick Rick's *Children's Story*	Def Jam DEFCD 07
02/09/1995	15	4		SOMETHIN' 4 DA HONEYZ Contains a sample of Kool & The Gang's *Summer Madness*	Def Jam DEFCD 10
19/10/1996	24	3		I LIKE MONTELL JORDAN FEATURING SLICK RICK Contains a sample of KC & The Sunshine Band's *Get Lifted*. This and above two singles featured in the 1996 film *The Nutty Professor*	Def Jam DEFCD 19
23/05/1998	25	2		LET'S RIDE MONTELL JORDAN FEATURING MASTER P AND SILKK THE SHOCKER	Def Jam 5686912
08/04/2000	15	4		GET IT ON TONITE Contains a sample of Claudja Barry's *Love For The Sake Of Love*. Featured in the 2001 film *Save The Last Dance*	Def Soul 5627222

RONNY JORDAN
UK guitarist (born Ronnie Simpson, 29/11/1962, London); he made his first solo album in 1991 for Island Records. He won the 2000 MOBO Award with Mos Def for Best Jazz Act.

01/02/1992	32	4		SO WHAT!	Antilles ANN 14
25/09/1993	72	1		UNDER YOUR SPELL	Island CID 565
15/01/1994	64	1		TINSEL TOWN	Island CID 566
28/05/1994	63	1		COME WITH ME	Island CID 584

JORDANAIRES – see ELVIS PRESLEY

JORIO
US producer Fred Jorio.

24/02/2001	54	1		REMEMBER ME	Wonderboy WBOYD 021

DAVID JOSEPH
UK singer (born London); lead singer with funk group Hi Tension before going solo in 1982.

26/02/1983	13	9		YOU CAN'T HIDE (YOUR LOVE FROM ME)	Island IS 101
28/05/1983	26	5		LET'S LIVE IT UP (NITE PEOPLE)	Island IS 116
18/02/1984	61	2		JOYS OF LIFE	Island IS 153
31/05/1986	58	5		EXPANSIONS '86 (EXPAND YOUR MIND) CHRIS PAUL FEATURING DAVID JOSEPH	Fourth & Broadway BRW 48

DAWN JOSEPH – see LOGO FEATURING DAWN JOSEPH

MARK JOSEPH
UK singer/songwriter (born 1980); he financed his debut hit after being turned down by major record companies. Support from selected Virgin stores helped it chart, leading to a contract with 14th Floor.

01/03/2003	38	1		GET THROUGH	Mark Joseph MJR 003
30/08/2003	28	1		FLY	14th Floor MJM01CD
27/03/2004	34	1		BRINGING BACK THOSE MEMORIES	14th Floor MJM02CD2

MARTYN JOSEPH
UK singer/songwriter (born Cardiff) who later recorded for Grapevine.

20/06/1992	34	4		DOLPHINS MAKE ME CRY	Epic 6581347
12/09/1992	65	1		WORKING MOTHER	Epic 6582937
09/01/1993	45	3		PLEASE SIRE	Epic 6588552
03/06/1995	43	2		TALK ABOUT IT IN THE MORNING	Epic 6613342

JOURNEY
US rock group formed in 1973 by Neal Schon (born 27/2/1954, guitar), George Tickner (guitar), Gregg Rolie (keyboards), Ross Valory (bass) and Aynsley Dunbar (drums). Tickner left in 1978, replaced by Steve Perry (born 22/1/1949, Hanford, CA, vocals). Rolie left in 1980, replaced by Jonathan Cain (born 26/2/1950). By 1986 the group was Schon, Cain and Perry, and after one more album they split with Schon and Cain, joining John Waite. Journey re-formed in 1996 with Perry, Schon, Cain, Valory and Steve Smith (drums). The group has a star on the Hollywood Walk of Fame.

27/02/1982	62	4		DON'T STOP BELIEVIN'	CBS A 1728
11/09/1982	46	5		WHO'S CRYING NOW	CBS A 2725

RUTH JOY
UK singer Ann Saunderson, who also sang with Krush and later with Octave One.

26/08/1989	66	2		DON'T PUSH IT	MCA RJOY 1
22/02/1992	67	1		FEEL	MCA MCS 1574

JOY DIVISION
UK group formed in Manchester in 1976 by Ian Curtis (born 15/7/1956, Macclesfield, vocals), Bernard Sumner (born Bernard Albrecht, 4/1/1956, Salford, guitar), Peter Hook (born 13/12/1956, Salford) and Steve Brotherdale (drums) as the Stiff Kittens, making their their live debut as Warsaw. Brotherdale left in 1977, replaced by Stephen Morris (born 28/10/1957, Macclesfield) shortly before they changed name again to Joy Division (taken from the Nazi-concentration camp novel *House Of Dolls*). Curtis committed suicide on 18/5/1980 with the surviving members re-emerging as New Order.

28/06/1980	13	9		LOVE WILL TEAR US APART	Factory FAC 23
29/10/1983	19	7		LOVE WILL TEAR US APART	Factory FAC 23
18/06/1988	34	5		ATMOSPHERE	Factory FAC 2137
17/06/1995	19	3		LOVE WILL TEAR US APART (remix)	London YOJCD 1

JOY STRINGS
UK vocal/instrumental group formed by Salvation Army captain Joy Webb. All but one of the eight-piece – trainee

❶9 Number of weeks single topped the UK chart ↑ Entered the UK chart at #1 ▲9 Number of weeks single topped the US chart

421

architect Wyncliffe Noble – were also in the Salvation Army.

| 27/02/1964 | 32 | 7 | | IT'S AN OPEN SECRET | Regal Zonophone RZ 501 |
| 17/12/1964 | 35 | 4 | | A STARRY NIGHT | Regal Zonophone RZ 504 |

JOY ZIPPER US duo formed in Long Island, NY by Vinny Cafiso and Tabitha Tindale.

| 24/04/2004 | 59 | 1 | | BABY YOU SHOULD KNOW | 13 Amp/Vertigo 9866235 |

JOYRIDER UK group formed in Northern Ireland by Phil Woolsey (guitar/vocals), Mitch (lead guitar), Simon (bass) and Buc (drums).

| 27/07/1996 | 22 | 3 | | RUSH HOUR | Paradox PDOXD 012 |
| 28/09/1996 | 54 | 1 | | ALL GONE AWAY | A&M 5819552 |

JT AND THE BIG FAMILY Italian vocal/instrumental group fronted by Joe T Vannelli.

| 03/03/1990 | 7 | 8 | | MOMENTS IN SOUL | Champion CHAMP 237 |

JT PLAYAZ UK production group formed by Giles Goodman. He also recorded as Powers That Be.

| 05/04/1997 | 30 | 3 | | JUST PLAYIN' | Pukka CDJTP 1 |
| 02/05/1998 | 64 | 1 | | LET'S GET DOWN Contains an interpolation of Kool & The Gang's Celebration | MCA MCSTD 40161 |

JTQ UK jazz-funk trio with James Taylor, David Taylor and John Willmott, formed in London in 1985 with vocalist Noel McKoy joining in 1992. He was later replaced by Yvonne Yaney. James Taylor was earlier in The Prisoners. The initials stand for James Taylor Quartet.

03/04/1993	34	3		LOVE THE LIFE	Big Life BLRD 93
03/07/1993	49	2		SEE A BRIGHTER DAY This and above single credited to JTQ WITH NOEL MCKOY	Big Life BLRDA 97
25/02/1995	63	1		LOVE WILL KEEP US TOGETHER JTQ FEATURING ALISON LIMERICK	Acid Jazz JAZID 112CD

JUCXI – see 2PLAY FEATURING RAGHAV AND JUCXI

JUDAS PRIEST UK heavy rock group formed in 1969 by Ken 'KK' Downing (born 25/8/1951, Birmingham, guitar) and Ian Hill (born 20/1/1952, Birmingham, bass). By 1971 the line-up consisted of Downing, Hill, Rob Halford (born 25/8/1951, Birmingham, vocals), John Hinch (drums), adding second guitarist Glenn Tipton (born 25/10/1948, Birmingham) in 1974. Signed with Gull in 1974, replacing Hinch with Alan Moore. Switched to CBS in 1977. Named after a Bob Dylan album track, The Ballad Of Frankie Lee And Judas Priest. Rob Halford later went solo, hitting the US album chart in 2001 with Resurrection.

20/01/1979	14	10		TAKE ON THE WORLD	CBS 6915
12/05/1979	53	4		EVENING STARS	CBS 7312
29/03/1980	12	7		LIVING AFTER MIDNIGHT	CBS 8379
07/06/1980	12	6		BREAKING THE LAW	CBS 8644
23/08/1980	26	8		UNITED	CBS 8897
21/02/1981	51	3		DON'T GO	CBS 9520
25/04/1981	60	3		HOT ROCKIN'	CBS A 1153
21/08/1982	66	2		YOU'VE GOT ANOTHER THING COMIN'	CBS A 2611
21/01/1984	42	3		FREEWHEEL BURNIN'	CBS A 4054
23/04/1988	64	2		JOHNNY B. GOODE	Atlantic A 9114
15/09/1990	74	1		PAINKILLER	CBS 6562737
23/03/1991	58	1		A TOUCH OF EVIL	Columbia 6565897
24/04/1993	63	1		NIGHT CRAWLER	Columbia 6590972

JUDGE DREAD UK singer (born Alex Hughes, 1945, Kent); he worked as a wrestler, bouncer and debt collector before fronting a mobile roadshow in the style of many Jamaican artists, singing over backing tapes. All his hits were banned by radio and TV because of the earthy lyrical content. He died from a heart attack while performing on stage on 13/3/1998.

26/08/1972	11	27		BIG SIX	Big Shot BI 608
09/12/1972	8	18		BIG SEVEN	Big Shot BI 613
21/04/1973	14	10		BIG EIGHT	Big Shot BI 619
05/07/1975	9	9		JE T'AIME (MOI NON PLUS)	Cactus CT 65
27/09/1975	14	7		BIG TEN	Cactus CT 77
06/12/1975	14	7		CHRISTMAS IN DREADLAND/COME OUTSIDE	Cactus CT 80
08/05/1976	35	4		THE WINKLE MAN	Cactus CT 90
28/08/1976	27	4		Y VIVA SUSPENDERS/CONFESSIONS OF A BOUNCER	Cactus CT 99
02/04/1977	31	4		5TH ANNIVERSARY EP Tracks on EP: Jamaica Jerk (Off), Bring Back The Skins, End Of The World and Big Everything	Cactus CT 98
14/01/1978	49	1		UP WITH THE COCK/BIG PUNK	Cactus CT 110
16/12/1978	59	4		HOKEY COKEY/JINGLE BELLS	EMI 2881

JUICE Danish vocal group formed by Maria, Anne and Eve-Louise.

| 18/04/1998 | 28 | 2 | | BEST DAYS | Chrysalis CDCHS 5081 |
| 22/08/1998 | 48 | 1 | | I'LL COME RUNNIN' | Chrysalis CDCHS 5090 |

JUICY US vocal duo, brother and sister Jerry (bass/vocals) and Katreese Barnes (keyboards/vocals). Their backing group featured Wyatt Staton (guitar/vocals), Allison Bragdon (keyboards/vocals) and John Tucker (drums).

| 22/02/1986 | 45 | 5 | | SUGAR FREE | Epic A 6917 |

JUICY LUCY UK rock group formed in 1969 by Glenn Campbell (guitar/mandolin/percussion/vocals), Peter Dobson (drums),

Keith Ellis (bass/vocals), Neil Hubbard (guitar), Chris Mercer (saxophone/keyboards) and Ray Owen (vocals). Later members included Mick Moody (guitar), Paul Williams (percussion/vocals), Rod Coombes (drums) and Jim Leverton (bass). The group split in 1973.

| 07/03/1970 | 14 | 12 | | WHO DO YOU LOVE | Vertigo V 1 |
| 10/10/1970 | 44 | 5 | | PRETTY WOMAN | Vertigo 6059 015 |

GARY JULES – see MICHAEL ANDREWS FEATURING GARY JULES

THOMAS JULES-STOCK UK singer.

| 15/08/1998 | 59 | 1 | | DIDN'T I TELL YOU TRUE | Mercury MERCD 501 |

JULIA AND COMPANY US singer (born Julia McGirt, 1955, Rowland, NC) teamed with David Ylvisaker.

| 03/03/1984 | 15 | 8 | | BREAKIN' DOWN (SUGAR SAMBA) | London LON 46 |
| 23/02/1985 | 56 | 2 | | I'M SO HAPPY | Next Plateau LON 61 |

JULUKA UK/South African group formed by Johnny Clegg (born 13/7/1953, Rochdale) who moved to South Africa in 1959 and formed Juluka (Zulu for 'sweat') with Sipho Mchunu in 1976. He formed Savuka in 1986.

| 12/02/1983 | 44 | 4 | | SCATTERLINGS OF AFRICA | Safari ZULU 1 |

JUMP UK instrumental group formed by Paul Kelly, Marc Kelly, Andrew Grimwood and John Viney.

| 01/03/1997 | 56 | 1 | | FUNKATARIUM | Heat Recordings HEATCD 005 |

WALLY JUMP JR AND THE CRIMINAL ELEMENT US groups formed by producer Arthur Baker for his label Criminal. Wally Jump Jr featured Will Downing as lead singer, Craig Derry, Donny Calvin, Dwight Hawkes, Rick Sher, Jeff Smith and toasters Michigan and Smily.

28/02/1987	60	2		TURN ME LOOSE	London LON 126
05/09/1987	63	3		PUT THE NEEDLE TO THE RECORD CRIMINAL ELEMENT ORCHESTRA	Cooltempo COOL 150
12/12/1987	24	7		TIGHTEN UP – I JUST CAN'T STOP DANCING	Breakout USA 621
19/03/1988	57	3		PRIVATE PARTY	Breakout USA 624
06/10/1990	30	4		EVERYBODY (RAP) CRIMINAL ELEMENT ORCHESTRA AND WENDELL WILLIAMS	Deconstruction PB 44701

JUMPING JACKS – see DANNY PEPPERMINT AND THE JUMPING JACKS

ROSEMARY JUNE US singer.

| 23/01/1959 | 14 | 9 | | I'LL BE WITH YOU IN APPLE BLOSSOM TIME | Pye International 7N 25005 |

JUNGLE BOOK US studio group with a disco version of the theme to the Walt Disney cartoon.

| 08/05/1993 | 14 | 8 | | THE JUNGLE BOOK GROOVE | Hollywood HWCD 128 |

JUNGLE BOYS UK vocal group formed by Mike Read (born 1/3/1951), Neil 'Razor' Ruddock (born 9/5/1968) and Lord Charles Brocket. The three first met while filming I'm A Celebrity Get Me Out Of Here and recorded their debut single for various charities.

| 20/03/2004 | 30 | 5 | | JUNGLE ROCK | Bushtucker JUNGLE001CD |
| 31/07/2004 | 72 | 1 | | IN THE SUMMERTIME | MCS JUNGLE002CD |

JUNGLE BROTHERS US rap group with Mike G (Michael Small), Afrika Baby Bam (Nathaniel Hall) and DJ Sammy B (Sammy Burwell) who have collaborated with De La Soul and A Tribe Called Quest.

22/10/1988	22	5		I'LL HOUSE YOU RICHIE RICH MEETS THE JUNGLE BROTHERS	Gee Street GEE 003
18/03/1989	72	1		BLACK IS BLACK/STRAIGHT OUT OF THE JUNGLE	Gee Street GEE 15
31/03/1990	35	5		WHAT 'U' WAITIN' '4' Contains a sample of People's Choice's Do It Any Way You Wanna	Eternal W 9865
21/07/1990	33	6		DOIN' OUR OWN DANG Features the uncredited vocals of De La Soul and Monie Love	Eternal W 9754
19/07/1997	52	1		BRAIN	Gee Street GEE 5000388
29/11/1997	56	1		JUNGLE BROTHER	Gee Street GEE 5000493
09/05/1998	18	4		JUNGLE BROTHER	Gee Street GEE 5000493
11/07/1998	26	5		I'LL HOUSE YOU '98 (REMIX)	Gee Street FCD 338
28/11/1998	32	2		BECAUSE I GOT IT LIKE THAT	Gee Street GEE 5003593
10/07/1999	33	3		V.I.P.	Gee Street GEE 5007958
06/11/1999	52	1		GET DOWN Contains a sample of Kool & The Gang's Get Down On It	Gee Street GEE 5010153
25/03/2000	70	1		FREAKIN' YOU Featured in the 2000 film Bring It On	Gee Street GEE 5008808
07/02/2004	21	5		BREATHE DON'T STOP MR ON VS THE JUNGLE BROTHERS	Positiva/Incentive CDTIVS 201

JUNGLE HIGH WITH BLUE PEARL German/UK production duo Johan Bley and Ben Watkins with female singer Durga McBroom and UK group Blue Pearl. Bley later recorded as Johan.

| 27/11/1993 | 71 | 1 | | FIRE OF LOVE | Logic 74321170292 |

JUNIOR UK singer (born Norman Giscombe, 10/11/1961, London); he made his recording debut in 1982, later recording in America.

24/04/1982	7	13	O	MAMA USED TO SAY	Mercury MER 98
10/07/1982	20	9		TOO LATE	Mercury MER 112
25/09/1982	53	3		LET ME KNOW/I CAN'T HELP IT	Mercury MER 116
23/04/1983	57	3		COMMUNICATION BREAKDOWN	Mercury MER 134
08/09/1984	64	2		SOMEBODY	London LON 50

❶⁹ Number of weeks single topped the UK chart ↑ Entered the UK chart at #1 ▲⁹ Number of weeks single topped the US chart

423

	09/02/1985	47	4		DO YOU REALLY (WANT MY LOVE)	London LON 60
	30/11/1985	74	3		OH LOUISE	London LON 75
	04/04/1987	6	11		**ANOTHER STEP CLOSER TO YOU** KIM WILDE AND JUNIOR	MCA KIM 5
	25/08/1990	63	3		STEP OFF	MCA 1432
	15/08/1992	32	5		THEN CAME YOU JUNIOR GISCOMBE	MCA MCS 1676
	31/10/1992	74	1		ALL OVER THE WORLD	MCA MCS 1691

JUNIOR – see FLIP & FILL

JUNIOR JACK Italian producer Vito Lucente. He also records as Mr Jack and Room 5. Robert Smith is lead singer with The Cure.

	16/12/2000	31	4		MY FEELING Contains a sample of Sister Sledge's *One More Time*	Defected DFECT 24CDS
	02/03/2002	29	3		THRILL ME	VC Recordings VCRD 102
	27/09/2003	34	3		E SAMBA	Defected DFTD 076CDS
	14/02/2004	25	4		DA HYPE JUNIOR JACK FEATURING ROBERT SMITH	Defected DFTD 083CDS
	03/07/2004	26	6		STUPIDISCO	Defected DFTD 089CDS

JUNIOR M.A.F.I.A. US rap group with Lil' Kim, Klepto, Trife, Larceny, Little Caesar, Chico and Nino Brown. Lil' Kim later recorded solo. Their name stands for Junior Masters At Finding Intelligent Attitudes.

	03/02/1996	66	1		I NEED YOU TONIGHT JUNIOR M.A.F.I.A. FEATURING AALIYAH	Big Beat A 8130CD
	19/10/1996	63	1		GETTING' MONEY Contains a sample of Dennis Edwards' *Don't Look Any Further*	Big Beat A 5674CD

JUNIOR SENIOR Danish vocal duo Jeeper Mortensen and Jeppe Breum.

	08/03/2003	3	17		**MOVE YOUR FEET** Featured in the 2003 film *Looney Tunes: Back In Action*	Mercury 0198192
	09/08/2003	22	3		RHYTHM BANDITS	Mercury 9810210

JUNIORS – see DANNY AND THE JUNIORS

JUNKIE XL Dutch producer Tom Holkenborg. His debut hit also featured Patrick Tilon. He had to amend his recording name to JXL for his Elvis remix after objections from the Presley estate. Solomon Burke is a US singer (born 1936, Philadelphia, PA).

	22/07/2000	63	1		ZEROTONINE	Manifesto FESCD 71
	22/02/2002	❶4	12	✪	**A LITTLE LESS CONVERSATION** ↑ ELVIS VS JXL A second posthumous #1 for Elvis Presley. Originally written in 1968 for Elvis' film *Live A Little Love A Little* it was revived in 2002 after being used in a TV advertisement for Nike. It might have remained at #1 for longer but the record company deleted it after four weeks at #1. Featured in the 2003 film *Bruce Almighty*	RCA 74321943572
	30/11/2002	56	1		OBSESSION TIESTO AND JUNKIE XL	Nebula NEBCD 029
	07/06/2003	63	1		CATCH UP TO MY STEP JUNKIE XL FEATURING SOLOMON BURKE	Roadrunner RR 20209

JUNO REACTOR UK/German production duo Ben Watkins and Stefan Holweck, with Mike Maguire, Johan Bley and Jens Waldenback occasional contributors. Watkins and Bley had previously recorded as Jungle High.

	08/02/1997	45	1		JUNGLE HIGH	Perfecto PERF 133CD

JURASSIC 5 US rap group formed in Los Angeles, CA by MC Mark 7even, MC Charli 2na, MC Zaakir, MC Akil, producer Cut Chemist and DJ Nu-Mark. The six had previously been in Unity Committee and Rebels of Rhythm before releasing *Unified Rebelution*.

	25/07/1998	56	1		JAYOU	Pan 018CD
	24/10/1998	35	3		CONCRETE SCHOOLYARD	Pan 020CD

CHRISTOPHER JUST Austrian producer.

	13/12/1997	72	1		I'M A DISCO DANCER	Slut Trax SLUT 001CD
	06/02/1999	69	1		I'M A DISCO DANCER (REMIX)	XL Recordings XLS 105CD

JUST 4 JOKES FEATURING MC RB UK garage group formed by DJ Butterfly and MC DT with MC RB.

	28/09/2002	67	1		JUMP UP	Serious SERR 050CD

JUST LUIS Spanish singer Luis Sierra Pizarro.

	14/10/1995	31	2		AMERICAN PIE	Pro-Activ CDPTV 1
	17/02/1996	70	1		AMERICAN PIE	Pro-Activ CDPTV 1

JIMMY JUSTICE UK singer (born James Little, 1940, Carshalton); signed to Pye in 1960 after recommendation from Emile Ford and dubbed the 'UK Ben E King'. Later moved to Sweden, forming the Excheckers. Rumoured he impersonated Elvis Presley on the successful *Top of the Pops* albums.

	29/03/1962	9	13		**WHEN MY LITTLE GIRL IS SMILING**	Pye 7N 15421
	14/06/1962	8	11		**AIN'T THAT FUNNY**	Pye 7N 15443
	23/08/1962	20	11		SPANISH HARLEM	Pye 7N 15457

JUSTIFIED ANCIENTS OF MU MU UK duo Bill Drummond (born William Butterworth, 29/4/1953, South Africa) and Jimmy Cauty (born 1954, London). They also recorded as the Timelords, KLF, 1300 Drums Featuring The Unjustified Ancients Of Mu and 2K.

	09/11/1991	10	6		**IT'S GRIM UP NORTH**	KLF Communications JAMS 028

JUSTIN UK singer Justin Osuji, he first came to prominence in the TV programme *The Fame Game*.

	22/08/1998	34	2		THIS BOY	Virgin STCDT 1

16/01/1999 . . . . . 11 . . . . . . 4 . . . . . . OVER YOU . . . . Virgin STCDT 2
17/07/1999 . . . . . 34 . . . . . . 3 . . . . . . IT'S ALL ABOUT YOU . . . . Virgin STCDT 3
22/01/2000 . . . . . 15 . . . . . . 4 . . . . . . LET IT BE ME . . . . Innocent STCDTX 4

BILL JUSTIS US saxophonist/arranger/producer (born 14/10/1926, Birmingham, AL); he led the house band at Sun Records, working with Elvis Presley, Johnny Cash, Jerry Lewis and Roy Orbison. He later scored the films *Smokey And The Bandit* and *Hooper*. He died from cancer on 15/7/1982.

10/01/1958 . . . . . 11 . . . . . . 8 . . . . RAUNCHY . . . . London HLS 8517

PATRICK JUVET French singer/songwriter discovered by producer Jacques Morali. He later composed the music to the film *Laura, Les Ombres De L'ete.*

02/09/1978 . . . . . 34 . . . . . . 7 . . . . . . GOT A FEELING . . . . Casablanca CAN 127
04/11/1978 . . . . . 12 . . . . . 12 . . . . . . I LOVE AMERICA . . . . Casablanca CAN 132

JX UK producer/designer Jake Williams.

02/04/1994 . . . . . 13 . . . . . . 6 . . . . . . SON OF A GUN . . . . Internal Dance IDC 5
01/04/1995 . . . . . 17 . . . . . . 5 . . . . . . YOU BELONG TO ME . . . . ffrreedom TABCD 227
19/08/1995 . . . . . 6 . . . . . . 6 . . . . **SON OF A GUN (REMIX)** . . . . ffrreedom TABCD 233
18/05/1996 . . . . . 4 . . . . . . 13 . . . . ○ **THERE'S NOTHING I WON'T DO** . . . . ffrreedom TABCD 241
08/03/1997 . . . . . 18 . . . . . . 3 . . . . . . CLOSE TO YOUR HEART . . . . ffrreedom TABCD 245
06/03/2004 . . . . . 22 . . . . . . 3 . . . . . . RESTLESS . . . . Tidy Two TIDYTWOJX1C

JXL – see JUNKIE XL

FRANK K FEATURING WISTON OFFICE Italian/US vocal/instrumental duo.

26/01/1991	61	1	EVERYBODY LETS SOMEBODY LOVE . . . . Urban URB 66

LEILA K Swedish singer/rapper (born Leila El Khalifi, 6/9/1971) of Moroccan parentage.

25/11/1989	8	14	**GOT TO GET** . . . . Arista 112696
17/03/1990	41	3	ROK THE NATION This and above single credited to **ROB 'N' RAZ FEATURING LEILA K** . . . . Arista 112971
23/01/1993	23	4	OPEN SESAME . . . . Polydor PQCD 1
03/07/1993	69	1	CA PLANE POUR MOI. . . . . Polydor PQCD 3

K-CI AND JOJO US duo of brothers Gedric 'K-Ci' (born 2/9/1969, Charlotte, NC) and Joel 'JoJo' Hailey (born 10/6/1971, Charlotte). The grandsons of Temptations member Ron Tyson, both are also in Jodeci.

27/07/1996	17	4	HOW DO YOU WANT IT? ▲² 2PAC FEATURING K-CI AND JOJO Contains a sample of Quincy Jones' *Body Heat*. 2Pac's estate was sued for intentional infliction of emotional distress, slander and invasion of privacy by C DeLores Tucker, a critic of gangsta rap lyrics, over the hit, in which she was mentioned by name. She also sued Interscope Records, Death Row Records, Time Warner, Seagram Co, Tower Records and other individuals and companies . . . . Death Row 228546532
23/08/1997	21	2	YOU BRING ME UP . . . . MCA MCSTD 48057
18/04/1998	8	11	**ALL MY LIFE ▲³** . . . . MCA MCSTD 48076
19/09/1998	16	3	DON'T RUSH (TAKE LOVE SLOWLY). . . . . MCA MCSD 48090
02/10/1999	40	2	TELL ME IT'S REAL . . . . MCA MCSXD 40211
23/09/2000	16	5	TELL ME IT'S REAL (REMIX) . . . . AM:PM CDAMPM 135
12/05/2001	35	2	CRAZY Featured in the 2001 film *Save The Last Dance* . . . . MCA MCSTD 40253

K CREATIVE UK vocal/instrumental group fronted by Dominic Oakenfull.

07/03/1992	58	2	THREE TIMES A MAYBE Listed flip side was *Feed The Feeling* by **PERCEPTION**. Talkin Loud TLK 17

ERNIE K-DOE US singer (born Ernest Kador Jr, 22/2/1936, New Orleans, LA) who sang gospel before recording with the Blue Diamonds in 1954. After his solo debut in 1956 (*Do Baby Do* on Specialty Records), his biggest hit was on the Minit label and he also recorded for Duke. Claimed his hit (with an uncredited contribution of bass singer Benny Spellman) 'will last to the end of the earth because someone is always going to get married', although he didn't acquire a mother-in-law until1996 when he married former Satin recording artist Annabelle Fox! He died from various internal diseases on 5/7/2001.

11/05/1961	29	7	MOTHER-IN-LAW ▲¹ . . . . London HLU 9330

K GEE UK male producer Karl Gordon.

04/11/2000	22	3	I DON'T REALLY CARE. . . . . Instant Karma 3CD

K-KLASS UK vocal/instrumental group formed by Andy Williams, Carl Thomas, Paul Roberts and Russ Morgan, with Bobbi Depasois providing vocals.

04/05/1991	61	2	RHYTHM IS A MYSTERY . . . . Deconstruction CREED 1
09/11/1991	3	10	**RHYTHM IS A MYSTERY** Re-issue of Deconstruction CREED 1 . . . . Deconstruction R 6302
25/04/1992	20	5	SO RIGHT. . . . . Deconstruction R 6309
07/11/1992	32	3	DON'T STOP . . . . Deconstruction R 6325
27/11/1993	13	7	LET ME SHOW YOU . . . . Deconstruction CDR 6367
28/05/1994	24	3	WHAT YOU'RE MISSING . . . . Deconstruction CDRS 6380
01/08/1998	45	1	BURNIN' . . . . Parlophone CDK 2001

K7 US rapper from New York (Louis 'Kayel' Sharpe, ex-TKA), with The Swing Kids – DJ Non-Stop, Prophet, Tre Duece and LOS.

11/12/1993	3	16	**COME BABY COME**. . . . . Big Life BLRD 105
02/04/1994	17	5	HI DE HO . . . . Big Life BLRD 108
25/06/1994	63	1	ZUNGA ZENG This and above single credited to **K7 AND THE SWING KIDS** . . . . Big Life BLRD 111

K3M Italian vocal/instrumental duo Franco Diafero and Guiseppe Isgro with singer Gale Robinson.

21/03/1992	71	1	LISTEN TO THE RHYTHM . . . . PWL Continental PWL 214

K-WARREN FEATURING LEE-O UK producer Kevin Warren Williams with singer Leo Ihenacho.

05/05/2001	32	2	COMING HOME . . . . Go Beat GOBCD 41

K2 FAMILY UK production/rap group formed in London by Don E Bravo, Uno Brown, Big D, Mad 'Millie' Gun and DJ Flex.

○ Silver disc ● Gold disc ✪ Platinum disc (additional platinum units are indicated by a figure following the symbol) ◎ Singles released prior to 1973 that are known to have sold over 1 million copies in the UK

27/10/2001.....27......3....... BOUNCING FLOW .... Relentless RELENT 22CD

KACI US singer (born Kaci Lynn Battaglia, 3/10/1987, Seminole, FL); she moved to Los Angeles at ten to pursue an acting career, subsequently presenting a Disney Christmas TV special. She made her first demo record at the age of eleven.

10/03/2001.....11......9....... PARADISE .... Curb CUBC 61
28/07/2001.....24......3....... TU AMOR... Curb CUBX 71
02/02/2002.....10......10...... **I THINK I LOVE YOU** .... Curb CUBC 076
09/08/2003.....55......1....... I'M NOT ANYBODY'S GIRL .... Curb CUBC 091

JOSHUA KADISON US singer (born 8/2/1965, Los Angeles, CA).

26/02/1994.....69......2....... JESSIE .... SBK CDSBK 43
01/10/1994.....48......3....... JESSIE .... SBK CDSBK 43
12/11/1994.....65......1....... BEAUTIFUL IN MY EYES .... SBK CDSBK 50
29/04/1995.....15......10...... JESSIE Re-issue of SBK CDSBK 43 .... SBK CDSBK 53
12/08/1995.....37......3....... BEAUTIFUL IN MY EYES Re-issue of SBK CDSBK 50. .... SBK CDSBKS 55

KADOC UK/Spanish vocal/ instrumental dance group formed by David Penin, JC Molina and Andreas Schneider.

06/04/1996.....14......8....... THE NIGHTTRAIN .... Positiva CDTIV 26
17/08/1996.....45......1....... YOU GOT TO BE THERE .... Positiva CDTIV 58
23/08/1997.....34......2....... ROCK THE BELLS .... Manifesto FESCD 30

BERT KAEMPFERT German orchestra leader/producer (born 16/10/1923, Hamburg) best known as the first to produce the Beatles, on the German sessions with Tony Sheridan that resulted in a belated UK hit after the group were superstars. He died in Spain while on holiday on 21/6/1980.

23/12/1965.....24......10...... BYE BYE BLUES .... Polydor BM 56 504

KAISER CHIEFS UK rock group formed in Leeds by Ricky Wilson (vocals), Andrew 'Whitey' White (guitar), Simon Rix (bass), Nick 'Peanut' Baines (keyboards) and Nick Hodgson (drums) who took their name in honour of the South African football club Lucas Redebe played for before joining Leeds United.

29/05/2004.....66......1....... OH MY GOD .... Drowned In Sound DIS03
13/11/2004.....22......2....... I PREDICT A RIOT .... B Unique BUN088CD

KAJAGOOGOO UK group from Leighton Buzzard with Steve Askew (guitar), Nick Beggs (born 15/12/1961, bass), Limahl (born Chris Hamill, 19/12/1958, his stage name an anagram of his real name, lead singer), Stuart Neale (keyboards) and Jez Strode (drums). Limahl went solo in 1983, Beggs taking over as lead singer. Later a trio, they shortened their name to Kaja. Beggs was later in Ellis, Beggs & Howard before becoming an A&R man in the record industry.

22/01/1983 ....❶²....13.....● **TOO SHY** Featured in the 1998 film *The Wedding Singer*................... EMI 5359
02/04/1983 .....7......8....... **OOH TO BE AH** .... EMI 5383
04/06/1983 .....13......7....... HANG ON NOW .... EMI 5394
17/09/1983 .....8......8....... **BIG APPLE** .... EMI 5423
03/03/1984.....25......7....... THE LION'S MOUTH .... EMI 5449
05/05/1984.....47......4....... TURN YOUR BACK ON ME .... EMI 5646
21/09/1985.....63......3....... SHOULDN'T DO THAT **KAJA** .... Parlophone R 6106

KALEEF UK group formed by 2Phaaan, Jabba Da Hype, Hogweed, Chokadoodle and SniffaDawg as Kaliphz, later name-changing to Kaleef and adding Twice Born and Travis Bickle.

30/03/1996.....23......3....... WALK LIKE A CHAMPION **KALIPHZ FEATURING PRINCE NASEEM** .... Payday KACD 5
07/12/1996.....22......4....... GOLDEN BROWN .... Unity 010CD
14/06/1997.....75......1....... TRIALS OF LIFE Contains a sample of The Pretenders' *Brass In Pocket* .... Unity 012CD
11/10/1997.....58......1....... I LIKE THE WAY (THE KISSING GAME) .... Unity 015CD
24/01/1998.....26......3....... SANDS OF TIME .... Unity 016CD

PREEYA KALIDAS UK singer (born 1980, Twickenham) best known as an actress, appearing in the films *Bollywood Queen* and *Bend It Like Beckham* (both 2002) before playing the role of Priya in the West End musical *Bombay Dreams*.

13/07/2002.....38......2....... SHAKALAKA BABY Featured in the musical *Bombay Dreams*.................... Sony Classical 6726322

KALIN TWINS US vocal duo Harold and Herbie Kalin (born 16/2/1934, Port Jarvis, NY), whose US record company Decca gave their year of birth as 1939 to make them seem younger than they actually were.

18/07/1958 ....❶⁵.....18...... **WHEN** .... Brunswick 05751

KALLAGHAN – see **N 'N' G FEATURING KALAGHAN**

KITTY KALLEN US singer (born 25/5/1922, Philadelphia, PA); she was a big band singer with Jack Teagarden, Jimmy Dorsey and Harry James, first charting in 1945 with Harry James. Her first solo hit was in 1949, she was still having US hits in 1963. She has a star on the Hollywood Walk of Fame.

02/07/1954 ....❶¹.....23...... **LITTLE THINGS MEAN A LOT** ▲⁹ .... Brunswick 05287

GUNTER KALLMAN CHOIR German vocal group under the direction of Gunter Kallman (born19/11/1930, Berlin).

24/12/1964.....45......3....... ELISABETH SERENADE .... Polydor NH 24678

❶⁹ Number of weeks single topped the UK chart ↑ Entered the UK chart at #1 ▲⁹ Number of weeks single topped the US chart

KAMASUTRA FEATURING JOCELYN BROWN Italian DJ/production duo Alex Neri and Marco Baroni with US singer Jocelyn Brown. Neri and Baroni were later in Planet Funk.

| 22/11/1997 | 45 | 1 | | HAPPINESS | Sony S2 KAMCD 2 |

NICK KAMEN UK singer (born 15/4/1962, London) first noticed via a Levi Jeans advertisement, stripping off in a laundrette, backed by Marvin Gaye's *I Heard It Through The Grapevine*. Madonna helped him get a recording deal.

08/11/1986	5	12	O	EACH TIME YOU BREAK MY HEART	WEA YZ 90
28/02/1987	16	9		LOVING YOU IS SWEETER THAN EVER	WEA YZ 106
16/05/1987	47	3		NOBODY ELSE	WEA YZ 122
28/05/1988	40	5		TELL ME	WEA YZ 184
28/04/1990	50	4		I PROMISED MYSELF	WEA YZ 454

INI KAMOZE Jamaican singer/author/playwright (born 9/10/1957, Kingston) whose name means 'mountain of the true God'.

| 07/01/1995 | 4 | 15 | ● | HERE COMES THE HOTSTEPPER ▲[2] Contains samples of Bobby Byrd's *Hot Pants – I'm Coming* and Taana Gardner's *Heartbeat* and incorporates *Land Of 1000 Dances*. Originally recorded in 1992, later featured in the 1994 film *Ready To Wear (Pret-A-Porter)* ... | Columbia 6610472 |

KANDI US singer (born Kandi Burruss, 17/5/1976, Atlanta, GA); in Xscape then a successful songwriter, penning hits for Destiny's Child, TLC and Pink. 1999 Grammy Award for Best Rhythm & Blues Song for *No Scrubs*, written with Kevin Briggs and Tameka Cottle.

| 11/11/2000 | 9 | 10 | | DON'T THINK I'M NOT Contains a sample of Isaac Hayes' *Ike's Mood* | Columbia 6705102 |

KANDIDATE UK soul group formed in London in 1976 by Ferdi Morris (bass/vocals), Teeroy Morris (keyboards/lead vocals), Alex Bruce (percussion), St Lloyd Phillips (drums), Bob Collins (guitar/percussion/vocals), Jascha Tambimuttu (rhythm guitar/vocals) and Phil Fearon (lead guitar/vocals). Fearon left in 1983 to form Galaxy, then went solo.

19/08/1978	47	6		DON'T WANNA SAY GOODNIGHT	RAK 280
17/03/1979	11	12		I DON'T WANNA LOSE YOU	RAK 289
04/08/1979	34	7		GIRLS GIRLS GIRLS	RAK 295
22/03/1980	58	3		LET ME ROCK YOU	RAK 306

KANE Dutch duo formed in 1998 by Dinand Woesthoff and Dennis van Leeuwen.

| 04/09/2004 | 38 | 2 | | RAIN DOWN ON ME | BMG 82876634262 |

EDEN KANE UK singer (born Richard Sarstedt, 29/3/1942, Delhi, India, came to Britain as a child). Took his stage name from the Bible. With songwriter Johnny Worth had a debut #1. Brothers Peter and Robin also had chart successes.

01/06/1961	❶[1]	21		WELL I ASK YOU	Decca F 11353
14/09/1961	10	11		GET LOST	Decca F 11381
18/01/1962	3	14		FORGET ME NOT	Decca F 11418
10/05/1962	7	13		I DON'T KNOW WHY	Decca F 11460
30/01/1964	8	14		BOYS CRY	Fontana TF 438

KANE GANG UK group formed in Newcastle-upon-Tyne by Martin Bramer (vocals), Paul Woods (vocals) and Dave Brewis (guitar) and named after the film *Citizen Kane*. Debuting in 1983, a year later they teamed with hit producer Pete Wingfield.

19/05/1984	60	2		SMALLTOWN CREED	Kitchenware SK 11
07/07/1984	12	11		CLOSEST THING TO HEAVEN	Kitchenware SK 15
10/11/1984	21	11		RESPECT YOURSELF	Kitchenware SK 16
09/03/1985	53	4		GUN LAW	Kitchenware SK 20
27/06/1987	45	5		MOTORTOWN	Kitchenware SK 30
16/04/1988	52	4		DON'T LOOK ANY FURTHER	Kitchenware SK 33

KANSAS US group formed in Topeka, KS by Steve Walsh (keyboards/vocals), Kerry Livgren (guitar), Rich Williams (guitar), Robby Steinhardt (violin), Dave Hope (bass) and Phil Ehart (drums). Walsh left in 1981, replaced by John Elefante.

| 01/07/1978 | 51 | 7 | | CARRY ON WAYWARD SON | Kirshner KIR 4932 |

MORY KANTE Guinean singer (born 1951, Kissidougou), one of the world's leading Mandingue musicians.

23/07/1988	29	9		YEKE YEKE	London LON 171
11/03/1995	25	3		YEKE YEKE Re-issue of London LON 171	ffrreedom TABCD 226
30/11/1996	28	2		YEKE YEKE – 96 REMIXES	ffrr FCD 288

KAOMA French pop group assembled by Jean-Claude Bonaventura featuring lead vocals of Loalwa Braz, a Paris-based Brazilian.

| 21/10/1989 | 4 | 18 | ● | LAMBADA Featured in the 1990 film of the same name | CBS 6550117 |
| 27/01/1990 | 62 | 2 | | DANCANDO LAMBADA | CBS 6552357 |

KAOTIC CHEMISTRY UK instrumental/production group formed by Robert Playford, Sean O'Keeffe and Simon Colebrooke.

| 31/10/1992 | 68 | 1 | | LSD (EP) Tracks on EP: *Space Cakes, LSD, Illegal Substances* and *Drumstrip II* | Moving Shadow SHADOW 20 |

KARAJA German singer (born 1978, Berlin).

| 19/10/2002 | 42 | 1 | | SHE MOVES (LALALA) | Substance SUBS 14CDS |

KARDINAL OFFISHALL – see TEXAS

O Silver disc ● Gold disc ✪ Platinum disc (additional platinum units are indicated by a figure following the symbol) ◎ Singles released prior to 1973 that are known to have sold over 1 million copies in the UK

KARIN — see **UNIQUE 3**

KARIYA US female singer.

08/07/1989.....44......9...... LET ME LOVE YOU FOR TONIGHT .... Sleeping Bag SBUK 4

MICK KARN UK singer/bass player (born Anthony Michaelide, 24/7/1958, London),and a founder member of Japan in 1977. When they disbanded in 1982, he went solo, then formed short-lived Dali's Car with Peter Murphy before returning to a solo career.

09/07/1983.....39......4...... AFTER A FASHION **MIDGE URE AND MICK KARN** .... Musicfest FEST 1
17/01/1987.....63......2...... BUOY **MICK KARN FEATURING DAVID SYLVIAN** .... Virgin VS 910

KARTOON KREW US rap/instrumental group assembled by Craig Bevan. They also recorded a tribute to Batman.

07/12/1985.....58......6...... INSPECTOR GADGET .... Champion CHAMP 6

KASABIAN UK rock group formed in Leicester in 1999 by Tom Meighan (vocals), Sergio Pizzorno (guitar/keyboards), Chris Edwards (bass) and Chris Karloff (keyboards).

22/05/2004.....19......3...... CLUB FOOT .... BMG PARADISE08
21/08/2004.....10......7...... **LSF** Title stands for Lost Souls Forever.. RCA PARADISE14
23/10/2004.....17......3...... PROCESSED BEATS .... RCA PARADISE21

KASENETZ-KATZ SINGING ORCHESTRAL CIRCUS US 'bubblegum' producers Jerry Kasenetz and Jeff Katz, (created 1910 Fruitgum Co and Ohio Express). The self-credited hit had vocals by Joey Levine.

20/11/1968.....19......15...... QUICK JOEY SMALL (RUN JOEY RUN)... Buddah 201 022

KATCHA UK DJ/producer also known as Red Jerry, the founder of Hooj Choons.

21/08/1999.....57......1...... TOUCHED BY GOD .... Hooj Choons HOOJ 77CD

KATOI Thai DJ Kat Henderson, raised in London, whose name is Thai for 'ladyboy'.

29/03/2003.....70......1...... TOUCH YOU .... Arista Dance 74321964492

KATRINA AND THE WAVES UK-based US group formed by Katrina Leskanich (vocals), Vince de la Cruz (bass), Alex Cooper (drums) and Kimberley Rew (guitar). They won the 1997 Eurovision Song Contest, Britain's first success since 1981.

04/05/1985.....8......12...... **WALKING ON SUNSHINE** Featured in the 1997 film *Bean: The Ultimate Disaster Movie*...................... Capitol CL 354
05/07/1986.....22......9...... SUN STREET .... Capitol CL 407
08/06/1996.....53......1...... WALKING ON SUNSHINE .... EMI Premier PRESCD 2
10/05/1997.....3......12...... **LOVE SHINE A LIGHT** The song won the 1997 Eurovision Song Contest................................ Eternal WEA 106CD1

KAVANA UK singer (born Anthony Kavanagh, 4/11/1977), he achieved his breakthrough after supporting Boyzone on tour.

11/05/1996.....35......3...... CRAZY CHANCE .... Nemesis NMSDG 1
24/08/1996.....26......2...... WHERE ARE YOU .... Nemesis NMSD 2
11/01/1997.....8......5...... **I CAN MAKE YOU FEEL GOOD** .... Nemesis NMSDX 3
19/04/1997.....8......4...... **MFEO** Title means 'made for each other' .... Nemesis NMSD 4
13/09/1997.....16......3...... CRAZY CHANCE '97 (RE-RECORDING) .... Nemesis NMSD 5
29/08/1998.....13......4...... SPECIAL KIND OF SOMETHING .... Virgin VSCDT 1704
12/12/1998.....32......3...... FUNKY LOVE .... Virgin VSCDT 1711
20/03/1999.....29......2...... WILL YOU WAIT FOR ME .... Virgin VSCDT 1726

NIAMH KAVANAGH Irish singer (born Dublin) who won the 1993 Eurovision Song Contest, beating Britain's entry by Sonia into second place. Worked in a bank before contributing three tracks to *The Commitments* soundtrack, later fronting The Illegals.

12/06/1993.....24......5...... IN YOUR EYES The song won the 1993 Eurovision Song Contest............................. Arista 74321154152

KAWALA UK group formed by Terry Mynott (vocals), George Matthews (vocals) and Pete Brazier (programming/production).

26/02/2000.....68......1...... HUMANISTIC Contains a sample of Simple Minds' *New Gold Dream*................................. Pepper 9230022

JANET KAY UK reggae singer (born Janet Kay Bogle, 17/1/1958, London); she first recorded for Stonehouse.

09/06/1979.....2......14......O **SILLY GAMES**.. Scope SC 2
11/08/1990.....22......7...... SILLY GAMES **LINDY LAYTON FEATURING JANET KAY** .... Arista 113452
11/08/1990.....62......3...... SILLY GAMES (REMIX) .... Music Factory Dance MFD 006

DANNY KAYE US singer/actor (born David Daniel Kominsky, 18/1/1913, Brooklyn, NYC) also known for his recordings with the Andrews Sisters. He began in vaudeville, making his Broadway starring debut in 1939, and films included *Hans Christian Andersen*, *White Christmas* and *The Secret Life Of Walter Mitty*. He died from internal bleeding on 3/3/1987. He has three stars on the Hollywood Walk of Fame for his contribution to recording, motion pictures and radio.

27/02/1953.....5......10...... **WONDERFUL COPENHAGEN** Featured in the 1952 film *Hans Christian Andersen* .... Brunswick 05023

KAYE SISTERS UK group (Carole Young, Sheila 'Shan' Palmer and Sheila Jones), who took their stage name after their organiser Carmen Kaye, first recording as The Three Kayes. Shan Palmer was later well known in TV soap operas. They reunited in 1992.

25/05/1956.....20......5...... IVORY TOWER **THREE KAYES** .... HMV POP 209
01/11/1957.....8......11...... **GOTTA HAVE SOMETHING IN THE BANK FRANK** FRANKIE VAUGHAN AND THE KAYE SISTERS .... Philips PB 751
03/01/1958.....27......1...... SHAKE ME I RATTLE/ALONE .... Philips PB 752

	DATE	POS	WKS	BPI	SINGLE TITLE	LABEL & NUMBER
	01/05/1959	9	9		**COME SOFTLY TO ME** FRANKIE VAUGHAN AND THE KAYE SISTERS	Philips PB 913
	07/07/1960	7	19		**PAPER ROSES**	Philips PB 1024

KAYESTONE UK DJ/production duo Derek Kaye and Ricky Stone, with David Jaye also an occasional member.

| | 29/07/2000 | 55 | 1 | | ATMOSPHERE | Distinctive DISNCD 62 |

KC AND THE SUNSHINE BAND US disco group formed in Florida in 1973 by Harry Casey (born 31/1/1951, Hialeah, FL, keyboards/vocals) and Richard Finch (born 25/1/1954, Indianapolis, IN, bass) as KC & The Sunshine Junkanoo Band. With a flexible line-up between seven and eleven strong, Casey and Finch primary writers, also for others on TK label, including George McCrae with *Rock Your Baby*. They won a 1975 Grammy Award for Best Rhythm & Blues Song with Willie Clarke and Betty Wright for *Where Is The Love*. Former guitarist Jerome Smith crushed to death by a bulldozer on 28/7/2000. They have a star on the Hollywood Walk of Fame.

	17/08/1974	7	12		**QUEEN OF CLUBS**	Jayboy BOY 88
	23/11/1974	17	9		SOUND YOUR FUNKY HORN	Jayboy BOY 83
	29/03/1975	21	9		GET DOWN TONIGHT ▲1 Featured in the films *Forrest Gump* (1994), *Picture Perfect* (1997), *Arlington Road* (1998) and *Deuce Bigalow: Male Gigolo* (1999)	Jayboy BOY 93
	02/08/1975	4	10		**THAT'S THE WAY (I LIKE IT)** ▲2 Featured in the films *The Stud* (1978), *Breast Men* (1997) and *Starsky & Hutch* (2004).	Jayboy BOY 99
	22/11/1975	34	3		I'M SO CRAZY ('BOUT YOU)	Jayboy BOY 101
	17/07/1976	22	8		(SHAKE SHAKE SHAKE) SHAKE YOUR BOOTY ▲1 Featured in the 1978 film *The Eyes Of Laura Mars*.	Jayboy BOY 110
	11/12/1976	31	8		KEEP IT COMIN' LOVE Featured in the films *Private Parts* (1996) and *Blow* (2001)	Jayboy BOY 112
	30/04/1977	41	4		I'M YOUR BOOGIE MAN ▲1	TK XB 2167
	06/05/1978	34	5		BOOGIE SHOES Featured in the films *Saturday Night Fever* (1978) and *Boogie Nights* (1998)	TK TKR 6025
	22/07/1978	47	5		IT'S THE SAME OLD SONG	TK TKR 6037
	08/12/1979	3	12	○	PLEASE DON'T GO ▲1	TK TKR 7558
	16/07/1983	❶3	14	●	GIVE IT UP	Epic EPC 3017
	24/09/1983	41	3		(YOU SAID) YOU'D GIMME SOME MORE	Epic A 2760
	11/05/1991	59	2		THAT'S THE WAY (I LIKE IT) (REMIX)	Music Factory Dance M7FAC 2

KE US singer/producer Kevin Grivois.

| | 13/04/1996 | 73 | 1 | | STRANGE WORLD | Venture 74321349412 |

KEANE UK group formed in Sussex by Tom Chaplin (vocals), Tim Rice-Oxley (keyboards) and Richard Hughes (drums).

	28/02/2004	3	12		**SOMEWHERE ONLY WE KNOW**	Island CID 849
	15/05/2004	4	9		**EVERYBODY'S CHANGING** Originally released in 2003 on Fierce Panda and failed to chart. This is a re-recording	Island CID 855
	28/08/2004	10	7		**BEDSHAPED**	Island CID 870
	04/12/2004	18	4+		THIS IS THE LAST TIME	Island CID880

JOHNNY KEATING UK orchestra leader (born 10/9/1927, Edinburgh); film music included *Robbery* and *Innocent Bystanders*.

| | 01/03/1962 | 8 | 14 | | **THEME FROM 'Z-CARS'** Theme to the TV series *Z-Cars*. | Piccadilly 7N 35032 |

RONAN KEATING Irish singer (born 3/3/1977, Dublin); lead singer with Boyzone. He also went into management with Westlife and took part in the *It's Only Rock 'N' Roll* project for the Children's Promise charity.

	07/08/1999	❶2	17	●	WHEN YOU SAY NOTHING AT ALL ↑ Featured in the 1999 film *Notting Hill*	Polydor 5612902
	22/07/2000	❶1	14	●	LIFE IS A ROLLERCOASTER ↑	Polydor 5619362
	02/12/2000	6	12		THE WAY YOU MAKE ME FEEL	Polydor 5878862
	28/04/2001	2	14	○	LOVIN' EACH DAY	Polydor 5876912
	18/05/2002	❶1	15	●	IF TOMORROW NEVER COMES ↑	Polydor 5707192
	21/09/2002	5	11		I LOVE IT WHEN WE DO	Polydor 5709042
	07/12/2002	4	13		WE'VE GOT TONIGHT RONAN KEATING FEATURING LULU	Polydor 0658612
	10/05/2003	3	10		THE LONG GOODBYE	Polydor 0657382
	22/11/2003	9	4		LOST FOR WORDS	Polydor 9813305
	21/02/2004	2	7		SHE BELIEVES (IN ME)	Polydor 9816653
	15/05/2004	5	9		LAST THING ON MY MIND RONAN KEATING AND LEANN RIMES	Polydor/Curb 9866595
	09/10/2004	2	7		I HOPE YOU DANCE	Polydor 9868261
	25/12/2004	2	1+		FATHER AND SON RONAN KEATING AND YUSUF ISLAM	Polydor 9869667

KEE – see BM DUBS PRESENT MR RUMBLE FEATURING BRASSTOOTH AND KEE

KEEDIE – see DUNCAN JAMES AND KEEDIE

KEVIN KEEGAN UK singer (born 14/2/1951, Doncaster), best known as a football player and later manager. At the time of his hit record he was playing in Germany for Hamburg and had just been voted European Footballer of the Year.

| | 09/06/1979 | 31 | 6 | | HEAD OVER HEELS IN LOVE | EMI 2965 |

YVONNE KEELEY – see SCOTT FITZGERALD

NELSON KEENE UK singer (born Malcolm Holland, 1942, Farnborough).

| | 25/08/1960 | 37 | 5 | | IMAGE OF A GIRL | HMV POP 771 |

○ Silver disc ● Gold disc ✪ Platinum disc (additional platinum units are indicated by a figure following the symbol) ◉ Singles released prior to 1973 that are known to have sold over 1 million copies in the UK

KEISHA – see **DESERT EAGLE DISCS FEATURING KEISHA**

KEITH US singer (born James Barry Keefer, 7/5/1949, Philadelphia, PA); he first recorded as Keith & The Admirations in 1965.

26/01/1967	24	7	98.6 Features the uncredited backing vocals of the Tokens.	Mercury MF 955
16/03/1967	50	1	TELL IT TO MY FACE	Mercury MF 968

KEITH 'N' SHANE Irish duo Keith Duffy (born 1/10/1974, Dublin) and Shane Lynch (born 3/7/1976, Dublin); both also in Boyzone. Lynch married Eternal's Easther Bennett in March 1998 and his two sisters, Edele and Keavy, are members of B*Witched. Thus the Lynch family and its offshoots have enjoyed eleven number #1 hits (six for Boyzone, four for B*Witched and one for Eternal)

23/12/2000	36	3	GIRL YOU KNOW IT'S TRUE Contains a sample of Belouis Some's *Imagination*	Polydor 5879462

LISA KEKAULA – see **BASEMENT JAXX**

KELIS US singer (born Kelis Rogers, 21/8/1980, Harlem, NYC). Named 2001 BRIT Awards Best International Newcomer, she also recorded with Moby.

26/02/2000	52	1	CAUGHT OUT THERE (IMPORT)	Virgin 8965102CD
04/03/2000	4	12	**CAUGHT OUT THERE**	Virgin VUSCD 158
17/06/2000	19	5	GOOD STUFF	Virgin VUSDX 164
08/07/2000	11	8	GOT YOUR MONEY **OL' DIRTY BASTARD FEATURING KELIS**	Elektra E 7077CD
21/10/2000	51	1	GET ALONG WITH YOU	Virgin VUSCD 174
03/11/2001	32	2	YOUNG FRESH N' NEW	Virgin VUSCD 212
05/10/2002	65	1	HELP ME **TIMO MAAS FEATURING KELIS**	Perfecto PERF 42CDS
23/08/2003	8	4	**FINEST DREAMS RICHARD X FEATURING KELIS** This song is effectively two songs: the lyrics from SOS Band's *The Finest* with the music from Human League's *Dreams*	Virgin RXCD 2
23/08/2003	25	4	LET'S GET ILL **P DIDDY FEATURING KELIS**	Bad Boy MCSTD 40331
17/01/2004	2	15	O	**MILKSHAKE** Featured in the 2004 film *Mean Girls*	Virgin VSCDX 1863
20/03/2004	5	9	NOT IN LOVE **ENRIQUE FEATURING KELIS**	Interscope 9862023
05/06/2004	2	14	**TRICK ME**	Virgin VSCDX 1872
30/10/2004	3	9+	**MILLIONAIRE KELIS FEATURING ANDRE 3000** Contains a sample of Doug E Fresh & Slick Rick's *La Di Da Di*	Virgin VSCDX 1885

JERRY KELLER US singer (born 20/6/1937, Fort Smith, AR); his first group, the Lads Of Note, formed in Tulsa in the early 1950s. Later a successful songwriter, he appeared in the films *You Light Up My Life* and *If I Ever See You Again*.

28/08/1959	❶[1]	14	**HERE COMES SUMMER**	London HLR 8890

FRANK KELLY Irish singer (born Francis O'Kelly). As an actor appeared in the TV comedy *Father Ted* as Father Jack Hackett.

24/12/1983	26	4	CHRISTMAS COUNTDOWN	Ritz 062
29/12/1984	54	1	CHRISTMAS COUNTDOWN	Ritz 062

FRANKIE KELLY US singer from Washington DC who began with sessions for Herbie Hancock, Melba Moore and Richard Pryor.

02/11/1985	65	2	AIN'T THAT THE TRUTH	10 TEN 87

GRACE KELLY – see **BING CROSBY**

KEITH KELLY UK singer (born Michael Pailthorpe, 1939, Selby). He was previously with the John Barry Seven.

05/05/1960	27	4	TEASE ME	Parlophone R 4640
18/08/1960	47	1	LISTEN LITTLE GIRL	Parlophone R 4676

R KELLY US singer (born Robert Kelly, 8/1/1969, Chicago, IL). He formed Public Announcement, a group of backing singers and dancers, but scored as a solo. Signed with Jive in 1991; he also writes and produces. Rumoured marriage to singer Aaliyah in August 1994 a publicity hoax on her part. Outstanding Achievement Award at the 2001 MOBOs. Big Tigger is US rapper/DJ Darian Morgan.

09/05/1992	57	2	SHE'S GOT THAT VIBE	Jive JIVET 292
20/11/1993	75	1	SEX ME This and above single credited to **R KELLY AND PUBLIC ANNOUNCEMENT**	Jive JIVECD 346
14/05/1994	19	4	YOUR BODY'S CALLIN'	Jive JIVECD 353
03/09/1994	23	3	SUMMER BUNNIES Contains a sample of The Gap Band's *Outstanding*	Jive JIVECD 358
22/10/1994	3	13	**SHE'S GOT THAT VIBE**	Jive JIVECD 364
21/01/1995	8	9	**BUMP N' GRIND** ▲[4]	Jive JIVECD 368
06/05/1995	23	3	THE 4 PLAYS EPS Available as two CDs, both of which featured *Your Body's Calling* and three additional tracks	Jive JIVECD 376
11/11/1995	24	3	YOU REMIND ME OF SOMETHING	Jive JIVECD 388
02/03/1996	23	3	DOWN LOW (NOBODY HAS TO KNOW) **R KELLY FEATURING RONALD ISLEY** Ronald Isley actually plays the part of Mr Biggs in the accompanying video.	Jive JIVERCD 392
22/06/1996	14	4	THANK GOD IT'S FRIDAY	Jive JIVERCD 395

❶[9] Number of weeks single topped the UK chart ↑ Entered the UK chart at #1 ▲[9] Number of weeks single topped the US chart

431

DATE	POS	WKS	BPI	SINGLE TITLE	LABEL & NUMBER
29/03/1997	❶[3]	17	✪	**I BELIEVE I CAN FLY** Featured in the 1996 film *Space Jam*. 1997 Grammy Awards for Best Male Rhythm & Blues Vocal Performance, Best Rhythm & Blues Song and Best Song Written Specifically for a Motion Picture for writer R Kelly. . . . Jive JIVECD 415	
19/07/1997	9	8		**GOTHAM CITY** Featured in the 1997 film *Batman And Robin*. . . . Jive JIVECD 428	
18/07/1998	7	7		**BE CAREFUL** SPARKLE FEATURING R KELLY . . . Jive 0521452	
26/09/1998	16	4		HALF ON A BABY . . . Jive 0521802	
14/11/1998	17	5		HOME ALONE R KELLY FEATURING KEITH MURRAY . . . Jive 0522392	
28/11/1998	3	13	○	**I'M YOUR ANGEL** ▲[6] CELINE DION AND R KELLY . . . Epic 6666282	
31/07/1999	20	5		DID YOU EVER THINK Features the uncredited vocal of Ma$e and contains a sample of Curtis Mayfield's *Right On For The Darkness* . . . Jive 0523612	
16/10/1999	57	2		IF I COULD TURN BACK THE HANDS OF TIME (IMPORT) . . . Jive 0523182	
30/10/1999	2	19	✪	**IF I COULD TURN BACK THE HANDS OF TIME** . . . Jive 0523182	
19/02/2000	73	2		SATISFY YOU (IMPORT) . . . Bad Boy/Arista 792832	
11/03/2000	8	8		**SATISFY YOU** PUFF DADDY FEATURING R KELLY Contains a sample of Club Nouveau's *Why You Treat Me So Bad*. . . . Puff Daddy 74321745592	
22/04/2000	24	3		ONLY THE LOOT CAN MAKE ME HAPPY/WHEN A WOMAN'S FED UP/I CAN'T SLEEP BABY (IF I) . . . Jive 9250282	
21/10/2000	12	6		I WISH . . . Jive 9251292	
31/03/2001	18	6		THE STORM IS OVER. . . . Jive 9251852	
23/06/2001	23	3		FIESTA R KELLY FEATURING JAY-Z . . . Jive 9252142	
02/03/2002	4	12		**THE WORLD'S GREATEST** Featured in the 2002 film *The Greatest* . . . Jive 9253242	
25/05/2002	35	2		HONEY R KELLY AND JAY-Z Contains a sample of The Bee Gees' *Love You Inside Out*. . . . Jive 9253662	
17/05/2003	❶[4]	20	●	**IGNITION** ↑ . . . Jive 9254982	
23/08/2003	8	5		**SNAKE** R KELLY FEATURING BIG TIGGER . . . Jive 82876547232	
15/11/2003	14	4		STEP IN THE NAME OF LOVE/THOIA THONG . . . Jive 82876573912	
29/05/2004	3	14		**HOTEL** CASSIDY FEATURING R KELLY . . . J Records 82876618612	
30/10/2004	6	9+		**HAPPY PEOPLE** . . . Jive 82876656182	
06/11/2004	❶[1]	8+		**WONDERFUL** ↑ JA RULE FEATURING R KELLY AND ASHANTI . . . Def Jam 9864606	
20/11/2004	28	3		SO SEXY TWISTA FEATURING R KELLY . . . Atlantic AT 0187CD	

RAMONA KELLY – see CEVIN FISHER

ROBERTA KELLY US singer discovered by producer Giorgio Moroder; she later sang backing vocals for Donna Summer.

21/01/1978	44	3		ZODIACS . . . Oasis/Hansa 3	

KELLY FAMILY Irish family group of Kathy, John, Patricia, Jimmy, Joey, Barby, Paddy, Maite and Angelo Kelly. They launched their own Kel-Life record label.

21/10/1995	69	1		AN ANGEL . . . EMI CDEM 390	

TRICIA LEE KELSHALL – see WAY OUT WEST

JOHNNY KEMP Bahamian singer (born 1966, Nassau, raised Harlem, NYC).

27/08/1988	68	1		JUST GOT PAID . . . CBS 6514707	

TARA KEMP US singer (born 11/5/1964, San Francisco).

20/04/1991	69	2		HOLD YOU TIGHT . . . Giant W 0020	

GRAHAM KENDRICK UK singer (born 2/8/1950, Northamptonshire); trained as a teacher, began a singing career in 1972.

09/09/1989	55	4		LET THE FLAME BURN BRIGHTER . . . Power P 30	

EDDIE KENDRICKS US singer (born 17/12/1939, Union Springs, AL); in the late 1950s joined the Primes in Detroit, MI, who were later the Temptations. Sang lead after David Ruffin's departure, then left in 1973 to go solo, rejoining them in 1982. In 1984 he dropped the 's' from his name, apparently because Motown owned the rights to it! He had a lung removed in 1989 after years of heavy smoking and died from cancer on 5/10/1992.

03/11/1973	18	14		KEEP ON TRUCKIN' ▲[2] . . . Tamla Motown TMG 873	
16/03/1974	39	4		BOOGIE DOWN . . . Tamla Motown TMG 888	
21/09/1985	58	2		A NIGHT AT THE APOLLO LIVE! DARYL HALL AND JOHN OATES FEATURING DAVID RUFFIN AND EDDIE KENDRICK . . . RCA PB 49935	

KENICKIE UK group formed in Sunderland in 1984 by Lauren Laverne (vocals), Marie Du Santiago (guitar), Emmy-Kate Montrose (bass) and Lauren's brother Johnny X (drums). Named after a character in *Grease*. Laverne later with Mint Royale and guest DJ for XFM.

14/09/1996	43	2		PUNKA. . . . Emidisc CDDISC 001	
16/11/1996	60	1		MILLIONAIRE SWEEPER . . . Emidisc CDDISC 002	
11/01/1997	24	3		IN YOUR CAR . . . Emidisc CDDISCX 005	
03/05/1997	27	2		NIGHTLIFE . . . Emidisc CDDISCX 006	
05/07/1997	38	2		PUNKA. . . . Emidisc CDDISCS 007	
06/06/1998	36	2		I WOULD FIX YOU . . . EMI CDEM 513	
22/08/1998	43	1		STAY IN THE SUN . . . EMI CDEMS 520	

JANE KENNAWAY AND STRANGE BEHAVIOUR UK singer/guitarist with instrumental group. The daughter of the late novelist James Kennaway, her debut hit was originally released on the Growing Up In Hollywood label.

DATE	POS	WKS	BPI	SINGLE TITLE	LABEL & NUMBER
24/01/1981	65	3		I.O.U	Deram DM 436

BRIAN KENNEDY Irish singer/songwriter (born 12/10/1966, Belfast), ex-Van Morrison's Blues & Soul Revue who co-writes with many other writers.

22/06/1996	28	3		A BETTER MAN	RCA 74321382642
21/09/1996	27	3		LIFE, LOVE AND HAPPINESS	RCA 74321409912
05/04/1997	37	2		PUT THE MESSAGE IN THE BOX	RCA 74321462272

KEVIN KENNEDY UK singer (born Kevin Williams, 4/9/1961, Manchester); since 1983 played *Coronation Street's* Curly Watts.

24/06/2000	70	1		BULLDOG NATION	D2m 74321759742

KENNY Irish singer (born Tony Kenny).

03/03/1973	11	13		HEART OF STONE	RAK 144
30/06/1973	38	3		GIVE IT TO ME NOW	RAK 153

KENNY UK pop group formed by Richard Driscoll (vocals), Jan Style (guitar), Christopher Lacklison (keyboards), Chris Redburn (bass) and Andy Walton (drums); their hits also featuring session musicians including Chris Spedding.

07/12/1974	3	15	O	THE BUMP	RAK 186
08/03/1975	4	9		FANCY PANTS	RAK 196
07/06/1975	12	7		BABY I LOVE YOU OK	RAK 207
16/08/1975	10	8		JULIE ANN	RAK 214

GERARD KENNY US singer/songwriter (born 8/7/1947, New York City).

09/12/1978	43	8		NEW YORK, NY	RCA PB 5117
21/06/1980	34	6		FANTASY	RCA PB 5256
18/02/1984	69	4		THE OTHER WOMAN, THE OTHER MAN	Impression IMS 3
04/05/1985	56	3		NO MAN'S LAND Theme to the TV series *Widows*	WEA YZ 38

PATSY KENSIT – see AVID MERRION, DAVINA McCALL AND PATSY KENSIT

KENT Swedish group formed in Eskilstuna in 1990 by Joakim Berg (vocals), Sami Sirvio (guitar), Martin Roos (guitar), Martin Skold (bass) and Markus Mustonen (drums).

13/03/1999	61	1		747	RCA 74321645912

KLARK KENT US singer/drummer (born Stewart Copeland, 16/7/1952, Alexandria, Egypt); founding member of The Police in 1977, later forming Animal Logic.

26/08/1978	48	4		DON'T CARE	A&M AMS 7376

KERBDOG Irish group originally formed in Kilkenny by Cormac Battle (guitar/vocals), Colin Fenelly (bass), Billy Dalton (guitar) and Darragh Butler (drums) as Rollercoaster. Dalton left in 1995 and the group continued as a trio.

12/03/1994	60	1		DRY RISER	Vertigo VERCC 83
06/08/1994	37	2		DUMMY CRUSHER	Vertigo VERCD 86
12/10/1996	69	1		SALLY	Fontana KERCD 2
29/03/1997	49	1		MEXICAN WAVE	Fontana KERCD 3

DICK KERR – see SLIM DUSTY

ANITA KERR SINGERS – see BOBBY HELMS

KERRI AND MICK Australian vocal duo Kerri Biddell and Mick Leyton.

28/04/1984	68	3		SONS AND DAUGHTERS' THEME Theme to the TV series of the same name	A1 286

KERRI-ANN Irish singer.

08/08/1998	58	1		DO YOU LOVE ME BOY?	Ragtan Road 5671012

LIZ KERSHAW AND BRUNO BROOKES UK vocal duo of radio DJs Liz Kershaw and Bruno Brookes (Trevor Brookes). Both their hits were in aid of the BBC's 'Children In Need' appeal.

02/12/1989	53	2		IT TAKES TWO BABY LIZ KERSHAW, BRUNO BROOKES, JIVE BUNNY AND LONDONBEAT	Spartan CIN 101
01/12/1990	54	1		LET'S DANCE BRUNO AND LIZ AND THE RADIO 1 POSSE	Jive BRUNO 1

NIK KERSHAW UK singer/writer/guitarist/keyboard player (born 1/3/1958, Bristol) who debuted in 1980 in Fusion. Later a songwriter, he wrote hits for Let Loose, The Hollies and Chesney Hawkes.

19/11/1983	47	5		I WON'T LET THE SUN GO DOWN ON ME	MCA 816
28/01/1984	4	14	O	WOULDN'T IT BE GOOD	MCA NIK 2
14/04/1984	13	9		DANCING GIRLS	MCA NIK 3
16/06/1984	2	13	O	I WON'T LET THE SUN GO DOWN ON ME	MCA NIK 4
15/09/1984	19	7		HUMAN RACING	MCA NIK 5
17/11/1984	3	11	O	THE RIDDLE	MCA NIK 6
16/03/1985	9	8		WIDE BOY	MCA NIK 7

❶⁹ Number of weeks single topped the UK chart ⬆ Entered the UK chart at #1 ▲⁹ Number of weeks single topped the US chart

433

DATE	POS	WKS	BPI	SINGLE TITLE	LABEL & NUMBER
03/08/1985	10	7		DON QUIXOTE	MCA NIK 8
30/11/1985	27	7		WHEN A HEART BEATS	MCA NIK 9
11/10/1986	44	3		NOBODY KNOWS	MCA NIK 10
13/12/1986	43	2		RADIO MUSICOLA	MCA NIK 11
04/02/1989	55	1		ONE STEP AHEAD	MCA NIK 12
27/02/1999	70	1		SOMEBODY LOVES YOU	Eagle EAGXA 023
07/08/1999	56	1		SOMETIMES LES RYTHMES DIGITALES FEATURING NIK KERSHAW	Wall Of Sound WALLD 054

KEVIN AND PERRY – see PRECOCIOUS BRATS FEATURING KEVIN AND PERRY

KEVIN THE GERBIL UK gerbil singer, the partner of Roland The Rat.

| 04/08/1984 | 50 | 6 | | SUMMER HOLIDAY | Magnet RAT 3 |

KEY WEST – see ERIK

KEYNOTES – see DAVE KING

ALICIA KEYS US singer (born Alicia Augello Cook, 25/1/1981, Manhattan) who began songwriting aged fourteen, having played the piano since the age of seven. Signed by Arista Records in 1998, she followed label boss Clive Davies when he set up J Records, with a debut album in 2001 that sold 50,000 copies on its first day of release in the US. Alicia had previously contributed to the soundtrack to *Shaft*. Five Grammies include Best Rhythm and Blues Album for *Songs In A Minor* and Best New Artist in 2001. She also won the 2002 MTV Europe Music Award for Best Rhythm and Blues Act (and repeated that success in 2004) and the 2002 MOBO Award for Best Album for *Songs In A Minor*.

10/11/2001	3	10		FALLIN' ▲⁶ 2001 Grammy Award for Best Rhythm & Blues Vocal Performance. 2001 Grammy Awards for Song of the Year and Best Rhythm & Blues Song for writer Alicia Keys	J Records 74321903692
09/03/2002	37	2		BROTHA PART II ANGIE STONE FEATURING ALICIA KEYS AND EVE Contains a sample of Albert King's *I'll Play The Blues For You* ... J Records 74321922142	
30/03/2002	18	8		A WOMAN'S WORTH	J Records 74321928692
20/07/2002	26	3		HOW COME YOU DON'T CALL ME	J Records 74321943122
05/10/2002	6	8		GANGSTA LOVIN' EVE FEATURING ALICIA KEYS Contains a sample of Yarbrough & Peoples' *Don't Stop The Music* ... Interscope 4978042	
07/12/2002	24	5		GIRLFRIEND	J Records 74321974972
20/12/2003	19	9		YOU DON'T KNOW MY NAME Contains a sample of The Main Ingredient's *Let Me Prove My Love To You*	J Records 82876588652
10/04/2004	18	5		IF I AIN'T GOT YOU	J Records 82876608172

CHAKA KHAN US singer (born Yvette Marie Stevens, 23/3/1953, Great Lakes, IL); she replaced Paulette McWilliams as lead singer with Ask Rufus in 1972. She signed solo with Atlantic in 1978, leaving the group in 1980 after fulfiling her contractual obligations. Her sister Taka Boom fronted Undisputed Truth. Six Grammy Awards include Best Rhythm & Blues Vocal Performance (1983) for *Chaka Khan*, Best Arrangement for Two or More Voices (1983) with Arif Mardin for *Be Bop Medley*, Best Rhythm & Blues Vocal Performance (1984) for *I Feel For You*, Best Rhythm & Blues Vocal Performance (1992) for *The Woman I Am* and Best Traditional Rhythm and Blues Vocal Performance (2002) with The Funk Brothers for *What's Going On*. Also Lifetime Achievement Award at 2002's MOBOs.

02/12/1978	11	13		I'M EVERY WOMAN Featured in the 2001 film *Bridget Jones's Diary*	Warner Brothers K 17269
31/03/1984	8	12	○	AIN'T NOBODY RUFUS AND CHAKA KHAN Featured in the 1984 film *Breakin'*. 1983 Grammy Award for Best Rhythm & Blues Vocal Performance by a Group	Warner Brothers RCK 1
20/10/1984	❶³	16	●	I FEEL FOR YOU Features the uncredited contributions of Grandmaster Melle Mel and Stevie Wonder. 1984 Grammy Award for Best Rhythm & Blues Song for writer Prince	Warner Brothers W 9209
19/01/1985	14	6		THIS IS MY NIGHT	Warner Brothers W 9097
20/04/1985	16	7		EYE TO EYE	Warner Brothers W 9009
12/07/1986	52	4		LOVE OF A LIFETIME	Warner Brothers W 8671
21/01/1989	71	2		IT'S MY PARTY	Warner Brothers W 7678
06/05/1989	8	8		I'M EVERY WOMAN (REMIX)	Warner Brothers W 2963
08/07/1989	6	9		AIN'T NOBODY (REMIX) RUFUS AND CHAKA KHAN	Warner Brothers W 2880
07/10/1989	45	2		I FEEL FOR YOU (REMIX)	Warner Brothers W 2764
13/01/1990	21	7		I'LL BE GOOD TO YOU QUINCY JONES FEATURING RAY CHARLES AND CHAKA KHAN 1990 Grammy Award for Best Rhythm & Blues Vocal Performance by a Duo	Qwest W 2697
28/03/1992	49	3		LOVE YOU ALL MY LIFETIME	Warner Brothers W 0087
17/07/1993	73	1		DON'T LOOK AT ME THAT WAY	Warner Brothers W 0192CD
19/08/1995	28	3		WATCH WHAT YOU SAY GURU FEATURING CHAKA KHAN	Cooltempo CDCOOL 308
01/03/1997	59	1		NEVER MISS THE WATER CHAKA KHAN FEATURING ME'SHELL NDEGEOCELLO	Reprise W 1393CD
11/11/2000	33	3		ALL GOOD DE LA SOUL FEATURING CHAKA KHAN	Tommy Boy TBCD 2154B

PRAGA KHAN Belgian producer Maurice Engelen, who also recorded as Lords of Acid, Channel X, Digital Orgasm. Jade 4 U is Belgian singer Nikki Danlierop.

04/04/1992	16	6		FREE YOUR BODY/INJECTED WITH A POISON PRAGA KHAN FEATURING JADE 4 U	Profile PROFT 347
11/07/1992	39	2		RAVE ALERT	Profile PROF 369
24/11/2001	52	1		INJECTED WITH A POISON (REMIX)	Nukleuz NUKC 0238

KHIA US singer (born Khia Finch but also known as Khia Chambers, 1973, Philadelphia, PA; raised in Tampa, FL).

| 16/10/2004 | 4 | 11+ | | MY NECK MY BACK (LICK IT) | Direction 6753802 |

MARY KIANI UK singer who was previously lead with Time Frequency before going solo.

12/08/1995	18	4		WHEN I CALL YOUR NAME	Mercury MERCD 440
23/12/1995	35	4		I GIVE IT ALL TO YOU/I IMAGINE	Mercury MERCD 449
27/04/1996	19	3		LET THE MUSIC PLAY	Mercury MERCD 456
18/01/1997	23	3		100%	Mercury MERCD 469
21/06/1997	46	1		WITH OR WITHOUT YOU	Mercury MERCD 487

KICK HORNS – see DODGY

KICK SQUAD UK/German vocal and instrumental group.

10/11/1990	59	2		SOUND CLASH (CHAMPION SOUND)	Kickin KICK 2

KICKING BACK WITH TAXMAN UK vocal/instrumental group with rapper Taxman.

17/03/1990	47	4		DEVOTION	10 TEN 297
07/07/1990	54	4		EVERYTHING	10 TEN 307

KICKS LIKE A MULE UK instrumental/production duo Nick Halkes and Richard Russell, Halkes launching Positiva Records.

01/02/1992	7	6		**THE BOUNCER**	Tribal Bass TRIBE 35

K.I.D. Antilles vocal/instrumental group assembled by producer Geoffrey Bastow.

28/02/1981	49	4		DON'T STOP	EMI 5143

KID CRÈME Belgian DJ Nicolas Scaravilli (born 1974). Charlise is Belgian singer Charlise Rookwood.

22/03/2003	55	1		DOWN AND UNDER (TOGETHER) **KID CRÈME FEATURING MC SHURAKANO**	Ink NIBNE 13CD
10/05/2003	31	2		HYPNOTISING **KID CRÈME FEATURING CHARLISE** Contains a sample of Monica De Lux's *Temperature's Rising*	Positiva CDTIV 189

KID 'N' PLAY US rap duo Christopher 'Kid' Reid (born 5/4/1964, New York) and Christopher 'Play' Martin (born 10/7/1962, New York).

18/07/1987	71	1		LAST NIGHT Contains a sample of Dexter Wansel's *Theme From The Planets*	Cooltempo COOL 148
26/03/1988	48	3		DO THIS MY WAY	Cooltempo COOL 164
17/09/1988	55	3		GITTIN' FUNKY	Cooltempo COOL 168

KID ROCK US rapper (born Robert Ritchie, 17/1/1971, Romeo, MI); he formed break dance crew the Furious Funkers, worked with Boogie Down Productions, producing debut album in 1990. In *It's Only Rock 'N' Roll* for the Children's Promise charity.

23/10/1999	36	2		COWBOY	Atlantic AT 0076CD
09/09/2000	25	4		AMERICAN BAD ASS	Atlantic AT 0085CD
12/05/2001	41	2		BAWITDABA	Atlantic AT 0098CD

KID UNKNOWN UK producer Paul Fitzpatrick.

02/05/1992	64	1		NIGHTMARE	Warp WAP 20CD

CAROL KIDD FEATURING TERRY WAITE UK vocal duo Carol Kidd and Terry Waite (born 31/5/1939, Cheshire). Kidd had worked with David Newton, Humphrey Lyttelton and Allan Ganley, Waite was famous as a hostage in Beirut during the 1980s.

17/10/1992	58	3		WHEN I DREAM	The Hit Label HLS 1

JOHNNY KIDD AND THE PIRATES UK group formed in London in 1959 by Johnny Kidd (born Frederick Heath, 23/12/1939, London), Alan Caddy (guitar), Johnny Gordon (bass), Ken McKay (drums) and backing singers Mike West and Tom Brown. By 1962 the line-up was Mick Green (guitar), Johnny Spence (bass) and Frank Farley (drums). Although a backing group for Johnny Kidd, The Pirates recorded without him from 1964. Green left in 1964, replaced by John Weider. The Pirates left Kidd in April 1966. Kidd formed a new group, disbanded when he was killed in a car crash on 7/10/1966. The Pirates re-formed in 1976.

12/06/1959	25	5		PLEASE DON'T TOUCH **JOHNNY KIDD**	HMV POP 615
12/02/1960	25	3		YOU GOT WHAT IT TAKES	HMV POP 698
16/06/1960	❶1	19		**SHAKIN' ALL OVER**	HMV POP 753
06/10/1960	22	7		RESTLESS	HMV POP 790
13/04/1961	47	1		LINDA LU	HMV POP 853
10/01/1963	48	1		SHOT OF RHYTHM AND BLUES	HMV POP 1088
25/07/1963	4	15		**I'LL NEVER GET OVER YOU**	HMV POP 1173
28/11/1963	20	10		HUNGRY FOR LOVE	HMV POP 1228
30/04/1964	46	1		ALWAYS AND EVER	HMV POP 1269

NICOLE KIDMAN Australian singer/actor (born 20/6/1967, Honolulu, HI, to Australian parents) whose family settled in Washington DC (her father, Anthony, was a pioneer in the study of breast cancer) before returning to Australia. After film debut in *Bush Christmas* (1983), she won an Australian Film Institute Award before her US debut in *Dead Calm* (1989). Following *Days Of Thunder* with Tom Cruise in 1990 she married him on Christmas Eve. They split early 2001, negotiating a lengthy divorce settlement. Nicole has a star on the Hollywood Walk of Fame.

06/10/2001	27	5		COME WHAT MAY **NICOLE KIDMAN AND EWAN MCGREGOR** Featured in the 2001 film *Moulin Rouge*	Interscope 4976302
22/12/2001	❶3	12	○	**SOMETHIN' STUPID** ↑ **ROBBIE WILLIAMS AND NICOLE KIDMAN**	Chrysalis CDCHS 5132

KIDS FROM 'FAME' US group, a spin-off from the TV series that featured Debbie Allen (as Lydia), Carlo Imperato (Danny), Valerie Landsburg (Doris), Carol Mayo (Coco), Lori Singer (Julie) and Gene Anthony Ray (Leroy). The series itself was inspired by the film

❶9 Number of weeks single topped the UK chart ↑ Entered the UK chart at #1 ▲9 Number of weeks single topped the US chart

435

Fame, the title track of which was a UK #1 by Irene Cara (for the TV series the same number was sung by Erica Gimpel). Ray suffered a stroke in June 2003 and died on 14/11/2003.

14/08/1982	5	10	○	**HI-FIDELITY** KIDS FROM FAME FEATURING VALERIE LANDSBERG	RCA 254
02/10/1982	3	10	●	**STARMAKER**	RCA 280
11/12/1982	50	6		MANNEQUIN KIDS FROM FAME FEATURING GENE ANTHONY RAY	RCA 299
09/04/1983	13	10		FRIDAY NIGHT (LIVE VERSION)	RCA 320

GREG KIHN BAND
US singer/guitarist (born 10/7/1950, Baltimore, MD); formed band in 1976 with Robbie Dunbar (guitar), Steve Wright (bass) and Larry Lynch (drums). Dunbar left after one LP, replaced by Dave Carpender, Gary Phillips (guitar) also joined in 1981.

| 23/04/1983 | 63 | 2 | | JEOPARDY | Beserkley E 9847 |

KILLAH PRIEST
US rapper (born William Reed, New York); he is also a member of Sunz Of Man.

| 07/02/1998 | 45 | 1 | | ONE STEP | Geffen GFSTD 22318 |

KILLCITY
UK group formed by Lisa Moorish (vocals), Tom Bowen (guitar), Rich (guitar), Pete Jones (bass) and Vas (drums). Rich and Vas later left and were replaced by Stuart Le Page (guitar) and a drum machine respectively.

| 14/08/2004 | 63 | 1 | | JUST LIKE BRUCE LEE | Poptones MC5091SCD |

KILLER MIKE
US rapper (born Mike Render, Adamsville, GA). Big Boi is a member of Outkast.

06/04/2002	19	5		THE WHOLE WORLD OUTKAST FEATURING KILLER MIKE 2002 Grammy Award for Best Rap Performance by a Duo or Group	
					LaFace 74321917592
27/07/2002	46	1		LAND OF A MILLION DRUMS OUTKAST FEATURING KILLER MIKE AND S BROWN	Atlantic AT 0134CD
10/05/2003	22	3		A.D.I.D.A.S. KILLER MIKE FEATURING BIG BOI	Columbia 6738652

KILLERS
US rock group formed in Las Vegas, NE by Brandon Flowers (vocals), David Keuning (guitar), Mark Steormer (bass) and Ronnie Vannucci (drums).

27/03/2004	28	2		SOMEBODY TOLD ME	Lizard King LIZARD009
05/06/2004	10	4		**MR BRIGHTSIDE**	Lizard King LIZARD010CD2
11/09/2004	18	4		ALL THESE THINGS THAT I'VE DONE	Lizard King LIZARD012

KILLING JOKE
UK group formed in London in 1979 by Jeremy 'Jaz' Coleman (born 26/2/1960, Cheltenham, vocals), 'Big' Paul Ferguson (born 31/3/1958, High Wycombe, drums), Geordie (born K Walker 18/12/1958, Newcastle, guitar) and Martin 'Pig Youth' Glover (born 27/12/1960, Africa).

23/05/1981	55	5		FOLLOW THE LEADERS	Malicious Damage EGMDS 101
20/03/1982	43	4		EMPIRE SONG	Malicious Damage EGO 4
30/10/1982	64	2		BIRDS OF A FEATHER	EG EGO 10
25/06/1983	51	3		LET'S ALL (GO TO THE FIRE DANCES)	EG EGO 11
15/10/1983	57	1		ME OR YOU?	EG EGO 14
07/04/1984	60	5		EIGHTIES Featured in the 1985 film *Weird Science*	EG EGO 16
21/07/1984	56	2		A NEW DAY	EG EGO 17
02/02/1985	16	9		LOVE LIKE BLOOD	EG EGO 20
30/03/1985	58	3		KINGS AND QUEENS	EG EGO 21
16/08/1986	42	6		ADORATIONS	EG EGO 27
18/10/1986	70	1		SANITY	EG EGO 30
07/05/1994	34	2		MILLENNIUM	Butterfly BFLD 12
16/07/1994	28	3		THE PANDEMONIUM SINGLE	Butterfly BFLDA 17
04/02/1995	54	1		JANA	Butterfly BFLDA 21
23/03/1996	39	1		DEMOCRACY	Butterfly BFLDB 33
26/07/2003	25	2		LOOSE CANNON	Zuma Recordings ZUMAD004

KILLS
UK duo formed in 2001 by VV (Alison Mosshart, vocals) and Hotel (Jamie Hince).

| 26/04/2003 | 55 | 1 | | FRIED MY LITTLE BRAINS | Domino Recordings RUG 154CD |

ANDY KIM
Canadian singer (born Andrew Joachim, 5/12/1946, Montreal). His limited US solo success in the late 1960s was followed by fame as the singer of the Archies, after which he resumed his solo career.

| 24/08/1974 | 2 | 12 | ○ | **ROCK ME GENTLY** ▲[1] | Capitol CL 15787 |

KINANE
Irish singer (born Bianca Kinane, 1977, Clonmel).

18/05/1996	59	1		ALL THE LOVER I NEED	Coliseum TOGA 003CD
21/09/1996	73	1		THE WOMAN IN ME This and above single credited to BIANCA KINANE	Coliseum TOGA 007CD
16/05/1998	49	1		HEAVEN	Coalition COLA 047CD
22/08/1998	63	1		SO FINE	Coalition COLA 055CD1

KINESIS
UK rock group formed in Bolton in 2000 by Michael Bromley (born 30/9/1983, guitar/vocals), Conor McGloin (born 14/12/1984, guitar/keyboards), Tom Marshall (born 14/4/1983, bass) and Neil Chow (born 28/6/1984, drums).

22/03/2003	63	1		AND THEY OBEY	Independiente ISOM 68MS
28/06/2003	65	1		FOREVER REELING	Independiente ISOM 74MS
27/09/2003	71	1		ONE WAY MIRROR	Independiente ISOM 77MS

○ Silver disc   ● Gold disc   ✪ Platinum disc (additional platinum units are indicated by a figure following the symbol)   ◎ Singles released prior to 1973 that are known to have sold over 1 million copies in the UK

KING UK group formed in Coventry by ex-Reluctant Stereotypes Paul King (born 20/1/1960, Coventry, vocals), Mick Roberts (keyboards), Tony Wall (bass) and Jim Jackal (born Jim Lantsbery, guitar). King later went solo before becoming a presenter on VH-1.

12/01/1985	2	14	●	**LOVE AND PRIDE**	CBS A 4988
23/03/1985	24	8		WON'T YOU HOLD MY HAND NOW	CBS A 6094
17/08/1985	8	9		**ALONE WITHOUT YOU**	CBS A 6308
19/10/1985	11	9		THE TASTE OF YOUR TEARS	CBS A 6618
11/01/1986	23	4		TORTURE	CBS A 6761

ALBERT KING – see **GARY MOORE**

BB KING US singer/guitarist (born Riley B King, 16/9/1925, Itta Bena, MS) who initially picked cotton alongside his parents and sang gospel in his spare time. In 1945 he moved to Memphis, sharing a room with a cousin, Bukka White (though he was unable to pay off his debts to the plantation owner until 1948) and busking on street corners. Appearing on radio stations KWEM and WDIA, the latter billed him as the 'Beale Street Blues Boy' (amended to Blues Boy King and then BB King); he debuted for Bullet Records in 1949. He was inducted into the Rock & Roll Hall of Fame in 1987 and has won twelve Grammy Awards: Best Rhythm and Blues Solo Vocal Performance, Male in 1970 for *The Thrill Is Gone*, Best Traditional Blues Recording in 1983 for *Blues 'N' Jazz*, Best Traditional Blues Recording in 1985 for *My Guitar Sings The Blues*, Best Traditional Blues Recording in 1990 for *Live At San Quentin*, Best Traditional Blues Album in 1991 for *Live At The Apollo*, Best Traditional Blues Album in 1993 for *Blues Summit*, Best Rock Instrumental in 1996 with Jimmie Vaughan, Eric Clapton, Bonnie Raitt, Robert Cray, Buddy Guy, Dr John and Art Neville for *SRV Shuffle*, Best Traditional Blues in 1999 for *Blues On The Bayou*, Best Pop Collaboration with Vocals in 2000 with Dr John for *Is You Is, Or Is You Ain't (My Baby)*, Best Traditional Blues Album with Eric Clapton for *Riding With The King* in 2000, Best Pop Instrumental Performance in 2002 for *Auld Lang Syne* and Best Traditional Blues Album the same year for *A Cristmas Celebration Of Hope*. He also won the 1998 MOBO Award for Lifetime Achievement. His guitar, usually a Gibson 335 or Gibson 355, has been known as 'Lucille' after a live date in Twist, AZ in the late 1940s. A fight broke out and a stove was knocked over, the building catching fire. BB rescued his guitar, later discovering the fight had been over a woman, Lucille. He has a star on the Hollywood Walk of Fame.

15/04/1989	6	7		**WHEN LOVE COMES TO TOWN** U2 WITH BB KING	Island IS 411
18/07/1992	59	3		SINCE I MET YOU BABY **GARY MOORE AND BB KING**	Virgin VS 1423

BEN E KING US singer (born Benjamin Earl Nelson, 23/9/1938, Henderson, NC) who was with the Four B's and Moonglows before the Five Crowns in 1957. Drifters' manager George Treadwell hired the Crowns as the new Drifters in 1958, King singing lead on hits before being sacked for complaining about low wages. He went solo, signing with Atco five months later. He was later in The Soul Clan with Solomon Burke, Arthur Conley, Don Covay and Joe Tex.

02/02/1961	27	11		FIRST TASTE OF LOVE	London HLK 9258
22/06/1961	27	7		STAND BY ME Featured in the films *The Wanderers* (1979) and *Stand By Me* (1986)	London HLK 9358
05/10/1961	38	4		AMOR AMOR	London HLK 9416
14/02/1987	❶³	11	●	**STAND BY ME** Revived following use in a Levi Jeans advertisement.	Atlantic A 9361
04/07/1987	69	2		SAVE THE LAST DANCE FOR ME	Manhattan MT 25

CAROLE KING US singer (born Carole Klein, 9/2/1942, Brooklyn, NYC); she began songwriting in 1958, teaming with lyricist (and future husband) Gerry Goffin on four US #1s: *Will You Love Me Tomorrow, Go Away Little Girl, Take Good Care Of My Baby* and *The Loco-Motion*. Her debut solo record was in 1959; she resumed her career in 1967 following divorce from Goffin. Four 1971 Grammy Awards included Album of the Year and Best Pop Vocal Performance for *Tapestry,* and Song of the Year for *You've Got A Friend*.

20/09/1962	3	13		**IT MIGHT AS WELL RAIN UNTIL SEPTEMBER**	London HLU 9591
07/08/1971	6	12		**IT'S TOO LATE** ▲⁵ 1971 Grammy Award for Record of the Year.	A&M AMS 849
28/10/1972	43	4		IT MIGHT AS WELL RAIN UNTIL SEPTEMBER Re-issue of London HLU 9591	London HL 10391

DAVE KING UK singer (born 23/6/1929, Twickenham), first known via TV shows *Showcase* and *Television Music Hall*. His earliest records were produced by George Martin for Parlophone. He had his own TV series in 1959, and died on 17/4/2002.

17/02/1956	5	15		**MEMORIES ARE MADE OF THIS**	Decca F 10684
13/04/1956	11	9		YOU CAN'T BE TRUE TO TWO This and above single credited to **DAVE KING FEATURING THE KEYNOTES**	Decca F 10720
21/12/1956	23	2		CHRISTMAS AND YOU	Decca F 10791
24/01/1958	20	3		THE STORY OF MY LIFE	Decca F 10973

DENIS KING – see **STUTZ BEARCATS AND THE DENIS KING ORCHESTRA**

DIANA KING Jamaican singer (born 8/11/1970, St Catherine's); played local clubs for eight years then toured as a backing singer with Shabba Ranks, relocating to New York in the process. She was signed as a solo artist by Sony in 1995.

08/07/1995	2	13	○	**SHY GUY** Featured in the 1995 film *Bad Boys*	Columbia 6621682
28/10/1995	13	5		AIN'T NOBODY	Work 6625495
01/11/1997	17	4		I SAY A LITTLE PRAYER Featured in the 1997 film *My Best Friend's Wedding*	Columbia 6651472

EVELYN KING US singer (born 29/6/1960, The Bronx, NYC); she moved to Philadelphia, PA in 1970. Discovered by producer T Life covering for her sister, who was a cleaner at Sigma Studios. Later worked with Kashif, who produced her biggest UK hit.

13/05/1978	39	23	○	SHAME Featured in the 1998 film *The Last Days Of Disco*	RCA PC 1122
03/02/1979	67	2		I DON'T KNOW IF IT'S RIGHT This and above single credited to **EVELYN 'CHAMPAGNE' KING**	RCA PB 1386
27/06/1981	27	11		I'M IN LOVE	RCA 95
26/09/1981	43	6		IF YOU WANT MY LOVIN'	RCA 131
28/08/1982	7	13	○	**LOVE COME DOWN**	RCA 249
20/11/1982	40	4		BACK TO LOVE	RCA 287

❶⁹ Number of weeks single topped the UK chart ↑ Entered the UK chart at #1 ▲⁹ Number of weeks single topped the US chart

437

DATE	POS	WKS	BPI	SINGLE TITLE	LABEL & NUMBER
19/02/1983	45	5		GET LOOSE	RCA 315
09/11/1985	37	5		YOUR PERSONAL TOUCH	RCA PB 49915
29/03/1986	55	3		HIGH HORSE	RCA PB 49891
23/07/1988	47	3		HOLD ON TO WHAT YOU'VE GOT	Manhattan MT 49
10/10/1992	74	1		SHAME (REMIX) ALTERN 8 VS EVELYN KING	Network NWKTEN 56

JONATHAN KING UK singer (born Kenneth George King, 6/12/1944, London); at university when he had his debut hit. After completing his degree he became a singer, songwriter, producer, broadcaster, record company executive and journalist. He named and produced Genesis, founded UK Records and was responsible for the selection of Britain's entry to the Eurovision Song Contest, helping the UK win in 1997. In November 2000 he was accused of sex attacks on boys dating back to 1970, and in January 2001 he was charged with seven counts of assaults against youths under 16. He was sentenced to seven years in prison, though he had already served two months in prison after being convicted of assault charges against the same youths.

DATE	POS	WKS	BPI	SINGLE TITLE	LABEL & NUMBER
29/07/1965	4	11		EVERYONE'S GONE TO THE MOON	Decca F 12187
10/01/1970	26	7		LET IT ALL HANG OUT	Decca F 12988
16/01/1971	19	9		IT'S THE SAME OLD SONG WEATHERMEN	B&C CB 139
03/04/1971	12	14		SUGAR SUGAR SAKKARIN	RCA 2064
29/05/1971	23	8		LAZY BONES	Decca F 13177
20/11/1971	23	10		HOOKED ON A FEELING	Decca F 13241
05/02/1972	22	9		FLIRT	Decca F 13276
14/10/1972	4	13		LOOP DI LOVE SHAG	UK 7
26/01/1974	29	5		(I CAN'T GET NO) SATISFACTION BUBBLEROCK	UK 53
06/09/1975	5	11		UNA PALOMA BLANCA	UK 105
20/09/1975	36	4		CHICK-A-BOOM (DON'T YA JES LOVE IT) 53RD AND 3RD FEATURING THE SOUND OF SHAG	UK 2012 002
07/02/1976	46	3		IN THE MOOD SOUND 9418	UK 121
26/06/1976	9	9		IT ONLY TAKES A MINUTE ONE HUNDRED TON AND A FEATHER	UK 135
07/10/1978	29	6		ONE FOR YOU ONE FOR ME	GTO GT 237
16/12/1978	58	4		LICK A SMURP FOR CHRISTMAS (ALL FALL DOWN) FATHER ABRAPHART AND THE SMURPS	Petrol GAS 1/Magnet MAG 139
16/06/1979	67	2		YOU'RE THE GREATEST LOVER	UK International INT 586
03/11/1979	65	3		GLORIA	Ariola ARO 198

NOSMO KING – see JAVELLS FEATURING NOSMO KING

PAUL KING UK singer (born 20/1/1960, Coventry), ex-lead with The Reluctant Stereotypes and King, later a presenter on VH1.

DATE	POS	WKS	BPI	SINGLE TITLE	LABEL & NUMBER
02/05/1987	59	3		I KNOW	CBS PKING 1

SOLOMON KING US singer (born in Lexington, KY) who later based himself in Prestwick, Manchester. His debut hit was based on the classical tune *Golandrina (The Swallow)*.

DATE	POS	WKS	BPI	SINGLE TITLE	LABEL & NUMBER
03/01/1968	3	18		SHE WEARS MY RING	Columbia DB 8325
01/05/1968	21	10		WHEN WE WERE YOUNG	Columbia DB 8402

TONY KING – see VISIONMASTERS AND KYLIE MINOGUE

KING ADORA UK rock group formed in Birmingham by Matt Browne (guitar/vocals), Martyn Nelson (guitar/vocals), Robbie Grimmitt (bass) and Dan Dabrowski (drums).

DATE	POS	WKS	BPI	SINGLE TITLE	LABEL & NUMBER
04/11/2000	62	1		SMOULDER	Superior Quality RQSD 010CD
03/03/2001	39	2		SUFFOCATE	Superior Quality RQS 11DD
26/05/2001	30	2		BIONIC	Superior Quality RQS 012DD
31/05/2003	68	1		BORN TO LOSE/KAMIKAZE	MHR MHRCD 001

KING BEE UK rapper. Michelle is singer Michelle Blackmon.

DATE	POS	WKS	BPI	SINGLE TITLE	LABEL & NUMBER
26/01/1991	44	4		MUST BEE THE MUSIC KING BEE FEATURING MICHELE	Columbia 6565827
23/03/1991	61	2		BACK BY DOPE DEMAND	First Bass 7RUFF 6X

KING BROTHERS UK family trio formed by Michael (guitar/vocals), Tony (bass/vocals) and Denis King (piano/vocals); first noticed after winning a TV talent show in 1953. Denis later became one of the top TV music writers.

DATE	POS	WKS	BPI	SINGLE TITLE	LABEL & NUMBER
31/05/1957	6	14		A WHITE SPORT COAT	Parlophone R 4310
09/08/1957	19	13		IN THE MIDDLE OF AN ISLAND	Parlophone R 4338
06/12/1957	22	3		WAKE UP LITTLE SUSIE	Parlophone R 4367
31/01/1958	25	4		PUT A LIGHT IN THE WINDOW	Parlophone R 4389
14/04/1960	4	11		STANDING ON THE CORNER	Parlophone R 4639
28/07/1960	16	10		MAIS OUI	Parlophone R 4672
12/01/1961	21	8		DOLL HOUSE	Parlophone R 4715
02/03/1961	19	11		76 TROMBONES	Parlophone R 4737

KING KURT UK rock group formed in 1983 by Bert, Rory Lyons, Maggit, John Reddington, Smeg and Thwack, produced by Dave Edmunds. By 1985 Bert and Reddington had left, replaced by Dick Crippen and Jim Piper.

DATE	POS	WKS	BPI	SINGLE TITLE	LABEL & NUMBER
15/10/1983	36	6		DESTINATION ZULULAND	Stiff BUY 189
28/04/1984	55	4		MACK THE KNIFE	Stiff BUY 199
04/08/1984	54	4		BANANA BANANA	Stiff BUY 206

○ Silver disc ● Gold disc ✪ Platinum disc (additional platinum units are indicated by a figure following the symbol) ◉ Singles released prior to 1973 that are known to have sold over 1 million copies in the UK

15/11/1986.....73......1.......	AMERICA...	Polydor KURT 1
02/05/1987.....67......1.......	THE LAND OF RING DANG DO...	Polydor KURT 2

KING SUN-D'MOET US rapper (born Todd Turnbrow, 23/2/1967, Paterson, NJ).
11/07/1987.....66......3.......	HEY LOVE.. Flame MELT 5

KING TRIGGER UK group with Sam Hodgkin (vocals), Martin Clapson (guitar/vocals), Stuart Kennedy (bass/vocals), Trudi Baptiste (keyboards/vocals) and Ian Cleverly (drums).
14/08/1982.....57......4.......	THE RIVER.. Chrysalis CHS 2623

KINGDOM COME German/US rock group formed by Lenny Wolf (vocals), Danny Stag (guitar), Rick Steier (guitar), Johnny Frank (bass) and James Kottak (drums). By 1991 it was effectively Wolf recording solo with studio musicians.
16/04/1988.....75......1.......	GET IT ON... Polydor KCS 1
06/05/1989.....73......1.......	DO YOU LIKE IT.. Polydor KCS 3

KINGMAKER UK group formed in Hull in 1990 by Lawrence 'Loz' Hardy (born 14/9/1970, Manchester, guitar/vocals), Myles Howell (born 23/1/1971, Rugby, bass) and John Andrew (born 27/5/1963, Hull, drums). First on Sacred Heart, switching to Scorch in 1991.
18/01/1992.....30......3.......	IDIOTS AT THE WHEEL EP Tracks on EP: *Really Scrape The Sky, Revelation, Every Teenage Suicide* and *Strip Away*....... Scorch 3
23/05/1992.....15......3.......	EAT YOURSELF WHOLE... Scorch SCORCHG 5
31/10/1992.....47......2.......	ARMCHAIR ANARCHIST.. Scorch SCORCHG 6
08/05/1993.....15......4.......	10 YEARS ASLEEP... Scorch CDSCORCHS 8
19/06/1993.....29......4.......	QUEEN JANE... Scorch CDSCORS 9
30/10/1993.....63......1.......	SATURDAY'S NOT WHAT IT USED TO BE................................... Scorch CDSCORCH 10
15/04/1995.....33......3.......	YOU AND I WILL NEVER SEE THINGS EYE TO EYE....................... Chrysalis CDSCORCHS 11
03/06/1995.....41......2.......	IN THE BEST POSSIBLE TASTE (PART 2).............................. Scorch CDSCORCHS 12

KINGS OF CONVENIENCE Norwegian duo from Bergen, Erik Glambek Boe (guitar/vocals) and Erlend Oye (guitar).
21/04/2001.....44......1.......	TOXIC GIRL... Source SOURCDSE 1025
14/07/2001.....63......1.......	FAILURE... Source SOURCD 036
04/09/2004.....60......1.......	I'D RATHER DANCE WITH YOU... Source SOURCDX 102

KINGS OF LEON US rock group formed in Tennessee by Caleb Followhill (guitar/vocals), his brothers Jared (bass) and Nathan (drums) and cousin Matthew (guitar).
08/03/2003.....53......1.......	HOLY ROLLER NOVACAINE.. Hand Me Down HMD21
14/06/2003.....22......3.......	WHAT I SAW... Hand Me Down HMD23
23/08/2003.....23......3.......	MOLLY'S CHAMBERS... Hand Me Down HMD30
01/11/2003.....51......2.......	WASTED TIME.. Hand Me Down HMD32
28/02/2004.....61......1.......	CALIFORNIA WAITING... Hand Me Down HMD37
06/11/2004.....16......3.......	THE BUCKET... Hand Me Down HMD41

KINGS OF SWING ORCHESTRA Australian studio orchestra.
01/05/1982.....48......5.......	SWITCHED ON SWING.. Philips Swing 1

KINGS OF TOMORROW US production duo Jay Finnister and Sandy Rivera. Rivera later recorded solo.
14/04/2001.....54......1.......	FINALLY.. Distance DI 2029
29/09/2001.....24......3.......	FINALLY (REMIX) This and above single credited to KINGS OF TOMORROW FEATURING JULIE MCKNIGHT... Defected DEFECT 37CDX
13/04/2002.....45......2.......	YOUNG HEARTS... Defected DFECT 46CDS
25/10/2003.....74......1.......	DREAMS/THROUGH... Defected DFTD 079
31/07/2004.....69......1.......	DREAMS KINGS OF TOMORROW FEATURING HAZE Remix of the above A-side.......................... Defected DFTD 090CDS

KINGSMEN US group formed in Portland, OR in 1957 by Jack Ely (guitar/vocals), Lynn Easton (drums/vocals), Mike Mitchell (guitar) and Bob Nordby (bass), taking the name Kingsmen when Easton's parents bought it from a disbanding local group. Their hit was recorded for $50 in 1963, sold locally (despite a rival version) then picked up nationally by Wand after a Boston DJ declared it the worst record he'd ever heard! A US #2, despite the Governor of Indiana banning it as 'pornographic', prompting an FBI investigation into the lyrical content – which they couldn't decipher at any speed they played it! Ely left after the hit.
30/01/1964.....26......7.......	LOUIE LOUIE Featured in the films *Animal House* (1978) and *Quadrophenia* (1979)................ Pye International 7N 25231

KINGSTON TRIO US folk group formed in San Francisco, CA in 1957 by Dave Guard (born 19/10/1934, San Francisco, banjo), Bob Shane (born 1/2/1934, Hilo, HI, guitar) and Nick Reynolds (born 27/7/1933, Coronado, CA, guitar). Guard left in 1961, replaced by John Stewart (born 5/9/1939, San Diego, CA). Disbanded in 1967. Shane later formed New Kingston Trio with Roger Gamble and George Grove. Second Grammy for 1959 Best Folk Performance for *The Kingston Trio At Large*. Guard died from lymphoma on 22/3/1991.
21/11/1958.....5......14......	**TOM DOOLEY** ▲[1] 1958 Grammy Award for Best Country & Western Performance........................... Capitol CL 14951
04/12/1959.....29......1.......	SAN MIGUEL... Capitol CL 15073

❶[9] Number of weeks single topped the UK chart ↑ Entered the UK chart at #1 ▲[9] Number of weeks single topped the US chart

439

KINKS UK group formed in London in 1962 by Ray Davies (born 21/6/1944, London, guitar/vocals), his brother Dave (born 3/2/1947, London), Pete Quaife (born 31/12/1943, Tavistock, bass) and John Start (drums) as the Ray Davies Quartet. As the Ravens in 1963, they replaced Start with Mick Avory (born 15/2/1944, London), and on 31/12/1963 appeared as The Kinks for the first time, signing with Pye in 1964. Numerous personnel changes came in the 1970s, Dave Davies recording solo. Ray Davies appeared in the film *Absolute Beginners*. They were inducted into the Rock & Roll Hall of Fame in 1990. In 2004, Ray Davies was shot by a mugger in New Orleans but survived, barely days after he was awarded the CBE.

DATE	POS	WKS	BPI	SINGLE TITLE	LABEL & NUMBER
13/08/1964	●²	12		YOU REALLY GOT ME Featured in the 1989 film *She's Out Of Control*	Pye 7N 15673
29/10/1964	2	14		ALL DAY AND ALL OF THE NIGHT	Pye 7N 15714
21/01/1965	●¹	10		TIRED OF WAITING FOR YOU	Pye 7N 15759
25/03/1965	17	8		EVERYBODY'S GONNA BE HAPPY Featured in the 2000 film *High Fidelity*	Pye 7N 15813
27/05/1965	9	11		SET ME FREE	Pye 7N 15854
05/08/1965	10	9		SEE MY FRIEND	Pye 7N 15919
02/12/1965	8	12		TILL THE END OF THE DAY	Pye 7N 15981
03/03/1966	4	11		DEDICATED FOLLOWER OF FASHION Featured in the 1993 film *In The Name Of The Father*	Pye 7N 17064
09/06/1966	●²	13		SUNNY AFTERNOON	Pye 7N 17125
24/11/1966	5	11		DEAD END STREET	Pye 7N 17222
11/05/1967	2	11		WATERLOO SUNSET	Pye 7N 17321
18/10/1967	3	11		AUTUMN ALMANAC	Pye 7N 17400
17/04/1968	36	5		WONDERBOY	Pye 7N 17468
17/07/1968	12	10		DAYS	Pye 7N 17573
16/04/1969	31	4		PLASTIC MAN	Pye 7N 17724
10/01/1970	33	4		VICTORIA	Pye 7N 17865
04/07/1970	2	14		LOLA	Pye 7N 17961
12/12/1970	5	14		APEMAN Featured in the 1986 film *Club Paradise*	Pye 7N 45016
03/06/1972	16	8		SUPERSONIC ROCKET SHIP	RCA 2211
27/06/1981	46	5		BETTER THINGS	Arista ARIST 415
06/08/1983	12	9		COME DANCING	Arista ARIST 502
15/10/1983	58	3		DON'T FORGET TO DANCE Featured in the 1986 film *Nothing In Common*	Arista ARIST 524
15/10/1983	47	4		YOU REALLY GOT ME Reissue of Pye 7N 15673	PRT KD1
18/01/1997	35	2		THE DAYS EP Tracks on EP: *You Really Got Me, Dead End Street* and *Lola*	When! WENX 1016
18/09/2004	42	2		YOU REALLY GOT ME Second re-issue of Pye 7N 15673	Sanctuary SANXD317

KINKY UK rapper (born Caron Geary, London); she was in the E-Zee Possee and also recorded with Erasure before going solo.

DATE	POS	WKS	BPI	SINGLE TITLE	LABEL & NUMBER
24/08/1996	71	1		EVERYBODY	Feverpitch CDFVR 1009

KINKY MACHINE UK group: Louis Elliot (guitar/vocals), Jon Bull (guitar), Malcolm Pardon (bass) and Julian Fenton (drums).

DATE	POS	WKS	BPI	SINGLE TITLE	LABEL & NUMBER
06/03/1993	70	1		SUPERNATURAL GIVER	Lemon 006CD
29/05/1993	70	1		SHOCKAHOLIC	Oxygen GASPD 5
14/08/1993	74	1		GOING OUT WITH GOD	Oxygen GASPD 9
02/07/1994	66	1		10 SECOND BIONIC MAN	Oxygen GASPD 14

FERN KINNEY US singer (born Fern Kinney-Lewis, Jackson, MS); she sang with Dorothy Moore in the Poppies before going solo with Atlantic in 1977. She also had a big club hit with *Groove Me*.

DATE	POS	WKS	BPI	SINGLE TITLE	LABEL & NUMBER
16/02/1980	●¹	11	●	TOGETHER WE ARE BEAUTIFUL	WEA K 79111

KINSHASA BAND — see JOHNNY WAKELIN

KIOKI Japanese singer discovered by producers Ridderhof and Garnefski working as a cocktail waiter at a Kewpie Doll bar in Tokyo.

DATE	POS	WKS	BPI	SINGLE TITLE	LABEL & NUMBER
17/08/2002	66	1		DO AND DON'T FOR LOVE	V2 VVR 5020803

KIRA Belgian singer (born Natasja De Witte) who began on the Belgian equivalent of *Stars In Their Eyes* aged thirteen, and reached the final of the Belgian *Popstars* competition.

DATE	POS	WKS	BPI	SINGLE TITLE	LABEL & NUMBER
01/03/2003	9	5		I'LL BE YOUR ANGEL	NuLife 74321970362

KATHY KIRBY UK singer (born 20/10/1940, Ilford). First noticed on tour with Cliff Richard and the Shadows in 1960, she became a regular on TV's *Stars And Garters*. She also had her own series on the BBC.

DATE	POS	WKS	BPI	SINGLE TITLE	LABEL & NUMBER
15/08/1963	11	13		DANCE ON	Decca F 11682
07/11/1963	4	18		SECRET LOVE	Decca F 11759
20/02/1964	10	11		LET ME GO LOVER	Decca F 11832
07/05/1964	17	9		YOU'RE THE ONE	Decca F 11892
04/03/1965	36	3		I BELONG Britain's entry for the 1965 Eurovision Song Contest (came second)	Decca F 12087

BO KIRKLAND AND RUTH DAVIS
US vocal duo Bo (born 11/10/1946, Yazoo City, MS) and Ruth (from Arkansas) were both solo artists when they were signed by Claridge Records. It was label boss Frank Slay's idea to team them up.

04/06/1977	12	9		YOU'RE GONNA GET NEXT TO ME	EMI International INT 532

KISS
US heavy rock group formed in New York in 1972 by Gene Simmons (born Chaim Witz, 25/8/1949, Haifa, Israel, bass/vocals), Paul Stanley (born Paul Elsen, 20/1/1950, New York, guitar/vocals), Peter Criss (born Peter Crisscoula, 27/12/1947, Brooklyn, NYC, drums/vocals) and Ace Frehley (born Paul Frehley, 22/4/1951, The Bronx, NYC, guitar/vocals) as Wicked Lester, becoming Kiss in 1973. They signed with Casablanca in 1974 and built a solid following with elaborate stage costumes and faces masked with make-up. All four released solo albums simultaneously in 1978. Criss left in 1980, replaced by Anton Fig and then Eric Carr (born 12/7/1950, Brooklyn, NYC). Frehley left in 1982 after a car accident (resurfacing with Frehley's Comet), replaced by Vinnie Vincent (born Vincent Cusano). They appeared without make-up for the first time in 1983. Vincent left in 1984, replaced by Mark St John (born Mark Norton), he in turn replaced by Bruce Kulick in 1985. Carr died from cancer on 24/11/1991, replaced by Eric Singer. In 1996 Frehley and Criss returned for an *Unplugged* performance on MTV, the original four members making the reunion permanent, appearing in the 1999 film *Detroit Rock City*. By 2003 they consisted of Simmons, Criss, Stanley and Tommy Thayer. The group has a star on the Hollywood Walk of Fame.

30/06/1979	50	7		I WAS MADE FOR LOVIN' YOU Featured in the 1981 film *Endless Love*	Casablanca CAN 152
20/02/1982	55	3		A WORLD WITHOUT HEROES	Casablanca KISS 002
30/04/1983	34	4		CREATURES OF THE NIGHT	Casablanca KISS 4
29/10/1983	31	5		LICK IT UP	Vertigo KISS 5
08/09/1984	43	3		HEAVEN'S ON FIRE	Vertigo VER 12
09/11/1985	57	2		TEARS ARE FALLING	Vertigo KISS 6
03/10/1987	4	9		CRAZY CRAZY NIGHTS	Vertigo KISS 7
05/12/1987	33	7		REASON TO LIVE	Vertigo KISS 8
10/09/1988	41	3		TURN ON THE NIGHT	Vertigo KISS 9
18/11/1989	59	2		HIDE YOUR HEART	Vertigo KISS 10
31/03/1990	65	2		FOREVER	Vertigo KISS 11
11/01/1992	4	8		GOD GAVE ROCK AND ROLL TO YOU II Featured in the 1991 film *Bill And Ted's Bogus Journey*	Interscope A 8696
09/05/1992	26	2		UNHOLY	Vertigo KISS 12

KISS AMC
UK rapper Anne Marie Copeland.

01/07/1989	58	2		A BIT OF... For copyright reasons it could not be given its full title. Contains a sample of U2's *New Year's Day*	Syncopate SY 29
19/08/1989	58	2		A BIT OF U2	Syncopate SY 29
03/02/1990	66	1		MY DOCS	Syncopate XAMC 1

KISSING THE PINK
UK group formed in 1981 by Nick Whitecross (guitar/vocals), Simon Aldridge (guitar/vocals), Peter Barnett (bass/vocals), Jon Kingsley-Hall (keyboards/vocals), George Stewart (keyboards/vocals), Jo Wells (saxophone/vocals) and Steve Cusack (drums).

05/03/1983	19	14		LAST FILM	Magnet KTP 3

MAC AND KATIE KISSOON
UK brother and sister duo Mac (born Gerald Farthing, 11/11/1943, Trinidad) and Kathleen Kissoon (born 11/3/1951, Trinidad) who moved to the UK in the late 1950s. Both in the Marionettes and the Rag Dolls, Kathleen recording solo as Peanut. A US hit with the original version of *Chirpy Chirpy Cheep Cheep*, a bigger UK hit for Middle of the Road.

19/06/1971	41	1		CHIRPY CHIRPY CHEEP CHEEP	Young Blood YB 1026
18/01/1975	3	10	O	SUGAR CANDY KISSES	Polydor 2058 531
03/05/1975	9	8		DON'T DO IT BABY	State STAT 4
30/08/1975	18	9		LIKE A BUTTERFLY	State STAT 9
15/05/1976	46	5		THE TWO OF US	State STAT 21

KEVIN KITCHEN
UK singer.

20/04/1985	64	3		PUT MY ARMS AROUND YOU	China WOK 1

JOY KITIKONTI
Italian producer Massimo Chiticonti.

17/11/2001	57	2		JOYENERGIZER	BXR BXRC 0347

EARTHA KITT
US singer (born 26/1/1928, Columbia, SC, raised in New York, later relocating to Paris). Break came on Broadway in *New Faces Of 1952*; subsequent films included *The Mark Of The Hawk* (1958), *Naughty Knights* (1971) and *Erik The Viking* (1989). She was also Catwoman in the TV series *Batman*. She has a star on the Hollywood Walk of Fame.

01/04/1955	7	10		UNDER THE BRIDGES OF PARIS	HMV B 10647
03/12/1983	36	11		WHERE IS MY MAN	Record Shack SOHO 11
07/07/1984	50	3		I LOVE MEN	Record Shack SOHO 21
12/04/1986	73	1		THIS IS MY LIFE	Record Shack SOHO 61
01/07/1989	32	7		CHA CHA HEELS EARTHA KITT AND BRONSKI BEAT	Arista 112331
05/03/1994	43	2		IF I LOVE YA THEN I NEED YA IF I NEED YA THEN I WANT YOU AROUND	RCA 74321190342

KITTIE
Canadian rock group formed in London, Ontario by Morgan Lander (guitar/vocals), her sister Mercedes (drums), Fallon Bowman (guitar) and Talena Atfield (bass).

25/03/2000	46	1		BRACKISH	Epic 6691292
22/07/2000	60	1		CHARLOTTE	Epic 6696222

❶⁹ Number of weeks single topped the UK chart ↑ Entered the UK chart at #1 ▲⁹ Number of weeks single topped the US chart

441

KLAXONS Belgian vocal/instrumental group.

10/12/1983.....45......6.......	THE CLAP CLAP SOUND .... PRT 7P 290

KLEA Dutch dance group formed by Diamond Geezer, Isis Rain and Arch Collision.

07/09/2002.....61......1.......	TIC TOC.. Incentive CENT 41CDS

KLEEER US R&B group formed in New York City by Paul Crutchfield (vocals/percussion), Richard Lee (guitar/keyboards), Norman Durham (bass) and Woddy Cunningham (drums) as heavy metal band Pipeline. Toured as The Universal Robot Band, brainchild of producer Patrick Adams, after which they became Kleeer. They later added David Frank (keyboards) and singers Isabelle Coles, Melanie Moore and Yvette Flowers. Lee, Durham and Cunningham were previously the backing group for The Choice Four in Baltimore, MD.

17/03/1979.....51......6......	KEEEP YOUR BODY WORKING .... Atlantic LV 21
14/03/1981.....49......4.......	GET TOUGH .... Atlantic 11560

D.D. KLEIN – see **ALIVE FEATURING D.D. KLEIN**

KLESHAY UK vocal group with Alani Gibbon, Leah and Candii. Alani later formed Anotherside with Celena Cherry (of Honeyz).

19/09/1998.....33......2......	REASONS.. Epic KLE 1CD
20/02/1999.....19......3......	RUSH .... Epic KLE 2CD

KLF UK duo Bill Drummond (born William Butterworth, 29/4/1953, South Africa) and Jimmy Cauty (born 1954, London) who teamed in 1987 and released records as the JAMs, Disco 2000, the Justified Ancients of Mu Mu, the Timelords, 1300 Drums Featuring The Unjustified Ancients Of Mu and KLF. Established the KLF Communication record label. KLF stands for Kopyright Liberation Front. They disbanded in 1992, returning in 1997 as 2K. They were named Best UK Group (jointly with Simply Red) at the 1992 BRIT Awards.

11/08/1990 .....5......12	**WHAT TIME IS LOVE (LIVE AT TRANCENTRAL)** .... KLF Communications KLF 004
19/01/1991 ....❶²....11 .....○	**3AM ETERNAL** This and above single credited to **KLF FEATURING THE CHILDREN OF THE REVOLUTION** .. KLF Communications KLF 005
04/05/1991 .....2......9......	LAST TRAIN TO TRANCENTRAL .... KLF Communications KLF 008
07/12/1991 .....2......12 .....○	**JUSTIFIED AND ANCIENT** KLF, GUEST VOCALS TAMMY WYNETTE .... KLF Communications KLF099
07/03/1992 .....4 ......7	**AMERICA: WHAT TIME IS LOVE (REMIX)** .... KLF Communications KLFUSA 004

KLUBHEADS Dutch instrumental/production group formed by Koen Groeneveld, Addy Van Der Zwan and Jan Voermans. They also recorded as Cooper, Drunkenmunky, Itty Bitty Boozy Woozy and Da Techno Bohemian.

11/05/1996.....10......6......	**KLUBHOPPING** .... AM:PM 5815572
16/08/1997.....35......2......	DISCOHOPPING Contains a sample of Patrick Hernandez's *Born To Be Alive* .... AM:PM 5823032
15/08/1998.....36......2......	KICKIN' HARD .... Wonderboy WBOYD 011

KLUSTER FEATURING RON CARROLL French DJ/production duo Robert Collado and Laurent Scimeca with US singer Ron Carroll.

28/04/2001.....73......1.......	MY LOVE Contains a sample of Odyssey's *Native New Yorker* .... Scorpio Music 1928112

KMC FEATURING DAHNY Italian dance group with DJ Benny Besmasse, his brother Alexander and singer Dahny Galli.

25/05/2002.....33......2......	I FEEL SO FINE .... Incentive CENT 39CDS

KNACK US rock group formed in Los Angeles, CA in 1978 by Doug Fieger (guitar/vocals), Bruce Gary (drums), Prescott Niles (bass) and Berton Averre (guitar), all ex-session players. They disbanded in 1982, re-forming in 1986 with Billy Ward replacing Gary.

30/06/1979 .....6......10	**MY SHARONA** ▲⁶ Featured in the 1994 film *Reality Bites* .... Capitol CL 16087
13/10/1979 .....66......2......	GOOD GIRLS DON'T .... Capitol CL 16097

KNACK – see **MOUNT RUSHMORE PRESENTS THE KNACK**

BEVERLEY KNIGHT UK singer (born Beverley Smith, 22/3/1973, Wolverhampton); she began singing in church, becoming known via local pirate radio. 1998 and 1999 MOBO Award for Best Rhythm and Blues Act, and 1999 award for Best Album for *Prodigal Sista*.

08/04/1995.....50......2......	FLAVOUR OF THE OLD SCHOOL... Dome CDDOME 101
02/09/1995.....55......1......	DOWN FOR THE ONE .... Dome CDDOME 102
21/10/1995.....33......2......	FLAVOUR OF THE OLD SCHOOL... Dome CDDOME 105
23/03/1996.....42......1......	MOVING ON UP (ON THE RIGHT SIDE) .... Dome CDDOME 107
30/05/1998.....21......3......	MADE IT BACK **BEVERLEY KNIGHT FEATURING REDMAN** Contains a sample of Chic's *Good Times*........................
	.... Parlophone Rhythm CDRHYTHM 11
22/08/1998.....40......2......	REWIND (FIND A WAY) .... Parlophone Rhythm CDRHYTHS 13
10/04/1999.....19......5......	MADE IT BACK 99 (REMIX) .... Parlophone Rhythm CDRHYTHS 18
17/07/1999.....14......5......	GREATEST DAY .... Parlophone Rhythm CDRHYTHS 22
04/12/1999.....31......2......	SISTA SISTA .... Parlophone Rhythm CDRHYTHS 26
17/11/2001.....17......4......	GET UP .... Parlophone CDRS 6564
09/03/2002.....10......8......	**SHOULDA WOULDA COULDA**.. Parlophone CDRS 6570
06/07/2002.....27......4......	GOLD .... Parlophone CDRS 6580
03/07/2004 .....9......10	**COME AS YOU ARE** .... Parlophone CDRS 6636
09/10/2004.....31......2......	NOT TOO LATE FOR LOVE .... Parlophone CDRS 6645

○ Silver disc ● Gold disc ✪ Platinum disc (additional platinum units are indicated by a figure following the symbol) ◉ Singles released prior to 1973 that are known to have sold over 1 million copies in the UK

FREDERICK KNIGHT
US singer (born 15/8/1944, Birmingham, AL) with Mercury and Capitol in New York before signing with Stax in 1972. After Stax's demise he launched Juana, writing/producing the Controllers and a UK #1 with Anita Ward's *Ring My Bell*.

10/06/1972	22	10		I'VE BEEN LONELY FOR SO LONG	Stax 2025 098

GLADYS KNIGHT AND THE PIPS

US family group formed in 1952 by Gladys (born 28/5/1944, Atlanta, GA), brother Merald (born 4/9/1942, Atlanta), sister Brenda and cousins William (born 2/6/1941, Atlanta) and Elenor Guest (born 1940). Another cousin, James 'Pips' Woods, gave them their name. Initially singing in church, they turned professional in 1957, recording a debut single in 1959. Brenda and Elenor left in 1959, replaced by another cousin, Edward Patten (born 2/8/1939, Atlanta), and Langston George. George left in 1962. They were the first act to appear on the US TV show *Soul Train*, on 17/8/1972. Legal wrangles stopped them recording together from 1977 to 1980: the Pips recorded two LPs for Casablanca and Gladys one for Buddah. They disbanded in 1989. Gladys appeared in the film *Pipe Dreams* in 1976. Elenor Guest died from heart failure on 23/8/1997. They were inducted into the Rock & Roll Hall of Fame in 1996. Gladys won a 2001 Grammy Award for Best Traditional Rhythm and Blues Album for *At Last*. Gladys has a star on the Hollywood Walk of Fame.

08/06/1967	13	15		TAKE ME IN YOUR ARMS AND LOVE ME	Tamla Motown TMG 604
27/12/1967	47	1		I HEARD IT THROUGH THE GRAPEVINE	Tamla Motown TMG 629
17/06/1972	35	8		JUST WALK IN MY SHOES	Tamla Motown TMG 813
25/11/1972	11	17		HELP ME MAKE IT THROUGH THE NIGHT	Tamla Motown TMG 830
03/03/1973	21	9		LOOK OF LOVE Featured in the films *Kevin And Perry Go Large* and *Beautiful People* (both 2000)	Tamla Motown TMG 844
26/05/1973	31	7		NEITHER ONE OF US 1973 Grammy Award for Best Pop Vocal Performance by a Group	Tamla Motown TMG 855
05/04/1975	4	15	O	**THE WAY WE WERE – TRY TO REMEMBER**	Buddah BDS 428
02/08/1975	7	10		**BEST THING THAT EVER HAPPENED TO ME**	Buddah BDS 432
15/11/1975	30	5		PART TIME LOVE	Buddah BDS 438
08/05/1976	10	9		**MIDNIGHT TRAIN TO GEORGIA** ▲² 1973 Grammy Award for Best Rhythm & Blues Vocal Performance by a Group	Buddah BDS 444
21/08/1976	35	4		MAKE YOURS A HAPPY HOME	Buddah BDS 447
06/11/1976	20	9		SO SAD THE SONG	Buddah BDS 448
15/01/1977	34	2		NOBODY BUT YOU This and above single featured in the 1976 film *Pipe Dreams*	Buddah BDS 451
28/05/1977	4	12	O	**BABY DON'T CHANGE YOUR MIND**	Buddah BDS 458
24/09/1977	35	4		HOME IS WHERE THE HEART IS	Buddah BDS 460
08/04/1978	32	5		THE ONE AND ONLY Featured in the 1978 film of the same name	Buddah BDS 470
24/06/1978	15	13		COME BACK AND FINISH WHAT YOU STARTED	Buddah BDS 473
30/09/1978	59	4		IT'S A BETTER THAN GOOD TIME	Buddah BDS 478
30/08/1980	35	6		TASTE OF BITTER LOVE	CBS 8890
08/11/1980	32	6		BOURGIE BOURGIE	CBS 9081
26/12/1981	74	1		WHEN A CHILD IS BORN JOHNNY MATHIS AND GLADYS KNIGHT	CBS S 1758
09/11/1985	16	9		THAT'S WHAT FRIENDS ARE FOR ▲⁴ DIONNE WARWICK AND FRIENDS FEATURING ELTON JOHN, STEVIE WONDER AND GLADYS KNIGHT The song was originally recorded by Rod Stewart in 1982 for the film *Night Shift*. 1986 Grammy Awards for Best Pop Vocal Performance by a Group, and Song of the Year for writers Burt Bacharach and Carole Bayer Sager	Arista ARIST 638
16/01/1988	42	4		LOVE OVERBOARD 1988 Grammy Award for Best Rhythm & Blues Vocal Performance by a Group	MCA 1223
10/06/1989	6	11		**LICENCE TO KILL** GLADYS KNIGHT Featured in the 1989 James Bond film of the same name	MCA 1339

JORDAN KNIGHT
US singer (born 17/5/1970, Worcester, MA); a member of New Kids On The Block before going solo.

16/10/1999	5	9		**GIVE IT TO YOU**	Interscope 4971672

ROBERT KNIGHT
US singer (born 21/4/1945, Franklin, TN) who formed the Paramounts in 1961 and signed with Dot but left music soon after. Heard singing at a party in 1967 and signed by Rising Sons (via Monument), his US hit *Everlasting Love* being covered in the UK by Love Affair. He later recorded for Elf and Private Stock before pursuing a career in chemical research!

17/01/1968	40	2		EVERLASTING LOVE	Monument MON 1008
24/11/1973	10	16		**LOVE ON A MOUNTAIN TOP**	Monument MNT 1875
09/03/1974	19	8		EVERLASTING LOVE Re-issue of Monument MON 1008	Monument MNT 2106

KNOC-TURN'AL – see DR DRE

MARK KNOPFLER
UK singer/guitarist (born 12/8/1949, Glasgow) who formed Dire Straits in 1977. He began solo projects in 1983 with the theme to the film *Local Hero*, also forming The Notting Hillbillies in 1986. He was awarded an OBE in the 2000 New Year's Honours List. Mark has collected five Grammy Awards: two as a member of Dire Straits and Best Country Instrumental Performance in 1985 with Chet Atkins for *Cosmic Square Dance*, Best Country Vocal Performance in 1990 with Chet Atkins for *Poor Boy Blues* and Best Country Instrumental Performance in 1990 with Chet Atkins for *So Soft Your Goodbye*.

12/03/1983	56	3		GOING HOME (THEME OF 'LOCAL HERO') Featured in the 1983 film *Local Hero*	Vertigo DSTR 4
16/03/1996	33	2		DARLING PRETTY Featured in the 1996 film *Twister*	Vertigo VERCD 88
25/05/1996	42	2		CANNIBALS	Vertigo VERCD 89
02/10/2004	34	2		BOOM LIKE THAT	Mercury 9867839

KNOWLEDGE
Italian production duo Stefano Gamma and Ranieri Senni.

08/11/1997	70	1		AS (UNTIL THE DAY)	ffrr FCD 312

BEYONCÉ KNOWLES
US singer (born 18/9/1981, Houston, TX); lead singer with Destiny's Child. Also an actress, she appeared in the film *Austin Powers – Goldmember*. She won the 2003 MTV Europe Music Award for Best Rhythm and Blues Female.

❶⁹ Number of weeks single topped the UK chart ↑ Entered the UK chart at #1 ▲⁹ Number of weeks single topped the US chart

443

Five Grammies include: Best Rhythm and Blues Performance by a Duo or Group with Vocals with Luther Vandross for *The Closer I Get To You*, Best Female Rhythm and Blues Vocal Performance for *Dangerously In Love* and Best Contemporary Rhythm and Blues Album for *Dangerously In Love* all in 2003. She was also named Best International Female at the 2004 BRIT Awards.

DATE	POS	WKS	BPI	SINGLE TITLE	LABEL & NUMBER
27/07/2002	7	11		**WORK IT OUT** BEYONCÉ Featured in the 2002 film *Goldmember*	Columbia 6729822
01/02/2003	2	12		**03 BONNIE AND CLYDE** JAY-Z FEATURING BEYONCÉ KNOWLES Contains samples of Prince's *If I Was Your Girlfriend* and Tupac's *Me And My Girlfriend*	Roc-A-Fella 0770102
12/07/2003	❶³	15		**CRAZY IN LOVE** ▲⁸ Contains a sample of The Chi-Lites' *Are You My* Woman and uncredited contribution of Jay-Z. The single won the 2003 MTV Europe Music Award for Best Song. 2003 Grammy Awards for Best Rhythm and Blues Song (for writers Shawn Carter, Rich Harrison, Beyoncé Knowles and Eugene Record) and Best Rap/Sung Collaboration. Featured in the 2004 film *Bridget Jones Diary 2: Edge Of Reason*	Columbia 6740675
18/10/2003	2	11		**BABY BOY** ▲⁹ BEYONCÉ KNOWLES FEATURING SEAN PAUL	Columbia 6744082
24/01/2004	11	7		ME, MYSELF & I	Columbia 6745445
17/04/2004	10	8		**NAUGHTY GIRL** Contains a sample of Shuggy Otis' *Strawberry Letter 23* and an interpolation of Bootsy Collins' *I'd Rather Be With You*. Featured in the 2004 film *Mean Girls*	Columbia 6748282

BUDDY KNOX
US singer (born Wayne Knox, 14/4/1933, Happy, TX); he formed the Rhythm Orchids in 1955 with Jimmy Bowen and Don Lanier. They released two numbers in 1956 (*Party Doll*, sung by Knox, and *I'm Sticking With You* by Bowen) on their own Triple-D label. It was heard by Roulette who signed them, and released two singles: *Party Doll* by Buddy Knox & The Rhythm Orchids and *I'm Sticking With You* by Jimmy Bowen & The Rhythm Orchids. Knox hit US #1, Bowen #14. Knox died from cancer on 14/2/1999.

DATE	POS	WKS	BPI	SINGLE TITLE	LABEL & NUMBER
10/05/1957	29	3		PARTY DOLL ▲¹	Columbia DB 3914
16/08/1962	45	2		SHE'S GONE	Liberty LIB 55473

FRANKIE KNUCKLES
US singer (born18/1/1955, the South Bronx, NYC) and a club DJ from 1971. He eventually owned his own club and became a noted remixer. He then launched his own recording career, and won the 1997 Grammy Award for Best Remixer.

DATE	POS	WKS	BPI	SINGLE TITLE	LABEL & NUMBER
17/06/1989	50	3		TEARS FRANKIE KNUCKLES PRESENTS SATOSHI TOMIIE	ffrr F 108
21/10/1989	59	4		YOUR LOVE	Trax TRAXT 3
27/07/1991	17	5		THE WHISTLE SONG	Virgin America VUS 47
23/11/1991	67	1		IT'S HARD SOMETIMES	Virgin America VUS 52
06/06/1992	48	2		RAIN FALLS FRANKIE KNUCKLES FEATURING LISA MICHAELIS	Virgin America VUST 60
27/05/1995	34	2		TOO MANY FISH	Virgin VUSCD 89
18/11/1995	36	2		WHADDA U WANT (FROM ME) This and above single credited to FRANKIE KNUCKLES FEATURING ADEVA	Virgin VUSCD 98

MOE KOFFMAN QUARTETTE
Canadian flautist (born Morris Koffman, 28/12/1928, Toronto) and big band saxophonist during the 1950s. He died on 28/3/2001.

DATE	POS	WKS	BPI	SINGLE TITLE	LABEL & NUMBER
28/03/1958	23	2		SWINGIN' SHEPHERD BLUES	London HLJ 8549

MIKE KOGLIN
German producer, remixer and keyboard player who worked with Todd Terry and The Sugarcubes before going solo. He later recorded as State One. Beatrice is German singer Beatrice A Mayeras.

DATE	POS	WKS	BPI	SINGLE TITLE	LABEL & NUMBER
28/11/1998	20	2		THE SILENCE	Multiply CDMULTY 44
29/05/1999	28	2		ON MY WAY MIKE KOGLIN FEATURING BEATRICE	Multiply CDMULTY 51

KOKOMO
US pianist Jimmy Wisner (born 8/12/1931, Philadelphia, PA).

DATE	POS	WKS	BPI	SINGLE TITLE	LABEL & NUMBER
13/04/1961	35	7		ASIA MINOR Based on Greig's *Piano Concerto In A Minor*	London HLU 9305

KOKOMO
UK group formed in Liverpool by Dyan Burch (born 25/1/1949, vocals), Paddy McHugh (born 28/8/1946, vocals), Frank Collins (born 25/10/1947, vocals), Neil Hubbard (guitar), Jim Mullen (guitar), Tony O'Malley (keyboards), Mel Collins (saxophone), Alan Spencer (bass), Joan Linscott (percussion) and Terry Stannard (drums). Burch, McHugh and Frank Collins all ex-members of Arrival.

DATE	POS	WKS	BPI	SINGLE TITLE	LABEL & NUMBER
29/05/1982	45	3		A LITTLE BIT FURTHER AWAY	CBS A 2064

KON KAN
Canadian duo Barry Harris (piano/guitar) and Kevin Wynne (vocals), although Wynne left shortly after their debut hit.

DATE	POS	WKS	BPI	SINGLE TITLE	LABEL & NUMBER
04/03/1989	5	13	O	I BEG YOUR PARDON Contains samples of Lynn Anderson's *Rose Garden* and GQ's *Disco Nights (Rock Freak)*	Atlantic A 8969

JOHN KONGOS
South African singer/multi-instrumentalist (born in Johannesburg). He settled in the UK in 1966 and led a group called Scrub. He left in 1969 to go solo, with Dawn Records and then Fly, where he was produced by Gus Dudgeon. Kongos was later a top session musician and also scored the film *The Greek Tycoon*.

DATE	POS	WKS	BPI	SINGLE TITLE	LABEL & NUMBER
22/05/1971	4	14		**HE'S GONNA STEP ON YOU AGAIN**	Fly BUG 8
20/11/1971	4	11		**TOKOLOSHE MAN**	Fly BUG 14

KONKRETE
UK production duo Miss Rock (born Manchester) and Electro Kid K (born Worthing).

DATE	POS	WKS	BPI	SINGLE TITLE	LABEL & NUMBER
22/09/2001	60	1		LAW UNTO MYSELF	Perfecto PERF 23CDS

LAURENT KONRAD – see FIGHT CLUB FEATURING LAURENT KONRAD

KONTAKT
UK production duo Scott Attrill and Jim Sullivan with singer Nicola Poustie. Attrill also records as Midas.

DATE	POS	WKS	BPI	SINGLE TITLE	LABEL & NUMBER
20/09/2003	19	4		SHOW ME A SIGN	NuLife 82876557432

KOOL AND THE GANG US group formed in New Jersey in 1964 by Robert 'Kool' Bell (born 8/10/1950, Youngstown, OH, bass), brother Ronald (born 1/11/1951, Youngstown, sax), Robert 'Spike' Mickens (trumpet), Dennis 'Dee Tee' Thomas (sax), Woody Sparrow (guitar) and Rick Westfield (keyboards) as the Jazziacs. Line-up and name-changes settled as Kool & The Gang in 1968, signing with De-Lite in 1969. Added singer James 'JT' Taylor (born 16/8/1953, South Carolina), and with producer Deodato moved from funk into mainstream. Taylor went solo in 1988, later returning. They won the 2003 MOBO Award for Outstanding Achievement.

27/10/1979	9	12		LADIES NIGHT Featured in the 1999 film *200 Cigarettes*	Mercury KOOL 7
19/01/1980	23	8		TOO HOT	Mercury KOOL 8
12/07/1980	52	4		HANGIN' OUT	Mercury KOOL 9
01/11/1980	7	13	O	CELEBRATION ▲²	De-Lite KOOL 10
21/02/1981	17	11		JONES VS JONES/SUMMER MADNESS	De-Lite KOOL 11
30/05/1981	15	9		TAKE IT TO THE TOP	De-Lite DE 2
31/10/1981	12	13		STEPPIN' OUT	De-Lite DE 4
19/12/1981	3	12	O	GET DOWN ON IT	De-Lite DE 5
06/03/1982	29	7		TAKE MY HEART (YOU CAN HAVE IT IF YOU WANT IT)	De-Lite DE 6
07/08/1982	14	8		BIG FUN	De-Lite DE 7
16/10/1982	6	9		OOH LA LA LA (LET'S GO DANCIN')	De-Lite DE 9
04/12/1982	29	8		HI DE HI, HI DE HO	De-Lite DE 14
10/12/1983	15	10		STRAIGHT AHEAD	De-Lite DE 15
11/02/1984	2	11	O	JOANNA/TONIGHT	De-Lite DE 16
14/04/1984	7	8		(WHEN YOU SAY YOU LOVE SOMEBODY) IN THE HEART	De-Lite DE 17
24/11/1984	11	12	O	FRESH	De-Lite DE 18
09/02/1985	28	5		MISLED Featured in the 1986 film *Jumpin' Jack Flash*	De-Lite DE 19
11/05/1985	4	22	O	CHERISH	De-Lite DE 20
02/11/1985	50	3		EMERGENCY	De-Lite DE 21
22/11/1986	30	12		VICTORY	Club JAB 44
21/03/1987	45	4		STONE LOVE	Club JAB 47
31/12/1988	56	5		CELEBRATION (REMIX)	Club JAB 78
06/07/1991	69	1		GET DOWN ON IT (REMIX)	Mercury MER 346
27/12/2003	8	11		LADIES NIGHT ATOMIC KITTEN FEATURING KOOL AND THE GANG Featured in the 2004 film *Confessions Of A Teenage Drama Queen*	Innocent SINDX 53

KOOL ROCK STEADY – see TYREE

KOON + STEPHENSON – see WESTBAM

KORGIS UK duo Andy Davis (drums/guitar) and James Warren (bass/guitar/vocals), both ex-Stackridge, joined by Phil Harrison (keyboards/percussion) and Stuart Gordon (guitar/violin).

23/06/1979	13	12		IF I HAD YOU	Rialto TREB 103
24/05/1980	5	12	O	EVERYBODY'S GOT TO LEARN SOMETIME	Rialto TREB 115
30/08/1980	56	3		IF IT'S ALRIGHT WITH YOU BABY	Rialto TREB 118

KORN US rock group formed in Bakersfield, CA in 1993 by Jonathan 'HIV' Davis (born 18/1/1971, Bakersfield, vocals), Brian 'Head' Welch (born 19/6/1970, Torrance, CA, guitar), James 'Munky' Shaffer (born 6/6/1970, Rosedale, CA, guitar), Reggie 'Fieldy Snuts' Arvizu (bass) and David Silveria (drums).

19/10/1996	26	2		NO PLACE TO HIDE	Epic 6638452
15/02/1997	22	2		A.D.I.D.A.S. Title is an acronym for 'all day I dream about sex'	Epic 6642042
07/06/1997	25	2		GOOD GOD	Epic 6646585
22/08/1998	23	2		GOT THE LIFE	Epic 6663912
08/05/1999	24	2		FREAK ON A LEASH 1999 Grammy Award for Best Video Short Form	Epic 6672525
12/02/2000	24	2		FALLING AWAY FROM ME	Epic 6688692
03/06/2000	25	2		MAKE ME BAD	Epic 6694332
01/06/2002	12	5		HERE TO STAY 2002 Grammy Award for Best Metal Performance	Epic 6727422
21/09/2002	37	2		THOUGHTLESS	Epic 6731572
23/08/2003	15	4		DID MY TIME	Epic 6741422

KOSHEEN UK production duo from Bristol, with Markee 'Substance' Morrison and Darren 'Decoder' Beale plus singer Sian Evans.

17/06/2000	73	1		EMPTY SKIES/HIDE U	Moksha Recordings MOKSHA 05CD
14/04/2001	50	2		(SLIP & SLIDE) SUICIDE	Moksha Recordings MOKSHA 07CD
01/09/2001	6	7		HIDE U (REMIX)	Moksha/Arista 74321879412
22/12/2001	15	8		CATCH	Moksha/Arista 74321913732
04/05/2002	13	4		HUNGRY	Moshka/Arista 74321934392
31/08/2002	53	1		HARDER	Moshka/Arista 74321954462

❶⁹ Number of weeks single topped the UK chart ↑ Entered the UK chart at #1 ▲⁹ Number of weeks single topped the US chart

445

09/08/2003 . . . . . 7 . . . . . . 7				**ALL IN MY HEAD**	Moksha/Arista 82876527252
01/11/2003 . . . . . 49 . . . . . . 1				WASTING MY TIME	Moksha/Arista 82876570032

KOWDEAN – see OXIDE AND NEUTRINO

KP AND ENVYI US vocal/rap duo Kia 'KP' Phillips and Susan 'Envyi' Hedgepeth.

13/06/1998 . . . . . 14 . . . . . . 4	SWING MY WAY Featured in the 1998 film Can't Hardly Wait. . . . . East West E 3849CD

KRAFTWERK German group formed in 1970 by Ralf Hutter (born 20/8/1946, Krefeld), Florian Schneider-Esleben (born 7/4/1947, Dusseldorf), Klaus Dinger and Thomas Homann, taking their name from the German for power plant. Dinger and Homann left in 1971, replaced two years later by Klaus Roeder-Bartos (born 31/5/1952, Berchtesgaden) and Wolfgang Flur (born 17/7/1947, Frankfurt).

10/05/1975 . . . . . 11 . . . . . . 9	AUTOBAHN . . . . Vertigo 6147 012
28/10/1978 . . . . . 53 . . . . . . 3	NEON LIGHTS . . . . Capitol CL 15998
09/05/1981 . . . . . 39 . . . . . . 6	POCKET CALCULATOR . . . . EMI 5175
11/07/1981 . . . . . 36 . . . . . . 8	THE MODEL/COMPUTER LOVE . . . . EMI 5207
26/12/1981 . . . . ❶¹ . . . . 13 . . . . . ●	**THE MODEL/COMPUTER LOVE** . . . . EMI 5207
20/02/1982 . . . . . 25 . . . . . . 5	SHOWROOM DUMMIES . . . . EMI 5272
06/08/1983 . . . . . 22 . . . . . . 8	TOUR DE FRANCE . . . . EMI 5413
25/08/1984 . . . . . 24 . . . . . . 11	TOUR DE FRANCE . . . . EMI 5413
01/06/1991 . . . . . 20 . . . . . . 4	THE ROBOTS . . . . EMI EM 192
02/11/1991 . . . . . 43 . . . . . . 2	RADIOACTIVITY . . . . EMI EM 201
23/10/1999 . . . . . 61 . . . . . . 1	TOUR DE FRANCE . . . . EMI 8874210
18/03/2000 . . . . . 27 . . . . . . 2	EXPO 2000 . . . . EMI CDEM 562
19/07/2003 . . . . . 20 . . . . . . 4	TOUR DE FRANCE 2003 . . . . EMI CDEM 626
27/03/2004 . . . . . 33 . . . . . . 3	AERODYNAMIK . . . . EMI CDEM 637

BILLY J KRAMER AND THE DAKOTAS UK singer (born William Ashton, 19/8/1943, Bootle) who was a British Rail apprentice fitter when signed by Brian Epstein in 1963. Epstein put Kramer with Manchester group the Dakotas – Mike Maxfield (born 23/2/1944, Manchester, guitar), Robin MacDonald (born 18/7/1943, Nairn, Scotland, rhythm guitar), Ray Jones (born 22/10/1939, Oldham, bass) and Tony Mansfield (born Anthony Bookbinder, 28/5/1943, Salford, drums) – recording various Lennon and McCartney compositions. Lennon suggested adding the 'J' to distinguish him from others with the same surname. The Dakotas split in 1968; by 1971 Kramer was recording under his real name.

02/05/1963 . . . . . 2 . . . . . . 15	**DO YOU WANT TO KNOW A SECRET?** First cover of a Lennon and McCartney song to chart . . . . Parlophone R 5023
01/08/1963 . . . . ❶³ 14	**BAD TO ME** Written specifically by John Lennon for the group . . . . Parlophone R 5049
07/11/1963 . . . . . 4 . . . . . . 13	**I'LL KEEP YOU SATISFIED** Also penned by Lennon and McCartney . . . . Parlophone R 5073
27/02/1964 . . . . ❶² 13	**LITTLE CHILDREN** . . . . Parlophone R 5105
23/07/1964 . . . . . 10 . . . . . . 8	**FROM A WINDOW** . . . . Parlophone R 5156
20/05/1965 . . . . . 12 . . . . . . 8	TRAINS AND BOATS AND PLANES . . . . Parlophone R 5285

KRANKIES UK duo Janette Krankie (born 16/5/1947, Queenzieburn, Scotland) and husband Ian, from kids' TV series The Krankies.

07/02/1981 . . . . . 46 . . . . . . 6	FAN'DABI'DOZI . . . . Monarch MON 21

LENNY KRAVITZ US singer/multi-instrumentalist (born 26/5/1964, New York), self-taught on guitar, bass, piano and drums as a child. Family moved to Los Angeles, CA in 1977 when his mother, actress Roxie Kravitz, landed a TV role. He went into acting, appearing in a Bill Cosby special before leaving home at 16 to pursue a musical career, initially as Romeo Blue. Signed with Virgin in 1989. He was named Best International Male at the 1994 BRIT Awards. Four Grammy Awards include Best Male Rock Vocal Performance in 1999 for American Woman, Best Male Rock Vocal Performance in 2000 for Again and Best Male Rock Vocal Performance in 2001 for Dig In.

02/06/1990 . . . . . 58 . . . . . . 2	MR CABDRIVER . . . . Virgin America VUS 20
04/08/1990 . . . . . 39 . . . . . . 4	LET LOVE RULE . . . . Virgin America VUS 26
30/03/1991 . . . . . 41 . . . . . . 3	ALWAYS ON THE RUN Featured in the 1998 film The Waterboy . . . . Virgin America VUS 34
15/06/1991 . . . . . 11 . . . . . . 8	IT AIN'T OVER TIL IT'S OVER . . . . Virgin America VUS 43
14/09/1991 . . . . . 55 . . . . . . 3	STAND BY MY WOMAN . . . . Virgin America VUS 45
20/02/1993 . . . . . 4 . . . . . . 11 . . . . . ○	**ARE YOU GONNA GO MY WAY** . . . . Virgin America VUSDG 65
22/05/1993 . . . . . 30 . . . . . . 5	BELIEVE . . . . Virgin America VUSCD 72
28/08/1993 . . . . . 20 . . . . . . 7	HEAVEN HELP . . . . Virgin America VUSDG 73
04/12/1993 . . . . . 35 . . . . . . 3	BUDDHA OF SUBURBIA DAVID BOWIE FEATURING LENNY KRAVITZ Theme to the TV series of the same name . . . .
	. . . . Arista 74321177052
04/12/1993 . . . . . 52 . . . . . . 2	IS THERE ANY LOVE IN YOUR HEART . . . . Virgin America VUSDG 76
09/09/1995 . . . . . 22 . . . . . . 3	ROCK AND ROLL IS DEAD . . . . Virgin America VUSCD 93
23/12/1995 . . . . . 54 . . . . . . 2	CIRCUS . . . . Virgin America VUSCD 96
02/03/1996 . . . . . 54 . . . . . . 2	CAN'T GET YOU OFF MY MIND . . . . Virgin America VUSCD 100
16/05/1998 . . . . . 48 . . . . . . 2	IF YOU CAN'T SAY NO . . . . Virgin VUSCD 130
10/10/1998 . . . . . 75 . . . . . . 1	I BELONG TO YOU . . . . Virgin VUSCD 138
20/02/1999 . . . . ❶¹ . . . . 10 . . . . . ○	**FLY AWAY** ↑ Originally used for an advertisement for Nissan in the US and Peugeot in the UK, and also by Sky Sports for their Scottish football coverage. 1998 Grammy Award for Best Male Rock Vocal Performance . . . . Virgin VUSCD 141
06/04/2002 . . . . . 44 . . . . . . 1	STILLNESS OF HEART . . . . Virgin VUSCD 236
07/02/2004 . . . . . 35 . . . . . . 2	SHOW ME YOUR SOUL P DIDDY, LENNY KRAVITZ, PHARRELL WILLIAMS AND LOON Featured in the 2003 film Bad Boys II . . . .
	. . . . Puff Daddy MCSTD 40350
24/07/2004 . . . . . 62 . . . . . . 1	CALIFORNIA . . . . Virgin VUSCD 294

○ Silver disc ● Gold disc ✪ Platinum disc (additional platinum units are indicated by a figure following the symbol) ◎ Singles released prior to 1973 that are known to have sold over 1 million copies in the UK

KRAZE US group comprising brothers and sisters Richard, Martine and Mirielle Laurent and Norris Burrows.

22/10/1988.....29......5......	THE PARTY .... MCA 1288
17/06/1989.....71......1......	LET'S PLAY HOUSE .... MCA 1337

KREUZ UK vocal group with Sean Cummings, Wayne Lawes and Ricardo Reid.

08/07/1995.....75......1......	PARTY ALL NIGHT .... Diesel DES 004C

CHANTAL KREVIAZUK Canadian singer/pianist (born 18/5/1973, Winnipeg).

06/03/1999.....59......1......	LEAVING ON A JET PLANE Featured in the 1998 film *Armageddon* .... Epic 6666272

KREW-KATS UK group. As the Wildcats they were Marty Wilde's backing group from 1959 until 1961 when they changed their name. They comprised Big Jim Sullivan (guitar), Tony Belcher (guitar), Brian 'Liquorice' Locking (bass) and Tony Belcher (drums).

09/03/1961.....33......10......	TRAMBONE .... HMV POP 840

KRIS KROSS US teenage rap duo Mack Daddy (born Chris Kelly, 1/5/1978) and Daddy Mack (born Chris Smith, 10/1/1979) from Atlanta, GA who wore their clothes back to front.

30/05/1992 .....2......8......	JUMP ▲[1] Based on The Jackson 5's *I Want You Back* .... Ruffhouse 6578547
25/07/1992.....16......6......	WARM IT UP .... Ruffhouse 6582187
17/10/1992.....57......1......	I MISSED THE BUS .... Ruffhouse 6583927
19/12/1992.....31......5......	IT'S A SHAME .... Ruffhouse 6588587
11/09/1993.....47......2......	ALRIGHT Contains a sample of Slave's *Just A Touch Of Love* and the uncredited contribution of Supercat..... Ruffhouse 6595652

MARTY KRISTIAN – see NEW SEEKERS

CHAD KROEGER FEATURING JOSEY SCOTT Canadian duo Chad Kroeger and Josey Scott. Kroeger is lead singer with Nickelback, Scott is lead singer with Saliva.

22/06/2002 .....4......14.....O	**HERO** Featured in the 2002 film *Spiderman* .... Roadrunner RR 20463

KROKUS Swiss rock group formed in Soluthurn in 1974 by Chris Von Rohr (vocals), Fernando Von Arb (guitar), Tommy Keifer (guitar), Jurg Naegeli (bass) and Freddie Steady (drums). Von Rohr switched to bass on arrival of lead singer Marc Storace. By 1983 the group was Storace, Von Arb, Von Rohr, Mark Kohler (guitar) and Steve Pace (drums). Pace left in 1984, replaced by Jeff Klaven. Rohr also left in 1984.

16/05/1981.....62......2......	INDUSTRIAL STRENGTH (EP) Tracks on EP: *Bedside Radio, Easy Rocker, Celebration* and *Bye Bye Baby* .... Ariola ARO 258

KRS-ONE US rapper (born Lawrence Kris Parker, 20/8/1966, The Bronx, NYC), with Boogie Down Productions with Scott LaRock before going solo when LaRock was shot to death. His name is an acronym for Knowledge Reigns Supreme Over Nearly Everyone; he later recorded with Goldie.

18/05/1996.....47......1......	RAPPAZ R N DAINJA... Jive JIVECD 396
08/02/1997.....70......1......	WORD PERFECT .... Jive JIVECD 418
26/04/1997.....24......2......	STEP INTO A WORLD (RAPTURE'S DELIGHT) Contains samples of Blondie's *Rapture* and The Mohawks' *The Champ*.............
	.... Jive JIVECD 411
20/09/1997.....66......1......	HEARTBEAT/A FRIEND .... Jive JIVECD 431
01/11/1997.....13......3......	DIGITAL GOLDIE FEATURING KRS ONE .... ffrr FCD 316

KRUSH UK house trio formed in Sheffield by Mark Gamble, Cassius Campbell and Ruth Joy. Their debut hit single also featured Kevin Clark (later a member of Definition of Sound as Kevvon).

05/12/1987 .....3......15.....O	**HOUSE ARREST** .... Club JAB 63
14/11/1992.....71......1......	WALKING ON SUNSHINE .... Network NWK 55

KRUSH PERSPECTIVE US vocal group.

16/01/1993.....61......2......	LET'S GET TOGETHER (SO GROOVY NOW)... Perspective PERD 7416

KRUST UK drum/bass act formed by DJ Krust (born Keith Thompson). He was previously with Fresh 4 and also launched Full Cycle Records with Roni Size.

23/10/1999.....66......1......	CODED LANGUAGE KRUST FEATURING SAUL WILLIAMS... Talkin Loud TLCD 51
26/01/2002.....58......1......	SNAPPED IT .... Full Cycle FCY 034

KUJAY DADA UK production group formed by four Ibiza-based DJs: Kurt, JC, Danny and David.

17/01/2004.....41......3......	YOUNG HEARTS .... Nebula NEBCD 057

KULA SHAKER UK rock group formed in 1994 by Crispian Mills (born 18/1/1973, London, guitar/vocals), Jay Darlington (born 3/5/1969, Sidcup, keyboards), Alonzo Bevin (born 24/10/1970, London, bass), Paul Winter-Hart (born 19/9/1971, London, drums) and Saul Dismont (vocals) as The Kays, name-changing to the Lovely Lads, and then Kula Shaker in 1995 (although minus Dismont). Won The City new band contest, signing with Columbia twelve days later. Named Best British Newcomer at the 1997 BRIT Awards. Mills is the son of actress Hayley Mills and grandson of actor Sir John Mills. They split in September 1999, Mills going solo.

04/05/1996.....35......3......	GRATEFUL WHEN YOU'RE DEAD – JERRY WAS THERE .... Columbia KULACD 2
06/07/1996 .....4......8......	TATTVA.. Columbia KULACD 3K
07/09/1996 .....2......7......	HEY DUDE... Columbia KULACD 4
23/11/1996 .....7......8......	GOVINDA.. Columbia KULACD 5

❶[9] Number of weeks single topped the UK chart ↑ Entered the UK chart at #1 ▲[9] Number of weeks single topped the US chart

447

	DATE	POS	WKS	BPI	SINGLE TITLE	LABEL & NUMBER
	08/03/1997	2	9	○	**HUSH** Featured in the 1997 film *I Know What You Did Last Summer*	Columbia KULACD 6
	02/05/1998	3	6		**SOUND OF DRUMS**	Columbia KULA 21CD
	06/03/1999	14	3		MYSTICAL MACHINE GUN	Columbia KULA 22CD
	15/05/1999	14	4		SHOWER YOUR LOVE	Columbia KULA 23CD

KULAY Philippine vocal group formed by Radha, Boom and Angel, whose name is Filipino for 'colour'.

| | 12/09/1998 | 73 | 1 | | DELICIOUS | INCredible INCRL 4CD |

KUMARA Dutch production duo Neeskens and Van De Jong.

| | 07/10/2000 | 70 | 1 | | SNAP YOUR FINGAZ | Y2K 018CD |

KUMARS – see GARETH GATES

CHARLIE KUNZ US pianist (born 18/8/1896, Allentown, PA) who played piano from the age of six, forming his own semi-pro band at sixteen. He came to England in 1922 (having spent World War I making shells), forming his own band in the early 1930s. Such was his popularity during World War II that he was the subject of German propaganda attempts to discredit him, including Goebbels claiming he was really a German and had left Britain to fight with the German Army in Russia, and claims that his piano playing during radio broadcasts contained morse code messages for the Germans! He died from respiratory problems on 17/3/1958.

| | 17/12/1954 | 16 | 4 | | PIANO MEDLEY NO. 114 Tracks on medley: *There Must Be A Reason, Hold My Hand, If I Give My Heart To You, Little Things Mean A Lot, Make Her Mine* and *My Son My Son* | Decca F 10419 |

KURSAAL FLYERS UK group formed in Southend in 1974 by Paul Shuttleworth (vocals), Graeme Douglas (guitar), Vic Collins (guitar), Richie Bull (bass) and Will Birch (drums). They disbanded in 1977.

| | 20/11/1976 | 14 | 10 | | LITTLE DOES SHE KNOW Track was subtitled *Little Does She Know That I Know That She Knows That I Know She's Cheating On Me* | CBS 4689 |

KURUPT US rapper (born Ricardo Brown, 23/11/1972, Philadelphia, PA), also a member of Tha Dogg Pound (with Delmar 'Daz Dillinger' Amaud).

| | 25/08/2001 | 14 | 7 | | WHERE I WANNA BE **SHADE SHEIST FEATURING NATE DOGG AND KURUPT** Contains a sample of Toto's *Waiting For Your Love* | London LONCD 461 |
| | 13/10/2001 | 21 | 3 | | IT'S OVER | PIAS Recordings PIASB 024CDX |

KUT KLOSE US vocal group with LaVonn Battle, Athena Cage and Tabitha Duncan. Cage later recorded with Keith Sweat.

| | 29/04/1995 | 72 | 1 | | I LIKE | Elektra EKR 200CD |

LI KWAN UK producer Dave Lee who also records as Joey Negro, Jakatta, Akubu, Hed Boys (with Andrew Livingstone), Z Factor, Il Padrinos (with Danny Rampling) and Raven Maize.

| | 17/12/1994 | 51 | 2 | | I NEED A MAN | Deconstruction 74321252192 |

TALIB KWELI FEATURING MARY J. BLIGE US vocal duo comprising male rapper Talib Kweli (born Talib Greene, Brooklyn, NY) and Mary J. Blige.

| | 18/12/2004 | 59 | 1 | | I TRY | Island MCSTD40390 |

KWS UK production duo (both ex-B Line) Chris King and Winston Williams (keyboards) with singer Delroy 'Mystic Meg' Joseph.

	25/04/1992	**●**5 1	16	●	**PLEASE DON'T GO/GAME BOY** Sued by another label over similarities between two versions of *Please Don't Go*	Network NWK 46
	22/08/1992	8	7		**ROCK YOUR BABY**	Network NWK 54
	12/12/1992	30	5		HOLD BACK THE NIGHT **KWS FEATURES GUEST VOCAL FROM THE TRAMMPS**	Network NWK 65
	05/06/1993	71	1		CAN'T GET ENOUGH OF YOUR LOVE	Network NWKCD 72
	09/04/1994	58	1		IT SEEMS TO HANG ON	X-clusive SCLU 006CD
	02/07/1994	21	4		AIN'T NOBODY (LOVES ME BETTER) **KWS AND GWEN DICKEY**	X-clusive XCLU 010CD
	19/11/1994	35	2		THE MORE I GET THE MORE I WANT **KWS FEATURING TEDDY PENDERGRASS**	X-clusive XCLU 011CD

KY-MANI – see PM DAWN

KYO – see BEDROCK

○ Silver disc   ● Gold disc   ✪ Platinum disc (additional platinum units are indicated by a figure following the symbol)   ⊚ Singles released prior to 1973 that are known to have sold over 1 million copies in the UK

L

JONNY L UK singer, instrumentalist and producer (Jonny Listners).

28/08/1993	73	1	OOH I LIKE IT .... XL Recordings XLS 44CD
31/10/1998	66	1	20 DEGREES JONNY L FEATURING SILVAH BULLET .... XL Recordings XLS 103CD

LA BELLE EPOQUE French vocal group of Marcia Briscue, Evelyne Lenton and Judy Lisboa, assembled by producer Albert Weyman.

27/08/1977	2	14	● BLACK IS BLACK .... Harvest HAR 5133

LA BIONDA Italian vocal/instrumental group formed by A and C La Bionda and R W Palmer James.

07/10/1978	54	4	ONE FOR YOU ONE FOR ME .... Philips 6198 227

LA BOUCHE US dance/rap duo Melanie Thornton and Lane McCray. They split in 2000, Thornton going solo; she was killed in a plane crash on 24/11/2001.

24/09/1994	63	1	SWEET DREAMS .... Bell 74321223912
15/07/1995	27	4	BE MY LOVER .... Arista 74321265402
30/09/1995	43	2	FALLING IN LOVE .... Arista 74321305102
02/03/1996	25	4	BE MY LOVER (REMIX) Featured in the 1998 film *A Night At The Roxbury* .... Arista 74321339822
07/09/1996	44	1	SWEET DREAMS Re-issue of Bell 74321223912 .... Arista 74321398542

LA FLEUR Belgian studio group assembled by Rutger Kroese, Errol Lafleur and Ben Liebrand.

30/07/1983	51	4	BOOGIE NIGHTS .... Proto ENA 111

LA GANZ US rap group formed in Louisville, KY by William Killebrew, Larry Young, Marcel and Puff.

09/11/1996	75	1	LIKE A PLAYA .... Jive JIVECD 405

L.A. GUNS US rock group formed in Los Angeles, CA in 1987 by Phil Lewis (vocals), Tracii Guns (guitar), Mick Cripps (guitar), Kelly Nickels (bass) and Steve Riley (drums). Guns had previously been a member of Guns N' Roses. The group disbanded in 1995 with Guns forming Killing Machine and Lewis forming Filthy Lucre.

30/11/1991	61	1	SOME LIE 4 LOVE .... Mercury MER 358
21/12/1991	53	3	THE BALLAD OF JAYNE .... Mercury MER 361

L.A. MIX UK trio formed by London DJ Les Adams, his wife Emma French and multi-instrumentalist Mike Stevens. Adams worked as a remixer for numerous other artists during the 1980s.

10/10/1987	47	4	DON'T STOP (JAMMIN') .... Breakout USA 615
21/05/1988	6	7	CHECK THIS OUT .... Breakout USA 629
08/07/1989	25	6	GET LOOSE L.A. MIX PERFORMED BY JAZZI P .... Breakout USA 659
16/09/1989	66	2	LOVE TOGETHER .... Breakout USA 662
15/09/1990	50	3	COMING BACK FOR MORE .... A&M AM 579
19/01/1991	46	2	MYSTERIES OF LOVE .... A&M AM 707
23/03/1991	69	1	WE SHOULDN'T HOLD HANDS IN THE DARK .... A&M AM 755

SAM LA MORE Australian DJ/producer (born Sam Littlemore, 1976, Sydney).

05/04/2003	70	1	TAKIN' HOLD .... Underwater H2O 023X

LA NA NEE NEE NOO NOO – see BANANARAMA

DANNY LA RUE Irish musical performer (born Daniel Patrick Carroll, 26/7/1927, Cork) who began his professional career in 1947 and is best known as a female impersonator. He was awarded an OBE in the Queen's Birthday Honours List in 2002.

18/12/1968	33	9	ON MOTHER KELLY'S DOORSTEP .... Page One POF 108

LA TREC – see SASH!

LABELLE US R&B vocal group comprising Patti LaBelle (born Patricia Holt, 24/5/1944, Philadelphia, PA), Cindy Birdsong (born 15/12/1939, Camden, NJ), Nona Hendryx (born 18/8/1945, Trenton, NJ) and Sarah Dash (born 24/5/1942, Trenton) formed in 1961 as the Blue Belles. Birdsong left in 1967 to join the Supremes. They disbanded in 1976, with all three remaining members recording solo.

22/03/1975	17	9	LADY MARMALADE (VOULEZ-VOUS COUCHER AVEC MOI CE SOIR) ▲¹ .... Epic EPC 2852

PATTI LABELLE
US singer (born Patricia Holt, 24/5/1944, Philadelphia, PA) in LaBelle from 1962 to 1976 when Nona Hendryx's departure ended the group. Patti went solo, also appeared in films and musicals, including *A Soldier's Story*. She won the 1998 Grammy Award for Best Rhythm & Blues Traditional Vocal Performance for *Live! One Night Only*. She has a star on the Hollywood Walk of Fame.

03/05/1986	2	13	O	**ON MY OWN** ▲³ PATTI LABELLE AND MICHAEL MCDONALD	MCA 1045
02/08/1986	26	6		OH, PEOPLE	MCA 1075
03/09/1994	50	2		THE RIGHT KINDA LOVER	MCA MCSTD 1995

TIFF LACEY
— see REDD SQUARE FEATURING TIFF LACEY

LADIES CHOICE
UK vocal/instrumental group whose debut hit was a cover of a Gwen McCrae US hit.

25/01/1986	41	4	FUNKY SENSATION	Sure Delight SD 01

LADIES FIRST
UK vocal trio Mel, Leanne and Sasha (who was born in Jamaica). Leanne also works as a DJ under the name DJ Precious and had her own radio show on BBC Radio Wales.

24/11/2001	30	2	MESSIN'	Polydor 5873422
13/04/2002	19	6	I CAN'T WAIT	Polydor 5706912

LADY G
— see B-15 PROJECT FEATURING CRISSY D AND LADY G

LADY J
— see RAZE

LADY OF RAGE
US rapper (born Robin Allen, Farmville, VA).

08/10/1994	72	1	AFRO PUFFS Featured in the 1994 film *Above The Rim*	Interscope A 8288CD

LADY SAW
Jamaican singer (born Marion Hall, 1972, St Mary's).

16/12/2000	59	1	BUMP N GRIND (I AM FEELING HOT TONIGHT) M DUBS FEATURING LADY SAW	Telstar CDSTAS 3129
20/10/2001	40	2	SINCE I MET YOU LADY/SPARKLE OF MY EYES UB40 FEATURING LADY SAW	DEP International DEPD 55

LADYSMITH BLACK MAMBAZO
South African group founded by lead vocalist Joseph Shabalala in 1960 (named after Shabalala's hometown and in honour of vocal group Black Mambazo, which means black axe) and turned professional in 1971, they were relatively unknown outside their homeland until Paul Simon invited them to perform on his 1986 *Graceland* album. Shabalala was shot to death on 10/12/1991. The group won the 1987 Grammy Award for Best Traditional Folk Recording for *Shaku Zulu*.

03/06/1995	15	6	SWING LOW SWEET CHARIOT LADYSMITH BLACK MAMBAZO FEATURING CHINA BLACK	Polygram TV SWLDW 2
03/06/1995	47	5	WORLD IN UNION '95 LADYSMITH BLACK MAMBAZO FEATURING PJ POWERS	Polygram TV RUGBY 2
15/11/1997	33	3	INKANYEZI NEZAZI (THE STAR AND THE WISEMAN)	A&M 5823892
11/07/1998	63	1	THE STAR AND THE WISEMAN Re-issue of A&M 5823892	AM:PM 5825692
16/10/1999	42	2	AIN'T NO SUNSHINE LADYSMITH BLACK MAMBAZO FEATURING DES'REE	Universal Music TV 1564332
18/12/1999	13	9	I SHALL BE THERE B*WITCHED FEATURING LADYSMITH BLACK MAMBAZO	Glow Worm 6683332

LADYTRON
UK group formed in Liverpool by Mira Aroyo (vocals), Helena Marnie (keyboards/vocals), Daniel Hunt (keyboards) and Reuben Wu (keyboards).

07/12/2002	68	1	SEVENTEEN	Invicta Hi-Fi/Telstar CDSTAS 3284
22/03/2003	43	1	BLUE JEANS	Invicta Hi-Fi/Telstar CDSTAS 3311
12/07/2003	44	1	EVIL	Invicta Hi-Fi/Telstar CXSTAS 3331

LAGUNA
Spanish production duo Cristiano Spiller and Tommaso Vianello. Cristiano later formed Spiller with Sophie Ellis-Bextor.

01/11/1997	40	2	SPILLER FROM RIO (DO IT EASY)	Positiva CDTIV 83

LAID BACK
Danish vocal/instrumental duo Tim Stahl (keyboards) and John Guldberg (guitar), their record debut was in 1980.

05/05/1990	44	4	BAKERMAN	Arista 112356

LAIN
— see WOOKIE

CLEO LAINE
UK singer (born Clementina Campbell, 28/10/1927, Southall, London) who began her career in 1952. Married to bandleader Johnny Dankworth, she was made a Dame in 1997. She won the 1985 Grammy Award for Best Jazz Vocal Performance for *Cleo At Carnegie – The 10th Anniversary Concert*.

29/12/1960	42	1	LET'S SLIP AWAY	Fontana H 269
14/09/1961	5	13	**YOU'LL ANSWER TO ME**	Fontana H 326

FRANKIE LAINE
US singer (born Frank Paul LoVecchio, 30/3/1913, Chicago, IL) who was in the choir at the Immaculate Conception Church in Chicago before leaving school for a career in show business. He was a dance instructor and singing waiter before he got his break replacing Perry Como as singer with the Freddie Carlone Band in 1937. He first recorded solo for Exclusive in 1945, and acted in films such as *When You're Smiling, Bring Your Smile Along* and *Rock 'Em Cowboy*. After his hits came to an end he toured in cabaret, and by the mid-1980s had retired to San Diego, California with his wife, former actress Nanette Gray. He has a star on the Hollywood Walk of Fame for his contribution to recording, and a second for TV

14/11/1952 . . . . . 7 . . . . . . 7	**HIGH NOON (DO NOT FORSAKE ME)** Featured in the 1952 film *High Noon* and won an Oscar for Best Film Song. . Columbia DB 3113
14/11/1952 . . . . . 8 . . . . . . 8	**SUGARBUSH** DORIS DAY AND FRANKIE LAINE. . . . . Columbia DB 3123
20/03/1953 . . . . . 11 . . . . . . 1	GIRL IN THE WOOD . . . . Columbia DB 2907
03/04/1953 . . . . ❶18 . . . . 36	**I BELIEVE** Reclaimed the #1 position on 3/7/1953 (for 6 weeks) and 21/8/1953 (3 weeks). The total of 18 weeks is the longest any single record has held the #1 position . . . . Philips PB 117
08/05/1953 . . . . . 5 . . . . 16	**TELL ME A STORY** FRANKIE LAINE AND JIMMY BOYD. . . . . Philips PB 126
04/09/1953 . . . . . 2 . . . . 12	**WHERE THE WINDS BLOW** . . . . Philips PB 167
16/10/1953 . . . . ❶2 . . . . 8	**HEY JOE** . . . . Philips PB 172
30/10/1953 . . . . ❶8 . . . . 17	**ANSWER ME** Reclaimed #1 position on 18/12/1953 . . . . Philips PB 196
08/01/1954 . . . . . 2 . . . . 12	**BLOWING WILD** Featured in the 1953 film *Blowing Wild* . . . . Philips PB 207
26/03/1954 . . . . . 9 . . . . . . 2	**GRANADA** . . . . Philips PB 242
16/04/1954 . . . . . 3 . . . . 10	**THE KID'S LAST FIGHT** . . . . Philips PB 258
13/08/1954 . . . . . 3 . . . . 15	**MY FRIEND** . . . . Philips PB 316
08/10/1954 . . . . . 9 . . . . . . 9	**THERE MUST BE A REASON** . . . . Philips PB 306
22/10/1954 . . . . . 8 . . . . 16	**RAIN RAIN RAIN** FRANKIE LAINE AND THE FOUR LADS . . . . Philips PB 311
11/03/1955 . . . . . 20 . . . . . . 1	IN THE BEGINNING . . . . Philips PB 404
24/06/1955 . . . . . 2 . . . . 22	**COOL WATER** FRANKIE LAINE WITH THE MELLOMEN . . . . Philips PB 465
15/07/1955 . . . . . 6 . . . . 13	**STRANGE LADY IN TOWN** Featured in the 1955 film *Strange Lady In Town* . . . . Philips PB 478
11/11/1955 . . . . . 16 . . . . . . 1	HUMMING BIRD . . . . Philips PB 498
25/11/1955 . . . . . 7 . . . . . . 8	**HAWKEYE** . . . . Philips PB 519
20/01/1956 . . . . . 10 . . . . . . 3	**SIXTEEN TONS** FRANKIE LAINE WITH THE MELLOMEN . . . . Philips PB 539
04/05/1956 . . . . . 28 . . . . . . 1	HELL HATH NO FURY Featured in the 1956 film *Meet Me In Las Vegas* which also starred Frankie Laine. . . . . Philips PB 585
07/09/1956 . . . . ❶4 . . . . 21	**A WOMAN IN LOVE** Featured in the 1955 film *Guys And Dolls* . . . . Philips PB 617
28/12/1956 . . . . . 13 . . . . 13	MOONLIGHT GAMBLER . . . . Philips PB 638
26/04/1957 . . . . . 19 . . . . . . 5	LOVE IS A GOLDEN RING FRANKIE LAINE AND THE EASY RIDERS . . . . Philips PB 676
04/10/1957 . . . . . 25 . . . . . . 4	GOOD EVENING FRIENDS/UP ABOVE MY HEAD I HEAR MUSIC IN THE AIR FRANKIE LAINE AND JOHNNIE RAY . . . . . . Philips PB 708
13/11/1959 . . . . . 6 . . . . 20	**RAWHIDE** Theme to the TV series of the same name . . . . Philips PB 965
11/05/1961 . . . . . 50 . . . . . . 1	GUNSLINGER Theme to the TV series of the same name . . . . Philips PB 1135

GREG LAKE
UK singer (born 10/11/1948, Bournemouth, Dorset) who was in King Crimson before forming eponymous band with Keith Emerson and Carl Palmer. He began recording solo while still a member of Emerson, Lake & Palmer.

06/12/1975 . . . . . 2 . . . . . . 7	I BELIEVE IN FATHER CHRISTMAS . . . . Manticore K 13511
25/12/1982 . . . . . 72 . . . . 3	I BELIEVE IN FATHER CHRISTMAS . . . . Manticore K 13511
24/12/1983 . . . . . 65 . . . . 2	I BELIEVE IN FATHER CHRISTMAS . . . . Manticore K 13511

LAMB
UK dance duo Louise Rhodes and Andrew Barlow who first linked in 1994. The pair are also in demand as remixers.

29/03/1997 . . . . . 30 . . . . . . 2	GORECKI . . . . Fontana LAMCD 4
03/04/1999 . . . . . 52 . . . . . . 1	B LINE . . . . Fontana LAMCD 5
22/05/1999 . . . . . 71 . . . . . . 1	ALL IN YOUR HANDS . . . . Fontana LAMCD 6

ANNABEL LAMB
UK singer born in Surrey in 1961; she was a nurse before becoming a singer. She is perhaps best remembered for the controversy surrounding her hit single: the record company launched it with an accompanying video as a 'free gift'.

| 27/08/1983 . . . . . 27 . . . . . . 7 . . . . . . | RIDERS ON THE STORM . . . . A&M AM 131 |

LAMBCHOP
US group formed by Kurt Wagner (vocals), Deanna Varagona (vocals), Paul Niehaus (vocals), Bill Killebrew (guitar), Jonathan Marx (saxophone), John Delworth (keyboards), Mike Doster (bass), Marc Trovillion (bass), Steve Goodhue (drums), Allen Lowrey (drums) and C Scott Chase (percussion).

| 20/05/2000 . . . . . 66 . . . . . . 1 . . . . . . | UP WITH THE PEOPLE. . . . . City Slang 201592 |

LAMBRETTAS
UK mod-revival group formed in Brighton by Jaz Bird (guitar/vocals), Mark Ellis (bass/vocals), Doug Sanders (guitar/vocals) and Paul Wincer (drums). They disbanded in 1981.

01/03/1980 . . . . . 7 . . . . . . 12 . . . . . O	POISON IVY . . . . Rocket XPRESS 25
24/05/1980 . . . . . 12 . . . . 8	D-A-A-ANCE . . . . Rocket XPRESS 33
23/08/1980 . . . . . 49 . . . . . . 4	ANOTHER DAY (ANOTHER GIRL) . . . . Rocket XPRESS 36

LAMPIES
US cartoon group featuring Bright Light, Livewire, Charge, Dustywugg and Contact. The series was created by Dave Bonner and James Caldwell.

| 22/12/2001 . . . . . 48 . . . . . . 3 . . . . . . | LIGHT UP THE WORLD FOR CHRISTMAS . . . . Bluecrest LAMPCD 001 |

❶9 Number of weeks single topped the UK chart ↑ Entered the UK chart at #1 ▲9 Number of weeks single topped the US chart

LANCASTRIANS UK group formed in Altrincham by Barry Langtree (guitar/vocals), Kevin Heywood (guitar/vocals), Terry Benson (bass) and John Fleury (drums).

24/12/1964.....47......2.......	WE'LL SING IN THE SUNSHINE .... Pye 7N 15732

MAJOR LANCE US singer (born 4/4/1939, Chicago, IL) who was a former amateur boxer before recording with Mercury in 1959. Jailed for four years in 1978 for selling cocaine, he then resumed his musical career. He suffered a heart attack in 1987 and by the time of his death was virtually blind from glaucoma. He died from heart failure on 3/9/1994.

13/02/1964.....40......2....... UM UM UM UM UM UM .... Columbia DB 7205

LANCERS – see **TERESA BREWER**

VALERIE LANDSBERG – see **KIDS FROM FAME**

LANDSCAPE UK technopop group formed by Richard James Burgess (drums), Chris Heaton (keyboards), Andy 'Captain Whorlix' Pask (bass), Peter Thomas (trombone and percussion) and John Walters (saxophone/percussion). Burgess later became a top producer.

28/02/1981.....5......13.....○	EINSTEIN A GO-GO .... RCA 22
23/05/1981.....40......7.......	NORMAN BATES .... RCA 60

DESMOND LANE UK penny whistler.

30/03/1956.....13......8.......	WILLIE CAN ALMA COGAN WITH DESMOND LANE – PENNY WHISTLE .... HMV POP 187
01/06/1956.....22......4.......	THE HAPPY WHISTLER CYRIL STAPLETON ORCHESTRA FEATURING DESMOND LANE, PENNY WHISTLE .... Decca F 10735

RONNIE LANE AND SLIM CHANCE UK group formed by Ronnie Lane (born 1/4/1946, Plaistow, London), formerly a member of The Faces, and featuring Steve Bingham (bass), Benny Gallagher (accordion/bass/guitar), Jimmy Jewell (saxophone), Billy Livsey (keyboards), Graham Lyle (banjo/guitar/mandolin/vocals), Ken Slaven (fiddle) and Kevin Westlake (guitar). Gallagher and Lyle had previously been members of McGuinness Flint and would go on to record as a duo. Lane died from multiple sclerosis on 4/6/1997.

12/01/1974.....11......8.......	HOW COME? .... GM GMS 011
15/06/1974.....36......4.......	THE POACHER .... GM GMS 024

EMMA LANFORD – see **MOUSSE T**

DON LANG UK singer (born Gordon Langhorn, 19/1/1925, Halifax), a trombonist with Peter Rose, Teddy Foster and Vic Lewis' bands. He went solo in the mid-1950s, forming TV regulars the Frantic Five. He died from cancer in London on 3/8/1992.

04/11/1955.....16......4.......	CLOUDBURST DON LANG AND THE MAIRANTS-LANGHORN BIG SIX .... HMV POP 115
05/07/1957.....26......2.......	SCHOOL DAY .... HMV POP 350
23/05/1958.....5......11......	WITCH DOCTOR This and above single credited to DON LANG AND HIS FRANTIC FIVE .... HMV POP 488
10/03/1960.....43......1.......	SINK THE BISMARK .... HMV POP 714

k.d. lang Canadian singer (born Kathryn Dawn Lang, 2/11/1961, Consort, Alberta); as a country artist she released her first album in 1983 (in Canada only) and signed with Sire in 1987. She won the Best International Female Award at the 1995 BRIT Awards, and her four Grammy Awards include Best Country Vocal Performance in 1989 for *Absolute Torch And Twang* and and Best Traditional Pop Vocal Album in 2003 with Tony Bennett for *A Wonderful World*.

16/05/1992.....52......4.......	CONSTANT CRAVING .... Sire W 0100
22/08/1992.....13......6.......	CRYING ROY ORBISON (DUET WITH k.d. lang) 1988 Grammy Award for Best Country Vocal Collaboration. Featured in the 1992 film *Holding Out* .... Virgin America VUS 63
27/02/1993.....15......8.......	CONSTANT CRAVING 1992 Grammy Award for Best Female Pop Vocal Performance .... Sire W 0157CD
01/05/1993.....72......1.......	THE MIND OF LOVE .... Sire W 0170CD1
26/06/1993.....68......2.......	MISS CHATELAINE .... Sire W 0181CDX
11/12/1993.....59......1.......	JUST KEEP ME MOVING Featured in the 1994 film *Even Cowgirls Get The Blues* .... Sire W 0227CD
30/09/1995.....53......1.......	IF I WERE YOU .... Sire W 0319CD
18/05/1996.....44......2.......	YOU'RE OK .... Warner Brothers W 0332CD

THOMAS LANG UK singer (born Tom Jones, Liverpool) who was a joiner for British Rail before recording. His backing band featured David Hughes, John Murphy, Andrew Redhead, Paul Thomas and Mark Vormawah.

30/01/1988.....67......3....... THE HAPPY MAN .... Epic VOW 4

LANGE UK producer Stuart Langelann who had previously been responsible for SuReal.

19/06/1999.....68......1.......	I BELIEVE LANGE FEATURING SARAH DWYER .... Addictive 12 ADD039
19/01/2002.....9......6.......	DRIFTING AWAY LANGE FEATURING SKYE .... VC Recordings VCRD 101
22/02/2003.....59......1.......	DON'T THINK IT (FEEL IT) LANGE FEATURING LEAH .... Nebula NEBCD 037

LANTERNS UK vocal/instrumental trio formed in Edinburgh and led by Jim Sutherland.

06/02/1999.....50......1....... HIGHRISE TOWN .... Columbia 6665712

MARIO LANZA US singer (born Alfredo Arnold Cocozza, 31/1/1921, Philadelphia, PA) whose stage surname was his mother's maiden name. Debuting on screen in 1949 in *That Midnight Kiss,* he was considered one of the world's finest operatic tenors. He died in Rome on 7/10/1959. He has two stars on the Hollywood Walk of Fame, for his contribution to recording and motion pictures.

14/11/1952.....3......24......	BECAUSE YOU'RE MINE Featured in the 1952 film *Because You're Mine* .... HMV DA 2017
04/02/1955.....13......1.......	DRINKING SONG Featured in the 1954 film *The Student Prince,* starring Edmund Purdom; Lanza dubbed his singing ... HMV DA 2065

○ Silver disc ● Gold disc ✪ Platinum disc (additional platinum units are indicated by a figure following the symbol) ◎ Singles released prior to 1973 that are known to have sold over 1 million copies in the UK

DATE	POS	WKS	BPI	SINGLE TITLE	LABEL & NUMBER
18/02/1955	18	2		I'LL WALK WITH GOD	HMV DA 2062
22/04/1955	15	3		SERENADE B-side to *Drinking Song*	HMV DA 2065
14/09/1956	25	2		SERENADE Different song to HMV DA 2065	HMV DA 2085

LAPTOP US singer/instrumentalist Jesse Hartman.

DATE	POS	WKS	BPI	SINGLE TITLE	LABEL & NUMBER
12/06/1999	74	1		NOTHING TO DECLARE	Island CID 744

JULIUS LAROSA US singer (born 2/1/1930, Brooklyn, NY) and a regular on the Arthur Godfrey TV show until he was fired on air and then went solo. He also appeared in films, including *Let's Rock*. He later became a popular DJ on WNEW, based in New York.

DATE	POS	WKS	BPI	SINGLE TITLE	LABEL & NUMBER
04/07/1958	15	9		TORERO	RCA 1063

LA'S UK rock group formed in Liverpool in 1986 by Lee Mavers (born 2/8/1962, Liverpool, guitar/vocals), John Power (born 14/9/1967, bass), Paul Hemmings (guitar) and John Timson (drums). They signed with Go Discs in 1987. By the time of their debut release in 1989 the line-up also included Neil Mavers on drums and Peter James 'Cammy' Cammel on guitar.

DATE	POS	WKS	BPI	SINGLE TITLE	LABEL & NUMBER
14/01/1989	59	4		THERE SHE GOES Featured in the films *So I Married An Axe Murderer* (1993) and *The Parent Trap* (1999)	Go Discs GOLAS 2
15/09/1990	57	2		TIMELESS MELODY	Go Discs GOLAS 4
03/11/1990	13	9		THERE SHE GOES Re-issue of Go Discs GOLAS 2	Go Discs GOLAS 5
16/02/1991	43	3		FEELIN'	Go Discs GOLAS 6
10/05/1997	65	1		FEVER PITCH THE EP Tracks on EP: *Goin' Back,* The Pretenders; *There She Goes,* The La's; *How Can We Hang On To A Dream,* Orlando; *Football,* Neil MacColl; and *Boo Hewerdine,* Nick Hornby	Blanco Y Negro NEG 104CD
02/10/1999	65	1		THERE SHE GOES Second re-issue of Go Discs GOLAS 2	Polydor 5614032

LAS KETCHUP Spanish vocal trio of sisters Pilar, Lola and Lucia Nunoz, the daughters of Spanish flamenco artist Tomate.

DATE	POS	WKS	BPI	SINGLE TITLE	LABEL & NUMBER
21/09/2002	49	4		KETCHUP SONG (ASEREJE) (IMPORT)	Columbia 9729602CD
19/10/2002	❶¹	22	✪	THE KETCHUP SONG (ASEREJE) ↑	Columbia 6731932

DENISE LASALLE US singer (born Denise Craig, 16/7/1939, Greenwood, MS); she moved to Chicago, IL at thirteen, taking her name from the city's Lasalle Avenue. Her 1969 debut single was for Parka, and she owns radio station WFXX in Jackson, TN.

DATE	POS	WKS	BPI	SINGLE TITLE	LABEL & NUMBER
15/06/1985	6	13		MY TOOT TOOT	Epic A 6334

LASGO Belgian production group formed by Peter Luts and David Vervoort and fronted by singer Evi Goffin.

DATE	POS	WKS	BPI	SINGLE TITLE	LABEL & NUMBER
09/03/2002	4	15	○	SOMETHING	Positiva CDTIV 169
24/08/2002	7	8		ALONE	Positiva CDTIV 176
30/11/2002	17	7		PRAY	Positiva CDTIVS 182
01/05/2004	24	4		SURRENDER	Positiva CDTIVS 205

LISA LASHES UK DJ/producer (born Lisa Dawn Rose-Wyatt) who is also a member of The Tidy Girls.

DATE	POS	WKS	BPI	SINGLE TITLE	LABEL & NUMBER
08/07/2000	63	1		UNBELIEVABLE	Tidy Trax TIDY 138CD
25/10/2003	52	2		WHAT CAN YOU DO 4 ME?	Tidy Trax TIDY 194C

JAMES LAST German orchestra leader (born Hans Last, 17/4/1929, Bremen) who joined the Hans-Gunther Osterreich Radio Bremen Dance Orchestra in 1946 as a bass player. After a spell fronting the Becker-Last Ensemble he was in-house arranger for Polydor Records, recording his first album, *Non-Stop Dancing* in 1965. His blend of well-known tunes over a dance beat proved immensely popular across Europe, and by 1990 he had released more than 50 albums of a similar style, selling more than 50 million copies. He later started working with a variety of guest musicians and singers, including Astrud Gilberto and Richard Clayderman.

DATE	POS	WKS	BPI	SINGLE TITLE	LABEL & NUMBER
03/05/1980	48	4		THE SEDUCTION (LOVE THEME)	Polydor PD 2071

LAST RHYTHM Italian instrumental/production group formed by Giulio Benedetti and Roberto Attarantato.

DATE	POS	WKS	BPI	SINGLE TITLE	LABEL & NUMBER
14/09/1996	62	1		LAST RHYTHM	Stress CDSTR 76

LATANZA WATERS – see E-SMOOVE FEATURING LATANZA WATERS

LATE SHOW UK vocal/ instrumental group.

DATE	POS	WKS	BPI	SINGLE TITLE	LABEL & NUMBER
03/03/1979	40	6		BRISTOL STOMP	Decca F 13822

LATIN QUARTER UK group formed in 1983 by Steve Skaith (guitar/vocals), Richard Wright (guitar) and Mike Jones (lyrics), adding Yona Dunsford (keyboards/vocals), Carol Douet (vocals), Greg Harewood (bass), Steve Jeffries (keyboards) and Richard Stevens (drums). Stevens and Jeffries left in 1987, replaced by Martin Lascalles (keyboards) and Darren Abraham (drums).

DATE	POS	WKS	BPI	SINGLE TITLE	LABEL & NUMBER
18/01/1986	19	9		RADIO AFRICA	Rockin' Horse RH 102
18/04/1987	73	1		NOMZAMO (ONE PEOPLE ONE CAUSE)	Rockin' Horse RH 113

LATIN RHYTHM – see TITO PUENTE JR AND THE LATIN RHYTHM FEATURING TITO PUENTE, INDIA AND CALI ALEMAN

LATIN THING Canadian/Spanish vocal/instrumental group formed by Poetro Tamames and Miguel Gomez.

DATE	POS	WKS	BPI	SINGLE TITLE	LABEL & NUMBER
13/07/1996	41	1		LATIN THING	Faze 2 CDFAZE 33

GINO LATINO Italian producer Giavomo Maiolini who also records as Lorenzo Cherubini.

DATE	POS	WKS	BPI	SINGLE TITLE	LABEL & NUMBER
20/01/1990	17	7		WELCOME	ffrr F 126

❶⁹ Number of weeks single topped the UK chart ↑ Entered the UK chart at #1 ▲⁹ Number of weeks single topped the US chart

LATINO RAVE – see VARIOUS ARTISTS (MONTAGES)

LATOUR US singer/producer William LaTour from Chicago, IL.

08/06/1991	15	7		PEOPLE ARE STILL HAVING SEX	Polydor PO 147

STACY LATTISHAW US singer (born 25/11/1966, Washington DC) who began singing professionally at eleven and recorded her first album in 1979. She also recorded with Johnny Gill, a childhood friend.

14/06/1980	3	11		JUMP TO THE BEAT	Cotillion K 11496
30/08/1980	51	3		DYNAMITE	Atlantic K 11554

DAVE LAUDAY – see HUSTLERS CONVENTION FEATURING DAVE LAUDAY AND ONDREA DUVERNEY

LAUNCHERS – see EZZ RECO AND THE LAUNCHERS WITH BOYSIE GRANT

CYNDI LAUPER US singer (born 20/6/1953, Queens, NYC) who joined local group Doc West as lead vocalist in 1974, then Flyer for three years. She formed Blue Angel with John Turi in 1978, releasing one album before disbanding and then signed as a solo artist with Portrait in 1983. She appeared in the 1988 film *Vibes* and won the 1984 Grammy Award for Best New Artist.

14/01/1984	2	12	O	GIRLS JUST WANT TO HAVE FUN Featured in the 1985 film *Girls Just Want To Have Fun*	Portrait A 3943
24/03/1984	54	4		TIME AFTER TIME ▲²	Portrait A 4290
16/06/1984	3	13	O	TIME AFTER TIME	Portrait A 4290
01/09/1984	46	5		SHE BOP	Portrait A 4620
17/11/1984	64	2		ALL THROUGH THE NIGHT	Portrait A 4849
27/09/1986	12	11		TRUE COLOURS ▲²	Portrait 65000267
27/12/1986	67	2		CHANGE OF HEART	Portrait CYNDI 1
28/03/1987	57	3		WHAT'S GOING ON	Portrait CYN 1
20/05/1989	7	12		I DROVE ALL NIGHT	Epic CYN 4
05/08/1989	53	4		MY FIRST NIGHT WITHOUT YOU	Epic CYN 5
30/12/1989	68	1		HEADING WEST	Epic CYN 6
06/06/1992	15	7		THE WORLD IS STONE Featured in the 1992 film *Tycoon*	Epic 6579707
13/11/1993	31	4		THAT'S WHAT I THINK	Epic 6598782
08/01/1994	32	4		WHO LET IN THE RAIN	Epic 6590392
17/09/1994	4	13	O	HEY NOW (GIRLS JUST WANT TO HAVE FUN) Re-recording of *Girls Just Want To Have Fun*. Featured in the 1995 film *To Wong Foo, Thanks For Everything! Julie Newmar*	Epic 6608072
11/02/1995	37	2		I'M GONNA BE STRONG	Epic 6611962
26/08/1995	39	2		COME ON HOME	Epic 6614255
01/02/1997	27	2		YOU DON'T KNOW	Epic 6641845

LAUREL AND HARDY UK vocal/instrumental reggae duo Dawkins and Robinson.

02/04/1983	65	2		CLUNK CLICK	CBS A 3213

LAUREL AND HARDY WITH THE AVALON BOYS FEATURING CHILL WILLS UK/US comedy duo Stan Laurel (born Arthur Stanley Jefferson, 16/6/1890, Ulverston, Cumbria) and Oliver 'Babe' Hardy (born Oliver Norvell Hardy, 18/1/1892, Harlem, GA). Although they appeared in the same films from 1919 (*The Lucky Dog* being one of the first), they didn't team up until 1926, with *Putting Pants On Philip* (1927) regarded as their first official film (although *Duck Soup* was released first). The Avalon Boys were Walter Trask, Art Green, Don Brookins and Chill Wills (born in 1903, died in 1978). Hardy died on 7/8/1957 after a stroke the previous September, Laurel from a heart attack on 23/2/1965. They have separate stars on the Hollywood Walk of Fame.

22/11/1975	2	10	O	THE TRAIL OF THE LONESOME PINE In the 1937 film *Way Out West*, uncredited vocal by Rosina Lawrence	United Artists UP 36026

LAURNEA US singer (born Laurnea Wilkinson, Omaha, NE), in Loose Ends and Bobby McFerrin's tour group before going solo.

12/07/1997	36	2		DAYS OF YOUTH	Epic 6646932

LAUREN LAVERNE – see MINT ROYALE

AVRIL LAVIGNE Canadian singer (born 27/9/1984, Napanee, Ontario) discovered by Antonio 'LA' Reid.

07/09/2002	64	2		COMPLICATED (IMPORT)	RCA 74321955782
05/10/2002	3	9		COMPLICATED	RCA 74321965962
28/12/2002	8	9		SK8ER BOI	RCA 74321979782
12/04/2003	7	10		I'M WITH YOU Featured in the 2003 film *Bruce Almighty*	Arista 82876506712
19/07/2003	22	6		LOSING GRIP	Arista 82876534542
22/05/2004	5	9		DON'T TELL ME	Arista 82876617322
14/08/2004	5	9		MY HAPPY ENDING	Arista 82876636492
27/11/2004	24	4		NOBODY'S HOME	Arista 82876663652

JOANNA LAW UK singer who began with brother Simon on Chrysalis Records and also worked with Slacker and Space Brothers.

07/07/1990	67	3		FIRST TIME EVER	Citybeat CBE 752
14/09/1996	15	3		THE GIFT WAY OUT WEST FEATURING MISS JOANNA LAW Contains a sample of Joanna Law's *First Time Ever*	Deconstruction 74321401912

LISA LAW – see CM2 FEATURING LISA LAW

O Silver disc ● Gold disc ✪ Platinum disc (additional platinum units are indicated by a figure following the symbol) ◉ Singles released prior to 1973 that are known to have sold over 1 million copies in the UK

STEVE LAWLER UK DJ/producer born in Birmingham.

11/11/2000	50	1		RISE 'IN	Bedrock BEDRCDS 008

BELLE LAWRENCE UK singer whose follow-up was a dance version of Shakira's *Whenever Wherever*.

30/03/2002	73	1		EVERGREEN	Euphoric CDUPH 024

BILLY LAWRENCE – see RAMPAGE FEATURING BILLY LAWRENCE

JOEY LAWRENCE US singer/actor (born 20/4/1976, Philadelphia, PA) who acted from the age of three. He appeared on *Gimme A Break* and *Blossom*.

26/06/1993	13	7		NOTHIN' MY LOVE CAN'T FIX	EMI CDEM 271
28/08/1993	27	4		I CAN'T HELP MYSELF	EMI CDEM 277
30/10/1993	41	3		STAY FOREVER	EMI CDEM 289
19/09/1998	49	1		NEVER GONNA CHANGE MY MIND	Curb CUBC 34

LEE LAWRENCE UK singer (born Leon Siroto, 1921, Salford) who made his broadcasting debut on *Beginners Please*. He later moved to America and died in February 1961.

20/11/1953	7	6		CRYING IN THE CHAPEL	Decca F 10177
02/12/1955	14	4		SUDDENLY THERE'S A VALLEY This and above single credited to LEE LAWRENCE WITH RAY MARTIN AND HIS ORCHESTRA	
					Columbia DB 3681

SOPHIE LAWRENCE UK singer/actress born in 1972, first well known in role of Diane Butcher in the TV series *Eastenders*.

03/08/1991	21	7		LOVE'S UNKIND	IQ ZB 44821

STEVE LAWRENCE US singer (born Sidney Leibowitz, 8/7/1935, Brooklyn, NYC) who made his first recordings for King in 1953. He married Eydie Gorme in 1957. They won the 1960 Best Performance by a Vocal Group Grammy Award for *We Got Us*.

21/04/1960	4	13		FOOTSTEPS	HMV POP 726
18/08/1960	49	1		GIRLS GIRLS GIRLS	London HLT 9166
22/08/1963	3	13		I WANT TO STAY HERE STEVE AND EYDIE (Gorme)	CBS AAG 163

LAYO AND BUSHWACKA UK dance group duo formed in London by Layo Paskin and Matthew 'Buskwacka' Benjamin. The pair are co-owner and resident DJ at The End respectively.

22/06/2002	30	2		LOVE STORY	XL Recordings XLS 144CD
25/01/2003	8	7		LOVE STORY (VS FINALLY) Remix of XL Recordings XLS 144CD and contains a sample of Kings Of Tomorrow's *Finally*	
					XL Recordings XLS 154CD
16/08/2003	25	3		IT'S UP TO YOU (SHINING THROUGH)	XL Recordings XLS 163CD

LINDY LAYTON UK singer (born Belinda Kimberley Layton, 7/12/1970, Chiswick, London) and former child actress who appeared in the children's TV show *Grange Hill* and numerous advertisements.

10/02/1990	❶⁴	13	●	DUB BE GOOD TO ME BEATS INTERNATIONAL FEATURING LINDY LAYTON	Go Beat GOD 39
11/08/1990	22	7		SILLY GAMES LINDY LAYTON FEATURING JANET KAY	Arista 113452
26/01/1991	42	2		ECHO MY HEART	Arista 113845
31/08/1991	71	2		WITHOUT YOU (ONE AND ONE)	Arista 114636
24/04/1993	38	3		WE GOT THE LOVE	PWL International PWCD 250
30/10/1993	47	1		SHOW ME	PWL International PWCD 275

PETER LAZONBY UK DJ and producer.

10/06/2000	49	1		SACRED CYCLES	Hooj Choons HOOJ 93CD

DOUG LAZY US rapper/producer (born Gene Finlay); as radio DJ Mean Gene he made one album before becoming a producer.

15/07/1989	27	5		LET IT ROLL RAZE PRESENTS DOUG LAZY	Atlantic A 8866
04/11/1989	45	3		LET THE RHYTHM PUMP	Atlantic A 8784
26/05/1990	63	1		LET THE RHYTHM PUMP (REMIX)	East West A 7919

LCD UK production group.

27/06/1998	20	5		ZORBA'S DANCE	Virgin VSCDT 1693
09/10/1999	22	4		ZORBA'S DANCE Re-issue of Virgin VSCO 1693	Virgin VSCDT 1757

LCD SOUNDSYSTEM US production duo Tim Goldsworthy and James Murphy who also record as The DFA.

20/11/2004	52	1		MOVEMENT	EMI DFAEMI2141CD

KEITH LE BLANC – see MALCOLM X

LE CLICK US dance group formed by DJ/producer Robert Haynes and Swedish-Nigerian female singer Kayo Shekoni.

30/08/1997	38	2		CALL ME	Logic 74321509672

KELE LE ROC UK singer (born Kelly Briggs, 5/10/1978, Jamaica) who later worked with Basement Jaxx, appearing on their hit *Romeo*. She won the 1999 MOBO Awards for Best Newcomer.

31/10/1998	8	7		LITTLE BIT OF LOVIN'	1st Avenue 5672812

❶⁹ Number of weeks single topped the UK chart ⬆ Entered the UK chart at #1 ▲⁹ Number of weeks single topped the US chart

455

DATE	POS	WKS	BPI	SINGLE TITLE	LABEL & NUMBER
27/03/1999	8	7		**MY LOVE** 1999 MOBO Award for Best Single	1st Avenue 5636112
30/09/2000	70	1		THINKING OF YOU CURTIS LYNCH JR FEATURING KELE LE ROC AND RED RAT	Telstar CDSTAS 3136
07/06/2003	34	2		FEELIN' U SHY FX AND T-POWER FEATURING KELE LE ROC	London FCD 409

LEAH – see LANGE

VICKY LEANDROS Greek singer born in 1950 and raised in Hamburg, Germany. She came to fame after winning the 1972 Eurovision Song Contest for Luxembourg! Recorded her debut at fifteen; at the height of her success she recorded in seven languages.

DATE	POS	WKS	BPI	SINGLE TITLE	LABEL & NUMBER
08/04/1972	2	16		**COME WHAT MAY** 1972 Eurovision Song Contest under its original title *Apres Toi*	Philips 6000 049
23/12/1972	40	8		THE LOVE IN YOUR EYES	Philips 6000 081
07/07/1973	44	5		WHEN BOUZOUKIS PLAYED	Philips 6000 111

DENIS LEARY US singer (born 20/4/1957, Boston, MA) who also made his name as a comic and actor.

DATE	POS	WKS	BPI	SINGLE TITLE	LABEL & NUMBER
13/01/1996	58	2		ASSHOLE	A&M 5813352

LEAVES Icelandic group formed in Reykjavik by Arna Gudjonsson (guitar/vocals), Arnar Olafsson (guitar/accordion), Hallur Hallson (bass) and Bjarni Grimsson (drums).

DATE	POS	WKS	BPI	SINGLE TITLE	LABEL & NUMBER
18/05/2002	66	1		RACE	B Unique BUN 020CDS

LED ZEPPELIN UK rock group formed in 1968 by Robert Plant (born 20/8/1948, West Bromwich, lead vocals), Jimmy Page (born 9/1/1944, Heston, guitar), John Paul Jones (born John Baldwin, 3/6/1946, Sidcup, bass) and John Bonham (born 31/5/1948, Birmingham, drums) as the New Yardbirds. The name changed shortly after, suggested by The Who's Keith Moon (although it wasn't meant to be complimentary, he thought they would 'go down like a lead balloon', hence the subtle change). Bonham died, choking in his sleep, on 25/9/1980; the group disbanded two months later. They briefly re-formed for Live Aid in 1985, Phil Collins guesting on drums. In 1970, during a Danish tour, they were forbidden to use their name at a Copenhagen gig after Eva von Zeppelin (relative of airship designer Ferdinand von Zeppelin) threatened to sue! They were inducted into the Rock & Roll Hall of Fame in 1995.

DATE	POS	WKS	BPI	SINGLE TITLE	LABEL & NUMBER
13/09/1997	21	2		WHOLE LOTTA LOVE Originally released in America in 1969 (reached position #4). The group was sued by Willie Dixon for plagiarising his song *You Need Love*: the suit was settled out of court in 1987	Atlantic AT 0013CD

ANGEL LEE UK R&B singer (born Angelique Beckford); she shared her name with a pornographic film star who starred in a film with the same name as her debut album – *Forbidden Angel*.

DATE	POS	WKS	BPI	SINGLE TITLE	LABEL & NUMBER
03/06/2000	39	1		WHAT'S YOUR NAME?	WEA 258CD1

ANN LEE UK singer (born Annerley Gordon, Sheffield) she later relocated to Italy.

DATE	POS	WKS	BPI	SINGLE TITLE	LABEL & NUMBER
11/09/1999	57	2		2 TIMES (IMPORT) The single was removed from the charts after it was discovered to be too long to qualify as a single	ZYX 90188
16/10/1999	2	16	●	**2 TIMES**	Systematic SYSX 31
04/03/2000	27	3		VOICES	Systematic SYSCD 32

BRENDA LEE US singer (born Brenda Mae Tarpley, 11/12/1944, Lithonia, GA) who began singing when she was six and signed with Decca in 1956. In 1959 a Paris date was cancelled when the promoter discovered her age. Her manager put out a story that she was a 32-year-old midget and then received even more publicity denying it! Still touring in the 1990s, she was inducted in the Rock and Roll Hall of Fame in 2002.

DATE	POS	WKS	BPI	SINGLE TITLE	LABEL & NUMBER
17/03/1960	4	19		**SWEET NOTHIN'S**	Brunswick 05819
30/06/1960	12	16		I'M SORRY ▲3 Featured in the 1996 film *Casino*	Brunswick 05833
20/10/1960	31	6		I WANT TO BE WANTED ▲1	Brunswick 05839
19/01/1961	12	15		LET'S JUMP THE BROOMSTICK	Brunswick 05823
06/04/1961	45	1		EMOTIONS	Brunswick 05847
20/07/1961	22	8		DUM DUM	Brunswick 05854
16/11/1961	38	3		FOOL NUMBER ONE	Brunswick 05860
08/02/1962	46	2		BREAK IT TO ME GENTLY	Brunswick 05864
05/04/1962	3	12		**SPEAK TO ME PRETTY** Featured in the 1961 film *The Two Little Bears*	Brunswick 05867
21/06/1962	5	12		**HERE COMES THAT FEELING**	Brunswick 05871
13/09/1962	15	11		IT STARTED ALL OVER AGAIN	Brunswick 05876
29/11/1962	6	7		**ROCKIN' AROUND THE CHRISTMAS TREE**	Brunswick 05880
17/01/1963	7	17		**ALL ALONE AM I**	Brunswick 05882
28/03/1963	10	16		**LOSING YOU**	Brunswick 05886
18/07/1963	14	9		I WONDER	Brunswick 05891
31/10/1963	28	6		SWEET IMPOSSIBLE YOU	Brunswick 05896
09/01/1964	5	15		**AS USUAL**	Brunswick 05899
09/04/1964	26	8		THINK	Brunswick 05903
10/09/1964	17	8		IS IT TRUE	Brunswick 05915
10/12/1964	29	5		CHRISTMAS WILL BE JUST ANOTHER LONELY DAY	Brunswick 05921

04/02/1965.....41......2...... THANKS A LOT .... Brunswick 05927
29/07/1965.....22......12...... TOO MANY RIVERS .... Brunswick 05936

BYRON LEE – see BORIS GARDINER

CURTIS LEE
US singer (born 28/10/1941, Yuma, AZ) who began his career in 1959 and signed with Dune Records the following year.

31/08/1961.....47......2...... PRETTY LITTLE ANGEL EYES .... London HLX 9397

DEE C. LEE
UK singer born Diane Sealey who joined Wham! as a backing singer in 1982. She left in October 1983 to join future husband Paul Weller (they married in December 1986 and separated in 1994) in Style Council.

09/11/1985 .....3......12......○ SEE THE DAY .... CBS A 6570
08/03/1986.....46......5...... COME HELL OR WATERS HIGH... CBS A 6869
13/11/1993.....25......3...... NO TIME TO PLAY GURU FEATURING D. C. LEE .... Cooltempo CDCOOL 282

GARRY LEE AND SHOWDOWN
Canadian vocal/instrumental group; their debut hit first released in Canada in 1982.

31/07/1993.....44......3...... THE RODEO SONG .... Party Dish VCD 101

JACKIE LEE
Irish singer (born Jacqueline Norah Flood), 29/5/1936, Dublin); recorded debut in 1956 and formed Jackie And The Raindrops.

10/04/1968.....10......14 ...... WHITE HORSES JACKY Theme to the TV series of the same name .... Philips BF 1674
02/01/1971.....14......17 ...... RUPERT Theme to the children's cartoon series *Rupert The Bear* .... Pye 7N 45003

LEAPY LEE
UK singer (born Lee Graham, 2/7/1942, Eastbourne) who was first nicknamed Leapy at school.

21/08/1968 .....2......21 ...... LITTLE ARROWS .... MCA MU 1028
20/12/1969.....29......7 ...... GOOD MORNING.. MCA MK 5021

MURPHY LEE – see NELLY and PUFF DADDY

PEGGY LEE
US singer (born Norma Jean Egstrom, 26/5/1920, Jamestown, ND); she began as a jazz singer with a number of bands before going solo in 1943, making her film debut in 1950 in *Mister Music*. Married four times, to Jack Del Rio, Dewey Martin, Dave Barbour and Brad Dexter. Numerous films included *Johnny Guitar, The Jazz Singer* and *Pete Kelly's Blues* (for which she was nominated for an Oscar for Best Supporting Actress). She suffered a stroke in October 1988 but recovered to collect a Grammy's Lifetime Achievement Award in 1995. She provided the singing voice to the Walt Disney animated film *The Lady And The Tramp* and was later awarded $4 million in video sale royalties after taking the company to court. She won the 1969 Grammy Award for Best Female Solo Vocal Performance for *Is That All There Is?* Her hit *Fever*, which has been covered by artists ranging from Helen Shapiro, Madonna and Ronnie Laws, was co-written by Eddie Cooley and John Davenport. Davenport was in fact a nom de plume of Otis Blackwell, who was under contract to Jay-Dee at the time. Peggy later sued Universal Music for underpaid royalties on her original Decca recordings. She won a settlement in January 2002, but died from cancer four days later on 22/1/2002. She has a star on the Hollywood Walk of Fame.

24/05/1957.....5......13 ...... MR WONDERFUL .... Brunswick 05671
15/08/1958.....5......11 ...... FEVER .... Capitol CL 14902
23/03/1961.....30......4....... TILL THERE WAS YOU.. Capitol CL 15184
22/08/1992.....75......1....... FEVER Re-issue of Capitol CL 14902 .... Capitol PEG 1

TONEY LEE
US singer born in New York City who also worked with Arthur Baker and the Criminal Element Orchestra.

29/01/1983.....64......4....... REACH UP .... TMT 2

TRACEY LEE
US rapper born in Philadelphia, PA who later worked with Queen Pen.

19/07/1997.....51......1....... THE THEME Contains a sample of Pieces Of A Dream's *Mt Airy Groove* .... Universal UND 56133

LEE-CABRERA
US duo producer/DJ Steven Lee and Albert Cabrera.

12/04/2003.....58......1....... SHAKE IT (NO TE MUEVAS TANTO) .... Credence 12CRED 035
06/09/2003.....16......6....... SHAKE IT (MOVE A LITTLE CLOSER) LEE CABRERA FEATURING ALEX CARTANA .... Credence CDCRED 039
15/11/2003.....45......2....... SPECIAL 2003.. Credence CDCRED 040
10/07/2004.....58......1....... VOODOO LOVE C2 CDC2001

LEEDS UNITED F.C.
UK football club formed in 1919 after the Football Association had ordered the winding up of Leeds City for making illegal payments to players.

29/04/1972.....10......10 ...... LEEDS UNITED .... Chapter One SCH 168
25/04/1992.....54......3...... LEEDS LEEDS LEEDS .... Q Music LUFC 2

CAROL LEEMING – see STAXX FEATURING CAROL LEEMING

LEE-O – see K-WARREN FEATURING LEE-O

RAYMOND LEFEVRE
French orchestra leader (born 1922, Paris) popular in Europe, who also had US hits during his career.

15/05/1968.....46......2...... SOUL COAXING .... Major Minor MM 559

❶⁹ Number of weeks single topped the UK chart ↑ Entered the UK chart at #1 ▲⁹ Number of weeks single topped the US chart

457

LEFTFIELD
UK instrumental/production duo Neil Barnes and Paul Daley (previously in A Man Called Adam). Originally Leftfield was Barnes recording solo; he issued one single for Outer Rhythm, *Not Forgotten*. When legal problems with Outer Rhythm prevented them recording, the duo made their names as remixers. They later set up the Hard Hands label, also recording as Herbal Infusion. They split in February 2002. Lydon is ex-Sex Pistol and PIL singer John Lydon, aka Johnny Rotten. Roots Manuva is singer Rodney Smith.

DATE	POS	WKS	SINGLE TITLE	LABEL & NUMBER
12/12/1992	59	1	SONG OF LIFE Featured in the 2001 film *Lara Croft: Tomb Raider*	Hard Hands HAND 002T
13/11/1993	13	5	OPEN UP LEFTFIELD LYDON	Hard Hands HAND 009CD
25/03/1995	18	3	ORIGINAL LEFTFIELD FEATURING TONI HALLIDAY	Hard Hands HAND 18CD
05/08/1995	22	3	THE AFRO-LEFT EP LEFTFIELD FEATURING DJUM DJUM Tracks on EP: *Afro-Left, Afro Ride, Afro Central* and *Afro Sol*	Hard Hands HAND 23CD
20/01/1996	13	3	RELEASE THE PRESSURE	Hard Hands HAND 29CD
18/09/1999	7	5	AFRIKA SHOX LEFTFIELD/BAMBAATAA	Hard Hands HAND 057CD1
11/12/1999	28	3	DUSTED LEFTFIELD/ROOTS MANUVA	Hard Hands HAND 058CD1

LEGEND B
German production duo Pete Blaze and Jens Ahrens.

DATE	POS	WKS	SINGLE TITLE	LABEL & NUMBER
22/02/1997	45	1	LOST IN LOVE	Perfecto PERF 132CD

JODY LEI
South African singer born in Johannesburg in 1984 who moved to London when she was fourteen.

DATE	POS	WKS	SINGLE TITLE	LABEL & NUMBER
22/02/2003	34	2	SHOWDOWN	Independiente ISOM 66SMS

LEILANI
UK singer born Leilani Sen in Potters Bar with Chinese, Maltese and Irish ancestry. She was working in a Happy Shopper while trying to become a professional singer and songwriter.

DATE	POS	WKS	SINGLE TITLE	LABEL & NUMBER
06/02/1999	19	4	MADNESS THING	ZTT 124CD
12/06/1999	40	2	DO YOU WANT ME?	ZTT 134CD
03/06/2000	73	1	FLYING ELVIS	ZTT 145CD

PAUL LEKAKIS
US singer (born 22/10/1965, Yonkers, NY) who is also a model and dancer.

DATE	POS	WKS	SINGLE TITLE	LABEL & NUMBER
30/05/1987	60	4	BOOM BOOM (LET'S GO BACK TO MY ROOM)	Champion CHAMP 43

LEMAR
UK singer (born Lemar Obika, in London) who first came to prominence as a competitor on BBC TV's *Fame Academy*. He was named Best Urban Act at the 2004 BRIT Awards.

DATE	POS	WKS	SINGLE TITLE	LABEL & NUMBER
30/08/2003	2	11	DANCE (WITH U)	Sony Music 6741322
29/11/2003	5	11	50:50/LULLABY	Sony Music 6744185
06/03/2004	9	6	ANOTHER DAY	Sony Music 6746595
27/11/2004	3	5+	IF THERE'S ANY JUSTICE	Sony Music 6756072

LEMON JELLY
UK production/DJ duo Nick Franglen and Fred Deakin.

DATE	POS	WKS	SINGLE TITLE	LABEL & NUMBER
19/10/2002	36	2	SPACE WALK	Impotent Fury/XL Recordings IFXLS 150CD
01/02/2003	16	3	NICE WEATHER FOR DUCKS	Impotent Fury/XL Recordings IFXL 156CD
04/12/2004	31	3	STAY WITH YOU	XL Recordings IFXLS201CD

LEMON PIPERS
US pop group formed in Oxford, OH by Ivan Browne (guitar/vocals), Bill Bartlett (guitar), Reg Nave (keyboards), Steve Walmsley (bass) and Bill Albaugh (drums). Bartlett later formed Ram Jam. Albaugh died on 20/1/1999.

DATE	POS	WKS	SINGLE TITLE	LABEL & NUMBER
07/02/1968	7	11	GREEN TAMBOURINE ▲[1]	Pye International 7N 25444
01/05/1968	41	5	RICE IS NICE	Pye International 7N 25454

LEMON TREES
UK vocal/instrumental group formed by Guy Chambers who later worked with Robbie Williams.

DATE	POS	WKS	SINGLE TITLE	LABEL & NUMBER
26/09/1992	75	1	LOVE IS IN YOUR EYES	Oxygen GASP 1
07/11/1992	62	2	THE WAY I FEEL	Oxygen GASP 2
13/02/1993	55	2	LET IT LOOSE	Oxygen GASPD 3
17/04/1993	55	3	CHILD OF LOVE	Oxygen GASPD 4
03/07/1993	52	1	I CAN'T FACE THE WORLD	Oxygen GASPD 6

LEMONESCENT
UK vocal group formed in Scotland by Sarah Cassidy (born 14/5/1981, Glasgow), Shonagh Strachan (born 23/2/1985, Irvine), Nikki MacLachlan (born 17/5/1981, Irvine) and Lisa Harrison (born 20/11/1981, Burnley).

DATE	POS	WKS	SINGLE TITLE	LABEL & NUMBER
29/06/2002	70	1	BEAUTIFUL	Supertone SUPTCD 1
09/11/2002	48	1	SWING MY HIPS (SEX DANCE)	Supertone SUPTCD 2
05/04/2003	36	1	HELP ME MAMA	Supertone SUPTCD 4
21/06/2003	31	1	CINDERELLA	Supertone SUPTCD 8
03/07/2004	37	1	ALL RIGHT NOW	Supertone SUPTCD 12

LEMONHEADS
US rock group formed in Boston, MA as the Whelps in 1985 by Evan Dando (born 4/3/1967, Boston, guitar/vocals), Ben Deily and Jesse Peretz. Dando adopted the name Lemonheads before settling on a line-up of himself, Nic Dalton (bass) and David Ryan (drums). The Lemonheads signed with Atlantic in 1990.

DATE	POS	WKS	SINGLE TITLE	LABEL & NUMBER
17/10/1992	70	1	IT'S A SHAME ABOUT RAY	Atlantic A 7423
05/12/1992	19	9	MRS ROBINSON/BEIN' AROUND A-side featured in the 1999 film *The Other Sister*	Atlantic A 7401
06/02/1993	44	2	CONFETTI/MY DRUG BUDDY	Atlantic A 7430CD
10/04/1993	31	3	IT'S A SHAME ABOUT RAY Re-issue of Atlantic A 7423	Atlantic A 5764CD
16/10/1993	14	4	INTO YOUR ARMS	Atlantic A 7302CD
27/11/1993	57	2	IT'S ABOUT TIME	Atlantic A 7296CD

14/05/1994	55	2		BIG GAY HEART	Atlantic A 7259CD
28/09/1996	39	2		IF I COULD TALK I'D TELL YOU Featured in the 1998 film *There's Something About Mary*	Atlantic A 5661CD1
14/12/1996	61	1		IT'S ALL TRUE	Atlantic A 5635CD

LEN Canadian rap group formed in Ontario by The Burger Pimp (Marc Costanzo), his sister Sharon Constanzo, D Rock, Philip Rae (also known as Planet Pea and Kudu5), DJ Moves and Drunkness Monster.

| 18/12/1999 | 8 | 13 | | **STEAL MY SUNSHINE** Contains a sample of Andrea True's *More More More*. Featured in the 1999 film *Go* | Columbia 6685062 |
| 10/06/2000 | 28 | 2 | | CRYPTIK SOULS CREW Contains a sample of Tony Camillo's *Bazuka* | Columbia 6693832 |

LENA – see **LENA FIAGBE**

JOHN LENNON UK singer (born John Winston Lennon, 9/10/1940, Woolton, Liverpool) and founding member of the Beatles. He began solo projects while still in the group, including an appearance in the film *How I Won The War* in 1967, writing a number of books and his debut solo album *Two Virgins* in 1968. He married Cynthia Powell in 1962 and met Yoko Ono in 1966, marrying her in Gibraltar in 1969. He formed the Plastic Ono Band in 1969 and moved to New York in 1971, although he was involved in a lengthy battle with US immigration until a resident visa was issued in 1976. He stopped recording in 1975 to become a 'house-husband' but returned to the studio in 1980. His return album *Double Fantasy* had just been released when he was shot dead outside his New York apartment by Mark David Chapman on 8/12/1980. In the immediate aftermath he scored three #1s in eight weeks, including *(Just Like) Starting Over*, which had already slipped down the charts to #21 at the time of his death. Awarded the MBE in 1964, he returned it in 1969 in protest at Britain's involvement in Nigeria-Biafra, their support for America in Vietnam and 'against *Cold Turkey* slipping down the charts'. His son Julian by Cynthia also recorded solo, while his son Sean by Yoko is a promising musician. He was inducted into the Rock & Roll Hall of Fame in 1994 (The Beatles had been inducted in 1988). John Lennon and Yoko Ono's *Double Fantasy* album won the 1981 Grammy Award for Album of the Year. He has a star on the Hollywood Walk of Fame.

09/07/1969	2	13		**GIVE PEACE A CHANCE** Featured in the 1970 film *The Strawberry Statement*	Apple 13
01/11/1969	14	8		COLD TURKEY This and above single credited to PLASTIC ONO BAND	Apple APPLES 1001
21/02/1970	5	9		INSTANT KARMA LENNON, ONO AND THE PLASTIC ONO BAND	Apple APPLES 1003
20/03/1971	7	9		**POWER TO THE PEOPLE** JOHN LENNON AND THE PLASTIC ONO BAND	Apple R 5892
09/12/1972	4	8		**HAPPY XMAS (WAR IS OVER)** JOHN AND YOKO AND THE PLASTIC ONO BAND WITH THE HARLEM COMMUNITY CHOIR	
					Apple R 5970
24/11/1973	26	9		MIND GAMES	Apple R 5994
19/10/1974	36	4		WHATEVER GETS YOU THROUGH THE NIGHT ▲[1] JOHN LENNON WITH THE PLASTIC ONO NUCLEAR BAND	Apple R 5998
04/01/1975	48	1		HAPPY XMAS (WAR IS OVER) JOHN AND YOKO AND THE PLASTIC ONO BAND WITH THE HARLEM COMMUNITY CHOIR	
					Apple R 5970
08/02/1975	23	8		#9 DREAM	Apple R 6003
03/05/1975	30	7		STAND BY ME	Apple R 6005
01/11/1975	6	11	O	**IMAGINE** Featured in the 1997 film *Mr Holland's Opus*	Apple R 6009
08/11/1980	❶[1]	15	●	**(JUST LIKE) STARTING OVER** ▲[5]	Geffen K 79186
20/12/1980	2	9		**HAPPY XMAS (WAR IS OVER)**	Apple R 5970
27/12/1980	❶[4]	13	O	**IMAGINE**	Apple R 6009
24/01/1981	❶[2]	11	O	**WOMAN** All the #1's were posthumous. *Woman* replaced *Imagine* at #1, the first time an artist had replaced themselves at #1 since The Beatles in 1963	Geffen K 79195
24/01/1981	33	5		GIVE PEACE A CHANCE PLASTIC ONO BAND	Apple 13
21/03/1981	40	4		I SAW HER STANDING THERE THE ELTON JOHN BAND FEATURING JOHN LENNON AND THE MUSCLE SHOALS HORNS	
					DJM DJS 10965
04/04/1981	30	6		WATCHING THE WHEELS Featured in the films *Never Been Kissed* (1999) and *Wonder Boys* (2000)	Geffen K 79207
19/12/1981	28	5		HAPPY XMAS (WAR IS OVER) JOHN AND YOKO AND THE PLASTIC ONO BAND WITH THE HARLEM COMMUNITY CHOIR	
					Apple R 5970
20/11/1982	41	7		LOVE	Parlophone R 6059
25/12/1982	56	3		HAPPY XMAS (WAR IS OVER) JOHN AND YOKO AND THE PLASTIC ONO BAND WITH THE HARLEM COMMUNITY CHOIR	
					Apple R 5970
21/01/1984	6	6		**NOBODY TOLD ME**	Ono Music/Polydor POSP 700
17/03/1984	32	6		BORROWED TIME	Polydor POSP 701
30/11/1985	65	2		JEALOUS GUY	Parlophone R 6117
10/12/1988	45	5		IMAGINE/JEALOUS GUY/HAPPY XMAS (WAR IS OVER)	Parlophone R 6199
25/12/1999	3	13	●	**IMAGINE** Re-issue of Apple R 6009	Parlophone CDR 6534
20/12/2003	33	3	●	HAPPY XMAS (WAR IS OVER) JOHN AND YOKO AND THE PLASTIC ONO BAND	Parlophone CDR 6627

JULIAN LENNON UK singer (born John Charles Julian Lennon, 8/4/1963, Liverpool); he is the son of John Lennon and the first child to be born to any of The Beatles. Paul McCartney penned *Hey Jude* in his honour.

06/10/1984	6	11		**TOO LATE FOR GOODBYES**	Charisma JL 1
15/12/1984	55	6		VALOTTE	Charisma JL 2
09/03/1985	75	1		SAY YOU'RE WRONG	Charisma JL 3
07/12/1985	40	7		BECAUSE	EMI 5538
11/03/1989	59	3		NOW YOU'RE IN HEAVEN	Virgin VS 1154
24/08/1991	6	13		**SALTWATER**	Virgin VS 1361
30/11/1991	53	2		HELP YOURSELF	Virgin VS 1379
25/04/1992	56	3		GET A LIFE	Virgin VS 1398
23/05/1998	66	1		DAY AFTER DAY	Music From Another JULIAN 4CD

❶[9] Number of weeks single topped the UK chart ↑ Entered the UK chart at #1 ▲[9] Number of weeks single topped the US chart

459

ANNIE LENNOX
UK singer (born 25/12/1954, Aberdeen) who met Dave Stewart in 1971 and teamed up with him in Catch, the Tourists and then the Eurythmics. She took a two-year sabbatical from the group in 1990, enabling Stewart to undertake a number of solo projects, but they disbanded in 1991. She returned as a solo artist in 1992. One of the biggest winners at the BRIT Awards, she won the Best British Female award in 1984, 1986, 1989, 1990 (all as lead vocalist with the Eurythmics), 1993 and 1996 and the Best Album Award (for *Diva*) in 1993. The Eurythmics received the Outstanding Contribution to British Music Award at the 1999 BRITS. She re-formed The Eurythmics with Stewart in 1999, and was in the *It's Only Rock 'N' Roll* project for the Children's Promise charity. Having won a Grammy Award with The Eurythmics, she collected two more, including Best Music Video Long Form in 1992 for *Diva*. She won the Oscar in 2004 for Best Original Score for *Lord Of The Rings – Return Of The King,* and Best Original Song with Fran Walsh and Howard Shore for *Into The West* from *Lord Of The Rings – Return Of The King*.

DATE	POS	WKS	BPI	SINGLE TITLE	LABEL & NUMBER
03/12/1988	28	8		PUT A LITTLE LOVE IN YOUR HEART **ANNIE LENNOX AND AL GREEN** Featured in the 1988 film *Scrooged*	A&M AM 484
28/03/1992	5	8		**WHY** Featured in the 1995 film *Boys On The Side*	RCA PB 45317
06/06/1992	23	5		PRECIOUS	RCA 74321100257
22/08/1992	8	8		**WALKING ON BROKEN GLASS**	RCA 74321107227
31/10/1992	26	4		COLD	RCA 74321116902
13/02/1993	3	12	O	**LITTLE BIRD/LOVE SONG FOR A VAMPIRE** B-side featured in the 1992 film *Bram Stoker's Dracula*	RCA 74321133832
18/02/1995	2	12	O	**NO MORE 'I LOVE YOUS'** 1995 Grammy Award for Best Female Pop Vocal Performance	RCA 74321257162
10/06/1995	16	6		A WHITER SHADE OF PALE	RCA 74321284822
30/09/1995	31	3		WAITING IN VAIN	RCA 74321316132
09/12/1995	44	2		SOMETHING SO RIGHT	RCA 74321332392

DINO LENNY
Italian producer (born in Cassino near Rome) who later moved to London and set up the Age One studio and label.

DATE	POS	WKS	BPI	SINGLE TITLE	LABEL & NUMBER
04/05/2002	60	1		I FEEL STEREO Contains a sample of Chaka Khan's *I Feel For You*	Incentive CENT 40CDS
10/05/2003	51	1		CHANGE THE WORLD **DINO LENNY VS THE HOUSEMARTINS** Contains a sample of The Housemartin's *Flag Day*	Free 2 Air 0146685 F2A

RULA LENSKA – see JULIE COVINGTON, RULA LENSKA, CHARLOTTE CORNWELL AND SUE JONES-DAVIES

PHILLIP LEO
UK reggae singer who began his career with Fashion Records.

DATE	POS	WKS	BPI	SINGLE TITLE	LABEL & NUMBER
23/07/1994	57	2		SECOND CHANCE	EMI CDEM 327
25/03/1995	64	1		THINKING ABOUT YOUR LOVE	EMI CDEM 358

KRISTIAN LEONTIOU
UK singer/songwriter (born 1982, London).

DATE	POS	WKS	BPI	SINGLE TITLE	LABEL & NUMBER
05/06/2004	9	7		**THE STORY OF MY LIFE**	Polydor 9866632
28/08/2004	13	6		SHINING Featured in the 2004 film *Win A Date With Tad Hamilton*	Polydor 9867640
04/12/2004	54	1		SOME SAY	Polydor 9868904

LES RHYTHMES DIGITALES
UK multi-instrumentalist Stuart Price who uses the French-sounding name Jacques Lu Cont for Les Rhythmes Digitales. He was born in Paris, but only because his parents were on holiday there from Reading!

DATE	POS	WKS	BPI	SINGLE TITLE	LABEL & NUMBER
25/04/1998	69	1		MUSIC MAKES YOU LOSE CONTROL	Wall Of Sound WALLD 037
07/08/1999	56	1		SOMETIMES **LES RYTHMES DIGITALES FEATURING NIK KERSHAW**	Wall Of Sound WALLD 054
30/10/1999	60	1		JACQUES YOUR BODY (MAKE ME SWEAT)	Wall Of Sound WALLD 060

LESHAUN – see LL COOL J

LESS THAN JAKE
US rock group formed in Gainesville, FL by Chris DeMakes (guitar/vocals), Roger Manganelli (bass) and Vinnie Fiorello (drums).

DATE	POS	WKS	BPI	SINGLE TITLE	LABEL & NUMBER
05/08/2000	51	1		ALL MY BEST FRIENDS ARE METALHEADS	Golf CDSHOLE 027
08/09/2001	57	1		GAINESVILLE ROCK CITY	Golf CDSHOLE 48
24/05/2003	39	1		SHE'S GONNA BREAK SOON	Sire W 606CD

LESTER – see NORMAN COOK

KETTY LESTER
US singer (born Revoyda Frierson, 16/8/1934, Hope, AR) who moved to Los Angeles, California in 1955 and acted in numerous films and TV shows, including *Little House On The Prairie*.

DATE	POS	WKS	BPI	SINGLE TITLE	LABEL & NUMBER
19/04/1962	4	12		LOVE LETTERS	London HLN 9527
19/07/1962	45	4		BUT NOT FOR ME	London HLN 9574

LET LOOSE
UK vocal trio Richie Wermerling, Rob Jeffrey and Lee Murray.

DATE	POS	WKS	BPI	SINGLE TITLE	LABEL & NUMBER
24/04/1993	44	3		CRAZY FOR YOU	Vertigo VERCD 74
09/04/1994	44	2		SEVENTEEN	Mercury MERCD 400
25/06/1994	2	24	●	**CRAZY FOR YOU** Re-issue of Vertigo VERCD 74	Mercury MERCD 402
22/10/1994	11	9		SEVENTEEN (REMIX)	Mercury MERCD 406
28/01/1995	12	6		ONE NIGHT STAND	Mercury MERCD 419
29/04/1995	8	5		**BEST IN ME**	Mercury MERDD 428
04/11/1995	29	4		EVERYBODY SAY EVERYBODY DO	Mercury MERDD 446
22/06/1996	7	6		**MAKE IT WITH YOU**	Mercury MERDD 464
07/09/1996	25	2		TAKE IT EASY	Mercury MERCD 472
16/11/1996	65	1		DARLING BE HOME SOON	Mercury MERCD 475

GERALD LETHAN – see WALL OF SOUND FEATURING GERALD LETHAN

O Silver disc ● Gold disc ✪ Platinum disc (additional platinum units are indicated by a figure following the symbol) ◎ Singles released prior to 1973 that are known to have sold over 1 million copies in the UK

LETTERMEN US vocal group formed in Los Angeles, California in 1960 by Tony Butala (born 20/11/1940, Sharon, PA), Jim Pike (born 6/11/1938, St Louis, MO) and Bob Engemann (born 19/2/1936, Highland Park, MI), who was replaced by Jim's brother Gary in 1968.

23/11/1961 . . . . . 36 . . . . . . 3 . . . . THE WAY YOU LOOK TONIGHT . . . . Capitol CL 15222

LEVEL 42 UK group formed in London in 1980 by Mark King (born 20/10/1958, Cowes, Isle of Wight, vocals/bass), Phil Gould (born 28/2/1957, Hong Kong, drums), Boon Gould (born 4/3/1955, Shanklin, Isle of Wight, guitar) and Mike Lindup (born 17/3/1959, London, keyboards/vocals). They debuted on the Elite label before signing with Polydor. The Gould brothers both left in 1987, replaced by Gary Husband (drums) and Alan Murphy (guitar). By 1991 they had a nucleus of King and Lindup with lead guitarist Jakko Jakszyk. They disbanded in 1995. Named from a Douglas Adams novel, *The Hitchhikers Guide To The Galaxy*, in which '42' was the answer to 'the meaning of life, the universe and everything'. Murphy died from AIDS-related pneumonia on 19/10/1989. Mark King has also recorded solo.

30/08/1980	61	4		LOVE MEETING LOVE	Polydor POSP 170
18/04/1981	38	6		LOVE GAMES	Polydor POSP 234
08/08/1981	57	6		TURN IT ON	Polydor POSP 286
14/11/1981	47	4		STARCHILD	Polydor POSP 343
08/05/1982	49	4		ARE YOU HEARING (WHAT I HEAR)?	Polydor POSP 396
02/10/1982	43	4		WEAVE YOUR SPELL	Polydor POSP 500
15/01/1983	24	8		THE CHINESE WAY	Polydor POSP 538
16/04/1983	41	4		OUT OF SIGHT, OUT OF MIND	Polydor POSP 570
30/07/1983	10	12		**THE SUN GOES DOWN (LIVING IT UP)**	Polydor POSP 622
22/10/1983	37	5		MICRO KID	Polydor POSP 643
01/09/1984	18	9		HOT WATER	Polydor POSP 697
03/11/1984	41	5		THE CHANT HAS BEGUN	Polydor POSP 710
21/09/1985	6	17	O	**SOMETHING ABOUT YOU**	Polydor POSP 759
07/12/1985	15	11		LEAVING ME NOW	Polydor POSP 776
26/04/1986	3	13	O	**LESSONS IN LOVE**	Polydor POSP 790
14/02/1987	6	10		**RUNNING IN THE FAMILY**	Polydor POSP 842
25/04/1987	10	7		**TO BE WITH YOU AGAIN**	Polydor POSP 855
12/09/1987	10	8		**IT'S OVER**	Polydor POSP 900
12/12/1987	22	6		CHILDREN SAY	Polydor POSP 911
03/09/1988	12	5		HEAVEN IN MY HANDS	Polydor PO 14
29/10/1988	32	4		TAKE A LOOK	Polydor PO 24
21/01/1989	25	5		TRACIE	Polydor PO 34
28/10/1989	39	3		TAKE CARE OF YOURSELF	Polydor PO 58
17/08/1991	17	4		GUARANTEED	RCA PB 44745
19/10/1991	62	2		OVERTIME	RCA PB 44997
18/04/1992	55	1		MY FATHER'S SHOES	RCA PB 45271
26/02/1994	19	4		FOREVER NOW	RCA 74321190272
30/04/1994	26	2		ALL OVER YOU	RCA 74321205662
06/08/1994	31	3		LOVE IN A PEACEFUL WORLD	RCA 74321220332

LEVELLERS UK group formed in Brighton in 1988 by Mark Chadwick (born 23/6/1966, Munster, Germany, vocals/banjo/ guitar), Alan Miles (vocals/guitar/mandolin/harmonica), Jeremy Cunningham (born 2/6/1965, Cuckfield, bass /bouzouki), Jon Sevink (born 15/5/1965, Harlow, violin) and Charlie Heather (born 2/2/1964, Beckenham, drums), and signed with HAG in 1989. Miles left in 1990, replaced by Simon Friend (born 17/5/1967, London).

21/09/1991	51	2		ONE WAY	China WOK 2008
07/12/1991	71	1		FAR FROM HOME	China WOK 2010
23/05/1992	11	5		15 YEARS (EP) Tracks on EP: *15 Years, Dance Before The Storm, The River Flow (Live)* and *Plastic Jeezus*	China WOKX 2020
10/07/1993	12	5		BELARUSE	China WOKCD 2034
30/10/1993	12	4		THIS GARDEN	China WOKCD 2039
14/05/1994	17	3		JULIE (EP) Tracks on EP: *Julie, English Civil War, Lowlands Of Holland* and *100 Years*	China WOKCD 2042
12/08/1995	12	5		HOPE ST	China WOKCD 2059
14/10/1995	16	3		FANTASY	China WOKCD 2067
23/12/1995	12	8		JUST THE ONE LEVELLERS, SPECIAL GUEST JOE STRUMMER	China WOKCD 2076
20/07/1996	24	2		EXODUS – LIVE	China WOKCD 2082
09/08/1997	13	5		WHAT A BEAUTIFUL DAY	China WOKCD 2088
18/10/1997	28	2		CELEBRATE	China WOKCD 2089
20/12/1997	24	5		DOG TRAIN	China WOKCD 2090
14/03/1998	46	1		TOO REAL	China WOKCD 2091
24/10/1998	44	2		BOZOS	China WOKCD 2096
06/02/1999	33	2		ONE WAY Re-recording	China WOKCD 2102
09/09/2000	57	1		HAPPY BIRTHDAY REVOLUTION	China EW 218CD
21/09/2002	44	1		COME ON	Eagle EHAGXS 001
18/01/2003	34	2		WILD AS ANGELS EP Tracks on EP: *Wild As Angels, American Air Do* and *Burn*	Eagle EHAGXS 003

❶⁹ Number of weeks single topped the UK chart   ↑ Entered the UK chart at #1   ▲⁹ Number of weeks single topped the US chart

461

LEVERT
US soul group from Ohio formed by Gerald (born 13/7/1966, Cleveland, OH) and Sean Levert (born 28/9/1969, Cleveland), and Marc Gordon. The Levert brothers are the sons of O'Jay vocalist Eddie Levert. They first recorded for Tempre in 1985 and have since become in demand as producers. Gerald Levert subsequently recorded solo. The group appeared in the 1991 Film *New Jack City*.

22/08/1987	9	10		CASANOVA .... Atlantic A 9217

LEVERT SWEAT GILL
US vocal trio Gerald Levert (born 13/7/1966, Cleveland, OH), Keith Sweat (born 22/7/1961, New York City) and Johnny Gill (born 22/5/1966, Washington DC). Gerald Levert had been in Levert, Keith Sweat in the Rhythm Makers (who evolved into GQ) and then a soloist, and Johnny Gill in New Edition before going solo. Sweat appeared in the 1991 film *New Jack City*.

14/03/1998	21	3		MY BODY .... East West E 3857CD
06/06/1998	23	2		CURIOUS .... East West E 3842CD
12/09/1998	45	2		DOOR #1 .... East West E 3817CD

HANK LEVINE
US orchestra leader (born 9/6/1932, Pittsburgh, PA) who later assembled The Miniature Men.

21/12/1961	45	4		IMAGE .... HMV POP 947

LEVITICUS
UK jungle producer Jumping Jack Frost. He launched the Philly Blunt record label.

25/03/1995	66	1		BURIAL Contains an interpolation of Foxy's *Madamoiselle* .... ffrr FCD 255

BARRINGTON LEVY
Jamaican singer born in Kingston in 1964; he made his first record in 1977.

02/02/1985	41	4		HERE I COME .... London LON 62
15/06/1991	20	6		TRIBAL BASE .... Desire WANT 44
24/09/1994	65	1		WORK .... MCA MCSTD 2003
13/10/2001	37	2		HERE I COME (SING DJ) .... NuLife 74321895622

JONA LEWIE
UK singer/songwriter and multi-instrumentalist (born John Lewis, 1943) who first hit the charts as Terry Dactyl & The Dinosaurs (the group evolved from Brett Marvin & The Thunderbolts). He adopted the name Jona Lewie in 1977.

10/05/1980	16	9		YOU'LL ALWAYS FIND ME IN THE KITCHEN AT PARTIES .... Stiff BUY 73
29/11/1980	3	11	●	STOP THE CAVALRY .... Stiff BUY 104

CJ LEWIS
UK reggae singer Steven James Lewis.

23/04/1994	3	13		SWEETS FOR MY SWEET .... Black Market BMITD 017
23/07/1994	10	7		EVERYTHING IS ALRIGHT (UPTIGHT) .... Black Market BMITD 019
08/10/1994	13	6		BEST OF MY LOVE .... Black Market BMITD 021
17/12/1994	34	4		DOLLARS .... Black Market BMITD 023
09/09/1995	34	2		R TO THE A .... Black Market BMITD 030

DANNY J LEWIS
UK producer and later a freelance lecturer for the Point Blank dance music college in London.

20/06/1998	29	2		SPEND THE NIGHT .... Locked On LOX 98CD

DARLENE LEWIS
US singer born in New York City, she later went into artist management.

16/04/1994	16	4		LET THE MUSIC (LIFT YOU UP) **LOVELAND FEATURING RACHEL MCFARLANE VS DARLENE LEWIS** All formats featured versions of *Let The Music Lift You Up* by Loveland Featuring Rachel McFarlane and also by Darlene Lewis .... KMS/Eastern Bloc KMSCD 10

DEE LEWIS
UK singer and later a backing singer for The Pet Shop Boys, Rick Astley, Peter Gabriel, Barry Manilow and Kylie Minogue.

18/06/1988	47	5		BEST OF MY LOVE .... Mercury DEE 3

DONNA LEWIS
UK singer/guitarist born in Cardiff, South Glamorgan; moved to New York where she began playing in piano bars.

07/09/1996	5	14	○	I LOVE YOU ALWAYS FOREVER .... Atlantic A 5495CD
08/02/1997	39	2		WITHOUT LOVE .... Atlantic A 5468CD

GARY LEWIS AND THE PLAYBOYS
US singer (born Gary Levitch, 31/7/1946, New York), son of comedian Jerry Lewis. He formed the Playboys in 1964 with Al Ramsey, John West, David Walker and David Costell.

08/02/1975	36	7		MY HEART'S SYMPHONY Originally a US hit in 1966 (position #13) .... United Artists UP 35780

HUEY LEWIS AND THE NEWS
US singer (born Hugh Creg III, 5/7/1950, New York); he joined Clover in 1976 and formed The News in 1980, with Chris Hayes (born 24/11/1957, California, guitar), Mario Cipollina (born 10/11/1954, California, bass), Bill Gibson (born 13/11/1951, California, drums), Sean Hopper (born 31/3/1953 California, keyboards) and Johnny Colla (born 2/7/1952, California, saxophone/guitar). They won the 1985 Grammy Award for Best Video Long Form for *The Heart Of Rock 'N' Roll*. They were also named Best International Group at the 1986 BRIT Awards.

27/10/1984	39	6		IF THIS IS IT .... Chrysalis CHS 2803
31/08/1985	11	10		THE POWER OF LOVE ▲² Featured in the 1985 film *Back To The Future* .... Chrysalis HUEY 1
23/11/1985	61	4		HEART AND SOUL (EP) Tracks on EP: *Heart And Soul, Hope You Love Me Like You Say You Do, Heart Of Rock And Roll* and *Buzz Buzz Buzz* .... Chrysalis HUEY 2
08/02/1986	9	12	○	THE POWER OF LOVE/DO YOU BELIEVE IN LOVE .... Chrysalis HUEY 3
10/05/1986	49	3		THE HEART OF ROCK AND ROLL .... Chrysalis HUEY 4
23/08/1986	12	12		STUCK WITH YOU ▲³ .... Chrysalis HUEY 5
06/12/1986	41	8		HIP TO BE SQUARE .... Chrysalis HUEY 6
21/03/1987	47	5		SIMPLE AS THAT .... Chrysalis HUEY 7
16/07/1988	48	6		PERFECT WORLD .... Chrysalis HUEY 10

○ Silver disc ● Gold disc ✪ Platinum disc (additional platinum units are indicated by a figure following the symbol) ◉ Singles released prior to 1973 that are known to have sold over 1 million copies in the UK

JERRY LEWIS
US singer/actor/comedian (born Joseph Levitch, 16/3/1925, Newark, NJ) who formed a comedy team with Dean Martin in 1946. They made 16 films together before separating. His son Gary is leader of The Playboys. He has two stars on the Hollywood Walk of Fame, for motion pictures and for TV.

08/02/1957	12	8		ROCK-A-BYE YOUR BABY (WITH A DIXIE MELODY)	Brunswick 05636

JERRY LEE LEWIS
US singer (born 29/9/1935, Ferriday, LA) who taught himself piano, aged nine. Debuted for Sun in 1956 (his single was banned for being vulgar); his film debut was in *Disc Jockey Jamboree* (1957). Known as 'The Killer' and well-known for his marriages, one of which caused the cancellation of his UK tour in 1958 when it was revealed that his 'wife' Myra Gale was his thirteen-year old cousin and he was not yet divorced from his second wife (also a bigamous marriage!). The 1989 film *Great Balls Of Fire* with Dennis Quaid is the story of his early career. He was inducted into the Rock & Roll Hall of Fame in 1986. He won the 1986 Grammy Award for Best Spoken Word Recording with various others for *Interviews From The Class Of '55* and has a star on the Hollywood Walk of Fame.

27/09/1957	8	11		WHOLE LOTTA SHAKIN' GOIN' ON Used in the films *American Hot Wax* (1978) and *Great Balls Of Fire* (1989)	London HLS 8457
20/12/1957	❶²	12		GREAT BALLS OF FIRE Featured in the films *Jamboree* (1957), *American Hot Wax* (1978), *Stand By Me* (1986) and *Great Balls Of Fire* (1989)	London HLS 8529
11/04/1958	8	7		BREATHLESS	London HLS 8592
23/01/1959	12	6		HIGH SCHOOL CONFIDENTIAL Featured in the 1958 film *High School Confidential*	London HLS 8780
01/05/1959	28	1		LOVIN' UP A STORM	London HLS 8840
09/06/1960	47	1		BABY BABY BYE BYE	London HLS 9131
04/05/1961	10	14		WHAT'D I SAY	London HLS 9335
06/09/1962	38	5		SWEET LITTLE SIXTEEN	London HLS 9584
14/03/1963	31	6		GOOD GOLLY MISS MOLLY	London HLS 9688
06/05/1972	33	5		CHANTILLY LACE	Mercury 6052 141

LINDA LEWIS
UK singer/songwriter born in London in 1950. In the early 1970s she was one of the top session singers working with artists such as David Bowie and Cat Stevens. She first recorded solo in 1971 for Bell.

02/06/1973	15	11		ROCK-A-DOODLE-DOO	Raft RA 18502
12/07/1975	6	8		IT'S IN HIS KISS	Arista 17
17/04/1976	33	6		BABY I'M YOURS	Arista 43
02/06/1979	40	5		I'D BE SURPRISINGLY GOOD FOR YOU	Ariola ARO 166
19/08/2000	61	1		REACH OUT MIDFIELD GENERAL FEATURING LINDA LEWIS	Skint 54CD

RAMSEY LEWIS
US pianist (born 27/5/1935, Chicago, IL); he formed the Gentlemen of Swing in 1956 with Eldes Young (bass) and Isaac 'Red' Holt (drums), changing their name to the Ramsey Lewis Trio upon signing with Chess. Young and Holt left in 1965 to form the Young-Holt Trio. Lewis re-formed his group the following year with Maurice White (drums) and Cleveland Eaton (bass). White left in 1970 to launch Earth, Wind & Fire, Eaton went solo. Lewis has won three Grammy Awards: Best Jazz Performance in 1965 for *The 'In' Crowd*, Best Rhythm & Blues Group Performance in 1965 for *Hold It Right There* and Best Rhythm & Blues Instrumental Performance in 1973 for *Hang On Sloopy*. His *Love Notes* album also won the 1977 Grammy Award for Best Album Package.

15/04/1972	31	8		WADE IN THE WATER Originally a US hit in 1966 (position #19)	Chess 6145 004

SHAZNAY LEWIS
UK singer (born Shaznay Tricia Lewis, 14/10/1975, London) who was a founding member of All Saints and went solo when the group disbanded.

17/07/2004	8	10		NEVER FELT LIKE THIS BEFORE	London LONCD484
30/10/2004	56	1		YOU	London LONCD486

SHIRLEY LEWIS – see ARTHUR BAKER

JOHN LEYTON
UK singer (born 17/2/1939, Fritton-on-Sea) who began by playing 'Ginger' in the TV series *Biggles* and then landed the role of singer Johnny St Cyr in *Harpers West One*. This exposure helped his recording career and he later appeared in the films *The Great Escape* and *Von Ryan's Express*.

03/08/1961	❶⁴	15		JOHNNY REMEMBER ME Song originally appeared in the TV series *Harpers West One*	Top Rank JAR 577
05/10/1961	2	10		WILD WIND	Top Rank JAR 585
28/12/1961	15	10		SON THIS IS SHE	HMV POP 956
15/03/1962	40	5		LONE RIDER	HMV POP 992
03/05/1962	14	11		LONELY CITY	HMV POP 1014
23/08/1962	42	3		DOWN THE RIVER NILE	HMV POP 1054
21/02/1963	22	12		CUPBOARD LOVE	HMV POP 1122
18/07/1963	36	3		I'LL CUT YOUR TAIL OFF	HMV POP 1175
20/02/1964	49	1		MAKE LOVE TO ME JOHN LEYTON AND THE LEROYS	HMV POP 1264

LEYTON BUZZARDS
UK group formed by Geoff Deane (vocals), Vernon Austin (guitar), David Jaymes (bass) and Kevin Steptoe (drums). The group later changed their name to The Buzzards and then evolved into Modern Romance.

03/03/1979	53	5		SATURDAY NIGHT (BENEATH THE PLASTIC PALM TREES)	Chrysalis CHS 2288

LFO
UK instrumental group formed by Jez Varley (keyboards), Mark Bell (keyboards/programming), Simon Hartley (drums) and Richie Brook (keyboards). They later added singer Susie Thorpe. The initials stand for Low Frequency Oscillation.

14/07/1990	12	10		LFO	Warp WAP 5
06/07/1991	47	3		WE ARE BACK/NURTURE	Warp 7WAP 14
01/02/1992	62	2		WHAT IS HOUSE (EP) Tracks on EP: *Tan Ta Ra*, *Mashed Potato*, *What Is House* and *Syndrome*	Warp WAP 17

❶⁹ Number of weeks single topped the UK chart ↑ Entered the UK chart at #1 ▲⁹ Number of weeks single topped the US chart

463

LIARS US group formed in Los Angeles, CA in 2000 by Angus Andrew (vocals), Aaron Hemphill (guitar), Pat Noecker (bass) and Ron Albertson (drums).

24/02/2004 . . . . . 74 . . . . . 1 . . . . . . THERE'S ALWAYS ROOM ON THE BROOM . . . . Mute CDMUTE 317

LIBERACE US pianist (born Wladzul Valentino Liberace, 16/5/1919, West Allis, WI) who began as Walter Busterkeys yet became one of the most flamboyant performers of the 1950s and certainly the best paid. He hosted his own TV show in 1952 and later appeared in films, including *Sincerely Yours* (rated the worst film ever made!) and *The Loved One*. His piano-playing style was emulated by the likes of Richard Clayderman. He died from an AIDS-related illness on 4/2/1987. He has two stars on the Hollywood Walk of Fame, for his contribution to recording and for TV.

17/06/1955 . . . . . 20 . . . . . 1 . . . . . . UNCHAINED MELODY . . . . Philips PB 430
19/10/1956 . . . . . 28 . . . . . 1 . . . . . . I DON'T CARE (AS LONG AS YOU CARE FOR ME) Track features Liberace as a vocalist too . . . . Columbia DB 3834

LIBERATION UK instrumental/production duo David Cooper and William Linch.

24/10/1992 . . . . . 28 . . . . . 3 . . . . . . LIBERATION . . . . ZYX 68657

LIBERTINES UK rock group formed in London by Carl Barat (guitar/vocals), Pete Doherty (guitar/vocals), John Hassall (bass) and Gary Powell (drums). Doherty was sacked in June 2003 because of a drug habit. He was later sentenced to six months in prison (reduced to two on appeal) for committing a burglary at Carl Barat's flat and re-admitted into the group in 2004.

15/06/2002 . . . . . 37 . . . . . 2 . . . . . . WHAT A WASTER Featured in the 2004 film *The Football Factory* . . . . Rough Trade RTRADESCD 054
12/10/2002 . . . . . 29 . . . . . 2 . . . . . . UP THE BRACKET. . . . . Rough Trade RTRADESCD 064
25/01/2003 . . . . . 20 . . . . . 2 . . . . . . TIME FOR HEROES Featured in the 2003 film *American Wedding* . . . . Rough Trade RTRADESCD 074
30/08/2003 . . . . . 11 . . . . . 4 . . . . . . DON'T LOOK BACK INTO THE SUN . . . . Rough Trade RTRADESCD 120
21/08/2004 . . . . 2 . . . . 6 . . . . . . **CAN'T STAND ME NOW**. . . . . Rough Trade RTRADSCDX 163
06/11/2004 . . . . 9 . . . . 4 . . . . . . **WHAT BECAME OF THE LIKELY LADS** . . . . Rough Trade RTRADSCD 215

LIBERTY X UK vocal group formed by Kelli Young (born 7/4/1981, Derby), Tony Lundon (born 13/4/1979, Galway, Ireland), Jessica Taylor (born 23/6/1980), Michelle Heaton (born 19/7/1980) and Kevin Simm (born 5/9/1980). The five were the runners-up in the Popstars TV series that gave rise to Hear'Say. Although they became the first group called Liberty to register a hit single, the name had previously been claimed by another group and in March 2002 they were forced to amend their name to Liberty X.

06/10/2001 . . . . . 5 . . . . . 8 . . . . . . **THINKING IT OVER** . . . . V2 VVR 5017773
15/12/2001 . . . . . 14 . . . . . 6 . . . . . . DOIN' IT This and above single credited to **LIBERTY** . . . . V2 VVR 5017798
25/05/2002 . . . . ❶¹ . . . . 16 . . . . ● **JUST A LITTLE** ↑ 2003 BRIT Award for Best UK Single . . . . V2 VVR 5018968
21/09/2002 . . . . . 2 . . . . . 12 . . . . . . **GOT TO HAVE YOUR LOVE** . . . . V2 VVR 5020508
14/12/2002 . . . . . 5 . . . . . 11 . . . . . . **HOLDING ON FOR YOU** . . . . V2 VVR 5020768
29/03/2003 . . . . . 3 . . . . . 11 . . . . . . **BEING NOBODY** RICHARD X VS LIBERTY X Effectively two songs with the lyrics from Rufus' *Ain't Nobody* and music from Human League's *Being Boiled* . . . . Virgin RXCD1
01/11/2003 . . . . . 6 . . . . . 7 . . . . . . **JUMPIN'** . . . . V2 VVR 5023549
24/01/2004 . . . . . 13 . . . . . 5 . . . . . . EVERYBODY CRIES . . . . V2 VVR 5023558

LIBIDO Norwegian vocal/instrumental group featuring Even Johansen and Martin Stone.

31/01/1998 . . . . . 53 . . . . . 1 . . . . . . OVERTHROWN . . . . Fire BLAZE 119CD

LIBRA PRESENTS TAYLOR US production/vocal duo Brian Transeau (aka BT) and DJ Taylor with singer Jan Johnston.

26/10/1996 . . . . . 71 . . . . . 1 . . . . . . ANOMALY – CALLING YOUR NAME Featured in the 2001 film *American Pie 2* . . . . Platipus PLATCD 24
18/03/2000 . . . . . 43 . . . . . 2 . . . . . . ANOMALY – CALLING YOUR NAME (REMIX) . . . . Platipus PLATCD 56

LICK THE TINS UK vocal/instrumental group formed in 1986 by Ronan Heenan (guitar/vocals), Alison Marr (vocals/penny whistle) and Simon Ryan (drums), later adding Aiden McCroary (keyboards) and Chris Haynes (bass). Named after a nickname given to a tramp in Heenan's hometown.

29/03/1986 . . . . . 42 . . . . . 8 . . . . . . CAN'T HELP FALLING IN LOVE Featured in the 1987 film *Some Kind Of Wonderful* . . . . Sedition EDIT 3308

OLIVER LIEB PRESENTS SMOKED German producer born in Frankfurt in 1969 who also recorded as LSG.

30/09/2000 . . . . . 72 . . . . . 1 . . . . . . METROPOLIS . . . . Duty Free DF 019CD

BEN LIEBRAND Dutch DJ and producer who had previously been a member of La Fleur.

09/06/1990 . . . . . 68 . . . . . 2 . . . . . . PULS(T)AR . . . . Epic LIEB 1

LIEUTENANT PIGEON UK group formed by Robert Woodward (piano), Steve Johnson (bass) and Nigel Fletcher (drums). By the time of their debut hit (recorded in the front room of Woodward's home) they had been joined by Fletcher's mother Hilda!

16/09/1972 . . . . ❶⁴ . . . . 19 . . . . . . **MOULDY OLD DOUGH** . . . . Decca F 13278
16/12/1972 . . . . . 17 . . . . . 10 . . . . . . DESPERATE DAN . . . . Decca F 13365

LIFEHOUSE US rock group formed in Malibu, California in 1996 by Jason Wade (guitar/vocals), Stuart Mathis (guitar), Sergio Andrade (bass) and Rick Woolstenhulme (drums).

08/09/2001 . . . . . 25 . . . . . 4 . . . . . . HANGING BY A MOMENT . . . . DreamWorks 4508942

LIFFORD – see **ARTFUL DODGER**

LIGHT OF THE WORLD UK funk group formed in 1978 by Canute 'Kenny' Wellington (trumpet), David 'Baps' Baptiste

○ Silver disc ● Gold disc ✪ Platinum disc (additional platinum units are indicated by a figure following the symbol) ◎ Singles released prior to 1973 that are known to have sold over 1 million copies in the UK

(trumpet), Jean Paul 'Bluey' Maunick (guitar), Everton McCalla (drums), Neville 'Breeze' McKreith (guitar), Chris Etienne (percussion), Paul 'Tubbs' Williams (bass) and Peter Hinds (keyboards). Splitting in 1981, Beggar & Co and Incognito were formed by ex-members.

14/04/1979	45	5		SWINGIN'	Ensign ENY 22
14/07/1979	72	1		MIDNIGHT GROOVIN'	Ensign ENY 29
18/10/1980	41	5		LONDON TOWN	Ensign ENY 43
17/01/1981	40	5		I SHOT THE SHERIFF	Ensign ENY 46
28/03/1981	35	6		I'M SO HAPPY/TIME	Ensign ENY 64
21/11/1981	49	3		RIDE THE LOVE TRAIN	EMI 5242

LIGHTER SHADE OF BROWN US rap duo ODM ('One Dope Mexican' Robert Guitterez) and DTTX ('Don't Try To Xerox' Bobby Ramirez).

09/07/1994	33	3		HEY DJ	Mercury MERCD 401

GORDON LIGHTFOOT Canadian singer (born 17/11/1938, Orillia, Ontario) who became a member of the Swinging Singing Eight in 1958. He recorded his solo debut in 1961 and relaunched his solo career in 1965 after finding success as a songwriter.

19/06/1971	30	9		IF YOU COULD READ MY MIND	Reprise K 20974
03/08/1974	33	7		SUNDOWN ▲¹	Reprise K 14327
15/01/1977	40	4		THE WRECK OF THE EDMUND FITZGERALD True story of the sinking of an ore vessel on Lake Superior on 11/11/1975 with the loss of all 29 crew	Reprise K 14451
16/09/1978	41	6		DAYLIGHT KATY	Warner Brothers K 17214

TERRY LIGHTFOOT AND HIS NEW ORLEANS JAZZMEN UK singer/clarinettist (born 21/5/1935, Potters Bar) who formed his first band in 1955 and by the 1960s was one of the top acts of the 'trad' boom appearing in the film *It's Trad, Dad*. He teamed up with Kenny Ball in 1967.

07/09/1961	33	4		TRUE LOVE	Columbia DB 4696
23/11/1961	29	12		KING KONG	Columbia SCD 2165
03/05/1962	49	1		TAVERN IN THE TOWN	Columbia DB 4822

LIGHTFORCE German production duo.

28/10/2000	53	1		JOIN ME	Slinky Music SLINKY 004CD

LIGHTHOUSE FAMILY UK group formed in Newcastle in 1993 by Tunde Baiyewu (born 25/11/1968, London, vocals) and Paul Tucker (born 12/8/1968, Crystal Palace, London, keyboards). The pair met while studying at college in Newcastle. Baiyewu went solo in 2004.

27/05/1995	61	2		LIFTED	Wild Card CARDW 17
14/10/1995	34	3		OCEAN DRIVE Featured in the 1995 film *Jack and Sarah*	Wild Card 5797072
10/02/1996	4	10	O	**LIFTED** Re-issue of Wild Card CARDW 17	Wild Card 5779432
01/06/1996	11	8		OCEAN DRIVE Re-issue of Wild Card 5797072	Wild Card 5766192
21/09/1996	14	6		GOODBYE HEARTBREAK	Wild Card 5753492
21/12/1996	20	7		LOVING EVERY MINUTE	Wild Card 5731012
11/10/1997	6	7		**RAINCLOUD**	Wild Card 5717932
10/01/1998	4	14	O	**HIGH** Featured in the 1998 film *Up 'N Under*	Wild Card 5691492
27/06/1998	6	8		**LOST IN SPACE** Featured in the 1998 film *Lost In Space*	Polydor 5670592
10/10/1998	21	5		QUESTION OF FAITH	Wild Card 5673932
09/01/1999	24	6		POSTCARD FROM HEAVEN	Wild Card 5633952
24/11/2001	6	9		**(I WISH I KNEW HOW IT WOULD FEEL TO BE) FREE/ONE**	Wild Card 5873812
09/03/2002	30	3		RUN	Wild Card 5705702
06/07/2002	51	1		HAPPY	Wild Card 5707912

LIGHTNING SEEDS UK group formed by ex-Big In Japan member Ian Broudie (born 4/8/1958, Liverpool). Initially a one-man band, it now features four members: Broudie, Martin Campbell (ex-Rain, bass), Chris Sharrock (ex-Icicle Works, drums) and Paul Hemmings (ex-La's, guitar). Broudie also took part in the *Perfect Day* project for the BBC's Children In Need charity.

22/07/1989	16	8		PURE	Ghetto GTG 4
14/03/1992	28	6		THE LIFE OF RILEY Used as the theme for 'Goal of the Month' on *Match Of The Day*	Virgin VS 1402
30/05/1992	31	5		SENSE	Virgin VS 1414
20/08/1994	43	2		LUCKY YOU	Epic 6606282
14/01/1995	13	6		CHANGE Featured in the 1995 film Clueless	Epic 6609865
15/04/1995	24	5		MARVELLOUS	Epic 6614265
22/07/1995	18	5		PERFECT	Epic 6621792
21/10/1995	15	6		LUCKY YOU	Epic 6625182
09/03/1996	20	4		READY OR NOT	Epic 6629672
01/06/1996	❶²	15	✪	**THREE LIONS (THE OFFICIAL SONG OF THE ENGLAND FOOTBALL TEAM)** ↑ **BADDIEL & SKINNER & LIGHTNING SEEDS** Reclaimed the #1 position on 6/7/1996	Epic 6632732
02/11/1996	14	4		WHAT IF	Epic 6638635
18/01/1997	12	4		SUGAR COATED ICEBERG	Epic 6640435
26/04/1997	8	5		**YOU SHOWED ME** Featured in the 1997 film *Austin Powers – International Man Of Mystery*	Epic 6643282
13/12/1997	41	5		WHAT YOU SAY	Epic 6653572
20/06/1998	❶³	13	✪	**THREE LIONS '98** ↑ **BADDIEL & SKINNER & LIGHTNING SEEDS** Re-written version of their first hit	Epic 6660982
27/11/1999	27	4		LIFE'S TOO SHORT	Epic 6681502
18/03/2000	67	1		SWEET SOUL SENSATIONS Contains a sample of Al Green's *Simply Beautiful*	Epic 6689422

❶⁹ Number of weeks single topped the UK chart   ↑ Entered the UK chart at #1   ▲⁹ Number of weeks single topped the US chart

15/06/2002 . . . . . 16 . . . . . . 6 . . . . THREE LIONS **BADDIEL & SKINNER & LIGHTNING SEEDS** Second re-written version and released to coincide with the 2002 FIFA
World Cup . . . . Epic 6728152

LIL BOW WOW US rapper (born Rashad Moss, 9/3/1987, Columbus, OH) and a protege of Snoop Doggy Dogg. He shortened
his name to Bow Wow in 2003.

14/04/2001 . . . . . 6 . . . . . . 9 . . . . **BOW WOW (THAT'S MY NAME)** Contains a sample of Andy Gibb's *Shadow Dancing* and an interpolation of George Clinton's
Atomic Dog . . . . So So Def 6709832

27/11/2004 . . . . . 8 . . . . . 5+ . . . . . **BABY IT'S YOU JOJO FEATURING BOW WOW** . . . . Mercury 9869056

LIL' DEVIOUS UK production duo Mark Baker and Gary Little.

15/09/2001 . . . . . 55 . . . . . . 1 . . . . COME HOME Contains samples of Imagination's *Flashback*, Mass Production's *Our Thought* and Double Exposure's *Ten Per Cent*.
. . . . Rulin 16CDS

LIL' FLIP US rapper (born Wesley Weston, 1983, Houston, TX), nicknamed The Freestyle King.

11/09/2004 . . . . . 44 . . . . . . 2 . . . . NEVER REALLY WAS **MARIO WINANS FEATURING LIL' FLIP** Contains a sample of Madonna's *Papa Don't Preach* . . . .
. . . . Bad Boy MCSTD 40372

30/10/2004 . . . . . 14 . . . . . . 4 . . . . SUNSHINE . . . . Columbia 6751842

LIL' JON — see USHER and LUDACRIS

LIL' KIM US rapper (born Kimberly Jones, 11/7/1975, New York) who is also a member of Junior M.A.F.I.A.

26/04/1997 . . . . . 45 . . . . . . 1 . . . . NO TIME **LIL' KIM FEATURING PUFF DADDY** Contains a sample of Lyn Collins' *Take Me Just As I Am* . . . . Atlantic A 5594CD

05/07/1997 . . . . . 36 . . . . . . 2 . . . . CRUSH ON YOU Contains a sample of Jeff Lorber's *Rain Dance* . . . . Atlantic AT 0002CD

16/08/1997 . . . . . 11 . . . . . . 5 . . . . NOT TONIGHT Contains a sample of Kool & The Gang's *Ladies Night*. Also features the uncredited contributions of Da Brat,
Lisa 'Left Eye' Lopes, Missy 'Misdemeanour' Elliott and Angie Martinez. Featured in the 1997 film *Nothing To Lose* . . . .
. . . . Atlantic AT 0007CD

25/10/1997 . . . . . 23 . . . . . . 3 . . . . CRUSH ON YOU Single re-promoted . . . . Atlantic AT 0002CD

22/08/1998 . . . . . 25 . . . . . . 3 . . . . HIT 'EM WIT DA HEE **MISSY 'MISDEMEANOR' ELLIOTT FEATURING LIL' KIM** Featured in the 1998 film *Can't Hardly Wait* . . . .
. . . . East West E 3824CD1

05/02/2000 . . . . . 16 . . . . . . 5 . . . . NOTORIOUS B.I.G. **NOTORIOUS B.I.G. FEATURING PUFF DADDY AND LIL' KIM** . . . . Puff Daddy 74321737312

02/09/2000 . . . . . 35 . . . . . . 2 . . . . NO MATTER WHAT THEY SAY Contains samples of Eric B & Rakim's *I Know I Got Soul*, Jose Feliciano's *Esto Es El Guaguanco*,
Special Ed's *I Got It Made* and The Sugarhill Gang's *Rappers Delight* . . . . Atlantic 7567846972

30/06/2001 . . . . ●[1] . . . . . 16 . . . . . ● LADY MARMALADE ↑ ▲[5] **CHRISTINA AGUILERA/LIL' KIM/MYA/PINK** Featured in the 2001 film *Moulin Rouge*. 2001 Grammy
Award for Best Pop Collaboration with Vocals. . . . . Interscope 4975612

11/08/2001 . . . . . 54 . . . . . . 1 . . . . WAIT A MINUTE **RAY J FEATURING LIL' KIM** . . . . Atlantic AT 0106CD

22/09/2001 . . . . . 26 . . . . . . 2 . . . . IN THE AIR TONITE **LIL' KIM FEATURING PHIL COLLINS** . . . . WEA 331CD

10/05/2003 . . . . . 16 . . . . . . 7 . . . . THE JUMP OFF **LIL' KIM FEATURING MR CHEEKS** . . . . Atlantic AT 0151CD

20/09/2003 . . . . . 6 . . . . . . 9 . . . . **CAN'T HOLD US DOWN** CHRISTINA AGUILERA FEATURING LIL' KIM . . . . RCA 82876556332

LIL' LOUIS US singer (born Louis Burns, Chicago, IL), the son of blues guitarist Bobby Sims (who played with BB King and Bobby
Bland) and began his career as a DJ at the age of 13. He has also recorded as Black Magic and as part of Lil' Mo Yin Yang.

29/07/1989 . . . . . 2 . . . . . . 11 . . . . . ○ **FRENCH KISS** Features the uncredited vocal of Shawn Christopher . . . . Ffrr FX 115

13/01/1990 . . . . . 16 . . . . . . 6 . . . . I CALLED U . . . . ffrr F 123

26/09/1992 . . . 74 . . . . . . 1 . . . . SAVED MY LIFE **LIL' LOUIS AND THE WORLD** . . . . ffrr FX 197

12/08/2000 . . . . . 23 . . . . . . 3 . . . . HOW'S YOUR EVENING SO FAR **JOSH WINK AND LIL' LOUIS** . . . . ffrr FCD 384

LIL' MISS MAX — see BLUE ADONIS FEATURING LIL' MISS MAX

LIL' MO US rapper (born Cindy Levin, 10/3/1976, Queens, NYC).

21/11/1998 . . . . . 72 . . . . . . 1 . . . . 5 MINUTES **LIL' MO FEATURING MISSY 'MISDEMEANOR' ELLIOTT** In the 1998 film *Why Do Fools Fall In Love* . . . . Elektra E 3803CD

23/09/2000 . . . . . 31 . . . . . . 3 . . . . WHATEVER **IDEAL U.S. FEATURING LIL' MO** . . . . Virgin VUSCD 172

06/04/2002 . . . . . 37 . . . . . . 2 . . . . WHERE'S MY **ADAM F FEATURING LIL' MO** . . . . EMI CDEMS 598

15/02/2003 . . . . . 61 . . . . . . 1 . . . . IF I COULD GO **ANGIE MARTINEZ FEATURING LIL' MO** . . . . Elektra E 7331CD

16/08/2003 . . . . . 14 . . . . . . 5 . . . . CAN'T LET YOU GO **FABOLOUS FEATURING MIKE SHOREY AND LIL' MO** . . . . Elektra E 7408CD

LIL MO' YIN YANG US instrumental/production duo Lil Louis Vega and Eric 'More' Morillo (who was also a member of Real
to Reel and Pianoheadz).

09/03/1996 . . . . . 28 . . . . . . 2 . . . . REACH . . . . Multiply CDMULTY 9

LIL' ROMEO US rapper (born Percy Romeo Miller, 19/8/1989, New Orleans, LA) who is the son of rapper Master P.

22/09/2001 . . . . . 67 . . . . . . 1 . . . . MY BABY . . . . Priority PTYCD 136

LIL' T — see MANIJAMA FEATURING MUKUPA AND LIL' T

LILYS US rock group formed in Philadelphia, PA in 1991 by Kurt Heasley. He disbanded the group after one single and re-formed it
in Washington in 1992, although it was to be another two years before they started working seriously.

21/02/1998 . . . . . 16 . . . . . . 4 . . . . A NANNY IN MANHATTAN Track first featured as an advertisement for Levi Jeans. . . . . Che 77CD

LIMA — see TOM NOVY

LIMAHL UK singer (born Christopher Hamill, 19/12/1958) whose stage name is an anagram of his surname. He first came to prominence as lead vocalist with Kajagoogoo and went solo six months after the group achieved their chart breakthrough.

05/11/1983	16	8		ONLY FOR LOVE	EMI LML 1
02/06/1984	64	3		TOO MUCH TROUBLE	EMI LML 2
13/10/1984	4	14	○	**NEVER ENDING STORY** Includes the uncredited vocal of Beth Anderson. Featured in the 1984 film *The Never Ending Story* . EMI LML 3

ALISON LIMERICK UK singer (born 1959, London) who began her career in musicals and appeared in the show *Starlight Express* before going solo.

30/03/1991	27	8		WHERE LOVE LIVES	Arista 114208
12/10/1991	53	2		COME BACK (FOR REAL LOVE)	Arista 114530
21/12/1991	42	4		MAGIC'S BACK (THEME FROM 'THE GHOSTS OF OXFORD STREET') MALCOLM MCLAREN FEATURING ALISON LIMERICK Theme to the TV series *The Ghosts Of Oxford Street*	RCA PB 45223
29/02/1992	16	6		MAKE IT ON MY OWN	Arista 114996
18/07/1992	57	2		GETTING' IT RIGHT	Arista 74321102867
28/11/1992	73	1		HEAR MY CALL	Arista 115337
08/01/1994	36	4		TIME OF OUR LIVES	Arista 74321180332
19/03/1994	36	2		LOVE COME DOWN	Arista 74321191952
25/02/1995	63	1		LOVE WILL KEEP US TOGETHER JTQ FEATURING ALISON LIMERICK	Acid Jazz JAZID 112CD
06/07/1996	9	6		**WHERE LOVE LIVES (REMIX)**	Arista 74321381592
14/09/1996	30	2		MAKE IT ON MY OWN (REMIX)	Arista 74321407812
23/08/1997	42	1		PUT YOUR FAITH IN ME	MBA XES 9001
15/03/2003	44	2		WHERE LOVE LIVES	Arista Dance 74321981442

LIMIT Dutch duo Bernard Oattes and Rob Van Schaik who first recorded as Future World Orchestra in 1981.

05/01/1985	17	8		SAY YEAH Features David Sanborn on saxophone and Gwen Guthrie on vocals	Portrait A 4808

LIMMIE AND THE FAMILY COOKIN' US singer (born Limmie Snell, Dalton, AL) who made his debut record at the age of eleven as Lemmie B Good. He formed Family Cookin' with brother Jimmy Thomas and sister Martha Stewart.

21/07/1973	3	13		**YOU CAN DO MAGIC**	Avco 6105 019
20/10/1973	31	5		DREAMBOAT	Avco 6105 025
06/04/1974	6	10		**A WALKIN' MIRACLE** Revival of The Essex's 1963 US hit (position #12)	Avco 6105 027

LIMP BIZKIT US rock group formed in Florida in 1994 by Fred Durst (born 20/8/1971, Jacksonville, FL, vocals), Sam Rivers (bass), Wes Borland (guitar) and John Otto (drums), later adding DJ Lethal (Leor DiMant) to the line-up. Wes Borland left in October 2001 and was replaced by Mike Smith. They won three awards at the 2001 MTV Europe Music Awards: Best Group, Best Album for *Chocolate Starfish And The Hot Dog Flavoured Water* and Best Website.

15/07/2000	3	13	○	**TAKE A LOOK AROUND (THEME FROM MI 2)** Featured in the 2000 film *Mission Impossible 2*	Interscope 4973692
11/11/2000	15	8		MY GENERATION	Interscope IND 97448
27/01/2001	❶²	13	○	**ROLLIN'** ↑ With the uncredited contributions of rappers DMX, Redman and Method Man. Featured in the 2001 film *The Fast And The Furious*	Interscope IND 97474
23/06/2001	6	10		**MY WAY**	Interscope 4975732
10/11/2001	18	5		BOILER	Interscope 4976362
27/09/2003	10	7		**EAT YOU ALIVE**	Interscope 9811757
06/12/2003	18	6		BEHIND BLUE EYES	Interscope 9814744

LINA US singer (born in Dallas, TX) who took her stage name from a Dinah Washington song. She later launched the MoodStar label before signing with Hidden Beach Recordings.

03/03/2001	46	1		PLAYA NO MO'	Atlantic AT 0094CD

BOB LIND US singer/songwriter (born 25/11/1944, Baltimore, MD), his debut UK hit was also covered by Val Doonican, and was originally the B-side in America of his recording debut *Cheryl's Going Home*.

10/03/1966	5	9		**ELUSIVE BUTTERFLY**	Fontana TF 670
26/05/1966	46	1		REMEMBER THE RAIN	Fontana TF 702

LINDA AND THE FUNKY BOYS – see LINDA CARR

LINDISFARNE UK group formed in Newcastle in 1967 by Alan Hull (born 20/2/1945, Newcastle-upon-Tyne, vocals/guitar/piano), Simon Cowe (born 1/4/1948, Jesmind Dene, guitar), Ray Jackson (born 12/12/1948, Wallsend, harmonica/mandolin), Rod Clements (born 17/11/1947, North Shields, bass/violin) and Ray Laidlaw (born 28/5/1948, North Shields, drums) as Downtown Faction. They changed their name the following year, Lindisfarne being an island off Northumberland. The group split in 1973 but reunited in 1978. Hull died on 17/11/1995 from a heart attack.

26/02/1972	5	11		**MEET ME ON THE CORNER**	Charisma CB 173
13/05/1972	3	11		**LADY ELEANOR**	Charisma CB 153
23/09/1972	34	5		ALL FALL DOWN	Charisma CB 191
03/06/1978	10	15	○	**RUN FOR HOME**	Mercury 6007 177
07/10/1978	56	4		JUKE BOX GYPSY	Mercury 6007 187
10/11/1990	2	9		**FOG ON THE TYNE (REVISITED)** GAZZA AND LINDISFARNE	Best ZB 44083

LINDSAY UK singer Lindsay Dracas was sixteen at the time of her debut hit: the British entry to the 2001 Eurovision Song Contest.

❶⁹ Number of weeks single topped the UK chart ↑ Entered the UK chart at #1 ▲⁹ Number of weeks single topped the US chart

467

It came fifteenth behind Estonia's entry, *Everybody*, by Tanel Padar and Dave Benton with 2XL. Had it finished one place lower then the UK would have been relegated from the competition until 2003!

12/05/2001 . . . . . 32 . . . . . 4 . . . . . . NO DREAM IMPOSSIBLE Britain's entry to the 2001 Eurovision Song Contest (came fifteenth) . . . . Universal TV 1589562

LINER UK group formed by Tom Farmer (bass/vocals), his brother Dave (drums) and Eddie Golga (guitar).

10/03/1979 . . . . . 49 . . . . . 3 . . . . . . KEEP REACHING OUT FOR LOVE . . . . Atlantic K 11235
26/05/1979 . . . . . 44 . . . . . 3 . . . . . . YOU AND ME . . . . Atlantic K 11285

ANDY LING UK/producer who has worked with Dave Ralh, Blue Amazone, Arkana and Tori Amos.

13/05/2000 . . . . . 55 . . . . . 1 . . . . . . FIXATION . . . . Hooj Choons HOOJ 094CD

LAURIE LINGO AND THE DIPSTICKS UK Radio 1 DJs Dave Lee Travis and Paul Burnett with a parody of C W McCall's hit. Although their debut single sold enough copies to qualify for a silver disc, State Records was not a member of the BPI.

17/04/1976 . . . . . 4 . . . . . 7 . . . . . . CONVOY G.B . . . . State STAT 23

LINK US rapper Lincoln Browder (born in Dallas, TX).

07/11/1998 . . . . . 48 . . . . . 1 . . . . . . WHATCHA GONE DO? . . . . Relativity 6666055

LINKIN PARK US rock group formed in Los Angeles by Chester Bennington (born 20/3/1976, vocals), Mike Shinoda (born 11/2/1977, raps/vocals), Joseph Hahn (born 15/3/1977, DJ), Brad Delson (born 1/12/1977, guitar), Dave 'Phoenix' Ferrel (born 8/2/1977, bass) and Rob Bourdon (born 20/1/1979, drums). Named Best Group and Best Hard Rock Act at the 2002 MTV Europe Music Awards, and Best Rock Act in 2004.

27/01/2001 . . . . . 24 . . . . . 4 . . . . . ONE STEP CLOSER . . . . Warner Brothers W 550CD
21/04/2001 . . . . . 16 . . . . . 8 . . . . . CRAWLING 2001 Grammy Award for Best Hard Rock Vocal Performance . . . . Warner Brothers W 556CD
30/06/2001 . . . . . 14 . . . . . 6 . . . . . PAPERCUT . . . . Warner Brothers W 562CD
20/10/2001 . . . . . 8 . . . . . 9 . . . . . IN THE END . . . . Warner Brothers W 569CD
03/08/2002 . . . . . 9 . . . . . 6 . . . . . HIGH VOLTAGE/POINTS OF AUTHORITY . . . . Warner Brothers W 588CD
29/03/2003 . . . . . 10 . . . . . 8 . . . . . SOMEWHERE I BELONG . . . . Warner Brothers W 602CD
21/06/2003 . . . . . 15 . . . . . 8 . . . . . FAINT . . . . Warner Brothers W 610CD
20/09/2003 . . . . . 14 . . . . . 6 . . . . . NUMB . . . . Warner Brothers W 622CD
19/06/2004 . . . . . 39 . . . . . 2 . . . . . BREAKING THE HABIT (IMPORT) . . . . Warner Brothers W 645CD
04/12/2004 . . . . . 14 . . . . . 4+ . . . . . NUMB/ENCORE JAY-Z VS LINKIN PARK . . . . WEA W660CD

LINOLEUM UK group formed by Caroline Finch (guitar/vocals), Paul Jones (guitar), Emma Tornaro (bass) and Dave Nice (drums). They also launched the Lino Vinyl label (their debut release, *Dissent/Twisted* featured a sleeve made of linoleum).

12/07/1997 . . . . . 73 . . . . . 1 . . . . . . MARQUIS . . . . Lino Vinyl LINO 004CD1

LINX UK funk duo David Grant (born 8/8/1956, Hackney, London) and Sketch (born Peter Martin, 1954, Antigua). They signed a deal with Chrysalis on the strength of a self-financed debut disc. They disbanded in 1982 and Grant went solo.

20/09/1980 . . . . . 15 . . . . . 10 . . . . . . YOU'RE LYING . . . . Chrysalis CHS 2461
07/03/1981 . . . . . 7 . . . . . 11 . . . . . O INTUITION . . . . Chrysalis CHS 2500
13/06/1981 . . . . . 21 . . . . . 9 . . . . . . THROW AWAY THE KEY . . . . Chrysalis CHS 2519
05/09/1981 . . . . . 15 . . . . . 9 . . . . . . SO THIS IS ROMANCE . . . . Chrysalis CHS 2546
21/11/1981 . . . . . 55 . . . . . 3 . . . . . . CAN'T HELP MYSELF . . . . Chrysalis CHS 2565
10/07/1982 . . . . . 48 . . . . . 3 . . . . . . PLAYTHING . . . . Chrysalis CHS 2621

LIONROCK UK producer Justin Robertson. A group was later assembled, which included MC Buzz B.

05/12/1992 . . . . . 63 . . . . . 1 . . . . . . LIONROCK . . . . Deconstruction 74321124381
08/05/1993 . . . . . 32 . . . . . 3 . . . . . . PACKET OF PEACE . . . . Deconstruction 74321144372
23/10/1993 . . . . . 34 . . . . . 2 . . . . . . CARNIVAL . . . . Deconstruction 74321164862
27/08/1994 . . . . . 44 . . . . . 1 . . . . . . TRIPWIRE . . . . Deconstruction 74321204702
06/04/1996 . . . . . 33 . . . . . 2 . . . . . . STRAIGHT AT YER HEAD . . . . Deconstruction 74321342972
27/07/1996 . . . . . 43 . . . . . 1 . . . . . . FIRE UP THE SHOESAW . . . . Deconstruction 74321382652
14/03/1998 . . . . . 20 . . . . . 3 . . . . . . RUDE BOY ROCK . . . . Concrete HARD 31CD
30/05/1998 . . . . . 54 . . . . . 1 . . . . . . SCATTER & SWING . . . . Concrete HARD 35CD

LIPPS INC US studio project formed by songwriter/producer/multi-instrumentalist Steven Greenberg with Cynthia Johnson (Miss Black Minnesota 1976) on lead vocals. Greenberg was later A&R Vice President for Mercury Records, signing Hanson, among other acts. He then formed S-Curve Records, home to The Baha Men.

17/05/1980 . . . . . 2 . . . . . 13 . . . . . O FUNKYTOWN ▲4 Featured in the 2004 film *Shrek 2* . . . . Casablanca CAN 194

LIQUID UK instrumental/production duo Eamon Downes and Shane Honegan. Honegan later left, Downes continuing on his own.

21/03/1992 . . . . . 15 . . . . . 6 . . . . . . SWEET HARMONY . . . . XL Recordings XLS 28
05/09/1992 . . . . . 59 . . . . . 2 . . . . . . THE FUTURE MUSIC (EP) Tracks on EP: *Liquid Is Liquid*, *Music, House (Is A Feeling)* and *The Year 3000* . . . . . XL Recordings XLT 33
20/03/1993 . . . . . 46 . . . . . 2 . . . . . . TIME TO GET UP . . . . XL Recordings XLS 40CD
08/07/1995 . . . . . 14 . . . . . 6 . . . . . . SWEET HARMONY/ONE LOVE FAMILY Re-issue of XL Recordings XLS 28 . . . . XL Recordings XLS 65CD
21/10/1995 . . . . . 47 . . . . . 2 . . . . . . CLOSER . . . . XL Recordings XLS 66CD
25/07/1998 . . . . . 59 . . . . . 1 . . . . . . STRONG . . . . Higher Ground HIGHS 7CD
21/10/2000 . . . . . 53 . . . . . 1 . . . . . . ORLANDO DAWN . . . . Xtravaganza XTRAV 16CDS

○ Silver disc ● Gold disc ✪ Platinum disc (additional platinum units are indicated by a figure following the symbol) ◎ Singles released prior to 1973 that are known to have sold over 1 million copies in the UK

LIQUID CHILD German production duo Thomas Menguser and Juergen Herbath.

23/10/1999.....25......2...... DIVING FACES .... Essential Recordings ESCD 9

LIQUID GOLD UK disco group with Ellie Hope (vocals), Syd Twynham (guitar), Ray Knott (bass), Tom Marshall (keyboards) and Wally Rothe (drums). The group came second in the UK heat of the 1981 Eurovision Song Contest.

02/12/1978.....41......7...... ANYWAY YOU DO IT .... Creole CR 159
23/02/1980.....2......14......O **DANCE YOURSELF DIZZY** .... Polo 1
31/05/1980.....8......9...... **SUBSTITUTE** .... Polo 4
01/11/1980.....32......7...... THE NIGHT THE WINE THE ROSES .... Polo 6
28/03/1981.....42......5...... DON'T PANIC The song came second in the UK's 'Song For Europe' competition. .... Polo 8
21/08/1982.....56......4...... WHERE DID WE GO WRONG .... Polo 23

LIQUID OXYGEN US DJ Frankie Bones recording under an assumed name. He also records as Break Boys and Looney Tunes.

28/04/1990.....56......2...... THE PLANET DANCE (MOVE YA BODY) .... Champion CHAMP 242

LIQUID PEOPLE UK production duo Dan Smith and Conan Manchester.

20/07/2002.....67......1...... MONSTER LIQUID PEOPLE VS SIMPLE MINDS .... Defected DFECT 49R
21/06/2003.....64......1...... IT'S MY LIFE LIQUID PEOPLE VS TALK TALK .... Nebula NEBCD 045

LIQUID STATE FEATURING MARCELLA WOODS UK production group formed by Andy Bury and Rich Mowatt with singer Marcella Woods. She has also sung with Matt Darey.

30/03/2002.....60......1...... FALLING .... Perfecto PERF 29CDS

LISA LISA US group formed by Lisa Lisa (born Lisa Velez, 15/1/1967), Mark Hughes and Alex 'Spanador' Mosely, with all their hits written and produced by Full Force.

04/05/1985.....12......17...... I WONDER IF I TAKE YOU HOME LISA LISA AND CULT JAM WITH FULL FORCE .... CBS A 6057
31/10/1987.....58......4...... LOST IN EMOTION ▲[1] .... CBS 6510367
13/07/1991.....17......6...... LET THE BEAT HIT 'EM .... Columbia 6572867
24/08/1991.....49......2...... LET THE BEAT HIT 'EM PART 2 This and above two singles credited to LISA LISA AND CULT JAM .... Columbia 6573747
26/03/1994.....34......3...... SKIP TO MY LU .... Chrysalis CDCHS 5006

LISA MARIE – see MALCOLM MCLAREN

LISA MARIE EXPERIENCE UK production duo DJs Neil Hinde and Dean Marriott.

27/04/1996.....7......13...... **KEEP ON JUMPIN'** .... ffrr FCD 271
10/08/1996.....33......2...... DO THAT TO ME .... Positiva CDTIV 57

LISBON LIONS FEATURING MARTIN O'NEILL AND CELTIC CHORUS UK vocal group assembled to record a single that pays tribute to the exploits of Celtic Football Club on the 35th anniversary of their winning the European Cup. The accompanying video also features celebrity Celtic fans Noel Gallagher (of Oasis), Billy Connolly, Rod Stewart, Ian McCulloch, Shane McGowan and Huey Morgan (Fun Lovin' Criminals). Martin O'Neill is the current manager of the club.

11/05/2002.....17......4...... THE BEST DAYS OF OUR LIVES .... Concept CDCON 32

LIT US group formed in California by A Jay Popoff (vocals), Jeremy Popoff (guitar), Kevin Blades (bass) and Allen Shellenberger (drums).

26/06/1999.....16......4...... MY OWN WORST ENEMY .... RCA 74321669992
25/09/1999.....60......1...... ZIP – LOCK Featured in the 2000 film *The Replacements* .... RCA 74321701852
19/08/2000.....37......2...... OVER MY HEAD .... Capitol 8889532

LITHIUM AND SONYA MADAN US/UK duo featuring Sonya Madan of Echobelly and Victor Imbres of Alcatraz.

01/03/1997.....40......2...... RIDE A ROCKET .... ffrr FCD 293

DE ETTA LITTLE AND NELSON PIGFORD US vocal duo; their hit was used in the first Sylvester Stallone *Rocky* film.

13/08/1977.....35......5...... YOU TAKE MY HEART AWAY Featured in the 1976 film *Rocky* .... United Artists UP 36257

LITTLE ANGELS UK heavy rock group formed by Toby Jepson (vocals), Bruce J Dickinson (guitar), Mark Plunkett (bass), Jim Dickinson (keyboards) and Michael Lee (drums). After a number of releases on Powerstation they signed with Polydor in 1988.

04/03/1989.....74......1...... BIG BAD EP Tracks on EP: *She's A Little Angel, Don't Waste My Time, Better Than The Rest* and *Sex In Cars*..... Polydor LTLEP 2
24/02/1990.....46......4...... KICKING UP DUST .... Polydor LTL 5
12/05/1990.....34......4...... RADICAL YOUR LOVER LITTLE ANGELS FEATURING THE BIG BAD HORNS .... Polydor LTL 6
04/08/1990.....21......3...... SHE'S A LITTLE ANGEL .... Polydor LTL 7
02/02/1991.....33......4...... BONEYARD .... Polydor LTL 8
30/03/1991.....40......2...... PRODUCT OF THE WORKING CLASS .... Polydor LTL 9
01/06/1991.....34......2...... YOUNG GODS .... Polydor LTL 10
20/07/1991.....26......3...... I AIN'T GONNA CRY .... Polydor LTL 11
07/11/1992.....22......3...... TOO MUCH TOO YOUNG .... Polydor LTL 12
09/01/1993.....12......5...... WOMANKIND. .... Polydor LTLCD 13
24/04/1993.....33......4...... SOAPBOX .... Polydor LTLCD 14
25/09/1993.....45......3...... SAIL AWAY .... Polydor LTLCD 15
09/04/1994.....18......3...... TEN MILES HIGH. .... Polydor LTLCD 16

❶[9] Number of weeks single topped the UK chart ↑ Entered the UK chart at #1 ▲[9] Number of weeks single topped the US chart

469

LITTLE ANTHONY AND THE IMPERIALS
US R&B vocal group formed by Little Anthony (born Anthony Gourdine 8/1/1940, Brooklyn, NYC) in 1958 and comprising Clarence Collins (born 17/3/1941, Brooklyn), Tracy Lord, Ernest Wright (born 24/8/1941, Brooklyn) and Nat Rogers (born 1940, Brooklyn). Little Anthony went solo in 1960 but re-formed the group in 1964 with Wright, Collins and Sammy Strain (born 9/12/1941, Brooklyn), who later became a member of the O'Jays. Both Little Anthony & The Imperials (in 1976) and The Imperials (in 1978) enjoyed UK hits. Clarence Collins assembled a third line-up to tour the country.

31/07/1976.....42......4....... BETTER USE YOUR HEAD .... United Artists UP 36141

LITTLE BENNY AND THE MASTERS
US go-go group formed in Washington DC in the mid-1980s by Little Benny (trumpet/ lead vocals), Rick Wellman (drums), Rick Holmes (bass), Tommy Crosby (guitar), Lowell Tucker (keyboards), Mark Lawson (keyboards), Tyrone Williams (percussion), Steve Colman (horns), Vernon McDonald (horns), Reggie Thomas (horns) and backing vocalists Diane Borg and Kim Anderson.

02/02/1985.....33......7....... WHO COMES TO BOOGIE.. Bluebird 10 BR 13

LITTLE CAESAR
UK singer whose single is a dance version of The Waterboys' hit.

09/06/1990.....68......3....... THE WHOLE OF THE MOON .... A1 EAU 1

LITTLE EVA
US singer (born Eva Narcissus Boyd, 29/6/1943, Bellhaven, NC) discovered by songwriters Carole King and Gerry Goffin (their babysitter). On a later single with Big Dee Irwin, her contribution is uncredited on the UK release. She died from cancer on 12/4/2003.

06/09/1962	2	17		**THE LOCO-MOTION** ▲[1]	London HL 9581
03/01/1963	30	5		KEEP YOUR HANDS OFF MY BABY	London HLU 9633
07/03/1963	13	12		LET'S TURKEY TROT	London HLU 9687
29/07/1972	11	11		THE LOCO-MOTION	London HL 9581

LITTLE LOUIE – see LOUIE VEGA

LITTLE MS MARCIE – see MELT FEATURING LITTLE MS MARCIE

LITTLE RICHARD
US singer (born Richard Wayne Penniman, 5/12/1932, Macon, GA) who first recorded for RCA Camden in 1951. He began recording with Specialty in 1955 and sold around 18 million singles over the next five years (although he sold the publishing rights to *Tutti Frutti* for $50) before recording gospel songs. He appeared in early rock 'n' roll films (including *Don't Knock The Rock,* 1956) and is regarded as one of the key figures in the development of rock 'n' roll. He denounced rock 'n' roll in 1957 and was ordained a Minister in 1961. Inducted into the Rock & Roll Hall of Fame in 1986, he has a star on the Hollywood Walk of Fame.

14/12/1956	30	1		RIP IT UP	London HLO 8336
08/02/1957	3	16		**LONG TALL SALLY** Featured in the films *Don't Knock The Rock* (1957) and *Predator* (1987)	London HLO 8366
22/02/1957	29	1		TUTTI FRUTTI B-side to *Long Tall Sally.* Featured in the films *American Hot Wax* (1978), *Down And Out In Beverly Hills* (1986) and *Cocktail* (1988)	London HLO 8366
08/03/1957	15	9		SHE'S GOT IT	London HLO 8382
15/03/1957	9	11		**THE GIRL CAN'T HELP IT** B-side to *She's Got It.* Featured in the 1956 film *The Girl Can't Help It*	London HLO 8382
28/06/1957	10	9		**LUCILLE**	London HLO 8446
13/09/1957	11	5		JENNY JENNY	London HLO 8470
29/11/1957	21	7		KEEP A KNOCKIN' Featured in the films *Mister Rock 'N' Roll* (1957), *Christine* (1983), and *Why Do Fools Fall In Love* (1998)	London HLO 8509
28/02/1958	8	9		**GOOD GOLLY MISS MOLLY** Featured in the 1984 film *The Flamingo Kid.*	London HLU 8560
11/07/1958	22	4		OOH MY SOUL	London HLO 8647
02/01/1959	2	15		**BABY FACE**	London HLU 8770
03/04/1959	17	5		BY THE LIGHT OF THE SILVERY MOON	London HLU 8831
05/06/1959	26	5		KANSAS CITY	London HLU 8868
11/10/1962	38	4		HE GOT WHAT HE WANTED	Mercury AMT 1189
04/06/1964	20	7		BAMA LAMA BAMA LOO	London HL 9896
02/07/1977	37	4		GOOD GOLLY MISS MOLLY/RIP IT UP Re-recordings of London HLU 8560 and London HLO 8336	Creole CR 140
14/06/1986	62	2		GREAT GOSH A'MIGHTY (IT'S A MATTER OF TIME)	MCA 1049
25/10/1986	67	2		OPERATOR	WEA YZ 89

LITTLE STEVEN
US singer/guitarist (born 22/11/1950, Boston, MA) who began with Steel Mill (featuring Bruce Springsteen) and then went on tour backing The Dovells. After a spell in Southside Johnny And The Asbury Jukes, he joined Bruce Springsteen's E Street Band in 1975 and stayed for six years. He left in 1981 to form Little Steven And The Disciples of Soul. He later masterminded The Artists United Against Apartheid single *Sun City* and, as a producer, worked with the likes of Gary US Bonds, Lone Justice and Ronnie Spector.

23/05/1987.....66......3....... BITTER FRUIT.. Manhattan MT 21

LITTLE T – see REBEL MC

LITTLE TONY AND HIS BROTHERS
Italian singer Antonio Ciacci, also an actor, appearing in *Pesci D'oro E Bikini D'Argento* and *Cuore Matto.*

15/01/1960.....19......3....... TOO GOOD.. Decca F 11190

LITTLE TREES
Danish vocal trio Marie Broebeck Mortensen (thirteen at the time of the debut hit), Stephanie Nguyen (fourteen) and Sofie Walbum Kring (fifteen). They met studying at a Copenhagen dance academy and were assembled by producer Ole Evenrude.

01/09/2001.....11......7....... HELP! I'M A FISH .... RCA 74321874652

○ Silver disc ● Gold disc ✪ Platinum disc (additional platinum units are indicated by a figure following the symbol) ◉ Singles released prior to 1973 that are known to have sold over 1 million copies in the UK

LIVE
US group formed in York, PA in 1991 by Ed Kowalcyzk (born 17/7/1971, Lancaster, PA, vocals), Patrick Dahlheimer (born 30/5/1971, York, bass), Chad Taylor (born 24/11/1970, York, guitar) and Chad Gracey (born 23/7/1971, York, drums). They signed with Radioactive in 1991.

18/02/1995	48	4		I ALONE	Radioactive RAXTD 13
01/07/1995	30	2		SELLING THE DRAMA	Radioactive RAXXD 17
07/10/1995	48	1		ALL OVER YOU	Radioactive RAXTD 20
13/01/1996	33	2		LIGHTNING CRASHES	Radioactive RAXXD 23
15/03/1997	29	2		LAKINI'S JUICE	Radioactive RAD 49023
12/07/1997	60	1		FREAKS	Radioactive RAXTD 29
05/02/2000	62	1		THE DOLPHINS' CRY	Radioactive RAXTD 39

LIVE ELEMENT
US DJ duo Greg Bahary and Chris Malinchak.

26/01/2002	26	2		BE FREE Contains a sample of Belinda Carlisle's Live Your Life Be Free	Strictly Rhythm SRUKCD 11

LIVE REPORT
UK vocal/instrumental group formed by Ray Carauna, Brian Hodgson, John Beeby, Peter May, Mike Bell and Maggie Jay. Their hit was Britain's entry to the 1989 Eurovision Song Contest and came second to Yugoslavia's entry, Rock Me, by Riva.

20/05/1989	73	1		WHY DO I ALWAYS GET IT WRONG Britain's entry to the 1989 Eurovision Song Contest	Brouhaha CUE 7

LIVERPOOL EXPRESS
UK group formed in Liverpool by Derek Cashin (drums), Tony Coates (guitar/vocals), Roger Craig (keyboards) and Billy Kinsley (bass). Kinsley had previously been in Liverpool groups the Merseybeats and Mersey.

26/06/1976	11	9		YOU ARE MY LOVE	Warner Brothers K 16743
16/10/1976	46	2		HOLD TIGHT	Warner Brothers K 16799
18/12/1976	17	11		EVERY MAN MUST HAVE A DREAM	Warner Brothers K 16854
04/06/1977	40	4		DREAMIN'	Warner Brothers K 16933

LIVERPOOL FC
UK professional football club formed in 1892 following Everton's switch from Anfield to Goodison Park.

28/05/1977	15	4		WE CAN DO IT (EP) Tracks on EP: We Can Do It, Liverpool Lou, We Shall Not Be Moved and You'll Never Walk Alone	State STAT 50
23/04/1983	54	4		LIVERPOOL (WE'RE NEVER GONNA…)/LIVERPOOL (ANTHEM)	Mean 102
17/05/1986	50	2		SITTING ON TOP OF THE WORLD	Columbia DB 9116
14/05/1988	3	6		ANFIELD RAP (RED MACHINE IN FULL EFFECT)	Virgin LFC 1
18/05/1996	4	5		PASS & MOVE (IT'S THE LIVERPOOL GROOVE) LIVERPOOL FC & THE BOOT ROOM BOYS	Telstar LFCCD 96

LIVIN' JOY
Italian dance group assembled by brothers Venturi and Giovanni Visnadi featuring the vocals of US singer Janice Robinson. The brothers are also responsible for Alex Party. Robinson left in 1996 and was replaced by fellow US singer Tameka Starr.

03/09/1994	18	6		DREAMER	Undiscovered MCSTD 1993
13/05/1995	❶¹ ↑	11		DREAMER (REMIX) ↑	Undiscovered MCSTD 2056
15/06/1996	5	14	○	DON'T STOP MOVIN'	Undiscovered MCSTD 40041
02/11/1996	9	5		FOLLOW THE RULES	Undiscovered MCSTD 40081
05/04/1997	12	4		WHERE CAN I FIND LOVE	Undiscovered MCSTD 40108
23/08/1997	17	4		DEEP IN YOU	Undiscovered MCSTD 40136

LIVING COLOUR
US rock group formed in New York in 1984 by Vernon Reid (born 22/8/1958, London, guitar), Corey Glover (born 6/11/1964, New York, vocals), Manuel 'Muzz' Skillings (born 6/1/1960, New York, bass) and William Calhoun (born 22/7/1964, New York, drums). Glover appeared in the film Platoon. Skillings left in 1992, replaced by Doug Wimbush (born 22/9/1956, Hartford, CT). They won two Grammy Awards before they disbanded in 1995: Best Hard Rock Performance (Vocal or Instrumental) in 1989 for Cult Of Personality and Best Hard Rock Performance (Vocal or Instrumental) in 1990 for Time's Up. Vernon Reid later recorded solo.

27/10/1990	75	1		TYPE	Epic LCL 7
02/02/1991	12	11		LOVE REARS ITS UGLY HEAD	Epic 6565937
01/06/1991	33	5		SOLACE OF YOU	Epic 6569087
26/10/1991	67	2		CULT OF PERSONALITY Featured in the 1989 film Say Anything	Epic 6575357
20/02/1993	34	2		LEAVE IT ALONE	Epic 6589762
17/04/1993	53	1		AUSLANDER	Epic 6591732

LIVING IN A BOX
UK group formed by Richard Darbyshire (born 8/3/1960, Stockport, vocals), Marcus Vere (born 29/1/1962, keyboards) and Anthony 'Tich' Critchlow (drums). Darbyshire later recorded solo.

04/04/1987	5	13		LIVING IN A BOX	Chrysalis LIB 1
13/06/1987	30	6		SCALES OF JUSTICE	Chrysalis LIB 2
26/09/1987	34	8		SO THE STORY GOES LIVING IN A BOX FEATURING BOBBY WOMACK	Chrysalis LIB 3
30/01/1988	45	4		LOVE IS THE ART	Chrysalis LIB 4
18/02/1989	10	9		BLOW THE HOUSE DOWN	Chrysalis LIB 5
10/06/1989	36	6		GATECRASHING	Chrysalis LIB 6
23/09/1989	5	13	○	ROOM IN YOUR HEART	Chrysalis LIB 7
30/12/1989	57	3		DIFFERENT AIR	Chrysalis LIB 8

DANDY LIVINGSTONE
Jamaican singer (born Robert Livingstone Thompson, 1943, St Andrews) who made his first recording in 1967 for Carnival Records. He moved to London at the end of the decade and worked for Trojan Records' A&R department.

02/09/1972	14	11		SUZANNE BEWARE OF THE DEVIL	Horse HOSS 16
13/01/1973	26	8		BIG CITY/THINK ABOUT THAT	Horse HOSS 26

❶⁹ Number of weeks single topped the UK chart ↑ Entered the UK chart at #1 ▲⁹ Number of weeks single topped the US chart

471

LL COOL J
US rapper (born James Todd Smith, 14/1/1968, Queens, NY) who began his career at the age of nine. His stage name stands for Ladies Love Cool James. He appeared in the films *Krush Groove, Toys, Halloween H2O, B*A*P*S, In Too Deep* and *Deep Blue Sea*. He won two Grammies including Best Rap Solo Performance in 1991 for *Mama Said Knock You Out*. He left music in 1997 for films, working on *Kingdom Come* and *Any Given Sunday*, returning in 2000 with the album *The G.O.A.T. (Greatest Of All Time)*.

DATE	POS	WKS	BPI	SINGLE TITLE	LABEL & NUMBER
04/07/1987	71	1		I'M BAD	Def Jam 6508567
12/09/1987	8	10		**I NEED LOVE**	Def Jam 6511017
21/11/1987	66	2		GO CUT CREATOR GO	Def Jam LLCJ 1
13/02/1988	37	4		GOING BACK TO CALI//JACK THE RIPPER A-side featured in the film 1987 *Less Than Zero*	Def Jam LLCJ 2
10/06/1989	43	5		I'M THAT TYPE OF GUY	Def Jam LLCJ 3
01/12/1990	41	4		AROUND THE WAY GIRL/MAMA SAID KNOCK YOU OUT	Def Jam 6564470
09/03/1991	36	4		AROUND THE WAY GIRL (REMIX) Contains a sample of The Mary Jane Girls' *All Night Long*	Columbia 6564470
10/04/1993	37	2		HOW I'M COMIN' Contains a sample of Bobby Byrd's *Hot Pants – I'm Coming*	Def Jam 6591692
20/01/1996	17	4		HEY LOVER **LL COOL J FEATURING BOYZ II MEN** Contains a sample of Michael Jackson's *The Lady In My Life*. 1996 Grammy Award for Best Rap Solo Performance	Def Jam DEFCD 14
01/06/1996	15	3		DOIN' IT Contains a sample of Grace Jones' *My Jamaican Guy*	Def Jam DEFCD 15
05/10/1996	7	8		**LOUNGIN'** Contains a sample of Bernard Edwards' *Who Do You Love*	Def Jam DEFCD 30
08/02/1997	❶¹	9		**AIN'T NOBODY** ↑ Featured in the 1996 film *Beavis And Butt-Head Do America*	Geffen GFSTD 22195
05/04/1997	8	6		HIT 'EM HIGH (THE MONSTARS' ANTHEM) **B REAL/BUSTA RHYMES/COOLIO/LL COOL J/METHOD MAN** Featured in the 1996 film *Space Jam*	Atlantic A 5449CD
01/11/1997	9	2		PHENOMENON Contains a sample of Creative Source's *Who Is He And What Is He To You*	Def Jam 5681172
28/03/1998	10	5		FATHER Contains a sample of George Michael's *Father Figure*	Def Jam 5685292
11/07/1998	15	3		ZOOM **DR DRE AND LL COOL J** Featured in the 1998 film *Bulworth*	Interscope IND 95594
05/12/1998	52	1		INCREDIBLE **KEITH MURRAY FEATURING LL COOL J** Contains a sample of James Brown's *Sportin' Life*	Jive 0522102
26/10/2002	7	7		**LUV U BETTER** Contains a sample of Hall & Oates' *Rich Girl*	Def Jam 0638722
22/02/2003	18	5		PARADISE **LL COOL J FEATURING AMERIE** Contains a sample of Keni Burke's *Risin' To The Top*	Def Jam 0637242
22/03/2003	2	13		ALL I HAVE ▲⁴ **JENNIFER LOPEZ FEATURING LL COOL J** Contains a sample of Debra Laws' *Very Special*	Epic 6736782
28/08/2004	25	4		HEADSPRUNG	Def Jam 9863759

LLAMA FARMERS
UK group: Bernie Simpson (vocals), Williams Briggs (guitar), Jenni Simpson (bass) and Brooke Rogers (drums).

DATE	POS	WKS	BPI	SINGLE TITLE	LABEL & NUMBER
06/02/1999	67	1		BIG WHEELS	Beggars Banquet BBQ 333CD
15/05/1999	74	1		GET THE KEYS AND GO	Beggars Banquet BBQ 335CD

KELLY LLORENNA
UK singer (born 1976, Manchester) who began her career (aged eighteen) with N-Trance before going solo. Although not credited, Kelly also appeared on both remixes of *Set You Free*, which hit the top five in 1995 and 2001.

DATE	POS	WKS	BPI	SINGLE TITLE	LABEL & NUMBER
07/05/1994	39	4		SET YOU FREE **N-TRANCE FEATURING KELLY LLORENNA** Originally released in September 1993 and failed to chart	All Around The World CDGLOBE 124
24/02/1996	43	2		BRIGHTER DAY	Pukka CDPUKKA 5
25/07/1998	55	1		HEART OF GOLD	Diverse VERSE 2CD
24/03/2001	34	3		TRUE LOVE NEVER DIES	All Around The World CDGLOBE 240
02/02/2002	7	10		**TRUE LOVE NEVER DIES (REMIX)** This and above single credited to **FLIP AND FULL FEATURING KELLY LLORENNA**	All Around The World CDGLOBE 248
06/07/2002	9	8		**TELL IT TO MY HEART**	All Around The World CDGLOBE 256
30/11/2002	19	4		HEART OF GOLD	All Around The World CXGLOBE 271
06/03/2004	14	4		THIS TIME I KNOW IT'S FOR REAL	All Around The World CXGLOBE 295

DON LLOYDIE — see SOUNDMAN AND DON LLOYDIE WITH ELISABETH TROY

LMC VS U2
UK duo comprising producer Lee Monteverde and singer Rachel Macfarlane (previously a member of Loveland).

DATE	POS	WKS	BPI	SINGLE TITLE	LABEL & NUMBER
07/02/2004	❶²	12		**TAKE ME TO THE CLOUDS ABOVE** ↑ This is effectively two songs: the melody of U2's *With Or Without You* and the lyrics to Whitney Houston's *How Will I Know*	All Around The World CXGLOBE 313

LNR
US vocal/instrumental house duo Robert Lenoir and Rev Thompson.

DATE	POS	WKS	BPI	SINGLE TITLE	LABEL & NUMBER
03/06/1989	64	2		WORK IT TO THE BONE	Kool Kat KOOL 501

LO FIDELITY ALLSTARS
UK group formed by Wrekked Train (Dave Randall, vocals), Albino Priest (decks), A One Man Crowd Called Gentile (bass), the Slammer (drums), Sheriff John Stone (keyboards) and the Many Tentacles (engineering/keyboards). Randall left the group in December 1998. Pigeonhed are a rock group from Seattle formed by Shawn Smith and Steve Fisk.

DATE	POS	WKS	BPI	SINGLE TITLE	LABEL & NUMBER
11/10/1997	50	1		DISCO MACHINE GUN	Skint 30CD
02/05/1998	30	2		VISION INCISION Contains samples of The Three Degrees' *A Woman Needs A Good Man* and Eric B and Rakim's *Follow The Leader*	Skint 33CD
28/11/1998	36	2		BATTLEFLAG **LO FIDELITY ALLSTARS FEATURING PIGEONHED**	Skint 38CD

LO-PRO — see X-PRESS 2

LOBO
US singer/songwriter/guitarist (born Roland Kent Lavoie, 31/7/1943, Tallahassee, FL) whose stage name is Spanish for wolf.

DATE	POS	WKS	BPI	SINGLE TITLE	LABEL & NUMBER
19/06/1971	4	14		**ME AND YOU AND A DOG NAMED BOO**	Philips 6073 801
08/06/1974	5	11		**I'D LOVE YOU TO WANT ME**	UK 68

LOBO
Dutch singer Imrich Lobo; his hit was inspired by Starsound's success and numerous well-known Caribbean calypso songs.

○ Silver disc ● Gold disc ✪ Platinum disc (additional platinum units are indicated by a figure following the symbol) ◎ Singles released prior to 1973 that are known to have sold over 1 million copies in the UK

25/07/1981 . . . . . 8 . . . . . . 11 . . . . . . **THE CARIBBEAN DISCO SHOW** . . . . Polydor POSP 302

TONE LOC US rapper (born Anthony Smith, 3/3/1966, Los Angeles, CA) who formed Triple A at school before going solo. *Loc'ed After Dark* was the first rap album to top US charts. Named from Spanish nickname 'Antonio Loco'. In the film *Ace Ventura: Pet Detective*.

11/02/1989 . . . . . 21 . . . . . . 8 . . . . . . WILD THING/LOC'ED AFTER DARK A-side contains a sample of Van Halen's *Jamie's Cryin'* . . . . Fourth & Broadway BRW 121

20/05/1989 . . . . . 13 . . . . . . 9 . . . . . . FUNKY COLD MEDINA/ON FIRE A-side contains samples of Free's *All Right Now,* Funkadelic's *(not just) Knee Deep* and Kiss' *Christine Sixteen* . . . . Fourth & Broadway BRW 129

05/08/1989 . . . . . 55 . . . . . . 2 . . . . . . I GOT IT GOIN' ON Contains a sample of Tom Browne's *Funkin' For Jamaica* . . . . Fourth & Broadway BRW 140

LOCK 'N' LOAD Dutch production group formed by Francis Rooijen and Nilz Pijpers.

15/04/2000 . . . . . 6 . . . . . . 11 . . . . ○ **BLOW YA MIND** . . . . Pepper 9230162

03/03/2001 . . . . . 45 . . . . . . 2 . . . . . . HOUSE SOME MORE . . . . Pepper 9230422

KIMBERLEY LOCKE US singer (born 3/1/1978, Hartsville, TN) who first came to prominence in the 2003 version of *American Pop Idol,* reaching the semi-final.

31/07/2004 . . . . . 49 . . . . . . 2 . . . . . . 8TH WORLD WONDER . . . . Curb CUBC097

HANK LOCKLIN US singer (born Lawrence Hankins Locklin, 15/2/1918, McLellan, FL) he had his own TV series in the 1970s.

11/08/1960 . . . . 9 . . . . . 19 . . . . . . **PLEASE HELP ME I'M FALLING** . . . . RCA 1188

15/02/1962 . . . . . 44 . . . . . . 3 . . . . . . FROM HERE TO THERE TO YOU . . . . RCA 1273

15/11/1962 . . . . . 18 . . . . . . 11 . . . . . . WE'RE GONNA GO FISHIN' . . . . RCA 1305

05/05/1966 . . . . . 29 . . . . . . 8 . . . . . . I FEEL A CRY COMING ON . . . . RCA 1510

LOCKSMITH US R&B instrumental group formed by Richard Steaker (guitar), James Simmons (keyboards), Tyrone Brown (bass), John Blake (violin), Leonard Gibbs (percussion) and Millard Yinson (drums).

23/08/1980 . . . . . 42 . . . . . . 6 . . . . . . UNLOCK THE FUNK . . . . Arista ARIST 364

LOCOMOTIVE UK group formed in Birmingham by Norman Haines (guitar/vocals) and also featuring Mick Taylor (trumpet), Bill Madge (saxophone), Mick Hincks (bass) and Bob Lamb (drums). Chris Wood, who later joined Traffic, was also briefly a member.

16/10/1968 . . . . . 25 . . . . . . 8 . . . . . . RUDI'S IN LOVE . . . . Parlophone R 5718

JOHN LODGE – see **JUSTIN HAYWARD**

LODGER UK group formed by Will Foster (piano), Neil Carhill (guitar/vocals) and singer Pearl.

02/05/1998 . . . . . 40 . . . . . 2 . . . . . . I'M LEAVING . . . . Island CID 693

LISA LOEB AND NINE STORIES US group based in New York and formed by Lisa Loeb (vocals), Tim Bright (guitar), Joe Quigley (bass) and Jonathan Feinberg (drums). Lisa won the Best International Newcomer award at the 1995 BRIT Awards.

03/09/1994 . . . . . 6 . . . . . . 15 . . . . . . **STAY (I MISSED YOU)** ▲³ Featured in the 1994 film *Reality Bites* . . . . RCA 74321212522

16/09/1995 . . . . . 45 . . . . . . 2 . . . . . . DO YOU SLEEP? . . . . Geffen GFSTD 96

NILS LOFGREN US singer/guitarist (born 21/6/1951, Chicago, IL); he first recorded as Paul Dowell And The Dolphin before forming Grin in the 1970s. After a spell with Neil Young's Crazy Horse, he was going to replace Mick Taylor in The Rolling Stones but signed a solo deal with A&M instead. In 1984 he joined Bruce Springsteen's E Street Band but kept a solo career, recording for Towerbell and Essential.

08/06/1985 . . . . . 53 . . . . . . 3 . . . . . . SECRETS IN THE STREET . . . . Towerbell TOW 68

JOHNNY LOGAN Irish singer (born Sean Sherrard, Australia) who became a naturalised Irishman and is the only artist to have won the Eurovision Song Contest more than one occasion.

03/05/1980 . . . ❶² . . 8 . . . . . . ○ **WHAT'S ANOTHER YEAR** The song won the 1980 Eurovision Song Contest . . . . Epic EPC 8572

23/05/1987 . . . . . 2 . . . . . . 11 . . . . . . ○ **HOLD ME NOW** The song won the 1987 Eurovision Song Contest . . . . Epic LOG 1

22/08/1987 . . . . . 51 . . . . . . 5 . . . . . . I'M NOT IN LOVE . . . . Epic LOG 2

KENNY LOGGINS US singer (born Kenneth Clarke Loggins, 7/1/1947, Everett, WA) who first signed solo with CBS in 1971. He later linked up with Jim Messina but then returned to being a solo artist. Kenny has won three Grammy Awards: Song of the Year in 1979 with Michael McDonald for *What A Fool Believes,* Best Pop Vocal Performance in 1980 for *This Is It* and Best Recording for Children in 1982 with various others for *In Harmony 2*. He has a star on the Hollywood Walk of Fame.

28/04/1984 . . . . . 6 . . . . . . 10 . . . . . . **FOOTLOOSE** ▲³ Featured in the 1984 film *Footloose* . . . . CBS A 4101

01/11/1986 . . . . . 45 . . . . . 11 . . . . . . DANGER ZONE Featured in the 1986 film *Top Gun* . . . . CBS A 7188

LOGO FEATURING DAWN JOSEPH UK production duo Mark Jolley and Andy Wright with singer Dawn Joseph.

08/12/2001 . . . . . 42 . . . . . . 1 . . . . . . DON'T PANIC . . . . Manifesto FESCD 89

LOLA US singer Lola Blank who toured with James Brown for ten years before going solo.

28/03/1987 . . . . . 65 . . . . . . 1 . . . . . . WAX THE VAN . . . . Syncopate SY 1

LOLLY UK teenage singer (born Anna Klumby, 27/6/1978, Sutton Coldfield).

10/07/1999 . . . . . 6 . . . . . . 9 . . . . . . **VIVA LA RADIO** . . . . Polydor 5639512

18/09/1999 . . . . . 4 . . . . . . 10 . . . . ○ **MICKEY** . . . . Polydor 5613692

04/12/1999 . . . . . 10 . . . . . . 9 . . . . . . **BIG BOYS DON'T CRY/ROCKIN' ROBIN** A-side is a cover version of The Four Seasons' hit *Big Girls Don't Cry* . . . . Polydor 5615552

❶⁹ Number of weeks single topped the UK chart ↑ Entered the UK chart at #1 ▲⁹ Number of weeks single topped the US chart

473

| 06/05/2000 | 11 | 10 | | PER SEMPRE AMORE (FOREVER IN LOVE) | Polydor 5617882 |
| 09/09/2000 | 14 | 6 | | GIRLS JUST WANNA HAVE FUN | Polydor 5619762 |

ALAIN LOMARD – see MADY MESPLE AND DANIELLE MILLET WITH THE PARIS OPERACOMIQUE ORCHESTRA CONDUCTED BY ALAIN LOMBARD

JULIE LONDON US singer (born June Webb, 26/9/1926, Santa Rose, CA) who made twenty albums and was a Second World War pinup girl, achieving later acclaim as Dixie McCall in the TV series *Emergency*. Married to actor Jack Webb from 1947 to 1952 and then jazz musician Bobby Troup. Her debut hit was in the film *The Girl Can't Help It*, for which her husband wrote the theme title. She died in hospital in California from heart failure on 18/10/2000. She has a star on the Hollywood Walk of Fame.

| 05/04/1957 | 22 | 3 | | CRY ME A RIVER Featured in the 1957 film *The Girl Can't Help It* | London HLU 8240 |

LAURIE LONDON UK singer (born 19/1/1944, London) who was thirteen years of age when he recorded this traditional gospel song hit with the Geoff Love orchestra.

| 08/11/1957 | 12 | 12 | | HE'S GOT THE WHOLE WORLD IN HIS HANDS | Parlophone R 4359 |

LONDON BOYS UK duo Dennis Fuller and Edem Ephraim who relocated to Germany before finding success in the hi-nrg market.

10/12/1988	59	6		REQUIEM	WEA YZ 345
01/04/1989	4	15	O	**REQUIEM**	WEA YZ 345
01/07/1989	2	9	O	**LONDON NIGHTS**	WEA YZ 393
16/09/1989	17	7		HARLEM DESIRE	WEA YZ 415
02/12/1989	46	6		MY LOVE	WEA YZ 433
16/06/1990	75	1		CHAPEL OF LOVE	East West YZ 458
19/01/1991	54	2		FREEDOM	East West YZ 554

LONDON COMMUNITY GOSPEL CHOIR – see SAL SOLO

LONDON PHILHARMONIC ORCHESTRA – see CLIFF RICHARD

LONDON STRING CHORALE UK orchestra and choir fronted by Denis King, who later formed his own orchestra and had a hit with Stutz Bearcats.

| 15/12/1973 | 31 | 13 | | GALLOPING HOME Theme to the TV series *The Adventures Of Black Beauty* | Polydor 2058 280 |

LONDON SYMPHONY ORCHESTRA UK orchestra conducted by US composer John Williams. They scored a US top ten hit with their theme from *Star Wars*, (written and conducted by Williams), and also recorded as The Armada Orchestra, a disco group!

| 06/01/1979 | 32 | 5 | | THEME FROM 'SUPERMAN' (MAIN TITLE) Featured in the 1979 film *Superman* | Warner Brothers K 17292 |

LONDONBEAT US/Trinidadian R&B vocal trio Jimmy Helms (born 1944, Florida), George Chandler (born in Atlanta, GA) and Jimmy Chambers (born 20/1/1946, Trinidad).

26/11/1988	19	10		9 A.M. (THE COMFORT ZONE)	AnXious ANX 008
18/02/1989	60	2		FALLING IN LOVE AGAIN	AnXious ANX 007
02/12/1989	53	2		IT TAKES TWO BABY LIZ KERSHAW, BRUNO BROOKES, JIVE BUNNY AND LONDONBEAT	Spartan CIN 101
01/09/1990	2	13	O	**I'VE BEEN THINKING ABOUT YOU** ▲[1]	AnXious ANX 14
24/11/1990	52	5		A BETTER LOVE	AnXious ANX 21
02/03/1991	64	2		NO WOMAN NO CRY	AnXious ANX 25
20/07/1991	23	6		A BETTER LOVE	AnXious ANX 32
27/06/1992	32	4		YOU BRING ON THE SUN	AnXious ANX 37
24/10/1992	69	1		THAT'S HOW I FEEL ABOUT YOU	AnXious ANX 40
08/04/1995	55	1		I'M JUST YOUR PUPPET ON A ... (STRING) The song came sixth in the UK's 'Song For Europe' competition	AnXious 74321270982
20/05/1995	69	1		COME BACK	AnXious 74321226682

LONE JUSTICE US group formed in Los Angeles, CA by Maria McKee (born 17/8/1964, Los Angeles, vocals), Ryan Hedgecock (guitar), Benmont Tench (keyboards), Marvin Etzioni (bass) and Don Effington (drums). By 1986 the line-up was McKee, Shayne Fontayne (guitar), Bruce Brody (keyboards), Greg Sutton (bass) and Rudy Richardson (drums). They disbanded in 1987 and McKee went solo.

| 07/03/1987 | 45 | 4 | | I FOUND LOVE | Geffen GEF 18 |

LONE STAR US country group formed in Nashville by Richie McDonald (guitar/vocals), John Rich (vocals/bass), Michael Britt (guitar), Dean Sams (keyboards) and Keech Rainwater (drums). Rich left in January 1998.

| 15/04/2000 | 21 | 22 | | AMAZED ▲[2] Despite reaching only #21, *Amazed* sold over 180,000 copies during its chart run | Grapevine 74321742582 |
| 07/10/2000 | 55 | 2 | | SMILE | Grapevine 74321786132 |

SHORTY LONG US singer (born Frederick Earl Long, 20/5/1940, Birmingham, AL); with Tri-Phi in 1962, he switched to Motown in 1964. His hit was from a sketch on the TV show *Rowan and Martin's Laugh In*. He died in a fishing accident in Canada on 29/6/1969.

| 17/07/1968 | 30 | 7 | | HERE COMES THE JUDGE | Tamla Motown TMG 663 |

LONG AND THE SHORT UK group formed by Bob McKinley (vocals), Bob Taylor (guitar), Les Saint (guitar), Alan Grundy (bass) and Gerry Waff (drums). They appeared in the 1965 film *Gonks Go Beat* with Lulu.

| 10/09/1964 | 35 | 5 | | THE LETTER | Decca F 11964 |
| 24/12/1964 | 49 | 3 | | CHOC ICE | Decca F 12043 |

O Silver disc ● Gold disc ✪ Platinum disc (additional platinum units are indicated by a figure following the symbol) ◎ Singles released prior to 1973 that are known to have sold over 1 million copies in the UK

LONG RYDERS US group formed in 1981 as The Long Riders by Sid Griffin (guitar /vocals), Barry Shank (bass/vocals) and Matt Roberts (drums), all previously in The Unclaimed. Steve Wynn (guitar) joined later but was replaced by Stephen McCarthy. By 1983 the line-up was Griffin, McCarthy, Des Brewer (bass) and Greg Sowders (drums), Brewer was replaced by Tom Stevens. They split in 1987.

05/10/1985	59	4		LOOKING FOR LEWIS AND CLARK	Island IS 237

LONGPIGS UK group formed in Sheffield in 1993 by Crispin Hunt (vocals), Richard Hawley (guitar), Simon Stafford (bass) and Dee Boyle (drums). They were initially signed by Elektra but did not release any records, switching to Mother Records in 1994.

22/07/1995	67	1		SHE SAID	Mother MUMCD 66
28/10/1995	61	1		JESUS CHRIST	Mother MUMCD 68
17/02/1996	37	2		FAR	Mother MUMCD 71
13/04/1996	16	3		ON AND ON	Mother MUMCD 74
22/06/1996	16	4		SHE SAID	Mother MUMXD 77
05/10/1996	22	3		LOST MYSELF	Mother MUMCD 82
09/10/1999	21	2		BLUE SKIES	Mother MUMCD 113
18/12/1999	57	1		THE FRANK SONATA	Mother MUMCD 114

JOE LONGTHORNE UK singer (born 31/5/1955, Hull) who made his TV debut on *Junior Showtime* in 1970.

30/04/1994	61	2		YOUNG GIRL	EMI CDEM 310
10/12/1994	34	4		PASSING STRANGERS JOE LONGTHORNE AND LIZ DAWN	EMI CDEM 362

LONGVIEW UK group formed in Manchester by Rob McVey (guitar/vocals), Doug Morch (guitar), Aidan Banks (bass) and Matt Dadds (drums).

26/10/2002	74	1		WHEN YOU SLEEP	4.45 Recordings LVIEW 02CD
08/02/2003	72	1		NOWHERE	4.45 Recordings LVIEW 03CD
19/07/2003	27	2		FURTHER	14th Floor 14FLR 01CD
11/10/2003	51	1		CAN'T EXPLAIN	14th Floor 14FLR 02CD
10/07/2004	38	1		IN A DREAM	14th Floor 14FLR 06CD

LONYO UK singer (born Lonyo Engele) who had previously been a vocalist on Dem 2's *Destiny*. MC Onyx Stone is a UK rapper.

08/07/2000	8	7		SUMMER OF LOVE LONYO – COMME CI COMME CA Contains a sample of Oscar D'Leon's *Madre*	Riverhorse RIVH CD3X
07/04/2001	39	2		GARAGE GIRLS LONYO FEATURING MC ONYX STONE	Riverhorse RIVHCD 12

LOOK UK group formed by Johnny Whetsone (guitar/vocals), Mick Bass (keyboards), Gus Goad (bass) and Trevor Walter (drums).

20/12/1980	6	12	O	I AM THE BEAT	MCA 647
29/08/1981	50	3		FEEDING TIME	MCA 736

LOON US rapper (born Chauncey Hawkins, 1975, Harlem, NY).

10/08/2002	4	11		I NEED A GIRL (PART ONE) P DIDDY FEATURING USHER AND LOON	Puff Daddy 74321947242
08/03/2003	29	3		HIT THE FREEWAY TONI BRAXTON FEATURING LOON	Arista 82876506372
07/02/2004	35	2		SHOW ME YOUR SOUL P DIDDY, LENNY KRAVITZ, PHARRELL WILLIAMS AND LOON Featured in the 2003 film *Bad Boys II* Puff Daddy MCSTD 40350	

LOOP DA LOOP UK producer Nick Destri; he also records as DJ Supreme and Space Cowboy.

07/06/1997	47	1		GO WITH THE FLOW	Manifesto FESCD 24
20/02/1999	20	3		HAZEL Contains a sample of Stetsasonic's *Sally*	Manifesto FESCD 53

LOOSE ENDS UK soul group formed by Carl McIntosh (guitar/bass), Jane Eugene (vocals) and Steve Nichol (keyboards/ trumpet). Eugene and Nichol left in 1990, replaced by Linda Carriere and Sunay Suleyman. Debut hit was the first record by a UK group to top the US R&B charts, a feat they repeated with *Slow Down*. Carl McIntosh won the 1998 MOBO Award for Contribution to Black Music.

23/02/1984	74	1		TELL ME WHAT YOU WANT	Virgin VS 658
28/04/1984	41	6		EMERGENCY (DIAL 999)	Virgin VS 677
21/07/1984	59	3		CHOOSE ME (RESCUE ME)	Virgin VS 697
23/02/1985	13	13		HANGIN' ON A STRING (CONTEMPLATING)	Virgin VS 748
11/05/1985	16	7		MAGIC TOUCH	Virgin VS 761
27/07/1985	59	4		GOLDEN TOUCH	Virgin VS 795
14/06/1986	52	5		STAY A LITTLE WHILE, CHILD	Virgin VS 819
20/09/1986	27	7		SLOW DOWN	Virgin VS 884
29/11/1986	42	7		NIGHTS OF PLEASURE	Virgin VS 919
04/06/1988	50	4		MR BACHELOR	Virgin VS 1080
01/09/1990	13	9		DON'T BE A FOOL	10 TEN 312
17/11/1990	40	4		LOVE'S GOT ME	10 TEN 330
20/06/1992	25	5		HANGIN' ON A STRING (CONTEMPLATING) (REMIX)	10 TEN 406
05/09/1992	75	1		MAGIC TOUCH (REMIX)	10 TEN 409

LISA 'LEFT EYE' LOPES US singer (born 27/5/1971, Philadelphia, PA) and a member of TLC when she launched a parallel solo career. Lopes was fined $10,000 and given five years probation in 1994 for setting fire to her boyfriend Andre Rison's home and vandalising his car, although they reconciled and he refused to press charges. Lopes was killed in a car crash while on holiday in Honduras on 26/4/2002. She was awarded a posthumous Outstanding Achievement Award at the 2002 MOBO Awards.

01/04/2000	❶[1]	16	●	NEVER BE THE SAME AGAIN MELANIE C AND LISA LEFT EYE LOPES	Virgin VSCDT 1786

❶[9] Number of weeks single topped the UK chart ↑ Entered the UK chart at #1 ▲[9] Number of weeks single topped the US chart

475

27/10/2001 . . . . . 16 . . . . . . 4				THE BLOCK PARTY . . . . LaFace 74321895912

JENNIFER LOPEZ US singer (born 24/7/1970, New York); first known as an actress, she appeared in the TV series *ER*, *In Living Color*, *Hotel Malibu* and was later one of the voices in the film *Antz*. Her first marriage to model Ojani Noa ended in divorce in 1998. Briefly engaged to producer Sean 'Puff Daddy' Combs, both were arrested in December 1999 after a nightclub shooting, charged with illegal possession of a firearm, although charges against Lopez were later dropped. Engagement ended soon after and Jennifer married dancer Cris Judd in September 2001 (this second marriage also ended in divorce). After a brief engagement to actor Ben Affleck, Jennifer married fellow singer Marc Anthony in June 2004. She appeared in the films *Out Of Sight* and *The Cell* and in the title role of the 1995 film *Selena*, the biopic of murdered Mexican singer Selena Quintanilla-Perez. She has won three MTV Europe Music Awards: Best Rhythm and Blues Act in 2000 and Best Female in 2001 and 2002. Big Pun is rapper Christopher Rios (born 9/11/1971, New York) who also recorded as Big Punisher, and died from a heart attack brought on from being overweight (698 pounds) on 7/2/2000.

DATE	POS	WKS	BPI	SINGLE TITLE	LABEL & NUMBER
03/07/1999	4	13		IF YOU HAD MY LOVE ▲5 . . . . Columbia 6675772
13/11/1999	5	12		WAITING FOR TONIGHT . . . . Columbia 6683072
01/04/2000	15	6		FEELIN' SO GOOD JENNIFER LOPEZ FEATURING BIG PUN AND FAT JOE Contains a sample of Strafe's *Set It Off* . . Columbia 6691972
20/01/2001	❶1	11	○	LOVE DON'T COST A THING ↑ . . . . Epic 6707282
12/05/2001	3	12		PLAY . . . . Epic 6712272
18/08/2001	3	9		AIN'T IT FUNNY JENNIFER LOPEZ FEATURING JA RULE AND CADILLAC TAH . . . . Epic 6717592
10/11/2001	4	15		I'M REAL ▲5 JENNIFER LOPEZ FEATURING JA RULE . . . . Epic 6720322
23/03/2002	4	13		AIN'T IT FUNNY (REMIX) ▲6 Contains a sample of Craig Mack's *Flava In Your Ear* and features the uncredited contributions of Ja Rule and Cadillac Tah . . . . Epic 6724922
13/07/2002	3	10		I'M GONNA BE ALRIGHT JENNIFER LOPEZ FEATURING NAS Contain samples of Club Nouveau's *Why You Treat Me So Bad* and Luniz's *I Got Five On It* . . . . Epic 6728442
30/11/2002	3	13		JENNY FROM THE BLOCK Contains a sample of Kool & The Gang's *Jungle Boogie* . . . . Epic 6733572
22/03/2003	2	13		ALL I HAVE ▲4 JENNIFER LOPEZ FEATURING LL COOL J Contains a sample of Debra Laws' *Very Special* . . . . Epic 6736782
21/06/2003	11	9		I'M GLAD . . . . Epic 6740152
20/03/2004	3	10		BABY I LOVE U . . . . Epic 6747902

TRINI LOPEZ US singer (born Trinidad Lopez, 15/5/1937, Dallas, TX) who was discovered by Don Costa when performing at a club in Los Angeles. He later appeared in a number of films, including *The Dirty Dozen* and *Marriage On The Rocks*.

DATE	POS	WKS	BPI	SINGLE TITLE	LABEL & NUMBER
12/09/1963	4	17		IF I HAD A HAMMER . . . . Reprise R 20198
12/12/1963	35	5		KANSAS CITY . . . . Reprise R 20236
12/05/1966	28	5		I'M COMING HOME CINDY . . . . Reprise R 20455
06/04/1967	41	5		GONNA GET ALONG WITHOUT YA NOW . . . . Reprise R 20547
19/12/1981	59	5		TRINI TRAX . . . . RCA 154

LORD ROCKINGHAM'S XI UK group led by Scottish bandleader Harry Robinson. They were the resident band on TV's *Oh Boy*. The programme's producer, Jack Good, came up with the name. Robinson later performed on Millie's *My Boy Lollipop*.

DATE	POS	WKS	BPI	SINGLE TITLE	LABEL & NUMBER
24/10/1958	❶3	17		HOOTS MON Saxophone player is Red Price . . . . Decca F 11059
06/02/1959	16	3		WEE TOM . . . . Decca F 11104
25/09/1993	60	1		HOOTS MON Re-issue of Decca F 11059 . . . . Decca 8820982

LORD TANAMO Trinidad & Tobago singer (born Joseph Abraham Gordon, 1934, Kingston, Jamaica) whose debut hit was originally released in 1965 and revived following use in a TV advertisement for Paxo.

DATE	POS	WKS	BPI	SINGLE TITLE	LABEL & NUMBER
01/12/1990	58	2		I'M IN THE MOOD FOR LOVE . . . . Mooncrest MOON 1009

LORD TARIQ AND PETER GUNZ US vocal/rap duo Sean Hamilton (Lord Tariq) and Peter Panky (Peter Gunz). They were first known as The Gunrunners. Tariq is also a member of Money Boss Players and the pair formed the Codeine label.

DATE	POS	WKS	BPI	SINGLE TITLE	LABEL & NUMBER
02/05/1998	21	3		DEJA VU (UPTOWN BABY) Contains a sample of Steely Dan's *Black Cow* . . . . Columbia 6658722

ERIN – see ERIN LORDAN

JERRY LORDAN UK singer (born 30/4/1934, London), also a noted songwriter, penning seventeen hits for the likes of Cliff Richard, Louise Cordet, Jet Harris and Tony Meehan, and Anthony Newley. Newley's success with *I've Waited So Long* earned Lordan a contract with Parlophone. Concentrating on writing through the 1960s, he returned to recording in 1970 with *Old Man And The Sea*, to no avail. Plagued by alcohol and financial problems, he sold the copyright to most of his major songs. He died on 24/7/1995.

DATE	POS	WKS	BPI	SINGLE TITLE	LABEL & NUMBER
08/01/1960	26	3		I'LL STAY SINGLE . . . . Parlophone R 4588
26/02/1960	16	11		WHO COULD BE BLUER . . . . Parlophone R 4627
02/06/1960	36	2		SING LIKE AN ANGEL . . . . Parlophone R 4653

TRACI LORDS US singer (born Nora Louise Kuzma, 7/5/1968, Steubenville, OH) who was initially a porn star. She made between 80 and 100 films. The FBI later revealed that she was under age when these were made and they were all pulled from the market! It did, however, prompt the formation of a something of a tribute group called Traci Lords' Ex-Lovers!

DATE	POS	WKS	BPI	SINGLE TITLE	LABEL & NUMBER
07/10/1995	72	1		FALLEN ANGEL . . . . Radioactive RAXTD 18

LEA LOREN – see DAVID MORALES

SOPHIA LOREN Italian singer/actress (born Sophia Scicolone, 1934, Rome); her film debut was a bit part in *Quo Vadis?* (1951), before being given the lead in *Aida* (1953). Her Hollywood debut was in *The Pride And The Passion* (1957) followed by *El Cid* and *A Breath Of Scandal*. She won an Oscar for *Two Women*. She also won the 2003 Grammy Award for Best Spoken Word Album for *Children*

with Bill Clinton (former President of the US) and Mikhail Gorbachev (former President of the USSR) for *Prokofiev: Peter And The Wolf/Beintus: Wolf Tracks*. Married to film director Carlo Ponti, she has a star on the Hollywood Walk of Fame.

| 10/11/1960 | 4 | 14 | | **GOODNESS GRACIOUS ME** Inspired by (but not in) the 1961 film *The Millionairess* with Peter Sellers and Loren . . . | Parlophone R 4702 |
| 12/01/1961 | 22 | 5 | | BANGERS AND MASH This and above single credited to **PETER SELLERS AND SOPHIA LOREN** | Parlophone R 4724 |

TREY LORENZ
US singer (born 19/1/1969, Florence, SC) who sang backing on Mariah Carey's first two albums and was the featured male vocalist on her *I'll Be There* hit. Carey produced his debut hit.

| 21/11/1992 | 65 | 2 | | SOMEONE TO HOLD | Epic 6587857 |
| 30/01/1993 | 38 | 3 | | PHOTOGRAPH OF MARY | Epic 6589542 |

LORI AND THE CHAMELEONS
UK singer Lori Larty whose backing group featured Bill Drummond (later of KLF) and David Balfe (later of Teardrop Explodes).

| 08/12/1979 | 70 | 1 | | TOUCH | Sire SIR 4025 |

LORRAINE – see BOMB THE BASS

LOS BRAVOS
Spanish/German group with Spaniards Manolo 'Manuel' Fernandez (born 29/9/1943, Seville, keyboards), Pablo 'Gomez' Samllehi (born 5/11/1943, Barcelona, drums), Antonio Martinez (born 3/10/1945, Madrid, guitar) and Miguel Vicens-Danus (born 21/6/1944, Palma de Mallona, bass) and German lead vocalist Mike Kogel (born 25/4/1945, Beuliu), whose Spanish language records caught the ear of Decca executive Ivor Raymonds. They were invited to London to record the English song *Black Is Black*.

| 30/06/1966 | 2 | 13 | | **BLACK IS BLACK** | Decca F 22419 |
| 08/09/1966 | 16 | 11 | | I DON'T CARE | Decca F 22484 |

LOS DEL CHIPMUNKS – see CHIPMUNKS

LOS DEL MAR FEATURING WIL VELOZ
Canadian studio group with Cuban singer Wil Veloz.

| 08/06/1996 | 43 | 7 | | MACARENA | Pulse 8 CDLOSE 101 |

LOS DEL RIO
Spanish flamenco guitar duo Antonio Romero Monge and Rafael Ruiz Perdigones whose sole hit was one of the world's biggest of the year, selling over 4 million copies in America alone and remaining on the charts for over a year. The version that became a hit did so after being remixed by The Bayside Boys – Miami-based production team Carlos A de Yarza and Mike Triay.

| 01/06/1996 | 2 | 19 | ● | **MACARENA** ▲[14] | RCA 74321345372 |

LOS INDIOS TABAJARAS
Brazilian Indian guitarist brothers Musiperi and Herundy, the sons of a Tabajaras Indian chieftain. For performing they used the names Natalicio and Antenor Lima.

| 31/10/1963 | 5 | 17 | | **MARIA ELENA** | RCA 1365 |

LOS LOBOS
US group formed in Los Angeles, CA in 1974 by Spanish Americans David Hidalgo (guitar/accordion/vocals), Cesar Rosas (guitar/vocals), Conrad Lozano (bass) and Luis Perez (drums). Steve Berlin (saxophone) was added to the line-up in 1983. They contributed eight tracks to the *La Bamba* soundtrack, the film of Ritchie Valens' life. Named after the Spanish word for 'wolves', they have three Grammy Awards: Best Mexican–American Performance in 1983 for *Anselma*, Best Mexican–American Performance in 1989 for *La Pistola Y El Corazon* and Best Pop Instrumental Performance in 1995 for *Mariachi Suite*.

06/04/1985	57	4		DON'T WORRY BABY/WILL THE WOLF SURVIVE	London LASH 4
18/07/1987	❶[2]	11		**LA BAMBA** ▲[3]	Slash LASH 13
26/09/1987	18	9		COME ON LET'S GO This and above single featured in the 1987 film *La Bamba*	Slash LASH 14

LOS POP TOPS
Spanish vocal group based in Spain and featuring Phil Trim (from the West Indies) on lead vocals.

| 09/10/1971 | 35 | 6 | | MAMY BLUE US version spelt *Mammy Blue* | A&M AMS 859 |

LOS UMBERELLOS
Multinational group formed by Ugandan-born Al Agami (who describes himself as an 'African cowboy from Denmark') and two former Danish models Mai-Britt Grondahl Vingsoe and Grith Hojfeldt. Agami was forced to flee Uganda by President Idi Amin and settled in Denmark.

| 03/10/1998 | 33 | 2 | | NO TENGO DINERO | Virgin VUSCD 139 |

JOE LOSS ORCHESTRA
UK bandleader (born 22/6/1909, Liverpool) who became a professional musician in 1926 and by the 1940s was acknowledged as the king of the ballroom. He was awarded the OBE in 1978. He died on 6/6/1990.

29/06/1961	21	21		WHEELS CHA CHA	HMV POP 880
19/10/1961	48	1		SUCU SUCU	HMV POP 937
29/03/1962	20	10		THE MAIGRET THEME	HMV POP 995
01/11/1962	20	13		MUST BE MADISON	HMV POP 1075
05/11/1964	31	8		MARCH OF THE MODS	HMV POP 1351

LOST
UK instrumental/production duo Steve Bicknell and Nigel Fairman.

| 22/06/1991 | 75 | 1 | | TECHNO FUNK | Perfecto PT 44560 |

LOST BOYZ
US rap group formed by Raymond 'Freaky Tah' Rogers, Terrance 'Mr Cheeks' Kelly, Eric 'Pretty Lou' Ruth and Ronald 'Spigg Nice' Blackwell. They signed with Uptown Records in 1995. Freaky Tah was murdered on 28/3/1999.

| 02/11/1996 | 42 | 1 | | MUSIC MAKES ME HIGH | Universal MCSTD 48015 |
| 12/07/1997 | 57 | 1 | | LOVE, PEACE & HAPPINESS | Universal UND 56131 |

❶[9] Number of weeks single topped the UK chart ↑ Entered the UK chart at #1 ▲[9] Number of weeks single topped the US chart

LOST BROTHERS FEATURING G TOM MAC UK dance group formed by Keiron McTernon, Harry Diamond and Sergei Hall with Gerald McMahon. McMahon had originally recorded *Cry Little Sister* for the 1987 film *The Lost Boys* and re-recorded his vocals on a dance interpretation in 2003.

20/12/2003 . . . . . 21 . . . . . . 9 . . . . CRY LITTLE SISTER (I NEED U NOW) . . . . Incentive CENT 60CDS

LOST IT.COM UK vocal/production duo John Vick and Jules Craig.

07/04/2001 . . . . . 70 . . . . . . 1 . . . . ANIMAL . . . . Perfecto PERF 13CDS

LOST TRIBE UK dance group formed by Matt Darey and Red Jerry. Darey also records under his own name and as a member of Sunburst and M3. Red Jerry also recorded with Westbam.

11/09/1999 . . . . . 24 . . . . . . 3 . . . . GAMEMASTER . . . . Hooj Choons HOOJ 81CD
06/12/2003 . . . . . 61 . . . . . . 1 . . . . GAMEMASTER . . . . Liquid Asset ASSETCD 12015

LOST WITNESS UK dance group fronted by Simon Paul and Simon Kemper.

29/05/1999 . . . . . 18 . . . . . . 4 . . . . HAPPINESS HAPPENING . . . . Ministry Of Sound MOSCDS 129
18/09/1999 . . . . . 22 . . . . . . 3 . . . . RED SUN RISING . . . . Sound Of Ministry MOSCDS 133
16/12/2000 . . . . . 28 . . . . . . 3 . . . . 7 COLOURS Contains a sample of Nino James' *After The Rain* . . . . Data 15CDS
18/05/2002 . . . . . 28 . . . . . . 3 . . . . DID I DREAM (SONG TO THE SIREN) Contains a sample of This Mortal Coil's *Song To The Siren*. . . . . Data 28CDS

LOSTPROPHETS UK nu-metal group formed in Pontypridd, Wales in 1997 by Ian Watkins (vocals), Mike Lewis (guitar), Lee Glaze (guitar) and Mike Chiplin (drums). Watkins and Lewis are both ex-Public Disturbance. After signing with Visible Noise in 1999 they added Stuart Richardson (bass) and Jamie Oliver (decks) to the line-up, releasing *The Fake Sound Of Progress* in 2000. The album was remixed in 2001 after the group had signed with Columbia for the US.

08/12/2001 . . . . . 41 . . . . . . 2 . . . . SHINOBI VS DRAGON NINJA . . . . Visible Noise TORMENT 17
23/03/2002 . . . . . 21 . . . . . . 3 . . . . THE FAKE SOUND OF PROGRESS . . . . Visible Noise TORMENT 20
15/11/2003 . . . . . 17 . . . . . . 3 . . . . BURN BURN . . . . Visible Noise TORMENT 30CD
07/02/2004 . . . . . 8 . . . . . . 7 . . . . LAST TRAIN HOME . . . . Visible Noise TORMENT 37CD
15/05/2004 . . . . . 18 . . . . . . 4 . . . . WAKE UP . . . . Visible Noise TORMENT 40CD
04/09/2004 . . . . . 13 . . . . . . 5 . . . . LAST SUMMER . . . . Visible Noise TORMENT 43CD
04/12/2004 . . . . . 42 . . . . . . 2 . . . . GOODBYE TONIGHT . . . . Visible Noise TORMENT47CD

LOTUS EATERS UK group formed in Liverpool by Peter Coyle (vocals), Gerard Quinn (keyboards), Alan Wills (drums) and Jeremy Kelly (guitar). Coyle and Kelly had previously been in the Wild Swans.

02/07/1983 . . . . . 15 . . . . . 12 . . . . . . THE FIRST PICTURE OF YOU . . . . Sylvan SYL 1
08/10/1983 . . . . . 53 . . . . . . 4 . . . . . . YOU DON'T NEED SOMEONE NEW . . . . Sylvan SYL 2

BONNIE LOU US singer (born Bonnie Lou Kath, 27/10/1924, Bloomington, IL).

05/02/1954 . . . . . . 4 . . . . . 10 . . . . . TENNESSEE WIG WALK . . . . Parlophone R 3730

LIPPY LOU UK female rapper.

22/04/1995 . . . . . 57 . . . . . . 2 . . . . . . LIBERATION . . . . More Protein PROCD 105

LOUCHIE LOU AND MICHIE ONE UK vocal duo, both born in London. Louchie Lou (Louise Gold) began her recording career with Rebel MC's own Tribal Bass label, while Michie One (Michelle Charles) first recorded for Gold.

29/05/1993 . . . . . 7 . . . . . 8 . . . . . . SHOUT (IT OUT) Based on Art Of Noise' *Peter Gunn* . . . . ffrr FCD 211
14/08/1993 . . . . . 54 . . . . . 2 . . . . . . SOMEBODY ELSE'S GUY . . . . ffrr FCD 216
26/08/1993 . . . . . 58 . . . . . 1 . . . . . . GET DOWN ON IT . . . . China WOKCD 2054
13/04/1996 . . . . . 4 . . . . . 19 . . . . . ○ CECILIA . . . . WEA 042CD1
15/06/1996 . . . . . 34 . . . . . 4 . . . . . . GOOD SWEET LOVIN' . . . . Indochina ID 050CD
21/09/1996 . . . . . 24 . . . . . 4 . . . . . . NO MORE ALCOHOL Contains a sample of The Champs' *Tequila*. This and above single credited to SUGGS FEATURING LOUCHIE LOU AND MICHIE ONE . . . . WEA 065CD1

LOUD UK group formed by Chris McLaughlin (guitar/vocals), Etch (guitar), Stuart Morrow (bass) and Ricky Howard (drums).

28/03/1992 . . . . . 67 . . . . . . 2 . . . . . . EASY . . . . China WOK 2016

JOHN D LOUDERMILK US singer (born 31/3/1934, Durham, NC) whose songwriting hits include *Indian Reservation* and *Tobacco Road*. He won the 1967 Grammy Award for Best Album Notes for his own album *Suburban Attitudes In Country Verse*.

04/01/1962 . . . . . 13 . . . . . 10 . . . . . . THE LANGUAGE OF LOVE . . . . RCA 1269

LOUIE LOUIE US singer/dancer/songwriter Louie Cordero who appeared in Madonna's *Borderline* video as her boyfriend.

19/12/1992 . . . . . 34 . . . . . . 5 . . . . . . THE THOUGHT OF IT . . . . Hardback YZ 724

LOUISE UK R&B singer (born Louise Elizabeth Nurding, 4/11/1974, Lewisham, London) and a founder member of Eternal before going solo in 1995. Married to Tottenham and England footballer Jamie Redknapp, son of former West Ham United manager Harry Redknapp.

07/10/1995 . . . . . 8 . . . . . 8 . . . . . . LIGHT OF MY LIFE . . . . EMI CDEMS 397
16/03/1996 . . . . . 17 . . . . . 6 . . . . . . IN WALKED LOVE . . . . EMI CDEMS 413
08/06/1996 . . . . . 5 . . . . . 8 . . . . . . NAKED . . . . EMI CDEM 431
31/08/1996 . . . . . 5 . . . . . 6 . . . . . . UNDIVIDED LOVE . . . . EMI CDEM 441

30/11/1996	9	7		ONE KISS FROM HEAVEN	EMI CDEM 454
04/10/1997	4	7		ARMS AROUND THE WORLD	EMI CDEM 490
29/11/1997	10	9		LET'S GO ROUND AGAIN	EMI CDEM 500
04/04/1998	11	6		ALL THAT MATTERS	1st Avenue CDEM 506
29/07/2000	3	8		2 FACED	1st Avenue CDEMS 570
11/11/2000	13	4		BEAUTIFUL INSIDE Contains a sample of Wu-Tang Clan's *Shame On A Nigga*	1st Avenue CDEMS 575
08/09/2001	4	9		STUCK IN THE MIDDLE WITH YOU	1st Avenue CDEM 600
27/09/2003	5	5		PANDORA'S KISS	Positive POSCDS002

COURTNEY LOVE
US guitarist/singer (born Love Michelle Harrison, 9/7/1965, San Francisco, CA), previously a member of Hole. Kurt Cobain of Nirvana's widow, she later became an actress, appearing in *Man On The Moon* and *The People Versus Larry Flint*.

27/03/2004	41	2		MONO	Virgin VUSDX 283

DARLENE LOVE
US singer (born Darlene Wright, 26/7/1938, Los Angeles, CA) who was lead singer with backing group the Blossoms, sang lead on the Crystals *He's A Rebel* and *He's Sure The Boy I Love,* and with Bob B Soxx & The Blue Jeans. She began recording solo in 1963 and later became an actress, appearing in the *Lethal Weapon* series.

19/12/1992	31	4		ALL ALONE ON CHRISTMAS Featured in the films *Home Alone 2: Lost In New York* (1992) and *Love Actually* (2003)	Arista 74321124767
01/01/1994	72	1		ALL ALONE ON CHRISTMAS	Arista 74321124767

HELEN LOVE
UK group formed in Swansea in 1992 by Helen Love (vocals), Sheena (guitar), Roxy (keyboards), Mark (keyboards) and Beth (keyboards).

20/09/1997	71	1		DOES YOUR HEART GO BOOM	Che 72CD
19/09/1998	65	1		LONG LIVE THE UK MUSIC SCENE	Che 82CD

MONIE LOVE
UK singer (born Simone Johnson, 2/7/1970, London) who signed to Cooltempo in 1988. She relocated to Brooklyn, NYC and worked with various American rappers.

04/02/1989	37	4		I CAN DO THIS Contains a sample of The Whispers' *And The Beat Goes On*	Cooltempo COOL 177
24/06/1989	16	9		GRANDPA'S PARTY	Cooltempo COOL 184
14/07/1990	46	3		MONIE IN THE MIDDLE	Cooltempo COOL 210
22/09/1990	12	8		IT'S A SHAME (MY SISTER) MONIE LOVE FEATURING TRUE IMAGE Rap version of Motown Spinners' hit	Cooltempo COOL 219
01/12/1990	31	6		DOWN TO EARTH	Cooltempo COOL 222
06/04/1991	20	5		RING MY BELL MONIE LOVE VS ADEVA	Cooltempo COOL 224
25/07/1992	34	4		FULL TERM LOVE Featured in the 1992 film *Class Act*	Cooltempo COOL 258
13/03/1993	18	5		BORN 2 B.R.E.E.D. Stands for Born To Build Relationships where Education and Enlightenment Dominate	Cooltempo CDCOOL 269
12/06/1993	33	3		IN A WORD OR 2/THE POWER	Cooltempo CDCOOL 273
21/08/1993	41	2		NEVER GIVE UP	Cooltempo CDCOOL 276
22/04/2000	29	2		SLICE OF DA PIE	Relentless RELENT 2CDS

VIKKI LOVE – see NUANCE FEATURING VIKKI LOVE

LOVE AFFAIR
UK group with Steve Ellis (lead vocals), Lynton Guest (keyboards), Morgan Fisher (keyboards), Maurice Bacon (drums), Rex Brayley (guitar) and Mick Jackson (bass), only Ellis appeared on the #1. The group did get to perform their other hits.

03/01/1968	❶²	12		EVERLASTING LOVE	CBS 3125
17/04/1968	5	13		RAINBOW VALLEY This and above single are both cover versions of Robert Knight songs	CBS 3366
11/09/1968	6	12		A DAY WITHOUT LOVE	CBS 3674
19/02/1969	16	9		ONE ROAD	CBS 3994
16/07/1969	9	10		BRINGING ON BACK THE GOOD TIMES	CBS 4300

LOVE AND MONEY
UK group formed by James Grant (guitar/vocals), Bobby Paterson (bass), Paul McGeechan (keyboards) and Stuart Kerr (drums). Grant, McGeechan and Kerr had previously been members of Friends Again. Kerr later left to join Texas.

24/05/1986	56	4		CANDYBAR EXPRESS	Mercury MONEY 1
25/04/1987	68	4		LOVE AND MONEY	Mercury MONEY 4
17/09/1988	63	4		HALLELUIAH MAN	Mercury MONEY 5
14/01/1989	45	5		STRANGE KIND OF LOVE	Mercury MONEY 6
25/03/1989	51	4		JOCELYN SQUARE	Mercury MONEY 7
16/11/1991	52	2		WINTER	Mercury MONEY 9

LOVE BITE
Italian production/vocal group formed by Daniele Tignino and Pat Legato.

07/10/2000	56	1		TAKE YOUR TIME	AM:PM CDAMPM 134

LOVE CITY GROOVE
UK group formed by Beanz (Stephen Rudden), Jay Williams, Paul Hardy and Reason. Jonathan King suggested that their eponymous single be entered for the Song For Europe competition. It won and so became Britain's entry in the Eurovision Song Contest. The contest wasn't ready for rap, the song came seventh, but it did better chartwise than winner Gunnhild Tvinnereim of Norway whose song *Nocturne* failed to chart.

15/04/1995	7	11		LOVE CITY GROOVE Britain's entry for the 1995 Eurovision Song Contest	Planet 3 GXY 2003CD

LOVE CONNECTION
Italian/German vocal and production group formed by R Djafer, O Lazouni and M Fages.

02/12/2000	53	1		THE BOMB Contains an interpolation of Davies' *Love Magic*	Multiply CDMULTY 63

❶⁹ Number of weeks single topped the UK chart ↑ Entered the UK chart at #1 ▲⁹ Number of weeks single topped the US chart

LOVE DECADE UK dance group led by Peter Gill. He later formed Lovestation.

06/07/1991	52	2	DREAM ON (IS THIS A DREAM)	All Around The World GLOBE 100
23/11/1991	14	7	SO REAL	All Around The World GLOBE 106
11/04/1992	34	3	I FEEL YOU	All Around The World GLOBE 107
06/02/1993	69	1	WHEN THE MORNING COMES	All Around The World CDGLOBE 114
17/02/1996	39	1	IS THIS A DREAM? Re-recording	All Around The World CDGLOBE 132

LOVE DECREE UK vocal/instrumental group formed by Robin Gow, Grant MacIntosh, Ian Stockdale and Mrs N.

16/09/1989	61	4	SOMETHING SO REAL (CHINHEADS THEME)	Ariola 112642

LOVE/HATE US heavy rock group formed by Jizzy Pearl (vocals), Jon E Love (guitar), Skid Rose (bass) and Joey Gold (drums).

30/11/1991	59	1	EVIL TWIN	Columbia 6575967
04/04/1992	38	3	WASTED IN AMERICA	Columbia 6578897

LOVE INC Jamaican/Canadian production duo Chris Sheppard and singer Simone Denny.

21/12/2002	7	13	YOU'RE A SUPERSTAR	NuLife 74321973842
31/05/2003	8	7	BROKEN BONES	NuLife 8286523172
06/03/2004	39	2	INTO THE NIGHT	NuLife 82876585782

LOVE INCORPORATED FEATURING MC NOISE UK vocal/production duo Dei Phillip Nardi and Bruce Smith.

09/02/1991	59	3	LOVE IS THE MESSAGE	Love EVOL 1

LOVE NELSON – see FIRE ISLAND

LOVE REACTION – see ZODIAC MINDWARP AND THE LOVE REACTION

LOVE SCULPTURE UK rock group formed in 1968 in Cardiff, South Glamorgan by Dave Edmunds (born 15/4/1944, Cardiff , guitar), Tommy Riley (drums) and John Williams (bass). Riley was replaced by Bob Jones the same year and the group disbanded in 1969.

27/11/1968	5	14	SABRE DANCE	Parlophone R 5744

LOVE SQUAD – see LINDA CARR

A LOVE SUPREME UK vocal/instrumental group whose hit was a tribute to Sunderland and Ireland footballer Niall Quinn and originated as a terrace chant.

17/04/1999	59	2	NIALL QUINN'S DISCO PANTS	A Love Supreme/Cherry Red CDVINNIE 3

[LOVE] TATTOO Australian producer Stephen Allkins.

06/10/2001	58	1	DROP SOME DRUMS	Positiva CDTIV 162

LOVE TO INFINITY UK dance group formed in Manchester by Andy and Peter Lee and featuring Louise Bailey on lead vocals. The Lee brothers later formed Soda Club.

24/06/1995	38	2	KEEP LOVE TOGETHER	Mushroom D 00467
18/11/1995	75	1	SOMEDAY	Mushroom D 1143
03/08/1996	69	1	PRAY FOR LOVE	Mushroom D 1213

LOVE TRIBE US group formed by Dewey Bullock, Latanya Waters and Victor Mitchell.

29/06/1996	23	3	STAND UP Contains an interpolation of Fire Island's *There But For The Grace Of God*	AM:PM 5816272

LOVE UNLIMITED US soul trio formed by sisters Glodean and Linda James and Diane Taylor. Glodean married the group's writer and producer Barry White in 1974.

17/06/1972	14	10	WALKIN' IN THE RAIN WITH THE ONE I LOVE Features the uncredited vocal of Barry White	Uni UN 539
25/01/1975	11	9	IT MAY BE WINTER OUTSIDE (BUT IN MY HEART IT'S SPRING)	20th Century BTC 2149

LOVE UNLIMITED ORCHESTRA US studio orchestra assembled by producer Barry White (born 12/9/1944, Galveston, TX) and arranger Gene Page (born 13/9/1938). Saxophonist Kenny Gorelick later recorded as Kenny G. Page died on 24/8/1998 and White on 4/7/2003.

02/02/1974	10	10	LOVE'S THEME ▲[1]	Pye International 7N 25635

LOVEBUG UK dance group: Lloydie Hadfield, Mark Smith and Lady Melika Hanley. Their hit was first used in a TV advertisement for Asda.

18/10/2003	35	2	WHO'S THE DADDY	Sony Music 6742705

LOVEBUG STARSKI US singer/rapper/DJ (born Kevin Smith, 13/7/1961, The Bronx, NYC) whose debut single was recorded in 1981 during his 1979–85 residency at the Disco Fever club. Named after the film *The Love Bug* and TV series *Starsky And Hutch*.

31/05/1986	12	9	AMITYVILLE (THE HOUSE ON THE HILL)	Epic A 7182

LOVEHAPPY US/UK house group featuring US/Australian singer Ellie Lawson.

18/02/1995	37	2	MESSAGE OF LOVE	MCA MCSTD 2040

○ Silver disc ● Gold disc ✪ Platinum disc (additional platinum units are indicated by a figure following the symbol) ◎ Singles released prior to 1973 that are known to have sold over 1 million copies in the UK

20/07/1996	70	1		MESSAGE OF LOVE (REMIX)	MCA MCSTD 40052

LOVEDEEJAY AKEMI – see YOSH PRESENTS LOVEDEEJAY AKEMI

BILL LOVELADY UK singer who later linked up with Julian Lloyd Webber, Mary Hopkin and Peter Skellern in 1983 to form Oasis, a group that scored one hit album.

18/08/1979	12	10		REGGAE FOR IT NOW	Charisma CB 337

LOVELAND FEATURING RACHEL MCFARLANE UK vocal/instrumental group with Mark Hadfield, Paul Taylor, Paul Waterman, Dave Ford and lead vocalist Rachel McFarlane. Their first hit generated lawsuits because the group, who were affiliated to Eastern Bloc, released the record on their own KMS label without any clearance. Finally, the labels agreed to a joint release.

16/04/1994	16	4		LET THE MUSIC (LIFT YOU UP) **LOVELAND FEATURING RACHEL MCFARLANE VS DARLENE LEWIS** All formats featured versions of *Let The Music Lift You Up* by Loveland Featuring Rachel McFarlane and also by Darlene Lewis	KMS/Eastern Bloc KMSCD 10
05/11/1994	37	2		(KEEP ON) SHINING/HOPE (NEVER GIVE UP)	Eastern Bloc BLOCCD 016
14/01/1995	21	3		I NEED SOMEBODY	Eastern Bloc BLOCCDX 019
10/06/1995	22	3		DON'T MAKE ME WAIT	Eastern Bloc BLOC 20CD
02/09/1995	53	1		THE WONDER OF LOVE	Eastern Bloc BLOC 22CD
11/11/1995	38	2		I NEED SOMEBODY	Eastern Bloc BLOC 23CD

LOVER SPEAKS UK vocal/instrumental duo Dave Freeman and Joseph Hughes.

16/08/1986	58	5		NO MORE 'I LOVE YOUS' The song became a bigger hit when revived by Annie Lennox in 1995	A&M AM 326

LINUS LOVES FEATURING SAM OBERNIK US DJ/producer with female singer Sam Obernik. Their debut hit was originally an instrumental called *The Terrace* and released on Loves' own Breast Fed Recordings label before vocals were added by Sam Obernik.

22/11/2003	31	3		STAND BACK	Data 62CDS

MICHAEL LOVESMITH US singer/songwriter/producer (born in St Louis, MO).

05/10/1985	75	1		AIN'T NOTHIN' LIKE IT	Motown ZB 40369

LOVESTATION UK dance group formed by producers Dave Morgan, Vikki Aspinall and Peter Gill with US singer Lisa Hunt. Gill had previously been a member of Love Decade.

13/03/1993	71	1		SHINE ON ME **LOVESTATION FEATURING LISA HUNT**	RCA 74321137912
13/11/1993	73	1		BEST OF MY LOVE	Fresh FRSHD 1
18/03/1995	42	2		LOVE COME RESCUE ME	Fresh FRSHD 22
01/08/1998	14	6		TEARDROPS	Fresh FRSHD 65
05/12/1998	16	7		SENSUALITY	Fresh FRSHD 71
05/02/2000	24	4		TEARDROPS (REMIX)	Fresh FRSHD 79

LENE LOVICH US singer (born Lili Premilovich, Detroit, MI) with a Yugoslavian father and an English mother. She was briefly a member of the Diversions before going solo. She also appeared in the films *Dandy* and *Cha-Cha*.

17/02/1979	3	11	O	**LUCKY NUMBER**	Stiff BUY 42
12/05/1979	19	10		SAY WHEN	Stiff BUY 46
20/10/1979	39	7		BIRD SONG	Stiff BUY 53
29/03/1980	58	3		WHAT WILL I DO WITHOUT YOU	Stiff BUY 69
14/03/1981	53	5		NEW TOY	Stiff BUY 97
27/11/1982	68	2		IT'S ONLY YOU (MEIN SCHMERZ)	Stiff BUY 164

LOVIN' SPOONFUL US group formed in New York in 1965 by John Sebastian (born 17/3/1944, New York, guitar/vocals), Zal Yanovsky (born 19/12/1944, Toronto, Canada, guitar), Steve Boone (born 23/9/1943, Camphejeune, NC, bass) and Joe Butler (born 19/1/1943, New York, drums). Yanovsky left in 1967 and was replaced by Jerry Yester (keyboards). They disbanded in 1968. Their name supposedly refers to the average male ejaculation, although some sources credit a phrase from *Coffee Blues* by Mississippi John Hurt. They were inducted into the Rock & Roll Hall of Fame in 2000.

14/04/1966	2	13		**DAYDREAM** Featured in the 1994 film *War*	Pye International 7N 25361
14/07/1966	8	11		**SUMMER IN THE CITY** ▲³	Kama Sutra KAS 200
05/01/1967	26	7		NASHVILLE CATS Featured in the 1973 film *Homer*	Kama Sutra KAS 204
09/03/1967	44	2		DARLING BE HOME SOON Featured in the 1966 film *You're A Big Boy Now*	Kama Sutra KAS 207

LOVINDEER Jamaican singer (full name Lloyd Lovindeer) who later worked with Shabba Ranks.

27/09/1986	69	3		MAN SHORTAGE	TSOJ TS 1

GARY LOW Italian singer.

08/10/1983	52	3		I WANT YOU	Savoir Faire FAIS 004

PATTI LOW – see BUG KANN AND THE PLASTIC JAM

JIM LOWE AND THE HIGH FIVES US singer (born 7/5/1927, Springfield, MO) who was working as a DJ in New York at the time he recorded his hit single. He has a star on the Hollywood Walk of Fame.

26/10/1956	8	9		**THE GREEN DOOR** ▲³	London HLD 8317

❶⁹ Number of weeks single topped the UK chart ↑ Entered the UK chart at #1 ▲⁹ Number of weeks single topped the US chart

481

NICK LOWE UK singer (born 25/3/1949, Woodbridge, Suffolk) who was in Brinsley Schwarz from 1970–75 and then in Rockpile. He was a founder member of Little Village with Ry Cooder, John Hiatt and Jim Keltner but later achieved greater success as a producer.

11/03/1978	7	8	**I LOVE THE SOUND OF BREAKING GLASS**	Radar ADA 1
09/06/1979	34	5	CRACKIN' UP	Radar ADA 34
25/08/1979	12	11	CRUEL TO BE KIND Featured in the 1999 film *200 Cigarettes*.	Radar ADA 43
26/05/1984	53	3	HALF A BOY HALF A MAN.	F. Beat XX 34

LOWGOLD UK group formed by Darren Ford (guitar/vocals), Dan Symons (guitar), Miles Willey (bass) and Scott Simon (drums). They signed with Nude Records in 1998 and released their debut album two years later.

30/09/2000	67	1	BEAUTY DIES YOUNG.	Nude NUD 52CD
10/02/2001	48	1	MERCURY	Nude NUD 53CD
12/05/2001	52	1	COUNTERFEIT	Nude NUD 55CD
08/09/2001	40	1	BEAUTY DIES YOUNG (REMIX)	Nude NUD 59CD1

LOWRELL US singer (born Lowrell Simon); previously in The Lost Generation, he later worked with Eugene Record of the Chi-Lites.

24/11/1979	37	9	MELLOW MELLOW RIGHT ON	AVI AVIS 108

LRS – see **D MOB**

L7 US rock group formed in 1985 in California by Donita Sparks (guitar/vocals), Suzi Gardner (guitar/vocals), Jennifer Finch (bass/vocals) and Dee Plakas (drums). They later added former Belly bassist, Gail Greenwood, to the line-up.

04/04/1992	21	7	PRETEND WE'RE DEAD.	Slash LASH 34
30/05/1992	27	3	EVERGLADE.	Slash LASH 36
12/09/1992	33	3	MONSTER	Slash LASH 38
28/11/1992	50	3	PRETEND WE'RE DEAD	Slash LASH 42
09/07/1994	34	2	ANDRES.	Slash LASCD 48

LSG German DJ/producer Oliver Lieb (born 1969, Frankfurt) who also recorded under his own name.

10/05/1997	63	1	NETHERWORLD	Hooj Choons HOOJCD 52

L.T.D. US R&B group formed in Greensboro, NC in 1970 by Jeffrey Osborne (born 9/3/1948, Providence, RI, vocals), John McGhee (guitar), Arthur 'Lorenzo' Carnegie (saxophone), Abraham 'Onion' Miller (saxophone), Jimmie 'JD' Davis (keyboards), Carle Vickers (trumpet), Jake Riley (trombone), Henry Davis (bass) and Alvino Bennett (drums). The Osborne brothers left in 1980 (Jeffrey went solo) and were replaced by Leslie Wilson and Andre Ray. The groups name stands for Love, Togetherness and Devotion.

09/09/1978	70	3	HOLDING ON (WHEN LOVE IS GONE)	A&M AMS 7378

LUCAS US rapper/producer (born Lucas Secon, 1970, Copenhagen), son of artist Berta Moltke and songwriter Paul Secon. He was later a member of Sprinkler.

06/08/1994	37	4	LUCAS WITH THE LID OFF.	WEA YZ 832CD

CARRIE LUCAS US singer (born in Los Angeles, CA) who signed with Solar after becoming label boss Dick Griffey's girlfriend. She later became dance consultant for the TV programme *For Their Own Good*.

16/06/1979	40	6	DANCE WITH YOU	Solar FB 1482

TAMMY LUCAS – see **TEDDY RILEY**

LUCIANA UK singer Luciana Caporaso who was a backing singer for artists such as Loketo before going solo. She later became a member of Crush (with Donna Air) and then fronted Shooter and Portobella.

23/04/1994	55	2	GET IT UP FOR LOVE	Chrysalis CDCHS 5008
06/08/1994	47	2	IF YOU WANT	Chrysalis CDCHS 5009
05/11/1994	67	1	WHAT GOES AROUND/ONE MORE RIVER	Chrysalis CDCHS 5015

LUCID UK vocal/instrumental group formed by Mark Hadfield and Ryan Carter with vocals by Clare Canty.

08/08/1998	7	8	**I CAN'T HELP MYSELF**	ffrr FCD 339
27/02/1999	14	5	CRAZY	ffrr FCDP 355
16/10/1999	25	2	STAY WITH ME TILL DAWN.	ffrr FCD 368

LUCKY MONKEYS UK instrumental/production group formed in 1989 by Mike Bryant (born1/5/1960, High Wycombe), Michael Tournier (born 24/5/1963, High Wycombe), and Jonathan Fugler (born 13/10/1962, St Austell, Cornwall). They also record as Fluke. Tournier and Fugler were both previously with Skin.

09/11/1996	50	1	BJANGO	Hi-Life 5757132

LUCY PEARL US rap group formed by ex-En Vogue Dawn Robinson (born 28/11/1968, New London, CT), Raphael Wiggins (also a member of Tony Toni Tone and also recorded as Raphael Saadiq) and Ali Shaheed Muhammad (born 11/8/1970, New York) formerly a member of A Tribe Called Quest. Robinson left after the group's debut album and was replaced by Joi.

29/07/2000	36	2	DANCE TONIGHT Featured in the 2000 film *Love And Basketball*	Virgin VSCDT 1775
25/11/2000	20	4	DON'T MESS WITH MY MAN.	Virgin VSCDT 1778
28/07/2001	51	1	WITHOUT YOU.	Virgin VSCDT 1805

○ Silver disc ● Gold disc ✪ Platinum disc (additional platinum units are indicated by a figure following the symbol) ◉ Singles released prior to 1973 that are known to have sold over 1 million copies in the UK

LUDACRIS
US rapper (born Chris Bridges, 11/9/1977, Champaign, IL) who was in the Loudmouth Hooligans before going solo.

DATE	POS	WKS	BPI	SINGLE TITLE	LABEL & NUMBER
09/06/2001	19	5		WHAT'S YOUR FANTASY Features the uncredited contribution of Shawna	Def Jam 5729842
18/08/2001	10	8		ONE MINUTE MAN MISSY ELLIOTT FEATURING LUDACRIS	The Gold Mind/Elektra E 7245CD
29/09/2001	25	3		AREA CODES LUDACRIS FEATURING NATE DOGG	Def Jam 5887722
22/06/2002	20	7		ROLLOUT (MY BUSINESS)	Def Jam 5829632
05/10/2002	31	2		SATURDAY (OOOH OOOH)	Def Jam 639142
09/11/2002	40	2		WHY DON'T WE FALL IN LOVE AMERIE FEATURING LUDACRIS	Columbia 6732212
22/03/2003	9	9		GOSSIP FOLKS MISSY ELLIOTT FEATURING LUDACRIS Featured in the 2003 film *Hollywood Homicide*	Elektra E 7380CD
22/11/2003	14	7		STAND UP ▲¹ Features the uncredited contribution of Shawnna	Def Jam South 9814001
27/03/2004	❶¹	14		YEAH ↑ ▲¹² USHER FEATURING LIL' JON AND LUDACRIS	Arista 82876606012

LUDES
UK rock group formed in London by David Ashby (vocals), Matt Allchin (guitar), James McCool (guitar), Dom Peach (bass) and Chris Morris (drums).

DATE	POS	WKS	BPI	SINGLE TITLE	LABEL & NUMBER
18/12/2004	68	1		RADIO	Double Dragon DD2018CD

BAZ LUHRMANN
Australian producer, better known for his movies (he produced the 1996 remake of *Romeo And Juliet* and *Strictly Ballroom*). His hit single was based on an article that first appeared in the *Chicago Sunday Tribune* by columnist Mary Schmich, although the article was originally wrongly credited as being Kurt Vonnegut's opening address to MIT.

DATE	POS	WKS	BPI	SINGLE TITLE	LABEL & NUMBER
12/06/1999	❶¹	16	●	EVERYBODY'S FREE (TO WEAR SUNSCREEN) ↑ Features the uncredited contribution of Lee Perry as well as samples of Quindon Tarver's gospel remake of the Rozalla hit *Everybody's Free (To Feel Good)*	EMI CDBAZ 001

ROBIN LUKE
US singer (born19/3/1942, Los Angeles, CA) whose one hit was inspired by his sister Susie and recorded in Hawaii.

DATE	POS	WKS	BPI	SINGLE TITLE	LABEL & NUMBER
17/10/1958	23	6		SUSIE DARLIN'	London HLD 8676

LUKK FEATURING FELICIA COLLINS
US vocal/instrumental group formed by Lenny Underwood and Ken Kramer with female singer Felicia Collins.

DATE	POS	WKS	BPI	SINGLE TITLE	LABEL & NUMBER
28/09/1985	72	1		ON THE ONE	Important TAN 6

LULU
UK singer (born Marie McDonald McLaughlin Lawrie, 3/11/1948, Glasgow) who joined the Gleneagles in 1963. The manager Marion Massey changed their name to Lulu & The Luvvers the same year. She married Maurice Gibb (of the Bee Gees) in 1969, was later divorced and married John Frieda. She appeared in the films *To Sir With Love* and *Gonks Go Beat* and recorded the theme to the James Bond film *The Man With The Golden Gun*. She was awarded an OBE in the 2000 Queen's Birthday Honours List.

DATE	POS	WKS	BPI	SINGLE TITLE	LABEL & NUMBER
14/05/1964	7	13		SHOUT LULU AND THE LUVVERS	Decca F 11884
12/11/1964	50	1		HERE COMES THE NIGHT	Decca F 12017
17/06/1965	8	11		LEAVE A LITTLE LOVE	Decca F 12169
02/09/1965	25	8		TRY TO UNDERSTAND	Decca F 12214
13/04/1967	6	11		THE BOAT THAT I ROW	Columbia DB 8169
29/06/1967	11	11		LET'S PRETEND	Columbia DB 8221
08/11/1967	32	6		LOVE LOVES TO LOVE LOVE	Columbia DB 8295
28/02/1968	9	9		ME THE PEACEFUL HEART	Columbia DB 8358
05/06/1968	15	7		BOY	Columbia DB 8425
06/11/1968	9	13		I'M A TIGER	Columbia DB 8500
12/03/1969	2	13		BOOM BANG-A-BANG The song jointly won the 1969 Eurovision Song Contest	Columbia DB 8550
22/11/1969	47	2		OH ME OH MY (I'M A FOOL FOR YOU BABY)	Atco 226 008
26/01/1974	3	9	○	THE MAN WHO SOLD THE WORLD Features songwriter/producer David Bowie on saxophone and backing vocals	Polydor 2001 490
19/04/1975	37	4		TAKE YOUR MAMA FOR A RIDE	Chelsea 2005 022
12/12/1981	62	5		I COULD NEVER MISS YOU (MORE THAN I DO)	Alfa 1700
19/07/1986	8	11		SHOUT Sales of the Jive re-recording and Decca original added together to calculate the chart position	Jive LULU 1/Decca SHOUT 1
30/01/1993	11	5		INDEPENDENCE	Dome CDDOME 1001
03/04/1993	27	5		I'M BACK FOR MORE LULU AND BOBBY WOMACK	Dome CDDOME 1002
04/09/1993	51	2		LET ME WAKE UP IN YOUR ARMS	Dome CDDOME 1005
09/10/1993	❶²	14	○	RELIGHT MY FIRE ↑ TAKE THAT FEATURING LULU	RCA 74321167722
27/11/1993	46	3		HOW 'BOUT US	Dome CDDOME 1007
27/08/1994	40	2		GOODBYE BABY AND AMEN	Dome CDDOME 1011
26/11/1994	44	2		EVERY WOMAN KNOWS	Dome CDDOME 1013
29/05/1999	42	2		HURT ME SO BAD	Rocket/Mercury 5726132
08/01/2000	59	1		BETTER GET READY Theme to the TV series *Red Alert*	Mercury 5625852
18/03/2000	24	5		WHERE THE POOR BOYS DANCE	Mercury 1568452
07/12/2002	4	13		WE'VE GOT TONIGHT RONAN KEATING FEATURING LULU	Polydor 0658612

❶⁹ Number of weeks single topped the UK chart ↑ Entered the UK chart at #1 ▲⁹ Number of weeks single topped the US chart

483

BOB LUMAN US country singer (born 15/4/1937, Nacogdoches, TX) who made his first records in 1957 and later appeared in films, including *Carnival Rock*. He died from pneumonia on 27/12/1978.

08/09/1960	6	18		**LET'S THINK ABOUT LIVING**	Warner Brothers WB 18
15/12/1960	46	1		WHY WHY BYE BYE	Warner Brothers WB 28
04/05/1961	49	2		THE GREAT SNOWMAN	Warner Brothers WB 37

LUMIDEE US female rapper (born Lumidee Cedeno, 1984, Spanish Harlem, NYC).

| 09/08/2003 | 2 | 13 | | **NEVER LEAVE YOU (UH OOOH UH OOOH)** | Universal MCSTD 40328 |
| 29/11/2003 | 55 | 1 | | CRASHIN' A PARTY **LUMIDEE FEATURING NORE** | Universal MCSTD 40341 |

LUMINAIRE – see JONATHAN PETERS PRESENTS LUMINAIRE

LUNIZ US rap duo Yukmouth (Jerold Ellis) and Knumskull (Garrick Husband). Melle Mel is US rapper Melvin Glover, a member of Grandmaster Flash & The Furious Five. Yo-Yo is US rapper Yolanda Whittaler (born 4/8/1971, Los Angeles, CA).

17/02/1996	3	13	O	**I GOT 5 ON IT** Contains a sample of Kool & The Gang's *Jungle Boogie*	Noo Trybe VUSCD 101
11/05/1996	20	3		PLAYA HATA Contains a sample of Bobby Caldwell's *What You Won't Do for Love*	Virgin VUSCDX 103
14/09/1996	28	2		STOMP – THE REMIXES **QUINCY JONES FEATURING MELLE MEL, COOLIO, YO-YO, SHAQUILLE O'NEAL & THE LUNIZ**	
					Qwest W 0372CD
31/10/1998	28	2		I GOT 5 ON IT (REMIX)	Virgin VCRD 41

LUPINE HOWL UK group formed by Mike Mooney (guitar/vocals), Sean Cook (bass) and Damon Reece (drums). All three were previously members of Spiritualized and formed Lupine Howl when they were sacked in 1999.

| 22/01/2000 | 68 | 1 | | VAPORIZER | Vinyl Hiss VHISSCD 001 |

LURKERS UK group formed by Howard Wall (vocals), Pete Stride (guitar), Arturo Bassick (born Arthur Billingsley, bass) and Manic Esso (born Pete Haynes, drums). Bassick left soon after their formation, replaced by Kim Bradshaw and then Nigel Moore. They split in 1980 but re-formed two years later with Stride, Moore, Mark Fincham (vocals) and Dan Tozer (drums). Esso and Bassick returned in 1988.

03/06/1978	45	3		AIN'T GOT A CLUE	Beggars Banquet BEG 6
05/08/1978	49	4		I DON'T NEED TO TELL HER	Beggars Banquet BEG 9
03/02/1979	66	2		JUST THIRTEEN	Beggars Banquet BEG 14
09/06/1979	72	1		OUT IN THE DARK/ CYANIDE	Beggars Banquet BEG 19
17/11/1979	72	1		NEW GUITAR IN TOWN	Beggars Banquet BEG 28

LUSCIOUS JACKSON US rock group formed by Gabby Glaser (born 21/12/1965, bass/vocals), Vivian Trimble (keyboards), Jill Cunniff (born 17/8/1966, guitar /vocals) and Kate Scheffenbach (born 5/1/1966, drums). They were named after Philadelphia '76ers basketball player Lucius Jackson.

18/03/1995	69	1		DEEP SHAG/CITYSONG	Capitol CDCL 739
21/10/1995	59	1		HERE Featured in the 1995 film *Clueless*	Capitol CDCL 758
12/04/1997	25	2		NAKED EYE	Capitol CDCL 786
03/07/1999	43	1		LADYFINGERS	Grand Royal CDCL 813

LUSH UK rock group formed in London in 1988 by Miki Berenyo (born 18/3/1967, London, guitar/vocals), Emma Anderson (born 10/6/1967, London, guitar), Steve Rippon (bass) and Christopher Acland (born 7/9/1966, Lancaster, drums). Rippon left in 1991 and was replaced by Philip King (born 29/4/1960, London). Acland committed suicide on 17/10/1996.

10/03/1990	55	1		MAD LOVE (EP) Tracks on EP: *De-Luxe, Leaves Me Cold, Downer* and *Thoughtforms*	4AD BAD 003
27/10/1990	47	2		SWEETNESS AND LIGHT	4AD BAD 0013
19/10/1991	43	2		NOTHING NATURAL	4AD AD 1016
11/01/1992	35	2		FOR LOVE (EP) Tracks on EP: *For Love, Starlust, Outdoor Miner* and *Astronaut*	4AD BAD 2001
11/06/1994	60	1		DESIRE LINES	4AD BAD 4010CD
11/06/1994	52	2		HYPOCRITE	4AD BAD 4008CD
20/01/1996	21	3		SINGLE GIRL	4AD BAD 6001CD
09/03/1996	22	3		LADYKILLERS	4AD BAD 6002CD
27/07/1996	21	3		500 (SHAKE BABY SHAKE)	4AD BADD 6009CD

LUSTRAL UK production duo Ricky Simmons and Stephen Jones, who also recorded as Ascension, Chakra, Oxygen and Space Brothers.

| 18/10/1997 | 60 | 1 | | EVERYTIME Contains a sample of Roberta Flack's *First Time Ever I Saw Your Face* | Hooj Choons HOOJCD 55 |
| 04/12/1999 | 30 | 2 | | EVERYTIME (REMIX) | Hooj Choons HOOJ 83CD |

LUVVERS – see LULU

LUZON US producer Stacy Burket.

| 14/07/2001 | 67 | 1 | | THE BAGUIO TRACK | Renaissance RENCDS 006 |

LV US singer/rapper (born Larry Sanders, Los Angeles, CA); his initials stand for Large Variety. He appeared in the 1997 film *Rhyme And Reason* along with just about everybody who is anybody in the world of rap.

28/10/1995	●[2]	20	✪	**GANGSTA'S PARADISE** ↑ ▲[3] **COOLIO FEATURING LV** Contains a sample of Stevie Wonder's *Pastime Paradise*. Featured in the 1995 film *Dangerous Minds*. 1995 Grammy Award for Best Rap Solo Performance	Tommy Boy MCSTD 2104
23/12/1995	24	4		THROW YOUR HANDS UP/GANGSTA'S PARADISE	Tommy Boy TBCD 699
04/05/1996	64	1		I AM LV	Tommy Boy TBCD 7724

ANNABELLA LWIN
Burmese singer (born Myant Myant Aye, 1966, Rangoon) who fronted Bow Wow Wow before going solo.

28/01/1995.....61......1.......	DO WHAT YOU DO..Sony S2 6611235

LWS
Italian instrumental group.

29/10/1994.....65......1....... GOSP ....Transworld TRANNY 4CD

JOHN LYDON
UK singer (born 31/1/1956, London); ex-Sex Pistols and Public Image Ltd and better known as Johnny Rotten.

13/11/1993.....13......5...... OPEN UP LEFTFIELD LYDON ....Hard Hands HAND 009CD
02/08/1997.....42......1....... SUN ....Virgin VUSCD 122

FRANKIE LYMON AND THE TEENAGERS
US singer (born 30/9/1942, Washington Heights, NYC); he joined the Premiers with Jimmy Merchant (born10/2/1940, The Bronx, NYC), Sharman Garnes (born 8/6/1940, NYC), Herman Santiago (born 18/2/1941, NYC) and Joe Negroni (born 9/9/1940, NYC) in 1955. They recorded *Why Do Fools Fall In Love*, based on a poem *Why Do Birds Sing So Gay* and renamed the group at the suggestion of the session saxophonist. They appeared in the films *Rock Rock Rock* and *Mister Rock 'N' Roll*. Lymon died on 28/2/1968 from a drug overdose, Garnes died in prison on 26/2/1977 and Negroni died from a cerebral haemorrhage on 5/9/1978. In 1992 a court ruled that their #1 hit had been co-written by Lymon, Santiago and Merchant and they (Santiago and Merchant) were entitled to $4 million in royalties backdated to 1969. The group was inducted into the Rock & Roll Hall of Fame in 1993, the same year Lymon was awarded a star on the Hollywood Walk of Fame.

29/06/1956 ....❶[3].....16 ...... WHY DO FOOLS FALL IN LOVE TEENAGERS FEATURING FRANKIE LYMON Featured in the films *American Graffiti* (1973) and *American Hot Wax* (1978) ....Columbia DB 3772
29/03/1957.....12......7...... I'M NOT A TEENAGE DELINQUENT ....Columbia DB 3878
12/04/1957 .....4......12 ...... BABY BABY B-side to *I'm Not A Teenage Delinquent*. Both sides featured in the 1956 film *Rock Rock Rock!* that starred Frankie Lymon & The Teenagers...Columbia DB 3878
20/09/1957.....24......3...... GOODY GOODY...Columbia DB 3983

DES LYNAM FEATURING WIMBLEDON CHORAL SOCIETY
UK singer (born 17/9/1942, County Clare) who is best known as a TV presenter, most notably on *Match of the Day* on BBC before switching to ITV.

12/12/1998.....45......3...... IF – READ TO FAURE'S 'PAVANE' ....BBC Worldwide WMSS 60062

CURTIS LYNCH JR FEATURING KELE LE ROC AND RED RAT
UK producer with singer Kele Le Roc and Jamaican singer Red Rat.

30/09/2000.....70......1....... THINKING OF YOU ....Telstar CDSTAS 3136

KENNY LYNCH
UK singer (born 18/3/1939, London) better known as a TV presenter and songwriter (he co-wrote The Small Faces' *Sha La La La Lee*). He was awarded an OBE.

30/06/1960.....33......3...... MOUNTAIN OF LOVE ....HMV POP 751
13/09/1962.....33......6...... PUFF ....HMV POP 1057
06/12/1962.....10......12...... UP ON THE ROOF ....HMV POP 1090
20/06/1963.....10......14...... YOU CAN NEVER STOP ME LOVING YOU.......................................HMV POP 1165
16/04/1964.....39......7...... STAND BY ME ....HMV POP 1280
27/08/1964.....37......6...... WHAT AM I TO YOU ....HMV POP 1321
17/06/1965.....29......7...... I'LL STAY BY YOU ....HMV POP 1430
20/08/1983.....50......4...... HALF THE DAY'S GONE AND WE HAVEN'T EARNT A PENNY ....Satril SAT 510

LIAM LYNCH
US singer first known as the creator of MTV's *Sifl & Olly*. Based in Los Angeles, CA, he graduated from the Liverpool music academy founded by Paul McCartney.

07/12/2002.....10......9...... UNITED STATES OF WHATEVER At 1.26 minutes, one of the shortest singles to have made the charts . . . Global Warming WARMCD 17

CHERYL LYNN
US singer (born 11/3/1957, Los Angeles, CA) who later recorded with Luther Vandross.

08/09/1984.....68......2...... ENCORE ....Streetwave KHAN 23

PATTI LYNN
UK singer.

10/05/1962.....37......5...... JOHNNY ANGEL ....Fontana H 391

TAMI LYNN
US singer (born 1945, New Orleans), discovered by Harold Battiste and signed to AFO Records, and who fronted the studio group AFO Executives. Her debut hit was originally recorded and released in America in 1964 and subsequently became popular on the UK Northern Soul scene. She later became a film executive and associate producer.

22/05/1971 .....4......14 ...... I'M GONNA RUN AWAY FROM YOU ....Mojo 2092 001
03/05/1975.....36......6....... I'M GONNA RUN AWAY FROM YOU Re-issue of Mojo 2092 001 ....Contempo Raries CS 9026

VERA LYNN
UK singer (born Vera Margaret Welsh, 20/3/1919, London) who began her singing career in her mid-teens, working briefly with Joe Loss and then Charlie Kunz before going solo in 1941. Her radio show *Sincerely Yours* was popular with UK servicemen around the world and led to her being dubbed 'the forces-sweetheart'. She made three films during the war: *We'll Meet Again* (the title track became her signature tune and one of the most famous songs of the war), *Rhythm Serenade* and *One Exciting Night*. She retained her popularity after the war and was awarded the OBE in 1969, subsequently becoming Dame Vera Lynn in 1975.

14/11/1952.....10......1...... AUF WIEDERSEHEN SWEETHEART ▲[9]..Decca F 9927
14/11/1952 .....5......6....... FORGET-ME-NOT ....Decca F 9985
14/11/1952 .....9......3....... HOMING WALTZ ....Decca F 9959
05/06/1953.....11......1...... THE WINDSOR WALTZ ....Decca F 10092

❶[9] Number of weeks single topped the UK chart ↑ Entered the UK chart at #1 ▲[9] Number of weeks single topped the US chart

L

DATE	POS	WKS	BPI	SINGLE TITLE	LABEL & NUMBER
15/10/1954	❶²	14		MY SON MY SON VERA LYNN WITH FRANK WEIR, HIS SAXOPHONE, HIS ORCHESTRA AND CHORUS	Decca F 10372
08/06/1956	30	1		WHO ARE WE	Decca F 10715
26/10/1956	17	13		A HOUSE WITH LOVE IN IT	Decca F 10799
15/03/1957	29	2		THE FAITHFUL HUSSAR (DON'T CRY MY LOVE)	Decca F 10846
21/06/1957	20	5		TRAVELLIN' HOME	Decca F 10903

JEFF LYNNE UK singer/guitarist (born 20/12/1947, Birmingham) and member of Roy Wood's group The Move in 1970, which became The Electric Light Orchestra the following year. When Wood left to form Wizzard after one album Lynne took over as group leader and was responsible for penning most of their hits. He was later in The Traveling Wilburys with Bob Dylan, George Harrison, Roy Orbison and Tom Petty and collected the 1989 Grammy Award for Best Rock Performance by a Group with Vocals for *Traveling Wilburys Volume One* (known as *Handle With Care* in the UK). He later recorded solo and also worked extensively as a producer for artists such as George Harrison, Roy Orbison, Randy Newman and The Beatles on their *Anthology* series.

DATE	POS	WKS	BPI	SINGLE TITLE	LABEL & NUMBER
30/06/1990	59	4		EVERY LITTLE THING	Reprise W 9799

SHELBY LYNNE US singer (born Shelby Lynn Moorer, 22/10/1966, Quantico, VA) who won 2000 Grammy Award for Best New Artist.

DATE	POS	WKS	BPI	SINGLE TITLE	LABEL & NUMBER
29/04/2000	73	1		LEAVIN'	Mercury 5627372

PHILIP LYNOTT Irish singer/guitarist (born 20/8/1951, Dublin) who formed Thin Lizzy in 1969. The group recorded their first album in 1971. He launched a parallel solo career in 1980 and later formed Grand Slam. He died from heart failure on 4/1/1986 although he had been in a coma for eight days following a drug overdose before his death.

DATE	POS	WKS	BPI	SINGLE TITLE	LABEL & NUMBER
05/04/1980	32	6		DEAR MISS LONELY HEARTS	Vertigo SOLO 1
21/06/1980	35	6		KING'S CALL	Vertigo SOLO 2
21/03/1981	56	3		YELLOW PEARL Theme to *Top Of The Pops* from 1982 until 1985	Vertigo SOLO 3
26/12/1981	14	9		YELLOW PEARL	Vertigo SOLO 3
18/05/1985	5	10		OUT IN THE FIELDS GARY MOORE AND PHIL LYNOTT	10 TEN 49
24/01/1987	68	2		KING'S CALL (REMIX)	Vertigo LYN 1

LYNYRD SKYNYRD US rock group formed in Jacksonville, FL in 1964 by Gary Rossington (born 4/12/1951, Jacksonville, guitar), Larry Jungstrom (bass), Bob Burns (drums), Ronnie Van Zant (born 15/1/1948, Jacksonville, vocals) and Allen Collins (born 19/7/1952, Jacksonville, guitar). They went under numerous names until settling on Lynyrd Skynyrd (after their school gym teacher Leonard Skinner) in 1970. They added Leon Wilkeson (born 2/4/1952, bass) in 1972 and Steve Gaines (born 14/9/1949, Seneca, MO, guitar) in 1976. Van Zant and Gaines were killed, along with four other passengers (including Gaines' sister Cassie, a member of the backing group) in a plane crash on 20/10/1977 when their plane ran out of fuel, although Rossington, Collins, Powell and Wilkeson all survived. Rossington and Collins left to form the Rossington Collins Band in 1980, which disbanded in 1982. Collins was paralysed in a car crash in 1986 that killed his girlfriend Debra Jean Watts (and was sent to prison after being held responsible for the crash). He died from pneumonia on 23/1/1990. Rossington and Johnny Van Zant (younger brother of Ronnie) assembled a version of Lynyrd Skynyrd in 1987 for a tribute tour. And in 1991 Rossington, Van Zant, Artimus Pyle (drums), Wilkeson, Billy Powell (keyboards), Randall Hall (guitar), Ed King (bass) and Custer (drums) regrouped. Pyle left the group for a second time in 1993 and was replaced by Mike Estes while Custer left the following year and was replaced by Owen Hale. Wilkeson died from chronic liver and lung disease on 27/7/2001.

DATE	POS	WKS	BPI	SINGLE TITLE	LABEL & NUMBER
11/09/1976	31	4		FREE BIRD EP Tracks on EP: *Free Bird, Sweet Home Alabama* and *Double Trouble*. *Free Bird* is a tribute to Duane Allman and featured in the 1994 film *Forrest Gump*. *Sweet Home Alabama* also featured in *Forrest Gump* and in the 1997 film *Con Air*. All three tracks were listed individually during the record's run in the charts	MCA 251
22/12/1979	43	8		FREE BIRD EP Tracks on EP as above	MCA 251
19/06/1982	21	9	○	FREE BIRD EP Tracks on EP as above	MCA 251

BARBARA LYON US singer (born in 1931) who later became an actress, appearing in *Life With The Lyons*. She died from a cerebral haemorrhage on 10/7/1985.

DATE	POS	WKS	BPI	SINGLE TITLE	LABEL & NUMBER
24/06/1955	12	8		STOWAWAY	Columbia DB 3619
21/12/1956	27	4		LETTER TO A SOLDIER	Columbia DB 3865

LYTE FUNKIE ONES US group formed by Richard Cronin, Brian Gillis and Bradley Fischetti.

DATE	POS	WKS	BPI	SINGLE TITLE	LABEL & NUMBER
22/05/1999	54	1		CAN'T HAVE YOU	Logic 74321649152
18/09/1999	16	7		SUMMER GIRLS	Logic 74321701162
05/02/2000	6	9		GIRL ON TV	Logic 74321717582
27/04/2002	24	3		EVERY OTHER TIME	Logic 74321925502

HUMPHREY LYTTELTON BAND UK bandleader (born 23/5/1921, Eton) who took up the trumpet when he was young and formed his own band, signed to EMI, in 1949. He played an important part in popularising traditional jazz in the 1950s. He later chaired the radio quiz *I Haven't Got A Clue*.

DATE	POS	WKS	BPI	SINGLE TITLE	LABEL & NUMBER
13/07/1956	19	6		BAD PENNY BLUES	Parlophone R 4184

KEVIN LYTTLE St Vincent soca singer (born 14/10/1976).

DATE	POS	WKS	BPI	SINGLE TITLE	LABEL & NUMBER
25/10/2003	2	19	○	TURN ME ON Contains a sample of 112's *All My Love*	Atlantic AT 0167CD
29/05/2004	22	4		LAST DROP	Atlantic AT 0176CD

○ Silver disc ● Gold disc ✪ Platinum disc (additional platinum units are indicated by a figure following the symbol) ◉ Singles released prior to 1973 that are known to have sold over 1 million copies in the UK

M UK singer/multi-instrumentalist (born Robin Scott, 1/4/1947) who later formed Do It Records.

07/04/1979	2	14	○	**POP MUZIK** ▲[1] .... MCA 413
08/12/1979	33	9		MOONLIGHT AND MUZAK. .... MCA 541
15/03/1980	45	5		THAT'S THE WAY THE MONEY GOES .... MCA 570
22/11/1980	64	2		OFFICIAL SECRETS .... MCA 650
10/06/1989	15	9		POP MUZIK (REMIX). .... Freestyle FRS 1

BOBBY M FEATURING JEAN CARN US vocal duo Bobby M (born Bobby Militello, Buffalo, NY) and Jean Carn (born Sarah Jean Perkins, Columbus, GA).

29/01/1983	53	3	LET'S STAY TOGETHER .... Gordy TMG 1288

M AND O BAND UK studio band assembled by Muff Murfin and Colin Owen to cover an import record that was just breaking on the charts. It was alleged in court that they had not played on the cover, lifting the music from the original by Eddie Drennon, an early example of sampling.

28/02/1976	16	6	LET'S DO THE LATIN HUSTLE .... Creole CR 120

M & S PRESENTS GIRL NEXT DOOR UK dance group formed by producers Ricky Morrison and Frank Sidoli and featuring singer Natasha Bryce.

07/04/2001	6	13	**SALSOUL NUGGET (IF U WANNA)** Contains samples of Double Exposure's *Everyman* and Loleatta Holloway's *Hit And Run* .... ffrr FCD 393

M-BEAT UK drummer/producer (born Marlon Hart, 1978) who was the first artist to sign with Renk Records. His debut single was *Let's Pop An E.*

18/06/1994	39	3	INCREDIBLE .... Renk 42CD
10/09/1994	8	9	**INCREDIBLE (REMIX)** This and above single credited to **M-BEAT FEATURING GENERAL LEVY** .... Renk CDRENK 44
17/12/1994	18	7	SWEET LOVE **M-BEAT FEATURING NAZLYN** .... Renk CDRENK 49
01/06/1996	12	5	DO U KNOW WHERE YOU'RE COMING FROM **M-BEAT FEATURING JAMIROQUAI** .... Renk CDRENK 63

M DUBS FEATURING LADY SAW UK producer Dennis M-Dubs with Jamaican singer Lady Saw. She also worked with UB40.

16/12/2000	59	1	BUMP N GRIND (I AM FEELING HOT TONIGHT) Contains a sample of Lady Saw's *No Long Talking* .... Telstar CDSTAS 3129

M FACTOR UK production duo Danny Harrison and Julian Jonah (born Danny Matlock). They also recorded as Congress, Nush, Nu-Birth, Stella Browne, Gant, Reflex and 187 Lockdown.

06/07/2002	18	4	MOTHER .... Serious SERR 042CD
26/07/2003	46	1	COME TOGETHER. .... Credence CDCRED 037

M1 UK producer Michael Woods. Previously in M3 with Matt Darey and Marcella Woods (his sister), he also teamed up with Australian model Imogen Bailey.

22/02/2003	72	1	HEAVEN SENT Features the uncredited contribution of vocalist Stacey Charles .... Inferno CDFERN 51

M PEOPLE UK dance group formed by Michael Pickering (born 21/2/1954, Manchester), Paul Heard (born 5/10/1960, London) and Heather Small (born 20/1/1965, London). They won awards for Best Dance Act at the 1994 and 1995 BRIT Awards. Small later launched a parallel solo career and also took part in the *Perfect Day* project for the BBC's Children In Need charity.

26/10/1991	29	9	HOW CAN I LOVE YOU MORE .... Deconstruction PB 44855
07/03/1992	35	4	COLOUR MY LIFE .... Deconstruction PB 45241
18/04/1992	38	3	SOMEDAY **M PEOPLE WITH HEATHER SMALL** .... Deconstruction PB 45369
10/10/1992	29	5	EXCITED .... Deconstruction 74321116337
06/02/1993	8	8	**HOW CAN I LOVE YOU MORE (REMIX)** .... Deconstruction 74321130232
26/06/1993	6	11	**ONE NIGHT IN HEAVEN** .... Deconstruction 74321151852
25/09/1993	2	11	**MOVING ON UP** Featured in the films *The First Wives Club* (1996) and *The Full Monty* (1997) ...... Deconstruction 74321166162
04/12/1993	9	10	**DON'T LOOK ANY FURTHER** .... Deconstruction 74321177112
12/03/1994	5	7	**RENAISSANCE** Theme to the TV series *The Living Soap* .... Deconstruction 74321194132
17/09/1994	31	2	ELEGANTLY AMERICAN: ONE NIGHT IN HEAVEN/MOVING ON UP .... Deconstruction 74321231882
19/11/1994	6	9	**SIGHT FOR SORE EYES** .... Deconstruction 74321245472
04/02/1995	9	7	**OPEN YOUR HEART** .... Deconstruction 74321261532
24/06/1995	9	7	**SEARCH FOR THE HERO** .... Deconstruction 74321287962
14/10/1995	32	4	LOVE RENDEZVOUS .... Deconstruction 74321319282

25/11/1995	11	8	ITCHYCOO PARK	Deconstruction 74321330732
04/10/1997	8	7	**JUST FOR YOU**	M People 74321523002
06/12/1997	33	9	FANTASY ISLAND	M People 74321542932
28/03/1998	8	6	**ANGEL STREET**	M People 74321564182
07/11/1998	12	6	TESTIFY	M People 74321621742
13/02/1999	13	4	DREAMING	M People 74321645362

M + M Canadian vocal duo Martha Johnson and Mark Gane, both of whom had been members of Martha And The Muffins.

28/07/1984	46	4	BLACK STATIONS WHITE STATIONS	RCA 426

M3 UK dance group formed by Matt Darey, Marcella Woods and Michael Woods. Matt Darey also records as Mash Up, Melt Featuring Little Ms Marcie and DSP and also recorded again with Marcella Woods, as well as being a member of Sunburst and Lost Tribe. Michael Woods later recorded as M1 and teamed up with Australian model Imogen Bailey.

30/10/1999	40	2	BAILAMOS	Inferno CDFERN 21

M2M Norwegian duo formed in Oslo by Marit Larsen (born 1/7/1983, Lorenskog) and Marion Raven (born 25/5/1984, Lorenskog). They linked in 1990 while still at school in a group called Hubba-bubba, named after their favourite bubble gum.

01/04/2000	16	6	DON'T SAY YOU LOVE ME Featured in the 2000 film *Pokemon – The First Movie*	Atlantic AT 0081CD1

TIMO MAAS German producer/DJ (born in Hanover) who was first known as a DJ at the Tunnel Club in Hamburg before going solo.

01/04/2000	50	1	DER SCHIEBER	48k/Perfecto SPECT 07CDS
30/09/2000	33	2	UBIK **TIMO MAAS FEATURING MARTIN BETTINGHAUS**	Perfecto PERF10CDS2
23/02/2002	14	4	TO GET DOWN (ROCK THING)	Perfecto PERF 30CDS
11/05/2002	38	2	SHIFTER **TIMO MAAS FEATURING MC CHICKABOO**	Perfecto PERF 31CDS
05/10/2002	65	1	HELP ME **TIMO MAAS FEATURING KELIS**	Perfecto PERF 42CDS

PETE MAC JR. US singer with a Japanese version of the TV theme that also charted in English with Godiego's version.

15/10/1977	37	4	THE WATER MARGIN	BBC RESL 50

SCOTT MAC – see SIGNUM

MAC BAND FEATURING THE McCAMPBELL BROTHERS US group formed in Flint, MI by brothers Charles, Kelvin, Ray and Derrick McCampbell (vocals), Mark Harper (guitar), Rodney Frazier (keyboards), Ray Flippin (bass) and Slye Fuller (drums). MAC stands for Men After Christ.

18/06/1988	8	13	**ROSES ARE RED**	MCA 1264
10/09/1988	40	4	STALEMATE	MCA 1271

KEITH MAC PROJECT UK vocal/instrumental group comprising Keith MacDonad and Matthew Clayden with singer Gwen Dupre. MacDonald and Clayden later recorded as Midi Xpress.

25/06/1994	66	1	DE DAH DAH (SPICE OF LIFE)	Public Demand PPDCD 3

LARA McALLEN – see ANGEL CITY FEATURING LARA McALLEN

DAVID McALMONT UK singer, ex-The Thieves, who also recorded with Bernard Butler and Ultramarine before going solo.

27/05/1995	8	8	YES	Hut HUTCD 57
04/11/1995	17	4	YOU DO This and above single credited to **McALMONT AND BUTLER**	Hut HUTDG 57
27/04/1996	65	1	HYMN **ULTRAMARINE FEATURING DAVID McALMONT**	Blanco Y Negro NEG 87CD
09/08/1997	40	2	LOOK AT YOURSELF	Hut HUTCD 87
22/11/1997	39	2	DIAMONDS ARE FOREVER **DAVID McALMONT AND DAVID ARNOLD**	East West EW 141CD
10/08/2002	23	3	FALLING	Chrysalis CDCHS 5141
09/11/2002	36	2	BRING IT BACK This and above single credited to **McALMONT AND BUTLER**	Chrysalis CDCHSS 5145

NEIL MacARTHUR UK singer Colin Blunstone (born 24/6/1945, Hatfield).

05/02/1969	34	5	SHE'S NOT THERE	Deram DM 225

DAVID MacBETH UK singer (born 1935, Newcastle-upon-Tyne) who was a youth player for Newcastle United FC before conscription into the army. Upon leaving he pursued a brief recording career, recording again in 1969 with Tony Hatch.

30/10/1959	18	4	MR BLUE	Pye 7N 15231

NICKO McBRAIN UK singer/drummer (born Michael McBrain, 5/6/1954, London) who joined Iron Maiden in 1983.

13/07/1991	72	1	RHYTHM OF THE BEAST	EMI NICK 1

FRANKIE McBRIDE Irish singer (born in Omagh, County Tyrone) who was formerly lead singer with the Polka Dots.

09/08/1967	19	15	FIVE LITTLE FINGERS	Emerald MD 1081

DAN McCAFFERTY UK singer (born 14/10/1946), lead singer with The Shadettes, who evolved into Nazareth. He launched a parallel solo career in 1975.

13/09/1975	41	3	OUT OF TIME	Mountain TOP 1

O Silver disc ● Gold disc ✪ Platinum disc (additional platinum units are indicated by a figure following the symbol) ◎ Singles released prior to 1973 that are known to have sold over 1 million copies in the UK

C.W. McCALL US country singer (born William Fries, 15/11/1928, Audubon, IA). C.W. McCall was created for a bread company for whom Fries was advertising manager.

14/02/1976 . . . . . 2 . . . . . . 10 . . . . . ○   **CONVOY** ▲¹ Featured in the 1978 film *Convoy* . . . . MGM 2006 560

DAVINA McCALL – see AVID MERRION, DAVINA McCALL AND PATSY KENSIT

NOEL McCALLA – see BIGFELLA FEATURING NOEL McCALLA

DAVID McCALLUM UK singer/actor (born 19/9/1933, Glasgow), best known for his portrayal of Illya Kuryakin in the TV series *The Man From U.N.C.L.E.* His debut hit (and accompanying albums) were masterminded by David Axelrod.

14/04/1966 . . . . . 32 . . . . . . 4 . . . .   COMMUNICATION . . . . Capitol CL 15439

McCAMPBELL BROTHERS – see MAC BAND FEATURING THE McCAMPBELL BROTHERS

LINDA McCARTNEY US singer (born Linda Eastman, 24/9/1942, Scarsdale, NY) who married Beatle Paul McCartney on 12/3/1969 and became a member of Wings when Paul formed the group in 1971. She died from breast cancer on 17/4/1998.

28/08/1971 . . . . . 39 . . . . . . 5 . . . . . .   BACK SEAT OF MY CAR **PAUL AND LINDA McCARTNEY** . . . . Apple R 5914
21/11/1998 . . . . . 74 . . . . . . 1 . . . . . .   WIDE PRAIRIE. . . . . Parlophone CDR 6510
06/02/1999 . . . . . 56 . . . . . . 1 . . . .   THE LIGHT COMES FROM WITHIN . . . . Parlophone CDR 6513

PAUL McCARTNEY UK singer (born James Paul McCartney, 18/6/1942, Liverpool) who was founding member of the Beatles with John Lennon and co-wrote most of their material. He released his first solo album in 1970, forming Wings the following year with wife Linda (keyboards/vocals), Denny Laine (guitar/vocals) and Denny Seiwell (drums). Henry McCullough (guitar) joined in 1972. Seiwell and McCullough left in 1973. The band became a five-piece again in 1974 with the addition of Jimmy McCullough and Geoff Britton (Britton left in 1975 and was replaced by Joe English). English and McCullough left in 1977, the group disbanding in 1981. Paul starred in the 1984 film *Give My Regards To Broad Street*. One of pop music's most honoured performers, he received the 1983 award for Best British Male at the BRIT Awards, the Sony Award for Technical Excellence at the 1983 BRIT Awards, countless Ivor Novello awards for his songwriting, the Outstanding Contribution Award at the 1983 BRIT Awards (as a Beatle), an MBE in 1964 (also as a Beatle) and was knighted in the 1996 New Year's Honours list. Linda died from breast cancer on 17/4/1998. He was inducted into the Rock & Roll Hall of Fame in 1999 (The Beatles were inducted in 1988). Having won ten Grammy Awards as a Beatle, three more included Best Arrangement Accompanying Singers in 1971 for *Uncle Albert/Admiral Halsey* and Best Rock Instrumental Performance in 1979 for *Rockestra Theme*. He has had more UK #1s than any other artist – seventeen were as a Beatle and four solo. *Mull Of Kintyre/Girls' School* is one of only five records to have sold more than 2 million copies in the UK. In July 2001 he was engaged to model Heather Mills (she had lost part of a leg after being hit by a police motorcycle), the pair marrying during 2002. In January 2002 he was named as pop music's first billionaire, his assets estimated at £1.1 billion. In December 2002 an argument with John Lennon's widow Yoko Ono ensued over changing the credit to a number of songs from Lennon/McCartney to McCartney/Lennon.

27/02/1971 . . . . . 2 . . . . . . 12 . . . . . .   ANOTHER DAY . . . . Apple R 5889
28/08/1971 . . . . . 39 . . . . . . 5 . . . . . .   BACK SEAT OF MY CAR **PAUL AND LINDA McCARTNEY** . . . . Apple R 5914
26/02/1972 . . . . . 16 . . . . . . 8 . . . . . .   GIVE IRELAND BACK TO THE IRISH . . . . Apple R 5936
27/05/1972 . . . . . 9 . . . . . . 11 . . . . . .   MARY HAD A LITTLE LAMB. . . . . Apple R 5949
09/12/1972 . . . . . 5 . . . . . . 13 . . . . . .   HI HI HI/C MOON This and above two singles credited to **WINGS** . . . . Apple R 5973
07/04/1973 . . . . . 9 . . . . . . 11 . . . . . .   MY LOVE ▲⁴ **PAUL McCARTNEY AND WINGS** . . . . Apple R 5985
09/06/1973 . . . . . 9 . . . . . . 14 . . . . . .   LIVE AND LET DIE **WINGS** Featured in the 1973 James Bond film *Live And Let Die* . . . . Apple R 5987
03/11/1973 . . . . . 12 . . . . . . 12 . . . . . .   HELEN WHEELS . . . . Apple R 5993
02/03/1974 . . . . . 7 . . . . . . 9 . . . . . . ●   JET . . . . Apple R 5996
06/07/1974 . . . . . 3 . . . . . . 11 . . . . . ○   BAND ON THE RUN ▲¹ 1974 Grammy Award for Best Pop Vocal Performance . . . . Apple R 5997
09/11/1974 . . . . . 16 . . . . . . 10 . . . . . .   JUNIOR'S FARM This and above three singles credited to **PAUL McCARTNEY AND WINGS** . . . . Apple R 5999
31/05/1975 . . . . . 6 . . . . . . 8 . . . . . .   LISTEN TO WHAT THE MAN SAID ▲¹ . . . . Capitol R 6006
18/10/1975 . . . . . 41 . . . . . . 3 . . . . . .   LETTING GO . . . . Capitol R 6008
15/05/1976 . . . . . 2 . . . . . . 11 . . . . . ○   SILLY LOVE SONGS ▲⁵ Featured in the 1984 film *Give My Regards To Broad Street* . . . . Parlophone R 6014
07/08/1976 . . . . . 2 . . . . . . 10 . . . . . ○   LET 'EM IN . . . . Parlophone R 6015
19/02/1977 . . . . . 28 . . . . . . 5 . . . . . .   MAYBE I'M AMAZED Live version of the song from his first solo album . . . . Parlophone R 6017
19/11/1977 . . . ❶⁹ . . . . . . 17 . . . . ✪²   MULL OF KINTYRE/GIRLS' SCHOOL . . . . Parlophone R 6018
08/04/1978 . . . . . 5 . . . . . . 9 . . . . . ○   WITH A LITTLE LUCK ▲² . . . . Parlophone R 6019
01/07/1978 . . . . . 42 . . . . . . 7 . . . . . .   I'VE HAD ENOUGH . . . . Parlophone R 6020
09/09/1978 . . . . . 60 . . . . . . 4 . . . . . .   LONDON TOWN . . . . Parlophone R 6021
07/04/1979 . . . . . 5 . . . . . . 10 . . . . . ○   GOODNIGHT TONIGHT . . . . Parlophone R 6023
16/06/1979 . . . . . 35 . . . . . . 6 . . . . . .   OLD SIAM SIR . . . . MPL R 6026
01/09/1979 . . . . . 60 . . . . . . 3 . . . . . .   GETTING CLOSER/BABY'S REQUEST This and above eleven singles credited to **WINGS** . . . . R 6027
01/12/1979 . . . . . 6 . . . . . . 8 . . . . . ○   WONDERFUL CHRISTMAS TIME . . . . Parlophone R 6029
19/04/1980 . . . . . 2 . . . . . . 9 . . . . . ○   COMING UP ▲³ . . . . Parlophone R 6035
21/06/1980 . . . . . 9 . . . . . . 8 . . . . . .   WATERFALLS . . . . Parlophone R 6037
10/04/1982 . . . ❶³ . . . . . . 10 . . . . . ●   EBONY AND IVORY ▲⁷ **PAUL McCARTNEY AND STEVIE WONDER** . . . . Parlophone R 6054
03/07/1982 . . . . . 15 . . . . . . 10 . . . . . .   TAKE IT AWAY . . . . Parlophone R 6056
09/10/1982 . . . . . 53 . . . . . . 3 . . . . . .   TUG OF WAR . . . . Parlophone R 6057
06/11/1982 . . . . . 8 . . . . . . 10 . . . . . .   THE GIRL IS MINE **MICHAEL JACKSON AND PAUL McCARTNEY** . . . . Epic A 2729
15/10/1983 . . . . . 2 . . . . . . 15 . . . . . ○   SAY SAY SAY ▲⁶ **PAUL McCARTNEY AND MICHAEL JACKSON** . . . . Parlophone R 6062
17/12/1983 . . . ❶² . . . . . . 12 . . . . . ○   PIPES OF PEACE . . . . Parlophone R 6064
06/10/1984 . . . . . 2 . . . . . . 15 . . . . . ○   NO MORE LONELY NIGHTS (BALLAD) Featured in the 1984 film *Give My Regards To Broad Street* . . . . Parlophone R 6080

---

❶⁹ Number of weeks single topped the UK chart   ↑ Entered the UK chart at #1   ▲⁹ Number of weeks single topped the US chart

24/11/1984	3	13	●	WE ALL STAND TOGETHER PAUL McCARTNEY AND THE FROG CHORUS	Parlophone R 6086
30/11/1985	13	10		SPIES LIKE US Featured in the 1985 film *Spies Like Us*	Parlophone R 6118
21/12/1985	32	5		WE ALL STAND TOGETHER	Parlophone R 6086
26/07/1986	25	8		PRESS	Parlophone R 6133
13/12/1986	34	5		ONLY LOVE REMAINS	Parlophone R 6148
28/11/1987	10	7		ONCE UPON A LONG AGO	Parlophone R 6170
20/05/1989	❶³	7		FERRY 'CROSS THE MERSEY ↑ CHRISTIANS, HOLLY JOHNSON, PAUL McCARTNEY, GERRY MARSDEN AND STOCK AITKEN WATERMAN Charity record to aid relatives of the Hillsborough football disaster victims	PWL 41
20/05/1989	18	5		MY BRAVE FACE	Parlophone R 6213
29/07/1989	18	6		THIS ONE	Parlophone R 6223
25/11/1989	42	3		FIGURE OF EIGHT	Parlophone R 6235
17/02/1990	32	2		PUT IT THERE	Parlophone R 6246
20/10/1990	29	3		BIRTHDAY	Parlophone R 6271
08/12/1990	35	5		ALL MY TRIALS	Parlophone R 6278
09/01/1993	18	6		HOPE OF DELIVERANCE	Parlophone CDR 6330
06/03/1993	41	3		C'MON PEOPLE	Parlophone CDRS 6338
10/05/1997	19	3		YOUNG BOY	Parlophone CDRS 6462
19/07/1997	23	2		THE WORLD TONIGHT This and above single featured in the 1997 film *Fathers' Day*	Parlophone CDR 6472
27/12/1997	25	4		BEAUTIFUL NIGHT	Parlophone CDR 6489
06/11/1999	42	2		NO OTHER BABY/BROWN EYED HANDSOME MAN	Parlophone CDR 6527
10/11/2001	45	2		FROM A LOVER TO A FRIEND	Parlophone CDR 6567
02/10/2004	21	3		TROPIC ISLAND HUM/WE ALL STAND TOGETHER	Parlophone CDR 6649

KIRSTY MacCOLL UK singer (born 10/10/1959), daughter of folk singer/songwriter Ewan MacColl (he wrote 1972 Song of the Year Grammy Award winner *The First Time Ever I Saw Your Face*) and married to producer Steve Lillywhite. Signed with Stiff at sixteen, she was also a songwriter, penning *They Don't Know* for Tracy Ullman. Hit by a speedboat in the Caribbean, she died on 19/12/2000.

13/06/1981	14	9		THERE'S A GUY WORKS DOWN THE CHIPSHOP SWEARS HE'S ELVIS	Polydor POSP 250
19/01/1985	7	10		A NEW ENGLAND	Stiff BUY 216
15/11/1986	58	2		GREETINGS TO THE NEW BRUNETTE	Go Discs GOD 15
05/12/1987	2	9	○	FAIRYTALE OF NEW YORK POGUES FEATURING KIRSTY MacCOLL	Pogue Mahone NY 7
08/04/1989	43	6		FREE WORLD	Virgin KMA 1
01/07/1989	12	9		DAYS	Virgin KMA 2
25/05/1991	23	7		WALKING DOWN MADISON	Virgin VS 1348
14/12/1991	56	1		MY AFFAIR	Virgin VS 1354
14/12/1991	36	5		FAIRYTALE OF NEW YORK POGUES FEATURING KIRSTY MacCOLL Re-issue of Pogue Mahone NY 7	PM YZ 628
04/03/1995	58	2		CAROLINE	Virgin VSCDX 1517
24/06/1995	75	1		PERFECT DAY KIRSTY MacCOLL AND EVAN DANDO	Virgin VSCDT 1552
29/07/1995	42	3		DAYS Re-issue of Virgin KMA 2	Virgin VSCDT 1558

NEIL MacCOLL – see LA'S AND PRETENDERS

MARILYN McCOO AND BILLY DAVIS JR US husband/wife team, both ex-5th Dimension. Marilyn (born 30/9/1943, Jersey City, NJ) and Billy (born 26/6/1939, St Louis, MO) split as an act in 1980. Marilyn then became a TV presenter and later an actress.

| 19/03/1977 | 7 | 9 | | YOU DON'T HAVE TO BE A STAR (TO BE IN MY SHOW) ▲¹ 1976 Grammy Award for Best Rhythm & Blues Vocal Performance by a Duo | ABC 4147 |

VAN McCOY US producer/orchestra leader (born 6/1/1944, Washington DC) who was singer with numerous groups before going solo in 1959. He was more successful as a songwriter and producer, especially with Gladys Knight & The Pips, The Drifters, The Stylistics, Jackie Wilson, Peaches And Herb and Faith Hope & Charity. He died from a heart attack on 6/7/1979.

31/05/1975	3	12	○	THE HUSTLE ▲¹ VAN McCOY WITH THE SOUL CITY SYMPHONY 1975 Grammy Award for Best Pop Instrumental Performance	Avco 6105 038
01/11/1975	36	4		CHANGE WITH THE TIMES	H&L 6105 042
12/02/1977	34	6		SOUL CHA CHA	H&L 6105 065
09/04/1977	4	14	○	THE SHUFFLE	H&L 6105 076

McCOYS US group formed in Union City, IN in 1962 by Rick Zehringer (born 5/8/1947, Fort Recovery, OH, lead guitar/vocals), his brother Randy (born 1951, Union City, IN, drums), Dennis Kelly (bass) and Ronnie Brandon (keyboards). Kelly and Brandon were replaced by Bobby Peterson and Randy Hobbs (born 5/8/1945) before their hit. Rick later changed his surname to Derringer and recorded solo. The group took their name from the B-side to The Ventures' 1962 hit *Walk Don't Run, The McCoy*. Hobbs died on 5/8/1993.

| 02/09/1965 | 5 | 14 | | HANG ON SLOOPY ▲¹ Featured in the films *More American Graffiti* (1976) and *The People Versus Larry Flynt* (1996) | Immediate IM 001 |
| 16/12/1965 | 44 | 4 | | FEVER | Immediate IM 021 |

GEORGE McCRAE US singer (born 19/10/1944, West Palm Beach, FL) who was with the Jivin' Jets before marrying Gwen McCrae and working and recording as a duet. His #1 hit had been intended for Gwen but she failed to show for the recording session.

29/06/1974	❶³	14	●	ROCK YOUR BABY ▲² Total worldwide sales exceed 11 million copies	Jayboy BOY 85
05/10/1974	9	9		I CAN'T LEAVE YOU ALONE	Jayboy BOY 90
14/12/1974	23	9		YOU CAN HAVE IT ALL	Jayboy BOY 92

○ Silver disc ● Gold disc ✪ Platinum disc (additional platinum units are indicated by a figure following the symbol) ◉ Singles released prior to 1973 that are known to have sold over 1 million copies in the UK

22/03/1975	38	4		SING A HAPPY SONG	Jayboy BOY 95
19/07/1975	4	11	O	**IT'S BEEN SO LONG**	Jayboy BOY 100
18/10/1975	12	7		I AIN'T LYIN'	Jayboy BOY 105
24/01/1976	33	4		HONEY I	Jayboy BOY 107
25/02/1984	57	4		ONE STEP CLOSER (TO LOVE)	President PT 522

GWEN McCRAE
US singer (born 21/12/1943, Pensacola, FL) who married fellow singer George McCrae (who later became her manager). Gwen first recorded for Columbia in 1970 and later for Cat, Atlantic and Black Jack.

30/04/1988	63	2		ALL THIS LOVE I'M GIVING	Flame MELT 7
13/02/1993	36	3		ALL THIS LOVE I'M GIVING MUSIC AND MYSTERY FEATURING GWEN McCRAE	KTDA CDKTDA 2

McCRARYS
US R&B vocal group formed by Alfred, Charity, Linda and Sam McCrary.

31/07/1982	52	4		LOVE ON A SUMMER NIGHT	Capitol CL 251

MINDY McCREADY
US country singer (born 30/11/1975, Fort Myers, FL).

01/08/1998	41	3		OH ROMEO	BNA 74321597242

IAN McCULLOCH
UK singer (born 5/5/1959, Liverpool) in The Crucial Three with Pete Wylie and Julian Cope. He formed Echo And The Bunnymen in 1978. They disbanded in 1988, McCulloch going solo, before re-forming in 1996.

15/12/1984	51	5		SEPTEMBER SONG	Korova KOW 40
02/09/1989	51	4		PROUD TO FALL	WEA YZ 417
12/05/1990	75	1		CANDLELAND (THE SECOND COMING) IAN McCULLOCH FEATURING ELIZABETH FRASER	East West YZ 452
22/02/1992	47	4		LOVER LOVER LOVER	East West YZ 643
26/04/2003	61	1		SLIDLING	Cooking Vinyl FRYCD 146X

MARTINE McCUTCHEON
UK singer (born 14/5/1976, London), best known as an actress playing Tiffany Raymond/Mitchell in *Eastenders*. Her character was killed in a road accident in 1999. By 2001 she was concentrating on acting again, appearing in the stage musical *My Fair Lady* in London.

18/11/1995	62	1		ARE YOU MAN ENOUGH UNO CLIO FEATURING MARTINE McCUTCHEON	Avex UK AVEXCD 14
17/04/1999	❶[2]	20	✪	**PERFECT MOMENT ↑**	Innocent SINCD 7
11/09/1999	6	10		**I'VE GOT YOU**	Innocent SINCD 12
04/12/1999	6	16	O	**TALKING IN YOUR SLEEP/LOVE ME** A-side recorded for the Children In Need charity	Innocent SINCD 14
04/11/2000	2	10		**I'M OVER YOU**	Innocent SINCD 20
03/02/2001	7	8		**ON THE RADIO**	Innocent SINCD 21

GENE McDANIELS
US singer (born 12/2/1935, Kansas City, KS) who was at the Omaha Conservatory of Music before recording. He appeared in the 1961 film *It's Trad, Dad*.

16/11/1961	49	2		TOWER OF STRENGTH	London HLG 9448

JULIE McDERMOTT
UK singer.

12/10/1996	34	2		DON'T GO THIRD DIMENSION FEATURING JULIE McDERMOTT	Soundprooof MCSTD 40082
26/10/1996	27	2		DON'T GO (2ND REMIX) AWESOME 3 FEATURING JULIE McDERMOTT	XL Recordings XLS 78CD

CHARLES McDEVITT SKIFFLE GROUP FEATURING NANCY WHISKEY
UK singer/guitarist (born 4/12/1934, Glasgow) who ran a London coffee bar in London called the Freight Train after his biggest hit. The group were in the 1957 film *The Tommy Steele Story*. Whiskey (born Anne Wilson, 4/3/1935, Glasgow) died on 1/2/2003.

12/04/1957	5	18		**FREIGHT TRAIN**	Oriole CB 1352
14/06/1957	28	2		GREENBACK DOLLAR	Oriole CB 1371

JANE McDONALD
UK singer (born 4/4/1963, Wakefield) who first became known as the resident singer on board *The Galaxy* in the BBC TV documentary *The Cruise Ship*. She is the first artist to have an album debut at #1 on the charts without first having a hit single.

26/12/1998	10	7		**CRUISE INTO CHRISTMAS MEDLEY**	Focus Music Int CDFM 2

MICHAEL McDONALD
US singer (born 2/12/1952, St Louis, MO) who recorded solo in 1972 before joining Steely Dan in 1974 and the Doobie Brothers the following year. He went solo again when the group disbanded in 1982. Michael won three Grammy Awards with the Doobie Brothers and two during his time with the group: for Song of the Year in 1979 with Kenny Loggins for *What A Fool Believes* and Best Arrangement Accompanying Vocalist in 1979 for *What A Fool Believes*.

18/02/1984	44	8		YAH MO BE THERE JAMES INGRAM WITH MICHAEL McDONALD 1984 Grammy Award for Best Rhythm & Blues Vocal Performance by a Duo	Qwest W 9394
19/01/1985	12	8		YAH MO B THERE	Qwest W 9394
03/05/1986	2	13	O	**ON MY OWN ▲[3]** PATTI LABELLE AND MICHAEL McDONALD	MCA 1045
26/07/1986	43	6		I KEEP FORGETTIN'	Warner Brothers K 17992
06/09/1986	12	10		SWEET FREEDOM Featured in the 1986 film *Running Scared*	MCA 1073
24/01/1987	57	3		WHAT A FOOL BELIEVES	Warner Brothers W 8451
05/10/2002	54	1		SWEET FREEDOM SAFRI DUO FEATURING MICHAEL McDONALD	Serious SERR 55CD

CARRIE McDOWELL
US singer (born 11/5/1963, Des Moines, IA).

26/09/1987	68	3		UH UH NO NO CASUAL SEX	Motown ZV 41501

❶[9] Number of weeks single topped the UK chart ↑ Entered the UK chart at #1 ▲[9] Number of weeks single topped the US chart

491

JOHN McENROE AND PAT CASH WITH THE FULL METAL RACKETS
US/Australian vocal duo John McEnroe (born 16/2/1959) and Pat Cash (born 27/5/1965, Melbourne), both former tennis stars. The Full Metal Rackets are a UK instrumental group.

13/07/1991	66	1	ROCK 'N' ROLL	Music For Nations KUT 141

REBA McENTIRE
US country singer (born 28/3/1954, Chockie, OK) who sang with brother Pake and sister Susie as The Singing McEntires, going solo in 1974. She appeared in the 1990 film *Tremors*. She has a star on the Hollywood Walk of Fame.

19/06/1999	62	1	DOES HE LOVE YOU .... MCA Nashville MCSTD 55569

MACEO AND THE MACKS
US saxophonist (born Maceo Parker, 14/2/1943, Kinston, NC) who was a member of James Brown's backing group and then joined Parliament.

16/05/1987	54	5	CROSS THE TRACK (WE BETTER GO BACK) .... Urban IRBX 1

BRIAN McFADDEN
Irish singer (born 12/4/1980, Dublin), previously a member of Westlife before going solo in 2004. He is married to former Atomic Kitten member Kerry Katona although the pair split in September 2004.

18/09/2004	●¹	12	**REAL TO ME** ↑ .... Modest/Sony Music 6753032
04/12/2004	6	4+	**IRISH SON** .... Modest/Sony Music 6754872

McFADDEN AND WHITEHEAD
US duo Gene McFadden (born 1948, Philadelphia, PA) and John Whitehead (born 2/7/1948, Philadelphia). They were both in The Epsilons before joining Philadelphia International as writers and producers. They penned and produced *Bad Luck* for Harold Melvin and *Back Stabbers* for the O'Jays. Whitehead recorded solo in 1988, while his sons also charted as The Whitehead Brothers. He was shot to death on 11/5/2004.

19/05/1979	5	10	○	**AIN'T NO STOPPIN' US NOW** Featured in the 1998 film *Boogie Nights* .... Philadelphia International PIR 7365

RACHEL McFARLANE
UK singer (born in Manchester) who was a member of Loveland before going solo.

01/08/1998	38	2	LOVER .... Multiply CDMULTY 37

BOBBY McFERRIN
US singer (born 11/3/1950, New York) who began singing professionally in the mid-1970s and signed with Elektra Musician in 1980. His debut album was released in 1982. Ten Grammy Awards include Best Jazz Vocal Performance in 1985 with Jon Hendricks for *Another Night In Tunisia*, Best Arrangement for Two or More Voices in 1985 with Cheryl Bentyne for *Another Night In Tunisia*, Best Jazz Vocal Performance in 1986 for *'Round Midnight*, Best Jazz Vocal Performance in 1987 for *What Is This Thing Called Love*, Best Recording for Children in 1987 with Jack Nicholson for *The Elephant's Child*, Record of the Year and Best Jazz Vocal Performance in 1988 for *Brothers* and Best Jazz Vocal Performance in 1992 for *'Round Midnight*.

24/09/1988	2	11	**DON'T WORRY BE HAPPY** ▲² Featured in the films *Cocktail* (1988) and *Casper – A Spirited Beginning* (1997). 1988 Grammy Awards for Best Pop Vocal Performance and Song of the Year for McFerrin as writer .... Manhattan MT 56
17/12/1988	46	4	THINKIN' ABOUT YOUR BODY .... Manhattan BLUE 6

McFLY
UK rock group formed in 2001 by Danny Jones (born 12/3/1986, Bolton, guitar/vocals), Tom Fletcher (born 17/7/1985, Harrow, guitar/vocals), Dougie Poynter (born 30/11/1987, Corringham, bass/vocals) and Harry Judd (born 23/1/1985, Chelmsford, drums). Tom originally auditioned to become a member of Busted and formed McFly (after the character in the *Back To The Future* films) after he was unsuccessful.

10/04/2004	●²	12	**FIVE COLOURS IN HER HAIR** ↑ .... Universal MCSXD 40357
03/07/2004	●¹	13	**OBVIOUSLY** ↑ .... Universal MCSXD 40364
18/09/2004	3	7	**THAT GIRL** .... Universal MCSXD 40378
27/11/2004	5	5+	**ROOM ON THE 3RD FLOOR** .... Island MCSXD40389

McGANNS
UK vocal trio formed by Joe, Mark and Stephen McGann.

14/11/1998	59	1	JUST MY IMAGINATION .... Coalition COLA 062CD
06/02/1999	42	3	A HEARTBEAT AWAY .... Coalition COLA 069CD

MIKE McGEAR
UK singer/songwriter/comedian (born Peter Michael McCartney, 7/1/1944, Liverpool) who was a member of Scaffold. Following the success of their first single, he revealed that his real name was Mike McCartney, younger brother of Beatle Paul. He had chosen his stage name to show he could achieve success without relying on his famous surname.

05/10/1974	36	4	LEAVE IT .... Warner Brothers K 16446

MAUREEN McGOVERN
US singer (born 27/7/1949, Youngstown, OH) who was chosen to sing *The Morning After*, the theme to the 1972 film *The Poseidon Adventure*, for which she won an Oscar.

05/06/1976	16	8	THE CONTINENTAL .... 20th Century BTC 2222

SHANE MacGOWAN
UK singer (born 25/12/1957, Tunbridge Wells, Kent, raised in Tipperary) who was with the Nipple Erectors before forming the Pogues in 1983. He went solo in 1993 and was in the *Perfect Day* project for BBC's Children In Need charity.

12/12/1992	72	1	WHAT A WONDERFUL WORLD NICK CAVE AND SHANE MacGOWAN .... Mute 151
03/09/1994	74	1	THE CHURCH OF THE HOLY SPOOK SHANE MacGOWAN AND THE POPES .... ZTT ZANG 57CD
15/10/1994	34	3	THAT WOMAN'S GOT ME DRINKING SHANE MacGOWAN AND THE POPES .... ZTT ZANG 57CD
29/04/1995	30	2	HAUNTED SHANE MacGOWAN AND SINEAD O'CONNOR .... ZTT BANG 65CD
20/04/1996	29	2	MY WAY .... ZTT ZANG 79CD

MARK McGRATH – see SHANIA TWAIN

○ Silver disc ● Gold disc ✪ Platinum disc (additional platinum units are indicated by a figure following the symbol) ◎ Singles released prior to 1973 that are known to have sold over 1 million copies in the UK

EWAN McGREGOR
UK singer/actor (born 31/3/1971, Crieff) who studied drama at Kirkcaldy and the Guildhall School of Music and Drama in London. After the TV series *Lipstick On Your Collar*, he made his name via the 1996 film *Trainspotting* and as Obi Wan Kenobi in the *Star Wars* prequel trilogy.

15/11/1997	6	11		**CHOOSE LIFE** PF PROJECT FEATURING EWAN McGREGOR Contains a sample of Ewan McGregor's dialogue from the 1996 film *Trainspotting*	Positiva CDTIV 84
06/10/2001	27	5		COME WHAT MAY NICOLE KIDMAN AND EWAN McGREGOR Featured in the 2001 film *Moulin Rouge*	Interscope 4976302

FREDDIE McGREGOR
Jamaican singer (born 1957, Clarendon) who debuted at seven, later working with Bob Marley.

27/06/1987	9	11		**JUST DON'T WANT TO BE LONELY**	Germain DG 24
19/09/1987	47	5		THAT GIRL (GROOVY SITUATION)	Polydor POSP 884

MARY MacGREGOR
US singer (born 6/5/1948, St Paul, MN) who worked as a session singer before going solo.

19/02/1977	4	10	O	**TORN BETWEEN TWO LOVERS** ▲[2]	Ariola America AA 111

McGUINNESS FLINT
UK group formed in 1969 by ex-Manfred Mann Tom McGuinness (born 2/12/1941, London, guitar/vocals), Hughie Flint (born 15/3/1942, drums), Benny Gallagher (born in Largs, guitar/vocals), Graham Lyle (born in Largs, guitar/vocals) and Dennis Coulson (keyboards). Gallagher and Lyle went on to record as a duo and with Ronnie Lane in Slim Chance.

21/11/1970	2	14		**WHEN I'M DEAD AND GONE**	Capitol CL 15662
01/05/1971	5	12		**MALT AND BARLEY BLUES**	Capitol CL 15682

BARRY McGUIRE
US singer (born 15/10/1935, Oklahoma City, OK) who joined the New Christy Minstrels in 1964 before going solo the following year. His hit was banned by most radio stations in the US but still reached #1. He later recorded gospel material.

09/09/1965	3	13		**EVE OF DESTRUCTION** ▲[1]	RCA 1469

McGUIRE SISTERS
US trio formed in Middlestown, OH by Christine (born 30/7/1929, Middletown, OH), Dorothy (born 13/2/1930, Middletown) and Phyllis McGuire (born 14/2/1931, Middletown). They replaced The Chordettes on the TV show *Arthur Godfrey And His Friends* in 1953, debuting on record the following year. Phyllis went solo in 1964, although the group reunited in 1986. They were the first recognised group to feature in an advertisement for Coca-Cola with *Pause For A Coke* in 1958.

01/04/1955	20	1		NO MORE	Vogue Coral Q 72050
15/07/1955	14	4		SINCERELY ▲[10] B-side to *No More*. Includes a writing credit for DJ Alan Freed	Vogue Coral Q 72050
01/06/1956	24	2		DELILAH JONES	Vogue Coral Q 72161
14/02/1958	14	6		SUGARTIME ▲[4]	Coral Q 72305
01/05/1959	15	11		MAY YOU ALWAYS	Coral Q 72356

MACHEL
Trinidadian singer Machel Montano (born in Port of Spain).

14/09/1996	56	2		COME DIG IT	London LONCD 386

MACHINE HEAD
US group formed in Oakland, CA in 1992 by Robb Flynn (guitar/vocals), Logan Mader (guitar), Adam Duce (bass) and Chris Kontos (drums).

27/05/1995	43	2		OLD	Roadrunner RR 23403
06/12/1997	73	1		TAKE MY SCARS	Roadrunner RR 22573
18/12/1999	74	1		FROM THIS DAY	Roadrunner RR 21383

BILLY MACK
UK singer (born Bill Nighy, 1949, Croydon). The name Billy Mack comes from a character in the film *Love Actually*. In the film the single made it to number one.

27/12/2003	26	3		CHRISTMAS ALL AROUND The song is The Troggs' *Love Is All Around* with lyrics re-written for Christmas. Featured in the 2003 film *Love Actually*	Island CID 841

CRAIG MACK
US rapper (born in Long Island, NY).

12/11/1994	57	2		FLAVA IN YOUR EAR	Bad Boy 74321242582
01/04/1995	54	1		GET DOWN	Puff Daddy 74321263402
07/06/1997	35	2		SPIRIT SOUNDS OF BLACKNESS FEATURING CRAIG MACK	Perspective 5822312

LIZZY MACK
UK singer.

05/11/1994	49	2		THE POWER OF LOVE FITS OF GLOOM FEATURING LIZZY MACK	Media MCSTD 2016
04/11/1995	52	1		DON'T GO	Power Station MCSTD 40004

LONNIE MACK
US guitarist (born Lonnie McIntosh, 18/7/1941, Harrison, IN) who formed Lonnie And The Twilighters and then worked with the Troy Seals Band before going solo.

14/04/1979	47	3		MEMPHIS Single was coupled with Chris Montez's *Let's Dance*	Lightning LIG 9011

MACK 10 – see ICE CUBE

MACK VIBE FEATURING JACQUELINE
US vocal/instrumental duo Al Mack and Jacqueline Stoudemire.

04/02/1995	53	1		I CAN'T LET YOU GO	MCA MCSTD 2020

McKAY
US singer (born Stephanie McKay, The Bronx, NYC).

23/08/2003	65	1		TAKE ME OVER Contains a sample of Dave & Ansil Collins' *Double Barrel*	Go! Beat GOBCD 57

❶[9] Number of weeks single topped the UK chart ↑ Entered the UK chart at #1 ▲[9] Number of weeks single topped the US chart

493

MARIA McKEE
US singer (born 17/8/1964, Los Angeles, CA) who followed her half-brother, ex-Love Bryan MacLean, into the recording industry. By the early 1980s Maria and Bryan were working together in the Maria McKee Band, which later changed name to the Bryan MacLean Band and disbanded in 1985. Maria then formed Lone Justice before going solo in 1987.

15/09/1990	●4	14			SHOW ME HEAVEN Featured in the 1990 film *Days Of Thunder*	Epic 6563037
26/01/1991	59	1			BREATHE	Geffen GFS 1
01/08/1992	45	4			SWEETEST CHILD	Geffen GFS 23
22/05/1993	35	3			I'M GONNA SOOTHE YOU	Geffen GFSTD 39
18/09/1993	74	1			I CAN'T MAKE IT ALONE	Geffen GFSTD 53

KENNETH McKELLAR
UK singer/arranger (born 1927, Paisley) who was popular in his homeland of Scotland from the 1950s and a regular on the EP charts when separate charts were compiled. His only UK hit came from the 1966 Eurovision Song Contest: McKellar was chosen by the BBC to represent the UK and sang six songs in the heats, postal votes selecting the final choice for the first time. The result was the UK's lowest placing in the competition since first entering in 1957.

10/03/1966	30	4			A MAN WITHOUT LOVE UK entry for the 1966 Eurovision Song Contest (came ninth)	Decca F 12341

TERENCE McKENNA – see SHAMEN

GISELE MacKENZIE
Canadian singer (born Gisele LeFleche, 10/1/1927, Winnipeg) who was first known on the TV show *Your Hit Paradise*. She later had her own variety show.

17/07/1953	6	6			SEVEN LONELY DAYS	Capitol CL 13920

SCOTT McKENZIE
US singer (born Philip Blondheim, 1/10/1939, Jacksonville, FL) who was a member of the Journeymen with John Phillips (later in The Mamas & The Papas). Phillips wrote McKenzie's hit.

12/07/1967	●4	17			SAN FRANCISCO (BE SURE TO WEAR SOME FLOWERS IN YOUR HAIR) Featured in the 1994 film *Forrest Gump*	CBS 2816
01/11/1967	50	1			LIKE AN OLD TIME MOVIE THE VOICE OF SCOTT McKENZIE	CBS 3009

KEN MACKINTOSH HIS SAXOPHONE AND HIS ORCHESTRA
UK orchestra leader (born 4/9/1919, Liversedge) who first played the saxophone as a child, forming his own group in 1948. Their success as a live group led to a recording contract with HMV in 1950. He later worked with Frankie Vaughan and Alma Cogan.

15/01/1954	10	2			THE CREEP	HMV BD 1295
07/02/1958	19	6			RAUNCHY	HMV POP 426
10/03/1960	45	1			NO HIDING PLACE	HMV POP 713

BRIAN McKNIGHT
US R&B singer (born 5/6/1969, Buffalo, NY) whose brother Claude is in the group Take 6.

06/06/1998	48	2			ANYTIME	Motown 8607752
03/10/1998	36	2			YOU SHOULD BE MINE BRIAN McKNIGHT FEATURING MA$E Contains a sample of James Brown's *I Got Ants In My Pants*	Motown 8608412

JULIE McKNIGHT
US singer (born in Memphis, TN; later relocated to Los Angeles, CA).

14/04/2001	54	1			FINALLY	Distance DI 2029
29/09/2001	24	3			FINALLY (REMIX) KINGS OF TOMORROW FEATURING JULIE McKNIGHT	Defected DEFECT 37CDX
15/06/2002	61	1			HOME	Defected DFECT 51CDS
23/11/2002	52	1			DIAMOND LIFE LOUIE VEGA AND JAY 'SINISTER' SEALEE STARRING JULIE McKNIGHT	Distance D12409

VIVIENNE McKONE
UK keyboardist/singer who was formerly at the Royal Ballet School. As an actress, she appeared in the TV series *Casualty*.

25/07/1992	47	4			SING (OOH-EE-OOH)	ffrr F 183
31/10/1992	69	1			BEWARE	ffrr F 202

McKOY
UK vocal group comprising brothers Noel, Cornell and Robin and their sister Junette McKoy. Noel McKoy also recorded with JTQ.

06/03/1993	54	2			FIGHT	Rightrack CDTUM 1

NOEL McKOY – see JTQ

CRAIG McLACHLAN
Australian actor/singer (born 1/9/1965) who first came to prominence as Henry Ramsey in *Neighbours*. He later relocated to the UK and appeared in the stage musical *Grease*.

23/06/1990	2	11			MONA	Epic 6557847
04/08/1990	19	6			AMANDA	Epic 6561707
10/11/1990	50	3			I ALMOST FELT LIKE CRYING This and above two singles credited to CRAIG McLACHLAN AND CHECK 1-2	Epic 6563107
23/05/1992	29	6			ONE REASON WHY	Epic 6580677
14/11/1992	59	2			ON MY OWN	Epic 6584677
24/07/1993	13	6			YOU'RE THE ONE THAT I WANT CRAIG McLACHLAN AND DEBBIE GIBSON	Epic 6595222
25/12/1993	44	4			GREASE	Epic 6600242
08/07/1995	65	2			EVERYDAY CRAIG McLACHLAN AND THE CULPRITS	MDMC DEVCS 6

SARAH McLACHLAN
Canadian vocalist (born 28/1/1968, Halifax, Nova Scotia) who was adopted and brought up by Jack and Dorice McLachlan, although it is believed that Judy James, a Nova Scotian jewellery craftswoman, was her biological mother. She has three Grammy Awards: Best Pop Instrumental Performance in 1997 for *Last Dance,* Best Female Pop Vocal Performance in 1997 for *Building A Mystery* and Best Female Pop Vocal Performance in 1999 for *I Will Remember You.*

○ Silver disc ● Gold disc ✪ Platinum disc (additional platinum units are indicated by a figure following the symbol) ◉ Singles released prior to 1973 that are known to have sold over 1 million copies in the UK

DATE	POS	WKS	BPI	SINGLE TITLE	LABEL & NUMBER
03/10/1998	18	5		ADIA Featured in the 2002 film *Once Upon A Time In The Midlands*	Arista 74321613902
14/10/2000	3	16	O	**SILENCE (REMIXES)** DELERIUM FEATURING SARAH McLACHLAN	Nettwerk 331082
02/02/2002	36	3		ANGEL	Nettwerk 331492
20/03/2004	50	1		FALLEN	Arista 82876599282
26/06/2004	72	1		WORLD ON FIRE	Arista 82876628632
27/11/2004	38	4		SILENCE 2004 DELERIUM FEATURING SARAH MCLACHLAN	Nettwerk 332422

TOMMY McLAIN US singer (born 15/3/1940, Jonesville, LA) who was bassist in Clint West And The Boogie Kings before going solo.

DATE	POS	WKS	BPI	SINGLE TITLE	LABEL & NUMBER
08/09/1966	49	1		SWEET DREAMS	London HL 10065

MALCOLM McLAREN UK producer (born 22/1/1946, London) who was best known as a manager, working with Adam Ant, The Sex Pistols and Bow Wow Wow, among others. The Bootzilla Orchestra was founded by former Parliament/Funkadelic member William 'Bootsy' Collins. The World Famous Supreme Team are a US vocal/rapping group formed by Jade, Anjou, Tammy, Rockafella and Asia.

DATE	POS	WKS	BPI	SINGLE TITLE	LABEL & NUMBER
04/12/1982	9	12	O	**BUFFALO GIRLS** MALCOLM McLAREN AND THE WORLD'S FAMOUS SUPREME TEAM	Charisma MALC 1
26/02/1983	32	5		SOWETO MALCOLM McLAREN AND THE McLARENETTES	Charisma MALC 2
02/07/1983	3	13	O	**DOUBLE DUTCH**	Charisma MALC 3
17/12/1983	54	5		DUCK FOR THE OYSTER	Charisma MALC 4
01/09/1984	13	9		MADAM BUTTERFLY (UN BEL DI VEDREMO)	Charisma MALC 5
27/05/1989	31	4		WALTZ DARLING MALCOLM McLAREN AND THE BOOTZILLA ORCHESTRA	Epic WALTZ 2
19/08/1989	29	7		SOMETHING'S JUMPIN' IN YOUR HEART MALCOLM McLAREN AND THE BOOTZILLA ORCHESTRA FEATURING LISA MARIE	Epic WALTZ 3
25/11/1989	73	1		HOUSE OF THE BLUE DANUBE MALCOLM McLAREN AND THE BOOTZILLA ORCHESTRA	Epic WALTZ 4
21/12/1991	42	4		MAGIC'S BACK (THEME FROM 'THE GHOSTS OF OXFORD STREET') MALCOLM McLAREN FEATURING ALISON LIMERICK Theme to the TV series *The Ghosts Of Oxford Street*	RCA PB 45223
03/10/1998	65	1		BUFFALO GALS STAMPEDE (REMIX) MALCOLM McLAREN AND THE WORLD'S FAMOUS SUPREME TEAM PLUS RAKIM AND ROGER SANCHEZ	Virgin VSCDT 1717

BITTY McLEAN UK singer (born 1972, Birmingham) who was a tape operator and later co-producer for UB40 before going solo.

DATE	POS	WKS	BPI	SINGLE TITLE	LABEL & NUMBER
31/07/1993	2	15	O	**IT KEEPS RAININ' (TEARS FROM MY EYES)**	Brilliant CDBRIL 1
30/10/1993	35	3		PASS IT ON	Brilliant CDBRIL 2
15/01/1994	10	6		**HERE I STAND**	Brilliant CDBRIL 3
09/04/1994	6	10		**DEDICATED TO THE ONE I LOVE**	Brilliant CDBRIL 4
06/08/1994	36	3		WHAT GOES AROUND	Brilliant CDBRIL 5
08/04/1995	27	4		OVER THE RIVER	Brilliant CDBRIL 9
17/06/1995	23	5		WE'VE ONLY JUST BEGUN	Brilliant CDBRIL 10
30/09/1995	55	2		NOTHING CAN CHANGE THIS LOVE	Brilliant CDBRIL 11
27/01/1996	63	1		NATURAL HIGH	Brilliant CDBRIL 12
05/10/1996	53	1		SHE'S ALRIGHT	Kuff KUFFD 9

DON McLEAN US singer (born 2/10/1945, New Rochelle, NY) who began performing in 1968 and made his debut album in 1970. The hit *Killing Me Softly With His Song* was written about him.

DATE	POS	WKS	BPI	SINGLE TITLE	LABEL & NUMBER
22/01/1972	2	16		**AMERICAN PIE** ▲4 Inspired by the death of Buddy Holly. Featured in the 1989 film *Born On The 4th Of July*	United Artists UP 35325
13/05/1972	❶2	15		**VINCENT** Tribute to the painter Vincent Van Gogh	United Artists UP 35359
14/04/1973	38	5		EVERYDAY	United Artists UP 35519
10/05/1980	❶3	14	O	**CRYING** Revival of Roy Orbison's 1961 hit. Featured in the 1987 film *Hiding Out*	EMI 5051
17/04/1982	47	8		CASTLES IN THE AIR	EMI 5258
05/10/1991	12	10		AMERICAN PIE Re-issue of United Artists UP 35325	Liberty EMCT 3

JACKIE McLEAN US saxophonist (born 17/5/1932, New York City) who worked with Sonny Rollins, Miles Davis and Charles Mingus before forming his own band.

DATE	POS	WKS	BPI	SINGLE TITLE	LABEL & NUMBER
07/07/1979	53	4		DR JACKYLL AND MISTER FUNK	RCA PB 1575

PHIL McLEAN US DJ (born in Detroit, MI).

DATE	POS	WKS	BPI	SINGLE TITLE	LABEL & NUMBER
18/01/1962	34	4		SMALL SAD SAM Parody of *Big Bad John*	Top Rank JAR 597

McLUSKY UK group formed by Andy Falkous (guitar/vocals), Jon Chapple (bass) and Jack Egglestone (drums).

DATE	POS	WKS	BPI	SINGLE TITLE	LABEL & NUMBER
08/05/2004	71	1		THAT MAN WILL NOT HANG	Too Pure PURE153CDS

IAN McNABB UK singer/guitarist (born 3/11/1960, Liverpool) who formed Icicle Works in 1980 with Chris Layhe and Chris Sharrock and recorded five albums with the group before going solo.

DATE	POS	WKS	BPI	SINGLE TITLE	LABEL & NUMBER
23/01/1993	67	1		IF LOVE WAS LIKE GUITARS	This Way Up WAY 233
02/07/1994	54	1		YOU MUST BE PREPARED TO DREAM IAN McNABB FEATURING RALPH MOLINA AND BILLY TALBOT	This Way Up WAY 3199
17/09/1994	66	2		GO INTO THE LIGHT	This Way Up WAY 3699
27/04/1996	72	1		DON'T PUT YOUR SPELL ON ME	This Way Up WAY 5033
06/07/1996	74	1		MERSEYBEAST	This Way Up WAY 5266

LUTRICIA McNEAL US singer (born in Oklahoma City, KS) who moved to Sweden where she first had top ten hits.
29/11/1997	6	18	O	**AIN'T THAT JUST THE WAY** .... Wildstar CDSTAS 2907
23/05/1998	3	12	O	**STRANDED** .... Wildstar CXSTAS 2973
26/09/1998	9	7		**SOMEONE LOVES YOU HONEY** .... Wildstar CDWILD 9
19/12/1998	17	6		THE GREATEST LOVE YOU'LL NEVER KNOW .... Wildstar CDWILD 11

PATRICK MacNEE AND HONOR BLACKMAN UK actor and actress duo Patrick MacNee (born 6/2/1922, London), best known for his portrayal of Steed in *The Avengers,* and Honor Blackman (born 22/8/1926, London), a regular in *The Upper Hand* and best known for having been Pussy Galore, the Bond Girl in the 1964 film *Goldfinger*. The name caused problems when the film was released in the US, with distributors insisting that the name be changed to Kitty Galore, although it was eventually retained.
| 01/12/1990 | 5 | 7 | | **KINKY BOOTS** Originally recorded in 1964 and first re-released in 1983. It failed to chart on both occasions .... Deram KINKY 1 |

RITA MacNEIL Canadian folk singer (born 1944, Big Pond, Cape Breton) who first became known at the 1985 Tokyo Expo.
| 06/10/1990 | 11 | 10 | | WORKING MAN. .... Polydor PO 98 |

CLYDE McPHATTER US singer (born 15/11/1931, Durham, NC) who joined the Dominoes in 1950, then formed The Drifters in 1953. Drafted the following year, he returned to record solo. He died from a heart attack brought on by alcohol abuse on 13/6/1972.
| 24/08/1956 | 27 | 1 | | TREASURE OF LOVE .... London HLE 8293 |

CARMEN McRAE – see SAMMY DAVIS JR

TOM McRAE UK singer/songwriter (born in Chelmsford) whose parents were Church of England vicars. He studied music politics at London Guildhall University and recorded his debut album in 2001.
| 24/05/2003 | 48 | 1 | | KARAOKE SOUL .... DB DB016CDE7JC2 |

RALPH McTELL UK singer/songwriter/guitarist (born Ralph May, 3/12/1944, Farnborough) who made his debut recording in 1968. He named himself after blues singer Blind Willie McTell.
| 07/12/1974 | 2 | 12 | O | **STREETS OF LONDON** .... Reprise K 14380 |
| 20/12/1975 | 36 | 6 | | DREAMS OF YOU .... Warner Brothers K 16648 |

MAD COBRA FEATURING RICHIE STEPHENS Jamaican reggae rapper (born Ewart Everton Brown, 31/3/1968, Kingston) with UK singer Richie Stephens.
| 15/05/1993 | 64 | 2 | | LEGACY .... Columbia 6592852 |

MAD DONNA US studio group from the Mother Goose Rocks educational company, with the old children's favourite performed in the style of Madonna's *Ray Of Light*, hence the artist credit. Mother Goose Rocks specialise in producing children's CDs.
| 04/05/2002 | 17 | 4 | | THE WHEELS ON THE BUS. .... Star Harbour/All Around The World DISCO 0202CR |

MAD JOCKS FEATURING JOCKMASTER B.A. UK vocal/instrumental group formed by ex-Shakatak Nigel Wright.
| 19/12/1987 | 46 | 5 | | JOCK MIX 1 .... Debut DEBT 3037 |
| 18/12/1993 | 57 | 4 | | PARTY FOUR (EP) Tracks on EP: *No Lager, Here We Go Again, Jock Party Mix* and *Jock Jak Mix* .... SMP CDSSKM 24 |

MAD MOSES US DJ/producer 'Mad' Mitch Moses.
| 16/08/1997 | 50 | 1 | | PANTHER PARTY .... Hi-Life 5744932 |

MAD STUNTMAN – see REEL 2 REAL

MADAM FRICTION – see CORTINA

SONYA MADAN – see LITHIUM AND SONYA MADAN

MADASUN UK vocal trio formed by Vicky Barratt, Vonda Barnes and Abby Norman.
11/03/2000	14	6		DON'T YOU WORRY .... V2 VVR 5011523
27/05/2000	14	4		WALKING ON WATER .... V2 VVR 5012418
02/09/2000	29	3		FEEL GOOD .... V2 VVR 5012983

DANNY MADDEN US singer (born in New York) who was a backing singer for Will Downing, Freddie Jackson and Mavis Staples.
| 14/07/1990 | 72 | 2 | | THE FACTS OF LIFE .... Eternal YZ 473 |

MADDER ROSE US group formed in Manhattan, NYC by Billy Cote (vocals), Mary Lorson (guitar), Matt Verta-Ray (bass) and Johnny Kick (drums). Verta-Ray left the group in 1994 and was replaced by Chris Giammalvo.
| 26/03/1994 | 65 | 1 | | PANIC ON. .... Atlantic A 8301CD |
| 16/07/1994 | 68 | 1 | | CAR SONG. .... Seed A 7256CD |

MADDOG – see STRETCH 'N' VERN PRESENT MADDOG

○ Silver disc ● Gold disc ✪ Platinum disc (additional platinum units are indicated by a figure following the symbol) ◉ Singles released prior to 1973 that are known to have sold over 1 million copies in the UK

MADE IN LONDON
Multinational vocal trio formed in London by Sherene Dyer (born in London; raised in Jamaica), Marianne Eide (born in Hammerfest, Norway) and Kelly Bryant (born in Bristol).

| 13/05/2000 | 15 | 5 | | DIRTY WATER | RCA 74321746192 |
| 09/09/2000 | 74 | 1 | | SHUT YOUR MOUTH | RCA 74321772602 |

MADELYNE
Dutch producer Carlo Resoort.

| 07/09/2002 | 63 | 1 | | BEAUTIFUL CHILD (A DEEPER LOVE) | Xtravaganza XTRAV 36CDS |

MADEMOISELLE
French production/instrumental duo Rami Mustakim and Frederi Chateau.

| 08/09/2001 | 56 | 1 | | DO YOU LOVE ME | RCA 74321878952 |

MADHOUSE
French production group formed by Bambi Mukendi and Stephane Durand, and fronted by Turkish singer Buse Unlu who was twenty years of age at the time of their debut hit.

| 17/08/2002 | 3 | 11 | | **LIKE A PRAYER** | Serious SERR 046CD |
| 09/11/2002 | 24 | 3 | | HOLIDAY | Serious SER 058CD |

MADISON AVENUE
Australian dance duo producer Andy Van Dorsselaar and vocalist Cheyne Coates.

13/11/1999	30	6		DON'T CALL ME BABY Contains a sample of Pino D'Anglo's *Ma-quale-idea*	VC Recordings VCRD 56
20/05/2000	❶1	12	○	**DON'T CALL ME BABY** ↑ Re-issue of VC Recordings VCRD 56	VC Recordings VCRD 64
21/10/2000	10	5		**WHO THE HELL ARE YOU**	VC Recordings VCRD 70
27/01/2001	33	2		EVERYTHING YOU NEED	VC Recordings VCRD 82

MADNESS
UK group formed in 1976 by Mike Barson (born 21/4/1958, London, keyboards), 'Chrissie Boy' Foreman (born 8/8/1958, London, guitar), Lee 'Kix' Thompson (born 5/10/1957, London, saxophone/vocals), John Hasler (drums), Chas Smash (born Cathal Smyth, 14/1/1959, London, horns), Suggs (born Graham McPherson, 13/1/1961, Hastings, vocals), Bedders (born Mark Bedford, 24/8/1961, London, bass) and Dan 'Woody' Woodgate (born 19/10/1960, London, drums) as The Invaders. They name-changed to Madness (after a Prince Buster song) in 1979 and signed a one-off deal with 2-Tone before linking with Stiff. They launched the Zarjazz label in 1984. Suggs later recorded solo and became a TV presenter. The group re-formed in 1999.

01/09/1979	16	11		THE PRINCE Inspired by reggae artist Prince Buster	2 Tone TT 3
10/11/1979	7	14	○	**ONE STEP BEYOND** Featured in the 1981 film *Dance Craze*	Stiff BUY 56
05/01/1980	3	10	○	**MY GIRL**	Stiff BUY 62
05/04/1980	6	8		**WORK REST AND PLAY EP** Tracks on EP: *Night Boat To Cairo, Deceives The Eye, The Young And The Old* and *Don't Quote Me On That. Night Boat To Cairo* was featured in the 1981 film *Dance Craze*	Stiff BUY 71
13/09/1980	3	20	●	**BAGGY TROUSERS** Featured in the 2001 film *Mean Machine*	Stiff BUY 84
22/11/1980	4	12	●	**EMBARRASSMENT**	Stiff BUY 102
24/01/1981	7	11	○	**RETURN OF THE LOS PALMAS SEVEN**	Stiff BUY 108
25/04/1981	4	10	○	**GREY DAY**	Stiff BUY 112
26/09/1981	7	9	○	**SHUT UP**	Stiff BUY 126
05/12/1981	4	12	●	**IT MUST BE LOVE** Featured in the 1989 film *The Tall Guy*	Stiff BUY 134
20/02/1982	14	10		CARDIAC ARREST	Stiff BUY 140
22/05/1982	❶2	9	○	**HOUSE OF FUN**	Stiff BUY 146
24/07/1982	4	8	○	**DRIVING IN MY CAR** Featured in the 1983 film *Party Party*	Stiff BUY 153
27/11/1982	5	13	●	**OUR HOUSE**	Stiff BUY 163
19/02/1983	8	9		**TOMORROW'S (JUST ANOTHER DAY)/MADNESS (IS ALL IN THE MIND)**	Stiff BUY 169
20/08/1983	2	10	○	**WINGS OF A DOVE** Featured in the 1999 film *10 Things I Hate About You*	Stiff BUY 181
05/11/1983	5	10		**THE SUN AND THE RAIN**	Stiff BUY 192
11/02/1984	11	8		MICHAEL CAINE Tribute to the actor Michael Caine	Stiff BUY 196
02/06/1984	17	7		ONE BETTER DAY	Stiff BUY 201
31/08/1985	18	7		YESTERDAY'S MEN	Zarjazz JAZZ 5
26/10/1985	21	11		UNCLE SAM	Zarjazz JAZZ 7
01/02/1986	35	6		SWEETEST GIRL	Zarjazz JAZZ 8
08/11/1986	18	8		(WAITING FOR) THE GHOST TRAIN	Zarjazz JAZZ 9
19/03/1988	44	4		I PRONOUNCE YOU **THE MADNESS**	Virgin VS 1054
15/02/1992	6	9		**IT MUST BE LOVE** Re-issue of Stiff BUY 134	Virgin VS 1405
25/04/1992	40	3		HOUSE OF FUN Re-issue of Stiff BUY 146	Virgin VS 1413
08/08/1992	27	4		MY GIRL Re-issue of Stiff BUY 62	Virgin VS 1425
28/11/1992	44	3		THE HARDER THEY COME	Go Discs GOD 93
27/02/1993	56	2		NIGHT BOAT TO CAIRO	Virgin VSCDT 1447
31/07/1999	10	7		**LOVESTRUCK**	Virgin VSCDT 1737
06/11/1999	44	2		JOHNNY THE HORSE	Virgin VSCDT 1740
11/03/2000	55	1		DRIP FED FRED **MADNESS FEATURING IAN DURY**	Virgin VSCDT 1768

❶9 Number of weeks single topped the UK chart ↑ Entered the UK chart at #1 ▲9 Number of weeks single topped the US chart

497

MADONNA US singer (born Madonna Louise Ciccone, 16/8/1958, Bay City, MI) who was with Patrick Hernandez's Revue before forming Breakfast Club in 1979. Her first records were backing Otto Van Wernherr in 1980, before signing solo with Sire in 1982. She made her lead film debut in *Desperately Seeking Susan* (1985), and later appeared in *Dick Tracy* (1990), *A League Of Their Own* (1992), *Body Of Evidence* (1993), *Evita* (1996) and *The Next Best Thing* (2000). As Eva Peron in *Evita*, she wore 85 costumes, 39 hats, 45 pairs of shoes and 56 pairs of earrings. She married actor Sean Penn in 1985; they divorced in 1989. She launched the Maverick label in 1992. Moving to London in 1999 with her daughter, Lourdes Maria Ciccone Leon, she married Guy Ritchie in January 2001, with whom she had a son, Rocco. While Sheena Easton was the first to record a James Bond theme and appear on screen, in 2002 Madonna was the first to perform the theme and appear in the film, in *Die Another Day*. Six Grammy Awards include Best Music Video Long Form in 1991 for *Blond Ambition World Tour Live* and Best Pop Album, Best Pop Dance Performance, Best Recording Package and Best Music Video Short Form in 1998 for *Ray Of Light*. She won Best International Female at the 2001 BRIT Awards, her first such award. She has, however, won four MTV Europe Music Awards: Best Female in 1998 and 2000, Best Album in 1998 for *Ray Of Light* and Best Dance Act in 2000. She was inducted into the UK Music Hall of Fame in 2004, one of its first inductees.

DATE	POS	WKS	BPI	SINGLE TITLE	LABEL & NUMBER
14/01/1984	6	11	●	**HOLIDAY** Featured in the 1998 film *The Wedding Singer*	Sire W 9405
17/03/1984	14	9		**LUCKY STAR** Featured in the 2000 film *Snatch*	Sire W 9522
02/06/1984	56	4		BORDERLINE	Sire W 9260
17/11/1984	3	18	●	**LIKE A VIRGIN** ▲[6]	Sire W 9210
02/03/1985	3	10	●	**MATERIAL GIRL**	Sire W 9083
08/06/1985	2	15	●	**CRAZY FOR YOU** ▲[1] Featured in the films *Vision Quest* (1985) and *13 Going On 30* (2004)	Geffen A 6323
08/06/1985	❶[4]	14		**INTO THE GROOVE** Featured in the 1985 film *Desperately Seeking Susan*	Sire W 8934
03/08/1985	2	10		**HOLIDAY** This and above single held #1 and #2 on 17/8/1985.	Sire W 9405
21/09/1985	5	9	○	**ANGEL**	Sire W 8881
12/10/1985	4	12	●	**GAMBLER** Featured in the 1985 film *Vision Quest*.	Geffen A 6585
07/12/1985	5	11	●	**DRESS YOU UP** Featured in the 1985 film *Desperately Seeking Susan*	Sire W 8848
25/01/1986	2	9	○	**BORDERLINE**	Sire W 9260
26/04/1986	2	12	○	**LIVE TO TELL** ▲[1] Featured in the 1986 film *At Close Range*	Sire W 8717
28/06/1986	❶[3]	14	●	**PAPA DON'T PREACH** ▲[2]	Sire W 8636
04/10/1986	❶[1]	15	●	**TRUE BLUE**	Sire W 8550
13/12/1986	4	9	○	**OPEN YOUR HEART** ▲[1]	Sire W 8480
04/04/1987	❶[2]	11	○	**LA ISLA BONITA**	Sire W 8378
18/07/1987	❶[1]	10	○	**WHO'S THAT GIRL** ▲[1]	Sire W 8341
19/09/1987	4	9		**CAUSING A COMMOTION**	Sire W 8224
12/12/1987	9	7		**THE LOOK OF LOVE** This and above two singles featured in the 1987 film *Who's That Girl*	Sire W 8115
18/03/1989	❶[3]	12	●	**LIKE A PRAYER** ▲[3]	Sire W 7539
03/06/1989	5	10	○	**EXPRESS YOURSELF**	Sire W 2948
16/09/1989	3	8		**CHERISH**	Sire W 2883
16/12/1989	5	9	○	**DEAR JESSIE**	Sire W 2668
07/04/1990	❶[4]	14	●	**VOGUE** ▲[3]	Sire W 9851
21/07/1990	2	9	○	**HANKY PANKY** This and above single featured in the 1990 film *Dick Tracy*	Sire W 9789
08/12/1990	2	10	○	**JUSTIFY MY LOVE** ▲[2] Songwriting credits were initially Madonna and Lenny Kravitz, but the following year Ingrid Chavez successfully sued Kravitz for omitting her name	Sire W 9000
02/03/1991	2	8	○	**CRAZY FOR YOU (REMIX)**	Sire W 0008
13/04/1991	3	8		**RESCUE ME**	Sire W 0024
08/06/1991	5	7		**HOLIDAY** Re-issue of Sire W 9405.	Sire W 0037
25/07/1992	3	9	○	**THIS USED TO BE MY PLAYGROUND** ▲[1] Featured in the 1992 film *A League Of Their Own*	Sire W 0122
17/10/1992	3	9		**EROTICA** Contains a sample of Kool & The Gang's *Jungle Boogie*	Maverick W 0138
12/12/1992	6	9		**DEEPER AND DEEPER**	Maverick W 0146
06/03/1993	10	7		**BAD GIRL**	Maverick W 0145CD
03/04/1993	6	6		**FEVER**	Maverick W 0168CD
31/07/1993	7	8		**RAIN**	Maverick W 0190CD
02/04/1994	7	8		**I'LL REMEMBER** Featured in the 1994 film *With Honors*	Maverick W 0240CD
08/10/1994	5	9		**SECRET**	Maverick W 0268CD
17/12/1994	16	9		TAKE A BOW ▲[7]	Maverick W 0278CD
25/02/1995	4	9		**BEDTIME STORY**	Maverick W 0285CD
26/08/1995	8	5		**HUMAN NATURE** Contains a sample of Main Source's *What You Need*	Maverick W 0300CD
04/11/1995	5	13		**YOU'LL SEE**	Maverick W 0324CDX
06/01/1996	16	6		**OH FATHER**	Maverick W 0326CDX
23/03/1996	11	4		ONE MORE CHANCE	Maverick W 0337CD
02/11/1996	10	6		**YOU MUST LOVE ME** 1996 Oscar for Best Song for writers Andrew Lloyd Webber and Tim Rice	Warner Brothers W 0378CD
28/12/1996	3	12	○	**DON'T CRY FOR ME ARGENTINA**.	Warner Brothers W 0384CD
29/03/1997	7	5		**ANOTHER SUITCASE IN ANOTHER HALL** This and above two singles featured in the 1996 film *Evita*	Warner Brothers W 0388CD
07/03/1998	❶[1]	13	●	**FROZEN** ↑	Maverick W 0433CD
09/05/1998	2	10	○	**RAY OF LIGHT**	Maverick W 0444CD
05/09/1998	10	5		**DROWNED WORLD (SUBSTITUTE FOR LOVE)**	Maverick W 0453CD1
05/12/1998	6	9		**THE POWER OF GOODBYE/LITTLE STAR**	Maverick W 459CD
13/03/1999	7	9	○	**NOTHING REALLY MATTERS**	Maverick W 471CD1
19/06/1999	2	16	●	**BEAUTIFUL STRANGER** Featured in the 1999 film *Austin Powers: The Spy Who Shagged Me*. 1999 Grammy Award for Best Song for a Motion Picture for writers Madonna and William Orbit	Maverick W 495CD
11/03/2000	❶[1]	14	●	**AMERICAN PIE** ↑ Featured in the 2000 film *The Next Best Thing*.	Maverick W 519CD
02/09/2000	❶[1]	23	●	**MUSIC** ↑ ▲[4]	Maverick W 537CD1

○ Silver disc ● Gold disc ✪ Platinum disc (additional platinum units are indicated by a figure following the symbol) ◎ Singles released prior to 1973 that are known to have sold over 1 million copies in the UK

09/12/2000	4	10		**DON'T TELL ME**	Maverick W 547CD1
28/04/2001	7	11		**WHAT IT FEELS LIKE FOR A GIRL**	Maverick W 533CD1
09/11/2002	3	16		**DIE ANOTHER DAY** Featured in the 2003 James Bond film *Die Another Day*	Warner Brothers W 595CD
19/04/2003	57	1		AMERICAN LIFE (IMPORT)	Maverick 166582
26/04/2003	2	11		**AMERICAN LIFE**...	Maverick W 603CD
19/07/2003	2	7		**HOLLYWOOD** Madonna was forced to pay an undisclosed sum to the estate of French photographer Guy Bourdin for failing to credit him as the inspiration for the accompanying video. The family also took action against video director Jean-Baptiste Mondino and Warner Brothers	Maverick W 614CD
22/11/2003	2	12		**ME AGAINST THE MUSIC** **BRITNEY SPEARS FEATURING MADONNA**	Jive 82876576432
20/12/2003	11	6		NOTHING FAILS/LOVE PROFUSION	Maverick W 634CD1

LISA MAFFIA
UK rapper (born 1979) who is also a member of So Solid Crew. She won the 2003 MOBO Awards for Best UK Act (jointly with Big Brovaz) and Best Garage Act.

| 03/05/2003 | 2 | 11 | | **ALL OVER** .... | Independiente ISOM 69SMS |
| 09/08/2003 | 13 | 4 | | IN LOVE .... | Independiente ISOM 75SMS |

MAGAZINE
UK group formed in 1977 by ex-Buzzcocks Howard Devoto (born Howard Trafford, vocals), John McGeoch (guitar), Barry Adamson (bass), Bob Dickinson (keyboards) and Martin Jackson (drums). Dickinson left late 1977, Dave Formula his eventual replacement. Jackson left in 1978 and was replaced by John Doyle. McGeoch left in 1980 and was replaced by Robin Simon, who was replaced shorty after by Ben Mandelson. Devoto's departure in May 1981 brought the group to an end. McGeoch died on 4/3/2004.

| 11/02/1978 | 41 | 4 | | SHOT BY BOTH SIDES .... | Virgin VS 200 |
| 26/07/1980 | 54 | 3 | | SWEET HEART CONTRACT .... | Virgin VS 368 |

MAGIC AFFAIR
US/German vocal/instrumental group formed by Mike Staab, Breiter and Kempf and fronted by rapper AK Swift and singer Franca.

04/06/1994	17	4		OMEN III.	EMI CDEM 317
27/08/1994	30	2		GIVE ME ALL YOUR LOVE	EMI CDEM 340
05/11/1994	38	2		IN THE MIDDLE OF THE NIGHT	EMI CDEM 349

MAGIC LADY
US vocal group formed in Detroit, MI by Jackie Ball, Kimberly Steele and Linda Strokes. Steele left in 1988.

| 14/05/1988 | 58 | 3 | | BETCHA CAN'T LOSE (WITH MY LOVE) .... | Motown ZB 42003 |

MAGIC LANTERNS
UK group formed in Manchester by Jimmy Bilsbury (vocals), Peter Shoesmith (guitar), Ian Moncur (bass) and Allan Wilson (drums). They disbanded in 1970, by which time the line-up was Bilsbury, Alistair Beveridge (guitar), Paul Garner (guitar), Mike Osbourne (bass) and Paul Ward (drums).

| 07/07/1966 | 44 | 3 | | EXCUSE ME BABY .... | CBS 202094 |

MAGNOLIA
Italian producer Nick Fernando with singer Kate Eloise.

| 24/07/2004 | 55 | 1 | | IT'S ALL VAIN. .... | Data 69CDS |

MAGNUM
UK heavy metal band formed in Birmingham in 1976 by Bob Catley (vocals), Tony Clarkin (guitar/vocals), Wally Lowe (bass), Mark Stanway (keyboards) and Mickey Barker (drums). They signed with Jet Records in 1978, FM Revolver for one album, then Polydor in 1985.

22/03/1980	47	6		MAGNUM (DOUBLE SINGLE) Tracks on double single: *Invasion, Kingdom Of Madness, All Of My Life* and *Great Adventure*	Jet 175
12/07/1986	70	2		LONELY NIGHT.	Polydor POSP 798
19/03/1988	32	4		DAYS OF NO TRUST	Polydor POSP 910
07/05/1988	22	4		START TALKING LOVE	Polydor POSP 920
02/07/1988	33	4		IT MUST HAVE BEEN LOVE	Polydor POSP 930
23/06/1990	27	4		ROCKIN' CHAIR	Polydor PO 88
25/08/1990	49	2		HEARTBROKE AND BUSTED	Polydor PO 94

MAGOO:MOGWAI
UK vocal/instrumental group. Magoo was formed in Norwich, Norfolk by Andrew Rayner (guitar/vocals), Owen Turner (guitar/keyboards), Andrew Hodge (bass) and David Bamford (drums). Mogwai was formed in Glasgow in 1996 by Stuart Braithwaite (guitar/vocals), Dominic Aitchison (guitar), John Cummings (guitar) and Martin Bulloch (drums).

| 04/04/1998 | 60 | 1 | | BLACK SABBATH/SWEET LEAF Double A-side that featured Mogwai's *Sweet Leaf* .... | Fierce Panda NING 47CD |

MAGOO
US rapper (born Melvin Barcliff, 12/7/1971, Norfolk, VA).

| 13/03/1999 | 43 | 1 | | HERE WE COME **TIMBALAND/MISSY ELLIOTT AND MAGOO** Contains samples from the cartoon series *Spiderman* .... | Virgin DINSD 179 |
| 13/03/2004 | 22 | 3 | | COP THAT SHIT **TIMBALAND/MAGOO/MISSY ELLIOTT** .... | Unique Corp TIMBACD001 |

SEAN MAGUIRE
UK actor/singer (born18/4/1976) who appeared in children's TV programmes such as *Grange Hill* as Terence Ratcliffe, *Dangerfield* as Marty Dangerfield and *Eastenders* as Aidan Brosnan. After a brief record career, he returned to TV in *Sunburn* and the US TV series *Off Centre*.

20/08/1994	14	7		SOMEONE TO LOVE	Parlophone CDRS 6390
05/11/1994	27	5		TAKE THIS TIME	Parlophone CDRS 6395
25/03/1995	18	5		SUDDENLY	Parlophone CDRS 6403
24/06/1995	22	3		NOW I'VE FOUND YOU	Parlophone CDLEEPYS 1

❶⁹ Number of weeks single topped the UK chart ↑ Entered the UK chart at #1 ▲⁹ Number of weeks single topped the US chart

499

DATE	POS	WKS	BPI	SINGLE TITLE	LABEL & NUMBER
18/11/1995	16	3		YOU TO ME ARE EVERYTHING	Parlophone CDR 6420
25/05/1996	12	4		GOOD DAY	Parlophone CDR 6432
03/08/1996	14	4		DON'T PULL YOUR LOVE	Parlophone CDRS 6440
29/03/1997	27	3		TODAY'S THE DAY	Parlophone CDR 6459

SIOBHAN MAHER – see OCEANIC

MAHLATHINI AND THE MAHOTELLA QUEENS – see ART OF NOISE

MAI TAI Dutch group formed in Amsterdam in 1983 by Jettie Wells, Carolien De Windt and Mildred Douglas, all from Guyana.

DATE	POS	WKS	BPI	SINGLE TITLE	LABEL & NUMBER
25/05/1985	8	13	O	HISTORY	Virgin VS 773
03/08/1985	9	13		BODY AND SOUL	Virgin VS 801
15/02/1986	54	4		FEMALE INTUITION	Virgin VS 844

MAIN INGREDIENT US R&B vocal group formed in New York in 1964 by Donald McPherson (born 9/7/1941, Indianapolis), Tony Sylvester (born 7/10/1941, Panama) and Luther Simmons (born 9/9/1942) as The Poets. McPherson died from leukaemia on 4/7/1971 and was replaced by Cuba Gooding (born 27/4/1944, New York). Gooding later recorded solo for Motown while his son became an actor. Simmons later became a stockbroker, although he has frequently returned to the group.

DATE	POS	WKS	BPI	SINGLE TITLE	LABEL & NUMBER
29/06/1974	27	7		JUST DON'T WANT TO BE LONELY	RCA APBO 0205

MAISONETTES UK group formed in Birmingham by ex-City Boy Lol Mason (vocals), Elaine Williams (vocals), Denise Ward (vocals), Mark Tibbenham (keyboards) and Nick Parry (drums).

DATE	POS	WKS	BPI	SINGLE TITLE	LABEL & NUMBER
11/12/1982	7	12	O	HEARTACHE AVENUE	Ready Steady Go! RSG 1

J MAJIK US producer Jamie Spratling who recorded as DJ Dextrous until 1994. Later in Infared, he launched Infared Records.

DATE	POS	WKS	BPI	SINGLE TITLE	LABEL & NUMBER
05/05/2001	34	2		LOVE IS NOT A GAME J MAJIK FEATURING KATHY BROWN	Defected DFECT 31CDS
27/04/2002	54	1		METROSOUND ADAM F AND J MAJIK	Kaos 001P
22/05/2004	67	1		SCOOBY DOO/SPYCATCHER J MAJIK AND WICKAMAN	Infared INFRA28

NIKI MAK – see TONY DE VIT

MAKADOPOULOS AND HIS GREEK SERENADERS Greek vocal/instrumental group whose hit was one of four versions vying for chart honours at the same time.

DATE	POS	WKS	BPI	SINGLE TITLE	LABEL & NUMBER
20/10/1960	36	14		NEVER ON SUNDAY	Palette PG 9005

MAKAVELI US rapper/actor Tupac Amara Shakur (born Lesane Crooks, 16/6/1971, Brooklyn, NYC) who was a member of Digital Underground. Brushes with the law included a gun battle with two off-duty policemen, an assault on Allen Hughes of Menace II Society a jail sentence for a sexual abuse conviction and a wrongful death suit for causing the death of a six-year-old child when his gun accidentally discharged. He was shot five times during a robbery in Manhattan in 1994 in which he was robbed of $40,000 and survived, but on 7/9/1996 he was shot four times while travelling to a boxing match between Mike Tyson and Bruce Seldon in Las Vegas and died as a result of gunshot wounds on 13/9/1996. He was on $1.4 million bail for a weapons conviction at the time of his death. He also recorded as 2Pac and appeared in films such as *Nothing But Trouble, Poetic Justice* and *Above The Rim*.

DATE	POS	WKS	BPI	SINGLE TITLE	LABEL & NUMBER
12/04/1997	10	4		TO LIVE AND DIE IN LA	Interscope IND 95529
09/08/1997	15	3		TOSS IT UP	Interscope IND 95521
14/02/1998	43	1		HAIL MARY	Interscope IND 95575

JACK E MAKOSSA US multi-instrumentalist (born Arthur Baker, 22/4/1955, Boston, MA) who also recorded as Wally Jump Jr and the Criminal Element Orchestra and under his own name. Jack E Makossa was supposedly a Kenyan producer.

DATE	POS	WKS	BPI	SINGLE TITLE	LABEL & NUMBER
12/09/1987	48	5		THE OPERA HOUSE	Champion CHAMP 50

MALA – see BOWA FEATURING MALA

MALAIKA US singer (born in Seattle, WA) whose name is Swahili for 'angel'.

DATE	POS	WKS	BPI	SINGLE TITLE	LABEL & NUMBER
31/07/1993	68	1		GOTTA KNOW (YOUR NAME)	A&M 5802732

CARL MALCOLM Jamaican reggae singer (born 1952, Black River, St Elizabeth) whose backing group at one time included Boris Gardiner, later a successful solo artist. Prior to recording his hit single he was a razor blade manufacturer.

DATE	POS	WKS	BPI	SINGLE TITLE	LABEL & NUMBER
13/09/1975	8	8		FATTIE BUM BUM Promotional copies of the record credited Max Romeo as the artist	UK 108

VALERIE MALCOLM – see CANDY GIRLS

STEPHEN MALKMUS US singer/guitarist (born 30/5/1963, Santa Monica, CA) who was in Pavement from 1989 to 2000 and then solo.

DATE	POS	WKS	BPI	SINGLE TITLE	LABEL & NUMBER
28/04/2001	60	1		DISCRETION GROVE	Domino RUG 123CD

RAUL MALO US guitarist/singer (born 7/8/1965, Miami, FL) who was also leader of The Mavericks, with a parallel solo career since 2002.

DATE	POS	WKS	BPI	SINGLE TITLE	LABEL & NUMBER
18/05/2002	57	1		I SAID I LOVE YOU	Gravity 74321923082

MAMA CASS
US singer (born Ellen Naomi Cohen, 19/9/1941, Baltimore, MD) who was one of The Mamas & The Papas (as Cass Elliott) from their formation in 1963 until they split in 1968. She died from a heart attack on 29/7/1974 (brought on by choking on a ham sandwich) at Flat 12, 9 Curzon Street in London's Mayfair – Keith Moon died at the same flat four years later.

14/08/1968	11	12		DREAM A LITTLE DREAM OF ME Featured in the 1989 film *Dream A Little Dream*	RCA 1726
16/08/1969	8	15		**IT'S GETTING BETTER**	Stateside SS 8021

MAMAS AND THE PAPAS
US group originally formed as the New Journeymen in St Thomas in the Virgin Islands in 1963 by John Phillips (born 30/8/1935, Parris Island, SC), Holly Michelle Gilliam Phillips (born 4/6/1945, Long Beach, CA) and Dennis 'Denny' Doherty (born 29/11/1941, Halifax, Novia Scotia), later adding Cass Elliot (born Ellen Naomi Cohen, 19/9/1941, Baltimore, MD) and becoming The Mamas & The Papas. They moved to Los Angeles, CA in 1964. They split in 1968, Mama Cass going solo. They reunited briefly in 1971 and then re-formed in 1982 with Phillips, Doherty, Phillips' daughter McKenzie and Spanky McFarlane. Michelle and John's daughter Chyna was later in Wilson Phillips. The group was inducted into the Rock & Roll Hall of Fame in 1998. Cass Elliot died from a heart attack on 29/7/1974. John Phillips died from heart failure on 18/3/2001.

28/04/1966	23	9		CALIFORNIA DREAMIN' Featured in the films *Air America* (1990) and *Forrest Gump* (1994)	RCA 1503
12/05/1966	3	13		**MONDAY MONDAY** ▲³ 1966 Grammy Award for Best Contemporary Rock & Roll Performance by a Group	RCA 1516
28/07/1966	11	11		I SAW HER AGAIN	RCA 1533
09/02/1967	47	3		WORDS OF LOVE	RCA 1564
06/04/1967	2	17		**DEDICATED TO THE ONE I LOVE**	RCA 1576
26/07/1967	9	11		**CREEQUE ALLEY**	RCA 1613
02/08/1997	9	7		**CALIFORNIA DREAMIN'** Re-issue of RCA 1503 following its use in an advertisement for Carling Premier Lager	MCA MCSTD 48058

MAMBAS – see MARC ALMOND

CHEB MAMI – see STING

A MAN CALLED ADAM
UK group formed by Sally Rodgers, Steve Jones and Paul Daley. When Daley left to form Leftfield, the group continued as a duo.

29/09/1990	60	4		BAREFOOT IN THE HEAD	Big Life BLR 28

MAN 2 MAN
US dance group formed in New York and featuring ex-strippers Paul and Miki Zone. The group members Miki and Michael Rudetski both died from AIDS.

13/09/1986	64	3		MALE STRIPPER	Bolts 4
03/01/1987	4	13	○	**MALE STRIPPER** This and above single credited to MAN 2 MAN MEETS MAN PARRISH	Bolts 4
04/07/1987	43	3		I NEED A MAN/ENERGY IS EUROBEAT	Bolts 5

MAN WITH NO NAME
UK producer Martin Freeland.

30/09/1995	68	1		FLOOR-ESSENCE	Perfecto PERF 108CD
20/01/1996	42	2		PAINT A PICTURE MAN WITH NO NAME FEATURING HANNAH	Perfecto PERF 114CD
12/10/1996	55	1		TELEPORT/SUGAR RUSH	Perfecto PERF 126CD
02/05/1998	43	1		VAVOOM!	Perfecto PERF 159CD1
18/07/1998	72	1		THE FIRST DAY (HORIZON)	Perfecto PERF 164CD

MELISSA MANCHESTER AND AL JARREAU
US vocal duo Melissa Manchester (born 15/2/1951, The Bronx, NYC) and Al Jarreau (born 12/3/1940, Milwaukee, WI). Melissa, backing singer for Bette Midler before going solo, has won one Grammy Award: Best Female Pop Vocal Performance in 1982 for *You Should Hear How She Talks About You*.

05/04/1986	75	1		THE MUSIC OF GOODBYE (LOVE THEME FROM 'OUT OF AFRICA') Featured in the 1985 film *Out Of Africa*	MCA 1038

MANCHESTER UNITED FOOTBALL CLUB
UK football club formed in 1878 as Newton Heath, changing their name in 1902. Their #1 was written by Status Quo's Francis Rossi and Rick Parfitt. They are the only club to have had a UK #1.

08/05/1976	50	1		MANCHESTER UNITED	Decca F 13633
21/05/1983	13	5		GLORY GLORY MAN. UNITED	EMI 5390
18/05/1985	10	5		**WE ALL FOLLOW MAN. UNITED**	Columbia DB 9107
19/06/1993	37	2		UNITED (WE LOVE YOU) MANCHESTER UNITED AND THE CHAMPIONS	Living Beat LBECD 026
30/04/1994	❶²	15	○	**COME ON YOU REDS**	Polygram TV MANU 2
13/05/1995	6	6		**WE'RE GONNA DO IT AGAIN** MANCHESTER UNITED FEATURING STRYKER	Polygram TV MANU 952
04/05/1996	6	15	○	**MOVE MOVE MOVE (THE RED TRIBE)** 1996 MANCHESTER UNITED FA CUP SQUAD	Music Collection MANUCD 1
29/05/1999	11	7		LIFT IT HIGH (ALL ABOUT BELIEF) 1999 MANCHESTER UNITED SQUAD	Music Collection MANUCD 4

MANCHILD
UK production duo Max Odell and Brett Parker with Rob Hinton, Dan Pye, Crowd Chaos Creator Kwam Chang and Rich Adlam.

16/09/2000	60	1		THE CLICHES ARE TRUE MANCHILD FEATURING KELLY JONES	One Little Indian 176 TP7CD
25/08/2001	40	1		NOTHING WITHOUT ME	One Little Indian 183 TP7CD

HENRY MANCINI
US orchestra leader (born 16/4/1924, Cleveland, OH, raised in Pennsylvania) who attended the Julliard School of Music in New York and became in-house composer for Universal Pictures in 1952. His twenty Grammy Awards, more than any other artist, include Album of the Year and Best Arrangement in 1958 for *The Music From Peter Gunn*, Best Performance by an Orchestra and Best Arrangement in 1960 for *Mr Lucky*, Best Jazz Performance by a Large Group in 1960 for *The Blues And The Beat*, Best Performance by an Orchestra and Best Soundtrack Album in 1961 for *Breakfast At Tiffany's*, Best Instrumental Arrangement in 1962 for *Baby Elephant Walk*, Record of the Year, Song of the Year (with Johnny Mercer) and Best Background Arrangement in 1963

❶⁹ Number of weeks single topped the UK chart ↑ Entered the UK chart at #1 ▲⁹ Number of weeks single topped the US chart

501

for *The Days Of Wine And Roses,* Best Instrumental Composition, Best Instrumental Performance and Best Instrumental Arrangement in 1964 for *The Pink Panther Theme,* Best Instrumental Arrangement in 1969 for *Romeo And Juliet,* and Best Contemporary Instrumental Performance and Best Instrumental Arrangement in 1970 for *Theme From 'Z'.* He also won four Oscars. He died from cancer on 14/6/1994. He has a star on the Hollywood Walk of Fame.

07/12/1961	44	3		MOON RIVER 1961 Grammy Awards for Record of the Year and Best Arrangement, plus Song of the Year for writers Henry Mancini and Johnny Mercer	RCA 1256
24/09/1964	10	12		HOW SOON	RCA 1414
25/03/1972	42	1		THEME FROM 'CADE'S COUNTY'	RCA 2182
11/02/1984	23	7		MAIN THEME FROM 'THE THORNBIRDS' Theme to the TV drama *The Thornbirds*	Warner Brothers 9677

MANFRED MANN UK group formed in London in 1962 by Manfred Mann (born Michael Lubowitz, 21/10/1940, Johannesburg, South Africa, keyboards), Mike Hugg (born 11/8/1942, Andover, drums), Paul Jones (born Paul Pond, 24/2/1942, Portsmouth, vocals), Mike Vickers (born 18/4/1941, Southampton, guitar) and Dave Richmond (bass) as the Mann-Hugg Blues Brothers, also adding a horn section. They name-changed in 1963 and signed to HMV. Richmond left in 1964 and was replaced by Tom McGuinness (born 2/12/1941, London). Jones went solo in 1966 and was replaced by Mike D'Abo (born 1/3/1944, Letchworth), Rod Stewart unsuccessfully auditioning for the job. They disbanded in 1969, Mann forming Manfred Mann's Earth Band in 1971 with Mick Rogers (guitar/vocals), Colin Pattenden (bass) and Chris Slade (drums).

23/01/1964	5	13		5-4-3-2-1 Theme to the TV series *Ready Steady Go!*	HMV POP 1252
16/04/1964	11	8		HUBBLE BUBBLE TOIL AND TROUBLE	HMV POP 1282
16/07/1964	❶²	14		DO WAH DIDDY DIDDY ▲² Featured in the 1991 film *My Girl*	HMV POP 1320
15/10/1964	3	12		SHA LA LA	HMV POP 1346
14/01/1965	4	9		COME TOMORROW	HMV POP 1381
15/04/1965	11	10		OH NO NOT MY BABY	HMV POP 1413
16/09/1965	2	12		IF YOU GOTTA GO GO NOW Cover of a Bob Dylan song	HMV POP 1466
21/04/1966	❶³	12		PRETTY FLAMINGO	HMV POP 1523
07/07/1966	36	4		YOU GAVE ME SOMEBODY TO LOVE	HMV POP 1541
04/08/1966	10	10		JUST LIKE A WOMAN Cover of a Bob Dylan song	Fontana TF 730
27/10/1966	2	12		SEMI-DETACHED SUBURBAN MR JAMES	Fontana TF 757
30/03/1967	4	11		HA HA SAID THE CLOWN	Fontana TF 812
25/05/1967	36	4		SWEET PEA	Fontana TF 828
24/01/1968	❶²	11		MIGHTY QUINN Written by Bob Dylan	Fontana TF 897
12/06/1968	8	11		MY NAME IS JACK	Fontana TF 943
18/12/1968	5	12		FOX ON THE RUN	Fontana TF 985
30/04/1969	8	11		RAGAMUFFIN MAN	Fontana TF 1013
08/09/1973	9	10		JOYBRINGER Based on Holt's *Jupiter Suite From 'The Planets'*	Vertigo 6059 083
28/08/1976	6	10		BLINDED BY THE LIGHT ▲¹ Written by Bruce Springsteen. Featured in the 2001 film *Blow*	Bronze BRO 29
20/05/1978	6	12	○	DAVY'S ON THE ROAD AGAIN Featured in the 1978 film *The Stud*	Bronze BRO 52
17/03/1979	54	5		YOU ANGEL YOU	Bronze BRO 68
07/07/1979	45	4		DON'T KILL IT CAROL This and above four singles credited to **MANFRED MANN'S EARTH BAND**	Bronze BRO 77

MANHATTAN TRANSFER US vocal group formed in New York in 1972 by Tim Hauser (born 1940, New York), Alan Paul (born 1949, New Jersey), Janis Siegel (born 1953, Brooklyn, NYC) and Cheryl Bentyne. Bentyne left in 1979 and was replaced by Laurel Masse (born 1954). They won eight Grammy Awards: Best Jazz Fusion Performance in 1980 for *Birdland,* Best Pop Vocal Performance by a Group in 1981 for *Boy From New York City,* Best Jazz Vocal Performance by a Group in 1981 for *Until I Met You (Corner Pocket),* Best Jazz Vocal Performance by a Group in 1982 for *Route 66,* Best Jazz Vocal Performance by a Group in 1983 for *Why Not!,* Best Jazz Vocal Performance by a Group in 1985 for *Vocalese,* Best Pop Vocal Performance by a Group in 1988 for *Brasil* and Best Contemporary Jazz Performance in 1991 for *Sassy.*

07/02/1976	24	6		TUXEDO JUNCTION	Atlantic K 10670
05/02/1977	❶³	13	●	CHANSON D'AMOUR	Atlantic K 10886
28/05/1977	32	6		DON'T LET GO	Atlantic K 10930
18/02/1978	12	12		WALK IN LOVE	Atlantic K 11075
20/05/1978	20	9		ON A LITTLE STREET IN SINGAPORE	Atlantic K 11136
16/09/1978	40	4		WHERE DID OUR LOVE GO/JE VOULAIS TE DIRE (QUE JE T'ATTENDS)	Atlantic K 11182
23/12/1978	49	6		WHO WHAT WHEN WHERE WHY	Atlantic K 11233
17/05/1980	25	8		TWILIGHT ZONE – TWILIGHT TONE (MEDLEY)	Atlantic K 11476
21/01/1984	19	8		SPICE OF LIFE	Atlantic A 9728

MANHATTANS US R&B vocal group formed in Jersey City, NJ in 1962 by George 'Smitty' Smith (born 16/11/1943), Winfred 'Blue' Lovett (born 16/11/1943), Edward 'Sonny' Bivins (born 15/1/1942), Kenneth 'Wally' Kelly (born 9/1/1943) and Richard Taylor (born 1940). Smith died from meningitis on 16/12/1970 and was replaced by Gerald Alston (born 8/11/1942). Taylor became a Muslim (adopting the name Abdul Rashid Tallah), left the group in 1976 and died on 7/12/1987. Alston later recorded solo.

19/06/1976	4	11	○	KISS AND SAY GOODBYE	CBS 4317
02/10/1976	4	11	○	HURT	CBS 4562
23/04/1977	43	3		IT'S YOU	CBS 5093
26/07/1980	45	4		SHINING STAR 1980 Grammy Award for Best Rhythm & Blues Vocal Performance by a Group	CBS 8624

06/08/1983	63	2		CRAZY	CBS A 3578

MANIA UK vocal duo Niara Scarlett and Giselle Sommerville. The pair first met while writing with Xenomania.

07/08/2004	29	2		LOOKING FOR A PLACE	RCA 82876617862

M.A.N.I.C. UK vocal/production duo Kieron Jolliffe and Lee Hudson.

18/04/1992	60	1		I'M COMIN' HARDCORE	Union City UCRT 2

MANIC MC'S FEATURING SARA CARLSON UK producers Colin Hudd and Richard Cottle with singer Sara Carlson.

12/08/1989	30	5		MENTAL	RCA PB 43037

MANIC STREET PREACHERS UK group formed in Blackwood, Gwent in 1988 by James Dean Bradfield (born 21/2/1969, Newport, Gwent, guitar/vocals), Nicky Wire (born Nick Jones, 20/1/1969, Tredegar, Gwent, bass), Sean Moore (born 30/7/1970, Pontypool, Gwent, drums) and Richey 'Manic' Edwards (born 22/12/1966, Blackwood, rhythm guitar), all graduates from Swansea University. They funded their debut in 1989, signing with CBS/Columbia in 1990. Edwards disappeared in February 1995, with his passport, credit cards and car being found near a notorious suicide spot at the Severn Bridge. Despite sightings in Wales and India, he was officially declared dead in 2002. They won Best UK Album (for *Everything Must Go*) and Best Group at the 1997 BRIT Awards, and Best Group at the 1999 BRIT Awards, while their *This Is My Truth Tell Me Yours* won Best UK Album.

25/05/1991	62	2		YOU LOVE US	Heavenly HVN 10
10/08/1991	40	3		STAY BEAUTIFUL	Columbia 6573377
09/11/1991	26	3		LOVE'S SWEET EXILE/REPEAT	Columbia 6575827
01/02/1992	16	4		YOU LOVE US	Columbia 6577247
28/03/1992	20	4		SLASH 'N' BURN	Columbia 6578737
13/06/1992	17	6		MOTORCYCLE EMPTINESS	Columbia 6580837
19/09/1992	7	6		**THEME FROM M.A.S.H. (SUICIDE IS PAINLESS)** Listed flip side was *(Everything I Do) I Do It For You* by FATIMA MANSIONS	
					Columbia 6583827
28/11/1992	29	3		LITTLE BABY NOTHING	Columbia 6587967
12/06/1993	25	4		FROM DESPAIR TO WHERE	Columbia 6593372
31/07/1993	22	5		LA TRISTESSE DURERA (SCREAM TO A SIGH)	Columbia 6594772
02/10/1993	15	3		ROSES IN THE HOSPITAL	Columbia 6597272
12/02/1994	36	2		LIFE BECOMING A LANDSLIDE	Columbia 6600702
11/06/1994	16	3		FASTER/PCP	Epic 6604472
13/08/1994	22	3		REVOL	Epic 6606862
15/10/1994	25	3		SHE IS SUFFERING	Epic 6608952
27/04/1996	2	11	O	**A DESIGN FOR LIFE**	Epic 6630705
03/08/1996	5	6		**EVERYTHING MUST GO**	Epic 6634685
12/10/1996	9	4		**KEVIN CARTER** Tribute to a photographer friend of the band who committed suicide	Epic 6637752
14/12/1996	7	7		**AUSTRALIA**	Epic 6640445
13/09/1997	52	1		STAY BEAUTIFUL	Epic MANIC 1CD
13/09/1997	55	1		LOVE'S SWEET EXILE	Epic MANIC 2CD
13/09/1997	49	1		YOU LOVE US	Epic MANIC 3CD
13/09/1997	54	1		SLASH 'N' BURN	Epic MANIC 4CD
13/09/1997	41	2		MOTORCYCLE EMPTINESS	Epic MANIC 5CD
13/09/1997	50	1		LITTLE BABY NOTHING	Epic MANIC 6CD
05/09/1998	❶¹	11	O	**IF YOU TOLERATE THIS YOUR CHILDREN WILL BE NEXT ↑**	Epic 6663452
12/12/1998	11	8		THE EVERLASTING	Epic 6666862
20/03/1999	5	8		**YOU STOLE THE SUN FROM MY HEART**	Epic 6669532
17/07/1999	11	5		TSUNAMI	Epic 6674112
22/01/2000	❶¹	7		**THE MASSES AGAINST THE CLASSES ↑**	Epic 6685302
10/03/2001	8	7		**SO WHY SO SAD**	Epic 6708322
10/03/2001	9	4		**FOUND THAT SOUL** This and above single were released on the same day	Epic 6708332
16/06/2001	15	4		OCEAN SPRAY	Epic 6712532
22/09/2001	19	2		LET ROBESON SING	Epic 6717732
26/10/2002	6	5		**THERE BY THE GRACE OF GOD**	Epic 6731662
30/10/2004	2	4		**THE LOVE OF RICHARD NIXON**	Sony Music 6753422

MANIJAMA FEATURING MUKUPA AND LIL' T Danish dance group formed by Nima Gorgi, Thomas Madvig, Jan Winther and Martin Ohrt.

08/02/2003	66	1		NO NO NO	Defected DFTD 058CDS

BARRY MANILOW US singer (born Barry Alan Pincus, 17/6/1946, Brooklyn, NYC) who was musical director for Bette Midler and a jingle writer before going solo, first recording as Featherbed. He has a star on the Hollywood Walk of Fame. Kevin DiSimone and James Jolis are both US singers.

22/02/1975	11	9		MANDY ▲¹ Originally written and record by Scott English as *Brandy*	Arista 1
06/05/1978	43	7		CAN'T SMILE WITHOUT YOU	Arista 176

❶⁹ Number of weeks single topped the UK chart ↑ Entered the UK chart at #1 ▲⁹ Number of weeks single topped the US chart

29/07/1978	42	10		SOMEWHERE IN THE NIGHT .... Arista 196
29/07/1978	42	10		COPACABANA (AT THE COPA) 1978 Grammy Award for Best Pop Vocal Performance. Featured in the films *Foul Play* (1977) and *The World Is Full Of Married Men* (1979) .... Arista 196
23/12/1978	25	10		COULD IT BE MAGIC Based on Chopin's *Prelude In C Minor* and originally recorded and released in the US in 1971 with the artist credit Featherbed Featuring Barry Manilow .... Arista ARIST 229
08/11/1980	21	13		LONELY TOGETHER .... Arista ARIST 373
07/02/1981	37	6		I MADE IT THROUGH THE RAIN .... Arista ARIST 384
11/04/1981	15	9		BERMUDA TRIANGLE .... Arista ARIST 406
26/09/1981	12	11	O	LET'S HANG ON .... Arista ARIST 429
12/12/1981	48	8		THE OLD SONGS .... Arista ARIST 443
20/02/1982	66	2		IF I SHOULD LOVE AGAIN .... Arista ARIST 453
17/04/1982	23	8		STAY **BARRY MANILOW FEATURING KEVIN DISIMONE AND JAMES JOLIS** .... Arista ARIST 464
16/10/1982	8	8		**I WANNA DO IT WITH YOU** .... Arista ARIST 495
04/12/1982	36	7		I'M GONNA SIT DOWN AND WRITE MYSELF A LETTER .... Arista ARIST 503
25/06/1983	48	2		SOME KIND OF FRIEND .... Arista ARIST 516
27/08/1983	47	6		YOU'RE LOOKING HOT TONIGHT .... Arista ARIST 542
10/12/1983	17	7		READ 'EM AND WEEP .... Arista ARIST 551
08/04/1989	35	5		PLEASE DON'T BE SCARED .... Arista 112186
10/04/1993	22	4		COPACABANA (AT THE COPA) (REMIX) .... Arista 74321136912
20/11/1993	36	3		COULD IT BE MAGIC Re-recording of ARIST 229 .... Arista 74321174882
06/08/1994	73	1		LET ME BE YOUR WINGS **BARRY MANILOW AND DEBRA BYRD** .... EMI CDEM 336

MANIX UK production group formed by Marc 'Mac' Clair and Iain Bardouille. Earlier in 4 Hero, they formed the Reinforced label.

23/11/1991	63	2		MANIC MINDS .... Reinforced RIVET 1209
07/03/1992	43	3		OBLIVION (HEAD IN THE CLOUDS) (EP) Tracks on EP: *Oblivion (Head In The Clouds), Never Been To Belgium (Gotta Rush), I Can't Stand It* and *You Held My Hand* .... Reinforced RIVET 1212
08/08/1992	57	1		RAINBOW PEOPLE .... Reinforced RIVET 1221

MANKEY UK producer Andy Manston.

16/11/1996	74	1		BELIEVE IN ME Contains a sample of Yazoo's *Situation* .... Frisky DISKY 3

MANKIND UK studio group assembled to record a cover version of the theme to the TV series *Dr Who*.

25/11/1978	25	12		DR WHO .... Pinnacle PIN 71

AIMEE MANN US singer/songwriter (born 9/8/1960, Richmond, VA) who was with punk group Young Snakes before leading 'Til Tuesday. She went solo in 1990 and married singer Michael Penn (brother of actors Sean, Christopher and Eileen Penn) in December 1997.

31/10/1987	42	3		TIME STAND STILL **RUSH WITH AIMEE MANN** .... Vertigo RUSH 13
28/08/1993	55	2		I SHOULD'VE KNOWN .... Imago 72787250437
20/11/1993	47	2		STUPID THING .... Imago 74321174227
05/03/1994	45	2		I SHOULD'VE KNOWN Re-issue of Imago 72787250437 .... Imago 72787250602

JOHNNY MANN SINGERS US choir led by the Joey Bishop Show musical director (born 30/8/1928, Baltimore, MD).

12/07/1967	6	13		**UP, UP AND AWAY** .... Liberty LIB 55972

MANSUN UK group formed in Chester in 1995 by Paul Draper (born 26/9/1972, Liverpool, guitar/vocals), Stove King (born 8/1/1974, Ellesmere Port, bass) and Dominic Chad (born 5/6/1973, Cheltenham, guitar/vocals) as Grey Lantern, later changing their name to A Man Called Sun. Discovering a group named A Man Called Adam, the name was shortened to Mansun (their debut release listed their name as Manson, which had the estate of Charles Manson threatening legal action). Andie Rathbone (born 8/9/1971, drums) joined in 1996. Technically all of their hits have been EPs, numbered *One* through to *Fourteen*.

06/04/1996	37	2		ONE EP Tracks on EP: *Egg Shaped Fred, Ski Jump Nose, Lemonade Secret Drinker* and *Thief (& Reprise)* .... Parlophone CDR 6430
15/06/1996	32	2		TWO EP Tracks on EP: *Take It Easy Chicken, Drastic Sturgeon, The Greatest Pain* and *Moronica* .... Parlophone CDR 6437
21/09/1996	19	3		THREE EP Tracks on EP: *An Open Letter To The Lyrical Trainspotter, No One Knows Us* and *Things Keep Falling Off Buildings*. The EP was also known as *Stripper Vicar* .... Parlophone CDR 6447
07/12/1996	15	4		WIDE OPEN SPACE .... Parlophone CDR 6453
15/02/1997	9	5		**SHE MAKES MY NOSE BLEED** .... Parlophone CDR 6458
10/05/1997	15	3		TAXLOSS .... Parlophone CDRS 6465
18/10/1997	10	3		**CLOSED FOR BUSINESS** .... Parlophone CDR 6482
11/07/1998	7	4		LEGACY EP Tracks on EP 1: *Legacy, I Can't Afford To Die, Spasm Of Identity* and *Check Under The Bed*. Tracks on EP 2: *Legazcy, Wide Open Space, GSOH* and *Face In The Crowd* .... Parlophone CDR 6497
05/09/1998	13	3		BEING A GIRL (PART ONE) EP Tracks on EP: *I Care, Been Here Before, Hideout* and *Railing* .... Parlophone CDR 6503
07/11/1998	27	2		NEGATIVE .... Parlophone CDR 6508
13/02/1999	16	3		SIX .... Parlophone CDRS 6511
12/08/2000	8	6		**I CAN ONLY DISAPPOINT U** .... Parlophone CDRS 6544
18/11/2000	23	2		ELECTRIC MAN .... Parlophone CDRS 6550
10/02/2001	28	2		FOOL .... Parlophone CDRS 6553
02/10/2004	55	1		SLIPPING AWAY .... Parlophone R 6650

O Silver disc ● Gold disc ✪ Platinum disc (additional platinum units are indicated by a figure following the symbol) ◎ Singles released prior to 1973 that are known to have sold over 1 million copies in the UK

MANTOVANI
UK orchestra leader (born Annunzio Paolo Mantovani, 15/11/1905, Venice, Italy) who moved to England with his parents in 1921. He formed his own orchestra in the early 1930s, had his first US hit in 1935 and was still in the album charts in the 1970s. He was given the Ivor Novello Oustanding Personal Services to Popular Music Award in 1956. He died in Kent on 29/3/1980. He has a star on the Hollywood Walk of Fame.

19/12/1952	6	3	**WHITE CHRISTMAS**	Decca F 10017
29/05/1953	❶¹	23	**THE SONG FROM MOULIN ROUGE**	Decca F 10094
23/10/1953	2	18	**SWEDISH RHAPSODY**	Decca F 10168
11/02/1955	16	4	LONELY BALLERINA	Decca F 10395
25/11/1955	7	11	**WHEN YOU LOSE THE ONE YOU LOVE** DAVID WHITFIELD WITH CHORUS AND MANTOVANI AND HIS ORCHESTRA	Decca F 10627
31/05/1957	20	4	AROUND THE WORLD Featured in the 1956 film *Around The World In 80 Days*	Decca F 10888
14/02/1958	22	3	CRY MY HEART DAVID WHITFIELD WITH CHORUS AND MANTOVANI AND HIS ORCHESTRA	Decca F 10978

MANTRONIX
US rap duo formed in New York by songwriters/producers Curtis Mantronik (born Kurtis Kahleel, 4/9/1965, Jamaica) and MC Tee (born Tooure Embden). They signed with Sleeping Bag Records in 1985. Embden joined the US Air Force in 1989 and was replaced by Bryce Wilson and DJ Dee. Wilson later formed Groove Theory. Mantronix disbanded in 1992, Kahleel returning as Kurtis Mantronik. Wondress is US singer Wondress Hutchinson.

22/02/1986	55	4	LADIES	10 TEN 116
17/05/1986	34	6	BASSLINE	10 TEN 118
07/02/1987	40	6	WHO IS IT	10 TEN 137
04/07/1987	46	4	SCREAM (PRIMAL SCREAM)	10 TEN 169
30/01/1988	61	2	SING A SONG (BREAK IT DOWN)	10 TEN 206
12/03/1988	72	2	SIMPLE SIMON (YOU GOTTA REGARD)	10 TEN 217
06/01/1990	4	11 ○	**GOT TO HAVE YOUR LOVE**	Capitol CL 559
12/05/1990	10	7	**TAKE YOUR TIME** This and above single credited to MANTRONIX FEATURING WONDRESS	Capitol CL 573
02/03/1991	22	5	DON'T GO MESSIN' WITH MY HEART	Capitol CL 608
22/06/1991	59	1	STEP TO ME (DO ME)	Capitol CL 613
15/08/1998	43	1	STRICTLY BUSINESS MANTRONIX VS EPMD Contains a sample of Eric Clapton's *I Shot The Sheriff*	Parlophone CDR 6502
09/11/2002	71	1	77 STRINGS	Southern Fried ECB 35
28/06/2003	16	4	HOW DID YOU KNOW This and above single credited to KURTIS MANTRONIK PRESENTS CHAMONIX *How Did You Know* is the same song as *77 Strings* with a vocal added by singer Miriam Gray	Southern Fried ECB 43CDS

MANUEL AND HIS MUSIC OF THE MOUNTAINS
UK orchestra leader (born Geoff Love, 4/9/1917, Todmorden) who debuted on radio in 1937, forming his own band in 1955 for the TV show *On The Town*. He first began recording as Manuel & His Music Of The Mountains in 1959 and later became a much-in-demand orchestra leader and arranger for artists such as Russ Conway, Connie Francis, Judy Garland and Frankie Vaughan, both in live concerts and on record. He died on 8/7/1991.

28/08/1959	22	9	THE HONEYMOON SONG	Columbia DB 4323
13/10/1960	29	10	NEVER ON SUNDAY	Columbia DB 4515
13/10/1966	42	2	SOMEWHERE MY LOVE	Columbia DB 7969
31/01/1976	3	10 ○	**RODRIGO'S GUITAR CONCERTO DE ARANJUEZ (THEME FROM 2ND MOVEMENT)** Topped the charts for three hours before it was noticed that a computer breakdown had occurred and the chart was re-calculated	EMI 2383

ROOTS MANUVA
UK rapper Rodney Hylton Smith. He won the 1999 MOBO Award for Best Hip Hop Act.

11/12/1999	28	3	DUSTED LEFTFIELD/ROOTS MANUVA	Hard Hands HAND 058CD1
04/08/2001	45	2	WITNESS (1 HOPE)	Big Dada BDCDS 022
20/10/2001	53	1	DREAMY DAYS	Big Dada BDCDS 033
08/05/2004	65	1	OH YOU WANT MORE TY FEATURING ROOTS MANUVA	Big Dada BDCDS 066

MARATHON
German/UK vocal/instrumental group formed by Thomas Fehlmann who also recorded as Schizophrenia.

25/01/1992	36	3	MOVIN'	10 TEN 395

MARAUDERS
UK group formed in Stoke-on-Trent by Bryn Martin (guitar), Danny Davis (guitar), Chris Renshaw (guitar), Kenny Sherratt (bass) and Barry Sargent (drums).

08/08/1963	43	4	THAT'S WHAT I WANT	Decca F 11695

MARBLES
UK duo formed by the Bee Gees' cousin Graham Bonnet (born 12/12/1947, Skegness) as lead vocalist and Trevor Gordon. The Bee Gees wrote and produced both hits, and Bonnet went on to become lead vocalist with Rainbow.

25/09/1968	5	12	**ONLY ONE WOMAN**	Polydor 56 272
26/03/1969	28	6	THE WALLS FELL DOWN	Polydor 56 310

MARC AND THE MAMBAS – see MARC ALMOND

MARC ET CLAUDE
German production group formed by Marc Romboy, Klaus Derichs and Jurgen Driessen. The trio also run the Alphabet City, Go For It and Slot Machine labels.

21/11/1998	28	3	LA	Positiva CDTIV 104
22/07/2000	12	7	I NEED YOUR LOVIN' (LIKE THE SUNSHINE) Contains a sample of The Korgis' *Everybody's Got To Learn Sometime*	Positiva CDTIV 136
06/04/2002	29	3	TREMBLE	Positiva CDTIV 170
19/04/2003	37	2	LOVING YOU '03	Positiva CDTIV 190

❶⁹ Number of weeks single topped the UK chart ↑ Entered the UK chart at #1 ▲⁹ Number of weeks single topped the US chart

505

MARCELS US R&B vocal group formed in Pittsburgh, PA by Cornelius 'Nini' Harp, Ronald 'Bingo' Mundy, Gene Bricker, Dick Knauss and Fred Johnson. Bricker and Knauss left in 1961 and were replaced by Walt Maddox and Allen Johnson (Fred's brother). Allen Johnson died from cancer on 28/9/1995. The group took their name from a hairstyle.

13/04/1961	❶²	13	**BLUE MOON** ▲³ Featured in the 1982 film *An American Werewolf In London*	Pye International 7N 25073
08/06/1961	46	4	SUMMERTIME	Pye International 7N 25083

LITTLE PEGGY MARCH US singer (born Margaret Battavio, 7/3/1948, Lansdale, PA) who moved to Germany in 1969. With her debut US hit *I Will Follow Him* at fifteen, she was the youngest female to top the US charts. Her *If You Love Me*, a vocal version of an instrumental by Raymond Lefevre, was a Northern Soul hit.

12/09/1963	29	7	HELLO HEARTACHE GOODBYE LOVE	RCA 1362

MARCO POLO Italian instrumental/production duo Marco Ceceve and Maurizo Pavesi.

08/04/1995	65	1	A PRAYER TO THE MUSIC	Hi-Life HICD 7

MARCY PLAYGROUND US rock group formed by John Wozniak (born 19/1/1971, guitar/vocals), Dylan Keefe (born 11/4/1970, bass) and Dan Rieser (drums). The group was formed at the Marcy Open School in Minneapolis, MN, hence their name.

18/04/1998	29	3	SEX AND CANDY	EMI CDEM 508

MARDI GRAS UK studio group assembled to record a cover version of Marvin Gaye's hit.

05/08/1972	19	9	TOO BUSY THINKING 'BOUT MY BABY	Bell 1226

MARIA – see **MARIA NAYLER**

KELLY MARIE UK singer (born Jacqueline McKinnon, 23/10/1957, Paisley, Scotland) who was first known as Keli Brown, winning the TV talent show *Opportunity Knocks* on four occasions. Her debut hit was penned by Ray Dorset, lead vocalist with Mungo Jerry.

02/08/1980	❶²	16	● **FEELS LIKE I'M IN LOVE** Originally released in February 1979 and failed to chart.	Calibre Plus 1
18/10/1980	21	7	LOVING JUST FOR FUN	Calibre Plus 4
07/02/1981	22	10	HOT LOVE	Calibre Plus 5
30/05/1981	51	3	LOVE TRIAL	Calibre Plus 7

ROSE MARIE Irish singer (born 1962) who was a hairdresser when she got her break on TV talent shows *New Faces* and *Search For A Star*.

19/11/1983	63	5	WHEN I LEAVE THE WORLD BEHIND	A1 284

TEENA MARIE US singer (born Mary Christine Brockett, 5/3/1956, Santa Monica, CA) who was one of the few white funk acts to record for Motown. She later recorded for Epic and worked with Soul II Soul 's Jazzie B.

07/07/1979	43	8	I'M A SUCKER FOR YOUR LOVE **TEENA MARIE, CO-LEAD VOCALS RICK JAMES**	Motown TMG 1146
31/05/1980	6	10	**BEHIND THE GROOVE**	Motown TMG 1185
11/10/1980	28	6	I NEED YOUR LOVIN'	Motown TMG 1203
26/03/1988	74	2	OOO LA LA LA	Epic 6514237
10/11/1990	69	2	SINCE DAY ONE	Epic 6564297

MARILLION UK rock group formed in Aylesbury in 1978 by Doug Irvine (bass), Mick Pointer (born 22/7/1956, drums) and Steve Rothery (born 25/11/1959, Brampton, guitar) as Silmarillion (title of a novel by JRR Tolkien). They shortened their name in 1979, adding keyboard player Brian Jelliman. Irvine left in 1980, shortly before Fish (born Derek Dick, 25/4/1958, Dalkeith, Midlothian, vocals) and Diz Minnitt (bass) joined. Fish remained the focal point during more changes. They signed with EMI in 1982. Fish later recorded solo.

20/11/1982	60	2	MARKET SQUARE HEROES	EMI 5351
12/02/1983	35	4	HE KNOWS YOU KNOW	EMI 5362
16/04/1983	53	6	MARKET SQUARE HEROES	EMI 5351
18/06/1983	16	5	GARDEN PARTY	EMI 5393
11/02/1984	29	4	PUNCH AND JUDY	EMI MARIL 1
12/05/1984	22	5	ASSASSING	EMI MARIL 2
18/05/1985	2	14	○ **KAYLEIGH**	EMI MARIL 3
07/09/1985	5	9	**LAVENDER**	EMI MARIL 4
30/11/1985	29	6	HEART OF LOTHIAN	EMI MARIL 5
23/05/1987	6	5	**INCOMMUNICADO**	EMI MARIL 6
25/07/1987	22	5	SUGAR MICE	EMI MARIL 7
07/11/1987	22	4	WARM WET CIRCLES	EMI MARIL 8
26/11/1988	24	3	FREAKS (LIVE)	EMI MARIL 9
09/09/1989	30	3	HOOKS IN YOU	Capitol MARIL 10
09/12/1989	53	2	UNINVITED GUEST	EMI MARIL 11
14/04/1990	34	2	EASTER	EMI MARIL 12
08/06/1991	34	4	COVER MY EYES (PAIN AND HEAVEN)	EMI MARIL 13
03/08/1991	33	2	NO ONE CAN.	EMI MARIL 14
05/10/1991	34	2	DRY LAND	EMI MARIL 15
23/05/1992	17	3	SYMPATHY	EMI MARIL 16
01/08/1992	26	4	NO ONE CAN Re-issue of EMI MARIL 14.	EMI MARIL 17
26/03/1994	30	2	THE HOLLOW MAN	EMI CDEMS 307
07/05/1994	53	3	ALONE AGAIN IN THE LAP OF LUXURY	EMI CDEMS 318

10/06/1995	29	2		BEAUTIFUL	EMI CDMARILS 18
01/05/2004	7	2		**YOU'RE GONE** Single was funded by donations of £10 each by fans via the internet.	Intact CXINTACT1
24/07/2004	16	2		DON'T HURT YOURSELF	Intact CXINTACT2

MARILYN
UK singer (born Peter Robinson, 3/11/1962, Kingston, Jamaica) who was a protégé of Boy George.

05/11/1983	4	12	O	**CALLING YOUR NAME**	Mercury MAZ 1
11/02/1984	31	6		CRY AND BE FREE	Mercury MAZ 2
21/04/1984	40	7		YOU DON'T LOVE ME	Mercury MAZ 3
13/04/1985	70	1		BABY U LEFT ME (IN THE COLD)	Mercury MAZ 4

MARILYN MANSON
US singer (born Brian Warner, 5/1/1969, Canton, OH) whose backing group comprises John 5 (born John Lowery, guitar), Twiggy Ramirez (born Jeordie White, 20/6/1972, bass), Madonna Wayne Gacy (born Stephen Bier, keyboards) and Ginger Fish (born Kenny Wilson, drums). Previous members included Olivia Newton-Bundy (born Brian Tutinuck, bass), Zsa Zsa Speck (born Perry Pandrea, keyboards), Zim Zum (born Michael Linton, guitar), Daisy Berkowitz (born Scott Mitchell, 28/4/1968, guitar) and Sara Lee Lucas (born Freddy Streithorst, drums).

07/06/1997	18	3		THE BEAUTIFUL PEOPLE	Interscope IND 95541
20/09/1997	28	2		TOURNIQUET	Interscope IND 95552
21/11/1998	12	3		THE DOPE SHOW	Interscope IND 95610
26/06/1999	23	2		ROCK IS DEAD	Maverick W 486CD
18/11/2000	12	3		DISPOSABLE TEENS	Nothing 4974372
03/03/2001	24	3		THE FIGHT SONG Featured in the 2001 film *Mean Machine*	Interscope 4974912
15/09/2001	34	2		THE NOBODIES	Interscope IND 97604
30/03/2002	5	11		**TAINTED LOVE** Featured in the 2002 film *Not Another Teen Movie*	Maverick W 579CD1
14/06/2003	13	6		MOBSCENE	Interscope 9807726
13/09/2003	29	2		THIS IS THE NEW SHIT	Interscope 9810793
16/10/2004	13	5		PERSONAL JESUS	Interscope 9864166

MARINO MARINI AND HIS QUARTET
Italian singer/pianist (born 11/5/1924, Seggiano) who formed his first quartet in 1954 with Ruggero Cori (bass/vocals), Tony 'Toto' Savio (guitar) and Sergio (drums). Marini ded in 1992.

03/10/1958	13	7		VOLARE	Durium DC 16632
10/10/1958	2	14		**COME PRIMA**	Durium DC 16632
20/03/1959	24	2		CIAO CIAO BAMBINA	Durium DC 16636

MARIO
US singer (born Mario Barrett, 1987, Baltimore, MD) who was signed by J Records at the age of fourteen.

12/04/2003	18	4		JUST A FRIEND	J Records 82876508082
12/07/2003	28	2		C'MON Contains samples of Lyn Collins' *Think (About It)* and Rob Base & DJ E-Z Rock's *It Takes Two*	J Records 82876528282

MARION
UK rock group formed by Jamie Harding (vocals), Anthony Grantham (guitar), Phil Cunningham (guitar), Julian Phillips (bass) and Murad Mousa (drums).

25/02/1995	53	1		SLEEP	London LONCD 360
13/05/1995	57	1		TOYS FOR BOYS	London LONCD 366
21/10/1995	37	2		LET'S ALL GO TOGETHER	London LONCD 371
03/02/1996	29	2		TIME	London LONCD 377
30/03/1996	17	2		SLEEP (REMIX)	London LONCD 381
07/03/1998	45	1		MIYAKO HIEAWAY	London LONCD 403

MARK' OH
German producer Marko Albrecht.

06/05/1995	24	3		TEARS DON'T LIE	Systematic SYSCD 9

PIGMEAT MARKHAM
US singer (born Dewey Markham, 18/4/1906, Durham, NC) who was better known as a stage and TV comedian, with his one hit single originating as a catchphrase in the *Rowan And Martin Laugh-In*. He died on 13/12/1981.

17/07/1968	19	8		HERE COMES THE JUDGE	Chess CRS 8077

BIZ MARKIE
US rapper (born Marcel Hall, Harlem, 8/4/1964, NYC).

26/05/1990	55	2		JUST A FRIEND Rap version of Freddie Scott's *(You) Got What I Need*	Cold Chillin' W 9823

YANNIS MARKOPOULOS
Greek orchestra leader/composer (born 1939, Heraclion, Crete).

17/12/1977	11	8		WHO PAYS THE FERRYMAN Theme to the TV series of the same name	BBC RESL 51

GUY MARKS
US singer/comedian/impressionist (born Mario Scarpa, 1923, Philadelphia, PA) who appeared on numerous TV series. He died on 28/11/1987.

13/05/1978	25	8		LOVING YOU HAS MADE ME BANANAS	ABC 4211

MARKSMEN
– see HOUSTON WELLS AND THE MARKSMEN

MARKY MARK AND THE FUNKY BUNCH
US singer (born Mark Wahlberg, 5/6/1971, Boston, MA) and younger brother of New Kid On The Block Donnie Wahlberg. The Funky Bunch are led by DJ Terry Yancey. Loleatta Holloway had been a solo singer on Salsoul. Mark Wahlberg later became an actor, appearing in the films *Boogie Nights* (1998) and the remake of *Planet Of The Apes* (2001).

❶⁹ Number of weeks single topped the UK chart   ↑ Entered the UK chart at #1   ▲⁹ Number of weeks single topped the US chart

507

31/08/1991	14	7		GOOD VIBRATIONS ▲¹ MARKY MARK AND THE FUNKY BUNCH FEATURING LOLEATTA HOLLOWAY Contains a sample of Loleatta Holloway's *Love Sensation*. Featured in the 2000 film *The Replacements*	Interscope A 8764
02/11/1991	42	3		WILDSIDE	Interscope A 8674
12/12/1992	54	4		YOU GOTTA BELIEVE	Interscope A 8680

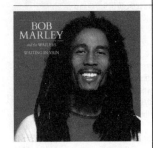

BOB MARLEY AND THE WAILERS Jamaican singer (born 6/2/1945, St Ann's, although his passport had date of birth as 6/4/1945) who first recorded in 1961. He formed the Wailin' Wailers in 1964 with Peter Tosh (born Winston McIntosh, 19/10/1944, Westmoreland), Bunny Livingston (born Neville O'Riley, 10/4/1947, Kingston, who changed his name again to Bunny Wailer), Junior Braithwaite, Cherry Smith and Beverley Kelso. Marley left Jamaica in 1966, returning in 1967 to set up the Wailin' Soul label, reuniting with Tosh and Wailer. He signed with Island in 1972, adding Aston 'Family Man' Barrett and his brother Carlton to the rhythm section. Tosh and Wailer left in 1974. Eric Clapton's cover of *I Shot The Sheriff* attracted attention to Marley, who became reggae's biggest star. He survived an assassination attempt in December 1976 (although he, his wife Rita and manager Don Taylor all suffered gunshot wounds, prompting Marley to leave Jamaica for eighteen months) but died from cancer on 11/5/1981. Pete Tosh was shot to death during a robbery at his home on 11/9/1987. (Tosh laughed as three men broke into his house, for which he was viciously beaten. When the intruders found insufficient valuables in the house, they shot three people through the back of the head, including Tosh. It was later suggested that the robbery was carried out merely to cover up a feud.) Carlton Barrett was shot to death on 17/4/1987 by a gunman hired by his wife and her lover. Junior Braithwaite was shot and killed by intruders in his home in 1999. Bob Marley was inducted into the Rock & Roll Hall of Fame in 1994. Pete Tosh won the 1987 Grammy Award for Best Reggae Recording for *No Nuclear War*. Bunny Wailer won the 1990 award for *Time Will Tell – A Tribute To Bob Marley,* the 1994 award for *Crucial Roots Classics* and the 1996 award for *Hall Of Fame – A Tribute To Bob Marley's 50th Anniversary,* all in the same category. Bob Marley has a star on the Hollywood Walk of Fame and was inducted into the UK Music Hall of Fame in 2004, one of its first inductees.

27/09/1975	22	7		NO WOMAN NO CRY Featured in the 2000 film *The Perfect Storm*	Island WIP 6244
25/06/1977	14	9		EXODUS	Island WIP 6390
10/09/1977	27	6		WAITING IN VAIN	Island WIP 6402
10/12/1977	9	12	○	JAMMING/PUNKY REGGAE PARTY	Island WIP 6410
25/02/1978	9	9		IS THIS LOVE Featured in the films *In The Name Of The Father* (1993) and *Lake Placid* (1999)	Island WIP 6420
10/06/1978	21	10		SATISFY MY SOUL	Island WIP 6440
20/10/1979	56	4		SO MUCH TROUBLE IN THE WORLD	Island WIP 6510
21/06/1980	5	12		COULD YOU BE LOVED	Island WIP 6610
13/09/1980	17	9		THREE LITTLE BIRDS	Island WIP 6641
13/06/1981	8	11	○	NO WOMAN NO CRY	Island WIP 6244
07/05/1983	4	12		BUFFALO SOLDIER	Island/Tuff Gong IS 180
21/04/1984	5	11		ONE LOVE – PEOPLE GET READY	Island IS 169
23/06/1984	31	7		WAITING IN VAIN Re-issue of Island WIP 6402	Island IS 180
08/12/1984	71	2		COULD YOU BE LOVED Re-issue of Island WIP 6610	Island IS 210
18/05/1991	42	3		ONE LOVE – PEOPLE GET READY Re-issue of Island IS 169	Tuff Gong TGX 1
19/09/1992	5	9		IRON LION ZION	Tuff Gong TGX 2
28/11/1992	42	4		WHY SHOULD I/EXODUS	Tuff Gong TFX 3
20/05/1995	17	4		KEEP ON MOVING	Tuff Gong TGXCD 4
08/06/1996	42	1		WHAT GOES AROUND COMES AROUND	Anansi ANACS 002
25/09/1999	3	10	○	SUN IS SHINING BOB MARLEY VERSUS FUNKSTAR DELUXE	Club Tools 0066895 CLU
11/12/1999	15	7		TURN YOUR LIGHTS DOWN LOW BOB MARLEY FEATURING LAURYN HILL Featured in the 1999 film *The Best Man*	Columbia 6684362
22/01/2000	11	6		RAINBOW COUNTRY BOB MARLEY VERSUS FUNKSTAR DELUXE	Club Tools 0067225 CLU

ZIGGY MARLEY AND THE MELODY MAKERS Jamaican family group formed by the children of Bob Marley – David 'Ziggy' (born 17/10/1968), Stephen, Cedella and Sharon Marley. Ziggy is married to singer Lauryn Hill. They have three Grammy Awards: Best Reggae Recording in 1988 for *Conscious Party,* Best Reggae Recording in 1989 for *One Bright Day* and Best Reggae Album in 1997 for *Fallen Is Babylon*.

11/06/1988	22	10		TOMORROW PEOPLE	Virgin VS 1049
23/09/1989	65	1		LOOK WHO'S DANCING	Virgin America VUS 5

LENE MARLIN Norwegian singer/songwriter (born Lene Marlin Pederson, 17/8/1980, Tromso) who began playing guitar at the age of fifteen. She was named Best Nordic Act at the 1999 MTV Europe Music Awards.

11/03/2000	5	11	○	SITTING DOWN HERE	Virgin DINSD 183
16/09/2000	13	6		UNFORGIVABLE SINNER	Virgin DINSCX 202
13/01/2001	31	2		WHERE I'M HEADED	Virgin DINSD 196
04/10/2003	59	1		YOU WEREN'T THERE	Virgin DINSD 262

MARLO UK vocal/instrumental group formed by Ben Chawner, Mark Eyden, Matthew Johnson and Dean Lanza.

24/07/1999	56	1		HOW DO I KNOW?	Polydor 5611362

MARLY Danish female singer (born 1985) discovered by production duo Jarob Johansen and Morten Lambertsen.

28/08/2004	23	2		YOU NEVER KNOW	All Around The World CDGLOBE 363

MARMALADE UK group formed in Glasgow in 1961 by Patrick Fairley (born 14/4/1946, Glasgow, guitar), Junior Campbell (born Wullie Campbell Jr, 31/5/1947, Glasgow, guitar/piano/vocals), Dean Ford (born Thomas McAleese, 5/9/1946, Glasgow, lead vocals), Raymond Duffy (drums) and Graham Knight (born 8/12/1946, Glasgow, bass) as Dean Ford And The Gaylords. They recorded for Columbia in 1965 with little success, re-forming and renaming the group in 1966, bringing in Alan Whitehead on drums (born 24/7/1946, Oswestry). Campbell quit in 1971 to record solo and was replaced by Hugh Nicholson, a former member of The Poets.

DATE	POS	WKS	BPI	SINGLE TITLE	LABEL & NUMBER
22/05/1968	6	13		**LOVIN' THINGS**	CBS 3412
23/10/1968	30	5		WAIT FOR ME MARIANNE	CBS 3708
04/12/1968	❶³	20		**OB-LA-DI OB-LA-DA** Reclaimed #1 position on 15/1/1969	CBS 3892
11/06/1969	9	13		**BABY MAKE IT SOON**	CBS 4287
20/12/1969	3	12		**REFLECTIONS OF MY LIFE**	Decca F 12982
18/07/1970	3	14		**RAINBOW**	Decca F 13035
27/03/1971	15	11		MY LITTLE ONE	Decca F 13135
04/09/1971	6	11		**COUSIN NORMAN**	Decca F 13214
27/11/1971	35	8		BACK ON THE ROAD	Decca F 13251
01/04/1972	6	12		**RADANCER**	Decca F 13297
21/02/1976	9	11		**FALLING APART AT THE SEAMS**	Target TGT 105

MARMION Spanish/Dutch instrumental/production duo Marcos Lopez and Mijk Van Dijk.

DATE	POS	WKS	BPI	SINGLE TITLE	LABEL & NUMBER
18/05/1996	53	1		SCHONEBERG	Hooj Choons HOOJCD 43
14/02/1998	56	1		SCHONEBERG (REMIX)	ffrr FCD 324

MAROON 5 US group formed in Los Angeles, CA in 1999 by Adam Levine (guitar/vocals), James Valentine (guitar), Jesse Carmichael (keyboards), Mickey Madden (bass) and Ryan Dusick (drums). They were named Best New Act at the 2004 MTV Europe Music Awards.

DATE	POS	WKS	BPI	SINGLE TITLE	LABEL & NUMBER
31/01/2004	13	7		HARDER TO BREATHE	J Records 82876566922
01/05/2004	3	14		**THIS LOVE**	J Records 82876608452
04/09/2004	4	10		**SHE WILL BE LOVED**	J Records 82876643632
18/12/2004	27	2+		SUNDAY MORNING	J Records 82876668042

JOHNNY MARR – see BILLY BRAGG AND KIRSTY MacCOLL

MARRADONA UK vocal/instrumental group formed by Richie Malone and Scott Rouse.

DATE	POS	WKS	BPI	SINGLE TITLE	LABEL & NUMBER
26/02/1994	38	3		OUT OF MY HEAD	Peach PWCD 282
26/07/1997	39	2		OUT OF MY HEAD (REMIX)	Soopa SPCD 1

M/A/R/R/S UK group formed by brothers Martyn and Steve Young and Alex and Rudi Kane, from 4AD bands Colourbox and A R Kane. The group also featured mixers Chris CJ Mackintosh and DJ Dave Dorrell. Their hit was the subject of an injunction that held up distribution for five days while clearance was sought for the use of three seconds of the Stock Aitken Waterman hit *Roadblock*.

DATE	POS	WKS	BPI	SINGLE TITLE	LABEL & NUMBER
05/09/1987	❶²	14	○	**PUMP UP THE VOLUME/ANITINA (THE FIRST TIME I SEE SHE DANCE)** A-side featured in the films *My Stepmother Is An Alien* (1988), *Bright Lights, Big City* (1988) and *The Replacements* (2000)	4AD AD 70

MARS VOLTA US group formed in El Paso, TX in 2001 by Cedric 'Bixler' Zavala (vocals), Omar Rodriguez-Lopez (guitar), Juan Alderate (bass), Isaiah Owens (keyboards) and Jon Theodore (drums). Bixler and Rodriguez had previously been in At The Drive In.

DATE	POS	WKS	BPI	SINGLE TITLE	LABEL & NUMBER
11/10/2003	42	2		INERTIATIC ESP	Universal MCSTD 40332
13/03/2004	41	1		TELEVATORS	Universal MCSTD 40352

GERRY MARSDEN – see GERRY AND THE PACEMAKERS

MATTHEW MARSDEN UK singer (born 3/3/1972, Walsall) who played Chris Collins in TV's *Coronation Street*.

DATE	POS	WKS	BPI	SINGLE TITLE	LABEL & NUMBER
11/07/1998	13	7		THE HEART'S LONE DESIRE	Columbia 6661152
07/11/1998	24	3		SHE'S GONE MATTHEW MARSDEN FEATURING DESTINY'S CHILD	Columbia 6664915

KYM MARSH UK singer (born 13/6/1976, Wiston) famous for winning a place in the group Hear'say on the TV show *Popstars*. She had previously sung with Solar Stone and left Hear'Say in January 2002 to go solo.

DATE	POS	WKS	BPI	SINGLE TITLE	LABEL & NUMBER
19/04/2003	2	12		**CRY**	Island MCSXD 40314
19/07/2003	10	7		**COME ON OVER**	Universal MCSXD 40323
08/11/2003	35	2		**SENTIMENTAL**	Universal MCSTD 40340

STEVIE MARSH UK female singer.

DATE	POS	WKS	BPI	SINGLE TITLE	LABEL & NUMBER
04/12/1959	24	4		IF YOU WERE THE ONLY BOY IN THE WORLD	Decca F 11181

MARSHA – see SHAGGY

JOY MARSHALL UK singer who also sang with the Gordon Beck Trio.

DATE	POS	WKS	BPI	SINGLE TITLE	LABEL & NUMBER
23/06/1966	34	2		THE MORE I SEE YOU	Decca F 12422

KEITH MARSHALL UK singer/guitarist who was in Hello from their formation in 1971, going solo when they disbanded in 1979.

DATE	POS	WKS	BPI	SINGLE TITLE	LABEL & NUMBER
04/04/1981	12	10		ONLY CRYING	Arrival PIK 2

LOUISE CLARE MARSHALL – see SILICONE SOUL FEATURING LOUISE CLARE MARSHALL

WAYNE MARSHALL UK singer.

DATE	POS	WKS	BPI	SINGLE TITLE	LABEL & NUMBER
01/10/1994	29	3		OOH AAH (G-SPOT)	Soultown SOULCDS 322

❶⁹ Number of weeks single topped the UK chart ↑ Entered the UK chart at #1 ▲⁹ Number of weeks single topped the US chart

509

03/06/1995	58	1		SPIRIT Featured in the 1995 film *Spirit Of The Pharoah*	Soultown SOULCDS 00352
24/02/1996	40	2		NEVER KNEW LOVE LIKE THIS PAULINE HENRY FEATURING WAYNE MARSHALL	Sony S2 6629382
07/12/1996	50	1		G SPOT (REMIX)	MBA INTER 9006

MARSHALL HAIN
UK duo of keyboard player/songwriter Julian Marshall and vocalist Kit Hain (born 15/12/1956, Cobham). Marshall later joined Deborah Berg in Eye To Eye, Hain going solo before moving to the US to become a successful songwriter.

03/06/1978	3	15	●	**DANCING IN THE CITY**	Harvest HAR 5157
14/10/1978	39	4		COMING HOME	Harvest HAR 5168

MARTAY FEATURING ZZ TOP
UK singer/rapper (born Melone McKenzy, 1977, Manchester) who is also a model under her real name.

16/10/1999	28	2		GIMME ALL YOUR LOVIN' 2000	Riverhorse RIVHCD 2

LENA MARTELL
UK singer (born Helen Thomson, Glasgow) who was in Billy McGregor's band before going solo. Her records were produced by manager George Elrick.

29/09/1979	❶³	18	●	**ONE DAY AT A TIME**	Pye 7N 46021

MARTHA AND THE MUFFINS
Canadian group formed by Martha Johnson (keyboards), Carl Finkle (bass), Mark Gane (guitar), Tim Gane (drums), Andy Haas (saxophone) and Martha Ladly (guitar/keyboards/trombone). They disbanded in 1982, Johnson and Gane re-forming as M+M in 1984.

01/03/1980	10	10		**ECHO BEACH**	Dindisc DIN 9

MARTHA AND THE VANDELLAS – see MARTHA REEVES AND THE VANDELLAS

MARTIKA
US singer (born Marta Marrera, 18/5/1969, Whittier, CA) with Cuban parents who appeared as a child in the musical *Annie* and TV shows.

29/07/1989	5	11	○	**TOY SOLDIERS ▲²**	CBS 6550497
14/10/1989	7	14		I FEEL THE EARTH MOVE	CBS 6552947
13/01/1990	15	7		MORE THAN YOU KNOW	CBS 6555267
17/03/1990	59	3		WATER	CBS 6557317
17/08/1991	9	9		**LOVE...THY WILL BE DONE**	Columbia 6573137
30/11/1991	17	10		MARTIKA'S KITCHEN This and above single co-written by Prince and Martika	Columbia 6575687
22/02/1992	41	3		COLOURED KISSES	Columbia 6577097

BILLIE RAY MARTIN
German singer (born Birgit Dieckmann, Hamburg) who came to the UK in 1985 and was lead vocalist with Electribe 101 before going solo.

19/11/1994	38	3		YOUR LOVING ARMS	Magnet MAG 1028CD
20/05/1995	6	10		**YOUR LOVING ARMS (REMIX)**	Magnet MAG 1031CD
02/09/1995	29	2		RUNNING AROUND TOWN	Magnet MAG 1035CD
06/01/1996	29	3		IMITATION OF LIFE	Magnet MAG 1040CD
06/04/1996	66	1		SPACE OASIS	Magnet MAG 1042CD
21/08/1999	54	1		HONEY	React CDREACT 129

DEAN MARTIN
US singer/actor (born Dino Paul Crocetti, 7/6/1917, Steubenville, OH) who moved to California in 1937, singing in local clubs. Teamed with comedian Jerry Lewis in 1946, they made sixteen films together, by which time Martin was established as a star in his own right. He was one of the first artists on Frank Sinatra's Reprise label (as befitted one of the infamous 'Ratpack', a hard-living and hard-drinking group comprising Sinatra, Martin, Sammy Davis Jr and Peter Crawford). He died from cancer on 25/12/1995. He has three stars on the Hollywood Walk of Fame, for his contribution to recording, motion pictures and TV.

18/09/1953	5	8		**KISS**	Capitol CL 13893
22/01/1954	2	11		**THAT'S AMORE** Featured in the 1953 film *The Caddy* starring Dean Martin and the 1987 film *Moonstruck*	Capitol CL 14008
01/10/1954	6	7		**SWAY** Featured in the 2000 film *Beautiful People*	Capitol CL 14138
22/10/1954	15	6		HOW DO YOU SPEAK TO AN ANGEL	Capitol CL 14150
28/01/1955	5	10		**NAUGHTY LADY OF SHADY LANE**	Capitol CL 14226
04/02/1955	14	2		MAMBO ITALIANO	Capitol CL 14227
25/02/1955	3	9		**LET ME GO LOVER**	Capitol CL 14226
01/04/1955	6	8		**UNDER THE BRIDGES OF PARIS**	Capitol CL 14255
10/02/1956	❶⁴	16		**MEMORIES ARE MADE OF THIS ▲⁶**	Capitol CL 14523
02/03/1956	20	1		YOUNG AND FOOLISH	Capitol CL 14519
27/04/1956	21	3		INNAMORATA Featured in the 1955 film *Artists And Models* starring Dean Martin	Capitol CL 14507
22/03/1957	21	2		THE MAN WHO PLAYS THE MANDOLINO Featured in the 1957 film *Ten Thousand Bedrooms* starring Dean Martin	Capitol CL 14690
13/06/1958	2	22		**RETURN TO ME** Featured in the 1996 film *Striptease*	Capitol CL 14844
29/08/1958	2	14		**VOLARE**	Capitol CL 14910

27/08/1964	11	13		EVERYBODY LOVES SOMEBODY ▲1	Reprise R 20281
12/11/1964	42	4		THE DOOR IS STILL OPEN TO MY HEART	Reprise R 20307
05/02/1969	2	24		**GENTLE ON MY MIND**	Reprise R 23343
22/06/1996	43	2		THAT'S AMORE Re-issue of Capitol CL 14008	EMI Premier PRESCD 3
21/08/1999	66	1		SWAY Re-issue of Capitol CL 14138	Capitol CDSWAY 001

JUAN MARTIN Spanish classical guitarist who later worked with Gordon Giltrap.

| 28/01/1984 | 10 | 7 | | **LOVE THEME FROM 'THE THORN BIRDS'** Featured in the TV series The Thorn Birds | WEA X 9518 |

LINDA MARTIN Irish singer whose debut hit won the 1992 Eurovision Song Contest, beating the UK's entry by Michael Ball One Step Out Of Time into second place. She later became a judge on the Irish version of Popstars.

| 30/05/1992 | 59 | 2 | | WHY ME 1992 Eurovision Song Contest winner | Columbia 6581317 |

LUCI MARTIN — see ROMINA JOHNSON

MARILYN MARTIN — see PHIL COLLINS

RAY MARTIN UK orchestra leader (born 11/10/1918, Vienna, Austria) who moved to the UK in 1937, already an accomplished composer, author, arranger and musical director. After service in the British Army during World War II (in the Intelligence Corps, his fluency in German being useful), he formed a string orchestra and started recording in 1949. He died in South Africa on 7/2/1988.

14/11/1952	8	4		**BLUE TANGO**	Columbia DB 3051
20/11/1953	7	6		**CRYING IN THE CHAPEL** LEE LAWRENCE WITH RAY MARTIN AND HIS ORCHESTRA	Decca F 10177
04/12/1953	4	4		**SWEDISH RHAPSODY**	Columbia DB 3346
02/12/1955	14	4		SUDDENLY THERE'S A VALLEY LEE LAWRENCE WITH RAY MARTIN AND HIS ORCHESTRA	Columbia DB 3681
15/06/1956	24	3		CAROUSEL WALTZ	Columbia DB 3771

RICKY MARTIN Puerto Rican singer (born Enrique Martin Morales, 24/12/1971, Hato Rey) who was in the boy group Menudo before becoming an actor on Mexican TV and working on Broadway in Les Miserables. He was named Best Male at the 2000 MTV Europe Music Awards.

20/09/1997	6	6		**(UN, DOS, TRES) MARIA**	Columbia 6649595
11/07/1998	29	3		THE CUP OF LIFE Official song of the 1998 FIFA World Cup	Columbia 6661502
17/07/1999	❶3	17	✪	**LIVIN' LA VIDA LOCA** ↑ ▲5	Columbia 6676402
20/11/1999	12	9		SHAKE YOUR BON-BON	Columbia 6683412
29/04/2000	9	9		**PRIVATE EMOTION** RICKY MARTIN FEATURING MEJA	Columbia 6692692
04/11/2000	3	15	◯	**SHE BANGS**	Columbia 6705422
10/03/2001	4	12		**NOBODY WANTS TO BE LONELY** RICKY MARTIN WITH CHRISTINA AGUILERA	Columbia 6709462
28/07/2001	19	4		LOADED	Columbia 6714642

TONY MARTIN US singer (born Alvin Morris Jr, 25/12/1913, Oakland, CA) who was a saxophonist with Tom Gerun's band before singing solo in 1938. His 1936 film debut in The Farmer In The Dell was uncredited, his first credited role being in Banjo On My Knee (1936). He was married to actress/singer Alice Faye, then in 1948 to actress Cyd Charisse. After the Japanese attack on Pearl Harbor in December 1941 he enlisted, first in the navy and later in the army, singing with the Armed Air Forces Training Command Orchestra, thus serving all three services in one way or another. He was awarded a Bronze Star during the war, after which he returned to Hollywood, appearing in the 1946 film Till The Clouds Roll By. He has a star on the Hollywood Walk of Fame.

| 22/04/1955 | 6 | 13 | | **STRANGER IN PARADISE** | HMV B 10849 |
| 13/07/1956 | 2 | 15 | | **WALK HAND IN HAND** | HMV POP 222 |

VINCE MARTIN — see TARRIERS

WINK MARTINDALE US singer (born Winston Conrad Martindale, 4/12/1933, Jackson, TN) who was a DJ in 1950 and later a TV host. He also appeared in the 1958 film Let's Rock.

04/12/1959	18	8		DECK OF CARDS	London HLD 8962
18/04/1963	5	21		**DECK OF CARDS**	London HLD 8962
20/10/1973	22	12		DECK OF CARDS Re-issue of London HLD 8962	Dot 109

ALICE MARTINEAU UK singer (born 8/6/1972) who suffered from cystic fibrosis, a condition requiring heart, lung and kidney transplants. She died on 6/3/2003.

| 23/11/2002 | 45 | 1 | | IF I FALL | Epic 6732332 |

ANGIE MARTINEZ FEATURING LIL' MO US vocal duo Angie Martinez (born in Brooklyn, NYC) and Lil' Mo (born Cindy Levin, Queens, NYC). Martinez began her career as a radio DJ before launching a singing career.

| 15/02/2003 | 61 | 1 | | IF I COULD GO | Elektra E 7331CD |

AL MARTINO US singer (born Alfred Cini, 7/10/1927, Philadelphia, PA) who, encouraged by the success of boyhood friend Mario Lanza, won Arthur Godfrey's Talent Scouts competition in 1952. He appeared in the 1972 film The Godfather as singer Johnny Fontane.

14/11/1952	❶9	18		**HERE IN MY HEART** ↑ ▲3 Entered the chart at #1 in the first chart compiled	Capitol CL 13779
21/11/1952	9	1		**TAKE MY HEART**	Capitol CL 13769
30/01/1953	3	12		**NOW**	Capitol CL 13835
10/07/1953	10	5		**RACHEL**	Capitol CL 13879

❶9 Number of weeks single topped the UK chart ↑ Entered the UK chart at #1 ▲9 Number of weeks single topped the US chart

511

04/06/1954	4	16		WANTED .... Capitol CL 14128
01/10/1954	10	8		THE STORY OF TINA .... Capitol CL 14163
23/09/1955	19	3		THE MAN FROM LARAMIE .... Capitol CL 14343
31/03/1960	49	1		SUMMERTIME .... Top Rank JAR 312
29/08/1963	48	1		I LOVE YOU BECAUSE .... Capitol CL 15300
22/08/1970	49	1		SPANISH EYES .... Capitol CL 15430
14/07/1973	5	21		**SPANISH EYES** Originally written by Bert Kaempfert as *Moon Over Naples,* which was released in 1965. The lyrics for Martino's version were written by Charles Singleton and Eddie Snyder .... Capitol CL 15430

JOHN MARTYN – see SISTER BLISS

MARVELETTES
US R&B vocal group formed in 1960 by Gladys Horton, Georgeanna Marie Tillman Gordon, Wanda Young, Katherine Anderson and Juanita Cowart. Cowart left in 1962, Gordon in 1965 and Horton in 1967 (replaced by Anne Bogan). They disbanded in 1969. Gordon died from lupus on 6/1/1980.

15/06/1967	13	10		WHEN YOU'RE YOUNG AND IN LOVE .... Tamla Motown TMG 609

HANK MARVIN
UK singer/guitarist (born Brian Rankin, 28/10/1941, Newcastle-upon-Tyne) who was co-founder of Cliff Richard's backing group the Drifters, later renamed the Shadows. He went solo when they split in 1968. The Young Ones are comedians Rik Mayall (Rik), Adrian Edmondson (Vivian), Nigel Planer (neil) and Christopher Ryan (Mike) from the TV series of the same name.

13/09/1969	7	9		THROW DOWN A LINE .... Columbia DB 8615
21/02/1970	25	8		JOY OF LIVING Theme to the TV series of the same name. This and above single credited to **CLIFF AND HANK** ..... Columbia DB 8657
06/03/1982	49	4		DON'T TALK .... Polydor POSP 420
22/03/1986	❶³	11	●	**LIVING DOLL CLIFF RICHARD AND THE YOUNG ONES FEATURING HANK B MARVIN** The record, a re-recording of Cliff Richard's 1962 hit, was released for Comic Relief .... WEA YZ 65
07/01/1989	52	3		LONDON KID **JEAN-MICHEL JARRE FEATURING HANK MARVIN** .... Polydor 32
17/10/1992	66	1		WE ARE THE CHAMPIONS **HANK MARVIN FEATURING BRIAN MAY** .... PolyGram TV PO 229

LEE MARVIN
US singer/actor (born 19/2/1924, New York) who saw action with the US Marines during World War II before being invalided home in 1944. He made his Broadway debut as Billy Budd and headed for Hollywood in 1950. He subsequently appeared in many films, usually cast in a 'tough-guy' role, including *You're In The Navy Now* (1951), *The Big Heat* (1953), *The Man Who Shot Liberty Valence* (1962), *The Dirty Dozen* (1967) and *Delta Force* (1986). He died from a heart attack on 28/8/1987.

07/02/1970	❶³	23		**WAND'RIN' STAR** The flip side was *I Talk To The Trees* by **CLINT EASTWOOD** Both sides were featured in the 1969 film *Paint Your Wagon* .... Paramount PARA 3004

MARVIN THE PARANOID ANDROID
UK robot in the Douglas Adams book *The Hitchhikers Guide To The Galaxy*.

16/05/1981	53	4		MARVIN .... Polydor POSP 261

MARVIN AND TAMARA
UK teenage vocal duo Marvin Simmonds from Croydon and Tamara Nicole from Walthamstow.

07/08/1999	11	5		GROOVE MACHINE .... Epic 6675582
25/12/1999	38	4		NORTH, SOUTH, EAST, WEST .... Epic 6684902

RICHARD MARX
US singer/songwriter (born 16/9/1963, Chicago, IL) who was a jingle writer before joining Lionel Richie's group as a backing singer. He went solo in 1987 and married Cynthia Rhodes of Animotion in August 1989. He won the 2003 Grammy Award for Song of the Year for *Dance With My Father* with co-writer Luther Vandross.

27/02/1988	50	5		SHOULD'VE KNOWN BETTER .... Manhattan MT 32
14/05/1988	50	3		ENDLESS SUMMER NIGHTS .... Manhattan MT 39
17/06/1989	52	4		SATISFIED ▲¹ .... EMI-USA MT 64
02/09/1989	2	10	○	RIGHT HERE WAITING ▲³ .... EMI-USA MT 72
11/11/1989	45	4		ANGELIA .... EMI-USA MT 74
24/03/1990	38	3		TOO LATE TO SAY GOODBYE .... EMI-USA MT 80
07/07/1990	54	2		CHILDREN OF THE NIGHT .... EMI-USA MT 84
01/09/1990	60	2		ENDLESS SUMMER NIGHTS/HOLD ON TO THE NIGHTS ▲¹ A-side was a re-issue of Manhattan MT 39. B-side topped the US charts .... EMI-USA MT 89
19/10/1991	55	2		KEEP COMING BACK .... Capitol CL 634
09/05/1992	3	15	○	HAZARD .... Capitol CL 654
29/08/1992	13	6		TAKE THIS HEART .... Capitol CL 667
28/11/1992	29	6		CHAINS AROUND MY HEART .... Capitol CL 676
29/01/1994	13	6		NOW AND FOREVER .... Capitol CDCLS 703
30/04/1994	32	4		SILENT SCREAM .... Capitol CDCLS 714
13/08/1994	38	3		THE WAY SHE LOVES ME .... Capitol CDCL 721

MARXMAN
UK left-wing political rap group formed by MC Hollis, Big Shouts and Phrase with musician Oisin 'Ollie' Lunny. Their debut single *Sad Affair* was banned by the BBC for being sympathetic to the IRA.

06/03/1993	28	4		ALL ABOUT EVE .... Talkin Loud TLKCD 35
01/05/1993	64	1		SHIP AHOY Features the uncredited contribution of Sinead O'Connor .... Talkin Loud TLKCD 39

MARY JANE GIRLS
US vocal group formed in 1983 by Joanne 'Jo-Jo' McDuffie, Candice 'Candi' Ghant, Kim 'Maxi' Wuletich and Cherri Wells. Wells was later replaced by Yvette 'Corvette' Marina.

21/05/1983	60	4		CANDY MAN .... Motown TMG 1301

25/06/1983	13	9		ALL NIGHT LONG	Gordy TMG 1309
08/10/1983	74	1		BOYS	Gordy TMG 1315
18/02/1995	51	1		ALL NIGHT LONG (REMIX)	Motown TMGCD 1436

MARY MARY US vocal duo formed in Inglewood, CA by sisters Erica and Tina Atkins. Both had been in the Michael Matthews travelling gospel show. As songwriters they have penned tracks for 702, Yomanda Adams and the soundtrack for the 1998 animated film *The Prince Of Egypt*. They won the 2000 Grammy Award for Best Contemporary Soul Gospel Album for *Thankful*, and Best Gospel Act at the 2000 and 2001 MOBOs.

10/06/2000	5	12		SHACKLES (PRAISE YOU)	Columbia 6694202
18/11/2000	32	2		I SINGS	Columbia 6699742

CAROLYNE MAS US singer/guitarist (born 20/10/1955, The Bronx, NYC).

02/02/1980	71	2		QUOTE GOODBYE QUOTE	Mercury 6167 873

MASAI UK vocal duo Sharon Amos (born in Nairobi, Kenya) and Anna Crane (born in London). The pair, who were 25 years of age at the time of their debut hit, first met in London in 1995. Anna's father Paul was a member of The Cryin' Shames.

01/03/2003	42	1		DO THAT THANG	Concept CDCON 36X

MA$E US rapper (born Mason Betha, 24/3/1970, Jacksonville, FL) who was discovered by Puff Daddy. He appeared on tracks by various other artists in the Puff Daddy stable before launching his own solo career in 1997. Blinky Blink is a US rapper.

29/03/1997	19	4		CAN'T NOBODY HOLD ME DOWN ▲6 PUFF DADDY FEATURING MA$E Contains samples of Grandmaster Flash's *The Message* and Matthew Wilder's *Break My Stride*	Puff Daddy 74321464552
09/08/1997	6	10		MO MONEY MO PROBLEMS ▲2 THE NOTORIOUS B.I.G. FEATURING PUFF DADDY AND MA$E Based on Diana Ross' *I'm Coming Out*	Puff Daddy 74321492492
27/12/1997	10	8		FEEL SO GOOD Contains a sample of Kool & The Gang's *Hollywood Swinging*. Featured in the 1997 film *Money Talks*	Puff Daddy 74321526442
18/04/1998	15	5		WHAT YOU WANT MA$E FEATURING TOTAL Contains a sample of Curtis Mayfield's *Right On For The Darkness*	Puff Daddy 74321578772
19/09/1998	12	4		HORSE AND CARRIAGE CAM'RON FEATURING MA$E	Epic 6662612
03/10/1998	36	2		YOU SHOULD BE MINE BRIAN McKNIGHT FEATURING MA$E Contains a sample of James Brown's *I Got Ants In My Pants*	Motown 8608412
10/10/1998	2	9	O	TOP OF THE WORLD BRANDY FEATURING MA$E	Atlantic AT 0046CD
12/12/1998	7	9		TAKE ME THERE BLACKSTREET AND MYA FEATURING MA$E AND BLINKY BLINK Featured in the 1998 film *The Rugrats Movie*	Interscope IND 95620
10/07/1999	32	4		GET READY MA$E FEATURING BLACKSTREET Contains a sample of Shalamar's *A Night To Remember*	Puff Daddy 74321682612
20/11/2004	29	2		WELCOME BACK/BREATHE STRETCH SHAKE	Bad Boy MCSTD40392

MASH US studio group. The hit 1970 film *M*A*S*H* spawned a TV spin-off series that began in 1972. Johnny Mandel's theme, arranged and conducted by Mandel himself, was belatedly a hit in the UK in 1980, the group all session musicians. The Manic Street Preachers later took a cover into the top ten. Mandel also won two Grammy Awards: Best Original Score in 1965 for *The Sandpiper* and Best Instrumental Arrangement Accompanying Vocals in 1992 for Shirley Horn's *Here's To Life*.

10/05/1980	❶3	12	O	THEME FROM M*A*S*H (SUICIDE IS PAINLESS) Featured in the 1970 film *M*A*S*H* and the TV series of the same name	CBS 8536

MASH! UK/US vocal/instrumental group fronted by Taffy and Merritt Crawford.

21/05/1994	37	2		U DON'T HAVE TO SAY U LOVE ME	React CDREACT 37
04/02/1995	66	1		LET'S SPEND THE NIGHT TOGETHER	Playa CDXPLAYA 2

MASH UP – see MATT DAREY

MASHONDA – see CASSIDY

MASON – see CHICANE

BARBARA MASON US R&B singer (born 9/8/1947, Philadelphia, PA) who first recorded for Crusader Records in 1964 and later recorded for Artic, National, Buddah, Prelude, WMOT and West End.

21/01/1984	45	5		ANOTHER MAN	Streetwave KHAN 3

GLEN MASON UK singer (born Tommy Lennon) who later became an actor, appearing in the 1962 film *The Cool Mikado*.

28/09/1956	28	2		GLENDORA	Parlophone R 4203
16/11/1956	24	5		GREEN DOOR	Parlophone R 4244

MARY MASON UK singer.

08/10/1977	27	6		ANGEL OF THE MORNING – ANY WAY THAT YOU WANT ME (MEDLEY)	Epic EPC 5552

MASQUERADE UK vocal/instrumental R&B group.

11/01/1986	54	6		ONE NATION	Streetwave KHAN 59
05/07/1986	64	4		(SOLUTION TO) THE PROBLEM	Streetwave KHAN 67

❶9 Number of weeks single topped the UK chart ↑ Entered the UK chart at #1 ▲9 Number of weeks single topped the US chart

513

MASS ORDER
US duo formed in Columbia, MD by Mark Valentine and Eugene Hayes. Their hit originally achieved notoriety after a DAT tape version was taken away from the New York New Music Seminar by David Cooper and William Lynch and released on bootleg as *Take Me Away*. The pair escaped prosecution because they claimed they did not know they were breaking the law.

14/03/1992	35	3		LIFT EVERY VOICE (TAKE ME AWAY)	Columbia 6577487
23/05/1992	45	2		LET'S GET HAPPY	Columbia 6580737

MASS PRODUCTION
US funk group formed in Richmond, VA by Agnes 'Tiny' Kelly (vocals), Larry Mareshall (vocals), Coy Bryant (guitar), Greg McCoy (saxophone), James Drumgole (trumpet), Tyrone Williams (keyboards), Kevin Douglas (bass), Emanuel Redding (percussion) and Ricardo Williams (drums). The group later recorded for Paran.

12/03/1977	44	3		WELCOME TO OUR WORLD (OF MERRY MUSIC)	Atlantic K 10898
17/05/1980	59	4		SHANTE	Atlantic K 11475

MASS SYNDICATE FEATURING SU SU BOBIEN
US producer Sandro Russo with singer Su Su Bobien.

24/10/1998	71	1		YOU DON'T KNOW	ffrr FCD 347

ZEITIA MASSIAH
UK singer who had previously been a backing vocalist for the likes of ABC, Thrashing Doves, Right Said Fred, Beverley Skeete and Richard O'Brien. She competed in the Song For Europe competition in 1996, coming third with *A Little Love*.

12/03/1994	74	1		I SPECIALIZE IN LOVE	Union City UCRCD 27
24/09/1994	62	1		THIS IS THE PLACE	Virgin VSCDT 1511

MASSIEL
Spanish singer (born Maria De Los Angeles Santamaia Espinosa, 2/8/1947, Madrid) who won the 1968 Eurovision Song Contest, beating the UK's entry *Congratulations* by Cliff Richard into second place. The song was originally to have been sung by Joan Manuel Serrat, but as she would only sing it in Catalan, Massiel was a late replacement.

24/04/1968	35	4		LA LA LA 1968 Eurovision Song Contest winner	Philips BF 1667

MASSIVE ATTACK
UK R&B group formed in Bristol in 1987 by 3-D (born Robert Del Naja, 21/1/1965, Brighton, vocals), Mushroom (born Andrew Vowles, 10/11/1967, Bristol, keyboards) and Daddy G (born Grant Marshall, 18/12/1959, Bristol, keyboards), all previously in the Wild Bunch. They were named Best Dance Act at the 1996 BRIT Awards. Mushroom announced he was to leave the group in September 1999.

23/02/1991	13	9		UNFINISHED SYMPATHY MASSIVE	Wild Bunch WBRS 2
08/06/1991	25	6		SAFE FROM HARM	Wild Bunch WBRS 3
22/02/1992	27	4		MASSIVE ATTACK EP Tracks on EP: *Hymn Of The Big Wheel, Home Of The Whale, Be Thankful* and *Any Love*	Wild Bunch WBRS 4
29/10/1994	24	4		SLY	Wild Bunch WBRDX 5
21/01/1995	14	4		PROTECTION MASSIVE ATTACK FEATURING TRACEY THORN Video won the 1995 MTV Europe Music Award for Best Director for Mark Gondry	Virgin WBRX 6
01/04/1995	28	4		KARMACOMA	Virgin WBRX 7
19/07/1997	11	3		RISINGSON Contains a sample of Velvet Underground's *I Found A Reason*	Circa WBRX 8
09/05/1998	10	6		TEARDROP Features the uncredited lead vocal of Elizabeth Fraser (of The Cocteau Twins). Video won the 1998 MTV Europe Music Award for Best Video	Virgin WBRX 9
25/07/1998	30	2		ANGEL Featured in the 1988 film *Pi*	Virgin WBRX 10
08/03/2003	15	2		SPECIAL CASES	Virgin VSCDT 1839

MASSIVO FEATURING TRACY
UK production group formed by Jon Jules and Steve McCutcheon with singer Tracy Ackerman. Ackerman also fronted Q and later became a successful songwriter.

26/05/1990	25	11		LOVING YOU	Debut DEBT 3097

MASTER BLASTER
Dutch production group formed by Sascha Van Holt, Mike De Ville and Rico Bass.

07/08/2004	64	1		HYPNOTIC TANGO	Mondo Pop 9867100

MASTER P – see MONTELL JORDAN

MASTER SINGERS
UK vocal group.

14/04/1966	25	6		HIGHWAY CODE	Parlophone R 5428
17/11/1966	45	2		WEATHER FORECAST	Parlophone R 5523

MASTERMIXERS – see JIVE BUNNY AND THE MASTERMIXERS

SAMMY MASTERS
US singer (born Sammy Lawmaster, 8/7/1930, Saskawa, OK) who moved to Los Angeles in 1947 and later appeared on TV.

09/06/1960	36	5		ROCKIN' RED WING	Warner Brothers WB 10

MASTERS AT WORK PRESENTS INDIA
US group with Little Louie Vega, Kenny 'Dope' Gonzalez and singer India.

05/08/1995	44	2		I CAN'T GET NO SLEEP	A&M 5811412
31/07/1999	23	3		TO BE IN LOVE MAW PRESENTS INDIA	Defected DEFECT 5CD
06/07/2002	62	1		BACKFIRED MASTERS AT WORK FEATURING INDIA	Susu CDSUSU 4

MASTERS OF CEREMONIES – see DJ PIED PIPER AND THE MASTERS OF CEREMONIES

PAUL MASTERSON PRESENTS SUSHI
UK producer who previously collaborated with Judge Jules (Julius O'Riordan) as Hi-Gate, with Rachel Auburn as Candy Girls and recorded as Sleazesisters and Yomanda.

| 02/11/2002 | 35 | 2 | | THE EARTHSHAKER | NuLife 74321970372 |

MATCH
UK vocal/instrumental group.

| 16/06/1979 | 48 | 3 | | BOOGIE MAN | Flamingo FM 2 |

MATCHBOX
UK rock 'n' roll revival group formed in 1971 by Fred Poke (bass), Jimmy Redhead, Steve Bloomfield (guitar), Wiffle Smith (vocals), Rusty Lipton (piano) and Bob Burgos (drums). Redhead left after their 1973 debut single, returning in 1979, when Graham Fenton (vocals) also joined. Dick Callan replaced Bloomfield for live appearances from 1980 onwards.

03/11/1979	18	12		ROCKABILLY REBEL	Magnet MAG 155
19/01/1980	22	8		BUZZ BUZZ A DIDDLE IT	Magnet MAG 157
10/05/1980	14	12		MIDNITE DYNAMOS	Magnet MAG 169
27/09/1980	4	12	O	WHEN YOU ASK ABOUT LOVE	Magnet MAG 191
29/11/1980	15	11		OVER THE RAINBOW – YOU BELONG TO ME (MEDLEY)	Magnet MAG 192
04/04/1981	46	6		BABES IN THE WOOD	Magnet MAG 193
01/08/1981	63	3		LOVE'S MADE A FOOL OF YOU	Magnet MAG 194
29/05/1982	63	2		ONE MORE SATURDAY NIGHT	Magnet MAG 223

MATCHBOX 20
US group with Rob Thomas (born 14/2/1972, vocals), Kyle Cook (born 29/8/1975, guitar/vocals), Adam Gaynor (born 26/11/1963, guitar/vocals), Brian Yale (born 14/11/1968, bass) and Paul Doucette (born 22/8/1972, drums). Thomas was later in Santana.

11/04/1998	38	2		PUSH	Atlantic AT 0021CD
04/07/1998	64	1		3AM	Atlantic AT 0034CD
17/02/2001	50	1		IF YOU'RE GONE	Atlantic AT 0090CD
22/02/2003	50	1		DISEASE	Atlantic AT 0145CD

MATCHROOM MOB – see CHAS AND DAVE

MIREILLE MATHIEU
French singer (born 22/7/1946, Avignon) discovered by Johnny Stark who made her first recordings for Barclay in 1965. She has since proved to be one of France's biggest stars and appeared in the 1973 film *La Bonne Annee*.

| 13/12/1967 | 26 | 7 | | LA DERNIERE VALSE | Columbia DB 8323 |

JOHNNY MATHIS
US singer (born John Royce Mathis, 30/9/1935, San Francisco, CA) who was a promising athlete at school, taking part in trials for the US Olympic team at the high jump. He was discovered by George Avakian and initially recorded jazz-style records in 1956, switching to pop ballads at the suggestion of Mitch Miller. In the early 1980s he worked with Chic's producers Nile Rodgers and Bernard Edwards, although nothing was ever released. He has a star on the Hollywood Walk of Fame.

23/05/1958	27	5		TEACHER TEACHER	Fontana H 130
26/09/1958	4	16		A CERTAIN SMILE Featured in the 1957 film *A Certain Smile*.	Fontana H 142
19/12/1958	17	3		WINTER WONDERLAND	Fontana H 165
07/08/1959	6	15		SOMEONE	Fontana H 199
27/11/1959	30	1		THE BEST OF EVERYTHING	Fontana H 218
29/01/1960	12	12		MISTY	Fontana H 219
24/03/1960	38	9		YOU ARE BEAUTIFUL	Fontana H 234
28/07/1960	47	2		STARBRIGHT	Fontana H 254
06/10/1960	9	18		MY LOVE FOR YOU	Fontana H 267
04/04/1963	49	1		WHAT WILL MARY SAY	CBS AAG 135
25/01/1975	10	12		I'M STONE IN LOVE WITH YOU	CBS 2653
13/11/1976	❶³	12	●	WHEN A CHILD IS BORN (SOLEADO)	CBS 4599
25/03/1978	3	14		TOO MUCH TOO LITTLE TOO LATE ▲¹	CBS 6164
29/07/1978	45	6		YOU'RE ALL I NEED TO GET BY This and above single credited to JOHNNY MATHIS AND DENIECE WILLIAMS	CBS 6483
11/08/1979	15	10		GONE GONE GONE	CBS 7730
26/12/1981	74	2		WHEN A CHILD IS BORN JOHNNY MATHIS AND GLADYS KNIGHT	CBS S 1758

IVAN MATIAS
US singer who studied at the LaGuardia High School of Music and also worked as a backing singer for En Vogue.

| 06/04/1996 | 69 | 1 | | SO GOOD (TO COME HOME TO)/I'VE HAD ENOUGH | Arista 74321345072 |

MATT BIANCO
UK pop group formed by Mark Reilly (born 20/2/1960, High Wycombe, vocals), Basia (born Basha Trzetrzelewska, 30/9/1954, Jaworzno, Poland, vocals) and Danny White (born 26/8/1959, High Wycombe, keyboards). Reilly and White are both ex-Blue Rondo A La Turk. Basia later went solo.

11/02/1984	15	8		GET OUT YOUR LAZY BED	WEA BIANCO 1
14/04/1984	44	7		SNEAKING OUT THE BACK DOOR/MATT'S MOOD	WEA YZ 3
10/11/1984	23	10		HALF A MINUTE	WEA YZ 26
02/03/1985	50	7		MORE THAN I CAN BEAR	WEA YZ 34
05/10/1985	13	10		YEH YEH	WEA YZ 46
01/03/1986	66	2		JUST CAN'T STAND IT	WEA YZ 62
14/06/1986	64	3		DANCING IN THE STREET	WEA YZ 72
04/06/1988	11	13		DON'T BLAME IT ON THAT GIRL/WAP-BAM-BOOGIE	WEA YZ 188
27/08/1988	55	3		GOOD TIMES	WEA YZ 302
04/02/1989	59	2		NERVOUS/WAP-BAM-BOOGIE (REMIX)	WEA YZ 328

---

❶⁹ Number of weeks single topped the UK chart ↑ Entered the UK chart at #1 ▲⁹ Number of weeks single topped the US chart

AL MATTHEWS US singer (born 2/9/1944, Brooklyn, NYC) who became the first black man to be promoted to sergeant while serving in the field in Vietnam. He later moved to Europe and signed with CBS. After a brief recording career he turned to DJ work – he was Radio 1's first black DJ – and acting, appearing in *Yanks* (1979), *Superman III* (1983) and *Aliens* (1986).

23/08/1975.....16......8.......FOOL .... CBS 3429

CERYS MATTHEWS UK singer (born 11/4/1969, Cardiff) who was lead vocalist with Catatonia. In September 2001 she returned from a rehabilitation unit and announced she was leaving the group to go solo, subsequently moving to the US.

07/03/1998 .....4......8......○ THE BALLAD OF TOM JONES SPACE WITH CERYS OF CATATONIA .... Gut CDGUT 18
18/12/1999.....17......7....... BABY, IT'S COLD OUTSIDE TOM JONES AND CERYS MATTHEWS .... Gut CDGUT 29
02/08/2003.....47......1....... CAUGHT IN THE MIDDLE .... Blanco Y Negro NEG 147CD

JOHN MATTHEWS – see UNDERCOVER

SUMMER MATTHEWS UK singer (born 1985, Newcastle-Upon-Tyne) who first came to prominence as an actress, appearing in *Byker Grove!* as Emma Miller (she acted under the name Holly Wilkinson).

28/02/2004.....32......2....... LITTLE MISS PERFECT .... Sony Music 6744732

DAVE MATTHEWS BAND South African singer/guitarist (born 9/1/1967, Johannesburg) who moved to New York with his family at two, then back to South Africa with his mother when his father died. He later settled in Charlottesville where he formed his multi-racial band with Carter Beauford (drums), Greg Howard (keyboards), Stefan Lessard (bass), Leroi Moore (saxophone), Tim Reynolds (guitar) and Boyd Tinsley (violin). Their self-funded debut album *Remember Two Things* sold over 100,000 copies, leading to an RCA contract in 1995. Matthews won the 2003 Grammy Award for Best Male Rock Vocal Performance for *Gravedigger*.

01/12/2001.....35......2....... THE SPACE BETWEEN .... RCA 74321883192

MATTHEWS' SOUTHERN COMFORT UK singer/guitarist (born Ian Matthew McDonald, 16/6/1946, Scunthorpe) who was an apprentice footballer with Bradford City. Turning to music, he co-founded Fairport Convention, then Matthews' Southern Comfort in 1969 with Mark Griffiths (guitar), Carl Barnwell (guitar), Gordon Huntley (steel guitar), Andy Leigh (bass) and Ramon Duffy (drums).

26/09/1970 ....❶³.....18....... WOODSTOCK .... Uni UNS 526

MATUMBI UK reggae group formed in London in 1972 by Ted Dixon (vocals), Uton Jones (drums), Dennis Bovell (guitar), Errol Pottinger (guitar), Bevin and Glaister Fagan and Nicholas Bailey (all vocals).

29/09/1979.....35......7....... POINT OF VIEW .... Matumbi RIC 101

SUSAN MAUGHAN UK singer (born 1/7/1942, Newcastle-upon-Tyne) who was launched as a rival to Helen Shapiro, with her debut hit being a cover version of Marcie Blane's US hit (which also stalled at #3). She was also with the Ray Ellington Quartet.

11/10/1962.....3......19....... BOBBY'S GIRL .... Philips 326544 BF
14/02/1963.....41......3....... HAND A HANDKERCHIEF TO HELEN .... Philips 326562 BF
09/05/1963.....45......3....... SHE'S NEW TO YOU... Philips 326586 BF

MAUREEN UK singer Maureen Walsh who began her career as vocalist with Bomb The Bass before going solo.

26/11/1988.....10......10....... SAY A LITTLE PRAYER BOMB THE BASS FEATURING MAUREEN .... Rhythm King DOOD 3
16/06/1990.....11......9....... THINKING OF YOU .... Urban URB 55
12/01/1991.....51......3....... WHERE HAS ALL THE LOVE GONE .... Urban URB 65

PAUL MAURIAT AND HIS ORCHESTRA French orchestra leader (born 1925, Marseille) who moved to Paris at ten and formed his first orchestra at seventeen, becoming one of the country's top arrangers for his work with Charles Aznavour.

21/02/1968.....12......14....... LOVE IS BLUE (L'AMOUR EST BLEU) ▲⁵ .... Philips BF 1637

MAVERICKS US country and western group from Florida formed by Raul Malo (guitar/vocals), Robert Reynolds (bass) and Paul Deakin (drums), adding Nick Kane (guitar) in 1994. After a self-financed 1990 debut album, they were signed by MCA before they finished their audition. They won the 1995 Grammy Award for Best Country Performance by a Group for *Here Comes The Rain*. Reynolds married country singer Trisha Yearwood in 1995.

02/05/1998 .....4......18.....● DANCE THE NIGHT AWAY .... MCA Nashville MCSTD 48081
26/09/1998.....27......4....... I'VE GOT THIS FEELING.. MCA Nashville MCSTD 48095
05/06/1999.....45......1......○ SOMEONE SHOULD TELL HER .... MCA Nashville MCSTD 55567

MAW – see MASTERS AT WORK

MAX LINEN UK production duo Leiam Sullivan and Rob Roar.

17/11/2001.....55......1....... THE SOULSHAKER.. Global Cuts GC 73CD

MAX Q Australian duo Michael Hutchence (born 22/1/1962, Sydney) and Ollie Olsen. Hutchence was in INXS and Olsen in No at the time of their hit. Hutchence was found hanged in a Sydney hotel room on 22/11/1997, a suicide verdict later being returned, although it was speculated that he died after an autoerotic sex act went wrong. He had been working on a solo album with producer Andy Gill at the time.

17/02/1990.....53......3....... SOMETIMES .... Mercury MXQ 2

MAX WEBSTER Canadian group formed in Sarnia, Ontario in 1973 by Kim Mitchell (guitar/vocals), Terry Watkinson (keyboard/vocals), Mike Tilka (bass) and Gary McCracken (drums).

DATE	POS	WKS	BPI	SINGLE TITLE	LABEL & NUMBER
19/05/1979	43	3		PARADISE SKIES	Capitol CL 16079

MAXEE US singer Charmayne Maxwell who was a member of Brownstone before going solo.

17/03/2001	55	1		WHEN I LOOK INTO YOUR EYES	Mercury 5628702

MAXIM UK singer/DJ Maxim Reality (born Keith Palmer, 21/3/1967) who was also in Prodigy before launching a parallel solo career.

10/06/2000	33	2		CARMEN QUEASY Features the uncredited vocal contribution of Skin of Skunk Anansie	XL Recordings XLS 119CD
23/09/2000	53	1		SCHEMING	XL Recordings XLS 121CD

MAXIMA FEATURING LILY UK/Spanish duo.

14/08/1993	55	2		IBIZA	Yo! Yo! CDLILY 1

MAXTREME Dutch production group.

09/03/2002	66	1		MY HOUSE IS YOUR HOUSE	Y2K 028CD

MAXWELL US R&B singer (born Maxwell Menard, 23/5/1974, Brooklyn, NYC) with West Indian and Puerto Rican parents.

11/05/1996	63	1		…TIL THE COPS COME KNOCKIN'	Columbia 6631792
24/08/1996	39	3		ASCENSION NO ONE'S GONNA LOVE YOU, SO DON'T EVER WONDER	Columbia 6636265
01/03/1997	27	3		SUMTHIN' SUMTHIN' THE MANTRA Featured in the 1997 film *Love Jones*	Columbia 6638642
24/05/1997	28	3		ASCENSION DON'T EVER WONDER Re-issue of Columbia 6636265 (although with a shorter title)	Columbia 6645952

MAXX UK/Swedish/German vocal/instrumental group formed by Dakota O'Neill, Dawhite, George Torpey and Gary Bokoe.

21/05/1994	4	12	○	**GET-A-WAY**	Pulse 8 CDLOSE 59
06/08/1994	8	8		**NO MORE (I CAN'T STAND IT)**	Pulse 8 CDLOSE 66
29/10/1994	21	3		YOU CAN GET IT	Pulse 8 CDLOSE 75
22/07/1995	56	1		I CAN MAKE YOU FEEL LIKE	Pulse 8 CDLOSE 88

TERRY MAXX – see FUNKSTAR DE LUXE

BILLY MAY US bandleader (born 10/11/1916, Pittsburgh, PA) who was also a composer and arranger (working on many of Frank Sinatra's early records) and trumpeter. He scored films and TV series, including the 1968 film *The Secret Life Of An American Wife*. He won Grammies for Best Performance by an Orchestra in 1958 for *Billy May's Big Fat Brass* and Best Arrangement in 1959 for *Come Dance With Me*. He died on 22/1/2004.

27/04/1956	9	10		**MAIN TITLE THEME FROM 'MAN WITH THE GOLDEN ARM'**	Capitol 14551

BRIAN MAY UK singer/guitarist (born 19/7/1947, Twickenham) who made his first guitar in 1963. He recorded with The Others, turning down a career in astronomy for music, before joining Queen in 1970. As well as his solo work he also co-wrote and co-produced the 1991 Comic Relief three-track charity CD *The Stonk*.

05/11/1983	65	3		STAR FLEET BRIAN MAY AND FRIENDS	EMI 5436
07/12/1991	6	9		DRIVEN BY YOU Originally a TV advertisement for Ford Motors	Parlophone R 6304
05/09/1992	5	9	○	**TOO MUCH LOVE WILL KILL YOU**	Parlophone R 6320
17/10/1992	66	1		WE ARE THE CHAMPIONS HANK MARVIN FEATURING BRIAN MAY	PolyGram TV PO 229
28/11/1992	19	4		BACK TO THE LIGHT	Parlophone R 6329
19/06/1993	23	3		RESURRECTION BRIAN MAY WITH COZY POWELL	Parlophone CDRS 6351
18/12/1993	51	2		LAST HORIZON	Parlophone CDR 6371
06/06/1998	51	1		THE BUSINESS	Parlophone CDR 6498
12/09/1998	44	1		WHY DON'T WE TRY AGAIN	Parlophone CDR 6504

LISA MAY UK singer who also worked with Richard Vission.

15/07/1995	61	1		WISHING ON A STAR 88.3 FEATURING LISA MAY	Urban Gorilla UG 3CD
14/09/1996	64	1		THE CURSE OF VOODOO RAY	Fontana VOOCD 1

MARY MAY UK singer.

27/02/1964	49	1		ANYONE WHO HAD A HEART	Fontana TF 440

SHERNETTE MAY UK singer (born 1974) who began her career as a gospel singer.

06/06/1998	50	1		ALL THE MAN THAT I NEED	Virgin VSCDT 1691

SIMON MAY UK orchestra leader/songwriter who is especially known for his TV themes.

09/10/1976	7	8	○	SUMMER OF MY LIFE	Pye 7N 45627
21/05/1977	49	2		WE'LL GATHER LILACS – ALL MY LOVING (MEDLEY)	Pye 7N 45688
26/10/1985	21	11		HOWARD'S WAY SIMON MAY ORCHESTRA Theme to the TV series of the same name	BBC RESL 174
09/08/1986	4	9	○	**ANYONE CAN FALL IN LOVE** ANITA DOBSON FEATURING THE SIMON MAY ORCHESTRA	BBC RESL 191
20/09/1986	13	12		ALWAYS THERE MARTI WEBB AND THE SIMON MAY ORCHESTRA Theme to the BBC TV series *Howard's Way*, with lyrics added by Don Black	BBC RESL 190

MAYA – see TAMPERER FEATURING MAYA

❶⁹ Number of weeks single topped the UK chart ↑ Entered the UK chart at #1 ▲⁹ Number of weeks single topped the US chart

JOHN MAYER
US singer (born16/10/1977, Atlanta, GA) who attended Berklee College of Music before releasing his debut album in 1999.

DATE	POS	WKS	SINGLE TITLE	LABEL & NUMBER
23/08/2003	42	1	NO SUCH THING	Columbia 6732322
28/02/2004	72	1	BIGGER THAN MY BODY	Columbia 6744392

CURTIS MAYFIELD
US singer (born, 3/6/1942, Chicago, IL) who joined the Impressions in 1957, writing many of their hits, as well as hits for Jerry Butler and others. He formed the Curtom label in 1968 with Emanuel Thomas (they adopted the slogan 'We're A Winner' from the last Impressions single on ABC) and went solo in 1970, being replaced in the Impressions by Leroy Hutson. He scored and appeared in the films *Superfly* (1972), its follow-up *Superfly TNT* (1973) and *Short Eyes* (1976). On 13/8/1990 he was performing outdoors in Brooklyn, NYC when the wind blew a lighting rig on top of him, leaving him paralysed from the neck down. The accident also led to diabetes, resulting in his right leg being amputated in 1998. He died on 26/12/1999 as a result of the injuries received in 1990 (although he had recorded one further album in 1996). He was awarded the Lifetime Achievement Award Grammy in 1995 and was inducted into the Rock & Roll Hall of Fame in 1999.

DATE	POS	WKS	SINGLE TITLE	LABEL & NUMBER
31/07/1971	12	10	MOVE ON UP Featured in the 2002 film *Bend It Like Beckham*	Buddah 2011 080
02/12/1978	65	3	NO GOODBYES	Atlantic LV 1
30/05/1987	52	2	(CELEBRATE) THE DAY AFTER YOU BLOW MONKEYS WITH CURTIS MAYFIELD As the single was anti-Margaret Thatcher (then UK Prime Minister) it was banned from all radio stations until after the General Election	RCA MONK 6
29/09/1990	48	3	SUPERFLY 1990 CURTIS MAYFIELD AND ICE-T	Capitol CL 586
16/06/2001	40	2	ASTOUNDED BRAN VAN 3000 FEATURING CURTIS MAYFIELD	Virgin VUSCD 194

MAYTALS
Jamaican reggae group formed in 1962 by Frederick 'Toots' Hibbert, Nathaniel 'Jerry' Matthias (who also used the surname McCarthy) and Henry 'Raleigh' Gordon.

DATE	POS	WKS	SINGLE TITLE	LABEL & NUMBER
25/04/1970	47	4	MONKEY MAN	Trojan TR 7711

MAYTE
US singer Mayte Garcia who was a dancer before being discovered by Prince. The pair wed on Valentine's Day in 1996, had the marriage annulled and then remarried on Valentine's Day in 1999.

DATE	POS	WKS	SINGLE TITLE	LABEL & NUMBER
18/11/1995	67	1	IF EYE LOVE U 2 NIGHT	NPG 0061635

MAZE FEATURING FRANKIE BEVERLY
US group formed in Philadelphia, PA in 1971 by Frankie Beverly (born 6/12/1946, Philadelphia) as Raw Soul, changing their name when they moved to San Francisco, CA. The line-up at the time of their debut album was Beverly (vocals), Wayne Thomas (guitar), Sam Porter (keyboards), Philip Woo (keyboards), Wayne 'Ziggy' Lindsay (keyboards), Robin Duke (bass), Roame Lowery (congas/vocals), McKinley 'Bug' Williams (percussion/vocals) and Aguna G Sun (drums).

DATE	POS	WKS	SINGLE TITLE	LABEL & NUMBER
20/07/1985	36	7	TOO MANY GAMES	Capitol CL 363
23/08/1986	55	3	I WANNA BE WITH YOU	Capitol CL 421
27/05/1989	57	4	JOY AND PAIN MAZE	Capitol CL 531

KYM MAZELLE
US singer (born Kimberley Grisby, Gary, IN) who lived just around the corner from the Jacksons before moving to Chicago, IL in 1985. She made her first recording in 1987 as lead vocalist with House To House and went solo the following year. Robert Howard is the lead singer with The Blow Monkeys.

DATE	POS	WKS	SINGLE TITLE	LABEL & NUMBER
12/11/1988	53	3	USELESS (I DON'T NEED YOU NOW)	Syncopate SY 18
14/01/1989	7	10	WAIT ROBERT HOWARD AND KYM MAZELLE	RCA PB 42595
25/03/1989	29	4	GOT TO GET YOU BACK	Syncopate SY 25
07/10/1989	52	3	LOVE STRAIN	Syncopate SY 30
20/01/1990	33	6	WAS THAT ALL IT WAS	Syncopate SY 32
26/05/1990	48	2	USELESS (I DON'T NEED YOU NOW) (REMIX)	Syncopate SY 36
24/11/1990	22	7	MISSING YOU SOUL II SOUL FEATURING KYM MAZELLE	10 TEN 345
25/05/1991	62	2	NO ONE CAN LOVE YOU MORE THAN ME	Parlophone R 6287
26/12/1992	22	10	LOVE ME THE RIGHT WAY RAPINATION AND KYM MAZELLE	Logic 74321128097
11/06/1994	13	7	NO MORE TEARS (ENOUGH IS ENOUGH)	Ding Dong 74321209032
08/10/1994	22	3	GIMME ALL YOUR LOVIN' This and above single credited to KYM MAZELLE AND JOCELYN BROWN	Ding Dong 74321231322
23/12/1995	40	3	SEARCHING FOR THE GOLDEN EYE MOTIV 8 AND KYM MAZELLE	Eternal 027CD
28/09/1996	55	1	LOVE ME THE RIGHT WAY (REMIX) RAPINATION AND KYM MAZELLE	Logic 74321404442
16/08/1997	20	4	YOUNG HEARTS RUN FREE Featured in the 1997 film *Romeo And Juliet*	EMI CDEM 488
19/02/2000	55	1	TRULY PESHAY FEATURING KYM MAZELLE	Island Blue PFACD 4

MAZZY STAR
US duo Hope Sandoval (vocals) and David Roback (guitar). Roback had previously been with Rain Parade and Sandoval with Going Home.

DATE	POS	WKS	SINGLE TITLE	LABEL & NUMBER
27/08/1994	48	1	FADE INTO YOU	Capitol CDCL 720
02/11/1996	40	2	FLOWERS IN DECEMBER	Capitol CDCL 781

MC ALISTAIR – see DREEM TEEM

MC CHICKABOO – see TIMO MAAS

MC DUKE
UK rapper Andrew Hilaire who later recorded for Shut Up And Dance and launched his own Bluntly Speaking Vinyl label.

DATE	POS	WKS	SINGLE TITLE	LABEL & NUMBER
11/03/1989	75	1	I'M RIFFIN (ENGLISH RASTA)	Music Of Life 7NOTE 25

MC ERIC – see TECHNOTRONIC

MC FIXX IT – see ANTICAPPELLA

MC HAMMER – see HAMMER

MC IMAGE – see JHAY PALMER FEATURING MC IMAGE

MC JIG German rapper discovered by producers Isy B and DJ Lil Tommy. His debut hit was a cover version of DJ Casper's hit.

21/02/2004.....37......3.......	CHA CHA SLIDE (IMPORT).. ZYX 95938
13/03/2004.....33......4.......	CHA CHA SLIDE.. NM Music SLIDE001

MC KIE – see TEEBONE FEATURING MC KIE AND MC SPARKS

MC LETHAL UK producer Lee Whitney who had previously been a DJ at Shelleys and Entropy.

14/11/1992.....66......1....... THE RAVE DIGGER... Network NWKT 60

MC LYTE US rapper (born Lana Moorer, 11/10/1971, New York). Gina Thompson is a US singer (born 1974, New Jersey).

15/01/1994.....67......1.......	RUFFNECK.. Atlantic A 8336CD
29/06/1996.....39......2.......	KEEP ON, KEEPIN' ON MC LYTE FEATURING XSCAPE Contains a sample of Michael Jackson's *Liberian Girl*. Featured in the 1996 film *Sunset Park*... East West A 4287CD
18/01/1997.....15......4.......	COLD ROCK A PARTY Contains a sample of Diana Ross' *Upside Down*................. East West A 3975CD
19/04/1997.....27......2.......	KEEP ON, KEEPIN' ON MC LYTE FEATURING XSCAPE Re-issue of East West A 4287CD .... East West A 3950CD1
05/09/1998.....46......1.......	I CAN'T MAKE A MISTAKE.. Elektra E 3813CD
19/12/1998.....36......4.......	IT'S ALL YOURS MC LYTE FEATURING GINA THOMPSON.............................. East West E 3789CD
24/06/2000.....42......2.......	JAMMIN' BOB MARLEY FEATURING MC LYTE.................................... Tuff Gong TGXCD 9
08/05/2004.....38......3.......	GIRLFRIEND'S STORY GEMMA FOX FEATURING MC LYTE................................. Polydor 9866362

MC MALIBU – see ROUND SOUND PRESENTS ONYX STONE AND MC MALIBU

MC MARIO – see AMBASSADORS OF FUNK FEATURING MC MARIO

MC MIKEE FREEDOM – see NOMAD

MC MIKER 'G' AND DEEJAY SVEN Dutch duo Lucien Witteveen and Sven Van Veen whose debut hit featured excerpts from Madonna's *Holiday* and Cliff Richard's *Summer Holiday*.

06/09/1986......6......7....... **HOLIDAY RAP**.. Debut DEBT 3008

MC NEAT – see DJ LUCK AND MC NEAT

MC NOISE – see LOVE INCORPORATED FEATURING MC NOISE

MC NUMBER 6 – see FAB

MC ONYX STONE UK rapper who also worked with Shola Ama.

07/04/2001.....39......2.....	GARAGE GIRLS LONYO FEATURING MC ONYX STONE................................. Riverhorse RIVHCD 12
16/03/2002.....69......1.....	WHADDA WE LIKE? ROUND SOUND PRESENTS ONYX STONE AND MC MALIBU.............. Cooltempo CDCOOL 358

MC PARKER – see FAB

MC RB UK rapper Ricky Benjamin who graduated from Brunel University with a degree in mathematics.

01/04/2000.....75......1.......	CHEQUE ONE-TWO SUNSHIP FEATURING MC RB.................................... Filter FILT 044
28/09/2002.....67......1.......	JUMP UP JUST 4 JOKES FEATURING MC RB....................................... Serious SERR 050CD

MC SAR – see REAL McCOY

MC SHURAKANO – see KID I

MC SKAT KAT AND THE STRAY MOB US cartoon cat that had first featured in Paula Abdul's *Opposites Attract* video. The Stray Mob feature Fatz, Katleen, Leo, Micetro, Taboo and Silk.

09/11/1991.....64......2....... SKAT STRUT Contains a sample of Earth Wind & Fire's *Let's Groove*................................. Virgin America VUS 51

MC SOLAAR French rapper (born in Dakar, Senegal).

20/08/1994.....47......2.......	LISTEN URBAN SPECIES FEATURING MC SOLAAR.................................... Talkin Loud TLKCD 50
25/09/1999.....20......4.......	ALL N MY GRILL MISSY 'MISDEMEANOR' ELLIOTT FEATURING MC SOLAAR............... Elektra E 3742CD

MC SPARKS – see TEEBONE FEATURING MC KIE AND MC SPARKS

MC SPY-D + FRIENDS UK vocal/instrumental group formed by ex-Queen guitarist Brian May (born19/7/1947, London).

11/03/1995.....37......2....... THE AMAZING SPIDER MAN.. Parlophone CDR 6404

---

❶⁹ Number of weeks single topped the UK chart ↑ Entered the UK chart at #1 ▲⁹ Number of weeks single topped the US chart

519

MC STYLES – see SCOTT GARCIA FEATURING MC STYLES

MC TUNES UK rapper from Manchester (born Nicky Lockett) who later formed the Dust Junkys.

02/06/1990	10	10		THE ONLY RHYME THAT BITES .... ZTT ZANG 3
15/09/1990	18	7		TUNES SPLITS THE ATOM This and above single credited to MC TUNES VERSUS 808 STATE .... ZTT ZANG 6
01/12/1990	67	1		PRIMARY RHYMING .... ZTT ZANG 10
06/03/1999	53	1		THE ONLY RHYME THAT BITES 99 MC TUNES VERSUS 808 STATE .... ZTT 125CD

MC WILDSKI UK rapper who later became a member of Beats International.

08/07/1989	29	6		BLAME IT ON THE BASSLINE NORMAN COOK FEATURING MC WILDSKI .... Go Beat GOD 33
03/03/1990	49	4		WARRIOR .... Arista 112956

MC VIPER – see REFLEX FEATURING MC VIPER

M-D-EMM UK producer Mark Ryder who also records under his own name and was previously a member of Fantasy UFO.

22/02/1992	55	2		GET DOWN .... Strictly Underground 7STUR 13
30/05/1992	67	1		MOVE YOUR FEET .... Strictly Underground 7STUR 15

MDM UK producer Matt Darey who is also a remixer for the likes of ATB, Moloko and Gabrielle. Darey recorded with Marcella Woods and Michael Woods as M3 for Inferno, as Sunburst and as a member of Lost Tribe and Melt Featuring Little Ms Marcie.

27/10/2001	66	1		MASH IT UP .... NuLife 74321870472

ME AND YOU FEATURING WE THE PEOPLE BAND UK studio group assembled by reggae star Dennis Brown.

28/07/1979	31	9		YOU NEVER KNOW WHAT YOU'VE GOT .... Laser LAS 8

ME ME ME UK vocal/instrumental group formed by artist Damien Hurst, Alex James (of Blur), Stephen Duffy, Justin Welch (of Elastica) and Charlie Bloor.

17/08/1996	19	4		HANGING AROUND .... Indolent DUFF 005CD

ABIGAIL MEAD AND NIGEL GOULDING UK/US duo. Abigail Mead (born Vivian Kubrick) is the daughter of the late film director Stanley Kubrick, while Goulding was an extra in the Kubrick film from which the hit originated.

26/09/1987	2	10	O	FULL METAL JACKET (I WANNA BE YOUR DRILL INSTRUCTOR) Featured in the 1987 film *Full Metal Jacket* . Warner Brothers W 8187

MEAT BEAT MANIFESTO UK production group formed by Marcus Adams, Jonny Stephens, Craig Morrison and rapper Jack Dangers.

20/02/1993	55	1		MINDSTREAM .... Play It Again Sam BIAS 232CD

MEAT LOAF US singer (born Marvin Lee Aday, 27/9/1951, Dallas, TX) who formed Meat Loaf Soul in 1966 before appearing in the stage musical *Hair*. He linked with Cheryl Murphy to form Stoney & Meat Loaf, with a debut US hit on the Motown label Rare Earth. He first met Jim Steinman in 1974, Steinman later penning the classic *Bat Out Of Hell* album. He appeared in a number of films, including *Roadie* (1979) and *Americathon* (1979). He won the 1993 Grammy Award for Best Rock Vocal Performance for *I'd Do Anything For Love (But I Won't Do That)*. His hit *Objects In The Mirror* is the longest song title without words or phrases in brackets to have hit the charts.

20/05/1978	33	8		YOU TOOK THE WORDS RIGHT OUT OF MY MOUTH .... Epic EPC 5980
19/08/1978	32	8		TWO OUT OF THREE AIN'T BAD .... Epic EPC 6281
10/02/1979	15	7		BAT OUT OF HELL .... Epic EPC 7018
26/09/1981	62	3		I'M GONNA LOVE HER FOR BOTH OF US .... Epic EPC A 1580
28/11/1981	5	17	O	DEAD RINGER FOR LOVE Features the uncredited vocal of Cher .... Epic EPC A 1697
24/09/1983	59	2		IF YOU REALLY WANT TO .... Epic A 3357
24/09/1983	17	8		MIDNIGHT AT THE LOST AND FOUND .... Epic A 3748
14/01/1984	41	3		RAZOR'S EDGE .... Epic A 4080
06/10/1984	17	9		MODERN GIRL .... Arista ARIST 585
22/12/1984	67	4		NOWHERE FAST .... Arista ARIST 600
23/03/1985	47	5		PIECE OF THE ACTION .... Arista ARIST 603
30/08/1986	31	6		ROCK 'N' ROLL MERCENARIES MEAT LOAF FEATURING JOHN PARR .... Arista ARIST 666
22/06/1991	53	2		DEAD RINGER FOR LOVE .... Epic 6569827
27/06/1992	69	1		TWO OUT OF THREE AIN'T BAD Re-issue of Epic EPC 6281 .... Epic 6574917
09/10/1993	●[7] 19		✪	I'D DO ANYTHING FOR LOVE (BUT I WON'T DO THAT) ▲[5] Features uncredtied vocals by Patti Russo .... Virgin VSCDT 1443
18/12/1993	8	9		BAT OUT OF HELL Re-issue of Epic EPC 7018 .... Epic 6600062
19/02/1994	11	7		ROCK AND ROLL DREAMS COME THROUGH .... Virgin VSCDT 1479
07/05/1994	26	4		OBJECTS IN THE REAR VIEW MIRROR MAY APPEAR CLOSER THAN THEY ARE .... Virgin VSCDT 1492
28/10/1995	2	11	O	I'D LIE FOR YOU (AND THAT'S THE TRUTH) .... Virgin VSCDT 1563
27/01/1996	7	6		NOT A DRY EYE IN THE HOUSE .... Virgin VSCDT 1567
27/04/1996	21	3		RUNNIN' FOR THE RED LIGHT (I GOTTA LIFE) .... Virgin VSCDX 1582
17/04/1999	15	4		IS NOTHING SACRED MEAT LOAF FEATURING PATTI RUSSO .... Virgin VSCDT 1734
26/04/2003	31	2		COULDN'T HAVE SAID IT BETTER .... Mercury 0656842
06/12/2003	21	4		MAN OF STEEL .... Mercury 9815114

MECHANICS – see MIKE AND THE MECHANICS

O Silver disc ● Gold disc ✪ Platinum disc (additional platinum units are indicated by a figure following the symbol) ◉ Singles released prior to 1973 that are known to have sold over 1 million copies in the UK

MECO US orchestra leader (born Meco Monardo, 29/11/1939, Johnsonburg, PA) who began his career as a session musican, arranger and producer, working with Gloria Gaynor on her hit *Never Can Say Goodbye* and Carol Douglas' *Doctor's Orders*. Inspired by the 1977 film *Star Wars* (which he saw eleven times in its opening weeks), he put together a disco medley of the theme and hit #1 in the US: higher than the official single release. Thereafter he recorded disco versions of almost all of John Williams' film scores, including *Close Encounters Of The Third Kind* (1977), *Superman* (1978), *The Empire Strikes Back* (1980) and *Return Of The Jedi* (1983).

01/10/1977 ..... 7 ...... 9 .... STAR WARS THEME – CANTINA BAND ▲² Inspired by the 1977 film *Star Wars* .... RCA XB 102

GLENN MEDEIROS US singer (born 24/6/1970, Hawaii) who received his first break winning a local radio talent contest. He later recorded with Bobby Brown and Ray Parker Jr.

18/06/1988 .... ❶⁴ ... 13 ..... ● NOTHING'S GONNA CHANGE MY LOVE FOR YOU Originally recorded in 1986 .... London LON 184
03/09/1988.... 42...... 4....... LONG AND LASTING LOVE (ONCE IN A LIFETIME) .... London LON 202
30/06/1990..... 12...... 9....... SHE AIN'T WORTH IT ▲² GLENN MEDEIROS FEATURING BOBBY BROWN .... London LON 265

PAUL MEDFORD – see LETITIA DEAN AND PAUL MEDFORD

MEDICINE HEAD UK duo John Fiddler (born 25/9/1947, Darlaston) and Peter Hope-Evans (born 28/9/1947, Brecon, Powys) whose 1970 debut album was on John Peel's Dandelion label. Hope-Evans left after their first hit, returning eighteen months later. Meantime Fiddler was joined by Keith Relf and John Davies. The group was later expanded by the addition of Roger Saunders (born 9/3/1947, Barking, guitar), Ian Sainty (bass) and Rob Townsend (born 7/7/1947, Leicester, drums).

26/06/1971..... 22...... 8....... (AND THE) PICTURES IN THE SKY .... Dandelion DAN 7003
05/05/1973..... 3...... 13 ...... ONE AND ONE IS ONE .... Polydor 2001 432
04/08/1973..... 11...... 9....... RISING SUN .... Polydor 2058 389
09/02/1974..... 22...... 7....... SLIP AND SLIDE .... Polydor 2058 436

MEDICINE SHOW – see DR. HOOK

BILL MEDLEY US singer (born 19/9/1940, Santa Ana, CA) who was with the Paramounts before joining Bobby Hatfield as the Righteous Brothers in 1962. Medley went solo in 1967, re-forming with Hatfield in 1974 and disbanding again in 1981.

31/10/1987 ..... 6...... 12 ...... (I'VE HAD) THE TIME OF MY LIFE ▲¹ BILL MEDLEY AND JENNIFER WARNES Featured in the 1987 film *Dirty Dancing*. 1987 Grammy Award for Best Vocal Performance by a Duo and 1987 Oscar for Best Film Song .... RCA PB 49625
27/08/1988..... 25...... 6....... HE AIN'T HEAVY, HE'S MY BROTHER Featured in the 1988 film *Rambo III* .... Scotti Brothers PO 10
15/12/1990 ..... 8...... 11 ..... ○ (I'VE HAD) THE TIME OF MY LIFE BILL MEDLEY AND JENNIFER WARNES Re-released following the TV screening of the 1987 film *Dirty Dancing* .... RCA PB 49625

MEDWAY US producer Jesse Skeens.

29/04/2000..... 69...... 1....... FAT BASTARD (EP) Tracks on EP: *Release, Flanker* and *Faith* .... Hooj Choons HOOJ 92CD
10/03/2001..... 67...... 1....... RELEASE .... Hooj Choons HOOJ 105CD

MICHAEL MEDWIN, BERNARD BRESSLAW, ALFIE BASS AND LESLIE FYSON UK vocal group formed by members of the radio series *The Army Game*. Michael Medwin (born 18/7/1923, London) played Corporal Springer. Bernard Bresslaw (born 25/2/1934, London) played Private 'Popeye' Popplewell and enjoyed a solo hit; he died in Manchester on 11/6/1993. Alfie Bass (born 8/4/1921, London) played Private 'Bootsie' Bisley; he died from a heart attack on 15/7/1987. Classical baritone singer Leslie Fyson appeared in numerous Gilbert & Sullivan shows.

30/05/1958 ..... 5...... 9....... THE SIGNATURE TUNE OF 'THE ARMY GAME' Theme to the TV series *The Army Game* .... HMV POP 490

MEECHIE US singer.

02/09/1995..... 74...... 1....... YOU BRING ME JOY .... Vibe MCSTD 2069

TONY MEEHAN COMBO UK drummer (born Daniel Meehan, 2/3/1943, London) who was with the Vipers before joining the Shadows. He had hits teamed with Jet Harris until they disbanded after a car accident, Meehan recovering and forming his own group.

16/01/1964..... 39...... 4....... SONG OF MEXICO .... Decca F 11801

MEEKER UK vocal/production duo Rachel Morrison (vocals) and Tom Morrison (guitar/loops).

26/02/2000..... 60...... 1....... SAVE ME .... Underwater H2O 009 CD

MEGA CITY FOUR UK thrash pop group formed in 1982 by Wiz (Darren Brown, guitar/vocals), Danny Brown (guitar), Gerry Bryant (bass) and Chris Jones (drums) as Capricorn, changing their name to Mega City Four in 1986.

19/10/1991..... 66...... 1....... WORDS THAT SAY .... Big Life MEGA 2
08/02/1992..... 36...... 2....... STOP (EP) Tracks on EP: *Stop, Desert Song, Back To Zero* and *Overlap* .... Big Life MEGA 3
16/05/1992..... 35...... 2....... SHIVERING SAND .... Big Life MEGA 4
01/05/1993..... 48...... 1....... IRON .... Big Life MEGAD 5
17/07/1993..... 69...... 1....... WALLFLOWER .... Big Life MEGAD 6

MEGABASS – see VARIOUS ARTISTS (MONTAGES)

MEGADETH US heavy rock group formed in Los Angeles, CA in 1983 by Dave Mustaine (born 13/9/1963, La Mesa, CA, lead guitar/vocals), Dave Ellefson (born 12/11/1964, Jackson, MN, bass), Gar Samuelson (drums) and Chris Poland (guitar). Samuelson and Poland left in 1987 and were replaced by Jeff Young and Chuck Behler. Young and Behler were replaced in 1990 by Marty Friedman (born

8/12/1962, Washington DC, guitar) and Nick Menza (born 23/7/1964, Munich, Germany, drums). Menza left in 1984 and was replaced by Jimmy DeGrasso. Mustaine had previously been with Metallica.

19/12/1987	65	2		WAKE UP DEAD	Capitol CL 476
27/02/1988	45	3		ANARCHY IN THE UK	Capitol CL 480
21/05/1988	46	1		MARY JANE	Capitol CL 489
13/01/1990	13	6		NO MORE MR NICE GUY	SBK 4
29/09/1990	24	3		HOLY WARS…THE PUNISHMENT DUE	Capitol CLP 588
16/03/1991	26	4		HANGAR 18	Capitol CLS 604
27/06/1992	15	3		SYMPHONY OF DESTRUCTION	Capitol CLS 662
24/10/1992	13	3		SKIN O' MY TEETH	Capitol CLP 669
29/05/1993	26	3		SWEATING BULLETS	Capitol CDCL 682
07/01/1995	22	3		TRAIN OF CONSEQUENCES	Capitol CDCL 730

MEGAMAN – see OXIDE AND NEUTRINO

MEHTA – see JOSE CARRERAS

MEJA Swedish singer/songwriter Meja Beckman who began writing songs in 1991 and recorded her debut album in 1992.

| 24/10/1998 | 12 | 5 | | ALL 'BOUT THE MONEY | Columbia 6665662 |
| 29/04/2000 | 9 | 9 | | **PRIVATE EMOTION** | Columbia 6692692 |

MEKKA UK producer Jake Williams.

| 24/03/2001 | 67 | 1 | | DIAMOND BACK | Perfecto PERF 12CDS |

MEKON UK producer John Gosling with US rapper Roxanne Shante (born Lolita Gooden, 8/3/1970, Long Island, NY).

| 23/09/2000 | 43 | 1 | | WHAT'S GOING ON MEKON FEATURING ROXANNE SHANTE Contains a sample of Globe & Wizzkid's *Play The Beat Mr DJ* . . . . Wall Of Sound WALD 064 |
| 13/03/2004 | 72 | 1 | | D-FUNKTIONAL MEKON FEATURING AFRIKA BAMBAATAA | Wall Of Sound WALLD092 |

MELLE MEL – see GRANDMASTER FLASH, MELLE MEL AND THE FURIOUS FIVE

MEL AND KIM UK duo of sisters Mel (born 11/7/1967) and Kim Appleby (born 1962). Both previously models, Mel died from spinal cancer on 18/1/1990 and Kim subsequently went solo.

20/09/1986	3	19	O	**SHOWING OUT (GET FRESH AT THE WEEKEND)**	Supreme SUPE 107
07/03/1987	❶¹	15	●	**RESPECTABLE**	Supreme SUPE 111
11/07/1987	7	10		**F.L.M.**	Supreme SUPE 113
27/02/1988	10	7		**THAT'S THE WAY IT IS** Featured in the 1988 film *Coming To America*	Supreme SUPE 117

MEL AND KIM – see MEL SMITH AND KIM WILDE

GEORGE MELACHRINO ORCHESTRA UK orchestra leader who scored films including *The Shop At Sly Corner* (1948), *Old Mother Riley's New Venture* (1949) and *Odongo* (1956). He also appeared in the 1948 film *House Of Darkness*. He died on 18/6/1965.

| 12/10/1956 | 18 | 9 | | AUTUMN CONCERTO | HMV B 10958 |

MELANIE US singer (born Melanie Safka, 3/2/1947, Long Island, NY) who recorded her debut single in 1967 and later formed the record company Neighbourhood Records with her husband Peter Schekeryk. She also recorded with The Edwin Hawkins Singers.

26/09/1970	9	15		**RUBY TUESDAY**	Buddah 2011 038
16/01/1971	39	1		WHAT HAVE THEY DONE TO MY SONG MA B-side to *Ruby Tuesday*	Buddah 2011 038
01/01/1972	4	12		**BRAND NEW KEY** ▲³ Featured in the 1998 film *Boogie Nights*	Buddah 2011 105
16/02/1974	37	5		WILL YOU LOVE ME TOMORROW	Neighbourhood NBH 9
24/09/1983	70	2		EVERY BREATH OF THE WAY	Neighbourhood HOOD NB1

MELKY SEDECK US vocal/instrumental duo Melky and Sedeck Jean, the sister and brother of Wyclef Jean.

| 08/05/1999 | 50 | 1 | | RAW | MCA MCSTD 48107 |
| 16/09/2000 | 3 | 8 | | **IT DOESN'T MATTER** WYCLEF JEAN FEATURING THE ROCK AND MELKY SEDECK Contains samples of Ricky Martin's *Livin' La Vida Loca* and John Denver's *Take Me Home Country Roads* | Columbia 6697782 |

JOHN MELLENCAMP US singer (born 7/10/1951, Seymour, IN) who recorded his first album in 1976. He was given the name Johnny Cougar by David Bowie's manager Tony De Fries. He won the 1982 Grammy Award for Best Rock Vocal Performance for *Hurts So Good*. Me'Shell Ndegeocello is a singer and bassist (born 29/8/1969, Berlin, Germany) whose surname is Swahili for 'free like a bird'.

23/10/1982	25	8		JACK AND DIANE ▲⁴ JOHN COUGAR	Riva 37
01/02/1986	53	4		SMALL TOWN Featured in the 1999 film *The Waterboy*	Riva JCM 5
10/05/1986	67	3		R.O.C.K. IN THE USA	Riva JCM 6
03/09/1994	34	3		WILD NIGHT JOHN MELLENCAMP FEATURING ME'SHELL NDEGEOCELLO	Mercury MERCD 409

MELLOMEN US vocal group formed by Thurl Ravenscroft, Max Smth, Bob Hamlin and Bill Lee. The group also worked with Mel Torme and Frank Sinatra and provided the singing voices to numerous Walt Disney films.

| 01/10/1954 | 4 | 11 | | **IF I GIVE MY HEART TO YOU** DORIS DAY WITH THE MELLOMEN | Philips PB 325 |

O Silver disc ● Gold disc ✪ Platinum disc (additional platinum units are indicated by a figure following the symbol) ◉ Singles released prior to 1973 that are known to have sold over 1 million copies in the UK

17/12/1954	❶³	16		**MAMBO ITALIANO** Reclaimed #1 position on 4/2/1955. Featured in the 1996 film *Big Night*	Philips PB 382
20/05/1955	6	13		**WHERE WILL THE BABY'S DIMPLE BE** This and above single credited to **ROSEMARY CLOONEY AND THE MELLOMEN**	Philips PB 428
24/06/1955	2	22		**COOL WATER**	Philips PB 465
20/01/1956	10	3		**SIXTEEN TONS** This and above single credited to **FRANKIE LAINE WITH THE MELLOMEN**	Philips PB 539
28/02/1963	12	9		ONE BROKEN HEART FOR SALE **ELVIS PRESLEY WITH THE MELLOMEN** Featured in the 1962 film *It Happened At The World's Fair*	RCA 1337

WILL MELLOR UK singer (born 3/4/1976, Stockport) who first came to prominence as an actor, playing the role of Jambo in *Hollyoaks*. He had previously been a member of the pop group Right Now.

| 28/02/1998 | 5 | 6 | | **WHEN I NEED YOU** | Unity 017RCD |
| 27/06/1998 | 23 | 3 | | NO MATTER WHAT I DO | Jive 0540012 |

MELLOW TRAX German producer Christian Schwarnweber.

| 14/10/2000 | 41 | 2 | | OUTTA SPACE Contains samples of Max Romeo and Lee Perry's *Chase The Devil* and The Prodigy's *Out Of Space* | Substance SUBS 3CDS |

MELODIANS Jamaican reggae group formed in 1960 by Brent Dow, Tony Brevett and Trevor McNaughton, with Robert Cogle also a member during their career. The group split in 1974, re-forming two years later.

| 10/01/1970 | 41 | 1 | | SWEET SENSATION | Trojan TR 695 |

MELODY MAKERS – see **ZIGGY MARLEY AND THE MELODY MAKERS**

MELT FEATURING LITTLE MS MARCIE UK producer Matt Darey. He has remixed for ATB, Moloko and Gabrielle, and recorded with Marcella Woods and Michael Woods as M3 for Inferno, as Sunburst and MDM, and as part of Lost Tribe.

| 08/04/2000 | 59 | 1 | | HARD HOUSE MUSIC | WEA 257CD |

MELTDOWN UK/US instrumental/production duo Richard Dekkard and Phil Dane with singer Hazel Watson.

| 27/04/1996 | 44 | 1 | | MY LIFE IS IN YOUR HANDS | Sony S3 DANU 7CD |

KATIE MELUA Russian singer (born 1984, Georgia) who moved to Northern Ireland while still a child and was subsequently discovered by Mike Batt.

13/12/2003	10	20		**THE CLOSEST THING TO CRAZY**	Dramatico DRAMCDS 0003
27/03/2004	19	4		CALL OFF THE SEARCH	Dramatico DRAMCDS 0005
31/07/2004	46	2		CRAWLING UP A HILL	Dramatico DRAMCDS 0007

HAROLD MELVIN AND THE BLUENOTES US R&B vocal group formed in Philadelphia, PA in 1954 by Harold Melvin (born 25/6/1939, Philadelphia), Bernard Wilson, Jesse Gillis Jr, Franklin Peaker and Roosevelt Brodie. They signed with Philadelphia International in 1970 with a line-up of Melvin, Wilson, Lawrence Brown, Lloyd Parkes and Theodore 'Teddy' Pendergrass (born 26/3/1950, Philadelphia), who had been the drummer before becoming lead singer. Pendergrass went solo in 1977 and was replaced by David Ebo. Pendergrass was paralysed from the neck down in a car crash in 1982. Melvin died in his sleep following a stroke on 24/3/1997.

13/01/1973	9	9		IF YOU DON'T KNOW ME BY NOW Featured in the films *My Girl* (1992) and *Scooby Doo 2: Monsters Unleashed* (2004)	CBS 8496
12/01/1974	21	8		THE LOVE I LOST Featured in the 1998 film *The Last Days Of Disco*	Philadelphia International PIR 1879
13/04/1974	32	6		SATISFACTION GUARANTEED (OR TAKE YOUR LOVE BACK)	Philadelphia International PIR 2187
31/05/1975	35	5		GET OUT (AND LET ME CRY)	Route RT 06
28/02/1976	23	7		WAKE UP EVERYBODY Featured in the 2004 film *Scooby Doo 2: Monsters Unleashed*	Philadelphia International PIR 3866
22/01/1977	5	10	O	**DON'T LEAVE ME THIS WAY HAROLD MELVIN AND THE BLUENOTES FEATURING THEODORE PENDERGRASS**	Philadelphia International PIR 4909
02/04/1977	48	1		REACHING FOR THE WORLD	ABC 4161
28/04/1984	59	4		DON'T GIVE ME UP	London LON 47
04/08/1984	66	2		TODAY'S YOUR LUCKY DAY **HAROLD MELVIN AND THE BLUENOTES FEATURING NIKKO**	London LON 52

MEMBERS UK rock group formed in Camberley in 1977 by Jean-Marie Carroll (guitar), Gary Baker (guitar), Adrian Lillywhite (drums), Chris Payne (bass) and Nicky Tesco (vocals). Baker left in 1978 and was replaced by Nigel Bennett.

| 03/02/1979 | 12 | 9 | | THE SOUND OF THE SUBURBS | Virgin VS 242 |
| 07/04/1979 | 31 | 5 | | OFFSHORE BANKING BUSINESS | Virgin VS 248 |

MEMBERS OF MAYDAY German production duo Maximilian Lenz and Klaus Jankuhn. Lenz also records as Westbam.

| 23/06/2001 | 31 | 3 | | 10 IN 01 | Deviant DVNT 42CDS |
| 13/04/2002 | 59 | 1 | | SONIC EMPIRE | Deviant DVNT 49CDS |

MEMPHIS BLEEK FEATURING JAY-Z US rapper (born Malik Cox, 23/6/1980, Memphis, TN) with rapper Jay-Z (born Jason Shawn Carter, 1970, Brooklyn, NYC).

| 04/12/1999 | 58 | 1 | | WHAT YOU THINK OF THAT Contains a sample of Keith Mansfield's *High Velocity* | Def Jam 8708292 |

MEN AT WORK Australian rock group formed in Melbourne in 1979 by Colin Hay (born 29/6/1953, Scotland, guitar/vocals), Ron Strykert (born 18/8/1957, guitar), Greg Ham (born 27/9/1953, saxophone/keyboards/flute), John Rees (bass) and Jerry Speiser (drums). Hay recorded solo in 1987 as Colin James Hay. The group was named Best New Artist at the 1982 Grammy Awards.

| 30/10/1982 | 45 | 5 | | WHO CAN IT BE NOW? ▲¹ Featured in the 1994 film *Valley Girl* | Epic A 2392 |
| 08/01/1983 | ❶³ | 12 | ● | **DOWN UNDER ▲⁴** | Epic EPC A 1980 |

❶⁹ Number of weeks single topped the UK chart   ↑ Entered the UK chart at #1   ▲⁹ Number of weeks single topped the US chart

	DATE	POS	WKS	BPI	SINGLE TITLE	LABEL & NUMBER
	09/04/1983	21	10		OVERKILL	Epic EPC A 3220
	02/07/1983	33	6		IT'S A MISTAKE	Epic EPC A 3475
	10/09/1983	31	6		DR HECKYLL AND MR JIVE	Epic EPC A 3668

MEN OF VIZION
US R&B vocal group formed in Brooklyn, NYC by George Spencer, Prathan 'Spanky' Williams, Brian L Deramus, Desmond T Greggs and Corley Randolph.

	DATE	POS	WKS	BPI	SINGLE TITLE	LABEL & NUMBER
	27/03/1999	36	2		DO YOU FEEL ME? (…FREAK YOU)	MJJ 6670912

MEN THEY COULDN'T HANG
UK group formed by Cush (vocals), Paul Simmonds (guitar), Shanne (bass), Phil (guitar/vocals) and his brother John (drums). They first signed with Imp in 1984. They added Nick Muir in 1990, disbanding soon after. They re-formed in 1996 with the addition of Kenny Harris (drums).

	DATE	POS	WKS	BPI	SINGLE TITLE	LABEL & NUMBER
	02/04/1988	61	4		THE COLOURS	Magnet SELL 6

MEN WITHOUT HATS
Canadian techno-rock group formed in Montreal, Quebec by brothers Ivan (vocals), Stefan (guitar) and Colin Doroschuk (keyboards) and Allan McCarthy (drums).

	DATE	POS	WKS	BPI	SINGLE TITLE	LABEL & NUMBER
	08/10/1983	6	11	O	**THE SAFETY DANCE**	Statik TAK 1

SERGIO MENDES
Brazilian conductor/pianist/singer (born 11/2/1941, Niteroi) who moved to the US in 1964, forming Brasil '66 with Lani Hall (later Herb Alpert's wife, vocals), Janis Hansen (vocals), Bob Matthews (bass), Joses Soares (percussion) and Jao Palma (drums).

	DATE	POS	WKS	BPI	SINGLE TITLE	LABEL & NUMBER
	09/07/1983	45	5		NEVER GONNA LET YOU GO Features the uncredited contribution of Joe Pizzulo and Leza Miller	A&M AM 118

ANDREA MENDEZ
UK singer.

	DATE	POS	WKS	BPI	SINGLE TITLE	LABEL & NUMBER
	03/08/1996	44	1		BRING ME LOVE	AM:PM 5817872

MENSWEAR
UK rock group formed in 1994 by Johnny Dean (born 12/12/1971, Salisbury, vocals), Chris Gentry (born 23/2/1977, Southend, guitar), Stuart Black (born 1/4/1974, London, bass), Matt Everett (born 13/8/1972, Birmingham, drums) and Simon White (born 1/7/1977, Birmingham, guitar). They performed on *Top Of The Pops* before even releasing a single. Everett left in 1997 and was briefly replaced by Tud Tudgate, the group disbanding soon after.

	DATE	POS	WKS	BPI	SINGLE TITLE	LABEL & NUMBER
	15/04/1995	49	1		I'LL MANAGE SOMEHOW	Laurel LAUCD 4
	01/07/1995	14	4		DAYDREAMER	Laurel LAUCD 5
	30/09/1995	16	3		STARDUST	Laurel LAUCD 6
	16/12/1995	24	3		SLEEPING IN	Laurel LAUCD 7
	23/03/1996	10	4		**BEING BRAVE**	Laurel LAUCD 8
	07/09/1996	22	3		WE LOVE YOU	Laurel LAUCD 11

MENTAL AS ANYTHING
Australian/New Zealand group formed in 1976 by Reg Mombasa (born Chris O'Doherty, guitar/vocals), Wayne Delisle (drums), Martin Plaza (born Martin Murphy, guitar/vocals), Greedy Smith (born Andrew Smith, keyboards/vocals) and Peter O'Doherty (bass).

	DATE	POS	WKS	BPI	SINGLE TITLE	LABEL & NUMBER
	07/02/1987	3	13	O	**LIVE IT UP** Featured in the 1987 film *Crocodile Dundee*	Epic ANY 1

FREDDIE MERCURY
UK singer (born Farookh Bulsara, 5/9/1946, Zanzibar, Tanzania) who moved to the UK in 1959, joining Queen as lead vocalist in 1970 and releasing his first single (as Larry Lurex) in 1973, shortly before Queen had their debut release. He launched a parallel solo career in 1984. With Queen he won the Outstanding Contribution Award at the 1990 BRIT Awards. Following his death, Queen's *Bohemian Rhapsody* was named Best British Single and Mercury was posthumously awarded the Outstanding Contribution Award at the 1992 BRIT Awards. Only John Lennon (solo in 1982, and 1983 as a Beatle) had previously been awarded two Outstanding Contribution Awards. Mercury died from AIDS on 24/11/1991.

	DATE	POS	WKS	BPI	SINGLE TITLE	LABEL & NUMBER
	22/09/1984	10	8		**LOVE KILLS** Featured in the 1984 reconstruction of the 1926 film *Metropolis* and the 1991 film *Love Kills*	CBS A 4735
	20/04/1985	11	10		I WAS BORN TO LOVE YOU	CBS A 6019
	13/07/1985	57	4		MADE IN HEAVEN	CBS A 6413
	21/09/1985	50	3		LIVING ON MY OWN	CBS A 6555
	24/05/1986	32	5		TIME	EMI 5559
	07/03/1987	4	9		**THE GREAT PRETENDER**	Parlophone R 6151
	07/11/1987	8	9		**BARCELONA** FREDDIE MERCURY AND MONTSERRAT CABALLE	Polydor POSP 887
	08/08/1992	2	8		**BARCELONA** FREDDIE MERCURY AND MONTSERRAT CABALLE Re-issue of Polydor POSP 887	Polydor PO 221
	12/12/1992	8	7		**IN MY DEFENCE**	Parlophone R 6331
	06/02/1993	29	3		THE GREAT PRETENDER Re-issue of Parlophone R 6151	Parlophone CDR 6336
	31/07/1993	●[2]	13	●	**LIVING ON MY OWN** Posthumous #1	Parlophone CDR 6355

MERCURY REV
US rock group originally formed by David Baker (guitar/vocals), Jonathan Donahue (guitar), Grasshopper (born Sean Mackowiak, guitar/clarinet), Suzanne Thorpe (flute), Dave Fridmann (bass) and Jimmy Chambers (drums).

	DATE	POS	WKS	BPI	SINGLE TITLE	LABEL & NUMBER
	14/11/1998	51	1		GODDESS ON A HIWAY	V2 VVR 5003323
	06/02/1999	26	2		DELTA SUN BOTTLENECK STOMP	V2 VVR 5005413
	22/05/1999	31	2		OPUS 40	V2 VVR 5006963
	28/08/1999	26	2		GODDESS ON A HIWAY	V2 VVR 5008498
	06/10/2001	47	1		NITE AND FOG	V2 VVR 5017728
	26/01/2002	16	3		THE DARK IS RISING	V2 VVR 5018713
	27/07/2002	51	1		LITTLE RHYMES	V2 VVR 5019788

MERCY MERCY
UK vocal/instrumental group formed by Luke Tunney and Colin Young.

O Silver disc ● Gold disc ✪ Platinum disc (additional platinum units are indicated by a figure following the symbol) ◉ Singles released prior to 1973 that are known to have sold over 1 million copies in the UK

21/09/1985 . . . . . 59 . . . . . . 2 . . . . WHAT ARE WE GONNA DO ABOUT IT? . . . . Ensign ENY 522

MERLIN UK rapper/singer who was in youth custody when The Beatmasters charted and had to have a police escort to the studio for *Top Of The Pops.*

27/08/1988 . . . . . 6 . . . . . . 9 . . . . . . **MEGABLAST/DON'T MAKE ME WAIT** BOMB THE BASS FEATURING MERLIN AND ANTONIA/BOMB THE BASS FEATURING LORRAINE . .
. . . . Mister-ron DOOD 2

22/04/1989 . . . . . 8 . . . . . . 9 . . . . . . **WHO'S IN THE HOUSE** BEATMASTERS FEATURING MERLIN . . . . Rhythm King LEFT 31

MERO UK vocal duo Tommy Clark and Derek McDonald. McDonald later recorded solo as Dmac.

25/03/2000 . . . . . 33 . . . . . . 2 . . . . IT MUST BE LOVE . . . . RCA 74321664772

TONY MERRICK UK singer (born in Scotland) who was leader of the Tony Merrick Scene before going solo.

02/06/1966 . . . . . 49 . . . . . . 1 . . . . LADY JANE . . . . Columbia DB 7913

AVID MERRION, DAVINA McCALL AND PATSY KENSIT UK vocal trio formed by Avid Merrion (born Leigh Francis, 30/5/1973), Davina McCall (born 16/10/1967, London) and Patsy Kensit (born 4/3/1968, London). Merrion had previously charted as Bo Selecta, Davina McCall is a TV presenter and Patsy Kensit was a member of Eighth Wonder before becoming an actress, appearing in *Emmerdale* as Sadie King.

25/12/2004 . . . . . 5 . . . . . 1+ . . . . . . **I GOT YOU BABE/SODA POP** . . . . BMG 82876669872

MERSEYBEATS UK group formed in Liverpool in 1960 as the Mavericks, changing their name to the Pacifics and finally the Merseybeats in 1962. The charting line-up was John Banks, Tony Crane, Johnny Gustafson and Aaron Williams. They disbanded in 1966, with Crane and another ex-Merseybeat, Billy Kinsley, forming The Merseys.

12/09/1963 . . . . . 24 . . . . . 12 . . . . . . IT'S LOVE THAT REALLY COUNTS . . . . Fontana TF 412
16/01/1964 . . . . . 5 . . . . . 17 . . . . . . **I THINK OF YOU** . . . . Fontana TF 431
16/04/1964 . . . . . 13 . . . . . 11 . . . . . . DON'T TURN AROUND . . . . Fontana TF 459
09/07/1964 . . . . . 13 . . . . . 10 . . . . . . WISHIN' AND HOPIN' . . . . Fontana TF 482
05/11/1964 . . . . . 40 . . . . . . 3 . . . . . . LAST NIGHT . . . . Fontana TF 504
14/10/1965 . . . . . 22 . . . . . . 8 . . . . . . I LOVE YOU, YES I DO . . . . Fontana TF 607
20/01/1966 . . . . . 38 . . . . . . 3 . . . . . . I STAND ACCUSED . . . . Fontana TF 645

MERSEYS UK vocal duo of ex-Merseybeats Tony Crane and Billy Kinsley. Kinsley was later in Liverpool Express.

28/04/1966 . . . . . 4 . . . . . 13 . . . . . . **SORROW** . . . . Fontana TF 694

MERTON PARKAS UK group formed in the Mod revival by Neil Hurrell (bass), Simon Smith (drums), Danny Talbot (vocals) and Mick Talbot (born 11/9/1958, London, keyboards). Talbot, also in the Chords, later formed Style Council with Paul Weller.

04/08/1979 . . . . . 40 . . . . . . 6 . . . . . . YOU NEED WHEELS . . . . Beggars Banquet BEG 22

MERZ UK singer/instrumentalist Conrad Lambert.

17/07/1999 . . . . . 48 . . . . . . 1 . . . . . . MANY WEATHERS APART . . . . Epic 6674972
16/10/1999 . . . . . 60 . . . . . . 1 . . . . . . LOVELY DAUGHTER . . . . Epic 6679132

MESCALEROS – see JOE STRUMMER

MADY MESPLE & DANIELLE MILLET WITH THE PARIS OPERACOMIQUE ORCHESTRA CONDUCTED BY ALAIN LOMBARD French vocal duo with an orchestra conducted by Alain Lombard.

06/04/1985 . . . . . 47 . . . . . . 4 . . . . . . FLOWER DUET (FROM LAKME) . . . . EMI 5481

MESSIAH UK dance duo Ali Ghani and Mark Davies, who met while students at the University of East Anglia. Precious Wilson is a US singer who used to be lead vocalist with Eruption.

20/06/1992 . . . . . 20 . . . . . . 5 . . . . . . TEMPLE OF DREAMS Contains a sample of This Mortal Coil's *Song To The Siren.* . . . . Kickin KICK 125
26/09/1992 . . . . . 19 . . . . . . 5 . . . . . . I FEEL LOVE MESSIAH FEATURING PRECIOUS WILSON . . . . Kickin KICK 225
27/11/1993 . . . . . 29 . . . . . . 3 . . . . . . THUNDERDOME . . . . WEA YZ 790CD1

METAL GURUS UK vocal/instrumental group formed by Wayne Hussey (guitar/vocals), Simon Hinkler (guitar), Craig Adams (bass) and Mick Brown (drums). This was effectively The Mission recording under a different name.

08/12/1990 . . . . . 55 . . . . . . 2 . . . . . . MERRY XMAS EVERYBODY . . . . Mercury GURU 1

METALHEADZ – see GOLDIE

METALLICA US heavy metal group formed in Los Angeles, CA in 1981 by Lars Ulrich (born 26/12/1963, Copenhagen, Denmark, drums), James Hetfield (born 3/8/1963, Los Angeles, vocals), Dave Mustaine (born 13/9/1963, La Mesa, CA, guitar) and Ron McGovney (bass). McGovney left in 1982 and was replaced by Cliff Burton (born 10/2/1962). Mustaine left in 1983 to form Megadeth and was replaced by Kirk Hammett (born 18/11/1962, San Francisco, CA). Burton was killed on 27/9/1986 when the tour bus crashed in Sweden; he was replaced by Jason Newsted (born 4/3/1963). Seven Grammy Awards include Best Metal Performance (Vocal or Instrumental) in 1990 for *Stone Cold Crazy,* Best Metal Performance with Vocal in 1991 for *Metallica,* Best Metal Performance in 1998 for *Better Than You* and Best Rock Instrumental Performance with Michael Kamen and the San Francisco Symphony Orchestra for *The Call Of The Ktulu.*

22/08/1987 . . . . . 27 . . . . . . 4 . . . . . . THE $5.98 EP – GARAGE DAYS REVISITED Tracks on EP: *Garage Days Revisited, Helpless, Crash Course In Brain Surgery, The Small Hours, Last Caress* and *Green Hell* . . . . Vertigo METAL 112

❶⁹ Number of weeks single topped the UK chart ↑ Entered the UK chart at #1 ▲⁹ Number of weeks single topped the US chart

525

03/09/1988	20	3		HARVESTER OF SORROW	Vertigo METAL 212
22/04/1989	13	7		ONE 1989 Grammy Award for Best Metal Performance (Vocal or Instrumental)	Vertigo METAL 5
10/08/1991	5	4		**ENTER SANDMAN**	Vertigo METAL 7
09/11/1991	15	4		THE UNFORGIVEN	Vertigo METAL 8
02/05/1992	6	6		**NOTHING ELSE MATTERS**	Vertigo METAL 10
31/10/1992	25	2		WHEREVER I MAY ROAM	Vertigo METAL 9
20/02/1993	20	3		SAD BUT TRUE	Vertigo METCD 11
01/06/1996	5	4		**UNTIL IT SLEEPS**	Vertigo UKMETCX 12
28/09/1996	17	4		HERO OF THE DAY	Vertigo METCD 13
07/12/1996	19	2		MAMA SAID	Vertigo METCD 14
22/11/1997	13	3		THE MEMORY REMAINS Features the uncredited contribution of Marianne Faithfull	Vertigo METCD 15
07/03/1998	15	4		THE UNFORGIVEN II	Vertigo METDD 17
04/07/1998	31	2		FUEL	Vertigo METCD 16
27/02/1999	29	2		WHISKEY IN THE JAR 1999 Grammy Award for Best Hard Rock Performance	Vertigo METCD 19
12/08/2000	35	3		I DISAPPEAR	Hollywood 0113875 HWR
05/07/2003	9	8		**ST ANGER** 2003 Grammy Award for Best Metal Performance	Vertigo 9865413
04/10/2003	16	3		FRANTIC	Vertigo 9811514
24/01/2004	42	2		THE UNNAMED FEELING	Vertigo 9815881

METEOR SEVEN German producer Jans Ebert.

18/05/2002	71	1		UNIVERSAL MUSIC	Bulletproof PROOF 16CD

METEORS UK group formed by Paul Fenech (guitar/vocals) and Nigel Lewis (double bass/vocals) as Rock Therapy. They added Mark Robertson (drums) in 1980 and became Raw Deal at the time they signed with Alligator Records. They changed their name again to The Meteors. By 1982 only Fenech remained from the original line-up, adding Mick White (bass), Russell Jones (guitar) and later Steve Meadham (drums). White left in 1983, was briefly replaced by Rick Ross and then by Ian 'Spider' Cubitt. Neville Hunt (bass) joined in 1985, with Cubitt leaving soon after to be ultimately replaced by Lee Brown. Mark Howe later took over on drums.

26/02/1983	66	2		JOHNNY REMEMBER ME	ID EYE 1

PAT METHENY GROUP – see DAVID BOWIE

METHOD MAN US rapper (born Clifford Smith, 1/4/1971, Staten Island, NYC) who is a member of rap supergroup Wu-Tang Clan and is also known as Johnny Blaze, Meth Tical, Shakwon, The MZA and Ticallion Stallion.

29/04/1995	46	1		RELEASE YO' SELF	Def Jam DEFCD 6
29/07/1995	10	5		**I'LL BE THERE FOR YOU/YOU'RE ALL I NEED TO GET BY METHOD MAN/MARY J. BLIGE** Both songs written by Ashford & Simpson. Method Man raps over *I'll Be There For You* while Blige sings the chorus of *You're All I Need To Get By*. 1995 Grammy Award for Best Rap Performance by a Duo	Def Jam DEFDX11
05/04/1997	8	6		**HIT 'EM HIGH (THE MONSTARS' ANTHEM) B REAL/BUSTA RHYMES/COOLIO/LL COOL J/METHOD MAN** Featured in the 1996 film *Space Jam*	Atlantic A 5449CD
22/05/1999	33	2		BREAK UPS 2 MAKE UPS **METHOD MAN FEATURING D'ANGELO**	Def Jam 8709272
27/09/2003	18	4		LOVE @ 1ST SIGHT **MARY J. BLIGE FEATURING METHOD MAN** Contains a sample of A Tribe Called Quest's *Hot Sex*	MCA MCSTD 40338
22/05/2004	17	5		WHAT'S HAPPENIN' **METHOD MAN FEATURING BUSTA RHYMES**	Def Jam 9862518

MEW Danish rock group formed in Copenhagen by Jonas Bjerre (vocals), Bo Madsen (guitar), Johan Wohlert (bass) and Silas Graae (drums). They launched their own label Evil Office.

05/04/2003	48	1		COMFORTING SOUNDS	Epic 6736432
28/06/2003	47	1		AM I WRY NO	Epic 6739395
27/12/2003	55	1		SHE CAME HOME FOR CHRISTMAS	Epic 6744942

MEZZOFORTE Icelandic group formed in 1977 by Johann Asmundsson (bass), Gunnlauger Briem (drums), Eythor Gunnarsson (keyboards), Fridrik Karlsson (guitar) and Kristin Svavarsson (saxophone).

05/03/1983	17	9		GARDEN PARTY	Steinar STE 705
11/06/1983	75	1		ROCKALL	Steinar STE 710

MFSB US studio group formed by producers Kenny Gamble and Leon Huff to back artists on Philadelphia International. Musicians included Larry Moore (bass), Lenny Pakula (keyboards), Norman Harris (guitar), James Herb Smith (guitar), Roland Chambers (guitar) and Earl Young (drums). The name stands for Mother Father Sister Brother. They had previously recorded as The Music Makers in 1967 for Kenny Gamble's eponymous label and scored a US hit with *United (Part 1)*.

27/04/1974	22	9	▲2	TSOP (THE SOUND OF PHILADELPHIA) **MFSB FEATURING THE THREE DEGREES** Theme to the US TV series *Soul Train*. 1974 Grammy Award for Best Rhythm & Blues Instrumental Performance	Philadelphia International PIR 2289
26/07/1975	37	5		SEXY	Philadelphia International PIR 3381
31/01/1981	41	4		MYSTERIES OF THE WORLD	Sound Of Philadelphia PIR 9501

MG'S – see BOOKER T AND THE MG'S

MIAMI SOUND MACHINE US group formed in Miami, FL in 1973 by Cuban exiles Emilio Estefan (born 4/3/1953, Havana, Cuba), Juan Avila (born 1956, Cuba) and Enrique E Garcia (born 1958, Cuba) as the Miami Latin Boys. Lead vocalist Gloria Fajardo (born 1/9/1957, Havana) joined in 1974, and the group changed their name to Miami Sound Machine. Estefan and Fajardo were married

in 1978, and by 1990 the group was basically Gloria Estefan's touring band. That same year their tour bus was hit by a tractor-trailer in Pennsylvania, leaving Gloria with fractures and dislocations. Although it was feared she was paralysed, she made a full recovery.

11/08/1984	6	14	○	DR BEAT	Epic A 4614
17/05/1986	16	11		BAD BOY	Epic A 6537
16/07/1988	10	16		ANYTHING FOR YOU ▲[2]	Epic 6516737
22/10/1988	9	10		1-2-3	Epic 6529587
17/12/1988	16	9		RHYTHM IS GONNA GET YOU	Epic 6545147
11/02/1989	7	12		CAN'T STAY AWAY FROM YOU This and above three singles credited to GLORIA ESTEFAN AND MIAMI SOUND MACHINE	Epic 6514447

GEORGE MICHAEL UK singer (born Georgios Panayiotou, 25/6/1963, London) who formed the Executive in 1979 with Andrew Ridgeley, the group later becoming Wham! He began recording solo while still in the group (*Careless Whisper* being released in the US as Wham! Featuring George Michael) before splitting the group in 1986. Legal wrangles with his record company stopped any new material from 1992 until 1996, when he switched to Virgin. He won the Best British Male Award at the 1988 and 1997 BRIT Awards and the Best Album category for *Listen Without Prejudice Volume 1* in 1991, and the 1996 MTV Europe Music Award for Best Male. While with Wham! he had collected the Best British Group award in 1985 and an Outstanding Contribution award (jointly with Elton John) in 1986. His two Grammy Awards include Album of the Year in 1988 for *Faith*. Toby Bourke is a UK singer.

04/08/1984	❶[3]	17	✪	CARELESS WHISPER ▲[3]	Epic A 4603
05/04/1986	❶[3]	10	●	A DIFFERENT CORNER	Epic A 7033
31/01/1987	❶[2]	9	●	I KNEW YOU WERE WAITING (FOR ME) ▲[2] ARETHA FRANKLIN AND GEORGE MICHAEL 1987 Grammy Award for Best Rhythm & Blues Vocal Performance by a Duo	Epic DUET 2
13/06/1987	3	10		I WANT YOUR SEX Featured in the 1987 film *Beverly Hills Cop II*	Epic LUST 1
24/10/1987	2	12		FAITH ▲[4]	Epic EMU 3
09/01/1988	11	6		FATHER FIGURE ▲[2]	Epic EMU 4
23/04/1988	8	7		ONE MORE TRY ▲[3]	Epic EMU 5
16/07/1988	13	6		MONKEY ▲[2]	Epic EMU 6
03/12/1988	18	6		KISSING A FOOL	Epic EMU 7
25/08/1990	6	7		PRAYING FOR TIME ▲[1]	Epic GEO 1
27/10/1990	23	5		WAITING FOR THAT DAY	Epic GEO 2
15/12/1990	28	6		FREEDOM 90	Epic GEO 3
16/02/1991	31	4		HEAL THE PAIN	Epic 6566477
30/03/1991	45	3		COWBOYS AND ANGELS	Epic 6567747
07/12/1991	❶[2]	10	○	DON'T LET THE SUN GO DOWN ON ME ↑ ▲[1] GEORGE MICHAEL AND ELTON JOHN Live version of 1974 Elton John hit	Epic 6576467
13/06/1992	4	9		TOOFUNKY ↑	Epic 6580587
01/05/1993	❶[3]	12	●	FIVE LIVE EP ↑ GEORGE MICHAEL AND QUEEN WITH LISA STANSFIELD Tracks on EP: *Somebody To Love, These Are The Days Of Our Lives, Calling You* and *Papa Was A Rolling Stone – Killer (Medley)*	Parlophone CDRS 6340
20/01/1996	❶[1]	13	○	JESUS TO A CHILD ↑	Virgin VSCDG 1571
04/05/1996	❶[3]	14	●	FASTLOVE ↑ Contains a sample of Patrice Rushen's *Forget Me Nots*	Virgin VSCDG 1579
31/08/1996	2	12	○	SPINNING THE WHEEL	Virgin VSCDG 1595
01/02/1997	3	9		OLDER/I CAN'T MAKE YOU LOVE ME	Virgin VSCDG 1626
10/05/1997	2	13		STAR PEOPLE '97	Virgin VSCDG 1641
07/06/1997	10	4		WALTZ AWAY DREAMING TOBY BOURKE/GEORGE MICHAEL	Aegean AECD 01
20/09/1997	2	8		YOU HAVE BEEN LOVED/THE STRANGEST THING '97	Virgin VSCD 1663
31/10/1998	2	16	○	OUTSIDE	Epic 6665625
13/03/1999	4	10	○	AS GEORGE MICHAEL AND MARY J. BLIGE	Epic 6670122
17/06/2000	9	11		IF I TOLD YOU THAT WHITNEY HOUSTON AND GEORGE MICHAEL	Arista 74321766282
30/03/2002	7	10		FREEEK! Contains a sample of Aaliyah's *Try Again*	Polydor 5706822
10/08/2002	12	5		SHOOT THE DOG Contains a sample of The Human League's *Love Action (I Believe In Love)*	Polydor 5709242
13/03/2004	4	11		AMAZING	Aegean 6747265
10/07/2004	8	10		FLAWLESS (GO TO THE CITY) Contains an interpolation of The Ones' *Flawless*	Aegean 6750682
13/11/2004	32	2		ROUND HERE	Aegean 6754702

MICHAELA UK singer Michaela Strachan who was first well known as a DJ on Radio 1.

02/09/1989	62	4		H-A-P-P-Y RADIO	London H 1
28/04/1990	66	2		TAKE GOOD CARE OF MY HEART	London WAC 90

LISA MICHAELIS – see FRANKIE KNUCKLES

PRAS MICHEL US rapper (born Prakazrel 'Pras' Micheal, 19/10/1972, NYC), also in The Fugees. Dante Thomas is a US singer.

27/06/1998	2	17	✪	GHETTO SUPERSTAR (THAT IS WHAT YOU ARE) PRAS MICHEL FEATURING OL' DIRTY BASTARD AND INTRODUCING MYA Contains a sample of James Brown's *Get Up, Get Into It, Get Involved* and an interpolation of the song *Islands In The Stream*. 1998 MOBO Award for Best International Single. Featured in the 1998 film *Bulworth*	Interscope IND 95593
07/11/1998	6	10		BLUE ANGELS PRAS	Ruffhouse 6666215
14/11/1998	5	6		ANOTHER ONE BITES THE DUST QUEEN WITH WYCLEF JEAN FEATURING PRAS MICHEL/FREE Featured in the 1998 film *Small Soldiers*	DreamWorks DRMCD 22364
01/09/2001	25	3		MISS CALIFORNIA DANTE THOMAS FEATURING PRAS	Elektra E 7192CD

❶[9] Number of weeks single topped the UK chart ↑ Entered the UK chart at #1 ▲[9] Number of weeks single topped the US chart

527

MICHELE – see **KING BEE**

KEITH MICHELL Australian actor/singer (born 1/12/1926, Adelaide) who was famous for his portrayal of Henry VIII in the TV drama *The Merry Wives of Henry VIII*.

27/03/1971.....30.....11.......	I'LL GIVE YOU THE EARTH (TOUS LES BATEAUX, TOUS LES OISEAUX)..Spark SRL 1046
26/01/1980.....5.....10.....O	**CAPTAIN BEAKY/WILFRED THE WEASEL**..Polydor POSP 106
29/03/1980.....53.....4.......	THE TRIAL OF HISSING SID **KEITH MICHELL, CAPTAIN BEAKY AND HIS BAND** ....Polydor HISS 1

MICHELLE Trinidadian singer.

08/06/1996.....69.....1.......	STANDING HERE ALL ALONE ....Positiva CDTIV 54

MICHELLE UK singer (born Michelle McManus, 1980 Bailleston, Lanarkshire) who won the 2003 *Pop Idols* competition.

17/01/2004.....❶³.....11......	ALL THIS TIME ↑ ....S 82876590652
17/04/2004.....16.....4......	THE MEANING OF LOVE ....S 82876604032

YVETTE MICHELLE US R&B singer (born Michele Bryant, Brooklyn, NYC) who worked with rapper O.C. and Full Force.

05/04/1997.....36.....3.......	I'M NOT FEELING YOU Contains a sample of Sylvester's *Was It Something I Said* ....Loud 74321465222

LLOYD MICHELS – see **MISTURA FEATURING LLOYD MICHELS**

MICROBE UK singer Ian Doody. The youngest artist to have a top 40 record, he was only three years of age at the time of his debut hit. The backing vocals on his hit were provided by Madeline Bell, Lesley Duncan and Dusty Springfield.

14/05/1969.....29.....7.......	GROOVY BABY ....CBS 4158

MICRODISNEY Irish group formed in Cork in 1980 by Sean O'Hagan and Cathal Coughlan. O'Hagan later recorded solo while Coughlan formed Fatima Mansions.

21/02/1987.....55.....3.......	TOWN TO TOWN ....Virgin VS 927

MIDDLE OF THE ROAD UK group formed in Glasgow by Sally Carr (born Sally Young, 28/3/1945), Ken Andrew and brothers Eric and Ian Campbell Lewis as Part Four. They changed their name to Middle Of The Road in 1970.

05/06/1971.....❶⁵.....34......	**CHIRPY CHIRPY CHEEP CHEEP** Total worldwide sales exceed 10 million copies ....RCA 2047
04/09/1971.....2.....17......	**TWEEDLE DEE TWEEDLE DUM** ....RCA 2110
11/12/1971.....5.....12......	**SOLEY SOLEY** ....RCA 2151
08/04/1972.....23.....7......	SACRAMENTO ....RCA 2184
29/07/1972.....26.....6......	SAMSON AND DELILAH ....RCA 2237

MIDDLESBROUGH FC FEATURING BOB MORTIMER AND CHRIS REA UK professional football club formed in 1875. Their hit single marked an appearance at the FA Cup Final. Bob Mortimer is a UK comic who usually works with Vic Reeves.

24/05/1997.....44.....1......	LET'S DANCE ....Magnet EW 112CD

MIDFIELD GENERAL FEATURING LINDA LEWIS UK producer Damian Harris with singer Linda Lewis.

19/08/2000.....61.....1.......	REACH OUT Contains a sample of Linda Lewis' *Reach For The Truth* ....Skint 54CD

MIDGET UK vocal/instrumental group formed in Stamford by Richard Gombault (guitar/vocals), Andy Hawkins (bass) and Lee Major (drums) as Smokin' Lizards. They signed with Radar in 1996 as Midget.

31/01/1998.....57.....1.......	ALL FALL DOWN ....Radarscope TINYCDS 6X
18/04/1998.....66.....1.......	INVISIBLE BALLOON ....Radarscope TINYCDS 7

MIDI XPRESS UK vocal/instrumental duo Matt Clayden and Keith MacDonald who previously recorded as Keith Mac Project.

11/05/1996.....73.....1.......	CHASE ....Labello Dance LAD 26CD

BETTE MIDLER US singer (born 1/12/1944, Paterson, NJ, raised in Hawaii) who moved to New York in 1966, appearing on Broadway before starting a singing career in 1969. Barry Manilow was her pianist during her early career. She later appeared in numerous films, including 1979's *The Rose,* for which she was nominated for an Oscar. Four Grammy Awards include Best New Artist in 1973, Best Pop Vocal Performance in 1980 for *The Rose* and Best Recording for Children in 1980 with various others for *In Harmony*. She has a star on the Hollywood Walk of Fame.

17/06/1989.....5.....12......	WIND BENEATH MY WINGS ▲¹ Featured in the 1988 film *Beaches*. 1989 Grammy Awards for Record of the Year plus Song of the Year for writers Larry Henley and Jeff Silbar ....Atlantic A 8972
13/10/1990.....45.....5......	FROM A DISTANCE ....Atlantic A 7820
15/06/1991.....6.....9......	**FROM A DISTANCE** ....Atlantic A 7820
05/12/1998.....58.....1......	MY ONE TRUE FRIEND Featured in the 1998 film *One True Thing* ....Warner Brothers W 460CD

MIDNIGHT COWBOY SOUNDTRACK US orchestra. The 1969 film was scored by UK composer John Barry and starred Dustin Hoffman and Jon Voight.

08/11/1980.....47.....4.......	MIDNIGHT COWBOY ....United Artists UP 634

MIDNIGHT OIL Australian rock group formed in 1976 by Jim Moginie (guitar), Rob Hirst (drums), Martin Rotsey (guitar), Andrew 'Bear' James (bass) and Peter Garrett (vocals). James left in 1980 and was replaced by Peter Gilford, who left in 1987 and was replaced

O Silver disc ● Gold disc ✪ Platinum disc (additional platinum units are indicated by a figure following the symbol) ◎ Singles released prior to 1973 that are known to have sold over 1 million copies in the UK

by Dwayne 'Bones' Hillman. Garrett later ran for the Australian Senate for the Nuclear Disarmament Party (he polled over 200,000 votes and was only narrowly defeated).

23/04/1988	48	5		BEDS ARE BURNING	Sprint OIL 1
02/07/1988	68	2		THE DEAD HEART	Sprint OIL 2
25/03/1989	6	13		**BEDS ARE BURNING** Re-issue of Sprint OIL 1	Sprint OIL 3
01/07/1989	62	4		THE DEAD HEART Re-issue of Sprint OIL 2	Sprint OIL 4
10/02/1990	66	2		BLUE SKY MINE	CBS OIL 5
17/04/1993	29	4		TRUGANINI	Columbia 6590492
03/07/1993	66	1		MY COUNTRY	Columbia 6593702
06/11/1993	60	1		IN THE VALLEY	Columbia 6598492

MIDNIGHT STAR
US R&B group formed at Kentucky State University in 1976 by Reggie Calloway (trumpet), Vincent Calloway (trombone), Belinda Lipscomb (lead vocals), Melvin Watson, Boaz 'Bo' Watson, Jeffrey Cooper, Kenneth Gentry, Bobby Lovelace and William Simmons. The Calloway brothers left in 1987 to form Calloway.

23/02/1985	66	2		OPERATOR	Solar MCA 942
28/06/1986	16	8		HEADLINES	Solar MCA 1065
04/10/1986	8	10		**MIDAS TOUCH**	Solar MCA 1096
07/02/1987	64	3		ENGINE NO 9	Solar MCA 1117
02/05/1987	60	3		WET MY WHISTLE	Solar MCA 1127

MIDNITE BAND – see TONY RALLO AND THE MIDNITE BAND

MIGHTY AVENGERS
UK vocal/instrumental group formed by Tony Campbell (born 24/6/1944, Rugby, guitar/vocals), Tony Machon (bass/lead vocals) and Biffo Beech (drums). The group was managed by Rolling Stone manager Andrew Loog Oldham. Campbell was later a member of Jigsaw.

26/11/1964	46	2		SO MUCH IN LOVE	Decca F 11962

MIGHTY AVONS – see LARRY CUNNINGHAM AND THE MIGHTY AVONS

MIGHTY DUB KATZ
UK singer Norman Cook (born Quentin Cook, 31/7/1963, Brighton). Formerly in The Housemartins, he formed Beats International and also recorded solo and as Pizzaman, Fatboy Slim and Freakpower.

07/12/1996	43	1		JUST ANOTHER GROOVE	ffrr FCD 287
02/08/1997	24	4		MAGIC CARPET RIDE	ffrr FCD 306
07/12/2002	73	1		LET THE DRUMS SPEAK	Southern Fried ECB 31X

MIGHTY LEMON DROPS
UK group formed in Wolverhampton by Paul Marsh (guitar/vocals), David Newton (guitar), Tony Linehan (bass) and Keith Rowley (drums). They signed with Chrysalis' Blue Guitar imprint in 1985.

13/09/1986	67	1		THE OTHER SIDE OF YOU	Blue Guitar AZUR 1
18/04/1987	66	3		OUT OF HAND	Blue Guitar AZUR 4
23/01/1988	74	2		INSIDE OUT	Blue Guitar AZUR 6

MIGHTY MIGHTY BOSSTONES
US rock group formed in 1985 by Nate Albert (guitar), Dicky Barrett, Joe Gittleman (bass) Tim 'Johnny Vegas' Burton (saxophone), Josh Dulcimer (drums) and 'Bosstone' Ben Carr as The Bosstones. By 1990 they had become the Mighty Mighty Bosstones and added drummer Joe Sirois and the beefed-up 'Hurtin' For Certain' horns, comprised of Vegas, trombonist and barrel-chested baritone Dennis Brockenborough and co-saxman Kevin Lenear.

25/04/1998	12	5		THE IMPRESSION THAT I GET Featured in the 1997 film *Fathers' Day*	Mercury 5748432
27/06/1998	63	1		THE RASCAL KING	Mercury 5661092

MIGHTY MORPH'N POWER RANGERS
US vocal group assembled by Kussa Mahchi, Shuki Levy and Haim Saban. The group also released the album *Island Of Illusion*.

17/12/1994	3	13	○	**POWER RANGERS**	RCA 74321253022

MIGHTY WAH – see WAH!

MIGIL FIVE
UK group formed in 1961 by Red Lambert (guitar), Gilbert Lucas (piano), Lenny Blanche (bass) and Mike Felix (drums) as the Migil Four. They added Alan Watson (saxophone/vocals) to become the Migil Five.

19/03/1964	10	13		**MOCKIN' BIRD HILL**	Pye 7N 15597
04/06/1964	31	7		NEAR YOU	Pye 7N 15645

MIG29
Italian instrumental/production group formed by M Aventino and F Scandolari.

22/02/1992	62	2		MIG29	Champion CHAMP 292

MIKAELA – see SUPERCAR

MIKE
UK producer Mark Jolley.

19/11/1994	40	2		TWANGLING THREE FINGERS IN A BOX	Pukka CDMIKE 100

MIKE AND THE MECHANICS
UK rock group formed by Genesis member Mike Rutherford (born 2/10/1950, Guildford, guitar) in 1986 with ex-Ace Paul Carrack (born 22/4/1951, Sheffield, keyboards/vocals), ex-Sad Café Paul Young (vocals), Peter Van

❶⁹ Number of weeks single topped the UK chart ↑ Entered the UK chart at #1 ▲⁹ Number of weeks single topped the US chart

529

Hooke (drums) and Adrian Lee (keyboards). Young died from a heart attack on 17/7/2000.

DATE	POS	WKS	BPI	SINGLE TITLE	LABEL & NUMBER
15/02/1986	21	9		SILENT RUNNING (ON DANGEROUS GROUND) Featured in the 1985 film *On Dangerous Ground*	WEA U 8908
31/05/1986	53	4		ALL I NEED IS A MIRACLE	WEA U 8765
14/01/1989	2	11	●	**THE LIVING YEARS** ▲¹	WEA U 7717
16/03/1991	13	10		WORD OF MOUTH	Virgin VS 1345
15/06/1991	58	3		A TIME AND PLACE	Virgin VS 1351
08/02/1992	56	4		EVERYBODY GETS A SECOND CHANCE	Virgin VS 1396
25/02/1995	12	9		OVER MY SHOULDER	Virgin VSCDX 1526
17/06/1995	33	5		A BEGGAR ON A BEACH OF GOLD	Virgin VSCD 1535
02/09/1995	51	4		ANOTHER CUP OF COFFEE	Virgin VSCDT 1554
17/02/1996	27	4		ALL I NEED IS A MIRACLE '96 (REMIX)	Virgin VSCDG 1576
01/06/1996	61	1		SILENT RUNNING Re-issue of WEA U 8908	Virgin VSCDT 1585
05/06/1999	35	2		NOW THAT YOU'VE GONE	Virgin VSCD 1732
28/08/1999	73	1		WHENEVER I STOP	Virgin VSCDT 1743

MIKI AND GRIFF UK duo Miki (born Barbara MacDonald Salisbury, 20/6/1920, Ayrshire) and Griff (born Emyr Morusa Griffiths, 9/5/1923, Holywell, Wales). They first met in the George Mitchell Choir and were married in 1950. Miki died from cancer on 20/4/1989; Griff died on 24/9/1995.

DATE	POS	WKS	BPI	SINGLE TITLE	LABEL & NUMBER
02/10/1959	26	2		HOLD BACK TOMORROW	Pye 7N 15213
13/10/1960	44	3		ROCKIN' ALONE	Pye 7N 15296
01/02/1962	16	13		LITTLE BITTY TEAR	Pye 7N 15412
22/08/1963	23	7		I WANNA STAY HERE	Pye 7N 15555

JOHN MILES UK singer/multi-instrumentalist (born 23/4/1949, Jarrow) who was a guest singer with the Alan Parsons Project, Parsons having produced Miles' debut album in 1975. His first job after leaving school was making lavatory signs.

DATE	POS	WKS	BPI	SINGLE TITLE	LABEL & NUMBER
18/10/1975	17	6		HIGH FLY	Decca F 13595
20/03/1976	3	9	○	**MUSIC**	Decca F 13627
16/10/1976	32	5		REMEMBER YESTERDAY	Decca F 13667
18/06/1977	10	10		**SLOW DOWN**	Decca F 13709

ROBERT MILES Italian DJ (born Roberto Concina, 3/11/1969, Fleurier, Switzerland) whose debut single, originally released in Italy in 1994, was recorded in a studio built by the artist in Venice. He was named Best International Newcomer at the 1997 BRIT Awards.

DATE	POS	WKS	BPI	SINGLE TITLE	LABEL & NUMBER
24/02/1996	2	18	✪	**CHILDREN** Total worldwide sales exceed 13 million copies	Deconstruction 74321348322
08/06/1996	7	9		**FABLE**	Deconstruction 74321382622
16/11/1996	3	17	●	**ONE & ONE** ROBERT MILES FEATURING MARIA NAYLER	Deconstruction 74321427692
29/11/1997	15	4		**FREEDOM** ROBERT MILES FEATURING KATHY SLEDGE	Deconstruction 74321536952
28/07/2001	74	1		**PATHS** ROBERT MILES FEATURING NINA MIRANDA	Salt 002CDX

JUNE MILES-KINGSTON – see JIMMY SOMERVILLE

PAUL MILES-KINGSTON – see SARAH BRIGHTMAN

CHRISTINA MILIAN US singer (born 26/9/1981, New Jersey, raised in Maryland) who started as an actress in the TV programmes *Sister Sister* and *Clueless* and worked for the Walt Disney Company. She wrote a number of hits, including Jennifer Lopez's *Play*, before going solo.

DATE	POS	WKS	BPI	SINGLE TITLE	LABEL & NUMBER
03/03/2001	26	3		**BETWEEN ME AND YOU** JA RULE FEATURING CHRISTINA MILIAN	Def Jam 5727402
26/01/2002	3	11		**AM TO PM**	Def Soul 5889332
29/06/2002	3	10		**WHEN YOU LOOK AT ME**	Def Soul 5829802
09/11/2002	9	6		**IT'S ALL GRAVY** ROMEO FEATURING CHRISTINA MILIAN Contains a sample of Mary J. Blige's *Real Love*	Relentless RELENT 32CD
15/05/2004	2	13		**DIP IT LOW**	Def Jam UK 9862395
16/10/2004	9	7		**WHATEVER U WANT** CHRSTINA MILIAN FEATURING JOE BUDDEN Contains a sample of The Bar-Kays' *Spellbound*	Def Jam 9864266

MILK – see JASON DOWNS FEATURING MILK

MILK AND HONEY FEATURING GALI ATARI Israeli group who won the 1979 Eurovision Song Contest, beating the UK's entry by Black Lace into seventh place.

DATE	POS	WKS	BPI	SINGLE TITLE	LABEL & NUMBER
14/04/1979	5	8	○	**HALLELUJAH** 1979 Eurovision Song Contest winner	Polydor 2001 870

MILK AND SUGAR German production duo Michael 'Milk' Kronenberger and Steffann 'Sugar' Harning.

DATE	POS	WKS	BPI	SINGLE TITLE	LABEL & NUMBER
12/01/2002	25	3		LOVE IS IN THE AIR MILK & SUGAR FEATURING JOHN PAUL YOUNG	Positiva CDTIV 166
11/10/2003	18	4		LET THE SUNSHINE IN MILK & SUGAR FEATURING LIZZY PATTINSON	Data 64CDS

MILK INC Belgian vocal/production group formed by Regi Penxten, Ivo Donkers and Filip Van Dueren with singer Nikki Van Lier. Van Lier was subsequently replaced by Sofie Winters, Ann Vervoort and then Linda Mertens.

DATE	POS	WKS	BPI	SINGLE TITLE	LABEL & NUMBER
28/02/1998	23	3		GOOD ENOUGH (LA VACHE) MILK INCORPORATED	Malarky MLKD 5
25/05/2002	9	8		**IN MY EYES**	All Around The World CDGLOBE 252
21/09/2002	10	6		**WALK ON WATER**	Positiva CDTIV 179
11/01/2003	18	4		LAND OF THE LIVING	Positiva CDTIV 184

○ Silver disc ● Gold disc ✪ Platinum disc (additional platinum units are indicated by a figure following the symbol) ◎ Singles released prior to 1973 that are known to have sold over 1 million copies in the UK

MILKY German singer Sabrina Elahl Aus Kassel (born in Egypt).

31/08/2002	8	6	JUST THE WAY YOU ARE	Multiply CDMULTY 87
07/12/2002	48	1	IN MY MIND	Multiply CDMULTY 92

MILL GIRLS – see BILLY COTTON AND HIS BAND

MILLA US singer (born Milla Jovovich, 1976, Los Angeles, CA) who began her career as a model.

18/06/1994	65	1	GENTLEMAN WHO FELL	SBK CDSBK 49

FRANKIE MILLER UK singer/songwriter/guitarist (born 1950, Glasgow) who moved to London in 1971 and was a member of the short-lived group Jude. He recorded his debut solo album in 1973 with backing provided by Brinsley Schwarz.

04/06/1977	27	6		BE GOOD TO YOURSELF	Chrysalis CHS 2147
14/10/1978	6	15	○	DARLIN'	Chrysalis CHS 2255
20/01/1979	42	5		WHEN I'M AWAY FROM YOU	Chrysalis CHS 2276
21/03/1992	45	6		CALEDONIA	MCS 2001

GARY MILLER UK singer (born Neville Williams, 1924, Blackpool) who began his career as a footballer and played for Blackpool as an amateur. After World War II he began the process of becoming a singing star and finally got his break when spotted by talent scout Norman Newell, who signed him to Columbia in 1953. He died from a heart attack at his London home in 1968.

21/10/1955	13	5	YELLOW ROSE OF TEXAS	Pye Nixa N 15004
13/01/1956	10	6	ROBIN HOOD	Pye Nixa N 15020
11/01/1957	14	7	GARDEN OF EDEN	Pye Nixa N 15070
19/07/1957	29	1	WONDERFUL WONDERFUL	Pye Nixa N 15094
17/01/1958	14	6	STORY OF MY LIFE	Pye Nixa N 15120
21/12/1961	29	10	THERE GOES THAT SONG AGAIN/THE NIGHT IS YOUNG *The Night Is Young* was only listed for three weeks of the record's run, peaking at #32	Pye Nixa N 15404

GLENN MILLER US orchestra leader/trombonist (born 1/3/1904, Clarinda, IA) who first learned to play the cornet and mandolin and then trombone, playing for the Grant City, MO town band. Forming his own orchestra in 1937, four years later he was the top band leader in the world: when *Billboard* published the first ever sales chart in July 1940 he had three of the top ten places. He entered the US forces in 1942 as a captain and was later promoted to major, touring the UK during World War II. Films included *Sun Valley Serenade* (1941) and *Orchestra Wives* (1942). On 15/12/1944 while en route to France his plane disappeared over the Channel. It was later believed that a bomber returning home had jettisoned its bombs, one striking Miller's plane (although one book claimed he died of a heart attack in a French brothel). *The Glenn Miller Story* starring James Stewart was made in 1953. His 1939 recording *In The Mood* was given a special Grammy Hall of Fame award. He has a star on the Hollywood Walk of Fame.

12/03/1954	12	1	MOONLIGHT SERENADE	HMV BD 5942
24/01/1976	13	8	MOONLIGHT SERENADE/LITTLE BROWN JUG/IN THE MOOD ▲13 Re-issue of HMV BD 5942. Only *In The Mood* topped the US chart	RCA 2644

JODY MILLER US singer (born Myrna Joy Brooks, 29/11/1941, Phoenix, AZ, raised in Oklahoma) who won the Grammy Award for Best Country & Western Vocal Performance for *Queen Of The House* in 1965.

21/10/1965	49	1	HOME OF THE BRAVE	Capitol CL 15415

LEZA MILLER – see SERGIO MENDES

MITCH MILLER US orchestra leader (born Mitchell William Miller, 4/7/1911, Rochester, NY) who was an oboe soloist with the CBS Symphony Orchestra from 1936 until 1947, then later an A&R executive for both Columbia and Mercury Records. He appeared in the 1961 film *Holiday Sing Along With Mitch*. He has a star on the Hollywood Walk of Fame.

07/10/1955	2	13	YELLOW ROSE OF TEXAS ▲6	Philips PB 505

NED MILLER US singer (born Henry Ned Miller, 12/4/1925, Rains, UT) who moved to California in 1956, signing with Fabor.

14/02/1963	2	21	FROM A JACK TO A KING Originally released in the US in 1957	London HL 9658
18/02/1965	48	1	DO WHAT YOU DO WELL	London HL 9937

ROGER MILLER US singer (born 2/1/1936, Fort Worth, TX, raised in Oklahoma) who moved to Nashville in the mid-1950s to begin songwriting. He worked with Faron Young in 1962 before going solo. He died from lung cancer on 25/10/1992. Ten Grammy Awards included Best Country & Western Album, Best Country & Western Single, Best Country & Western Song and Best Country & Western Vocal Performance in 1964 for *Dang Me*, and Best New Country & Western Artist the same year.

18/03/1965	❶1	15	KING OF THE ROAD Featured in the 1966 film *Big T.N.T. Show* and the 1996 film *Swingers*. 1965 Grammy Awards for Best Contemporary Rock & Roll Single, Best Contemporary Rock & Roll Vocal Performance, Best Country & Western Single and Best Country & Western Vocal Performance, plus Best Country & Western Song for writer Roger Miller	Philips BF 1397
03/06/1965	33	5	ENGINE ENGINE NO. 9	Philips BF 1416
21/10/1965	48	1	KANSAS CITY STAR	Philips BF 1437
16/12/1965	13	8	ENGLAND SWINGS	Philips BF 1456
27/03/1968	19	10	LITTLE GREEN APPLES	Mercury MF 1021
02/04/1969	39	3	LITTLE GREEN APPLES	Mercury MF 1021

STEVE MILLER BAND US rock group formed in San Francisco, CA in 1966 by Steve Miller (born 5/10/1943, Milwaukee, WI, guitar/vocals), James 'Curley' Cooke (guitar/vocals), Lonnie Turner (bass/vocals) and Tim Davis (drums/vocals). They signed to Capitol in

❶9 Number of weeks single topped the UK chart ↑ Entered the UK chart at #1 ▲9 Number of weeks single topped the US chart

531

1967 and recorded their debut album in 1968. The group has a star on the Hollywood Walk of Fame.

DATE	POS	WKS	BPI	SINGLE TITLE	LABEL & NUMBER
23/10/1976	11	9		ROCK 'N ME ▲[1]	Mercury 6078 804
19/06/1982	2	11	○	**ABRACADABRA** ▲[2]	Mercury STEVE 3
04/09/1982	52	3		KEEPS IN ME IN WONDERLAND	Mercury STEVE 4
11/08/1990	❶[2]	13	○	**THE JOKER** ▲[1] Originally #1 in the US in 1973, it was revived in the UK after use in a Levi Jeans advertisement	Capitol CL 583

SUZI MILLER AND THE JOHNSTON BROTHERS UK singer (born Renee Lester) with vocal group.

21/01/1955	14	2		HAPPY DAYS AND LONELY NIGHTS	Decca F 10389

LISA MILLETT UK singer, also in Baby Bumps, who has worked with Lo Fidelity Allstars, The All Seeing I, Mojave 3 and Little Louie Vega.

03/09/1994	63	1		WALKIN' ON SHEER BRONZE FEATURING LISA MILLETT	Go Beat GODCD 115
16/09/2000	17	3		BAD HABIT A.T.F.C. PRESENTS ONEPHATDEEVA FEATURING LISA MILLETT Contains samples of Bad Habits' *Bad Habits* and Chaka Khan's *I Know You – I Love You*	Defected DFECT 19CDX
21/07/2001	27	2		SOUL HEAVEN GOODFELLAS FEATURING LISA MILLETT	Direction 6713852
09/02/2002	33	2		SLEEP TALK A.T.F.C. FEATURING LISA MILLETT	Defected DFECT 43CDS

MILLI VANILLI French/German vocal duo producerd by Frank Farian (who previously produced Boney M) with Rob Pilatus (born 8/6/1965) and Fabrice Morvan. Rob and Fab (as they became known) were later involved in financial wrangles with Farian, revealing that they had not sung on either of their first two hits, the actual vocalists being Charles Shaw, John Davis and Brad Howe. They were forced to give back their 1989 Best New Artist Grammy Award as a result. Pilatus was found dead from a drug overdose on 3/4/1998.

01/10/1988	3	13	○	**GIRL YOU KNOW IT'S TRUE**	Cooltempo COOL 170
17/12/1988	16	11		BABY DON'T FORGET MY NUMBER ▲[1]	Cooltempo COOL 178
22/07/1989	53	5		BLAME IT ON THE RAIN ▲[2]	Cooltempo COOL 180
30/09/1989	2	15	○	**GIRL I'M GONNA MISS YOU** ▲[2]	Cooltempo COOL 191
02/12/1989	52	5		BLAME IT ON THE RAIN	Cooltempo COOL 180
10/03/1990	74	1		ALL OR NOTHING	Cooltempo COOL 199

MILLICAN AND NESBITT UK vocal duo Alan Millican and Tom Nesbitt, two coal miners who won the TV talent show *Opportunity Knocks*.

01/12/1973	20	11		VAYA CON DOS	Pye 7N 45310
18/05/1974	38	3		FOR OLD TIME'S SAKE	Pye 7N 45357

MILLIE Jamaican singer (born Millicent Small, 6/10/1946, Clarendon) who was a juvenile star in Jamaica before finding worldwide acclaim.

12/03/1964	2	18		**MY BOY LOLLIPOP**	Fontana TF 449
25/06/1964	30	9		SWEET WILLIAM	Fontana TF 479
11/11/1965	48	1		BLOODSHOT EYES	Fontana TF 617
25/07/1987	46	5		MY BOY LOLLIPOP Re-issue of Fontana TF 449	Island WIP 6574

MILLION DAN UK producer Michael Dunn who was previously a member of Demon Boyz.

27/09/2003	66	1		DOGZ N SLEDGEZ	Gut CDGUT 52

MILLION DEAD UK rock group formed in London in 2001 by Frank Turner (vocals), Cameron Dean (guitar), Julia Ruzicka (bass) and Ben Dawson (drums).

29/05/2004	72	1		I GAVE MY EYES TO STEVIE WONDER	Xtra Mile XMR101

MILLIONAIRE HIPPIES UK producer Danny Rampling.

18/12/1993	52	3		I AM THE MUSIC HEAR ME!	Deconstruction 74321175432
10/09/1994	59	1		C'MON	Deconstruction 74321229372

GARRY MILLS UK singer (born 13/10/1941, West Wickham, Kent) who made his name with cover versions of US hits. Ironically, his biggest hit was heavily covered in the US, where four versions charted. His debut was the first hit for writer Mark Anthony, better known as Tony Hatch. He later recorded the theme to the TV puppet series *Stingray* and *Aqua Marina*.

07/07/1960	7	14		**LOOK FOR A STAR** Featured in the 1960 film *Circus Of Horrors*	Top Rank JAR 336
20/10/1960	24	12		TOP TEEN BABY	Top Rank JAR 500
22/06/1961	39	5		I'LL STEP DOWN	Decca F 11358

HAYLEY MILLS UK singer/actress (born 18/4/1946, London). Daughter of actor John Mills, she became a noted actress herself, appearing in the 1960 film *Pollyana*, among others, while in her teens. Her son Crispian formed Kula Shaker.

19/10/1961	17	11		LET'S GET TOGETHER Featured in the 1961 film *The Parent Trap*	Decca F 21396

STEPHANIE MILLS US singer (born 22/3/1957, Brooklyn, NYC) who appeared in the Broadway production of *Maggie Flynn* at the age of nine and toured with the Isley Brothers the following year. She won awards in the role of Dorothy in the Broadway show *The Wiz* and debuted on record in 1974 for Paramount. She was briefly married to Jeffrey Daniels of Shalamar.

18/10/1980	4	14	○	**NEVER KNEW LOVE LIKE THIS BEFORE** 1980 Grammy Awards for Best Rhythm & Blues Vocal Performance plus Best Rhythm & Blues Song for writers Reggie Lucas and James Mtume.	20th Century TC 2460
23/05/1981	49	5		TWO HEARTS STEPHANIE MILLS FEATURING TEDDY PENDERGRASS	20th Century TC 2492

15/09/1984.....29......9...... THE MEDICINE SONG..Club JAB 8
05/09/1987.....62......2...... (YOU'RE PUTTIN') A RUSH ON ME.......................................MCA 1187
01/05/1993.....57......2...... NEVER DO YOU WRONG...................................MCA MCSTD 1767
10/07/1993.....68......1...... ALL DAY ALL NIGHT..MCA MCSTD 1778

WARREN MILLS Zambian singer.
28/09/1985.....74......1...... SUNSHINE...Jive 99

MILLS BROTHERS US family vocal group formed in Pique, OH by John Jr (born 11/2/1911), Herbert (born 2/4/1912), Harry (born 9/8/1913) and Donald Mills (born 29/4/1915). Father John Sr (born 11/2/1889) joined the group in 1936, replacing John Jr. John Sr retired in 1956, the group continuing as a trio until 1982, when Donald and his son John III continued as a duo. The group, who began in the 1920s and were first famous for their vocal style of imitating instruments, had their first US hit in 1931. John Jr died in 1936, John Sr died on 8/12/1967, Harry died on 28/6/1982, Herbert died on 12/4/1989 and Donald died on 13/11/1999. They have a star on the Hollywood Walk of Fame.
30/01/1953.....10......1....... **GLOW WORM** Written in 1902 by Paul Lincke and Lilla Cayley Robinson. New lyrics by Johnny Mercer in 1952.....Brunswick 05007

MILLTOWN BROTHERS UK rock group formed in Burnley by Matt Nelson (vocals), Simon Nelson (guitar), James Fraser (bass), Nian Brindle (drums) and Barney James (keyboards).
02/02/1991.....38......5...... WHICH WAY SHOULD I JUMP...A&M AM 711
13/04/1991.....41......4...... HERE I STAND..A&M AM 758
06/07/1991.....43......4...... APPLE GREEN..A&M AM 787
22/05/1993.....55......1...... TURN OFF...A&M 5802692
17/07/1993.....48......2...... IT'S ALL OVER NOW BABY BLUE...A&M 5803332

MILLWALL FC UK professional football club formed in London in 1885 as Millwall Rovers, changing to Millwall Athletic and then Millwall. Their debut hit was released to coincide with an appearance in the FA Cup final.
29/05/2004.....41......1...... OH MILLWALL...Absolute CDAME4

CB MILTON Dutch singer.
21/05/1994.....49......2...... IT'S A LOVING THING..Logic 74321208062
25/03/1995.....34......2...... IT'S A LOVING THING (REMIX)...................................Logic 74321267212
19/08/1995.....62......1...... HOLD ON...Logic 74321292112

GARNET MIMMS AND TRUCKIN' CO US singer (born 16/11/1933, Ashland, WV, raised in Philadelphia, PA) who formed The Gainors in 1958, then fronted Garnet Mimms & The Enchanters, before going solo in 1964.
25/06/1977.....44......1...... WHAT IT IS...Arista 109

MIND OF KANE UK producer David Hope. He also recorded as Hope AD.
27/07/1991.....64......1...... STABBED IN THE BACK...Déjà Vu DJV 007

MINDBENDERS UK group formed in Manchester in 1963 by Wayne Fontana as his backing group, comprising Eric Stewart (born 20/1/1945, Manchester, lead guitar/vocals), Bob Lang (born 10/1/1946, Manchester, bass) and Ric Rothwell (born Eric Rothwell, 11/3/1944, Stockport, drums). Fontana left acrimoniously to go solo in 1965, the group adding Graham Gouldman in 1968. Gouldman and Stewart were later members of 10cc.
11/07/1963.....46......2...... HELLO JOSEPHINE...Fontana TF 404
28/05/1964.....37......4...... STOP LOOK AND LISTEN...Fontana TF 451
08/10/1964.....5......15...... UM UM UM UM UM UM...Fontana TF 497
04/02/1965.....2......11...... **GAME OF LOVE** ▲[1] Featured in the 1988 film *Good Morning Vietnam*................Fontana TF 535
17/06/1965.....20......7...... JUST A LITTLE BIT TOO LATE..Fontana TF 579
30/09/1965.....32......6...... SHE NEEDS LOVE This and above five singles credited to WAYNE FONTANA AND THE MINDBENDERS.............Fontana TF 611
13/01/1966.....2......14...... **A GROOVY KIND OF LOVE**..Fontana TF 644
05/05/1966.....28......7...... CAN'T LIVE WITH YOU (CAN'T LIVE WITHOUT YOU).....................Fontana TF 697
25/08/1966.....14......9...... ASHES TO ASHES...Fontana TF 731
20/09/1967.....42......4...... THE LETTER..Fontana TF 869

MINDS OF MEN UK group formed by Paul Birtles, Piers Sanderson and Kevin Edwards with singer Tracey Riggan.
22/06/1996.....41......1...... BRAND NEW DAY...Perfecto PERF 121CD

ZODIAC MINDWARP AND THE LOVE REACTION UK heavy rock group formed in 1986 by Zodiac Mindwarp (born Mark Manning, vocals), Cobalt Stargazer (guitar), Kid Chaos (bass) and Slam Thunderhide (drums). They disbanded in 1989.
09/05/1987.....18......6...... PRIME MOVER...Mercury ZOD 1
14/11/1987.....49......3...... BACKSEAT EDUCATION..Mercury ZOD 2
02/04/1988.....63......2...... PLANET GIRL..Mercury ZOD 3

SAL MINEO US singer (born 10/1/1939, New York) who appeared in numerous Broadway musicals and Hollywood films, including *Rebel Without A Cause* (1955), for which he received an Oscar nomination for Best Supporting Actor, *Escape From The Planet Of The Apes* and *Exodus* (1960), receiving a second Oscar nomination. Nicknamed The Switchblade Kid, he was stabbed to death on his way home from a theatre in Los Angeles on 12/2/1976; his killer was sentenced to life imprisonment in 1979.
12/07/1957.....16......11...... START MOVIN' (IN MY DIRECTION)....................................Philips PB 707

❶[9] Number of weeks single topped the UK chart ↑ Entered the UK chart at #1 ▲[9] Number of weeks single topped the US chart

533

MARCELLO MINERBI Italian orchestra leader.

22/07/1965 . . . . . 6 . . . . . . 16 . . . . . .   ZORBA'S DANCE Featured in the 1964 film *Zorba The Greek* . . . . Durium DRS 54001

MINI POPS UK children's vocal group assembled by producer Martin Wyatt and TV programme-maker Mike Mansfield. The group featured Zoe Hart, Joanna Wyatt, Joanna Fisher, Abby Kimber and Paul Hardy.

26/12/1987 . . . . . 39 . . . . . . 2 . . . . . .   SONGS FOR CHRISTMAS '87 EP Tracks on EP: *Thanks For Giving Us Christmas, The Man In Red, Christmas Time Around The World* and *Shine On*. . . . . Bright BULB 9

MINIMAL CHIC FEATURING MATT GOSS Italian production duo Gianluca Motta and Max Castrezzati with former Bros singer Matt Goss.

02/10/2004 . . . . . 54 . . . . . . 1 . . . . . .   I NEED THE KEY . . . . Inferno CDFERN63

MINIMAL FUNK 2 Italian production duo Gianfranco Randone and Rana. Randone is also a member of Eiffel 65.

18/07/1998 . . . . . 65 . . . . . . 1 . . . . . .   THE GROOVY THANG . . . . Cleveland City CLECD 13046
18/05/2002 . . . . . 63 . . . . . . 1 . . . . . .   DEFINITION OF HOUSE MINIMAL FUNK . . . . Junior BRG 033

MINIMALISTIX Belgian production trio Brian Koner, Steve Sidewinder and Joey Morton with vocalist Poison IV.

16/03/2002 . . . . . 12 . . . . . . 5 . . . . . .   CLOSE COVER. . . . . Data 32CDS
19/07/2003 . . . . . 36 . . . . . . 2 . . . . . .   MAGIC FLY . . . . Data 48CDS

MINISTERS DE LA FUNK US production trio Jose Nunez, Harry 'Choo Choo' Romero and Erick 'More' Morillo.

11/03/2000 . . . . . 45 . . . . . . 2 . . . . . .   BELIEVE. . . . . Defected DFECT 14CDS
27/01/2001 . . . . . 42 . . . . . . 2 . . . . . .   BELIEVE (REMIX) MINISTERS DE LA FUNK FEATURING JOCELYN BROWN . . . . Defected DFECT 26CDS

MINISTRY US rock group formed by Alain Jourgensen (guitar/keyboards/vocals), Paul Barker (bass/keyboards) and Bill Reiflin (drums). Reiflin left the group in 1994 and was replaced by Ray Washam. Jourgensen is also a member of The Revolting Cocks.

08/08/1992 . . . . . 49 . . . . . . 1 . . . . . .   NWO . . . . Sire W 0125TE
06/01/1996 . . . . . 53 . . . . . . 2 . . . . . .   THE FALL . . . . Warner Brothers W 0328CD

MINK DE VILLE UK rock group formed by guitarist/songwriter Willy DeVille (born 27/8/1953, New York) with Ruben Siguenza (bass) and Thomas Allen (drums), later adding Louie X Erlanger on guitar.

06/08/1977 . . . . . 20 . . . . . . 9 . . . . . .   SPANISH STROLL . . . . Capitol CLX 103

MINKY UK producer Gary Dedman.

30/10/1999 . . . . . 70 . . . . . . 1 . . . . . .   THE WEEKEND HAS LANDED . . . . Offbeat OFFCD 1001

LIZA MINNELLI US actress/singer (born 12/3/1946, Los Angeles, CA), daughter of singer Judy Garland and film director Vincente Minnelli, who hit the UK album charts for the first time in 1973, almost ten years after her US breakthrough. She debuted in public at two-and-a-half in the 1949 film *The Good Old Summer Time* (which also starred her mother). Her debut hit single was written and produced by the Pet Shop Boys. In October 2000 she was discovered in a coma and rushed to hospital, recovering a few days later (she was reunited with her estranged step-sister Lorna Luft as a result). She has been married four times: to singer/songwriter Peter Allen (he won the 1982 Best Film Song Oscar with Burt Bacharach, Carole Bayer Sager and Christopher Cross for *Arthur's Theme* and died from an AIDS-related illness on 18/6/1992) in 1967; filmmaker Jack Haley in 1974; sculptor Mark Gero in 1979 and producer David Gest in November 2001. She has a star on the Hollywood Walk of Fame and won an Oscar in 1972 for Best Actress for the role of Sally Bowles in *Cabaret*.

12/08/1989 . . . . . 6 . . . . . . 7 . . . . . .   **LOSING MY MIND** . . . . Epic ZEE 1
07/10/1989 . . . . . 46 . . . . . . 3 . . . . . .   DON'T DROP BOMBS. . . . . Epic ZEE 2
25/11/1989 . . . . . 62 . . . . . . 3 . . . . . .   SO SORRY I SAID . . . . Epic ZEE 3
03/03/1990 . . . . . 41 . . . . . . 3 . . . . . .   LOVE PAINS . . . . Epic ZEE 4

DANNII MINOGUE Australian singer/actress (born 20/10/1970, Melbourne) who was first known via the TV series *Skyways* at the age of seven (a star in Australia before older sister Kylie) and later *Home And Away*. She was engaged to racing driver Jacques Villeneuve (her marriage to actor Julian McMahon lasted a year) although the pair had split up by January 2001.

30/03/1991 . . . . . 8 . . . . . . 8 . . . . . .   **LOVE AND KISSES** . . . . MCA MCS 1529
18/05/1991 . . . . . 11 . . . . . . 7 . . . . . .   SUCCESS . . . . MCA MCS 1538
27/07/1991 . . . . . 8 . . . . . . 6 . . . . . .   **JUMP TO THE BEAT** . . . . MCA MCS 1556
19/10/1991 . . . . . 14 . . . . . . 6 . . . . . .   BABY LOVE. . . . . MCA MCS 1580
14/12/1991 . . . . . 40 . . . . . . 5 . . . . . .   I DON'T WANNA TAKE THIS PAIN . . . . MCA MCS 1600
01/08/1992 . . . . . 30 . . . . . . 3 . . . . . .   SHOW YOU THE WAY TO GO . . . . MCA MCS 1671
12/12/1992 . . . . . 44 . . . . . . 4 . . . . . .   LOVE'S ON EVERY CORNER . . . . MCA MCSR 1723
17/07/1993 . . . . . 10 . . . . . . 8 . . . . . .   **THIS IS IT** . . . . MCA MCSTD 1790
02/10/1993 . . . . . 27 . . . . . . 3 . . . . . .   THIS IS THE WAY . . . . MCA MCSTD 1935
11/06/1994 . . . . . 36 . . . . . . 2 . . . . . .   GET INTO YOU DANNII . . . . Mushroom D 11751
23/08/1997 . . . . . 4 . . . . . . 8 . . . . . .   **ALL I WANNA DO** . . . . Eternal WEA 119CD
01/11/1997 . . . . . 15 . . . . . . 4 . . . . . .   EVERYTHING I WANTED . . . . Eternal WEA 137CD
28/03/1998 . . . . . 21 . . . . . . 3 . . . . . .   DISREMEMBRANCE. . . . . Eternal WEA 153CD
01/12/2001 . . . . . 3 . . . . . . 15 . . . . . .   **WHO DO YOU LOVE NOW (STRINGER)** RIVA FEATURING DANNII MINOGUE . . . . ffrr DFCD 002
16/11/2002 . . . . . 7 . . . . . . 11 . . . . . .   **PUT THE NEEDLE ON IT** . . . . London LONCD 470
15/03/2003 . . . . . 2 . . . . . . 11 . . . . . .   **I BEGIN TO WONDER** . . . . London LONCD 473

  ○ Silver disc   ● Gold disc   ✪ Platinum disc (additional platinum units are indicated by a figure following the symbol)   ◉ Singles released prior to 1973 that are known to have sold over 1 million copies in the UK

21/06/2003 . . . . . 5 . . . . . . 9	DON'T WANNA LOSE THIS FEELING . . . . London LONCD 478		
06/11/2004 . . . . . 7 . . . . . . 5	YOU WON'T FORGET ABOUT ME DANNII MINOGUE VS FLOWER POWER . . . . All Around The World CXGLOBE379		

KYLIE MINOGUE Australian singer/actress (born 28/5/1968, Melbourne) whose first acting role was in *The Sullivans* in 1979, later appearing in the hit TV series *Neighbours* as Charlene. She hit #1 in Australia with *The Loco-Motion* in 1987, travelling to London to record with Stock Aitken Waterman. When *Kylie! – The Album* hit the #1 spot on 27/8/1988 she was the youngest woman to have topped the UK album charts. Kylie won two awards at the inaugural Top Of The Pops Awards in 2001 including Best Tour; and won two BRIT Awards at the 2002 ceremony: Best International Female and Best International Album for *Fever*. She also won two awards at the MTV Europe Music Awards in 2002: Best Dance and Best Pop Act; and a Grammy in 2003. Kylie is Dannii Minogue's elder sister. Keith Washington is an US R&B singer born in Detroit, MI.

23/01/1988 . . . . ❶⁵ . . . . 16 . . . . . ●	I SHOULD BE SO LUCKY . . . . PWL 8		
14/05/1988 . . . . . 2 . . . . . . 12 . . . . . ○	GOT TO BE CERTAIN . . . . PWL 12		
06/08/1988 . . . . . 2 . . . . . . 11	THE LOCO-MOTION Remixed version of her Australian #1 from 1987. Featured in the 1989 film *Arthur 2: On The Rocks* . . . . PWL 14		
22/10/1988 . . . . . 2 . . . . . . 13 . . . . . ○	JE NE SAIS PAS POURQUOI . . . . PWL 21		
10/12/1988 . . . . ❶³ . . . . 14 . . . . . ●	ESPECIALLY FOR YOU KYLIE MINOGUE AND JASON DONOVAN . . . . PWL 24		
06/05/1989 . . . . ❶¹ . . . . 11 . . . . . ●	HAND ON YOUR HEART . . . . PWL 35		
05/08/1989 . . . . . 2 . . . . . . 9	WOULDN'T CHANGE A THING . . . . PWL 42		
04/11/1989 . . . . . 4 . . . . . . 10 . . . . . ○	NEVER TOO LATE . . . . PWL 45		
20/01/1990 . . . . ❶¹ . . . . 8 . . . . . ○	TEARS ON MY PILLOW . . . . PWL 47		
12/05/1990 . . . . . 2 . . . . . . 10 . . . . . ○	BETTER THE DEVIL YOU KNOW . . . . PWL 56		
03/11/1990 . . . . . 4 . . . . . . 8	STEP BACK IN TIME . . . . PWL 64		
02/02/1991 . . . . . 6 . . . . . . 8	WHAT DO I HAVE TO DO . . . . PWL 72		
01/06/1991 . . . . . 6 . . . . . . 7	SHOCKED . . . . PWL 81		
07/09/1991 . . . . . 16 . . . . . 5	WORD IS OUT . . . . PWL 204		
02/11/1991 . . . . . 4 . . . . . . 7	IF YOU WERE WITH ME NOW KYLIE MINOGUE AND KEITH WASHINGTON . . . . PWL 208		
30/11/1991 . . . . . 49 . . . . . 1	KEEP ON PUMPIN' IT . . . . PWL 207		
25/01/1992 . . . . . 2 . . . . . . 8	GIVE ME JUST A LITTLE MORE TIME . . . . PWL 212		
25/04/1992 . . . . . 11 . . . . . 6	FINER FEELINGS . . . . PWL International PWL 227		
22/08/1992 . . . . . 14 . . . . . 5	WHAT KIND OF FOOL (HEARD IT ALL BEFORE) . . . . PWL International PWL 241		
28/11/1992 . . . . . 20 . . . . . 7	CELEBRATION . . . . PWL International PWL 257		
10/09/1994 . . . . . 2 . . . . . . 9 . . . . . ○	CONFIDE IN ME . . . . Deconstruction 74321227482		
26/11/1994 . . . . . 11 . . . . . 9	PUT YOURSELF IN MY PLACE . . . . Deconstruction 74321246572		
22/07/1995 . . . . . 16 . . . . . 3	WHERE IS THE FEELING? . . . . Deconstruction 74321293612		
14/10/1995 . . . . . 11 . . . . . 4	WHERE THE WILD ROSES GROW NICK CAVE + KYLIE MINOGUE . . . . Mute CDMUTE 185		
20/09/1997 . . . . . 22 . . . . . 5	SOME KIND OF BLISS . . . . Deconstruction 74321517252		
06/12/1997 . . . . . 14 . . . . . 6	DID IT AGAIN . . . . Deconstruction 74321535702		
21/03/1998 . . . . . 14 . . . . . 4	BREATHE . . . . Deconstruction 74321570132		
31/10/1998 . . . . . 63 . . . . . 1	GBI TOWA TEI FEATURING KYLIE MINOGUE . . . . Athrob ART 021CD		
01/07/2000 . . . . ❶¹ . . . . 11 . . . . . ○	SPINNING AROUND ↑ Co-written by Paula Abdul . . . . Parlophone CDRS 6542		
23/09/2000 . . . . . 2 . . . . . . 8	ON A NIGHT LIKE THIS . . . . Parlophone CDRS 6546		
21/10/2000 . . . . . 2 . . . . . . 19 . . . . . ○	KIDS ROBBIE WILLIAMS AND KYLIE MINOGUE . . . . Chrysalis CDCHSS 5119		
23/12/2000 . . . . . 10 . . . . . 7	PLEASE STAY . . . . Parlophone CDRS 6551		
29/09/2001 . . . . ❶⁴ . . . . 25 . . . . . ✪	CAN'T GET YOU OUT OF MY HEAD ↑ 2001 Top Of The Pops Award for Best Single. Featured in the 2004 film *Bridget Jones Diary 2: Edge Of Reason* . . . . Parlophone CDRS 6562		
02/03/2002 . . . . . 3 . . . . . . 17 . . . . . ○	IN YOUR EYES . . . . Parlophone CDRS 6569		
22/06/2002 . . . . . 2 . . . . . . 12	LOVE AT FIRST SIGHT . . . . Parlophone CDRS 6577		
23/11/2002 . . . . . 8 . . . . . . 10	COME INTO MY WORLD 2003 Grammy Award for Best Dance Recording . . . . Parlophone CDR 6590		
15/11/2003 . . . . ❶¹ 10	SLOW ↑ . . . . Parlophone CDRS 6625		
13/03/2004 . . . . . 5 . . . . . . 9	RED BLOODED WOMAN . . . . Parlophone CDRS 6633		
10/07/2004 . . . . . 6 . . . . . . 7	CHOCOLATE . . . . Parlophone CDRS 6639		
18/12/2004 . . . . . 2 . . . . . . 2+	I BELIEVE IN YOU . . . . Parlophone CDRS 6656		

MORRIS MINOR AND THE MAJORS UK comedy group with Tony Hawks, Phil Judge and Paul Baross who later recorded for Pacific Minor. Hawks was later a stand-up comedian and author, penning *Round Ireland With A Fridge* and *Playing The Moldovans At Tennis*.

19/12/1987 . . . . . 4 . . . . . . 11	STUTTER RAP (NO SLEEP 'TIL BEDTIME) . . . . 10 TEN 203		

SUGAR MINOTT Jamaican singer (born Lincoln Minott, 25/5/1956, Kingston) who came to the UK in the late 1970s.

28/03/1981 . . . . . 4 . . . . . . 12 . . . . . ○	GOOD THING GOING (WE'VE GOT A GOOD THING GOING) Written by Motown boss Berry Gordy and recorded by Michael Jackson . . . RCA 58		
17/10/1981 . . . . . 52 . . . . . 4	NEVER MY LOVE . . . . RCA 138		

MINT CONDITION US group formed in Minneapolis, MN by Stokley Williams (drums/vocals), Homer O'Dell (guitar), Larry Waddell (keyboards), Jeffrey Allen (saxophone), Keri Lewis (keyboards) and Ricky Kinchen (bass). Lewis wed singer Toni Braxton in 2001.

21/06/1997 . . . . . 38 . . . . . 2	WHAT KIND OF MAN WOULD I BE . . . . Wild Card 5710492		
04/10/1997 . . . . . 63 . . . . . 1	LET ME BE THE ONE . . . . Wild Card 5717132		

❶⁹ Number of weeks single topped the UK chart   ↑ Entered the UK chart at #1   ▲⁹ Number of weeks single topped the US chart

MINT JULEPS
UK vocal group from London: sisters Debbie, Lizzie, Sandra and Marcia Charles, Julie Isaac and Debbie Longworth.

22/03/1986	62	2		ONLY LOVE CAN BREAK YOUR HEART	Stiff BUY 241
30/05/1987	58	5		EVERY KINDA PEOPLE	Stiff BUY 257

MINT ROYALE
UK production duo formed in Manchester by Neil Claxton and Chris Baker. Lauren Laverne sings with Kenickie.

05/02/2000	15	4		DON'T FALTER	Faith & Hope FHCD 014
06/05/2000	66	1		TAKE IT EASY This and above single credited to MINT ROYALE FEATURING LAUREN LAVERNE	Faith & Hope FHCD 016
07/09/2002	20	3		SEXIEST MAN IN JAMAICA	Faith & Hope FHCD 025
08/02/2003	35	2		BLUE SONG	Illustrious/Epic FHCD 030

MINTY
Australian singer Angela Kelly.

23/01/1999	67	1		I WANNA BE FREE	Virgin VSCDT 1728

MINUTEMAN
Swiss group formed by Eva Staub, Yann Becker and Nicolas Jones.

20/07/2002	69	1		BIGBOY	Ignition IGNSCD 225
21/09/2002	75	1		5000 MINUTES OF PAIN	Ignition IGNSCD 27
15/02/2003	45	1		BIGBOY/MOTHER FIXATION Re-issue of Ignition IGNSCD 225	Ignition IGNSCD 28X

MIRACLES
US R&B vocal group formed in Detroit, MI in 1954 by Smokey Robinson (born William Robinson, 19/2/1940), Ronnie White (born 5/4/1939, Detroit), Pete Moore (born 19/11/1939, Detroit) and Bobby Rogers (born 19/2/1940, Detroit) with guitarist Marv Tarplin as the Matadors. Rogers' sister Claudette (born 1942, Detroit, later Robinson's wife) joined in 1957. They changed their name at the suggestion of Berry Gordy in 1957. First recording for End Records, they then leased product to Chess before joining Gordy's Motown and releasing their debut on the Tamla imprint, *Way Over There*. Claudette stopped touring in 1963 (still appearing on their records) and Smokey went solo in 1972. He was replaced by Billy Griffin (born 15/8/1950, Detroit). They moved to CBS in 1976 but split after one album. White died from leukaemia on 26/8/1995.

24/02/1966	44	5		GOING TO A GO-GO	Tamla Motown TMG 547
22/12/1966	45	2		(COME 'ROUND HERE) I'M THE ONE YOU NEED	Tamla Motown TMG 584
10/01/1968	27	11		I SECOND THAT EMOTION	Tamla Motown TMG 631
03/04/1968	50	1		IF YOU CAN WANT	Tamla Motown TMG 648
07/05/1969	9	13		**TRACKS OF MY TEARS** Featured in the films *The Big Chill* (1984), *Platoon* (1987) and *The Walking Dead* (1995) Tamla Motown TMG 696	
01/08/1970	❶[1]	14		**TEARS OF A CLOWN** ▲[2] Originally released in 1967 without success	Tamla Motown TMG 745
30/01/1971	13	9		(COME 'ROUND HERE) I'M THE ONE YOU NEED	Tamla Motown TMG 761
05/06/1971	11	10		I DON'T BLAME YOU AT ALL This and above seven singles credited to SMOKEY ROBINSON AND THE MIRACLES Tamla Motown TMG 774	
10/01/1976	3	10	O	**LOVE MACHINE (PART 1)** ▲[1] Featured in the films *Donnie Brasco* (1997) and *54* (1998) ▲ Tamla Motown TMG 1015	
16/10/1976	34	6		TEARS OF A CLOWN SMOKEY ROBINSON AND THE MIRACLES Re-issue of Tamla Motown TMG 745	Tamla Motown TMG 1048

MIRAGE
UK studio group created by producer Nigel Wright and featuring the vocals of Kiki Billy.

14/01/1984	49	4		GIVE ME THE NIGHT	Passion PASH 15
09/05/1987	4	11		**JACK MIX II/III**	Debut DEBT 3022
25/07/1987	42	4		SERIOUS MIX	Debut DEBT 3028
07/11/1987	8	10		**JACK MIX IV**	Debut DEBT 3035
27/02/1988	50	3		JACK MIX VII	Debut DEBT 3042
02/07/1988	67	2		PUSH THE BEAT	Debut DEBT 3050
11/11/1989	70	1		LATINO HOUSE	Debut DEBT 3085

NINA MIRANDA – see ROBERT MILES

DANNY MIRROR
Dutch singer Eddy Ouwens who later recorded with the Jordinaires (Elvis Presley's backing group). He had previously produced Teach-In's Eurovision Song Contest winner.

17/09/1977	4	9	O	**I REMEMBER ELVIS PRESLEY (THE KING IS DEAD)**	Sonet SON 2121

MIRRORBALL
UK production duo Jamie Ford and Jamie White who also record as The Cool, The Fab & The Groovy . White had previously been a member of PF Project and Tzant.

13/02/1999	12	4		GIVEN UP Contains a sample of The Three Degrees' *Givin' Up Givin' In*	Multiply CDMULTY 46
24/06/2000	47	1		BURNIN' Contains a sample of Thelma Houston's *Don't Leave Me This Way*	Multiply CDMULTY 56

MIRWAIS
French producer Mirwais Ahmadzaïs who first came to prominence producing Madonna.

20/05/2000	68	1		DISCO SCIENCE	Epic 6693102
23/12/2000	50	2		NAÏVE SONG	Epic 6706922

MIS-TEEQ
UK R&B group formed by Alesha Dixon (born 7/10/1979, Welwyn Garden City), Su-Elise Nash (born 27/10/1978, Harlesden, London), Sabrena Washington (born 22/5/1981, West Dulwich, London) and Zena Playford. Co-lead singer Zena left the group after their first single due to illness but later went solo. They won the 2002 MOBO Award for Best British Garage Act.

20/01/2001	8	7		**WHY**	Inferno CDFERN 35
23/06/2001	2	11		**ALL I WANT**	Telstar CDSTAS 3184
27/10/2001	5	12		**ONE NIGHT STAND**	Inferno/Telstar CDTAS 3208
02/03/2002	5	8		**B WITH ME**	Inferno/Telstar CDSTAS 3243

29/06/2002 . . . . . 7 . . . . . . 7	ROLL ON/THIS IS HOW WE DO IT . . . . Inferno/Telstar CDSTAS 3255
29/03/2003 . . . . . 2 . . . . . . 11	SCANDALOUS . . . . Telstar CDSTAS 3319
12/07/2003 . . . . . 8 . . . . . . 9	CAN'T GET IT BACK . . . . Telstar CXSTAS 3337
29/11/2003 . . . . . 13 . . . . . . 5	STYLE Contains a sample of The Pet Shop Boys' *West End Girls* . . . . Telstar CDSTAS 3369

MISHKA Bermudan singer Alexander Mishka Frith who represented Bermuda in the 1991 and 1992 windsurfing World Championships.

15/05/1999 . . . . . 34 . . . . . . 2	GIVE YOU ALL THE LOVE . . . . Creation CRESCD 311

MISS BEHAVIN' UK DJ Nichola Potterton who is also a member of The Tidy Girls.

18/01/2003 . . . . . 62 . . . . . . 1	SUCH A GOOD FEELIN' . . . . Tidy Two 115C

MISS JANE UK singer.

30/10/1999 . . . . . 62 . . . . . . 1	IT'S A FINE DAY . . . . G1 Recordings G 1001CD

MISS SHIVA German singer Khadra Bungardt.

10/11/2001 . . . . . 30 . . . . . . 3	DREAMS . . . . VC Recordings VCRCD 99

MISS KITTIN — see GOLDEN BOY FEATURING MISS KITTIN

MISS X UK singer Joyce Blair. She is also an actress, appearing in the films *Jazz Boat* (1960), *The Wild Affair* (1965) *Mister Ten Percent* (1967) and others.

01/08/1963 . . . . . 37 . . . . . . 6	CHRISTINE . . . . Ember S 175

MISSION UK group formed in 1986 by Wayne Hussey (born Jerry Lovelock, 26/5/1959, Bristol, guitar/vocals) and Craig Adams (born 4/4/1962, Otley, bass) following the temporary demise of Sisters Of Mercy and also featuring Simon Hinkler (guitar) and Mick Brown (drums). Hinkler left in 1990 and was replaced by guitarist Paul Etchells in 1991.

14/06/1986 . . . . . 70 . . . . . . 3	SERPENTS KISS . . . . Chapter 22 CHAP 6
26/07/1986 . . . . . 49 . . . . . . 4	GARDEN OF DELIGHT/LIKE A HURRICANE . . . . Chapter 22 CHAP 7
18/10/1986 . . . . . 30 . . . . . . 4	STAY WITH ME . . . . Mercury MYTH 1
17/01/1987 . . . . . 11 . . . . . . 6	WASTELAND . . . . Mercury MYTH 2
14/03/1987 . . . . . 25 . . . . . . 5	SEVERINA . . . . Mercury MYTH 3
13/02/1988 . . . . . 12 . . . . . . 7	TOWER OF STRENGTH . . . . Mercury MYTH 4
23/04/1988 . . . . . 32 . . . . . . 4	BEYOND THE PALE . . . . Mercury MYTH 6
13/01/1990 . . . . . 12 . . . . . . 4	BUTTERFLY ON A WHEEL . . . . Mercury MYTH 8
10/03/1990 . . . . . 27 . . . . . . 4	DELIVERANCE . . . . Mercury MYTH 9
02/06/1990 . . . . . 32 . . . . . . 3	INTO THE BLUE . . . . Mercury MYTH 10
17/11/1990 . . . . . 28 . . . . . . 2	HANDS ACROSS THE OCEAN . . . . Mercury MYTH 11
25/04/1992 . . . . . 34 . . . . . . 3	NEVER AGAIN . . . . Mercury MYTH 12
20/06/1992 . . . . . 30 . . . . . . 2	LIKE A CHILD AGAIN . . . . Mercury MYTH 13
17/10/1992 . . . . . 49 . . . . . . 2	SHADES OF GREEN. . . . . Vertigo MYTH 14
08/01/1994 . . . . . 33 . . . . . . 3	TOWER OF STRENGTH (REMIX) . . . . Vertigo MYTCD 15
26/03/1994 . . . . . 53 . . . . . . 1	AFTERGLOW . . . . Vertigo MYTCD 16
04/02/1995 . . . . . 73 . . . . . . 1	SWOON . . . . Neverland HOOKCD 002

MISS JONES US singer (born Tarsha Jones, 1969, New York City).

10/10/1998 . . . . . 49 . . . . . . 1	2 WAY STREET . . . . Motown 8608572

MRS MILLS UK pianist Gladys Mills (born 1922); she was a civil servant and part-time pianist before she went solo. She died in February 1978.

14/12/1961 . . . . . 18 . . . . . . 5	MRS MILLS MEDLEY Medley of *I Want To Be Happy, Sheik Of Araby, Baby Face, Somebody Stole My Gal, Ma (He's Making Eyes At Me), Swanee, Ain't She Sweet* and *California Here I Come* . . . . Parlophone R 4856
31/12/1964 . . . . . 50 . . . . . . 1	MRS MILLS PARTY MEDLEY . . . . Parlophone R 5214

MRS WOODS UK singer/pianist/DJ Jane Rolink, from Barnsley, who also recorded with Marc Almond.

16/09/1995 . . . . . 40 . . . . . . 2	JOANNA . . . . React CDREACT 066
06/07/1996 . . . . . 44 . . . . . . 1	HEARTBREAK MRS WOODS FEATURING EVE GALLAGHER. . . . . React CDREACT 78
04/10/1997 . . . . . 34 . . . . . . 2	JOANNA (REMIX) . . . . React CDXREACT 107
15/08/1998 . . . . . 54 . . . . . . 1	1234 . . . . React CDREACT 121

MISTA E UK producer Damon Rochefort who was also a member of Nomad.

10/12/1988 . . . . . 41 . . . . . . 5	DON'T BELIEVE THE HYPE . . . . Urban URB 28

MR AND MRS SMITH UK instrumental/production group formed by DJ Randy and DJ The Freak.

12/10/1996 . . . . . 70 . . . . . . 1	GOTTA GET LOOSE . . . . Hooj Choons HOOJCD 46

MR BEAN AND SMEAR CAMPAIGN FEATURING BRUCE DICKINSON UK comedian/actor Rowan Atkinson (born 6/1/1955, Newcastle-upon-Tyne) re-creating his TV character Mr Bean with Iron Maiden's Bruce Dickenson on a cover of an Alice Cooper hit. The character later appeared in the 1997 film *Bean: The Ultimate Disaster Movie.*

04/04/1992 . . . . . 9 . . . . . . 5	(I WANT TO BE) ELECTED Released in aid of the Comic Relief charity . . . . London LON 319

❶⁹ Number of weeks single topped the UK chart   ↑ Entered the UK chart at #1   ▲⁹ Number of weeks single topped the US chart

537

MR BIG UK group formed in Oxford by Jeff Dicken (vocals), Peter Crowther (guitar), Edee Carter (bass) and John Marter (drums).

12/02/1977.....4......10.....○	**ROMEO**..EMI 2567
21/05/1977.....35......4.......	FEEL LIKE CALLING HOME..EMI 2610

MR BIG US group from San Francisco, CA formed by Eric Martin (vocals), Paul Gilbert (guitar), Billy Sheehan (bass) and Pat Torpey (drums).

07/03/1992.....3......11......	**TO BE WITH YOU** ▲³...Atlantic A 7514
23/05/1992.....26......4......	JUST TAKE MY HEART..Atlantic A 7490
08/08/1992.....72......1......	GREEN TINTED SIXTIES MIND..Atlantic A 7468
20/11/1993.....59......1......	WILD WORLD...Atlantic A 7310CD

MR BLOBBY UK character created for the TV series *Noel Edmonds' House Party* at the instigation of producer Mike Leggo.

04/12/1993 ....❶³......12 .....✪	**MR BLOBBY** Reclaimed #1 position on 25/12/1993.........................Destiny Music CDDMUS 104
16/12/1995.....36......4......	CHRISTMAS IN BLOBBYLAND..Destiny DMUSCD 108

MR BLOE UK session group assembled by pianist Zack Lawrence. The single was originally recorded in 1969 as a B-side by Wind, a US studio group featuring Tony Orlando, prompting a cover version by another studio group Cool Heat.

09/05/1970 .....2......18	**GROOVIN' WITH MR BLOE**...DJM DJS 216

MR CHEEKS – see LIL' KIM

MR FINGERS US producer Larry Heard.

17/03/1990.....74......1......	WHAT ABOUT THIS LOVE...ffrr F 131
07/03/1992.....50......3......	CLOSER..MCA MCS 1601
23/05/1992.....71......1......	ON MY WAY...MCA MCS 1630

MR FOOD UK singer.

09/06/1990.....62......3......	...AND THAT'S BEFORE ME TEA!...Tangible TGB 005

MR HAHN – see X-ECUTIONERS FEATURING MIKE SHINODA AND MR HAHN OF LINKIN PARK

MR HANKEY US cartoon excrement character from the TV series *South Park*.

25/12/1999 .....4......6......	**MR HANKEY THE CHRISTMAS POO**...Columbia 6685582

MR JACK Italian producer Vito Lucente whose initial release, *Only House Muzik*, was banned due to the use of an uncleared sample of Tom Wilson's *Technocat*. Lucente also records as Junior Jack and Room 5.

25/01/1997.....32......2......	WIGGLY WORLD...Xtravaganza 0090965

MR LEE US producer Leroy Haggard (born Chicago, IL).

06/08/1988.....64......2......	PUMP UP LONDON...Breakout USA 639
11/11/1989.....71......1......	GET BUSY..Jive 231
24/02/1990.....41......3......	GET BUSY..Jive 231

MR MISTER US rock group formed in Phoenix, AZ by Richard Page (bass/vocals), Steve George (keyboards), Pat Mastelotto (drums) and Steve Farris (guitar) and relocated to Los Angeles, CA. Farris left in 1989 and was replaced by Buzzy Feiten.

21/12/1985 .....4......13	**BROKEN WINGS** ▲²...RCA PB 49945
01/03/1986.....11......9	KYRIE ▲²..RCA PB 49927

MR OIZO French musician Quentin Dupieux, Mr Oizo being a puppet. The act began as a TV advertisement for Levi's Sta-Prest Jeans.

03/04/1999 ....❶²......15 .....✪	**FLAT BEAT** ↑ First featured in an advertisement for Levi Jeans...........F Communications/PIAS Recordings F 104CDUK

MR ON VS THE JUNGLE BROTHERS UK producer from London (his name is a variation on the Mysterons, the characters from the TV series *Captain Scarlet*) with US vocal group The Jungle Brothers.

07/02/2004.....21......5......	BREATHE DON'T STOP...Positiva/Incentive CDTIVS 201

MR PINK PRESENTS THE PROGRAM US producer Leiam Sullivan. His debut hit was a dance version of Joan Armatrading's hit.

19/01/2002.....22......4......	LOVE AND AFFECTION...Manifesto FESCD 90

MR PRESIDENT German Europop trio formed by Kai Matthiesen, T-Seven and Lady Danii with UK rapper DJ Lazy Dee.

14/06/1997 .....8......11 .....○	**COCO JAMBOO**...WEA 110CD
20/09/1997.....52......1......	I GIVE YOU MY HEART...WEA 126CD
25/04/1998.....73......1......	JOJO ACTION...WEA 156CD

MR REDZ VS DJ SKRIBBLE UK/US duo Mr Redz and DJ Skribble (Scott Ialacci). Skribble was previously in Young Black Teenagers.

24/05/2003.....13......6......	EVERYBODY COME ON (CAN U FEEL IT) Contains a sample of Bob James's *Take Me To The Mardi Gras*............ffrr FCD 410

MR ROY UK instrumental/production group with Alun Harrison, Mark Mumford and Graham Simmons. Mumford also recorded as Time Of The Mumph.

07/05/1994.....74......1.......			SOMETHING ABOUT YOU .... Fresh FRSHD 11
21/01/1995.....24......4.......			SAVED .... Fresh FRSHD 21
16/12/1995.....49......1.......			SOMETHING ABOUT YOU (CAN'T BE BEAT) (REMIX) Contains a sample of Nikita Warren's *I Need You*........... Fresh FRSHD 33

MR RUMBLE – see BM DUBS PRESENT MR RUMBLE FEATURING BRASSTOOTH AND KEE

MR SCRUFF UK dance artist (born Andrew Carthy, 10/2/1972, Macclesfield).

14/12/2002.....75......1...... SWEETSMOKE .... Ninja Tune ZEN 12124

MR SHABZ – see SO SOLID CREW

MR SMASH AND FRIENDS UK producer Charles Smash (born Cathal Smyth, 14/1/1959, London) who was previously a member of Madness. He also formed the RGR record label.

08/06/2002.....67......1....... WE'RE COMING OVER .... RGR RGRCD 2

MR V UK producer Rob Villiers.

06/08/1994.....40......2...... GIVE ME LIFE .... Cheeky CHEKCD 005

MR VEGAS Jamaican reggae artist (born Clifford Smith, 1975, Kingston) who was nicknamed Mr Vegas because his football-playing style and pink shorts reminded friends of a go-go dancer from Las Vegas. He won the 1999 MOBO Award for Best International Reggae Act.

22/08/1998.....71......1.......			HEADS HIGH .... Greensleeves GRECD 650
13/11/1999.....16......6.......			HEADS HIGH Re-issue of GRECD 650 .... Greensleeves GRECD 785

MISTURA FEATURING LLOYD MICHELS US instrumental group featuring Lloyd Michels on trumpet. Their debut hit was originally released by the Fusion label of New York.

15/05/1976.....23......10...... THE FLASHER .... Route RT 30

DES MITCHELL UK/Belgian production trio Johan Gielen, Sven Maes and Des Mitchell. Gielen and Maes were also responsible for Aircaspe, Balaeric Bill, Blue Bamboo and Svenson & Gielen.

29/01/2000 .....5......5...... (WELCOME) TO THE DANCE .... Code Blue BLU 008CD1

GUY MITCHELL US singer (born Albert Cernik, 27/2/1927, Detroit, MI) who was a child actor with Warner Brothers before World War II, turning to music after he left the US Navy. He was named Guy Mitchell at the suggestion of producer Mitch Miller. His films included *Red Garters* (1954, with Rosemary Clooney) and *Those Red Heads From Seattle* (1953, with Theresa Brewer). He died on 1/7/1999. He has a star on the Hollywood Walk of Fame.

14/11/1952 .....2......10......			**FEET UP** .... Columbia DB 3151
13/02/1953 .....❶⁴......16......			**SHE WEARS RED FEATHERS** .... Columbia DB 3238
24/04/1953 .....2......11......			**PRETTY LITTLE BLACK EYED SUSIE** .... Columbia DB 3255
28/08/1953 .....❶⁶......14......			**LOOK AT THAT GIRL** .... Philips PB 162
06/11/1953 .....4......15......			**CHICKA BOOM** Featured in the 1953 film *Those Redheads From Seattle*, also starring Guy Mitchell .... Philips PB 178
18/12/1953 .....2......16......			**CLOUD LUCKY SEVEN** .... Philips PB 210
19/02/1954 .....9......3......			**CUFF OF MY SHIRT** .... Philips PB 225
26/02/1954 .....11......1......			SIPPIN' SODA.. Philips PB 210
30/04/1954 .....8......5......			**DIME AND A DOLLAR** Featured in the 1954 film *Red Garters*, also starring Guy Mitchell....................... Philips PB 248
07/12/1956 .....❶³......22......			**SINGING THE BLUES** ▲¹⁰ Reclaimed #1 on 18/1/1957 for one week and on 1/2/1957 for one week .... Philips PB 650
15/02/1957 .....3......12......			**KNEE DEEP IN THE BLUES** .... Philips PB 669
26/04/1957 .....❶¹......14......			**ROCK-A-BILLY** .... Philips PB 685
26/07/1957 .....25......4......			IN THE MIDDLE OF A DARK DARK NIGHT/SWEET STUFF .... Philips PB 712
11/10/1957 .....17......6......			CALL ROSIE ON THE PHONE .... Philips PB 743
27/11/1959 .....5......16......			**HEARTACHES BY THE NUMBER** ▲² .... Philips PB 964

JONI MITCHELL Canadian singer (born Roberta Joan Anderson, 7/11/1943, Fort McLeod, Alberta) who moved to New York and adopted her married name (married to Chuck Mitchell in June 1965, the marriage later dissolved). Her 1968 debut album had David Crosby producing. Inducted into the Rock & Roll Hall of Fame in 1997, she has five Grammy Awards: Best Folk Recording in 1969 for *Clouds*, Best Arrangement Accompanying Singers in 1974 with Tom Scott for *Down To You*, Best Pop Album in 1995 for *Turbulent Indigo*, for which she also collected an award for Best Album Package with Robbie Cavolina, and Best Traditional Pop Vocal Album in 2000 for *Both Sides Now*.

13/06/1970 .....11 .....15......			BIG YELLOW TAXI .... Reprise RS 20906
04/10/1997 .....6......9......O			**GOT 'TIL IT'S GONE** JANET FEATURING Q-TIP AND JONI MITCHELL Contains a sample of Joni Mitchell's *Big Yellow Taxi* .... Virgin VSCDG 1666

❶⁹ Number of weeks single topped the UK chart ↑ Entered the UK chart at #1 ▲⁹ Number of weeks single topped the US chart

539

WILLIE MITCHELL US singer/guitarist (born 3/1/1928, Ashland, MS) who was also producer for the likes of Al Green and Ann Peebles.

24/04/1968.....43......1......	SOUL SERENADE .... London HLU 10186
11/12/1976.....47......2......	THE CHAMPION .... London HL 10545

MIX FACTORY UK vocal/instrumental group formed by Paul Higgins and Iain McArthur with singer Alison Williamson.

30/01/1993.....51......2......	TAKE ME AWAY (PARADISE) .... All Around The World CDGLOBE 120

MIXMASTER Italian producer Daniele 'DJ Lelewel' Davoli who had previously been responsible for Black Box and Starlight.

04/11/1989 .....9......10......	GRAND PIANO .... BCM 344

MIXTURES Australian group formed by Mick Flynn, Idris Jones, Gary Howard, John Creech, Greg Cook, Mick Holden, Peter Williams, Don Lebler and Fred Wieland.

16/01/1971 .....2......21......	THE PUSHBIKE SONG .... Polydor 2058 083

HANK MIZELL US songwriter/producer (born Bill Mizell) whose one UK hit was originally recorded in 1957 for the EKO label and later released by King. By the time it was revived, Mizell was a preacher and had retired from music. He died in December 1992.

20/03/1976 .....3......13.....O	JUNGLE ROCK .... Charly CS1005

MK US producer Mark Kinchen whose debut hit featured singer Alana Simon.

04/02/1995.....69......1......	ALWAYS MK FEATURING ALANA... Activ CDTV 3
27/05/1995.....44......2......	BURNING.. Activ CDTVR 6

MN8 UK vocal R&B group formed by KG, Kule-T, Dee-Tails and G-Man.

04/02/1995 .....2......13.....O	I'VE GOT A LITTLE SOMETHING FOR YOU Featured in the 1995 film Bad Boys .... Columbia 6608802
29/04/1995.....6......7......	IF YOU ONLY LET ME IN... Columbia 6613252
15/07/1995.....8......7......	HAPPY .... Columbia 6622192
04/11/1995.....22......3......	BABY IT'S YOU .... Columbia 6624522
24/02/1996.....25......2......	PATHWAY TO THE MOON... Columbia 6629212
31/08/1996.....15......3......	TUFF ACT TO FOLLOW .... Columbia 6635345
26/10/1996.....21......3......	DREAMING .... Columbia 6638302

MNO Belgian dance group formed by Praga Khan and Jade and featuring Maurice Engelen and Nikki Van Lierop. They also recorded as Digital Orgasm.

28/09/1991.....66......2......	GOD OF ABRAHAM .... A&M AM 820

MOBILES UK group formed in Brighton by Anna Marie (vocals), Jon (keyboards), Chris Downton (guitar), Russ Madge (guitar), David Blundell (bass) and Eddie Fragile (drums). They were all sacked from their jobs after appearing on Top Of The Pops to promote their debut single. They later recorded for MCA.

09/01/1982 .....9......10......	DROWNING IN BERLIN .... Rialto RIA 3
27/03/1982.....45......4......	AMOUR AMOUR .... Rialto RIA 5

MOBO ALLSTARS UK/US group comprising members of Another Level, Shola Ama, Kelle Bryan, Celetia, Cleopatra, Damage, Des'ree, D'Influence, E17, Michelle Gayle, Glamma Kid, Lynden David Hall, Hinda Hicks, Honeyz, Kle'Shay, Kele Le Roc, Beverley Knight, Tony Momrelle, Nine Yards, Mica Paris, Karen Ramirez, Connor Reeves, Roachford, 7th Son, Byron Stingily, Truce, Soundproof and Ultimate Kaos.

26/12/1998.....47......3......	AIN'T NO STOPPING US NOW In aid of the Sickle Cell Society and the Royal Marsden Hospital Charity Leukaemia Research Fund ... . PolyGram TV 5632302

MOBY US singer (born Richard Melville Hall, 11/9/1966, New York) nicknamed Moby because he is an ancestor of Herman Melville, the author of the Captain Ahab whaling story Moby Dick. His track Thousand (the B-side to I Feel It) earned him a place in the Guinness Book Of Records: at 1,015 beats per minute it is the fastest single ever. He won the 2000 MTV Europe Music Award for Best Video for Natural Blues and the 2002 award for Best Website.

27/07/1991.....46......3......	GO Theme to the TV series Twin Peaks .... Outer Rhythm FOOT 15
19/10/1991...10......7......	GO .... Outer Rhythm FOOT 15
03/07/1993.....38......3......	I FEEL IT .... Equator AXISCD 001
11/09/1993.....21......5......	MOVE .... Mute CDMUTE 158
28/05/1994.....31......2......	HYMN .... Mute CDMUTE 161
29/10/1994.....30......2......	FEELING SO REAL.. Mute CDMUTE 173
25/02/1995.....28......3......	EVERY TIME YOU TOUCH ME .... Mute CDMUTE 176
01/07/1995.....34......2......	INTO THE BLUE.. Mute CDMUTE 179A
07/09/1996.....50......1......	THAT'S WHEN I REACH FOR MY REVOLVER .... Mute CDMUTE 184
15/11/1997.....8......8......	JAMES BOND THEME Featured in the 1997 James Bond film Tomorrow Never Dies .... Mute CDMUTE 210
05/09/1998.....33......2......	HONEY Contains a sample of Bessie Jones' Sometimes .... Mute CDMUTE 218
08/05/1999.....33......2......	RUN ON.. Mute LCDMUTE 221
24/07/1999.....38......2......	BODYROCK Contains a sample of Spoony Gee's Love Rap .... Mute LCDMUTE 225
23/10/1999...16......4......	WHY DOES MY HEART FEEL SO BAD .... Mute CDMUTE 230
18/03/2000.....11......6......	NATURAL BLUES Contains a sample of Vera Hall's Trouble So Hard .... Mute CDMUTE 251
24/06/2000 .....5......6......	PORCELAIN Featured in the 2000 film The Beach .... Mute LCDMUTE 252

○ Silver disc ● Gold disc ✪ Platinum disc (additional platinum units are indicated by a figure following the symbol) ◉ Singles released prior to 1973 that are known to have sold over 1 million copies in the UK

28/10/2000	17	5		WHY DOES MY HEART FEEL SO BAD Re-issue of CDMUTE 230	Mute LCDMUTE 255
11/05/2002	11	4		WE ARE ALL MADE OF STARS	Mute LCDMUTE 268
31/08/2002	39	1		EXTREME WAYS	Mute LCDMUTE 270
16/11/2002	35	2		IN THIS WORLD	Mute LCDMUTE 276

MOCA — see **DAVID MORALES**

MOCHA — see **MISSY 'MISDEMEANOR' ELLIOTT AND NICOLE RAY**

MOCK TURTLES UK rock group formed in Manchester in 1987 by former Judge Happiness member Martin Coogan (guitar/vocals) with Steve Green (bass), Krzysztof Korab (keyboards) and Steve Cowen (drums). Martin Glyn Murray (guitar) joined in 1989. When he left for an acting career the group disbanded.

09/03/1991	18	11		CAN YOU DIG IT	Siren SRN 136
29/06/1991	44	4		AND THEN SHE SMILES	Siren SRN 139
15/03/2003	19	3		CAN YOU DIG IT Re-issue of Siren SRN 136, revived after use in a TV advertisement for Vodaphone	Virgin CDMOCK 001

MODERN LOVERS — see **JONATHAN RICHMAN AND THE MODERN LOVERS**

MODERN ROMANCE UK pop group formed as the Leyton Buzzards, changing their name in 1980 to Modern Romance. The line-up at the time of their success was Geoff Deane (born10/12/1954, vocals), Paul Gendler (born 11/8/1960, guitar), Robbie James (born 3/10/1962, keyboards), David Jaymes (born 28/11/1954, bass), Andy Kyriacou (born 19/4/1958, drums) and John du Prez (trumpet). Deane left at the end of 1982 and was replaced by Michael Mullins (born 9/11/1956). They disbanded in 1985.

15/08/1981	12	10		EVERYBODY SALSA	WEA K 18815
07/11/1981	10	12		AY AY AY AY MOOSEY	WEA K 18883
30/01/1982	37	8		QUEEN OF THE RAPPING SCENE (NOTHING EVER GOES THE WAY YOU PLAN)	WEA K 18928
14/08/1982	15	8		CHERRY PINK AND APPLE BLOSSOM WHITE MODERN ROMANCE FEATURING JOHN DU PREZ	WEA K 19245
13/11/1982	4	13	O	BEST YEARS OF OUR LIVES	WEA ROM 1
26/02/1983	8	8		HIGH LIFE	WEA ROM 2
07/05/1983	14	6		DON'T STOP THAT CRAZY RHYTHM	WEA ROM 3
06/08/1983	7	12	O	WALKING IN THE RAIN	WEA X 9733

MODERN TALKING German duo Thomas Anders and Dieter Bohlen.

15/06/1985	56	7		YOU'RE MY HEART, YOU'RE MY SOUL	Magnet MAG 277
12/10/1985	70	2		YOU CAN WIN IF YOU WANT	Magnet MAG 282
16/08/1986	4	10	O	BROTHER LOUIE	RCA PB 40875
04/10/1986	55	3		ATLANTIS IS CALLING (S.O.S. FOR LOVE)	RCA PB 40969

MODEST MOUSE US rock group formed in Issaquah, WI in 1993 by Isaac Brock (guitar/vocals), Eric Judy (bass) and Jeremiah Green (drums). Brock is also a member of Ugly Casanova.

24/07/2004	46	1		FLOAT ON	Epic 6750692

MODETTES UK/US group formed by Kate Korus (born Katherine Corris, New York, guitar), Ramona Carlier (vocals), Jane Crockford (bass) and June Miles-Kingston (drums). Carlier left in 1981 and was replaced by Sue Slack. Korus left later the same year and was replaced by Melissa Ritter. They disbanded in 1982. Miles-Kingston later sang with The Communards.

12/07/1980	42	5		PAINT IT BLACK	Deram DET-R 1
18/07/1981	68	1		TONIGHT	Deram DET 3

MODEY LEMON US duo formed in Oakland, CA in 1999 by Philander Boyd (guitar/vocals) and Paul Quattrone (drums).

22/05/2004	75	1		CROWS	Mute CDMUTE 328

MODJO French dance group formed by Romain Tranchart (aged 23 at the time of their debut hit) and Yann Destagnol (aged 21). After 48 years, they were the first French group to top the UK charts. They were named Best French Act at the 2000 MTV Europe Music Awards.

16/09/2000	❶2	20	●	LADY (HEAR ME TONIGHT) ↑ Features a sample of Chic's *Soup For One*	Sound Of Barclay 5877582
14/04/2001	12	8		CHILLIN'	Polydor 5870092
06/10/2001	59	1		WHAT I MEAN	Polydor 5873462

DOMENICO MODUGNO Italian singer (born 9/1/1928, Polignano a Mare) who studied with Sophia Loren at college. He made his film debut in *Filumena Marturano* (1951) and his final film appearance in *Maestro Di Violino* (1976). He died from a heart attack on 6/8/1994.

05/09/1958	10	12		VOLARE ▲5 Original Italian title was *Nel Blu, Dipento Di Blu* (In The Blue Sky Painted Blue [To Fly]). Finished third in the 1958 Eurovision Song Contest. 1958 Grammy Awards for Record of the Year plus Song of the Year for writers Domenico Modugno and Franco Migliacci	Oriole ICB 5000
27/03/1959	29	1		CIAO CIAO BAMBINA (PIOVE)	Oriole ICB 1489

MOFFATTS Canadian vocal group with Scott Moffatt (born 30/3/1984) and his triplet brothers Clint, Dave and Bob (born 8/3/1985).

20/02/1999	16	3		CRAZY	Chrysalis CDEM 533
26/06/1999	36	2		UNTIL YOU LOVED ME Featured in the 1999 film *Never Been Kissed*	Chrysalis CDEMS 541
23/10/1999	47	1		MISERY	EMI CDEM 551

❶9 Number of weeks single topped the UK chart ↑ Entered the UK chart at #1 ▲9 Number of weeks single topped the US chart

MOGUAI German DJ (born Andre Tegeler) who also records as Dial M For Moguai and Punx.

08/02/2003	62	1		U KNOW Y	Hope Recordings HOPECDS 038

MOGWAI UK group formed in Glasgow in 1996 by Stuart Braithwaite (guitar/vocals), Dominic Aitchison (guitar), John Cummings (guitar) and Martin Bulloch (drums). After releases on independent labels they added Brendan O'Hare in time for their debut album for Chemikal Underground, although he left after the recording sessions were complete.

04/04/1998	60	1	SWEET LEAF/BLACK SABBATH Double A-side featuring Magoo's *Black Sabbath*	Fierce Panda NING 47CD
11/04/1998	57	1	FEAR SATAN	Eye-Q EYEUK 032CD
11/07/1998	68	1	NO EDUCATION NO FUTURE (F**K THE CURFEW)	Chemikal Underground CHEM 026CD

MOHAWKS UK keyboard player Alan Hawkshaw who had previously been a member of Emile Ford's Checkmates.

24/01/1987	58	2	THE CHAMP	Pama PM 1

FRANK'O MOIRAGHI FEATURING AMNESIA Italian producer/remixer/DJ Frank'O Moiraghi and studio group.

01/06/1996	39	2	FEEL MY BODY	Multiply CDMULTY 10
26/10/1996	40	2	FEEL MY BODY (REMIX)	Multiply CDMULTY 15

MOIST Canadian group formed in Vancouver in 1992 by David Usher (guitar/vocals), Jeff Pearce (bass), Mark Makoway (guitar), Kevin Young (keyboards) and Paul Wilcox (drums). Their February 1994 own-label self-funded debut was picked up by EMI Canada a month later.

12/11/1994	35	3	PUSH	Chrysalis CDCHS 5016
25/02/1995	50	2	SILVER	Chrysalis CDCHS 5019
29/04/1995	47	2	FREAKY BE BEAUTIFUL	Chrysalis CDCHS 5022
19/08/1995	20	3	PUSH Re-issue of Chrysalis CDCHS 5016	Chrysalis CDCHS 5024

MOJO UK instrumental group assembled by Nigel Wright.

22/08/1981	70	3	DANCE ON Medley of *Apache*, *Man Of Mystery*, *Foot Tapper*, *Dance On*, *Atlantis*, *Wonderful Land*, *Stingray*, *The Rise And Fall Of Flingell Bunt* and *FBI*	Creole CR 17

MOJOLATORS FEATURING CAMILLA US producers Justin Nichols and Drew Robustelli with singer Camilla Hamblin.

06/10/2001	52	1	DRIFTING	Multiply CDMULTY 81

MOJOS UK group formed in Liverpool in 1962 by Nicky Crouch (guitar), Stu James (vocals), Keith Karlson (bass), John Konrad (drums) and Terry O'Toole (piano) as the Nomads, changing their name to the Mojos the following year.

26/03/1964	9	11	EVERYTHING'S ALRIGHT	Decca F 11853
11/06/1964	25	10	WHY NOT TONIGHT	Decca F 11918
10/09/1964	30	5	SEVEN DAFFODILS	Decca F 11959

MOKENSTEF US vocal group formed in Los Angeles, CA by Monifa Bethune, Kenya Hadley and Stephanie Sinclair, all previously high school cheerleaders.

23/09/1995	70	1	HE'S MINE	Def Jam DEFCD 13

MOLELLA FEATURING THE OUTHERE BROTHERS Italian singer/DJ with accompaniment provided by The Outhere Brothers. He was later responsible for writing and producing Gala's hit.

16/12/1995	9	10	IF YOU WANNA PARTY	Stip 030CD

SOPHIA MOLETA – see HUMAN MOVEMENT FEATURING SOPHIA MOLETA

RALPH MOLINA – see IAN McNABB

BRIAN MOLKO – see ALPINESTARS FEATURING BRIAN MOLKO

SAM MOLLISON – see SASHA

MOLLY HALF HEAD UK group formed in Manchester by Paul Bardsley (vocals), Phil Murphy (guitar), Graham Atkinson (bass) and Andy Pickering (drums).

03/06/1995	73	1	SHINE	Columbia 6620732

MOLOKO UK/Irish vocal/instrumental duo formed in Sheffield in 1993 by Mark Brydon and Roisin Murphy. They were named after a drug-laced milk drink in the Anthony Burgess novel and 1971 Stanley Kubrick film *A Clockwork Orange*. Murphy later recorded with Boris Dlugosch and The Psychedelic Waltons.

24/02/1996	65	1		DOMINOID	Echo ECSCD 016
25/05/1996	36	2		FUN FOR ME Featured in the 1997 film *Batman And Robin*	Echo ECSCD 20
20/06/1998	53	1		THE FLIPSIDE	Echo ECSCD 54
27/03/1999	45	2		SING IT BACK	Echo ECSCD 71
04/09/1999	4	9	O	SING IT BACK (REMIX)	Echo ECSCD 82
01/04/2000	2	10	O	THE TIME IS NOW	Echo ECSCD 88
05/08/2000	21	5		PURE PLEASURE SEEKER	Echo ECSCD 99
25/11/2000	51	1		INDIGO	Echo ECSCD 104

O Silver disc ● Gold disc ✪ Platinum disc (additional platinum units are indicated by a figure following the symbol) ⊚ Singles released prior to 1973 that are known to have sold over 1 million copies in the UK

01/03/2003	10	4		FAMILIAR FEELING	Echo ECSCD 131
05/07/2003	17	4		FOREVER MORE	Echo ECSCD 136

MOMBASSA UK production duo Phil Nicholas and Simon Gannon.

08/03/1997	63	1		CRY FREEDOM	Soundproof SPCD 021

MOMENTS US R&B vocal trio formed in Washington DC in 1968 by Mark Greene, Richie Horsely and John Morgan. Greene and Horsely were sacked soon after their debut R&B hit (*Not On The Outside*) by label owners Sylvia and Joe Robinson (who also owned the name The Moments) and were replaced by Al Goodman (born 31/3/1947, Jackson, MS) and Billy Brown (born 30/6/1946, Atlanta, GA). Six months later Morgan was replaced by John Moore, who in turn was replaced by Harry Ray (born 15/12/1946, Longbranch, NJ). The group recorded for Polydor as Ray Goodman & Brown from 1978. Ray left in 1982 and was replaced by Kevin Owens. The Whatnauts are Baltimore, MD vocal trio Billy Herndon, Garrett Jones and Gerald Pinkney. Ray died from a stroke on 1/12/1992. Al Goodman's wife Retta Young enjoyed a solo career. Al has a star on the Hollywood Walk of Fame.

08/03/1975	3	10	O	GIRLS MOMENTS AND WHATNAUTS	All Platinum 6146 302
19/07/1975	10	9		DOLLY MY LOVE	All Platinum 6146 306
25/10/1975	42	4		LOOK AT ME (I'M IN LOVE)	All Platinum 6146 309
22/01/1977	7	9	O	JACK IN THE BOX	All Platinum 6146 318

TONY MOMRELLE UK singer who also took part in the Mobo Allstars recording.

15/08/1998	67	1		LET ME SHOW YOU	Art & Soul ART 1CDS

MONACO UK duo Peter Hook (born 13/2/1956, Salford) and David Potts (born in Manchester). Hook was previously bass player with New Order, and first teamed up with Potts in Revenge in 1990.

15/03/1997	11	6		WHAT DO YOU WANT FROM ME?	Polydor 5731912
31/05/1997	18	4		SWEET LIPS	Polydor 5710552
20/09/1997	55	1		SHINE (SOMEONE WHO NEEDS ME)	Polydor 5714182

PHAROAHE MONCH US rapper (born Troy Jamerson, Queens, NYC) who was previously in Organised Konfusion with Prince Poetry.

19/02/2000	24	2		SIMON SAYS	Rawkus RWK 205CD
19/08/2000	72	1		LIGHT	Rawkus RWK 259CD
03/03/2001	24	4		OH NO MOS DEF AND NATE DOGG FEATURING PHAROAHE MONCH	Rawkus RWK 302
01/12/2001	27	3		GOT YOU	Priority PTYCD 145
14/09/2002	50	1		THE LIFE STYLES AND PHAROAHE MONCH	MCA MCSTD 40292

JAY MONDI AND THE LIVING BASS UK vocal/instrumental group with singer Juliie Zee (born in London) who later recorded with Mobius Loop.

24/03/1990	63	3		ALL NIGHT LONG	10 TEN 304

MONDO KANE UK vocal/instrumental group assembled by Mike Stock, Matt Aitken and Pete Waterman and featuring Dee Lewi and Coral Gordon with Georgie Fame.

16/08/1986	70	3		NEW YORK AFTERNOON	Lisson DOLE 2

MONE US singer.

12/08/1995	64	1		WE CAN MAKE IT	A&M 5811592
16/03/1996	48	1		MOVIN'	AM:PM 5814392

ZOOT MONEY AND THE BIG ROLL BAND UK R&B artist (born George Bruno, 17/7/1942, Bournemouth, piano/vocals) who formed the Big Roll Band in 1961 with Roger Collis (guitar), Kevin Drake (saxophone), Johnny King (bass) and Peter Brooks (drums). By 1963 they were Money, Andy Somers (later as Summers a member of The Police, guitar), Nick Newall (saxophone) and Colin Allen (drums), later adding Paul Williams (bass) and Clive Burrows (saxophone). Burrows left in 1966 and was replaced by Johnny Almond. Money (and Andy Somers) joined Eric Burdon's New Animals in 1968. Money has also appeared in various TV dramas.

18/08/1966	25	8		BIG TIME OPERATOR	Columbia DB 7975

MONEY MARK US rapper (born Mark Ramos Nishita, Detroit, MI) who first became known with The Beastie Boys, effectively becoming the fourth, unofficial member after recording with them in 1988. His debut album, recorded at home, originally appeared as a set of three ten-inch singles released by Los Angeles label Love Kit before being re-issued on Mo Wax.

28/02/1998	40	2		HAND IN YOUR HEAD	Mo Wax MW 066CD
06/06/1998	45	1		MAYBE I'M DEAD	Mo Wax MW 089CD1

MONICA US singer (born Monica Arnold, 24/10/1980, Atlanta, GA) who was discovered winning a talent contest. She recorded her debut album at fourteen.

29/07/1995	32	3		DON'T TAKE IT PERSONAL (JUST ONE OF DEM DAYS) Contains a sample of LL Cool J's *Back Seat (Of My Jeep)* .... Arista 74321301452	
17/02/1996	33	2		LIKE THIS AND LIKE THAT Contains a sample of Sugarhill Gang's *Spoonin' Rap*	Rowdy 74321344222
08/06/1996	22	3		BEFORE YOU WALK OUT OF MY LIFE	Rowdy 74321374042
24/05/1997	27	2		FOR YOU I WILL Featured in the 1996 film *Space Jam*	Atlantic A 5437CD
06/06/1998	2	20	O	THE BOY IS MINE ▲[13] BRANDY AND MONICA 1998 Grammy Award for Best Rhythm & Blues Performance by a Duo .... Atlantic AT 0036CD	

❶[9] Number of weeks single topped the UK chart ↑ Entered the UK chart at #1 ▲[9] Number of weeks single topped the US chart

543

| 17/10/1998 | 6 | 6 | | THE FIRST NIGHT ▲5 Contains a sample of Diana Ross' *Love Hangover* | Rowdy 74321619342 |
| 04/09/1999 | 55 | 1 | | ANGEL OF MINE ▲4 | Arista 74321692892 |

MONIFAH US singer/actress (born Monifah Carter, 28/1/1968, New York City) who was a backing singer for Maxi Priest.

| 30/01/1999 | 29 | 2 | | TOUCH IT Contains a sample of Laid Back's *White Horse* | Universal UMD 56218 |

TS MONK US vocal/instrumental group formed in 1976 by Thelonious Sphere Monk Jr (son of legendary jazz pianist Thelonious Monk), his sister Boo Boo and Yvonne Fletcher as Cycles, changing name in 1980. Thelonious Monk later recorded with Eric Mercury.

| 07/03/1981 | 63 | 2 | | BON BON VIE | Mirage K 11653 |
| 25/04/1981 | 58 | 4 | | CANDIDATE FOR LOVE | Mirage K 11648 |

MONKEES UK/US group formed in Los Angeles, CA in 1965 by writer/director/producer Bob Rafelson and Bert Schneider for a TV series. From 437 applicants, the four chosen were Davy Jones (born 30/12/1945, Manchester) who had appeared on British TV in *Coronation Street* and *Z Cars*, Michael Nesmith (born 30/12/1942, Houston, TX), Peter Tork (born Peter Thorkelson, 13/2/1944, Washington DC) and Mickey Dolenz (born 8/3/1945, Los Angeles). The TV series ran from 1966 to 1968, with a film, *Head*, in 1968. Tork left in 1968, the group continuing as a trio until 1969 when they disbanded. They re-formed in 1986 minus Nesmith and again in 1996 with all four original members. They took their name in honour of The Beatles. Tork served three months in prison for possession of hashish In the early 1970s. They have a star on the Hollywood Walk of Fame.

05/01/1967	❶4	17		I'M A BELIEVER ▲7 Worldwide sales exceed 10 million copies. Featured in the 1999 film *Austin Powers: The Spy Who Shagged Me*	RCA 1560
26/01/1967	23	7		LAST TRAIN TO CLARKSVILLE ▲1	RCA 1547
06/04/1967	3	12		A LITTLE BIT ME A LITTLE BIT YOU	RCA 1580
22/06/1967	2	12		ALTERNATE TITLE Was to have been called *Randy Scouse Git*, inspired by the TV comedy *'Til Death Us Do Part*, but changed at the insistence of the record company	RCA 1604
16/08/1967	11	8		PLEASANT VALLEY SUNDAY	RCA 1620
15/11/1967	5	17		DAYDREAM BELIEVER ▲4 Featured in the 1996 film *Now and Then*	RCA 1645
27/03/1968	12	8		VALLERI	RCA 1673
26/06/1968	17	6		D. W. WASHBURN	RCA 1706
26/03/1969	46	1		TEARDROP CITY	RCA 1802
25/06/1969	47	1		SOMEDAY MAN	RCA 1824
15/03/1980	33	9		THE MONKEES EP Tracks on EP: *I'm A Believer*, *Daydream Believer*, *Last Train To Clarksville* and *A Little Bit Me A Little Bit You*	Arista ARIST 326
18/10/1986	68	1		THAT WAS THEN, THIS IS NOW	Arista ARIST 673
01/04/1989	62	2		THE MONKEES EP Tracks on EP: *Daydream Believer*, *Monkees Theme* and *Last Train to Clarksville*	Arista 112157

MONKEY BARS FEATURING GABRIELLE WIDMAN US production duo Doron Orenstein and Gabriel Vine with Gabrielle Widman.

| 08/05/2004 | 61 | 1 | | SHUGGIE LOVE | Subliminal SUB117CD |

MONKEY MAFIA UK production duo Daniel Peppe and Jon Carter. Carter initially recorded as Artery and Junior Cartier and is married to Radio 1 DJ Sara Cox, while Peppe records as Agent Dan and Themroc.

10/08/1996	75	1		WORK MI BODY	Heavenly HVN 53CD
07/06/1997	67	1		15 STEPS (EP) Tracks on EP: *Lion In The Hall*, *Krash The Decks: Slaughter The Vinyl*, *Metro Love* and *Beats In The Hall*	Heavenly HVN 67CD
02/05/1998	51	1		LONG AS I CAN SEE THE LIGHT	Heavenly HVN 84CD

MONKS UK duo Richard Hudson (born 9/5/1948, London, guitar/vocals) and John Ford (born 1/7/1948, London, bass/vocals), previously both in Velvet Opera and The Strawbs before leaving in 1973 and recording as Hudson-Ford.

| 21/04/1979 | 19 | 9 | | NICE LEGS SHAME ABOUT HER FACE | Carrere CAR 104 |

MONO UK vocal/instrumental duo Siobhan De Mare (vocals) and producer Martin Virgo.

| 02/05/1998 | 60 | 1 | | LIFE IN MONO | Echo ECSCD 64 |

MONOBOY FEATURING DELORES Irish producer Ian Masterson with singer Delores.

| 07/07/2001 | 50 | 1 | | THE MUSIC IN YOU | Perfecto PERF 18CDS |

MATT MONRO UK singer (born Terence Parsons, 1/12/1932, London) who was a bus driver who sang in his spare time, usually under the name Al Jordan until adopting the name Monro, supposedly in honour of Winifred Atwell's father. After singing on a Camay advertisement he was asked by George Martin to perform on a Peter Sellers album and was noticed for his Frank Sinatra impersonation. He represented the UK in the 1964 Eurovision Song Contest, coming second behind Italy with *I Love The Little Things* which failed to chart in the UK. He moved to the US in 1965 and died from liver cancer on 7/2/1985.

15/12/1960	3	16		PORTRAIT OF MY LOVE	Parlophone R 4714
09/03/1961	5	12		MY KIND OF GIRL Featured in the 1988 film *Scandal*	Parlophone R 4755
18/05/1961	24	9		WHY NOT NOW/CAN THIS BE LOVE	Parlophone R 4775
28/09/1961	44	3		GONNA BUILD A MOUNTAIN	Parlophone R 4819
08/02/1962	10	18		SOFTLY AS I LEAVE YOU	Parlophone R 4868
14/06/1962	46	3		WHEN LOVE COMES ALONG	Parlophone R 4911
08/11/1962	29	5		MY LOVE AND DEVOTION	Parlophone R 4954
14/11/1963	20	13		FROM RUSSIA WITH LOVE Featured in the 1964 James Bond film *From Russia With Love*	Parlophone R 5068

○ Silver disc ● Gold disc ✪ Platinum disc (additional platinum units are indicated by a figure following the symbol) ◎ Singles released prior to 1973 that are known to have sold over 1 million copies in the UK

17/09/1964	4	20		**WALK AWAY** Originally recorded as *Warum Nur Warum* by Udo Jurgens, Austria's entry in the 1964 Eurovision Song Contest where it came sixth	Parlophone R 5171
24/12/1964	36	4		FOR MAMA	Parlophone R 5215
25/03/1965	37	4		WITHOUT YOU Originally *Sag Ihr, Ich Lass Sie Grussen* by Udo Jurgens, Austria's entry in the 1965 Eurovision Song Contest where it came fourth	Parlophone R 5251
21/10/1965	8	12		**YESTERDAY**	Parlophone R 5348
24/11/1973	28	8		AND YOU SMILED	EMI 2091

MONROE UK vocal group formed in London by Gemma, Hannah, Sian and Celetia.

31/07/2004	60	1		SMILE	Zu ZUDB001

GERRY MONROE UK singer, a contestant on the TV talent show *Opportunity Knocks* where he registered the highest number of votes. He was 37 at the time of his chart debut.

23/05/1970	4	20		**SALLY**	Chapter One CH 122
19/09/1970	38	5		CRY	Chapter One CH 128
14/11/1970	9	12		**MY PRAYER**	Chapter One CH 132
17/04/1971	13	12		IT'S A SIN TO TELL A LIE	Chapter One CH 144
21/08/1971	37	6		LITTLE DROPS OF SILVER	Chapter One CH 152
12/02/1972	43	2		GIRL OF MY DREAMS	Chapter One CH 159

HOLLIS P MONROE Canadian producer who later worked with Matt Jackson, David Duriez and DJ Hardware.

24/04/1999	51	1		I'M LONELY Contains a sample of Terence Trent D'Arby's *And I Need To Be With Someone Tonight*	City Beat CBE 778CD

MONSOON UK group formed by Sheila Chandra (born 14/3/1965, London), Steve Coe, Dan Mankoo and Martin Smith. Chandra, a former child actress (she appeared in TV's *Grange Hill*), later recorded solo.

03/04/1982	12	9		EVER SO LONELY	Mobile Suit Corporation CORP 2
05/06/1982	41	3		SHAKTI (THE MEANING OF WITHIN)	Mobile Suit Corporation CORP 4

MONSTA BOY FEATURING DENZIE UK production duo Dave Edwards and Denzie.

07/10/2000	25	3		SORRY (I DIDN'T KNOW)	Locked On LOX 125C

MONSTER MAGNET US rock group formed in New Jersey in 1989 by Dave Wyndorf (guitar/vocals), John McBain (guitar), Joe Calandra (bass), Jon Kleinman (drums) and Tim Cronin (visuals/propaganda). McBain left in 1993 and was replaced by Ed Mundell.

29/05/1993	67	1		TWIN EARTH	A&M 5802812
18/03/1995	49	1		NEGASONIC TEENAGE WARHEAD	A&M 5809812
06/05/1995	58	1		DOPES TO INFINITY	A&M 5810332
23/01/1999	39	2		POWERTRIP Featured in the 1999 film *Soldiers*	A&M 5828232
06/03/1999	45	1		SPACE LORD	A&M 5632752

MONTAGE UK vocal trio Roberta Forgie, Eve Horne and Lorraine Pryce.

15/02/1997	64	1		THERE AIN'T NOTHIN' LIKE THE LOVE	Wild Card 5733172

MONTANA SEXTET US instrumental group with vibes player Vince Montana, who began as an arranger for Philly Groove and Philadelphia International.

15/01/1983	59	1		HEAVY VIBES	Virgin VS 560

MONTANO VS THE TRUMPET MAN UK instrumental/production duo Gordon Matthewman and Adam Routh.

18/09/1999	46	1		ITZA TRUMPET THING	Serious SERR 010CD

HUGO MONTENEGRO US orchestra leader (born 2/9/1925, New York) who moved to California after serving in the US Navy. He made his name as the composer of numerous film and TV themes. He died from emphysema on 6/2/1981.

11/09/1968	❶4	25		**THE GOOD THE BAD THE UGLY**	RCA 1727
08/01/1969	50	1		HANG 'EM HIGH This and above single featured in the 1968 film *The Good, The Bad And The Ugly*	RCA 1771

CHRIS MONTEZ US singer (born Christopher Montanez, 17/1/1943, Los Angeles, CA) who was a protégé of Ritchie Valens and later worked with Herb Alpert.

04/10/1962	2	18		**LET'S DANCE** Featured in the 1978 film *Animal House*	London HLU 9596
17/01/1963	10	9		**SOME KINDA FUN**	London HLU 9650
30/06/1966	3	13		**THE MORE I SEE YOU** Originally appeared in the 1945 film *Billy Rose's Diamond Horseshoe*	Pye International 7N 25369
22/09/1966	37	4		THERE WILL NEVER BE ANOTHER YOU Originally appeared in the 1943 film *Iceland*	Pye International 7N 25381
14/10/1972	9	14		**LET'S DANCE** Re-issue of London HLU 9596	London HL 10205
14/04/1979	47	3		LET'S DANCE Second re-issue of London HLU 9596 coupled with *Memphis* by Lonnie Mack	Lightning LIG 9011

MONTROSE US rock group formed in 1973 by Ronnie Montrose (guitar), Sammy Hagar (born 13/10/1947, Monterey, CA, vocals), Bill Church (bass) and Denny Carmassi (drums). Church left in 1974 and was replaced by Alan Fitzgerald, while Hagar was sacked in 1975 (promptly going solo) and was replaced by Bob James, with Jim Alcivar joining on keyboards at the same time. Ronnie Montrose dissolved the group in 1976 and initially went solo as a jazz-rock artist before forming Gamma. In 1983 he resumed a solo career.

28/06/1980	71	2		SPACE STATION NO. 5/GOOD ROCKIN' TONIGHT	WB HM 9

❶⁹ Number of weeks single topped the UK chart ↑ Entered the UK chart at #1 ▲⁹ Number of weeks single topped the US chart

545

MONTROSE AVENUE
UK group formed by Scott James (guitar/piano/vocals), Paul Williams (guitar/vocals), Rob Lindsey-Clarke (guitar/vocals), Jimmy Taylor (bass) and Matthew Everitt (drums).

28/03/1998	38	2	WHERE DO I STAND?	Columbia 6656072
20/06/1998	58	1	SHINE	Columbia 6660012
17/10/1998	59	1	START AGAIN	Columbia 6664255

MONTY PYTHON
UK film/TV comedy team formed by John Cleese (born 27/10/1939, Weston-super-Mare), Graham Chapman (born 8/1/1941, Leicester), Terry Jones (born 1/2/1942, Colwyn Bay), Terry Gilliam (born 22/11/1940, Minneapolis, MN), Eric Idle (born 29/3/1943, South Shields) and Michael Palin (born 5/5/1943, Sheffield). Most of the Python songs were written in conjunction with Neil Innes (born 9/12/1944, Danbury). Chapman died from throat cancer on 4/10/1989. Palin was awarded a CBE in the 2000 New Year's Honours List. The distinctive theme to the TV series was John Phillip Sousa's *Liberty Bell March*.

05/10/1991	3	9	**ALWAYS LOOK ON THE BRIGHT SIDE OF LIFE** Featured in the 1979 film *Life Of Brian*. Revived as an anthem on football terraces	Virgin PYTH 1

MONYAKA
US group formed in New York in 1974 comprising Errol Moore (lead guitar), Beres Barnet (guitar/vocals), Paul Henton (bass/vocals), William Brown (keyboards), John Allen (keyboards) and Richard Bertram (drums). The name means 'good luck' in Swahili.

10/09/1983	14	8	GO DEH YAKA (GO TO THE TOP)	Polydor POSP 641

MOOD
UK vocal/instrumental trio with a guest appearance by Roy Hay of Culture Club.

06/02/1982	59	4	DON'T STOP	RCA 171
22/05/1982	42	5	PARIS IS ONE DAY AWAY	RCA 211
30/10/1982	74	1	PASSION IN DARK ROOMS	RCA 276

MOOD II SWING
US production duo Lem Springsteen and John Ciafone.

31/01/2004	45	2	CAN'T GET AWAY	Defected DFTD 078CDS

MOODSWINGS/CHRISSIE HYNDE
UK group with JFT 'Fred' Hood, Grant Showbiz and US singer Chrissie Hynde.

12/10/1991	66	2	SPIRITUAL HIGH (STATE OF INDEPENDENCE) Featured in the 1992 film *Single White Female*	Arista 114528
23/01/1993	47	2	SPIRITUAL HIGH (STATE OF INDEPENDENCE) (REMIX)	Arista 74321127712

MOODY BLUES
UK group formed in Birmingham in 1964 by Denny Laine (born Brian Hines, 29/10/1944, Tyseley, Birmingham), Ray Thomas (born 29/12/1942, Stourport-on-Severn), Mike Pinder (born 27/12/1941, Birmingham), Graeme Edge (born 30/3/1942, Roxeter) and Clint Warwick (born Clinton Eccles, 25/6/1940) as the Moody Blues Five. Laine and Warwick left in 1966 and the group disbanded, quickly re-forming with the three remaining members and Justin Hayward (born 14/10/1946, Swindon) and John Lodge (born 20/7/1945, Birmingham). Pinder left in 1978 and was replaced by Patrick Moraz (born 24/6/1948). Laine joined Wings in 1971 and Hayward, Lodge and Thomas recorded projects outside the group. They launched the Threshold label in 1970. Originally called M&B5, after the local Mitchell & Butler brewery sponsored the group, later the M became Moody, the B Blues and the 5 was dropped.

10/12/1964	❶[1]	14	**GO NOW**	Decca F 12022
04/03/1965	33	9	I DON'T WANT TO GO ON WITHOUT YOU	Decca F 12095
10/06/1965	22	9	FROM THE BOTTOM OF MY HEART	Decca F 12166
18/11/1965	44	2	EVERYDAY	Decca F 12266
27/12/1967	19	11	NIGHTS IN WHITE SATIN Featured in the films *A Bronx Tale* (1994) and *Casino* (1995)	Deram DM 161
07/08/1968	27	10	VOICES IN THE SKY	Deram DM 196
04/12/1968	42	1	RIDE MY SEE-SAW	Deram DM 213
02/05/1970	2	12	**QUESTION**	Threshold TH 4
06/05/1972	13	10	ISN'T LIFE STRANGE	Threshold TH 9
02/12/1972	9	11	**NIGHTS IN WHITE SATIN**	Deram DM 161
10/02/1973	36	4	I'M JUST A SINGER (IN A ROCK 'N' ROLL BAND)	Threshold TH 13
10/11/1979	14	12	NIGHTS IN WHITE SATIN	Deram DM 161
20/08/1983	35	5	BLUE WORLD	Threshold TH 30
25/06/1988	52	4	I KNOW YOU'RE OUT THERE SOMEWHERE	Polydor POSP 921

MICHAEL MOOG
US DJ/producer Shivaun Gaines.

11/12/1999	32	2	THAT SOUND	ffrr FCD 374
25/08/2001	62	1	YOU BELONG TO ME	Strictly Rhythm SRUKECD 04

MOOGWAI
Swiss/Dutch production duo Francois Chabolis and Armin Van Buuren. Van Buuren also recorded solo.

06/05/2000	55	1	VIOLA	Platipus PLATCD 71
26/05/2001	68	1	THE LABYRINTH	Platipus PLATCD 83

MOONMAN
Dutch DJ/singer Ferry Corsten who earlier recorded as Gouryella, Starparty, Moonman and System F as well as under his own name.

09/08/1997	60	1	DON'T BE AFRAID	Heat Recordings HEATCD 009
27/11/1999	41	2	DON'T BE AFRAID '99 (REMIX)	Heat Recordings HEATCD 022
07/10/2000	50	1	GALAXIA **MOONMAN FEATURING CHANTAL**	Heat Recordings HEATCD 025

MOONTREKKERS
UK instrumental group with Gary LePort and Ron Winskill. They were discovered by producer Joe Meek who sacked the group's singer and harmonica player, Rod Stewart, before they recorded their debut hit. They disbanded in 1964.

02/11/1961	50	1	NIGHT OF THE VAMPIRE	Parlophone R 4814

MOONY Italian singer (born Monica Bragato, Venice) who was first known as featured vocalist with DB Boulevard.

15/06/2002	9	8		DOVE (I'LL BE LOVING YOU)	Positiva/Cream CDMNY1
01/03/2003	64	1		ACROBATS (LOOKING FOR BALANCE)	WEA 363CD

CHANTE MOORE US R&B singer (born 17/2/1967, San Francisco, CA).

20/03/1993	54	3		LOVE'S TAKEN OVER	MCA MCSTD 1744
04/03/1995	69	1		FREE/SAIL ON	MCA MCSTD 2042
07/04/2001	11	7		STRAIGHT UP	MCA MCSTD 40250

DOROTHY MOORE US singer (born 13/10/1947, Jackson, MS), a member of the Poppies (along with Fern Kinney), who first recorded solo for GSF and Chimneyville before linking with Malaco.

19/06/1976	5	12	O	MISTY BLUE Featured in the 1996 film *Phenomenon*	Contempo CS 2087
16/10/1976	38	3		FUNNY HOW TIME SLIPS AWAY	Contempo CS 2092
15/10/1977	20	9		I BELIEVE YOU	Epic EPC 5573

DUDLEY MOORE – see PETER COOK

GARY MOORE UK singer/guitarist (born 4/4/1952, Belfast) who formed his first band, Skid Row, in 1968 before joining Thin Lizzy in 1974. Later a member of Colusseum II, he rejoined Thin Lizzy, recording his debut solo album at the same time. Moore also joined Jack Bruce and Ginger Baker to form BBM.

21/04/1979	8	11	O	PARISIENNE WALKWAYS Features the uncredited vocal of Phil Lynott	MCA 419
21/01/1984	65	3		HOLD ON TO LOVE	10 TEN 13
11/08/1984	51	5		EMPTY ROOMS	10 TEN 25
18/05/1985	5	10		OUT IN THE FIELDS GARY MOORE AND PHIL LYNOTT	10 TEN 49
27/07/1985	23	8		EMPTY ROOMS	10 TEN 58
20/12/1986	20	8		OVER THE HILLS AND FAR AWAY	10 TEN 134
28/02/1987	35	5		WILD FRONTIER	10 TEN 159
09/05/1987	26	6		FRIDAY ON MY MIND	10 TEN 164
29/08/1987	53	5		THE LONER	10 TEN 178
05/12/1987	75	1		TAKE A LITTLE TIME (DOUBLE SINGLE)	10 TEN 190
14/01/1989	37	4		AFTER THE WAR	Virgin GMS 1
18/03/1989	56	2		READY FOR LOVE	Virgin GMS 2
24/03/1990	48	3		OH PRETTY WOMAN GARY MOORE FEATURING ALBERT KING	Virgin VS 1233
12/05/1990	31	7		STILL GOT THE BLUES (FOR YOU)	Virgin VS 1267
18/08/1990	48	5		WALKING BY MYSELF	Virgin VS 1281
15/12/1990	71	1		TOO TIRED	Virgin VS 1306
22/02/1992	24	5		COLD DAY IN HELL	Virgin VS 1393
09/05/1992	40	4		STORY OF THE BLUES	Virgin VS 1412
18/07/1992	59	3		SINCE I MET YOU BABY GARY MOORE AND BB KING	Virgin VS 1423
24/10/1992	59	1		SEPARATE WAYS	Virgin VS 1437
08/05/1993	32	4		PARISIENNE WALKWAYS Re-recording	Virgin VSCDX 1456
17/06/1995	48	2		NEED YOUR LOVE SO BAD	Virgin VSCDG 1546

JACKIE MOORE US singer (born 1946, Jacksonville, FL).

15/09/1979	49	5		THIS TIME BABY	CBS 7722

LYNSEY MOORE – see RAMSEY AND FEN FEATURING LYNSEY MOORE

MANDY MOORE US singer (born 10/4/1984, Nashua, NH) whose family moved to Orlando, FL when she was two months old. She appeared in the 2002 film *A Walk To Remember*.

06/05/2000	6	13		CANDY	Epic 6693452
19/08/2000	21	5		I WANNA BE WITH YOU Featured in the 2000 film *Center Stage*	Epic 6695922

MARK MOORE – see S EXPRESS

MELBA MOORE US singer (born Melba Hill, 29/10/1945, New York) who first came to prominence in the Broadway production of *Hair* before signing with Philadelphia International and then Buddah. She appeared in a number of films, including *Seasonal Differences* (1987) and *Def By Temptation* (1990), and won a Tony Award for her portrayal of Lutiebelle in the stage musical *Purdie*.

15/05/1976	9	8		THIS IS IT	Buddah BDS 443
26/05/1979	48	5		PICK ME UP I'LL DANCE	Epic EPC 7234
09/10/1982	15	8		LOVE'S COMIN' AT YA	EMI America EA 146
15/01/1983	22	6		MIND UP TONIGHT	Capitol CL 272
05/03/1983	60	2		UNDERLOVE	Capitol CL 281

RAY MOORE UK singer/DJ (born 1942, Liverpool) who was an announcer for Granada Television in 1962 and later on Radio 2 at its launch. He died in January 1989.

29/11/1986	24	7		O' MY FATHER HAD A RABBIT	Play 213
05/12/1987	61	2		BOG EYED JOG	Play 224

❶⁹ Number of weeks single topped the UK chart   ↑ Entered the UK chart at #1   ▲⁹ Number of weeks single topped the US chart

547

SAM MOORE AND LOU REED
US vocal duo Sam Moore (born 12/10/1935, Miami, FL) and Lou Reed (born Louis Firbank, 2/3/1943, Freeport, Long Island, NY). Moore had previously been with Sam And Dave.

17/01/1987.....30.....10...... SOUL MAN Featured in the 1986 film *Soul Man*...........................A&M AM 364

TINA MOORE
US singer (born in Milwaukee, WI) who made her first album in 1994 with producer Steve 'Silk' Hurley.

30/08/1997.....7.....15......O **NEVER GONNA LET YOU GO**...........................Delirious 74321511052
25/04/1998.....20.....3....... NOBODY BETTER...........................Delirious 74321571612

LISA MOORISH
UK singer. It was rumoured that George Michael guested on her cover version of *I'm Your Man*, especially as both singers were known to be using the same studio at the same time. She later became a member of Killcity and had a child with Liam Gallagher (shortly after he had married Patsy Kensit).

07/01/1995.....42.....3....... JUST THE WAY IT IS...........................Go Beat GODCD 123
19/08/1995.....24.....3....... I'M YOUR MAN...........................Go Beat GODCD 128
03/02/1996.....24.....3....... MR FRIDAY NIGHT...........................Go Beat GODCD 137
18/05/1996.....37.....2....... LOVE FOR LIFE...........................Go Beat GODCD 145

M.O.P.
US rap duo formed in Brownsville, Brooklyn in 1993 by Lil' Fame and Billy Danzenie. The name stands for Mashed Out Posse.

12/05/2001.....4.....10...... **COLD AS ICE** Contains a sample of Foreigner's *Cold As Ice*...........................Epic 6711762
18/08/2001.....7.....8....... **ANTE UP** M.O.P. FEATURING BUSTA RYMES...........................Epic 6717882
01/12/2001.....43.....1....... STAND CLEAR...........................Chrysalis CDEM 597
08/06/2002.....50.....1....... STAND CLEAR This and above single credited to ADAM F FEATURING M.O.P....................Kaos KAOSCD 002

ANGEL MORAES
US producer (born in Brooklyn, NYC) of Puerto Rican descent. He launched his own Hot N Spycy label.

16/11/1996.....72.....1....... HEAVEN KNOWS – DEEP DEEP DOWN...........................ffrr FCD 282
17/05/1997.....70.....1....... I LIKE IT...........................AM:PM 5871792

DAVID MORALES
US producer (born 21/8/1961, New York) with Puerto Rican parents who was first known as a DJ and remixer before launching his recording career. He also recorded as Pulse, Bad Yard Club and Boss. He won the 1998 Grammy Award for Best Remixer.

10/07/1993.....37.....3....... GIMME LUV (EENIE MEENIE MINY MO) DAVID MORALES AND THE BAD YARD CLUB.....................Mercury MERCD 390
20/11/1993.....66.....1....... THE PROGRAM...........................Mercury MERCD 396
24/08/1996.....35.....2....... IN DE GHETTO DAVID MORALES AND THE BAD YARD CLUB FEATURING CRYSTAL WATERS AND DELTA..........Manifesto FESCD 12
15/08/1998.....8.....8....... **NEEDIN' U** DAVID MORALES PRESENTS THE FACE Contains samples of The Chi-Lites' *My First Mistake* and Rare Pleasure's *Let Me Down Easy*...........................Manifesto FESCD 46
24/06/2000.....41.....2....... HIGHER DAVID MORALES AND ALBERT CABRERA PRESENT MOCA FEATURING DEANNA....................Azuli AZNYCDX 120
20/01/2001.....11.....5....... NEEDIN' YOU II (REMIX) DAVID MORALES PRESENTS THE FACE FEATURING JULIET ROBERTS...............Manifesto FESCD 78
02/10/2004.....71.....1....... HOW WOULD U FEEL DAVID MORALES FEATURING LEA LORIEN...........................DMI DM102

MIKE MORAN – see LYNSEY DE PAUL

MORCHEEBA
UK psychedelic blues group formed by brothers Paul and Ross Godfrey and lead vocalist Skye Edwards. Edwards took part in the *Perfect Day* project for the BBC's Children In Need charity.

13/07/1996.....42.....1....... TAPE LOOP...........................Indochina ID 045CD
05/10/1996.....40.....2....... TRIGGER HIPPIE...........................Indochina ID 052CDR
15/02/1997.....47.....1....... THE MUSIC THAT WE HEAR (MOOG ISLAND)...........................Indochina ID 054CD
11/10/1997.....53.....1....... SHOULDER HOLSTER...........................Indochina ID 064CD
11/04/1998.....56.....1....... BLINDFOLD...........................Indochina ID 070CD
20/06/1998.....46.....1....... LET ME SEE...........................Indochina ID 076CD
29/08/1998.....38.....2....... PART OF THE PROCESS...........................China WOKCD 2097
05/08/2000.....34.....3....... ROME WASN'T BUILT IN A DAY...........................East West EW 214CD
31/03/2001.....48.....1....... WORLD LOOKING IN...........................East West EW 225CD
06/07/2002.....64.....1....... OTHERWISE...........................East West EW 247CD

MORE
UK rock group formed by Paul Mario Day (vocals), Kenny Cox (guitar), Laurie Mansworth (guitar), Brian Day (bass) and Frank Darch (drums). By 1981 the line-up consisted of Cox, Nick Stratton (vocals), Barry Nicholls (bass) and Andy Burton (drums).

14/03/1981.....59.....2....... WE ARE THE BAND...........................Atlantic K 11561

MORE FIRE CREW
UK garage group formed in London by Lethal B, Neeko and Ozzie B.

16/03/2002.....8.....8....... **OI** PLATINUM 45 FEATURING MORE FIRE CREW...........................Go! Beat GOBCD 48
25/01/2003.....45.....2....... BACK THEN...........................Go! Beat GOBCD 54

MOREL
US singer/producer Richard Morel.

12/08/2000.....64.....1....... TRUE (THE FAGGOT IS YOU)...........................Hooj Choons HOOJ 097CD

GEORGE MOREL FEATURING HEATHER WILDMAN
US singer (born in New York) who first recorded as Morel's Grooves in 1992 for the Strictly Rhythm label.

26/10/1996.....42.....2....... LET'S GROOVE...........................Positiva CDTIV 62

MORGAN UK vocal/instrumental duo Wiliam Nicholls and Jack Shillacker.

27/11/1999 . . . . . 74 . . . . . . 1	MISS PARKER	Source CDSOUR 002

DEBELAH MORGAN US singer (born 29/9/1977, Detroit, MI) who won the Miss Teen Black Arizona and Miss Black Teenage World beauty competitions at the age of fifteen and made her first record in 1994.

| 24/02/2001 . . . . . 10 . . . . . . 9 . . . . | **DANCE WITH ME** Contains an interpolation of Archie Bleyer's *Hernando's Hideaway* . . . . Atlantic AT 0087CD |

DERRICK MORGAN Jamaican singer (born 1940, Stewarton).

| 17/01/1970 . . . . . 49 . . . . . . 1 . . . . | MOON HOP . . . . Crab 32 |

JAMIE J. MORGAN US R&B singer who began as a stylist and photographer before starting a solo singing career.

| 10/02/1990 . . . . . 27 . . . . . . 6 . . . . | WALK ON THE WILD SIDE . . . . Tabu 6555967 |

JANE MORGAN US singer (born Jane Currier, 1920, Boston, MA, raised in Florida) who initially achieved greater success in Europe before becoming a major US star via numerous TV appearances. She died in 1974.

05/12/1958 . . . . ❶¹ 16	**THE DAY THE RAINS CAME** . . . . London HLR 8751
22/05/1959 . . . . . 27 . . . . . . 1	IF ONLY I COULD LIVE MY LIFE AGAIN . . . . London HLR 8810
21/07/1960 . . . . . 39 . . . . . . 5	ROMANTICA . . . . London HLR 9120

MELI'SA MORGAN US singer (born in Queens, NYC) who later worked with Kashif.

| 09/08/1986 . . . . . 41 . . . . . . 5 . . . . | FOOL'S PARADISE . . . . Capitol CL 415 |
| 25/06/1988 . . . . . 59 . . . . . . 2 . . . . | GOOD LOVE . . . . Capitol CL 483 |

RAY MORGAN UK singer (born 1947) who began his singing career in 1955.

| 25/07/1970 . . . . . 32 . . . . . . 6 . . . . | THE LONG AND WINDING ROAD . . . . B&C CB 128 |

ERICK 'MORE' MORILLO US DJ/producer who is also a member of Lil Mo' Yin Yang and Ministers De La Funk.

| 04/02/1995 . . . . . 74 . . . . . . 1 . . . . | HIGHER (FEEL IT) **ERICK 'MORE' MORILLO PRESENTS RAW** . . . . A&M 5809412 |
| 26/06/2004 . . . . . 44 . . . . . . 2 . . . . | BREAK DOWN THE DOORS **MORILLO FEATURING AUDIO BULLYS** . . . . Subliminal SUB124CD |

ALANIS MORISSETTE Canadian singer (born Nadine Morissette, 1/6/1974, Ottawa, Ontario) who began her career as an actress, appearing on Nickelodeon TV in 1984. She recorded her first single at eleven, and by 1992 was recording material similar to Paula Abdul. She switched styles in 1994 following a teaming with songwriter Glen Ballard and signed with Madonna's Maverick label. She won Best International Newcomer at the 1996 BRIT Awards and Best Female at the 1996 MTV Europe Music Awards. Seven Grammy Awards include Album of the Year and Best Rock Album in 1995 for *Jagged Little Pill* (which has sold more than 29 million copies worldwide, the most by any female performer), Best Music Video Long Form in 1997 for *Jagged Little Pill Live* and Best Rock Song and Best Female Rock Vocal Performance in 1998 for *Uninvited*.

05/08/1995 . . . . . 22 . . . . . . 7	YOU OUGHTA KNOW 1995 Grammy Awards for Best Female Rock Vocalist plus Best Rock Song for writers Alanis Morissette and Glen Ballard . . . . Maverick W 03070CD
28/10/1995 . . . . . 26 . . . . . . 3	HAND IN MY POCKET . . . . Maverick W 0312CD1
24/02/1996 . . . . . 24 . . . . . . 4	YOU LEARN . . . . Maverick W 0334CD
20/04/1996 . . . . . 11 . . . . . . 9	IRONIC . . . . Maverick W 0343CD
03/08/1996 . . . . 7 . . . . . . 7	**HEAD OVER FEET** . . . . Maverick W 0355CD
07/12/1996 . . . . . 59 . . . . . . 1	ALL I REALLY WANT . . . . Maverick W 0382CD
31/10/1998 . . . . 5 . . . . . . 10	**THANK U** . . . . Maverick W 0458CD
13/03/1999 . . . . . 28 . . . . . . 2	JOINING YOU . . . . Maverick W 472CD
31/07/1999 . . . . . 38 . . . . . . 2	SO PURE . . . . Maverick W 492CD1
02/03/2002 . . . . . 12 . . . . . . 7	HANDS CLEAN . . . . Maverick W 574CD1
17/08/2002 . . . . . 53 . . . . . . 1	PRECIOUS ILLUSIONS . . . . Maverick W 582CD
22/05/2004 . . . . . 22 . . . . . . 3	EVERYTHING . . . . Maverick W 641CD
31/07/2004 . . . . . 56 . . . . . . 1	OUT IS THROUGH . . . . Maverick W 647CD

MORJAC FEATURING RAZ CONWAY Danish production duo Jarob Johansen and Morten Lambertsen with singer Raz Conway.

| 11/10/2003 . . . . . 38 . . . . . . 2 . . . . . . | STARS . . . . Credence CDCRED 036 |

GIORGIO MORODER Italian producer/synthesiser player (born 26/4/1940, Ortisel) who was first known as a songwriter and producer, notably on Donna Summer's early albums. He won an Oscar in 1978 for *Midnight Express*. He has also won three Grammy Awards: Best Instrumental Composition in 1983 for *Theme For Flashdance*, Best Album of Original Score Written for a Motion Picture in 1983 for *Flashdance* and Best Dance Recording in 1997 with Donna Summer for *Carry On*. Phil Oakey (born 2/10/1955, Leicester) was lead vocalist with Human League.

24/09/1977 . . . . . 16 . . . . . 10	FROM HERE TO ETERNITY **GIORGIO** . . . . Oasis 1
17/03/1979 . . . . . 48¹ 6	CHASE Featured in the 1978 film *Midnight Express* . . . . Casablanca CAN 144
22/09/1984 . . . . . 3 . . . . . . 13 . . . . . O	**TOGETHER IN ELECTRIC DREAMS GIORGIO MORODER AND PHIL OAKEY** Featured in the 1984 film *Electric Dreams* . . . . Virgin VS 713
29/06/1985 . . . . . 44 . . . . . . 5	GOODBYE BAD TIMES **PHILIP OAKEY AND GIORGIO MORODER** . . . . Virgin VS 772
11/07/1998 . . . . . 65 . . . . . . 1	CARRY ON **DONNA SUMMER AND GIORGIO MORODER** . . . . Almighty CDALMY 120
12/02/2000 . . . . . 46 . . . . . . 1	THE CHASE **DJ EMPIRE PRESENTS GIORGIO MORODER** . . . . Logic 74321732112

❶⁹ Number of weeks single topped the UK chart ↑ Entered the UK chart at #1 ▲⁹ Number of weeks single topped the US chart

ENNIO MORRICONE
Italian orchestra leader/conductor/composer (born 11/10/1928, Rome) who scored over 400 films and TV themes during his long and illustrious career, including the 1964 film *A Fistful Of Dollars,* for which he is best known. He won an Oscar in 1984 for his music to the film *The Mission* and the 1987 Grammy Award for Best Album of Original Instrumental Background Score Written for a Motion Picture for *The Untouchables.*

11/04/1981	2	12	●	CHI MAI (THEME FROM THE TV SERIES THE LIFE AND TIMES OF DAVID LLOYD GEORGE) .... BBC RESL 92

SARAH JANE MORRIS – see COMMUNARDS

DIANA MORRISON – see MICHAEL BALL

DOROTHY COMBS MORRISON – see EDWIN HAWKINS SINGERS FEATURING DOROTHY COMBS MORRISON

MARK MORRISON
UK R&B singer (born 3/5/1972, Hanover, Germany) who was raised in Leicester and also spent a number of years in Florida before returning to England in 1993. He was jailed for three months in 1997 for threatening an off-duty policeman with a stun gun and later arrested and held in custody for failing to turn up at court on three occasions: when the case came before court he was sentenced to a further year in prison. He won the 1996 MOBO Award for Best Rhythm & Blues Act.

DATE	POS	WKS	BPI	SINGLE TITLE / LABEL & NUMBER
22/04/1995	19	4		CRAZY .... WEA YZ 907CD
16/09/1995	39	2		LET'S GET DOWN .... WEA 001CD
16/03/1996	❶²	24	✪	RETURN OF THE MACK Contains a sample of Kool & The Gang's *N.T.* .... WEA 040CD
27/07/1996	6	9		CRAZY (REMIX) Featured in the 1997 film *Speed 2 – Cruise Control* .... WEA 054CD1
19/10/1996	8	6		TRIPPIN' .... WEA 079CD1
21/12/1996	5	9		HORNY .... WEA 090CD1
15/03/1997	7	6		MOAN AND GROAN .... WEA 096CD1
20/09/1997	13	5		WHO'S THE MACK .... WEA 128CD1
04/09/1999	23	3		BEST FRIEND MARK MORRISON AND CONNOR REEVES Originally recorded by Mark Morrison and Gary Barlow, although Barlow later changed his mind about releasing it due to Morrison's numerous clashes with the law .... WEA 221CD1
14/08/2004	48	1		JUST A MAN/BACKSTABBERS .... 2 Wikid WKDCD007

VAN MORRISON
UK singer (born George Ivan Morrison, 31/8/1945, Belfast) who joined his first band Deannie Sands And The Javelins at twelve and two years later joined The Monarchs. He formed Them in 1963, disbanding the group in 1966 following a traumatic US tour. He signed solo with Bert Bern's Bang label in 1967 and scored a US top ten hit with *Brown Eyed Girl.* He has achieved considerably more success as an album artist. He was presented with the Outstanding Contribution Award at the 1994 BRIT Awards and in 1996 was awarded an MBE. He was inducted into the Rock & Roll Hall of Fame in 1993 and won the 1997 Grammy Award for Best Pop Collaboration with Vocals with John Lee Hooker for *Don't Look Back.*

DATE	POS	WKS	SINGLE TITLE / LABEL & NUMBER
20/10/1979	63	3	BRIGHT SIDE OF THE ROAD Featured in the 1996 film *Michael* .... Mercury 6001 121
01/07/1989	74	1	HAVE I TOLD YOU LATELY Featured in the 1997 film *One Fine Day* .... Polydor VANS 1
09/12/1989	20	6	WHENEVER GOD SHINES HIS LIGHT VAN MORRISON WITH CLIFF RICHARD .... Polydor VANS 2
15/05/1993	31	3	GLORIA VAN MORRISON AND JOHN LEE HOOKER .... Exile VANCD 11
18/03/1995	71	1	HAVE I TOLD YOU LATELY THAT I LOVE YOU CHIEFTAINS WITH VAN MORRISON ... RCA 74321271702
10/06/1995	65	1	DAYS LIKE THIS .... Exile VANCD 12
02/12/1995	54	1	NO RELIGION .... Exile 5775792
01/03/1997	46	1	THE HEALING GAME .... Exile 5733912
06/03/1999	36	2	PRECIOUS TIME .... Pointblank POBDX 14
22/05/1999	69	1	BACK ON TOP .... Exile/Pointblank/Virgin POBD 15
18/05/2002	58	1	HEY MR DJ .... Exile 5705962

MORRISSEY
UK singer (born Steven Morrissey, 22/5/1959, Davyhulme) who was a journalist for *Record Mirror* before forming The Smiths with Johnny Marr in 1982. He went solo in 1988.

DATE	POS	WKS	SINGLE TITLE / LABEL & NUMBER
27/02/1988	5	6	SUEDEHEAD .... HMV POP 1618
11/06/1988	9	6	EVERYDAY IS LIKE SUNDAY .... HMV POP 1619
11/02/1989	6	5	LAST OF THE FAMOUS INTERNATIONAL PLAYBOYS .... HMV POP 1620
29/04/1989	9	4	INTERESTING DRUG .... HMV POP 1621
25/11/1989	18	4	OUIJA BOARD OUIJA BOARD .... HMV POP 1622
05/05/1990	12	4	NOVEMBER SPAWNED A MONSTER .... HMV POP 1623
20/10/1990	18	2	PICCADILLY PALARE .... HMV POP 1624
23/02/1991	26	3	OUR FRANK .... HMV POP 1625
13/04/1991	33	2	SING YOUR LIFE .... HMV POP 1626
27/07/1991	25	4	PREGNANT FOR THE LAST TIME .... HMV POP 1627
12/10/1991	29	2	MY LOVE LIFE .... HMV POP 1628
09/05/1992	17	3	WE HATE IT WHEN OUR FRIENDS BECOME SUCCESSFUL. .... HMV POP 1629
18/07/1992	19	3	YOU'RE THE ONE FOR ME, FATTY .... HMV POP 1630
19/12/1992	35	4	CERTAIN PEOPLE I KNOW .... HMV POP 1631
12/03/1994	8	3	THE MORE YOU IGNORE ME THE CLOSER I GET .... Parlophone CDR 6372
11/06/1994	47	2	HOLD ON TO YOUR FRIENDS .... Parlophone CDR 6383
20/08/1994	25	2	INTERLUDE MORRISSEY AND SIOUXSIE .... Parlophone CDR 6365
28/01/1995	23	3	BOXERS .... Parlophone CDR 6400
02/09/1995	26	2	DAGENHAM DAVE .... RCA Victor 74321299802
09/12/1995	36	2	THE BOY RACER .... RCA Victor 74321332952
23/12/1995	42	2	SUNNY .... Parlophone CDR 6243

○ Silver disc   ● Gold disc   ✪ Platinum disc (additional platinum units are indicated by a figure following the symbol)   ◎ Singles released prior to 1973 that are known to have sold over 1 million copies in the UK

DATE	POS	WKS	BPI	SINGLE TITLE	LABEL & NUMBER
02/08/1997	16	3		ALMA MATTERS	Island CID 667
18/10/1997	42	1		ROY'S KEEN	Island CID 671
10/01/1998	39	2		SATAN REJECTED MY SOUL	Island CID 686
22/05/2004	3	5		**IRISH BLOOD ENGLISH HEART**	Attack ATKXS002
24/07/2004	6	7		**FIRST OF THE GANG TO DIE**	Attack ATKXS003
23/10/2004	8	3		**LET ME KISS YOU**	Attack ATKXS008
25/12/2004	10	1+		**I HAVE FORGIVEN JESUS**	Attack ATKXS011

MORRISTON ORPHEUS MALE VOICE CHOIR – see ALARM

BUDDY MORROW
US orchestra leader (born Muni Zudekoff, 8/2/1919, New Haven, CT) who played trombone with Paul Whiteman, Artie Shaw, Tommy Dorsey, Bob Crosby and Jimmy Dorsey before forming his own band in 1951. He later played with the house band on Johnny Carson's *Tonight Show*.

DATE	POS	WKS	BPI	SINGLE TITLE	LABEL & NUMBER
20/03/1953	12	1		NIGHT TRAIN	HMV B 10347

MORTIIS
Norwegian male singer/bass player (born 1975, Notodden) who was a member of Emperor before going solo.

DATE	POS	WKS	BPI	SINGLE TITLE	LABEL & NUMBER
28/08/2004	51	1		THE GRUDGE	Earache MOSH284CD

BOB MORTIMER
UK comic (born 23/5/1959, Middlesbrough) and co-host of the TV show *Shooting Stars* with Vic Reeves.

DATE	POS	WKS	BPI	SINGLE TITLE	LABEL & NUMBER
08/07/1995	3	8		**I'M A BELIEVER** EMF AND REEVES AND MORTIMER	Parlophone CDR 6412
24/05/1997	44	1		LET'S DANCE MIDDLESBROUGH FC FEATURING BOB MORTIMER AND CHRIS REA	Magnet EW 112CD

MOS DEF
US rapper (born Dante Smith, New York City) who is also a member of rap duo Black Star with Talib Kweli. He won the 2000 MOBO Award with Ronny Jordan for Best Jazz Act.

DATE	POS	WKS	BPI	SINGLE TITLE	LABEL & NUMBER
24/06/2000	60	1		UMI SAYS	Rawkus RWK 232CD
04/11/2000	64	1		MISS FAT BOOTY – PART II MOS DEF FEATURING GHOSTFACE KILLAH Contains a sample of Aretha Franklin's *One Step*	Rawkus RWK 282CD
03/03/2001	24	4		OH NO MOS DEF AND NATE DOGG FEATURING PHAROAHE MONCH	Rawkus RWK 302

MICKIE MOST
UK singer (born Michael Hayes, 20/6/1938, Aldershot) who was better known as a producer for the likes of The Animals, Lulu, Jeff Beck, Donovan and Herman's Hermits before launching his own label, RAK. He was also a regular member of the *New Faces* TV talent show panel. He died from cancer on 31/5/2003.

DATE	POS	WKS	BPI	SINGLE TITLE	LABEL & NUMBER
25/07/1963	45	1		MISTER PORTER	Decca F 11664

MOTELS
US group formed in Berkeley, CA by Martha Davis (born 15/1/1951, vocals), Jeff Jourard (guitar), Martin Jourard (keyboards), Michael Goodroe (bass) and Brian Glascock (drums). Scott Thurston (guitar) joined in 1983. The group disbanded in 1987.

DATE	POS	WKS	BPI	SINGLE TITLE	LABEL & NUMBER
11/10/1980	42	4		WHOSE PROBLEM?	Capitol CL 16162
10/01/1981	41	3		DAYS ARE O.K.	Capitol CL 16149

WENDY MOTEN
US singer (born in Memphis, TN) who is one of six children born to Elder James and Viola Moten. She began her singing career in the church, performing at the Grace Tabernacle Church and St Stephen's B Church.

DATE	POS	WKS	BPI	SINGLE TITLE	LABEL & NUMBER
05/02/1994	8	9		**COME IN OUT OF THE RAIN**	EMI-USA CDMT 105
14/05/1994	35	4		SO CLOSE TO LOVE	EMI-USA CDMTS 106

MOTHER
UK instrumental/production duo Lee Fisher and Jools Brettle.

DATE	POS	WKS	BPI	SINGLE TITLE	LABEL & NUMBER
12/06/1993	34	2		ALL FUNKED UP	Bosting BYSNCD 101
01/10/1994	73	1		GET BACK	Six6 SIXT 119
31/08/1996	66	1		ALL FUNKED UP (REMIX)	Six6 SIXXCD 1

MOTHER'S PRIDE
UK DJ/production duo Andy Cato and Andy Guise. Cato is also a member of Groove Armada.

DATE	POS	WKS	BPI	SINGLE TITLE	LABEL & NUMBER
21/03/1998	42	1		FLORIBUNDA	Heat Recordings HEATCD 013
06/11/1999	54	1		LEARNING TO FLY	Devolution DEVR 001CDS

MOTIV 8
UK producer/remixer Steve Rodway. In 1996 he set up FX Music, which signed Australian singer Gina G and sububsequently licensed her product to Warner. Her single *Ooh Aah…Just A Little Bit* won the Eurovision Song Contest, reached #1 in the UK (selling over 800,000 copies) and hit the US top twenty. However, Gina G, the song's writer Simon Taube and producers Richard Burton and Bob Wainwright were forced to launch court proceedings in order to retrieve royalties. Rodway was ordered to surrender his passport, pay £88,000 to the producers and £350,000 to Taube, while Gina G was looking for £500,000 (by June 1999 she had received just £26,000, her career having been on hold for two years). Rodway, who had put FX Music into liquidation, was personally made bankrupt for 'having acted improperly and dishonestly in knowingly swearing false evidence'.

DATE	POS	WKS	BPI	SINGLE TITLE	LABEL & NUMBER
17/07/1993	67	1		ROCKIN' FOR MYSELF MOTIV 8 FEATURING ANGIE BROWN	Nuff Respect NUFF 002CD
07/05/1994	18	4		ROCKIN' FOR MYSELF	WEA YZ 814CD
21/10/1995	31	2		BREAK THE CHAIN	Eternal 010CD
23/12/1995	40	3		SEARCHING FOR THE GOLDEN EYE MOTIV 8 AND KYM MAZELLE	Eternal 027CD

MOTIVATION
Dutch producer Francis Louwers.

DATE	POS	WKS	BPI	SINGLE TITLE	LABEL & NUMBER
17/11/2001	71	1		PARA MI	Definitive CDDEF 1

MOTIVO – see SNAP

❶[9] Number of weeks single topped the UK chart ⬆ Entered the UK chart at #1 ▲[9] Number of weeks single topped the US chart

551

MOTLEY CRUE

US heavy rock group formed in Los Angeles, CA in 1981 by Nikki Sixx (born Frank Carlton Serafino Ferrano, 11/12/1958, San Jose, CA, bass), Tommy Lee (born Thomas Lee Bass, 3/10/1962, Athens, Greece, drums), Vince Neil (born Vincent Neil Wharton, 8/2/1961, Hollywood, CA, vocals) and Mick Mars (born Bob Deal, 3/4/1955, Terre Haute, guitar). On 8/12/1984 a car driven by Neil was involved in a crash, killing Hanoi Rocks drummer Nicholas 'Razzle' Dingley and injuring two others, for which Neil was jailed and fined. Neil was sacked from the group in 1992 (and issued a $5 million lawsuit for breach of contract) and replaced by John Corabi (born 26/4/1959, Philadelphia, PA), although Corabi later left (replaced by the returning Neil) and launched a $7 million lawsuit for breach of contract. Lee was married to actress Heather Locklear and then *Baywatch* actress Pamela Anderson (both marriages ended in divorce, although Lee and Anderson later remarried). Lee was sentenced to six months for assaulting Pamela Anderson during their first marriage and subsequently jailed a second time for breaching the terms of his parole after being caught drinking. Sixx was married to *Playboy* Playmate Brandi Brandt and then *Baywatch* actress Donna D'Errico. Neil married mud wrestler Sharisse Rudell.

24/08/1985.....71......2.......	SMOKIN' IN THE BOYS ROOM	Elektra EKR 16
08/02/1986.....51......3.......	HOME SWEET HOME	Elektra EKR 33
08/02/1986.....51......3.......	SMOKIN' IN THE BOYS ROOM	Elektra EKR 33
01/08/1987.....26......6.......	GIRLS GIRLS GIRLS Featured in the 1987 film *Like Father Like Son*	Elektra EKR 59
16/01/1988.....23......4.......	YOU'RE ALL I NEED/WILD SIDE	Elektra EKR 65
04/11/1989.....50......3.......	DR FEELGOOD	Elektra EKR 97
12/05/1990.....39......3.......	WITHOUT YOU	Elektra EKR 109
07/09/1991.....32......2.......	PRIMAL SCREAM	Elektra EKR 133
11/01/1992.....37......2.......	HOME SWEET HOME	Elektra EKR 136
05/03/1994.....36......2.......	HOOLIGAN'S HOLIDAY	Elektra EKR 180CDX
19/07/1997.....58......1.......	AFRAID	Elektra E 3936 CD1

MIKKI MOTO — see BOBBY BLANCO AND MIKKI MOTO

MOTORCYCLE

US group formed in San Francisco, CA by production duo Dave Dresden and Josh Gabriel with female singer Jes.

17/01/2004.....11......9.......	AS THE RUSH COMES	Positiva CDTIVS 203

MOTORHEAD

UK heavy rock group formed in 1975 by Lemmy (born Ian Kilmister, 24/12/1945, Stoke-on-Trent) after he had been sacked from Hawkwind. The original line-up was Lemmy (bass/vocals), Larry Wallis (guitar) and Lucas Fox (drums). Fox was replaced by Philthy Animal (born Phil Taylor, 21/9/1954, Chesterfield) in 1975 and 'Fast' Eddie Clarke (born 5/10/1950, guitar) joined just before Wallis left in 1976. Clarke left in 1982 and was replaced by Brian Robertson (born 12/9/1956, Glasgow). Robertson and Taylor left in 1983 and were replaced by Phil Campbell (born 7/5/1961, Pontypridd) and Wurzel (born Michael Burston, 23/10/1949, Cheltenham). Taylor briefly returned but left again in 1992, this time being replaced by Mikkey Dee (born 31/10/1963, Olundby, Sweden).

16/09/1978.....68......2.......	LOUIE LOUIE	Bronze BRO 60
10/03/1979.....39......7.......	OVERKILL	Bronze BRO 67
30/06/1979.....61......4.......	NO CLASS	Bronze BRO 78
01/12/1979.....34......7.......	BOMBER	Bronze BRO 85
03/05/1980 .....8......7.......	THE GOLDEN YEARS EP Tracks on EP: *Dead Men Tell No Tales, Too Late Too Late, Leaving Here* and *Stone Dead Forever* .... Bronze BRO 92
01/11/1980.....15......12.......	ACE OF SPADES	Bronze BRO 106
22/11/1980.....43......4.......	BEER DRINKERS AND HELL RAISERS	Big Beat SWT 61
21/02/1981 .....5......8.....O	ST VALENTINE'S DAY MASSACRE EP MOTORHEAD AND GIRLSCHOOL (also known as HEADGIRL) Tracks on EP: *Please Don't Touch, Emergency* and *Bomber* .... Bronze BRO 116
11/07/1981 .....6......7.......	MOTORHEAD LIVE	Bronze BRO 124
03/04/1982.....29......5.......	IRON FIST	Bronze BRO 146
21/05/1983.....46......2.......	I GOT MINE	Bronze BRO 165
30/07/1983.....59......2.......	SHINE	Bronze BRO 167
01/09/1984.....51......2.......	KILLED BY DEATH	Bronze BRO 185
05/07/1986.....67......1.......	DEAF FOREVER	GWR 2
05/01/1991.....45......3.......	THE ONE TO SING THE BLUES	Epic 6565787
14/11/1992.....63......1.......	92 TOUR (EP) Tracks on EP: *Hellraiser, You Better Run, Going To Brazil* and *Ramones*	Epic 6588096
11/09/1993.....23......5.......	ACE OF SPADES (THE CNN REMIX)	WGAF CDWGAF 101
10/12/1994.....47......2.......	BORN TO RAISE HELL MOTORHEAD/ICE-T/WHITFIELD CRANE Featured in the 1994 film *Airheads*	Fox 74321230152

MOTORS

UK rock group formed by Nick Garvey (born 26/4/1951, Stoke-on-Trent, guitar), Andy McMaster (born 27/7/1947, Glasgow, guitar), Rob Hendry (guitar) and Ricky Wernham (aka Ricky Slaughter, drums). Hendry left soon after their formation and was replaced by Bram Tchaikovsky (born Peter Bramall, 10/11/1950, Lincolnshire). The group dissolved by the end of the 1970s.

24/09/1977.....42......4.......	DANCING THE NIGHT AWAY	Virgin VS 186
10/06/1978 .....4......13.....O	AIRPORT	Virgin VS 219
19/08/1978.....13......9.......	FORGET ABOUT YOU	Virgin VS 222
12/04/1980.....58......3.......	LOVE AND LONELINESS	Virgin VS 263

MOTOWN SPINNERS — see DETROIT SPINNERS

MOTT THE HOOPLE

UK rock group formed in 1968 by Overend Watts (born Peter Watts, 13/5/1949, Birmingham, bass), Dale 'Buffin' Griffin (born 24/10/1948, Ross-on-Wye, drums), Verden Allen (born 26/5/1944, keyboards), Mick Ralphs (born 31/5/1944, Hereford, guitar) and Stan Tippins (vocals) as the Shakedown Sound. Tippins was replaced the following year by Ian Hunter (born 3/6/1946, Oswestry) shortly after the group signed with Island Records. They were on the verge of splitting in 1972 having had little success, when David Bowie urged them to carry on and record a couple of tracks he had written. Allen left in 1972, Ralphs in 1973

(replaced by Luther Grosvenor, born 23/12/1949, Evesham). Grosvenor left in 1974 and was replaced by former David Bowie guitarist Mick Ronson (born 26/5/1949, Hull), although the group disbanded three months later. Hunter and Ronson formed the Hunter-Ronson Band, which lasted six months before splitting (they re-formed in 1990). Mott The Hoople were named after a 1967 novel by Willard Manus. Ronson died from cancer 29/4/1993.

12/08/1972	3	11		**ALL THE YOUNG DUDES** Written by and featuring David Bowie on saxophone. Featured in the 1995 film *Among Friends*. . .	CBS 8271
16/06/1973	12	9		HONALOOCHIE BOOGIE	CBS 1530
08/09/1973	10	8		**ALL THE WAY FROM MEMPHIS**	CBS 1764
24/11/1973	8	12		**ROLL AWAY THE STONE**	CBS 1895
30/03/1974	16	7		GOLDEN AGE OF ROCK AND ROLL	CBS 2177
22/06/1974	33	5		FOXY FOXY	CBS 2439
02/11/1974	41	3		SATURDAY GIGS	CBS 2754

MOUNT RUSHMORE PRESENTS THE KNACK UK production duo Lukas Burton and Miles 'Ahead' Morgan with singer Kate Cameron.

03/04/1999	53	1		YOU BETTER	Universal MCSTD 40192

NANA MOUSKOURI Greek singer (born 10/10/1936, Athens) who began recording in 1959 and relocated to Germany in 1960 to break into the European market. After scoring several European hits, Nana undertook a US college tour in 1967 in an attempt to crossover into the US. Despite her nationality she represented Luxembourg in the 1963 Eurovision Song Contest. She became a Member of the European Parliament in 1994.

11/01/1986	2	11		**ONLY LOVE**	Philips PH 38

MOUSSE T German remixer (born Mustafa Gundogdu) whose debut hit featured vocal accompaniment from UK singers Nadine Richardson and Emma Southam.

06/06/1998	2	17	●	**HORNY MOUSSE T VERSUS HOT 'N' JUICY**	AM:PM 5826712
20/05/2000	3	10		**SEX BOMB** TOM JONES AND MOUSSE T Contains a sample of Sister Sledge's *All-American Girls*	Gut CXGUT 33
10/08/2002	58	1		FIRE	Serious SERR 44CDX
04/09/2004	9	9		**IS IT COS I'M COOL?**	Free 2 Air F2A1CDX
18/12/2004	28	2+		RIGHT ABOUT NOW This and above two singles credited to MOUSSE T FEATURING EMMA LANFORD	Free2Air F2A2CDX

MOUTH AND MACNEAL Dutch duo Willem Duyn and Maggie Macneal (born Sjoukje Van't Spijker), who represented Holland in the 1974 Eurovision Song Contest, which was won by Sweden's Abba. Despite this their entry hit the top ten in the UK.

04/05/1974	8	10		**I SEE A STAR** Dutch entry in the 1974 Eurovision Song Contest	Decca F 13504

MOVE UK rock group formed in Birmingham in 1966 by Roy Wood (born Ulysses Wood, 8/11/1946, Birmingham, guitar/vocals), Carl Wayne (born 18/8/1944, Birmingham, vocals), Bev Bevan (born 24/11/1944, Birmingham, drums), Christopher 'Ace' Kefford (born 10/12/1946, Birmingham, bass) and Trevor Burton (born 9/3/1944, Birmingham, lead guitar). Kefford left in 1968, Burton in 1969 and Wayne in 1970. Their replacements were Rick Price and Jeff Lynne (born 20/12/1947, Birmingham, guitar/vocals). By 1971 the Move began evolving into the Electric Light Orchestra, a transformation completed in 1972. Wayne died from cancer on 31/8/2004.

05/01/1967	2	10		**NIGHT OF FEAR**	Deram DM 109
06/04/1967	5	10		**I CAN HEAR THE GRASS GROW**	Deram DM 117
06/09/1967	2	13		**FLOWERS IN THE RAIN** First record played on Radio 1 on 30/9/1967. In promoting the record the Move sent out postcards bearing a nude caricature of then Prime Minister Harold Wilson, who successfully sued the band and won an injunction, with a proportion of the royalties being handed to charity	Regal Zonophone RZ 3001
07/02/1968	3	11		**FIRE BRIGADE**	Regal Zonophone RZ 3005
25/12/1968	●[1]	12		**BLACKBERRY WAY**	Regal Zonophone RZ 3015
23/07/1969	12	12		CURLY	Regal Zonophone RZ 3021
25/04/1970	7	10		**BRONTOSAURUS**	Regal Zonophone RZ 3026
03/07/1971	11	10		TONIGHT	Harvest HAR 5038
23/10/1971	23	8		CHINATOWN	Harvest HAR 5043
13/05/1972	7	14		**CALIFORNIA MAN**	Harvest HAR 5050

MOVEMENT US group formed by Hazze (rapper), AJ Mra (keyboards) and Richard 'Humpty' Vission (turntables).

24/10/1992	57	2		JUMP!	Arista 74321116677

MOVEMENT 98 FEATURING CARROLL THOMPSON UK vocal/instrumental group assembled by Paul Oakenfold (born 30/8/1963, London). Carroll Thompson also recorded with Courtney Pine. Oakenfold also recorded as Perfecto Allstarz and Planet Perfecto. The group were so named because Oakenfold believed dance music should be at 98 BPM (beats per minute).

19/05/1990	27	5		JOY AND HEARTBREAK	Circa YR 45
15/09/1990	58	3		SUNRISE	Circa YR 51

MOVIN' MELODIES Dutch producer Patrick Prinz who also records as Artemesia, Ethics and Subliminal Cuts.

22/10/1994	64	1		LA LUNA MOVIN' MELODIES PRODUCTION	Effective EFFS 017CD
29/06/1996	62	1		INDICA	Hooj Choons HOOJCD 44
26/07/1997	71	1		ROLLERBLADE	Movin' Melodies 5822352

ALISON MOYET UK singer (born Genevieve Alison Moyet, 18/6/1961, Basildon) who had sung with a number of Southend groups before accepting an invitation from Vince Clarke (ex-Depeche Mode) to help form Yazoo in 1982. The group split after two

❶[9] Number of weeks single topped the UK chart   ↑ Entered the UK chart at #1   ▲[9] Number of weeks single topped the US chart

553

albums, with Moyet going solo. After going into semi-retirement in 1995 she returned in 2001, appearing in the West End musical *Chicago*. She has twice been a winner at the BRIT Awards, having won the Best British Female Award in 1985 and 1988.

DATE	POS	WKS	BPI	SINGLE TITLE	LABEL & NUMBER
23/06/1984	10	11		**LOVE RESURRECTION**	CBS A 4497
13/10/1984	8	11	O	**ALL CRIED OUT**	CBS A 4757
01/12/1984	21	10		INVISIBLE	CBS A 4930
16/03/1985	2	10	O	**THAT OLE DEVIL CALLED LOVE**	CBS A 6044
29/11/1986	3	16	O	**IS THIS LOVE?**	CBS MOYET 1
07/03/1987	6	10		**WEAK IN THE PRESENCE OF BEAUTY**	CBS MOYET 2
30/05/1987	43	4		ORDINARY GIRL	CBS MOYET 3
28/11/1987	4	10	O	**LOVE LETTERS**	CBS MOYET 5
06/04/1991	50	4		IT WON'T BE LONG	Columbia 6567577
01/06/1991	72	1		WISHING YOU WERE HERE	Columbia 6569397
12/10/1991	40	5		THIS HOUSE	Columbia 6575157
16/10/1993	42	3		FALLING	Columbia 6595962
12/03/1994	18	7		WHISPERING YOUR NAME	Columbia 6601622
28/05/1994	51	2		GETTING INTO SOMETHING	Columbia 6603565
22/10/1994	59	1		ODE TO BOY	Columbia 6607952
26/08/1995	44	2		SOLID WOOD	Columbia 6623265

MOZAIC UK vocal group.

DATE	POS	WKS	BPI	SINGLE TITLE	LABEL & NUMBER
05/08/1995	14	4		SING IT (THE HALLELUJAH SONG)	Perfecto PERF 106CD
10/08/1996	32	2		RAYS OF THE RISING SUN	Perfecto PERF 123CD
30/11/1996	62	1		MOVING UP MOVING ON	Perfecto PERF 131CD

MS DYNAMITE UK garage singer (born Niomi McLean-Daley, 1981) who won the 2002 MOBO Awards for Best British Act, Best Newcomer and Best Single for *It Takes More* and the Mercury Music Prize for her debut album *A Little Deeper*. She then won two BRIT Awards at the 2003 ceremony: Best British Female Solo Artist and Best British Urban Act.

DATE	POS	WKS	BPI	SINGLE TITLE	LABEL & NUMBER
23/06/2001	12	6		BOOO! STICKY FEATURING MS DYNAMITE	ffrr FCD 399
01/06/2002	7	10		**IT TAKES MORE** 2002 MOBO Award for Best Single	Polydor 5707982
07/09/2002	5	10		**DY-NA-MI-TEE**	Polydor 5709782
14/12/2002	19	6		PUT HIM OUT	Polydor 0658942

MS THING – see BEENIE MAN

MS TOI – see ICE CUBE

MTUME US R&B group formed in 1980 by James Mtume (born in Philadelphia, PA), previously with Miles Davis' group, and featuring Tawatha Agee, Ed Moore and Roger Parker at the time of their hit. Mtume and Reggie Lucas won the 1980 Grammy Award for Best Rhythm & Blues Song for *Never Knew Love Like This Before*, a hit for Stephanie Mills.

DATE	POS	WKS	BPI	SINGLE TITLE	LABEL & NUMBER
14/05/1983	34	9		JUICY FRUIT	Epic A 3424
22/09/1984	57	3		PRIME TIME	Epic A 4720

MUD UK pop group formed in 1966 by Les Gray (born 9/4/1946, Carshalton, vocals), Rob Davis (born 1/10/1947, Carshalton, guitar/vocals), Dave Mount (born 3/3/1947, Carshalton, drums/vocals) and Ray Stiles (born 20/11/1946, Carshalton, bass/vocals). They turned professional in 1968 and in 1972 were spotted by producer Mickie Most, who signed them to his label with songwriters Nicky Chinn and Mike Chapman. Gray later recorded solo and Stiles joined the Hollies. Davis later wrote dance hits including Coco's *I Need A Miracle* and Spiller's *Groovejet*. Gray died from cancer on 21/2/2004.

DATE	POS	WKS	BPI	SINGLE TITLE	LABEL & NUMBER
10/03/1973	12	12		CRAZY	RAK 146
23/06/1973	16	13		HYPNOSIS	RAK 152
27/10/1973	4	12	O	**DYNA-MITE**	RAK 159
19/01/1974	❶⁴	11	●	**TIGER FEET**	RAK 166
13/04/1974	2	9	O	**THE CAT CREPT IN**	RAK 170
27/07/1974	6	9		**ROCKET**	RAK 178
30/11/1974	❶⁴	10	●	**LONELY THIS CHRISTMAS**	RAK 187
15/02/1975	3	9	O	**THE SECRETS THAT YOU KEEP**	RAK 194
26/04/1975	❶²	9	O	**OH BOY**	RAK 201
21/06/1975	10	7		**MOONSHINE SALLY**	RAK 208
02/08/1975	32	4		ONE NIGHT	RAK 213
04/10/1975	10	6		**L-L-LUCY**	Private Stock PVT 41
29/11/1975	8	8		**SHOW ME YOU'RE A WOMAN**	Private Stock PVT 45
15/05/1976	12	8		SHAKE IT DOWN	Private Stock PVT 65
27/11/1976	7	9	O	**LEAN ON ME**	Private Stock PVT 85
21/12/1985	61	3		LONELY THIS CHRISTMAS	RAK 187

MUDHONEY US group formed in Seattle, WA by Mark Arm (vocals), Steve Turner (guitar), Matt Lukin (bass) and Dan Peters (drums). Arm and Turner had previously been in Green River and Thrown Ups, Lukin in The Melvins and Peters in Bundles Of Hiss.

DATE	POS	WKS	BPI	SINGLE TITLE	LABEL & NUMBER
17/08/1991	60	1		LET IT SLIDE	Subpop SP 15154
24/10/1992	65	1		SUCK YOU DRY	Reprise W 0137

MUDLARKS UK vocal group formed by Mary, Fred and Jeff Mudd as the Mud Trio in 1951. They were named Best British Vocal Group in the 1958 NME Readers' Poll. Jeff Mudd left in 1959 to do his national service and was replaced by David Lane. They disbanded in 1961.

02/05/1958	2	9		**LOLLIPOP**	Columbia DB 4099
06/06/1958	8	9		**BOOK OF LOVE**	Columbia DB 4133
27/02/1959	30	1		THE LOVE GAME	Columbia DB 4250

MUFFINS – see MARTHA AND THE MUFFINS

IDRIS MUHAMMAD US drummer (born Leo Morris, 13/11/1939, New Orleans, LA) who began as a session musician, becoming house drummer for Prestige Records in 1970.

17/09/1977	42	3		COULD HEAVEN EVER BE LIKE THIS	Kudu 935

MUKKAA UK instrumental/production duo Michael Kiltie and Stuart Crichton. They also record as Deep Piece. Crichton was later a member of Umboza and Eye To Eye.

27/02/1993	74	1		BURUCHACCA	Limbo 008

MUKUPA – see MANIJAMA FEATURING MUKUPA AND LIL' T

MARIA MULDAUR US singer (born Maria Grazia Rosa Domenica D'Amato, 12/9/1943, New York) who was a member of the Jug Band with husband Geoff Muldaur and later recorded gospel material.

29/06/1974	21	8		MIDNIGHT AT THE OASIS Featured in the 1989 film *Perfect Witness*	Reprise K 14331

MULL HISTORICAL SOCIETY UK group formed in Scotland in 2000 by Colin MacIntyre (guitar/vocals) and Alan Malloy (bass). They signed with independent label Tugboat the same year.

21/07/2001	53	1		ANIMAL CANNABUS	Rough Trade RTRADESCD 021
09/02/2002	36	2		WATCHING XANADU	Blanco Y Negro NEG 138CD
01/03/2003	32	2		THE FINAL ARREARS	Blanco Y Negro NEG 144CD
14/06/2003	51	1		AM I WRONG	Blanco Y Negro NEG 146CD
24/07/2004	37	1		HOW 'BOUT I LOVE YOU MORE	B Unique BUN080CDS

ARTHUR MULLARD – see HYLDA BAKER AND ARTHUR MULLARD

LARRY MULLEN – see ADAM CLAYTON AND LARRY MULLEN

SHAWN MULLINS US singer/acoustic guitarist (born 8/3/1968, Atlanta, GA) who also runs the SMG independent record label. He later became a member of The Thorns with Matthew Sweet and Pete Droge.

06/03/1999	9	10		**LULLABY**	Columbia 6669595
02/10/1999	62	1		WHAT IS LIFE Featured in the 1999 film *Big Daddy*	Columbia 6678212

MULU UK vocal/instrumental duo Alan Edmunds and Bob Kraushaar with singer Laura Campbell.

02/08/1997	50	1		PUSSYCAT	Dedicated MULU 003CD1

OMERO MUMBA Irish singer (born 2/7/1989, Dublin) and younger brother of Samantha Mumba. He made his film debut in 2002 in *The Time Machine*.

20/07/2002	42	2		LIL' BIG MAN	Polydor 5708862

SAMANTHA MUMBA Irish singer (born 18/1/1983, Dublin) with a Zambian aircraft engineer father and Irish office worker mother. She was just fifteen when she first signed with Wild Card. She later made her film debut in 2002 in *The Time Machine*.

08/07/2000	2	12		**GOTTA TELL YOU**	Wild Card 5618832
28/10/2000	5	12		**BODY II BODY** Contains a sample of David Bowie's *Ashes To Ashes*	Wild Card 5877752
03/03/2001	3	15	○	**ALWAYS COME BACK TO YOUR LOVE**	Wild Card 5879252
22/09/2001	5	10		**BABY COME ON OVER**	Wild Card 5872352
22/12/2001	6	12		**LATELY**	Wild Card 5705232
26/10/2002	5	8		**I'M RIGHT HERE**	Wild Card 0659372

COATI MUNDI – see KID CREOLE AND THE COCONUTS

MUNDY Irish singer/songwriter (born 1975, Burr) who moved to Dublin while still a teenager.

03/08/1996	60	1		TO YOU I BESTOW	Epic MUNDY 1CD
05/10/1996	75	1		LIFE'S A CINCH	Epic MUNDY 2CD

MUNGO JERRY UK group formed in the late 1960s as a skiffle and pub-rock group by Ray Dorset (born 21/3/1946, Middlesex, guitar/vocals), Colin Earl (keyboards), Paul King (banjo/guitar) and Mike Cole (bass). Cole left in 1971 and was replaced by John Godfrey. King and Earl left in 1972 and were replaced by Jon Pope (keyboards) and Tim Reeves (drums). After their chart career ended Dorset recorded solo and also teamed up with Peter Green (ex-Fleetwood Mac) and Vincent Crane (ex-Atomic Rooster) as Katmandu. As a songwriter he penned Kelly Marie's chart topper *Feels Like I'm In Love*.

06/06/1970	❶7	20		**IN THE SUMMERTIME** Featured in the 1996 film *Flipper*	Dawn DNX 2502
06/02/1971	❶2	13		**BABY JUMP**	Dawn DNX 2505

❶9 Number of weeks single topped the UK chart ↑ Entered the UK chart at #1 ▲9 Number of weeks single topped the US chart

555

29/05/1971	5	12		**LADY ROSE** .... Dawn DNX 2510
18/09/1971	13	8		YOU DON'T HAVE TO BE IN THE ARMY TO FIGHT IN THE WAR .... Dawn DNX 2513
22/04/1972	21	8		OPEN UP .... Dawn DNX 2514
07/07/1973	3	12	○	**ALRIGHT ALRIGHT ALRIGHT** .... Dawn DNS 1037
10/11/1973	32	5		WILD LOVE .... Dawn DNS 1051
06/04/1974	13	9		LONG LEGGED WOMAN DRESSED IN BLACK .... Dawn DNS 1061
29/05/1999	57	1		SUPPORT THE TOON – IT'S YOUR DUTY (EP) **MUNGO JERRY AND TOON TRAVELLERS** Tracks on EP: *Blaydon Races, Going To Wembley* and *Bottle Of Beer* .... Saraja TOONCD 001

MUNICH MACHINE German studio group assembled by producer Giorgio Moroder.

10/12/1977	41	4		GET ON THE FUNK TRAIN .... Oasis 2
04/11/1978	42	4		A WHITER SHADE OF PALE .... Oasis 5

DAVID MUNROW – see **EARLY MUSIC CONSORT DIRECTED BY DAVID MUNROW**

MUPPETS US puppet group created for TV by Jim Henson (born 24/9/1936, Greenville, MS). Henson had already achieved considerable success with *Sesame Street* aimed at children. The Muppets were aimed at an older market and featured Kermit The Frog, Miss Piggy, Fozzie Bear, Animal (who enjoyed a solo hit), Gonzo and others. Henson died from pneumonia on 16/5/1990. The Muppets have won eight Grammy Awards, all in the Best Recording for Children category: in 1977, 1978, 1979, 1980, 1981, 1985, 1986 and 1998. The Muppets' debut hit was performed by Jerry Nelson as Kermit's nephew Robin. Both Jim Henson and Kermit The Frog have a star on the Hollywood Walk of Fame.

28/05/1977	7	8		**HALFWAY DOWN THE STAIRS** .... Pye 7N 45698
17/12/1977	19	7		THE MUPPET SHOW MUSIC HALL EP Tracks on EP: *Don't Dilly Dally On The Way, Waiting At The Church, The Boy In The Gallery* and *Wotcher (Knocked 'Em In The Old Kent Road)* .... Pye 7NX 8004

MURDERDOLLS US rock group formed by Joey Jordison (guitar), Tripp Eisen (guitar), Wednesday 13 (vocals), Eric Griffin (bass) and Ben Graves (drums). Jordison is also a member of Slipknot while Eisen is a member of Static-X.

16/11/2002	54	1		DEAD IN HOLLYWOOD .... Roadrunner RR 20223
26/07/2003	24	3		WHITE WEDDING .... Roadrunner RR 20155

LYDIA MURDOCK US R&B singer (born in New Jersey) whose one hit was an 'answer' record to Michael Jackson's *Billie Jean*.

24/09/1983	14	9		SUPERSTAR .... Korova KOW 30

SHIRLEY MURDOCK US singer (born in Toledo, OH) who was discovered by Roger Troutman and began as a backing singer for Zapp.

12/04/1986	60	2		TRUTH OR DARE .... Elektra EKR 36

ANNE MURRAY Canadian singer (born Moma Anne Murray, 20/6/1945, Springhill, Nova Scotia) who was a physical education teacher before singing professionally. Debuting on record in 1969, her four Grammy Awards include Best Country & Western Vocal Performance in 1974 for *Love Song,* Best Country Vocal Performance in 1980 for *Could I Have This Dance* and Best Country Vocal Performance in 1983 for *A Little Good News*. She has a star on the Hollywood Walk of Fame.

24/10/1970	23	17		SNOWBIRD .... Capitol CL 15654
21/10/1972	41	4		DESTINY .... Capitol CL 15734
09/12/1978	22	14		YOU NEEDED ME ▲¹ 1978 Grammy Award for Best Pop Vocal Performance .... Capitol CL 16011
21/04/1979	58	2		I JUST FALL IN LOVE AGAIN .... Capitol CL 16069
19/04/1980	61	3		DAYDREAM BELIEVER .... Capitol CL 16123

EDDIE MURPHY FEATURING SHABBA RANKS US/Jamaican vocal duo Eddie Murphy and Shabba Ranks. Murphy (born 3/4/1961, New York) is best known as an actor, on the TV series *Saturday Night Live* and then films such as *48 Hours* (1982), *Trading Places* (1983), *Beverly Hills Cop* (1984) and *The Nutty Professor* (1996). His recording career was masterminded by Rick James. He has a star on the Hollywood Walk of Fame.

06/03/1993	64	1		I WAS A KING .... Motown TMGCD 1414

KEITH MURRAY US rapper/singer (born 1972, Long Island, NY) who appeared uncredited on hits by Boyz II Men, LL Cool J, Mary J. Blige and Total before launching his own career.

02/11/1996	59	1		THE RHYME Contains samples of Frankie Beverly & Maze's *Before I Let Go* and Run DMC's *Sucker MCs* .... Jive JIVECD 407
27/06/1998	22	3		SHORTY (YOU KEEP PLAYIN' WITH MY MIND) **IMAJIN FEATURING KEITH MURRAY** .... Jive 0521212
14/11/1998	17	5		HOME ALONE **R KELLY FEATURING KEITH MURRAY** .... Jive 0522392
05/12/1998	52	1		INCREDIBLE **KEITH MURRAY FEATURING LL COOL J** Contains a sample of James Brown's *Sportin' Life* .... Jive 0522102

NOEL MURPHY Irish singer.

27/06/1987	57	4		MURPHY AND THE BRICKS .... Murphy's STACK 1

PAULINE MURRAY AND THE INVISIBLE GIRLS UK singer Murray with a group that at times featured Robert Blamire (guitar), Vini Reilly, Bernard Sumner, John Maher, Wayne Hussey and Martin Hannett. Murray was earlier in Durham punk group Penetration.

02/08/1980	67	2		DREAM SEQUENCE (ONE) .... Illusive IVE 1

ROISIN MURPHY UK singer (born in Sheffield) who is also a member of Moloko with Mark Brydon.

○ Silver disc ● Gold disc ✪ Platinum disc (additional platinum units are indicated by a figure following the symbol) ◉ Singles released prior to 1973 that are known to have sold over 1 million copies in the UK

16/06/2001.....16......4...... NEVER ENOUGH **BORIS DLUGOSCH FEATURING ROISIN MURPHY**..........................Positiva CDTIV 156
19/01/2002.....37......2...... WONDERLAND **PSYCHEDELIC WALTONS FEATURING ROISIN MURPHY** ....Echo ECSCD 120

RUBY MURRAY
UK singer (born 29/3/1935, Belfast) who was the first female to dominate the charts in a single year, with seven top ten records in 1955. Her name has entered folklore as Cockney rhyming slang for curry. She died from liver cancer on 17/12/1996.

03/12/1954.....3......16...... **HEARTBEAT**..........................Columbia DB 3542
28/01/1955....❶³.....23..... **SOFTLY SOFTLY**..........................Columbia DB 3558
04/02/1955.....6......8...... **HAPPY DAYS AND LONELY NIGHTS**..........................Columbia DB 3577
04/03/1955.....5......7...... **LET ME GO LOVER** B-side to *Happy Days And Lonely Nights*..........................Columbia DB 3577
18/03/1955.....4......11..... **IF ANYONE FINDS THIS I LOVE YOU RUBY MURRAY WITH ANNE WARREN**..........................Columbia DB 3580
01/07/1955.....3......17..... **EVERMORE**..........................Columbia DB 3617
14/10/1955.....6......7...... **I'LL COME WHEN YOU CALL**..........................Columbia DB 3643
31/08/1956.....16.....5...... YOU ARE MY FIRST LOVE..........................Columbia DB 3770
12/12/1958.....18.....6...... REAL LOVE..........................Columbia DB 4192
05/06/1959.....10.....14..... **GOODBYE JIMMY GOODBYE**..........................Columbia DB 4305

WALTER MURPHY AND THE BIG APPLE BAND
US orchestra leader (born 1952, New York) who studied both classical and jazz music piano at the Manhattan School of Music.

10/07/1976.....28......9....... A FIFTH OF BEETHOVEN ▲¹ Based on Beethoven's *Fifth Symphony*. Featured in the 1978 film *Saturday Night Fever*..........................
..........................Private Stock PVT 59

JUNIOR MURVIN
Jamaican singer (born Mervin Smith, 1949, Port Antonio) who originally recorded under the name Junior Soul.

03/05/1980.....23......9....... POLICE AND THIEVES Originally released in 1976 and revived after use in the 1980 film *Rockers*..........................Island WIP 6539

MUSE
UK rock group formed in Teignmouth by Matt Bellamy (guitar/vocals), Chris Wolstenholme (bass) and Dominic Howard (drums), originally called Gothic Plague, Fixed Penalty and Rocket Baby Dolls. Named Best Newcomer in the 2000 NME Premier Awards, they were initially signed by Maverick Records in the US. They also won the 2004 MTV Europe Music Awards for Best Alternative Artist and Best UK & Ireland Act.

26/06/1999.....73......1...... UNO..........................Mushroom/Taste Media MUSH 50CDS
18/09/1999.....52......1...... CAVE Featured in the 2000 film *Little Nicky*..........................Mushroom/Taste Media MUSH 58CDS
04/12/1999.....43......2...... MUSCLE MUSEUM..........................Mushroom/Taste Media MUSH 66CDS
04/03/2000.....22......2...... SUNBURN..........................Mushroom/Taste Media MUSH 68CDS
17/06/2000.....20......4...... UNINTENDED..........................Mushroom/Taste Media MUSH 72CDS
21/10/2000.....25......3...... MUSCLE MUSEUM Re-issue of Mushroom/Taste Media MUSH 66CDS..........................Mushroom/Taste Media MUSH 84CDS
24/03/2001.....11......5...... PLUG IN BABY..........................Mushroom/Taste Media MUSH 89CDS
16/06/2001.....12......4...... NEW BORN..........................Mushroom/Taste Media MUSH 92CDS
01/09/2001.....22......2...... BLISS..........................Mushroom/Taste Media MUSH 96CDS
01/12/2001.....24......3...... HYPER MUSIC/FEELING GOOD..........................Mushroom MUSH 97CDS
29/06/2002.....13......3...... DEAD STAR/IN YOUR WORLD..........................Mushroom MUSH 104CDS
20/09/2003.....8......8...... **TIME IS RUNNING OUT**..........................East West EW 272CD
13/12/2003.....17......6...... HYSTERIA..........................Taste Media/East West EW 278CD
29/05/2004.....16......4...... SING FOR ABSOLUTION..........................Taste Media/East West EW 285CD
02/10/2004.....14......3...... BUTTERFLIES AND HURRICANES..........................Atlantic ATUK003CD

MUSIC
UK rock group formed in Leeds by Robert Harvey (vocals), Adam Nutter (guitar), Stuart Coleman (bass) and Phil Jordan (drums).

31/08/2002.....14......3...... TAKE THE LONG ROAD AND WALK IT..........................Hut HUTDX 158
30/11/2002.....26......2...... GETAWAY..........................Hut HUTCD 162
01/03/2003.....18......2...... THE TRUTH IS NO WORDS..........................Hut HUTCD 164
18/09/2004.....15......4...... FREEDOM FIGHTERS..........................Virgin VSCDX 1883

MUSIC AND MYSTERY FEATURING GWEN McCRAE
UK production duo Stevie Vincent and Martin Greenwood with US singer Gwen McCrae (born 21/12/1943, Pensacola, FL), who made her debut record in 1969 for Alston. She married singer George McCrae, who was later her manager. Their hit was a re-recording of Gwen's 1988 hit *All This Love That I'm Giving* (position #63).

13/02/1993.....36......3...... ALL THIS LOVE I'M GIVING..........................KTDA CDKTDA 2

MUSIC RELIEF '94
UK vocal/instrumental group assembled to record a charity record for Rwanda.

05/11/1994.....70......1....... WHAT'S GOING ON..........................Jive RWANDACD 1

MUSICAL YOUTH
UK reggae group formed by Dennis Seaton (lead vocals), Kelvin (guitar) and his brother Michael Grant (keyboards) and Patrick (bass) and his brother Junior Waite (drums), five pupils of Duddeston Manor School in Birmingham. At the time of their debut hit their ages ranged from eleven to sixteen. Patrick Waite, who later served time in prison for drug offences, died after collapsing at a friend's house and hitting his head on 18/2/1993 at the age of 24 years.

25/09/1982....❶³.....13.....● **PASS THE DUTCHIE** Featured in the 1998 film *The Wedding Singer*..........................MCA YOU 1
20/11/1982.....13......9....... YOUTH OF TODAY..........................MCA YOU 2
12/02/1983.....6......10...... **NEVER GONNA GIVE YOU UP**..........................MCA YOU 3
16/04/1983.....44......3...... HEARTBREAKER..........................MCA YOU 4
09/07/1983.....33......6....... TELL ME WHY..........................MCA YOU 5

❶⁹ Number of weeks single topped the UK chart ↑ Entered the UK chart at #1 ▲⁹ Number of weeks single topped the US chart

557

DATE	POS	WKS	BPI	SINGLE TITLE	LABEL & NUMBER
22/10/1983	26	6		007	MCA YOU 6
14/01/1984	23	8		SIXTEEN	MCA YOU 7

MUSIQ – see ROOTS

MUSIQUE
US studio creation of producer Patrick Adams and featuring Christine Wiltshire (lead vocals), Gina Tharps and Mary Seymour. Adams later stated that Jocelyn Brown also sang on their hit.

DATE	POS	WKS	BPI	SINGLE TITLE	LABEL & NUMBER
18/11/1978	16	12		IN THE BUSH	CBS 6791

MUSIQUE VS U2
UK production duo Moussa Clarke and Nick Hanson. Clarke had previously been a member of PF Project with Jamie White. Their debut hit also features a rap from Barney C over the guitar riff by The Edge on U2's 1983 hit *New Year's Day*.

DATE	POS	WKS	BPI	SINGLE TITLE	LABEL & NUMBER
02/06/2001	15	5		NEW YEARS DUB Contains a sample of U2's *New Year's Day*	Serious SERRO 030CD

MUSTAFAS – see STAIFFI AND HIS MUSTAFAS

MUTINY UK
UK production duo Dylan Barnes and Rob Davy.

DATE	POS	WKS	BPI	SINGLE TITLE	LABEL & NUMBER
19/05/2001	47	1		SECRETS VOCALS BY LORRAINE CATO Contains a sample of First Choice's *Dr Love*	Sunflower VCRD 86
25/08/2001	42	2		VIRUS	VC Recordings VCRD 91

MXM
Italian vocal/instrumental group.

DATE	POS	WKS	BPI	SINGLE TITLE	LABEL & NUMBER
02/06/1990	68	1		NOTHING COMPARES 2 U	London LON 267

MY BLOODY VALENTINE
UK rock group formed in Northern Ireland in 1984 by Kevin Shields (born 21/5/1963, New York, guitar/vocals), Colin O'Ciosoig (born 31/10/1964, Dublin, drums), Dave Conway (vocals) and Tina (keyboards). They later added Belinda Butcher (born 16/9/1961, London, vocals) and Debbie Googe (born 24/10/1962, Somerset, bass).

DATE	POS	WKS	BPI	SINGLE TITLE	LABEL & NUMBER
05/05/1990	41	3		SOON	Creation CRE 073
16/02/1991	29	2		TO HERE KNOWS WHEN	Creation CRE 085

MY CHEMICAL ROMANCE
US rock group formed in New Jersey by Gerard Way (vocals), Ray Toto (guitar), Frank Iero (guitar), Mikey Way (bass) and Matt Pelissier (drums).

DATE	POS	WKS	BPI	SINGLE TITLE	LABEL & NUMBER
25/12/2004	71	1+		THANK YOU FOR THE VENOM	Reprise W661

MY LIFE STORY
UK group formed by Jake Shillingford. For live dates the group is augmented by an eleven-piece orchestra.

DATE	POS	WKS	BPI	SINGLE TITLE	LABEL & NUMBER
17/08/1996	32	2		12 REASONS WHY I LOVE HER	Parlophone CDR 6442
09/11/1996	34	2		SPARKLE	Parlophone CDR 6450
01/03/1997	35	1		THE KING OF KISSINGDOM	Parlophone CDRS 6457
17/05/1997	27	2		STRUMPET	Parlophone CDR 6464
23/08/1997	39	1		DUCHESS	Parlophone CDR 6474
19/06/1999	37	2		IT'S A GIRL THING	IT ITR 001
30/10/1999	58	1		EMPIRE LINE	IT ITR 003
19/02/2000	48	1		WALK/DON'T WALK	IT ITR 007

MY RED CELL
UK rock group formed in Barry, Wales by Russell Toney (guitar/vocals), Adam Cook (guitar), Ginger (bass) and Phil Myles (drums).

DATE	POS	WKS	BPI	SINGLE TITLE	LABEL & NUMBER
12/06/2004	61	1		IN A CAGE (ON PROZAC)	V2 VVR 5027133

MY VITRIOL
UK rock group formed by Som Wijay-Wardner (born in Sri Lanka, guitar/vocals), Seth Taylor (guitar), Carolyn Bannister (bass) and Ravi Kesevaram (drums), taking the group's name from a passage in Graham Greene's book *Brighton Rock*. They first recorded for ORG Records before being snapped up by Infectious.

DATE	POS	WKS	BPI	SINGLE TITLE	LABEL & NUMBER
22/07/2000	65	1		CEMENTED SHOES	Infectious INFECT 89CDS
11/11/2000	56	1		PIECES	Infectious INFECT 94CDS
24/02/2001	31	2		ALWAYS YOUR WAY	Infectious INFECT 95CDSX
19/05/2001	29	2		GROUNDED	Infectious INFECT 97CD
27/07/2002	39	1		MOODSWINGS/THE GENTLE ART OF CHOKING	Infectious INFEC 107CDSX

MYA
US singer (born Mya Harrison, 10/10/1979, Washington DC) who was named after writer Maya Angelou. She began as a tap dancer with TWA (Tappers With Attitude) before turning to singing. Blinky Blink is a US rapper.

DATE	POS	WKS	BPI	SINGLE TITLE	LABEL & NUMBER
27/06/1998	2	17	✪	GHETTO SUPERSTAR (THAT IS WHAT YOU ARE) PRAS MICHEL FEATURING OL' DIRTY BASTARD AND INTRODUCING MYA Contains a sample of James Brown's *Get Up, Get Into It, Get Involved* and an interpolation of the song *Islands In The Stream*. 1998 MOBO Award for Best International Single. Featured in the 1998 film *Bulworth*	Interscope IND 95593
12/12/1998	7	9		TAKE ME THERE BLACKSTREET AND MYA FEATURING MA$E AND BLINKY BLINK Featured in the 1998 animated film *The Rugrats Movie*	Interscope IND 95620
10/02/2001	3	11		CASE OF THE EX	Interscope 4974772
24/03/2001	13	5		GIRLS DEM SUGAR BEENIE MAN FEATURING MYA	Virgin VUSCD173
09/06/2001	11	6		FREE Featured in the 2000 film *Bait*	Interscope 4975002
30/06/2001	●¹	16	●	LADY MARMALADE ↑ ▲⁵ CHRISTINA AGUILERA/LIL' KIM/MYA/PINK Featured in the 2001 film *Moulin Rouge*. 2001 Grammy Award for Best Pop Collaboration with Vocals	Interscope 4975612
20/09/2003	33	2		MY LOVE IS LIKE...WO!	Interscope 9810302

○ Silver disc ● Gold disc ✪ Platinum disc (additional platinum units are indicated by a figure following the symbol) ◉ Singles released prior to 1973 that are known to have sold over 1 million copies in the UK

TIM MYCROFT – see SOUNDS NICE FEATURING TIM MYCROFT

ALICIA MYERS US singer (born in Detroit, MI) who had previously been lead vocalist with One Way.

01/09/1984 . . . . . 58 . . . . . . 3 . . . . YOU GET THE BEST FROM ME (SAY SAY SAY) . . . . MCA 914

BILLIE MYERS UK singer (born 14/6/1971, Coventry) of English and Jamaican parentage.

11/04/1998 . . . . . 4 . . . . . . 9 . . . . **KISS THE RAIN** . . . . Universal UND 56182
25/07/1998 . . . . . 28 . . . . . . 3 . . . . TELL ME . . . . Universal UND 56201

RICHARD MYHILL UK singer.

01/04/1978 . . . . . 17 . . . . . . 9 . . . . IT TAKES TWO TO TANGO . . . . Mercury 6007 167

ALANNAH MYLES Canadian singer (born 25/12/1955, Toronto, raised in Buckhorn, Canada).

17/03/1990 . . . . . 2 . . . . . . 15 . . . . . ○ **BLACK VELVET ▲²** . . . . East West A 8742
16/06/1990 . . . . . 61 . . . . . . 2 . . . . LOVE IS . . . . East West A 8918

MYLO UK male producer (born Myles MacInnes, Isle of Skye).

30/10/2004 . . . . . 19 . . . . . . 6 . . . . DROP THE PRESSURE . . . . Breastfed BFD009CD

MARIE MYRIAM French singer (born Myriam Lopes) whose debut hit won the 1977 Eurovision Song Contest, beating the UK's entry by Lynsey De Paul and Mike Moran into second place.

28/05/1977 . . . . . 42 . . . . . . 4 . . . . L'OISEAU ET L'ENFANT 1977 Eurovision Song Contest winner . . . . Polydor 2056 634

MYRON US singer (born Myron Davis, Cleveland, OH).

22/11/1997 . . . . . 74 . . . . . . 1 . . . . WE CAN GET DOWN . . . . Island Black Music CID 677

MYSTERIANS – see ? (QUESTION MARK) AND THE MYSTERIANS

MYSTERY Dutch production duo Veldman and Van Den Beuken.

06/10/2001 . . . . . 56 . . . . . . 1 . . . . MYSTERY . . . . Inferno CDFERN 42
10/08/2002 . . . . . 57 . . . . . . 1 . . . . ALL I EVER WANTED (DEVOTION) . . . . Xtravaganza XTRAV 33CDS

MYSTI – see CAMOUFLAGE FEATURING MYSTI

MYSTIC MERLIN US group formed in New York as a novelty act of R&B music and magic by Clyde Bullard, Jerry Anderson, Keith Gonzales, Sly Randolph and Barry Strutt, later adding Freddie Jackson as lead vocalist.

26/04/1980 . . . . . 20 . . . . . . 9 . . . . JUST CAN'T GIVE YOU UP . . . . Capitol CL 16133

MYSTIC 3 UK/Italian production trio that features Brandon Block. He also records as Blockster and Grifters.

24/06/2000 . . . . . 63 . . . . . . 1 . . . . SOMETHING'S GOIN' ON . . . . Rulin 2CDS

MYSTICA Israeli production trio formed by Charli Ben-Moha, Avi Pe'er and Yossef Master.

24/01/1998 . . . . . 62 . . . . . . 1 . . . . EVER REST . . . . Perfecto PERF 152CD
09/05/1998 . . . . . 59 . . . . . . 1 . . . . AFRICAN HORIZON . . . . Perfecto PERF 161CD

MYSTIKAL US rapper (born Michael Tyler, 22/9/1975, New Orleans) who was previously a member of No Limit and served in the US Army, seeing action in Operation Desert Storm. In January 2004 he was sentenced to six years in prison for sexual assault.

09/12/2000 . . . . . 30 . . . . . . 5 . . . . SHAKE YA ASS . . . . Jive 9251552
17/02/2001 . . . . . 7 . . . . . . 8 . . . . **STUTTER ▲⁴** JOE FEATURING MYSTIKAL Contains a sample of The Pharcyde's *Passin' Me By*. Featured in the 2000 film *Double Take*
. . . . Jive 9251632
03/03/2001 . . . . . 28 . . . . . . 3 . . . . DANGER (BEEN SO LONG) MYSTIKAL FEATURING NIVEA . . . . Jive 9251722
29/12/2001 . . . . . 32 . . . . . . 4 . . . . NEVER TOO FAR/DON'T STOP (FUNKIN' 4 JAMAICA) MARIAH CAREY/MARIAH CAREY FEATURING MYSTIKAL *Don't Stop (Funkin' 4 Jamaica)* contains a sample of Tom Browne's *Funkin' for Jamaica* . . . . Virgin VUSCD 228
23/02/2002 . . . . . 45 . . . . . . 1 . . . . BOUNCIN' BACK . . . . Jive 9253272

MYTOWN Irish vocal group formed in Dublin by Terry Daly, Danny O'Donoghue, Marc Sheehan and Paul Walker. They were runners-up in the 1999 *Smash Hits* Newcomers Award.

13/03/1999 . . . . . 22 . . . . . . 2 . . . . PARTY ALL NIGHT . . . . Universal UND 56231

MZ MAY – see DREEM TEEM

🌑⁹ Number of weeks single topped the UK chart   ↑ Entered the UK chart at #1   ▲⁹ Number of weeks single topped the US chart

559

N-JOI British dance group formed in Essex by Mark Franklin, Nigel Champion and female vocalist Saffron. Saffron later recorded solo.

27/10/1990	45	5	ANTHEM .... Deconstruction PB 44041
02/03/1991	23	5	ADRENALIN (EP) Tracks on EP: *Adrenalin, The Kraken, Rhythm Zone* and *Phoenix*.................. Deconstruction PT 44344
06/04/1991	8	8	**ANTHEM** .... Deconstruction PB 44445
22/02/1992	12	5	LIVE IN MANCHESTER (PARTS 1 + 2) .... Deconstruction PT 45252
24/07/1993	33	3	THE DRUMSTRUCK (EP) Tracks on EP: *The Void, Boom Bass* and *Drumstruck* .... Deconstruction 74321154832
17/12/1994	70	1	PAPILLON .... Deconstruction 74321252132
08/07/1995	57	1	BAD THINGS .... Deconstruction 74321277292

N' + G FEATURING KALLAGHAN AND MC NEAT UK production duo Norris 'Da Boss' Windross and Grant Nelson, with male vocalists Kallaghan and MC Neat (born Michael Rose). MC Neat also records with DJ Luck.

01/04/2000	12	6	RIGHT BEFORE MY EYES .... Urban Heat UHTCD003

'N SYNC US vocal group formed in Orlando, FL by James Lance 'Lantsen' Bass (born 4/5/1979, Clinton, MS), Joshua Scott 'JC' Chasez (born 8/8/1976, Washington DC), Joseph 'Joey' Anthony Fatone (born 28/1/1977, Brooklyn, NY), Christopher Alan Kirkpatrick (born 17/10/1971, Clarion, PA) and Justin Randall Timberlake (born 31/1/1981, Memphis, TN). The name is derived from the last letters of the members' first names: JustiN, ChriS, JoeY, LantseN and JC. In 1999 ex-manager Louis J Pearlman, his company Trans Continental Media, Trans Continental Records and BMG (which owns Trans Continental Records) launched a $150 million lawsuit claiming the group and Jive Records were using the name 'N Sync illegally. It was eventually settled out of court. Justin Timberlake allegedly got engaged to Britney Spears in June 2000, although they actually got engaged a year later in July 2001, and split in March 2002. Bass briefly trained as an astronaut in 2002. Fatone appeared in the film *My Big Fat Greek Wedding*. Timberlake went solo in 2002, Chasez in 2004.

13/09/1997	40	2		TEARIN' UP MY HEART .... Arista 74321505152
22/11/1997	62	1		I WANT YOU BACK .... Arista 74321541122
27/02/1999	5	10		**I WANT YOU BACK** Re-issue of Arista 74321541122 .... Transcontinental 74321646982
26/06/1999	9	10		**TEARIN' UP MY HEART** Re-issue of Arista 74321505152 .... Northwestside 74321675832
08/01/2000	34	3	○	MUSIC OF MY HEART **'N SYNC AND GLORIA ESTEFAN** Featured in the 1999 film *Music Of The Heart* .... Epic 6678052
11/03/2000	3	8	○	**BYE BYE BYE** .... Jive 9250202
22/07/2000	13	6		I'LL NEVER STOP .... Jive 9250762
16/09/2000	9	8		**IT'S GONNA BE ME** .... Jive 9251082
02/12/2000	21	7		THIS I PROMISE YOU .... Jive 9251302
21/07/2001	9	8		**POP** .... Jive 9252422
08/12/2001	24	4		GONE Contains a sample of Teddy Pendergrass's *Believe In Love* .... Jive 9252772
27/04/2002	2	12		**GIRLFRIEND 'N SYNC FEATURING NELLY** .... Jive 9253312

N-TRANCE UK rave group featuring Ricardo Da Force (born Ricardo Lyte, raps), Jerome Stokes (vocals), Viveen Wray (vocals), Vinny Burns (guitar), Kevin O'Toole (synthesiser), Dale Longworth (programming) and Lee Limer (dancing).

07/05/1994	39	4		SET YOU FREE **N-TRANCE FEATURING KELLY LLORENNA** Originally released in September 1993 and failed to chart .... All Around The World CDGLOBE 124
22/10/1994	23	3		TURN UP THE POWER Features the uncredited vocals of Rachel McFarlane .... All Around The World CDGLOBE 125
14/01/1995	2	15	●	**SET YOU FREE (REMIX)** .... All Around The World CXGLOBE 126
16/09/1995	2	11	○	**STAYIN' ALIVE N-TRANCE FEATURING RICARDO DA FORCE** .... All Around The World CDGLOBE 131
24/02/1996	11	4		ELECTRONIC PLEASURE .... All Around The World CDGLOBE 135
05/04/1997	11	6		D.I.S.C.O. .... All Around The World CDGLOBE 153
23/08/1997	15	4		THE MIND OF THE MACHINE Features the uncredited vocal of Steven Berkoff .... All Around The World CDGLOBE 159
01/11/1997	7	10		**DO YA THINK I'M SEXY? N-TRANCE FEATURING ROD STEWART** Featured in the 1998 film *A Night At The Roxbury* .... All Around The World CDGLOBE 150
12/09/1998	28	3		PARADISE CITY .... All Around The World CDGLOBE 140
19/12/1998	53	1		TEARS IN THE RAIN .... All Around The World CDGLOBE 185
20/05/2000	37	1		SHAKE YA BODY .... All Around The World CDGLOBE 204
22/09/2001	4	11		**SET YOU FREE (2ND REMIX)** .... All Around The Globe CXGLOBE 242
14/09/2002	6	8		**FOREVER** .... All Around The World CXGLOBE 257
19/07/2003	37	2		DESTINY .... All Around The World CDGLOBE 282
04/12/2004	46	2		I'M IN HEAVEN .... All Around The World CDGLOBE343

N-TYCE UK R&B vocal group formed by Donna Stubbs, Chantal Kerzner, Ario Odubore and M'chelle Robinson.

05/07/1997	20	2	HEY DJ! (PLAY THAT SONG) .... Telstar CDSTAS 2885

○ Silver disc ● Gold disc ✪ Platinum disc (additional platinum units are indicated by a figure following the symbol) ◎ Singles released prior to 1973 that are known to have sold over 1 million copies in the UK

DATE	POS	WKS	BPI	SINGLE TITLE	LABEL & NUMBER
13/09/1997	12	4		WE COME TO PARTY	Telstar CDSTAS 2915
28/02/1998	16	5		TELEFUNKIN'	Telstar CXSTAS 2944
06/06/1998	18	4		BOOM BOOM Features the uncredited contribution of Damon Elliott (the son of Dionne Warwick)	Telstar CDSTAS 2971

NADA SURF US grunge group formed in New York by Matthew Caws (guitar/vocals), Daniel Lorca (bass) and Ira Elliott (drums).

24/05/2003	73	1		INSIDE OF LOVE	Heavenly HVN 133CD

NADIA Portuguese singer (born Jorge Leodoro, 28/1/1977, Madeira) who underwent a sex change in December 2003 and became Nadia Almada. She won the 2004 *Big Brother* TV series.

11/12/2004	27	3+		A LITTLE BIT OF ACTION	Virgin/EMI VTSCDX6

JIMMY NAIL UK singer (born James Michael Aloysius Bradford, 16/3/1954, Newcastle-upon-Tyne); he first came to prominence as an actor, appearing in the TV series *Auf Wiedersehen Pet* as Oz and later in *Spender* and *Crocodile Shoes*, both of which he also wrote. He also appeared in the films *Evita* and *Still Crazy*.

27/04/1985	3	11	○	LOVE DON'T LIVE HERE ANYMORE	Virgin VS 764
11/07/1992	❶3	12	●	AIN'T NO DOUBT	East West YZ 686
03/10/1992	58	2		LAURA	East West YZ 702
26/11/1994	4	20	●	CROCODILE SHOES	East West YZ 867CD
11/02/1995	13	7		COWBOY DREAMS	East West YZ 878CD
06/05/1995	65	1		CALLING OUT YOUR NAME This and above two titles featured in the TV series *Crocodile Shoes*	East West YZ 935CD
28/10/1995	18	5		BIG RIVER	East West EW 008CD
23/12/1995	33	4		LOVE	East West EW 018CD1
03/02/1996	72	2		BIG RIVER (REMIX)	East West EW 024CD
16/11/1996	25	8		COUNTRY BOY Featured in the TV series *Crocodile Shoes 2*	East West EW 070CD
21/11/1998	47	1		THE FLAME STILL BURNS JIMMY NAIL WITH STRANGE FRUIT Featured in the 1998 film *Still Crazy*	London LONCD 420

NAKATOMI Dutch production group formed by Dennis Van Den Driesschen and Wessel Van Diepen.

07/02/1998	47	2		CHILDREN OF THE NIGHT	Peach PCHCD 006
26/10/2002	31	2		CHILDREN OF THE NIGHT (REMIX)	Jive 9254212

NAKED EYES UK duo Pete Byrne (vocals) and Rob Fisher (born 5/11/1959, keyboards). The pair disbanded in 1984; Fisher went on to link up with Simon Climie in Climie Fisher but died from complications brought on by stomach surgery on 25/8/1999.

23/07/1983	59	3		ALWAYS SOMETHING THERE TO REMIND ME Featured in the 1997 film *Romy And Michele's High School Reunion*	EMI 5334

NALIN I.N.C. German production duo fronted by Andry Nalin. He is also a member of Nalin and Kane.

28/03/1998	51	1		PLANET VIOLET	Logic 74321565702

NALIN AND KANE German DJ/production duo Andry Nalin and Harry Cane. Nalin also recorded as Nalin I.n.c.

01/11/1997	48	1		BEACHBALL	ffrr FCD 318
13/09/1998	17	5		BEACHBALL (REMIX)	London FCD 349

NANA – see **ARCHITECHS**

NAPOLEON XIV US recording engineer and composer Jerry Samuels (born 1938, New York).

04/08/1966	4	10		THEY'RE COMING TO TAKE ME AWAY HA-HAAA!	Warner Brothers WB 5831

NARADA – see **NARADA MICHAEL WALDEN**

NARCOTIC THRUST UK dance group formed by Stuart Crichton and Andy Morris with vocals by Yvonne John Lewis.

10/08/2002	24	3		SAFE FROM HARM Contains a sample of Instant Funk's *Got My Mind Made Up*	ffrr FCD 406
17/04/2004	9	6		I LIKE IT	Free 2 Air 0153656F2A

MICHELLE NARINE – see **BIG BASS VS MICHELLE NARINE**

NAS US singer (born Nasir Jones, 14/9/1974, Long Island, NY) who made his recording debut in 1989. He is also a member of The Firm with AZ, Foxy Brown and Dawn Robinson.

28/05/1994	64	1		IT AIN'T HARD TO TELL Contains samples of Michael Jackson's *Human Nature* and Kool & The Gang's *N.T.*	Columbia 6604702
17/08/1996	12	7		IF I RULED THE WORLD Contains samples of Whodini's *Friends* and Kurtis Blow's *If I Ruled The World* and features the uncredited contribution of Lauryn Hill	Columbia 6634022
25/01/1997	13	4		STREET DREAMS Contains a sample of Linda Clifford's *Never Gonna Stop* and an interpolation of The Eurythmics' *Sweet Dreams*	Columbia 6641302
14/06/1997	18	3		HEAD OVER HEELS ALLURE FEATURING NAS Contains a sample of Frankie Beverly and Maze's *Before I Let Go*	Epic 6645942
29/05/1999	14	6		HATE ME NOW NAS FEATURING PUFF DADDY Based on the classical piece *The First Movement From Carmina Burana – O Fortuna!* Puff Daddy was unhappy with the accompanying video that depicted him being crucified on a cross and he was later arrested and charged with second-degree assault and criminal mischief after he attacked a Columbia employee	Columbia 6672565
15/01/2000	24	3		NASTRADAMUS Contains a sample of The JB's' *(It's Not The Express) It's The J.B.'s Monorail*	Columbia 6685572
22/01/2000	18	3		HOT BOYZ MISSY 'MISDEMEANOR' ELLIOTT FEATURING NAS, EVE & Q TIP	Elektra E 7002CD
21/04/2001	30	3		OOCHIE WALLY QB FINEST FEATURING NAS AND BRAVEHEARTS	Columbia 6710852
02/02/2002	30	5		GOT UR SELF A Contains a sample of The Alabama Three's *Woke Up This Morning*	Columbia 6723022

❶9 Number of weeks single topped the UK chart ↑ Entered the UK chart at #1 ▲9 Number of weeks single topped the US chart

561

DATE	POS	WKS	BPI	SINGLE TITLE	LABEL & NUMBER
13/07/2002	3	10		**I'M GONNA BE ALRIGHT** JENNIFER LOPEZ FEATURING NAS Contains samples of Club Nouveau's *Why You Treat Me So Bad* and Luniz's *I Got Five On It*	Epic 6728442
25/01/2003	27	3		MADE YOU LOOK Contains a sample of The Incredible Bongo Band's *Apache*	Columbia 6734792
05/04/2003	19	7		I CAN Contains a sample of The Honeydrippers' *Impeach The President*	Columbia 6737385
20/11/2004	18	4		BRIDGING THE GAP	Columbia 6754682

JOHNNY NASH US singer (born 19/8/1940, Houston, TX) who began his recording career in 1958, scoring a number of US hits with pop material. He set up the Jad and Joda labels in 1965 and in 1968 began recording regularly in Jamaica. He appeared in a number of films, including *Take A Giant Step, Key Witness* and the Swedish sex film *Love Is Not A Game!*

DATE	POS	WKS	BPI	SINGLE TITLE	LABEL & NUMBER
07/08/1968	5	16		**HOLD ME TIGHT**	Regal Zonophone RZ 3010
08/01/1969	6	12		**YOU GOT SOUL**	Major Minor MM 586
02/04/1969	6	12		**CUPID**	Major Minor MM 603
01/04/1972	13	12		STIR IT UP	CBS 7800
24/06/1972	5	15		**I CAN SEE CLEARLY NOW** ▲4 Features Bob Marley's Wailers (backing) and used in the 1997 film *Grosse Pointe Blank*	CBS 8113
07/10/1972	9	9		**THERE ARE MORE QUESTIONS THAN ANSWERS**	CBS 8351
14/06/1975	❶1	11	○	**TEARS ON MY PILLOW**	CBS 3220
11/10/1975	42	3		LET'S BE FRIENDS	CBS 3597
12/06/1976	25	7		(WHAT A) WONDERFUL WORLD	Epic EPC 4294
09/11/1985	47	4		ROCK ME BABY	2000 AD FED 19
15/04/1989	54	5		I CAN SEE CLEARLY NOW (REMIX)	Epic JN 1

LEIGH NASH – see DELERIUM

NASHVILLE TEENS UK rock group formed by Arthur 'Art' Sharp (born 26/5/1941, Woking), Ray Phillips (born Ramon John Phillips, 16/1/1944, Cardiff), Michael Dunford (guitar), John Hawken (born 9/5/1940, Bournemouth, piano), Pete Shannon (born Peter Shannon Harris, 23/8/1941, Antrim, bass) and Roger Groom (drums). Dunford and Groom left to be replaced by John Allen (born 23/4/1945, St Albans, guitar), Barrie Jenkins (born 22/12/1944, Leicester, drums) and Terry Crow (vocals). Jenkins was later a member of The Animals.

DATE	POS	WKS	BPI	SINGLE TITLE	LABEL & NUMBER
09/07/1964	6	13		**TOBACCO ROAD**	Decca F 11930
22/10/1964	10	11		**GOOGLE EYE**	Decca F 12000
04/03/1965	34	6		FIND MY WAY BACK HOME	Decca F 12089
20/05/1965	38	4		THIS LITTLE BIRD	Decca F 12143
03/02/1966	45	3		THE HARD WAY	Decca F 12316

NATASHA UK singer (full name Natasha England) who was previously a member of The Flirts before going solo in 1980.

DATE	POS	WKS	BPI	SINGLE TITLE	LABEL & NUMBER
05/06/1982	10	11		**IKO IKO**	Towerbell TOW 22
04/09/1982	44	5		THE BOOM BOOM ROOM	Towerbell TOW 25

ULTRA NATE US singer (born Ultra Nate Wyche, 1968, Havre De Grace, Maryland) raised in Boston, MA and Baltimore, Maryland. She began her career with the Basement Boys and made her debut album in 1989. She is also a member of Stars On 54, a group assembled to record parts of the soundtrack to the film *54*.

DATE	POS	WKS	BPI	SINGLE TITLE	LABEL & NUMBER
09/12/1989	62	3		IT'S OVER NOW	Eternal YZ 440
23/02/1991	71	1		IS IT LOVE BASEMENT BOYS PRESENT ULTRA NATE	Eternal YZ 509
29/01/1994	62	1		SHOW ME	Warner Brothers W 0219CD
14/06/1997	4	17	●	**FREE**	AM:PM 5822432
24/01/1998	33	2		FREE (REMIX)	AM:PM 5825012
18/04/1998	6	7		**FOUND A CURE**	AM:PM 5826452
25/07/1998	14	5		NEW KIND OF MEDICINE	AM:PM 5827492
22/07/2000	40	2		DESIRE	AM:PM CDAMPM 133
09/06/2001	51	1		GET IT UP (THE FEELING) Contains a sample of The Isley Brothers' *Tell Me When You Need It Again*	AM:PM CDAMPM 140

NATIONAL PHILHARMONIC ORCHESTRA – see JAMES GALWAY

NATIVE UK production duo Rob Tissera and Ian Bland, who had previously recorded as Quake.

DATE	POS	WKS	BPI	SINGLE TITLE	LABEL & NUMBER
10/02/2001	46	2		FEEL THE DRUMS	Slinky Music SLINKY 009CD

NATURAL US group formed by Patrick Jr King (guitar/keyboards/vocals), Marc Terenzi (guitar/keyboards/saxophone), Josh 'J' Horn (keyboards/trombone), Ben Bledsoe (bass/saxophone) and Michael Johnson (drums).

DATE	POS	WKS	BPI	SINGLE TITLE	LABEL & NUMBER
10/08/2002	32	2		PUT YOUR ARMS AROUND ME	Ariola 74321947892

NATURAL BORN CHILLERS UK production duo Gavin King and Arif Salih. King also records as Aphrodite.

DATE	POS	WKS	BPI	SINGLE TITLE	LABEL & NUMBER
01/11/1997	30	3		ROCK THE FUNKY BEAT	East West EW 138CD1

NATURAL BORN GROOVES Belgian production group formed by Burn Boon and Jaco van Rijsvijck and fronted by vocalist Bibi. The group also launched the Experimental label.

DATE	POS	WKS	BPI	SINGLE TITLE	LABEL & NUMBER
02/11/1996	64	1		FORERUNNER	XL Recordings XLS 76CD
19/04/1997	21	2		GROOVEBIRD	Positiva CDTIV 75

NATURAL LIFE UK vocal/instrumental group formed by Jon Spong, Darren Hunter, John Locko, Peter Holdforth, Andrew Lovell, Mark Matthews and Raymond Wilson.

07/03/1992.....47......3....... NATURAL LIFE .... Tribe NLIFE 3

NATURAL SELECTION US duo Elliott Erikson (keyboards) and Frederick Thomas (vocals).

09/11/1991.....69......2....... DO ANYTHING .... East West A 8724

NATURALS UK group formed in Harlow by Ricki Potter (vocals), Curt Cresswell (guitar), Bob O'Neale (harmonica), Mike Wakelin (bass), Douglas Ellis (guitar) and Roy Heather (drums) as the Blue Beats, changing to The Naturals upon signing with Parlophone. They disbanded after two further singles.

20/08/1964.....24......9....... I SHOULD HAVE KNOWN BETTER .... Parlophone R 5165

DAVID NAUGHTON US singer/songwriter (born 13/2/1952, Hartford, CT) who later became an actor, appearing in the film *An American Werewolf In London*.

25/08/1979.....44......6....... MAKIN' IT Theme to the TV series of the same name .... RSO 32

NAUGHTY BY NATURE US rap group from New Jersey comprising Anthony 'Treach' Criss, Vincent Brown and Kier 'DJ KG' Gist. Treach appeared in the film *Jason's Lyric* and married Sandra 'Pepa' Denton of Salt-N-Pepa in 1999. The group also appeared in the films *The Meteor Man* and *Who's The Man*. They won the 1995 Grammy Award for Best Rap Album for *Poverty's Paradise*.

09/11/1991.....73......1....... O.P.P. Stands for Other People's Property and contains a sample of The Jackson 5's *ABC* .... Big Life BLR 62
20/06/1992.....35......3....... O.P.P. Re-issue of Big Life BLR 62 .... Big Life BLR 74
30/01/1993.....22......3....... HIP HOP HOORAY .... Big Life BLRD 89
19/06/1993.....48......2....... IT'S ON .... Big Life BLRD 99
27/11/1993.....20......4....... HIP HOP HOORAY (REMIX) .... Big Life BLRDA 104
29/04/1995.....23......3....... FEEL ME FLOW Contains a sample of The Meters' *Find Yourself*................... Big Life BLRD 115
11/09/1999.....51......1....... JAMBOREE **NAUGHTY BY NATURE FEATURING ZHANE** Contains a sample of Benny Golson's *I'm Always Dancin' To The Music* ..... Arista 74321692882
19/10/2002.....44......1....... FEELS GOOD (DON'T WORRY BOUT A THING) **NAUGHTY BY NATURE FEATURING 3LW** Contains a sample of Tony! Toni! Tone!'s *Feel's Good*.............................. Island CID 806

NAVIGATOR – see **FREESTYLERS**

MARIA NAYLER UK singer who began her professional career with Ultraviolet and also recorded with Tilt.

09/03/1996.....17......4....... BE AS ONE **SASHA AND MARIA** 7pm 74321342962
16/11/1996.....3......17.....● ONE AND ONE **ROBERT MILES FEATURING MARIA NAYLER** .... Deconstruction 74321427692
07/03/1998.....32......3....... NAKED AND SACRED .... Deconstruction 74321534242
05/09/1998.....65......1....... WILL YOU BE WITH ME/LOVE IS THE GOD .... Deconstruction 74321591772
27/05/2000.....42......1....... ANGRY SKIES .... Deconstruction 74321759492

NAZARETH UK rock group formed in Dunfermline in 1969 by Dan McCafferty (lead vocals), Manny Charlton (guitar), Pete Agnew (bass) and Darrell Sweet (born 16/5/1947, Bournemouth, drums). McCafferty released his debut solo album in 1975 and went solo when the group disbanded in the mid-1980s. They reunited in 1992. Sweet died from a heart attack on 30/4/1999.

05/05/1973.....9......11...... **BROKEN DOWN ANGEL** .... Mooncrest MOON 1
21/07/1973.....10......9...... **BAD BAD BOY** .... Mooncrest MOON 9
13/10/1973.....11......13...... THIS FLIGHT TONIGHT... Mooncrest MOON 14
23/03/1974.....41......4...... SHANGHAI'D IN SHANGHAI... Mooncrest MOON 22
14/06/1975.....14......8...... MY WHITE BICYCLE .... Mooncrest MOON 47
15/11/1975.....36......4...... HOLY ROLLER .... Mountain TOP 3
24/09/1977.....15......11...... HOT TRACKS EP Tracks on EP: *Love Hurts, This Flight Tonight, Broken Down Angel* and *Hair Of The Dog*. *Love Hurts* was featured in the 1993 film *Dazed And Confused* .... Mountain NAZ 1
18/02/1978.....49......2...... GONE DEAD TRAIN.. Mountain NAZ 002
13/05/1978.....70......2...... PLACE IN YOUR HEART .... Mountain TOP 37
27/01/1979.....22......8...... MAY THE SUN SHINE .... Mountain NAZ 003
28/07/1979.....54......3...... STAR .... Mountain TOP 45

NAZLYN – see **M-BEAT**

ME'SHELL NDEGEOCELLO US singer/bass player (born Michelle Johnson, 29/8/1969, Berlin, Germany) who was raised in Maryland. Her name is Swahili for 'free like a bird'.

12/02/1994.....74......1....... IF THAT'S YOUR BOYFIEND (HE WASN'T LAST NIGHT)............................... Maverick W 0223CD1
03/09/1994.....34......3....... WILD NIGHT **JOHN MELLENCAMP FEATURING ME'SHELL NDEGEOCELLO**............ Mercury MERCD 409
01/03/1997.....59......1....... NEVER MISS THE WATER **CHAKA KHAN FEATURING ME'SHELL NDEGEOCELLO** ...... Reprise W 1393CD

YOUSSOU N'DOUR Senegalese singer (born 1/10/1959, Medina, Dakar region) who began singing traditional music at the age of twelve and joined the Star Band at the age of sixteen. He relocated to Paris and worked with Peter Gabriel in 1986.

03/06/1989.....61......3....... SHAKING THE TREE Re-issue of Virgin VS 1322 .... Virgin VS 1167
22/12/1990.....57......4....... SHAKING THE TREE This and above single credited to **YOUSSOU N'DOUR AND PETER GABRIEL** .... Virgin VS 1322
25/06/1994.....3......25.....○ **7 SECONDS YOUSSOU N'DOUR (FEATURING NENEH CHERRY)** The song won the 1994 MTV Europe Music Award for Best Song for writers Youssou N'Dour, Neneh Cherry and Cameron McVey .... Columbia 6605082
14/01/1995.....53......2....... UNDECIDED .... Columbia 6609712
10/10/1998.....52......1....... HOW COME **YOUSSOU N'DOUR AND CANIBUS** Featured in the 1998 film *Bulworth*..................... Interscope IND 95598

❶[9] Number of weeks single topped the UK chart ↑ Entered the UK chart at #1 ▲[9] Number of weeks single topped the US chart

563

NEARLY GOD UK rapper Tricky (born Adrian Thaws).

20/04/1996	28	2		POEMS .... Durban Poison DPCD 3

TERRY NEASON UK singer/comedienne/actress (born Glasgow) who has appeared in TV shows such as *The Bill* and *Casualty*.

25/06/1994	72	1		LIFEBOAT .... WEA YZ 830

NEBULA II UK instrumental/production group formed in Nottingham by Joe Shotter, Tony Thomas, Matt Lawless, Paul Smith and Richard McCormack.

01/02/1992	55	2		SÉANCE/ATHEAMA .... Reinforced RIVET 1211
16/05/1992	54	1		FLATLINERS J4M 12NEBULA 2

NED'S ATOMIC DUSTBIN UK rock group formed in Stourbridge in 1988 by Jonn Penney (vocals), Rat (guitar), Matt Cheslin (bass), Alex Griffin (bass) and Dan Warton (drums).

14/07/1990	53	2		KILL YOUR TELEVISION .... Chapter 22 CHAP 48
27/10/1990	51	2		UNTIL YOU FIND OUT .... Chapter 22 CHAP 52
09/03/1991	16	4		HAPPY .... Columbia 6566807
21/09/1991	21	4		TRUST .... Furtive 6574627
10/10/1992	19	3		NOT SLEEPING AROUND .... Furtive 6583866
05/12/1992	36	6		INTACT .... Furtive 6588166
25/03/1995	33	2		ALL I ASK OF MYSELF IS THAT I HOLD TOGETHER .... Furtive 6613565
15/07/1995	64	1		STUCK .... Furtive 6620562

RAJA NEE US female R&B singer discovered by James 'Jimmy Jam' Harris and Terry Lewis.

04/03/1995	42	2		TURN IT UP Contains a sample of The Isley Brothers' *Make Me Say It Again, Girl*. Featured in the 1994 film *A Low Down Dirty Shame* .... Perspective 5874872

NEEDLE DAMAGE – see DJ DAN PRESENTS NEEDLE DAMAGE

JOEY NEGRO UK producer and remixer Dave Lee; he is also a member of Hed Boys and has recorded as Z Factor, Akabu, Phase II, Jakatta, Il Padrinos, Turntable Orchestra and Raven Maize.

16/11/1991	36	3		DO WHAT YOU FEEL .... 10 TEN 391
21/12/1991	70	1		REACHIN' (REMIX) JOEY NEGRO PRESENTS PHASE II .... Republic LICT 160
18/07/1992	35	3		ENTER YOUR FANTASY EP Tracks on EP: *Love Fantasy, Get Up, Enter Your Mind* and *Everybody* .... 10 TEN 397
25/09/1993	51	2		WHAT HAPPENED TO THE MUSIC .... Virgin VSCD 1466
19/02/2000	8	5		MUST BE THE MUSIC JOEY NEGRO FEATURING TAKA BOOM .... Incentive CENT 4CDS
16/09/2000	41	1		SATURDAY Contains a sample of Norma Jean's *Saturday* .... Yola CDX03

neil UK actor (born Nigel Planer, 22/2/1955) who first came to prominence in the comedy series *The Young Ones,* playing the role of neil, a born-again hippie. The BRIT Award was the only time the category was included.

14/07/1984	2	10	O	HOLE IN MY SHOE The single won the 1985 BRIT Award for Best Comedy Record. .... WEA YZ 10

VINCE NEIL US singer (born Vince Neil Wharton, 8/2/1961, Los Angeles, CA) who was a founder member of Motley Crue in 1981. In 1992 he was sacked, the reason given was that motor racing had become his main priority. Neil rejected this and issued a $5 million lawsuit against the band for breach of contract, although he went solo during the litigation. By 1997 he had rejoined Motley Crue, replacing his replacement John Corabi (who issued a $7 million lawsuit against the band also for breach of contract but he did not name Neil as a defendant). On 8/12/1984 a car driven by Neil was involved in a crash, killing Hanoi Rocks drummer Nicholas 'Razzle' Dingley and injuring two others. Neil was jailed for 20 days, ordered to serve 200 hours community service and to pay $2.6 million in compensation. He appeared in the film *The Adventures Of Ford Fairlane* in 1990 and is married to mud wrestler Sharisse Rudell.

03/10/1992	63	1		YOU'RE INVITED (BUT YOUR FRIEND CAN'T COME) Featured in the 1992 film *Encino Man* .... Hollywood HWD 123

NEJA Italian singer (born Agnese Cacciola, Turin) who later recorded for Universal.

26/09/1998	47	1		RESTLESS (I KNOW YOU KNOW) .... Panorama CDPAN 1

NEK Italian singer (born Filippo Neviani, 6/1/1972, Montegibbio) who was a member of Winchester before going solo.

29/08/1998	59	1		LAURA .... Coalition COLA 054CD

NELLY US rapper (born Cornell Haynes, 2/11/1974, Travis, TX) who relocated to St Louis. He has won two Grammy Awards

11/11/2000	7	9		(HOT S**T) COUNTRY GRAMMAR .... Universal MCSTD 40242
24/02/2001	11	5		EI Featured in the 2003 film *Marci X* .... Universal MCSTD 40249
19/05/2001	3	12	O	RIDE WIT ME NELLY FEATURING CITY SPUD .... Universal MCSTD 40252
15/09/2001	28	2		BATTER UP NELLY AND ST LUNATICS .... Universal MCSTD 40261
27/10/2001	25	3		WHERE'S THE PARTY AT JAGGED EDGE FEATURING NELLY .... Columbia 6719012
27/04/2002	2	12		GIRLFRIEND 'N SYNC FEATURING NELLY .... Jive 9253312
29/06/2002	4	15	O	HOT IN HERRE ▲7 Contains an interpolation of Chuck Brown's *Bustin' Loose*. 2002 Grammy Award for Best Male Rap Solo Performance .... Universal MCSTD 40289
26/10/2002	❶²	21	✪	DILEMMA ↑ ▲10 NELLY FEATURING KELLY ROWLAND Contains an interpolation of *Love, Need And Want You*. 2002 Grammy Award for Best Rap/Sung Collaboration .... Universal MCSTD 40299
15/03/2003	7	11		WORK IT NELLY FEATURING JUSTIN TIMBERLAKE .... Universal MCSXD 40312
20/09/2003	10	7		SHAKE YA TAILFEATHER ▲4 NELLY, P DIDDY AND MURPHY LEE Featured in the 2003 film *Bad Boys II*. 2003 Grammy Award for Best

○ Silver disc ● Gold disc ✪ Platinum disc (additional platinum units are indicated by a figure following the symbol) ◎ Singles released prior to 1973 that are known to have sold over 1 million copies in the UK

				Rap Performance by a Duo or Group	Bad Boy MCSTD 40337
13/12/2003	36	4		IZ U Contains a sample of Alan Tew's *The Big One*	Universal MCSTD 40346
11/09/2004	❶¹	11		**MY PLACE/FLAP YOUR WINGS** ↑	Universal MCSTD 40379
04/12/2004	5	4+		**TILT YA HEAD BACK** NELLY AND CHRISTINA AGUILERA Contains a sample of Curtis Mayfield's *Superfly*	Universal MCSTD40396

NELSON US duo Gunnar Nelson (born 20/9/1967, bass/vocals) and his twin brother Matthew (guitar/vocals). They are the sons of Ricky Nelson.

27/10/1990	54	3		(CAN'T LIVE WITHOUT YOUR) LOVE AND AFFECTION ▲¹	DGC GEF 82

BILL NELSON UK singer/multi-instrumentalist (born 18/12/1948, Wakefield); he formed Be Bop Deluxe in 1971, which he fronted for most of the decade. When they disbanded in 1978, Nelson formed Red Noise for a brief time and then went solo. He proved in demand as a producer and session musician and appeared on recordings by the likes of The Skids, A Flock Of Seagulls and David Sylvian.

24/02/1979	59	3		FURNITURE MUSIC	Harvest HAR 5176
05/07/1980	52	4		REVOLT INTO STYLE This and above single credited to BILL NELSON'S BIG NOISE	Cocteau COQ 1
05/07/1980	52	4		DO YOU DREAM IN COLOUR?	Cocteau COQ 1
13/06/1981	73	3		YOUTH OF NATION ON FIRE	Mercury WILL 2

PHYLLIS NELSON US singer (born Jacksonville, FL) and a member of family group the Nelson Five. She was later a backing singer for Major Harris and Philly Cream. Her son Marc also enjoyed a recording career.

23/03/1985	❶¹	21	●	**MOVE CLOSER** Originally released in April 1984 and failed to chart	Carrere CAR 337
21/05/1994	34	3		MOVE CLOSER Re-issue of Carrere CAR 337	EMI CDEMCT 9

RICKY NELSON US singer (born Eric Hillard Nelson, 8/5/1940, Teaneck, NJ) who began on radio in 1949, with his first single in 1957 for Verve. He moved to Imperial the same year (despite US success, Verve had not passed on any royalties) and signed a $1 million deal with Decca in 1963. He appeared in numerous films, including *A Tale Of Four Wishes, Here Come The Nelsons, Rio Bravo, The Wackiest Ship In The Army* and *Love And Kisses*. He was one of seven people who died when his chartered plane caught fire and crashed on 31/12/1985. It was rumoured that he and his fellow passengers had been 'freebasing' cocaine, causing the fire, but later revealed that no drugs had been found and that they had died through smoke inhalation. The fire was subsequently blamed on a faulty gasoline heater that had caused the plane to make two emergency landings in the previous six months. He won the 1986 Grammy Award for Best Spoken Word Recording with various others for *Interviews From The Class Of '55*. He was inducted into the Rock & Roll Hall of Fame in 1987. He has a star on the Hollywood Walk of Fame. His twin sons, Matthew and Gunnar, recorded as Nelson.

21/02/1958	27	2		STOOD UP	London HLP 8542
22/08/1958	4	14		**POOR LITTLE FOOL** ▲²	London HLP 8670
07/11/1958	9	13		**SOMEDAY**	London HLP 8732
21/11/1958	27	1		I GOT A FEELING B-side to *Someday*	London HLP 8732
17/04/1959	3	20		**IT'S LATE**	London HLP 8817
15/05/1959	14	10		NEVER BE ANYONE ELSE BUT YOU B-side to *It's Late*	London HLP 8817
04/09/1959	19	3		SWEETER THAN YOU	London HLP 8927
11/09/1959	11	8		JUST A LITTLE TOO MUCH B-side to *Sweeter Than You*	London HLP 8927
15/01/1960	30	1		I WANNA BE LOVED	London HLP 9021
07/07/1960	48	1		YOUNG EMOTIONS	London HLP 9121
01/06/1961	2	18		**HELLO MARY LOU/TRAVELLIN' MAN** ▲²	London HLP 9347
16/11/1961	23	5		EVERLOVIN' RICK NELSON	London HLP 9440
29/03/1962	19	13		YOUNG WORLD RICK NELSON	London HLP 9524
30/08/1962	39	4		TEENAGE IDOL	London HLP 9583
17/01/1963	22	9		IT'S UP TO YOU	London HLP 9648
17/10/1963	12	9		FOOLS RUSH IN	Brunswick 05895
30/01/1964	14	10		FOR YOU	Brunswick 05900
21/10/1972	41	4		GARDEN PARTY This and above five singles credited to RICK NELSON	MCA MU 1165
24/08/1991	45	5		HELLO MARY LOU (GOODBYE HEART) RICKY NELSON Re-issue of London HLP 9347	Liberty EMCT 2

SANDY NELSON US drummer (born Sander Nelson, 1/12/1938, Santa Monica, CA) who started out as a session drummer, appearing on several Phil Spector recordings. He financed his first recording, *Teen Beat*, in 1959 and leased it to Original Sound. He lost his right foot and part of his leg in a motorcycle accident in 1963, but returned to drumming in 1964. He later formed Veebletronics label.

06/11/1959	9	12		**TEEN BEAT**	Top Rank JAR 197
14/12/1961	3	16		**LET THERE BE DRUMS**	London HLP 9466
22/03/1962	30	6		DRUMS ARE MY BEAT	London HLP 9521
07/06/1962	39	8		DRUMMIN' UP A STORM	London HLP 9558

SHARA NELSON UK singer/songwriter (born London) who began her career with Massive Attack before going solo in 1993.

24/07/1993	19	6		DOWN THAT ROAD	Cooltempo CDCOOL 275
18/09/1993	21	5		ONE GOODBYE IN TEN	Cooltempo CDCOOL 279
12/02/1994	19	5		UPTIGHT	Cooltempo CDCOOL 286
04/06/1994	49	1		NOBODY	Cooltempo CDCOOL 290
10/09/1994	34	3		INSIDE OUT/DOWN THAT ROAD (REMIX)	Cooltempo CDCOOLX 295
16/09/1995	30	2		ROUGH WITH THE SMOOTH	Cooltempo CDCOOL 311
05/12/1998	61	1		SENSE OF DANGER PRESENCE FEATURING SHARA NELSON	Pagan 024CDS

SHELLEY NELSON – see TIN TIN OUT

❶⁹ Number of weeks single topped the UK chart ↑ Entered the UK chart at #1 ▲⁹ Number of weeks single topped the US chart

565

WILLIE NELSON US singer/songwriter (born 30/4/1933, Abbott, TX) who cut his first record, *Lumberjack,* in Washington in 1956 with copies being offered for sale over the radio. He has appeared in a number of films, including *Honeysuckle Rose, Thief, Red Headed Stranger* (in the lead role which Robert Redford had hoped to land!) and *Three Of A Kind*. He has won six Grammy Awards: Best Country Vocal Performance, Male in 1975 for *Blue Eyes Crying In The Rain,* Best Country Vocal Performance, Male in 1978 for *Georgia On My Mind,* Best Country Performance By A Duo Or Group in 1978 with Waylon Jennings for *Mommas, Don't Let Your Babies Grow Up To Be Cowboys,* Best Country Song in 1980 for *On The Road Again,* Best Country Vocal Performance, Male in 1982 for *Always On My Mind* and Best Country Collaboration With Vocals in 2002 with Lee Ann Womack for *Mendocino County Line*.

31/07/1982	49	3		ALWAYS ON MY MIND	CBS A 2511
07/04/1984	17	10		TO ALL THE GIRLS I'VE LOVED BEFORE **JULIO IGLESIAS AND WILLIE NELSON**	CBS A 4252

NENA German rock group formed in Berlin by Gabriele 'Nena' Kerner (born 26/3/1960) and featuring Rolf Brendel (drums), Jurgen Dehmel (bass), Joern-Uwe Fahrenkrog-Peterson (keyboards) and Carlo Karges (guitar).

04/02/1984	❶³	12	●	**99 RED BALLOONS** Original German title *99 Luftballons* (English translation by Kevin McAlea)	Epic A 4074
05/05/1984	70	2		JUST A DREAM	Epic A 3249

NEO CORTEX Danish production trio formed by Lars Böge, Jan Miesner and Heiko Lempio.

23/10/2004	67	1	ELEMENTS	All Around The World CDGLOBE332

NEPTUNES – see **N*E*R*D**

N*E*R*D US hip hop group The Neptunes, formed by Pharrell Williams (born 5/4/1973, Virginia Beach, VI) and Chad Hugo (born 24/2/1974, Portsmouth, VI). Based in Virginia, Williams and Hugo first came to prominence as songwriters, penning and producing hits for Kelis, Ol' Dirty Bastard and Jay-Z. The name stands for No-one Ever Really Dies. They won the 2002 and 2003 MOBO Awards for Best Producers and the 2003 Grammy Award in the same category.

09/06/2001	33	2		LAPDANCE **N*E*R*D FEATURING LEE HARVEY AND VITA** Featured in the 2003 film *Daredevil*	Virgin VUSCD 196
26/01/2002	19	4		DIDDY **P DIDDY FEATURING THE NEPTUNES**	Puff Daddy 74321911652
08/06/2002	16	7		PASS THE COURVOISIER – PART II **BUSTA RHYMES, P DIDDY AND PHARRELL**	J Records 74321937902
10/08/2002	7	8		**BOYS BRITNEY SPEARS FEATURING PHARRELL WILLIAMS** Featured in the 2002 film *Goldmember*	Jive 9253912
10/08/2002	15	4		ROCK STAR	Virgin VUSCD 253
29/03/2003	20	4		PROVIDER/LAPDANCE	Virgin VUSCD 262
05/04/2003	23	20		BEAUTIFUL **SNOOP DOGG FEATURING PHARRELL**	Capitol CDCL 842
16/08/2003	6	10		**FRONTIN' PHARRELL WILLIAMS FEATURING JAY-Z** Contains a sample of Michael Jackson's *Human Nature*	Arista 82876553332
29/11/2003	62	1		LIGHT YOUR ASS ON FIRE **BUSTA RHYMES FEATURING PHARRELL**	Arista 82876572512
07/02/2004	35	2		SHOW ME YOUR SOUL **P DIDDY, LENNY KRAVITZ, PHARRELL WILLIAMS AND LOON** Featured in the 2003 film *Bad Boys II* .... Puff Daddy MCSTD 40350
27/03/2004	5	12		**SHE WANTS TO MOVE**	Virgin VUSDX 284
15/05/2004	71	1		PASS THE COURVOISIER - PART II **BUSTA RHYMES, P DIDDY AND PHARRELL**	J Records 74321937902
26/06/2004	25	5		MAYBE	Virgin VUSDX 291
11/12/2004	10	3+		**DROP IT LIKE IT'S HOT ▲³ SNOOP DOGG FEATURING PHARRELL**	Geffen 2103461

NERIO'S DUBWORK – see **DARRYL PANDY**

FRANCES NERO US R&B singer (born Detroit, MI) who began her career as a teenager after winning a talent contest in 1965 and signing with Motown. After three years with them (when only one single was released) and a brief stint with the Crazy Horse label, she retired. She re-emerged in 1989 with the Motorcity label, her one hit being a remixed version of a 1990 Motorcity original.

13/04/1991	17	9	FOOTSTEPS FOLLOWING ME	Debut DEBT 3109

NERO AND THE GLADIATORS UK instrumental group formed by Mike O'Neill (as Nero, keyboards), Colin Green (guitar), Boots Slade (bass) and Laurie Jay (drums).

23/03/1961	37	5	ENTRY OF THE GLADIATORS	Decca F 11329
27/07/1961	48	1	IN THE HALL OF THE MOUNTAIN KING	Decca F 11367

ANN NESBY US singer (born Joliet, IL) who is also lead singer with Sounds Of Blackness and has provided backing vocals for Janet Jackson and Patti LaBelle.

21/12/1996	42	2	WITNESS (EP) Tracks on EP: *Can I Get A Witness, In The Spirit* and *I'm Still Wearing Your Name*	AM:PM 5875612
17/05/1997	75	1	HOLD ON (EP) Tracks on EP: *Hold On (Mousse T's Uplifting Garage Edit), Hold (Moose T's Hard Soul Remix), Hold On (Klub Head Mix)* and *This Weekend (Laidback Mix)*	AM:PM 5822332

MICHAEL NESMITH US singer (born Robert Michael Nesmith, 30/12/1942, Houston, TX) who released several singles as Michael Blessing prior to winning an audition to join The Monkees. He left them in 1970 following the completion of his contractual obligations, recorded solo and formed the Second National Band. He is the only ex-member of The Monkees to chart in the UK, and the only one to have won a Grammy Award, in the Video of the Year category in 1981 for *Michael Nesmith In Elephant Parts*.

26/03/1977	28	6	RIO	Island WIP 6373

NETWORK UK vocal/instrumental group.

12/12/1992	46	4	BROKEN WINGS	Chrysalis CHS 3923

NEVADA UK vocal/instrumental group.

08/01/1983	71	1	IN THE BLEAK MID WINTER	Polydor POSP 203

○ Silver disc ● Gold disc ✪ Platinum disc (additional platinum units are indicated by a figure following the symbol) ◎ Singles released prior to 1973 that are known to have sold over 1 million copies in the UK

NEVADA – see STEREOPOL FEATURING NEVADA

NEVE – see Y-TRAXX

ROBBIE NEVIL US singer/songwriter/guitarist (born 10/1/1961, Los Angeles, CA); he appeared in the TV series *Beverly Hills 90210*.

20/12/1986	3	11		C'EST LA VIE	Manhattan MT 14
02/05/1987	26	6		DOMINOES	Manhattan MT 19
11/07/1987	43	7		WOT'S IT TO YA	Manhattan MT 24

AARON NEVILLE – see LINDA RONSTADT

TOM NEVILLE UK DJ/producer, previously a member of Sentience.

06/03/2004	60	1		JUST FUCK	Nukleuz 0555PNUK

NEVILLE BROTHERS US group formed in New Orleans, LA in 1978 by Art (born 17/12/1937, New Orleans, keyboards/vocals), Charles (born 28/12/1938, New Orleans, saxophone/flute), Aaron (born 24/1/1941, New Orleans, keyboards/vocals) and Cyril Neville (born 10/1/1948, New Orleans, vocals). All had previously been heavily involved in the New Orleans music scene: Art had formed The Meters, Aaron had sung with The Avalons and Charles and Cyril had been members of various bands. They won the 1989 Grammy Award for Best Pop Instrumental Performance for *Healing Chant* from the album *Yellow Moon*. Additionally, Aaron Neville won the 1989 Grammy Award for Best Pop Vocal Performance by a Duo or Group with Linda Ronstadt for *Don't Know Much*, Best Pop Vocal Performance by a Duo or Group with Linda Ronstadt the following year for *All My Life* and Best Country Vocal Collaboration in 1994 with Trisha Yearwood for *I Fall To Pieces*. Art won the 1996 Grammy Award for Best Rock instrumental with Jimmie Vaughan, Eric Clapton, Bonnie Raitt, Robert Cray, B.B. King, Buddy Guy and Dr. John for *SRV Shuffle*.

25/11/1989	47	6		WITH GOD ON OUR SIDE	A&M AM 545
07/07/1990	72	1		BIRD ON A WIRE	A&M AM 568

JASON NEVINS US DJ/producer/remixer from Long Island, NY. Holly James was previously a member of Tymes 4.

21/02/1998	63	3		IT'S LIKE THAT (GERMAN IMPORT)	Epidrome EPD 665293-20
14/03/1998	65	1		IT'S LIKE THAT (AMERICAN IMPORT)	Sm:)e SM 9069-2
21/03/1998	❶[6]	16	✪	**IT'S LIKE THAT** ↑	Sm:)e Communications SM 90652
18/04/1998	74	1		IT'S TRICKY (IMPORT) This and above three singles credited to RUN DMC VERSUS JASON NEVINS	Epidrome EPD 6656982
26/06/1999	19	3		INSANE IN THE BRAIN JASON NEVINS VERSUS CYPRESS HILL	INCredible INCRL 17CD
16/08/2003	9	5		**I'M IN HEAVEN** JASON NEVINS PRESENTS UKNY FEATURING HOLLY JAMES Contains a sample of Michael Jackson's *Human Nature*	Free 2 Air/Incentive 0148665 F2A

NEW ATLANTIC UK instrumental/production duo Richard Lloyd and Cameron Saunders.

29/02/1992	12	7		I KNOW	3 Beat 3BT 1
03/10/1992	70	1		INTO THE FUTURE NEW ATLANTIC FEATURING LINDA WRIGHT	3 Beat 3BT 2
13/02/1993	64	1		TAKE OFF SOME TIME	3 Beat 3BTCD 14
26/11/1994	26	6		THE SUNSHINE AFTER THE RAIN NEW ATLANTIC/U4EA FEATURING BERRI	3 Beat TABCD 223

NEW BOHEMIANS – see EDIE BRICKELL AND THE NEW BOHEMIANS

NEW EDITION US R&B vocal group formed in Boston, MA in 1982 by manager and producer Maurice Starr and comprising Ricky Bell (born 18/9/1967, Boston), Michael Bivins (born 10/8/1968, Boston), Bobby Brown (born 5/2/1969, Roxbury, MA), Ronald DeVoe (born 17/11/1967, Boston) and Ralph Tresvant (born 16/5/1968, Boston). They were all aged between thirteen and fifteen at the time of their formation and were moulded as an '80s version of the Jackson 5. The group split acrimoniously with Starr in 1984. Brown left in 1987 to go solo, and was replaced by Johnny Gill (born 22/5/1966, Washington DC). Bell, Bivins and DeVoe recorded as Bell Biv Devoe in 1990, while both Tresvant and Gill recorded solo. All six members reunited in 1996. Starr later created New Kids On The Block.

16/04/1983	❶[1]	13	○	**CANDY GIRL**	London LON 21
13/08/1983	43	5		POPCORN LOVE	London LON 31
23/02/1985	19	9		MR TELEPHONE MAN	MCA 938
15/04/1989	70	1		CRUCIAL	MCA 23934
10/08/1996	20	4		HIT ME OFF Contains a sample of Black Moon's *I Got Cha Opin*	MCA MCSTD 48014
07/06/1997	16	4		SOMETHING ABOUT YOU Contains a sample of Edie Brickell's *What I Am*	MCA MCSTD 48032

NEW FOUND GLORY US rock group formed in Coral Springs, FL by Jordan Pundik (vocals), Chad Gilbert (guitar), Steve Klein (guitar), Ian Grushka (bass) and Cyrus Bolooki (drums).

16/06/2001	58	1		HIT OR MISS (WAITED TOO LONG)	MCA 1558232
03/08/2002	30	3		MY FRIENDS OVER YOU	MCA MCSXD 40286
19/10/2002	64	1		HEAD ON COLLISION	MCA MCSXD 40298
12/06/2004	58	1		ALL DOWNHILL FROM HERE	Geffen 9862523
11/09/2004	67	1		FAILURE'S NOT FLATTERING	Geffen MCSTD 40380

A NEW GENERATION UK group formed by Ian Sutherland (guitar/vocals), Gavin Sutherland (bass/vocals), Christopher Kemp (keyboards/vocals) and John Wright (drums). Ian and Gavin later recorded as The Sutherland Brothers.

26/06/1968	38	5		SMOKEY BLUES AWAY	Spark SRL 1007

NEW KIDS ON THE BLOCK US vocal group formed in 1984 by manager Maurice Starr as a 'white New

Edition' and comprising Donnie Wahlberg (born 17/8/1969, Dorchester, MA), Danny Wood (born 14/5/1969, Boston, MA), Jordan Knight (born 17/5/1970, Worcester, MA), his brother Jonathan (born 29/11/1968, Worcester) and Joey McIntyre (born 31/12/1972, Needham, MA). Originally called Nynuk, they changed to New Kids On The Block on signing with CBS Records' Black Division. They shortened their name to New Kids and then NKOTB in 1993. They disbanded in 1995 with McIntyre and Jordan Knight subsequently recording solo and Wahlberg and Wood becoming producers. McIntyre also became an actor, appearing in the film *The Fantasticks*.

DATE	POS	WKS	BPI	SINGLE TITLE	LABEL & NUMBER
16/09/1989	52	4		HANGIN' TOUGH	CBS BLOCK 1
11/11/1989	❶³	13	●	**YOU GOT IT (THE RIGHT STUFF)**	CBS BLOCK 2
06/01/1990	❶²	9		**HANGIN' TOUGH** ▲¹ Re-issue of CBS BLOCK 1	CBS BLOCK 3
17/03/1990	5	8		**I'LL BE LOVING YOU (FOREVER)** ▲¹	CBS BLOCK 4
12/05/1990	4	8		**COVER GIRL**	CBS BLOCK 5
16/06/1990	2	7	○	**STEP BY STEP** ▲³	CBS BLOCK 6
04/08/1990	3	10		**TONIGHT**	CBS BLOCK 7
13/10/1990	8	5		LET'S TRY AGAIN/DIDN'T I BLOW YOUR MIND	CBS BLOCK 8
08/12/1990	9	7		**THIS ONE'S FOR THE CHILDREN**	CBS BLOCK 9
09/02/1991	14	4		GAMES	CBS 6566267
18/05/1991	12	5		CALL IT WHAT YOU WANT	Columbia 6567857
14/12/1991	9	5		**IF YOU GO AWAY**	Columbia 6576667
19/02/1994	27	3		DIRTY DAWG Contains a sample of James Brown's *Papa Don't Take No Mess*	Columbia 6600362
26/03/1994	42	2		NEVER LET YOU GO This and above single credited to NKOTB	Columbia 6602072

NEW MODEL ARMY UK rock group formed in Bradford in 1980 by Justin 'Slade The Leveller' Sullivan (born 8/4/1956, Jordans, guitar/vocals), Jason 'Moose' Harris (born 22/9/1958, Colchester, bass) and Robb Heaton (born 6/7/1961, Knutsford, drums). The group attracted considerable controversy from *Top Of The Pops* for wearing t-shirts with the slogan 'Only Stupid Bastards Use Heroin'. The group took their name from the army raised by Oliver Cromwell in the English Civil War. Heaton died from pancreatic cancer on 4/11/2004.

DATE	POS	WKS	BPI	SINGLE TITLE	LABEL & NUMBER
27/04/1985	28	5		NO REST	EMI NMA 1
03/08/1985	49	2		THE ACOUSTICS (EP) Tracks on EP: *Better Than Them, No Sense, Adrenalin* and *Trust*	EMI NMA 2
30/11/1985	57	1		BRAVE NEW WORLD	EMI NMA 3
08/11/1986	71	2		51ST STATE	EMI NMA 4
28/02/1987	64	1		POISON STREET	EMI NMA 5
26/09/1987	50	3		WHITE COATS (EP) Tracks on EP: *White Coats, The Charge, Chinese Whispers* and *My Country*	EMI NMA 6
21/01/1989	31	3		STUPID QUESTION	EMI NMA 7
11/03/1989	37	3		VAGABONDS	EMI NMA 8
10/06/1989	37	3		GREEN AND GREY	EMI NMA 9
08/09/1990	34	3		GET ME OUT	EMI NMA 10
03/11/1990	61	2		PURITY	EMI NMA 11
08/06/1991	39	2		SPACE	EMI NMA 12
20/02/1993	25	2		HERE COMES THE WAR	Epic 6589352
24/07/1993	51	1		LIVING IN THE ROSE (THE BALLADS EP) Tracks on EP: *Living In The Rose, Drummy B, Marry The Sea* and *Sleepwalking* .... Epic 6592492

NEW MUSIK UK technopop group formed by Clive Gates (keyboards), Tony Hibbert (bass), Tony Mansfield (guitar/keyboards/vocals) and Phil Towner (drums). Mansfield later became a successful producer (Captain Sensible and Naked Eyes).

DATE	POS	WKS	BPI	SINGLE TITLE	LABEL & NUMBER
06/10/1979	53	5		STRAIGHT LINES	GTO GT 255
19/01/1980	13	8		LIVING BY NUMBERS	GTO GT 261
26/04/1980	31	7		THIS WORLD OF WATER	GTO GT 268
12/07/1980	31	7		SANCTUARY	GTO GT 275

NEW ORDER UK group formed in 1980 following the sudden demise of Joy Division (brought about by Ian Curtis' suicide) and comprising Barney Sumner (born Bernard Dicken, 4/1/1956, Salford, guitar/vocals), Peter Hook (born 13/2/1956, Manchester, bass) and Stephen Morris (born 28/10/1957, Macclesfield, drums), adding Gillian Gilbert (born 27/1/1961, Macclesfield, keyboards) to the line-up five months later. Sumner later formed Electronic.

DATE	POS	WKS	BPI	SINGLE TITLE	LABEL & NUMBER
14/03/1981	34	5		CEREMONY	Factory FAC 33
03/10/1981	38	5		PROCESSION/EVERYTHING'S GONE GREEN	Factory FAC 53
22/05/1982	29	7		TEMPTATION Featured in the 1996 film *Trainspotting*	Factory FAC 63
19/03/1983	12	17		BLUE MONDAY Featured in the 1998 film *The Wedding Singer*	Factory FAC 73
13/08/1983	9	21		**BLUE MONDAY**	Factory FAC 73
03/09/1983	12	7		CONFUSION	Factory FAC 93
28/04/1984	18	5		THIEVES LIKE US	Factory FAC 103
25/05/1985	46	4		THE PERFECT KISS	Factory FAC 123
09/11/1985	63	4		SUB-CULTURE	Factory FAC 133
29/03/1986	28	5		SHELLSHOCK Featured in the 1986 film *Pretty In Pink*	Factory FAC 143

DATE	POS	WKS	BPI	SINGLE TITLE	LABEL & NUMBER
27/09/1986	30	3		STATE OF THE NATION	Factory FAC 153
27/09/1986	54	1		THE PEEL SESSIONS EP (1ST JUNE 1982) Tracks on EP: *Turn The Heater On, We All Stand, Too Late* and *5-8-6*	
					Strange Fruit SFPS 001
15/11/1986	56	2		BIZARRE LOVE TRIANGLE	Factory FAC 163
01/08/1987	4	10		**TRUE FAITH** 1988 BRIT Award for Best Video and featured in the 1988 film *Bright Lights, Big City*	Factory FAC 183/7
19/12/1987	20	7		TOUCHED BY THE HAND OF GOD	Factory FAC 1937
07/05/1988	3	11		**BLUE MONDAY (REMIX)** This was the first time this single had been available on 7-inch vinyl	Factory FAC 737
10/12/1988	11	8		FINE TIME	Factory FAC 2237
11/03/1989	21	7		ROUND AND ROUND	Factory FAC 2637
09/09/1989	49	2		RUN 2	Factory FAC 273
02/06/1990	❶[2]	12	●	**WORLD IN MOTION** ENGLANDNEWORDER	Factory/MCA FAC 2937
17/04/1993	4	7		**REGRET**	Centredate Co NUOCD 1
03/07/1993	22	4		RUINED IN A DAY	Centredate Co NUOCD 2
04/09/1993	13	5		WORLD (THE PRICE OF LOVE)	Centredate Co NUOCD 3
18/12/1993	22	4		SPOOKY	Centredate Co NUOCD 4
19/11/1994	9	8		**TRUE FAITH (REMIX)**	Centredate Co NUOCD 5
21/01/1995	21	4		NINETEEN63	London NUOCD 6
05/08/1995	17	4		BLUE MONDAY (2ND REMIX)	London NUOCD 7
25/08/2001	8	4		**CRYSTAL**	London NUOCD 8
01/12/2001	29	2		60 MILES AN HOUR	London NUOCD 9
27/04/2002	15	3		HERE TO STAY	London NUOCD 11
15/06/2002	43	2		WORLD IN MOTION ENGLANDNEWORDER	London NUOCD 12
30/11/2002	64	1		CONFUSION ARTHUR BAKER VERSUS NEW ORDER	Whacked WACKT 002CD

NEW ORLEANS JAZZMEN – see TERRY LIGHTFOOT'S NEW ORLEANS JAZZMEN

NEW POWER GENERATION
US group formed by Prince as his backing group in 1991 and featuring Levi Seacer Jr (guitar), Tony M (raps), Tommy Barbarella (keyboards), Kirk Johnson (percussion/vocals), Damon Dickson (percussion/vocals), Sonny T (bass/vocals), Michael B (drums), Rosie Gaines (vocals) and Mayte Garcia (vocals and later Prince's wife), with Prince penning and producing their releases. By 1997 the group was fronted by Tora Tora (a pseudonym for Prince). Gaines later went solo.

DATE	POS	WKS	BPI	SINGLE TITLE	LABEL & NUMBER
31/08/1991	4	8		**GETT OFF**	Paisley Park W 0056
21/09/1991	15	7		CREAM	Paisley Park W 0061
07/12/1991	25	6		DIAMONDS AND PEARLS	Paisley Park W 0075
28/03/1992	19	5		MONEY DON'T MATTER 2 NIGHT	Paisley Park W 0091
27/06/1992	28	3		THUNDER	Paisley Park W 01132P
18/07/1992	4	7		**SEXY MF/STROLLIN'**	Paisley Park W 0123
10/10/1992	7	5		**MY NAME IS PRINCE**	Paisley Park W 0132
14/11/1992	51	1		MY NAME IS PRINCE (REMIX)	Paisley Park W 0142T
05/12/1992	27	6		7 This and above eight singles credited to PRINCE AND THE NEW POWER GENERATION	Paisley Park W 0147
13/03/1993	52	3		THE MORNING PAPERS	Paisley Park W 0162CD
01/04/1995	19	4		GET WILD Featured in the 1994 film *Ready To Wear (Pret-A-Porter)*	NPG 0061045
19/08/1995	29	3		THE GOOD LIFE	NPG 0061515
05/07/1997	15	5		THE GOOD LIFE	NPG 0061515
21/11/1998	65	1		COME ON	RCA 74321634722

NEW RADICALS
US rock group fronted by singer/songwriter Gregg Alexander (born Grosse Pointe, MI). After brief success, Alexander announced he was leaving the group in order to concentrate on writing and producing on a freelance basis.

DATE	POS	WKS	BPI	SINGLE TITLE	LABEL & NUMBER
03/04/1999	5	17	O	**YOU GET WHAT YOU GIVE** Featured in the 2004 film *Scooby Doo 2: Monsters Unleashed*	MCA MCSTD 48111
25/09/1999	48	1		SOMEDAY WE'LL KNOW	MCA MCSTD 40217

NEW RHODES
UK rock group formed in Bristol in 2001 by James Williams (guitar/vocals), Joe Gascoigne (guitar), Jack Ashdown (bass) and Chun Leek (drums). Leek was later replaced by Steve.

DATE	POS	WKS	BPI	SINGLE TITLE	LABEL & NUMBER
07/08/2004	63	1		I WISH I WAS YOU	Moshi Moshi MOSHI11CD

NEW SEEKERS
UK/Australian group formed by Keith Potger after the demise of The Seekers in 1969. The line-up for their hits consisted of Eve Graham (born 19/4/1943, Perth), Lyn Paul (born 16/2/1949, Manchester), Peter Doyle (born 28/7/1949, Melbourne), Marty Kristian (born 27/5/1947, Leipzig, Germany) and Paul Layton (born 4/8/1947, Beaconsfield). Doyle left in 1974 and was replaced by Peter Oliver (born 15/1/1952, Southampton). Disbanding in 1975, each member went solo (Kristian was a member of Prima Donna, UK's entrant in the 1980 Eurovision Song Contest). They re-formed in 1975 (minus Paul). Doyle died from cancer in Australia on 22/10/2001.

DATE	POS	WKS	BPI	SINGLE TITLE	LABEL & NUMBER
17/10/1970	44	2		WHAT HAVE THEY DONE TO MY SONG MA	Philips 6006 027
10/07/1971	2	19		**NEVER ENDING SONG OF LOVE**	Philips 6006 125
18/12/1971	❶[4]	21		**I'D LIKE TO TEACH THE WORLD TO SING (IN PERFECT HARMONY)** Originally written as an advertisement for Coca Cola – *I'd Like To Buy The World A Coke*	Polydor 2058 184
04/03/1972	2	13		**BEG STEAL OR BORROW** Britain's entry for the 1972 Eurovision Song Contest (came second to Vicki Leandros of Greece's entry, *Apres Toi*)	Polydor 2058 201
10/06/1972	4	16		**CIRCLES**	Polydor 2058 242
02/12/1972	20	11		COME SOFTLY TO ME NEW SEEKERS FEATURING MARTY KRISTIAN	Polydor 2058 315
24/02/1973	16	8		PINBALL WIZARD – SEE ME FEEL ME (MEDLEY)	Polydor 2058 338

❶[9] Number of weeks single topped the UK chart ↑ Entered the UK chart at #1 ▲[9] Number of weeks single topped the US chart

07/04/1973	34	5		NEVERTHELESS EVE GRAHAM AND THE NEW SEEKERS	Polydor 2058 340
16/06/1973	36	5		GOODBYE IS JUST ANOTHER WORD	Polydor 2058 368
24/11/1973	❶¹	16	●	YOU WON'T FIND ANOTHER FOOL LIKE ME	Polydor 2058 421
09/03/1974	5	9	○	I GET A LITTLE SENTIMENTAL OVER YOU This and above single credited to NEW SEEKERS FEATURING LYN PAUL	Polydor 2058 439
14/08/1976	44	4		IT'S SO NICE (TO HAVE YOU HOME)	CBS 4391
29/01/1977	25	4		I WANNA GO BACK	CBS 4786
15/07/1978	21	10		ANTHEM (ONE DAY IN EVERY WEEK)	CBS 6413

NEW TONE AGE FAMILY – see DREAD FLIMSTONE AND THE MODERN TONE AGE FAMILY

NEW VAUDEVILLE BAND
UK group masterminded by songwriter/producer Geoff Stephens. Following the success of their debut single, a group was assembled with Alan Klein (born 29/6/1942, also known as Tristram), Henry Harrison (born 6/6/1943, Watford), Stan Haywood (born 23/8/1947, Dagenham), Robert 'Pops' Kerr (born 14/2/1943, London), Neil Korner (born 6/8/1942, Ashford), Hugh 'Shuggy' Watts (born 25/7/1941, Watford), Chris Eddy (born 4/3/1942) and Mick Wilsher (born 21/12/1945, Sutton).

08/09/1966	4	19		WINCHESTER CATHEDRAL ▲³ 1966 Grammy Award for Best Contemporary Rock & Roll Recording	Fontana TF 741
26/01/1967	7	11		PEEK-A-BOO NEW VAUDEVILLE BAND FEATURING TRISTRAM	Fontana TF 784
11/05/1967	11	9		FINCHLEY CENTRAL	Fontana TF 824
02/08/1967	37	4		GREEN STREET GREEN	Fontana TF 853

NEW VISION
US duo Samuel Morales and Albert Cabrerra.

29/01/2000	23	2		(JUST) ME AND YOU	AM:PM CDAMPM 128

NEW WORLD
Australian pop group formed by John 'Fuzz' Lee, John Kane and Mel Noonan after they won a TV talent contest.

27/02/1971	15	11		ROSE GARDEN	RAK 111
03/07/1971	6	15		TOM-TOM TURNAROUND	RAK 117
04/12/1971	17	13		KARA KARA	RAK 123
13/05/1972	9	13		SISTER JANE	RAK 130
12/05/1973	50	1		ROOF TOP SINGING	RAK 148

NEW YORK CITY
US R&B vocal group formed in the mid-1960s by John Brown (ex-The Five Satins), Tim McQueen, Edward Schell and Claude Johnson (born 17/5/1938) as Triboro Exchange, changing to New York City in 1972. Before becoming a singer, Johnson had been a jukebox revenue collector and later became an actor. Their backing band, the Big Apple Band, included future Chic members Nile Rodgers and Bernard Edwards. Schell died on 16/7/1997 at the age of 56.

21/07/1973	20	11		I'M DOING FINE NOW	RCA 2351

NEW YORK SKYY
US soul group formed in Brooklyn, NY by Solomon Roberts Jr (guitar/vocals), three sisters: Denise Dunning-Crawford (vocals), Delores Dunning-Milligan (vocals) and Bonnie Dunning (vocals), Anibal Anthony (guitar), Gerald La Bon (bass), Larry Greenberg (keyboards) and Tommy McConnel (drums). After backing Charles Earland on Let The Music Play, they signed with Salsoul and had a hit single (with the artist credit New York Skyy, to avoid confusion with Sky, in the UK), written and produced by Randy Muller.

16/01/1982	67	2		LET'S CELEBRATE	Epic EPC A 1898

NEWBEATS
US pop trio formed in Nashville, TN by Larry Henley (born 30/6/1941, Arp, TX), and brothers Dean (born 17/3/1939, Hahira, GA) and Marc Mathis (born 9/2/1942, Hahira). The group disbanded in 1974 and Henley concentrated on a solo career and later became a songwriter, penning Wind Beneath My Wings.

10/09/1964	15	9		BREAD AND BUTTER	Hickory 1269
23/10/1971	10	13		RUN BABY RUN Originally a hit in the US in 1965 (position #12)	London HL 10341

BOOKER NEWBURY III
US singer (born 19/1/1956, Youngstown, OH) who formed Sweet Thunder in 1975 and went solo in 1983.

28/05/1983	6	8		LOVE TOWN	Polydor POSP 613
08/10/1983	44	3		TEDDY BEAR	Polydor POSP 637

MICKEY NEWBURY
US singer (born Milton Newbury Jr, 19/5/1940, Houston, TX) who moved to Nashville, TN in 1963 and worked as a staff writer for publishers' Acuff-Rose before launching a singing career. He died on 28/9/2002.

01/07/1972	42	5		AMERICAN TRILOGY Medley of Dixie, Battle Hymn Of The Republic and All My Trials	Elektra K 12047

NEWCLEUS
US rap group formed in Brooklyn, NY by Ben 'Cozmo D' Cenad and his sister Yvette with Bob 'Chilly B' Crafton and his sister Monique.

03/09/1983	44	6		JAM ON REVENGE (THE WIKKI WIKKI SONG)	Beckett BKS 8

ANTHONY NEWLEY
UK singer/actor (born 24/9/1931, Hackney, London) who was a successful child actor. He starred in Vice Versa with Petula Clark and began his singing career after appearing in the film Idle On Parade, the story of a singer conscripted into the army (topical because of Terry Dene and Elvis Presley). He and Leslie Bricusse were successful songwriters, penning the lyrics to Goldfinger for Shirley Bassey, the film Willy Wonka And The Chocolate Factory and the musicals The Good Old Bad Old Days and Stop The World – I Want To Get Off (featuring What Kind Of Fool Am I?) as well as appearing in films such as Dr Doolittle. He was married to actress Joan Collins (their daughter Tara Newley released her debut record in 1994), and died from cancer on 14/4/1999.

01/05/1959	3	15		I'VE WAITED SO LONG Featured in the 1959 film Idle On Parade	Decca F 11127
08/05/1959	13	4		IDLE ON PARADE EP Tracks on EP: I've Waited So Long, Idle Rock-A-Boogie, Idle On Parade and Saturday Night Rock-A-Boogie	Decca DFE 6566

○ Silver disc ● Gold disc ✪ Platinum disc (additional platinum units are indicated by a figure following the symbol) ◉ Singles released prior to 1973 that are known to have sold over 1 million copies in the UK

DATE	POS	WKS	SINGLE TITLE	LABEL & NUMBER
12/06/1959	6	12	PERSONALITY	Decca F 11142
15/01/1960	❶⁴	18	WHY	Decca F 11194
24/03/1960	❶¹	15	DO YOU MIND	Decca F 11220
14/07/1960	4	15	IF SHE SHOULD COME TO YOU	Decca F 11254
24/11/1960	3	11	STRAWBERRY FAIR	Decca F 11295
16/03/1961	6	12	AND THE HEAVENS CRIED	Decca F 11331
15/06/1961	12	9	POP GOES THE WEASEL/BEE BOM	Decca F 11362
03/08/1961	36	8	WHAT KIND OF FOOL AM I? The song was featured in the musical *Stop The World I Want To Get Off* and won the 1962 Grammy Award for Song of the Year for writers Anthony Newley and Leslie Bricusse	Decca F 11376
25/01/1962	25	6	D-DARLING	Decca F 11419
26/07/1962	34	5	THAT NOISE	Decca F 11486

TARA NEWLEY – see E-ZEE POSSEE

BRAD NEWMAN UK singer and pianist (born Charles Melvyn Thomas, 1938, Yorkshire) who began his career as a member of The Kingpins. He died in Spain on 18/1/1999.

DATE	POS	WKS	SINGLE TITLE	LABEL & NUMBER
22/02/1962	47	1	SOMEBODY TO LOVE	Fontana H 357

DAVE NEWMAN UK singer whose debut hit was originally released in 1970. He made three further (unsuccessful) singles for Pye.

DATE	POS	WKS	SINGLE TITLE	LABEL & NUMBER
15/04/1972	34	6	THE LION SLEEPS TONIGHT	Pye 7N 45134

NEWS – see HUEY LEWIS AND THE NEWS

NEWS UK group: Trevor Midgley (guitar/vocals), Alan Quinn (bass/vocals), Ivor Dawmer (keyboards) and Roger Harrison (drums).

DATE	POS	WKS	SINGLE TITLE	LABEL & NUMBER
29/08/1981	52	3	AUDIO VIDEO	George 1

NEWTON UK singer from Manchester (born Billy Myers); he was a fireman before launching a singing career.

DATE	POS	WKS	SINGLE TITLE	LABEL & NUMBER
15/07/1995	56	2	SKY HIGH	Bags Of Fun BAGSCD 6
15/02/1997	32	3	SOMETIMES WHEN WE TOUCH	Dominion CDDMIN 202
16/08/1997	61	1	DON'T WORRY	Dominion CDDMIN 206

JUICE NEWTON US country singer (born Judy Kay Newton, 18/2/1952, New Jersey); raised in Virginia Beach and moving to Los Angeles in 1974 to form the Silver Spur band. They disbanded in 1978 and she went solo. She is an accomplished equestrian rider.

DATE	POS	WKS	SINGLE TITLE	LABEL & NUMBER
02/05/1981	43	6	ANGEL OF THE MORNING	Capitol CL 16189

OLIVIA NEWTON-JOHN UK singer (born 26/9/1948, Cambridge) who moved to Melbourne, Australia at the age of five. She won a talent contest in 1964; the prize was a trip to the UK but she postponed it for a year to finish school. She came over with Pat Carroll and performed as Pat & Olivia, remaining when Carroll's visa expired. She recorded her debut single in 1966 (for Decca), was a member of Toomorrow and in 1971 sang her first duet with Cliff Richard. She signed to Pye International (via Festival Records in Australia) in 1971 and appeared in the films *Grease* and *Xanadu*. It was revealed in 1992 that she had breast cancer. She has won four Grammy Awards including Best Country & Western Vocal Performance in 1973 for *Let Me Be There*. She was voted Female Vocalist of the Year in 1975 by the Country Music Association, the first UK artist to be afforded the honour. Not everyone in the CMA agreed and some members defected to form the Association of Country Entertainers. She has a star on the Hollywood Walk of Fame.

DATE	POS	WKS	BPI	SINGLE TITLE	LABEL & NUMBER
20/03/1971	7	11		IF NOT FOR YOU	Pye International 7N 25543
23/10/1971	6	17		BANKS OF THE OHIO	Pye International 7N 25568
11/03/1972	16	8		WHAT IS LIFE	Pye International 7N 25575
13/01/1973	15	13		TAKE ME HOME COUNTRY ROADS	Pye International 7N 25599
16/03/1974	11	8		LONG LIVE LOVE Britain's entry for the 1974 Eurovision Song Contest (came fourth)	Pye International 7N 25638
12/10/1974	22	6		I HONESTLY LOVE YOU ▲² 1974 Grammy Awards for Record of the Year and Best Pop Vocal Performance	EMI 2216
11/06/1977	6	11		SAM	EMI 2616
20/05/1978	❶⁹	26	✪	YOU'RE THE ONE THAT I WANT ▲¹	RSO 006
16/09/1978	❶⁷	19	✪	SUMMER NIGHTS This and above single credited to JOHN TRAVOLTA AND OLIVIA NEWTON-JOHN	RSO 18
04/11/1978	2	11	●	HOPELESSLY DEVOTED TO YOU This and above two singles featured in the 1978 film *Grease*	RSO 17
16/12/1978	4	12	○	A LITTLE MORE LOVE	EMI 2879
30/06/1979	64	3		DEEPER THAN THE NIGHT	EMI 2954
21/06/1980	❶²	11	○	XANADU OLIVIA NEWTON-JOHN AND ELECTRIC LIGHT ORCHESTRA	Jet 185
23/08/1980	32	7		MAGIC ▲⁴	Jet 196
25/10/1980	15	7		SUDDENLY OLIVIA NEWTON-JOHN AND CLIFF RICHARD This and above two singles featured in the 1980 film *Xanadu*	Jet 7002
10/10/1981	7	16	○	PHYSICAL ▲¹⁰ 1982 Grammy Award for Video of the Year	EMI 5234
16/01/1982	18	9		LANDSLIDE	EMI 5257
17/04/1982	43	3		MAKE A MOVE ON ME	EMI 5291
23/10/1982	46	4		HEART ATTACK	EMI 5347
15/01/1983	52	4		I HONESTLY LOVE YOU Re-issue of EMI 2216	EMI 5360
12/11/1983	57	2		TWIST OF FATE Featured in the 1983 film *Twist Of Fate*	EMI 5438
22/12/1990	3	10		THE GREASE MEGAMIX JOHN TRAVOLTA AND OLIVIA NEWTON-JOHN	Polydor PO 114
23/03/1991	47	2		GREASE – THE DREAM MIX FRANKIE VALLI, JOHN TRAVOLTA AND OLIVIA NEWTON-JOHN	PWL/Polydor PO 136

❶⁹ Number of weeks single topped the UK chart ↑ Entered the UK chart at #1 ▲⁹ Number of weeks single topped the US chart

	DATE	POS	WKS	BPI	SINGLE TITLE	LABEL & NUMBER
	04/07/1992	75	1		I NEED LOVE	Mercury MER 370
	09/12/1995	22	4		HAD TO BE CLIFF RICHARD AND OLIVIA NEWTON-JOHN	EMI CDEMS 410
	25/07/1998	4	9		YOU'RE THE ONE THAT I WANT JOHN TRAVOLTA AND OLIVIA NEWTON-JOHN Re-issue of RSO 006	Polydor 0441332

NEXT US R&B vocal group formed in Minneapolis, MN by Raphael 'Tweety' Brown (born 28/1/1977), his brother Terry 'T-Low' Brown (born 7/6/1974) and Robert 'R.L.' Huggar, the three having first met when they were part of the same gospel choir.

	06/06/1998	24	3		TOO CLOSE ▲5 Contains a sample of Kurtis Blow's *Christmas Rappin'* and the uncredited contribution of female vocalist Coffee Brown	Arista 74321580672
	16/09/2000	19	5		WIFEY	Arista 74321790912

NEXT OF KIN UK vocal group formed by brothers Kieran, Mark and Nathan Bass, who were thirteen, fifteen and eighteen respectively at the time of their debut hit. They were discovered by former Spice Girls manager Simon Fuller.

	20/02/1999	13	4		24 HOURS FROM YOU	Universal MCSTD 40201
	19/06/1999	33	2		MORE LOVE	Universal MCSTD 40207

NIAGRA UK DJ/production duo Mike Plaw and Chris Anslow.

	27/09/1997	65	1		CLOUDBURST	Freeflow FLOW CD2

NICE UK rock group formed in 1967 as PP Arnold's backing group before evolving into an autonomous band. They comprised Keith Emerson (born 2/11/1944, Todmorden, keyboards), Lee Jackson (born 8/1/1943, Newcastle-upon-Tyne, bass/vocals), Brian 'Blinky' Davison (born 25/5/1942, Leicester, guitar/vocals) and David O'List (born 13/12/1948, London, drums). O'List left in 1968; the remaining members continued as a trio until disbanding in 1970. Emerson then became a founding member of Emerson Lake & Palmer.

	10/07/1968	21	15		AMERICA This song is from the musical *West Side Story*	Immediate IM 068

PAUL NICHOLAS UK singer/actor (born Oscar Beuselinck, 3/12/1945, Peterborough) who was a pianist with the Savages in 1964 and later joined the musical *Hair* before going solo as Paul Dean. He changed his name briefly back to Oscar before settling on Paul Nicholas. A successful actor, he appeared in the TV series *Just Good Friends*, the musical *Cats* and the film *Sgt Pepper's Lonely Hearts Club Band*.

	17/04/1976	17	8		REGGAE LIKE IT USED TO BE	RSO 2090 185
	09/10/1976	8	9		DANCING WITH THE CAPTAIN	RSO 2090 206
	04/12/1976	9	11	○	GRANDMA'S PARTY	RSO 2090 216
	09/07/1977	40	3		HEAVEN ON THE 7TH FLOOR	RSO 2090 249

SUE NICHOLLS UK actress (born 23/11/1943, Walsall) who appeared in the TV series *Crossroads,* as Joan Greengross in *Reginald Perrin* and later as Audrey Roberts in the long-running *Coronation Street* (and in real life is married to former *Coronation Street* actor Mark Eden). Her full name is The Honourable Susan Frances Harmer-Nicholls, the daughter of a former Tory MP.

	03/07/1968	17	8		WHERE WILL YOU BE Featured in the TV series *Crossroads*	Pye 7N 17565

NICKELBACK Canadian rock group formed in Vancouver in 1996 by Chad Kroeger (guitar/vocals), his brother Mike (bass), Ryan Peake (guitar/vocals) and Ryan Vikedal (drums). Chad Kroeger later recorded solo on the soundtrack to *Spiderman*.

	23/02/2002	65	2		HOW YOU REMIND ME (IMPORT)	Roadrunner 23203323CD
	09/03/2002	4	21	●	HOW YOU REMIND ME	Roadrunner 23203325
	07/09/2002	9	9		TOO BAD	Roadrunner RR 20375
	07/12/2002	30	2		NEVER AGAIN	Roadrunner RR 20255
	27/09/2003	6	9		SOMEDAY Featured in 2004 the film *Torque*	Roadrunner RR 20088
	27/03/2004	39	2		FEELIN' WAY TOO DAMN GOOD	Roadrunner RR 39983

STEVIE NICKS US singer (born 26/5/1948, Phoenix, AZ) who was raised in California. After performing with San Francisco-based group Fritz she formed a duo with boyfriend Lindsey Buckingham and they both subsequently joined Fleetwood Mac in 1975. Nicks stopped touring with the group in 1990 and left in 1993, although she has made appearances with them since.

	15/08/1981	50	4		STOP DRAGGIN' MY HEART AROUND STEVIE NICKS WITH TOM PETTY AND THE HEARTBREAKERS	WEA K 79231
	25/01/1986	54	4		I CAN'T WAIT	Parlophone R 6110
	29/03/1986	68	2		TALK TO ME	Parlophone R 6124
	06/05/1989	16	7		ROOMS ON FIRE	EMI EM 90
	12/08/1989	60	2		LONG WAY TO GO	EMI EM 97
	11/11/1989	62	2		WHOLE LOTTA TROUBLE	EMI EM 114
	24/08/1991	40	4		SOMETIMES IT'S A BITCH	EMI EM 203
	09/11/1991	47	2		I CAN'T WAIT Re-issue of Parlophone R 6110	EMI EM 214
	02/07/1994	42	3		MAYBE LOVE	EMI CDEMS 328

NICOLE German singer (full name Nicole Hohloch) who came to prominence at the age of seventeen by winning the 1982 Eurovision Song Contest, beating Britain's entry by Bardo into seventh place.

	08/05/1982	❶2	9	○	A LITTLE PEACE The song won the 1982 Eurovision Song Contest	CBS A 2365
	21/08/1982	75	1		GIVE ME MORE TIME	CBS A 2467

NICOLE US R&B singer/songwriter (born Nicole McLeod, 1960, Rochester, NY).

	28/12/1985	41	7		NEW YORK EYES NICOLE WITH TIMMY THOMAS	Portrait A 6805
	26/12/1992	63	1		ROCK THE HOUSE SOURCE FEATURING NICOLE	React 12REACT 12
	06/07/1996	69	1		RUNNIN' AWAY	Ore AG 18CD

○ Silver disc ● Gold disc ✪ Platinum disc (additional platinum units are indicated by a figure following the symbol) ⓜ Singles released prior to 1973 that are known to have sold over 1 million copies in the UK

NICOLETTE UK singer born in Scotland and raised in Nigeria; she made her debut record for Shut Up And Dance in 1992.

23/12/1995.....67......1....... NO GOVERNMENT Contains a sample of Tom Waits' *Shore Leave* .... Talkin Loud TLCD 1

KURT NIELSEN Norwegian singer (born 29/9/1978, Bergren) who was the winner of the Norwegian TV talent contest *Pop Idol* and then went on to win the 2003 *World Idol* contest (a competition for all the international winners).

29/05/2004.....25......3....... SHE'S SO HIGH .... RCA 82876610882

NIGEL AND MARVIN Trinidad & Tobago duo formed by brothers Nigel and Marvin Lewis, ex-members of calypso band Charlie Roots.

18/05/2002 .....5......10...... **FOLLOW DA LEADER** Contains a sample of Chocolate Puma's *I Wanna Be U* .... Relentless RELENT 19CD

NIGHTBREED UK drum/bass act who also recorded for Frequency.

09/10/2004.....45......1....... PACK OF WOLVES .... Ram RAMM52CD

NIGHTCRAWLERS FEATURING JOHN REID UK instrumental/production duo Alysha Warren and John Reid.

15/10/1994.....22......5....... PUSH THE FEELING ON **NIGHTCRAWLERS** .... ffrr FCD 245
04/03/1995 ....3......11...... **PUSH THE FEELING ON (REMIX)** .... ffrr FCD 257
27/05/1995 .....7......7....... **SURRENDER YOUR LOVE** .... Final Vinyl 74321283982
09/09/1995.....13......4....... DON'T LET THE FEELING GO .... Final Vinyl 74321298822
20/01/1996.....23......4....... LET'S PUSH IT .... Final Vinyl 74321328142
20/04/1996.....34......2....... SHOULD I EVER (FALL IN LOVE) .... Arista 74321358072
27/07/1996.....30......2....... KEEP ON PUSHING OUR LOVE **NIGHTCRAWLERS FEATURING JOHN REID AND ALYSHA WARREN**............. Arista 74321390422
03/07/1999.....59......1....... NEVER KNEW LOVE **NIGHTCRAWLERS** .... Riverhorse RIVHCD 1

MAXINE NIGHTINGALE UK singer (born 2/11/1952, Wembley, London) who appeared in numerous stage musicals before going solo. She later recorded in the US.

01/11/1975 .....8......8....... **RIGHT BACK WHERE WE STARTED FROM** Featured in the films *Slap Shot* (1977) and *Starsky & Hutch* (2004) .... United Artists UP 36015
12/03/1977.....11......8....... LOVE HIT ME.. United Artists UP 36215

NIGHTMARES ON WAX UK dance duo George 'E.A.S.E.' Evelyn and Kevin 'Boy Wonder' Harper. Vocalist Desoto later joined the group.

27/10/1990.....38......5....... AFTERMATH/I'M FOR REAL... Warp WAP 6
26/06/1999.....63......1....... FINER.. Warp WAP 123CD

NIGHTWISH Finnish rock group formed in Kitee in 1997 by Tarja Turunen (vocals), Emppo Vuorinen (guitar), Sami Vanska (bass), Tuomas Holopainen (keyboards) and Jukka Nevalainen (drums).

09/10/2004.....60......1....... WISH I HAD AN ANGEL.. Nuclear Blast NB1336CD

NIGHTWRITERS US vocal/ instrumental duo formed in Chicago, IL by Henry Watson and Alan Walker.

23/05/1992.....51......2....... LET THE MUSIC USE YOU .... ffrreedom TABX 112

NIKKE? NICOLE! US rapper (born Nicole Miller).

01/06/1991.....73......1....... NIKKE DOES IT BETTER .... Love EVOL 5

MARKUS NIKOLAI German producer.

06/10/2001.....74......1....... BUSHES .... Southern Fried ECB 24CD

NILSSON US singer (born Harry Edward Nelson III, 15/6/1941, Brooklyn, NY) who moved to Los Angeles to work for the Security First National Bank as a supervisor, writing songs in his spare time. The Monkees recorded one of his songs in 1967 that prompted RCA to sign him the following year (although his biggest hits were scored with other writers' material). He effectively retired from the music industry in the 1980s to concentrate on other business interests, including a film distribution company, although he recorded sporadically throughout the decade. He suffered a heart attack in February 1993 and died on 15/1/1994 without having fully recovered.

27/09/1969.....23......15...... EVERYBODY'S TALKIN' Featured in the films *Midnight Cowboy* (1969) and *Forrest Gump* (1994). It won the 1969 Grammy Award for Best Solo Vocal Performance .... RCA 1876
05/02/1972 ....❶5.....20...... **WITHOUT YOU** ▲4 Featured in the films *Son Of Dracula* (1974) and *Casino* (1996). It won the 1972 Grammy Award for Best Pop Vocal Performance .... RCA 2165
03/06/1972.....42......5....... COCONUT Featured in the 1999 film *Practical Magic* .... RCA 2214
16/10/1976.....22......8....... WITHOUT YOU Re-issue of RCA 2165 .... RCA 2733
20/08/1977.....43......3....... ALL I THINK ABOUT IS YOU .... RCA PB 9104
19/02/1994.....47......4....... WITHOUT YOU Second re-issue of RCA 2165 .... RCA 74321193092

CHARLOTTE NILSSON Swedish singer (born Southern Sweden) whose debut hit won the Eurovision Song Contest in 1999, beating Britain's entry by Precious into twelfth place. Charlotte is lead singer with Wisex, a well-known dance orchestra in Sweden.

03/07/1999.....20......4....... TAKE ME TO YOUR HEAVEN The song won the 1999 Eurovision Song Contest.......................... Arista 74321686952

NINA AND FREDERICK Danish vocal duo, husband and wife Baron Frederick Jan Gustav Floris van Pallandt (born 14/5/1934, Copenhagen) and Baroness Nina Moller. They hosted their own TV series in the UK in the 1960s. They divorced in 1976. Frederick was shot to death by a robber on 15/5/1994. Nina was of the opinion that he had been the victim of a professional killing.

18/12/1959.....26......1....... MARY'S BOY CHILD.. Columbia DB 4375

❶9 Number of weeks single topped the UK chart ↑ Entered the UK chart at #1 ▲9 Number of weeks single topped the US chart

DATE	POS	WKS	BPI	SINGLE TITLE	LABEL & NUMBER
10/03/1960	46	2		LISTEN TO THE OCEAN	Columbia DB 4332
17/11/1960	3	10		**LITTLE DONKEY**	Columbia DB 4536
28/09/1961	43	3		LONGTIME BOY	Columbia DB 4703
05/10/1961	23	13		SUCU SUCU	Columbia DB 4632

NINA SKY US vocal duo formed in New York by twin sisters Nicole and Natalie Albino, who took their name from the first two letters of their names and to reflect their aspirations.

17/07/2004	6	11		**MOVE YA BODY** Contains samples of Full Force's *Can You Feel The Beat* and Cordell Burrell's *Coolie Dance Rhythm* .... Universal MCSTD40373	

NINE INCH NAILS US rock group formed in Cleveland, OH in 1988 and fronted by Michael Trent Reznor (born 17/5/1965, Mercer, PA). By the 1990s the group was effectively Reznor working as a solo artist in the studio and employing musicians for live dates. The group has won two Grammy Awards: Best Metal Performance with Vocal in 1992 for *Wish* and Best Metal Performance in 1995 for *Happiness In Slavery*.

14/09/1991	45	4		HEAD LIKE A HOLE	TVT IS 484
16/11/1991	35	2		SIN	TVT IS 508
09/04/1994	45	3		MARCH OF THE PIGS	TVT CID 592
18/06/1994	25	3		CLOSER	TVT CID 596
13/09/1997	43	1		THE PERFECT DRUG Featured in the 1997 film *The Lost Highway*	Interscope IND 95542
18/12/1999	39	2		WE'RE IN THIS TOGETHER	Island 4971832

999 UK rock group formed in London in 1977 by Nick Cash (born Keith Lucas, 6/5/1950, Gosport, guitar/vocals), Guy Days (guitar), John Watson (bass) and Pablo LaBrittain (drums). After a self-funded single release they signed with United Artists in late 1977 and issued their debut album in 1978. They also recorded for Radarscope and Polydor. Watson left in 1985 and was replaced by Danny Palmer.

25/11/1978	40	3		HOMICIDE	United Artists UP 36467
27/10/1979	69	2		FOUND OUT TOO LATE	Radar ADA 46
16/05/1981	71	1		OBSESSED	Albion ION 1011
18/07/1981	59	3		LIL RED RIDING HOOD	Albion ION 1017
14/11/1981	51	4		INDIAN RESERVATION	Albion ION 1023

911 UK vocal trio assembled in 1996 by Lee Brennan (born 27/9/1975, Carlisle), Simon 'Spike' Dawbarn (born 5/8/1974, Warrington) and Jimmy Constable (born 21/9/1973, Liverpool) after they won GMTV's 'Search for the next big thing' contest. Brennan later wentsolo.

11/05/1996	38	2		NIGHT TO REMEMBER	Ginga CDGINGA 1
10/08/1996	21	4		LOVE SENSATION Featured in the 1997 film *Casper – A Spirited Beginning*	Ginga CDGINGA 2
09/11/1996	10	8		**DON'T MAKE ME WAIT**	Ginga VSCDT 1618
22/02/1997	4	8		**THE DAY WE FIND LOVE**	Virgin VSCDG 1619
03/05/1997	3	7		**BODYSHAKIN'**	Virgin VSCDT 1634
12/07/1997	3	7		**THE JOURNEY**	Virgin VSCDT 1645
01/11/1997	5	10		**PARTY PEOPLE...FRIDAY NIGHT**	Ginga VSCDT 1658
04/04/1998	4	7		**ALL I WANT IS YOU**	Virgin VSCDT 1681
04/07/1998	10	9		**HOW DO YOU WANT ME TO LOVE YOU?**	Ginga VSCDT 1686
24/10/1998	2	13		**MORE THAN A WOMAN**	Virgin VSCDT 1707
23/01/1999	●1	9	○	**A LITTLE BIT MORE ↑**	Virgin VSCDT 1719
15/05/1999	3	7		**PRIVATE NUMBER**	Virgin VSCDT 1730
23/10/1999	13	3		WONDERLAND	Virgin VSCDT 1755

9.9 US R&B vocal group formed in Boston, MA by Leslie Jones, Wanda Perry and Margo Thunder. Thunder had previously recorded solo.

06/07/1985	53	3		ALL OF ME FOR ALL OF YOU	RCA PB 49951

NINE YARDS UK group formed by Wayne Beckford, Clevedon Buntyn and Ian Thomas.

21/11/1998	70	1		LONELINESS IS GONE	Virgin VSCDT 1696
10/04/1999	59	1		MATTER OF TIME	Virgin VSCDT 1723
28/08/1999	50	1		ALWAYS FIND A WAY	Virgin VSCDT 1746

1910 FRUITGUM CO US group formed in New Jersey by Mark Gutkowski (keyboards/vocals), Floyd Marcus (drums/vocals), Pat Karwan (guitar/vocals), Steve Mortkowitz (bass/vocals) and Frank Jeckell (guitar/vocals). They were part of the bubblegum explosion and were produced by Jerry Kasenetz and Jeff Katz, also responsible for Ohio Express. They took their name from a chewing-gum vending machine developed by the Mills Novelty Company — believed to be the first slot machine in the world. Gutkowski died in 1998.

20/03/1968	2	16		**SIMON SAYS**	Pye International 7N 25447

1927 Australian group formed by Eric Weidman (vocals), Garry Frost (guitar), Bill Frost (bass) and James Barton (drums), later adding Charlie Cole (keyboards) to the line-up. The group disbanded in 1993.

22/04/1989	46	6		THAT'S WHEN I THINK OF YOU	WEA YZ 351

98° US R&B vocal group formed in Cincinnati, OH by Jeff Timmons (born 30/4/1973, Canton, OH), Nick Lachey (born 9/11/1973, Harlan, KY), Drew Lachey (born Andrew Lachey, 8/8/1976, Cincinnati) and Justin Jeffre (born 25/2/1973, Mount Clemens, MI). Nick Lachey married fellow singer Jessica Simpson in 2002 (their marriage was the subject of the MTV documentary series *The Newlyweds*). Both Nick Lachey and Jeff Timmons launched solo careers during 2004 (although the group had not disbanded).

29/11/1997	66	1		INVISIBLE MAN	Motown 8607092

○ Silver disc ● Gold disc ✪ Platinum disc (additional platinum units are indicated by a figure following the symbol) ◎ Singles released prior to 1973 that are known to have sold over 1 million copies in the UK

31/10/1998.....51......1...... TRUE TO YOUR HEART **98 DEGREES FEATURING STEVIE WONDER** Featured in the 1998 Walt Disney film *Mulan*... Motown 8608832

13/03/1999.....36......2...... BECAUSE OF YOU .... Motown 8609012

11/03/2000.....10.....10...... **THANK GOD I FOUND YOU ▲**[1] **MARIAH CAREY FEATURING JOE & 98 DEGREES** Features the uncredited contribution of Trey Lorenz. In 2000 Seth Swirsky and Warryn Campbell filed a suit against the song's writers, James Harris III, Terry Lewis and Mariah, claiming they had infringed their copyright on *One Of Those Love Songs* recorded in 1998 by Xscape .... Columbia 6690582

11/03/2000.....29......2...... THE HARDEST THING .... Universal MCSTD 40228

02/12/2000.....61......1...... GIVE ME JUST ONE MORE NIGHT (UNA NOCHE) .... Universal MCSTD 40243

99TH FLOOR ELEVATORS UK dance group fronted by producer Tony De Vit.

12/08/1995.....28......2...... HOOKED.. Labello Dance LAD 18CD

30/03/1996.....37......2...... I'LL BE THERE This and above single credited to **99TH FLOOR ELEVATORS FEATURING TONY DE VIT**....... Labello Dance LAD 25CD2

08/04/2000.....66......1...... HOOKED (REMIX) .... Tripoli Trax TTRAX 061CD

NIO Irish singer/remixer Robert Medcalf (born 1985, London).

23/08/2003.....52......1...... DO YOU THINK YOU'RE SPECIAL? .... Echo ECSCX 132

NIRVANA UK/Irish psychedelic rock group formed in 1967 by Patrick Campbell-Lyons, George Alex Spyropoulos, Ray Singer, Brian Henderson, Michael Coe and Sylvia Schuster. They split in 1970, although Campbell-Lyons continued to record under the Nirvana name.

15/05/1968.....34......6...... RAINBOW CHASER .... Island WIP 6029

NIRVANA US rock group formed in Seattle, WA in 1987 by Kurt Cobain (born 20/2/1967, Hoquiam, WA, guitar/vocals), Kris Novoselic (born 16/5/1965, Seattle, bass) and Dale Crover (drums) as Skid Row. The name changed the same year firstly to Ed Ted & Fred, then to Fecal Matter and finally to Nirvana as it means 'the extinction of individuality and absorption into supreme spirit as Buddhist highest good.' They released their debut album in 1989 for Sub Pop and brought in drummer Dave Grohl (born 14/1/1969, Warren, OH) in 1990. They were named Best International Newcomers at the 1993 BRIT Awards. Cobain, who was married to Hole member Courtney Love, committed suicide on 5/4/1994 – his body wasn't discovered for three days. Nirvana won the 1995 Grammy Award for Best Alternative Music Performance for *MTV Unplugged In New York*. Grohl later formed The Foo Fighters.

30/11/1991 .....7......6....... **SMELLS LIKE TEEN SPIRIT** Featured in the film *1991: The Year That Punk Broke* .... DGC DGCS 5

14/03/1992 .....9......5....... **COME AS YOU ARE**.................................... DGC DGCS 7

25/07/1992.....11......6...... LITHIUM .... DGC DGCS 9

12/12/1992.....28......7...... IN BLOOM .... Geffen GFS 34

06/03/1993.....12......2...... OH THE GUILT Listed flip side was *Puss* by **JESUS LIZARD** .... Touch And Go TG 83CD

11/09/1993 .....5......5...... **HEART-SHAPED BOX** .... Geffen GFSTD 54

18/12/1993.....32......5...... ALL APOLOGIES/RAPE ME .... Geffen GFSTD 66

NITRO DELUXE US multi-instrumentalist Lee Junior recording under an assumed group name.

14/02/1987.....47......7...... THIS BRUTAL HOUSE .... Cooltempo COOL 142

13/06/1987.....62......4...... THIS BRUTAL HOUSE (REMIX) .... Cooltempo COOL 142

06/02/1988.....24......5...... LET'S GET BRUTAL .... Cooltempo COOL 142

NITZER EBB UK group formed by Douglas McCarthy (born 1/9/1966, Chelmsford, vocals) and Bon Harris (born 12/8/1965, Chelmsford, drums/vocals), with David Gooday an early member. Gooday left in 1988 and was replaced by Julian Beeston.

11/01/1992.....56......1...... GODHEAD .... Mute 1MUTE 135T

11/04/1992.....52......1...... ASCEND .... Mute CDMUTE 145

04/03/1995.....75......1...... KICK IT .... Mute LCDMUTE 155

NIVEA US singer (born Nivea Hamilton, 1982, Atlanta, GA).

03/03/2001.....28......3...... DANGER (BEEN SO LONG) **MYSTIKAL FEATURING NIVEA**.................... Jive 9251722

04/05/2002.....48......1...... RUN AWAY (I WANNA BE WITH U)/DON'T MESS WITH THE RADIO .... Jive 9253362

21/09/2002.....41......2...... DON'T MESS WITH MY MAN **NIVEA FEATURING BRIAN AND BRANDON CASEY** .... Jive 9254082

10/05/2003.....33......2...... LAUNDROMAT/DON'T MESS WITH MY MAN.......................... Jive 9254822

NKOTB – see NEW KIDS ON THE BLOCK

NO AUTHORITY US vocal group formed in California by Ricky Felix, Josh Keaton, Eric Stretch and Danny Zavatsky.

14/03/1998.....54......1....... DON'T STOP Contains a sample of Teddy Riley's *Don't Stop* .... Epic 6655592

NO DICE UK group formed by Roger Ferris (vocals), Dave Martin (guitar/vocals), Gary Strange (bass) and Chris Wyles (drums). Ferris and Strange later formed Shooting Party.

05/05/1979.....65......2...... COME DANCING .... EMI 2927

NO DOUBT US rock group formed in Anaheim, CA in 1986 by John Spence (born 1969, Orange County, CA, vocals), Eric Stefani (keyboards), Tony Kanal (born 27/8/1970, bass), Adrian Young (born 26/8/1969, drums) and Tom Dumont (born 11/1/1968, guitar). Spence committed suicide on 21/12/1987 by shooting himself in the head and was initially replaced by Alan Meade and then Gwen Stefani (born 3/10/1969, Anaheim). Stefani later recorded with Eve and won the 2001 Grammy Award for Best Rap/Sung Performance for *Let Me Blow Ya Mind*.

26/10/1996.....38......2....... JUST A GIRL... Interscope IND 80034

22/02/1997 ....❶[3].....18 .....● **DON'T SPEAK** ↑ .... Interscope IND 95515

05/07/1997 .....3 ......7....... **JUST A GIRL** Re-issue of Interscope IND 80034 .... Interscope IND 95539

❶[9] Number of weeks single topped the UK chart ↑ Entered the UK chart at #1 ▲[9] Number of weeks single topped the US chart

04/10/1997	16	3		SPIDERWEBS	Interscope IND 95551
20/12/1997	50	3		SUNDAY MORNING	Interscope IND 95566
12/06/1999	30	2		NEW Featured in the 1999 film *Go*	Higher Ground HIGHS 22CD
25/03/2000	23	3		EX-GIRLFRIEND	Interscope 4972992
07/10/2000	69	1		SIMPLE KIND OF LIFE	Interscope 4974162
16/02/2002	2	9		**HEY BABY** 2002 Grammy Award for Best Pop Performance By A Duo Or Group With Vocal. Featured in the 2004 film *New York Minute*	Interscope 4976682
15/06/2002	12	7		HELLA GOOD	Interscope 4977362
12/10/2002	18	5		UNDERNEATH IT ALL 2003 Grammy Award for Best Pop Performance by a Duo or Group with Vocal	Interscope 4977792
06/12/2003	20	7		IT'S MY LIFE	Interscope 9813724
13/03/2004	17	7		IT'S MY LIFE/BATHWATER A-side re-issue of Interscope 9813724	Interscope 9861993

NO MERCY
US group featuring Marty Cintron on lead vocals and twins Ariel and Gabriel Hernandez. The group originally worked as waiters in Gloria Estefan's restaurant.

18/01/1997	2	15	●	**WHERE DO YOU GO** Featured in the 1998 film *A Night At The Roxbury*	Arista 74321401502
24/05/1997	4	7		**PLEASE DON'T GO**	Arista 74321481372
06/09/1997	16	4		KISS YOU ALL OVER	Arista 74321514452

NO ONE DRIVING – see NOVACANE VS NO ONE DRIVING

NO REASON
UK vocal group formed in Scotland by Craig Chalmers, Paul Martin, Tony Elliott and Craig Cavanah. Chalmers had previously been a contestant on *Pop Idol* while Elliott had been a professional footballer with East Stirling and Kilmarnock.

11/09/2004	53	1		MAN LIKE ME	Mad As Toast TOAST001

NO SWEAT
Irish group formed in Dublin by Paul Quinn (vocals), Dave Gooding (guitar), Jim Phillips (guitar), PJ Smith (keyboards), Jon Angel (bass) and Ray Fearn (drums).

13/10/1990	64	4		HEART AND SOUL	London LON 274
02/02/1991	61	1		TEAR DOWN THE WALLS	London LON 257

NO WAY JOSE
US group formed by Jose (guitar/vocals), Flaco (bass) and Al Pastor (drums).

03/08/1985	47	6		TEQUILA	Fourth & Broadway BRW 28

NO WAY SIS
US tribute group to Oasis formed by Joel McKay, Gerry McKay, James McLardy, Tony McCarthy and Mick Reilly.

21/12/1996	27	4		I'D LIKE TO TEACH THE WORLD TO SING	EMI CDEM 461

NODDY
UK cartoon character created by Enid Blyton (born 11/8/1897, died in 1968). The vocals on the hit were supplied by Caroline Gill, Carrie Mullan and Alison Orbaum.

20/12/2003	29	4		MAKE WAY FOR NODDY	BMG 82876582142

NODESHA
US female singer (born 1985, San Bernardino, CA).

06/09/2003	5	7		**MISS PERFECT** ABS FEATURING NODESHA	BMG 82876556742
01/11/2003	55	1		GET IT WHILE IT'S HOT Contains a sample of Chic's *I Want Your Love*	Arista 82876559592

NOISE NEXT DOOR
UK group formed in Portsmouth by triplets Scott, Ed and Craig Sutton.

06/11/2004	12	4		LOCK UP YA DAUGHTERS/MINISTRY OF MAYHEM	Us & Them USTHEMS10

BERNIE NOLAN
Irish singer/actress (born 17/10/1960) who was a member of The Nolans with her sisters before launching an acting career, appearing in *Brookside* as Diane Murray and *The Bill* as Sgt Shelagh Murphy. Her debut hit originally appeared in the *The Bill*.

06/03/2004	38	3		MACUSHLA	Laurel Bank 4KATECD1

NOLANS
Irish group formed by sisters Anne (born 12/11/1950), Denise (born 1952), Linda (born 23/2/1959), Bernadette (born 17/10/1961) and Maureen Nolan (born 14/6/1954). Denise left the group in 1978 to go solo. Anne left the group to get married and was replaced by Coleen (born 12/3/1965). Anne returned and the group became a quintet for a while until Linda left to get married.

06/10/1979	34	6		SPIRIT BODY AND SOUL NOLAN SISTERS	Epic EPC 7796
22/12/1979	3	15	●	**I'M IN THE MOOD FOR DANCING**	Epic EPC 8068
12/04/1980	12	11		DON'T MAKE WAVES	Epic EPC 8349
13/09/1980	9	13	○	**GOTTA PULL MYSELF TOGETHER**	Epic EPC 8878
06/12/1980	12	11		WHO'S GONNA ROCK YOU	Epic EPC 9325
14/03/1981	9	13	○	**ATTENTION TO ME**	Epic EPC 9571
15/08/1981	15	8		CHEMISTRY	Epic EPC A 1485
20/02/1982	14	12		DON'T LOVE ME TOO HARD	Epic EPC A 1927
01/04/1995	51	1		I'M IN THE MOOD FOR DANCING Re-recording	Living Beat LBECD 31

NOMAD
UK duo formed by songwriter/producer/keyboard player Damon Rochefort (from Cardiff, South Glamorgan) and vocalist Sharon Dee Clarke, who previously recorded as FPI Project. Nomad is Damon spelt backwards. Rochefort also recorded as Spirits.

02/02/1991	2	10	○	**(I WANNA GIVE YOU) DEVOTION** NOMAD FEATURING MC MIKEE FREEDOM	Rumour RUMA 25
04/05/1991	16	6		JUST A GROOVE	Rumour RUMA 33
28/09/1991	73	1		SOMETHING SPECIAL	Rumour RUMA 35

○ Silver disc   ● Gold disc   ✪ Platinum disc (additional platinum units are indicated by a figure following the symbol)   ◎ Singles released prior to 1973 that are known to have sold over 1 million copies in the UK

25/04/1992.....60......2.......	YOUR LOVE IS LIFTING ME...	Rumour RUMA 48
07/11/1992.....61......1.......	24 HOURS A DAY	Rumour RUMA 60
25/11/1995.....42......2.......	(I WANNA GIVE YOU) DEVOTION (REMIX).................................	Rumour RUMACD 75

NONCHALANT US singer/songwriter (born Tanya Pointer, Washington DC).

29/06/1996.....44......1.......	5 O'CLOCK	MCA MCSTD 48011

PETER NOONE
UK singer (born 5/11/1947, Davyhulme) who appeared in TV's *Coronation Street* before becoming lead vocalist with Herman's Hermits in 1963. He left to go solo in 1971, briefly reuniting with the group in 1973. He later returned to acting, appearing in the American TV series *Quantum Leap*.

14/11/1970.....13.....12......	LADY BARBARA PETER NOONE AND HERMAN'S HERMITS.........................	RAK 106
22/05/1971.....12......9.......	OH YOU PRETTY THING	RAK 114

NOOTROPIC UK instrumental/production duo Rich Dekkard and Spencer Williams, with singer Ruth Campbell.

16/03/1996.....42......1.......	I SEE ONLY YOU	Hi-Life 5779832

KEN NORDENE – see BILLY VAUGHN AND HIS ORCHESTRA

N.O.R.E.
US rapper (born Victor Santiago, New York City) who is a member of Capone-N-Noreaga. He won the 1998 MOBO Award for Best International Hip Hop Act.

21/09/2002.....11......7.......	NOTHIN'..	Def Jam 639262
29/11/2003.....55......1.......	CRASHIN' A PARTY LUMIDEE FEATURING NORE..............................	Universal MCSTD 40341
22/05/2004.....72......1.......	NOTHIN'..	Def Jam 639262

CHRIS NORMAN – see SUZI QUATRO

NORTH AND SOUTH
UK group formed by Lee Otter (vocals), Samuel Chapman (keyboards), James Hurst (guitar) and Thomas Lowe (keyboards/saxophone).

17/05/1997 .....7......5.......	I'M A MAN NOT A BOY	RCA 74321461142
09/08/1997.....18......5.......	TARANTINO'S NEW STAR	RCA 74321501242
08/11/1997.....27......2.......	BREATHING	RCA 74321528422
04/04/1998.....29......4.......	NO SWEAT '98	RCA 74321562212

NORTHERN HEIGHTZ
UK production group formed by Pez Tellett, Ian Bland and Martin Neary with singer Katie Halliday. They previously recorded as PNK.

20/03/2004.....29......3.......	LOOK AT US..	Iconic CDXIC002

NORTHERN LINE UK vocal group formed by Dan, Zak, Michael, Andy and Warren.

09/10/1999.....18......4.......	RUN FOR YOUR LIFE	Global Talent GTR 002CDS1
11/03/2000.....15......5.......	LOVE ON THE NORTHERN LINE	Global Talent GTR 003CDS1
17/06/2000.....27......3.......	ALL AROUND THE WORLD	Global Talent GTR 004CDS1

NORTHERN UPROAR
UK rock group formed in Manchester by Leon Meya (born 31/5/1978, bass/vocals), Paul Kelly (born 19/9/1977, guitar), Jeff Fletcher (born 14/12/1977, guitar) and Keith Chadwick (born 30/5/1977, drums).

21/10/1995.....41......2.......	ROLLERCOASTER/ROUGH BOYS..	Heavenly HVN 047CD
03/02/1996.....17......3.......	FROM A WINDOW/THIS MORNING...	Heavenly HVN 051CD
20/04/1996.....24......2.......	LIVIN' IT UP	Heavenly HVN 52CD
22/06/1996.....48......1.......	TOWN	Heavenly HVN 54CD
07/06/1997.....36......2.......	ANY WAY YOU LOOK	Heavenly HVN 70CD
23/08/1997.....63......1.......	A GIRL I ONCE KNEW	Heavenly HVN 73CD

NORTHSIDE UK group: Warren 'Dermo' Dermody (vocals), Cliff Ogier (bass), Timmy Walsh (guitar) and Paul Walsh (drums).

09/06/1990.....50......5.......	SHALL WE TAKE A TRIP/MOODY PLACES	Factory FAC 268
03/11/1990.....32......3.......	MY RISING STAR	Factory FAC 2987
01/06/1991.....40......4.......	TAKE 5	Factory FAC 3087

FREDDIE NOTES AND THE RUDIES
Jamaican reggae group formed by Freddie Notes and Danny Smith. They originally backed Dandy Livingstone before launching their own career. They subsequently evolved into Greyhound, although Notes left in the early 1970s and was replaced by Glenroy Oakley.

10/10/1970.....45......2.......	MONTEGO BAY	Trojan TR 7791

NOTORIOUS B.I.G.
US rapper (born Christopher Wallace, 21/5/1972, Brooklyn, NY) also known as Biggy Smallz. He originally recorded with rap group OGB and was then discovered by Mister Cee and subsequently signed by Puff Daddy. He was shot dead on 9/3/1997 after attending the *Soul Train* awards in circumstances similar to those of 2Pac, prompting rumours of a feud between East and West Coast rapping crews (recent evidence suggests possible involvement of the Los Angeles Police Department in his death).

29/10/1994.....72......1.......	JUICY	Bad Boy 74321240102
01/04/1995.....63......1.......	BIG POPPA Contains a sample of The Isley Brothers' *Between The Sheets*	Puff Daddy 74321263412
15/07/1995.....43......2.......	CAN'T YOU SEE TOTAL FEATURING THE NOTORIOUS B.I.G. Featured in the 1995 film *New Jersey Drive*.......	Tommy Boy TBCD 700
19/08/1995.....34......2.......	ONE MORE CHANCE/STAY WITH ME Contains a sample of DeBarge's *Stay With Me*	Puff Daddy 74321300782

❶⁹ Number of weeks single topped the UK chart ↑ Entered the UK chart at #1 ▲⁹ Number of weeks single topped the US chart

577

03/05/1997.....10......4.......	**HYPNOTIZE ▲³** Contains samples of Slick Rick's *La Di Da Di* and Herb Alpert's *Rise* .... Puff Daddy 74321466412
09/08/1997.....6......10.......	**MO MONEY MO PROBLEMS ▲²** THE NOTORIOUS B.I.G. FEATURING PUFF DADDY AND MA$E Contains a sample of Diana Ross' *I'm Coming Out* .... Puff Daddy 74321492492
14/02/1998.....35......2.......	SKY'S THE LIMIT THE NOTORIOUS B.I.G. FEATURING 112 .... Puff Daddy 74321587992
18/07/1998.....15......3.......	RUNNIN' 2PAC AND THE NOTORIOUS B.I.G. Contains a sample of Bobby Caldwell's *My Flame* .... Black Jam BJAM 9005
05/02/2000.....16......5.......	NOTORIOUS B.I.G. NOTORIOUS B.I.G. FEATURING PUFF DADDY AND LIL' KIM Contains a sample of Duran Duran's *Notorious* .... Puff Daddy 74321737312
31/01/2004.....17......6.......	RUNNIN' (DYIN' TO LIVE) 2PAC AND THE NOTORIOUS B.I.G. .... Interscope 9815329

NOTTINGHAM FOREST FC AND PAPER LACE
UK football club formed in 1865; their hit record was released to coincide with an appearance in the League Cup final. Musical accompaniment was provided by local hitmakers Paper Lace.

04/03/1978.....24......6.......	WE'VE GOT THE WHOLE WORLD IN OUR HANDS .... Warner Brothers K 17110

HEATHER NOVA
US singer/guitarist born on an island in the Bermuda Sound and raised on a sailboat in the Caribbean. She later relocated to London.

25/02/1995.....69......1.......	WALK THIS WORLD .... Butterfly BFLD 19

NANCY NOVA
UK singer who previously recorded for Siamese.

04/09/1982.....63......2.......	NO NO NO. .... EMI 5328

NOVACANE VS NO ONE DRIVING
German production team of Trancey Spacer and Spacey Trancer, although in reality it was the work of Jam El Mar and DJ Mark Spoon. They also record as Tokyo Ghetto Pussy, Storm and Jam And Spoon.

15/06/2002.....69......1.......	LOVE BE MY LOVER (PLAYA SOL) .... Direction 6727792

NOVASPACE
German producer Felix Gauder who was previously responsible for E-Rotic.

22/02/2003.....29......3.......	TIME AFTER TIME. .... Substance SUBS 15CDS

TOM NOVY
German producer/DJ (born in Munich) who first recorded for Kosmotune in 1995.

02/05/1998.....32......3.......	SUPERSTAR .... D:disco 74321569352
03/06/2000.....19......3.......	PUMPIN' This and above single credited to NOVY VS ENIAC. .... Positiva CDTIVS 132
02/09/2000.....55......1.......	I ROCK TOM NOVY FEATURING VIRGINIA .... Rulin 3CDS
04/08/2001.....64......1.......	NOW OR NEVER TOM NOVY FEATURING LIMA .... Rulin 14CDS

NRG
UK DJ/production duo Neil Rumney and Paul Lundon.

29/03/1997.....71......1.......	NEVER LOST HIS HARDCORE .... Top Banana TOPCD 04
12/12/1998.....61......1.......	NEVER LOST HIS HARDCORE (REMIX). .... Top Banana TOPCD 010
20/03/2004.....59......1.......	NEVER LOST HIS HARDCORE Second remix. .... Tidy Trax TIDY200T2

NT GANG
German vocal/instrumental group.

02/04/1988.....71......1.......	WAM BAM .... Cooltempo COOL 163

NU-BIRTH
UK production duo Danny Harrison and Julian Jonah (born Danny Matlock). They also recorded as Congress, Nush, Stella Browne, Gant, M Factor, Reflex and 187 Lockdown.

06/09/1997.....48......1.......	ANYTIME .... XL Recordings XLS 85CD
06/06/1998.....41......1.......	ANYTIME Re-issue of XL Recordings XLS 85CD .... Locked On LOX 97CD

NU CIRCLES FEATURING EMMA B
UK dance duo Andy Lysandrou and Emma Blocksage. Lysandrou also records as Truesteppers and is a member of 5050, while Emma B came to prominence as a model and radio DJ.

08/02/2003.....46......1.......	WHAT YOU NEED (TONIGHT) .... East West EW 258CD

NU COLOURS
UK R&B vocal group formed by Lawrence Johnson, Fay Simpson, Lain Grey, Patricia Knight and Carol Riley.

06/06/1992.....55......2.......	TEARS .... Wild Card CARD 1
10/10/1992.....64......1.......	POWER .... Wild Card CARD 3
05/06/1993.....57......2.......	WHAT IN THE WORLD .... Wild Card CARDD 4
27/11/1993.....40......2.......	POWER (REMIX). .... Wild Card CARDD 5
25/05/1996.....31......2.......	DESIRE .... Wild Card 5763652
24/08/1996.....38......2.......	SPECIAL KIND OF LOVER .... Wild Card 5752012

NU GENERATION
UK producer Aston Harvey who is also a member of the Freestylers.

29/01/2000.....8......8.......	**IN YOUR ARMS (RESCUE ME)** Contains a sample of Fontella Bass' *Rescue Me* .... Concept CDCON 7
21/10/2000.....66......1.......	NOWHERE TO RUN 2000 Contains a sample of Martha Reeves' *Nowhere To Run* .... Concept CDCON 16

NU MATIC
UK instrumental/production duo fronted by Matthew Edwards.

08/08/1992.....58......1.......	SPRING IN MY STEP .... XL Recordings XLS 31

NU SHOOZ
US duo formed in Portland, OR by husband and wife John Smith and Valerie Day.

24/05/1986.....2......14.....○	**I CAN'T WAIT** .... Atlantic A 9446
26/07/1986.....48......3.......	POINT OF NO RETURN .... Atlantic A 9392

○ Silver disc ● Gold disc ✪ Platinum disc (additional platinum units are indicated by a figure following the symbol) ◉ Singles released prior to 1973 that are known to have sold over 1 million copies in the UK

NU SOUL FEATURING KELLI RICH US vocal/instrumental duo Spike Rebel (born Carnell Condon Newbill) and Kelli Richardson.

13/01/1996	27	2		HIDE-A-WAY	ffrr FCD 269

NUANCE FEATURING VIKKI LOVE US vocal/instrumental group fronted by Vikki Love who later went solo.

19/01/1985	59	3		LOVERIDE	Fourth & Broadway BRW 20

NUBIAN JUICE – see POWERCUT FEATURING NUBIAN PRINCE

NUFF JUICE – see D MOB

NUKLEUZ DJ's UK techno group formed by Dave Randall and BK (full name Ben Keen).

24/08/2002	40	2		DJ NATION	Nukleuz NUKFB 0440
08/02/2003	33	2		DJ NATION (BOOTLEG EDITION)	Nukleuz 0468 FNUK
09/08/2003	59	2		SUMMER EDITION DJ NATION	Nukleuz 0542 FNUK
15/11/2003	48	3		DJ NATION - HARDER EDITION	Nukleuz 0572 FBNUK
17/01/2004	63	2		DJ NATION (BOOTLEG EDITION)	Nukleuz 0468 FNUK
27/03/2004	52	3		X-RATED DJ NATION	Amato 0501FBNUK

GARY NUMAN UK singer (born Gary Anthony James Webb, 8/3/1958, London) who formed Tubeway Army in 1977, with Paul 'Scarlett' Gardiner (bass) and Gerald 'Rael' Lidyard (drums). Numan quit his job with WH Smith on the day his debut release was issued in 1978. He formed the Numa label in 1984. A keen aviator, he attempted to fly around the world in his light aircraft in 1982 but was arrested in India on suspicion of spying. The charge was later dropped. Gardiner died from a drug overdose on 4/2/1984.

DATE	POS	WKS	BPI	SINGLE TITLE	LABEL & NUMBER
19/05/1979	❶4	16	●	ARE 'FRIENDS' ELECTRIC? TUBEWAY ARMY	Beggars Banquet BEG 18
01/09/1979	❶1	11	●	CARS	Beggars Banquet BEG 23
24/11/1979	6	9	○	COMPLEX	Beggars Banquet BEG 29
24/05/1980	5	7		WE ARE GLASS	Beggars Banquet BEG 35
30/08/1980	6	7		I DIE: YOU DIE	Beggars Banquet BEG 46
20/12/1980	20	7		THIS WRECKAGE	Beggars Banquet BEG 50
29/08/1981	6	6		SHE'S GOT CLAWS Features guest appearances by Mick Karn and Roger Taylor (of Queen)	Beggars Banquet BEG 62
05/12/1981	33	7		LOVE NEEDS NO DISGUISE GARY NUMAN AND DRAMATIS	Beggars Banquet BEG 33
06/03/1982	19	7		MUSIC FOR CHAMELEONS	Beggars Banquet BEG 70
19/06/1982	9	4		WE TAKE MYSTERY (TO BED)	Beggars Banquet BEG 77
28/08/1982	20	4		WHITE BOYS AND HEROES	Beggars Banquet BEG 81
03/09/1983	20	5		WARRIORS	Beggars Banquet BEG 95
22/10/1983	32	3		SISTER SURPRISE	Beggars Banquet BEG 101
03/11/1984	32	5		BERSERKER	Numa NU 4
22/12/1984	66	1		MY DYING MACHINE	Numa NU 6
09/02/1985	17	8		CHANGE YOUR MIND (Bill) SHARPE AND NUMAN	Polydor POSP 722
25/05/1985	27	4		THE LIVE EP Tracks on EP: Are 'Friends' Electric, Berserker and We Are Glass	Numa NUM 7
10/08/1985	46	5		YOUR FASCINATION	Numa NU 9
21/09/1985	49	2		CALL OUT THE DOGS	Numa NU 11
16/11/1985	49	3		MIRACLES	Numa NU 13
19/04/1986	28	3		THIS IS LOVE	Numa NU 16
28/06/1986	27	4		I CAN'T STOP	Numa NU 17
04/10/1986	52	3		NEW THING FROM LONDON TOWN	Numa NU 19
06/12/1986	74	1		I STILL REMEMBER	Numa NU 21
28/03/1987	35	6		RADIO HEART	GFM 109
13/06/1987	48	2		LONDON TIMES This and above single credited to RADIO HEART FEATURING GARY NUMAN	GFM 112
19/09/1987	16	7		CARS (E REG MODEL)/ARE 'FRIENDS' ELECTRIC? (REMIX)	Beggars Banquet BEG 199
30/01/1988	34	3		NO MORE LIES SHARPE AND NUMAN	Polydor POSP 894
01/10/1988	46	2		NEW ANGER	Illegal ILS 1003
03/12/1988	49	1		AMERICA	Illegal ILS 1004
03/06/1989	44	2		I'M ON AUTOMATIC SHARPE AND NUMAN	Polydor PO 43
16/03/1991	43	2		HEART	IRS NUMAN 1
21/03/1992	68	1		THE SKIN GAME	Numa NU 23
01/08/1992	72	1		MACHINE + SOUL	Numa NUM 124
04/09/1993	53	1		CARS (2ND REMIX)	Beggars Banquet BEG 264CD
16/03/1996	19	4		CARS (PREMIER MIX) Re-issue of Beggars Banquet BEG 264CD and revived following use in a TV advertisement for Carling Premier Lager	Polygram TV PRMCD 1
13/07/2002	29	2		RIP	Jagged Halo JHCD5
05/07/2003	13	3		CRAZIER GARY NUMAN VS RICO	Jagged Halo JHCDX6

❶9 Number of weeks single topped the UK chart ↑ Entered the UK chart at #1 ▲9 Number of weeks single topped the US chart

NUMBER ONE CUP US group formed in Chicago, IL by Seth Cohen (guitar/vocals), Patrick O'Connell (guitar) and Michael Lenzi (drums). They later added Jenni Snyder (bass). Snyder was subsequently replaced by John Przyborowski and then Kurt Volk.

02/03/1996.....61......1....... DIVEBOMB Featured in the 1995 film *Learning Curves* .... Blue Rose BRRC 10032

JOSE NUNEZ FEATURING OCTAHVIA US DJ and producer with singer Octahvia Lambert who later became a member of Choo Choo Project.

05/09/1998.....56......1....... IN MY LIFE .... Ministry Of Sound MOSCDS 126
05/06/1999.....44......1....... HOLD ON .... Ministry Of Sound MOSCDS 130

BOBBY NUNN US R&B singer/songwriter/keyboard player (born Buffalo, NY) who later relocated to Los Angeles where he formed Splendor, although they disbanded after one album and Nunn signed a solo deal with Motown. He died on 5/11/1986.

04/02/1984.....65......3....... DON'T KNOCK IT (UNTIL YOU TRY IT) .... Motown TMG 1323

NUSH UK production duo Danny Harrison and Julian Jonah (born Danny Matlock). They also record as Congress, Gant, Nu-Birth, Stella Browne, M Factor, Reflex and 187 Lockdown.

23/07/1994.....58......1....... U GIRLS .... Blunted Vinyl BLNCDX 006
22/04/1995.....46......2....... MOVE THAT BODY .... Blunted Vinyl BLNCD 012
16/09/1995.....15......4....... U GIRLS (LOOK SO SEXY) (REMIX) .... Blunted Vinyl BLNCD 13

NUT UK singer (born in Northumberland to Russian parents); Nut is her real name and she was named after an Egyptian god.

08/06/1996.....64......1....... BRAINS .... Epic NUTCD 2
21/09/1996.....56......1....... CRAZY .... Epic NUTCD 5
11/01/1997.....43......2....... SCREAM .... Epic NUTCD 6

NUTTIN' NYCE US R&B vocal group formed in Sacramento, CA by Eboni Foster, Onnie Ponder and Teece Wallace. Foster later recorded solo.

10/06/1995.....62......1....... DOWN 4 WHATEVA Contains a sample of Soul II Soul's *Back To Life*. Featured in the 1995 film *A Low Down Dirty Shame* .... Jive JIVECD 365
12/08/1995.....68......1....... FROGGY STYLE Contains samples of Yarbrough & Peoples' *Don't Stop The Music*, George Clinton's *Atomic Dog* and The Gap Band's *Shake* .... Jive JIVECD 381

NUYORICAN SOUL US R&B group formed by Masters At Work (Little Louie Vega and Kenny 'Dope' Gonzalez) and featuring Roy Ayers, George Benson, Jocelyn Brown, Jazzy Jeff, India, Vincent Montana Jr, Eddie Palmieri and Tito Puente.

08/02/1997.....24......6....... RUNAWAY NUYORICAN SOUL FEATURING INDIA .... Talkin Loud TLCD 20
10/05/1997.....26......2....... IT'S ALRIGHT, I FEEL IT! .... Talkin Loud TLCD 22
25/10/1997.....31......2....... I AM THE BLACK GOLD OF THE SUN This and above single credited to NUYORICAN SOUL FEATURING JOCELYN BROWN .... Talkin Loud TLCD 26

NWA US rap group formed in Compton, Los Angeles, CA in 1987 by Ice Cube (born O'Shea Jackson, 15/6/1969, Los Angeles), Eric 'Eazy-E' Wright (born 7/9/1964, Compton), MC Ren (born Lorenzo Patterson, 16/6/1966, Los Angeles), Dr Dre (born Andre Young, 18/2/1965, Los Angeles) and DJ Yella (born Antoine Carraby, 11/12/1967, Los Angeles). Ice Cube, Dr Dre and Eazy-E all released solo recordings. The group's name stands for Niggaz With Attitude (although according to some sources it stands for No Whiteboys Allowed). Eazy-E died from an AIDS-related illness on 26/3/1995. The group's 1991 album *EFIL4ZAGGIN* (Niggaz4Life spelt backwards) was seized by the British government under the Obscene Publications Act. Distributors Island Records went to court in order to get the ban overturned and were represented by Geoffrey Robertson QC, who had previously represented the infamous magazine *Oz* in 1971.

09/09/1989.....50......4....... EXPRESS YOURSELF .... Fourth & Broadway BRW 144
26/05/1990.....26......5....... EXPRESS YOURSELF .... Fourth & Broadway BRW 144
01/09/1990.....70......1....... GANGSTA, GANGSTA .... Fourth & Broadway BRW 191
10/11/1990.....38......3....... 100 MILES AND RUNNIN' .... Fourth & Broadway BRW 200
23/11/1991.....60......2....... ALWAYZ INTO SOMETHIN' .... Fourth & Broadway BRW 238

NYCC German rap group formed in Hamburg.

30/05/1998.....14......5....... FIGHT FOR YOUR RIGHT (TO PARTY) .... Control 0042645 CON
19/09/1998.....68......1....... CAN YOU FEEL IT (ROCK DA HOUSE) .... Control 0042785 CON

JOE NYE – see DNA

NYLON MOON Italian instrumental duo Donald 'Gas' Maffei and Michele Gernerale.

13/04/1996.....43......2....... SKY PLUS .... Positiva CDTIV 50

MICHAEL NYMAN UK composer/pianist (born 23/3/1944, London) who studied at the Royal Academy of Music and later King's College in London. Although he has made his name as the composer of film themes and scores, including *The Draughtsman's Contract* (1982), *The Cook, The Thief, His Wife And Her Lover* (1989) and *Prospero's Books* (1991), he has also composed various operas, including *The Man Who Mistook His Wife For A Hat*.

19/03/1994.....60......2....... THE HEART ASKS PLEASURE FIRST/THE PROMISE These tracks featured in the 1994 film *The Piano* .... Virgin VEND 3

O

O-TOWN
US group formed by Ashley Angel (born 1/8/1981), Jacob Underwood (born 25/4/1980), Trevor Penick (born 16/11/1979), Erik-Michael Estrada (born 23/9/1979) and Dan Miller (born 4/9/1980). They were the US winners of *Making The Band*.

Date	Pos	Wks		Title	Label
28/04/2001	3	10		**LIQUID DREAMS**	J Records 74321853212
04/08/2001	4	10		**ALL OR NOTHING**	J Records 74321877952
03/11/2001	20	4		WE FIT TOGETHER	J Records 74321893692
23/02/2002	38	2		LOVE SHOULD BE A CRIME	J Records 74321920232
15/02/2003	36	1		THESE ARE THE DAYS	J Records 82876503052

O-ZONE
Moldovan vocal group (although they later relocated to Romania) formed by Dan Balan (born 6/2/1979), Radu Alexei Sarbu (born 14/12/1978) and Arsenie Toderas (born 22/7/1983).

Date	Pos	Wks		Title	Label
19/06/2004	3	17		**DRAGOSTEA DIN TEI**	Jive 82876618412

PAUL OAKENFOLD
UK producer (born 30/8/1963, London) who also records as Perfecto Allstars, Element Four, Planet Perfecto and Movement 98 and is a member of Rise.

Date	Pos	Wks		Title	Label
25/08/2001	47	1		PLANET ROCK **PAUL OAKENFOLD PRESENTS AFRIKA BAMBAATAA** Contains a sample of Kraftwerk's *Trans Europe Express*	Tommy Boy TBCD 2266
22/06/2002	16	4		SOUTHERN SUN/READY STEADY GO	Perfecto PERF 17CDS
31/08/2002	6	8		**STARRY EYED SURPRISE** Features the uncredited contribution of Shifty Shellshock (of Crazy Town)	Perfecto PERF 27CDS
22/02/2003	38	2		THE HARDER THEY COME	Perfecto PERF 49CDSX
27/09/2003	57	1		HYPNOTISED	Perfecto EW 271CD

PHILIP OAKEY
UK singer (born 2/10/1955, Leicester) who was previously the lead singer with Human League.

Date	Pos	Wks		Title	Label
22/09/1984	3	13	O	**TOGETHER IN ELECTRIC DREAMS GIORGIO MORODER AND PHIL OAKEY** Featured in the 1984 film *Electric Dreams*	Virgin VS 713
29/06/1985	44	5		GOODBYE BAD TIMES **PHILIP OAKEY AND GIORGIO MORODER**	Virgin VS 772
26/04/2003	68	1		LA TODAY **ALEX GOLD FEATURING PHILIP OAKEY**	Xtravaganza XTRAV 37CDS

OASIS

UK group formed in Manchester by Liam Gallagher (born 21/9/1972, Manchester, vocals), Paul 'Bonehead' Arthurs (born 23/6/1965, Manchester, guitar), Tony McCarroll (drums) and Paul 'Guigsy' McGuigan (born 9/5/1971, Manchester, bass). With ex-Inspiral Carpets roadie Noel Gallagher (born 29/5/1967, Manchester, guitar), Liam's brother, they were catapulted into stardom. McCarroll was sacked in 1995 (getting a £500,000 settlement from the group), replaced by Alan White (born 26/5/1972, London). 1995 BRIT award for Best British Newcomer, they were the major winners of 1996, awards including Best British Group and Best Album (for *(What's The Story) Morning Glory?*). Three MTV Europe Music Awards include Best Group in 1996 and Best Rock Act in 1997. Liam Gallagher married actress Patsy Kensit in April 1997; they divorced in September 2000. Bonehead left in August 1999 and two weeks later Guigsy also quit. They were replaced by Andy Bell (born 11/8/1970, Cardiff), formerly of Ride and Hurricane #1 on bass, and Gem Archer (guitar). They launched Big Brother label in 2000. Noel Gallagher quit in May 2000 during a world tour, temporarily replaced by Matt Deighton, later returning. Nicole Appleton (a member of All Saints, later Appleton) and Liam had a son, Gene, in July 2001.

Date	Pos	Wks		Title	Label
23/04/1994	31	14		SUPERSONIC	Creation CRESCD 176
02/07/1994	11	15		SHAKERMAKER	Creation CRESCD 182
20/08/1994	10	18	O	**LIVE FOREVER**	Creation CRESCD 185
22/10/1994	7	35	O	**CIGARETTES AND ALCOHOL**	Creation CRESCD 190
31/12/1994	3	50	●	**WHATEVER**	Creation CRESCD 195
06/05/1995	❶¹	27	●	**SOME MIGHT SAY** ↑	Creation CRESCD 204
13/05/1995	71	1		SOME MIGHT SAY	Creation CRE 204T
26/08/1995	2	18	●	**ROLL WITH IT**	Creation CRESCD 212
11/11/1995	2	34	✪	**WONDERWALL** 1996 BRIT Award for Best Video. 1996 MTV Europe Music Award for Best Song	Creation CRESCD 215
25/11/1995	52	2		WIBBLING RIVALRY (INTERVIEWS WITH NOEL AND LIAM GALLAGHER) **OAS●S**	Fierce Panda NING 12CD
02/03/1996	❶¹	24	✪	**DON'T LOOK BACK IN ANGER** ↑	Creation CRESCD 221
19/07/1997	❶¹	18	✪	**D'YOU KNOW WHAT I MEAN?** ↑ The track was later used by Sky TV for their Scottish football coverage	Creation CRESCD 256
04/10/1997	2	18	●	**STAND BY ME**	Creation CRESCD 273
24/01/1998	❶¹	9		**ALL AROUND THE WORLD** ↑ At 9 minutes 38 seconds, the longest single to have topped the UK charts	Creation CRESCD 282
19/02/2000	❶¹	12	O	**GO LET IT OUT** ↑	Big Brother RKIDSCD 001
29/04/2000	4	8		**WHO FEELS LOVE?**	Big Brother RKIDSCD 003
15/07/2000	4	6		**SUNDAY MORNING CALL**	Big Brother RKIDSCD 004
27/04/2002	❶¹	11	O	**THE HINDU TIMES** ↑	Big Brother RKIDSCD 23
29/06/2002	2	10	O	**STOP CRYING YOUR HEART OUT** Featured in the 2004 film *The Butterfly Effect*	Big Brother RKIDSCD 24
05/10/2002	2	8		**LITTLE BY LITTLE/SHE IS LOVE**	Big Brother RKIDSCD 26

❶⁹ Number of weeks single topped the UK chart   ↑ Entered the UK chart at #1   ▲⁹ Number of weeks single topped the US chart

581

15/02/2003	3	10		**SONGBIRD** Written by Liam Gallagher, the first Oasis single he has written	Big Brother RKIDSCD 27

JOHN OATES – see **DARYL HALL AND JOHN OATES**

SAM OBERNIK Irish female singer who launched a solo career on East West as well as guesting on other records.

20/07/2002	14	7	IT JUST WON'T DO **TIM DELUXE FEATURING SAM OBERNIK**	Underwater H2O 016CD
22/11/2003	31	3	STAND BACK **LINUS LOVES FEATURING SAM OBERNIK**	Data 62CDS

OBERNKIRCHEN CHILDREN'S CHOIR German school choir from the town of Oberkirnchen. The original German title of the hit was *Der Frohliche Wanderer*.

22/01/1954	2	26	**HAPPY WANDERER**	Parlophone R 3799

OBI PROJECT FEATURING HARRY, ASHER D AND DJ WHAT? UK rap group, from So Solid Crew.

04/08/2001	75	1	BABY, CAN I GET YOUR NUMBER	East West EW 235CD

DERMOT O'BRIEN AND HIS CLUBMEN Irish singer/accordionist who played for Louth in the 1957 All-Ireland Gaelic football final.

20/10/1966	46	2	THE MERRY PLOUGHBOY	Envoy ENV 016

BILLY OCEAN UK singer (born Leslie Sebastian Charles, 21/1/1950, Trinidad) who moved to London at four and signed with GTO in 1975. He later relocated to America.

21/02/1976	2	10	O	**LOVE REALLY HURTS WITHOUT YOU**	GTO GT 52
10/07/1976	19	8		L.O.D. (LOVE ON DELIVERY)	GTO GT 62
13/11/1976	12	11		STOP ME (IF YOU'VE HEARD IT ALL BEFORE)	GTO GT 72
12/03/1977	2	10	O	**RED LIGHT SPELLS DANGER**	GTO GT 85
01/09/1979	54	5		AMERICAN HEARTS	GTO GT 244
19/01/1980	42	7		ARE YOU READY	GTO GT 259
13/10/1984	6	14	O	**CARIBBEAN QUEEN (NO MORE LOVE ON THE RUN)** ▲² 1984 Grammy Award for Best Rhythm & Blues Vocal Performance	Jive 77
19/01/1985	15	10		LOVERBOY	Jive 80
11/05/1985	4	14	O	**SUDDENLY**	Jive 90
17/08/1985	49	4		MYSTERY LADY	Jive 98
25/01/1986	❶⁴	13	●	**WHEN THE GOING GETS TOUGH, THE TOUGH GET GOING** Featured in the 1985 film *The Jewel Of The Nile*. The video was banned as it included non-US musician's union members Michael Douglas, Kathleen Turner and Danny De Vito (all starred in the film).	Jive 114
12/04/1986	12	13		**THERE'LL BE SAD SONGS (TO MAKE YOU CRY)** ▲¹	Jive 117
09/08/1986	49	3		LOVE ZONE	Jive 124
11/10/1986	44	4		BITTERSWEET	Jive 133
10/01/1987	34	7		LOVE IS FOREVER	Jive 134
06/02/1988	3	11	O	**GET OUTTA MY DREAMS GET INTO MY CAR** ▲² Featured in the 1996 film *Striptease*.	Jive BOS 1
07/05/1988	35	4		CALYPSO CRAZY	Jive BOS 2
06/08/1988	65	3		THE COLOUR OF LOVE	Jive BOS 3
06/02/1993	55	2		PRESSURE	Jive BOSCD 6

OCEAN COLOUR SCENE UK group formed by Simon Fowler (born 25/4/1965, Birmingham, guitar/vocals), Steve Craddock (born 22/8/1969, Birmingham, guitar/keyboards/vocals), Damon Minchella (born 1/6/1969, Liverpool, bass) and Oscar Harrison (born 15/4/1965, Birmingham, drums/keyboards). They took part in the *It's Only Rock 'N' Roll* project for the Children's Promise charity.

23/03/1991	49	1	YESTERDAY TODAY	!Phfft FIT 2
17/02/1996	15	5	THE RIVERBOAT SONG	MCA MCSTD 40021
06/04/1996	7	4	**YOU'VE GOT IT BAD**	MCA MCSTD 40036
15/06/1996	4	11	**THE DAY WE CAUGHT THE TRAIN**	MCA MCSTD 40046
28/09/1996	6	6	**THE CIRCLE**	MCA MCSTD 40077
28/06/1997	4	7	**HUNDRED MILE HIGH CITY** Featured in the 1998 film *Lock Stock And Two Smoking Barrels*.	MCA MCSTD 40133
06/09/1997	5	5	**TRAVELLERS TUNE**	MCA MCSTD 40144
22/11/1997	9	5	**BETTER DAY**	MCA MCSTD 40151
28/02/1998	12	4	IT'S A BEAUTIFUL THING	MCA MCSTD 40157
04/09/1999	13	5	PROFIT IN PEACE	Island CID 757
27/11/1999	34	2	SO LOW	Island CID 759
08/07/2000	31	2	JULY/I AM THE NEWS	Island CID 763
07/04/2001	19	3	UP ON THE DOWN SIDE	Island CID 774
14/07/2001	49	1	MECHANICAL WONDER	Island CID 779
22/12/2001	64	1	CRAZY LOWDOWN WAYS	Island CID 787
12/07/2003	13	3	I JUST NEED MYSELF	Sanctuary SANXD 159X
06/09/2003	35	2	MAKE THE DEAL	Sanctuary SANXD 219
10/01/2004	40	3	GOLDEN GATE BRIDGE	Sanctuary SANXD 244

OCEANIC UK group formed by Siobhan Maher (vocals), Sarah Miller (vocals), Amanda Williams (vocals), Jorinda Williams (vocals), Jorinde Williams (vocals), Frank Crofts (keyboards) and David Harry (keyboards).

24/08/1991	3	15	O	**INSANITY**	Dead Dead Good GOOD 4
30/11/1991	25	5		WICKED LOVE	Dead Dead Good GOOD 5
13/06/1992	14	5		CONTROLLING ME	Dead Dead Good GOOD 14

O Silver disc ● Gold disc ✪ Platinum disc (additional platinum units are indicated by a figure following the symbol) ◉ Singles released prior to 1973 that are known to have sold over 1 million copies in the UK

14/11/1992	72	1		IGNORANCE OCEANIC FEATURING SIOBHAN MAHER	Dead Dead Good GOOD 22

OCEANLAB FEATURING JUSTINE SUISSA
UK/Dutch production group formed by Jono Grant, Tony McGuinness and Paavo Siljamaki (who also produce as Above & Beyond) with singer Justine Suissa. Grant and Siljamaki also record as Dirt Devils.

27/04/2002	48	1		CLEAR BLUE WATER	Code Blue BLU 024CD1
01/05/2004	19	4		SATELLITE OCEAN LAB	NuLife 82876614002

OCEANSIZE
UK group formed in Manchester by Mike Vennart (guitar/vocals), Steve Durose (guitar/vocals), Gambler (guitar), Jon Ellis (bass) and Mark Heron (drums).

14/02/2004	73	1		CATALYST	Beggars Banquet BBQ 375CD

DES O'CONNOR
UK singer (born 12/1/1932, London); he was a Butlin's Red Coat before making his stage debut in 1953. He compered *Sunday Night At The London Palladium* in the early 1960s, later hosting his own TV show and a revival of *Take Your Pick*.

01/11/1967	6	17		CARELESS HANDS DES O'CONNOR WITH THE MICHAEL SAMMES SINGERS	Columbia DB 8275
08/05/1968	❶¹	36		I PRETEND	Columbia DB 8397
20/11/1968	4	11		1-2-3 O'LEARY	Columbia DB 8492
07/05/1969	14	10		DICK-A-DUM-DUM (KING'S ROAD)	Columbia DB 8566
29/11/1969	18	11		LONELINESS	Columbia DB 8632
14/03/1970	30	7		I'LL GO ON HOPING	Columbia DB 8661
03/10/1970	15	15		THE TIPS OF MY FINGERS	Columbia DB 8713
08/11/1986	10	10		THE SKYE BOAT SONG ROGER WHITTAKER AND DES O'CONNOR	Tembo TML 119

HAZEL O'CONNOR
UK singer (born 16/5/1955, Coventry) who joined Albion Records in 1978, coming to prominence after appearing in the film *Breaking Glass* in 1980. She later appeared in *Car Trouble*.

16/08/1980	5	11	O	EIGHTH DAY	A&M AMS 7553
25/10/1980	41	4		GIVE ME AN INCH This and above single featured in the 1980 film *Breaking Glass*.	A&M AMS 7569
21/03/1981	10	9	O	D-DAYS	Albion ION 1009
23/05/1981	8	10	O	WILL YOU Featured in the 1980 film *Breaking Glass*	A&M AMS 8131
01/08/1981	41	6		(COVER PLUS) WE'RE ALL GROWN UP	Albion ION 1018
03/10/1981	45	3		HANGING AROUND	Albion ION 1022
23/01/1982	60	3		CALLS THE TUNE Featured in the 1980 film *Breaking Glass*	A&M AMS 8203

SINEAD O'CONNOR
Irish singer (born 12/12/1966, Glenageary) who started with local group Ton Ton Macoute. She first appeared on record on the soundtrack to *Captive*, releasing her debut in 1988. Best International Newcomer at the 1991 BRIT Awards and 1990 Grammy Award winner for Best Alternative Music Performance for *I Do Not Want What I Haven't Got*.

16/01/1988	17	9		MANDINKA	Ensign ENY 611
20/01/1990	❶⁴	14	✪	NOTHING COMPARES 2 U ▲⁴ Cover version of a Prince song originally recorded by his Paisley Park act Family	Ensign ENY 630
21/07/1990	31	5		THE EMPEROR'S NEW CLOTHES	Ensign ENY 633
20/10/1990	42	4		THREE BABIES	Ensign ENY 635
08/06/1991	42	3		MY SPECIAL CHILD	Ensign ENY 646
14/12/1991	60	4		SILENT NIGHT	Ensign ENY 652
12/09/1992	18	4		SUCCESS HAS MADE A FAILURE OF OUR HOME	Ensign ENY 656
12/12/1992	53	4		DON'T CRY FOR ME ARGENTINA	Ensign ENY 657
19/02/1994	42	3		YOU MADE ME THE THIEF OF YOUR HEART Featured in the 1993 film *In The Name Of The Father*	Island CID 588
26/11/1994	13	7		THANK YOU FOR HEARING ME	Ensign CDENYS 662
29/04/1995	30	2		HAUNTED SHANE MACGOWAN AND SINEAD O'CONNOR	ZTT BANG 65CD
26/08/1995	51	1		FAMINE	Ensign CDENY 663
17/05/1997	28	1		GOSPEL OAK EP Tracks on EP: *This Is To Mother You, I Am Enough For Myself, Petit Poulet* and *4 My Love*	Chrysalis CDCHS 5051
06/12/1997	60	1		THIS IS A REBEL SONG	Columbia 6652992
24/08/2002	48	1		TROY (THE PHOENIX FROM THE FLAME)	Devolution DEVR 003CDS

OCTOPUS
UK group formed by Marc Shearer, Alan McSeveney, Cameron Miller and Oliver Grasset. The group's line-up sometimes increases to eight with the addition of a brass section.

22/06/1996	42	2		YOUR SMILE	Food CDFOODS 78
14/09/1996	40	2		SAVED	Food CDFOODS 84
23/11/1996	59	1		JEALOUSY	Food CDFOODS 87

OCTAHVIA – see JOSE NUNEZ FEATURING OCTAHVIA

OCTAVE ONE FEATURING ANN SAUNDERSON
US group formed in Detroit, Michigan by Lawrence Burden, his brothers Lynell and Lenny, Anthony Shakir, Jay Denham and Juan Atkins with singer Ann Saunderson. They formed the 430 West label (named after the location of the original offices – 430 West 8 Mile Road in Detroit). Saunderson earlier recorded solo as Ruth Joy.

16/02/2002	47	1		BLACKWATER	Concept/430 West CDCON 26
28/09/2002	69	1		BLACKWATER Remix of Concept/430 West CDCON 26.	Concept/430 West CDCON 34

ALAN O'DAY
US pianist/singer (born 3/10/1940, Hollywood, CA) who as a songwriter penned hits for Helen Reddy.

02/07/1977	43	3		UNDERCOVER ANGEL ▲¹	Atlantic K 10926

❶⁹ Number of weeks single topped the UK chart   ↑ Entered the UK chart at #1   ▲⁹ Number of weeks single topped the US chart

ODETTA – see **HARRY BELAFONTE**

DANIEL O'DONNELL Irish singer (born12/12/1961, Kincasslagh, County Donegal); he is a hugely popular Irish country artist. Initially big in Scotland, he first recorded for Ritz in 1985. An MBE in the 2002 New Year's Honours List. Mary Duff is an Irish singer.

DATE	POS	WKS	SINGLE TITLE	LABEL & NUMBER
12/09/1992	20	7	I JUST WANT TO DANCE WITH YOU	Ritz 250P
02/01/1993	71	1	THE THREE BELLS	Ritz RITZCD 239
08/05/1993	47	3	THE LOVE IN YOUR EYES	Ritz RITZCD 257
07/08/1993	21	5	WHAT EVER HAPPENED TO OLD FASHIONED LOVE	Ritz RITZCD 262
16/04/1994	23	3	SINGING THE BLUES	Ritz RITZCD 270
26/11/1994	46	3	THE GIFT	Ritz RITZCD 275
10/06/1995	28	3	SECRET LOVE	Ritz RITZCD 285
09/03/1996	32	3	TIMELESS This and above single credited to **DANIEL O'DONNELL AND MARY DUFF**	Ritz RITZCD 293
28/09/1996	25	5	FOOTSTEPS	Ritz RITZCD 300
07/06/1997	27	4	THE LOVE SONGS EP Tracks on EP: *Save The Last Dance For Me, I Can't Stop Loving You, You're The Only Good Thing (That's Happened To Me)* and *Limerick You're A Lady*	Ritz RITZCD 306
11/04/1998	7	5	**GIVE A LITTLE LOVE** A charity single with proceeds donated to The Romanian Challenge Appeal	Ritz RITZCD 315
17/10/1998	16	4	THE MAGIC IS THERE	Ritz RZCD 320
20/03/1999	18	3	THE WAY DREAMS ARE	Ritz RZCD 325
24/07/1999	25	3	UNO MAS	Ritz RZCD 326
18/12/1999	20	4	A CHRISTMAS KISS	Ritz RZCD 330
15/04/2000	23	4	LIGHT A CANDLE	Ritz RZCD 335
16/12/2000	32	4	MORNING HAS BROKEN	Ritz RZCD 341
13/12/2003	22	4	YOU RAISE ME UP	Rosette ROSCD 310

ODYSSEY US R&B vocal group originally formed by sisters Lillian, Louise and Carmen Lopez as the Lopez Sisters. Carmen left in 1968, replaced by Tony Reynolds, who left in 1977, replaced by Bill McEarchern who in turn was replaced by Al Jackson in 1982.

DATE	POS	WKS	BPI	SINGLE TITLE	LABEL & NUMBER
24/12/1977	5	11	O	NATIVE NEW YORKER Featured in the films *The Stud* (1978), *The Eyes Of Laura Mars* (1978) and *54* (1998)	RCA PC 1129
21/06/1980	O[2]	12	O	**USE IT UP AND WEAR IT OUT**	RCA PB 1962
13/09/1980	6	15	O	**IF YOU'RE LOOKING FOR A WAY OUT**	RCA 5
17/01/1981	36	7		HANG TOGETHER	RCA 23
30/05/1981	4	12	O	**GOING BACK TO MY ROOTS**	RCA 85
19/09/1981	43	5		IT WILL BE ALRIGHT	RCA 128
12/06/1982	3	11	O	**INSIDE OUT**	RCA 226
11/09/1982	41	5		MAGIC TOUCH	RCA 275
17/08/1985	51	4		(JOY) I KNOW IT	Mirror BUTCH 12

ESTHER AND ABI OFARIM Israeli husband and wife duo Esther (born Esther Zaled, 13/6/1943, Safed) and Abi (born Abraham Reichstadt, 5/10/1939, Tel Aviv) Ofarim. Esther represented Switzerland in the 1963 Eurovision Song Contest.

DATE	POS	WKS	SINGLE TITLE	LABEL & NUMBER
14/02/1968	O[3]	13	**CINDERELLA ROCKEFELLA**	Philips BF 1640
19/06/1968	13	9	ONE MORE DANCE	Philips BF 1678

OFF-SHORE German instrumental/production duo Jens Lissat and Peter Harder.

DATE	POS	WKS	SINGLE TITLE	LABEL & NUMBER
22/12/1990	7	11	**I CAN'T TAKE THE POWER**	CBS 6565707
17/08/1991	64	1	I GOT A LITTLE SONG	Dance Pool 6568257

WISTON OFFICE – see **FRANK K FEATURING WISTON OFFICE**

OFFSPRING US punk group formed in 1984 by songwriter Bryan Dexter Holland (born 29/12/1966, Orange County, CA, guitar/vocals), Greg Kriesel (born 20/1/1965, Glendale, CA, bass), Doug Thompson (vocals) and Jim Benton (drums) as Manic Subsidal. Thompson left, with Holland taking over as lead vocalist and Benton being replaced by James Lilja. Kevin 'Noodles' Wasserman (born 4/2/1963, Los Angeles, CA, guitar) joined shortly before they changed their name in 1985. Lilja left in 1987, replaced by Ron Welty (born 1/2/1971, Long Beach, CA). Named Best Rock Act at the 1999 MTV Europe Music Awards.

DATE	POS	WKS	BPI	SINGLE TITLE	LABEL & NUMBER
25/02/1995	37	3		SELF ESTEEM	Epitaph CDSHOLE 001
19/08/1995	43	2		GOTTA GET AWAY	Out Of Step WOOS 2CDS
01/02/1997	31	2		ALL I WANT	Epitaph 64912
26/04/1997	42	1		GONE AWAY	Epitaph 64982
30/01/1999	O[1]	11	●	**PRETTY FLY (FOR A WHITE GUY)** ↑ Popular on the internet, has been downloaded more than 22 million times!	Columbia 6668802
08/05/1999	2	8		**WHY DON'T YOU GET A JOB**	Columbia 6673545
11/09/1999	11	6		THE KIDS AREN'T ALRIGHT Featured in the 1999 film *The Faculty*	Columbia 6677632
04/12/1999	41	2		SHE'S GOT ISSUES	Columbia 6683772
18/11/2000	6	8		**ORIGINAL PRANKSTER** Contains a sample of War's *Low Rider*	Columbia 6699972
31/03/2001	15	9		WANT YOU BAD Featured in the 2001 film *American Pie 2*	Columbia 6709292
07/07/2001	21	4		MILLION MILES AWAY	Columbia 6714082
31/01/2004	11	7		HIT THAT	Columbia 6745475
05/06/2004	48	1		(CAN'T GET MY) HEAD AROUND YOU	Columbia 6748262

OH WELL German producer Ackim Faulker.

DATE	POS	WKS	SINGLE TITLE	LABEL & NUMBER
14/10/1989	28	6	OH WELL	Parlophone R 6236
03/03/1990	65	1	RADAR LOVE	Parlophone R 6244

OHIO EXPRESS US bubblegum group with Douglas Grassel (rhythm guitar), Dale Powers (lead guitar), Jim Pfahler (organ), Tim Corwin (drums) and Dean Kastran (bass). Tracks created by singer/songwriter Joey Levine, co-writer Artie Resnick and studio musicians.

05/06/1968 . . . . . 5 . . . . . . 15 . . . . . . **YUMMY YUMMY YUMMY** . . . . Pye International 7N 25459

OHIO PLAYERS US R&B group formed in Dayton, OH in 1959 by Leroy 'Sugarfoot' Bonner (guitar/vocals), Clarence 'Satch' Satchell (saxophone/vocals) and Marshall 'Rock' Jones (bass) as The Ohio Untouchables. By 1968 they had added Marvin 'Merv' Pierce (horns), Ralph 'Pee-Wee' Middlebrooks (saxophone), David Johnson (keyboards), Vincent 'Vennie' Thomas and Jimmy Sampson (drums).

10/07/1976 . . . . . 43 . . . . . . 4 . . . . WHO'D SHE COO . . . . Mercury PLAY 001

O'JAYS US R&B vocal group formed in 1958 by Eddie Levert (born 16/6/1942, Canton, OH), Walter Williams (born 25/8/1942, Canton), William Powell (born 20/1/1942, Canton), Bill Isles and Bobby Massey as the Triumphs. Later recording as the Mascots, they became the O'Jays (after Cleveland DJ Eddie O'Jay) in 1963. Isles left in 1965, Massey in 1972 and they continued as a trio. Powell gave up live work owing to ill health in 1975 (but continued to record with them), replaced by Sammy Strain (born 20/1/1942, Brooklyn, NYC). Powell died from cancer on 26/5/1977. Strain left in 1990, replaced by Nathaniel Best (born 13/12/1960, Miami, FL). Best left in 1996, replaced by Eric Grant. Levert's sons Gerald and Sean are members of Levert.

23/09/1972 . . . . . 14 . . . . . . 9 . . . . BACK STABBERS Featured in the 1977 film *Looking For Mr Goodbar* . . . . CBS 8270
03/03/1973 . . . . . 9 . . . . . . 13 . . . . . . **LOVE TRAIN** ▲[1] Featured in the films *Dead Presidents* (1995) and *The Last Days Of Disco* (1998) . . . . CBS 1181
31/01/1976 . . . . . 13 . . . . . . 9 . . . . I LOVE MUSIC . . . . Philadelphia International PIR 3879
12/02/1977 . . . . . 24 . . . . . . 6 . . . . DARLIN' DARLIN' BABY (SWEET, TENDER, LOVE) . . . . Philadelphia International PIR 4834
08/04/1978 . . . . . 36 . . . . . . 3 . . . . I LOVE MUSIC Re-issue of Philadelphia International PIR 3879 . . . . Philadelphia International PIR 6093
17/06/1978 . . . . . 12 . . . . . . 12 . . . . . . USED TA BE MY GIRL . . . . Philadelphia International PIR 6332
30/09/1978 . . . . . 21 . . . . . . 9 . . . . BRANDY . . . . Philadelphia International PIR 6658
29/09/1979 . . . . . 39 . . . . . . 6 . . . . SING A HAPPY SONG . . . . Philadelphia International PIR 7825
30/07/1983 . . . . . 45 . . . . . . 5 . . . . PUT OUR HEADS TOGETHER . . . . Philadelphia International A 3642

OK GO US group formed in Chicago, IL in 1998 by Damian Kulash (vocals), Andrew Duncan (guitar), Tim Nordwind (bass) and Dan Konopka (drums).

22/03/2003 . . . . . 21 . . . . . . 3 . . . . GET OVER IT . . . . Capitol CDR 6603

JOHN O'KANE UK singer born in Glasgow who was a member of Millions Like Us before going solo.

09/05/1992 . . . . . 41 . . . . . . 4 . . . . STAY WITH ME . . . . Circa YR 88

OL' DIRTY BASTARD US rapper (born Russell Jones, 15/11/1968, Brooklyn, NYC), aka Dirt McGirt, in rap supergroup Wu-Tang Clan. He collapsed and died on 13/11/2004.

27/06/1998 . . . . . 2 . . . . . . 17 . . . . . ✪ **GHETTO SUPERSTAR (THAT IS WHAT YOU ARE)** PRAS MICHEL FEATURING OL' DIRTY BASTARD AND INTRODUCING MYA Contains a sample of James Brown's *Get Up, Get Into It, Get Involved* and an interpolation of the song *Islands In The Stream*. 1998 MOBO Award for Best International Single. Featured in the 1998 film *Bulworth* . . . . Interscope IND 95593
08/07/2000 . . . . . 11 . . . . . . 8 . . . . GOT YOUR MONEY OL' DIRTY BASTARD FEATURING KELIS . . . . Elektra E 7077CD

OLD SKOOL ORCHESTRA UK DJ/production duo Stuart 'Stretch' Collins and Julian Peake who also record as Stretch 'N' Vern Present Maddog.

23/01/1999 . . . . . 55 . . . . . . 1 . . . . B-BOY HUMP Contains a sample of Engelbert Humperdinck's *Can't Take My Eyes Off You* . . . . East West EW 186CD1

MIKE OLDFIELD UK singer/multi-instrumentalist (born 15/5/1953, Reading) who released his first album in 1968 as Sallyangie with his sister Sally. He went solo in 1971 and his debut album was released in 1973, the first release on Virgin. Maggie Reilly is a UK soprano singer.

13/07/1974 . . . . . 31 . . . . . . 6 . . . . MIKE OLDFIELD'S SINGLE (THEME FROM TUBULAR BELLS) Featured in the 1973 film *The Exorcist*. 1974 Grammy Award for Best Instrumental Composition for Mike Oldfield as writer . . . . Virgin VS 101
20/12/1975 . . . . . 4 . . . . . . 10 . . . . . . **IN DULCE JUBILO/ON HORSEBACK** . . . . Virgin VS 131
27/11/1976 . . . . . 3 . . . . . . 12 . . . . . O **PORTSMOUTH** . . . . Virgin VS 163
23/12/1978 . . . . . 72 . . . . . . 3 . . . . TAKE 4 (EP) Tracks on EP: *Portsmouth, In Dulce Jubilo, Wrekorder Wrongdo* and *Sailors Hornpipe* . . . . Virgin VS 238
21/04/1979 . . . . . 22 . . . . . . 8 . . . . GUILTY . . . . Virgin VS 245
08/12/1979 . . . . . 19 . . . . . . 9 . . . . BLUE PETER Cover of the children's TV show theme, a charity single in aid of the Blue Peter Cambodia Appeal . . . . . . Virgin VS 317
20/03/1982 . . . . . 43 . . . . . . 5 . . . . FIVE MILES OUT . . . . Virgin VS 464
12/06/1982 . . . . . 45 . . . . . . 6 . . . . FAMILY MAN This and above single credited to MIKE OLDFIELD FEATURING MAGGIE REILLY . . . . Virgin VS 489
28/05/1983 . . . . . 4 . . . . . . 17 . . . . . O **MOONLIGHT SHADOW** MIKE OLDFIELD WITH VOCALS BY MAGGIE REILLY . . . . Virgin VS 586
14/01/1984 . . . . . 61 . . . . . . 3 . . . . CRIME OF PASSION . . . . Virgin VS 648
30/06/1984 . . . . . 48 . . . . . . 7 . . . . TO FRANCE This and above single credited to MIKE OLDFIELD FEATURING MAGGIE REILLY . . . . Virgin VS 686
14/12/1985 . . . . . 50 . . . . . . 6 . . . . PICTURES IN THE DARK MIKE OLDFIELD FEATURING ALED JONES, ANITA HEGERLAND AND BARRY PALMER . . . . Virgin VS 836
03/10/1992 . . . . . 10 . . . . . . 6 . . . . **SENTINEL** . . . . WEA YZ 698
19/12/1992 . . . . . 33 . . . . . . 5 . . . . TATTOO . . . . WEA YZ 708
17/04/1993 . . . . . 50 . . . . . . 2 . . . . THE BELL . . . . WEA YZ 737CD
09/10/1993 . . . . . 52 . . . . . . 2 . . . . MOONLIGHT SHADOW Re-issue of Virgin VS 586. . . . . Virgin VSCDT 1477
17/12/1994 . . . . . 47 . . . . . . 3 . . . . HIBERNACULUM. . . . . WEA YZ 871CD
02/09/1995 . . . . . 51 . . . . . . 1 . . . . LET THERE BE LIGHT . . . . WEA YZ 880CD
22/11/1997 . . . . . 70 . . . . . . 1 . . . . WOMEN OF IRELAND . . . . WEA YZ 093CD
24/04/1999 . . . . . 53 . . . . . . 1 . . . . FAR ABOVE THE CLOUDS . . . . WEA 206CD1

❶[9] Number of weeks single topped the UK chart ↑ Entered the UK chart at #1 ▲[9] Number of weeks single topped the US chart

585

SALLY OLDFIELD UK singer; she is the older sister of Mike Oldfield who recorded with him as Sallyangie in 1968. She also appeared on his *Tubular Bells* album as part of the 'girlie chorus'.

09/12/1978 . . . . . 19 . . . . . 13 . . . . . . MIRRORS . . . . Bronze BRO 66

MISTY OLDLAND UK singer born in London; she was a member of duo Oldland Montana before going solo.

16/10/1993 . . . . . 59 . . . . . 2 . . . . . . GOT ME A FEELING . . . . Columbia 6597872
12/03/1994 . . . . . 49 . . . . . 4 . . . . . . A FAIR AFFAIR (JE T'AIME) . . . . Columbia 6601612
09/07/1994 . . . . . 73 . . . . . 1 . . . . . . I WROTE YOU A SONG . . . . Columbia 6603732

OLGA Italian female singer.

01/10/1994 . . . . . 68 . . . . . 1 . . . . . . I'M A BITCH . . . . UMM 144UKCD

OLIVE UK group with ex-Simply Red Tim Kellett, Robin Taylor-Firth and vocalist Ruth-Ann Boyle.

07/09/1996 . . . . . 42 . . . . . 4 . . . . . . YOU'RE NOT ALONE . . . . RCA 74321406272
15/03/1997 . . . . . 41 . . . . . 2 . . . . . . MIRACLE . . . . RCA 74321461242
17/05/1997 . . . . . ❶² . . . . . 13 . . . . . . **YOU'RE NOT ALONE ↑** Re-issue of RCA 74321406272 . . . . RCA 74321473232
16/08/1997 . . . . . 14 . . . . . 4 . . . . . . OUTLAW . . . . RCA 74321508372
08/11/1997 . . . . . 41 . . . . . 1 . . . . . . MIRACLE (REMIX) . . . . RCA 74321530842

OLIVER US singer (born William Oliver Swofford, 22/2/1945, North Wilkesboro, NC), produced by Bob Crewe. He died from cancer on 12/2/2000.

09/08/1969 . . . . . 6 . . . . . 18 . . . . . . **GOOD MORNING STARSHINE** From the musical *Hair* . . . . CBS 4435

FRANKIE OLIVER UK singer who later studied business administration and sound engineering at college.

07/06/1997 . . . . . 58 . . . . . 1 . . . . . . GIVE HER WHAT SHE WANTS . . . . Island Jamaica IJCD 2011

OLLIE AND JERRY US duo drummer Ollie Brown and Jerry Knight, both of whom had previously been in Raydio.

23/06/1984 . . . . . 5 . . . . . 11 . . . . . . **BREAKIN'...THERE'S NO STOPPING US** Featured in the 1984 film *Breakin'* . . . . Polydor POSP 690
09/03/1985 . . . . . 57 . . . . . 3 . . . . . . ELECTRIC BOOGALOO . . . . Polydor POSP 730

OLYMPIC ORCHESTRA UK studio orchestra assembled to record the theme to the TV drama *Reilly – Ace Of Spies*.

01/10/1983 . . . . . 26 . . . . . 15 . . . . . . REILLY Theme to the TV series *Reilly – Ace Of Spies* . . . . Red Bus RBUS 82

OLYMPIC RUNNERS UK funk group with DeLisle Harber (bass), Glen LeFleur (drums), Pete Wingfield (keyboards), Joe Hammer (guitar) and George Chandler (vocals). Wingfield later recorded solo while Chandler was a member of Londonbeat.

13/05/1978 . . . . . 61 . . . . . 2 . . . . . . WHATEVER IT TAKES . . . . RCA PC 5078
14/10/1978 . . . . . 35 . . . . . 6 . . . . . . GET IT WHILE YOU CAN . . . . Polydor RUN 7
20/01/1979 . . . . . 35 . . . . . 6 . . . . . . SIR DANCEALOT . . . . Polydor POSP 17
28/07/1979 . . . . . 37 . . . . . 7 . . . . . . THE BITCH Featured in the 1979 film *The Bitch* . . . . Polydor POSP 63

OLYMPICS US R&B group formed in California in 1954 by Walter Ward (born 1940, Jackson, MA), Eddie Lewis (born 1937, Houston, TX), Charles Fizer (born 1940, Shreveport, LA) and Walter Hammond (born 1940, Shreveport) as The Challengers. Fizer left in 1958, replaced by Melvin King. Fizer returned in 1959 when Hammond left and, having spent time in jail for drug dealing, was shot and killed in 1965 in the Watts race riots. He was replaced by Julian McMichael.

03/10/1958 . . . . . 12 . . . . . 8 . . . . . . WESTERN MOVIES . . . . HMV POP 528
19/01/1961 . . . . . 40 . . . . . 1 . . . . . . I WISH I COULD SHIMMY LIKE MY SISTER KATE Although credited to A.J. Piron, was Louis Armstrong's 1914 debut song . Vogue V 9174

OMAR UK singer (born Omar Lye Fook, 1969, Canterbury) who debuted with the Kongo label in 1990, then with Talkin' Loud in 1991.

22/06/1991 . . . . . 14 . . . . . 7 . . . . . . THERE'S NOTHING LIKE THIS . . . . Talkin Loud TLK 9
23/05/1992 . . . . . 47 . . . . . 2 . . . . . . YOUR LOSS MY GAIN . . . . Talkin Loud TLK 22
26/09/1992 . . . . . 53 . . . . . 2 . . . . . . MUSIC . . . . Talkin Loud TLK 28
23/07/1994 . . . . . 43 . . . . . 2 . . . . . . OUTSIDE/SATURDAY . . . . RCA 74321213982
15/10/1994 . . . . . 57 . . . . . 1 . . . . . . KEEP STEPPIN' . . . . RCA 74321233682
02/08/1997 . . . . . 29 . . . . . 2 . . . . . . SAY NOTHIN' . . . . RCA 74321502872
18/10/1997 . . . . . 37 . . . . . 2 . . . . . . GOLDEN BROWN . . . . RCA 74321525122

OMC New Zealand singer Paul Fuemana-Lawrence. OMC stands for Otara Millionaires Club.

20/07/1996 . . . . . 5 . . . . . 16 . . . . O **HOW BIZARRE** . . . . Polydor 5776202
18/01/1997 . . . . . 56 . . . . . 1 . . . . . . ON THE RUN . . . . Polydor 5732452

OMD – see **ORCHESTRAL MANOEUVRES IN THE DARK**

OMNI TRIO UK producer Rob Haigh.

07/07/2001 . . . . . 44 . . . . . 3 . . . . . . THE ANGELS & SHADOWS PROJECT . . . . Moving Shadow SHADOW 150CD
26/07/2003 . . . . . 61 . . . . . 1 . . . . . . RENEGADE SNARES . . . .

ONE UK four-piece vocal group who began as a TV group for a series on GMTV. The group comprised Billy, Tim, Thomas and Trevor.

11/01/1997 . . . . . 31 . . . . . 2 . . . . . . ONE MORE CHANCE . . . . Mercury MERDD 478

◯ Silver disc   ● Gold disc   ✪ Platinum disc (additional platinum units are indicated by a figure following the symbol)   ◎ Singles released prior to 1973 that are known to have sold over 1 million copies in the UK

MICHIE ONE – see LOUCHIE LOU AND MICHELE ONE

PHOEBE ONE UK singer/producer/DJ (born Phoebe Espirit, London) who won the 1998 MOBO Award for Best Hip Hop Act. She is also an accomplished writer having penned songs for Kavana and Robyn.

12/12/1998	59	1		DOIN' OUR THING/ONE MAN'S BITCH	Mecca Recordings MECX 1020
15/05/1999	38	2		GET ON IT Contains a sample of Rod Stewart's *Baby Jane*	Mecca Recordings MECX 1026

ONE DOVE UK dance group with Ian Carmichael (born 1/6/1960, Glasgow), Jim McKinven (born 1959, Glasgow) and Dot Allison (born 17/8/1969, Edinburgh). McKinven had previously been in the Bluebells and Altered Images. Allison later went solo.

07/08/1993	43	3		WHITE LOVE	Boy's Own BOICD 14
16/10/1993	24	3		BREAKDOWN	Boy's Own BOICD 15
15/01/1994	30	3		WHY DON'T YOU TAKE ME	Boy's Own BOICD 16

187 LOCKDOWN UK production duo Danny Harrison and Julian Jonah (born Danny Matlock); they are named after the US police code for a murder (187) and slang for prison (lockdown), aka Congress, Nush, Nu-Birth, Gant, Reflex, Stella Browne and M Factor.

15/11/1997	16	4		GUNMAN	East West EW 140CD
25/04/1998	9	5		**KUNG-FU**	East West EW 155CD
25/07/1998	17	4		GUNMAN (REMIX)	East West EW 176CD
03/10/1998	29	2		THE DON	East West EW 180CD
13/02/1999	43	1		ALL 'N' ALL 187 LOCKDOWN (FEATURING D'EMPRESS)	East West EW 194CD

1 GIANT LEAP FEATURING MAXI JAZZ AND ROBBIE WILLIAMS UK production group formed by Duncan Bridgeman and Jamie Catto. Catto is a member of Faithless, as is guest vocalist Maxi Jazz.

20/04/2002	9	6		**MY CULTURE**	Palm Pictures PPCD 70732

100% FEATURING JENNIFER JOHN UK production duo Mike Cave and Gary Wilkinson, with singer Jennifer John.

25/12/2004	28	1+		JUST CAN'T WAIT (SATURDAY)	CR2 CDC2X005

ONE HUNDRED TON AND A FEATHER UK singer Jonathan King (born Kenneth King, 6/12/1944, London).

26/06/1976	9	9		**IT ONLY TAKES A MINUTE**	UK 135

ONE MINUTE SILENCE UK group: Brian 'Yap' Barry (vocals), Chris Ignatiou (guitar), Glenn Diani (bass), Eddie Stratton (drums).

20/01/2001	56	1		FISH OUT OF WATER	V2 VVR 5013213
05/07/2003	44	1		I WEAR MY SKIN	Taste Media TMCDSX 5005

112 US R&B group formed in Atlanta, GA by Daron Jones (born 27/12/1977, keyboards/vocals), Marvin 'Slim' Scandrick (born 25/9/1979, strings/vocals), Mike Keith (born 18/12/1978, keyboards/vocals) and Quinees 'Q' Parker (born 24/3/1977, drums/vocals).

28/06/1997	**❶**[6]	21	**❷**[2]	I'LL BE MISSING YOU ↑ ▲[11] PUFF DADDY AND FAITH EVANS AND 112 Contains a sample of The Police's *Every Breath You Take*. A tribute to The Notorious B.I.G., the single entered the chart at #1, being the first record to have entered both the US and UK charts at #1. Reclaimed #1 position on 24/7/1997. 1997 Grammy Award for Best Rap Performance by a Group	Puff Daddy 74321499102
10/01/1998	12	5		ALL CRIED OUT ALLURE FEATURING 112	Epic 6652715
14/02/1998	35	2		SKY'S THE LIMIT THE NOTORIOUS B.I.G. FEATURING 112 Contains a sample of Bobby Caldwell's *My Flame*	Puff Daddy 74321587992
30/06/2001	22	3		IT'S OVER NOW ONE TWELVE Contains an interpolation of *White Lines*	Puff Daddy 74321849912
08/09/2001	32	3		PEACHES AND CREAM	Arista 74321882632

ONE THE JUGGLER UK group with Rokko (guitar/vocals) and Lushi (bass), later Lin Minchin (guitar) and Steve Nicol (drums).

19/02/1983	71	1		PASSION KILLER	Regard RG 107

1000 CLOWNS US dance group formed by songwriter/producer Kevi Krakower and singers Anita and Michelle Kopacz. Their hit also featured DJ Mr Pao, Karl Denson (flute), Ricardo Harnright (flute), Stuart Wylen (flute), John Coz (guitar) and Mott Smith (bass).

22/05/1999	23	4		(NOT THE) GREATEST RAPPER	Elektra E 3759CD

ONE TRIBE – see OUR TRIBE/ONE TRIBE

ONE TRUE VOICE UK vocal group formed by Anton Gordon, Daniel Pearce, Jamie Shaw, Keith Semple and Matt Johnson. They were the male winners in the TV programme *Popstars: The Rivals,* disbanding after their second single.

21/12/2002	2	9	●	**SACRED TRUST/AFTER YOU'RE GONE**	Ebul/Jive 9201532
14/06/2003	10	5		**SHAKESPEARE'S WAY WITH WORDS**	Ebul/Jive 9201582

ONE 2 MANY Norwegian group with Camilla Griehsel (vocals), Dag Kolsrud (keyboards/production) and Jan Gisle Ytterdal (guitar).

12/11/1988	65	4		DOWNTOWN	A&M AM 476
03/06/1989	43	7		DOWNTOWN Re-issue of A&M AM 476	A&M AM 456

ONE WAY US R&B group formed in Detroit, Michigan (until 1979 as The Soul Partners) by Al Hudson (vocals), Alicia Myers (vocals), Dave Roberson (guitar), Kevin McCord (bass) and Gregory Green (drums). Myers went solo in 1980, replaced by Candyce Edwards.

08/12/1979	56	6		MUSIC ONE WAY FEATURING AL HUDSON	MCA 542
29/06/1985	64	2		LET'S TALK ABOUT SHHH	MCA 972

❶[9] Number of weeks single topped the UK chart ↑ Entered the UK chart at #1 ▲[9] Number of weeks single topped the US chart

587

ALEXANDER O'NEAL
US singer (born 14/11/1954, Natchez, MS) who was the lead vocalist with Flyte Tyme that later became Time. He went solo in 1980 and later relocated to London.

DATE	POS	WKS	BPI	SINGLE TITLE	LABEL & NUMBER
28/12/1985	6	11		SATURDAY LOVE CHERRELLE WITH ALEXANDER O'NEAL	Tabu A 6829
15/02/1986	13	10		IF YOU WERE HERE TONIGHT	Tabu A 6391
05/04/1986	53	4		A BROKEN HEART CAN MEND	Tabu A 6244
06/06/1987	33	6		FAKE	Tabu 6508917
31/10/1987	4	14		CRITICIZE	Tabu 6512117
06/02/1988	26	7		NEVER KNEW LOVE LIKE THIS ALEXANDER O'NEAL FEATURING CHERRELLE	Tabu 6513827
28/05/1988	28	4		THE LOVERS	Tabu 6515957
23/07/1988	27	5		(WHAT CAN I SAY) TO MAKE YOU LOVE ME	Tabu 6528527
24/09/1988	16	7		FAKE '88	Tabu 6529497
10/12/1988	30	5		CHRISTMAS SONG (CHESTNUTS ROASTING ON AN OPEN FIRE)/THANK YOU FOR A GOOD YEAR	Tabu 6531827
25/02/1989	56	2		HEARSAY '89	Tabu 6544667
02/09/1989	72	1		SUNSHINE	Tabu 6551917
09/12/1989	19	7		HITMIX (OFFICIAL BOOTLEG MEGA-MIX)	Tabu 6555047
24/03/1990	55	2		SATURDAY LOVE (REMIX) CHERRELLE WITH ALEXANDER O'NEAL	Tabu 6558007
12/01/1991	18	6		ALL TRUE MAN	Tabu 6565717
23/03/1991	53	2		WHAT IS THIS THING CALLED LOVE	Tabu 6567317
11/05/1991	71	1		SHAME ON ME	Tabu 6568737
09/05/1992	53	2		SENTIMENTAL	Tabu 6580147
30/01/1993	26	6		LOVE MAKES NO SENSE	Tabu AMCD 7708
03/07/1993	32	3		IN THE MIDDLE	Tabu 5877152
25/09/1993	67	1		ALL THAT MATTERS TO ME	Tabu 6577232
02/11/1996	38	2		LET'S GET TOGETHER	EMI Premier PRESCD 11
02/08/1997	56	1		BABY COME TO ME ALEXANDER O'NEAL FEATURING CHERRELLE	One World Entertainment OWECD 1
12/12/1998	51	1		CRITICIZE '98 MIX (RE-RECORDING)	One World Entertainment OWECD 3

SHAQUILLE O'NEAL
US singer (born 6/3/1972, New Jersey). A basketball player with Orlando Magic and Los Angeles Lakers, he was in the film *Blue Chips* (1994), debuting on record in 1993. Yo-Yo is US rapper Yolanda Whittaler (born 4/8/1971, Los Angeles, CA).

DATE	POS	WKS	BPI	SINGLE TITLE	LABEL & NUMBER
26/03/1994	70	1		I'M OUTSTANDING Contains samples of The Gap Band's *Outstanding,* Yarbrough & Peoples' *Don't Stop The Music* and Tom Browne's *Funkin' For Jamaica*	Jive JIVECD 349
14/09/1996	28	2		STOMP – THE REMIXES QUINCY JONES FEATURING MELLE MEL, COOLIO, YO-YO, SHAQUILLE O'NEAL & THE LUNIZ	Qwest W 0372CD
01/02/1997	40	2		YOU CAN'T STOP THE REIGN	Interscope IND 95522
17/10/1998	62	1		THE WAY IT'S GOIN' DOWN (T.W.I.S.M. FOR LIFE)	A&M 5827932

MARTIN O'NEILL – see LISBON LIONS FEATURING MARTIN O'NEILL AND CELTIC CHORUS

ONEPHATDEEVA – see A.T.F.C. PRESENTS ONEPHATDEEVA

ONES
US trio formed in New York by Paul Alexander, JoJo America and Nashorn Benjamin. Alexander earlier sang on David Morales' hit *Gimme Luv*, America had written for Danny Tenaglia and Benjamin appeared in the 1999 film *Flawless*.

DATE	POS	WKS	BPI	SINGLE TITLE	LABEL & NUMBER
20/10/2001	7	13		FLAWLESS Featured in the 1999 film *Flawless*	Positiva CDTIV 164
01/03/2003	45	1		SUPERSTAR	Positiva CDTIVS 186

ONLY ONES
UK group formed in 1976 by Peter Perrett (guitar/vocals), John Perry (guitar), Alan Mair (bass) and Mike Killie (drums) who signed with CBS in 1977. They disbanded in 1981 after being dropped by the label.

DATE	POS	WKS	BPI	SINGLE TITLE	LABEL & NUMBER
01/02/1992	57	2		ANOTHER GIRL – ANOTHER PLANET	Columbia 6577507

YOKO ONO
Japanese singer (born 18/2/1933, Tokyo) who was married to John Lennon in 1969 and credited on most of his later songs, this delaying the release of some singles and albums. Her single was released in the aftermath of his murder in December 1980.

DATE	POS	WKS	BPI	SINGLE TITLE	LABEL & NUMBER
28/02/1981	35	5		WALKING ON THIN ICE	Geffen K 79202
14/06/2003	35	2		WALKING ON THIN ICE (REMIX)	Parlophone CDMINDS 002

BEN ONONO
UK singer.

DATE	POS	WKS	BPI	SINGLE TITLE	LABEL & NUMBER
15/03/2003	51	1		ON MY MIND FUTURESHOCK FEATURING BEN ONONO	Junior/Parlophone CDR 6595
17/05/2003	28	3		MY LOVE IS ALWAYS SAFFRON HILL FEATURING BEN ONONO	Illustrious CDILL 016

ONSLAUGHT
UK group formed in Bristol, Avon in 1983 by Paul Mahoney (vocals), Nigel Rocket (guitar), Jason Stallord (bass) and Steve Grice (drums). After a release on the indie label Cor, they were signed by Under One Flag, part of the Music For Nations group. Their debut for the label saw Sy Keeler join on vocals, Mahoney switching to bass and Stallord to rhythm guitar. Soon after the album release Mahoney left, replaced by James Hinder. Keeler and Stallord left before the recording of the next album, replaced by Rob Trottman and Steve Grimmett. Grimmett left in 1990, replaced by Tony O'Hara, and the group disbanded in 1991.

DATE	POS	WKS	BPI	SINGLE TITLE	LABEL & NUMBER
06/05/1989	50	3		LET THERE BE ROCK	London LON 224

ONYX
US rap group from New York, with Sticky Fingaz (born Kirk Jones), Big DS, Fredro Starr and Suave Sonny Caesar. After one single for Profile, switched to Columbia. Big DS left in 1995, Fredro Starr appeared in films, including *Strapped*, *Dead Presidents* and *Clockers*.

DATE	POS	WKS	BPI	SINGLE TITLE	LABEL & NUMBER
28/08/1993	31	4		SLAM	Columbia 6596302
27/11/1993	34	3		THROW YA GUNZ	Columbia 6598312
20/02/1999	59	1		ROC-IN-IT DEEJAY PUNK-ROC VS ONYX	Independiente ISOM 21MS

○ Silver disc ● Gold disc ✪ Platinum disc (additional platinum units are indicated by a figure following the symbol) ◎ Singles released prior to 1973 that are known to have sold over 1 million copies in the UK

ONYX FEATURING GEMMA J
UK/US production group formed by Lee S, Anton Powers, Bruce Elliot Smith and Phil Larsen with singer Gemma J (born Gemma Louise Campson, 29/7/1982, Reading).

11/12/2004.....66......1....... EVERY LITTLE TIME .... Data 78CDS

ONYX STONE – see MC ONYX STONE

OO LA LA
UK vocal/instrumental group assembled by ex-Gygafo Eddie Stringer, a tribute to footballer Eric Cantona.

05/09/1992.....64......2....... OO…AH…CANTONA .... North Speed OOAH 1

OOBERMAN
UK group formed by Andy Flett (guitar), Steve Flett (bass), Danny Popplewell (vocals), Sophia Churney (vocals/keyboards) and Alan Kelly (drums). They first recorded for the Transcopic label.

08/05/1999.....39......2.......	BLOSSOMS FALLING .... Independiente ISOM 26MS
17/07/1999.....43......1.......	MILLION SUNS .... Independiente ISOM 30MS
23/10/1999.....63......1.......	TEARS FROM A WILLOW .... Independiente ISOM 37MS
08/04/2000.....47......1.......	SHORLEY WALL .... Independiente ISOM 41MS

OOE – see COLUMBO FEATURING OOE

OPEN
UK rock group formed by Steven Bayley (vocals), Jon Winter (guitar), Jim Reynolds (bass), Alan Dutton (keyboards) and Scott Holland (drums).

13/03/2004.....46......1.......	CLOSE MY EYES .... Polydor 9817294
03/07/2004.....52......1.......	JUST WANT TO LIVE .... Loog 9866489
11/09/2004.....54......1.......	ELEVATION .... Loog 9867495
13/11/2004.....53......1.......	NEVER ENOUGH .... Loog 9868779

OPEN ARMS FEATURING ROWETTA
UK vocal/instrumental group: Graham Turner, Mark Hall and singer Rowetta.

15/06/1996.....62......1....... HEY MR DJ... All Around The World CDGLOBE 136

OPERABABES
UK vocal duo Karen England and Rebecca Knight, first spotted busking in Covent Garden and invited to perform at the 2002 FA Cup Final.

06/07/2002.....54......1....... ONE FINE DAY .... Sony Classical 6727062

OPTICAL – see ED RUSH AND OPTICAL/UNIVERSAL PROJECT

OPM
US rock group formed by Matthew Lo (guitar/vocals), John Necro (bass) and Geoff Turney (drums).

| 14/07/2001 .....4......14.....O | HEAVEN IS A HALFPIPE Contains a sample of The Honeydrippers' *Impeach The President* .... Atlantic AT 0107CD |
| 12/01/2002.....20......4....... | EL CAPITAN .... East West AT 0118CD |

OPTIMYSTIC
UK group formed by Ian McKeith, Stuart McKeith, Brin Downing, Shola Finni and Felina Charlier.

17/09/1994.....49......3.......	CAUGHT UP IN MY HEART... WEA YZ 841CD
10/12/1994.....37......2.......	NOTHING BUT LOVE .... WEA YZ 864CD1
13/05/1995.....70......1.......	BEST THING IN THE WORLD .... WEA YZ 920CD

OPUS
Austrian rock group with Herwig Rudlsser (vocals), Ewald Pfleger (guitar), Kurt Trene Plisnier (keyboards), Niki Gruber (bass) and Gunter Grasmuck (drums).

15/06/1985 .....6......15.....O LIVE IS LIFE .... Polydor POSP 743

OPUS III
UK dance group formed by Ian Dodds, Kevin Walters, Nigel Munro and vocalist Kirsty Hawkshaw, who later went solo.

22/02/1992 .....5......8.......	IT'S A FINE DAY .... PWL International PWL 215
27/06/1992.....52......1.......	I TALK TO THE WIND .... PWL International PWL 235
11/06/1994.....71......1.......	WHEN YOU MADE THE MOUNTAIN. .... PWL International PWL 302

ORANGE
UK vocal/instrumental group with Rick Corcoran, Steve Manders, Alan Strawbridge and Anthony Wilson. Corcoran later recorded as The Orgone Box.

08/10/1994.....73......1....... JUDY OVER THE RAINBOW .... Chrysalis CDCHS 5012

ORANGE JUICE
UK group formed in Glasgow in 1977 by Edwyn Collins (born 23/8/1959, Edinburgh, guitar/vocals), David McClymont (bass), Steve Daly (drums) and James Kirk (guitar); they originally recorded for indie label Postcard. Kirk and Daly left in 1982 and were replaced by Malcolm Ross and Zeke Manyika. Collins later recorded solo.

07/11/1981.....65......2.......	L.O.V.E…LOVE .... Polydor POSP 357
30/01/1982.....63.....3.......	FELICITY .... Polydor POSP 386
21/08/1982.....60......2.......	TWO HEARTS TOGETHER/HOKOYO .... Polydor POSP 470
23/10/1982.....42......3.......	I CAN'T HELP MYSELF... Polydor POSP 522
19/02/1983 .....8......11	RIP IT UP .... Polydor POSP 547
04/06/1983.....41......6.......	FLESH OF MY FLESH .... Polydor OJ 4
25/02/1984.....67......2.......	BRIDGE .... Polydor OJ 5
12/05/1984.....47......4.......	WHAT PRESENCE? .... Polydor OJ 6
27/10/1984.....74......1.......	LEAN PERIOD .... Polydor OJ 7

❶[9] Number of weeks single topped the UK chart ↑ Entered the UK chart at #1 ▲[9] Number of weeks single topped the US chart

589

ORB

UK house group formed in 1988 by Dr Alex Paterson (born Duncan Robert Alex Paterson, initials giving him his Dr title) and Jimmy Cauty. Cauty left in 1990 for KLF, Paterson assuming lead role. By 1996 they were Paterson, Andy Hughes and Thomas Fehlmann.

DATE	POS	WKS	TITLE	LABEL & NUMBER
15/06/1991	61	1	PERPETUAL DAWN	Big Life BLRD 46
20/06/1992	8	6	**BLUE ROOM**	Big Life BLRT 75
17/10/1992	12	5	ASSASSIN	Big Life BLRT 81
13/11/1993	10	5	**LITTLE FLUFFY CLOUDS**	Big Life BLRD 98
05/02/1994	18	5	PERPETUAL DAWN	Big Life BLRD 46
27/05/1995	38	2	OXBOW LAKES	Island CID 609
08/02/1997	4	4	**TOXYGENE**	Island CID 652
24/05/1997	20	2	ASYLUM	Island CID 657
24/02/2001	38	2	ONCE MORE	Island CIDX 767

ROY ORBISON

US singer (born 23/4/1936, Vernon, TX); his first group, the Wink Westerners, formed in 1952. He released his debut record in 1955 with the Teen Kings for Je-Wel with his first solo recordings for Sun in 1956. He moved to Nashville to concentrate on songwriting in 1957, signing with RCA with little success before joining Monument. He later recorded as 'Lefty' in the Traveling Wilburys. His wife Claudette was killed in a motorcycle accident in 1966, while two of his three sons were killed in a fire in 1968. He died from a heart attack on 6/12/1988. He was inducted into the Rock & Roll Hall of Fame in 1987. Four Grammy Awards included Best Country Performance by a Duo in 1980 with Emmylou Harris for *That Lovin' You Feelin' Again*, Best Spoken Word Documentary in 1986 with various others for *Interviews From The Class Of '55*, and Best Pop Vocal Performance in 1990 for *Oh Pretty Woman*. In 1989 he also recieved a Grammy Award for Best Rock Performance by a Group with Vocals with the Traveling Wilburys for *Traveling Wilburys Volume One* (the album was known as *Handle With Care* in the UK).

DATE	POS	WKS	BPI	TITLE	LABEL & NUMBER
28/07/1960	◎ 2	24		**ONLY THE LONELY** Orbison composition turned down earlier by both Elvis Presley and The Everly Brothers	London HLU 9149
27/10/1960	11	16		BLUE ANGEL	London HLU 9207
25/05/1961	9	15		**RUNNING SCARED** ▲1	London HLU 9342
28/09/1961	25	9		CRYIN'	London HLU 9405
08/03/1962	2	14		**DREAM BABY**	London HLU 9511
28/06/1962	40	4		THE CROWD	London HLU 9561
08/11/1962	50	1		WORKIN' FOR THE MAN	London HLU 9607
28/02/1963	6	23		**IN DREAMS** Featured in the 1987 film *Blue Velvet*	London HLU 9676
30/05/1963	9	11		**FALLING**	London HLU 9727
19/09/1963	3	19		**BLUE BAYOU/MEAN WOMAN BLUES**	London HLU 9777
20/02/1964	15	10		BORNE ON THE WIND	London HLU 9845
30/04/1964	◎ 2	18		**IT'S OVER**	London HLU 9882
10/09/1964	◎ 3	18		**OH PRETTY WOMAN** ▲3 Reclaimed #1 position 12/11/1964. In the films *Pretty Woman* (1990), *Dumb And Dumber* (1994) and *Au Pair* (1999)	London HLU 9919
19/11/1964	6	11		**PRETTY PAPER**	London HLU 9930
11/02/1965	14	9		GOODNIGHT	London HLU 9951
22/07/1965	23	8		(SAY) YOU'RE MY GIRL	London HLU 9978
09/09/1965	34	6		RIDE AWAY	London HLU 9986
04/11/1965	19	9		CRAWLIN' BACK	London HLU 10000
27/01/1966	22	6		BREAKIN' UP IS BREAKIN' MY HEART	London HLU 10015
07/04/1966	29	5		TWINKLE TOES	London HLU 10034
16/06/1966	15	9		LANA	London HLU 10051
18/08/1966	3	17		**TOO SOON TO KNOW**	London HLU 10067
01/12/1966	18	9		THERE WON'T BE MANY COMING HOME	London HLU 10096
23/02/1967	32	6		SO GOOD	London HLU 10113
24/07/1968	39	10		WALK ON	London HLU 10206
25/09/1968	44	4		HEARTACHE	London HLU 10222
07/05/1969	35	4		MY FRIEND	London HLU 10261
13/09/1969	27	14		PENNY ARCADE	London HLU 10285
14/01/1989	3	10	○	**YOU GOT IT**	Virgin VS 1166
01/04/1989	27	5		SHE'S A MYSTERY TO ME	Virgin VS 1173
04/07/1992	7	10		**I DROVE ALL NIGHT**	MCA MCS 1652
22/08/1992	13	6		CRYING **ROY ORBISON (DUET WITH k.d. lang)** Featured in the 1992 film *Holding Out*. 1988 Grammy Award for Best Country Vocal Collaboration	Virgin America VUS 63
07/11/1992	36	3		HEARTBREAK RADIO	Virgin America VUS 68
13/11/1993	47	2		I DROVE ALL NIGHT Re-issue of MCA MCS 1652	Virgin America VUSCD 79

WILLIAM ORBIT

UK producer (born William Wainwright) who also records as Bass-O-Matic and founded Guerilla and O Records. As a producer, he handled Madonna's *Ray Of Light* album. He was awarded Best Selling Classical Album for *Pieces In A Modern Style* at the inaugural Classical BRIT Awards in 2000. The eligibility of his album, from which the remixed *Barber's Adagio For Strings* was a big club and pop single, was the subject of considerable debate in the classical sector.

DATE	POS	WKS	BPI	TITLE	LABEL & NUMBER
26/06/1993	59	1		WATER FROM A VINE LEAF	Guerilla VSCDT 1465
18/12/1999	4	15	○	**BARBER'S ADAGIO FOR STRINGS**	WEA 247CD
06/05/2000	31	2		RAVEL'S PAVANE POUR UNE INFANTE DEFUNTE	WEA 269CD
19/07/2003	4	11		**FEEL GOOD TIME PINK FEATURING WILLIAM ORBIT** Featured in the 2003 film *Charlie's Angels: Full Throttle*	Columbia 6741062

○ Silver disc ● Gold disc ✪ Platinum disc (additional platinum units are indicated by a figure following the symbol) ◎ Singles released prior to 1973 that are known to have sold over 1 million copies in the UK

ORBITAL
UK duo, brothers Paul (born 19/5/1968, Dartford) and Phil Hartnoll (born 9/1/1964, Dartford) who are named after the M25 – London's orbital motorway.

DATE	POS	WKS	BPI	SINGLE TITLE	LABEL & NUMBER
24/03/1990	17	7		CHIME	ffrr F 85
22/09/1990	46	3		OMEN	ffrr 145
19/01/1991	31	4		SATAN	ffrr FX 149
15/02/1992	24	3		MUTATIONS EP Tracks on EP: *Chime Chime, Oolaa, Fahrenheit 3D 3* and *Speed Freak*	ffrr FX 181
26/09/1992	37	2		RADICCIO EP Tracks on EP: *Halcyon, The Naked And The Dead* and *Sunday*	Internal LIARX 1
21/08/1993	43	2		LUSH	Internal LIECD 7
24/09/1994	33	2		ARE WE HERE	Internal LIECD 15
27/05/1995	53	1		BELFAST	Volume VOLCD 1
27/04/1996	11	4		THE BOX	Internal LIECD 30
11/01/1997	3	6		**SATAN** Live version of ffrr FX 149	Internal LIECD 37
19/04/1997	3	7		**THE SAINT** Featured in the 1997 film *The Saint*	ffrr FCD 296
20/03/1999	13	4		STYLE	ffrr FCD 358
17/07/1999	32	2		NOTHING LEFT	ffrr FCDP 365
11/03/2000	36	3		BEACHED **ORBITAL AND ANGELO BADALAMENTI** Featured in the 2000 film *The Beach*	ffrr FCD 377
28/04/2001	21	3		FUNNY BREAK (ONE IS ENOUGH) Features the uncredited contribution of singer Naomi Bedford	ffrr FCDP 395
08/06/2002	33	3		REST AND PLAY EP Tracks on EP: *Frenetic, Illuminate* and *Chime*	ffrr FCD 407
17/07/2004	29	2		ONE PERFECT SUNRISE	Orbital Music ORBITALCD03X

ORCHESTRA ON THE HALF SHELL
US vocal/instrumental group assembled by David Frank and John Du Prez.

DATE	POS	WKS	BPI	SINGLE TITLE	LABEL & NUMBER
15/12/1990	36	6		TURTLE RHAPSODY	SBK 17

ORCHESTRAL MANOEUVRES IN THE DARK
UK group formed in Liverpool in 1977 by Andy McCluskey (born 24/6/1959, Liverpool, vocals) and Paul Humphreys (born 27/2/1960, Liverpool, keyboards) as Id with Gary Hodgson (guitar), Steve Hollis (bass) and Malcolm Hughes (drums). They disbanded in 1978, re-forming the same year with the addition of Dave Hughes (keyboards) and Malcolm Homes (drums). They are also sometimes known as OMD.

DATE	POS	WKS	BPI	SINGLE TITLE	LABEL & NUMBER
09/02/1980	67	2		RED FRAME WHITE LIGHT	Dindisc DIN 6
10/05/1980	13	11		MESSAGES	Dindisc DIN 15
04/10/1980	8	15	O	**ENOLA GAY** The name of the aeroplane that dropped the first atomic bomb on Hiroshima	Dindisc DIN 22
29/08/1981	3	12	O	**SOUVENIR**	Dindisc DIN 24
24/10/1981	5	14	O	**JOAN OF ARC**	Dindisc DIN 36
23/01/1982	4	10	O	**MAID OF ORLEANS (THE WALTZ JOAN OF ARC)**	Dindisc DIN 40
19/02/1983	20	8		GENETIC ENGINEERING	Virgin VS 527
09/04/1983	42	4		TELEGRAPH	Virgin VS 580
14/04/1984	5	11		**LOCOMOTION**	Virgin VS 660
16/06/1984	11	10		TALKING LOUD AND CLEAR	Virgin VS 685
08/09/1984	21	8		TESLA GIRLS	Virgin VS 705
10/11/1984	70	2		NEVER TURN AWAY	Virgin VS 727
25/05/1985	27	7		SO IN LOVE	Virgin VS 766
20/07/1985	34	7		SECRET	Virgin VS 796
26/10/1985	42	4		LA FEMME ACCIDENT	Virgin VS 811
03/05/1986	48	4		IF YOU LEAVE Featured in the 1986 film *Pretty In Pink*	Virgin VS 843
06/09/1986	11	10		(FOREVER) LIVE AND DIE	Virgin VS 888
15/11/1986	54	5		WE LOVE YOU	Virgin VS 911
02/05/1987	52	3		SHAME	Virgin VS 938
06/02/1988	50	3		DREAMING	Virgin VS 987
02/07/1988	60	3		DREAMING	Virgin VS 987
30/03/1991	3	13		**SAILING ON THE SEVEN SEAS**	Virgin VS 1310
06/07/1991	7	10		**PANDORA'S BOX**	Virgin VS 1331
14/09/1991	50	4		THEN YOU TURN AWAY	Virgin VS 1368
07/12/1991	50	2		CALL MY NAME	Virgin VS 1380
15/05/1993	21	4		STAND ABOVE ME	Virgin VSCDG 1444
17/07/1993	24	5		DREAM OF ME (BASED ON LOVE'S THEME)	Virgin VSCDT 1461
18/09/1993	59	2		EVERYDAY	Virgin VSCDT 1471
17/08/1996	17	5		WALKING ON THE MILKY WAY	Virgin VSCDT 1599
02/11/1996	55	1		UNIVERSAL	Virgin VSCDT 1606
26/09/1998	35	2		THE OMD REMIXES (EP) Tracks on EP: *Enola Gay, Souvenir* and *Electricity*	Virgin VSCDT 1694

ORDINARY BOYS
UK rock group formed in 2002 by Preston (guitar/vocals), William J Brown (guitar), James Gregory (bass) and Charlie Stanley (drums).

DATE	POS	WKS	BPI	SINGLE TITLE	LABEL & NUMBER
17/04/2004	36	2		WEEK IN WEEK OUT	B Unique WEA372CD

❶⁹ Number of weeks single topped the UK chart ↑ Entered the UK chart at #1 ▲⁹ Number of weeks single topped the US chart

591

10/07/2004	17	3		TALK TALK TALK	B Unique WEA377CD
02/10/2004	27	2		SEASIDE	B Unique WEA379CD

RAUL ORELLANA Spanish multi-instrumentalist/producer.

30/09/1989	29	8		THE REAL WILD HOUSE	RCA BCM 322

O.R.G.A.N. Spanish DJ/producer Vidana Crespo.

16/05/1998	33	2		TO THE WORLD	Multiply CDMULTY 34

ORIGIN UK production duo Dave Wood and Anthony Mein.

12/08/2000	73	1		WIDE EYED ANGEL	Lost Language LOST 001CD

ORIGIN UNKNOWN UK production duo Andy Clarke and Ant Miles who also record as Ram Trilogy (with Shimon Alcovy).

13/07/1996	60	1		VALLEY OF THE SHADOWS	Ram RAMM 16CD
11/05/2002	53	1		TRULY ONE	Ram RAMM 38CD
20/09/2003	66	1		HOTNESS DYNAMITE MC AND ORIGIN UNKNOWN	Ram RAMM 45

ORIGINAL US dance duo Everett Bradley and Walter Taieb who both come from New York.

14/01/1995	31	3		I LUV U BABY	Ore AG 8CD
19/08/1995	2	9	O	I LUV U BABY (REMIX)	Ore/XL Recordings AGR 8CD
11/11/1995	29	2		B 2 GETHER	Ore/XL Recordings AG 12CD

ORIGINOO GUNN CLAPPAZ – see HELTAH SKELTAH AND ORIGINOO GUNN CLAPPAZ AS THE FABULOUS FIVE

ORION UK production duo Darren Tate and vocalist Sarah J. Tate was later in Angelic and recorded as Jurgen Vries and DT8.

07/10/2000	38	2		ETERNITY	Incentive CENT 11CDS

ORION TOO Belgian dance group formed by producers J Serge Ramaekers (aka Mr Vinx) and Gery Francois with singer Caitlin (born Kathleen Goossens, 23/5/1976, Heist op den Berg).

09/11/2002	46	1		HOPE AND WAIT	Data 4CDS

ORLANDO – see LA'S AND PRETENDERS

TONY ORLANDO US singer (born Michael Anthony Orlando Cassavitis, 3/4/1944, New York) who was with local group the Five Gents when discovered by Don Kirshner. After brief success he retired from performing and worked in music publishing before being asked to sing the lead with Dawn on *Candida*. He resumed his solo career in 1977 and has a star on the Hollywood Walk of Fame.

05/10/1961	5	11		BLESS YOU	Fontana H 330

ORLONS US R&B group formed in Philadelphia, PA by Rosetta Hightower (born 23/6/1944), Marlena Davis (born 4/10/1944), Steve Caldwell (born 22/11/1942) and Shirley Brickley (born 9/12/1944). The group disbanded in 1968. Brickley was shot to death at her home in Philadelphia on 13/10/1977. Davis died from lung cancer on 27/2/1993.

27/12/1962	39	3		DON'T HANG UP	Cameo Parkway C 231

ORN UK DJ/producer Omio Nourizadeh.

01/03/1997	61	1		SNOW	Deconstruction 74321447612

STACIE ORRICO US singer (born 3/3/1986, Seattle, WA).

23/08/2003	9	8		STUCK	Virgin VUSCD 269
01/11/2003	12	8		THERE'S GOTTA BE MORE TO LIFE	Virgin VUSCD 275
24/01/2004	22	4		I PROMISE	Virgin VUSDX 280
12/06/2004	34	2		I COULD BE THE ONE	Virgin VUSDX 289

CLAUDETTE ORTIZ – see WYCLEF JEAN

BETH ORTON UK singer/songwriter (born 1974, Norwich). She began her career guesting on albums by other artists, including The Chemical Brothers and William Orbit. She was named Best British Female Solo Artist at the 2000 BRIT Awards.

01/02/1997	60	1		TOUCH ME WITH YOUR LOVE	Heavenly HVN 64CD
05/04/1997	49	1		SOMEONE'S DAUGHTER	Heavenly HVN 65CD
14/06/1997	40	2		SHE CRIES YOUR NAME	Heavenly HVN 68CD
13/12/1997	36	3		BEST BIT EP BETH ORTON FEATURING TERRY CALLIER Tracks on EP: *Best Bit, Skimming Stone, Dolphins* and *Lean On Me*	
					Heavenly HVN 72CD
13/03/1999	34	2		STOLEN CAR	Heavenly HVN 89CD
25/09/1999	37	2		CENTRAL RESERVATION	Heavenly HVN 92CD1
16/11/2002	55	1		ANYWHERE	Heavenly HVN 125CDS
12/04/2003	57	1		THINKING ABOUT TOMORROW	Heavenly HVN 129CD

ORVILLE – see KEITH HARRIS AND ORVILLE

O Silver disc ● Gold disc ✪ Platinum disc (additional platinum units are indicated by a figure following the symbol) ◎ Singles released prior to 1973 that are known to have sold over 1 million copies in the UK

JEFFREY OSBORNE
US singer (born 9/3/1948, Providence, RI); he was the lead singer with LTD from 1970 to 1980 before going solo.

Date	Pos	Wks	Title	Label & Number
17/09/1983	54	2	DON'T YOU GET SO MAD	A&M AM 140
14/04/1984	18	11	STAY WITH ME TONIGHT	A&M AM 188
23/06/1984	11	14	ON THE WINGS OF LOVE	A&M AM 198
20/10/1984	61	2	DON'T STOP	A&M AM 222
26/07/1986	44	6	SOWETO	A&M AM 334
15/08/1987	63	3	LOVE POWER DIONNE WARWICK AND JEFFREY OSBORNE	Arista RIS 27

JOAN OSBORNE
US singer (born 8/7/1962, Anchorage, KY); she was a film student who took to singing as a dare at the Abilene Bar in New York in 1988. She formed the Womanly Hips label.

Date	Pos	Wks	Title	Label & Number
10/02/1996	6	10	ONE OF US	Blue Gorilla JOACD 1
08/06/1996	33	3	ST TERESA	Blue Gorilla JOACD 3

TONY OSBORNE SOUND
UK orchestra fronted by Tony Osborne. They were regulars on the BBC radio show *Saturday Club* (their tune *Saturday Jump* was theme to the programme). Osborne's son Gary later wrote with Elton John.

Date	Pos	Wks	Title	Label & Number
23/02/1961	50	1	MAN FROM MADRID	HMV POP 827
03/02/1973	46	2	THE SHEPHERD'S SONG TONY OSBORNE SOUND FEATURING JOANNE BROWN	Philips 6006 266

KELLY OSBORNE
UK singer (born 27/10/1984); she is the daughter of Ozzy and Sharon Osbourne.

Date	Pos	Wks	Title	Label & Number
24/08/2002	65	3	PAPA DON'T PREACH (IMPORT)	Epic 6729152CD
21/09/2002	3	10	PAPA DON'T PREACH	Epic 6731602
08/02/2003	12	6	SHUT UP	Epic 6735552
20/12/2003	❶¹	16	●	CHANGES ↑ OZZY AND KELLY OSBOURNE	Sanctuary SANXD 34

OZZY OSBOURNE
UK singer (born John Osbourne, 3/12/1948, Birmingham) who was the lead singer with Black Sabbath from their formation in 1970 until leaving in 1980. He formed Blizzard of Oz with an ever-changing line-up. He appeared in the film *Trick Or Treat* in 1987. In 1982 he was banned from the city of San Antonio after being caught urinating on a wall of the monument to the Alamo, the ban finally being lifted ten years later when he donated $20,000 towards its restoration. Osbourne also took part in the *It's Only Rock 'N' Roll* project for the Children's Promise charity. 1993 Grammy Award for Best Metal Performance with vocal for *I Don't Want To Change The World*. He has a star on the Hollywood Walk of Fame.

Date	Pos	Wks	Title	Label & Number
13/09/1980	49	4	CRAZY TRAIN	Jet 197
15/11/1980	46	3	MR CROWLEY	Jet 7003
26/11/1983	21	8	BARK AT THE MOON	Epic A 3915
02/06/1984	20	9	SO TIRED	Epic A 4452
01/02/1986	20	6	SHOT IN THE DARK	Epic A 6859
09/08/1986	72	1	THE ULTIMATE SIN/LIGHTNING STRIKES	Epic A 7311
20/05/1989	47	3	CLOSE MY EYES FOREVER	Dreamland PB 49409
28/09/1991	32	3	NO MORE TEARS	Epic 6574407
30/11/1991	46	2	MAMA I'M COMING HOME	Epic 6576177
25/11/1995	23	2	PERRY MASON	Epic 6626395
31/08/1996	43	1	I JUST WANT YOU	Epic 6635702
08/06/2002	18	6	DREAMER/GETS ME THROUGH	Epic 6724122
20/12/2003	❶¹	16	●	CHANGES ↑ OZZY AND KELLY OSBOURNE	Sanctuary SANXD 34

OSIBISA
Ghanaian/Nigerian group formed in Britain in the early 1970s by Teddy Osei, (flute/percussion), Kofi Ayivor (congas), Kiki Gyan (keyboards), Mike Odumosa (bass), Sol Amarfio (drums), Marc Tontoh (horns) and Wendell Richardson (guitar).

Date	Pos	Wks	Title	Label & Number
17/01/1976	17	6	SUNSHINE DAY	Bronze BRO 20
05/06/1976	31	6	DANCE THE BODY MUSIC	Bronze BRO 26

DONNY OSMOND
US singer (born 9/12/1957, Ogden, UT); he joined the family vocal group in 1963, appearing on the *Andy Williams Show*. He first recorded solo in 1971 and later teamed with sister Marie. He returned with a new image and a US #2 in 1988.

Date	Pos	Wks	Title	Label & Number
17/06/1972	❶⁵	23	PUPPY LOVE	MGM 2006 104
16/09/1972	5	15	TOO YOUNG	MGM 2006 113
11/11/1972	3	20	WHY	MGM 2006 119
10/03/1973	❶¹	14	THE TWELFTH OF NEVER	MGM 2006 199
18/08/1973	❶⁴	10	○	YOUNG LOVE	MGM 2006 300
10/11/1973	4	13	○	WHEN I FALL IN LOVE	MGM 2006 365
16/11/1974	18	10	WHERE DID ALL THE GOOD TIMES GO	MGM 2006 468
26/09/1987	70	1	I'M IN IT FOR LOVE	Virgin VS 994
06/08/1988	29	8	SOLDIER OF LOVE	Virgin VS 1094
12/11/1988	70	2	IF IT'S LOVE THAT YOU WANT	Virgin VS 1140
09/02/1991	64	2	MY LOVE IS A FIRE	Capitol CL 600
02/10/2004	8	5	BREEZE ON BY	Decca 9863140

DONNY AND MARIE OSMOND
US brother and sister duo Donny (born 9/12/1957, Ogden, UT) and Marie Osmond (born 13/10/1959, Ogden). They hosted their own TV show 1976–78, and appeared in the film *Goin' Coconuts* in 1978.

Date	Pos	Wks	Title	Label & Number
03/08/1974	2	12	○	I'M LEAVING IT (ALL) UP TO YOU	MGM 2006 446
14/12/1974	5	12	○	MORNING SIDE OF THE MOUNTAIN	MGM 2006 274

❶⁹ Number of weeks single topped the UK chart ↑ Entered the UK chart at #1 ▲⁹ Number of weeks single topped the US chart

593

21/06/1975.....18......6......	MAKE THE WORLD GO AWAY	MGM 2006 523
17/01/1976.....25......7......	DEEP PURPLE Featured in the 1987 film *Stardust*	MGM 2006 561

LITTLE JIMMY OSMOND
US singer (born 16/4/1963, Canoga Park, CA); he is the youngest member of the Osmond family. After a brief singing career he turned his attentions to business, including tour promoting. He is also the youngest solo artist ever to top the UK charts, a feat accomplished at the age of 9 years 8 months. His brother Donny holds second place, achieved when aged 14 years 6 months.

25/11/1972 .....❶⁵...27	LONG HAIRED LOVER FROM LIVERPOOL .... MGM 2006 109
31/03/1973 .....4......13	TWEEDLE DEE .... MGM 2006 175
23/03/1974.....11.....10	I'M GONNA KNOCK ON YOUR DOOR .... MGM 2006 389

MARIE OSMOND
US singer (born Olive Marie Osmond, 13/10/1959, Ogden, UT) who began performing with her brothers at 14. She teamed up with brother Donny for a number of hits and hosted their own TV show. She hosted her own show in 1980.

17/11/1973 .....2.....15	PAPER ROSES .... MGM 2006 315

OSMOND BOYS
US vocal group formed by David, Doug, Nathan and Michael Osmond, the four sons of Alan Osmond.

09/11/1991.....65......2......	BOYS WILL BE BOYS .... Curb 6573847
11/01/1992.....60......4......	SHOW ME THE WAY .... Curb 6577227

OSMONDS
US family group formed in Ogden, UT in 1959 by Alan (born 22/6/1949, Ogden), Wayne (born 28/8/1951, Ogden), Merrill (born 30/4/1953, Ogden) and Jay Osmond (born 2/3/1955, Ogden) as the Osmond Brothers who won a contract to appear on the weekly *Andy Williams Show* in 1962. They added brother Donny (born 9/10/1959, Ogden) in 1963. The group later had their own UK TV series and a cartoon series. The original four brothers went on to record country music in the 1980s. The group has a star on the Hollywood Walk of Fame.

25/03/1972.....40......5......	DOWN BY THE LAZY RIVER .... MGM 2006 096
11/11/1972 .....2.....18	CRAZY HORSES .... MGM 2006 142
14/07/1973 .....4.....10	GOING HOME .... MGM 2006 288
27/10/1973 .....2.....14 .....O	LET ME IN .... MGM 2006 321
20/04/1974.....12.....10	I CAN'T STOP .... MCA 129
24/08/1974 .....❶³......9...... ●	LOVE ME FOR A REASON .... MGM 2006 458
01/03/1975.....28......8......	HAVING A PARTY .... MGM 2006 492
24/05/1975 .....5......8...... O	THE PROUD ONE .... MGM 2006 520
15/11/1975.....32......4......	I'M STILL GONNA NEED YOU .... MGM 2006 551
30/10/1976.....37......5......	I CAN'T LIVE A DREAM .... Polydor 2066 726
23/09/1995.....50......1......	CRAZY HORSES (REMIX) .... Polydor 5793212
12/06/1999.....34......2......	CRAZY HORSES (REMIX) Re-issue of Polydor 5793212 .... Polydor 5611372

GILBERT O'SULLIVAN
Irish singer (born Raymond O'Sullivan, 1/12/1946, Waterford) who was in bands before having two songs recorded by the Tremeloes in 1967. He recorded as Gilbert for CBS in 1968, sending out demos. He was signed by Tom Jones/Engelbert Humperdinck manager Gordon Mills to MAM and re-named Gilbert O'Sullivan. Back with CBS in 1980, he later sued Mills over his original contract.

28/11/1970 .....8......11	NOTHING RHYMED .... MAM 3
03/04/1971.....40......4......	UNDERNEATH THE BLANKET GO .... MAM 13
24/07/1971.....16......11	WE WILL Covered in US by Andy Williams who changed the line 'I bagsy be in goal', not understanding what it meant! .... MAM 30
27/11/1971 .....5......15	NO MATTER HOW I TRY .... MAM 53
04/03/1972 .....3......12	ALONE AGAIN (NATURALLY) ▲⁶ .... MAM 66
17/06/1972 .....8......11	OOH-WAKKA-DOO-WAKKA-DAY .... MAM 78
21/10/1972 .....❶²......14	CLAIR Written by O'Sullivan as a tribute to the daughter of his manager Gordon Mills .... MAM 84
17/03/1973 .....❶²......13	GET DOWN .... MAM 96
15/09/1973.....18......7......	OOH BABY .... MAM 107
10/11/1973 .....6......14 .....O	WHY OH WHY OH WHY .... MAM 111
09/02/1974.....19......7......	HAPPINESS IS ME AND YOU .... MAM 114
24/08/1974.....42......3......	A WOMAN'S PLACE .... MAM 122
14/12/1974.....12......6......	CHRISTMAS SONG .... MAM 124
14/06/1975.....14......6......	I DON'T LOVE YOU BUT I THINK I LIKE YOU .... MAM 130
27/09/1980.....19......9......	WHAT'S IN A KISS? .... CBS 8929
24/02/1990.....70......2......	SO WHAT .... Dover ROJ 3

O.T. QUARTET – see OUR TRIBE/ONE TRIBE

OTHER TWO
UK vocal/instrumental duo Stephen Morris (born 28/10/1957, Macclesfield) and Gillian Gilbert (born 27/1/1961, Manchester); they were both previously members of New Order.

09/11/1991.....41......3......	TASTY FISH .... Factory FAC 3297
06/11/1993.....46......2......	SELFISH .... London TWOCD 1

OTHERS
UK rock group formed in London by Dominic Masters (vocals), James Portinari (guitar), Jon Endersby (bass) and Martin Oldham (drums).

29/05/2004.....42......1......	THIS IS FOR THE POOR .... Poptones MC5090SCD
06/11/2004.....36......2......	STAN BOWLES Stan Bowles is a former professional footballer who played for QPR .... Vertigo 9868521

O Silver disc ● Gold disc ✪ Platinum disc (additional platinum units are indicated by a figure following the symbol) ◉ Singles released prior to 1973 that are known to have sold over 1 million copies in the UK

JOHNNY OTIS SHOW
US singer (born John Veliotes, 8/12/1921, Vallejo, CA) who began in big band jazz before turning to R&B. Known as the Godfather of Rhythm & Blues with his Johnny Otis R&B Caravan, a touring revue of big R&B names of the 1950s. Later a broadcaster, he founded numerous recording companies. He was inducted into the Rock & Roll Hall of Fame in 1994.

22/11/1957	2	15		MA HE'S MAKING EYES AT ME JOHNNY OTIS AND HIS ORCHESTRA WITH MARIE ADAMS AND THE THREE TONS OF JOY
					Capitol CL 14794
10/01/1958	20	7		BYE BYE BABY JOHNNY OTIS SHOW, VOCALS BY MARIE ADAMS AND JOHNNY OTIS	Capitol CL 14817

OTT
Irish vocal group featuring Glen, Alan, Adam, Niall and Keith. Keith left the group in March 1997.

15/02/1997	12	5		LET ME IN	Epic 6642052
17/05/1997	24	3		FOREVER GIRL	Epic 6645082
23/08/1997	11	4		ALL OUT OF LOVE	Epic 6649152
24/01/1998	10	6		THE STORY OF LOVE	Epic OTT 1CD

OTTAWAN
Martinique vocal duo Jean Patrick (born 6/4/1954) and Annette (born 1/11/1958); their hits were produced by the same team responsible for the Gibson Brothers, Daniel Vangarde and Jean Kluger.

13/09/1980	2	18	●	D.I.S.C.O.	Carrere CAR 161
13/12/1980	56	6		YOU'RE OK	Carrere CAR 168
05/09/1981	3	15	O	HANDS UP (GIVE ME YOUR HEART)	Carrere CAR 183
05/12/1981	49	6		HELP, GET ME SOME HELP!	Carrere CAR 215

JOHN OTWAY AND WILD WILLY BARRETT
UK duo John Otway (born 2/10/1952, Aylesbury, vocals) and Wild Willy Barrett (guitar/fiddle).

03/12/1977	27	8		REALLY FREE	Polydor 2058 951
05/07/1980	45	4		DK 50-80 OTWAY AND BARRETT	Polydor 2059 250
12/10/2002	9	3		BUNSEN BURNER JOHN OTWAY Based on The Trammps' Disco Inferno	U-vibe OTWAY 02Z

OUI 3
US dance trio Blair Booth (vocals/programming), Philip Erb (keyboards) and Trevor Miles (rapping).

20/02/1993	28	6		FOR WHAT IT'S WORTH	MCA MCSTD 1736
24/04/1993	54	2		ARMS OF SOLITUDE	MCA MCSTD 1759
17/07/1993	17	6		BREAK FROM THE OLD ROUTINE	MCA MCSTD 1793
23/10/1993	26	3		FOR WHAT IT'S WORTH	MCA MCSTD 1941
29/01/1994	38	2		FACT OF LIFE	MCA MCSTD 1939
27/05/1995	55	2		JOY OF LIVING	MCA MCSTD 2057

OUR DAUGHTER'S WEDDING
US vocal/instrumental group formed in NYC by Scott Simon, Layne Rico and Keith Silva.

| 01/08/1981 | 49 | 6 | | LAWNCHAIRS | EMI America EA 124 |

OUR HOUSE
Australian instrumental/production duo Kasey Taylor and Sean Quinn.

| 31/08/1996 | 52 | 1 | | FLOOR SPACE | Perfecto PERF 125CD |

OUR KID
UK teenage pop group from Liverpool fronted by Kevin Rown who was first known after winning New Faces on TV. Because of their average age of twelve, they fell foul of the educational authorities over time they were able to devote to TV and promotional work.

| 29/05/1976 | 2 | 11 | O | YOU JUST MIGHT SEE ME CRY | Polydor 2058 729 |

OUR LADY PEACE
Canadian rock group formed in Toronto by Raine Maida (vocals), Mike Turner (guitar), Duncan Coutts (bass) and Jeremy Taggart (drums).

| 15/01/2000 | 70 | 1 | | ONE MAN ARMY Contains a sample of Terminalhead's Underfire | Epic 6688662 |

OUR TRIBE/ONE TRIBE
UK/US duo Rob Dougan and Rollo Armstrong. They also recorded as Our Tribe and Rollo was later in Faithless.

20/06/1992	52	2		WHAT HAVE YOU DONE (IS THIS ALL) ONE TRIBE FEATURING GEM	Inner Rhythm HEART 03
27/03/1993	42	2		I BELIEVE IN YOU OUR TRIBE	ffrreedom TABCD 117
30/04/1994	24	3		HOLD THAT SUCKER DOWN OT QUARTET	Cheeky CHEKCD 004
21/05/1994	73	1		LOVE COME HOME OUR TRIBE WITH FRANKIE PHAROAH AND KRISTINE W	Triangle BLUESCD 001
13/05/1995	55	1		HIGH AS A KITE ONE TRIBE FEATURING ROGER	ffrr FCD 259
30/09/1995	26	3		HOLD THAT SUCKER DOWN (REMIX)	Cheeky CHEKCD 009
09/12/2000	45	1		HOLD THAT SUCKER DOWN Re-issue of Cheeky CHEKCD 009. This and above single credited to OT QUARTET
					Champion CHAMPCD 786

OUT OF MY HAIR
UK vocal/instrumental group formed in 1993 by Simon Eugene (bass/vocals), Sean Elliott (guitar), George Muranyi (keyboards) and Kenny Rumbles (drums). They split in 1996, Eugene going solo as Comfort. The group revived in 1999.

| 01/07/1995 | 73 | 1 | | MISTER JONES | RCA 74321267812 |

OUTHERE BROTHERS
US dance group formed by Malik E Martel, W Phillips, Hula Mahone and K Fingers. The CD which contained six mixes of their debut hit was reported to the Crown Prosecution Service for obscenity. The version in question, OHB Club Version, contained references to oral sex, although the CPS took no further action. Then the follow-up Boom Boom Boom also hit #1 and once again the club version on the CD attracted attention. The CPS also received a copy of the pair's album 1 Polish, 2 Biscuits And A Fish Sandwich from Cleveland police, querieing whether it contravened the Obscene Publications Act. Menwhile the head of

❶⁹ Number of weeks single topped the UK chart ↑ Entered the UK chart at #1 ▲⁹ Number of weeks single topped the US chart

595

Wroughton Middle School in Gorleston, Norfolk, banned his pupils from bringing the record to the school! For publicity purposes, Hula and Malik assumed the roles of the brothers. They were later a production outfit, handling hits for Indo among others.

DATE	POS	WKS	BPI	SINGLE TITLE	LABEL & NUMBER
18/03/1995	●¹	15	●	**DON'T STOP (WIGGLE WIGGLE)**	Stip YZ 917CD
17/06/1995	●⁴	15	●	**BOOM BOOM BOOM**	Stip YZ 938CD
23/09/1995	7	7		**LA LA LA HEY HEY**	Stip YZ 974CD
16/12/1995	9	10		**IF YOU WANNA PARTY** MOELLA FEATURING THE OUTHERE BROTHERS	Stip 030CD
25/01/1997	18	3		LET ME HEAR YOU SAY 'OLE OLE'	Stip 089CD

OUTKAST US rap duo formed in Atlanta, GA by Big Boi (born Antoine Patton) and Dre (born Andre Benjamin). Dre is the partner of fellow rapper Erykah Badu and the pair have a young son. The two also have outside interests: Big Boi runs Pitfall Kennels, which breeds and sells Pitbull Terriers, while Dre is a painter who runs Andre Classic Paintings! They first recorded for LaFace in 1994. Six Grammy Awards include Best Rap Album in 2001 for *Stankonia*, and Album of the Year and Best Rap Album in 2003 for *Speakerboxx/The Love Below*. They also won the Best Group at the 2004 MTV Europe Music Awards.

DATE	POS	WKS	BPI	SINGLE TITLE	LABEL & NUMBER
23/12/2000	61	1		B.O.B. (BOMBS OVER BAGHDAD)	LaFace 74321822942
03/02/2001	48	4		MS JACKSON (IMPORT)	LaFace 73008245252
03/03/2001	2	10	O	**MS JACKSON** ▲¹ 2001 Grammy Award for Best Rap Performance by a Duo or Group	LaFace 74321836822
09/06/2001	16	8		SO FRESH SO CLEAN	LaFace 74321863402
06/04/2002	19	5		THE WHOLE WORLD OUTKAST FEATURING KILLER MIKE 2002 Grammy Award for Best Rap Performance by a Duo or Group	LaFace 74321917592
27/07/2002	46	1		LAND OF A MILLION DRUMS OUTKAST FEATURING KILLER MIKE AND SLEEPY BROWN	Atlantic AT 0134CD
04/10/2003	55	1		GHETTO MUSICK	Arista 82876567232
22/11/2003	3	21		**HEY YA!** ▲⁹ 2003 Grammy Award for Best Urban/Alternative Performance. 2004 MTV Europe Music Awards for Best Song and Best Video	Arista 82876580102
03/04/2004	7	10		**THE WAY YOU MOVE** ▲¹ OUTKAST FEATURING SLEEPY BROWN	Arista 82876605672
03/07/2004	4	7		**ROSES**	Arista 82876624392

OUTLANDER Belgian producer Marcos Salon.

DATE	POS	WKS	BPI	SINGLE TITLE	LABEL & NUMBER
31/08/1991	51	2		VAMP	R&S RSUK 1
07/02/1998	62	1		THE VAMP (REVISITED)	R&S RS 97113CDX

OUTLANDISH Multinational hip hop trio formed in Denmark by Isam (from Morocco), Waqas (Pakistan) and Lenny (Honduras).

DATE	POS	WKS	BPI	SINGLE TITLE	LABEL & NUMBER
31/05/2003	31	2		GUANTANAMO	RCA 82876517702

OUTLAWS UK instrumental group, ex-Mike Berry accompanists who once included Richie Blackmore (later of Deep Purple) and Chas Hodges (of Chas and Dave).

DATE	POS	WKS	BPI	SINGLE TITLE	LABEL & NUMBER
13/04/1961	46	2		SWINGIN' LOW	HMV POP 844
08/06/1961	43	2		AMBUSH	HMV POP 877

OUTRAGE US singer Fabio Paras.

DATE	POS	WKS	BPI	SINGLE TITLE	LABEL & NUMBER
11/03/1995	57	1		TALL 'N' HANDSOME	Effective ECFL 001CD
23/11/1996	51	1		TALL 'N' HANDSOME (REMIX)	Positiva CDTIV 64

OUTSIDAZ FEATURING RAH DIGGA AND MELANIE BLATT US rap group formed in New Jersey by Young Zee, Pace Won, Leun One, Yah Ya, D.U., Az-Izz, Slang Ton, NawShis, DJ Muhammed and Denton with UK singer Melanie Blatt.

DATE	POS	WKS	BPI	SINGLE TITLE	LABEL & NUMBER
02/03/2002	41	2		I'M LEAVIN'	Rufflife RLCDM 03

OVERLANDERS UK vocal trio formed in 1963 by Laurie Mason, Paul Arnold and Pete Bartholomew, adding Terry Widlake and David Walsh when signing with Pye in 1965. Lead Arnold went solo in 1966 and was replaced by Ian Griffiths before they split the same year.

DATE	POS	WKS	BPI	SINGLE TITLE	LABEL & NUMBER
13/01/1966	●³	10		**MICHELLE** First cover of a Beatles album track to hit #1	Pye 7N 17034

OVERWEIGHT POOCH FEATURING CE CE PENISTON US female rapper with female singer Ce Ce Peniston.

DATE	POS	WKS	BPI	SINGLE TITLE	LABEL & NUMBER
18/01/1992	58	2		I LIKE IT	A&M AM 847

MARK OWEN UK singer (born 27/1/1974, Manchester) who was a founder member of Take That, staying with the group until they disbanded in 1996, then going solo. He also took part in the *It's Only Rock 'N' Roll* project for the Children's Promise charity.

DATE	POS	WKS	BPI	SINGLE TITLE	LABEL & NUMBER
30/11/1996	3	15	O	**CHILD**	RCA 74321424422
15/02/1997	3	6		**CLEMENTINE**	RCA 74321454992
23/08/1997	29	3		I AM WHAT I AM	RCA 74321501222
16/08/2003	4	9		**FOUR MINUTE WARNING**	Universal MCSTD 40329
08/11/2003	26	2		ALONE WITHOUT YOU	Universal MCSXD 40342
19/06/2004	30	1		MAKIN' OUT	Sedna CXSEDNA1

REG OWEN UK orchestra leader (born February 1928; died 1978).

DATE	POS	WKS	BPI	SINGLE TITLE	LABEL & NUMBER
27/02/1959	20	8		MANHATTAN SPIRITUAL	Pye International 7N 25009
27/10/1960	43	2		OBSESSION	Palette PG 9004

SID OWEN UK singer (born David Sutton, 12/1/1972) who was first known as an actor in TV's *Eastenders* as Ricky Butcher. He has also been in a number of films, including *Revolution*. Patsy Palmer, with whom he first charted, played Bianca Butcher in *Eastenders*.

O Silver disc ● Gold disc ✪ Platinum disc (additional platinum units are indicated by a figure following the symbol) ⊚ Singles released prior to 1973 that are known to have sold over 1 million copies in the UK

16/12/1995.....60......1....... BETTER BELIEVE IT (CHILDREN IN NEED) **SID OWEN AND PATSY PALMER** In aid of the BBC's 'Children In Need' appeal ....
.... Trinity TDM 001CD

08/07/2000.....14......5....... GOOD THING GOING .... Mushroom MUSH 74CDS

ROBERT OWENS
US dance artist who worked with David Morales, and previously with The It and Finger's Inc. He was brought up by his mother in Los Angeles, CA and his father in Chicago, IL, his musical style being influenced by both cities.

07/12/1991.....75......2....... I'LL BE YOUR FRIEND .... Perfecto PB 45161

26/04/1997.....25......2....... I'LL BE YOUR FRIEND (REMIX) .... Perfecto PERF 137CD1

24/02/2001.....44......1....... MINE TO GIVE **PHOTEK FEATURING ROBERT OWENS** .... Science QEDCD 10

15/02/2003.....34......1....... LAST NIGHT A DJ BLEW MY MIND **FAB FOR FEATURING ROBERT OWENS**................................ Illustrious CDILL 013

OXIDE AND NEUTRINO
UK garage duo formed by Londoners Oxide (born Alex Rivers, seventeen at the time of their debut hit) and Neutrino (born Mark Oseitutu, eighteen at debut hit). Their first hit was an adaptation of the theme to the TV series *Casualty*, originally on a self-financed white label before being picked up by East West. They are also members of The So Solid Crew, as are Megaman, Romeo and Lisa Maffia. They won the 2001 MOBO Award for Best Video for *Up Middle Finger*.

06/05/2000 ....❶[1].....11.....○ **BOUND 4 DA RELOAD (CASUALTY)** ↑ Contains an interpolation of the theme to the TV series *Casualty* ...... East West OXIDE01CD1

30/12/2000 .....6......8....... **NO GOOD 4 ME OXIDE AND NEUTRINO FEATURING MEGAMAN, ROMEO AND LISA MAFFIA** Contains a sample of The Prodigy's *No Good (Start The Dance)* .... East West OXIDE 02CD

26/05/2001 .....7......7....... **UP MIDDLE FINGER** .... East West OXIDE 03CD

28/07/2001.....16......5....... DEVIL'S NIGHTMARE Featured in the 2001 film *Lara Croft: Tomb Raider*............................ East West OXIDE 07CD1

08/12/2001.....12......8....... RAP DIS/ONLY WANNA KNOW U COS URE FAMOUS .... East West OXIDE 08CD

28/09/2002.....10......6....... **DEM GIRLZ (I DON'T KNOW WHY) OXIDE AND NEUTRINO FEATURING KOWDEAN** .... East West OXIDE 09CD

OXYGEN FEATURING ANDREA BRITTON
UK production duo Ricky Simmons and Stephen Jones. They also record as Ascension, Lustral, Oxygen and Space Brothers. Singer Andrea Britton comes from London, and was 28 at their debut hit.

11/01/2003.....30......3....... AM I ON YOUR MIND .... Innocent SINCD 40

OZOMATLI
US vocal/instrumental group formed by Ulises Bella, Pablo Castorena, Cut Chemist, Jose 'Crunchy' Espinosa, William 'Echo' Marrufo, Raul 'El Bully' Pacheco, Justin 'Nino' Poree, Asdru Sierra, Charli 2na, Wil-Dog and Jiro Yamaguchi.

20/03/1999.....58......1....... CUT CHEMIST SUITE .... Almo Sounds CDALM 62

22/05/1999.....68......1....... SUPER BOWL SUNDAE .... Almo Sounds CDALM 63

❶[9] Number of weeks single topped the UK chart ↑ Entered the UK chart at #1 ▲[9] Number of weeks single topped the US chart

597

P

JAZZI P UK rapper Pauline Bennett.

08/07/1989	25	6	GET LOOSE LA MIX FEATURING JAZZI P .... Breakout USA 659
09/06/1990	51	3	FEEL THE RHYTHM .... A&M USA 691
03/08/1991	42	4	REBEL WOMAN DNA FEATURING JAZZI P Contains a sample of David Bowie's *Rebel Rebel* .... DNA 7DNA 001

TALISMAN P FEATURING BARRINGTON LEVY UK/Jamaican duo formed by UK DJ Talisman P and Jamaican singer Barrington Levy (born 1964, Kingston). Their debut hit single had originally been a hit for Levy in 1985 (position #41).

13/10/2001	37	2	HERE I COME (SING DJ) .... NuLife 74321895622

P J B FEATURING HANNAH AND HER SISTERS US group assembled by Pete Bellotte and fronted by singer Hannah Jones.

14/09/1991	21	8	BRIDGE OVER TROUBLED WATER .... Dance Pool 6565467

PETEY PABLO US rapper (born Moses Barrett, Greenville, NC) who worked with Black Rob, Mystikal, Heavy D and Queen Latifah before signing a solo deal with Jive.

09/02/2002	51	1	I Featured in the 2001 film *The Fast And The Furious* .... Jive 9253092

THOM PACE US singer (born Boise, ID) who wrote the music for numerous films before leaving the industry and conducting helicopter tours around Hawaii.

19/05/1979	14	15	MAYBE Featured in the 1975 film *The Life And Times Of Grizzly Adams* .... RSO 34

PACEMAKERS – see **GERRY AND THE PACEMAKERS**

PACIFICA UK production duo formed in Glasgow by Donald McDonald and Stuart McCredie.

31/07/1999	54	1	LOST IN THE TRANSLATION Contains a sample of Blondie's *Heart Of Glass* .... Wildstar CDWILD 25

PACK FEATURING NIGEL BENN UK vocal/instrumental group formed by Lesley Shone, Vicky Steer, Tim Stone and David Scanes with UK boxer Nigel Benn.

08/12/1990	61	2	STAND AND FIGHT .... IQ ZB 44237

PACKABEATS UK group formed by Dave Cameron (vocals), Mick Flynn (guitar), Ken Eade (guitar), Brian Lewis (bass) and Ian Stewart (drums).

23/02/1961	49	1	GYPSY BEAT .... Parlophone R 4729

PADDINGTONS UK rock group formed in Hull by Tom Atkins (vocals), Marv (guitar), Josh Hubbard (guitar), Lloyd Dobbs (bass) and Grant Dobbs (drums).

23/10/2004	47	1	21/SOME OLD GIRL .... Poptones MC5093SCD

JOSE PADILLA FEATURING ANGELA JOHN Spanish DJ with UK singer Angela John.

08/08/1998	59	1	WHO DO YOU LOVE .... Manifesto FESCD 45

PAFFENDORF German group formed in Cologne by Gottfried Engels and Ramon Zenker who is also responsible for Fragma, Ariel and Bellini.

15/06/2002	7	7	BE COOL .... Data 29CDS
26/04/2003	52	1	CRAZY SEXY MARVELLOUS .... Data 51CDS

PAGANINI TRAXX Italian DJ/producer Sam Paganini (born 27/9/1972, Vittorio Veneto).

01/02/1997	47	1	ZOE .... Sony S3 DANCUCD 18X

JIMMY PAGE UK guitarist (born 9/1/1944, Heston) and founder member of Led Zeppelin in 1968, one of the most successful groups of all time. Page (ex-Yardbirds) and Robert Plant formed the Honeydrippers in 1984 and later undertook numerous solo projects.

17/12/1994	35	3	GALLOWS POLE JIMMY PAGE AND ROBERT PLANT .... Fontana PPCD 2
11/04/1998	26	2	MOST HIGH PAGE AND PLANT 1998 Grammy Award for Best Hard Rock Song for Jimmy Page and Robert Plant ... Mercury 5687512
01/08/1998	75	1	COME WITH ME (IMPORT) Featured in the 1998 film *Godzilla* .... Epic 34K78954
08/08/1998	2	10	**COME WITH ME** This and above single credited to PUFF DADDY FEATURING JIMMY PAGE .... Epic 6662842

PATTI PAGE US singer (born Clara Ann Fowler, 8/11/1927, Muskogee, OK) who began her career on radio before joining Jimmy

○ Silver disc ● Gold disc ✪ Platinum disc (additional platinum units are indicated by a figure following the symbol) ⓜ Singles released prior to 1973 that are known to have sold over 1 million copies in the UK

Joy's band as singer in 1947. She started recording solo in 1949 and later had her own TV series *The Patti Page Show*. She appeared in films, including *Dondi* (1961) and *Boys Night Out* (1962) and was still recording in the late 1980s. She is reckoned to have sold more records than any other female performer of the 1950s. She won the 1998 Grammy Award for Best Traditional Pop Vocal Performance for *Live At Carnegie Hall – The 50th Anniversary Concert*. Despite limited UK chart success, Patti scored 81 US hits from 1948–68, including four #1's (*All My Love [Bolero]*, *The Tennessee Waltz*, *I Went To Your Wedding* and *The Doggie In The Window*) and a further twenty top ten hits. She has a star on the Hollywood Walk of Fame.

| 27/03/1953 | 9 | 5 | | **HOW MUCH IS THAT DOGGIE IN THE WINDOW** ▲[8] Dog barks supplied by 'Jon and Mac' | Oriole CB 1156 |

TOMMY PAGE US singer (born 24/5/1969, New Jersey).

| 26/05/1990 | 53 | 3 | | I'LL BE YOUR EVERYTHING ▲[1] | Sire W 9959 |

WENDY PAGE – see TIN TIN OUT

PAGLIARO Canadian singer (born Michel Pagliaro, 9/11/1948, Montreal); he was a member of Les Chancelliers, who scored on the Canadian charts in 1966, before going solo. He spent some time in France during the 1980s producing acts such as Jacques Hagelin.

| 19/02/1972 | 31 | 6 | | LOVING YOU AIN'T EASY | Pye 7N 45111 |

PAID AND LIVE FEATURING LAURYN HILL US production duo Hakim Moore and Chad Moore with rapper and singer Lauryn Hill.

| 27/12/1997 | 57 | 1 | | ALL MY TIME | World Entertainment OWECD 2 |

ELAINE PAIGE UK singer (born Elaine Bickerstaff, 5/3/1948, Barnet) who was initially known for her lead role in *Evita*, although Julie Covington scored the hit single. She left the show after a few months in order to concentrate on a recording career.

21/10/1978	46	5		DON'T WALK AWAY TILL I TOUCH YOU	EMI 2862
13/06/1981	6	12	●	**MEMORY** From the musical *Cats*	Polydor POSP 279
30/01/1982	67	3		MEMORY	Polydor POSP 279
14/04/1984	72	1		SOMETIMES (THEME FROM 'CHAMPIONS')	Island IS 174
05/01/1985	❶[4]	16	●	**I KNOW HIM SO WELL** ELAINE PAIGE AND BARBARA DICKSON From the musical *Chess*	RCA CHESS 3
21/11/1987	69	1		THE SECOND TIME (THEME FROM 'BILITIS')	WEA YZ 163
21/01/1995	68	1		HYMNE A L'AMOUR	WEA YZ 899CD
24/10/1998	36	2		MEMORY Re-recording of Polydor POSP 279	WEA 197CD

HAL PAIGE AND THE WHALERS US vocal/instrumental group fronted by guitarist Hal Paige. They also recorded for Fury and Atlantic Records. Paige also formed The Blue Boys.

| 25/08/1960 | 50 | 1 | | GOING BACK TO MY HOME TOWN | Melodisc MEL 1553 |

JENNIFER PAIGE US singer/songwriter (born 3/9/1975, Atlanta, GA) who began performing duets with her brother at the age of eight and learned to play piano at ten. She moved to Los Angeles, CA in 1997.

| 12/09/1998 | 4 | 12 | ○ | **CRUSH** | EAR 0039425 ERE |
| 20/03/1999 | 68 | 1 | | SOBER | EAR 0044185 ERE |

ORCHESTRE DE CHAMBRE JEAN-FRANCOIS PAILLARD French orchestra leader (born 12/4/1928, Vitry-Le-Francois).

| 20/08/1988 | 61 | 3 | | THEME FROM 'VIETNAM' (CANON IN D) | Debut DEBT 3053 |

PALE Irish group formed in Dublin by Matthew Devereaux (vocals), Shane Wearen (mandolin) and Sean Malloy (bass).

| 13/06/1992 | 51 | 2 | | DOGS WITH NO TAILS | A&M AM 866 |

PALE FOUNTAINS UK group formed in Liverpool in 1981 by Michael Head (guitar/vocals), Chris McCaffrey (bass), Andy Diagram (trumpet) and Thomas Whelan (drums). They first recorded for the Operation Twilight label in 1982. The group disbanded in 1985; Head went on to form Shack with his brother John.

| 27/11/1982 | 48 | 6 | | THANK YOU | Virgin VS 557 |

PALE SAINTS UK group formed in Leeds in 1989 by Graeme Naysmith (born 9/2/1967, Edinburgh, guitar), Ian Masters (born 4/1/1964, Potters Bar, bass) and Chris Cooper (born 17/11/1966, Portsmouth, drums), with Ashley Horner (guitar) an occasional member. Horner was later replaced on a more permanent basis by Meriel Barham (born 15/10/1964).

| 06/07/1991 | 72 | 1 | | KINKY LOVE | 4AD AD 1009 |

PALE X Dutch trance producer Michael Pollen.

| 03/02/2001 | 74 | 1 | | NITRO | Nukleuz NUKP 0280 |

NERINA PALLOT UK singer (born 1975) who signed her first contract at the age of nineteen while at art school in London.

| 18/08/2001 | 61 | 1 | | PATIENCE | Polydor 5872122 |

BARRY PALMER – see MIKE OLDFIELD

JHAY PALMER FEATURING MC IMAGE Jamaican/UK vocal duo; Palmer had a number of Jamaican hits before breaking in the UK, while MC Image appeared in the TV series *Ayia Napa Fantasy Island*.

| 27/04/2002 | 69 | 1 | | HELLO | Bagatrix CDBTX 002 |

PATSY PALMER – see SID OWEN

ROBERT PALMER UK singer (born Alan Palmer, 19/1/1949, Scarborough); he joined the Alan Bown Set in 1969 before forming Vinegar Joe in 1971 and signing with Island. Palmer remained with Island as a solo artist when the group disbanded in 1974. He was lead singer for Power Station in 1985. He died from a heart attack on 26/9/2003.

DATE	POS	WKS	BPI	SINGLE TITLE	LABEL & NUMBER
20/05/1978	53	4		EVERY KINDA PEOPLE	Island WIP 6425
07/07/1979	61	2		BAD CASE OF LOVIN' YOU (DOCTOR DOCTOR)	Island WIP 6481
06/09/1980	44	8		JOHNNY AND MARY	Island WIP 6638
22/11/1980	33	9		LOOKING FOR CLUES	Island WIP 6651
13/02/1982	16	8		SOME GUYS HAVE ALL THE LUCK	Island WIP 6754
02/04/1983	53	4		YOU ARE IN MY SYSTEM	Island IS 104
18/06/1983	66	2		YOU CAN HAVE IT (TAKE MY HEART)	Island IS 121
10/05/1986	5	15	○	ADDICTED TO LOVE ▲[1] 1986 Grammy Award for Best Rock Vocal Performance	Island IS 270
19/07/1986	9	9		I DIDN'T MEAN TO TURN YOU ON	Island IS 283
01/11/1986	68	1		DISCIPLINE OF LOVE	Island IS 242
26/03/1988	58	3		SWEET LIES	Island IS 352
11/06/1988	44	4		SIMPLY IRRESISTIBLE 1988 Grammy Award for Best Rock Vocal Performance	EMI EM 61
15/10/1988	6	12		SHE MAKES MY DAY	EMI EM 65
13/05/1989	28	7		CHANGE HIS WAYS	EMI EM 85
26/08/1989	71	1		IT COULD HAPPEN TO YOU	EMI EM 99
03/11/1990	6	10		I'LL BE YOUR BABY TONIGHT ROBERT PALMER AND UB40	EMI EM 167
12/01/1991	9	9		MERCY MERCY ME – I WANT YOU Cover versions of two Marvin Gaye songs	EMI EM 173
15/06/1991	68	1		DREAMS TO REMEMBER	EMI EM 193
07/03/1992	43	3		EVERY KINDA PEOPLE (REMIX)	Island IS 498
17/10/1992	50	3		WITCHCRAFT	EMI EM 251
09/07/1994	57	2		GIRL U WANT	EMI CDEMS 331
03/09/1994	25	5		KNOW BY NOW	EMI CDEMS 343
24/12/1994	38	4		YOU BLOW ME AWAY	EMI CDEMS 350
14/10/1995	45	2		RESPECT YOURSELF	EMI CDEMS 399
18/01/2003	42	1		ADDICTED TO LOVE SHAKE B4 USE VS ROBERT PALMER	Serious SER 606CD

SUZANNE PALMER US singer (born in Chicago, IL).

DATE	POS	WKS	BPI	SINGLE TITLE	LABEL & NUMBER
18/01/1997	38	1		I BELIEVE ABSOLUTE FEATURING SUZANNE PALMER	AM:PM 5820752
14/11/1998	70	1		ALRIGHT CLUB 69 FEATURING SUZANNE PALMER	Twisted UK TWCD 10039
29/06/2002	36	1		643 (LOVE'S ON FIRE) DJ TIESTO FEATURING SUZANNE PALMER	Nebula VCRD 106

TYRONE 'VISIONARY' PALMER – see SLAM

PAN POSITION Italian/Venezuelan instrumental/production group formed by Ottorino Menardi, Lino Lodi and Stefano Mango.

DATE	POS	WKS	BPI	SINGLE TITLE	LABEL & NUMBER
18/06/1994	55	1		ELEPHANT PAW (GET DOWN TO THE FUNK)	Positiva CDTIV 13

PANDORA'S BOX US vocal/instrumental group assembled by Jim Steinman and featuring singers Ellen Foley, Paula Pierce, Kim Shattuck and Melanie Vammen.

DATE	POS	WKS	BPI	SINGLE TITLE	LABEL & NUMBER
21/10/1989	51	3		IT'S ALL COMING BACK TO ME NOW	Virgin VS 1216

DARRYL PANDY US singer based in Chicago. Big Room Girl are a UK and Maltese production duo who also record as the Rhythm Masters.

DATE	POS	WKS	BPI	SINGLE TITLE	LABEL & NUMBER
14/12/1996	40	2		LOVE CAN'T TURN AROUND FARLEY JACKMASTER FUNK FEATURING DARRYL PANDY	4 Liberty LIBTCD 27R
20/02/1999	40	2		RAISE YOUR HANDS BIG ROOM GIRL FEATURING DARRYL PANDY	VC Recordings VCRD 44
02/10/1999	68	1		SUNSHINE & HAPPINESS DARRYL PANDY/NERIO'S DUBWORK	Azuli AZNYCD 103

JOHNNY PANIC UK group formed in London by Rob Solly (guitar/vocals), Matt James (guitar/vocals), Nash Francis (bass/vocals) and Jonny Shock (drums).

DATE	POS	WKS	BPI	SINGLE TITLE	LABEL & NUMBER
18/09/2004	69	1		BURN YOUR YOUTH	Concept CDCON59

JOHNNY PANIC AND THE BIBLE OF DREAMS UK group formed by Roland Orzabal (born Roland Orzabal de la Quintana, 22/8/1961, Portsmouth) and David Bascombe. Orzabal is an ex-member of Graduate and Tears For Fears.

DATE	POS	WKS	BPI	SINGLE TITLE	LABEL & NUMBER
02/02/1991	70	2		JOHNNY PANIC AND THE BIBLE OF DREAMS	Fontana PANIC 1

PANJABI MC UK DJ/singer (born Rajinder Rai, 1975, Coventry); he won the 2003 MTV Europe Music Award for Best Dance Act.

DATE	POS	WKS	BPI	SINGLE TITLE	LABEL & NUMBER
04/01/2003	59	3		MUNDIAN TO BACH KE (IMPORT) Contains a sample of the theme to the TV series Knightrider	Big Star BigCDM 076CD
25/01/2003	5	13		MUNDIAN TO BACH KE Featured in the 2003 film Bend It Like Beckham	Showbiz/Instant Karma KARMA 28CD
05/07/2003	25	3		JOGI/BEWARE OF THE BOYS PANJABI MC FEATURING JAY-Z	Showbiz/Dharma DHARMA 1CDS

PANTERA US heavy metal group formed in Arlinton, TX in 1983 by Terry Glaze (guitar/vocals), 'Dimebag' Darrell Abbot (born 20/8/1966, Dallas, TX, guitar), Vince Abbott (born 11/3/1964, Dallas, drums) and Rex Rocker (born 27/7/1964, Graham, TX, bass). Glaze was replaced by Philip Anselmo (born 30/6/1968, New Orleans, LA) in 1988. Pantera disbanded in 2004 and Abbott formed Damageplan, but at a Damageplan concert in Columbus, OH on 10/12/2004, deranged Pantera fan Nathan Gale leapt on stage and shot and killed Abbott, two band workers and a fan before he was shot dead by police. It was later revealed that Gale blamed Abbott for the demise of Pantera.

10/10/1992	73	1		MOUTH FOR WAR	Atco A 5845T
27/02/1993	35	2		WALK	Atco B 6076CD
19/03/1994	19	2		I'M BROKEN	Atco B 5832CD1
22/10/1994	26	3		PLANET CARAVAN	East West A 5836CD1

PAPA ROACH US rock group formed in California in 1993 by Coby Dick (vocals), Jerry Horton (guitar), Will James (bass) and Dave Buckner (drums). James was replaced by Tobin Esperance in 1996.

17/02/2001	3	10		LAST RESORT	DreamWorks 4509212
05/05/2001	17	6		BETWEEN ANGELS AND INSECTS	DreamWorks 4509092
22/06/2002	14	8		SHE LOVES ME NOT	DreamWorks 4508182
02/11/2002	54	1		TIME AND TIME AGAIN	DreamWorks 4508052
18/09/2004	45	2		GETTING AWAY WITH MURDER	Geffen 9863647

PAPER DOLLS UK vocal trio formed in Northampton by Pauline 'Spider' Bennett, Sue 'Copper' Marshall and Suzi 'Tiger' Mathis, all of whom wore blonde wigs and matching satin dresses. Kim Goody later joined the group.

13/03/1968	11	13		SOMETHING HERE IN MY HEART (KEEPS A-TELLIN' ME NO)	Pye 7N 17456

PAPER LACE UK pop group formed in Nottingham in 1968 by Phil Wright (born 9/4/1950, Nottingham, drums/lead vocals), Cliff Fish (born 13/8/1949, Ripley, bass), Michael Vaughan (born 27/7/1950, Sheffield, guitar), Chris Morris (born 1/11/1954, Nottingham, guitar) and Carlo Santanna (born 29/7/1947, Rome, Italy, guitar). They appeared on a number of TV shows before winning *Opportunity Knocks* in 1974 and signing for Pete Callender and Mitch Murray's new Bus Stop label.

23/02/1974	❶[3]	14	●	BILLY DON'T BE A HERO Featured in the 1994 film *The Adventures Of Priscilla: Queen Of The Desert*	Bus Stop BUS 1014
04/05/1974	3	11	○	THE NIGHT CHICAGO DIED ▲[1]	Bus Stop BUS 1016
24/08/1974	11	10		THE BLACK EYED BOYS	Bus Stop BUS 1019
04/03/1978	24	6		WE'VE GOT THE WHOLE WORLD IN OUR HANDS NOTTINGHAM FOREST FC AND PAPER LACE	Warner Brothers K 17110

PAPERDOLLS UK vocal trio formed by Hollie, Debbie and Lucy.

12/09/1998	65	1		GONNA MAKE YOU BLUSH	MCA MCSTD 40175

PAPPA BEAR FEATURING VAN DER TOORN German rapper with a Dutch singer.

16/05/1998	47	1		CHERISH	Universal UMD 70316

PAR-T-ONE VS INXS Italian DJ Serio Casu.

03/11/2001	19	6		I'M SO CRAZY Track is based on the INXS song *Just Keep Walking*	Credence CDCRED 016

VANESSA PARADIS French singer (born 22/12/1972, St Maur) who became an actress; her screen debut was in *Noce Blanche*.

13/02/1988	3	10		JOE LE TAXI	FA Productions POSP 902
10/10/1992	6	15		BE MY BABY	Remark PO 235
27/02/1993	49	4		SUNDAY MORNINGS	Remark PZCD 251
24/07/1993	57	1		JUST AS LONG AS YOU ARE THERE	Remark PZCD 272

PARADISE UK group formed by Paul Johnson (vocals), David Aiyeola (guitar), Junior Edwards (bass), Phillip Edwards (keyboards) and Bobby Clarke (drums).

10/09/1983	42	4		ONE MIND, TWO HEARTS	Priority P 1

PARADISE LOST UK death metal group formed in Yorkshire in 1989 by Nick Holmes (vocals), Gregor MacKintosh (guitar), Aaron Aedy (guitar), Stephen Edmonson (bass) and Mathew Archer (drums). They were originally signed by Peaceville. Archer left in 1994, replaced by Lee Morris.

20/05/1995	60	1		THE LAST TIME	Music For Nations CDKUT 165
07/10/1995	66	1		FOREVER FAILURE	Music For Nations CDKUT 169
28/06/1997	53	1		SAY JUST WORDS	Music For Nations CDKUT 174

PARADISE ORGANISATION UK vocal/instrumental group formed by Jonathan Helmer and David Yowell.

23/01/1993	70	1		PRAYER TOWER	Cowboy RODEO 13

PARADOX UK producer Dev Pandya who also records as Alaska.

24/02/1990	66	2		JAILBREAK	Ronin 7R2

NORRIE PARAMOR UK producer/arranger/orchestra leader and conductor (born 1914) who began his career with Gracie Fields. He is best known as a producer, having been responsible for 27 #1's in the UK 1954–69. He died on 9/9/1979.

17/03/1960	36	2		THEME FROM 'A SUMMER PLACE'	Columbia DB 4419
22/03/1962	33	6		THEME FROM 'Z CARS'	Columbia DB 4789

PARAMOUNT JAZZ BAND – see MR ACKER BILK AND HIS PARAMOUNT JAZZ BAND

PARAMOUNTS UK group formed in Southend in 1961 by Gary Brooker (born 29/5/1945, Southend, keyboard/vocals), Robin Trower (born 9/3/1945, Southend, guitar), Chris Copping (born 29/8/1945, Southend, bass) and Mick Brownlee (drums), replaced in 1963 by Barrie 'BJ' Wilson (born 18/3/1947, Southend). They disbanded in 1966; Brooker, Trower and Wilson formed Procol Harum.

16/01/1964	35	7		POISON IVY	Parlophone R 5093

❶[9] Number of weeks single topped the UK chart ↑ Entered the UK chart at #1 ▲[9] Number of weeks single topped the US chart

PARCHMENT UK gospel group formed in 1970 by John Pac (born John Pacalabo); they disbanded in 1980.

16/09/1972.....31......5....... LIGHT UP THE FIRE .... Pye 7N 45178

PARIS UK vocal group.

19/06/1982.....49......4....... NO GETTING OVER YOU .... RCA 222

PARIS US singer (born Oscar Jackson, 29/10/1967, San Francisco, CA); he is the son of a bandleader and made his first recordings in the mid-1980s with producer Carl Davis.

21/01/1995.....38......2....... GUERRILLA FUNK .... Virgin PTYCD 100

MICA PARIS UK singer (born Michelle Wallen, 27/4/1969, London) who was a member of the Spirit of Watts gospel choir and later toured and recorded with Hollywood Beyond. She went solo in 1988. In February 2001 her brother Jason Phillips was killed in a gangland-style shooting; three months later Mica was declared bankrupt.

07/05/1988 ......7.....11	MY ONE TEMPTATION	.... Fourth & Broadway BRW 85
30/07/1988.....26......5......	LIKE DREAMERS DO MICA PARIS FEATURING COURTNEY PINE	.... Fourth & Broadway BRW 108
22/10/1988.....26.....10......	BREATHE LIFE INTO ME	.... Fourth & Broadway BRW 115
21/01/1989.....19......7......	WHERE IS THE LOVE MICA PARIS AND WILL DOWNING	... Fourth & Broadway BRW 122
06/10/1990.....33......4......	CONTRIBUTION	.... Fourth & Broadway BRW 188
01/12/1990.....50......2......	SOUTH OF THE RIVER	.... Fourth & Broadway BRW 199
23/02/1991.....43......3......	IF I LOVE U 2 NITE	.... Fourth & Broadway BRW 207
31/08/1991.....61......3......	YOUNG SOUL REBELS	.... Big Life BLR 57
03/04/1993.....15......5......	I NEVER FELT LIKE THIS BEFORE	.... Fourth & Broadway BRCD 263
05/06/1993.....27......3......	I WANNA HOLD ON TO YOU	.... Fourth & Broadway BRCD 275
07/08/1993.....51......2......	TWO IN A MILLION	.... Fourth & Broadway BRCD 285
04/12/1993.....65......1......	WHISPER A PRAYER	.... Fourth & Broadway BRCD 287
08/04/1995.....29......4......	ONE	.... Cooltempo CDCOOL 304
16/05/1998.....40......2......	STAY	.... Cooltempo CDCOOL 334
14/11/1998.....72......1......	BLACK ANGEL	.... Cooltempo CDCOOL 341

RYAN PARIS Italian singer (born Fabio Roscioli) based in Rome who began his career over a decade before making his UK chart breakthrough.

03/09/1983 .....5......10 ...... DOLCE VITA .... Carrere CAR 289

PARIS AND SHARP UK production duo Luis Paris and Martin Sharp.

01/12/2001.....61......1...... APHRODITE .... Cream 16CD

PARIS ANGELS Irish group formed by Rikki Turner, Jayne Gill, Paul 'Wags' Wagstaffe, Scott Carey and Mark Adge. Wags later became a member of Black Grape.

03/11/1990.....75......1......	SCOPE	.... Sheer Joy SHEER 0047
20/07/1991.....55......3......	PERFUME	.... Virgin VS 1360
21/09/1991.....70......1......	FADE	.... Virgin VS 1365

PARIS RED US/German vocal/instrumental duo produced by Torsten Fenslau and Juergen Katzmann of Culture Beat.

29/02/1992.....61......1......	GOOD FRIEND	.... Columbia 6569417
15/05/1993.....59......1......	PROMISES	.... Columbia 6592342

JOHN PARISH + POLLY JEAN HARVEY UK guitarist Parish and singer Harvey (born 9/10/1969, Yeovil, Somerset) were members of PJ Harvey, the group launched by Polly in 1991. They met while members of Automatic Diamini in the late 1980s.

23/11/1996.....75......1...... THAT WAS MY VEIL .... Island CID 648

SIMON PARK ORCHESTRA UK orchestra leader (born 1946, Market Harborough) who began playing the piano at the age of five and graduated from Winchester College in music. The TV theme was written by Dutch composer Jules Staffaro, although the official credit was given to Jack Trombey, and was recorded in France.

25/11/1972.....41......2......	EYE LEVEL Theme to the TV series Van Der Valk	.... Columbia DB 8946
15/09/1973 ...❶⁴.....22 .....✪	EYE LEVEL	.... Columbia DB 8946

GRAHAM PARKER AND THE RUMOUR UK singer (born 18/11/1950, London) who was teamed up with the Rumour in 1975 and signed with Vertigo in 1976. The Rumour comprised Brinsley Schwarz (guitar), Bob Andrews (keyboards), Andrew Rodnar (bass) and Steve Goulding (drums).

19/03/1977.....24......5......	THE PINK PARKER EP Tracks on EP: Hold Back The Night, (Let Me Get) Sweet On You, White Honey, Soul Shoes . Vertigo PARK 001
22/04/1978.....32......7......	HEY LORD DON'T ASK ME QUESTIONS	.... Vertigo PARK 002
20/03/1982.....50......4......	TEMPORARY BEAUTY GRAHAM PARKER	.... RCA PARK 100

RAY PARKER JR. US singer/guitarist (born 1/5/1954, Detroit, MI); he learned to play the guitar while laid up with a broken leg and went on to become a prominent session guitarist in California, including spells working with Stevie Wonder, the Rolling Stones and Barry White. He formed Raydio in 1977 and began recording solo in 1982.

25/08/1984 .....2......31 .....●	GHOSTBUSTERS ▲³ Featured in the 1984 film Ghostbusters. 1984 Grammy Award for Best Pop Instrumental Performance. Parker was subsequently sued for plagiarism by Huey Lewis over the similarities between this and I Want A New Drug. .. Arista ARIST 580
18/01/1986.....46......4......	GIRLS ARE MORE FUN	.... Arista ARIST 641

| 03/10/1987 | 13 | 10 | | I DON'T THINK THAT MAN SHOULD SLEEP ALONE | Geffen GEF 27 |
| 30/01/1988 | 65 | 2 | | OVER YOU | Geffen GEF 33 |

ROBERT PARKER
US singer (born 14/10/1930, Crescent City, LA) and an accomplished saxophonist. He was in Professor Longhair's band from 1949. He appeared on numerous sessions with the likes of Irma Thomas, Ernie K-Doe and Joe Tex while undertaking his own solo recordings.

| 04/08/1966 | 24 | 8 | | BAREFOOTIN' | Island WI 286 |

SARA PARKER
US singer who was previously with Rumourz before going solo.

| 12/04/1997 | 22 | 2 | | MY LOVE IS DEEP | Manifesto FESCD 22 |

JIMMY PARKINSON
Australian singer who appeared in the 1957 film *The Secret Place*.

02/03/1956	9	13		THE GREAT PRETENDER	Columbia DB 3729
17/08/1956	26	2		WALK HAND IN HAND	Columbia DB 3775
09/11/1956	26	4		IN THE MIDDLE OF THE HOUSE	Columbia DB 3833

ALEX PARKS
UK singer (born 26/7/1984, Mount Hawke, Truro); she was the winner of the second series of *Fame Academy*.

| 29/11/2003 | 3 | 9 | | MAYBE THAT'S WHAT IT TAKES | Polydor 9814581 |
| 28/02/2004 | 13 | 4 | | CRY | Polydor 9816986 |

PARKS AND WILSON
UK production duo Michael Parks and Michael Wilson.

| 09/09/2000 | 71 | 1 | | FEEL THE DRUM (EP) Tracks on EP: *My Orbit, The Dragon, My Orbit (Remix), Drum Parade (No UFOs)* | Hooj Choons HOOJ 099CD |

PARLIAMENT – see SCOTT GROOVES

JOHN PARR
UK singer/songwriter (born 18/11/1954, Nottingham) who appeared in the films *Bible!* and *Valet Girls* and wrote the themes to films such as *American Anthem* and *St Elmo's Fire*.

14/09/1985	6	13	O	ST ELMO'S FIRE (MAN IN MOTION) ▲² Featured in the 1985 film *St Elmo's Fire*	London LON 73
18/01/1986	58	3		NAUGHTY NAUGHTY	London 80
30/08/1986	31	6		ROCK 'N' ROLL MERCENARIES MEAT LOAF FEATURING JOHN PARR	Arista ARIST 666

DEAN PARRISH
US singer (born Phil Anastasi, 1942, Brooklyn, NY) who scored one US hit – *Tell Her* in 1966 (position #97).

| 08/02/1975 | 38 | 5 | | I'M ON MY WAY | UK USA 2 |

MAN PARRISH
US DJ/producer (born Manny Parrish, New York).

26/03/1983	41	6		HIP HOP, BE BOP (DON'T STOP) Featured in the 2004 film *Shaun Of The Dead*	Polydor POSP 575
23/03/1985	56	4		BOOGIE DOWN (BRONX)	Boiling Point POSP 731
13/09/1986	64	3		MALE STRIPPER	Bolts 4
03/01/1987	4	13	O	MALE STRIPPER This and above single credited to MAN 2 MAN MEET MAN PARRISH	Bolts 4

KAREN PARRY
UK singer who also worked with DJ Ian Gordon.

| 21/12/2002 | 23 | 5 | | I THINK WE'RE ALONE NOW PASCAL FEATURING KAREN PARRY | All Around The World CDGLOBE267 |
| 24/07/2004 | 11 | 7 | | DISCOLAND FLIP & FILL FEATURING KAREN PARRY | All Around The World CDGLOBE 346 |

BILL PARSONS
US singer (born Robert Joseph Bare, 7/4/1935, Ironton, OH); he was drafted into the US Army and left a demo tape of *All American Boy* with Fraternity Records, intending it to be recorded by his friend Bill Parsons. They subsequently released it erroneously credited to Bill Parsons, as did London on the UK release. Bare later recorded as Bobby Bare for Mercury, RCA and CBS and appeared in the 1964 film *A Distant Trumpet*. He won one Grammy Award: 1963 Best Country & Western Recording for *Detroit City*.

| 10/04/1959 | 22 | 2 | | ALL AMERICAN BOY | London HL 8798 |

ALAN PARSONS PROJECT
UK producer/guitarist/keyboard player (born 1949) who worked as a staff engineer at Abbey Road Studios and made his reputation for engineering The Beatles' *Abbey Road* album, subsequently working on projects by artists such as Pink Floyd and Al Stewart. He then linked with songwriter Eric Woolfson in the Alan Parsons Project, adapting the works of Edgar Allan Poe and utilising a host of studio musicians.

| 15/01/1983 | 74 | 1 | | OLD AND WISE | Arista ARIST 494 |
| 10/03/1984 | 58 | 3 | | DON'T ANSWER ME | Arista ARIST 553 |

PARTIZAN
UK dance group formed by Craig Daniel-Yefet and 'Tall' Paul Newman. Newman has also recorded solo and under the names Escrima and Camisra and with Brandon Block in Grifters.

| 08/02/1997 | 36 | 2 | | DRIVE ME CRAZY | Multiply CDMULTY 17 |
| 06/12/1997 | 53 | 1 | | KEEP YOUR LOVE PARTIZAN FEATURING NATALIE ROBB | Multiply CDMULTY 29 |

PARTNERS IN KRYME
US group formed in 1986 by James Alpern (stage name Keymaster Snow) and Richard Usher (MC Golden Voice), with Kryme standing for 'keeping rhythm your motivating energy'. The pair were asked to write and record a song for the film *Teenage Mutant Hero Turtles* (originally created as comic-book heroes by Kevin Eastman and Peter Laird in 1984, and by 1989 a teenage phenomenon, with a TV cartoon series and a film in the pipeline). The single subsequently sold 2 million copies worldwide.

| 21/07/1990 | ❶4 | 10 | O | TURTLE POWER Featured in the films *Teenage Mutant Ninja Turtles* (1990), *Teenage Mutant Ninja Turtles 2: Secret Of The Ooze* (1991) and *Teenage Mutant Ninja Turtles III* (1993) | SBK TURTLE 1 |

❶⁹ Number of weeks single topped the UK chart ↑ Entered the UK chart at #1 ▲⁹ Number of weeks single topped the US chart

603

DAVID PARTON
UK singer (born in Newcastle-under-Lyme) and successful songwriter who was penning hits for Sweet Sensation at the time Stevie Wonder's *Songs In The Key Of Life* album was released. The outstanding track on the record was *Isn't She Lovely*. Wonder refused to release it as a single so Parton and producer Tony Hatch recorded a cover version.

15/01/1977	4	9	○	ISN'T SHE LOVELY	Pye 7N 45663

DOLLY PARTON
US singer (born 19/1/1946, Sevier County, TN); the fourth of twelve children, she made her own guitar at the age of five and sang on radio at eleven. She recorded her first single in 1955 for Gold Band and relocated to Nashville in 1964. She replaced Norma Jean on the Porter Wagoner TV show in 1967 and joined the Grand Ole Opry in 1968. She hosted her own TV variety show in 1976 and appeared in the films *9 To 5* and *Best Little Whorehouse In Texas* (her country #1 *I Will Always Love You* was featured in this film and later covered by Whitney Houston for *The Bodyguard*). She also appeared in an episode of *The Simpsons*, releasing all the male cast from a jail cell while on her way to sing at half time at the Super Bowl. She has won seven Grammy Awards: Best Country Vocal Performance in 1978 for *Here You Come Again,* Best Country Song and Best Country Vocal Performance in 1981 for *9 To 5,* Best Country Performance by a Group in 1987 with Linda Ronstadt and Emmylou Harris for *Trio,* Best Country Vocal Collaboration in 1999 with Linda Ronstadt and Emmylou Harris for *After The Gold Rush,* Best Bluegrass Album in 2000 for *The Grass Is Blue* and Best Female Country Vocal Performance in 2001 for *Shine*. She has a star on the Hollywood Walk of Fame.

15/05/1976	7	10		JOLENE	RCA 2675
21/02/1981	47	5		9 TO 5 ▲² Featured in the 1981 film *9 To 5.*	RCA 325
12/11/1983	7	15	○	ISLANDS IN THE STREAM ▲² KENNY ROGERS AND DOLLY PARTON	RCA 378
07/04/1984	75	1		HERE YOU COME AGAIN	RCA 395
16/04/1994	64	2		THE DAY I FALL IN LOVE DOLLY PARTON AND JAMES INGRAM	Columbia 6600282
19/10/2002	73	1		IF	Sanctuary SANX 139X

STELLA PARTON
US singer (born 4/5/1949, Sevier County, TN) and younger sister of Dolly Parton. She sang with Dolly on radio in 1955 and relocated to Nashville in 1972, later moving to California and working on TV.

22/10/1977	35	4		THE DANGER OF A STRANGER	Elektra K 12272

DON PARTRIDGE
UK singer (born 1945, Bournemouth) who began his career as a street busker in London. After his run of hits came to an end, he quit the music business and returned to entertaining the public in the streets.

07/02/1968	4	12		ROSIE	Columbia DB 8330
29/05/1968	3	13		BLUE EYES	Columbia DB 8416
19/02/1969	26	7		BREAKFAST ON PLUTO	Columbia DB 8538

PARTRIDGE FAMILY
US group named after a TV series loosely based on the real-life Cowsills. The Partridge Family members were Shirley (Shirley Jones, born 31/3/1934, Smithton, PA), Keith (David Cassidy, Jones' stepson, born 12/4/1950, New York), Laurie (Susan Dey), Danny (Danny Bonaduce), Christopher (Jeremy Gelbwaks) and Tracy (Suzanne Crough), with only Jones and Cassidy featuring on the resultant records. The TV series first aired on ABC TV on 25/9/1970 and by October Bell Records had signed up the 'group', linking them with top songwriting teams. The series ended in 1974, by which time Cassidy was already recording solo.

13/02/1971	18	9		I THINK I LOVE YOU ▲³	Bell 1130
26/02/1972	11	11		IT'S ONE OF THOSE NIGHTS (YES LOVE)	Bell 1203
08/07/1972	3	13		BREAKING UP IS HARD TO DO This and above two singles credited to PARTRIDGE FAMILY STARRING SHIRLEY JONES FEATURING DAVID CASSIDY	Bell MABEL 1
03/02/1973	9	9		LOOKING THROUGH THE EYES OF LOVE	Bell 1278
19/05/1973	10	11		WALKING IN THE RAIN This and above single credited to PARTRIDGE FAMILY STARRING DAVID CASSIDY	Bell 1293

PARTY ANIMALS
Dutch instrumental/production duo Jeff Porter and Jeroen Flamman.

01/06/1996	56	1		HAVE YOU EVER BEEN MELLOW	Mokum DB 17553
19/10/1996	43	2		HAVE YOU EVER BEEN MELLOW (EP) Tracks on EP: *Have You Ever Been Mellow, Hava Naquilla* and *Aquarius.*	Mokum DB 17413

PARTY BOYS
UK dance group formed by Dale Towl, Andy Hoe and Steve Hodgkinson.

10/01/2004	44	2		BUILD ME UP BUTTERCUP 2003	Liberty CDUP 001

PARTY FAITHFUL
UK vocal/instrumental group assembled by producers Mousse and Juicy Lucy.

22/07/1995	54	1		BRASS, LET THERE BE HOUSE	Ore AG 10CD

PASADENAS
UK soul group formed in 1987 by Jeff Aaron Brown (born 12/12/1964), Michael Milliner (born 16/2/1962), David Milliner (born 16/2/1962), John Andrew Banfield (born 4/12/1964) and Hammish Seelochan (born 11/8/1964), all of whom were previously with dance outfit Finesse since 1982.

28/05/1988	5	14		TRIBUTE (RIGHT ON) Tribute to Little Richard, Elvis Presley, Sam Cooke, Jackie Wilson, Otis Redding, James Brown, Marvin Gaye, Stevie Wonder, Smokey Robinson, the Supremes, Jimi Hendrix and the Jackson 5	CBS PASA 1
17/09/1988	13	9		RIDING ON A TRAIN	CBS PASA 2
26/11/1988	31	6		ENCHANTED LADY	CBS PASA 3
12/05/1990	22	5		LOVE THING	CBS PASA 4
01/02/1992	4	10	○	I'M DOING FINE NOW	Columbia 6577187
04/04/1992	20	4		MAKE IT WITH YOU	Columbia 6579257
06/06/1992	34	3		I BELIEVE IN MIRACLES	Columbia 6580567
29/08/1992	49	2		MOVING IN THE RIGHT DIRECTION	Columbia 6583417
21/11/1992	22	3		LET'S STAY TOGETHER	Columbia 6587747
14/07/1993	75	1		REELING	CBS PASA 5

○ Silver disc ● Gold disc ✪ Platinum disc (additional platinum units are indicated by a figure following the symbol) ⓜ Singles released prior to 1973 that are known to have sold over 1 million copies in the UK

PASCAL FEATURING KAREN PARRY UK production group fronted by singer Karen Parry; she was also with Flip & Fill.

21/12/2002.....23......5....... I THINK WE'RE ALONE NOW .... All Around The World CDGLOBE267

PASSENGERS Multinational album project that began as a combination between U2 and Brian Eno and which also featured guest appearances by Luciano Pavarotti, DJ Howie B and Japanese singer Holi. The single features Bono and Pavarotti.

02/12/1995 .....6.....9.....O **MISS SARAJEVO** .... Island CID 625

PASSION UK reggae group.

25/01/1997.....62......1....... SHARE YOUR LOVE (NO DIGGITY) .... Charm CRTCDS 269

PASSIONS UK group formed in 1978 by Mitch Barker (vocals), Barbara Gogan (guitar/vocals), Clive Timperley (guitar/vocals), Claire Bidwell (bass) and Richard Williams (drums). Barker left in 1979 (owing to a broken leg), Bidwell left in 1980, replaced by David Agar. Timperley left in 1981, replaced by Kevin Armstrong, with Jeff Smith (keyboards) also joining. Armstrong left the following year, replaced by Steve Wright.

31/01/1981.....25......8....... I'M IN LOVE WITH A GERMAN FILM STAR .... Polydor POSP 222

PAT AND MICK UK vocal duo Pat Sharp and Mick Brown. Both were DJs on Capitol Radio and recorded their hits in aid of the 'Help A London Child' charity.

09/04/1988.....11......9.......	LET'S ALL CHANT/ON THE NIGHT MICK AND PAT .... PWL 10
25/03/1989 .....9.....8.......	I HAVEN'T STOPPED DANCING YET .... PWL 33
14/04/1990.....22......6.......	USE IT UP AND WEAR IT OUT .... PWL 55
23/03/1991.....53......2.......	GIMME SOME .... PWL 75
15/05/1993.....47......2.......	HOT HOT HOT .... PWL International PARKCD 1

PATIENCE AND PRUDENCE US duo formed by sisters Patience and Prudence McIntyre who were aged eleven and fourteen respectively at the time of their debut hit. Both hits were recorded with their father Mack McIntyre's orchestra.

| 02/11/1956.....28......3....... | TONIGHT YOU BELONG TO ME .... London HLU 8321 |
| 01/03/1957.....22......5....... | GONNA GET ALONG WITHOUT YA NOW .... London HLU 8369 |

PATRA Jamaican singer (born Dorothy Smith, 22/11/1972) who originally recorded as Lady Patra.

25/12/1993.....18......8.......	FAMILY AFFAIR SHABBA RANKS FEATURING PATRA AND TERRI AND MONICA .... Polydor PZCD 304
30/09/1995.....50......2.......	PULL UP TO THE BUMPER .... Epic 6623942
10/08/1996....75......1.......	WORK MI BODY MONKEY MAFIA FEATURING PATRA .... Heavenly HVN 53CD

PATRIC UK singer Patric Osborne and an ex-member of Worlds Apart.

09/07/1994.....54......2....... LOVE ME .... Bell 74321215352

DEE PATTEN UK DJ/producer.

30/01/1999.....42......1....... WHO'S THE BAD MAN .... Higher Ground HIGHS 15CD

KELLEE PATTERSON US singer (born in Gary, IN) who also became an actress and was crowned Miss Indiana in 1971.

18/02/1978.....44......7....... IF IT DON'T FIT DON'T FORCE IT .... EMI International INT 544

RAHSAAN PATTERSON US singer (born 11/1/1974, New York) who began his career as a backing singer for the likes of Brandy and Martika.

| 26/07/1997.....50......1....... | STOP BY .... MCA MCSTD 48055 |
| 21/03/1998.....55......1....... | WHERE YOU ARE .... MCA MCSTD 48073 |

LIZZY PATTINSON – see MILK AND SUGAR

BILLY PAUL US singer (born Paul Williams, 1/12/1934, Philadelphia, PA); he made his first recordings for Jubilee in 1952 and established himself as a jazz singer throughout the 1950s and 1960s. He was first linked with Kenny Gamble on the Neptune label and became one of the first signings to Philadelphia International in 1971.

13/01/1973.....12......9.......	ME AND MRS JONES ▲³ 1972 Grammy Award for Best Rhythm & Blues Vocal Performance. Featured in the 1996 film *Beautiful Girls* .... Epic EPC 1055
12/01/1974.....33......6.......	THANKS FOR SAVING MY LIFE .... Philadelphia International PIR 1928
22/05/1976.....30......5.......	LET'S MAKE A BABY .... Philadelphia International PIR 4144
30/04/1977.....26......5.......	LET 'EM IN .... Philadelphia International PIR 5143
16/07/1977.....37......7.......	YOUR SONG .... Philadelphia International PIR 5391
19/11/1977.....33......7.......	ONLY THE STRONG SURVIVE .... Philadelphia International PIR 5699
14/07/1979.....51......5.......	BRING THE FAMILY BACK .... Philadelphia International PIR 7456

CHRIS PAUL UK producer/guitarist who also records as Isotonik.

31/05/1986.....58......5.......	EXPANSIONS '86 (EXPAND YOUR MIND) CHRIS PAUL FEATURING DAVID JOSEPH .... Fourth & Broadway BRW 48
21/11/1987.....74......2.......	BACK IN MY ARMS .... Syncopate SY 5
13/08/1988.....73......1.......	TURN THE MUSIC UP .... Syncopate SY 13

FRANKIE PAUL – see APACHE INDIAN

❶⁹ Number of weeks single topped the UK chart ↑ Entered the UK chart at #1 ▲⁹ Number of weeks single topped the US chart

605

LES PAUL AND MARY FORD

US duo Les (born Lester Polfus, 9/6/1916) and Mary (born Colleen Summer, 7/7/1928) were married in 1949 and divorced in 1963. Les Paul played guitar with Fred Waring in 1938 and later for Bing Crosby. He became best known for his innovations in the development of the electric guitar. He and Mary began recording together in 1950. Mary died on 30/9/1977 after being in a diabetic coma. Les was inducted into the Rock & Roll Hall of Fame in 1988. He also won the 1976 Grammy Award for Best Country Instrumental Performance with Chet Atkins for *Chester And Lester*. Les and Mary's 1951 recording *How High The Moon* was honoured with a Grammy Hall of Fame award. They have a star on the Hollywood Walk of Fame.

20/11/1953 . . . . . 7 . . . . . . 4 . . . . **VAYA CON DIOS** ▲[11] . . . . Capitol CL 13943

LYN PAUL

UK singer (born Lynda Belcher, 16/2/1949, Manchester) who was a founder member of the New Seekers in 1969. They disbanded in 1974 with all five going solo; Lyn Paul scored the only chart hit, which sold considerably less than its title implied. She did not rejoin the group when they re-formed in 1975.

28/06/1975 . . . . . 37 . . . . . . 6 . . . . IT OUGHTA SELL A MILLION . . . . Polydor 2058 602

OWEN PAUL

UK singer (born Owen McGhee, 1/5/1962) who was originally an apprentice footballer with Celtic before turning to music and joining The Venigmas, subsequently going solo in 1985.

31/05/1986 . . . . . 3 . . . . . . 14 . . . . . ○ **MY FAVOURITE WASTE OF TIME** . . . . Epic A 7125

SEAN PAUL

Jamaican singer (born Sean Paul Henriques, 8/1/1975, Kingston). He won the 2002 and 2004 MOBO Award for Best Reggae Act and the 2003 MTV Europe Music Award for Best New Act.. He also won the 2003 Grammy Award for Best Reggae Album for *Dutty Rock*.

21/09/2002 . . . . . 32 . . . . . . 7	GIMME THE LIGHT . . . . VP VPCD 6400
15/02/2003 . . . . . 5 . . . . . . 10	**GIMME THE LIGHT** Remix of VP VPCD 6400 and features the uncredited contribution of Busta Rhymes . . . . . . VP/Atlantic AT 0146CD
24/05/2003 . . . . . 4 . . . . . . 7	**GET BUSY** ▲[3] Featured in the 2003 film *Grind*. . . . . VP/Atlantic AT 0155CD
19/07/2003 . . . . . 59 . . . . . 3	BREATHE (IMPORT) Contains a sample of Dr Dre's *What's The Difference* . . . . Arista 82876534002
09/08/2003 . . . . . ❶[4] . . . . . 18 . . . . . ○	**BREATHE** ↑ This and above single credited to BLU CANTRELL FEATURING SEAN PAUL . . . . Arista 82876545722
06/09/2003 . . . . . 3 . . . . . . 10	**LIKE GLUE** This and above single were #2 and #3 in the charts on 6/9/2003 . . . . VP/Atlantic AT 0162CD
18/10/2003 . . . . . 2 . . . . . . 11	**BABY BOY** ▲[9] BEYONCÉ KNOWLES FEATURING SEAN PAUL . . . . Columbia 6744082
17/01/2004 . . . . . 6 . . . . . . 14	**I'M STILL IN LOVE WITH YOU** SEAN PAUL FEATURING SASHA . . . . VP/Atlantic AT 0170CDX

PAUL AND PAULA

US duo of Paul (born Ray Hildebrand, 21/12/1940, Joshua, TX) and Paula (born Jill Jackson, 20/5/1942, McCaney, TX); they first teamed up for a benefit show on local radio in Texas. Despite the image, they were never romantically linked.

14/02/1963 . . . . . 8 . . . . . . 17 . . . . . . **HEY PAULA** ▲[3] First released in the US in 1962, credited to Jill & Ray. Featured in the 1978 film *Animal House* . . . Philips 304012 BF
18/04/1963 . . . . . 9 . . . . . . 14 . . . . . . YOUNG LOVERS . . . . Philips 304016 BF

LUCIANO PAVAROTTI

Italian singer (born 12/10/1935, Modena) who made his professional debut as an operatic tenor in 1961 (in *Reggio Emilia*) and became one of the leading operatic singers in the world. He has had two close brushes with death: in 1947 he suffered a blood infection and in 1975 survived an air crash in Milan. He has won five Grammy Awards: Best Classical Performance Vocal Soloist in 1978 for *Hits From Lincoln Center*, Best Classical Performance Vocal Soloist in 1979 for *O Sole Mio*, Best Classical Performance Vocal Soloist in 1981 with Joan Sutherland and Marilyn Horne for *Live From Lincoln Center*, Best Classical Performance Vocal Soloist in 1988 for *Luciano Pavarotti In Concert*, Best Classical Performance Vocal Soloist in 1990 with Jose Carreras and Placido Domingo for *Carreras, Domingo, Pavarotti In Concert*. Mehta is Indian conductor Zubin Mehta (born 29/4/1936, Bombay).

16/06/1990 . . . . . 2 . . . . . . 11 . . . . . ●	**NESSUN DORMA** Theme to BBC TV's 1990 World Cup coverage . . . . Decca PAV 03
24/10/1992 . . . . . 15 . . . . . 5	MISERERE ZUCCHERO WITH LUCIANO PAVAROTTI . . . . London LON 329
30/07/1994 . . . . . 21 . . . . . 4	LIBIAMO/LA DONNA E MOBILE JOSE CARRERAS, PLACIDO DOMINGO AND LUCIANO PAVAROTTI . . . . Teldec YZ 843CD
14/12/1996 . . . . . 9 . . . . . . 6	**LIVE LIKE HORSES** ELTON JOHN AND LUCIANO PAVAROTTI . . . . Rocket LLHDD 1
25/07/1998 . . . . . 35 . . . . . 4	YOU'LL NEVER WALK ALONE CARRERAS/DOMINGO/PAVAROTTI WITH MEHTA . . . . Decca 4607982

PAVEMENT

US rock group formed in California 1989 by Stephen Malkmus (born 1967, Santa Monica, CA, guitar/vocals) and Scott Kannberg (born 1967, Stockton, CA, guitar/vocals); Gary Young (drums) joined in 1990 and bass player Mark Ibold (born 1967, Cincinnati, OH) and second drummer Bob Nastanovich (born 1968, Rochester, NY) in 1991. Young left in 1993, replaced by Steve West (born 1967, Richmond, VA). They disbanded in 2000 and Malkmus and Kannberg both went solo.

28/11/1992 . . . . . 58 . . . . . 1 . . . . . . WATERY, DOMESTIC (EP) Tracks on EP: *Texas Never Whispers, Frontwards, Feed 'Em, The Linden Lions* and *Shoot The Singer (1 Sick Verse)*. . . . . Big Cat ABB 38T
12/02/1994 . . . . . 52 . . . . . 1 . . . . . . CUT YOUR HAIR . . . . Big Cat ABB 55SCD
08/02/1997 . . . . . 48 . . . . . 1 . . . . . . STEREO . . . . Domino RUG 51CD
03/05/1997 . . . . . 40 . . . . . 1 . . . . . . SHADY LANE . . . . Domino RUG 53CD
22/05/1999 . . . . . 27 . . . . . 2 . . . . . . CARROT ROPE . . . . Domino RUG 90CD1

RITA PAVONE

Italian singer (born 23/8/1945, Turin) who signed with RCA Italy in 1962 after winning a talent contest. She became a big-selling star in Italy and recorded in French, German, Spanish and English. At only 5 feet tall and weighing 80 pounds, she was given the nickname 'Little Queen of Italian Song'. She also became an actress, appearing in the Italian film *Rita The Mosquito*.

01/12/1966 . . . . . 27 . . . . . 12 . . . . . . HEART . . . . RCA 1553
19/01/1967 . . . . . 21 . . . . . 7 . . . . . . YOU ONLY YOU . . . . RCA 1561

PAY AS U GO

UK garage group formed by DJs Slimzee, Target, Geeneus and Carnage and MCs Maxwell 'D' Donaldson, Plague, Wiley, Major Ace, Godsgift and Flo Dan; they were originally formed out of two groups, Pay As U Go Kartel and The Ladies Hit Squad.

27/04/2002 . . . . . 13 . . . . . 4 . . . . . . CHAMPAGNE DANCE. . . . . So Urban 6721362

FREDA PAYNE
US singer (born 19/9/1945, Detroit, MI) who sang with the Pearl Bailey Revue and later Quincy Jones. She made her debut album for MGM in 1963 and in 1965 with ABC as a jazz artist before switching to Holland/Dozier/Holland's Invictus label in 1969. Her sister Scherrie was a member of the Supremes. Freda was married to fellow soul singer Gregory Abbott.

05/09/1970	❶⁶	19		**BAND OF GOLD** Featured in the 1996 film Now And Then	Invictus INV 502
21/11/1970	33	9		DEEPER AND DEEPER	Invictus INV 505
27/03/1971	46	2		CHERISH WHAT IS DEAR TO YOU	Invictus INV 509

TAMMY PAYNE
UK singer who later worked with Rob Smith and Ray Mighty.

20/07/1991	55	2		TAKE ME NOW	Talkin Loud TLK 12

HEATHER PEACE
UK singer (born 6/6/1975, Bradford) who also made her name as an actress, appearing in London's Burning as Sally Fields.

13/05/2000	56	1		THE ROSE	RCA 74321742892

PEACE BY PIECE
UK vocal group.

21/09/1996	46	1		SWEET SISTER	Blanco Y Negro 94CD
25/04/1998	50	1		NOBODY'S BUSINESS	Blanco Y Negro 110CD1

PEACH
UK/Belgium vocal/production group formed by Lisa Lamb, Pascal Gabriel and Paul Statham.

17/01/1998	69	1		ON MY OWN	Mute CDMUTE 215

PEACHES
Canadian singer Merrill Nisker who began her career as a folk singer.

15/06/2002	36	2		SET IT OFF	Epic 6726862
17/01/2004	39	3		KICK IT **PEACHES FEATURING IGGY POP**	XL Recordings XLS 176CD

PEACHES AND HERB
US R&B vocal duo formed in Washington DC in 1965 by Herb Fame (born Herbert Feemster, 1/10/1942) and Francine Barker (born Francine Hurd, 1947). Fame was recording solo when he auditioned for Van McCoy who paired him with Francine. Although Barker appeared on recordings in the mid-1960s, Marlene Mack (born Virginia, 1945) joined Fame for live performances. When Barker got married in 1970, Fame left the music business and joined the police. He returned in 1975 with Linda Green.

20/01/1979	26	10		SHAKE YOUR GROOVE THING Featured in the films The Adventures Of Priscilla: Queen Of The Desert (1994) and The Sweetest Thing (2002)	Polydor 2066 992
21/04/1979	4	13	O	**REUNITED** ▲⁴ Featured in the 2001 film Jack	Polydor POSP 43

MARY PEARCE – see UP YER RONSON FEATURING MARY PEARCE

NATASHA PEARL – see TASTE XPERIENCE FEATURING NATASHA PEARL

PEARL JAM
US group formed in Seattle, WA in 1990 by Jeff Ament (born 10/3/1963, Big Sandy, MT, bass), Stone Gossard (born 20/7/1966, Seattle, guitar), Mike McCready (born 5/4/1965, Seattle, guitar) and Eddie Vedder (born Edward Mueller, 23/12/1964, Evanston, IL, vocals), adding Dave Krusen (drums) the following year. Ament and Gossard were ex-members of Mother Love Bone, Green River and Temple Of The Dog, the latter also included McCready and Vedder. Krusen left after the debut album, replaced by Dave Abbruzzese (born 17/5/1964). They signed with Epic in 1991. Abbruzzese left in 1994, replaced by Jack Irons (born 18/7/1962, Los Angeles, CA). Pearl Jam portrayed the band Citizen Dick in the 1992 film Singles.

15/02/1992	16	6		ALIVE	Epic 6575727
18/04/1992	27	3		EVEN FLOW	Epic 6578577
26/09/1992	15	4		JEREMY	Epic 6582587
01/01/1994	18	5		DAUGHTER	Epic 6600202
28/05/1994	14	4		DISSIDENT	Epic 6604415
26/11/1994	10	3		**SPIN THE BLACK CIRCLE** Won the 1995 Grammy Award for Best Hard Rock Performance	Epic 6610362
25/02/1995	34	2		NOT FOR YOU	Epic 6612032
16/12/1995	25	3		MERKINBALL EP Tracks on EP: I Got ID and Long Road	Epic 6627162
17/08/1996	18	2		WHO YOU ARE	Epic 6635392
31/01/1998	12	3		GIVEN TO FLY	Epic 6653942
23/05/1998	30	2		WISHLIST	Epic 6657902
14/08/1999	42	1		LAST KISS Cover of a 1962 song by Wayne Cochran and released to raise funds for Kosovo	Epic 6674792
13/05/2000	22	2		NOTHING AS IT SEEMS	Epic 6693742
22/07/2000	52	1		LIGHT YEARS	Epic 6696282
09/11/2002	26	2		I AM MINE	Epic 6733082

PEARLS
UK vocal duo Lynn Cornell and Ann Simmons. Cornell was an ex-member of the Vernons Girls.

27/05/1972	31	6		THIRD FINGER, LEFT HAND	Bell 1217
23/09/1972	32	5		YOU CAME YOU SAW YOU CONQUERED	Bell 1254
24/03/1973	41	3		YOU ARE EVERYTHING	Bell 1284
08/06/1974	10	10		**GUILTY**	Bell 1352

JOHNNY PEARSON
UK orchestra leader/pianist (born 18/6/1925, London) who began playing the piano at the age of seven and two years later won a scholarship to the London Academy of Music. He went on to become a regular on TV and radio.

18/12/1971	8	15		**SLEEPY SHORES** Theme to the BBC TV series Owen MD	Penny Farthing PEN 778

---

❶⁹ Number of weeks single topped the UK chart　↑ Entered the UK chart at #1　▲⁹ Number of weeks single topped the US chart

PEBBLES
US singer (born Perri Alette McKissack, 29/8/1965, Oakland, CA) who was nicknamed 'Pebbles' because she resembled the cartoon character Pebbles Flintstone. She sang with Bill Summers before teaming up with Con Funk Shun and signed with MCA in 1987. She married producer and songwriter Antonio Reid in 1989; they later divorced. She later assembled and managed TLC.

19/03/1988	8	11	**GIRLFRIEND** .... MCA 1233
28/05/1988	42	4	MERCEDES BOY .... MCA 1248
27/10/1990	73	2	GIVING YOU THE BENEFIT .... MCA 1448

PEDDLERS
UK group formed in 1964 by Tab Martin (born 24/12/1944, Liverpool, bass), Roy Phillips (born 5/5/1943, Poole, Dorset, keyboards) and Trevor Morris (born 16/10/1943, Liverpool, drums). The group disbanded in the mid-1970s with Martin becoming a session musician, Phillips emigrating to Australia and Morris joining Quantum Jump.

07/01/1965	50	1	LET THE SUNSHINE IN .... Philips BF 1375
23/08/1969	17	9	BIRTH .... CBS 4449
31/01/1970	34	4	GIRLIE .... CBS 4720

PEE BEE SQUAD
UK singer Paul Burnett whose debut hit was a spoof on the film character Rambo.

05/10/1985	52	3	RUGGED AND MEAN, BUTCH AND ON SCREEN .... Project PRO 3

ANN PEEBLES
US singer (born 27/4/1947, East St Louis, MO) who began her career singing with the gospel group The Peebles Choir from the age of eight.

20/04/1974	41	3	I CAN'T STAND THE RAIN .... London HL 10428

PEECH BOYS
US funk group formed in New York by Bernard Fowler, Robert Kasper, Michael De Benedictus, Daryl Short and Steven Brown; they also recorded as New York Citi Peech Boys.

30/10/1982	49	3	DON'T MAKE ME WAIT .... TMT 7001

DONALD PEERS
UK singer (born 1919, Ammanford, Dyfed, Wales) who began making radio broadcasts in 1927, first recorded in 1944 and became popular during the late 1940s and early 1950s. He toured Australia, South Africa and India extensively, hence his lack of UK hits until the late 1960s. He appeared in the films *The Balloon Goes Up* and *Sing Along With Me*. He died in August 1973.

29/12/1966	46	1	GAMES THAT LOVERS PLAY .... Columbia DB 8079
18/12/1968	3	21	**PLEASE DON'T GO** .... Columbia DB 8502
24/06/1972	36	6	GIVE ME ONE MORE CHANCE .... Decca F 13302

PELE
UK group formed in Liverpool in 1990 by Ian Prowse (vocals), Nico (violin and guitar), Jimmy McAllister (bass), Andrew 'Robbo' Roberts (keyboards) and Dally (drums). McAllister left in 1998, replaced by Wayne Morgan. Prowse later formed Amersterdam.

15/02/1992	73	1	MEGALOMANIA .... M&G MAGS 20
13/06/1992	62	1	FAIR BLOWS THE WIND FOR FRANCE .... M&G MAGS 24
31/07/1993	75	1	FAT BLACK HEART .... M&G MAGCD 43

MARTI PELLOW
UK singer (born Mark McLoughlin, 23/3/1966, Clydebank) who was lead singer with Vortex Motion, a group that subsequently became Wet Wet Wet. He left the group to go solo in 1999.

16/06/2001	9	6	**CLOSE TO YOU** .... Mercury MERDD 532
01/12/2001	28	2	I'VE BEEN AROUND THE WORLD .... Mercury 5887772
22/11/2003	59	1	A LOT OF LOVE .... Universal TV 9813763

DEBBIE PENDER
US singer who worked with production duo Blaze.

30/05/1998	41	1	MOVIN' ON .... AM:PM 5826492

TEDDY PENDERGRASS
US singer (born Theodore Pendergrass, 26/3/1950, Philadelphia, PA) who was a member of The Cadillacs before joining Harold Melvin & The Bluenotes (as did the rest of the group) in 1969. Initially the drummer, he became featured singer in 1970. Personality clashes with Melvin led to him to go solo in 1976. A road accident on 18/3/1982 left him paralysed from the neck down, although he subsequently resumed his recording career. In 1982 he appeared in the film *Soup For One*. He won the 1982 Grammy Award for Best Recording for Children, along with Billy Joel, Bruce Springsteen, James Taylor, Kenny Loggins, Carly and Lucy Simon, Crystal Gayle, Lou Rawls, Deniece Williams, Janis Ian and Dr. John, for *In Harmony 2*.

21/05/1977	44	3	THE WHOLE TOWN'S LAUGHING AT ME .... Philadelphia International PIR 5116
28/10/1978	41	6	ONLY YOU/CLOSE THE DOOR .... Philadelphia International PIR 6713
23/05/1981	49	5	TWO HEARTS STEPHANIE MILLS FEATURING TEDDY PENDERGRASS .... 20th Century TC 2492
25/01/1986	44	5	HOLD ME TEDDY PENDERGRASS WITH WHITNEY HOUSTON .... Asylum EKR 32
28/05/1988	58	3	JOY .... Elektra EKR 75
19/11/1994	35	2	THE MORE I GET THE MORE I WANT KWS FEATURING TEDDY PENDERGRASS ...... X-clusive XCLU 011CD

PENDULUM
UK production trio formed by Rob Swire, Gareth McGrillen and Paul Harding.

06/03/2004	46	2	ANOTHER PLANET/VOYAGER .... Breakbeat Kaos BBK003

CE CE PENISTON
US singer (born Cecelia Peniston, 6/9/1969, Dayton, OH) who moved to Phoenix in 1977, appeared in numerous talent and beauty contests, and was crowned Miss Black Arizona and Miss Galaxy in 1989. She then worked as a backing singer before going solo and scoring a major debut hit with a song she had written while still at school.

12/10/1991	29	7	FINALLY Featured in the 1994 film *The Adventures Of Priscilla: Queen Of The Desert* .... A&M AM 822
11/01/1992	6	8	**WE GOT A LOVE THANG** .... A&M AM 846
18/01/1992	58	2	I LIKE IT OVERWEIGHT POOCH FEATURING CE CE PENISTON .... A&M AM 847

○ Silver disc ● Gold disc ✪ Platinum disc (additional platinum units are indicated by a figure following the symbol) ◉ Singles released prior to 1973 that are known to have sold over 1 million copies in the UK

DATE	POS	WKS	BPI	SINGLE TITLE	LABEL & NUMBER
21/03/1992	2	8	O	FINALLY Re-issue of A&M AM822	A&M AM 858
23/05/1992	10	6		KEEP ON WALKIN'	A&M AM 878
05/09/1992	44	3		CRAZY LOVE	A&M AM 0060
12/12/1992	42	2		INSIDE THAT I CRIED	A&M AM 0121
15/01/1994	16	4		I'M IN THE MOOD	A&M 5804552
02/04/1994	36	2		KEEP GIVIN' ME YOUR LOVE	A&M 5805492
06/08/1994	33	2		HIT BY LOVE	A&M 5806932
13/09/1997	26	5		FINALLY (REMIX)	AM:PM 5823432
07/02/1998	13	4		SOMEBODY ELSE'S GUY	AM:PM 5825112

DAWN PENN Jamaican singer (born Dawn Pickering, 1952, Kingston) discovered by Coxone Dodd and session singer for the likes of Johnny Nash before going solo. Her 1969 debut hit was written and recorded by Sonny and Cher. She has penned over 400 songs.

DATE	POS	WKS	BPI	SINGLE TITLE	LABEL & NUMBER
11/06/1994	3	12	O	YOU DON'T LOVE ME (NO NO NO)	Big Beat A 8295CD

BARBARA PENNINGTON US singer (born in Chicago, IL) who was discovered by producer Ian Levine.

DATE	POS	WKS	BPI	SINGLE TITLE	LABEL & NUMBER
27/04/1985	62	3		FAN THE FLAME	Record Shack SOHO 37
27/07/1985	57	5		ON A CROWDED STREET	Record Shack SOHO 49

TRICIA PENROSE UK singer (born 6/4/1970, Liverpool); she was initially known as an actress, appearing in *Heartbeat* and *The Royal* as Gina Ward.

DATE	POS	WKS	BPI	SINGLE TITLE	LABEL & NUMBER
07/12/1996	71	1		WHERE DID OUR LOVE GO	RCA 74321428152
04/03/2000	44	1		DON'T WANNA BE ALONE	Doop DP 2001CD

PENTANGLE UK group formed in 1967 by Bert Jansch (born 3/11/1943, Glasgow, guitar), Jacqui McShee (vocals), John Renbourn (guitar/vocals), Danny Thompson (bass) and Terry Cox (drums). This version of Pentangle dissolved in 1972, but re-formed in 1984 with Mike Piggott replacing Renbourn. By 1991 Piggott had left and the group had been joined by Nigel Portman-Smith (bass) and Gerry Conway (drums).

DATE	POS	WKS	BPI	SINGLE TITLE	LABEL & NUMBER
28/05/1969	46	1		ONCE I HAD A SWEETHEART	Big T BIG 124
14/02/1970	43	3		LIGHT FLIGHT	Big T BIG 128

PENTHOUSE 4 UK vocal/instrumental duo formed by Stephen Warwick.

DATE	POS	WKS	BPI	SINGLE TITLE	LABEL & NUMBER
23/04/1988	56	3		BUST THIS HOUSE DOWN	Syncopate SY 10

PEOPLE'S CHOICE US group formed in 1971 by Frank Brunson (vocals/keyboards), David Thompson (drums), Valerie Brown (vocals), Marc Reed (vocals), Darnell Jordan (guitar), Johnnie Hightower (guitar), Clifton Gamble (keyboards), Bill Rodgers (keyboards) and Stanley Thomas (bass). Signed to Philadelphia International by Kenny Gamble, but Leon Huff worked with them as writer and producer.

DATE	POS	WKS	BPI	SINGLE TITLE	LABEL & NUMBER
20/09/1975	36	5		DO IT ANY WAY YOU WANNA	Philadelphia International PIR 3500
21/01/1978	40	4		JAM JAM JAM	Philadelphia International PIR 5891

PEPE DELUXE Finnish production/DJ trio formed by JA Jazz, Super Jock Slow and Spectrum.

DATE	POS	WKS	BPI	SINGLE TITLE	LABEL & NUMBER
26/05/2001	20	3		BEFORE YOU LEAVE	Catskills 6712392

DANNY PEPPERMINT AND THE JUMPING JACKS US vocal/instrumental group fronted by Danny Peppermint (born Danny Kamego). Peppermint died after being electrocuted on stage.

DATE	POS	WKS	BPI	SINGLE TITLE	LABEL & NUMBER
18/01/1962	26	8		PEPPERMINT TWIST	London HLL 9478

PEPPERS French studio duo of synthesiser player Mat Camison and drummer Pierre Dahan.

DATE	POS	WKS	BPI	SINGLE TITLE	LABEL & NUMBER
26/10/1974	6	12		PEPPER BOX	Spark SRL 1100

PEPSI AND SHIRLIE UK duo Lawrie 'Pepsi' DeMacque (born 10/12/1958, London) and Shirlie Holliman (born 18/4/1962, Watford). They first teamed up as backing singers and dancers for Wham!

DATE	POS	WKS	BPI	SINGLE TITLE	LABEL & NUMBER
17/01/1987	2	12	O	HEARTACHE	Polydor POSP 837
30/05/1987	9	7		GOODBYE STRANGER	Polydor POSP 865
26/09/1987	58	3		CAN'T GIVE ME NOW	Polydor POSP 885
12/12/1987	50	2		ALL RIGHT NOW	Polydor POSP 896

PERAN Dutch DJ Peran Van Dijk.

DATE	POS	WKS	BPI	SINGLE TITLE	LABEL & NUMBER
23/03/2002	37	2		GOOD TIME	Incentive CENT 37CDS

PERCEPTION UK vocal group formed by Sean Daly, Stephen Forde, Joy Rose and Anthony Campbell.

DATE	POS	WKS	BPI	SINGLE TITLE	LABEL & NUMBER
07/03/1992	58	2		FEED THE FEELING Listed flip side was *Three Times A Maybe* by K CREATIVE	Talkin Loud TLK 17

LANCE PERCIVAL UK singer (born 26/7/1933), better known as an actor, who made his debut in 1961 in *What A Whopper!* and later appeared in *Up The Chastity Belt, Confessions From A Holiday Camp* and *Rosie Dixon – Night Nurse*.

DATE	POS	WKS	BPI	SINGLE TITLE	LABEL & NUMBER
28/10/1965	37	3		SHAME AND SCANDAL IN THE FAMILY	Parlophone R 5335

PERCY FILTH UK production duo Mark Baker and Gary Little. They also record as Lil' Devious.

DATE	POS	WKS	BPI	SINGLE TITLE	LABEL & NUMBER
09/08/2003	72	1		SHOW ME THE MONKEY	Southern Fried ECB 53CDS

O[9] Number of weeks single topped the UK chart ↑ Entered the UK chart at #1 ▲[9] Number of weeks single topped the US chart

A PERFECT CIRCLE US rock group formed by Maynard James Keenan (vocals), Billy Howerdel (guitar), Troy Van Leeuwen (guitar), Paz Lenchantin (bass) and Josh Freese (drums). Keenan and Howerdel were ex-members of Tool and formed A Perfect Circle after Tool ran into legal difficulties with their record label.

18/11/2000 . . . . . 72 . . . . . . 1 . . . . THE HOLLOW . . . . Virgin VUSCD 181

13/01/2001 . . . . . 49 . . . . . . 1 . . . . 3 LIBRAS . . . . Virgin VUSCD 184

PERFECT DAY UK vocal/instrumental group formed by Mark Jones, Kevin Howard, Andrew Wood and Mark Stott.

21/01/1989 . . . . . 58 . . . . . . 3 . . . . LIBERTY TOWN . . . . London LON 214

01/04/1989 . . . . . 68 . . . . . . 1 . . . . JANE . . . . London LON 188

PERFECT PHASE Dutch production duo Jeff Roach and Mac Zimms.

25/12/1999 . . . . . 21 . . . . . . 7 . . . . HORNY HORNS Contains a sample of The 49ers Featuring Anne Marie Smith's *Move Your Feet* . . . . Positiva CDTIV 123

12/06/2004 . . . . . 75 . . . . . . 1 . . . . BLOW YOUR HORNY HORNS . . . . Feverpitch 12FEV3

PERFECTLY ORDINARY PEOPLE UK vocal/instrumental group formed by Martin Freland and Mike Morrison.

22/10/1988 . . . . . 61 . . . . . . 3 . . . . THEME FROM P.O.P. . . . . Urban URB 25

PERFECTO ALLSTARZ UK group assembled by Paul Oakenfold (born 30/8/1963, London) and Steve Osborne. Oakenfold also records as Planet Perfecto and Movement 98.

04/02/1995 . . . . . 6 . . . . . . 11 . . . . O   **REACH UP (PAPA'S GOT A BRAND NEW PIG BAG)** . . . . Perfecto YZ 892CD

PERFUME UK vocal/instrumental group fronted by Mick McCarthy.

10/02/1996 . . . . . 71 . . . . . . 1 . . . . HAVEN'T SEEN YOU . . . . Aromasound AROMA 005CDS

EMILIO PERICOLI Italian singer/actor (born 1928, Cesenatico). *Al di la* won the San Remo Song Festival in 1961 and was used in the film *Lovers Must Learn* starring Angie Dickinson and Troy Donahue. Pericoli's single then became an international success.

28/06/1962 . . . . . 30 . . . . . 14 . . . . . . AL DI LA Featured in the 1962 film *Lovers Must Learn* (US title *Rome Adventure*) . . . . Warner Brothers WB 69

CARL PERKINS US singer (born Carl Lee Perkins, although his surname was misspelled on his birth certificate as Perkings, 9/4/1932, Tiptonville, TN); he was a member of the Perkins Brothers Band with brothers Jay (born 1930) and Clayton (born 1935) in 1950. He turned professional in 1954 and moved to Memphis to audition for Sun Records after hearing Elvis Presley. He joined Johnny Cash' touring band in 1967. The Beatles covered three of his songs in their early career (and earned Perkins more in royalties than he had earned from all his post-hit sales). Jay, a member of Carl's touring band, was badly injured in a car crash in 1956 (Carl was in the car at the time) and never fully recovered, dying on 21/10/1958. Clayton was also a member of the touring band, but was sacked in 1963 and shot himself on 25/12/1973. Carl Perkins was inducted into the Rock & Roll Hall of Fame in 1987. He won the 1986 Grammy Award for Best Spoken Word Recording with various others for *Interviews From The Class Of '55*. He died from a stroke on 19/1/1998.

18/05/1956 . . . . . 10 . . . . . . 8 . . . . **BLUE SUEDE SHOES** . . . . London HLU 8271

PERPETUAL MOTION UK instrumental/production group formed by Andy Marston of Clockwork Orange and Julian Napolitano, who is also a member of JDS and produces under the moniker Quo Vadis.

02/05/1998 . . . . . 12 . . . . . . 5 . . . . KEEP ON DANCIN' (LET'S GO) Contains a sample of D.O.P.'s *Here I Go* . . . . Positiva CDTIV 90

STEVE PERRY UK singer.

04/08/1960 . . . . . 41 . . . . . . 1 . . . . STEP BY STEP . . . . HMV POP 745

NINA PERSSON AND DAVID ARNOLD Swedish singer (born 1975) with UK pianist/composer David Arnold. Persson is also lead singer with The Cardigans while Arnold is a well known film composer.

29/04/2000 . . . . . 49 . . . . . . 1 . . . . THEME FROM 'RANDALL & HOPKIRK (DECEASED)' Theme to the TV series of the same name, the remake of which starred Vic Reeves and Bob Mortimer. . . . . Island CID 762

JON PERTWEE UK actor (born 7/7/1919) who was *Dr Who* for 128 episodes and later starred as *Worzel Gummidge*. He died from a heart attack on 20/5/1996.

01/03/1980 . . . . . 33 . . . . . . 7 . . . . WORZEL SONG . . . . Decca F 13885

PESHAY UK producer Paul Pesce.

09/05/1998 . . . . . 75 . . . . . . 1 . . . . MILES FROM HOME. . . . . Mo Wax MW 092

17/07/1999 . . . . . 59 . . . . . . 1 . . . . SWITCH . . . . Island Blue PFACD 1

19/02/2000 . . . . . 55 . . . . . . 1 . . . . TRULY **PESHAY FEATURING KYM MAZELLE** . . . . Island Blue PFACD 4

04/05/2002 . . . . . 41 . . . . . . 2 . . . . YOU GOT ME BURNING/FUZION **PESHAY FEATURING CO-ORDINATE** . . . . Cubik Music CUBIKSAMPCD 001

24/08/2002 . . . . . 67 . . . . . . 1 . . . . SATISFY MY LOVE **PESHAY VERSUS FLYTRONIX** . . . . Cubik Music CUBIK 002CD

○ Silver disc   ● Gold disc   ✪ Platinum disc (additional platinum units are indicated by a figure following the symbol)   ◉ Singles released prior to 1973 that are known to have sold over 1 million copies in the UK

PET SHOP BOYS

PET SHOP BOYS UK duo formed in 1981 by Neil Tennant (born 10/7/1954, Gosforth, Tyne and Wear, vocals) and Chris Lowe (born 4/10/1959, Blackpool, keyboards). Tennant was then assistant editor of *Smash Hits*, a position he held for a further two years while the group wrote and made demos. They were signed by Epic for their debut release, *West End Girls*, which became a big European success but failed in the UK. They re-recorded the single for Parlophone and took three months to make the top ten. They launched the Spaghetti label in 1992. They were named Best British Group at the 1988 BRIT Awards.

DATE	POS	WKS	BPI	SINGLE TITLE	LABEL & NUMBER
23/11/1985	❶²	15	●	**WEST END GIRLS** ▲¹ Won the 1987 BRIT Award for Best Single (although the single had originally been recorded and released on Epic Records – this version is a re-recording).	Parlophone R 6115
08/03/1986	19	9		LOVE COMES QUICKLY	Parlophone R 6116
31/05/1986	11	8		OPPORTUNITIES (LET'S MAKE LOTS OF MONEY) Remix; originally released in July 1985 and failed to chart.	Parlophone R 6129
04/10/1986	8	9		**SUBURBIA**	Parlophone R 6140
27/06/1987	❶³	11	○	**IT'S A SIN**	Parlophone R 6158
22/08/1987	2	9	○	**WHAT HAVE I DONE TO DESERVE THIS** PET SHOP BOYS AND DUSTY SPRINGFIELD	Parlophone R 6163
24/10/1987	8	7		RENT	Parlophone R 6168
12/12/1987	❶⁴	11	●	**ALWAYS ON MY MIND**	Parlophone R 6171
02/04/1988	❶³	10	○	**HEART**	Parlophone R 6177
24/09/1988	7	8		**DOMINO DANCING**	Parlophone R 6190
26/11/1988	4	8		**LEFT TO MY OWN DEVICES**	Parlophone R 6198
08/07/1989	5	8		**IT'S ALRIGHT**	Parlophone R 6220
06/10/1990	4	6		**SO HARD**	Parlophone R 6269
24/11/1990	20	8		BEING BORING	Parlophone R 6275
23/03/1991	4	8		**WHERE THE STREETS HAVE NO NAME – CAN'T TAKE MY EYES OFF YOU/ HOW CAN YOU EXPECT ME TO BE TAKEN SERIOUSLY**	Parlophone R 6285
08/06/1991	12	5		JEALOUSY	Parlophone R 6283
26/10/1991	13	3		DJ CULTURE	Parlophone R 6301
23/11/1991	40	2		DJ CULTURE (REMIX)	Parlophone 12RX 6301
21/12/1991	24	4		WAS IT WORTH IT	Parlophone R 6306
12/06/1993	7	7		**CAN YOU FORGIVE HER**	Parlophone CDR 6348
18/09/1993	2	9		**GO WEST**	Parlophone CDR 6356
11/12/1993	13	7		I WOULDN'T NORMALLY DO THIS KIND OF THING	Parlophone CDR 6370
16/04/1994	14	5		LIBERATION	Parlophone CDR 6377
11/06/1994	6	7		**ABSOLUTELY FABULOUS** ABSOLUTELY FABULOUS Single recorded for *Comic Relief*.	Spaghetti CDR 6382
10/09/1994	13	4		YESTERDAY WHEN I WAS MAD	Parlophone CDRS 6386
05/08/1995	15	4		PANINARO '95	Parlophone CDRS 6414
04/05/1996	7	5		**BEFORE**	Parlophone CDRS 6431
24/08/1996	8	8		**SE A VIDA E (THAT'S THE WAY LIFE IS)**	Parlophone CDR 6443
23/11/1996	14	3		SINGLE	Parlophone CDRS 6452
29/03/1997	9	3		**RED LETTER DAY**	Parlophone CDR 6460
05/07/1997	9	5		**SOMEWHERE** Cover version of a song originally featured in the musical *West Side Story*	Parlophone CDR 6470
31/07/1999	15	3		I DON'T KNOW WHAT YOU WANT BUT I CAN'T GIVE IT TO YOU	Parlophone CDR 6523
09/10/1999	14	4		NEW YORK CITY BOY	Parlophone CDR 6525
15/01/2000	8	4		**YOU ONLY TELL ME YOU LOVE ME WHEN YOU'RE DRUNK**	Parlophone CDR 6533
30/03/2002	14	6		HOME AND DRY	Parlophone CDRS 6572
27/07/2002	18	3		I GET ALONG	Parlophone CDRS 6581
29/11/2003	10	4		**MIRACLES**	Parlophone CDRS 6620
10/04/2004	12	4		FLAMBOYANT	Parlophone CDRS 6629

PETER AND GORDON

PETER AND GORDON UK duo formed in London in 1963 by Peter Asher (born 22/6/1944, London) and Gordon Waller (born 4/6/1945, Braemar, Scotland). Asher had been a child actor and is the brother of actress Jane Asher, Paul McCartney's one-time girlfriend. McCartney was invited to Peter & Gordon's first recording session in 1964 and wrote their two debut hits. The duo disbanded in 1967 with Asher moving into production.

DATE	POS	WKS	BPI	SINGLE TITLE	LABEL & NUMBER
12/03/1964	❶²	14		**A WORLD WITHOUT LOVE** ▲¹	Columbia DB 7225
04/06/1964	10	11		**NOBODY I KNOW** This and above single written by Paul McCartney (but credited to Lennon/McCartney).	Columbia DB 7292
08/04/1965	2	15		**TRUE LOVE WAYS**	Columbia DB 7524
24/06/1965	5	10		**TO KNOW YOU IS TO LOVE YOU**	Columbia DB 7617
21/10/1965	19	9		BABY I'M YOURS	Columbia DB 7729
24/02/1966	28	7		WOMAN Written by Paul McCartney but given the credit Bernard Webb to see whether it would still be a hit if the true identity of the writer was not revealed (the US release gave the writer's credit to A Smith). McCartney also wrote *I Don't Want To See You Again* for the duo that failed to chart	Columbia DB 7834
22/09/1966	16	11		LADY GODIVA	Columbia DB 8003

PETER, PAUL AND MARY

PETER, PAUL AND MARY US folk group formed in New York in 1961 by Peter Yarrow (born 31/5/1938, New York), Paul Stookey (born 30/11/1937, Baltimore, MD) and Mary Travers (born 7/11/1937, Louisville, KY), and assembled by future Bob Dylan manager Albert Grossman. They disbanded in the mid-1970s but re-formed in 1978. Yarrow later became a successful

❶⁹ Number of weeks single topped the UK chart ↑ Entered the UK chart at #1 ▲⁹ Number of weeks single topped the US chart

611

writer and producer. They won four Grammy Awards including Best Performance by a Vocal Group and Best Folk Recording in 1962 for *If I Had A Hammer*.

10/10/1963.....13.....16......	BLOWING IN THE WIND 1963 Grammy Awards for Best Performance by a Vocal Group and Best Folk Recording. Featured in the 1979 film *Banjo Man*	Warner Brothers WB 104
16/04/1964.....33.....4......	TELL IT ON THE MOUNTAIN	Warner Brothers WB 127
15/10/1964.....44.....2......	THE TIMES THEY ARE A-CHANGIN'	Warner Brothers WB 142
17/01/1970 .....2.....16.....	**LEAVIN' ON A JET PLANE** ▲[1]	Warner Brothers WB 7340

PETERS AND LEE
UK duo Lennie Peters (born 1939, London, piano/vocals) and Dianne Lee (born 1950, Sheffield, vocals) who first teamed up in 1970. Peters had been a pianist in a London pub; Lee half of a dance group called the Hailey Twins. They appeared on *Opportunity Knocks* in 1972, and proved a sensation, winning week after week and were then signed by Philips. Peters, uncle of Rolling Stone Charlie Watts and blind since he was sixteen, died of bone cancer on 10/10/1992.

26/05/1973 ...❶[1].....24......	**WELCOME HOME**..	Philips 6006 307
03/11/1973.....39.....4......	BY YOUR SIDE	Philips 6006 339
20/04/1974 .....3.....15.....○	**DON'T STAY AWAY TOO LONG**	Philips 6006 388
17/08/1974.....17.....7......	RAINBOW	Philips 6006 406
06/03/1976.....16.....7......	HEY MR. MUSIC MAN	Philips 6006 502

JONATHAN PETERS PRESENTS LUMINAIRE
US DJ/producer.

24/07/1999.....75.....1......	FLOWER DUET	Pelican PELID 001

RAY PETERSON
US singer (born 23/4/1939, Denton, TX) who began singing to take his mind off treatment for polio in hospital. He later formed the Dunes record label. His biggest US success, *Tell Laura I Love Her*, was not released in the UK, so Ricky Valence recorded a cover version and hit #1.

04/09/1959.....23.....1......	THE WONDER OF YOU	RCA 1131
24/03/1960.....47.....1......	ANSWER ME	RCA 1175
19/01/1961.....41.....7......	CORRINE, CORRINA	London HLX 9246

TOM PETTY AND THE HEARTBREAKERS
US singer (born 20/10/1953, Gainesville, FL) who formed his first group, the Sundowners, in 1968, later changing the name to the Epics and then Mudcrutch. The line-up comprised Petty (bass and guitar), Tommy Leadon (guitar), Mike Campbell (guitar) and Randall Marsh (drums). Signed by Shelter in 1973, they released only one single before the group split up in 1975, but Petty was retained and formed the Heartbreakers with Campbell, Benmont Tench (keyboards), Ron Blair (guitar), Jeff Jourard (guitar) and Stan Lynch (drums). Jourard left soon after. Petty later became a member of The Traveling Wilburys. He collected the 1989 Grammy Award for Best Rock Performance by a Group with Vocals as a member of the Traveling Wilburys for *Traveling Wilburys Volume One* (the album was known as *Handle With Care* in the UK). Petty also won the 1995 Grammy Award for Best Male Rock Vocal Performance for *You Don't Know How It Feels*. He has a star on the Hollywood Walk of Fame.

25/06/1977.....36.....3.......	ANYTHING THAT'S ROCK 'N' ROLL..	Shelter WIP 6396
13/08/1977.....40.....5....	AMERICAN GIRL..	Shelter WIP 6403
15/08/1981.....50.....4....	STOP DRAGGIN' MY HEART AROUND **STEVIE NICKS WITH TOM PETTY AND THE HEARTBREAKERS**	WEA K 79231
13/04/1985.....50.....4....	DON'T COME AROUND HERE NO MORE	MCA 926
13/05/1989.....28.....10....	I WON'T BACK DOWN	MCA 1334
12/08/1989.....55.....4....	RUNNIN' DOWN A DREAM	MCA 1359
25/11/1989.....64.....2....	FREE FALLIN' This and above two singles credited to **TOM PETTY**	MCA 1381
29/06/1991.....46.....4....	LEARNING TO FLY	MCA MCS 1555
04/04/1992.....34.....3....	TOO GOOD TO BE TRUE	MCA MCS 1616
30/10/1993.....53.....2....	SOMETHING IN THE AIR **TOM PETTY**	MCA MCSTD 1945
12/03/1994.....52.....2....	MARY JANE'S LAST DANCE	MCA MCSTD 1966

PEYTON
US singer with producer Eric 'K-Scope' Kupper.

22/05/2004.....68.....1.......	A HIGHER PLACE	Hed Kandi HEDK12006

PF PROJECT FEATURING EWAN MCGREGOR
UK group featuring songwriters and producers Jamie White and Moussa 'Moose' Clarke and fronted by actor and singer Ewan McGregor. White had also been a member of Tzant, Mirrorball and the PF Project. Moussa Clarke later recorded as Musique.

15/11/1997 .....6.....11......	**CHOOSE LIFE** Contains a sample of Ewan McGregor's dialogue from the 1996 film *Trainspotting*	Positiva CDTIV 84

PHANTOMS – see JOHNNY BRANDON WITH THE PHANTOMS

PHARAO
German group formed by Kyr Pharao, Marcus Deon Thomas, Hanz Marathon and JPS.

04/03/1995.....43.....2.......	THERE IS A STAR	Epic 6611832

PHARAOHS – see SAM THE SHAM AND THE PHARAOHS

PHARCYDE
US rap group formed in Los Angeles, CA by Romye 'Booty Brown' Robinson, Tre 'Slim Kid' Hardson, Imani 'Darky Boy' Wilcox, Derek 'Fat Lip' Stewart, DJ Mark Luv and J-Swift.

31/07/1993.....55.....3.......	PASSIN' ME BY Contains a sample of Quincy Jones' *Summer In The City*. Featured in the 1999 film *Big Daddy* ..	Atlantic A 8360CD
06/04/1996.....36.....2.......	RUNNIN' Contains samples of Stan Getz' *Saudade Ven Correndo* and Run DMC's *Rock Box*................	Go Beat GODCD 142
10/08/1996.....51.....1.......	SHE SAID	Go Beat GODCD 144

FRANKE PHAROAH – see FRANKE

PHARRELL – see N*E*R*D

PHASE II
UK producer and remixer Dave Lee who is also a member of Hed Boys and has recorded as Z Factor, Akabu, Joey Negro, Jakatta and Raven Maize.

| 18/03/1989 | 70 | 1 | | REACHIN'. | Republic LICT 006 |
| 21/12/1991 | 70 | 1 | | REACHIN' (REMIX) | Republic LICT 160 |

PHAT 'N' PHUNKY
UK production duo.

| 14/06/1997 | 61 | 1 | | LET'S GROOVE | Chase CDCHASE 8 |

PHATS AND SMALL
UK dance/production duo Jason 'Phats' Hayward and Richard Small. The pair are also much in-demand as remixers. They added singer Tony Thompson in 2001.

10/04/1999	2	16	●	TURN AROUND Contains samples of Toney Lee's *Reach Up* and Change's *The Glow Of Love*	Multiply CDMULTY 49
14/08/1999	7	8		FEEL GOOD Contains a sample of BT Express' *Does It Feel Good*	Multiply CDMULTY 54
04/12/1999	11	6		TONITE Contains a sample of Delegation's *Heartache No9*.	Multiply CDMULTY 57
30/06/2001	15	5		THIS TIME AROUND Contains a sample of S.O.U.L. Featuring Larry Hancock's *This Time Around*.	Multiply CDMULTY 75
24/11/2001	45	1		CHANGE	Multiply CDMULTY 80

PHATT B
Dutch producer Bernsquil Verndoom.

| 11/11/2000 | 58 | 1 | | AND DA DRUM MACHINE | NuLife 74321801902 |

PHD
UK duo formed by classically trained pianist Tony Hymas and singer Jim Diamond (born 28/9/1953). Diamond later recorded solo.

| 03/04/1982 | 3 | 14 | ○ | I WON'T LET YOU DOWN | WEA K 79209 |

BARRINGTON PHELOUNG
Australian conductor/arranger (born 1954, Sydney) who began his career playing in blues bands before moving to London, aged eighteen, to attend the Royal College of Music. He was appointed Musical Advisor to the London Contemporary Dance Theatre in 1979 before moving into film and TV work. His credits also include *Boon*, *The Politician's Wife*, *Truly Madly Deeply* and *Portrait Of A Marriage*.

| 13/03/1993 | 61 | 2 | | INSPECTOR MORSE' THEME Theme to the TV series of the same name. | Virgin VSCDT 1458 |

PHILADELPHIA INTERNATIONAL ALL-STARS
US charity ensemble formed by Lou Rawls, Archie Bell, the O'Jays (Eddie Levert, Walter Williams and Sammy Strain), Billy Paul, Teddy Pendergrass, The Three Degrees (Fayette Pinkney, Sheila Ferguson and Valerie Holiday), Harold Melvin and Dee Dee Sharp. The song was originally written by Kenny Gamble for a Lou Rawls album in 1975 but shelved because it was out of context with the other material. It was revived in 1977, Rawls sang the opening lines.

| 13/08/1977 | 34 | 8 | | LET'S CLEAN UP THE GHETTO | Philadelphia International PIR 5451 |

PHILHARMONIA ORCHESTRA, CONDUCTOR LORIN MAAZEL
UK orchestra with US conductor.

| 30/07/1969 | 33 | 7 | | THUS SPAKE ZARATHUSTRA Featured in the 1968 film *2001: A Space Odyssey* | Columbia DB 8607 |

CHYNA PHILLIPS
US singer (born 12/2/1968, Los Angeles, CA), the daughter of ex-Mama & Papas members John and Michelle Phillips, she was a member of Wilson Phillips before going solo.

| 03/02/1996 | 62 | 1 | | NAKED AND SACRED | EMI CDEM 409 |

ESTHER PHILLIPS
US singer (born Esther Mae Jones, 23/12/1935, Galveston, TX) who recorded with the Johnny Otis Orchestra as Little Esther from 1948 until 1954 and scored numerous R&B hits. Ill health brought about by drug addiction forced her into virtual retirement between 1954 and 1962 and she died from liver and kidney failure on 7/8/1984.

| 04/10/1975 | 6 | 8 | | WHAT A DIFFERENCE A DAY MAKES | Kudu 925 |

PHIXX
UK vocal group formed by Nikk Mager, Pete Smith, Chris Park, Andrew Kilochan and Mikey Green; they first came to prominence as competitors on *Popstars: The Rivals* and formed their own group when they all missed out on being voted into One True Voice.

08/11/2003	10	4		HOLD ON ME	Concept CDCON 51X
20/03/2004	13	5		LOVE REVOLUTION	Concept CDCON 55X
03/07/2004	12	3		WILD BOYS	Concept CON 56X

PHOENIX
French vocal/instrumental group formed by Thomas Mars (vocals), Christian Mazzalai (guitar) and Deck Darcy (bass).

03/02/2001	65	1		IF I EVER FEEL BETTER Contains a sample of Toshiyuki Honda's *Lament*	Source DINSD 210
01/05/2004	66	1		RUN RUN RUN.	Source SOURCD094
24/07/2004	74	1		EVERYTHING IS EVERYTHING	Source SOURCDX097

PAUL PHOENIX
UK singer who later sang with the St Paul's Cathedral Choir.

| 03/11/1979 | 56 | 4 | | NUNC DIMITTIS Theme to the TV series *Tinker Tailor Soldier Spy*. Full artist credit on the single is 'Paul Phoenix (treble)' with Instrumental Ensemble – James Watson (trumpet), John Scott (organ), conducted by Barry Rose. | Different HAVE 20 |

PHOTEK
UK jungle/drum and bass artist Rupert Parkes who began his career with a £2,000 loan from the Prince's Trust.

22/03/1997	37	2		NI-TEN-ICHI-RYU (TWO SWORDS TECHNIQUE).	Science QEDCD 2
28/02/1998	66	1		MODUS OPERANDI	Virgin QEDCD 6
24/02/2001	44	1		MINE TO GIVE PHOTEK FEATURING ROBERT OWENS	Science QEDCD 10

PHOTOS UK group from Worcestershire: Wendy Wu (vocals), Steve Eagles (guitar), Dave Sparrow (bass) and Oily Harrison (drums).

17/05/1980.....56......4....... IRENE...Epic EPC 8517

PHUNKY PHANTOM UK producer Lawrence Nelson.

16/05/1998.....27......3....... GET UP STAND UP ....Club For Life DISNCD 44

PHUTURE ASSASSINS UK instrumental/production group formed by Austin Reynolds, Terry Holt and Bernard Simon.

06/06/1992.....64......1....... FUTURE SOUND (EP) Tracks on EP: *Future Sound, African Sanctus, Rydim Come Forward* and *Freedom Sound* ....
....Suburban Base SUBBASE 010

PIA – see **PIA ZADORA**

EDITH PIAF French singer (born Edith Giovanna Gassion, 19/12/1915, Paris); discovered singing on the streets by Louis Leplee, owner of a cabaret club. During the Second World War she was as important to French soldiers as Vera Lynn was to British, giving numerous concerts to French prisoners in Germany. After the war she had hits in both the US and UK charts. She died on 11/10/1963.

| 12/05/1960.....41......4....... | MILORD ....Columbia DC 754 |
| 03/11/1960.....24......11...... | MILORD ....Columbia DC 754 |

PIANOHEADZ US production/DJ duo Erick 'More' Morillo and Jose Nunez. Morillo was an ex-member of Real To Reel and Lil Mo' Yin Yang.

11/07/1998.....39......2....... IT'S OVER (DISTORTION)...Incredible Music INCRL 3CD

PIANOMAN UK producer James Sammon who also records as Bass Boyz.

| 15/06/1996 .....6......7....... | **BLURRED** Contains a sample of Blur's *Girls And Boys*...Ffrreedom TABCD 243 |
| 26/04/1997.....43......1....... | PARTY PEOPLE (LIVE YOUR LIFE BE FREE) ....3 Beat 3 BTDCD 1 |

MARK PICCHIOTTI – see **BASSTOY**

BOBBY 'BORIS' PICKETT AND THE CRYPT-KICKERS US singer (born 11/2/1940, Somerville, Massachusetts); he began recording while trying to become an actor. The Crypt-Kickers comprised Leon Russell, Johnny MacCrae, Rickie Page and Gary Paxton. After his recording career came to an end Pickett became a taxi driver.

01/09/1973 .....3......13.....O **MONSTER MASH** ▲[2] Originally released in America in 1962...London HL 10320

WILSON PICKETT US singer (born 18/3/1941, Prattville, AL) who sang with gospel groups before relocating to Detroit, MI in 1955. He joined the Falcons in 1961 and replaced Eddie Floyd on lead vocals until 1963 when he recorded solo. Signed by Double L records (Atlantic subsequently bought his contract), he was sent to Memphis to record with the Stax stalwarts. He was sentenced to one year in prison (and five years probation) in 1993 for driving while drunk and hitting a pedestrian. Since his release he has been arrested twice for cocaine possession. He appeared in the film *Blues Brothers 2000*. He was inducted into the Rock & Roll Hall of Fame in 1991.

23/09/1965.....12......11......	IN THE MIDNIGHT HOUR Featured in the 1985 film *Into The Night* ....Atlantic AT 4036
25/11/1965.....29......8.......	DON'T FIGHT IT ....Atlantic AT 4052
10/03/1966.....36......5.......	634-5789..Atlantic AT 4072
01/09/1966.....22......9.......	LAND OF 1000 DANCES Used in the films *Soul to Soul* (1971), *Forrest Gump* (1994) and *The Full Monty* (1997) ....Atlantic 584-039
15/12/1966.....28......7.......	MUSTANG SALLY ....Atlantic 584-066
27/09/1967.....43......2.......	FUNKY BROADWAY Featured in the 1971 film *Soul To Soul*..Atlantic 584 130
11/09/1968.....38......6.......	I'M A MIDNIGHT MOVER ....Atlantic 584 203
08/01/1969.....16......9.......	HEY JUDE...Atlantic 584 236
21/11/1987.....62......3.......	IN THE MIDNIGHT HOUR Re-recording ....Motown ZB 41583

PICKETTYWITCH UK group formed by Polly Brown (born 18/4/1947, Birmingham) and Maggie Farren who, after appearing on *Opportunity Knocks* in 1969, became protégées of songwriters/producers Tony Macauley and John McLeod. Brown later recorded solo and with Sweet Dreams, replaced by Sheila Rossall (who was reported in 1980 to be suffering from an allergy to the 20th century).

28/02/1970 .....5......14......	**THAT SAME OLD FEELING** ....Pye 7N 17887
04/07/1970.....16......10......	(IT'S LIKE A) SAD OLD KINDA MOVIE ....Pye 7N 17951
07/11/1970.....27......10......	BABY I WON'T LET YOU DOWN ....Pye 7N 45002

MAURO PICOTTO Italian dance producer based in Turin who also worked with Gianfranco Bortolotti of Cappella and 49ers. He also recorded as CRW and RAF.

12/06/1999.....27......3.......	LIZARD (GONNA GET YOU) ....VC Recordings VCRD 50
20/11/1999.....33......2.......	LIZARD (GONNA GET YOU) (REMIX) ....VC Recordings VCRD 57
15/07/2000.....33......3.......	IGUANA..VC Recordings VCRD 68
13/01/2001.....13......5.......	KOMODO (SAVE A SOUL)..VC Recordings VCRDX 85
11/08/2001.....21......4.......	LIKE THIS LIKE THAT ....VC Recordings VCRD 92
25/08/2001.....74......1.......	VERDI ....BXR BXRP 0318
16/03/2002.....35......3.......	PULSAR 2002 ....BXR/Nukleuz BXRCA 0162
03/08/2002.....42......2.......	BACK TO CALI ....BXR BXRC 0433

PIGBAG
UK group formed in Cheltenham in 1980 by Chris Hamlyn (clarinet), Mark Smith (bass), Roger Freeman (trombone), James Johnstone (saxophone/guitar), Chris Lee (trumpet), Ollie Moore (saxophone), Simon Underwood (bass) and Andrew 'Chip' Carpenter (drums). Hamlyn left them in 1981, Freeman left in 1982, replaced by Oscar Verden, with Brian Nevill (drums) also joining. Singer Angela Jaeger joined in 1983, but the group disbanded soon after.

Date	Pos	Wks	Title	Label
07/11/1981	53	3	SUNNY DAY	Y Records Y 12
27/02/1982	61	3	GETTING UP	Y Records Y 16
03/04/1982	3	11	**PAPA'S GOT A BRAND NEW PIGBAG** Single released in May 1981 and took nine months to chart	Y Records Y 10
10/07/1982	40	3	THE BIG BEAN	Y Records Y 24

PIGEON HED – see LO FIDELITY ALLSTARS

NELSON PIGFORD – see DE ETTA LITTLE AND NELSON PIGFORD

PIGLETS
UK studio group assembled by producer Jonathan King. The lead vocal was by Barbara Kay, although King has always maintained it had been by him.

Date	Pos	Wks	Title	Label
06/11/1971	3	12	**JOHNNY REGGAE**	Bell 1180

DICK PIKE – see RUBY WRIGHT

P.I.L. – see PUBLIC IMAGE LIMITED

PILOT
UK group formed by David Paton (born 29/10/1951, Edinburgh, bass/guitar/vocals), Bill Lyall (born 26/3/1953, Edinburgh, keyboards/vocals), Stuart Tosh (born 26/9/1951, Aberdeen, drums/vocals) and Ian Bairnson (born 3/8/1953, Shetland Isles, guitar). When the group disbanded Bairnson, Paton and Tosh became part of the Alan Parsons Project (Parsons produced *January*) and Tosh later joined 10CC. Lyall died from an AIDS-related illness in December 1989.

Date	Pos	Wks	BPI	Title	Label
02/11/1974	11	11		MAGIC	EMI 2217
18/01/1975	❶³	10	○	JANUARY	EMI 2255
19/04/1975	34	4		CALL ME ROUND	EMI 2287
27/09/1975	31	4		JUST A SMILE	EMI 2338

PILTDOWN MEN
US group of session musicians assembled by Ed Cobb and Lincoln Mayorga. Cobb was ex-Four Preps and penned *Tainted Love*, later a smash for Soft Cell and Marilyn Manson.

Date	Pos	Wks	Title	Label
08/09/1960	14	18	MACDONALD'S CAVE Based on the kid's song *Old MacDonald Had A Farm*	Capitol CL 15149
12/01/1961	14	10	PILTDOWN RIDES AGAIN	Capitol CL 15175
09/03/1961	18	8	GOODNIGHT MRS. FLINTSTONE	Capitol CL 15186

COURTNEY PINE
UK saxophonist (born 18/3/1964, London) who played with Dwarf Steps before providing musical backing for a number of reggae artists. He made his reputation in the jazz field, performing with the likes of Elvin Jones, Charlie Watts and Art Blakey. After turning down an opportunity to be in Art Blakey's Jazz Messengers he went solo in 1987. He later formed his own quartet with Kenny Kirkland (piano), Charnett Moffett (bass) and Marvin Smith (drums). He won the 1996 MOBO Award for Best Jazz Act.

Date	Pos	Wks	Title	Label
30/07/1988	26	5	LIKE DREAMERS DO **MICA PARIS FEATURING COURTNEY PINE**	Fourth & Broadway BRW 108
07/07/1990	66	1	I'M STILL WAITING **COURTNEY PINE FEATURING CARROLL THOMPSON**	Mango MNG 749

PING PING AND AL VERLAINE
Belgian vocal duo. Verlaine later sang with the Ricco Zorroh Trio.

Date	Pos	Wks	Title	Label
28/09/1961	41	4	SUCU SUCU	Oriole CB 1589

P!NK
US singer (born Alecia Moore, 6/9/1979, Philadelphia, PA) who was previously lead singer with Basic Instinct and then Choice before going solo. She attained her name because of her pink hair, although by the time of her fifth hit single had reverted to blonde. She won Best International Female Artist at the 2003 BRIT Awards.

Date	Pos	Wks	BPI	Title	Label
10/06/2000	6	9		**THERE YOU GO** Features the uncredited contribution of Kandi on backing vocals	LaFace 74321757602
30/09/2000	5	8		**MOST GIRLS**	LaFace 74321792012
27/01/2001	9	6		**YOU MAKE ME SICK** Featured in the 2001 film *Save The Last Dance*	LaFace 74321828702
30/06/2001	❶¹	16	●	**LADY MARMALADE** ↑ ▲⁵ **CHRISTINA AGUILERA/LIL' KIM/MYA/PINK** Featured in the 2001 film *Moulin Rouge*. 2001 Grammy Award for Best Pop Collaboration with Vocals	Interscope 4975612
26/01/2002	2	15	○	**GET THE PARTY STARTED** 2002 MTV Europe Music Award for Best Song	Arista 74321913372
25/05/2002	6	11		**DON'T LET ME GET ME**	Arista 74321939212
28/09/2002	❶¹	11		**JUST LIKE A PILL** ↑	Arista 74321959652
14/12/2002	66	1		FAMILY PORTRAIT (IMPORT)	Arista 74321982102
21/12/2002	11	9		FAMILY PORTRAIT	Arista 74321982052
19/07/2003	4	11		**FEEL GOOD TIME** **PINK FEATURING WILLIAM ORBIT** Featured in the 2003 film *Charlie's Angels: Full Throttle*	Columbia 6741062
08/11/2003	7	12		**TROUBLE** 2003 Grammy Award for Best Female Rock Vocal Performance	Arista 82876572172
07/02/2004	11	6		GOD IS A DJ Featured in the 2004 film *Mean Girls*	Arista 82876589472
01/05/2004	21	4		LAST TO KNOW	Arista 82876611732

PINK FLOYD
UK rock group formed in London in 1965 by Roger Waters (born 6/9/1944, Great Bookham, vocals/bass), Rick Wright (born 28/7/1945, London, keyboards), Syd Barrett (born Roger Barrett, 6/1/1946, Cambridge, guitar/vocals) and Nick Mason (born 27/1/1945, Birmingham, drums) as Pink Floyd Sound (the name came from Georgia bluesmen Pink Anderson and Floyd Council). Barrett's erratic behaviour in 1968 led to Dave Gilmour (born 6/3/1947, Cambridge, guitar/vocals) replacing him. Their 1973 album *Dark Side Of The Moon* sold over 23 million copies worldwide, the most by a UK group, although this was matched by *The Wall*, which

❶⁹ Number of weeks single topped the UK chart   ↑ Entered the UK chart at #1   ▲⁹ Number of weeks single topped the US chart

615

sold in excess of 23 million copies in America alone. Waters left acrimoniously in 1983 and made numerous attempts to prevent the remaining three from using the name Pink Floyd. They won the 1994 Grammy Award for Best Rock Instrumental Performance for *Marooned* and were inducted into the Rock & Roll Hall of Fame in 1996. Gilmour was awarded a CBE in the Queen's 2003 Honours List.

30/03/1967	20	8		ARNOLD LAYNE............Columbia DB 8156
22/06/1967	6	12		SEE EMILY PLAY............Columbia DB 8214
01/12/1979	❶⁵	12	✪	ANOTHER BRICK IN THE WALL (PART 2) ▲⁴............Harvest HAR 5194
07/08/1982	39	5		WHEN THE TIGERS BROKE FREE This and above single featured in the 1982 film *The Wall*............Harvest HAR 5222
07/05/1983	30	4		NOT NOW JOHN............Harvest HAR 5224
19/12/1987	55	4		ON THE TURNING AWAY............EMI EM 34
25/06/1988	50	3		ONE SLIP............EMI EM 52
04/06/1994	23	4		TAKE IT BACK............EMI CDEMS 309
29/10/1994	26	3		HIGH HOPES/KEEP TALKING............EMI CDEMS 342

PINK GREASE UK rock group formed in Sheffield in 2001 by Rory Lewarne (vocals), Steve Santacruz (guitar), Nick Collier (keyboards), John Lynch (saxophone/guitar/keyboards), Stuart Faulkner (bass) and Marc Hoad (drums).

26/06/2004	75	1	THE PINK GREASE............Mute CDMUTE 316

PINKEES UK group formed by Paul Egholm (guitar/vocals), Andy Price (guitar/vocals), Max Reinsch (guitar/keyboards), Nevil Kiddier (bass) and Paul Reynolds (drums). Their one hit single was investigated by Scotland Yard when it suddenly zoomed up the charts from #27 to #8: it was later revealed that the record company had conspired with a representative of the chart compilers.

18/09/1982	8	9	DANGER GAMES............Creole CR 39

PINKERTON'S ASSORTED COLOURS UK group formed in Rugby by Barrie Bernard (born 27/11/1944, Coventry, bass), Dave Holland (drums), Samuel 'Pinkerton' Kemp (vocals/autoharp), Tom Long (guitar) and Tony Newman (guitar). After their hit Bernard was replaced by Stuart Coleman (born Harrogate). The group later evolved into Flying Machine, Bernard became a member of Jigsaw while Coleman became a noted producer.

13/01/1966	9	11	MIRROR MIRROR............Decca F 12307
21/04/1966	50	1	DON'T STOP LOVIN' ME BABY............Decca F 12377

PINKY AND PERKY UK puppet duo created by Jan Dalibor in 1964. They had their own children's TV series in the 1960s and were revived in the 1990s.

29/05/1993	47	3	REET PETITE............Telstar CDPIGGY 1

LISA PIN-UP UK DJ Lisa Chilcott who also worked with fellow producer BK and is a member of The Tidy Girls.

25/05/2002	60	1	TURN UP THE SOUND............Nukleuz NUKC 0406
21/12/2002	60	3	BLOW YOUR MIND (I AM THE WOMAN)............Nukleuz 0450 FNUK

PIONEERS Jamaican reggae group formed in 1962 by Sidney and Derrick Crooks and Glen Adams. Sydney teamed up with Jackie Robinson in 1968 and they later added George Dekker (brother of Desmond) to the line-up.

18/10/1969	21	11	LONG SHOT KICK DE BUCKET Based on the true story about two horses, Long Shot and Combat, which died in a race at Kingston's Caymanas Park............Trojan TR 672
31/07/1971	5	12	LET YOUR YEAH BE YEAH............Trojan TR 7825
15/01/1972	35	6	GIVE AND TAKE............Trojan TR 7846
29/03/1980	42	5	LONG SHOT KICK DE BUCKET Re-issue of Trojan TR 672 and coupled with Harry J All Stars' *Liquidator*............Trojan TRO 9063

BILLIE PIPER UK singer (born 9/9/1982, Swindon) who was fifteen years old at the time of her debut hit, having been singing since the age of four. She took part in the BRITS Trust *Thank Abba For The Music* project. In May 2001 she married former Virgin Radio DJ/entrepreneur Chris Evans and later became an actress.

11/07/1998	❶¹	12	◯	BECAUSE WE WANT TO ↑............Innocent SINCD 2
17/10/1998	❶¹	12	◯	GIRLFRIEND ↑............Innocent SINCD 3
19/12/1998	3	13	◯	SHE WANTS YOU............Innocent SINDXX 6
03/04/1999	3	11	◯	HONEY TO THE BEE This and above three singles credited to BILLIE............Innocent SINCD 8
27/05/2000	❶¹	12	◯	DAY & NIGHT ↑............Innocent SINDX 11
30/09/2000	4	9		SOMETHING DEEP INSIDE............Innocent SINDX 19
23/12/2000	25	5		WALK OF LIFE............Innocent SINDX 23

PIPKINS UK duo of Roger Greenaway (born 19/8/1940, Bristol), better known as a songwriter and producer, and Tony Burrows (born 14/4/1942, Exeter), the leading session singer of the time, although live the roles were fulfilled by Davey Sands and Len Marshall.

28/03/1970	6	10	GIMME DAT DING............Columbia DB 8662

PIPS – see GLADYS KNIGHT AND THE PIPS

PIRANHAS UK group formed by 'Boring' Bob Grover (vocals), Johnny Helmer (guitar), Reginald Hornsbury (bass), Zoot Alors (saxophone) and Dick Slexia (drums).

02/08/1980	6	12	◯	TOM HARK............Sire SIR 4044
16/10/1982	17	9		ZAMBESI PIRANHAS FEATURING BORING BOB GROVER............Dakota DAK 6

PIRATES – see JOHNNY KIDD AND THE PIRATES

PIRATES, ENYA, SHOLA AMA, NAILA BOSS & ISHANI UK group formed by production duo Ryan Perera and Man De Lev with singers Shola Ama, Naila Boss and Ishana. Their debut hit was an answer record to Mario Winans' *I Don't Wanna Know*.

11/09/2004	8	8		**YOU SHOULD REALLY KNOW** Contains a sample of Enya's *Boadicea*	Relentless RELCD9

PITCHSHIFTER UK group formed in Nottingham by Jonathan Clayden (vocals), Jonathan Carter (guitar/programming), Mark Clayden (bass) and D (drums). They signed with Peaceville Records in 1991. By the time their debut album appeared D had departed and Stuart Toolin (guitar) joined. They subsequently added guitarist Jim Davies and also recorded for Earache and Geffen Records.

28/02/1998	71	1		GENIUS	Geffen GFSTD 22324
26/09/1998	54	1		MICROWAVED	Geffen GFSTD 22348
21/10/2000	71	1		DEAD BATTERY	MCA MCSTD 40241
29/06/2002	66	1		SHUTDOWN	Mayan MYNX 008X

GENE PITNEY US singer (born 17/2/1941, Hartford, CT, raised in Rockville) who recorded his first single in 1959 and shortly after became a successful writer, penning *Rubber Ball* under the name Annie Orlowski (his wife's name) because of publishing difficulties. His other song writing credits include *He's A Rebel* (The Crystals), *Hello Mary Lou* (Ricky Nelson) and *Loneliness* (Des O'Connor). In 1961 he quit university to concentrate on music and signed with Musicor. He was inducted into the Rock & Roll Hall of Fame in 2002.

23/03/1961	26	11		(I WANNA) LOVE MY LIFE AWAY	London HL 9270
08/03/1962	32	6		TOWN WITHOUT PITY Featured in the films *Town Without Pity* (1961) and *Hairspray* (1988)	HMV POP 952
05/12/1963	5	19		**TWENTY FOUR HOURS FROM TULSA**	United Artists UP 1035
05/03/1964	7	12		**THAT GIRL BELONGS TO YESTERDAY**	United Artists UP 1045
15/10/1964	36	4		IT HURTS TO BE IN LOVE	United Artists UP 1063
12/11/1964	2	14		**I'M GONNA BE STRONG**	Stateside SS 358
18/02/1965	6	10		**I MUST BE SEEING THINGS**	Stateside SS 390
10/06/1965	3	12		**LOOKING THROUGH THE EYES OF LOVE**	Stateside SS 420
04/11/1965	9	12		**PRINCESS IN RAGS**	Stateside SS 471
17/02/1966	4	10		**BACKSTAGE**	Stateside SS 490
09/06/1966	2	13		**NOBODY NEEDS YOUR LOVE**	Stateside SS 518
10/11/1966	8	12		**JUST ONE SMILE**	Stateside SS 558
23/02/1967	38	6		(IN THE) COLD LIGHT OF DAY	Stateside SS 597
15/11/1967	5	13		**SOMETHING'S GOTTEN HOLD OF MY HEART**	Stateside SS 2060
03/04/1968	19	9		SOMEWHERE IN THE COUNTRY	Stateside SS 2103
27/11/1968	34	7		YOURS UNTIL TOMORROW	Stateside SS 2131
05/03/1969	25	6		MARIA ELENA	Stateside SS 2142
14/03/1970	37	5		A STREET CALLED HOPE	Stateside SS 2164
03/10/1970	29	8		SHADY LADY	Stateside SS 2177
28/04/1973	34	7		24 SYCAMORE	Pye International 7N 25606
02/11/1974	39	4		BLUE ANGEL	Bronze BRO 11
14/01/1989	❶⁴	12	○	**SOMETHING'S GOTTEN HOLD OF MY HEART** MARC ALMOND FEATURING SPECIAL GUEST STAR GENE PITNEY	Parlophone R 6201

MARIO PIU Italian producer featuring German/Indonesian singer Sinta who was also a dancer for Robbie Williams and appeared in a James Bond film.

11/12/1999	5	9		**COMMUNICATION (SOMEBODY ANSWER THE PHONE)**	Incentive CENT 2CDS
10/03/2001	16	5		THE VISION **MARIO PIU PRESENTS DJ ARABESQUE**	BXR BXRC 0253

PIXIES US rock group formed in Boston, Massachusetts by Black Francis (born Charles Michael Kittridge Thompson IV, 1965, Long Beach, CA, guitar/vocals), Joey Santiago (born 10/6/1965, Manila, Philippines, guitar), Kim Deal (born 10/6/1961,Dayton, OH, bass) and David Lovering (born 6/12/1961, Boston, drums) as Pixies In Panoply. Francis subsequently changed his name to Frank Black and went solo in 1993. Deal was later a member of The Breeders.

01/04/1989	60	3		MONKEY GONE TO HEAVEN	4AD AD 904
01/07/1989	54	1		HERE COMES YOUR MAN	4AD AD 909
28/07/1990	28	3		VELOURIA	4AD AD 0009
10/11/1990	62	1		DIG FOR FIRE	4AD AD 0014
08/06/1991	27	3		PLANET OF SOUND	4AD AD 1008
04/10/1997	23	2		DEBASER	4AD BADO 7010CD

PIZZAMAN UK instrumental/production group assembled by Norman Cook (born Quentin Cook, 31/7/1963, Brighton), ex-Housemartins. Cook has also been responsible for Beats International and Freakpower, among others.

27/08/1994	33	2		TRIPPIN' ON SUNSHINE	Loaded CDLOAD 16
10/06/1995	24	4		SEX ON THE STREETS	Cowboy CDLOAD 24
18/11/1995	19	4		HAPPINESS	Cowboy CDLOAD 29
06/01/1996	23	4		SEX ON THE STREETS	Cowboy CDLOAD 24

❶⁹ Number of weeks single topped the UK chart ↑ Entered the UK chart at #1 ▲⁹ Number of weeks single topped the US chart

| 01/06/1996 | 18 | 3 | | TRIPPIN' ON SUNSHINE Re-issue of Loaded CDLOAD 16 | Cowboy CDLOAD 32 |
| 14/09/1996 | 41 | 1 | | HELLO HONKY TONKS (ROCK YOUR BODY) | Cowboy CDLOAD 39 |

PIZZICATO FIVE Japanese vocal/instrumental group formed by Konishi (born 3/2/1959), Maki Nomiya and Bravo.

| 01/11/1997 | 72 | 1 | | MON AMOUR TOKYO | Matador OLE 2902 |

JOE PIZZULO – see **SERGIO MENDES**

PJ Canadian producer Paul Jacobs.

| 20/09/1997 | 72 | 1 | | HAPPY DAYS | Deconstruction 74321511822 |
| 04/09/1999 | 57 | 1 | | HAPPY DAYS (REMIX) | Defected DFECT 6CDS |

PJ AND DUNCAN – see **ANT AND DEC**

PKA UK producer Phil Kelsey.

| 20/04/1991 | 68 | 1 | | TEMPERATURE RISING | Stress SS 4 |
| 07/03/1992 | 70 | 1 | | POWERSIGN (ONLY YOUR LOVE) | Stress PKA 1 |

PLACEBO UK rock group formed in London in 1994 by Brian Molko (guitar/vocals), Stefan Olsdal (bass) and Robert Schultzberg (drums). Schultzberg left in 1996 and was replaced by Steve Hewitt.

28/09/1996	30	3		TEENAGE ANGST	Elevator Music FLOORCD 3
01/02/1997	4	6		**NANCY BOY**	Elevator Music FLOORCD 4
24/05/1997	14	3		BRUISE PRISTINE	Elevator Music FLOORCD 5
15/08/1998	4	6		**PURE MORNING**	Hut FLOORCD 6
10/10/1998	5	5		**YOU DON'T CARE ABOUT US**	Hut FLOORCD 7
06/02/1999	11	5		EVERY YOU EVERY ME Featured in the 1999 film *Cruel Intentions*	Hut FLOORDX 9
29/07/2000	16	6		TASTE IN MEN	Hut FLOORD 11
07/10/2000	19	3		SLAVE TO THE WAGE Contains a sample of Pavement's *Texas Never Whispers*	Hut FLOORDX 12
22/03/2003	12	5		BITTER END	Hut FLOORDX 16
28/06/2003	23	2		THIS PICTURE	Hut FLOORCD 18
27/09/2003	27	2		SPECIAL NEEDS	Hut FLOORCD 19
06/03/2004	23	2		ENGLISH SUMMER RAIN	Hut FLOORDX 21
30/10/2004	18	3		TWENTY YEARS	Virgin FLOORDX24

PLANET FUNK Italian dance group formed by Alex Neri, Marco Baroni, Andrea Cozzani, Sergio Bella Monica, Domenico Canu, Alessandro Sommella and singer Auli Cocco. Neri and Baroni had previously recorded as Kamasutra.

10/02/2001	5	9		**CHASE THE SUN**	Virgin VSCDT 1749
26/04/2003	36	2		WHO SAID (STUCK IN THE UK) Contains samples of Gary Numan's *Machine* and Medium Medium's *Hungry So Angry*	Illustrious/Bustin L CDILL 015
16/08/2003	52	1		THE SWITCH	Illustrious/Epic CDILL 017

PLANET PATROL US vocal group formed in Boston, MA by Rodney Butler, Melvin Franklin, Herb Jackson, Michael Jones and Joseph Lites.

| 17/09/1983 | 64 | 3 | | CHEAP THRILLS | Polydor POSP 639 |

PLANET PERFECTO UK DJ Paul Oakenfold (born 30/8/1963, London) recording under an assumed name. He owns the Perfecto label and also records as Perfecto Allstarz with Steve Osborne and as Movement 98.

14/08/1999	16	4		NOT OVER YET 99 **PLANET PERFECTO FEATURING GRACE**	Code Blue BLU 004CD
13/11/1999	15	4		BULLET IN THE GUN	Perfecto PERF 3CDS
16/09/2000	7	6		**BULLET IN THE GUN 2000 (REMIX)**	Perfecto PERF 03CDSX
29/09/2001	52	1		BITES DA DUST	Perfecto PERF 19CDS

PLANETS UK vocal/instrumental group fronted by Steve Lindsey who was previously a member of Deaf School.

| 18/08/1979 | 36 | 6 | | LINES | Rialto TREB 104 |
| 25/10/1980 | 66 | 2 | | DON'T LOOK DOWN | Rialto TREB 116 |

PLANK 15 UK dance group formed by Kelvin Andrews, Danny Spencer, Chris Bourne, Andy Holt and Mark Ralph.

| 02/02/2002 | 60 | 1 | | STRINGS OF LIFE | Multiply CDMULTY 82 |

ROBERT PLANT UK singer (born 20/8/1948, West Bromwich) who began his career with the New Memphis Bluesbreakers (a Birmingham-based group, despite their name), Crawling King Snakes and then Listen before going solo in 1967. He had spells with Band Of Joy and Hobstweedle before being invited to join Led Zeppelin in 1969 (he was not the original choice). In August 1975 he and his wife were in a serious car accident while on holiday in Rhodes, which forced Led Zeppelin to cancel plans for a world tour that year. The death of John Bonham in 1980 effectively brought Led Zeppelin to an end and Plant relaunched his solo career. In 1984 he and Jimmy Page formed The Honeydrippers with Jeff Beck and Nile Rodgers, and he has since recorded both solo and with Jimmy Page.

09/10/1982	73	1		BURNING DOWN ONE SIDE	Swansong SSK 19429
16/07/1983	11	10		BIG LOG	WEA B 9848
30/01/1988	33	5		HEAVEN KNOWS	Es Paranza A 9373
28/04/1990	45	3		HURTING KIND (I'VE GOT MY EYES ON YOU)	Es Paranza A 8985

○ Silver disc ● Gold disc ✪ Platinum disc (additional platinum units are indicated by a figure following the symbol) ◎ Singles released prior to 1973 that are known to have sold over 1 million copies in the UK

08/05/1993	21	5		29 PALMS	Fontana FATEX 1
03/07/1993	64	2		I BELIEVE	Fontana FATEX 2
25/12/1993	63	2		IF I WERE A CARPENTER	Fontana FATEX 4
17/12/1994	35	3		GALLOWS POLE **JIMMY PAGE AND ROBERT PLANT**	Fontana PPCD 2
11/04/1998	26	2		MOST HIGH **PAGE AND PLANT** 1998 Grammy Award for Best Hard Rock Song	Mercury 5687512

PLASMATICS US punk rock group formed in 1979 by former sex show star Wendy O Williams (born 28/5/1949, Rochester, NY, vocals) with Richie Stotts (guitar), Wes Beech (guitar), Chosei Funahara (bass) and Stu Deutsch (drums). The group was the brainchild of pornographic mogul Rod Swenson – Wendy's stage 'outfit' was either see-through lingerie or topless with little more than strategically placed tape. After a number of recordings for Stiff and Capitol Records, the Plasmatics disbanded in 1982; Wendy subsequently went solo. She committed suicide on 6/4/1998.

26/07/1980	55	4		BUTCHER BABY	Stiff BUY 76

PLASTIC BERTRAND Belgian punk-rock singer (born Roger Jouret, 1958), an ex-member of Stalag 6 and Hubble Bubble.

13/05/1978	8	12		**CA PLANE POUR MOI**	Sire 6078 616
05/08/1978	39	5		SHA LA LA LA LEE	Vertigo 6059 209

PLASTIC BOY FEATURING ROZALLA Belgian producer Dirk 'M.I.K.E.' Dierickx (born 20/2/1973) recording under an assumed name. He also records as Push.

22/11/2003	55	1		LIVE ANOTHER LIFE	Inferno CDFERN 59

PLASTIC JAM – see **BUG KANN AND THE PLASTIC JAM**

PLASTIC ONO BAND – see **JOHN LENNON**

PLASTIC PENNY UK group formed by Brian Keith (vocals), Mick Graham (guitar), Paul Raymond (keyboards), Tony Murray (bass) and Nigel Olsson (drums). Olsson later became a member of the Spencer Davis Group.

03/01/1968	6	10		**EVERYTHING I AM**	Page One POF 051

PLASTIC POPULATION – see **YAZZ**

PLATINUM 45 FEATURING MORE FIRE CREW UK producer with London MC trio More Fire Crew, who were formed by Lethal B, Neeko and Ozzie B.

16/03/2002	8	8		**OI**	Go! Beat GOBCD 48

PLATINUM HOOK US R&B group formed by Stephen Daniels (drums/vocals), Tina Renee Stanford (percussion/vocals), Robert Douglas (keyboards), Elisha 'Skipp' Ingram (bass), Victor Jones (guitar), Robin David Corley (saxophone) and Glenn Wallace (trombone).

02/09/1978	72	1		STANDING ON THE VERGE (OF GETTING IT ON)	Motown TMG 1115

PLATTERS US R&B vocal group formed in Los Angeles, CA in 1953 by Tony Williams (born 5/4/1928, Elizabeth, NJ, lead vocals), David Lynch (born 3/7/1929, St Louis, MO), Paul Robi (born 1931, New Orleans, LA), Herb Reed (born 1931, Kansas City, MO) and Zola Taylor (born 1934). The group was managed by Buck Ram (born Samuel Ram, 18/12/1908, Chicago, IL), who also penned *Only You*. Williams went solo in 1961, replaced by Sonny Turner. Williams' departure led to problems with Mercury, who initially refused to accept recordings without his lead vocal; Ram argued that their contract did not stipulate who should sing lead. Lynch died from cancer on 2/1/1981, Robi died from pancreatic cancer on 1/2/1989, Ram died on 1/1/1991 and Williams died from diabetes and emphysema on 14/8/1992. Due to the many personnel changes over the course of 25 years, numerous singers laid claim to the Platters name. The matter was settled in April 1999 when Herb Reed won ownership of the name. The group was inducted into the Rock & Roll Hall of Fame in 1990.

07/09/1956	5	16		THE GREAT PRETENDER/ONLY YOU ▲2 A-side featured in the 1973 film *American Graffiti*. B-side featured in the films *Rock Around The Clock* (1956), *This Angry Age* (1958) and *American Graffiti* (1973)	Mercury MT 117
02/11/1956	4	13		MY PRAYER ▲5	Mercury MT 120
25/01/1957	23	3		YOU'LL NEVER NEVER KNOW/IT ISN'T RIGHT	Mercury MT 130
17/05/1957	18	8		I'M SORRY	Mercury MT 145
16/05/1958	3	18		TWILIGHT TIME ▲1	Mercury MT 214
16/01/1959	❶1	20		SMOKE GETS IN YOUR EYES ▲3 Featured in the films *American Graffiti* (1973), *La Bamba* (1987), *Always* (1989) and *Backfire* (1995)	Mercury AMT 1016
28/08/1959	25	2		REMEMBER WHEN	Mercury AMT 1053
29/01/1960	11	12		HARBOUR LIGHTS	Mercury AMT 1081

PLAVKA – see **JAM AND SPOON FEATURING PLAVKA**

PLAYBOY BAND – see **JOHN FRED AND THE PLAYBOY BAND**

PLAYBOYS – see **GARY LEWIS AND THE PLAYBOYS**

PLAYER US rock group formed in Los Angeles, CA by Peter Beckett (guitar/vocals), John Crowley (guitar/vocals), Ronn Moss (bass), John Friesen (drums) and Wayne Cooke (keyboards). Moss later became an actor.

25/02/1978	32	7		BABY COME BACK ▲3	RSO 2090 254

❶9 Number of weeks single topped the UK chart ↑ Entered the UK chart at #1 ▲9 Number of weeks single topped the US chart

619

PLAYERS ASSOCIATION
US dance group initially assembled as a studio aggregation by producer Danny Weiss and multi-instrumentalist Chris Hills. Performers on the hits included Chris Hills, Bob Berg (tenor saxophone), Bob Mover (alto saxophone), Karl Ratzer (guitar), Tom Harrell (trumpet), Pat Rebillot (keyboards), Mike Mandel (keyboards), Herb Bushler (bass), David Earle Johnson (percussion), Ray Mantilla (percussion), Gary Anderson (reeds), Marvin Stamm (trumpet), Victor Paz (trumpet) and Ed Byrne (trombone). A touring band was later formed. Weiss and Hills had previously recorded as Everything Is Everything and later recorded as Feel.

10/03/1979	8	9	**TURN THE MUSIC UP**	Vanguard VS 5011
05/05/1979	42	5	RIDE THE GROOVE	Vanguard VS 5012
09/02/1980	61	3	WE GOT THE GROOVE	Vanguard VS 5016

PLAYGROUP
UK producer Trevor Jackson.

24/11/2001	66	1	NUMBER ONE	Source SOURCD 026

PLAYTHING
Italian production duo Luca Moretti and Riccardo Romanini. They also record as Triple X.

05/05/2001	48	1	INTO SPACE	Manifesto FESCD 81
24/08/2002	14	5	DO YOU SEE THE LIGHT **SNAP VERSUS PLAYTHING**	Data 33CDS

PLUMB
US singer Tiffany Arbuckle (born in Indianapolis) who formed Plumb in 1996 and assumed the name for her own solo career when the group disbanded in 2000.

14/02/2004	41	2	REAL	Curb CUBC 095

PLUMMET
US duo producer Eric Muniz and singer Nikki. Muniz also records as DJ X and runs the Xquizit and EBM record labels.

26/04/2003	12	10	DAMAGED	Serious SER 68CD
08/05/2004	35	2	CHERISH THE DAY	Manifesto 9866389

PLUS ONE FEATURING SIRRON
UK vocal/instrumental group formed by Dexter Roberts, Sam Roberts and Sirron.

19/05/1990	40	4	IT'S HAPPENIN'	MCA 1405

PLUTO – see PLUTO SHERVINGTON

PLUX FEATURING GEORGIA JONES
US vocal/instrumental group fronted by Georgia Jones.

04/05/1996	33	2	OVER & OVER Contains samples of Rufus & Chaka Khan's *Ain't Nobody,* The Bucketheads' *The Bomb* and Patrick Juvet's *Got A Feeling*	ffrr FCD 277

PM DAWN
US rap duo of brothers Atrell 'Prince B' Cordes (born 19/5/1970, Jersey City, NJ) and Jarrett 'DJ Minutemix' Cordes (born 17/7/1971, Jersey City). They began their recording career straight from leaving school. The group's name is defined as 'from the darkest hour comes the light'. They were named Best International Newcomers at the 1992 BRIT Awards.

08/06/1991	36	5	A WATCHER'S POINT OF VIEW (DON'T CHA THINK)	Gee Street GEE 32
17/08/1991	3	8	**SET ADRIFT ON A MEMORY BLISS** ▲[1] Contains a sample of Spandau Ballet's *True*	Gee Street GEE 33
19/10/1991	49	3	PAPER DOLL	Gee Street GEE 35
22/02/1992	29	4	REALITY USED TO BE A GOOD FRIEND OF MINE	Gee Street GEE 37
07/11/1992	30	5	I'D DIE WITHOUT YOU Featured in the 1992 film *Boomerang*	Gee Street GEE 39
13/03/1993	11	7	LOOKING THROUGH PATIENT EYES Contains a sample of George Michael's *Father Figure*	Gee Street GESCD 47
12/06/1993	40	3	MORE THAN LIKELY **PM DAWN FEATURING BOY GEORGE**	Gee Street GESCD 49
30/09/1995	58	2	DOWNTOWN VENUS Contains a sample of Deep Purple's *Hush*	Gee Street GESCD 63
06/04/1996	58	1	SOMETIMES I MISS YOU SO MUCH	Gee Street GESCD 65
31/10/1998	68	1	GOTTA…MOVIN' ON UP Contains a sample of Imagination's *Just An Illusion*	Gee Street GEE 5003933

POB FEATURING DJ PATRICK REID
UK producer Paul Brogden recording under an assumed name.

11/12/1999	74	1	BLUEBOTTLE/FLY	Platipus PLAT 63CD

P.O.D.
US Christian rock group formed in San Diego, CA in 1992 by Sonny Sandoval (vocals), Marcos Curiel (guitar), Traa Daniels (bass) and Noah 'Wuv' Bernado (drums). The group's name is short for Payable On Death.

02/02/2002	19	6	ALIVE	Atlantic AT 0119CD
18/05/2002	36	2	YOUTH OF THE NATION	East West AT 0127CD
07/06/2003	42	1	SLEEPING AWAKE Featured in the 2003 film *The Matrix Reloaded*	Maverick W 608CD
24/01/2004	68	1	WILL YOU	Atlantic AT 0169CD

POETS
UK group formed in Glasgow in 1961 by George Gallagher (vocals), Hume Paton (guitar), Tony Myles (guitar), John Dawson (bass) and Alan Weir (drums) and signed by manager Andrew Loog Oldham (manager of the Rolling Stones) in 1964. By 1967 the line-up consisted of Andy Mulvey (vocals), Fraser Watson (guitar), Ian McMillan (guitar), Norrie MacLean (bass) and Raymond Duffy (drums). Later member Hugh Nicholson joined Marmalade as replacement for Junior Campbell.

29/10/1964	31	5	NOW WE'RE THRU	Decca F 11995

POGUES
UK group formed in London in 1983 by Shane MacGowan (born 25/12/1957, Tunbridge Wells, guitar/vocals), Jem Finer (born 20/7/1955, Stoke-on-Trent, banjo), James Fearnley (born 9/10/1954, Manchester, accordion), Andrew Ranken (born 13/11/1953, London, drums) and Caitlin O'Riordan (born 4/1/1965, Nigeria, bass) as Pogiue Mo Chone (Gaelic for 'kiss my arse'). They signed with Stiff in 1984, who shortened the name to make it less offensive. They later added Philip Chevron (born 17/6/1957, Dublin, guitar) and Peter 'Spider' Stacy (born 14/12/1958, Eastbourne, tin whistle), with ex-Clash member Joe Strummer (born

○ Silver disc ● Gold disc ✪ Platinum disc (additional platinum units are indicated by a figure following the symbol) ◎ Singles released prior to 1973 that are known to have sold over 1 million copies in the UK

John Mellors, 21/8/1952, Ankara, Turkey) becoming a member and taking over as lead singer when MacGowan was sacked. MacGowan later recorded solo.

DATE	POS	WKS	BPI	SINGLE TITLE	LABEL & NUMBER
06/04/1985	72	2		A PAIR OF BROWN EYES	Stiff BUY 220
22/06/1985	51	4		SALLY MACLENNANE	Stiff BUY 224
14/09/1985	62	3		DIRTY OLD TOWN	Stiff BUY 229
08/03/1986	29	6		POGUETRY IN MOTION EP Tracks on EP: *London Girl, The Body Of An American, A Rainy Night In Soho* and *Planxty Noel Hill*... Stiff BUY 243	
30/08/1986	42	4		HAUNTED	MCA 1084
28/03/1987	8	8		**THE IRISH ROVER** POGUES AND THE DUBLINERS	Stiff BUY 258
05/12/1987	2	9	O	**FAIRYTALE OF NEW YORK** POGUES FEATURING KIRSTY MACCOLL	Pogue Mahone NY 7
05/03/1988	58	3		IF I SHOULD FALL FROM GRACE WITH GOD	Pogue Mahone PG 1
16/07/1988	24	5		FIESTA	Pogue Mahone PG 2
17/12/1988	43	4		YEAH YEAH YEAH YEAH YEAH	Pogue Mahone YZ 355
08/07/1989	41	3		MISTY MORNING, ALBERT BRIDGE	PM YZ 407
16/06/1990	63	2		JACK'S HEROES/WHISKEY IN THE JAR	Pogue Mahone YZ 500
15/09/1990	64	2		SUMMER IN SIAM	PM YZ 519
21/09/1991	67	1		A RAINY NIGHT IN SOHO	PM YZ 603
14/12/1991	36	5		FAIRYTALE OF NEW YORK POGUES FEATURING KIRSTY MACCOLL Re-issue of Pogue Mahone NY 7	PM YZ 628
30/05/1992	56	2		HONKY TONK WOMEN	PM YZ 673
21/08/1993	18	5		TUESDAY MORNING	PM YZ 758CD
22/01/1994	66	2		ONCE UPON A TIME	PM YZ 771CD

POINT BREAK
UK vocal group formed by Brett Adams (born 29/12/1976), David 'Ollie' Oliver (born 28/7/1976) and Declan Bennett (born 20/3/1981, Coventry). Brett and Ollie met working on the TV series *Byker Grove* (as Noddy and Marcus respectively).

DATE	POS	WKS	BPI	SINGLE TITLE	LABEL & NUMBER
09/10/1999	29	2		DO WE ROCK	Eternal WEA 216CD1
22/01/2000	7	5		**STAND TOUGH**	Eternal WEA 248CD2
22/04/2000	13	6		FREAKY TIME	Eternal WEA 265CD1
05/08/2000	14	5		YOU	Eternal WEA 290CD1
02/12/2000	24	3		WHAT ABOUT US	Eternal WEA 314CD1

POINTER SISTERS
US R&B vocal group formed in Oakland, CA in 1971 by sisters Anita (born 23/1/1948, Oakland), Bonnie (born 11/7/1950, Oakland), Ruth (born 19/3/1946, Oakland) and June (born 30/11/1954, Oakland) Pointer who first teamed up to sing at the church where their parents were ministers. They disbanded briefly in 1977; Bonnie signed solo with Motown and the remaining trio linked with Richard Perry's Planet label. The group appeared in the film *Car Wash*. They have won three Grammy Awards including Best Country & Western Performance by a Group in 1974 for *Fairy Tale*. They have a star on the Hollywood Walk of Fame.

DATE	POS	WKS	BPI	SINGLE TITLE	LABEL & NUMBER
03/02/1979	61	3		EVERYBODY IS A STAR	Planet K 12324
17/03/1979	34	8		FIRE	Planet K 12339
22/08/1981	10	11		**SLOWHAND**	Planet K 12530
05/12/1981	50	5		SHOULD I DO IT?	Reprise K 12578
14/04/1984	2	15	O	**AUTOMATIC** 1984 Grammy Award for Best Arrangement for Two or More Voices	Planet RPS 105
23/06/1984	6	10		**JUMP (FOR MY LOVE)** 1984 Grammy Award for Best Pop Vocal Performance by a Group. Featured in the 2003 film *Love Actually*... Planet RPS 106	
11/08/1984	25	9		I NEED YOU	Planet RPS 107
27/10/1984	11	11		I'M SO EXCITED Featured in the films *Working Girl* (1988) and *The Nutty Professor* (1996)	Planet RPS 108
12/01/1985	31	7		NEUTRON DANCE Featured in the 1985 film *Beverly Hills Cop*	Planet RPS 109
20/07/1985	17	8		DARE ME	RCA PB 49957

POISON
US heavy rock group formed in Pittsburgh, PA in 1984 by Bret Michaels (born Bret Michael Sychak, 15/3/1963, Harrisburg, PA, vocals), Rikki Rockett (born Richard Ream, 9/8/1959, Mechanicsburg, PA, drums), Bobby Dall (born 2/11/1965, Miami, FL, bass) and Matt Smith (guitar) as Paris. They relocated to Los Angeles, CA (in an ambulance bought by Michaels for $700), replaced Smith with CC DeVille (born Bruce Anthony Johannesson, 14/5/1962, Brooklyn, NY) and name-changed to Poison. They signed with Enigma (through Capitol) in 1986. DeVille left in 1992, replaced by Richie Kotzen (born 3/2/1970, Birdsboro, PA), although he was fired after a year and replaced by Blues Saraceno (born 17/10/1971). They disbanded in 1994 and re-formed in 1999.

DATE	POS	WKS	BPI	SINGLE TITLE	LABEL & NUMBER
23/05/1987	67	1		TALK DIRTY TO ME	Music For Nations KUT 125
07/05/1988	35	3		NOTHIN' BUT A GOOD TIME	Capitol CL 486
05/11/1988	59	1		FALLEN ANGEL	Capitol CL 500
11/02/1989	13	9		EVERY ROSE HAS ITS THORN ▲[3]	Capitol CL 520
29/04/1989	13	7		YOUR MAMA DON'T DANCE	Capitol CL 523
23/09/1989	48	3		NOTHIN' BUT A GOOD TIME Re-issue of Capitol CL 486	Capitol CL 539
30/06/1990	15	7		UNSKINNY BOP	Capitol CL 582
27/10/1990	35	4		SOMETHING TO BELIEVE IN	Enigma CL 594
23/11/1991	25	2		SO TELL ME WHY	Capitol CL 640
13/02/1993	25	3		STAND	Capitol CDCL 679
24/04/1993	32	3		UNTIL YOU SUFFER SOME (FIRE AND ICE)	Capitol CDCL 685

POKEMON ALLSTARS – see 50 GRIND FEATURING POKEMON ALLSTARS

O[9] Number of weeks single topped the UK chart   ↑ Entered the UK chart at #1   ▲[9] Number of weeks single topped the US chart

POLECATS UK group formed by Tim Worman (vocals), Martin Boorer (guitar), Philip Bloomberg (bass) and Neil Rooney (drums).

07/03/1981	35	8		JOHN I'M ONLY DANCING/BIG GREEN CAR	Mercury POLE 1
16/05/1981	35	6		ROCKABILLY GUY	Mercury POLE 2
22/08/1981	53	4		JEEPSTER/MARIE CELESTE	Mercury POLE 3

POLICE UK/US rock group formed in London in 1977 by Stewart Copeland (born 16/7/1952, Alexandria, Egypt, drums), Sting (born Gordon Sumner, 2/10/1951, Wallsend, Tyne and Wear, vocals/bass) and Henry Padovani (guitar), funding the recording of their first single *Fall Out*. They added Andy Summers (born Andrew Somers, 31/12/1942, Poulton-le-Fylde) in June and Padovani left in August 1977. They signed with A&M in 1978. Copeland recorded as Klark Kent and later formed Animal Logic. They were named Best British Group at the 1982 BRIT Awards and picked up an Outstanding Contribution Award in 1985. Sting began recording solo in 1985. The group has won five Grammy Awards including Best Rock Instrumental Performance in 1980 for *Regatta De Blanc, and* Best Rock Instrumental Performance in 1982 for *Behind My Camel*. The group was inducted into the Rock & Roll Hall of Fame in 2003. Sting was awarded a CBE in the Queen's 2003 Birthday Honours List.

07/10/1978	42	5		ROXANNE Originally released April 1978 and failed to chart	A&M AMS 7381
28/04/1979	12	9		ROXANNE	A&M AMS 7348
07/07/1979	2	11	○	**CAN'T STAND LOSING YOU**	A&M AMS 7381
22/09/1979	❶³	11	●	**MESSAGE IN A BOTTLE**	A&M AMS 7474
17/11/1979	47	4		FALL OUT	Illegal IL 001
01/12/1979	❶¹	10	●	**WALKING ON THE MOON**	A&M AMS 7494
16/02/1980	6	10	○	**SO LONELY**	A&M AMS 7402
14/06/1980	17	4		SIX PACK Six Pack consisted of this and the above four singles plus *The Bed's Too Big Without You*	A&M AMPP 6001
27/09/1980	❶⁴	10	●	**DON'T STAND SO CLOSE TO ME** ↑ 1981 Grammy Award for Best Rock Vocal Performance by a Group	A&M AMS 7564
13/12/1980	5	8	●	**DE DO DO DO, DE DA DA DA**	A&M AMS 7578
26/09/1981	2	8	○	INVISIBLE SUN The accompanying video, which featured footage of sectarian riots in Northern Ireland, was banned across UK TV, prompting the rush-release of *Every Little Thing She Does Is Magic*	A&M AMS 8164
24/10/1981	❶¹	13	○	**EVERY LITTLE THING SHE DOES IS MAGIC** Featured in the 1998 film *The Wedding Singer*	A&M AMS 8174
12/12/1981	12	8	○	SPIRITS IN THE MATERIAL WORLD	A&M AMS 8194
28/05/1983	❶⁴	11	○	**EVERY BREATH YOU TAKE** ▲⁸ 1983 Grammy Award for Best Pop Vocal Performance by a Group and the 1983 Grammy Award for Best New Song of the Year for writer Sting. Featured in the 2000 film *The Replacements*	A&M AM 117
23/07/1983	7	7		**WRAPPED AROUND YOUR FINGER**	A&M AM 127
05/11/1983	17	4		SYNCHRONICITY II Won the 1983 Grammy Award for Best Rock Vocal Performance by a Group	A&M AM 153
14/01/1984	17	5		KING OF PAIN	A&M AM 176
11/10/1986	24	4		DON'T STAND SO CLOSE TO ME (REMIX)	A&M AM 354
13/05/1995	27	2		CAN'T STAND LOSING YOU (LIVE)	A&M 5810372
20/12/1997	17	6		ROXANNE '97 STING AND THE POLICE Remix of A&M AMS 7348 by Puff Daddy and contains a sample of The Real Roxanne's *Roxanne Roxanne*	A&M 5824552
05/08/2000	28	3		WHEN THE WORLD IS RUNNING DOWN DIFFERENT GEAR VERSUS THE POLICE Featured in the 2000 film *Red Planet*. The single originally appeared as an illegal bootleg before being picked up by Pagan	Pagan 039CDS

SU POLLARD UK actress (born 1949); she is best known for her role of Peggy Ollerenshaw in *Hi De Hi*. Her biggest UK hit came from a song used in a TV documentary about a couple getting married.

05/10/1985	71	1		COME TO ME (I AM WOMAN)	Rainbow RBR 1
01/02/1986	2	10	○	**STARTING TOGETHER**	Rainbow RBR 4

JIMI POLO US singer.

09/11/1991	51	2		NEVER GOIN' DOWN ADAMSKI FEATURING JIMI POLO Flip side was *Born to Be Alive* by Adamski Featuring Soho	MCA MCS 1578
01/08/1992	59	2		EXPRESS YOURSELF	Perfecto 74321101827
09/08/1997	62	1		EXPRESS YOURSELF Re-issue of Perfecto 74321101827	Perfecto PERF 146CD1

POLOROID UK singer Danielle Rowe.

11/10/2003	28	2		SO DAMN BEAUTIFUL	Decode/Telstar CXSTAS 3351

POLTERGEIST UK producer Simon Berry.

06/07/1996	32	2		VICIOUS CIRCLES	Manifesto FESCD 8

PETER POLYCARPOU UK singer (born in Brighton) who also made his name as an actor, appearing in the TV series *Birds Of A Feather* (as Chris Theodopolopoudos) and films such as *Evita* and *Julie And The Cadillacs*.

20/02/1993	26	4		LOVE HURTS Theme to the TV series of the same name	Soundtrack Music CDEM 259

POLYGON WINDOW UK producer (born Richard James, 18/8/1971, Limerick) who also records as Aphex Twin and Powerpill.

03/04/1993	49	1		QUOTH	Warp WAP 33CD

POLYPHONIC SPREE US symphonic group formed in Dallas, TX by Tim DeLaughter with 24 other members. DeLaughter had previously been a member of Tripping Daisy and disbanded the group following the death of fellow member Wes Berggren.

02/11/2002	39	1		HANGING AROUND	679 Recordings 679L 012CD
22/02/2003	40	1		LIGHT AND DAY	679 Recordings 679L 015CD
26/07/2003	26	2		SOLDIER GIRL	679 Recordings 679L 014CD
07/08/2004	72	1		HOLD ME NOW	Good CDPOLY1

PONI-TAILS
US vocal trio formed in Ohio by Toni Cistone, LaVerne Novak and Karen Topinka. They first recorded for the Point label in 1957. Topinka left in 1958, replaced by Patti McCabe (born 6/7/1939). McCabe died from cancer on 17/1/1989.

DATE	POS	WKS	SINGLE TITLE	LABEL & NUMBER
19/09/1958	5	11	**BORN TOO LATE**	HMV POP 516
10/04/1959	26	3	EARLY TO BED	HMV POP 596

BRIAN POOLE AND THE TREMELOES
UK pop group formed in Dagenham in 1959 by Brian Poole (born 2/11/1941, Barking, guitar/vocals), Alan Blakely (born 1/4/1942, Bromley, drums), Alan Howard (born 17/10/1941, Dagenham, saxophone) and Brian Scott (lead guitar), later adding Dave Munden (born 12/12/1943, Dagenham) on drums and switching Blakley to rhythm guitar, Howard to bass and allowing Poole to sing. They added Rick West (born Richard Westwood, 7/5/1943, Dagenham, lead guitar) in 1961 and signed with Decca in 1962. They disbanded in 1966. Poole and the (re-formed) Tremeloes subsequently recorded autonomously. Blakely died from cancer on 10/6/1996.

DATE	POS	WKS	SINGLE TITLE	LABEL & NUMBER
04/07/1963	4	14	**TWIST AND SHOUT**	Decca F 11694
12/09/1963	❶³	14	**DO YOU LOVE ME**	Decca F 11739
28/11/1963	31	8	I CAN DANCE	Decca F 11771
30/01/1964	6	13	**CANDY MAN**	Decca F 11823
07/05/1964	2	17	**SOMEONE SOMEONE**	Decca F 11893
20/08/1964	32	7	TWELVE STEPS TO LOVE	Decca F 11951
07/01/1965	17	10	THREE BELLS	Decca F 12037
22/07/1965	25	8	I WANT CANDY	Decca F 12197

GLYN POOLE
UK singer best known for the TV show *Junior Showtime*.

DATE	POS	WKS	SINGLE TITLE	LABEL & NUMBER
03/11/1973	35	8	MILLY MOLLY MANDY	York SYK 565

IAN POOLEY
German DJ/producer.

DATE	POS	WKS	SINGLE TITLE	LABEL & NUMBER
10/03/2001	57	1	900 DEGREES Contains a sample of Rene & Angela's *I Love You More*	V2 VVR 5015143
11/08/2001	65	1	BALMES **IAN POOLEY FEATURING ESTHERO**	V2 VVR 5016613
23/11/2002	53	1	PIHA **IAN POOLEY AND MAGIK J**	Honchos Music HONM019CD

POP!
UK vocal group assembled by producer Pete Waterman and manager Tim Byrne and comprising Jade McGuire (born 17/2/1985), Glenn Ball (born 27/6/1985), Jamie Tinkler (born 28/1/1981) and Hannah Lewis (born 17/7/1979).

DATE	POS	WKS	SINGLE TITLE	LABEL & NUMBER
12/06/2004	14	2	HEAVEN AND EARTH	Jive 82876619582
11/09/2004	26	3	CAN'T SAY GOODBYE	Jive 82876639492

IGGY POP
US singer (born James Jewel Osterberg, 21/4/1947, Muskegan, MI) who formed the Psychedelic Stooges in 1967 with his brother Scott and Ron Asheton. They disbanded in 1971, re-formed in 1972, disbanding for good in 1974. He later worked with Death In Vegas and also took part in the *It's Only Rock 'N' Roll* project for the Children's Promise charity.

DATE	POS	WKS	SINGLE TITLE	LABEL & NUMBER
13/12/1986	10	11	**REAL WILD CHILD (WILD ONE)**	A&M AM 368
10/02/1990	51	4	LIVIN' ON THE EDGE OF THE NIGHT	Virgin America VUS 18
13/10/1990	67	1	CANDY	Virgin America VUS 29
05/01/1991	42	4	WELL DID YOU EVAH!	Chrysalis CHS 3646
04/09/1993	63	1	THE WILD AMERICA (EP) Tracks on EP: *Wild America, Credit Card, Come Back Tomorrow, My Angel*	Virgin America VUSCD 74
21/05/1994	47	2	BESIDE YOU	Virgin America VUSCD 77
23/11/1996	26	2	LUST FOR LIFE Featured in the 1996 film *Trainspotting*	Virgin VUSCD 116
07/03/1998	22	3	THE PASSENGER	Virgin VSCDT 1689
17/01/2004	39	3	KICK IT **PEACHES FEATURING IGGY POP**	XL Recordings XLS 176CD

POP WILL EAT ITSELF
UK group formed in Wolverhampton in 1986 by Clint Mansell (born 7/11/1962, Coventry, guitar/vocals), Adam Mole (born 8/4/1962, Stourbridge, keyboards), Graham Crabbe (born 10/10/1964, Sutton Coldfield, drums) and Richard Marsh (born 4/3/1965, York, bass); they took their name from a headline in the *New Musical Express*. Robert 'Fuzz' Townshend (born 31/7/1964, Birmingham) joined on drums in 1992, with Crabbe moving to vocals.

DATE	POS	WKS	SINGLE TITLE	LABEL & NUMBER
30/01/1988	66	1	THERE IS NO LOVE BETWEEN US ANYMORE	Chapter 22 CHAP 20
23/07/1988	63	4	DEF CON ONE	Chapter 22 PWEI 001
11/02/1989	38	4	CAN U DIG IT	RCA PB 42621
22/04/1989	41	3	WISE UP! SUCKER	RCA PB 42761
02/09/1989	45	3	VERY METAL NOISE POLLUTION (EP) Tracks on EP: *Def Con 1989 AD Inclusing The Twilight Zone, Preaching To The Perverted, PWEI-zation* and *92°F*	RCA PB 42883
09/06/1990	28	4	TOUCHED BY THE HAND OF CICCIOLINA	RCA PB 43735
13/10/1990	32	2	DANCE OF THE MAD	RCA PB 44023
12/01/1991	15	4	X Y & ZEE	RCA PB 44243
01/06/1991	23	3	92 DEGREES	RCA PB 44555
06/06/1992	17	2	KARMADROME/EAT ME DRINK ME LOVE ME	RCA PB 45467
29/08/1992	24	3	BULLETPROOF!	RCA 74321110137
16/01/1993	9	4	**GET THE GIRL! KILL THE BADDIES!**	RCA 74321128802
16/10/1993	27	2	RSVP/FAMILIUS HORRIBILUS	Infectious INFECT 1CD
12/03/1994	28	2	ICH BIN EIN AUSLANDER	Infectious INFECT 4CD
10/09/1994	23	2	EVERYTHING'S COOL	Infectious INFECT 9CD

POPES
– see SHANE MACGOWAN

❶⁹ Number of weeks single topped the UK chart ↑ Entered the UK chart at #1 ▲⁹ Number of weeks single topped the US chart

623

POPPERS PRESENTS AURA
UK production trio with singer Aura.

25/10/1997.....44......1....... EVERY LITTLE TIME .... VC Recordings VCRD 26

POPPY FAMILY
Canadian pop group formed by husband and wife Terry (born 29/3/1944, Winnipeg, guitar) and Susan Jacks (born Susan Pesklevits, Vancouver, lead vocals), Craig MacCaw (guitar) and Satwan Singh (percussion). The group dissolved when the Jacks' marriage ended in 1973, with both Susan and Terry going solo.

15/08/1970.....7......14...... **WHICH WAY YOU GOIN' BILLY** .... Decca F 22976

POPPYFIELDS
UK rock group formed in Rhyl in 1977 as The Toilets and comprising Mike Peters (born 25/2/1959, Prestatyn, guitar/vocals), Dave Sharp (born 28/1/1959, Salford, guitar), Eddie MacDonald (born 1/11/1959, St Asaph, bass) and Nigel Twist (born 18/7/1958, Manchester, drums). They changed their name to Alarm in 1981. They disbanded in 1991 with Peters going solo and Twist forming Fringe.. The group re-formed in 2003 and initially recorded as The Poppyfields.

21/02/2004.....28......2....... 45 RPM .... Snapper Music SMASCD055

PORN KINGS
UK instrumental/production group fronted by Kenny 'Colors' Hayes.

28/09/1996.....28......2.......	UP TO NO GOOD	All Around The World CDGLOBE 145
21/06/1997.....17......3.......	AMOUR (C'MON)	All Around The World CDGLOBE 152
16/01/1999.....10......4.......	UP TO THE WILDSTYLE PORN KINGS VERSUS DJ SUPREME	All Around The World CDGLOBE 170
10/02/2001.....71......1.......	SLEDGER	All Around The World CDGLOBE 229
22/03/2003.....28......2.......	SHAKE YA SHIMMY PORN KINGS VERSUS FLIP & FILL FEATURING 740 BOYZ ...	All Around The World CXGLOBE 213

PORNO FOR PYROS
US rock group formed in 1992 by Perry Farrell (vocals), Peter DiStephano (guitar), Martyn Lenoble (bass) and Stephen Perkins (drums), following the demise of Farrell's previous group Jane's Addiction. The group were later joined by Matt Hyde (keyboards).

05/06/1993.....53......2....... PETS .... Warner Brothers W 0177CD

PORTISHEAD
UK group formed in Bristol in 1992 by Geoff Barrow (born 9/12/1971, Somerset, numerous instruments/producer), Beth Gibbons (born 4/1/1965, Devon, vocals), Adrian Utley (guitar) and Dave McDonald (sound engineer).

13/08/1994.....57......1.......	SOUR TIMES	Go Beat GOLCD 116
14/01/1995.....13......7.......	GLORY BOX Contains a sample of Isaac Hayes' Ike's Mood	Go Beat GODCD 120
22/04/1995.....13......4.......	SOUR TIMES	Go Beat GOLCD 116
20/09/1997.....8......4.......	**ALL MINE**	Go Beat 5715972
22/11/1997.....25......2.......	OVER	Go Beat 5710932
14/03/1998.....35......2.......	ONLY YOU	Go Beat 5694752

GARY PORTNOY
US singer/songwriter from Valley Stream, NY.

25/02/1984.....58......3....... THEME FROM 'CHEERS' Featured in the TV series *Cheers*. The full title is *Where Everybody Knows Your Name (The Theme From 'Cheers')* .... Starblend CHEER 1

PORTOBELLA
UK quartet formed in London by Luciana Caporaso (vocals), Adam Evans (guitar), Mark Ferguson (bass) and Simon Merry (drums). They first recorded for Eye Industries and later featured on MTV's *Breaking Point*. Caporaso had previously been a member of Crush and Shooter and also recorded solo.

26/06/2004.....54......1....... COVERED IN PUNK .... Island CID 862

PORTRAIT
US R&B vocal group formed by Eric Kirkland, Michael Angelo Saulsberry, Irving Washington III and Philip Johnson. Johnson left in 1995 and was replaced by Kurt Jackson.

27/03/1993.....37......3.......	HERE WE GO AGAIN	Capitol CDCL 683
08/04/1995.....61......1.......	I CAN CALL YOU	Capitol CDCL 740
08/07/1995.....41......2.......	HOW DEEP IS YOUR LOVE	Capitol CDCL 751

PORTSMOUTH SINFONIA
UK orchestra formed in Portsmouth, whose claim to fame was that they either couldn't play their instruments or that they could but never in time with the tune they were supposed to be playing!

12/09/1981.....38......4....... CLASSICAL MUDDLEY .... Island WIP 6736

SANDY POSEY
US singer (born Martha Sharp, 18/6/1947, Jasper, AL, raised in Arkansas) who worked as a session singer in Nashville and Memphis in the early 1960s.

15/09/1966.....24......11......	BORN A WOMAN	MGM 1321
05/01/1967.....15......13......	SINGLE GIRL...	MGM 1330
13/04/1967.....48......3.......	WHAT A WOMAN IN LOVE WON'T DO	MGM 1335
06/09/1975.....35......5.......	SINGLE GIRL Re-issue of MGM 1330.	MGM 2006 533

POSIES
US rock group formed in Seattle, WA by Jonathan Auer (guitar/vocals), Ken Stringfellow (guitar/vocals), Dave Fox (bass) and Mike Musburger (drums).

19/03/1994.....67......1....... DEFINITE DOOR .... Geffen GFSTD 68

POSITIVE FORCE
US funk group formed in Pennsylvania and fronted by singers Brenda Reynolds and Vicki Drayton. They also provided the musical accompaniment to The Sugarhill Gang.

22/12/1979.....18......9....... WE GOT THE FUNK .... Sugarhill SHL 102

○ Silver disc ● Gold disc ✪ Platinum disc (additional platinum units are indicated by a figure following the symbol) ◎ Singles released prior to 1973 that are known to have sold over 1 million copies in the UK

POSITIVE GANG UK vocal/instrumental group.

| 17/04/1993 | 34 | 4 | | SWEET FREEDOM | PWL Continental PWCD 261 |
| 31/07/1993 | 67 | 1 | | SWEET FREEDOM PART 2 | PWL Continental PWCD 264 |

POSITIVE K US rapper (born Darryl Gibson, The Bronx, NY) who changed his name to Positive Knowledge Allah upon becoming a Muslim in 1982.

| 15/05/1993 | 43 | 2 | | I GOT A MAN | Fourth & Broadway BRCD 280 |

MIKE POST US orchestra leader (born 29/9/1944, Los Angeles, CA) who was orchestra leader for a couple of TV variety shows and then composed the themes to numerous TV series and films. Larry Carlton (born 2/3/1948) was formerly guitarist with the Crusaders (1971–76) and was shot in the throat by a burglar at his studio in 1988 but survived after an emergency operation. He later joined jazz group Fourplay. Mike Post has won five Grammy Awards including Best Instrumental Arrangement in 1968 for *Classical Gas,* Best Instrumental Arrangement in 1975 with Pete Carpenter for *The Rockford Files,* and Best Instrumental Composition in 1988 for *Theme From L.A. Law.* Larry Carlton also won the 1987 Grammy Award for Best Pop Instrumental Performance for *Minute By Minute* and the 2001 Grammy Award for Best Pop Instrumental Album with Steve Lukather for *No Substitutions – Live In Osaka.*

09/08/1975	47	2		AFTERNOON OF THE RHINO MIKE POST COALITION	Warner Brothers K 16588
16/01/1982	25	11		THEME FROM 'HILL STREET BLUES' MIKE POST FEATURING LARRY CARLTON Theme to the TV series of the same name. 1981 Grammy Award for Best Pop Instrumental Performance and the 1981 Grammy Award for Best Instrumental Composition for writer Mike Post	Elektron K 12576
29/09/1984	45	5		THE A TEAM Theme to the TV series of the same name	RCA 443

POTTERS UK vocal group formed by the supporters of Stoke City Football Club, who had reached the League Cup Final that season. Stoke City beat Chelsea 2–1 in the final to win their only major trophy since their formation in 1863.

| 01/04/1972 | 34 | 2 | | WE'LL BE WITH YOU | Pye JT 100 |

P.O.V. FEATURING JADE US vocal group formed in New Jersey by Hakim Bell (son of Kool & The Gang's Robert Bell), Lincoln DeVlkught, Mark Sherman and Ewarner Mills. The group's name stands for Points Of View. Jade are a vocal trio formed in Los Angeles, CA by Joi Marshall, Tonya Kelly and Di Reed.

| 05/02/1994 | 32 | 3 | | ALL THRU THE NITE | Giant 74321187552 |

POWDER UK group formed by Pearl Lowe (vocals), Mark Thomas (guitar), Tim McTighe (bass) and James Walden (drums).

| 24/06/1995 | 72 | 1 | | AFRODISIAC | Parkway PARK 002CD |

BRYAN POWELL UK singer/producer/keyboard player who also worked with Nu Colours.

13/03/1993	73	1		IT'S ALRIGHT	Talkin Loud TLKCD 34
15/05/1993	61	1		I THINK OF YOU	Talkin Loud TLKCD 38
07/08/1993	73	1		NATURAL	Talkin Loud TLKCD 41

COZY POWELL UK drummer (born Colin Flooks, 29/12/1947, Cirencester) who was a member of Bedlam before recording solo. He retired from the music industry for a while, racing cars for Hitachi before joining Rainbow in 1975. He was killed in a road crash on 5/4/1998, with an autopsy revealing excess alcohol in his bloodstream.

08/12/1973	3	15	O	DANCE WITH THE DEVIL	RAK 164
25/05/1974	18	8		THE MAN IN BLACK	RAK 173
10/08/1974	10	10		NA NA NA	RAK 180
10/11/1979	62	2		THEME ONE	Ariola ARO 189
19/06/1993	23	3		RESURRECTION BRIAN MAY WITH COZY POWELL	Parlophone CDRS 6351

KOBIE POWELL – see US3

POWER CIRCLE – see CHICANE

POWER OF DREAMS Irish group formed by Craig Walker (guitar/vocals), Michael Lennox (bass) and Keith Walker (drums).

| 19/01/1991 | 74 | 1 | | AMERICAN DREAM | Polydor PO 117 |
| 11/04/1992 | 65 | 1 | | THERE I GO AGAIN | Polydor PO 200 |

POWER STATION UK/US rock group formed by Robert Palmer (born Alan Palmer, 19/1/1949, Scarborough, vocals), Tony Thompson (born 15/11/1954), drummer with Chic, John Taylor (born Nigel John Taylor, 20/6/1960, Birmingham), bass player with Duran Duran, and Andy Taylor (born 16/2/1961, Wolverhampton), guitarist with Duran Duran, initially as a one-album outfit. Palmer left and was replaced by Michael Des Barres as the group wanted to work live. Palmer died from a heart attack on 26/9/2003. Thompson died from renal cell cancer on 12/11/2003.

16/03/1985	14	8		SOME LIKE IT HOT	Parlophone R 6091
11/05/1985	22	7		GET IT ON	Parlophone R 6096
09/11/1985	75	1		COMMUNICATION	Parlophone R 6114
12/10/1996	63	1		SHE CAN ROCK IT	Chrysalis CDCHS 5039

POWERCUT FEATURING NUBIAN PRINZ US vocal/instrumental group formed by Brian Mitchell, Michael Power and Courtney Coulson.

| 22/06/1991 | 50 | 4 | | GIRLS | Eternal YZ 570 |

O[9] Number of weeks single topped the UK chart ↑ Entered the UK chart at #1 ▲[9] Number of weeks single topped the US chart

625

POWERHOUSE UK production duo Hamilton Dean and Julian Slatter.

20/12/1997.....38......4...... RHYTHM OF THE NIGHT Contains a sample of DeBarge's *Rhythm Of The Night*..........................Satellite 74321522592

POWERHOUSE FEATURING DUANE HARDEN US producer Lenny Fontana with singer Duane Harden.

22/05/1999.....13......5....... WHAT YOU NEED...Defected DEFECT 3CDS

POWERPILL UK producer (born Richard James, 18/8/1971, Limerick) who also records as Aphex Twin and Polygon Window.

06/06/1992.....43......3...... PAC-MAN...ffrreedom TABX 110

PJ POWERS – see LADYSMITH BLACK MAMBAZO

WILL POWERS US singer (born Lynn Goldsmith, Detroit, MI) who was initially known as a photographer, doing album covers for Carly Simon (who returned the compliment by appearing on her hit single) and Frank Zappa.

01/10/1983.....17......9...... KISSING WITH CONFIDENCE Features the uncredited contribution of Carly Simon....................................Island IS 134

POWERS THAT BE UK producer Giles Goodman.

26/07/2003.....63......1....... PLANET ROCK/FUNKY PLANET..Defected DFTD 074

PPK Russian dance group formed in Rostov in 1998 by Sergey Pimenov and Alexander Polyakov, later adding singer Sveta.

08/12/2001.....3......15...... RESURRECTION Contains a sample of the theme to the film *Sibiriada*.....................................Perfecto PERF 32CDS
26/10/2002.....39......2...... RELOAD..Perfecto PERF 41CDS

PQM FEATURING CICA US producer with singer Cica.

09/12/2000.....68......1...... THE FLYING SONG..Renaissance/Yoshitoshi RENCD 004

PEREZ 'PREZ' PRADO AND HIS ORCHESTRA Cuban orchestra leader (born Damaso Perez Prado, 11/12/1916, Mantanzas) who moved to Mexico City in 1949 and formed his orchestra. He began touring America in 1954 and was bestowed with the nickname 'The King Of The Mambo'. He died on 14/9/1989 after suffering a stroke. He has a star on the Hollywood Walk of Fame.

25/03/1955....❶².....17...... CHERRY PINK AND APPLE BLOSSOM WHITE ▲¹⁰ PEREZ 'PREZ' PRADO AND HIS ORCHESTRA, THE KING OF THE MAMBO Featured in the 1955 film *Underwater!*...HMV B 10833
25/07/1958.....8......16...... PATRICIA ▲¹..RCA 1067
10/12/1994.....41......6....... GUAGLIONE...RCA 74321250192
08/04/1995.....2......18.....● GUAGLIONE Revived following use in an advertisement for Guinness.................................RCA 74321250192

PRAISE UK vocal/instrumental group fronted by Simon Goldenberg and Geoff MacCormack, featuring singer Miriam Stockley.

02/02/1991.....4......7....... ONLY YOU...Epic 6566117

PRAISE CATS US producer (born Eric Miller, Chicago, IL) who also records as E-Smoove and Thick Dick.

26/10/2002.....56......1....... SHINED ON ME...PIAS Recordings PIASX 028CD

PRAS – see PRAS MICHEL

PRATT AND MCCLAIN WITH BROTHERLOVE US duo Truett Pratt and Jerry McLain who recorded a cover version of the theme to the hit TV series *Happy Days*; the version on the show was sung by a studio chorus. The series began in 1974 and originally featured Bill Haley's *Rock Around The Clock* as its theme and changed to *Happy Days* in 1976.

01/10/1977.....31......6....... HAPPY DAYS Theme to the TV series of the same name....................................Reprise K 14435

PRAXIS US duo producer David Shaw and singer Kathy Brown.

25/11/1995.....44......2...... TURN ME OUT (TURN TO SUGAR)...Stress CDSTR 40
20/09/1997.....35......3...... TURN ME OUT (TURN TO SUGAR) (REMIX) PRAXIS FEATURING KATHY BROWN......................ffrr FCD 314

PRAYING MANTIS UK group formed in London in 1977 by Tino Troy Neophytou (guitar/vocals), Robert Angelo (guitar), Chris Troy Neophytou (bass/vocals) and Mick Ransome (drums). By the time they signed with Arista in 1981 Angelo and Ransome had been replaced by Steve Carroll and Dave Potts respectively. Carroll left after their debut album for the label, replaced by Bernie Shaw, with Jon Bavin (keyboards) joining at the same time. By the mid-1980s they had become Stratus, although they re-formed as Praying Mantis in 1990 with both Troy Neophytou brothers, Paul Di'Anno (vocals), Dennis Stratton (guitar) and Bruce Bisland (drums).

31/01/1981.....69......2....... CHEATED...Arista ARIST 378

PRECIOUS UK vocal group formed by Kelli Clarke-Stenberg, Louise Rose, Anya Lahiri, Sophie McDonnell and Jenny Frost. Jenny Frost left them in January 2001 to replace Kerry Katona in Atomic Kitten.

29/05/1999.....6......11.....○ SAY IT AGAIN Britain's entry for the 1999 Eurovision Song Contest (finished twelfth).........................EMI CDEM 544
01/04/2000.....11......5...... REWIND..EMI CDEM 557
15/07/2000.....27......3...... IT'S GONNA BE MY WAY...EMI CDEMS 569
25/11/2000.....50......1...... NEW BEGINNING...EMI CDEM 573

PRECOCIOUS BRATS FEATURING KEVIN AND PERRY UK production duo Judge Jules (born Julius O'Riordan) and Matt Smith, with UK vocal duo Kevin (played by Harry Enfield) and Perry (played by Kathy Burke). Kevin and Perry featured in the TV series *Harry Enfield And Chums*.

06/05/2000.....16......4...... BIG GIRL Featured in the 2000 film *Kevin And Perry Go Large*...Virgin VTSCD 1

○ Silver disc ● Gold disc ✪ Platinum disc (additional platinum units are indicated by a figure following the symbol) Ⓜ Singles released prior to 1973 that are known to have sold over 1 million copies in the UK

PREFAB SPROUT
UK rock group formed in Newcastle-upon-Tyne in 1982 by Paddy McAloon (born 7/6/1957, Consett, Co. Durham, guitar/vocals), his brother Martin (born 4/1/1962, Durham, bass), Wendy Smith (born 31/5/1963, Durham, guitar/vocals) and Mick Salmon (drums). They signed with Kitchenware in 1983. Salmon left in 1984, replaced by Graham Lant and then Neil Conti (born 12/2/1959, London).

DATE	POS	WKS	SINGLE TITLE	LABEL & NUMBER
28/01/1984	62	2	DON'T SING	Kitchenware SK 9
20/07/1985	74	1	FARON YOUNG	Kitchenware SK 22
09/11/1985	25	10	WHEN LOVE BREAKS DOWN Single released three times before it became a hit	Kitchenware SK 21
08/02/1986	64	2	JOHNNY JOHNNY	Kitchenware SK 24
13/02/1988	44	5	CARS AND GIRLS	Kitchenware SK 35
30/04/1988	7	10	**THE KING OF ROCK 'N' ROLL**	Kitchenware SK 37
23/07/1988	72	2	HEY MANHATTAN	Kitchenware SK 38
18/08/1990	51	3	LOOKING FOR ATLANTIS	Kitchenware SK 47
20/10/1990	50	3	WE LET THE STARS GO	Kitchenware SK 48
05/01/1991	35	4	JORDAN: THE EP Tracks on EP: *Carnival 2000*, *The Ice Maiden*, *One Of The Broken* and *Jordan: The Comeback*	Kitchenware SK 49
13/06/1992	23	5	THE SOUND OF CRYING	Kitchenware SK 58
08/08/1992	33	4	IF YOU DON'T LOVE ME	Kitchenware SK 60
03/10/1992	61	2	ALL THE WORLD LOVES LOVERS	Kitchenware SK 62
09/01/1993	24	4	LIFE OF SURPRISES	Kitchenware SKCD 63
10/05/1997	30	2	A PRISONER OF THE PAST	Columbia SKZD 70
02/08/1997	53	1	ELECTRIC GUITARS	Columbia SKZD 71

PRELUDE
UK folk trio formed in Gateshead in 1970 by Ian Vardy (born 21/3/1947, Gateshead, guitar/vocals) and husband and wife team Brian (born 21/6/1947, Gateshead, guitar/vocals) and Irene Hume (born Irene Marshall, 5/8/1948, Gateshead, percussion /vocals).

DATE	POS	WKS	SINGLE TITLE	LABEL & NUMBER
26/01/1974	21	9	AFTER THE GOLDRUSH	Dawn DNS 1052
26/04/1980	45	7	PLATINUM BLONDE	EMI 5046
22/05/1982	28	7	AFTER THE GOLDRUSH Re-recording	After Hours AFT 02
31/07/1982	55	3	ONLY THE LONELY	After Hours AFT 06

PRESENCE
UK vocal/production group formed by Charles Webster, Steve Edwards and Del St Joseph.

DATE	POS	WKS	SINGLE TITLE	LABEL & NUMBER
05/12/1998	61	1	SENSE OF DANGER PRESENCE FEATURING SHARA NELSON	Pagan 024CDS
19/06/1999	66	1	FUTURE LOVE	Pagan 028CDS

PRESIDENT BROWN – see SABRE FEATURING PRESIDENT BROWN

PRESIDENTS OF THE UNITED STATES OF AMERICA
US trio formed in Seattle in 1994 by Chris Ballew (vocals/two-string guitar), Dave Dederer (vocals/three-string bass) and Dave Thiele (vocals/no-string drums). Thiele subsequently moved to Boston, MA and was replaced by Jason Finn. They disbanded in 1998.

DATE	POS	WKS	SINGLE TITLE	LABEL & NUMBER
06/01/1996	15	7	LUMP	Columbia 6624962
20/04/1996	8	7	**PEACHES**	Columbia 6631072
20/07/1996	15	4	DUNE BUGGY	Columbia 6634892
02/11/1996	29	2	MACH 5	Columbia 6638812
01/08/1998	52	1	VIDEO KILLED THE RADIO STAR	Maverick W 0450CD

ELVIS PRESLEY
US singer (born Elvis Aaron Presley, 8/1/1935, East Tupelo, MS, to Gladys and Vernon; his twin brother Jesse Garon was stillborn) who entered a singing contest in 1945 and came second behind Shirley Jones Gallentine. The family moved to Memphis in 1948 and upon graduation he worked as a truck driver at Crown Electric Co. He paid for his first recording (*My Happiness* and *That's When Your Heartaches Begin*) at Memphis Recording Service, a copy being later handed to Sam Phillips of Sun Records. He signed with Sun in 1954 and released his first single, *That's All Right Mama* backed with *Blue Moon Of Kentucky* (catalogue number Sun 209), then signed with manager Colonel Tom Parker (born Andreas Cornelius Van Kuijk, 26/6/1909, Breda, Holland) in 1955 as bidding for his Sun contract got underway. He signed with RCA in November 1955, with Sun collecting $35,000 for Presley's contract and Presley himself $5,000 for future royalties on Sun material. His first single with RCA, *Heartbreak Hotel* backed with *I Was The One* (catalogue number RCA Victor 47-6420), topped the US charts for eight weeks. He was drafted into the US Army in 1958 (as US Private Presley 53310761) and subsequently stationed in Germany where he first met future wife Priscilla Beaulieu. He was demobbed in 1960. (The flight from Frankfurt made a refuelling stop at Prestwick Airport in Scotland, the only occasion Presley set foot in Britain. He did not tour outside America because Parker was an illegal immigrant and feared being refused re-entry; since this fact did not become public knowledge until after Presley's death, it has been suggested that Presley did not know of his manager's background.) He returned to America with his popularity having been maintained by a steady flow of releases. He married Priscilla in 1967 (their only child, Lisa Marie, was born in 1968); they divorced in 1973. He starred in 31 films (plus two others of live performances), beginning with *Love Me Tender* in 1956. His last recordings were made in April 1977 and his last live appearance was at the Market Square Arena, Indianapolis on 26/6/1977. He was found unconscious by girlfriend Ginger Alden on 16/8/1977 and pronounced dead on arrival at hospital. The cause of death given as heart failure brought on by prescription drug abuse. Over 75,000 flocked to Graceland for his funeral; his body was laid next to his mother's at Forest Hills Cemetery in Memphis. After several break-ins, the body was moved to Graceland. He won three Grammy Awards: Best Sacred Recording in 1967 for *How Great Thou Art*, Best Inspirational Recording in 1972 for *He Touched Me* and Best Inspirational Recording in 1974 for *How Great Thou Art*. He is the biggest selling solo artist in the world with sales of over 1 billion records. In 1993 the US postal service issued an Elvis Presley postage stamp: many were sent by fans to fictitious addresses so that they could be stamped 'Return To Sender'! Even 25 years after his death, there are more Elvis Presley fan clubs around the world (over 480) than for any other act. This is despite the fact that he only

❶⁹ Number of weeks single topped the UK chart ⬆ Entered the UK chart at #1 ▲⁹ Number of weeks single topped the US chart

627

recorded in English and only did one concert outside America, in Canada in 1957. He was inducted into the Rock & Roll Hall of Fame in 1986 and has a star on the Hollywood Walk of Fame. Parker died from a stroke on 21/1/1997. The Jordanaires are a US vocal quartet formed by Gordon Stocker, Neal Matthews, Hoyt Hawkins and Hugh Jarrett. JXL is Dutch producer Tom Holkenborg. He normally records as Junkie XL but after objections from the estate of Elvis Presley amended his recording name. In topping the charts with *A Little Less Conversation* Elvis became the first artist to top the UK charts eighteen times. Elvis was inducted into the UK Music Hall of Fame in 2004, one of its first inductees.

DATE	POS	WKS	BPI	SINGLE TITLE	LABEL & NUMBER
11/05/1956	2	22		**HEARTBREAK HOTEL** ▲[8] Featured in the films *Elvis* (1979) and *Heartbreak Hotel* (1988)	HMV POP 182
25/05/1956	9	10		**BLUE SUEDE SHOES** Featured in the films *G.I. Blues* (1960), *Elvis* (1979) and *Porky's Revenge* (1985).	HMV POP 213
03/08/1956	14	11		I WANT YOU I NEED YOU I LOVE YOU ▲[1]	HMV POP 235
21/09/1956	2	23		**HOUND DOG** ▲[11] Total worldwide sales exceed 9 million. Featured in the 1994 film *Forrest Gump*	HMV POP 249
16/11/1956	9	11		**BLUE MOON** Featured in the 1999 film *Liberty Heights*	HMV POP 272
23/11/1956	23	4		I DON'T CARE IF THE SUN DON'T SHINE B-side to *Blue Moon*	HMV POP 272
07/12/1956	11	9		LOVE ME TENDER ▲[5] Featured in the films *Love Me Tender* (1956) and *F.M.* (1978)	HMV POP 253
15/02/1957	25	5		MYSTERY TRAIN	HMV POP 295
08/03/1957	27	1		RIP IT UP	HMV POP 305
10/05/1957	6	9		**TOO MUCH** ▲[3]	HMV POP 330
14/06/1957	●[7]	21		**ALL SHOOK UP** ▲[9] Featured in the films *Look Who's Talking Too* (1990) and *Honeymoon In Las Vegas* (1992). The single originally charted on import — EMI manufactured copies for sale to American G.I.'s that subsequently sold enough copies to debut at #24 in the charts	HMV POP 359
12/07/1957	3	19		**(LET ME BE YOUR) TEDDY BEAR** ▲[7] This and above two singles credited to **ELVIS PRESLEY WITH THE JORDANAIRES** Featured in the 1957 film *Loving You*	RCA 1013
30/08/1957	8	10		**PARALYSED**	HMV POP 378
04/10/1957	2	15		**PARTY**	RCA 1020
18/10/1957	17	4		GOT A LOT O' LIVIN' TO DO This and above single credited to **ELVIS PRESLEY WITH THE JORDANAIRES** B-side to *Party*	RCA 1020
01/11/1957	16	4		TRYING TO GET TO YOU	HMV POP 408
01/11/1957	24	2		LOVING YOU **ELVIS PRESLEY WITH THE JORDANAIRES** B-side to *(Let Me Be Your) Teddy Bear*. Featured in the 1957 film *Loving You*	RCA 1013
08/11/1957	15	5		LAWDY MISS CLAWDY B-side to *Trying To Get To You*	HMV POP 408
15/11/1957	7	8		**SANTA BRING MY BABY BACK TO ME**	RCA 1025
17/01/1958	21	3		I'M LEFT YOU'RE RIGHT SHE'S GONE	HMV POP 428
24/01/1958	●[3]	14		**JAILHOUSE ROCK** ↑ ▲[7] Featured in the 1957 film *Jailhouse Rock*	RCA 1028
31/01/1958	18	5		JAILHOUSE ROCK EP Tracks on EP: *Jailhouse Rock, Young And Beautiful, I Want To Be Free, Don't Leave Me Now* and *Baby I Don't Care*	RCA RCX 106
28/02/1958	2	11		**DON'T** ▲[5]	RCA 1043
02/05/1958	3	10		**WEAR MY RING AROUND YOUR NECK**	RCA 1058
25/07/1958	2	11		**HARD HEADED WOMAN** ▲[2]	RCA 1070
03/10/1958	2	15		**KING CREOLE** This and above four singles credited to **ELVIS PRESLEY WITH THE JORDANAIRES** This and above single featured in the 1958 film *King Creole*	RCA 1081
23/01/1959	●[3]	12		**ONE NIGHT/I GOT STUNG** A-side featured in the 1988 film *Heartbreak Hotel*	RCA 1100
24/04/1959	●[5]	15		**A FOOL SUCH AS I/I NEED YOUR LOVE TONIGHT**	RCA 1113
24/07/1959	4	9		**A BIG HUNK O' LOVE** ▲[2] This and above single credited to **ELVIS PRESLEY WITH THE JORDANAIRES**	RCA 1136
12/02/1960	26	1		STRICTLY ELVIS EP Tracks on EP: *Old Shep, Any Place Is Paradise, Paralysed* and *Is It So Strange*	RCA RCX 175
07/04/1960	3	14		**STUCK ON YOU** ▲[4]	RCA 1187
28/07/1960	2	18		**A MESS OF BLUES**	RCA 1194
03/11/1960	●[8]	19	◎	**IT'S NOW OR NEVER** ↑ ▲[5] Based on the Italian song *O Sole Mio*. Total worldwide sales exceed 20 million	RCA 1207
19/01/1961	●[4]	15		**ARE YOU LONESOME TONIGHT** ▲[6] This and above three singles credited to **ELVIS PRESLEY WITH THE JORDANAIRES** Featured in the 1990 film *Look Who's Talking Too*	RCA 1216
09/03/1961	●[6]	27		**WOODEN HEART** Featured in the 1960 film *G.I. Blues*	RCA 1226
25/05/1961	●[4]	15		**SURRENDER** ▲[2] Until overtaken by Captain Sensible, this held the record for the biggest leap within the charts to #1: from 27 to 1. The record is based on a 1911 Italian composition *Torna A Sorrento* with English lyrics by Doc Pumus and Mort Shuman	RCA 1227
07/09/1961	4	12		**WILD IN THE COUNTRY/I FEEL SO BAD** This and above single credited to **ELVIS PRESLEY WITH THE JORDANAIRES** A-side featured in the 1961 film *Wild In The Country*	RCA 1244
02/11/1961	●[4]	13		**(MARIE'S THE NAME) HIS LATEST FLAME/LITTLE SISTER**	RCA 1258
01/02/1962	●[4]	20		**ROCK A HULA BABY/CAN'T HELP FALLING IN LOVE** B-side based on Martini's *Plaisir D'Amour*. Featured in the 1962 film *Blue Hawaii*	RCA 1270
10/05/1962	●[5]	17		**GOOD LUCK CHARM** ▲[2] This and above single credited to **ELVIS PRESLEY WITH THE JORDANAIRES**	RCA 1280
21/06/1962	34	2		FOLLOW THAT DREAM EP Tracks on EP: *Follow That Dream, Angel, What A Wonderful Life* and *I'm Not The Marrying Kind*. The EP's relatively poor chart position was due to it being effectively pulled from the chart by the compilers on the grounds of difficulties in assessing sales returns	RCA RCX 211
30/08/1962	●[3]	14		**SHE'S NOT YOU**	RCA 1303
29/11/1962	●[3]	14		**RETURN TO SENDER** This and above single credited to **ELVIS PRESLEY WITH THE JORDANAIRES** Featured in the 1962 film *Girls! Girls! Girls!*	RCA 1320
28/02/1963	12	9		ONE BROKEN HEART FOR SALE **ELVIS PRESLEY WITH THE MELLOMEN** Featured in the 1962 film *It Happened At The World's Fair*	RCA 1337
04/07/1963	●[1]	12		**(YOU'RE THE) DEVIL IN DISGUISE** Featured in the 1989 film *She-Devil*	RCA 1355
24/10/1963	13	8		BOSSA NOVA BABY Featured in the 1963 film *Fun In Acapulco*	RCA 1374
19/12/1963	14	10		KISS ME QUICK	RCA 1375
12/03/1964	17	12		VIVA LAS VEGAS Featured in the 2003 film *Looney Tunes: Back In Action*	RCA 1390
25/06/1964	10	11		**KISSIN' COUSINS** Featured in the 1963 film *Kissin' Cousins*	RCA 1404

DATE	POS	WKS	BPI	SINGLE TITLE	LABEL & NUMBER
20/08/1964	13	10		SUCH A NIGHT This and above five singles credited to **ELVIS PRESLEY WITH THE JORDANAIRES**	RCA 1411
29/10/1964	15	8		AIN'T THAT LOVIN' YOU BABY	RCA 1422
03/12/1964	11	7		BLUE CHRISTMAS **ELVIS PRESLEY WITH THE JORDANAIRES**	RCA 1430
11/03/1965	19	8		DO THE CLAM **ELVIS PRESLEY WITH THE JORDANAIRES JUBILEE FOUR AND CAROL LOMBARD TRIO** Featured in the 1965 film *Girl Happy*	RCA 1443
27/05/1965	❶²	15		**CRYING IN THE CHAPEL** Reclaimed #1 position on 1/7/1965. Featured in the 1973 film *American Graffiti*.	RCA 1455
11/11/1965	15	10		TELL ME WHY This and above single credited to **ELVIS PRESLEY WITH THE JORDANAIRES**.	RCA 1489
24/02/1966	22	7		BLUE RIVER	RCA 1504
07/04/1966	21	9		FRANKIE AND JOHNNY	RCA 1509
07/07/1966	6	10		**LOVE LETTERS**	RCA 1526
13/10/1966	18	8		ALL THAT I AM **ELVIS PRESLEY WITH THE JORDANAIRES**	RCA 1545
01/12/1966	13	7		IF EVERY DAY WAS LIKE CHRISTMAS	RCA 1557
09/02/1967	21	5		INDESCRIBABLY BLUE This and above single credited to **ELVIS PRESLEY WITH THE JORDANAIRES AND IMPERIALS QUARTET**	RCA 1565
11/05/1967	38	5		YOU GOTTA STOP/LOVE MACHINE	RCA 1593
16/08/1967	49	2		LONG LEGGED GIRL (WITH THE SHORT DRESS ON) **ELVIS PRESLEY WITH THE JORDANAIRES**	RCA 1616
21/02/1968	19	9		GUITAR MAN Featured in the 1967 film *Clambake*	RCA 1663
15/05/1968	15	8		U.S. MALE	RCA 1688
17/07/1968	22	11		YOUR TIME HASN'T COME YET BABY	RCA 1714
16/10/1968	44	3		YOU'LL NEVER WALK ALONE This and above two singles credited to **ELVIS PRESLEY WITH THE JORDANAIRES**.	RCA 1747
26/02/1969	11	10		IF I CAN DREAM Featured in the 1988 film *Heartbreak Hotel*	RCA 1795
11/06/1969	2	17		**IN THE GHETTO**	RCA 1831
06/09/1969	21	7		CLEAN UP YOUR OWN BACK YARD Featured in the 1969 film *Trouble With Girls (And How To Get Into It)*	RCA 1869
29/11/1969	2	14		**SUSPICIOUS MINDS** ▲¹ Featured in the 2003 film *Intolerable Cruelty*	RCA 1900
28/02/1970	8	11		**DON'T CRY DADDY**	RCA 1916
16/05/1970	21	12		KENTUCKY RAIN	RCA 1949
11/07/1970	❶⁶	21		**THE WONDER OF YOU** Recorded live	RCA 1974
14/11/1970	9	12		I'VE LOST YOU	RCA 1999
09/01/1971	9	10		**YOU DON'T HAVE TO SAY YOU LOVE ME**	RCA 2046
20/03/1971	6	11		**THERE GOES MY EVERYTHING ELVIS PRESLEY, VOCAL ACCOMPANIMENT: THE IMPERIALS QUARTET**	RCA 2060
15/05/1971	9	11		**RAGS TO RICHES**	RCA 2084
17/07/1971	10	12		**HEARTBREAK HOTEL/HOUND DOG** Re-issue of HMV POP 182 and HMV POP 249	RCA Maximillion 2104
02/10/1971	23	9		I'M LEAVIN' **ELVIS PRESLEY, VOCAL ACCOMPANIMENT: THE IMPERIALS QUARTET**	RCA 2125
04/12/1971	6	16		**I JUST CAN'T HELP BELIEVING ELVIS PRESLEY, VOCAL ACCOMPANIMENT: THE IMPERIALS QUARTET & THE SWEET INSPIRATIONS**	RCA 2158
11/12/1971	42	5		JAILHOUSE ROCK Re-issue of RCA 1028.	RCA Maximillion 2153
01/04/1972	5	9		**UNTIL IT'S TIME FOR YOU TO GO ELVIS PRESLEY, VOCAL ACCOMPANIMENT: THE IMPERIALS QUARTET**	RCA 2188
17/06/1972	8	11		**AMERICAN TRILOGY**	RCA 2229
30/09/1972	7	9		**BURNING LOVE** Featured in the 1988 film *Heartbreak Hotel*	RCA 2267
16/12/1972	9	13		**ALWAYS ON MY MIND ELVIS PRESLEY, VOCAL ACCOMPANIMENT: JD SUMNER AND THE STAMPS** Featured in the films *A Life Less Ordinary* (1998) and *Practical Magic* (1999)	RCA 2304
26/05/1973	23	7		POLK SALAD ANNIE	RCA 2359
11/08/1973	15	10		FOOL	RCA 2393
24/11/1973	36	7		RAISED ON ROCK	RCA 2435
16/03/1974	33	5		I'VE GOT A THING ABOUT YOU BABY **ELVIS PRESLEY, VOCAL ACCOMPANIMENT: JD SUMNER AND THE STAMPS**	RCA APBO 0196
13/07/1974	40	3		IF YOU TALK IN YOUR SLEEP	RCA APBO 0280
16/11/1974	5	13	○	**MY BOY**	RCA 2458
18/01/1975	9	8		**PROMISED LAND**	RCA PB 10074
24/05/1975	31	4		T.R.O.U.B.L.E. Featured in the 1958 film *King Creole*	RCA 2562
29/11/1975	29	7		GREEN GREEN GRASS OF HOME	RCA 2635
01/05/1976	37	5		HURT	RCA 2674
04/09/1976	9	12		**GIRL OF MY BEST FRIEND**	RCA 2729
25/12/1976	9	12		**SUSPICION**	RCA 2768
05/03/1977	6	9		MOODY BLUE **ELVIS PRESLEY, VOCAL ACCOMPANIMENT: JD SUMNER AND THE STAMPS QUARTET, KATHY WESTMORELAND, MYRNA SMITH**	RCA PB 0857
13/08/1977	❶⁵	13	●	**WAY DOWN ELVIS PRESLEY, VOCAL ACCOMPANIMENT: JD SUMNER AND THE STAMPS QUARTET, K WESTMORELAND, S NEILSON AND M SMITH** Posthumous #1	RCA PB 0998
03/09/1977	41	2		ALL SHOOK UP Re-issue of HMV POP 359	RCA PB 2694
03/09/1977	46	1		ARE YOU LONESOME TONIGHT Re-issue of RCA 1216	RCA PB 2699
03/09/1977	43	2		CRYING IN THE CHAPEL Re-issue of RCA 1455	RCA PB 2708
03/09/1977	39	2		IT'S NOW OR NEVER Re-issue of RCA 1207	RCA PB 2698
03/09/1977	44	1		JAILHOUSE ROCK Second re-issue of RCA 1028	RCA PB 2695
03/09/1977	42	3		RETURN TO SENDER This and above five singles credited to **ELVIS PRESLEY WITH THE JORDANAIRES** Re-issue of RCA 1320	RCA PB2706
03/09/1977	48	1		THE WONDER OF YOU Re-issue of RCA 1974	RCA PB 2709
03/09/1977	49	1		WOODEN HEART Re-issue of RCA 1226.	RCA PB 2700
10/12/1977	9	8		**MY WAY ELVIS PRESLEY, VOCAL ACCOMPANIMENT: JD SUMNER AND THE STAMPS, THE SWEET INSPIRATIONS AND KATHY WESTMORELAND** Recorded live.	RCA PB 1165

❶⁹ Number of weeks single topped the UK chart ↑ Entered the UK chart at #1 ▲⁹ Number of weeks single topped the US chart

DATE	POS	WKS	BPI	SINGLE TITLE	LABEL & NUMBER
24/06/1978	24	12		DON'T BE CRUEL Featured in the 1982 film *Diner*	RCA PB 9265
15/12/1979	13	6		IT WON'T SEEM LIKE CHRISTMAS (WITHOUT YOU)	RCA PB 9464
30/08/1980	3	10	○	**IT'S ONLY LOVE/BEYOND THE REEF**	RCA 4
06/12/1980	41	6		SANTA CLAUS IS BACK IN TOWN Featured in the 2001 film *Miracle On 34th Street*	RCA 16
14/02/1981	43	4		GUITAR MAN	RCA 43
18/04/1981	47	6		LOVING ARMS	RCA 48
13/03/1982	25	7		ARE YOU LONESOME TONIGHT **ELVIS PRESLEY, VOCAL ACCOMPANIMENT: JD SUMNER AND THE STAMPS, THE SWEET INSPIRATIONS AND KATHY WESTMORELAND** Recorded live in Las Vegas in 1969	RCA 196
26/06/1982	59	2		THE SOUND OF YOUR CITY	RCA 232
05/02/1983	27	6		JAILHOUSE ROCK	RCA 1028
07/05/1983	61	3		BABY I DON'T CARE	RCA 332
03/12/1983	30	9		I CAN HELP	RCA 369
10/11/1984	48	6		THE LAST FAREWELL	RCA 459
19/01/1985	51	3		THE ELVIS MEDLEY **ELVIS PRESLEY WITH THE JORDANAIRES** Tracks on medley: *Jailhouse Rock, (Let Me Be Your) Teddy Bear, Hound Dog, Don't Be Cruel, Burning Love* and *Suspicious Minds*	RCA 476
10/08/1985	59	4		ALWAYS ON MY MIND Re-recording	RCA PB 49944
11/04/1987	47	5		AIN'T THAT LOVIN' YOU BABY/BOSSA NOVA BABY Re-issue of RCA 1422 and RCA 1374	RCA ARON 1
22/08/1987	56	3		LOVE ME TENDER/IF I CAN DREAM Re-issue of HMV POP 253 and RCA 1795	RCA ARON 2
16/01/1988	58	2		STUCK ON YOU **ELVIS PRESLEY WITH THE JORDANAIRES** Re-issue of RCA 1187	RCA PB 49595
17/08/1991	68	2		ARE YOU LONESOME TONIGHT (LIVE) Re-issue of RCA 196	RCA PB 49177
29/08/1992	42	2		DON'T BE CRUEL **ELVIS PRESLEY WITH THE JORDANAIRES** Re-issue of RCA PB 9265	RCA 74321110777
11/11/1995	21	3		THE TWELFTH OF NEVER **ELVIS PRESLEY, VOCAL ACCOMPANIMENT THE VOICE**	RCA 74321320122
18/05/1996	45	1		HEARTBREAK HOTEL/I WAS THE ONE Second re-issue of HMV POP 182	RCA 74321336862
24/05/1997	13	6		ALWAYS ON MY MIND Re-issue of RCA 2304	RCA 74321485412
14/04/2001	15	4		SUSPICIOUS MINDS (LIVE) Limited to 30,000 copies	RCA 74321855822
10/11/2001	69	1		AMERICA THE BEAUTIFUL	RCA 74321904022
22/06/2002	❶⁴	12	✪	**A LITTLE LESS CONVERSATION** ↑ **ELVIS VS JXL** A second posthumous #1 for Elvis Presley. Originally written in 1968 for Elvis' film *Live A Little Love A Little* and was revived for the 2001 film *Ocean's Eleven* and then in 2002 after being used in a TV advertisement for Nike. It might have remained at #1 for longer but for a decision by the record company to delete it after four weeks. Featured in the 2003 film *Bruce Almighty*	RCA 74321943572
04/10/2003	5	8		**RUBBERNECKIN'** Featured in the 2004 film *New York Minute*	RCA 82876543412
17/07/2004	3	5		**THAT'S ALL RIGHT** Originally released in the US in July 1954 on Sun Records, his first single	RCA 82876619212

LISA MARIE PRESLEY
US singer (born 1/2/1968, Memphis, TN) and the only child of legendary singer Elvis Presley and Priscilla Presley. Although she began writing songs at the age of eighteen she did not pursue a musical career until into her 30s. She married Danny Keough in 1988 (by whom she had two children before they divorced), singer Michael Jackson in 1994 (they divorced in 1997) and actor Nicholas Cage in 2002 (they separated in 2003). Initially encouraged by producer Glen Ballard to return to music (he helped her get a contract with Capitol in 2000), she released her debut in 2003.

DATE	POS	WKS	BPI	SINGLE TITLE	LABEL & NUMBER
12/07/2003	16	5		LIGHTS OUT	Capitol CDCL 844

PRESSURE DROP
UK vocal/instrumental group formed by Justin Langlands and Dave Henley.

DATE	POS	WKS	BPI	SINGLE TITLE	LABEL & NUMBER
21/03/1998	53	1		SILENTLY BAD MINDED	Higher Ground HIGHS 6CD
17/03/2001	72	1		WARRIOR SOUND	Higher Ground 6697192

BILLY PRESTON
US singer and keyboard player (born 9/9/1946, Houston, TX) who first recorded for Derby and Vee-Jay before joining Ray Charles touring band. Spotted playing in the UK by the Beatles who signed him to Apple in 1969, he later signed with A&M and then Motown. He won the 1972 Grammy Award for Best Pop Instrumental Performance with *Outa Space*. He was placed on probation in 1992 after pleading guilty to assault with a deadly weapon and possession of cocaine. In November 1997 he was sent to prison after he tested positive for cocaine.

DATE	POS	WKS	BPI	SINGLE TITLE	LABEL & NUMBER
23/04/1969	❶⁶	17		**GET BACK** ↑ ▲⁵ **BEATLES WITH BILLY PRESTON**	Apple R 5777
02/07/1969	11	10		THAT'S THE WAY GOD PLANNED IT	Apple 12
16/09/1972	44	3		OUTA SPACE	A&M AMS 7007
03/04/1976	28	5		GET BACK **BEATLES WITH BILLY PRESTON**	Apple R 5777
15/12/1979	2	11	○	**WITH YOU I'M BORN AGAIN** Featured in the 1979 film *Fastbreak*	Motown TMG 1159
08/03/1980	47	4		IT WILL COME IN TIME This and above single credited to **BILLY PRESTON AND SYREETA**	Motown TMG 1175
22/04/1989	74	1		GET BACK **BEATLES WITH BILLY PRESTON**	Apple R 5777

JOHNNY PRESTON
US singer (born John Preston Courville, 18/8/1939, Port Arthur, TX) who was discovered by the Big Bopper while singing in the Twilight Club, Port Neches, Texas in 1958.

DATE	POS	WKS	BPI	SINGLE TITLE	LABEL & NUMBER
12/02/1960	❶²	16		**RUNNING BEAR** ▲³ Indian sounds by the Big Bopper and George Jones. Its release in America was delayed by six months as Big Bopper had been killed in a plane crash	Mercury AMT 1079
21/04/1960	2	16		**CRADLE OF LOVE**	Mercury AMT 1092
28/07/1960	49	1		I'M STARTING TO GO STEADY	Mercury AMT 1104
11/08/1960	18	10		FEEL SO FINE	Mercury AMT 1104
08/12/1960	34	3		CHARMING BILLY	Mercury AMT 1114

MIKE PRESTON
UK singer (born Jack Davis, 14/5/1934, London) who had previously served in the Irish Guards.

DATE	POS	WKS	BPI	SINGLE TITLE	LABEL & NUMBER
30/10/1959	12	8		MR BLUE	Decca F 11167
25/08/1960	23	10		I'D DO ANYTHING	Decca F 11255

○ Silver disc ● Gold disc ✪ Platinum disc (additional platinum units are indicated by a figure following the symbol) ◉ Singles released prior to 1973 that are known to have sold over 1 million copies in the UK

22/12/1960.....41......5......		TOGETHERNESS	Decca F 11287
09/03/1961.....14.....10......		MARRY ME	Decca F 11335

PRETENDERS
UK/US rock group formed in 1978 by Chrissie Hynde (born 7/9/1951, Akron, OH, guitar/vocals), Pete Farndon (born 12/6/1952, Hereford, bass), Gerry Mackleduff (drums) and James Honeyman-Scott (born 4/11/1956, Hereford, guitar). After recording the first single Mackleduff was replaced by Martin Chambers (born 4/9/1951, Hereford). Farndon was fired in June 1982 and replaced by Billy Bremner (born 1947, Scotland, lead guitar) and Malcolm Foster (bass). Hynde had a daughter by Ray Davies (of the Kinks) and was due to marry him, but the vicar postponed the wedding after the pair argued just before the ceremony. Their relationship ended, and Hynde married Jim Kerr (Simple Minds) in 1984. By 1994 the group comprised Hynde, Chambers, Adam Seymour (guitar) and Andy Hobson (bass). Honeyman-Scott died from cocaine and heroin addiction on 16/6/1982. Farndon died from a drug overdose on 14/4/1983.

10/02/1979.....34......9......		STOP YOUR SOBBING	Real ARE 6
14/07/1979.....33......7......		KID	Real ARE 9
17/11/1979 ....❶²....17.....●		BRASS IN POCKET	Real ARE 11
05/04/1980.....8......8......		TALK OF THE TOWN Featured in the 1980 film Times Square.................	Real ARE 12
14/02/1981.....11......7......		MESSAGE OF LOVE	Real ARE 15
12/09/1981.....45......4......		DAY AFTER DAY	Real ARE 17
14/11/1981 ....7......10......		I GO TO SLEEP	Real ARE 18
02/10/1982.....17......9......		BACK ON THE CHAIN GANG Featured in the 1982 film King Of Comedy.........	Real ARE 19
26/11/1983.....15......9......		2000 MILES	Real ARE 20
09/06/1984.....49......3......		THIN LINE BETWEEN LOVE AND HATE	Real ARE 22
11/10/1986.....10......9......		DON'T GET ME WRONG Featured in the 2001 film Bridget Jones's Diary.......	Real YZ 85
13/12/1986.....8......12......		HYMN TO HER	Real YZ 93
15/08/1987.....49......6......		IF THERE WAS A MAN PRETENDERS FOR 007 Featured in the 1987 James Bond film The Living Daylights (although A-Ha recorded the theme)	Real YZ 149
23/04/1994.....10......10......		I'LL STAND BY YOU	Real YZ 815CD
02/07/1994.....25......5......		NIGHT IN MY VEINS	Real YZ 825CD
15/10/1994.....66......2......		977	WEA YZ 848CD1
14/10/1995.....73......1......		KID	WEA 014CD
10/05/1997.....65......1......		FEVER PITCH THE EP Tracks on EP: Goin' Back – The Pretenders, There She Goes – The La's, How Can We Hang On To A Dream – Orlando, Football – Neil MacColl and Boo Hewerdine – Nick Hornby	Blanco Y Negro NEG 104CD
15/05/1999.....33......3......		HUMAN	WEA 207CD

PRETTY BOY FLOYD
US rock group formed by Steve Summers (vocals), Kristy Majors (guitar), Vinnie Chase (bass) and Karl Kane (drums).

10/03/1990.....75......1......		ROCK AND ROLL (IS GONNA SET THE NIGHT ON FIRE)	MCA 1393

PRETTY THINGS
UK rock group formed in Sidcup in 1963 by Dick Taylor (born 28/1/1943, Dartford, lead guitar), Phil May (born 9/11/1944, Dartford, vocals), Viv Prince (born 9/8/1944, Loughborough, drums), Brian Pendleton (born 13/4/1944, Wolverhampton, rhythm guitar) and John Stax (born John Fullegar, 6/4/1944, Crayford, bass); they signed with Fontana the same year. Prince was replaced by Skip Alan (born Alan Skipper, 11/6/1948, London) in 1965. They then added Wally Allen (bass/vocals) and John Povey (born 20/8/1944, London, keyboards/vocals). The group disbanded in 1977 (following numerous personnel changes), but re-formed in 1980 with May, Taylor, Povey, Allen, Alan and Peter Tolson (born 10/9/1951, Bishops Stortford, guitar). Pendleton died from liver cancer on 16/5/2001.

18/06/1964.....41......5......		ROSALYN	Fontana TF 469
22/10/1964.....10.....11......		DON'T BRING ME DOWN	Fontana TF 503
25/02/1965.....13.....10......		HONEY I NEED	Fontana TF 537
15/07/1965.....28......7......		CRY TO ME	Fontana TF 585
20/01/1966.....46......1......		MIDNIGHT TO SIX MAN	Fontana TF 647
05/05/1966.....43......5......		COME SEE ME	Fontana TF 688
21/07/1966.....50......2......		A HOUSE IN THE COUNTRY	Fontana TF 722

ALAN PRICE
UK singer/keyboard player (born 19/4/1941, Fairfield) who formed the Alan Price Trio in 1960 with Chas Chandler and John Steel; the group later evolved into the Alan Price Combo and then the Animals. He left them in 1965 to re-form the Combo with Boots Slade (bass), Roy Mills (drums), John Walters (trumpet), Terry Childs (saxophone), Steve Gregor (saxophone) and Pete Kirtley, changing the name to the Alan Price Set before the release of their first single.

31/03/1966 .....9......10......		I PUT A SPELL ON YOU	Decca F 12367
14/07/1966.....11......12......		HI LILI HI LO	Decca F 12442
02/03/1967 .....4......12......		SIMON SMITH AND HIS AMAZING DANCING BEAR	Decca F 12570
02/08/1967 .....4......10......		THE HOUSE THAT JACK BUILT	Decca F 12641
15/11/1967.....45......2......		SHAME	Decca F 12691
31/01/1968.....13......8......		DON'T STOP THE CARNIVAL THis and above five singles credited to ALAN PRICE SET	Decca F 12731
10/04/1971.....11......10......		ROSETTA (Georgie) FAME AND PRICE TOGETHER	CBS 7108
25/05/1974 .....6......9......		JARROW SONG	Warner Brothers K 16372
29/04/1978.....43......7......		JUST FOR YOU	Jet UP 36358
17/02/1979.....32......3......		BABY OF MINE/JUST FOR YOU...	Jet 135
30/04/1988.....54......4......		CHANGES	Ariola 109911

KELLY PRICE
US singer (born 4/4/1973, New York); she was a backing singer for Mariah Carey and then worked with the likes of Puff Daddy, The Notorious B.I.G. and Aretha Franklin before being signed as a solo artist by Ronald Isley.

07/11/1998.....25......3......		FRIEND OF MINE Contains a sample of Seals & Crofts' Summer Breeze..........	Island Black Music CID 723

❶⁹ Number of weeks single topped the UK chart ↑ Entered the UK chart at #1 ▲⁹ Number of weeks single topped the US chart

631

| 08/05/1999 | 26 | 2 | | SECRET LOVE Features the uncredited contribution of rapper Da Brat | Island Black Music CID 739 |
| 30/12/2000 | 26 | 5 | | HEARTBREAK HOTEL WHITNEY HOUSTON FEATURING FAITH EVANS AND KELLY PRICE | Arista 74321820572 |

LLOYD PRICE
US singer (born 9/3/1933, Kenner, LA) who formed an R&B quintet in 1950 and signed as a solo artist with Specialty in 1952. He served in the US Army from 1953–56 and moved to Washington DC to form his own record label KRC. He leased early material to ABC and signed with the label in 1958. He was inducted into the Rock & Roll Hall of Fame in 1998.

13/02/1959	7	14		STAGGER LEE ▲4	HMV POP 580
15/05/1959	15	6		WHERE WERE YOU (ON OUR WEDDING DAY)?	HMV POP 598
12/06/1959	9	10		PERSONALITY	HMV POP 626
11/09/1959	23	5		I'M GONNA GET MARRIED	HMV POP 650
21/04/1960	45	1		LADY LUCK	HMV POP 712

PRICKLY HEAT
UK male producer.

| 26/12/1998 | 57 | 1 | | OOOIE, OOOIE, OOOIE Theme to the TV series *Prickly Heat* | Virgin VSCDT 1727 |

DICKIE PRIDE
UK singer (born Richard Knellar, London) who was discovered singing in a public house by Russ Conway and recommended to Norrie Paramour and Larry Parnes. He became known as 'The Sheikh of Shake' because of his gyrations on stage. He died from drug abuse in May 1969.

| 30/10/1959 | 28 | 1 | | PRIMROSE LANE | Columbia DB 4340 |

MAXI PRIEST
UK singer (born Max Elliott, 10/6/1960, London) of Jamaican parentage. He was christened Max because his mother was a fan of Max Bygraves and took his professional name after his conversion to Rastafarianism. He began his career building sound systems and then he toured with the Saxon Assembly. His biggest solo hit was a record produced by Sly and Robbie in Jamaica; he later worked with Soul II Soul.

29/03/1986	32	9		STROLLIN' ON	10 TEN 84
12/07/1986	54	3		IN THE SPRINGTIME	10 TEN 127
08/11/1986	67	5		CRAZY LOVE	10 TEN 135
04/04/1987	49	4		LET ME KNOW	10 TEN 156
24/10/1987	12	12		SOME GUYS HAVE ALL THE LUCK Featured in the 1989 film *Slaves Of New York*	10 TEN 198
20/02/1988	41	6		HOW CAN WE EASE THE PAIN	10 TEN 207
04/06/1988	5	9		WILD WORLD	10 TEN 221
27/08/1988	57	3		GOODBYE TO LOVE AGAIN	10 TEN 238
09/06/1990	7	10		CLOSE TO YOU ▲1	10 TEN 294
01/09/1990	41	4		PEACE THROUGHOUT THE WORLD	10 TEN 317
01/12/1990	71	4		HUMAN WORK OF ART	10 TEN 328
24/08/1991	31	7		HOUSECALL SHABBA RANKS FEATURING MAXI PRIEST	Epic 6573477
05/10/1991	62	3		THE MAXI PRIEST EP Tracks on EP: *Just A Little Bit Longer, Best Of Me, Searching* and *Fever*	10 TEN 343
26/09/1992	50	2		GROOVIN' IN THE MIDNIGHT	10 TEN 412
28/11/1992	33	3		JUST WANNA KNOW/FE' REAL MAXI PRIEST/MAXI PRIEST FEATURING APACHE INDIAN	10 TEN 416
20/03/1993	40	3		ONE MORE CHANCE	10 TENCD 420
08/05/1993	8	8		HOUSECALL (REMIX) SHABBA RANKS FEATURING MAXI PRIEST	Epic 6592842
31/07/1993	65	2		WAITING IN VAIN	GRP MCSTD 1921
22/06/1996	15	7		THAT GIRL MAXI PRIEST/SHAGGY Contains a sample of Booker T & The MG's' *Green Onions*	Virgin VUSDX 106
21/09/1996	36	2		WATCHING THE WORLD GO BY	Virgin VUSD 108

PRIMA DONNA
UK vocal group formed by June Robins, Kate Robins, Sally-Ann Triplet, Danny Finn, Marty Kristian (ex-The New Seekers) and Paul Layton. They were assembled for the 1980 Eurovision Song Contest, where they were beaten by Johnny Logan of Ireland's entry *What's Another Year*. Triplett later became a member of Bardo, another of Britain's Eurovision Song Contest entrants.

| 26/04/1980 | 48 | 4 | | LOVE ENOUGH FOR TWO Britain's entry for the 1980 Eurovision Song Contest (finished third) | Ariola ARO 221 |

LOUIS PRIMA
US singer/trumpeter/bandleader (born 7/12/1911, New Orleans, LA); he married Dorothy Keely Smith (with whom he scored a US chart hit) in 1952 and was divorced in 1961. The pair won a Grammy Award in 1958 for Best Performance by a Vocal Group or Chorus for *That Old Black Magic*. Louis supplied the voice of King Louis in the 1967 Walt Disney animated film *The Jungle Book*. He underwent surgery for a brain tumour in 1975 and was left in a coma until he died on 24/8/1978.

| 21/02/1958 | 25 | 1 | | BUONA SERA Featured in the 1996 film *Big Night* | Capitol CL 14841 |

PRIMAL SCREAM
UK rock group formed in Glasgow in 1984 by Bobby Gillespie (born 22/6/1964, Glasgow, vocals), the only constant member. The line-up has featured Robert Young, Andrew Innes, Henry Olsen, Tobay Toman, Jim Beattie, Hugo Nicolson, Martin Duffy, Denise Johnson and two DJs as it evolved from a metal band to a dance-fusion act. They signed with Creation in 1985, spent a brief spell at Warner's and then returned to Creation in 1989. They added ex-Stone Roses bass player Gary Mountfield in 1996. They took their name from Arthur Janov's book *Prisoner Of Pain* that referred to primal therapy. On U-Sound is UK reggae artist Adrian Sherwood.

03/03/1990	16	9		LOADED Featured in the 2004 film *Bridget Jones Diary 2: Edge Of Reason*	Creation CRE 070
18/08/1990	26	6		COME TOGETHER	Creation CRE 078
22/06/1991	40	2		HIGHER THAN THE SUN	Creation CRE 096
24/08/1991	41	2		DON'T FIGHT IT FEEL IT	Creation CRE 110
08/02/1992	11	6		DIXIE-NARCO EP Tracks on EP: *Movin' On Up, Stone My Soul, Carry Me Home* and *Screamadelica*	Creation CRE 117
12/03/1994	7	5		ROCKS/FUNKY JAM	Creation CRESCD 129

○ Silver disc ● Gold disc ✪ Platinum disc (additional platinum units are indicated by a figure following the symbol) ◎ Singles released prior to 1973 that are known to have sold over 1 million copies in the UK

18/06/1994.....29......2......				JAILBIRD..	Creation CRESCD 145
10/12/1994.....49......2......				(I'M GONNA) CRY MYSELF BLIND..	Creation CRESCD 183
15/06/1996.....17......2......				THE BIG MAN AND THE SCREAM TEAM MEET THE BARMY ARMY UPTOWN **PRIMAL SCREAM, IRVINE WELSH & ON U-SOUND**.....	
				....	Creation CRESCD 194
17/05/1997 .....8......3......				**KOWALSKI**..	Creation CRESCD 245
28/06/1997.....16......3......				STAR	Creation CRESCD 263
25/10/1997.....17......2......				BURNING WHEEL...	Creation CRESCD 272
20/11/1999.....22......2......				SWASTIKA EYES Featured in the 2004 film *The Football Factory*	Creation CRESCD 326
01/04/2000.....24......2......				KILL ALL HIPPIES Contains a sample of Linda Manz' dialogue from the film *Out Of The Blue*................	Creation CRESCD 332
23/09/2000.....34......1......				ACCELERATOR	Creation CRESCD 333
03/08/2002.....25......2......				MISS LUCIFER Featured in the 2004 film *The Football Factory*	Columbia 6728252
09/11/2002.....44......1......				AUTOBAHN 66...	Columbia 6733122
29/11/2003.....44......2......				SOME VELVET MORNING..	Columbia 6744022

PRIME MOVERS
US rock group formed by Severs Ramsey, Gary Putman, Curt Lichter and Gregory Markel. They later contributed to the soundtrack of the film *Manhunter*.

08/02/1986.....74......1......				ON THE TRAIL..	Island IS 263

PRIMITIVE RADIO GODS
US singer Chris O'Connor.

30/03/1996.....74......1......				STANDING OUTSIDE A BROKEN PHONE BOOTH WITH MONEY IN MY HAND	Columbia 6627692

PRIMITIVES
UK group formed in 1985 by Keiron (vocals), Paul Court (guitar/vocals), Steve Dullaghan (bass) and Pete Tweedie (drums). Keiron was subsequently replaced by Australian singer Tracy Tracy and the group launched the Lazy label in 1988. Tweedie was subsequently replaced by Tig Williams and Dullaghan by Andy Hobson.

27/02/1988 .....5......10				**CRASH**..	Lazy PB 41761
30/04/1988.....25......4......				OUT OF REACH	Lazy PB 42011
03/09/1988.....36......4......				WAY BEHIND ME	Lazy PB 42209
29/07/1989.....24......4......				SICK OF IT	Lazy PB 42947
30/09/1989.....49......3......				SECRETS	Lazy PB 43173
03/08/1991.....58......2......				YOU ARE THE WAY	RCA PB 44481

PRINCE
US singer/guitarist/producer (born Prince Rogers Nelson, 7/6/1958, Minneapolis, MN) who began writing songs in 1970 and joined Grand Central in 1972 (with Prince's friend Andre Cymon). He formed Flyte Tyme in 1974 with Morris Day, Jellybean Johnson, Terry Lewis and Alexander O'Neal among the members. After a brief spell with 94 East (who also featured Colonel Abrams) he signed a solo deal with Warner's in 1977, with an agreement that he could produce himself, then almost unheard of in the industry, and his debut album appeared in 1988. One of the first black artists to receive extensive airplay on MTV, he later changed his name to a hieroglyphic (known as symbol) and then Artist Formerly Known As Prince (or AFKAP for short). Prince has won seven BRIT Awards: Best International Male in 1985, 1992, 1993, 1995 and 1996, and the Best Soundtrack Album category in 1985 (for *Purple Rain*) and 1990 (for *Batman*). He also won an Oscar in 1984 for *Purple Rain* in the Best Original Song Score category. He married dancer Mayte Garcia on Valentine's Day in 1996, had the marriage annulled and then remarried her on Valentine's Day in 1999. He has won four Grammy Awards including Best Rock Vocal Performance by a Group and Best Album of Original Score Written for a Motion Picture in 1984 for *Purple Rain, and* Best Rhythm & Blues Song in 1984 for *I Feel For You*. He was inducted into the Rock & Roll Hall of Fame in 2004.

19/01/1980.....41......3......				I WANNA BE YOUR LOVER..	Warner Brothers K 17537
29/01/1983.....25......7......				1999	Warner Brothers W 9896
30/04/1983.....54......6......				LITTLE RED CORVETTE..	Warner Brothers W 9688
26/11/1983.....66......2......				LITTLE RED CORVETTE Re-issue of Warner Brothers W 9688	Warner Brothers W 9436
30/06/1984 .....4......15 ....O				**WHEN DOVES CRY** ▲5 **PRINCE AND THE REVOLUTION**:...............................	Warner Brothers W 9286
22/09/1984 .....8......9......				**PURPLE RAIN** This and above single featured in the 1984 film *Purple Rain*.......	Warner Brothers W 9174
08/12/1984.....58......6......				I WOULD DIE 4 U	Warner Brothers W 9121
19/01/1985 .....2......10 ....O				**1999/LITTLE RED CORVETTE** Re-issue of Warner Brothers W 9896	Warner Brothers W 1999
23/02/1985 .....7......9......				**LET'S GO CRAZY/TAKE ME WITH YOU** ▲2 Featured in the 1984 film *Purple Rain*....	Warner Brothers W 2000
25/05/1985.....18......10				PAISLEY PARK	WEA W 9052
27/07/1985.....25......8......				RASPBERRY BERET	WEA W 8929
26/10/1985.....60......2......				POP LIFE	Paisley Park W 8858
08/03/1986 .....6......9......				**KISS** ▲2 1986 Grammy Award for Best Rhythm & Blues Vocal Performance......	Paisley Park W 8751
14/06/1986.....45......4......				MOUNTAINS	Paisley Park W 8711
16/08/1986.....11......8......				GIRLS AND BOYS Featured in the 1996 film *Girl 6*..................................	Paisley Park W 8586
01/11/1986.....36......3......				ANOTHERLOVERHOLENYOHEAD This and above three titles featured in the 1986 film *Under The Cherry Moon*. This and above eleven singles credited to **PRINCE AND THE REVOLUTION**..................................	Paisley Park W 8521
14/03/1987.....10......9......				**SIGN O' THE TIMES**	Paisley Park W 8399
20/06/1987.....20......6......				IF I WAS YOUR GIRLFRIEND Featured in the 1996 film *Striptease*	Paisley Park W 8334
15/08/1987.....11......9......				U GOT THE LOOK Features the uncredited vocal of Sheena Easton	Paisley Park W 8289
28/11/1987.....29......6......				I COULD NEVER TAKE THE PLACE OF YOUR MAN Featured in the 1987 film *Sign O' The Times*	Paisley Park W 8288
07/05/1988 .....9......6......				**ALPHABET STREET** Featured in the 1986 film *Under The Cherry Moon*............	Paisley Park W 7900
23/07/1988.....29......4......				GLAM SLAM...	Paisley Park W 7806
05/11/1988.....24......5......				I WISH U HEAVEN	Paisley Park W 7745
17/06/1989 .....2......12 ....O				**BATDANCE** ▲1	Warner Brothers W 2924
09/09/1989 .....14......6......				PARTYMAN This and above title featured in the 1989 film *Batman* and feature dialogue from Jack Nicholson, Michael Keaton and Kim Bassinger..	Warner Brothers W 2814

❶9 Number of weeks single topped the UK chart ↑ Entered the UK chart at #1 ▲9 Number of weeks single topped the US chart

633

18/11/1989.....27......5......	THE ARMS OF ORION **PRINCE WITH SHEENA EASTON** Featured in the 1989 film *Batman*.................Warner Brothers W 2757
04/08/1990.....7......6......	**THIEVES IN THE TEMPLE**.................Paisley Park W 9751
10/11/1990.....26......4......	NEW POWER GENERATION This and above title featured in the 1990 film *Graffiti Bridge*.................Paisley Park W 9525
31/08/1991.....4......8......	**GETT OFF**.................Paisley Park W 0056
21/09/1991.....15......7......	CREAM ▲² ....Paisley Park W 0061
07/12/1991.....25......6......	DIAMONDS AND PEARLS.................Paisley Park W 0075
28/03/1992.....19......5......	MONEY DON'T MATTER 2 NIGHT.................Paisley Park W 0091
27/06/1992.....28......3......	THUNDER.................Paisley Park W 01132P
18/07/1992.....4......7......	**SEXY MF/STROLLIN'**.................Paisley Park W 0123
10/10/1992.....7......5......	**MY NAME IS PRINCE**.................Paisley Park W 0132
14/11/1992.....51......1......	MY NAME IS PRINCE (REMIX).................Paisley Park W 0142T
05/12/1992.....27......6......	7 Contains a sample of Jimmy McCracklin and Lowell Fulson's *Tramp*. This and above eight singles credited to **PRINCE AND THE NEW POWER GENERATION**.................Paisley Park W 0147
13/03/1993.....52......3......	THE MORNING PAPERS.................Paisley Park W 0162CD
16/10/1993.....14......5......	PEACH.................Paisley Park W 0210CD
11/12/1993.....5......5......	**CONTROVERSY**.................Paisley Park W 0215CD1
09/04/1994.....❶²......12.....○	**THE MOST BEAUTIFUL GIRL IN THE WORLD**.................NPG 60155
04/06/1994.....18......3......	THE BEAUTIFUL EXPERIENCE.................NPG 60212
10/09/1994.....30......4......	LETITGO This and above two singles credited to ♀ ....Warner Brothers W 0260CD
18/03/1995.....33......2......	PURPLE MEDLEY.................Warner Brothers W 0289CD
23/09/1995.....20......3......	EYE HATE U.................Warner Brothers W 0315CD
09/12/1995.....10......9......	**GOLD** This and above two singles credited to **ARTIST FORMERLY**.................Warner Brothers W 0325CDX
03/08/1996.....36......2......	DINNER WITH DELORES.................Warner Brothers 9362437422
14/12/1996.....11......7......	BETCHA BY GOLLY WOW! This and above single credited to **THE ARTIST**.................NPG CDEMS 463
08/03/1997.....19......3......	THE HOLY RIVER **PRINCE**.................EMI CDEM 467
09/01/1999.....10......4......	**1999** Re-issue of Warner Brothers W 1999.................Warner Brothers W 467CD
18/12/1999.....40......5......	1999.................Warner Brothers W 467CD
26/02/2000.....65......1......	THE GREATEST ROMANCE EVER SOLD.................NPG 74321745002
20/11/2004.....43......1......	CINNAMON GIRL.................Columbia 6751422

PRINCE BUSTER
Jamaican singer (born Cecil Bustamante Campbell, 28/5/1938, Kingston) who was named after the leader of the Jamaican Labour Party Alexandra Bustamante. He started his career as a boxer, earning the nickname Prince, before turning to music and becoming one of the leading pioneers of the 'blue beat' style. He recorded a single called *Madness*, from which the group took their name. Madness paid tribute to him in their debut hit, *The Prince*. He was also indirectly responsible for Judge Dread, who took his name in honour of the single *Judge Dread*.

23/02/1967.....18......13......	AL CAPONE.................Blue Beat BB 324
04/04/1998.....21......3......	WHINE AND GRINE Originally recorded in 1968 and revived following its use in a Levi Jeans advertisement.........Island CID 691

PRINCE CHARLES AND THE CITY BEAT BAND
US group formed in New York City; they also recorded for Greyhound and Solid Platinum Records.

22/02/1986.....56......2......	WE CAN MAKE IT HAPPEN.................PRT 7P 348

PRINCE NASEEM – see KALEEF

PRINCESS
UK singer Desiree Heslop (born 28/11/1962) who was a backing singer for Osibisa, Evelyn Thomas and Precious Wilson before teaming up with Stock Aitken Waterman and the Supreme label. She later returned to being a backing singer, appearing on Vanilla Ice's *To The Extreme* album.

03/08/1985.....7......12......	**SAY I'M YOUR NO. 1**.................Supreme SUPE 101
09/11/1985.....28......13......	AFTER THE LOVE HAS GONE.................Supreme SUPE 103
19/04/1986.....16......8......	I'LL KEEP ON LOVING YOU.................Supreme SUPE 105
05/07/1986.....34......5......	TELL ME TOMORROW Featured in the 1986 film *Knights And Emeralds*.................Supreme SUPE 106
25/10/1986.....74......1......	IN THE HEAT OF A PASSIONATE MOMENT.................Supreme SUPE 109
13/06/1987.....58......5......	RED HOT.................Polydor POSP 868

PRINCESS IVORI
US rapper Taryn Gresham who was discovered by producer Jurgen Korduletsch.

17/03/1990.....69......2......	WANTED.................Supreme SUPE 163

PRINCESS SUPERSTAR
US rapper (born Concetta Kirshner, New York); she adopted the name Princess Superstar in 1994 and after signing with 5th Beetle Records assembled a backing band of Art 'F' Levis (guitar), Doug Pressman (bass) and Kirsten 'Pro' Jansen (drums). She formed her own label, A Big Rich Major, in 1996 and put together a new band with Ski Love Ski (bass), Mike Linn (drums) and DJ Science Center. By 1999 the label was known as The Corrupted Conglomerate and her band consisted of Walter Sipser (bass), Money Mike Linn (drums) and DJ Cutless Supreme (guitar/turntables).

02/03/2002.....11......7......	BAD BABYSITTER.................Rapster/!K7 RR 007CDM

MADDY PRIOR – see STATUS QUO

PRIVATE LIVES
UK group formed by John Adams (drums/vocals), Rick Lane (keyboards) and John Read (bass).

11/02/1984.....53......4......	LIVING IN A WORLD (TURNED UPSIDE DOWN).................EMI PRIV 2

PRIZNA FEATURING DEMOLITION MAN UK vocal/instrumental group.

29/04/1995.....33......2.......	FIRE .... Labello Blanco NLBCDX 18

P.J. PROBY US singer (born James Marcus Smith, 6/11/1938, Houston, TX) who first recorded under the name Jeff Powers in 1958. Introduced by Jack Good to UK audiences in the TV special *Around The Beatles* in May 1964, he signed with Decca shortly after and was promoted in America as part of the British invasion. He caused controversy when his trousers split during a live performance in Luton in 1965. In 1973 his fiancée Claudia Martin (daughter of Dean Martin) ran off with another man, prompting Proby to chase after the couple brandishing a gun. He fired off a couple of warning shots and was subsequently jailed for three months.

Date	Pos	Wks	Title	Label
28/05/1964 .....3......15	**HOLD ME** .... Decca F 11904
03/09/1964 .....8......11	**TOGETHER** .... Decca F 11967
10/12/1964 .....6......12	**SOMEWHERE** Cover version of a song originally featured in the musical *West Side Story* .... Liberty LIB 10182
25/02/1965 .....11......8	I APOLOGISE .... Liberty LIB 10188
08/07/1965 .....19......8	LET THE WATER RUN DOWN .... Liberty LIB 10206
30/09/1965 .....30......6	THAT MEANS A LOT Written by John Lennon and Paul McCartney .... Liberty LIB 10215
25/11/1965 .....8......9	**MARIA** .... Liberty LIB 10218
10/02/1966 .....25......7	YOU'VE COME BACK .... Liberty LIB 10223
16/06/1966 .....34......3	TO MAKE A BIG MAN CRY .... Liberty LIB 10236
27/10/1966 .....37......5	I CAN'T MAKE IT ALONE .... Liberty LIB 10250
06/03/1968 .....32......5	IT'S YOUR DAY TODAY .... Liberty LIB 15046
28/12/1996 .....58......2	YESTERDAY HAS GONE .... EMI Premier CDPRESX 13

PROCLAIMERS UK duo formed by twin brothers Charlie and Craig Reid (born 5/3/1962, Edinburgh). They worked with Pete Wingfield on their second album, then took a break to concentrate on saving Hibernian Football Club, becoming shareholders in the club.

Date	Pos	Wks	BPI	Title	Label
14/11/1987 .....3......10 .....O	**LETTER FROM AMERICA** .... Chrysalis CHS 3178
05/03/1988 .....63......3	MAKE MY HEART FLY .... Chrysalis CLAIM 1
27/08/1988 .....11......11	I'M GONNA BE (500 MILES) Featured in the 1993 film *Benny & Joon* .... Chrysalis CLAIM 2
12/11/1988 .....41......5	SUNSHINE ON LEITH .... Chrysalis CLAIM 3
11/02/1989 .....43......4	I'M ON MY WAY Featured in the 2001 animated film *Shrek* .... Chrysalis CLAIM 4
24/11/1990 .....9......8	**KING OF THE ROAD (EP)** Tracks on EP: *King Of The Road, Long Black Veil, Lulu Selling Tea* and *Not Ever* .... Chrysalis CLAIM 5
19/02/1994 .....21......4	LET'S GET MARRIED .... Chrysalis CDCLAIMS 6
23/04/1994 .....38......3	WHAT MAKES YOU CRY .... Chrysalis CDCLAIMS 7
22/10/1994 .....51......2	THESE ARMS OF MINE .... Chrysalis CDCLAIM 8

PROCOL HARUM UK rock group formed in 1959 by Gary Brooker (born 29/5/1945, Southend, vocals/piano), Robin Trower (born 9/3/1945, Southend, guitar), Chris Copping (born 29/8/1945, Southend, bass), Bob Scott (vocals) and Mick Brownlee (drums) as the Paramounts. Brownlee left when the group turned professional, replaced by Barry 'BJ' Wilson (born 18/3/1947, Southend). The Paramounts split in 1966 and re-formed as Procol Harum in 1967 with Brooker, Matthew Fisher (born 7/3/1946, Croydon, keyboards), Ray Royer (born 8/10/1945, guitar), Dave Knights (born 28/6/1945, London, bass) and Bobby Harrison (born 28/6/1943, drums). Following the success of their debut single Royer and Harrison were asked to leave and Trower and Wilson replaced them, with numerous personnel changes until they disbanded in 1977. Wilson died from pneumonia in October 1990. The group's name was either derived from the Latin word 'procul', meaning 'far from these things', or from the birth certificate of impresario Guy Steven's pedigree cat 'Procul Harun'. *A Whiter Shade Of Pale* was named Best Single (jointly with Queen's *Bohemian Rhapsody*) at the 1977 BRIT Awards.

Date	Pos	Wks	Title	Label
25/05/1967 .....❶6......15	**A WHITER SHADE OF PALE** Won the 1977 BRIT Award for Best Single. Total worldwide sales exceed 10 million copies. Featured in the 1984 film *The Big Chill* .... Deram DM 126
04/10/1967 .....6......10	**HOMBURG** .... Regal Zonophone RZ 3003
24/04/1968 .....50......1	QUITE RIGHTLY SO .... Regal Zonophone RZ 3007
18/06/1969 .....44......3	SALTY DOG .... Regal Zonophone RZ 3109
22/04/1972 .....13......13	A WHITER SHADE OF PALE Re-issue of Deram DM 126. .... Magnify ECHO 10
05/08/1972 .....22......7	CONQUISTADOR .... Chrysalis CHS 2003
23/08/1975 .....16......7	PANDORA'S BOX .... Chrysalis CHS 2073

MICHAEL PROCTOR – see URBAN BLUES PROJECT PRESENTS MICHAEL PROCTOR

PRODIGY UK rave group formed in Essex in 1991 by Liam Howlett (born 21/8/1971, Braintree, musical instruments), Maxim Reality (born Keith Palmer, 21/3/1967, MC), Leeroy Thornhill (born 7/10/1969, Peterborough, dancer) and Keith Flint (born 17/9/1969, Braintree, vocals and dancer). The group was signed by Madonna's Maverick label for America. Prodigy was named Best Dance Act at the 1997 MOBO Awards and won the same category at the 1997 and 1998 BRIT Awards. The group has also won six MTV Europe Music Awards: Best Dance Act in 1994, 1996, 1997, 1998, Best Alternative Act in 1997 and Best Video for *Breathe* in 1997 (directed by Walter Stern). Howlett married ex-All Saints member Nicole Appleton in June 2002.

Date	Pos	Wks	BPI	Title	Label
24/08/1991 .....3......10 .....O	**CHARLY** .... XL Recordings XLS 21
04/01/1992 .....2......9	**EVERYBODY IN THE PLACE (EP)** Tracks on EP: *Everybody In The Place, Crazy Man, G-Force* and *Rip Up The Sound System* ...... XL Recordings XLS 26
26/09/1992 .....11......4	FIRE/JERICHO .... XL Recordings XLS 30
21/11/1992 .....5......12 .....O	**OUT OF SPACE/RUFF IN THE JUNGLE BIZNESS** .... XL Recordings XLS 35

❶9 Number of weeks single topped the UK chart ↑ Entered the UK chart at #1 ▲9 Number of weeks single topped the US chart

635

DATE	POS	WKS	BPI	SINGLE TITLE	LABEL & NUMBER
17/04/1993	11	7		WIND IT UP (REWOUND)	XL Recordings XLS 39CD
16/10/1993	8	6		**ONE LOVE**	XL Recordings XLS 47CD
28/05/1994	4	12		**NO GOOD (START THE DANCE)** Contains a sample of Kelly Charles' *No Good For Me*	XL Recordings XLS 51CD
24/09/1994	13	5		VOODOO PEOPLE	XL Recordings XLS 54CD
18/03/1995	15	6		POISON Featured in the 1999 film *End Of Days*	XL Recordings XLS 58CD
30/03/1996	❶³	19	●	**FIRESTARTER** ↑ Contains a sample of The Breeders' *SOS*. Following the success of *Firestarter,* all the group's previous singles were re-promoted and all but *One Love* re-entered the top 75	XL Recordings XLS 70CD
20/04/1996	66	1		CHARLY	XL Recordings XLS 21
20/04/1996	63	1		FIRE/JERICHO	XL Recordings XLS 30
20/04/1996	57	2		NO GOOD (START THE DANCE)	XL Recordings XLS 51CD
20/04/1996	52	2		OUT OF SPACE	XL Recordings XLS 35
20/04/1996	62	1		POISON	XL Recordings XLS 58CD
20/04/1996	52	2		RUFF IN THE JUNGLE BIZNESS	XL Recordings XLS 35
20/04/1996	75	1		VOODOO PEOPLE	XL Recordings XLS 54CD
20/04/1996	71	1		WIND IT UP (REWOUND)	XL Recordings XLS 39CD
27/04/1996	69	1		EVERYBODY IN THE PLACE (EP)	XL Recordings XLS 26
23/11/1996	❶²	17	✪	**BREATHE** ↑ The video won the 1997 MVT Europe Music Award for Best Video	XL Recordings XLS 80CD
14/12/1996	53	11		FIRESTARTER	XL Recordings XLS 70CD
29/11/1997	8	10		**SMACK MY BITCH UP** Contains a sample of Ultramagnetic MC's *Give The Drummer Some*. Featured in the 2000 film *Charlie's Angels*. Release of the single was delayed by two months following the death of Princess Diana	XL Recordings XLS 90CD
13/07/2002	5	6		**BABY'S GOT A TEMPER**	XL Recordings XLS 145CD
11/09/2004	19	4		GIRLS	XL Recordings XLS 195CD
04/12/2004	73	1		CHARLY Re-issue of XL Recordings XLS 21	XL Recordings XLXV1506

PRODUCT G&B – see SANTANA

PROFESSIONALS UK rock group formed by Steve Jones (guitar), Ray McVeigh (guitar), Paul Meyers (bass) and Paul Cook (drums). Jones and Cook were ex-members of The Sex Pistols.

DATE	POS	WKS	BPI	SINGLE TITLE	LABEL & NUMBER
11/10/1980	43	4		1-2-3	Virgin VS 376

PROFESSOR – see DJ PROFESSOR

PROFESSOR T – see SHUT UP AND DANCE

PROGRAM – see MR PINK PRESENTS THE PROGRAM

PROGRAM 2 BELTRAM – see BELTRAM

PROGRESS FUNK Italian production group formed by Chicco Secci.

DATE	POS	WKS	BPI	SINGLE TITLE	LABEL & NUMBER
11/10/1997	73	1		AROUND MY BRAIN	Deconstruction 74321518182

PROGRESS PRESENTS THE BOY WUNDA UK DJ Robert Webster from Derby's Progress Club recording under an assumed group name. Webster, 22 at the time of his debut hit, began going to Progress at age 15 and later became DJ at the club.

DATE	POS	WKS	BPI	SINGLE TITLE	LABEL & NUMBER
18/12/1999	7	10		**EVERYBODY** Contains a sample of Madonna's *Papa Don't Preach*	Manifesto FESCD 65

PROJECT FEATURING GERIDEAU US vocal/instrumental duo Jose Burgos and Gerideau.

DATE	POS	WKS	BPI	SINGLE TITLE	LABEL & NUMBER
27/08/1994	65	1		BRING IT BACK 2 LUV	Fruittree FTREE 10CD

PROJECT 1 UK producer Mark Williams.

DATE	POS	WKS	BPI	SINGLE TITLE	LABEL & NUMBER
16/05/1992	49	2		ROUGHNECK (EP) Tracks on EP: *Come My Selector, I Can't Take The Heartbreak, Live Vibe 4 (Summer Vibes)*	Rising High RSN 22
29/08/1992	64	1		DON GARGON COMIN'	Rising High RSN 35

PRONG US heavy metal group formed in New York by Tommy Victor (guitar/vocals), Mike Kirkland (bass) and Ted Parsons (drums). Kirkland left in 1991, replaced by Troy Gregory who soon left and was replaced by Paul Raven, with John Bechdel (keyboards) also joining. They disbanded in 1996.

DATE	POS	WKS	BPI	SINGLE TITLE	LABEL & NUMBER
25/04/1992	58	1		WHOSE FIST IS THIS ANYWAY EP Tracks on EP: *Prove You Wrong, Hell If I Could, (Get A) Grip (On Yourself)* and *Prove You Wrong (remix)*	Epic 6580026

PROPAGANDA German synthesiser pop band formed in Britain by Claudia Brucken (vocals), Michael Mertens (percussion), Susanne Freytag (keyboards) and Ralf Dorper (keyboards). Brucken later married ZTT label boss Paul Morley and formed Act. The group left ZTT for Virgin in 1990, with Brucken remaining at ZTT for a solo career.

DATE	POS	WKS	BPI	SINGLE TITLE	LABEL & NUMBER
17/03/1984	27	9		DR MABUSE	ZTT ZTAS 2
04/05/1985	21	12		DUEL	ZTT ZTAS 8
10/08/1985	50	5		P MACHINERY	ZTT ZTAS 12
28/04/1990	36	5		HEAVEN GIVE ME WORDS	Virgin VS 1245
08/09/1990	71	4		ONLY ONE WORD	Virgin VS 1271

PROPELLERHEADS UK dance duo Alex Gifford (born 29/12/1963) and Will White (born 16/5/1973). Gifford had previously performed with The Grid.

○ Silver disc ● Gold disc ✪ Platinum disc (additional platinum units are indicated by a figure following the symbol) ⊚ Singles released prior to 1973 that are known to have sold over 1 million copies in the UK

07/12/1996.....69......1......	TAKE CALIFORNIA .... Wall Of Sound WALLD 024
17/05/1997.....40......1......	SPYBREAK! Featured in the 1997 film *Playing God* .... Wall Of Sound WALLD 029X
18/10/1997 .....7 .....5......	**ON HER MAJESTY'S SECRET SERVICE** **PROPELLERHEADS AND DAVID ARNOLD** Cover version of the theme to the James Bond film of the same name. .... East West EW 136CD
20/12/1997... 19......7......	HISTORY REPEATING **PROPELLERHEADS AND SHIRLEY BASSEY** Featured in the 1998 film *There's Something About Mary*.. Wall Of Sound WALLD 036
27/06/1998.....53......1......	BANG ON!.. Wall Of Sound WALLD 039

PROPHETS OF SOUND UK instrumental/production duo Dylan Barnes and Jem Panufnik.

14/11/1998.....73......1......	HIGH .... Distinctive DISNCD 47
23/02/2002.....51......1......	NEW DAWN .... Ink NIBNE 10CD

PROSPECT PARK/CAROLYN HARDING UK vocal/production duo Michele Chiavarini (keyboards) and Carolyn Harding (vocals).

08/08/1998.....55......1......	MOVIN' ON .... AM:PM 5827312

SHAILA PROSPERE – see RIMES FEATURING SHAILA PROSPERE

BRIAN PROTHEROE UK singer (born Salisbury) who also made numerous appearances in various TV series including *Reilly – Ace Of Spies* and *Not A Penny More, Not A Penny Less*.

07/09/1974.....22......6.......	PINBALL .... Chrysalis CHS 2043

PROUD MARY UK vocal/instrumental group formed in Manchester by Greg Griffin (vocals), Paul Newsome (guitar), Adam Gray (guitar) and Nev Cottee (bass); they took their name from a Creedence Clearwater Revival song. They were the first signing to Noel Gallagher's (of Oasis) Sour Mash label.

25/08/2001.....75......1......	VERY BEST FRIEND .... Sour Mash JDNCSCD 004

DOROTHY PROVINE US singer (born 20/1/1937, Deadwood, SD) who was also an actress, appearing in the long-running TV series *77 Sunset Strip*.

07/12/1961.....17.....12......	DON'T BRING LULU .... Warner Brothers WB 53
28/06/1962.....45......3.......	CRAZY WORDS CRAZY TUNE .... Warner Brothers WB 70

ERIC PRYDZ Swedish DJ/producer who also records as Dukes Of Sluca and The Sheridan and with Marcus Stork and later launched the Pryda label. Steve Angello is a member of Outfunk.

21/08/2004.....55......1.......	WOZ NOT WOZ **ERIC PRYDZ AND STEVE ANGELLO** C2 CDC2002
25/09/2004 ....❶⁵....14+	**CALL ON ME** ↑ Contains a sample of Steve Winwood's *Valerie*. Winwood re-recorded his vocal parts for the record. Reclaimed #1 position on 23/10/2004 .... Data 68CDS

PSEUDO ECHO Australian pop group formed in Melbourne in 1982 by Bruce Canham (guitar/vocals), James Leigh (keyboards), Pierre Gigliotti (bass) and Vince Leigh (drums).

18/07/1987 .....8......12......	**FUNKY TOWN** .... RCA PB 49705

PSG – see COLOUR GIRL

PSYCHEDELIC FURS UK rock group formed in 1979 by Richard Butler (born 5/6/1956, Kingston-upon-Thames, vocals), Vince Ely (drums), Roger Morris (guitar), Tim Butler (born 7/12/1958, Kingston-upon-Thames, bass) and Duncan Kilburn (woodwinds) and signed to CBS in 1980. They later added John Ashton (born 30/11/1957, guitar), although by the end of the 1980s the Furs were a trio of the Butler brothers and Ashton. They disbanded in 1993 with Richard Butler going on to form Love Spit Love.

02/05/1981.....59......2......	DUMB WAITERS .... CBS A 1166
27/06/1981.....43......5......	PRETTY IN PINK... CBS A 1327
31/07/1982.....42......6......	LOVE MY WAY Featured in the films *Valley Girl* (1994) and *The Wedding Singer* (1998) .... CBS A 2549
31/03/1984.....29......6......	HEAVEN .... CBS A 4300
16/06/1984.....68......2......	GHOST IN YOU... CBS A 4470
23/08/1986.....18......9......	PRETTY IN PINK Re-recording. .... CBS A 7242
09/07/1988.....75......1......	ALL THAT MONEY WANTS .... CBS FURS 4

PSYCHEDELIC WALTONS UK production duo Nelle Hooper and Fabien Waltman.

19/01/2002.....37......2......	WONDERLAND **PSYCHEDELIC WALTONS FEATURING ROISIN MURPHY** .... Echo ECSCD 120
12/04/2003.....48......1......	PAYBACK TIME **DYSFUNCTIONAL PSYCHEDELIC WALTONS** Track first appeared as an advertisement for Levi Jeans and features the uncredited contribution of Kalli Ali, formerly of Sneaker Pimps.................................... Sony Music 6737622

PSYCHIC TV UK group formed by Genesis P-Orridge, Peter Christopherson, Cosey Fanni Tutt and Geoff Rushton.

26/04/1986.....67......2......	GODSTAR **PSYCHO TV AND THE ANGELS OF LIGHT**.. Temple TOPY 009
20/09/1986.....65......2......	GOOD VIBRATIONS/ROMAN P .... Temple TOPY 23

PSYCHO RADIO – see LC ANDERSON VS PSYCHO RADIO

PSYCHOTROPIC – see FREEFALL FEATURING PSYCHOTROPIC

---

❶⁹ Number of weeks single topped the UK chart ↑ Entered the UK chart at #1 ▲⁹ Number of weeks single topped the US chart

PUBLIC ANNOUNCEMENT
US R&B and hip hop group formed in Chicago, IL by Earl Robinson, Felony Davis, Euclid Gray and Glen Wright. The group was originally the backing group for R Kelly.

DATE	POS	WKS	SINGLE TITLE	LABEL & NUMBER
09/05/1992	57	2	SHE'S GOT THAT VIBE	Jive JIVET 292
20/11/1993	75	1	SEX ME This and above single credited to **R KELLY AND PUBLIC ANNOUNCEMENT**	Jive JIVECD 346
04/07/1998	38	2	BODY BUMPIN' (YIPPIE-YI-YO)	A&M 5826972

PUBLIC DEMAND UK vocal group.

DATE	POS	WKS	SINGLE TITLE	LABEL & NUMBER
15/02/1997	41	2	INVISIBLE	ZTT ZANG 85CD

PUBLIC DOMAIN
UK dance group formed in Scotland by Mallorca Lee and David Forbes with James Allen and Alistair MacIsaac. Lee had previously been a member of Ultra-Sonic.

DATE	POS	WKS	BPI	SINGLE TITLE	LABEL & NUMBER
02/12/2000	5	13	O	**OPERATION BLADE (BASS IN THE PLACE)** Contains a sample of New Order's *Confusion*	Xtravaganza X2H1 CDS
23/06/2001	19	3		ROCK DA FUNKY BEATS **PUBLIC DOMAIN FEATURING CHUCK D**	Xtrahard X2H3 CDS
12/01/2002	34	2		TOO MANY MC'S/LET ME CLEAR MY THROAT	Xtrahard X2H 8CDS

PUBLIC ENEMY
US rap group formed in 1984 by Chuck D (born Carlton Douglas Ridenhour, 1/8/1960, Long Island, NY), Hank Shocklee and Flavour Flav (born William Drayton, 16/3/1959 Long Island), later adding Professor Griff, Minister of Information (born Richard Griffin) and DJ Terminator X (born Norman Rogers, 25/8/1966, New York). They signed to Def Jam in 1986 and released their first album in 1987. Griff was sacked from the group in 1989 for allegedly making anti-Semitic remarks in a newspaper interview. The group took their name from the 1930s' FBI phrase 'Public Enemy Number One.'

DATE	POS	WKS	SINGLE TITLE	LABEL & NUMBER
21/11/1987	37	7	REBEL WITHOUT A PAUSE Contains a sample of The JB's *The Grunt*	Def Jam 6512457
09/01/1988	32	5	BRING THE NOISE Featured in the 1987 film *Less Than Zero*	Def Jam 6513357
02/07/1988	18	5	DON'T BELIEVE THE HYPE	Def Jam 6528337
15/10/1988	63	2	NIGHT OF THE LIVING BASEHEADS	Def Jam 6530460
24/06/1989	29	5	FIGHT THE POWER Featured in the 1989 film *Do The Right Thing*	Motown ZB 42877
20/01/1990	18	4	WELCOME TO THE TERRORDOME	Def Jam 6554760
07/04/1990	41	3	911 IS A JOKE Contains a sample of Lyn Collins' *Think About It* and is an attack on the emergency service response time in ghetto areas	Def Jam 6558377
23/06/1990	46	2	BROTHERS GONNA WORK IT OUT	Def Jam 6560181
03/11/1990	53	2	CAN'T DO NUTTIN' FOR YA MAN	Def Jam 6563857
12/10/1991	22	4	CAN'T TRUSS IT Contains samples of James Brown's *Get Up Get Into It Get Involved,* George Clinton's *Atomic Dog,* Slave's *Slide* and Sly & The Family Stone's *Sing A Simple Song*	Def Jam 6575307
25/01/1992	21	3	SHUT 'EM DOWN	Def Jam 6577617
11/04/1992	55	2	NIGHTTRAIN	Def Jam 6578647
13/08/1994	18	3	GIVE IT UP Contains a sample of Albert King, Steve Cropper and Pop Staples' *Opus De Soul*	Def Jam DEFCD1
29/07/1995	50	1	SO WATCHA GONNA DO NOW	Def Jam DEFCD5
06/06/1998	16	4	HE GOT GAME **PUBLIC ENEMY FEATURING STEPHEN STILLS** Featured in the 1998 film *He Got Game*	Def Jam 5689852
25/09/1999	66	1	DO YOU WANNA GO OUR WAY???	PIAS Recordings PIASX 005CDX

PUBLIC IMAGE LTD
UK rock group formed in 1978 by John Lydon (born 31/1/1956, London) who had just finished touring with Sex Pistols under the name Johnny Rotten, Keith Levene (ex-Clash), Jah Wobble (born John Wardle) and Jim Walker. They signed with the same label as the Sex Pistols and often released their singles as P.I.L.

DATE	POS	WKS	SINGLE TITLE	LABEL & NUMBER
21/10/1978	9	8	**PUBLIC IMAGE**	Virgin VS 228
07/07/1979	20	7	DEATH DISCO (PARTS 1 & 2)	Virgin VS 274
20/10/1979	60	2	MEMORIES	Virgin VS 299
04/04/1981	24	7	FLOWERS OF ROMANCE	Virgin VS 397
17/09/1983	5	10	**THIS IS NOT A LOVE SONG**	Virgin VS 529
19/05/1984	71	2	BAD LIFE	Virgin VS 675
01/02/1986	11	8	RISE	Virgin VS 841
03/05/1986	75	1	HOME	Virgin VS 855
22/08/1987	47	4	SEATTLE	Virgin VS 988
06/05/1989	38	5	DISAPPOINTED	Virgin VS 1181
20/10/1990	22	5	DON'T ASK ME	Virgin VS 1231
22/02/1992	49	2	CRUEL	Virgin VS 1390

GARY PUCKETT – see UNION GAP FEATURING GARY PUCKETT

PUDDLE OF MUDD
US rock group formed by Wesley Scantlin (guitar/vocals), Paul Phillips (guitar/vocals), Douglas Ardito (bass/vocals) and Greg Upchurch (drums/vocals).

DATE	POS	WKS	SINGLE TITLE	LABEL & NUMBER
23/02/2002	15	5	CONTROL	Geffen 4976822
15/06/2002	8	9	**BLURRY**	Geffen 4977352
28/09/2002	14	7	SHE HATES ME	Geffen 4978052
13/12/2003	55	1	AWAY FROM ME	Geffen 9814810

TITO PUENTE JR AND THE LATIN RHYTHM FEATURING TITO PUENTE, INDIA AND CALI ALEMAN
American Tito Puente (born Ernesto Antonio Puente Jr, 20/4/1923, New York) has been one of the leading Latin music players of the last four decades. His son is following in his footsteps. Tito Puente Jr has won five Grammy Awards: Best Latin Recording in 1978 for *Homenaje A Beny More,* Best Tropical Latin Performance in 1983 for *On Broadway,* Best Tropical Latin Performance in 1985 for *Mambo Diablo,* Best Tropical Latin Performance in 1990 for *Lambada Timbales* and Best Traditional Latin

○ Silver disc ● Gold disc ✪ Platinum disc (additional platinum units are indicated by a figure following the symbol) ◎ Singles released prior to 1973 that are known to have sold over 1 million copies in the UK

Performance in 1999 for *Mambo Birdland*. He also 'appeared' in an episode of *The Simpsons*, becoming a music teacher at Springfield school. Tito Puente Jr died from heart trouble on 1/6/2000. He has a star on the Hollywood Walk of Fame. His son then won the 2000 Grammy Award for Best Salsa Album with Eddie Palmieri for *Masterpiece*.

16/03/1996	36	2		OYE COMO VA	Media MCSTD 40013
19/07/1997	56	1		OYE COMO VA (REMIX)	Nukleuz MCSTD 40120

PUFF DADDY

US rapper/record company boss/producer (born Sean Combs, 4/11/1970, New York) who launched the Bad Boy and Puff Daddy labels. He produced The Notorious B.I.G. and Mariah Carey. In September 1999 he was arrested after beating up a record company representative following an argument over a promotional video. In December 1999 he was arrested and charged with illegal possession of a firearm after a nightclub shooting left three people injured. He later amended his name to P Diddy. He has won three Grammy Awards including Best Rap Album in 1997 with The Family for *No Way Out*. He has also won three MOBO Awards: Best Producer in 1997 and Best International Act and Outstanding Achievement in 1998. Hurricane G is a female rapper called Gloria from Puerto Rico. Mario Winans (born Detroit) is a brother to but not a member of the family group The Winans. The Neptunes are US producers and songwriters Pharrell Williams and Chad Hugo, who also record as N*E*R*D. Black Rob (born Robert Ross) and Mark Curry are both US rappers.

29/03/1997	19	4		CAN'T NOBODY HOLD ME DOWN ▲⁶ **PUFF DADDY FEATURING MA$E** Contains samples of Grandmaster Flash's *The Message* and Matthew Wilder's *Break My Stride*	Puff Daddy 74321464552
26/04/1997	45	1		NO TIME **LIL' KIM FEATURING PUFF DADDY** Contains a sample of Lyn Collins' *Take Me Just As I Am*	Atlantic A 5594CD
28/06/1997	❶⁶	21	✪²	I'LL BE MISSING YOU ↑ ▲¹¹ **PUFF DADDY AND FAITH EVANS AND 112** Contains a sample of The Police's *Every Breath You Take*, is a tribute to The Notorious B.I.G. and entered the chart at #1. It was the first record to enter both the US and UK charts at pole position. Reclaimed #1 position on 24/7/1997. 1997 Grammy Award for Best Rap Performance by a Group	Puff Daddy 74321499102
09/08/1997	6	10		MO MONEY MO PROBLEMS ▲² **THE NOTORIOUS B.I.G. FEATURING PUFF DADDY AND MA$E** Contains a sample of Diana Ross' *I'm Coming Out*	Puff Daddy 74321492492
13/09/1997	34	2		SOMEONE **SWV FEATURING PUFF DADDY** Contains samples of The Notorious B.I.G.'s *Ten Crack Commandments* and The Notorious B.I.G.'s *The World Is Filled*	RCA 74321513942
01/11/1997	20	6		BEEN AROUND THE WORLD Contains a sample of David Bowie's *Let's Dance*	Puff Daddy 74321539442
07/02/1998	18	3		IT'S ALL ABOUT THE BENJAMINS This and above single credited to **PUFF DADDY AND THE FAMILY** Contains a sample of The Love Unlimited Orchestra's *I Did It For Love*	Puff Daddy 74321561972
01/08/1998	75	1		COME WITH ME (IMPORT)	Epic 34K78954
08/08/1998	2	10		**COME WITH ME PUFF DADDY FEATURING JIMMY PAGE** Featured in the 1998 film *Godzilla*	Epic 6662842
01/05/1999	23	3		ALL NIGHT LONG **FAITH EVANS FEATURING PUFF DADDY** Contains a sample of Unlimited Touch's *I Hear Music In The Streets*	Puff Daddy 74321625592
29/05/1999	14	6		HATE ME NOW **NAS FEATURING PUFF DADDY** Based on the classical piece *The First Movement from Carmina Burana – O Fortuna!* Puff Daddy was unhappy with the accompanying video, which depicted him being crucified on a cross and was later arrested and charged with second-degree assault and criminal mischief after he attacked a Columbia employee	Columbia 6672565
21/08/1999	13	4		PE 2000 **PUFF DADDY FEATURING HURRICANE G** Contains a sample of Public Enemy's *Public Enemy No.1*	Puff Daddy 74321694982
20/11/1999	24	4		BEST FRIEND **PUFF DADDY FEATURING MARIO WINANS** Contains a sample of Christopher Cross' *Sailing*	Puff Daddy 74321712312
05/02/2000	16	5		NOTORIOUS B.I.G. **NOTORIOUS B.I.G. FEATURING PUFF DADDY AND LIL' KIM** Contains a sample of Duran Duran's *Notorious*	Puff Daddy 74321737312
19/02/2000	73	2		SATISFY YOU (IMPORT)	Bad Boy/Arista 792832
11/03/2000	8	8		**SATISFY YOU PUFF DADDY FEATURING R KELLY** Contains a sample of Club Nouveau's *Why You Treat Me So Bad*	Puff Daddy 74321745592
06/10/2001	13	6		BAD BOY FOR LIFE **P DIDDY/BLACK ROB/MARK CURRY** Featured in the 2003 film *The Fighting Temptations*	Arista 74321889982
26/01/2002	19	4		DIDDY **P DIDDY FEATURING THE NEPTUNES**	Puff Daddy 74321911652
08/06/2002	16	7		PASS THE COURVOISIER – PART II **BUSTA RHYMES, P DIDDY AND PHARRELL**	J Records 74321937902
10/08/2002	4	11		I NEED A GIRL (PART ONE) **P DIDDY FEATURING USHER AND LOON**	Puff Daddy 74321947242
29/03/2003	11	8		BUMP BUMP BUMP ▲¹ **B2K FEATURING P DIDDY**	Epic 6736452
23/08/2003	25	3		LET'S GET ILL **P DIDDY FEATURING KELIS**	Bad Boy MCSTD 40331
20/09/2003	10	7		SHAKE YA TAILFEATHER ▲⁴ **NELLY, P DIDDY AND MURPHY LEE** 2003 Grammy Award for Best Rap Performance by a Duo or Group	Bad Boy MCSTD 40337
07/02/2004	35	2		SHOW ME YOUR SOUL **P DIDDY, LENNY KRAVITZ, PHARRELL WILLIAMS AND LOON** This and above single featured in the 2003 film *Bad Boys II*	Puff Daddy MCSTD 40350
15/05/2004	71	1		PASS THE COURVOISIER – PART II **BUSTA RHYMES, P DIDDY AND PHARRELL**	J Records 74321937902
05/06/2004	71	1		I DON'T WANNA KNOW (IMPORT) Contains a sample of Enya's *Boadicea*	Universal 9862372PMI
12/06/2004	❶²	14	○	**I DON'T WANNA KNOW** ↑ Above two singles credited to **MARIO WINANS FEATURING ENYA AND P DIDDY**	Bad Boy MCSTD 40369

PULP

UK rock group formed in 1981 by Jarvis Cocker (born 19/9/1963, Sheffield, guitar/vocals), Peter Dalton (keyboards), Jamie Pinchbeck (bass) and Wayne Furniss (drums). The line-up by 1992 consisted of Cocker, Russell Senior (born 18/5/1961, Sheffield, guitar), Candida Doyle (born 25/8/1963, Belfast, keyboards), Stephen Mackay (born 10/11/1966, Sheffield, bass) and Nicholas Banks (born 28/7/1965, Rotherham, drums). Senior left in 1995, replaced by Mark Webber (born 14/9/1970).

27/11/1993	50	2		LIP GLOSS	Island CID 567
02/04/1994	33	4		DO YOU REMEMBER THE FIRST TIME	Island CID 574
04/06/1994	19	4		THE SISTERS EP Tracks on EP: *Babies, Your Sister's Clothes, Seconds* and *His 'N' Hers*	Island CID 595
03/06/1995	2	13	○	**COMMON PEOPLE**	Island CID 613
07/10/1995	2	11	○	**MIS-SHAPES/SORTED FOR ES & WIZZ**	Island CIDX 620
09/12/1995	7	11	○	**DISCO 2000**	Island CID 623
06/04/1996	10	7		**SOMETHING CHANGED**	Island CID 632

❶⁹ Number of weeks single topped the UK chart ↑ Entered the UK chart at #1 ▲⁹ Number of weeks single topped the US chart

639

DATE	POS	WKS	BPI	SINGLE TITLE	LABEL & NUMBER
07/09/1996	73	1		DO YOU REMEMBER THE FIRST TIME	Island CID 574
22/11/1997	8	9		**HELP THE AGED**	Island CID 679
28/03/1998	12	4		THIS IS HARDCORE Contains a sample of The Peter Thomas Sound Orchester's *Bolero On The Moon Rocks*	Island CID 695
20/06/1998	22	2		A LITTLE SOUL	Island CID 708
19/09/1998	29	2		PARTY HARD	Island CID 719
20/10/2001	23	2		THE TREES/SUNRISE	Island CID 786
27/04/2002	27	2		BAD COVER VERSION	Island CIDX 794

PULSE FEATURING ANTOINETTE ROBERTSON US vocal/instrumental duo David Morales and Antoinette Robertson. Morales also recorded under his own name.

DATE	POS	WKS	BPI	SINGLE TITLE	LABEL & NUMBER
25/05/1996	22	3		THE LOVER THAT YOU ARE	ffrr FCD 278

PUNK CHIC Swedish producer Johan Strandkvist.

DATE	POS	WKS	BPI	SINGLE TITLE	LABEL & NUMBER
06/10/2001	69	1		DJ SPINNIN'	WEA 333CD

PUNX German DJ Andre Tegeler who also records as Dial M For Moguai and Moguai.

DATE	POS	WKS	BPI	SINGLE TITLE	LABEL & NUMBER
16/11/2002	59	1		THE ROCK	Data 38CDS

PURE REASON REVOLUTION UK rock group formed in Reading by Jon Courtney (guiter/vocals), Greg Jong (guitar/vocals), James Dodson (keyboards/vocals), Chloe Alper (bass/vocals) and Andrew Courtney (drums).

DATE	POS	WKS	BPI	SINGLE TITLE	LABEL & NUMBER
01/05/2004	74	1		APPRENTICE OF THE UNIVERSE	Poptones MC5089SCD

PURE SUGAR US dance group formed in Los Angeles, CA by Jennifer Starr (vocals), Peter Lorimer and Richard 'Humpty' Vission.

DATE	POS	WKS	BPI	SINGLE TITLE	LABEL & NUMBER
24/10/1998	70	1		DELICIOUS Contains a sample of A Taste Of Honey's *Boogie Oogie Oogie*	Geffen GFSTD 22355

PURESSENCE UK group formed in Manchester by James Murdriezki (vocals), Tony Szuminski (drums), Neil McDonald (guitar) and Kevin Matthews (bass).

DATE	POS	WKS	BPI	SINGLE TITLE	LABEL & NUMBER
23/05/1998	33	2		THIS FEELING	Island CID 688
08/08/1998	47	1		IT DOESN'T MATTER ANYMORE	Island CID 703
21/11/1998	39	2		ALL I WANT	Island CID 722
05/10/2002	40	1		WALKING DEAD	Island CIDX 803

PURETONE Australian producer Josh Abrahams whose debut hit originally charted a week before its official release date at #68 owing to a number of stores selling early. Its rise to #2 was the biggest rise in the charts since Steps rose from #70 to #2. Had copies not been sold a week early, it would have hit the #1 spot.

DATE	POS	WKS	BPI	SINGLE TITLE	LABEL & NUMBER
12/01/2002	2	15		**ADDICTED TO BASS**	Gut GDGUS 6
10/05/2003	26	2		STUCK IN A GROOVE	Illustrious CDILL 014

JAMES AND BOBBY PURIFY US R&B duo formed by cousins James Purify (born 12/5/1944, Pensacola, FL) and Robert Lee Dickey (born 2/9/1939, Tallahassee, FL), who first teamed up in 1965. Dickey retired in the late 1960s and James Purify worked as a solo artist until 1974 when he was joined by Ben Moore.

DATE	POS	WKS	BPI	SINGLE TITLE	LABEL & NUMBER
24/04/1976	12	10		I'M YOUR PUPPET Originally a US hit in 1966 (position #6) when recorded by James and Robert. This version was recorded by James and Ben	Mercury 6167 324
07/08/1976	27	6		MORNING GLORY	Mercury 6167 380

PURPLE HEARTS UK group formed in Romford by Robert Manton (vocals), Simon Stebbing (guitar), Jeff Shadbolt (bass) and Gary Sparks (drums).

DATE	POS	WKS	BPI	SINGLE TITLE	LABEL & NUMBER
22/09/1979	57	3		MILLIONS LIKE US	Fiction FICS 003
08/03/1980	60	2		JIMMY	Fiction FICS 9

PURPLE KINGS UK vocal/instrumental duo Rob Tillen and Dodo, with singer Glen Williamson.

DATE	POS	WKS	BPI	SINGLE TITLE	LABEL & NUMBER
15/10/1994	26	3		THAT'S THE WAY YOU DO IT Contains an interpolation of Dire Straits' *Money For Nothing*	Positiva CDTIV 21

PUSH Belgian producer Dirk 'M.I.K.E.' Dierickx (born 20/2/1973) recording under an assumed name.

DATE	POS	WKS	BPI	SINGLE TITLE	LABEL & NUMBER
15/05/1999	36	2		UNIVERSAL NATION	Inferno CDFERN 16
09/10/1999	35	2		UNIVERSAL NATION (REMIX)	Inferno CDFERN 20
23/09/2000	46	1		TILL WE MEET AGAIN	Inferno CDFERN 29
12/05/2001	21	4		STRANGE WORLD	Inferno CDFERN 38
20/10/2001	36	2		PLEASE SAVE ME SUNSCREEM VS PUSH	Five AM/Inferno FAMFERN 1CD
03/11/2001	22	4		THE LEGACY	Inferno CDFERN 43
04/05/2002	31	2		TRANZY STATE OF MIND	Inferno CDFERN 45
05/10/2002	55	1		STRANGE WORLD/THE LEGACY	Inferno CDFERN 49
15/03/2003	54	1		UNIVERSAL NATION	Inferno CDFERN 53

PUSSY 2000 UK production duo Sterling Void and Paris Robinson.

DATE	POS	WKS	BPI	SINGLE TITLE	LABEL & NUMBER
03/11/2001	70	1		IT'S GONNA BE ALRIGHT	Ink NIBNE 9CD

PUSSYCAT Dutch pop group formed by Lou Wille, his wife Tony, Marianne Hensen, Betty Dragstra (Hensen and Dragstra were Tony Wille's sisters), Theo Wetzels, Theo Coumans and John Theunissen.

○ Silver disc ● Gold disc ✪ Platinum disc (additional platinum units are indicated by a figure following the symbol) ◎ Singles released prior to 1973 that are known to have sold over 1 million copies in the UK

28/08/1976 .... ❶⁴ ..... 22 ..... ●				MISSISSIPPI	Sonet SON 2077
25/12/1976 ..... 24 ...... 8				SMILE	Sonet SON 2096

PYRAMIDS Jamaican ska and rock steady group formed by Josh Roberts, Ray Knight, Roy Barrington, Monty Naismith, Ray Ellis, Mick Thomas and Frank Pitter. Their one hit was written and produced by Eddy Grant of the Equals. Ellis, Naismith and Thomas were later members of Symarip.

22/11/1967 ..... 35 ...... 4				TRAIN TOUR TO RAINBOW CITY	President PT 161

PYTHON LEE JACKSON Australian studio group formed by David Bentley (keyboards), Mike Liber (guitar), Gary Boyle (guitar), Tony Cahill (bass) and David Montgomery (drums) for which Rod Stewart provided the guide vocals on a demo in 1970, and was paid a fee sufficient to buy seat covers for his car! The single was released two years later with Stewart's vocals still in place although he received no credit.

30/09/1972 ..... 3 ...... 12				IN A BROKEN DREAM Features the uncredited vocals of Rod Stewart....................................	Young Blood YB 1002

❶⁹ Number of weeks single topped the UK chart ↑ Entered the UK chart at #1 ▲⁹ Number of weeks single topped the US chart

641

Q UK instrumental/production duo Mark Taylor and Tracy Ackerman. Tracy Ackerman later became a successful songwriter, with hits for Dana Dawson, Geri Halliwell and B*Witched among others.

05/06/1993	37	4	GET HERE **Q FEATURING TRACY ACKERMAN** .... Arista 74321145972
12/03/1994	47	2	(EVERYTHING I DO) I DO IT FOR YOU **Q FEATURING TONY JACKSON** .... Bell 74321193062

Q UNIQUE – see **C & C MUSIC FACTORY**

QATTARA UK production duo Andy Cato and Alex Whitcombe who were joined by singer Sarah Dwyer. Cato was later in Groove Armada, and Whitcombe recorded under his own name.

15/03/1997	31	2	COME WITH ME .... Positiva CDTIV 71

QB FINEST FEATURING NAS AND BRAVEHEARTS US rap group formed by Nas (born Nasir Jones, 1974, Long Island, NY) with Capone, Mobb Deep, Tragedy, MC Shan, Marley Marl, Nature, Cormega and Millennium Thug.

21/04/2001	30	3	OOCHIE WALLY .... Columbia 6710852

Q-BASS UK instrumental/production group formed by Dan Donnelly.

08/02/1992	64	1	HARDCORE WILL NEVER DIE .... Suburban Base SUBBASE 007

Q-CLUB Italian vocal/instrumental group formed by Corrado Vacondio, Mauro Gazzotti and Gianluca Lul.

06/01/1996	28	3	TELL IT TO MY HEART .... Manifesto FESCD 5

QFX UK producer Kirk Turnbull.

06/05/1995	41	3	FREEDOM (EP) Tracks on EP: *Freedom, Metropolis, Sianora Baby* and *The Machine*. .... Epidemic EPICD 004
03/02/1996	22	4	EVERYTIME YOU TOUCH ME .... Epidemic EPICD 006
03/08/1996	33	3	YOU GOT THE POWER. .... Epidemic EPICD 007
18/01/1997	21	4	FREEDOM 2 (REMIX). .... Epidemic EPICD 008
20/03/1999	34	2	SAY YOU'LL BE MINE .... Quality Recordings QUAL 005CD
23/08/2003	36	2	FREEDOM .... Data 57CDS

Q-TEE UK rapper (born Tatiana Mais, 1975).

21/04/1990	42	5	AFRIKA **HISTORY FEATURING Q-TEE** .... SBK 7008
10/02/1996	40	2	GIMME THAT BODY .... Heavenly HVN 48CD

Q-TEX UK vocal/instrumental group with Scott Brown, Gordon Anderson and Alan Todd, later joined by Gillian Tennant.

09/04/1994	65	1	THE POWER OF LOVE .... Stoatin' VSCDG 1666
26/11/1994	41	2	BELIEVE .... 23rd Precinct THIRD 2CD
15/06/1996	30	2	LET THE LOVE .... 23rd Precinct THIRD 4CD
30/11/1996	48	1	DO YOU WANT ME. .... 23rd Precinct THIRD 5CD
28/06/1997	49	1	POWER OF LOVE '97 (REMIX). .... 23rd Precinct THIRD 7CD

Q-TIP US rapper (born Jonathan Davis, 10/4/1970, Brooklyn, NYC), also a member of A Tribe Called Quest. He and Raphael Saadiq also write and produce for other acts, including Whitney Houston.

04/10/1997	6	9	○	**GOT 'TIL IT'S GONE** JANET **FEATURING Q-TIP AND JONI MITCHELL** Contains a sample of Joni Mitchell's *Big Yellow Taxi* .... Virgin VSCDG 1666
19/06/1999	36	2		GET INVOLVED **RAPHAEL SAADIQ AND Q-TIP** .... Hollywood 0101185 HWR
22/01/2000	18	3		HOT BOYZ **MISSY 'MISDEMEANOR' ELLIOTT FEATURING NAS, EVE & Q-TIP** .... Elektra E 7002CD
12/02/2000	12	7		BREATHE AND STOP Contains a sample of Kool & The Gang's *N.T.* .... Arista 74321727062
06/05/2000	39	2		VIVRANT THING Contains a sample of Barry White's *I Wanna Stay*. .... Arista 74321751302

QPR MASSIVE – see **SOOPA HOOPZ FEATURING QPR MASSIVE**

QUAD CITY DJS US dance group formed in Orlando, FL by Lana LeFleur, Johnny 'Jay Ski' McGowan and Nathaniel Orange.

15/11/1997	57	1	SPACE JAM Featured in the 1997 film *Space Jam* .... Atlantic EW 773

QUADROPHONIA Belgian instrumental/production group featuring Oliver Abbelous and Lucien 'RIV-Master' Foort.

13/04/1991	14	9	QUADROPHONIA. .... ARS 6567687
06/07/1991	40	3	THE WAVE OF THE FUTURE. .... ARS 6569937

○ Silver disc ● Gold disc ✪ Platinum disc (additional platinum units are indicated by a figure following the symbol) ◎ Singles released prior to 1973 that are known to have sold over 1 million copies in the UK

| 21/12/1991 | 41 | 3 | | FIND THE TIME (PART ONE) | ARS 6576260 |

QUADS UK vocal/instrumental group formed by Josh Jones, Johnny Jones, Jack Jones and James Doherty.

| 22/09/1979 | 66 | 2 | | THERE MUST BE THOUSANDS | Big Bear BB 23 |

QUAKE FEATURING MARCIA RAE UK producer Ian Bland and Rob Tissera with singer Marcia Rae. Bland and Tissera later recorded as Native.

| 29/08/1998 | 53 | 1 | | THE DAY WILL COME | ffrr FCD 344 |

QUANTUM JUMP UK group formed by Rupert Hine (keyboards/vocals), John Parry (bass), Mark Warner (guitar/vocals) and Trevor Morais (drums).

| 02/06/1979 | 5 | 10 | O | THE LONE RANGER | Electric WOT 33 |

QUARTERFLASH US group formed by Cindy Ross (vocals/saxophone), husband Marv Ross (guitar), Jack Charles (guitar), Rich Gooch (bass), Rick DiGiallonardo (keyboards) and Brian Willis (drums). They disbanded in 1985 and re-formed in 1990.

| 27/02/1982 | 49 | 5 | | HARDEN MY HEART | Geffen GEF A 1838 |

QUARTZ UK instrumental group formed in London by David Rawlings and Ronnie Herel.

17/03/1990	65	2		WE'RE COMIN' AT YA QUARTZ FEATURING STEPZ	Mercury ITMR 2
02/03/1991	8	14		IT'S TOO LATE QUARTZ INTRODUCING DINA CARROLL	Mercury ITM 3
15/06/1991	39	3		NAKED LOVE (JUST SAY YOU WANT ME) QUARTZ AND DINA CARROLL	Mercury ITM 4

JACKIE QUARTZ French singer (born in Brittany).

| 11/03/1989 | 55 | 3 | | A LA VIE, A L'AMOUR | PWL 30 |

QUARTZ LOCK FEATURING LONNIE GORDON UK production duo formed by Marc Andrews and Donald Lynch with US singer Lonnie Gordon. She had previously recorded with Stock Aitken and Waterman and launched a solo career.

| 07/10/1995 | 32 | 2 | | LOVE EVICTION | X-Plode BANG 2CD |

SUZI QUATRO US singer/bass player (born Susan Kay Quatrocchio, 3/6/1950, Detroit, MI) who left school in 1964 and formed the Pleasure Seekers with her sisters, and later progressive rock act Cradle. In 1970 she relocated to London and signed with Mickie Most at RAK. She signed with Dreamland (the label set up by her hit writers Nicky Chinn and Mike Chapman) in 1980, but re-signed with RAK in 1983. Quatro also made her name as an actress, appearing as Leather Tuscadero in the TV series *Happy Days*.

19/05/1973	❶¹	14	O	CAN THE CAN	RAK 150
28/07/1973	3	9		48 CRASH	RAK 158
27/10/1973	14	13		DAYTONA DEMON	RAK 161
09/02/1974	❶²	11	●	DEVIL GATE DRIVE	RAK 167
29/06/1974	14	6		TOO BIG	RAK 175
09/11/1974	7	10		THE WILD ONE	RAK 185
08/02/1975	31	5		YOUR MAMA WON'T LIKE ME	RAK 191
05/03/1977	27	6		TEAR ME APART	RAK 248
18/03/1978	4	13	O	IF YOU CAN'T GIVE ME LOVE	RAK 271
22/07/1978	43	5		THE RACE IS ON	RAK 278
11/11/1978	41	8		STUMBLIN' IN SUZI QUATRO AND CHRIS NORMAN	RAK 285
20/10/1979	11	9		SHE'S IN LOVE WITH YOU	RAK 299
19/01/1980	34	5		MAMA'S BOY	RAK 303
05/04/1980	56	3		I'VE NEVER BEEN IN LOVE	RAK 307
25/10/1980	68	2		ROCK HARD Featured in the 1980 film *Times Square*	Dreamland DLSP 6
13/11/1982	60	3		HEART OF STONE	Polydor POSP 477

FINLEY QUAYE UK singer (born 25/3/1974, Edinburgh) of Ghanaian ancestry and from a musical background: he is Tricky's uncle and his father is a jazz composer. He was named Best Reggae Act at the 1997 MOBO Awards and Best British Male Artist at the 1998 BRIT Awards.

21/06/1997	16	6		SUNDAY SHINING	Epic 6644552
13/09/1997	10	5		EVEN AFTER ALL	Epic 6649712
29/11/1997	29	3		IT'S GREAT WHEN WE'RE TOGETHER	Epic 6653382
07/03/1998	16	5		YOUR LOVE GETS SWEETER	Epic 6656065
15/08/1998	51	1		ULTRA STIMULATION	Epic 6660792
23/09/2000	26	3		SPIRITUALIZED	Epic 6698032

❶⁹ Number of weeks single topped the UK chart ↑ Entered the UK chart at #1 ▲⁹ Number of weeks single topped the US chart

QUEEN UK group formed in London in 1970 by Brian May (born 19/7/1947, London, guitar), Roger Taylor (born Roger Meddows-Taylor, 26/1/1949, King's Lynn, Norfolk, drums), John Deacon (born 19/8/1951, Leicester, bass) and Freddie Mercury (born Farookh Bulsura, 5/9/1946, Zanzibar, Tanzania, vocals). They played their first date in 1971, signed with EMI in 1972 and were subsequently managed by Elton John's manager John Reid. All members undertook outside projects: Mercury recorded solo from 1985; Taylor produced actor Jimmy Nail; May formed the Immortals and he and Deacon worked with Elton John. Queen were the biggest hit at Live Aid in 1985. Mercury died from AIDS on 24/11/1991. The group were honoured with the Outstanding Contribution Award at the 1990 BRIT Awards and Mercury was posthumously given a further Outstanding Contribution Award in 1992 (he and John Lennon being the only artists to have received it twice). *Bohemian Rhapsody* is one of only five singles to have sold more than 2 million copies in the UK. Inducted into the Rock & Roll Hall of Fame in 2001, Queen have a star on the Hollywood Walk of Fame. They were inducted into the UK Music Hall of Fame in 2004, one of its first inductees. Vanguard are German producers Asem Shama and Axel Bartsch.

DATE	POS	WKS	BPI	SINGLE TITLE	LABEL & NUMBER
09/03/1974	10	10		**SEVEN SEAS OF RHYE**	EMI 2121
26/10/1974	2	12	O	**KILLER QUEEN**	EMI 2229
25/01/1975	11	7		NOW I'M HERE	EMI 2256
08/11/1975	❶⁹	17	✪	**BOHEMIAN RHAPSODY** 1977 BRIT Award for Best Single, won jointly with Procol Harum's *Whiter Shade Of Pale*	EMI 2375
03/07/1976	7	8		**YOU'RE MY BEST FRIEND** Featured in the 2004 film *Shaun Of The Dead*	EMI 2494
27/11/1976	2	9		**SOMEBODY TO LOVE**	EMI 2565
19/03/1977	31	4		TIE YOUR MOTHER DOWN	EMI 2593
04/06/1977	17	10		QUEEN'S FIRST EP Tracks on EP: *Good Old Fashioned Lover Boy, Death On Two Legs (Dedicated To…), Tenement Funster* and *White Queen (As It Began)*	EMI 2623
22/10/1977	2	12	●	**WE ARE THE CHAMPIONS** Although not listed, the B-side *We Will Rock You* contributed to the success of the single. Both sides were featured in the 1994 film *D2: The Mighty Ducks. We Will Rock You* was featured in the films *F.M.* (1978), *The Replacements* (2000) and *A Knight's Tale* (2001)	EMI 2708
25/02/1978	34	4		SPREAD YOUR WINGS	EMI 2757
28/10/1978	11	12	O	BICYCLE RACE/FAT BOTTOMED GIRLS	EMI 2870
10/02/1979	9	12	O	**DON'T STOP ME NOW** Featured in the 2004 film *Shaun Of The Dead*	EMI 2910
14/07/1979	63	2		LOVE OF MY LIFE	EMI 2959
20/10/1979	2	14	●	**CRAZY LITTLE THING CALLED LOVE** ▲⁴ Featured in the 1993 film *Son In Law*	EMI 5001
02/02/1980	11	6		SAVE ME	EMI 5022
14/06/1980	14	8		PLAY THE GAME	EMI 5076
06/09/1980	7	9		**ANOTHER ONE BITES THE DUST** ▲⁴ Featured in the 1998 film *Small Soldiers*	EMI 5102
06/12/1980	10	13	O	**FLASH** Featured in the 1981 film *Flash Gordon*	EMI 5126
14/11/1981	❶²	11	O	**UNDER PRESSURE** QUEEN AND DAVID BOWIE Featured in the 1997 film *Grosse Pointe Blank*	EMI 5250
01/05/1982	25	6		BODY LANGUAGE	EMI 5293
12/06/1982	17	8		LAS PALABRAS DE AMOR	EMI 5316
21/08/1982	40	4		BACKCHAT	EMI 5325
04/02/1984	2	9	O	**RADIO GA GA**	EMI QUEEN 1
14/04/1984	3	15	O	**I WANT TO BREAK FREE**	EMI QUEEN 2
28/07/1984	6	9		**IT'S A HARD LIFE**	EMI QUEEN 3
22/09/1984	13	7		HAMMER TO FALL	EMI QUEEN 4
08/12/1984	21	6		THANK GOD IT'S CHRISTMAS	EMI QUEEN 5
16/11/1985	7	10		**ONE VISION** Featured in the 1985 film *Iron Eagle*	EMI QUEEN 6
29/03/1986	3	11		**A KIND OF MAGIC**	EMI QUEEN 7
21/06/1986	14	8		FRIENDS WILL BE FRIENDS This and above single featured in the 1986 film *Highlander*	EMI QUEEN 8
27/09/1986	24	5		WHO WANTS TO LIVE FOREVER	EMI QUEEN 9
13/05/1989	3	7	O	**I WANT IT ALL**	Parlophone QUEEN 10
01/07/1989	7	7		**BREAKTHRU'**	Parlophone QUEEN 11
19/08/1989	12	6		THE INVISIBLE MAN	Parlophone QUEEN 12
21/10/1989	25	4		SCANDAL	Parlophone QUEEN 14
09/12/1989	21	5		THE MIRACLE	Parlophone QUEEN 15
26/01/1991	❶¹	6	O	**INNUENDO** ↑	Parlophone QUEEN 16
16/03/1991	22	5		I'M GOING SLIGHTLY MAD	Parlophone QUEEN 17
25/05/1991	14	4		HEADLONG	Parlophone QUEEN 18
26/10/1991	16	10		THE SHOW MUST GO ON	Parlophone QUEEN 19
21/12/1991	❶⁵	14	✪	**BOHEMIAN RHAPSODY/THESE ARE THE DAYS OF OUR LIVES** ↑ 1992 BRIT Award for Best Single, the only record to have won it twice. It was also featured in the 1992 film *Wayne's World*. Total UK sales exceed 2.5 million copies	Parlophone QUEEN 20
01/05/1993	❶³	12	●	**FIVE LIVE EP** ↑ GEORGE MICHAEL AND QUEEN WITH LISA STANSFIELD Tracks on EP: *Somebody To Love, These Are The Days Of Our Lives, Calling You* and *Papa Was A Rolling Stone – Killer (Medley)*	Parlophone CDRS 6340
04/11/1995	2	12	O	**HEAVEN FOR EVERYONE**	Parlophone CDQUEEN 21
23/12/1995	6	6		**A WINTER'S TALE**	Parlophone CDQUEENS 22
09/03/1996	15	6		TOO MUCH LOVE WILL KILL YOU	Parlophone CDQUEENS 23
29/06/1996	9	4		**LET ME LIVE**	Parlophone CDQUEENS 24
30/11/1996	17	4		YOU DON'T FOOL ME – THE REMIXES	Parlophone CDQUEEN 25
17/01/1998	13	4		NO-ONE BUT YOU/TIE YOUR MOTHER DOWN	Parlophone CDQUEEN 27
14/11/1998	5	6		**ANOTHER ONE BITES THE DUST** QUEEN WITH WYCLEF JEAN FEATURING PRAS MICHEL/FREE Featured in the 1998 film *Small Soldiers*	DreamWorks DRMCD 22364
18/12/1999	14	7		UNDER PRESSURE (REMIX) QUEEN AND DAVID BOWIE	Parlophone CDQUEEN 28
29/07/2000	❶¹	13		**WE WILL ROCK YOU** ↑ FIVE AND QUEEN	RCA 74321774022
29/03/2003	15	4		FLASH QUEEN AND VANGUARD	Nebula NEBCD 041

O Silver disc ● Gold disc ✪ Platinum disc (additional platinum units are indicated by a figure following the symbol) ◉ Singles released prior to 1973 that are known to have sold over 1 million copies in the UK

QUEEN LATIFAH
US rapper (born Dana Owens, 18/3/1970, Newark, NJ) and a successful actress. Her films include *The Bone Collector* (1999) and *Chicago* (2002). Latifah is Arabic for 'delicate and sensitive'.

24/03/1990.....14......7.......				MAMA GAVE BIRTH TO THE SOUL CHILDREN QUEEN LATIFAH + DE LA SOUL..........................	Gee Street GEE 26
26/05/1990.....52......2......				FIND A WAY COLDCUT FEATURING QUEEN LATIFAH	Ahead Of Our Time CCUT 8
31/08/1991.....67......1......				FLY GIRL	Gee Street GEE 34
26/06/1993.....21......4......				WHAT'CHA GONNA DO SHABBA RANKS FEATURING QUEEN LATIFAH	Epic 6593072
26/03/1994.....74......1......				U.N.I.T.Y. 1994 Grammy Award for Best Rap Solo Performance. Contains a sample of The Crusaders' *Message From The Inner City*	Motown TMGCD 1422
12/04/1997.....31......2.......				MR BIG STUFF QUEEN LATIFAH, SHADES AND FREE	Motown 5736572

QUEEN PEN
US rapper (born Lynise Walters, Brooklyn, NYC) discovered by BLACKstreet singer and songwriter Teddy Riley, making her debut on the BLACKstreet hit *No Diggety*. She was the first artist to be signed to Riley's Lil 'Man record label.

07/03/1998.....38......2......				MAN BEHIND THE MUSIC Features the uncredited contribution of Teddy Riley	Interscope IND 95562
09/05/1998.....11......5......				ALL MY LOVE QUEEN PEN FEATURING ERIC WILLIAMS Contains a sample of Luther Vandross' *Never Too Much*	Interscope IND 95584
05/09/1998.....24......3.......				IT'S TRUE Contains a sample of Spandau Ballet's *True*.	Interscope IND 95597

QUEENS OF THE STONE AGE
US rock group formed by Josh Homme (guitar/vocals), Nick Oliveri, Dave Catching and Alfredo Hernandez (drums). By 2002 former Foo Fighters and Nirvana member Dave Grohl was drumming for the group.

26/08/2000.....31......2......				THE LOST ART OF KEEPING A SECRET	Interscope 4973922
16/11/2002.....15......7......				NO ONE KNOWS..	Interscope 4978122
19/04/2003.....21......3......				GO WITH THE FLOW	Interscope 4978702
30/08/2003.....33......2......				FIRST IT GIVETH..	Interscope 9810505

QUEENSRYCHE
US heavy metal group formed in 1981 by Geoff Tate (born 14/1/1959, Stuttgart, Germany, vocals), Chris DeGarmo (born 14/6/1963, Wenatchee, WA, guitar), Michael Wilton (born 23/2/1962, San Francisco, CA, guitar), Eddie Jackson (born 29/1/1961, Robstown, TX, bass) and Scott Rockenfield (born 15/6/1963, Seattle, WA, drums). All five had been classmates in Bellevue, WA.

13/05/1989.....59......1......				EYES OF A STRANGER	EMI USA MT 65
10/11/1990.....61......1......				EMPIRE	EMI USA MT 90
20/04/1991.....34......5......				SILENT LUCIDITY..	EMI USA MT 94
06/07/1991.....36......3......				BEST I CAN	EMI USA MT 97
07/09/1991.....39......2......				JET CITY WOMAN	EMI USA MT 98
08/08/1992.....18......4......				SILENT LUCIDITY Re-issue of EMI USA MT 94	EMI USA MT 104
28/01/1995.....40......2......				I AM I	EMI CDMT 109
25/03/1995.....40......3......				BRIDGE..	EMI CDMTS 111

QUENCH
Australian instrumental/production duo CJ Dolan and Sean Quinn.

17/02/1996.....75......1......				DREAMS..	Infectious INFECT 3CD

QUENTIN AND ASH
UK duo Caroline Quentin (born 11/6/1961) and Leslie Ash (born 19/2/1960), actresses in the TV comedy *Men Behaving Badly* playing Dorothy and Deborah, respectively. Quentin was married to comedian Paul Merton, while Ash is married to former Stoke City, Arsenal and Leeds United footballer Lee Chapman.

06/07/1996.....25......3.......				TELL HIM	East West EW 049CD

? (QUESTION MARK) AND THE MYSTERIANS
US rock group fronted by Rudy Martinez (born 1945, Mexico, raised in Michigan) and featuring Frankie Rodriguez (born 9/3/1951, Crystal Cty, TX, keyboards), Robert Lee 'Bobby' Balderrama (born 1950, Mexico, guitar), Francisco Hernandez 'Frank' Lugo (born 15/3/1947, Welasco, TX, bass) and Eduardo Delgardo 'Eddie' Serrato (born 1947, Mexico, drums). Their hit, a US #1, was originally the B-side before being flipped by DJs.

17/11/1966.....37......4.......				96 TEARS ▲[1] Originally written as *69 Tears* but changed because the group feared a radio ban. Featured in the 1979 film *More American Graffiti*	Cameo Parkway C 428

QUESTIONS
UK group formed by Paul Barry (bass/vocals), John Robinson (guitar), Stephen Lennon (guitar) and Frank Mooney (drums).

23/04/1983.....56......3......				PRICE YOU PAY	Respond KOB 702
17/09/1983.....66......1......				TEAR SOUP	Respond KOB 705
10/03/1984.....46......4.......				TUESDAY SUNSHINE...	Respond KOB 707

QUICK
UK duo Colin Campsie (vocals) and George McFarlane (guitar/bass/keyboards).

15/05/1982.....41......7.......				RHYTHM OF THE JUNGLE	Epic EPC A 2013

TOMMY QUICKLY
UK singer (born 1943, Liverpool) who was a member of his sister's group The Challengers before signing with Brian Epstein and joining a Beatles UK package tour. At the end of his recording career he developed a drug habit and later fell from a ladder, suffering severe brain damage.

22/10/1964.....33......8.......				WILD SIDE OF LIFE..	Pye 7N 15708

QUIET FIVE
UK group formed by Kris Ife (guitar/vocals), Roger McKew (guitar), Richard Barnes (bass/vocals), John Howell (keyboards), John Gaswell (saxophone) and Roger Marsh (drums).

13/05/1965.....45......1......				WHEN THE MORNING SUN DRIES THE DEW..................................	Parlophone R 5273

❶[9] Number of weeks single topped the UK chart ↑ Entered the UK chart at #1 ▲[9] Number of weeks single topped the US chart

645

| 21/04/1966.....44......2....... | HOMEWARD BOUND .... Parlophone R 5421 |

QUIET RIOT US heavy metal group formed in 1975 by Kevin DuBrow (vocals), Randy Rhoads (guitar), Kelly Garni (bass) and Drew Forsyth (drums). Their first two albums were available only in Japan, after which Garni left and was replaced by Rudy Sarzo. Rhoads left in 1979 to join Ozzy Osbourne (and was later killed in a plane crash) and Quiet Riot disbanded. The group later re-formed with DuBrow, Sarxo, Carlos Cavazo (guitar) and Frankie Banali (drums). DuBrow left in 1988 and was replaced by Paul Shortino. After one more album the group disbanded a second time.

03/12/1983.....45......5....... METAL HEALTH/CUM ON FEEL THE NOIZE .... Epic A 3968

ELMEAR QUINN Irish singer whose *The Voice* won the 1996 Eurovision Song Contest, beating the UK entry by Gina G into seventh place. Her hit was written by Brendan Graham, a Eurovision winner in 1994 with *Rock 'n' Roll Kids*.

15/06/1996.....40......2....... THE VOICE.. Polydor 5768842

PAUL QUINN AND EDWYN COLLINS UK instrumental/vocal duo. Edwyn Collins had previously been a member of Orange Juice.

11/08/1984.....72......2....... PALE BLUE EYES... Swamplands SWP 1

SINEAD QUINN Irish singer (born 1980, Irvinestown) who studied musical technology at Hull University and appeared on TV's *Fame Academy*, finishing second behind David Sneddon.

22/02/2003 .....2......12....... **I CAN'T BREAK DOWN**.. Mercury 0637282
12/07/2003.....19......3....... WHAT YOU NEED IS .... Fontana 9808972

QUIREBOYS UK heavy metal group formed in Newcastle-upon-Tyne in 1986 by Nigel Mogg (bass), Chris Johnstone (piano), Gus Bailey (guitar), Jonathon 'Spike' Grey (vocals) and Coze (drums). Originally known as the Queerboys, this name was quickly changed. They were joined by guitarist Ginger who later left to form the Wildhearts and who was replaced by Guy 'Griff' Griffin. The first two singles were on Survival before they switched to Parlophone.

04/11/1989.....36......4....... 7 O'CLOCK .... Parlophone R 6230
06/01/1990.....14......7....... HEY YOU .... Parlophone R 6241
07/04/1990.....24......6....... I DON'T LOVE YOU ANYMORE.. Parlophone R 6248
08/09/1990.....37......4....... THERE SHE GOES AGAIN/MISLED .... Parlophone R 6267
10/10/1992.....41......3....... TRAMPS AND THIEVES .... Parlophone R 6323
20/02/1993.....31......3....... BROTHER LOUIE .... Parlophone CDR 6335

QUIVER – see **SUTHERLAND BROTHERS**

QUIVVER UK instrumental/production duo John Graham and Neil Barry. Barry left after one single and Graham continued under the Quivver name as well as becoming a member of Tilt.

05/03/1994.....56......2....... SAXY LADY... A&M 5805152
18/11/1995.....56......1....... BELIEVE IN ME .... Perfecto PERF 111CD

QUO VADIS UK production trio formed by Andy Manston, Fionn Lucas and Julian Napolitano. Napolitano is also a member of JDS and Perpetual Motion.

16/12/2000.....49......1....... SONIC BOOM (LIFE'S TOO SHORT) .... Serious SERR 028CD

QWILO AND FELIX DA HOUSECAT US DJ with producer Felix Da Housecat (real name Felix Stallings Jr).
06/09/1997.....66......1....... DIRTY MOTHA .... Manifesto FESCD 29

○ Silver disc ● Gold disc ✪ Platinum disc (additional platinum units are indicated by a figure following the symbol) ◉ Singles released prior to 1973 that are known to have sold over 1 million copies in the UK

R

EDDIE RABBITT
US country singer/guitarist (born 27/11/1941, Brooklyn, NYC, raised in New Jersey) who died from cancer on 7/5/1998.

27/01/1979.....41......9......	EVERY WHICH WAY BUT LOOSE Featured in the 1978 film of the same name .... Elektra K 12331
28/02/1981.....53......5......	I LOVE A RAINY NIGHT ▲² .... Elektra K 12498

STEVE RACE
UK pianist/TV presenter (born 1921) who composed the music to the films *Brass Monkey* (1948) and *Plan 9 From Outer Space* (1959).

28/02/1963.....29......9......	PIED PIPER (THE BEEJE) .... Parlophone R 4981

RACEY
UK group formed in 1974 by Phil Fursdon (guitar/vocals), Richard Gower (vocals/keyboards), Pete Miller (vocals/bass) and Clive Wilson (vocals/drums).

25/11/1978 .....3......14.....●	LAY YOUR LOVE ON ME .... RAK 284
31/03/1979 .....2......11.....●	SOME GIRLS .... RAK 291
18/08/1979 .....22......9......	BOY OH BOY .... RAK 297
20/12/1980 .....13......10.....	RUNAROUND SUE .... RAK 325

RACING CARS
UK group formed in Manchester in 1975 by ex-Mindbenders Bob Lang (born 10/1/1946, bass) and comprising Graham Headley Williams (guitar), Gareth 'Monty' Mortimer (vocals), Roy Edwards (bass) and Robert Wilding (drums), with Geraint Watkins (piano), Jerry Jumonville (saxophone) and Ray Ennis (guitar) also appearing on the sessions for their debut album.

12/02/1977.....14......7.......	THEY SHOOT HORSES DON'T THEY .... Chrysalis CHS 2129

RACKETEERS – see ELBOW BONES AND THE RACKETEERS

JIMMY RADCLIFFE
US singer (born 18/11/1936, New York City) who was first signed by Musicor Records in 1959, but didn't release anything until 1962. He died on 27/7/1973.

04/02/1965.....40......2......	LONG AFTER TONIGHT IS ALL OVER .... Stateside SS 374

RADHA KRISHNA TEMPLE
Multinational group who were disciples of the London Radha Krishna Temple in Oxford Street and were signed to the Apple label by George Harrison, who also produced their hits. The holy maha-mantra was introduced to Western culture by Swani Prabhupada in 1965. He died in November 1977.

13/09/1969.....12......9......	HARE KRISHNA MANTRA .... Apple 15
28/03/1970.....23......8......	GOVINDA .... Apple 25

RADICAL ROB
UK producer Rob McLuan.

11/01/1992.....67......1......	MONKEY WAH .... R&S RSUK 8

JACK RADICS
Jamaican singer (born Jordan Bailey, Kingston) who made one record before moving to London and signing for Island. He later returned to Jamaica.

18/12/1993 ....❶²....14.....●	TWIST AND SHOUT CHAKA DEMUS AND PLIERS FEATURING JACK RADICS AND TAXI GANG .... Mango CIDM 814
06/05/1995.....22......4......	MY GIRL JOSEPHINE SUPERCAT FEATURING JACK RADICS Featured in the 1994 film *Ready To Wear (Pret-A-Porter)* .... Columbia 6614702

RADIO 4
US rock group formed in New York in 1999 by Tommy Williams (guitar), Anthony Roman (bass), Gerard Garone (keyboards), Greg Collins (drums) and PJ O'Connor (percussion). They took their name from a song by Public Image Limited.

24/07/2004.....75......1......	PARTY CRASHERS .... City Slang 5494920
18/09/2004.....61......1......	ABSOLUTE AFFIRMATION .... Labels 5498032

RADIO HEART FEATURING GARY NUMAN
UK instrumental group formed by Hugh Nicholson and fronted by singer/keyboard player Gary Numan.

28/03/1987.....35......6......	RADIO HEART .... GFM 109
13/06/1987.....48......2.......	LONDON TIMES .... GFM 112

RADIO 1 POSSE – see LIZ KERSHAW AND BRUNO BROOKES

RADIO REVELLERS – see ANTHONY STEEL AND THE RADIO REVELLERS

RADIO STARS UK rock group formed in 1977 by Andy Ellison (vocals), Ian McLeod (guitar) and Martin Gordon (bass), later adding Steve Parry (drums) and Trevor White. Ellison, McLeod and Gordon were all ex-members of Jet. Gordon left in December 1978 and the group disbanded in 1979, although Ellison later tried to revive the group but with little success.

04/02/1978	39	3		NERVOUS WRECK	Chiswick NS 23

RADIOHEAD UK rock group formed in Oxford by Thom Yorke (born 7/10/1968, Wellingborough, guitar/vocals), Jonny Greenwood (born 5/11/1971, Oxford, guitar), his brother Colin (born 26/6/1969, Oxford, bass), Ed O'Brien (born 15/4/1968, Oxford, guitar) and Phil Selway (born 23/5/1967, Hemmingford Grey, drums) as On A Friday, name-changing in 1991 to Radiohead (the name came from a Talking Heads song). They won the 1997 Grammy Award for Best Alternative Music Performance for *OK Computer* and the 2000 Award for the Best Alternative Music Album for *Kid A. Amnesiac (Special Limited Edition)* won the 2001 Grammy Award for Best Recording Package.

13/02/1993	32	2	ANYONE CAN PLAY GUITAR	Parlophone CDR 6333
22/05/1993	42	2	POP IS DEAD	Parlophone CDR 6345
18/09/1993	7	6	**CREEP**	Parlophone CDR 6359
08/10/1994	24	2	MY IRON LUNG	Parlophone CDR 6394
11/03/1995	17	4	HIGH AND DRY/PLANET TELEX	Parlophone CDRS 6405
27/05/1995	20	4	FAKE PLASTIC TREES Featured in the 1995 film *Clueless*	Parlophone CDR 6411
02/09/1995	19	3	JUST	Parlophone CDR 6415
03/02/1996	5	4	**STREET SPIRIT (FADE OUT)**	Parlophone CDR 6419
07/06/1997	3	5	**PARANOID ANDROID**	Parlophone CDODATA 01
06/09/1997	8	4	**KARMA POLICE**	Parlophone CDODATAS 03
24/01/1998	4	7	**NO SURPRISES**	Parlophone CDODATAS 04
02/06/2001	5	5	**PYRAMID SONG**	Parlophone CDSFHEIT 45102
18/08/2001	13	4	KNIVES OUT	Parlophone CDFEIT 45103
07/06/2003	4	4	**THERE THERE**	Parlophone CDR 6608
30/08/2003	12	4	GO TO SLEEP	Parlophone CDRS 6613
29/11/2003	15	3	2 + 2 = 5	Parlophone CDRS 6623

RADISH US rock group formed in Greenville, TX by Ben Kweller (guitar/vocals), John Kent (drums/vocals) and Bryan Bradford (bass). Kweller was fifteen at the time of their debut hit.

30/08/1997	32	2	LITTLE PINK STARS	Mercury MERCD 494
15/11/1997	50	1	SIMPLE SINCERITY	Mercury MERCD 498

FONDA RAE US dance singer (born Fonda Rae Woods, New York) who was a session singer before going solo with the Vanguard and Telescope labels.

06/10/1984	49	4	TUCH ME	Streetwave KHAN 28

JESSE RAE UK singer who was previously a member of The Space Cadets.

11/05/1985	65	2	OVER THE SEA	Scotland Video YZ 36

MARCIA RAE – see QUAKE FEATURING MARCIA RAE

RAE AND CHRISTIAN FEATURING VEBA UK production duo formed in 1995 by Mark Rae and Steve Christian with singer Veba.

06/03/1999	67	1	ALL I ASK Contains a sample of Brian & Brenda Russell's *World Called Love*	Grand Central GCD 120

RAF Italian producer Mauro Picotto who has also recorded as CRW and under his own name.

14/03/1992	34	3	WE'VE GOT TO LIVE TOGETHER Contains a sample of Enya's *Orinoco Flow*	PWL Continental PWL 218
05/03/1994	71	1	TAKE ME HIGHER	Media MRLCD 0012
23/03/1996	59	1	TAKE ME HIGHER (REMIX)	Media MCSTD 40026
27/07/1996	73	1	ANGEL'S SYMPHONY	Media MCSTD 40051

GERRY RAFFERTY UK singer/guitarist (born 16/4/1947, Paisley, Scotland) who joined the Humblebums in 1968 (a group that also included comic Billy Connolly), recording two albums for Transatlantic. The group disbanded in 1970 and Rafferty remained with Transatlantic for one solo album, released in 1971, before forming Stealers Wheel in 1972. He left them after recording their debut album, although he was persuaded back when *Stuck In The Middle With You* hit the top ten. He left again in 1975 and resurfaced as a solo artist in 1978. He later became a producer.

18/02/1978	3	15	●	**BAKER STREET** Saxophone by session player Raphael Ravenscroft	United Artists UP 36346
26/05/1979	5	13	○	**NIGHT OWL**	United Artists UP 36512
18/08/1979	30	9	GET IT RIGHT NEXT TIME	United Artists BP 301
22/03/1980	54	4	BRING IT ALL HOME	United Artists BP 340
21/06/1980	67	2	ROYAL MILE	United Artists BP 354
10/03/1990	53	4	BAKER STREET (REMIX)	EMI EM 132

RAGE UK production group formed by Barry Leng and Duncan Hannant.

31/10/1992	3	11	**RUN TO YOU**	Pulse 8 LOSE 33
27/02/1993	44	2	WHY DON'T YOU	Pulse 8 CDLOSE 39
15/05/1993	41	2	HOUSE OF THE RISING SUN	Pulse 8 CDLOSE 43

RAGE AGAINST THE MACHINE US group formed in California in 1991 by Tom Morello (born 30/5//1964, New York, guitar), Brad Wilk (born 5/9/1968, Portland, OR, drums), Zack de la Rocha (born 13/1/1970, Long Beach, CA, vocals) and Timmy C (born Tim Commerford, bass). They signed with Epic in 1992 (having rejected advances from Madonna's Maverick label) and won the 1996 Grammy Award for Best Metal Performance for *Tire Me*. They disbanded in October 2000 but still won their 2000 Grammy Award, at the ceremony held in February 2001.

27/02/1993.....25......4......				KILLING IN THE NAME...	Epic 6584922
08/05/1993.....16......4......				BULLET IN THE HEAD...	Epic 6592582
04/09/1993.....37......2......				BOMBTRACK..	Epic 6594712
13/04/1996 .....8......3......				BULLS ON PARADE..	Epic 6631522
07/09/1996.....26......2......				PEOPLE OF THE SUN	Epic 6636282
06/11/1999.....32......2......				GUERRILLA RADIO 2000 Grammy Award for Best Hard Rock Performance...............	Epic 6683142
15/04/2000.....43......2......				SLEEP NOW IN THE FIRE...	Epic 6691362

RAGGA TWINS UK vocal duo formed in 1990 by Flinty Badman and Deman Rocker.

10/11/1990.....51......2......				ILLEGAL GUNSHOT/SPLIFFHEAD	Shut Up And Dance SUAD 7
06/04/1991.....71......2......				WIPE THE NEEDLE/JUGGLING	Shut Up And Dance SUAD 12S
06/07/1991.....56......2......				HOOLIGAN 69...	Shut Up And Dance SUAD 16S
07/03/1992.....65......2......				MIXED TRUTH/BRING UP THE MIC SOME MORE	Shut Up And Dance SUAD 27S
11/07/1992.....63......2......				SHINE EYE RAGGA TWINS FEATURING JUNIOR REID	Shut Up And Dance SUAD 32S

RAGHAV Canadian singer who was educated at Paul McCartney's LIPA school of performing arts.

24/01/2004 .....6......13......				SO CONFUSED 2PLAY FEATURING RAGHAV AND JUCXI 2004 MOBO Award for Best Collaboration	2PSL 2PSLCD02
28/02/2004 .....10......8......				CAN'T GET ENOUGH	A&R ANR1CDS
22/05/2004 .....8......7......				IT CAN'T BE RIGHT 2PLAY FEATURING RAGHAV AND NAILA BOSS	2PSL/inferno 2PSLCD04
04/09/2004.....15......3......				LET'S WORK IT OUT RAGHAV FEATURING JAHAZIEL	V2 ARV5028628

RAGING SPEEDHORN UK metal group formed in Corby, Northants in 1998 by Jon Loughlin (vocals), Frank Regan (vocals), Tony Loughlin (guitar), Gareth Smith (guitar), Darren Smith (bass/vocals) and Gordon Morrison (drums).

16/06/2001.....47......1......				THE GUSH...	ZTT GIR004CD
06/07/2002.....69......1......				THE HATE SONG	ZTT RSH001CD

RAGTIMERS UK studio group whose one hit single was a cover version of Scott Joplin's *The Entertainer*, with the title changed to reflect the 1973 film that contributed to its popularity.

16/03/1974.....31......8......				THE STING	Pye 7N 45323

RAH BAND UK multi-instrumentalist Richard Anthony Hewson (born in Stockton-in-Tees) whose initials formed the name of the band. He was an arranger for Apple and was responsible for hits by Mary Hopkin, James Taylor and The Beatles.

09/07/1977 .....6......12......				THE CRUNCH	Good Earth GD 7
01/11/1980.....35......7......				FALCON..	DJM DJS 10954
07/02/1981.....50......7......				SLIDE...	DJM DJS 10964
01/05/1982.....45......7......				PERFUMED GARDEN	KR 5
09/07/1983.....42......5......				MESSAGES FROM THE STARS	TMT 5
19/01/1985.....70......2......				ARE YOU SATISFIED? (FUNKA NOVA)..	RCA 470
30/03/1985 .....6......10......				CLOUDS ACROSS THE MOON	RCA PB 40025

RAHSAAN – see US3

RAHZEL – see RONI SIZE REPRAZENT

RAILWAY CHILDREN UK rock group formed in 1985 by Gary Newby (born 5/6/1966, Australia, guitar/vocals), Brian Bateman (born 3/8/1966, Wigan, guitar), Stephen Hull (born 7/7/1966, Wigan, bass) and Guy Keegan (born 16/6/1966, Wigan, drums); they added Tony Martin (keyboards) in 1987 and were initially linked with Factory Records, albeit without a contract. They signed with Virgin towards the end of the year, but had disbanded by 1995.

24/03/1990.....68......2......				EVERY BEAT OF THE HEART..	Virgin VS 1237
02/06/1990.....66......2......				MUSIC STOP	Virgin VS 1255
20/10/1990.....68......1......				SO RIGHT..	Virgin VS 1289
02/02/1991.....24......6......				EVERY BEAT OF THE HEART..	Virgin VS 1237
20/04/1991.....57......2......				SOMETHING SO GOOD	Virgin VS 1318

RAIN – see STEPHANIE DE SYKES

RAIN BAND UK rock group formed in Manchester by Richard Nancollis (vocals), Mark Lee (guitar) and Stephen Taylor (bass) with session drummer Danny.

01/03/2003.....63......1......				EASY RIDER	Temptation TEMPTCD 003
19/07/2003.....56......1......				KNEE DEEP AND DOWN	Temptation TEMPTCD 007

RAIN TREE CROW UK group formed in 1991 by David Sylvian (born David Batt, 23/2/1958, London, guitar/vocals), Steve Jansen (born Stephen Batt, 1/12/1959,London, drums), Richard Barbieri (born 30/11/1957, keyboards) and Mick Karn (born Anthony Michaelides, 24/7/1958, London, bass). The four had been members of Japan between 1977 and 1982,

❶⁹ Number of weeks single topped the UK charts ↑ Entered the UK chart at #1 ▲⁹ Number of weeks single topped the US chart

649

with Sylvian and Karn subsequently recording solo. Karn also linked with Peter Murphy (formerly of Bauhaus) to record one album as Dali's Car.

| 30/03/1991 | 62 | 1 | | BLACKWATER | Virgin VS 1340 |

RAINBOW
UK heavy rock group formed in 1975 by ex-Deep Purple guitarist Ritchie Blackmore (born 14/4/1945, Weston-super-Mare), Ronnie James Dio (born 10/7/1949, Cortland, NY, vocals), Mickey Lee Soule (keyboards), Craig Gruber (bass) and Gary Driscoll (drums) as Ritchie Blackmore's Rainbow. Blackmore re-formed the group in 1976 with Dio, Tony Carey (born 16/10/1953, Fresno, CA, keyboards), Cozy Powell (born 29/12/1947, Cirencester, drums) and Jimmy Bain (bass). Bain was fired in 1977 and replaced by Mark Clarke. Carey and Clarke were fired in May 1977 and replaced by David Stone (keyboards) and Bob Daisley (bass). In 1978 Blackmore sacked all of the band except Powell and brought in Don Airey (keyboards), Graham Bonnet (born 12/12/1947, Skegness, vocals) and Roger Glover (born 30/11/1945, Brecon, Powys, bass). Powell resigned in 1980 (replaced by Bobby Rondinelli), Bonnet left a month later (replaced by Joe Lynn Turne), Airey left in 1981 (replaced by Dave Rosenthal) and Rondinelli left soon after (replaced by Chuck Burgi). Blackmore disbanded the group in 1984 and rejoined Deep Purple. Powell was killed in a car crash on 5/4/1998.

17/09/1977	44	3		KILL THE KING	Polydor 2066 845
08/04/1978	33	3		LONG LIVE ROCK 'N' ROLL	Polydor 2066 913
30/09/1978	40	4		L.A. CONNECTION	Polydor 2066 968
15/09/1979	6	10	○	**SINCE YOU'VE BEEN GONE**	Polydor POSP 70
16/02/1980	5	11	○	**ALL NIGHT LONG**	Polydor POSP 104
31/01/1981	3	10	○	**I SURRENDER**	Polydor POSP 221
20/06/1981	20	8		CAN'T HAPPEN HERE	Polydor POSP 251
11/07/1981	41	4		KILL THE KING Re-issue of Polydor 2066 845	Polydor POSP 274
03/04/1982	34	4		STONE COLD	Polydor POSP 421
27/08/1983	52	3		STREET OF DREAMS	Polydor POSP 631
05/11/1983	43	2		CAN'T LET YOU GO	Polydor POSP 654

RAINBOW COTTAGE
UK group formed in Wigan by Brian Gibbs (guitar), Tony Houghton (guitar/keyboards), Graham Hill (bass) and Steve Morris (drums).

| 06/03/1976 | 33 | 4 | | SEAGULL | Penny Farthing PEN 906 |

RAINBOW (GEORGE AND ZIPPY)
UK singer Geoffrey Hayes with puppet characters Bungle The Bear, Zippy and George. *Rainbow* was a popular kids' TV show during the 1970s and 1980s, ending in 1992. Hayes revived it as a stage show towards the end of the 1990s.

| 14/12/2002 | 15 | 6 | | IT'S A RAINBOW | BBC Music ZIPPCD1X |

RAINMAKERS
US group formed by Bob Walkenhorst (guitar/keyboards/vocals), Steve Phillips (guitar/vocals), Rich Ruth (bass/vocals) and Pat Tomek (drums).

| 07/03/1987 | 18 | 11 | | LET MY PEOPLE GO-GO | Mercury MER 238 |

MARVIN RAINWATER
US singer (born Marvin Karlton Percy, 2/7/1925, Wichita, KS) who is of Cherokee Indian extraction. He was spotted on the *Arthur Godfrey Talent Scout* TV show and signed with Coral during the 1950s. He later recorded for Warwick, United Artists, Warner Brothers, Wesco, Philips, Westwood and Sonet and formed his own Brave label.

| 07/03/1958 | ●³ | 15 | | **WHOLE LOTTA WOMAN** | MGM 974 |
| 06/06/1958 | 19 | 7 | | I DIG YOU BABY | MGM 980 |

RAISSA
UK singer Raissa Khan-Panni.

| 12/02/2000 | 47 | 1 | | HOW LONG DO I GET | Polydor 5616282 |

BONNIE RAITT
US singer (born 8/11/1949, Burbank, CA) who signed with Warner Brothers in 1971, her debut album covering blues, early R&B and country material. She went into semi-retirement in the mid-1980s (mainly to battle alcoholism), but re-emerged at the end of the decade with a new record deal. She has won nine Grammy Awards: Album of the Year, Best Pop Vocal Performance and Best Rock Vocal Performance in 1989 for *Nick Of Time,* Best Traditional Blues Recording in 1989 with John Lee Hooker for *I'm In The Mood,* Best Female Pop Vocal Performance in 1991 for *Something To Talk About,* Best Rock Solo Vocal Performance in 1991 for *Luck Of The Draw,* Best Rock Performance by a Duo in 1991 with Delbert McClinton for *Good Man, Good Woman,* Best Pop Album in 1994 for *Longing In Their Hearts* and Best Rock Instrumental in 1996 with Jimmie Vaughan, Eric Clapton, Robert Cray, BB King, Buddy Guy, Dr John and Art Neville for *SRV Shuffle.* She was inducted into the Rock & Roll Hall of Fame in 2000 and has a star on the Hollywood Walk of Fame.

14/12/1991	50	4		I CAN'T MAKE YOU LOVE ME	Capitol CL 639
09/04/1994	69	1		LOVE SNEAKIN' UP ON YOU	Capitol CDCL 713
18/06/1994	31	2		YOU	Capitol CDCLS 718
11/11/1995	50	2		ROCK STEADY **BONNIE RAITT AND BRYAN ADAMS**	Capitol CDCL 763

DIONNE RAKEEM
UK dance singer from Birmingham.

| 04/08/2001 | 46 | 2 | | SWEETER THAN WINE | Virgin VSCDT 1809 |

RAKES
UK rock group formed in London by Alan Donohoe (guitar/vocals), Matthew Swinnerton (guitar), Jamie Hornsmith (bass) and Lasse Petersen (drums).

| 09/10/2004 | 57 | 1 | | STRASBOURG | City Rockers ROCKERS28CD |

○ Silver disc ● Gold disc ✪ Platinum disc (additional platinum units are indicated by a figure following the symbol) ◉ Singles released prior to 1973 that are known to have sold over 1 million copies in the UK

RAKIM US rapper (born William Griffin, 28/1/1968, Long Island, NY) who was originally with Erik B And Rakim with Eric Barrier. The pair later produced a number of acts for MCA including Jody Watley and appeared in the 1994 film *Gunmen*. Rakim later went solo.

27/12/1997.....32......3....... GUESS WHO'S BACK ....Universal UND 56151
22/08/1998.....53......1....... STAY A WHILE Contains a sample of Loose End's *Stay A Little While Child*............................Universal UND 56203
03/10/1998.....65......1....... BUFFALO GALS STAMPEDE **MALCOLM McLAREN AND THE WORLD'S FAMOUS SUPREME TEAM PLUS RAKIM AND ROGER SANCHEZ**
....Virgin VSCDT 1717
31/08/2002.....3......12...... **ADDICTIVE TRUTH HURTS FEATURING RAKIM** Contains a sample of B.T. Express' *Do It 'Til You're Satisfied* ......Interscope 497782

TONY RALLO AND THE MIDNIGHT BAND French jazz funk group fronted by singer/songwriter Tony Rallo. Rallo had previously co-written and produced France's entry for the 1976 Eurovision Song Contest, *Un Deux Trois* by Catherine Ferry (it came second behind Brotherhood Of Man).

23/02/1980.....34......8....... HOLDIN' ON...Calibre CAB 150

SHERYL LEE RALPH US singer/actress (born 30/12/1956, Waterbury, CT) who appeared in the original *Dreamgirls* show on Broadway (for which she was nominated for a Tony Award) and films including *The Flintstones* (1994) and *Baby Of The Family* (2002).

26/01/1985.....64......2....... IN THE EVENING ....Arista ARIST 595

RAM JAM US rock group formed by Bill Bartlett (ex-The Lemon Pipers, guitar), Howie Blauvelt (bass), Myke Scavone (vocals) and Pete Charles (drums). Blauvelt, an ex-member of Billy Joel's group The Hassles, died from a heart attack on 25/10/1993, aged 44.

10/09/1977.....7......12.....O **BLACK BETTY** Featured in the 2001 film *Blow*...Epic EPC 5492
17/02/1990.....13......8....... BLACK BETTY (REMIX)..Epic 6554307

RAM JAM BAND – see **GENO WASHINGTON AND THE RAM JAM BAND**

RAM TRILOGY UK trio formed by Andy Clarke, Shimon Alcovy and Ant Miles. Clarke and Miles were ex-members of Origin Unknown, while Alcovy and Clarke had recorded together. The three launched the Ram Records label.

06/07/2002.....71......1....... CHAPTER FOUR...Ram RAMM 39
20/07/2002.....62......1....... CHAPTER FIVE...Ram RAMM 40
03/08/2002.....60......1....... CHAPTER SIX..Ram RAMM 41

RAMBLERS – see **PERRY COMO**

RAMBLERS (FROM THE ABBEY HEY JUNIOR SCHOOL) UK kids' school group that released a number of singles throughout the 1980s although not with the same line-up. Their hit was written by their teacher Maurice Jordan and produced by Kevin Parrott, who had previously been responsible for Brian & Michael's hit.

13/10/1979.....11......15.....O THE SPARROW ....Decca F 13860

KAREN RAMIREZ UK dance singer (born Karen Ramelize).

28/03/1998.....50......1....... TROUBLED GIRL ....Manifesto FESCD 31
27/06/1998.....8......11.....O **LOOKING FOR LOVE** ....Manifesto FESCD 44
21/11/1998.....23......3....... IF WE TRY ....Manifesto FESCD 50

RAMMSTEIN German rock group formed by Till Lindemann (born 1/4/1963, vocals), Richard Kruspe-Bernstein (born 12/9/1964, guitar), Christian 'Flake' Lorenz (born 11/6/1966, keyboards), Oliver Riedel (born 4/11/1971, bass) and Christoph 'Doom' Schneider (born 5/11/1966, drums).

25/05/2002.....30......2....... ICH WILL...Universal MCSXD 40280
23/11/2002.....35......2....... FEUER FREI...Universal MCSXD 40302
14/08/2004.....61......2....... MEIN TEIL (IMPORT) ....Universal 9866978
30/10/2004.....38......2....... AMERIKA ....Universal MCSTD 40394

RAMONES US rock group formed in New York in 1974 by Johnny (born John Cummings, 8/10/1951, Long Island, NY, guitar), Joey (born Jeffrey Hyman, 19/5/1952, Forest Hills, NY, vocals) and Ritchie Ramone. Ritchie was soon replaced by Dee Dee (born Douglas Colvin, 18/9/1952, Fort Lee, VA, bass) and Tommy (born Thomas Erdelyi, 29/1/1952, Budapest, Hungary, drums) was added. They signed with Sire in 1975 and released their debut album in 1976. Tommy left the group in 1978 (but remained their producer) and was replaced by Marc Bell (born 15/7/1956, New York), who adopted the name Marky Ramone. Dee Dee left the group in 1989 and was replaced by CJ Ramone (born Christopher Joseph Ward, 8/10/1965, Long Island). The group disbanded in 1996. Joey Ramone died from cancer on 16/4/2001. Dee Dee Ramone was found dead from a drug overdose on 5/6/2002. Johnny Ramone died from prostate cancer on 15/9/2004. The group was inducted into the Rock & Roll Hall of Fame in 2002.

21/05/1977.....22......7...... SHEENA IS A PUNK ROCKER..Sire RAM 001
06/08/1977.....36......3...... SWALLOW MY PRIDE ....Sire 6078 607
30/09/1978.....39......5...... DON'T COME CLOSE ....Sire SRE 1031
08/09/1979.....67......2...... ROCK 'N' ROLL HIGH SCHOOL Featured in the 1979 film *Rock 'N' Roll High School* starring The Ramones.........Sire SRE 4021
26/01/1980.....8......9...... **BABY I LOVE YOU**..Sire SIR 4031
19/04/1980.....54......3...... DO YOU REMEMBER ROCK 'N' ROLL RADIO ....Sire SIR 4037
10/05/1986.....69......1...... SOMEBODY PUT SOMETHING IN MY DRINK/SOMETHING TO BELIEVE IN....................Beggars Banquet BEG 157
19/12/1992.....69......2...... POISON HEART ....Chrysalis CHS 3917

RAMP UK instrumental/production duo Shem McCauley and Simon Rogers. They later recorded as Slacker.

08/06/1996.....49......1....... ROCK THE DISCOTEK...Loaded LOADCD 30

❶⁹ Number of weeks single topped the UK charts ↑ Entered the UK chart at #1 ▲⁹ Number of weeks single topped the US chart

651

RAMPAGE
UK DJ/production group formed by Mike Anthony and Mike Fletcher.

25/11/1995	51	1	THE MONKEES	Almo Sounds CDALMOS 017

RAMPAGE FEATURING BILLY LAWRENCE
US rapper Roger McNair with singer Billy Lawrence.

| 18/10/1997 | 58 | 1 | TAKE IT TO THE STREETS | Elektra E 3914CD |

RAMRODS
US instrumental group formed in Connecticut in 1956 by Vincent Bell Lee (guitar), Eugene Morrow (guitar), Richard Lane (saxophone) and his sister Claire (drums/vocals).

| 23/02/1961 | 8 | 12 | RIDERS IN THE SKY Originally recorded by Vaughan Monroe in 1949 as *Riders In The Sky (A Cowboy Legend)* | London HLU 9282 |

RAMSEY AND FEN FEATURING LYNSEY MOORE
UK production duo with singer Lynsey Moore. Ramsey and Fen began their careers on Freek FM radio.

| 10/06/2000 | 75 | 1 | LOVE BUG | Nebula VCNEBD 4 |

RANCID
US rock group formed in 1989 by Tim 'Lint' Armstrong (guitar/vocals), Lars Frederiksen (guitar), Matt Freeman (bass) and Brett Reed (drums). Armstrong and Freeman were ex-Operation Ivy and formed Rancid when that band split up. Armstrong was later a member of The Transplants.

| 07/10/1995 | 56 | 1 | TIME BOMB | Out Of Step WOOS 8CDS |
| 27/09/2003 | 42 | 2 | FALL BACK DOWN | Hellcat W 618CD |

RANGE – see BRUCE HORNSBY AND THE RANGE

RANGERS FC
UK professional football club formed in Glasgow in 1873. They have won the Scottish League 50 times and the European Cup Winners' Cup once. Their debut hit was to honour their record-equalling ninth League championship in a row.

| 04/10/1997 | 54 | 2 | GLASGOW RANGERS (NINE IN A ROW) | Gers GERSCD 1 |

RANI – see DELERIUM

RANK 1
Dutch production duo Piet Bervoets and Benno de Goeij. They were later responsible for the debut hit by Jonah.

| 15/04/2000 | 10 | 5 | AIRWAVE | Manifesto FESCD 69 |

RANKING ANN – see SCRITTI POLITTI

RANKING ROGER – see PATO BANTON

SHABBA RANKS
Jamaican singer (born Rexton Rawlson Fernando Gordon, 17/1/1966, Sturgetown) who began recording in 1980 as Jamaican DJ Don, building up a strong following on the island. He signed with Epic in 1990 and has won the Grammy Award for Best Reggae Album twice: in 1991 for *As Raw As Ever* and 1992 for *X-Tra Naked*. While he was collecting his first award thieves broke into his Jamaican home and virtually emptied it of all belongings. Johnny Gill is a US singer (born 22/5/1966, Washington DC). Patra is a dancer/singer (born Dorothy Smith 22/11/1972, Kingston, Jamaica). Terry and Monica are Jamaican singers.

16/03/1991	20	7	SHE'S A WOMAN SCRITTI POLITTI FEATURING SHABBA RANKS	Virgin VS 1333
18/05/1991	63	2	TRAILER LOAD A GIRLS	Epic 6568747
24/08/1991	31	7	HOUSECALL SHABBA RANKS FEATURING MAXI PRIEST	Epic 6573477
08/08/1992	23	7	MR LOVERMAN Featured in the 1992 film *Deep Cover*	Epic 6582517
28/11/1992	17	7	SLOW AND SEXY SHABBA RANKS FEATURING JOHNNY GILL	Epic 6587727
06/03/1993	64	1	I WAS A KING EDDIE MURPHY FEATURING SHABBA RANKS	Motown TMGCD 1414
13/03/1993	3	11	MR LOVERMAN Re-issue of Epic 6582517.	Epic 6590782
08/05/1993	8	8	HOUSECALL (REMIX) SHABBA RANKS FEATURING MAXI PRIEST	Epic 6592842
26/06/1993	21	4	WHAT'CHA GONNA DO SHABBA RANKS FEATURING QUEEN LATIFAH	Epic 6593072
25/12/1993	18	8	FAMILY AFFAIR SHABBA RANKS FEATURING PATRA AND TERRY & MONICA Featured in the 1993 film *Addams Family Values*	Polydor PZCD 304
29/04/1995	22	3	LET'S GET IT ON	Epic 6614122
05/08/1995	46	2	SHINE EYE GAL SHABBA RANKS (FEATURING MYKAL ROSE)	Epic 6622332

BUBBLER RANX – see PETER ANDRE

RAPINATION
Italian instrumental/production duo Charlie Mallozzi and Marco Sabiu.

26/12/1992	22	10	LOVE ME THE RIGHT WAY RAPINATION FEATURING KYM MAZELLE	Logic 74321128097
10/07/1993	69	1	HERE'S MY A RAPINATION FEATURING CAROL KENYON	Logic 74321153092
28/09/1996	55	1	LOVE ME THE RIGHT WAY (REMIX) RAPINATION FEATURING KYM MAZELLE	Logic 74321404442

RAPPIN' 4-TAY
US rapper (born Anthony Forte, 1969, San Francisco, CA) who served time in prison, which inspired his 1996 album *Off Parole*.

| 24/06/1995 | 30 | 4 | I'LL BE AROUND RAPPIN' 4-TAY FEATURING THE SPINNERS Rappin' 4-Tay raps a new verse over the Detroit Spinners' 1972 US hit, with the original music and chorus. | Cooltempo CDCOOL 306 |
| 30/09/1995 | 63 | 1 | PLAYAZ CLUB | Cooltempo CDCOOL 310 |

RAPTURE
US rock group formed in New York City in 1998 by Luke Jenner (guitar/vocals), Matt Safer (bass) and Vito Roccoforte (drums). They later added Gabriel Abdruzzi (multi-instruments).

○ Silver disc ● Gold disc ✪ Platinum disc (additional platinum units are indicated by a figure following the symbol) ◎ Singles released prior to 1973 that are known to have sold over 1 million copies in the UK

06/09/2003 . . . . . 27 . . . . . 2			HOUSE OF JEALOUS LOVERS Featured in the 2004 film *The Football Factory* . . . . XL Recordings XLS 167CD
13/12/2003 . . . . . 51 . . . . . 1			SISTER SAVIOUR . . . . DFA/Output/Vertigo 9814181
21/02/2004 . . . . . 38 . . . . . 1			LOVE IS ALL . . . . DFA/Output/Vertigo 9816876

RARE UK group formed by Mary Gallagher (vocals), Locky Morris (various instruments), Sean O'Neill (various instruments), Damian O'Neill (guitar) and David Whiteside (drums).

17/02/1996 . . . . . 57 . . . . . 1	SOMETHING WILD . . . . Equator AXISCD 011

RARE BIRD UK group formed by Steve Gould (vocals/saxophone/bass), Dave Kaffinette (keyboards), Graham Field (organ) and Mark Ashton (drums). Gould and Kaffinette were joined by Andy Curtis (guitar) and Fred Kelly (drums) for the group's second album.

14/02/1970 . . . . . 27 . . . . . 8	SYMPATHY . . . . Charisma CB 120

O RASBURY – see **RAHNI HARRIS AND F.L.O.**

DIZZEE RASCAL UK rapper (born Dylan Mills, London) who was eighteen at the time of his debut hit. He is also a member of The Roll Deep Crew. His debut album *Boy In Da Corner* won the 2003 Mercury Music Prize; he was named UK Act of the Year at the 2004 MOBO Awards (jointly with Jamelia).

07/06/2003 . . . . . 29 . . . . . 3	I LUV U . . . . XL Recordings XLS 165CD
30/08/2003 . . . . . 17 . . . . . 5	FIX UP LOOK SHARP Contains a sample of Billy Squire's *The Big Beat* . . . . XL Recordings XLS 167CD
22/11/2003 . . . . . 23 . . . . . 4	LUCKY STAR **BASEMENT JAXX FEATURING DIZZEE RASCAL** . . . . XL Recordings XLS 172CD
06/12/2003 . . . . . 30 . . . . . 3	JUS' A RASCAL . . . . XL Recordings XLS 175CD
04/09/2004 . . . . . 10 . . . . . 6	**STAND UP TALL** . . . . XL Recordings XLS 198CD
20/11/2004 . . . . . 14 . . . . . 6+	DREAM . . . . XL Recordings XLS 204CD1

RASMUS Finnish rock group formed in 1995 by schoolfriends Lauri Johannes Ylönen (born 23/4/1979, vocals), Eero Aleksi Heinonen (born 27/11/1979, guitar), Pauli Antero Rantasalmi (born 1/5/1979, guitar) and Aki Markus Hakala (born 28/10/1979, drums).

17/04/2004 . . . . . 3 . . . . . 16	**IN THE SHADOWS** . . . . Universal MCSXD 40351
21/08/2004 . . . . . 15 . . . . . 6	GUILTY . . . . Universal MCSTD 40376
13/11/2004 . . . . . 50 . . . . . 1	FIRST DAY OF MY LIFE . . . . Universal MCSTD 40391

ROLAND RAT SUPERSTAR UK puppet first introduced to TV audiences via the early morning show *TV AM*. Roland Rat's voice was supplied by David Claridge.

19/11/1983 . . . . . 14 . . . . . 12	RAT RAPPING . . . . Rodent RAT 1
28/04/1984 . . . . . 32 . . . . . 7	LOVE ME TENDER . . . . Rodent RAT 2
02/03/1985 . . . . . 72 . . . . . 1	NO. 1 RAT FAN . . . . Rodent RAT 4

RATPACK UK production duo Mark McKee and Evenson Allen.

06/06/1992 . . . . . 58 . . . . . 3	SEARCHIN' FOR MY RIZLA . . . . Big Giant BIGT 02

RATTLES German rock group formed by Achim Reishel (guitar/vocals), Hajo Kreutzfeldt (guitar), Herbert Hildebrandt (bass/vocals) and Reinhard Tarrach (drums). Although this line-up scored a domestic hit with the original German language version of their hit, the English language version was recorded by Frank Mille (guitar), Zappo Luengen (bass), Herbert Bornhold (drums) and 'Edna' (vocals) under the guidance of Hildebrandt.

03/10/1970 . . . . . 8 . . . . . 15	**THE WITCH** . . . . Decca F 23058

RATTY German/UK production group formed by Leslie Silvokos and David Smith.

24/03/2001 . . . . . 51 . . . . . 1	SUNRISE (HERE I AM) . . . . Neo NEOCD 051

RAVEN MAIZE UK producer/remixer Dave Lee. He is also a member of Hed Boys and has recorded as Z Factor, Jakatta and Joey Negro.

05/08/1989 . . . . . 67 . . . . . 1	FOREVER TOGETHER . . . . Republic LIC 014
18/08/2001 . . . . . 12 . . . . . 6	THE REAL LIFE Contains samples of Queen's *Bohemian Rhapsody* and Simple Minds' *Theme From Great Cities* . . . . . Rulin 18CDS
17/08/2002 . . . . . 37 . . . . . 2	FASCINATED . . . . Rulin 27CDS

RAVEONETTES Danish duo Sune Rose Wagner (vocals) and Sharin Foo (bass/vocals), with Manoj Ramdas (guitar) and Jakob Hoyer (drums) appearing on live dates.

21/12/2002 . . . . . 73 . . . . . 1	ATTACK OF THE GHOSTRIDERS . . . . Columbia 6733892
30/08/2003 . . . . . 34 . . . . . 2	THAT GREAT LOVE SOUND . . . . Columbia RAVEON005
20/12/2003 . . . . . 49 . . . . . 1	HEARTBREAK STROLL . . . . Columbia RAVEON008
22/05/2004 . . . . . 52 . . . . . 1	THAT GREAT LOVE SOUND Re-issue of Columbia RAVEON005 . . . . Columbia RAVEON010

RAVESIGNAL III UK producer (born Christian Jay Bolland, 18/6/1971, Stockton-on-Tees, raised in Antwerp, Belgium) who has also recorded as Sonic Solution, Pulse, The Project, CJ Bolland and Space Opera.

14/12/1991 . . . . . 61 . . . . . 2	HORSEPOWER . . . . R&S RSUK 6

RAW – see **ERICK 'MORE' MORILLO PRESENTS RAW**

RAW SILK US studio group assembled by Ronald Dean Miller in 1980.

16/10/1982 . . . . . 18 . . . . . 9	DO IT TO THE MUSIC . . . . KR 14
10/09/1983 . . . . . 49 . . . . . 3	JUST IN TIME . . . . West End WEND 2

❶[9] Number of weeks single topped the UK charts ↑ Entered the UK chart at #1 ▲[9] Number of weeks single topped the US chart

653

RAW STYLUS
UK duo Jules Brookes and Ron Aslan with singer Donna Gardier. Gardier later went solo.

| 26/10/1996 | 66 | 1 | BELIEVE IN ME | Wired 234 |

RAWHILL CRU – see BAD COMPANY

LOU RAWLS
US singer (born 1/12/1935, Chicago, IL) who began his career as a gospel singer and toured with the Pilgrim Travellers. He went solo with Shardee and then Colpix, scoring a number of US hits on Capitol and MGM. He signed to Philadelphia International in 1976. He has won four Grammy Awards: Best Rhythm & Blues Solo Vocal Performance in 1967 for *Dead End Street*, Best Rhythm & Blues Solo Vocal Performance in 1971 for *A Natural Man*, Best Rhythm & Blues Solo Vocal Performance in 1977 for *Unmistakably Lou* and Best Recording for Children in 1982 with various others for *In Harmony 2*. He has a star on the Hollywood Walk of Fame.

| 31/07/1976 | 10 | 10 | YOU'LL NEVER FIND ANOTHER LOVE LIKE MINE | Philadelphia International PIR 4372 |

GENE ANTHONY RAY – see KIDS FROM FAME

JIMMY RAY
UK singer (born James Edwards, 1976, Walthamstow, London) who collaborated with Con Fitzpatrick (of Shampoo) for his debut album.

| 25/10/1997 | 13 | 5 | ARE YOU JIMMY RAY? | Sony S2 6650125 |
| 14/02/1998 | 49 | 1 | GOIN' TO VEGAS | Sony S2 6654652 |

JOHNNIE RAY
US singer (born 10/1/1927, Dallas, OR) who was partially deafened at the age of nine and had to wear a hearing aid from fourteen. Spotted on a nightclub tour by a representative of Columbia Records, he was signed in 1951; his first record *Cry* sold over 1 million copies. He appeared in the films *There's No Business Like Show Business* (1954) and *Rogues' Gallery* (1968). He died from liver failure on 25/2/1990. He has a star on the Hollywood Walk of Fame.

14/11/1952	12	1	WALKING MY BABY BACK HOME	Columbia DB 3060
19/12/1952	7	3	FAITH CAN MOVE MOUNTAINS JOHNNIE RAY AND THE FOUR LADS	Columbia DB 3154
03/04/1953	12	1	MA SAYS PA SAYS DORIS DAY AND JOHNNIE RAY	Columbia DB 3242
10/04/1953	6	7	SOMEBODY STOLE MY GAL	Philips PB 123
17/04/1953	11	1	FULL TIME JOB	Columbia DB 3242
24/07/1953	4	14	LET'S WALK THATA-WAY This and above single credited to DORIS DAY AND JOHNNIE RAY	Philips PB 157
09/04/1954	●¹	18	SUCH A NIGHT	Philips PB 244
08/04/1955	7	11	IF YOU BELIEVE Featured in the 1954 film *There's No Business Like Show Business* starring Johnnie Ray	Philips PB 379
20/05/1955	20	1	PATHS OF PARADISE	Philips PB 441
07/10/1955	11	5	HERNANDO'S HIDEAWAY	Philips PB 495
14/10/1955	5	9	HEY THERE B-side to *Hernando's Hideaway*. Both sides featured in the 1957 film *The Pajama Game*	Philips PB 495
28/10/1955	10	5	SONG OF THE DREAMER	Philips PB 516
17/02/1956	17	2	WHO'S SORRY NOW	Philips PB 546
20/04/1956	17	7	AIN'T MISBEHAVIN'	Philips PB 580
12/10/1956	●⁷	19	JUST WALKIN' IN THE RAIN Song written by Johnny Bragg and Robert S Riley and originally recorded by The Prisonaires, a group of inmates at Tennessee State Penitentiary, where Bragg was serving 99 years for six rapes (later found to have been falsely convicted)	Philips PB 624
18/01/1957	12	15	YOU DON'T OWE ME A THING	Philips PB 655
08/02/1957	7	16	LOOK HOMEWARD ANGEL	Philips PB 655
10/05/1957	●³	16	YES TONIGHT JOSEPHINE	Philips PB 686
06/09/1957	17	7	BUILD YOUR LOVE	Philips PB 721
04/10/1957	25	4	GOOD EVENING FRIENDS/UP ABOVE MY HEAD I HEAR MUSIC IN THE AIR FRANKIE LAINE AND JOHNNIE RAY	Philips PB 708
04/12/1959	26	6	I'LL NEVER FALL IN LOVE AGAIN	Philips PB 952

NICOLE RAY
US rapper (born in Salinas, CA, later moving with her family to Portsmouth, VA) who was discovered by fellow rapper Missy 'Misdemeanor' Elliott and made her debut album shortly after her seventeenth birthday.

| 22/08/1998 | 22 | 4 | MAKE IT HOT NICOLE FEATURING MISSY 'MISDEMEANOR' ELLIOTT AND MOCHA | East West E 3821CD |
| 05/12/1998 | 55 | 1 | I CAN'T SEE | East West E 3801CD |

RAYDIO
US R&B group formed in 1977 by Ray Parker Jr (born 1/5/1954, Detroit, MI, guitar/vocals), Arnell Carmichael (keyboards), Jerry Knight (bass) and Vincent Bonham (piano). Parker later recorded solo while Jerry Knight linked with Ollie Brown to form the duo Ollie and Jerry.

| 08/04/1978 | 11 | 12 | JACK AND JILL | Arista 161 |
| 08/07/1978 | 27 | 9 | IS THIS A LOVE THING | Arista 193 |

RAYVON
Barbadian singer Bruce Brewster.

| 08/07/1995 | 5 | 9 | IN THE SUMMERTIME | Virgin VSCDT 1542 |
| 09/06/2001 | ●³ | 16 | ● | ANGEL ↑ ▲¹ This and above single credited to SHAGGY FEATURING RAYVON Contains samples of Merrilee Rush' *Angel Of The Morning* and Steve Miller's *The Joker* | MCA MCSTD 40257 |

○ Silver disc ● Gold disc ✪ Platinum disc (additional platinum units are indicated by a figure following the symbol) ◉ Singles released prior to 1973 that are known to have sold over 1 million copies in the UK

03/08/2002.....67......1....... 2-WAY .... MCA MCSTD 40287

RAZE US house group comprising Vaughn Mason and singer Keith Thompson. Their later singers included Pamela Frazier and rapper Doug Lazy.

01/11/1986.....20.....15.....	JACK THE GROOVE.. Champion CHAMP 23
28/02/1987.....57......3......	LET THE MUSIC MOVE U .... Champion CHAMP 27
31/12/1988.....28.....11.....	BREAK 4 LOVE .... Champion CHAMP 67
15/07/1989.....27......5.....	LET IT ROLL **RAZE PRESENTS DOUG LAZY** .... Atlantic A 8866
02/09/1989.....59......5.....	BREAK 4 LOVE .... Champion CHAMP 67
27/01/1990.....30......5.....	ALL 4 LOVE (BREAK 4 LOVE 1990) **RAZE FEATURING LADY J AND SECRETARY OF ENTERTAINMENT** .... Champion CHAMP 228
10/02/1990.....62......1.....	CAN YOU FEEL IT/CAN YOU FEEL IT **RAZE/CHAMPIONSHIP LEGEND** .... Champion CHAMP 227
24/09/1994.....44......2.....	BREAK 4 LOVE (2ND REMIX) .... Champion CHAMPCD 314
29/03/2003.....64......1.....	BREAK 4 LOVE (3RD REMIX) .... Champion CHAMPCD 784

RAZORLIGHT UK rock group formed in London in 2002 by Johnny Borrell (vocals), Bjorn Agren (guitar), Carl Dalemo (bass) and Christian Smith (drums).

30/08/2003.....56......1......	ROCK 'N' ROLL LIES .... Vertigo 9800413
22/11/2003.....42......1......	RIP IT UP .... Vertigo 9814046
07/02/2004.....27......3......	STUMBLE AND FALL Featured in the 2004 film *The Football Factory* .... Vertigo 9816397
26/06/2004.....9......7......	**GOLDEN TOUCH** .... Vertigo 9866836
25/09/2004.....18......4.....	VICE .... Vertigo 9867759
11/12/2004.....20......3+.....	RIP IT UP Re-issue of Vertigo 9814046 .... Vertigo 9869077

RE-FLEX UK techno-rock group from London formed by Baxter (guitar/vocals), Paul Fishman (keyboards), Nigel Ross-Scott (bass) and Roland Vaughan Kerridge (drums).

28/01/1984.....28......9....... THE POLITICS OF DANCING .... EMI FLEX 2

REA – see **JAM AND SPOON**

CHRIS REA UK singer (born 4/3/1951, Middlesbrough) who joined Magdelene as replacement for David Coverdale in 1973 and recorded with them for Magnet. The group name-changed to the Beautiful Lovers but disbanded in 1977. Rea signed solo with Magnet and also appeared on Hank Marvin's solo project the same year. He later became an actor, starring in *Parting Shots* (1999).

07/10/1978.....30......7.......	FOOL (IF YOU THINK IT'S OVER)..................................... Magnet MAG 111
21/04/1979.....44......3.....	DIAMONDS .... Magnet MAG 144
27/03/1982.....65......3.....	LOVING YOU .... Magnet MAG 215
01/10/1983.....60......2.....	I CAN HEAR YOUR HEARTBEAT .... Magnet MAG 244
17/03/1984.....65......2.....	I DON'T KNOW WHAT IT IS BUT I LOVE IT.............................. Magnet MAG 255
30/03/1985.....26.....10.....	STAINSBY GIRLS .... Magnet MAG 276
29/06/1985.....67......2.....	JOSEPHINE .... Magnet MAG 280
29/03/1986.....69......1.....	IT'S ALL GONE .... Magnet MAG 283
31/05/1986.....57......8.....	ON THE BEACH .... Magnet MAG 294
06/06/1987.....12.....10.....	LET'S DANCE .... Magnet MAG 299
29/08/1987.....47......4.....	LOVING YOU AGAIN .... Magnet MAG 300
05/12/1987.....67......1.....	JOYS OF CHRISTMAS .... Magnet MAG 314
13/02/1988.....73......2.....	QUE SERA .... Magnet MAG 318
13/08/1988.....12......6.....	ON THE BEACH SUMMER '88 .... WEA YZ 195
22/10/1988.....74......2.....	I CAN HEAR YOUR HEARTBEAT .... WEA YZ 320
17/12/1988.....53......3.....	DRIVING HOME FOR CHRISTMAS (EP) Tracks on EP: *Driving Home For Christmas, Footsteps In The Snow, Joys Of Christmas*
	and *Smile* .... WEA YZ 325
18/02/1989.....53......3.....	WORKING ON IT .... WEA YZ 350
14/10/1989.....10......9.....	**THE ROAD TO HELL (PART 2)** Featured in the 1994 film *Beyond The Law* .... WEA YZ 431
10/02/1990.....24......6.....	TELL ME THERE'S A HEAVEN .... East West YZ 455
05/05/1990.....69......1.....	TEXAS .... East West YZ 468
16/02/1991.....16......6.....	AUBERGE .... East West YZ 555
06/04/1991.....57......2.....	HEAVEN .... East West YZ 566
29/06/1991.....49......3.....	LOOKING FOR THE SUMMER .... East West YZ 584
09/11/1991.....27......4.....	WINTER SONG .... East West YZ 629
24/10/1992.....16......4.....	NOTHING TO FEAR .... East West YZ 699
28/11/1992.....31......3.....	GOD'S GREAT BANANA SKIN .... East West YZ 706
30/01/1993.....53......2.....	SOFT TOP HARD SHOULDER Featured in the 1993 film of the same name .... East West YZ 710CD
23/10/1993.....18......5.....	JULIA .... East West YZ 722CD
12/11/1994.....28......3.....	YOU CAN GO YOUR OWN WAY .... East West YZ 835CD
24/12/1994.....70......1.....	TELL ME THERE'S A HEAVEN Re-issue of East West YZ 455 .... East West YZ 885CD
16/11/1996.....41......1.....	DISCO' LA PASSIONE **CHRIS REA AND SHIRLEY BASSEY** Featured in the 1996 film *La Passione*............ East West EW 072CD
24/05/1997.....44......1.....	LET'S DANCE **MIDDLESBROUGH FC FEATURING BOB MORTIMER AND CHRIS REA** .... Magnet EW 112CD

REACT 2 RHYTHM UK production duo Richard Dight and Lawrence Hammond who previously recorded for IRS.

28/06/1997.....73......1....... INTOXICATION.. Jackpot WIN 014CD

❶⁹ Number of weeks single topped the UK charts ↑ Entered the UK chart at #1 ▲⁹ Number of weeks single topped the US chart

655

REACTOR
UK rock group formed by Dave O'Brien (vocals), his brother Ewan (guitar/vocals), Kev Browne (bass) and Evan Jenkins (drums).

10/04/2004.....56......1.......	FEELING THE LOVE Track first appeared as an advertisement for Lynx Touch deodorant....................	Liberty CDREACT001

EILEEN READ – see CADETS WITH EILEEN READ

EDDI READER
UK singer (born 28/8/1959, Glasgow) who was a street busker for eight years before fronting Fairground Attraction. She went solo in 1994 and won Best British Female at the 1995 BRIT Awards.

04/06/1994.....33......5.......	PATIENCE OF ANGELS .... Blanco Y Negro NEG 68CD
13/08/1994.....42......3.......	JOKE (I'M LAUGHING) .... Blanco Y Negro NEG 72CD
05/11/1994.....48......2.......	DEAR JOHN...................................... Blanco Y Negro NEG 75CD1
22/06/1996.....26......3.......	TOWN WITHOUT PITY .... Blanco Y Negro NEG 90CDX
21/08/1999.....69......1.......	FRAGILE THING BIG COUNTRY FEATURING EDDI READER .... Track 0004A

READY FOR THE WORLD
US R&B group formed in Flint, MI by Melvin Riley (vocals), Gordon Strozier (guitar), John Eaton (bass), Greg Potts (keyboards), Willie Triplett (percussion) and Gerald Valentine (drums). They originally recorded for their own Blue Lake label before being signed by MCA. Riley later recorded solo.

26/10/1985.....50......5.......	OH SHEILA ▲[1] .... MCA 1005
14/03/1987.....60......3.......	LOVE YOU DOWN .... MCA 1110

REAL & RICHARDSON FEATURING JOBABE
UK production duo Ed Real and Mark Richardson. Their debut hit originally appeared in January 2003 as part of the *DJ Nation (Bootleg Edition)* by Nukleuz DJs.

10/05/2003.....69......1.......	SUNSHINE ON A RAINY DAY .... Nukleuz 0489 CNUK

REAL EMOTION
UK vocal/instrumental group assembled by producer Simon Harris.

01/07/1995.....67......1.......	BACK FOR GOOD .... Living Beat LBECD 34

REAL McCOY
German/US trio Olaf 'OJ' Jeglitza, Patricia 'Patsy' Petersen and Vanessa Mason. Petersen was later replaced by Lisa Cork.

06/11/1993.....61......1.......	ANOTHER NIGHT .... Logic 74321173732
05/11/1994 .....2......12......O	ANOTHER NIGHT Re-issue of Logic 74321173732 .... Logic 74321236992
28/01/1995.....6......10......O	RUN AWAY Featured in the 1994 film *Asterix In America* .... Logic 74321258822
22/04/1995.....11......8.......	LOVE AND DEVOTION This and above three singles credited to (MC SAR &) THE REAL McCOY.......... Logic 74321272702
26/08/1995.....19......4.......	COME AND GET YOUR LOVE .... Logic 74321301272
11/11/1995.....58......1.......	AUTOMATIC LOVER (CALL FOR LOVE) .... Logic 74321325042

REAL PEOPLE
UK pop group formed in 1989 by Tony Griffiths (born 7/4/1966, Liverpool, bass/vocals), his brother Chris (born 30/3/1968, Liverpool, guitar/vocals), Sean Simpson (born 9/10/1969, Liverpool, guitar) and Tony Elson (born 2/1/1966, Liverpool, drums). A previous attempt known as Jo Jo And The Real People recorded with Stock Aitken Waterman without success.

16/02/1991.....70......1.......	OPEN YOUR MIND (LET ME IN).. CBS 6566127
20/04/1991.....73......1.......	THE TRUTH .... Columbia 6567877
06/07/1991.....60......1.......	WINDOW PANE (EP) Tracks on EP: *Window Pane, See Through You* and *Everything Must Change* .... Columbia 6569327
11/01/1992.....41......3.......	THE TRUTH .... Columbia 6576987
23/05/1992.....38......2.......	BELIEVER.. Columbia 6580067

REAL ROXANNE
US rapper (born Adelaida Joanne Martinez, Puerto Rico, based in New York) who took her stage name after the Roxanne craze started by Hitman Howie Tee.

28/06/1986.....11......9.......	BANG ZOOM (LET'S GO GO) REAL ROXANNE WITH HITMAN HOWIE TEE .... Cooltempo COOL 124
12/11/1988.....71......1.......	RESPECT .... Cooltempo COOL 176

REAL THING
UK R&B group formed in Liverpool by Chris Amoo, Ray Lake, Dave Smith and Kenny Davis. They spent two years on the cabaret circuit and appeared on the TV talent show *Opportunity Knocks* before signing with Bell Records. Davis left and was replaced by Chris' brother Eddie, and the group switched to Pye after a brief spell with EMI. They appeared in the 1978 film *The Stud*. Remixed versions of their early hits revived interest in them and they recorded for Jive in 1986. Chris Amoo's Afghan hound Gable was Crufts Supreme Champion in 1987.

05/06/1976 .....❶[3]......11.....O	YOU TO ME ARE EVERYTHING .... Pye International 7N 25709
04/09/1976 .....2......10.....O	CAN'T GET BY WITHOUT YOU.. Pye 7N 45618
12/02/1977.....16......9.......	YOU'LL NEVER KNOW WHAT YOU'RE MISSING .... Pye 7N 45662
30/07/1977.....33......5.......	LOVE'S SUCH A WONDERFUL THING.. Pye 7N 45701
04/03/1978.....18......9.......	WHENEVER YOU WANT MY LOVE .... Pye 7N 46045
03/06/1978.....39......7.......	LET'S GO DISCO Featured in the 1978 film *The Stud*.. Pye 7N 46078
12/08/1978.....40......8.......	RAININ' THROUGH MY SUNSHINE .... Pye 7N 46113
17/02/1979 .....5......11.....O	CAN YOU FEEL THE FORCE .... Pye 7N 46147
21/07/1979.....33......6.......	BOOGIE DOWN (GET FUNKY NOW).. Pye 7P 109
22/11/1980.....52......4.......	SHE'S A GROOVY FREAK .... Calibre CAB 105
08/03/1986.....5......13.......	YOU TO ME ARE EVERYTHING (THE DECADE REMIX 78–86) .... PRT 7P 349
24/05/1986.....6......13.......	CAN'T GET BY WITHOUT YOU (THE SECOND DECADE REMIX).. PRT 7P 352
02/08/1986.....24......6.......	CAN YOU FEEL THE FORCE ('86 REMIX).. PRT 7P 358
25/10/1986.....71......2.......	STRAIGHT TO THE HEART .... Jive 129

O Silver disc ● Gold disc ✪ Platinum disc (additional platinum units are indicated by a figure following the symbol) ◉ Singles released prior to 1973 that are known to have sold over 1 million copies in the UK

REAL TO REEL
US group formed in Los Angeles, CA in 1980 by brothers Matthew (vocals), Dominic (guitar) and Peter Leslie (guitar), Billy Smith (bass) and Daniel Morgan (drums).

21/04/1984 . . . . . 68 . . . . . . 2 . . . . LOVE ME LIKE THIS . . . . Arista ARIST 565

REBEL MC
UK rapper/singer (born Mike West, 27/8/1965, Tottenham, London) who was an ex-member of Double Trouble And The Rebel MC. He later set up the Tribal Bass label and recorded as Conquering Lion.

27/05/1989 . . . . . 11 . . . . . 12	JUST KEEP ROCKIN' DOUBLE TROUBLE AND THE REBEL MC . . . . Desire WANT 9
07/10/1989 . . . . . 3 . . . . . 14	STREET TUFF REBEL MC AND DOUBLE TROUBLE . . . . Desire WANT 18
31/03/1990 . . . . . 20 . . . . . . 6	BETTER WORLD . . . . Desire WANT 25
02/06/1990 . . . . . 53 . . . . . . 2	REBEL MUSIC . . . . Desire WANT 31
06/04/1991 . . . . . 43 . . . . . . 6	WICKEDEST SOUND REBEL MC FEATURING TENOR FLY . . . . Desire WANT 40
15/06/1991 . . . . . 20 . . . . . . 6	TRIBAL BASE REBEL MC FEATURING TENOR FLY AND BARRINGTON LEVY . . . . Desire WANT 44
31/08/1991 . . . . . 73 . . . . . . 1	BLACK MEANING GOOD . . . . Desire WANT 47
21/03/1992 . . . . . 48 . . . . . . 4	RICH AH GETTING RICHER REBEL MC INTRODUCING LITTLE T . . . . Big Life BLR 70
08/08/1992 . . . . . 62 . . . . . . 1	HUMANITY REBEL MC FEATURING LINCOLN THOMPSON . . . . Big Life BLR 78

REBEL ROUSERS – see CLIFF BENNETT AND THE REBEL ROUSERS

REBELETTES – see DUANE EDDY

REBELS – see DUANE EDDY

EZZ RECO AND THE LAUNCHERS WITH BOYSIE GRANT
Jamaican trombonist (born Emmanuel Rodriguez, 17/10/1934, Kingston) with singer Boysie Grant.

05/03/1964 . . . . . 44 . . . . . . 4 . . . . KING OF KINGS . . . . Columbia DB 7217

RECOIL
UK vocal/instrumental group formed by Alan Wilder (born 1/6/1959) with assistance from Toni Halliday, Douglas McCarthy, Jimmy Hughes, Bukka White, Moby and Diamanda Glass. Wilder is also a member of Depeche Mode.

21/03/1992 . . . . . 60 . . . . . . 1 . . . . FAITH HEALER. . . . . Mute 110

RED
UK production duo Ian Bland and Paul Fitzgerald. The pair also record as Beat Renegades and Dejure.

20/01/2001 . . . . . 41 . . . . . . 1 . . . . HEAVEN & EARTH . . . . Slinky Music SLINKY 008CD

RED BOX
UK group formed in 1982 by Simon Toulson-Clarke (guitar/vocals), Julian Close (saxophone), Martin Nickson (drums), Rob Legge (drums) and Paddy Talbot (keyboards). By the time of their hits the group were a duo of Toulson-Clarke and Close.

24/08/1985 . . . . . 3 . . . . . 14 . . . . . O	LEAN ON ME (AH-LI-AYO) . . . . Sire W 8926
25/10/1986 . . . . . 10 . . . . . 12	FOR AMERICA . . . . Sire YZ 84
31/01/1987 . . . . . 71 . . . . . . 2	HEART OF THE SUN . . . . Sire YZ 100

RED CAR AND THE BLUE CAR
UK vocal/instrumental group.

14/12/1991 . . . . . 44 . . . . . . 4 . . . . HOME FOR CHRISTMAS DAY. . . . . Virgin VS 1394

RED CARPET
Belgian production duo Patrick Bruyndonx (who also records as Den Hetrix) and Raffaele Brescia.

11/12/2004 . . . . . 58 . . . . . . 2 . . . . ALRIGHT . . . . Positiva CDTIVS212

RED DRAGON WITH BRIAN AND TONY GOLD
Jamaican singer (born Leroy May, Kingston) who began his career as a DJ and changed his name to Red Dragon in 1984 following the success of the local hit *The Laughing Dragon*.

30/07/1994 . . . . . 2 . . . . . 15 . . . . . O . COMPLIMENTS ON YOUR KISS . . . . Mango CIDM 820

RED EYE
UK instrumental/production duo Francis Hendy and Sean Bastie.

03/12/1994 . . . . . 62 . . . . . . 1 . . . . KUT IT . . . . Champion CHAMPCD 315

RED 5
German producer/DJ Thomas Kukula.

10/05/1997 . . . . . 11 . . . . . . 5	I LOVE YOU...STOP! Contains a sample of Maxine Harvey's *I Love You...Stop!* . . . . Multiply CDMULTY 20
20/12/1997 . . . . . 26 . . . . . . 5	LIFT ME UP . . . . Multiply CDMULTY 30

RED HED – see VINYLGROOVER AND THE RED HED

RED HILL CHILDREN
UK vocal group.

30/11/1996 . . . . . 40 . . . . . . 2 . . . . WHEN CHILDREN RULE THE WORLD . . . . Really Useful 5797262

RED HOT CHILI PEPPERS
US rock group formed in Los Angeles, CA in 1978 by Anthony 'Antoine The Swann' Kiedis (born 1/11/1962, Grand Rapids, MI, vocals), Flea (born Michael Balzary, 16/10/1962, Melbourne, Australia, bass), Jack Irons (drums) and Hillel Slovak (guitar) as Los Faces and then Anthem. Slovak and Irons briefly left to join What Is This? and could not appear on the Peppers' first album for EMI America imprint Enigma in 1984. Slovak died of a drug overdose on 25/6/1988 and was replaced by John Frusciante (born 5/3/1970, New York). Irons left the same year and was replaced by Chad Smith (born 25/10/1962, St Paul, MN). Frusciante resigned in 1992 and was eventually replaced by Arik Marshall (born 13/2/1967, Los Angeles). Dave Navarro (born 7/6/1967, Santa Monica, CA) replaced Marshall in 1993. Navarro left the group in 1998 to go solo and was replaced by the returning Frusciante. The group appeared in an episode of the TV animation *The Simpsons,* performing *Give It Away* at both Moe's bar and at a Krusty The

❶⁹ Number of weeks single topped the UK charts ↑ Entered the UK chart at #1 ▲⁹ Number of weeks single topped the US chart

657

Klown special. They were named Best Rock Act at the 2000 and 2002 MTV Europe Music Awards and collected the 2002 award for Best Live Act. They won their first BRIT Award in 2003 for Best International Group.

DATE	POS	WKS	SINGLE TITLE	LABEL & NUMBER
10/02/1990	55	3	HIGHER GROUND Featured in the 2000 film *Center Stage*	EMI-USA MT 75
23/06/1990	29	3	TASTE THE PAIN Featured in the 1989 film *Say Anything*	EMI-USA MT 85
08/09/1990	54	3	HIGHER GROUND	EMI-USA MT 88
14/03/1992	26	4	UNDER THE BRIDGE	Warner Brothers W 0084
15/08/1992	41	3	BREAKING THE GIRL	Warner Brothers W 0126
05/02/1994	9	4	**GIVE IT AWAY** 1992 Grammy Award for Best Hard Rock Performance with Vocal	Warner Brothers W 0225CD1
30/04/1994	13	6	UNDER THE BRIDGE Re-issue of Warner Brothers W 0084	Warner Brothers W 0237CDX
02/09/1995	31	2	WARPED	Warner Brothers W 0316CD
21/10/1995	29	2	MY FRIENDS	Warner Brothers W 0317CD
17/02/1996	11	3	AEROPLANE	Warner Brothers W 0331CD
14/06/1997	7	8	**LOVE ROLLERCOASTER** Cover version of the Ohio Players' 1975 US #1. Featured in the 1997 film *Beavis And Butt-Head Do America*	Geffen GFSTD 22188
12/06/1999	15	6	SCAR TISSUE 1999 Grammy Award for Best Rock Song for writers Anthony Kiedis, Michael Balzary, John Frusciante and Chad Smith	Warner Brothers W 490CD
04/09/1999	35	2	AROUND THE WORLD	Warner Brothers W 500CD1
12/02/2000	33	2	OTHERSIDE	Warner Brothers W 510CD1
19/08/2000	16	5	CALIFORNICATION	Warner Brothers W 534CD1
13/01/2001	30	2	ROAD TRIPPIN'	Warner Brothers W 546CD1
13/07/2002	2	10	**BY THE WAY**	Warner Brothers W 580CD1
02/11/2002	11	10	THE ZEPHYR SONG	Warner Brothers W 592CD
22/02/2003	22	6	CAN'T STOP	Warner Brothers W 599CD
28/06/2003	27	2	UNIVERSALLY SPEAKING	Warner Brothers W 609CD
22/11/2003	11	5	FORTUNE FADED	Warner Brothers W 630CD

RED JERRY – see WESTBAM

RED 'N' WHITE MACHINES UK vocal/instrumental group assembled by supporters of Southampton Football Club.

DATE	POS	WKS	SINGLE TITLE	LABEL & NUMBER
24/05/2003	16	1	SOUTHAMPTON BOYS	Centric CEN 008

RED RAT Jamaican singer.

DATE	POS	WKS	SINGLE TITLE	LABEL & NUMBER
12/09/1998	51	1	ALL OF THE GIRLS (ALL AI-DI-GIRL DEM) **CARNIVAL FEATURING RIP VS RED RAT**	Pepper 0530072
30/09/2000	70	1	THINKING OF YOU **CURTIS LYNCH JR FEATURING KELE LE ROC AND RED RAT**	Telstar CDSTAS 3136

RED RAW FEATURING 007 UK vocal/instrumental duo Pete Pritchard and Stu Allen with ragga singer 007. They also recorded as Clock.

DATE	POS	WKS	SINGLE TITLE	LABEL & NUMBER
28/10/1995	59	1	OOH LA LA LA	Media MCSTD 2065

RED SNAPPER UK group formed in 1993 by David Ayers (guitar), Ali Friend (double bass) and Richard Thair (drums). They funded their own debut EP.

DATE	POS	WKS	SINGLE TITLE	LABEL & NUMBER
21/11/1998	60	1	IMAGE OF YOU	Warp WAP 111CD

RED VENOM – see BIG BOSS STYLUS PRESENTS RED VENOM

REDBONE US/Indian swamp rock group formed in Los Angeles, CA in 1968 by Lolly Vegas (born Fresno, CA, guitar/vocals), his brother Pat (born Fresno, vocals/bass), Anthony Bellamy (born Los Angeles, guitar/vocals) and Peter De Poe (born in Neah Bay Indian Reservation, WA and given the Indian name 'Last Walking Bear', drums). De Poe left in 1973 and was replaced by Butch Rillera.

DATE	POS	WKS	SINGLE TITLE	LABEL & NUMBER
25/09/1971	2	12	**THE WITCH QUEEN OF NEW ORLEANS**	Epic EPC 7351

REDD KROSS US group formed in Los Angeles, CA in 1979 by Jeff McDonald (vocals), Greg Hetson (guitar), Steve McDonald (bass) and Ron Reyes (drums) as The Tourists, name-changing shortly after to Red Cross (they subsequently amended the spelling after the International Red Cross organisation threatened to sue). Hetson and Reyes later left the group, with the Hetson brothers utilising various musicians.

DATE	POS	WKS	SINGLE TITLE	LABEL & NUMBER
05/02/1994	75	1	VISIONARY	This Way Up WAY 2733
10/09/1994	45	2	YESTERDAY ONCE MORE Listed flip side was Sonic Youth's *Superstar*. Both tracks were taken from a tribute album to The Carpenters, *If I Were A Carpenter*	A&M 5807932
01/02/1997	63	1	GET OUT OF MYSELF	This Way Up WAY 5466

REDD SQUARE FEATURING TIFF LACEY UK duo producer Chris Dececio and vocalist Tiff Lacey.

DATE	POS	WKS	SINGLE TITLE	LABEL & NUMBER
26/10/2002	64	1	IN YOUR HANDS	Inferno CDFERN 50

SHARON REDD US singer (born 19/10/1945, Norfolk, VA) who began her career in musicals and landed the lead role in *Hair* in Australia. She signed as a solo artist with Prelude in 1980. She died from AIDS on 1/5/1992.

DATE	POS	WKS	SINGLE TITLE	LABEL & NUMBER
28/02/1981	31	8	CAN YOU HANDLE IT	Epic EPC 9572
02/10/1982	20	9	NEVER GIVE YOU UP	Prelude PRL A 2755
15/01/1983	31	5	IN THE NAME OF LOVE	Prelude PRL A 2905
22/10/1983	39	5	LOVE HOW YOU FEEL	Prelude A 3868
01/02/1992	17	5	CAN YOU HANDLE IT **DNA FEATURING SHARON REDD**	EMI EM 219

OTIS REDDING
US singer (born 9/9/1941, Dawson, GA) who began his career backing Johnny Jenkins And The Pinetoppers and made his first recordings as Otis & The Shooters (The Shooters being The Pinetoppers) for Finer Arts. He went with Jenkins to Stax for a recording session and persuaded the label to let him use available studio time, subsequently releasing *These Arms Of Mine* on Volt (a Stax subsidiary). As Atlantic had paid for the Jenkins session they technically had Redding under contract (and signed him to their Atco label), but under a special arrangement all his early releases appeared on Volt. He was killed in a plane crash while en route to Madison, WI on 10/12/1967, the crash also killing most members of his backing group the Bar-Kays, the only survivor being Bar-Kay Ben Cauley. Otis Redding was inducted into the Rock & Roll Hall of Fame in 1989. Carla Thomas is a US singer (born 21/12/1942, Memphis, TN) and daughter of Rufus Thomas.

DATE	POS	WKS		SINGLE TITLE	LABEL & NUMBER
25/11/1965	11	16		MY GIRL	Atlantic AT 4050
07/04/1966	33	4		SATISFACTION	Atlantic AT 4080
14/07/1966	37	6		MY LOVER'S PRAYER	Atlantic 584 019
25/08/1966	29	8		I CAN'T TURN YOU LOOSE	Atlantic 584 030
24/11/1966	23	9		FA FA FA FA FA (SAD SONG)	Atlantic 584 049
26/01/1967	46	4		TRY A LITTLE TENDERNESS	Atlantic 584 070
23/03/1967	43	6		DAY TRIPPER	Stax 601 005
04/05/1967	48	1		LET ME COME ON HOME	Stax 601 007
15/06/1967	28	10		SHAKE	Stax 601 011
19/07/1967	18	11		TRAMP	Stax 601 012
11/10/1967	35	5		KNOCK ON WOOD This and above single credited to **OTIS REDDING AND CARLA THOMAS**	Stax 601 021
14/02/1968	36	9		MY GIRL	Atlantic 584 092
21/02/1968	3	15		**(SITTIN' ON) THE DOCK OF THE BAY** ▲[4] Recorded three days before Redding was killed. 1968 Grammy Awards for Best Rhythm & Blues Performance, plus Best Rhythm & Blues Song for writers Otis Redding and Steve Cropper. Featured in the 1987 film *Platoon* ..	Stax 601 031
29/05/1968	24	5		HAPPY SONG	Stax 601 040
31/07/1968	15	12		HARD TO HANDLE	Atlantic 584 199
09/07/1969	43	3		LOVE MAN	Atco 226 001

HELEN REDDY
Australian singer (born 25/10/1942, Melbourne) who made her stage debut at the age of four and later hosted her own TV series. She won a talent contest in 1966 that included a trip to New York and relocated to the city, later switching to Los Angeles, CA. Signed by Capitol in 1971, she won the 1972 Grammy Award for Best Pop Vocal Performance with *I Am Woman*. She has a star on the Hollywood Walk of Fame.

DATE	POS	WKS		SINGLE TITLE	LABEL & NUMBER
18/01/1975	5	10		**ANGIE BABY** ▲[1]	Capitol CL 15799
28/11/1981	43	8		I CAN'T SAY GOODBYE TO YOU	MCA 744

REDHEAD KINGPIN AND THE FBI
US singer (born David Guppy, 1970, Englewood, NJ) who took his stage name from his red hair. Unlike most rappers, he does not swear on record as his mother is a serving police officer. FBI stands for For Black Intelligence and comprised DJ Wildstyle, Bo Roc, Lieutenant Squeak, Buzz and Poochie. The group later name-changed to Private Investigations.

DATE	POS	WKS		SINGLE TITLE	LABEL & NUMBER
22/07/1989	13	10		DO THE RIGHT THING	10 TEN 271
02/12/1989	68	1		SUPERBAD SUPERSLICK	10 TEN 286

REDMAN
US rapper (born Reggie Noble, 17/4/1970, Newark, NJ).

DATE	POS	WKS		SINGLE TITLE	LABEL & NUMBER
25/04/1998	42	1		RAP SCHOLAR **DAS EFX FEATURING REDMAN**	East West E 3853CD
30/05/1998	21	3		MADE IT BACK **BEVERLEY KNIGHT FEATURING REDMAN** Contains a sample of Chic's *Good Times*	Parlophone Rhythm CDRHYTHM 11
24/10/1998	9	8		**HOW DEEP IS YOUR LOVE DRU HILL FEATURING REDMAN**	Island Black Music CID 725
12/06/1999	52	1		DA GOODNESS Contains a sample of Duke Ellington's *Caravan*	Def Jam 8709232
22/07/2000	29	2		OOOH DE LA SOUL **FEATURING REDMAN** Contains an interpolation of Run DMC's *Together Forever*	Tommy Boy TBCD 2102B
15/09/2001	11	2		SMASH SUMTHIN' **REDMAN FEATURING ADAM F**	Def Jam 5886932
31/08/2002	47	2		SMASH SUMTHIN (REMIX) **ADAM F FEATURING REDMAN**	Kaos KOASCD 003
23/11/2002	❶[2]	9	✪	**DIRRTY** ↑ **CHRISTINA AGUILERA FEATURING REDMAN** 2003 MOBO Award for Best Video	RCA 74321962722
11/01/2003	14	5		REACT **ERICK SERMON FEATURING REDMAN**	J Records 74321988492

REDNEX
Swedish studio group featuring Goran Danielsson, Annika Ljungberg, Cool James, Pat Reinioz, Bosse Nilsson, General Custer and Animal.

DATE	POS	WKS		SINGLE TITLE	LABEL & NUMBER
17/12/1994	❶[2]	16	✪	**COTTON EYE JOE**	Internal Affairs KGBCD 016
25/03/1995	12	6		OLD POP IN AN OAK	Internal Affairs KGBCD 019
21/10/1995	55	1		WILD 'N FREE	Internal Affairs KGBCD 024

REDS UNITED
UK vocal group formed by 40 supporters of Manchester United FC.

DATE	POS	WKS		SINGLE TITLE	LABEL & NUMBER
06/12/1997	12	9	O	SING UP FOR THE CHAMPIONS	Music Collection MANUCD 2
09/05/1998	33	4		UNITED CALYPSO '98	Music Collection MANUCD 3

REDSKINS
UK rock group formed in York by Chris Dean (who assumed the identity X Moore, guitar/vocals), Lloyd Dwyer (saxophone), Steve Nichol (trumpet), Martin Hewes (bass) and Nick King (drums) as No Swastikas. King was later replaced by Paul Hookham. They disbanded in 1986.

DATE	POS	WKS		SINGLE TITLE	LABEL & NUMBER
10/11/1984	43	5		KEEP ON KEEPIN' ON	Decca F 1
22/06/1985	33	5		BRING IT DOWN (THIS INSANE THING)	Decca F 2
22/02/1986	59	2		THE POWER IS YOURS	Decca F 3

❶[9] Number of weeks single topped the UK charts ↑ Entered the UK chart at #1 ▲[9] Number of weeks single topped the US chart

ALEX REECE
UK producer from London who is also a keyboard player, bass player, drummer and in demand as a remixer.

DATE	POS	WKS	BPI	SINGLE TITLE	LABEL & NUMBER
16/12/1995	69	1		FEEL THE SUNSHINE	Blunted Vinyl BLNCD 016
11/05/1996	26	3		FEEL THE SUNSHINE (REMIX) Uncredited singer is Deborah Anderson	Fourth & Broadway BRCD 332
27/07/1996	33	2		CANDLES	Fourth & Broadway BRCD 333
16/11/1996	64	1		ACID LAB	Fourth & Broadway BRCD 344

JIMMY REED
US blues singer/guitarist (born Mathis James Reed, 6/9/1925, Leland, MS) who began his recording career with Vee-Jay in 1953. Afflicted by epilepsy from 1957, he died from a seizure on 29/8/1976. He was inducted into the Rock & Roll Hall of Fame in 1991.

DATE	POS	WKS	SINGLE TITLE	LABEL & NUMBER
10/09/1964	45	2	SHAME SHAME SHAME	Stateside SS 330

LOU REED
US singer (born Louis Firbank, 2/3/1943, Freeport, Long Island, NY) who was a founder member of Velvet Underground in 1965, leaving in 1970. He released his solo debut in 1972. He took part in the *Perfect Day* project for the BBC's Children In Need charity. He won the 1998 Grammy Award for Best Music Video Long Form for *Rock And Roll Heart*. Sam Moore is a US singer (born 12/10/1935, Miami, FL) and a member of Sam And Dave.

DATE	POS	WKS	SINGLE TITLE	LABEL & NUMBER
12/05/1973	10	9	**WALK ON THE WILD SIDE** Featured in the 1980 film *Times Square*	RCA 2303
17/01/1987	30	10	SOUL MAN **SAM MOORE AND LOU REED** Featured in the 1986 film of the same name	A&M AM 364
31/07/2004	10	7	**SATELLITE OF LOVE 04** Remix of a track originally released in 1972	NuLife 82876636472

DAN REED NETWORK
US funk-rock group formed in Portland, OR by Dan Reed (vocals), Melvin Brannon II (bass), Brion James (guitar), Daniel Pred (drums) and Blake Sakamoto (keyboards).

DATE	POS	WKS	SINGLE TITLE	LABEL & NUMBER
20/01/1990	51	3	COME BACK BABY	Mercury DRN 2
17/03/1990	60	3	RAINBOW CHILD	Mercury DRN 3
21/07/1990	39	4	STARDATE 1990/RAINBOW CHILD	Mercury DRN 4
08/09/1990	45	3	LOVER/MONEY	Mercury DRN 5
13/07/1991	49	2	MIX IT UP	Mercury MER 345
21/09/1991	65	1	BABY NOW	Mercury MER 352

MICHAEL REED ORCHESTRA – see RICHARD HARTLEY/MICHAEL REED ORCHESTRA

REEF
UK rock group formed in Wolverhampton in 1993 by Gary Stringer (vocals), Kenwyn House (guitars), Jack Bessant (bass), Benmont Tench (keyboards) and Dominic Greensmith (drums) as Naked, name-changing upon signing with Sony.

DATE	POS	WKS	SINGLE TITLE	LABEL & NUMBER
15/04/1995	24	4	GOOD FEELING	Sony S2 6613602
03/06/1995	11	5	NAKED	Sony S2 6620622
05/08/1995	19	3	WEIRD	Sony S2 6622772
02/11/1996	6	7	**PLACE YOUR HANDS**	Sony S2 6635712
25/01/1997	8	5	**COME BACK BRIGHTER**	Sony S2 6640972
05/04/1997	13	4	CONSIDERATION	Sony S2 6643125
02/08/1997	21	3	YER OLD	Sony S2 6647032
10/04/1999	15	6	I'VE GOT SOMETHING TO SAY	Sony S2 6669545
05/06/1999	46	1	SWEETY	Sony S2 6673732
11/09/1999	73	1	NEW BIRD	Sony S2 6678512
12/08/2000	19	5	SET THE RECORD STRAIGHT	Sony S2 6695952
16/12/2000	55	1	SUPERHERO	Sony S2 6699382
19/05/2001	51	1	ALL I WANT	Sony S2 6708222
25/01/2003	44	1	GIVE ME YOUR LOVE	Sony S2 6731645
28/06/2003	56	1	WASTER	Reef Recordings SMASCD 051X

REEL
Irish group formed by Philip J Gargan, Matthew Keaney, Garry O'Meara and twins Colin and Joseph O'Halloran.

DATE	POS	WKS	SINGLE TITLE	LABEL & NUMBER
24/11/2001	39	1	LIFT ME UP	Universal TV 0154632
08/06/2002	31	2	YOU TAKE ME AWAY	Universal TV 0190182

REEL BIG FISH
US group formed by Aaron Barrett (guitar/vocals), Matt Wong (bass) and Andrew Gonzales (drums), later adding Tavis Werts (trumpet), Scot Klopfenstein (trumpet), Grant Barry (trombone) and Dan Regan (trombone).

DATE	POS	WKS	SINGLE TITLE	LABEL & NUMBER
06/04/2002	62	1	SOLD OUT EP Tracks on EP: *Sell Out, Take On Me* and *Hungry Like The Wolf*	Jive 9270002

REEL 2 REAL FEATURING THE MAD STUNTMAN
US duo producer Erick 'More' Morillo and rapper Mark 'The Mad Stuntman' Quashie. Stuntman took his name from the Lee Majors character in *The Fall Guy* TV series. Morillo later launched the Subliminal label and was a member of Pianoheadz.

DATE	POS	WKS	BPI	SINGLE TITLE	LABEL & NUMBER
12/02/1994	5	20	○	**I LIKE TO MOVE IT**	Positiva CDTIV 10
02/07/1994	7	9		**GO ON MOVE**	Positiva CDTIV 15
01/10/1994	13	5		CAN YOU FEEL IT	Positiva CDTIV 22
03/12/1994	14	6		RAISE YOUR HANDS	Positiva CDTIV 27
01/04/1995	27	4		CONWAY	Positiva CDTIVS 30
06/07/1996	7	7		**JAZZ IT UP**	Positiva CDTIV 59
05/10/1996	24	2		ARE YOU READY FOR SOME MORE? This and above two singles credited to **REEL 2 REAL**	Positiva CDTIV 56

REELISTS
UK production duo Saif 'Sef' Naqui and Kaywan 'K1' Qazzaz. Sef is the brother of So Solid Crew member Mr Shabz.

DATE	POS	WKS	SINGLE TITLE	LABEL & NUMBER
25/05/2002	16	6	FREAK MODE	Go! Beat GOBCD 45

○ Silver disc ● Gold disc ✪ Platinum disc (additional platinum units are indicated by a figure following the symbol) ◉ Singles released prior to 1973 that are known to have sold over 1 million copies in the UK

MAUREEN REES
UK singer who first came to prominence in a TV documentary covering her efforts to pass her driving test (she managed it at the seventh attempt).

20/12/1997	49	4		DRIVING IN MY CAR	Eagle EAGXS 014

TONY REES AND THE COTTAGERS
UK vocal group assembled by followers of Fulham FC, with their debut hit released to coincide with team's appearance in the FA Cup Final.

10/05/1975	46	1		VIVA EL FULHAM	Sonet SON 2059

REESE PROJECT
US producer Kevin Saunderson (born 9/5/1964, New York City) who was previously a member of Inner City.

08/08/1992	52	2		THE COLOUR OF LOVE	Network NWK 1
12/12/1992	74	1		I BELIEVE	Network NWKT 63
13/03/1993	54	2		SO DEEP	Network NWKCD 68
24/09/1994	55	1		THE COLOUR OF LOVE (REMIX)	Network NWKCD 81
06/05/1995	44	1		DIRECT-ME	Network NWKCD 87

CONNOR REEVES
UK R&B singer (born 1971, London) who was initally known as a songwriter, penning tracks for Tina Turner, MN8, Brand New Heavies and Carleen Anderson.

30/08/1997	12	5		MY FATHER'S SON	Wildstar CDWILD 1
22/11/1997	14	4		EARTHBOUND	Wildstar CDWILD 2
11/04/1998	19	4		READ MY MIND	Wildstar CXWILD 4
03/10/1998	28	2		SEARCHING FOR A SOUL	Wildstar CDWILD 6
04/09/1999	23	3		BEST FRIEND **MARK MORRISON AND CONNOR REEVES** Originally recorded by Mark Morrison and Gary Barlow, although Barlow later changed his mind about releasing it due to Morrison's numerous clashes with the law	WEA 221CD1

JIM REEVES
US country singer (born 20/8/1923, Panola County, TX) who hoped to become a professional baseball player until an ankle injury ended his career. His year of birth is sometimes given as 1924 – the discrepancy occurred when Reeves lied about his age when trying out for the St Louis Cardinals. He became a DJ in Louisiana and made his first recordings for Macy's in 1950. He appeared in the 1963 film *Kimberley Jim*. He was killed in a plane crash in Nashville on 31/7/1964, although his body was not found for three days, despite over 500 people being involved in the search. He is buried in a specially landscaped area alongside Highway 79, along with his collie Cheyenne, who died in 1967.

24/03/1960	12	31		HE'LL HAVE TO GO	RCA 1168
16/03/1961	50	1		WHISPERING HOPE	RCA 1223
23/11/1961	17	19		YOU'RE THE ONLY GOOD THING (THAT HAPPENED TO ME)	RCA 1261
28/06/1962	23	21		ADIOS AMIGO	RCA 1293
22/11/1962	42	2		I'M GONNA CHANGE EVERYTHING	RCA 1317
13/06/1963	6	15		**WELCOME TO MY WORLD**	RCA 1342
17/10/1963	29	7		GUILTY	RCA 1364
20/02/1964	5	39		**I LOVE YOU BECAUSE**	RCA 1385
18/06/1964	3	26		**I WON'T FORGET YOU**	RCA 1400
05/11/1964	6	13		**THERE'S A HEARTACHE FOLLOWING ME**	RCA 1423
04/02/1965	8	10		**IT HURTS SO MUCH (TO SEE YOU)**	RCA 1437
15/04/1965	13	12		NOT UNTIL NEXT TIME	RCA 1446
06/05/1965	45	5		HOW LONG HAS IT BEEN	RCA 1445
15/07/1965	22	9		THIS WORLD IS NOT MY HOME	RCA 1412
11/11/1965	17	9		IS IT REALLY OVER	RCA 1488
18/08/1966	❶5	25		**DISTANT DRUMS** Posthumous #1. Originally written by Cindy Walker for Roy Orbison and Reeves' recording was merely a demo, but accompaniment was added following his death and the single subsequently released	RCA 1537
02/02/1967	12	11		I WON'T COME IN WHILE HE'S THERE	RCA 1563
26/07/1967	33	5		TRYING TO FORGET	RCA 1611
22/11/1967	38	6		I HEARD A HEART BREAK LAST NIGHT	RCA 1643
27/03/1968	33	5		PRETTY BROWN EYES	RCA 1672
25/06/1969	17	17		WHEN TWO WORLDS COLLIDE	RCA 1830
06/12/1969	15	16		BUT YOU LOVE ME, DADDY	RCA 1899
21/03/1970	32	5		NOBODY'S FOOL	RCA 1915
12/09/1970	32	3		ANGELS DON'T LIE	RCA 1997
26/06/1971	34	8		I LOVE YOU BECAUSE/HE'LL HAVE TO GO/MOONLIGHT & ROSES	RCA Maximillion 2092
19/02/1972	48	2		YOU'RE FREE TO GO	RCA 2174

MARTHA REEVES AND THE VANDELLAS
US R&B vocal group formed in Detroit, MI as The Delphis and featuring Martha Reeves (born 18/7/1941, Eufaula, AL), Annette Sterling Beard and Rosalind Ashford (born 2/9/1943, Detroit, MI) by the time the trio joined Motown (initially as secretaries, although all three later sang backing vocals). They got their break when Mary Wells failed to show for a recording session and were dubbed the Vandellas. Beard left in 1964 and was replaced by Betty Kelly (born 16/9/1944, Detroit). Kelly left in 1968 and was replaced by Lois Reeves, Martha's sister. The group re-formed in 1971 with Martha and Lois Reeves and Sandra Tilley (born 1945, Cleveland, OH). Martha Reeves went solo in 1972, although the original line-up regrouped in 1989 to

❶9 Number of weeks single topped the UK charts   ↑ Entered the UK chart at #1   ▲9 Number of weeks single topped the US chart

661

record for Ian Levine's Nightmare/Motor City labels. Depending on sources, the Vandellas got their name from Marvin Gaye (they appeared as backing singers on the *Stubborn Kind Of Fellow* sessions and virtually hijacked the show) or an amalgamation of Van Dyke Street in Detroit with singer Della Reese. Tilley died from a brain haemorrhage on 9/9/1983. The group was inducted into the Rock & Roll Hall of Fame in 1995.

DATE	POS	WKS	BPI	SINGLE TITLE	LABEL & NUMBER
29/10/1964	28	8		DANCING IN THE STREET Featured in the 1984 film *The Big Chill*	Stateside SS 345
01/04/1965	26	8		NOWHERE TO RUN Featured in the films *Platoon* (1987), *Good Morning Vietnam* (1988) and *Bringing Out The Dead* (1999)	Tamla Motown TMG 502
01/12/1966	29	8		I'M READY FOR LOVE	Tamla Motown TMG 582
30/03/1967	21	9		JIMMY MACK This and above three singles credited to **MARTHA AND THE VANDELLAS**	Tamla Motown TMG 599
17/01/1968	30	9		HONEY CHILE	Tamla Motown TMG 636
15/01/1969	4	12		**DANCING IN THE STREET** Re-issue of Stateside SS 345	Tamla Motown TMG 684
16/04/1969	42	3		NOWHERE TO RUN Re-issue of Tamla Motown TMG 502	Tamla Motown TMG 694
29/08/1970	21	12		JIMMY MACK	Tamla Motown TMG 599
13/02/1971	11	8		FORGET ME NOT	Tamla Motown TMG 762
08/01/1972	33	5		BLESS YOU	Tamla Motown TMG 794
23/07/1988	52	3		NOWHERE TO RUN Listed flip side was *I Got You (I Feel Good)* by **JAMES BROWN**. Released following the use of both songs in the 1988 film *Good Morning Vietnam*	A&M AM 444

VIC REEVES UK singer/comedian (born Jim Moir, 24/1/1959, Darlington) who established himself as one of the top 'alternative' comedians in UK and has his own series on national TV, with Bob Mortimer his usual sidekick.

DATE	POS	WKS	BPI	SINGLE TITLE	LABEL & NUMBER
27/04/1991	6	6		**BORN FREE** VIC REEVES AND THE ROMAN NUMERALS	Sense SIGH 710
26/10/1991	❶²	12	○	**DIZZY** VIC REEVES AND THE WONDER STUFF	Sense SIGH 712
14/12/1991	47	3		ABIDE WITH ME	Sense SIGH 713
08/07/1995	3	8		**I'M A BELIEVER** EMF/REEVES & MORTIMER	Parlophone CDR 6412

REFLEX FEATURING MC VIPER UK production duo Danny Harrison and Julian Jonah (born Danny Matlock) with rapper MC Viper. Harrison and Jonah also recorded as Congress, Nush, Nu-Birth, Gant, Stella Browne, M Factor and 187 Lockdown.

DATE	POS	WKS	BPI	SINGLE TITLE	LABEL & NUMBER
19/05/2001	72	1		PUT YOUR HANDS UP	Gusto CDGUS 2

REFUGEE ALLSTARS US group that is effectively The Fugees. It therefore features Wyclef 'Clef' Jean (born 17/10/1972, Haiti), Lauryn 'L-Boogie' Hill (born 25/5/1975, East Orange, NJ) and Prakazrel 'Pras' Michel (born 19/10/1972, Haiti).

DATE	POS	WKS	BPI	SINGLE TITLE	LABEL & NUMBER
28/06/1997	13	5		WE TRYING TO STAY ALIVE WYCLEF JEAN AND THE REFUGEE ALLSTARS Based on The Bee Gees' *Stayin' Alive*	Columbia 6646815
06/09/1997	18	4		THE SWEETEST THING REFUGEE ALLSTARS FEATURING LAURYN HILL Featured in the 1997 film *Love Jones*	Columbia 6649785
27/09/1997	25	2		GUANTANAMERA WYCLEF JEAN AND THE REFUGEE ALLSTARS	Columbia 6650852
27/10/2001	20	3		LOVING YOU (OLE OLE OLE) BRIAN HARVEY FEATURING THE REFUGEE CREW	Blacklist 0133045 ERE

JOAN REGAN UK singer (born 19/1/1928, Romford) who made private recordings of two numbers (*Too Young* and *I'll Walk Alone*) and gained a contract with Decca on their strength. She became one of the most popular female singers of the decade, although she suffered various troubles towards the end of the 1950s and early 1960s: in July 1957 she married Harry Claff and in November a newspaper claimed she was expecting a child in February (seven months after the wedding). She received a number of abusive letters from the public but successfully sued the newspaper for libel. In 1963 Harry was sent to prison for defrauding his employers out of £62,000 and she suffered a nervous breakdown. Joan later remarried and settled in Florida. The Squadronaires are a UK military band formed by members of the Royal Air Force, and had all previously worked with orchestra leader Bert Ambrose.

DATE	POS	WKS	BPI	SINGLE TITLE	LABEL & NUMBER
11/12/1953	8	5		**RICOCHET** JOAN REGAN AND THE SQUADRONAIRES	Decca F 10193
14/05/1954	5	8		**SOMEONE ELSE'S ROSES**	Decca F 10257
01/10/1954	3	11		**IF I GIVE MY HEART TO YOU**	Decca F 10373
05/11/1954	18	1		WAIT FOR ME DARLING JOAN REGAN AND THE JOHNSTON BROTHERS	Decca F 10362
25/03/1955	6	8		**PRIZE OF GOLD** Featured in the 1955 film of the same name	Decca F 10432
06/05/1955	19	1		OPEN UP YOUR HEART JOAN AND RUSTY REGAN	Decca F 10474
01/05/1959	9	16		**MAY YOU ALWAYS**	HMV POP 593
05/02/1960	29	2		HAPPY ANNIVERSARY	Pye 7N 15238
28/07/1960	29	8		PAPA LOVES MAMA	Pye 7N 15278
24/11/1960	47	1		ONE OF THE LUCKY ONES	Pye 7N 15310
05/01/1961	42	1		IT MUST BE SANTA	Pye 7N 15303

REGENTS UK group formed by Damian Pew (drums/guitar/vocals), Martin Sheller (bass/keyboards) and singers Kath Best and Bic Brac.

DATE	POS	WKS	BPI	SINGLE TITLE	LABEL & NUMBER
22/12/1979	11	12		7TEEN	Rialto TREB 111
07/06/1980	55	2		SEE YOU LATER	Arista ARIST 350

REGGAE BOYZ Jamaican vocal/instrumental group formed by the members of the Jamaican national team competing in the FIFA World Cup Finals in France.

DATE	POS	WKS	BPI	SINGLE TITLE	LABEL & NUMBER
27/06/1998	59	1		KICK IT	Universal MCSTD 40167

REGGAE PHILHARMONIC ORCHESTRA UK reggae group formed by Steel Pulse member Mykaell Riley.

DATE	POS	WKS	BPI	SINGLE TITLE	LABEL & NUMBER
19/11/1988	35	9		MINNIE THE MOOCHER	Mango IS 378
28/07/1990	71	2		LOVELY THING FEATURING JAZZY JOYCE	Mango MNG 742

REGGAE REVOLUTION – see PATO BANTON

○ Silver disc ● Gold disc ✪ Platinum disc (additional platinum units are indicated by a figure following the symbol) ◉ Singles released prior to 1973 that are known to have sold over 1 million copies in the UK

REGGIE – see **TECHNOTRONIC**

REGINA US dance singer (born Regina Richards, New York City) whose debut hit featured Siedah Garrett on backing vocals and David Sanborn on saxophone.

01/02/1986	50	3		BABY LOVE	Funkin' Marvellous MARV 01

REID UK vocal group formed by brothers Tony, Ivor and Mark Reid.

08/10/1988	66	2		ONE WAY OUT	Syncopate SY 16
11/02/1989	65	2		REAL EMOTION	Syncopate SY 24
15/04/1989	55	6		GOOD TIMES	Syncopate SY 27
21/10/1989	71	2		LOVIN' ON THE SIDE	Syncopate REID 1

ELLEN REID – see **CRASH TEST DUMMIES**

JOHN REID – see **NIGHTCRAWLERS FEATURING JOHN REID**

JUNIOR REID Jamaican reggae singer (born Delroy Reid, 1965, Kingston) who first recorded in 1979 for the Rockers label. In 1985 he became a member of Black Uhuru, remaining with them until 1988 when he went solo. He later set up the RAS Records label.

10/09/1988	21	7		STOP THIS CRAZY THING COLDCUT FEATURING JUNIOR REID AND THE AHEAD OF OUR TIME ORCHESTRA	Ahead Of Our Time CCUT 4
14/07/1990	5	11		I'M FREE SOUP DRAGONS FEATURING JUNIOR REID Featured in the 1999 film *The Other Sister*	Raw TV RTV 9
11/07/1992	63	2		SHINE EYE RAGGA TWINS FEATURING JUNIOR REID	Shut Up And Dance SUAD 32S

MIKE REID UK singer/actor/comedian (born 19/1/1940, London) who began his career as a stand-up comedian with much success and scored a one-off comedy hit single. He later appeared in the BBC TV soap *Eastenders* as Frank Butcher.

22/03/1975	10	8		UGLY DUCKLING	Pye 7N 45434
24/04/1999	46	2		THE MORE I SEE YOU BARBARA WINDSOR AND MIKE REID	Telstar TV CDSTAS 3049

NEIL REID UK singer discovered singing at a Christmas party for old-age pensioners in 1968 who then worked various clubs, usually around school holidays. He won the TV talent show *Opportunity Knocks* three times at the age of eleven and later became the youngest artist to top the album charts with *Neil Reid*.

01/01/1972	2	20		MOTHER OF MINE	Decca F 13264
08/04/1972	45	6		THAT'S WHAT I WANT TO BE	Decca F 13300

PATRICK REID – see **POB FEATURING DJ PATRICK REID**

MAGGIE REILLY – see **MIKE OLDFIELD**

KEITH RELF UK singer (born 22/3/1943, Richmond), initially known as a member of The Yardbirds, who launched a parallel solo career in 1966. He died on 14/5/1976 after being electrocuted while playing his guitar at home.

26/05/1966	50	1		MR ZERO	Columbia DB 7920

R.E.M. US rock group formed in Athens, GA in 1980 by Michael Stipe (born 4/1/1960, Decatur, GA, vocals), Peter Buck (born 6/12/1956, Berkeley, CA, guitar), Bill Berry (born 31/7/1958, Duluth, MN, drums) and Mike Mills (born 17/12/1956, Orange County, CA, bass), taking their name from the abbreviation for Rapid Eye Movement (a psychological term for the stage of sleep in which the most intense dreams occur). They made their first recording for Hib-Tone in 1981, signing with IRS in 1982 and linking with Warner's in 1988. The group has won the Best International Group at the BRIT Awards on three occasions: 1992, 1993 and 1995. They have also won three Grammy Awards including Best Alternative Music Album in 1991 for *Out Of Time*.

28/11/1987	51	8		THE ONE I LOVE	IRS IRM 46
30/04/1988	50	2		FINEST WORKSONG	IRS IRM 161
04/02/1989	51	3		STAND	Warner Brothers W 7577
03/06/1989	28	5		ORANGE CRUSH	Warner Brothers W 2960
12/08/1989	48	2		STAND	Warner Brothers W 2833
09/03/1991	19	9		LOSING MY RELIGION 1991 Grammy Awards for Best Pop Performance by a Group with Vocal and Best Music Video Short Form	Warner Brothers W 0015
18/05/1991	6	11		SHINY HAPPY PEOPLE	Warner Brothers W 0027
17/08/1991	27	4		NEAR WILD HEAVEN	Warner Brothers W 0055
21/09/1991	16	6		THE ONE I LOVE Re-issue of IRS IRM 46	IRS IRM 178
16/11/1991	28	3		RADIO SONG	Warner Brothers W 0072
14/12/1991	39	4		IT'S THE END OF THE WORLD AS WE KNOW IT Featured in the 1989 film *Dream A Little Dream*	IRS IRM 180
03/10/1992	11	5		DRIVE	Warner Brothers W 0136
28/11/1992	18	8		MAN ON THE MOON Featured in the 1999 film of the same name, the story of alternative comedian Andy Kaufman	Warner Brothers W 0143
20/02/1993	17	6		THE SIDEWINDER SLEEPS TONITE	Warner Brothers W 0152CD1
17/04/1993	7	12	O	EVERYBODY HURTS	Warner Brothers W 0169CD1

❶⁹ Number of weeks single topped the UK charts ↑ Entered the UK chart at #1 ▲⁹ Number of weeks single topped the US chart

663

				SINGLE TITLE	LABEL & NUMBER
24/07/1993	27	5		NIGHTSWIMMING	Warner Brothers W 0184CD
11/12/1993	54	1		FIND THE RIVER	Warner Brothers W 0211CD
17/09/1994	9	7		WHAT'S THE FREQUENCY, KENNETH Featured in the 1999 film *Bringing Out The Dead*	Warner Brothers W 0265CD
12/11/1994	15	4		BANG AND BLAME	Warner Brothers W 0275CD
04/02/1995	23	3		CRUSH WITH EYELINER	Warner Brothers W 0281CD
15/04/1995	9	4		**STRANGE CURRENCIES**	Warner Brothers W 0290CD
29/07/1995	13	5		TONGUE	Warner Brothers W 0308CD
31/08/1996	4	5		**E – BOW THE LETTER**	Warner Brothers W 0369CD
02/11/1996	19	2		BITTERSWEET ME	Warner Brothers W 0377CDX
14/12/1996	29	2		ELECTROLITE	Warner Brothers W 0383CDX
24/10/1998	6	6		**DAYSLEEPER**	Warner Brothers W 0455CD
19/12/1998	26	5		LOTUS	Warner Brothers W 466CD
20/03/1999	10	4		**AT MY MOST BEAUTIFUL**	Warner Brothers W 477CD
05/02/2000	3	10		**THE GREAT BEYOND** Featured in the 1999 film *Man On The Moon*	Warner Brothers W 516CD
12/05/2001	6	9		**IMITATION OF LIFE**	Warner Brothers W 559CD
04/08/2001	24	3		ALL THE WAY TO RENO	Warner Brothers W 568CDX
01/12/2001	44	1		I'LL TAKE THE RAIN	Warner Brothers W 573CD
25/10/2003	8	7		**BAD DAY**	Warner Brothers W 624CD1
17/01/2004	33	2		ANIMAL	Warner Brothers W 633CD
09/10/2004	5	5		**LEAVING NEW YORK**	Warner Brothers W 654CD1
11/12/2004	41	2		AFTERMATH	Warner Brothers W658CD2

REMBRANDTS US vocal duo Danny Wilde and Phil Solem who first linked in 1990. Solem left in 1996 and Wilde put together another band with Graham Edwards, Dorian Crozier and Mark Karan.

02/09/1995	3	12	O	**I'LL BE THERE FOR YOU** Theme to the TV series *Friends*	Elektra A 4390CD
20/01/1996	58	1		THIS HOUSE IS NOT A HOME	East West A 4336CD
24/05/1997	5	15	O	**I'LL BE THERE FOR YOU** Re-issue of Elektra A 4390CD and re-promoted following the release of the series on video	East West A 4390CD

REMO FOUR – see TOMMY QUICKLY AND THE REMO FOUR

REMY – see TERROR SQUAD FEATURING FAT JOE AND REMY

REMY ZERO US rock group formed in Birmingham, AL by Cinjun Tate (vocals), Shelby Tate (guitar), Jeffrey Cain (guitar), Cedric LeMoyne (bass) and Gregory Slay (drums).

27/04/2002	55	1		SAVE ME	Elektra E 7297CD

RENAISSANCE UK rock group formed in 1969 by Keith Relf (born 22/3/1943, Richmond, harmonica/vocals), Jim McCarty (born 25/7/1943, Liverpool, drums), Louis Cennamo (bass), John Hawken (keyboards) and Jane Relf (vocals). Both Keith Relf and McCarty had been with the Yardbirds. By 1971 the group consisted of Jon Camp (bass), John Tout (keyboards), Terry Sullivan (drums) and Annie Haslam (vocals). Later members included Michael Dunford (guitar) and Andy Powell (guitar). The group disbanded in the early 1980s, although Haslam, Dunford and Jane Relf attempted to revive separate versions of the group bearing the name. Keith Relf died on 14/5/1976 after being electrocuted while playing his guitar at home.

15/07/1978	10	11	O	**NORTHERN LIGHTS**	Warner Brothers K 17177

RENE AND ANGELA US R&B duo Rene Moore and Angela Winbush who first teamed up as songwriters, penning cuts for Lenny Williams and Lamont Dozier. They signed with Capitol and released their debut album in 1980. Angela Winbush married Ronald Isley of the Isley Brothers in 1993.

15/06/1985	66	2		SAVE YOUR LOVE (FOR NUMBER 1) **RENE AND ANGELA FEATURING KURTIS BLOW**	Club JAB 14
07/09/1985	22	10		I'LL BE GOOD	Club JAB 18
02/11/1985	54	3		SECRET RENDEZVOUS	Champion CHAMP 5

RENE AND YVETTE UK vocal duo Gordon Kaye (born 7/4/1941, Huddersfield) and Vicki Michelle (born 14/12/1950, Chigwell), who played the characters of Rene and Yvette in the TV comedy *'Allo 'Allo*.

22/11/1986	57	4		JE T'AIME (ALLO ALLO)/RENE DMC (DEVASTATING MACHO CHARISMA)	Sedition EDIT 3319

NICOLE RENEE US R&B singer/songwriter (born 1975, Philadelphia, PA).

12/12/1998	55	1		STRAWBERRY Contains a sample of Grover Washington Jr's *Paradise*	Atlantic AT 0050CD

RENEE AND RENATO UK duo Renato Pagliari (born in Romania, based in Birmingham) and Renee (born Hilary Lester). Renato was working as a waiter at the time of his hit, while Renee left before the record became a hit, with the result that Val Penny had to mime for the accompanying video. Renee returned for their second record.

30/10/1982	●4	16	●	**SAVE YOUR LOVE**	Hollywood HWD 003
12/02/1983	48	6		JUST ONE MORE KISS	Hollywood HWD 006

RENEGADE SOUNDWAVE UK dance group formed in London by Danny Briotett (bass), Carl Bonnie (guitar) and Gary Asquith (vocals) and initially signed with Rhythm King. Bonnie went solo in 1992.

03/02/1990	38	6		PROBABLY A ROBBERY	Mute 102
05/02/1994	64	1		RENEGADE SOUNDWAVE	Mute CDMUTE 146

O Silver disc ● Gold disc O Platinum disc (additional platinum units are indicated by a figure following the symbol) ◎ Singles released prior to 1973 that are known to have sold over 1 million copies in the UK

REO SPEEDWAGON
US rock group formed in Champaign, IL in 1968 by Alan Gratzer (born 9/11/1948, Syracuse, NY, drums), Neal Doughty (born 29/7/1946, Evanston, IL, keyboards), Gary Richrath (born 18/10/1949, Peoria, IL, guitar), Terry Luttrell (vocals) and Craig Philbin (bass). They signed with Epic in 1970 and released their debut album in 1971. Kevin Cronin (born 6/10/1951, Evanston) replaced Luttrell as singer in 1972, briefly left the group at the end of the year but returned in 1976. Bruce Hall (born 3/5/1953, Champaign, IL) replaced Philbin in 1976. By 1990 the line-up consisted of Cronin, Doughty, Hall and new members Bryan Hitt, Dave Amato and Jesse Harms. They took their name from a 1911 fire engine.

11/04/1981	7	14		KEEP ON LOVING YOU ▲[1]	Epic EPC 9544
27/06/1981	19	14		TAKE IT ON THE RUN	Epic EPC A 1207
16/03/1985	16	10		CAN'T FIGHT THIS FEELING ▲[3]	Epic A 4880

REPARATA AND THE DELRONS
US vocal group formed in Brooklyn, NYC by Reparata Elise, Sheila Reilly and Carol Drobnicki. The group later name-changed to Lady Flash and became Barry Manilow's backing group.

| 20/03/1968 | 13 | 10 | | CAPTAIN OF YOUR SHIP | Bell 1002 |
| 18/10/1975 | 43 | 2 | | SHOES REPARATA | Dart 2066 562 |

REPRAZENT – see RONI SIZE REPRAZENT

REPUBLICA
UK rock group formed in London by Saffron (born Samantha Sprackling, 3/6/1968, Lagos, Nigeria, vocals), Tim Dorney (born 30/3/1965, Ascot, keyboards), Andy Todd (keyboards), Johnny Male (born 10/10/1963, Windsor, guitar) and ex-Bow Wow Wow Dave Barbarossa (drums). Barbarossa left Republica after their first album.

27/04/1996	43	2		READY TO GO Later used as the theme to Sky TV's Scottish football coverage	Deconstruction 74321326132
01/03/1997	13	6		READY TO GO Re-issue of Deconstruction 74321326132	Deconstruction 74321421332
03/05/1997	7	7		DROP DEAD GORGEOUS Featured in the 1997 film Scream	Deconstruction 74321408442
03/10/1998	20	3		FROM RUSH HOUR WITH LOVE	Deconstruction 74321610472

RESEARCH
UK group formed in Leeds by Russell Searle (keyboards/vocals), Georgie Lashbrook (bass/vocals) and Sarah William (drums/vocals).

| 27/11/2004 | 73 | 1 | | SHE'S NOT LEAVING | At Large FUGCD005 |

RESONANCE FEATURING THE BURRELLS
US producer Michael Moog with vocal duo formed by twins Ronald and Rheji Burrell.

| 26/05/2001 | 67 | 1 | | DJ | Strictly Rhythm SRUKCD 02 |

RESOURCE
German production group fronted by 24-year-old former model Georgios Karolidis (born in Stuttgart).

| 31/05/2003 | 41 | 2 | | I JUST DIED IN YOUR ARMS | Substance SUBS17CDS |

REST ASSURED
UK production group formed by Laurence Nelson, Alistair Johnson and Nick Carter with singer Shelley Nelson.

| 28/02/1998 | 14 | 7 | | TREAT INFAMY | ffrr FCD 333 |

REUBEN
UK rock group formed in Surrey in 1998 by Jamie Lenman (guitar/vocals), Jon Pearce (bass) and Jason Wilcock (drums) as Angel. Wilcock left in 2000 and was replaced by Mark Lawton and the group changed name to Reuben. Lawton was subsequently replaced by Guy Davis.

| 19/06/2004 | 53 | 1 | | FREDDY KREUGER | Xtra Mile XMR102 |
| 28/08/2004 | 59 | 1 | | MOVING TO BLACKWATER | Xtra Mile XMR104 |

REUNION
US studio group assembled by songwriters Norman Dolph and Paul DiFranco, with Joey Levine (of Ohio Express) handling lead vocals.

| 21/09/1974 | 33 | 4 | | LIFE IS A ROCK (BUT THE RADIO ROLLED ME) | RCA PB 10056 |

REVELATION
UK production group fronted by singer Clare Pearce.

| 10/05/2003 | 36 | 2 | | JUST BE DUB TO ME | Multiply CDMULTY 99 |

REVILLOS – see REZILLOS

REVIVAL 3000
UK DJ/production trio formed by Leon Roberts, Matthews Roberts and Chris Reynolds.

| 01/11/1997 | 47 | 1 | | THE MIGHTY HIGH Contains a sample of The Mighty Clouds Of Joy's Mighty High | Hi-Life 5718092 |

REVOLTING COCKS
US rock group formed by Alain Jourgenson, Richard 23 and Luc Van Acker, later adding William Rieflin. Richard 23 left in 1986 and was replaced by Chris Connelly. Later members of the group included Roland Barker, Mike Scaccia and Louie Svitek. Jourgenson is also a member of Ministry.

| 18/09/1993 | 61 | 1 | | DA YA THINK I'M SEXY | Devotion CDDVN 111 |

REVOLUTION – see PRINCE

DEBBIE REYNOLDS
US singer (born Mary Frances Reynolds, 1932, El Paso, TX) who won a beauty contest in 1948 (Miss Burbank) and landed a screen contract as a result. She made her name as the star of musicals and later in comedies, including Singing In The Rain (1953), The Mating Game (1959) and The Singing Nun (1966). She married Eddie Fisher in 1955 and divorced 1959. Their daughter is actress Carrie Fisher (of Star Wars fame).

❶[9] Number of weeks single topped the UK charts ↑ Entered the UK chart at #1 ▲[9] Number of weeks single topped the US chart

665

30/08/1957 . . . . . 2 . . . . . . 17 . . . . . .   **TAMMY** ▲[5] Featured in the films *Tammy And The Bachelor* (1957) and *Fear And Loathing In Las Vegas* (1998). Berry Gordy, founder of Motown Records, wanted to call his label Tammy in honour of the record but was forced to amend the name to Tamla
. . . . Coral Q 72274

JODY REYNOLDS US singer (born 3/12/1938, Denver, CO, raised in Oklahoma).

14/04/1979 . . . . . 66 . . . . . . 1 . . . .   ENDLESS SLEEP Features Al Casey on guitar and was originally a US hit in 1958 (#5). Coupled with The Teddy Bears' *To Know Him Is To Love Him* . . . . Lightning LIG 9015

LJ REYNOLDS US R&B singer/songwriter/producer (born Larry J Reynolds, 1953, Detroit, MI) who was a member of Chocolate Syrup and then The Dramatics before going solo. His sister Jeannie Reynolds also launched a singing career.

30/06/1984 . . . . . 53 . . . . . . 3 . . . .   DON'T LET NOBODY HOLD YOU DOWN . . . . Club JAB 5

REYNOLDS GIRLS UK duo Linda and Aisling Reynolds who later formed their own Reynotone label.

25/02/1989 . . . . . 8 . . . . . . 12 . . . . . .   **I'D RATHER JACK** . . . . PWL 25

REZILLOS UK rock group formed in Edinburgh by Eugene Reynolds (born Alan Forbes, vocals), Fay Fife (born Sheila Hynde, vocals), Luke Warm (aka Jo Callis, guitar), Hi Fi Harris (born Mark Harris, guitar), Dr D.K. Smythe (bass), Angel Patterson (born Alan Patterson, drums) and Gale Warning (backing vocals). The group disbanded in 1978, with Fife and Reynolds forming the Revillos.

12/08/1978 . . . . . 17 . . . . . . 9	TOP OF THE POPS . . . . Sire SIR 4001
25/11/1978 . . . . . 43 . . . . . . 4	DESTINATION VENUS . . . . Sire SIR 4008
18/08/1979 . . . . . 71 . . . . . . 2	I WANNA BE YOUR MAN/I CAN'T STAND MY BABY . . . . Sensible SAB 1
26/01/1980 . . . . . 45 . . . . . . 6	MOTORBIKE BEAT **REVILLOS** . . . . Dindisc DIN 5

REZONANCE Q UK production/vocal duo formed in Liverpool by Mike Di Scala and singer Nazene.

01/03/2003 . . . . . 29 . . . . . . 2 . . . . . .   SOMEDAY . . . . All Around The World CXGLOBE 266

RHAPSODY FEATURING WARREN G AND SISSEL US rap group formed by Warren Griffith (born 1971, Long Beach, CA) and Norwegian singer Sissel Kyrkjebo (born 1969, Bergen).

10/01/1998 . . . . . 15 . . . . . . 7 . . . . . .   PRINCE IGOR . . . . Def Jam 5749652

RHC Belgian vocal/instrumental duo Caspar Pound and Plavka Lonich.

11/01/1992 . . . . . 65 . . . . . . 1 . . . . . .   FEVER CALLED LOVE . . . . R&S RSUK 9

RHIANNA UK singer (born Rhianna Kenny, 1983, Leeds).

01/06/2002 . . . . . 18 . . . . . . 5	OH BABY . . . . Sony S2 6726232
14/09/2002 . . . . . 41 . . . . . . 1	WORD LOVE . . . . Sony S2 6730115

RHODA WITH THE SPECIAL AKA UK singer Rhoda Dakar with UK ska group The Special AKA.

23/01/1982 . . . . . 35 . . . . . . 5 . . . . . .   THE BOILER . . . . 2 Tone CHSTT 18

BUSTA RHYMES US rapper (born Trevor Smith, 20/5/1972, Brooklyn, NYC) who is also a member of rap group Leaders Of The New School And The Flipmode Squad.

11/05/1996 . . . . 8 . . . . . . 7	**WOO-HAH!! GOT YOU ALL IN CHECK** Contains a sample of Galt McDermot's *Space* . . . . Elektra EKR 220CD
21/09/1996 . . . . 23 . . . . . . 2	IT'S A PARTY **BUSTA RHYMES FEATURING ZHANE** Contains a sample of Con Funk Shun's *Too Tight* . . . . Elektra EKR 226CD
05/04/1997 . . . . . 8 . . . . . . 6	HIT 'EM HIGH (THE MONSTARS' ANTHEM) **B REAL/BUSTA RHYMES/COOLIO/LL COOL J/METHOD MAN** Featured in the 1996 film *Space Jam* . . . . Atlantic A 5449CD
03/05/1997 . . . . . 39 . . . . . . 1	DO MY THING . . . . Elektra EKR 235CD
18/10/1997 . . . . 16 . . . . . . 3	PUT YOUR HANDS WHERE MY EYES COULD SEE Contains a sample of Seals & Crofts' *Sweet Green Fields* . . . . . . Elektra E 3900CD
20/12/1997 . . . . 32 . . . . . . 4	DANGEROUS Contains a sample of Extra T's *ET Boogie*, even though the original record (released in 1982) had to be withdrawn due to legal problems . . . . Elektra E 3877CD
18/04/1998 . . . . . 2 . . . . . . 10 . . . . . O	**TURN IT UP/FIRE IT UP** Contains a sample of the theme to TV's *Knight Rider*. Featured in the 1998 film *Can't Hardly Wait* . . . . Elektra E 3847CD
11/07/1998 . . . . . 23 . . . . . . 3	ONE **BUSTA RHYMES FEATURING ERYKAH BADU** Contains a sample of Stevie Wonder's *Love's In Need Of Love Today* . . . . Elektra E 3833CD1
30/01/1999 . . . . . 5 . . . . . . 6	**GIMME SOME MORE** . . . . Elektra E 3782CD
01/05/1999 . . . . . 6 . . . . . . 7	**WHAT'S IT GONNA BE?!** **BUSTA RHYMES FEATURING JANET** (Jackson) . . . . Elektra E 3762CD1
22/07/2000 . . . . . 57 . . . . . . 1	GET OUT Contains a sample of Richard Wolfe Children's Chorus' *The Ugly Duckling* . . . . Elektra E 7075CD
16/12/2000 . . . . . 60 . . . . . . 1	FIRE Featured in the 2003 film *Marci X* . . . . East West E 7136CD
18/08/2001 . . . . . 7 . . . . . . 8	**ANTE UP** **M.O.P. FEATURING BUSTA RYMES** . . . . Epic 6717882
16/03/2002 . . . . . 11 . . . . . . 6	BREAK YA NECK . . . . J Records 74321922332
08/06/2002 . . . . . 16 . . . . . . 7	PASS THE COURVOISIER – PART II **BUSTA RHYMES, P DIDDY AND PHARRELL** . . . . J Records 74321937902
08/02/2003 . . . . . 16 . . . . . . 4	MAKE IT CLAP **BUSTA RHYMES FEATURING SPLIFF STAR** . . . . J Records 82876502062
07/06/2003 . . . . . 3 . . . . . . 13	**I KNOW WHAT YOU WANT** **BUSTA RHYMES AND MARIAH CAREY** . . . . J Records 82876528292
29/11/2003 . . . . . 62 . . . . . . 1	LIGHT YOUR ASS ON FIRE **BUSTA RHYMES FEATURING PHARRELL** . . . . Arista 82876572512
15/05/2004 . . . . . 71 . . . . . . 1	PASS THE COURVOISIER – PART II **BUSTA RHYMES, P DIDDY AND PHARRELL** . . . . J Records 74321937902
22/05/2004 . . . . . 17 . . . . . . 5	WHAT'S HAPPENIN' **METHOD MAN FEATURING BUSTA RHYMES** . . . . Def Jam 9862518

RHYTHIM IS RHYTHIM US producer Derrick May who formed the Transmat label.

11/11/1989 . . . . . 74 . . . . . . 1 . . . . . .   STRINGS OF LIFE . . . . Kool Kat KOOL 509

  ○ Silver disc ● Gold disc ✪ Platinum disc (additional platinum units are indicated by a figure following the symbol) ◎ Singles released prior to 1973 that are known to have sold over 1 million copies in the UK

RHYTHM BANGERS – see ROBBIE RIVERA

RHYTHM ETERNITY UK vocal/instrumental group formed by Paul Spencer, Scott Rosser and Lynsey Davenport. Spencer and Rosser later formed Dario G.

23/05/1992 . . . . . 72 . . . . . . 1 . . . . PINK CHAMPAGNE . . . . Dead Dead Good GOOD 15T

RHYTHM FACTOR UK vocal/instrumental group formed by Shank Thompson and Paul Scott.

29/04/1995 . . . . . 53 . . . . . . 2 . . . . YOU BRING ME JOY . . . . Multiply CDMULTY 4

RHYTHM MASTERS UK/Maltese production duo Robert Chetcutti and Steve McGuinness, who also record as Big Room Girl and RM Project.

16/08/1997 . . . . . 49 . . . . . . 1 . . . . COME ON YALL . . . . Faze 2 CDFAZE 37
06/12/1997 . . . . . 49 . . . . . . 1 . . . . ENTER THE SCENE DJ SUPREME VS THE RHYTHM MASTERS . . . . Distinctive DISNCD 40
18/08/2001 . . . . . 50 . . . . . . 1 . . . . UNDERGROUND . . . . Black & Blue NEOCD 056
30/03/2002 . . . . . 71 . . . . . . 1 . . . . GHETTO RHYTHM MASTERS FEATURING JOE WATSON . . . . Black & Blue NEOCD 074

RHYTHM-N-BASS UK vocal group.

19/09/1992 . . . . . 56 . . . . . . 2 . . . . ROSES . . . . Epic 6582907
03/07/1993 . . . . . 59 . . . . . . 2 . . . . CAN'T STOP THIS FEELING . . . . Epic 6592002

RHYTHM OF LIFE UK DJ/producer Steve Burgess.

13/05/2000 . . . . . 24 . . . . . . 2 . . . . YOU PUT ME IN HEAVEN WITH YOUR TOUCH Contains a sample of Debbie Shaw's *You Put Me In Heaven With Your Touch* . . . . . .
. . . . Xtravaganza XTRAV 4CDS

RHYTHM ON THE LOOSE UK producer Geoff Hibbert.

19/08/1995 . . . . . 36 . . . . . . 2 . . . . BREAK OF DAWN Contains a sample of First Choice's *Let No Man Put Asunder* . . . . Six6 SIXCD 126

RHYTHM QUEST UK producer Mark Hadfield.

20/06/1992 . . . . . 45 . . . . . . 2 . . . . CLOSER TO ALL YOUR DREAMS . . . . Network NWK 40

RHYTHM SECTION UK vocal/instrumental group formed by Renie Pilgrem.

18/07/1992 . . . . . 66 . . . . . . 1 . . . . MIDSUMMER MADNESS (EP) Tracks on EP: *Dreamworld, Burnin' Up, Perfect Love 2am* and *Perfect Love 8am* . . . .
. . . . Rhythm Section RSEC 006

RHYTHM SOURCE UK vocal/instrumental group formed by Helen Mason (vocals) and Bradley Stone (keyboards).

17/06/1995 . . . . . 74 . . . . . . 1 . . . . LOVE SHINE . . . . A&M 5810672

RHYTHM SPINNERS – see ROLF HARRIS

RHYTHMATIC UK techno group fronted by former Krush member Mark Gamble.

12/05/1990 . . . . . 71 . . . . . . 2 . . . . TAKE ME BACK . . . . Network NWK 8
03/11/1990 . . . . . 62 . . . . . . 1 . . . . FREQUENCY . . . . Network NWK 13

RHYTHMATIC JUNKIES UK vocal/production group formed by Steve Rowe, Steve McGuinness and Robert Bruce. McGuinness is also a member of Big Time Charlie, Rhythm Masters and RM Project.

15/05/1999 . . . . . 67 . . . . . . 1 . . . . THE FEELIN (CLAP YOUR HANDS) . . . . Sound Of Ministry RIDE 2CDS

RHYTHMKILLAZ Dutch instrumental/production duo DJ Ziki (born Rene Terhorst) and Dobre (born Gaston Steenkist). They also record as Chocolate Puma, DJ Manta, Tomba Vira, Jark Prongo, Goodmen and Riva.

31/03/2001 . . . . . 32 . . . . . . 2 . . . . WACK ASS MF . . . . Incentive CENT 18CDS

RIALTO UK rock group formed in 1991 by Louis Eliot (vocals), Jonny Bull (guitar), Julian Taylor (bass), Pete Cuthbert (drums), Antony Christmas (drums) and Toby Hounsham (keyboards). They were originally formed in 1991 as Kinky Machine by Eliot and Bull.

08/11/1997 . . . . . 37 . . . . . . 2 . . . . MONDAY MORNING 5:19 . . . . East West EW 116CD
17/01/1998 . . . . . 20 . . . . . . 3 . . . . UNTOUCHABLE . . . . East West EW 107CD1
28/03/1998 . . . . . 39 . . . . . . 2 . . . . DREAM ANOTHER DREAM . . . . East West EW 156CD1
17/10/1998 . . . . . 60 . . . . . . 1 . . . . SUMMER'S OVER . . . . China WOKCDR 2099

ROSIE RIBBONS UK singer (born 1982, Alltwen, Wales) who came to prominence as one of the entrants in *Pop Idol*.

02/11/2002 . . . . . 12 . . . . . . 4 . . . . BLINK . . . . T2 CDSTAS 3288
25/01/2003 . . . . . 19 . . . . . . 3 . . . . A LITTLE BIT . . . . T2 CDSTAS 3312

DAMIEN RICE Irish singer/guitarist (born 1974, Celbridge, County Kildare) who was a member of Juniper before going solo.

01/11/2003 . . . . . 32 . . . . . . 2 . . . . CANNONBALL . . . . DRM/14th Floor DR03CD1
17/07/2004 . . . . . 19 . . . . . . 7 . . . . CANNONBALL . . . . DRM/14th Floor DR03CD1
25/12/2004 . . . . . 27 . . . . . . 1+ . . . . . . THE BLOWER'S DAUGHTER . . . . 14th Floor DR06CD1

REVA RICE AND GREG ELLIS UK vocal duo who first came to prominence in the musical *Starlight Express*.

27/03/1993 . . . . . 59 . . . . . . 2 . . . . NEXT TIME YOU FALL IN LOVE Featured in the musical *Starlight Express* . . . . Really Useful RURCD 12

❶⁹ Number of weeks single topped the UK charts ↑ Entered the UK chart at #1 ▲⁹ Number of weeks single topped the US chart

667

CHARLIE RICH
US singer (born 14/12/1932, Colt, AR) who began his career performing jazz and blues, but made his breakthrough performing country music. He died from an acute blood clot on 25/7/1995.

16/02/1974 . . . . . 2 . . . . . 14	**THE MOST BEAUTIFUL GIRL** ▲² Featured in the 1979 film *Every Which Way But Loose* . . . . CBS 1897
13/04/1974 . . . . . 16 . . . . . 10	BEHIND CLOSED DOORS 1973 Grammy Awards for Best Country & Western Vocal Performance plus Best Country Song for writer Kenny O'Dell. Featured in the films *Every Which Way But Loose* (1979) and *Scooby Doo 2: Monsters Unleashed* (2004) . . . .
	. . . . Epic EPC 1539
01/02/1975 . . . . . 37 . . . . . . 5	WE LOVE EACH OTHER . . . . Epic EPC 2868

KELLI RICH – see NU SOUL FEATURING KELLI RICH

RICHIE RICH
UK singer who helped set up Gee Street Records with John Baker and the Stereo MC's.

16/07/1988 . . . . . 48 . . . . . . 3	TURN IT UP . . . . Club JAR 68
22/10/1988 . . . . 22 . . . . . . 5	I'LL HOUSE YOU **RICHIE RICH MEETS THE JUNGLE BROTHERS** . . . . Gee Street GEE 003
10/12/1988 . . . . 74 . . . . . . 1	MY DJ (PUMP IT UP SOME) . . . . Gee Street GEE 7
02/09/1989 . . . . 50 . . . . . . 3	SALSA HOUSE . . . . ffrr F 113
09/03/1991 . . . . 52 . . . . . . 3	YOU USED TO SALSA **RICHIE RICH FEATURING RALPHI ROSARIO** . . . . ffrr F 156
29/03/1997 . . . . 58 . . . . . . 1	STAY WITH ME **RICHIE RICH AND ESERA TUAOLO** . . . . Castle CATX 1001

RISHI RICH PROJECT FEATURING JAY SEAN
UK producer with singers Jay Sean and Juggy D.

20/09/2003 . . . . 12 . . . . . . 5	**DANCE WITH YOU (NACHNA TERE NAAL)** . . . . Relentless RELCD1
03/07/2004 . . . . . 6 . . . . . 10	**EYES ON YOU** JAY SEAN FEATURING RISHI RICH PROJECT . . . . Relentless RELDX5

TONY RICH PROJECT
US singer (born Anthony Jeffries, 19/11/1971, Detroit, MI) who began his career as a songwriter, penning four songs for Pebbles. Through her he was introduced to LA Reid (Pebbles' then husband) and signed with LaFace in 1994. He won the 1996 Grammy Award for Best Rhythm & Blues Album for *Words*.

04/05/1996 . . . . . 4 . . . . . 17	**NOBODY KNOWS** . . . . LaFace 74321356422
31/08/1996 . . . . 27 . . . . . . 4	LIKE A WOMAN . . . . LaFace 74321401612
14/12/1996 . . . . 52 . . . . . . 1	LEAVIN' . . . . LaFace 74321438382

RICH KIDS
UK rock group formed in London in 1977 by Glen Matlock (born 27/8/1956, London, bass/vocals), Steve New (guitar) and Rusty Egan (born 19/9/1957, drums), with Midge Ure (born 10/10/1953, Gambusland, Scotland, guitar/vocals) joining later. Matlock was ex-Sex Pistols, Ure ex-Slik. The group disbanded in 1978; Ure and Egan formed Visage, although Ure ultimately found greater success with Ultravox.

28/01/1978 . . . . 24 . . . . . . 5	RICH KIDS . . . . EMI 2738

EXPRESSO BONGO · CLIFF RICHARD mono

CLIFF RICHARD
UK singer (born Harry Webb, 14/10/1940, Lucknow, India) who came to the UK in 1948. He joined the Dick Teague Skiffle Group in 1957, leaving in 1958 with drummer Terry Smart to form Harry Webb & The Drifters. He was renamed Cliff Richard prior to an engagement in Ripley that year. He auditioned for Norrie Paramour in August 1958 and signed with EMI, quitting his job with Atlas Lamps. He made his TV debut on Jack Good's *Oh Boy*, performing his debut release (originally released with *Schoolboy Crush* the A-side, *Move It* the B-side). His backing group in 1958 featured Hank Marvin, Bruce Welch, Ian Samwell and Terry Smart. He appeared in the 1959 film *Serious Charge*, then made numerous starring roles, and also appeared in the puppet film *Thunderbirds Are Go* (1966). The Drifters name-changed to The Shadows in 1959 to avoid confusion with the US R&B act of the same name. Richard later recorded inspirational material. He has received many awards and honours, including the Lifetime Achievement Award at the 35th Ivor Novello Awards (even though he isn't a songwriter), the Best British Male Award at the 1977 and 1982 BRIT Awards, the Outstanding Contribution Award at the 1989 BRIT Awards and, the crowning glory, a knighthood in 1995. In July 1996 he gave an impromptu 'concert' on Centre Court at the Wimbledon Tennis Championships when rain caused a delay. He performed four numbers with a 'backing group' that included tennis players Pam Shriver, Virginia Wade, Martina Navratilova, Hana Mandlikova, Conchita Martinez, Gig Fernandez and Rosalyn Nideffer. The Young Ones are TV comedians Rik Mayall (Rik), Adrian Edmondson (Vivian), Nigel Planer (Neil) and Christopher Ryan (Mike) from the TV series of the same name. Cliff was inducted into the UK Music Hall of Fame in 2004, one of its first inductees.

12/09/1958 . . . . . 2 . . . . . 17	**MOVE IT** . . . . Columbia DB 4178
21/11/1958 . . . . . 7 . . . . . 10	**HIGH CLASS BABY** . . . . Columbia DB 4203
30/01/1959 . . . . 20 . . . . . . 6	LIVIN' LOVIN' DOLL . . . . Columbia DB 4249
08/05/1959 . . . . 10 . . . . . . 9	**MEAN STREAK** . . . . Columbia DB 4290
15/05/1959 . . . . 21 . . . . . . 2	NEVER MIND B-side to *Mean Streak* . . . . Columbia DB 4290
10/07/1959 . . . ❶⁶ 23	**LIVING DOLL** Featured in the films *Serious Charge* (1959) and *The Young Ones* (1962), both starring Cliff Richard . . . .
	. . . . Columbia DB 4306
09/10/1959 . . . ❶⁵ 17	**TRAVELLIN' LIGHT** . . . . Columbia DB 4351
09/10/1959 . . . . 16 . . . . . . 4	DYNAMITE B-side to *Travellin' Light* . . . . Columbia DB 4351
15/01/1960 . . . . 14 . . . . . . 7	EXPRESSO BONGO EP Tracks on EP: *Love, A Voice In The Wilderness, The Shrine On The Second Floor* and *Bongo Blues* . . . . . .
	. . . . Columbia SEG 7971
22/01/1960 . . . . . 2 . . . . . 16	**A VOICE IN THE WILDERNESS** This and above single featured in the 1960 film *Expresso Bongo* starring Cliff Richard . . . .
	. . . . Columbia DB 4398
24/03/1960 . . . . . 2 . . . . . 15	**FALL IN LOVE WITH YOU** . . . . Columbia DB 4431
30/06/1960 . . . ❶³ 18	**PLEASE DON'T TEASE** Reclaimed #1 position on 11/8/1960 . . . . Columbia DB 4479
22/09/1960 . . . . . 3 . . . . . 12	**NINE TIMES OUT OF TEN** . . . . Columbia DB 4506
01/12/1960 . . . ❶² 16	**I LOVE YOU** . . . . Columbia DB 4547
02/03/1961 . . . . . 3 . . . . . 14	**THEME FOR A DREAM** . . . . Columbia DB 4593
30/03/1961 . . . . . 4 . . . . . 14	**GEE WHIZ IT'S YOU** Export single that sold sufficient copies in the UK to chart . . . . Columbia DC 756
22/06/1961 . . . . . 3 . . . . . 14	**A GIRL LIKE YOU** This and all the above singles feature The Shadows . . . . Columbia DB 4667

DATE	POS	WKS	BPI	SINGLE TITLE	LABEL & NUMBER
19/10/1961	3	15		WHEN THE GIRL IN YOUR ARMS IS THE GIRL IN YOUR HEART	Columbia DB 4716
11/01/1962	❶⁶	21	◎	THE YOUNG ONES ↑ Features The Shadows. This and above single featured in the 1961 film *The Young Ones* starring Cliff Richard	Columbia DB 4761
10/05/1962	2	17		I'M LOOKING OUT THE WINDOW/DO YOU WANNA DANCE B-side features The Shadows	Columbia DB 4828
06/09/1962	2	12		IT'LL BE ME	Columbia DB 4886
06/12/1962	❶³	18		THE NEXT TIME/BACHELOR BOY	Columbia DB 4950
21/02/1963	❶³	18		SUMMER HOLIDAY Reclaimed #1 position on 4/4/1963. This and above single featured in the 1962 film *Summer Holiday* starring Cliff Richard	Columbia DB 4977
09/05/1963	4	15		LUCKY LIPS This and above three singles feature The Shadows	Columbia DB 7034
22/08/1963	2	13		IT'S ALL IN THE GAME	Columbia DB 7089
07/11/1963	2	14		DON'T TALK TO HIM	Columbia DB 7150
06/02/1964	8	10		I'M THE LONELY ONE This and above single features The Shadows	Columbia DB 7203
30/04/1964	4	13		CONSTANTLY	Columbia DB 7272
02/07/1964	7	13		ON THE BEACH Features The Shadows. Featured in the 1964 film *Wonderful Life* starring Cliff Richard	Columbia DB 7305
08/10/1964	8	11		THE TWELFTH OF NEVER	Columbia DB 7372
10/12/1964	9	11		I COULD EASILY FALL Features The Shadows	Columbia DB 7420
11/03/1965	❶¹	14		THE MINUTE YOU'RE GONE	Columbia DB 7496
10/06/1965	12	10		ON MY WORD	Columbia DB 7596
19/08/1965	22	8		THE TIME IN BETWEEN Features The Shadows	Columbia DB 7660
04/11/1965	2	16		WIND ME UP (LET ME GO)	Columbia DB 7745
24/03/1966	15	9		BLUE TURNS TO GREY Features The Shadows	Columbia DB 7866
21/07/1966	7	12		VISIONS	Columbia DB 7968
13/10/1966	10	12		TIME DRAGS BY	Columbia DB 8017
15/12/1966	6	10		IN THE COUNTRY This and above single features The Shadows	Columbia DB 8094
16/03/1967	9	10		IT'S ALL OVER	Columbia DB 8150
08/06/1967	26	8		I'LL COME RUNNING	Columbia DB 8210
16/08/1967	10	14		THE DAY I MET MARIE	Columbia DB 8245
15/11/1967	6	12		ALL MY LOVE	Columbia DB 8293
20/03/1968	❶²	13		CONGRATULATIONS UK entry for the 1968 Eurovision Song Contest (came second)	Columbia DB 8376
26/06/1968	27	6		I'LL LOVE YOU FOREVER TODAY Featured in the 1967 film *Two A Penny* starring Cliff Richard	Columbia DB 8437
25/09/1968	22	8		MARIANNE	Columbia DB 8476
27/11/1968	21	10		DON'T FORGET TO CATCH ME Features The Shadows	Columbia DB 8503
26/02/1969	12	11		GOOD TIMES (BETTER TIMES)	Columbia DB 8548
28/05/1969	8	10		BIG SHIP	Columbia DB 8581
13/09/1969	7	9		THROW DOWN A LINE CLIFF AND HANK (MARVIN)	Columbia DB 8615
06/12/1969	20	11		WITH THE EYES OF A CHILD	Columbia DB 8641
21/02/1970	25	8		JOY OF LIVING CLIFF AND HANK (MARVIN) Theme to the TV series of the same name	Columbia DB 8657
06/06/1970	6	15		GOODBYE SAM HELLO SAMANTHA	Columbia DB 8685
05/09/1970	21	7		I AIN'T GOT TIME ANYMORE	Columbia DB 8708
23/01/1971	19	8		SUNNY HONEY GIRL	Columbia DB 8747
10/04/1971	27	6		SILVERY RAIN	Columbia DB 8774
17/07/1971	37	7		FLYING MACHINE	Columbia DB 8797
13/11/1971	13	12		SING A SONG OF FREEDOM	Columbia DB 8836
11/03/1972	35	3		JESUS	Columbia DB 8864
26/08/1972	12	10		LIVING IN HARMONY	Columbia DB 8917
17/03/1973	4	12		POWER TO ALL OUR FRIENDS UK entry for the 1973 Eurovision Song Contest (came third)	EMI 2012
12/05/1973	29	6		HELP IT ALONG/TOMORROW RISING	EMI 2022
01/12/1973	27	12		TAKE ME HIGH Featured in the 1973 film of the same name starring Cliff Richard	EMI 2088
18/05/1974	13	8		(YOU KEEP ME) HANGIN' ON	EMI 2150
07/02/1976	15	10		MISS YOU NIGHTS	EMI 2376
08/05/1976	9	8		DEVIL WOMAN	EMI 2458
21/08/1976	17	8		I CAN'T ASK FOR ANY MORE THAN YOU	EMI 2499
04/12/1976	31	5		HEY MR. DREAM MAKER	EMI 2559
05/03/1977	15	8		MY KINDA LIFE	EMI 2584
16/07/1977	46	3		WHEN TWO WORLDS DRIFT APART	EMI 2633
31/03/1979	57	3		GREEN LIGHT	EMI 2920
21/07/1979	❶⁴	14	●	WE DON'T TALK ANYMORE	EMI 2975
03/11/1979	46	5		HOT SHOT	EMI 5003
02/02/1980	4	10	○	CARRIE	EMI 5006
16/08/1980	8	10	○	DREAMIN' Featured in the 1981 film *Endless Love*	EMI 5095
25/10/1980	15	7		SUDDENLY OLIVIA NEWTON-JOHN AND CLIFF RICHARD Featured in the 1980 film *Xanadu*	Jet 7002
24/01/1981	15	8		A LITTLE IN LOVE	EMI 5123
29/08/1981	4	9	○	WIRED FOR SOUND	EMI 5221
21/11/1981	2	12	●	DADDY'S HOME	EMI 5251
17/07/1982	10	9		THE ONLY WAY OUT	EMI 5318
25/09/1982	60	3		WHERE DO WE GO FROM HERE	EMI 5341
04/12/1982	11	7		LITTLE TOWN	EMI 5348
19/02/1983	9	9		SHE MEANS NOTHING TO ME PHIL EVERLY AND CLIFF RICHARD	Capitol CL 276
16/04/1983	8	8		TRUE LOVE WAYS CLIFF RICHARD WITH THE LONDON PHILHARMONIC ORCHESTRA	EMI 5385

❶⁹ Number of weeks single topped the UK charts   ↑ Entered the UK chart at #1   ▲⁹ Number of weeks single topped the US chart

DATE	POS	WKS	BPI	SINGLE TITLE	LABEL & NUMBER
04/06/1983	64	2		DRIFTING SHEILA WALSH AND CLIFF RICHARD	DJM SHEILA 1
03/09/1983	15	7		NEVER SAY DIE (GIVE A LITTLE BIT MORE)	EMI 5415
26/11/1983	7	9	○	**PLEASE DON'T FALL IN LOVE**	EMI 5437
31/03/1984	27	7		BABY YOU'RE DYNAMITE/OCEAN DEEP	EMI 5457
03/11/1984	51	4		SHOOTING FROM THE HEART	EMI RICH 1
09/02/1985	46	3		HEART USER	EMI RICH 2
14/09/1985	17	9		SHE'S SO BEAUTIFUL Features the uncredited contribution of Stevie Wonder (all instruments).	EMI 5531
07/12/1985	45	6		IT'S IN EVERY ONE OF US This and above single featured in the musical *Time*.	EMI 5537
22/03/1986	❶³	11	●	**LIVING DOLL** CLIFF RICHARD AND THE YOUNG ONES FEATURING HANK B MARVIN Re-recording of Cliff Richard's 1959 hit released for Comic Relief.	WEA YZ 65
04/10/1986	3	16	○	**ALL I ASK OF YOU** CLIFF RICHARD AND SARAH BRIGHTMAN Featured in the musical *Phantom Of The Opera*	Polydor POSP 802
29/11/1986	44	8		SLOW RIVERS ELTON JOHN AND CLIFF RICHARD	Rocket EJS 13
20/06/1987	6	10		**MY PRETTY ONE**	EMI EM 4
29/08/1987	3	10	○	**SOME PEOPLE**	EMI EM 18
31/10/1987	35	4		REMEMBER ME	EMI EM 31
13/02/1988	34	3		TWO HEARTS	EMI EM 42
03/12/1988	❶⁴	8	●	**MISTLETOE AND WINE**	EMI EM 78
10/06/1989	2	7	○	**THE BEST OF ME** The single was tagged as Cliff's 100th single when in fact it represented his 101st appearance on the chart!	EMI EM 92
26/08/1989	3	8	○	**I JUST DON'T HAVE THE HEART**	EMI EM 101
14/10/1989	17	6		LEAN ON YOU	EMI EM 105
09/12/1989	20	6		WHENEVER GOD SHINES HIS LIGHT VAN MORRISON WITH CLIFF RICHARD	Polydor VANS 2
24/02/1990	14	5		STRONGER THAN THAT	EMI EM 129
25/08/1990	10	7		**SILHOUETTES**	EMI EM 152
13/10/1990	11	6		FROM A DISTANCE	EMI EM 155
08/12/1990	❶¹	7	○	**SAVIOUR'S DAY**	EMI XMAS 90
14/09/1991	23	5		MORE TO LIFE Theme to the TV series *Trainer*.	EMI EM 205
07/12/1991	10	6		**WE SHOULD BE TOGETHER**	EMI XMAS 91
11/01/1992	30	2		THIS NEW YEAR	EMI EMS 216
05/12/1992	7	6		**I STILL BELIEVE IN YOU**	EMI EM 255
27/03/1993	8	5		PEACE IN OUR TIME	EMI CDEMS 265
12/06/1993	24	4		HUMAN WORK OF ART	EMI CDEMS 267
02/10/1993	32	3		NEVER LET GO	EMI CDEM 281
18/12/1993	19	5		HEALING LOVE	EMI CDEM 294
10/12/1994	14	9		ALL I HAVE TO DO IS DREAM/MISS YOU NIGHTS CLIFF RICHARD WITH PHIL EVERLY/CLIFF RICHARD	EMI CDEMS 359
21/10/1995	19	3		MISUNDERSTOOD MAN	EMI CDEM 394
09/12/1995	22	4		HAD TO BE CLIFF RICHARD AND OLIVIA NEWTON-JOHN	EMI CDEMS 410
30/03/1996	40	1		THE WEDDING CLIFF RICHARD FEATURING HELEN HOBSON	EMI CDEM 422
25/01/1997	52	1		BE WITH ME ALWAYS	EMI CDEM 453
24/10/1998	10	4		**CAN'T KEEP THIS FEELING IN**	EMI CDEM 526
07/08/1999	23	2		THE MIRACLE	Blacknight CDEM 546
27/11/1999	❶³	16	✪²	**THE MILLENNIUM PRAYER** The song is *The Lord's Prayer* combined with the melody to *Auld Lang Syne*. Released in aid of the Children's Promises charity.	Papillon PROMISECD 01
15/12/2001	11	6		SOMEWHERE OVER THE RAINBOW/WHAT A WONDERFUL WORLD	Papillon CLIFFCX 1
13/04/2002	29	3		LET ME BE THE ONE	Papillon CLIFFCD 2
20/12/2003	5	5		**SANTA'S LIST**	EMI SANTA 02
23/10/2004	9	3		**SOMETHIN' IS GOIN' ON**	Decca/UCJ 4756419
25/12/2004	13	1		I CANNOT GIVE YOU MY LOVE	Decca/UCJ 4756611

CALVIN RICHARDSON US singer (born in Monroe, NC) who first began singing with the gospel group The Willing Wonders and formed Undacova before going solo.

DATE	POS	WKS	BPI	SINGLE TITLE	LABEL & NUMBER
27/03/2004	74	1		I'VE GOT TO MOVE	Hollywood HOL004CD

LIONEL RICHIE US singer (born 20/6/1949, Tuskegee, AL) who was a founding member of The Commodores in 1967 and quickly emerged as an accomplished songwriter, penning their biggest hits (usually ballads). He began writing for other artists in 1980, penning Kenny Rogers' hit *Lady* and left the group in 1982. He also co-wrote (with Michael Jackson) the USA For Africa single *We Are The World*. He has won four Grammy Awards including Album of the Year in 1984 for *Can't Slow Down*, Producer of the Year in 1984 with James Anthony Carmichael and Song of the Year in 1985 with Michael Jackson for *We Are The World*. He was given a Lifetime Achievement Award at the 1996 MOBO Awards, and he has a star on the Hollywood Walk of Fame.

DATE	POS	WKS	BPI	SINGLE TITLE	LABEL & NUMBER
12/09/1981	7	12		**ENDLESS LOVE** ▲⁹ DIANA ROSS AND LIONEL RICHIE Featured in the 1981 film of the same name	Motown TMG 1240
20/11/1982	6	11	○	**TRULY** ▲² 1982 Grammy Award for Best Pop Vocal Performance	Motown TMG 1284
29/11/1983	43	7		YOU ARE	Motown TMG 1290
07/05/1983	70	3		MY LOVE	Motown TMG 1300
01/10/1983	2	16		**ALL NIGHT LONG (ALL NIGHT)** ▲⁴	Motown TMG 1319

○ Silver disc ● Gold disc ✪ Platinum disc (additional platinum units are indicated by a figure following the symbol) ◉ Singles released prior to 1973 that are known to have sold over 1 million copies in the UK

03/12/1983	9	12		RUNNING WITH THE NIGHT	Motown TMG 1324
10/03/1984	❶⁶	15	●	HELLO ▲²	Motown TMG 1330
23/06/1984	12	12		STUCK ON YOU	Motown TMG 1341
20/10/1984	18	7		PENNY LOVER	Motown TMG 1356
16/11/1985	8	11		SAY YOU, SAY ME ▲⁴ Featured in the 1985 film *White Nights*. 1985 Oscar for Best Original Song	Motown ZB 40421
26/07/1986	7	11		DANCING ON THE CEILING	Motown LIO 1
11/10/1986	45	5		LOVE WILL CONQUER ALL	Motown LIO 2
20/12/1986	17	8		BALLERINA GIRL/DEEP RIVER WOMAN B-side features the uncredited vocals of Alabama	Motown LIO 3
28/03/1987	43	6		SELA	Motown LIO 4
09/05/1992	33	6		DO IT TO ME	Motown TMG 1407
22/08/1992	7	13		MY DESTINY	Motown TMG 1408
28/11/1992	52	4		LOVE OH LOVE	Motown TMG 1413
06/04/1996	17	5		DON'T WANNA LOSE YOU	Mercury MERDD 461
23/11/1996	66	1		STILL IN LOVE	Mercury MERDD 477
27/06/1998	26	2		CLOSEST THING TO HEAVEN	Mercury 5661312
21/10/2000	18	5		ANGEL	Mercury 5726702
23/12/2000	34	5		DON'T STOP THE MUSIC	Mercury 5688992
17/03/2001	29	3		TENDER HEART	Mercury 5728462
23/06/2001	34	2		I FORGOT	Mercury 5729922
26/04/2003	19	4		TO LOVE A WOMAN LIONEL RICHIE FEATURING ENRIQUE IGLESIAS	Mercury 0779082
20/03/2004	20	4		JUST FOR YOU	Mercury 9862072

SHANE RICHIE UK singer (born 11/3/1964, London); he is better known as an actor, appearing as Alfie Moon in *Eastenders*. He was also married to Colleen Nolan.

06/12/2003	2	14	●	I'M YOUR MAN Released to raise funds for the BBC Children In Need Fund	BMG 82876576932

JONATHAN RICHMAN AND THE MODERN LOVERS US singer (born 16/5/1951, Boston, MA) who formed The Modern Lovers with Jerry Harrison (born 21/2/1949, Milwaukee, WI, guitar), Ernie Brooks (bass) and David Robinson (drums). By 1977 the Modern Lovers consisted of Leroy Radcliffe (guitar), Greg 'Curly' Kerenen (bass) and D Sharpe (drums).

16/07/1977	11	9		ROADRUNNER	Beserkley BZZ 1
29/10/1977	5	14	○	EGYPTIAN REGGAE	Beserkley BZZ 2
21/01/1978	29	4		MORNING OF OUR LIVES MODERN LOVERS	Beserkley BZZ 7

ADAM RICKITT UK singer (born 29/5/1978, Crewe) who first came to prominence as an actor, playing the role of Nicky Tilsley in the TV soap *Coronation Street*.

26/06/1999	5	10	○	I BREATHE AGAIN	Polydor 5611862
16/10/1999	15	6		EVERYTHING MY HEART DESIRES	Polydor 5614492
05/02/2000	25	3		BEST THING	Polydor 5616142

RICKY UK group formed in Portsmouth by James Lines (vocals), Darren Richardson (guitar/vocals), Gary Rex (guitar) and Guy Gyngell (bass/vocals).

18/09/2004	50	1		THAT EXTRA MILE	Garcia GARCIA005CD

RICO – see SPECIALS

RICO – see GARY NUMAN

RIDE UK rock group formed in Oxford by Mark Gardner (born 6/12/1969, Oxford, guitar/vocals), Andy Bell (born 11/8/1970, Cardiff, guitar/vocals), Stephan Queralt (born 4/2/1968, Oxford, bass) and Laurence 'Loz' Colbert (born 27/6/1970, Kingston, drums). All four had met while at art school. They disbanded in 1996, with Bell forming Hurricane #1 and later joining Oasis, and Gardner and Colbert forming Animalhouse.

27/01/1990	71	2		RIDE (EP) Tracks on EP: *Chelsea Girl, Drive Blind, All I Can See* and *Close My Eyes*	Creation CRE 072T
14/04/1990	32	3		PLAY EP Tracks on EP: *Like A Daydream, Silver, Furthest Sense* and *Perfect Time*	Creation CRE 07T2
29/09/1990	34	3		FALL EP Tracks on EP: *Dreams Burn Down, Taste, Hear And Now* and *Nowhere*	Creation CRE 075T
16/03/1991	14	4		TODAY FOREVER	Creation CRE 100T
15/02/1992	9	3		LEAVE THEM ALL BEHIND	Creation CRE 123T
25/04/1992	36	2		TWISTERELLA	Creation CRE 150T
30/04/1994	38	2		BIRDMAN	Creation CRESCD 155
25/06/1994	58	1		HOW DOES IT FEEL TO FEEL	Creation CRESCD 184
08/10/1994	46	1		I DON'T KNOW WHERE IT COMES FROM	Creation CRESCD 189R
24/02/1996	67	1		BLACK NITE CRASH	Creation CRESCD 199

RIDER WITH TERRY VENABLES UK instrumental group with former footballer Terry Venables. Venables (born 6/1/1943, Bethnal Green, London) played for Chelsea, Tottenham Hotspur, Queens Park Rangers and Crystal Palace as well as representing England (he is the only player to have represented the country at schoolboy, youth, amateur, Under-23 and full level). He went into management with Crystal Palace, Queens Park Rangers, Barcelona and Tottenham, and became England manager for the 1996 European Championships. He then had spells as chief coach to Portsmouth, Australia and Middlesbrough before becoming a TV pundit. He went back into club management with Leeds United in July 2002 and was sacked before the end of his first season.

01/06/2002	46	2		ENGLAND CRAZY	East West EW 248CD

❶⁹ Number of weeks single topped the UK charts ↑ Entered the UK chart at #1 ▲⁹ Number of weeks single topped the US chart

671

ANDREW RIDGELEY
UK singer (born 26/1/1963, Bushey) and founding member of Wham! with George Michael. He went solo when the pair split in 1986. He also had a spell as a racing car driver and married former Bananarama member Keren Woodward.

31/03/1990	58	3		SHAKE	Epic AJR 1

STAN RIDGWAY
US singer (born Stanard Ridgway, 1954, Los Angeles, CA) who began playing the banjo at the age of ten before switching to the guitar. A founder member of Wall Of Voodoo, he left in 1983 and spent two years building his own studio.

05/07/1986	4	12		**CAMOUFLAGE**	IRS IRM 114

RIGHEIRA
Italian group formed by Dana Moray (vocals), Mats Bjoerklund (guitar), Gunther Gebauer (bass) and Kurt Crass (drums).

24/09/1983	53	3		VAMOS A LA PLAYA	A&M AM 137

RIGHT SAID FRED
UK group formed in London in 1990 by Fred Fairbrass (born Christopher Abbott Bernard Fairbrass, 2/11/1956, East Grinstead, bass), his brother Richard (born 22/9/1953, East Grinstead, vocals) and Rob Manzoli (born 29/1/1954, London, guitar) following the failure of the brothers' previous group, the Actors. They took their name from the Bernard Cribbins' hit of the same name.

27/07/1991	2	16	●	I'M TOO SEXY ▲3	Tug SNOG 1
07/12/1991	3	11		DON'T TALK JUST KISS RIGHT SAID FRED, GUEST VOCALS: JOCELYN BROWN	Tug SNOG 2
21/03/1992	❶3	14	○	DEEPLY DIPPY	Tug SNOG 3
01/08/1992	29	5		THOSE SIMPLE THINGS/DAYDREAM	Tug SNOG 4
27/02/1993	4	7		STICK IT OUT RIGHT SAID FRED AND FRIENDS Released in aid of the Comic Relief charity	Tug CDCOMIC 1
23/10/1993	32	4		BUMPED	Tug CDSNOG 7
18/12/1993	60	3		HANDS UP (4 LOVERS)	Tug CDSNOG 8
19/03/1994	55	1		WONDERMAN	Tug CDSNOG 9
13/10/2001	18	5		YOU'RE MY MATE	Kingsize 74321895632

RIGHTEOUS BROTHERS
US vocal duo formed in 1962 by ex-Paramours Bill Medley (born 19/9/1940, Santa Ana, CA) and ex-Variations Bobby Hatfield (born 10/8/1940, Beaver Dam, WI). They were dubbed the Righteous Brothers by black marines. They first recorded for Moonglow in 1963 and were contracted to that label when Phil Spector expressed an interest in signing them (their US releases subsequently appeared on Philles, UK ones through London). Medley left in 1967 to go solo and Hatfield teamed up with Jimmy Walker but was not able to use the name Righteous Brothers for legal reasons. Hatfield and Medley re-formed in 1974. They were inducted into the Rock & Roll Hall of Fame in 2003. Hatfield was found dead in a hotel room on 5/11/2003 shortly before the pair were to perform on stage in Kalamazoo, MI.

14/01/1965	❶2	10		YOU'VE LOST THAT LOVIN' FEELIN' ▲2 One of the most popular records of all time, having received over 7 million plays on US radio (over 35,000 hours of airtime). Featured in the 1986 film *Top Gun*	London HLU 9943
12/08/1965	14	12		UNCHAINED MELODY	London HL 9975
13/01/1966	48	2		EBB TIDE	London HL 10011
14/04/1966	15	10		(YOU'RE MY) SOUL AND INSPIRATION ▲3	Verve VS 535
10/11/1966	21	9		WHITE CLIFFS OF DOVER	London HL 10086
22/12/1966	36	5		ISLAND IN THE SUN	Verve VS 547
12/02/1969	10	11		YOU'VE LOST THAT LOVIN' FEELIN' Re-issue of London HLU 9943	London HL 10241
19/11/1977	42	4		YOU'VE LOST THAT LOVIN' FEELIN' Second re-issue of London HLU 9943	Phil Spector International 2010 022
27/10/1990	❶4	14	✪	UNCHAINED MELODY Re-issue of London HL 9975 after being featured in the 1990 film *Ghost*	Verve/Polydor PO 101
15/12/1990	3	9		YOU'VE LOST THAT LOVIN' FEELIN'/EBB TIDE Third re-issue of London HLU 9943	Verve/Polydor PO 116

RIKKI AND DAZ FEATURING GLEN CAMPBELL
UK production duo Ricardo Autobahn (born John Matthews) and Darren 'Daz' Sampson. Ricardo is also a member of The Cuban Boys while Daz sang with Clock.

30/11/2002	12	8		RHINESTONE COWBOY (GIDDY UP GIDDY UP)	Serious SER 059CD

RIKROK
US singer Ricardo Ducent.

11/03/2001	❶1	20	✪	IT WASN'T ME ↑ SHAGGY FEATURING RIKROK	MCA 1558022
03/07/2004	57	1		YOUR EYES RIKROK FEATURING SHAGGY	VP VPCD6415

CHERYL PEPSII RILEY
US R&B singer (born in New York City) who was discovered by Full Force.

28/01/1989	75	1		THANKS FOR MY CHILD	CBS 6531537

JEANNIE C. RILEY
US singer (born Jeanne Carolyn Stephenson, 19/10/1945, Anson, TX) who scored a US #1 with her only hit single. However, the hit inspired a successful film and spin-off TV series of the same name.

16/10/1968	12	15		HARPER VALLEY P.T.A. ▲1 Featured in the 1972 film of the same name. 1968 Grammy Award for Best Country & Western Vocal Performance	Polydor 56 748

TEDDY RILEY
US singer/producer (born 8/10/1966, Harlem, NYC) who formed Guy in 1988, then formed BLACKstreet and re-formed Guy in 1999. He won the 1992 Grammy Award for Best Engineered Album with Bruce Swedien for Michael Jackson's *Dangerous*.

21/03/1992	53	2		IS IT GOOD TO YOU TEDDY RILEY FEATURING TAMMY LUCAS	MCA MCS 1611
19/06/1993	37	3		BABY BE MINE BLACKSTREET FEATURING TEDDY RILEY	MCA MCSTD 1772

RIMES FEATURING SHAILA PROSPERE
UK rapper Julian Johnson.

22/05/1999	51	1		IT'S OVER Contains a sample of Odyssey's *Don't Tell Me Tell Her*	Universal MCSTD 40199

○ Silver disc ● Gold disc ✪ Platinum disc (additional platinum units are indicated by a figure following the symbol) ⦿ Singles released prior to 1973 that are known to have sold over 1 million copies in the UK

LeANN RIMES
US country singer (born 28/8/1982) who made her first album at the age of eleven for the independent Nor Va Jak label. She subsequently signed with Curb and her major label debut sold over 7 million copies in the US. She has also won two Grammy Awards including Best New Artist in 1996.

07/03/1998	7	34	✪	**HOW DO I LIVE** Originally written for the 1997 film *Con Air* in which it was performed by Trisha Yearwood	Curb CUBCX 30
12/09/1998	38	2		LOOKING THROUGH YOUR EYES/COMMITMENT A-side featured in the 1998 animated film *Quest For Camelot*	Curb CUBC 32
12/12/1998	23	6		BLUE 1996 Grammy Award for Best Female Country Vocal Performance	Curb CUBC 39
06/03/1999	10	8		**WRITTEN IN THE STARS** ELTON JOHN AND LEANN RIMES Featured in the 1999 Walt Disney film *Aida*	Mercury EJSDD 45
18/12/1999	36	3		CRAZY	Curb CUBC 52
25/11/2000	❶¹	17	●	**CAN'T FIGHT THE MOONLIGHT** ↑ Featured in the 2000 film *Coyote Ugly*	Curb CUBCX 58
31/03/2001	13	7		I NEED YOU Featured in the 2000 TV film *Jesus*	Curb CUBCX 60
23/02/2002	20	4		BUT I DO LOVE YOU Featured in the 2000 film *Coyote Ugly*	Curb CUBC 075
12/10/2002	11	8		LIFE GOES ON	Curb CUBCX 085
08/03/2003	47	1		SUDDENLY	Curb CUBC 088
23/08/2003	27	2		WE CAN Featured in the 2003 film *Legally Blonde 2*	Curb CUBC 092
14/02/2004	54	1		THIS LOVE	Curb CUNC 096
15/05/2004	5	8		**LAST THING ON MY MIND** RONAN KEATING AND LeANN RIMES	Polydor/Curb 9866595

RIMSHOTS
US R&B group formed in 1972 by Nate 'Gator' Edmonds (guitar), Curtis McTeer (bass), Mike Watson (guitar), Joe 'Groundhog' Richardson (guitar) and Ronald Smith (drums). By 1974 the group comprised Billy Jones (guitar), Michael Burton (guitar/vocals), Frankie Prescord (bass), Yogi Horton (drums) and Craig Derry (percussion), with later members including Jonathan Williams (bass), Mozart Pierre-Louis (organ), Walter Morris (guitar), Tommy Keith (guitar), Bernadette Randall (keyboards) and Clarence 'Foot' Oliver (drums). The group was also All Platinum's house band, backing the likes of the Moments and Retta Young on their hits.

19/07/1975	26	5		7-6-5-4-3-2-1 (BLOW YOUR WHISTLE) Originally recorded as *Get Up* by Blue Mink	All Platinum 6146 304

RIO AND MARS
French/UK vocal/instrumental duo Rio Adrian Zerbini and Marcia Wilkinson.

28/01/1995	43	2		BOY I GOTTA HAVE YOU	Dome CDDOME 1014
13/04/1996	46	1		BOY I GOTTA HAVE YOU Re-issue of Dome CDDOME 1014	Feverpitch CDFVR 1007

MIGUEL RIOS
Spanish singer (born 7/6/1944, Granada) who began singing at the age of eight. His hit is with the orchestra and chorus conducted by Waldo De Los Rios. He had previously appeared in a couple of films, including *Hamelin* in 1967.

11/07/1970	16	12		SONG OF JOY Based on Beethoven's *Symphony No.9*	A&M AMS 790

RIP PRODUCTIONS
UK production team formed by Tim 'Deluxe' Liken and DJ Omar Adimora. They also record as Double 99 and Carnival Featuring RIP Vs Red Rat.

29/11/1997	50	1		THE CHANT (WE R)/RIP PRODUCTIONS A-side contains a sample of Lennie De-Ice's *We Are I.E.*	Satellite 74321534022

MINNIE RIPERTON
US singer (born 8/11/1947, Chicago, IL) who first recorded for Chess in 1966 under the name Andrea Davis and as a member of the Gems before joining Rotary Connection in 1967. She signed as a soloist with Janus in 1970 and switched to Epic in 1975. She died from cancer on 12/7/1979.

12/04/1975	2	10	○	**LOVING YOU** ▲¹ Featured in the 2004 film *Bridget Jones Diary 2: Edge Of Reason*	Epic EPC 3121

RISE
UK production duo producer Paul Oakenfold (born 30/8/1963, London) and Steve Osborne. Oakenfold also records as Perfecto Allstars, Element Four, Planet Perfecto and Movement 98.

03/09/1994	70	1		THE SINGLE	East West YZ 839CD

RITCHIE FAMILY
US studio group assembled by songwriter/producer Ritchie Rome to record *Brazil* in 1975. Following its US success a group was hired featuring Cheryl Mason Jacks, Cassandra Wooten and Gwendolyn Oliver. A later line-up featured Jacqueline Smith-Lee, Theodosia Draher and Ednah Holt.

23/08/1975	41	4		BRAZIL	Polydor 2058 625
18/09/1976	10	9		**THE BEST DISCO IN TOWN**	Polydor 2058 777
17/02/1979	49	6		AMERICAN GENERATION	Mercury 6007 199

LEE RITENOUR AND MAXI PRIEST
US guitarist Ritenour (born 1/11/1953, Los Angeles, CA), also known as 'Captain Fingers'; he was a member of Fourplay until 1997. Maxi Priest is a UK singer (born Max Elliott, 10/6/1960, London).

31/07/1993	65	2		WAITING IN VAIN	GRP MCSTD 1921

RITMO DYNAMIC
French DJ Laurent Wolf recording under an assumed name.

15/11/2003	68	1		CALINDA	Xtravaganza XTRAV42CDS

TEX RITTER
US singer (born Maurice Woodward Ritter, 12/1/1905, near Murvaul, TX) who made his name as an actor, appearing in over 80 western films between 1935 and 1945, including *Trouble In Texas* (1937), *Marshall Of Gunsmoke* (1944) and *Riders Of The Rockies* (1958). He made his first recordings in 1934 and in 1942 became the first country artist to sign with Capitol. He died from a heart attack on 3/1/1974. He has a star on the Hollywood Walk of Fame.

22/06/1956	8	14		**WAYWARD WIND**	Capitol CL 14581

RIVA FEATURING DANNII MINOGUE
Dutch instrumental/production duo DJ Ziki (born Rene Terhorst) and Dobre (born Gaston Steenkist). They also record as Chocolate Puma, DJ Manta, Tomba Vira, Jark Prongo, Goodmen and Rhythmkillaz. Their hit *Who Do You Love* was originally an instrumental called *Stringer* and became a major hit with the addition of lyrics sung by Dannii.

❶⁹ Number of weeks single topped the UK charts   ↑ Entered the UK chart at #1   ▲⁹ Number of weeks single topped the US chart

673

01/12/2001	3	15		WHO DO YOU LOVE NOW (STRINGER)		ffrr DFCD 002

RIVAL SCHOOLS US group formed by Walter Schreifels (guitar/vocals), Ian Love (guitar), Cache 'Utah Slim' Tolman (bass) and Sam Seigler (drums).

30/03/2002	42	1		USED FOR GLUE		Mercury 5889652
20/07/2002	74	1		GOOD THINGS		Mercury 5829662

PACO RIVAZ – see GAMBAFREAKS

RIVER CITY PEOPLE UK group formed in Liverpool in 1986 by Siobhan Maher (born 11/1/1964, Liverpool, vocals), Tim Speed (born 17/11/1961, Chester, guitar), his brother Paul (born 27/10/1964, Chester, drums) and Dave Snell (bass). They were signed by EMI in 1988 but disbanded during the 1990s, with Paul and Tim going on to form Speed.

12/08/1989	70	3		(WHAT'S WRONG WITH) DREAMING		EMI EM 95
03/03/1990	62	2		WALKING ON ICE		EMI EM 130
30/06/1990	13	10		CARRY THE BLAME/CALIFORNIA DREAMIN'		EMI EM 145
22/09/1990	40	3		(WHAT'S WRONG WITH) DREAMING		EMI EM 156
02/03/1991	62	2		WHEN I WAS YOUNG		EMI EM 176
28/09/1991	44	3		SPECIAL WAY		EMI EM 207
29/02/1992	36	4		STANDING IN THE NEED OF LOVE		EMI EM 216

RIVER DETECTIVES UK vocal/instrumental duo Sam Corry and Dan O'Neill.

29/07/1989	51	4		CHAINS		WEA YZ 383

RIVER OCEAN FEATURING OCEAN US producer Louie Vega recording with singer India.

26/02/1994	50	2		LOVE AND HAPPINESS (YEMAYA Y OCHUN)		Cooltempo CDCOOL 287

ROBBIE RIVERA Italian DJ/remixer who later recorded with Marc Sachell as Wicked Phunker. Billy Paul W is US singer Billy Paul Williams.

02/09/2000	13	7		BANG ROBBIE RIVERA PRESENTS RHYTHM BANGERS		Multiply CDMULTY 64
12/10/2002	55	1		SEX ROBBIE RIVERA FEATURING BILLY PAUL W		352 Recordings 352 CD001

SANDY RIVERA US DJ/producer who is also a member of Kings Of Tomorrow.

18/01/2003	48	2		CHANGES SANDY RIVERA FEATURING HAZE		Defected DFTD 059R
05/04/2003	58	1		I CAN'T STOP		Defected DFTD 063R

DANNY RIVERS UK singer (born David Lee Baker, Liverpool) who worked with Joe Meek and was one of the stars of Jack Good's TV show *Wham*.

12/01/1961	36	3		CAN'T YOU HEAR MY HEART		Decca F 11294

RM PROJECT UK/Maltese production duo Robert Chetcufi and Steve McGuinness who also record as Big Room Girl and Rhythm Masters.

03/07/1999	49	1		GET IT UP		Inferno CDFERN 15

RMXCRW FEATURING EBON-E PLUS AMBUSH Dutch production duo Affie and Chuckie.

17/01/2004	52	2		TURN ME ON		Digi Dance 871486697203

ROACH MOTEL UK duo Pete Heller and Terry Farley. They were initially known as part of the Boy's Own collective. They also recorded as Fire Island and under their own names.

21/08/1993	73	1		AFRO SLEEZE/TRANSATLANTIC		Junior Boy's Own JBO 1412
10/12/1994	75	1		HAPPY BIZZNESS/WILD LUV		Junior Boy's Own JBO 24

ROACHFORD UK R&B group formed by Andrew Roachford (keyboards/vocals) and comprising Chris Taylor (drums), Hawi Gonwe (guitar) and Derrick Taylor (bass). They made their debut album for CBS in 1988.

18/06/1988	61	4		CUDDLY TOY		CBS ROA 2
14/01/1989	4	9		CUDDLY TOY Re-issue of CBS ROA 2.		CBS ROA 4
18/03/1989	25	6		FAMILY MAN		CBS ROA 5
01/07/1989	43	5		KATHLEEN		CBS ROA 6
13/04/1991	22	8		GET READY!		Columbia 6567057
19/03/1994	21	7		ONLY TO BE WITH YOU		Columbia 6601562
18/06/1994	36	5		LAY YOUR LOVE ON ME		Columbia 6603722
20/08/1994	38	4		THIS GENERATION		Columbia 6607452
03/12/1994	46	2		CRY FOR ME		Columbia 6610742
01/04/1995	42	2		I KNOW YOU DON'T LOVE ME		Columbia 6612525
11/10/1997	20	4		THE WAY I FEEL		Columbia 6650142
14/02/1998	34	3		HOW COULD I? (INSECURITY)		Columbia 6653462
11/07/1998	53	2		NAKED WITHOUT YOU		Columbia 6659362

ROB 'N' RAZ FEATURING LEILA K Swedish production duo Robert Watz and Rasmus Lindvall with rapper Leila El Kahalifi.

25/11/1989	8	14		GOT TO GET	Arista 112696
17/03/1990	41	3		ROK THE NATION	Arista 112971

KATE ROBBINS AND BEYOND
UK actress/comedienne/singer/impersonator (and cousin of Paul McCartney) whose single began life in the TV series *Crossroads*: the hotel built a studio in the basement and *More Than In Love* was supposedly recorded there. It was subsequently released due to public demand.

30/05/1981	2	10	●	MORE THAN IN LOVE	RCA 69

MARTY ROBBINS
US singer (born Martin David Robinson, 26/9/1925, Glendale, AZ) who began his career in local clubs, usually under the name Jack Robinson as his mother disapproved of him performing at such venues. He first broke through on radio and then local TV, hosting his own *Western Caravan* on KPHO Phoenix. He made his first recordings for Columbia in 1952 and later appeared in eight films, including *Guns Of A Stranger* (1973). He also raced stock cars in Nashville. He won two Grammy Awards including Best Country & Western Song in 1970 for *My Woman, My Woman, My Wife*. He suffered three heart attacks and died from cardiac arrest on 8/12/1982. He has a star on the Hollywood Walk of Fame.

29/01/1960	19	9		EL PASO ▲² 1960 Grammy Award for Best Country & Western Performance	Fontana H 233
26/05/1960	48	1		BIG IRON	Fontana H 229
27/09/1962	5	17		DEVIL WOMAN	CBS AAG 114
17/01/1963	24	6		RUBY ANN	CBS AAG 128

ANTOINETTE ROBERSON – see PULSE FEATURING ANTOINETTE ROBERSON

AUSTIN ROBERTS
US singer (born 19/9/1945, Newport News, VA) who also provided voices to cartoons including *Scooby-Doo*. He was a member of The Buchanan Brothers before going solo.

25/10/1975	22	7		ROCKY	Private Stock PVT 33

JOE ROBERTS
UK singer based in Manchester who was in the local group Risk before forming a songwriting partnership with Eric Gooden.

28/08/1993	59	1		BACK IN MY LIFE	ffrr FCD 215
29/01/1994	22	5		LOVER	ffrr FCD 220
14/05/1994	39	3		BACK IN MY LIFE	ffrr FCD 230
06/08/1994	45	3		ADORE	ffrr FCD 240
18/02/1995	28	4		YOU ARE EVERYTHING MELANIE WILLIAMS AND JOE ROBERTS	Columbia 6611755
24/02/1996	63	1		HAPPY DAYS SWEET MERCY FEATURING JOE ROBERTS	Grass Green GRASS 10CD

JULIET ROBERTS
UK singer (born in London) who joined the reggae outfit Black Jade and then recorded solo for Bluebird. She was lead singer for Funk Masters on their top ten hit and later Working Week as well as maintaining a solo career.

31/07/1993	24	6		CAUGHT IN THE MIDDLE	Cooltempo CDCOOL 272
06/11/1993	25	3		FREE LOVE	Cooltempo CDCOOL 281
19/03/1994	33	3		AGAIN/I WANT YOU	Cooltempo CDCOOL 285
02/07/1994	14	5		CAUGHT IN THE MIDDLE (REMIX)	Cooltempo CDCOOL 291
15/10/1994	28	3		I WANT YOU	Cooltempo CDCOOL 297
31/01/1998	15	4		SO GOOD/FREE LOVE 98 (REMIX)	Delirious 74321554002
23/01/1999	17	5		BAD GIRLS/I LIKE	Delirious DELICD 11
20/01/2001	11	5		NEEDIN' YOU II DAVID MORALES PRESENTS THE FACE FEATURING JULIET ROBERTS	Manifesto FESCD 78

MALCOLM ROBERTS
UK singer (born 31/3/1945, Manchester) who later recorded for Columbia, EMI, Cheapskate and Dakota. He appeared in the TV series *Coronation Street*. He died from a heart attack on 7/2/2003.

11/05/1967	45	2		TIME ALONE WILL TELL	RCA 1578
30/10/1968	8	15		MAY I HAVE THE NEXT DREAM WITH YOU	Major Minor MM 581
22/11/1969	12	12		LOVE IS ALL	Major Minor MM 637

B.A. ROBERTSON
UK singer/songwriter (born Brian Alexander Robertson, Glasgow) who was also responsible for penning hits by Brown Sauce and Mike + The Mechanics.

28/07/1979	2	12	O	BANG BANG	Asylum K 13152
27/10/1979	8	12	O	KNOCKED IT OFF	Asylum K 12396
01/03/1980	17	12		KOOL IN THE KAFTAN	Asylum K 12427
31/05/1980	9	11		TO BE OR NOT TO BE	Asylum K 12449
17/10/1981	11	8		HOLD ME B.A. ROBERTSON AND MAGGIE BELL	Swansong BAM 1
17/12/1983	45	5		TIME FRIDA AND B.A. ROBERTSON	Epic A 3983

DON ROBERTSON
US pianist/whistler (born 5/12/1922, Peking, China) who moved to Chicago, IL with his family at the age of four. He began composing at the age of seven and wrote twelve songs for Elvis Presley, including five featured in his films, and also penned hits for The Chordettes, Lorne Greene and Dave Edmunds. He also created the Nashville piano style.

11/05/1956	8	9		THE HAPPY WHISTLER	Capitol CL 14575

ROBBIE ROBERTSON
Canadian singer (born 5/7/1944, Toronto, Ontario) who had previously been guitarist with Ronnie Hawkins' backing group and then guitarist and singer with The Band before going solo.

23/07/1988	15	10		SOMEWHERE DOWN THE CRAZY RIVER	Geffen GEF 40
11/04/1998	74	1		TAKE YOUR PARTNER BY THE HAND HOWIE B FEATURING ROBBIE ROBERTSON	Polydor 5693272

❶⁹ Number of weeks single topped the UK charts ↑ Entered the UK chart at #1 ▲⁹ Number of weeks single topped the US chart

675

IVO ROBIC Yugoslavian singer (born 29/1/1927, near Zagreb, now part of Croatia) whose one hit was a German song also known as *One More Sunrise*. He later starred in the 1981 film *Samo Jednom Se Ijubi* and composed the music for the 1998 film *Zwickel Auf Bizyckel*. He died from cancer on 10/3/2000.

| 06/11/1959.....23......1....... | MORGEN... Polydor 23923 |

DAWN ROBINSON – see FIRM

FLOYD ROBINSON US singer (born 1937, Nashville) who was a member of the Eagle Rangers at the age of twelve and later hosted his own radio programmes and composed the music for the 1962 film *Los Secretos Del Sexo Debil*.

| 16/10/1959 .....9......9....... | **MAKIN' LOVE** .... RCA 1146 |

SMOKEY ROBINSON US singer (born William Robinson, 19/2/1940, Detroit, MI) who formed the Matadors in 1954, changing the group's name to the Miracles at the suggestion of Berry Gordy. They made their first record for End in 1958, leased other product to Chess and became one of the first acts signed to Gordy's Motown company. Smokey wrote for many of the acts signed to the label, including the Temptations, Mary Wells and the Marvelettes. He was vice president of Motown from 1961 until 1988 and wrote the company's theme song. He was inducted into the Rock & Roll Hall of Fame in 1987 and has a star on the Hollywood Walk of Fame. He won the 1987 Grammy Award for Best Rhythm & Blues Vocal Performance for *Just To See Her*.

23/02/1974.....35......6.......	JUST MY SOUL RESPONDING.................................. Tamla Motown TMG 883
24/02/1979.....66......5.......	POPS WE LOVE YOU DIANA ROSS, MARVIN GAYE, SMOKEY ROBINSON AND STEVIE WONDER Recorded to honour Berry Gordy's father's 90th birthday... Motown TMG 1136
09/05/1981 ....❶².....13.....●	**BEING WITH YOU** .... Motown TMG 1223
13/03/1982.....51......4.......	TELL ME TOMORROW .... Motown TMG 1255
28/03/1987.....52......6.......	JUST TO SEE HER .... Motown ZB 41147
17/09/1988.....55......4.......	INDESTRUCTIBLE FOUR TOPS FEATURING SMOKEY ROBINSON.................. Arista 111717
25/02/1989.....30......7.......	INDESTRUCTIBLE FOUR TOPS FEATURING SMOKEY ROBINSON.................. Arista 112074

SMOKEY ROBINSON AND THE MIRACLES US R&B vocal group formed in Detroit, MI in 1954 by Smokey Robinson (born William Robinson, 19/2/1940, Detroit), Ronnie White (born 5/4/1939, Detroit), Pete Moore (born 19/11/1939, Detroit), Bobby Rogers (born 19/2/1940, Detroit) and guitarist Marv Tarplin as the Matadors. Rogers' sister Claudette (born 1942, Detroit, and later Robinson's wife) joined in 1957. They name-changed at the suggestion of Berry Gordy in 1957. They first recorded for End Records, then leased product to Chess before joining Gordy's Motown label and releasing the first record on the Tamla imprint, *Way Over There*. Claudette stopped touring in 1963 (although she continued to appear on their records) and Smokey left to go solo in 1972, being replaced by Billy Griffin (born 15/8/1950, Detroit). The group switched from Motown to CBS in 1976, but disbanded after one album. White died from leukaemia on 26/8/1995.

27/12/1967.....27......11......	I SECOND THAT EMOTION .... Tamla Motown TMG 631
03/04/1968.....50......1.......	IF YOU CAN WANT .... Tamla Motown TMG 648
07/05/1969 .....9......13......	TRACKS OF MY TEARS Featured in the films *The Big Chill* (1984), *Platoon* (1987) and *The Walking Dead* (1995).............. .... Tamla Motown TMG 696
01/08/1970 ....❶¹.....14......	TEARS OF A CLOWN ▲² Originally released in 1967 without success........... Tamla Motown TMG 745
30/01/1971.....13......9.......	(COME 'ROUND HERE) I'M THE ONE YOU NEED.................... Tamla Motown TMG 761
05/06/1971.....11......10......	I DON'T BLAME YOU AT ALL .... Tamla Motown TMG 774
02/10/1976.....34......6.......	TEARS OF A CLOWN Re-issue of Tamla Motown TMG 745 .... Tamla Motown TMG 1048

TOM ROBINSON UK singer (born 1/7/1950, Cambridge) who formed his own band with Danny Kustow (guitar), 'Dolphon' Taylor (drums) and Mark Ambler (keyboards). He later moved to Germany.

22/10/1977 .....5......9......○	**2-4-6-8 MOTORWAY** .... EMI 2715
18/02/1978.....18......6.......	DON'T TAKE NO FOR AN ANSWER .... EMI 2749
13/05/1978.....33......6.......	UP AGAINST THE WALL .... EMI 2787
17/03/1979.....68......2.......	BULLY FOR YOU This and above three singles credited to TOM ROBINSON BAND ..... EMI 2916
25/06/1983 .....6......9.......	**WAR BABY** .... Panic NIC 2
12/11/1983.....39......6.......	LISTEN TO THE RADIO: ATMOSPHERICS .... Panic NIC 3
15/09/1984.....58......3.......	RIKKI DON'T LOSE THAT NUMBER .... Castaway TR 2

VICKI SUE ROBINSON US singer (born 31/5/1954, Philadelphia, PA) who appeared in the original Broadway cast of *Hair* before going solo. She died from cancer on 27/4/2000.

| 27/09/1997.....48......1....... | HOUSE OF JOY .... Logic 74321511492 |

ROBO BABE – see SIR KILLALOT VS ROBO BABE

ROBSON AND JEROME – see ROBSON GREEN AND JEROME FLYNN

ROBYN Swedish singer (born Robin Mirriam Carlsson, 12/6/1979, Stockholm) who modelled her vocal style on US R&B artists, most notably Etta James and Aretha Franklin. She made her debut album in 1995.

20/07/1996.....54......1.......	YOU'VE GOT THAT SOMETHIN'................................ RCA 74321393462
16/08/1997.....26......3.......	DO YOU KNOW (WHAT IT TAKES) .... RCA 74321509932
07/03/1998 .....8......6.......	**SHOW ME LOVE**.. RCA 74321555032
30/05/1998.....20......4.......	DO YOU REALLY WANT ME .... RCA 74321582982

ROC PROFECT FEATURING TINA ARENA
US/Australian duo Ray Roc (born Ramon Checo) and singer Tina Arena (born Phillipa Arena, 1/11/1967, Melbourne).

12/04/2003.....42......1....... NEVER (PAST TENSE) Contains a sample of Fused's *Twisted* .... Illustrious CDILL 010

JOHN ROCCA – see FREEEZ

ERIN ROCHA
UK singer (born 1987, Poole); she was doing work experience at a studio when asked to sing a demo of her debut hit which was intended for Norah Jones. Erin's version sounded so good it was decided to release it as it was.

27/12/2003.....36......5....... CAN'T DO RIGHT FOR DOING WRONG .... Flying Sparks TDBCDS76

ROCHELLE
US singer (born Hamilton, Bermuda) who formed the Mellotones and then moved to New York to go solo.

01/02/1986.....27......6....... MY MAGIC MAN .... Warner Brothers W 8838

ROCK – see WYCLEF JEAN

CHUBB ROCK
US rapper (born Richard Simpson, 28/5/1968, Jamaica, raised in Brooklyn, NYC) who later appeared in the film *Private Times*. He is a cousin of fellow rapper Hitman Howie Tee.

19/01/1991.....67......1....... TREAT 'EM RIGHT .... Champion CHAMP 272

SIR MONTI ROCK III – see DISCO TEX AND THE SEX-O-LETTES

ROCK AID ARMENIA
UK charity ensemble comprising Ian Gillan, Brian May, Bruce Dickenson and Robert Plant to raise funds for the victims of the Armenian earthquake. The album featured thirteen classic rock tracks and the single sold over 100,000 copies.

16/12/1989.....39......5....... SMOKE ON THE WATER .... Life Aid Armenia ARMEN 001

ROCK CANDY
UK vocal/instrumental group formed by Mike Lovatt, Martin O'Mahony, Butch Osborn and Bob Stuart.

11/09/1971.....32......6....... REMEMBER .... MCA MK 5069

ROCK GODDESS
UK rock group formed in London in 1977 by Jody Turner (guitar), her sister Julie (drums) and Tracey Lamb (bass), subsequently adding Kate Burbela (guitar). Lamb left in 1986 and was replaced by Dee O'Malley, who left the group in 1988 in order to start a family. Lamb later became a member of Girlschool.

05/03/1983.....64......2....... MY ANGEL .... A&M AMS 8311
24/03/1984.....57......3....... I DIDN'T KNOW I LOVED YOU (TILL I SAW YOU ROCK 'N' ROLL) .... A&M AMS 185

ROCKER'S REVENGE
US studio group assembled by producer Arthur Baker (born 22/4/1955, Boston, MA) and featuring singer Donnie Calvin.

14/08/1982.....4......13.....O **WALKING ON SUNSHINE** ROCKER'S REVENGE FEATURING DONNIE CALVIN .... London LON 11
29/01/1983.....30......7....... THE HARDER THEY COME .... London LON 18

ROCKET FROM THE CRYPT
US group formed in San Diego, CA in 1990 by John 'Speedo' Reis (guitar/vocals), ND (guitar), Petey X (bass), Atom (drums), Apollo 9 (saxophone) and JC 2000 (trumpet).

27/01/1996.....68......1....... BORN IN 69 .... Elemental ELM 32CD
13/04/1996.....67......1....... YOUNG LIVERS .... Elemental ELM 33CDS
14/09/1996.....12......4....... ON A ROPE Featured in the 1996 film *Supercop* .... Elemental ELM 38CDS1
29/08/1998.....64......1....... LIPSTICK .... Elemental ELM 48CDS1

ROCKETS – see TONY CROMBIE AND HIS ROCKETS

ROCKFORD FILES
UK instrumental/production duo fronted by Ben McColl.

11/03/1995.....34......3....... YOU SEXY DANCER .... Escapade/Rumour CDJAPE 7
06/04/1996.....59......1....... YOU SEXY DANCER Re-issue of Escapade/Rumour CDJAPE 7 .... Escapade CDJAPE 14

ROCKIN' BERRIES
UK group formed in Birmingham by Geoff Turton (born 11/3/1944, Birmingham, guitar), Clive Lea (born 16/2/1942, Birmingham, vocals), Bryan Charles 'Chuck' Botfield (born 14/11/1943, Birmingham, guitar), Roy Austin (born 27/12/1943, Birmingham, guitar) and Terry Bond (born 22/3/1943, Birmingham, drums). The group later recorded as The Berries while Turton recorded as Jefferson.

01/10/1964.....43......1....... I DIDN'T MEAN TO HURT YOU .... Piccadilly 7N 35197
15/10/1964.....3......13....... **HE'S IN TOWN** .... Piccadilly 7N 35203
21/01/1965.....23......7....... WHAT IN THE WORLD'S COME OVER YOU .... Piccadilly 7N 35217
13/05/1965.....5......11....... **POOR MAN'S SON** .... Piccadilly 7N 35236
26/08/1965.....40......7....... YOU'RE MY GIRL .... Piccadilly 7N 35254
06/01/1996.....43......2....... THE WATER IS OVER MY HEAD .... Piccadilly 7N 35270

ROCKNEY – see CHAS AND DAVE

ROCKSTEADY CREW
US singing/breakdancing group featuring Crazy Legs (born Richie Colon), Baby Love and Prince Ken Swift.

01/10/1983.....6......12.....O **(HEY YOU) THE ROCKSTEADY CREW** .... Charisma/Virgin RSC 1
05/05/1984.....64......4....... UPROCK .... Charisma/Virgin RSC 2

❶⁹ Number of weeks single topped the UK charts ↑ Entered the UK chart at #1 ▲⁹ Number of weeks single topped the US chart

677

ROCKWELL US singer (born Kennedy Gordy, 15/3/1964, Detroit, MI) who is the son of Motown founder Berry Gordy.

04/02/1984	6	11	SOMEBODY'S WATCHING ME .... Motown TMG 1331

ROCKY V FEATURING JOEY B. ELLIS AND TYNETTA HARE US dance group formed by rapper/producer Joey B Ellis (born Philadelphia, PA) and ex-Soft Touch singer Tynetta Hare (born Charlotte, NC).

16/02/1991	20	8	GO FOR IT (HEART AND FIRE) Featured in the 1990 film *Rocky V* .... Capitol CL 601

ROCOCO UK/Italian vocal/instrumental group.

16/12/1989	54	5	ITALO HOUSE MIX .... Mercury MER 314

RODEO JONES UK/Grenadine vocal/instrumental group formed by Benson Copland, Jayne Tretton and Graham Plato.

30/01/1993	75	1	NATURAL WORLD .... A&M AMCD 0165
03/04/1993	59	1	SHADES OF SUMMER .... A&M AMCD 212

CLODAGH RODGERS UK singer (born in Northern Ireland, later based in London) who made her debut in 1957 with Michael Holliday. She also recorded as Cloda Rodgers for Decca in 1962 and later recorded for Polydor and Precision.

26/03/1969	3	14	**COME BACK AND SHAKE ME** .... RCA 1792
09/07/1969	4	12	**GOODNIGHT MIDNIGHT** .... RCA 1852
08/11/1969	22	9	BILJO .... RCA 1891
04/04/1970	47	2	EVERYBODY GO HOME THE PARTY'S OVER .... RCA 1930
20/04/1971	4	10	**JACK IN THE BOX** UK entry for the 1971 Eurovision Song Contest (came fourth) .... RCA 2066
09/10/1971	28	12	LADY LOVE BUG .... RCA 2117

JIMMIE RODGERS US singer (born 18/9/1933, Camas, WA) who formed his first group while serving in the US Air Force. His career was halted in 1967 when he was found on the San Diego freeway with a fractured skull, the victim of a mysterious assault (he could recall nothing of the incident), but he returned to performing in 1968. He was inducted into the Rock & Roll Hall of Fame in 1986.

01/11/1957	30	1	HONEYCOMB ▲4 .... Columbia DB 3986
20/12/1957	7	11	**KISSES SWEETER THAN WINE** .... Columbia DB 4052
28/03/1958	18	6	OH OH, I'M FALLING IN LOVE AGAIN .... Columbia DB 4078
19/12/1958	18	6	WOMAN FROM LIBERIA .... Columbia DB 4206
14/06/1962	5	13	**ENGLISH COUNTRY GARDEN** .... Columbia DB 4847

PAUL RODGERS UK singer (born 12/12/1949, Middlesbrough, Cleveland) who was a founding member of Free in 1968 with Andy Fraser, Paul Kossoff and Simon Kirke. He and Kirke then linked up in Bad Company in 1973; Rodgers was later a member of The Firm and The Law.

12/02/1994	45	2	MUDDY WATER BLUES .... Victory ROGCD 1

RODRIGUEZ – see **SASH!**

RODS – see **EDDIE AND THE HOT RODS**

TOMMY ROE US singer (born 9/5/1943, Atlanta, GA) who formed the Satins while still at school and first recorded for Judd in 1960. He later moved to the UK, returning to the US in 1969. He later recorded country material and scored a number of country hits.

06/09/1962	3	14	SHEILA ▲2 .... HMV POP 1060
06/12/1962	37	5	SUSIE DARLIN' .... HMV POP 1092
21/03/1963	4	13	**THE FOLK SINGER** .... HMV POP 1138
26/09/1963	9	14	**EVERYBODY** .... HMV POP 1207
16/04/1969	●1	19	DIZZY ▲4 .... Stateside SS 2143
23/07/1969	24	9	HEATHER HONEY .... Stateside SS 2152

ROFO UK instrumental/production duo Ray Muylie and Fonny De Wulf.

01/08/1992	44	3	ROFO'S THEME .... PWL Continental PWLT 236

ROGER US singer (born 29/11/1951, Hamilton, OH) who formed Zapp with his brothers Larry, Lester and Tony and then recorded solo. Roger was shot to death by Larry on 25/4/1999, who then committed suicide.

17/10/1987	61	4	I WANT TO BE YOUR MAN .... Reprise W 8229
12/11/1988	55	3	BOOM! THERE SHE WAS SCRITTI POLITTI FEATURING ROGER .... Virgin VS 1143
13/05/1995	55	1	HIGH AS A KITE ONE TRIBE FEATURING ROGER .... ffrr FCD 259

JULIE ROGERS UK singer (born Julie Rolls, 6/4/1943, London) who auditioned for bandleader Teddy Foster and subsequently toured as a cabaret duo. Spotted by Johnny Franz, she was signed as a solo artist.

13/08/1964	3	23	**THE WEDDING** JULIE ROGERS WITH JOHNNY ARTHEY AND HIS ORCHESTRA AND CHORUS Cover version of the Argentinean song *La Novia* .... Mercury MF 820
10/12/1964	21	9	LIKE A CHILD .... Mercury MF 838
25/03/1965	31	6	HAWAIIAN WEDDING SONG .... Mercury MF 849

KENNY ROGERS US singer (born 21/8/1938, Houston, TX) who formed First Edition in 1967 with Mike Settle, Terry Williams and Thelma Camacho, all of whom had previously been members of the New Christy Minstrels. The group disbanded in 1974 with Rogers signing with Capitol as a solo artist in 1975. He has won three Grammy Awards including Best Country Vocal Performance in

○ Silver disc ● Gold disc ✪ Platinum disc (additional platinum units are indicated by a figure following the symbol) ◎ Singles released prior to 1973 that are known to have sold over 1 million copies in the UK

1979 for *The Gambler* (which also won the Best Country Song category for writer Don Schlitz) and Best Country Vocal Performance by a Duo in 1987 with Ronnie Milsap for *Make No Mistake, She's Mine*. He has a star on the Hollywood Walk of Fame.

DATE	POS	WKS	BPI	SINGLE TITLE	LABEL & NUMBER
18/10/1969	2	23		**RUBY DON'T TAKE YOUR LOVE TO TOWN**	Reprise RS 20829
07/02/1970	8	14		**SOMETHING'S BURNING** This and above single credited to KENNY ROGERS AND THE FIRST EDITION	Reprise RS 20888
30/04/1977	❶[1]	14	○	**LUCILLE** Featured in the 1978 film *Convoy*. 1977 Grammy Award for Best Country Vocal Performance	United Artists UP 36242
17/09/1977	39	4		**DAYTIME FRIENDS**	United Artists UP 36289
02/06/1979	42	7		**SHE BELIEVES IN ME**	United Artists UP 36533
26/01/1980	❶[2]	12	●	**COWARD OF THE COUNTY**	United Artists UP 614
15/11/1980	12	12		**LADY** ▲[6]	United Artists UP 635
12/02/1983	28	7		**WE'VE GOT TONIGHT** KENNY ROGERS AND SHEENA EASTON	Liberty UP 658
22/10/1983	61	1		**EYES THAT SEE IN THE DARK**	RCA 358
12/11/1983	7	15	○	**ISLANDS IN THE STREAM** ▲[2] KENNY ROGERS AND DOLLY PARTON	RCA 378

ROKOTTO
UK soul group formed by Sister B (vocals), Hugh Paul (vocals), Cleveland Walker (vocals), Derek Henderson (guitar), Owen 'Lloyd' Wisdom (bass), Stewart Garden (keyboards) and Howard 'Bongo' McLeod (drums).

DATE	POS	WKS	BPI	SINGLE TITLE	LABEL & NUMBER
22/10/1977	40	4		**BOOGIE ON UP**	State STAT 62
10/06/1978	49	6		**FUNK THEORY**	State STAT 80

ROLLERGIRL
German dance artist (born Nicci Juice, 1976, Waltrop).

DATE	POS	WKS	BPI	SINGLE TITLE	LABEL & NUMBER
16/09/2000	22	3		**DEAR JESSIE**	Neo NEOCD038

ROLLING STONES

UK rock group formed in London in 1963 by Mick Jagger (born 26/7/1943, Dartford, vocals), Keith Richards (born 18/12/1943, Dartford, guitar), Brian Jones (born Lewis Brian Hopkin-Jones, 28/2/1942, Cheltenham, guitar), Bill Wyman (born William Perks, 24/10/1936, London, bass), Ian Stewart (born 1938, Pittenween, Scotland, keyboards) and Charlie Watts (born 2/6/1941, London), making their debut live appearance at the Flamingo Jazz Club on 14/1/1963. They signed with Decca in May 1963 and released their first single, a cover of Chuck Berry's *Come On,* in June (Decca rejected the first version of *Come On* as 'dreadful'). They made their first UK tour in 1963 supporting the Everly Brothers, Bo Diddley and Little Richard. Stewart appeared on many of their recordings but was not an official member of the group when they signed with Decca (he subsequently became road manager). Jones resigned from the group in June 1969 and drowned on 3/7/1969. He was replaced by Mick Taylor (born 17/1/1948, Welwyn Garden City). Taylor left in 1974 and was replaced by Ron Wood (born 1/6/1947, Hillingdon). Wyman left in 1993. Stewart died from a heart attack on 12/12/1985 in his doctor's waiting room. Jagger recorded solo and made appearances in a number of films, including *Ned Kelly* in 1970, and was knighted in the 2002 Queen's Birthday Honours List. The documentary film *Gimme Shelter* (1970) covers the events at the Altamont concert where fan Meredith Hunter was stabbed to death by Hell's Angels. The group was inducted into the Rock & Roll Hall of Fame in 1989. Jagger and Richards took part in the *It's Only Rock 'N' Roll* project for the Children's Promise charity. The group has won two Grammy Awards: Best Rock Album in 1994 for *Voodoo Lounge* and Best Music Video Short Form in 1994 for *Love Is Strong*. They were inducted into the UK Music Hall of Fame in 2004, one of its first inductees.

DATE	POS	WKS	BPI	SINGLE TITLE	LABEL & NUMBER
25/07/1963	21	14		**COME ON**	Decca F 11675
14/11/1963	12	16		**I WANNA BE YOUR MAN** Written by John Lennon and Paul McCartney	Decca F 11764
27/02/1964	3	15		**NOT FADE AWAY**	Decca F 11845
02/07/1964	❶[1]	15		**IT'S ALL OVER NOW**	Decca F 11934
19/11/1964	❶[1]	12		**LITTLE RED ROOSTER**	Decca F 12014
04/03/1965	❶[3]	13		**THE LAST TIME**	Decca F 12104
26/08/1965	❶[2]	12		**(I CAN'T GET NO) SATISFACTION** ▲[4] Featured in the 1979 film *Apocalypse Now*	Decca F 12220
28/10/1965	❶[3]	12		**GET OFF OF MY CLOUD** ▲[2]	Decca F 12263
10/02/1966	2	8		**NINETEENTH NERVOUS BREAKDOWN**	Decca F 12331
19/05/1966	❶[1]	10		**PAINT IT, BLACK** ▲[2]	Decca F 12395
29/09/1966	5	8		**HAVE YOU SEEN YOUR MOTHER BABY STANDING IN THE SHADOW**	Decca F 12497
19/01/1967	3	10		**LET'S SPEND THE NIGHT TOGETHER/RUBY TUESDAY** ▲[1] Title was changed to *Let's Spend Some Time Together* for an appearance on the Ed Sullivan Show. *Ruby Tuesday* was a US chart topper	Decca F 12546
23/08/1967	8	8		**WE LOVE YOU/DANDELION**	Decca F 12654
29/05/1968	❶[2]	11		**JUMPING JACK FLASH** Featured in the 1986 film *Jumpin' Jack Flash*	Decca F 12782
09/07/1969	❶[5]	17		**HONKY TONK WOMEN** ▲[4]	Decca F 12952
24/04/1971	2	13	○	**BROWN SUGAR/BITCH/LET IT ROCK** ▲[2] Subsequently re-released in 1974 and qualified for a silver disc award, despite not re-charting	Rolling Stones RS 19100
03/07/1971	21	8		**STREET FIGHTING MAN**	Decca F 13195
29/04/1972	5	8		**TUMBLING DICE**	Rolling Stones RS 19103
01/09/1973	5	10	○	**ANGIE** ▲[1] Tribute to David Bowie's wife Angie Barnet	Rolling Stones RS 19105
03/08/1974	10	7		**IT'S ONLY ROCK AND ROLL**	Rolling Stones RS 19114
20/09/1975	45	2		**OUT OF TIME**	Decca F 13597
01/05/1976	6	10		**FOOL TO CRY**	Rolling Stones RS 19121
03/06/1978	3	13	○	**MISS YOU/FAR AWAY EYES** ▲[1]	Rolling Stones EMI 2802
30/09/1978	23	9		**RESPECTABLE**	Rolling Stones EMI 2861
05/07/1980	9	9		**EMOTIONAL RESCUE**	Rolling Stones RSR 105
04/10/1980	33	6		**SHE'S SO COLD**	Rolling Stones RSR 106
29/08/1981	7	9		**START ME UP** Subsequently used by Microsoft for their Windows '95 advertising for $8 million	Rolling Stones RSR 108
12/12/1981	50	6		**WAITING ON A FRIEND**	Rolling Stones RSR 109
12/06/1982	26	6		**GOING TO A GO GO** Cover version of The Miracles' 1965 US hit	Rolling Stones RSR 110
02/10/1982	62	2		**TIME IS ON MY SIDE**	Rolling Stones RSR 111
12/11/1983	11	9		**UNDER COVER OF THE NIGHT** Accompanying video was banned by the BBC for being too violent	Rolling Stones RSR 113

❶[9] Number of weeks single topped the UK charts ↑ Entered the UK chart at #1 ▲[9] Number of weeks single topped the US chart

679

				SINGLE TITLE	LABEL & NUMBER
11/02/1984	42	4		SHE WAS HOT	Rolling Stones RSR 114
21/07/1984	58	2		BROWN SUGAR Re-issue of Rolling Stones RS 19100	Rolling Stones SUGAR 1
15/03/1986	13	7		HARLEM SHUFFLE	Rolling Stones A 6864
02/09/1989	36	5		MIXED EMOTIONS	Rolling Stones 6551937
02/12/1989	63	1		ROCK AND A HARD PLACE	Rolling Stones 6554227
23/06/1990	61	3		PAINT IT, BLACK Re-issue of Decca F 12395	London LON 264
30/06/1990	31	5		ALMOST HEAR YOU SIGH	Rolling Stones 6560657
30/03/1991	29	4		HIGHWIRE	Rolling Stones 6567567
01/06/1991	59	2		RUBY TUESDAY (LIVE)	Rolling Stones 6568927
16/07/1994	14	5		LOVE IS STRONG	Virgin VSCDT 1503
08/10/1994	23	3		YOU GOT ME ROCKING	Virgin VSCDG 1518
10/12/1994	36	4		OUT OF TEARS	Virgin VSCDT 1524
15/07/1995	29	3		I GO WILD	Virgin VSCDX 1539
11/11/1995	12	5		LIKE A ROLLING STONE Featured in the 1995 film *Assassins*	Virgin VSCDT 1562
04/10/1997	22	3		ANYBODY SEEN MY BABY?	Virgin VSCDT 1653
07/02/1998	26	2		SAINT OF ME	Virgin VSCDT 1667
22/08/1998	51	1		OUT OF CONTROL	Virgin VSCDT 1700
21/12/2002	36	2		DON'T STOP	Virgin VSCDT 1838
13/09/2003	14	6		SYMPATHY FOR THE DEVIL	Mercury 9810612

ROLLINS BAND US group formed and fronted in 1987 by ex-Black Flag Henry Rollins (born Henry Garfield, 13/2/1961, Washington DC) with Chris Haskett, Andrew Weiss and Sim Cain. By 1999 the group consisted of Rollins, Jim Wilson (guitar), Marcus Blake (bass) and Jason Mackenroth (drums).

12/09/1992	54	2		TEARING	Imago 72787250187
10/09/1994	27	2		LIAR/DISCONNECTED	Imago 74321213052

ROLLO UK producer Roland Armstrong who later became a member of Faithless. Pauline Taylor is a UK singer.

29/01/1994	43	2		GET OFF YOUR HIGH HORSE	Cheeky CHEKCD 003
01/10/1994	47	2		GET OFF YOUR HIGH HORSE This and above single credited to **ROLLO GOES CAMPING**	Cheeky CHEKCD 003
10/06/1995	32	2		LOVE, LOVE, LOVE – HERE I COME **ROLLO GOES MYSTIC**	Cheeky CHEKCD 007
08/06/1996	26	2		LET THIS BE A PRAYER **ROLLO GOES SPIRITUAL WITH PAULINE TAYLOR**	Cheeky CHEKCD 013

ROMAN HOLIDAY UK group formed by Steve Lambert (vocals), his brother Rob (saxophone), Brian Bonhomme (guitar), Jon Durno (bass), Adrian York (keyboards), John Escott (trumpet) and Simon Cohen (drums).

02/04/1983	61	3		STAND BY	Jive 31
02/07/1983	14	9		DON'T TRY TO STOP IT	Jive 39
24/09/1983	40	7		MOTORMANIA	Jive 49

ROMAN NUMERALS – see **VIC REEVES**

ROMANTICS – see **RUBY AND THE ROMANTICS**

ROMEO UK rapper (born Marvin Dawkins) who is also a member of So Solid Crew.

30/12/2000	6	8		**NO GOOD 4 ME OXIDE AND NEUTRINO FEATURING MEGAMAN, ROMEO AND LISA MAFFIA** Contains a sample of The Prodigy's *No Good (Start The Dance)*	East West OXIDE 02CD
24/08/2002	3	9		**ROMEO DUNN**	Relentless RELENT 29CD
09/11/2002	9	6		**IT'S ALL GRAVY ROMEO FEATURING CHRISTINA MILIAN** Contains a sample of Mary J. Blige's *Real Love*	Relentless RELENT 32CD
06/12/2003	52	1		I SEE GIRLS (CRAZY) **STUDIO B/ROMEO AND HARRY BROOKS**	Multiply CDMULTY 109

MAX ROMEO Jamaican singer (born Max Smith, 1947, Kingston) who made his first recording in 1965 and after the success of his risqué hit single recorded a number of spiritual releases. By the 1990s he was back recording reggae music in Jamaica.

28/05/1969	10	25		**WET DREAM**	Unity UN 503

HARRY 'CHOO CHOO' ROMERO US DJ/producer based in New York who worked with Erick 'More' Morillo and his Subliminal Records label. He also records as Choo Choo Project.

22/05/1999	39	2		JUST CAN'T GET ENOUGH **HARRY 'CHOO CHOO' ROMERO PRESENTS INAYA DAY**	AM:PM CDAMPM 121
01/09/2001	51	1		I WANT OUT (I CAN'T BELIEVE)	Perfecto PERF 22CDS

RONALDO'S REVENGE UK dance group formed by producers Mike Gray and Jon Pearn. They also recorded as Arizona, Hustlers Convention, Full Intention, Disco Tex Presents Cloudburst and Sex-O-Sonique.

01/08/1998	37	2		MAS QUE MANCADA Song is also known as *Ronaldo's Revenge*	AM:PM 5827532

RONDO VENEZIANO Italian orchestral group formed in 1980 by Gian Piero Reverberi (born 29/7/1939, Genoa) as a chamber orchestra. The group members all wear authentic 18th-century Italian costumes (complete with wigs) when performing.

22/10/1983	58	3		LA SERENISSIMA (THEME FROM 'VENICE IN PERIL')	Ferroway 7 RON 1

RONETTES US R&B vocal group formed in 1961 by Veronica 'Ronnie' Bennett (born 10/8/1943, New York), her sister Estelle (born 22/7/1944, New York) and cousin Nedra Talley (born 27/1/1946, New York) as dance troupe The Dolly Sisters. They released their first record in 1961 as Ronnie & The Relatives for Colpix, becoming The Ronettes in 1962. They were spotted by Phil Spector and signed

○ Silver disc ● Gold disc ✪ Platinum disc (additional platinum units are indicated by a figure following the symbol) ◉ Singles released prior to 1973 that are known to have sold over 1 million copies in the UK

with his Philles label in 1963. They disbanded in 1966. Ronnie married Phil Spector in 1968; they divorced in 1974 (his first alimony payment to her for $1,300 was paid in 5 cent pieces). In November 2001 the New York Supreme Court's appellate division upheld a lower court ruling that ordered Phil Spector to pay $3 million in back royalties. Although a 1963 agreement between Spector and The Ronettes did not include synchronisation and domestic licensing rights, the court ruled that The Ronettes were entitled to payment for such usage in accordance with industry customs and practices.

17/10/1963	4	13		BE MY BABY Featured in the films *Big T.N.T. Show* (1966), *Quadrophenia* (1979) and *Dirty Dancing* (1987)	London HLU 9793
09/01/1964	11	14		BABY I LOVE YOU	London HLU 9826
27/08/1964	43	3		(THE BEST PART OF) BREAKING UP	London HLU 9905
08/10/1964	35	4		DO I LOVE YOU	London HLU 9922

RONNETTE – see FIDELFATTI FEATURING RONNETTE

MARK RONSON US DJ (born in New York City) and stepson of Foreigner's Mick Jones.

01/11/2003	15	7		OOH WEE Features the uncredited contributions of Ghostface Killah and Nate Dogg	Elektra E 7490CD

MICK RONSON WITH JOE ELLIOTT UK instrumental/vocal duo Mick Ronson (born 26/5/1949, Hull, Humberside) and Joe Elliott (born 1/8/1959, Sheffield). Ex-Mott The Hoople Ronson died from cancer on 29/4/1993. Elliott is a member of Def Leppard.

07/05/1994	55	1		DON'T LOOK DOWN	Epic 6603582

LINDA RONSTADT US singer (born 15/7/1946, Tucson, AZ) who formed the Three Ronstadts with her brother Mike and sister Suzi in 1960. They name-changed to the New Union Ramblers before Linda left to join the Kimmel Brothers. Bob Kimmel, Linda and Kenny Edwards then formed the Stone Poneys and recorded for Capitol. Ronstadt went solo in 1968 with her 1971 touring band, including future Eagles Glenn Frey, Bernie Leadon, Randy Meisner and Don Henley. She appeared in the 1983 film *The Pirates Of Penzance*, having also appeared in the Broadway production, and 'appeared' in an episode of the TV cartoon *The Simpsons*, singing the Plow King Theme jingle. She has won eleven Grammy Awards including Best Country Vocal Performance in 1975 for *I Can't Help It (If I'm Still In Love With You)*, Best Pop Vocal Performance in 1976 for *Hasten Down The Wind*, Best Recording for Children in 1980 with various others for *In Harmony*, Best Country Performance by a Group in 1987 with Dolly Parton and Emmylou Harris for *Trio*, Best Mexican-American Performance in 1988 for *Canciones De Mi Padre*, Best Pop Vocal Performance by a Duo in 1990 with Aaron Neville for *All My Life*, Best Tropical Latin Album in 1992 for *Frenesi*, Best Mexican-American Album in 1992 for *Mas Canciones*, Best Children's Music in 1996 for *Dedicated To The One I Love* and Best Country Vocal Collaboration in 1999 with Emmylou Harris and Dolly Parton for *After The Gold Rush*. Aaron Neville (born 21/1/1941, New Orleans, LA) was originally with the Hawketts before linking with his brothers in the Neville Family Band; he then went solo.

08/05/1976	42	3		TRACKS OF MY TEARS	Asylum K 13034
28/01/1978	35	4		BLUE BAYOU	Asylum K 13106
26/05/1979	66	2		ALISON	Asylum K 13149
11/07/1987	8	13		SOMEWHERE OUT THERE LINDA RONSTADT AND JAMES INGRAM Featured in the 1987 film *An American Tail*	MCA 1132
11/11/1989	2	12	O	DON'T KNOW MUCH LINDA RONSTADT AND AARON NEVILLE 1989 Grammy Award for Best Pop Vocal Performance by a Duo	
					Elektra EKR 101

ROOFTOP SINGERS US folk group formed in New York by Erik Darling (born 25/9/1933, Baltimore, MD), Willard Svanoe and Lynne Taylor. They disbanded in 1967, the same year Taylor died. Following the success of the group's debut single, efforts were made to locate songwriter Gus Cannon, then aged 79, living in a small house near a railway track and virtually penniless, having recently sold his banjo for $20 to raise money for coal. As a result of *Walk Right In*, Gus picked up a recording contract with Stax and a 'Gus Cannon Story' was broadcast across the world by The Voice Of America.

31/01/1963	10	12		WALK RIGHT IN ▲2 Originally recorded in 1929 by (Gus) Cannon's Jug Stompers. This version featured in the 1994 film *Forrest Gump*	Fontana TF 271700

ROOM 5 FEATURING OLIVER CHEATHAM Italian DJ/producer Vito Lucente whose debut hit was originally recorded with a sample of Oliver Cheatham's *Get Down Saturday Night*, but Cheatham later re-recorded his vocal parts for the single. Lucente also records as Junior Jack and Mr Jack.

05/04/2003	❶4	15	O	MAKE LUV ↑ First came to prominence after being used in a TV advertisement for Lynx deodorant	Positiva CDTIV 187
06/12/2003	38	2		MUSIC AND YOU	Positiva CDTIVS 197

ROONEY US group formed in New York City by Robert Carmine (guitar/vocals), Taylor Locke (guitar), Matt Winter (bass) and Ned Brower (drums).

26/06/2004	73	1		I'M SHAKIN'	Geffen 9862557

ROOSTER UK rock group formed in London by Nick Atkinson (vocals), Luke Potashnick (guitar), Ben Smyth (bass) and David Neale (drums).

23/10/2004	7	6		COME GET SOME	Brightside 82876652382

ROOTJOOSE UK group formed in Cornwall by James Crowe (guitar/vocals), Rob Elton (guitar/vocals), Harry Collier (bass/vocals) and Fez (drums). They later name-changed to Rarebirds.

17/05/1997	73	1		CAN'T KEEP LIVING THIS WAY	Rage RAGECD 2
02/08/1997	54	1		MR FIXIT	Rage RAGECDX 3
04/10/1997	68	1		LONG WAY	Rage RAGECD 5

ROOTS US rap group formed in Philadelphia, PA by Tariq Trotter, Ahmir-Khalib Thompson, Malik Abdul-Basil and Leonard Hubbard.

03/05/1997	49	1		WHAT THEY DO	Geffen GFSTD 22240

❶9 Number of weeks single topped the UK charts ↑ Entered the UK chart at #1 ▲9 Number of weeks single topped the US chart

681

06/03/1999	31	2		YOU GOT ME **THE ROOTS FEATURING ERYKAH BADU** 1999 Grammy Award for Best Rap Group Performance .... MCA MCSTD 48110
12/04/2003	33	2		THE SEED (2.0) **ROOTS FEATURING CODY CHESTNUTT** .... MCA MCSTD 40316
16/08/2003	59	1		BREAKS YOU OFF **ROOTS FEATURING MUSIQ** .... MCA MCSTD 40330

RALPHI ROSARIO – see RICHIE RICH

MYKAL ROSE – see SHABBA RANKS

ROSE OF ROMANCE ORCHESTRA UK orchestra.

09/01/1982	71	1		TARA'S THEME FROM 'GONE WITH THE WIND' .... BBC RESL 108

ROSE ROYCE

US soul group formed in Los Angeles, CA in 1972 by Kenji Chiba Brown (guitar), Lequient 'Duke' Jobe (bass), Victor Nix (keyboards), Kenny Copeland (trumpet), Freddie Dunn (trumpet), Michael Moore (saxophone) and Terral Santiel (congas). First known as Total Concept Unlimited, they were used by producer Norman Whitfield as Edwin Starr's backing band, later name-changing to Magic Wand and supporting Yvonne Fair, the Temptations and Undisputed Truth. They added lead singer Gwen Dickey and name-changed to Rose Royce in 1975. The first act to sign to Whitfield's eponymous label, their big break came with the recording of the soundtrack to the 1976 film *Car Wash*. Dickey left in 1977 and was replaced by Rose Norwalt. Dickey returned in 1978 for two years and was subsequently replaced by Ricci Benson. Nix left in 1977 (replaced by Michael Nash) and Brown left in 1980 (replaced by Walter McKinney). *Car Wash* won the 1976 Grammy Award for Best Album of Original Score Written for a Motion Picture.

25/12/1976	9	12		**CAR WASH** ▲¹ Featured in the 1978 film *The Stud* .... MCA 267
22/01/1977	44	5		PUT YOUR MONEY WHERE YOUR MOUTH IS .... MCA 259
02/04/1977	14	8		I WANNA GET NEXT TO YOU This and above two singles featured in the 1976 film *Car Wash*. This hit also featured in the films *Friday* (1995) and *Never Die Alone* (2004). .... MCA 278
24/09/1977	30	6		DO YOUR DANCE .... Whitfield K 17006
14/01/1978	3	14	○	**WISHING ON A STAR** Featured in the 1998 film *54* .... Whitfield K 17060
06/05/1978	16	10		IT MAKES YOU FEEL LIKE DANCIN' .... Whitfield K 17148
16/09/1978	2	10	●	**LOVE DON'T LIVE HERE ANYMORE** .... Whitfield K 17236
03/02/1979	51	4		I'M IN LOVE (AND I LOVE THE FEELING) .... Whitfield K 17291
17/11/1979	13	13		IS IT LOVE YOU'RE AFTER Featured in the 2000 film *The Most Fertile Man In Ireland* .... Whitfield K 17456
08/03/1980	46	7		OOH BOY .... Whitfield K 17575
21/11/1981	52	3		R.R. EXPRESS .... Warner Brothers K 17875
01/09/1984	43	8		MAGIC TOUCH .... Streetwave KHAN 21
06/04/1985	60	3		LOVE ME RIGHT NOW .... Streetwave KHAN 39
11/06/1988	20	7		CAR WASH/IS IT LOVE YOU'RE AFTER Re-issue of MCA 267 and Whitfield K 17456. .... MCA 1253
31/10/1998	18	3		CAR WASH **ROSE ROYCE FEATURING GWEN DICKEY** Re-recording of MCA 267 .... MCA MCSTD 48096

ROSE TATTOO

Australian group formed in Sydney in 1977 by Angry Anderson (born Gary Stephen Anderson, 5/8/1948, vocals), Peter Wells (guitar/vocals), Michael Cocks (guitar), Mick 'Geordie' Leech (bass) and Dallas 'Digger' Royall (drums). They released their debut album in 1978. Cocks left in 1982 and was replaced by Robin Riley. Anderson and Leech then re-assembled the group with Greg Jordan (guitar), John Meyer (guitar) and Robert Bowron (drums) for one album before the group disbanded. Although another Rose Tattoo album appeared, this was a contractual obligation album that was effectively Anderson recording solo. The original line-up re-formed in 1993 (minus Royall who had died three years previously).

11/07/1981	60	4		ROCK 'N' ROLL OUTLAW .... Carrere CAR 200

JIMMY ROSELLI Italian singer (born 1925) who later relocated to US and grew up in Hoboken, NJ.

05/03/1983	51	5		WHEN YOUR OLD WEDDING RING WAS NEW A1 282
20/06/1987	52	3		WHEN YOUR OLD WEDDING RING WAS NEW Re-issue of A1 282 .... First Night SCORE 9

ROSIE – see G NATION FEATURING ROSIE

DIANA ROSS

US singer (born Diane Ernestine Ross, 26/3/1944, Detroit, MI) who joined the Primettes in 1959, the group subsequently becoming the Supremes when signed by Motown in 1960. She took over from Florence Ballard as lead singer and was given top billing in 1967. She left the group to go solo in 1970 and was replaced by Jean Terrell. She appeared in films including the biopic of singer Billie Holiday *Lady Sings The Blues* (1972) , for which she was nominated for an Oscar, *Mahogany* (1975), *The Wiz* (1978) and alongside Brandy in *Double Platinum* (1999). She left Motown in 1981, signing with RCA for the US and EMI/Capitol for the UK. She had a relationship with Motown founder Berry Gordy with whom she had a son. She has a star on the Hollywood Walk of Fame.

30/08/1967	5	14		**REFLECTIONS** Featured in the 1989 film *Arthur 2: On The Rocks*. .... Tamla Motown TMG 616
29/11/1967	13	13		IN AND OUT OF LOVE .... Tamla Motown TMG 632
10/04/1968	28	8		FOREVER CAME TODAY .... Tamla Motown TMG 650
03/07/1968	34	6		SOME THINGS YOU NEVER GET USED TO .... Tamla Motown TMG 662
20/11/1968	15	14		LOVE CHILD ▲² This and above four singles credited to **DIANA ROSS AND THE SUPREMES** .... Tamla Motown TMG 677
29/01/1969	3	12		**I'M GONNA MAKE YOU LOVE ME** DIANA ROSS AND THE SUPREMES AND THE TEMPTATIONS Featured in the 1996 film *Now And Then*. .... Tamla Motown TMG 685
23/04/1969	14	10		I'M LIVING IN SHAME .... Tamla Motown TMG 695

DATE	POS	WKS	BPI	SINGLE TITLE	LABEL & NUMBER
16/07/1969	37	7		NO MATTER WHAT SIGN YOU ARE This and above single credited to **DIANA ROSS AND THE SUPREMES**	Tamla Motown TMG 704
20/09/1969	18	8		I SECOND THAT EMOTION **DIANA ROSS AND THE SUPREMES AND THE TEMPTATIONS**	Tamla Motown TMG 709
13/12/1969	13	13		SOMEDAY WE'LL BE TOGETHER ▲1 **DIANA ROSS AND THE SUPREMES**	Tamla Motown TMG 721
21/03/1970	31	7		WHY (MUST WE FALL IN LOVE) **DIANA ROSS AND THE SUPREMES AND THE TEMPTATIONS**	Tamla Motown TMG 730
18/07/1970	33	5		REACH OUT AND TOUCH	Tamla Motown TMG 743
12/09/1970	6	12		**AIN'T NO MOUNTAIN HIGH ENOUGH ▲3**	Tamla Motown TMG 751
03/04/1971	7	12		**REMEMBER ME**	Tamla Motown TMG 768
31/07/1971	❶4	14		**I'M STILL WAITING**	Tamla Motown TMG 781
30/10/1971	10	11		**SURRENDER**	Tamla Motown TMG 792
13/05/1972	12	9		DOOBEDOOD'NDOOBE DOOBEDOOD'NDOOBE	Tamla Motown TMG 812
14/07/1973	9	13		**TOUCH ME IN THE MORNING ▲1**	Tamla Motown TMG 861
05/01/1974	9	13		**ALL OF MY LIFE**	Tamla Motown TMG 880
23/03/1974	5	12	○	**YOU ARE EVERYTHING DIANA ROSS AND MARVIN GAYE**	Tamla Motown TMG 890
04/05/1974	35	4		LAST TIME I SAW HIM	Tamla Motown TMG 893
20/07/1974	25	8		STOP LOOK LISTEN (TO YOUR HEART) **DIANA ROSS AND MARVIN GAYE** Featured in the 2001 film *Bridget Jones's Diary* Tamla Motown TMG 906	
24/08/1974	12	10		BABY LOVE **DIANA ROSS AND THE SUPREMES**	Tamla Motown TMG 915
28/09/1974	38	5		LOVE ME	Tamla Motown TMG 917
29/03/1975	23	9		SORRY DOESN'T ALWAYS MAKE IT RIGHT	Tamla Motown TMG 941
03/04/1976	5	8		**THEME FROM MAHOGANY (DO YOU KNOW WHERE YOU'RE GOING TO) ▲1** Featured in the 1975 film *Mahogany* Tamla Motown TMG 1010	
24/04/1976	10	10		**LOVE HANGOVER ▲2** Featured in the 1977 film *Looking For Mr Goodbar*	Tamla Motown TMG 1024
10/07/1976	32	5		I THOUGHT IT TOOK A LITTLE TIME	Tamla Motown TMG 1032
16/10/1976	41	4		I'M STILL WAITING Re-issue of Tamla Motown TMG 781	Tamla Motown TMG 1041
19/11/1977	23	7		GETTING' READY FOR LOVE	Motown TMG 1090
22/07/1978	54	6		LOVIN' LIVIN' AND GIVIN' Featured in the 1978 film *Thank God It's Friday*	Motown TMG 1112
18/11/1978	45	4		EASE ON DOWN THE ROAD **DIANA ROSS AND MICHAEL JACKSON** Featured in the 1978 film *The Wiz*	MCA 396
24/02/1979	66	5		POPS WE LOVE YOU **DIANA ROSS, MARVIN GAYE, SMOKEY ROBINSON AND STEVIE WONDER** Recorded to honour Berry Gordy's father's 90th birthday	Motown TMG 1136
21/07/1979	40	7		THE BOSS Featured in the 1998 film *54*	Motown TMG 1150
06/10/1979	59	3		NO ONE GETS THE PRIZE	Motown TMG 1160
24/11/1979	32	10		IT'S MY HOUSE	Motown TMG 1169
19/07/1980	2	12	○	**UPSIDE DOWN ▲4**	Motown TMG 1195
20/09/1980	5	9	○	**MY OLD PIANO**	Motown TMG 1202
15/11/1980	13	10		I'M COMING OUT Featured in the films *The Last Days Of Disco* (1998) and *Maid In Manhattan* (2002)	Motown TMG 1210
17/01/1981	16	8		IT'S MY TURN Featured in the 1980 film *It's My Turn*	Motown TMG 1217
28/03/1981	49	5		ONE MORE CHANCE	Motown TMG 1227
13/06/1981	58	3		CRYIN' MY HEART OUT FOR YOU	Motown TMG 1233
12/09/1981	7	12		ENDLESS LOVE ▲9 **DIANA ROSS AND LIONEL RICHIE** Featured in the 1981 film *Endless Love*	Motown TMG 1240
07/11/1981	4	12	○	**WHY DO FOOLS FALL IN LOVE**	Capitol CL 226
23/01/1982	73	2		TENDERNESS	Motown TMG 1248
30/01/1982	36	5		MIRROR MIRROR	Capitol CL 234
29/05/1982	7	11		**WORK THAT BODY**	Capitol CL 241
07/08/1982	41	4		IT'S NEVER TOO LATE	Capitol CL 256
23/10/1982	15	9		MUSCLES Written and produced by Michael Jackson	Capitol CL 268
15/01/1983	43	4		SO CLOSE	Capitol CL 277
23/07/1983	46	3		PIECES OF ICE	Capitol CL 298
07/07/1984	43	8		ALL OF YOU **JULIO IGLESIAS AND DIANA ROSS**	CBS A 4522
15/09/1984	47	6		TOUCH BY TOUCH	Capitol CL 337
28/09/1985	71	1		EATEN ALIVE Written and produced by Michael Jackson	Capitol CL 372
25/01/1986	❶3	17	●	**CHAIN REACTION**	Capitol CL 386
03/05/1986	47	3		EXPERIENCE	Capitol CL 400
13/06/1987	49	3		DIRTY LOOKS	EMI EM 2
08/10/1988	58	2		MR LEE	EMI EM 73
26/11/1988	75	1		LOVE HANGOVER (REMIX)	Motown ZB 42307
18/02/1989	62	1		STOP! IN THE NAME OF LOVE **DIANA ROSS AND THE SUPREMES**	Motown ZB 41963
06/05/1989	32	5		WORKIN' OVERTIME	EMI EM 91
29/07/1989	61	2		PARADISE	EMI EM 94
07/07/1990	21	6		I'M STILL WAITING (REMIX)	Motown ZB 43781
30/11/1991	2	11	○	**WHEN YOU TELL ME THAT YOU LOVE ME**	EMI EM 217
15/02/1992	27	3		THE FORCE BEHIND THE POWER	EMI EM 221
20/06/1992	10	8		**ONE SHINING MOMENT**	EMI EM 239
28/11/1992	11	10		IF WE HOLD ON TOGETHER Featured in the 1988 film *The Land Before Time*	EMI EM 257
13/03/1993	31	3		HEART (DON'T CHANGE MY MIND)	EMI CDEM 261
09/10/1993	20	5		CHAIN REACTION Re-issue of Capitol CL 386	EMI CDEM 290
11/12/1993	14	8		YOUR LOVE	EMI CDEM 299
02/04/1994	28	4		THE BEST YEARS OF MY LIFE	EMI CDEM 305
09/07/1994	36	4		WHY DO FOOLS FALL IN LOVE/I'M COMING OUT (REMIX)	EMI CDEM 332
02/09/1995	32	4		TAKE ME HIGHER	EMI CDEM 388

❶9 Number of weeks single topped the UK charts ↑ Entered the UK chart at #1 ▲9 Number of weeks single topped the US chart

25/11/1995	36	3		I'M GONE	EMI CDEMS 402
17/02/1996	14	4		I WILL SURVIVE DIANA Accompanying video features RuPaul	EMI CDEM 415
21/12/1996	34	4		IN THE ONES YOU LOVE	EMI CDEM 457
06/11/1999	9	7		**NOT OVER YOU YET**	EMI CDEM 553

RICKY ROSS UK singer (born 22/12/1957, Dundee, Scotland) who was a member of Deacon Blue before going solo.

18/05/1996	35	2		RADIO ON	Epic 6631352
10/08/1996	58	1		GOOD EVENING PHILADELPHIA	Epic 6635335

FRANCIS ROSSI UK singer/guitarist (born 29/4/1949, London) who is also a member of Status Quo.

11/05/1985	54	4		MODERN ROMANCE (I WANT TO FALL IN LOVE AGAIN) FRANCIS ROSSI AND BERNARD FROST	Vertigo FROS 1
03/08/1996	42	2		GIVE MYSELF TO LOVE FRANCIS ROSSI OF STATUS QUO	Virgin VSCDT 1594

NATALIE ROSSI – see FOUNDATION FEATURING NATALIE ROSSI

NINI ROSSO Italian singer (born Celeste Rosso, 19/9/1926, Turin) who learned to play the trumpet while still at school and became one of Italy's leading jazz musicians.

26/08/1965	8	14		**IL SILENZIO**	Durium DRS 54000

DAVID LEE ROTH US singer (born 10/10/1955, Bloomington, IN) who was lead singer with Van Halen from their formation in 1975 until 1985 when he left to go solo.

23/02/1985	68	2		CALIFORNIA GIRLS	Warner Brothers W 9102
05/03/1988	27	7		JUST LIKE PARADISE	Warner Brothers W 8119
03/09/1988	72	1		DAMN GOOD/STAND UP	Warner Brothers W 7753
12/01/1991	32	3		A LIL' AIN'T ENOUGH	Warner Brothers W 0002
19/02/1994	64	1		SHE'S MY MACHINE	Reprise W 0229CD
28/05/1994	72	1		NIGHT LIFE	Reprise W 0249CD

ROTTERDAM TERMINATION SOURCE Dutch instrumental/production duo Danny Scholte and Maurice Steenbergen.

07/11/1992	27	4		POING	SEP EDGE 74
25/12/1993	73	2		MERRY X-MESS	React CDREACT 33

ROULA – see 20 FINGERS

ROULETTES – see ADAM FAITH

ROUND SOUND PRESENTS ONYX STONE AND MC MALIBU UK garage group featuring Onyx Stone and MC Malibu.

16/03/2002	69	1		WHADDA WE LIKE?	Cooltempo CDCOOL 358

DEMIS ROUSSOS Greek singer (born 15/6/1947, Alexandria, Egypt) who was a member of Aphrodite's Child with Vangelis and Lucas Sideras from 1963 until they disbanded in the mid-1970s. He then went solo and became a big hit across Europe. He was one of the passengers hijacked and held hostage at Beirut Airport in 1985.

22/11/1975	5	10	O	**HAPPY TO BE ON AN ISLAND IN THE SUN**	Philips 6042 033
28/02/1976	35	5		CAN'T SAY HOW MUCH I LOVE YOU	Philips 6042 114
26/06/1976	❶[1]	12	O	**THE ROUSSOS PHENOMENON EP** Tracks on EP: *Forever And Ever, Sing An Ode To Love, So Dreamy* and *My Friend The Wind*	Philips DEMIS 001
02/10/1976	2	10	O	**WHEN FOREVER HAS GONE**	Philips 6042 186
19/03/1977	39	4		BECAUSE	Philips 6042 245
18/06/1977	33	3		KYRILA (EP) Tracks on EP: *Kyrila, I'm Gonna Fall In Love, I Dig You* and *Sister Emilyne*	Philips DEMIS 002

ROUTERS US rock 'n' roll instrumental group formed by Leon Russell (keyboards), Tommy Tedesco (guitar), Mike Gordon (guitar) and Hal Blaine (drums). The group was assembled by Gordon and producer Joe Saraceno.

27/12/1962	32	7		LET'S GO	Warner Brothers WB 77

MARIA ROWE UK singer.

20/05/1995	67	2		SEXUAL	ffrr FCD 248

ROWETTA – see OPEN ARMS FEATURING ROWETTA

KELLY ROWLAND US singer (born Kelendria Rowland, 11/2/1981, Houston, TX) who is also a member of Destiny's Child and launched a parallel solo career in 2002. Kelly became engaged to Dallas Cowboys' football player Roy Williams in May 2003.

26/10/2002	❶[2]	21	✪	**DILEMMA** ↑ ▲[10] NELLY FEATURING KELLY ROWLAND Contains an interpolation of *Love, Need And Want You*. 2002 Grammy Award for Best Rap/Sung Collaboration	Universal MCSTD 40299
21/12/2002	57	5		STOLE (IMPORT)	Columbia 6732122
08/02/2003	2	14		**STOLE**	Columbia 6735182
10/05/2003	5	10		**CAN'T NOBODY**	Columbia 6738142
16/08/2003	20	4		TRAIN ON A TRACK Featured in the 2002 film Maid In Manhattan	Columbia 6742155

O Silver disc ● Gold disc ✪ Platinum disc (additional platinum units are indicated by a figure following the symbol) ◉ Singles released prior to 1973 that are known to have sold over 1 million copies in the UK

KEVIN ROWLAND – see DEXY'S MIDNIGHT RUNNERS

JOHN ROWLES New Zealand singer who later recorded for Columbia and scored a minor hit in the US in 1971.

Date	Pos	Wks		Title	Label & Number
13/03/1968	3	18		**IF I ONLY HAD TIME**	MCA MU 1000
19/06/1968	12	10		HUSH NOT A WORD TO MARY	MCA MU 1023

LISA ROXANNE UK singer (born Lisa Roxanne Naraine, London); she is the daughter of ex-Loose Ends singer Trisha Naraine. Lisa was fourteen at the time of her debut hit and was discovered by former Island Records boss Chris Blackwell.

09/06/2001	18	2		NO FLOW	Palm Pictures PPCD 70542

ROXETTE Swedish duo formed in 1986 by Per Gessle (born 12/2/1959, Halmstad, guitar/vocals) and Marie Frederiksson (born 29/5/1958, Ostra Ljungby, vocals). Gessle was ex-member of the group Gyllene Tyler while Frederiksson was a successful solo artist.

22/04/1989	7	10		**THE LOOK** ▲[1]	EMI EM 87
15/07/1989	48	5		DRESSED FOR SUCCESS	EMI EM 96
28/10/1989	62	3		LISTEN TO YOUR HEART ▲[1]	EMI EM 108
02/06/1990	3	14	○	**IT MUST HAVE BEEN LOVE** ▲[2] Featured in the 1990 film *Pretty Woman*	EMI EM 141
11/08/1990	6	9		LISTEN TO YOUR HEART/DANGEROUS Re-issue of EMI EM 108	EMI EM 149
27/10/1990	18	7		DRESSED FOR SUCCESS Re-issue of EMI EM 96	EMI EM 162
09/03/1991	4	10		**JOYRIDE** ▲[1]	EMI EM 177
11/05/1991	12	6		FADING LIKE A FLOWER	EMI EM 190
07/09/1991	21	6		THE BIG L	EMI EM 204
23/11/1991	22	4		SPENDING MY TIME	EMI EM 215
28/03/1992	21	4		CHURCH OF YOUR HEART	EMI EM 227
01/08/1992	13	7		HOW DO YOU DO!	EMI EM 241
07/11/1992	28	4		QUEEN OF RAIN	EMI EM 253
24/07/1993	7	9		**ALMOST UNREAL** Featured in the 1993 film *Super Mario Brothers*	EMI CDEM 268
18/09/1993	10	8		**IT MUST HAVE BEEN LOVE** Re-issue of EMI EM 141	EMI CDEM 285
26/03/1994	14	6		SLEEPING IN MY CAR	EMI CDEM 314
04/06/1994	26	5		CRASH! BOOM! BANG!	EMI CDEM 324
17/09/1994	30	4		FIREWORKS	EMI CDEM 345
03/12/1994	27	4		RUN TO YOU	EMI CDEMS 360
08/04/1995	44	2		VULNERABLE	EMI CDEM 369
25/11/1995	28	3		THE LOOK '95 (REMIX)	EMI CDEMS 406
30/03/1996	42	2		YOU DON'T UNDERSTAND ME	EMI CDEM 418
20/07/1996	52	1		JUNE AFTERNOON	EMI CDEM 437
20/03/1999	11	7		WISH I COULD FLY	EMI CDEM 537
09/10/1999	56	1		STARS	EMI CDEM 550

ROXY MUSIC UK group formed in 1971 by Bryan Ferry (born 26/9/1945, Washington, Tyne and Wear, vocals/keyboards), Andy Mackay (born 23/7/1946, London, saxophone), Brian Eno (born Brian Peter George St John le Baptiste de la Salle Eno, 15/5/1948, Woodbridge, Suffolk, synthesiser), Davy O'List (born 13/12/1950, London, guitar), Graham Simpson (bass) and Paul Thompson (born 13/5/1951, Jarrow, Northumberland). O'List left in 1972 and was replaced by Phil Manzanera (born Philip Targett Adams, 31/1/1951, London); Simpson was replaced by Rik Kenton the same year. Thereafter they went through a succession of bass guitarists, including John Porter, John Gustafson, John Wetton, Rik Kenton, Sal Maida, Rick Wills and Gary Tibbs (later a member of Adam And The Ants). They signed with management company EG in 1971, with their initial recordings licensed to Island. Ferry later recorded solo, while Eno moved into production. Eno was named Best Producer at the 1994 and 1996 BRIT Awards and also collected the 1992 Grammy Award with Daniel Lanois in the same category (jointly with Babyface).

19/08/1972	4	12		**VIRGINIA PLAIN**	Island WIP 6144
10/03/1973	10	12		**PYJAMARAMA**	Island WIP 6159
17/11/1973	9	12		**STREET LIFE**	Island WIP 6173
12/10/1974	12	8		ALL I WANT IS YOU	Island WIP 6208
11/10/1975	2	10	○	**LOVE IS THE DRUG**	Island WIP 6248
27/12/1975	25	7		BOTH ENDS BURNING	Island WIP 6262
22/10/1977	11	6		VIRGINIA PLAIN	Polydor 2001 739
03/03/1979	40	6	●	TRASH	Polydor POSP 32
28/04/1979	2	14	●	**DANCE AWAY**	Polydor POSP 44
11/08/1979	4	11	○	**ANGEL EYES**	Polydor POSP 67
17/05/1980	5	9	○	**OVER YOU**	Polydor POSP 93
02/08/1980	5	8		**OH YEAH (ON THE RADIO)**	Polydor 2001 972
08/11/1980	12	7		THE SAME OLD SCENE Featured in the 1980 film *Times Square*	Polydor ROXY 1
21/02/1981	❶[2]	11	●	**JEALOUS GUY** Tribute to John Lennon	EG ROXY 2
03/04/1982	6	8	○	**MORE THAN THIS** Featured in the 1999 film *200 Cigarettes*	EG ROXY 3
19/06/1982	13	6		AVALON	EG ROXY 4
25/09/1982	26	6		TAKE A CHANCE WITH ME	EG ROXY 5
27/04/1996	33	2		LOVE IS THE DRUG (REMIX)	EG VSCDT 1580

❶[9] Number of weeks single topped the UK charts ↑ Entered the UK chart at #1 ▲[9] Number of weeks single topped the US chart

685

BILLY JOE ROYAL
US singer (born 1942, Valdosta, GA) who formed the Corvettes while still at school and made his first recordings in 1962.

07/10/1965.....38......4....... DOWN IN THE BOONDOCKS.. CBS 201802

CENTRAL BAND OF THE ROYAL AIR FORCE, CONDUCTOR W/CDR. A.E. SIMS OBE
UK military band that were still recording and releasing records into the 1990s.

21/10/1955.....18......1....... THE DAMBUSTERS MARCH Featured in the 1954 film *The Dam Busters* .... HMV B 10877

ROYAL GIGOLOS
UK production duo DJ Mike Moore and DJ Tyson with singers Mel and Romeo.

31/07/2004.....44......3....... CALIFORNIA DREAMIN'.. Manifesto 9866931

ROYAL GUARDSMEN
US pop group formed in Florida by Barry Winslow (guitar/vocals), Chris Nunley (vocals), Tom Richards (guitar), Bill Balough (bass) and Billy Taylor (organ).

19/01/1967.....8......13...... **SNOOPY VS THE RED BARON**.. Stateside SS 574
06/04/1967.....37......4....... RETURN OF THE RED BARON.. Stateside SS 2010

ROYAL HOUSE
US group formed by Dena Spurling, Dwight Mitchell, Carlos Savoury and DJ Tony D with production handled by Todd Terry.

10/09/1988.....14......14...... CAN YOU PARTY.. Champion CHAMP 79
07/01/1989.....35......4...... YEAH! BUDDY.. Champion CHAMP 91

ROYAL PHILHARMONIC ORCHESTRA ARRANGED AND CONDUCTED BY LOUIS CLARK
UK orchestra formed in 1946 by Sir Thomas Beecham; following his death in 1961 Rudolf Kempe became musical director. Sir Thomas Beecham and the Royal Philharmonic Orchestra won the 1960 Grammy Award for Best Classical Performance, Choral (including Oratorio) for *Handel's Messiah*. In 1966 Queen Elizabeth II conferred the Royal title on the orchestra. Conductor Louis Clark was born in Birmingham. Among the musical directors since 1975 (when Kempe retired) are Andre Previn, Walter Weller and Vladimir Ashkenazy.

25/07/1981.....2......11.....O **HOOKED ON CLASSICS** Medley of *Tchaikovsky Piano Concerto No1, Flight Of The Bumble Bee, Mozart Symphony No40 In G Minor, Rhapsody In Blue, Karelia Suite, The Marriage Of Figaro, Romeo & Juliet, Trumpet Voluntary, Hallelujah Chorus, Grieg Piano Concerto In A Minor* and *March Of The Toreadors* .... RCA 109
24/10/1981.....47......3....... HOOKED ON CAN-CAN.. RCA 151
10/07/1982.....61......3....... BBC WORLD CUP GRANDSTAND Theme to the BBC's coverage of the 1982 FIFA World Cup. Louis Clark was not present on this hit . ... BBC RESL 116
07/08/1982.....71......2....... IF YOU KNEW SOUSA (AND FRIENDS) .... RCA 256

PIPES AND DRUMS AND MILITARY BAND OF THE ROYAL SCOTS DRAGOON GUARDS
UK military band formed in 1971 by the amalgamation of the Royal Scots Greys Band and the 3rd Carabineers (Prince of Wales Dragoon Guards). Their initial recording used 20 pipes and drums and a 30-piece military band with Pipe Major Tony Crease on 'lead' bagpipes.

01/04/1972.....●5.....27...... **AMAZING GRACE** Tune originally written in 1779 by John Newton. Featured in the 1978 film *Invasion Of The Bodysnatchers* .... RCA 2191
19/08/1972.....30......7....... HEYKENS SERENADE/THE DAY IS ENDED .... RCA 2251
02/12/1972.....13......9....... LITTLE DRUMMER BOY .... RCA 2301

ROYALLE DELITE
US vocal group formed by Lonnie Johnson, K Moore, K Belle and D Staler.

14/09/1985.....45......6...... (I'LL BE A) FREAK FOR YOU .... Streetwave KHAN 51

ROYCE DA 5' 9" – see BAD MEETS EVIL FEATURING EMINEM AND ROYCE DA 5' 9"

ROYKSOPP
Norwegian production duo formed in Tromso by Svein Berge and Torbjrn Brundtland.

15/12/2001.....59......1....... POOR LENO.. Wall Of Sound WALLD 073
17/08/2002.....21......3....... REMIND ME/SO EASY *Remind Me* won the 2002 MTV Europe Music Award for Best Video. *So Easy* contains a sample of Gals & Pals' *Blue On Blue* .... Wall Of Sound WALLD 074X
30/11/2002.....38......2....... POOR LENO.. Wall Of Sound WALLD 079V
08/03/2003.....16......3....... EPLE.. Wall Of Sound WALLD 080V
28/06/2003.....41......1....... SPARKS.. Wall Of Sound WALLD 084V

LITA ROZA
UK singer (born 1926, Liverpool) who sang with the Ted Heath orchestra from 1950 to 1954. She appeared in the films *Cast A Dark Shadow* (1957) and *My Way Home* (1978), and was still recording in the 1980s.

13/03/1953.....●1.....11...... **(HOW MUCH IS) THAT DOGGIE IN THE WINDOW**.. Decca F 10070
07/10/1955.....17......2....... HEY THERE.. Decca F 10611
23/03/1956.....15......5....... JIMMY UNKNOWN.. Decca F 10679

ROZALLA
Zambian singer (born Rozalla Miller, 18/3/1964, Ndola) who was lead singer with the Band Of Gypsies before going solo. She lives in Zimbabwe and London.

27/04/1991.....65......2....... FAITH (IN THE POWER OF LOVE).. Pulse 8 LOSE 7
07/09/1991.....6......11.....O **EVERYBODY'S FREE (TO FEEL GOOD)** Featured in the 1996 film *Romeo And Juliet* .... Pulse 8 LOSE 13
16/11/1991.....11......6....... FAITH (IN THE POWER OF LOVE) Re-issue of Pulse 8 LOSE 7.. Pulse 8 LOSE 15
22/02/1992.....14......6....... ARE YOU READY TO FLY .... Pulse 8 LOSE 21
09/05/1992.....65......2....... LOVE BREAKDOWN .... Pulse 8 LOSE 25

O Silver disc ● Gold disc ✪ Platinum disc (additional platinum units are indicated by a figure following the symbol) ◎ Singles released prior to 1973 that are known to have sold over 1 million copies in the UK

15/08/1992	50	2		IN 4 CHOONS LATER	Pulse 8 LOSE 29
30/10/1993	50	1		DON'T PLAY WITH ME	Pulse 8 CDLOSE 52
05/02/1994	18	5		I LOVE MUSIC Featured in the 1993 film *Carlito's Way*	Epic 6598932
06/08/1994	33	3		THIS TIME I FOUND LOVE	Epic 6603742
29/10/1994	16	5		YOU NEVER LOVE THE SAME WAY TWICE	Epic 6609052
04/03/1995	26	3		BABY	Epic 6611955
31/08/1996	30	2		EVERYBODY'S FREE (TO FEEL GOOD) (REMIX)	Pulse 8 CDLOSE 110
22/11/2003	55	1		LIVE ANOTHER LIFE **PLASTIC BOY FEATURING ROZALLA**	Inferno CDFERN 59

RTE CONCERT ORCHESTRA – see BILL WHELAN FEATURING ANUNA AND THE RTE CONCERT ORCHESTRA

RUBBADUBB UK vocal/instrumental group formed by Peter Oxendale, Kevin Armstrong, Peter Gordeno and Paul 'Max' Bloom.

18/07/1998	56	1		TRIBUTE TO OUR ANCESTORS	Perfecto PERF 165CD

RUBETTES UK pop group formed in 1974 after the success of their debut single (sung by Paul Da Vinci). They comprised Alan Williams (born 22/12/1948, Welwyn Garden City, guitar/flute/piano), Tony Thorpe (born 20/7/1947, London, guitar/piano/drums), Mick Clarke (born 10/8/1946, Grimsby, Humberside, bass), Bill Hurd (born 11/8/1948, London, keyboards) and John Richardson (born 3/5/1948, Dagenham, drums), all of whom had been in Barry Blue's backing band. Williams was later a member of The Firm.

04/05/1974	❶⁴	10	●	SUGAR BABY LOVE Featured in the 1995 film *Muriel's Wedding*	Polydor 2058 442
13/07/1974	12	9		TONIGHT	Polydor 2058 499
16/11/1974	3	12	○	**JUKE BOX JIVE**	Polydor 2058 529
08/03/1975	7	9		**I CAN DO IT**	State STAT 1
21/06/1975	15	6		FOE-DEE-O-DEE	State STAT 7
22/11/1975	30	5		LITTLE DARLING	State STAT 13
01/05/1976	28	4		YOU'RE THE REASON WHY	State STAT 20
25/09/1976	40	3		UNDER ONE ROOF	State STAT 27
12/02/1977	10	10		**BABY I KNOW**	State STAT 37

MARIA RUBIA UK singer who was 23 at the time of her debut hit. She moved to the south of France while in her teens and then to Marbella in Spain. Rubia is a stage name meaning 'blonde' in Spanish.

13/01/2001	3	11	○	**EVERYTIME YOU NEED ME FRAGMA FEATURING MARIA RUBIA**	Positiva CDTIVS 147
19/05/2001	40	2		SAY IT	Neo NEOCD 055

PAULINA RUBIO Mexican singer, daughter of actress Susana Dosamantes, who began her career in 1982 as a member of Timbiriche and went solo in 1992.

28/09/2002	68	1		DON'T SAY GOODBYE	Universal MCSXD 40291

RUBY AND THE ROMANTICS US R&B vocal group formed in Akton, OH by Ruby Nash Curtis (born 12/11/1939, New York), Ed Roberts (born 24/4/1936, Akron), George Lee (born 24/3/1936, Akron), Ronald Mosley and Leroy Fann (born 9/11/1936, Akron) as The Supremes. They name-changed in 1962 because of another group with the same name. Ruby re-formed the Romantics in 1965 with Bill Evans, Ronald Jackson, Robert Lewis, Vincent McLeod and Richard Pryor. Fann died from a heart attack in November 1973, Roberts died from cancer on 15/8/1993 and Lee also died from cancer on 25/10/1994.

28/03/1963	38	6		OUR DAY WILL COME ▲¹	London HLR 9679

RUDE BOY OF HOUSE – see HOUSEMASTER BOYZ AND THE RUDE BOY OF HOUSE

RUDIES – see FREDDIE NOTES AND THE RUDIES

RUFF DRIVERZ UK production group formed by Chris Brown and Bradley Carter, with singer Katherine Ellis.

07/02/1998	30	2		DON'T STOP	Inferno CDFERN 003
23/05/1998	19	3		DEEPER LOVE	Inferno CDFERN 006
24/10/1998	51	2		SHAME	Inferno CXFERN 9
28/11/1998	10	8		**DREAMING** Featured in the 1999 film *The Big Tease*	Inferno CXFERN 11
24/04/1999	14	4		LA MUSICA This and above single credited to **RUFF DRIVERZ PRESENTS ARROLA**	Inferno CDFERN 14
02/10/1999	37	2		WAITING FOR THE SUN	Inferno CDFERN 19

RUFF ENDZ US vocal group formed in Baltimore, MD by David 'Davinch' Chance and Dante 'Chi' Jordan.

19/08/2000	11	5		NO MORE	Epic 6696202

FRANCES RUFFELLE UK singer who represented the UK in the 1994 Eurovision Song Contest (won by Ireland's *Rock 'N' Roll Kids* performed by Paul Harrington and Charlie McGettigan). She had previously made her name as an actress, winning a Tony Award for her portrayal of Eponine in *Les Miserables* on Broadway.

16/04/1994	25	6		LONELY SYMPHONY UK entry for the 1994 Eurovision Song Contest (came tenth)	Virgin VSCDT 1499

BRUCE RUFFIN Jamaican reggae singer (born Bernado Constantine Balderamus, 17/2/1952, St Catherine) who began his career with The Techniques before going solo.

01/05/1971	19	11		RAIN	Trojan TR 7814
24/06/1972	9	12		**MAD ABOUT YOU**	Rhino RNO 101

❶⁹ Number of weeks single topped the UK charts ↑ Entered the UK chart at #1 ▲⁹ Number of weeks single topped the US chart

687

DAVID RUFFIN US singer (born Davis Eli Ruffin, 18/1/1941, Meridian, MS) who was the younger brother of Jimmy Ruffin. He joined The Temptations in 1963 and soon assumed the role of lead singer, leaving in 1968 to go solo. He died from a drug overdose on 1/6/1991. Some $40,000 worth of cash and travellers cheques that he had on him at the time of his death later disappeared from police custody. As Ruffin was otherwise destitute at the time of his death, Michael Jackson offered to pay for his funeral.

17/01/1976	10	8		**WALK AWAY FROM LOVE**	Tamla Motown TMG 1017
21/09/1985	58	2		A NIGHT AT THE APOLLO LIVE! DARYL HALL AND JOHN OATES FEATURING DAVID RUFFIN AND EDDIE KENDRICK	RCA PB 49935

JIMMY RUFFIN US singer (born 7/5/1939, Collinsville, MS) and older brother of David Ruffin who joined Motown in 1961, recording one single before he was drafted. He returned in 1963 and turned down the opportunity to join The Temptations, recommending his brother David instead. He later relocated to the UK and took part in the Paul Weller project Council Collective.

27/10/1966	10	15		**WHAT BECOMES OF THE BROKENHEARTED**	Tamla Motown TMG 577
09/02/1967	29	7		I'VE PASSED THIS WAY BEFORE	Tamla Motown TMG 593
20/04/1967	26	6		GONNA GIVE HER ALL THE LOVE I'VE GOT	Tamla Motown TMG 603
09/08/1969	33	6		I'VE PASSED THIS WAY BEFORE Re-issue of Tamla Motown TMG 593	Tamla Motown TMG 703
28/02/1970	8	16		**FAREWELL IS A LONELY SOUND**	Tamla Motown TMG 726
04/07/1970	7	12		**I'LL SAY FOREVER MY LOVE**	Tamla Motown TMG 740
17/10/1970	6	14		**IT'S WONDERFUL (TO BE LOVED BY YOU)**	Tamla Motown TMG 753
27/07/1974	4	12	O	**WHAT BECOMES OF THE BROKENHEARTED** Re-issue of Tamla Motown TMG 577	Tamla Motown TMG 911
02/11/1974	30	5		FAREWELL IS A LONELY SOUND Re-issue of Tamla Motown TMG 726	Tamla Motown TMG 922
16/11/1974	39	4		TELL ME WHAT YOU WANT	Polydor 2058 433
03/05/1980	7	8		**HOLD ON TO MY LOVE**	RSO 57
26/01/1985	68	1		THERE WILL NEVER BE ANOTHER YOU	EMI 5541

KIM RUFFIN – see CHUBBY CHUNKS

RUFFNECK FEATURING YAVAHN US vocal/instrumental group formed in New Jersey by Dwayne Richardson, Derek Jenkins, Stephen Wilson and Joanne 'Yavahn' Thomas.

11/11/1995	13	4		EVERYBODY BE SOMEBODY Contains a sample of Yello's *Bostich*	Positiva CDTIV 46
07/09/1996	60	1		MOVE YOUR BODY	Positiva CDTIV 61
01/12/2001	66	1		EVERYBODY BE SOMEBODY (REMIX)	Strictly Rhythm SRUKCD 08

RUFUS AND CHAKA KHAN US inter-racial R&B group formed in Chicago, IL in 1970 by Al Ciner (guitar), Charles Colbert (bass), Kevin Murphy (keyboards), Lee Graziano (drums), Paulette McWilliams (vocals), Ron Stockard and Dennis Belfield as Smoke, with Andre Fisher subsequently replacing Graziano. The group evolved from American Breed, and after further name (Ask Rufus and then Rufus) and personnel changes settled on a line-up of Chaka Khan (born Yvette Marie Stevens, 23/3/1953, Great Lakes, IL), Murphy, Tony Maiden (guitar), Dave Wolinski (keyboards), Bobby Watson (bass) and John Robinson (drums). Khan went solo in 1978. The group took their name from a help column in the US magazine *Mechanics Illustrated*, called 'Ask Rufus.' They have won two Grammy Awards including Best Rhythm & Blues Vocal Performance by a Group in 1974.

31/03/1984	8	12	O	**AIN'T NOBODY** Featured in the 1984 film *Breakin'*. 1983 Grammy Award for Best Rhythm & Blues Vocal Performance by a Group	Warner Brothers RCK 1
08/07/1989	6	9		**AIN'T NOBODY (REMIX)**	Warner Brothers W 2880

RUKMANI – see SNAP

DICK RULES – see SCOOTER

RUMOUR – see GRAHAM PARKER AND THE RUMOUR

RUMPLE-STILTS-SKIN US vocal/instrumental group formed by brothers Sam, Leroy, James and Chris McCant as The Chicago Gangsters, name-changing upon signing with Polydor in 1983. They later name-changed again to Ivy.

24/09/1983	51	4		I THINK I WANT TO DANCE WITH YOU	Polydor POSP 649

RUN D.M.C. US rap group formed in New York in 1983 by Joseph 'Run' Simmons (born 24/11/1964, Queens, NYC), MC Darryl 'D' McDaniels (born 31/5/1964, Queens) and Jam Master Jay (born Jason Mizell, 21/1/1965, Queens). They signed with Profile the same year. Their eponymous debut album became the first rap album to achieve gold status in the US. Run's brother Russell Simmons co-founded Def Jam Records. Jason Mizell was shot to death on 31/10/2002.

19/07/1986	62	2		MY ADIDAS/PETER PIPER	London LON 101
06/09/1986	8	10		**WALK THIS WAY** Features the uncredited contributions of Steve Tyler and Joe Perry of Aerosmith, the song's writers	London LON 104
07/02/1987	42	4		YOU BE ILLIN'	Profile LON 118
30/05/1987	16	7		IT'S TRICKY Featured in the 1998 film *Can't Hardy Wait*	Profile LON 130
12/12/1987	56	4		CHRISTMAS IN HOLLIS	Profile LON 163
21/05/1988	37	4		RUN'S HOUSE	London LON 177
02/09/1989	65	2		GHOSTBUSTERS	MCA 1360
01/12/1990	48	3		WHAT'S IT ALL ABOUT	Profile PROF 315
27/03/1993	69	2		DOWN WITH THE KING	Profile PROFCD 39
21/02/1998	63	3		IT'S LIKE THAT (GERMAN IMPORT)	Epidrome EPD 665293-20
14/03/1998	65	1		IT'S LIKE THAT (AMERICAN IMPORT)	Sm:)e SM 9069-2
21/03/1998	❶⁶	16	✪	**IT'S LIKE THAT** ↑	Sm:)e Communications SM 90652
18/04/1998	74	1		IT'S TRICKY (IMPORT) This and above three singles credited to RUN DMC VERSUS JASON NEVINS	Epidrome EPD 6656982

○ Silver disc ● Gold disc ✪ Platinum disc (additional platinum units are indicated by a figure following the symbol) ◎ Singles released prior to 1973 that are known to have sold over 1 million copies in the UK

19/04/2003 . . . . . 20 . . . . . . 3 . . . . IT'S TRICKY 2003 **RUN DMC FEATURING JACKNIFE LEE** . . . . Arista 82876513712

RUN TINGS UK instrumental/production duo Winston Meikle and Austin Reynolds.

16/05/1992 . . . . . 58 . . . . . . 1 . . . . FIRES BURNING . . . . Suburban Base SUBBASE 009

TODD RUNDGREN US singer (born 22/6/1948, Upper Darby, PA) who was in the groups Nazz and Utopia. He later became a successful producer, including Meat Loaf's *Bat Out Of Hell* album.

30/06/1973 . . . . . 36 . . . . . . 6 . . . . I SAW THE LIGHT Featured in the 1996 film *Kingpin*. . . . . Bearsville K 15506

14/12/1985 . . . . . 73 . . . . . . 2 . . . . LOVING YOU'S A DIRTY JOB BUT SOMEBODY'S GOTTA DO IT **BONNIE TYLER, GUEST VOCALS TODD RUNDGREN** . . . . CBS A 6662

RUNRIG UK group formed by Iain Bayne (born 22/1/1960, St Andrews, Scotland), Bruce Guthro (born 31/8/1961, Canada), Rory MacDonald (born 27/7/1949, Dornoch, Scotland), Peter Wishart (born 3/3/1962, Dunfirmline, Scotland), Malcolm Jones (born 12/7/1959, Inverness, Scotland), Calum MacDonald (born 12/11/1953, Lochmaddy, Scotland) and Donnie Munro (born 2/8/1953, Uig, Isle of Skye) who often record in Gaelic and who have established a big cult following in the US. Lead singer Donnie Munro stood for election in the 1997 General Election as a Labour candidate for Ross, Sky and Inverness West but lost to the Liberal Democrats. Wishart, however, was returned as the MP for North Tayside.

29/09/1990 . . . . . 49 . . . . . . 2 . . . . CAPTURE THE HEART (EP) Tracks on EP: *Stepping Down The Glory Road, Satellite Flood, Harvest Moon* and *The Apple Came Down* . . . . Chrysalis CHS 3594

07/09/1991 . . . . . 25 . . . . . . 4 . . . . HEARTHAMMER (EP) Tracks on EP: *Hearthammer, Pride Of The Summer (Live), Loch Lomond (Live)* and *Solus Na Madainn* . . . . Chrysalis CHS 3754

09/11/1991 . . . . . 43 . . . . . . 2 . . . . FLOWER OF THE WEST . . . . Chrysalis CHS 3805

06/03/1993 . . . . . 29 . . . . . . 3 . . . . WONDERFUL . . . . Chrysalis CDCHS 3952

15/05/1993 . . . . . 36 . . . . . . 3 . . . . THE GREATEST FLAME . . . . Chrysalis CDCHS 3975

07/01/1995 . . . . . 38 . . . . . . 2 . . . . THIS TIME OF YEAR . . . . Chrysalis CDCHS 5018

06/05/1995 . . . . . 18 . . . . . . 5 . . . . AN UBHAL AS AIRDE (THE HIGHEST APPLE) . . . . Chrysalis CDCHS 5021

04/11/1995 . . . . . 40 . . . . . . 2 . . . . THINGS THAT ARE . . . . Chrysalis CDCHS 5029

12/10/1996 . . . . . 24 . . . . . . 2 . . . . RHYTHM OF MY HEART . . . . Chrysalis CDCHS 5035

11/01/1997 . . . . . 30 . . . . . . 3 . . . . THE GREATEST FLAME Re-issue of Chrysalis CDCHS 3975 . . . . Chrysalis CDCHSS 5045

RUPAUL US transsexual singer (born RuPaul Andre Charles, 17/11/1960, San Diego, CA) who first made his name as a female impersonator. He appeared in the films *Crooklyn* (1994) and *The Brady Bunch Movie* (1995).

26/06/1993 . . . . . 39 . . . . . . 4 . . . . SUPERMODEL (YOU BETTER WORK) Featured in the 1995 film *The Brady Bunch Movie* . . . . Union City UCRD 21

18/09/1993 . . . . . 40 . . . . . . 2 . . . . HOUSE OF LOVE/BACK TO MY ROOTS. . . . . Union City UCRD 23

22/01/1994 . . . . . 61 . . . . . . 2 . . . . SUPERMODEL/LITTLE DRUMMER BOY (REMIX) . . . . Union City UCRD 25

26/02/1994 . . . 7 . . . . . . 7 . . . . **DON'T GO BREAKING MY HEART ELTON JOHN WITH RuPAUL**. . . . . Rocket EJCD 33

28/02/1998 . . . . . 21 . . . 3 . . . . IT'S RAINING MEN...THE SEQUEL **MARTHA WASH FEATURING RuPAUL** . . . . Logic 74321555412

RUPEE Barbadian soca singer (born Rupert Clarke, 1975).

23/10/2004 . . . . . 44 . . . . . . 2 . . . . TEMPTED TO TOUCH . . . . Atlantic AT0185CD

RUSH Canadian rock group formed in Toronto, Ontario in 1969 by Alex Lifeson (born Alex Zivojinovic, 27/8/1953, Fernie, British Columbia, guitar), Geddy Lee (born Gary Lee Weinrib, 29/7/1953, Toronto, vocals/bass) and John Rutsey (drums). They funded the release of their debut album on their Moon label and were signed by Mercury as a result. Rutsey left in 1974 and was replaced by Neil Peart (born 12/9/1952, Hamilton, Ontario). They switched to Atlantic in 1989.

11/02/1978 . . . . . 36 . . . . . . 3 . . . . CLOSER TO THE HEART . . . . Mercury RUSH 7

15/03/1980 . . . . . 13 . . . . . . 7 . . . . SPIRIT OF RADIO . . . . Mercury RADIO 7

28/03/1981 . . . . . 41 . . . . . . 4 . . . . VITAL SIGNS/A PASSAGE TO BANGKOK . . . . Mercury VITAL 7

31/10/1981 . . . . . 25 . . . . . . 6 . . . . TOM SAWYER Featured in the films *Small Soldiers* (1999) and *The Waterboy* (1999). . . . . Mercury Exit 7

04/09/1982 . . . . . 42 . . . . . . 3 . . . . NEW WORLD MAN . . . . Mercury RUSH 8

30/10/1982 . . . . . 53 . . . . . . 2 . . . . SUBDIVISIONS . . . . Mercury RUSH 9

07/05/1983 . . . . . 36 . . . . . . 5 . . . . COUNTDOWN/NEW WORLD MAN (LIVE) . . . . Mercury RUSH 10

26/05/1984 . . . . . 56 . . . . . . 3 . . . . THE BODY ELECTRIC . . . . Mercury RUSH 11

12/10/1985 . . . . . 46 . . . . . . 3 . . . . THE BIG MONEY . . . . Vertigo RUSH 12

31/10/1987 . . . . . 42 . . . . . . 3 . . . . TIME STAND STILL **RUSH WITH AIMEE MANN** . . . . Vertigo RUSH 13

23/04/1988 . . . . . 43 . . . . . . 3 . . . . PRIME MOVER. . . . . Vertigo RUSH 14

07/03/1992 . . . . . 49 . . . . . . 1 . . . . ROLL THE BONES. . . . . Atlantic A 7524

DONELL RUSH US singer who also worked as a backing singer for the likes of Katie Webster, Kym Sims and Chantay Savage.

05/12/1992 . . . . . 66 . . . . . . 1 . . . . SYMPHONY. . . . . ID 6587977

ED RUSH AND OPTICAL/UNIVERSAL US DJ/production duo Ed Rush and Nico Sykes. Rush first recorded for the No U-Turn and Nu Black labels.

01/06/2002 . . . . . 61 . . . . . . 1 . . . . PACMAN/VESSEL . . . . Virus VRS 010

20/11/2004 . . . . . 69 . . . . . . 1 . . . . REMIXES - VOLUME 2 **ED RUSH AND OPTICAL** . . . . Virus VRS014B

JENNIFER RUSH US singer (born Heidi Stern, 29/9/1960, Queens, NYC); daughter of opera singer Maurice Stern. She had relocated to Germany by the time of her debut hit. It became the first single by a female soloist to sell over 1 million copies in the UK.

29/06/1985 . . . . . ❶⁵ . . . 36 . . . . . ✪ **THE POWER OF LOVE** . . . . CBS A 5003

14/12/1985 . . . . . 14 . . . . 10 . . . . . . RING OF ICE. . . . . CBS A 4745

❶⁹ Number of weeks single topped the UK charts ↑ Entered the UK chart at #1 ▲⁹ Number of weeks single topped the US chart

689

				SINGLE TITLE	LABEL & NUMBER
20/06/1987	59	3		FLAMES OF PARADISE JENNIFER RUSH AND ELTON JOHN	Columbia 6508657
27/05/1989	24	9		TILL I LOVED YOU PLACIDO DOMINGO AND JENNIFER RUSH	CBS 6548437

PATRICE RUSHEN
US singer/pianist (born 30/9/1954, Los Angeles, CA) who won the Monterey Jazz Festival in 1972 and was signed by Prestige as a result. She also played with Donald Byrd, Sonny Rollins and Abbey Lincoln before joining Lee Ritenour's group in 1977.

01/03/1980	62	3		HAVEN'T YOU HEARD	Elektra K 12414
24/01/1981	66	3		NEVER GONNA GIVE YOU UP (WON'T LET YOU BE)	Elektra K 12494
24/04/1982	8	11		**FORGET ME NOTS** Featured in the 1988 film *Big*	Elektra K 13173
10/07/1982	39	5		I WAS TIRED OF BEING ALONE	Elektra K 13184
09/06/1984	51	3		FEELS SO REAL (WON'T LET GO)	Elektra E 9742

RUSLANA
Ukrainian singer Ruslana Luzychko; she won the Ukrainian Festival of Modern Songs in 1999 and 2000 and then went on to win the 2004 Eurovision Song Contest.

19/06/2004	47	1		WILD DANCES Winning entry in the 2004 Eurovision Song Contest	Liberty 5490542

RUSSELL
US singer Russell Taylor (born in Chicago, IL).

27/05/2000	52	1		FOOL FOR LOVE	Rulin ICDS

BRENDA RUSSELL
US singer (born Brenda Gordon, Brooklyn, NYC) whose father was a member of the Ink Spots. She met her husband Brian Russell in Canada and as Brian & Brenda recorded two albums for Rocket Records, having been spotted by Elton John. Following her divorce in 1978 she recorded solo.

19/04/1980	51	5		SO GOOD SO RIGHT/IN THE THICK OF IT	A&M AM 7515
12/03/1988	23	12		PIANO IN THE DARK	Breakout USA 623

PATTI RUSSO – see MEAT LOAF

RUSTIN MAN – see BETH GIBBONS AND RUSTIN MAN

RUTH
UK group formed by Matt Hales (keyboards/vocals), Ben Hales (guitar), Stephen Cousins (bass) and Matt Vincent-Brown (drums).

12/04/1997	66	1		I DON'T KNOW	Arc 5737812

PAUL RUTHERFORD
UK singer (born 8/12/1959, Liverpool) who was a founder member of Frankie Goes To Hollywood and went solo in 1988.

08/10/1988	47	3		GET REAL	Fourth & Broadway BRW 113
19/08/1989	61	3		OH WORLD	Fourth & Broadway BRW 136

RUTHLESS RAP ASSASINS
UK rap group formed by Dangerous 'C' Carsonova, Paul 'Kermit' Leverage and Jed Bithwhistle. Kermit and Bithwhistle were later members of Black Grape.

09/06/1990	75	1		JUST MELLOW	Syncopate SY 35
01/09/1990	75	1		AND IT WASN'T A DREAM RUTHLESS RAP ASSASINS FEATURING TRACEY CARMEN	Syncopate SY 38

RUTLES
UK group officially formed at 43 Egg Lane, Liverpool in 1959 by Ron Nasty (rhythm guitar/vocals), Dirk McQuickly (bass/vocals), Stig O'Hara (lead guitar/vocals) and Barry Wom (born Barrington Womble, drums/vocals), later acquiring a fifth member in Leppo (standing at the back of the stage) as the Quarrelmen, name-changing to The Rutles in 1961. Unofficially, this was a parody of The Beatles assembled by ex-Bonzo Dog Neil Innes (born 9/12/1944, Danbury) and Monty Python member Eric Idle (born 29/3/1943, South Shields) for the TV documentary *All You Need Is Cash*.

15/04/1978	39	4		I MUST BE IN LOVE	Warner Brothers K 17125
16/11/1996	68	1		SHANGRI-LA	Virgin America VUSCD 117

RUTS
UK group formed by Malcolm Owen (vocals), Paul Fox (guitar/vocals), Dave Ruffy (drums) and John 'Segs' Jennings (bass). The group effectively came to an end after Owen's sudden death from a drug overdose on 14/7/1980.

16/06/1979	7	11		**BABYLON'S BURNING** Featured in the 1980 film *Times Square*	Virgin VS 271
08/09/1979	29	5		SOMETHING THAT I SAID	Virgin VS 285
19/04/1980	22	8		STARING AT THE RUDE BOYS	Virgin VS 327
30/08/1980	43	4		WEST ONE (SHINE ON ME)	Virgin VS 370

BARRY RYAN
UK singer (born Barry Sapherson, 24/10/1948, Leeds); son of 1950s UK star Marion Ryan. Together with his twin brother Paul, he enjoyed a number of hits before going solo (with Paul penning his biggest hit).

23/10/1968	2	12		**ELOISE**	MGM 1442
19/02/1969	25	4		LOVE IS LOVE	MGM 1464
04/10/1969	34	5		HUNT	Polydor 56 348
21/02/1970	49	1		MAGICAL SPIEL	Polydor 56 370
16/05/1970	37	6		KITSCH	Polydor 2001 035
15/01/1972	32	5		CAN'T LET YOU GO	Polydor 2001 256

JOSHUA RYAN
US singer/songwriter (born in Sicily, moved to the US) who originally recorded for Slinkey Records.

27/01/2001	29	3		PISTOL WHIP	NuLife 74321825482

MARION RYAN
UK singer (born Marion Sapherson, 4/2/1933, although the year is more likely to have been 1931, Middlesbrough, Cleveland) who sang with Ray Ellington's orchestra and became a successful singer during the 1950s and 1960s. Her twin sons, Paul and Barry, also enjoyed successful recording careers. She retired from singing in 1965 following her marriage to impresario Harold Davidson. She died from a heart attack on 15/1/1999.

24/01/1958	5	11		**LOVE ME FOREVER** MARION RYAN WITH THE PETER KNIGHT ORCHESTRA AND THE BERYL STOTT CHORUS	Pye Nixa N 15121

PAUL AND BARRY RYAN
UK duo of twin brothers Paul and Barry Sapherson (born 24/10/1948, Leeds); the sons of popular 1950s star Marion Ryan. Barry later went solo, enjoying his biggest hit with a song written by Paul. Paul died from cancer on 29/11/1992.

11/11/1965	13	9		DON'T BRING ME YOUR HEARTACHES	Decca F 12260
03/02/1966	18	6		HAVE PITY ON THE BOY	Decca F 12319
12/05/1966	17	8		I LOVE HER	Decca F 12391
14/07/1966	21	7		I LOVE HOW YOU LOVE ME	Decca F 12445
29/09/1966	49	1		HAVE YOU EVER LOVED SOMEBODY	Decca F 12494
08/12/1966	43	4		MISSY MISSY	Decca F 12520
02/03/1967	30	6		KEEP IT OUT OF SIGHT	Decca F 12567
29/06/1967	47	2		CLAIRE	Decca F 12633

REBEKAH RYAN
UK singer (born 2/8/1976, Kansas City, MO, relocated with her family to Tamworth) who also became an actress, appearing in the TV series *Charmed*. She later recorded for Jive.

18/05/1996	26	3		YOU LIFT ME UP	MCA MCSTD 40022
07/09/1996	51	1		JUST A LITTLE BIT OF LOVE	MCA MCSTD 40063
17/05/1997	64	1		WOMAN IN LOVE	MCA MCSTD 40109

BOBBY RYDELL
US singer (born Robert Ridarelli, 26/4/1942, Philadelphia, PA) who was drummer with Rocco & His Saints in 1956 before making his first solo record in 1957 for Veko. He appeared in the films *Bye Bye Birdie* (1963) and *That Lady From Peking* (1970).

10/03/1960	7	15		**WILD ONE**	Columbia DB 4429
30/06/1960	44	1		SWINGING SCHOOL Featured in the 1960 film *Because They're Young*	Columbia DB 4471
01/09/1960	22	6		VOLARE	Columbia DB 4495
15/12/1960	12	13		SWAY	Columbia DB 4545
23/03/1961	42	7		GOOD TIME BABY	Columbia DB 4600
19/04/1962	45	1		TEACH ME TO TWIST	Columbia DB 4802
20/12/1962	40	3		JINGLE BELL ROCK This and above single credited to **CHUBBY CHECKER AND BOBBY RYDELL**	Cameo Parkway C 205
23/05/1963	13	14		FORGET HIM	Cameo Parkway C 108

MARK RYDER
UK producer and ex-Fantasy UFO who also records as M-D-Emm.

31/03/2001	34	2		JOY	Relentless/Public Demand RELENT 9CDS

MITCH RYDER AND THE DETROIT WHEELS
US singer (born William Levise Jr, 26/2/1945, Detroit, MI) who formed Billy Lee & The Rivieras in 1963 with John Badanjek (drums), Jim McCarty (guitar), Joe Kubert (guitar) and Earl Elliott (bass). They name-changed in 1965 to Mitch Ryder & The Detroit Wheels, with Elliott and Kubeck leaving in 1966. They were replaced by Mark Manko and Jim McCallister.

10/02/1966	33	5		JENNY TAKE A RIDE Medley of Little Richard's *Jenny, Jenny* and Chuck Willis' *C. C. Rider*. Featured in the 2000 film *The Replacements*	Stateside SS 481

SHAUN RYDER
UK singer (born 23/8/1962, Little Hulton) who formed Happy Mondays in 1984 and then Black Grape before re-forming Happy Mondays.

09/11/1996	60	1		DON'T TAKE MY KINDNESS FOR WEAKNESS HEADS WITH SHAUN RYDER	Radioactive MCSTD 48024
22/07/2000	68	1		BARCELONA (FRIENDS UNTIL THE END) RUSSELL WATSON AND SHAUN RYDER	Decca 46672772

RHYTHM SYNDICATE
US group formed by Evan Rogers (vocals), Carl Sturken (guitar), John Nevin (bass), Rob Mingrino (saxophone) and Kevin Cloud (drums).

27/07/1991	58	5		P.A.S.S.I.O.N.	Impact American EM 197

RYZE
UK R&B group formed by Angel, Blaze and Orion.

02/11/2002	46	1		IN MY LIFE	Inferno Cool CDFERN 48

❶⁹ Number of weeks single topped the UK charts ↑ Entered the UK chart at #1 ▲⁹ Number of weeks single topped the US chart

691

S

ROBIN S
US dance singer (born Robin Stone, Jamaica, NY).

16/01/1993	59	4	SHOW ME LOVE	Champion CHAMPCD 300
13/03/1993	6	13	**SHOW ME LOVE**	Champion CHAMPCD 300
31/07/1993	11	7	LUV 4 LUV	Champion CHAMPCD 301
04/12/1993	43	2	WHAT I DO BEST	Champion CHAMPCD 307
19/03/1994	48	1	I WANT TO THANK YOU	Champion CHAMPCD 310
05/11/1994	43	2	BACK IT UP	Champion CHAMPCD 312
08/03/1997	9	5	**SHOW ME LOVE (REMIX)**	Champion CHAMPCD 326
12/07/1997	37	2	IT MUST BE LOVE	Atlantic A 5596CD
04/10/1997	62	1	YOU GOT THE LOVE T2 FEATURING ROBIN S	Champion CHAMPCD 330
07/12/2002	61	1	SHOW ME LOVE (2ND REMIX)	Champion CHAMPCD 796

S CLUB JUNIORS
UK vocal group formed by Stacey McClean (born 17/2/1989, Blackpool), Calvin Goldspink (born 24/1/1989, Great Yarmouth), Rochelle Wiseman (born 21/3/1989, Barking), Aaron Renfree (born 19/12/1987, Truro), Jay Asforis (born 30/10/1989, Waltham Forest), Hannah Richings (born 30/11/1990, Birmingham), Daisy Evans (born 30/11/1989, Chadwell Heath) and Frankie Sandford (born 14/1/1989, Havering). They were assembled by Simon Fuller as a younger version of Fuller's other major act S Club 7 and were selected after over 10,000 children auditioned. When S Club 7/S Club disbanded in 2003, S Club Juniors became S Club 8.

04/05/2002	2	16	○	**ONE STEP CLOSER**	Polydor 5707332
03/08/2002	2	13		**AUTOMATIC HIGH**	Polydor 5708922
19/10/2002	2	13		**NEW DIRECTION**	Polydor 0659702
21/12/2002	6	10		**PUPPY LOVE/SLEIGH RIDE** A-side featured in the 2003 film Love Actually	Polydor 0658442
12/07/2003	4	8		**FOOL NO MORE**	Polydor 9808754
11/10/2003	4	10		**SUNDOWN**	19/Universal 9811790
10/01/2004	11	8		DON'T TELL ME YOU'RE SORRY This and above two singles credited to S CLUB 8	Polydor 9815342

S CLUB 7
UK vocal group formed by Paul Cattermole (born 7/3/1977), Jon Lee (born 26/4/1982), Rachel Stevens (born 9/4/1978), Joanne O'Meara (born 29/4/1979), Bradley McIntosh (born 8/8/1981), Hannah Spearitt (born 1/4/1981) and Tina Barrett (born 16/9/1976). Best British Newcomer at the 2000 BRIT Awards, they took part in the It's Only Rock 'N' Roll project for the Children's Promise charity. Cattermole left in August 2002, and they shortened their name to S Club. They disbanded in May 2003, shortly after the release of their film Seeing Double.

19/06/1999	●¹	15	✪	**BRING IT ALL BACK** ↑ Theme tune to the BBC TV show Miami 7, a series that featured the group's exploits	Polydor 5610852
02/10/1999	2	14	●	**S CLUB PARTY**	Polydor 5614172
25/12/1999	2	11	○	**TWO IN A MILLION/YOU'RE MY NUMBER ONE**	Polydor 5615962
03/06/2000	2	17	●	**REACH**	Polydor 5618302
23/09/2000	3	16		**NATURAL**	Polydor 5677602
09/12/2000	●¹	18	●	**NEVER HAD A DREAM COME TRUE** ↑ Released to raise funds for the BBC Children In Need Fund	Polydor 5879032
05/05/2001	●²	19	✪	**DON'T STOP MOVIN'** ↑ Reclaimed #1 position on 26/5/01. Record of the Year and also won the 2002 BRIT Award for Best Single. Featured in the 2001 film The Parole Officer	Polydor 5870842
01/12/2001	●¹	14		**HAVE YOU EVER** ↑ Released to raise funds for the BBC Children In Need Fund. The single also features 275,000 children singers from 3,616 schools, the greatest number of people to sing on one single	Polydor 5705002
23/02/2002	2	14		**YOU**	Polydor 5705822
30/11/2002	5	16		**ALIVE**	Polydor 0658912
07/06/2003	2	12		**SAY GOODBYE/LOVE AIN'T GONNA WAIT FOR YOU** This and above single credited to S CLUB	Polydor 9807140

S-EXPRESS
UK dance group formed by producer/DJ Mark Moore, singer Michelle and vocalist/percussionist/dancer Chilo Harlo. The group later included female singer Sonique who subsequently enjoyed a successful solo career.

16/04/1988	●²	13	○	**THEME FROM S-EXPRESS**	Rhythm King LEFT 21
23/07/1989	5	9		**SUPERFLY GUY**	Rhythm King LEFT 28
18/02/1989	6	10		**HEY MUSIC LOVER**	Rhythm King LEFT 30
16/09/1989	21	8		MANTRA FOR A STATE OF MIND	Rhythm King LEFT 35
15/09/1990	32	4		NOTHING TO LOSE	Rhythm King SEXY 01

○ Silver disc ● Gold disc ✪ Platinum disc (additional platinum units are indicated by a figure following the symbol) ◉ Singles released prior to 1973 that are known to have sold over 1 million copies in the UK

DATE	POS	WKS	BPI	SINGLE TITLE	LABEL & NUMBER
30/05/1992	43	2		FIND 'EM, FOOL 'EM, FORGET 'EM	Rhythm King 6580137
11/05/1996	14	4		THEME FROM S-EXPRESS (REMIX) **MARK MOORE PRESENTS S-EXPRESS**	Rhythm King SEXY 9CD

S-J UK singer (born Sarah Jane Jimenez-Heany, Spain) who is also known as The Diva Divine.

DATE	POS	WKS	BPI	SINGLE TITLE	LABEL & NUMBER
11/01/1997	46	1		FEVER	React CDREACT 93
24/01/1998	30	2		I FEEL DIVINE	React CDREACT 113
07/11/1998	59	1		SHIVER	React CDREACT 138

RAPHAEL SAADIQ US singer (born Raphael Wiggins) who is also a member of Tony! Toni! Tone! He made his first public appearance at the age of seven with his father's blues band. He and Q-Tip also write and produce for other acts, including Whitney Houston. He was later in Lucy Pearl with Dawn Robinson (of En Vogue) and Ali Shaheed Muhammad (of A Tribe Called Quest).

DATE	POS	WKS	BPI	SINGLE TITLE	LABEL & NUMBER
23/11/1996	33	2		STRESSED OUT **A TRIBE CALLED QUEST FEATURING FAITH EVANS AND RAPHAEL SAADIQ**	Jive JIVECD 404
19/06/1999	36	2		GET INVOLVED **RAPHAEL SAADIQ AND Q-TIP** Contains a sample of The Intruders' *I'll Always Love My Mama*. Featured in the animated TV series *The P.J.Y.*	Hollywood 0101185 HWR

SABRE FEATURING PREZIDENT BROWN Jamaican vocal duo. Brown (born Fitzroy Cotterell, Colonel Ridge, Clarendon) was named Prezident Brown by Burning Spear's producer Jack Ruby.

DATE	POS	WKS	BPI	SINGLE TITLE	LABEL & NUMBER
19/08/1995	71	1		WRONG OR RIGHT	Greensleeves GRECD 485

SABRES – see **DENNY SEYTON AND THE SABRES**

SABRES OF PARADISE UK dance group formed by Andy Weatherall, Nina Walsh, Jagz Kooner and Gary Burns.

DATE	POS	WKS	BPI	SINGLE TITLE	LABEL & NUMBER
02/10/1993	55	3		SMOKEBELCH II	Sabres Of Paradise PT 009CD
09/04/1994	56	3		THEME	Sabres Of Paradise PT 014CD
17/09/1994	36	2		WILMOT	Warp WAP 50CD

SABRINA Italian singer (born Sabrina Salerno, 15/3/1968, Genoa) whose film appearances have included *Grandi Maggazzini* and *Jolly Blu*.

DATE	POS	WKS	BPI	SINGLE TITLE	LABEL & NUMBER
06/02/1988	60	3		BOYS (SUMMERTIME LOVE)	Ibiza IBIZ 1
11/06/1988	3	11	○	**BOYS (SUMMERTIME LOVE)**	Ibiza IBIZ 1
01/10/1988	25	7		ALL OF ME	PWL 19
01/07/1989	72	1		LIKE A YO-YO	Videogram DCUP 1

SACRED SPIRIT European producer/composer The Fearsome Brave who mixed the chants of North American Indians with contemporary beats. The album projects also featured the vocals of John Lee Hooker and Lightning Hopkins, among others.

DATE	POS	WKS	BPI	SINGLE TITLE	LABEL & NUMBER
15/04/1995	71	1		YEHA-NOHA (WISHES OF HAPPINESS AND PROSPERITY)	Virgin VSCDT 1514
18/11/1995	37	2		YEHA-NOHA (WISHES OF HAPPINESS AND PROSPERITY)	Virgin VSCDT 1514
16/03/1996	45	2		WINTER CEREMONY (TOR-CHENEY-NAHANA)	Virgin VSCDT 1574

SAD CAFÉ UK rock group formed in Manchester in 1976 by Paul Young (vocals), Ian Wilson (guitar), Mike Hehir (guitar), Lennie (saxophone), Vic Emerson (keyboards), John Stimpson (bass) and David Irving (drums). Stimpson was later their manager and was replaced by Des Tong. Young later joined Mike + The Mechanics and died from a heart attack on 17/7/2000.

DATE	POS	WKS	BPI	SINGLE TITLE	LABEL & NUMBER
22/09/1979	3	12	○	**EVERY DAY HURTS**	RCA PB 5180
19/01/1980	32	5		STRANGE LITTLE GIRL	RCA PB 5202
15/03/1980	14	11		MY OH MY	RCA SAD 3
21/06/1980	62	4		NOTHING LEFT TOULOUSE	RCA SAD 4
27/09/1980	41	6		LA-DI-DA	RCA SAD 5
20/12/1980	40	6		I'M IN LOVE AGAIN	RCA SAD 6

SADE UK group formed in London in 1983 by Sade Adu (born Helen Folasade Adu, 16/1/1959, Ibadan, Nigeria), Stewart Matthewman (saxophone), Paul Denman (bass) and Andrew Hale (keyboards); they were all previously in Pride. Sade was signed solo to Epic in 1984, the band signing to her in turn. She appeared in the 1987 film *Absolute Beginners*. *Diamond Life* was named Best Album at the 1985 BRIT Awards. The backing group later recorded as Sweetback. Three Grammy Awards include Best New Artist in 1985 and Best Pop Vocal Album in 2001 for *Lovers Rock*. Sade was awarded an OBE in the 2002 New Year's Honours List.

DATE	POS	WKS	BPI	SINGLE TITLE	LABEL & NUMBER
25/02/1984	6	12		**YOUR LOVE IS KING**	Epic A 4137
26/05/1984	36	5		WHEN AM I GONNA MAKE A LIVING	Epic A 4437
15/09/1984	19	10		SMOOTH OPERATOR	Epic A 4655
12/10/1985	31	5		THE SWEETEST TABOO	Epic A 6609
11/01/1986	49	3		IS IT A CRIME	Epic A 6742
02/04/1988	44	3		LOVE IS STRONGER THAN PRIDE	Epic SADE 1
04/06/1988	29	7		PARADISE	Epic SADE 2
10/10/1992	26	6		NO ORDINARY LOVE 1993 Grammy Award for Best Rhythm & Blues Performance by a Group	Epic 6583567
28/11/1992	56	2		FEEL NO PAIN	Epic 6588297
08/05/1993	44	3		KISS OF LIFE	Epic 6591162
05/06/1993	14	8		NO ORDINARY LOVE Re-issue of Epic 6583567 and re-promoted following use in the 1993 film *Indecent Proposal*	Epic 6583562
31/07/1993	53	2		CHERISH THE DAY	Epic 6594812
18/11/2000	17	5		BY YOUR SIDE	Epic 6699992
24/03/2001	59	1		KING OF SORROW	Epic 6708672

❶⁹ Number of weeks single topped the UK charts ↑ Entered the UK chart at #1 ▲⁹ Number of weeks single topped the American charts

693

STAFF SERGEANT BARRY SADLER US singer (born 1/11/1940, Carlsbad, NM); he served in the US Army Special Forces (the Green Berets) in Vietnam until suffering a leg injury in a booby trap. He was shot in the head during a robbery attempt at his home in Guatemala in 1988 and returned to America where he died from heart failure the following year on 5/11/1989.

24/03/1966......24......8....... BALLAD OF THE GREEN BERETS ▲5 Featured in the 1979 film *More American Graffiti* ....RCA 1506

SAFFRON UK singer (born Samantha Sprackling, 3/6/1968, Lagos, Nigeria); she was later lead vocalist with Republica.

16/01/1993......60......2....... CIRCLES ....WEA SAFF 9CD

SAFFRON HILL FEATURING BEN ONONO UK producer Tim 'Deluxe' Liken with UK singer Ben Onono. Liken also recorded as Tim Deluxe and Double 99.

17/05/2003......28......3....... MY LOVE IS ALWAYS Contains a sample of The Sylvers' *Come Back Love* ....Illustrious CDILL 016

SAFFRONS – see CINDY AND THE SAFFRONS

ALESSANDRO SAFINA – see ELTON JOHN

SAFRI DUO Danish dance group formed by Morten Friis, Uffe Savery and Michael Parsberg.

03/02/2001......6......9....... **PLAYED A LIVE (THE BONGO SONG)** ....AM:PM CDAMPM 141
05/10/2002......54......1....... SWEET FREEDOM SAFRI DUO FEATURING MICHAEL MCDONALD ....Serious SERR 55CD

MIKE SAGAR AND THE CRESTERS UK group formed by Mike Sagar (born in Leeds, vocals), Malcolm Clarke (guitar), John Harding (guitar), Richard Harding (bass) and Johnny Casson (drums). Sagar later became a country music singer.

08/12/1960......44......5....... DEEP FEELING ....HMV POP 819

SAGAT US rapper (born Faustin Lenon, Baltimore, MD); he also produces under the name Jump Chico Slamm.

04/12/1993......25......5....... FUNK DAT ....ffrr FCD 224
03/12/1994......71......1....... LUVSTUFF ....ffrr FCD 250

CAROLE BAYER SAGER US singer (born 8/3/1946, New York) and songwriter who penned hits for numerous artists before going solo. She married composer Burt Bacharach in 1982 but divorced in 1992. Together they won the 1986 Grammy Award for Song of the Year for *That's What Friends Are For*. She later recorded for Boardwalk. She has a star on the Hollywood Walk of Fame.

28/05/1977......6......9....... **YOU'RE MOVING OUT TODAY** ....Elektra K 12257

BALLY SAGOO Indian singer/record producer (born 1964); he produced his first single in 1990 and became house producer for the Oriental Star label.

03/09/1994......64......1....... CHURA LIYA ....Columbia 6607092
22/04/1995......45......1....... CHOLI KE PEECHE...Columbia 6613352
19/10/1996......12......3....... DIL CHEEZ (MY HEART)...Higher Ground 6634882
01/02/1997......21......3....... TUM BIN JIYA ....Higher Ground 6641372

SAILOR UK group formed in 1974 by Georg Kajanus (guitar/vocals), Henry Marsh (keyboard/vocals), Grant Serpell (drums/vocals) and Phil Pickett (bass/vocals). Pickett later worked with Culture Club and wrote *Karma Chameleon*.

06/12/1975......2......12......○ **A GLASS OF CHAMPAGNE** ....Epic EPC 3770
27/03/1976......7......8....... **GIRLS GIRLS GIRLS**...Epic EPC 3858
19/02/1977......35......4....... ONE DRINK TOO MANY ....Epic EPC 4804

SAINT FEATURING SUZANNA DEE UK dance group with Mark Smith, Dave Pickard and singer Suzanna Dee.

12/04/2003......36......2....... SHOW ME HEAVEN...Inferno CXFERN 52

ST. ANDREWS CHORALE UK church choir.

14/02/1976......31......5....... CLOUD 99...Decca F 13617

ST. CECILIA UK singer Jonathan King (born Kenneth King, 6/12/1944, London); he regards this as the worst record he ever made!

19/06/1971......12......17....... LEAP UP AND DOWN (WAVE YOUR KNICKERS IN THE AIR) ....Polydor 2058 104

SAINT ETIENNE UK group formed in 1988 by Peter Wiggs (born 15/5/1966, Reigate) and Bob Stanley (born 25/12/1965, Horsham), with Moira Lambert of Faith Over Reason fronting their debut hit. Donna Savage of Dead Famous People sang the lead on their second hit before Sarah Cracknell (born12/4/1967, Chelmsford) became permanent vocalist in 1992. Cracknell later recorded solo. Tim Burgess (born 30/5/1968, Salford) is lead singer with The Charlatans.

18/05/1991......54......3....... NOTHING CAN STOP US/SPEEDWELL ....Heavenly HVN 009
07/09/1991......39......4....... ONLY LOVE CAN BREAK YOUR HEART/FILTHY.....................................Heavenly HVN 12
16/05/1992......21......3....... JOIN OUR CLUB/PEOPLE GET REAL ....Heavenly HVN 15
17/10/1992......40......2....... AVENUE ....Heavenly HVN 2312
13/02/1993......12......5....... YOU'RE IN A BAD WAY ....Heavenly HVN 25CD
22/05/1993......23......5....... HOBART PAVING/WHO DO YOU THINK YOU ARE...................................Heavenly HVN 29CD
18/12/1993......37......5....... I WAS BORN ON CHRISTMAS DAY SAINT ETIENNE CO-STARRING TIM BURGESS..........Heavenly HVN 36CD
19/02/1994......28......3....... PALE MOVIE ....Heavenly HVN 37CD
28/05/1994......47......2....... LIKE A MOTORWAY ....Heavenly HVN 40CD
01/10/1994......32......2....... HUG MY SOUL Contains an interpolation of Andrea True Connection's *More More More* ....Heavenly HVN 42CD

11/11/1995	11	5		HE'S ON THE PHONE SAINT ETIENNE FEATURING ETIENNE DAHO	Heavenly HVN 50CDR
07/02/1998	12	3		SYLVIE	Creation CRESCD 279X
02/05/1998	27	2		THE BAD PHOTOGRAPHER	Creation CRESCD 290
20/05/2000	7	5		TELL ME WHY (THE RIDDLE) PAUL VAN DYK FEATURING SAINT ETIENNE	Deviant DVNT 36CDS
24/06/2000	50	1		HEART FAILED (IN THE BACK OF A TAXI)	Mantra MNT 54CD
20/01/2001	34	2		BOY IS CRYING	Mantra MNT 60CD1
07/09/2002	41	1		ACTION	Mantra MNT 73CD
29/03/2003	40	1		SOFT LIKE ME	Manta MNT 78CD

ST. GERMAIN
French group formed by Ludovic Navarre (conductor), Pascal Ohse (trumpet), Edouard Labor (saxophone/flute), Idrissa Diop (drums), Carneiro (percussion), Claudio De Qeiroz (baritone) and special guest Ernest Raglin.

| 31/08/1996 | 50 | 1 | | ALABAMA BLUES (REVISITED) | F Communications F 050CD |
| 10/03/2001 | 54 | 2 | | ROSE ROUGE Contains a sample of Marlena Shaw's *Live At Montreaux* | Blue Note CDROSE 001 |

BARRY ST JOHN
UK singer from Glasgow who sang backing for Pink Floyd, Elton John, Rick Wakeman and the Tom Robinson Band.

| 09/12/1965 | 47 | 1 | | COME AWAY MELINDA | Columbia DB 7783 |

ST. JOHN'S COLLEGE SCHOOL CHOIR AND THE BAND OF THE GRENADIER GUARDS
UK school choir and the military band of the Grenadier Guards whose debut hit was a tribute to Queen Elizabeth II's 60th birthday.

| 03/05/1986 | 40 | 3 | | THE QUEEN'S BIRTHDAY SONG | Columbia Q1 |

ST. LOUIS UNION
UK group with Tony Cassidy (vocals), Keith Miller (guitar), Alex Kirby (saxophone), David Tomlinson (organ), John Nichols (bass) and Dave Webb (drums). They won the 1965 *Melody Maker* contest, the prize a recording contract with Decca.

| 13/01/1966 | 11 | 10 | | GIRL | Decca F 12318 |

ST LUNATICS – see NELLY

CRISPIAN ST. PETERS
UK singer/guitarist (born Robin Peter Smith, 5/4/1944, Swanley). He began with the skiffle group the Hard Travellers and then Beat Formula Three before being persuaded to turn solo by manager David Nicholson.

06/01/1966	2	14		YOU WERE ON MY MIND Featured in the 1996 film *Jenseits Der Stille*	Decca F 12287
31/03/1966	5	13		PIED PIPER	Decca F 12359
15/09/1966	47	4		CHANGES	Decca F 12480

ST PHILIPS CHOIR UK choir.

| 12/12/1987 | 49 | 4 | | SING FOR EVER | BBC RESL 222 |

ST THOMAS MORE SCHOOL CHOIR – see SCOTT FITZGERALD

ST. WINIFRED'S SCHOOL CHOIR
UK girls school choir who previously appeared on the hit single by Brian and Michael. Their single was written by Gordon Lorenz and the lead vocalist was Dawn Ralph.

| 22/11/1980 | ●2 | 11 | ● | THERE'S NO ONE QUITE LIKE GRANDMA | MFP FP 900 |

BUFFY SAINTE-MARIE
Canadian singer (born 20/2/1941, Piaport Indian Reserve, Saskatchewan) who is part North American Indian. She emerged during the late 1960s' folk boom. As a songwriter she penned *Until It's Time For You To Go*, a hit for both The Four Pennies and Elvis Presley. She was married at one time to record producer Jack Nitzsche who died in August 2000.

17/07/1971	7	18		SOLDIER BLUE Featured in the 1970 film *Soldier Blue*	RCA 2081
18/03/1972	34	5		I'M GONNA BE A COUNTRY GIRL AGAIN	Vanguard VRS 35143
08/02/1992	39	5		THE BIG ONES GET AWAY	Ensign ENY 650
04/07/1992	57	1		FALLEN ANGELS	Ensign ENY 655

SAINTS
Australian punk group formed in 1975 by Chris Bailey (guitar/vocals), Kym Bradshaw (bass), Ed Kuepper (guitar) and Ivor Hay (drums). Bradshaw left in 1977, replaced by Alisdair Ward.

| 23/07/1977 | 34 | 4 | | THIS PERFECT DAY | Harvest HAR 5130 |

KYU SAKAMOTO
Japanese singer (born 1941, Kawasaki); he was signed by the Toshiba label in 1960 and two years later scored a huge domestic hit with his record originally titled *Ueo Muite Aruko* ('Walk With Your Chin Up'). A cover version by Kenny Ball titled *Sukiyaki* attracted interest in the original version. Sakamoto was killed in a Japan Airlines 747 crash near Tokyo on 12/8/1985.

| 27/06/1963 | 6 | 13 | | SUKIYAKI ▲3 | HMV POP 1171 |

RYUICHI SAKAMOTO
Japanese synthesiser player (born 17/1/1952, Tokyo); he was a member of The Yellow Magic Orchestra before going solo and later recording with ex-Japan David Sylvian. As an actor he appeared in *Merry Christmas Mr Lawrence* with David Bowie. He won an Oscar for his music to the (1987) film *The Last Emperor*. He also won the 1988 Grammy Award for Best Album of Original Instrumental Background Score written for a Motion Picture with David Byrne and Cong Su for *The Last Emperor*.

07/08/1982	30	4		BAMBOO HOUSES/BAMBOO MUSIC SYLVIAN SAKAMOTO	Virgin VS 510
02/07/1983	16	8		FORBIDDEN COLOURS DAVID SYLVIAN AND RYUICHI SAKAMOTO	Virgin VS 601
13/06/1992	58	3		HEARTBEAT (TAINAI KAIKI II) RETURNING TO THE WOMB DAVID SYLVIAN/RYUICHI SAKAMOTO FEATURING INGRID CHAVEZ	
					Virgin America VUS 57

●9 Number of weeks single topped the UK chart ↑ Entered the UK chart at #1 ▲9 Number of weeks single topped the US chart

695

SAKKARIN UK singer Jonathan King (born Kenneth King, 6/12/1944, London).

| 03/04/1971 | 12 | 14 | | SUGAR SUGAR | RCA 2064 |

SALAD UK/Dutch group with Marijne Van Der Vlugt (vocals), Paul Kennedy (guitar), Peter Brown (bass) and Rob Wakeman (drums).

11/03/1995	66	1		DRINK THE ELIXIR	Island Red CIRD 104
13/05/1995	42	1		MOTORBIKE TO HEAVEN	Island Red CIRD 106
16/09/1995	50	1		GRANITE STATUE	Island Red CIRD 108
26/10/1996	60	1		I WANT YOU	Island CID 646
17/05/1997	65	1		CARDBOY KING	Island CID 654

SALFORD JETS UK group formed in 1976 by Mike Sweeney (vocals), Rod Gerrard (guitar), Diccon Hubbard (bass), Geoff Kerry (keyboards) and 'Shaky' Dave Morris (drums). Morris left in 1981, replaced by Mike Twigg.

| 31/05/1980 | 72 | 2 | | WHO YOU LOOKING AT? | RCA PB 5239 |

SALIVA US rock group formed in Memphis, TN in 1996 by Josey Scott (vocals), Chris Dibaldo (guitar), Wayne Swinny (guitar), Dave Novotny (bass) and Paul Crosby (drums).

| 15/03/2003 | 47 | 1 | | ALWAYS | Mercury 0637082 |

SALSOUL ORCHESTRA – see **CHARO AND THE SALSOUL ORCHESTRA**

SALT TANK UK production duo Malcolm Stanners and David R Gates; Stanners previously with Derrick May and Kevin Saunderson.

11/05/1996	40	2		EUGINA	Internal LIECD 29
03/07/1999	52	1		DIMENSION	Hooj Choons HOOJ 74CD
09/12/2000	58	1		EUGINA (REMIX)	Lost Language LOST 004CD

SALT-N-PEPA US rap duo formed in New York in 1985 by Salt (born Cheryl James, 28/3/1969, Brooklyn, NYC) and Pepa (born Sandra Denton, 9/11/1969, Kingston, Jamaica) as Super Nature, with a US R&B chart hit the same year, name-changing to Salt-N-Pepa in 1986. They later launched Jireh Records. On stage they were usually augmented by DJ Spinderella, originally Latoya Hanson, then replaced by Deirdre Roper (born 3/8/1971, NYC) in 1988. Denton married Anthony 'Treach' Criss of Naughty By Nature in 1999. E.U. is an R&B group from Washington led by Gregory 'Sugar Bear' Elliott (the name stands for Experience Unlimited).

26/03/1988	41	6		PUSH IT/I AM DOWN	ffrr FFR 2
25/06/1988	2	13	◯	**PUSH IT/TRAMP** Featured in the 1989 film *True Love*. Previously available as *Push It* with *I Am Down* on the B side on ffrr 2, it was re-released by Champion with *Tramp* as B side. Sales of both were added together for the chart Champion CHAMP 51/ffrr FFR 2
03/09/1988	22	8		SHAKE YOUR THANG (IT'S YOUR THING) **SALT-N-PEPA FEATURING E.U.**	ffrr FFR 11
12/11/1988	4	9		**TWIST AND SHOUT**	ffrr FFR 16
14/04/1990	40	6		EXPRESSION	ffrr F 127
25/05/1991	5	12		**DO YOU WANT ME** Features the uncredited contribution of Hurby Luv Bug	ffrr F 151
31/08/1991	2	13	◯	**LET'S TALK ABOUT SEX SALT-N-PEPA FEATURING PSYCHOTROPIC**	ffrr F 162
30/11/1991	15	9		YOU SHOWED ME	ffrr F 174
28/03/1992	23	4		EXPRESSION (REMIX)	ffrr F 182
03/10/1992	39	3		START ME UP Featured in the 1992 film *Stay Tuned*	ffrr F 196
09/10/1993	29	3		SHOOP Contains samples of The Sweet Inspirations' *I'm Blue* and Captain Sky's *Super Sporm*	ffrr FCD 219
19/03/1994	7	10		**WHATTA MAN SALT-N-PEPA WITH EN VOGUE** Contains a sample of Linda Lyndell's *What A Man*	ffrr FCD 222
28/05/1994	13	8		SHOOP (REMIX)	ffrr FCD 234
12/11/1994	19	5		NONE OF YOUR BUSINESS 1994 Grammy Award for Best Rap Performance by a Group	ffrr FCD 244
21/12/1996	23	6		CHAMPAGNE Featured in the 1996 film *Bulletproof*	MCA MCSTD 48025
29/11/1997	24	2		R U READY	ffrr FCDP 322
11/12/1999	22	4		THE BRICK TRACK VERSUS GITTY UP **SALTNPEPA** Contains samples of Rick James' *Give It To Me Baby* and Pink Floyd's *Another Brick In The Wall*	ffrr FCD 373

SAM AND DAVE US R&B vocal duo formed in 1961 by Sam Moore (born 12/10/1935, Miami, FL) and Dave Prater (born 9/5/1937, Ocilla, GA) and signed by Roulette in 1962. They switched to Atlantic in 1965, their material appearing on the Stax label. They split in 1970, re-forming in 1972. Moore re-recorded *Soul Man* with Lou Reed as the theme to the film of the same name. Prater was killed in a car crash on 9/4/1988. They were inducted into the Rock & Roll Hall of Fame in 1992.

16/03/1967	35	8		SOOTHE ME	Stax 601 004
01/11/1967	24	14		SOUL MAN 1967 Grammy Award for Best Rhythm & Blues Group Performance	Stax 601 023
13/03/1968	34	9		I THANK YOU	Stax 601 030
29/01/1969	15	8		SOUL SISTER BROWN SUGAR	Atlantic 584 237

SAM AND MARK UK vocal duo Sam Nixon (born 21/3/1986, Barnsley) and Mark Rhodes (born 11/9/1981, Darlaston) who first came to prominence as runners-up in the 2003 *Pop Idol* contest.

| 21/02/2004 | ❶[1] | 10 | | **WITH A LITTLE HELP FROM MY FRIENDS/MEASURE OF A MAN** ↑ | 19 19RECS9 |
| 05/06/2004 | 19 | 3 | | THE SUN HAS COME YOUR WAY | 19/UMTV 9866906 |

SAM THE SHAM AND THE PHARAOHS US group formed in Dallas, TX in the early 1960s by Domingo 'Sam' Samudio (born 1940, Dallas, vocals), Ray Stinnet (guitar), David Martin (bass), Jerry Patterson (drums) and Butch Gibson (saxophone). Samudio recorded solo for Atlantic in 1970, re-formed The Pharaohs in 1974 and later became a street preacher. Martin died from a heart attack on 2/8/1987. Samudio won the 1971 Grammy Award for Best Album Notes for *Sam Hard And Heavy*.

◯ Silver disc ● Gold disc ✪ Platinum disc (additional platinum units are indicated by a figure following the symbol) ◉ Singles released prior to 1973 that are known to have sold over 1 million copies in the UK

DATE	POS	WKS	BPI	SINGLE TITLE	LABEL & NUMBER
24/06/1965	11	15		WOOLY BULLY Featured in the 1987 film *Full Metal Jacket*	MGM 1269
04/08/1966	46	3		LIL' RED RIDING HOOD	MGM 1315

RICHIE SAMBORA US vocalist/guitarist (born 11/7/1959, New Jersey) who was a founder of Bon Jovi in 1983 and went solo from 1998.

DATE	POS	WKS	BPI	SINGLE TITLE	LABEL & NUMBER
07/09/1991	59	1		BALLAD OF YOUTH	Mercury MER 350
07/03/1998	37	2		HARD TIMES COME EASY	Mercury 5686972
01/08/1998	58	1		IN IT FOR LOVE	Mercury 5660632

MIKE SAMMES SINGERS UK vocal group formed and fronted by Mike Sammes (born 19/2/1928, Reigate). The group was frequently used by other artists for backing purposes.

DATE	POS	WKS	BPI	SINGLE TITLE	LABEL & NUMBER
03/05/1957	30	1		ROUND AND ROUND JIMMY YOUNG WITH THE MICHAEL SAMMES SINGERS	Decca F 10875
21/03/1958	14	12		TO BE LOVED MALCOLM VAUGHAN WITH THE MICHAEL SAMMES SINGERS	HMV POP 459
18/04/1958	27	3		I MAY NEVER PASS THIS WAY AGAIN RONNIE HILTON WITH THE MICHAEL SAMMES SINGERS	HMV POP 468
17/10/1958	5	14		MORE THAN EVER (COME PRIMA) MALCOLM VAUGHAN WITH THE MICHAEL SAMMES SINGERS	HMV POP 538
09/01/1959	18	6		THE WORLD OUTSIDE RONNIE HILTON WITH THE MICHAEL SAMMES SINGERS	HMV POP 559
27/02/1959	20	3		LITTLE DRUMMER BOY MICHAEL FLANDERS WITH THE MICHAEL SAMMES SINGERS	Parlophone R 4528
01/01/1960	❶[1]	13		STARRY EYED MICHAEL HOLLIDAY WITH THE MICHAEL SAMMES SINGERS	Columbia DB 4378
15/12/1960	37	1		DONALD WHERE'S YOUR TROOSERS	Top Rank JAR 427
12/01/1961	19	40		A SCOTTISH SOLDIER	Top Rank JAR 512
01/06/1961	28	13		THE BATTLE'S O'ER This and above two singles credited to ANDY STEWART AND THE MICHAEL SAMMES SINGERS	Top Rank JAR 565
26/03/1964	43	3		UNCHAINED MELODY JIMMY YOUNG WITH THE MICHAEL SAMMES SINGERS	Columbia DB 7234
15/09/1966	22	19		SOMEWHERE MY LOVE	HMV POP 1546
12/07/1967	14	19		SOMEWHERE MY LOVE	HMV POP 1546
01/11/1967	6	17		CARELESS HANDS DES O'CONNOR WITH THE MICHAEL SAMMES SINGERS	Columbia DB 8275

DAVE SAMPSON UK singer (born 9/1/1941) who was discovered by Cliff Richard's manager and backed by his group The Hunters.

DATE	POS	WKS	BPI	SINGLE TITLE	LABEL & NUMBER
19/05/1960	29	6		SWEET DREAMS	Columbia DB 4449

SAMSON UK heavy metal group formed in 1978 by Paul Samson (guitar), Bruce Bruce (vocals), Chris Aylmer (bass) and Clive Burr (drums). Burr left soon after their formation to join Iron Maiden, replaced by Thundersticks. Bruce left in 1981 (assuming his real name of Bruce Dickinson, he resurfaced as lead singer with Iron Maiden), as did Thundersticks, with Nicky Moore (vocals) and Mel Gaynor (drums) replacements. Gaynor then left, with Pete Jupp his replacement. Aylmer left in 1984, replaced by Merv Goldsworthy. After Nicky Moore left in 1986 Samson disbanded the group and went solo, re-forming it in 1988. Samson died from cancer on 9/8/2002.

DATE	POS	WKS	BPI	SINGLE TITLE	LABEL & NUMBER
04/07/1981	55	3		RIDING WITH THE ANGELS	RCA 67
24/07/1982	63	2		LOSING MY GRIP	Polydor POSP 471
05/03/1983	65	1		RED SKIES	Poolydor POSP 554

SAN JOSE FEATURING RODRIGUEZ ARGENTINA UK instrumental group fronted by Rodriguez Argentina, with keyboard player Rod Argent (born 14/6/1945, St Albans).

DATE	POS	WKS	BPI	SINGLE TITLE	LABEL & NUMBER
17/06/1978	14	8		ARGENTINE MELODY (CANCION DE ARGENTINA) Theme to the BBC TV coverage of the 1978 football World Cup in Argentina	MCA 369

SAN REMO STRINGS US group of master violinists fronted by Bob Wilson who first recorded for Ric Tic as the San Remo Golden Strings and later moved to Motown when it bought the Ric Tic label. They scored their first US hits in 1965 with their UK hit being originally released in the States in 1966.

DATE	POS	WKS	BPI	SINGLE TITLE	LABEL & NUMBER
18/12/1971	39	8		FESTIVAL TIME	Tamla Motown TMG 795

JUNIOR SANCHEZ FEATURING DAJAE US DJ/producer based in New York who worked with Erick 'More' Morillo and his Subliminal Records label.

DATE	POS	WKS	BPI	SINGLE TITLE	LABEL & NUMBER
16/10/1999	31	2		B WITH U	Manifesto FESCD 62

ROGER SANCHEZ US producer/remixer (born 1/6/1967, NYC); he previously recorded as El Mariachi, Funk Junkeez and Transatlantic Soul and records as Roger S or the S Man in America and runs the R-Senal record label. He won the 2002 Grammy Award for Best Remixed Recording, Non-Classical for *Hella Good* by No Doubt.

DATE	POS	WKS	BPI	SINGLE TITLE	LABEL & NUMBER
03/10/1998	65	1		BUFFALO GALS STAMPEDE MALCOLM MCLAREN AND THE WORLD'S FAMOUS SUPREME TEAM PLUS RAKIM AND ROGER SANCHEZ	Virgin VSCDT 1717
20/02/1999	31	2		I WANT YOUR LOVE ROGER SANCHEZ PRESENTS TWILIGHT	Perpetual PERPCDS 001
29/01/2000	24	2		I NEVER KNEW	INCredible INCS 4CD

❶[9] Number of weeks single topped the UK chart ↑ Entered the UK chart at #1 ▲[9] Number of weeks single topped the US chart

697

| 14/07/2001 | ❶¹ | 12 | | ANOTHER CHANCE ↑ Contains a sample of Toto's *I Won't Hold You Back* | Defected DFECT 35CD |
| 15/12/2001 | 25 | 4 | | YOU CAN'T CHANGE ME ROGER SANCHEZ FEATURING ARMAND VAN HELDEN AND N'DEA DAVENPORT | Defected DFECT 41CDS |

CHRIS SANDFORD UK singer and actor who appeared in *Coronation Street*. He was later a member of Yin and Yan and also recorded as Chris Sandford Friendship and Chris Sandford Rag 'n' Bone Band.

| 12/12/1963 | 17 | 9 | | NOT TOO LITTLE NOT TOO MUCH | Decca F 11778 |

SANDPIPERS US vocal group formed in Los Angeles, CA by Jim Brady (born 24/8/1944), Michael Piano (born 26/10/1944) and Richard Shoff (born 30/4/1944) as the Four Seasons, name-changing because of another group so titled. All three were previously in the Mitchell Boys Choir.

15/09/1966	7	17		GUANTANAMERA	Pye International 7N 25380
05/06/1968	33	6		QUANDO M'INNAMORO (A MAN WITHOUT LOVE)	A&M AMS 723
26/03/1969	38	2		KUMBAYA	A&M AMS 744
27/11/1976	32	8		HANG ON SLOOPY	Satril SAT 114

SANDRA German singer (born Sanda Lauer, 18/5/1962, Saarbrucken); she later backed Camouflage, Enigma and Thirteen Mg.

| 17/12/1988 | 45 | 8 | | EVERLASTING LOVE | Siren SRN 85 |

JODIE SANDS US singer (born Philadelphia, PA); she appeared in the 1957 film *Jamboree*.

| 17/10/1958 | 14 | 10 | | SOMEDAY (YOU'LL WANT ME TO WANT YOU) | HMV POP 533 |

TOMMY SANDS US singer (born 27/8/1937, Chicago, IL); he was a DJ in Houston, TX at twelve and then a successful singer and actor, whose films included *Babes In Toyland* (1961) and *The Longest Day* (1962). He married Nancy Sinatra in 1960; they divorced in 1965. He has a star on the Hollywood Walk of Fame.

| 04/08/1960 | 25 | 7 | | OLD OAKEN BUCKET | Capitol CL 15143 |

SANDSTORM US producer Mark Picchiotti. He is also a member of Absolute and recorded under his own name and as Basstoy.

| 13/05/2000 | 54 | 1 | | THE RETURN OF NOTHING | Renaissance Recordings RENCDS 001 |

SAMANTHA SANG Australian singer (born Cheryl Gray, 5/8/1953, Melbourne); she began on radio at the age of eight.

| 04/02/1978 | 11 | 13 | | EMOTION | Private Stock PVT 128 |

SANTA CLAUS AND THE CHRISTMAS TREES UK studio group inspired by the success of Starsound.

| 11/12/1982 | 19 | 5 | | SINGALONG-A-SANTA | Polydor IVY 1 |
| 10/12/1983 | 39 | 5 | | SINGALONG-A-SANTA AGAIN | Polydor IVY 2 |

SANTA ESMERALDA FEATURING LEROY GOMEZ US dance group assembled by producers Nicolas Skorsky and Jean-Manuel De Scarano and fronted by Leroy Gomez.

| 12/11/1977 | 41 | 5 | | DON'T LET ME BE MISUNDERSTOOD | Philips 6042 325 |

SANTANA US rock group formed in Los Angeles, CA in 1966 by a nucleus of Carlos Santana (born 20/7/1947, Autlan de Navarro, Mexico, guitar/vocals), Gregg Rolie (born 17/6/1947, Seattle, WA, keyboards) and David Brown (born 15/2/1947, New York, bass) as Santana Blues Band. They added percussionists Jose Chepitos Areas (born 17/6/1947, Leon, Nicaragua), Mike Carrabello and Mike Shrieve (born 6/7/1949, San Francisco, CA) in 1969 and shortened the name to Santana. They signed to CBS in 1969, and remained with the label until 1989 when Carlos launched the Guts & Grace label. There have been numerous personnel changes since, including most notably Neal Schon (born 27/2/1954, San Mateo, CA) on guitar who joined in 1971. They were inducted into the Rock & Roll Hall of Fame in 1998. Carlos Santana's nine Grammy Awards include Best Rock Instrumental Performance in 1988 for *Blues For Salvador*, Record of the Year, Album of the Year and Best Rock Album in 1999 for *Supernatural*, Best Pop Instrumental in 1999 for *El Farol*, Best Rock Group in 1999 with Everlast for *Put Your Lights On* and Best Rock Instrumental in 1999 with Eric Clapton for *The Calling*. His eight awards in 1999 equalled Michael Jackson's tally of 1984. He also won the 2000 MOBO Award for Best World Music Act. He has a star on the Hollywood Walk of Fame. Rob Thomas is lead singer with Matchbox 20.

28/09/1974	27	7		SAMBA PA TI	CBS 2561
15/10/1977	11	12		SHE'S NOT THERE	CBS 5671
25/11/1978	53	3		WELL ALL RIGHT	CBS 6755
22/03/1980	57	3		ALL I EVER WANTED	CBS 8160
23/10/1999	75	1		SMOOTH ▲¹² SANTANA FEATURING ROB THOMAS 1999 Grammy Awards for Record of the Year, Best Pop Collaboration with Vocals, and Song of the Year for writers Rob Thomas and Itaal Shur. Featured in the 2003 film *Love Actually*	Arista 74321709492
01/04/2000	3	10		SMOOTH Re-issue of Arista 74321709492	Arista 74321748762
05/08/2000	6	9		MARIA MARIA SANTANA FEATURING THE PRODUCT G&B 1999 Grammy Award for Best Pop Group Performance and subsequently became the bestselling single in America during 2000, shifting more than 1.3 million copies	Arista 74321769372
23/11/2002	16	8		THE GAME OF LOVE SANTANA FEATURING MICHELLE BRANCH 2002 Grammy Award for the Best Pop Collaboration With Vocals	Arista 74321959442

JUELZ SANTANA — see CAM'RON

SANTO AND JOHNNY US guitar duo Santo Farina (born 24/10/1937, Brooklyn, NYC, steel guitar) and his brother Johnny (born 30/4/1941, Brooklyn, rhythm guitar). The pair went their own way in the 1970s.

| 16/10/1959 | 22 | 4 | | SLEEP WALK ▲² Featured in the films *La Bamba* (1987) and *Mermaids* (1990) | Pye International 7N 25037 |
| 31/03/1960 | 50 | 1 | | TEARDROP | Parlophone R 4619 |

○ Silver disc ● Gold disc ✪ Platinum disc (additional platinum units are indicated by a figure following the symbol) ◎ Singles released prior to 1973 that are known to have sold over 1 million copies in the UK

SANTOS Italian producer Sante Pucello. Pucello is based in Rome.

| 20/01/2001 | 9 | 6 | | CAMELS | Incentive CENT 15CDS |

MIKE SARNE UK singer (born Michael Scheur, 6/8/1939) of German extraction. He later became a film producer. His first recording partner, Wendy Richard, became a well-known actress in the TV comedy *Are You Being Served* and as Pauline Fowler in *Eastenders,* and was awarded an MBE in the 2000 Queen's Birthday Honours List.

10/05/1962	❶²	19		COME OUTSIDE MIKE SARNE WITH WENDY RICHARD	Parlophone R 4902
30/08/1962	18	10		WILL I WHAT MIKE SARNE WITH BILLIE DAVIS	Parlophone R 4932
10/01/1963	22	7		JUST FOR KICKS	Parlophone R 4974
28/03/1963	29	7		CODE OF LOVE	Parlophone R 5010

JOY SARNEY UK singer (born Southend). Her debut hit was a duet between Joy and a Punch & Judy performer as the song was a love song between Joy and Mr Punch!

| 07/05/1977 | 26 | 6 | | NAUGHTY NAUGHTY NAUGHTY | Alaska ALA 2005 |

SARR BAND Italian/UK/French studio group.

| 16/09/1978 | 68 | 1 | | MAGIC MANDRAKE | Calendar Day 111 |

PETER SARSTEDT UK singer (born 10/12/1942); brother of Richard (who recorded as Eden Kane) and Clive (who recorded as Robin Sartsedt) Sarstedt. He still performs regularly in clubs around the country.

| 05/02/1969 | ❶⁴ | 16 | | WHERE DO YOU GO TO MY LOVELY | United Artists UP 2262 |
| 04/06/1969 | 10 | 9 | | FROZEN ORANGE JUICE | United Artists UP 35021 |

ROBIN SARSTEDT UK singer (born Clive Sarstedt); brother of Peter and Richard (who recorded as Eden Kane) Sarstedt.

| 08/05/1976 | 3 | 9 | | MY RESISTANCE IS LOW | Decca F 13624 |

SARTORELLO Italian vocal/instrumental duo formed by Sartorello Fornityre.

| 10/08/1996 | 56 | 1 | | MOVE BABY MOVE | Multiply CDMULTY 12 |

SASH! German producer/DJ Sascha Lappessen and a dance group that features Thomas Ludke, Thomas Alisson and Ralf Kappmeier.

01/03/1997	2	15	●	ENCORE UNE FOIS Features the uncredited vocals of Sabine Ohms	Multiply CDMULTY 18
05/07/1997	2	12	●	ECUADOR SASH! FEATURING RODRIGUEZ	Multiply CDMULTY 23
18/10/1997	2	14	●	STAY SASH! FEATURING LA TREC	Multiply CDMULTY 26
04/04/1998	3	12	○	LA PRIMAVERA	Multiply CXMULTY 32
15/08/1998	2	12	○	MYSTERIOUS TIMES SASH! FEATURING TINA COUSINS	Multiply CDMULTY 40
28/11/1998	8	10		MOVE MANIA SASH! FEATURING SHANNON	Multiply CDMULTY 45
03/04/1999	15	6		COLOUR THE WORLD	Multiply CDMULTY 48
12/02/2000	2	10		ADELANTE	Multiply CDMULTY 60
22/04/2000	8	7		JUST AROUND THE HILL SASH! FEATURING TINA COUSINS	Multiply CDMULTY 62
23/09/2000	10	5		WITH MY OWN EYES	Multiply CDMULTY 67

SASHA UK producer (born Alexander Coe, 4/9/1969, Bangor, Wales, raised in Manchester); he was known as a remixer before signing a solo deal with DeConstruction. Sam Mollison is a UK singer and a member of Bone. Darren Emerson was previously in Underworld.

31/07/1993	57	1		TOGETHER DANNY CAMPBELL AND SASHA	ffrr FCD 212
19/02/1994	19	3		HIGHER GROUND	Deconstruction 74321189002
27/08/1994	32	4		MAGIC This and above single credited to SASHA WITH SAM MOLLISON	Deconstruction 74321221862
09/03/1996	17	4		BE AS ONE SASHA AND MARIA	7pm 74321342962
23/09/2000	23	3		SCORCHIO SASHA/EMERSON	Arista 74321788222
31/08/2002	64	1		WAVY GRAVY	Arista 74321960602

SASHA – see SEAN PAUL

JOE SATRIANI US guitarist (born 15/7/1957, Carle Place, NY); he began a solo career in 1984, although his work with other artists, including Greg Kihn, Mick Jagger and Deep Purple, made his reputation. He formed a touring band in 1988 with Stu Hamm (bass) and Jonathan Moyer (drums).

| 13/02/1993 | 53 | 1 | | THE SATCH EP Tracks on EP: *The Extremist, Cryin, Banana Bongo* and *Crazy* | Relativity 6589532 |

SATURATED SOUL FEATURING MISS BUNTY US production duo Ian Carey and Eddie Amador with Dutch singer Miss Bunty.

| 14/08/2004 | 56 | 1 | | GOT TO RELEASE | Defected DFTD093 |

SATURDAY NIGHT BAND US studio group assembled by producers Jessie Boyce and Moses Dillard with vocalists Donna McElroy, Vicki Hampton and Jessie Boyce.

| 01/07/1978 | 16 | 9 | | COME ON DANCE DANCE | CBS 6367 |

DEION SAUNDERS – see HAMMER

ANN SAUNDERSON – see OCTAVE ONE FEATURING ANN SAUNDERSON

❶⁹ Number of weeks single topped the UK chart ↑ Entered the UK chart at #1 ▲⁹ Number of weeks single topped the US chart

699

KEVIN SAUNDERSON – see INNER CITY

ANNE SAVAGE
UK DJ who had her first residency aged nineteen in Bolzano, Italy and also records as Destiny Angel.

19/04/2003	74	1		HELLRAISER	Tidy Trax TIDY 186T

CHANTAY SAVAGE
US R&B singer/keyboard player (born 16/7/1967, Chicago, IL); she is the daughter of jazz musician parents. She had been a session backing singer for the likes of Kym Sims before going solo.

04/05/1996	12	8		I WILL SURVIVE Featured in the 1996 film *First Wives Club*	RCA 74321377682
08/11/1997	59	1		REMINDING ME (OF SEF) **COMMON FEATURING CHANTAY SAVAGE**	Relativity 6560762

EDNA SAVAGE
UK singer; briefly married to singer Terry Dene. She had a role in the 1956 film *It's Great To Be Young* and died on 31/12/2000.

13/01/1956	19	1		ARRIVEDERCI DARLING	Parlophone R 4097

SAVAGE GARDEN
Australian duo Darren Hayes (vocals) and Daniel Jones (all instruments). Debut album *Savage Garden* sold over 11 million worldwide. Jones set up the Meridienmusik label, Brisbane duo Aneiki the debut signing, while Hayes went solo.

21/06/1997	11	7		I WANT YOU	Columbia 6645452
27/09/1997	55	1		TO THE MOON AND BACK	Columbia 6648932
28/02/1998	4	23	✪	**TRULY MADLY DEEPLY ▲²**	Columbia 6656022
22/08/1998	3	16	●	**TO THE MOON AND BACK** Re-issue of Columbia 6648932	Columbia 6662882
12/12/1998	12	10		I WANT YOU '98 (REMIX)	Columbia 6667332
10/07/1999	16	6		THE ANIMAL SONG Featured in the 1999 film *The Other Sister*	Columbia 6675882
13/11/1999	10	12		**I KNEW I LOVED YOU ▲⁴**	Columbia 6683102
01/04/2000	14	6		CRASH AND BURN	Columbia 6690442
29/07/2000	8	10		**AFFIRMATION**	Columbia 6696882
25/11/2000	16	7		HOLD ME	Columbia 6706032
31/03/2001	35	3		THE BEST THING	Columbia 6709852

TELLY SAVALAS
US singer/actor (born Aristotle Savalas, 21/1/1925, New York); he was in his late 30s when he became an actor, first on TV and then in films, before returning to TV where he created the detective *Kojak*. He died from cancer on 22/1/1994 and has a star on the Hollywood Walk of Fame.

22/02/1975	❶²	9	○	IF	MCA 174
31/05/1975	47	3		YOU'VE LOST THAT LOVIN' FEELIN'	MCA 189

SAVANA
Reggae singer (born in Jamaica; based in London).

24/07/2004	48	1		PRETTY LADY	Jetstar JECDS1805

SAVANNA
UK vocal group formed by Joe Williams.

10/10/1981	61	4		I CAN'T TURN AWAY	R&B RBS 203

SAVUKA – see JOHNNY CLEGG AND SAVUKA

SAW DOCTORS
Irish rock group formed in Tuam, County Galway in 1987 by Leo Moran (vocals), Davy Corton (guitar/vocals), John 'Turps' Burke (mandolin/vocals), Pierce Doherty (bass) and John Donnelly (drums). Tony Lambert joined on keyboards in 1993 and later won £1 million on the Irish lottery.

12/11/1994	24	3		SMALL BIT OF LOVE	Shamtown SAW 001CD
27/01/1996	15	3		WORLD OF GOOD	Shamtown SAW 002CD
13/07/1996	14	2		TO WIN JUST ONCE Inspired by Tony Lambert's win on the Irish national lottery	Shamtown SAW 004CD
06/12/1997	56	1		SIMPLE THINGS	Shamtown SAW 006CD
01/06/2002	31	1		THIS IS ME	Shamtown SAW 012CD

NITIN SAWHNEY FEATURING ESKA
UK singer/producer who created *Secret Asians* with Sanjeev Bhaskar for BBC Radio and co-devised *Goodness Gracious Me*. He was named Best World Music Act at the 2001 MOBO Awards.

28/07/2001	65	1		SUNSET	V2 VVR 5016768

SAXON
UK heavy rock group formed in Yorkshire in 1977 by Peter 'Biff' Byford (born 5/1/1951, vocals), Paul Quinn (guitar), Graham Oliver (guitar), Steve Lawson (bass) and Pete Gill (drums). Gill left in 1980, replaced by Nigel Glockler.

22/03/1980	20	11		WHEELS OF STEEL	Carrere CAR 143
21/06/1980	13	9		747 (STRANGERS IN THE NIGHT)	Carrere CAR 151
28/06/1980	64	2		BACKS TO THE WALL	Carrere HM 6
28/06/1980	66	2		BIG TEASER/RAINBOW THEME	Carrere HM 5
29/11/1980	63	3		STRONG ARM OF THE LAW	Carrere CAR 170
11/04/1981	12	8		AND THE BANDS PLAYED ON	Carrere CAR 180
18/07/1981	18	6		NEVER SURRENDER	Carrere CAR 204
31/10/1981	57	3		PRINCESS OF THE NIGHT	Carrere CAR 208
23/04/1983	32	5		POWER AND THE GLORY	Carrere SAXON 1
30/07/1983	50	3		NIGHTMARE	Carrere CAR 284
31/08/1985	75	1		BACK ON THE STREETS	Parlophone R 6103
29/03/1986	71	1		ROCK 'N' ROLL GYPSY	Parlophone R 6112

30/08/1986	66	2		WAITING FOR THE NIGHT	EMI 5575
05/03/1988	52	4		RIDE LIKE THE WIND	EMI EM 43
30/04/1988	71	1		I CAN'T WAIT ANYMORE	EMI EM 54

AL SAXON UK singer (born Allan Fowler) who later sang with Doug Sheldon. He also sang the theme to the Peter Sellers film *I'm All Right Jack*.

16/01/1959	17	4		YOU'RE THE TOP CHA	Fontana H 164
28/08/1959	24	3		ONLY SIXTEEN	Fontana H 205
22/12/1960	39	2		BLUE-EYED BOY	Fontana H 278
07/09/1961	48	1		THERE I'VE SAID IT AGAIN	Piccadilly 7N 35011

LEO SAYER UK singer (born Gerard Hugh Sayer, 21/5/1948, Shoreham-by-Sea); he formed Jester in 1972, later changing the name to Patches. Songwriting with David Courtney the same year, they penned Roger Daltrey's solo debut before Sayer launched his own career under the guidance of Adam Faith. He later had his own BBC TV series. Groove Generation are a UK production duo.

15/12/1973	2	13	●	THE SHOW MUST GO ON	Chrysalis CHS 2023
15/06/1974	6	9		ONE MAN BAND	Chrysalis CHS 2045
14/09/1974	4	9		LONG TALL GLASSES	Chrysalis CHS 2052
30/08/1975	2	8	○	MOONLIGHTING	Chrysalis CHS 2076
30/10/1976	2	12	○	YOU MAKE ME FEEL LIKE DANCING ▲[1] 1977 Grammy Award for Best Rhythm & Blues Song for writers Leo Sayer and Vinnie Poncia. Featured in the films *Slap Shot* (1977) and *Charlie's Angels* (2000)	Chrysalis CHS 2119
29/01/1977	●[3]	13	●	WHEN I NEED YOU ▲[1]	Chrysalis CHS 2127
09/04/1977	10	8		HOW MUCH LOVE	Chrysalis CHS 2140
10/09/1977	22	8		THUNDER IN MY HEART	Chrysalis CHS 2163
16/09/1978	6	11	○	I CAN'T STOP LOVIN' YOU (THOUGH I TRY)	Chrysalis CHS 2240
25/11/1978	21	10		RAINING IN MY HEART	Chrysalis CHS 2277
05/07/1980	2	11	○	MORE THAN I CAN SAY	Chrysalis CHS 2442
13/03/1982	10	9		HAVE YOU EVER BEEN IN LOVE	Chrysalis CHS 2596
19/06/1982	22	10		HEART (STOP BEATING IN TIME)	Chrysalis CHS 2616
12/03/1983	16	8		ORCHARD ROAD	Chrysalis CHS 2677
15/10/1983	51	3		TILL YOU COME BACK TO ME	Chrysalis LEO 01
08/02/1986	54	4		UNCHAINED MELODY	Chrysalis LEO 3
13/02/1993	65	2		WHEN I NEED YOU	Chrysalis CDCHS 3926
08/08/1998	32	3		YOU MAKE ME FEEL LIKE DANCING THE GROOVE GENERATION FEATURING LEO SAYER	Brothers Organisation CDBRUV 8

ALEXEI SAYLE UK singer/comedian (born 7/8/1952, Liverpool); he has had his own TV series and appeared in a number of films, including *Gorky Park*, *Indiana Jones And The Last Crusade* and *Siesta*.

25/02/1984	15	8		'ULLO JOHN GOT A NEW MOTOR?	Island IS 162

SCAFFOLD UK group formed in Liverpool by John Gorman (born 4/1/1937, Liverpool), Roger McGough (born 9/11/1937, Liverpool) and Mike McGear (born Michael McCartney, 7/1/1944, Liverpool). McGear was later revealed to be Paul McCartney's younger brother. McGough was awarded an OBE in the 1996 New Year's Honours list. Gorman was later a member of the Four Bucketeers.

22/11/1967	4	12		THANK U VERY MUCH	Parlophone R 5643
27/03/1968	34	5		DO YOU REMEMBER	Parlophone R 5679
06/11/1968	●[4]	24		LILY THE PINK Reclaimed #1 position on 8/1/1969	Parlophone R 5734
01/11/1969	38	12		GIN GAN GOOLIE	Parlophone R 5812
01/06/1974	7	9		LIVERPOOL LOU	Warner Brothers K 16400

BOZ SCAGGS US singer (born William Royce Scaggs, 8/6/1944, Ohio); he joined Steve Miller's band the Marksmen in 1959. He later formed Wigs which disbanded while on tour in Europe: Scaggs headed for Sweden and recorded his debut solo album, only available in Sweden. He returned to America in 1967, signing solo with Atlantic in 1969. After one album he switched to CBS.

30/10/1976	28	4		LOWDOWN 1976 Grammy Award for Best Rhythm & Blues Song for writers Boz Scaggs and David Paich. Featured in the 1977 film *Looking For Mr Goodbar*	CBS 4563
22/01/1977	10	10		WHAT CAN I SAY	CBS 4869
14/05/1977	13	9		LIDO SHUFFLE Featured in the 1978 film *F.M.*	CBS 5136
10/12/1977	33	8		HOLLYWOOD	CBS 5836

SCANTY SANDWICH UK producer Richard Marshall.

29/01/2000	3	8		BECAUSE OF YOU Contains a sample of Michael Jackson's *Shoo-Be-Doo-Be-Doo-Da-Day*	Southern Fried ECB 18CDS

SCARFACE US rapper (born Brad Jordan, 9/11/1969, Houston, TX) who is also a member of the Getto Boys.

11/03/1995	41	2		HAND OF THE DEAD BODY SCARFACE FEATURING ICE CUBE	Virgin America VUSCD 88
05/08/1995	55	2		I SEEN A MAN DIE	Virgin America VUSCD 94
05/07/1997	34	2		GAME OVER Contains a sample of Indeep's *Last Night A DJ Saved MY Life*	Virgin VUSCD 121

SCARFO UK group fronted by Jamie Hince. They split in 1999, Hince forming the Impresario Records label and recording as Fiji.

19/07/1997	61	1		ALKALINE	Deceptive BLUFF 044CD
18/10/1997	67	1		COSMONAUT NO. 7	Deceptive BLUFF 053CD

● [9] Number of weeks single topped the UK chart   ↑ Entered the UK chart at #1   ▲[9] Number of weeks single topped the US chart

SCARLET UK duo Joe Youle (keyboards) and Cheryl Parker (vocals). The Hull school friends began writing songs together at sixteen.

21/01/1995	12	12	INDEPENDENT LOVE SONG	WEA YZ 820CD
29/04/1995	21	4	I WANNA BE FREE (TO BE WITH HIM)	WEA YZ 913CD
05/08/1995	54	1	LOVE HANGOVER	WEA YZ 969CD
06/07/1996	54	1	BAD GIRL	WEA 046CD

SCARLET FANTASTIC UK group formed by Maggie De Monde (keyboards/vocals), Robert Shaw (guitar/vocals) and Rick Jones (guitar/keyboards). De Monde and Shaw had previously been in Swans Way.

03/10/1987	24	10	NO MEMORY	Arista RIS 36
23/01/1988	67	2	PLUG ME IN (TO THE CENTRAL LOVE LINE)	Arista 109693

SCARLET PARTY UK group formed by Graham Dye (guitar/vocals), Mark Gilmour (guitar), Steve Dye (keyboards/bass/vocals) and Sean Heaphy (drums). Their debut hit was intended as a Beatles' soundalike on the 20th anniversary of the release of *Love Me Do*.

16/10/1982	44	5	101 DAM-NATIONS	Parlophone R 6058

SCATMAN JOHN US singer (born John Larkin, 13/3/1942, El Monte, CA) who used his stutter as the basis for his first hit. He is now a resident in Britain.

13/05/1995	3	12	O	SCATMAN (SKI-BA-BOP-BA-DOP-BOP)	RCA 74321281712
02/09/1995	10	7		SCATMAN'S WORLD	RCA 74321289952

SCENT Italian/UK production and vocal group formed by Daniele Davoli and Andrea Mazzali with singer Miss Motif (born Mandy Darcy). Davoli was previously responsible for Black Box while Mazzali had been a member of Flickman.

21/08/2004	23	3	UP AND DOWN	Positiva CDTIVS209

MICHAEL SCHENKER GROUP German/UK heavy metal group formed by Michael Schenker (born 10/1/1955, Savstedt, Germany), with a fluctuating line-up. Schenker had previously been the founder of The Scorpions and briefly a member of UFO before forming the Michael Schenker Group. He later shortened the group's name to MSG.

13/09/1980	53	3	ARMED AND READY	Chrysalis CHS 2455
08/11/1980	56	3	CRY FOR THE NATIONS	Chrysalis CHS 2471
11/09/1982	52	3	DANCER	Chrysalis CHS 2636

LALO SCHIFRIN Argentinean orchestra leader (born Boris Schifrin, 21/6/1932, Buenos Aires); he joined Dizzy Gillespie's quintet in 1958 and relocated to Los Angeles, CA. He became a top film and TV theme composer and signed with CTI in 1976. He has won four Grammy Awards: Best Original Jazz Composition in 1964 for *The Cat*, Best Original Jazz Composition in 1965 for *Jazz Suite On The Mass Texts* and Best Instrumental Theme and Best Original Score in 1967 for *Mission Impossible Theme*. He has a star on the Hollywood Walk of Fame.

09/10/1976	14	9	JAWS Jazz-funk version of the theme to the film of the same name	CTI CTSP 005
25/10/1997	36	2	BULLITT Featured in the 1968 film of the same name, revived via a Ford cars advertisement with footage from the film	Warner. esp WESP 002CD

SCHILLER German production duo Christopher Von Deylen and Mirko Von Schlieffen.

28/04/2001	17	3	DAS GLOCKENSPIEL	Data 22CDS

PETER SCHILLING German singer (born 28/1/1956, Stuttgart).

05/05/1984	42	6	MAJOR TOM (COMING HOME)	PSP/WEA X 9438

SCHOOL OF ROCK US group formed by the cast of the film *School Of Rock*, led by Jack Black as Dewey Finn. Black is also a member of Tenacious D.

21/02/2004	51	2	SCHOOL OF ROCK Featured in the 2003 film *School Of Rock*	Atlantic AT 0172CD

PHILIP SCOFIELD UK singer (born 1962, Manchester); he was a children's TV presenter before going into musicals.

05/12/1992	27	6	CLOSE EVERY DOOR	Really Useful RUR 11

SCIENCE DEPARTMENT FEATURING ERIRE UK production duo Danny Howells and female singer Erire.

10/11/2001	64	1	BREATHE	Renaissance RENCDS 010

SCIENTIST UK producer Phil Sebastiene.

06/10/1990	62	3	THE EXORCIST	Kickin KICK 1
01/12/1990	46	3	THE EXORCIST (REMIX)	Kickin KICK 1TR
15/12/1990	47	6	THE BEE	Kickin KICK 35
11/05/1991	74	1	SPIRAL SYMPHONY	Kickin KICK 5

SCISSOR SISTERS US rock group formed in New York City by Jake Shears (vocals), Ana Mantronic (vocals), Babydaddy (keyboards/bass), Del Marquis (guitar), Derek G (guitar) and Paddy Boom (drums).

08/11/2003	54	2	LAURA	Polydor 9812788
31/01/2004	10	7	**COMFORTABLY NUMB**	Polydor 9815883
10/04/2004	17	6	TAKE YOUR MAMA	Polydor 9866277
19/06/2004	12	10	LAURA Re-issue of Polydor 9812788	Polydor 9866833
23/10/2004	14	6	MARY	Polydor 9868282

SCOOBIE
UK group formed by Ewan 'Big Euri' Gallagher (vocals), Lisa Lane (keyboards), Ziggi De Beers (guitars), Stanton Drew (tambourine) and Diamond Whitey (Svengali).

22/12/2001	58	2		THE MAGNIFICENT 7 Song is a tribute to Celtic football player Henrik Larsson	Big Tongue BTR 001CDS
01/06/2002	71	1		THE MAGNIFICENT 7 (REMIX)	Big Tongue BTR 001CDSX

SCOOCH
UK vocal group formed by Natalie Powers (born 26/7/1977, Birmingham), Caroline Barnes (born 15/4/1979, Leeds), Russ Spencer (born 1/3/1980, Bournemouth) and David Ducasse (born 3/11/1978, South Shields).

06/11/1999	29	4		WHEN MY BABY	Accolade CDACS 002
22/01/2000	5	5		**MORE THAN I NEEDED TO KNOW**	Accolade CDACS 003
06/05/2000	12	5		THE BEST IS YET TO COME	Accolade CDAC 004
05/08/2000	15	6		FOR SURE	Accolade CDACS 005

SCOOTER
UK/German rock group formed in Hamburg by HP Baxter, Rick Jordan and Ferris Bueller as Celebrate The Nun before name-changing to Scooter. Bueller left in 1998, and was replaced by Axel Cohn.

21/10/1995	23	4		MOVE YOUR ASS	Club Tools 0061675 CLU
17/02/1996	18	3		BACK IN THE UK	Club Tools 0061955 CLU
25/05/1996	30	2		REBEL YELL	Club Tools 0062575 CLU
19/10/1996	33	3		I'M RAVING	Club Tools 0063015 CLU
17/05/1997	45	2		FIRE	Club Tools 0060005 CLU
22/06/2002	2	15	●	**THE LOGICAL SONG**	Sheffield Tunes 0139295 STU
21/09/2002	4	9		**NESSAJA**	Sheffield Tunes 0142165 STU
07/12/2002	15	7		POSSE (I NEED YOU ON THE FLOOR)	Sheffield Tunes 0143775 STU
05/04/2003	12	10		WEEKEND	Sheffield Tunes 0147315 STU
05/07/2003	16	5		THE NIGHT	Sheffield Tunes 0149005 STU
18/10/2003	16	4		MARIA (I LIKE IT LOUD) **SCOOTER VS MARC ACARDIPANE AND DICK RULES**	Sheffield Tunes 0151135 STU
10/07/2004	48	1		JIGGA JIGGA	All Around The World CXGLOBE 348

SCORPIONS
German heavy rock group formed in Hanover in 1971 by Klaus Meine (born 25/5/1948, Hanover, vocals), Rudolf Schenker (born 31/8/1948, Hildesheim, guitar), Michael Schenker (born 10/1/1955, Savstedt, guitar) and Rudy Lenners (drums). By 1980 the line-up was Meine, Rudolf Schenker, Mathias Jabs (born 25/10/1955, Hanover, guitar), Francis Bucholz (born 19/1/1950, bass) and Herman Rarebell (born 18/11/1949, Lubeck, drums). By 1999 James Kottak (born 26/12/1962, Louisville, KY) was drummer. One-time member Ulrich Roth later formed Electric Sun, while Michael Schenker formed the Michael Schenker Group.

26/05/1979	39	4		IS THERE ANYBODY THERE/ANOTHER PIECE OF MEAT	Harvest HAR 5185
25/08/1979	69	2		LOVEDRIVE	Harvest HAR 5188
31/05/1980	72	2		MAKE IT REAL	Harvest HAR 5206
20/09/1980	75	1		THE ZOO	Harvest HAR 5212
03/04/1982	64	4		NO ONE LIKE YOU	Harvest HAR 5219
17/07/1982	63	2		CAN'T LIVE WITHOUT YOU	Harvest HAR 5221
04/06/1988	59	2		RHYTHM OF LOVE	Harvest HAR 5240
18/02/1989	74	1		PASSION RULES THE GAME	Harvest HAR 5242
01/06/1991	53	3		WIND OF CHANGE	Vertigo VER 54
28/09/1991	2	9	○	**WIND OF CHANGE** Re-issue of Vertigo VER 54	Vertigo VER 58
30/11/1991	27	5		SEND ME AN ANGEL	Vertigo VER 60

SCOTLAND WORLD CUP SQUAD
UK vocal group. Like their English counterparts, the Scottish football team has made records to capitalise on appearances in the World Cup. Also like England, they have had more success on the charts than on the field!

22/06/1974	20	4		EASY EASY	Polydor 2058 452
27/05/1978	4	6		**OLE OLA (MULHER BRASILEIRA) ROD STEWART FEATURING THE SCOTTISH WORLD CUP FOOTBALL SQUAD**	Riva 15
01/05/1982	5	9		**WE HAVE A DREAM**	WEA K 19145
09/06/1990	45	3		SAY IT WITH PRIDE This and above single credited to **SCOTTISH WORLD CUP SQUAD**	RCA PB 43791
15/06/1996	16	5		PURPLE HEATHER **ROD STEWART WITH THE SCOTTISH EURO '96 SQUAD** Official anthem of the Scottish 1996 European Championship football squad, in aid of the Dunblane Appeal (launched after Thomas Hamilton shot and killed fourteen children, their teacher and himself on 13/3/1996 in Dunblane)	Warner Brothers W 0354CD

JACK SCOTT
Canadian singer (born Jack Scafone Jr, 28/1/1936, Windsor, Ontario); he moved to Michigan in 1946 and made his first recordings for ABC-Paramount in 1957. He later set up Ponie Records and recorded country material.

10/10/1958	9	10		**MY TRUE LOVE**	London HLU 8626
25/09/1959	30	1		THE WAY I WALK	London HLL 8912
10/03/1960	11	15		WHAT IN THE WORLD'S COME OVER YOU	Top Rank JAR 280
02/06/1960	32	2		BURNING BRIDGES Featured in the 1970 film *Kelly's Heroes*	Top Rank JAR 375

JAMIE SCOTT
UK soul singer (born 12/2/1983, Rowtown, Surrey).

04/09/2004	29	2		JUST	Sony Music 6752282

JILL SCOTT
US soul singer (born 13/4/1972, Philadelphia, PA).

04/11/2000	30	3		GETTIN' IN THE WAY	Epic 6705272
07/04/2001	54	1		A LONG WALK	Epic 6710382
06/11/2004	59	1		GOLDEN	Epic 6751772

❶⁹ Number of weeks single topped the UK chart ↑ Entered the UK chart at #1 ▲⁹ Number of weeks single topped the US chart

703

JOEY SCOTT — see CHAD KROEGER FEATURING JOEY SCOTT

LINDA SCOTT
US singer (born Linda Joy Sampson, 1/6/1945, Queens, NYC); she sang on Arthur Godfrey's radio show in the late 1950s and co-hosted the TV show *Where The Action Is*.

DATE	POS	WKS	SINGLE TITLE	LABEL & NUMBER
18/05/1961	7	13	I'VE TOLD EVERY LITTLE STAR	Columbia DB 4638
14/09/1961	50	1	DON'T BET MONEY HONEY	Columbia DB 4692

MIKE SCOTT
UK singer/multi-instrumentalist (born 14/12/1958, Edinburgh, Scotland); he was a founder member of The Waterboys in 1981 and launched a parallel solo career in 1995.

DATE	POS	WKS	SINGLE TITLE	LABEL & NUMBER
16/09/1995	56	1	BRING 'EM ALL IN	Chrysalis CDCHS 5025
11/11/1995	60	1	BUILDING THE CITY OF LIGHT	Chrysalis CDCHS 5026
27/09/1997	50	1	LOVE ANYWAY	Chrysalis CDCHS 5064
14/02/1998	74	1	RARE, PRECIOUS AND GONE	Chrysalis CDCHS 5073

MILLIE SCOTT
US R&B singer (born Savannah, GA).

DATE	POS	WKS	SINGLE TITLE	LABEL & NUMBER
12/04/1986	52	4	PRISONER OF LOVE	Fourth & Broadway BRW 45
23/08/1986	56	3	AUTOMATIC	Fourth & Broadway BRW 51
21/02/1987	63	4	EV'RY LITTLE BIT	Fourth & Broadway BRW 58

SIMON SCOTT
UK singer (born Darjeeling, India) who came to Britain in 1962. His debut hit also featured The LeRoys.

DATE	POS	WKS	SINGLE TITLE	LABEL & NUMBER
13/08/1964	37	8	MOVE IT BABY	Parlophone R 5164

TONY SCOTT
Dutch rapper.

DATE	POS	WKS	SINGLE TITLE	LABEL & NUMBER
15/04/1989	48	4	THAT'S HOW I'M LIVING/THE CHIEF TONI SCOTT	Champion CHAMP 97
10/02/1990	63	2	GET INTO IT/THAT'S HOW I'M LIVING	Champion CHAMP 232

SCOTT AND LEON
UK dance/production duo Scott Anderson and Leon McCormack. The vocals on their second hit were by Sylvia Mason-James. They also record as Deep Cover.

DATE	POS	WKS	SINGLE TITLE	LABEL & NUMBER
30/09/2000	19	4	YOU USED TO HOLD ME	AM:PM CDAMPM 137
19/05/2001	34	2	SHINE ON	AM:PM CDAMPM 143

LISA SCOTT-LEE
UK singer (born 5/11/1975). A founding member of Steps, she went solo when they disbanded in 2002.

DATE	POS	WKS	SINGLE TITLE	LABEL & NUMBER
24/05/2003	6	8	LATELY	Fontana 9800295
20/09/2003	11	4	TOO FAR GONE	Fontana 9811643
04/12/2004	23	3	GET IT ON INTENSO PROJECT FEATURING LISA SCOTT-LEE	Inspired INSPMOS1CDS

SCOTTISH RUGBY TEAM WITH RONNIE BROWNE
UK rugby team singers.

DATE	POS	WKS	SINGLE TITLE	LABEL & NUMBER
02/06/1990	73	1	FLOWER OF SCOTLAND	Greentrax STRAX 1001

SCREAMING BLUE MESSIAHS
UK rock group formed by Bill Carter (guitar/vocals), Kenny Harris (drums) and Chris Thompson (bass). The group disbanded in 1989, Thompson and Harris going on to form Lerue.

DATE	POS	WKS	SINGLE TITLE	LABEL & NUMBER
16/01/1988	28	6	I WANNA BE A FLINTSTONE	WEA YZ 166

SCREAMING TREES
US rock group formed in Ellensburg, WA by Gary Lee Connor (guitar), his brother Van Connor (bass), Mark Lanegan (vocals) and Mark Pickerell (drums). Pickerell was later replaced by Barrett Martin, while Lanegan later recorded solo.

DATE	POS	WKS	SINGLE TITLE	LABEL & NUMBER
06/03/1993	50	1	NEARLY LOST YOU Tracks on EP: *E.S.K., Song Of A Baker* and *Winter Song*	Epic 6582372
01/05/1993	52	1	DOLLAR BILL	Epic 6591792

SCRITTI POLITTI
UK group formed in Leeds in 1977 by Green Gartside (born Green Strohmeyer-Gartside, 22/6/1956, Cardiff, vocals), Niall Jinks (bass) and Tom Morley (drums). Debuting in 1979 on their own St Pancras label, after a spell with Rough Trade they signed with Virgin in 1983 with the group now consisting of Green, David Gamson (keyboards) and Fred Maher (drums).

DATE	POS	WKS	SINGLE TITLE	LABEL & NUMBER
21/11/1981	64	3	THE SWEETEST GIRL	Rough Trade RT 091
22/05/1982	56	4	FAITHLESS	Rough Trade RT 101
07/08/1982	43	5	ASYLUMS IN JERUSALEM/JACQUES DERRIDA	Rough Trade RT 111
10/03/1984	10	12	WOOD BEEZ (PRAY LIKE ARETHA FRANKLIN)	Virgin VS 657
09/06/1984	17	9	ABSOLUTE	Virgin VS 680
17/11/1984	68	2	HYPNOTIZE	Virgin VS 725
11/05/1985	6	12	THE WORD GIRL SCRITTI POLITTI FEATURING RANKING ANN	Virgin VS 747
07/09/1985	48	5	PERFECT WAY	Virgin VS 780
07/05/1988	13	9	OH PATTI (DON'T FEEL SORRY FOR LOVERBOY) Features the uncredited contribution of Miles Davis	Virgin VS 1006
27/08/1988	63	3	FIRST BOY IN THIS TOWN (LOVE SICK)	Virgin VS 1082
12/11/1988	55	3	BOOM! THERE SHE WAS SCRITTI POLITTI FEATURING ROGER	Virgin VS 1143
16/03/1991	20	7	SHE'S A WOMAN SCRITTI POLITTI FEATURING SHABBA RANKS	Virgin VS 1333
03/08/1991	47	3	TAKE ME IN YOUR ARMS AND LOVE ME SCRITTI POLITTI AND SWEETIE IRIE	Virgin VS 1346
31/07/1999	46	1	TINSELTOWN TO THE BOOGIEDOWN	Virgin VSCDT 1731

EARL SRUGGS — see LESTER FLATT AND EARL SCRUGGS

SCUMFROG
Dutch producer Jesse Houk (born in Amsterdam) who also records as Dutch.

○ Silver disc ● Gold disc ✪ Platinum disc (additional platinum units are indicated by a figure following the symbol) ◉ Singles released prior to 1973 that are known to have sold over 1 million copies in the UK

11/05/2002.....41......1.......				LOVING THE ALIEN **SCUMFROG VS DAVID BOWIE** Contains a sample of David Bowie's *Loving The Alien* .... Positiva CDTIV 172
31/05/2003.....46......2.......				MUSIC REVOLUTION.. Positiva CDTIV 191

SEA FRUIT UK group formed in 1998 by Geoff Barradale (vocals), Alan Smyth (guitars), Joe Newman (keyboards), Stuarty Doughty (drums) and Tom Hogg (images).

24/07/1999.....59......1.......	HELLO WORLD.. Electric Canyon ECCD 3055

SEA LEVEL US group formed by Chuck Leavell (keyboards/vocals), Jimmy Nalls (guitar), Davis Causey (guitar), Randall Bramblett (saxophone), Lamar Williams (bass) and George Weaver (drums). Weaver left in 1978, replaced by Joe English.

17/02/1979.....63......4.......	FIFTY-FOUR .... Capricorn POSP 28

SEAFOOD UK group formed in London by David Line (guitar/vocals), Kev Penny (guitar/vocals), Kevin Hendrick (bass/vocals) and Caroline Banks (drums/vocals).

28/07/2001.....71......1.......	CLOAKING.. Infectious INFEC 103CDS
01/05/2004.....65......1.......	GOOD REASON.. Cooking Vinyl FRYCD189

SEAHORSES UK rock group formed by Chris Helme (born 22/7/1971, York, guitar), John Squire (born 24/11/1962, Manchester, guitar), Stuart Fletcher (born 16/1/1976, York, bass) and Andy Watts (drums). Ex-Stone Roses Squire denied any significance in the name being an anagram of 'he hates roses'!! He disbanded the group after their debut album and went solo.

10/05/1997 .....3......7.......	**LOVE IS THE LAW** .... Geffen GFSTD 22243
26/07/1997 .....7......7.......	**BLINDED BY THE SUN** .... Geffen GFSTD 22266
11/10/1997.....16......4.......	LOVE ME AND LEAVE ME .... Geffen GFSTD 22292
13/12/1997.....15......8.......	YOU CAN TALK TO ME.. Geffen GFSTD 22297

SEAL UK singer (born Sealhenry Samuel, 19/2/1963, Paddington, London) who spent nearly ten years recording demos before meeting Adamski and co-writing *Killer*, a UK #1. On the strength of this he was signed by ZTT as a solo artist in 1990. He was the big winner at the 1992 BRITs ceremony with three awards including Best Album (*Seal*) and Best British Male. He also collected an International Achievement Award at the 1996 MOBO Awards.

08/12/1990 .....2......15......O	**CRAZY** 1992 BRIT Award for Best Video. Featured in the 1994 film *Naked In New York* .... ZTT ZANG 8
04/05/1991.....12......6.......	FUTURE LOVE EP Tracks on EP: *Future Love Paradise, A Minor Groove* and *Violet* .... ZTT ZANG 11
20/07/1991.....24......6.......	THE BEGINNING .... ZTT ZANG 21
16/11/1991 .....8......8.......	**KILLER (EP)** Tracks on EP: *Killer, Hey Joe* and *Come See What Love Has Done. Killer* featured in 1992 film *Gladiator*............
	.... ZTT ZANG 23
29/02/1992.....39......2.......	VIOLET.. ZTT ZANG 27
21/05/1994.....14......5.......	PRAYER FOR THE DYING .... ZTT ZANG 51CD
30/07/1994.....20......5.......	KISS FROM A ROSE .... ZTT ZANG 52CD1
05/11/1994.....45......2.......	NEWBORN FRIEND .... ZTT ZANG 58CD
15/07/1995 .....4......13......O	**KISS FROM A ROSE/I'M ALIVE** ▲[1] A-side re-issued after featuring in the 1995 film *Batman Forever*. 1996 Grammy Awards for Best Pop Vocal Performance, Record of the Year and Song of the Year for writer Seal .... ZTT ZANG 70CD
09/12/1995.....51......2.......	DON'T CRY/PRAYER FOR THE DYING.. ZTT ZANG 75CD
29/03/1997.....13......5.......	FLY LIKE AN EAGLE Featured in the 1996 film *Space Jam* .... ZTT ZEAL 1CD
14/11/1998.....50......1.......	HUMAN BEINGS .... Warner Brothers W 464CD
12/10/2002 .....6......8.......	**MY VISION JAKATTA FEATURING SEAL** .... Rulin 26CDS
20/09/2003.....25......3.......	GET IT TOGETHER .... Warner Brothers W 620CD
22/11/2003.....68......1.......	LOVE'S DIVINE.. Warner Brothers W 629CD

JAY 'SINISTER' SEALEE – see LOUIE VEGA

JAY SEAN UK singer (born 1982, Hounslow) who was originally a member of Compulsive Disorder and then attended medical school until 2003 when he left for a musical career.

20/09/2003.....12......5.......	DANCE WITH YOU (NACHNA TERE NAAL) **RISHI RICH PROJECT FEATURING JAY SEAN** .... Relentless RELCD1
03/07/2004 .....6......10	**EYES ON YOU JAY SEAN FEATURING RISHI RICH PROJECT**.. Relentless RELDX5
06/11/2004 .....4......6.......	**STOLEN** .... Relentless RELDX11

SEARCHERS UK group formed in Liverpool in 1961 by John McNally (born 30/8/1941, Liverpool, guitar/vocals), Mike Pender (born Michael Prendergast, 3/3/1942, Liverpool, guitar/vocals), Tony Jackson (born 16/7/1940, Liverpool, vocals/bass) and Norman McGarry (drums), with McGarry replaced by Chris Curtis (born Christopher Crummy, 26/8/1941, Oldham) in 1962. Jackson left in 1964, replaced by ex-Rebel Rousers Frank Allen (born Francis McNeice, 14/12/1943, Hayes), Curtis left in 1966, initially replaced by John Blunt (born 28/3/1947, Croydon), Blunt later replaced by Billy Adamson. Pender left in 1985 to form Mike Pender's Searchers (prompting a legal battle), replaced by Spencer James. Fred Nightingale, who is credited with penning *Sugar And Spice*, is none other than Tony Hatch writing under a pseudonym. Jackson died on 20/8/2003.

27/06/1963 ...O[2]......16	**SWEETS FOR MY SWEET** Featured in the 1988 film *Buster*... Pye 7N 15533
10/10/1963.....48......2......	SWEET NOTHINS .... Phillips BF 1274
24/10/1963 .....2......13	**SUGAR AND SPICE** Featured in the 1988 film *Good Morning Vietnam*................................... Pye 7N 15566
16/01/1964 ...O[3]......15	**NEEDLES AND PINS**.. Pye 7N 15594
16/04/1964 ...O[2]......11	**DON'T THROW YOUR LOVE AWAY** .... Pye 7N 15630
16/07/1964.....11......8.......	SOMEDAY WE'RE GONNA LOVE AGAIN .... Pye 7N 15670
17/09/1964 .....3......12	**WHEN YOU WALK IN THE ROOM** .... Pye 7N 15694
03/12/1964.....13......11	WHAT HAVE THEY DONE TO THE RAIN .... Pye 7N 15739

O[9] Number of weeks single topped the UK chart ↑ Entered the UK chart at #1 ▲[9] Number of weeks single topped the US chart

705

04/03/1965 ..... 4 ...... 11	GOODBYE MY LOVE	Pye 7N 15794
08/07/1965 ..... 12 ...... 10	HE'S GOT NO LOVE	Pye 7N 15878
14/10/1965 ..... 35 ...... 3	WHEN I GET HOME	Pye 7N 15950
16/12/1965 ..... 20 ...... 8	TAKE ME FOR WHAT I'M WORTH	Pye 7N 15992
21/04/1966 ..... 31 ...... 6	TAKE IT OR LEAVE IT	Pye 7N 17094
13/10/1966 ..... 48 ...... 2	HAVE YOU EVER LOVED SOMEBODY	Pye 7N 17170

SEASHELLS UK vocal group.

09/09/1972 ..... 32 ...... 5	MAYBE I KNOW	CBS 8218

SEB UK keyboard player.

18/02/1995 ..... 61 ...... 1	SUGAR SHACK	React CDREACT 50

SEBADOH US group formed in 1989 by Lou Barlow (guitar/bass/vocals), Jason Loewenstein (bass/guitar/vocals) and Bob Fay (drums). Fay left in 1998 and was replaced by Russ Pollard.

27/07/1996 ..... 74 ...... 1	BEAUTY OF THE RIDE	Domino RUG 47CD
30/01/1999 ..... 30 ...... 3	FLAME	Domino RUG 80CD1

JON SECADA US singer/songwriter (born Juan Secada, 4/10/1963, Havana, Cuba); he was raised in Miami, where he moved to in 1971 aged eight. First known as a songwriter, he penned six songs for Gloria Estefan, touring with her as a backing singer. He has a masters degree in jazz from Miami University. He has won two Grammy Awards: Best Latin Pop Album in 1992 for *Otro Dia Mas Sin Verte* and Best Latin Pop Performance in 1995 for *Amor*.

18/07/1992 ..... 5 ...... 15 ...... ○	JUST ANOTHER DAY	SBK 35
31/10/1992 ..... 30 ...... 4	DO YOU BELIEVE IN US	SBK 37
06/02/1993 ..... 23 ...... 5	ANGEL	SBK CDSBK 39
17/07/1993 ..... 30 ...... 4	DO YOU REALLY WANT ME	SBK CDSBK 41
16/10/1993 ..... 50 ...... 2	I'M FREE	SBK CDSBK 44
14/05/1994 ..... 39 ...... 5	IF YOU GO	SBK CDSBK 51
04/02/1995 ..... 44 ...... 2	MENTAL PICTURE Featured in the 1995 film *The Specialist*	SBK CDSBK 54
16/12/1995 ..... 51 ...... 4	IF I NEVER KNEW YOU (LOVE THEME FROM 'POCAHONTAS') JON SECADA AND SHANICE Featured in the 1995 film *Pocahontas*	Walt Disney WD 7023C
14/06/1997 ..... 43 ...... 1	TOO LATE, TOO SOON	SBK CDSBK 57

SECCHI FEATURING ORLANDO JOHNSON Italian/US vocal/instrumental duo Stefano Secchi and Orlando Johnson.

04/05/1991 ..... 46 ...... 3	I SAY YEAH	Epic 6568467

HARRY SECOMBE UK singer (born 8/9/1921, Swansea) who formed the Goons with Spike Milligan, Peter Sellers and Michael Bentine in 1949 and began his recording career in 1952. He later became presenter of the religious programme *Highway* on TV. He was appointed a CBE in 1963 and knighted in 1981. He died from cancer on 11/4/2001.

09/12/1955 ..... 16 ...... 3	ON WITH THE MOTLEY	Philips PB 523
03/10/1963 ..... 18 ...... 17	IF I RULED THE WORLD	Philips BF 1261
23/02/1967 ..... 2 ...... 15	THIS IS MY SONG	Philips BF 1539

SECOND CITY SOUND UK instrumental group formed by ex-Overlanders Dave Walsh, later adding singer Jeannie Darren.

20/01/1966 ..... 22 ...... 7	TCHAIKOVSKY ONE	Decca F 12310
02/04/1969 ..... 43 ...... 1	DREAM OF OLWEN	Major Minor MM 600

SECOND IMAGE UK soul group formed in London by Simon Eyre (guitar), Weston Foster (guitar), Ozie Selcuck (guitar), Junior Bromfield (bass), Rem Fiori (keyboards), Frank Burke (trumpet) and Tom 'Zoot' Heritage (saxophone/flute). Bromfield and Burke designed their own skateboards and also represented Britain at the sport.

24/07/1982 ..... 60 ...... 2	STAR	Polydor POSP 457
02/04/1983 ..... 67 ...... 2	BETTER TAKE TIME	Polydor POSP 565
26/11/1983 ..... 68 ...... 2	DON'T YOU	MCA 848
11/08/1984 ..... 53 ...... 3	SING AND SHOUT	MCA 882
02/02/1985 ..... 65 ...... 2	STARTING AGAIN	MCA 936

SECOND PHASE US production duo Joey Beltram and Mundo Muzique.

21/09/1991 ..... 48 ...... 2	MENTASM	R&S RSUK 2

SECOND PROTOCOL UK production duo Justin Fry and Brian Johnson.

23/09/2000 ..... 58 ...... 2	BASSLICK	East West 216CD

SECOND SUN – see PAUL VAN DYK

SECRET AFFAIR UK mod revival group formed by Ian Page (vocals/trumpet/piano), David Cairns (guitar/vocals), Dennis Smith (bass/vocals) and Seb Shelton (drums). They also set up the I-Spy label. Shelton left in 1980, replaced by Paul Bultitude, although the group disbanded after a further two singles.

01/09/1979 ..... 13 ...... 10	TIME FOR ACTION	I-Spy SEE 1
10/11/1979 ..... 32 ...... 6	LET YOUR HEART DANCE	I-Spy SEE 3

DATE	POS	WKS	BPI	SINGLE TITLE	LABEL & NUMBER
08/03/1980	16	9		MY WORLD	I-Spy SEE 5
23/08/1980	45	5		SOUND OF CONFUSION	I-Spy SEE 8
17/10/1981	57	4		DO YOU KNOW	I-Spy SEE 10

SECRET KNOWLEDGE UK/US duo producer Kris Needs and female singer Wonder.

DATE	POS	WKS	BPI	SINGLE TITLE	LABEL & NUMBER
27/04/1996	66	1		LOVE ME NOW	Deconstruction 74321342432
24/08/1996	75	1		SUGAR DADDY	Deconstruction 74321400242

SECRET LIFE UK dance group with Paul Bryant and Andy Throup, with Steve Anderson and Greg Bone added on their second hit.

DATE	POS	WKS	BPI	SINGLE TITLE	LABEL & NUMBER
12/12/1992	45	4		AS ALWAYS	Cowboy 7RODEO 9
07/08/1993	38	2		LOVE SO STRONG	Cowboy RODEO 18CD
07/05/1994	63	1		SHE HOLDS THE KEY	Pulse 8 CDLOSE 58
29/10/1994	70	1		I WANT YOU	Pulse 8 CDLOSE 71
28/01/1995	37	2		LOVE SO STRONG (REMIX)	Pulse 8 CDLOSE 79

SECRET MACHINES US rock group formed in Dallas, TX in 2000 by Brandon Curtis (bass/vocals), his brother Benjamin (drums) and Josh Garza (guitar/vocals).

DATE	POS	WKS	BPI	SINGLE TITLE	LABEL & NUMBER
07/08/2004	49	1		NOWHERE AGAIN	Reprise W648CD

SECRETARY OF ENTERTAINMENT – see RAZE

SECTION-X French instrumental duo Francois Cribier and Patrice Pezet.

DATE	POS	WKS	BPI	SINGLE TITLE	LABEL & NUMBER
08/03/1997	42	1		ATLANTIS	Perfecto PERF 136CD

NEIL SEDAKA US singer (born 13/3/1939, Brooklyn, NYC); he began writing with Howard Greenfield in 1952 and was a member of the original Tokens in 1955. He began his own record career in 1957 with Legion, still writing for other artists, and signed with RCA in 1958. His US popularity revived in the 1970s with Elton John's Rocket label. He has a star on the Hollywood Walk of Fame.

DATE	POS	WKS	BPI	SINGLE TITLE	LABEL & NUMBER
24/04/1959	9	13		I GO APE	RCA 1115
13/11/1959	3	17		OH CAROL Tribute to singer/songwriter Carole King (she in turn wrote a song entitled *Oh Neil*)	RCA 1152
14/04/1960	8	15		STAIRWAY TO HEAVEN	RCA 1178
01/09/1960	45	3		YOU MEAN EVERYTHING TO ME	RCA 1198
02/02/1961	8	14		CALENDAR GIRL	RCA 1220
18/05/1961	9	12		LITTLE DEVIL	RCA 1236
21/12/1961	3	18		HAPPY BIRTHDAY SWEET SIXTEEN	RCA 1266
19/04/1962	23	11		KING OF CLOWNS	RCA 1282
19/07/1962	7	16		BREAKING UP IS HARD TO DO ▲[2]	RCA 1298
22/11/1962	29	4		NEXT DOOR TO AN ANGEL	RCA 1319
30/05/1963	42	3		LET'S GO STEADY AGAIN	RCA 1343
07/10/1972	19	14		OH CAROL/BREAKING UP IS HARD TO DO/LITTLE DEVIL Re-issue of RCA 1152, RCA 1298 and RCA 1236	RCA Maximillion 2259
04/11/1972	43	3		BEAUTIFUL YOU	RCA 2269
24/02/1973	18	10		THAT'S WHEN THE MUSIC TAKES ME	RCA 2310
02/06/1973	26	9		STANDING ON THE INSIDE	MGM 2006 267
25/08/1973	31	8		OUR LAST SONG TOGETHER	MGM 2006 307
09/02/1974	34	6		A LITTLE LOVIN'	Polydor 2058 434
22/06/1974	15	9		LAUGHTER IN THE RAIN ▲[1]	Polydor 2058 494
22/03/1975	35	5		THE QUEEN OF 1964	Polydor 2058 546

MAX SEDGLEY UK producer/drummer who performed with the likes of Roni Size, King Kooba, Organic Audio and Noel McKoy before going solo.

DATE	POS	WKS	BPI	SINGLE TITLE	LABEL & NUMBER
17/07/2004	30	3		HAPPY	Sunday Best SBESTC14

SEDUCTION US vocal group formed in New York City by April Harris, Idalis Leon and Michelle Visage (born 20/9/1968, NYC). Visage later worked with Cliville & Coles.

DATE	POS	WKS	BPI	SINGLE TITLE	LABEL & NUMBER
21/04/1990	75	1		HEARTBEAT	Breakout USA 685

SEEKERS Australian group formed in Melbourne in the early 1960s by Judith Durham (born 3/7/1943, Melbourne, lead vocals), Keith Potger (born 2/3/1941, Colombo, Sri Lanka, guitar), Bruce Woodley (born 25/7/1942, Melbourne, Spanish guitar) and Athol Guy (born 5/1/1940, Victoria, bass). They disbanded in 1968 and Potger formed the New Seekers, although he wasn't in the group.

DATE	POS	WKS	BPI	SINGLE TITLE	LABEL & NUMBER
07/01/1965	❶[2]	23		I'LL NEVER FIND ANOTHER YOU	Columbia DB 7431
15/04/1965	3	18		A WORLD OF OUR OWN	Columbia DB 7532
28/10/1965	❶[3]	17	◎	THE CARNIVAL IS OVER	Columbia DB 7711

❶[9] Number of weeks single topped the UK chart ↑ Entered the UK chart at #1 ▲[9] Number of weeks single topped the US chart

	DATE	POS	WKS	BPI	SINGLE TITLE	LABEL & NUMBER
	24/03/1966	11	11		SOMEDAY ONE DAY	Columbia DB 7867
	08/09/1966	10	12		**WALK WITH ME**	Columbia DB 8000
	24/11/1966	2	15		**MORNINGTOWN RIDE**	Columbia DB 8060
	23/02/1967	3	11		**GEORGY GIRL** Featured in the 1966 film *Georgy Girl*	Columbia DB 8134
	20/09/1967	11	12		WHEN WILL THE GOOD APPLES FALL	Columbia DB 8273
	13/12/1967	50	1		EMERALD CITY	Columbia DB 8313

SEELENLUFT FEATURING MICHAEL SMITH Swiss producer Beat Soler.

	DATE	POS	WKS	BPI	SINGLE TITLE	LABEL & NUMBER
	04/10/2003	70	1		MANILA	Back Yard BACK 10CSC1

BOB SEGER AND THE SILVER BULLET BAND US singer (born 6/5/1945, Dearborn, MI); he joined the Omens in 1964, first recording under his own name in 1966. He formed the Silver Bullet Band in 1975 with Drew Abbott (guitar), Robyn Robbins (keyboards), Alto Reed (saxophone), Chris Campbell (bass) and Charlie Allen Martin (drums). Campbell would be the only member to remain with the Silver Bullet Band for the next twenty years as they underwent personnel changes. The group won the 1980 Grammy Award for Best Rock Vocal Performance by a Group for *Against The Wind* and has a star on the Hollywood Walk of Fame. He was inducted into the Rock & Roll Hall of Fame in 2003.

	DATE	POS	WKS	BPI	SINGLE TITLE	LABEL & NUMBER
	30/09/1978	42	6		HOLLYWOOD NIGHTS	Capitol CL 16004
	03/02/1979	41	6		WE'VE GOT TONITE	Capitol CL 16028
	24/10/1981	49	3		HOLLYWOOD NIGHTS Live recording	Capitol CL 223
	06/02/1982	60	4		WE'VE GOT TONITE Live recording	Capitol CL 235
	09/04/1983	73	2		EVEN NOW	Capitol CL 284
	28/01/1995	22	5		WE'VE GOT TONIGHT Re-issue of Capitol CL 16028	Capitol CDCLS 734
	29/04/1995	45	2		NIGHT MOVES	Capitol CDCL 741
	29/07/1995	52	1		HOLLYWOOD NIGHTS Re-issue of Capitol CL 16004	Capitol CDCL 749
	10/02/1996	57	1		LOCK AND LOAD	Capitol CDCL 765

SHEA SEGER US singer (born 1981, Quitman, TX).

	DATE	POS	WKS	BPI	SINGLE TITLE	LABEL & NUMBER
	05/05/2001	47	1		CLUTCH	RCA 74321828142

SEIKO AND DONNIE WAHLBERG Japanese female singer with former New Kids On The Block member Donnie Wahlberg (born 17/8/1969, Dorchester, MA). Seiko is married to Japanese actor Masaki Kanda.

	DATE	POS	WKS	BPI	SINGLE TITLE	LABEL & NUMBER
	18/08/1990	44	5		THE RIGHT COMBINATION	Epic 6562037

SELECTER UK ska group formed in Coventry in 1979 by Noel Davis (guitar), Prince Rimshot (born John Bradbury, drums) and Barry Jones (trombone). Following the success of their first record (B-side to The Specials debut), a touring group was assembled featuring Davis, Pauline Black (vocals), Crompton Amanor (drums), Charles Bainbridge (drums), Gappa Hendricks (keyboards), Desmond Brown (keyboards) and Charlie Anderson (bass), with Rico Rodriguez also appearing on their debut album. Black later recorded solo and hosted the children's TV show *Hold Tight*. The group re-formed in 1990.

	DATE	POS	WKS	BPI	SINGLE TITLE	LABEL & NUMBER
	13/10/1979	8	9		**ON MY RADIO**	2 Tone CHSTT 4
	02/02/1980	16	6		THREE MINUTE HERO	2 Tone CHSTT 8
	29/03/1980	23	8		MISSING WORDS	2 Tone CHSTT 10
	23/08/1980	36	5		THE WHISPER	Chrysalis CHS 1

SELENA VS X MEN UK singer with a production duo.

	DATE	POS	WKS	BPI	SINGLE TITLE	LABEL & NUMBER
	14/07/2001	61	1		GIVE IT UP	Go Beat GOBCD 40

SELFISH C**T UK duo Martin Tomlinson (vocals) and Patrick Constable (guitar). Their name was spelt out in full on both the charts and their single.

	DATE	POS	WKS	BPI	SINGLE TITLE	LABEL & NUMBER
	17/07/2004	66	1		AUTHORITY CONFRONTATION	Horseglue UHU008

PETER SELLERS UK comedian/actor (born Richard Henry Sellers, 8/9/1925, Southsea); he was a member of The Goons who later had international success as Inspector Clouseau in the *Pink Panther* series of films. He died from a heart attack on 24/7/1980.

	DATE	POS	WKS	BPI	SINGLE TITLE	LABEL & NUMBER
	02/08/1957	17	11		ANY OLD IRON	Parlophone R 4337
	10/11/1960	4	14		**GOODNESS GRACIOUS ME** Inspired by (but not in) the1961 Peter Sellers/Sophia Loren film *The Millionairess*	Parlophone R 4702
	12/01/1961	22	5		BANGERS AND MASH This and above single credited to **PETER SELLERS AND SOPHIA LOREN**	Parlophone R 4724
	23/12/1965	14	7		A HARD DAY'S NIGHT	Parlophone R 5393
	27/11/1993	52	2		A HARD DAY'S NIGHT Re-issue of Parlophone R 5393	EMI CDEMS 293

MICHAEL SEMBELLO US singer/guitarist (born 17/4/1954, Philadelphia, PA) who was first known as a session guitarist, working with the likes of Stevie Wonder, David Sanborn and Donna Summer.

	DATE	POS	WKS	BPI	SINGLE TITLE	LABEL & NUMBER
	20/08/1983	43	6		MANIAC ▲² Featured in the 1983 film *Flashdance*	Casablanca CAN 1017

SEMISONIC US group formed in Minnesota in 1993 by Dan Wilson (guitar/vocals), John Munson (bass) and Jake Slichter (drums).

	DATE	POS	WKS	BPI	SINGLE TITLE	LABEL & NUMBER
	10/07/1999	13	11		SECRET SMILE	MCA MCSTD 40210
	06/11/1999	25	5		CLOSING TIME	MCA MCDXD 40221
	01/04/2000	39	2		SINGING IN MY SLEEP	MCA MCSTD 40227
	03/03/2001	35	2		CHEMISTRY	MCA MCSTD 40248

SEMPRINI UK pianist Fernando Riccardo Alberto Semprini who died on 4/2/1982.

○ Silver disc ● Gold disc ✪ Platinum disc (additional platinum units are indicated by a figure following the symbol) ◉ Singles released prior to 1973 that are known to have sold over 1 million copies in the UK

16/03/1961.....25......8...... THEME FROM 'EXODUS' ....HMV POP 842

SENSELESS THINGS
UK rock group formed by Mark Keds (guitar/vocals), Morgan Nicholls (bass) and Cass 'Cade' Browne (drums) as the Psychotics, changing their name in 1986. By 1987 Nicholls had switched to bass, Ben Harding taking over on guitar.

22/06/1991.....73......1......	EVERYBODY'S GONE ....Epic 6569807
28/09/1991.....50......3......	GOT IT AT THE DELMAR ....Epic 6574497
11/01/1992.....18......4......	EASY TO SMILE ....Epic 6576957
11/04/1992.....19......4......	HOLD IT DOWN ....Epic 6579267
05/12/1992.....52......2......	HOMOPHOBIC ASSHOLE ....Epic 6588337
13/02/1993.....41......2......	PRIMARY INSTINCT ....Epic 6589402
12/06/1993.....69......1......	TOO MUCH KISSING ....Epic 6592502
05/11/1994.....56......1......	CHRISTINE KEELER ....Epic 6609572
28/01/1995.....57......1......	SOMETHING TO MISS ....Epic 6611162

SENSER
UK group formed in London in 1987 by Heitham Al-Sayed (raps/vocals/percussion), Nick Michaelson (guitar), Andy 'Awe' (DJ), Haggis (engineer), James Barrett (bass), John Morgan (drums) and Kersten Haigh (vocals/flute).

25/09/1993.....47......1......	THE KEY ....Ultimate TOPP 019CD
19/03/1994.....39......2......	SWITCH ....Ultimate TOPP 022CD
23/07/1994.....52......1......	AGE OF PANIC ....Ultimate TOPP 027CD
17/08/1996.....42......1......	CHARMING DEMONS ....Ultimate TOPP 045CD

NICK SENTIENCE – see BK

SEPULTURA
Brazilian heavy metal group formed in 1984 by Max Cavalera (born 4/8/1969, Belo Horizonte, guitar/vocals), Jairo T (guitar), Paolo Jr (born Paulo Xisto Pinto Jr, 30/4/1969, Belo Horizonte, bass) and Igor Cavalera (born 4/9/1970, Belo Horizonte, drums). Jairo left in 1987, replaced by Andreas Kisser (born 24/8/1968, San Bernado Do Campo). Their name is Portuguese for 'grave'. Cavalera later formed Soulfly.

02/10/1993.....66......2......	TERRITORY ....Roadrunner RR 23823
26/02/1994.....51......2......	REFUSE-RESIST ....Roadrunner RR 23773
04/06/1994.....46......2......	SLAVE NEW WORLD ....Roadrunner RR 23745
24/02/1996.....19......2......	ROOTS BLOODY ROOTS ....Roadrunner RR 23205
17/08/1996.....23......2......	RATAMAHATTA ....Roadrunner RR 23145
14/12/1996.....46......2......	ATTITUDE ....Roadrunner RR 22995

SERAFIN
UK group formed by Ben Fox (guitar/vocals), Darryn Harkness (guitar/vocals), Ben Ellis (bass) and Ronny Growler (drums).

17/05/2003.....49......1......	THINGS FALL APART ....Taste Media TMCDSX 5003
16/08/2003.....49......1......	DAY BY DAY ....Taste Media TMCDSX 5006

SERAPHIM SUITE
UK production group formed by Ricard Berg, Jeremy Healy (born 18/1/1962, Woolwich, London) and Amos Pizzey with singer Monie Love.

27/03/2004.....45......2...... HEART ....Inferno CDFERN61

SERIAL DIVA
UK production group fronted by singer Chantelle Phillips.

18/01/1997.....57......1......	KEEP HOPE ALIVE ....Sound Of Ministry SOMCD 26
15/05/1999.....32......2......	PEARL RIVER THREE 'N' ONE PRESENTS JOHNNY SHAKER FEATURING SERIAL DIVA ....Low Sense SENSECD 24

SERIOUS DANGER
UK producer Richard Phillips.

20/12/1997.....40......3......	DEEPER ....Fresh FRSHD 68
02/05/1998.....54......1......	HIGH NOON ....Fresh FRSHD 69

SERIOUS INTENTION
UK vocal/instrumental group formed by Anthony Molloy and Paul Simpson.

16/11/1985.....75......1......	YOU DON'T KNOW (OH-OH-OH) ....Important TAN 8
05/04/1986.....51......5......	SERIOUS ....Pow Wow LON 93

SERIOUS ROPE
UK vocal/production group formed by Damon Rochefort and Sharon Dee Clarke, both of whom had previously been in Nomad. Clarke was later a member of Six Chix.

22/05/1993.....54......2......	HAPPINESS SERIOUS ROPE PRESENTS SHARON DEE CLARKE ....Rumour RUMACD 64
01/10/1994.....70......1......	HAPPINESS – YOU MAKE ME HAPPY (REMIX) ....Mercury MERCD 407

ERICK SERMON
US singer (born 25/11/1968, Brentwood, NY) who was previously a member of EPMD with Parrish Smith (their name was an acronym for Erick and Parrish Making Dollars) before going solo in 1993.

06/10/2001.....36......2......	MUSIC ERICK SERMON FEATURING MARVIN GAYE Featured in the 2001 film What's The Worst That Could Happen? ....Polydor 4976222
11/01/2003.....14......5......	REACT ERICK SERMON FEATURING REDMAN ....J Records 74321988492
19/04/2003.....72......1......	LOVE IZ Contains samples of Al Green's Love And Happiness and Run DMC's Here We Go ....J Records 82876510971

SERTAB
Turkish singer (born Sertab Erener, 1964, Istanbul); she represented Turkey in the Eurovision Song Contest twice (1989 and 1990) before winning the contest in 2003, beating Britain's entry by Jemini into last place.

21/06/2003.....72......1...... EVERY WAY THAT I CAN The song won the 2003 Eurovision Song Contest ....Columbia 6739621

❶⁹ Number of weeks single topped the UK chart ↑ Entered the UK chart at #1 ▲⁹ Number of weeks single topped the US chart

709

SET THE TONE UK vocal/instrumental group formed by Chris Morgan, Kenneth Hyslop and Robert Paterson.

22/01/1983.....62......2.......	DANCE SUCKER..Island WIP 6836
26/03/1983.....67......2.......	RAP YOUR LOVE...Island IS 110

SETTLERS UK vocal/instrumental studio group.

16/10/1971.....36......5....... THE LIGHTNING TREE Theme to the children's TV programme *Follyfoot* ....York SYK 505

BRIAN SETZER ORCHESTRA US singer/guitarist (born 10/4/1959, Long Island, NY), previously in The Stray Cats. Three Grammies include Best Pop Instrumental Performance for *Sleepwalk* and Best Pop Instrumental Performance for *Caravan* in 2000.

03/04/1999.....34......3....... JUMP JIVE AN' WAIL 1998 Grammy Award for Best Pop Group Performance ....Interscope IND 95601

TAJA SEVELLE US singer/DJ (born Minneapolis, MN) discovered by Prince. After her debut album she moved to Los Angeles, CA and wrote with Burt Bacharach, Thom Bell and Nile Rodgers. By 1999 she was working with RJ Rice and was signed to 550 Music.

20/02/1988.....7......9.......	LOVE IS CONTAGIOUS..Paisley Park W 8257
14/05/1988.....59......4.......	WOULDN'T YOU LOVE TO LOVE ME...Paisley Park W 8127

702 US vocal group formed in Las Vegas, NV by Kameelah Williams, Irish Grinstead and her sister Lemisha Grinstead. The group's name is derived from the Las Vegas area telephone code.

14/12/1996.....41......2.......	STEELO...Motown 8606072
29/11/1997.....59......1.......	NO DOUBT...Motown 8607052
07/08/1999.....22......4.......	WHERE MY GIRLS AT?...Motown TMGCD 1500
27/11/1999.....36......3.......	YOU DON'T KNOW...Motown TMGCD 1502

740 BOYZ US duo Winston Rosa and Eddie Rosa.

04/11/1995.....54......1.......	SHIMMY SHAKE..MCA MCSTD 40002
22/03/2003.....28......2.......	SHAKE YA SHIMMY **PORN KINGS VERSUS FLIP & FILL FEATURING 740 BOYZ**.................All Around The World CXGLOBE 213

SEVEN GRAND HOUSING AUTHORITY UK producer Terence Parker.

23/10/1993.....70......1....... THE QUESTION...Olympic ELYCD 010

7669 US vocal group formed in New York City by Big Ang, Thicknezz, El-Boog-E and Shorti 1 Forti.

18/06/1994.....60......1....... JOY...Motown TMGCD 1429

7TH HEAVEN UK vocal group; their follow-up was *Hanky Panky*.

14/09/1985.....47......5....... HOT FUN..Mercury MER 199

SEVERINE French singer who won the 1971 Eurovision Song Contest at the age of 21 representing Monaco, beating Britain's entry by Clodagh Rodgers into fourth place.

24/04/1971......9......11...... UN BANC, UN ARBRE, UNE RUE The song won the 1971 Eurovision Song Contest ....Philips 6009 135

DAVID SEVILLE US singer (born Ross Bagdasarian, 27/1/1919, Fresno, CA); he moved to Los Angeles in 1950 and later appeared in a number of films. He created the Chipmunks and also scored as Alfi & Harry. Numerous Grammy Awards include Best Comedy Performance and Best Recording for Children in 1958 for *The Chipmunk Song* and Best Recording For Children in 1960 for *Let's All Sing With The Chipmunks*. He died from a heart attack on 16/1/1972.

23/05/1958.....11......6....... WITCH DOCTOR ▲[3]..London HLU 8619

JANETTE SEWELL – see **DOUBLE TROUBLE**

SEX CLUB FEATURING BROWN SUGAR US vocal/instrumental duo from Chicago, IL, DJ Pepe and Amos Smith.

28/01/1995.....67......1....... BIG DICK MAN Answer record to 20 Fingers' *Small Dick Man*...................................Club Tools CLU 60775

SEX-O-LETTES – see **DISCO TEX AND THE SEX-O-LETTES**

SEX-O-SONIQUE UK dance group formed by producers Mike Gray and Jon Pearn. They also recorded as Arizona, Hustlers Convention, Full Intention, Disco Tex Presents Cloudburst and Ronaldo's Revenge.

06/12/1997.....32......3....... I THOUGHT IT WAS YOU..ffrr FCD 321

SEX PISTOLS UK punk rock group assembled in 1973 by manager Malcom McLaren with Paul Cook (born 20/7/1956, London, drums), Steve Jones (born 3/5/1955, London, guitar) and Glen Matlock (born 27/8/1956, London, bass) as the Swankers. After one gig they disbanded, but McLaren re-formed them, added Johnny Rotten (born John Lydon, 31/1/1956, London, vocals) and changed their name to the Sex Pistols in 1975. Signed by EMI in October 1976 for a £40,000 advance, they were dropped by the company in January 1977 after only one single as a result of their interview on the early evening TV show *Today* when, goaded by presenter Bill Grundy, they launched into an outburst of swearing. The following month Sid Vicious (born John Ritchie, 10/5/1957, London) replaced Matlock. They were signed by A&M on 10th March for a £75,000 advance. After protests by other acts on the label (most notably Rick Wakeman), they were dropped by A&M on 16th March without releasing a record, although copies of *God Save The Queen* were pressed. They were signed by Virgin in May 1977 for £15,000 advance. Their Virgin debut, *God Save The Queen*, was released on Jubilee Day. They disbanded in 1978 with Rotten forming Public Image Ltd. Vicious died from a drug overdose on 2/2/1979 while on bail for murdering his girlfriend Nancy Spungen (though recent evidence suggests that they may have been the victims of a robbery).

○ Silver disc ● Gold disc ✪ Platinum disc (additional platinum units are indicated by a figure following the symbol) ◉ Singles released prior to 1973 that are known to have sold over 1 million copies in the UK

The group re-formed in 1996 for a world tour. Ronald Biggs (born 8/8/1929) achieved notoriety as a member of the Great Train Robbery gang of 1963. He was sentenced to 30 years in prison, but escaped from Wandsworth Prison on 8/7/1965, surfacing in Brazil. He gave himself up on 7/5/2001 after 35 years on the run.

18/12/1976.....38......4....... ANARCHY IN THE U.K. Withdrawn by EMI after they dropped the group, the record had sold 55,000 copies .... EMI 2566

04/06/1977 .....2......9......O **GOD SAVE THE QUEEN** It was claimed that the single sold more copies than the #1 by Rod Stewart (*I Don't Want To Talk About It/First Cut Is The* Deepest) on the week of 11/6/1977, but was deliberately marked down to #2. The sleeve to the single was adjudged to be the best sleeve of all time by *Q* magazine in 2001 .... Virgin VS 181

09/07/1977 .....6......8......O **PRETTY VACANT** .... Virgin VS 184

22/10/1977 .....8......6....... **HOLIDAYS IN THE SUN** .... Virgin VS 191

08/07/1978 .....7......10...... **NO ONE IS INNOCENT/MY WAY** SEX PISTOLS, PUNK PRAYER BY RONALD BIGGS The A-side was to have been entitled *Cosh The Driver* but Virgin Records objected .... Virgin VS 220

03/03/1979 .....3......12.....O **SOMETHING ELSE/FRIGGIN' IN THE RIGGIN'** .... Virgin VS 240

07/04/1979 .....6......8......O **SILLY THING** Flip side was *Who Killed Bambi* by TEN POLE TUDOR... Virgin VS 256

30/06/1979 .....3......9......O **C'MON EVERYBODY** .... Virgin VS 272

13/10/1979 .....21......6...... THE GREAT ROCK 'N' ROLL SWINDLE Flip side was *Rock Around The Clock* by TEN POLE TUDOR. This and above four singles featured in the 1980 film *The Great Rock 'N' Roll Swindle* which starred The Sex Pistols......................... Virgin VS 290

14/06/1980.....21......8...... (I'M NOT YOUR) STEPPING STONE .... Virgin VS 339

03/10/1992.....33......3...... ANARCHY IN THE UK Re-issue of EMI 2566... Virgin VS 1431

05/12/1992.....56......2...... PRETTY VACANT Re-issue of Virgin VS 184. .... Virgin VS 1448

27/07/1996.....18......3...... PRETTY VACANT (LIVE) Recorded at Finsbury Park on 23/6/1996.............................. Virgin VUSCD 113

08/06/2002.....15......3...... GOD SAVE THE QUEEN Re-issue of Virgin VS 181. The single was originally released to coincide with Queen Elizabeth II's Silver Jubilee and was re-issued to coincide with the Golden Jubilee... Virgin VSCDT 1832

RON SEXSMITH – see ALEX CUBA BAND FEATURING RON SEXSMITH

DENNY SEYTON AND THE SABRES UK vocal/instrumental group formed by Denny Seyton (born Brian Tarr, vocals), John Francis (guitar), Dave Maher (guitar), John Boyle (bas) and Bernie Rogers (drums).

17/09/1964.....48......1....... THE WAY YOU LOOK TONIGHT .... Mercury MF 824

SFX UK instrumental/production group formed by Ian Richardson, Nicholas Coler, Hubert Humphrey and Bryan Johnston. Their debut hit was inspired by the computer game Lemmings 2 – The Tribes.

15/05/1993.....51......3....... LEMMINGS... Parlophone CDR 6343

SFX BOYS CHOIR – see FARM

SHABOOM UK instrumental/production group with Mark Bell, Ben Davi, Dick Johnson and Paul Birchall and US singer Taka Boom on lead vocals.

31/07/1999.....64......1....... SWEET SENSATION .... WEA 218CD1

SHACK UK vocal/instrumental group formed in 1988 by Michael Head (vocals) with brother John (guitar). Shortly after finishing their second album, *Waterpistol*, the studio where it was recorded (Star Street in London) burned to the ground and the master tapes destroyed. A DAT copy was found, the album appearing four years later in 1995, by which time the group had disbanded and Michael Head had formed Strands. He revived Shack in 1999 with his brother John, Ren Perry (bass) and Iain Templeton (drums).

26/06/1999.....44......1...... COMEDY .... London LONCD 427

14/08/1999.....63......1...... NATALIE'S PARTY... London LONCD 436

11/03/2000.....67......1...... OSCAR .... London LONCD 445

04/10/2003.....63......1...... BYRDS TURN TO STONE .... North Country NCCDB 002

SHADES US vocal group formed by Monique Peoples, Danielle Andrews, Tiffanie Cardwell and Shannon Walker Williams. The four first got together while at university in Boston, MA.

12/04/1997.....31......2...... MR BIG STUFF QUEEN LATIFAH, SHADES AND FREE .... Motown 5736572

20/09/1997.....75......1...... SERENADE .... Motown 8606892

SHADES OF LOVE US instrumental/production duo Johnny Vicious and Junior Vasquez with keyboard player Gomi.

22/04/1995.....64......1...... KEEP IN TOUCH (BODY TO BODY) .... Vicious Muzik MUZCD 102

SHADES OF RHYTHM UK production/instrumental group formed by Kevin Lancaster, Nick Slater and Rayan Hepburn.

02/02/1991.....53......3...... HOMICIDE/EXORCIST.. ZTT ZANG 13

13/04/1991.....54......4...... SWEET SENSATION... ZTT ZANG 18

20/07/1991.....35......5...... THE SOUND OF EDEN... ZTT ZANG 22

30/11/1991.....16......7...... EXTACY .... ZTT ZANG 24

20/02/1993.....61......1...... SWEET REVIVAL (KEEP IT COMIN'). .... ZTT ZANG 40CD

11/09/1993.....37......3...... THE SOUND OF EDEN Re-issue of ZTT ZANG 22............................... ZTT ZANG 44CD

05/11/1994.....55......1...... THE WANDERING DRAGON .... Public Demand PPDCD 5

21/06/1997.....57......1...... PSYCHO BASE .... Coalition CRUM 002CD

❶⁹ Number of weeks single topped the UK chart ↑ Entered the UK chart at #1 ▲⁹ Number of weeks single topped the US chart

711

SHADOWS UK group formed in 1960 by Hank Marvin (born Brian Rankin, 28/10/1941, Newcastle-upon-Tyne, lead guitar), Bruce Welch (born Bruce Cripps, 2/11/1941, Bognor Regis, rhythm guitar), Jet Harris (born Terence Harris, 6/7/1939, London, bass) and Tony Meehan (born Daniel Meehan, 2/3/1943, London) as The Drifters. The withdrawal of the record (*Feelin' Fine*) from the US market was forced by an injunction placed by the US R&B group The Drifters. The (UK) Drifters' second US release was credited the Four Jets but prompted a name-change to The Shadows. Meehan left in 1961, replaced by Brian Bennett (born 9/2/1940, London). Harris left in 1962, initially replaced by Brian 'Liquorice' Locking, who left in 1963 to become a Jehovah's Witness and was replaced by John Rostill (born 16/6/1942, Birmingham). They disbanded in 1968, re-forming on a number of occasions with Marvin, Welch, Bennett and John Farrar. Rostill died on 26/11/1973 after being accidentally electrocuted while playing guitar in his home studio. Welch discovered the body when he arrived to continue writing songs with Rostill. Bennett and Welch were awarded OBEs in the 2004 Queen's Birthday Honours List.

DATE	POS	WKS	BPI	SINGLE TITLE	LABEL & NUMBER
12/09/1958	2	17		**MOVE IT**	Columbia DB 4178
21/11/1958	7	10		**HIGH CLASS BABY**	Columbia DB 4203
30/01/1959	20	6		LIVIN' LOVIN' DOLL	Columbia DB 4249
08/05/1959	10	9		**MEAN STREAK**	Columbia DB 4290
15/05/1959	21	2		NEVER MIND	Columbia DB 4290
10/07/1959	●[6]	23		**LIVING DOLL** Featured in the films *Serious Charge* (1959) and *The Young Ones* (1961).	Columbia DB 4306
09/10/1959	●[5]	17		**TRAVELLIN' LIGHT**	Columbia DB 4351
09/10/1959	16	4		DYNAMITE B-side to *Travellin' Light*. This and all above singles credited to **CLIFF RICHARD AND THE DRIFTERS**	Columbia DB 4351
15/01/1960	14	7		EXPRESSO BONGO EP Tracks on EP: *Love, A Voice In The Wilderness, The Shrine On The Second Floor* and *Bongo Blues*	Columbia SEG 7971
22/01/1960	2	16		**A VOICE IN THE WILDERNESS**	Columbia DB 4398
24/03/1960	2	15		**FALL IN LOVE WITH YOU**	Columbia DB 4431
30/06/1960	●[3]	18		**PLEASE DON'T TEASE** This and above three singles credited to **CLIFF RICHARD AND THE SHADOWS**	Columbia DB 4479
21/07/1960	●[5]	21		**APACHE** Featured in the films *Baby Love* (1968) and *Scandal* (1988).	Columbia DB 4484
22/09/1960	3	12		**NINE TIMES OUT OF TEN** CLIFF RICHARD AND THE SHADOWS	Columbia DB 4506
10/11/1960	5	15		**MAN OF MYSTERY/THE STRANGER**	Columbia DB 4530
01/12/1960	●[2]	16		**I LOVE YOU** CLIFF RICHARD AND THE SHADOWS	Columbia DB 4547
09/02/1961	6	19		**F.B.I.**	Columbia DB 4580
02/03/1961	3	14		**THEME FOR A DREAM**	Columbia DB 4593
30/03/1961	4	14		**GEE WHIZ IT'S YOU** This and above single credited to **CLIFF RICHARD AND THE SHADOWS**	Columbia DC 756
11/05/1961	3	20		**FRIGHTENED CITY** Featured in the 1961 film *Frightened City*	Columbia DB 4637
22/06/1961	3	14		**A GIRL LIKE YOU** CLIFF RICHARD AND THE SHADOWS	Columbia DB 4667
07/09/1961	●[1]	12		**KON-TIKI**	Columbia DB 4698
16/11/1961	10	8		**THE SAVAGE** Featured in the 1961 film *The Young Ones*	Columbia DB 4726
11/01/1962	●[6]	21	◎	**THE YOUNG ONES ↑** CLIFF RICHARD AND THE SHADOWS Featured in the 1961 film *The Young Ones*	Columbia DB 4761
01/03/1962	●[8]	19		**WONDERLAND**	Columbia DB 4790
10/05/1962	2	17		**I'M LOOKING OUT THE WINDOW/DO YOU WANNA DANCE** CLIFF RICHARD AND THE SHADOWS	Columbia DB 4828
02/08/1962	4	15		**GUITAR TANGO**	Columbia DB 4870
06/09/1962	2	12		**IT'LL BE ME**	Columbia DB 4886
06/12/1962	●[3]	18		**THE NEXT TIME/BACHELOR BOY** Featured in the 1962 film *Summer Holiday*. This and above single credited to **CLIFF RICHARD AND THE SHADOWS**	Columbia DB 4950
13/12/1962	●[1]	15		**DANCE ON!** *Dance On!* Replaced *The Next Time/Bachelor Boy* by Cliff Richard and The Shadows at #1	Columbia DB 4948
21/02/1963	●[3]	18		**SUMMER HOLIDAY** Reclaimed #1 position on 4/4/1963. Featured in the 1962 film *Summer Holiday*	Columbia DB 4977
07/03/1963	●[1]	16		**FOOT TAPPER** Featured in the 1962 film *Summer Holiday*. *Foot Tapper* replaced *Summer Holiday* by Cliff Richard and The Shadows at #1. A week later, *Summer Holiday* returned to #1	Columbia DB 4984
09/05/1963	4	15		**LUCKY LIPS** CLIFF RICHARD AND THE SHADOWS	Columbia DB 7034
06/06/1963	2	17		**ATLANTIS**	Columbia DB 7047
19/09/1963	6	12		**SHINDIG**	Columbia DB 7106
07/11/1963	2	14		**DON'T TALK TO HIM** CLIFF RICHARD AND THE SHADOWS	Columbia DB 7150
05/12/1963	11	12		GERONIMO	Columbia DB 7163
06/02/1964	8	10		**I'M THE LONELY ONE** CLIFF RICHARD AND THE SHADOWS	Columbia DB 7203
05/03/1964	12	10		THEME FOR YOUNG LOVERS	Columbia DB 7231
07/05/1964	5	14		**THE RISE AND FALL OF FLINGEL BUNT**	Columbia DB 7261
02/07/1964	7	13		**ON THE BEACH** CLIFF RICHARD AND THE SHADOWS	Columbia DB 7305
03/09/1964	22	7		RHYTHM AND GREENS	Columbia DB 7342
03/12/1964	17	10		GENIE WITH THE LIGHT BROWN LAMP	Columbia DB 7416
10/12/1964	9	11		**I COULD EASILY FALL** CLIFF RICHARD AND THE SHADOWS	Columbia DB 7420
11/02/1965	17	10		MARY ANNE	Columbia DB 7476
10/06/1965	19	7		STINGRAY	Columbia DB 7588
05/08/1965	10	10		**DON'T MAKE MY BABY BLUE**	Columbia DB 7650
19/08/1965	22	8		THE TIME IN BETWEEN CLIFF RICHARD AND THE SHADOWS	Columbia DB 7660
25/11/1965	18	9		WAR LORD Featured in the 1965 film *War Lord*	Columbia DB 7769
17/03/1966	22	5		I MET A GIRL	Columbia DB 7853
24/03/1966	15	9		BLUE TURNS TO GREY CLIFF RICHARD AND THE SHADOWS	Columbia DB 7866
07/07/1966	24	6		A PLACE IN THE SUN	Columbia DB 7952
13/10/1966	10	12		**TIME DRAGS BY** CLIFF RICHARD AND THE SHADOWS	Columbia DB 8017
03/11/1966	42	6		THE DREAMS I DREAM	Columbia DB 8034

15/12/1966 .....6......10				**IN THE COUNTRY** CLIFF RICHARD AND THE SHADOWS .... Columbia DB 8094
13/04/1967.....24.....8......				MAROC 7 Featured in the 1967 film of the same name .... Columbia DB 8170
27/11/1968.....21.....10......				DON'T FORGET TO CATCH ME CLIFF RICHARD AND THE SHADOWS .... Columbia DB 8503
08/03/1975.....12.....9......				LET ME BE THE ONE Britain's entry for the 1975 Eurovision Song Contest (came second) .... EMI 2269
16/12/1978 .....5......14 .....○				**DON'T CRY FOR ME ARGENTINA** .... EMI 2890
28/04/1979 .....9......14 .....○				**THEME FROM THE DEER HUNTER (CAVATINA)** .... EMI 2939
26/01/1980.....12.....12......				RIDERS IN THE SKY .... EMI 5027
23/08/1980.....50.....3......				EQUINOXE (PART V) .... Polydor POSP 148
02/05/1981.....44.....4......				THE THIRD MAN .... Polydor POSP 255

SHAFT UK producer Mark Pritchard.

21/12/1991 .....7......8......			**ROOBARB AND CUSTARD** .... ffrreedom TAB 100
25/07/1992.....61......1......			MONKEY .... ffrreedom TAB 114

SHAFT UK production/instrumental duo Alex Rizzo and Elliott Ireland, friends since school in Yeovil, who also record as Da Muttz.

04/09/1999 .....2......12 .....○			**(MUCHO MAMBO) SWAY** The original version of this single featured a sample of Rosemary Clooney's *Mucho Mambo*, but after permission was refused the vocals were re-created by Claire Vaughan .... Wonderboy WBYD 015
20/05/2000.....12.....6......			MAMBO ITALIANO .... Wonderboy WBDD 017
21/07/2001.....62......1......			KIKI RIRI BOOM .... Wonderboy WBOYD 026

SHAG UK singer Jonathan King (born Kenneth King, 6/12/1944, London).

14/10/1972 .....4......13			LOOP DI LOVE .... UK 7

SHAGGY Jamaican singer (born Orville Richard Burrell, 22/10/1968, Kingston); he moved to New York at fifteen and formed the Sting International Posse. He later joined the US Marines, maintaining a parallel recording career. He won a 1995 Grammy Award for Best Reggae Album for *Boombastic*, 2001 MOBO Award for Best Reggae Act and 2002 BRIT Award for Best International Male. The Grand Puba is US rapper Maxwell Dixon. Rikrok is US singer Ricardo Ducent. Ali G is UK TV comedian Saccha Baron-Cohen.

06/02/1993 ....❶[2]......19 .....●			**OH CAROLINA** Featured in the 1993 film *Sliver*... Greensleeves GRECD 361
10/07/1993.....46.....3......			SOON BE DONE .... Greensleeves GRECD 380
08/07/1995 .....5......9......			**IN THE SUMMERTIME** SHAGGY FEATURING RAYVON .... Virgin VSCDT 1542
23/09/1995 ....❶[1]......12 .....●			**BOOMBASTIC** ↑ First appeared as an advertisement for Levi Jeans. Contains a sample of King Floyd's *Baby Let Me Kiss You*....... .... Virgin VSCDT 1536
13/01/1996.....11.....5......			WHY YOU TREAT ME SO BAD SHAGGY FEATURING GRAND PUBA Contains a sample of Bob Marley's *Mr Brown*.... Virgin VSCDT 1566
23/03/1996.....21.....5......			SOMETHING DIFFERENT/THE TRAIN IS COMING SHAGGY FEATURING WAYNE WONDER/SHAGGY *Something Different* contains samples of First Choice's *Love Thang* and Stetsasonic's *Go Stetsa*. *The Train Is Coming* featured in the 1996 film *Money Train*.... .... Virgin VSCDX 1581
22/06/1996.....15......7......			THAT GIRL MAXI PRIEST/SHAGGY Contains a sample of Booker T & The MG's ' *Green Onions* .... Virgin VUSDX 106
19/07/1997 .....7......6......			**PIECE OF MY HEART** SHAGGY FEATURING MARSHA Contains a sample of Erma Franklin's *Piece Of My Heart* .... Virgin VSCDT 1647
17/02/2001.....31......3......			IT WASN'T ME (IMPORT) ▲[2] .... MCA 1558032
11/03/2001 ....❶[1]......20 .....✪			**IT WASN'T ME** ↑ SHAGGY FEATURING RIKROK .... MCA 1558022
09/06/2001 ....❶[3]......16 .....●			**ANGEL** ↑ ▲[1] SHAGGY FEATURING RAYVON Contains samples of Merrilee Rush' *Angel Of The Morning* and Steve Miller's *The Joker* .... MCA MCSTD 40257
29/09/2001 .....5......10			**LUV ME LUV ME** Features the uncredited contribution of Samantha Cole and contains a sample of The Honeydrippers' *Impeach The President* and elements of Norman Whitfield's *Ooh Boy*. Featured in the 1998 film *How Stella Got Her Groove Back* .... MCA MCSTD 40263
01/12/2001.....19.....7......			DANCE AND SHOUT/HOPE. .... MCA MCSTD 40272
23/03/2002 .....2......14 .....○			**ME JULIE** SHAGGY AND ALI G Featured in the 2002 film *Ali G Indahouse*........................ Island CID 793
09/11/2002.....10......7......			**HEY SEXY LADY** SHAGGY FEATURING BRIAN AND TONY GOLD .... MCA MCSTD 40304
03/07/2004.....57......1......			YOUR EYES RIKROK FEATURING SHAGGY .... VP VPCD6415

SHAH UK female singer.

06/06/1998.....69......1.......			SECRET LOVE .... Evocative EVOKE 5CDS

SHAI US R&B vocal group formed at Howard University, Washington DC, by Marc Gay, Darnell Van Rensalier, Carl 'Groove' Martin and Garfield Bright.

19/12/1992.....36.....6......			IF I EVER FALL IN LOVE .... MCA MCS 1727

SHAKATAK UK group formed in London, 1980 by Bill Sharpe (keyboards), Jill Saward (vocals), Keith Winter (guitar), George Anderson (bass), Roger Odell (drums) and Nigel Wright (keyboards). Wright left, but stayed as producer. Sharpe later recorded with Gary Numan.

08/11/1980.....41......5......			FEELS LIKE THE RIGHT TIME .... Polydor POSP 188
07/03/1981.....52.....4......			LIVING IN THE UK .... Polydor POSP 230
25/07/1981.....48.....3......			BRAZILIAN DAWN. .... Polydor POSP 282
21/11/1981.....12.....17......			EASIER SAID THAN DONE. .... Polydor POSP 375
03/04/1982 .....9......8......			**NIGHT BIRDS** .... Polydor POSP 407
19/06/1982.....38.....6......			STREETWALKIN' .... Polydor POSP 452
04/09/1982.....24......7......			INVITATIONS .... Polydor POSP 502
06/11/1982.....43.....3......			STRANGER. .... Polydor POSP 530
04/06/1983.....15.....8......			DARK IS THE NIGHT. .... Polydor POSP 595
27/08/1983.....49......4......			IF YOU COULD SEE ME NOW .... Polydor POSP 635

❶[9] Number of weeks single topped the UK chart ↑ Entered the UK chart at #1 ▲[9] Number of weeks single topped the US chart

07/07/1984 . . . . . 9 . . . . . . 11				DOWN ON THE STREET . . . . Polydor POSP 688
15/09/1984 . . . . . 55 . . . . . . 3				DON'T BLAME IT ON LOVE . . . . Polydor POSP 699
16/11/1985 . . . . . 53 . . . . . . 3				DAY BY DAY SHAKATAK FEATURING AL JARREAU . . . . Polydor POSP 770
24/10/1987 . . . . . 56 . . . . . . 3				MR MANIC AND SISTER COOL . . . . Polydor MANIC 1

SHAKE B4 USE VS ROBERT PALMER UK production group from London with UK singer Robert Palmer (born 19/1/1949, Scarborough).

18/01/2003 . . . . . 42 . . . . . . 1				ADDICTED TO LOVE . . . . Serious SER 606CD

SHAKEDOWN Swiss dance group with brothers Stephan 'Mandrax' Kohler and Sebastien 'Seb K' Kohler and US singer Terra Deva.

11/05/2002 . . . . . 6 . . . . . 8				AT NIGHT . . . . Defected DFECT 50CDS
28/06/2003 . . . . . 46 . . . . . . 2				DROWSY WITH HOPE . . . . Defected DFTD 071CDS

JOHNNY SHAKER – see THREE 'N' ONE

SHAKESPEARS SISTER UK/US duo formed in 1989 by ex-Bananarama Siobhan Fahey (born 10/9/1958, London, vocals) and Marcella Detroit (born Marcella Levy, 21/6/1959, Detroit, MI, vocals/guitar/programming), who had toured and written with Eric Clapton. After a two year 'maternity' break following their debut hit, they disbanded in 1993, Detroit going solo. Fahey revived the name in 1996.

29/07/1989 . . . . . 7 . . . . . 9				YOU'RE HISTORY . . . . ffrr F 112
14/10/1989 . . . . . 54 . . . . . . 3				RUN SILENT . . . . ffrr F 119
10/03/1990 . . . . . 71 . . . . . . 1				DIRTY MIND . . . . ffrr F 128
12/10/1991 . . . . . 59 . . . . . . 2				GOODBYE CRUEL WORLD . . . . London LON 309
25/01/1992 . . . . ❶[8] . . . . 16 . . . . ●				STAY 1993 BRIT Award for Best Video . . . . London LON 314
16/05/1992 . . . . . 7 . . . . . 7				I DON'T CARE . . . . London LON 318
18/07/1992 . . . . . 32 . . . . . . 4				GOODBYE CRUEL WORLD Re-issue of London LON 309 . . . . London LON 322
07/11/1992 . . . . . 14 . . . . . . 6				HELLO (TURN YOUR RADIO ON) . . . . London LON 330
27/02/1993 . . . . . 61 . . . . . . 1				MY 16TH APOLOGY (EP) Tracks on EP: My 16th Apology, Catwoman, Dirty Mind and Hot Love. . . . . London LONCD 337
22/06/1996 . . . . . 30 . . . . . . 3				I CAN DRIVE . . . . London LONCD 383

SHAKIRA Colombian singer (born Shakira Isabel Mebarak Ripoll, 9/2/1977, Barranquilla): first known in Spanish-speaking world before widening her appeal by recording in English. 2000 Grammy Award for Best Latin Pop Album for Shakira – MTV Unplugged.

09/03/2002 . . . . . 2 . . . 19 . . . . ●				WHENEVER WHEREVER . . . . Epic 6724262
03/08/2002 . . . . . 3 . . . . . 15				UNDERNEATH YOUR CLOTHES . . . . Epic 6729532
23/11/2002 . . . . . 17 . . . . . . 8				OBJECTION (TANGO) . . . . Epic 6733402

SHAKY AND BONNIE – see SHAKIN' STEVENS AND BONNIE TYLER

SHALAMAR US group initially formed as a studio group in 1977. Following their debut success an actual group was assembled featuring Jody Watley (born 30/1/1959, Chicago, IL, god-daughter of Jackie Wilson), Jeffrey Daniels (born 24/8/1957, Los Angeles, CA) and Gerald Brown. Brown left in 1979, replaced by Howard Hewett (born 1/10/1955, Akron, OH). Both Watley and Daniel went solo in 1984, replaced by Delisa Davies and Micki Free. Hewett left in 1985, replaced by Sydney Justin (previously a defensive back for American football side the Los Angeles Rams). Daniels was briefly married to singer Stephanie Mills. Hewett, Watley and Daniels reunited in 1996 to contribute to a Babyface single.

14/05/1977 . . . . . 30 . . . . . 5				UPTOWN FESTIVAL Medley of the following tracks: Going To A Go Go, I Can't Help Myself (Sugar Pie Honey Bunch), Uptight (Everything's Alright), Stop In The Name Of Love and It's The Same Old Song . . . . Soul Train FB 0885
09/12/1978 . . . . . 20 . . . . . 12				TAKE THAT TO THE BANK . . . . RCA FB 1379
24/11/1979 . . . . . 45 . . . . . . 9				THE SECOND TIME AROUND . . . . Solar FB 1709
09/02/1980 . . . . . 44 . . . . . . 6				RIGHT IN THE SOCKET . . . . Solar SO 2
30/08/1980 . . . . . 13 . . . . . 10				I OWE YOU ONE . . . . Solar SO 11
28/03/1981 . . . . . 30 . . . . . 10				MAKE THAT MOVE . . . . Solar SO 17
27/03/1982 . . . . . 7 . . . . . 11				I CAN MAKE YOU FEEL GOOD . . . . Solar K 12599
12/06/1982 . . . . . 5 . . . . . 12				A NIGHT TO REMEMBER . . . . Solar K 13162
04/09/1982 . . . . . 5 . . . . . 10 . . . . ○				THERE IT IS . . . . Solar K 13194
27/11/1982 . . . . . 12 . . . . . 10				FRIENDS . . . . Solar CHUM 1
11/06/1983 . . . . . 8 . . . . . 10				DEAD GIVEAWAY . . . . Solar E 9819
13/08/1983 . . . . . 18 . . . . . . 8				DISAPPEARING ACT . . . . Solar E 9807
15/10/1983 . . . . . 23 . . . . . . 6				OVER AND OVER . . . . Solar E 9792
24/03/1984 . . . . . 41 . . . . . . 3				DANCING IN THE SHEETS Featured in the 1984 film Footloose . . . . CBS A 4171
31/03/1984 . . . . . 52 . . . . . . 3				DEADLINE USA . . . . MCA 866
24/11/1984 . . . . . 61 . . . . . . 2				AMNESIA . . . . Solar/MCA SHAL 1
02/02/1985 . . . . . 45 . . . . . . 3				MY GIRL LOVES ME . . . . MCA SHAL 2
26/04/1986 . . . . . 52 . . . . . . 4				A NIGHT TO REMEMBER (REMIX) . . . . MCA SHAL 3

SHAM ROCK Irish vocal/instrumental group assembled by producers John Harrison and Philip Larsen.

07/11/1998 . . . . . 13 . . . . . 11				TELL ME MA . . . . Jive 0522352

SHAM 69 UK rock group formed in 1977 by Jimmy Pursey (vocals), Dave Parsons (guitar), Albie Slider (bass) and Mark Cain

○ Silver disc ● Gold disc ✪ Platinum disc (additional platinum units are indicated by a figure following the symbol) ◉ Singles released prior to 1973 that are known to have sold over 1 million copies in the UK

(drums). Slider and Cain left in 1978, replaced by Dave Treganna and Rick Goldstein. They split in 1979, re-forming in 1980 for one album, then in 1987 attempted another comeback with a line-up of Pursey, Parsons, Andy Prince (bass), Ian Whitehead (drums), Tony Black (keyboards) and Linda Paganelli (saxophone). Pursey also recorded solo.

13/05/1978	19	10		ANGELS WITH DIRTY FACES	Polydor 2059 023
29/07/1978	9	9		**IF THE KIDS ARE UNITED**	Polydor 2059 050
14/10/1978	10	8		**HURRY UP HARRY**	Polydor POSP 7
24/03/1979	18	5		QUESTIONS AND ANSWERS	Polydor POSP 27
04/08/1979	6	9		**HERSHAM BOYS**	Polydor PSOP 64
27/10/1979	49	5		YOU'RE A BETTER MAN THAN I	Polydor POSP 82
12/04/1980	45	3		TELL THE CHILDREN	Polydor POSP 136

SHAMEN
UK group formed in Scotland in 1985 by Colin Angus (born 24/8/1961, Aberdeen, vocals/bass), Derek MacKenzie (born 27/2/1964, Aberdeen), Keith MacKenzie (born 30/8/1961, Aberdeen) and Peter Stephenson (born 1/3/1962, Ayr). They signed with Moshka in 1987, adding sampling and keyboards player Will Sin (born William Sinnott, 23/12/1960, Glasgow) in 1987. The MacKenzie brothers left in 1988. Sin was drowned on 22/5/1991 while filming a video for *Pro-Gen*.

07/04/1990	55	4		PRO-GEN	One Little Indian 36 TP7
22/09/1990	42	5		MAKE IT MINE	One Little Indian 46 TP7
06/04/1991	29	5		HYPERREAL	One Little Indian 48 TP7
27/07/1991	4	10		**MOVE ANY MOUNTAIN/PRO-GEN '91**	One Little Indian 52 TP7
18/07/1992	6	8		**LSI** Single stands for 'Love, Sex, Intelligence.'.	One Little Indian 68 TP7
05/09/1992	❶⁴	10	○	**EBENEEZER GOODE**	One Little Indian 78 TP7
07/11/1992	4	7		**BOSS DRUM**	One Little Indian 88 TP7
07/11/1992	58	1		BOSS DRUM (REMIX)	One Little Indian 88 TP12
19/12/1992	5	10	○	**PHOREVER PEOPLE**	One Little Indian 98 TP7
06/03/1993	18	2		RE:EVOLUTION **SHAMEN WITH TERENCE MCKENNA**	One Little Indian 118 TP7CD
06/11/1993	14	4		THE SOS EP Tracks on EP: *Comin' On, Make It Mine* and *Possible Worlds*	One Little Indian 108 TP7CD
19/08/1995	15	4		DESTINATION ESCHATON	One Little Indian 128 TP7CDL
21/10/1995	28	2		TRANSAMAZONIA	One Little Indian 138 TP7CD
10/02/1996	31	2		HEAL (THE SEPARATION)	One Little Indian 158 TP7CDL
21/12/1996	35	3		MOVE ANY MOUNTAIN (2ND REMIX)	One Little Indian 169 TP7CD

SHAMPOO
UK duo Jacqui Blake (born November 1974) and Carrie Askew (born May 1977) who first met at Plumstead Manor High School in London and first recorded for Icerink (Saint Etienne's label). Despite limited UK success, they were very popular in Japan.

30/07/1994	11	12		TROUBLE	Food CDFOOD 51
15/10/1994	27	4		VIVA LA MEGABABES	Food CDFOOD 54
18/02/1995	21	4		DELICIOUS Featured in the 1997 film *Casper – A Spirited Beginning*	Food CDFOOD 58
05/08/1995	36	3		TROUBLE Re-issue of Food CDFOOD 51 and featured in the 1995 film *Mighty Morphin Power Rangers*	Food CDFOODS 66
13/07/1996	25	4		GIRL POWER	Food CDFOOD 76
21/09/1996	42	1		I KNOW WHAT BOYS LIKE	Food CDFOOD 83

JIMMY SHAND BAND
UK accordionist (born 29/1/1908, East Wenyss, Fife). A miner who was made redundant after the 1926 General Strike, he went to work in a music shop. He made his first recording in 1933. He was awarded the MBE in 1962 and was knighted in 1999. He died on 23/12/2000.

23/12/1955	20	2		BLUEBELL POLKA	Parlophone R 3436

PAUL SHANE AND THE YELLOWCOATS
UK actor/singer (born 19/6/1940, Rotherham); he played the role of Ted Bovis in the TV comedy series *Hi De Hi*.

16/05/1981	36	5		HI DE HI (HOLIDAY ROCK) Theme to the TV series *Hi De Hi*	EMI 5180

SHANGRI-LAS
US vocal group formed in New York by two pairs of sisters: Mary and Betty Weiss and twins Mary Ann and Marge Ganser. Discovered by George 'Shadow' Morton, they first recorded for Spokane as the Bon Bons, issuing two singles before changing their name and signing with Red Bird. Marge Ganser left in 1966. Mary Ann died from encephalitis in 1976, Marge died from breast cancer on 28/7/1996. Initially *Leader Of The Pack* was banned by the BBC because of the 'death disc' lyrics.

08/10/1964	14	13		REMEMBER (WALKIN' IN THE SAND)	Red Bird RB 10008
14/01/1965	11	9		LEADER OF THE PACK ▲¹ Featured in the 1965 film *Leader Of The Pack*	Red Bird RB 10014
14/10/1972	3	14		**LEADER OF THE PACK**	Kama Sutra 2013 024
05/06/1976	7	11		**LEADER OF THE PACK** Both label's releases were bracketed together from 19th June	Charly CS 1009/Contempo CS 7032

SHANICE
US R&B singer (born Shanice Wilson, 14/5/1973, Pittsburgh, PA) who debuted at the age of three and was singing with Ella Fitzgerald in a TV advertisement at eight. She signed with A&M in 1984 at the age of eleven, switching to Motown in 1989.

23/11/1991	55	4		I LOVE YOUR SMILE	Motown ZB 44907
22/02/1992	2	10		**I LOVE YOUR SMILE (REMIX)**	Motown TMG 1401
14/11/1992	54	1		LOVIN' YOU	Motown TMG 1409
16/01/1993	42	3		SAVING FOREVER FOR YOU	Giant W 0148CD
13/08/1993	49	2		I LIKE	Motown TMGCD 1427
16/12/1995	51	4		IF I NEVER KNEW YOU (LOVE THEME FROM 'POCAHONTAS') **JON SECADA AND SHANICE** Featured in the 1995 Walt Disney film *Pocahontas*	Walt Disney WD 7023C

❶⁹ Number of weeks single topped the UK chart   ↑ Entered the UK chart at #1   ▲⁹ Number of weeks single topped the US chart

715

SHANKS AND BIGFOOT
UK production duo Shanks (born Stephen Mead) and Bigfoot (Daniel Langsman), with vocals provided by Sharon Woolf. Mead had trained as a barrister and worked as a magazine sub-editor prior to becoming a producer. The duo also recorded as Doolally. They won the 1999 MOBO Award for Best Dance Act.

DATE	POS	WKS	BPI	SINGLE TITLE	LABEL & NUMBER
29/05/1999	●²	16	✪	**SWEET LIKE CHOCOLATE** ↑	Chocolate Boy 0530352
29/07/2000	12	8		SING-A-LONG	Pepper 9230232

SHANNON
US R&B singer (born Brenda Shannon Greene, 12/5/1958, Washington DC) who began in 1978 with the New York Jazz Ensemble. She sang with Brownstone in the early 1980s.

DATE	POS	WKS	BPI	SINGLE TITLE	LABEL & NUMBER
19/11/1983	14	15		LET THE MUSIC PLAY	Club LET 1
07/04/1984	24	7		GIVE ME TONIGHT Featured in the 2003 film *Party Monster*	Club JAB 1
30/06/1984	25	8		SWEET SOMEBODY	Club JAB 3
20/07/1985	46	6		STRONGER TOGETHER	Club JAB 15
06/12/1997	16	8		IT'S OVER LOVE **TODD TERRY PRESENTS SHANNON**	Manifesto FESCD 37
28/11/1998	8	10		**MOVE MANIA SASH! FEATURING SHANNON**	Multiply CDMULTY 45

DEL SHANNON
US singer (born Charles Westover, 30/12/1934, Cooperville, MI). Shannon claimed his birthdate was in 1939 to improve his teen market appeal, an 'error' not revealed until years later. He signed with Big Top in 1960 and set up the Berlee label in 1963. His debut hit featured the 'musitron', a forerunner of the synthesiser developed by Max Crook. He died from a self-inflicted gunshot wound on 8/2/1990 having been prescribed the anti-depressant drug Prozac prior to his suicide. He was inducted into the Rock & Roll Hall of Fame in 1999.

DATE	POS	WKS	BPI	SINGLE TITLE	LABEL & NUMBER
27/04/1961	●³	22		**RUNAWAY** ▲⁴ Featured in the 1973 film *American Graffiti*	London HLX 9317
14/09/1961	6	12		**HATS OFF TO LARRY**	London HLX 9402
07/12/1961	10	11		**SO LONG BABY**	London HLX 9462
15/03/1962	2	15		**HEY LITTLE GIRL**	London HLX 9515
06/09/1962	29	6		CRY MYSELF TO SLEEP	London HLX 9587
18/10/1962	2	17		**SWISS MAID**	London HLX 0609
17/01/1963	4	13		**LITTLE TOWN FLIRT**	London HLX 9653
25/04/1963	5	13		**TWO KINDS OF TEARDROPS**	London HLX 9710
22/08/1963	23	8		TWO SILHOUETTES	London HLX 9761
24/10/1963	21	8		SUE'S GOTTA BE MINE	London HLU 9800
12/03/1964	35	5		MARY JANE	Stateside SS 269
30/07/1964	36	4		HANDY MAN	Stateside SS 317
14/01/1965	3	11		**KEEP SEARCHIN' (WE'LL FOLLOW THE SUN)**	Stateside SS 368
18/03/1965	40	2		STRANGER IN TOWN	Stateside SS 395

ROXANNE SHANTE
US R&B singer (born Lolita Gooden, 8/3/1970, Long Island, NY).

DATE	POS	WKS	BPI	SINGLE TITLE	LABEL & NUMBER
01/08/1987	58	3		HAVE A NICE DAY Contains a sample of King Erricsson's *Well, Have A Nice Day*	Breakout USA 612
04/06/1988	55	3		GO ON GIRL	Breakout USA 633
29/10/1988	45	3		SHARP AS A KNIFE **BRANDON COOKE FEATURING ROXANNE SHANTE**	Club JAB 73
14/04/1990	74	1		GO ON GIRL (REMIX)	Breakout USA 689
23/09/2000	43	1		WHAT'S GOING ON **MEKON FEATURING ROXANNE SHANTE**	Wall Of Sound WALLD 064

SHAPESHIFTERS
UK/Swedish production group formed by Simon Marlin and DJ Max Reich with female gospel singer Cookie.

DATE	POS	WKS	BPI	SINGLE TITLE	LABEL & NUMBER
24/07/2004	●¹	14	○	**LOLA'S THEME** ↑ Contains a sample of Johnnie Taylor's *What About My Love*. Lola is Simon Marlin's wife	Positiva CDTIVS 207

HELEN SHAPIRO
UK singer (born 28/9/1946, London); she signed with EMI while still at school and released her first single when aged fourteen. Appeared in the film *It's Trad Dad* and after her hits came to an end became an actress. She is the youngest female artist to have topped the UK charts, a feat accomplished when she was fourteen years and ten months.

DATE	POS	WKS	BPI	SINGLE TITLE	LABEL & NUMBER
23/03/1961	3	20		**DON'T TREAT ME LIKE A CHILD**	Columbia DB 4589
29/06/1961	●³	23		**YOU DON'T KNOW**	Columbia DB 4670
28/09/1961	●³	19		**WALKIN' BACK TO HAPPINESS**	Columbia DB 4715
15/02/1962	2	15		**TELL ME WHAT HE SAID**	Columbia DB 4782
03/05/1962	23	7		LET'S TALK ABOUT LOVE	Columbia DB 4824
12/07/1962	8	11		**LITTLE MISS LONELY**	Columbia DB 4869
18/10/1962	40	6		KEEP AWAY FROM OTHER GIRLS	Columbia DB 4908
07/02/1963	33	5		QUEEN FOR TONIGHT	Columbia DB 4966
25/04/1963	35	6		WOE IS ME	Columbia DB 7026
24/10/1963	47	3		LOOK WHO IT IS	Columbia DB 7130
23/01/1964	38	4		FEVER	Columbia DB 7190

SHARADA HOUSE GANG
Italian vocal/instrumental group formed by Mario Scalambrin, Massimo Perona, Samuel Scaboro, Roberto Arduini and Gianfranco Bortolotti with singer Anne Marie Smith.

DATE	POS	WKS	BPI	SINGLE TITLE	LABEL & NUMBER
12/08/1995	36	2		KEEP IT UP	Media MCSTD 2071
11/05/1996	50	1		LET THE RHYTHM MOVE YOU	Media MCSTD 40035
18/10/1997	52	1		GYPSY BOY, GYPSY GIRL	Gut CXGUT 12

SHARKEY
UK DJ/producer Jonathan Sharkey.

DATE	POS	WKS	BPI	SINGLE TITLE	LABEL & NUMBER
08/03/1997	53	1		REVOLUTIONS (EP) Tracks on EP: *Revolution Part One, Revolution Part Two* and *Revolution Part Two (remix)*.	React CDREACT 95

○ Silver disc ● Gold disc ✪ Platinum disc (additional platinum units are indicated by a figure following the symbol) ◉ Singles released prior to 1973 that are known to have sold over 1 million copies in the UK

FEARGAL SHARKEY
UK singer (born 13/8/1958, Londonderry, Northern Ireland); lead singer with the Undertones from their formation in 1975 until they split in 1983. He was the first artist to sign with Madness' Zarjazz label in 1984, switching to Virgin in 1985.

DATE	POS	WKS	BPI	SINGLE TITLE	LABEL & NUMBER
13/10/1984	23	7		LISTEN TO YOUR FATHER	Zarjazz JAZZ 1
29/06/1985	26	10		LOVING YOU	Virgin VS 770
12/10/1985	❶²	16	●	**A GOOD HEART**	Virgin VS 808
04/01/1986	5	9		**YOU LITTLE THIEF**	Virgin VS 840
05/04/1986	64	3		SOMEONE TO SOMEBODY	Virgin VS 828
16/01/1988	44	5		MORE LOVE	Virgin VS 992
16/03/1991	12	8		I'VE GOT NEWS FOR YOU	Virgin VS 1294

SHARONETTES
UK vocal group assembled by producer Simon Soussan, their debut hit a cover of The Rivington's 1962 US hit.

DATE	POS	WKS	BPI	SINGLE TITLE	LABEL & NUMBER
26/04/1975	26	5		PAPA OOM MOW MOW	Black Magic BM 102
12/07/1975	46	3		GOING TO A GO-GO	Black Magic BM 104

DEBBIE SHARP – see DREAM FREQUENCY

DEE DEE SHARP
US singer (born 9/9/1945, Philadelphia, PA), wed to producer Kenny Gamble, recording as Dee Dee Sharp Gamble.

DATE	POS	WKS	BPI	SINGLE TITLE	LABEL & NUMBER
25/04/1963	46	2		DO THE BIRD	Cameo Parkway C 244

BARRIE K SHARPE – see DIANA BROWN AND BARRIE K SHARPE

SHARPE AND NUMAN
UK duo Bill Sharpe and Gary Numan (born Gary Anthony James Webb, 8/3/1958, London). Sharpe was keyboard player with Shakatak while Numan had formed Tubeway Army and enjoyed a successful solo career.

DATE	POS	WKS	BPI	SINGLE TITLE	LABEL & NUMBER
09/02/1985	17	8		CHANGE YOUR MIND	Polydor POSP 722
04/10/1986	52	3		NEW THING FROM LONDON TOWN	Numa NU 19
30/01/1988	34	3		NO MORE LIES	Polydor POSP 894
03/06/1989	44	2		I'M ON AUTOMATIC	Polydor PO 43

ROCKY SHARPE AND THE REPLAYS
UK group formed by Rocky Sharpe (born Den Hegarty, formerly in the Darts), Helen Highwater, Johnny Stud and Eric Rondo. Hegarty later became a kid's TV presenter.

DATE	POS	WKS	BPI	SINGLE TITLE	LABEL & NUMBER
16/12/1978	17	10		RAMA LAMA DING DONG	Chiswick CHIS 104
24/03/1979	39	6		IMAGINATION	Chiswick CHIS 110
25/08/1979	60	4		LOVE WILL MAKE YOU FAIL IN SCHOOL	Chiswick CHIS 114
09/02/1980	55	4		MARTIAN HOP This and above single credited to **ROCKY SHARPE AND THE REPLAYS FEATURING THE TOP LINERS**	Chiswick CHIS 121
17/04/1982	19	9		SHOUT SHOUT (KNOCK YOURSELF OUT)	Chiswick DICE 3
07/08/1982	54	3		CLAP YOUR HANDS	RAK 345
26/02/1983	46	5		IF YOU WANNA BE HAPPY	Polydor POSP 560

BEN SHAW FEATURING ADELE HOLNESS
UK producer with a female singer.

DATE	POS	WKS	BPI	SINGLE TITLE	LABEL & NUMBER
14/07/2001	72	1		SO STRONG	Fire Recordings ERIF 009CDS

MARK SHAW
UK singer (born 10/6/1961, Chesterfield); he was the lead singer with Then Jerico before going solo.

DATE	POS	WKS	BPI	SINGLE TITLE	LABEL & NUMBER
17/11/1990	54	1		LOVE SO BRIGHT	EMI EM 161

SANDIE SHAW
UK singer (born Sandra Goodrich, 26/2/1947, Dagenham). She was a machine operator when discovered by Adam Faith's manager Eve Taylor. Signed with Pye in 1964, her trademark of always singing barefoot was initially a publicity stunt devised by Taylor. She married fashion designer Jeff Banks in 1968 and later entertainment mogul Nik Powell.

DATE	POS	WKS	BPI	SINGLE TITLE	LABEL & NUMBER
08/10/1964	❶³	11		**(THERE'S) ALWAYS SOMETHING THERE TO REMIND ME** Featured in the 1985 film *A Letter To Brezhnev*	Pye 7N 15704
10/12/1964	3	12		**GIRL DON'T COME**	Pye 7N 15743
18/02/1965	4	11		**I'LL STOP AT NOTHING**	Pye 7N 15783
13/05/1965	❶³	14		**LONG LIVE LOVE**	Pye 7N 15841
23/09/1965	6	10		**MESSAGE UNDERSTOOD**	Pye 7N 15940
18/11/1965	21	9		HOW CAN YOU TELL	Pye 7N 15987
27/01/1966	9	9		**TOMORROW**	Pye 7N 17036
19/05/1966	14	9		NOTHING COMES EASY	Pye 7N 17086
08/09/1966	32	5		RUN	Pye 7N 17163
24/11/1966	32	4		THINK SOMETIMES ABOUT ME	Pye 7N 17212
19/01/1967	50	1		I DON'T NEED ANYTHING	Pye 7N 17239
16/03/1967	❶³	18		**PUPPET ON A STRING** The song won the 1967 Eurovision Song Contest	Pye 7N 17272
12/07/1967	21	6		TONIGHT IN TOKYO	Pye 7N 17346
04/10/1967	18	12		YOU'VE NOT CHANGED	Pye 7N 17378

❶⁹ Number of weeks single topped the UK chart ↑ Entered the UK chart at #1 ▲⁹ Number of weeks single topped the US chart

07/02/1968	27	7	TODAY	Pye 7N 17441
12/02/1969	6	15	**MONSIEUR DUPONT**	Pye 7N 17675
14/05/1969	42	4	THINK IT ALL OVER	Pye 7N 17726
21/04/1984	27	5	HAND IN GLOVE	Rough Trade RT 130
14/06/1986	68	1	ARE YOU READY TO BE HEARTBROKEN	Polydor POSP 793
12/11/1994	66	2	NOTHING LESS THAN BRILLIANT	Virgin VSCDT 1521

TRACY SHAW UK singer (born 27/7/1973, Belper, Derbyshire) who is best known as an actress in *Coronation Street* playing Maxine Heavey Elliott. Her debut hit single was first performed on the *Coronation Street* special, 'Viva Las Vegas'.

04/07/1998	46	1	HAPPENIN' ALL OVER AGAIN	Recognition CDREC 2

WINIFRED SHAW US singer (born 25/2/1899, Hawaii) who was the voice of non-singing stars in many Warner Brothers' musicals during the 1930s and also appeared in a number of films herself, including *Three On A Honeymoon, Gold Diggers Of 1935, In Caliente* and *Melody For Two*. She died on 2/5/1982.

14/08/1976	42	4	LULLABY OF BROADWAY Featured in the 1935 film *Gold Diggers Of 1935* and won an Oscar for Best Film Song for writers Harry Warren and Al Dubin	United Artists UP 36131

SHE – see URBAN DISCHARGE FEATURING SHE

SHE ROCKERS UK group formed by Alison Clarkson, Donna McConnell and Antonia Jolly. Clarkson went solo as Betty Boo.

13/01/1990	58	2	JAM IT JAM	Jive 233

GEORGE SHEARING UK pianist (born 13/8/1919, London). Born blind, he learned piano from the age of three. After playing for names like Harry Parry and Stephane Grappelli, he moved to America in 1946 forming his own quartet, a group that would include Cal Tjader, Joe Pass, Gary Burton and Denzil Best among others. He also worked with numerous singers, including Peggy Lee, Nat 'King' Cole, Carmen McRae and Mel Torme, and also performed classical music. He has a star on the Hollywood Walk of Fame.

19/07/1962	11	14	LET THERE BE LOVE NAT 'KING' COLE WITH GEORGE SHEARING	Capitol CL 15257
04/10/1962	49	1	BAUBLES, BANGLES AND BEADS	Capitol CL 15269

GARY SHEARSTON Australian pop singer (born 1939, New South Wales); he later recorded for the Larrikin label.

05/10/1974	7	8	**I GET A KICK OUT OF YOU**	Charisma CB 234

SHED SEVEN UK rock group formed in York in 1991 by Rick Witter (vocals), Tim Gladwin (bass), Paul Banks (guitar) and Alan Leach (drums). They fell out with their record label Polydor in 1999 and left in September of that year to sign with Artful.

25/06/1994	28	4	DOLPHIN	Polydor YORCD 2
27/08/1994	24	3	SPEAKEASY	Polydor YORCD 3
12/11/1994	33	2	OCEAN PIE	Polydor YORCD 4
13/05/1995	23	2	WHERE HAVE YOU BEEN TONIGHT?	Polydor YORCD 5
27/01/1996	14	3	GETTING BETTER	Polydor 5778912
23/03/1996	8	5	**GOING FOR GOLD**	Polydor 5762152
18/05/1996	22	3	BULLY BOY	Polydor 5765972
31/08/1996	12	4	ON STANDBY	Polydor 5752732
23/11/1996	17	5	CHASING RAINBOWS	Polydor 5759292
14/03/1998	11	4	SHE LEFT ME ON FRIDAY	Polydor 5695412
23/05/1998	18	3	THE HEROES	Polydor 5699172
22/08/1998	37	2	DEVIL IN YOUR SHOES (WALKING ALL OVER)	Polydor 5672072
05/06/1999	13	6	DISCO DOWN	Polydor 5638752
05/05/2001	30	2	CRY FOR HELP	Artful CDX 35ARTFUL
24/05/2003	23	2	WHY CAN'T I BE YOU?	Taste Media TMCDSX 5004

SHEEP ON DRUGS UK duo formed in London in 1991 by 'Dead' Lee Fraser (electronics/guitar) and 'King' Duncan Gil-Rodriguez (vocals). Lee later changed his name to Lee 303. They launched their own The Drug Squad label.

27/03/1993	44	2	15 MINUTES OF FAME	Transglobal CID 564
30/10/1993	40	2	FROM A TO H AND BACK AGAIN	Transglobal CID 575
14/05/1994	56	1	LET THE GOOD TIMES ROLL	Transglobal CID 576

SHEER BRONZE FEATURING LISA MILLETT UK vocal/instrumental duo Charles Eve and Lisa Millett.

03/09/1994	63	1	WALKIN' ON	Go Beat GODCD 115

SHEER ELEGANCE UK R&B vocal trio Dennis Robinson, Bev Gordon (ex-Earthquake, aka Little Henry) and Herbie Watkins.

20/12/1975	18	10	MILKY WAY	Pye International 7N 25697
03/04/1976	9	9	**LIFE IS TOO SHORT GIRL**	Pye International 7N 25703
24/07/1976	41	4	IT'S TEMPTATION	Pye International 7N 25717

SHADE SHEIST FEATURING NATE DOGG AND KURUPT US rap group formed by Shade Sheist (Tremayne Thompson), Nate Dogg (Nathan Hale) and Kurupt (Ricardo Brown).

25/08/2001	14	7	WHERE I WANNA BE	London LONCD 461

DOUG SHELDON UK singer, his hits all covers of US hits by Dion, Kenny Dino and Dickey Lee. He later recorded with Al Saxon.

○ Silver disc ● Gold disc ✪ Platinum disc (additional platinum units are indicated by a figure following the symbol) ◎ Singles released prior to 1973 that are known to have sold over 1 million copies in the UK

09/11/1961	36	3		RUNAROUND SUE	Decca F 11398
04/01/1962	29	6		YOUR MA SAID YOU CRIED IN YOUR SLEEP LAST NIGHT	Decca F 11416
07/02/1963	36	6		I SAW LINDA YESTERDAY	Decca F 11564

MICHELLE SHELLERS – see SOUL PROVIDERS FEATURING MICHELLE SHELLERS

PETE SHELLEY UK singer/guitarist (born Peter McNeish, 17/4/1955); formerly in The Buzzcocks whom he re-formed in 1990.

| 12/03/1983 | 66 | 1 | | TELEPHONE OPERATOR | Genetic XX1 |

PETER SHELLEY UK singer/songwriter; he also worked in-house for Magnet Records and penned hits for Alvin Stardust.

| 14/09/1974 | 4 | 10 | | GEE BABY | Magnet MAG 12 |
| 22/03/1975 | 3 | 10 | O | LOVE ME LOVE MY DOG | Magnet MAG 22 |

ANNE SHELTON UK singer (born Patricia Sibley, 10/11/1924, Dulwich, London). Debuting on radio aged twelve, she worked with Glenn Miller and Bing Crosby during Second World War. Films included *Miss London* (1943), *Bees In Paradise* (1943) and *King Arthur Was A Gentleman* (1942) with comedian Arthur Askey and *Yanks* (1979). Awarded an OBE in 1990, she died on 31/7/1994.

16/12/1955	17	4		ARRIVEDERCI DARLING	HMV POP 146
13/04/1956	20	4		SEVEN DAYS	Philips PB 567
24/08/1956	❶4	14		LAY DOWN YOUR ARMS	Philips PB 616
20/11/1959	27	1		VILLAGE OF ST. BERNADETTE	Philips PB 969
26/01/1961	10	8		SAILOR	Philips PB 1096

SHENA UK female singer.

02/08/1997	28	2		LET THE BEAT HIT 'EM	VC Recordings VCRD 24
01/09/2001	44	1		I'LL BE WAITING FULL INTENTION PRESENTS SHENA	Rulin 17CDS
04/10/2003	20	3		WILDERNESS JURGEN VRIES FEATURING SHENA	Direction 6742692

VIKKI SHEPARD – see SLEAZESISTERS

VONDA SHEPARD US singer (born 1963, NYC); her songs' first exposure was via the TV show *Ally McBeal*. She was originally signed by Reprise but dropped after one release. She first hit the US charts in 1987 with a duet with Dan Hill (*Can't We Try*).

| 05/12/1998 | 10 | 9 | | SEARCHIN' MY SOUL Theme to the US TV series *Ally McBeal* | Epic 6666332 |

SHEPHERD SISTERS US group Martha, Mary Lou, Gayle and Judy Shepherd from Middletown, OH who later moved to NYC.

| 15/11/1957 | 14 | 6 | | ALONE | HMV POP 411 |

SHERBET Australian pop group formed in Sydney in 1969 who at the time of their hit comprised Daryl Braithwaite (born 11/1/1949, Melbourne, vocals), Harvey James (guitar/vocals), Tony Mitchell (born 21/10/1951, bass/vocals), Garth Porter (keyboards) and Alan Sandow (born 28/2/1958, drums). They later shortened their name to The Sherbs.

| 25/09/1976 | 4 | 10 | O | HOWZAT | Epic EPC 4574 |

TONY SHERIDAN AND THE BEATLES UK singer (born Anthony Sheridan McGinnity, 2/5/1940, Norwich). He joined Vince Taylor & The Playboys, moving to Hamburg in 1959 where he formed The Beat Brothers, with Sheridan (guitar/vocals), Ken Packwood (guitar), Rick Richards (guitar), Colin Melander (bass), Ian Hines (keyboards) and Jimmy Doyle (drums). The line-up who recorded *My Bonnie*, however, featured John Lennon, Paul McCartney, Ringo Starr, Roy Young and Rikky Barnes, released as Tony Sheridan & The Beat Brothers. The subsequent popularity of The Beatles saw the record re-released as Tony Sheridan & The Beatles. Sheridan later converted to the Sannyasin religion and changed his name to Swami Probhu Sharan.

| 06/06/1963 | 48 | 1 | | MY BONNIE | Polydor NH 66833 |

ALLAN SHERMAN US singer/comedian (born Allan Copelon, 30/1/1924, Chicago, IL); he began as a writer for comedians Jackie Gleason and Joe E Lewis among others. He died on 21/11/1973.

| 12/09/1963 | 14 | 10 | | HELLO MUDDAH HELLO FADDAH Based on Ponchielli's *Dance Of The Hours*. 1963 Grammy Award for Best Comedy Recording | Warner Brothers WB 106 |

BOBBY SHERMAN US singer/actor (born 18/7/1943, Santa Monica, CA); he regularly appeared on TV as an actor before moving into TV production.

| 31/10/1970 | 28 | 4 | | JULIE DO YA LOVE ME | CBS 5144 |

SHERRICK US singer (born 6/7/1957, Sacramento, CA) who backed Stevie Wonder, The Temptations and Rick James and such before going solo.

| 01/08/1987 | 23 | 8 | | JUST CALL | Warner Brothers W 8380 |
| 21/11/1987 | 63 | 2 | | LET'S BE LOVERS TONIGHT | Warner Brothers W 8146 |

PLUTO SHERVINGTON Jamaican reggae singer/writer/producer (born Leighton Shervington, August 1950) who was with Tomorrow's Children before going solo.

07/02/1976	6	8		DAT	Opal Pal 5
10/04/1976	43	4		RAM GOAT LIVER	Trojan TR 7978
06/03/1982	19	8		YOUR HONOUR PLUTO	KR 4

❶9 Number of weeks single topped the UK chart ↑ Entered the UK chart at #1 ▲9 Number of weeks single topped the US chart

719

HOLLY SHERWOOD US singer whose hit featured in the musical *Godspell*. She later sang with Fire Inc and as a backing vocalist.

05/02/1972 . . . . . 29 . . . . . . 7 . . . . DAY BY DAY . . . . Bell 1182

TONY SHEVETON UK singer who toured with The Kinks, Manfred Mann and The Honeycombs; still touring into the 1990s.

13/02/1964 . . . . . 49 . . . . . . 1 . . . . MILLION DRUMS . . . . Oriole CB 1895

SHIFTY US singer (born Seth Binzer, Los Angeles, CA) who is also a member of Crazy Town (as Shifty Shellshock).

11/09/2004 . . . . . 29 . . . . . . 3 . . . . SLIDE ALONG SIDE . . . . Maverick W649CD

SHIMMON AND WOOLFSON UK DJ/production duo of DJ Mark Shimmon and musician Nick Woolfson; they also recorded as Sundance.

10/01/1998 . . . . . 69 . . . . . . 1 . . . . WELCOME TO THE FUTURE . . . . React CDREACT 119

SHIMON AND ANDY C UK drum/bass duo Shimon Alcovy and Andy Clarke. Clarke was previously a member of Origin Unknown and formed Ram Records with Ant Miles, with the pair subsequently linking with Alcovy to form Ram Trilogy.

15/09/2001 . . . . . 58 . . . . . . 2 . . . . BODY ROCK . . . . Ram RAMM 34CD
12/01/2002 . . . . . 28 . . . . . . 3 . . . . BODY ROCK . . . . Ram RAMM 34CD

SHINEHEAD Jamaican singer (born Edmund Carl Aitken, 10/4/1962, Kent). His family emigrated to Jamaica when he was two and then to New York in 1976. He also provided the raps for former Shalamar member Howard Hewett's *Allegiance* album.

03/04/1993 . . . . . 30 . . . . . . 5 . . . . JAMAICAN IN NEW YORK . . . . Elektra EKR 161CD
26/06/1993 . . . . . 70 . . . . . . 1 . . . . LET 'EM IN . . . . Elektra EKR 168CD

SHINING UK group with Duncan Baxter (vocals), Simon Tong (guitar/keyboards), Dan MacBean (guitar), Simon Jones (born 29/7/1972, bass) and Mark Heaney (drums). Jones and Tong had previously been members of The Verve.

06/07/2002 . . . . . 58 . . . . . . 1 . . . . I WONDER HOW . . . . Zuma ZUMAD 002
14/09/2002 . . . . . 52 . . . . . . 1 . . . . YOUNG AGAIN . . . . Zuma ZUMASCD 03B

MIKE SHINODA – see X-ECUTIONERS FEATURING MIKE SHINODA AND MR HAHN OF LINKIN PARK

SHINS US rock group formed in Albequerque, NM by James Mercer (guitar/vocals), Neal Langford (bass) and Jesse Sandoval (drums). All three had previously been members of Flake. Langford left in 2002 and was replaced by Dave Hernandez.

13/03/2004 . . . . . 73 . . . . . . 1 . . . . SO SAYS I . . . . Sub Pop SPCD621

SHIRELLES US R&B vocal group formed in Passiac, NJ in 1957 by Shirley Owens Alston (born 10/6/1941, New Jersey), Addi 'Micki' Harris (born 22/1/1940, New Jersey), Doris Coley Kenner (born 2/8/1941, New Jersey) and Beverley Lee (born 3/8/1941, New Jersey) as the Poquellos. All classmates at junior high school, they signed to Florence Greenberg's Tiara Records in 1957 who suggested name-change to the Shirelles. The success of their first single *I Met Him On A Sunday* led to Tiara leasing the record to Decca for national distribution and Greenberg later setting up the Scepter label (although after the trust fund supposedly set up by Scepter was never going to materialise, the group left the label). Kenner left in 1968, returning in 1975 to replace Owens who went solo (she later recorded as Lady Rose). Harris died from a heart attack on 10/6/1982. Doris Kenner died from breast cancer on 4/2/2000. The group was inducted into the Rock & Roll Hall of Fame in 1996.

09/02/1961 . . . . . 4 . . . . . . 15 . . . . . . **WILL YOU LOVE ME TOMORROW** ▲² Features songwriter Carole King on drums. Featured in the films *Police Academy* (1984) and *Dirty Dancing* (1987) . . . . Top Rank JAR 540
31/05/1962 . . . . . 23 . . . . . . 9 . . . . SOLDIER BOY ▲³ Featured in the films *The Wanderers* (1979) and *Born On The 4th Of July* (1989) . . . . HMV POP 1019
23/05/1963 . . . . . 38 . . . . . . 5 . . . . FOOLISH LITTLE GIRL . . . . Stateside SS 181

SHIRLEY AND COMPANY US singer (born Shirley Goodman, 19/6/1936, New Orleans, LA). She first recorded as one half of Shirley & Lee with Leonard Lee. The duo split in 1963. The 'Company' were Jesus Alvarez (vocals), Walter Morris (guitar), Bernadette Randle (keyboards), Seldon Powell (saxophone), Jonathan Williams (bass) and Clarence Oliver (drums), later adding singer Kenneth Jeremiah, a former member of the Soul Survivors.

08/02/1975 . . . . . 6 . . . . . . 9 . . . . **SHAME SHAME SHAME** . . . . All Platinum 6146 301

SHIVA UK dance group formed by Paul Ross, Gino Piscitelli and singer Louise Dean. Originally called Shine, they were threatened with injunctions from other groups of that name so changed to Shiva, the mythical 'Lord of the Dance'. Dean had previously been backing singer for Urban Cookie Collective and Rozalla.

13/05/1995 . . . . . 36 . . . . . . 2 . . . . WORK IT OUT . . . . ffrr FCD 261
19/08/1995 . . . . . 18 . . . . . . 3 . . . . FREEDOM . . . . ffrr FCD 263

SHIVAREE US group formed by Ambrosia Parsley (vocals), Duke McVinnie (guitar) and Danny McGough (keyboards).

17/02/2001 . . . . . 63 . . . . . . 1 . . . . GOODNIGHT MOON . . . . Capitol CDCL 825

SHO NUFF US group formed in Mississippi by Frederick Young (vocals), Lawrence Lewis (guitar), James Lewis (keyboards), Sky Chambers (bass), Albert Bell (percussion), Jerod Minnis (percussion) and Bruce Means (drums).

24/05/1980 . . . . . 53 . . . . . . 4 . . . . IT'S ALRIGHT . . . . Ensign ENY 37

MICHELLE SHOCKED US singer/guitarist (born Michelle Johnston, 24/2/1962, Dallas, TX). Her debut album *The Texas Campfire Tapes* was recorded on a Walkman at a campfire in Texas (crickets and passing lorries audible in the background). Later albums were recorded more conventionally. In 1995 she took legal action to be released from her contract with London after various disagreements.

08/10/1988 . . . . . 60 . . . . . . 4 . . . . ANCHORAGE . . . . Cooking Vinyl LON 193

| 14/01/1989 | 63 | 3 | | IF LOVE WAS A TRAIN | Cooking Vinyl LON 212 |
| 11/03/1989 | 67 | 3 | | WHEN I GROW UP | Cooking Vinyl LON 219 |

SHOCKING BLUE
Dutch rock group formed in 1967 by Robbie Van Leeuwen (born 1944, guitar), Fred De Wilde (vocals), Cor Van Beek (drums) and Klaasje Van Der Wal (bass). De Wilde was replaced after one local hit (*Lucy Brown Is Back In Town*) by Mariska Veres (born 1949). They disbanded in 1974.

| 17/01/1970 | 8 | 11 | | VENUS ▲[1] | Penny Farthing PEN 702 |
| 25/04/1970 | 43 | 3 | | MIGHTY JOE | Penny Farthing PEN 713 |

SHOLAN
UK/German dance duo female singer Sholan (born 1982, Winchester) and producer Matti Schwartz. Sholan is the Buddhist term for a Chinese flower.

| 05/04/2003 | 47 | 1 | | CAN YOU FEEL (WHAT I'M GOING THROUGH) | Data 39CDS |

TROY SHONDELL
US singer (born Gary Schelton, 14/5/1944, Fort Wayne, IN); his only hit was released on three different US labels (Gaye, Liberty and his own Goldcrest) before charting. He later moved to Nashville and recorded country music.

| 02/11/1961 | 22 | 11 | | THIS TIME | London HLG 9432 |

SHONDELLS – see TOMMY JAMES AND THE SHONDELLS

SHOOTING PARTY
UK vocal duo Roger 'Russell Sprout' Ferris and Gary Strange, both previously members of No Dice.

| 31/03/1990 | 66 | 2 | | LET'S HANG ON | Lisson DOLE 15 |

MIKE SHOREY – see FABOLOUS

SHORTIE VS BLACK LEGEND
Italian production duo Alex Effe and Claudio Rossi with singer Elroy 'Spoon Face' Powell.

| 04/08/2001 | 37 | 2 | | SOMEBODY Contains a sample of First Choice's *Dr Love* | WEA 328CDX |

SHOWADDYWADDY
UK rock 'n' roll revival group formed in Leicester in 1973 by Dave Bartram (vocals), Buddy Gask (vocals), Romeo Challenger (drums), Malcolm Allured (drums), Trevor Oakes (guitar), Russ Field (guitar), Rod Deas (bass) and Al James (bass). An amalgamation of two groups, the Hammers and the Choice, they were signed by Bell after winning *Opportunity Knocks*.

18/05/1974	2	14	O	HEY ROCK AND ROLL	Bell 1357
17/08/1974	15	9		ROCK 'N' ROLL LADY	Bell 1374
30/11/1974	13	8		HEY MR. CHRISTMAS	Bell 1387
22/02/1975	14	9		SWEET MUSIC	Bell 1403
17/05/1975	2	11	O	THREE STEPS TO HEAVEN	Bell 1426
06/09/1975	7	7		HEARTBEAT	Bell 1450
15/11/1975	34	6		HEAVENLY	Bell 1460
29/05/1976	32	3		TROCADERO	Bell 1476
06/11/1976	❶[3]	15	●	UNDER THE MOON OF LOVE	Bell 1495
05/03/1977	3	11	O	WHEN	Arista 91
23/07/1977	2	10	O	YOU GOT WHAT IT TAKES	Arista 126
05/11/1977	4	11	O	DANCIN' PARTY	Arista 149
25/03/1978	2	11	O	I WONDER WHY	Arista 174
24/06/1978	5	12	O	A LITTLE BIT OF SOAP	Arista 191
04/11/1978	5	12	O	PRETTY LITTLE ANGEL EYES	Arista ARIST 222
31/03/1979	17	8		REMEMBER THEN	Arista 247
28/07/1979	15	9		SWEET LITTLE ROCK 'N' ROLLER	Arista 278
10/11/1979	39	5		A NIGHT AT DADDY GEE'S	Arista 314
27/09/1980	22	10		WHY DO LOVERS BREAK EACH OTHER'S HEARTS	Arista ARIST 359
29/11/1980	32	9		BLUE MOON	Arista ARIST 379
13/06/1981	39	4		MULTIPLICATION	Arista ARIST 416
28/11/1981	31	9		FOOTSTEPS	Bell 1499
28/08/1982	37	6		WHO PUT THE BOMP (IN THE BOMP-A-BOMP-A-BOMP)	RCA 236

SHOWDOWN – see GARRY LEE AND SHOWDOWN

SHOWDOWN
US studio group assembled by Meco Monardo (born 29/11/1939, Johnsonburg, PA).

| 17/12/1977 | 41 | 3 | | KEEP DOIN' IT | State STAT 63 |

SHOWSTOPPERS
US R&B vocal group comprising two sets of brothers: Laddie and Alec Burke (also brothers of Solomon Burke) and Earl (lead singer) and Timmy Smith.

❶[9] Number of weeks single topped the UK chart ↑ Entered the UK chart at #1 ▲[9] Number of weeks single topped the US chart

721

13/03/1968.....11.....15......	AIN'T NOTHING BUT A HOUSEPARTY	Beacon 3-100
13/11/1968.....33.....7......	EENY MEENY	MGM 1436
30/01/1971.....33.....3......	AIN'T NOTHING BUT A HOUSEPARTY Re-issue of Beacon 3-100	Beacon BEA 100

SHRIEKBACK UK group formed by Barry Andrews (vocals), Carl Marsh (guitar) and Dave Allen (bass). Marsh later left, the remaining pair recruiting Martyn Baker (drums) plus assorted session musicians and singers.

28/07/1984.....52.....4......	HAND ON MY HEART .... Arista SHRK 1

SHRINK Dutch DJ/production trio R Fiolet, Bobellow and HJ Lookers.

10/10/1998.....42.....2......	NERVOUS BREAKDOWN .... VC Recordings VCRD 42
19/08/2000.....39.....2......	ARE YOU READY TO PARTY Contains a sample of Bizz Nizz' *Don't Miss The Partyline* .... NuLife 74321783772

SHUT UP AND DANCE UK hip hop/house duo formed in London in 1988 by Philip 'PJ' Johnson and Carl 'Smiley' Hyman. The duo also set up the Shut Up And Dance label.

21/04/1990.....56.....3......	£20 TO GET IN.. Shut Up And Dance SUAD 3
28/07/1990.....55.....2......	LAMBORGHINI .... Shut Up And Dance SUAD 4
08/02/1992.....43.....2......	AUTOBIOGRAPHY OF A CRACKHEAD/THE GREEN MAN... Shut Up And Dance SUAD 21
30/05/1992 .....2.....2......	**RAVING I'M RAVING** SHUT UP AND DANCE FEATURING PETER BOUNCER Contains a sample of Marc Cohn's *Walking In Memphis*, although clearance to do so was not received. Proceeds from the sale of the offending single were ordered to be donated to charity .... Shut Up And Dance SUAD 30S
15/08/1992.....69.....1......	THE ART OF MOVING BUTTS SHUT UP AND DANCE FEATURING ERIN................................ Shut Up And Dance SUAD 34S
01/04/1995.....25.....3......	SAVE IT 'TIL THE MOURNING AFTER Contains a sample of Duran Duran's *Save A Prayer*.................... Pulse 8 PULS 84CD
08/07/1995.....68.....1......	I LUV U SHUT UP AND DANCE FEATURING RICHIE DAVIS AND PROFESSOR T Contains a sample of Perez Prado's *Guaglione* .... Pulse 8 PULS 90CD

SHY UK rock group formed in Birmingham by Tony Mills (vocals), Steve Harris (guitar), Roy Davis (bass), Pat McKenna (keyboards) and Alan Kelly (drums). Mills later went on to join Siam.

19/04/1980.....60.....3......	GIRL (IT'S ALL I HAVE) .... Gallery GA 1

SHY FX UK producer Andre Williams.

01/10/1994.....39.....3......	ORIGINAL NUTTAH UK APACHI WITH SHY FX Contains samples of Cypress Hill's *I Ain't Going Out Like That* and the vocal introduction to the film *Goodfellas* .... Sound Of Underground SOUR 008CD
20/03/1999.....60.....1......	BAMBAATA 2012.. Ebony EBR 020CD
06/04/2002 .....7.....11......	**SHAKE UR BODY** SHY FX AND T POWER FEATURING DI .... Positiva CDTIV 171
23/11/2002.....19.....4......	DON'T WANNA KNOW SHY FX/T POWER/DI & SKIBADEE .... ffrr FCD 408
21/12/2002.....60.....1......	WOLF .... Ebony Dubs EBD001
07/06/2003.....34.....2......	FEELIN' U SHY FX AND T-POWER FEATURING KELE LE ROC .... London FCD 409

SHYEIM US rapper (born Shyeim Franklin, 1980, Staten Island, NYC) who is also known as The Rugged Child.

08/06/1996.....61.....1......	THIS IZ REAL .... Noo Trybe VUSCD 105

SHYSTIE UK rappe/MC Chanelle Calica (born 1983, London).

17/07/2004.....40.....2......	ONE WISH .... Polydor 9866875
02/10/2004.....59.....1......	MAKE IT EASY .... Polydor 9867988

SIA Australian singer/songwriter Sia Furler; she later guested on Zero 7's album.

03/06/2000.....10.....5......	**TAKEN FOR GRANTED** Contains a sample of Prokofiev's *Romeo And Juliet* .... Long Lost Brother S002CD1
18/08/2001.....30.....3......	DESTINY ZERO 7 FEATURING SIA AND SOPHIE... Ultimate Dilemma UDRCDS 043
01/05/2004.....71.....1......	BREATHE ME .... Go! Beat 9866392
29/05/2004.....56.....1......	SOMERSAULT ZERO 7 FEATURING SIA... Ultimate Dilemma EW290CD

LABI SIFFRE UK singer (born 25/6/1945, London) with an English mother and Nigerian father. He spent some time working in Cannes, France before returning to the UK and going solo.

27/11/1971.....14.....12......	IT MUST BE LOVE .... Pye International 7N 25572
25/03/1972.....11.....9......	CRYING LAUGHING LOVING LYING.. Pye International 7N 25576
29/07/1972.....29.....6......	WATCH ME .... Pye International 7N 25586
04/04/1987 .....4.....13......	**(SOMETHING INSIDE) SO STRONG** .... China WOK 12
21/11/1987.....52.....4......	NOTHIN'S GONNA CHANGE .... China WOK 16

SIGNUM Dutch production duo Pascal Minnaard and Ronald Hagen.

28/11/1998.....70.....1......	WHAT YA GOT 4 ME .... Tidy Trax TIDY 118CD
31/07/1999.....66.....1......	COMING ON STRONG SIGNUM FEATURING SCOTT MAC... Tidy Trax TIDY 128T
09/02/2002.....35.....3......	WHAT YA GOT 4 ME .... Tidy Trax TIDY 163CD
29/06/2002.....50.....1......	COMING ON STRONG SIGNUM FEATURING SCOTT MAC... Tidy Two TIDYTWO 104CD

SIGUE SIGUE SPUTNIK UK rock group formed in the mid-1980s by ex-Generation X Tony James (guitar), Martin Degville (vocals), Neal X (born Neil Whitmore, guitar), Chris Kavanagh (drums), Ray Mayhew (drums) and Miss Yana Ya Ya (keyboards). They disbanded in 1988, James joining Sisters Of Mercy.

01/03/1986 .....3.....9......O	**LOVE MISSILE F1-11** Featured in the films *Ferris Bueller's Day Off* (1987) and *Mean Machine* (2001) .... Parlophone SSS 1

07/06/1986	20	5		TWENTY-FIRST CENTURY BOY	Parlophone SSS 2
19/11/1988	31	3		SUCCESS	Parlophone SSS 3
01/04/1989	50	2		DANCERAMA	Parlophone SSS 5
20/05/1989	75	1		ALBINONI VS STAR WARS	Parlophone SSS 4

SIGUR ROS Icelandic rock group formed in Reykjavic in 1994 by Jon Thor Birgisson (guitar/vocals), Georg Holm (bass) and August (drums). Kjartan Sveinsson (keyboards) joined in 1997 while August left in 1999, replaced by Orri Pall Dyrason. Their name means Victory Rose. Their debut hit and video had no title and is taken from an album that similarly had no title, comprising eight tracks with no titles.

24/05/2003	72	1		() Won the 2003 MTV Europe Music Award for Best Video	Pias Recordings CD10FAT02

SIL Dutch production duo Olav Basoski and DJ Ziki (Rene Terhost). Ziki is also a member of Chocolate Puma and Goodmen.

11/04/1998	58	1		WINDOWS '98	Hooj Choons HOOJCD 60

SILENCERS UK group formed by Jimmie O'Neill (guitar/vocals), Cha Burns (guitar), Joe Donnelly (bass) and Martin Hanlin (drums).

25/06/1988	57	4		PAINTED MOON	RCA HUSH 1
27/05/1989	71	2		SCOTTISH RAIN	RCA PB 42701
15/05/1993	62	1		I CAN FEEL IT	RCA 74321147112

SILENT UNDERDOG UK producer Paul Hardcastle (born 10/12/1957, London). He played with Direct Drive and First Light and formed the Total Control record company in 1984. He also recorded as the Def Boys, Beeps International, Jazzmasters and Kiss The Sky, the latter with singer Jaki Graham.

16/02/1985	73	1		PAPA'S GOT A BRAND NEW PIGBAG	Kaz 50

SILICONE SOUL FEATURING LOUISE CLARE MARSHALL UK production duo formed in Glasgow by Graeme Reddie and Craig Morrison. They had originally formed Dead City Radio as a punk group, but switched styles in the early 1990s. They formed Depth Perception Records in 1996 and re-formed as Silicone Soul soon after, linking with Soma Records in 1998.

06/10/2001	15	5		RIGHT ON SILICONE SOUL FEATURING LOUISE CLARE MARSHALL Contains a sample of Curtis Mayfield's *Right On For The Darkness*	Soma/VC Recordings VCRD 96

SILJE Norwegian female singer Silje Nergaard.

15/12/1990	55	6		TELL ME WHERE YOU'RE GOING	EMI EM 159

SILK US R&B vocal group formed in Atlanta, GA by Timothy Cameron, Jimmy Gates Jr, Gary Glenn, Gary Jenkins and Johnathen Rasboro.

24/04/1993	46	5		FREAK ME ▲²	Elektra EKR 165CD
05/06/1993	67	2		GIRL U FOR ME	Elektra EKR 167CD
09/10/1993	44	2		BABY IT'S YOU	Elektra EKR 173CD
26/02/1994	72	1		FREAK ME	Elektra EKR 165CD

SILKIE UK folk quartet formed at Hull University in 1963 by Silvia Tatler (vocals), Mike Ramsden (born 21/6/1943, guitar/vocals), Ivor Aylesbury (guitar/vocals) and Kevin Cunningham (double bass). Their hit had contributions from The Beatles on composition, musical accompaniment and production. Ramsden died on 17/1/2004.

23/09/1965	28	6		YOU'VE GOT TO HIDE YOUR LOVE AWAY	Fontana TF 603

SILKK THE SHOCKER – see **MONTELL JORDAN**

SILSOE UK keyboard player Rod Argent (born 14/6/1945, St Albans). Previously in Argent, he also recorded as Rodriguez Argentina.

21/06/1986	48	4		AZTEC GOLD Theme to ITV's coverage of the 1986 FIFA World Cup	CBS A 7231

LUCIE SILVAS UK singer (born 1978) who was a backing singer for Judie Tzuke (along with her sister Mia) before going solo. She then turned to songwriting, penning *Jumpin'* for Liberty X before relaunching her solo career.

17/06/2000	62	1		IT'S TOO LATE	EMI CDEM 565
16/10/2004	7	7		**WHAT YOU'RE MADE OF**	Mercury 9867463

JOHN SILVER German DJ.

25/01/2003	35	2		COME ON OVER	Cream 20CD

SILVER BULLET UK duo Richard Brown and DJ Mo.

02/09/1989	70	1		BRING FORTH THE GUILLOTINE	Tam Tam TTT 013
09/12/1989	11	10		20 SECONDS TO COMPLY	Tam Tam 7TTT 019
03/03/1990	45	5		BRING FORTH THE GUILLOTINE	Tam Tam TTT 013
13/04/1991	33	4		UNDERCOVER ANARCHIST	Parlophone R 6284

SILVER BULLET BAND – see **BOB SEGER AND THE SILVER BULLET BAND**

SILVER CITY UK vocal/instrumental duo Greg Fenton and Simon Bradshaw.

30/10/1993	62	1		LOVE INFINITY	Silver City GFJMCD 1

SILVER CONVENTION German/US group initially formed as a studio project by producer Michael Kunze and writer/arranger

❶⁹ Number of weeks single topped the UK chart ↑ Entered the UK chart at #1 ▲⁹ Number of weeks single topped the US chart

723

Silvester Levay. Following the success of the single a group was assembled comprising singers Penny McLean, Ramona Wolf and Linda Thompson. Thompson left in 1976, replaced by Rhonda Heath, although the group had split by the end of the decade.

DATE	POS	WKS	BPI	SINGLE TITLE	LABEL & NUMBER
05/04/1975	30	7		SAVE ME	Magnet MAG 26
15/11/1975	28	8		FLY ROBIN FLY ▲³ 1975 Grammy Award for Best Rhythm & Blues Instrumental Performance. Featured in the 1998 film *54* .... Magnet MAG 43	
03/04/1976	7	11		**GET UP AND BOOGIE**	Magnet MAG 55
19/06/1976	41	4		TIGER BABY/NO NO JOE	Magnet MAG 69
29/01/1977	25	5		EVERYBODY'S TALKIN' 'BOUT LOVE	Magnet MAG 81

SILVER SUN
UK rock group formed in Darlington by James Broad (guitar/vocals), Paul Smith (guitar), Richard Kane (bass) and Richard Sayce (drums). Sayce left in 1999, replaced by Merlin Matthews. They later relocated to London.

DATE	POS	WKS	BPI	SINGLE TITLE	LABEL & NUMBER
02/11/1996	54	1		LAVA	Polydor 5756872
22/02/1997	48	1		LAST DAY	Polydor 5732432
03/05/1997	32	2		GOLDEN SKIN	Polydor 5738272
05/07/1997	51	1		JULIA	Polydor 5711752
18/10/1997	35	2		LAVA Re-issue of Polydor 5756872	Polydor 5714242
20/06/1998	20	4		TOO MUCH, TOO LITTLE, TOO LATE	Polydor 5699152
26/09/1998	26	2		I'LL SEE YOU AROUND	Polydor 5674532

SILVERCHAIR
Australian rock group formed in Newcastle by Ben Gillies (born 24/11/1979, drums), Chris Joannou (born 10/11/1979, USA, bass) and Daniel Johns (born 22/4/1979, guitar/vocals) in 1992 as Innocent Criminals. After winning a national Talent Quest contest they recorded a single and video for Sony Australia (*Tomorrow* which reached #1 in their home country).

DATE	POS	WKS	BPI	SINGLE TITLE	LABEL & NUMBER
29/07/1995	71	1		PURE MASSACRE	Murmur 6622642
09/09/1995	59	2		TOMORROW	Murmur 6623952
05/04/1997	34	2		FREAK	Murmur 6640765
19/07/1997	40	2		ABUSE ME	Murmur 6647905
15/05/1999	45	1		ANA'S SONG	Columbia 6673452

DOOLEY SILVERSPOON
US singer (born 31/10/1946, Lancaster, SC); he originally recorded as Little Dooley.

DATE	POS	WKS	BPI	SINGLE TITLE	LABEL & NUMBER
31/01/1976	44	3		LET ME BE THE NUMBER 1 (LOVE OF YOUR LIFE)	Seville SEV 1020

HARRY SIMEONE CHORALE
US choir leader (born 9/5/1911, Newark, NJ); he began as arranger for Fred Waring in 1939.

DATE	POS	WKS	BPI	SINGLE TITLE	LABEL & NUMBER
13/02/1959	13	7		LITTLE DRUMMER BOY	Top Rank JAR 101
22/12/1960	35	2		ONWARD CHRISTIAN SOLDIERS	Ember EMBS 118
21/12/1961	36	3		ONWARD CHRISTIAN SOLDIERS	Ember EMBS 118
20/12/1962	38	2		ONWARD CHRISTIAN SOLDIERS Re-issue of Ember EMBS 118 and re-released for the Christmas market	Ember EMBS 144

SIMIAN
UK group formed by Simon Lord, James Ford, Alex MacNaughton and Jason Shaw.

DATE	POS	WKS	BPI	SINGLE TITLE	LABEL & NUMBER
14/06/2003	55	1		LA BREEZE	Source SOURCD 069

GENE SIMMONS
US singer/bass player (born Chaim Witz, 25/8/1949, Haifa, Israel); he was a founding member of Kiss in 1972. He later appeared in films, including *Runaway* (1984) and *Trick Or Treat* (1986).

DATE	POS	WKS	BPI	SINGLE TITLE	LABEL & NUMBER
27/01/1979	41	4		RADIOACTIVE	Casablanca CAN 134

SIMON
UK producer Simon Pearson.

DATE	POS	WKS	BPI	SINGLE TITLE	LABEL & NUMBER
31/03/2001	36	2		FREE AT LAST Contains samples of Martin Luther King's *I Have A Dream* speech of 28/8/1963 and Soft Cell's *Tainted Love*. .... Positiva CDTIV 152	

CARLY SIMON
US singer (born 25/6/1945, New York) who began as one half of the Simon Sisters with sister Lucy. She made her first solo recordings in 1966, but had nothing released until 1971. Married James Taylor in 1972 and divorced in 1983. She won an Oscar in 1988 for *Let The River Run*, the theme to *Working Girl* in the Best Original Song category. She has also won four Grammy Awards: Best New Artist in 1971, Best Recording For Children in 1980 with various others for *In Harmony*, Best Recording for Children in 1982 with various others for *In Harmony 2* and Best Song Written Specifically for a Motion Picture in 1989 for *Let The River Run*.

DATE	POS	WKS	BPI	SINGLE TITLE	LABEL & NUMBER
16/12/1972	3	15		**YOU'RE SO VAIN ▲³**	Elektra K 12077
31/03/1973	17	9		THE RIGHT THING TO DO	Elektra K 12095
16/03/1974	34	5		MOCKINGBIRD **CARLY SIMON AND JAMES TAYLOR**	Elektra K 12134
06/08/1977	7	12	O	**NOBODY DOES IT BETTER** Featured in the films *The Spy Who Loved Me* (1977) and *Bridget Jones Diary 2: Edge Of Reason* (2004) .... Elektra K 12261	
21/08/1982	10	13		**WHY** Featured in the 1982 film *Soup For One*	WEA K 79300
24/01/1987	10	12		**COMING AROUND AGAIN** Featured in the 1987 film *Heartburn*	Arista ARIST 687
10/06/1989	56	5		WHY Re-issue of WEA K 79300	WEA U 7501
20/04/1991	41	5		YOU'RE SO VAIN Re-issue of Elektra K 12077	Elektra EKR 123
22/12/2001	13	10		SON OF A GUN (BETCHA THINK THIS SONG) **JANET JACKSON WITH CARLY SIMON FEATURING MISSY ELLIOTT** Contains a sample of Carly Simon's *You're So Vain*	Virgin VUSCDX 232

JOE SIMON
US singer (born 2/9/1943, Simmesport, LA). He grew up in Oakland, CA, singing with the Goldentones in 1960 before going solo in 1964. He recorded for Vee-Jay, Sound Stage 7, Spring, Posse and Compleat, later moving to Nashville and working with John Richbourg, pioneering a fusion of soul and country. He won the 1969 Grammy Award for Best Rhythm & Blues

Solo Vocal Performance for *The Chokin' Kind*. He retired from recording in 1986 following Richbourg's death from cancer and took to religion.

16/06/1973.....14.....10......	STEP BY STEP	Mojo 2093 030

PAUL SIMON
US singer (born 13/10/1941, Newark, NJ). He met up with Art Garfunkel in 1955; they first recorded as Tom & Jerry for Big Records in 1957 (Garfunkel called himself Tom Graph, Simon was Jerry Landis). They first recorded as Simon & Garfunkel in 1964 and split in 1970. Simon had recorded as Jerry Landis, Tico and Tico & The Temples during his early career with Garfunkel and under his own name in 1970. Following the split with Garfunkel he remained with CBS, switching to Warner's in 1979. He married singer Edie Brickell in May 1992, having previously been married to actress Carrie Fisher (Princess Leia in *Star Wars*). Having won five Grammy Awards with Garfunkel and three for his songwriting with the duo, Simon has gone on to win a further four: Album of the Year (at the ceremony, he thanked Stevie Wonder, who had won the award the two years previously, for not releasing an album that year!) and Best Pop Vocal Performance in 1975 for *Still Crazy After All These Years*, Album of the Year in 1986 for *Graceland* and Record of the Year in 1987 for *Graceland*. Named Best International Male at the 1987 BRIT Awards. He was inducted into the Rock & Roll Hall of Fame in 2001 having previously been inducted in 1990 as a member of Simon & Garfunkel.

19/02/1972.....5......12......	**MOTHER AND CHILD REUNION** .... CBS 7793
29/04/1972.....15......9......	ME AND JULIO DOWN BY THE SCHOOLYARD Featured in the 2002 film *Maid In Manhattan* .... CBS 7964
16/06/1973 .....7......11......	**TAKE ME TO THE MARDI GRAS** .... CBS 1578
22/09/1973.....39......5......	LOVES ME LIKE A ROCK.. CBS 1700
10/01/1976.....23......6......	50 WAYS TO LEAVE YOUR LOVER ▲3 .... CBS 3887
03/12/1977.....36......5......	SLIP SLIDIN' AWAY .... CBS 5770
06/09/1980.....58......4......	LATE IN THE EVENING .... Warner Brothers K 17666
13/09/1986.....4......13......O	**YOU CAN CALL ME AL**.. Warner Brothers W 8667
13/12/1986.....26......8......	THE BOY IN THE BUBBLE .... Warner Brothers W 8509
06/10/1990.....15......10......	THE OBVIOUS CHILD .... Warner Brothers W 9549
09/12/1995.....44......2......	SOMETHING SO RIGHT ANNIE LENNOX FEATURING PAUL SIMON .... RCA 74321332392

RONNI SIMON
UK singer who also sang with Inner City.

13/08/1994.....73......1......	B GOOD 2 ME.. Network NWKCD 80
10/06/1995.....58......1......	TAKE YOU THERE .... Network NWKCD 85

TITO SIMON
Jamaican reggae singer Keith Foster.

08/02/1975.....45......4.......	THIS MONDAY MORNING FEELING .... Horse HOSS 57

SIMON AND GARFUNKEL
US folk-rock duo Paul Simon (born 13/10/1941, Newark, NJ) and Art Garfunkel (born 5/11/1941, Forest Hills, NY) who first teamed up at school in 1955. They recorded for Big Top in 1957 as Tom & Jerry (Garfunkel was Tom Graph, Simon was Jerry Landis) but split after leaving high school. Teaming again in 1960 as Simon & Garfunkel, their debut album was on CBS in 1964. They disbanded in 1970, Garfunkel concentrating on acting and Simon on a solo career. They have reunited for concerts and recorded their 1982 concert in Central Park. They were inducted into the Rock & Roll Hall of Fame in 1990. Five Grammy Awards included Album of the Year, Record of the Year and Best Arrangement Accompanying Singers in 1970 for *Bridge Over Troubled Water*. Their two 1977 BRIT Awards included Best International Album for *Bridge Over Troubled Water*.

24/03/1966 .....9......12......	**HOMEWARD BOUND**.. CBS 202045
16/06/1966.....17......10......	I AM A ROCK .... CBS 202303
10/07/1968 .....4......12......	**MRS. ROBINSON** ▲3 Featured in the films *The Graduate* (1967) and *Forrest Gump* (1994)........................ CBS 3443
08/01/1969 .....9......5......	**MRS. ROBINSON (EP)** Tracks on EP: *Mrs Robinson, Scarborough Fair – Canticle, Sounds Of Silence* and *April Come She Will*. All these tracks were featured in the 1967 film *The Graduate*. All EPs were excluded from the chart from February 1969. *The Sounds Of Silence* was featured in the films *More American Graffiti* (1979) and *Kingpin* (1996). *Mrs Robinson* won the 1968 Grammy Awards for Record of the Year and Best Contemporary Pop Vocal Performance by a Duo. *The Graduate* won the Grammy Award for Best Original Score Written for a Motion Picture for writer Paul Simon the same year .... CBS EP 6400
30/04/1969 .....6......14......	**THE BOXER** Featured in the film *Intolerable Cruelty* (2003) .... CBS 4162
21/02/1970 ...❶3.....20......	**BRIDGE OVER TROUBLED WATER** ▲6 1968 Grammy Award for Record of the Year, plus Grammy Award for Best Contemporary Song for writer Paul Simon the same year. 1977 BRIT Award for Best International Single.......................... CBS 4790
07/10/1972.....25......7.......	AMERICA Featured in the 2000 film *Almost Famous*.................................. CBS 8336
07/12/1991.....30......6.......	A HAZY SHADE OF WINTER/SILENT NIGHT/SEVEN O'CLOCK NEWS .... Columbia 6576537
15/02/1992.....75......1.......	THE BOXER Re-issue CBS 4162 .... Columbia 6578067

SIMONE
US singer who also worked as a backing singer for the likes of George Duke, Zhigge and Milton Nascimento.

23/11/1991.....75......1.......	MY FAMILY DEPENDS ON ME.................................... Strictly Rhythm A 8678

NINA SIMONE
US singer (born Eunice Waymon, 21/2/1933, Tryon, SC); her first US hit was with *I Love You Porgy* in 1959. Towards the end of the 1960s she began devoting more time to political activities (including penning *To Be Young Gifted And Black*, which was a tribute to playwright Lorraine Hansberry) and later relocated to France. She died on 21/4/2003.

05/08/1965.....49......1.......	I PUT A SPELL ON YOU .... Philips BF 1415
16/10/1968 .....2......18......	**AIN'T GOT NO – I GOT LIFE/DO WHAT YOU GOTTA DO** A-side featured in the 2001 film *The Parole Officer* .... RCA 1743
16/10/1968 .....2......18......	**DO WHAT YOU GOTTA DO** .... RCA 1743
15/01/1969 .....5......9.......	**TO LOVE SOMEBODY**... RCA 1779
15/01/1969 .....28......4.......	I PUT A SPELL ON YOU Re-issue of Philips BF 1415..................................... Philips BF 1736
31/10/1987 .....5......11......O	**MY BABY JUST CARES FOR ME** Originally recorded in 1959 and revived following use in an advertisement for Chanel No5 perfume. Featured in the 1996 film *Shallow Grave*.............................. Charly CYZ 7112
09/07/1994.....40......3.......	FEELING GOOD .... Mercury MERCD 403

❶9 Number of weeks single topped the UK chart ↑ Entered the UK chart at #1 ▲9 Number of weeks single topped the US chart

725

VICTOR SIMONELLI PRESENTS SOLUTION
US producer, previously in Colourblind with Tommy Musto.

02/11/1996	63	1	FEELS SO RIGHT	Soundproof MCSTD 40068

SIMPLE KID
Irish singer Ciaran McFeely. He had previously been a member of Young Offenders.

13/09/2003	72	1	THE AVERAGE MAN	2M 2M005CD
14/02/2004	38	2	TRUCK ON	2M 2M007CD

SIMPLE MINDS

UK rock group formed in Glasgow in 1978 by Jim Kerr (born 9/7/1959, Glasgow, vocals), Charlie Burchill (born 27/11/1959, Glasgow, guitar), Mike McNeil (born 20/7/1958, Glasgow, keyboards), Derek Forbes (born 22/6/1956, Glasgow, bass), Brian McGhee (drums) and Duncan Barnwell (guitar), most of whom had been in Johnny and the Self Abusers. They first recorded for Zoom in 1978, their product licensed to Arista, switching to Virgin in 1981. Barnwell left in 1978, but was not replaced. McGhee left in 1981, replaced by Kenny Hyslop (born 14/2/1951, Helensburgh, Strathclyde), Mark Ogeltree and then Mel Gaynor (born 29/5/1959, Glasgow). Forbes left in 1984, replaced by John Giblin. Kerr married Chrissie Hynde in 1984 and, following their divorce, married Patsy Kensit (of Eighth Wonder) in 1992. This also ended in divorce. By 1995 the line-up was Kerr, Burchill, Foster, Mark Taylor (keyboards/acoustic guitar) and Mark Schulman (drums). In 1999 Kerr joined a consortium (along with Kenny Dalglish) taking over Glasgow Celtic Football Club.

12/05/1979	62	2		LIFE IN A DAY	Zoom ZUM 10
23/05/1981	59	3		THE AMERICAN	Virgin VS 410
15/08/1981	47	4		LOVE SONG	Virgin VS 434
07/11/1981	52	3		SWEAT IN A BULLET	Virgin VS 451
10/04/1982	13	11		PROMISED YOU A MIRACLE	Virgin VS 488
28/08/1982	16	11		GLITTERING PRIZE	Virgin VS 511
13/11/1982	36	5		SOMEONE SOMEWHERE (IN SUMMERTIME)	Virgin VS 538
26/11/1983	13	10		WATERFRONT	Virgin VS 636
28/01/1984	20	4		SPEED YOUR LOVE TO ME	Virgin VS 649
24/03/1984	27	5		UP ON THE CATWALK	Virgin VS 661
20/04/1985	7	24	○	**DON'T YOU FORGET ABOUT ME** ▲[1] Featured in the 1985 film *The Breakfast Club*	Virgin VS 749
12/10/1985	7	11		**ALIVE AND KICKING**	Virgin VS 817
01/02/1986	10	7		**SANCTIFY YOURSELF**	Virgin SM 1
12/04/1986	9	9		**ALL THE THINGS SHE SAID**	Virgin VS 860
15/11/1986	13	8		GHOSTDANCING	Virgin VS 907
20/06/1987	19	7		PROMISED YOU A MIRACLE Live recording	Virgin SM 2
18/02/1989	❶[2]	11	○	**BELFAST CHILD**	Virgin SMX 3
22/04/1989	13	4		THIS IS YOUR LAND	Virgin SMX 4
29/07/1989	15	5		KICK IT IN	Virgin SM 5
09/12/1989	18	6		THE AMSTERDAM EP Tracks on EP: *Let It All Come Down, Jerusalem* and *Sign Of The Times*	Virgin SMX 6
23/03/1991	6	7		**LET THERE BE LOVE**	Virgin VS 1332
25/05/1991	20	4		SEE THE LIGHTS	Virgin VS 1343
31/08/1991	13	4		STAND BY LOVE	Virgin VS 1358
26/10/1991	34	3		REAL LIFE	Virgin VS 1382
10/10/1992	6	6		**LOVE SONG/ALIVE AND KICKING**	Virgin VS 1440
28/01/1995	9	5		**SHE'S A RIVER**	Virgin VSCDX 1509
08/04/1995	18	5		HYPNOTISED	Virgin VSCDX 1534
14/03/1998	18	2		GLITTERBALL	Chrysalis CDCHSS 5078
30/05/1998	43	1		WAR BABIES	Chrysalis CDCHSS 5088
02/02/2002	74	1		BELFAST TRANCE **JAMES '00' FLEMING VS SIMPLE MINDS**	Nebula BELFCD 001
30/03/2002	47	1		CRY	Eagle EAGXS 218
20/07/2002	67	1		MONSTER **LIQUID PEOPLE VS SIMPLE MINDS**	Defected DFECT 49R

SIMPLE PLAN
Canadian rock group formed in Montreal in 1999 by Pierre Bouvier (vocals), Jeff Stinco (guitar), Sebastien Lefebvre (guitar), David Desrosiers (bass) and Chuck Comeau (drums).

05/07/2003	65	3	LET HER FEEL IT	Lava/Atlantic AT 0158CD

SIMPLICIOUS
US R&B group from Miami featuring eight members of the Broomfield family, including Ron Bloomfield who changed his name to Eugene Wilde and recorded solo. They were originally known as La Voyage and also recorded as Tight Connection.

29/09/1984	65	3	LET HER FEEL IT	Fourth & Broadway BRW 13
02/02/1985	34	6	LET HER FEEL IT Re-issue of Fourth & Broadway BRW 13. B-side was *Personality* by **EUGENE WILDE**	Fourth & Broadway BRW 18

SIMPLY RED UK group fronted by singer/songwriter Mick Hucknall (born 8/6/1960, Manchester). He had formed new-wave band the Frantic Elevators in 1979, disbanding it in 1984 in favour of the soul-styled Simply Red. The initial line-up featured Hucknall, David Fryman, Eddie Sherwood, Ojo and Mog. The following year Hucknall re-formed the group with Fritz McIntyre (born 2/9/1958, Birmingham, keyboards), Tim Kellet (born 23/7/1964, Knaresborough, horns), Tony Bowers (born 31/10/1956, bass), Sylvan Richardson (guitar) and Chris Joyce (born 10/11/1957, Manchester, drums). Richardson left in 1987, replaced by Aziz Ibrahim, with Ian Kirkham (saxophone) and Janette Sewell (vocals) also joining. Sewell and Ibrahim left in 1988, Heitor TP joining on guitar. The line-up in 1996 was Hucknall, McIntyre, Heitor, Joyce and Ian Kirkham (keyboards). Hucknall was named Best British Male at the 1993 BRIT Awards while the group have won the Best British Group category in 1992 (jointly with KLF) and 1993. Hucknall also won the 1997 MOBO Award for Outstanding Achievement.

DATE	POS	WKS	BPI	SINGLE TITLE	LABEL & NUMBER
15/06/1985	13	12		MONEY'S TOO TIGHT TO MENTION	Elektra EKR 9
21/09/1985	66	2		COME TO MY AID	Elektra EKR 19
16/11/1985	51	4		HOLDING BACK THE YEARS ▲[1] Originally recorded by the Frantic Elevators in 1979	Elektra EKR 29
08/03/1986	53	3		JERICHO	WEA YZ 63
17/05/1986	2	13	○	**HOLDING BACK THE YEARS** Re-issue of Elektra EKR 29. Featured in the 2001 film *Door To Door*	WEA YZ 70
09/08/1986	61	4		OPEN UP THE RED BOX	WEA YZ 75
14/02/1987	11	10		THE RIGHT THING	WEA YZ 103
23/05/1987	31	5		INFIDELITY	Elektra YZ 114
28/11/1987	11	9		EV'RY TIME WE SAY GOODBYE	Elektra YZ 161
12/03/1988	68	3		I WON'T FEEL BAD	Elektra YZ 172
28/01/1989	13	8		IT'S ONLY LOVE	Elektra YZ 349
08/04/1989	2	10	○	**IF YOU DON'T KNOW ME BY NOW** ▲[1] Featured in the 1991 film *My Girl*. The song (written in 1972) won the 1989 Grammy Award for Best Rhythm & Blues Song for writers Kenny Gamble and Leon Huff	Elektra YZ 377
08/07/1989	17	8		A NEW FLAME	WEA YZ 404
28/10/1989	46	3		YOU'VE GOT IT	WEA YZ 424
21/09/1991	11	8		SOMETHING GOT ME STARTED	East West YZ 614
30/11/1991	8	10		**STARS**	East West YZ 626
08/02/1992	9	8		**FOR YOUR BABIES**	East West YZ 642
02/05/1992	33	5		THRILL ME	East West YZ 671
25/07/1992	17	4		YOUR MIRROR	East West YZ 689
21/11/1992	11	10		MONTREAUX EP Tracks on EP: *Drowning In My Own Tears, Granma's Hands, Lady Godiva's Room* and *Love For Sale* .... East West YZ 716	
30/09/1995	❶[4]	14	✪	**FAIRGROUND** ↑	East West EW 001CD2
16/12/1995	22	6		REMEMBERING THE FIRST TIME	East West EW 015CD1
24/02/1996	18	4		NEVER NEVER LOVE	East West EW 029CD1
22/06/1996	11	6		WE'RE IN THIS TOGETHER Official theme of the 1996 European Football Championships	East West EW 046CDX
09/11/1996	4	13	○	**ANGEL** Featured in the 1996 film *Set It Off*	East West EW 074CD1
20/09/1997	14	8		NIGHT NURSE SLY AND ROBBIE FEATURING SIMPLY RED	East West EW 129CD1
16/05/1998	7	7		**SAY YOU LOVE ME**	East West EW 164CD
22/08/1998	6	7		**THE AIR I BREATHE**	East West EW 181CD1
12/12/1998	34	2		GHETTO GIRL	East West EW 191CD1
30/10/1999	14	6		AIN'T THAT A LOT OF LOVE	East West EW 208CD1
19/02/2000	26	2		YOUR EYES	East West EW 212CD1
29/03/2003	7	11		**SUNRISE** Contains a sample of Hall & Oates *I Can't Go For That (No Can Do)*	Simplyred.com SRS 001CD2
19/07/2003	21	4		FAKE	Simplyred.com SRS 002CD
13/12/2003	7	9		**YOU MAKE ME FEEL BRAND NEW**	Simplyred.com SRS 003CD1
10/04/2004	40	2		HOME	Simplyred.com SRS 004CD

SIMPLY RED AND WHITE UK vocal group formed by Sunderland FC supporters and fronted by Sean Vasey; their debut hit was a tribute to manager Peter Reid to the tune of The Monkees' *Daydream Believer*. All profits were given to the Malcolm Sargent Cancer Fund for Children.

DATE	POS	WKS	BPI	SINGLE TITLE	LABEL & NUMBER
06/04/1996	41	4		DAYDREAM BELIEVER (CHEER UP PETER REID) Only available as a one-track cassette	Ropery SHAYISGOD 1D

SIMPLY SMOOTH US vocal group formed by Marlin Jones, Raymond Frank and Dion McIntosh.

DATE	POS	WKS	BPI	SINGLE TITLE	LABEL & NUMBER
17/10/1998	70	1		LADY (YOU BRING ME UP)	Big Bang CDBANG 07

ASHLEE SIMPSON US singer (born 30/10/1984, Dallas, TX) who is the younger sister of Jessica Simpson. She began her career as an actress, appearing in *Malcolm In The Middle* and *Seventh Heaven* before launching a singing career.

DATE	POS	WKS	BPI	SINGLE TITLE	LABEL & NUMBER
09/10/2004	4	10		**PIECES OF ME**	Geffen 9863812

JESSICA SIMPSON US singer (born 10/7/1980, Dallas, TX); she moved to Los Angeles, making her debut album at seventeen. She married fellow singer Nick Lachey of 98 Degrees in 2002 (their marriage was the subject of the MTV documentary series *The Newlyweds*).

DATE	POS	WKS	BPI	SINGLE TITLE	LABEL & NUMBER
22/04/2000	7	11		**I WANNA LOVE YOU FOREVER**	Columbia 6691272
15/07/2000	15	7		I THINK I'M IN LOVE WITH YOU Contains a sample of John Mellencamp's *Jack And Diane*	Columbia 6695942
14/07/2001	11	6		IRRESISTIBLE	Columbia 6714102
26/06/2004	7	8		**WITH YOU**	Columbia 6748302

❶[9] Number of weeks single topped the UK chart ↑ Entered the UK chart at #1 ▲[9] Number of weeks single topped the US chart

PAUL SIMPSON FEATURING ADEVA US producer/singer based in New York with female singer Adeva.

25/03/1989.....22......8....... MUSICAL FREEDOM (MOVING ON UP) .... Cooltempo COOL 182

VIDA SIMPSON US singer who also worked with Erick Morillo, Armand Van Helden and Todd Edwards.

18/02/1995.....70......1....... OOHHH BABY .... Hi-Life HICD 6

SIMPSONS US cartoon TV series that first appeared in April 1987 as a short slot in Tracey Ullman's comedy show, leading to the Simpsons being given their own series. Created by Matt Groening, the family consists of Homer (the father, voice supplied by Dan Castellaneta), Marge (mother, Julie Kavner), Bart (son, Nancy Cartwright), Lisa (daughter, Yeardley Smith) and Maggie (youngest daughter, Liz Taylor). Aside from the success of the Simpsons themselves on the pop charts, a slew of acts have also 'appeared' in the programme, including Michael Jackson, Barry White, Tom Jones, Red Hot Chili Peppers, Sting, Ringo Starr, Spinal Tap, Aerosmith, Radiohead, Paul and Linda McCartney and Tony Bennett and more recently Britney Spears and 'N Sync. They have a star on the Hollywood Walk of Fame.

26/01/1991 .... ❶³.....12.....● DO THE BARTMAN Although the single was written by Bryan Loren and sung by Nancy Cartwright, there is speculation that the song was really written by Michael Jackson .... Geffen GEF 87

06/04/1991 .....7......7....... DEEP DEEP TROUBLE SIMPSONS FEATURING BART AND HOMER.. Geffen GEF 88

W/CDR AE SIMS – see THE CENTRAL BAND OF THE ROYAL AIR FORCE, CONDUCTOR W/CDR AE SIMS OBE

JOYCE SIMS US singer (born 1959, Rochester, NY). After working in a hamburger bar, she signed with Sleeping Bag Records in 1986.

19/04/1986.....16......10......	ALL AND ALL	London LON 94
13/06/1987.....34......6......	LIFETIME LOVE	London LON 137
09/01/1988 .....7......9......	COME INTO MY LIFE	London LON 161
23/04/1988.....24......6......	WALK AWAY	London LON 176
17/06/1989.....39......4......	LOOKING FOR A LOVE	ffrr F 109
27/05/1995.....72......1......	COME INTO MY LIFE (REMIX).........................	Club Tools 0060435 CLU

KYM SIMS US singer (born 28/12/1966, Chicago, IL); she began as a jingle singer. She also recorded with Ce Ce Peniston.

07/12/1991 .....5......12.....O	TOO BLIND TO SEE IT Contains a sample of First Choice's Let No Man Put Asunder	Atco B 8667
28/03/1992.....13......7......	TAKE MY ADVICE	Atco B 8591
27/06/1992.....30......3......	A LITTLE BIT MORE..................................	Atco B 8528
08/06/1996.....58......1......	WE GOTTA LOVE	Pulse 8 CDLOSE 104

SIN WITH SEBASTIAN German singer Sebastian Roth.

16/09/1995.....44......1...... SHUT UP (AND SLEEP WITH ME) .... Sing Sing 74321253592

27/01/1996.....46......1...... SHUT UP (AND SLEEP WITH ME) (REMIX)... Sing Sing 74321337972

FRANK SINATRA US singer (born 12/12/1915, Hoboken, NJ). He joined Harry James' band in 1939 then Tommy Dorsey in 1940. He went solo in 1942 with Columbia, later switching to Capitol and forming the Reprise label in 1961. He began his film career in 1941 in Las Vegas Nights and landed his first starring role in Higher And Higher in 1943. He sold Reprise to Warner Brothers in 1963, being made Vice President and Consultant of Warner Brothers Picture Corp. the same year. He won an Oscar for the film From Here To Eternity (for Best Supporting Actor) in 1953. Eight Grammy Awards include Best Album Cover in 1958 for Only The Lonely, Album of the Year in 1965 for September Of My Years, Album of the Year in 1966 for A Man And His Music and the Best Traditional Pop Album in 1995 for Duets II. Daughter Nancy Sinatra is also an actress and singer. He died from a heart attack after a lengthy illness on 14/5/1998. He has three stars on the Hollywood Walk of Fame, for his contribution to recording, motion pictures and TV.

09/07/1954.....12......1......	YOUNG AT HEART Featured in the 1999 film Liberty Heights	Capitol CL 14064
16/07/1954 .... ❶³.....19......	THREE COINS IN THE FOUNTAIN Featured in the 1954 film Three Coins In The Fountain winning Oscar for Best Film Song.........	Capitol CL 14120
10/06/1955.....13......7......	YOU MY LOVE	Capitol CL 14240
05/08/1955 .....2......13......	LEARNIN' THE BLUES ▲²	Capitol CL 14296
02/09/1955.....18......1......	NOT AS A STRANGER.................................	Capitol CL 14326
13/01/1956 .....3......8......	LOVE AND MARRIAGE Featured in the TV production Our Town	Capitol CL 14503
20/01/1956 .....2......9......	(LOVE IS) THE TENDER TRAP Featured in the 1955 film The Tender Trap and the 1995 film Miami Rhapsody.....	Capitol CL 14511
15/06/1956.....12......8......	SONGS FOR SWINGING LOVERS (LP) Tracks on LP: You Make Me Feel So Young, It Happened In Monterey, You're Getting To Be A Habit With Me, You Brought A New Kind Of Love To Me, Too Marvelous For Words, Old Devil Moon, Pennies From Heaven, Love Is Here To Stay, I've Got You Under My Skin, I Thought About You, We'll Be Together Again, Making Whoopee, Swingin' Down The Lane, Anything Goes and How About You. I've Got You Under My Skin and Too Marvelous For Words featured in the 2000 film What Women Want...................................	Capitol LCT 6106
22/11/1957 .....3......20......	ALL THE WAY Featured in the 1957 film The Joker Is Wild winning an Oscar for Best Film Song...............	Capitol CL 14800
29/11/1957.....21......2......	CHICAGO	Capitol CL 14800
07/02/1958.....12......8......	WITCHCRAFT	Capitol CL 14819
14/11/1958.....25......4......	MR. SUCCESS.......................................	Capitol CL 14956
10/04/1959.....18......5......	FRENCH FOREIGN LEGION	Capitol CL 14997
16/05/1959.....30......1......	COME DANCE WITH ME (LP) FRANK SINATRA WITH BILLY MAY AND HIS ORCHESTRA Tracks on EP: Something's Gotta Give, Just In Time, Dancing In The Dark, Too Close For Comfort, I Could Have Danced All Night, Saturday Night Is The Loneliest Night Of The Week, Day In Day Out, Cheek To Cheek, Baubles Bangles And Beads, The Song Is You and The Last Dance. 1959 Grammy Awards for Album of the Year, Best Vocal Performance and Special Trustees Award for Artists & Repertoire Contribution	Capitol LCT 6179

28/08/1959	6	15		**HIGH HOPES** Featured in the 1959 film *A Hole In The Head* for which it won an Oscar for Best Film Song. A parody of the song was adopted by John F Kennedy for his successful 1960 presidential campaign . . . . Capitol CL 15052
07/04/1960	48	2		IT'S NICE TO GO TRAV'LING . . . . Capitol CL 15116
16/06/1960	18	9		RIVER STAY 'WAY FROM MY DOOR . . . . Capitol CL 15135
08/09/1960	15	12		NICE 'N' EASY . . . . Capitol CL 15150
24/11/1960	11	8		OL' MACDONALD . . . . Capitol CL 15168
20/04/1961	33	7		MY BLUE HEAVEN . . . . Capitol CL 15193
28/09/1961	15	8		GRANADA . . . . Reprise R 20010
23/11/1961	39	3		THE COFFEE SONG . . . . Reprise R 20035
05/04/1962	22	12		EVERYBODY'S TWISTING . . . . Reprise R 20063
13/12/1962	20	9		ME AND MY SHADOW **FRANK SINATRA AND SAMMY DAVIS JR** . . . . Reprise R 20128
07/03/1963	35	6		MY KIND OF GIRL . . . . Reprise R 20148
24/09/1964	47	1		HELLO DOLLY This and above single credited to **FRANK SINATRA WITH COUNT BASIE**. . . Reprise R 20351
12/05/1966	●3	20		**STRANGERS IN THE NIGHT** ▲1 1966 Grammy Awards for Record of the Year and Best Male Solo Vocal Performance. Featured in the 1966 film *A Man Could Get Killed* . . . . Reprise R 23052
29/09/1966	36	5		SUMMER WIND . . . . Reprise R 20509
15/12/1966	46	5		THAT'S LIFE . . . . Reprise RS 20531
23/03/1967	●2	18		**SOMETHIN' STUPID** ▲4 **NANCY SINATRA AND FRANK SINATRA** . . . . Reprise RS 23166
23/08/1967	33	11		THE WORLD WE KNEW . . . . Reprise R 20610
02/04/1969	5	122		**MY WAY** The longest any record has been on the charts, departing on 8/1/1972. It also spent 73 weeks in the top 40 . . . . Reprise R 20817
04/10/1969	8	18		**LOVE'S BEEN GOOD TO ME** . . . . Reprise R 20852
06/03/1971	16	12		I WILL DRINK THE WINE . . . . Reprise R 23487
20/12/1975	34	7		I BELIEVE I'M GONNA LOVE YOU . . . . Reprise K 14400
09/08/1980	59	4		THEME FROM NEW YORK, NY Featured in the 1999 film *Summer Of Sam* . . . . Reprise K 14502
22/03/1986	4	10	○	**THEME FROM NEW YORK, NY** . . . . Reprise K 14502
04/12/1993	4	9		**I'VE GOT YOU UNDER MY SKIN FRANK SINATRA WITH BONO** Listed flip side was *Stay (Faraway, So Close)* by **U2**. It made Frank Sinatra the oldest singer to have enjoyed a chart hit – he was 78 years of age at the time . . . . Island CID 578
16/04/1994	45	2		MY WAY Re-issue of Reprise R 20817 . . . . Reprise W 0163CD
30/01/1999	41	1		THEY ALL LAUGHED . . . . Reprise W 469CD

NANCY SINATRA
US singer (born 8/6/1940, Jersey City, NY), the first child of Frank and Nancy Sinatra; she moved with her parents to Los Angeles, CA while still a child. She sang with her father and Elvis Presley on TV in 1959, signing with Reprise in 1961. Various films included *Marriage On The Rocks* with her father and Dean Martin. Married to singer Tommy Sands in 1960, divorced in 1965.

27/01/1966	●4	14		**THESE BOOTS ARE MADE FOR WALKIN'** ▲1 Featured in the 1987 film *Full Metal Jacket*. . . . . Reprise R 20432
28/04/1966	19	8		HOW DOES THAT GRAB YOU DARLIN'. . . . . Reprise R 20461
19/01/1967	8	10		**SUGAR TOWN**. . . . . Reprise RS 20527
23/03/1967	●2	18		**SOMETHIN' STUPID** ▲4 **NANCY SINATRA AND FRANK SINATRA** . . . . Reprise RS 23166
05/07/1967	11	19		YOU ONLY LIVE TWICE/JACKSON **NANCY SINATRA/NANCY SINATRA AND LEE HAZLEWOOD** A-side featured in the 1967 James Bond film *You Only Live Twice* . . . . Reprise RS 20595
08/11/1967	47	1		LADYBIRD. . . . . Reprise RS 20629
29/11/1969	21	10		THE HIGHWAY SONG . . . . Reprise RS 20869
21/08/1971	2	19		**DID YOU EVER NANCY AND LEE** (Hazlewood) . . . . Reprise K 14093
23/10/2004	46	1		LET ME KISS YOU . . . . Attack ATKXS005

SINCLAIR
UK singer Mike Sinclair.

21/08/1993	28	5		AIN'T NO CASANOVA . . . . Dome CDDOME 1004
26/02/1994	58	2		(I WANNA KNOW) WHY. . . . . Dome CDDOME 1009
06/08/1994	70	1		DON'T LIE . . . . Dome CDDOME 1010

BOB SINCLAR
French DJ/producer (born in Paris).

20/03/1999	56	1		MY ONLY LOVE **BOB SINCLAR FEATURING LEE A GENESIS** . . . . East West EW 196CD
19/08/2000	9	5		**I FEEL FOR YOU** Contains a sample of Cerrone's *Look For Love* . . . . Defected DFECT 18CDS
07/04/2001	46	1		DARLIN' **BOB SINCLAR FEATURING JAMES WILLIAMS**. . . . . Defected DFECT 30CDS
25/01/2003	33	2		THE BEAT GOES ON. . . . . Defected DFTD 062CDS
02/08/2003	67	1		KISS MY EYES . . . . Defected DFTD 070CDX

SINDY
UK doll singer. The doll was first manufactured by Pedigree in 1963 and was launched as Top Pop Sindy in 1972, although her debut hit was still 24 years away!

05/10/1996	70	1		SATURDAY NIGHT . . . . Love This LUVTHISCD 13

SINE
US studio dance group created by songwriter/producer Patrick Adams who was also responsible for Musique. The vocals were by Craig Derry, Venus Dobson and Kenny Simmons.

10/06/1978	33	9		JUST LET ME DO MY THING. . . . . CBS 6351

SINFONIA OF LONDON – see PETER AUTY AND THE SINFONIA OF LONDON CONDUCTED BY HOWARD BLAKE

SINGING CORNER MEETS DONOVAN
UK duo Trevor Neal and Simon Hickson from TV's *Going Live* with Donovan.

01/12/1990	68	1		JENNIFER JUNIPER . . . . Fontana SYP 1

●9 Number of weeks single topped the UK chart ↑ Entered the UK chart at #1 ▲9 Number of weeks single topped the US chart

729

SINGING DOGS Danish record made in Copenhagen by producer Don Charles of dogs barking. The four dogs were named Dolly, Pearl, Caesar and King.

25/11/1955 . . . . . 13 . . . . . . 4 . . . . THE SINGING DOGS (MEDLEY)/OH SUSANNA **DON CHARLES PRESENTS THE SINGING DOGS** Tracks on medley: *Pat-A-Cake, Three Blind Mice* and *Jingle Bells* . . . . Nixa N 15009

SINGING NUN Belgian singer (born Jeanine Deckers, 1928). She entered the Fichermont Convent near Brussels and was given the name Sister Luc-Gabrielle. She recorded an album for private purposes in 1962 but label executives at the studio decided to release them commercially as Soeur Sourire (Sister Smile), with *Dominique* issued as a single, topping the US charts. She left the convent in 1966 and committed suicide on 31/3/1985 along with her partner Annie Pescher.

05/12/1963 . . . . . 7 . . . . . . 14 . . . . . . **DOMINIQUE** ▲4 1963 Grammy Award for Best Gospel and Religious Recording . . . . Philips BF 1293

SINGING SHEEP UK computerised sheep vocals.

18/12/1982 . . . . . 42 . . . . . . 5 . . . . BAA BAA BLACK SHEEP . . . . Sheep BAA 1

MAXINE SINGLETON US singer discovered by producer Curtis Hudson.

02/04/1983 . . . . . 57 . . . . . . 3 . . . . YOU CAN'T RUN FROM LOVE . . . . Creole CR 50

SINITTA US singer (born Sinitta Renay Malone, 19/10/1966, Seattle, WA). UK-based daughter of Miquel Brown who began in musicals.

08/03/1986	2	28	●	**SO MACHO/CRUISING**	Fanfare FAN 7
11/10/1986	45	5		FEELS LIKE THE FIRST TIME	Fanfare FAN 8
25/07/1987	4	14	O	**TOY BOY**	Fanfare FAN 12
12/12/1987	15	9		G.T.O.	Fanfare FAN 14
19/03/1988	6	9	O	**CROSS MY BROKEN HEART**	Fanfare FAN 15
24/09/1988	22	8		I DON'T BELIEVE IN MIRACLES	Fanfare FAN 16
03/06/1989	4	10	O	**RIGHT BACK WHERE WE STARTED FROM**	Fanfare FAN 18
07/10/1989	20	6		LOVE ON A MOUNTAIN TOP	Fanfare FAN 21
21/04/1990	24	6		HITCHIN' A RIDE	Fanfare FAN 24
22/09/1990	62	3		LOVE AND AFFECTION	Fanfare FAN 31
04/07/1992	28	4		SHAME SHAME SHAME	Arista 74321100327
17/04/1993	49	2		THE SUPREME EP Tracks on EP: *Where Did Our Love Go, Stop! In The Name Of Love, You Can't Hurry Love* and *Remember Me*	Arista 74321139592

SINNAMON US vocal group of Bernard Fowler, Melissa Bell, Marsha Carter and Barbara Fowler, the hit a remix of a 1978 single.

28/09/1996 . . . . . 70 . . . . . . 1 . . . . I NEED YOU NOW . . . . Worx WORXCD 003

SIOUXSIE AND THE BANSHEES UK punk group formed in London in 1976 by Siouxsie Sioux (born Susan Dallion, 27/5/1957, Bromley, vocals), Steve 'Havoc' Severin (born Steven Bailey, 25/9/1955, London, bass), Sid Vicious (born John Ritchie, 10/5/1957, London, drums) and Marco Pirroni (born 27/4/1959, London, guitar). They disbanded after one gig, Vicious joining the Sex Pistols and Pirroni later joining Adam & The Ants. Sioux and Severin re-formed with Pete Fenton (guitar) and Kenny Morris (drums) in 1977. Fenton left after four months, replaced by John McKay. Morris and McKay left in 1979, replaced by Budgie (born Peter Clark, 21/8/1957, St Helens, drums) and an on-loan Robert Smith from The Cure. John McGeoch joined on guitar but left in 1982, Smith again filling in. He was eventually replaced by John Carruthers in 1984. Two years later Carruthers left, replaced by John Klein, with Martin McCarrick added on keyboards. They split in 1996. Sioux and Budgie, who later married, also recorded as the Creatures. Severin later linked with Robert Smith in a one-off project The Glove.

26/08/1978	7	10	O	HONG KONG GARDEN	Polydor 2059 052
31/03/1979	24	8		THE STAIRCASE (MYSTERY)	Polydor POSP 9
07/07/1979	28	6		PLAYGROUND TWIST	Polydor POSP 59
29/09/1979	47	3		MITTAGEISEN (METAL POSTCARD)	Polydor 2059 151
15/03/1980	17	8		HAPPY HOUSE	Polydor POSP 117
07/06/1980	22	8		CHRISTINE	Polydor 2059 249
06/12/1980	41	8		ISRAEL	Polydor POSP 205
30/05/1981	22	8		SPELLBOUND	Polydor POSP 273
01/08/1981	32	7		ARABIAN KNIGHTS	Polydor PSOP 309
29/05/1982	22	6		FIRE WORKS	Polydor POSPG 450
09/10/1982	41	4		SLOWDIVE	Polydor POSP 510
04/12/1982	49	5		MELT/IL EST NE LE DIVIN ENFANT	Polydor POSP 539
01/10/1983	3	8	O	**DEAR PRUDENCE**	Wonderland SHE 4
24/03/1984	28	4		SWIMMING HORSES	Wonderland SHE 6
02/06/1984	33	3		DAZZLE	Wonderland SHE 7
27/10/1984	47	3		THE THORN EP Tracks on EP: *Overground, Voices, Placebo Effect* and *Red Over White*	Wonderland SHE 8
26/10/1985	21	6		CITIES IN DUST	Wonderland SHE 9
08/03/1986	34	5		CANDYMAN	Wonderland SHE 10
17/01/1987	14	6		THIS WHEEL'S ON FIRE	Wonderland SHE 11
28/03/1987	41	6		THE PASSENGER	Wonderland SHE 12
25/07/1987	59	3		SONG FROM THE EDGE OF THE WORLD	Wonderland SHE 13
30/07/1988	16	6		PEEK-A-BOO	Wonderland SHE 14
08/10/1988	41	3		THE KILLING JAR	Wonderland SHE 15

O Silver disc ● Gold disc ✪ Platinum disc (additional platinum units are indicated by a figure following the symbol) ◉ Singles released prior to 1973 that are known to have sold over 1 million copies in the UK

03/12/1988	44	1		THE LAST BEAT OF MY HEART	Wonderland SHE 16
25/05/1991	32	4		KISS THEM FOR ME	Wonderland SHE 19
13/07/1991	57	1		SHADOWTIME	Wonderland SHE 20
25/07/1992	21	4		FACE TO FACE Featured in the 1992 film *Batman Returns*	Wonderland SHE 21
20/08/1994	25	2		INTERLUDE MORRISSEY AND SIOUXSIE	Parlophone CDR 6365
07/01/1995	34	3		O BABY	Wonderland SHECD 22
18/02/1995	64	1		STARGAZER	Wonderland SHECD 23

SIR DOUGLAS QUINTET
US Tex-Mex rock group formed in San Antonio, TX in 1964 by Doug Sahm (born 6/11/1941, San Antonio, guitar/vocals), Augie Meyers (born 31/5/1940, San Antonio, organ), Jack Barber (bass), Johnny Perez (born 8/11/1942, drums) and Frank Morin (born 13/8/1946, horns). Sahm had recorded as Little Doug in 1955. They initially pretended they were British to attract publicity. By 1968 the line-up was Sahm, Morin, Martin Fierro (horns), George Rains (drums) and Wayne Talbert (piano). Sahm later recorded solo, appeared in the film *More American Hot Wax*, re-formed the group, recorded solo again and formed The Almost Brothers and then the Texas Tornados.

17/06/1965	15	10		SHE'S ABOUT A MOVER	London HLU 9964

SIR KILLALOT VS ROBO BABE
UK robot rapper with female singer Robo Babe. Sir Killalot is one of the house robots in BBC TV's *Robot Wars*.

30/12/2000	51	3		ROBOT WARS (ANDROID LOVE)	Polydor 5879362

SIR MIX-A-LOT
US rapper (born Anthony Ray, 12/8/1963, Seattle, WA).

08/08/1992	56	2		BABY GOT BACK ▲5 Featured in the films *Charlie's Angels* (2000) and *Scooby Doo 2: Monsters Unleashed* (2004)	Def American DEFA 20

SIRENS
UK vocal group formed in Newcastle-Upon-Tyne by Karina Brians, Kat Haslam, Lynsey Schofield and Lea Cummings. An early member was Michelle Heaton, who later auditioned for Popstars and joined Liberty X.

28/08/2004	49	1		BABY (OFF THE WALL)	Kitchenware SKCD742

SIRRON — see PLUS ONE FEATURING SIRRON

SISQO
US singer (born Mark Andrews, 9/11/1977, Baltimore, MD); he is also a member of Dru Hill.

12/02/2000	14	4		GOT TO GET IT Features the uncredited contribution of Make It Hot	Def Soul 5626442
22/04/2000	3	14	○	THONG SONG Contains a sample of Ricky Martin's *Livin' La Vida Loca*. Featured in the 2000 film *The Nutty Professor II: The Klumps*	Def Soul 5688902
30/09/2000	6	7		UNLEASH THE DRAGON	Def Soul 5726432
16/12/2000	13	8		INCOMPLETE ▲2	Def Soul 5727542
28/07/2001	6	10		DANCE FOR ME	Def Soul 5887002

SISSEL — see WARREN G

SISTER BLISS
UK producer/instrumentalist Ayalah Ben-Tovim. She later joined Faithless. Collette is a UK singer. John Martyn (born Ian McGeachy, 11/9/1948, New Malden) is a UK singer/guitarist who made his first album in 1968.

15/10/1994	31	4		CANTGETAMAN CANTGETAJOB (LIFE'S A BITCH)	Go Beat GODCD 124
15/07/1995	40	2		OH! WHAT A WORLD This and above single credited to SISTER BLISS FEATURING COLLETTE	Go Beat GODCD 126
29/06/1996	51	1		BADMAN	Junk Dog JDOGCD 1
07/10/2000	34	2		SISTER SISTER	Multiply CDMULTY 68
24/03/2001	31	2		DELIVER ME SISTER BLISS FEATURING JOHN MARTYN	Multiply CXMULTY 72

SISTER SLEDGE
US R&B vocal group formed in Philadelphia, PA by sisters Kathy (born 6/1/1959, Philadelphia), Joni (born 1957, Philadelphia), Kim (born 21/8/1958, Philadelphia) and Debbie Sledge (born 9/7/1955, Philadelphia). They began as The Sisters Sledge for the Money Back label in 1971, worked as backing singers and signed with Cotillion in 1974. Kathy Sledge later recorded solo.

21/06/1975	20	6		MAMA NEVER TOLD ME	Atlantic K 10619
17/03/1979	6	11		HE'S THE GREATEST DANCER Featured in the 1998 film *The Last Days Of Disco*	Cotillion K 11257
26/05/1979	8	10		WE ARE FAMILY Featured in the films *The Birdcage* (1996) and *The Full Monty* (1997)	Cotillion K 11293
11/08/1979	17	10		LOST IN MUSIC	Cotillion K 11337
19/01/1980	34	4		GOT TO LOVE SOMEBODY	Cotillion K 11404
28/02/1981	41	5		ALL AMERICAN GIRLS	Atlantic K 11656
26/05/1984	11	13		THINKING OF YOU	Cotillion B 9744
08/09/1984	4	12	○	LOST IN MUSIC (REMIX)	Cotillion B 9718
24/11/1984	33	4		WE ARE FAMILY (REMIX)	Cotillion B 9692
01/06/1985	❶4	16	●	FRANKIE	Atlantic A 9547
31/08/1985	50	3		DANCING ON THE JAGGED EDGE	Atlantic A 9520
23/01/1993	5	8		WE ARE FAMILY (2ND REMIX)	Atlantic A 4508CD
13/03/1993	14	5		LOST IN MUSIC (2ND REMIX)	Atlantic A 4509CD
12/06/1993	17	4		THINKING OF YOU (REMIX)	Atlantic A 4515CD

SISTER 2 SISTER
Australian duo of sisters Christine (born 27/2/1981, New Zealand) and Sharon Muscat (born 23/8/1984, Australia). They are now based in Melbourne.

22/04/2000	18	4		SISTER	Mushroom MUSH 70CDS
28/10/2000	61	1		WHAT'S A GIRL TO DO	Mushroom MUSH 76CDS

❶9 Number of weeks single topped the UK chart ↑ Entered the UK chart at #1 ▲9 Number of weeks single topped the US chart

731

SISTERS OF MERCY UK rock group formed in Leeds in 1980 by Andrew Eldritch (born Andrew Taylor, 15/5/1959, Ely, vocals), Gary Marx (born Mark Pearman, guitar) and a drum machine called Doktor Avalanche. They set up the Merciful Release label the same year. They added Ben Gunn (guitar) and Craig Adams (born 4/4/1962, Otley, Yorkshire, bass) in 1980 in order to perform live. Gunn left in 1983, replaced by Wayne Hussey (born Jerry Lovelock, 26/5/1958, Bristol). They temporarily split in 1985, Hussey and Adams going on to form the Mission and Eldritch adopting the name Sisterhood for one album. Eldritch re-formed the group in 1987 with Patricia Morrison (born 14/1/1962), and by 1990 the line-up was Eldritch, Tony James (ex-Sigue Sigue Sputnik, guitar), Tim Bricheno (born 6/7/1963, Huddersfield, bass) and Andreas Bruhn (born 5/11/1967, Hamburg, Germany, drums). James left in 1991.

	DATE	POS	WKS	BPI	SINGLE TITLE	LABEL & NUMBER
	16/06/1984	46	3		BODY AND SOUL/TRAIN	Merciful Release MR 029
	20/10/1984	45	3		WALK AWAY	Merciful Release MR 033
	09/03/1985	63	2		NO TIME TO CRY	Merciful Release MR 035
	03/10/1987	7	6		**THIS CORROSION**	Merciful Release MR 39
	27/02/1988	13	6		DOMINION	Merciful Release MR 43
	18/06/1988	20	4		LUCRETIA MY REFLECTION	Merciful Release MR 45
	13/10/1990	14	4		MORE	Merciful Release MR 47
	22/12/1990	37	4		DOCTOR JEEP	Merciful Release MR 51
	02/05/1992	3	5		**TEMPLE OF LOVE**	Merciful Release MR 53
	28/08/1993	19	3		UNDER THE GUN	Merciful Release MR 59CDX

SIVUCA Brazilian accordion player who had previously worked with Paul Simon and Airto Moreira before going solo.

	DATE	POS	WKS	BPI	SINGLE TITLE	LABEL & NUMBER
	28/07/1984	56	3		AIN'T NO SUNSHINE	London LON 51

SIX BY SEVEN UK rock group formed in Nottingham by Chris Olley (guitar/vocals), Sam Hempton (guitar), James Flower (keyboards/saxophone), Paul Douglas (bass) and Chris Davis (drums). Hempton left the group after the Glastonbury Festival in 2000.

	DATE	POS	WKS	BPI	SINGLE TITLE	LABEL & NUMBER
	09/05/1998	70	1		CANDLELIGHT	Mantra MNT 34CD
	02/03/2002	48	1		IOU LOVE	Mantra MNT 68CD1

6 BY SIX UK instrumental/production duo fronted by Andre S.

	DATE	POS	WKS	BPI	SINGLE TITLE	LABEL & NUMBER
	04/05/1996	51	1		INTO YOUR HEART	Six6 SIXCD 130

SIX CHIX UK vocal group with Laura Witcombe (seventeen at the time of their debut hit), Becky McCormack (twenty), Cheri Nicolette (25), Sharon Dee Clarke (34), Lynda Hayes (42) and Linda Taylor (51); their debut hit first came to prominence as a competitor to Britain's 'Song For Europe' competition (the song was written by Kimerley Rew, herself a Eurovision Song Contest winner in 1997).

	DATE	POS	WKS	BPI	SINGLE TITLE	LABEL & NUMBER
	26/02/2000	72	1		ONLY THE WOMEN KNOW	EMI CDCHIX 001

666 German dance group formed by Thomas Detert, Mike Griesheimer, Andreas Hoetter and Alexander Stiepel.

	DATE	POS	WKS	BPI	SINGLE TITLE	LABEL & NUMBER
	03/10/1998	58	1		ALARMA	Danceteria CDDAN 001
	25/11/2000	18	4		DEVIL	Echo ECSCD 102

SIXPENCE NONE THE RICHER US group formed in Austin, TX by Leigh Nash (born Leigh Bingham, New Braunfels, TX, vocals), Matt Slocum (guitar), Sean Kelly (guitar), Justin Cary (bass) and Dale Baker (drums). Nash later recorded solo and contributed to the soundtrack for the film *Bounce*.

	DATE	POS	WKS	BPI	SINGLE TITLE	LABEL & NUMBER
	29/05/1999	4	12	O	**KISS ME** Featured in the 1998 film *Dawson's Creek* and the 1998 film *She's All That*	Elektra E 3750CD
	18/09/1999	14	5		THERE SHE GOES Featured in the 2000 film *Snow Day*	Elektra E 3728CD

60FT DOLLS UK vocal/instrumental group from Newport, Wales with Richard Parfitt (guitar/vocals), Mike Cole (bass/vocals) and Carl Bevan (drums).

	DATE	POS	WKS	BPI	SINGLE TITLE	LABEL & NUMBER
	03/02/1996	48	1		STAY	Indolent DOLLS 002CD
	11/05/1996	37	1		TALK TO ME	Indolent DOLLS 003CD
	20/07/1996	38	1		HAPPY SHOPPER	Indolent DOLLS 005CD
	09/05/1998	61	1		ALISON'S ROOM	Indolent DOLLS 007CD1

SIZE 9 US dance singer Josh Wink from Philadelphia, PA; he also recorded as Firefly, Just King & Wink, Winc, E-Culture, Wink and Winx.

	DATE	POS	WKS	BPI	SINGLE TITLE	LABEL & NUMBER
	17/06/1995	52	1		I'M READY Contains samples of B-Beat Girls' *For The Same Man* and Raw Silk's *Do It To The Music*	Virgin America VUSCD 92
	11/11/1995	30	3		I'M READY **JOSH WINK'S SIZE 9** Re-issue of Virgin America VUSCD 92	VC Recordings VCRD 2

RONI SIZE REPRAZENT UK dance group from Bristol, Avon formed by Roni Size (born Ryan Williams, 29/10/1969, Bristol) with Krust, DJ Die, Suv, MC Dynamite and singer Onallee. Their *New Forms* album was the 1997 Mercury Music Prize winner. They also won the 1997 MOBO Award for Best Jungle Act. Size and DJ Die are also in Breakbeat Era. Size later formed the Full Cycle label.

	DATE	POS	WKS	BPI	SINGLE TITLE	LABEL & NUMBER
	14/06/1997	37	2		SHARE THE FALL	Talkin Loud TLCD 21
	13/09/1997	31	2		HEROES	Talkin Loud TLCD 25
	15/11/1997	20	3		BROWN PAPER BAG	Talkin Loud TLCD 28
	14/03/1998	28	2		WATCHING WINDOWS	Talkin Loud TLCD 31
	07/10/2000	17	3		WHO TOLD YOU	Talkin Loud TLCD 61
	24/03/2001	32	3		DIRTY BEATS	Talkin Loud TLCDD 63
	23/06/2001	58	1		LUCKY PRESSURE **RONI SIZE**:	Talkin Loud TLCD 64
	19/10/2002	69	1		SOUND ADVICE	Full Cycle FCY 044
	09/11/2002	53	2		PLAYTIME	Full Cycle FCY 045
	07/12/2002	57	1		SCRAMBLED EGGS/SWINGS & ROUNDABOUTS	Full Cycle FCY 046
	18/01/2003	55	1		FEEL THE HEAT	Full Cycle FCY 048

○ Silver disc ● Gold disc ✪ Platinum disc (additional platinum units are indicated by a figure following the symbol) ◎ Singles released prior to 1973 that are known to have sold over 1 million copies in the UK

22/02/2003.....61......1......	SNAPSHOT 3/SORRY FOR YOU	Full Cycle FCY 033
12/07/2003.....67......1......	SIREN SOUNDS/AT THE MOVIES	Full Cycle FCY 054
06/09/2003.....61......1......	SOUND ADVICE/FORGET ME KNOTS	Full Cycle FCY 056
17/04/2004.....70......1......	STRICTLY SOCIAL/AUTUMN	Liquid V LQD001
24/04/2004.....60......1......	BAMBAKITA/FASSY HOLE	V Recordings V045
09/10/2004.....44......2......	OUT OF BREATH RONI SIZE FEATURING RAHZEL	V Recordings VRECUK002X

SIZZLA Jamaican rapper Miguel Collins.

17/04/1999.....51......2......	RAIN SHOWERS...	Xterminator EXTCDS 76

SKANDAL UK vocal group formed by Matty MacKenzie (born 10/8/1979, Milton Keynes), James Cohen (born 22/12/1979, Twickenham), Matt Baldwin (born 11/9/1980, Middlesex) and Darren Keating (born 10/10/1978, Herne Bay).

14/10/2000.....53......1......	CHAMPAGNE HIGHWAY	Prestige Management CDGING 1

SKANDI GIRLS Scandinavian vocal group formed by Jessica (born 6/2/1981, Finland), Hege (born 22/2/1981, Norway), Helena (born 5/8/1982, Sweden) and Lene (born 29/5/1980, Norway).

25/12/2004.....38......1+......	DO THE CAN CAN	Intelligent IR001CDX

SKATALITES Jamaican reggae group formed in 1964 by Don Drummond (born 1943, Kingston, trombone), Tommy McCook (born 4/3/1927, Cuba, saxophone), Roland Alphonso (born 1936, Clarendon, saxophone), Johnny 'Dizzy' Moore (trumpet), Lester Sterling (saxophone), Jackie Mittoo (born 1948, piano), Jah Jerry (guitar), Lloyd Brevett (bass) and Lloyd Nibbs (drums). They disbanded in August 1965. Drummond committed suicide at Kingston's Bellevue Asylum on 6/5/1969, having been admitted following the murder of his common-law wife in 1965 (she had given him the wrong medication so he would be asleep while she went out dancing. He missed a gig as a result and stabbed her in the neck when she returned the next morning). Mittoo died in 1990. McCook died from heart failure and pneumonia on 5/5/1998. Alphonso collapsed on stage in November 1998, fell into a coma and died on 20/11/1998.

20/04/1967.....36......6......	GUNS OF NAVARONE Originally recorded in 1965	Island WI 168

SKEE-LO US rapper/producer (born Antoine Roundtree, 5/3/1975, Riverside, CA).

09/12/1995.....15......8......	I WISH	Wild Card 5777752
27/04/1996.....38......2......	TOP OF THE STAIRS Featured in the 1995 film *Money Train*........	Wild Card 5763352

BEVERLI SKEETE – see DE-CODE FEATURING BEVERLI SKEETE

PETER SKELLERN UK singer (born 1947, Bury); he sang with Harlan County before signing solo with Decca. He later linked with Julian Lloyd Webber, Mary Hopkin and Bill Lovelady in 1983 to form Oasis, a group who scored one hit album.

23/09/1972.....3......11......	YOU'RE A LADY	Decca F 13333
29/03/1975.....14......9......	HOLD ON TO LOVE	Decca F 13568
28/10/1978.....60......4......	LOVE IS THE SWEETEST THING PETER SKELLERN FEATURING GRIMETHORPE COLLIERY BAND	Mercury 6008 603

SKIBADEE UK MC/rapper (born 1/2/1975, London).

23/11/2002.....19......4......	DON'T WANNA KNOW SHY FX/T POWER/DI & SKIBADEE	ffrr FCD 408
28/06/2003.....35......3......	TWIST 'EM OUT DILLINJA FEATURING SKIBADEE.....................	Trouble On Vinyl TOV 56CD

SKID ROW US heavy rock group formed in New Jersey in 1986 by Rachel Bolan (born 9/2/1964, bass), Dave Sabo (born 16/9/1962, guitar), Rob Affuso (born 1/3/1963, drums), Scotti Hill (born 31/5/1964, guitar) and Sebastian Bach (born Sebastian Bierk, 3/4/1968, Bahamas, vocals). They signed with Atlantic Records in 1988.

18/11/1989.....42......3......	YOUTH GONE WILD	Atlantic A 8935
03/02/1990.....12......6......	18 AND LIFE...	Atlantic A 8883
31/03/1990.....36......4......	I REMEMBER YOU	East West A 8836
15/06/1991.....19......3......	MONKEY BUSINESS	Atlantic A 7673
14/09/1991.....43......2......	SLAVE TO THE GRIND	Atlantic A 7603
23/11/1991.....20......3......	WASTED TIME	Atlantic A 7570
29/08/1992.....22......4......	YOUTH GONE WILD/DELIVERING THE GOODS Re-issue of Atlantic A 8935	Atlantic A 7444
18/11/1995.....48......2......	BREAKIN' DOWN Featured in the 1995 film *The Prophecy*...........	Atlantic A 7135CD1

SKIDS UK rock group formed in Scotland in 1977 by Stuart Adamson (born 11/4/1958, Manchester, guitar), Bill Simpson (bass), Tom Kellichan (drums) and Richard Jobson (vocals). Simpson and Webb left in 1980, replaced by Russell Webb and Mike Baillie. Adamson left in 1981 to form Big Country. After Big Country disbanded in 2000 Adamson became a country singer/songwriter but on 17/12/2001 his body was found hanged in a hotel room in Hawaii – he had been dead for two days. He had been depressed after his second marriage collapsed and had been declared missing from Nashville by his wife on 26/11/2001. Arranging to meet her, he changed his mind and flew to Honolulu and checked into a hotel on December 4th, rarely venturing out of his room thereafter.

23/09/1978.....70......3......	SWEET SUBURBIA...	Virgin VS 227
04/11/1978.....48......3......	THE SAINTS ARE COMING	Virgin VS 232
17/02/1979.....10......11......	INTO THE VALLEY..	Virgin VS 241
26/05/1979.....14......9......	MASQUERADE	Virgin VS 262
29/09/1979.....31......6......	CHARADE	Virgin VS 288
24/11/1979.....20......11......	WORKING FOR THE YANKEE DOLLAR	Virgin VS 306
01/03/1980.....56......3......	ANIMATION	Virgin VS 323
16/08/1980.....32......7......	CIRCUS GAMES	Virgin VS 359

❶⁹ Number of weeks single topped the UK chart ↑ Entered the UK chart at #1 ▲⁹ Number of weeks single topped the US chart

733

18/10/1980.....52......4......	GOODBYE CIVILIAN .... Virgin VS 373
06/12/1980.....49......3......	WOMAN IN WINTER .... Virgin VSK 101

SKIN German/UK rock group formed in Hamburg by Neville MacDonald (vocals), Myke Gray (born 12/5/1968, London, guitar), Andy Robbins (bass) and Dicki Fliszar (drums) as Taste, name-changing as another group had the same name. Gray and Robbins had previously been in Jagged Edge.

25/12/1993.....67......2......	THE SKIN UP (EP) Tracks on EP: *Look But Don't Touch, Shine Your Light* and *Monkey* .... Parlophone CDR 6363
12/03/1994.....45......2......	HOUSE OF LOVE .... Parlophone CDR 6374
30/04/1994.....18......3......	MONEY/UNBELIEVABLE .... Parlophone CDRS 6381
23/07/1994.....19......3......	TOWER OF STRENGTH.. Parlophone CDRS 6387
15/10/1994.....33......3......	LOOK BUT DON'T TOUCH (EP) Tracks on EP: *Look But Don't Touch, Should I Stay Or Should I Go, Pump It Up* and *Monkey* .....
	.... Parlophone CDRS 6391
20/05/1995.....26......2......	TAKE ME DOWN TO THE RIVER .... Parlophone CDRS 6409
23/03/1996.....32......2......	HOW LUCKY YOU ARE .... Parlophone CDR 6425
18/05/1996.....33......2......	PERFECT DAY .... Parlophone CDR 6433

SKIN UK singer (born Deborah Anne Dyer, 3/8/1967, London); she had previously been lead vocalist with Skunk Anansie. She took part in the *It's Only Rock 'N' Roll* project for the Children's Promise charity.

20/07/2002.....49......1......	GOOD TIMES ED CASE AND SKIN .... Columbia 6727672
07/06/2003.....30......2......	TRASHED .... EMI CDEM 622
20/09/2003.....64......1......	FAITHFULNESS.. EMI CDEM 624

SKIN UP UK producer Jason Cohen.

07/09/1991.....48......2......	IVORY .... Love EVOL 4
14/03/1992.....32......4......	A JUICY RED APPLE .... Love EVOL 11
18/07/1992.....45......2......	ACCELERATE .... Love EVOL 17

SKINNER – see LIGHTNING SEEDS

SKINNY UK duo formed in London by Paul Herman (vocals/guitar/programming) and Matt Benbrook (vocals/drums/programming) who had met a year earlier while vacationing in India.

11/04/1998.....31......2......	FAILURE .... Cheeky CHEKCD 023

SKIP RAIDERS FEATURING JADA US producer/DJ Dave Aude with singer Deanna Della Cioppa.

15/07/2000.....46......1......	ANOTHER DAY .... Perfecto PERF 4CDS

SKIPWORTH AND TURNER US R&B vocal duo Rodney Skipworth (born Syracuse, NY) and Phil Turner (born Memphis, TN), both formerly lead singers with rival Syracuse groups: Skipworth with New Sound Express and Turner with Sunrise.

27/04/1985.....24......10	THINKING ABOUT YOUR LOVE .... Fourth & Broadway BRW 23
21/01/1989.....60......2......	MAKE IT LAST.. Fourth & Broadway BRW 118

NICK SKITZ – see FUNKY CHOAD FEATURING NICK SKITZ

SKUNK ANANSIE UK rock group formed in London in 1994 by Skin (born Deborah Anne Dyer, 3/8/1967, London, vocals), Ace (born Martin Ivor Kent, 30/3/1967, Cheltenham, guitar), Cass Lewis (born Richard Keith Lewis, 1/9/1960, London, bass) and Mark Richardson (born 28/5/1970, Leeds, drums). Skin took part in the *It's Only Rock 'N' Roll* project for the Children's Promise charity.

25/03/1995.....46......1......	SELLING JESUS Featured in the 1995 film *Strange Days*.. One Little Indian 101 TP7CD
17/06/1995.....41......2......	I CAN DREAM.. One Little Indian 121 TP7CD
02/09/1995.....40......2......	CHARITY .... One Little Indian 131 TP7CD
27/01/1996.....20......5......	WEAK .... One Little Indian 141 TP7CD
27/04/1996.....20......3......	CHARITY Re-issue of One Little Indian 131 TP7CD .... One Little Indian 151 TP7CD
28/09/1996.....14......4......	ALL I WANT .... One Little Indian 161 TP7CD
30/11/1996.....26......4......	TWISTED (EVERYDAY HURTS) .... One Little Indian 171 TP7CDL
01/02/1997.....13......6......	HEDONISM (JUST BECAUSE YOU FEEL GOOD) .... One Little Indian 181 TP7CD
14/06/1997.....11......5......	BRAZEN 'WEEP'... One Little Indian 191 TP7CD1
13/03/1999.....17......3......	CHARLIE BIG POTATO .... Virgin VSCDT 1725
22/05/1999.....16......4......	SECRETLY Featured in the 1999 film *Cruel Intentions* .... Virgin VSCDT 1733
07/08/1999.....33......2......	LATELY .... Virgin VSCDT 1738

SKY UK rock group formed in 1978 by John Williams (born 24/4/1941, Melbourne, Australia, guitar), Herbie Flowers (bass), Francis Monkman (keyboards), Kevin Peek (guitar) and Tristan Fry (drums). Monkman left in 1980, replaced by Steve Gray, Williams left in 1983.

05/04/1980 .....5......11	TOCCATA .... Ariola ARO 300

SKYE – see LANGE

SKYHOOKS Australian vocal/instrumental group formed by Graeme 'Shirley' Strachan, Redmond Symonds, Bob Starkie, Greg McCainsh and Fred Strauks. Strachan left in 1978, replaced by Tony Williams, and was killed in a helicopter crash on 29/8/2001.

09/06/1979.....73......1.......	WOMEN IN UNIFORM .... United Artists UP 36508

○ Silver disc ● Gold disc ✪ Platinum disc (additional platinum units are indicated by a figure following the symbol) ◉ Singles released prior to 1973 that are known to have sold over 1 million copies in the UK

SKYLARK UK DJ Nic Fanciulli (born in Maidstone) who is a DJ on Radio 1 and also formed Portent Records.

27/03/2004.....62......1.......	THAT'S MORE LIKE IT .... Credence CDCRED042

SLACKER UK dance group formed by Shem McCauley and Simon Rogers and featuring Joanna Law on vocals. Law also recorded with Way Out West while McCauley and Rogers had previously recorded as Ramp.

26/04/1997.....36......2......	SCARED Contains a sample of Peter Gabriel's *Of These, Hope – Reprise* .... XL Recordings XLS 84CD
30/08/1997.....33......2......	YOUR FACE Contains a sample of Roberta Flack's *First Time Ever I Saw Your Face* .... XL Recordings XLS 87CD

SLADE UK rock group formed in Wolverhampton in 1969 by Noddy Holder (born Neville Holder, 15/6/1950, Walsall, guitar/vocals), Dave Hill (born 4/4/1952, Fleet Castle, guitar), Don Powell (born 10/9/1950, Bilston, drums) and Jimmy Lea (born 14/6/1952, Wolverhampton, bass/piano), all four having originally teamed up in the 'N Betweens in 1966. They name-changed to Ambrose Slade in 1969, adopted a 'skinhead' look and released a debut album with Fontana. They shortened their name to Slade the same year and switched to Polydor in 1970. They split in 1988 but re-formed in 1991. Holder later became an actor, appearing in the TV series *The Grimleys*. He was awarded an MBE in the 2000 New Year's Honours List.

19/06/1971.....16.....14......	GET DOWN AND GET WITH IT .... Polydor 2058 112
30/10/1971.....❶⁴.....15......	**COZ I LUV YOU** .... Polydor 2058 155
05/02/1972.....4......10......	**LOOK WOT YOU DUN** .... Polydor 2058 195
03/06/1972.....❶¹.....13......	**TAKE ME BAK 'OME** .... Polydor 2058 231
02/09/1972.....❶³.....10......	**MAMA WEER ALL CRAZEE NOW** .... Polydor 2058 274
25/11/1972.....2......13......	**GUDBUY T' JANE** .... Polydor 2058 312
03/03/1973.....❶⁴.....12......	**CUM ON FEEL THE NOIZE** ↑ .... Polydor 2058 339
30/06/1973.....❶³.....10......○	**SKWEEZE ME PLEEZE ME** ↑ The first artist to have consecutive releases enter at #1 .... Polydor 2058 377
06/10/1973.....2......8......○	**MY FREND STAN** .... Polydor 2058 407
15/12/1973.....❶⁵.....9......✪	**MERRY XMAS EVERYBODY** ↑ .... Polydor 2058 422
06/04/1974.....3......7......○	**EVERYDAY** .... Polydor 2058 453
06/07/1974.....3......7......	**THE BANGIN' MAN** .... Polydor 2058 492
19/10/1974.....2......6......○	**FAR FAR AWAY** .... Polydor 2058 522
15/02/1975.....15......7......	HOW DOES IT FEEL .... Polydor 2058 547
17/05/1975.....7......7......	**THANKS FOR THE MEMORY (WHAM BAM THANK YOU MAM)** .... Polydor 2058 585
22/11/1975.....11......8......	IN FOR A PENNY .... Polydor 2058 663
07/02/1976.....11......7......	LET'S CALL IT QUITS .... Polydor 2058 690
05/02/1977.....48......2......	GYPSY ROAD HOG .... Barn 2014 105
29/10/1977.....32......4......	MY BABY LEFT ME – THAT'S ALL RIGHT (MEDLEY) .... Barn 2014 114
18/10/1980.....44......5......	SLADE LIVE AT READING '80 (EP) .... Cheapskate CHEAP 5
27/12/1980.....70......2......	MERRY XMAS EVERYBODY SLADE AND THE READING CHOIR Re-recording .... Cheapskate CHEAP 11
31/01/1981.....10......9......	**WE'LL BRING THE HOUSE DOWN** .... Cheapskate CHEAPO 16
04/04/1981.....60......3......	WHEELS AIN'T COMING DOWN .... Cheapskate CHEAPO 21
19/09/1981.....29......8......	LOCK UP YOUR DAUGHTERS .... RCA 124
19/12/1981.....32......4......	MERRY XMAS EVERYBODY .... Polydor 2058 422
27/03/1982.....51......3......	RUBY RED.. RCA 191
27/11/1982.....50......6......	(AND NOW – THE WALTZ) C'EST LA VIE .... RCA 291
25/12/1982.....67......3......	MERRY XMAS EVERYBODY .... Polydor 2058 422
19/11/1983.....2.....11......●	**MY OH MY** .... RCA 373
10/12/1983.....20......5......	MERRY XMAS EVERYBODY .... Polydor 2058 422
04/02/1984.....7......10......	**RUN RUN AWAY** .... RCA 385
17/11/1984.....15......9......	ALL JOIN HANDS .... RCA 455
15/12/1984.....47......4......	MERRY XMAS EVERYBODY .... Polydor 2058 422
26/01/1985.....60......3......	7 YEAR BITCH .... RCA 475
23/03/1985.....50......5......	MYZSTERIOUS MIZSTER JONES .... RCA PB 40027
30/11/1985.....54......6......	DO YOU BELIEVE IN MIRACLES .... RCA PB 40449
21/12/1985.....48......3......	MERRY XMAS EVERYBODY Re-issue of Polydor 2058 422..................................... Polydor POSP 780
27/12/1986.....71......1......	MERRY XMAS EVERYBODY .... Polydor POSP 780
21/02/1987.....73......2......	STILL THE SAME .... RCA PB 41137
19/10/1991.....21......5......	RADIO WALL OF SOUND.. Polydor PO 180
26/12/1998.....30......3......	MERRY XMAS EVERYBODY '98 REMIX SLADE VERSUS FLUSH .... Polydor 5633532

SLAM UK production duo Orde Meikle and Stuart McMillan.

17/02/2001.....44......2......	POSITIVE EDUCATION .... VC Recordings VCRD 84
17/03/2001.....66......1......	NARCO TOURISTS SLAM VS UNKLE... Soma 100CD
07/07/2001.....61......1......	LIFETIMES SLAM FEATURING TYRONE 'VISIONARY' PALMER................................... Soma 107CDS

SLAMM UK group: John (vocals), Julee (guitar), Jase (bass), Dave (keyboards) and Scotty (drums), later name-changed to The Children.

17/07/1993.....57......2......	ENERGIZE .... PWL International PWCD 266
23/10/1993.....60......1......	VIRGINIA PLAIN .... PWL International PWCD 274

❶⁹ Number of weeks single topped the UK chart ↑ Entered the UK chart at #1 ▲⁹ Number of weeks single topped the US chart

735

22/10/1994	68	1		THAT'S WHERE MY MIND GOES	PWL International PWCD 310
04/02/1995	47	2		CAN'T GET BY	PWL International PWCD 316

SLARTA JOHN – see HATIRAS FEATURING SLARTA JOHN

LUKE SLATER UK producer who previously recorded as Clementine, 7th Plain and Planetary Assault Systems before signing with Nova mute in 1997.

16/09/2000	74	1		ALL EXHALE	Novamute CDNOMU 79
06/04/2002	70	1		NOTHING AT ALL	Mute CDMUTE 261

SLAUGHTER US rock group formed in Las Vegas, NV in 1988 by Mark Slaughter (vocals), Tim Kelly (guitar), Dana Strum (bass) and Blas Elias (drums). Slaughter and Strum were previously in Vinnie Vincent's Invasion. Kelly was killed in a car crash on 5/2/1998.

29/09/1990	62	1		UP ALL NIGHT	Chrysalis CHS 3556
02/02/1991	55	1		FLY TO THE ANGELS	Chrysalis CHS 3634

SLAVE US funk group formed in Dayton, OH by Mike Williamson (vocals), Danny Webster (guitar), Mark Hicks (keyboards), Mark Adams (bass), Steve Washington (horns), Floyd Miller (horns) and Rodger Parker (drums), later adding Orion Wilhoite (saxophone) and Charles Bradley (keyboards). Steve Arrington took over as lead singer in 1979, then left to form Aurra and later went solo.

08/03/1980	64	3		JUST A TOUCH OF LOVE	Atlantic/Cotillion K 11442

SLAYER US rock group formed in Huntington Beach, CA in 1982 by Tom Araya (bass/vocals), Kerry King (guitar), Jeff Hanneman (guitar) and Dave Lombardo (drums). Lombardo left in 1982, replaced by Paul Bostaph.

13/06/1987	64	1		CRIMINALLY INSANE	Def Jam LON 133
26/10/1991	51	1		SEASONS IN THE ABYSS	Def American DEFA 9
09/09/1995	50	1		SERENITY IN MURDER	American Recordings 74321312482

SLEAZESISTERS UK producer Paul Masterson, also a member of Amen! UK, The Dope Smugglaz and Hi-Gate and Candy Girls.

29/07/1995	53	1		SEX	Pulse 8 CDLOSE 92
30/03/1996	46	1		LET'S WHIP IT UP (YOU GO GIRL) This and above single credited to SLEAZESISTERS WITH VIKKI SHEPARD	Pulse 8 CDLOSE 102
26/09/1998	74	1		WORK IT UP SLEAZE SISTERS	Logic 74321616622

KATHY SLEDGE US singer (born 6/1/1959, Philadelphia, PA); founded Sister Sledge with her sisters in 1970 before going solo.

16/05/1992	62	2		TAKE ME BACK TO LOVE AGAIN	Epic 6579837
18/02/1995	54	1		ANOTHER STAR	NRC DEACD
29/11/1997	15	4		FREEDOM ROBERT MILES FEATURING KATHY SLEDGE	Deconstruction 74321536952

PERCY SLEDGE US singer (born 25/11/1941, Leighton, AL); a member of the Esquires Combo before going solo in 1966. Recommended to Quin Ivy, owner of Norala Sound Studio, he wrote When A Man Loves A Woman around an Esquires song Why Did You Leave Me Baby?, with Cameron Lewis (bass) and Andrew Wright (organ), although session man Spooner Oldham has been credited for the organ sound. He later recorded for Capricorn (with a minor R&B hit I'll Be Your Everything), Monument and Pointblank.

19/05/1966	4	17		WHEN A MAN LOVES A WOMAN ▲² Featured in films More American Graffiti (1979), The Big Chill (1984), Platoon (1987) .... Atlantic 584 001	
04/08/1966	34	7		WARM AND TENDER LOVE	Atlantic 584 034
14/02/1987	2	10	O	WHEN A MAN LOVES A WOMAN Revived following use in a Levi Jeans advertisement	Atlantic YZ 96

SLEEPER UK group formed in London in 1992 by Louise Wener (born 30/7/1968, Ilford, guitar/vocals), Jon Stewart (born 12/9/1967, Sheffield, guitar), Kenediid 'Diid' Osman (born 10/4/1968, Mogadishu, Somalia, bass) and Andy Maclure (born 4/7/1970, Manchester, drums).

21/05/1994	75	1		DELICIOUS	Indolent SLEEP 003CD
21/01/1995	16	4		INBETWEENER	Indolent SLEEP 006CD
08/04/1995	33	3		VEGAS	Indolent SLEEP 008CD
07/10/1995	14	4		WHAT DO I DO NOW?	Indolent SLEEP 009CD
04/05/1996	10	5		SALE OF THE CENTURY	Indolent SLEEP 011CD
13/07/1996	10	5		NICE GUY EDDIE	Indolent SLEEP 013CD
05/10/1996	17	3		STATUESQUE	Indolent SLEEP 014CD1
04/10/1997	28	2		SHE'S A GOOD GIRL	Indolent SLEEP 015CD
06/12/1997	39	2		ROMEO ME	Indolent SLEEP 17CD1

SLEEPY JACKSON Australian group formed in Perth in 1997 by brothers Luke and Jesse Steele and Matt O'Connor.

19/07/2003	50	1		VAMPIRE RACECOURSE	Virgin DINSD 261
25/10/2003	71	1		GOOD DANCERS	Virgin DINSD 265

SLIM CHANCE – see RONNIE LANE AND SLIM CHANCE

SLICK US studio dance group assembled by Larry James (of Fat Larry's Band) and his wife Doris James. The lead vocals were by Brandi Wells and the musical accompaniment by Fat Larry's Band. Wells died on 25/3/2003.

16/06/1979	16	10		SPACE BASS	Fantasy FTC 176
15/09/1979	47	5		SEXY CREAM	Fantasy FTC 182

GRACE SLICK US singer (born Grace Wing, 30/10/1939, Chicago, IL); she was with Jefferson Airplane from 1965 until 1978 when alcohol problems saw her departure. She returned in 1981 and departed a second final time, in 1988.

24/05/1980 . . . . . 50 . . . . . . 4 . . . . DREAMS . . . . RCA PB 9534

SLICK RICK US rapper (born Ricky Walters, 14/1/1965, London), also a member of Doug E Fresh & The Get Fresh Crew. He also recorded as MC Ricky D. Jailed in 1991 for attempted murder, he served five years before being released in 1996. In 2001 he was re-arrested by the INS (Immigration & Naturalization Service) who wished to deport him to England for his original crime.

10/06/1989 . . . . . 54 . . . . . . 3 . . . . IF I'M NOT YOUR LOVER **AL B SURE FEATURING SLICK RICK** . . . . Uptown W 2908
19/10/1996 . . . . . 24 . . . . . . 3 . . . . I LIKE **MONTELL JORDAN FEATURING SLICK RICK** Contains a sample of KC & The Sunshine Band's *I Get Lifted*. Featured in the 1996 film *The Nutty Professor* . . . . Def Jam DEFCD 19

SLIK UK pop group formed in Scotland by Midge Ure (born 10/10/1953, Gambusland, guitar), Billy McIsaac (keyboards), Kenny Hyslop (drums) and Jim McGinlay (bass). Ure was later in the Rich Kids, Visage, Ultravox and recorded solo, Hyslop was later in Simple Minds.

17/01/1976 . . . . ❶¹ . . . . . 9 . . . . . . ● **FOREVER AND EVER** . . . . Bell 1464
08/05/1976 . . . . . 24 . . . . . . 9 . . . . REQUIEM . . . . Bell 1478

SLEEPY BROWN – see OUTKAST

SLIPKNOT US rock group formed in Des Moines, IA by DJ Sid Wilson, Joey Jordison (drums), Paul Gray (bass), Chris Fehn (percussion), James Root (guitar), Craig Jones (samples), Shawn Crahan (percussion), Mic Thompson (guitar) and Corey Taylor (vocals). Root and Taylor had previously been members of Stone Sour and revived the group in 2002 while Jordison formed Murderdolls.

11/03/2000 . . . . . 27 . . . . . . 3 . . . . WAIT AND BLEED . . . . Roadrunner RR21125
16/09/2000 . . . . . 28 . . . . . . 2 . . . . SPIT IT OUT . . . . Roadrunner RR20903
10/11/2001 . . . . . 24 . . . . . . 4 . . . . LEFT BEHIND . . . . Roadrunner 23203352
20/07/2002 . . . . . 43 . . . . . . 2 . . . . MY PLAGUE . . . . Roadrunner RR 20453
26/06/2004 . . . . . 15 . . . . . . 6 . . . . DUALITY . . . . Roadrunner RR 39880
30/10/2004 . . . . . 31 . . . . . . 2 . . . . VERMILION. . . . . Roadrunner RR 39770

SLIPMATT UK DJ/producer (born Matthew Nelson, Loughton) who was previously a member of SL2.

19/04/2003 . . . . . 41 . . . . . . 2 . . . . SPACE . . . . Concept CDCON 37

SLIPSTREAM UK group: Mark Refoy (guitar/vocals), Gary Lennon (bass), Steve Beswick (drums) and Johnny Mattock (percussion).

19/12/1992 . . . . . 18 . . . . . . 7 . . . . WE ARE RAVING – THE ANTHEM . . . . Boogie Food 7BF 1

SLITS UK punk group formed in 1976 by Ari-Up (vocals), Kate Korus (guitar), Suzi Gutsy (bass) and Palmolive (drums). Korus and Gutsy left soon after, replaced by Viv Albertine (guitar) and Tessa Pollitt (bass). Palmolive left in 1978, replaced by Budgie (born Peter Clark, 21/8/1957, St Helens). Budgie left to join Siouxsie & The Banshees in 1979, replaced by Bruce Smith. They split in 1981.

13/10/1979 . . . . . 60 . . . . . . 3 . . . . TYPICAL GIRLS/I HEARD IT THROUGH THE GRAPEVINE . . . . Island WIP 6505

P.F. SLOAN US singer/songwriter (born Philip Sloan – the F stands for Faith – 1946, Los Angeles, CA) who teamed up with Steve Barrik as the Fantastic Baggies. They became better known as songwriters, penning *Eve Of Destruction* for Barry Maguire.

04/11/1965 . . . . . 38 . . . . . . 3 . . . . SINS OF THE FAMILY . . . . RCA 1482

SLO-MOSHUN UK production/instrumental duo Mark Archer and Danny Taurus. Archer was previously in Altern 8.

05/02/1994 . . . . . 29 . . . . . . 3 . . . . BELLS OF NY . . . . Six6 SIXCD 108
30/07/1994 . . . . . 52 . . . . . . 1 . . . . HELP MY FRIEND. . . . . Six6 SIXCD 117

SLOWDIVE UK group formed in 1989 by Rachel Goswell (born 16/5/1971, guitar/vocals), Neil Halstead (born 7/10/1970, Luton, guitar/vocals), Brook Christian Savill (born 6/12/1977, Bury, guitar), Nicholas Chaplin (born 23/12/1970, Slough, bass) and Adrian Sell (drums). Sell left soon after, replaced by first Neil Carter and then Simon Scott (born 3/3/1971, Cambridge).

15/06/1991 . . . . . 52 . . . . . . 1 . . . . CATCH THE BREEZE/SHINE . . . . Creation CRE 112
29/05/1993 . . . . . 69 . . . . . . 1 . . . . OUTSIDE YOUR ROOM (EP) Tracks on EP: *Outside Your Room, Alison, So Tired* and *Souvlaki Space Station* . . . Creation CRESCD 119

SL2 UK production/instrumental duo Slipmatt (Matthew Nelson) and Lime (John Fernandez). Slipmatt later recorded solo.

02/11/1991 . . . . . 11 . . . . . . 6 . . . . DJS TAKE CONTROL/WAY IN MY BRAIN . . . . XL Recordings XLS 24
18/04/1992 . . . . . 2 . . . . . . 11 . . . . . . ○ **ON A RAGGA TIP** . . . . XL Recordings XLS 29
19/12/1992 . . . . . 26 . . . . . . 6 . . . . WAY IN MY BRAIN (REMIX)/DRUMBEATS . . . . XL Recordings XLS 36
15/02/1997 . . . . . 31 . . . . . . 2 . . . . ON A RAGGA TIP '97 (REMIX). . . . . XL Recordings XLSR 29CD

SLUSNIK LUNA Finnish production duo Niko Nyman and Nicklas Renqvist.

01/09/2001 . . . . . 40 . . . . . . 2 . . . . SUN . . . . Incentive CENT 29CDS

SLY AND THE FAMILY STONE US singer (born Sylvester Stewart, 15/3/1944, Dallas, TX); he formed Family Stone in 1966 with brother Freddie (born 5/6/1946, Dallas, guitar), sister Rosemary (born 21/3/1945, Vallejo, CA, vocals/piano), cousin Larry Graham (born 14/8/1946, Beaumont, TX, bass), Jerry Martini (born 1/10/1943, Colorado, saxophone), Cynthia Robinson (born 12/1/1946, Sacramento, CA, trumpet) and Greg Errico (born 1/9/1946, San Francisco, CA, drums). Graham left in 1972, forming Graham Central Station. Sly jailed in 1989 for driving under the influence of cocaine. They were inducted into the Rock & Roll Hall of Fame in 1993.

10/07/1968 . . . . . 7 . . . . . . 14 . . . . . . **DANCE TO THE MUSIC**. . . . . Direction 58 3568
02/10/1968 . . . . . 32 . . . . . . 7 . . . . M'LADY . . . . Direction 58 3707

❶⁹ Number of weeks single topped the UK chart ↑ Entered the UK chart at #1 ▲⁹ Number of weeks single topped the US chart

737

19/03/1969.....36......5......	EVERYDAY PEOPLE ▲4 Featured in the 1994 film *Crooklyn*	Direction 58 3938
08/01/1972.....15......8......	FAMILY AFFAIR ▲3	Epic EPC 7632
15/04/1972.....17......8......	RUNNIN' AWAY	Epic EPC 7810

SLY FOX
US duo Gary 'Mudbone' Cooper and Michael Camacho. Cooper had previously been with Parliament and Funkadelic.

31/05/1986 .....3......16	**LET'S GO ALL THE WAY** .... Capitol CL 403

SLY AND ROBBIE
Jamaican duo Lowell 'Sly' Charles Dunbar (born 10/5/1952, Kingston, drums) and Robbie Shakespeare (born 27/9/1953, Kingston, bass) who first teamed up in the Aggravators. 1998 Grammy Award for Best Reggae Performance for *Friends*.

04/04/1987.....12......11	BOOPS (HERE TO GO)... Fourth & Broadway BRW 61
25/07/1987.....60......4	FIRE .... Fourth & Broadway BRW 71
20/09/1997.....14......8.......	NIGHT NURSE **SLY AND ROBBIE FEATURING SIMPLY RED**............................. East West EW 129CD1

HEATHER SMALL
UK singer (born 20/1/1965, London); she was the lead singer with M People before going solo.

20/05/2000.....16......5......	PROUD .... Arista 74321757112
19/08/2000.....58......1......	HOLDING ON .... Arista 74321781332
18/11/2000.....24......3......	YOU NEED LOVE LIKE I DO **TOM JONES AND HEATHER SMALL**........................... Gut CXGUT 36

SMALL ADS
UK vocal/instrumental group fronted by Nick Dickman.

18/04/1981.....63......3......	SMALL ADS .... Bronze BRO 115

SMALL FACES
UK rock group formed in London in 1965 by Ronnie 'Plonk' Lane (born 1/4/1946, London, bass), Kenny Jones (born 16/9/1948, London, drums), Jimmy Winston (born James Langwith, 20/4/1945, London, organ) and Steve Marriott (born 30/1/1947, London, guitar/vocals). Winston left shortly after they signed with Decca in 1965, replaced by Ian McLagan (born 12/5/1945, Middlesex). They disbanded in 1969, Marriott forming Humble Pie and Lane, Jones and McLagan linking up with Ron Wood and Rod Stewart as the Faces. Marriott was killed in a house fire on 20/4/1991 while Lane died from multiple sclerosis on 4/6/1997.

02/09/1965.....14......12	WHATCHA GONNA DO ABOUT IT .... Decca F 12208
10/02/1966 .....3......11	**SHA LA LA LA LEE** .... Decca F 12317
12/05/1966.....10......9......	**HEY GIRL** .... Decca F 12393
11/08/1966 .....◉1......12	**ALL OR NOTHING** .... Decca F 12470
17/11/1966 .....4......11	**MY MIND'S EYE** .... Decca F 12500
09/03/1967.....26......7......	I CAN'T MAKE IT .... Decca F 12565
08/06/1967.....12......10	HERE COME THE NICE .... Immediate IM 050
09/08/1967 .....3......14	**ITCHYCOO PARK** .... Immediate IM 057
06/12/1967 .....9......12	**TIN SOLDIER** .... Immediate IM 062
17/04/1968 .....2......11	**LAZY SUNDAY** .... Immediate IM 064
10/07/1968.....16......11	UNIVERSAL .... Immediate IM 069
19/03/1969.....36......1......	AFTERGLOW OF YOUR LOVE... Immediate IM 077
13/12/1975 .....9......11	**ITCHYCOO PARK** Re-issue of Immediate IM 057 .... Immediate IMS 102
20/03/1976.....39......5......	LAZY SUNDAY Re-issue of Immediate IM 064 .... Immediate IMS 106

SMALLER
UK group formed in Liverpool by Digsy (vocals), Paul Cavanagh (guitar), Jason Riley (bass) and Steven Dreary (drums).

28/09/1996.....72......1......	WASTED... Better BETSCD 006
29/03/1997.....55......1......	IS .... Better BETSCD 008

SMART E'S
UK production/instrumental group formed in Romford by Tom Orton, Chris 'Luna C' Howell and Nick Arnold, with singer Jayde guesting on their hit single, which is based on the theme to the kids' TV show *Sesame Street*.

11/07/1992 .....2......9.......	**SESAME'S TREET** .... Suburban Base SUBBASE 125

S*M*A*S*H
UK rock group formed in Welwyn Garden City by Ed Borrie (guitar/vocals), Rob Hague (drums) and Salvador Alessi (bass) as Smash At The Blues. They name-changed after spotting it misspelled on a hoarding.

06/08/1994.....26......1.......	(I WANT TO) KILL SOMEBODY The single, only available for one day, had to be edited for radio as it contains a list of Tory MPs the group wanted to kill! .... Hi-Rise FLATSCD 5

SMASH MOUTH
US rock group formed in San Jose, CA in 1994 by Steve Harwell (born 9/1/1967, vocals), Greg Camp (born 2/4/1967, guitar), Paul De Lisle (born 14/6/1963, bass) and Kevin Coleman (drums). Coleman had back problems that resulted in him missing shows, and was sacked from the group in November 1999.

25/10/1997.....19......4.......	WALKIN' ON THE SUN .... Interscope IND 95555
31/07/1999.....24......5.......	ALL STAR Featured in the films *Mystery Men* (1999) and animated film *Shrek* (2001) .... Interscope IND 4971182

SMASHING PUMPKINS
US rock group formed in Chicago, IL in 1989 by Billy Corgan (born 17/3/1967, Chicago, guitar/vocals), James Iha (born 26/3/1968, Elk Grove, IL, guitar), D'Arcy Wretzky (born 1/5/1968, South Haven, MI, bass) and Jimmy Chamberlin (born 10/6/1964, Joliet, IL, drums). They signed with Caroline Records in America in 1991. On 12/7/1996 touring keyboard player Jonathan Melvoin died from a heroin overdose, Chamberlin just waking up in time from his own drug-induced sleep to alert paramedics; he was subsequently sacked for continued drug use. They added drummer Matt Walker and keyboard player Dennis Flemion the following month. They won the 1996 MTV Europe Music Award for Best Rock Act. They split in May 2000, Corgan forming Zwan.

05/09/1992.....73......1.......	I AM ONE .... Hut HUTT 18
03/07/1993.....31......2.......	CHERUB ROCK .... Hut HUTCD 31

○ Silver disc ● Gold disc ✪ Platinum disc (additional platinum units are indicated by a figure following the symbol) ◉ Singles released prior to 1973 that are known to have sold over 1 million copies in the UK

25/09/1993	44	2		TODAY	Hut HUTCD 37
05/03/1994	11	3		DISARM	Hut HUTCD 43
28/10/1995	20	3		BULLET WITH BUTTERFLY WINGS 1996 Grammy Award for Best Hard Rock Performance	Virgin HUTCD 63
10/02/1996	16	3		1979 Featured in the 2000 film *On The Edge*	Virgin HUTCD 67
18/05/1996	7	6		**TONIGHT TONIGHT**	Virgin HUTDX 69
23/11/1996	21	2		THIRTY THREE	Virgin HUTCD 78
14/06/1997	10	4		**THE END IS THE BEGINNING IS THE END** Featured in the 1997 film *Batman & Robin*. 1997 Grammy Award for Best Hard Rock Performance	Warner Brothers W 0404CD
23/08/1997	72	1		THE END IS THE BEGINNING IS THE END (REMIX)	Warner Brothers W 0410CD
30/05/1998	11	4		AVA ADORE	Hut HUTCD 101
19/09/1998	24	2		PERFECT	Hut HUTCD 106
04/03/2000	23	2		STAND INSIDE YOUR LOVE	Hut HUTCD 127
23/09/2000	73	1		TRY TRY TRY	Hut HUTCD 140

SMEAR CAMPAIGN – see MR BEAN AND SMEAR CAMPAIGN FEATURING BRUCE DICKINSON

SMELLS LIKE HEAVEN Italian producer Fabio Paras.

10/07/1993	57	1		LONDRES STRUTT	Deconstruction 74321154312

ANNE-MARIE SMITH UK singer.

23/01/1993	34	2		MUSIC FARGETTA AND ANNE-MARIE SMITH	Synthetic CDR 6334
18/03/1995	31	2		ROCKIN' MY BODY 49ERS FEATURING ANNE-MARIE SMITH	Media MCSTD 2021
15/07/1995	46	1		(YOU'RE MY ONE AND ONLY) TRUE LOVE	Media MCSTD 2060

ELLIOTT SMITH US singer/songwriter (born Portland, OR); he began writing songs at fourteen and later joined Heatmiser. He went solo in 1994 with the Cavity Search label, contributing music to the 1997 film *Good Will Hunting* (his track *Miss Misery* was nominated for an Oscar for Best Original Song). He signed with DreamWorks in 1998.

19/12/1998	52	1		WALTZ #2 (XO)	DreamWorks DRMCD 22347
01/05/1999	55	1		BABY BRITAIN	DreamWorks DRMDM 50950
08/07/2000	55	1		SON OF SAM	DreamWorks DRMCD 4509492

'FAST' EDDIE SMITH – see DJ 'FAST' EDDIE

HURRICANE SMITH UK singer/producer/engineer/trumpeter (born Norman Smith, 1923); he produced Pink Floyd's early albums, later appearing on albums by Teardrop Explodes and Julian Cope.

12/06/1971	2	12		**DON'T LET IT DIE**	Columbia DB 8785
29/04/1972	4	16		**OH BABE WHAT WOULD YOU SAY?**	Columbia DB 8878
02/09/1972	23	7		WHO WAS IT	Columbia DB 8916

JIMMY SMITH US organist (born 8/12/1925, Norristown, PA). After learning to play the piano and bass as a child, he concentrated on Hammond organ, forming his own trio. He recorded for Blue Note in the 1950s, moving to Verve in 1962.

28/04/1966	48	3		GOT MY MOJO WORKING	Verve VS 536

KEELY SMITH US singer (born Dorothy Keely Smith, 9/3/1932, Norfolk, VA); she married jazz trumpeter and singer Louis Prima in 1952 and recorded with both her husband and Frank Sinatra. Prima and Smith won the Best Performance by a Vocal Group Grammy Award in 1958 for *That Old Black Magic*. The couple divorced in 1961. She has a star on the Hollywood Walk of Fame.

18/03/1965	14	10		YOU'RE BREAKIN' MY HEART	Reprise R 20346

LONNIE LISTON SMITH – see WAG YA TAIL FEATURING LONNIE LISTON SMITH

MANDY SMITH UK singer (born 17/7/1970) who is famous for marrying ex-Rolling Stone Bill Wyman, which attracted controversy when it was revealed she had been involved with Wyman since she was fourteen years of age.

20/05/1989	59	2		DON'T YOU WANT ME BABY	PWL 37

MARK E SMITH UK singer (born 5/3/1957, Manchester). He formed The Fall in 1977.

05/03/1994	18	3		I WANT YOU INSPIRAL CARPETS FEATURING MARK E SMITH	Cow DUNG 24CD
23/03/1996	50	1		PLUG MYSELF IN D.O.S.E. FEATURING MARK E SMITH	Coliseum TOGA 001CD1

MEL SMITH UK singer/comedian (born 3/12/1952, London) who was first known via the TV series *Not The Nine O'Clock News* then teaming with Griff Rhys Jones in *Alas Smith And Jones*. Smith and Jones later linked with Rowan Atkinson to form Talkback Productions. The Kim with whom he enjoyed his debut hit is singer Kim Wilde.

05/12/1987	3	7	O	**ROCKIN' AROUND THE CHRISTMAS TREE** MEL AND KIM Single released in aid of the Comic Relief Charity	10 TEN 2
21/12/1991	59	3		ANOTHER BLOOMING CHRISTMAS	Epic 6576877

MICHAEL SMITH – see SEELENLUFT FEATURING MICHAEL SMITH

MURIEL SMITH WITH WALLY STOTT AND HIS ORCHESTRA US singer (born 23/2/1923, NYC); she was also an actress, appearing in *Moulin Rouge* in 1952. She died on 13/9/1985.

15/05/1953	3	17		**HOLD ME THRILL ME KISS ME**	Philips PB 122

❶⁹ Number of weeks single topped the UK chart ↑ Entered the UK chart at #1 ▲⁹ Number of weeks single topped the US chart

739

O.C. SMITH
US singer (born Ocie Lee Smith, 21/6/1936, Mansfield, LA) who replaced Joe Williams as singer in Count Basie's band in 1961. He began recording country music in 1965, switching to soul in 1973. He died from a heart attack on 23/11/2001.

29/05/1968 . . . . . 2 . . . . . . 15	**SON OF HICKORY HOLLER'S TRAMP** . . . . CBS 3343
26/03/1977 . . . . . 25 . . . . . . 8	TOGETHER . . . . Caribou CRB 4910

PATTI SMITH GROUP
US singer (born 31/12/1946, Chicago, IL); she debuted on record in 1974 for the Mer label. The group was Lenny Kaye (guitar), Richard Sohl (piano), Jay Dee Daughtery (drums) and Ivan Kral (guitar). Smith broke her neck when she fell off stage in Tampa, FL in 1977. They disbanded in 1980 after Patti had married Fred 'Sonic' Smith, formerly of the MC5, and retired to have a family. She resumed recording in 1988. Sohl died from a heart attack on 3/6/1990. Fred Smith died in 1995.

29/04/1978 . . . . . 5 . . . . . . 12 . . . . . O	**BECAUSE THE NIGHT** . . . . Arista 181
19/08/1978 . . . . . 72 . . . . . . 1	PRIVILEGE (SET ME FREE) . . . . Arista 197
02/06/1979 . . . . . 63 . . . . . . 3	FREDERICK . . . . Arista 264

REX SMITH AND RACHEL SWEET
US vocal duo Rex Smith (born 19/9/1956, Jacksonville, FL) and Rachel Sweet (born 28/7/1963, Akron, OH). Both appeared in various musicals on Broadway and went on to pursue acting careers.

22/08/1981 . . . . . 35 . . . . . . 7	EVERLASTING LOVE . . . . CBS A 1405

RICHARD JON SMITH
South African singer (born in Cape Town).

16/07/1983 . . . . . 63 . . . . . . 2	SHE'S THE MASTER OF THE GAME . . . . Jive 38

ROBERT SMITH – see JUNIOR JACK

ROSE SMITH – see DELAKOTA

SHEILA SMITH – see CEVIN FISHER

SIMON BASSLINE SMITH – see DRUMSOUND/SIMON BASSLINE SMITH

STEVE SMITH – see PAUL JACKSON AND STEVE SMITH

WHISTLING JACK SMITH
UK group originally a studio production by the Mike Sammes Singers, whistling provided by producer Ivor Raymonde. Following the success of the single, Billy Moeller (born 2/2/1946, Liverpool) toured as Whistling Jack Smith.

02/03/1967 . . . . . 5 . . . . . . 12	**I WAS KAISER BILL'S BATMAN** . . . . Deram DM 112

WILL SMITH
US singer (born Willard Christopher Smith Jr, 25/9/1968, Philadelphia, PA); he first recorded as The Fresh Prince with DJ Jazzy Jeff, and as an actor appeared in the TV comedy *Fresh Prince Of Bel-Air* and the films *Independence Day, Men In Black* and *Wild Wild West*. His two Grammy Awards were preceded by two with DJ Jazzy Jeff and the Fresh Prince. He has also won two MTV Europe Music Awards: Best Rap Act in 1997 and Best Male in 1999, and the 1997 MOBO Award for Best Video for *Men In Black*.

16/08/1997 . . . . ❶⁴ . . . 16 . . . . . ✪	**MEN IN BLACK** ↑ Contains a sample of Patrice Rushen's *Forget Me Nots*. Featured in the 1997 film *Men In Black*. 1997 Grammy Award for Best Rap Performance . . . . Columbia 6648682
13/12/1997 . . . . . 23 . . . . . . 6	JUST CRUISIN' Contains a sample of Al Johnson's *I'm Back For More*. . . . . Columbia 6653482
07/02/1998 . . . . . 3 . . . . . . 10 . . . . . O	**GETTIN' JIGGY WIT IT** ▲³ Contains samples of Sister Sledge's *He's The Greatest Dancer,* The Bar-Kays *Sang And Dance* and Spoonie Gee's *Love Rap*. 1998 Grammy Award for Best Rap Solo Performance . . . . Columbia 6655605
01/08/1998 . . . . . 2 . . . . . . 10	JUST THE TWO OF US Contains a sample of Grover Washington's *Just The Two Of Us*. . . . . Columbia 6662092
05/12/1998 . . . . . 3 . . . . . . 14	MIAMI Contains a sample of The Whispers' *And The Beat Goes On* . . . . Columbia 6666782
19/06/1999 . . . . . 3 . . . . . . 9 . . . . . O	BOY YOU KNOCK ME OUT TATYANA ALI FEATURING WILL SMITH Contains a sample of Bobby Caldwell's *What You Won't Do For Love* . . . . MJJ 6674742
10/07/1999 . . . . . 2 . . . . . . 16 . . . . . ●	**WILD WILD WEST** ▲¹ WILL SMITH FEATURING DRU HILL Contains a sample of Stevie Wonder's *I Wish*. Featured in the 1999 film *Wild Wild West*. Stevie Wonder appeared in the accompanying video . . . . Columbia 6675962
20/11/1999 . . . . . 2 . . . . . . 11	WILL 2K Contains a sample of The Clash's *Rock The Casbah* and features the uncredited contribution of K-Ci . . Columbia 6684452
25/03/2000 . . . . . 15 . . . . . . 8	FREAKIN' IT Contains samples of Diana Ross' *Love Hangover* and The Sugarhill Gang's *Rapper's Delight* . . . . . . Columbia 6691052
10/08/2002 . . . . . 3 . . . . . . 10	**BLACK SUITS COMIN' (NOD YA HEAD)** WILL SMITH FEATURING TRA-KNOX Featured in the 2002 film *Men In Black 2* . . . . Columbia 6730135

SMITHS
UK rock group formed in Manchester in 1982 by Johnny Marr (born John Maher, 31/10/1963, Manchester, guitar), Morrissey (born Stephen Morrissey, 22/5/1959, Manchester, vocals), Andy Rourke (born 1963, Manchester, bass) and Mike Joyce (born 1/6/1963, Manchester, drums). They signed with Rough Trade in 1983 and announced they were moving to EMI in 1987, although only Morrissey as a solo artist actually made the move. Marr subsequently formed Electronic.

12/11/1983 . . . . . 25 . . . . . 12	THIS CHARMING MAN . . . . Rough Trade RT 136
28/01/1984 . . . . . 12 . . . . . . 9	WHAT DIFFERENCE DOES IT MAKE . . . . Rough Trade RT 146
02/06/1984 . . . . . 10 . . . . . . 8	**HEAVEN KNOWS I'M MISERABLE NOW** . . . . Rough Trade RT 156
01/09/1984 . . . . . 17 . . . . . . 6	WILLIAM, IT WAS REALLY NOTHING . . . . Rough Trade RT 166
09/02/1985 . . . . . 24 . . . . . . 6	HOW SOON IS NOW? Featured in the 1998 film *The Wedding Singer* . . . . Rough Trade RT 176
30/03/1985 . . . . . 26 . . . . . . 4	SHAKESPEARE'S SISTER . . . . Rough Trade RT 181
13/07/1985 . . . . . 49 . . . . . . 3	THE JOKE ISN'T FUNNY ANYMORE . . . . Rough Trade RT 186
05/10/1985 . . . . . 23 . . . . . . 5	THE BOY WITH THE THORN IN HIS SIDE . . . . Rough Trade RT 191
31/05/1986 . . . . . 26 . . . . . . 4	BIG MOUTH STRIKES AGAIN . . . . Rough Trade RT 192
02/08/1986 . . . . . 11 . . . . . . 8	PANIC Featured in the 2004 film *Shaun Of The Dead* . . . . Rough Trade RT 193
01/11/1986 . . . . . 14 . . . . . . 5	ASK . . . . Rough Trade RT 194

○ Silver disc ● Gold disc ✪ Platinum disc (additional platinum units are indicated by a figure following the symbol) ◉ Singles released prior to 1973 that are known to have sold over 1 million copies in the UK

07/02/1987	12	4		SHOPLIFTERS OF THE WORLD UNITE	Rough Trade RT 195
25/04/1987	10	5		**SHEILA TAKE A BOW**	Rough Trade RT 196
22/08/1987	13	5		GIRLFRIEND IN A COMA	Rough Trade RT 197
14/11/1987	23	4		I STARTED SOMETHING I COULDN'T FINISH	Rough Trade RT 198
19/12/1987	30	4		LAST NIGHT I DREAMT THAT SOMEBODY LOVED ME	Rough Trade RT 200
15/08/1992	8	5		**THIS CHARMING MAN** Re-issue of Rough Trade RT 136	WEA YZ 0001
12/09/1992	16	4		HOW SOON IS NOW Re-issue of Rough Trade RT 176	WEA YX 0002
24/10/1992	25	3		THERE IS A LIGHT THAT NEVER GOES OUT	WEA YZ 0003
18/02/1995	62	1		ASK Re-issue of Rough Trade RT 194	WEA YZ 0004CDX

SMOKE
UK group formed in Yorkshire by Mick Rowley (vocals), Mal Luker (guitar), Phil Peacock (guitar), John 'Zeke' Lund (bass) and Geoff Gill (drums) as The Shots, Peacock leaving after one failed single. The remaining members renamed themselves The Smoke.

09/03/1967	45	3		MY FRIEND JACK The single was effectively banned by UK radio stations who believed it praised drug abuse	Columbia DB 8115

SMOKE CITY
UK group formed by Anglo-Brazilian singer Nina Miranda, Marc Brown (producer/programmer) and Chris Franck (multi-instrumentalist). Their debut hit was originally released on the Rita label in 1996.

12/04/1997	4	5		**UNDERWATER LOVE** Originally in an advertisement for Levi jeans, it contains an interpolation of Luiz Bonfa's *Bahia Soul*	Jive JIVECD 422

SMOKE 2 SEVEN
UK vocal group formed by Jo Perry, Bev Clarke (both aged 22 at the time of their debut hit) and Nikki O'Neill (aged seventeen). They were originally called Holy Smoke, but name-changed after discovering another group with the same name.

16/03/2002	26	2		BEEN THERE DONE THAT	Curb CUBCX 077

SMOKED – see OLIVER LIEB PRESENTS SMOKED

SMOKIE
UK pop group formed in 1968 by Chris Norman (vocals), Alan Silson (guitar), Terry Utley (bass) and Peter Spencer (drums) as Kindness. They name-changed to Smokey, amending the spelling to Smokie to avoid confusion with Smokey Robinson. Norman and Spencer were later successful as songwriters, penning hits for Kevin Keegan and the England World Cup Squad. Norman left, replaced by Alan Barton who was killed in a road crash in 1995. Roy Chubby Brown is UK comedian Royston Vasey.

19/07/1975	3	9		**IF YOU THINK YOU KNOW HOW TO LOVE ME**	RAK 206
04/10/1975	8	7		**DON'T PLAY YOUR ROCK 'N' ROLL TO ME** This and above single credited to **SMOKEY**	RAK 217
31/01/1976	17	8		SOMETHING'S BEEN MAKING ME BLUE	RAK 227
25/09/1976	11	9		I'LL MEET YOU AT MIDNIGHT	RAK 241
04/12/1976	5	11	O	**LIVING NEXT DOOR TO ALICE**	RAK 244
19/03/1977	12	9		LAY BACK IN THE ARMS OF SOMEONE	RAK 251
16/07/1977	5	9		**IT'S YOUR LIFE**	RAK 260
15/10/1977	10	9	O	**NEEDLES AND PINS**	RAK 263
28/01/1978	17	6		FOR A FEW DOLLARS MORE	RAK 267
20/05/1978	5	13	O	**OH CAROL**	RAK 276
23/09/1978	19	9		MEXICAN GIRL	RAK 283
19/04/1980	34	7		TAKE GOOD CARE OF MY BABY	RAK 309
13/05/1995	64	2		LIVING NEXT DOOR TO ALICE (WHO THE F**K IS ALICE)	NOW CDWAG 245
12/08/1995	3	17	O	**LIVING NEXT DOOR TO ALICE (WHO THE F**K IS ALICE)** This and above single credited to **SMOKIE FEATURING ROY CHUBBY BROWN** Re-recording of RAK 244	NOW CDWAG 245

SMOKIN' BEATS FEATURING LYN EDEN
UK DJ/production team Paul Landon and Neil Rumney and singer Lyn Eden.

17/01/1998	23	3		DREAMS	AM:PM 5624711

SMOKIN' MOJO FILTERS
UK/US charity ensemble with Paul McCartney (born 18/6/1942 Liverpool), Paul Weller (born 25/5/1958, Woking) and Noel Gallagher (born 29/5/1967, Manchester) plus Beautiful South, Black Grape and Dodgy.

23/12/1995	19	5		COME TOGETHER (WAR CHILD)	Go Discs GODCD 136

SMOOTH
US singer/rapper Juanita Stokes (born in Los Angeles, CA); she originally recorded as MC Smooth. Immature are Los Angeles vocal trio Marques Houston, Jerome Jones and Kelton Kessee.

22/07/1995	36	2		MIND BLOWIN' Contains a sample of the Isley Brothers' *For The Love Of You*	Jive JIVECD 379
07/10/1995	46	1		IT'S SUMMERTIME (LET IT GET INTO YOU)	Jive JIVECD 383
16/03/1996	46	1		LOVE GROOVE (GROOVE WITH YOU)	Jive JIVECD 390
16/03/1996	26	2		WE GOT IT **IMMATURE FEATURING SMOOTH**	MCA MCSTD 48009
06/07/1996	41	1		UNDERCOVER LOVER	Jive JIVECD 397

JOE SMOOTH
US producer from Chicago, IL; his debut hit featured singer Anthony Thomas.

04/02/1989	56	4		PROMISED LAND	DJ international DJIN 6

SMOOTH TOUCH
US instrumental/production duo Erick 'More' Morillo and Kenny Lewis.

02/04/1994	58	1		HOUSE OF LOVE (IN MY HOUSE)	Six6 SIXCD 112

JEAN JACQUES SMOOTHIE
UK DJ Steve Robson. His debut hit, originally released at the beginning of 2001, charted after it was remixed by Mirwais Ahmadzai.

13/10/2001	12	7		2 PEOPLE Contains a sample of Minnie Riperton's *Inside My Love*	Echo ECSCD 112

❶⁹ Number of weeks single topped the UK chart ↑ Entered the UK chart at #1 ▲⁹ Number of weeks single topped the US chart

741

SMUJJI Jamaican singer Sean McLeod (born 1983, Clarendon) who got his nickname after pinching someone else's girlfriend.

13/03/2004	13	7		MUST BE LOVE **FYA FEATURING SMUJJI**	Def Jam UK 9817508
31/07/2004	43	2		KO	Def Jam 9867077

THE SMURFS Dutch novelty act assembled by Pierre Kartner who were popular in Holland in the early 1970s, charting in the UK when Smurf cartoon characters became popular.

03/06/1978	2	17	●	**THE SMURF SONG**	Decca F 13759
30/09/1978	13	12	○	DIPPETY DAY This and above single credited to **FATHER ABRAHAM AND THE SMURFS**	Decca F 13798
02/12/1978	19	7		CHRISTMAS IN SMURFLAND	Decca F 13819
07/09/1996	4	10		**I'VE GOT A LITTLE PUPPY**	EMI TV CDSMURF 100
21/12/1996	8	6		**YOUR CHRISTMAS WISH**	EMI TV CDSMURF 102

PATTY SMYTH WITH DON HENLEY US singer (born 26/6/1957, NYC); lead singer with Scandal before going solo.

03/10/1992	22	6		SOMETIMES LOVE JUST AIN'T ENOUGH	MCA MCS 1692

SNAKEBITE Italian dance group formed by Guido Callandro and Bologna production duo Pagano-Mazzavallani.

09/08/1997	25	2		THE BIT GOES ON The actual title should be *The Beat Goes On* but the Italian record company misspelled the label copy and the new title was retained for the UK	Multiply CDMULTY 22

SNAP US/German dance act assembled by producers Michael Muenzing and Luca Anzilotti, who appeared in the group as Benito Benitez and John 'Virgo' Garrett III, the other members being Turbo B (Durron Butler) and Penny Ford. Interviews for the group were handled by Jackie Harris owing to Ford's reluctance. Ford left in 1991, replaced by Thea Austin and then Niki Haris.

24/03/1990	❶²	15	○	**THE POWER** Featured in the films *Coyote Ugly* (2000) and *Bruce Almighty* (2003)	Arista 113133
16/06/1990	5	12	○	**OOOPS UP**	Arista 113296
22/09/1990	8	7		**CULT OF SNAP**	Arista 113596
08/12/1990	8	10		**MARY HAD A LITTLE BOY**	Arista 113831
30/03/1991	10	6		**SNAP MEGAMIX**	Arista 114169
21/12/1991	54	3		THE COLOUR OF LOVE	Arista 114678
04/07/1992	❶⁶	19	●	**RHYTHM IS A DANCER**	Arista 115309
09/01/1993	2	11		**EXTERMINATE!** Featured in the 1992 film *Batman Returns*	Arista 74321106962
12/06/1993	10	8		DO YOU SEE THE LIGHT (LOOKING FOR) This and above single credited to **SNAP FEATURING NIKI HARIS**	Arista 74321147622
17/09/1994	6	14	○	**WELCOME TO TOMORROW**	Arista 74321223852
01/04/1995	15	7		THE FIRST THE LAST THE ETERNITY (TIL THE END)	Arista 74321254672
28/10/1995	44	1		THE WORLD IN MY HANDS This and above two singles credited to **SNAP FEATURING SUMMER**	Arista 74321314792
13/04/1996	50	1		RAME **SNAP FEATURING RUKMANI**	Arista 74321368902
24/08/1996	42	1		THE POWER 96 **SNAP FEATURING EINSTEIN**	Arista 74321398672
24/08/2002	14	5		DO YOU SEE THE LIGHT **SNAP VERSUS PLAYTHING**	Data 33CDS
17/05/2003	17	4		RHYTHM IS A DANCER Remix of Arista 115309	Data 47CDS
06/09/2003	34	2		THE POWER (OF BHANGRA) **SNAP VERSUS MOTIVO**	Data 60CDS

SNEAKER PIMPS UK rock group formed in 1992 by Liam Howe (keyboards) and Chris Corner (guitar) as F.R.I.S.K. They later added singer Keli Ali and name-changed to Sneaker Pimps. Ali left in 1998 to go solo.

19/10/1996	15	4		6 UNDERGROUND Featured in the 1997 film *The Saint*	Clean Up CUP 023CDD
15/03/1997	21	3		SPIN SPIN SUGAR	Clean Up CUP 033CDS
07/06/1997	9	4		**6 UNDERGROUND** Re-issue of Clean Up CUP 023CDD following the release of the film *The Saint*	Clean Up CUP 036CDS
30/08/1997	22	3		POST MODERN SLEAZE	Clean Up CUP 038CDM
07/02/1998	46	2		SPIN SPIN SUGAR (REMIX)	Clean Up CUP 037X
21/08/1999	39	2		LOW FIVE	Clean Up CUP 052CDS
30/10/1999	56	1		TEN TO TWENTY	Clean Up CUP 054CDS

DAVID SNEDDON UK singer (born 15/9/1978, Glasgow), winner of BBC TV's *Fame Academy*, who joined the show two weeks later than the other contestants as a replacement for Naomi Roper. In the final he received 3.5 million of the 6.9 million votes.

25/01/2003	❶²	18		**STOP LIVING THE LIE** ↑	Mercury 0637292
03/05/2003	3	10		**DON'T LET GO**	Mercury 9800069
23/08/2003	19	3		BEST OF ORDER	Fontana 9810277
08/11/2003	38	2		BABY GET HIGHER	Fontana 9813422

SNIFF 'N' THE TEARS UK group with Paul Roberts (vocals), Mick Dyche (guitar), Laurence Netto (guitar), Leith Miller (keyboards), Nick South (bass) and Luigi Salvoni (drums). Roberts, an accomplished painter, did most of their distinctive album artwork.

23/06/1979	42	5		DRIVER'S SEAT	Chiswick CHIS 105

SNOOP DOGGY DOGG US rapper (born Calvin Broadus, 20/10/1972, Long Beach, CA); he began rapping while serving a year in prison for selling cocaine, then was discovered by Dr Dre. He was arrested following a drive-by shooting and killing in 1993. He and his bodyguard were acquitted of murder in 1996, and as the jury could not agree on charges of manslaughter, the judge ordered a mistrial. As an actor he appeared in films including *Murder Was The Case*, *Half Baked* and *Hot Boyz*. He later formed rap supergroup 213 with Nate Dogg and Warren G. Charlie Wilson is in The Gap Band.

04/12/1993	20	8		WHAT'S MY NAME?	Death Row A 8337CD
12/02/1994	39	3		GIN AND JUICE Contains a sample of Slave's *Watching You*. Featured in the 2001 film *Down To Earth*	Death Row A 8316CD

○ Silver disc ● Gold disc ✪ Platinum disc (additional platinum units are indicated by a figure following the symbol) ◎ Singles released prior to 1973 that are known to have sold over 1 million copies in the UK

DATE	POS	WKS	BPI	SINGLE TITLE	LABEL & NUMBER
20/08/1994	32	3		DOGGY DOGG WORLD	Death Row A 8289CD
14/12/1996	12	7		SNOOP'S UPSIDE YA HEAD SNOOP DOGGY DOGG FEATURING CHARLIE WILSON	Interscope IND 95520
26/04/1997	16	3		WANTED DEAD OR ALIVE 2PAC AND SNOOP DOGGY DOGG	Def Jam 5744052
03/05/1997	18	2		VAPORS	Interscope IND 95530
20/09/1997	21	2		WE JUST WANNA PARTY WITH YOU SNOOP DOGGY DOGG FEATURING JD Featured in the 1997 film *Men In Black*	
					Columbia 6649902
24/01/1998	36	2		THA DOGGFATHER	Interscope IND 95550
12/12/1998	58	1		COME AND GET WITH ME	Elektra E 3787CD
25/03/2000	6	10		**STILL DRE**	Interscope 4972862
03/02/2001	3	10		**THE NEXT EPISODE** This and above single credited to DR DRE FEATURING SNOOP DOGGY DOGG	Interscope 4974762
17/03/2001	14	7		X XZIBIT FEATURING SNOOP DOGG	Epic 6709072
28/04/2001	13	5		SNOOP DOGG	Priority PTYCD 134
30/11/2002	27	6		FROM THA CHUUUCH TO DA PALACE This and above single credited to SNOOP DOGG	Priority 5516102
01/03/2003	48	2		THE STREETS WC FEATURING SNOOP DOGG AND NATE DOGG	Def Jam 0779852
05/04/2003	23	20		BEAUTIFUL SNOOP DOGG FEATURING PHARRELL	Capitol CDCL 842
14/02/2004	58	2		THE NEXT EPISODE DR DRE FEATURING SNOOP DOGGY DOGG	Interscope 4974762
14/08/2004	31	3		I WANNA THANK YOU ANGIE STONE FEATURING SNOOP DOGG Contains interpolations of *Come Into My Life* and *All This Love*	
					J Records 82876624782
11/12/2004	10	3+		**DROP IT LIKE IT'S HOT** ❶³ SNOOP DOGG FEATURING PHARRELL	Geffen 2103461

SNOW Canadian rapper/reggae singer (born Darren O'Brien, 30/10/1969, Toronto, Ontario). He was in prison awaiting trial for manslaughter (he was later acquitted) at the time of his debut hit.

DATE	POS	WKS	BPI	SINGLE TITLE	LABEL & NUMBER
13/03/1993	2	15	○	**INFORMER** ▲⁷	East West America A 8436CD
05/06/1993	48	2		GIRL I'VE BEEN HURT	East West America A 8417CD
04/09/1993	67	1		UHH IN YOU	Atlantic A 8378CD

MARK SNOW US composer/pianist (born 26/8/1946, Brooklyn, NYC). He relocated to Los Angeles, CA in 1974 and has written the scores to many TV series and films, including *The Day Lincoln Was Shot*, *Murder Between Friends* and *Hart To Hart*.

DATE	POS	WKS	BPI	SINGLE TITLE	LABEL & NUMBER
30/03/1996	2	15	○	**THE X FILES** Theme to the TV series of the same name	Warner Brothers W 0341CD

PHOEBE SNOW US singer (born Phoebe Laub, 17/7/1952, New York; she began performing in Greenwich Village in the early 1970s. She briefly retired in the early 1980s in order to look after her mentally handicapped child.

DATE	POS	WKS	BPI	SINGLE TITLE	LABEL & NUMBER
06/01/1979	37	7		EVERY NIGHT	CBS 6842

SNOW PATROL UK rock group formed in Dundee, Scotland by Gary Lightbody (guitar/vocals), Mark McClelland (bass/keyboards) and John Quinn (drums). They first recorded for Jeepster in 1998.

DATE	POS	WKS	BPI	SINGLE TITLE	LABEL & NUMBER
27/09/2003	54	1		SPITTING GAMES	Polydor 9809350
07/02/2004	5	11		**RUN**	Fiction/Polydor 9816353
24/04/2004	24	6		CHOCOLATE	Fiction/Polydor 9866355
24/07/2004	23	5		SPITTING GAMES Re-issue of Polydor 9809350	Fiction/Polydor 9867126
06/11/2004	39	2		HOW TO BE DEAD	Polydor 9868777

SNOWMEN UK studio group inspired by the success of Star Sound and assembled by Martin Kershaw.

DATE	POS	WKS	BPI	SINGLE TITLE	LABEL & NUMBER
12/12/1981	18	8		HOKEY COKEY	Stiff ODB 1
18/12/1982	44	4		XMAS PARTY	Solid STOP 006

SNUG UK vocal/instrumental group formed by Ed Harcourt, James Deane, Ed Groves and Johnny Lewsley.

DATE	POS	WKS	BPI	SINGLE TITLE	LABEL & NUMBER
18/04/1998	55	1		BEATNIK GIRL	WEA 151CDX

SO UK group formed by Mark Long (vocals) and Marcus Bell (keyboards).

DATE	POS	WKS	BPI	SINGLE TITLE	LABEL & NUMBER
13/02/1988	62	3		ARE YOU SURE	Parlophone R 6173

SO SOLID CREW UK rap/garage group that features 22 members, including MC Harvey, MC Romeo, Shane 'Kaish' Neil, Megaman, Jason 'G Man' Phillips, Ashley 'Asher D' Walters, Lisa Maffia and Dan Da Man. The group's debut hit *21 Seconds* was so named because each of the ten rappers are given 21 seconds in which to impress! After live dates in November 2001 were marred by violence, including one at London's Astoria Theatre that resulted in a shooting, the rest of their UK tour was scrapped. They won the 2001 MOBO Awards for Best British Garage Act and Best Newcomer. In March 2002 Asher D was jailed for 18 months for possessing a loaded revolver. In December 2002 Kaish and G Man were similarly questioned about gun and drug offences, G Man being sentenced to four years in June 2003 for possessing a loaded firearm.

DATE	POS	WKS	BPI	SINGLE TITLE	LABEL & NUMBER
18/08/2001	❶¹	15	○	**21 SECONDS** ↑ 2002 BRIT Award for Best Video	Relentless RELENT 16CD
17/11/2001	3	9		**THEY DON'T KNOW**	Relentless RELENT 26CD
19/01/2002	8	7		HATERS SO SOLID CREW PRESENTS MR SHABZ FEATURING MBD AND THE REELISTS	Relentless/Independiente RELENT 23CD
20/04/2002	19	6		RIDE WID US	Relentless ISOM 55SMS
27/09/2003	9	5		**BROKEN SILENCE**	Independiente ISOM 71MS
03/04/2004	62	1		SO GRIMEY	Independiente ISOM 82MS

S.O.A.P. Danish instrumental/production duo formed by sisters Heidi and Line Sorensen.

DATE	POS	WKS	BPI	SINGLE TITLE	LABEL & NUMBER
25/07/1998	36	2		THIS IS HOW WE PARTY	Columbia 6661295

❶⁹ Number of weeks single topped the UK chart ↑ Entered the UK chart at #1 ▲⁹ Number of weeks single topped the US chart

743

SOAPY UK instrumental/production duo Dan Bewick and Jak Kaleniuk.

14/09/1996.....35......2....... HORNY AS FUNK ....WEA 074CD

GINO SOCCIO Canadian singer/keyboard player (born 1955, Montreal).

28/04/1979.....46......5....... DANCER ....Warner Brothers K 17357

SODA CLUB FEATURING HANNAH ALETHA UK production duo formed by brothers Andy and Pete Lee with singer Hannah Aletha. The Lee brothers had previously recorded as Love To Infinity.

09/11/2002.....16......4.......	TAKE MY BREATH AWAY..Concept CDCON 33
08/03/2003.....13......4.......	HEAVEN IS A PLACE ON EARTH ....Concept CDCON 39
23/08/2003.....31......2.......	KEEP LOVE TOGETHER SODA CLUB EATURING ANDREA ANATOLA..................Concept CDCON 44X
28/08/2004.....40......2.......	AIN'T NO LOVE (AIN'T NO USE) SODA CLUB FEATURING ASHLEY JADE ....Concept CDCON58X

SOFT CELL UK techno-pop duo Marc Almond (born Peter Marc Almond, 9/7/1957, Southport, vocals) and Peter Ball (born 3/5/1959, Blackpool, keyboards), who teamed up in 1979. They funded their debut release on their Big Frock label before signing with Some Bizzare in 1980. They split in 1984, Almond recording as Marc & The Mambas and solo and Ball forming Grid.

01/08/1981 .... ❶².....30 .....●	TAINTED LOVE 1982 BRIT Award for Best Single. Featured in the films *Coneheads* (1993) and *13 Going On 30* (2004) ....
	....Some Bizzare BZS 2
14/11/1981 .....4......12 .....○	BED SITTER ....Some Bizzare BZS 6
06/02/1982 ....3......9......○	SAY HELLO WAVE GOODBYE ....Some Bizzare BZS 7
29/05/1982 ....2......9......○	TORCH ....Some Bizzare BZS 9
21/08/1982 ....3......8......○	WHAT..Some Bizzare BZS 11
04/12/1982.....21......7.......	WHERE THE HEART IS ....Some Bizzare BZS 16
05/03/1983.....25......4.......	NUMBERS/BARRIERS..Some Bizzare BZS 17
24/09/1983.....16......5.......	SOUL INSIDE..Some Bizzare BZS 20
25/02/1984.....24......6.......	DOWN IN THE SUBWAY ....Some Bizzare BZS 22
09/02/1985.....43......6.......	TAINTED LOVE ....Some Bizzare BZS 2
23/03/1991.....38......3.......	SAY HELLO WAVE GOODBYE '91...Mercury SOFT 1
18/05/1991.....5......8.......	TAINTED LOVE This and above single credited to SOFT CELL/MARC ALMOND ....Mercury SOFT 2
28/09/2002.....52......1.......	MONOCULTURE ....Cooking Vinyl FRYCD 132X
08/02/2003.....39......2.......	THE NIGHT ....Cooking Vinyl FRYCD 135X

SOFT PARADE – see ELECTRIC SOFT PARADE

SOHO UK trio formed by Timothy Brinkhurst (born 20/11/1960, London, guitar), Jacqueline Cuff (born 25/11/1962, Wolverhampton, vocals) and her twin sister Pauline (vocals). The group re-emerged in 1994 as Oosh.

05/05/1990.....47......1.......	HIPPY CHICK Contains a sample of The Smiths' *How Soon Is Now* ....Savage 7SAV 106
19/01/1991 .....8......8.......	HIPPY CHICK ....Savage 7SAV 106
09/11/1991.....51......2.......	BORN TO BE ALIVE ADAMSKI FEATURING SOHO The listed flip side was *Never Goin' Down* by Adamski Featuring Jimi Polo ....
	....MCA MCS 1578

SOHO DOLLS UK group formed by Maya Y (guitar/vocals), Patricia X (bass) and Shannon X (keyboards).

27/11/2004.....57......1....... PRINCE HARRY ....Poptones MC5096SCD

SOIL US rock group formed in Chicago, IL by Ryan McCombs (vocals), Adam Zadel (guitar/vocals), Shaun Glass (guitar), Tim King (bass) and Tom Schofield (drums).

09/11/2002.....74......1.......	HALO..J Records 74321970132
05/06/2004.....68......1.......	REDEFINE ....J Records 82876618512

SOLAR STONE UK production duo formed in Birmingham by Rich Mowatt and Andy Bury. They also produce under the names Z2 and Skyscraper. *The Impressions EP* featured vocal contributions from future *Popstars* winner and Hear'Say member Kym Marsh.

21/02/1998.....75......1.......	THE IMPRESSIONS EP Tracks on EP: *The Calling, Day By Day* and *So Clear* ....Hooj Choons HOOJCD 57
06/11/1999.....39......2.......	SEVEN CITIES ....Hooj Choons HOOJ 85CD
28/09/2002.....44......2.......	SEVEN CITIES Remix of Hooj Choons HOOJ 85CD ....Lost Language LOST 018CD

SOLID GOLD CHARTBUSTERS UK vocal/production group formed by Jimmy Cauty (born 1954, London) and Guy Pratt. Cauty had also been in JAMs, Disco 2000, the Justified Ancients of Mu Mu, the Timelords, 1300 Drums Featuring The Unjustified Ancients Of Mu and KLF with Bill Drummnd.

25/12/1999.....62......1....... I WANNA 1-2-1 WITH YOU ....Virgin VSCDT 1765

SOLID HARMONIE UK/US vocal group with Becki Onslow, Elisa Cariera, Mariama Goodman and Melissa Graham. Goodman later joined Honeyz and Graham went solo. The remaining two members were joined by Jenilca Guisti.

31/01/1998.....18......3.......	I'LL BE THERE FOR YOU ....Jive JIVECD 437
18/04/1998.....16......3.......	I WANT YOU TO WANT ME ....Jive JIVECD 452
15/08/1998.....20......4.......	I WANNA LOVE YOU ....Jive 0521742
21/11/1998.....55......1.......	TO LOVE ONCE AGAIN ....Jive 0522472

SOLID SESSIONS Dutch production duo DJ San and vocalist Natalie Smith.

14/09/2002.....47......1....... JANEIRO..Positiva CDTIV 175

○ Silver disc ● Gold disc ✪ Platinum disc (additional platinum units are indicated by a figure following the symbol) ◉ Singles released prior to 1973 that are known to have sold over 1 million copies in the UK

SOLITAIRE UK DJ/producer Lewis Dene, who also records as Westway.

29/11/2003.....57......2....... I LIKE LOVE (I LOVE LOVE) ....SuSu CDSUSU21

SOLO UK producer Stuart Crichton.

20/07/1991.....59......2....... RAINBOW (SAMPLE FREE) ....Reverb RVBT 003
18/01/1992.....75......1....... COME ON! ....Reverb RVBT 008
11/09/1993.....63......1....... COME ON! (REMIX)..Stoatin' STOAT 003CD

ED SOLO — see BROCKIE/ED SOLO

SAL SOLO UK singer (born 5/9/1954, Hatfield); previously lead singer with Classix Nouveaux before (appropriately) going solo.

15/12/1984.....15......10...... SAN DAMIANO (HEART AND SOUL) ....MCA 930
06/04/1985.....52......3....... MUSIC AND YOU SAL SOLO WITH THE LONDON COMMUNITY GOSPEL CHOIR ....MCA 946

SOLO (US) US R&B vocal group formed in New York by Eunique Mack, Darnell Chavis and Daniele Stokes with jazz bassist Robert Anderson. The group was discovered by songwriters and producer Jimmy Jam and Terry Lewis.

03/02/1996.....35......2....... HEAVEN Contains a sample of The Isley Brothers' *Between The Sheets*......................Perspective 5875212
30/03/1996.....45......1....... WHERE DO U WANT ME TO PUT IT ....Perspective 5875312

SOLUTION — see VICTOR SIMONELLI PRESENTS SOLUTION

MARTIN SOLVEIG French DJ/producer (born 1977, Paris).

24/04/2004.....35......4....... ROCKING MUSIC ....Defected DFTD082CDS
26/06/2004.....57......1....... I'M A GOOD MAN..Defected DFTD091CDS

BELOUIS SOME UK singer (born Neville Keighley, 1960).

27/04/1985.....50......7....... IMAGINATION...Parlophone R 6097
18/01/1986.....17......10...... IMAGINATION Re-issue of Parlophone R 6097.............................Parlophone R 1986
12/04/1986.....33......7....... SOME PEOPLE...Parlophone R 6130
16/05/1987.....53......2....... LET IT BE WITH YOU..Parlophone R 6154

JIMMY SOMERVILLE UK singer (born 22/6/1961, Glasgow) who was a founder member of Bronski Beat in 1984. He left the following year to form the Communards. He disbanded them in 1988, going solo in 1989. June Miles-Kingston is a UK singer.

11/11/1989.....14......9....... COMMENT TE DIRE ADIEU JIMMY SOMERVILLE FEATURING JUNE MILES-KINGSTON......................London LON 241
13/01/1990 ....5......8....... YOU MAKE ME FEEL (MIGHTY REAL) ....London LON 249
17/03/1990.....26......6....... READ MY LIPS (ENOUGH IS ENOUGH) ....London LON 254
03/11/1990 .....8......11...... TO LOVE SOMEBODY ....London LON 281
02/02/1991.....32......4....... SMALLTOWN BOY (REMIX) JIMMY SOMERVILLE WITH BRONSKI BEAT.......................London LON 287
10/08/1991.....52......2....... RUN FROM LOVE ....London LON 301
28/01/1995.....24......4....... HEARTBEAT ....London LONCD 358
27/05/1995.....15......6....... HURT SO GOOD ....London LONCD 364
28/10/1995.....41......2....... BY YOUR SIDE ....London LONCD 372
13/09/1997.....66......1....... DARK SKY ....Gut CXGUT 11

SOMETHIN' FOR THE PEOPLE FEATURING TRINA AND TAMARA US vocal group formed in Oakland, CA by Rochad 'Cat Daddy' Holiday, Curtis 'Sauce' Wilson and Jeff 'Fuzzy' Young with singers Trina and Tamara Powell.

07/02/1998.....64......1....... MY LOVE IS THE SHHH! ....Warner Brothers W 0427CD

SOMETHING CORPORATE US rock group formed in Orange County, CA by Andrew McMahon (piano/vocals), Josh Partington (guitar), William Tell (guitar), Clutch (bass) and Brian Ireland (drums).

29/03/2003.....33......2....... PUNK ROCK PRINCESS..MCA MCSTD 40315
12/07/2003.....68......1....... IF YOU C JORDAN ....MCA MCSTD 40324

SOMORE FEATURING DAMON TRUEITT US production group with Wayne Gardiner, Filthy Rich Crisco and singer Damon Trueitt.

24/01/1998.....21......2....... I REFUSE (WHAT YOU WANT) ....XL Recordings XLS 93CD

SONGSTRESS US vocal/production duo Kerri Chandler and Jerome Sydenham.

27/02/1999.....64......1....... SEE LINE WOMAN '99...Locked On LOX 106CD

SONIA UK singer (born Sonia Evans, 13/2/1971, Liverpool). After attending drama school she made a brief appearance in the TV comedy *Bread*. She introduced herself to producer Pete Waterman, securing a place on his TV show *Hitman And Her*, with Waterman writing and producing her early hits. She left PWL Management in 1991 and later represented Britain in the Eurovision Song Contest in 1993. Gary Barnacle is a UK saxophonist.

24/06/1989 ....❶[2].....13...... YOU'LL NEVER STOP ME LOVING YOU ....Chrysalis CHS 3385
07/10/1989.....17......6....... CAN'T FORGET YOU...Chrysalis CHS 3419
09/12/1989.....10......10...... LISTEN TO YOUR HEART ....Chrysalis CHS 3465
07/04/1990.....16......7....... COUNTING EVERY MINUTE..Chrysalis CHS 3492
23/06/1990.....14......6....... YOU'VE GOT A FRIEND BIG FUN AND SONIA FEATURING GARY BARNACLE........................Jive CHILD 90

❶[9] Number of weeks single topped the UK chart ↑ Entered the UK chart at #1 ▲[9] Number of weeks single topped the US chart

745

25/08/1990	18	7		END OF THE WORLD	Chrysalis CHS 3557
01/06/1991	10	8		**ONLY FOOLS (NEVER FALL IN LOVE)**	IQ ZB 44613
31/08/1991	22	5		BE YOUNG BE FOOLISH BE HAPPY	IQ ZB 44935
16/11/1991	13	5		YOU TO ME ARE EVERYTHING	IQ ZB 45121
12/09/1992	30	3		BOOGIE NIGHTS	Arista 74321113467
01/05/1993	15	7		BETTER THE DEVIL YOU KNOW Britain's entry for the 1993 Eurovision Song Contest (came second)	Arista 74321146872
30/07/1994	61	1		HOPELESSLY DEVOTED TO YOU	Cockney COCCD 2

SONIC SOLUTION UK/Belgian production duo CJ Bolland (born Christian Jay Bolland, 18/6/1971, Stockton-On-Tees) and Steve Cop. Bolland has also recorded as Pulse, The Project, CJ Bolland and Space Opera.

04/04/1992	59	1		BEATSTIME	R&S RSUK 11

SONIC SURFERS Dutch instrumental/production duo Ian Anthony Stephens and Rew.

20/03/1993	61	1		TAKE ME UP SONIC SURFERS FEATURING JOCELYN BROWN	A&M AMCD 210
30/07/1994	54	1		DON'T GIVE IT UP	Brilliant CDBRIL 6

SONIC THE HEDGEHOG – see HWA FEATURING SONIC THE HEDGEHOG

SONIC YOUTH US rock group formed in the mid-1980s by Thurston Moore (born 25/7/1958, Coral Gables, FL, guitar), Kim Gordon (born 28/4/1953, New York, bass), Lee Renaldo (born 3/2/1956, New York, guitar) and Bob Bert (drums). Bert left in 1986, replaced by Steve Shelley (born 23/6/1962, Midland, MI). They switched to the Geffen label in 1990.

11/07/1992	28	4		100%	DGC DGCS 11
07/11/1992	52	2		YOUTH AGAINST FASCISM	Geffen GFS 26
03/04/1993	26	3		SUGAR KANE Featured in the 1999 film *End Of Days*	Geffen GFSTD 37
07/05/1994	24	2		BULL IN THE HEATHER	Geffen GFSTD 72
10/09/1994	45	2		SUPERSTAR Listed flip side was Redd Kross' *Yesterday Once More*. Both tracks were taken from a tribute album to The Carpenters, *If I Were A Carpenter*	A&M 5807932
11/07/1998	72	1		SUNDAY	Geffen GFSTD 22332

SONIQUE UK singer/DJ (born Sonia Clarke, London); she previously worked with Bass-O-Matic and S-Express before relaunching her solo career. She first recorded solo for Cooltempo Records while still a teenager and scored a big club hit with *Let Me Hold You*. Her UK #1 was re-released in the UK after it had hit the US top ten. She was named Best British Female Artist at the 2001 BRIT Awards.

13/06/1998	36	2		I PUT A SPELL ON YOU	Serious SERR 001CD
05/12/1998	24	3		IT FEELS SO GOOD	Serious SERR 004CD1
03/06/2000	●³	17	✪	**IT FEELS SO GOOD ((REMIX) ↑**	Universal MCSTD 40233
16/09/2000	2	10		**SKY**	Universal MCSTD 40240
09/12/2000	5	10		**I PUT A SPELL ON YOU** Re-issue of SERR 001CD	Universal MCSTD 40245
31/05/2003	17	4		CAN'T MAKE MY MIND UP	Serious 9807217
13/09/2003	70	1		ALIVE	Serious 9811500

SONNY US singer (born Salvatore Bono, 16/2/1935, Detroit, MI). He moved to Los Angeles, CA in 1954 and joined Specialty Records in 1957 as a record-packer. He developed his songwriting and recorded as Don Christy for the label. After Specialty's demise he recorded as Sonny Christie and Ronny Sommers for a number of labels before meeting Cher in 1963. After the pair dissolved both their marriage and partnership in 1974, Sonny became an actor (appearing in *Hairspray*), was Mayor of Palm Springs and later opened a restaurant. In 1994 he was elected to the House of Representatives after winning California's 44th district congressional seat. He was killed in a skiing accident on 5/1/1998.

19/08/1965	9	11		**LAUGH AT ME**	Atlantic AT 4038

SONNY AND CHER US husband and wife duo Sonny Bono (born Salvatore Bono, 16/2/1935, Detroit, MI) and Cher (born Cherilyn Sarkasian La Pierre, 20/5/1946, El Centro, CA). They first recorded together with Phil Spector as Caesar & Cleo in 1964, reverting to their real names in 1965. They were married in 1964, divorced 1965. Both recorded solo and appeared in films; Cher won an Oscar for her performance in *Moonstruck*. Sonny was killed in a skiing accident on 5/1/1998. They have a star on the Hollywood Walk of Fame.

12/08/1965	●²	12		**I GOT YOU BABE ▲³** Featured in the films *Buster* (1988) and *Look Who's Talking Too* (1990)	Atlantic AT 4035
16/09/1965	11	9		BABY DON'T GO	Reprise R 20309
21/10/1965	17	8		BUT YOU'RE MINE	Atlantic AT 4047
17/02/1966	13	11		WHAT NOW MY LOVE	Atlantic AT 4069
30/06/1966	42	3		HAVE I STAYED TOO LONG	Atlantic 584 018
08/09/1966	4	10		**LITTLE MAN**	Atlantic 584 040
17/11/1966	44	4		LIVING FOR YOU	Atlantic 584 057
02/02/1967	29	8		THE BEAT GOES ON	Atlantic 584 078
15/01/1972	8	12		**ALL I EVER NEED IS YOU**	MCA MU 1145
22/05/1993	66	1		I GOT YOU BABE Re-issue of Atlantic AT 4035	Epic 6592402

SONO German production duo Florian Sikorski and Martin Weiland, with singer Lenart Salomon.

16/06/2001	66	1		KEEP CONTROL	Code Blue BLU 020CD1

SON'Z OF A LOOP DA LOOP ERA UK producer Danny Breaks.

15/02/1992	36	3		FAR OUT	Suburban Base SUBBASE 008
17/10/1992	60	1		PEACE + LOVEISM	Suburban Base SUBBASE 14

○ Silver disc ● Gold disc ✪ Platinum disc (additional platinum units are indicated by a figure following the symbol) ◉ Singles released prior to 1973 that are known to have sold over 1 million copies in the UK

SONS AND DAUGHTERS
UK group formed in Glasgow by Adele Bethel (guitar), Scott Paterson (guitar/bass), Ailidh Lennon (mandolin/bass) and David Gow (drums).

16/10/2004 . . . . . 68 . . . . . . 1 . . . . JOHNNY CASH . . . . Domino RUG186CD

SOOPA HOOPZ FEATURING QPR MASSIVE
UK group formed by supporters of Queens Park Rangers football club and fronted by Phil Parry.

16/10/2004 . . . . . 54 . . . . . . 1 . . . . . . ○ SOOPA HOOPZ . . . . Sniper Alley SNIPER001

SOOZY Q – see BIG TIME CHARLIE

SOPHIE – see ZERO 7

SORROWS
UK group formed in Coventry in 1963 by Don Maughn (born 19/8/1943, Coventry, vocals), Pip Whitcher (guitar), Wez Price (guitar), Philip Packham (bass) and Bruce Finley (drums). Maughn later name-changed to Don Fardon, enjoying solo success.

16/09/1965 . . . . . 21 . . . . . . 8 . . . . TAKE A HEART . . . . Piccadilly 7N 35260

S.O.S. BAND
US R&B group formed in Atlanta, GA by Mary Davis (vocals), Jason Bryant (keyboards), Abdul Raoof (trumpet), Billy Ellis (saxophone), John Simpson (bass), Bruno Speight (guitar), Jerome 'JT' Thomas (drums) and Willie 'Sonny' Killebrew (saxophone) as Santa Monica. They name-changed in 1980 (SOS stands for 'Sounds Of Success') upon signing with Tabu.

19/07/1980 . . . . . 51 . . . . . . 4	TAKE YOUR TIME (DO IT RIGHT) PART 1 Featured in the 1998 film *54*.	Tabu TBU 8564
26/02/1983 . . . . . 72 . . . . . . 1	GROOVIN' (THAT'S WHAT WE'RE DOIN')	Tabu TBU A 3120
07/04/1984 . . . . . 13 . . . . . 11	JUST BE GOOD TO ME	Tabu A 3626
04/08/1984 . . . . . 32 . . . . . . 7	JUST THE WAY YOU LIKE IT	Tabu A 4621
13/10/1984 . . . . . 51 . . . . . . 5	WEEKEND GIRL	Tabu A 4785
29/03/1986 . . . . . 17 . . . . . 10	THE FINEST	Tabu A 6997
05/07/1986 . . . . . 50 . . . . . . 5	BORROWED LOVE	Tabu A 7241
02/05/1987 . . . . . 64 . . . . . . 3	NO LIES	Tabu 6504447

AARON SOUL
UK singer (born Aaron Anyia, London); his mother sang in a group with Soul II Soul's Caron Wheeler before moving to Southampton when Aaron was fourteen.

02/06/2001 . . . . . 14 . . . . . . 4 . . . . RING RING RING Featured in the 2001 film *Bridget Jones' Diary* . . . . Def Soul 5689042

DAVID SOUL
US singer/actor (born David Solberg, 28/8/1943, Chicago, IL). As a folk singer he appeared on TV as 'The Covered Man' wearing a ski mask. As an actor best known as Ken Hutchinson in *Starsky & Hutch*, he maintained a parallel career as a singer.

18/12/1976 . . . . ❶⁴ . . . . 16 . . . . ✪	DON'T GIVE UP ON US ▲¹	Private Stock PVT 84
26/03/1977 . . . . . 2 . . . . . . 8 . . . . ○	GOING IN WITH MY EYES OPEN	Private Stock PVT 99
27/08/1977 . . . . ❶³ . . . . 14 . . . . ●	SILVER LADY Featured in the 1978 film *The Stud*.	Private Stock PVT 115
17/12/1977 . . . . . 8 . . . . . . 9	LET'S HAVE A QUIET NIGHT IN	Private Stock PVT 130
27/05/1978 . . . . . 12 . . . . . . 9	IT SURE BRINGS OUT THE LOVE IN YOUR EYES	Private Stock PVT 137

JIMMY SOUL
US singer (born James McCleese, 24/8/1942, New York). He worked with numerous gospel groups including The Nightingales. He died from a heart attack while serving time in prison on a drug conviction on 25/6/1988 (his third spell inside).

11/07/1963 . . . . . 39 . . . . . . 2 . . . . IF YOU WANNA BE HAPPY ▲² Featured in the films *Mermaids* (1990) and *My Best Friend's Wedding* (1997) . . . . Stateside SS 178
15/06/1991 . . . . . 68 . . . . . . 3 . . . . IF YOU WANNA BE HAPPY Re-issue of Stateside SS 178 and released after being featured in the film *Mermaids* . . . . . Epic 6569647

SOUL ASYLUM
US rock group formed in Minneapolis, MN in 1983 by Dave Pirner (born 16/4/1964, Green Bay, WI, guitar/vocals), Daniel Murphy (born 12/7/1962, Duluth, MN, guitar), Karl Mueller (born 27/7/1962, Minneapolis, bass) and Grant Young (born 5/1/1964, Iowa City, IA, drums). Young left in 1995, replaced by Sterling Campbell.

19/06/1993 . . . . . 37 . . . . . . 8	RUNAWAY TRAIN	Columbia 6593902
04/09/1993 . . . . . 34 . . . . . . 3	SOMEBODY TO SHOVE	Columbia 6596492
13/11/1993 . . . . . 7 . . . . . 11	RUNAWAY TRAIN	Columbia 6593902
22/01/1994 . . . . . 26 . . . . . . 4	BLACK GOLD	Columbia 6598442
26/03/1994 . . . . . 32 . . . . . . 3	SOMEBODY TO SHOVE Re-issue of Columbia 6596492	Columbia 6602245
15/07/1995 . . . . . 30 . . . . . . 3	MISERY	Columbia 6621092
02/12/1995 . . . . . 52 . . . . . . 1	JUST LIKE ANYONE	Columbia 6624785

SOUL BROTHERS
UK vocal/instrumental group who also recorded for Parlophone.

22/04/1965 . . . . . 42 . . . . . . 3 . . . . I KEEP RINGING MY BABY . . . . Decca F 12116

SOUL CITY ORCHESTRA
UK instrumental/production group.

11/12/1993 . . . . . 70 . . . . . . 1 . . . . IT'S JURASSIC . . . . London JURCD 1

SOUL CITY SYMPHONY – see VAN MCCOY

SOUL CONTROL
Dutch production duo formed in Amsterdam by Jobbe Strobosch and Olaf Boswijk.

18/09/2004 . . . . . 25 . . . . . . 3 . . . . CHOCOLATE (CHOCO CHOCO) . . . . Tug CDSNOG12

❶⁹ Number of weeks single topped the UK chart ↑ Entered the UK chart at #1 ▲⁹ Number of weeks single topped the US chart

747

SOUL FAMILY SENSATION
UK/US group formed by Jhelisa Anderson (vocals), Jonathon Male (guitar), Pete Zivkovic (keyboards) and Gary Batson (keyboards). Anderson (a cousin of fellow singer Carleen Anderson) later went solo.

11/05/1991	49	4		I DON'T EVEN KNOW IF I SHOULD CALL YOU BABY . . . . One Little Indian 47 TP7

SOUL FOR REAL
US vocal group formed in Long Island by the four Dalyrimple brothers: Christopher 'Choc', Andre 'Dre', Brian and Jason. Their sisters Nicole and Desiree provided backing vocals.

08/07/1995	23	2		CANDY RAIN . . . . Uptown MCSTD 2052
23/03/1996	31	2		EVERY LITTLE THING I DO . . . . Uptown MCSTD 48005

SOUL SONIC FORCE
US vocal group formed by MC G.L.O.B.E. (born John Miller), Mr Biggs (Ellis Williams), Pow Wow (Robert Allen) and DJ Jazzy Jay.

28/08/1982	53	3		PLANET ROCK Contains a sample of Kraftwerk's Trans Euro Express . . . . Polydor POSP 497
10/03/1984	30	4		RENEGADES OF FUNK This and above single credited to AFRIKA BAMBAATAA AND THE SONIC SOUL FORCE . . . . . . Tommy Boy AFR 1
25/08/2001	47	1		PLANET ROCK PAUL OAKENFOLD PRESENTS AFRIKA BAMBAATAA AND SOULSONIC FORCE . . . . Tommy Boy TBCD 2266

SOUL II SOUL
UK R&B group formed in London in 1982 as a sound system for dance clubs by Jazzie B (born Beresford Romeo, 26/1/1963, London) and Philip 'Daddae' Harvey (born 28/2/1964, London). Nellee Hooper (born Paul Andrew Hooper) joined in 1985, the group debuting on record in 1987. They achieved their chart breakthrough in 1989 with Caron Wheeler (born 19/1/1963, London) on lead vocals. Earlier lead singer Do'Reen (born Doreen Waddell, 1966, Southend) was killed on 1/3/2002 after being hit by a number of cars while trying to flee a shop after being caught shoplifting. Two Grammy Awards include Best Rhythm & Blues Instrumental Performance in 1989 for African Dance. Jazzie B was given a Outstanding Contribution Award at the 1996 MOBO Awards.

21/05/1988	63	3		FAIRPLAY SOUL II SOUL FEATURING ROSE WINDROSS . . . . 10 TEN 228
17/09/1988	64	2		FEEL FREE SOUL II SOUL FEATURING DO'REEN . . . . 10 TEN 239
18/03/1989	5	12		KEEP ON MOVING . . . . 10 TEN 263
10/06/1989	●⁴	14	○	BACK TO LIFE (HOWEVER DO YOU WANT ME) This and above single credited to SOUL II SOUL FEATURING CARON WHEELER 1989 Grammy Award for Best Rhythm & Blues Vocal Performance by a Group . . . . 10 TEN 265
09/12/1989	3	13	○	GET A LIFE . . . . 10 TEN 284
05/05/1990	6	6		A DREAM'S A DREAM . . . . 10 TEN 300
24/11/1990	22	7		MISSING YOU SOUL II SOUL FEATURING KYM MAZELLE . . . . 10 TEN 345
04/04/1992	4	7		JOY . . . . 10 TEN 350
13/06/1992	31	4		MOVE ME NO MOUNTAIN SOUL II SOUL, LEAD VOCALS KOFI . . . . 10 TEN 400
26/09/1992	38	2		JUST RIGHT . . . . 10 TEN 410
06/11/1993	24	4		WISH . . . . Virgin VSCDG 1480
22/07/1995	12	6		LOVE ENUFF . . . . Virgin VSCDT 1527
21/10/1995	17	4		I CARE . . . . Virgin VSCDT 1560
19/10/1996	31	2		KEEP ON MOVING . . . . Virgin VSCDT 1612
30/08/1997	39	2		REPRESENT . . . . Island CID 668
08/11/1997	51	1		PLEASURE DOME . . . . Island CID 669

SOUL PROVIDERS FEATURING MICHELLE SHELLERS
UK/US production duo Jason Pailon and Ian Carey with US singer Michelle Shellers. Carey later formed Saturated Soul with Eddie Amador.

14/07/2001	59	1		RISE . . . . AM:PM CDAMPM 147

S.O.U.L. S.Y.S.T.E.M. INTRODUCING MICHELLE VISAGE
US dance group assembled by David Cole (born 3/6/1962, Johnson City, TN) and Robert Clivilles (born 30/8/1964, NYC) and featuring Michelle Visage (born 20/9/1968, NYC) as lead singer. They also recorded as C&C Music Factory and Clivilles and Coles. Visage had previously been a member of Seduction.

16/01/1993	17	5		IT'S GONNA BE A LOVELY DAY Rap version of Bill Wither's Lovely Day. Featured in the 1992 film The Bodyguard . . . . Arista 74321125692

SOUL U✱NIQUE
UK vocal group formed by Kate, Ben, Marc and Kwashaan.

19/02/2000	53	1		BE MY FRIEND . . . . M&J MAJCD 2
29/07/2000	66	1		3IL (THRILL) . . . . M&J MAJCD 3

SOUL VISION – see EVERYTHING BUT THE GIRL

SOULED OUT
Italian/US/UK group formed by Sarah Warwick, Kerome Stokes and Rio with production team Sergio Della, Monica Gigi Canu and Sandro Sommella. The group was also known as Souled Out International.

09/05/1992	75	1		IN MY LIFE . . . . Columbia 6578367

SOULSEARCHER
UK production duo Marc Pomerby and Brian Tapperts, with singer Thea Austin.

13/02/1999	8	7		CAN'T GET ENOUGH Contains an interpolation of The Gibson Brothers' Cuba and a sample of Gary's Gang's Let's Love Dance Tonite . . . . Defected DEFECT 1CDS
08/04/2000	32	2		DO IT TO ME AGAIN . . . . Defected DEFECT 15CDS

SOULSONIC FORCE – see SOUL SONIC FORCE

SOULWAX
Belgian dance group formed by Stephen Dewaele (vocaliser/harmonies), David Dewaele (guitar/keyboards/loops), Piet Dierickx (keyboards), Stefaan Van Leuven (bass) and Stephane (drums).

25/03/2000	65	1		CONVERSATION INTERCOM . . . . Pias Recordings PIASB 018CD

○ Silver disc ● Gold disc ✪ Platinum disc (additional platinum units are indicated by a figure following the symbol) ◎ Singles released prior to 1973 that are known to have sold over 1 million copies in the UK

24/06/2000.....56......1...... MUCH AGAINST EVERYONE'S ADVICE .... Pias Recordings PIASB 026CD
30/09/2000.....40......2...... TOO MANY DJ'S The accompanying video featured 20 small-town public house DJ's playing the song while fake telephone numbers for booking purposes was striped across them! .... Pias Recordings PIASB 036CD
03/03/2001.....50......1...... CONVERSATION INTERCOM (REMIX) .... Pias Recordings PIASB 046CD
21/08/2004.....34......2...... ANY MINUTE NOW .... Pias Recordings PIASB 126CDM

SOUND BLUNTZ Canadian production group formed by DJ Lil Pete and Cory Cash.
30/11/2002.....32......2...... BILLIE JEAN Contains a sample of Jay Dee's *Plastic Dreams* .... Incentive CENT 51CDS

SOUND-DE-ZIGN Dutch DJ/production duo Adri Blok and Arjen Rietvink. They also record as Souvenance.
14/04/2001.....19......5...... HAPPINESS Contains a sample of Shena's *Let The Beat Hit 'Em* .... NuLife 74321844002

SOUND FACTORY Swedish vocal/instrumental duo Emil Hellman and St James.
05/06/1993.....72......1...... 2 THE RHYTHM .... Logic 74321149422

SOUND 5 UK vocal/instrumental duo Rick Peet (born Richard Anderson-Peet, 1970, Liverpool) and Daniel 'Dizzy' Dee (born Daniel Spencer, 1970, Stoke-on-Trent). Both had previously been in house band This Ain't Chicago and recorded as Candy Flip.
24/04/1999.....69......1...... ALA KABOO .... Gut CDGUT 23

SOUND 9418 UK singer Jonathan King (born Kenneth King, 6/12/1944, London).
07/02/1976.....46......3...... IN THE MOOD .... UK 121

SOUND OF ONE FEATURING GLADEZZ US vocal/instrumental duo Allen George and Fred McFarlane.
20/11/1993.....65......1...... AS I AM .... Cooltempo CDCOOL 280

SOUNDGARDEN US rock group formed in Seattle, WA in 1984 by Kim Thayil (born 4/9/1960, Seattle, guitar), Hiro Yamamoto (born 20/9/1968, Okinawa, Japan, bass), Chris Cornell (born 20/7/1964, Seattle, guitar/vocals) and Scott Sundquist (drums). Sundquist left soon after, replaced by Matt Cameron (born 28/11/1962, San Diego, CA). Yamamoto left in 1990, replaced by Ben 'Hunter' Shepherd (born 20/9/1968). They disbanded in 1997 with Chris Cornell going solo and later forming Audioslave. Two Grammy Awards included Best Metal Performance with Vocal in 1994 for *Superunknown*.
11/04/1992.....30......3...... JESUS CHRIST POSE .... A&M AM 862
20/06/1992.....41......1...... RUSTY CAGE .... A&M AM 874
21/11/1992.....50......1...... OUTSHINED .... A&M AM 0102
26/02/1994.....20......3...... SPOONMAN .... A&M 5805392
30/04/1994.....42......2...... THE DAY I TRIED TO LIVE .... A&M 5805952
20/08/1994.....12......5...... BLACK HOLE SUN 1994 Grammy Award for Best Hard Rock Performance with Vocal .... A&M 5807532
28/01/1995.....24......2...... FELL ON BLACK DAYS .... A&M 5809472
18/05/1996.....14......3...... PRETTY NOOSE .... A&M 5816202
28/09/1996.....33......2...... BURDEN IN MY HAND .... A&M 5818552
28/12/1996.....40......2...... BLOW UP THE OUTSIDE WORLD .... A&M 5819862

SOUNDMAN AND DON LLOYDIE WITH ELISABETH TROY UK vocal/production group with singer Elisabeth Troy.
25/02/1995.....49......2...... GREATER LOVE .... Sound Of Underground SOJURCD 016

SOUNDS INCORPORATED UK instrumental group formed by Alan Holmes (flute/saxophone), John St John (guitar), Wes Hunter (bass), Barrie Cameron (keyboards) and Tony Newman (drums). They disbanded at the end of the 1960s.
23/04/1964.....30......6...... THE SPARTANS .... Columbia DB 7239
30/07/1964.....35......5...... SPANISH HARLEM .... Columbia DB 7321

SOUNDS NICE FEATURING TIM MYCROFT UK studio group fronted by organist Tim Mycroft to produce a cover version of the Jane Birkin and Serge Gainsbourg hit that had been banned by radio.
06/09/1969.....18......11...... LOVE AT FIRST SIGHT (JE T'AIME...MOI NON PLUS) .... Parlophone R 5797

SOUNDS OF BLACKNESS US gospel choir formed in Minnesota in 1969 as the Macalester College Black Choir and which later came under the direction of former body builder Gary Hines (once crowned Mr Minnesota) in 1971. The 40-strong choir and 10-piece orchestra was eventually spotted by Jimmy Jam and Terry Lewis and provided backing vocals for Alexander O'Neill before recording their debut album. They won the 1991 Grammy Award for Best Gospel Album by a Choir for *The Evolution Of Gospel*.
22/06/1991.....45......4...... OPTIMISTIC .... Perspective PERSS 786
28/09/1991.....71......1...... THE PRESSURE PART 1 .... Perspective PERSS 816
15/02/1992.....28......4...... OPTIMISTIC Re-issue of Perspective PERSS 786 .... Perspective PERSS 849
25/04/1992.....49......2...... THE PRESSURE PART 1 (REMIX) .... Perspective PERSS 867
08/05/1993.....27......3...... I'M GOING ALL THE WAY .... Perspective 5874252
26/03/1994.....17......4...... I BELIEVE Contains a sample of The Ohio Players' *Pain* .... A&M 5874512
02/07/1994.....36......4...... GLORYLAND DARYL HALL AND THE SOUNDS OF BLACKNESS The official song of the 1994 FIFA World Cup ..... Mercury MERCD 404
20/08/1994.....29......3...... EVERYTHING IS GONNA BE ALRIGHT Contains a sample of Isaac Hayes' *Walk On By* .... A&M 5874672
14/01/1995.....14......4...... I'M GOING ALL THE WAY .... A&M 5874832
07/06/1997.....35......2...... SPIRIT SOUNDS OF BLACKNESS FEATURING CRAIG MACK .... Perspective 5822312
14/02/1998.....46......1...... THE PRESSURE (2ND REMIX) .... AM:PM 5824872

❶[9] Number of weeks single topped the UK chart ↑ Entered the UK chart at #1 ▲[9] Number of weeks single topped the US chart

749

SOUNDS ORCHESTRAL UK studio group assembled by producer John Schroeder and comprising John Pearson, Kenny Clare and Tony Reeves. Schroeder had previously been in-house producer for Oriole and later formed Alaska Records.

03/12/1964	5	16	CAST YOUR FATE TO THE WIND	Piccadilly 7N 35206
08/07/1965	43	2	MOONGLOW	Piccadilly 7N 35248

SOUNDSATION UK production group formed by Warren Clark, Peter Lunn and Martyn The Hat.

14/01/1995	48	1	PEACE AND JOY	ffrreedom TABCD 224

SOUNDSCAPE UK DJ/production group with singer Tempo O'Neil.

14/02/1998	61	1	DUBPLATE CULTURE	Satellite 74321552002

SOUNDSOURCE UK/Swedish production group formed by Morgan King and Nick Hook.

11/01/1992	62	1	TAKE ME UP	ffrr FX 177

SOUP DRAGONS UK rock group formed in Glasgow by Sean Dickinson (vocals), Jim McCulloch (guitar), Sushil Dade (bass) and Paul Quinn (drums).

20/06/1987	65	1	CAN'T TAKE NO FOR AN ANSWER	Raw TV RTV 3
05/09/1987	66	1	SOFT AS YOUR FACE	Raw TV RTV 4
14/07/1990	5	12	I'M FREE SOUP DRAGONS FEATURING JUNIOR REID Featured in the 1999 film *The Other Sister*	Raw TV RTV 9
20/10/1990	26	5	MOTHER UNIVERSE	Big Life BLR 30
11/04/1992	53	3	DIVINE THING	Big Life BLR 68

SOURCE UK producer John Truelove.

02/02/1991	4	11	○	YOU GOT THE LOVE SOURCE FEATURING CANDI STATON	Truelove TLOVE 7001
26/12/1992	63	1		ROCK THE HOUSE SOURCE FEATURING NICOLE	React 12REACT 12
01/03/1997	3	8		YOU GOT THE LOVE (REMIX) SOURCE FEATURING CANDI STATON	React CDREACT 89
23/08/1997	38	2		CLOUDS	XL Recordings XLS 83CD

SOURMASH UK production trio formed by Doug Osborne, David Wesson and Steve Jones.

23/12/2000	73	1	PILGRIMAGE/MESCALITO	Hooj Choons HOOJ 102CD

SOUTH UK vocal/instrumental group formed by Joel Cadbury, Brett Shaw and Jamie McDonald.

17/03/2001	69	1	PAINT THE SILENCE	Mo Wax MWR 134CD
23/08/2003	73	1	LOOSEN YOUR HOLD	Double Dragon DD 2010CD
03/04/2004	60	1	COLOURS IN WAVES	Sanctuary SANXD249
14/08/2004	72	1	MOTIVELESS CRIMS	Sanctuary SANXD286

JOE SOUTH US singer (born Joe Souter, 28/2/1940, Atlanta, GA). He began as a session guitarist and songwriter in Nashville.

05/03/1969	6	11	GAMES PEOPLE PLAY 1969 Grammy Awards for Song of the Year and Best Contemporary Song for writer Joe South	Capitol CL 15579

SOUTH ST. PLAYER US singer/producer Roland Clark.

02/09/2000	49	1	WHO KEEPS CHANGING YOUR MIND	Cream 4CD

JERI SOUTHERN US singer/jazz pianist (born Genevieve Hering, 5/8/1926, Royal, NE); she began her recording career with Decca in 1950. She died from pneumonia in Los Angeles, CA on 4/8/1991.

21/06/1957	22	3	FIRE DOWN BELOW Featured in the 1957 film of the same name	Brunswick 05665

SOUTHLANDERS UK vocal group formed in 1954 by Vernon Nesbeth, Frank Mannah, Alan Wilmot and his brother Harry. They are best known for the novelty record *Mole In A Hole*.

22/11/1957	17	10	ALONE	Decca F 10946

SOUTHSIDE SPINNERS Dutch production/DJ duo Marvo Verkuylen and Benjamin Kuyten whose debut hit was originally released by the District label in November 1999. It also features singer Janny.

27/05/2000	9	7	LUVSTRUCK	AM:PM CDAMPM 132

SOUVERNANCE Dutch DJ/production duo Adri Blok and Arjen Rietvink with vocalist Delano Girigorie. They also record as Sound-De-Zign.

31/08/2002	63	1	HAVIN' A GOOD TIME Contains a sample of Mass Order's *Let's Get Happy*	Positiva CDTIV 174

SOUVLAKI UK producer Mark Summers. He had previously recorded under his own name.

15/02/1997	24	3	INFERNO	Wonderboy WBOYD 003
08/08/1998	63	1	MY TIME	Wonderboy WBOYD 009

SOVEREIGN COLLECTION UK orchestra.

03/04/1971	27	6	MOZART 40	Capitol CL 15676

RED SOVINE US singer (born Woodrow Wilson Sovine, 17/1/1918, Charleston, WV). He began as a session guitarist and songwriter. He died from a heart attack on 4/4/1980.

13/06/1981	4	8	○	TEDDY BEAR	Starday SD 142

○ Silver disc ● Gold disc ✪ Platinum disc (additional platinum units are indicated by a figure following the symbol) ◎ Singles released prior to 1973 that are known to have sold over 1 million copies in the UK

SOX UK vocal/instrumental group that featured Samantha Fox on lead vocals and whose debut hit first came to prominence as a competitor to Britain's 'Song For Europe' competition.

15/04/1995......47......1....... GO FOR THE HEART... Living Beat LBECD 33

BOB B SOXX AND THE BLUE JEANS US vocal group formed by producer Phil Spector (born 26/12/1940, New York) with Bobby Sheen (born 17/5/1941, St Louis, MO), Darlene Love (born Darlene Wright, 26/7/1938, Los Angeles, CA) and Fanita James. Love and James were members of The Blossoms and when they left were replaced by Gloria Jones (another member of The Blossoms) and Carolyn Willis. Sheen died on 23/11/2000.

31/01/1963......45......2....... ZIP-A-DEE-DOO-DAH... London HLU 9646

SPACE French group originally put together as a studio group, the success of the single prompting the creation of a band that featured Didier Marouani and Roland Romanelli (both on keyboards), Joe Hammer (drums) and singer Madeline Bell.

13/08/1977.....2......12.....O **MAGIC FLY**... Pye International 7N 25746

SPACE UK rock group formed in Liverpool by Tommy Scott (born 18/2/1967, Liverpool, bass/vocals), Andrew Parle (drums), James Murphy (guitar/vocals) and Francis Griffiths (keyboards).

06/04/1996.....56......1.......	NEIGHBOURHOOD... Gut CDGUT 1
08/06/1996.....14......10.......	FEMALE OF THE SPECIES Featured in the 1997 film *Austin Powers – International Man Of Mystery* .... Gut CDGUT 2
07/09/1996.....9......6.......	ME AND YOU VERSUS THE WORLD... Gut CXGUT 4
02/11/1996.....11......6.......	NEIGHBOURHOOD... Gut GXGUT 5
22/02/1997.....14......4.......	DARK CLOUDS... Gut CDGUT 6
10/01/1998.....6......8.......	AVENGING ANGELS .... Gut CDGUT 16
07/03/1998.....4......8.....O	THE BALLAD OF TOM JONES SPACE WITH CERYS OF CATATONIA... Gut CDGUT 18
04/07/1998.....21......4.......	BEGIN AGAIN... Gut CDGUT 019
05/12/1998.....20......3.......	THE BAD DAYS EP Tracks on EP: *Bad Days, The Unluckiest Man In The World* and *We Gotta Get Out Of This Place* .... Gut CDGUT 22
08/07/2000.....49......1.......	DIARY OF A WIMP... Gut CDGUT 34
06/03/2004.....67......1.......	SUBURBAN ROCK 'N' ROLL... R&M Entertainment RAMCDS001

SPACE BABY UK dance producer/instrumentalist Matt Darey. As a remixer he works with the likes of ATB, Moloko and Gabrielle. Darey and Marcella Woods also recorded with Michael Woods as M3 for Inferno, Darey also recording as Sunburst and in Lost Tribe.

08/07/1995.....55......1....... FREE YOUR MIND... Hooj Choons HOOJ 34CD

SPACE BROTHERS UK production duo Ricky Simmons and Stephen Jones, also recording as Ascension, Lustral, Oxygen and Space Brothers.

17/05/1997.....23......3.......	SHINE... Manifesto FESCD 23
13/12/1997.....27......7.......	FORGIVEN (I FEEL YOUR LOVE)... Manifesto FESCD 36
10/07/1999.....31......3.......	LEGACY (SHOW ME LOVE)... Manifesto FESCD 55
09/10/1999.....25......2.......	HEAVEN WILL COME... Manifesto FESCD 61
05/02/2000.....18......4.......	SHINE 2000 (REMIX)... Manifesto FESCD 67

SPACE COWBOY UK producer Nick Destri who also records as DJ Supreme. His debut hit should have charted much higher (within the top ten), but there were too many tracks on the CD version, thus disqualifying it for consideration on the singles chart (it did top the budget albums chart instead!). The records' chart position was therefore based entirely on sales of the 12-inch vinyl version.

06/07/2002.....55......2.......	I WOULD DIE 4 U... Southern Fried ECB 29
02/08/2003.....71......1.......	JUST PUT YOUR HAND IN MINE... Southern Fried ECB 37CDS

SPACE FROG German producer from Frankfurt. His debut hit was originally released in 1997.

16/03/2002.....70......1....... X RAY FOLLOW ME... Tripoli Trax TTRAX 082CD

SPACE KITTENS UK instrumental/production group formed by Sam Tierney, Andy Bury and Richard Mowatt.

13/04/1996.....58......1....... STORM... Hooj Choons HOOJCD 41

SPACE MANOEUVRES UK producer John Graham. He also records as Stoneproof.

29/01/2000.....25......2....... STAGE ONE... Hooj Choons HOOJ 79CD

SPACE MONKEY UK producer Paul Goodchild.

08/10/1983.....53......4....... CAN'T STOP RUNNING... Innervision A 3742

SPACE MONKEY VS GORILLAZ UK production group formed by D-Zire, Dubversive and Gavva.

03/08/2002.....73......1....... LIL' DUB CHEFIN'... Parlophone CDR 6584

SPACE RAIDERS UK production trio Mark Hornby, Martin Jenkins and Gary Bradford.

28/03/1998.....68......1....... GLAM RAID Contains a sample of Kenny's *The Bump* .... Skint 32CD

SPACE 2000 UK instrumental/production group formed by Liam May.

12/08/1995.....50......1....... DO U WANNA FUNK... Wired 218

❶⁹ Number of weeks single topped the UK chart ↑ Entered the UK chart at #1 ▲⁹ Number of weeks single topped the US chart

751

SPACECORN Swedish DJ/producer Daniel Ellenson.

28/04/2001	74	1		AXEL F	69 SN 069CD

SPACEDUST UK production duo Paul Glancey and Duncan Glasson.

| 24/10/1998 | ❶¹ | 10 | ○ | GYM AND TONIC ↑ | East West EW 188CD |
| 27/03/1999 | 20 | 2 | | LET'S GET DOWN Contains a sample of Chic's *I Want Your Love* | East West EW 195CD |

SPACEHOG UK rock group formed in Leeds by brothers Ant (guitar/vocals) and Royston Langlands (vocals/bass), Richard Steel (guitar) and Jonny Cragg (drums).

11/05/1996	70	1		IN THE MEANTIME	Sire 7559643162
28/12/1996	29	6		IN THE MEANTIME	Sire 7559643162
07/02/1998	43	1		CARRY ON	Sire W 0428CD

SPACEMAID UK group formed in Hull, Humberside in 1992 by Lonnie Evans (vocals), Alan Jones (guitar), Mat Tennant (guitar), Andy Burgess (bass) and Chris Black (drums).

| 05/04/1997 | 70 | 1 | | BABY COME ON | Big Star STARC 105 |

SPAGHETTI SURFERS UK instrumental/production duo fronted by Ian Stephens.

| 22/07/1995 | 55 | 1 | | MISIRLOU (THE THEME TO THE MOTION PICTURE 'PULP FICTION') | Tempo Toons CDTOON 4 |

SPAGNA Italian singer from Verona (born Ivana Spagna). She later became a successful songwriter, penning hits for Corona.

25/07/1987	2	12		CALL ME	CBS 6502797
17/10/1987	62	3		EASY LADY	CBS 6511697
20/08/1988	23	8		EVERY GIRL AND BOY	CBS SPAG 1

SPAN Norwegian rock group formed in Oslo by Jarle Bernhoft (guitar/vocals), Joff Nilsen (guitar), Wes Stawnes (bass) and Fredrik Wallumrod (drums)

| 21/02/2004 | 52 | 1 | | DON'T THINK THE WAY THEY DO | Island CID 846 |

SPANDAU BALLET UK pop group formed in London in 1976 by Tony Hadley (born 2/6/1960, London, vocals), Gary Kemp (born 16/10/1959, London, guitar), Steve Norman (born 25/3/1960, London, guitar), John Keeble (born 6/7/1959, London, drums) and Richard Miller as the Makers. They re-formed the following year as Spandau Ballet with Kemp, his brother Martin (born 10/10/1961, London, bass), Keeble, Hadley and Norman establishing their own 'New Romantic' image. They set up the Reformation label in 1980 with a licensing deal with Chrysalis. Both Kemp brothers appeared in the 1990 film *The Krays*. In 1998 Hadley, Norman and Keeble sued Gary Kemp, the chief songwriter, for a greater share of the royalties, but lost their case. They were awarded the Sony Technical Excellence Award at the 1984 BRIT Awards. Martin Kemp later concentrated on acting, appearing in the TV series *Eastenders* as Steve Owen. In 2003 Tony Hadley won ITV's *Reborn In The USA* competition.

15/11/1980	5	11	○	TO CUT A LONG STORY SHORT	Reformation CHS 2473
24/01/1981	17	8		THE FREEZE	Reformation CHS 2486
04/04/1981	10	10		MUSCLEBOUND/GLOW	Reformation CHS 2509
18/07/1981	3	10	○	CHANT NO. 1 (I DON'T NEED THIS PRESSURE ON) Features the uncredited accompaniment of Beggar & Co	Reformation CHS 2528
14/11/1981	30	5		PAINT ME DOWN	Reformation CHS 2560
30/01/1982	49	4		SHE LOVED LIKE DIAMOND	Reformation CHS 2585
10/04/1982	10	11		INSTINCTION	Reformation CHS 2602
02/10/1982	7	9		LIFELINE	Reformation CHS 2642
12/02/1983	12	10		COMMUNICATION	Reformation CHS 2662
23/04/1983	❶⁴	12	●	TRUE Featured in the films *The Wedding Singer* (1998) and *Charlie's Angels* (2000)	Reformation SPAN 1
13/08/1983	2	9	○	GOLD	Reformation SPAN 2
09/06/1984	3	10		ONLY WHEN YOU LEAVE	Reformation SPAN 3
25/08/1984	9	9		I'LL FLY FOR YOU	Reformation SPAN 4
20/10/1984	15	5		HIGHLY STRUNG	Reformation SPAN 5
08/12/1984	18	8		ROUND AND ROUND	Reformation SPAN 6
26/07/1986	15	7		FIGHT FOR OURSELVES	Reformation A 7264
08/11/1986	6	10		THROUGH THE BARRICADES	Reformation SPANS 1
14/02/1987	34	4		HOW MANY LIES	Reformation SPANS 2
03/09/1988	47	3		RAW	CBS SPANS 3
26/08/1989	42	4		BE FREE WITH YOUR LOVE	CBS SPANS 4

SPANKOX Italian DJ producer Agostino Carollo (born in Rovereto). He had previously recorded as X-Treme, Eyes Cream and Ago.

| 09/10/2004 | 69 | 1 | | TO THE CLUB | Inferno CDFERN62 |

SPARKLE US singer (born New York City) who was discovered by R Kelly. She won't reveal her full name although her first name is Stephanie. She was given the nickname 'Sparkle' by R Kelly after he spotted her wearing a distinctive sparkling jacket.

18/07/1998	7	7		BE CAREFUL SPARKLE FEATURING R KELLY	Jive 0521452
07/11/1998	40	2		TIME TO MOVE ON	Jive 0522032
28/08/1999	65	1		LOVIN' YOU Featured in the 1999 film *Life*	Jive 0523452

SPARKLEHORSE US group formed by Mark Linkous (vocals), David Charles (guitar/keyboards/drums), Bob Rupe (bass/vocals) and Johnny Hott (drums). In 1996 Linkous nearly died after mixing Valium with prescription anti-depressants and spent 14 hours lying unconscious on the bathroom floor at his hotel.

31/08/1996	61	1		RAINMAKER	Capitol CDCL 777
17/10/1998	57	1		SICK OF GOODBYES	Parlophone CDCLS 808

SPARKS US rock group formed in Los Angeles, CA in 1968 by brothers Ron (born 12/8/1948, Culver City, CA, keyboards) and Russell Mael (born 5/10/1953, Santa Monica, CA, vocals) as Halfnelson. They evolved into Sparks by 1971 and featured both Mael brothers, Earle Mankay (guitar), Jim Mankay (bass) and Harley Fernstein (drums). The pair moved to Britain in 1973, enlisting Adrian Fisher (guitar), Martin Gordon (bass) and Dinky Diamond (drums) to re-form Sparks. They returned to America in 1976. Fisher died from a possible drugs overdose in May 2000.

04/05/1974	2	10	○	THIS TOWN AIN'T BIG ENOUGH FOR THE BOTH OF US	Island WIP 6193
20/07/1974	7	9		AMATEUR HOUR	Island WIP 6203
19/10/1974	13	7		NEVER TURN YOUR BACK ON MOTHER EARTH	Island WIP 6211
18/01/1975	17	7		SOMETHING FOR THE GIRL WITH EVERYTHING	Island WIP 6221
19/07/1975	27	7		GET IN THE SWING	Island WIP 6236
04/10/1975	26	4		LOOKS LOOKS LOOKS	Island WIP 6249
21/04/1979	14	12		THE NUMBER ONE SONG IN HEAVEN	Virgin VS 244
21/07/1979	10	9		BEAT THE CLOCK	Virgin VS 270
27/10/1979	45	5		TRYOUTS FOR THE HUMAN RACE	Virgin VS 289
29/10/1994	38	3		WHEN DO I GET TO SING 'MY WAY'	Logic 74321234472
11/03/1995	36	2		WHEN I KISS YOU (I HEAR CHARLIE PARKER)	Logic 74321264272
20/05/1995	32	2		WHEN DO I GET TO SING 'MY WAY' Re-issue of Logic 74321234472	Logic 74321274002
09/03/1996	60	1		NOW THAT I OWN THE BBC	Logic 74321348672
25/10/1997	70	1		THE NUMBER ONE SONG IN HEAVEN	Roadrunner RR 22692
13/12/1997	40	2		THIS TOWN AIN'T BIG ENOUGH FOR THE BOTH OF US SPARKS VERSUS FAITH NO MORE	Roadrunner RR 22513

BUBBA SPARXXX US rapper (born Warren Mathis, 6/3/1977, LaGrange, GA) who was discovered by Timbaland, and signed to his Beat Club label.

24/11/2001	7	10		UGLY Contains a sample of Missy Elliott's *Get Ur Freak On*	Interscope 4976542
09/03/2002	24	2		LOVELY	Interscope 4976752
20/03/2004	55	1		DELIVERANCE	Interscope 9862013

SPEAR OF DESTINY UK rock group formed by Kirk Brandon (born 3/8/1956, London, guitar/vocals), Chris Bell (drums), Lasettes Ames (saxophone) and Stan Stammers (bass). Bell and Ames left in 1983, replaced by John Lennard and Nigel Preston. The group later added Alan St Clair (guitar) and Nicky Donnelly (saxophone).

21/05/1983	59	5		THE WHEEL	Epic A 3372
21/01/1984	59	3		PRISONER OF LOVE	Epic A 4068
14/04/1984	67	2		LIBERATOR	Epic A 4310
15/06/1985	61	3		ALL MY LOVE (ASK NOTHING)	Epic A 6333
10/08/1985	55	3		COME BACK	Epic A 6445
07/02/1987	49	4		STRANGERS IN OUR TOWN	10 TEN 148
04/04/1987	14	11		NEVER TAKE ME ALIVE	10 TEN 162
25/07/1987	55	4		WAS THAT YOU	10 TEN 173
03/10/1987	44	3		THE TRAVELLER	10 TEN 189
24/09/1988	36	5		SO IN LOVE WITH YOU	Virgin VS 1123

SPEARHEAD US hip hop group formed in San Francisco, CA by Michael Franti (vocals), Trinna Simmons (vocals), Sub Commander Ras Zulu (vocals), David James (guitar), Carl Young (keyboards), Oneida James (bass) and James Gray (drums). Franti had previously been a member of The Disposable Heroes Of Hiphoprisy.

17/12/1994	74	1		OF COURSE YOU CAN	Capitol CDCL 733
22/04/1995	55	1		HOLE IN THE BUCKET	Capitol CDCL 742
15/07/1995	49	2		PEOPLE IN THA MIDDLE	Capitol CDCLS 752
15/03/1997	45	1		WHY OH WHY Contains a sample of Isaac Hayes' *The End Theme (Tough Guys)*	Capitol CDCL 785

BILLIE JO SPEARS US singer (born 14/1/1937, Beaumont, TX) who was discovered by Jack Rhodes, first recording for Abbot in 1953 as Billie Jo Moore. She began recording regularly for United Artists in 1964, and later occasionally with Brite Star and Cutlass.

12/07/1975	6	13		BLANKET ON THE GROUND Featured in the 1978 film *Convoy*	United Artists UP 35805
17/07/1976	4	13		WHAT I'VE GOT IN MIND	United Artists UP 36118
11/12/1976	34	9		SING ME AN OLD FASHIONED SONG	United Artists UP 36179
21/07/1979	47	5		I WILL SURVIVE	United Artists UP 601

❶⁹ Number of weeks single topped the UK chart ↑ Entered the UK chart at #1 ▲⁹ Number of weeks single topped the US chart

753

BRITNEY SPEARS US singer (born 2/12/1981, Kentwood, LA). Her first break was on the Disney Channel's *Mickey Mouse Club* at the age of eleven, having been turned down three years previously. She 'appeared' in an episode of *The Simpsons*, presenting Montgomery Burns with an award for being the oldest citizen in the city at the Springfield Awards Fair. She allegedly got engaged to Justin Timberlake of N' Sync in June 2000, it later being revealed that they got engaged in July 2001. At the same time she began filming her movie debut, *Cross Roads*. In September 2001 she fell foul of sponsors Pepsi Cola, with whom she had signed a £75 million deal, after she was photographed clutching a bottle of rival Coca Cola! She split with Timberlake in March 2002. In January 2004 she married former school friend Jason Alexander, but later revealed it was a drunken act and had the marriage annulled two days later. She then married dancer Kevin Federline in November 2004, this time supposedly for real, but a few days later it was revealed that the pair had signed a 'pre-marriage contract' agreeing to go through a ceremony but without becoming legally married. Five MTV Europe Music Awards include Best Female, Breakthrough Artist and Best Pop Act, all in 1999, and Best Female Artist in 2004. She has a star on the Hollywood Walk of Fame.

DATE	POS	WKS	BPI	SINGLE TITLE	LABEL & NUMBER
27/02/1999	❶²	22	✪²	**BABY ONE MORE TIME** ↑ ▲² Total worldwide sales exceed 9 million copies. Its sales in its first week in the UK topped 464,000 copies, a record for a debut act. 1999 MTV Europe Music Award for Best Song.	Jive 0521692
26/06/1999	3	16	●	**SOMETIMES**	Jive 0523202
02/10/1999	5	11	○	**(YOU DRIVE ME) CRAZY** Featured in the 2000 film *Drive Me Crazy*	Jive 0550582
29/01/2000	❶¹	12	○	**BORN TO MAKE YOU HAPPY** ↑	Jive 9250022
13/05/2000	❶¹	14	●	**OOPS!…I DID IT AGAIN** ↑	Jive 9250542
26/08/2000	5	11	○	**LUCKY**	Jive 9251022
16/12/2000	7	10		**STRONGER**	Jive 9251502
07/04/2001	12	8		DON'T LET ME BE THE LAST TO KNOW	Jive 9252032
27/10/2001	4	14		**I'M A SLAVE 4 U**	Jive 9252892
02/02/2002	4	12		**OVERPROTECTED**	Jive 9253072
13/04/2002	2	10		**I'M NOT A GIRL NOT YET A WOMAN** Featured in the 2002 film *Crossroads*	Jive 9253472
10/08/2002	7	8		**BOYS** BRITNEY SPEARS FEATURING PHARRELL WILLIAMS Featured in the 2002 film *Goldmember*	Jive 9253912
16/11/2002	13	8		I LOVE ROCK 'N' ROLL	Jive 9254222
22/11/2003	2	12		**ME AGAINST THE MUSIC** BRITNEY SPEARS FEATURING MADONNA	Jive 82876576432
13/03/2004	❶¹	14	○	**TOXIC** ↑	Jive 82876602092
26/06/2004	❶¹	14		**EVERYTIME** ↑	Jive 82876626202
13/11/2004	3	7+		**MY PREROGATIVE**	Jive 82876652582

SPECIAL D German singer Dennis Horstmann; he is also a member of Dickheadz.

DATE	POS	WKS	BPI	SINGLE TITLE	LABEL & NUMBER
17/04/2004	6	11		**COME WITH ME**	All Around The World CDGLOBE 340

SPECIAL NEEDS UK group formed in London by Zac Stephenson (vocals), Andrew Pearson (guitar), Daniel Shack (guitar), Philip James (bass) and Neil 'Skipper' Allan (drums).

DATE	POS	WKS	BPI	SINGLE TITLE	LABEL & NUMBER
16/10/2004	69	1		FRANCESCA – THE MADDENING GLARE/WINTER	Poptones MC5092SCD

SPECIALS UK ska group formed in Coventry in 1977 by Jerry Dammers (born Gerald Dankin, 22/5/1954, India, keyboards), Lynval Golding (born 7/7/1952, St Catherines, Jamaica, guitar), Terry Hall (born 19/3/1959, Coventry, vocals), Neville Staples (born 11/4/1956, Christiana, Jamaica, vocals), Roddy Radiation (born Rod Byers, guitar), Sir Horace Gentleman (born Horace Panter, bass) and a drummer named Silverton. Silverton left in 1978, replaced by John Bradbury. They funded the recording of their debut record and set up the 2 Tone label, distributed by Chrysalis. Staples, Hall and Golding left in 1981 to form the Fun Boy Three. In July 2001 the group's 1979 debut album, *The Specials*, re-charted on the album chart for the first time in more than twenty years after the RRP had been slashed to £2.99 and sold 11,000 copies in a single week (it re-charted at #22).

DATE	POS	WKS	BPI	SINGLE TITLE	LABEL & NUMBER
28/07/1979	6	12	○	**GANGSTERS** SPECIAL A.K.A. SPECIALS (FEATURING RICO)	2 Tone CHSTT 1
27/10/1979	10	14	○	**A MESSAGE TO YOU RUDY/NITE CLUB** SPECIALS (FEATURING RICO)	2 Tone CHSTT 5
26/01/1980	❶²	10	○	**THE SPECIAL A.K.A. LIVE! EP** SPECIAL A.K.A. Tracks on EP: *Too Much Too Young, Guns Of Navarone, Long Shot Kick De Bucket, Liquidator* and *Skinhead Moonstomp*	2 Tone CHSTT 7
24/05/1980	5	9		**RAT RACE/RUDE BUOYS OUTA JAIL**	2 Tone CHSTT 11
20/09/1980	6	8		**STEREOTYPE/INTERNATIONAL JET SET**	2 Tone CHSTT 13
13/12/1980	4	11	○	**DO NOTHING/MAGGIE'S FARM**	2 Tone CHSTT 16
20/06/1981	❶³	14	●	**GHOST TOWN** Featured in the films *Snatch* (2000) and *Shaun Of The Dead* (2004)	2 Tone CHSTT 17
23/01/1982	35	5		**THE BOILER** RHODA WITH THE SPECIAL A.K.A.	2 Tone CHSTT 18
03/09/1983	60	3		RACIST FRIENDS/BRIGHT LIGHTS	2 Tone CHSTT 25
17/03/1984	9	10		**NELSON MANDELA** Nelson Mandela was leader of the African National Congress (ANC), imprisoned for life by the South African government in 1962. Released in February 1990, he became State President of South Africa in 1994.	2 Tone CHSTT 26
08/09/1984	51	4		WHAT I LIKE MOST ABOUT YOU IS YOUR GIRLFRIEND This and above two singles credited to SPECIAL A.K.A.	2 Tone CHSTT 27
10/02/1996	66	1		HYPOCRITE	Kuff KUFFD 3

SPECTRUM UK instrumental/production group formed by Pete 'Sonic Boom' Kember, Richard Formby and Mike Stout. Formby was replaced by Kevin Cowan, the group also adding Scott Riley, Alf Hardy and Pete Bassman. Kember was previously in Spacemen 3.

DATE	POS	WKS	BPI	SINGLE TITLE	LABEL & NUMBER
26/09/1992	70	1		TRUE LOVE WILL FIND YOU IN THE END	Silvertone ORE 44

CHRIS SPEDDING UK singer/guitarist (born 17/6/1944, Sheffield) who was previously guitarist with Sharks (with former Free member Andy Fraser) and The Vulcans, and also played with Cozy Powell. He is now a session guitarist based in Los Angeles, CA.

DATE	POS	WKS	BPI	SINGLE TITLE	LABEL & NUMBER
23/08/1975	14	8		MOTOR BIKING	RAK 210

SPEECH US rapper (born Todd Thomas, 25/10/1968, Milwaukee, WI) who was lead singer with Arrested Development before going solo. Originally known as Dr Peech, he had formed DLR (Disciples of Lyrical Rebellion) which he renamed Secret Society before forming

Arrested Development in 1988. His debut hit was recorded for the *Inner City Blues: The Tribute To Marvin Gaye* album.

17/02/1996 . . . . . 35 . . . . . . 2 . . . . LIKE MARVIN GAYE SAID (WHAT'S GOING ON) . . . . Cooltempo CDCOOL 314

SPEEDWAY UK rock group formed in Scotland by Jill Jackson (guitar/vocals), Dan Sells (guitar), Graeme Smillie (bass) and Jim Duguid (drums).

06/09/2003 . . . . . 10 . . . . . . 4	**GENIE IN A BOTTLE/SAVE YOURSELF** . . . . Innocent SINCD 47
21/02/2004 . . . . . 12 . . . . . . 4	CAN'T TURN BACK . . . . Innocent SINDX 55
19/06/2004 . . . . . 31 . . . . . . 2	IN AND OUT . . . . Innocent SINDX 61

SPEEDY UK vocal/instrumental group.

09/11/1996 . . . . . 56 . . . . . . 1 . . . . . . BOY WONDER . . . . Boiler House! BOIL 2CD

SPEKTRUM UK group formed by Gabriel Olegavich, Lola Olafisoye, Isaac Tucker and Teia Williams.

18/09/2004 . . . . . 70 . . . . . . 1 . . . . . . KINDA NEW . . . . Non Stop SPEKD004

SPELLBOUND Indian vocal duo of sisters Meneka and Sheenu (born Allahabad, Uttar Pradesh).

31/05/1997 . . . . . 73 . . . . . . 1 . . . . . . HEAVEN ON EARTH . . . . East West EW 098CD

JOHNNIE SPENCE UK orchestra leader; he backed and arranged for Tom Jones, Matt Monro and such, and led The Family Tree.

01/03/1962 . . . . . 15 . . . . . 15 . . . . . . THEME FROM DR KILDARE . . . . Parlophone R 4872

DON SPENCER Australian singer; he was later an actor and kid's TV presenter. He is the father-in-law of actor Russell Crowe.

21/03/1963 . . . . . 32 . . . . . 12 . . . . . . FIREBALL Theme to the TV series *Fireball XL5* . . . . HMV POP 1087

TRACIE SPENCER US R&B singer (born 12/7/1976, Waterloo, IA).

| 04/05/1991 . . . . . 65 . . . . . . 2 . . . . . . | THIS HOUSE . . . . Capitol CL 612 |
| 06/11/1999 . . . . . 65 . . . . . . 1 . . . . . . | IT'S ALL ABOUT YOU (NOT ABOUT ME) . . . . Parlophone Rhythm Series CDCL 815 |

JON SPENCER BLUES EXPLOSION US group assembled by producer Jon Spencer and featuring contributions from Rob K (vocals), Hollis Queens (vocals), Kurt Hoffman (saxophone) and Doug Easley (keyboards).

10/05/1997 . . . . . 66 . . . . . . 1	WAIL . . . . Mute CDMUTE 204
06/04/2002 . . . . . 58 . . . . . . 1	SHE SAID . . . . Mute LCDMUTE 263
06/07/2002 . . . . . 66 . . . . . . 1	SWEET N SOUR . . . . Mute LCDMUTE 271

SPHINX US group formed in Chicago, IL by Nick Langis (vocals), George Langis (guitar), Tim Mattefs (bass) and Pete Stegios (drums).

25/03/1995 . . . . . 43 . . . . . . 2 . . . . . . WHAT HOPE HAVE I . . . . Champion CHAMPCD 318

SPICE GIRLS UK vocal group formed in June 1994 by Michelle Stephenson, Geraldine Halliwell (aka Geri/Ginger Spice, born 6/8/1972, Watford), Melanie Brown (aka Mel B/Scary Spice, born 29/5/1973, Leeds), Victoria Adams (aka Posh Spice, born 7/4/1974, Essex) and Melanie Chisholm (aka Mel C/Sporty Spice, born 12/1/1974, Liverpool) as Touch, later name-changing to The Spice Girls. Stephenson left after a month to return to university, replaced by Emma Bunton (aka Baby Spice, born 21/1/1976, London). They were the first act to top the charts with their first six singles, repeating their success in America, topping the singles chart with *Wannabe* and then becoming the first British female act to top the album charts. They appeared in the film *Spiceworld: The Movie* in 1997. They were awarded a Special Achievement Award at the 1998 BRIT Awards and a Lifetime Achievement Award at the 2000 BRIT Awards. They have also won three MTV Europe Music Awards: Best Group in 1997 and 1998 and Best Pop Act in 1998. They took part in the England United recording for the 1998 World Cup Finals. Geri announced she was going solo on 31/5/1998, although both Mel B (with Missy Misdemeanor Elliott) and Mel C (with Bryan Adams) preceded her into the charts. Victoria married Manchester United and England football star David Beckham in July 1999. Emma Bunton also recorded with Tin Tin Out while Victoria recorded with True Steppers and Dane Bowers. They had a packet of crisps named after them by Walker's (the company sold over 16 million bags in its first year). They also took part in the *It's Only Rock 'N' Roll* project for the Children's Promise charity. In June 2000 the girls were ordered to pay £45,000 to motor scooter company Aprilla, relating to an earlier sponsorship deal the group signed in May 1998 where hundreds of 'Sonic Spice' scooters were produced featuring the likeness of all five. Three weeks after the deal was signed, Geri Halliwell left to go solo. A subsequent appeal failed and the girls were left with a legal bill of nearly £1 million as a result.

20/07/1996 . . . . ❶[7] . . . . 26 . . . . . ✪	**WANNABE** ▲[4] 1997 BRIT Award for Best Single. Featured in the 1998 film *Small Soldiers* . . . . Virgin VSCDX 1588
26/10/1996 . . . . ❶[2] . . . . 17 . . . . . ✪	**SAY YOU'LL BE THERE** ↑ 1997 BRIT Award for Best Video . . . . Virgin VSCDT 1601
28/12/1996 . . . . ❶[3] . . . . 23 . . . . . ✪	**2 BECOME 1** ↑ . . . . Virgin VSCDT 1607
15/03/1997 . . . . ❶[3] . . . . 15 . . . . . ✪	**MAMA/WHO DO YOU THINK YOU ARE** ↑ In topping the charts with their first four releases, the Spice Girls became the most successful debut act of all time, beating Gerry and the Pacemakers, Frankie Goes To Hollywood, Jive Bunny and the Mastermixers and Robson and Jerome, all of whom topped the charts with their first three releases (The Spice Girls extended their record to six, a tally that was itself beaten in 2000 by Westlife). Single released in aid of the Comic Relief Charity . . . . Virgin VSCDT 1623
25/10/1997 . . . . ❶[1] . . . . 15 . . . . . ✪	**SPICE UP YOUR LIFE** ↑ . . . . Virgin VSCDT 1660
27/12/1997 . . . . ❶[2] . . . . 15 . . . . . ✪	**TOO MUCH** ↑ This and above five titles featured in the 1997 film *Spiceworld: The Movie* . . . . Virgin VSCDR 1669
21/03/1998 . . . . . 2 . . . . . . 17 . . . . . ○	**STOP** . . . . Virgin VSCDT 1679
01/08/1998 . . . . ❶[2] . . . . 13 . . . . . ✪	**VIVA FOREVER** ↑ . . . . Virgin VSCDT 1692
26/12/1998 . . . . ❶[1] . . . . 21 . . . . . ✪	**GOODBYE** ↑ The Spice Girls are only the second act (after The Beatles) to have held the Christmas #1 on three separate (and consecutive) occasions . . . . Virgin VSCDT 1721
04/11/2000 . . . . ❶[1] . . . . 17 . . . . . ○	**HOLLER/LET LOVE LEAD THE WAY** ↑ . . . . Virgin VSCDT 1788

❶[9] Number of weeks single topped the UK chart   ↑ Entered the UK chart at #1   ▲[9] Number of weeks single topped the US chart

SPIDER US rock group formed in New York by Amanda Blue (vocals), Keith Lenthin (guitar), Holly Knight (keyboards), Jimmy Lowell (bass) and Anton Fig (drums). Knight later joined Device and subsequently went solo.

05/03/1983.....65......2.......	WHY D'YA LIE TO ME .... RCA 313
10/03/1984.....57......3.......	HERE WE GO ROCK 'N' ROLL .... A&M AM 180

SPIKEY TEE – see **BOMB THE BASS**

SPILLER UK/Italian dance group formed by singer Sophie Ellis Bextor (daughter of former *Blue Peter* presenter Janet Ellis) and Italian DJ Cristiano Spiller. Sophie was previously lead singer with Theaudience, in October 2000 signing with Polydor as a solo artist. Cristiano had previously been a member of Laguna.

26/08/2000 .....❶¹.....24 .....●	GROOVEJET (IF THIS AIN'T LOVE) ↑ Contains a sample of Carol Williams' *Love Is You* .... Positiva CDTIV 137
02/02/2002.....40......2.......	CRY BABY .... Positiva CDTIVS 167

SPIN CITY Irish vocal group formed by Nathan Quist, Ashley Crowther, Conor O'Connor and Kristan Gilroy.

26/08/2000.....30......3.......	LANDSLIDE .... Epic 6696132

SPIN DOCTORS US rock group formed in New York in 1987 by Chris Barron (born 5/2/1968, Hawaii, vocals), Eric Schenkman (born 12/12/1963, Massachusetts, guitar), Mark White (born 7/7/1962, New York, bass) and Aaron Comes (born 24/4/1968, Arizona, drums). They signed with Epic in 1990. Schenkman left in 1994, replaced by Anthony Krizan (born 25/8/1965, Plainfield, NJ). White left in 1998.

15/05/1993 .....3......15 .....○	TWO PRINCES Featured in the 1993 film *So I Married An Axe Murderer* .... Epic 6591452
14/08/1993.....23......5.......	LITTLE MISS CAN'T BE WRONG .... Epic 6584892
09/10/1993.....40......2.......	JIMMY OLSEN'S BLUES .... Epic 6597582
04/12/1993.....56......1.......	WHAT TIME IS IT. .... Epic 6599552
25/06/1994.....29......2.......	CLEOPATRA'S CAT .... Epic 6604192
30/07/1994.....66......1.......	YOU LET YOUR HEART GO TOO FAST .... Epic 6606612
29/10/1994.....55......1.......	MARY JANE .... Epic 6609772
08/06/1996.....55......1.......	SHE USED TO BE MINE. .... Epic 6632682

SPINAL TAP UK/US rock group 'officially' formed in 1964 by Derek Smalls (played by Harry Shearer, born 23/12/1943, bass), David St Hubbins (played by Michael McKean, born 17/10/1947, vocals) and Nigel Tufnell (played by Christopher Guest, born 5/2/1948, guitar) as a beat combo, changing their name and musical style in 1967. During their career they had 22 names, never had a permanent drummer and charted only one album. In reality, the 'group' was a satire on heavy metal that was first aired on TV in the late 1970s and the subject of the 1984 film *This Is Spinal Tap*. They provided the voices of the Gorgons in the 1998 film *Small Soldiers*.

28/03/1992.....35......2.......	BITCH SCHOOL .... MCA 1624
02/05/1992.....61......1.......	THE MAJESTY OF ROCK .... MCA MCS 1629

SPIRAL TRIBE UK vocal/instrumental group with Simone Feeney, Sebastian Vaughan, Mark Harrison and Laurence Hammond.

29/08/1992.....66......1.......	BREACH THE PEACE (EP) Tracks on EP: *Breach The Peace, Do It, Seven* and *25 Minute Warning* .... Butterfly BLRT 79
21/11/1992.....70......1.......	FORWARD THE REVOLUTION .... Butterfly BLRT 85

SPIRITS UK vocal group with Damon Rochefort, Beverley Thomas and Osmond Wright. Rochefort also recorded as Nomad

19/11/1994.....31......3.......	DON'T BRING ME DOWN. .... MCA MCSTD 2018
08/04/1995.....39......2.......	SPIRIT INSIDE .... MCA MCSTD 2045

SPIRITUAL COWBOYS – see **DAVE STEWART**

SPIRITUALIZED UK group formed in 1990 by Jason Pierce (born 19/11/1965, Rugby, guitar/vocals), Mark Refoy (guitar), Willie Carruthers (bass) and John Mattock (drums), later adding Kate Radley (born 19/2/1965, piano/vocals). Pierce was previously in Spacemen 3, forming Spiritualized after falling out with the other spaceman, Sonic Boom. By 1995 their name had been extended to Spiritualized Electric Mainline and the group trimmed down to Jason Pierce, Kate Radley and Sean Cook (born 16/4/1969, bass/harmonica), although a year later the name shortened again to Spiritualized. They later launched their own Spaceman label.

30/06/1990.....75......1.......	ANYWAY THAT YOU WANT ME/STEP INTO THE BREEZE .... Dedicated ZB 43783
17/08/1991.....59......1.......	RUN. .... Dedicated SPIRT 002
25/07/1992.....55......1.......	MEDICATION .... Dedicated SPIRT 005T
23/10/1993.....49......1.......	ELECTRIC MAINLINE .... Dedicated SPIRT 007CD
04/02/1995.....30......2.......	LET IT FLOW SPIRITUALIZED ELECTRIC MAINLINE .... Dedicated SPIRT 009CD
09/08/1997.....32......2.......	ELECTRICITY .... Dedicated SPIRIT 012CD1
14/02/1998.....27......2.......	I THINK I'M IN LOVE .... Dedicated SPIRIT 014CD
06/06/1998.....39......2.......	THE ABBEY ROAD EP Tracks on EP: *Abbey Road, Broken Heart* and *Death In Vegas* .... Dedicated SPIRT 015CD
15/09/2001.....18......3.......	STOP YOUR CRYING .... Spaceman OPM 002
08/12/2001.....65......1.......	OUT OF SIGHT. .... Spaceman OPM 005
23/02/2002.....31......2.......	DO IT ALL OVER AGAIN .... Spaceman OPM 007
13/09/2003.....38......1.......	SHE KISSED ME (IT FELT LIKE A HIT) .... Sanctuary SANXD 222

SPIRO AND WIX UK instrumental duo Steve Spiro and Paul 'Wix' Wickens.

10/08/1996.....29......2.......	TARA'S THEME Theme to BBC's TV coverage of the 1996 Atlanta Olympic Games .... EMI Premier PRESCD 4

SPITTING IMAGE UK TV puppets created by Peter Fluck and Roger Law that lampooned political and public figures. The first record was written by Philip Pope (star of the TV comedy *KYTV*), Doug Naylor and Robert Grant (the creators of *Red Dwarf*).

○ Silver disc ● Gold disc ✪ Platinum disc (additional platinum units are indicated by a figure following the symbol) ⊚ Singles released prior to 1973 that are known to have sold over 1 million copies in the UK

10/05/1986 .... **❶**³ ..... 11 ..... ○   **THE CHICKEN SONG** .... Virgin SPIT 1
06/12/1986 ..... 22 ..... 7 ......   SANTA CLAUS IS ON THE DOLE/FIRST ATHEIST TABERNACLE CHOIR .... Virgin VS 921

SPLIFF STAR – see BUSTA RHYMES

SPLINTER
UK duo formed in Newcastle-upon-Tyne by Bill Elliott (born 1950, Newcastle-upon-Tyne) and Bob Purvis (born 1950, Newcastle-upon-Tyne). They were discovered by George Harrison who produced their hit.

02/11/1974 ..... 17 ..... 10 ......   COSTAFINE TOWN .... Dark Horse AMS 7135

SPLIT ENZ
New Zealand rock group formed in Auckland in 1972 by Tim Finn (born 25/6/1952, Te Awamuta, piano/vocals), Phil Judd (guitar/mandolin/vocals), Mike Chunn (born 8/6/1952, Auckland, bass/keyboards), Geoff Chunn (drums), Rob Gillies (saxophone), Miles Golding (violin) and Michael Howard (flute) as Split Ends. Moved to Australia in 1975 and name-changed to Split Enz, relocating to the UK in 1976. Later members included Tim's brother Neil (born 27/5/1958, Te Awamuta, guitar/vocals), Wally Wilkinson, Nigel Griggs (born 18/8/1949, bass), Malcolm Green (born 25/1/1953, drums), Paul Crowther (born 2/10/1949, Dunedin, drums) and Noel Crombie. Neil Finn later formed Crowded House, the brothers formed Finn and both subsequently recorded solo.

16/08/1980 ..... 12 ..... 11 ......   I GOT YOU .... A&M AMS 7546
23/05/1981 ..... 63 ..... 4 ......   HISTORY NEVER REPEATS .... A&M AMS 8128

A SPLIT SECOND
Belgian/Italian instrumental/production group formed by Chismar Chavall and Marc Icky.

14/12/1991 ..... 68 ...... 1 ......   FLESH .... ffrr FX 178

SPLODGENESSABOUNDS
UK rock/comedy group: Max Splodge, Baby Greensleeves, Pat Thetic, Miles Flat and Wiffy Arsher.

14/06/1980 ..... 7 ..... 8 ......   **SIMON TEMPLAR/TWO PINTS OF LAGER AND A PACKET OF CRISPS PLEASE** .... Deram BUM 1
06/09/1980 ..... 26 ..... 7 ......   TWO LITTLE BOYS/HORSE .... Deram ROLF 1
13/06/1981 ..... 69 ..... 2 ......   COWPUNK MEDLUM .... Deram BUM 3

SPOILED AND ZIGO
Israeli dance group formed by Elad Avnon and Ziv Goland.

12/08/2000 ..... 31 ..... 3 ......   MORE & MORE .... Manifesto FESCD 72

SPONGE
US rock group formed in Detroit, MI by Vinnie Dombrowski (vocals), Mike Cross (guitar), Joe Mazzola (guitar), Tim Cross (bass) and Jimmy Paluzzi (drums). Paluzzi left in 1996, replaced by Charlie Glover.

19/08/1995 ..... 74 ...... 1 ......   PLOWED .... Work 6623162

SPOOKS
US hip hop group formed in 1995 by MCs Mr Booka-T aka Bookaso (born Booker T Tucker), Water Water aka Aqua Dinero, Hypno, JD aka Vengeance (born Joseph Davis) and singer Ming-Xia with the addition of a live band.

27/01/2001 ..... 6 ..... 10 ......   **THINGS I'VE SEEN** Featured in the 2001 film *Once In The Life* .... Artemis ANTCD 6706722
05/05/2001 ..... 15 ..... 6 ......   KARMA HOTEL .... Artemis ANTCD 6709012
15/09/2001 ..... 67 ..... 1 ......   SWEET REVENGE .... Artemis 6718072

SPOOKY
UK vocal/instrumental duo Charlie May (born 7/3/1969, Gillingham) and Duncan Forbes (born 29/1/1969, Yeovil).

13/03/1993 ..... 72 ..... 1 ......   SCHMOO .... Guerilla GRRR 45CD

SPORTY THIEVZ
US rap group formed by King Kirk (aka Thievin' Stealburg), Big Dubez (Safebreaker) and Marlon Brando (Robin Hood). Brando was killed in a car crash on 11/5/2001.

10/07/1999 ..... 21 ..... 6 ......   NO PIGEONS Features the uncredited contribution of Mr Woods and is an answer record to TLC's *No Scrubs* .... Columbia 6676022

SPOTNICKS
Swedish instrumental group formed in 1957 by Bo Winberg (born 27/3/1939, Gothenburg), Bob Lander (born 11/3/1942, Bo Starander), Bjorn Thelin (born 11/6/1942) and Ole Johannsson as The Frazers. They name-changed to The Spotnicks in 1961 and wore spacesuits on stage.

14/06/1962 ..... 29 ..... 10 ......   ORANGE BLOSSOM SPECIAL .... Oriole CB 1724
06/09/1962 ..... 38 ..... 9 ......   ROCKET MAN .... Oriole CB 1755
31/01/1963 ..... 13 ..... 12 ......   HAVA NAGILA .... Oriole CB 1790
25/04/1963 ..... 36 ..... 6 ......   JUST LISTEN TO MY HEART .... Oriole CB 1818

DUSTY SPRINGFIELD
UK singer (born Mary Isabel Catherine Bernadette O'Brien, 16/4/1939, Hampstead, London). She was a member of vocal trio the Lana Sisters before teaming with her brother Dion O'Brien and Tim Field in the Springfields in 1960. The group disbanded in 1963, Springfield signing with Philips as a solo artist. She relocated to America in 1972 and became an in-demand session singer. She was awarded the OBE in the 1999 New Year's Honours List; the presentation took place while Dusty was lying in hospital shortly before her death from breast cancer on 2/3/1999. She was inducted into the Rock & Roll Hall of Fame in 1999 (the ceremony was held eleven days after she died). She was the first act to appear on *Top of the Pops*, on 1/1/1964, when she performed her debut hit.

21/11/1963 ..... 4 ..... 18 ......   **I ONLY WANT TO BE WITH YOU** First record played on *Top Of The Pops* .... Philips BF 1292
20/02/1964 ..... 13 ..... 10 ......   STAY AWHILE .... Philips BF 1313
02/07/1964 ..... 3 ..... 12 ......   **I JUST DON'T KNOW WHAT TO DO WITH MYSELF** Featured in the 1988 film *Buster* .... Philips BF 1348

DATE	POS	WKS	BPI	SINGLE TITLE	LABEL & NUMBER
22/10/1964	9	13		LOSING YOU	Philips BF 1369
18/02/1965	37	4		YOUR HURTIN' KIND OF LOVE	Philips BF 1396
01/07/1965	8	10		IN THE MIDDLE OF NOWHERE	Philips BF 1418
16/09/1965	8	12		SOME OF YOUR LOVIN'	Philips BF 1430
27/01/1966	17	9		LITTLE BY LITTLE	Philips BF 1466
31/03/1966	❶¹	13		YOU DON'T HAVE TO SAY YOU LOVE ME	Philips BF 1482
07/07/1966	10	10		GOING BACK	Philips BF 1502
15/09/1966	9	12		ALL I SEE IS YOU	Philips BF 1510
23/02/1967	13	9		I'LL TRY ANYTHING	Philips BF 1553
25/05/1967	24	6		GIVE ME TIME	Philips BF 1577
10/07/1968	4	12		I CLOSE MY EYES AND COUNT TO TEN	Philips BF 1682
04/12/1968	9	9		SON OF A PREACHER MAN Featured in the 1994 film *Pulp Fiction*	Philips BF 1730
20/09/1969	43	4		AM I THE SAME GIRL	Philips BF 1811
19/09/1970	36	4		HOW CAN I BE SURE	Philips 6006 045
20/10/1979	61	5		BABY BLUE	Mercury DUSTY 4
22/08/1987	2	9	○	WHAT HAVE I DONE TO DESERVE THIS PET SHOP BOYS AND DUSTY SPRINGFIELD	Parlophone R 6163
25/02/1989	16	7		NOTHING HAS BEEN PROVED Featured in the 1988 film *Scandal*	Parlophone R 6207
02/12/1989	14	10		IN PRIVATE	Parlophone R 6234
26/05/1990	38	6		REPUTATION	Parlophone R 6253
24/11/1990	70	2		ARRESTED BY YOU	Parlophone R 6266
30/10/1993	75	1		HEART AND SOUL CILLA BLACK WITH DUSTY SPRINGFIELD	Columbia 6598562
10/06/1995	44	3		WHEREVER WOULD I BE DUSTY SPRINGFIELD AND DARYL HALL	Columbia 6620592
04/11/1995	68	1		ROLL AWAY	Columbia 6623682

RICK SPRINGFIELD Australian singer (born 23/8/1949, Sydney). In Zoot before going solo in 1972, later a successful actor.

DATE	POS	WKS	BPI	SINGLE TITLE	LABEL & NUMBER
14/01/1984	23	7		HUMAN TOUCH/SOULS	RCA RICK 1
24/03/1984	43	6		JESSIE'S GIRL ▲² 1981 Grammy Award for Best Rock Vocal Performance. Featured in the 2004 film *13 Going On 30*	RCA RICK 2

SPRINGFIELDS UK folk trio formed in 1960 by Dusty Springfield (born Mary O'Brien, 16/4/1939, Hampstead, London), her brother Dion O'Brien (born 2/7/1934, Hampstead) and Tim Field. Dion O'Brien assumed the name Tom Springfield, his sister similarly taking her stage name from the group. Field left in 1962, replaced by Mike Hurst (born Mike Pickworth). They disbanded in 1963 with Dusty going solo, Tom becoming a songwriter and Hurst a producer. Tom Springfield formed Springfield Revival in the 1970s.

DATE	POS	WKS	BPI	SINGLE TITLE	LABEL & NUMBER
31/08/1961	31	8		BREAKAWAY	Philips BF 1168
16/11/1961	16	11		BAMBINO	Philips BF 1178
13/12/1962	5	26		ISLAND OF DREAMS	Philips 326557 BF
28/03/1963	5	15		SAY I WON'T BE THERE	Philips 326577 BF
25/07/1963	31	6		COME ON HOME	Philips BF 1253

BRUCE SPRINGSTEEN US singer/guitarist (born Frederick Joseph Springsteen, 23/9/1949, Freehold, NJ). He joined the Castiles in 1965 and then Earth in 1967. He formed Child in 1969, who name-changed to Steel Mills shortly after, and assembled his first band in 1971. He signed with producers/managers Mike Appel and Jim Cretecos in 1972 shortly before linking with CBS and re-forming his band with David Sancious (keyboards), Garry Tallent (bass), Vini Lopez (drums), Clarence Clemons (saxophone) and Danny Federici (keyboards). They were renamed the E Street Band in 1973. Legal wrangles with Appel prevented the release of any new albums after *Born To Run* in 1975 to 1978, by which time Jon Landau had taken over as manager and co-producer. A motorcycle accident in April 1979 forced a three-month break and delayed his new album. He split with the E Street Band in 1989. He married actress Juliane Phillips in 1985, divorced in 1989 and then married former backing singer Patti Sciaffa in 1991. Bruce was named Best International Male at the 1986 BRIT Awards. He was inducted into the Rock & Roll Hall of Fame in 1999. Twelve Grammy Awards include Best Recording for Children in 1982 with various others for *In Harmony 2*, Best Male Rock Vocal Performance and Best Rock Song for *The Rising*, and Best Rock Album for *The Rising* in 2002 and Best Rock Performance by a Duo or Group with Vocal with Warren Zevon for *Disorder In The House* in 2003. In 2000 he wrote and recorded *American Skin (41 Shots)*, a song that criticised the New York police department over the shooting and killing of Amadiu Diallo. The African immigrant was hit by nineteen of the 41 bullets fired at him by the police who mistook his wallet for a gun. Four policemen were later cleared of his murder. Following the song's release, the New York police department called for a boycott of Springsteen's concerts in the city.

DATE	POS	WKS	BPI	SINGLE TITLE	LABEL & NUMBER
22/11/1980	44	4		HUNGRY HEART Featured in the 2000 film *The Perfect Storm*	CBS 9309
13/06/1981	35	6		THE RIVER	CBS A 1179
26/05/1984	28	7		DANCING IN THE DARK The promotional video features actress Courtney Cox, later a star of *Friends*. 1984 Grammy Award for Best Rock Vocal Performance	CBS A 4436
06/10/1984	38	5		COVER ME	CBS A 4662
12/01/1985	4	16	○	DANCING IN THE DARK	CBS A 4436
23/03/1985	16	8		COVER ME	CBS A 4662
15/06/1985	5	12	○	I'M ON FIRE/BORN IN THE USA	CBS A 6342
03/08/1985	17	6		GLORY DAYS	CBS A 6375
14/12/1985	9	5	○	SANTA CLAUS IS COMIN' TO TOWN/MY HOMETOWN A-side was recorded live on 12/12/1975 in New York	CBS A 6773
29/11/1986	18	7		WAR Recorded live in 1985 in Los Angeles	CBS 6501937
07/02/1987	54	2		FIRE	CBS 6503817
23/05/1987	16	4		BORN TO RUN	CBS BRUCE 2
03/10/1987	20	5		BRILLIANT DISGUISE	CBS 6511417
12/12/1987	45	4		TUNNEL OF LOVE 1997 Grammy Award for Best Rock Vocal Performance	CBS 6512957
18/06/1988	13	8		TOUGHER THAN THE REST	CBS BRUCE 3

○ Silver disc ● Gold disc ✪ Platinum disc (additional platinum units are indicated by a figure following the symbol) ◎ Singles released prior to 1973 that are known to have sold over 1 million copies in the UK

24/09/1988	32	3		SPARE PARTS	CBS BRUCE 4
21/03/1992	11	5		HUMAN TOUCH	Columbia 6578727
23/05/1992	34	3		BETTER DAYS	Columbia 6578907
25/07/1992	32	4		57 CHANNELS (AND NOTHIN' ON)	Columbia 6581387
24/10/1992	46	3		LEAP OF FAITH	Columbia 6583697
10/04/1993	48	3		LUCKY TOWN (LIVE)	Columbia 6592282
19/03/1994	2	12	O	**STREETS OF PHILADELPHIA** Featured in the 1994 film *Philadelphia*. 1994 Grammy Award for Best Rock Vocal Performance. The song won the Grammy Awards for Song of the Year, Best Rock Song and Best Song Written Specifically for a Motion Picture for writer Bruce Springsteen the same year. The song then went on to win an Oscar for Best Film Song	Columbia 6600652
22/04/1995	44	3		SECRET GARDEN Featured in the 1997 film *Jerry Maguire*	Columbia 6612955
11/11/1995	28	3		HUNGRY HEART	Columbia 6626252
04/05/1996	26	2		THE GHOST OF TOM JOAD 1996 Grammy Award for Best Contemporary Folk Performance	Columbia 6630315
19/04/1997	17	4		SECRET GARDEN Re-promoted after being featured in the 1997 film *Jerry Maguire*	Columbia 6643245
14/12/2002	39	2		LONESOME DAY	Columbia 6734082

SPRINGWATER
UK instrumentalist Phil Cordell. He later recorded for Motown's Prodigal label.

23/10/1971	5	12		**I WILL RETURN**	Polydor 2058 141

SPRINKLER
US rap group formed by Lucas Secon and Chardel. Secon had previously recorded solo.

11/07/1998	45	2		LEAVE 'EM SOMETHING TO DESIRE	Island CID 706

(SPUNGE)
UK group formed in 1994 by Alex Copeland (vocals), Damon Robins (guitar), Paul Gurney (guitar), Chris Murphy (bass) and Jeremy King (drums).

15/06/2002	39	2		JUMP ON DEMAND	B Unique BUN 022CDS
24/08/2002	52	1		ROOTS	B Unique BUN 030CDX

SPYRO GYRA
US jazz-fusion group formed in Buffalo, NY in 1975 by Jay Beckenstein (born 14/5/1951, saxophone), Jeremy Wall (keyboards), Jim Kurzdorfer (bass), Tom Schuman (piano), Chet Catallo (guitar), Ed Konikoff (drums) and Richard Calandra (percussion). Catallo was later replaced by Jay Azzolina.

21/07/1979	17	10		MORNING DANCE	Infinity INF 111

SQUADRONAIRES – see JOAN REGAN

SQUEEZE
UK rock group formed in London in 1974 by Chris Difford (born 4/11/1954, London, guitar/vocals), Glenn Tilbrook (born 31/8/1957, London, guitar/vocals), Jools Holland (born Julian Holland, 24/1/1955, London, keyboards) and Paul Gunn (drums). Gunn left the same year, replaced by Gilson Lavis (born 27/6/1951, Bedford), with bass player Harry Kakoulli joining at the same time. Kakoulli left in 1980, replaced by John Bentley (born 16/4/1951, London). Holland also left in 1980, replaced by Paul Carrack (born 22/4/1951, Sheffield). Carrack left in 1981, replaced by Don Snow (born 13/1/1957, Kenya). They split in 1982, re-forming in 1985. Holland hosted 80s' TV series *The Tube* and subsequently *Later With Jools Holland*, and was awarded an OBE in the Queen's 2003 Birthday Honours List.

08/04/1978	19	9		TAKE ME I'M YOURS	A&M AMS 7335
10/06/1978	49	5		BANG BANG	A&M AMS 7360
18/11/1978	63	2		GOODBYE GIRL	A&M AMS 7398
24/03/1979	2	11	●	**COOL FOR CATS**	A&M AMS 7426
02/06/1979	2	11	O	**UP THE JUNCTION**	A&M AMS 7444
08/09/1979	24	8		SLAP AND TICKLE	A&M AMS 7466
01/03/1980	17	9		ANOTHER NAIL IN MY HEART	A&M AMS 7507
10/05/1980	44	6		PULLING MUSSELS (FROM THE SHELL)	A&M AMS 7523
16/05/1981	35	8		IS THAT LOVE	A&M AMS 8129
25/07/1981	41	5		TEMPTED	A&M AMS 8147
10/10/1981	4	10	O	**LABELLED WITH LOVE**	A&M AMS 8166
24/04/1982	51	4		BLACK COFFEE IN BED	A&M AMS 8219
23/10/1982	43	4		ANNIE GET YOUR GUN	A&M AMS 8259
15/06/1985	45	5		LAST TIME FOREVER	A&M AM 255
08/08/1987	16	10		HOURGLASS	A&M AM 4000
17/10/1987	72	1		TRUST ME TO OPEN MY MOUTH	A&M AM 412
25/04/1992	62	2		COOL FOR CATS	A&M AM 860
24/07/1993	39	3		THIRD RAIL	A&M 5803372
11/09/1993	73	1		SOME FANTASTIC PLACE	A&M 5803792
09/09/1995	36	3		THIS SUMMER	A&M 5811912
18/11/1995	44	2		ELECTRIC TRAINS	A&M 5812692
15/06/1996	27	2		HEAVEN KNOWS Featured in the 1996 film *Hackers*	A&M 5816052
24/08/1996	32	2		THIS SUMMER (REMIX)	A&M 5818412

BILLY SQUIRE
US singer/songwriter/guitarist (born 12/5/1950, Wellesley Hills, MA).

03/10/1981	52	3		THE STROKE	Capitol CL 214

JOHN SQUIRE
UK singer/guitarist (born 24/11/1962, Manchester); he was a member of Stone Roses before leaving to form The Seahorses. He disbanded the group after one album and went solo.

02/11/2002	43	1		JOE LOUIS	North Country NCCDB 001

❶⁹ Number of weeks single topped the UK chart   ↑ Entered the UK chart at #1   ▲⁹ Number of weeks single topped the US chart

759

				SINGLE TITLE	LABEL & NUMBER

14/02/2004.....44......1....... ROOM IN BROOKLYN .... North Country NCCDA 003

DOROTHY SQUIRES UK singer (born Edna May Squires, 25/3/1915 – although she claimed it was 1918 – Llanelli, Wales). Starting professionally aged eighteen, she was still performing 50 years later. Married to actor Roger Moore 1953–68. She died from cancer on 14/4/1998.

05/06/1953.....12......1....... I'M WALKING BEHIND YOU .... Polygon P 1068
24/08/1961.....23......10...... SAY IT WITH FLOWERS **DOROTHY SQUIRES AND RUSS CONWAY** .... Columbia DB 4665
20/09/1969.....24......11...... FOR ONCE IN MY LIFE .... President PT 267
21/02/1970.....25......11...... TILL.. President PT 281
08/08/1970.....25......23...... MY WAY... President PT 305

STABBS Finnish producer Kosky.
24/12/1994.....65......1....... JOY AND HAPPINESS... Hi-Life HICD 3

STACCATO UK/Dutch vocal/instrumental duo.
20/07/1996.....65......1....... I WANNA KNOW .... Multiply CDMULTY 11

WARREN STACEY UK singer (born 1980, London). First known as one of the 10,000-plus entrants into the TV talent search *Popstars*. His habit of choosing gospel material rather than pop songs saw him eliminated from the competition early on, but he emerged barely months later with a recording contract.
23/03/2002.....26......3....... MY GIRL MY GIRL... Def Soul 5889932

JIM STAFFORD US singer (born 16/1/1944, Eloise, FL); he moved to Nashville soon after graduating from high school. He hosted his own TV series and married singer Bobbie Gentry in 1978.
27/04/1974.....14......8....... SPIDERS AND SNAKES... MGM 2006 374
06/07/1974.....20......8....... MY GIRL BILL .... MGM 2006 423

JO STAFFORD US singer (born 12/11/1920, Coalings, CA); a member of Tommy Dorsey's group The Pied Pipers. She later sang with Johnny Mercer, Frankie Laine and Liberace. She hosted her own series on TV and scored over 70 US chart hits. She and her husband Paul Weston (born 12/3/1912, Springfield, MA, formerly arranger for Tommy Dorsey) also recorded as Jonathan and Darlene Edwards and had their own Corinthian label. Three stars on the Hollywood Walk of Fame are for her contribution to recording, radio and TV.
14/11/1952 .....❶1.....19...... **YOU BELONG TO ME** ▲12 Features the uncredited contribution of The Paul Weston Orchestra................. Columbia DB 3152
19/12/1952.....11......2...... JAMBALAYA... Columbia DB 3169
07/05/1954 .....8......1....... **MAKE LOVE TO ME** ▲7 .... Philips PB 233
09/12/1955.....12......6....... SUDDENLY THERE'S A VALLEY .... Philips PB 509

TERRY STAFFORD US singer (born 22/11/1941, Hollis, OK, raised in Amarillo, TX). He began by singing impersonations of Elvis Presley and Buddy Holly at high school dances (his only UK hit was a cover of an Elvis Presley album track from 1962). He was signed by Crusader Records in 1964 and later appeared in films, including *Wild Wheels* (1969). He died on 17/3/1996.
07/05/1964.....31......9....... SUSPICION .... London HLU 9871

STAGECOACH FEATURING PENNY FOSTER UK charity group formed by 3,000 members of the Stagecoach Theatre Arts group. They are the UK's largest network of part-time performing arts schools for young people aged between four and sixteen. Their debut hit, written and sung by Penny Foster, was in aid of Milly's Fund, in memory of murdered schoolgirl Milly Dowler.
18/10/2003.....59......1....... ANGEL LOOKING THROUGH.. Stagecoach Theatre SCR00001

STAIFFI AND HIS MUSTAFAS French vocal/instrumental group.
28/07/1960.....43......1....... MUSTAFA CHA CHA CHA.. Pye International 7N 25057

STAIND US rock group formed in 1993 by Aaron Lewis (vocals), Mike Mushok (guitar) and Jon Wysocki (drums). They financed their own debut release, the cover of which nearly got them thrown off a Limp Bizkit tour because of the Satanic images. Limp Bizkit leader Fred Durst later relented and helped get them a deal with Flip Records.
15/09/2001.....15......6...... IT'S BEEN A WHILE... Elektra E 7252CD1
01/12/2001.....33......2...... OUTSIDE... Elektra E 7277CD
23/02/2002.....55......1...... FOR YOU .... Elektra E 7281CD
24/05/2003.....36......2...... PRICE TO PAY .... Elektra E 7417CD

STAKKA BO Swedish record producer Johan Renck, whose debut hit also featured Nanna Hedin (vocals) and MC Oscar Franzen.
25/09/1993.....13......8...... HERE WE GO .... Polydor PZCD 280
18/12/1993.....64......4...... DOWN THE DRAIN .... Polydor PZCD 301

FRANK STALLONE US singer (born 30/7/1950, Philadelphia, PA); he is the brother of actor Sylvester Stallone.
22/10/1983.....68......2...... FAR FROM OVER Featured in the 1983 film *Staying Alive* (directed by Sylvester Stallone)............................ RSO 95

STAMFORD AMP UK group formed by Mark Kilminster (26 at the time of the hit, vocals), Chris Leonard (23, guitar), Tim Jackson (20, bass), David Tench (25, keyboards) and Guy Anderton (27, drums). First known as the houseband on BBC TV series *The Saturday Show*.
12/10/2002.....33......2....... ANYTHING FOR YOU.. Mercury 638982

○ Silver disc ● Gold disc ✪ Platinum disc (additional platinum units are indicated by a figure following the symbol) ◎ Singles released prior to 1973 that are known to have sold over 1 million copies in the UK

STAMFORD BRIDGE UK vocal group of Chelsea Football Club supporters.

16/05/1970	47	1		CHELSEA Released to concide with Chelsea's appearance in the FA Cup Final.	Penny Farthing PEN 715

STAMINA MC UK producer and DJ Linden Reeves.

20/07/2002	17	6		LK (CAROLINA CAROL BELA).	V Recordings V 035
16/11/2002	45	1		LK (REMIX) This and above single credited to DJ MARKY AND XRS AND STAMINA MC.	V Recordings V 038
30/08/2003	14	2		BARCELONA D KAY AND EPSILON FEATURING STAMINA MC	Alphamagic/BC/BMG BCAU001CD

STAMPS QUARTET – see ELVIS PRESLEY

STAN UK vocal/instrumental duo Simon Andrew and Kevin Stagg.

31/07/1993	40	3		SUNTAN	Hug CDBUM 1

STANDS UK group from Liverpool: Howie Payne (guitar/vocals), Luke Thomson (guitar), Dean Ravera (bass) and Steve Pilgrim (drums).

16/08/2003	32	1		WHEN THIS RIVER ROLLS OVER YOU.	Echo ECSCD 142
25/10/2003	39	2		I NEED YOU	Echo ECSCX 146
21/02/2004	25	2		HERE SHE COMES AGAIN.	Echo ECSCX 148
05/06/2004	49	1		OUTSIDE YOUR DOOR	Echo ECSCX 151

LISA STANSFIELD UK singer (born 11/4/1966, Rochdale); she formed Blue Zone in 1984 with Andy Morris (trumpet) and Ian Devaney (keyboards/trombone). They were signed by Rocking Horse in 1986 and released one album. Stansfield was invited to provide the lead vocals to Coldcut's third single in 1989, its success gaining her a solo deal with Arista via Big Life. Best British Newcomer at the 1990 BRIT Awards and Best British Female in 1991 and 1992. Dirty Rotten Scoundrels are a UK production/remixing group.

25/03/1989	11	9		PEOPLE HOLD ON COLDCUT FEATURING LISA STANSFIELD	Ahead Of Our Time CCUT 5
12/08/1989	13	8		THIS IS THE RIGHT TIME	Arista 112512
28/10/1989	●²	14	●	ALL AROUND THE WORLD	Arista 112693
10/02/1990	10	6		LIVE TOGETHER	Arista 112914
12/05/1990	25	4		WHAT DID I DO TO YOU (EP) Tracks on EP: *What Did I Do To You, My Apple Heart, Lay Me Down* and *Something's Happenin'*.	Arista 113168
19/10/1991	10	7		CHANGE	Arista 114820
21/12/1991	20	8		ALL WOMAN	Arista 115000
14/03/1992	14	8		TIME TO MAKE YOU MINE	Arista 115113
06/06/1992	28	4		SET YOUR LOVING FREE	Arista 74321100587
19/12/1992	10	9		SOMEDAY (I'M COMING BACK) Featured in the 1992 film *The Bodyguard*	Arista 74321123567
01/05/1993	●³	12	●	FIVE LIVE EP ↑ GEORGE MICHAEL AND QUEEN WITH LISA STANSFIELD Tracks on EP: *Somebody To Love, These Are The Days Of Our Lives, Calling You* and *Papa Was A Rolling Stone – Killer (Medley)*	Parlophone CDRS 6340
05/06/1993	8	11		IN ALL THE RIGHT PLACES Featured in the 1995 film *Indecent Proposal*	MCA MCSTD 1780
23/10/1993	15	5		SO NATURAL	Arista 74321169132
11/12/1993	32	4		LITTLE BIT OF HEAVEN.	Arista 74321178202
18/01/1997	4	6		PEOPLE HOLD ON (THE BOOTLEG MIXES) LISA STANSFIELD VS THE DIRTY ROTTEN SCOUNDRELS	Arista 74321452012
22/03/1997	9	7		THE REAL THING.	Arista 74321463222
21/06/1997	25	3		NEVER NEVER GONNA GIVE YOU UP	Arista 74321490392
04/10/1997	64	1		THE LINE	RCA 74321511372
23/06/2001	48	1		LET'S CALL IT LOVE	Arista 74321863422

VIVIAN STANSHALL – see MIKE OLDFIELD

STANTON WARRIORS UK production duo Dominic B and Mark Yardley.

22/09/2001	69	1		DA ANTIDOTE	Mob MOBCD 006

STAPLE SINGERS US R&B/gospel group formed by Roebuck 'Pops' Staples (born 28/12/1915, Winoma, MS) and four of his children: Mavis (born 1940, Chicago, IL), Yvonne (born 1939, Chicago), Cleotha (born 1934, Chicago) and Pervis (born 1935, Chicago). Pervis left in 1971, Mavis recorded solo in 1970. They group first recorded for United in 1953. Mavis appeared in the Prince film *Graffiti Bridge* in 1990. The group was inducted into the Rock & Roll Hall of Fame in 1999. Pops Staples won the 1994 Grammy Award for Best Contemporary Blues Album for *Father Father*. He died on 19/12/2000 following a fall.

10/06/1972	30	8		I'LL TAKE YOU THERE ▲¹ Featured in the 1996 film *Casino*	Stax 2025 110
08/06/1974	34	6		IF YOU'RE READY (COME GO WITH ME) Featured in the 1996 film *Private Parts*	Stax 2025 224

CYRIL STAPLETON UK orchestra leader (born 31/12/1914, Nottingham); he died on 25/2/1974.

27/05/1955	19	4		ELEPHANT TANGO.	Decca F 10488
23/09/1955	2	12		BLUE STAR (THE MEDIC THEME) CYRIL STAPLETON ORCHESTRA FEATURING JULIE DAWN	Decca F 10599
06/04/1956	18	2		THE ITALIAN THEME.	Decca F 10703
01/06/1956	22	4		THE HAPPY WHISTLER CYRIL STAPLETON ORCHESTRA FEATURING DESMOND LANE, PENNY WHISTLE	Decca F 10735
19/07/1957	27	5		FORGOTTEN DREAMS	Decca F 10912

STAR SPANGLES US rock group formed in New York by Ian Wilson (vocals), Tommy Volume (guitar), Nick Price (bass) and Joey Valentine (drums).

19/04/2003	52	1		STAY AWAY FROM ME.	Parlophone CDR 6604
12/07/2003	60	1		I LIVE FOR SPEED	Capitol CDR 6609

●⁹ Number of weeks single topped the UK chart ↑ Entered the UK chart at #1 ▲⁹ Number of weeks single topped the US chart

761

STAR TURN ON 45 (PINTS) UK studio group assembled by Steve O'Donnell. He died on 4/8/1997.

24/10/1981.....45......4.......	STARTURN ON 45 (PINTS)	V Tone 003
30/04/1988.....12......5.......	PUMP UP THE BITTER	Pacific DRINK 1

STARCHASER Italian production group formed by Danny JC, Speedcity and Fausto Fanizzia.

22/06/2002.....24......4.......	LOVE WILL SET YOU FREE (JAMBE MYTH)	Rulin 23CDS

STARDUST French vocal/instrumental group.

08/10/1977.....42......3.......	ARIANA	Satril SAT 120

STARDUST French group formed in Paris by Thomas Bangalter (born 1/1/1975), Alan 'Braxe' Queme and Benjamin 'Diamond' Cohen, with Cohen on lead vocals. Bangalter is also a member of Daft Punk. Stardust won the 1998 MOBO Award for Best Dance Act.

01/08/1998.....55......3.......	MUSIC SOUNDS BETTER WITH YOU (IMPORT)	Roule 305
22/08/1998 .....2......23.....✪	**MUSIC SOUNDS BETTER WITH YOU** Contains a sample of Chaka Khan's *Fate*.	Virgin DINSD 175

ALVIN STARDUST UK singer (born Bernard William Jewry, 27/9/1942, London); he was road manager and occasional singer for Johnny Theakston & the Fentones when they made an audition tape as Shane Fenton & The Fentones. Theakston died soon after, Jewry assuming the Fenton name, signing with Parlophone in 1961. He quit recording in 1964, returning in 1973 as Alvin Stardust.

03/11/1973 .....2......21.....●	MY COO-CA-CHOO	Magnet MAG 1
16/02/1974 ....❶¹....11.....	JEALOUS MIND	Magnet MAG 5
04/05/1974 ....7......8.......	RED DRESS	Magnet MAG 8
31/08/1974 .....6......10.....○	YOU YOU YOU	Magnet MAG 13
30/11/1974.....16......8.......	TELL ME WHY	Magnet MAG 19
01/02/1975.....11......9.......	GOOD LOVE CAN NEVER DIE.	Magnet MAG 21
12/07/1975.....37......4.......	SWEET CHEATIN' RITA	Magnet MAG 32
05/09/1981 .....4......10.....○	PRETEND	Stiff BUY 124
21/11/1981.....56......8.......	A WONDERFUL TIME UP THERE.	Stiff BUY 132
05/05/1984 .....7......11.....	I FEEL LIKE BUDDY HOLLY	Chrysalis CHS 2784
27/10/1984 .....7......13.....	I WON'T RUN AWAY	Chrysalis CHS 2829
15/12/1984.....29......8.......	SO NEAR TO CHRISTMAS	Chrysalis CHS 2835
23/03/1985.....55......2.......	GOT A LITTLE HEARTACHE	Chrysalis CHS 2856

STARFIGHTER Belgian producer Philip Dirix.

05/02/2000.....31......3.......	APACHE	Sound Of Ministry MOSCDS 136

STARGARD US R&B trio formed in Los Angeles, CA in the late 1970s by Rochelle Runnells, Debra Anderson and Janice Williams. They later appeared as The Diamonds in the 1978 film *Sgt Pepper's Lonely Hearts Club Band*. Anderson left the group in 1980.

28/01/1978.....19......7.......	THEME FROM 'WHICH WAY IS UP' Featured in the 1977 film of the same name.	MCA 346
15/04/1978.....45......1.......	LOVE IS SO EASY.	MCA 354
09/09/1978.....39......6.......	WHAT YOU WAITING FOR	MCA 382

STARGATE Norwegian production group Mikkel S Eriksen, Hallgeir Rustan and Tor Erik Hermansen, singer Anna and rapper D Flex.

07/09/2002.....55......1.......	EASIER SAID THAN DONE	Telstar CDSTAS 3269

STARGAZERS UK group formed in 1949 by Dick James (born Isaac Vapnick, 1919, London), Cliff Adams, Marie Benson, Fred Datchler and Ronnie Milne. Milne left in 1953, replaced by David Carey. James went solo, forming the DJM record and publishing company. Adams led his own orchestra, and Datchler's son Clark was a member of Johnny Hates Jazz. James died from a heart attack on 1/2/1986.

13/02/1953 ....❶¹....12.....	BROKEN WINGS	Decca F 10047
19/02/1954 ....❶⁶....15.....	I SEE THE MOON Reclaimed #1 position on 23/4/1954	Decca F 10213
09/04/1954.....12......1.....	HAPPY WANDERER	Decca F 10259
17/12/1954 ....❶³....15.....	FINGER OF SUSPICION DICKIE VALENTINE WITH THE STARGAZERS Reclaimed #1 position on 21/1/1955	Decca F 10394
04/03/1955.....20......1.....	SOMEBODY	Decca F 10437
03/06/1955.....18......3.....	CRAZY OTTO RAG	Decca F 10523
09/09/1955 .....6......9.....	CLOSE THE DOOR.	Decca F 10594
11/11/1955 .....4......11.....	TWENTY TINY FINGERS	Decca F 10626
22/06/1956.....28......1.....	HOT DIGGITY (DOG ZIGGITY BOOM)	Decca F 10731

STARGAZERS UK rock 'n' roll revival group formed in 1980 by Danny Brittain (vocals), John Wallace (saxophone), Peter Davenport (guitar), Anders Janes (bass) and Ricky Lee Brawn (drums).

06/02/1982.....56......3.......	GROOVE BABY GROOVE (EP) Tracks on EP: *Groove Baby Groove, Jump Around, La Rock 'N' Roll (Quelques Uns A La Lune)* and *Red Light Green Light*	Epic EPC A 1924

STARJETS UK group formed in Belfast in 1976 by Paul Bowen (guitar/vocals), Terry Sharpe (guitar/vocals), John Martin (bass/vocals) and Liam L'Estrange (drums/vocals). The group disbanded in 1980.

08/09/1979.....51......5.......	WAR STORIES	Epic EPC 7770

STARLAND VOCAL BAND US pop group formed in Washington DC by Bill Danoff and his wife Taffy, John Carroll and Margot Chapman. Carroll and Chapman were later married. Their two 1976 Grammy Awards included Best New Artist.

07/08/1976 . . . . . 18 . . . . . 10 . . . . . . AFTERNOON DELIGHT ▲² 1976 Grammy Award for Best Arrangement for Vocals. Featured in the 2004 film *Starsky & Hutch* . . . . RCA 2716

STARLIGHT Italian studio project masterminded by Daniele 'DJ Lelewel' Davoli, who also produced for Black Box and Mixmaster.
19/08/1989 . . . . . 9 . . . . . . 11 . . . . . . **NUMERO UNO** . . . . Citybeat CBE 742

STARLIGHTERS – see **JOE DEE AND THE STARLIGHTERS**

STARPARTY Dutch dance group assembled by Ferry Corsten (he also records as Gouryella, Veracocha and System F) and Robert Smit.
26/02/2000 . . . . . 26 . . . . . . 2 . . . . I'M IN LOVE Contains a sample of Gwen Guthrie's *Peanut Butter* . . . . Incentive CENT 5CDS

EDWIN STARR US singer (born Charles Hatcher, 21/1/1942, Nashville, TN, raised in Cleveland, OH). He formed the Future Tones in 1957 and signed with Ric Tic in 1965. He switched to Motown in 1967 when the label bought Ric Tic, recording an album with Sandra 'Blinky' Williams in 1969. He left Motown in 1975, later moving to the UK. He died from a heart attack on 2/4/2003.

12/05/1966 . . . . . 35 . . . . . . 8	STOP HER ON SIGHT (SOS)	Polydor BM 56 702
18/08/1966 . . . . . 39 . . . . . . 3	HEADLINE NEWS	Polydor 56 717
11/12/1968 . . . . . 11 . . . . . . 11	STOP HER ON SIGHT (SOS)/HEADLINE NEWS	Polydor 56 753
13/09/1969 . . . . . 36 . . . . . . 6	25 MILES	Tamla Motown TMG 672
24/10/1970 . . . . . 3 . . . . . . 12	WAR ▲³ Featured in the films *Backdraft* (1991), *Small Soldiers* (1998) and *New York Minute* (2004)	Tamla Motown TMG 754
20/02/1971 . . . . . 33 . . . . . . 1	STOP THE WAR NOW	Tamla Motown TMG 764
27/01/1979 . . . . . 6 . . . . . . 12 . . . . . . ○	**CONTACT** Sold over 100,000 copies on 12-inch. Featured in the 1998 film *54*	20th Century BTC 2396
26/05/1979 . . . . . 9 . . . . . . 11	**H.A.P.P.Y. RADIO**	20th Century TC 2408
01/06/1985 . . . . . 56 . . . . . . 4	IT AIN'T FAIR	Hippodrome HIP 101
30/10/1993 . . . . . 69 . . . . . . 2	WAR **EDWIN STARR AND SHADOW** Listed flip side was *Wild Thing* by **TROGGS AND WOLF**	Weekend CDWEEK 103

FREDDIE STARR UK comedian/singer (born Fred Smith, 9/1/1944, Liverpool). He began as a singer, making his first single for Decca in 1963. Nationally known via the TV series *Who Do You Do?* and then his own series, he later achieved notoriety for supposedly eating a fan's pet, prompting the classic *Sun* headline 'Freddie Starr Ate My Hamster'!

23/02/1974 . . . . . 9 . . . . . . 10	IT'S YOU	Tiffany 6121 501
20/12/1975 . . . . . 41 . . . . . . 4	WHITE CHRISTMAS	Thunderbird THE 102

KAY STARR US singer (born Katherine LaVerne Starks, 21/7/1922, Dougherty, OK). She joined Joe Venuti's orchestra in 1937 and later Glenn Miller before going solo in 1945. Films included *Make Believe Ballroom* and *When You're Smiling*. She has a star on the Hollywood Walk of Fame.

05/12/1952 . . . . . ❶¹ 16	**COMES A-LONG A-LOVE**	Capitol CL 13808
24/04/1953 . . . . . 7 . . . . . . 4	**SIDE BY SIDE**	Capitol CL 13871
19/03/1954 . . . . . 4 . . . . . . 14	**CHANGING PARTNERS**	Capitol CL 14050
15/10/1954 . . . . . 17 . . . . . . 4	AM I A TOY OR A TREASURE	Capitol CL 14151
17/02/1956 . . . . . ❶¹ 20	**ROCK AND ROLL WALTZ** ▲⁶	HMV POP 168

RINGO STARR UK singer/drummer (born Richard Starkey, 7/7/1940, Liverpool). Drummer with Rory Storm & The Hurricanes, in 1962 he replaced Pete Best in the Beatles. He made his first solo album in 1970 and appeared in a number of films, including *Candy* (filmed in 1967, released in 1969), *Born To Boogie* and *That'll Be The Day*. He married Maureen Cox, and then actress Barbara Bach in 1981. He spoke the voiceover to the children's TV series *Thomas The Tank Engine* and launched the Ring'O and Able record labels.

17/04/1971 . . . . . 4 . . . . . . 11	**IT DON'T COME EASY** Features Badfinger on backing vocals	Apple R 5898
01/04/1972 . . . . . 2 . . . . . . 10	**BACK OFF BOOGALOO** This and above single produced by George Harrison	Apple R 5944
27/10/1973 . . . . . 8 . . . . . . 13	**PHOTOGRAPH** ▲¹ Features George Harrison on guitar and vocals	Apple R 5992
23/02/1974 . . . . . 4 . . . . . . 10 . . . . . . ○	**YOU'RE SIXTEEN** ▲¹ Features Nilsson on backing vocals and Paul McCartney on kazoo . . .	Apple R 5995
30/11/1974 . . . . . 28 . . . . . . 11	ONLY YOU	Apple R 6000
06/06/1992 . . . . . 74 . . . . . . 1	WEIGHT OF THE WORLD	Private Music 115392

STARS ON 54 US vocal group formed by Ultra Nate (born 1968, Havre De Grace, MD), Jocelyn Enriquez (born 28/12/1974, San Francisco) and Amber (born in Holland). The single (hence their name) was for the film *54*, based on New York nightclub Studio 54.
28/11/1998 . . . . . 23 . . . . . . 3 . . . . IF YOU COULD READ MY MIND Featured in the 1998 film *54* . . . . Tommy Boy TBCD 7497

STARSAILOR UK rock group formed in Chorley in 2000 by James Walsh (guitar/vocals), James Stelfox (bass), Barry Westhead (keyboards) and Ben Byrne (drums). The group took their name from a 1971 album by folk singer Tim Buckley.

17/02/2001 . . . . . 18 . . . . . . 3	FEVER	Chrysalis 555123
05/05/2001 . . . . . 12 . . . . . . 6	GOOD SOULS	Chrysalis CDCHS 5125
29/09/2001 . . . . . 10 . . . . . . 6	**ALCOHOLIC**	Chrysalis CDCHSS 5130
22/12/2001 . . . . . 36 . . . . . . 4	LULLABY	Chrysalis CDCHS 5131
30/03/2002 . . . . . 23 . . . . . . 3	POOR MISGUIDED FOOL	Chrysalis CDCHS 5136
13/09/2003 . . . . . 9 . . . . . . 8	**SILENCE IS EASY**	EMI CDEM 625
29/11/2003 . . . . . 40 . . . . . . 2	BORN AGAIN	EMI CDEMS 632
13/03/2004 . . . . . 24 . . . . . . 4	FOUR TO THE FLOOR	EMI CDEM 634

STARSHIP US rock group formed in San Francisco, CA in 1965 by Marty Balin (born Martyn Buchwald, 30/1/1942, Cincinnati, OH, vocals), Paul Kantner (born 12/3/1941, San Francisco, guitar), Jorma Kaukonen (born 23/12/1940, Washington DC, guitar), Bob Harvey

❶⁹ Number of weeks single topped the UK chart ↑ Entered the UK chart at #1 ▲⁹ Number of weeks single topped the US chart

763

(bass), Jerry Peloguin (drums) and Sigue Anderson (vocals) as Jefferson Airplane. They added singer Grace Slick (born Grace Wing 30/10/1939, Chicago, IL) in 1965 and replaced Harvey with Jack Casady (born 13/4/1944, Washington DC) the same year. They first recorded for RCA in 1966. They name-changed to Jefferson Starship in 1974, shortening it to Starship in 1985 following the departure of Kantner. Grace Slick left in 1978 with alcohol problems, returning in 1981, departing for good in 1988. Jefferson Airplane reunited in 1989 with the 1966 line-up. As Jefferson Airplane they were inducted into the Rock & Roll Hall of Fame in 1996.

26/01/1980	21	9		JANE **JEFFERSON STARSHIP**		Grunt FB 1750
16/11/1985	12	12		WE BUILT THIS CITY ▲[2]		RCA PB 49929
08/02/1986	66	3		SARA ▲[1]		RCA PB 49893
11/04/1987	❶[4]	17	●	NOTHING'S GONNA STOP US NOW ▲[2] Featured in the 1987 film *Mannequin*		Grunt FB 49757

STARSOUND Dutch studio project assembled by ex-Golden Earring and producer Jaap Eggermont. The concept originally appeared on an American bootleg 12-inch called *Bits & Pieces* – 16 minutes of segued hits from the 1960s, including some from the Beatles. Since copyright matters ruled it out officially, Eggermont assembled studio musicians and singers to recreate the record (with Bas Muys, Okkie Huysdens and Hans Vermoulen singing the John Lennon, Paul McCartney and George Harrison vocals respectively).

18/04/1981	2	14	●	**STARS ON 45** ▲[1] Medley tracks: *Stars On 45, Venus, Sugar Sugar, No Reply, I'll Be Back, Do You Want To Know A Secret, We Can Work It Out, I Should Have Known Better, Nowhere Man, You're Going To Lose That Girl* and *Stars On 45*		CBS A 1102
04/07/1981	2	10	○	**STARS ON 45 VOL 2** Medley tracks: *Stars On 45, Voulez Vous, SOS, Bang-A-Boomerang, Money Money Money, Knowing Me Knowing You, Fernando, The Winner Takes It All, Super Trouper* and *Stars On 45*		CBS A 1407
19/09/1981	17	6		STARS ON 45 VOL 3 Tracks on medley: *Stars On 45, Papa Was A Rolling Stone, Dance To The Music, Sugar Baby Love, Let's Go To San Francisco, A Horse With No Name, Monday Monday, Tears Of A Clown, Stop In The Name Of Love, Cracklin' Rosie, Do Wah Diddy-Diddy, A Lover's Concerto, Reach Out I'll Be There, Sounds Of Silence* and *Stars On 45*		CBS A 1521
27/02/1982	14	7		STARS ON STEVIE Tracks on medley: *Everything's All Right, My Cherie Amour, Yester-Me, Yester-You, Yesterday, Master Blaster, You Are The Sunshine Of My Life, Isn't She lovely, Stars On 45, Sir Duke, I Wish, I Was Made To Love Her, Superstition* and *Fingertips*		CBS A 2041

STARTRAX UK studio group assembled by Bruce Baxter with a medley of songs made famous by The Bee Gees.

01/08/1981	18	8		STARTRAX CLUB DISCO Tracks on medley: *Startrax Club Disco, More Than A Woman, Night Fever, Tragedy, Massachusetts, How Deep Is Your Love, Stayin' Alive, Nights On Broadway, Saved By The Bell, Words, Jive Talkin', If I Can't Have You, New York Mining Disaster 1941, First Of May, You Should Be Dancing* and *Startrax Club Disco*		Picksy KSY 1001

STARVATION Multinational charity group with Madness, UB40, the Specials and General Public in aid of Ethiopian famine relief.

09/03/1985	33	6		STARVATION/TAM-TAM POUR L'ETHIOPE		Zarjazz JAZZ 3

STARVING SOULS UK rapper (born Adrian Thaws, 27/1/1968, Bristol). He began contributing tracks to Massive Attack and made his debut single in 1994. He also recorded under the names Nearly God and Tricky.

21/10/1995	66	1		I BE THE PROPHET		Durban Poison DPCD 1

STATE OF MIND UK dance group formed by producers Ricky Morrison and Frank Sidoli. They are also responsible for M&S.

18/04/1998	30	2		THIS IS IT		Ministry Of Sound MOSCDS 123
25/07/1998	46	1		TAKE CONTROL		Ministry Of Sound MOSCDS 124

STATE ONE German producer/remixer/keyboard player Mike Koglin, with Todd Terry and The Sugarcubes before going solo.

27/09/2003	62	1		FOREVER AND A DAY		Incentive CENT 54CDS

STATIC REVENGER US producer/remixer (born Dennis White, Detroit, MI). A graduate of Berklee College of Music, Boston, MA in 1988, he signed debut deal with KMS Records the same year. He joined Inner City in 1989, becoming Static Revenger in 1998.

07/07/2001	23	3		HAPPY PEOPLE		Incentive/Rulin CENRUL 1CDS

STATIC-X US group formed by Wayne Static (guitar/vocals), Koicki Fukada (guitar), Tony Campos (bass) and Ken Jay (drums). They signed with Warner Brothers in 1998. Fukada left the group in 1999, replaced by Tripp Elsen.

06/10/2001	65	1		BLACK AND WHITE		Warner Brothers W 560CD

STATLER BROTHERS US country vocal group formed in Staunton, VA by Harold Reid, his brother Don, Phil Balsley and Lew DeWitt. DeWitt left in 1983, replaced by Jimmy Fortune. DeWitt died on 15/8/1990. Three Grammy Awards include Best New Country & Western Artist in 1965 and Best Country & Western Performance in 1972 for *Class Of '57*.

24/02/1966	38	4		FLOWERS ON THE WALL 1965 Grammy Award for Best Contemporary Rock & Roll Performance by a Group		CBS 201976

CANDI STATON US R&B singer (born Canzetta Maria Staton, 13/3/1943, Hanceville, AL); she was discovered by Bishop ML Jewell who formed the Jewell Gospel Trio with Candi, her sister Maggie and Naomi Harrison. Candi left at seventeen when she got married, but returned to music four children later, discovered a second time by Clarence Carter (who later became her second husband). She first recorded solo for Fame in 1969 and switched to Warner's in 1974. She later formed her own gospel label Beracah Records.

29/05/1976	2	13	○	**YOUNG HEARTS RUN FREE** Featured in the films *Romeo And Juliet* (1996) and *54* (1996)		Warner Brothers K 16730
18/09/1976	41	3		DESTINY		Warner Brothers K 16806
23/07/1977	6	12	○	**NIGHTS ON BROADWAY**		Warner Brothers K 16972
03/06/1978	48	5		HONEST I DO LOVE YOU		Warner Brothers K 17164
24/04/1982	31	9		SUSPICIOUS MINDS		Sugarhill SH 112
31/05/1986	47	5		YOUNG HEARTS RUN FREE (REMIX)		Warner Brothers W 8680
02/02/1991	4	11	○	**YOU GOT THE LOVE**		Truelove TLOVE 7001

○ Silver disc ● Gold disc ✪ Platinum disc (additional platinum units are indicated by a figure following the symbol) ◎ Singles released prior to 1973 that are known to have sold over 1 million copies in the UK

DATE	POS	WKS	BPI	SINGLE TITLE	LABEL & NUMBER
01/03/1997	3	8		**YOU GOT THE LOVE (REMIX)** This and above single credited to **SOURCE FEATURING CANDI STATON**	React CDREACT 89
17/04/1999	27	3		LOVE ON LOVE	React CDREACT 143
07/08/1999	29	2		YOUNG HEARTS RUN FREE Re-recording	React CDREACT 158

STATUS IV US gospel group formed in NYC in 1982 by Jerome Brooks, Lorenzo Lawrence, Sylvester McLain III and Derek Wyche.

DATE	POS	WKS	BPI	SINGLE TITLE	LABEL & NUMBER
09/07/1983	56	3		YOU AIN'T REALLY DOWN	TMT 4

STATUS QUO UK rock group formed in Beckenham in 1962 by Alan Lancaster (born 7/2/1949, Peckham, London, bass), Francis Rossi (born 29/4/1949, London, guitar/vocals), John Coghlan (born 19/9/1946, Dulwich, London, drums) and Jess Jaworski (organ) as the Spectres. Jaworski left in 1965, replaced by Roy Lynes (born 25/11/1943, Redhill). They signed to Pye via Piccadilly in 1966 (still as the Spectres), after three singles changing their name to Traffic Jam. After one single they changed to Status Quo, signing direct to Pye. Rick Parfitt (born Richard Harrison, 12/10/1948, Woking, guitar/vocals) joined at the same time. They switched to Vertigo in 1972. Lancaster left in 1984. They gained the Outstanding Contribution Award at the 1991 BRIT Awards, and also took part in the *It's Only Rock 'N' Roll* project for the Children's Promise charity. Rossi and Parfitt penned Manchester United's number one hit *Come On You Reds*. In 1991 the group entered the *Guinness Book Of Records* after playing four venues in one day (Sheffield International Centre, Glasgow Scottish Exhibition & Conference Centre, Birmingham National Exhibition Centre and Wembley Arena) as part of a 'Rock 'Til You Drop' tour to commemorate their 25th anniversary.

DATE	POS	WKS	BPI	SINGLE TITLE	LABEL & NUMBER
24/01/1968	7	12		**PICTURES OF MATCHSTICK MEN**	Pye 7N 17449
21/08/1968	8	12		**ICE IN THE SUN**	Pye 7N 17581
28/05/1969	46	3		ARE YOU GROWING TIRED OF MY LOVE	Pye 7N 17728
02/05/1970	12	17		DOWN THE DUSTPIPE	Pye 7N 17907
07/11/1970	21	14		IN MY CHAIR	Pye 7N 17998
13/01/1973	8	11		**PAPER PLANE**	Vertigo 6059 071
14/04/1973	20	11		MEAN GIRL	Pye 7N 45229
08/09/1973	5	13	○	**CAROLINE**	Vertigo 6059 085
04/05/1974	8	8		**BREAK THE RULES**	Vertigo 6059 101
07/12/1974	❶[1]	11	○	**DOWN DOWN**	Vertigo 6059 114
10/05/1975	9	8		**ROLL OVER LAY DOWN**	Vertigo QUO 13
14/02/1976	7	7		**RAIN**	Vertigo 6059 133
10/07/1976	11	9		MYSTERY SONG	Vertigo 6059 146
11/12/1976	9	12	○	**WILD SIDE OF LIFE**	Vertigo 6059 153
08/10/1977	3	16	●	**ROCKIN' ALL OVER THE WORLD**	Vertigo 6059 184
02/09/1978	13	9		AGAIN AND AGAIN	Vertigo QUO 1
25/11/1978	36	8		ACCIDENT PRONE	Vertigo QUO 2
22/09/1979	4	9	○	**WHATEVER YOU WANT**	Vertigo 6059 242
24/11/1979	16	10		LIVING ON AN ISLAND	Vertigo 6059 248
11/10/1980	2	11	○	**WHAT YOU'RE PROPOSING**	Vertigo QUO 3
06/12/1980	11	10	○	LIES/DON'T DRIVE MY CAR	Vertigo QUO 4
28/02/1981	9	7		SOMETHING 'BOUT YOU BABY I LIKE	Vertigo QUO 5
28/11/1981	8	11	○	**ROCK 'N' ROLL**	Vertigo QUO 6
27/03/1982	10	8		**DEAR JOHN**	Vertigo QUO 7
12/06/1982	36	5		SHE DON'T FOOL ME	Vertigo QUO 8
30/10/1982	13	7		CAROLINE (LIVE AT THE NEC)	Vertigo QUO 10
10/09/1983	9	8		**OL' RAG BLUES**	Vertigo QUO 11
05/11/1983	15	6		A MESS OF THE BLUES	Vertigo QUO 12
10/12/1983	3	11	○	**MARGUERITA TIME**	Vertigo QUO 14
19/05/1984	20	6		GOING DOWN TOWN TONIGHT	Vertigo QUO 15
27/10/1984	7	11		**THE WANDERER**	Vertigo QUO 16
17/05/1986	9	6		**ROLLIN' HOME**	Vertigo QUO 18
26/07/1986	19	8		RED SKY	Vertigo QUO 19
04/10/1986	2	14	○	**IN THE ARMY NOW**	Vertigo QUO 20
06/12/1986	15	8		DREAMIN'	Vertigo QUO 21
26/03/1988	19	6		AIN'T COMPLAINING	Vertigo QUO 22
21/05/1988	34	4		WHO GETS THE LOVE	Vertigo QUO 23
20/08/1988	17	6		RUNNING ALL OVER THE WORLD	Vertigo QUAID 1
03/12/1988	5	10	○	**BURNING BRIDGES (ON AND OFF AND ON AGAIN)**	Vertigo QUO 25
28/10/1989	50	2		NOT AT ALL	Vertigo QUO 26
29/09/1990	2	9	○	**ANNIVERSARY WALTZ – PART 1**	Vertigo QUO 28
15/12/1990	16	7		ANNIVERSARY WALTZ – PART 2	Vertigo QUO 29
07/09/1991	37	3		CAN'T GIVE YOU MORE	Vertigo QUO 30
18/01/1992	38	3		ROCK 'TIL YOU DROP	Vertigo QUO 32
10/10/1992	21	4		ROADHOUSE MEDLEY (ANNIVERSARY WALTZ PART 25)	Vertigo QUO 33
06/08/1994	21	4		I DIDN'T MEAN IT	Vertigo QUOCD 34
22/10/1994	38	2		SHERRI DON'T FAIL ME NOW	Vertigo QUOCD 35
03/12/1994	39	2		RESTLESS	Polydor QUOCD 36
04/11/1995	34	2		WHEN YOU WALK IN THE ROOM	Polygram TV 5775122
02/03/1996	24	4		FUN FUN FUN **STATUS QUO WITH THE BEACH BOYS**	Polygram TV 5762972
13/04/1996	35	2		DON'T STOP	Polygram TV 5766352

❶[9] Number of weeks single topped the UK chart ↑ Entered the UK chart at #1 ▲[9] Number of weeks single topped the US chart

DATE	POS	WKS	BPI	SINGLE TITLE	LABEL & NUMBER
09/11/1996	47	1		ALL AROUND MY HAT	Polygram TV 5759452
20/03/1999	39	2		THE WAY IT GOES	Eagle EAGXS 075
12/06/1999	47	1		LITTLE WHITE LIES	Eagle EAGXS 101
02/10/1999	53	1		TWENTY WILD HORSES	Eagle EAGXS 105
13/05/2000	48	1		MONY MONY	Universal TV 1580132
17/08/2002	17	3		JAM SIDE DOWN	Universal TV 0192352
09/11/2002	51	1		ALL STAND UP (NEVER SAY NEVER)	Universal TV 0194872
25/09/2004	14	3		YOU'LL COME 'ROUND	Universal TV 9868038
04/12/2004	21	3		THINKING OF YOU	Universal TV 9825824

STAXX UK production group formed by Tommy Jones and Simon Thorne and fronted by Carol Leeming.

DATE	POS	WKS	BPI	SINGLE TITLE	LABEL & NUMBER
02/10/1993	25	6		JOY	Champion CHAMPCD 303
20/05/1995	50	1		YOU	Champion CHAMPCD 316
13/09/1997	14	4		JOY (REMIX)	Champion CHAMPCD 328

STEALERS WHEEL UK rock group formed in London in 1972 by Gerry Rafferty (born 16/4/1946, Paisley), Joe Egan (born 1946), Rab Noakes, Ian Campbell and Roger Brown. By the time they signed with A&M that year they were Rafferty (lead guitar/vocals) Egan (lead vocals/keyboards), Rod Coombes (drums), Tony Williams (bass) and Paul Pilnick (guitar). Rafferty left after their debut album, replaced by Luther Grosvenor, and Williams was replaced by Delisle Harper.

DATE	POS	WKS	BPI	SINGLE TITLE	LABEL & NUMBER
26/05/1973	8	10		STUCK IN THE MIDDLE WITH YOU Featured in the 1992 film *Reservoir Dogs*	A&M AMS 7036
01/09/1973	33	6		EVERYTHING'L TURN OUT FINE	A&M AMS 7079
26/01/1974	25	6		STAR	A&M AMS 7094

STEAM US studio group assembled by NYC producer/pianist Paul Leka with Gary DeCarlo (drums) and Dale Frashuer. After the success of the single (originally written in 1961) Leka put together a touring group as Steam which did not include DeCarlo or Frashuer.

DATE	POS	WKS	BPI	SINGLE TITLE	LABEL & NUMBER
31/01/1970	9	14		NA NA HEY HEY KISS HIM GOODBYE ▲2 Featured in the films *Eddie* (1996) and *Remember The Titans* (2000)	Fontana TF 1058

STEEL – see UNITONE ROCKERS FEATURING STEEL

ANTHONY STEEL AND THE RADIO REVELLERS UK singer (born 21/5/1920 London); he was primarily an actor, appearing in such films as *The Malta Story, West Of Zanzibar* and *The World Is Full Of Married Men*. Married three times during his lifetime, most notably to actress Anita Ekberg. He died from heart failure on 21/3/2001.

DATE	POS	WKS	BPI	SINGLE TITLE	LABEL & NUMBER
10/09/1954	11	6		WEST OF ZANZIBAR	Polygon P 1114

STEEL HORSES – see TRUMAN AND WOLFF FEATURING STEEL HORSES

STEEL PULSE UK reggae group formed in Birmingham in 1976 by David Hinds (born 15/6/1956, Birmingham, guitar/vocals), Basil Gabbidon (guitar/vocals) and Ronnie McQueen (bass), later adding Selwyn 'Bumbo' Brown (born 4/6/1958, London, keyboards), Steve 'Grizzly' Nesbitt (born 15/3/1948, Nevis, West Indies, drums), Fonso Martin (vocals) and Michael Riley (vocals). 1986 Grammy Award for Best Reggae Recording for *Babylon The Bandit*.

DATE	POS	WKS	BPI	SINGLE TITLE	LABEL & NUMBER
01/04/1978	41	4		KU KLUX KHAN	Island WIP 6428
08/07/1978	35	6		PRODIGAL SON	Island WIP 6449
23/06/1979	71	2		SOUND SYSTEM	Island WIP 6490

TOMMY STEELE UK singer (born Thomas Hicks, 17/12/1936, London); he was a member of skiffle group The Cavemen with Lionel Bart and Mike Pratt before being discovered singing in a coffee shop and signed by Decca. After appearing in the autobiographical *Tommy Steele Story* in 1957 he starred in a number of films and musicals, becoming an all-round entertainer. He was awarded an OBE in 1980. He has also published a novel (*The Final Run*), is a sculptor, and has had a painting exhibited at the Royal Academy.

DATE	POS	WKS	BPI	SINGLE TITLE	LABEL & NUMBER
26/10/1956	13	5		ROCK WITH THE CAVEMAN	Decca F 10795
14/12/1956	❶1	15		SINGING THE BLUES	Decca F 10819
15/02/1957	15	9		KNEE DEEP IN THE BLUES	Decca F 10849
03/05/1957	8	18		BUTTERFINGERS	Decca F 10877
16/08/1957	5	17		WATER WATER/HANDFUL OF SONGS This and above single credited to TOMMY STEELE AND THE STEELMEN Both featured in the 1957 film *The Tommy Steele Story*	Decca F 10923
30/08/1957	11	4		SHIRALEE Featured in the 1957 film *Shiralee*	Decca F 10896
22/11/1957	28	1		HEY YOU	Decca F 10941
07/03/1958	3	11		NAIROBI	Decca F 10991
25/04/1958	20	5		HAPPY GUITAR	Decca F 10976
18/07/1958	16	8		THE ONLY MAN ON THE ISLAND	Decca F 11041
14/11/1958	10	13		COME ON, LET'S GO	Decca F 11072
14/08/1959	16	5		TALLAHASSEE LASSIE	Decca F 11152
28/08/1959	28	2		GIVE GIVE GIVE	Decca F 11152
04/12/1959	6	17		LITTLE WHITE BULL Featured in the 1959 film *Tommy The Toreador*	Decca F 11177
23/06/1960	5	11		WHAT A MOUTH	Decca F 11245
29/12/1960	40	1		MUST BE SANTA	Decca F 11299
17/08/1961	30	5		WRITING ON THE WALL	Decca F 11372

STEELEYE SPAN UK folk-rock group formed in 1969 by ex-Fairport Convention Ashley Hutchings, Terry Woods, Gay Woods, Tim Hart and Maddy Prior. When they charted they were Tim Hart (born 9/1/1948, Lincoln, guitar/vocals), Maddy Prior (born 14/8/1947,

○ Silver disc ● Gold disc ✪ Platinum disc (additional platinum units are indicated by a figure following the symbol) ◉ Singles released prior to 1973 that are known to have sold over 1 million copies in the UK

Blackpool, vocals), Peter Knight (born 27/5/1947, London, vocals), Bob Johnson (born 17/3/1944, Enfield, London, guitar), Rick Kemp (born 15/11/1941, Little Hanford, Dorset, bass) and Nigel Pegrum (drums). Prior was made an MBE in the 2001 New Year's Honours list.

08/12/1973	14	9		GAUDETE	Chrysalis CHS 2007
15/11/1975	5	9	◯	**ALL AROUND MY HAT**	Chrysalis CHS 2078

STEELY DAN
US pop group formed in Los Angeles, CA by Donald Fagen (born 10/1/1948, Passiac, NJ, vocals/keyboards), Walter Becker (born 20/2/1950, Queens, NYC, bass), Jeff 'Skunk' Baxter (born 13/12/1948, guitar), Jim Hodder (born 17/12/1947, Boston, MA, drums), David Palmer (vocals) and Denny Dias (guitar). Baxter later joined the Doobie Brothers, briefly replaced by Michael McDonald, who also went on to join the Doobie Brothers. Fagen and Becker, the nucleus of the group, parted company in 1981 but reunited in 1990. Hodder drowned on 5/6/1990. They took their name from the William Burroughs novel *The Naked Lunch,* Steely Dan being a steam-powered dildo. They have three Grammy Awards: Album of the Year and Best Pop Vocal Album for *Two Against Nature* and Best Pop Performance by a Duo or Group with Vocal for *Cousin Dupree* all in 2000. Additionally, their *Two Against Nature* album won the Best Engineered album award the same year. The group was inducted into the Rock & Roll Hall of Fame in 2001.

30/08/1975	39	4		DO IT AGAIN Featured in the films *F.M.* (1978), *Air America* (1990) and *Flipper* (1996)	ABC 4075
11/12/1976	17	9		HAITIAN DIVORCE	ABC 4152
29/07/1978	49	5		FM (NO STATIC AT ALL) Featured in the 1978 film *F.M.*	MCA 374
10/03/1979	58	3		RIKKI DON'T LOSE THAT NUMBER	ABC 4241

GWEN STEFANI
US singer (born 3/10/1969, Anaheim, CA), lead vocalist with No Doubt, who went solo in 2004.

25/08/2001	4	12		**LET ME BLOW YA MIND** EVE FEATURING GWEN STEFANI 2001 Grammy Award for Best Rap/Sung Performance	Interscope 4976052
27/11/2004	4	5+		**WHAT YOU WAITING FOR**	Interscope 9864986

STEFY – see DJH FEATURING STEFY

JIM STEINMAN
US singer/producer (born 1/11/1947, NYC); he was first known as the musical arranger for National Lampoon. He then wrote the *Bat Out Of Hell* album for Meat Loaf, produced by Todd Rundgren. Steinman intended producing the follow-up album himself, but with Meat Loaf unavailable at the time ended up recording *Bad For Good* as well. He also produced hit albums for Bonnie Tyler and Barry Manilow and eventually resumed his relationship with Meat Loaf on *Dead Ringer* and *Bat Out Of Hell 2*.

04/07/1981	52	7		ROCK 'N' ROLL DREAMS COME THROUGH JIM STEINMAN, VOCALS BY RORY DODD	Epic EPC A 1236
23/06/1984	67	2		TONIGHT IS WHAT IT MEANS TO BE YOUNG JIM STEINMAN AND FIRE INC	MCA 889

STEINSKI AND MASS MEDIA
US production group formed by Steve Stein, who previously recorded with Douglas DiFranco as Double Dee & Steinski.

31/01/1987	63	2		WE'LL BE RIGHT BACK	Fourth & Broadway BRW 59

MIKE STEIPHENSON – see BURUNDI STEIPHENSON BLACK

STELLA BROWNE
UK production duo Danny Harrison and Julian Jonah (Danny Matlock) with singer Yvonne John Lewis. They also recorded as Congress, Nush, Nu-Birth, M Factor, Reflex, Gant and 187 Lockdown.

20/05/2000	55	1		EVERY WOMAN NEEDS LOVE	Perfecto PERF 06
09/02/2002	42	2		NEVER KNEW LOVE	Perfecto PERF 26CDS

STELLAR PROJECT FEATURING BRANDI EMMA
Italian production group formed by Steffano Sorrentino and Phunk Investigation with US singer Brandi Emma, who is also an actress, having appeared in *Night Stalker*.

14/08/2004	14	4		GET UP STAND UP	Data 74CDS

STELLASTARR*
US rock group formed in New York in 2000 by Shawn Christensen (guitar/vocals), Michael Jurin (guitar), Amanda Tannen (bass) and Arthur Kremer (drums).

31/05/2003	73	1		SOMEWHERE ACROSS FOREVER	Twenty-20 TWENTYCDS001
27/09/2003	61	1		JENNY	Twenty-20 TWENTYCDS002
20/03/2004	46	1		MY COCO	RCA 82876599082

DOREEN STEPHENS – see BILLY COTTON AND HIS BAND

RICHIE STEPHENS
Jamaican singer who also worked with Soul II Soul.

15/05/1993	64	2		LEGACY MAD COBRA FEATURING RICHIE STEPHENS	Columbia 6592852
09/08/1997	62	1		COME GIVE ME YOUR LOVE RICHIE STEPHENS AND GENERAL DEGREE	Delirious 74321450442

MARTIN STEPHENSON AND THE DAINTEES
UK singer/songwriter/guitarist (born 1965, Durham). He formed the Daintees in his teens, a line-up finally settling in 1985 with Anthony Dunn (bass/vocals), John Steel (keyboards) and Paul Smith (drums).

08/11/1986	70	2		BOAT TO BOLIVIA	Kitchenware SL 27
17/01/1987	58	3		TROUBLE TOWN	Kitchenware SK 13
27/06/1992	71	2		BIG SKY NEW LIGHT	Kitchenware SK 57

STEPPENWOLF
Canadian rock group formed in 1967 by John Kay (born Joachim Krauledat, 12/4/1944, Tilsit, Germany, guitar/vocals), Michael Monarch (born 5/7/1950, Los Angeles, CA, guitar), Rushton Moreve (born 1948, Los Angeles, bass), Goldy McJohn (born John Goadsby, 2/5/1945, organ) and Jerry Edmonton (born Jerry McCrohan, 24/10/1946, drums) as Sparrow. They recorded one single for Columbia before relocating to Los Angeles, CA, name-changing to Steppenwolf and signing with Dunhill. Record producer Gabriel Mekler suggested the name, from a novel by Herman Hesse. Moreve left after their debut album, replaced by John

❶⁹ Number of weeks single topped the UK chart ↑ Entered the UK chart at #1 ▲⁹ Number of weeks single topped the US chart

767

Russell Morgan. Monarch and Morgan left in 1969, replaced by Larry Byrom (born 27/12/1948) and Nick St Nicholas (born Klaus Karl Kassbaum, 28/9/1943, Hamburg, Germany). They disbanded in 1972, re-forming two years later. Moreve was killed in a car crash on 1/7/1981. Edmonton was killed in a car crash on 28/11/1993.

| 11/06/1969 | 30 | 9 | | BORN TO BE WILD Featured in the 1969 films *Easy Rider* (1969) and *American Motorcycle* | Stateside SS 8017 |
| 27/02/1999 | 18 | 5 | | BORN TO BE WILD Revived following use in an advertisement for Ford cars | MCA MCSTD 48104 |

STEPS
UK vocal group formed by Faye Tozer (born 14/11/1975), Lee Latchford-Evans (born 28/1/1975), Claire Richards (born 17/8/1977), Ian Watkins (aka H, born 8/5/1976) and Lisa Scott-Lee (born 5/11/1975). They also took part in the BRITS Trust *Thank Abba For The Music* project. The group received a Special Achievement Award for Best Selling Live Act at the 2000 BRIT Awards. They split in December 2001, Lisa Scott Lee announcing plans to manage her three brothers' group 3SL, Faye Tozer recording solo and Ian Watkins and Claire Richards forming H & Claire.

22/11/1997	14	17	○	5, 6, 7, 8.	Jive JIVECD 438
02/05/1998	6	14	○	LAST THING ON MY MIND	Jive 0518492
05/09/1998	2	11	○	ONE FOR SORROW Featured in the 2000 film *Drive Me Crazy*	Jive 0519092
21/11/1998	❶¹	30	✪	HEARTBEAT/TRAGEDY	Ebul/Jive 0519142
20/03/1999	2	17	●	BETTER BEST FORGOTTEN	Ebul/Jive 0519242
24/07/1999	2	12	○	LOVE'S GOT A HOLD ON MY HEART	Ebul/Jive 0519372
23/10/1999	5	11	○	AFTER THE LOVE HAS GONE	Ebul/Jive 0519462
25/12/1999	4	17	●	SAY YOU'LL BE MINE/BETTER THE DEVIL YOU KNOW	Ebul/Jive 9201008
15/04/2000	4	9		DEEPER SHADE OF BLUE	Ebul/Jive 9201022
15/07/2000	5	11		WHEN I SAID GOODBYE/SUMMER OF LOVE	Ebul/Jive 9201162
28/10/2000	❶¹	11		STOMP ↑	Ebul/Jive 9201212
13/01/2001	2	11		IT'S THE WAY YOU MAKE ME FEEL/TOO BUSY THINKING ABOUT MY BABY The single charted at #72 due to a small number of stores selling the single before it was officially released. Its jump to #2 therefore is the biggest rise in chart history	Ebul/Jive 9201232
16/06/2001	4	10		HERE AND NOW/YOU'LL BE SORRY	Ebul/Jive 9201372
06/10/2001	2	12	○	CHAIN REACTION/ONE FOR SORROW	Ebul/Jive 9201442
15/12/2001	5	11		WORDS ARE NOT ENOUGH/I KNOW HIM SO WELL	Ebul/Jive 9201452

STEREO MC'S
UK rap group formed in London by Rob Birch (born 11/6/1961, Nottingham), Nick 'The Head' Hallam (born 11/6/1960, Nottingham) and Owen 'If' Rossiter (born 20/3/1959, Newport), with singer Cath Coffey (born 1965, Kenya) joining them on tours. Named Best British Group at the 1994 BRIT Awards, their *Connected* album won the Best Album category the same year.

29/09/1990	74	1		ELEVATE MY MIND	Fourth & Broadway BRW 186
09/03/1991	46	3		LOST IN MUSIC	Fourth & Broadway BRW 198
26/09/1992	18	6		CONNECTED Contains a sample of Jimmy Bo Horne's *Let Me (Let Me Be Your Lover)*	Fourth & Broadway BRW 262
05/12/1992	12	12		STEP IT UP	Fourth & Broadway BRW 266
20/02/1993	19	5		GROUND LEVEL	Fourth & Broadway BRCD 268
29/05/1993	19	4		CREATION	Fourth & Broadway BRCD 276
26/05/2001	17	5		DEEP DOWN AND DIRTY	Island CID 777
01/09/2001	59	1		WE BELONG IN THIS WORLD TOGETHER	Island CID 782

STEREO NATION
UK vocal duo Tarsame Singh and DJ Kendall. Singh had previously recorded as Johnny Zee. Kendall later left and Taz (as Singh had become known) continued to record as Stereo Nation alone.

| 17/08/1996 | 53 | 1 | | I'VE BEEN WAITING | EMI Premier PRESCD 5 |
| 27/10/2001 | 44 | 2 | | LAILA TAZ AND STEREO NATION | Wizard WIZ 015 |

STEREOLAB
UK group formed in London in 1990 by Tim Gane (guitar), Letitia Sadier (vocals), Martin Kean (bass) and Joe Dilworth (drums), with Russell Yates (guitar) and Gina Morris (vocals) also on early live dates. They formed their own Duophonic Ultra High Frequency label (the name Stereolab was taken from an imprint of the US label Vanguard used as a hi-fi testing label). Mary Hansen (keyboards/vocals) joined in 1992, Andy Ramsay replacing Dilworth. Duncan Brown (bass) and Sean O'Hagan (guitar) joined in 1993.

08/01/1994	75	1		JENNY ONDIOLINE/FRENCH DISCO	Duophonic UHF DUHFCD 01
30/07/1994	45	2		PING PONG	Duophonic UHF DUHFCD 04
12/11/1994	70	1		WOW AND FLUTTER	Duophonic UHF DUHFCD 07
02/03/1996	62	1		CYBELE'S REVERIE	Duophonic UHF DUHFCD 10
13/09/1997	60	1		MISS MODULAR	Duophonic UHF DUHFCD 16

STEREOPHONICS
UK rock group formed in Aberdare, Wales in 1996 by Kelly Jones (born 3/6/1974, Aberdare, guitar/vocals), Richard Jones (born 23/5/1974, Aberdare, bass) and Stuart Cable (born 19/5/1970, Aberdare, drums) as Tragic Love Company, name-changing on signing with V2 in 1996. They were named Best British Newcomer at the 1998 BRIT Awards. Cable was sacked in September 2003 and temporarily replaced by ex-Black Crowes Steve Gorman. In December 2004 the group announced that Javier Weyler was to be his permanent replacement.

29/03/1997	51	1		LOCAL BOY IN THE PHOTOGRAPH	V2 SPHD 2
31/05/1997	33	2		MORE LIFE IN A TRAMP'S VEST	V2 SPHD 4
23/08/1997	22	3		A THOUSAND TREES	V2 VVR 5000443

DATE	POS	WKS	BPI	SINGLE TITLE	LABEL & NUMBER
08/11/1997	20	3		TRAFFIC	V2 VVR 5000948
21/02/1998	14	4		LOCAL BOY IN THE PHOTOGRAPH	V2 VVR 5001283
21/11/1998	3	12		**THE BARTENDER AND THE THIEF**	V2 VVR 5004653
06/03/1999	4	9		**JUST LOOKING**	V2 VVR 5005310
15/05/1999	4	9		**PICK A PART THAT'S NEW**	V2 VVR 5006778
04/09/1999	11	7		I WOULDN'T BELIEVE YOUR RADIO	V2 VVR 5008823
20/11/1999	11	8		HURRY UP AND WAIT	V2 VVR 5009323
18/03/2000	4	7		**MAMA TOLD ME NOT TO COME** TOM JONES AND STEREOPHONICS	Gut CXGUT 031
31/03/2001	5	12		**MR WRITER**	V2 VVR 5015938
23/06/2001	5	9		**HAVE A NICE DAY**	V2 VVR 5016248
06/10/2001	16	5		STEP ON MY OLD SIZE NINES	V2 VVR 5016253
15/12/2001	4	15	O	**HANDBAGS AND GLADRAGS**	V2 VVR 5017752
13/04/2002	23	2		**VEGAS TWO TIMES**	V2 VVR 5019173
31/05/2003	4	4		**MADAME HELGA**	V2 VVR 5021743
02/08/2003	3	8		**MAYBE TOMORROW**	V2 VVR 5021898
22/11/2003	16	4		SINCE I TOLD YOU IT'S OVER	V2 VVR 5022628
21/02/2004	5	5		**MOVIESTAR**	V2 VVR 5024658

STEREOPOL FEATURING NEVADA
UK dance group formed in Stockholm, Sweden by Eric Amarillo, Michael Feiner and vocalists Steve Lee, Gary Miller and Nevada Cato.

DATE	POS	WKS	BPI	SINGLE TITLE	LABEL & NUMBER
29/03/2003	36	2		DANCIN' TONIGHT	Rulin 28CDS

STERIOGRAM
New Zealand rock group formed by Tyson Kennedy (vocals), Brad Carter (guitar/vocals), Tim Youngson (guitar), Jake Adams (bass) and Jared Wrennall (drums).

DATE	POS	WKS	BPI	SINGLE TITLE	LABEL & NUMBER
20/11/2004	19	4		WALKIE TALKIE MAN	EMI CDEMS652

STETSASONIC
US rap group formed in Brooklyn, NYC by Glenn 'Daddy-O' Bolton, Arnold Hamilton, Paul Huston, Martin Nemley, Leonardo Roman and Marvin Wright. Hamilton and Huston later formed Gravediggaz.

DATE	POS	WKS	BPI	SINGLE TITLE	LABEL & NUMBER
24/09/1988	73	2		TALKIN' ALL THAT JAZZ Contains samples of Donald Byrd's *Dominoes* and Banbara's *Shack Up*.	Breakout USA 640
07/11/1998	54	1		TALKIN' ALL THAT JAZZ (REMIX)	Tommy Boy TBCD 7310A

STEVE AND EYDIE – see STEVE LAWRENCE AND EYDIE GORME

APRIL STEVENS – see NINO TEMPO AND APRIL STEVENS

CAT STEVENS
UK singer (born Steven Georgiou, 21/7/1947, London) who was discovered by ex-Springfields-turned-producer Mike Hurst in 1966. He signed to Deram (an imprint of Decca designed as a showcase for British talent) in July 1966 and switched to Island in 1970. He converted to the Islamic faith in 1977, taking the name Yusuf Islam.

DATE	POS	WKS	BPI	SINGLE TITLE	LABEL & NUMBER
20/10/1966	28	7		I LOVE MY DOG	Deram DM 102
12/01/1967	2	10		**MATTHEW AND SON**	Deram DM 110
30/03/1967	6	10		**I'M GONNA GET ME A GUN**	Deram DM 118
02/08/1967	20	8		A BAD NIGHT	Deram DM 140
20/12/1967	47	1		KITTY	Deram DM 156
27/06/1970	8	13		**LADY D'ARBANVILLE**	Island WIP 6086
28/08/1971	22	11		MOON SHADOW	Island WIP 6092
01/01/1972	9	13		**MORNING HAS BROKEN**	Island WIP 6121
09/12/1972	13	12		CAN'T KEEP IT IN	Island WIP 6152
24/08/1974	19	8		ANOTHER SATURDAY NIGHT	Island WIP 6206
02/07/1977	44	3		(REMEMBER THE DAYS OF THE) OLD SCHOOL YARD	Island WIP 6387
25/12/2004	2	1+		**FATHER AND SON** RONAN KEATING AND YUSUF ISLAM	Polydor 9869667

CONNIE STEVENS
US singer (born Concetta Ann Ingolia, 8/4/1938, Brooklyn, NYC). After four years in the TV series *Hawaiian Eye* films included *Young And Dangerous, Susan Slade* and *Love Is All There Is*. She has a star on the Hollywood Walk of Fame.

DATE	POS	WKS	BPI	SINGLE TITLE	LABEL & NUMBER
05/05/1960	27	8		KOOKIE KOOKIE (LEND ME YOUR COMB) EDWARD BYRNES AND CONNIE STEVENS Song originally featured in the TV series *77 Sunset Strip*	Warner Brothers WB 5
05/05/1960	9	12		**SIXTEEN REASONS**	Warner Brothers WB 3

RACHEL STEVENS
UK singer (born 9/4/1978). Previously a member of S Club 7, she went solo when they disbanded in 2003.

DATE	POS	WKS	BPI	SINGLE TITLE	LABEL & NUMBER
27/09/2003	2	10	O	**SWEET DREAMS MY LA EX**	Polydor 9811874
20/12/2003	26	4		FUNKY DORY Contains a sample of David Bowie's *Andy Warhol*	Polydor 9814984
24/07/2004	2	12		**SOME GIRLS** Single released to raise funds for Sport Relief	Polydor 9867433
16/10/2004	3	8		**MORE MORE MORE**	Polydor 9868325

RAY STEVENS
US singer (born Ray Ragsdale, 24/1/1939, Clarksdale, GA) who started as a DJ at fifteen and began making novelty records in the early 1960s.

DATE	POS	WKS	BPI	SINGLE TITLE	LABEL & NUMBER
16/05/1970	6	16		**EVERYTHING IS BEAUTIFUL** ▲2 1970 Grammy Award for Best Contemporary Vocal Performance	CBS 4953
13/03/1971	2	14		**BRIDGET THE MIDGET (THE QUEEN OF THE BLUES)**	CBS 7070
25/03/1972	33	4		TURN YOUR RADIO ON	CBS 7634
25/05/1974	❶1	12	O	**THE STREAK** ▲3	Janus 6146 201

❶9 Number of weeks single topped the UK chart ↑ Entered the UK chart at #1 ▲9 Number of weeks single topped the US chart

769

21/06/1975.....2......10.....O				**MISTY** 1975 Grammy Award for Best Arrangement Accompanying Singer .... Janus 6146 204
27/09/1975.....34......4.......				INDIAN LOVE CALL .... Janus 6146 205
05/03/1977.....31......4.......				IN THE MOOD .... Warner Brothers K 16875

RICKY STEVENS UK singer; he later recorded for Bronze.

14/12/1961.....34......7.......	I CRIED FOR YOU .... Columbia DB 4739

SHAKIN' STEVENS UK singer (born Michael Barratt, 4/3/1948, Ely, Wales); lead singer with the Backbeats before changing the group's (and his) name to Shakin' Stevens and the Sunsets at the end of the 1960s. They recorded unsuccessfully for a number of labels before disbanding in 1976. He then starred in the musical *Elvis* before going solo, recording similar-style music.

16/02/1980.....24......9......	HOT DOG .... Epic EPC 8090
16/08/1980.....19......10......	MARIE MARIE .... Epic EPC 8725
28/02/1981.....❶³......17.....●	**THIS OLE HOUSE** .... Epic EPC 9555
02/05/1981.....2......12.....●	**YOU DRIVE ME CRAZY** .... Epic A 1165
25/07/1981.....❶⁴......12.....●	**GREEN DOOR** .... Epic A 1354
10/10/1981.....10......9.....O	**IT'S RAINING** .... Epic A 1643
16/01/1982.....❶¹......10.....●	**OH JULIE** .... Epic EPC A 1742
24/04/1982.....6......6......	**SHIRLEY** .... Epic EPC A 2087
21/08/1982.....11......10......	GIVE ME YOUR HEART TONIGHT .... Epic EPC A 2656
16/10/1982.....10......8......	**I'LL BE SATISFIED** .... Epic EPC A 2846
11/12/1982.....2......7.....O	**THE SHAKIN' STEVENS EP** Tracks on EP: *Blue Christmas, Que Sera Sera, Josephine* and *Lawdy Miss Clawdy* .... Epic SHAKY 1
23/07/1983.....11......7......	IT'S LATE .... Epic A 3565
05/11/1983.....3......12.....O	**CRY JUST A LITTLE BIT** .... Epic A 3774
07/01/1984.....5......9......	**A ROCKIN' GOOD WAY** SHAKY AND BONNIE (Tyler) .... Epic A 4071
24/03/1984.....2......10.....O	**A LOVE WORTH WAITING FOR** .... Epic A 4291
15/09/1984.....10......8......	**A LETTER TO YOU** .... Epic A 4677
24/11/1984.....5......9.....O	**TEARDROPS** .... Epic A 4882
02/03/1985.....14......7......	BREAKING UP MY HEART .... Epic A 6072
12/10/1985.....11......9......	LIPSTICK POWDER AND PAINT .... Epic A 6610
07/12/1985.....❶²......8.....●	**MERRY CHRISTMAS EVERYONE** .... Epic A 6769
08/02/1986.....15......7......	TURNING AWAY .... Epic A 6819
01/11/1986.....14......10......	BECAUSE I LOVE YOU .... Epic SHAKY 2
20/12/1986.....58......3......	MERRY CHRISTMAS EVERYONE .... Epic A 6769
27/06/1987.....12......10......	A LITTLE BOOGIE WOOGIE (IN THE BACK OF MY MIND) .... Epic SHAKY 3
19/09/1987.....24......6......	COME SEE ABOUT ME .... Epic SHAKY 4
28/11/1987.....5......8......	**WHAT DO YOU WANT TO MAKE THOSE EYES AT ME FOR** .... Epic SHAKY 5
23/07/1988.....26......5......	FEEL THE NEED IN ME .... Epic SHAKY 6
15/10/1988.....47......4......	HOW MANY TEARS CAN YOU HIDE .... Epic SHAKY 7
10/12/1988.....23......6......	TRUE LOVE .... Epic SHAKY 8
18/02/1989.....58......2......	JEZEBEL .... Epic SHAKY 9
13/05/1989.....28......4......	LOVE ATTACK .... Epic SHAKY 10
24/02/1990.....18......6......	I MIGHT .... Epic SHAKY 11
12/05/1990.....60......2......	YES I DO .... Epic SHAKY 12
18/08/1990.....59......2......	PINK CHAMPAGNE .... Epic SHAKY 13
13/10/1990.....75......1......	MY CUTIE CUTIE .... Epic SHAKY 14
15/12/1990.....19......4......	THE BEST CHRISTMAS OF THEM ALL .... Epic SHAKY 15
07/12/1991.....34......5......	I'LL BE HOME THIS CHRISTMAS .... Epic 6576507
10/10/1992.....37......3......	RADIO SHAKY FEATURING ROGER TAYLOR .... Epic 6584367

STEVENSON'S ROCKET UK vocal/instrumental group formed in Coventry by Kevin Harris, Alan Twigg, Steve Bray, David Reid and Mike Croshaw.

29/11/1975.....37......5......	ALRIGHT BABY .... Magnet MAG 47

AL STEWART UK singer (born 5/9/1945, Glasgow). Single debut on Decca 1966, first album on CBS '67, moved to RCA '77.

29/01/1977.....31......6......	YEAR OF THE CAT .... RCA 2771

AMII STEWART US singer (born 1956, Washington DC); as an actress was in the Broadway musical *Bubbling Brown Sugar*. Turning to cabaret, she was on tour when she recorded her debut hit, a disco version of Eddie Floyd's classic. She later moved to Italy.

07/04/1979.....6......12......	**KNOCK ON WOOD** ▲¹ Featured in the 1998 film *The Last Days Of Disco* .... Atlantic/Hansa K 11214
16/06/1979.....5......11......	**LIGHT MY FIRE/137 DISCO HEAVEN (MEDLEY)** .... Atlantic/Hansa K 11278
03/11/1979.....58......3......	**JEALOUSY** .... Atlantic/Hansa K 11386

19/01/1980.....39.....4....... THE LETTER/PARADISE BIRD..Atlantic/Hansa K 11424
19/07/1980.....39.....5....... MY GUY – MY GIRL (MEDLEY) AMII STEWART AND JOHNNY BRISTOL ....Atlantic/Hansa K 11550
29/12/1984.....12.....11...... FRIENDS ....RCA 471
17/08/1985.....7.....12...... **KNOCK ON WOOD/LIGHT MY FIRE (REMIX)**..Sedition EDIT 3303
25/01/1986.....63.....3....... MY GUY – MY GIRL (MEDLEY) AMII STEWART AND DEON ESTUS ....Sedition EDIT 3310

ANDY STEWART
UK singer (born 20/12/1933, Scotland); best known as compere of TV's *White Heather Club*. Ill health plagued his career, and he later underwent a triple heart bypass. Awarded an MBE in 1976, he died from a heart attack on 11/10/1993.

15/12/1960.....37......1....... DONALD WHERE'S YOUR TROOSERS ....Top Rank JAR 427
12/01/1961.....19.....40...... A SCOTTISH SOLDIER ....Top Rank JAR 512
01/06/1961.....28.....13...... THE BATTLE'S O'ER This and above two singles credited to ANDY STEWART AND THE MICHAEL SAMMES SINGERS Top Rank JAR 565
12/08/1965.....43.....5....... DR FINLAY ....HMV POP 1454
09/12/1989.....4⁵.....8.....O **DONALD WHERE'S YOUR TROOSERS** Re-issue of Top Rank JAR 427 ....Stone SON 2353

BILLY STEWART
US R&B singer (born 24/3/1937, Washington DC). He sang with Marvin Gaye and Don Covay in the Rainbows in the 1950s. Discovered by Bo Diddley, he made his first recordings for Chess in 1956. He was killed in a car accident when his car plunged into the River Neuse in North Carolina on 17/1/1970 with three of his band also perishing: Rico Hightower, Norman Rich and William Cathey. The wheels on his week-old Ford Thunderbird had locked up; his family sued Ford Motors, who settled out of court.

08/09/1966.....39......2....... SUMMERTIME ....Chess CRS 8040

DAVE STEWART
UK keyboard player (born 30/12/1950, London) who was previously a member of Uriel, Khan, Egg and Hatfield & The North. The latter two groups also included Barbara Gaskin.

14/03/1981.....13.....10...... WHAT BECOMES OF THE BROKENHEARTED DAVE STEWART. GUEST VOCALS: COLIN BLUNSTONE................Stiff BROKEN 1
19/09/1981....❶⁴.....13.....● **IT'S MY PARTY** ....Stiff BROKEN 2
13/08/1983.....49.....4....... BUSY DOING NOTHING ....Broken 5
14/06/1986.....70.....3....... THE LOCOMOTION This and above two singles credited to DAVE STEWART WITH BARBARA GASKIN ....Broken 8

DAVID A STEWART
UK singer/guitarist (born 9/9/1952, Sunderland); he was a founder member of Catch in 1977, the group later becoming the Tourists. When they split in 1980 he and Annie Lennox formed the Eurythmics, having a string of hits until Lennox took a sabbatical in 1990. Stewart was involved in various outside projects, including the Spiritual Cowboys in 1990. He married former Bananarama's Siobhan Fahey in 1987, this ending in divorce. He directed the 2000 film *Honest*, which starred All Saints' Natalie and Melanie Appleton and Melanie Blatt. He has won the Best Producer category at the BRIT Awards on three occasions: 1986, 1987 and 1990. The Eurythmics received the Outstanding Contribution to British Music Award at the 1999 BRIT Awards and then re-formed.

24/02/1990.....6......12...... **LILY WAS HERE** DAVID A STEWART FEATURING CANDY DULFER Featured in the 1989 film *Lily Was Here* ....RCA ZB 43045
18/08/1990.....69.....2....... JACK TALKING DAVE STEWART AND THE SPIRITUAL COWBOYS ....RCA PB 43907
03/09/1994.....36.....5....... HEART OF STONE DAVE STEWART ....East West YZ 845CD
06/11/2004.....45.....2....... OLD HABITS DIE HARD MICK JAGGER AND DAVE STEWART Featured in the 2004 film *Alfie* ....Virgin VSCDX1887

JERMAINE STEWART
US R&B singer (born 7/9/1957, Columbus, OH; raised in Chicago, IL). A backing singer for Shalamar, the Temptations, Millie Jackson and Gladys Knight before signing solo with US Arista. He died from liver cancer on 17/3/1996.

09/08/1986.....2.....14.....O **WE DON'T HAVE TO…** ....10 TEN 96
01/11/1986.....50.....4....... JODY ....10 TEN 143
16/01/1988.....7.....12...... **SAY IT AGAIN** ....10 TEN 188
02/04/1988.....13.....9....... GET LUCKY ....Siren SRN 82
24/09/1988.....61.....3....... DON'T TALK DIRTY TO ME ....Siren SRN 86

JOHN STEWART
US singer/songwriter (born 5/9/1939, San Diego, CA); a member of The Kingston Trio before going solo.

30/06/1979.....43......6....... GOLD ....RSO 35

ROD STEWART
UK singer (born 10/1/1945, Highgate, London). He was an apprentice footballer with Brentford FC, quitting after three weeks to travel Europe busking, arriving back in the UK and joining the Five Dimensions in 1963. Discovered by Long John Baldry, he sang with his band before signing solo with Decca in 1964 (and dropped after one single). After the Soul Agents and Steampacket, he spent two years with the Jeff Beck Group, still recording the odd solo single, and failing an audition to join Manfred Mann replacing Paul Jones. He joined the Faces in 1969, signed a solo deal with Phonogram and charted two years later. He married actress Alana Hamilton in 1979, divorced in 1984. He married model Rachel Hunter in 1990 (which prompted the quote 'I found the girl I want, and it's all up to me now. I won't be putting my banana in anybody's fruit bowl from now on') although they later separated. Received the Outstanding Contribution Award at the 1993 BRIT Awards, and was inducted into the Rock & Roll Hall of Fame in 1994.

04/09/1971....❶⁵.....21...... **REASON TO BELIEVE/MAGGIE MAY** ▲⁵ *Reason To Believe* was two weeks into its chart run and had reach #19 when the single was flipped and *Maggie May* promoted as the lead track ....Mercury 6052 097
12/08/1972....❶¹.....12...... **YOU WEAR IT WELL** Featured in the 1978 film *The Stud* ....Mercury 6052 171
18/11/1972.....4......11...... **ANGEL/WHAT MADE MILWAUKEE FAMOUS (HAS MADE A LOSER OUT OF ME)** ....Mercury 6052 198
05/05/1973.....27.....6....... I'VE BEEN DRINKING JEFF BECK AND ROD STEWART ....RAK RR4
08/09/1973.....6.....9....... **OH NO NOT MY BABY** ....Mercury 6052 371
05/10/1974.....7.....7....... **FAREWELL – BRING IT ON HOME TO ME/YOU SEND ME**..Mercury 6167 033
07/12/1974.....12.....9....... YOU CAN MAKE ME DANCE SING OR ANYTHING (EVEN TAKE THE DOG FOR A WALK, MEND A FUSE, FOLD AWAY THE IRONING

❶⁹ Number of weeks single topped the UK chart ↑ Entered the UK chart at #1 ▲⁹ Number of weeks single topped the US chart

				BOARD, OR ANY OTHER DOMESTIC SHORTCOMINGS) **ROD STEWART AND THE FACES**	Warner Brothers K 16494
16/08/1975 ....❶⁴..11.....●				**SAILING**	Warner Brothers K 16600
15/11/1975 .....4......9.......				**THIS OLD HEART OF MINE**	Riva 1
05/06/1976 .....5......9.......				**TONIGHT'S THE NIGHT** ▲⁸ Features background whispering by then-girlfriend Britt Ekland. Featured in the 1985 film *The Sure Thing*	
					Riva 3
21/08/1976 .....2.....10......				**THE KILLING OF GEORGIE**	Riva 4
04/09/1976 .....3.....20......O				**SAILING** Re-released following its use as the theme to a TV documentary about HMS Ark Royal	Warner Brothers K 16600
20/11/1976....11......9.......				GET BACK Featured in the 1976 film *All This And World War II*	Riva 6
04/12/1976....31......7.......				MAGGIE MAY Re-issue of Mercury 6052 097	Mercury 6160 006
23/04/1977 ....❶⁴..13......O				**I DON'T WANT TO TALK ABOUT IT/FIRST CUT IS THE DEEPEST**	Riva 7
15/10/1977 .....3.....10......O				**YOU'RE IN MY HEART**	Riva 9
28/01/1978 .....5......8......O				**HOTLEGS/I WAS ONLY JOKING**	Riva 10
27/05/1978 .....4......6......				**OLE OLA (MULHER BRASILEIRA) ROD STEWART FEATURING THE SCOTTISH WORLD CUP FOOTBALL SQUAD**	Riva 15
18/11/1978 ....❶¹..13.....●				**DA YA THINK I'M SEXY?** ▲⁴	Riva 17
03/02/1979....11......8......O				AIN'T LOVE A BITCH	Riva 18
05/05/1979....63......3.......				BLONDES (HAVE MORE FUN)	Riva 19
31/05/1980....23......9.......				IF LOVING YOU IS WRONG (I DON'T WANT TO BE RIGHT)..	Riva 23
08/11/1980....17.....10......				PASSION	Riva 26
20/12/1980....32......7.......				MY GIRL	Riva 28
17/10/1981 .....8.....13......				**TONIGHT I'M YOURS (DON'T HURT ME)**	Riva 33
12/12/1981....11......9.......				YOUNG TURKS	Riva 34
27/02/1982....41......4.......				HOW LONG	Riva 35
04/06/1983 ....❶³..14......O				**BABY JANE**	Warner Brothers W 9608
27/08/1983 .....3......8.......				**WHAT AM I GONNA DO**	Warner Brothers W 9564
10/12/1983....23......9.......				SWEET SURRENDER	Warner Brothers W 9440
26/05/1984....27......7.......				INFATUATION Featured in the 1985 film *The Sure Thing*...	Warner Brothers W 9256
28/07/1984....15.....10......				SOME GUYS HAVE ALL THE LUCK...	Warner Brothers W 9204
24/05/1986....27......8.......				LOVE TOUCH Featured in the 1986 film *Legal Eagles*...	Warner Brothers W 8668
12/07/1986 .....2......9......O				**EVERY BEAT OF MY HEART**	Warner Brothers W 8625
20/09/1986....54......2.......				ANOTHER HEARTACHE	Warner Brothers W 8631
28/03/1987....41......3.......				SAILING Proceeds from this re-entry were in aid of the Zeebrugge Channel Ferry Disaster Fund after the *Herald Of Free Enterprise* sank soon after sailing from Zeebrugge on 6/3/1987 with the loss of more than 200 passengers	Warner Brothers K 16600
28/05/1988....21......6.......				LOST IN YOU..	Warner Brothers W 7927
13/08/1988....57......3.......				FOREVER YOUNG...	Warner Brothers W 7796
06/05/1989....49......4.......				MY HEART CAN'T TELL YOU NO	Warner Brothers W 7729
11/11/1989....51......3.......				THIS OLD HEART OF MINE **ROD STEWART FEATURING RONALD ISLEY**	Warner Brothers W 2686
13/01/1990....10.....12......				**DOWNTOWN TRAIN**	Warner Brothers W 2647
24/11/1990 .....5......8.......				**IT TAKES TWO ROD STEWART AND TINA TURNER**	Warner Brothers ROD 1
16/03/1991 .....3.....11......O				**RHYTHM OF MY HEART**	Warner Brothers W 0017
15/06/1991....10......8.......				**THE MOTOWN SONG ROD STEWART WITH BACKING VOCALS BY THE TEMPTATIONS**	Warner Brothers W 0030
07/09/1991....54......3.......				BROKEN ARROW	Warner Brothers W 0059
07/03/1992....49......3.......				PEOPLE GET READY	Epic 6577567
18/04/1992....41......4.......				YOUR SONG/BROKEN ARROW B-side is a re-issue of Warner Brothers W 0059	Warner Brothers W 0104
05/12/1992 .....6......9......O				**TOM TRAUBERT'S BLUES (WALTZING MATILDA)**	Warner Brothers W 0144
20/02/1993....11......6.......				RUBY TUESDAY...	Warner Brothers W 0158CD
17/04/1993....21......4.......				SHOTGUN WEDDING	Warner Brothers W 0171CD
26/06/1993 .....5......9.......				**HAVE I TOLD YOU LATELY**	Warner Brothers W 0185CD
21/08/1993....51......3.......				REASON TO BELIEVE...	Warner Brothers W 0198CD1
18/12/1993....45......4.......				PEOPLE GET READY	Warner Brothers W 0226CD1
15/01/1994 .....2.....13......O				**ALL FOR LOVE** ▲³ **BRYAN ADAMS, ROD STEWART AND STING** Featured in the 1993 film *The Three Musketeers*.....	A&M 5804772
20/05/1995....19......5.......				YOU'RE THE STAR...	Warner Brothers W 0296CD
19/08/1995....56......1.......				LADY LUCK	Warner Brothers W 0310CD1
15/06/1996....16......5.......				PURPLE HEATHER **ROD STEWART WITH THE SCOTTISH EURO '96 SQUAD** Official anthem of the Scottish 1996 European Championship football squad, in aid of the Dunblane Appeal (launched after Thomas Hamilton shot and killed 14 children, their teacher and himself on 13/3/1996 in Dunblane)	Warner Brothers W 0354CD
14/12/1996....58......1.......				IF WE FALL IN LOVE TONIGHT	Warner Brothers W 0380CD
01/11/1997 .....7......10......				**DO YA THINK I'M SEXY? N-TRANCE FEATURING ROD STEWART** Featured in the 1998 film *A Night At The Roxbury*	
					All Around The World CDGLOBE 150
30/05/1998....16......5.......				OOH LA LA	Warner Brothers W 0446CD
05/09/1998....55......1.......				ROCKS..	Warner Brothers W 0452CD1
17/04/1999....60......1.......				FAITH OF THE HEART Featured in the 1999 film *Patch Adams*	Universal UND 56235
24/03/2001....26......2.......				I CAN'T DENY IT	Atlantic AT 0096CD

STEX UK vocal/instrumental group formed by Steve White and Andrew Enamejewa.

19/01/1991....63......2.......	STILL FEEL THE RAIN	Some Bizzare SBZ 7002

STICKY FEATURING MS DYNAMITE UK producer Richard Forbes.

23/06/2001.....12......6.......	BOOO!	Ffrr FCD 399

STIFF LITTLE FINGERS
Irish rock group formed by Jake Burns (guitar/vocals), Henry Cluney (guitar), Ali McMordie (bass) and Brian Falloon (drums). They formed the Rigid Digits label for their debut release.

29/09/1979	44	4		STRAW DOGS	Chrysalis CHS 2368
16/02/1980	15	9		AT THE EDGE	Chrysalis CHS 2406
24/05/1980	36	5		NOBODY'S HERO/TIN SOLDIERS	Chrysalis CHS 2424
02/08/1980	49	4		BACK TO FRONT	Chrysalis CHS 2447
28/03/1981	47	6		JUST FADE AWAY	Chrysalis CHS 2510
30/05/1981	68	3		SILVER LINING	Chrysalis CHS 2517
23/01/1982	33	6		LISTEN EP Tracks on EP: *That's When Your Blood Pumps, Two Guitars Clash, Listen* and *Sad-Eyed People*	Chrysalis CHS 2580
18/09/1982	73	2		BITS OF KIDS	Chrysalis CHS 2637

CURTIS STIGERS
US singer (born 1968, Los Angeles, CA, raised in Boise ID); he formed the High Tops and moved to New York when they disbanded. He signed with Arista in 1991.

18/01/1992	5	10		**I WONDER WHY**	Arista 114716
28/03/1992	6	12		**YOU'RE ALL THAT MATTERS TO ME**	Arista 115273
11/07/1992	53	4		SLEEPING WITH THE LIGHTS ON	Arista 74321102307
17/10/1992	34	4		NEVER SAW A MIRACLE	Arista 74321117257
03/06/1995	28	3		THIS TIME	Arista 74321286962
02/12/1995	57	1		KEEP ME FROM THE COLD	Arista 74321319162

STILLS
Canadian rock group formed in Montreal in 2000 with Tim Fletcher (vocals), Greg Paquet (guitar), Oliver Crow (bass) and Dave Hamelin (drums).

06/09/2003	75	1		REMEMBERESE	679 Recordings 679L 026CD
28/02/2004	39	2		LOLA STARS AND STRIPES	679 Recordings 679L 036CD1
08/05/2004	51	1		CHANGES ARE NO GOOD	679 Recordings 679L 072CD2
28/08/2004	45	1		STILL IN LOVE SONG	679 Recordings 679L079CD2

STEPHEN STILLS
US singer (born 3/1/1945, Dallas, TX); he was a member of Buffalo Springfield and later formed Crosby Stills & Nash with David Crosby and Graham Nash. He also auditioned for the Monkees, being turned down because he had bad teeth.

13/03/1971	37	4		LOVE THE ONE YOU'RE WITH	Atlantic 2091 046
06/06/1998	16	4		HE GOT GAME **PUBLIC ENEMY FEATURING STEPHEN STILLS** Featured in the 1998 film *He Got Game*	Def Jam 5689852

STILTSKIN
UK group formed in Glasgow by Ray Wilson (born 1969, Edinburgh, vocals), James Finnigan (bass), Peter Lawlor (guitar) and Ross McFarlane (drums). Their debut single was chosen for a Levi Jeans advertisement, the first time a classic had not been used. Wilson later became lead singer with Genesis.

07/05/1994	❶1	13	O	**INSIDE** Track first appeared as an advertisement for Levi Jeans	White Water LEV 1CD
24/09/1994	34	2		FOOTSTEPS	White Water WWRD 2

STING
UK singer (born Gordon Sumner, 2/10/1951, Wallsend, Newcastle-upon-Tyne) who was in various local groups while teaching full time. He joined Police in 1977 as lead singer and bass player, emerging as chief songwriter. He began a parallel solo career in 1982 and after the Police disbanded in 1985 he formed a backing group, the Blue Turtles. He appeared in the films *Radio Man, Quadrophenia* and *Plenty*, among others. He was named Best British Male at the 1994 BRIT Awards, and received the Outstanding Contribution Award in 1985, as a member of Police. He then won a second Outstanding Contribution BRIT Award in 2002 as a solo artist. His album *Nothing Like The Sun* gained Best Album in 1988. He 'appeared' in an episode of *The Simpsons*, organising the charity record *We're Sending Our Love Down The Well*. Six Grammy Awards with The Police (five with the group, one as songwriter) have been followed by a further ten including Best Rock Instrumental Performance in 1983 for *Brimstone And Treacle,* Best Video Long Form and Best Pop Vocal Performance in 1986 for *Bring On The Night*, Best Rock Song in 1991 for *Soul Cages*, Best Music Video Long Form in 1993 for *Ten Summoner's Tales*, Best Pop Album and Best Pop Male Performance in 1999 for *Brand New Day,* and Best Pop Male Performance in 2000 for *She Walks This Earth (Soberana Rosa)*. He has a star on the Hollywood Walk of Fame and was made a CBE in the Queen's 2003 Birthday Honours List.

14/08/1982	16	8		SPREAD A LITTLE HAPPINESS Featured in the 1982 film *Brimstone And Treacle*	A&M AMS 8242
08/06/1985	26	7		IF YOU LOVE SOMEBODY SET THEM FREE	A&M AM 258
24/08/1985	41	5		LOVE IS THE SEVENTH WAVE	A&M AM 272
19/10/1985	49	3		FORTRESS AROUND YOUR HEART	A&M AM 286
07/12/1985	12	12		RUSSIANS	A&M AM 292
15/02/1986	44	4		MOON OVER BOURBON STREET	A&M AM 305
07/11/1987	41	4		WE'LL BE TOGETHER	A&M AM 410
20/02/1988	51	3		ENGLISHMAN IN NEW YORK Tribute to Quentin Crisp	A&M AM 431
09/04/1988	70	2		FRAGILE	A&M AM 439
11/08/1990	15	7		ENGLISHMAN IN NEW YORK (REMIX)	A&M AM 580
12/01/1991	22	4		ALL THIS TIME	A&M AM 713
09/03/1991	56	2		MAD ABOUT YOU	A&M AM 721
04/05/1991	57	1		THE SOUL CAGES	A&M AM 759
29/08/1992	30	5		IT'S PROBABLY ME **STING WITH ERIC CLAPTON** Featured in the 1992 film *Lethal Weapon 3*	A&M AM 883
13/02/1993	14	6		IF I EVER LOSE MY FAITH IN YOU 1993 Grammy Award for Best Male Pop Vocal Performance	A&M AMCD 0172
24/04/1993	25	4		SEVEN DAYS	A&M 5802232
19/06/1993	16	6		FIELDS OF GOLD	A&M 5803012
04/09/1993	57	1		SHAPE OF MY HEART	A&M 5803532
20/11/1993	21	4		DEMOLITION MAN Featured in the 1993 film of the same name	A&M 5804512

❶9 Number of weeks single topped the UK chart ↑ Entered the UK chart at #1 ▲9 Number of weeks single topped the US chart

	DATE	POS	WKS	BPI	SINGLE TITLE	LABEL & NUMBER
	15/01/1994	2	13	O	**ALL FOR LOVE** ▲³ **BRYAN ADAMS, ROD STEWART AND STING** Featured in the 1993 film *The Three Musketeers*	A&M 5804772
	26/02/1994	32	3		NOTHING 'BOUT ME	A&M 5805292
	29/10/1994	9	7		**WHEN WE DANCE**	A&M 5808612
	11/02/1995	15	6		THIS COWBOY SONG **STING FEATURING PATO BANTON** Featured in the 1995 film *Terminal Velocity*. Originally written for Jimmy Nail's *Crocodile Shoes* TV series but submitted too late for either the series or soundtrack album	A&M 5809652
	20/01/1996	36	2		SPIRITS IN THE MATERIAL WORLD **PATO BANTON WITH STING** Featured in the 1995 film *Ace Ventura: When Nature Calls*	MCA MCSTD 2113
	02/03/1996	15	4		LET YOUR SOUL BE YOUR PILOT	A&M 5813312
	11/05/1996	27	3		YOU STILL TOUCH ME	A&M 5815472
	22/06/1996	53	2		LIVE AT TFI FRIDAY EP	A&M 5817652
	14/09/1996	31	2		I WAS BROUGHT TO MY SENSES	A&M 5818912
	30/11/1996	54	1		I'M SO HAPPY I CAN'T STOP CRYING	A&M 5820312
	20/12/1997	17	6		ROXANNE '97 (REMIX) **STING AND THE POLICE** Puff Daddy remix, it contains a sample of the Real Roxanne's *Roxanne*	A&M 5824552
	25/09/1999	13	5		BRAND NEW DAY	A&M 4971522
	29/01/2000	15	6		DESERT SONG **STING FEATURING CHEB MAMI**	A&M 4972412
	22/04/2000	31	4		AFTER THE RAIN HAS FALLEN	A&M 4973262
	10/05/2003	2	10		**RISE & FALL** **CRAIG DAVID AND STING**	Wildstar CDWILD 45
	27/09/2003	30	2		SEND YOUR LOVE	A&M 9810103
	20/12/2003	60	1		WHENEVER I SAY YOUR NAME **STING AND MARY J. BLIGE** 2003 Grammy Award for Best Pop Collaboration with Vocals	A&M 9815304
	29/05/2004	66	1		STOLEN CAR (TAKE ME DANCING)	A&M 9862266

STINGERS – see B BUMBLE AND THE STINGERS

BYRON STINGILY US singer from Chicago, IL who was previously lead singer with Ten City.

	DATE	POS	WKS	BPI	SINGLE TITLE	LABEL & NUMBER
	25/01/1997	14	5		GET UP (EVERYBODY)	Manifesto FESCD 19
	01/11/1997	38	2		SING A SONG	Manifesto FESCD 35
	31/01/1998	13	4		YOU MAKE ME FEEL (MIGHTY REAL) Featured in the 1998 film *54*	Manifesto FESCD 38
	13/06/1998	48	1		TESTIFY	Manifesto FESCD 42
	12/02/2000	32	2		THAT'S THE WAY LOVE IS	Manifesto FESCD 66

STINX UK vocal duo Natalie James and Lesley I'Anson; the hit is from an anti-smoking advertisement for the Health Education Board of Scotland.

	DATE	POS	WKS	BPI	SINGLE TITLE	LABEL & NUMBER
	24/03/2001	49	3		WHY DO YOU KEEP ON RUNNING BOY	HEBS 1

STIX 'N' STONED UK instrumental/production duo Judge Jules (born Julius O'Riordan) and Jon Kelly.

	DATE	POS	WKS	BPI	SINGLE TITLE	LABEL & NUMBER
	20/07/1996	39	2		OUTRAGEOUS	Positiva CDTIV 52

CATHERINE STOCK UK singer.

	DATE	POS	WKS	BPI	SINGLE TITLE	LABEL & NUMBER
	18/10/1986	17	6		TO HAVE AND TO HOLD	Sierra FED 29

STOCK AITKEN WATERMAN UK songwriting/production trio formed by Mike Stock (born 3/12/1951), Matt Aitken (born 25/8/1956) and Pete Waterman (born 15/1/1947). Stock and Aitken had first linked in 1981 when Aitken was recruited for Stock's covers band Mirage. Three years later they disbanded Mirage to move into production, at the same time being introduced to Pete Waterman (who had enjoyed a hit as 14-18). The trio's first production #1 came in 1985 (Dead Or Alive's *You Spin Me Round*) and their first composition and production #1 in 1987 (Mel & Kim's *Respectable*). Aitken left in 1991. Stock left Waterman in 1993, resuming production with Aitken. Waterman later married Tight Fit's Denise Gyngell. Named Best Producers at the 1988 BRIT Awards.

	DATE	POS	WKS	BPI	SINGLE TITLE	LABEL & NUMBER
	25/07/1987	13	9		ROADBLOCK	Breakout USA 611
	24/10/1987	3	10	O	**MR SLEAZE** A-side credited to **BANANARAMA** – *Love In The First Degree*	London NANA 14
	12/12/1987	41	6		PACKJAMMED (WITH THE PARTY POSSE)	Breakout USA 620
	21/05/1988	64	2		ALL THE WAY	MCA GOAL 1
	03/12/1988	68	2		SS PAPARAZZI	PWL 22
	20/05/1989	❶³	7		**FERRY 'CROSS THE MERSEY** ↑ **CHRISTIANS, HOLLY JOHNSON, PAUL McCARTNEY, GERRY MARSDEN AND STOCK AITKEN WATERMAN** Charity record to aid relatives of the Hillsborough football disaster victims	PWL 41

RHET STOLLER UK guitarist (born Barry Stuart Stoller, London).

	DATE	POS	WKS	BPI	SINGLE TITLE	LABEL & NUMBER
	12/01/1961	26	8		CHARIOT	Decca F 11302

MORRIS STOLOFF US orchestra leader (born 1/8/1898, Philadelphia, PA) and musical director of Columbia Pictures from 1936. He went on to win three Academy Awards and has a star on the Hollywood Walk of Fame. He died on 16/4/1980.

	DATE	POS	WKS	BPI	SINGLE TITLE	LABEL & NUMBER
	01/06/1956	7	11		**MOONGLOW/THEME FROM PICNIC** ▲³ Featured in the 1956 film *Picnic*	Brunswick 05553

ANGIE STONE US singer (born Angie Williams, 30/1/1964, Columbia, SC), previously a member of Vertical Hold and Sequence.

	DATE	POS	WKS	BPI	SINGLE TITLE	LABEL & NUMBER
	15/04/2000	22	3		LIFE STORY	Arista 74321748492
	16/12/2000	57	1		KEEP YOUR WORRIES **GURU'S JAZZAMATAZZ FEATURING ANGIE STONE**	Virgin VUSCD 177
	09/03/2002	37	2		BROTHA PART II **ANGIE STONE FEATURING ALICIA KEYS AND EVE** Contains a sample of Albert King's *I'll Play The Blues For You*	J Records 74321922142
	27/07/2002	30	5		WISH I DIDN'T MISS YOU Contains a sample of The O'Jays' *Back Stabbers*	J Records 74321939182

27/12/2003	11	10		SIGNED SEALED DELIVERED I'M YOURS BLUE FEATURING STEVIE WONDER & ANGIE STONE	Innocent SINCD 54
14/08/2004	31	3		I WANNA THANK YOU ANGIE STONE FEATURING SNOOP DOGG Contains interpolations of *Come Into My Life* and *All This Love*. . . .	
				. . . .	J Records 82876624782

JOSS STONE UK soul singer Joscelyn Eve Stoker (born 11/4/1987, Dover) who won the BBC talent show *Star For A Night* at the age of fourteen. Her debut album was produced by soul legend Betty Everett. When her second album *Mind Body & Soul* topped the charts she became the youngest female to top the album charts.

07/02/2004	18	5		FELL IN LOVE WITH A BOY	Relentless RELCD3
22/05/2004	18	4		SUPER DUPER LOVE (ARE YOU DIGGIN ON ME) Featured in the 2004 film *Bridget Jones Diary 2: Edge of Reason* . . .	Relentless RELCD4
25/09/2004	9	8		YOU HAD ME	Relentless RELDX10
11/12/2004	29	3+		RIGHT TO BE WRONG	Relentless RELDX13

R & J STONE US/UK husband and wife duo Russell and Joanne Stone who met while in James Last's choir. Joanne died in 1979.

10/01/1976	5	9	O	WE DO IT	RCA 2616

STONE ROSES UK rock group formed in Manchester in 1984 by Ian Brown (born 20/2/1963, Manchester, vocals), John Squire (born 24/11/1962, Manchester, guitar), Andy Couzens (guitar/vocals), Pete Garner (bass) and Alan 'Reni' Wren (born 10/4/1964, Manchester, drums). They signed with Thin Line in 1985, later recording for FM Revolver before Silvertone in 1988. Garner left in 1987, replaced by Gary 'Mani' Mountfield (born 16/11/1962, Manchester). A move to Geffen Records was delayed by an injunction taken out by Silvertone, although Stone Roses eventually signed a deal worth a reported $4 million in 1992. Wren left in 1995, replaced by Robbie Maddix. They disbanded in 1996. Brown later recorded solo, while Squire formed The Seahorses (denying there was any significance in the name being an anagram of 'he hates roses').

29/07/1989	36	3		SHE BANGS THE DRUMS	Silvertone ORE 6
25/11/1989	8	14	O	WHAT THE WORLD IS WAITING FOR/FOOL'S GOLD	Silvertone ORE 13
06/01/1990	46	5		SALLY CINNAMON	Revolver REV 36
03/03/1990	8	6		ELEPHANT STONE	Silvertone ORE 1
17/03/1990	20	4		MADE OF STONE	Silvertone ORE 2
31/03/1990	34	3		SHE BANGS THE DRUMS	Silvertone ORE 6
14/07/1990	4	7		ONE LOVE	Silvertone ORE 17
15/09/1990	22	5		WHAT THE WORLD IS WAITING FOR/FOOL'S GOLD	Silvertone ORE 13
14/09/1991	20	3		I WANNA BE ADORED	Silvertone ORE 31
11/01/1992	27	4		WATERFALL	Silvertone ORE 35
11/04/1992	33	2		I AM THE RESURRECTION	Silvertone ORE 40
30/05/1992	73	1		FOOL'S GOLD Re-issue of Silvertone ORE 13	Silvertone ORET 13
03/12/1994	2	8		LOVE SPREADS	Geffen GFSTD 84
11/03/1995	11	3		TEN STOREY LOVE SONG	Geffen GFSTD 87
29/04/1995	25	3		FOOL'S GOLD Second re-issue of Silvertone ORE 13	Silvertone ORECD 71
11/11/1995	15	3		BEGGING YOU	Geffen GFSTD 22060
06/03/1999	25	3		FOOL'S GOLD (REMIX)	Jive Electro 0523092

STONE SOUR US group formed in Des Moines, IA in 1992 by Corey Taylor (vocals) and James Root (guitar). They disbanded when the pair joined Slipknot, revived in 2002 by Taylor, Root, Josh Rand (guitar), Sean Economaki (bass), Joel Ekman (drums) and DJ Sid Wilson.

15/03/2003	28	2		BOTHER	Roadrunner RR 20243
19/07/2003	63	1		INHALE	Roadrunner RR 20093

STONE TEMPLE PILOTS US rock group formed in San Diego, CA in 1987 by Scott Weiland (born 27/10/1967, Santa Cruz, CA, vocals), Robert DeLeo (born 2/2/1966, New Jersey, bass), Dean DeLeo (born 23/8/1961, New Jersey, guitar) and Eric Krez (born 7/6/1966, Santa Cruz, drums) as Mighty Joe Young. They name-changed to Shirley Temple's Pussy before settling on Stone Temple Pilots in 1990, signing to Atlantic in 1992.

27/03/1993	60	2		SEX TYPE THING	Atlantic A 5769CD
04/09/1993	23	4		PLUSH 1993 Grammy Award for Best Hard Rock Performance with Vocal	Atlantic A 7349CD
27/11/1993	55	2		SEX TYPE THING Re-issue of Atlantic A 5769CD	Atlantic A 7293CD
20/08/1994	48	2		VASOLINE	Atlantic A 5650CD
10/12/1994	53	1		INTERSTATE LOVE SONG	Atlantic A 7192CD

STONEBRIDGE Swedish DJ/producer Sten Hallstrom; he founded the StoneBridge, Stoney Boy Music, BTB, Clubvision and Monday Bar Experience labels.

13/03/2004	59	2		PUT EM HIGH	Hed Kandi HEDK12004
28/08/2004	6	10		PUT EM HIGH STONEBRIDGE FEATURING THERESE Re-issue of Hed Kandi HEDK12004	Hed Kandi HEDKCDS008

STONEBRIDGE McGUINNESS UK duo Lou Stonebridge (keyboards) and Tom McGuinness (born 2/12/1941, London). Both had previously been members of McGuinness Flint and later joined The Blues Band.

14/07/1979	54	2		OO-EEH BABY	RCA PB 5163

STONEFREE UK singer Tony Stone.

23/05/1987	73	1		CAN'T SAY 'BYE	Ensign ENY 607

STONEPROOF UK producer John Graham.

15/05/1999	68	1		EVERYTHING'S NOT YOU	VC Recordings VCRD 47

❶⁹ Number of weeks single topped the UK chart ↑ Entered the UK chart at #1 ▲⁹ Number of weeks single topped the US chart

775

STONKERS – see HAL AND PACE AND THE STONKERS

STOP THE VIOLENCE MOVEMENT US rap group with KRS-One, D-Nice, Kool Moe Dee, MC Lyte, Doug E Fresh, Heavy D, Chuck D and Glenn 'Daddy-O' Bolton.

18/02/1989.....75......1....... SELF DESTRUCTION..Jive BDPST 1

AXEL STORDAHL – see JUNE HUTTON

STORM UK group whose one hit was a reggae version of Diana Ross' hit.

17/11/1979.....36.....10...... IT'S MY HOUSE...Scope SC 10

STORM German production duo Jam El Mar (Rolf Ellmer) and DJ Mark Spoon (Markus Loeffel). They also recorded as Jam & Spoon and Tokyo Ghetto Pussy.

29/08/1998.....32......2...... STORM..Postiva CDTIV 94
12/08/2000.....3......10......○ **TIME TO BURN**...Data 16CDS
23/12/2000.....21......5...... STORM ANIMAL...Data 20CDS
26/05/2001.....32......2...... STORM (REMIX)...Postiva CDTIV 154

DANNY STORM UK singer (born Leicester); he formed The Strollers as his backing group.

12/04/1962.....42......4...... HONEST I DO...Piccadilly 7N 35025

REBECCA STORM UK singer/actress (born Ripley). She later appeared in the TV film *Tanya*.

13/07/1985.....22.....13...... THE SHOW (THEME FROM 'CONNIE') Theme to the TV series *Connie*......................Towerbell TVP 3

STORY OF THE YEAR US rock group formed in St Louis, MI in 1995 by Dan Marsala (vocals), Ryan Phillips (guitar), Philip Sneed (guitar), Adam Russell (bass) and Joshua Willis (drums) as Big Blue Monkey, changing their name to Story Of The Year when they relocated to California in 2002.

12/06/2004.....62......1...... UNTIL THE DAY I DIE..Maverick W 643CD

STORYVILLE JAZZ BAND – see BOB WALLIS AND HIS STORYVILLE JAZZ BAND

IZZY STRADLIN' US guitarist (born Jeffrey Isbell, 8/4/1962, Lafayette, IN) who was a founder member of Guns N' Roses in 1985, remaining with them until 1991. He then formed the Ju Ju Hounds with Rick Richards (guitar), Jimmy Ashhirst (bass) and Charlie Quintana (drums). After briefly standing in for his replacement in Guns N' Roses, Gilbey Clarke, when he broke his wrist in 1993, Stradlin' returned to the group on a more permanent basis in 1995.

26/09/1992.....45......2...... PRESSURE DROP...Geffen GFS 25

NICK STRAKER BAND UK group formed by keyboard player Nick Straker (born Nick Bailey), Tony Mansfield (guitar), Tony Hibbert (bass) and Phil Towner (bass). Mansfield, Hibbert and Towner were later members of New Musik while Straker recorded as PJQ.

02/08/1980.....20.....12...... A WALK IN THE PARK...CBS 8525
15/11/1980.....61......3....... LEAVING ON THE MIDNIGHT TRAIN..CBS 9088

PETER STRAKER AND THE HANDS OF DR. TELENY UK group fronted by Peter Straker (born Jamaica). Straker later made his name as an actor, appearing in *Doctor Who* as Commander Sharrel.

19/02/1972.....40......4....... THE SPIRIT IS WILLING..RCA 2163

STRANGE BEHAVIOUR – see JANE KENNAWAY AND STRANGE BEHAVIOUR

STRANGE FRUIT – see JIMMY NAIL

STRANGELOVE UK group formed in 1991 by Patrick Duff (vocals), Alex Lee (guitar/keyboards), Julian Pransky-Poole (guitar), Joe Allen (bass) and John Langley (drums).

20/04/1996.....53......1....... LIVING WITH THE HUMAN MACHINES...Food CDFOOD 70
15/06/1996.....35......2....... BEAUTIFUL ALONE..Food CDFOOD 81
19/10/1996.....47......1....... SWAY...Food CDFOOD 82
26/07/1997.....36......2....... THE GREATEST SHOW ON EARTH...Food CDFOOD 97
11/10/1997.....43......1....... FREAK..Food CDFOOD 105
21/02/1998.....46......1....... ANOTHER NIGHT IN...Food CDFOOD 110

○ Silver disc ● Gold disc ✪ Platinum disc (additional platinum units are indicated by a figure following the symbol) ◎ Singles released prior to 1973 that are known to have sold over 1 million copies in the UK

STRANGLERS

STRANGLERS UK punk-rock group formed in Surrey in 1974 by Hugh Cornwell (born 28/8/1949, London, guitar/vocals), Jet Black (born Brian Duffy, 26/8/1948, Ilford, drums) and Jean-Jacques Burnel (born 21/2/1952, London, vocals/bass), with Dave Greenfield (born 29/3/1949, Brighton, keyboards) joining the following year. Signed with United Artists in 1976, one of the first punk groups to link with a major company. They switched to Epic in 1982.

DATE	POS	WKS	BPI	SINGLE TITLE	LABEL & NUMBER
19/02/1977	44	4		(GET A) GRIP (ON YOURSELF)	United Artists UP 36211
21/05/1977	8	14	○	**PEACHES/GO BUDDY GO**	United Artists UP 36248
30/07/1977	9	8		**SOMETHING BETTER CHANGE/STRAIGHTEN OUT**	United Artists UP 36277
24/09/1977	8	9		**NO MORE HEROES**	United Artists UP 36300
04/02/1978	11	9		FIVE MINUTES	United Artists UP 36350
06/05/1978	18	8		NICE 'N' SLEAZY	United Artists UP 36379
12/08/1978	21	8		WALK ON BY	United Artists UP 36429
18/08/1979	14	9		DUCHESS	United Artists BP 308
20/10/1979	36	4		NUCLEAR DEVICE (THE WIZARD OF AUS)	United Artists BP 318
01/12/1979	41	3		DON'T BRING HARRY (EP) Tracks on EP: *Don't Bring Harry, Wired, Crabs (Live)* and *In The Shadows (Live)*	United Artists STR 1
22/03/1980	36	5		BEAR CAGE	United Artists BP 344
07/06/1980	39	4		WHO WANTS THE WORLD	United Artists BPX 355
31/01/1981	42	4		THROWN AWAY	Liberty BP 383
14/11/1981	42	3		LET ME INTRODUCE YOU TO THE FAMILY	Liberty BP 405
09/01/1982	2	12	●	**GOLDEN BROWN** Featured in the 2000 film *Snatch*	Liberty BP 407
24/04/1982	47	3		LA FOLIE	Liberty BP 410
24/07/1982	7	9		**STRANGE LITTLE GIRL**	Liberty BP 412
08/01/1983	9	6		**EUROPEAN FEMALE**	Epic EPC A 2893
26/02/1983	35	4		MIDNIGHT SUMMER DREAM	Epic EPC A 3167
06/08/1983	48	3		PARADISE	Epic A 3387
06/10/1984	15	7		SKIN DEEP	Epic A 4738
01/12/1984	37	7		NO MERCY	Epic A 4921
16/02/1985	48	4		LET ME DOWN EASY	Epic A 6045
23/08/1986	30	5		NICE IN NICE	Epic 6500557
18/10/1986	30	5		ALWAYS THE SUN	Epic SOLAR 1
13/12/1986	48	6		BIG IN AMERICA	Epic HUGE 1
07/03/1987	58	4		SHAKIN' LIKE A LEAF	Epic SHEIK 1
09/01/1988	7	7		**ALL DAY AND ALL OF THE NIGHT** Featured in the 1988 film *Permanent Record*	Epic VICE 1
28/01/1989	33	3		GRIP '89 (GET A) GRIP (ON YOURSELF) (REMIX)	EMI EM 84
17/02/1990	17	6		96 TEARS	Epic TEARS 1
21/04/1990	65	2		SWEET SMELL OF SUCCESS	Epic TEARS 2
05/01/1991	29	5		ALWAYS THE SUN (REMIX)	Epic 6564307
30/03/1991	68	2		GOLDEN BROWN (REMIX)	Epic 6567617
22/08/1992	46	2		HEAVEN OR HELL	Psycho WOK 2025
14/02/2004	31	2		BIG THING COMING	Liberty 5480692
24/04/2004	51	1		LONG BLACK VEIL	EMI 05489062

STRAW

STRAW UK rock group formed in Bristol, Avon by Mattie Bennett (guitar/vocals), Roger Power (vocals/bass), Duck (keyboards/ electronics) and Andy Dixon (drums).

DATE	POS	WKS	BPI	SINGLE TITLE	LABEL & NUMBER
06/02/1999	37	2		THE AEROPLANE SONG	WEA 196CD
24/04/1999	50	1		MOVING TO CALIFORNIA	WEA 205CD
03/03/2001	52	1		SAILING OFF THE EDGE OF THE WORLD	Columbia 6708452

STRAWBERRY SWITCHBLADE

STRAWBERRY SWITCHBLADE UK punk duo Rose McDowell (guitar/vocals) and Jill Bryson (guitar/vocals) who took their name from the title of an Orange Juice song. They disbanded in the late 1980s, Rose later recording as Candy Cane.

DATE	POS	WKS	BPI	SINGLE TITLE	LABEL & NUMBER
17/11/1984	5	17		**SINCE YESTERDAY**	Korova KOW 38
23/03/1985	59	5		LET HER GO	Korova KOW 39
21/09/1985	53	4		JOLENE	Korova KOW 42

STRAWBS

STRAWBS UK folk-rock group formed in 1967 by Dave Cousins (born 7/1/1945, guitar/banjo/piano) and Tony Hooper as the Strawberry Hill Boys, shortening the name to Strawbs in 1970. The group at this time featured Cousins, Hooper, Richard Hudson (born 9/5/1948, London, drums/guitar/sitar), John Ford (born 1/7/1948, London, bass) and Rick Wakeman (born 18/5/1949, London, keyboards). Wakeman left in 1971, replaced by Blue Weaver (born 11/3/1947, Cardiff, guitar/autoharp/piano). Hooper left soon after, replaced by Dave Lambert (born 8/3/1949, Hounslow). Sandy Denny (born 6/1/1947, London) was also briefly a member. Hudson and Ford recorded as a duo, while Wakeman recorded solo and was a member of Yes.

DATE	POS	WKS	BPI	SINGLE TITLE	LABEL & NUMBER
28/10/1972	12	13		LAY DOWN	A&M AMS 7035
27/01/1973	2	11		**PART OF THE UNION**	A&M AMS 7047
06/10/1973	34	3		SHINE ON SILVER SUN	A&M AMS 7082

● ⁹ Number of weeks single topped the UK chart ↑ Entered the UK chart at #1 ▲⁹ Number of weeks single topped the US chart

777

STRAY CATS
US rockabilly group formed in New York by Brian Setzer (born 10/4/1959, Long Island, NYC, guitar/vocals), Lee Rocker (born Leon Drucher, 1961, bass) and Slim Jim Phantom (born Jim McDonnell, 20/3/1961, drums). They moved to the UK in 1979 and signed with Arista the same year. They disbanded in 1984 and reunited 1986. Setzer and Phantom appeared in films: Setzer portrayed Eddie Cochran in *La Bamba* and Phantom appeared in *Bird*. Setzer later formed The Brian Setzer Orchestra. Slim Jim Phantom later joined Colonel Parker with Gilbey Clarke (ex-Guns N' Roses), Muddy Stardust (ex-L.A. Guns) and Teddy Andreadis (ex-Slash's Snakepit), the first contemporary act signed to actor Mel Gibson's Icon Records label.

29/11/1980	9	10	O	RUNAWAY BOYS	Arista SCAT 1
07/02/1981	9	8		ROCK THIS TOWN	Arista SCAT 2
25/04/1981	11	10		STRAY CAT STRUT	Arista SCAT 3
20/06/1981	34	6		THE RACE IS ON DAVE EDMUNDS AND THE STRAY CATS	Swansong SSK 19425
07/11/1981	57	3		YOU DON'T BELIEVE ME	Arista SCAT 4
06/08/1983	29	9		(SHE'S) SEXY AND 17	Arista SCAT 6
04/03/1989	64	3		BRING IT BACK AGAIN	EMI USA MT 62

STRAY MOB – see MC SKAT KAT AND THE STRAY MOB

STREETBAND
UK rock group formed in Luton by Paul Young (born 17/1/1956, Luton, vocals), Roger Kelly (guitar), John Gifford (guitar), Mick Pearl (bass) and Vince Chaulk (drums). After two albums Young, Gifford and Pearl formed Q-Tips, Young later going solo.

| 04/11/1978 | 18 | 6 | | TOAST/HOLD ON | Logo GO 325 |

STREETS
UK DJ Mike Skinner (born Birmingham, later moved to London). He also records as Grafiti.

20/10/2001	18	5		HAS IT COME TO THIS	679 Recordings 679L 001CD1
27/04/2002	30	3		LET'S PUSH THINGS FORWARD	Locked On/679 Recordings 679005CD
03/08/2002	27	3		WEAK BECOME HEROES	Locked On/679 Recordings 679007CD
02/11/2002	21	3		DON'T MUG YOURSELF	Locked On/679 Recordings 008CDX
08/05/2004	4	10		FIT BUT YOU KNOW IT Skinner later dedicated the single to Rachel Stevens. Featured in the 2004 film *The Football Factory*	Locked On/679 Recordings 679L071CD2
31/07/2004	❶¹	13		DRY YOUR EYES ↑	Locked On/679 Recordings 679L077CD1
09/10/2004	10	7		BLINDED BY THE LIGHTS	Locked On/679 Recordings 679L085CD
11/12/2004	30	3+		COULD WELL BE IN	Locked On/679 679L092CD

BARBRA STREISAND

US singer/actress (born Barbara Joan Streisand, 24/4/1942, Brooklyn, NYC); she began as an actress, appearing in the Broadway musical *I Can Get It For You Wholesale* in 1962. She made her film debut in *Funny Girl* in 1968 (for which she won the Oscar for Best Actress) and has since appeared in numerous films as well as undertaking production and directing. Her *Love Songs* album was named Best Album at the 1983 BRIT Awards. Eight Grammy Awards include Album of the Year and Best Female Solo Vocal Performance 1963 for *The Barbra Streisand Album*, Best Female Solo Vocal Performance 1964 for *People*, Best Female Solo Vocal Performance 1965 for *My Name Is Barbra*, and Best Female Pop Vocal Performance 1986 for *The Broadway Album*. She has therefore won an Oscar, an Emmy, a Grammy, a BRIT and a special 'Star of the Decade' Tony award, and has a star on the Hollywood Walk of Fame.

20/01/1966	14	13		SECOND HAND ROSE Song originally a US hit in 1922 for Fanny Brice, the subject of the film *Funny Girl*	CBS 202025
30/01/1971	27	11		STONEY END	CBS 5321
30/03/1974	31	6		THE WAY WE WERE ▲³ Featured in the 1973 film *The Way We Were*. 1973 Grammy Award for Song of the Year for writers Marvin Hamlisch, Marilyn Bergman and Alan Bergman and then went on to win an Oscar for Best Film Song	CBS 1915
09/04/1977	3	19	O	LOVE THEME FROM 'A STAR IS BORN' (EVERGREEN) ▲³ Featured in the 1976 film *A Star Is Born*. 1977 Grammy Award for Best Female Pop Vocal Performance. The song won the Grammy Award for Song of the Year the same year and then went on to win an Oscar for Best Film Song for writers Barbra Streisand and Paul Williams	CBS 4855
25/11/1978	5	12	●	YOU DON'T BRING ME FLOWERS ▲² BARBRA AND NEIL (Diamond)	CBS 6803
03/11/1979	3	13	O	NO MORE TEARS (ENOUGH IS ENOUGH) ▲² DONNA SUMMER AND BARBRA STREISAND The 7-inch version was available through Casablanca, the 12-inch on CBS	Casablanca CAN 174/CBS 8000
04/10/1980	❶³	16	●	WOMAN IN LOVE ▲³	CBS 8966
06/12/1980	34	10		GUILTY BARBRA STREISAND AND BARRY GIBB 1980 Grammy Award for Best Pop Vocal Performance by a Duo	CBS 9315
30/01/1982	66	3		COMIN' IN AND OUT OF YOUR LIFE	CBS A 1789
20/03/1982	34	6		MEMORY	CBS A 1903
05/11/1988	16	7		TILL I LOVED YOU (LOVE THEME FROM 'GOYA') BARBRA STREISAND AND DON JOHNSON Featured in 1988 film *Goya*	CBS BARB 2
07/03/1992	17	5		PLACES THAT BELONG TO YOU	Columbia 6577947
05/06/1993	30	3		WITH ONE LOOK	Columbia 6593422
15/01/1994	54	3		THE MUSIC OF THE NIGHT BARBRA STREISAND (DUET WITH MICHAEL CRAWFORD)	Columbia 6597382
30/04/1994	20	3		AS IF WE NEVER SAID GOODBYE (FROM SUNSET BOULEVARD)	Columbia 6603572
08/02/1997	10	7		I FINALLY FOUND SOMEONE BARBRA STREISAND AND BRYAN ADAMS Featured in the 1996 film *The Mirror Has Two Faces*	A&M 5820832
15/11/1997	3	15	●	TELL HIM BARBRA STREISAND AND CELINE DION	Epic 6653052
30/10/1999	26	3		IF YOU EVER LEAVE ME BARBRA STREISAND/VINCE GILL	Columbia 6681242

STRESS
UK group formed by Wayne Binite (guitar/vocals), Mitchell Amachi Ogugua (bass) and Ian Mussington (drums).

| 13/10/1990 | 74 | 1 | | BEAUTIFUL PEOPLE | Eternal YZ 495 |

STRETCH
UK group formed by Elmer Gantry, Gregory Kirby, Steve Emery, Tweek Lewis and Jeff Rich. Initial copies of their hit were wrongly labelled and appeared to feature the B-side on both sides.

08/11/1975 . . . . . 16 . . . . . . 9 . . . . WHY DID YOU DO IT Featured in the 1998 film *Lock Stock And Two Smoking Barrels* . . . . Anchor ANC 1021

STRETCH 'N' VERN PRESENT MADDOG
UK production/instrumental duo Julian Peake and Stuart 'Stretch' Collins. Peake is also a well known remixer and DJ, while Collins is co-owner of the Funk Essentials label.

14/09/1996 . . . . . 6 . . . . . . 9 . . . . I'M ALIVE Based on Earth Wind & Fire's *Boogie Wonderland* . . . . Ffrr FCD 284
09/08/1997 . . . . . 17 . . . . . . 5 . . . . GET UP! GO INSANE! Contains a sample of House Of Pain's *Jump Around* . . . . Ffrr FCD 304

STRICT INSTRUCTOR
Russian female singer.

24/10/1998 . . . . . 49 . . . . . . 1 . . . . STEP-TWO-THREE-FOUR . . . . All Around The World CDGLOBE 155

STRIKE
UK/Australian dance group formed by Matt Cantor and Andy Gardner and singer Victoria Newton.

24/12/1994 . . . . . 31 . . . . . . 5 . . . . U SURE DO . . . . Fresh FRSHD 19
01/04/1995 . . . . . 4 . . . . . . 9 . . . . U SURE DO . . . . Fresh FRSHD 19
23/09/1995 . . . . . 38 . . . . . . 1 . . . . THE MORNING AFTER (FREE AT LAST) . . . . Fresh FRSHD 37
29/06/1996 . . . . . 27 . . . . . . 2 . . . . INSPIRATION . . . . Fresh FRSHD 45
16/11/1996 . . . . . 35 . . . . . . 2 . . . . MY LOVE IS FOR REAL . . . . Fresh FRSHD 46
31/05/1997 . . . . . 17 . . . . . . 4 . . . . I HAVE PEACE . . . . Fresh FRSHD 58
25/09/1999 . . . . . 53 . . . . . . 1 . . . . U SURE DO (REMIX) . . . . Fresh FRSHD 78

STRIKERS
US funk group formed in New York City by Ruben Faison (vocals), Robert Gilliom (guitar), Robert Rodriguez (guitar), Howie Young (keyboards), Willie Slaughter (bass), Darryl Gibbs (saxophone) and Milton Brown (drums).

06/06/1981 . . . . . 45 . . . . . . 5 . . . . BODY MUSIC . . . . Epic A 1290

STRING-A-LONGS
US instrumental group with guitarists Keith McCormack, Aubrey Lee de Cordova, Richard Stephens and Jimmy Torres and drummer Don Allen.

23/02/1961 . . . . . 8 . . . . . . 16 . . . . . . WHEELS . . . . London HLU 9278

STRINGS OF LOVE
Italian vocal/instrumental group with Max and Frank Minoia and Corrado Rizza, also recording as Jam Machine.

03/03/1990 . . . . . 59 . . . . . . 2 . . . . NOTHING HAS BEEN PROVED . . . . Breakout USA 688

STROKES
US rock group formed in New York City in 1999 by Julian Casablancas (vocals), Nick Valensi (guitar), Albert Hammond (guitar), Nikolai Fraiture (bass) and Fabrizo Moretti (drums). They were named Best New International Act at the 2002 BRIT Awards.

07/07/2001 . . . . . 16 . . . . . . 5 . . . . HARD TO EXPLAIN/NEW YORK CITY COPS . . . . Rough Trade RTRADESCD 023
07/07/2001 . . . . . 68 . . . . . . 3 . . . . MODERN AGE . . . . Rough Trade RTRADESCD 010
17/11/2001 . . . . . 14 . . . . . . 5 . . . . LAST NITE . . . . Rough Trade RTRADESCD 041
05/10/2002 . . . . . 27 . . . . . . 2 . . . . SOMEDAY . . . . Rough Trade RTRADESCD 063
18/10/2003 . . . . . 7 . . . . . . 4 . . . . 12:15 . . . . Rough Trade RTRADESCD 140
21/02/2004 . . . . . 17 . . . . . . 5 . . . . REPTILLA . . . . Rough Trade RTRADESCD 155
13/11/2004 . . . . . 27 . . . . . . 2 . . . . THE END HAS NO END . . . . Rough Trade RTRADESCD 205

JOE STRUMMER
UK singer/guitarist (born John Mellors, 21/8/1952, Ankara, Turkey); a founder of The Clash in 1976 after being lured from the R&B group The 101ers. He went solo in 1988 after the demise of The Clash and later fronted The Pogues and then formed The Mescaleros with Scott Shields, Martin Slattery, Pablo Cook and Tymonn Dogg, with Roger Daltrey also guesting on their album *Global A Go Go*. He also appeared in the films *Straight To Hell* and *Mystery Train*. He died from a heart attack on 22/12/2002.

02/08/1986 . . . . . 69 . . . . . . 1 . . . . LOVE KILLS . . . . CBS A 7244
23/12/1995 . . . . . 12 . . . . . . 8 . . . . JUST THE ONE LEVELLERS, SPECIAL GUEST JOE STRUMMER . . . . China WOKCD 2076
29/06/1996 . . . . . 6 . . . . . . 4 . . . . ENGLAND'S IRIE BLACK GRAPE FEATURING JOE STRUMMER AND KEITH ALLEN . . . . Radioactive RAXTD 25
18/10/2003 . . . . . 33 . . . . . . 2 . . . . COMA GIRL JOE STRUMMER AND THE MESCALEROS . . . . Hellcat 11362
27/12/2003 . . . . . 46 . . . . . . 2 . . . . REDEMPTION SONG/ARMS ALOFT JOE STRUMMER AND THE MESCALEROS . . . . Hellcat 11482

STRYKER
– see MANCHESTER UNITED FC

STUART
Dutch DJ/producer with singer Lara McAllen.

05/04/2003 . . . . . 41 . . . . . . 2 . . . . FREE (LET IT BE) . . . . Product/Incentive PFT 07CDS

CHAD STUART AND JEREMY CLYDE
UK vocal duo Chad Stuart (born 10/12/1943) and Jeremy Clyde (born 22/3/1944). They first met at the London Central School of Speech and Drama in the early 1960s. They disbanded in 1967 but briefly re-formed in 1982. Clyde subsequently became an actor while Stuart wrote musicals.

28/11/1963 . . . . . 37 . . . . . . 7 . . . . YESTERDAY'S GONE . . . . Ember EMBS 180

STUDIO B/ROMEO AND HARRY BROOKS
UK production group formed by So Solid Crew's MC Romeo, Harry Brooks and JD (aka Dready); they adoped their name from the studio at Abbey Road where they recorded their debut hit.

06/12/2003 . . . . . 52 . . . . . . 1 . . . . I SEE GIRLS (CRAZY) STUDIO B/ROMEO AND HARRY BROOKS . . . . Multiply CDMULTY 109

STUDIO 45
German DJ/production duo Tilo Cielsa and Jens Brachvogel.

20/02/1999 . . . . . 36 . . . . . . 2 . . . . FREAK IT! Contains a sample of Aquarian Dream's *Phoenix* . . . . Azuli AZNYCD 090

---

❶⁹ Number of weeks single topped the UK chart ↑ Entered the UK chart at #1 ▲⁹ Number of weeks single topped the US chart

STUDIO 2 Jamaican singer Errol Jones.

27/06/1998	40	1		TRAVELLING MAN	Multiply CDMULTY 35

AMY STUDT UK singer/guitarist/pianist/songwriter (born 22/3/1986, London) who was discovered by Simon Fuller.

13/07/2002	14	6		JUST A LITTLE GIRL	Polydor 5708802
21/06/2003	6	10		**MISFIT**	Polydor 9800107
11/10/2003	10	6		**UNDER THE THUMB**	Polydor 9811793
24/01/2004	21	4		ALL I WANNA DO	19/Polydor 9815012

STUMP UK group formed by Mick Lynch (vocals), Chris Salmon (guitar), Kevin Hopper (bass) and Rob McKahey (drums).

| 13/08/1988 | 72 | 1 | | CHARLTON HESTON | Ensign ENY 614 |

STUNTMASTERZ UK production duo Steve Harris and Pete Cook.

| 03/03/2001 | 10 | 9 | | **THE LADYBOY IS MINE** Contains a sample of Chic's *Soup For One* | East West EW 226CD |

STUTZ BEARCATS AND THE DENIS KING ORCHESTRA UK vocal group with the Denis King Orchestra. King had previously fronted the London String Chorale on their hit *Galloping Home*.

| 24/04/1982 | 36 | 6 | | THE SONG THAT I SING (THEME FROM 'WE'LL MEET AGAIN') Theme to the TV series *We'll Meet Again* | Multi-Media Tapes MMT 6 |

STYLE COUNCIL UK group formed in 1983 by former Jam leader Paul Weller (born John Weller, 25/5/1958, Woking, guitar/vocals), ex-Merton Parkas keyboard player Mick Talbot (born 11/9/1958, London) and drummer Steve White (born 31/5/1965, London). The following year they added singer Dee C Lee (born Diane Sealey, 6/6/1961, London) as a full time member. Weller and Lee married in 1986. The Style Council disbanded in 1989, Weller going on to form the Paul Weller Movement and then record solo.

19/03/1983	4	8	○	**SPEAK LIKE A CHILD**	Polydor TSC 1
28/05/1983	11	7		MONEY GO ROUND (PART 1)	Polydor TSC 2
13/08/1983	3	9	○	**LONG HOT SUMMER/PARIS MATCH**	Polydor TSC 3
19/11/1983	11	8		SOLID BOND IN YOUR HEART	Polydor TSC 4
18/02/1984	5	7		**MY EVER CHANGING MOODS**	Polydor TSC 5
26/05/1984	5	8		**GROOVIN' (YOU'RE THE BEST THING)/BIG BOSS GROOVE**	Polydor TSC 6
13/10/1984	7	8		**SHOUT TO THE TOP** Featured in the 1985 film *Vision Quest*	Polydor TSC 7
11/05/1985	6	7		**WALLS COME TUMBLING DOWN!**	Polydor TSC 8
06/07/1985	23	5		COME TO MILTON KEYNES	Polydor TSC 9
28/09/1985	13	6		THE LODGERS	Polydor TSC 10
05/04/1986	14	6		HAVE YOU EVER HAD IT BLUE Featured in the 1986 film *Absolute Beginners*	Polydor CINE 1
17/01/1987	9	5		**IT DIDN'T MATTER**	Polydor TSC 12
14/03/1987	52	3		WAITING	Polydor TSC 13
31/10/1987	20	4		WANTED	Polydor TSC 14
28/05/1988	28	3		LIFE AT A TOP PEOPLE'S HEALTH FARM	Polydor TSC 15
23/07/1988	41	2		HOW SHE THREW IT ALL AWAY (EP) Tracks on EP: *How She Threw It All Away, Love The First Time, Long Hot Summer* and *I Do Like To B-Side The A-Side*	Polydor TSC 16
18/02/1989	27	5		PROMISED LAND	Polydor TSC 17
27/05/1989	48	2		LONG HOT SUMMER 89 (REMIX)	Polydor LHS 1

STYLES AND PHAROAHE MONCH US rap duo David Styles (ex-LOX – Living Off Experience) and Pharoahe Monch.

| 14/09/2002 | 50 | 1 | | THE LIFE | MCA MCSTD 40292 |

DARREN STYLES/MARK BREEZE UK production duo who also record as Infextious.

| 05/04/2003 | 59 | 1 | | LET ME FLY | Nukleuz 0432 CNUK |
| 31/07/2004 | 19 | 4 | | YOU'RE SHINING | All Around The World CDGLOBE 346 |

STYLISTICS US R&B vocal group formed in Philadelphia, PA in 1968 by the members of two groups, the Percussions and the Monarchs. They comprised Herb Murrell (born 27/4/1949, Lane, SC), James Dunn (born 4/2/1950, Philadelphia), Russell Thompkins Jr (born 21/3/1951, Philadelphia), Airrion Love (born 8/8/1949, Philadelphia) and James Smith (born 16/6/1950, New York). After local success with Sebring Records they were signed by Avco, teamed initially with writer/producer Thom Bell and later Van McCoy. Dunn left with ill-health in 1978. They switched to Philadelphia International in 1980. When Smith later left they continued as a trio.

24/06/1972	13	12		BETCHA BY GOLLY WOW	Avco 6105 011
04/11/1972	9	10		**I'M STONE IN LOVE WITH YOU**	Avco 6105 015
17/03/1973	34	5		BREAK UP TO MAKE UP	Avco 6105 020
30/06/1973	35	6		PEEK-A-BOO	Avco 6105 023
19/01/1974	6	9		ROCKIN' ROLL BABY	Avco 6105 026
13/07/1974	2	14	○	**YOU MAKE ME FEEL BRAND NEW**	Avco 6105 028
19/10/1974	9	9		LET'S PUT IT ALL TOGETHER	Avco 6105 032
25/01/1975	12	8		STAR ON A TV SHOW	Avco 6105 035
10/05/1975	3	10	○	**SING BABY SING**	Avco 6105 036
26/07/1975	❶³	11	●	**CAN'T GIVE YOU ANYTHING (BUT MY LOVE)**	Avco 6105 039
15/11/1975	5	10	○	**NA NA IS THE SADDEST WORD**	Avco 6105 041
14/02/1976	10	7		**FUNKY WEEKEND**	Avco 6105 044
24/04/1976	4	7		**CAN'T HELP FALLING IN LOVE**	Avco 6105 050

07/08/1976 . . . . . 7 . . . . . 9 . . . . **16 BARS** . . . . H&L 6105 059

27/11/1976 . . . . .24 . . . . . 9 . . . . YOU'LL NEVER GET TO HEAVEN EP Tracks on EP: *You'll Never Get To Heaven*, *Country Living*, *You Are Beautiful* and *The Miracle*

. . . . H&L STYL 001

26/03/1977 . . . . .24 . . . . . . 7 . . . . 7000 DOLLARS AND YOU . . . . H&L 6105 073

STYLUS TROUBLE UK producer Pete Heller. He is also a member of Heller & Farley Project.

23/06/2001 . . . . .63 . . . . . . 1 . . . . SPUTNIK . . . . Junior London BRG 014

STYX US rock group formed in Chicago, IL in 1971 by Dennis De Young (born 18/2/1947, Chicago, keyboards/vocals), James Young (born 14/11/1948, Chicago, guitar/vocals), Chuck Panozzo (born 20/9/1947, Chicago, bass), his twin brother John (drums) and John Curulewski (guitar). Curulewski left in 1976, replaced by Tommy Shaw (born 11/9/1950, Montgomery, AL). They disbanded in 1984, and reunited in 1990. John Panozzo died from alcoholism on 16/7/1996.

05/01/1980 . . . . . 6 . . . . . .10 . . . . .O BABE ▲² Featured in the 1999 film *Big Daddy* . . . . A&M AMS 7489

24/01/1981 . . . . .42 . . . . . 5 . . . . THE BEST OF TIMES . . . . A&M AMS 8102

18/06/1983 . . . . .56 . . . . . 3 . . . . DON'T LET IT END . . . . A&M AM 120

SUB SUB UK dance group formed in Manchester in 1989 by Jimi Goodwin, Jezz Williams, Andy Williams and singer Melanie Williams. Sub Sub subsequently became The Doves.

10/04/1993 . . . . . 3 . . . . . .11 . . . . .O **AIN'T NO LOVE (AIN'T NO USE)** SUB SUB FEATURING MELANIE WILLIAMS . . . . Rob's CDROB 9

19/02/1994 . . . . .49 . . . . . 1 . . . . RESPECT Contains a sample of The Fatback Band's *Double Dutch* . . . . Rob's CDROB 19

SUBCIRCUS UK/Danish group with Peter Bradley Jr (vocals), Nikolaj Bloch (guitar), George 'Funky' Brown (bass) and Tommy Arnby (drums).

26/04/1997 . . . . .61 . . . . . 1 . . . . YOU LOVE YOU . . . . Echo ECSCD 34

12/07/1997 . . . . .56 . . . . . 1 . . . . 86'D . . . . Echo ECSCX 43

SUBLIME US ska group formed in San Francisco, CA by Brad Nowell (guitar/vocals), Eric Wilson (bass) and Bud Gaugh (drums). Nowell died from a drugs overdose on 25/5/1996.

05/07/1997 . . . . .71 . . . . . 1 . . . . WHAT I GOT . . . . Gasoline Alley MCSTD 48045

SUBLIMINAL CUTS Dutch producer Patrick Prinz. He also records as Artemesia, Ethics and Movin' Melodies.

15/10/1994 . . . . .69 . . . . . 1 . . . . LE VOIE LE SOLEIL . . . . XL Recordings XLS 53CD

20/07/1996 . . . . .23 . . . . . 2 . . . . LE VOIE LE SOLEIL (REMIX) . . . . XL Recordings XLSR 53CD

SUBMERGE FEATURING JAN JOHNSTON US instrumentalist/producer with singer Jan Johnston.

08/02/1997 . . . . .28 . . . . . 2 . . . . TAKE ME BY THE HAND . . . . AM:PM 5821012

SUBSONIC 2 UK rap duo Robin Morley and Donald Brown.

13/07/1991 . . . . .63 . . . . . 3 . . . . THE UNSUNG HEROES OF HIP HOP . . . . Unity 6577947

SUBTERRANIA FEATURING ANN CONSUELO Swedish vocal/instrumental duo Nick Nice and Ann Consuelo.

05/06/1993 . . . . .68 . . . . . 1 . . . . DO IT FOR LOVE . . . . Champion CHAMPCD 297

SUEDE UK rock group formed in London in 1990 by Brett Anderson (born 27/9/1967, Haywards Heath, vocals), Mat Osman (born 9/10/1967, Haywards Heath) and Bernard Butler (born 1/5/1970, guitar). They signed with RMI the same year but left the label without any releases. They added drummer Simon Gilbert (born 23/5/1965, Stratford-on-Avon), signed with Nude Records in 1992 and later added Neil Codling on keyboards. Butler left in 1994, replaced by Richard Oakes (born 10/10/1976). In April 1992 they appeared on the cover of *Melody Maker*, even though they hadn't released any records.

23/05/1992 . . . . .49 . . . . . 2 . . . . THE DROWNERS/TO THE BIRDS . . . . Nude NUD 1CD

26/09/1992 . . . . .17 . . . . . 3 . . . . METAL MICKEY . . . . Nude NUD 3CD

06/03/1993 . . . . . 7 . . . . . . 7 . . . . **ANIMAL NITRATE** . . . . Nude NUD 4CD

29/05/1993 . . . . .22 . . . . . 3 . . . . SO YOUNG . . . . Nude NUD 5CD

26/02/1994 . . . . . 3 . . . . . . 6 . . . . **STAY TOGETHER** . . . . Nude NUD 9CD

24/09/1994 . . . . .18 . . . . . 3 . . . . WE ARE THE PIGS . . . . Nude NUD 10CD

19/11/1994 . . . . .18 . . . . . 4 . . . . THE WILD ONES . . . . Nude NUD 11CD1

11/02/1995 . . . . .21 . . . . . 4 . . . . NEW GENERATION . . . . Nude NUD 12CD2

10/08/1996 . . . . . 3 . . . . . . 6 . . . . **TRASH** . . . . Nude NUD 21CD1

26/10/1996 . . . . . 8 . . . . . . 5 . . . . **BEAUTIFUL ONES** . . . . Nude NUD 23CD1

25/01/1997 . . . . . 6 . . . . . . 4 . . . . **SATURDAY NIGHT** . . . . Nude NUD 24CD1

19/04/1997 . . . . . 9 . . . . . . 3 . . . . **LAZY** . . . . Nude NUD 27CD

23/08/1997 . . . . . 9 . . . . . . 4 . . . . **FILMSTAR** . . . . Nude NUD 30CD1

24/04/1999 . . . . . 5 . . . . . . 5 . . . . **ELECTRICITY** . . . . Nude NUD 43CD1

03/07/1999 . . . . .13 . . . . . 5 . . . . SHE'S IN FASHION . . . . Nude NUD 44CD1

18/09/1999 . . . . .24 . . . . . 2 . . . . EVERYTHING WILL FLOW . . . . Nude NUD 45CD1

20/11/1999 . . . . .23 . . . . . 2 . . . . CAN'T GET ENOUGH . . . . Nude NUD 47CD1

28/09/2002 . . . . .16 . . . . . 2 . . . . POSITIVITY . . . . Epic 6729495

30/11/2002 . . . . .29 . . . . . 2 . . . . OBSESSIONS . . . . Epic 6732942

18/10/2003 . . . . .14 . . . . . 3 . . . . ATTITUDE/GOLDEN GUN . . . . Sony Music 6743585

❶⁹ Number of weeks single topped the UK chart ↑ Entered the UK chart at #1 ▲⁹ Number of weeks single topped the US chart

781

SUENO LATINO
Italian production duo Massimo Lippoli and Angelino Albanese with singer Carolina Damas.

23/09/2000	47	5	SUENO LATINO	BCM 323
11/11/2000	68	1	SUENO LATINO (REMIX)	Distinctive DISNCD 64

SUGABABES
UK group formed by Keisha Buchanan (born 30/9/1985, London), Mutya Buena (born 21/5/1985, London) and Siobhan Donaghy (born 19/6/1984, London). Donaghy left in August 2001 to go solo and was replaced by Heidi Range (born 23/5/1984), who had been a founding member of Atomic Kitten. Sugababes were named Best British Dance Act at the 2003 BRIT Awards.

23/09/2000	6	8	**OVERLOAD**	London LONCD 449
30/12/2000	12	9	NEW YEAR	London LONCD 455
21/04/2001	13	7	RUN FOR COVER	London LONCD 459
28/07/2001	30	2	SOUL SOUND	London LONCD 460
04/05/2002	❶¹	14	○ **FREAK LIKE ME** ↑ Contains an interpolation of Gary Numan's *Are Friends Electric*. The single had originally been put together as a bootleg by mixing Adina Howard's *Freak Like Me* with Gary Numan's *Are Friends Electric* and circulated on white label as *We Don't Give A Damn About Are Friends* by Girls On Top (in reality Richard X under an assumed name). Adina Howard refused permission for her vocals to be used on a legitimate version, hence the re-recording by Sugababes	Island CID 798
24/08/2002	❶¹	13	○ **ROUND ROUND** ↑ Contains a sample of Dublex Inc's *Tangoforte*. Featured in the 2003 film *American Wedding*	Island CIDX 804
23/11/2002	7	13	**STRONGER/ANGELS WITH DIRTY FACES**	Island CIDX 813
22/03/2003	11	9	SHAPE Contains a sample of Sting's *Shape Of My Heart*	Island CIDX 817
25/10/2003	❶¹	13	**HOLE IN THE HEAD** ↑	Island CIDX 836
27/12/2003	10	13	**TOO LOST IN YOU** Featured in the 2003 film *Love Actually*	Island CID 844
03/04/2004	8	8	**IN THE MIDDLE** Contains a sample of Moguai's *U Know Y*	Island MCSXD 40360
04/09/2004	8	7	**CAUGHT IN A MOMENT**	Universal MCSXD 40371

SUGACOMA
UK rock group formed in Romford by Jess Mayers (vocals), Claire Simson (guitar), Heidi McEwen (bass) and James Cuthbert (drums).

13/04/2002	57	1	YOU DRIVE ME CRAZY/WINGDINGS	Music For Nations CDKUT 190

SUGAR
US rock group formed in 1991 by ex-Husker Du singer/writer Bob Mould (born 16/10/1960, Malone, NY, guitar/vocals), David Barbe (born 30/9/1963, Atlanta, GA, bass) and Malcolm Travis (born 15/2/1953, Niskayuna, NY, drums). They split in 1995.

31/10/1992	65	1	A GOOD IDEA	Creation CRE 143
30/01/1993	30	2	IF I CAN'T CHANGE YOUR MIND	Creation CRESCD 149
21/08/1993	48	1	TILTED	Creation CRECD 156
03/09/1994	40	2	YOUR FAVOURITE THING	Creation CRESCD 186
29/10/1994	73	1	BELIEVE WHAT YOU'RE SAYING	Creation CRESCD 193

SUGAR CANE
US studio group assembled by producer Pete Bellotte.

30/09/1978	54	5	MONTEGO BAY	Ariola Hansa AHA 524

SUGAR RAY
US group formed in Orange County in 1995 by Mark Sayers McGrath (vocals), Rodney Sheppard (guitar), Murphy Karges (bass), Craig 'DJ Homocide' Bullock (born 17/12/1970, DJ) and Stan Frazier (born 23/4/1968, drums). They appeared in the 1997 film *Fathers' Day* with Billy Crystal and Robin Williams.

31/01/1998	58	1	FLY	Atlantic AT 0008CD
29/05/1999	10	9	**EVERY MORNING**	Lava AT 0065CD
20/10/2001	32	2	WHEN IT'S OVER Featured in the 2002 film *The Sweetest Thing*	Atlantic 020114CD

SUGARCUBES
Icelandic rock group formed in Reykjavik in 1986 by Bjork Gundmundsdottir (born 21/11/1965, Reykjavik, vocals/keyboards), Bragi Olaffson (born 11/8/1962, bass), Einar Orn Benediktsson (born 29/10/1962, Copenhagen, Denmark, vocals/trumpet), Margret Ornolfsdottir (born 21/11/1967, Reykjavik, keyboards), Sigtryggur Balduresson (born 2/10/1962, Stavanger, Norway, drums) and Thor Eldon (born 2/6/1962, Reykjavik, guitar). Bjork went solo in 1992.

14/11/1987	65	3	BIRTHDAY	One Little Indian 7TP 7
30/01/1988	56	4	COLD SWEAT	One Little Indian 7TP 9
16/04/1988	51	3	DEUS	One Little Indian 7TP 10
03/09/1988	65	3	BIRTHDAY Re-recording	One Little Indian 7TP 11
16/09/1989	55	2	REGINA	One Little Indian 26 TP7
11/01/1992	17	6	HIT	One Little Indian 62 TP7
03/10/1992	64	1	BIRTHDAY (REMIX)	One Little Indian 104 TP12

SUGARHILL GANG
US rap group formed in Harlem in 1979 by Michael 'Wonder Mike' Wright, Guy 'Master Gee' O'Brien and Henry 'Big Bank Hank' Jackson who were assembled by record executive Sylvia Robinson. They were successfully sued by Chic for using a segment of *Good Times* without permission (the reason the single carries the writing credit of Edwards and Rodgers, even though they were not responsible for writing the rap). Their debut hit was the first commercially successful rap record.

01/12/1979	3	11	○ **RAPPER'S DELIGHT** Based on Chic's *Good Times* and features musical accompaniment from Positive Force	Sugarhill SHL 101
11/09/1982	54	3	THE LOVER IN YOU	Sugarhill SH 116
25/11/1989	58	2	RAPPER'S DELIGHT (REMIX)	Sugarhill SHRD 0007

SUGGS
UK singer (born Graham McPherson, 13/1/1961, Hastings) who was lead singer with Madness from 1978. He later managed the Farm and went solo in 1995. He also presents the TV pop quiz *Night Fever* on Channel 5.

12/08/1995	7	6	**I'M ONLY SLEEPING/OFF ON HOLIDAY**	WEA YZ 975CD

○ Silver disc ● Gold disc ✪ Platinum disc (additional platinum units are indicated by a figure following the symbol) ◎ Singles released prior to 1973 that are known to have sold over 1 million copies in the UK

DATE	POS	WKS	BPI	SINGLE TITLE	LABEL & NUMBER
14/10/1995	14	6		CAMDEN TOWN	WEA 019CD
16/12/1995	33	3		THE TUNE	WEA 031CD
13/04/1996	4	19	○	**CECILIA**	WEA 042CD1
21/09/1996	24	4		NO MORE ALCOHOL This and above single credited to **SUGGS FEATURING LOUCHIE LOU AND MICHIE ONE** Contains a sample of The Champs' *Tequila*	WEA 065CD1
17/05/1997	22	5		BLUE DAY **SUGGS AND CO FEATURING CHELSEA TEAM**	WEA 112CD
05/09/1998	38	3		I AM Featured in the 1998 film *Avengers*	WEA 174CD

JUSTINE SUISSA Dutch singer who also recorded with Chicane before helping to form Oceanlab.

DATE	POS	WKS	BPI	SINGLE TITLE	LABEL & NUMBER
27/04/2002	48	1		CLEAR BLUE WATER **OCEANLAB FEATURING JUSTINE SUISSA**	Code Blue BLU 024CD1
20/03/2004	45	2		BURNED WITH DESIRE **ARMIN VAN BUUREN FEATURING JUSTINE SUISSA**	Nebula NEBCDX 055

SULTANA Italian instrumental/production group formed by El Zigeuner, DJ Carletto and Julio.

DATE	POS	WKS	BPI	SINGLE TITLE	LABEL & NUMBER
26/03/1994	57	1		TE AMO	Union City UCRD 28

SULTANS OF PING Irish rock group formed in 1989 by Niall O'Flaherty (vocals), Paddy O'Connell (guitar), Morty McCarthy (drums) and Alan 'Dat' McFeely (bass).

DATE	POS	WKS	BPI	SINGLE TITLE	LABEL & NUMBER
08/02/1992	67	2		WHERE'S ME JUMPER	Divine ATHY 01
09/05/1992	67	1		STUPID KID	Divine ATHY 02
10/10/1992	69	1		VERONICA	Divine ATHY 03
09/01/1993	26	3		YOU TALK TOO MUCH This and above three singles credited to **SULTANS OF PING FC**	Rhythm King 6588872
11/09/1993	49	2		TEENAGE PUNKS	Epic 6595792
30/10/1993	43	2		MICHIKO	Epic 6598222
19/02/1994	50	1		WAKE UP AND SCRATCH ME	Epic 6601122

SUM 41 Canadian group formed in Ontario by Derick Whibley (guitar/vocals), Dave Baksh (guitar/vocals), Cone McCaslin (bass) and Steve Jocz (drums). They signed with Island Records in 1999.

DATE	POS	WKS	BPI	SINGLE TITLE	LABEL & NUMBER
13/10/2001	8	9		**FAT LIP**	Def Jam 5888012
15/12/2001	13	11		IN TOO DEEP This and above single featured in the 2001 film *American Pie 2*	Mercury 5888982
06/04/2002	21	7		MOTIVATION	Mercury 5889452
29/06/2002	32	3		IT'S WHAT WE'RE ALL ABOUT	Columbia 6728642
30/11/2002	16	7		STILL WAITING	Mercury 0638342
22/02/2003	35	3		THE HELL SONG	Mercury 0637202

SUMMER – see SNAP

DONNA SUMMER US singer (born Adrian Donna Gaines, 31/12/1948, Dorchester, MA). She began in the German production of *Hair*, relocating to Austria in 1971. She married actor Helmut Sommer, keeping an anglicised version of his name when they divorced. After meeting producer Giorgio Moroder she recorded solo for the Oasis label in 1973, with numerous European hits, and worldwide breakthrough in 1975. She appeared in the 1978 film *Thank God It's Friday* and married singer Bruce Sudano (of Brooklyn Dreams) in 1980. Five Grammy Awards include Best Inspirational Performance in 1983 for *He's A Rebel*, Best Inspirational Performance in 1984 for *Forgive Me* and Best Dance Recording in 1999 with Giorgio Moroder for *Carry On*. She has a star on the Hollywood Walk of Fame.

DATE	POS	WKS	BPI	SINGLE TITLE	LABEL & NUMBER
17/01/1976	4	9		**LOVE TO LOVE YOU BABY**	GTO GT 17
29/05/1976	40	7		COULD IT BE MAGIC Featured in the 1977 film *Looking For Mr Goodbar*	GTO GT 60
25/12/1976	27	6		WINTER MELODY	GTO GT 76
09/07/1977	❶⁴	11	●	**I FEEL LOVE**	GTO GT 100
20/08/1977	5	10	○	**DOWN DEEP INSIDE (THEME FROM 'THE DEEP')** Featured in the 1977 film *The Deep*	Casablanca CAN 111
24/09/1977	14	7		I REMEMBER YESTERDAY	GTO GT 107
03/12/1977	3	13	●	**LOVE'S UNKIND**	GTO GT 113
10/12/1977	10	9		**I LOVE YOU**	Casablanca CAN 114
25/02/1978	19	8		RUMOUR HAS IT	Casablanca CAN 122
22/04/1978	29	7		BACK IN LOVE AGAIN	GTO GT 117
10/06/1978	51	9		LAST DANCE Featured in the films *Thank God It's Friday* (1978) and *Charlie's Angels: Full Throttle* (2003). 1978 Grammy Awards for Best Rhythm & Blues Vocal Performance, and Best Rhythm & Blues Song category for writer Paul Jabara. The song also won an Oscar for Best Film Song for writer Paul Jabara	Casablanca TGIF 2
14/10/1978	5	10	○	**MACARTHUR PARK** ▲³	Casablanca CAN 131
17/02/1979	34	8		HEAVEN KNOWS	Casablanca CAN 141
12/05/1979	11	10		HOT STUFF ▲³ Features The Doobie Brothers' Jeff 'Skunk' Baxter on guitar. Featured in the films *The Full Monty* (1997) and *Door To Door* (2001). 1979 Grammy Award for Best Rock Vocal Performance	Casablanca CAN 151
07/07/1979	14	10	○	BAD GIRLS ▲⁵ Featured in the films *Picture Perfect* (1997) and *The Replacements* (2000)	Casablanca CAN 155
01/09/1979	29	9		DIM ALL THE LIGHTS	Casablanca CAN 162
03/11/1979	3	13	○	**NO MORE TEARS (ENOUGH IS ENOUGH)** ▲² **DONNA SUMMER AND BARBRA STREISAND** The 7-inch version was available through Casablanca, the 12-inch on CBS	Casablanca CAN 174/CBS 8000
16/02/1980	32	6		ON THE RADIO Featured in the 1980 film *Foxes*	Casablanca NB 2236

❶⁹ Number of weeks single topped the UK chart   ↑ Entered the UK chart at #1   ▲⁹ Number of weeks single topped the US chart

21/06/1980 . . . . . 46 . . . . . 5	SUNSET PEOPLE . . . . Casablanca CAN 198
27/09/1980 . . . . . 48 . . . . . 6	THE WANDERER . . . . Geffen K 79180
17/01/1981 . . . . . 44 . . . . . 3	COLD LOVE . . . . Geffen K 79193
10/07/1982 . . . . . 18 . . . . . 11	LOVE IS IN CONTROL (FINGER ON THE TRIGGER) . . . . Warner Brothers K 79302
06/11/1982 . . . . . 14 . . . . . 11	STATE OF INDEPENDENCE . . . . Warner Brothers K 79344
04/12/1982 . . . . . 21 . . . . . 10	I FEEL LOVE (REMIX) . . . . Casablanca FEEL 7
05/03/1983 . . . . . 62 . . . . . 2	THE WOMAN IN ME . . . . Warner Brothers U 9983
18/06/1983 . . . . . 25 . . . . . 8	SHE WORKS HARD FOR THE MONEY Featured in the 1996 film *The Birdcage* . . . . Mercury DONNA 1
24/09/1983 . . . . . 14 . . . . . 12	UNCONDITIONAL LOVE Features the uncredited vocals of Musical Youth . . . . Mercury DONNA 2
21/01/1984 . . . . . 57 . . . . . 2	STOP LOOK AND LISTEN . . . . Mercury DONNA 3
24/10/1987 . . . . . 13 . . . . . 11	DINNER WITH GERSHWIN . . . . Warner Brothers U 8237
23/01/1988 . . . . . 54 . . . . . 3	ALL SYSTEMS GO . . . . WEA U 8122
25/02/1989 . . . . . 3 . . . . . 14 . . . . . ○	**THIS TIME I KNOW IT'S FOR REAL** . . . . Warner Brothers U 7780
27/05/1989 . . . . . 7 . . . . . 9	**I DON'T WANNA GET HURT** . . . . Warner Brothers U 7567
26/08/1989 . . . . . 20 . . . . . 6	LOVE'S ABOUT TO CHANGE MY HEART . . . . Warner Brothers U 7494
25/11/1989 . . . . . 72 . . . . . 1	WHEN LOVE TAKES OVER YOU . . . . WEA U 7361
17/11/1990 . . . . . 45 . . . . . 3	STATE OF INDEPENDENCE . . . . Warner Brothers U 2857
12/01/1991 . . . . . 49 . . . . . 4	BREAKAWAY . . . . Warner Brothers U 3308
30/11/1991 . . . . . 74 . . . . . 1	WORK THAT MAGIC . . . . Warner Brothers U 5937
12/11/1994 . . . . . 21 . . . . . 3	MELODY OF LOVE (WANNA BE LOVED) . . . . Mercury MERCD 418
09/09/1995 . . . . . 8 . . . . . 5	**I FEEL LOVE** Re-recording . . . . Manifesto FESCD 1
06/04/1996 . . . . . 13 . . . . . 5	STATE OF INDEPENDENCE (REMIX) **DONNA SUMMER FEATURING THE ALL STAR CHOIR** All Star Choir consists of Dara Bernard, Dyan Cannon, Christopher Cross, James Ingram, Michael Jackson, Peggy Lipton Jones, Quincy Jones, Kenny Loggins, Michael McDonald, Lionel Richie, Brenda Russell, Donna Summer, Dionne Warwick and Stevie Wonder . . . . Manifesto FESCD 7
11/07/1998 . . . . . 65 . . . . . 1	CARRY ON **DONNA SUMMER and GIORGIO MORODER** . . . . Almighty CDALMY 120
30/10/1999 . . . . . 44 . . . . . 1	I WILL GO WITH YOU (CON TE PARTIRO) . . . . Epic 6682092

SUMMER DAZE UK instrumental/production duo Felix Buxton and Simon Ratcliffe. They later recorded as Basement Jaxx.

26/10/1996 . . . . . 61 . . . . . 1	SAMBA MAGIC . . . . VC Recordings VCRD 14

MARK SUMMERS UK producer who also recorded as Souvlaki.

26/01/1991 . . . . . 27 . . . . . 6	SUMMER'S MAGIC Contains a sample of the theme to the TV series *The Magic Roundabout* . . . . Fourth & Broadway BRW 205

JD SUMNER – see ELVIS PRESLEY

SUNBURST UK dance producer/instrumentalist Matt Darey. He has also remixed for the likes of ATB, Moloko and Gabrielle. Darey and Marcella Woods also recorded with Michael Woods as M3 for Inferno, Darey also recording as Space Baby and in Lost Tribe.

08/07/2000 . . . . . 48 . . . . . 1	EYEBALL (EYEBALL PAUL'S THEME) Featured in the 2000 film *Kevin And Perry Go Large* . . . . Virgin/EMI VTSCD 4

SUNDANCE – see DJ 'FAST' EDDIE

SUNDANCE UK production duo Mark Shimmon and Nick Woolfson. They also recorded as Shimmon & Woolfson.

08/11/1997 . . . . . 33 . . . . . 2	SUNDANCE . . . . React CDREACT 109
03/10/1998 . . . . . 37 . . . . . 2	SUNDANCE '98 (REMIX) . . . . React CDREACTX 136
27/02/1999 . . . . . 56 . . . . . 1	THE LIVING DREAM . . . . React CDREACT 134
05/02/2000 . . . . . 40 . . . . . 2	WON'T LET THIS FEELING GO . . . . Inferno CDFERN 23

SUNDAYS UK rock group formed in London in 1987 by David Gavurin (born 4/4/1963, guitar), Harriet Wheeler (born 26/6/1963, vocals), Paul Brindley (born 6/11/1963, bass) and Patrick Hannan (born 4/3/1966, drums).

11/02/1989 . . . . . 45 . . . . . 5	CAN'T BE SURE . . . . Rough Trade RT 218
03/10/1992 . . . . . 27 . . . . . 2	GOODBYE . . . . Parlophone R 6319
20/09/1997 . . . . . 15 . . . . . 4	SUMMERTIME . . . . Parlophone CDRS 6475
22/11/1997 . . . . . 43 . . . . . 1	CRY . . . . Parlophone CDR 6487

SUNDRAGON UK vocal/instrumental duo who had previously been members of Sands.

21/02/1968 . . . . . 50 . . . . . 1	GREEN TAMBOURINE . . . . MGM 1380

SUNFIRE US group formed by Rowland Smith (vocals), ex-Mtume Reggie Lucas (keyboards) and Raymond Calhoun (bass).

12/03/1983 . . . . . 20 . . . . . 11	YOUNG, FREE AND SINGLE . . . . Warner Brothers W 9897

SUNKIDS FEATURING CHANCE US production duo Eric Wilkman and James Donaldson with female singer Chance.

13/11/1999 . . . . . 50 . . . . . 2	RESCUE ME . . . . AM:PM CDAMPM 126

SUNNY UK session singer Sunny Leslie. She had previously recorded in the duo Sue & Sunny in 1965.

30/03/1974 . . . . . 7 . . . . . 10	**DOCTOR'S ORDERS** . . . . CBS 2068

SUNSCREEM UK group formed by Lucia Holm (vocals), Darren Woodford (guitar), Paul Carnell (keyboards), Rob Fricker (bass) and Sean Wright (drums).

29/02/1992 . . . . . 60 . . . . . 2	PRESSURE . . . . Sony S2 6578017

○ Silver disc ● Gold disc ✪ Platinum disc (additional platinum units are indicated by a figure following the symbol) ◉ Singles released prior to 1973 that are known to have sold over 1 million copies in the UK

DATE	POS	WKS	BPI	SINGLE TITLE	LABEL & NUMBER
18/07/1992	23	6		LOVE U MORE	Sony S2 6581727
17/10/1992	18	5		PERFECT MOTION	Sony S2 6584057
09/01/1993	13	5		BROKEN ENGLISH	Sony S2 6589032
27/03/1993	19	5		PRESSURE US (REMIX)	Sony S2 6591102
02/09/1995	47	2		WHEN	Sony S2 6623222
18/11/1995	40	2		EXODUS	Sony S2 6625342
20/01/1996	25	3		WHITE SKIES	Sony S2 6627425
23/03/1996	36	2		SECRETS	Sony S2 6629342
06/09/1997	55	1		CATCH	Pulse 8 CDLOSE 117
20/10/2001	36	2		PLEASE SAVE ME SUNSCREEM VS PUSH	Five AM/Inferno FAMFERN 1CD
16/11/2002	71	1		PERFECT MOTION	Five AM FAM 15CD

MONTY SUNSHINE – see CHRIS BARBER'S JAZZ BAND

SUNSHINE BAND – see KC AND THE SUNSHINE BAND

SUNSHINE GIRLS – see GUNTHER AND THE SUNSHINE GIRLS

SUNSHIP FEATURING MCRB UK producer Ceri Evans with singer Ricky Benjamin.

| 01/04/2000 | 75 | 1 | | CHEQUE ONE-TWO | Filter FILT 044 |

SUPATONIC UK duo formed in Leyland by brothers Jon and Yew Han Baker. They previously performed as Kindred and The Baker Brothers.

| 06/11/2004 | 69 | 1 | | I WISH IT WASN'T TRUE | Fluff Alley FLUFFA0001 |

SUPER FURRY ANIMALS UK rock group formed in Cardiff in 1993 by Gruff Rhys (born 18/7/1970, Haverfordwest, guitar/vocals), Cian Claran (born 16/6/1976, Bangor, electronics/keyboards), Guto Pryce (born 4/9/1972, Cardiff, bass), Huw Bunford (born 15/9/1967, Cardiff, guitar/vocals) and Dafydd Ieuan (born 16/6/1976, Bangor, drums) who previously recorded for Ankst Records.

09/03/1996	47	1		HOMETOWN UNICORN	Creation CRESCD 222
11/05/1996	33	2		GOD! SHOW ME MAGIC	Creation CRESCD 231
13/07/1996	18	3		SOMETHING 4 THE WEEKEND	Creation CRESCD 235
12/10/1996	18	2		IF YOU DON'T WANT ME TO DESTROY YOU	Creation CRESCD 243
14/12/1996	22	2		THE MAN DON'T GIVE A FUCK Contains a sample of Steely Dan's *Showbiz Kids*, and is a tribute to ex- Reading footballer Robin Friday	Creation CRESCD 247
24/05/1997	26	2		HERMANN LOVES PAULINE	Creation CRESCD 252
26/07/1997	24	2		THE INTERNATIONAL LANGUAGE OF SCREAMING	Creation CRESCD 269
04/10/1997	27	2		PLAY IT COOL	Creation CRESCD 275
06/12/1997	27	2		DEMONS	Creation CRESCD 283
06/06/1998	12	3		ICE HOCKEY HAIR	Creation CRESCD 288
22/05/1999	11	4		NORTHERN LITES	Creation CRESCD 314
21/08/1999	25	3		FIRE IN MY HEART	Creation CRESCD 323
29/01/2000	20	2		DO OR DIE	Creation CRESCD 329
21/07/2001	14	4		JUXTAPOZED WITH U	Epic 6712242
20/10/2001	28	2		(DRAWING) RINGS AROUND THE WORLD	Epic 6719082
26/01/2002	30	2		IT'S NOT THE END OF THE WORLD?	Epic 6721752
26/07/2003	13	3		GOLDEN RETRIEVER	Epic 6739062
01/11/2003	31	2		HELLO SUNSHINE	Epic 6743602
09/10/2004	16	2		THE MAN DON'T GIVE A FUCK Live version	Epic 6753041

SUPERCAR Italian production duo Alberto Pizarelli and Ricki Pagano.

| 13/02/1999 | 15 | 5 | | TONITE | Pepper 0530202 |
| 21/08/1999 | 67 | 1 | | COMPUTER LOVE SUPERCAR FEATURING MIKAELA | Pepper 0530392 |

SUPERCAT Jamaican singer (born William Maragh, 25/6/1953, Kingston). He began as a DJ and later became a producer.

| 01/08/1992 | 66 | 1 | | IT FE DONE | Columbia 6582737 |
| 06/05/1995 | 22 | 4 | | MY GIRL JOSEPHINE SUPERCAT FEATURING JACK RADICS Featured in the 1994 film *Ready To Wear (Pret-A-Porter)* | Columbia 6614702 |

SUPERFUNK French production trio Fafa Monteco, Mike 303 and Stephane B.

| 04/03/2000 | 42 | 1 | | LUCKY STAR SUPERFUNK FEATURING RON CARROLL Contains a sample of Chris Rea's *Josephine* | Virgin DINSD 198 |
| 10/06/2000 | 62 | 1 | | THE YOUNG MC Contains a sample of Musical Youth's *Pass The Dutchie* | Virgin DINSD 206 |

SUPERGRASS UK rock group:Danny Goffey (born 7/2/1974, Oxford, drums), Gareth 'Gaz' Coombes (born 8/3/1976, Oxford, guitar/vocals) and Mickey Quinn (born 17/12/1969, Oxford, bass). Debuted with Nude Records in 1992 and signed with Parlophone in 1994. In 1995 they added Bob Coombes (born 27/4/1972, Oxford, keyboards). Best British Newcomers at the 1996 BRIT Awards.

29/10/1994	43	2		CAUGHT BY THE FUZZ	Parlophone CDR 6396
18/02/1995	20	3		MANSIZE ROOSTER Featured in the 1997 film *Casper – A Spirited Beginning*	Parlophone CDR 6402
25/03/1995	75	1		LOSE IT	Sub Pop SP 281
13/05/1995	10	3		LENNY	Parlophone CDR 6410

15/07/1995	2	10	○	ALRIGHT/TIME A-side featured in the films *Clueless* (1995) and *On The Edge* (2000) ... Parlophone CDR 6413
09/03/1996	5	6		GOING OUT ... Parlophone CDR 6428
12/04/1997	2	5		RICHARD III ... Parlophone CDR 6461
21/06/1997	10	4		SUN HITS THE SKY ... Parlophone CDR 6469
18/10/1997	18	4		LATE IN THE DAY ... Parlophone CDRS 6484
05/06/1999	11	7		PUMPING ON YOUR STEREO ... Parlophone CDR 6518
18/09/1999	9	5		MOVING ... Parlophone CDR 6524
04/12/1999	36	4		MARY ... Parlophone CDR 6531
13/07/2002	75	1		NEVER DONE NOTHING LIKE THAT BEFORE ... Parlophone R 6583
28/09/2002	13	4		GRACE ... Parlophone CDRS 6586
08/02/2003	22	3		SEEN THE LIGHT ... Parlophone CDR 6592
05/06/2004	23	3		KISS OF LIFE ... Parlophone CDR 6638

SUPERMEN LOVERS FEATURING MANI HOFFMAN
French dance group formed by producer Guillaume Atlan and singer Mani Hoffman. The accompanying video to their debut hit single featured an animated potato!

15/09/2001	2	17	○	STARLIGHT ... Independiente ISOM 53MS

SUPERNATURALS
UK group formed by James McColl (guitar/lead vocals), Derek McManus (guitar), Mark Guthrie (bass), Ken McAlpine (keyboards) and Alan Tilston (drums). The group formed the OFL label before signing with Food.

26/10/1996	34	2	LAZY LOVER ... Food CDFOOD 85
08/02/1997	25	3	THE DAY BEFORE YESTERDAY'S MAN ... Food CDFOODS 88
26/04/1997	23	2	SMILE ... Food CDFOOD 92
12/07/1997	38	2	LOVE HAS PASSED AWAY ... Food CDFOOD 99
25/10/1997	48	1	PREPARE TO LAND ... Food CDFOODS 106
01/08/1998	25	3	I WASN'T BUILT TO GET UP ... Food CDFOOD 112
24/10/1998	45	1	SHEFFIELD SONG ... Food CDFOODS 115
13/03/1999	52	1	EVEREST ... Food CDFOOD 119

SUPERNOVA
UK vocal/instrumental group formed by Art, Dave and Joey.

11/05/1996	55	1	SOME MIGHT SAY ... Sing Sing 74321369442

SUPERSISTER
UK vocal group formed in Sheffield by Louise Fudge, Tina Peacock and Eleanor Phillips.

14/10/2000	16	5	COFFEE ... Gut CXGUT 35
25/08/2001	36	2	SHOPPING ... Gut CXGUT 37
17/11/2001	51	1	SUMMER GONNA COME AGAIN ... Gut CDGUT 38

SUPERSTAR
UK group formed in 1992 by Joe McAlinden (guitar/vocals), Nellie Grant and Raymond Prior. McAlinden re-formed the group in 1996 with Jim McCulloch (guitar), Alan Hutchison (bass) and Quentin McAfee (drums).

07/02/1998	66	1	EVERY DAY I FALL APART ... Camp Fabulous CFAB 003CD
25/04/1998	49	1	SUPERSTAR ... Camp Fabulous CFAB 007CD

SUPERTRAMP
UK rock group formed in 1969 by Richard Davies (born 22/7/1944, Swindon, vocals/keyboards), Roger Hodgson (born 21/3/1950, London, bass), Richard Palmer (born June 1947, Bournemouth, guitar) and Bob Miller (drums). They signed with A&M, adding saxophonist Dave Winthrop (born 27/11/1948, New Jersey, USA) in 1970. Palmer and Miller left in 1971, replaced by Kevin Currie (drums) and Frank Farrell (bass), Hodgson switching to guitar. John Helliwell (born 15/2/1945, Todmorden, saxophone) and Bob C Benberg joined in 1973. Hodgson went solo in 1982. They were named after a book by W H Davis, *Diary Of A Supertramp*.

15/02/1975	13	10	DREAMER Featured in the 2001 film *The Parole Officer* ... A&M AMS 7132
25/06/1977	29	7	GIVE A LITTLE BIT ... A&M AMS 7293
31/03/1979	7	11	THE LOGICAL SONG ... A&M AMS 7427
30/06/1979	9	10	BREAKFAST IN AMERICA ... A&M AMS 7451
27/10/1979	57	3	GOODBYE STRANGER ... A&M AMS 7481
30/10/1982	26	11	IT'S RAINING AGAIN SUPERTRAMP FEATURING VOCALS BY ROGER HODGSON ... A&M AMS 8255

SUPREME DREAM TEAM – see CK AND SUPREME DREAM TEAM

SUPREMES
US R&B vocal group formed in 1959 by Mary Wilson (born 6/3/1944, Greenville, MS), Florence Ballard (born 30/6/1943, Detroit, MI) and Betty Travis as the Primettes, a sister group to manager Milton Jenkins' act the Primes (who became the Temptations). They added Diana Ross (born Diane Ross, 26/3/1944, Detroit) the same year, Travis also leaving, replaced by Barbara Martin. They debuted on record for Lupine in 1960 shortly before signing with Motown, changing their name (at Berry Gordy's request) to Ballard's suggestion The Supremes. Martin left and the group remained a trio. Original lead Ballard was fired in 1967, replaced by Cindy Birdsong (born 15/12/1939, Camden, NJ). Ross went solo in 1970, replaced by Jean Terrell (born 26/11/1944, Texas, sister of boxer Ernie). Birdsong left in 1972, replaced by Lynda Laurence; Terrell left in 1972, replaced by Scherrie Payne (born 14/11/1944, Detroit, sister of Freda Payne). Laurence left in 1974, replaced by Susaye Greene. They disbanded in 1976, although Wilson formed a new Supremes with Karen Jackson and Karen Ragland. Ross and Wilson accepted an invitation to re-form the group for a series of live concerts in 2000. Ballard died on 21/2/1976 from a heart attack. They were inducted into the Rock & Roll Hall of Fame in 1988. Diana Ross was awarded a star on the Hollywood Walk of Fame in 1982, Mary Wilson in 1990.

03/09/1964	3	14	WHERE DID OUR LOVE GO ▲² ... Stateside SS 327
22/10/1964	❶²	15	BABY LOVE ▲⁴ Featured in the 1997 film *Jackie Brown* ... Stateside SS 350
21/01/1965	27	6	COME SEE ABOUT ME ▲² Featured in the 1994 film *Beverly Hills Cop 3* ... Stateside SS 376

25/03/1965	7	12		**STOP IN THE NAME OF LOVE** ▲² Featured in the 1979 film *More American Graffiti*	Tamla Motown TMG 501
10/06/1965	40	5		BACK IN MY ARMS AGAIN ▲¹	Tamla Motown TMG 516
09/12/1965	39	5		I HEAR A SYMPHONY ▲²	Tamla Motown TMG 543
08/09/1966	3	12		**YOU CAN'T HURRY LOVE** ▲² Featured in the 1986 film *Jumpin' Jack Flash*	Tamla Motown TMG 575
01/12/1966	8	10		**YOU KEEP ME HANGIN' ON** ▲²	Tamla Motown TMG 585
02/03/1967	17	10		LOVE IS HERE AND NOW YOU'RE GONE ▲¹	Tamla Motown TMG 597
11/05/1967	6	12		**THE HAPPENING** ▲¹ Featured in the 1967 film *The Happening*. **DIANA ROSS AND THE SUPREMES:**	Tamla Motown TMG 607
30/08/1967	5	14		**REFLECTIONS** Featured in the 1989 film *Arthur 2: On The Rocks*.	Tamla Motown TMG 616
29/11/1967	13	13		IN AND OUT OF LOVE	Tamla Motown TMG 632
10/04/1968	28	8		FOREVER CAME TODAY	Tamla Motown TMG 650
03/07/1968	34	6		SOME THINGS YOU NEVER GET USED TO	Tamla Motown TMG 662
20/11/1968	15	14		LOVE CHILD ▲²	Tamla Motown TMG 677
29/01/1969	3	12		**I'M GONNA MAKE YOU LOVE ME** DIANA ROSS AND THE SUPREMES AND THE TEMPTATIONS Featured in the 1996 film *Now And Then*	Tamla Motown TMG 685
23/04/1969	14	10		I'M LIVING IN SHAME	Tamla Motown TMG 695
16/07/1969	37	7		NO MATTER WHAT SIGN YOU ARE	Tamla Motown TMG 704
20/09/1969	18	8		I SECOND THAT EMOTION DIANA ROSS AND THE SUPREMES AND THE TEMPTATIONS	Tamla Motown TMG 709
13/12/1969	13	13		SOMEDAY WE'LL BE TOGETHER ▲¹	Tamla Motown TMG 721
21/03/1970	31	7		WHY (MUST WE FALL IN LOVE) DIANA ROSS AND THE SUPREMES AND THE TEMPTATIONS SUPREMES:	Tamla Motown TMG 730
02/05/1970	6	15		**UP THE LADDER TO THE ROOF**	Tamla Motown TMG 735
16/01/1971	3	13		**STONED LOVE** Featured in the 1994 film *Forrest Gump*	Tamla Motown TMG 760
26/06/1971	11	10		RIVER DEEP MOUNTAIN HIGH SUPREMES AND THE FOUR TOPS	Tamla Motown TMG 777
21/08/1971	5	11		**NATHAN JONES**	Tamla Motown TMG 782
20/11/1971	25	10		YOU GOTTA HAVE LOVE IN YOUR HEART SUPREMES AND THE FOUR TOPS	Tamla Motown TMG 793
04/03/1972	9	10		**FLOY JOY**	Tamla Motown TMG 804
15/07/1972	10	9		**AUTOMATICALLY SUNSHINE**	Tamla Motown TMG 821
21/04/1973	37	4		BAD WEATHER	Tamla Motown TMG 847
24/08/1974	12	10		BABY LOVE Re-issue of Stateside SS 350	Tamla Motown TMG 915
18/02/1989	62	1		STOP! IN THE NAME OF LOVE Re-issue of Tamla Motown TMG 501 This and previous hit credited to DIANA ROSS AND THE SUPREMES	Motown ZB 41963

AL B SURE! US singer (born Al Brown, Boston, MA, 1969, raised in New York).

16/04/1988	44	5		NITE AND DAY	Uptown W 8192
30/07/1988	70	2		OFF ON YOUR OWN (GIRL)	Uptown W 7870
10/06/1989	54	3		IF I'M NOT YOUR LOVER AL B SURE FEATURING SLICK RICK	Uptown W 2908
31/03/1990	67	1		SECRET GARDEN QUINCY JONES FEATURING AL B SURE! JAMES INGRAM, EL DEBARGE AND BARRY WHITE Featured in the 1997 film *Sprung*	Qwest W 9992
12/06/1993	36	2		BLACK TIE WHITE NOISE DAVID BOWIE FEATURING AL B SURE!	Arista 74321148682

SUREAL UK dance group formed by Stuart Lange featuring vocals by Billie Godfrey. Lange later recorded as Lange Featuring Skye.

07/10/2000	15	4		YOU TAKE MY BREATH AWAY	Cream 7CD

SURFACE US R&B group: Bernard Jackson (bass/vocals), David Townsend (guitar/keyboards) and David Conley (saxophone/drums).

23/07/1983	67	3		FALLING IN LOVE	Salsoul SAL 104
23/06/1984	52	4		WHEN YOUR 'EX' WANTS YOU BACK	Salsoul SAL 106
28/02/1987	56	5		HAPPY	CBS 6503937
12/01/1991	60	2		THE FIRST TIME ▲²	Columbia 6564767

SURFACE NOISE UK songwriter/producer Chris Palmer. Initial releases were via his own Groove Productions label.

31/05/1980	26	8		THE SCRATCH	WEA K 18291
30/08/1980	59	3		DANCIN' ON A WIRE	Groove Productions GP 102

SURFARIS US surf group formed in Glendora, CA by Ron Wilson (drums), Jim Fuller (guitar), Bob Berryhill (guitar), Pat Connolly (bass) and Jim Pash (clarinet). Their one hit was released on three different US labels before charting (DFS, Princess and Dot). The distinctive opening laugh was provided by their manager Dale Smallin. Wilson died from a heart attack on 19/5/1989.

25/07/1963	5	14		WIPE OUT Featured in the films *The Wanderers* (1979), *Dirty Dancing* (1987), *Disorderlies* (1987), *George Of The Jungle* (1997). They were successfully sued by Impacts guitarist Merrell Frankhauser over similarities with his tune of the same name	London HLD 9751

SURPRISE SISTERS UK vocal group formed by Ellen, Linda, Patricia and Susan Sutcliffe. They were discovered by Tony Visconti while performing in an East London public house.

13/03/1976	38	3		LA BOOGA ROOGA	Good Earth GD 1

SURVIVOR US rock group formed by Dave Bickler (keyboards/vocals), Jim Peterik (born 1/11/1950, keyboards/guitar/vocals), Frankie Sullivan (guitar/vocals), Gary Smith (drums) and Dennis Johnson (bass). Smith and Johnson left in 1981, replaced by Marc Droubay and Stephen Ellis. Bickler left in 1984, replaced by Jimi Jamison. Droubay and Ellis left in 1988, the group disbanding the following year. They reunited in 1994.

31/07/1982	❶⁴	15	●	**EYE OF THE TIGER** ▲⁶ In 1982 film *Rocky III*. 1982 Grammy for Best Rock Vocal Performance by a Group.	Scotti Brothers SCT A 2411
01/02/1986	5	11		**BURNING HEART** Featured in the 1985 film *Rocky IV*	Scotti Brothers A 6708

SUSHI – see PAUL MASTERSON PRESENTS SUSHI

SUTHERLAND BROTHERS AND QUIVER
UK folk-rock group formed in 1972 by Iain (guitar/vocals) and Gavin Sutherland (bass/vocals), Willie Wilson (drums/vocals), Bruce Thomas (bass), Pete Wood (keyboards) and Tim Renwick (guitar/vocals). The group disbanded in 1977.

03/04/1976.....5......12	ARMS OF MARY..	CBS 4001
20/11/1976.....35......4.......	SECRETS..	CBS 4668
02/06/1979.....50......4.......	EASY COME EASY GO SUTHERLAND BROTHERS....................................	CBS 7121

PAT SUZUKI
US singer (born Chiyoko Suzuki, 23/9/1930, Cressy, CA) with Japanese parents, interned during World War II.

14/12/1974.....49......1.......	I ENJOY BEING A GIRL Song featured in the musical *Flower Drum Song*.........................	RCA 1171

SVENSON AND GIELEN
Belgian duo producer Johan Gielen and singer Sven Maes. Both are also members of Airscape, Balearic Bill and Cubic 22 while Gielen records as Blue Bamboo and under his own name.

22/09/2001.....41......2	THE BEAUTY OF SILENCE..	Xtrahard X2H5 CDS

BILLY SWAN
US singer/songwriter (born 12/5/1942, Cape Girardeau, MO); he also produced three albums for Tony Joe White.

14/12/1974.....6......9......O	I CAN HELP ▲[2]..	Monument MNT 2752
24/05/1975.....42......4.......	DON'T BE CRUEL..	Monument MNT 3244

SWAN LAKE
US remixer/producer (born Todd Terry, 18/4/1967, Brooklyn, NYC); he mixed hits by Everything But The Girl, Brownstone, 3T and Jimmy Somerville among others, before going solo. He has also recorded as Royal House, Gypsymen and Black Riot.

17/09/1988.....53......4.......	IN THE NAME OF LOVE...	Champion CHAMP 86

SWANS WAY
UK group formed in Birmingham in 1982 by Rick Jones (double bass), Maggie De Monde (vocals) and Robert Shaw (guitar/vocals). De Monde and Shaw went on to form Scarlet Fantastic.

04/02/1984.....20......7......	SOUL TRAIN...	Exit EXT 3
26/05/1984.....57......5......	ILLUMINATIONS..	Balgier PH 5

PATRICK SWAYZE FEATURING WENDY FRASER
US singer/actor (born 18/8/1952, Houston, TX); he made his name as an actor in *Red Dawn, Ghost* and *Dirty Dancing* among other films. Actress Wendy Fraser appeared in *Dirty Dancing*.

26/03/1988.....17......11......	SHE'S LIKE THE WIND Featured in the 1987 film *Dirty Dancing*......................	RCA PB 49565

KEITH SWEAT
US R&B singer (born 22/7/1961, Harlem, NYC). He was a member of the Rhythm Makers and GQ before going solo as both a singer and producer. He appeared in the 1991 film *New Jack City* and later linked with Gerald Levert and Johnny Gill to form Levert Sweat Gill. Athena Cage is a US singer.

20/02/1988.....26......10......	I WANT HER..	Vintertainment EKR 68
14/05/1988.....55......3......	SOMETHING JUST AIN'T RIGHT...	Vintertainment EKR 72
14/05/1994.....71......1......	HOW DO YOU LIKE IT..	Elektra EKR 185CD
22/06/1996.....39......2......	TWISTED...	Elektra EKR 223CD
23/11/1996.....35......2......	JUST A TOUCH..	Elektra EKR 227CD
03/05/1997.....30......2......	NOBODY KEITH SWEAT FEATURING ATHENA CAGE..........................	Elektra EKR 233CD
06/12/1997.....44......1......	I WANT HER (REMIX)...	Elektra E 3887CD
12/12/1998.....58......1......	COME AND GET WITH ME KEITH SWEAT FEATURING SNOOP DOGG..........	Elektra E 3787CD
27/03/1999.....53......1......	I'M NOT READY..	Elektra E 3767CD

MICHELLE SWEENEY
US singer, also an actress, appearing in the films *The Company Of Strangers* and *The List*.

29/10/1994.....57......1......	THIS TIME..	Big Beat A 8229CD

SWEET
UK pop group formed in London in 1968 by Brian Connolly (born Brian McManus, 5/10/1949, Hamilton, vocals), Mick Tucker (born 17/7/1949, London, drums), Steve Priest (born 23/2/1950, Hayes, bass) and Frank Torpey (guitar) as Sweetshop. After unsuccessful singles with Fontana and Parlophone, they group shortened their name and replaced Torpey with Andy Scott (born 30/6/1951, Wrexham). They signed with RCA in 1971. Connolly went solo in 1979, the group dissolving in 1981. A series of heart attacks (including 14 in one 24-hour spell) effectively brought Connolly's career to an end, and he died from kidney failure on 10/2/1997. After battling with leukaemia for five years, Mick Tucker died on 14/2/2002.

13/03/1971.....13......14......	FUNNY FUNNY..	RCA 2051
12/06/1971.....2......15......	CO-CO..	RCA 2087
16/10/1971.....33......5......	ALEXANDER GRAHAM BELL..	RCA 2121
05/02/1972.....11......12......	POPPA JOE..	RCA 2164
10/06/1972.....4......14......	LITTLE WILLY Featured in the 1999 film *Detroit Rock City*..........................	RCA 2225
09/09/1972.....4......13......	WIG-WAM BAM..	RCA 2260
13/01/1973.....❶[5]......15......	BLOCKBUSTER Featured in the 2000 film *Gangster No 1*.........................	RCA 2305
05/05/1973.....2......11......	HELL RAISER...	RCA 2357
22/09/1973.....2......9......O	BALLROOM BLITZ..	RCA 2403

○ Silver disc ● Gold disc ✪ Platinum disc (additional platinum units are indicated by a figure following the symbol) ◎ Singles released prior to 1973 that are known to have sold over 1 million copies in the UK

19/01/1974	2	8	O	**TEENAGE RAMPAGE**	RCA LPBO 5004
13/07/1974	9	7		**THE SIX TEENS**	RCA LPBO 5037
09/11/1974	41	2		TURN IT DOWN	RCA 2480
15/03/1975	2	10	O	**FOX ON THE RUN** Featured in the 1993 film *Dazed And Confused*	RCA 2524
12/07/1975	15	6		ACTION	RCA 2578
24/01/1976	35	4		LIES IN YOUR EYES	RCA 2641
28/01/1978	9	9	O	**LOVE IS LIKE OXYGEN** Featured in the 1979 film *The Bitch*	Polydor POSP 1
26/01/1985	45	5		IT'S…IT'S…THE SWEET MIX Tracks on medley: *Blockbuster, Fox On The Run, Teenage Rampage, Hell Raiser* and *Ballroom Blitz*	Anagram ANA 28

RACHEL SWEET
US rock singer (born 28/7/1963, Akron, OH); she began singing professionally at five and recorded her first single at twelve for the Derrick label. She later pursued an acting career.

09/12/1978	35	8		B-A-B-Y	Stiff BUY 39
22/08/1981	35	7		EVERLASTING LOVE REX SMITH AND RACHEL SWEET	CBS A 1405

SWEET DREAMS
UK duo of top session singers Tony Jackson and Polly Brown (born 18/4/1947, Birmingham). Brown had previously been in Pickettywitch and also recorded solo while Jackson later became a member of Paul Young's backing group.

20/07/1974	10	12		**HONEY HONEY**	Bradley's BRAD 7408

SWEET DREAMS
UK vocal group formed by Bobby McVey, Carrie Gray and Helen Cray to represent Britain in the 1983 Eurovision Song Contest where they finished sixth. The winner was Luxembourg's *Si La Vie Est Cadeau*, performed by Corinna Hermes.

09/04/1983	21	7		I'M NEVER GIVING UP Britain's entry for the 1983 Eurovision Song Contest (came sixth)	Ariola ARO 333

SWEET FEMALE ATTITUDE
UK garage group formed by Leanne Brown and Catherine Cassidy who were both born in Manchester and twenty years of age at the time of their debut hit.

15/04/2000	2	12	O	**FLOWERS**	Milkk 267CD
07/10/2000	43	4		8 DAYS A WEEK	WEA 296 CD

SWEET MERCY FEATURING JOE ROBERTS
UK instrumental/production duo Melanie Williams and Eric Gooden with singer Joe Roberts.

24/02/1996	63	1		HAPPY DAYS	Grass Green GRASS 10CD

SWEET PEOPLE
French pop group fronted by keyboard player Alain Morisod.

04/10/1980	4	8		**ET LES OISEAUX CHANTAIENT (AND THE BIRDS WERE SINGING)**	Polydor POSP 179
29/08/1987	73	2		ET LES OISEAUX CHANTAIENT (AND THE BIRDS WERE SINGING)	Polydor POSP 179

SWEET PUSSY PAULINE – see CANDY GIRLS

SWEET SENSATION
UK soul group formed in Manchester by singers Marcel King, Vincent James, Junior Faye and St Clair Palmer and musicians Barry Johnson (bass), Leroy Smith (piano), Roy Flowers (drums) and Gary Shaughnessy (guitar). After winning *New Faces*, they were signed by Pye with most of their material written by David Parton. King was later replaced by Rikki Patrick.

14/09/1974	●1	10	O	**SAD SWEET DREAMER**	Pye 7N 45385
18/01/1975	11	7		PURELY BY COINCIDENCE	Pye 7N 45421

SWEET TEE
US rapper (born Toi Jackson, New York). She later changed her name to Suga.

16/01/1988	31	6		IT'S LIKE THAT Y'ALL/I GOT DA FEELIN'	Cooltempo COOL 160
13/08/1994	32	2		THE FEELING TIN TIN OUT FEATURING SWEET TEE	Deep Distraxion OILYCD 029

SWEETBACK
UK vocal/instrumental group formed by Paul Deman, Andrew Hale and Stuart Matthewman. All three are also members of Sade's backing band. Their debut hit also featured Amel Larrieux.

29/03/1997	64	1		YOU WILL RISE	Epic 6643155

SWEETBOX
US rapper Tina Harris from Maryland with German producer Rosan Roberto. Her debut hit is based on the classical composition *Air from Suite No3* by Johann Sebastian Bach and features the Babelsberg Symphony Orchestra. By 2001 Harris had left the project and was replaced by Jade.

22/08/1998	5	12		**EVERYTHING'S GONNA BE ALRIGHT**	RCA 74321606842

SALLY SWEETLAND – see EDDIE FISHER

SWERVEDRIVER
UK group formed in 1990 by Adam Franklin (born 19/7/1968, guitar/vocals), Jimmy Hartridge (born 27/11/1967, guitar/vocals), Adi Vines (born 25/1/1968, bass) and Graham Bonner (born 28/4/1967, drums). By 1993 the group was a trio of Franklin, Hartridge and drummer Jez, Bonner and Vines going on to form Skyscraper.

10/08/1991	67	1		SANDBLASTED (EP) Tracks on EP: *Sandblaster, Flawed, Out* and *Laze It Up*	Creation CRE 102
30/05/1992	62	1		NEVER LOST THAT FEELING	Creation CRE 120
14/08/1993	60	1		DUEL	Creation CRESCD 136

MAMPI SWIFT
UK DJ/producer (born Philip Anim, 1978) who recorded for True Playaz, Suburban Base, Frontline, Sour and K Power before launching Charge Recordings in 1990.

05/06/2004	72	1		HI-TEK/DRUNKEN STARS	Charge Recordings CHRG024

●9 Number of weeks single topped the UK charts ↑ Entered the UK chart at #1 ▲9 Number of weeks single topped the American charts

789

SWIMMING WITH SHARKS German vocal duo Inga and Anette Humpe.

07/05/1988.....63......3....... CARELESS LOVE .... WEA YZ 173

SWING FEATURING DR ALBAN US rapper with Nigerian singer Dr Alban.

29/04/1995.....59......1....... SWEET DREAMS .... Logic 74321251552

SWING 52 US vocal/instrumental group formed by Arnold Jarvis, Benji Candelario and Wayne Rollins.

25/02/1995.....60......1....... COLOR OF MY SKIN .... ffrr FCD 256

SWING KIDS – see K7

SWING OUT SISTER UK jazz-pop group formed by Andy Connell (keyboards), Martin Jackson (percussion) and Corrine Drewery (vocals). Jackson left in 1989 and they continued as a duo. In 1994 they were joined by Derick Johnson (bass), Myke Wilson (drums), Tim Cansfield (guitar), John Thrikell (trumpet) and Gary Plumey (saxophone).

25/10/1986.....4......14......○ **BREAKOUT** .... Mercury SWING 2
10/01/1987.....7......8....... **SURRENDER** .... Mercury SWING 3
18/04/1987.....32......6....... TWILIGHT WORLD .... Mercury SWING 4
11/07/1987.....43......4....... FOOLED BY A SMILE .... Mercury SWING 5
08/04/1989.....28......9....... YOU ON MY MIND .... Fontana SWING 6
08/07/1989.....47......4....... WHERE IN THE WORLD .... Fontana SWING 7
11/04/1992.....21......6....... AM I THE SAME GIRL .... Fontana SWING 9
20/06/1992.....49......2....... NOTGONNACHANGE .... Fontana SWING 10
27/08/1994.....37......2....... LA LA (MEANS I LOVE YOU) Featured in the 1994 film *Four Weddings And A Funeral* .... Fontana SWIDD 11

SWINGING BLUE JEANS UK rock group formed in Liverpool in 1958 by Ray Ennis (born 26/5/1942, Liverpool, guitar/vocals), Ralph Ellis (born 8/3/1942, Liverpool, guitar/vocals), Les Braid (born 15/9/1941, Liverpool, bass) and Norman Kuhlke (born 17/6/1942, Liverpool, drums). Ellis left in 1966, replaced by Terry Sylvester (born 8/1/1945, Liverpool). Braid left soon after, replaced by Mike Gregory. They disbanded in 1968, Ennis putting together a new line-up in 1973 for an American nostalgia tour.

20/06/1963.....30......9....... IT'S TOO LATE NOW .... HMV POP 1170
12/12/1963.....2......17....... **HIPPY HIPPY SHAKE** .... HMV POP 1242
19/03/1964.....11......10....... GOOD GOLLY MISS MOLLY .... HMV POP 1273
04/06/1964.....3......13....... **YOU'RE NO GOOD** .... HMV POP 1304
20/01/1966.....31......8....... DON'T MAKE ME OVER .... HMV POP 1501

SWIRL 360 US vocal duo formed in Jacksonville, FL by Denny Scott and his brother Kenny.

14/11/1998.....61......1....... HEY NOW NOW .... Mercury 5665352

SWITCH US R&B group formed in Mansfield, OH by Philip Ingram (vocals), Bobby DeBarge (keyboards), his brother Tommy (bass), Eddie Fluellen (horns), Greg Williams (horns) and Jody Sims (drums). The DeBarge brothers were later members of DeBarge, while Bobby died from AIDS on 16/8/1995.

10/11/1984.....61......3....... KEEPING SECRETS .... Total Experience RCA XE 502

SWITCHFOOT US rock group formed in San Diego, CA by Jon Foreman (guitar/vocals), his brother Tim (bass/vocals), Jerome Fontamillas (guitar/keyboards/vocals) and Chad Butler (drums).

14/08/2004.....29......2....... MEANT TO LIVE Featured in the 2004 film *Spider Man 2* .... Columbia 6750812

SWIZZ BEATZ – see DMX

S.W.V. US R&B vocal group formed by Cheryl 'Coko' Gamble (born 1974, lead vocals), Tamara 'Taj' Johnson (born 1974) and Leanne 'Lelee' Lyons (born 1976). The group's name is short for Sisters With Voices. Coko later recorded solo.

01/05/1993.....17......6....... I'M SO INTO YOU .... RCA 74321144972
26/06/1993.....33......3....... WEAK ▲² .... RCA 74321153352
28/08/1993.....3......12....... **RIGHT HERE** Contains a sample of Michael Jackson's *Human Nature*. Featured in the 1993 film *Free Willy* ..... RCA 74321160482
26/02/1994.....19......5....... DOWNTOWN .... RCA 74321189012
11/06/1994.....24......3....... ANYTHING Featured in the 1994 film *Above The Rim* .... RCA 74321212212
25/05/1996.....13......3....... YOU'RE THE ONE Contains a sample of Tanya Gardner's *Heartbeat* .... RCA 74321383312
21/12/1996.....36......5....... IT'S ALL ABOUT U .... RCA 74321442152
12/04/1997.....18......4....... CAN WE Featured in the 1997 film *Booty Call* .... Jive JIVECD 423
13/09/1997.....34......2....... SOMEONE **SWV FEATURING PUFF DADDY** Contains samples of Notorious B.I.G.'s *Ten Crack Commandments* and *The World Is Filled* .... RCA 74321513942

SYBIL US singer (born Sybil Lynch, 1963, Paterson, NJ); first known in Ce Ce & Company with Ce Ce Rogers before going solo in 1986.

01/11/1986.....68......3....... FALLING IN LOVE .... Champion CHAMP 22
25/04/1987.....32......6....... LET YOURSELF GO .... Champion CHAMP 42
29/08/1987.....42......5....... MY LOVE IS GUARANTEED .... Champion CHAMPX 55
22/07/1989.....59......5....... DON'T MAKE ME OVER .... Champion CHAMP 213
14/10/1989.....19......6....... DON'T MAKE ME OVER .... Champion CHAMP 213
27/01/1990.....6......9....... **WALK ON BY** .... PWL 48
21/04/1990.....71......1....... CRAZY FOR YOU .... PWL 53

○ Silver disc ● Gold disc ✪ Platinum disc (additional platinum units are indicated by a figure following the symbol) ◉ Singles released prior to 1973 that are known to have sold over 1 million copies in the UK

16/01/1993	3	13		THE LOVE I LOST WEST END FEATURING SYBIL	PWL Sanctuary PWCD 253
20/03/1993	5	13		WHEN I'M GOOD AND READY	PWL International PWCD 260
26/06/1993	41	2		BEYOND YOUR WILDEST DREAMS	PWL International PWCD 265
11/09/1993	41	2		STRONGER TOGETHER	PWL International PWCD 269
11/12/1993	48	1		MY LOVE IS GUARANTEED (REMIX)	PWL International PWCD 277
09/03/1996	53	1		SO TIRED OF BEING ALONE	PWL International PWL 324CD
08/03/1997	66	1		WHEN I'M GOOD AND READY (REMIX)	Next Plateau NP 14183
26/07/1997	55	1		STILL A THRILL	Coalition COLA 007CD

SYLK 130 US vocal group assembled by Philadelphia, PA-based rapper and DJ King Britt and producer John Wicks.

25/04/1998	33	2		LAST NIGHT A DJ SAVED MY LIFE	Sony S2 SYLK 1CD

SYLVER Belgian vocal/production duo singer Silvy De Bie and musician/DJ Wout Van Dessel.

01/06/2002	56	1		TURN THE TIDE	Pepper 9230562

SYLVESTER US singer (born Sylvester James, 6/9/1947, Los Angeles, CA). He joined the Cockettes in 1970 and signed solo with Blue Thumb in 1973. He formed the Two Tons of Fun (later known as the Weather Girls) and switched to Fantasy in 1977. He died from an AIDS-related illness on 16/12/1988. Patrick Cowley is an American producer.

19/08/1978	8	15	O	YOU MAKE ME FEEL (MIGHTY REAL) Featured in the 1991 film *Young Soul Rebels* even though the film is set around the Queen's Silver Jubilee in 1977, before the track was recorded	Fantasy FTC 160
18/11/1978	29	12		DANCE (DISCO HEAT)	Fantasy FTC 163
31/03/1979	46	5		I (WHO HAVE NOTHING)	Fantasy FTC 171
07/07/1979	47	3		STARS	Fantasy FTC 177
11/09/1982	32	8		DO YOU WANNA FUNK SYLVESTER WITH PATRICK COWLEY	London LON 13
03/09/1983	67	2		BAND OF GOLD	London LON 33

SYLVIA US singer (born Sylvia Vanderpool, 6/3/1936, New York); part of duo Mickey & Sylvia with McHouston 'Mickey' Baker before going solo in 1973. She married record executive Joe Robinson, helped run the All Platinum label group and assembled the Sugarhill Gang.

23/06/1973	14	11		PILLOW TALK	London HL 10415

SYLVIA Swedish singer Sylvia Vrethammer. The song had originally been written by two Belgians, recorded by Samantha and become a big domestic hit. A Dutch version by Imca Marina sold over 1 million copies and topped the charts in Germany, Sweden and Spain despite there being 56 cover versions! The biggest UK hit, however, was by Sylvia.

10/08/1974	4	28	●	Y VIVA ESPANA	Sonet SON 2037
26/04/1975	38	5		HASTA LA VISTA	Sonet SON 2055

DAVID SYLVIAN UK singer (born David Batt, 23/2/1958, Lewisham) who was a founder member of Japan in 1977 until they disbanded in 1982 when he went solo.

07/08/1982	30	4		BAMBOO HOUSES/BAMBOO MUSIC SYLVIAN SAKAMOTO	Virgin VS 510
02/07/1983	16	8		FORBIDDEN COLOURS DAVID SYLVIAN AND RYUICHI SAKAMOTO	Virgin VS 601
02/06/1984	17	5		RED GUITAR	Virgin VS 633
18/08/1984	36	3		THE INK IN THE WELL	Virgin VS 700
03/11/1984	56	2		PULLING PUNCHES	Virgin VS 717
14/12/1985	72	1		WORDS WITH THE SHAMEN	Virgin VS 835
09/08/1986	53	3		TAKING THE VEIL	Virgin VS 815
17/01/1987	63	2		BUOY MICK KARN FEATURING DAVID SYLVIAN	Virgin VS 910
10/10/1987	66	1		LET THE HAPPINESS IN	Virgin VS 1001
13/06/1992	58	3		HEARTBEAT (TAINAI KAIKI II) RETURNING TO THE WOMB DAVID SYLVIAN/RYUICHI SAKAMOTO FEATURING INGRID CHAVEZ	Virgin America VUS 57
28/08/1993	68	2		JEAN THE BIRDMAN DAVID SYLVIAN AND ROBERT FRIPP	Virgin VSCDG 1462
27/03/1999	40	2		I SURRENDER	Virgin VSCDT 1722

SYMARIP UK group with Ray Ellis, Monty Naismith and Mick Thomas, all previously members of The Pyramids.

02/02/1980	54	3		SKINHEAD MOONSTOMP	Trojan TRO 9062

SYMBOLS UK group formed by Mick Clarke (bass/vocals), Clive Graham (drums), Rikki Smith (guitar) and Johnny Milton (vocals) as Johnny Milton & The Condors. They name-changed to The Symbols in 1965.

02/08/1967	44	3		BYE BYE BABY	President PT 144
03/01/1968	25	12		BEST PART OF BREAKING UP	President PT 173

TERRI SYMON UK singer (born Su Neil) who began backing the likes of David Grant before going solo in 1986.

10/06/1995	54	1		I WANT TO KNOW WHAT LOVE IS	A&M 5810592

SYMPOSIUM UK rock group formed in London in 1995 by Ross Cummins (vocals), William McGonagle (guitar), Hagop Tchaparian (guitar), Wojtek Godzisz (bass) and Joe Birch (drums).

22/03/1997	25	2		FAREWELL TO TWILIGHT	Infectious INFECT 34CD
31/05/1997	32	2		THE ANSWER TO WHY I HATE YOU	Infectious INFECT 37CD
30/08/1997	25	3		FAIRWEATHER FRIEND	Infectious INFECT 44CD
14/03/1998	45	1		AVERAGE MAN	Infectious INFECT 52CD

❶⁹ Number of weeks single topped the UK charts ↑ Entered the UK chart at #1 ▲⁹ Number of weeks single topped the American charts

791

16/05/1998	41	1		BURY YOU	Infectious INFECT 55CDS
18/07/1998	48	1		BLUE	Infectious INFECT 57CD

SYNTAX UK DJ/producer (born Michael Tournier, 24/5/1963, High Wycombe); he was previously in Fluke, Lucky Monkeys and Skin.

08/02/2003	28	3		PRAY	Illustrious/Epic CDILL 012
28/02/2004	69	1		BLISS	Illustrious/Epic CDILLX 020

SYREETA US singer (born Rita Wright, 3/8/1946, Pittsburgh, PA); she was a secretary at Motown in the early 1960s before becoming a session singer. She made her first single (as Rita Wright) in 1967, and began writing songs with Stevie Wonder in 1968. He produced her breakthrough album in 1972. They were married in 1970 and divorced in 1972. She later recorded for the Motorcity label and died from cancer on 6/7/2004.

21/09/1974	49	3		SPINNIN' AND SPINNIN'	Tamla Motown TMG 912
01/02/1975	12	8		YOUR KISS IS SWEET	Tamla Motown TMG 933
12/07/1975	32	4		HARMOUR LOVE	Tamla Motown TMG 954
15/12/1979	2	11	O	**WITH YOU I'M BORN AGAIN** Featured in the 1979 film *Fastbreak*	Motown TMG 1159
08/03/1980	47	4		IT WILL COME IN TIME This and above single credited to **BILLY PRESTON AND SYREETA**	Motown TMG 1175

SYSTEM US duo Mic Murphy (guitar/vocals) and David Frank (keyboards). Murphy later recorded solo.

09/06/1984	73	2		I WANNA MAKE YOU FEEL GOOD	Polydor POSP 685

SYSTEM F Dutch producer Ferry Corste. He is also a member of Gouryella and Veracocha, and records as Albion and Moonman.

03/04/1999	14	6		OUT OF THE BLUE	Essential Recordings 5704052
06/05/2000	19	4		CRY	Essential Recordings ESCD 14

SYSTEM OF A DOWN US rock group formed in Los Angeles, CA by Serj Tankian (vocals), Daron Malakian (guitar), Shavo Odadjian (bass) and John Doolayan (drums). After a three-song demo attracted interest they signed with American (distributed by Columbia) in 1997 and released their eponymous debut album the following year.

03/11/2001	17	4		CHOP SUEY	Columbia 6720342
23/03/2002	25	3		TOXICITY	Columbia 6725022
27/07/2002	34	2		ARIELS	Columbia 6728692

SYSTEM OF LIFE UK production group.

29/05/2004	63	1		LUV IS COOL	Freedream CDFDREAM1

SYSTEM PRESENTS KERRI B UK dance group.

08/11/2003	55	1		IF YOU LEAVE ME NOW	All Around The World CDGLOBE 288

SYSTEM 7 French/UK dance duo Miquette Giraudy and Steve Hillage (born 2/8/1951, London). The group has also featured contributions from DJ Paul Oakenfold, Alex Paterson (of The Orb) and Simple Minds' Mike McNeil (born 20/7/1958, Glasgow).

13/02/1993	39	1		7:7 EXPANSION	Butterfly BFLD 2
17/07/1993	74	1		SINBAD QUEST	Butterfly BFLD 8

T

T-BOZ
US singer (born Tionne Watkins, 26/4/1970, Des Moines, IA); she is a member of TLC and launched a parallel solo career in 1996.

23/11/1996	48	1	TOUCH MYSELF Featured in the 1996 film *Fled* . . . . LaFace 74321422882
14/04/2001	44	1	MY GETAWAY TIONNE 'T-BOZ' WATKINS . . . . Maverick W 549CD

T-CONNECTION
US soul group formed in the Bahamas in 1975 by Theopilus Coakley (vocals/keyboards), his brother Kirkwood (bass/drums), Anthony Flowers (drums) and David Mackey (guitar).

18/06/1977	11	8	DO WHAT YOU WANNA DO . . . . TK XC 9109
14/01/1978	16	5	ON FIRE . . . . TK TKR 6006
10/06/1978	52	3	LET YOURSELF GO . . . . TK TKR 6024
24/02/1979	53	5	AT MIDNIGHT . . . . TK TKR 7517
05/05/1979	41	6	SATURDAY NIGHT . . . . TK TKR 7536

T-COY – see VARIOUS ARTISTS (EPS AND LPS)

T-EMPO
UK producer (born Tim Lennox, 1966, Birmingham).

07/05/1994	19	3	SATURDAY NIGHT SUNDAY MORNING . . . . ffrr FCD 232
09/11/1996	71	1	THE LOOK OF LOVE/THE BLUE ROOM A-side contains a sample of New Order's *Blue Monday* . . . . ffrr FCD 281

T FACTORY
Italian production group. Their debut hit was originally to be called *Massage In A Brothel* and performed by a session singer, but Sting (of The Police) gave permission for his original vocals to be added to the track. It was originally released in 2000 with the artist credited to Tomato's Factory.

13/04/2002	51	2	MESSAGE IN A BOTTLE Contains a sample of The Police's *Message In A Bottle* . . . . Inferno CDFERN 44

T-POWER
UK producer Mark Royal.

13/04/1996	63	1	POLICE STATE . . . . Sound Of Underground TPOWCD 001
06/04/2002	7	11	SHAKE UR BODY SHY FX AND T POWER FEATURING DI . . . . Positiva CDTIV 171
23/11/2002	19	4	DON'T WANNA KNOW SHY FX/T POWER/DI & SKIBADEE . . . . ffrr FCD 408
07/06/2003	34	2	FEELIN' U SHY FX AND T-POWER FEATURING KELE LE ROC . . . . London FCD 409

T. REX
UK rock group formed in London in 1967 by Marc Bolan (born Mark Feld, 30/9/1947, Hackney, London, guitar/vocals), Steve Peregrine Took (born Stephen Porter, 28/7/1949, Eltham, percussion) and Ben Cartland. Took left in 1969, replaced by Mickey Finn (born 3/6/1947, Thornton Heath), with Steve Currie (bass) and Bill Legend (drums) also being recruited. Bolan appeared in the 1972 film *Born To Boogie*. He was killed when a car driven by his then-girlfriend Gloria Jones hit a tree on 16/9/1977. Took choked to death on a cherry on 27/10/1980 after eating 'magic mushrooms' that had numbed the senses in his throat. Currie was killed in a road crash on 28/4/1981. Finn died on 11/1/2003.

MARC BOLAN and T-REX

08/05/1968	34	7	DEBORA . . . . Regal Zonophone RZ 3008
04/09/1968	28	7	ONE INCH ROCK . . . . Regal Zonophone RZ 3011
09/08/1969	44	1	KING OF THE RUMBLING SPIRES This and above two singles credited to TYRANNOSAURUS REX . . . . Regal Zonophone RZ 3022
24/10/1970	2	20	RIDE A WHITE SWAN Featured in the 2000 film *Billy Elliott* . . . . Fly BUG 1
27/02/1971	❶6	17	HOT LOVE . . . . Fly BUG 6
10/07/1971	❶4	13	GET IT ON Featured in the 2000 film *Billy Elliott* . . . . Fly BUG 10
13/11/1971	2	15	JEEPSTER . . . . Fly BUG 16
29/01/1972	❶2	12	TELEGRAM SAM . . . . T Rex 101
01/04/1972	7	10	DEBORA/ONE INCH ROCK TYRANNOSAURUS REX Re-issue of Regal Zonophone RZ 3008 and Regal Zonophone RZ 3011 . . . .
			. . . . Magnifly ECHO 102
13/05/1972	❶4	14	METAL GURU . . . . EMI MARC 1
16/09/1972	2	10	CHILDREN OF THE REVOLUTION Featured in the 2000 film *Billy Elliott* . . . . EMI MARC 2
09/12/1972	2	11	SOLID GOLD EASY ACTION . . . . EMI MARC 3
10/03/1973	3	9	20TH CENTURY BOY . . . . EMI MARC 4
16/06/1973	4	9	THE GROOVER . . . . EMI MARC 5
24/11/1973	12	11	TRUCK ON (TYKE) . . . . EMI MARC 6
09/02/1974	13	5	TEENAGE DREAM MARC BOLAN AND T REX . . . . EMI MARC 7

❶9 Number of weeks single topped the UK chart ↑ Entered the UK chart at #1 ▲9 Number of weeks single topped the US chart

13/07/1974.....22.....5.....	LIGHT OF LOVE	EMI MARC 8
16/11/1974.....41.....3.....	ZIP GUN BOOGIE	EMI MARC 9
12/07/1975.....15.....8.....	NEW YORK CITY	EMI MARC 10
11/10/1975.....30.....5.....	DREAMY LADY T REX DISCO PARTY	EMI MARC 11
06/03/1976.....40.....3.....	LONDON BOYS	EMI MARC 13
19/06/1976.....13.....9.....	I LOVE TO BOOGIE Featured in the 2000 film Billy Elliott	EMI MARC 14
02/10/1976.....41.....4.....	LASER LOVE	EMI MARC 15
02/04/1977.....42.....4.....	THE SOUL OF MY SUIT	EMI MARC 16
09/05/1981.....50.....4.....	RETURN OF THE ELECTRIC WARRIOR (EP) Tracks on EP: Sing Me A Song, Endless Sleep Extended and The Lilac Hand Of Menthol Dan	Rarn MBSF 001
19/09/1981.....51.....4.....	YOU SCARE ME TO DEATH This and above single credited to MARC BOLAN	Cherry Red CHERRY 29
27/03/1982.....69.....2.....	TELEGRAM SAM...	T Rex 101
18/05/1985.....72.....2.....	MEGAREX Tracks on medley: Truck On (Tyke), The Groover, Telegram Sam, Shock Rock, Metal Guru, 20th Century Boy, Children Of The Revolution and Hot Love	Marc On Wax TANX 1
09/05/1987.....54.....4.....	GET IT ON (REMIX)	Marc On Wax MARC 10
24/08/1991.....13.....8.....	20TH CENTURY BOY This and above two singles credited to MARC BOLAN AND T REX Revived following use in a Levi Jeans advertisement	Marc On Wax MARC 501
07/10/2000.....59.....1.....	GET IT ON BUS STOP FEATURING T REX.......................................	All Around The World CDGLOBE 225

T-SHIRT UK vocal duo formed in London by Chloe Treend and Miranda Cooper.

13/09/1997.....63.....1.....	YOU SEXY THING..	Eternal WEA 122CD

T-SPOON Dutch vocal/instrumental group formed by Remy de Groot (also known as Prince Peration), Linda Estelle and Shamrock. Shamrock left the group in 1998, replaced by Greg Dillard. On stage the group is supplemented by numerous dancers.

19/09/1998 .....2.....13 .....O	SEX ON THE BEACH	Control 0042395 CON
23/01/1999.....27.....2.....	TOM'S PARTY..	Control 0043505 CON

T2 FEATURING ROBIN S US duo Todd Terry (born 18/4/1967, Brooklyn, NY) and Robin Stone (born Jamaica, NY). Terry also recorded as The Todd Terry Project.

04/10/1997.....62.....1.....	YOU GOT THE LOVE	Champion CHAMPCD 330

TABERNACLE UK instrumental/production group featuring singer Bessie Griffin.

04/03/1995.....62.....1.....	I KNOW THE LORD	Good Groove CDGG 1
03/02/1996.....55.....1.....	I KNOW THE LORD (REMIX)	Good Groove CDGGX 1

TACK HEAD US production/rap group formed in New York in 1984 by Keith LeBlanc, Bernard Fowler, Skip McDonald, Adrian Sherwood and Doug Wimbish.

30/06/1990.....48.....3.....	DANGEROUS SEX	SBK 7014

TAFFY UK singer Catherine Quaye.

10/01/1987 .....6.....10.....	I LOVE MY RADIO (MY DEE JAY'S RADIO)	Transglobal TYPE 1
18/07/1987.....59.....4.....	STEP BY STEP	Transglobal TYPE 5

TAG TEAM US hip-hop duo formed in Atlanta, GA by Cecil Glenn ('DC The Brain Supreme') and Steve Gibson ('Steve Rollin'). The pair first met when they were classmates in Denver.

08/01/1994.....34.....5.....	WHOOMP! (THERE IT IS) Contains a sample of Kano's I'm Ready. Featured in the 1994 film D2: The Mighty Ducks.............	CluTools SHXCD 1
29/01/1994.....53.....1.....	ADDAMS FAMILY (WHOOMP!)	Atlas PZCD 305
10/09/1994.....48.....2.....	WHOOMP! (THERE IT IS) (REMIX)	Club Tools SHXR 1

CADILLAC TAH — see JENNIFER LOPEZ AND JA RULE

TAIKO German production duo Stephan Bodzin and Oliver Huntemann.

29/06/2002.....72.....1.....	SILENCE..	Nukleuz NUKC 0330

TAK TIX US vocal/production group formed by Asha Elfenbein.

20/01/1996.....33.....2.....	FEEL LIKE SINGING	Dub Dub 5813212

TAKE 5 US vocal group formed in Minneapolis, MN by Clay Goodell, T.J. Christofore, Stevie Sculthorpe, Tilky Jones and Ryan Goodell.

07/11/1998.....70.....1.....	I GIVE	Edel 0039635 ERE
27/03/1999.....34.....3.....	NEVER HAD IT SO GOOD	Edel 0043975 ERE

O Silver disc ● Gold disc ✪ Platinum disc (additional platinum units are indicated by a figure following the symbol) ⓜ Singles released prior to 1973 that are known to have sold over 1 million copies in the UK

TAKE THAT
UK vocal group formed in Manchester in 1990 by Gary Barlow (born 20/1/1971, Frodsham), Howard Donald (born 27/4/1970, Manchester), Jason Orange (born 10/7/1974, Manchester), Mark Owen (born 27/1/1974, Oldham) and Robbie Williams (born 13/2/1974, Stoke-on-Trent) who took their name from a newspaper headline. Their initial single (*Do What U Like*) failed to chart but did secure them a major record deal with RCA. Williams had an acrimonious split with the group in 1995 and legal wrangles delayed his own solo career. The group announced they were to split in 1996 with their sign-off single *How Deep Is Your Love,* and with various solo projects awaiting the remaining members. *Back For Good*, for which they won a 1996 BRIT Award, was also their US chart debut. They also won two MTV Europe Music Awards: Best Group in 1994 and Best Live Act in 1995.

DATE	POS	WKS	BPI	SINGLE TITLE	LABEL & NUMBER
23/11/1991	38	2		PROMISES	RCA PB 45085
08/02/1992	47	3		ONCE YOU'VE TASTED LOVE	RCA PB 45257
06/06/1992	7	8		**IT ONLY TAKES A MINUTE**	RCA 74321101007
15/08/1992	15	6		I FOUND HEAVEN	RCA 74321108137
10/10/1992	7	9		**A MILLION LOVE SONGS**	RCA 74321116307
12/12/1992	3	12	O	**COULD IT BE MAGIC** 1993 BRIT Award for Best Single	RCA 74321123137
20/02/1993	2	10	O	**WHY CAN'T I WAKE UP WITH YOU**	RCA 74321133102
17/07/1993	❶⁴	11	●	**PRAY ↑** 1994 BRIT Award for Best Single. The video won the 1994 BRIT Award for Best Video	RCA 74321154502
09/10/1993	❶²	14	O	**RELIGHT MY FIRE ↑** TAKE THAT FEATURING LULU	RCA 74321167722
18/12/1993	❶¹	10	✪	**BABE ↑**	RCA 74321182122
09/04/1994	❶²	10	O	**EVERYTHING CHANGES ↑**	RCA 74321167732
09/07/1994	3	12	O	**LOVE AIN'T HERE ANYMORE**	RCA 74321214832
15/10/1994	❶²	15	O	**SURE ↑**	RCA 74321236622
08/04/1995	❶⁴	13	✪	**BACK FOR GOOD ↑** 1996 BRIT Award for Best Single	RCA 74321271462
05/08/1995	❶³	9	●	**NEVER FORGET ↑**	RCA 74321299572
09/03/1996	❶³	14	✪	**HOW DEEP IS YOUR LOVE ↑**	RCA 74321355592

TAKING BACK SUNDAY
US group formed in Amityville, NY in 1999 by Adam Lazzara (vocals), Ed Reyes (guitar), John Nolan (guitar), Shaun Cooper (bass) and Mark O'Connell (drums). Cooper and Nolan left in 2003 and were replaced by Fred Mascherino (guitar/vocals) and Matt Rubano (bass).

DATE	POS	WKS	BPI	SINGLE TITLE	LABEL & NUMBER
02/10/2004	70	1		A DECADE UNDER THE INFLUENCE	Victory VR236CD

BILLY TALBOT – see IAN McNABB

TALI
New Zealand female singer/rapper MC Tali who was discovered by Roni Size.

DATE	POS	WKS	BPI	SINGLE TITLE	LABEL & NUMBER
10/08/2002	75	1		LYRIC ON MY LIP	Full Cycle FCY 042
07/02/2004	42	2		BLAZIN'	Full Cycle FCYCDS 059
15/05/2004	39	2		LYRIC ON MY LIP Re-issue of Full Cycle FCY 042	Full Cycle FCYCDS 065

TALK TALK
UK rock group formed in London in 1981 by Mark Hollis (born 1955, London, vocals/guitar/keyboards), Lee Harris (drums), Simon Bremner (keyboards) and Paul Webb (born 16/1/1962, bass). They signed with EMI the same year, with Bremner leaving in 1983. They switched to Polydor in 1990 but disbanded the following year.

DATE	POS	WKS	BPI	SINGLE TITLE	LABEL & NUMBER
24/04/1982	52	4		TALK TALK	EMI 5284
24/07/1982	14	13		TODAY	EMI 5314
13/11/1982	23	10		TALK TALK (REMIX)	EMI 5352
19/03/1983	57	3		MY FOOLISH FRIEND	EMI 5373
14/01/1984	46	5		IT'S MY LIFE	EMI 5443
07/04/1984	49	6		SUCH A SHAME	EMI 5433
11/08/1984	74	1		DUM DUM GIRL	EMI 5480
18/01/1986	16	9		LIFE'S WHAT YOU MAKE IT	EMI 5540
15/03/1986	48	4		LIVING IN ANOTHER WORLD	EMI 5551
17/05/1986	59	3		GIVE IT UP	Parlophone R 6131
19/05/1990	13	9		IT'S MY LIFE Re-issue of EMI 5443	Parlophone R 6254
01/09/1990	23	6		LIFE'S WHAT YOU MAKE IT Re-issue of EMI 5540	Parlophone R 6264
21/06/2003	64	1		IT'S MY LIFE LIQUID PEOPLE VS TALK TALK	Nebula NEBCD 045

TALKING HEADS
US rock group formed in New York in 1974 by David Byrne (born 14/5/1952, Dumbarton, Scotland, guitar/vocals), Tina Weymouth (born 22/11/1950, Coronado, CA, bass) and Chris Frantz (born 8/5/1951, Fort Campbell, KY, drums). They signed with Sire in 1976 having added Jerry Harrison (born 21/2/1949, Milwaukee, WI, keyboards) to the line-up. Byrne won the 1988 Grammy Award for Best Album of Original Instrumental Background Score written for a Motion Picture with Ryuichi Sakamoto and Cong Su for *The Last Emperor*. The group was inducted into the Rock & Roll Hall of Fame in 2002.

DATE	POS	WKS	BPI	SINGLE TITLE	LABEL & NUMBER
07/02/1981	14	10		ONCE IN A LIFETIME Featured in the 1986 film *Down And Out In Beverly Hills*	Sire SIR 4048
09/05/1981	50	3		HOUSES IN MOTION	Sire SIR 4050
21/01/1984	51	3		THIS MUST BE THE PLACE	sire W 9451
03/11/1984	68	2		SLIPPERY PEOPLE	EMI 5504
12/10/1985	6	16		**ROAD TO NOWHERE**	EMI 5530
08/02/1986	17	8		AND SHE WAS	EMI 5543
06/09/1986	43	4		WILD WILD LIFE	EMI 5567

❶⁹ Number of weeks single topped the UK chart ↑ Entered the UK chart at #1 ▲⁹ Number of weeks single topped the US chart

16/05/1987	52	2	RADIO HEAD	EMI EM 1
13/08/1988	59	3	BLIND	EMI EM 68
10/10/1992	50	3	LIFETIME PILING UP	EMI EM 250

TALL PAUL
UK DJ/producer 'Tall Paul' Newman who previously recorded as Escrima and Camisra and is also a member of Partizan.

29/03/1997	12	4	ROCK DA HOUSE Contains a sample of Homeboys Only's *Turn It Out*	VC Recordings VCRD 18
29/05/1999	45	1	BE THERE	Duty Free DF 009CD
08/04/2000	43	2	FREEBASE	Duty Free DF 015CD
02/06/2001	29	2	ROCK DA HOUSE (REMIX)	VC Recordings VCRD 89
18/08/2001	14	5	PRECIOUS HEART TALL PAUL VS INXS	Duty Freee/Decode DFTELCD 001
13/04/2002	60	1	EVERYBODY'S A ROCK STAR	Duty Free DFTELCD 003

TAMBA TRIO
Argentinian group formed by Luis Eca (piano), Bebeto Castilho (flute/saxophone) and Heldo Milito (percussion).

18/07/1998	34	2	MAS QUE NADA	Talkin Loud TLCD 34

TAMIA – see FABOLOUS

TAMPERER FEATURING MAYA
Italian production team of Mario Fargetta, Alex Farolfi and Giuliano Saglia with US singer Maya, who was a make-up artist at the time of their debut hit.

25/04/1998	●¹ 17	○	FEEL IT Based on The Jacksons' *Can You Feel It*	Pepper 0530032
14/11/1998	3 14	○	IF YOU BUY THIS RECORD YOUR LIFE WILL BE BETTER Contains a sample of Madonna's *Material Girl*	Pepper 0530082
12/02/2000	6 7		HAMMER TO THE HEART Featured in the 2000 film *Drive Me Crazy*	Pepper 9230038

TAMS
US R&B vocal group formed in Atlanta, GA in 1952 by Joseph Pope (born 6/11/1933, Atlanta), Charles Pope (born 7/8/1936, Atlanta), Robert Lee Smith (born 18/3/1936) and Horace Kay (born 13/4/1934) as the Four Dots. They added a further singer in Floyd Ashton (born 15/8/1933, Atlanta) prior to signing their first recording deal with Swan in 1960 and name-changed to the Tams (because they wore Tam O'Shanter hats on stage). Ashton left in 1964, replaced by Albert Cottle (born 2/8/1941, Atlanta). Horace Key died in 1991, replaced by Robert Arnold (born 21/4/1954, Atlanta), Joseph Pope died from heart failure on 16/3/1996. Reginald Preston (born 6/7/1969) joined the group in 1998.

14/02/1970	32	7	BE YOUNG BE FOOLISH BE HAPPY Originally released in the US in 1968 (position #61)	Stateside SS 2123
31/07/1971	●³ 17		HEY GIRL DON'T BOTHER ME Originally released in the US in 1964 (position #41)	Probe PRO 532
21/11/1987	21	7	THERE AIN'T NOTHING LIKE SHAGGIN' Banned by the BBC because of the title, though it refers to a dance style	Virgin VS 1029

NORMA TANEGA
US singer/songwriter/pianist/guitarist (born 30/1/1939, Vallejo, CA).

07/04/1966	22	8	WALKING MY CAT NAMED DOG	Stateside SS 496

CHILDREN OF TANSLEY SCHOOL
UK children's school choir who also recorded an album of similar material.

28/03/1981	27	4	MY MUM IS ONE IN A MILLION	EMI 5151

JIMMY TARBUCK
UK singer (born 6/2/1940, Liverpool), best known as a comedian.

16/11/1985	68	2	AGAIN	Safari SAFE 68

TARLISA – see CO-RO FEATURING TARLISA

BILL TARMEY
UK actor/singer (born William Cleworth Piddington, 4/4/1941, Manchester) whose most prominent role has been that of Jack Duckworth in the TV series *Coronation Street*.

03/04/1993	16	4	ONE VOICE	Arista 74321140852
19/02/1994	40	3	WIND BENEATH MY WINGS	EMI CDEM 304
19/11/1994	55	2	IOU	EMI CDEM 361

TARRIERS
US folk trio formed by Erik Darling (banjo/vocals), Bob Carey (bass) and Alan Arkin (guitar/vocals). Their debut hit with Vince Martin was adapted from a sailor's sea shanty. Arkin became better known as an actor and appeared in films such as *Freebie And The Bean*.

14/12/1956	26	1	CINDY OH CINDY VINCE MARTIN AND THE TARRIERS	London HLN 8340
01/03/1957	15	5	BANANA BOAT SONG	Columbia DB 3891

TARTAN ARMY
UK vocal group formed by supporters of the Scottish World Cup squad.

06/06/1998	54	4	SCOTLAND BE GOOD	Precious Organisation JWLCD 33

A TASTE OF HONEY
US R&B group formed in Los Angeles, CA in 1972 by Janice Marie Johnson (guitar/vocals), Hazel Payne (vocals/bass), Perry Kibble (born 10/6/1949, keyboards) and Donald Johnson (drums). The two female members re-formed the group in 1980. The group won the 1978 Grammy Award for Best New Artist. Kibble died on 22/2/1999.

17/06/1978	3 16	○	BOOGIE OOGIE OOGIE ▲³ Featured in the 1997 film *Breast Men*	Capitol CL 15988
18/05/1985	59	3	BOOGIE OOGIE OOGIE (REMIX)	Capitol CL 357

TASTE XPERIENCE FEATURING NATASHA PEARL
UK instrumental/production group formed by Russell Barker and Richard Cornish with singer Natasha Pearl.

06/11/1999	66	1	SUMMERSAULT	Manifesto FESCD 64

○ Silver disc ● Gold disc ✪ Platinum disc (additional platinum units are indicated by a figure following the symbol) ◉ Singles released prior to 1973 that are known to have sold over 1 million copies in the UK

TATA BOX INHIBITORS
Dutch production duo Jamez and Dobre (Gaston Steenkist); they also record as Trancesetters. Steenkist is also a member of DJ Manta, Goodmen, Chocolate Puma, Tomba Vira, Jark Prongo, Rhythmkillaz and Riva.

03/02/2001 . . . . . 67 . . . . . . 1 . . . . FREET . . . . Hooj Choons HOOJ 103CD

TATJANA
Croatian model/actress/singer (born Tatjana Simic, Zagreb) who moved to Holland with her family in 1979. She appeared in *Baywatch Nights* and the *Charlie's Angels* remake. Her debut hit was removed from the charts under suspicions it had been hyped.

21/09/1996 . . . . . 40 . . . . . . 2 . . . . SANTA MARIA . . . . Love This LUVTHISCDX 4

TATU
Russian vocal duo Lena Katina (born Katina Elana Sergheeva, 4/10/1984, Moscow) and Julia Volkova Olegovna (born 20/2/1985, Moscow). Their name means This Girl Loves That Girl, reflecting their lesbian stance (later revealed as a marketing ploy instigated by their manager, especially when it was announced in May 2004 that Julia was pregnant by her long-term boyfriend).

25/01/2003 . . . . . 44 . . . . . . 2				ALL THE THINGS SHE SAID (IMPORT)	Interscope 0193332
08/02/2003 . . . . . ❶⁴ . . . . . 15 . . . . . ○				**ALL THE THINGS SHE SAID** ↑	Interscope 0196972
31/05/2003 . . . . . 7 . . . . . . 8				**NOT GONNA GET US**	Interscope 9806961

TAVARES
US R&B vocal group formed in New Bedford, MA in 1964 by brothers Ralph, Antone 'Chubby', Feliciano 'Butch', Arthur 'Pooch' and Perry Lee 'Tiny' Tavares as Chubby & The Turnpikes. They changed their name to Tavares in 1969.

10/07/1976 . . . . . 4 . . . . . . 11 . . . . . ○ **HEAVEN MUST BE MISSING AN ANGEL** Featured in the 2000 film *Charlie's Angels* . . . . Capitol CL 15876
09/10/1976 . . . . . 4 . . . . . . 10 . . . . . ○ **DON'T TAKE AWAY THE MUSIC** . . . . Capitol CL 15886
05/02/1977 . . . . . 25 . . . . . . 6 . . . . . . MIGHTY POWER OF LOVE . . . . Capitol CL 15905
09/04/1977 . . . . . 5 . . . . . . 10 . . . . . . **WHODUNNIT** . . . . Capitol CL 15914
02/07/1977 . . . . . 16 . . . . . . 7 . . . . . . ONE STEP AWAY . . . . Capitol CL 15930
18/03/1978 . . . . . 29 . . . . . . 6 . . . . . . THE GHOST OF LOVE . . . . Capitol CL 15968
06/05/1978 . . . . . 7 . . . . . . 11 . . . . . . **MORE THAN A WOMAN** Featured in the 1978 film *Saturday Night Fever* . . . . Capitol CL 15977
12/08/1978 . . . . . 62 . . . . . . 3 . . . . . . SLOW TRAIN TO PARADISE . . . . Capitol CL 15996
22/02/1986 . . . . . 12 . . . . . . 9 . . . . . . HEAVEN MUST BE MISSING AN ANGEL (REMIX) . . . . Capitol TAV 1
03/05/1986 . . . . . 46 . . . . . . 4 . . . . . . IT ONLY TAKES A MINUTE . . . . Capitol TAV 2

TAXMAN – see KICKING BACK WITH TAXMAN

TAYLOR – see LIBRA PRESENTS TAYLOR

ANDY TAYLOR
UK singer/guitarist (born 16/2/1961, Wolverhampton) who was a founder member of Duran Duran in 1978 and remained with the group until 1984. He then helped form Power Station with fellow Duran Duran member John Taylor, Robert Palmer and Tony Thompson. He launched a parallel solo career in 1987.

20/10/1990 . . . . . 60 . . . . . . 2 . . . . LOLA . . . . A&M AM 596

BECKY TAYLOR
UK singer (born 1988, London) who appeared in the West End musical *Les Miserables,* aged seven, and won the British Arts Awards final for dancing, aged nine. She was signed by EMI Classics a week after her father sent in a demo tape of her singing.

16/06/2001 . . . . . 60 . . . . . . 1 . . . . SONG OF DREAMS . . . . EMI Classics 8794880

DINA TAYLOR – see BBG

FELICE TAYLOR
US singer (born 29/1/1948, Richmond, CA) who was discovered by Barry White. She also recorded the original version of *It May Be Winter Outside* in 1967, later a major hit for Love Unlimited (and a top 50 pop and R&B hit for Felice).

25/10/1967 . . . . . 11 . . . . . . 13 . . . . . . I FEEL LOVE COMIN' ON . . . . President PT 155

JAMES TAYLOR
US singer (born 12/3/1948, Boston, MA) who formed the Flying Machine in 1966. When they split in 1967 he moved to the UK and was signed as a solo artist to Apple Records, releasing one album before returning to the US and signing with Warner's. He married Carly Simon in 1972 and was divorced in 1983. He 'appeared' in an episode of *The Simpsons* offering advice when Homer became an astronaut. James has won six Grammy Awards including Best Pop Vocal Performance in 1977 for *Handyman,* Best Recording For Children in 1980 with various others for *In Harmony,* Best Recording for Children in 1982 with various others for *In Harmony 2,* Best Pop Album in 1997 for *Hourglass* and Best Male Pop Vocal Performance in 2001 for *Don't Let Me Be Lonely Tonight.* He was inducted into the Rock & Roll Hall of Fame in 2000.

21/11/1970 . . . . . 42 . . . . . . 3 . . . . FIRE AND RAIN . . . . Warner Brothers WB 6104
28/08/1971 . . . . . 4 . . . . . . 15 . . . . . . **YOU'VE GOT A FRIEND** ▲¹ 1971 Grammy Award for Best Pop Vocal Performance . . . . Warner Brothers K 16085
16/03/1974 . . . . . 34 . . . . . . 5 . . . . . . MOCKINGBIRD CARLY SIMON AND JAMES TAYLOR . . . . Elektra K 12134

JAMES TAYLOR QUARTET – see JTQ

JOHN TAYLOR
UK singer (born Nigel John Taylor, 20/6/1960, Birmingham) and a founder member of Duran Duran in 1978. He later became a member of Power Station.

15/03/1986 . . . . . 42 . . . . . . 4 . . . . I DO WHAT I DO...THEME FOR '9½ WEEKS' Featured in the 1986 film *9½ Weeks* . . . . Parlophone R 6125

JOHNNIE TAYLOR
US singer (born 5/5/1938, Crawfordsville, AR) who replaced Sam Cooke in the Soul Stirrers and then joined Cooke's Sar label as a solo artist in 1963. He switched to Stax in 1966, then to CBS in 1976. His hit was the first single certified platinum by the R.I.A.A. (Recording Industry Association of America), indicating sales over 2 million units. He later recorded for Malaco, scoring a number of US R&B hits. He had his first heart attack in 1980 and died from a massive heart attack on 31/5/2000.

❶⁹ Number of weeks single topped the UK chart ↑ Entered the UK chart at #1 ▲⁹ Number of weeks single topped the US chart

797

24/04/1976	25	7		DISCO LADY ▲⁴	CBS 4044

JT TAYLOR US singer (born James Taylor, 16/8/1953, South Carolina) who joined Kool & The Gang as lead singer in 1979 and remained with the group until he went solo in 1988. He rejoined the group in the 1990s.

24/08/1991	63	2		LONG HOT SUMMER NIGHT	MCA MCS 1567
30/11/1991	57	1		FEEL THE NEED	MCA MCS 1592
18/04/1992	59	2		FOLLOW ME	MCA MCS 1617

PAULINE TAYLOR UK singer who sang with Faithless before going solo.

08/06/1996	26	2		LET THIS BE A PRAYER ROLLO GOES SPIRITUAL WITH PAULINE TAYLOR	Cheeky CHEKCD 013
09/11/1996	51	1		CONSTANTLY WAITING	Cheeky CHEKCD 015

R. DEAN TAYLOR Canadian singer (born 1939, Toronto) who made his first recordings for Parry in 1960, but was first known as a songwriter at Motown (he wrote *Love Child* for The Supremes) before resuming his singing career. He later launched the Jane label.

19/06/1968	17	12		GOTTA SEE JANE	Tamla Motown TMG 656
03/04/1971	2	15		INDIANA WANTS ME	Tamla Motown TMG 763
11/05/1974	3	12	O	THERE'S A GHOST IN MY HOUSE	Tamla Motown TMG 896
31/08/1974	36	5		WINDOW SHOPPING	Polydor 2058 502
21/09/1974	41	4		GOTTA SEE JANE Re-issue of Tamla Motown TMG 656	Tamla Motown TMG 918

ROGER TAYLOR UK singer/drummer (born Roger Meddows Taylor, 26/7/1949, King's Lynn, Norfolk) who was a founder member of Queen in 1970 and launched a parallel solo career in 1981.

18/04/1981	49	4		FUTURE MANAGEMENT	EMI 5157
16/06/1984	66	2		MAN ON FIRE	EMI 5478
10/10/1992	37	3		RADIO SHAKY FEATURING ROGER TAYLOR	Epic 6584367
14/05/1994	22	2		NAZIS	Parlophone CDR 6379
01/10/1994	26	2		FOREIGN SAND ROGER TAYLOR AND YOSHIKI	Parlophone CDR 6389
26/11/1994	32	2		HAPPINESS	Parlophone CDRS 6399
10/10/1998	45	1		PRESSURE ON	Parlophone CDR 6507
10/04/1999	38	2		SURRENDER	Parlophone CDRS 6517

TAZ AND STEREO NATION UK vocal duo Tarsame Singh and DJ Kendall. Singh had previously recorded as Johnny Zee. Kendall later left and Taz (as he had become known) continued to record alone under the Stereo Nation moniker.

27/10/2001	44	2		LAILA	Wizard WIZ 015
26/06/2004	46	2		CAN'T CONTAIN ME TAZ	Def Jam UK/Mercury 9866825

TC Italian instrumental/production duo led by Marco Fratty.

14/03/1992	73	1		BERRY TC 1991	Union City UCRT 13
21/11/1992	40	2		FUNKY GUITAR TC 1992	Union City UCRT 13
10/07/1993	51	2		HARMONY TC 1993	Union City UCRD 20

KIRI TE KANAWA New Zealand singer (born 6/3/1944, Gisborne) who sang at the 1981 wedding of HRH Prince Charles and Lady Diana Spencer. She was made a Dame of the British Empire in 1982.

28/09/1991	4	11		WORLD IN UNION Theme to ITV's coverage of the 1991 Rugby World Cup	Columbia 6574817

TEACH-IN Dutch group formed in Enschede in 1973, fronted by Austrian singer Getty Kaspers. They won the 1975 Eurovision Song Contest, beating UK entry by the Shadows into second place. The single was produced by Eddy Ouwens, who later hit as Danny Mirror.

12/04/1975	13	7		DING-A-DONG 1975 Eurovision Song Contest winning entry	Polydor 2058 570

TEAM UK vocal/instrumental group.

01/06/1985	55	5		WICKY WACKY HOUSE PARTY	EMI 5519

TEAM DEEP Belgian production duo.

17/05/1997	42	1		MORNINGLIGHT	Multiply CDMULTY 19

TEARDROP EXPLODES UK rock group formed in Liverpool in 1978 by Julian Cope (born 21/10/1957, Deri, Mid-Glamorgan, vocals/bass), Paul Simpson (keyboards), Michael Simpson (guitar) and Gary Dwyer (drums) and signed with Zoo in 1979. Simpson left in 1979, replaced by Dave Balfe. They disbanded in 1982 with Cope recording solo. Balfe later formed Food records, discovering Blur and Shampoo before selling the label to EMI Records.

27/09/1980	47	6		WHEN I DREAM	Mercury TEAR 1
31/01/1981	6	13	O	REWARD	Vertigo TEAR 2
02/05/1981	18	8		TREASON (IT'S JUST A STORY)	Mercury TEAR 3
29/08/1981	25	10		PASSIONATE FRIEND	Mercury TEAR 5
21/11/1981	54	3		COLOURS FLY AWAY	Mercury TEAR 6
19/06/1982	44	7		TINY CHILDREN	Mercury TEAR 7
19/03/1983	41	3		YOU DISAPPEAR FROM VIEW	Mercury TEAR 8

TEARS FOR FEARS UK group formed in 1981 by Roland Orzabal (born Roland Orzabal de la Quintana, 22/8/1961, Portsmouth, guitar/keyboards) and Curt Smith (born 24/6/1961, Bath, vocals/bass), both ex-Graduate, a five-piece ska band. Initially

O Silver disc ● Gold disc ✪ Platinum disc (additional platinum units are indicated by a figure following the symbol) ◉ Singles released prior to 1973 that are known to have sold over 1 million copies in the UK

called History of Headaches, they took their name from Arthur Janov's book *Prisoners Of Pain* in which fears have to be confronted in order to be eliminated. They signed with Mercury in 1981 and worked with producer Chris Hughes (former member of Adam and the Ants). They split in 1992 with Smith recording solo and Orzabal retaining the group name; by 2000 they had effectively re-formed. Smith later launched the Zerodisc label.

02/10/1982 . . . . . 3 . . . . . . 16 . . . . . O	**MAD WORLD** . . . . Mercury IDEA 3
05/02/1983 . . . . . 4 . . . . . . 9 . . . . . O	**CHANGE** . . . . Mercury IDEA 4
30/04/1983 . . . . . 5 . . . . . . 8	**PALE SHELTER** . . . . Mercury IDEA 5
03/12/1983 . . . . . 24 . . . . . . 8	THE WAY YOU ARE . . . . Mercury IDEA 6
18/08/1984 . . . . . 14 . . . . . . 8	MOTHER'S TALK . . . . Mercury IDEA 7
01/12/1984 . . . . . 4 . . . . . . 16 . . . . . O	**SHOUT ▲²** . . . . Mercury IDEA 8
30/03/1985 . . . . . 2 . . . . . . 14 . . . . . O	**EVERYBODY WANTS TO RULE THE WORLD ▲³** 1986 BRIT Award for Best Single. Featured in the 1997 film *Romy And Michele's High School Reunion* . . . . Mercury IDEA 9
22/06/1985 . . . . . 12 . . . . . . 9	HEAD OVER HEELS . . . . Mercury IDEA 10
31/08/1985 . . . . . 52 . . . . . . 4	SUFFER THE CHILDREN . . . . Mercury IDEA 1
07/09/1985 . . . . . 73 . . . . . . 2	PALE SHELTER . . . . Mercury IDEA 2
12/10/1985 . . . . . 23 . . . . . . 4	I BELIEVE (A SOULFUL RECORDING) . . . . Mercury IDEA 11
22/02/1986 . . . . . 73 . . . . . . 1	EVERYBODY WANTS TO RULE THE WORLD . . . . Mercury IDEA 9
31/05/1986 . . . . . 5 . . . . . . 7	**EVERYBODY WANTS TO RUN THE WORLD** Charity remake of *Everybody Wants To Rule The World* . . . . Mercury RACE 1
02/09/1989 . . . . . 5 . . . . . . 9	**SOWING THE SEEDS OF LOVE** . . . . Fontana IDEA 12
18/11/1989 . . . . . 26 . . . . . . 8	WOMAN IN CHAINS Features Oleta Adams on backing vocals and Phil Collins on drums. . . . . Fontana IDEA 13
03/03/1990 . . . . . 36 . . . . . . 4	ADVICE FOR THE YOUNG AT HEART . . . . Fontana IDEA 14
22/02/1992 . . . . . 17 . . . . . . 5	LAID SO LOW (TEARS ROLL DOWN) . . . . Fontana IDEA 17
25/04/1992 . . . . . 57 . . . . . . 1	WOMAN IN CHAINS . . . . Fontana IDEA 16
29/05/1993 . . . . . 20 . . . . . . 5	BREAK IT DOWN AGAIN . . . . Mercury IDECD 18
31/07/1993 . . . . . 72 . . . . . . 1	COLD . . . . Mercury IDECD 19
07/10/1995 . . . . . 31 . . . . . . 3	RAOUL AND THE KINGS OF SPAIN . . . . Epic 6624765
29/06/1996 . . . . . 61 . . . . . . 1	GOD'S MISTAKE . . . . Epic 6634185

TECHNATION UK production duo.

07/04/2001 . . . . . 56 . . . . . . 1	SEA OF BLUE . . . . Slinky Music SLINK 012CD

TECHNICIAN 2 UK instrumental/production group formed by Toby Jarvis and Ben Keen with singer Georgia Lewis.

14/11/1992 . . . . . 70 . . . . . . 1	PLAYING WITH THE BOY . . . . MCA MCS 1710

TECHNIQUE UK vocal/instrumental duo Stephen Hague and Richard Norris.

10/04/1999 . . . . . 64 . . . . . . 1	SUN IS SHINING . . . . Creation CRESCD 306
28/08/1999 . . . . . 56 . . . . . . 1	YOU + ME . . . . Creation CRESCD 315

TECHNO TWINS UK vocal/instrumental duo Bev Sage and Steve Fairnie.

16/01/1982 . . . . . 70 . . . . . . 2	FALLING IN LOVE AGAIN . . . . PRT 7P 224

TECHNOHEAD UK duo formed by remixer/producer Michael Wells with female singer Lee Newman. Wells has also recorded as Tricky Disco and GTO.

03/02/1996 . . . . . 6 . . . . . . 14 . . . . . O	**I WANNA BE A HIPPY** . . . . Mokum DB 17703
27/04/1996 . . . . . 18 . . . . . . 5	HAPPY BIRTHDAY . . . . Mokum DB 17593
12/10/1996 . . . . . 64 . . . . . . 1	BANANA-NA-NA (DUMB DI DUMB) . . . . Mokum DB 17473

TECHNOTRONIC Belgian dance group assembled by producer and DJ Jo 'Thomas DeQuincy' Bogaert and rapper Manuella 'Ya Kid K' Komosi with MC Eric. The group's videos also feature model Felly. They also recorded as Hi-Tek 3 Featuring Ya Kid K.

02/09/1989 . . . . . 2 . . . . . . 15 . . . . . ●	**PUMP UP THE JAM** TECHNOTRONIC FEATURING FELLY . . . . Swanyard SYR 4
03/02/1990 . . . . . 2 . . . . . . 10 . . . . . O	**GET UP (BEFORE THE NIGHT IS OVER)** TECHNOTRONIC FEATURING YA KID K . . . . Swanyard SYR 8
07/04/1990 . . . . . 14 . . . . . . 7	THIS BEAT IS TECHNOTRONIC TECHNOTRONIC FEATURING MC ERIC. . . . . Swanyard SYR 9
14/07/1990 . . . . . 9 . . . . . . 9	ROCKIN' OVER THE BEAT TECHNOTRONIC FEATURING YA KID K Featured in the 1993 film *Teenage Mutant Ninja Turtles III* . . . . Swanyard SYR 14
06/10/1990 . . . . . 6 . . . . . . 8	**MEGAMIX** . . . . Swanyard SYR 19
15/12/1990 . . . . . 42 . . . . . . 4	TURN IT UP TECHNOTRONIC FEATURING MELISSA AND EINSTEIN . . . . Swanyard SYD 9
25/05/1991 . . . . . 12 . . . . . . 7	MOVE THAT BODY . . . . ARS 6568377
03/08/1991 . . . . . 40 . . . . . . 4	WORK This and above single credited to TECHNOTRONIC FEATURING REGGIE . . . . ARS 6573317
14/12/1996 . . . . . 36 . . . . . . 2	PUMP UP THE JAM (REMIX) . . . . Worx WORXCD 004

TEDDY BEARS US pop group formed in Los Angeles, CA by Phil Spector (born 26/12/1940, New York), Carol Connors and Marshall Leib. Spector later became one of the most prominent producers in the history of pop music. He married Ronette member Ronnie Bennett in 1968 and divorced in 1974 (Spector made his first alimony payment of $1,300 to her in 26,000 nickels). In November 2001 the New York Supreme Court's appellate division upheld a lower court ruling ordering Spector to pay $3 million in back royalties. Although a 1963 agreement between Spector and The Ronettes did not include synchronisation and domestic licensing rights, the court ruled The Ronettes were entitled to payment for such usage in accordance with industry customs and practices.

19/12/1958 . . . . . 2 . . . . . . 16	**TO KNOW HIM IS TO LOVE HIM ▲³** . . . . London HLN 8733
14/04/1979 . . . . . 66 . . . . . . 1	TO KNOW HIM IS TO LOVE HIM Coupled with Jody Reynolds' *Endless Sleep* . . . . Lightning LIG 9015

❶⁹ Number of weeks single topped the UK chart   ↑ Entered the UK chart at #1   ▲⁹ Number of weeks single topped the US chart

799

TEEBONE FEATURING MC KIE AND MC SPARKS
UK producer Leon Thompson with rap duo MC Kie and MC Sparks.

05/08/2000	43	2	FLY BI	East West EW 217CD

TEENAGE FANCLUB
UK rock group formed in Scotland in 1989 by Norman Blake (born 20/10/1965, Glasgow, guitar/vocals), Raymond McGinley (born 3/1/1964, Glasgow, guitar/vocals) and Francis MacDonald (born 21/11/1970, Bellshill, drums), later adding Gerard Love (born 31/8/1967, Motherwell, bass) to the line-up. Most of the band were ex-Boy Hairdressers. MacDonald left in 1989, replaced by Brendan O'Hare (born 16/1/1970, Motherwell). By 1995 Paul Quinn had taken over on drums.

24/08/1991	44	2	STAR SIGN	Creation CRE 105
02/11/1991	51	1	THE CONCEPT	Creation CRE 111
08/02/1992	31	2	WHAT YOU DO TO ME (EP) Tracks on EP: *What You Do To Me, B-side, Life's A Gas* and *Filler*	Creation CRE 115
26/06/1993	31	2	RADIO	Creation CRESCD 130
02/10/1993	50	1	NORMAN 3	Creation CRESCD 142
02/04/1994	59	1	FALLIN' TEENAGE FANCLUB AND DE LA SOUL Contains a sample of Tom Petty's *Free Fallin'*. Featured in the 1994 film *Judgement Night*	Epic 6602622
08/04/1995	34	2	MELLOW DOUBT	Creation CRESCD 175
27/05/1995	40	2	SPARKY'S DREAM	Creation CRESCD 201
02/09/1995	62	1	NEIL JUNG	Creation CRESCD 210
16/12/1995	53	1	HAVE LOST IT (EP) Tracks on EP: *120 Mins, Don't Look Back, Everything Flows* and *Star Sign*	Creation CRESCD 216
12/07/1997	17	3	AIN'T THAT ENOUGH	Creation CRESCD 228
30/08/1997	43	1	I DON'T WANT CONTROL OF YOU	Creation CRESCD 238
29/11/1997	54	1	START AGAIN	Creation CRESCD 280
28/10/2000	48	1	I NEED DIRECTION	Columbia 6699512
02/03/2002	68	1	NEAR TO ME TEENAGE FANCLUB AND JAD FAIR	Geographic GEOG 013CD
04/09/2004	75	1	ASSOCIATION INTERNATIONAL AIRPORT/TEENAGE FANCLUB	Geographic GEOG 29CD

TEENAGERS – see FRANKIE LYMON AND THE TEENAGERS

TOWA TEI FEATURING KYLIE MINOGUE
Japanese DJ/producer with Australian singer Kylie Minogue.

31/10/1998	63	1	GBI	Athrob ART 021CD

TEKNO TOO
UK instrumental/production duo.

13/07/1991	56	2	JET-STAR	D-Zone DANCE 012

TELEPOPMUSIK
French electronic group formed in 1997 by Fabrice Dumont, Stephan Haeri and Christophe Hetier.

02/03/2002	42	1	BREATHE	Chrysalis CDCHS 5133

TELETUBBIES
UK children's TV characters featuring Tinky Winky, Po, Dipsy and Laa-Laa. The characters are played by Dave Thompson, Pui Fan Lee, John Simmit and Nikky Sedley respectively. Simon Shelton replaced Thompson in 1998.

13/12/1997	●²	32	✪²	TELETUBBIES SAY EH-OH! ↑	BBC Worldwide Music WMXS 00092

TELEVISION
US rock group formed in New York in 1973 by Richard Hell (born Richard Myers, 2/10/1949, Lexington, KY, bass), Tom Verlaine (born Thomas Miller, 13/12/1949, New Jersey, guitar/vocals), Billy Ficca (drums) and Richard Lloyd (guitar). Hell left in 1975, replaced by Fred Smith (born 10/4/1948, New York). They disbanded in 1978, but re-formed in 1990.

16/04/1977	30	4	MARQUEE MOON	Elektra K 12252
30/07/1977	25	4	PROVE IT	Elektra K 12262
22/04/1978	36	2	FOXHOLE	Elektra K 12287

TELEX
Belgian vocal/instrumental trio formed by Dan Lacksman, Marc Moulin and Michel Moers. The year after their debut hit they represented Belgium in the Eurovision Song Contest and came second but last with one point (Turkey were bottom with no points!).

21/07/1979	34	7	ROCK AROUND THE CLOCK	Sire SIR 4020

SYLVIA TELLA – see BLOW MONKEYS

TEMPERANCE SEVEN
UK group formed in 1950s by Captain Cephas Howard (trumpet/euphonium), Sheikh Haroun Wadi el John R T Davies (trombone/saxophone), Frank Paverty (sousaphone), Mr Philip 'Fingers' Harrison (saxophone), Alan Swainston-Cooper (clarinet), Canon Colin Bowles (piano), Brian Innes (drums), Dr John Grieves-Watson (banjo) and Whispering Paul McDowell (vocals).

30/03/1961	●¹	16		YOU'RE DRIVING ME CRAZY	Parlophone R 4757
15/06/1961	4	17		PASADENA	Parlophone R 4781
28/09/1961	28	4		HARD HEARTED HANNAH/CHILI BOM BOM	Parlophone R 4823
07/12/1961	22	8		CHARLESTON	Parlophone R 4851

TEMPLE OF THE DOG
US group formed by Soundgarden members: Chris Cornell (born 20/7/1964, Seattle) and Matt Cameron (born 28/11/1962, San Diego, CA); Pearl Jam members: Stone Gossard (born 20/7/1966, Seattle), Mike McCready (born 5/4/1965, Seattle), Jeff Ament (born 10/3/1963, Big Sandy, MT) and Eddie Vedder (born Edward Mueller, 23/12/1964, Evanston, IL), and Rick Parashar as a tribute to Andrew Wood, former lead of Mother Love Bone, who died from a heroin overdose.

24/10/1992	51	2	HUNGER STRIKE	A&M AM 0091

NINO TEMPO AND APRIL STEVENS
US family duo formed by Nino (born Antonio Lo Tempio, 6/1/1935, Niagara

○ Silver disc ● Gold disc ✪ Platinum disc (additional platinum units are indicated by a figure following the symbol) ◉ Singles released prior to 1973 that are known to have sold over 1 million copies in the UK

Falls, NY) and April (born Carol Lo Tempio, 29/4/1936). Both had previously recorded solo and Nino was a top session saxophonist. He later teamed up with 5th Avenue Sax.

07/11/1963.....17.....11......				DEEP PURPLE ▲[1] 1963 Grammy Award for Best Rock & Roll Recording	London HLK 9782
16/01/1964.....20.....8......				WHISPERING...	London HLK 9829

TEMPTATIONS US R&B vocal group formed in 1960 by Eddie Kendricks (born 17/12/1939, Union Springs, AL), Paul Williams (born 2/7/1939, Birmingham, AL), Melvin Franklin (born David English, 12/10/1942, Montgomery, AL), Otis Williams (born Otis Miles, 30/10/1939, Texarkana, TX) and Eldridge Bryant from two other groups, The Primes and The Distants. They signed with Motown as The Elgins in 1961 and name-changed to The Temptations (suggested by Otis Williams). Bryant left in 1962, replaced by David Ruffin (born 18/1/1941, Meridian, MS). They scored their first hits with Smokey Robinson handling production and later switched to Norman Whitfield. Ruffin left in 1968 because the group would not give him individual credit as had happened with Diana Ross and the Supremes; he was replaced by Dennis Edwards (born 3/2/1943, Birmingham). Kendricks left in 1971, replaced by Richard Owens and then Damon Harris (born 3/7/1950, Baltimore, MD). Williams also left in 1971, replaced by Richard Street (born 5/10/1942, Detroit, MI). The group left Motown in 1976 for Atlantic but returned two albums later. By 1988 the line-up consisted of Otis Williams, Melvin Franklin, Richard Street, Dennis Edwards (who returned to the line-up in 1987) and Ron Tyson. Edwards subsequently left the group a second time and became embroiled in a legal dispute with them over the use of the name. Their line-up in 2001 was Otis Williams (last surviving original member), Ron Tyson, Barrington Henderson, Terry Weeks and Harry McGilberry. Paul Williams committed suicide on 17/8/1973, Ruffin died from a drugs overdose on 1/6/1991, Kendricks from cancer on 5/10/1992 and Franklin from emphysema on 23/2/1995. The group was inducted into the Rock & Roll Hall of Fame in 1989 and has a star on the Hollywood Walk of Fame. They won four Grammy Awards during their career including the 2000 Grammy Award for Best Traditional Rhythm & Blues Vocal Album for *Ear-Resistible*.

18/03/1965.....43.....1......				MY GIRL ▲[1] Featured in the films *The Big Chill* (1984), *Born On The 4th Of July* (1989) and *My Girl* (1991)	Stateside SS 378
01/04/1965.....45.....2......				IT'S GROWING..	Tamla Motown TMG 504
14/07/1966.....21.....11......				AIN'T TOO PROUD TO BEG Featured in the 1984 film *The Big Chill*	Tamla Motown TMG 565
06/10/1966.....18.....10......				BEAUTY IS ONLY SKIN DEEP...	Tamla Motown TMG 578
15/12/1966.....19.....9......				(I KNOW) I'M LOSING YOU..	Tamla Motown TMG 587
06/09/1967.....26.....15......				YOU'RE MY EVERYTHING..	Tamla Motown TMG 620
06/03/1968.....45.....1......				I WISH IT WOULD RAIN..	Tamla Motown TMG 641
12/06/1968.....47.....1......				I COULD NEVER LOVE ANOTHER...	Tamla Motown TMG 658
29/01/1969.....3.....12......				**I'M GONNA MAKE YOU LOVE ME** DIANA ROSS AND THE SUPREMES AND THE TEMPTATIONS Featured in the 1996 film *Now And Then*..	Tamla Motown TMG 685
05/03/1969.....10.....9......				**GET READY** Featured in the 1990 film *Air America*	Tamla Motown TMG 688
23/08/1969.....15.....10......				CLOUD NINE 1968 Grammy Award for Best Rhythm & Blues Group Performance	Tamla Motown TMG 707
20/09/1969.....18.....8......				I SECOND THAT EMOTION DIANA ROSS AND THE SUPREMES AND THE TEMPTATIONS..................	Tamla Motown TMG 709
17/01/1970.....13.....9......				I CAN'T GET NEXT TO YOU ▲[2]..	Tamla Motown TMG 722
21/03/1970.....31.....7......				WHY (MUST WE FALL IN LOVE) DIANA ROSS AND THE SUPREMES AND THE TEMPTATIONS.............	Tamla Motown TMG 730
13/06/1970.....33.....7......				PSYCHEDELIC SHACK..	Tamla Motown TMG 741
19/09/1970.....7.....15......				**BALL OF CONFUSION**..	Tamla Motown TMG 749
22/05/1971.....8.....16......				**JUST MY IMAGINATION (RUNNING AWAY WITH ME)** ▲[2]....................................	Tamla Motown TMG 773
05/02/1972.....32.....5......				SUPERSTAR (REMEMBER HOW YOU GOT WHERE YOU ARE)..	Tamla Motown TMG 800
15/04/1972.....13.....10......				TAKE A LOOK AROUND..	Tamla Motown TMG 808
13/01/1973.....14.....8......				PAPA WAS A ROLLIN' STONE ▲[1] Because of the first line, the single was originally released in the US on 3rd September 1972. 1972 Grammy Awards for Best Rhythm & Blues Performance by a Group, Best Rhythm & Blues Instrumental Performance, and Best Rhythm & Blues Song for writers Norman Whitfield and Barrett Strong...	Tamla Motown TMG 839
29/09/1973.....41.....4......				LAW OF THE LAND	Tamla Motown TMG 866
12/06/1982.....53.....3......				STANDING ON THE TOP (PART 1) TEMPTATIONS FEATURING RICK JAMES	Motown TMG 1263
17/11/1984.....12.....10......				TREAT HER LIKE A LADY...	Motown TMG 1365
15/08/1987.....31.....6......				PAPA WAS A ROLLIN' STONE (REMIX)..	Motown ZB 41431
06/02/1988.....63.....2......				LOOK WHAT YOU STARTED...	Motown ZB 41733
21/10/1989.....71.....1......				ALL I WANT FROM YOU..	Motown ZB 43233
15/02/1992.....2.....10......				**MY GIRL** Re-issue of Stateside SS 378	Epic 6576767
22/02/1992.....69.....1......				THE JONES'...	Motown TMG 1403

10 CC UK rock group formed in 1972 by Eric Stewart (born 20/1/1945, Manchester, guitar/vocals), Graham Gouldman (born 10/5/1946, Manchester, guitar/vocals), Kevin Godley (born 7/10/1945, Manchester, vocals/drums) and Lol Creme (born 19/9/1947, Manchester, guitar/vocals). All four were ex-Hotlegs and had set up Strawberry Studios in Manchester. After working on two demos they were offered a deal with Jonathan King's UK label (he gave them their name – supposedly the amount of the average UK male ejaculation). Godley and Creme left in 1976 to form a new partnership; Gouldman and Stewart recruited Paul Burgess (drums), later adding Duncan Mackay (keyboards), Rick Fenn (guitar), Tony O'Malley (keyboards) and Stuart Tosh (drums). They disbanded in 1983.

23/09/1972.....2.....13......				**DONNA**...	UK 6
19/05/1973.....❶[1].....15......				**RUBBER BULLETS**...	UK 36
25/08/1973.....10.....8......				**THE DEAN AND I**...	UK 48
15/06/1974.....10.....10......				**WALL STREET SHUFFLE**...	UK 69
14/09/1974.....24.....7......				**SILLY LOVE**...	UK 77
05/04/1975.....7.....8......				**LIFE IS A MINESTRONE**...	Mercury 6008 010
31/05/1975.....❶[2].....11.....○				**I'M NOT IN LOVE** Featured in the films *The Stud* (1978), *Deuce Bigalow: Male Gigolo* (1999) and *Bridget Jones Diary 2: Edge Of Reason* (2004)...	Mercury 6008 014
29/11/1975.....5.....10......				**ART FOR ART'S SAKE**...	Mercury 6008 017
20/03/1976.....6.....9......				**I'M MANDY FLY ME**..	Mercury 6008 019
11/12/1976.....6.....11.....●				**THINGS WE DO FOR LOVE**...	Mercury 6008 022

❶[9] Number of weeks single topped the UK chart　↑ Entered the UK chart at #1　▲[9] Number of weeks single topped the US chart

16/04/1977	5	12	O	GOOD MORNING JUDGE	Mercury 6008 025
12/08/1978	**❶**[1]	13	●	DREADLOCK HOLIDAY Featured in the 2000 film *Snatch*	Mercury 6008 035
07/08/1982	50	4		RUN AWAY	Mercury MER 113
18/03/1995	29	2		I'M NOT IN LOVE Re-recording	Avex UK AVEXCD 2

TEN CITY
US soul group formed in Chicago, IL by Byron Stingily (vocals), Herb Lawson (guitar) and Byron Burke (keyboards) as Ragtyme. They disbanded in 1994 and Stingily went solo.

21/01/1989	8	10		THAT'S THE WAY LOVE IS	Atlantic A 8963
08/04/1989	29	4		DEVOTION	Atlantic A 8916
22/07/1989	60	1		WHERE DO WE GO	Atlantic A 8864
27/10/1990	60	2		WHATEVER MAKES YOU HAPPY	Atlantic A 7819
15/08/1992	63	2		ONLY TIME WILL TELL/MY PEACE OF HEAVEN	East West America A 8516
11/09/1993	45	2		FANTASY	Columbia 6595042

TEN POLE TUDOR
UK punk rock group formed by Eddie Tenpole (born 6/12/1955, London, also known as Eddie Tudor-Pole), Garry Long (drums), Dick Crippen (bass) and Bob Kingston (guitar). Eddie later turned to acting and appeared in *Sid And Nancy* and *Absolute Beginners,* and recorded solo.

07/04/1979	6	8	O	WHO KILLED BAMBI Flip side was *Silly Thing* by THE SEX PISTOLS	Virgin VS 256
13/10/1979	21	6		ROCK AROUND THE CLOCK Flip side was *The Great Rock 'N' Roll Swindle* by THE SEX PISTOLS	Virgin VS 290
25/04/1981	6	12	O	SWORDS OF A THOUSAND MEN	Stiff BUY 109
01/08/1981	16	9		WUNDERBAR	Stiff BUY 120
14/11/1981	49	5		THROWING MY BABY OUT WITH BATHWATER	Stiff BUY 129

10 REVOLUTIONS
UK dance group formed by producer Dave Lambert and singer Shena McSween. Their debut hit fused Members of Mayday's *10 In 01* with Superchumbo's *Revolution.*

| 30/08/2003 | 59 | 1 | | TIME FOR THE REVOLUTION | Incentive CENT 53CDS |

TEN SHARP
Dutch duo Marcel Kapteijn (guitar/vocals) and Niels Hermes (keyboards), with Ton Groen (bass), Nick Bult (keyboards), Jelle Sieswerda (guitar), Bennie Top (drums) and Hubert Heeringa (saxophone) supplementing on live dates.

| 21/03/1992 | 10 | 13 | | YOU | Columbia 6566647 |
| 20/06/1992 | 63 | 2 | | AIN'T MY BEATING HEART | Columbia 6580947 |

10,000 MANIACS
US group formed in Jamestown, NY in 1981 by Natalie Merchant (born 26/10/1963, Jamestown, vocals), Robert Buck (guitar), Steven Gustafson (bass), Dennis Drew (keyboards) and Jerome Augustyniak (drums) and signed by Elektra in 1985. In 1990 Merchant announced her intention to go solo, finally departing in 1992. Elektra promptly dropped the group from their roster! Buck died from liver failure on 19/12/2000 aged 42.

12/09/1992	58	3		THESE ARE DAYS	Elektra EKR 156
10/04/1993	47	3		CANDY EVERYBODY WANTS	Elektra EKR 160CD1
23/10/1993	65	1		BECAUSE THE NIGHT	Elektra EKR 175CD

TEN YEARS AFTER
UK rock group formed in Nottingham in 1965 by Alvin Lee (born 19/12/1944, Nottingham, guitar/vocals), Leo Lyons (born 30/11/1943, Standbridge, bass), Ric Lee (born 20/10/1945, Cannock, drums) and Chick Churchill (born 2/1/1949, Flint, Wales, keyboards) as The Jaybirds. They name-changed to Ten Years After in 1966 and signed with Decca in 1967. They stopped recording in 1975 and disbanded in 1980. In 2001 Ric Lee launched an investigation into the alleged missing royalty earnings from countless Woodstock compilations featuring the band's live or recorded versions of their perennial favourite *Goin' Home.*

| 06/06/1970 | 10 | 18 | | LOVE LIKE A MAN | Deram DM 299 |

TENACIOUS D
US duo formed by comedians Kyle Glass (also known as KG or Kage) and Jack Black (also known as JB or Jables). Black had previously appeared in the film *Shallow Hal.*

| 23/11/2002 | 34 | 2 | | WONDERBOY | Epic 6733512 |

DANNY TENAGLIA
US DJ and producer (born March 1951, New York) who left school at 17 to pursue a career as a DJ and began producing during the 1980s, later turning to recording. He has recorded as Deep State, Soulboy, The Look and Datar.

05/09/1998	36	3		MUSIC IS THE ANSWER (DANCING' & PRANCIN') DANNY TENAGLIA AND CELEDA	Twisted UK TWCD 10038
10/04/1999	53	1		TURN ME ON DANNY TENAGLIA FEATURING LIZ TORRES	Twisted UK TWCD 10045
23/10/1999	50	1		MUSIC IS THE ANSWER (REMIX) DANNY TENAGLIA AND CELEDA	Twisted UK TWCD 10052

TENNESSEE THREE – see JOHNNY CASH

TENOR FLY
UK reggae singer (born Jonathan Sutter, London) who later appeared on the *Regatta Mondata* project.

06/04/1991	43	6		WICKEDEST SOUND REBEL MC FEATURING TENOR FLY	Desire WANT 40
15/06/1991	20	6		TRIBAL BASE REBEL MC FEATURING TENOR FLY AND BARRINGTON LEVY	Desire WANT 44
07/01/1995	51	2		BRIGHT SIDE OF LIFE Contains a sample of Nina Simone's *My Baby Just Cares For Me*	Mango CIDM 825
07/02/1998	23	3		B-BOY STANCE FREESTYLERS FEATURING TENOR FLY	Freskanova FND 7

TENTH PLANET
UK vocal/production group formed by Nick Hale, Gez Dewar and Clare Pearce.

| 14/04/2001 | 59 | 1 | | GHOSTS | Nebula NEBCD 015 |

BRYN TERFEL – see SHIRLEY BASSEY

O Silver disc   ● Gold disc   ✪ Platinum disc (additional platinum units are indicated by a figure following the symbol)   ⦿ Singles released prior to 1973 that are known to have sold over 1 million copies in the UK

TERMINATORS – see **ARNEE AND THE TERMINATORS**

TERRA DEVA – see **WHO DA FUNK FEATURING JESSICA EVE**

TERRA FIRMA Italian producer Claudio Guissani who is an ex-member of Urban Shakedown.

18/05/1996	64	1		FLOATING	Platipus PLAT 21CD

TAMMI TERRELL US singer (born Tammy Montgomery, 21/1/1946, Philadelphia, PA) who made her first recordings for Wand in 1961 and toured with the James Brown Revue before signing as a solo artist with Motown. All her hits came while singing with Marvin Gaye: she would undoubtedly have gone on to enjoy solo success but for a brain tumour, first diagnosed after she collapsed on stage in 1967. Briefly married to boxer Ernie Terrell, she died on 16/3/1970. It has been widely claimed that her brain disorders were the result of regular beatings by someone within the Motown hierarchy. The accusations formed the basis of the novel *Number One With A Bullet* by former Marvin Gaye aide Elaine Jesmer. Having been unsuccessful in getting the book blocked, Motown bought the film rights and the project never saw light of day again.

17/01/1968	41	7		IF I COULD BUILD MY WHOLE WORLD AROUND YOU	Tamla Motown TMG 635
12/06/1968	34	7		AIN'T NOTHING LIKE THE REAL THING	Tamla Motown TMG 655
02/10/1968	19	19		YOU'RE ALL I NEED TO GET BY	Tamla Motown TMG 668
22/01/1969	21	8		YOU AIN'T LIVIN' TILL YOU'RE LOVIN'	Tamla Motown TMG 681
04/06/1969	26	8		GOOD LOVIN' AIN'T EASY TO COME BY	Tamla Motown TMG 697
15/11/1969	9	12		**ONION SONG** This and above singles credited to **MARVIN GAYE AND TAMMI TERRELL** although the female singer on the last two is Valerie Ashford as Terrell was too ill to record the songs	Tamla Motown TMG 715

TERRIS UK group formed by Gavin Goodwin (vocals), Alun Bound (guitar), Neil Dugmore (keyboards) and Owen Matthews (drums).

17/03/2001	62	1		FABRICATED LUNACY	Blanco Y Negro NEG 130CD

TERROR SQUAD FEATURING FAT JOE AND REMY US rap group formed in New York by Big Punisher (born Christopher Rios, 9/11/1971, New York City, who also recorded as Big Pun and died from a heart attack brought on by his weight – he was 698 pounds – on 7/2/2000), Fat Joe (born Joseph Cartagena in The Bronx, NY to Puerto Rican and Cuban parents), Cuban Link, Prospect, Triple Seis and Tony Sunshine. Following the death of Big Pun the group disbanded but was reassembled by Armageddon, Tony Sunshine, Prospect and Remy.

16/10/2004	24	5		LEAN BACK	Universal MCSTD 40385

TERRORIZE UK producer Shaun Imrei.

02/05/1992	52	3		IT'S JUST A FEELING	Hamster STER 1
22/08/1992	69	1		FEEL THE RHYTHM	Hamster 12STER2
14/11/1992	47	2		IT'S JUST A FEELING	Hamster STER 8

TERRORVISION UK group formed in Bradford in 1986 by Tony Wright (born 6/5/1968, vocals), Mark Yates (born 4/4/1968, guitar), Leigh Marklew (born 10/8/1968, bass) and Shutty (born David Shuttleworth, 20/3/1967, drums) as Spoiled Bratz. They name-changed to Terrorvision in 1991 upon signing with EMI via their own Total Vegas label.

19/06/1993	63	1		AMERICAN TV	Total Vegas CDVEGAS 3
30/10/1993	42	2		NEW POLICY ONE	Total Vegas CDVEGAS 4
08/01/1994	29	4		MY HOUSE	Total Vegas CDVEGAS 5
09/04/1994	21	5		OBLIVION	Total Vegas CDVEGAS 6
25/06/1994	25	4		MIDDLEMAN	Total Vegas CDVEGAS 7
03/09/1994	25	3		PRETEND BEST FRIEND	Total Vegas CDVEGASS 8
29/10/1994	24	4		ALICE WHAT'S THE MATTER	Total Vegas CDVEGAS 9
18/03/1995	22	3		SOME PEOPLE SAY	Total Vegas CDVEGAS 10
02/03/1996	5	4		**PERSEVERANCE**	Total Vegas CDVEGAS 11
04/05/1996	20	3		CELEBRITY HIT LIST	Total Vegas CDVEGAS 12
20/07/1996	10	3		**BAD ACTRESS**	Total Vegas CDVEGAS 13
11/01/1997	12	4		EASY	Total Vegas CDVEGAS 14
03/10/1998	23	2		JOSEPHINE	Total Vegas CDVEGAS 15
30/01/1999	2	10		**TEQUILA**	Total Vegas CDVEGAS 16
15/05/1999	42	1		III WISHES	Total Vegas CDVEGAS 17
27/01/2001	28	2		D'YA WANNA GO FASTER	Papillon BTFLYX0007

HELEN TERRY UK singer (born 24/5/1956), who was a former backing singer for Culture Club before going solo.

12/05/1984	34	6		LOVE LIES LOST	Virgin VS 678

TODD TERRY PROJECT US remixer/producer (born 18/4/1967, Brooklyn, NY) who was responsible for mixing hits by Everything But The Girl, Brownstone, 3T and Jimmy Somerville, among others, before going solo. He has also recorded as Swan Lake, Royal House, Gypsymen, T2 and Black Riot.

12/11/1988	56	3		WEEKEND	Sleeping Bag SBUK 1T
14/10/1995	28	3		WEEKEND (REMIX)	Ore AG 13CD
13/07/1996	8	6		**KEEP ON JUMPIN'**	Manifesto FESCD 11
12/07/1997	5	10		**SOMETHING GOIN' ON** This and above single credited to **TODD TERRY FEATURING MARTHA WASH AND JOCELYN BROWN**	
					Manifesto FESCD 25
06/12/1997	16	8		IT'S OVER LOVE **TODD TERRY PRESENTS SHANNON**	Manifesto FESCD 37

❶[9] Number of weeks single topped the UK chart ↑ Entered the UK chart at #1 ▲[9] Number of weeks single topped the US chart

803

11/04/1998	20	2		READY FOR A NEW DAY **TODD TERRY FEATURING MARTHA WASH**	Manifesto FESCD 40
03/07/1999	58	1		LET IT RIDE	Innocent RESTCD 1

TONY TERRY US R&B singer (born 12/3/1964, Pinehurst, North Carolina).

27/02/1988	44	6		LOVEY DOVEY	Epic TONY 2

TESLA US group formed in Sacramento, CA in 1985 by Jeff Keith (vocals), Tommy Skeoch (guitar/vocals), Frank Hannon (guitar/vocals), Brian Wheat (bass) and Troy Lucketta (drums) as City Kid. They name-changed in honour of the scientist Nikola Tesla.

27/04/1991	70	1		SIGNS	Geffen GFS 3

JOE TEX US singer (born Joseph Arrington Jr, 8/8/1933, Rogers, TX) who won a talent contest at the Apollo in 1954 and gained a recording contract with King as a result. He achieved his US chart breakthrough in 1965 with a series of hits. He converted to the Muslim faith in 1966, adopted the name Yusef Hazziez and later retired from the industry. Later he became a member of The Soul Clan with Solomon Burke, Arthur Conley, Don Covay and Ben E King. He died from a heart attack on 13/8/1982.

23/04/1977	2	11	◯	**AIN'T GONNA BUMP NO MORE (WITH NO BIG FAT WOMAN)**	Epic EPC 5035

TEXAS UK rock group formed in Glasgow in 1988 by Sharleen Spiteri (born 7/11/1967, Glasgow, vocals), Ally McErlaine (born 31/10/1968, Glasgow, guitar), Eddie Campbell (born 6/7/1965, keyboards), John McElhone (born 21/4/1963, Glasgow, bass) and Richard Hynd (born 17/6/1965, Aberdeen, drums). McElhone was ex-member of Altered Images and Hipsway.

04/02/1989	8	11		**I DON'T WANT A LOVER** Featured in the 2000 film *Beautiful People*	Mercury TEX 1
06/05/1989	60	3		THRILL HAS GONE	Mercury TEX 2
05/08/1989	44	5		EVERYDAY NOW	Mercury TEX 3
02/12/1989	73	1		PRAYER FOR YOU	Mercury TEX 4
07/09/1991	66	1		WHY BELIEVE IN YOU	Mercury TEX 5
26/10/1991	74	1		IN MY HEART	Mercury TEX 6
08/02/1992	32	4		ALONE WITH YOU	Mercury TEX 7
25/04/1992	19	6		TIRED OF BEING ALONE	Mercury TEX 8
11/09/1993	30	3		SO CALLED FRIEND	Mercury TEXCD 9
30/10/1993	39	3		YOU OWE IT ALL TO ME	Vertigo TEXCD 10
12/02/1994	28	2		SO IN LOVE WITH YOU	Vertigo TEXCD 11
18/01/1997	3	10	◯	**SAY WHAT YOU WANT** Featured in the 1997 film *Picture Perfect*	Mercury MERDD 480
19/04/1997	10	7		**HALO**	Mercury MERCD 482
09/08/1997	5	6		**BLACK EYED BOY**	Mercury MERCD 490
15/11/1997	10	8		**PUT YOUR ARMS AROUND ME** Featured in the 1998 film *Ever After*	Mercury MERCD 497
21/03/1998	4	7		**SAY WHAT YOU WANT/INSANE** **TEXAS FEATURING THE WU TANG CLAN**	Mercury MERCD 499
01/05/1999	4	9	◯	**IN OUR LIFETIME**	Mercury MERCD 517
28/08/1999	5	9		**SUMMER SON**	Mercury MERDD 520
27/11/1999	12	9		WHEN WE ARE TOGETHER	Mercury MERDD 525
14/10/2000	6	10		**IN DEMAND**	Mercury MERDD 528
20/01/2001	6	8		**INNER SMILE** Featured in the 2002 film *Bend It Like Beckham*	Mercury MERDD 531
21/07/2001	16	4		I DON'T WANT A LOVER (REMIX)	Mercury MERCD 533
18/10/2003	9	5		**CARNIVAL GIRL** **TEXAS FEATURING KARDINAL OFFISHALL**	Mercury 9812254
20/12/2003	40	3		I'LL SEE IT THROUGH Featured in the 2003 film *Love Actually*	Mercury 9815221

THAT KID CHRIS US DJ/producer Chris Staropoli.

22/02/1997	52	1		FEEL THA VIBE	Manifesto FESCD 16

THAT PETROL EMOTION UK group formed by Sean O'Neill (born 26/8/1957, Londonderry, guitar, previously known as John O'Neill), his brother Damian 'Dee' O'Neill (born 15/1/1961, Belfast, bass), Steve Mack (vocals), Reamman O'Gormain (guitar) and Ciaran McLaughlin (drums). The O'Neill brothers were ex-members of The Undertones. Sean O'Neill left in 1989, Damian switched to guitar and John Marchini (bass) joined as his replacement. They were dropped by Virgin in 1992 and after one release on their own Koogat label disbanded in 1994.

11/04/1987	43	7		BIG DECISION	Polydor TPE 1
11/07/1987	64	2		DANCE	Polydor TPE 2
17/10/1987	65	2		GENIUS MOVE	Virgin VS 1002
31/03/1990	73	1		ABANDON	Virgin VS 1242
01/09/1990	49	4		HEY VENUS	Virgin VS 1290
09/02/1991	49	4		TINGLE	Virgin VS 1312
27/04/1991	55	4		SENSITIZE	Virgin VS 1261

THE THE UK rock group formed in 1980 by Matt Johnson (born 15/8/1961, London, guitar/vocals) with an ever-changing list of supporting musicians.

04/12/1982	68	3		UNCERTAIN SMILE	Epic EPC A 2787
17/09/1983	71	3		THIS IS THE DAY	Epic A 3710
09/08/1986	29	10		HEARTLAND	Some Bizzare TRUTH 2
25/10/1986	48	5		INFECTED	Some Bizzare TRUTH 3
24/01/1987	64	2		SLOW TRAIN TO DAWN	Some Bizzare TENSE 1
23/05/1987	55	2		SWEET BIRD OF TRUTH	Epic TENSE 2
01/04/1989	18	5		THE BEAT(EN) GENERATION	Epic EMU 8

◯ Silver disc ● Gold disc ✪ Platinum disc (additional platinum units are indicated by a figure following the symbol) ◉ Singles released prior to 1973 that are known to have sold over 1 million copies in the UK

22/07/1989	63	3		GRAVITATE TO ME	Epic EMU 9
07/10/1989	70	2		ARMAGEDDON DAYS ARE HERE (AGAIN)	Epic EMU 10
02/03/1991	54	1		SHADES OF BLUE (EP) Tracks on EP: *Jealous Of Youth, Another Boy Drowning (Live)* and *Solitude and Dolphins*	Epic 6557968
16/01/1993	25	4		DOGS OF LUST	Epic 6584572
17/04/1993	35	3		SLOW EMOTION REPLAY	Epic 6590772
19/06/1993	39	3		LOVE IS STRONGER THAN DEATH	Epic 6593712
15/01/1994	17	4		DIS-INFECTED EP Tracks on EP: *That Was The Day, Dis-Infected, Helpline Operator* and *Dogs Of Lust*	Epic 6598112
04/02/1995	31	2		I SAW THE LIGHT	Epic 6610912

THEATRE OF HATE
UK rock group formed in 1981 by Kirk Brandon (born 3/8/1956, London, guitar/vocals), John Lennard (saxophone), Stan Stammers (bass), Bill Duffy (guitar) and Nigel Preston (drums). Duffy was later a member of The Cult while the bulk of the group later became Spear Of Destiny.

23/01/1982	40	7		DO YOU BELIEVE IN THE WESTWORLD	Burning Rome BRR 2
29/05/1982	70	2		THE HOP	Burning Rome BRR 3

THEAUDIENCE
UK rock group formed by Sophie Ellis Bextor (lead vocals), Kerin Smith (bass), Patrick Hannan (drums), Nyge Butler (keyboards) and Dean Molle (guitar). Billy Reeves had been a member of the group but left to concentrate on songwriting and later linked with Catherine Turner to form Yours. Sophie Ellis Bextor linked with Italian DJ Cristiano Spiller to form Spiller and then signed as a solo artist with Polydor in October 2000.

07/03/1998	48	1		IF YOU CAN'T DO IT WHEN YOU'RE YOUNG, WHEN CAN YOU DO IT?	Mercury AUDCD 2
23/05/1998	27	2		A PESSIMIST IS NEVER DISAPPOINTED	Mercury AUDCD 3
08/08/1998	25	2		I KNOW ENOUGH (I DON'T GET ENOUGH)	Elleffe AUCD 4

THEE UNSTRUNG
UK rock group formed by Steve Holbrock (guitar/vocals), Ben Bailey (guitar/vocals), Bobby Cooper (bass) and Ben Tweedy (drums).

13/11/2004	59	1		CONTRARY MARY/YOU	Poptones MC5094SCD

THEM
UK rock group formed in Belfast in 1963 by Van Morrison (born George Ivan, 31/8/1945, vocals/harmonica/saxophone), Billy Harrison (guitar), Alan Henderson (bass), Eric Wickson (piano) and Ronnie Millings (drums). They disbanded in 1966 with Morrison going solo.

07/01/1965	10	9		**BABY PLEASE DON'T GO** Featured in the 1988 film *Good Morning Vietnam*	Decca F 12018
25/03/1965	2	12		**HERE COMES THE NIGHT**	Decca 12094
09/02/1991	65	2		BABY PLEASE DON'T GO Re-issue of Decca F 12018	London LON 292

THEN JERICO
UK group formed by Mark Shaw (born 10/6/1961, Chesterfield, vocals), Scott Taylor (born 31/12/1961, Redhill, guitar), Rob Downes (born 7/12/1961, Cheadle Hulme, guitar), Jasper Stanthorpe (born 18/2/1958, Tonbridge, bass), Keith Airey (keyboards) and Steve Wren (born 26/10/1962, London, drums).

31/01/1987	65	3		LET HER FALL	London LON 97
25/07/1987	18	12		THE MOTIVE (LIVING WITHOUT YOU)	London LON 145
24/10/1987	48	4		MUSCLE DEEP	London LON 156
28/01/1989	13	7		BIG AREA	London LON 204
08/04/1989	33	4		WHAT DOES IT TAKE	London LON 223
12/08/1989	22	6		SUGAR BOX	London LON 235

THERAPY?
UK rock band formed in Northern Ireland in 1989 by Andy Cairns (born 22/9/1965, Antrim, guitar/vocals), Michael McKeegan (born 25/3/1971, Antrim, bass) and Fyfe Ewing (drums). They launched the label Multifuckingnational when their original demos had been rejected by others, but signed with A&M in 1992. They later added Martin McCarrick (born 29/7/1962, Luton, guitar) and Graham Hopkins (born 20/12/1975, Dublin, drums).

31/10/1992	30	2		TEETHGRINDER	A&M AM 0097
20/03/1993	9	4		**SHORTSHARPSHOCK EP** Tracks on EP: *Screamager, Auto Surgery, Totally Random Man* and *Accelerator*	A&M AMCD 208
12/06/1993	18	3		FACE THE STRANGE EP Tracks on EP: *Turn, Speedball, Bloody Blue* and *Neckfreak*	A&M 5803052
28/08/1993	13	3		OPAL MANTRA	A&M 5803612
29/01/1994	18	4		NOWHERE	A&M 5805052
12/03/1994	22	3		TRIGGER INSIDE	A&M 5805352
11/06/1994	29	2		DIE LAUGHING	A&M 5805892
27/05/1995	53	1		INNOCENT X Listed flip side was Orbital's *Belfast*	Volume VOLCD 1
03/06/1995	14	3		STORIES	A&M 5811052
05/08/1995	25	3		LOOSE	A&M 5811652
18/11/1995	26	2		DIANE	A&M 5812912
14/03/1998	29	2		CHURCH OF NOISE	A&M 5825392
30/05/1998	32	1		LONELY, CRYIN', ONLY	A&M 0441212

THERESE – see STONEBRIDGE

THESE ANIMAL MEN
UK group formed in Brighton by Hooligan (born Julian Hewings, guitar/vocals), Patrick (bass), Boag (vocals) and Stevie (drums).

24/09/1994	72	1		THIS IS THE SOUND OF YOUTH	Hi-Rise FLATSCD 7
08/02/1997	62	1		LIFE SUPPORTING MACHINE	Hut HUTCD 76
12/04/1997	72	1		LIGHT EMITTING ELECTRICAL WAVE	Hut HUTCD 81

❶⁹ Number of weeks single topped the UK chart   ↑ Entered the UK chart at #1   ▲⁹ Number of weeks single topped the US chart

805

THEY MIGHT BE GIANTS
US rock group formed in Boston, MA in 1983 by John Flansburgh (guitar/vocals) and John Linnell (accordion/keyboards/vocals), later adding Brian Doherty (drums), Tony Maimone (bass), Kurt Hoffman (saxophone) and Steven Bernstein (trumpet). Dan Hickey later replaced Doherty.

DATE	POS	WKS	BPI	SINGLE TITLE	LABEL & NUMBER
03/03/1990	6	11		**BIRDHOUSE IN YOUR SOUL**	Elektra EKR 104
02/06/1990	61	2		ISTANBUL (NOT CONSTANTINOPLE)	Elektra EKR 110
28/07/2001	21	5		BOSS OF ME Theme to the US TV series *Malcolm In The Middle*. 2001 Grammy Award for Best Song Written for a Motion Picture, Television or Other Visual Media	PIAS PIASREST 001CD

THICK D
US producer (born Eric Miller, Chicago, IL) with female singer Latanza Waters. The group name is short for Thick Dick and the pair also record as E-Smoove.

DATE	POS	WKS	BPI	SINGLE TITLE	LABEL & NUMBER
12/10/2002	35	3		INSATIABLE	Multiply CDMULTY 88

THIN LIZZY
Irish rock group formed in Dublin in 1969 by Phil Lynott (born 20/8/1951, Dublin, vocals/bass), Brian Downey (born 27/1/1951, Dublin, drums) and Eric Bell (born 3/9/1947, Belfast, guitar). They signed with Decca in 1970. Bell left in 1972, briefly replaced by Gary Moore then Scott Gorman (born 17/3/1951, Santa Monica, CA) and Brian Robertson (born 12/9/1956, Glasgow). Robertson left in 1980 and the group disbanded in 1983. Lynott recorded solo from 1980 and died from heart failure on 4/1/1986. According to legend, they took their name either from a kids' comic character or it was a reference to the Model-T Ford car.

DATE	POS	WKS	BPI	SINGLE TITLE	LABEL & NUMBER
20/01/1973	6	12		**WHISKEY IN THE JAR** Featured in the 1993 film *In The Name Of The Father*	Decca F 13355
29/05/1976	8	10		**THE BOYS ARE BACK IN TOWN** Featured in the 2001 film *A Knight's Tale*	Vertigo 6059 139
14/08/1976	31	4		JAILBREAK Featured in the 1999 film *Detroit Rock City*	Vertigo 6059 150
15/01/1977	12	7		DON'T BELIEVE A WORD	Vertigo LIZZY 001
13/08/1977	14	8		DANCIN' IN THE MOONLIGHT (IT'S CAUGHT ME IN THE SPOTLIGHT)	Vertigo 6059 177
13/05/1978	20	13		ROSALIE – COWGIRLS' SONG (MEDLEY)	Vertigo LIZZY 2
03/03/1979	9	8		**WAITING FOR AN ALIBI**	Vertigo LIZZY 003
16/06/1979	14	9		DO ANYTHING YOU WANT TO	Vertigo LIZZY 004
20/10/1979	24	13		SARAH	Vertigo LIZZY 5
24/05/1980	21	9		CHINATOWN	Vertigo LIZZY 6
27/09/1980	10	7		**KILLER ON THE LOOSE**	Vertigo LIZZY 7
02/05/1981	19	7		KILLERS LIVE EP Tracks on EP: *Bad Reputation, Are You Ready* and *Dear Miss Lonely Hearts*	Vertigo LIZZY 8
08/08/1981	53	4		TROUBLE BOYS	Vertigo LIZZY 9
06/03/1982	53	3		HOLLYWOOD (DOWN ON YOUR LUCK)	Vertigo LIZZY 10
12/02/1983	27	5		COLD SWEAT	Vertigo LIZZY 11
07/05/1983	39	2		THUNDER AND LIGHTNING	Vertigo LIZZY 12
06/08/1983	52	3		THE SUN GOES DOWN	Vertigo LIZZY 13
26/01/1991	35	3		DEDICATION	Vertigo LIZZY 14
23/03/1991	63	1		THE BOYS ARE BACK IN TOWN Re-issue of Vertigo 6059 139	Vertigo LIZZY 15

3RD BASS
US rap group formed in Queens, NY by MC Serch (born Michael Berrin, 6/5/1967, Queens), Prime Minister Pete Nice (born Peter Nash, 5/2/1967, Brooklyn, NY) and DJ Richie Rich (born Richard Lawson). They disbanded in 1992 with Nash and Lawson linking to form Prime Minister Pete Nice and DJ Daddy Rich, while Berrin became A&R Vice President for Wild Pitch Records.

DATE	POS	WKS	BPI	SINGLE TITLE	LABEL & NUMBER
10/02/1990	71	1		THE GAS FACE	Def Jam 6556270
07/04/1990	61	2		BROOKLYN-QUEENS	Def Jam 6558307
22/06/1991	64	2		POP GOES THE WEASEL Contains samples of Peter Gabriel's *Sledgehammer* and Stevie Wonder's *You Haven't Done Nothin'*	Def Jam 6569547

THIRD DIMENSION FEATURING JULIE McDERMOTT
UK vocal/instrumental group fronted by Julie McDermott. She also fronted The Awesome 3's recording of the same song.

DATE	POS	WKS	BPI	SINGLE TITLE	LABEL & NUMBER
12/10/1996	34	2		DON'T GO	Soundprooof MCSTD 40082

THIRD EDGE
UK garage trio formed by Jamie Thompson, Thomas Jules Stock and Dan Grant.

DATE	POS	WKS	BPI	SINGLE TITLE	LABEL & NUMBER
31/08/2002	15	5		IN AND OUT	Q Zone/Parlophone CDR 6568
08/02/2003	17	4		KNOW YOU WANNA	Parlophone CDRS 6596

THIRD EYE BLIND
US group formed by Stephan Jenkins (born 27/9/1966, guitar/vocals), Kevin Cadogan (born 14/8/1970, guitar/vocals), Arion Salazar (born 9/8/1972, bass), Brad Hargreaves (born 30/7/1972, drums) and Eric Valentine (programming). Jenkins was previously a producer, including The Braids' hit *Bohemian Rhapsody*. Steve Bowman (born 14/1/1967) later took over on drums.

DATE	POS	WKS	BPI	SINGLE TITLE	LABEL & NUMBER
27/09/1997	33	5		SEMI-CHARMED LIFE Featured in the 1999 film *American Pie*	Elektra E 3907CD
21/03/1998	51	1		HOW'S IT GOING TO BE	Elektra E 3863CD

3RD STOREE
US R&B vocal group formed in Los Angeles, CA by D-Smoove, KJ, Jay-R and Lil' Man.

DATE	POS	WKS	BPI	SINGLE TITLE	LABEL & NUMBER
05/06/1999	53	1		IF EVER Contains a sample of Unlimited Touch's *I Can Hear Music In The Street*	Yab Yum E 3752CD

3RD WISH
US vocal group formed in 2003 by Alex Acosta (born 17/2/1981, Miami, FL), Ricky Gonzalez (born 7/1/1981, Orlando, FL) and Justin Martin (born 3/5/1982, Orlando); they are based in Germany.

DATE	POS	WKS	BPI	SINGLE TITLE	LABEL & NUMBER
18/12/2004	15	2+		OBSESSION (SI ES AMOR)	Three8 CXTHREE8004

THIRD WORLD
Jamaican reggae group formed in Kingston in 1973 by Michael 'Ibo' Cooper (keyboards), Stephen 'Cat' Coore (guitar), Irving 'Carrot' Jarrett (percussion), Richie Daley (bass) and Carl Barovier (drums). By 1975 Willie 'Root' Stewart had taken over

○ Silver disc　● Gold disc　✪ Platinum disc (additional platinum units are indicated by a figure following the symbol)　◉ Singles released prior to 1973 that are known to have sold over 1 million copies in the UK

on drums and William 'Rugs' Clark joined as lead singer. By 1999 the group consisted of Richie Daley, William Clark, Stephen Coore, Leroy Romans, Lenworth Williams and Rupert Bent.

23/09/1978	10	9		**NOW THAT WE'VE FOUND LOVE**	Island WIP 6457
06/01/1979	17	10		COOL MEDITATION	Island WIP 6469
16/06/1979	56	5		TALK TO ME	Island WIP 6496
06/06/1981	10	15		**DANCING ON THE FLOOR (HOOKED ON LOVE)**	CBS A 1214
17/04/1982	47	6		TRY JAH LOVE	CBS A 2063
09/03/1985	22	8		NOW THAT WE'VE FOUND LOVE Re-issue of Island WIP 6457	Island IS 219

THIRST UK vocal/instrumental group formed by Martin Brammah and Karl Burns, both briefly members of The Fall.

| 06/07/1991 | 61 | 2 | | THE ENEMY WITHIN | 10 TEN 379 |

1300 DRUMS FEATURING THE UNJUSTIFIED ANCIENTS OF MU UK group featuring ex-KLF members Bill Drummond (born William Butterworth, 29/4/1953, South Africa) and Jimmy Cauty (born 1954, London). The single had previously been a hit for Oo La La (position #62 in 1992). The pair also recorded as KLF, 2K, the Timelords, the Jams and the Justified Ancients Of Mu Mu.

| 18/05/1996 | 11 | 4 | | OOH! AAH! CANTONA | Dynamo DYND 5 |

THIRTEEN SENSES UK rock group formed in Cornwall by Will South (guitar/keyboards/vocals), Tom Welham (guitar), Adam Wilson (bass) and Brendon James (drums).

| 12/06/2004 | 38 | 2 | | DO NO WRONG | Vertigo 9866746 |
| 25/09/2004 | 35 | 2 | | INTO THE FIRE | Vertigo 9867851 |

THIS ISLAND EARTH UK vocal/instrumental group.

| 05/01/1985 | 47 | 5 | | SEE THAT GLOW | Magnet MAG 266 |

THIS MORTAL COIL UK group formed by Ivo Watts-Russell, with contributions from Heidi Berry, Caroline Crawley, Kim Deal, Howard Devoto, Tanya Donelly and Gordon Sharp. Watts-Russell was the founder of 4AD Records, with most of the contributors to This Mortal Coil being acts signed to the label.

| 22/10/1983 | 66 | 3 | | SONG TO THE SIREN | 4AD AD 310 |

THIS WAY UP UK vocal/instrumental duo Roy Hay (born 12/8/1961, Southend) and John Reid. Hay had previously been a member of Culture Club.

| 22/08/1987 | 72 | 2 | | TELL ME WHY | Virgin VS 954 |

THIS YEAR'S BLONDE UK studio group featuring singer Tracy Ackerman (from Enigma).

| 10/10/1981 | 46 | 5 | | PLATINUM POP Medley of Blondie covers | Creole CR 19 |
| 14/11/1987 | 62 | 3 | | WHO'S THAT MIX Medley of Madonna covers | Debut DEBT 3034 |

B.J. THOMAS US singer (born Billy Joe Thomas, 7/8/1942, Hugo, OK) who joined the Triumphs while still at high school. He has won five Grammy Awards: Best Inspirational Recording in 1977 for *Home Where I Belong,* Best Inspirational Recording in 1978 for *Happy Man,* Best Inspirational Recording in 1979 for *You Gave Me Love (When Nobody Gave Me A Prayer),* Best Gospel Performance in 1980 with various others for *The Lord's Prayer* and Best Inspirational Recording in 1981 for *Amazing Grace.*

| 21/02/1970 | 38 | 4 | | RAINDROPS KEEP FALLING ON MY HEAD ▲⁴ Featured in the films *Butch Cassidy And The Sundance Kid* (1969), *Forrest Gump* (1994) and *Spider-Man 2* (2004). Oscar for Best Film Song | Wand WN 1 |

CARLA THOMAS – see **OTIS REDDING**

DANTE THOMAS FEATURING PRAS US singer (born Darin Espinoza, 7/1/1978, Salt Lake City, UT); he later relocated to New York where he was discovered by Fugee member Pras.

| 01/09/2001 | 25 | 3 | | MISS CALIFORNIA | Elektra E 7192CD |

EVELYN THOMAS US singer (born 22/8/1953, Chicago, IL) who first teamed up with producer Ian Levine in 1975. After later releases on Casablanca and AVI she reunited with Levine for the hi-nrg anthem *High Energy.* She later recorded with the Fatback Band and for Vanguard Records.

24/01/1976	26	7		WEAK SPOT	20th Century BTC 1014
17/04/1976	41	2		DOOMSDAY	20th Century BTC 1017
21/04/1984	5	17		**HIGH ENERGY**	Record Shack SOHO 18
25/08/1984	60	3		MASQUERADE	Record Shack SOHO 25

JAMO THOMAS AND HIS PARTY BROTHERS ORCHESTRA US singer (born Bahamas), he moved to Chicago in the early 1960s and first recorded for the Conlo label.

| 26/02/1969 | 44 | 2 | | I SPY FOR THE FBI | Polydor 56 755 |

KENNY THOMAS UK R&B singer/songwriter/keyboard player/producer from Essex who also played keyboards on an album by Sherman Hemsley and produced Laurie Roth.

26/01/1991	12	10		OUTSTANDING	Cooltempo COOL 227
01/06/1991	4	13		**THINKING ABOUT YOUR LOVE**	Cooltempo COOL 235
05/10/1991	11	7		BEST OF YOU	Cooltempo COOL 243

30/11/1991.....26......6......	TENDER LOVE	Cooltempo COOL 247
10/07/1993.....22......6......	STAY	Cooltempo CDCOOL 271
04/09/1993.....17......5......	TRIPPIN' ON YOUR LOVE	Cooltempo CDCOOL 277
06/11/1993.....36......3......	PIECE BY PIECE	Cooltempo CDCOOL 283
14/05/1994.....59......1......	DESTINY	Cooltempo CDCOOL 289
02/09/1995.....27......3......	WHEN I THINK OF YOU	Cooltempo CDCOOL 309

LILLO THOMAS US singer (born Brooklyn, NY); he was an outstanding athlete as a child, later setting a world record for the 200 metres. He would have appeared at the 1984 Olympics but for a car crash in Brazil and pursued a musical career thereafter.

27/04/1985.....66......2.....	SETTLE DOWN	Capitol CL 356
21/03/1987.....23......5.....	SEXY GIRL	Capitol CL 445
30/05/1987.....54......3.....	I'M IN LOVE	Capitol CL 450

MICKEY THOMAS – see ELVIN BISHOP

MILLARD THOMAS – see HARRY BELAFONTE

NICKY THOMAS Jamaican reggae singer (born Cecil Nicholas Thomas, 1949, Portland) who was working as a labourer on a building site prior to being discovered.

13/06/1970.....9......14......	LOVE OF THE COMMON PEOPLE	Trojan TR 7750

ROB THOMAS – see SANTANA

RUFUS THOMAS US singer (born 17/3/1917, Cayce, MS, raised in Memphis) who began his career as a comedian. He made his first recordings for Talent in 1950 and was still touring and recording as he approached his 80th birthday. He died on 15/12/2001.

11/04/1970.....18......12......	DO THE FUNKY CHICKEN	Stax 144

TASHA THOMAS US singer (born 1950, Jeutyn, AK); she was in the Broadway show *The Wiz* and died from cancer on 8/11/1984.

20/01/1979.....59......3......	SHOOT ME (WITH YOUR LOVE)	Atlantic LV 4

TIMMY THOMAS US singer/keyboard player (born 13/11/1944, Evansville, IN) who was an in-house keyboard player for Gold Wax in Memphis before moving to Texas to become a teacher. He moved to Miami in 1970 and became a session player at TK.

24/02/1973.....12......11......	WHY CAN'T WE LIVE TOGETHER Featured in the films *Boys Don't Cry* (1999) and *Scooby Doo 2: Monsters Unleashed* (2004) ...	Mojo 2027 012
28/12/1985.....41......7......	NEW YORK EYES NICOLE WITH TIMMY THOMAS	Portrait A 6805
14/07/1990.....54......2......	WHY CAN'T WE LIVE TOGETHER (REMIX)	TK TKR 1

THOMAS AND TAYLOR US vocal duo Lamar Thomas and Judy Taylor. They also worked as producers for the likes of Ronnie Dyson and Johnny Bristol.

17/05/1986.....53......5......	YOU CAN'T BLAME LOVE	Cooltempo COOL 123

AMANDA THOMPSON – see LESLEY GARRETT AND AMANDA THOMPSON

CARROLL THOMPSON UK singer.

19/05/1990.....27......5......	JOY AND HEARTBREAK MOVEMENT 98 FEATURING CARROLL THOMPSON	Circa YR 45
07/07/1990.....66......1......	I'M STILL WAITING COURTNEY PINE FEATURING CARROLL THOMPSON	Mango MNG 749
15/09/1990.....58......3......	SUNRISE MOVEMENT 98 FEATURING CARROLL THOMPSON	Circa YR 51

CHRIS THOMPSON UK singer who had been lead singer with Manfred Mann's Earth Band and then formed Night in 1979. In the US his debut hit single was credited to Chris Thompson & Night.

27/10/1979.....42......5......	IF YOU REMEMBER ME Featured in the 1979 film *The Champ*	Planet K 12389

GINA THOMPSON – see MC LYTE

LINCOLN THOMPSON – see REBEL MC

SUE THOMPSON US singer (born Eva Sue McKee, 19/7/1926, Nevada, MO) who was raised in San Jose, CA and appeared regularly on Dude Martin's country TV show. A single recorded with Martin led to a solo contract with Mercury, but it wasn't until she signed with Hickory Records that she scored any hits.

02/11/1961.....46......2......	SAD MOVIES (MAKE ME CRY)	Polydor NH 66967
21/01/1965.....30......7......	PAPER TIGER	Hickory 1284

THOMPSON TWINS UK/New Zealand group formed by Tom Bailey (born 18/6/1957, Halifax, vocals/keyboards), Joe Leeway (born 15/11/1957, London, percussion) and Alannah Currie (born 20/9/1959, Auckland, New Zealand, vocals/saxophone). They took their name from the detective twins in Herge's cartoon series *Tintin*. They first recorded for their Dirty Discs label in 1980. Leeway left in 1986.

06/11/1982.....67......3......	LIES	Arista ARIST 486
29/01/1983.....9......12......	LOVE ON YOUR SIDE	Arista ARIST 504
16/04/1983.....7......9......	WE ARE DETECTIVE	Arista ARIST 526

○ Silver disc ● Gold disc ✪ Platinum disc (additional platinum units are indicated by a figure following the symbol) ◉ Singles released prior to 1973 that are known to have sold over 1 million copies in the UK

DATE	POS	WKS	BPI	SINGLE TITLE	LABEL & NUMBER
16/07/1983	33	6		WATCHING	Arista TWINS 1
19/11/1983	4	15	●	**HOLD ME NOW** Featured in the 1998 film *The Wedding Singer*	Arista TWINS 2
04/02/1984	3	10	○	**DOCTOR DOCTOR**	Arista TWINS 3
31/03/1984	2	9	○	**YOU TAKE ME UP**	Arista TWINS 4
07/07/1984	11	9		SISTER OF MERCY	Arista TWINS 5
08/12/1984	13	9	○	LAY YOUR HANDS ON ME Featured in the 1985 film *Perfect*	Arista TWINS 6
31/08/1985	15	6		DON'T MESS WITH DOCTOR DREAM	Arista TWINS 9
19/10/1985	22	6		KING FOR A DAY	Arista TWINS 7
07/12/1985	56	4		REVOLUTION	Arista TWINS 10
21/03/1987	66	3		GET THAT LOVE	Arista TWINS 12
15/10/1988	46	3		IN THE NAME OF LOVE '88	Arista 111808
28/09/1991	56	4		COME INSIDE	Warner Brothers W 0058
25/01/1992	53	2		THE SAINT	Warner Brothers W 0080

TRACEY THORN – see **MASSIVE ATTACK**

DAVID THORNE US singer who recorded for the Riverside label. His hit features the Richard Wolfe Orchestra.

24/01/1963	21	8		ALLEY CAT SONG	Stateside SS 141

KEN THORNE UK keyboard player who was with Vic Lewis' orchestra until 1950 when he left to play the organ at Ely Cathedral. His one hit was a rush-released version of Nini Rosso's film theme. His hit also features Ray Davies on trumpet.

18/07/1963	4	15		**THEME FROM THE FILM 'THE LEGION'S LAST PATROL'**	HMV POP 1176

THOSE 2 GIRLS UK vocal duo Denise Van Outen (born 1974) and Cathy Warwick. Van Outen later became a TV presenter, hosting the *Big Breakfast* on Channel Four and appearing in *Babes In The Wood*. She also linked with fellow *Big Breakfast* presenter Johnny Vaughan for one single and was briefly engaged to Jamiroquai lead singer Jay Kay.

05/11/1994	74	1		WANNA MAKE YOU GO…UUH!	Final Vinyl 74321233782
04/03/1995	36	3		ALL I WANT	Final Vinyl 74321254202

THOUSAND YARD STARE UK group formed in Windsor in 1988 by Stephen Barnes (vocals), Giles Duffy (guitar), Kevin Moxon (guitar), Sean McDonough (bass) and Dominic Bostock (drums).

26/10/1991	65	1		SEASONSTREAM (EP) Tracks on EP: *O-O AET, Village End, Keepsake* and *Worse For Wear*	Stifled Aardvark AARD 5T
08/02/1992	37	2		COMEUPPANCE	Stifled Aardvark AARD 007
11/07/1992	58	1		SPINDRIFT (EP) Tracks on EP: *Wideshire Two, Hand Son, Happenstance* and *Mocca Pune*	Stifled Aardvark AARDT 010
08/05/1993	57	1		VERSION OF ME	Polydor AARDC 012

THRASHING DOVES UK group formed in London by Ken Foreman (guitar/vocals), Ian Button (bass), Brian Foreman (keyboards) and Kevin Sargent (drums).

24/01/1987	50	3		BEAUTIFUL IMBALANCE	A&M TDOVE 1

THREE AMIGOS UK production group formed by Edgardo Lintron and Mike Ianieri.

03/07/1999	15	6		LOUIE LOUIE Featured in the 1999 film *American Pie*	Inferno CDFERN 17
24/03/2001	30	2		25 MILES 2001 Contains a sample of Edwin Starr's *25 Miles*	Wonderboy WBOYD 25

3 COLOURS RED UK rock group featuring Pete Vuckovic (born 16/2/1971, Tiverton, vocals/ bass), Chris McCormack (born 21/6/1973, South Shields, guitar), Ben Harding (born 31/1/1965, Stoke-on-Trent, guitar) and Keith Baxter (born 19/2/1971, Morecambe, drums). Chris McCormack is brother of The Wildhearts' Danny McCormack and launched the Limited record label in 1997.

18/01/1997	22	2		NUCLEAR HOLIDAY	Creation CRESCD 250
15/03/1997	20	3		SIXTY MILE SMILE	Creation CRESCD 254
10/05/1997	28	1		PURE	Creation CRESCD 265
12/07/1997	30	2		COPPER GIRL	Creation CRESCD 270
08/11/1997	48	1		THIS IS MY HOLLYWOOD	Creation CRESCD 277
23/01/1999	11	6		BEAUTIFUL DAY	Creation CRESCD 308
29/05/1999	36	2		THIS IS MY TIME	Creation CRESCD 313

THREE DEGREES US R&B vocal group, formed in Philadelphia, PA in 1963 by Fayette Pickney, Linda Turner and Shirley Porter, who scored their first hit for Swan in 1965. Turner and Porter left in 1966, replaced by Sheila Ferguson (born 8/10/1947, Philadelphia) and Valerie Holiday (born 2/12/1947, Newark). Ferguson left to become an actress in 1986, replaced by Victoria Wallace (who was later replaced by Cynthia Garrison). The group appeared in the 1971 film *The French Connection*. It was claimed they were Prince Charles' favourite group and they performed at his 30th birthday celebration at Buckingham Palace.

13/04/1974	13	10		YEAR OF DECISION	Philadelphia International PIR 2073
27/04/1974	22	9		TSOP (THE SOUND OF PHILADELPHIA) ▲2 **MFSB FEATURING THE THREE DEGREES**	Philadelphia International PIR 2289
13/07/1974	❶2	16	●	**WHEN WILL I SEE YOU AGAIN** Gold disc presentation was made by HRH Princess Anne	Philadelphia International PIR 2155
02/11/1974	34	4		GET YOUR LOVE BACK	Philadelphia International PIR 2737
12/04/1975	9	9	○	**TAKE GOOD CARE OF YOURSELF**	Philadelphia International PIR 3177
05/07/1975	40	4		LONG LOST LOVER	Philadelphia International PIR 3352
01/05/1976	36	4		TOAST OF LOVE	Epic EPC 4215
07/10/1978	12	10		GIVIN' UP GIVIN' IN	Ariola ARO 130
13/01/1979	3	11	●	**WOMAN IN LOVE**	Ariola ARO 141

❶9 Number of weeks single topped the UK chart   ↑ Entered the UK chart at #1   ▲9 Number of weeks single topped the US chart

809

DATE	POS	WKS	BPI	SINGLE TITLE	LABEL & NUMBER
24/03/1979	10	10	○	**THE RUNNER**	Ariola ARO 154
23/06/1979	56	3		THE GOLDEN LADY Featured in the 1979 film *The Golden Lady*	Ariola ARO 170
29/09/1979	48	5		JUMP THE GUN	Ariola ARO 183
24/11/1979	9	11	○	**MY SIMPLE HEART**	Ariola ARO 202
05/10/1985	42	5		THE HEAVEN I NEED	Supreme SUPE 102
26/12/1998	54	2		LAST CHRISTMAS ALIEN VOICES FEATURING THE THREE DEGREES	Wildstar CDWILD 15

THREE DOG NIGHT US rock group formed in Los Angeles, CA in 1968 by Danny Hutton (born 10/9/1946, Buncrana, Ireland, vocals), Cory Wells (born 5/2/1944, New York, vocals), Chuck Negron (born 8/6/1942, New York, vocals), Jimmy Greenspoon (born 7/2/1948, Los Angeles, CA, organ), Floyd Sneed (born 22/11/1943, Calgary, Canada, drums), Mike Allsup (born 8/3/1947, Modesto, CA, guitar) and Joe Schermie (born 12/2/1945, Madison, WI, bass). The group took their name from an Aborigine term relating to how cold it was, with a 'three dog night' the coldest. They disbanded in 1976 and re-formed in 1981. Schermie died in March 2002.

DATE	POS	WKS	BPI	SINGLE TITLE	LABEL & NUMBER
08/08/1970	3	14		**MAMA TOLD ME NOT TO COME** ▲² Featured in the films *G.I. Jane* (1997), *Boogie Nights* (1998) and *Fear and Loathing In Las Vegas* (1998).	Stateside SS 8052
29/05/1971	24	9		JOY TO THE WORLD ▲⁶ Featured in the films *The Big Chill* (1984) and *Forrest Gump* (1994)	Probe PRO 523

THREE DRIVES Dutch dance group formed by Ton TB and DJ Enrico and featuring Jules Harrington on vocals.

DATE	POS	WKS	BPI	SINGLE TITLE	LABEL & NUMBER
27/06/1998	44	1		GREECE 2000	Hooj Choons HOOJCD 63
30/01/1999	12	4		GREECE 2000 (REMIX)	Hooj Choons HOOJ 70CD
17/11/2001	44	2		SUNSET ON IBIZA THREE DRIVES ON A VINYL	Xtravaganza XTRAV 27CDS
07/06/2003	57	1		CARRERA 2	Nebula NEBCD 043
14/08/2004	75	1		AIR TRAFFIC	Nebula NEBCD 056

THREE GOOD REASONS UK vocal/instrumental group formed in Bradford by Annette Clegg, Pete Clegg and Radivoj Danic. Danic left in 1966, replaced by Noel Finn.

DATE	POS	WKS	BPI	SINGLE TITLE	LABEL & NUMBER
10/03/1966	47	3		NOWHERE MAN	Mercury MF 899

3 JAYS UK dance trio formed in London by Jeff Patterson, Jamie White and Jim Lee. White was ex-member of Tzant, Mirrorball and the PF Project.

DATE	POS	WKS	BPI	SINGLE TITLE	LABEL & NUMBER
31/07/1999	17	5		FEELING IT TOO	Multiply CDMULTY 53

THREE KAYES – see KAYE SISTERS

3LW US vocal group formed in New Jersey by Kiely Alexis Williams (also known as Keylay Keylay, born 9/7/1986, Alexandria, VA), Naturi Cora Maria Naughton (born 20/5/1984, East Orange, NJ) and Adrienne Eliza Bailon (born 24/10/1983, of Puerto Rican and Ecuadorian descent). The group's name stands for Three Little Women. Naughton left in October 2002 and filed suit against her former bandmates and management company claiming she was forced out of the group.

DATE	POS	WKS	BPI	SINGLE TITLE	LABEL & NUMBER
02/06/2001	6	9		**NO MORE (BABY I'MA DO RIGHT)** Contains a sample of Eric B & Rakim's *Eric B For President*	Epic 6712722
08/09/2001	21	3		PLAYAS GON' PLAY	Epic 6717932
19/10/2002	44	1		FEELS GOOD (DON'T WORRY BOUT A THING) NAUGHTY BY NATURE FEATURING 3LW Contains a sample of Tony! Toni! Tone!'s *Feel's Good*	Island CID 806

THREE 'N' ONE German production duo Sharam 'Jey' Khososi and Andre Strasser. Khososi also recorded as Billy Hendrix.

DATE	POS	WKS	BPI	SINGLE TITLE	LABEL & NUMBER
07/06/1997	66	1		REFLECT	ffrr FCD 301
15/05/1999	32	2		PEARL RIVER THREE 'N' ONE PRESENTS JOHNNY SHAKER FEATURING SERIAL DIVA	Low Sense SENSECD 24

3 OF A KIND UK production/vocal group formed by Miz Tipzta, Devine and Marky P.

DATE	POS	WKS	BPI	SINGLE TITLE	LABEL & NUMBER
21/08/2004	❶¹	14	○	**BABYCAKES** ↑	Relentless RELDX6

3SL UK vocal group formed by Steve, Andy and Ant Scott-Lee, younger brothers of former Steps member Lisa Scott-Lee (who was initially their manager). They were dropped by Epic after their two hits; Andy Scott-Lee then auditioned for the third series of *Pop Idols*.

DATE	POS	WKS	BPI	SINGLE TITLE	LABEL & NUMBER
20/04/2002	11	6		TAKE IT EASY	Epic 6724042
07/09/2002	16	4		TOUCH ME TEASE ME	Epic 6727875

3T US R&B vocal trio formed in Los Angeles by Tariano 'Taj' Adaryll (born 4/8/1973, Hollywood, CA), Tarryll Adren (born 8/8/1975, Hollywood) and Tito Joe 'TJ' Jackson (born 16/7/1978, Hollywood). They are the sons of Tito Jackson and nephews of Michael Jackson.

DATE	POS	WKS	BPI	SINGLE TITLE	LABEL & NUMBER
27/01/1996	2	14	●	**ANYTHING**	MJJ 6627152
04/05/1996	11	7		24/7	MJJ 6631995
24/08/1996	2	9		WHY 3T FEATURING MICHAEL JACKSON	Epic 6636482
07/12/1996	3	10	○	I NEED YOU	Epic 6639912
05/04/1997	10	5		GOTTA BE YOU 3T: RAP BY HERBIE	Epic 6643645

THREE TONS OF JOY – see JOHNNY OTIS SHOW

THRICE US rock group formed in California by Dustin Kensrue (guitar/vocals), Teppei Teranishi (guitar), Edward Breckenridge (bass) and Riley Breckenridge (drums).

DATE	POS	WKS	BPI	SINGLE TITLE	LABEL & NUMBER
18/10/2003	69	1		ALL THAT'S LEFT	Island US 9811957

○ Silver disc ● Gold disc ✪ Platinum disc (additional platinum units are indicated by a figure following the symbol) ◉ Singles released prior to 1973 that are known to have sold over 1 million copies in the UK

THRILLS Irish group formed in Dublin by Conor Deasey (vocals), Daniel Ryan (guitar), Padraic McMahon (bass), Kevin Horan (keyboards) and Ben Carrigan (drums).

22/03/2003	18	3		ONE HORSE TOWN	Virgin VSCDT 1845
21/06/2003	17	4		BIG SUR	Virgin VSCDT 1852
06/09/2003	33	2		SANTA CRUZ (YOU'RE NOT THAT FAR)	Virgin VSCDT 1862
06/12/2003	45	1		DON'T STEAL OUR SUN	Virgin VSCDT 1864
11/09/2004	22	4		WHATEVER HAPPENED TO COREY HAIM? Corey Haim is a US actor who appeared in the film *Lost Boys*	Virgin VSCDX 1876
27/11/2004	39	2		NOT FOR ALL THE LOVE IN THE WORLD	Virgin VSCDX 1890

THRILLSEEKERS UK producer Steve Helstrip.

17/02/2001	28	2		SYNAESTHESIA (FLY AWAY) **THRILLSEEKERS FEATURING SHERYL DEANE**	Neo NEOCD1 050
07/09/2002	48	1		DREAMING OF YOU	Data 36CDS

THROWING MUSES US group formed in Newport, Long Island in 1986 by Kristin Hersh (born 1966, Atlanta, GA, guitar/vocals), her step sister Tanya Donelly (born 14/8/1966, Newport, guitar/vocals), Elaine Adamedes (bass) and David Narcizo (drums). Adamedes left and was replaced by Leslie Langston. The band then relocated to Boston, MA. Langston left in 1991, replaced by Fred Abong. Donelly, also a member of The Breeders, announced her departure in 1991 and by 1992 the group comprised Hersh, Narcizo and Bernard Georges (bass). They disbanded in 1993 but re-formed in 1994, although Hersh also undertook a solo career.

09/02/1991	70	2		COUNTING BACKWARDS	4AD AD 1001
01/08/1992	46	1		FIREPILE (EP) Tracks on EP: *Firepile, Manic Depression, Snailhead* and *City Of The Dead*	4AD BAD 2012
24/12/1994	51	2		BRIGHT YELLOW GUN	4AD BAD 4018CD
10/08/1996	53	1		SHARK	4AD BAD 6016CD

THS – THE HORN SECTION US vocal/instrumental group formed in Philadelphia, PA in 1983 by Roger Garnett (born 28/12/1958, Philadelphia, vocals/percussion) and Henry Horne (born 9/12/1960, Philadelphia, songwriter/producer).

18/08/1984	54	3		LADY SHINE (SHINE ON)	Fourth & Broadway BRW 10

HARRY THUMANN German keyboard player who also recorded as Wonder Dogs and was an engineer for Rondo Veneziano.

21/02/1981	41	6		UNDERWATER	Decca F 13901

THUNDER UK heavy rock group formed in 1989 by Danny Bowes (vocals), Luke Morley (guitar), Gary James (drums), Mark Lockhurst (bass) and Ben Matthews (guitar). Bowes, Morley and James were ex-members of Terraplane. Lockhurst left in 1993.

17/02/1990	32	4		DIRTY LOVE	EMI EM 126
12/05/1990	25	4		BACKSTREET SYMPHONY	EMI EM 137
14/07/1990	36	3		GIMME SOME LOVIN'	EMI EM 148
29/09/1990	34	3		SHE'S SO FINE	EMI EM 158
23/02/1991	21	4		LOVE WALKED IN	EMI EM 175
15/08/1992	22	5		LOW LIFE IN HIGH PLACES	EMI EM 242
10/10/1992	36	4		EVERYBODY WANTS HER	EMI EM 249
13/02/1993	18	4		A BETTER MAN	EMI CDBETTER 1
19/06/1993	28	2		LIKE A SATELLITE (EP) Tracks on EP: *Like A Satellite, The Damage Is Done, Like A Satellite (Live)* and *Gimme Shelter*	EMI CDEM 272
07/01/1995	23	4		STAND UP	EMI CDEM 365
25/02/1995	31	2		RIVER OF PAIN	EMI CDEM 367
06/05/1995	30	3		CASTLES IN THE SAND	EMI CDEMS 372
23/09/1995	26	2		IN A BROKEN DREAM	EMI CDEMS 384
25/01/1997	27	2		DON'T WAIT UP	Raw Power RAWX 1020
05/04/1997	60	1		LOVE WORTH DYING FOR	Raw Power RAWX 1043
07/02/1998	31	2		THE ONLY ONE	Eagle EAGXA 016
27/06/1998	39	2		PLAY THAT FUNKY MUSIC	Eagle EAGXS 030
20/03/1999	49	1		YOU WANNA KNOW	Eagle EAGXA 037
31/05/2003	48	1		LOSER	STC Recordings STC20032
04/12/2004	27	2		I LOVE YOU MORE THAN ROCK N ROLL	STC STC20044

THUNDERBIRDS – see **CHRIS FARLOWE**

THUNDERBUGS UK/French/German group formed by Jane Vaughan (England, vocals), Nick Shaw (England, drums), Brigitta Jansen (Germany, guitar) and Stef Maillard (France, bass).

18/09/1999	5	10		**FRIENDS FOREVER** Featured in the 2000 film *Center Stage*	1st Avenue 6676932
18/12/1999	43	5		IT'S ABOUT TIME YOU WERE MINE	1st Avenue 6683972

THUNDERCLAP NEWMAN UK rock group formed by Andy 'Thunderclap' Newman (keyboards), John 'Speedy' Keen (born 29/3/1945, London, vocals/drums) and Jimmy McCulloch (guitar). They were discovered by Pete Townshend. McCulloch later joined Wings. He died from heart failure on 27/9/1979.

11/06/1969	❶[3]	12		**SOMETHING IN THE AIR** Featured in the films *The Magic Christian* (1969), *The Strawberry Statement* (1970), *Kingpin* (1996) and *Almost Famous* (2000)	Track 604 031
27/06/1970	46	1		ACCIDENTS	Track 2094 001

❶[9] Number of weeks single topped the UK chart ↑ Entered the UK chart at #1 ▲[9] Number of weeks single topped the US chart

811

THUNDERTHIGHS UK vocal group formed by Karen Friedman, Dari Lalou and Casey Synge.

22/06/1974	30	5		CENTRAL PARK ARREST .... Philips 6006 386

THURSDAY US rock group formed in New Brunswick, NJ in 1998 by Geoff Rickly (vocals), Tom Keeley (guitar), Steve Pedulla (guitar), Tim Payne (bass) and Tucker Rule (drums). They first recorded for Eyeball Records.

25/10/2003	62	1		SIGNALS OVER THE AIR .... Island US 9812292

BOBBY THURSTON US singer (born 1954, Washington DC), he originally sang with Spectrum Ltd while working in the Washington State Department until signing as a solo singer with Mainstream in 1978 and then Prelude in 1980.

29/03/1980	10	10		**CHECK OUT THE GROOVE** .... Epic EPC 8348

TIFFANY US singer (born Tiffany Renee Darwish, 2/10/1971, Norwalk, CA) who started singing aged nine and was signed by her manager at the age of thirteen. She signed with MCA in 1986 and was sent out touring shopping malls to promote her debut album. She provided the voice of Judy Jetson in the film *Jetsons: The Movie* in 1990.

16/01/1988	❶³	13	●	**I THINK WE'RE ALONE NOW** ▲² .... MCA 1211
19/03/1988	4	9		**COULD'VE BEEN** ▲² .... MCA TIFF 2
04/06/1988	8	7		**I SAW HIM STANDING THERE** .... MCA TIFF 3
06/08/1988	52	2		FEELINGS OF FOREVER .... MCA TIFF 4
12/11/1988	13	11		RADIO ROMANCE .... MCA TIFF 5
11/02/1989	47	3		ALL THIS TIME .... MCA TIFF 6

TIGA AND ZYNTHERIUS Canadian dance duo formed in Montreal by producers Tiga Sontag and Jori Hulkkonen.

11/05/2002	25	3		SUNGLASSES AT NIGHT .... City Rockers ROCKERS 15CD
06/09/2003	46	2		HOT IN HERRE Contains a sample of Chuck Brown's *Bustin' Loose*.................... Skint 90CD
19/06/2004	57	1		PLEASURE FROM THE BASS This and above single credited to **TIGA** .... Different DIFB1028CDM

TIGER UK/Irish group formed by Dan Laidler (guitar/vocals), Julie Sims (guitar/vocals), Tina Whitlow (keyboards), Dido Hallett (keyboards) and Seamus Feeney (drums).

31/08/1996	37	2		RACE .... Trade 2 TRDCD 004
16/11/1996	62	1		MY PUPPET PAL .... Trade 2 TRDCD 005
22/02/1997	57	1		ON THE ROSE .... Trade 2 TRDCD 008
22/08/1998	72	1		FRIENDS .... Trade 2 TRDCD 013

TIGERTAILZ US vocal/instrumental group formed in 1985 by Pepsi Tate, Jay Pepper, Steevie Jaimz and Ian Welsh. They subsequently added Ace Finchum and signed with Music For Nations in 1987. Jaimz left in 1987, replaced by Kim Hooker; Finchum left in 1991, replaced by Andy Skinner.

24/06/1989	75	1		LOVE BOMB BABY .... Music For Nations KUT 132
16/02/1991	71	1		HEAVEN .... Music For Nations KUT 137

TIGHT FIT UK group originally assembled as session musicians to record their first two hits, inspired by the success of Starsound. A trio was put together in 1982 comprising Steve Grant, Julie Harris and Denise Gyngell, with Gyngell and Harris later replaced by Vicki Pemberton and Carol Stevens. Denise later married producer Pete Waterman.

18/07/1981	4	11		**BACK TO THE SIXTIES** Tracks on medley: *Dancing In The Street, (I Can't Get No) Satisfaction, You Really Got Me, Do Wah Diddy, Black Is Black, Bend Me Shape Me, When You Walk In The Room* and *Mony Mony* .... Jive 002
26/09/1981	33	5		BACK TO THE SIXTIES PART 2 .... Jive 005
23/01/1982	❶³	15	●	**THE LION SLEEPS TONIGHT** .... Jive 9
01/05/1982	5	12	○	**FANTASY ISLAND** .... Jive 13
31/07/1982	41	6		SECRET HEART .... Jive 20

TIJUANA BRASS – see HERB ALPERT

TIK AND TOK UK vocal/instrumental duo. They were ex-members of Shock, also appeared as Ronnie and Reggie Dome and recorded with Gary Numan. Tik played guitars/keyboards/bass/vocals while Tok played keyboards/vocals.

08/10/1983	69	2		COOL RUNNING .... Survival SUR 0116

TANITA TIKARAM UK singer (born 12/8/1969, Munster, Germany, of Malaysian and Fijian parentage) whose first album was produced by Rod Argent and Peter Van Hoote.

30/07/1988	10	10		**GOOD TRADITION** .... WEA YZ 196
22/10/1988	22	8		TWIST IN MY SOBRIETY .... WEA YZ 321
14/01/1989	48	3		CATHEDRAL SONG .... WEA YZ 331
18/03/1989	58	2		WORLD OUTSIDE YOUR WINDOW .... WEA YZ 363
13/01/1990	52	3		WE ALMOST GOT IT TOGETHER .... WEA YZ 443
09/02/1991	69	1		ONLY THE ONES WE LOVE .... East West YZ 558
04/02/1995	64	2		I MIGHT BE CRYING .... East West YZ 879CD
06/06/1998	67	1		STOP LISTENING .... Mother MUMCD 102
29/08/1998	73	1		I DON'T WANNA LOSE AT LOVE .... Mother MUMCD 105

TILLMAN AND REIS German production duo Tillman Uhrmacher and Peter Reis. Uhrmacher later recorded solo.

16/09/2000	70	1		BASSFLY .... Liquid Asset ASSETCD 004

○ Silver disc ● Gold disc ✪ Platinum disc (additional platinum units are indicated by a figure following the symbol) ⊛ Singles released prior to 1973 that are known to have sold over 1 million copies in the UK

JOHNNY TILLOTSON
US singer (born 20/4/1939, Jacksonville, FL) who began his career on local radio aged nine. He later appeared on Toby Dowdy's TV show before being given his own show. He first recorded for Cadence Records in 1958.

DATE	POS	WKS	BPI	SINGLE TITLE	LABEL & NUMBER
01/12/1960	❶²	15		POETRY IN MOTION	London HLA 9231
02/02/1961	43	2		JIMMY'S GIRL	London HLA 9275
12/07/1962	31	10		IT KEEPS RIGHT ON A HURTIN'	London HLA 9550
04/10/1962	21	10		SEND ME THE PILLOW YOU DREAM ON	London HLA 9598
27/12/1962	41	6		I CAN'T HELP IT	London HLA 9642
09/05/1963	34	5		OUT OF MY MIND	London HLA 9695
14/04/1979	67	2		POETRY IN MOTION Re-issue of London HLA 9231	Lightning LIG 9016

TILT
UK production group formed by John Graham, Mick Parks and Mick Wilson. They later recorded with Maria Nayler. Graham was an ex-member of Quivver and left Tilt in 2001.

DATE	POS	WKS	BPI	SINGLE TITLE	LABEL & NUMBER
02/12/1995	69	1		I DREAM	Perfecto PERF 112CD
10/05/1997	61	1		MY SPIRIT	Perfecto PERF 139CD
13/09/1997	64	1		PLACES	Perfecto PERF 149CD
07/02/1998	41	1		BUTTERFLY TILT FEATURING ZEE	Perfecto PERF 154CD1
27/03/1999	51	1		CHILDREN	Deconstruction 74321648172
08/05/1999	20	2		INVISIBLE	Hooj Choons HOOJ 73CD
12/02/2000	55	1		DARK SCIENCE (EP) Tracks on EP: *36* (two mixes) and *Seduction Of Orpheus* (two mixes)	Hooj Choons HOOJ 87CD

TIMBALAND
US rapper (born Timothy Mosley, 10/3/1971, Norfolk, VA) who originally linked with fellow rapper Magoo before recording with a succession of other artists.

DATE	POS	WKS	BPI	SINGLE TITLE	LABEL & NUMBER
23/01/1999	15	5		GET ON THE BUS DESTINY'S CHILD FEATURING TIMBALAND Featured in the 1998 film *Why Do Fools Fall In Love*	East West E 3780CD
13/03/1999	43	1		HERE WE COME TIMBALAND/MISSY ELLIOTT AND MAGOO Contains a sample from the cartoon series *Spiderman*	Virgin DINSD 179
19/06/1999	48	1		LOBSTER & SCRIMP TIMBALAND FEATURING JAY-Z	Virgin DINSD 186
21/07/2001	20	6		WE NEED A RESOLUTION AALIYAH FEATURING TIMBALAND	Blackground VUSCD 206
13/03/2004	22	3		COP THAT SHIT TIMBALAND/MAGOO/MISSY ELLIOTT	Unique Corp TIMBACD001

JUSTIN TIMBERLAKE
US singer (born 31/1/1981, Memphis, TN) who was previously a member of N Sync before going solo. He was briefly engaged to fellow singer Britney Spears and won the 2003 MOBO Award for Best Rhythm & Blues Act. He then won the MTV Europe Music Awards for Best Male, Best Pop and Best Album for *Justified* in the same year. He has two Grammy Awards including Best Pop Vocal Album in 2003 for *Justified*, and won two BRIT Awards in 2004: Best International Male and Best International Album for *Justified*.

DATE	POS	WKS	BPI	SINGLE TITLE	LABEL & NUMBER
02/11/2002	2	16	○	LIKE I LOVE YOU Featured in the 2003 film *Love Actually*	Jive 9254342
15/02/2003	2	12		CRY ME A RIVER 2003 Grammy Award for Best Male Pop Vocal Performance	Jive 9254632
15/03/2003	7	11		WORK IT NELLY FEATURING JUSTIN TIMBERLAKE	Universal MCSXD 40312
24/05/2003	46	1		ROCK YOUR BODY (IMPORT)	Jive 9254962
31/05/2003	2	13		ROCK YOUR BODY	Jive 9254952
27/09/2003	13	8		SENORITA	Jive 82876563442

TIMBUK 3
US husband and wife duo Pat and Barbara Kooyman MacDonald, and a tape machine. They first linked in Madison, WI in 1978 and are now based in Texas. They later added Wally Ingram on drums and Courtney Audain on bass.

DATE	POS	WKS	BPI	SINGLE TITLE	LABEL & NUMBER
31/01/1987	21	7		THE FUTURE'S SO BRIGHT I GOTTA WEAR SHADES	IRS IRM 126

TIME FREQUENCY
UK instrumental/production group formed by John Campbell and Debbie Muller.

DATE	POS	WKS	BPI	SINGLE TITLE	LABEL & NUMBER
06/06/1992	60	1		REAL LOVE	Jive JIVET 307
09/01/1993	36	6		NEW EMOTION	Internal Affairs KGBCD 009
12/06/1993	17	11		THE ULTIMATE HIGH/THE POWER ZONE	Internal Affairs KGBCD 010
06/11/1993	8	8		REAL LOVE (REMIX)	Internal Affairs KGBCD 011
28/05/1994	25	4		SUCH A PHANTASY	Internal Affairs KGBCD 013
08/10/1994	32	3		DREAMSCAPE '94	Internal Affairs KGBCD 015
31/08/2002	43	1		REAL LOVE 2002	Jive 9253782

TIME OF THE MUMPH
UK producer Mark Mumford.

DATE	POS	WKS	BPI	SINGLE TITLE	LABEL & NUMBER
11/02/1995	69	1		CONTROL	Fresh FRSHD 24

TIME UK
UK vocal/instrumental group formed by Rick Buckler, Danny Kustow, Jimmy Edwards, Ray Simone and Nick South. Buckler was an ex-member of The Jam.

DATE	POS	WKS	BPI	SINGLE TITLE	LABEL & NUMBER
08/10/1983	63	3		THE CABARET	Red Bus/Aroadia TIM 123

TIME ZONE
UK/US group formed by John Lydon (born 31/1/1956, London, vocals), formerly a member of The Sex Pistols under the name Johnny Rotten, Afrika Bambaataa (born Kevin Donovan, 10/4/1960, The Bronx, NY, vocals), Bill Laswell (bass), Bernie Worrell (keyboards), Nicky Skopelitis (guitar) and Anyb Dieng (percussion).

DATE	POS	WKS	BPI	SINGLE TITLE	LABEL & NUMBER
19/01/1985	44	9		WORLD DESTRUCTION	Virgin VS 743

TIMEBOX
UK group formed in 1966 by Mike Patto (vocals), Peter 'Ollie' Halsall (guitar), Chris Holmes (piano), Clive Griffiths (bass) and John Halsey (drums). The group name-changed to Patto in 1969.

DATE	POS	WKS	BPI	SINGLE TITLE	LABEL & NUMBER
24/07/1968	38	4		BEGGIN'	Deram DM 194

❶⁹ Number of weeks single topped the UK chart ↑ Entered the UK chart at #1 ▲⁹ Number of weeks single topped the US chart

813

TIMELORDS UK duo Bill Drummond (born William Butterworth, 29/4/1953, South Africa) and Jim Cauty (born 1954, London), better known as the KLF. They produced one hit single under the banner of Timelords: a mixture of Gary Glitter's *Rock And Roll Part 2* and the theme to the TV series *Dr Who*. Gary Glitter lent the project further respectability by appearing with the duo on some of their rare live appearances as the Timelords.

04/06/1988 .... ●¹ .... 9 .... DOCTORIN' THE TARDIS .... KLF Communications KLF 003

TIMEX SOCIAL CLUB US rap group formed by Gregory Thomas, Marcus Thompson, Kevin Moore, Craig Samuel, Darrien Cleage and Alex Hill and featuring singer Michael Marshall. Producer Jay King later formed Club Nouveau.

13/09/1986 ..... 13 ...... 9 .... RUMORS .... Cooltempo COOL 133

TIN MACHINE UK/US rock group formed in 1989 by David Bowie (born David Robert Jones, 8/1/1947, Brixton, London) with Tony Sales (bass), Reeves Gabrels (born Boston, MA, guitar) and Hunt Sales (drums).

01/07/1989 ..... 51 ..... 2	UNDER THE GOD	EMI-USA MT 68
09/09/1989 ..... 48 ..... 2	TIN MACHINE/MAGGIE'S FARM (LIVE)	EMI-USA MT 73
24/08/1991 ..... 33 ..... 3	YOU BELONG IN ROCK 'N' ROLL	London LON 305
02/11/1991 ..... 48 ..... 3	BABY UNIVERSAL	London LON 310

TIN TIN OUT UK instrumental/production duo Darren Stokes and Lindsay Edwards. Sweet Tee is US female rapper Toi Jackson. Espiritu are UK duo Chris Taplin and Vanessa Quinnones. Tony Hadley (born 2/6/1960, London) is the former lead singer with Spandau Ballet. Shelley Nelson also recorded with Ed Case. Wendy Page is a UK singer. Emma Bunton is a singer (born 21/1/1976, London) and was a member of The Spice Girls.

13/08/1994 ..... 32 ..... 2	THE FEELING TIN TIN OUT FEATURING SWEET TEE Contains a sample of Sweet Tee's *I Got Da Feelin* ... Deep Distraxion OILYCD 029
25/03/1995 ..... 14 ..... 5	ALWAYS SOMETHING THERE TO REMIND ME TIN TIN OUT FEATURING ESPIRITU .... WEA YZ 911CD
08/02/1997 ..... 31 ..... 2	ALL I WANNA DO .... VC Recordings VCRD 15
10/05/1997 ..... 35 ..... 2	DANCE WITH ME TIN TIN OUT FEATURING TONY HADLEY .... VC Recordings VCRD 17
20/09/1997 ..... 31 ..... 3	STRINGS FOR YASMIN First featured in a TV advertisement for Sky's football coverage and contains a sample of Liberty City's *If You Really Want Somebody*. Featured in the 2001 film *Mean Machine* .... VC Recordings VCRD 20
28/03/1998 ..... 7 ..... 10	HERE'S WHERE THE STORY ENDS .... VC Recordings VCRD 30
12/09/1998 ..... 20 ..... 4	SOMETIMES This and above single credited to TIN TIN OUT FEATURING SHELLEY NELSON .... VC Recordings VCRD 34
11/09/1999 ..... 26 ..... 2	ELEVEN TO FLY TIN TIN OUT FEATURING WENDY PAGE .... VC Recordings VCRDX 52
13/11/1999 ..... 2 ..... 12 ..... ○	WHAT I AM TIN TIN OUT FEATURING EMMA BUNTON .... VC Recordings VCRD 53

TINDERSTICKS UK rock group formed in Nottingham by Stuart Staples (born 14/11/1965, Nottingham, vocals), Dickon Hinchcliffe (born 9/7/1967, Nottingham, violin), Dave Boulter (born 27/2/1965, Nottingham, keyboards), Neil Fraser (born 22/11/1962, London, guitar), Mark Cornwill (born 15/5/1967, Nottingham, bass) and Al McCauley (born 2/8/1965, Nottingham, drums).

05/02/1994 ..... 61 ..... 1	KATHLEEN (EP) Tracks on EP: *Kathleen, Summat Moon, A Sweet Sweet Man* and *E-Type Joe* .... This Way Up WAY 2833CD
18/03/1995 ..... 58 ..... 1	NO MORE AFFAIRS .... This Way Up WAY 3833
12/08/1995 ..... 51 ..... 1	TRAVELLING LIGHT .... This Way Up WAY 4533
07/06/1997 ..... 38 ..... 1	BATHTIME .... This Way Up WAY 6166
01/11/1997 ..... 56 ..... 1	RENTED ROOMS .... This Way Up WAY 6566
04/09/1999 ..... 54 ..... 1	CAN WE START AGAIN? .... Island CID 756
02/08/2003 ..... 60 ..... 1	SOMETIMES IT HURTS .... Beggars Banquet BBQ369CD

TINGO TANGO UK instrumental group.

21/07/1990 ..... 68 ..... 2 .... IT IS JAZZ .... Champion CHAMP 250

TINMAN UK producer Paul Dakeyne.

20/08/1994 ..... 9 ..... 8	EIGHTEEN STRINGS Contains a sample of The Monkees' *(I'm Not Your) Steppin' Stone,* although it was originally recorded a year earlier with a sample of Nirvana's *Smells Like Teen Spirit* but permission to use the sample was refused .... ffrr FCD 242
03/06/1995 ..... 49 ..... 1	GUDVIBE Contains a sample of Yello's *The Race* .... ffrr FCD 262

TINY TIM US singer (born Herbert Khaury, 12/4/1930, New York City) who first came to prominence on the TV show *Rowan And Martin's Laugh-In* and best known for the song *Tip-Toe Thru' The Tulips With Me*. He married 'Miss Vicky' (Victoria May Budinger) live on the *Johnny Carson Show* in 1969, divorced in 1977 (they had a daughter, Tulip) and died from heart failure on 30/11/1996.

05/02/1969 ..... 45 ..... 1 ...... GREAT BALLS OF FIRE .... Reprise RS 20802

ROB TISSERA AND VINYLGROOVER UK production duo Rob Tissera and Nick Sentience.

10/07/2004 ..... 61 ..... 1 ...... STAY .... Tidy Trax TIDYTWO133C

TITANIC Norwegian/UK group formed by Roy Robinson (vocals), Janny Loseth (guitar), Kenny Aas (keyboards), Kjell Asperud (drums) and John Lorck (drums).

25/09/1971 ..... 5 ..... 12 ...... SULTANA .... CBS 5365

TITIYO Swedish singer, daughter of Ahmadu Jah and half-sister of Neneh Cherry who also provided backing vocals for the likes of Army Of Lovers and Papa Dee.

03/03/1990 ..... 60 ..... 3	AFTER THE RAIN .... Arista 112722
06/10/1990 ..... 71 ..... 1	FLOWERS .... Arista 113212
05/02/1994 ..... 45 ..... 2	TELL ME I'M NOT DREAMING .... Arista 74321185622

○ Silver disc ● Gold disc ✪ Platinum disc (additional platinum units are indicated by a figure following the symbol) ◉ Singles released prior to 1973 that are known to have sold over 1 million copies in the UK

CARA TIVEY – see BILLY BRAGG

TJR FEATURING XAVIER UK dance group formed by Xavier, Gavin 'DJ Face' Mills, Brian Thorne, Karl 'Tuff Enuff' Brown and Matt 'Jam' Lamont.

27/09/1997.....28......2........ JUST GETS BETTER .... Multiply CDMULTY 25

TLC US female rap group formed by Tionne 'T-Boz' Watkins (born 26/4/1970, Des Moines, IA), Lisa 'Left Eye' Lopes (born 27/5/1971, Philadelphia, PA) and Rozonda 'Chilli' Thomas (born 27/2/1971, Atlanta, GA). They were founded and managed by Pebbles (then married to songwriter, producer and record label owner Antonio 'LA' Reid). Lopes was fined $10,000 and given five years probation in 1994 for setting fire to her boyfriend Andre Rison's home and vandalising his car, although the pair reconciled and he refused to press charges. In 1995 the group filed for Chapter 11 bankruptcy claiming liabilities of $3.5 million ($1.5 million of this related to an unpaid insurance claim by Lloyd's of London for Lopes' arson attack). Lisa Lopes later sang with a number of other acts, including Melanie C, and recorded solo, as did T-Boz. They have also won five Grammy Awards including Best Rhythm & Blues Album on 1995 for *Crazysexycool* and Best Rhythm & Blues Album in 1999 for *Fanmail*. The group was named Best International Group at the 2000 BRIT Awards. Lopes was killed in a car crash while on holiday in Honduras on 26/4/2002. She was awarded a posthumous Outstanding Achievement Award at the 2002 MOBO Awards.

20/06/1992.....13......5....... AIN'T 2 PROUD 2 BEG Contains samples of James Brown's *Escape-ism*, Kool & The Gang's *Jungle Boogie*, Average White Band's School Boy Crush, Silver Convention's *Fly Robin Fly* and Bob James' *Take Me To The Mardi Gras* .... Arista 115265

22/08/1992.....55......3....... BABY-BABY-BABY .... LaFace 74321111297

24/10/1992.....59......2....... WHAT ABOUT YOUR FRIENDS .... LaFace 74321118177

21/01/1995.....22......4....... CREEP ▲4 Contains a sample of Slick Rick's *Hey Young World*. 1995 Grammy Award for Best Rhythm & Blues Performance by a Group .... LaFace 74321254212

22/04/1995.....18......4....... RED LIGHT SPECIAL .... LaFace 74321273662

05/08/1995.....4......14....○ **WATERFALLS** ▲7 .... LaFace 74321298812

04/11/1995.....18......5....... DIGGIN' ON YOU .... LaFace 74321319252

13/01/1996.....6......7....... **CREEP** Re-issue of LaFace 74321254212 .... LaFace 74321340942

03/04/1999.....3......19....✪ **NO SCRUBS** ▲4 1999 Grammy Awards for Best Rhythm & Blues Group Performance and Best Rhythm & Blues Song for writers Kevin Briggs, Kandi Burruss and Tameka Cottle. The video won the 1999 MOBO Award for Best Video .... LaFace 74321660952

28/08/1999.....6......11....... **UNPRETTY** ▲3 Contains a sample of Dennis Edwards' *Don't Look Any Further* .... LaFace 74321695842

18/12/1999.....31......9....... DEAR LIE .... LaFace 74321724012

14/12/2002.....30......2....... GIRL TALK .... Arista 74321983502

T99 Belgian instrumental/production group formed by Patrick De Meyer and Oliver Abeloos, with Perla Den Boer (vocals).

11/05/1991.....14......6....... ANASTHASIA .... XL XLS 19

19/10/1991.....33......4....... NOCTURNE .... Emphasis 6574097

TOADS – see STAN FREBERG

ART AND DOTTY TODD US husband and wife vocal duo Art (born 11/3/1920, Elizabeth, NJ) and Dotty Todd (born 22/6/1923, Elizabeth, NJ) who married in 1941. Dotty died on 12/12/2000.

13/02/1953.....6......7....... **BROKEN WINGS** .... HMV B 10399

TOGETHER UK vocal/instrumental group formed by Jonathan Donaghy and Suddi Raval.

04/08/1990.....12......8....... HARDCORE UPROAR .... ffrr F 143

TOKENS US vocal group formed in Brooklyn, NY in 1955 by Hank Medress (born 19/11/1938, Brooklyn), Neil Sedaka (born 13/3/1939, Brooklyn), Eddie Rabkin and Cynthia Zolitin as the Linc-Tones. Rabkin left in 1956, replaced by Jay Siegel (born 20/10/1939, Brooklyn). Zolitin and Sedaka left in 1958 and the group became Daryl & the Oxfords, re-forming in 1958 as the Tokens with Medress, Siegel, Mitch Margo (born 25/5/1947, Brooklyn) and Phil Margo (born 1/4/1942, Brooklyn). They launched the BT Puppy (BT standing for Big Time) label in 1964 with The Happenings scoring hits.

21/12/1961.....11......12...... THE LION SLEEPS TONIGHT ▲3 Featured in the 1996 film *Private Parts* .... RCA 1263

TOKYO DRAGONS UK rock group formed in London by Steve Lomax (guitar/vocals), Mal Bruck (guitar/vocals), Ade Easily (bass) and Phil Martini (drums/vocals).

26/06/2004.....61......1....... TEENAGE SCREAMERS.. Island CID 864

23/10/2004.....75......1....... GET 'EM OFF.. Island CID 876

TOKYO GHETTO PUSSY German production duo Jam El Mar (born Rolf Ellmer) and DJ Mark Spoon (born Markus Loeffel). They also recorded as Jam & Spoon and Storm.

16/09/1995.....26......2....... EVERYBODY ON THE FLOOR (PUMP IT) .... Epic 6611132

16/03/1996.....55......2....... I KISS YOUR LIPS... Epic 6623212

TOL AND TOL Dutch vocal/instrumental duo formed by brothers Cees and Thomas Tol.

14/04/1990.....73......2....... ELENI .... Dover ROJ 5

TOM TOM CLUB US studio group assembled by Chris Frantz (born 8/5/1951, Fort Campbell, KY), his wife Tina Weymouth (born 22/11/1950, Coronado, CA), Stephen Stanley (keyboards) and Monty Brown (drums). Frantz and Weymouth were members of Talking Heads while Brown was with T-Connection.

20/06/1981.....7......9....... **WORDY RAPPINGHOOD** .... Island WIP 6694

❶9 Number of weeks single topped the UK chart   ↑ Entered the UK chart at #1   ▲9 Number of weeks single topped the US chart

815

	10/10/1981	65	2		GENIUS OF LOVER	Island WIP 6735
	07/08/1982	22	9		UNDER THE BOARDWALK	Island WIP 6762

TOMBA VIRA Dutch instrumental/production duo DJ Ziki (Rene Terhorst) and Dobre (Gaston Steenkist). They also recorded as Chocolate Puma, DJ Manta, Jark Prongo, Goodmen, Rhythmkillaz and Riva.

| 16/06/2001 | 51 | 1 | | THE SOUND OF OH YEAH Contains a sample of OMD's *Enola Gay* | VC Recordings VCRD 88 |

TOMCAT UK vocal/instrumental group formed in Liverpool and London.

| 14/10/2000 | 48 | 1 | | CRAZY | Virgin VSCSDT 1785 |

TOMCRAFT German DJ Thomas Bruckner (born in Munich).

| 10/05/2003 | ❶¹ | 13 | | LONELINESS ↑ Contains a sample of Andrea Martin's *Share The Love* | Data 52CDS |
| 25/10/2003 | 43 | 2 | | BRAINWASHED (CALL YOU) | Data 63CDS |

SATOSHI TOMIIE – see FRANKIE KNUCKLES

RICKY TOMLINSON UK singer (born Eric Tomlinson, 26/9/1939, Liverpool), best known as an actor, appearing as Bobby Grant in *Brookside*, Jim Royle in *The Royle Family* and as England manager Mike Bassett in the film of the same name.

| 10/11/2001 | 28 | 3 | | ARE YOU LOOKIN' AT ME Features the uncredited contribution of Noddy Holder (of Slade) on backing vocals | All Around The World CDRICKY 1 |

TOMMI UK group formed by Bambi, Lil Chill, Peekaboo, Mi$ Thang and Stylus.

| 05/07/2003 | 12 | 8 | | LIKE WHAT | Sony Music 6739095 |

TOMSKI UK producer Tom Jankiewicz.

| 18/04/1998 | 42 | 1 | | 14 HOURS TO SAVE THE EARTH Contains a sample from the 1980 film *Flash Gordon* | Xtravaganza 0091515 EXT |
| 12/02/2000 | 31 | 2 | | LOVE WILL COME TOMSKI FEATURING JAN JOHNSTON | Xtravaganza XTRAV 6CDS |

TONGUE 'N' CHEEK UK R&B group, discovered by Total Contrast, who wrote and produced their debut album in 1990.

27/02/1988	59	6		NOBODY (CAN LOVE ME) TONGUE IN CHEEK	Criminal BUS 6
25/11/1989	41	4		ENCORE	Syncopate SY 33
14/04/1990	20	7		TOMORROW	Syncopate SY 34
04/08/1990	37	5		NOBODY Re-recording	Syncopate SY 37
19/01/1991	26	6		FORGET ME NOTS	Syncopate SY 39

TONIGHT UK group formed by Chris Turner (vocals), Dave Cook (guitar), Phil Cambon (guitar), Russ Strothard (bass) and Gary Thompson (drums).

| 28/01/1978 | 14 | 8 | | DRUMMER MAN | Target TDS 1 |
| 20/05/1978 | 66 | 2 | | MONEY THAT'S YOUR PROBLEM | Target TDS 2 |

TONY! TONI! TONE! US R&B group from Oakland, CA formed by brothers Dwayne and Raphael Wiggins and cousin Timothy Christian. DJ Quik is a rapper from Compton, California (born David Blake, 18/1/1970). Wiggins also recorded as Raphael Saadiq and later joined Lucy Pearl with Dawn Robinson (of En Vogue) and Ali Shaheed Muhammad (of A Tribe Called Quest).

30/06/1990	50	5		OAKLAND STROKE	Wing 7
09/03/1991	69	2		IT NEVER RAINS (IN SOUTHERN CALIFORNIA)	Wing 10
04/09/1993	44	3		IF I HAD NO LOOT	Polydor PZCD 292
03/05/1997	33	2		LET'S GET DOWN TONY TONI TONE FEATURING DJ QUICK	Mercury MERCD 485

TOO TOUGH TEE – see DYNAMIX II FEATURING TOO TOUGH TEE

TOON TRAVELLERS – see MUNGO JERRY

TOP UK group formed in Liverpool by Paul Cavanagh (guitar/vocals), Joseph Fearon (bass) and Alan Wills (drums). Wills and Fearon were ex-members of Wild Swans.

| 20/07/1991 | 67 | 2 | | NUMBER ONE DOMINATOR | Island IS 496 |

TOPLOADER UK rock group formed in Eastbourne by Joseph Washbourn (born 24/12/1975, Sidcup, keyboards/vocals), Dan Hipgrave (born 5/8/1975, Brighton, guitar), Matt Knight (born 18/11/1972, Portsmouth, bass), Julian Deane (born 31/3/1971, Bristol, guitar) and Rob Green (born 24/10/1969, London, drums). Hipgrave is engaged to model and TV presenter Gail Porter.

22/05/1999	64	1		ACHILLES HEEL	Sony S2 6671612
07/08/1999	52	1		LET THE PEOPLE KNOW	Sony S2 6677132
04/03/2000	19	7		DANCING IN THE MOONLIGHT	Sony S2 6689412
13/05/2000	8	7		ACHILLES HEEL	Sony S2 6691872
02/09/2000	20	4		JUST HOLD ON	Sony S2 6696242
25/11/2000	7	25	○	DANCING IN THE MOONLIGHT Re-issue of Sony S2 6689412	Sony S2 6699852
21/04/2001	19	4		ONLY FOR A WHILE	Sony S2 6708612
17/08/2002	18	7		TIME OF MY LIFE	Sony S2 6728862

○ Silver disc ● Gold disc ✪ Platinum disc (additional platinum units are indicated by a figure following the symbol) ◉ Singles released prior to 1973 that are known to have sold over 1 million copies in the UK

TOPOL Israeli singer (born Chaim Topol, 9/9/1935, Tel Aviv) who came to prominence in the musical *Fiddler On The Roof*, later turned into a successful film. At the time of his birth Tel Aviv was part of Palestine.

20/04/1967	9	20		**IF I WERE A RICH MAN** From the musical *Fiddler on the Roof*	CBS 202651

MEL TORME US singer (born Melvin Howard, 13/9/1925, Chicago, IL) who made his name as a songwriter, singer and actor. Nicknamed The Velvet Fog (a moniker he was not happy with), The Kid With The Gauze In his Jaws and Mr Butterscotch, he made his film debut in 1944 in *Pardon My Rhythm* and hosted his own TV series in 1951. He won two Grammy Awards: Best Jazz Vocal Performance in 1982 with George Shearing for *An Evening With George Shearing And Mel Torme* and Best Jazz Vocal Performance in 1983 for *Top Drawer*. He died from a stroke on 15/6/1999. He has a star on the Hollywood Walk of Fame.

27/04/1956	4	24		**MOUNTAIN GREENERY**	Vogue Coral Q 72150
03/01/1963	13	8		COMING HOME BABY	London HLK 9643

TORNADOS UK surf group assembled by producer Joe Meek (born 5/4/1929, Newent), comprising Alan Caddy (born 2/2/1940, London, guitar), Georgy Bellamy (born 8/10/1941, Sunderland, guitar), Roger Lavern (born Roger Jackson, 11/11/1938, Kidderminster, keyboards), Heinz Burt (born 24/7/1942, Hargin, Germany, bass) and Clem Cattini (born 28/8/1939, London, drums). Their debut hit was also a #1 in the US, the first UK group to accomplish the feat. Burt went solo in 1963, replaced by Chas Hodges and then Tab Hunter. Meek committed suicide on 3/2/1967 after first shooting dead his landlady. Heinz died from motor neurone disease on 7/4/2000.

30/08/1962	❶⁵	25		**TELSTAR** ▲³ Featured in the film *Beloved Invaders*	Decca F 11494
10/01/1963	5	11		**GLOBETROTTER**	Decca F 11562
21/03/1963	17	12		ROBOT	Decca F 11606
06/06/1963	18	9		THE ICE CREAM MAN	Decca F 11662
10/06/1963	41	2		DRAGONFLY	Decca F 11745

MITCHELL TOROK US singer (born 28/10/1929, Houston, TX) who made his first recordings in 1948.

28/09/1956	6	18		**WHEN MEXICO GAVE UP THE RUMBA**	Brunswick 05586
11/01/1957	29	1		RED LIGHT GREEN LIGHT	Brunswick 05626

LIZ TORRES – see **DANNY TENAGLIA**

EMILIANA TORRINI Norwegian singer born to Italian and Icelandic parents; she later relocated to England and worked with Roland Orzabal of Tears For Fears on her debut album.

10/06/2000	63	1		EASY	One Little Indian 274 TP7CD
09/09/2000	63	1		UNEMPLOYED IN SUMMERTIME	One Little Indian 275 TP7CD
03/02/2001	44	1		TO BE FREE	One Little Indian 276TP 7CDL

PETE TOSH Jamaican singer (born Winston Hubert McIntosh, 19/10/1944, Westmoreland) who was a founder member of The Wailin' Wailers with Bob Marley, Bunny Livingston, Junior Braithwaite, Cherry Smith and Beverley Kelso in 1964, the group subsequently became The Wailers and backed Bob Marley on his hits. Tosh recorded solo throughout his time with Marley and later launched his own label, Intel Diplo HIM (short for Intelligent Diplomat for His Imperial Majesty). He won the 1987 Grammy Award for Best Reggae Recording for *No Nuclear War*, the first time reggae had been included as a separate category at the awards. On 11/9/1987 Tosh laughed as three men broke into his house, for which he was viciously beaten. When the intruders found insufficient valuables, they shot Tosh dead through the back of the head, and killed two others. It was later suggested the robbery was carried out to cover up a feud.

21/10/1978	43	7		(YOU GOTTA WALK) DON'T LOOK BACK	Rolling Stones 2859
02/04/1983	48	5		JOHNNY B GOODE	EMI RIC 115

TOTAL US vocal trio formed in New York City by JaKima Raynor, Keisha Spivey and Pam Long.

15/07/1995	43	2		CAN'T YOU SEE **TOTAL FEATURING THE NOTORIOUS B.I.G.** Featured in the 1995 film *New Jersey Drive*	Tommy Boy TBCD 700
14/09/1996	29	2		KISSIN' YOU	Arista 74321404172
15/02/1997	49	1		DO YOU THINK ABOUT US	Puff Daddy 74321458492
18/04/1998	15	5		WHAT YOU WANT **MASE FEATURING TOTAL** Contains a sample of Curtis Mayfield's *Right On For The Darkness* .... Puff Daddy 74321578772	
30/09/2000	68	1		I WONDER WHY HE'S THE GREATEST DJ **TONY TOUCH FEATURING TOTAL** Contains a sample of Sister Sledge's *He's The Greatest Dancer*	Tommy Boy TBCD 2100

TOTAL CONTRAST UK R&B group formed in 1983 by Robin Achampong (bass/vocals) and Delroy Murray (keyboards/vocals). They later concentrated on production and songwriting.

03/08/1985	17	10		TAKES A LITTLE TIME	London LON 71
19/10/1985	41	5		HIT AND RUN	London LON 76
01/03/1986	44	3		THE RIVER	London LON 83
10/05/1986	63	4		WHAT YOU GONNA DO ABOUT IT	London LON 95

TOTO US rock group formed in Los Angeles, CA in 1978 by Bobby Kimball (born Robert Toteaux, 29/3/1947, Vinton, LA, vocals), Jeff Pocaro (born 1/4/1954, Hartford, CT, drums), his brother Steve (born 2/9/1957, Hartford, keyboards/vocals), David Hungate (bass), Steve Lukather (born 21/10/1957, Los Angeles, guitar) and David Paich (born 25/6/1954, Los Angeles, keyboards/vocals), all of whom were noted session musicians. They were named after Dorothy's dog in the film *The Wizard Of Oz*. Hungate left in 1983, replaced by Mike Pocaro (born 29/5/1955, Hartford). Kimball left in 1984, was initially replaced by Dennis 'Fergie' Frederiksen (born 15/5/1951) and then by Joseph Williams. Steve Pocaro left in 1988. Jeff Pocaro died on 5/8/1992 from heart failure brought about by drugs, although it was claimed he suffered an allergic reaction to garden pesticides (an autopsy found no traces of pesticide in his body). David Paich has won four Grammy Awards including Best Rhythm & Blues Song in 1976 with Boz Scaggs for *Lowdown* and Best Engineered

❶⁹ Number of weeks single topped the UK chart ↑ Entered the UK chart at #1 ▲⁹ Number of weeks single topped the US chart

Recording in 1982 with Steve Pocaro and others for *Toto IV*. Steve Lukather won the 1982 Grammy Award for Best Rhythm & Blues Song with Jay Graydon and Bill Champlin for *Turn Your Love Around* and the 2001 Grammy Award for Best Pop Instrumental Album with Larry Carlton for *No Substitutions – Live In Osaka*. The group won three Grammy Awards including Album of the Year in 1982 for *Toto IV* and Producer of the Year in 1982.

DATE	POS	WKS	BPI	SINGLE TITLE	LABEL & NUMBER
10/02/1979	14	11		HOLD THE LINE	CBS 6784
05/02/1983	3	10	O	**AFRICA** ▲[1]	CBS A 2510
09/04/1983	12	8		ROSANNA Inspired by the actress Rosanna Arquette, then Steve Pocaro's girlfriend. 1982 Grammy Awards for Record of the Year, Best Arrangement for Voices and Best Instrumental Arrangement Accompanying Vocals with Jerry Hey	CBS A 2079
18/06/1983	37	5		I WON'T HOLD YOU BACK	CBS A 3392
18/11/1995	64	1		I WILL REMEMBER	Columbia 6626552

TOTO COELO UK group formed by Roz Holness, Anita Mahadervan, Lindsey Danvers, Lacey Bond and Sheen Doran.

DATE	POS	WKS	BPI	SINGLE TITLE	LABEL & NUMBER
07/08/1982	8	10		**I EAT CANNIBALS PART 1**	Radialchoice TIC 10
13/11/1982	54	4		DRACULA'S TANGO/MUCHO MACHO	Radialchoice TIC 11

TOTTENHAM HOTSPUR F.A. CUP FINAL SQUAD UK professional football club formed in London in 1882 as Hotspur FC, name-changed in 1885 to Tottenham Hotspur. They have won the League title twice (1951 and 1961), the FA Cup eight times (1901, 1921, 1961, 1962, 1967, 1981, 1982 and 1991), the League Cup three times (1971, 1973 and 1999), the European Cup Winners Cup once (1963) and the UEFA Cup twice (1972 and 1984). All their hits feature Cockney duo Chas and Dave.

DATE	POS	WKS	BPI	SINGLE TITLE	LABEL & NUMBER
09/05/1981	5	8		**OSSIE'S DREAM (SPURS ARE ON THEIR WAY TO WEMBLEY)**	Rockney SHELF 1
01/05/1982	19	7		TOTTENHAM TOTTENHAM	Rockney SHELF 2
09/05/1987	18	5		HOT SHOT TOTTENHAM	Rainbow RBR 16
11/05/1991	44	3		WHEN THE YEAR ENDS IN 1	A1 A 1324

TONY TOUCH FEATURING TOTAL US producer Joseph Anthony Hernandez (born 1970, Brooklyn, NYC) with US female trio Total.

DATE	POS	WKS	BPI	SINGLE TITLE	LABEL & NUMBER
30/09/2000	68	1		I WONDER WHY HE'S THE GREATEST DJ Contains a sample of Sister Sledge's *He's The Greatest Dancer*	Tommy Boy TBCD 2100

TOUCH & GO UK vocal/production group formed by David Lowe (keyboards/bass/drums/vocals) with various session musicians.

DATE	POS	WKS	BPI	SINGLE TITLE	LABEL & NUMBER
07/11/1998	3	12	O	**WOULD YOU...?**	V2 VVR 5003083

TOUCH OF SOUL UK vocal/instrumental group.

DATE	POS	WKS	BPI	SINGLE TITLE	LABEL & NUMBER
19/05/1990	46	3		WE GOT THE LOVE	Cooltempo COOL 204

TOUR DE FORCE UK production group formed by John Dennis, Adrian Clarida, Jamie Henry and Mark Ryder.

DATE	POS	WKS	BPI	SINGLE TITLE	LABEL & NUMBER
16/05/1998	71	1		CATALAN	East West EW 161CD

TOURISTS UK rock group formed in 1977 by Dave Stewart (born 9/9/1952, Sunderland), Annie Lennox (born 25/12/1954, Aberdeen) and Peet Coombes as Catch. They changed their name in 1979 to Tourists with the addition of Jim Toomey (drums) and Eddie Chin (bass) but disbanded in 1980 with Lennox and Stewart forming the Eurythmics.

DATE	POS	WKS	BPI	SINGLE TITLE	LABEL & NUMBER
09/06/1979	52	5		BLIND AMONG THE FLOWERS	Logo GO 350
08/09/1979	32	7		THE LONELIEST MAN IN THE WORLD	Logo GO 360
10/11/1979	4	14	●	**I ONLY WANT TO BE WITH YOU**	Logo GO 370
09/02/1980	8	9		**SO GOOD TO BE BACK HOME AGAIN**	Logo TOUR 1
18/10/1980	40	5		DON'T SAY I TOLD YOU SO	RCA TOUR 2

TOUTES LES FILLES UK female vocal trio.

DATE	POS	WKS	BPI	SINGLE TITLE	LABEL & NUMBER
04/09/1999	44	1		THAT'S WHAT LOVE CAN DO	London LONCD 434

CAROL LYNN TOWNES US singer based in New York who was lead singer with Fifth Avenue before going solo.

DATE	POS	WKS	BPI	SINGLE TITLE	LABEL & NUMBER
04/08/1984	47	4		991/2 Featured in the 1984 film *Breakin'*	Polydor POSP 693
19/01/1985	56	3		BELIEVE IN THE BEAT Featured in the 1985 film *Breakin' 2*	Polydor POSP 720

FUZZ TOWNSHEND UK male producer with a backing group that includes James Atkin (bass) and two rappers.

DATE	POS	WKS	BPI	SINGLE TITLE	LABEL & NUMBER
06/09/1997	51	1		HELLO DARLIN'	Echo ECSCD 46

PETE TOWNSHEND UK singer (born 19/5/1945, London) and a founder member of The Who. He recorded his first solo album in 1972. Awarded a Lifetime Achievement Award at the 1983 BRIT Awards. He also won the 1993 Grammy Award for Best Music Show Album for *The Who's Tommy – Original Cast Recording*.

DATE	POS	WKS	BPI	SINGLE TITLE	LABEL & NUMBER
05/04/1980	39	6		ROUGH BOYS	Atco K 11460
21/06/1980	46	6		LET MY LOVE OPEN YOUR DOOR	Atco k 11486
21/08/1982	48	5		UNIFORMS (CORPS D'ESPRIT)	Atco K 11751

TOXIC TWO US instrumental/production duo Ray Love and Damon Wild.

DATE	POS	WKS	BPI	SINGLE TITLE	LABEL & NUMBER
07/03/1992	13	6		RAVE GENERATOR	PWL International PWL 223

TOY-BOX Danish vocal duo Anila and Ami. They made their debut album in 1999.

DATE	POS	WKS	BPI	SINGLE TITLE	LABEL & NUMBER
18/09/1999	41	2		BEST FRIENDS	Edel 0058245 ERE

TOY DOLLS UK trio formed in Sunderland in 1980 by Olga, Flip and Happy Bob. Their one hit was the perennial kids' favourite. They later composed the theme to *Razzmatazz*.

01/12/1984 . . . . . 4 . . . . . 12 . . . . . . **NELLIE THE ELEPHANT** . . . . Volume VOL 11

TOYAH UK singer (born Toyah Ann Wilcox, 18/5/1958, Birmingham) who was one of the most successful new-wave female singers and later appeared in the films *Jubilee* and *Quadrophenia*. Married to Robert Fripp, she became a successful TV presenter.

14/02/1981 . . . . . 4 . . . . . 14 . . . . . ○	**FOUR FROM TOYAH EP** Tracks on EP: *It's A Mystery, Revelations, War Boys* and *Angels And Demons* . . . . Safari TOY 1			
16/05/1981 . . . . . 8 . . . . . 11 . . . . . ○	**I WANT TO BE FREE** . . . . Safari SAFE 34			

16/05/1981 . . . . . 8 . . . . . 11 . . . . . ○ **I WANT TO BE FREE** . . . . Safari SAFE 34
03/10/1981 . . . . . 4 . . . . . 9 . . . . . ○ **THUNDER IN THE MOUNTAINS** . . . . Safari SAFE 38
28/11/1981 . . . . 14 . . . . . 9 . . . . . . FOUR MORE FROM TOYAH EP Tracks on EP: *Good Morning Universe, Urban Tribesman, In The Fairground* and *The Furious Futures*. . . . . Safari TOY 2
22/05/1982 . . . . 21 . . . . . 8 . . . . . . BRAVE NEW WORLD . . . . Safari SAFE 45
17/07/1982 . . . . 48 . . . . . 5 . . . . . . IEYA . . . . Safari SAFE 28
09/10/1982 . . . . 30 . . . . . 7 . . . . . . BE LOUD BE PROUD (BE HEARD). . . . . Safari SAFE 52
24/09/1983 . . . . 24 . . . . . 5 . . . . . . REBEL RUN . . . . Safari SAFE 56
19/11/1983 . . . . 50 . . . . . 5 . . . . . . THE VOW . . . . Safari SAFE 58
27/04/1985 . . . . 22 . . . . . 6 . . . . . . DON'T FALL IN LOVE (I SAID) . . . . Portrait A 6160
29/06/1985 . . . . 57 . . . . . 3 . . . . . . SOUL PASSING THROUGH SOUL. . . . . Portrait A 6359
25/04/1987 . . . . 54 . . . . . 5 . . . . . . ECHO BEACH . . . . EG EGO 31

TOYS US soul group formed in Jamaica, NY by Barbara Harris, June Moniero and Barbara Parritt. They appeared in the film *The Girl In Daddy's Bikini* and disbanded in 1968.

04/11/1965 . . . . . 5 . . . . . 13 . . . . . **A LOVER'S CONCERTO** Based on Bach's *Minuet In G*. Featured in the films *Andre* (1995) and *Mr Holland's Opus* (1997). . . . . Stateside SS 460
27/01/1966 . . . . 36 . . . . . 4 . . . . . ATTACK . . . . Stateside SS 483

FAYE TOZER UK singer (born 14/11/1975) who was a member of Steps before going solo.

18/05/2002 . . . . 10 . . . . . 4 . . . . . . **SOMEONE LIKE YOU** RUSSELL WATSON AND FAYE TOZER. . . . . Decca 4730002

T'PAU UK rock group formed in Shrewsbury in 1986 by Carol Decker (born 10/9/1957, London, vocals), Ronnie Rogers (born 13/3/1959, Shrewsbury, guitar), Paul Jackson (born 8/8/1961, Shrewsbury, bass), Tim Burgess (born 6/10/1961, Shrewsbury, drums), Michael Chetwood (born 26/8/1954, Shrewsbury, keyboards) and Taj Wyzgowski (guitar). The group was named after a *Star Trek* character. Wyzgowski left in 1988, replaced by Dean Howard. They disbanded in 1994 with Decker going solo.

08/08/1987 . . . . . 4 . . . . . 13 . . . . . **HEART AND SOUL** . . . . Siren SRN 41
24/10/1987 . . . ❶[5] . . . 15 . . . . . ● **CHINA IN YOUR HAND** . . . . Siren SRN 64
30/01/1988 . . . . . 9 . . . . . 8 . . . . . . **VALENTINE** . . . . Siren SRN 69
02/04/1988 . . . . 23 . . . . . 7 . . . . . . SEX TALK (LIVE) . . . . Siren SRN 80
25/06/1988 . . . . 14 . . . . . 6 . . . . . . I WILL BE WITH YOU . . . . Siren SRN 87
01/10/1988 . . . . 18 . . . . . 7 . . . . . . SECRET GARDEN. . . . . Siren SRN 93
03/12/1988 . . . . 42 . . . . . 5 . . . . . . ROAD TO OUR DREAM . . . . Siren SRN 100
25/03/1989 . . . . 28 . . . . . 6 . . . . . . ONLY THE LONELY . . . . Siren SRN 107
18/05/1991 . . . . 16 . . . . . 6 . . . . . . WHENEVER YOU NEED ME. . . . . Siren SRN 140
27/07/1991 . . . . 62 . . . . . 2 . . . . . . WALK ON AIR . . . . Siren SRN 142
20/02/1993 . . . . 53 . . . . . 1 . . . . . . VALENTINE Re-issue of Siren SRN 69 . . . . Virgin VALEG 1

TQ US rapper (born Terrance Quaites, Mobile, AL) who moved with his family to Compton in California and was subsequently influenced by NWA, among other rap acts. He was briefly lead singer with Coming Of Age before going solo.

30/01/1999 . . . . . 4 . . . . . 9 . . . . . . **WESTSIDE** Contains samples of Kurtis Blow's *The Breaks* and Joe Sample's *In All My Wildest Dreams* . . . . Epic 6668105
01/05/1999 . . . . . 7 . . . . . 7 . . . . . . **BYE BYE BABY** . . . . Epic 6672372
21/08/1999 . . . . 32 . . . . . 2 . . . . . . BETTER DAYS . . . . Epic 6677535
04/09/1999 . . . . . 7 . . . . . 7 . . . . . . **SUMMERTIME** ANOTHER LEVEL FEATURING TQ. . . . . Northwestside 74321694672
29/04/2000 . . . . 14 . . . . . 5 . . . . . . DAILY Contains an interpolation of *Just A Friend* . . . . Epic 6692752
13/10/2001 . . . . 16 . . . . . 5 . . . . . . LET'S GET BACK TO BED…BOY SARAH CONNOR FEATURING TQ. . . . . Epic 6718662

TRA-KNOX – see WILL SMITH

TRACIE UK singer (full name Tracie Young) discovered by Paul Weller and signed with his Respond label in 1983.

26/03/1983 . . . . . 9 . . . . . 8 . . . . . . **THE HOUSE THAT JACK BUILT** . . . . Respond KOB 701
16/07/1983 . . . . 24 . . . . . 9 . . . . . . GIVE IT SOME EMOTION . . . . Respond KOB 704
14/04/1984 . . . . 73 . . . . . 2 . . . . . . SOUL'S ON FIRE. . . . . Respond KOB 708
09/06/1984 . . . . 59 . . . . . 3 . . . . . . (I LOVE YOU) WHEN YOU SLEEP. . . . . Respond KOB 710
17/08/1985 . . . . 60 . . . . . 2 . . . . . . I CAN'T LEAVE YOU ALONE TRACIE YOUNG . . . . Respond SBS 1

TRACY – see MASSIVO FEATURING TRACY

JEANIE TRACY US singer (born Houston, TX) who began her career as a backing singer for the likes of Aretha Franklin, Diana Ross, Michael Bolton, Tevin Campbell and Sylvester before going solo.

11/06/1994 . . . . 73 . . . . . 1 . . . . . . IF THIS IS LOVE . . . . Pulse 8 CDLOSE 63
05/11/1994 . . . . 57 . . . . . 1 . . . . . . DO YOU BELIEVE IN THE WONDER . . . . Pulse 8 CDLOSE 74

❶[9] Number of weeks single topped the UK chart ↑ Entered the UK chart at #1 ▲[9] Number of weeks single topped the US chart

819

13/05/1995.....73......1.......	IT'S A MAN'S MAN'S MAN'S WORLD **JEANIE TRACY AND BOBBY WOMACK**..............................	Pulse 8 CDLOSE 89

TRAFFIC UK rock group formed in 1967 by Steve Winwood (born 12/5/1948, Birmingham, vocals/keyboards/guitar), Dave Mason (born 10/5/1947, Worcester, guitar/vocals), Chris Wood (born 24/6/1944, Birmingham, flute/saxophone) and Jim Capaldi (born 24/8/1944, Evesham, drums/vocals) following Winwood's departure from the Spencer Davis Group. The group disbanded in 1974 with Winwood and Capaldi subsequently recording solo. Wood died from liver failure on 12/7/1983. They were inducted into the Rock & Roll Hall of Fame in 2004.

01/06/1967 .....5......10	**PAPER SUN** .... Island WIP 6002
06/09/1967 .....2......14	**HOLE IN MY SHOE**... Island WIP 6017
29/11/1967.....8......12	**HERE WE GO ROUND THE MULBERRY BUSH** .... Island WIP 6025
06/03/1968.....40......4.......	NO FACE, NO NAME, NO NUMBER .... Island WIP 6030

TRAIN US rock group formed in San Francisco, CA in 1994 by Patrick Monahan (vocals), Ron Hotchkiss (guitar/vocals), Jim Stafford (guitar), Charlie Colin (bass) and Scott Underwood (drums). Although initially signed by Columbia Records, they were effectively farmed out to Aware Records before recording their debut album in 1998.

11/08/2001.....10......8	**DROPS OF JUPITER (TELL ME)** 2001 Grammy Awards for Best Rock Song for writers Charlie Colin, Rob Hotchkiss, Pat Monahan, Jimmy Stafford and Scott Underwood; and Best Instrumental Arrangement Accompanying Singers for arranger Paul Buckmaster .... Columbia 6714472
02/03/2002.....49......2.......	SHE'S ON FIRE.. Columbia 6722812

TRAMAINE US gospel singer (born Tramaine Hawkins, 11/10/1957, Los Angeles, CA) who began her career singing in the Edwin Hawkins Singers (where she met and married Edwin's younger brother Walter) and later went solo.

05/10/1985.....60......2.......	FALL DOWN (SPIRIT OF LOVE).. A&M AM 281

TRAMMPS US soul group formed in Philadelphia, PA in 1971 by Earl Young (drums), Jimmy Ellis (vocals), Dennis Harris (guitar), Ron 'Have Mercy' Kersey (keyboards), John Hart (organ), Stanley Wade (bass) and Michael Thompson (drums). They formed the Golden Fleece label in 1973 and the bulk of the group were also members of MFSB, the house band for Philadelphia International.

23/11/1974.....29 .....10	ZING WENT THE STRINGS OF MY HEART Revival of Judy Garland's 1943 US pop hit .... Buddah BDS 405
01/02/1975.....40 .....4	SIXTY MINUTE MAN... Buddah BDS 415
11/10/1975.....5......8......	**HOLD BACK THE NIGHT** .... Buddah BDS 437
13/03/1976.....35......8......	THAT'S WHERE THE HAPPY PEOPLE GO .... Atlantic K 10703
24/07/1976.....42......3......	SOUL SEARCHIN' TIME .... Atlantic K 10797
14/05/1977.....16......7.......	DISCO INFERNO Featured in the films *Saturday Night Fever* (1978), *Backfire* (1995), *Kingpin* (1996) and *Donnie Brasco* (1997) ... . Atlantic K 10914
24/06/1978.....47 .....10	DISCO INFERNO Re-issue of Atlantic K 10914 .... Atlantic K 11135
12/12/1992.....30......5......	HOLD BACK THE NIGHT **KWS FEATURING GUEST VOCALS FROM THE TRAMMPS** .... Network NWK 65

TRANCESETTERS Dutch production duo Jamez and Dobre (Gaston Steenkist). They also record as Tata Box Inhibitors. Steenkist is also a member of Goodmen, DJ Manta, Chocolate Puma, Tomba Vira, Jark Prongo, Rhythmkillaz and Riva.

04/03/2000.....55......1......	ROACHES .... Hooj Choons HOOJ 89CD
09/06/2001.....72......1......	SYNERGY .... Hooj Choons HOOJ 107CD

TRANS-X Canadian trio fronted by Pascal Languirand and featuring the vocals of Laurie Gill.

13/07/1985 .....9 .....9.......	**LIVING ON VIDEO** .... Boiling Point POSP 650

TRANSA UK DJ/production duo Dave Webster and Brendan Webster.

30/08/1997.....65......1......	PROPHASE .... Perfecto PERF 147CD
21/02/1998.....42......1......	ENERVATE .... Perfecto PERF 155CD

TRANSATLANTIC SOUL US producer and remixer (born Roger Sanchez, 1/6/1967, New York City) who previously recorded as El Mariachi, Funk Junkeez and under his own name. He records as Roger S or the S Man in the US and runs the R-Senal record label.

22/03/1997.....43......1......	RELEASE YO SELF .... Deconstruction 74321459102

TRANSFER UK production duo Mark Jolley and Andy Wright, with female singer Karine.

03/11/2001.....54......1......	POSSESSION .... Multiply CDMULTY 76

TRANSFORMER 2 Belgian instrumental/production duo Peter Ramson and Danny Van Wauwe. They also record as Convert.

24/02/1996.....45......1......	JUST CAN'T GET ENOUGH .... Positiva CDTIV 49

TRANSISTER UK/US vocal/instrumental group formed by Gary Clark (formerly of Danny Wilson) and Eric Pressley, with female singer Keeley Hawkes.

28/03/1998.....56......1......	LOOK WHO'S PERFECT NOW .... Virgin VSCDT 1678

TRANSPLANTS US rock group formed in 1999 by Tim 'Lint' Armstrong (guitar/vocals), Travis Barker (drums) and Rob 'SR' Ashton (raps). Armstrong was an ex-member of Rancid while Barker was with Blink 182.

19/04/2003.....27......2.......	DIAMONDS AND GUNS .... Hellcat 11082
19/07/2003.....49......1.......	DJ DJ .... Hellcat 11122

TRANSVISION VAMP UK rock group formed by singer Wendy James (born 21/1/1966, London, vocals), Nick Christian

○ Silver disc ● Gold disc ✪ Platinum disc (additional platinum units are indicated by a figure following the symbol) ◉ Singles released prior to 1973 that are known to have sold over 1 million copies in the UK

Sayer (born 1/8/1964, guitar), Tex Axile (born 30/7/1963, keyboards), Dave Parsons (born 2/7/1962, bass) and Pol Burton (born 1/7/1964, drums). James later went solo while Parsons became a member of Bush.

DATE	POS	WKS	SINGLE TITLE	LABEL & NUMBER
16/04/1988	45	3	TELL THAT GIRL TO SHUT UP	MCA TVV 2
25/06/1988	5	13	**I WANT YOUR LOVE**	MCA TVV 3
17/09/1988	30	5	REVOLUTION BABY	MCA TVV 4
19/11/1988	41	5	SISTER MOON	MCA TVV 5
01/04/1989	3	11	**BABY I DON'T CARE**	MCA TVV 6
10/06/1989	15	6	THE ONLY ONE	MCA TVV 7
05/08/1989	14	5	LANDSLIDE OF LOVE	MCA TVV 8
04/11/1989	22	4	BORN TO BE SOLD	MCA TVV 9
13/04/1991	30	4	(I JUST WANNA) B WITH U	MCA TVV 10
22/06/1991	41	3	IF LOOKS COULD KILL	MCA TVV 11

TRASH UK group formed by Ian Crawford Clews (vocals), Neil McCormick (guitar), Colin Hunter Morrison (guitar), Ronnie Leahy (keyboards) and Timi Donald (drums) as The Pathfinders. McCormick left in 1967, replaced by Fraser Watson. Signed to the Beatles' Apple label, they were originally dubbed White Trash but dropped the 'White' moniker after complaints from the BBC! The group disbanded in 1970 with Donald going on to become a successful studio musician.

25/10/1969	35	3	GOLDEN SLUMBERS/CARRY THAT WEIGHT	Apple 17

TRASH CAN SINATRAS UK group formed in Glasgow in 1987 by Frank Reader (guitar/vocals), John Douglas (guitar), Paul Livingston (guitar), George McDaid (bass) and Stephen Douglas (drums). McDaid left in 1992, replaced by David Hughes. Reader is the brother of Fairground Attraction's Eddi Reader.

24/04/1993	61	1	HAYFEVER	Go Discs GODCD 98

TRAVEL French producer Laurent Gutbier.

24/04/1999	67	2	BULGARIAN	Tidy Trax TIDY 121CD

TRAVELING WILBURYS UK/US group formed in 1988 by George Harrison (born 24/2/1943, Liverpool, who assumed the names Nelson and Spike for the Wilburys), Roy Orbison (born 23/4/1936, Vernon, TX, Lefty), Tom Petty (born 20/10/1953, Gainesville, FL, Charlie T Junior or Muddy), Bob Dylan (born 24/5/1941, Duluth, MN, Lucky or Boo) and Jeff Lynne (born 30/12/1947, Birmingham, Otis or Clayton). The group won the 1989 Grammy Award for Best Rock Performance by a Group with Vocals for *Traveling Wilburys Volume One* (the album was originally known as *Handle With Care* in the UK). Orbison died from a heart attack on 6/12/1988, Harrison from cancer on 29/11/2001.

29/10/1988	21	13	HANDLE WITH CARE	Wilbury W 7732
11/03/1989	52	4	END OF THE LINE	Wilbury W 7637
30/06/1990	44	2	NOBODY'S CHILD	Wilbury W 9773

TRAVIS UK rock quartet formed in Glasgow in 1990 by Francis Healy (born 23/7/1973, Stafford, guitar/vocals), Douglas Payne (born 14/11/1972, Glasgow, guitar), Andrew Dunlop (born 1/3/1972, Glasgow, bass) and Neil Primrose (born 20/2/1972, Glasgow, drums). They were named Best British Group at the 2000 and 2002 BRIT Awards, and their album *The Man Who* Best British Album at the 2000 BRIT Awards.

12/04/1997	40	2	U16 GIRLS	Independiente ISOM 1MS
28/06/1997	39	2	ALL I WANT TO DO IS ROCK Originally released in 1996 on the Red Telephone Box label and failed to chart because the pressing was limited to 500 copies	Independiente ISOM 3MS
23/08/1997	30	2	TIED TO THE 90'S	Independiente ISOM 5MS
25/10/1997	38	2	HAPPY	Independiente ISOM 6SMS
11/04/1998	16	3	MORE THAN US EP Tracks on EP: *More Than Us, Give Me Some Truth, All I Want To Do Is Rock* and *Funny Thing*	Independiente ISOM 11MS
20/03/1999	14	5	WRITING TO REACH YOU	Independiente ISOM 22MS
29/05/1999	13	5	DRIFTWOOD	Independiente ISOM 27SMS
14/08/1999	10	8	**WHY DOES IT ALWAYS RAIN ON ME**	Independiente ISOM 33MS
20/11/1999	8	11	**TURN**	Independiente ISOM 39SMS
17/06/2000	5	10	**COMING AROUND**	Independiente ISOM 45SMS
09/06/2001	3	14	**SING**	Independiente ISOM 49SMS
29/05/2001	14	8	SIDE	Independiente ISOM 54SMS
06/04/2002	18	7	FLOWERS IN THE WINDOW	Independiente ISOM 56SMS
11/10/2003	7	4	**RE-OFFENDER**	Independiente ISOM 78SMS
27/12/2003	48	3	THE BEAUTIFUL OCCUPATION	Independiente ISOM 81SMS
03/04/2004	28	3	LOVE WILL COME THROUGH	Independiente ISOM 84MS
30/10/2004	20	3	WALKING IN THE SUN	Independiente ISOM 88SMS

RANDY TRAVIS US singer (born Randy Bruce Traywick, 4/5/1959, Marshville, NC) who was frequently in trouble with the law as a teenager, including drunkenness, theft, drugs and motoring offences (one for speeding at 135 miles per hour). He was on probation in 1977 when he got a break at the Country City club in Charlotte and was subsequently signed by Warner Brothers in 1984. He has won four Grammy Awards: Best Country Vocal Performance, Male in 1987 for *Always And Forever,* Best Country Vocal Performance, Male in 1988 for *Old 8 x 10,* Best Country Vocal collaboration in 1998 with Clint Black, Joe Diffie, Merle Haggard, Emmylou Harris, Alison Krauss, Patty Loveless, Earl Scruggs, Ricky Skaggs, Marty Stuart, Pam Tillis, Travis Tritt and Dwight Yoakam for *Same Old Train* and Best Southern, Country or Bluegrass Gospel Album in 2003 for *Rise And Shine.* He has a star on the Hollywood Walk of Fame.

21/05/1988	55	6	FOREVER AND EVER, AMEN	Warner Brothers W 8384

❶⁹ Number of weeks single topped the UK chart   ↑ Entered the UK chart at #1   ▲⁹ Number of weeks single topped the US chart

821

JOHN TRAVOLTA
US singer/actor (born 18/2/1954, Englewood, NJ), first became known in the film *Saturday Night Fever* and subsequently appeared in *Grease, Look Who's Talking, Face/Off* and many others. He has a star on the Hollywood Walk of Fame.

DATE	POS	WKS	BPI	SINGLE TITLE	LABEL & NUMBER
20/05/1978	❶[9]	26	✪	**YOU'RE THE ONE THAT I WANT** ▲[1]	RSO 006
16/09/1978	❶[7]	19	✪	**SUMMER NIGHTS** This and above single credited to JOHN TRAVOLTA AND OLIVIA NEWTON-JOHN	RSO 18
07/10/1978	2	15	●	**SANDY**	Polydor POSP 6
02/12/1978	11	9	○	GREASED LIGHTNIN' This and above three singles featured in the 1978 film *Grease*	Polydor POSP 14
22/12/1990	3	10		**GREASE MEGAMIX** JOHN TRAVOLTA AND OLIVIA NEWTON-JOHN	Polydor PO 114
23/03/1991	47	2		GREASE – THE DREAM MIX FRANKIE VALLI, JOHN TRAVOLTA AND OLIVIA NEWTON-JOHN	PWL/Polydor PO 136
25/07/1998	4	9		**YOU'RE THE ONE THAT I WANT** JOHN TRAVOLTA AND OLIVIA NEWTON-JOHN Re-issue of RSO 008	Polydor 0441332

TREMELOES
UK group formed in 1959 by Brian Poole (born 2/11/1941, Barking, guitar/vocals), Alan Blakley (born 1/4/1942, Bromley, drums), Alan Howard (born 17/10/1941, Dagenham, saxophone) and Brian Scott (lead guitar), later adding Dave Munden (born 12/12/1943, Dagenham) on drums and switching Blakley to rhythm guitar, Howard to bass and allowing Poole to sing. They added Rick West (born Richard Westwood, 7/5/1943, Dagenham, lead guitar) in 1961 and signed with Decca in 1962. They split with Poole in 1966, by which time they comprised Blakely, Munden, West and Len 'Chips' Hawkes (born 11/11/1946, London). The group disbanded in 1974, by which time Blakley and Howard had established themselves as successful songwriters, but re-formed in the 1980s for numerous concerts. Blakley died from cancer on 10/6/1996.

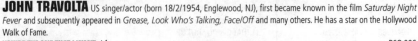

me and my life

DATE	POS	WKS	BPI	SINGLE TITLE	LABEL & NUMBER
04/07/1963	4	14		**TWIST AND SHOUT**	Decca F 11694
12/09/1963	❶[3]	14		**DO YOU LOVE ME**	Decca F 11739
28/11/1963	31	8		I CAN DANCE	Decca F 11771
30/01/1964	6	13		**CANDY MAN**	Decca F 11823
07/05/1964	2	17		**SOMEONE SOMEONE**	Decca F 11893
20/08/1964	32	7		TWELVE STEPS TO LOVE	Decca F 11951
07/01/1965	17	10		THREE BELLS	Decca F 12037
22/07/1965	25	8		I WANT CANDY This and above seven singles credited to BRIAN POOLE AND THE TREMELOES	Decca F 12197
02/02/1967	4	11		**HERE COMES MY BABY**	CBS 202519
27/04/1967	❶[3]	15		**SILENCE IS GOLDEN**	CBS 2723
02/08/1967	4	13		**EVEN THE BAD TIMES ARE GOOD**	CBS 2930
08/11/1967	39	2		BE MINE	CBS 3043
17/01/1968	6	11		**SUDDENLY YOU LOVE ME**	CBS 3234
08/05/1968	14	9		HELULE HELULE	CBS 2889
18/09/1968	6	12		**MY LITTLE LADY**	CBS 3680
11/12/1968	29	5		I SHALL BE RELEASED	CBS 3873
19/03/1969	14	8		HELLO WORLD	CBS 4065
01/11/1969	2	14		**(CALL ME) NUMBER ONE**	CBS 4582
21/03/1970	35	6		BY THE WAY	CBS 4815
12/09/1970	4	18		**ME AND MY LIFE**	CBS 5139
10/07/1971	32	7		HELLO BUDDY	CBS 7294

JACKIE TRENT
UK singer (born Yvonne Burgess, 6/9/1940, Staffordshire) who achieved more success as a songwriter, usually in conjunction with her husband, Tony Hatch.

DATE	POS	WKS	BPI	SINGLE TITLE	LABEL & NUMBER
22/04/1965	❶[1]	11		**WHERE ARE YOU NOW (MY LOVE)**	Pye 7N 15776
01/07/1965	39	2		WHEN THE SUMMERTIME IS OVER	Pye 7N 15865
02/04/1969	38	4		I'LL BE THERE	Pye 7N 17693

RALPH TRESVANT
US singer (born 16/5/1968, Boston, MA) and a founder member of New Edition in 1981. He went solo when the group disbanded in 1989.

DATE	POS	WKS	BPI	SINGLE TITLE	LABEL & NUMBER
12/01/1991	18	8		SENSITIVITY	MCA MCS 1462
15/08/1992	2	13	○	**THE BEST THINGS IN LIFE ARE FREE** LUTHER VANDROSS AND JANET JACKSON WITH SPECIAL GUESTS BBD AND RALPH TRESVANT Featured in the 1992 film *Mo' Money*	Perspective PERSS 7400
16/12/1995	7	7		**THE BEST THINGS IN LIFE ARE FREE (REMIX)** LUTHER VANDROSS AND JANET JACKSON WITH SPECIAL GUESTS BBD AND RALPH TRESVANT	A&M 5813092

DICK TREVOR
– see DANNY HOWELLS AND DICK TREVOR

TREVOR AND SIMON
UK production duo Trevor Reilly and Simon Foy.

DATE	POS	WKS	BPI	SINGLE TITLE	LABEL & NUMBER
10/06/2000	12	5		HANDS UP Contains a sample of Black And White Brothers' *Put Your Hands Up*	Substance SUBS 1CDS

TRI
UK vocal/instrumental group.

DATE	POS	WKS	BPI	SINGLE TITLE	LABEL & NUMBER
02/09/1995	61	1		WE GOT THE LOVE	Epic 6623642

TRIBAL HOUSE
US vocal/instrumental group formed by Winston Jones, Pierre Salandy, Danny Miller and Karen Bernod.

DATE	POS	WKS	BPI	SINGLE TITLE	LABEL & NUMBER
03/02/1990	57	2		MOTHERLAND-A-FRI-CA	Cooltempo COOL 198

○ Silver disc ● Gold disc ✪ Platinum disc (additional platinum units are indicated by a figure following the symbol) ◎ Singles released prior to 1973 that are known to have sold over 1 million copies in the UK

TONY TRIBE Jamaican singer.

16/07/1969	46	2		RED RED WINE	Downtown DT 419

A TRIBE CALLED QUEST US rap group formed by rappers Q-Tip (born Jonathan Davis, 10/4/1970, Brooklyn, NY) and Phife Dog (born Malik Taylor, 20/11/1970, Brooklyn) and sound system controller Ali Shaheed Muhammad (born 11/8/1970, New York). Q-Tip has also recorded solo. Ali Shaheed Muhammad later became a member of Lucy Pearl with Dawn Robinson (of En Vogue) and Raphael Saadiq (of Tony! Toni! Tone!).

18/08/1990	47	3	BONITA APPLEBUM	Jive 256
19/01/1991	15	7	CAN I KICK IT Based on Lou Reed's *Walk On The Wild Side*	Jive 265
11/06/1994	68	1	OH MY GOD	Jive JIVECD 355
13/07/1996	34	2	1NCE AGAIN	Jive JIVECD 399
23/11/1996	33	2	STRESSED OUT A TRIBE CALLED QUEST FEATURING FAITH EVANS AND RAPHAEL SAADIQ	Jive JIVECD 404
23/08/1997	61	1	THE JAM EP Tracks on EP: *Jam, Get A Hold, Mardi Gras At Midnight* and *Same Ol' Thing. Same Ol' Thing* featured in the 1997 film *Men In Black*	Jive JIVECD 427
29/08/1998	41	2	FIND A WAY Contains a sample of Towa Tei's *Dubnova (Parts 1 & 2)*	Jive 0518982

TRIBE OF TOFFS UK group formed in Sunderland by Stephen Cousins (guitar/vocals), Andrew Stephenson (bass/vocals) and Philip Rodgers (drums). They later added Michael Haggerton (guitar/vocals). Their debut hit was a tribute to TV weatherman John Ketley and they later recorded *Terry Wogan's On TV (Again!)*.

24/12/1988	21	5	JOHN KETLEY (IS A WEATHERMAN)	Completely Different DAFT 1

OBIE TRICE US rapper (born 14/11/1978, Detroit, MI) who was discovered by Eminem.

01/11/2003	8	11	GOT SOME TEETH	Interscope 9813061
14/02/2004	32	3	THE SET UP (YOU DON'T KNOW) OBIE TRICE FEATURING NATE DOGG	Interscope 9815333

TRICKBABY UK group formed by Saira Hussain (vocals) and Steve Ager (guitar/keyboards/bass) with Jeevan Rihal (keyboards), Renu Hossain (percussion) and Vikaash Sankadecha (drums).

12/10/1996	47	2	INDIE-YARN	Logic 74321423152

TRICKSTER UK producer Liam Sullivan.

04/04/1998	19	3	MOVE ON UP	AM:PM 5825812

TRICKY UK rapper (born Adrian Thaws, 27/1/1968, Bristol, Avon) who began his career contributing tracks to Massive Attack and made his debut single in 1994. He also recorded under the names Nearly God and Starving Souls. The Gravediggaz are rappers Robert 'RZA' Diggs (of Wu-Tang Clan), Poetic, Paul Hutson (of Stetsasonic) and Arnold Hamilton.

05/02/1994	69	1	AFTERMATH	Fourth & Broadway BRCD 288
28/01/1995	34	3	OVERCOME	Fourth & Broadway BRCD 304
15/04/1995	28	3	BLACK STEEL	Fourth & Broadway BRCDX 320
05/08/1995	12	3	THE HELL EP TRICKY VS THE GRAVEDIGGAZ Tracks on EP: *Hell Is Around The Corner, Hell Is Around The Corner (remix), Psychosis* and *Tonite Is A Special Nite*	Fourth & Broadway BRCD 326
11/11/1995	26	2	PUMPKIN	Fourth & Broadway BRCD 330
09/11/1996	36	2	CHRISTIANSANDS	Fourth & Broadway BRCD 340
23/11/1996	10	8	MILK GARBAGE FEATURING TRICKY	Mushroom D 1494
11/01/1997	28	2	TRICKY KID Contains a sample of The Commodores' *The Zoo (The Human Zoo)*	Fourth & Broadway BRCD 341
03/05/1997	29	2	MAKES ME WANNA DIE	Fourth & Broadway BRCD 348
30/05/1998	25	2	MONEY GREEDY/BROKEN HOMES	Island CID 701
21/08/1999	45	1	FOR REAL	Island CID 753

TRICKY DISCO UK remixer and producer Michael Wells who has also recorded as Technohead and GTO.

28/07/1990	14	8	TRICKY DISCO	Warp WAP 7
20/04/1991	55	2	HOUSE FLY	Warp 7WAP 11

TRIFFIDS Australian group formed in Perth by David McComb (guitar/keyboards/vocals), 'Evil' Graham Lee (guitar), Jill Burt (keyboards/vocals), Robert McComb (guitar/violin/vocals), Martyn Casey (bass) and Alsy MacDonald (drums).

06/02/1988	73	1	A TRICK OF THE LIGHT	Island IS 350

TRINA AND TAMARA US R&B vocal duo formed in Gary, IN by sisters Trina and Tamara Powell. Their brother Jesse Powell also enjoyed a successful recording career.

07/02/1998	64	1	MY LOVE IS THE SHHH! SOMETHIN' FOR THE PEOPLE FEATURING TRINA AND TAMARA	Warner Brothers W 0427CD
12/06/1999	46	2	WHAT'D YOU COME HERE FOR?	Columbia 6673382
19/10/2002	45	1	NO PANTIES TRINA	Atlantic AT 0141CD

TRINIDAD OIL COMPANY Trinidad vocal/instrumental group based in Holland and produced by Hans Grevelt.

21/05/1977	34	5	THE CALENDAR SONG (JANUARY, FEBRUARY, MARCH, APRIL, MAY)	Harvest HAR 5122

TRINITY – see JULIE DRISCOLL, BRIAN AUGER AND THE TRINITY

TRINITY-X UK group formed in London by Thorn, Julian Irani and Emma Dean.

19/10/2002	19	3	FOREVER	All Around The World CXGLOBE 255

❶⁹ Number of weeks single topped the UK chart ↑ Entered the UK chart at #1 ▲⁹ Number of weeks single topped the US chart

823

TRIO German trio formed in 1979 by Stephan Remmler, Peter Behrens and Kralle Krawinkel. They disbanded in 1984.
03/07/1982 . . . . . 2 . . . . . . 10 . . . . . O DA DA DA . . . . Mobile Suit Corporation CORP 5

TRIPLE EIGHT UK group formed by David Wilcox (born 23/8/1981, Blackpool), Josh Barnett (born 2/2/1983), Jamie Bell (born 17/5/1985), Justin (born 9/4/1982, Bristol, Avon) and Sparx (born 20/2/1980, Bristol).
03/05/2003 . . . . . 8 . . . . . . 4 . . . . KNOCK OUT . . . . Polydor 9800048
02/08/2003 . . . . . 9 . . . . . . 5 . . . . GIVE ME A REASON . . . . Polydor 9809137

TRIPLE X Italian production duo Luca Morretti and Ricky Romanini. They also record as Plaything.
30/10/1999 . . . . . 32 . . . . . 2 . . . . . FEEL THE SAME Contains a sample of Delegation's *You And I* . . . . Ministry Of Sound MOSCDS 135

TRIPPING DAISY US group formed in Dallas, TX by Tim DeLaughter (vocals), Wes Berggren (guitar), Mark Pirro (bass) and Bryan Wakeland (drums). Berggren died from a drugs overdose on 28/10/1999, with DeLaughter disbanding Tripping Daisy and going on to form Polyphonic Spree.
30/03/1996 . . . . . 72 . . . . . . 1 . . . . . . PIRANHA . . . . Island CID 638

TRISCO UK production duo Harvey Dawson and Rupert Edwards.
30/06/2001 . . . . . 28 . . . . . 2 . . . . . . MUSAK . . . . Positiva CDTIV 155

TRIUMPH Canadian rock group formed in Toronto in 1975 by Rik Emmett (guitar/vocals), Mike Levine (bass/keyboards) and Gil Moore (drums). Emmett left the group in 1988, replaced by Phil Xenides, with Moore becoming lead singer.
22/11/1980 . . . . . 59 . . . . . . 2 . . . . . . I LIVE FOR THE WEEKEND . . . . RCA 13

TROGGS UK rock group formed in Andover in 1964 by Howard Mansfield (guitar/vocals), Reg Presley (born Reginald Ball, 12/6/1943, Andover, bass), Dave Wright (guitar) and Ronnie Bond (born Ronald Bullis, 4/5/1943, Andover, drums) as the Troglodytes. Wright and Mansfield left soon after, replaced by Pete Staples (born 3/5/1944, Andover) and Chris Britton (born 21/1/1945, Watford). As Staples played bass Presley switched to lead vocals. They signed with manager Larry Page in 1965 who leased their releases first to CBS then to Fontana. Ball adopted the name of Presley as a publicity stunt in 1966. Bond died on 13/11/1992.
05/05/1966 . . . . . 2 . . . . . 12 . . . . . . WILD THING ▲² Featured in the 1994 film *D2: The Mighty Ducks* . . . . Fontana TF 689
14/07/1966 . . . . ❶² . . . . . 12 . . . . . . WITH A GIRL LIKE YOU . . . . Fontana TF 717
29/09/1966 . . . . . 2 . . . . . 14 . . . . . . I CAN'T CONTROL MYSELF . . . . Page One POF 001
15/12/1966 . . . . . 8 . . . . . 10 . . . . . . ANY WAY YOU WANT ME . . . . Page One POF 010
16/02/1967 . . . . . 12 . . . . . 10 . . . . . . GIVE IT TO ME . . . . Page One POF 015
01/06/1967 . . . . . 17 . . . . . . 6 . . . . . . NIGHT OF THE LONG GRASS . . . . Page One POF 022
26/07/1967 . . . . . 42 . . . . . . 3 . . . . . . HI HI HAZEL . . . . Page One POF 030
18/10/1967 . . . . . 5 . . . . . 14 . . . . . . LOVE IS ALL AROUND . . . . Page One POF 040
28/02/1968 . . . . . 37 . . . . . . 4 . . . . . . LITTLE GIRL . . . . Page One POF 056
30/10/1993 . . . . . 69 . . . . . . 2 . . . . . . WILD THING **TROGGS AND WOLF** Listed flip side was *War* by **EDWIN STARR AND SHADOW** . . . . Weekend CDWEEK 103

TRONIKHOUSE US producer Kevin Saunderson.
14/03/1992 . . . . . 68 . . . . . . 1 . . . . . . UP TEMPO . . . . KMS UK KMSUK 1

TROUBADOURS DU ROI BAUDOUIN Zairian vocal group formed by Father Uudo Haazen, a Belgian priest who went to the Congo in the 1950s.
19/03/1969 . . . . . 28 . . . . . 11 . . . . . . SANCTUS (MISSA LUBA) Featured in the 1969 film *If...* . . . . Philips BF 1732

TROUBLE FUNK US funk group formed in Washington DC by Mack Carey (percussion/vocals), with Robert Reed (keyboards), James Avery (keyboards), Chester Davis (guitar), Tony Fisher (bass), Taylor Reed (trumpet), David Rudd (saxophone), Gerald Reed (trombone), Robert Reed (trombone), Timothy David (percussion) and Emmett Nixon (drums).
27/06/1987 . . . . . 65 . . . . . . 3 . . . . . . WOMAN OF PRINCIPLE . . . . Fourth & Broadway BRW 70

ROGER TROUTMAN – see **2PAC**

DORIS TROY US singer (born Doris Higginson, 6/1/1937, New York) who was taken to Atlantic Records by James Brown. She later recorded for the Beatles' Apple label and provided backing vocals for Pink Floyd. She died from emphysema on 16/2/2004.
19/11/1964 . . . . . 37 . . . . . 12 . . . . . . WHATCHA GONNA DO ABOUT IT . . . . Atlantic AT 4011

ELISABETH TROY UK garage singer (full name Elisabeth Troy Antwi).
25/02/1995 . . . . . 49 . . . . . 2 . . . . . . GREATER LOVE **SOUNDMAN AND DON LLOYDIE WITH ELISABETH TROY** . . . . Sound Of Underground SOJURCD 016
18/12/1999 . . . . . 49 . . . . . 3 . . . . . . ENOUGH IS ENOUGH **Y-TRIBE FEATURING ELISABETH TROY** . . . . Northwest 10 NORTHCD 002
02/12/2000 . . . . . 35 . . . . . 2 . . . . . . HOLD ON TO ME **MJ COLE FEATURING ELISABETH TROY** . . . . Talkin Loud TLCD 62
18/05/2002 . . . . . 75 . . . . . 1 . . . . . . FOREVER YOUNG **4 VINI FEATURING ELISABETH TROY** . . . . Botchit & Scarper BOS2CD 033

TRU FAITH AND DUB CONSPIRACY UK production group featuring female singer Imaani.
09/09/2000 . . . . . 12 . . . . . 5 . . . . . . FREAK LIKE ME . . . . Public Demand CDTIV 138

TRUBBLE UK female singer Cherzia. The 'dancing baby' is a computer-generated digital image that began on the internet and subsequently appeared on mainstream TV via the *Ally McBeal Show*.
26/12/1998 . . . . . 21 . . . . . . 5 . . . . . . DANCING BABY (OOGA-CHAKA) Contains a sample of Blue Swede's *Hooked On A Feeling* . . . . Island YYCD 1

O Silver disc ● Gold disc ✪ Platinum disc (additional platinum units are indicated by a figure following the symbol) ◉ Singles released prior to 1973 that are known to have sold over 1 million copies in the UK

TRUCE UK vocal group formed by Diane Joseph, Janine Linton and Michelle Escoffery. Escoffery later worked with The Artful Dodger.

02/09/1995	54	1		THE FINEST	Big Life BLRD 118
30/03/1996	51	1		CELEBRATION OF LIFE	Big Life BLRD 126
29/11/1997	71	1		NOTHIN' BUT A PARTY	Big Life BLRD 138
05/09/1998	20	3		EYES DON'T LIE	Big Life BLRD 146

TRUCKIN' CO – see GARNET MIMMS AND TRUCKIN' CO

TRUCKS UK/Norwegian group formed by Olav Iversen (vocals), Mark Remmington (guitar), Steve Ryan (bass) and Tor Bjelland (drums).

| 05/10/2002 | 35 | 2 | | IT'S JUST PORN MUM | Gut CDGUT 43 |

ANDREA TRUE CONNECTION US singer (born Nashville, TN) who moved to New York in 1968 and wrote jingles for radio and TV before making her debut as a pornographic actress in *Illusions Of A Lady* in 1972 (she also made films under the names Inger Kissen, Singh Low and Andrea Travis). After winning the Most Versatile Actress award from the Adult Motion Picture Association in 1975 she turned to music and enlisted the assistance of producer, pianist and drummer Gregg Diamond, Jim Gregory (bass), Steve Love (guitar) and Jimmy Maelin (percussion). She later became a drug counsellor in Florida.

| 17/04/1976 | 5 | 10 | | MORE MORE MORE Featured in the 1998 film *The Last Days Of Disco* | Buddah BDS 442 |
| 04/03/1978 | 34 | 6 | | WHAT'S YOUR NAME WHAT'S YOUR NUMBER | Buddah BDS 467 |

TRUE FAITH AND BRIDGETTE GRACE WITH FINAL CUT US vocal/instrumental group.

| 02/03/1991 | 51 | 4 | | TAKE ME AWAY | Network NWK 20 |

TRUE IMAGE – see MONIE LOVE

TRUE PARTY UK studio group assembled by Adrienne Aiken and Jackie Khan whose debut hit was inspired by an advertisement for Budweiser beer. The song contained elements of *Pop Muzik*, previously a hit for M, with writer Robin Scott unhappy at having the song linked to an alcoholic drink.

| 02/12/2000 | 13 | 6 | | WHAZZUP | Positiva CDBUD 001 |

TRUE STEPPERS UK producers Andy Lysandrou and Jonny Linders recording with Another Level singer Dane Bowers. Victoria Beckham is Spice Girl member Posh Spice (born Victoria Adams, 7/4/1973, Essex). Brian Harvey is a former singer with East 17 (born 8/8/1974, London) who subsequently went solo. Lysandrou is also a member of 5050.

29/04/2000	6	8		BUGGIN' TRUE STEPPERS FEATURING DANE BOWERS	NuLife 74321753342
26/08/2000	2	20	●	OUT OF YOUR MIND TRUE STEPPERS AND DANE BOWERS FEATURING VICTORIA BECKHAM Features the uncredited contribution of Victoria's husband, England footballer David Beckham	NuLife 74321782942
02/12/2000	25	3		TRUE STEP TONIGHT TRUE STEPPERS FEATURING BRIAN HARVEY AND DONELL JONES	NuLife 74321811312

DAMON TRUEITT – see SOMORE FEATURING DAMON TRUEITT

TRUMAN AND WOLFF FEATURING STEEL HORSES UK production duo Mike Truman and Darren Wolff with UK rap group Steel Horses.

| 22/08/1998 | 57 | 1 | | COME AGAIN | Multiply CDMULTY 38 |

TRUMPET MAN – see MONTANO VS THE TRUMPET MAN

TRUSSEL US R&B group formed in Petersburg, VA by Michael Spratley (vocals), Michael Gray (guitar), Hannon Lane (guitar), Lorenzo Maclin (bass), Larry Tynes (keyboards), Lynwood Jones (saxophone), William McGhee (flugelhorn) and Ronald Smith (drums).

| 08/03/1980 | 43 | 4 | | LOVE INJECTION | Elektra K 12412 |

TRUTH UK vocal duo Frank Aiello and Stephen Jameson. Jameson later recorded as Nosmo King.

| 03/02/1966 | 27 | 6 | | GIRL | Pye 7N 17035 |

TRUTH UK group formed by Dennis Greaves (guitar/vocals), Mark Lester (guitar/vocals), Brian Bethell (bass) and Gary Wallis (drums).

11/06/1983	22	7		CONFUSION (HITS US EVERY TIME)	Formation TRUTH 1
27/08/1983	32	7		A STEP IN THE RIGHT DIRECTION	Formation TRUTH 2
04/02/1984	66	2		NO STONE UNTURNED	Formation TRUTH 3

TRUTH HURTS FEATURING RAKIM US R&B singer Shari Watson (from St Louis, MO) with US rapper Rakim.

| 31/08/2002 | 3 | 12 | | ADDICTIVE Contains a sample of B.T. Express' *Do It 'Til Your Satisfied* | Interscope 4977782 |

TSD UK vocal group formed by Bonnie, Cossie and Claire Richards (born 17/8/1977, later a member of Steps and H & Claire).

| 17/02/1996 | 69 | 1 | | HEART AND SOUL | Avex UK AVEXCD 21 |
| 30/03/1996 | 64 | 1 | | BABY I LOVE YOU | Avex UK AVEXCD 34 |

ESERA TUAOLO – see RICHIE RICH

TUBBY T UK garage singer (born Anthony Robinson, 1975, London).

| 21/09/2002 | 47 | 1 | | TALES OF THE HOOD | Go Beat GOBCD 51 |
| 24/05/2003 | 45 | 2 | | BIG N BASHY FALLACY FEATURING TUBBY T | Virgin VSCDT 1847 |

❶[9] Number of weeks single topped the UK chart **↑** Entered the UK chart at #1 **▲**[9] Number of weeks single topped the US chart

TUBE AND BERGER FEATURING CHRISSIE HYNDE
Belgian production duo Arndt Rorig and Marco Vidovic with singer Chrissie Hynde. Rorig and Vidovic had previously worked with Technotronic.

07/02/2004.....29......3....... STRAIGHT AHEAD .... Direction 6746222

TUBES
US rock group formed in Phoenix, AZ in the late 1960s and relocated to San Francisco, CA in the early 1970s. They comprised Rick Anderson (born 1/8/1947, St Paul, MN, bass), Bill 'Sputnik' Spooner (born 16/4/1949, Phoenix, guitar), Vince Welnick (born 21/2/1951, Phoenix, keyboards), 'Fee' Waybill (born John Waldo, 17/9/1950, Omaha, NE, vocals), Michael Cotten (born 25/1/1950, Kansas City, MO, synthesiser), Prairie Prince (born 7/5/1950, Charlotte, NC, drums), Roger Steen (born 13/11/1949, Pipestone, MN, guitar) and Re Styles (born 3/3/1950, guitar/vocals). They signed with A&M in 1975. Welnick later joined the Grateful Dead.

19/11/1977.....28......4...... WHITE PUNKS ON DOPE .... A&M AMS 7323
28/04/1979.....34......10...... PRIME TIME .... A&M AMS 7423
12/09/1981.....60......4...... DON'T WANT TO WAIT ANYMORE .... Capitol CL 208

TUBEWAY ARMY — see GARY NUMAN

BARBARA TUCKER
US singer (born New York), she was discovered by producers Tommy Musto and Victor Simonelli.

05/03/1994.....23......3...... BEAUTIFUL PEOPLE .... Positiva CDTIV 11
26/11/1994.....33......2...... I GET LIFTED .... Positiva CDTIV 23
23/09/1995.....46......1...... STAY TOGETHER.................................... Positiva CDTIV 39
08/08/1998.....28......2...... EVERYBODY DANCE (THE HORN SONG) .... Positiva CDTIV 96
18/03/2000.....17......4...... STOP PLAYING WITH MY MIND BARBARA TUCKER FEATURING DARYL D'BONNEAU .... Positiva CDTIV 127

JUNIOR TUCKER
UK singer who also sang background vocals for Maxi Priest and later based himself in Los Angeles, CA.

02/06/1990.....54......2...... DON'T TEST .... 10 TEN 299

LOUISE TUCKER
UK classical singer; the male vocals on her debut hit were provided by Charlie Skarbek.

09/04/1983.....59......5...... MIDNIGHT BLUE Adapted from Beethoven's Sonata Pathetique .... Ariola ARO 289

TOMMY TUCKER
US singer (born Robert Higginbotham, 5/3/1939, Springfield, OH) who made his first recordings for Hi in 1959. He died of poisoning on 22/1/1982.

26/03/1964.....23......10...... HI-HEEL SNEAKERS .... Pye 7N 25238

TUFF JAM
UK production duo Karl 'Tuff Enuff' Brown and Matt 'Jam' Lamont.

10/10/1998.....44......1...... NEED GOOD LOVE .... Locked On LOX 99CD

TUKAN
Danish production duo Soren Weile and Lars Fredriksen, and fronted by 25-year-old female model and singer Mischa.

15/12/2001.....38......3...... LIGHT A RAINBOW .... Incentive CENT 33CDS

TURIN BRAKES
UK duo formed in South London by Olly Knights and Gale Paridjanian.

03/03/2001.....67......1...... THE DOOR.. Source SOURCDS 024
12/05/2001.....39......2...... UNDERDOG (SAVE ME) .... Source SOURCDSE 1015
11/08/2001.....31......2...... MIND OVER MONEY .... Source SOURCD 038
27/10/2001.....41......1...... EMERGENCY 72 .... Source SOURCD 041
02/11/2002.....22......2...... LONG DISTANCE .... Source SOURCDX 064
01/03/2003.....5......3...... PAIN KILLER .... Source SOURCD 068
07/06/2003.....35......2...... AVERAGE MAN.................................... Source SOURCD 085
11/10/2003.....31......2...... 5 MILE (THESE ARE THE DAYS)................... Source SOURCD 089

IKE AND TINA TURNER
US husband and wife duo Ike (born Izear Turner, 5/11/1931, Clarksdale, MS) and Tina Turner (born Annie Mae Bullock, 26/11/193, Brownsville, TN). They met in 1956 when Ike's band the Kings of Rhythm took a residency at a club in St Louis. They married in 1958 and at Ike's suggestion she took the stage name Tina. They first recorded as Ike & Tina Turner in 1960 for Sue Records. Backing band became the Ike & Tina Turner Revue and assembled three backing singers as the Ikettes. They linked with Phil Spector in 1966 (the lack of success in the US for River Deep prompted Spector to shut down his Philles label and go into semi-retirement) and later recorded for Blue Thumb. They separated in 1975, divorced in 1978 and officially ended their professional relationship in October 1976. Tina later went solo. Ike Turner served eighteen months of a four-year prison sentence for driving under the influence of cocaine (in a later interview, he claimed to have spent $11 million on his habit). They were inducted into the Rock & Roll Hall of Fame in 1991. They won the 1971 Grammy Award for Best Rhythm & Blues Vocal Performance by a Duo for Proud Mary.

09/06/1966.....3......13...... RIVER DEEP MOUNTAIN HIGH .... London HL 10046
28/07/1966.....48......1...... TELL HER I'M NOT HOME .... Warner Brothers WB 5753
27/10/1966.....16......10...... A LOVE LIKE YOURS .... London HL 10083
12/02/1969.....33......7...... RIVER DEEP MOUNTAIN HIGH Re-issue of London HL 10046 .... London HLU 10242
08/09/1973.....4......13...... NUTBUSH CITY LIMITS .... United Artists UP 35582

RUBY TURNER
UK singer (born 1958, Jamaica, raised in Birmingham) who formed her first band with Bob Lamb, Billy Paul and Geoff Pearse before signing with Jive in 1985. She later became a noted session singer, appearing on albums by UB40, Lulu and Joshua Kadison and sang with Full Flava. She also became an actress, appearing in Eastenders.

25/01/1986.....30......7...... IF YOU'RE READY (COME GO WITH ME) RUBY TURNER FEATURING JONATHAN BUTLER .... Jive 109
29/03/1986.....61......4...... I'M IN LOVE .... Jive 118

○ Silver disc ● Gold disc ✪ Platinum disc (additional platinum units are indicated by a figure following the symbol) ◉ Singles released prior to 1973 that are known to have sold over 1 million copies in the UK

13/09/1986.....52.....3......				BYE BABY..	Jive 126
14/03/1987.....24.....8......				I'D RATHER GO BLIND..	Jive RTS 1
16/05/1987.....57.....2......				I'M IN LOVE..	Jive RTS 2
13/01/1990.....57.....3......				IT'S GONNA BE ALRIGHT...	Jive RTS 7
05/02/1994.....39.....3......				STAY WITH ME BABY...	M&G MAGCD 53
09/12/1995.....64.....1......				SHAKABOOM! **HUNTER FEATURING RUBY TURNER**.....................................	Telstar HUNTCD 1

SAMMY TURNER US singer (born Samuel Black, 2/6/1932, Paterson, NJ).

13/11/1959.....26.....2......				ALWAYS...	London HLX 8963

TINA TURNER

TINA TURNER US singer (born Annie Mae Bullock, 26/11/1939, Brownsville, TN), she teamed up with Ike Turner in 1956, becoming singer with his Kings of Rhythm group. Following their marriage in 1958 she adopted the stage name Tina Turner and recorded as Ike & Tina Turner from 1960 until their professional relationship dissolved in 1976. Signed with Capitol in 1982 as a solo artist. She appeared in numerous films, including *Mad Max 3 – Beyond Thunderdome*. Her autobiography *I, Tina* was turned into the film *What's Love Got To Do With It* with Angela Bassett as Tina and Lawrence Fishburne as Ike. She was inducted into the Rock & Roll Hall of Fame in 1991 (as part of Ike & Tina Turner). She won one Grammy Award with Ike and six further Grammies including Best Rock Vocal Performance in 1984 for *Better Be Good To Me*, Best Rock Vocal Performance in 1985 for *One Of The Living*, Best Rock Vocal Performance in 1986 for *Back Where You Started* and Best Rock Vocal Performance in 1988 for *Tina Live In Europe*. She also won the 1999 MOBO Award for Lifetime Achievement. She has a star on the Hollywood Walk of Fame.

19/11/1983 .....6.....13.....O				**LET'S STAY TOGETHER**...	Capitol CL 316
25/02/1984.....40.....6......				HELP..	Capitol CL 325
16/06/1984 .....3.....16.....O				**WHAT'S LOVE GOT TO DO WITH IT** ▲3 1984 Grammy Awards for Record of the Year, Best Pop Vocal Performance and Song of the Year for writers Graham Lyle and Terry Britten. Featured in the 1993 film of the same name	Capitol CL 334
15/09/1984.....45.....5......				BETTER BE GOOD TO ME..	Capitol CL 338
17/11/1984.....26.....9......				PRIVATE DANCER..	Capitol CL 343
02/03/1985.....57.....3......				I CAN'T STAND THE RAIN..	Capitol CL 352
20/07/1985 .....3.....12.....O				**WE DON'T NEED ANOTHER HERO (THUNDERDOME)** Featured in the 1985 film *Mad Max 3 – Beyond Thunderdome* .	Capitol CL 364
12/10/1985.....55.....2......				ONE OF THE LIVING...	Capitol CL 376
02/11/1985.....29.....6......				IT'S ONLY LOVE **BRYAN ADAMS AND TINA TURNER**..................................	A&M AM 285
23/08/1986.....33.....6......				TYPICAL MALE..	Capitol CL 419
08/11/1986.....43.....4......				TWO PEOPLE..	Capitol CL 430
14/03/1987.....30.....7......				WHAT YOU GET IS WHAT YOU SEE..	Capitol CL 439
13/06/1987.....43.....3......				BREAK EVERY RULE..	Capitol CL 452
20/06/1987.....56.....3......				TEARING US APART..	Duck W 8299
19/03/1988.....71.....2......				ADDICTED TO LOVE (LIVE)...	Capitol CL 484
02/09/1989 .....5.....12.....O				**THE BEST** Saxophone solo is by Edgar Winter.................................	Capitol CL 543
18/11/1989 .....8.....11......				**I DON'T WANNA LOSE YOU**..	Capitol CL 553
17/02/1990.....13.....6......				STEAMY WINDOWS..	Capitol CL 560
11/08/1990.....31.....6......				LOOK ME IN THE HEART..	Capitol CL 584
13/10/1990.....28.....4......				BE TENDER WITH ME BABY..	Capitol CL 593
24/11/1990 .....5.....8......				**IT TAKES TWO ROD STEWART AND TINA TURNER** Cover version of Marvin Gaye & Tammi Terrell's hit and recorded for a Pepsi Cola advertisement..	Warner Brothers ROD 1
21/09/1991.....23.....5......				NUTBUSH CITY LIMITS Featured in the 1993 film *What's Love Got To Do With It* ...	Capitol CL 630
23/11/1991.....13.....7......				WAY OF THE WORLD..	Capitol CL 637
15/02/1992.....29.....4......				LOVE THING..	Capitol CL 644
06/06/1992.....22.....4......				I WANT YOU NEAR ME..	Capitol CL 659
22/05/1993 .....7.....9......				**I DON'T WANNA FIGHT**...	Parlophone CDRS 6346
28/08/1993.....12.....6......				DISCO INFERNO This and above single featured in the 1993 film *What's Love Got To Do With It*	Parlophone CDR 6357
30/10/1993.....16.....4......				WHY MUST WE WAIT UNTIL TONIGHT..	Parlophone CDR 6366
18/11/1995.....10.....9......				**GOLDENEYE** Featured in the 1995 James Bond film *GoldenEye*..................	Parlophone CDR 007 1001
23/03/1996.....23.....6......				WHATEVER YOU WANT...	Parlophone CDRS 6429
08/06/1996.....13.....6......				ON SILENT WINGS...	Parlophone CDR 6434
27/07/1996.....12.....5......				MISSING YOU...	Parlophone CDRS 6441
19/10/1996.....27.....2......				SOMETHING BEAUTIFUL REMAINS...	Parlophone CDR 6448
21/12/1996.....32.....3......				IN YOUR WILDEST DREAMS **TINA TURNER FEATURING BARRY WHITE**....................	Parlophone CDR 6451
30/10/1999.....10.....7......				**WHEN THE HEARTACHE IS OVER**..	Parlophone CDR 6529
12/02/2000.....27.....3......				WHATEVER YOU NEED...	Parlophone CDRS 6532
06/11/2004.....25.....3......				OPEN ARMS...	Parlophone CDCLS862

TURNTABLE ORCHESTRA UK producer/remixer Dave Lee, although the label was designed to make the listener think this was a US duo of Hippie Torrales and Paul Scott. Lee is also a member of Hed Boys and recorded as Z Factor, Akabu, Phase II, Jakatta, Il Padrinos, Joey Negro and Raven Maize.

21/01/1989.....52.....4......				YOU'RE GONNA MISS ME..	Republic LIC 012

TURTLES US group formed in Los Angeles, CA by Howard Kaylan (born 22/6/1947, New York, vocals), Al Nichol (born 31/3/1946, Winston Salem, NC, guitar), Jim Tucker (born 17/10/1946, Los Angeles, guitar), Chuck Portz (born 28/3/1945, Santa Monica, CA, bass), Mark Volman (born 19/4/1947, Los Angeles, vocals) and Don Murray (born 8/11/1945, Los Angeles, drums) as the Nightriders, later

❶9 Number of weeks single topped the UK chart ↑ Entered the UK chart at #1 ▲9 Number of weeks single topped the US chart

827

name-changing to the Crossfires. They became The Turtles upon signing with White Whale in 1965. Murray left in 1966, replaced by John Barbata (born 1/4/1946, New Jersey). Portz left soon after, replaced by Jim Pons (born 14/3/1943, Santa Monica). Barbata left in 1969, replaced by John Seiter (born 17/8/1944, St Louis, MO). The group disbanded in 1970. Murray set up a computer graphics company and died on 22/3/1996 from complications brought on by surgery.

23/03/1967	12	12		HAPPY TOGETHER ▲³ Featured in the 1995 film *Muriel's Wedding*	London HL 10115
15/06/1967	4	15		**SHE'D RATHER BE WITH ME**	London HLU 10135
30/10/1968	7	12		**ELENORE**	London HL 10223

TUXEDOS – see BOBBY ANGELO AND THE TUXEDOS

TWA UK instrumental/production group formed by John Themis and featuring Lady JoJo, Queen of the GoGo. Their name stands for Trannies With Attitude.

16/09/1995	51	1		NASTY GIRLS	Mercury MERCD 441

SHANIA TWAIN Canadian country singer (born Eilleen Regina Edwards, 28/8/1965, Windsor, Ontario) whose stage name means 'I'm on my way' in the Ojibwa Indian language. She signed with Mercury in 1992 and released her first single in 1993. She married record producer Robert John 'Mutt' Lange in 1993 and gave birth to their first son, Eja, in August 2001. Her *Come On Over* album is the biggest selling CD by a solo female artist, with sales of 26 million worldwide by March 2000. She has won five Grammy Awards including Best Country Album in 1995 for *The Woman In Me* and Best Country Song in 1999 for *Come On Over*. Mark McGrath is lead singer with Sugar Ray.

28/02/1998	10	10		**YOU'RE STILL THE ONE** 1998 Grammy Awards for Best Female Country Vocal Performance, and Best Country Song for writers Shania Twain and Robert 'Mutt' Lange	Mercury 5684932
13/06/1998	18	4		WHEN	Mercury 5661192
28/11/1998	9	8		**FROM THIS MOMENT ON**	Mercury 5665632
22/05/1999	3	21	✪	**THAT DON'T IMPRESS ME MUCH**	Mercury 8708032
02/10/1999	3	18	○	**MAN! I FEEL LIKE A WOMAN** 1999 Grammy Award for Best Female Country Vocal Performance	Mercury 5623242
26/02/2000	5	11		**DON'T BE STUPID (YOU KNOW I LOVE YOU)**	Mercury 1721492
16/11/2002	4	15		**I'M GONNA GETCHA GOOD!**	Mercury 1722732
22/03/2003	8	8		**KA-CHING**	Mercury 1722872
14/06/2003	6	10		**FOREVER AND FOR ALWAYS**	Mercury 9807734
06/09/2003	11	7		THANK YOU BABY!	Mercury 9810628
29/11/2003	21	5		WHEN YOU KISS ME/UP!	Mercury 9814004
04/12/2004	10	4+		**PARTY FOR TWO** SHANIA TWAIN & MARK McGRATH	Mercury 2103240

TWEENIES UK kids' TV characters featuring Jake, Fizz, Milo, Bella and Doodles the dog.

11/11/2000	5	23	○	**NUMBER 1**	BBC Music WMSS 60332
31/03/2001	12	10		BEST FRIENDS FOREVER	BBC Music WMSS 60382
04/08/2001	17	8		DO THE LOLLIPOP	BBC Music WMSS 60452
15/12/2001	9	6		**I BELIEVE IN CHRISTMAS**	BBC Music WMSS 60502
14/09/2002	20	7		HAVE FUN GO MAD	BBC Music WMSS 60572

TWEET US singer (born Charlene Keys, 4/3/1971, Rochester, NY) who was discovered by and sang with Missy Elliott and with Ja Rule before going solo.

11/05/2002	5	8		**OOPS (OH MY)** Features the uncredited contribution of Missy Elliott	Elektra E 7306CD
07/09/2002	35	2		CALL ME	Elektra E 7326CD

TWEETS UK session musicians assembled by Henry Hadaway covering a song that had been a huge European hit by Electronicas.

12/09/1981	2	23	●	**THE BIRDIE SONG (BIRDIE DANCE)**	PRT 7P 219
05/12/1981	44	6		LET'S ALL SING LIKE THE BIRDIES SING	PRT 7P 226
18/12/1982	46	5		THE BIRDIE SONG (BIRDIE DANCE)	PRT 7P 219

20 FINGERS FEATURING GILLETTE US trio formed by Chicago, IL-based producers Charles Babie and Manfred Mohr with singer Sandra Gillette (born 16/9/1973, Chicago).

26/11/1994	21	4		SHORT DICK MAN Inspired an answer record by Sex Club – *Big Dick Man*	Multiply CDMULT 12
30/09/1995	48	3		LICK IT	ZYX 75908
30/09/1995	11	7		SHORT SHORT MAN Cleaned up version of Multiply CDMULT 12	Multiply CXMULTY 7

21ST CENTURY GIRLS UK group formed by Kate Turley, Meriam 'Mim' Mohammed, Leanne Garner and Fiona Garner.

12/06/1999	16	4		21ST CENTURY GIRLS	EMI NTNCDS 001

TWEN2Y 4 SE7EN Irish vocal group formed by Andy Keelaghan (born 5/10/1984), Niall Keelaghan (born 19/7/1983), Radon Reynolds (born 10/5/1985) and Thom Evans (born 2/4/1985).

12/06/2004	42	1		HIDE	Diablo Music MND2

TWENTY 4 SEVEN FEATURING CAPTAIN HOLLYWOOD German duo Stay-C and Stella, with Captain Hollywood (Tony Harrison).

22/09/1990	7	10		**I CAN'T STAND IT**	BCM BCMR 395
24/11/1990	17	10		ARE YOU DREAMING	BCM 07504

29 PALMS UK producer Pete Lorimar.
25/05/2002.....51......1....... TOUCH THE SKY .... Mushroom PERF 35CDS

22-20'S UK group formed by Martin Trimble (guitar/vocals), Glen Bartup (bass) and James Irving (bass).
17/04/2004.....41......2....... WHY DON'T YOU DO IT FOR ME .... Heavenly HVN 138CD
10/07/2004.....30......2....... SHOOT YOUR GUN .... Heavenly HVN 141CD
25/09/2004.....34......2....... 22 DAYS... Heavenly HVN 144CDS

TWICE AS MUCH UK vocal/songwriting duo Dave Skinner and Andrew Rose.
16/06/1966.....25......9...... SITTIN' ON A FENCE.. Immediate IM 033

TWIGGY UK singer (born Lesley Hornby, 1949, London); she first came to prominence as a model during the 1960s.
14/08/1976.....17.....10...... HERE I GO AGAIN... Mercury 6007 100

TWILIGHT – see ROGER SANCHEZ

TWIN HYPE US rap duo Hollywood Impact and King Shameek.
15/07/1989.....65......2....... DO IT TO THE CROWD... Profile PROF 255

TWINKLE UK singer/songwriter (born Lynne Annette Ripley, 15/7/1947, Surbiton) who retired from recording at the end of the 1960s to raise a family. She returned briefly in 1972, without success, but after The Smiths covered *Golden Lights* in 1993 she undertook live appearances.
26/11/1964 .....4......15...... TERRY .... Decca F 12013
25/02/1965.....21......5....... GOLDEN LIGHTS... Decca F 12076

TWISTA US rapper (born Carl Mitchell, Chicago, IL) known as Tung Twista after the *Guinness Book of Records* named him the world's fastest rapper in 1992.
10/04/2004 .....3......10 ...... SLOW JAMZ ▲[1] .... Atlantic AT 0174CD
03/07/2004.....16......7....... OVERNIGHT CELEBRITY... Atlantic AT 0180CD
14/08/2004.....60......3....... SUNSHINE (IMPORT) Contains a sample of Bill Withers' *Lovely Day* .... Atlantic 7567932652CD
11/09/2004 .....3......10 ...... SUNSHINE Features the uncredited contribution of Anthony Hamilton. .... Atlantic AT 0181CD
20/11/2004.....28......3....... SO SEXY TWISTA FEATURING R KELLY .... Atlantic AT 0187CD

TWISTED INDIVIDUAL UK drum/bass producer Lee Greenaway.
09/08/2003.....51......1....... BANDWAGON BLUES.. Formation FORM 12102

TWISTED SISTER US heavy rock group formed in New York in 1982 by Dee Snider (vocals), Jay Jay French (guitar), Eddie Ojeda (guitar), Mark Mendoza (bass) and AJ Pero (drums). Pero left in 1987, replaced by Joey Franco, although the group disbanded later the same year. Snider later appeared in the film *Strangeland*.
26/03/1983.....18......9...... I AM (I'M ME) .... Atlantic A 9854
28/05/1983.....32......6...... THE KIDS ARE BACK .... Atlantic A 9827
20/08/1983.....43......4...... YOU CAN'T STOP ROCK 'N' ROLL .... Atlantic A 9792
02/06/1984.....58......6...... WE'RE NOT GONNA TAKE IT .... Atlantic A 9657
18/01/1986.....47......3...... LEADER OF THE PACK .... Atlantic A 9478

TWISTED X UK group assembled by XFM DJ Christian O'Connell and featuring members of The Libertines, The Wheatleys, Supergrass, The Delays and actor James Nesbitt. The single was released to raise funds for the Help A Local Child charity.
19/06/2004 .....9 .....3...... BORN IN ENGLAND .... Universal TV 9867021

CONWAY TWITTY US singer (born Harold Lloyd Jenkins, 1/9/1933, Friars Point, MS) who formed his first group at the age of ten. He changed his name in 1957 upon signing with Sun (although nothing was released), switching to MGM in 1958. He changed his musical style to country in 1965 and moved to Nashville, TN in 1968. He appeared in a number of films such as *Platinum High School* and *Sex Kittens Go To College*. He also opened his own leisure complex Twitty City in Hendersonville, TN, selling Twittyburgers. He won the 1971 Grammy Award for Best Country & Western Performance by a Duo with Loretta Lynn for *After The Fire Is Gone*. He scored 41 chart toppers on the country charts and died from a blood clot on 5/6/1993.
14/11/1958 .... ❶[5].....15...... IT'S ONLY MAKE BELIEVE ▲[2] .... MGM 992
27/03/1959.....30......1...... STORY OF MY LOVE .... MGM 1003
21/08/1959 .....5......14...... MONA LISA .... MGM 1029
21/07/1960.....43......3...... IS A BLUE BIRD BLUE .... MGM 1082
23/02/1961.....40......3...... C'EST SI BON .... MGM 1118

2 BAD MICE UK instrumental/production group formed by Sean O'Keefe, Simon Colebrooke and Rob Playford. Playford was later a member of Metalheadz.
15/02/1992.....70......1...... HOLD IT DOWN .... Moving Shadow SHADOW 14
08/08/1992.....48......2...... HOLD IT DOWN .... Moving Shadow SHADOW 14
07/09/1996.....46......1...... BOMBSCARE .... Arista 74321397662

TWO COWBOYS Italian instrumental/production group fronted by Maurizio Braccagni and Robert Gallo Sagotto.
09/07/1994 .....7......11 ...... EVERYBODY GONFI-GON .... 3 Beat TABCD 221

❶[9] Number of weeks single topped the UK chart ↑ Entered the UK chart at #1 ▲[9] Number of weeks single topped the US chart

829

2 EIVISSA German vocal duo Pascale Jean Louis and Ellen Helbig.

04/10/1997.....13......6..... OH LA LA LA Contains a sample of Crystal Waters' *Gypsy Woman* .... Club Tools 0063475 CLU

2 FOR JOY UK instrumental/production duo Mark Hall and Stuart Quinn. Hall later formed Bus Stop.

01/12/1990.....61......1....... IN A STATE .... Mercury MER 333

09/11/1991.....67......2....... LET THE BASS KICK .... All Around The World GLOBE 102

2 FUNKY 2 FEATURING KATHRYN DION UK vocal/instrumental group fronted by Kathryn Dion.

06/11/1993.....56......2....... BROTHERS AND SISTERS .... Logic 74321170772

30/11/1996.....36......2....... BROTHERS AND SISTERS (REMIX) .... All Around The World CDGLOBE 138

2 HOUSE US instrumental/production duo Todd Terry (born 18/4/1967, Brooklyn, NY) and Tony Humphries. Terry also recorded as Swan Lake, Royal House, Gypsymen, T2 and Black Riot.

21/03/1992.....65......1....... GO TECHNO... Atlantic A 7519

2 IN A ROOM US dance duo rapper Rafael 'Dose' Vargas and remixer Roger 'Rog Nice' Pauletta who teamed up in Washington Heights in New York.

18/11/1989.....66......1....... SOMEBODY IN THE HOUSE SAY YEAH! .... Big Life BLR 12

26/01/1991.....3.....8......○ **WIGGLE IT** .... Positiva CDTIV 18

06/04/1991.....54......2....... SHE'S GOT ME GOING CRAZY .... SBK 23

22/10/1994.....34......2....... EL TRAGO (THE DRINK)... SBK 19

08/04/1995.....43......1....... AHORA ES (NOW IS THE TIME) .... Positiva CDTIV 32

17/08/1996.....74......1....... GIDDY-UP .... Encore CDCOR 008

2 IN A TENT UK production duo Mike Stock (born 3/12/1951) and Matt Aitken (born 25/8/1956). They had previously worked with Pete Waterman and later linked with Jive Bunny member Andy Pickles.

17/12/1994.....25......5....... WHEN I'M CLEANING WINDOWS (TURNED OUT NICE AGAIN) Contains a sample of George Formby's *When I'm Cleaning Windows (Turned Out Nice Again)* .... Love This SPONCD 1

13/05/1995.....48......1....... BOOGIE WOOGIE BUGLE BOY (DON'T STOP) **2 IN A TANK** .... Bald Cat BALCD 1

06/01/1996.....62......1....... WHEN I'M CLEANING WINDOWS (TURNED OUT NICE AGAIN) .... Love This SPONCD 1

2K UK duo Bill Drummond (born William Butterworth, 29/4/1953, South Africa) and Jimmy Cauty (born 1954, London) who also recorded as the Timelords, the Justified Ancients of Mu Mu and KLF.

25/10/1997.....28......2....... ***K THE MILLENNIUM Contains a sample of Isaac Hayes' *Theme From Shaft*....................... Blast First BFFP 146CDK

2 MAD UK vocal/instrumental duo.

09/02/1991.....43......4....... THINKING ABOUT YOUR BODY .... Big Life BLR 37

TWO MAN SOUND Belgian vocal/instrumental group formed in Brussels by Nico Gomez, Benito DiPaula, A Ward and Lou Deprijck.

20/01/1979.....46......7....... QUE TAL AMERICA .... Miracle M 1

TWO MEN, A DRUM MACHINE AND A TRUMPET UK production duo Andy Cox and David Steele, both of whom were members of the Fine Young Cannibals at the time.

09/01/1988.....18......8....... I'M TIRED OF GETTING PUSHED AROUND .... London LON 141

25/06/1988.....21......9....... HEAT IT UP **WEE PAPA GIRL RAPPERS FEATURING TWO MEN AND A DRUM MACHINE** .... Jive 174

TWO NATIONS UK vocal/instrumental group.

20/06/1987.....74......1....... THAT'S THE WAY IT FEELS .... 10 TEN 168

TWO PEOPLE UK vocal/instrumental group formed by Mark Stevenson and Noel Ram.

31/01/1987.....63......2....... HEAVEN .... Polydor POSP 844

2WO THIRD3 UK vocal group formed in 1993 by Victor, Lee and Justin. Justin left the group soon after their formation, replaced by Danny. All three were twenty years of age at the time the group formed. A fourth member, Biff, provided all of the music and appeared with the group as a cartoon character.

19/02/1994.....48......3....... HEAR ME CALLING Features the uncredited vocal contribution of Helen Terry .... Epic 6600642

11/06/1994.....45......2....... EASE THE PRESSURE .... Epic 6604782

08/10/1994.....20......5....... I WANT THE WORLD .... Epic 6608542

17/12/1994.....29......5....... I WANT TO BE ALONE .... Epic 6610852

2-4 FAMILY Multinational rap and vocal group formed by Miss Jo (born Joanna Biscardine, London), The Fly Thai (born Essence Woods, Dallas, TX), Jazz (born Joseph Bellamy, Queens, NY), Jay Dogg (born, Detroit, MI) and Lil' Bit (born Ladwida Jackson).

29/05/1999.....69......1....... LEAN ON ME (WITH THE FAMILY)... Epic 6670132

2 UNLIMITED Dutch dance duo Anita Dels (born 28/12/1971, Amsterdam) and Ray 'Kid Ray' Slijngaard (born 28/6/1971, Amsterdam) who teamed up in 1991 with Belgian production duo Phil Wilde and Jean-Paul De Coster. Wilde and De Coster had previously been responsible for Bizz Nizz.

05/10/1991.....2......15..... **GET READY FOR THIS** Featured in the films *Eddie* (1996) and *Scooby Doo 2: Monsters Unleashed* (2004)......................
.... PWL Continental PWL 206

25/01/1992	2	10		TWILIGHT ZONE	PWL Continental PWL 211
02/05/1992	4	7		WORKAHOLIC	PWL Continental PWL 228
15/08/1992	11	7		THE MAGIC FRIEND	PWL Continental PWL 240
30/01/1993	❶5	16		NO LIMIT	PWL Continental PWCD 256
08/05/1993	4	11		TRIBAL DANCE	PWL Continental PWCD 262
04/09/1993	8	7		FACES	PWL Continental PWCD 268
20/11/1993	15	8		MAXIMUM OVERDRIVE	PWL Continental PWCD 276
19/02/1994	6	9		LET THE BEAT CONTROL YOUR BODY	PWL Continental PWCD 280
21/05/1994	6	7		THE REAL THING	PWL Continental PWCD 306
01/10/1994	17	6		NO ONE	PWL Continental PWCD 314
25/03/1995	22	3		HERE I GO	PWL Continental PWCD 317
21/10/1995	16	4		DO WHAT'S GOOD FOR ME	PWL 322CD
11/07/1998	38	2		WANNA GET UP	Big Life BLRD 143

2PAC US rapper/actor Tupac Amara Shakur (born Lesane Crooks, 16/6/1971, Brooklyn, NY) who was a member of Digital Underground. He has had numerous brushes with the law, including a gun battle with two off-duty policemen, an assault on Allen Hughes of Menace II Society, receiving a jail sentence for a sexual abuse conviction and causing the death of a six-year old child when his gun accidentally discharged. He was shot five times, had $40,000 stolen, and survived during a robbery in Manhattan in 1994. Two years later, on 7/9/1996 he was shot four times while travelling to the boxing match between Mike Tyson and Bruce Seldon in Las Vegas and died as a result of gunshot wounds on 13/9/1996. He was on $1.4 million bail for a weapons conviction at the time of his death. He also recorded as Makaveli and appeared in films such as *Nothing But Trouble, Poetic Justice* and *Above The Rim*. He won the 1996 MOBO Award for Best Video for *California Love*.

13/04/1996	6	8		CALIFORNIA LOVE 2PAC FEATURING DR DRE Contains samples of Roger's *So Ruff So Tuff* and Joe Cocker's *Woman To Woman*, and features the uncredited contribution of Roger Troutman. 1996 MOBO Award for Best Video	Death Row DRWCD 3
27/07/1996	17	4		HOW DO YOU WANT IT? ▲2 2PAC FEATURING K-CI AND JOJO Contains a sample of Quincy Jones' *Body Heat*. 2Pac's estate was sued for intentional infliction of emotional distress, slander and invasion of privacy by C DeLores Tucker over the lyrics to this hit in which she was mentioned by name. Tucker, an outspoken critic and lobbyist against gangsta rap lyrics, also sued Interscope Records, Death Row Records, Time Warner, Seagram Co, Tower Records and various individuals connected with the companies	Death Row 228546532
30/11/1996	13	9		I AIN'T MAD AT CHA	Death Row DRWCD 5
26/04/1997	16	3		WANTED DEAD OR ALIVE 2PAC AND SNOOP DOGGY DOGG	Def Jam 5744052
10/01/1998	21	4		I WONDER IF HEAVEN GOT A GHETTO Contains a sample of Cameo's *Two Of Us*	Jive JIVECD 446
13/06/1998	12	4		DO FOR LOVE 2PAC FEATURING ERIC WILLIAMS Contains a sample of Bobby Caldwell's *What You Won't Do For Love*	Jive 0518512
18/07/1998	15	3		RUNNIN' 2PAC AND THE NOTORIOUS B.I.G	Black Jam BJAM 9005
28/11/1998	17	2		HAPPY HOME	Eagle EAGXS 058
20/02/1999	3	12	○	CHANGES Contains a sample of Bruce Hornsby & The Range's *The Way It Is*	Jive 0522832
03/07/1999	27	3		DEAR MAMA Contains samples of The Detroit Spinners' *Sadie* and Joe Sample's *In My Wildest Dreams*. Featured in the 2003 film *The Fighting Temptations*	Jive 0523702
23/06/2001	4	11		UNTIL THE END OF TIME Contains a sample of Mr Mister's *Broken Wings*	Interscope 4975812
10/11/2001	21	5		LETTER 2 MY UNBORN Contains a sample of Michael Jackson's *Liberian Girl*	Interscope 4976142
22/02/2003	24	5		THUGZ MANSION	Interscope 4978542
31/01/2004	17	6		RUNNIN' (DYIN' TO LIVE) 2PAC AND THE NOTORIOUS B.I.G	Interscope 9815329

2PLAY FEATURING RAGHAV UK production/vocal group formed by 2Play (born Wesley Johnson) and Raghav with rapper MC Jucxi Dee on their debut hit and singer Naila Boss on their follow-up.

24/01/2004	6	13		SO CONFUSED 2PLAY FEATURING RAGHAV AND JUCXI 2004 MOBO Award for Best Collaboration	2PSL 2PSLCD02
22/05/2004	8	1		IT CAN'T BE RIGHT 2PLAY FEATURING RAGHAV AND NAILA BOSS	2PSL/Inferno 2PSLCD04
04/12/2004	29	3		CARELESS WHISPER 2PLAY FEATURING THOMAS JULES & JUCXI D	Inferno 2PSLCD06

TY FEATURING ROOTS MANUVA UK rapper (born Ben Chijioke, 1971) with fellow rapper Roots Manuva (born Rodney Hylton Smith).

| 08/05/2004 | 65 | 1 | | OH YOU WANT MORE | Big Dada BDCDS 066 |

TYGERS OF PAN TANG UK rock group formed in Whitley Bay in 1979 by Jess Cox (vocals), Robb Weir (guitar), Rocky (bass) and Brian Dick (drums). They added John Sykes (guitar) in 1980, with Cox leaving the group at the end of the same year, replaced by Jon Deverill. Sykes left in 1981, replaced by Fred Purser, but the group disbanded in 1983. Deverill and Dick re-formed the group in 1985 with Steve Lamb (guitar), Neil Shepard (guitar) and Dave Donaldson (bass), although after two albums they disbanded again in 1987. They took their name from the Michael Moorcock novel *Stormbringer*.

14/02/1981	48	3		HELLBOUND	MCA 672
27/03/1982	45	6		LOVE POTION NO. 9	MCA 769
10/07/1982	49	4		RENDEZVOUS	MCA 777
11/09/1982	63	2		PARIS BY AIR	MCA 790

BONNIE TYLER UK singer (born Gaynor Hopkins, 8/6/1951, Swansea) who was a club singer before being discovered by producers Steve Wolfe and Ronnie Scott.

30/10/1976	9	10		LOST IN FRANCE	RCA 2734
19/03/1977	27	6		MORE THAN A LOVER	RCA PB 5008
03/12/1977	4	12	●	IT'S A HEARTACHE	RCA PB 5057

❶9 Number of weeks single topped the UK chart ↑ Entered the UK chart at #1 ▲9 Number of weeks single topped the US chart

831

	DATE	POS	WKS	BPI	SINGLE TITLE	LABEL & NUMBER
	30/06/1979	35	6		MARRIED MEN Featured in the 1979 film *The World Is Full Of Married Men*	RCA PB 5164
	19/02/1983	❶²	12	●	**TOTAL ECLIPSE OF THE HEART** ▲⁴	CBS TYLER 1
	07/05/1983	43	4		FASTER THAN THE SPEED OF NIGHT	CBS A 3338
	25/06/1983	47	3		HAVE YOU EVER SEEN THE RAIN	CBS A 3517
	07/01/1984	5	9		**A ROCKIN' GOOD WAY SHAKY** (Stevens) **AND BONNIE**	Epic A 4071
	31/08/1985	2	13	○	**HOLDING OUT FOR A HERO** Featured in the 1984 film *Footloose* and the 1989 film *Who's Harry Crumb*	CBS A 4251
	14/12/1985	73	2		LOVING YOU'S A DIRTY JOB BUT SOMEBODY'S GOTTA DO IT **BONNIE TYLER, GUEST VOCALS TODD RUNDGREN**	CBS A 6662
	28/12/1991	69	2		HOLDING OUT FOR A HERO Re-issue of CBS A 4251	Total TYLER 10
	27/01/1996	45	2		MAKING LOVE (OUT OF NOTHING AT ALL)	East West EW 010CD

TYMES US R&B group formed in Philadelphia, PA by Norman Burnett, George Hilliard, Donald Banks and Albert 'Caesar' Berry as the Latineers, adding George Williams and becoming the Tymes in 1960. They first recorded for Cameo-Parkway in 1962. By the time they recorded for RCA in the 1970s, Berry and Hilliard had been replaced by female singers Terri Gonzalez and Melanie Moore.

	DATE	POS	WKS	BPI	SINGLE TITLE	LABEL & NUMBER
	25/07/1963	21	8		SO MUCH IN LOVE ▲¹	Cameo Parkway P 871
	15/01/1969	16	10		PEOPLE Featured in the 1968 film *Funny Girl*	Direction 58 3903
	21/09/1974	18	9		YOU LITTLE TRUSTMAKER	RCA 2456
	21/12/1974	❶¹	11	○	**MS GRACE**	RCA 2493
	17/01/1976	41	3		GOD'S GONNA PUNISH YOU	RCA 2626

TYMES 4 UK R&B vocal group formed in London by Holly James Mallett (born 8/11/1981, London), Taymah Gaye (born 18/2/1980, London), Melissa Garrick (born 20/8/1980, London) and Natalie Edwards (born 12/10/1983, London). Mallett was replaced by Leah Tribe.

	DATE	POS	WKS	BPI	SINGLE TITLE	LABEL & NUMBER
	25/08/2001	23	3		BODYROCK	Edel 0118635 ERE
	15/12/2001	40	2		SHE GOT GAME	Blacklist 0133135 EREP

TYPICALLY TROPICAL UK session musicians assembled by recording engineers-turned songwriters Jeffrey Calvert and Max West. Their first song, *The Ghost Song*, a Christmas novelty item, was recorded too late for the Christmas market and they therefore released *Barbados* in time for the summer market. The hit features the spoken vocals of 'Captain Tobias Wilcock of Coconut Airways'.

	DATE	POS	WKS	BPI	SINGLE TITLE	LABEL & NUMBER
	05/07/1975	❶¹	11	○	**BARBADOS**	Gull GULS 14

TYREE US producer Tyree Cooper who began his career as a DJ in Chicago and made his debut single in 1987.

	DATE	POS	WKS	BPI	SINGLE TITLE	LABEL & NUMBER
	25/02/1989	12	7		TURN UP THE BASS **TYREE FEATURING KOOL ROCK STEADY**	ffrr FFR 24
	06/05/1989	70	2		HARDCORE HIP HOUSE	DJ international DJIN 11
	02/12/1989	72	1		MOVE YOUR BODY **TYREE FEATURING JMD**	CBS 6554707

TYRESE US singer/actor (born Tyrese Gibson, 1979, Los Angeles, CA) who appeared in the 2003 film *2 Fast 2 Furious*.

	DATE	POS	WKS	BPI	SINGLE TITLE	LABEL & NUMBER
	31/07/1999	59	1		NOBODY ELSE	RCA 74321688282
	25/09/1999	55	1		SWEET LADY	RCA 74321700842
	26/07/2003	30	4		HOW YOU GONNA ACT LIKE THAT	J Records 82876544892

TYRREL CORPORATION UK vocal/instrumental duo Joe Watson and Tony Barry.

	DATE	POS	WKS	BPI	SINGLE TITLE	LABEL & NUMBER
	14/03/1992	71	1		THE BOTTLE	Volante TYR 1
	15/08/1992	58	2		GOING HOME	Volante TYR 2
	10/10/1992	59	1		WAKING WITH A STRANGER/ONE DAY	Volante TYRS 3
	24/09/1994	42	2		YOU'RE NOT HERE	Cooltempo CDCOOL 292
	14/01/1995	29	3		BETTER DAYS AHEAD	Cooltempo CDCOOLS 303

TZANT UK vocal/instrumental duo Jamie White and Marcus Thomas. Thomas left in 1998 and was replaced by Marcel Atteen. White was later a member of Mirrorball, The 3 Jays and the PF Project.

	DATE	POS	WKS	BPI	SINGLE TITLE	LABEL & NUMBER
	07/09/1996	36	2		HOT AND WET (BELIEVE IT)	Logic 74321376832
	25/04/1998	11	6		SOUNDS OF WICKEDNESS	Logic 74321568842
	22/08/1998	39	2		BOUNCE WITH THE MASSIVE	Logic 74321602102

JUDIE TZUKE UK singer (born Judie Myers, 3/4/1955, London) who reverted to the former surname of her Polish father when she launched a singing career. She first recorded with Mike Paxman as Tzuke and Paxo in 1975 before joining Elton John's Rocket label. She formed Big Moon Records in 1996.

	DATE	POS	WKS	BPI	SINGLE TITLE	LABEL & NUMBER
	14/07/1979	16	10		STAY WITH ME TILL DAWN	Rocket XPRES 17

○ Silver disc ● Gold disc ✪ Platinum disc (additional platinum units are indicated by a figure following the symbol) ◉ Singles released prior to 1973 that are known to have sold over 1 million copies in the UK

U

UB40 UK reggae group formed in Birmingham in 1978 by Ali Campbell (born 15/2/1959, Birmingham, vocals/rhythm guitar), Earl Falconer (born 23/1/1959, Birmingham, bass), Robin Campbell (born 25/12/1954, Birmingham, guitar/vocals), Mickey Virtue (born 19/1/1957, Birmingham, keyboards), Brian Travers (born 7/2/1959, Birmingham, saxophone), Jim Brown (born 20/11/1957, Birmingham, drums), Norman Hassan (born 26/1/1957, Birmingham, percussion) and Yomi Babayemi (percussion), taking their name from the unemployment benefit form. Babayemi was deported to Nigeria after only two live dates and Astro (born Terence Wilson, 24/6/1957, Birmingham, reggae toaster/singer) joined them shortly before they began recording in 1979. They left indie label Graduate in 1980 (in protest against an anti-apartheid song, *Burden Of Shame*, being deleted from the South African release of their debut album *Signing Off*) and set up DEP International through Virgin. Falconer was jailed for six months in July 1988 for driving offences (he was driving with over twice the legal alcohol limit and his brother was killed) and the group were forced to use a replacement bass player for their world tour. Ali Campbell recorded solo in the 1990s. The group appeared in the 1997 film *Speed 2 – Cruise Control*.

08/03/1980	4	13	○	**KING/FOOD FOR THOUGHT** A-side dedicated to Martin Luther King .... Graduate GRAD 6
14/06/1980	6	10		**MY WAY OF THINKING/I THINK IT'S GOING TO RAIN** .... Graduate GRAD 8
01/11/1980	10	12		**THE EARTH DIES SCREAMING/DREAM A LIE** .... Graduate GRAD 10
23/05/1981	16	9		DON'T LET IT PASS YOU BY/DON'T SLOW DOWN .... DEP International DEP 1
08/08/1981	7	10		**ONE IN TEN** .... DEP International DEP 2
13/02/1982	32	6		I WON'T CLOSE MY EYES .... DEP International DEP 3
15/05/1982	29	7		LOVE IS ALL IS ALRIGHT .... DEP International DEP 4
28/08/1982	25	9		SO HERE I AM .... DEP International DEP 5
05/02/1983	45	4		I'VE GOT MINE. .... DEP International DEP 6
20/08/1983	❶³	14	●	**RED RED WINE** ▲¹ Featured in the 1999 film *Bringing Out The Dead* .... DEP International DEP 7
15/10/1983	10	8		**PLEASE DON'T MAKE ME CRY** .... DEP International DEP 8
10/12/1983	16	8		MANY RIVERS TO CROSS .... DEP International DEP 9
17/03/1984	12	8		CHERRY OH BABY. .... DEP International DEP 10
22/09/1984	9	8		**IF IT HAPPENS AGAIN** .... DEP International DEP 11
01/12/1984	59	2		RIDDLE ME .... DEPInternational DEP 15
03/08/1985	❶¹	13	●	**I GOT YOU BABE** UB40 FEATURING CHRISSIE HYNDE .... DEP International DEP 20
26/10/1985	3	13	○	**DON'T BREAK MY HEART** Song writer Jahid Khan was sued by Deborah Banks for taking her work and passing it off as his own .... DEP International DEP 22
12/07/1986	5	9		**SING OUR OWN SONG**. .... DEP International DEP 23
27/09/1986	41	4		ALL I WANT TO DO .... DEP International DEP 24
17/01/1987	12	7		RAT IN MI KITCHEN .... DEP International DEP 25
09/05/1987	39	4		WATCHDOGS .... DEP International DEP 26
10/10/1987	14	8		MAYBE TOMORROW .... DEP International DEP 27
27/02/1988	17	8		RECKLESS AFRIKA BAMBAATAA FEATURING UB4J AND FAMILY .... EMI EM 41
18/06/1988	6	11		**BREAKFAST IN BED** UB40 FEATURING CHRISSIE HYNDE. .... DEP International DEP 29
20/08/1988	26	6		WHERE DID I GO WRONG .... DEP International DEP 30
17/06/1989	45	4		I WOULD DO FOR YOU .... DEP International DEP 32
18/11/1989	6	10		**HOMELY GIRL**. .... DEP International DEP 33
27/01/1990	46	3		HERE I AM (COME AND TAKE ME). .... DEP International DEP 34
31/03/1990	4	12	○	**KINGSTON TOWN** .... DEP International DEP 35
28/07/1990	35	6		WEAR YOU TO THE BALL .... DEP International DEP 36
03/11/1990	6	10		**I'LL BE YOUR BABY TONIGHT** ROBERT PALMER AND UB40 .... EMI EM 167
01/12/1990	47	2		IMPOSSIBLE LOVE. .... DEP International DEP 37
02/02/1991	49	3		THE WAY YOU DO THE THINGS YOU DO .... DEP International DEP 38
12/12/1992	17	8		ONE IN TEN 808 STATE VS UB40 .... ZTT ZANG 39
22/05/1993	❶²	16	✪	**(I CAN'T HELP) FALLING IN LOVE WITH YOU** ▲⁷ Featured in the films *Sliver* (1993, although originally intended for *Honeymoon In Vegas*) and *Speed 2 – Cruise Control* (1997) .... DEP International DEPDG 40
21/08/1993	8	9		**HIGHER GROUND**. .... DEP International DEPD 41
11/12/1993	24	6		BRING ME YOUR CUP .... DEP International DEPD 42
02/04/1994	37	3		C'EST LA VIE .... DEP International DEPD 43
27/08/1994	28	2		REGGAE MUSIC. .... DEP International DEPDG 44
04/11/1995	15	6		UNTIL MY DYING DAY .... DEP International DEPD 45
30/08/1997	14	4		TELL ME IS IT TRUE Featured in the 1997 film *Speed 2 – Cruise Control* .... DEP International DEPD 48
15/11/1997	53	1		ALWAYS THERE. .... DEP International DEPD 49
10/10/1998	10	6		**COME BACK DARLING** .... DEP International DEPD 50
19/12/1998	31	3		HOLLY HOLY .... DEP International DEPD 51

❶⁹ Number of weeks single topped the UK chart ↑ Entered the UK chart at #1 ▲⁹ Number of weeks single topped the US chart

	DATE	POS	WKS	BPI	SINGLE TITLE	LABEL & NUMBER
	01/05/1999	30	2		THE TRAIN IS COMING	DEP International DEPD 52
	09/12/2000	63	1		LIGHT MY FIRE	DEP International DEPD 53
	20/10/2001	40	2		SINCE I MET YOU LADY/SPARKLE OF MY EYES **UB40 FEATURING LADY SAW**	DEP International DEPD 55
	02/03/2002	54	1		COVER UP	DEP International DEPD 56
	08/11/2003	15	14		SWING LOW **UB40 FEATURING UNITED COLOURS OF SOUND** Official theme to the 2003 Rugby World Cup	DEP International DEPX 58

UBM German vocal/instrumental group formed by Uli Brenner, Uwe Wagenknecht and Misar (born Mike Staab) with vocalist Andrea Rincon.

	23/05/1998	46	1		LOVIN' YOU	Logic 74321571692

UCC – see **URBAN COOKIE COLLECTIVE**

UD PROJECT Multinational group formed by producers DJ F.R.A.N.K., Andy Jansen, Tone Def, Triple S and singers Vic Krishna and Craig Smart. Their debut hit began as a bootleg of the track *Sunclub* by Fiesta with the vocals of *Summer Jam* by Vic Krishna and Craig Smart. UD stands for Underdog.

	04/10/2003	14	6		SUMMER JAM	Free 2 Air/Kontor 0150795KON
	21/02/2004	19	4		SATURDAY NIGHT	Free 2 Air/Kontor 0152955KON

UFO UK/German heavy metal group formed by Phil Mogg (born 1951, London, vocals), Mick Bolton (guitar), Pete Way (bass) and Andy Parker (drums) as Hocus Pocus, changing their name to UFO in 1969. Michael Schenker (born 10/1/1955, Savstedt, Germany) replaced Bolton in 1974, remaining with the group until 1979 when he rejoined the Scorpions, Paul Chapman being his replacement. They added Paul Raymond (keyboards) in 1977, and disbanded in 1983. Re-forming in 1985 without success, Way and Mogg attempted another revival in 1991.

	05/08/1978	50	4		ONLY YOU CAN ROCK ME	Chrysalis CHS 2241
	27/01/1979	35	6		DOCTOR DOCTOR	Chrysalis CHS 2287
	31/03/1979	48	5		SHOOT SHOOT	Chrysalis CHS 2318
	12/01/1980	36	5		YOUNG BLOOD	Chrysalis CHS 2399
	17/01/1981	41	5		LONELY HEART	Chrysalis CHS 2482
	30/01/1982	62	3		LET IT RAIN	Chrysalis CHS 2576
	19/03/1983	70	3		WHEN IT'S TIME TO ROCK	Chrysalis CHS 2672

U4EA FEATURING BERRI – see **NEW ATLANTIC**

UGLY DUCKLING US production/rap trio formed in Los Angeles, CA in 1993 by Dizzy Dustin, Young Einstein and Andy 'Andycat' Cooper.

	13/10/2001	70	1		A LITTLE SAMBA	XL Recordings XLS 135CD

UGLY KID JOE US rock group formed in California by Whitfield Crane (vocals), Klaus Eichstadt (guitar), Roger Lahr (guitar), Cordell Crockett (bass) and Mark Davis (drums). In 1992 Lahr was replaced by Dave Fortman. Davis left in 1994 and was replaced by Shannon Larkin.

	16/05/1992	3	9		**EVERYTHING ABOUT YOU** Featured in the 1992 film *Wayne's World*	Mercury MER 367
	22/08/1992	28	4		NEIGHBOUR	Mercury MER 374
	31/10/1992	44	2		SO DAMN COOL	Mercury MER 383
	13/03/1993	7	9		**CAT'S IN THE CRADLE**	Mercury MERCD 385
	19/06/1993	39	2		BUSY BEE	Mercury MERCD 389
	08/07/1995	39	2		MILKMAN'S SON	Mercury MERDD 435

UHF US singer (born Richard Melville Hall, 11/9/1966 , New York) who was given the nickname Moby because he is a descendant of Herman Melville, the author of the Captain Ahab whaling story *Moby Dick*. He was later better known as Moby.

	14/12/1991	46	4		UHF/EVERYTHING	XL Recordings XLS 25

TILLMANN UHRMACHER German DJ/producer who also worked with Uwe Wagenknecht, Peter Reis, Misar, George Acosta and Judge Jules.

	23/03/2002	16	3		ON THE RUN	Direction 6721352

U.K. UK group formed in 1977 by Allan Holdsworth (guitar), Eddie Jobson (keyboards/violin), John Wetton (born 12/7/19, Derby, bass/vocals) and Bill Bruford (born 17/5/1948, London, drums). Holsworth and Bruford left after one album, Bruford being replaced by Terry Bozzio. They disbanded in 1979.

	30/06/1979	67	2		NOTHING TO LOSE	Polydor POSP 55

UK Canadian/Spanish vocal/instrumental group formed by Moucho Tamares and De Palma.

	03/08/1996	74	1		SMALL TOWN BOY	Media MCSTD 40049

U.K. APACHI/APACHE UK singer Lafta Wahab.

	01/10/1994	39	3		ORIGINAL NUTTAH **UK APACHI WITH SHY FX** Contains samples of Cypress Hill's *I Ain't Going Out Like That* and the vocal introduction to the 1990 film *Goodfellas*	Sound Of Underground SOUR 008CD
	28/07/2001	63	1		SIGNS **DJ BADMARSH AND SHRI FEATURING UK APACHE**	Outcaste OUT 38CD1

U.K. MIXMASTERS UK producer Nigel Wright who was also responsible for Mirage.

	02/02/1991	23	5		THE NIGHT FEVER MEGAMIX **MIXMASTERS** Features songs from the 1977 film *Saturday Night Fever*	IQ ZB 44339

27/07/1991	43	3		LUCKY 7 MEGAMIX Features songs that were hits for Kylie Minogue	IQ ZB 44731
07/12/1991	14	7		BARE NECESSITIES MEGAMIX Features songs from the 1967 film *The Jungle Book*	Connect ZB 35135

UK PLAYERS UK funk group formed in Stevenage, Hertfordshire by James Ross (guitar/vocals), Phil Bishop (guitar), Sedley Francis (bass), Patrick Seymour (keyboards) and Rusty Jones (drums).

14/05/1983	52	3		LOVE'S GONNA GET YOU	RCA 326

U.K. SUBS UK group formed in London in 1976 by Charlie Harper (born David Charles Perez, 25/4/1944, London, vocals), Nicky Garratt (guitar), Paul Slack (bass) and Pete Davies (drums). Harper also recorded solo.

23/06/1979	26	8		STRANGLEHOLD	Gem GEMS 5
08/09/1979	28	6		TOMORROW'S GIRLS	Gem GEMS 10
01/12/1979	36	7		SHE'S NOT THERE/KICKS EP Tracks on EP: *She's Not There, Kicks, Victim* and *The Same Thing*	Gem GEMS 14
08/03/1980	30	4		WARHEAD	Gem GEMS 23
17/05/1980	32	5		TEENAGE	Gem GEMS 30
25/10/1980	37	4		PARTY IN PARIS	Gem GEMS 42
18/04/1981	41	5		KEEP ON RUNNIN' (TILL YOU BURN)	Gem GEMS 45

UKNY – see JASON NEVINS

TRACEY ULLMAN UK singer (born 30/12/1959, Burham, Buckinghamshire) who first came to prominence in the BBC TV show *Three Of A Kind* with David Copperfield and Lenny Henry. She launched a record career after meeting the wife of Stiff Records' boss. She appeared in a number of films and then relocated to the US where she starred in her own TV series.

19/03/1983	4	11	O	**BREAKAWAY**	Stiff BUY 168
24/09/1983	2	11	O	**THEY DON'T KNOW**	Stiff BUY 180
03/12/1983	8	9		**MOVE OVER DARLING**	Stiff BUY 195
03/03/1984	23	6		MY GUY Accompanying video featured Neil Kinnock, then leader of the Labour Party	Stiff BUY 205
28/07/1984	18	9		SUNGLASSES	Stiff BUY 205
27/10/1984	61	3		HELPLESS	Stiff BUY 211

ULTIMATE KAOS UK R&B vocal group formed in London by Haydon Eshun, Ryan Elliot, Jomo Baxter, Nicky Grant and Jayde Delpratt Spence.

22/10/1994	9	9		**SOME GIRLS**	Wild Card CARDD 12
21/01/1995	17	4		HOOCHIE BOOTY	Wild Card CARDW 14
01/04/1995	23	5		SHOW A LITTLE LOVE	Wild Card CARDW 18
01/07/1995	18	4		RIGHT HERE	Wild Card 5795832
08/03/1997	24	3		CASANOVA	Polydor 5759312
18/07/1998	29	2		CASANOVA Re-issue of Polydor 5759312	Mercury MERCD 505
05/06/1999	52	1		ANYTHING YOU WANT (I'VE GOT IT)	Mercury MERCD 510

ULTRA UK group formed by James Hearn (born 19/6/1976, vocals), Michael Harwood (born 12/12/1975, guitar), Nick Keynes (born 3/5/1974, bass) and Jon O'Mahoney (born 10/8/1974, drums).

18/04/1998	11	7		SAY YOU DO	East West EW 124CD
04/07/1998	16	6		SAY IT ONCE	East West EW 171CD
10/10/1998	28	3		THE RIGHT TIME	East West EW 182CD
16/01/1999	8	6		**RESCUE ME**	East West EW 193CD1

ULTRA HIGH UK singer Michael McLeod.

02/12/1995	36	2		STAY WITH ME	MCA MCSTD 40007
20/07/1996	45	1		ARE YOU READY FOR LOVE	MCA MCSTD 40039

ULTRABEAT UK group formed in Liverpool by Mike Di Scala, Ian Redman and Chris Henry.

19/08/2003	2	14		**PRETTY GREEN EYES**	All Around The World CXGLOBE 281
27/12/2003	12	12		FEELIN' FINE	All Around The World CXGLOBE 320
11/09/2004	23	5		BETTER THAN LIFE	All Around The World CDGLOBE 360

ULTRACYNIC UK vocal/instrumental group formed by Alex Moran, Tim Brennan and Gerard McGrath.

29/08/1992	50	2		NOTHING IS FOREVER	380 PEW 2
19/04/1997	47	1		NOTHING IS FOREVER (REMIX)	All Around The World CDGLOBE 139

ULTRAMARINE UK dance duo formed in London by Paul Hammond (born 12/12/1965, Chelmsford, Essex, bass/keyboards) and Ian Cooper (born 15/8/1966, Derby, guitars/programming). They first recorded in 1989 for the Belgian label Les Disques Du Crepuscule, then Brainiak and Rough Trade, before switching to Blanco Y Negro.

24/07/1993	46	2		KINGDOM	Blanco Y Negro NEG 65CD
29/01/1994	61	1		BAREFOOT (EP) Tracks on EP: *Hooter, The Badger, Urf* and *Happy Land*	Blanco Y Negro NEG 67CD
27/04/1996	65	1		HYMN ULTRAMARINE FEATURING DAVID McALMONT	Blanco Y Negro NEG 87CD

ULTRA-SONIC UK instrumental/production duo formed in 1990 by Rodger Hughes and Mallorca Lee. Lee was later a member of Public Domain.

03/09/1994	75	1		OBSESSION	Clubscene DCSRT 027

❶⁹ Number of weeks single topped the UK chart ↑ Entered the UK chart at #1 ▲⁹ Number of weeks single topped the US chart

835

	DATE	POS	WKS	BPI	SINGLE TITLE	LABEL & NUMBER
	21/09/1996	47	1		DO YOU BELIEVE IN LOVE	Clubscene DCSRT 070

ULTRASOUND UK group formed by Andy 'Tiny' Wood (guitar/vocals), Richard Green (guitar), Vanessa West (bass), Matt Jones (keyboards/programming) and Andy Pearce (drums).

	DATE	POS	WKS	BPI	SINGLE TITLE	LABEL & NUMBER
	07/03/1998	68	1		BEST WISHES	Nude NUD 33CD
	13/06/1998	30	2		STAY YOUNG	Nude NUD 35CD1
	10/04/1999	39	2		FLOODLIT WORLD	Nude NUD 41CD1

ULTRAVOX UK group formed in 1973 by John Foxx and Chris Cross (born Christopher St John, 14/7/1952, London, bass/synthesiser), with early recruits Warren Cann (born 20/5/1952, Victoria, Canada, drums) and Steve Shears (guitar) as Tiger Lily. Billy Currie (born 1/4/1952, Huddersfield, synthesiser/piano) joined prior to their debut recording, with the group's name changed to Ultravox in 1976. Foxx went solo in 1979 and ex-Slik and Visage member Midge Ure (born 10/10/1953, Gambusland, Scotland, guitar/vocals) replaced him. They moved from Island to Chrysalis in 1980, where later Ure pursued a solo career. Ure was one of the prime movers behind Band Aid with Bob Geldof. Tony Fenneller was recruited as lead singer in 1993.

	DATE	POS	WKS	BPI	SINGLE TITLE	LABEL & NUMBER
	05/07/1980	29	11		SLEEPWALK	Chrysalis CHS 2441
	18/10/1980	57	4		PASSING STRANGERS	Chrysalis CHS 2457
	17/01/1981	2	14	●	**VIENNA**	Chrysalis CHS 2481
	28/03/1981	33	4		SLOW MOTION	Island WIP 6691
	06/06/1981	8	10	○	**ALL STOOD STILL**	Chrysalis CHS 2522
	22/08/1981	14	8		THE THIN WALL	Chrysalis CHS 2540
	07/11/1981	16	12		THE VOICE	Chrysalis CHS 2559
	25/09/1982	12	9		REAP THE WILD WIND	Chrysalis CHS 2639
	27/11/1982	11	11	○	HYMN	Chrysalis CHS 2657
	19/03/1983	15	6		VISIONS IN BLUE	Chrysalis CHS 2676
	04/06/1983	18	7		WE CAME TO DANCE	Chrysalis VOX 1
	11/02/1984	27	6		ONE SMALL DAY	Chrysalis VOX 2
	19/05/1984	3	11		**DANCING WITH TEARS IN MY EYES**	Chrysalis UV 1
	07/07/1984	22	7		LAMENT	Chrysalis UV 2
	20/10/1984	12	9		LOVE'S GREAT ADVENTURE	Chrysalis UV 3
	27/09/1986	31	4		SAME OLD STORY	Chrysalis UV 4
	22/11/1986	30	5		ALL FALL DOWN	Chrysalis UV 5
	06/02/1993	13	4		VIENNA Re-issue of Chrysalis CHS 2481	Chrysalis CDCHSS 3936

UMBOZA UK instrumental/production duo Stuart Crichton and Bryan Chamberlyn. Crichton had previously been a member of Mukkaa and Deep Piece.

	DATE	POS	WKS	BPI	SINGLE TITLE	LABEL & NUMBER
	23/09/1995	19	4		CRY INDIA Contains a sample of Lionel Richie's *All Night Long*	Positiva CDTIV 43
	20/07/1996	14	5		SUNSHINE Contains a sample of Gipsy King's *Bomboleo*	Positiva CDTIV 47

PIERO UMILIANI Italian orchestra/chorus leader (born 1926, Florence) whose debut single originally charted in the US in 1969 and was revived after a version was featured in TV programme *The Muppet Show*. He died from a heart attack on 23/2/2001.

	DATE	POS	WKS	BPI	SINGLE TITLE	LABEL & NUMBER
	30/04/1977	8	8		**MAH NA MAH NA**	EMI International INT 530

UN-CUT UK dance group formed by Darren Lewis and 2D with singer Jenna G.

	DATE	POS	WKS	BPI	SINGLE TITLE	LABEL & NUMBER
	29/03/2003	26	3		MIDNIGHT Contains a sample of Shirley Bassey's *Light My Fire*	WEA 364CD2
	28/06/2003	63	1		FALLIN'	WEA 368CD

UNATION UK vocal/instrumental group formed by Damien Johnson, Joanna Nye and Steve Kane.

	DATE	POS	WKS	BPI	SINGLE TITLE	LABEL & NUMBER
	05/06/1993	42	2		HIGHER AND HIGHER	MCA MCSTD 1773
	07/08/1993	75	1		DO YOU BELIEVE IN LOVE	MCA MCSTD 1796

UNBELIEVABLE TRUTH UK group with Andy Yorke (guitar/vocals), Jason Moulster (bass) and Nigel Powell (drums). Yorke is the brother of Radiohead's Thom Yorke.

	DATE	POS	WKS	BPI	SINGLE TITLE	LABEL & NUMBER
	14/02/1998	38	2		HIGHER THAN REASON	Virgin VSCDT 1676
	09/05/1998	39	2		SOLVED	Virgin VSCDT 1684
	18/07/1998	46	1		SETTLE DOWN/DUNE SEA	Virgin VSCDT 1697

UNCANNY ALLIANCE US vocal/instrumental duo formed in Queens, NYC by Yvette Mustique and Brinsley Evans.

	DATE	POS	WKS	BPI	SINGLE TITLE	LABEL & NUMBER
	19/12/1992	39	5		I GOT MY EDUCATION	A&M AM 0128

UNCLE KRACKER US DJ/rapper (born Matthew Shafer, 6/6/1974, Mount Clemens, MI) who is also a member of Twisted Brown Trucker, Kid Rock's backing group.

	DATE	POS	WKS	BPI	SINGLE TITLE	LABEL & NUMBER
	08/09/2001	3	18		**FOLLOW ME**	Atlantic AT 0108CD

UNCLE SAM US singer (born Sam Turner, Detroit, MI) who was signed to Boyz II Men's label Stonecreek. His debut hit was written and produced by Wanya Morris.

	DATE	POS	WKS	BPI	SINGLE TITLE	LABEL & NUMBER
	16/05/1998	30	2		I DON'T EVER WANT TO SEE YOU AGAIN	Epic 6656382

UNDERCOVER UK group formed by John Matthews (vocals), John Jules (bass) and Steve McCutcheon (keyboards). McCutcheon later linked with Wayne Hector to form a successful songwriting partnership.

15/08/1992 . . . . . 2 . . . . . 14	**BAKER STREET** . . . . PWL International PWL 239
14/11/1992 . . . . . 5 . . . . . . 11	**NEVER LET HER SLIP AWAY** . . . . PWL International PWL 255
06/02/1993 . . . . . 28 . . . . 3	I WANNA STAY WITH YOU . . . . PWL International PWL 258
14/08/1993 . . . . . 62 . . . . . 1	LOVESICK **UNDERCOVER FEATURING JOHN MATTHEWS** . . . . PWL International PWCD 271
03/07/2004 . . . . . 49 . . . . . 1	VIVA ENGLAND Theme to the TV comedy series *Only Fools And Horses* with re-written lyrics for the 2004 Euro Championships . . . .
	. . . . MCS MCSRECS1

UNDERTAKERS UK group formed in Wallasey, Merseyside in 1961 by Jimmy McManus (vocals), Chris Huston (guitar), Geoff Nugent (guitar), Brian 'Boots' Jones (saxophone), Dave 'Mushy' Cooper (bass) and Bob Evans (drums), originally known as The Vegas Five. They changed their name after a local newspaper wrongly advertised them as The Undertakers. By 1962 the line-up consisted of Jones, Huston, Nugent, Jackie Lomax (bass) and Bugs Pemberton (drums). They disbanded in 1965.

09/04/1964 . . . . . 49 . . . . . . 1	JUST A LITTLE BIT . . . . Pye 7N 15607

UNDERTONES UK group formed in Londonderry, Northern Ireland in 1975 by Feargal Sharkey (born 13/8/1958, Londonderry, vocals) and John O'Neill (born 26/8/1957, Londonderry, guitar) and including Damian 'Dee' O'Neill (born 15/1/1961, Belfast, guitar), Michael Bradley (born 13/8/1959, Londonderry, bass) and Billy Doherty (drums). They released their debut single on local independent label Good Vibrations. Radio exposure on John Peel's show attracted major record company interest, with the manager-less group negotiating a deal with Sire and re-issuing *Teenage Kicks*. They launched the Ardeck label in 1981 but disbanded in 1983, with Sharkey going solo (he was the first signing to Madness' Zarjazz label). The O'Neill brothers later formed That Petrol Emotion.

21/10/1978 . . . . . 31 . . . . . 6	TEENAGE KICKS . . . . Sire SIR 4007
03/02/1979 . . . . . 57 . . . . . 4	GET OVER YOU . . . . Sire SIR 4010
28/04/1979 . . . . . 16 . . . . . 10	JIMMY JIMMY . . . . Sire SIR 4015
21/07/1979 . . . . . 34 . . . . . 6	HERE COMES THE SUMMER . . . . Sire SIR 4022
20/10/1979 . . . . . 32 . . . . . 6	YOU'VE GOT MY NUMBER (WHY DON'T YOU USE IT) . . . . Sire SIR 4024
05/04/1980 . . . . . 9 . . . . . 10	**MY PERFECT COUSIN** . . . . Sire SIR 4038
05/07/1980 . . . . . 11 . . . . . 9	WEDNESDAY WEEK . . . . Sire SIR 4042
02/05/1981 . . . . . 18 . . . . . 9	IT'S GOING TO HAPPEN! . . . . Ardeck ARDS 8
25/07/1981 . . . . . 41 . . . . . 5	JULIE OCEAN . . . . Ardeck ARDS 9
09/07/1983 . . . . . 60 . . . . . 2	TEENAGE KICKS Re-issue of Sire SIR 4007 . . . . Ardeck ARDS 1

UNDERWORLD UK group formed in Romford, Essex in the late 1980s by Karl Hyde (born 10/5/1957, Worcester, guitar/vocals), Alfie Thomas, Rick Smith (born 25/5/1959, Ammanford, Wales, keyboards), Baz Allen and John Warwicker. By 1992 the band comprised Hyde, Smith and Darren Emerson (born 3/4/1971, Hornchurch, Essex, keyboards). Emerson left in April 2000, subsequently recording with Sasha.

18/12/1993 . . . . . 63 . . . . . 1	SPIKEE/DOGMAN GO WOOF . . . . Junior Boy's Own JBO 17CD
25/06/1994 . . . . . 57 . . . . . 1	DARK AND LONG . . . . Junior Boy's Own JBO 19CDS
13/05/1995 . . . . . 52 . . . . . 2	BORN SLIPPY . . . . Junior Boy's Own JBO 29CDS
18/05/1996 . . . . . 24 . . . . . 1	PEARL'S GIRL Featured in the 1997 film *The Saint* . . . . Junior Boy's Own JBO 38CDS1
13/07/1996 . . . 2 . . . . 21 . . . . . . ●	**BORN SLIPPY (REMIX)** Featured in the 1996 film *Trainspotting* . . . . Junior Boy's Own JBO 44CDS1
09/11/1996 . . . . . 22 . . . . . 3	PEARL'S GIRL Re-issue of Junior Boy's Own JBO 38CDS1 . . . . Junior Boy's Own JBO 45CDS1
27/03/1999 . . . . . 12 . . . . . 4	PUSH UPSTAIRS . . . . Junior Boy's Own JBO 5006173
05/06/1999 . . . . . 21 . . . . . 2	JUMBO . . . . JBO 5007193
28/08/1999 . . . . . 17 . . . . . 3	KING OF SNAKE . . . . JBO 5008798
02/09/2000 . . . . . 24 . . . . . 2	COWGIRL . . . . JBO 5012518
14/09/2002 . . . . . 12 . . . . . 4	TWO MONTHS OFF . . . . JBO 5020098
01/02/2003 . . . . . 34 . . . . . 1	DINOSAUR ADVENTURE 3D . . . . JBO 05020528
08/11/2003 . . . . . 27 . . . . . 3	BORN SLIPPY NUXX . . . . JBO 5024703

UNDISPUTED TRUTH US R&B vocal group formed in 1970 by Joe Harris, Billie Calvin and Brenda Evans. By 1973 the line-up consisted of Harris, Tyrone Berkeley, Tyrone Douglas, Virginia McDonald and Calvin Stevens. The group were down to a trio again by 1976, featuring Harris, Berkeley and Taka Boom.

22/01/1977 . . . . . 43 . . . . . . 4	YOU + ME = LOVE . . . . Warner Brothers K 16804

U96 German producer Alex Christiansen.

29/08/1992 . . . . . 18 . . . . . 5	DAS BOOT Featured in the 1992 film *Das Boot* . . . . M&G MAGS 28
04/06/1994 . . . . . 44 . . . . . 1	INSIDE YOUR DREAMS . . . . Logic 74321209722
29/06/1996 . . . . . 70 . . . . . 1	CLUB BIZARRE . . . . Urban 5750152

UNION FEATURING THE ENGLAND WORLD CUP SQUAD UK/Dutch group and the 1991 England rugby team. Following the successes of football teams with cup final records, Union and the England team recorded the traditional rugby song *Swing Low* as their anthem for the 1991 World Cup held in England.

12/10/1991 . . . . . 16 . . . . . 7	SWING LOW (RUN WITH THE BALL) . . . . Columbia 6575317

UNION GAP FEATURING GARY PUCKETT US singer/guitarist Gary Puckett (born 17/10/1942, Hibbing, MN) formed Union Gap in San Diego, CA in 1967, taking the name from a town in Washington. Other members included Kerry Chater (bass), Paul Whitebread (drums), Dwight Bement (saxophone) and Gary Withem (keyboards).

17/04/1968 . . . . ❶4 . . . . . 17	**YOUNG GIRL** . . . . CBS 3365
07/08/1968 . . . . . 5 . . . . . 16	**LADY WILLPOWER** . . . . CBS 3551
28/08/1968 . . . . . 48 . . . . . 1	WOMAN WOMAN . . . . CBS 3110
15/06/1974 . . . . . 6 . . . . 13 . . . . . ○	**YOUNG GIRL** **GARY PUCKETT AND THE UNION GAP** Re-issue of CBS 3365 . . . . CBS 8202

❶9 Number of weeks single topped the UK chart ↑ Entered the UK chart at #1 ▲9 Number of weeks single topped the US chart

837

UNIQUE US studio group assembled in New York in 1982 by producer Deems J Smith.

10/09/1983	27	7	WHAT I GOT IS WHAT YOU NEED	Prelude A 3707

UNIQUE 3 UK rap group formed by Patrick Cargill and DJs Edzy and Delroy.

04/11/1989	61	3	THE THEME	10 TEN 285
14/04/1990	29	5	MUSICAL MELODY/WEIGHT FOR THE BASS	10 TEN 298
10/11/1990	41	3	RHYTHM TAKES CONTROL UNIQUE 3 FEATURING KARIN	10 TEN 327
16/11/1991	74	1	NO MORE	10 TEN 387

UNIT FOUR PLUS TWO UK pop sextet with Rod Garwood (born 27/3/1944, bass), Hugh Halliday (born 12/12/1944, drums), Howard Lubin (piano), David 'Buster' Miekle (born 1/3/1942, guitar/vocals), Pete Moules (born 14/10/1944, guitar/banjo/autoharp/vocals) and Tommy Moeller (born 23/2/1945, lead vocals).

13/02/1964	48	2	GREEN FIELDS	Decca F 11821
25/02/1965	●[1]	15	CONCRETE AND CLAY Featured in the 1998 film *Rushmore*	Decca F 12071
13/05/1965	14	11	YOU'VE NEVER BEEN IN LOVE LIKE THIS BEFORE	Decca F 12144
17/03/1966	49	1	BABY NEVER SAY GOODBYE	Decca F 12333

UNITED CITIZEN FEDERATION FEATURING SARAH BRIGHTMAN UK production group formed by Frank Petersen with singer Sarah Brightman.

14/02/1998	58	1	STARSHIP TROOPERS	Coalition COLA 040CD

UNITED COLOURS OF SOUND – see UB40

UNITED KINGDOM SYMPHONY UK orchestra.

27/07/1985	68	4	SHADES (THEME FROM THE CROWN PAINT TELEVISION COMMERCIAL)	Food For Thought YUM 108

UNITING NATIONS UK duo Darren 'Daz' Sampson (ex-Rikki & Daz) and Paul Keenan.

04/12/2004	12	4+	OUT OF TOUCH	Gusto CDGUS13

UNITONE – see LAUREL AITKEN AND THE UNITONE

UNITONE ROCKERS FEATURING STEEL UK vocal/instrumental group who later worked with former Sweet singer Brian Connolly.

26/06/1993	60	1	CHILDREN OF THE REVOLUTION	The Hit Label HLC 4

UNITY UK vocal/instrumental group formed by Robert Manley and Paul Witts.

31/08/1991	64	2	UNITY	Cardiac CNY 6

UNIVERSAL Australian vocal trio.

02/08/1997	19	4	ROCK ME GOOD	London LONCD 397
18/10/1997	33	2	MAKE IT WITH YOU	London LONCD 404

UNIVERSAL PROJECT – see ED RUSH AND OPTICAL/UNIVERSAL PROJECT

UNJUSTIFIED ANCIENTS OF M U – see 1300 DRUMS FEATURING THE UNJUSTIFIED ANCIENTS OF M U

UNKLE UK DJ/production duo Josh Davis and James Lavelle.

20/02/1999	8	6	BE THERE UNKLE FEATURING IAN BROWN	Mo Wax MW 108CD1
17/03/2001	66	1	NARCO TOURISTS SLAM VS UNKLE	Soma 100CD
06/09/2003	31	2	EYE FOR AN EYE Contains samples of The Undisputed Truth's *Ball Of Confusion* and James Asher's *Fairground Music*.	Mo Wax/Island CIDX 826
15/11/2003	44	2	IN A STATE	Mo Wax/Island CID 839
27/11/2004	40	2	REIGN UNKLE FEATURING IAN BROWN	Mo Wax GUSIN007CDS

UNO CLIO FEATURING MARTINE McCUTCHEON UK instrumental group formed by Paul Woods and Gareth Cooke with singer/actress Martine McCutcheon.

18/11/1995	62	1	ARE YOU MAN ENOUGH	Avex UK AVEXCD 14

UNO MAS UK production duo Simon Law and Lee Hambin. Their name is Spanish for 'one more'.

06/04/2002	55	1	I WILL FOLLOW	Defected DFECT 47CDS

UNTOUCHABLES US group formed by Chuck Askerneese (vocals), Clyde Grimes (guitar/vocals), Derek Breakfield (bass), Brewster (keyboards) and various drummers.

06/04/1985	26	11	FREE YOURSELF	Stiff BUY 221
27/07/1985	59	5	I SPY FOR THE FBI	Stiff BUY 227

UP YER RONSON FEATURING MARY PEARCE UK vocal/instrumental group formed by Andy Wood and Richie Malone, fronted by singer Mary Pearce.

05/08/1995	27	3	LOST IN LOVE	Hi-Life 5795572

30/03/1996	27	2		ARE YOU GONNA BE THERE?	Hi-Life 5763272
19/04/1997	32	2		I WILL BE RELEASED	Hi-Life 5737352

PHIL UPCHURCH COMBO
US R&B/jazz guitarist (born 19/7/1941, Chicago, IL) who was a house guitarist with Chess Records and also formed his own combo, scoring a US million seller with his one hit single. As a much-in-demand session guitarist he has recorded with Michael Jackson, The Crusaders and Chaka Khan.

05/05/1966	39	2		YOU CAN'T SIT DOWN	Sue WI 4005

UPSETTERS
Jamaican reggae group formed by Lee Perry (born 28/3/1936, Hanover), Jackie Robinson, Val Bennett, Glenroy Adams, Winston Wright (organ), Aston 'Family Man' Barrett, Boris Gardiner (bass), Carlton Barrett, Lloyd 'Tinleg' Adams, Mikey 'Boo' Richards, Sly Dunbar, Hux Brown (guitar) and Clevie Browne (drums).

04/10/1969	5	15		**RETURN OF DJANGO/DOLLAR IN THE TEETH**	Upsetter US 301

UPSIDE DOWN
UK vocal group formed by Giles Upton, Richard Micaleff, Chris Leng and Jamie Browne. Their formation and recording debut was the subject of a TV documentary, but by 1997 the label had folded, the group was without a deal and couldn't use the name Upside Down.

20/01/1996	11	7		CHANGE YOUR MIND	World CDWORLD 1A
13/04/1996	18	4		EVERY TIME I FALL IN LOVE	World CDWORLD 2A
29/06/1996	19	3		NEVER FOUND A LOVE LIKE THIS BEFORE	World CDWORLD 3A
23/11/1996	27	2		IF YOU LEAVE ME NOW	World CDWORLD 4A

URBAN ALL STARS
UK producer/instrumentalist (born Quentin 'Norman' Cook, 31/7/1963, Brighton) recording with US vocal/instrumental groups.

27/08/1988	64	2		IT BEGAN IN AFRICA	Urban URB 23

URBAN BLUES PROJECT PRESENT MICHAEL PROCTER
US vocal/instrumental group formed by Marc Pomeroy and Brian Tappert with Michael Procter.

10/08/1996	55	1		LOVE DON'T LIVE	AM:PM 5817932

URBAN COOKIE COLLECTIVE
UK vocal/instrumental group formed by Rohan Heath, Diane Charlemagne, Marty and DJ Pete Hayes.

10/07/1993	2	16	O	**THE KEY THE SECRET**	Pulse 8 CDLOSE 48
13/11/1993	5	9		**FEELS LIKE HEAVEN**	Pulse 8 CDLOSE 55
19/02/1994	18	4		SAIL AWAY	Pulse 8 CDLOSE 56
23/04/1994	31	3		HIGH ON A HAPPY VIBE	Pulse 8 CDLOSE 60
15/10/1994	56	1		BRING IT ON HOME	Pulse 8 CDLOSE 73
27/05/1995	59	1		SPEND THE DAY	Pulse 8 CDLOSE 85
09/09/1995	67	1		REST OF MY LOVE	Pulse 8 CDLOSE 93
16/12/1995	68	1		SO BEAUTIFUL	Pulse 8 CDLOSE 100
24/08/1996	52	1		THE KEY THE SECRET (REMIX) UCC	Pulse 8 CDLOSE 109

URBAN DISCHARGE FEATURING SHE
US vocal/instrumental group formed by Jim Dyke and Junior Vasquez.

27/01/1996	51	1		WANNA DROP A HOUSE (ON THAT BITCH)	MCA MCSTD 40020

URBAN HYPE
UK production/instrumental group formed by Robert Dibden and Mark Chitty.

11/07/1992	6	8		**A TRIP TO TRUMPTON** Contains a sample from the BBC children's TV show *Trumpton*	Faze 2 FAZE 5
17/10/1992	67	1		THE FEELING	Faze 2 FAZE 10
09/01/1993	57	3		LIVING IN A FANTASY	Faze 2 CDFAZE 13

URBAN SHAKEDOWN
UK/Italian production group formed by Gavin King and Claudio Guissani. Guissani later recorded as Terra Firma.

27/06/1992	23	5		SOME JUSTICE Contains a sample of CeCe Rogers' *Someday*	Urban Shakedown URBST 1
12/09/1992	59	2		BASS SHAKE URBAN SHAKEDOWN FEATURING MICKEY FINN	Urban Shakedown URBST 2
10/06/1995	49	1		SOME JUSTICE URBAN SHAKEDOWN FEATURING D BO GENERAL Re-recording	Urban Shakedown URBCD 3

URBAN SOUL
UK/US vocal/production group fronted by Roland Clark.

30/03/1991	60	4		ALRIGHT	Cooltempo COOL 231
21/09/1991	43	3		ALRIGHT (REMIX)	Cooltempo COOL 244
28/03/1992	41	3		ALWAYS	Cooltempo COOL 251
13/06/1998	75	1		LOVE IS SO NICE	VC Recordings VCRD 33

URBAN SPECIES
UK rap group formed in London in the 1980s by Mintos (Peter Akinrinola) and DJ Renegade (Winston Small), joined later by Dr Slim (Rodney Green).

12/02/1994	35	4		SPIRITUAL LOVE	Talkin Loud TLKCD 45
23/04/1994	40	3		BROTHER	Talkin Loud TLKCD 47
20/08/1994	47	2		LISTEN URBAN SPECIES FEATURING MC SOLAAR	Talkin Loud TLKCD 50
06/03/1999	56	1		BLANKET URBAN SPECIES FEATURING IMOGEN HEAP	Talkin Loud TLDD 39

❶⁹ Number of weeks single topped the UK chart ↑ Entered the UK chart at #1 ▲⁹ Number of weeks single topped the US chart

839

MIDGE URE

MIDGE URE UK singer (born 10/10/1953, Gambusland, Scotland) who was a member of Slik and Visage and formed the Rich Kids with ex-Sex Pistol member Glen Matlock before joining Ultravox in 1979. He ran his own solo career in tandem from 1982 and co-wrote (with Bob Geldof) the Band Aid single *Do They Know It's Christmas?* He was subsequently active in staging Live Aid in 1985.

DATE	POS	WKS	BPI	SINGLE TITLE	LABEL & NUMBER
12/06/1982	9	10		NO REGRETS	Chrysalis CHS 2618
09/07/1983	39	4		AFTER A FASHION MIDGE URE AND MICK KARN	Musicfest FEST 1
14/09/1985	●1	11	O	IF I WAS	Chrysalis URE 1
16/11/1985	28	4		THAT CERTAIN SMILE	Chrysalis URE 2
08/02/1986	46	3		WASTELANDS	Chrysalis URE 3
07/06/1986	27	8		CALL OF THE WILD	Chrysalis URE 4
20/08/1988	49	4		ANSWERS TO NOTHING	Chrysalis URE 5
19/11/1988	55	4		DEAR GOD	Chrysalis URE 6
17/08/1991	17	7		COLD COLD HEART	Arista 114555
25/05/1996	70	1		BREATHE	Arista 74321371172

URGE OVERKILL

URGE OVERKILL US group formed in Chicago, IL in 1986 by National 'Nash' Kato (guitar/vocals), Blackie 'Black Caesar' Onassis (born Johnny Rowan, drums/vocals) and Eddie 'King' Roeser (bass/vocals). They took their name from a Funkadelic song.

DATE	POS	WKS	BPI	SINGLE TITLE	LABEL & NUMBER
21/08/1993	67	1		SISTER HAVANA	Geffen GFSTD 51
16/10/1993	61	1		POSITIVE BLEEDING	Geffen GFSTD 57
19/11/1994	37	4		GIRL, YOU'LL BE A WOMAN SOON Featured in the 1994 film *Pulp Fiction*	MCA MCSTD 2024

URUSEI YATSURA

URUSEI YATSURA UK group formed by Graham Kemp (born 3/12/1968, guitar/vocals), Fergus Lawrie (born 23/11/1968, guitar/vocals), Elaine Graham (born 1970, bass) and Ian Graham (born 19/10/1972, drums).

DATE	POS	WKS	BPI	SINGLE TITLE	LABEL & NUMBER
22/02/1997	64	1		STRATEGIC HAMLETS	Che 67CD
28/06/1997	58	1		FAKE FUR	Che 70CD
21/02/1998	40	1		HELLO TIGER	Che 75CD1
06/06/1998	63	1		SLAIN BY ELF	Che 80CD1

USA FOR AFRICA

USA FOR AFRICA Multinational group inspired by the success of Band Aid. Veteran singer Harry Belafonte put together a US version with a song written by Lionel Richie and Michael Jackson, produced by Quincy Jones and released as USA For Africa (which stood for United Support of Artists) and featuring (in order) Lionel Richie, Stevie Wonder, Paul Simon, Kenny Rogers, James Ingram, Tina Turner, Billy Joel, Michael Jackson, Diana Ross, Dionne Warwick, Willie Nelson, Al Jarreau, Bruce Springsteen, Kenny Loggins, Steve Perry, Daryl Hall, Huey Lewis, Cyndi Lauper, Kim Carnes, Bob Dylan and Ray Charles.

DATE	POS	WKS	BPI	SINGLE TITLE	LABEL & NUMBER
13/04/1985	●2	9	O	WE ARE THE WORLD ▲4 1985 Grammy Awards for Record of the Year and Best Pop Vocal Performance by a Group, Song of the Year for writers Michael Jackson and Lionel Richie, and Best Video Short Form with *We Are The World: The Video Event*. Total worldwide sales exceed 7 million	CBS USAID 1

USED

USED US rock group formed in Orem, UT by Bert McCracken (vocals), Quinn Allman (guitar), Jeph Howard (bass) and Branden Steinckert (drums).

DATE	POS	WKS	BPI	SINGLE TITLE	LABEL & NUMBER
22/03/2003	52	1		THE TASTE OF INK	Reprise W 601CD

USHER

USHER US singer (born Usher Raymond, 14/10/1978, Chattanooga, TN) who was discovered by LA Reid and Babyface and began his recording career in 1994 aged fifteen. His *8701* album, released in July 2001, was to have been issued six months earlier as *All About U* but was withdrawn after pre-release copies became available on the internet. He has won MOBO Awards for Best Rhythm & Blues Act in 2001 and 2004, and Best Album for *8701* in 2001. His two Grammies include the 2002 Award for Best Male Rhythm & Blues Vocal Performance for *U Don't Have To Call*. He was named Best Male Artist at the 2004 MTV Europe Music Awards, while *Confessions* was named Best Album.

DATE	POS	WKS	BPI	SINGLE TITLE	LABEL & NUMBER
18/03/1995	70	1		THINK OF YOU Contains a sample of Ronnie Laws' *Tidal Wave* and features the uncredited contributions of Biz Marks and Faith Evans	LaFace 74321269252
31/01/1998	●1	13	O	YOU MAKE ME WANNA... ↑	LaFace 74321560652
02/05/1998	24	5		NICE & SLOW ▲2 Features the uncredited contribution of Jagged Edge	LaFace 74321579102
03/02/2001	2	9		POP YA COLLAR	LaFace 74321828692
07/07/2001	3	9		U REMIND ME ▲4 2001 Grammy Award for Best Male Rhythm & Blues Vocal Performance	LaFace 74321863382
20/10/2001	5	8		U GOT IT BAD ▲6 Featured in the 2002 film *The Sweetest Thing*	LaFace 74321898552
20/04/2002	16	6		U TURN	LaFace 74321934092
10/08/2002	4	11		I NEED A GIRL (PART ONE) P DIDDY FEATURING USHER AND LOON	Puff Daddy 74321947242
27/03/2004	●1	14		YEAH ↑ ▲12 USHER FEATURING LIL' JON AND LUDACRIS	Arista 82876606012
10/07/2004	●2	12		BURN ↑ ▲8	LaFace 82876624362
13/11/2004	5	7+		CONFESSIONS PART II/MY BOO ●2/●6 Both sides of this release topped the US charts. *My Boo* features the uncredited contribution of Alica Keys	LaFace 82876655292

US3

US3 UK duo Mel Simpson (keyboards) and Geoff Wilkinson (samples). They first linked on another jazz sample experiment *And The Band Played Boogie* that was released on Coldcut's Ninja Tune label. It came to the attention of Blue Note Records since most of the samples came from their repertoire, and the pair were invited to produce a legitimate version with access to the entire catalogue. The resulting album featured rappers Tukka Yoot, Kobie Powell and Rahsaan and jazz musicians Gerald Presencer, Dennisa Rollins, Tony Remy and Steve Williamson.

DATE	POS	WKS	BPI	SINGLE TITLE	LABEL & NUMBER
10/07/1993	34	6		RIDDIM US3 FEATURING TUKKA YOOT	Blue Note CDCL 686
25/09/1993	23	5		CANTALOOP US3 FEATURING RAHSAAN Contains samples of Herbie Hancock's *Cantaloupe Island* and The Art Blakey Quintet's *A Night In Birdland, Volume 1*. Featured in the 1993 film *Super Mario Bros*	Blue Note CDCL 696

O Silver disc ● Gold disc ✪ Platinum disc (additional platinum units are indicated by a figure following the symbol) ◉ Singles released prior to 1973 that are known to have sold over 1 million copies in the UK

28/05/1994	52	2		I GOT IT GOIN' ON US3 FEATURING KOBIE POWELL AND RAHSAAN	Blue Note CDCL 708
01/03/1997	38	1		COME ON EVERYBODY (GET DOWN)	Blue Note CDCL 784

USURA Italian vocal/instrumental group assembled by Giacomo Maiolini, Walter Cremonini, Michele Comis, Claudio Varaola, Elisa Spreafichi and C Calvello.

23/01/1993	7	9		**OPEN YOUR MIND**	Deconstruction 74321128042
10/07/1993	29	3		SWEAT	Deconstruction 74321154602
06/12/1997	21	3		OPEN YOUR MIND (REMIX) U.S.U.R.A.	Malarky MLKD 4

UTAH SAINTS UK production/instrumental duo Jez Willis (born 14/8/1963, Brampton, Cumbria) and Tim Garbutt (born 6/1/1969, London), both previously members of MDMA.

24/08/1991	10	11		**WHAT CAN YOU DO FOR ME** Contains samples of The Eurythmics' *There Must Be An Angel (Playing With My Heart)* and Gwen Guthrie's *Ain't Nothing Goin' On But The Rent*	ffrr F 164
06/06/1992	4	9		**SOMETHING GOOD** Contains a sample of Kate Bush's *Cloudbursting*	ffrr F 187
08/05/1993	8	6		**BELIEVE IN ME** Contains samples of Human League's *Love Action,* Crown Heights Affair's *You Gave Me Love* and Sylvester's *Do You Wanna Funk*	ffrr FCD 209
17/07/1993	25	5		I WANT YOU Contains a sample of Slayer's *War Ensemble*	ffrr FCD 213
25/06/1994	32	2		I STILL THINK OF YOU Featured in the 1994 film *Shopping*	ffrr FCD 225
02/09/1995	42	2		OHIO Contains a sample of Jocelyn Brown's *Somebody Else's Guy*	ffrr FCD 264
05/02/2000	37	2		LOVE SONG Contains a sample of Average White Band's *Pick Up The Pieces*	Echo ECSCD 83
20/05/2000	23	2		FUNKY MUSIC Features the uncredited contribution of Edwin Starr	Echo ECSCX 96

U2 Irish rock group initially formed in school in 1976 by Bono (born Paul Hewson, 10/5/1960, Dublin, vocals), The Edge (born David Evans, 8/8/1961, Wales, guitar), Adam Clayton (born 13/3/1960, Chinnor, Oxfordshire, bass), Larry Mullen Jr (born 31/10/1961, Dublin, drums) and Dick Evans (guitar) as Feedback. The name was changed to the Hype, Evans left to form the Virgin Prunes and there was a final name change to U2. After a talent contest win they signed to CBS Ireland in 1978 (CBS in the UK did not take up their option, with Island snapping them up in 1980 following live dates), and by 1987 they were world stars. Bono subsequently recorded with Clannad and Frank Sinatra, The Edge solo and Clayton and Mullen did film score work in the 1990s. They won the Best International Group Award at the 1988, 1989, 1990, 1998 and 2001 BRIT Awards, and a special award for Best Live Act in 1993, subsequently being awarded the Outstanding Contribution Award at the 2001 ceremony. Fourteen Grammy Awards include Album of the Year and Best Rock Performance by a Group in 1987 for *The Joshua Tree,* Best Rock Performance by a Group in 1992 for *Achtung Baby,* Best Alternative Music Album in 1993 for *Zooropa,* Best Music Video Long Form in 1994 for *Zoo TV – Live From Sydney* and Best Rock Album in 2001 for *All That You Can't Leave Behind.* The group has won two MTV Europe Music Awards – Best Group in 1995 and Best Live Act in 1997 – and Bono was awarded the Free Your Mind Award in 1999 in recognition of his charitable work. The group was inducted into the UK Music Hall of Fame in 2004, one of its first inductees.

08/08/1981	35	6		FIRE	Island WIP 6679
17/10/1981	55	4		GLORIA	Island WIP 6733
03/04/1982	47	4		A CELEBRATION	Island WIP 6770
22/01/1983	10	8		**NEW YEARS DAY**	Island WIP 6848
02/04/1983	18	5		TWO HEARTS BEAT AS ONE	Island IS 109
15/09/1984	3	11		**PRIDE (IN THE NAME OF LOVE)** Dedicated to Martin Luther King	Island IS 202
04/05/1985	6	6		**THE UNFORGETTABLE FIRE**	Island IS 220
28/03/1987	4	11		**WITH OR WITHOUT YOU** ▲³	Island IS 319
06/06/1987	6	11		**I STILL HAVEN'T FOUND WHAT I'M LOOKING FOR** ▲² Featured in the 1999 film *Runaway Bride*	Island IS 328
12/09/1987	4	6		**WHERE THE STREETS HAVE NO NAME** 1988 Grammy Award for Best Performance Music Video	Island IS 340
26/12/1987	48	4		IN GOD'S COUNTRY (IMPORT)	Island 7-99385
01/10/1988	❶¹	8	O	**DESIRE** 1988 Grammy Award for Best Rock Performance by a Group	Island IS 400
17/12/1988	9	6		ANGEL OF HARLEM Tribute to Billie Holiday	Island IS 402
15/04/1989	6	7		**WHEN LOVE COMES TO TOWN** U2 FEATURING BB KING	Island IS 411
17/06/1989	4	6		ALL I WANT IS YOU Featured in the 1994 film *Reality Bites*	Island IS 422
02/11/1991	❶¹	6	O	**THE FLY** ↑	Island IS 500
14/12/1991	13	7		MYSTERIOUS WAYS	Island IS 509
07/03/1992	7	6		**ONE**	Island IS 515
20/06/1992	12	7		EVEN BETTER THAN THE REAL THING	Island IS 525
11/07/1992	8	7		**EVEN BETTER THAN THE REAL THING (REMIX)**	Island REAL U2
05/12/1992	14	8		WHO'S GONNA RIDE YOUR WILD HORSES	Island IS 550
04/12/1993	4	9	O	**STAY (FARAWAY, SO CLOSE)** Featured in the 1994 film *Faraway, So Close.* Listed flip side was *I've Got You Under My Skin* by **FRANK SINATRA WITH BONO**	Island CID 578
17/06/1995	2	14	●	**HOLD ME, THRILL ME, KISS ME, KILL ME** Featured in the 1995 film *Batman Forever*	Atlantic A 7131CD
15/02/1997	❶¹	11	O	**DISCOTHEQUE** ↑	Island CID 649
26/04/1997	3	6		**STARING AT THE SUN**	Island CID 658
02/08/1997	10	5		**LAST NIGHT ON EARTH**	Island CID 664
04/10/1997	7	4		**PLEASE**	Island CIDX 673
20/12/1997	12	6		IF GOD WILL SEND HIS ANGELS Featured in the 1998 film *City Of Angels*	Island CID 684
31/10/1998	3	13	O	**SWEETEST THING** Features the uncredited vocal contribution of Boyzone	Island CID 727
21/10/2000	❶¹	16	O	**BEAUTIFUL DAY** ↑ 2000 Grammy Awards for Record of the Year, Song of the Year (for writers Paul Hewson, David Evans, Adam Clayton and Larry Mullen) and Best Rock Group Performance with Vocal. The track was subsequently used by ITV for their *Premiership* programme	Island CIDX 766
10/02/2001	2	8		**STUCK IN A MOMENT YOU CAN'T GET OUT OF** 2001 Grammy Award for Best Pop Performance by a Duo or Group with Vocal	Island CIDX 770

❶⁹ Number of weeks single topped the UK chart   ↑ Entered the UK chart at #1   ▲⁹ Number of weeks single topped the US chart

841

	DATE	POS	WKS	BPI	SINGLE TITLE	LABEL & NUMBER
	02/06/2001	15	5		NEW YEAR'S DUB MUSIQUE VS U2	Serious SERRO 030CD
	28/07/2001	3	8		ELEVATION Featured in the 2001 film *Lara Croft: Tomb Raider*. 2001 Grammy Award for Best Rock Performance by a Duo or Group with Vocal	Island CIDX 780
	01/12/2001	5	8		WALK ON 2001 Grammy Award for Record of the Year	Island CIDX 788
	02/11/2002	5	13		ELECTRICAL STORM	Island CIDX 808
	07/02/2004	●²	12		TAKE ME TO THE CLOUDS ABOVE ↑ LMC VS U2 This is effectively two songs: the melody of U2's *With Or Without You* and the lyrics to Whitney Houston's *How Will I Know*	All Around The World CXGLOBE 313
	20/11/2004	●¹	6+		VERTIGO ↑	Island CIDX 878

○ Silver disc ● Gold disc ✪ Platinum disc (additional platinum units are indicated by a figure following the symbol) ◎ Singles released prior to 1973 that are known to have sold over 1 million copies in the UK

V UK vocal group formed by Leon Pisani, Antony Brant, Mark Harle, Kevin McDaid and Aaron Buckingham.

05/06/2004	6	5	**BLOOD SWEAT & TEARS** . . . . Universal MCSXD 40362
21/08/2004	5	6	**HIP TO HIP/CAN YOU FEEL IT** . . . . Universal MCSXD 40374
20/11/2004	12	4	YOU STOOD UP . . . . Universal MCSXD 40388

STEVIE V – see ADVENTURES OF STEVIE V

VERNA V – see HELIOTROPIC FEATURING VERNA V

V-BIRDS UK animated cartoon group formed by Bling (who was aged seventeen at their debut hit and changes her name every year), Wow (aged eighteen), Boom (aged sixteen) and D'Lin (aged fifteen). The characters were designed by Ali Campbell (son of the UB40 singer of the same name) and Dann Hanks and have their own series on the Cartoon Network.

03/05/2003	21	3	VIRTUALITY . . . . Liberty CDVIRT001

VAGABONDS – see JIMMY JAMES AND THE VAGABONDS

HOLLY VALANCE Australian singer (born Holly Vukadinovic, 11/5/1983, Melbourne) who first came to prominence as an actress, starring in *Neighbours* as Felicity 'Flick' Scully. Her debut hit was an English re-write of a Turkish hit by Tarkan.

11/05/2002	❶1	16	○ **KISS KISS** ↑ . . . . London LONCD 464
12/10/2002	2	14	**DOWN BOY** . . . . London LONCD 469
21/12/2002	16	9	**NAUGHTY GIRL** . . . . London LONCD 472
08/11/2003	8	10	**STATE OF MIND** . . . . London LONCD 482

RICKY VALANCE UK singer (born David Spencer, 1940, Ynysddu, Wales) who recorded a cover version of Ray Peterson's huge US 'death disc' hit after Peterson's label RCA decided against a UK release because of its content. The BBC banned Valence's version too, but plays from the mainland Europe-based Radio Luxembourg ensured its success.

25/08/1960	❶3	16	**TELL LAURA I LOVE HER** . . . . Columbia DB 4493

RITCHIE VALENS US singer (born Richard Steve Valenzuela, 13/5/1941, Pacoima, CA) who began his career with a home-made guitar. His record debut was in 1958. He scored a US top five hit with *Donna* before being killed in the plane crash that also claimed the lives of Buddy Holly and the Big Bopper on 3/2/1959. (It was later reported that the crash was due to pilot error: after a successful take-off, pilot Roger Peterson experienced vertigo and flew straight into the ground.) The 1987 film *La Bamba* was based on Valens' life. He was inducted into the Rock & Roll Hall of Fame in 2001 and has a star on the Hollywood Walk of Fame.

06/03/1959	29	1	DONNA Written by Valens about his high school friend Donna Ludwig. . . . . London HL 8803
01/08/1987	49	4	LA BAMBA This and above single featured in the 1987 film *La Bamba* . . . . RCA PB 41435

CATERINA VALENTE French singer (born 14/1/1931, Paris) of Italian parentage, a popular concert star throughout Europe able to sing in six languages. She was married to film composer Roy Budd between 1972 and 1979.

19/08/1955	5	14	THE BREEZE AND I CATERINA VALENTE WITH WERNER MULLER & THE RIAS DANCE ORCHESTRA . . . . Polydor BM 6002

VALENTINE BROTHERS US vocal duo formed in Columbus, OH by John and Billy Valentine.

23/04/1983	73	1	MONEY'S TOO TIGHT TO MENTION Later successfully covered by Simply Red. . . . . Energy NRG 1

DICKIE VALENTINE UK singer (born Richard Bryce, 4/11/1929, London) who was invited to work with the Ted Heath Band in 1949, then the most popular big band in the country, and voted Top UK Male Singer during his spell with the orchestra. He went solo in 1954 and quickly became a teen idol: in 1957 he had to hire the Royal Albert Hall to accommodate all the members of his fan club for its annual party. He was killed in a car crash in Wales on 6/5/1971.

20/02/1953	12	1	BROKEN WINGS . . . . Decca F 9954
13/03/1953	9	3	ALL THE TIME AND EVERYWHERE . . . . Decca F 10038
05/06/1953	7	1	IN A GOLDEN COACH . . . . Decca F 10098
05/11/1954	19	1	ENDLESS . . . . Decca F 10346
17/12/1954	5	12	**MR SANDMAN** . . . . Decca F 10415
17/12/1954	❶3	15	**FINGER OF SUSPICION** DICKIE VALENTINE WITH THE STARGAZERS Reclaimed #1 position on 21/1/1955 . . . . Decca F 10394
18/02/1955	9	10	A BLOSSOM FELL . . . . Decca F 10430
03/06/1955	4	15	I WONDER . . . . Decca F 10493
25/11/1955	❶3	7	**CHRISTMAS ALPHABET** . . . . Decca F 10628
16/12/1955	15	5	OLD PIANO RAG . . . . Decca F 10645

❶9 Number of weeks single topped the UK chart ↑ Entered the UK chart at #1 ▲9 Number of weeks single topped the US chart

843

07/12/1956	8	5		CHRISTMAS ISLAND	Decca F 10798
27/12/1957	28	1		SNOWBOUND FOR CHRISTMAS	Decca F 10950
13/03/1959	20	8		VENUS	Pye Nixa 7N 15192
23/10/1959	14	8		ONE MORE SUNRISE (MORGEN)	Pye 7N 15221

JOE VALINO US vocalist (born 9/3/1929, Philadelphia, PA) who appeared in a number of films after his singing career, including *Girl In Gold Boots* (1969) and *The Commitment* (1976). He died on 26/12/1996.

18/01/1957	23	2	THE GARDEN OF EDEN	HMV POP 283

FRANKIE VALLI US singer (born Francis Castellucio, 3/5/1937, Newark, NJ) who made his first solo single as Frank Valley in 1953. His first group the Variatones were formed in 1955. They changed their name to the Four Lovers in 1956 and evolved into the Four Seasons. Valli began recording solo again in 1965.

12/12/1970	11	13		YOU'RE READY NOW ▲	Philips 320226
01/02/1975	5	11	○	MY EYES ADORED YOU ▲[1]	Private Stock PVT 1
21/06/1975	31	5		SWEARIN' TO GOD	Private Stock PVT 21
17/04/1976	11	7		FALLEN ANGEL	Private Stock PVT 51
26/08/1978	3	14	●	GREASE ▲[2] Featured in the 1978 film *Grease* and appears over the credits in the film	RSO 012
23/03/1991	47	2		GREASE – THE DREAM MIX	PWL/Polydor PO 136

MARK VAN DALE WITH ENRICO Dutch DJ/producer (born 13/11/1964, Rotterdam) with singer Enrico (born Erik De Koning).

03/10/1998	71	1	WATER WAVE	Club Tools 0065815 CLU

DAVID VAN DAY UK singer (born 28/11/1957) who was a member of Guys And Dolls before forming Dollar with fellow member Thereze Bazar. After a brief solo career Van Day joined a re-formed Bucks Fizz, but by 2000 was operating a burger van in Brighton.

14/05/1983	43	3	YOUNG AMERICANS TALKING	WEA DAY 1

VAN DER TOORN – see **PAPPA BEAR FEATURING VAN DER TOORN**

RON VAN DEN BEUKEN Dutch DJ/producer; he also works with John Van Dongen.

19/06/2004	65	1	TIMELESS (KEEP ON MOVIN')	Manifesto 9866717

GEORGE VAN DUSEN UK singer/yodeler (born George Harrington, 1905) whose debut hit was originally released in 1937. It became a hit after a music publisher found a copy on a market stall and arranged for its re-release. He died in 1992.

17/12/1988	43	4	IT'S PARTY TIME AGAIN	Bri-Tone 7BT 001

PAUL VAN DYK German DJ/remixer (born 16/12/1971, Eisenhüttenstadt) who also worked with Toni Halliday and Cosmic Baby, the latter in a group called Visions Of Shiva. He is also a member of Humate.

17/05/1997	69	1	FORBIDDEN FRUIT	Deviant DVNT 18CDR
15/11/1997	54	1	WORDS PAUL VAN DYK FEATURING TONI HALLIDAY	Deviant DVNT 26CDS
05/09/1998	28	4	FOR AN ANGEL	Deviant DVNT 24CDS
20/11/1999	13	7	ANOTHER WAY/AVENUE	Deviant DVNT 35CDS
20/05/2000	7	5	TELL ME WHY (THE RIDDLE) PAUL VAN DYK FEATURING SAINT ETIENNE	Deviant DVNT 36CDS
02/12/2000	15	6	WE ARE ALIVE	Deviant DVNT 38CDS
12/07/2003	14	5	NOTHING BUT YOU PAUL VAN DYK FEATURING HEMSTOCK	Positiva CDTIVS 192
18/10/2003	28	2	TIMES OF OUR LIVES/CONNECTED PAUL VAN DYK FEATURING VEGA 4	Positiva CDTIVS 196
17/04/2004	42	3	CRUSH PAUL VAN DYK FEATURING SECOND SUN	Positiva CDTIVS 204

LEROY VAN DYKE US singer (born 4/10/1929, Spring Fork, MO) who learned to play the guitar while in the US Army in Korea. On his return to the US he became a livestock auctioneer, which prompted him in 1956 to write a song about his work. A novelty top twenty hit, it led to two further US hits and brief success in the UK.

04/01/1962	5	17	WALK ON BY	Mercury AMT 1166
26/04/1962	34	3	BIG MAN IN A BIG HOUSE	Mercury AMT 1173

NIELS VAN GOGH German DJ/producer who was resident at the Ausburger Pleasure Dome Club from 1997 to 2000 and then moved on to the Poison Club in Dusseldorf.

10/04/1999	75	1	PULVERTURM	Logic 74321649192

VAN HALEN US rock group formed in Pasadena, California in 1974 by David Lee Roth (born 10/10/1955, Bloomington, IN, lead vocals), Alex Van Halen (born 8/5/1955, Nijmegen, Holland, drums), Eddie Van Halen (born 26/1/1957, Nijmegen, guitar) and Michael Anthony (born Michael Sobolewski, 20/6/1955, Chicago, IL, bass). Roth quit in 1985 to go solo, and the Van Halen brothers then recruited Sammy Hagar (born 13/10/1947, Monterey, CA) as lead singer. They won the 1991 Grammy Award for Best Hard Rock Performance with Vocal for *For Unlawful Carnal Knowledge*.

28/06/1980	52	3	RUNNIN' WITH THE DEVIL Featured in the 1999 film *Detroit Rock City*	Warner Brothers HM 10
04/02/1984	7	13	JUMP ▲[5] Featured in the 1999 film *Big Daddy*	Warner Brothers W 9384
19/05/1984	61	2	PANAMA	Warner Brothers W 9273
05/04/1986	8	14	WHY CAN'T THIS BE LOVE	Warner Brothers W 8740
12/07/1986	62	2	DREAMS	Warner Brothers W 8642
06/08/1988	28	7	WHEN IT'S LOVE	Warner Brothers W 7816
01/04/1989	63	1	FEELS SO GOOD	Warner Brothers W 7565

22/06/1991	74	1		POUNDCAKE	Warner Brothers W 0045
19/10/1991	63	1		TOP OF THE WORLD	Warner Brothers W 0066
27/03/1993	26	3		JUMP (LIVE)	Warner Brothers W 0155CD
21/01/1995	27	2		DON'T TELL ME	Warner Brothers W 0280CD
01/04/1995	33	2		CAN'T STOP LOVING YOU	Warner Brothers W 0288CD

ARMAND VAN HELDEN
US producer/remixer (born 1972, Boston, MA) who also worked with Nuyorican Soul and CJ Bolland.

08/03/1997	38	2		THE FUNK PHENOMENA	ZYX 8523U8
08/11/1997	46	1		ULTRAFUNKULA	ffrr FCD 317
06/02/1999	❶¹	11	○	**YOU DON'T KNOW ME** ↑ ARMAND VAN HELDEN FEATURING DUANE HARDEN	ffrr FCD 357
01/05/1999	18	6		FLOWERZ ARMAND VAN HELDEN FEATURING ROLAND CLARK	ffrr FCD 361
20/05/2000	4	7		KOOCHY Adaptation of Gary Numan's *Cars*.	ffrr FCDP 379
03/11/2001	34	2		WHY CAN'T YOU FREE SOME TIME	ffrr FCD 402
15/12/2001	25	4		YOU CAN'T CHANGE ME ROGER SANCHEZ FEATURING ARMAND VAN HELDEN AND N'DEA DAVENPORT	Defected DFECT 41CDS
01/05/2004	34	2		HEAR MY NAME	Southern Fried ECB64CDS
11/09/2004	15	11		MY MY MY	Southern Fried ECB67CDS

DENISE VAN OUTEN
UK singer (born 27/5/1974, Basildon, Essex) who was a member of Those Two Girls before presenting TV's *The Big Breakfast*. Her single with co-presenter Johnny Vaughan (born 16/7/1966) was a charity record.

26/12/1998	3	12		**ESPECIALLY FOR YOU** DENISE AND JOHNNY	RCA 74321644722
29/06/2002	23	4		CAN'T TAKE MY EYES OFF YOU ANDY WILLIAMS AND DENISE VAN OUTEN	Columbia 6721052

VAN TWIST
Belgian/Zairian vocal/instrumental group assembled by Carlos Radia.

16/02/1985	57	2		SHAFT	Polydor POSP 729

VANDELLAS – see MARTHA REEVES AND THE VANDELLAS

DESPINA VANDI
Greek singer (born 22/7/1969, Tipigen, Germany); she studied philosophy, education and psychology at Aristoteleio University of Thessaloniki before launching a singing career.

20/03/2004	63	1		GIA	Positiva CDTIVS 199

LUTHER VANDROSS
US singer (born 20/4/1951, New York) who began his professional career as a commercial jingles singer, graduating to being one of New York's top session singers on records by David Bowie, Bette Midler, Barbra Streisand, Carly Simon, Change and many others. The group Luther were signed to Cotillion (a division of Atlantic) but dropped after two albums. A new recording contract with Epic led to his becoming one of the top R&B singers of the late 1980s and 1990s. He appeared in the 1993 film *The Meteor Man*. In 1992 Vandross filed a suit in Los Angeles Superior Court, Santa Monica, against his record label Sony Entertainment, citing the California Labor Code section 2855, which states that personal service contracts cannot exceed seven years. He subsequently signed with Clive Davis' J Records imprint. He has won eight Grammy Awards including: Best Rhythm & Blues Album in 2003 for *Dance With My Father* and Best Rhythm & Blues Performance by a Duo or Group with Vocals with Beyoncé for *The Closer I Get To You* the same year. He was also given a Lifetime Achievement Award at the 2001 MOBO Awards. On 8/6/1987 his drummer Yogi Horton committed suicide by jumping out of a seventeenth-floor window in New York City shortly after a performance at Madison Square Garden.

19/02/1983	44	6		NEVER TOO MUCH	Epic EPC A 3101
26/07/1986	60	3		GIVE ME THE REASON Featured in the 1986 film *Ruthless People*	Epic A 7288
21/02/1987	71	2		GIVE ME THE REASON Re-issue of Epic A 7288	Epic 6502167
28/03/1987	60	4		SEE ME	Epic LUTH 1
11/07/1987	16	10		I REALLY DIDN'T MEAN IT	Epic LUTH 3
05/09/1987	24	7		STOP TO LOVE	Epic LUTH 2
07/11/1987	33	6		SO AMAZING	Epic LUTH 4
23/01/1988	26	6		GIVE ME THE REASON Second re-issue of Epic A 7288	Epic LUTH 5
16/04/1988	28	5		I GAVE IT UP (WHEN I FELL IN LOVE)	Epic LUTH 6
09/07/1988	72	1		THERE'S NOTHING BETTER THAN LOVE LUTHER VANDROSS, DUET WITH GREGORY HINES	Epic LUTH 7
08/10/1988	31	4		ANY LOVE	Epic LUTH 8
04/02/1989	34	4		SHE WON'T TALK TO ME	Epic LUTH 9
22/04/1989	53	3		COME BACK	Epic LUTH 10
28/10/1989	13	7		NEVER TOO MUCH (REMIX)	Epic LUTH 12
06/01/1990	43	3		HERE AND NOW 1990 Grammy Award for Best Rhythm & Blues Vocal Performance	Epic LUTH 13
27/04/1991	46	5		POWER OF LOVE – LOVE POWER 1991 Grammy Awards for Best Rhythm & Blues Song (with co-writers Marcus Miller and Teddy Van), and Best Rhythm & Blues Vocal Performance	Epic 6568227
18/01/1992	53	3		THE RUSH	Epic 6577237
15/08/1992	2	13	○	**THE BEST THINGS IN LIFE ARE FREE** LUTHER VANDROSS AND JANET JACKSON WITH SPECIAL GUESTS BBD AND RALPH TRESVANT Featured in the 1992 film *Mo' Money*	Perspective PERSS 7400
22/05/1993	28	3		LITTLE MIRACLES (HAPPEN EVERY DAY)	Epic 6590442
18/09/1993	34	3		HEAVEN KNOWS	Epic 6596522
04/12/1993	38	2		LOVE IS ON THE WAY	Epic 6599592
17/09/1994	3	16		**ENDLESS LOVE** LUTHER VANDROSS AND MARIAH CAREY	Epic 6608062
26/11/1994	31	4		LOVE THE ONE YOU'RE WITH	Epic 6610612
04/02/1995	20	5		ALWAYS AND FOREVER	Epic 6611942
15/04/1995	22	3		AIN'T NO STOPPING US NOW	Epic 6614242

❶⁹ Number of weeks single topped the UK chart ↑ Entered the UK chart at #1 ▲⁹ Number of weeks single topped the US chart

845

DATE	POS	WKS	BPI	SINGLE TITLE	LABEL & NUMBER
11/11/1995	31	3		POWER OF LOVE – LOVE POWER (REMIX)	Epic 6625902
16/12/1995	7	7		**THE BEST THINGS IN LIFE ARE FREE (REMIX)** LUTHER VANDROSS AND JANET JACKSON WITH SPECIAL GUESTS BBD AND RALPH TRESVANT	A&M 5813092
23/12/1995	43	2		EVERY YEAR EVERY CHRISTMAS	Epic 6627762
12/10/1996	14	5		YOUR SECRET LOVE 1996 Grammy Award for Best Rhythm & Blues Vocal Performance	Epic 6638385
28/12/1996	44	2		I CAN MAKE IT BETTER	Epic 6640632
20/10/2001	59	1		TAKE YOU OUT	J Records 74321899442
28/02/2004	21	4		DANCE WITH MY FATHER 2003 Grammy Awards for Song of the Year (for writers Richard Marx and Luther Vandross) and Best Male Rhythm & Blues Vocal Performance	J Records 82876569982

VANESSA-MAE
UK classical violinist (born Vanessa-Mae Nicholson, 27/10/1968, Singapore) who is now resident in the UK.

DATE	POS	WKS	BPI	SINGLE TITLE	LABEL & NUMBER
28/01/1995	16	10		TOCCATA AND FUGUE	EMI Classics MAE 886812
20/05/1995	37	2		RED HOT	EMI CDMAE 2
18/11/1995	41	2		CLASSICAL GAS	EMI CDEM 404
26/10/1996	28	2		I'M A DOUN FOR LACK O' JOHNNIE (A LITTLE SCOTTISH FANTASY)	EMI CDMAE 3
25/10/1997	54	1		STORM	EMI CDEM 497
20/12/1997	41	2		I FEEL LOVE	EMI CDEM 503
05/12/1998	53	1		DEVIL'S THRILL/REFLECTION Reflection featured in the 1998 Walt Disney film Mulan	EMI CDEM 530
28/07/2001	66	1		WHITE BIRD	EMI CDVAN 002

VANGELIS
Greek keyboard player (born Evangelos Papathanassiou, 29/3/1943, Valos) who moved to Paris in the early 1960s, forming Aphrodite's Child with Demis Roussos in 1968. Based in London from the the mid-1970s, he worked with Jon Anderson as Jon And Vangelis. In 1981 he received an Oscar for Chariots Of Fire.

DATE	POS	WKS	BPI	SINGLE TITLE	LABEL & NUMBER
09/05/1981	12	10		CHARIOTS OF FIRE – TITLES ▲¹ Featured in the films Chariots Of Fire (1981) and Bruce Almighty (2003)	Polydor POSP 246
11/07/1981	48	6		HEAVEN AND HELL, THIRD MOVEMENT (THEME FROM THE BBC-TV SERIES 'THE COSMOS') Theme to the TV series Cosmos	BBC 1
24/04/1982	41	7		CHARIOTS OF FIRE – TITLES	Polydor POSP 246
31/10/1992	60	2		CONQUEST OF PARADISE Featured in the 1992 film 1492: Conquest Of Paradise	East West YZ 704

VANILLA
UK vocal group formed in London by Francis, Sharon, Alida and Alison.

DATE	POS	WKS	BPI	SINGLE TITLE	LABEL & NUMBER
22/11/1997	14	8		NO WAY NO WAY	EMI CDEM 487
23/05/1998	36	2		TRUE TO US	EMI CDEM 509

VANILLA FUDGE
US psychedelic rock group formed in New York in 1966 by Mark Stein (born 11/3/1947, New Jersey, keyboards/vocals), Vinnie Martell (born 11/11/1945, New York, guitar), Tim Bogart (born 27/8/1944, Richfield, NJ, bass) and Joey Brennan (drums). Brennan was soon replaced by Carmine Appice (born 15/12/1946, New York). They disbanded in 1970.

DATE	POS	WKS	BPI	SINGLE TITLE	LABEL & NUMBER
09/08/1967	18	11		YOU KEEP ME HANGIN' ON	Atlantic 584 123

VANILLA ICE
US rapper (born Robert Van Winkle, 31/10/1968, Miami Lakes, FL) who appeared in the 1991 films Cool As Ice and Teenage Mutant Ninja Turtles II.

DATE	POS	WKS	BPI	SINGLE TITLE	LABEL & NUMBER
24/11/1990	❶⁴	13	✪	**ICE ICE BABY** ▲¹ Bass line sampled from Under Pressure by Queen and David Bowie. Featured in the 2004 film 13 Going On 30	SBK 18
02/02/1991	10	6		**PLAY THAT FUNKY MUSIC** Based on Play That Funky Music by Wild Cherry. Vanilla Ice was subsequently sued by Robert Parissi (the writer of Play That Funky Music) and forced to hand over $500,000 in royalties	SBK 20
30/03/1991	45	5		I LOVE YOU	SBK 22
29/06/1991	27	4		ROLLIN' IN MY 5.0	SBK 27
10/08/1991	22	4		SATISFACTION	SBK 29

VANITY FARE
UK pop group formed by Trevor Brice (born 12/2/1945, Rochester, Kent, vocals), Tony Jarrett (born 4/9/1944, bass/guitar), Tony Goulden (born 21/11/1944, Rochester, guitar), Barry Landeman (born 25/10/1947, Woodbridge, Suffolk, keyboards) and Dick Allix (born 3/5/1945, Gravesend, Kent, drums). Goulden was elected Mayor of Medway, Kent in 2001, vowing to fight poverty.

DATE	POS	WKS	BPI	SINGLE TITLE	LABEL & NUMBER
28/08/1968	20	9		I LIVE FOR THE SUN	Page One POF 075
23/07/1969	8	12		**EARLY IN THE MORNING**	Page One POF 142
27/12/1969	16	13		HITCHIN' A RIDE Featured in the 1996 film Now and Then	Page One POF 158

JOE T VANNELLI
Italian DJ/producer who began his career as a club DJ in 1977 and later launched the Dreambeat, DBX, Music Without Control and Rush labels.

DATE	POS	WKS	BPI	SINGLE TITLE	LABEL & NUMBER
17/06/1995	45	2		SWEETEST DAY OF MAY	Positiva CDTIV 36

RANDY VANWARMER
US singer (born Randall Van Wormer, 30/3/1955, Indian Hills, CO) who moved to the UK in 1967 and returned to the US in 1979. Died from leukemia on 12/01/04.

DATE	POS	WKS	BPI	SINGLE TITLE	LABEL & NUMBER
04/08/1979	8	11	O	**JUST WHEN I NEEDED YOU MOST**	Bearsville WIP 6516

VAPORS
UK pub-rock group formed by David Fenton (vocals), Ed Bazalgette (guitar), Steve Smith (bass) and Howard Smith (drums). When the group disbanded, Fenton became a pub landlord in Woking.

DATE	POS	WKS	BPI	SINGLE TITLE	LABEL & NUMBER
09/02/1980	3	13	O	**TURNING JAPANESE** Featured in the films Romy And Michele's High School Reunion (1997) and Charlie's Angels (2000)	United Artists BP 334
05/07/1980	44	4		NEWS AT TEN	United Artists BP 345
11/07/1981	44	6		JIMMIE JONES	Liberty BP 401

VARDIS UK group formed in Wakefield, Yorkshire by Steve Zodiac (guitar/vocals), Alan Selway (bass) and Gary Pearson (drums) as Quo Vardis, dropping the 'Quo' in 1979. Selway left in 1982 and was replaced by Terry Horbury.

27/09/1980.....59......4....... LET'S GO...Logo VAR 1

HALO VARGA US producer Brian Vargas.

09/12/2000.....67......1....... FUTURE...Hooj Choons HOOJ 101CD

VARIOUS ARTISTS (EPS AND LPS)

15/06/1956.....26......2....... CAROUSEL – ORIGINAL SOUNDTRACK (LP) Tracks on LP: Orchestra conducted by Alfred Newman, *Carousel Waltz*; Barbara Ruick and Shirley Jones, *You're A Queer One Julie Jordan*; Barbara Ruick, *Mister Snow*; Shirley Jones and Gordon MacRae, *If I Loved You*; Claramae Mitchell, *June Is Busting Out All Over*; Gordon MacRae, *Soliloquy*; Cameron Mitchell, *Blow High Blow Low*; Robert Rounseville and Barbara Ruick, *When The Children Are Asleep*; Barbara Ruick, Claramae Turner, Robert Rounseville and Cameron Mitchell, *This Was A Real Nice Clambake*; Cameron Mitchell, *Stonecutters Cut It On Stone (There's Nothing So Bad For A Woman)*; Shirley Jones, *What's The Use Of Wonderin'*; Claramae Turner, *You'll Never Walk Alone*; Gordon MacRae, *If I Loved You*; and Shirley Jones, *You'll Never Walk Alone*..Capitol LCT 6105

29/06/1956 .....2 ......9....... **ALL STAR HIT PARADE** Tracks as follows: Winifred Atwell, *Theme From The Threepenny Opera*; Dave King, *No Other Love*; Joan Regan, *My September Love*; Lita Roza, *A Tear Fell*; Dickie Valentine, *Out Of Town*; and David Whitfield, *It's Almost Tomorrow* ... .Decca F 10752

26/07/1957.....15......7....... ALL STAR HIT PARADE NO. 2 Tracks as follows: Johnston Brothers, *Around The World*; Billy Cotton, *Puttin' On The Style*; Jimmy Young, *When I Fall In Love*; Max Bygraves, *A White Sport Coat*; Beverley Sisters, *Freight Train*; and Tommy Steele, *Butterfly* ....Decca 10915

09/12/1989.....63......1....... FOOD CHRISTMAS EP Tracks on EP: Crazyhead, *Like Princes Do*; Jesus Jones, *I Don't Want That Kind Of Love*; and Diesel Park West, *Info Freako* ....Food 23

20/01/1990.....64......2....... THE FURTHER ADVENTURES OF THE NORTH Tracks on EP: Annette, *Dream 17*; T-Coy, *Carino 90*; Frequency 9, *The Way I Feel*; and Dynasty Of Two Featuring Rowetta, *Stop This Thing*...Deconstruction PT 43372

02/11/1991.....60......1....... THE APPLE EP Tracks on EP: Mary Hopkin, *Those Were The Days*; Billy Preston, *That's The Way God Planned It*; Jackie Lomax, *Sour Milk Sea*; and Badfinger, *Come And Get It* ....Apple APP 1

11/07/1992.....45......2....... FOURPLAY (EP) Tracks on EP: Glide, *DJs Unite, Alright*; Noisy Factory, *Be Free*; and EQ, *True Devotion* .... XL Recordings XLFP 1

07/11/1992.....26......3....... THE FRED EP Tracks on EP: Rockingbirds, *Deeply Dipply*; Flowered Up, *Don't Talk Just Kiss*; and Saint Etienne, *I'm Too Sexy*. The single was a charity record with proceeds going to the Terence Higgins Trust for AIDS research..................Heavenly HVN 19

24/04/1993.....23......4....... GIMME SHELTER (EP) Available in four formats, each featuring an interview with the featured artist who also performed a version of the track *Gimme Shelter*. The versions and artists available were: (cassette) Jimmy Somerville and Voice Of The Beehive and Heaven 17; (12-inch) Blue Pearl, 808 State and Robert Owens, Pop Will Eat Itself Vs Gary Clail, Ranking Roger and the Mighty Diamonds; (CD 1) Thunder, Little Angels, Hawkwind and Sam Fox; (CD 2) Cud with Sandie Shaw, Kingmaker, New Model Army and Tom Jones. The single was released to raise funds for the Putting Our House In Order charity ....Food CDORDERA 1

05/06/1993.....69......1....... SUBPLATES VOLUME 1 (EP) Tracks on EP: Son'z Of A Loop Da Loop Era, *Style Warz*; Q-Bass, *Funky Dope Track*; DJ Hype, *The Chopper*; and Run Tings, *Look No Further* ....Suburban Base SUBBASE 24CD

09/10/1993.....30......3....... THE TWO TONE EP Tracks on EP: Special AKA, *Gangsters*; Madness, *The Prince*; Selecter, *On My Radio*; and The Beat, *Tears Of A Clown* ....2 Tone CHSTT 31

04/11/1995.....51......2....... HELP (EP) Tracks on EP: Radiohead, *Lucky*; PJ Harvey, *50th Queenie (Live)*; Guru Featuring Big Shug, *Momentum*; and an unnamed piece of incidental music...Go Discs GODCD 135

16/03/1996.....39......1....... NEW YORK UNDERCOVER 4-TRACK EP Tracks on EP: Guy, *Tell Me What You Like*; Little Shawn, *Dom Perignon*; Monifah, *I Miss You*; and The Lost Boyz, *Jeeps, Lex Coups, Bimaz & Menz*. All four tracks were featured in the US TV series *New York Undercover* ....Uptown MCSTD 48002

30/03/1996.....35......1....... THE DANGEROUS MINDS EP Tracks on EP: Aaron Hall, *Curiosity*; De Vante, *Gin & Dance*; and Sista Featuring Craig Mack, *It's Alright*. All three tracks were featured in the 1995 film *Dangerous Minds*......................................MCA MCSTD 48007

29/11/1997 .....❶3.....21.....✪2 **PERFECT DAY** ↑ Charity record for the BBC's Children In Need charity. Reclaimed the #1 position on 10/1/1998. The artists include Lou Reed (who originally wrote and recorded the song); Bono; Skye Edwards; David Bowie; Burning Spear (born Winston Rodney); Thomas Allen; Brodsky Quartet; Sheona White; Dr John; Robert Cray; Evan Dando; Emmylou Harris; Courtney Pine; Andrew Davis and the BBC Symphony Orchestra; Heather Small; Tom Jones; Visual Ministry Choir; Suzanne Vega; Elton John; Boyzone (Ronan Keating, Stephen Gately, Keith Duffy, Shane Lynch and Mikey Graham); Lesley Garrett; Tammy Wynette; Shane MacGowan; Huey; Ian Broudie; Gabrielle; Brett Anderson; Joan Armatrading; and Laura Anderson ....Chrysalis CDNEED 01

12/09/1998.....62......1....... THE FULL MONTY – MONSTER MIX Medley of Hot Chocolate's *You Sexy Thing*, Donna Summer's *Hot Stuff*, and Tom Jones' *You Can Leave Your Hat On*. The CD version of the single also contained the full length version of Tom Jones' *You Can Leave Your Hat On* and David Rose's *The Stripper* ....RCA Victor 74321602582

26/09/1998.....75......1....... TRADE (EP) (DISC 2) Tracks on EP: Steve Thomas, *Put Your House In Order* and Tony De Vit, *The Dawn* ....Tidy Trax TREP 2

10/04/1999 .....4......13.....○ **THANK ABBA FOR THE MUSIC** Medley of *Take A Chance On Me*, *Dancing Queen*, *Mamma Mia* and *Thank You For The Music*. Multinational artists Steps (Faye Tozer, Lee Latchford-Evans, Claire Richards, Ian Watkins and Lisa Scott-Lee), Tina Cousins, Cleopatra (sisters Yonah, Cleopatra and Zainam Higgins), B*Witched (Sinead O'Carroll, Lindsay Armaou and twin sisters Edele and Keavy Lynch) and Billie (Billie Piper) with a tribute to Abba. The single was released to support the BRITS Trust..................Epic ABCD 1

25/12/1999.....19......10....... IT'S ONLY ROCK 'N' ROLL Multinational charity ensemble for Children's Promise formed by Mick Jagger; Keith Richards; Spice Girls (Melanie Brown, Victoria Addams, Melanie Chisholm and Emma Bunton); The Corrs (Andrea, Caroline, Sharon and Jim Corr); Jon Bon Jovi; Annie Lennox; Kid Rock; Mary J. Blige; Kelly Jones; Kelle Bryan; Jay Kay; Ozzy Osbourne; James Brown; Robin Williams; Jackson Browne; Iggy Pop; Chrissie Hynde; Skin; Mark Owen; Natalie Imbruglia; Fun Lovin' Criminals (Huey, Steve Borovini and Brian 'Fast'); Dina Carroll; Gavin Rossdale; BB King; Joe Cocker; Ocean Colour Scene (Simon Fowler, Steve Craddock, Damon Minchella and Oscar Harrison); Ronan Keating; Ray Barretto; Herbie Hancock; Status Quo (Francis Rossi and Rick Parfitt); S Club 7 (Paul Cattermole, Jon Lee, Rachel Stevens, Joanne O'Meara, Bradley McIntosh, Hannah Spearitt and Tina Barrett); and Eric Idle ....Universal TV 1566012

17/06/2000.....69......1....... PERFECT DAY (RE-RECORDING)..Chrysalis 8887840

10/11/2001.....71......1....... HARD BEAT EP 19 Tracks on EP: Eternal Rhythm, *Eternal 99*; BK, *Tragic*; BK, *F**k Me*; and BK, *Don't Give Up* ....Nukleuz NUKPA 0369

❶9 Number of weeks single topped the UK chart ↑ Entered the UK chart at #1 ▲9 Number of weeks single topped the US chart

847

VARIOUS ARTISTS (MONTAGES)

17/05/1980	75	2	**CALIBRE CUTS** Contains samples of the following tracks: Black Ivory, *Big Apples Rock;* Chanson, *Don't Hold Back;* Jupiter Beyond, *The River Drive;* LAX, *Dancing In The Disco;* Lowrell, *Mellow Mellow Right On;* Osibisa, *Pata Pata;* Players Association, *I Like It;* Positive Force, *We Got The Funk;* Tony Rallo And The Midnight Band, *Holdin' On;* Real Thing, *Can You Feel The Force;* Seventh Avenue, *Miami Heatwave;* Sugarhill Gang, *Rappers Delight;* Two Man Sound, *Que Tel America;* and studio musician remakes of *Ain't No Stoppin' Us Now, Bad Girls* and *We Are Family* .... Calibre CAB 502
25/11/1989	12	11	**DEEP HEAT '89** Contains samples of the following tracks: Technotronic, *Pump Up The Jam;* Humanoid, *Stakker Humanoid;* Black Riot, *A Day In The Life;* LNR, *Work It To The Bone;* DJ 'Fast' Eddie, *I Can Make U Dance;* A Guy Called Gerald, *Voodoo Ray;* Starlight, *Numero Uno;* Todd Terry, *Bango (To The Batmobile);* Raze, *Break 4 Love;* and Sugar Bear, *Don't Scandalize Mine* .... Deep Heat DEEP 10
03/03/1990	2	7	**THE BRITS 1990** Contains samples of the following tracks: Double Trouble And The Rebel MC, *Street Tuff;* A Guy Called Gerald, *Voodoo Ray;* S Express, *Theme From S Express;* Beatmasters, *Hey DJ I Can't Dance To That Music You're Playing;* Jeff Wayne, *Eve Of The War;* 808 State, *Pacific State;* D Mob, *We Call It Acieed;* and Cookie Crew, *Got To Keep On* .... RCA PB 43565
28/04/1990	49	2	**THE SIXTH SENSE** Contains samples of the following tracks: Technotronic, *Get Up;* De La Soul, *The Magic Number;* Anna G, *G'Ding G'Ding (Do Wanna Wanna);* MC Miker G, *Show 'M The Bass;* Project D, *Eve Of The War;* and 2 To The Power, *Moments In Love* .... Deep Heat DEEP 12
10/11/1990	16	9	**TIME TO MAKE THE FLOOR BURN** Contains samples of the following tracks: Kid 'N' Play, *Do This My Way;* Double Trouble And The Rebel MC, *Street Tuff;* Lake Eerie, *Sex 4 Daze;* Black Box, *Ride On Time;* Jomanda, *Make My Body Rock;* Bizz Nizz, *Don't Miss The Partyline;* Hypnotek, *Pump Pump It Up;* Inner City, *Big Fun;* Mr Lee, *Pump That Body;* Technotronic, *Pump Up The Jam;* Technotronic, *This Beat Is Technotronic;* Mr Lee, *Get Busy;* 49ers, *Touch Me;* and FAB, *Thunderbirds Are Go* .... Megabass MEGAX 1

JUNIOR VASQUEZ
US DJ/producer Donald Gregory Jerome Pattern who began his career as a dancer at Paradise Garage before graduating to DJing. He also recorded as Shades Of Love.

15/07/1995	22	3	GET YOUR HANDS OFF MY MAN!	Tribal UK/Positiva CDTIV 37
31/08/1996	24	2	IF MADONNA CALLS Features the voice of Madonna recorded on an answerphone	Multiply CDMULTY 13

ELAINE VASSELL – see BEATMASTERS

VAST
Australian group formed by Thomas Froggatt (born 19/1/1979, Byron Bay, bass/vocals), Justin Cotter (guitar) and Steve Clark (drums).

16/09/2000	55	1	FREE	Mushroom MUSH 79CDS

SVEN VATH
German DJ/producer (born 26/10/1964, Offenbach).

24/07/1993	63	2	L'ESPERANZA	Eye Q YZ 757
06/11/1993	57	2	AN ACCIDENT IN PARADISE	Eye Q YZ 778CD
22/10/1994	72	1	HARLEQUIN – THE BEAUTY AND THE BEAST	Eye Q YZ 857

FRANKIE VAUGHAN
UK singer (born Frank Abelson, 3/2/1928, Liverpool) whose chart success was equalled by that as a top cabaret act. He appeared in the film *Let's Make Love* with Marilyn Monroe in 1960 (and turned down the opportunity of a romantic liaison with her during filming!) and was awarded the OBE in 1965. He was also awarded a CBE in the 1996 New Year's Honours list. He died on 17/9/1999.

29/01/1954	11	1	ISTANBUL (NOT CONSTANTINOPLE) FRANKIE VAUGHAN WITH THE PETER KNIGHT SINGERS	HMV B 10599
28/01/1955	12	3	HAPPY DAYS AND LONELY NIGHTS	HMV B 10783
22/04/1955	17	1	TWEEDLE DEE	Philips PB 423
02/12/1955	18	3	SEVENTEEN	Philips PB 511
03/02/1956	20	2	MY BOY FLAT TOP	Philips PB 544
09/11/1956	2	15	**GREEN DOOR**	Philips PB 640
11/01/1957	○4	13	**THE GARDEN OF EDEN** Reclaimed #1 position on 8/2/1957	Philips PB 660
04/10/1957	6	12	**MAN ON FIRE/WANDERIN' EYES**	Philips PB 729
01/11/1957	8	11	**GOTTA HAVE SOMETHING IN THE BANK FRANK** FRANKIE VAUGHAN AND THE KAYE SISTERS	Philips PB 751
20/12/1957	8	11	**KISSES SWEETER THAN WINE**	Philips PB 775
07/03/1958	11	6	CAN'T GET ALONG WITHOUT YOU/WE ARE NOT ALONE	Philips PB 793
09/05/1958	10	12	**KEWPIE DOLL**	Philips PB 825
01/08/1958	22	6	WONDERFUL THINGS	Philips PB 834
10/10/1958	25	4	AM I WASTING MY TIME ON YOU	Philips PB 865
30/01/1959	28	2	THAT'S MY DOLL	Philips PB 895
01/05/1959	9	9	**COME SOFTLY TO ME** FRANKIE VAUGHAN AND THE KAYE SISTERS	Philips PB 913
24/07/1959	5	14	**THE HEART OF A MAN**	Philips PB 930
18/09/1959	28	2	WALKIN' TALL	Philips PB 931
29/01/1960	25	2	WHAT MORE DO YOU WANT	Philips PB 985
22/09/1960	31	5	KOOKIE LITTLE PARADISE	Philips PB 1054

27/10/1960	34	6		MILORD	Philips PB 1066
09/11/1961	❶[3]	13		**TOWER OF STRENGTH**	Philips PB 1195
01/02/1962	22	7		DON'T STOP TWIST	Philips PB 1219
27/09/1962	42	4		HERCULES	Philips 326542 BF
24/01/1963	5	21		**LOOP-DE-LOOP**	Philips 326566 BF
20/06/1963	21	9		HEY MAMA	Philips BF 1254
04/06/1964	18	11		HELLO DOLLY	Philips BF 1339
11/03/1965	46	1		SOMEONE MUST HAVE HURT YOU A LOT	Philips BF 1394
23/08/1967	7	21		**THERE MUST BE A WAY**	Columbia DB 8248
15/11/1967	21	9		SO TIRED	Columbia DB 8298
28/02/1968	29	5		NEVERTHELESS	Columbia DB 8354

MALCOLM VAUGHAN UK singer (born in Abercynon, Wales) who began his career with comedian Kenny Earle when he was spotted by an A&R scout from EMI. Signed to HMV, he made his record debut in 1955 and was still touring northern night clubs into the 1990s.

01/07/1955	5	16		**EVERY DAY OF MY LIFE**	HMV B 10874
27/01/1956	18	3		WITH YOUR LOVE MALCOLM VAUGHAN WITH THE PETER KNIGHT SINGERS	HMV POP 130
26/10/1956	3	20		**ST. THERESE OF THE ROSES**	HMV POP 250
12/04/1957	29	3		THE WORLD IS MINE	HMV POP 303
10/05/1957	13	8		CHAPEL OF THE ROSES	HMV POP 325
29/11/1957	3	14		**MY SPECIAL ANGEL**	HMV POP 419
21/03/1958	14	12		TO BE LOVED	HMV POP 459
17/10/1958	5	14		**MORE THAN EVER (COME PRIMA)** This and above single credited to MALCOLM VAUGHAN WITH THE MICHAEL SAMMES SINGERS	
					HMV POP 538
27/02/1959	13	15		WAIT FOR ME/WILLINGLY	HMV POP 590

NORMAN VAUGHAN UK comedian/TV presenter (born 10/4/1927, Liverpool) who also made numerous advertisements: his 'roses grow on you' became a popular 1960s catchphrase. He died on 17/5/2002, four weeks after being knocked down by a car.

17/05/1962	34	5		SWINGING IN THE RAIN	Pye 7N 15438

SARAH VAUGHAN US singer (born 27/3/1924, Newark, NJ) who studied piano from 1931 to 1939, won a talent contest at the Apollo Theater in 1942 and with it an engagement with the Earl Hines band as singer and second pianist. Her record debut was in 1944, the same year she joined Billy Eckstine's band. She married trumpeter George Treadwell in 1947 (subsequently her manager), and later married Clyde Atkins and Waymon Reed. She won the 1982 Grammy Award for Best Female Jazz Performance for *Gershwin Live* and died from cancer on 3/4/1990. She has two stars on the Hollywood Walk of Fame.

27/09/1957	22	2		PASSING STRANGERS BILLY ECKSTINE AND SARAH VAUGHAN	Mercury MT 164
11/09/1959	7	13		**BROKEN HEARTED MELODY**	Mercury AMT 1057
29/12/1960	37	4		LET'S/SERENATA	Columbia DB 4542
12/03/1969	20	15		PASSING STRANGERS BILLY ECKSTINE AND SARAH VAUGHAN Re-issue of Mercury MT 164	Mercury MF 1082

BILLY VAUGHN US singer (born Richard Vaughn, 12/4/1919 Glasgow, KY) who formed the Hilltoppers in 1952 and was later musical director for Dot Records, where he arranged or conducted for the likes of Pat Boone, Gale Storm and The Fontane Sisters. He died from cancer on 26/9/1991.

27/01/1956	20	1		SHIFTING WHISPERING SANDS BILLY VAUGHN ORCHESTRA AND CHORUS, NARRATION BY KEN NORDENE	London HLD 8205
23/03/1956	12	7		THEME FROM THE 'THREEPENNY OPERA' Tune later known as *Mack The Knife*	London HLD 8238

VAULTS UK rock group formed in Stowbridge by Beaz Harper (vocals), Jimmy Vandel (guitar/vocals), Richie Kicks (bass/vocals) and Eddie Treasure (drums).

20/03/2004	70	1		NO SLEEP NO NEED EP Tracks on EP: *Ladyhell*, *No Sleep No Need* and *Leaving Here*	Red Flag RFO9CDS

VDC – see BLAST FEATURING VDC

VEBA – see RAE AND CHRISTIAN FEATURING VEBA

BOBBY VEE US singer (born Robert Velline, 30/4/1943, Fargo, ND) inspired by Buddy Holly. He formed the Shadows in 1958, filling in for Holly, the Big Bopper and Ritchie Valens in Fargo the night after the fatal plane crash. The group recorded their first single in 1959, financing the session themselves, which led to a contract with Liberty Records (Vee signed a solo deal at the same time). He appeared in numerous films and was still appearing on the 'oldies' circuit into the 1990s.

19/01/1961	4	11		**RUBBER BALL**	London HLG 9255
13/04/1961	4	16		**MORE THAN I CAN SAY/STAYING IN**	London HLG 9316
03/08/1961	10	13		**HOW MANY TEARS**	London HLG 9389
26/10/1961	3	16		**TAKE GOOD CARE OF MY BABY** ▲[3]	London HLG 9438
21/12/1961	6	15		**RUN TO HIM**	London HLG 9470
08/03/1962	29	9		PLEASE DON'T ASK ABOUT BARBARA	Liberty LIB 55419
07/06/1962	10	13		**SHARING YOU**	Liberty LIB 55451
27/09/1962	13	19		A FOREVER KIND OF LOVE	Liberty LIB 10046
07/02/1963	3	12		**THE NIGHT HAS A THOUSAND EYES**	Liberty LIB 10069
20/06/1963	21	10		BOBBY TOMORROW	Liberty LIB 55530

❶[9] Number of weeks single topped the UK chart ⬆ Entered the UK chart at #1 ▲[9] Number of weeks single topped the US chart

LOUIE VEGA US producer (born 12/7/1965, The Bronx, NYC) and also a member of Lil Mo' Yin Yang, Masters At Work and Nuyorican Soul.

05/10/1991.....71......1.......	RIDE ON THE RHYTHM LITTLE LOUIE VEGA AND MARC ANTHONY..	Atlantic A 7602
23/05/1992.....70......1.......	RIDE ON THE RHYTHM	Atlantic A 7486
31/01/1998.....36......2.......	RIDE ON THE RHYTHM (REMIX) LITTLE LOUIE AND MARK ANTHONY	Perfecto PERF 151CD1
23/11/2002.....52......1.......	DIAMOND LIFE LOUIE VEGA AND JAY 'SINISTER' SEALEE STARRING JULIE MCKNIGHT	Distance D12409

SUZANNE VEGA US singer (born 12/8/1959, New York) who began her career on the New York folk circuit, signing with A&M in 1984. A debut album the following year greeted with critical acclaim. Her biggest hit (*Tom's Diner*) was remixed by UK remixers DNA who sampled Vega's original. Initially only on bootleg it was then snapped up by Vega's own company A&M! Vega apparently less than happy with the release. She took part in the *Perfect Day* project for the BBC's Children In Need charity and won the 1990 Grammy Award for Best Album Package with Len Peltier and Jeffrey Gold for *Days Of Open Hand*.

18/01/1986.....65......3.......	SMALL BLUE THING	A&M AM 294
22/03/1986.....21......9.......	MARLENE ON THE WALL	A&M AM 309
07/06/1986.....32......9.......	LEFT OF CENTER SUZANNE VEGA FEATURING JOE JACKSON Featured in the 1986 film *Pretty In Pink*	A&M AM 320
23/05/1987.....23......8.......	LUKA	A&M VEGA 1
18/07/1987.....58......3.......	TOM'S DINER	A&M VEGA 2
19/05/1990.....66......1.......	BOOK OF DREAMS...	A&M AM 559
28/07/1990 .....2......10 .....○	TOM'S DINER DNA FEATURING SUZANNE VEGA	A&M AM 592
22/08/1992.....52......2.......	IN LIVERPOOL	A&M AM 0029
24/10/1992.....46......2.......	99.9°F.	A&M AM 0085
19/12/1992.....60......3.......	BLOOD MAKES NOISE	A&M AM 0112
06/03/1993.....58......1.......	WHEN HEROES GO DOWN	A&M AMCD 0158
22/02/1997.....40......1.......	NO CHEAP THRILL	A&M 5818692

TATA VEGA US singer (born Carmen Rose Vega, 7/10/1951, Queens, NYC).

26/05/1979.....52......4.......	GET IT UP FOR LOVE/I JUST KEEP THINKING ABOUT YOU BABY	Motown TMG 1140

VEGA 4 – see PAUL VAN DYK

VEGAS UK vocal/instrumental duo Terry Hall (born 19/3/1959, Coventry) and David A. Stewart (born 9/9/1952, Sunderland). Hall had previously been in The Specials and Fun Boy Three, Dave Stewart in The Tourists and Eurythmics.

19/09/1992.....32......4.......	POSSESSED...	RCA 74321110437
28/11/1992.....43......4.......	SHE	RCA 74321124657
03/04/1993.....65......2.......	WALK INTO THE WIND	RCA 74321122462

VEILS New Zealand group formed by Finn Andrews (vocals), Oli Drake (guitar), Adam Kinsella (bass) and Ben Woollacott (drums).

07/02/2004.....74......1.......	THE WILD SON...	Rough Trade RTRADESCD 154
19/06/2004.....63......1.......	THE TIDE THAT LEFT AND NEVER CAME BACK	Rough Trade RTRADSCD 164

ROSIE VELA US singer (born 18/12/1952, Galveston, TX) who made her name as a model, later appearing in the films *Heaven's Gate* and *Inside Edge*.

17/01/1987.....27......7.......	MAGIC SMILE	A&M AM 369

WIL VELOZ – see LOS DEL MAR FEATURING WIL VELOZ

VELVELETTES US vocal group formed in Detroit, MI by Carolyn Gil, Mildred Gill-Arbour, Bertha Barbee-McNeil and Norma Barbee-Fairhurst. Recorded their debut single for IPG in 1962, then signed by Motown's VIP subsidiary in 1964. Gill and the Barbee sisters left in 1965 to be replaced by Sandra Tilley, Betty Kelly (both later in Martha and the Vandellas) and Annette McCullen. Best known in the UK for *He Was Really Saying Something* (later covered by Bananarama) and *Needle In A Haystack*, neither of which made the top forty either side of the Atlantic! Disbanding in 1970, they re-formed in 1984, returning to recording in 1987 for Ian Levine's Nightmare/Motor City labels.

31/07/1971.....34......7.......	THESE THINGS WILL KEEP ME LOVING YOU	Tamla Motown TMG 780

VELVET REVOLVER US rock group formed in 2002 by former Guns N' Roses members Slash (born Saul Hudson, 23/7/1965, Stoke-on-Trent, guitar), Michael 'Duff' McKagan (born 5/2/1964, Seattle, bass) and Matt Sorum (born 19/11/1960, drums), later adding Dave Kushner (guitar) and Scott Weiland (born 27/10/1967, Santa Cruz, CA, vocals, ex-member of Stone Temple Pilots).

24/07/2004.....35......3.......	SLITHER...	RCA 82876633312
23/10/2004.....32......2.......	FALL TO PIECES..	RCA 82876647692

VELVET UNDERGROUND US rock group formed in New York in 1965 by Lou Reed (born 2/3/1942, Freeport, Long Island, NY, guitar/vocals), John Cale (born 9/3/1940, Cryant, various instruments), Sterling Morrison (born 29/8/1942, East Meadow, Long Island, guitar) and Angus MacLise (drums), the latter suggesting the group's name, which he had seen on a paperback book. Despite MacLise's role in the development of the group he left soon after and was replaced by Maureen Tucker. The group met Andy Warhol the same year, who was to play an integral part in their development, including introducing them to lead singer Nico (born Christa Paffgen 16/10/1938, Cologne, Germany). Nico left after one album and then Warhol began to lose interest. Cale left to be replaced by Billy Yule in 1969 and Reed left in 1970 to go solo, although the group carried on for a further two years before disbanding. There was a brief reunion in 1991 and a subsequent live album was made in 1993. Nico fell off her bicycle while on holiday in Ibiza and subsequently died of a brain haemorrhage on 18/7/1988. Morrison died from Non-Hodgkin's lymphoma on 30/8/1995. The group was inducted into the Rock & Roll Hall of Fame in 1996.

12/03/1994.....71......1.......	VENUS IN FURS (LIVE) Recorded at the Olympia, Paris in 1993	Sire W 0224CD

○ Silver disc   ● Gold disc   ✪ Platinum disc (additional platinum units are indicated by a figure following the symbol)   ◉ Singles released prior to 1973 that are known to have sold over 1 million copies in the UK

VELVETS
US R&B vocal group formed in Odessa, TX by Virgil Johnson, Will Soloman, Mark Prince, Bob Thursby and Clarence Rigsby. Rigsby was killed in a car crash in 1978.

11/05/1961	46	1	THAT LUCKY OLD SUN	London HLU 9328
17/08/1961	50	1	TONIGHT (COULD BE THE NIGHT)	London HLU 9372

TERRY VENABLES – see RIDER AND TERRY VENABLES

VENGABOYS
Multinational group initially formed by DJs Danski (Dennis Van Den Driesschen) and DJ Delmundo (Wessel Van Diepen), later joined by singers and dancers Kim, Robin, Roy and Denice. Robin left in 1999 and was replaced by Yorick. Danski and Delmundo also recorded as Nakatomi.

28/11/1998	4	15	●	UP AND DOWN	Positiva CDTIV 105
13/03/1999	3	14	●	WE LIKE TO PARTY (THE VENGABUS)	Positiva CDTIV 108
26/06/1999	❶¹	15	●	BOOM BOOM BOOM BOOM!! ↑	Positiva CDTIV 114
11/09/1999	69	1		WE'RE GOING TO IBIZA! (IMPORT) Based on Typically Tropical's *Barbados*	Jive 550422
18/09/1999	❶¹	12	●	WE'RE GOING TO IBIZA! ↑	Positiva CDTIVS 119
18/12/1999	3	18	○	KISS (WHEN THE SUN DON'T SHINE)	Positiva CDTIV 122
11/03/2000	5	10	○	SHALALA LALA	Positiva CDTIV 126
08/07/2000	6	7		UNCLE JOHN FROM JAMAICA	Positiva CDTIV 135
14/10/2000	19	5		CHEEKAH BOW WOW (THAT COMPUTER SONG)	Positiva CDTIV 142
24/02/2001	28	2		FOREVER AS ONE	Positiva CDTIV 148

VENT 414
UK group formed by Miles Hunt (formerly of Wonder Stuff), Pete Howard and Morgan Nicholls.

28/09/1996	71	1	FIXER	Polydor 5753292

VENTURES
US rock 'n' roll band formed in 1960 in Seattle, Washington by Don Wilson (born 10/2/1937, Tacoma, WA, guitar), Nokie Edwards (born 9/5/1939, WA, guitar), Howie Johnson (born 1938, WA, drums) and Bob Bogle (born 16/1/1937, Portland, OR, guitar/bass) as The Versatones. Formed the Blue Horizon label and name-changed for their second single *Walk Don't Run*, the master being bought by Liberty subsidiary Dolton. Johnson left in 1962 following a car accident and was replaced by Mel Taylor (born 24/9/1933 in Brooklyn, NYC), who left in 1973 to form his own group, returning in 1978. Edwards left in 1967 and his replacement was Gerry McGee. Edwards returned in 1972 and left for good in 1985, and keyboard player John Durrill joined in 1969. The group still tours and are very big in Japan. Johnson died in January 1988, while Taylor died from cancer on 11/8/1996.

08/09/1960	8	13	WALK DON'T RUN Featured in the 1999 film *American Pie*	Top Rank JAR 417
01/12/1960	4	13	PERFIDIA	London HLG 9232
09/03/1961	45	1	RAM-BUNK-SHUSH	London HLG 9292
11/05/1961	43	4	LULLABY OF THE LEAVES	London HLG 9344

VERACOCHA
Dutch dance group formed by Ferry Corsten and Vincent De Moor. Corsten is also a member of Gouryella, Starparty and System F and also records under his own name and as Albion and Moonman. De Moor also records under his own name.

15/05/1999	22	4	CARTE BLANCHE	Positiva CDTIV 110

AL VERLAINE – see PING PING AND AL VERLAINE

VERNONS GIRLS
UK group formed in Liverpool, featuring Maureen Kennedy, Jean Owen and Frances Lee at the time of their hits. They were later fronted by Lynn Cornell, who became a member of the Pearls and recorded solo. They took their name from their sponsor, the pools company Vernons.

17/05/1962	16	9	LOVER PLEASE	Decca F 11450
23/08/1962	39	11	LOVER PLEASE/YOU KNOW WHAT I MEAN	Decca F 11450
06/09/1962	47	1	LOCO-MOTION	Decca F 11495
03/01/1963	31	8	FUNNY ALL OVER	Decca F 11549
18/04/1963	44	2	DO THE BIRD	Decca F 11629

VERNON'S WONDERLAND
German producer Matthias Hoffmann.

25/05/1996	59	1	VERNON'S WONDERLAND	Eye Q Classics EYECL 004CD

VERONIKA – see CRW

VERTICAL HORIZON
US rock group formed in Boston, MA by Matt Scannell (vocals), Keith Kane (guitar), Sean Hurley (bass) and Ed Toth (drums).

26/08/2000	42	2	EVERYTHING YOU WANT ▲¹	RCA 74321748692

VERUCA SALT
US group formed in Chicago, IL in 1992 by Nina Gordon (guitar/vocals), Louise Post (guitar/vocals), Steve Lack (bass) and Jim Shapiro (drums). Debut recordings for Minty Fresh in 1993 and subsequently linked with Geffen Records (who had already snapped up Jim Powers, the founder of Minty Fresh Records).

02/07/1994	61	1	SEETHER	Scared Hitless FRET 003CD
03/12/1994	73	1	SEETHER Re-issue of Scared Hitless FRET 003CD	Hi-Rise FLATSDG 12
04/02/1995	68	1	NUMBER ONE BLIND	Hi-Rise FLATSDG 16
22/02/1997	56	1	VOLCANO GIRLS	Outpost OPRCD 22197
30/08/1997	75	1	BENJAMIN	Outpost OPRCD 22261

❶⁹ Number of weeks single topped the UK chart ↑ Entered the UK chart at #1 ▲⁹ Number of weeks single topped the US chart

851

VERVE UK group formed in 1989 by Richard Ashcroft (born 11/9/1971, Wigan, vocals), Peter Salisbury (born 24/9/1971, drums), Simon Jones (born 29/7/1972, bass) and Nick McCabe (born 14/7/1971, guitar). Their debut album was released in 1993. They were named Best British Group and Best Producer at the 1998 BRIT Awards, while their album *Urban Hymns* was named Best Album. They disbanded in April 1999 with Ashcroft going solo and Jones joining The Shining.

04/07/1992	66	1		SHE'S A SUPERSTAR .... Hut 16
22/05/1993	69	1		BLUE .... Hut HUTCD 29
13/05/1995	35	3		THIS IS MUSIC .... Hut HUTCD 54
24/06/1995	28	2		ON YOUR OWN .... Hut HUTCD 55
30/09/1995	24	3		HISTORY .... Hut HUTDX 59
28/06/1997	2	13	O	**BITTER SWEET SYMPHONY** Contains a sample of Andrew Loog Oldham's *The Last Time*. Featured in the 1999 film *Cruel Intentions* .... Hut HUTDG 82
13/09/1997	❶[1]	13	O	**THE DRUGS DON'T WORK** ↑ .... Hut HUTDG 88
06/12/1997	7	13		**LUCKY MAN** .... Hut HUTDG 92
30/05/1998	74	1		SONNET (IMPORT) .... Hut 8950752

A VERY GOOD FRIEND OF MINE Italian vocal/instrumental/production group formed by Mario Caminita and Dario Caminita with singer Joy.

03/07/1999	55	1		JUST ROUND Contains a sample of Stevie Wonder's *Uptight* .... Positiva CDTIV 109

VEX RED UK rock group formed in Aldershot by Terry Abbott (guitar and vocals), Keith Lambert (bass and programming), Ant Forbes (guitar and keyboards), Nick Goulding (guitar and bass) and Ben Calvert (drums).

02/03/2002	45	1		CAN'T SMILE .... Virgin VUSCD 237

VIBRATIONS – see **TONY JACKSON AND THE VIBRATIONS**

VIBRATORS UK punk group formed by Knox (born Ian Carnochan, 4/4/1945, guitar/vocals), John Ellis (born 1/6/1952, guitar), Pat Collier (born October 1951, bass) and Eddie (born 1/4/1951, drums), later adding Chris Spedding (born 17/6/1944, Sheffield). They pulled out of the Sex Pistols' Anarchy In The UK tour following the furore over the Pistols' TV appearance with Bill Grundy.

18/03/1978	35	5		AUTOMATIC LOVER .... Epic EPC 6137
17/06/1978	70	3		JUDY SAYS (KNOCK YOU IN THE HEAD) .... Epic EPC 6393

VICE SQUAD UK group formed in Bristol in 1978 by Beki Bondage (born Rebecca Bond, vocals), Dave Bateman (guitar), Mark Hambly (bass) and Shane Baldwin (drums). Bondage left in 1984 to form Ligotage and later Beki And The Bomshells while Vice Squad recruited Lia (vocals) and Sooty (guitar) for one album before disbanding in 1985.

13/02/1982	68	1		OUT OF REACH .... Zonophone Z 26

VICIOUS CIRCLES UK producer Simon Berry who also records as Poltergeist.

16/12/2000	68	1		VICIOUS CIRCLES .... Platipus PLATCD 82

VICIOUS PINK UK vocal/instrumental duo Josie Warden and Brian Moss.

15/09/1984	67	4		CCCAN'T YOU SEE .... Parlophone R 6074

MIKE VICKERS – see **KENNY EVERETT**

MARIA VIDAL US singer also in demand as a backing singer for the likes of Belinda Carlisle, Stevie Nicks and Celine Dion, and also an accomplished songwriter, usually in conjunction with Robert Seidman.

24/08/1985	11	13		BODY ROCK Featured in the 1985 film *Body Rock* .... EMI America EA 189

VIDEO KIDS Dutch vocal duo formed by Peter Slaghuis, later to record under the name Hithouse.

05/10/1985	72	1		WOODPECKERS FROM SPACE .... Epic A 6504

VIDEO SYMPHONIC UK orchestra.

24/10/1981	42	3		THE FLAME TREES OF THIKA Theme to the TV series of the same name .... EMI 5222

VIENNA PHILHARMONIC ORCHESTRA Austrian orchestra established in 1842; it moved to the Grosser Musikvereinssaal in 1870 and is also the Vienna Staatsoper orchestra. Debut hit was conducted by Aram Khachaturian.

18/12/1971	15	14		THEME FROM 'THE ONEDIN LINE' Theme to the TV series *The Onedin Line* .... Decca F 13259

VIEW FROM THE HILL UK group formed by Angela Wynter (vocals), Patrick Patterson (guitar and vocals) and Trevor White (bass and vocals).

19/07/1986	58	3		NO CONVERSATION .... EMI 5565
21/02/1987	59	3		I'M NO REBEL .... EMI 5580

VIKKI UK singer (full name Vikki Watson) whose debut hit was Britain's entry in the 1985 Eurovision Song Contest, won by Norway's Bobbysocks with *Let It Swing*.

04/05/1985	49	3		LOVE IS Britain's entry in the 1985 Eurovision Song Contest that came fourth .... PRT 7P 326

VILLAGE PEOPLE US group formed in New York by French producer Jacques Morali, each member representing gay stereotypes (although only one was actually gay): Randy Jones (cowboy), David 'Scar' Hodo (construction worker), Felipe Rose (Red Indian), Glenn

O Silver disc ● Gold disc ✪ Platinum disc (additional platinum units are indicated by a figure following the symbol) ◎ Singles released prior to 1973 that are known to have sold over 1 million copies in the UK

Hughes (leather biker), Alexander Briley (soldier) and Victor Willis (policeman). Willis was later replaced by Ray Simpson (brother of Valerie Ashford). The group appeared in the film *Can't Stop The Music*. Morali died from AIDS on 15/11/1991 (his mother, who had dressed him as a girl while he was growing up, was barred from his funeral in Paris). Hughes died from lung cancer on 14/3/2001 at the age of 51. Although he had left the group in 1995, he asked to be buried wearing his biker outfit.

03/12/1977	45	5		SAN FRANCISCO (YOU'VE GOT ME)	DJM DJS 10817
25/11/1978	❶³	16	✪	**Y.M.C.A.** Featured in the films *Wayne's World 2* (1993) and *A Night At McCools* (2000)	Mercury 6007 192
17/03/1979	2	9	○	**IN THE NAVY**	Mercury 6007 209
16/06/1979	15	8		GO WEST Featured in the films *Can't Stop The Music* (1980) and *The Adventures Of Priscilla: Queen Of The Desert* (1994)	Mercury 6007 221
09/08/1980	11	11		CAN'T STOP THE MUSIC Featured in the 1980 film *Can't Stop The Music*	Mercury MER 16
09/02/1985	59	5		SEX OVER THE PHONE	Record Shack SOHO 34
04/12/1993	12	7		Y.M.C.A. (REMIX)	Bell 74321177182
28/05/1994	36	2		IN THE NAVY (REMIX)	Bell 74321198192
27/11/1999	35	3		Y.M.C.A. (2ND REMIX)	Wrasse WRASX 002

V.I.M. UK instrumental/production group formed by Peter Harman, Andrew Harman, Casper Pound and Tarquin Boyesen.

26/01/1991	68	1		MAGGIE'S LAST PARTY	F2 BOZ 1

GENE VINCENT US singer (born Vincent Eugene Craddock, 11/2/1935, Norfolk, VA) who was discharged from the US Navy in 1956 following a motorcycle accident and had to wear a steel brace thereafter. Debut recordings in 1956 with his group the Blue Caps (Cliff Gallup, guitar, Willie Williams, guitar, Jack Neal, bass and Dickie Harrell on drums), scoring a US top ten hit with the B-side *Be Bop A Lula*. The Blue Caps split in 1958 (Vincent had been unable to pay them their wages, which prompted the Musicians Union to withdraw his card). He was injured in the car crash that killed Eddie Cochran in 1960. Vincent died from a bleeding ulcer on 12/9/1970, Gallup dying from a heart attack on 9/10/1988 aged 58 years. Gene Vincent was inducted into the Rock & Roll Hall of Fame in 1998.

13/07/1956	16	7		BE BOP A LULA Featured in the 1957 film *The Girl Can't Help It*	Capitol CL 14599
12/10/1956	28	1		RACE WITH THE DEVIL	Capitol CL 14628
19/10/1956	16	5		BLUE JEAN BOP	Capitol CL 14637
08/01/1960	21	6		WILD CAT	Capitol CL 15099
10/03/1960	16	8		MY HEART	Capitol CL 15115
16/06/1960	15	9		PISTOL PACKIN' MAMA	Capitol CL 15136
01/06/1961	22	11		SHE SHE LITTLE SHEILA	Capitol CL 15202
31/08/1961	36	4		I'M GOING HOME (TO SEE MY BABY)	Capitol CL 15215

VINDALOO SUMMER SPECIAL UK vocal/instrumental group formed by Robert Lloyd (born 1959, Cannock, Staffordshire). He had previously formed The Prefects and Nightingales and launched the Vindaloo label in 1980.

19/07/1986	56	3		ROCKIN' WITH RITA (HEAD TO TOE)	Vindaloo UGH 13

VINES Australian rock group formed by Craig Nicholls (guitar/vocals), Ryan Griffiths (guitar), Patrick Matthews (bass) and David Olliffe (drums). Olliffe appeared on their debut album but left the group as he disliked touring and was replaced by Hamish Rosser.

20/04/2002	32	2		HIGHLY EVOLVED	Heavenly HVN 112CD
29/06/2002	24	3		GET FREE	Heavenly HVN 113CD
19/10/2002	20	2		OUTTATHAWAY	Heavenly HVN 120CDS
20/03/2004	25	3		RIDE	Heavenly HVN 137CD
05/06/2004	42	2		WINNING DAYS	Heavenly HVN 139CDS

BOBBY VINTON US singer (born Stanley Robert Vinton, 16/4/1935 Canonsburg, PA) who formed his own band, The Tempos, while still at high school. The band recorded two albums for Epic. Vinton went solo in 1962 and had his own TV series 1975–78. He has a star on the Hollywood Walk of Fame.

02/08/1962	15	8		ROSES ARE RED (MY LOVE) ▲⁴	Columbia DB 4878
19/12/1963	34	10		THERE I'VE SAID IT AGAIN ▲⁴	Columbia DB 7179
29/09/1990	2	10		**BLUE VELVET** ▲³ Originally a US hit in 1963 and revived following use in a Nivea advertisement. Featured in the 1987 film *Blue Velvet*	Epic 6505240
17/11/1990	71	1		ROSES ARE RED (MY LOVE) Re-issue of Columbia DB 4878	Epic 6564677

VINYLGROOVER AND THE RED HED UK production duo Nick Sentience (born Nick Fryer) and BK (Brian Keen).

27/01/2001	72	1		ROK DA HOUSE	Nukleuz NUKP 0285
10/07/2004	61	1		STAY ROB TISSERA AND VINYLGROOVER	Tidy Trax TIDYTWO133C

VIOLENT DELIGHT UK rock group formed in London in 1999 by Rodney Henderson (vocals), VD Tom Steenvoorden (guitar), MC Ben Macrow (bass) and DJ Ken Hayakawa (drums). Tom left in November 2003.

01/03/2003	25	3		I WISH I WAS A GIRL	WEA 362CD
21/06/2003	38	1		ALL YOU EVER DO	WEA 367CD
13/09/2003	64	1		TRANSMISSION	WEA 370CD

VIOLINSKI UK instrumental group formed by Electric Light Orchestra member Mik Kaminski and also featuring Michael D'Albuquerque, Baz Dunnery, John Hodson, Paul Mann, John Marcangelo, Iain Whitmore and Andrew Brown.

17/02/1979	17	9		CLOG DANCE	Jet 136

❶⁹ Number of weeks single topped the UK chart ↑ Entered the UK chart at #1 ▲⁹ Number of weeks single topped the US chart

853

VIPER Belgian production group formed by Ilse Leonaer, Marc Guillaume and Suzanne Coolkens.

07/02/1998.....55......1....... THE TWISTER Contains a sample of Nina Simone's *Feeling Good* .... Hooj Choons HOOJCD 59

VIPER UK rapper.

19/05/2001.....72......1....... PUT YOUR HANDS UP **REFLEX FEATURING MC VIPER** .... Gusto CDGUS 2
14/09/2002.....51......1....... SELECTA (URBAN HEROES) **JAMESON AND VIPER** .... Soundproof SPR 1CD

VIPERS SKIFFLE GROUP UK skiffle group whose hit-making line-up in 1956 included founder Wally Whyton (born 23/9/1929, guitar/vocals), guitarists Johnny Booker and Jean Van Der Bosch, bassist Tony Tolhurst and John Pilgrim on washboard. Singer Tommy Steele (born Thomas Hicks, 17/12/1936, London) was briefly involved before they began recording. A later line-up included Hank Marvin (born Brian Rankin, 28/10/1941, Newcastle-upon-Tyne), Jet Harris (born Terence Harris, 6/7/1939, Kingsbury, Middlesex) and Bruce Welch (born Bruce Cripps, 2/11/1941 Bognor Regis). Steele became a solo star, while Marvin, Harris and Welch formed The Shadows. Tony Meehan, another future Shadow, was also a member at one point. Whyton later became a radio presenter and died from cancer on 22/1/1997.

25/01/1957.....10......9...... **DON'T YOU ROCK ME DADDY-O** Written by Wally Whyton, Lonnie Donegan's cover version charted at # 4 .... Parlophone R 4261
22/03/1957.....10......6...... **CUMBERLAND GAP** .... Parlophone R 4289
31/05/1957.....23......3...... STREAMLINE TRAIN .... Parlophone R 4308

VIPS UK group formed in 1978 by Jed Dmochowski (guitar and vocals), Guy Morley (guitar), Andrew Price (bass) and Paul Shurey (drums).

06/09/1980.....55......4....... THE QUARTER MOON .... Gem GEMS 39

VIRGINIA – see **TOM NOVY**

VIRUS UK production duo Paul Oakenfold and Steve Osborne, and featuring Stephanie Dosen on vocals.

26/08/1995.....62......1...... SUN .... Perfecto PERF 107CD
25/01/1997.....36......2...... MOON .... Perfecto PERF 134CD

VISAGE UK electronic dance group formed by Steve Strange (born Steve Harrington, 28/5/1959), Rusty Egan (born 19/9/1957) and Midge Ure. Ure later left to join Ultravox, with Strange and Egan opening London's Camden Palace venue.

20/12/1980.....8......15.....O **FADE TO GREY** .... Polydor POSP 194
14/03/1981.....13......8...... MIND OF A TOY .... Polydor POSP 236
11/07/1981.....21......7...... VISAGE .... Polydor POSP 293
13/03/1982.....11......8...... DAMNED DON'T CRY .... Polydor POSP 390
26/06/1982.....12......10..... NIGHT TRAIN .... Polydor POSP 441
13/11/1982.....44......3...... PLEASURE BOYS .... Polydor POSP 523
01/09/1984.....54......3...... LOVE GLOVE .... Polydor POSP 691
28/08/1993.....39......2...... FADE TO GREY (REMIX) .... Polydor PZCD 282

MICHELLE VISAGE US singer (born 20/9/1968, New York) who was a member of Seduction before going solo.

16/01/1993.....17......5....... IT'S GONNA BE A LOVELY DAY **S.O.U.L. S.Y.S.T.E.M. INTRODUCING MICHELLE VISAGE** Rap version of Bill Wither's hit *Lovely Day*. Featured in the 1992 film *The Bodyguard*. .... Arista 74321125692

VISCOUNTS UK group formed by three of the Morton Fraser Harmonica Gang – Gordon Mills, Don Paul and Ronnie Wells. Mills later became a successful songwriter and manager, founding the MAM label.

13/10/1960.....16......8...... SHORT'NIN' BREAD... Pye 7N 15287
14/09/1961.....21......10..... WHO PUT THE BOMP .... Pye 7N 15379

VISION UK group formed by Pete Dineley (bass/vocals), Andy Beaumont (keyboards) and Chip Gillott (drums).

09/07/1983.....74......1....... LOVE DANCE .... MVM 2886

VISIONMASTERS WITH TONY KING AND KYLIE MINOGUE UK DJ/production duo Mike Stock and Pete Waterman, with DJ Tony King and Australian singer Kylie Minogue.

30/11/1991.....49......1....... KEEP ON PUMPIN' IT.. PWL 207

VITA US singer (born Lavita Rayer, Brooklyn, NYC) who is also a member of Irv Gotti's Murderers.

09/06/2001.....33......2...... LAPDANCE **N*E*R*D FEATURING LEE HARVEY AND VITA**... Virgin VUSCD 196
12/10/2002.....4......10...... **DOWN 4 U IRV GOTTI PRESENTS JA RULE, ASHANTI, CHARLI BALTIMORE AND VITA**................. Murder Inc 0639002

VITAMIN C US singer (born Colleen Fitzpatrick, 20/7/1972, Old Bridge, NJ) who was a member of Eve's Plum before going solo. She also made her name as an actress, appearing in the 1988 film *Hairspray*.

19/07/2003.....70......1....... LAST NITE Contains samples of The Strokes' *Last Night* and Blondie's *Heart Of Glass* .... V2 VVR 5023283

SORAYA VIVIAN UK singer (born in Hull).

16/03/2002.....59......1....... WHEN YOU'RE GONE.. Activ 8 ACT 501

VIXEN US heavy rock group formed in Los Angeles, CA in 1986 by Janet Gardner (vocals), Janet Kushnemund (guitar), Pia Koko (bass) and Roxy Petrucci (drums). Koko left before their record debut and was replaced by Share Pedersen (bass). Pedersen later joined Contraband.

03/09/1988.....51......4...... EDGE OF A BROKEN HEART... Manhattan MT 48
04/03/1989.....27......4...... CRYIN' .... EMI Manhattan MT 60
03/06/1989.....36......4...... LOVE MADE ME .... EMI-USA MT 66

02/09/1989	59	2		EDGE OF A BROKEN HEART Re-issue of Manhattan MT 48	EMI-USA MT 48
28/07/1990	35	3		HOW MUCH LOVE	EMI-USA MT 87
20/10/1990	41	2		LOVE IS A KILLER	EMI-USA MT 91
16/03/1991	37	2		NOT A MINUTE TOO SOON	EMI America MT 93

VOGGUE Canadian vocal duo Denis Le Page and Denys Le Page.

18/07/1981	39	6		DANCIN' THE NIGHT AWAY	Mercury MER 76

VOICE OF THE BEEHIVE UK/US group formed by Tracey Bryn (guitar/vocals), her sister Melissa Brooke Belland (guitar), Mick Jones (guitar), Dan Woodgate (drums) and Mark Bedford (bass). They first signed with the Food label.

14/11/1987	45	5		I SAY NOTHING	London LON 151
05/03/1988	42	4		I WALK THE EARTH	London LON 169
14/05/1988	15	10		DON'T CALL ME BABY	London LON 175
23/07/1988	22	6		I SAY NOTHING	London LON 190
22/10/1988	46	4		I WALK THE EARTH	London LON 206
13/07/1991	17	10		MONSTERS AND ANGELS	London LON 302
28/09/1991	25	6		I THINK I LOVE YOU	London LON 308
25/01/1992	37	6		PERFECT PLACE	London LON 312

VOICES OF LIFE US vocal/production duo Steve 'Silk' Hurley (born 9/11/1962, Chicago, IL) and Sharon Pass.

21/03/1998	26	2		THE WORD IS LOVE (SAY THE WORD)	AM:PM 5825272

STERLING VOID UK instrumentalist and singer who also made his name as a songwriter, with hits for The Pet Shop Boys.

04/02/1989	53	3		RUNAWAY GIRL/IT'S ALL RIGHT	ffrr FFR 21

VOLATILE AGENTS FEATURING SIMONE BENN UK garage duo formed by Kiss FM DJ Bamster and singer Simone Benn, the latter discovered via a breakfast show competition.

15/12/2001	54	3		HOOKED ON YOU	Melting Pot MPRCD 10

VOLCANO Norwegian vocal/instrumental group formed by Rune Lindbaek, Bjorn Torkse and Ole Mjos.

23/07/1994	32	3		MORE TO LOVE	Deconstruction 74321221832
18/11/1995	72	1		THAT'S THE WAY LOVE IS VOLCANO WITH SAM CARTWRIGHT	EXP EXPCD 002

VON BONDIES US rock group formed in Detroit, MI by Jason Stollsteimer (guitar/vocals), Marcie Bolen (guitar), Carrie Smith (bass) and Don Blum (drums).

14/02/2004	21	2		C'MON C'MON	Sire W 635CD
15/05/2004	43	1		TELL ME WHAT YOU SEE	Sire W 639CD

VOODOO AND SERANO German production duo Reinhard Raith and Tommy Serano.

03/02/2001	19	4		BLOOD IS PUMPIN'	Xtrahard X2H2 CDS
16/08/2003	30	2		OVERLOAD	All Around The World CDGLOBE 284

VOYAGE French/UK group comprising Marc Chantereau (keyboards/vocals), Pierre-Alain Dahan (drums/vocals), Slim Pezin (guitar/vocals), Sylvia Mason (lead vocals) and Sauveur Mallia (bass).

17/06/1978	13	13		FROM EAST TO WEST/SCOTS MACHINE	GTO GT 224
25/11/1978	56	7		SOUVENIRS	GTO GT 241
24/03/1979	38	7		LET'S FLY AWAY	GTO GT 245

VOYAGER UK group formed in 1977 by Paul French (keyboards/vocals), Paul Hirsh (guitar/keyboards), Chris Hook (bass) and John Marter (drums). They disbanded in 1981.

26/05/1979	33	8		HALFWAY HOTEL	Mountain VOY 001

JURGEN VRIES UK producer Darren Tate who is also a member of Angelic and DT8 and records as Citizen Caned. CMC is UK singer Charlotte Church.

14/09/2002	13	4		THE THEME	Direction 6730952
01/02/2003	3	10		THE OPERA SONG (BRAVE NEW WORLD) JURGEN VRIES FEATURING CMC	Direction 6734642
04/10/2003	20	3		WILDERNESS JURGEN VRIES FEATURING SHENA	Direction 6742692
19/06/2004	23	3		TAKE MY HAND JURGEN VRIES FEATURING ANDREA BRITTON	Direction 6749932

VS UK vocal group formed by Jamie Summaz, Chinyere McKenzie, Blimi, Marvin Humes and Rayan Taylor.

06/03/2004	7	7		LOVE YOU LIKE MAD	Innocent SINCD 59
19/06/2004	11	6		CALL U SEXY Contains a sample of Imagination's Body Talk	Innocent SINDX 62
23/10/2004	29	2		MAKE IT HOT	Innocent SINDX 66

VYBE US vocal group formed in Los Angeles, CA by Pam Olivia, Tanya Robinson, Debbie Mitchell and Stacey Dove-Daniels.

07/10/1995	60	1		WARM SUMMER DAZE Contains a sample of Judy Clay and William Bell's Private Number	Fourth & Broadway BRCD 315

VYBZ KARTEL – see ZENA

---

❶[9] Number of weeks single topped the UK chart   ↑ Entered the UK chart at #1   **▲**[9] Number of weeks single topped the US chart

BILLY PAUL W – see ROBBIE RIVERA

KRISTINE W US singer (born Kristine Weitz, Pasco, WA) who began performing from the age of eight. A former beauty queen (Miss Tri Citie 1980, Miss Washington 1981), she is also an accomplished saxophonist, guitarist, drummer and pianist.

21/05/1994	73	1	LOVE COME HOME . . . . Triangle BLUESCD 001
25/06/1994	33	3	FEEL WHAT YOU WANT . . . . Champion CHAMPCD 304
25/05/1996	41	1	ONE MORE TRY . . . . Champion CHAMPCD 317
21/12/1996	57	1	LAND OF THE LIVING . . . . Champion CHAMPCD 324
05/07/1997	40	2	FEEL WHAT YOU WANT Re-issue of Champion CHAMPCD 304 . . . . Champion CHAMPCD 329

BILL WADDINGTON – see CORONATION STREET CAST FEATURING BILL WADDINGTON

ADAM WADE WITH THE GEORGE PAXTON ORCHESTRA AND CHORUS US singer (born 17/3/1937, Pittsburgh, PA) who was later an actor and TV gameshow and talkshow host. Wade's films included *Shaft* (1971), *Claudine* (1974) and *Kiss Me Goodbye* (1982).

08/06/1961	38	6	TAKE GOOD CARE OF HER . . . . HMV POP 843

WAG YA TAIL FEATURING LONNIE LISTON SMITH UK vocal/instrumental group with US keyboard player Lonnie Liston Smith (born 28/12/1940, Richmond, VA).

03/10/1992	49	1	XPAND YA MIND (EXPANSIONS) . . . . PWL International PWL 238

WAH! UK rock group formed in Liverpool in 1979 by Pete Wylie after being in the Crucial Three with Julian Cope and Ian McCulloch.

25/12/1982	3	12	**THE STORY OF THE BLUES** . . . . Eternal JF 1
19/03/1983	37	5	HOPE (I WISH YOU'D BELIEVE ME) . . . . WEA X 9880
30/06/1984	20	9	COME BACK MIGHTY WAH . . . . Beggars Banquet BEG 111

DONNIE WAHLBERG – see SEIKO AND DONNIE WAHLBERG

WAIKIKIS Belgian instrumental group formed by Willy Albimoor.

11/03/1965	41	2	HAWAII TATTOO . . . . Pye International 7N 25286

WAILERS – see BOB MARLEY AND THE WAILERS

RUFUS WAINWRIGHT Canadian singer (born 1973), son of Loudon Wainwright III and Kate McGarrigle. When his parents divorced, he was brought up by his mother in Montreal and sang with her in her group McGarrigle Sisters with his aunt Anna from the age of thirteen.

07/08/2004	74	1	I DON'T KNOW WHAT IT IS . . . . DreamWorks 9863229

JOHN WAITE UK singer (born 4/7/1955, London) who was lead singer with the Babys and Bad English before going solo in 1981.

29/09/1984	9	11	**MISSING YOU ▲1** . . . . EMI America EA 182
13/02/1993	56	2	MISSING YOU Re-issue of EMI America EA 182 . . . . Chrysalis CDCHS 3938

WAITRESSES US group formed in Akron, OH in 1978 by Patty Donahue (vocals), Chris Butler (guitar), Dan Kleyman (keyboards), Mars Williams (saxophone), Tracy Wormworth (bass) and Billy Ficca (drums). Donahue died from cancer on 9/12/1996.

18/12/1982	45	4	CHRISTMAS WRAPPING . . . . Ze/Island WIP 6821

JOHNNY WAKELIN UK singer/songwriter (born 1939) whose ambition to become a professional footballer was dashed at sixteen after losing a leg in a road accident. Both hits were tributes to US boxer Muhammad Ali (formerly Cassius Clay).

18/01/1975	7	10	**BLACK SUPERMAN (MUHAMMAD ALI)** JOHNNY WAKELIN AND THE KINSHASA BAND . . . . Pye 7N 45420
24/07/1976	4	10	**IN ZAIRE** . . . . Pye 7N 45595

NARADA MICHAEL WALDEN US singer/producer (born Michael Anthony Walden, 23/4/1952, Kalamazoo, MI) who was a drummer with the Mahavishnu Orchestra 1973–1975 before going solo. Later a successful writer and producer, he was given the name Narada (which means 'supreme musician') by Sri Chinmoy. He has won two Grammy Awards: Best Rhythm & Blues Song in 1985 for *Freeway Of Love* and Producer of the Year in 1987.

23/02/1980	34	9	TONIGHT I'M ALL RIGHT . . . . Atlantic K 11437
26/04/1980	8	9	**I SHOULDA LOVED YA** . . . . Atlantic K 11413

○ Silver disc ● Gold disc ✪ Platinum disc (additional platinum units are indicated by a figure following the symbol) ◎ Singles released prior to 1973 that are known to have sold over 1 million copies in the UK

DATE	POS	WKS	BPI	SINGLE TITLE	LABEL & NUMBER
23/04/1988	8	10		**DIVINE EMOTIONS** NARADA Featured in the 1988 film *Bright Lights, Big City*	Reprise W 7967

GARY WALKER
US singer (born Gary Leeds, 3/9/1944, Glendale, CA) who was drummer with PJ Proby's band and The Standells before joining The Walker Brothers in 1964. The group disbanded in 1967, re-forming in 1976.

DATE	POS	WKS	BPI	SINGLE TITLE	LABEL & NUMBER
24/02/1966	26	6		YOU DON'T LOVE ME	CBS 202036
26/05/1966	26	6		TWINKIE LEE	CBS 202081

JOHN WALKER
US singer (born John Maus, 12/11/1943, NYC) who was in the Walker Brothers from 1964. The group disbanded in 1967, re-forming in 1976.

DATE	POS	WKS	BPI	SINGLE TITLE	LABEL & NUMBER
05/07/1967	24	6		ANNABELLA	Philips BF 1593

SCOTT WALKER
US singer (born Noel Scott Engel, 9/1/1944, Hamilton, OH) who was a member of the Walker Brothers from 1964. The group disbanded in 1967, re-forming in 1976.

DATE	POS	WKS	BPI	SINGLE TITLE	LABEL & NUMBER
06/12/1967	22	9		JACKIE	Philips BF 1628
01/05/1968	7	11		**JOANNA**	Philips BF 1662
11/06/1969	13	10		LIGHTS OF CINCINNATI	Philips BF 1793

JUNIOR WALKER AND THE ALL-STARS
US singer/saxophonist (born Autry DeWalt Jr, 14/6/1931, Blytheville, AR), nicknamed Junior by his stepfather. Signed by Harvey Fuqua to his Harvey label in 1962 and moving to Motown in 1964, they later recorded briefly for Norman Whitfield's before returning to Motown. The All-Stars also included Willie Woods (guitar), Vic Thomas (organ) and James Graves (drums). Graves was killed in a car crash in 1967, Walker died from cancer on 23/11/1995 and Woods died from lung cancer on 27/5/1997. Walker appeared in the 1988 film *Tapeheads*.

DATE	POS	WKS	BPI	SINGLE TITLE	LABEL & NUMBER
18/08/1966	22	10		HOW SWEET IT IS	Tamla Motown TMG 571
02/04/1969	12	12		(I'M A) ROAD RUNNER	Tamla Motown TMG 691
18/10/1969	13	12		WHAT DOES IT TAKE (TO WIN YOUR LOVE)	Tamla Motown TMG 712
26/08/1972	16	11		WALK IN THE NIGHT	Tamla Motown TMG 824
27/01/1973	16	9		TAKE ME GIRL I'M READY	Tamla Motown TMG 840
30/06/1973	35	5		WAY BACK HOME	Tamla Motown TMG 857

TERRI WALKER
UK R&B singer (born 1980, London) who was a studio singer for Xosa before being signed by Def Soul.

DATE	POS	WKS	BPI	SINGLE TITLE	LABEL & NUMBER
01/03/2003	60	1		GUESS YOU DIDN'T LOVE ME	Def Soul 779962
17/05/2003	38	2		CHING CHING (LOVIN' YOU STILL)	Def Soul 9800075

WALKER BROTHERS
US vocal group formed in 1964 by Noel Scott Engel (born 9/1/1944, Hamilton, OH), John Maus (born 12/11/1943, NYC) and Gary Leeds (born 3/9/1944, Glendale, CA), all adopting Walker as a stage surname. Signed by Smash in the US, they disbanded in 1967, by which time both John and Gary had begun solo careers. They re-formed in 1976 for three albums.

DATE	POS	WKS	BPI	SINGLE TITLE	LABEL & NUMBER
29/04/1965	20	13		LOVE HER	Philips BF 1409
19/08/1965	❶1	14		**MAKE IT EASY ON YOURSELF**	Philips BF 1428
02/12/1965	3	12		**MY SHIP IS COMING IN**	Philips BF 1454
03/03/1966	❶4	11		**THE SUN AIN'T GONNA SHINE ANYMORE**	Philips BF 1473
14/07/1966	13	8		(BABY) YOU DON'T HAVE TO TELL ME	Philips BF 1497
22/09/1966	12	8		ANOTHER TEAR FALLS	Philips BF 1514
15/12/1966	34	6		DEADLIER THAN THE MALE Featured in the 1967 film *Deadlier Than The Male*	Philips BF 1537
09/02/1967	26	6		STAY WITH ME BABY	Philips BF 1548
18/05/1967	26	6		WALKING IN THE RAIN	Philips BF 1576
17/01/1976	7	9		**NO REGRETS**	GTO GT 42

WALKMEN
US rock group formed in New York, NYC in 2000 by Walter Martin (keyboards/vocals), Paul Maroon (guitar), Hamilton Leithauser, Peter Bauer and Matt Barrick (drums). Martin, Maroon and Barrick had previously been with Jonathan Fire Eater, Leithauser and Bauer with The Recoys.

DATE	POS	WKS	BPI	SINGLE TITLE	LABEL & NUMBER
01/05/2004	45	1		THE RAT	WEA W640CD
10/07/2004	72	1		LITTLE HOUSE OF SAVAGES	Record Collection W646CD

WALL OF SOUND FEATURING GERALD LETHAN
US vocal/instrumental group formed by Lem Springsteen and Gerald Lethan. Springsteen was later a member of Mood II Swing.

DATE	POS	WKS	BPI	SINGLE TITLE	LABEL & NUMBER
31/07/1993	73	1		CRITICAL (IF ONLY YOU KNEW)	Positiva CDTIV 4

WALL OF VOODOO
US rock group formed in Los Angeles, CA in 1977 by Stan Ridgway (keyboards/vocals), Bill Noland (guitar/vocals), Charles Gray (bass/keyboards) and Joe Nanini (drums). Noland left in 1981 and was replaced by Marc Moreland, Bruce Moreland (bass) joining at the same time. Ridgway went solo in 1985 and was replaced by Andy Prieboy. Moreland died from kidney failure on 13/3/2002.

DATE	POS	WKS	BPI	SINGLE TITLE	LABEL & NUMBER
19/03/1983	64	3		MEXICAN RADIO	Illegal ILS 36

JERRY WALLACE
US singer (born 15/12/1928, Guilford, MO) who made his first recordings for Allied in 1951.

DATE	POS	WKS	BPI	SINGLE TITLE	LABEL & NUMBER
23/06/1960	46	1		YOU'RE SINGING OUR LOVE SONG TO SOMEBODY ELSE	London HLH 9110

RIK WALLER
UK singer (born 1982, Gillingham) who took part in the *Pop Idol* TV series, subsequently won by Will Young. He was forced to withdraw from the final ten with a throat infection (his replacement, Darius, came third). After soloing briefly, he formed Souled As Seen.

---

❶9 Number of weeks single topped the UK chart ↑ Entered the UK chart at #1 ▲9 Number of weeks single topped the US chart

16/03/2002 . . . . . 6 . . . . . . 8 . . . . . . **I WILL ALWAYS LOVE YOU** . . . . Liberty CDRIK 001
06/07/2002 . . . . . 25 . . . . . 4 . . . . SOMETHING INSIDE (SO STRONG) . . . . Liberty CDRIK 002

WALLFLOWERS US rock group formed in Los Angeles, CA by Jakob Dylan (son of Bob Dylan, vocals), Michael Ward (guitar), Rami Jaffe (keyboards), Greg Richling (bass) and Mario Calire (drums).

12/07/1997 . . . . . 54 . . . . . . 1 . . . . ONE HEADLIGHT 1997 Grammy Awards for Best Rock Performance By A Duo Or Group with Vocal, plus Best Rock Song for writer
Jakob Dylan . . . . Interscope IND 95532

BOB WALLIS AND HIS STORYVILLE JAZZ BAND UK singer/trumpeter (born 3/6/1934, Bridlington) who formed The Storyville Jazz Band in 1950. He died on 10/1/1997.

06/07/1961 . . . . . 44 . . . . . . 2 . . . . I'M SHY MARY ELLEN (I'M SHY) . . . . Pye Jazz 7NJ 2043
04/01/1962 . . . . . 33 . . . . . 5 . . . . COME ALONG PLEASE . . . . Pye Jazz 7NJ 2048

JOE WALSH US singer (born 20/11/1947, Wichita, KS) who was in The James Gang 1969–71 and The Eagles 1975–82, fronting his own band in between. He also tried twice for the nomination of Vice President in the US Presidential race.

16/07/1977 . . . . . 39 . . . . . . 4 . . . . ROCKY MOUNTAIN EP Tracks on EP: *Rocky Mountain Way, Turn To Stone, Meadows* and *Walk Away* . . . . ABC ABE 12002
08/07/1978 . . . . . 14 . . . . . 11 . . . . . . LIFE'S BEEN GOOD Featured in the 1978 film *F.M.* . . . . Asylum K 13129

MAUREEN WALSH – see MAUREEN

SHEILA WALSH AND CLIFF RICHARD UK vocal duo Sheila Walsh (born in Ayr, Scotland) and Cliff Richard (born Harry Webb, 14/10/1940, Lucknow, India). Walsh later moved to the US, where she hosted several Christian TV shows.

04/06/1983 . . . . . 64 . . . . . . 2 . . . . DRIFTING . . . . DJM SHEILA 1

STEVE WALSH UK singer (born 1959) who began as a club DJ on the UK soul scene. He broke a leg in Spain while filming a video and was rushed home to England for an operation. He died from a heart attack while undergoing surgery on 3/7/1988.

18/07/1987 . . . . . 9 . . . . . 13 . . . . . . **I FOUND LOVIN'** A1 299
12/12/1987 . . . . . 74 . . . . . 1 . . . . LET'S GET TOGETHER (TONITE) A1 303
30/07/1988 . . . . . 44 . . . . . . 4 . . . . AIN'T NO STOPPING US NOW (PARTY FOR THE WORLD) A1 304

TREVOR WALTERS UK reggae singer who began as a singer with Santic.

24/10/1981 . . . . . 27 . . . . . . 8 . . . . LOVE ME TONIGHT . . . . Magnet MAG 198
21/07/1984 . . . . . 9 . . . . . 12 . . . . . . **STUCK ON YOU** . . . . Sanity IS 002
01/12/1984 . . . . . 73 . . . . . . 2 . . . . NEVER LET HER SLIP AWAY . . . . Polydor POSP 716

WAMDUE PROJECT US dance group formed by Atlanta, GA producer Chris Bann featuring Argentinian singer Victoria Frigerio. Brann had already recorded as Wamdue Kids. The debut single was originally released in the summer of 1998, failing to chart.

20/11/1999 . . . . . 61 . . . . . . 1 . . . . KING OF MY CASTLE (IMPORT) . . . . Orange ORCDM 53584CD
27/11/1999 . . . ❶¹ . . . . 16 . . . . . ● **KING OF MY CASTLE ↑** . . . . AM:PM CDAMPM 127
15/04/2000 . . . . . 39 . . . . . . 2 . . . . YOU'RE THE REASON . . . . AM:PM CDAMPM 130

WANG CHUNG UK rock group formed in 1980 by Jack Hues (guitar/keyboards/vocals), Nick Feldman (bass) and Darren Costin (drums) as Huang Chung. They recorded for Arista, changing name and label in 1982. Costin left in 1985 and they continued as a duo.

28/01/1984 . . . . . 21 . . . . . 12 . . . . . . DANCE HALL DAYS Featured in the films *To Live And Die In L.A.* (1985) and *Romy And Michele's High School Reunion* (1997)
. . . . Geffen A 3837

WANNADIES Swedish rock group formed in 1989 by Par Wiksten (guitar/vocals), Stefan Schonfeldt (guitar), Fredrik Schonfeldt (bass), Cristina Bergmark (percussion) and Gunnar Karlsson (drums).

18/11/1995 . . . . . 51 . . . . . . 2 . . . . MIGHT BE STARS . . . . Indolent DIE 003CD1
24/02/1996 . . . . . 53 . . . . . . 1 . . . . HOW DOES IT FEEL . . . . Indolent DIE 004CD1
20/04/1996 . . . . . 18 . . . . . . 3 . . . . YOU & ME SONG . . . . Indolent DIE 005CD
07/09/1996 . . . . . 38 . . . . . . 1 . . . . SOMEONE SOMEWHERE . . . . Indolent DIE 006CD
26/04/1997 . . . . . 20 . . . . . . 2 . . . . HIT . . . . Indolent DIE 009CD1
05/07/1997 . . . . . 41 . . . . . . 2 . . . . SHORTY . . . . Indolent DIE 010CD1
04/03/2000 . . . . . 56 . . . . . . 1 . . . . YEAH . . . . RCA 74321745552

DEXTER WANSELL US keyboard player (born in Philadelphia, PA) who was in Yellow Sunshine before joining Philadelphia International as an in-house producer, arranger and songwriter. He launched his own solo career in 1976.

20/05/1978 . . . . . 59 . . . . . 3 . . . . . . ALL NIGHT LONG . . . . Philadelphia International PIR 6255

WAR US soul group formed in Long Beach, CA in 1969 by Lonnie Jordan (born 21/11/1948, San Diego, CA, keyboards), Howard Scott (born 15/3/1946, San Pedro, CA, guitar), Charles Miller (born 2/6/1939, Olathe, KS, saxophone), Morris 'BB' Dickerson (born 3/8/1949, Torrence, CA, bass), Harold Brown (born 17/3/1946, Long Beach, CA, drums), Thomas 'Papa Dee' Allen (born 18/7/1931, Wilmington, DE, percussion) and Lee Oskar (born 24/3/1948, Copenhagen, Denmark, harmonica). They were backing group for ex-Animal Eric Burdon before launching their own career in 1971, adding singer Alice Tweed Smith in 1978. Miller was murdered in June 1980 after being shot by a robber, while Allen died from a brain haemorrhage on 29/8/1988.

24/01/1976 . . . . . 12 . . . . . . 7 . . . . LOW RIDER Featured in the films *Dazed And Confused* (1993), *Gone In 60 Seconds* (2000) and *A Knight's Tale* (2001). . . . .
. . . . Island WIP 6267
26/06/1976 . . . . . 21 . . . . . . 7 . . . . ME AND BABY BROTHER Originally released in the US in 1973 (position #15) . . . . Island WIP 6303

○ Silver disc ● Gold disc ✪ Platinum disc (additional platinum units are indicated by a figure following the symbol) ◎ Singles released prior to 1973 that are known to have sold over 1 million copies in the UK

14/01/1978	14	7		GALAXY Featured in the films *54* (1998) and *Summer Of Sam* (1999)	MCA 339
15/04/1978	40	2		HEY SENORITA	MCA 359
10/04/1982	58	4		YOU GOT THE POWER	RCA 201
06/04/1985	43	5		GROOVIN'	Bluebird BR 16

ANITA WARD
US singer (born 20/12/1957, Memphis, TN) discovered by writer/producer Frederick Knight and signed with his Juana label in 1979. Her hit single was originally intended for Stacy Lattishaw and was only recorded by Ward, who disliked the song, because Knight insisted that her album needed one more dance number.

| 02/06/1979 | ❶² | 11 | ● | RING MY BELL ▲² | TK TKR 7543 |

BILLY WARD AND HIS DOMINOES
US pianist (born 19/9/1921, Los Angeles, CA) who founded the Dominoes in 1950 with Clyde McPhatter (born 15/11/1932, Durham, NC), Charlie White (born 1930, Washington DC), Joe Lamont and Bill Brown (born 1936, died 1958). McPhatter was later replaced by Jackie Wilson (born 9/6/1934, Detroit, MI) and then Eugene Mumford (born 24/6/1925, North Carolina). Ward was the only constant member through the 1950s. McPhatter later formed The Drifters. He died from a heart attack on 13/6/1972. He was inducted into the Rock & Roll Hall of Fame in 1987. Mumford died in May 1977, and Wilson lapsed into a coma in 1975 and died on 20/1/1984. Ward died on 15/2/2002.

| 13/09/1957 | 13 | 12 | | STARDUST | London HLU 8465 |
| 29/11/1957 | 30 | 1 | | DEEP PURPLE | London HLU 8502 |

CHRISSY WARD
US singer.

| 24/06/1995 | 62 | 1 | | RIGHT AND EXACT | Ore AG 6CD |
| 08/02/1997 | 59 | 1 | | RIGHT AND EXACT (REMIX) | Ore AG 21CD |

CLIFFORD T. WARD
UK singer (born 10/2/1946, Kidderminster) who was a schoolteacher before recording for John Peel's Dandelion label in the early 1970s. After over twenty years suffering from multiple sclerosis, he died from pneumonia on 18/12/2001.

| 30/06/1973 | 8 | 11 | | GAYE | Charisma CB 205 |
| 26/01/1974 | 37 | 5 | | SCULLERY | Charisma CB 221 |

MICHAEL WARD
UK singer, first known via *Opportunity Knocks*, the TV show's youngest ever winner.

| 29/09/1973 | 15 | 13 | | LET THERE BE PEACE ON EARTH (LET IT BEGIN WITH ME) | Philips 6006 340 |

WARD BROTHERS
UK vocal/instrumental group formed in Barnsley by Graham, Dave and Derek Ward.

| 10/01/1987 | 32 | 8 | | CROSS THAT BRIDGE | Siren 37 |

MATHIAS WARE FEATURING ROB TAYLOR
German producer with singer Rob Taylor. Their debut hit was a cover version of an Icehouse track.

| 09/03/2002 | 42 | 1 | | HEY LITTLE GIRL | Manifesto FESCD 91 |

WARM JETS
UK rock group formed by Louis Jones (guitar/vocals), Paul Noble (guitar/sound effects), Colleen Brown (bass) and Ed Grimshaw (drums). Brown was subsequently replaced by Aki Shibahara.

| 14/02/1998 | 37 | 2 | | NEVER NEVER | Island WAY 6766 |
| 25/04/1998 | 34 | 2 | | HURRICANE | Island CID 697 |

WARM SOUNDS
UK vocal duo Denver Gerrard (born 1945, Johannesburg, South Africa) and Barry Husband, later adding John Carr.

| 04/05/1967 | 27 | 6 | | BIRDS AND BEES | Deram DM 120 |

TONI WARNE
UK singer (born 1979, Ipswich) who was first noticed after winning a TV talent contest.

| 25/04/1987 | 50 | 4 | | BEN | Mint CHEW 110 |

JENNIFER WARNES
US singer (born 3/3/1947, Seattle, WA) who appeared in the Smothers Brothers TV show as Jennifer Warren before playing the lead role in the musical *Hair* in 1968. She signed with Decca in 1968 and later with Reprise and Arista.

15/01/1983	7	13	O	UP WHERE WE BELONG ▲³ JOE COCKER AND JENNIFER WARNES Featured in the 1982 film *An Officer And A Gentleman*, where it was credited as 'love theme', though over the end titles. 1982 Grammy for Best Vocal Performance by a Duo and an Oscar for Best Film Song	Island WIP 6830
25/07/1987	74	1		FIRST WE TAKE MANHATTAN	Cypress PB 49709
31/10/1987	6	12		(I'VE HAD) THE TIME OF MY LIFE ▲¹ Featured in the 1987 film *Dirty Dancing*. 1987 Grammy Award for Best Vocal Performance by a Duo and an Oscar for Best Film Song	RCA PB 49625
15/12/1990	8	11	O	(I'VE HAD) THE TIME OF MY LIFE This and above single credited to BILL MEDLEY AND JENNIFER WARNES Re-released following the TV screening of the 1987 film *Dirty Dancing*	RCA PB 49625

WARP BROTHERS
German DJ/production group formed by Dennis Bierbrodt, Guido Kramer, Olly Goedicke and Jurgen Dohr.

11/11/2000	58	3		PHATT BASS (IMPORT) Featured in the 2000 film *The Blade*	Dos Or Die BMSCDM 40009
09/12/2000	9	8		PHATT BASS WARP BROTHERS VERSUS AQUAGEN	NuLife 74321817102
17/02/2001	19	4		WE WILL SURVIVE Contains a sample of Josh Wink's *Higher State Of Consciousness*	NuLife 74321832722
29/12/2001	40	3		BLAST THE SPEAKERS	NuLife 74321899162

WARRANT
US heavy rock group formed in Los Angeles, CA by Jani Lane (born 1/2/1964, Akron, OH, vocals), Erik Turner (born 31/3/1964, Omaha, NE, guitar), Joey Allan (born 23/6/1964, Fort Wayne, IN, guitar), Jerry Dixon (born 15/9/1967, Pasadena, CA, bass)

❶⁹ Number of weeks single topped the UK chart ↑ Entered the UK chart at #1 ▲⁹ Number of weeks single topped the US chart

859

and Steven Sweet (born 29/10/1965, Weadsworth, OH, drums). They signed with Columbia in 1988. Lane went solo in 1992, later returning. Allen and Sweet also left and were replaced by Rick Steier and James Kottak.

17/11/1990	59	2		CHERRY PIE	CBS 6562587
09/03/1991	35	5		CHERRY PIE Re-issue of CBS 6562587	Columbia 6566867

ALYSHA WARREN UK singer, previously a member of The Nightcrawlers.

24/09/1994	61	1		I'M SO IN LOVE	Wild Card CARDD 10
25/03/1995	40	1		I THOUGHT I MEANT THE WORLD TO YOU	Wild Card CARDD 16
27/07/1996	30	2		KEEP ON PUSHING OUR LOVE NIGHTCRAWLERS FEATURING JOHN REID AND ALYSHA WARREN	Arista 74321390422

ANN WARREN – see RUBY MURRAY

NIKITA WARREN Italian singer who originally recorded for Atmo Records in Italy.

13/07/1996	48	1		I NEED YOU	VC Recordings VCRD 12

WARRIOR UK dance duo Michael Woods and Stacey Charles. Woods, also a member of M3, later recorded as M1. He also teamed up with Australian model Imogen Bailey.

21/10/2000	19	4		WARRIOR	Incentive CENT 12CDS
30/06/2001	37	2		VOODOO	Incentive CENT 26CDS
04/10/2003	64	1		X	Incentive CENT 56CDS

DIONNE WARWICK US singer (born Marie Dionne Warrick, 12/12/1940, East Orange, NJ) who formed the Gospelaires with sister Dee Dee, cousin Cissy Houston and Doris Troy, working as backing singers in New York. Heard by Burt Bacharach on a Drifters session in 1961, she was signed by Scepter in 1962. Her name was misspelled on the Scepter contract, hence her stage name (she was also briefly Dionne Warwicke, adding the 'e' after a visit to a psychic). She made her acting debut in the 1969 film *Slave* and also launched her own label, Sonday, distributed through Scepter. Five Grammy Awards include Best Contemporary Vocal Performance in 1970 for *I'll Never Fall In Love Again* and Best Rhythm & Blues Vocal Performance in 1979 for *Déjà Vu*. She has a star on the Hollywood Walk of Fame.

13/02/1964	42	3		ANYONE WHO HAD A HEART Featured in the 2001 film *Door To Door*	Pye International 7N 25234
16/04/1964	9	14		WALK ON BY	Pye International 7N 25241
30/07/1964	20	8		YOU'LL NEVER GET TO HEAVEN	Pye International 7N 25256
08/10/1964	23	7		REACH OUT FOR ME	Pye International 7N 25265
01/04/1965	37	5		YOU CAN HAVE HIM	Pye International 7N 25290
13/03/1968	28	8		(THEME FROM) VALLEY OF THE DOLLS Featured in the 1967 film of the same name	Pye International 7N 25445
15/05/1968	8	10		DO YOU KNOW THE WAY TO SAN JOSE 1968 Grammy Award for Best Female Solo Vocal Performance	Pye International 7N 25457
19/10/1974	29	6		THEN CAME YOU ▲¹ DIONNE WARWICK AND THE DETROIT SPINNERS	Atlantic K 10495
23/10/1982	2	13	○	HEARTBREAKER	Arista ARIST 496
11/12/1982	10	10	○	ALL THE LOVE IN THE WORLD	Arista ARIST 507
26/02/1983	66	2		YOURS	Arista ARIST 518
28/05/1983	62	3		I'LL NEVER LOVE THIS WAY AGAIN 1979 Grammy Award for Best Pop Vocal Performance	Arista ARIST 530
09/11/1985	16	9		THAT'S WHAT FRIENDS ARE FOR ▲⁴ DIONNE WARWICK AND FRIENDS FEATURING ELTON JOHN, STEVIE WONDER AND GLADYS KNIGHT Originally recorded by Rod Stewart for the 1982 film *Night Shift*. 1986 Grammy Awards for Best Pop Vocal Performance by a Group, plus Song of the Year for writers Burt Bacharach and Carole Bayer Sager	Arista ARIST 638
15/08/1987	63	3		LOVE POWER DIONNE WARWICK AND JEFFREY OSBORNE	Arista RIS 27

WAS (NOT WAS) US rock group formed in Detroit, MI in 1980 by Don Was (born Don Fagenson, 13/9/1952, Detroit, bass/synthesiser/vocals) and David Was (born David Weiss, 26/10/1952, Detroit, keyboards/vocals) with guest vocals from Sweet Pea Atkinson (born 20/9/1945, Oberlin, OH), Donald Ray Mitchell (born 12/4/1957, Detroit) and Sir Harry Bowens (born 8/10/1949, Detroit). They first recorded for Ze Records. Don Was was named Producer of the Year at the 1994 Grammy Awards.

03/03/1984	41	5		OUT COME THE FREAKS	Ze/Geffen A 4178
18/07/1987	51	7		SPY IN THE HOUSE OF LOVE	Fontana WAS 2
03/10/1987	10	10		WALK THE DINOSAUR Featured in the films *Super Mario Bros* (1993) and *Meet The Flintstones* (1994)	Fontana WAS 3
06/02/1988	21	8		SPY IN THE HOUSE OF LOVE	Fontana WAS 2
07/05/1988	44	3		OUT COME THE FREAKS (AGAIN)	Fontana WAS 4
16/07/1988	67	3		ANYTHING CAN HAPPEN	Fontana WAS 5
26/05/1990	12	7		PAPA WAS A ROLLING STONE	Fontana WAS 7
11/08/1990	53	3		HOW THE HEART BEHAVES	Fontana WAS 8
23/05/1992	58	2		LISTEN LIKE THIEVES	Fontana WAS 10
11/07/1992	4	9		SHAKE YOUR HEAD Features the uncredited vocals of Ozzy Osbourne and Kim Basinger	Fontana WAS 11
26/09/1992	57	1		SOMEWHERE IN AMERICA (THERE'S A STREET NAMED AFTER MY DAD)	Fontana WAS 12

MARTHA WASH US R&B singer (born in San Francisco) who was one of Two Tons Of Fun, Sylvester's backing singers who became the Weather Girls, before going solo. She is also much in demand as a session singer.

28/11/1992	74	1		CARRY ON	RCA 74321125457
06/03/1993	37	4		GIVE IT TO YOU	RCA 74321136562
10/07/1993	49	2		RUNAROUND/CARRY ON (REMIX)	RCA 74321153702
18/02/1995	26	2		I FOUND LOVE/TAKE A TOKE C & C MUSIC FACTORY FEATURING ZELMA DAVIS/C & C MUSIC FACTORY FEATURING MARTHA WASH A-side featured in the 1992 film *Gladiator*	Columbia 6612112
13/07/1996	8	6		KEEP ON JUMPIN'	Manifesto FESCD 11

○ Silver disc   ● Gold disc   ✪ Platinum disc (additional platinum units are indicated by a figure following the symbol)   ◉ Singles released prior to 1973 that are known to have sold over 1 million copies in the UK

12/07/1997	5	10		**SOMETHING GOIN' ON** This and above single credited to **TODD TERRY FEATURING MARTHA WASH AND JOCELYN BROWN**	
				. . . . Manifesto FESCD 25	
25/10/1997	49	1		CARRY ON (2ND REMIX) . . . . Delirious DELICD 6	
28/02/1998	21	3		IT'S RAINING MEN…THE SEQUEL **MARTHA WASH FEATURING RUPAUL** . . . . Logic 74321555412	
11/04/1998	20	2		READY FOR A NEW DAY **TODD TERRY FEATURING MARTHA WASH** . . . . Manifesto FESCD 40	
15/08/1998	45	1		CATCH THE LIGHT . . . . Logic 74321587912	
03/07/1999	64	1		COME . . . . Logic 74321653942	
05/02/2000	56	1		IT'S RAINING MEN (RE-RECORDING) . . . . Logic 74321726282	

DINAH WASHINGTON US singer (born Ruth Lee Jones, 29/8/1924, Tuscaloosa, AL, raised in Chicago, IL) who sang in local clubs from 1941. Spotted by Lionel Hampton, she joined his group in 1943, making debut recordings for Keynote the same year. She won the 1959 Grammy Award for Best Female Jazz Performance for *What A Diff'rence A Day Makes*. She enjoyed success to the full, was married seven times, had countless other relationships and spent a fortune on cars, drugs, drink and men. She died from an overdose of alcohol and pills on 14/12/1963. She was inducted into the Rock & Roll Hall of Fame in 1993.

30/11/1961	35	4		SEPTEMBER IN THE RAIN . . . . Mercury AMT 1162	
04/04/1992	41	4		MAD ABOUT THE BOY Revived following use in a Levi Jeans advertisement . . . . Mercury DINAH 1	

GENO WASHINGTON AND THE RAM JAM BAND US singer (born in Evansville, IN) who came to the UK while serving in the US Air Force and began singing while still in service. He remained in the UK and formed the Ram Jam Band with Pete Gage (guitar), Lionel Kingham (saxophone), Buddy Beadle (saxophone), Jeff Wright (organ), John Roberts (bass) and Herb Prestige (drums). His live act produced two top ten albums. He later returned to the US, forming a rock trio, while Gage joined Vinegar Joe.

19/05/1966	39	8		WATER . . . . Piccadilly 7N 35312	
21/07/1966	45	4		HI HI HAZEL . . . . Piccadilly 7N 35329	
06/10/1966	43	3		QUE SERA SERA . . . . Piccadilly 7N 35346	
02/02/1967	39	5		MICHAEL . . . . Piccadilly 7N 35359	

GROVER WASHINGTON JR US saxophonist (born 12/12/1943, Buffalo, NY) who played saxophone from childhood. A prolific session musician, he recorded his debut album for Kudu in 1971. He won the 1981 Grammy Award for Best Jazz Fusion Performance for *Winelight*. He died from a heart attack while recording an appearance on a TV show on 17/12/1999.

16/05/1981	34	7		JUST THE TWO OF US Features the uncredited vocal contribution of Bill Withers. 1981 Grammy Award for Best Rhythm & Blues Song for writers William Salter, Bill Withers and Ralph MacDonald . . . . Elektra K 12514	

KEITH WASHINGTON – see **KYLIE MINOGUE**

SARAH WASHINGTON UK singer/guitarist (born in London, raised in Dorset).

14/08/1993	12	7		I WILL ALWAYS LOVE YOU . . . . Almighty CDALMY 33	
27/11/1993	45	2		CARELESS WHISPER . . . . Almighty CDALMY 43	
25/05/1996	28	2		HEAVEN . . . . AM:PM 5815332	
12/10/1996	30	2		EVERYTHING . . . . AM:PM 5818872	

W.A.S.P. US heavy rock group formed in 1982 by Blackie Lawless (born Steve Duren, 4/9/1954, Florida, vocals/bass), Chris Holmes (born 23/6/1961, guitar), Randy Piper (guitar) and Tony Richards (drums). Piper and Richards left and were replaced by Steve Riley and Johnny Rod (Lawless moving to guitar). Holmes left in 1990 and Lawless later recorded solo. Their name is an acronym for We Are Sexual Perverts.

31/05/1986	71	2		WILD CHILD . . . . Capitol CL 388	
11/10/1986	70	1		95 – NASTY . . . . Capitol CL 432	
29/08/1987	32	5		SCREAM UNTIL YOU LIKE IT Featured in the 1987 film *Ghoulies 2* . . . . Capitol CL 458	
31/10/1987	31	5		I DON'T NEED NO DOCTOR (LIVE) . . . . Capitol CL 469	
20/02/1988	61	3		LIVE ANIMAL (F**K LIKE A BEAST) . . . . Music For Nations KUT 109	
04/03/1989	21	5		MEAN MAN . . . . Capitol CL 521	
27/05/1989	23	5		THE REAL ME . . . . Capitol CL 534	
09/09/1989	25	5		FOREVER FREE . . . . Capitol CL 546	
04/04/1992	17	2		CHAINSAW CHARLIE (MURDERS IN THE NEW MORGUE) . . . . Parlophone RS 6308	
06/06/1992	41	2		THE IDOL . . . . Parlophone RPD 6314	
31/10/1992	56	1		I AM ONE . . . . Parlophone 10RG 6324	
23/10/1993	38	2		SUNSET AND BABYLON . . . . Capitol CDCL 698	

WATERBOYS UK rock group formed in London in 1981 by Mike Scott (born 14/12/1958, Edinburgh, guitar/vocals) and Anthony Thistlewaite (born 31/8/1955, Leicester, multi-instrumentalist), signing with Ensign. They later added guitarist Karl Wallinger (born 19/10/1957, Prestatyn, Wales), fiddler Steve Wickham and drummer Kevin Wilkinson. Wallinger left in 1986, forming World Party.

02/11/1985	26	7		THE WHOLE OF THE MOON . . . . Ensign ENY 520	
14/01/1989	32	6		FISHERMAN'S BLUES . . . . Ensign ENY 621	
01/07/1989	51	4		AND A BANG ON THE EAR . . . . Ensign ENY 624	
06/04/1991	3	9		**THE WHOLE OF THE MOON** Re-issue of Ensign ENY 520 . . . . Ensign ENY 642	
08/06/1991	75	1		FISHERMAN'S BLUES . . . . Ensign ENY 645	
15/05/1993	24	3		THE RETURN OF PAN . . . . Geffen GFSTD 42	
24/07/1993	29	3		GLASTONBURY SONG . . . . Geffen GFSTD 49	

WATERFRONT UK duo formed in Cardiff, South Glamorgan by singer Chris Duffy and guitarist Phil Cilla.

15/04/1989	63	2		BROKEN ARROW . . . . Polydor WON 3	

❶⁹ Number of weeks single topped the UK chart ↑ Entered the UK chart at #1 ▲⁹ Number of weeks single topped the US chart

861

27/05/1989.....17.....13......	CRY..Polydor WON 1
09/09/1989.....63......4......	NATURE OF LOVE..Polydor WON 2

WATERGATE Turkish/Belgian production group formed by Orhan Terzi, Tommaso De Donatis and David Haid. Terzi and De Donatis also record as DJ Quicksilver.

13/05/2000.....3......10......	**EAST OF ASIA** Contains a sample of Riuichi Sakamoto's *Merry Christmas Mr Lawrence*.....................Positiva CDTIV 129

DENNIS WATERMAN UK actor/singer (born 24/2/1948, London) who came to fame in the TV roles of Carter in *The Sweeney* and Terry in *Minder*. He was married to fellow actress (and hitmaker) Rula Lenska, although this ended in divorce in 2000. George Cole is also an actor, most notably in the role of Arthur Daley in *Minder*, the series that featured Waterman as Terry McCann.

25/10/1980.....3......12.....O	**I COULD BE SO GOOD FOR YOU** DENNIS WATERMAN WITH THE DENNIS WATERMAN BAND Theme to the TV series *Minder*....EMI 5009
17/12/1983.....21......5......	WHAT ARE WE GONNA GET 'ER INDOORS DENNIS WATERMAN AND GEORGE COLE...........................EMI MIN 101

CRYSTAL WATERS US R&B singer (born 1964, New Jersey) who originally intended pursuing a career in computers, having graduated from Howard University in computer science. She appeared in the 1995 film *Wigstock: The Movie*.

18/05/1991.....2......10.....O	**GYPSY WOMAN (LA DA DEE)** Title was listed as *Gypsy Woman (She's Homeless)* in the US......................A&M AM 772
07/09/1991.....18......6......	MAKIN' HAPPY..A&M AM 790
11/01/1992.....39......3......	MEGAMIX..A&M AM 843
03/10/1992.....35......2......	GYPSY WOMAN (REMIX) Listed flip side was *Peace* by SABRINA JOHNSTON.....................Epic 6584377
23/04/1994.....15......7......	100% PURE LOVE..A&M 8586692
02/07/1994.....40......2......	GHETTO DAY..A&M 8589592
25/11/1995.....37......2......	RELAX..Manifesto FESCD 4
24/08/1996.....35......2......	IN DE GHETTO DAVID MORALES AND THE BAD YARD CLUB FEATURING CRYSTAL WATERS AND DELTA.........Manifesto FESCD 12
19/04/1997.....45......1......	SAY...IF YOU FEEL ALRIGHT..Mercury 5742912
20/09/2003.....22......4......	MY TIME DUTCH FEATURING CRYSTAL WATERS..Illustrious/Epic CDILL 018

MUDDY WATERS US blues singer/guitarist (born McKinley Morganfield, 4/4/1915, Rolling Fork, MS) who first recorded for the Library of Congress in 1941 and signed his first record contract in 1948 with Aristocrat, which later became Chess. He was inducted into the Rock & Roll Hall of Fame in 1987 and won a Grammy Lifetime Achievement Award in 1992. He died from a heart attack on 30/4/1983.

16/07/1988.....51......6.......	MANNISH BOY..Epic MUD 1

ROGER WATERS UK singer (born 6/9/1944, Great Bookham) who was a founder member of Pink Floyd in 1965, leaving the group in 1983. He first recorded solo in 1970: the soundtrack to *The Body*.

30/05/1987.....74......1......	RADIO WAVES..Harvest EM 6
26/12/1987.....54......4......	THE TIDE IS TURNING (AFTER LIVE AID)..Harvest EM 37
05/09/1992.....35......3......	WHAT GOD WANTS PART 1..Columbia 6581395

LAUREN WATERWORTH UK singer (born 1989, Wigan) who was discovered by producer Pete Waterman at eleven years of age.

01/06/2002.....24......3......	BABY NOW THAT I'VE FOUND YOU..Jive 9253622

MICHAEL WATFORD US singer (born 1959, Virginia) who also worked as a backing singer for Freedom Williams.

26/02/1994.....53......2......	SO INTO YOU..East West A 8309CD

TIONNE 'T-BOZ' WATKINS – see T-BOZ

JODY WATLEY US singer (born 30/1/1959, Chicago, IL) who was a dancer on TV's *Soul Train* and then a singer with Shalamar from 1978 until 1983, when she went solo. She won the 1987 Grammy Award for Best New Artist.

09/05/1987.....13......11......	LOOKING FOR A NEW LOVE..MCA 1107
17/10/1987.....55......3......	DON'T YOU WANT ME..MCA 1198
08/04/1989.....31......7......	REAL LOVE..MCA 1324
12/08/1989.....21......6......	FRIENDS JODY WATLEY WITH ERIC B AND RAKIM..MCA 1352
10/02/1990.....74......2......	EVERYTHING..MCA 1395
11/04/1992.....50......3......	I'M THE ONE YOU NEED..MCA MCS 1608
21/05/1994.....33......2......	WHEN A MAN LOVES A WOMAN..MCA MCSTD 1964
25/04/1998.....51......1......	OFF THE HOOK..Atlantic AT 0024CD1

JOE WATSON – see RHYTHM MASTERS

JOHNNY 'GUITAR' WATSON US singer/guitarist (born 3/2/1935, Houston, TX) who moved to Los Angeles, CA at thirteen and was discovered by Johnny Otis. He first recorded for Federal in 1953. He died on stage in Japan from a heart attack on 18/5/1996.

28/08/1976.....35......5......	I NEED IT..DJM DJS 10694
23/04/1977.....44......3......	A REAL MOTHER FOR YA..DJM DJS 10762

RUSSELL WATSON UK operatic singer (born 20/11/1966, although he routinely knocks six years off his age) whose debut album *The Voice* went double platinum in March 2001 (sales in excess of 600,000 copies), the first classical album to do so since 1998. *The Voice* won the 2001 Classical BRIT Award for Best Selling Debut Album and was also named Album of the Year.

30/10/1999.....38......2......	SWING LOW '99..Universal TV 4669502
22/07/2000.....68......1.......	BARCELONA (FRIENDS UNTIL THE END) RUSSELL WATSON AND SHAUN RYDER...........................Decca 46672772

O Silver disc ● Gold disc ✪ Platinum disc (additional platinum units are indicated by a figure following the symbol) ◎ Singles released prior to 1973 that are known to have sold over 1 million copies in the UK

| 18/05/2002 | 10 | 4 | | SOMEONE LIKE YOU RUSSELL WATSON AND FAYE TOZER | Decca 4730002 |
| 21/12/2002 | 17 | 5 | | NOTHING SACRED – A SONG FOR KIRSTY Released to raise funds for the Francis House Children's Hospice Appeal in aid of terminally ill children. Kirsty is Kirsty Howard, a six-year-old girl born with her heart back to front | Decca 4737402 |

BARRATT WAUGH UK singer (born 30/8/1979, Swindon).

| 26/07/2003 | 56 | 1 | | SKIP A BEAT | BNW Records BNWCD02 |

WAVELENGTH UK vocal group formed by Phil Fisher, John Kirby, Raymond Howard, Danny Daniels and Lee Hersh.

| 10/07/1982 | 17 | 12 | | HURRY HOME | Ariola ARO 281 |

WAX US/UK duo Andrew Gold (born 2/8/1951, Burbank, CA) and Graham Gouldman (born 10/5/1946, Manchester). Gold had previously enjoyed solo success while Gouldman had been in Hotlegs, a group that evolved into 10cc.

| 12/04/1986 | 60 | 5 | | RIGHT BETWEEN THE EYES | RCA PB 40509 |
| 01/08/1987 | 12 | 11 | | BRIDGE TO YOUR HEART | RCA PB 41405 |

ANTHONY WAY UK singer (born 1982, London) who was discovered as a soprano chorister at St Paul's Cathedral choir and appeared in the role of Henry Ashworth in the TV production The Choir.

| 15/04/1995 | 55 | 2 | | PANIS ANGELICUS Featured in the TV series The Choir | Decca 4481642 |

A WAY OF LIFE US vocal/instrumental group.

| 21/04/1990 | 55 | 3 | | TRIPPIN' ON YOUR LOVE | Eternal YZ 4664 |

WAY OF THE WEST UK new wave group that also recorded for MCA.

| 25/04/1981 | 54 | 5 | | DON'T SAY THAT'S JUST FOR WHITE BOYS | Mercury MER 66 |

WAY OUT WEST UK dance duo Nick Warren and Jody Wisternoff, both of whom began as DJs. The pair first got together in 1993 and signed with Deconstruction in 1994. Joanna Law has also recorded with Slacker.

03/12/1994	52	1		AJARE	Deconstruction 74321243802
02/03/1996	38	2		DOMINATION	Deconstruction 74321342822
14/09/1996	15	5		THE GIFT WAY OUT WEST FEATURING MISS JOANNA LAW Contains a sample of Joanna Law's First Time Ever	Deconstruction 74321401912
30/08/1997	41	2		BLUE	Deconstruction 74321477512
29/11/1997	36	2		AJARE (REMIX)	Deconstruction 74321521352
09/12/2000	61	1		THE FALL Contains a sample of Coldcut's Autumn Leave	Wow 005CD
18/08/2001	46	1		INTENSIFY	Distinctive Breaks DISNCD 74
30/03/2002	39	2		MINDCIRCUS WAY OUT WEST FEATURING TRICIA LEE KELSHALL	Distinctive Breaks DISNCD 80
21/09/2002	67	1		STEALTH WAY OUT WEST FEATURING KIRSTY HAWKSHAW	Distinctive Breaks DISNCD 90

BRUCE WAYNE German DJ/producer.

| 13/12/1997 | 44 | 1 | | READY | Logic 74321527012 |
| 04/07/1998 | 70 | 1 | | NO GOOD FOR ME | Logic 74321587052 |

JAN WAYNE German DJ (born Jan Christiansen, 11/1/1974).

| 09/11/2002 | 14 | 5 | | BECAUSE THE NIGHT | Product PDT 02CDS |
| 29/03/2003 | 28 | 3 | | TOTAL ECLIPSE OF THE HEART | Product PDT 10CDS |

JEFF WAYNE US producer/songwriter/keyboard player (born in NYC) who was David Essex's producer in the 1970s.

09/09/1978	36	8		THE EVE OF THE WAR JEFF WAYNE'S WAR OF THE WORLDS	CBS 6496
10/07/1982	57	3		MATADOR Theme to ITV's coverage of the 1982 FIFA World Cup in Spain	CBS A 2493
25/11/1989	3	10		THE EVE OF THE WAR (REMIX) JEFF WAYNE'S WAR OF THE WORLDS Features the uncredited vocal of Justin Hayward	CBS 6551267

WC US rapper William Calhoun (born in Los Angeles, CA) who was a member of Low Profile and Westside Connection before going solo.

| 01/03/2003 | 48 | 2 | | THE STREETS WC FEATURING SNOOP DOGG AND NATE DOGG | Def Jam 0779852 |

WEATHER GIRLS US R&B duo Martha Wash and Izora Redman-Armstead, first together in NOW (News Of The World) before backing Sylvester. Recording for Fantasy as the Two Tons Of Fun (because of their size), they moved to CBS as the Weather Girls in 1982. Redman-Armstead died from heart failure on 16/9/2004.

| 27/08/1983 | 73 | 3 | | IT'S RAINING MEN | CBS A 2924 |
| 10/03/1984 | 2 | 11 | O | IT'S RAINING MEN | CBS A 2924 |

WEATHER PROPHETS UK group with Pete Astor (guitar/vocals), Greenwood Goulding (bass), Ooisin Little (bass) and Dave Morgan (drums).

| 28/03/1987 | 62 | 2 | | SHE COMES FROM THE RAIN | Elevation ACID 1 |

WEATHERMEN UK singer Jonathan King (born Kenneth King, 6/12/1944, London).

| 16/01/1971 | 19 | 9 | | IT'S THE SAME OLD SONG | B&C CB 139 |

J WEAV – see CHINGY

❶⁹ Number of weeks single topped the UK chart ↑ Entered the UK chart at #1 ▲⁹ Number of weeks single topped the US chart

863

MARTI WEBB UK singer (born 1944, London), selected by composer Andrew Lloyd-Webber and lyricist Don Black to front the TV musical *Tell Me On A Sunday,* Webber's first project after his split with Tim Rice. She had previously replaced Elaine Paige in *Evita.*

09/02/1980	3	12	O	TAKE THAT LOOK OFF YOUR FACE	Polydor POSP 100
19/04/1980	67	2		TELL ME ON A SUNDAY	Polydor POSP 111
20/09/1980	61	4		YOUR EARS SHOULD BE BURNING NOW This and above two singles from the musical *Tell Me On A Sunday*	Polydor POSP 166
08/06/1985	5	11		BEN Released to raise funds for the Ben Hardwick Memorial Fund	Starblend STAR 6
20/09/1986	13	12		ALWAYS THERE MARTI WEBB AND THE SIMON MAY ORCHESTRA Theme to BBC TV's *Howard's Way*, with lyrics added by Don Black	
					BBC RESL 190
06/06/1987	65	1		I CAN'T LET GO	Rainbow RBR 12

WEBB BROTHERS US duo Justin (guitar/vocals) and Christian Webb (keyboards/vocals), sons of songwriter Jimmy Webb.

17/02/2001	69	1		I CAN'T BELIEVE YOU'RE GONE	WEA 320CD

JOAN WEBER US singer (born 1936, Paulsboro, NJ) who was with her husband's dance band when discovered by Mitch Miller. She was giving birth when her debut hit #1 in the US, so was unable to promote a follow-up. She was dropped by label Columbia. She died on 13/5/1981.

18/02/1955	16	1		LET ME GO LOVER ▲4	Philips PB 389

NIKKI WEBSTER Australian singer (born 29/4/1987, Sydney) who performed at the opening and closing ceremonies of the 2000 Olympics in Sydney.

08/06/2002	64	1		STRAWBERRY KISSES	Gotham 74321943642

WEDDING PRESENT UK rock group formed 1984 by David Gedge (born 23/4/1960, Leeds, guitar/vocals), Pete Solowka (born in Manchester, guitar), Keith Gregory (born 2/1/1963, Darlington, bass) and Paul Charman (born in Brighton, drums). Debuting on their own Reception label, they signed with RCA in 1989. Charman left soon after their debut and was replaced by Simon Smith (born 3/5/1965, Lincolnshire). Solowka left in 1991 and was replaced by Paul Dorrington. In 1992 they released a single a month, each of which made the top 40 for one week.

05/03/1988	46	2		NOBODY'S TWISTING YOUR ARM	Reception REC 009
01/10/1988	42	2		WHY ARE YOU BEING SO REASONABLE NOW	Reception REC 011
07/10/1989	33	3		KENNEDY	RCA PB 43117
17/02/1990	24	3		BRASSNECK	RCA PB 43403
29/09/1990	25	4		3 SONGS EP Tracks on EP: *Corduroy, Crawl* and *Make Me Smile (Come Up And See Me)*	RCA PB 44021
11/05/1991	29	3		DALLIANCE	RCA PB 44495
27/07/1991	58	1		LOVENEST	RCA PT 44750
18/01/1992	26	2		BLUE EYES	RCA PB 45185
15/02/1992	20	1		GO-GO DANCER	RCA PB 45183
14/03/1992	14	2		THREE	RCA PB 45181
18/04/1992	14	1		SILVER SHORTS	RCA PB 45311
16/05/1992	10	2		COME PLAY WITH ME	RCA PB 45313
13/06/1992	16	1		CALIFORNIA	RCA PB 43515
18/07/1992	22	1		FLYING SAUCER	RCA 74321101157
15/08/1992	19	1		BOING!	RCA 74321101177
19/09/1992	17	1		LOVE SLAVE	RCA 74321101167
17/10/1992	17	1		STICKY	RCA 74321116917
14/11/1992	23	1		THE QUEEN OF OUTER SPACE	RCA 74321116927
19/12/1992	25	1		NO CHRISTMAS	RCA 74321116937
10/09/1994	51	2		YEAH YEAH YEAH YEAH	Island CID 585
26/11/1994	71	1		IT'S A GAS	Island CID 591
31/08/1996	67	1		2, 3, GO	Cooking Vinyl FRYCD 048
25/01/1997	40	1		MONTREAL	Cooking Vinyl FRYCD 053
27/11/2004	62	1		INTERSATE 5	Scopitones TONECD018

FRED WEDLOCK UK singer (born 23/5/1942, Bristol), a long-time regular on the UK folk circuit prior to his hit single.

31/01/1981	6	10	O	OLDEST SWINGER IN TOWN	Rocket XPRES 46

WEE PAPA GIRL RAPPERS UK rap duo Ty Tim and Total S (Samantha and Sandra Lawrence).

12/03/1988	60	4		FAITH	Jive 164
25/06/1988	21	9		HEAT IT UP WEE PAPA GIRL RAPPERS FEATURING TWO MEN AND A DRUM MACHINE	Jive 174
01/10/1988	6	9		WEE RULE	Jive 185
24/12/1988	45	4		SOULMATE	Jive 193
25/03/1989	65	1		BLOW THE HOUSE DOWN	Jive 197

BERT WEEDON UK guitarist (born 10/5/1921, London) who made his recording debut for Parlophone in 1956. He then became an in-demand session musician and signed with the Top Rank label in 1959.

15/05/1959	10	9		GUITAR BOOGIE SHUFFLE	Top Rank JAR 117
20/11/1959	29	2		NASHVILLE BOOGIE	Top Rank JAR 221
10/03/1960	37	4		BIG BEAT BOOGIE	Top Rank JAR 300
09/06/1960	47	2		TWELFTH STREET RAG	Top Rank JAR 360
28/07/1960	24	4		APACHE	Top Rank JAR 415

27/10/1960	28	11		SORRY ROBBIE	Top Rank JAR 517
02/02/1961	35	5		GINCHY	Top Rank JAR 537
04/05/1961	47	1		MR GUITAR	Top Rank JAR 559

WEEKEND Multinational vocal/instrumental group.

| 14/12/1985 | 47 | 5 | | CHRISTMAS MEDLEY/AULD LANG SYNE | Lifestyle XY 1 |

WEEKEND PLAYERS UK dance group formed in Nottingham by singer Rachel Foster and Andy Cato of Groove Armada.

| 08/09/2001 | 22 | 4 | | 21ST CENTURY | Multiply CXMULTY 78 |
| 16/03/2002 | 42 | 1 | | INTO THE SUN | Multiply CXMULTY 84 |

MICHELLE WEEKS US singer who had previously appeared in the 1986 film *Little Shop Of Horrors*.

02/08/1997	23	3		MOMENT OF MY LIFE BOBBY D'AMBROSIO FEATURING MICHELLE WEEKS	Ministry Of Sound MOSCDS 1
08/11/1997	28	2		DON'T GIVE UP	Ministry Of Sound MOSCDS 2
11/07/1998	59	1		GIVE ME LOVE DJ DADO VS MICHELLE WEEKS	VC Recordings VCRD 37
03/05/2003	69	1		THE LIGHT	Defected DFTD 064X

WEEN US duo formed in New Hope, PA by Gene (born Aaron Freeman) and Dean Ween (born Micky Melchiondo).

| 29/08/1998 | 20 | 3 | | WALKING AFTER YOU:BEACON LIGHT FOO FIGHTERS:WEEN Featured in the 1998 film *The X Files* | Elektra E 4100CD |

WEEZER US rock group formed in Los Angeles, CA in 1992 by Rivers Cuomo (born 1971, Connecticut, guitar/vocals), Brian Bell (born in Tennessee, guitar), Matt Sharp (bass) and Patrick Wilson (born in Buffalo, NY, drums). They signed with DGC Records in June 1993.

11/02/1995	35	2		UNDONE – THE SWEATER SONG	Geffen GFSTD 85
06/05/1995	12	7		BUDDY HOLLY	Geffen GFSTD 88
22/07/1995	37	2		SAY IT AIN'T SO	Geffen GFSTD 95
05/10/1996	50	1		EL SCORCHO	Geffen GFSTD 22167
14/07/2001	21	2		HASH PIPE Featured in the 2001 film *American Pie 2*	Geffen 4975642
03/11/2001	31	2		ISLAND IN THE SUN	Geffen 4976162
14/09/2002	29	2		KEEP FISHIN'	Geffen 04977922

FRANK WEIR UK saxophonist/orchestra leader. He died on 12/5/1981.

| 15/10/1954 | ❶² | 14 | | MY SON MY SON VERA LYNN WITH FRANK WEIR, HIS SAXOPHONE, HIS ORCHESTRA AND CHORUS | Decca F 10372 |
| 15/09/1960 | 42 | 4 | | CARIBBEAN HONEYMOON | Oriole CB 1559 |

WEIRD SCIENCE UK DJ/production duo who also record as The Lab Rats. Their debut single also features Anne Marie Smith, Angie Brown and Anna Ross on vocals.

| 01/07/2000 | 62 | 1 | | FEEL THE NEED | NuLife 74321751982 |

DENISE WELCH UK actress/singer (born 22/5/1958, Ebchester, County Durham) who was first known in TV's *Soldier Soldier* as Marsha Stubbs (at the same time as Robson & Jerome) and later played Natalie Horrocks in *Coronation Street*. She is married to fellow actor Tim Healy (*Auf Wiedersehen Pet*).

| 04/11/1995 | 23 | 3 | | YOU DON'T HAVE TO SAY YOU LOVE ME/CRY ME A RIVER | Virgin VSCDT 1569 |

PAUL WELLER UK singer (born John Paul Weller, 25/5/1958, Woking), a founder member of the Jam in 1976, who also wrote most of their material. They split in 1982, Weller forming the Style Council with Mick Talbot, later adding Weller's wife Dee C Lee (born Diane Sealey). He launched the Respond label with artists such as The Questions and Tracie Young. Weller disbanded Style Council in 1989, emerging in 1990 with the Paul Weller Movement. He was named Best British Male at the 1995 and 1996 BRIT Awards.

18/05/1991	36	3		INTO TOMORROW PAUL WELLER MOVEMENT	Freedom High FHP 1
15/08/1992	18	5		UH HUH OH YEH	Go Discs GOD 86
10/10/1992	47	2		ABOVE THE CLOUDS	Go Discs GOD 91
17/07/1993	16	5		SUNFLOWER	Go Discs GODCD 102
04/09/1993	14	3		WILD WOOD	Go Discs GODCD 104
13/11/1993	18	3		THE WEAVER (EP) Tracks on EP: *The Weaver, There Is No Time, Another New Day* and *Ohio*	Go Discs GODCD 107
09/04/1994	11	3		HUNG UP	Go Discs GODCD 111
05/11/1994	20	3		OUT OF THE SINKING (RE-RECORDING)	Go Discs GODCD 121
06/05/1995	7	4		THE CHANGINGMAN	Go Discs GODCD 127
22/07/1995	9	6		YOU DO SOMETHING TO ME	Go Discs GODCD 130
30/09/1995	20	4		BROKEN STONES	Go Discs GODCD 132
09/03/1996	16	2		OUT OF THE SINKING	Go Discs GODCD 143
17/08/1996	5	5		PEACOCK SUIT	Go Discs GODCD 149
09/08/1997	14	3		BRUSHED	Island CID 666
11/10/1997	21	2		FRIDAY STREET	Island CID 676
06/12/1997	30	2		MERMAIDS	Island CID 683
14/11/1998	16	3		BRAND NEW START	Island CID 711
09/01/1999	22	3		WILD WOOD Re-issue of Go Discs GODCD 104	Island CID 734
02/09/2000	44	1		SWEET PEA, MY SWEET PEA	Island CID 764
14/09/2002	7	3		IT'S WRITTEN IN THE STARS	Independiente ISOM 63SMS
30/11/2002	23	2		LEAFY MYSTERIES	Independiente ISOM 65SMS
26/06/2004	13	3		THE BOTTLE	V2 VVR 5026913

	11/09/2004	11	5		WISHING ON A STAR	V2 VVR 5026928
	27/11/2004	18	3		THINKING OF YOU	V2 VVR5028463

BRANDI WELLS US singer (born Marguerite Pinder Bannister, 1955, Philadelphia, PA) who was lead singer with Slick before going solo. She died on 25/3/2003.

| | 20/02/1982 | 74 | 1 | | WATCH OUT | Virgin VS 479 |

HOUSTON WELLS AND THE MARKSMEN UK singer (born Andrew Smith, 1938).

| | 01/08/1963 | 22 | 10 | | ONLY THE HEARTACHES | Parlophone R 5031 |

MARY WELLS US singer (born 13/5/1943, Detroit, MI) whose initial songwriting ambitions with *Bye Bye Baby* (intended for Jackie Wilson) led to her being signed by Motown boss (and Wilson's producer) Berry Gordy as a singer, becoming the label's first star. She left for 20th Century in 1965, encouraged by her then husband to ask for a bigger royalty. She was diagnosed as having throat cancer in 1990 and died on 26/7/1992.

	21/05/1964	5	14		MY GUY ▲² Featured in the 1979 film *More American Graffiti*	Stateside SS 288
	30/07/1964	50	1		ONCE UPON A TIME MARVIN GAYE AND MARY WELLS	Stateside SS 316
	08/07/1972	14	10		MY GUY Re-issue of Stateside SS 288	Tamla Motown TMG 820

TERRI WELLS US singer (born in Philadelphia, PA) who became a session singer at Philadelphia International after the demise of her City Limits group. At the time of her hit she was working full-time as an insurance underwriter.

| | 02/07/1983 | 53 | 2 | | YOU MAKE IT HEAVEN | Phillyworld PWS 111 |
| | 05/05/1984 | 17 | 7 | | I'LL BE AROUND Cover version of Detroit Spinners' 1972 US hit on which Wells was a backing singer | Phillyworld LON 48 |

ALEX WELSH BAND UK group formed by Alex Welsh (trumpet), Archie Semple (clarinet), Roy 'Boy' Crimmins (trombone), Fred Hunt (piano), Jim Douglas (guitar), Ron Mathewson (bass) and Lennie Hastings (drums). Welsh died on 25/6/1982.

| | 10/08/1961 | 45 | 4 | | TANSY | Columbia DB 4686 |

IRVINE WELSH – see PRIMAL SCREAM

WENDY AND LISA US soul duo Wendy Melvoin (born 1964, guitar) and Lisa Coleman (born 1960, keyboards), who teamed up in 1986 following the demise of Prince's backing group the Revolution. They had been childhood friends in Los Angeles, CA.

	05/09/1987	66	4		WATERFALL	Virgin VS 999
	16/01/1988	49	5		SIDE SHOW	Virgin VS 1012
	18/02/1989	70	3		ARE YOU MY BABY	Virgin VS 1156
	29/04/1989	64	3		LOLLY LOLLY	Virgin VS 1175
	08/07/1989	27	8		SATISFACTION	Virgin VS 1194
	18/11/1989	69	2		WATERFALL (REMIX)	Virgin VS 1223
	30/06/1990	44	5		STRUNG OUT	Virgin VS 1272
	10/11/1990	70	1		RAINBOW LAKE	Virgin VS 1280

WES French singer Wes Madiko. He is an African Griot and his name in Bantou means 'root from the land of the ancestors'.

| | 14/02/1998 | 11 | 6 | | ALANE | Epic 6654682 |
| | 27/06/1998 | 75 | 1 | | I LOVE FOOTBALL Official song for the Cameroon FIFA World Cup squad | Epic 6660772 |

DODIE WEST UK singer whose hit was a cover of Little Anthony And The Imperials' US hit. She based her vocal style on Mary Wells.

| | 14/01/1965 | 39 | 4 | | GOING OUT OF MY HEAD | Decca F 12046 |

KANYE WEST US rapper (born 8/6/1977, Chicago, IL) who first worked with Roc-A-Fella as a producer before going solo. He won the 2004 MOBO Awards for Best Hip Hop Artist, Best Producer and Best Album for *The College Dropout*. His debut hit referred to the fact that his vocals were recorded with his jaw wired almost completely shut after a near fatal road crash.

	03/04/2004	9	9		THROUGH THE WIRE Contains a sample of Chaka Khan's *Through The Fire*	Roc-A-Fella 9862270
	19/06/2004	10	8		ALL FALLS DOWN KANYE WEST FEATURING SYLEENA JOHNSON	Roc-A-Fella 9862670
	26/06/2004	6	10		TALK ABOUT OUR LOVE BRANDY FEATURING KANYE WEST	Atlantic AT 0177CD
	11/09/2004	16	6		JESUS WALKS	Roc-A-Fella 9863964

KEITH WEST UK singer (born Keith Hopkins, 6/12/1943, Dagenham) who had previously been a member of Four Plus One, the In Crowd and Tomorrow before linking with songwriter/producer Mark Wirtz. His biggest hit is probably better known as *Grocer Jack*. He later became a backing singer, appearing on projects by Steve Howe (also ex-In Crowd) among others.

| | 09/08/1967 | 2 | 15 | | EXCERPT FROM A TEENAGE OPERA | Parlophone R 5623 |
| | 22/11/1967 | 38 | 3 | | SAM | Parlophone R 5651 |

KIT WEST – see DEGREES OF MOTION FEATURING BITI

WEST END UK vocal group.

| | 19/08/1995 | 44 | 2 | | LOVE RULES | RCA 74321292702 |

WEST END FEATURING SYBIL UK production duo Mike Stock and Pete Waterman with US singer Sybil Lynch.

| | 16/01/1993 | 3 | 13 | | THE LOVE I LOST | PWL Sanctuary PWCD 253 |

○ Silver disc ● Gold disc ✪ Platinum disc (additional platinum units are indicated by a figure following the symbol) ◉ Singles released prior to 1973 that are known to have sold over 1 million copies in the UK

WEST HAM UNITED CUP SQUAD UK professional football club formed in London in 1895 as Thames Ironworks FC, changing their name to West Ham United in 1900. Their record was released to capitalise on an appearance in the FA Cup final.

| 10/05/1975 | 31 | 2 | | I'M FOREVER BLOWING BUBBLES | Pye 7N 45470 |

WEST STREET MOB US DJ/production trio formed in Englewood, NJ by Sebrina Gillison, Warren Moore and Joey Robinson (the son of singer Sylvia Robinson).

| 08/10/1983 | 64 | 3 | | BREAK DANCIN' – ELECTRIC BOOGIE | Sugarhill SH 128 |

WESTBAM German producer Maximilian Lenz who first charted in 1994 with *Celebration Generation*. He later recorded as Members of Mayday.

09/07/1994	48	2		CELEBRATION GENERATION	Low Spirit PQCD 5
19/11/1994	57	1		BAM BAM BAM	Low Spirit PZCD 329
03/06/1995	32	2		WIZARDS OF THE SONIC	Urban PZCD 344
23/03/1996	51	1		ALWAYS MUSIC WESTBAM/KOON + STEPHENSON	Low Spirit 5779152
13/06/1998	43	2		WIZARDS OF THE SONIC (REMIX) WESTBAM VS RED JERRY	Wonderboy WBOYD 010
28/11/1998	58	1		ROOF IS ON FIRE	Logic 74321633162

WESTLIFE Irish vocal group formed by Nicky Byrne (born 9/10/1978, Dublin), Shane Filan (born 5/7/1979, Sligo), Kian Egan (born 29/4/1980, Sligo), Bryan McFadden (born 12/4/1980, Dublin) and Mark Feehily (born 28/5/1980, Sligo). Called Westside, they had to change their name because of a US group of the same name. Co-managed by Boyzone's Ronan Keating, they were the first 'boy band' to have their first two hit singles enter the charts at #1. They were also the first group to have their first seven singles all hit #1 (and achieving seven #1s quicker than any other act ever, including Elvis Presley). They were named Best Pop Act at the 2001 and 2002 BRIT Awards, having previously won the Select UK & Ireland Award at the 2000 MTV Europe Music Awards. McFadden left the group in March 2004.

01/05/1999	❶²	13	●	SWEAR IT AGAIN ↑	RCA 74321662062
21/08/1999	❶¹	11	○	IF I LET YOU GO ↑	RCA 74321692352
30/10/1999	❶¹	13	○	FLYING WITHOUT WINGS ↑ Voted Record of the Year in the BBC poll	RCA 74321709162
25/12/1999	❶⁴	17	✪	I HAVE A DREAM/SEASONS IN THE SUN ↑	RCA 74321726012
08/04/2000	❶¹	12		FOOL AGAIN ↑	RCA 74321751562
30/09/2000	❶²	12	○	AGAINST ALL ODDS ↑ MARIAH CAREY FEATURING WESTLIFE	Columbia 6698872
11/11/2000	❶¹	10		MY LOVE ↑ Voted Record of the Year in the BBC poll	RCA 74321802802
30/12/2000	2	13	●	WHAT MAKES A MAN	RCA 74321826252
17/03/2001	❶¹	16	○	UPTOWN GIRL ↑ Released in aid of the Comic Relief charity	RCA 74321841692
17/11/2001	❶¹	15	○	QUEEN OF MY HEART ↑	RCA 74321899142
02/03/2002	❶¹	13	○	WORLD OF OUR OWN ↑	RCA 74321919242
01/06/2002	5	10		BOP BOP BABY	S 74321940452
16/11/2002	❶¹	16	○	UNBREAKABLE ↑	S 74321975222
05/04/2003	3	10		TONIGHT/MISS YOU NIGHTS	S 74321986802
27/09/2003	4	7		HEY WHATEVER	S 82876560862
29/11/2003	❶¹	9		MANDY ↑ Voted Record of the Year	S 82876570742
06/03/2004	3	8		OBVIOUS	S 82876596322

KIM WESTON – see MARVIN GAYE

WESTWORLD UK/US vocal/instrumental group formed by Derwood Andrews, Elizabeth Westwood and Ralph Jezzard.

21/02/1987	11	7		SONIC BOOM BOY	RCA BOOM 1
02/05/1987	37	5		BA-NA-NA-BAM-BOO	RCA BOOM 2
25/07/1987	54	4		WHERE THE ACTION IS	RCA BOOM 3
17/10/1987	42	5		SILVERMAC	RCA BOOM 4
15/10/1988	72	2		EVERYTHING GOOD IS BAD	RCA PB 42243

WET WET WET UK group formed in Glasgow in 1982 by Graeme Clark (born 15/4/1966, Glasgow, bass), Tom Cunningham (born 22/6/1965, Glasgow, drums), Neil Mitchell (born 8/6/1967, Helensburgh, keyboards) and Marti Pellow (born Mark McLoughlin, 23/3/1966, Clydebank, vocals) as Vortex Motion. They launched the Precious Organisation label in 1984, signing with Phonogram in 1985. They were named Best British Newcomer at the 1988 BRIT Awards. Cunningham was sacked in 1997 and Pellow went solo in 1999. They took their name from a line in the Scritti Politti song *Getting Having And Holding*.

11/04/1987	6	14		WISHING I WAS LUCKY	Precious Organisation JEWEL 3
25/07/1987	5	12		SWEET LITTLE MYSTERY	Precious Organisation JEWEL 4
05/12/1987	5	12		ANGEL EYES (HOME AND AWAY)	Precious Organisation JEWEL 6

❶⁹ Number of weeks single topped the UK chart   ↑ Entered the UK chart at #1   ▲⁹ Number of weeks single topped the US chart

DATE	POS	WKS	BPI	SINGLE TITLE	LABEL & NUMBER
19/03/1988	12	8		TEMPTATION	Precious Organisation JEWEL 7
14/05/1988	❶⁴	11	○	**WITH A LITTLE HELP FROM MY FRIENDS** Flip side was *She's Leaving Home* by BILLY BRAGG WITH CARA TIVEY	Childline CHILD 1
30/09/1989	6	8		**SWEET SURRENDER**	Precious Organisation JEWEL 9
09/12/1989	19	7		BROKE AWAY	Precious Organisation JEWEL 10
10/03/1990	31	4		HOLD BACK THE RIVER	Precious Organisation JEWEL 11
11/08/1990	30	4		STAY WITH ME HEARTACHE/I FEEL FINE	Precious Organisation JEWEL 13
14/09/1991	37	3		MAKE IT TONIGHT	Precious Organisation JEWEL 15
02/11/1991	56	2		PUT THE LIGHT ON	Precious Organisation JEWEL 16
04/01/1992	❶⁴	11		**GOODNIGHT GIRL**	Precious Organisation JEWEL 17
21/03/1992	19	5		MORE THAN LOVE	Precious Organisation JEWEL 18
11/07/1992	15	5		LIP SERVICE (EP) Tracks on EP: *Lip Service, High On The Happy Side, Lip Service (Live)*, and *More Than Love (Live)*	Precious Organisation JEWEL 19
08/05/1993	38	2		BLUE FOR YOU/THIS TIME (LIVE)	Precious Organisation JWLCD 20
06/11/1993	22	5		SHED A TEAR	Precious Organisation JWLCD 21
08/01/1994	20	4		COLD COLD HEART	Precious Organisation JWLCD 22
21/05/1994	❶¹⁵	37	✪²	**LOVE IS ALL AROUND** Cover version of The Troggs' 1967 hit. Featured in the 1994 film *Four Weddings And A Funeral*. It might have remained at #1 and in the charts for much longer but the group decided to delete it one week before they would have equalled Bryan Adams' record of most consecutive weeks at #1	Precious Organisation JWLCD 23
25/03/1995	3	9	○	**JULIA SAYS**	Precious Organisation JWLDD 24
17/06/1995	7	8		**DON'T WANT TO FORGIVE ME NOW**	Precious Organisation JWLDD 25
30/09/1995	7	7		**SOMEWHERE SOMEHOW**	Precious Organisation JWLDD 26
02/12/1995	17	7		SHE'S ALL ON MY MIND	Precious Organisation JWLDD 27
30/03/1996	16	4		MORNING	Precious Organisation JWLDD 28
22/03/1997	3	9		**IF I NEVER SEE YOU AGAIN**	Precious Organisation JWLCD 29
14/06/1997	13	5		STRANGE	Precious Organisation JWLCD 30
16/08/1997	4	6		**YESTERDAY** Cover version of The Beatles record. Featured in the 1997 film *Bean: The Ultimate Disaster Movie*	Precious Organisation JWLCD 31
13/11/2004	14	3		ALL I WANT	Mercury 9868448

WE'VE GOT A FUZZBOX AND WE'RE GONNA USE IT UK rock group formed in Birmingham in 1985 by Maggie Dunne (vocals/keyboards/guitar), Jo Dunne (bass/piano), Vickie Perks (vocals) and Tina O'Neill (drums). Later called just Fuzzbox, they disbanded in 1990.

DATE	POS	WKS	BPI	SINGLE TITLE	LABEL & NUMBER
26/04/1986	41	7		XX SEX/RULES AND REGULATIONS	Vindaloo UGH 11
15/11/1986	31	4		LOVE IS THE SLUG	Vindaloo UGH 14
07/02/1987	51	2		WHAT'S THE POINT FUZZBOX	Vindaloo YZ 101
25/02/1989	11	10		INTERNATIONAL RESCUE	WEA YZ 347
20/05/1989	14	10		PINK SUNSHINE	WEA YZ 401
05/08/1989	24	6		SELF! This and above single credited to FUZZBOX	WEA YZ 408

WHALE Swedish group formed by Cia Berg (vocals), her fiancé Henrik Schyffert (guitar) and Gordon Cyrus (bass). They said their debut hit *Hobo Humpin' Slobo Babe* was dedicated to 'affluent women who bring homeless men home to have their way with them'. The accompanying video won director Mark Pellington the 1994 MTV Europe Music Award for Best Director.

DATE	POS	WKS	BPI	SINGLE TITLE	LABEL & NUMBER
19/03/1994	46	2		HOBO HUMPIN' SLOBO BABE	East West YZ 798CD
15/07/1995	53	1		I'LL DO YA	Hut HUTDG 51
25/11/1995	15	4		HOBO HUMPIN' SLOBO BABE Re-issue of East West YZ 798CD	Hut HUTCD 64
04/07/1998	69	1		FOUR BIG SPEAKERS WHALE FEATURING BUS 75	Hut HUTCD 96

WHALERS – see HAL PAIGE AND THE WHALERS

WHAM! UK pop group formed in 1981 by George Michael (born Georgios Panayiotou, 25/6/1963, Bushey) and Andrew Ridgeley (born 26/1/1963, Bushey). Signed by Innervision in 1982, they recruited backing singers Shirlie Holliman (born 18/4/1962, Watford) and Mandy Washburn (soon replaced by Dee C Lee, born Diane Sealey). They switched to Epic in 1984 following a court case against Innervision, by which time Dee C Lee had gone solo and been replaced by Pepsi DeMacque (born 10/12/1958, London). They split in 1986 with a farewell concert at Wembley Stadium, Michael and Ridgeley later recording solo, while Pepsi and Shirlie also recorded as a duo. Michael and Ridgeley reunited for a concert in Rio in 1991. They were named Best British Group at the 1985 BRIT Awards and picked up an Outstanding Contribution Award at the 1986 ceremony, jointly with Elton John.

DATE	POS	WKS	BPI	SINGLE TITLE	LABEL & NUMBER
16/10/1982	3	17	○	**YOUNG GUNS (GO FOR IT)**	Innervision IVL A 2766
15/01/1983	8	11		**WHAM RAP** Originally released in April 1982 and failed to chart. Featured in the 1985 film *Perfect*	Innervision IVL A 2442
14/05/1983	2	14	○	**BAD BOYS**	Innervision A 3143
30/07/1983	4	11		**CLUB TROPICANA**	Innervision A 3613
03/12/1983	15	8		CLUB FANTASTIC MEGAMIX	Innervision A 3586
26/05/1984	❶²	16	●	**WAKE ME UP BEFORE YOU GO GO** ▲³ Featured in the 2000 film *Charlie's Angels*	Epic A 4440
13/10/1984	❶³	14	●	**FREEDOM**	Epic A 4743
15/12/1984	2	13	✪	**LAST CHRISTMAS/EVERYTHING SHE WANTS** ▲²	Epic A 4949
23/11/1985	❶²	12	●	**I'M YOUR MAN**	Epic A 6716
14/12/1985	6	7		**LAST CHRISTMAS** Re-issue of Epic A 4949	Epic WHAM 1
21/06/1986	❶²	10	○	**THE EDGE OF HEAVEN/WHERE DID YOUR HEART GO**	Epic FIN 1
20/12/1986	45	4		LAST CHRISTMAS Second re-issue of Epic A 4949	Epic 6502697

○ Silver disc ● Gold disc ✪ Platinum disc (additional platinum units are indicated by a figure following the symbol) ◎ Singles released prior to 1973 that are known to have sold over 1 million copies in the UK

SARAH WHATMORE UK singer (born 1982, Manchester) who first became known competing on TV's *Pop Idol*. Although she did not make the final ten, she was signed by RCA. She also developed a parallel career as a songwriter.

21/09/2002	6	9		WHEN I LOST YOU	RCA 74321965952
22/02/2003	11	8		AUTOMATIC	RCA 82876504612

WHATNAUTS – see MOMENTS

REBECCA WHEATLEY UK singer (born 1965) who first came to prominence as an actress, appearing as Amy Howard in the TV drama series *Casualty*. She also played the same role in an episode of the spin-off series *Holby City*.

26/02/2000	10	8		STAY WITH ME (BABY)	BBC Music WMSS 60222

WHEATUS US rock group formed in Long Island, NY by Brendan Brown (guitar/vocals), Rich Leigey (bass), Phil A Jimenez (guitar) and Peter Brown (Brendan's brother, drums). Leigey was replaced by Mike McCabe in July 2000.

17/02/2001	2	20	●	TEENAGE DIRTBAG Featured in the 2001 film *Loser*	Columbia 6707962
14/07/2001	3	12		A LITTLE RESPECT	Columbia 6714282
26/01/2002	22	5		WANNABE GANGSTER/LEROY	Columbia 6721272
06/09/2003	59	1		AMERICAN IN AMSTERDAM	Columbia 6741072

CARON WHEELER UK singer (born 19/1/1963, London) who sang with Soul II Soul before going solo with RCA.

18/03/1989	5	12		KEEP ON MOVING	10 TEN 263
10/06/1989	❶[4]	14	○	BACK TO LIFE (HOWEVER DO YOU WANT ME) This and above single credited to SOUL II SOUL FEATURING CARON WHEELER 1989 Grammy Award for Best Rhythm & Blues Vocal Performance by a Group	10 TEN 265
08/09/1990	14	6		LIVIN' IN THE LIGHT	RCA PB 43939
10/11/1990	40	4		UK BLAK	RCA PB 43719
09/02/1991	53	3		DON'T QUIT	RCA PB 44259
07/11/1992	59	2		I ADORE YOU	Perspective PERSS 7407
11/09/1993	75	1		BEACH OF THE WAR GODDESS	EMI CDEM 282

BILL WHELAN FEATURING ANUNA AND THE RTE CONCERT ORCHESTRA Irish composer Bill Whelan fronting the RTE (Irish TV company) Orchestra. The Riverdance first became popular after the 1994 Eurovision Song Contest when Ireland, represented by Paul Harrington and Charlie McGettigan, had triumphed with *Rock 'N' Roll Kids*, prompting a number of riverdance shows across the country.

17/12/1994	9	16	○	RIVERDANCE	Son RTEBUACD 1

WHEN IN ROME UK group formed in Manchester by Clive Farrington, Andrew Mann and Bob Andrew.

28/01/1989	58	3		THE PROMISE	10 TEN 244

WHIGFIELD Danish model (born Sannie Charlotte Carlson, 11/4/1970, Skaelskor).

17/09/1994	❶[4]	18	✪	SATURDAY NIGHT ↑ First instance of an artist debuting at #1 on the singles chart	Systematic SYSCD 3
10/12/1994	7	10	○	ANOTHER DAY	Systematic SYSCD 6
10/06/1995	7	11		THINK OF YOU	Systematic SYCDP 10
09/09/1995	13	7		CLOSE TO YOU	Systematic SYCDP 18
16/12/1995	21	5		LAST CHRISTMAS/BIG TIME	Systematic SYSCD 24
10/10/1998	68	1		SEXY EYES – REMIXES	ZYX 8085R8

WHIPPING BOY Irish group with Fearghal McKee (vocals), Paul Page (guitar), Myles McDonnell (bass) and Colm Hassett (drums).

14/10/1995	51	1		WE DON'T NEED NOBODY ELSE	Columbia 6622205
03/02/1996	46	2		WHEN WE WERE YOUNG	Columbia 6628062
25/05/1996	55	1		TWINKLE	Columbia 6632272

NANCY WHISKEY – see CHARLES McDEVITT SKIFFLE GROUP FEATURING NANCY WHISKEY

WHISPERS US R&B vocal group formed in Los Angeles, CA in 1964 by Wallace Scott (born 23/9/1943, Fort Worth, TX), his twin brother Walter, Nicholas Caldwell (born 5/4/1944, Loma Linda, CA), Marcus Hutson (born 8/1/1943, Kansas City, MO) and Gordy Harmon. Debuting on Dore in 1964, they first made the R&B chart with Janus in 1970. They signed to Soul Train in 1975, by which time Harmon had left. He was replaced by Leavell Degree (born 31/7/1948, New Orleans, LA). Soul Train became Solar (Sound Of Los Angeles Records) in 1977. They later signed with Capitol Records.

02/02/1980	2	12	○	AND THE BEAT GOES ON	Solar SO 1
10/05/1980	55	3		LADY	Solar SO 4
12/07/1980	26	6		MY GIRL	Solar SO 8
14/03/1981	9	11		IT'S A LOVE THING	Solar SO 16
13/06/1981	44	5		I CAN MAKE IT BETTER	Solar SO 19
19/01/1985	56	3		CONTAGIOUS	MCA 937
28/03/1987	45	4		AND THE BEAT GOES ON Re-issue of Solar SO 1	Solar MCA 1126
13/06/1987	38	6		ROCK STEADY	Solar MCA 1152
15/08/1987	69	2		SPECIAL F/X	Solar MCA 1178

WHISTLE US group formed in Brooklyn, NYC in 1985 by Garvin Dublin, Brian Faust and Rickford Bennett as a rap group. They added Kerry 'Kraze' Hodge in 1988 and switched style to R&B. Dublin left in 1988 and was replaced by Tarek Stevens.

❶[9] Number of weeks single topped the UK chart ↑ Entered the UK chart at #1 ▲[9] Number of weeks single topped the US chart

869

01/03/1986 . . . . . 7 . . . . . 8 . . . .   **(NOTHIN' SERIOUS) JUST BUGGIN'** . . . . Champion CHAMP 12

ALEX WHITCOMBE AND BIG C UK DJ with a singer. Whitcombe had previously been a member of Qattara.

23/05/1998 . . . . . 44 . . . . . . 1 . . . .   ICE RAIN . . . . Xtravaganza 0091075 EXT

BARRY WHITE US singer/producer (born 12/9/1944, Galveston, TX) who formed the Atlantics in 1963 and then (with Carl Carlton) the Majestics in 1964. His first solo singles were for Downey in 1965 and Jeep (as Barry Lee) before becoming A&R man for Mustang and Bronco in 1966. Discovering Love Unlimited in 1968, he formed a production company to handle them, linking with 20thCentury Records in 1972. He first recorded as Barry White in 1973, forming the Love Unlimited Orchestra in 1974. As a youth he served three months in prison for stealing 300 tyres from a car dealer. Early in his career he wrote songs for *The Banana Splits* TV series. In 1999 he published his autobiography *Insights On Life & Love*. His Grammy Awards were Best Male Rhythm & Blues Vocal Performance and Best Rhythm & Blues Traditional Vocal Performance in 1999, both for *Staying Power*. He died from kidney failure on 4/7/2003.

09/06/1973 . . . . . 23 . . . . . . 7 . . . .   I'M GONNA LOVE YOU JUST A LITTLE BIT MORE BABY Featured in the 2003 film *Bruce Almighty* . . . . . Pye International 7N 25610
26/01/1974 . . . . . 14 . . . . . 11 . . . . .   NEVER NEVER GONNA GIVE YA UP Featured in the 1995 film *Dead Presidents*. . . . . Pye International 7N 25633
17/08/1974 . . . . . 8 . . . . . 12 . . . . .   **CAN'T GET ENOUGH OF YOUR LOVE BABE ▲¹** . . . . Pye International 7N 25661
02/11/1974 . . . . ❶² . . . . . 14 . . . . . O   **YOU'RE THE FIRST THE LAST MY EVERYTHING** Featured in the 2004 film *Bridget Jones Diary 2: Edge Of Reason* . . . .
   . . . . 20th Century BTC 2133
08/03/1975 . . . . . 5 . . . . . . 8 . . . .   **WHAT AM I GONNA DO WITH YOU** . . . . 20th Century BTC 2177
24/05/1975 . . . . . 20 . . . . . . 6 . . . .   I'LL DO ANYTHING YOU WANT ME TO . . . . 20th Century BTC 2208
27/12/1975 . . . . . 9 . . . . . . 8 . . . .   **LET THE MUSIC PLAY** . . . . 20th Century BTC 2265
06/03/1976 . . . . . 2 . . . . . 10 . . . . . O   **YOU SEE THE TROUBLE WITH ME** . . . . 20th Century BTC 2277
21/08/1976 . . . . . 15 . . . . . . 7 . . . .   BABY, WE BETTER TRY TO GET IT TOGETHER . . . . 20th Century BTC 2298
13/11/1976 . . . . . 17 . . . . . . 8 . . . .   DON'T MAKE ME WAIT TOO LONG . . . . 20th Century BTC 2309
05/03/1977 . . . . . 37 . . . . . . 5 . . . .   I'M QUALIFIED TO SATISFY . . . . 20th Century BTC 2328
15/10/1977 . . . . . 40 . . . . . . 3 . . . .   IT'S ECSTASY WHEN YOU LAY DOWN NEXT TO ME Featured in the 1999 film *Summer Of Sam* . . . . 20th Century BTC 2350
16/12/1978 . . . . . 12 . . . . . 12 . . . . . O   JUST THE WAY YOU ARE . . . . 20th Century BTC 2380
24/03/1979 . . . . . 55 . . . . . . 6 . . . .   SHA LA LA MEANS I LOVE YOU . . . . 20th Century BTC 1041
07/11/1987 . . . . . 14 . . . . . . 7 . . . .   SHO' YOU RIGHT . . . . Breakout USA 614
16/01/1988 . . . . . 63 . . . . . . 2 . . . .   NEVER NEVER GONNA GIVE YA UP (REMIX) . . . . Club JAB 59
31/03/1990 . . . . . 67 . . . . . . 1 . . . .   SECRET GARDEN QUINCY JONES FEATURING AL B SURE! JAMES INGRAM, EL DEBARGE AND BARRY WHITE Featured in the 1997
   film *Sprung*. . . . . Qwest W 9992
21/01/1995 . . . . . 20 . . . . . . 4 . . . .   PRACTICE WHAT YOU PREACH/LOVE IS THE ICON . . . . A&M 5808992
08/04/1995 . . . . . 36 . . . . . . 2 . . . .   I ONLY WANT TO BE WITH YOU . . . . A&M 5810252
21/12/1996 . . . . . 32 . . . . . . 3 . . . .   IN YOUR WILDEST DREAMS TINA TURNER FEATURING BARRY WHITE. . . . . Parlophone CDR 6451
04/11/2000 . . . . . 45 . . . . . . 2 . . . .   LET THE MUSIC PLAY (REMIX) . . . . Wonderboy WBOYD 020

CHRIS WHITE UK singer/bass player (born 7/3/1943, Barnet) who was previously a member of The Zombies.

20/03/1976 . . . . . 37 . . . . . . 4 . . . .   SPANISH WINE . . . . Charisma CB 272

KARYN WHITE US singer (born 14/10/1965, Los Angeles, CA) who was a touring backing singer with O'Bryan and recorded with Jeff Lorber in 1986. She landed a solo deal with Warner's in 1988 and is married to producer Terry Lewis.

05/11/1988 . . . . . 42 . . . . . . 5 . . . .   THE WAY YOU LOVE ME . . . . Warner Brothers W 7773
18/02/1989 . . . . . 52 . . . . . . 3 . . . .   SECRET RENDEZVOUS. . . . . Warner Brothers W 7562
10/06/1989 . . . . . 11 . . . . . 13 . . . .   SUPERWOMAN . . . . Warner Brothers W 2920
09/09/1989 . . . . . 22 . . . . . . 9 . . . .   SECRET RENDEZVOUS . . . . Warner Brothers W 2855
17/08/1991 . . . . . 23 . . . . . . 5 . . . .   ROMANTIC ▲¹ . . . . Warner Brothers W 0028
18/01/1992 . . . . . 65 . . . . . . 2 . . . .   THE WAY I FEEL ABOUT YOU . . . . Warner Brothers W 0073
24/09/1994 . . . . . 69 . . . . . . 1 . . . .   HUNGAH . . . . Warner Brothers W 0264CD

KEISHA WHITE UK singer (born 1987, London) who first guested on hits by Paul Oakenfold and Desert Eagle Disc before going solo.

27/03/2004 . . . . . 53 . . . . . . 1 . . . .   WATCHA GONNA DO . . . . Radar RAD005CD

SNOWY WHITE UK singer/guitarist (raised on the Isle of Wight) who played guitar with Pink Floyd's live band. He worked with Peter Green and joined Thin Lizzy in 1979. He left in 1982 to go solo.

24/12/1983 . . . . . 6 . . . . . 10 . . . . . O   **BIRD OF PARADISE** . . . . Towerbell TOW 42
28/12/1985 . . . . . 65 . . . . . . 2 . . . .   FOR YOU. . . . . R4 FOR 3

TAM WHITE UK singer (born in Edinburgh) who was in the Boston Dexters (despite their name they were based in Edinburgh) before going solo. He won the TV talent show *New Faces* in 1974, which led to a recording contract with RAK.

15/03/1975 . . . . . 36 . . . . . . 4 . . . .   WHAT IN THE WORLD'S COME OVER YOU . . . . RAK 193

TONY JOE WHITE US singer (born 23/7/1943, Oak Grove, LA) who, as a songwriter, penned Brook Benton's US hit *Rainy Night In Georgia* and *Polk Salad Annie*, later a hit for Elvis Presley.

06/06/1970 . . . . . 22 . . . . . 10 . . . .   GROUPIE GIRL. . . . . Monument MON 1043

WHITE AND TORCH UK vocal/instrumental duo Roy White and Steve Torch.

02/10/1982 . . . . . 54 . . . . . . 4 . . . .   PARADE. . . . . Chrysalis CHS 2641

O Silver disc ● Gold disc ✪ Platinum disc (additional platinum units are indicated by a figure following the symbol) ◉ Singles released prior to 1973 that are known to have sold over 1 million copies in the UK

WHITE PLAINS
UK pop group initially formed as a studio project by songwriters Roger Greenaway (born 23/8/1938, Bristol) and Roger Cook (born 19/8/1940, Bristol) with Tony Burrows (born 14/4/1942, Exeter, lead vocals). After the first two hits a group was assembled with Pete Nelson, Robin Cox, Roger Hills, Ricky Wolff and Robin Shaw. Burrows later fronted Brotherhood Of Man and was lead singer on hits by Edison Lighthouse, First Class and the Pipkins.

DATE	POS	WKS	SINGLE TITLE	LABEL & NUMBER
07/02/1970	9	11	**MY BABY LOVES LOVIN'** Featured in the 1994 film *The Adventures Of Priscilla: Queen Of The Desert*	Deram DM 280
18/04/1970	17	11	I'VE GOT YOU ON MY MIND	Deram DM 291
24/10/1970	8	14	**JULIE DO YA LOVE ME**	Deram DM 315
12/06/1971	13	11	WHEN YOU ARE A KING	Deram DM 333
17/02/1973	21	9	STEP INTO A DREAM	Deram DM 371

WHITE STRIPES
US rock duo formed in Detroit, MI in 1997 by (apparent) brother and sister Jack (born 9/7/1975, guitar/vocals) and Meg White (born 16/12/1974, drums). They later revealed they weren't brother and sister but husband and wife, their 1996 marriage certificate showing Jack's real name to be John Anthony Gillis. They divorced in March 2000. In 2003 they won the MTV Europe Music Award for Best Rock Act, and two Grammy Awards including Best Alternative Music Album for *Elephant*. They were named Best International Group at the 2004 BRIT Awards.

DATE	POS	WKS	SINGLE TITLE	LABEL & NUMBER
24/11/2001	26	2	HOTEL YORBA	XL Recordings XLS 139CD
09/03/2002	21	2	FELL IN LOVE WITH A GIRL	XL Recordings XLS 142CD
14/09/2002	25	2	DEAD LEAVES AND THE DIRTY GROUND	XL Recordings XLS 148CD
03/05/2003	7	4	**7 NATION ARMY** 2003 Grammy Award for Best Rock Song	XL Recordings XLS 162CD
13/09/2003	13	5	I JUST DON'T KNOW WHAT TO DO WITH MYSELF	XL Recordings XLS 166CD
29/11/2003	23	3	THE HARDEST BUTTON TO BUTTON	XL Recordings XLS 173CD
27/11/2004	16	4	JOLENE – LIVE UNDER BLACKPOOL LIGHTS	XL Recordings XLS207CD

WHITE TOWN
Indian singer Jyoti Mishra (born 30/7/1966, Rourkela, India). Recording his debut hit in his bedroom in Derby, it was originally released on the Parasol label, then snapped up by Chrysalis. It made #1 despite his refusal to appear in a video or *Top Of The Pops*.

DATE	POS	WKS	SINGLE TITLE	LABEL & NUMBER
25/01/1997	❶¹ 9 ○		**YOUR WOMAN ↑**	Chrysalis CDCHS 5052
24/05/1997	57	1	UNDRESSED	Chrysalis CDCHS 5058

WHITE ZOMBIE
US group formed by Rob Zombie (born Rob Straker, 12/1/1966, vocals), Tom Guay (guitar), Sean Yseult (bass) and Ivan DePlume (drums). Guay was later replaced by John Ricci.

DATE	POS	WKS	SINGLE TITLE	LABEL & NUMBER
20/05/1995	51	2	MORE HUMAN THAN HUMAN	Geffen GFSTD 92
18/05/1996	31	2	ELECTRIC HEAD PART 2 (THE ECSTASY)	Geffen GFSXD 22140

WHITEHEAD BROTHERS
US R&B group with Johnny and Kenny Whitehead, Crystal Alford and Nicole Renee Harris. The Whitehead brothers are the sons of prolific songwriter John Whitehead of McFadden And Whitehead.

DATE	POS	WKS	SINGLE TITLE	LABEL & NUMBER
14/01/1995	32	3	YOUR LOVE IS A 187 Contains a sample of Dr Dre & Snoop Doggy Dogg's *Deep Cover*	Motown TMGCD 1434
13/05/1995	40	2	FORGET I WAS A G Featured in the 1994 film *Jason's Lyric*	Motown TMGCD 1441

WHITEHOUSE
US/UK instrumenta/production duo William Bennett and Philip Best.

DATE	POS	WKS	SINGLE TITLE	LABEL & NUMBER
15/08/1998	60	1	AIN'T NO MOUNTAIN HIGH ENOUGH	Beautiful Noise BNOISE 2CD

WHITEOUT
UK vocal/instrumental group formed by Andrew Caldwell, Paul Carroll, Eric Lindsay and Stuart Smith.

DATE	POS	WKS	SINGLE TITLE	LABEL & NUMBER
24/09/1994	73	1	DETROIT	Silvertone ORECD 66
18/02/1995	72	1	JACKIE'S RACING	Silvertone ORECD 68

WHITESNAKE
UK heavy rock group formed in 1978 by David Coverdale (born 22/9/1949, Saltburn-by-the-Sea, Cleveland, vocals), Mickey Moody (guitar), Bernie Marsden (guitar), Brian Johnston (keyboards), Neil Murray (bass) and John Dowie (drums). Coverdale had been with Deep Purple, leaving them in 1976 and making two solo albums as Whitesnake. Marsden later recorded solo.

DATE	POS	WKS	SINGLE TITLE	LABEL & NUMBER
24/06/1978	61	3	SNAKE BITE (EP) **DAVID COVERDALE'S WHITESNAKE** Tracks on EP: *Bloody Mary, Steal Away, Ain't No Love Lost In The Heart Of The City* and *Come On*	EMI International INEP 751
10/11/1979	55	2	LONG WAY FROM HOME	United Artists BP 324
26/04/1980	13	9	FOOL FOR YOUR LOVING	United Artists BP 352
12/07/1980	43	4	READY AN' WILLING (SWEET SATISFACTION)	United Artists BP 363
22/11/1980	51	4	AIN'T NO LOVE IN THE HEART OF THE CITY	Sunburst/Liberty BP 381
11/04/1981	17	9	DON'T BREAK MY HEART AGAIN	Liberty BP 395
06/06/1981	37	6	WOULD I LIE TO YOU	Liberty BP 399
06/11/1982	34	10	HERE I GO AGAIN/BLOODY LUXURY ▲¹	Liberty BP 416
13/08/1983	31	5	GUILTY OF LOVE	Liberty BP 420
14/01/1984	29	4	GIVE ME MORE TIME	Liberty BP 422
28/04/1984	62	2	STANDING IN THE SHADOW	Liberty BP 423
09/02/1985	44	2	LOVE AIN'T NO STRANGER	Liberty BP 424
28/03/1987	16	8	STILL OF THE NIGHT	EMI 5606
06/06/1987	9	11	**IS THIS LOVE**	EMI EM 3
31/10/1987	9	11	**HERE I GO AGAIN (REMIX)**	EMI EM 35
06/02/1988	18	6	GIVE ME ALL YOUR LOVE	EMI EM 23
02/12/1989	43	2	FOOL FOR YOUR LOVING	EMI EM 123
10/03/1990	35	3	THE DEEPER THE LOVE	EMI EM 128
25/08/1990	31	4	NOW YOU'RE GONE	EMI EM 150
06/08/1994	25	4	IS THIS LOVE/SWEET LADY LUCK (REMIX)	EMI CDEM 329

❶⁹ Number of weeks single topped the UK chart ↑ Entered the UK chart at #1 ▲⁹ Number of weeks single topped the US chart

07/06/1997 . . . . . 46 . . . . . . 1 . . . . TOO MANY TEARS **DAVID COVERDALE AND WQHITESNAKE** . . . . EMI CDEM 471

DAVID WHITFIELD UK singer (born 2/2/1925, Hull) who began as a singer on the Hughie Green show on Radio Luxembourg while working in a pre-cast stonemaker's yard. Green introduced him to Cecil Landeau and he was signed by Decca in 1953, turning to an operatic career in 1963. Although the writers of his biggest hit *Cara Mia* were listed as Lee Lange and Tulio Trapani, they were in fact Bunny Lewis (Whitfield's producer) and Mantovani (his arranger). He died on 15/1/1980.

02/10/1953 . . . . . 9 . . . . . . 1	**BRIDGE OF SIGHS**	Decca F 10129
16/10/1953 . . . . . ❶² 14	**ANSWER ME** Reclaimed #1 position on 11/12/1953	Decca F 10192
11/12/1953 . . . . . 3 . . . . . . 11	**RAGS TO RICHES DAVID WHITFIELD WITH STANLEY BLACK AND HIS ORCHESTRA**	Decca F 10207
19/02/1954 . . . . . 5 . . . . . . 15	**THE BOOK**	Decca F 10242
18/06/1954 . . . . . ❶¹⁰ . . . 25	**CARA MIA DAVID WHITFIELD WITH CHORUS AND MANTOVANI AND HIS ORCHESTRA**	Decca F 10327
12/11/1954 . . . . . 2 . . . . . . 10	**SANTO NATALE (MERRY CHRISTMAS)**	Decca F 10399
11/02/1955 . . . . . 8 . . . . . . 9	**BEYOND THE STARS**	Decca F 10458
27/05/1955 . . . . . 12 . . . . . 11	MAMA	Decca F 10515
08/07/1955 . . . . . 3 . . . . . . 20	**EV'RYWHERE DAVID WHITFIELD WITH THE ROLAND SHAW ORCHESTRA**	Decca F 10515
25/11/1955 . . . . . 7 . . . . . . 11	**WHEN YOU LOSE THE ONE YOU LOVE DAVID WHITFIELD WITH CHORUS AND MANTOVANI AND HIS ORCHESTRA**	Decca F 10627
02/03/1956 . . . . . 3 . . . . . . 24	**MY SEPTEMBER LOVE**	Decca F 10690
24/08/1956 . . . . . 22 . . . . . 4	MY SON JOHN	Decca F 10769
31/08/1956 . . . . . 29 . . . . . 1	MY UNFINISHED SYMPHONY	Decca F 10769
25/01/1957 . . . . . 9 . . . . . . 11	**ADORATION WALTZ DAVID WHITFIELD WITH THE ROLAND SHAW ORCHESTRA**	Decca F 10833
05/04/1957 . . . . . 27 . . . . . 4	I'LL FIND YOU Featured in the 1957 film *Sea Wife*	Decca F 10864
14/02/1958 . . . . . 22 . . . . . 3	CRY MY HEART **DAVID WHITFIELD WITH CHORUS AND MANTOVANI AND HIS ORCHESTRA**	Decca F 10978
16/05/1958 . . . . . 16 . . . . . 14	ON THE STREET WHERE YOU LIVE **DAVID WHITFIELD WITH CYRIL STAPLETON AND HIS ORCHESTRA** . . .	Decca F 11018
08/08/1958 . . . . . 30 . . . . . 1	THE RIGHT TO LOVE	Decca F 11039
24/11/1960 . . . . . 49 . . . . . 1	I BELIEVE	Decca F 11289

SLIM WHITMAN US singer (born Otis Dewey Whitman Jr, 20/1/1924, Tampa, FL) who was a shipfitter when he turned professional in 1948. After his UK #1, as one of the first country artists to tour the UK he was largely responsible for introducing country music to UK audiences. His concentration on the UK market marred his US chart career, but he was still having UK album hits into the 1970s. He appeared in the 1957 film *Jamboree* and has a star on the Hollywood Walk of Fame.

15/07/1955 . . . . . ❶¹¹ 19	**ROSE MARIE** Originally recorded in 1925 by Jesse Crawford	London HL 8061
29/07/1955 . . . . . 7 . . . . . . 12	**INDIAN LOVE CALL**	London L 1149
23/09/1955 . . . . . 15 . . . . . 2	CHINA DOLL	London L 1149
09/03/1956 . . . . . 19 . . . . . 2	TUMBLING TUMBLEWEEDS	London HLU 8230
13/04/1956 . . . . . 16 . . . . . 4	I'M A FOOL	London HLU 8252
22/06/1956 . . . . . 8 . . . . . . 15	**SERENADE**	London HLU 8287
12/04/1957 . . . . . 7 . . . . . . 13	**I'LL TAKE YOU HOME AGAIN KATHLEEN**	London HLP 8403
05/10/1974 . . . . . 14 . . . . . 10	HAPPY ANNIVERSARY	United Artists UP 35728

ROGER WHITTAKER Kenyan singer (born 22/3/1936, Nairobi) who came to the UK (his parents were of British origin) to attend university, turning to music after graduating in 1960. He hosted a radio series that led to his biggest hit *The Last Farewell*. He invited listeners to submit lyrics that he would put to music, Ron Webster, a Birmingham silversmith, penning *The Last Farewell*.

08/11/1969 . . . . . 12 . . . . . 18	DURHAM TOWN (THE LEAVIN')	Columbia DB 8613
11/04/1970 . . . . . 8 . . . . . . 18	**I DON'T BELIEVE IN 'IF' ANYMORE**	Columbia DB 8664
10/10/1970 . . . . . 17 . . . . . 14	NEW WORLD IN THE MORNING	Columbia DB 8718
03/04/1971 . . . . . 47 . . . . . 1	WHY	Columbia DB 8752
02/10/1971 . . . . . 31 . . . . . 10	MAMMY BLUE	Columbia DB 8822
26/07/1975 . . . . . 2 . . . . . . 14 . . . . ○	**THE LAST FAREWELL**	EMI 2294
08/11/1986 . . . . . 10 . . . . . 10	**THE SKYE BOAT SONG ROGER WHITTAKER AND DES O'CONNOR**	Tembo TML 119

WHO UK rock group formed in London in 1962 by Roger Daltrey (born 1/4/1944, London, vocals), Pete Townshend (born 19/5/1945, London, guitar), John Entwistle (born 9/10/1944, London, bass) and Doug Sandom (drums) as the Detours, name-changing to the High Numbers in 1964 and recruiting Keith Moon (born 23/8/1947, London) as drummer. They became The Who in 1964 because manager Kit Lambert thought that 'High Numbers' on a poster would suggest it was a bingo session. They signed with Brunswick in 1965. Moon died on 7/9/1978 from a drug overdose (at Flat 12, 9 Curzon Street, London, the apartment where Mama Cass had died four years previously). He was replaced by ex-Small Faces Kenny Jones (born 16/9/1948, London). In 1979 eleven fans were trampled to death in Cincinnati during a stampede for unreserved seats. Their 1969 album *Tommy* was made into a film in 1975, as was 1973's *Quadrophenia* in 1979. They split in 1983, re-forming for Live Aid in 1985. Entwistle, Daltrey and Townshend reunited in 1989 for a North American tour. They were presented with the Outstanding Contribution Award at the 1988 BRIT Awards, while Pete Townshend was given the Lifetime Achievement Award in 1983. They were inducted into the Rock & Roll Hall of Fame in 1990.

18/02/1965 . . . . . 8 . . . . . . 13 . . . . . . **I CAN'T EXPLAIN** . . . . Brunswick 05926

DATE	POS	WKS	BPI	SINGLE TITLE	LABEL & NUMBER
27/05/1965	10	12		**ANYWAY ANYHOW ANYWHERE** Theme to the TV series *Ready Steady Go*	Brunswick 05935
04/11/1965	2	13		**MY GENERATION** Featured in the films *The Kids Are Alright* (1979) and *Austin Powers: The Spy Who Shagged Me* (1999)	Brunswick 05944
10/03/1966	5	13		**SUBSTITUTE**	Reaction 591 001
24/03/1966	32	6		A LEGAL MATTER	Brunswick 05956
01/09/1966	2	13		**I'M A BOY**	Reaction 591 004
01/09/1966	41	3		THE KIDS ARE ALRIGHT	Brunswick 05965
15/12/1966	3	11		**HAPPY JACK**	Reaction 591 010
27/04/1967	4	10		**PICTURES OF LILY**	Track 604 002
26/07/1967	44	3		THE LAST TIME/UNDER MY THUMB	Track 604 006
18/10/1967	10	12		**I CAN SEE FOR MILES** Featured in the 1997 film *Apollo 13*	Track 604 011
19/06/1968	25	5		DOGS	Track 604 023
23/10/1968	26	6		MAGIC BUS Featured in the films *Romeo And Juliet* (1996) and *Jerry Maguire* (1997)	Track 604 024
19/03/1969	4	13		**PINBALL WIZARD** Featured in the films *Tommy* (1975) and *The Kids Are Alright* (1979)	Track 604 027
04/04/1970	19	11		THE SEEKER Featured in the 1999 film *American Beauty*	Track 604 036
08/08/1970	38	4		SUMMERTIME BLUES	Track 2094 002
10/07/1971	9	12		**WON'T GET FOOLED AGAIN**	Track 2094 009
23/10/1971	16	12		LET'S SEE ACTION	Track 2094 012
24/06/1972	9	9		**JOIN TOGETHER**	Track 2094 102
13/01/1973	21	5		RELAY	Track 2094 106
13/10/1973	20	6		5.15	Track 2094 115
24/01/1976	10	9		**SQUEEZE BOX**	Polydor 2121 275
30/10/1976	7	7		**SUBSTITUTE** Re-issue of Reaction 591 001	Polydor 2058 803
22/07/1978	18	12		WHO ARE YOU	Polydor WHO 1
28/04/1979	48	5		LONG LIVE ROCK	Polydor WHO 2
07/03/1981	9	8		**YOU BETTER YOU BET**	Polydor WHO 004
09/05/1981	47	4		DON'T LET GO THE COAT	Polydor WHO 005
02/10/1982	40	4		ATHENA	Polydor WHO 6
26/11/1983	58	2		READY STEADY WHO (EP) Tracks on EP: *Disguises, Circles, Batman, Bucket 'T'* and *Barbara Ann*	Polydor WHO 7
20/02/1988	68	2		MY GENERATION Re-issue of Brunswick 05944	Polydor POSP 907
27/07/1996	31	2		MY GENERATION Second re-issue of Brunswick 05944	Polydor 8546372

WHO DA FUNK FEATURING JESSICA EVE
US production group formed in New York by Alex Alicea and Jorge 'DJ Lace' Jaramillo with singer Jessica Eve. Eve is the wife of fellow hitmaker Harry 'Choo Choo' Romero.

DATE	POS	WKS	BPI	SINGLE TITLE	LABEL & NUMBER
26/10/2002	69	1		SHINY DISCO BALLS (IMPORT)	Subusa 5000007432304
02/11/2002	15	5		SHINY DISCO BALLS	Cream 22CD
15/02/2003	32	2		STING ME RED (YOU THINK YOU'RE SO) **WHO DA FUNK FEATURING TERRA DEVA**	Cream 19CDS

WHODINI
US rap group formed in NYC by Jalil 'Whodini' Hutchins and John 'Ecstasy' Fletcher, adding Grandmaster Dee in 1986.

DATE	POS	WKS	BPI	SINGLE TITLE	LABEL & NUMBER
25/12/1982	47	6		MAGIC'S WAND	Jive 28
17/03/1984	63	4		MAGIC'S WAND (THE WHODINI ELECTRIC EP) Tracks on EP: *Jive Magic Wand, Nasty Lady, Rap Machine* and *The Haunted House Of Rock*	Jive 61

WHOOLIGANZ
US rap duo Mad Skillz (born Scott Caan, son of actor James Caan, 1975) and Mudfoot (born Alan Maman, 1977).

DATE	POS	WKS	BPI	SINGLE TITLE	LABEL & NUMBER
13/08/1994	53	2		PUT YOUR HANDZ UP	Positiva CDTIV 17

WHOOSH
UK production trio Spencer Hickson, Mike Bell and DMW.

DATE	POS	WKS	BPI	SINGLE TITLE	LABEL & NUMBER
13/09/1997	72	1		WHOOSH	Wonderboy WBOYD 006

WHYCLIFFE
UK R&B singer Bramwell Donovan Whycliffe.

DATE	POS	WKS	BPI	SINGLE TITLE	LABEL & NUMBER
20/11/1993	56	1		HEAVEN	MCA MCSTD 1944
02/04/1994	72	1		ONE MORE TIME	MCA MCSTD 1955

WIDEBOYS FEATURING DENNIS G
UK dance group formed in Southampton by Jim Sullivan and Ed Craig with singer Dennis Gordon, a former basketball player.

DATE	POS	WKS	BPI	SINGLE TITLE	LABEL & NUMBER
27/10/2001	15	6		SAMBUCA	Locked On/679 Recordings 679L 002CD

GABRIELLE WIDMAN – see MONKEY BARS FEATURING GABRIELLE WIDMAN

JANE WIEDLIN
US singer (born 20/5/1958, Oconomowoc, WI). She was guitarist with all-girl group The Go-Go's, who disbanded in 1985.

DATE	POS	WKS	BPI	SINGLE TITLE	LABEL & NUMBER
06/08/1988	12	11		RUSH HOUR	Manhattan MT 36
29/10/1988	64	3		INSIDE A DREAM	Manhattan MT 55

WIGAN'S CHOSEN FEW
Canadian instrumental track recorded by unknown group Chosen Few. The UK single release had additional crowd noises from the 1966 FA Cup Final between Everton and Sheffield Wednesday. When the record made the charts and earned an appearance on *Top Of The Pops*, dancers from the Wigan Casino gave a demonstration of Northern Soul dancing.

DATE	POS	WKS	BPI	SINGLE TITLE	LABEL & NUMBER
18/01/1975	9	11		**FOOTSEE**	Pye Disco Demand DDS 111

WIGAN'S OVATION
UK group formed by brothers Pete and Phil Preston, Jim McCluskey and Alf Brooks, and previously called The Wigan Peer and Forum before settling on Wigan's Ovation.

DATE	POS	WKS		SINGLE TITLE	LABEL & NUMBER
15/03/1975	12	10		SKIING IN THE SNOW	Spark SRL 1122
28/06/1975	38	6		PER-SO-NAL-LY	Spark SRL 1129
29/11/1975	41	3		SUPER LOVE	Spark SRL 1133

WILCO
US group formed by Daniel Corrigan (vocals), Jeff Tweedy (bass/vocals), John Stirratt (keyboards/vocals), Max Johnston (banjo/fiddle), Lloyd Maines (guitar), Brian Henneman (guitar) and Ken Coomer (drums).

DATE	POS	WKS		SINGLE TITLE	LABEL & NUMBER
17/04/1999	67	1		CAN'T STAND IT	Reprise W 475CD1

JACK WILD
UK singer (born 30/9/1952, Oldham) who was first known via the 1968 film musical *Oliver!* and later the children's TV programme *HR Puffenstuff*.

DATE	POS	WKS		SINGLE TITLE	LABEL & NUMBER
02/05/1970	46	2		SOME BEAUTIFUL	Capitol CL 15635

WILD BOYS – see HEINZ

WILD CHERRY
US funk group formed in Steubenville, OH in the early 1970s by Robert Parissi (guitar/vocals), Allen Wentz (bass/synthesiser/vocals), Ronald Beitle (drums/vocals) and Bryan Bassett (guitar/vocals). Mark Avsec was later added on keyboards.

DATE	POS	WKS		SINGLE TITLE	LABEL & NUMBER
09/10/1976	7	11		PLAY THAT FUNKY MUSIC ▲³ Featured in the 2004 film *Scooby Doo 2: Monsters Unleashed*	Epic EPC 4593

WILD COLOUR
UK vocal/instrumental group formed by Paul Oakenfold and Steve Osborne with vocalists Davis and Dane.

DATE	POS	WKS		SINGLE TITLE	LABEL & NUMBER
14/10/1995	25	2		DREAMS	Perfecto PERF 105CD

WILD PAIR – see PAULA ABDUL

WILD WEEKEND
UK vocal/instrumental group formed by Jon Bull and Alan Scott.

DATE	POS	WKS		SINGLE TITLE	LABEL & NUMBER
29/04/1989	74	1		BREAKIN' UP	Parlophone R 6204
05/05/1990	70	1		WHO'S AFRAID OF THE BIG BAD LOVE	Parlophone R 6249

WILDCHILD
UK producer/DJ Roger McKenzie (born 1971). He died from a heart condition on 25/11/1995.

DATE	POS	WKS		SINGLE TITLE	LABEL & NUMBER
22/04/1995	34	3		LEGENDS OF THE DARK BLACK – PART 2	Hi-Life HICD 9
21/10/1995	11	4		RENEGADE MASTER Same record as *Legends Of The Dark Black – Part 2* but with a different title	Hi-Life 5771312
23/11/1996	30	2		JUMP TO MY BEAT Contains samples of Mark Ryder's *Get Down,* Aretha Franklin's *Jump To It* and Lisa Lisa's *Let The Beat Hit 'Em*	Hi-Life 5757372
17/01/1998	3	10	O	RENEGADE MASTER (REMIX)	Hi-Life 5692792
25/04/1998	38	1		BAD BOY WILDCHILD FEATURING JOMALSKI	Polydor 5716072

EUGENE WILDE
US singer (born Ronald Bloomfield, Miami, FL) with the family group La Voyage, which became Tight Connection and recorded for TK in the 1970s. Wilde recorded solo in 1979, at the same time that the group changed their name to Simplicious. Both acts were signed to the same label. Wilde later recorded for MCA and as a songwriter penned tracks for the likes of Britney Spears.

DATE	POS	WKS		SINGLE TITLE	LABEL & NUMBER
13/10/1984	18	9		GOTTA GET YOU HOME TONIGHT	Fourth & Broadway BRW 15
02/02/1985	34	6		PERSONALITY Listed flip side was *Let Her Feel It* by SIMPLICIOUS	Fourth & Broadway BRW 18

KIM WILDE
UK singer (born Kim Smith, 18/11/1960, London) who began as backing vocalist for her father Marty on live dates. She signed with RAK in 1980, her early material written by brother Ricky and produced by him and Marty, and switched to MCA in 1984. Engaged to Mickie Most's son Calvin Hayes (of Johnny Hates Jazz) for a time, she was named Best British Female at the 1983 BRIT Awards.

DATE	POS	WKS		SINGLE TITLE	LABEL & NUMBER
21/02/1981	2	13	●	KIDS IN AMERICA	RAK 327
09/05/1981	4	9	O	CHEQUERED LOVE	RAK 330
01/08/1981	11	8		WATER ON GLASS/BOYS	RAK 334
14/11/1981	12	12		CAMBODIA	RAK 336
17/04/1982	16	7		VIEW FROM A BRIDGE	RAK 342
16/10/1982	43	4		CHILD COME AWAY	RAK 352
30/07/1983	23	8		LOVE BLONDE	RAK 360
12/11/1983	67	2		DANCING IN THE DARK	RAK 365
13/10/1984	29	6		THE SECOND TIME	MCA KIM 1
08/12/1984	56	3		THE TOUCH	MCA KIM 2
27/04/1985	19	8		RAGE TO LOVE	MCA KIM 3
25/10/1986	2	14	O	YOU KEEP ME HANGIN' ON ▲¹	MCA KIM 4
04/04/1987	6	11		ANOTHER STEP CLOSER TO YOU KIM WILDE AND JUNIOR	MCA KIM 5
08/08/1987	29	5		SAY YOU REALLY WANT ME Featured in the 1986 film *Running Scared*	MCA KIM 6
05/12/1987	3	7	O	ROCKIN' AROUND THE CHRISTMAS TREE MEL AND KIM (Mel Smith)	10 TEN 2

14/05/1988	31	5		HEY MISTER HEARTACHE	MCA KIM 7
16/07/1988	3	11	○	**YOU CAME**	MCA KIM 8
01/10/1988	7	9		**NEVER TRUST A STRANGER**	MCA KIM 9
03/12/1988	6	12		**FOUR LETTER WORD**	MCA KIM 10
04/03/1989	32	6		LOVE IN THE NATURAL WAY	MCA KIM 11
14/04/1990	42	4		IT'S HERE	MCA KIM 12
16/06/1990	71	3		TIME	MCA KIM 13
15/12/1990	51	3		I CAN'T SAY GOODBYE	MCA KIM 14
02/05/1992	16	6		LOVE IS HOLY	MCA KIM 15
27/06/1992	34	3		HEART OVER MIND	MCA KIM 16
12/09/1992	49	3		WHO DO YOU THINK YOU ARE	MCA KIM 17
10/07/1993	12	8		IF I CAN'T HAVE YOU	MCA KIMTD 18
13/11/1993	54	1		IN MY LIFE	MCA KIMTD 19
14/10/1995	43	2		BREAKIN' AWAY	MCA KIMTD 21
10/02/1996	46	1		THIS I SWEAR	MCA KIMTD 22

MARTY WILDE
UK singer (born Reginald Smith, 15/4/1939, London) who began as Reginald Patterson before being introduced to Larry Parnes. Parnes re-christened him Marty Wilde, signing him to Philips in 1957. He formed backing group the Wildcats in 1959 with Big Jim Sullivan (guitar), Tony Belcher (guitar), Brian 'Liquorice' Locking (bass) and Tony Belcher (drums). They split to become the Krew-Kats in 1961. In the 1980s he was co-writer/producer of daughter Kim's hits. He was the first act to appear on pioneering TV rock 'n' roll show *Oh Boy!* on 15/6/1958.

11/07/1958	4	14		**ENDLESS SLEEP**	Philips PB 835
06/03/1959	3	18		**DONNA**	Philips PB 902
05/06/1959	2	17		**A TEENAGER IN LOVE** Originally called *Great To Be In Love*	Philips PB 926
25/09/1959	3	12		**SEA OF LOVE**	Philips PB 959
11/12/1959	7	8		**BAD BOY**	Philips PB 972
10/03/1960	30	4		JOHNNY ROCCO	Philips PB 1002
19/05/1960	47	1		THE FIGHT	Philips PB 1022
22/12/1960	16	9		LITTLE GIRL	Philips PB 1078
26/01/1961	9	9		**RUBBER BALL**	Philips PB 1101
27/07/1961	47	2		HIDE AND SEEK	Philips PB 1240
09/11/1961	33	5		TOMORROW'S CLOWN	Philips PB 1191
24/05/1962	19	11		JEZEBEL	Philips PB 1240
25/10/1962	31	7		EVER SINCE YOU SAID GOODBYE	Philips 326546 BF

ROXANNE WILDE – see DT8 FEATURING ROXANNE WILDE

MATTHEW WILDER
US singer (born 24/1/1953, Manhattan, NYC) who relocated to Los Angeles, CA in the late 1970s, singing backing for Rickie Lee Jones and Bette Midler before going solo. He later became a noted producer for the likes of No Doubt.

21/01/1984	4	11	○	**BREAK MY STRIDE**	Epic A 3908

WILDFLOWER – see APHRODITE FEATURING WILDFLOWER

WILDHEARTS
UK group formed by Ginger (born David Walls, 17/12/1964, South Shields, guitar/vocals), Danny McCormack (born 28/2/1972, South Shields, bass/vocals), Jeff Streatham (born 8/6/1973, Southampton, guitar) and Richie Battersby (born 29/6/1968, Birmingham, drums). They originally signed with East West in 1992, consisting of Ginger, Mark Kedds, CJ and Willie Dowling, the latter two going on to form Honeycrack. Danny McCormack is the brother of 3 Colours Red's Chris McCormack.

20/11/1993	53	2		TV TAN	Bronze YZ 784CD
19/02/1994	31	3		CAFFEINE BOMB	Bronze YZ 794CD
09/07/1994	38	2		SUCKERPUNCH	Bronze YZ 828CD
28/01/1995	31	3		IF LIFE IS LIKE A LOVE BANK I WANT AN OVERDRAFT/GEORDIE IN WONDERLAND	Bronze YZ 874CD
06/05/1995	16	3		I WANNA GO WHERE THE PEOPLE GO	East West YZ 923CD
29/07/1995	28	2		JUST IN LUST	East West YZ 967CD
20/04/1996	14	3		SICK OF DRUGS	Round WILD 1CDX
29/06/1996	30	2		RED LIGHT GREEN LIGHT EP Tracks on EP: *Red Light – Green Light, Got It On Tuesday, Do Anything* and *The British All-American Homeboy Crowd*	Round WILD 2CD
16/08/1997	21	2		ANTHEM	Mushroom MUSH 6CD
18/10/1997	26	2		URGE	Mushroom MUSH 14CD
12/10/2002	26	2		VANILLA RADIO	Round/Snapper SMASCD 048X
01/02/2003	17	2		STORMY IN THE NORTH KARMA IN THE SOUTH	Snapper Music SMASCD 049X
24/05/2003	22	2		SO INTO YOU	Gut CXGUT 49
15/11/2003	26	2		TOP OF THE WORLD	Gut CXGUT 54

WILEY
UK rapper Richard Cowie (born in London) who was formerly a member of Pay As U Go and Roll Deep Crew.

17/04/2004	31	4		WOT DO U CALL IT?	XL Recordings XLS179CD
21/08/2004	45	2		PIES	XL Recordings XLS188CD

JONATHAN WILKES
UK singer (born 1/8/1978), initially known as a TV presenter. He shares a flat with singer Robbie Williams.

17/03/2001	24	2		JUST ANOTHER DAY	Innocent SINCD 25

❶[9] Number of weeks single topped the UK chart ↑ Entered the UK chart at #1 ▲[9] Number of weeks single topped the US chart

875

SUE WILKINSON UK singer who later became stage manager for the TV series *Emmerdale*.

02/08/1980 . . . . . 25 . . . . . . 8	YOU GOTTA BE A HUSTLER IF YOU WANNA GET ON . . . . Cheapskate CHEAP 2

WILL TO POWER US group, originally a trio, with producer Bob Rosenberg, Dr J and Maria Mendez. Dr J and Mendez left in 1990 and were replaced by Elin Michaels.

| 07/01/1989 . . . . . 6 . . . . . 9 . . . . . . | **BABY I LOVE YOUR WAY – FREEBIRD** ▲[1] . . . . Epic 6530947 |
| 22/12/1990 . . . . . 29 . . . . . . 9 . . . . . . | I'M NOT IN LOVE . . . . Epic 6565377 |

ALYSON WILLIAMS US singer (born in Harlem, NYC), daughter of trumpeter Bobby Booker and a backing singer before joining High Fashion in 1982. She debuted solo for Profile in 1986. Nikki D is hip hop singer Nichelle Strong (born 10/9/1968, Los Angeles, CA).

04/03/1989 . . . . . 17 . . . . . . 9	SLEEP TALK . . . . Def Jam 6546567
06/05/1989 . . . . . 34 . . . . . . 5	MY LOVE IS SO RAW ALYSON WILLIAMS FEATURING NIKKI D . . . . Def Jam 6548987
19/08/1989 . . . . . 8 . . . . . 11	**I NEED YOUR LOVIN'** . . . . Def Jam 6551437
18/11/1989 . . . . . 44 . . . . . . 3	I SECOND THAT EMOTION ALYSON WILLIAMS WITH CHUCK STANLEY . . . . Def Jam 6554567

ANDY WILLIAMS US singer (born Howard Andrew Williams, 3/12/1928, Wall Lake, IA), who sang with his three brothers on radio before moving with the family to California. The group then teamed up with comedienne Kay Thompson for six years before Williams went solo in 1952. He appeared on Steve Allen's *Tonight* show for two and half years and hosted his own TV show from 1959, introducing the Osmonds to the record-buying public. He has a star on the Hollywood Walk of Fame.

19/04/1957 . . . . ❶[2] 16	BUTTERFLY ▲[3] . . . . London HLA 8399
21/06/1957 . . . . . 16 . . . . 10	I LIKE YOUR KIND OF LOVE Features the uncredited vocals of Peggy Powers . . . . London HLA 8437
14/06/1962 . . . . . 30 . . . . 10	STRANGER ON THE SHORE . . . . CBS AAG 103
21/03/1963 . . . . . 2 . . . . 18	**CAN'T GET USED TO LOSING YOU** . . . . CBS AAG 138
27/02/1964 . . . . . 40 . . . . . 4	A FOOL NEVER LEARNS . . . . CBS AAG 182
16/09/1965 . . . . . 2 . . . . 17	**ALMOST THERE** . . . . CBS 201813
24/02/1966 . . . . . 19 . . . . . 8	MAY EACH DAY . . . . CBS 202042
22/09/1966 . . . . . 33 . . . . . 7	IN THE ARMS OF LOVE Featured in the 1966 film *What Did You Do In The War, Daddy* . . . . CBS 202300
04/05/1967 . . . . . 33 . . . . . 6	MUSIC TO WATCH GIRLS BY . . . . CBS 2675
02/08/1967 . . . . . 45 . . . . . 1	MORE AND MORE . . . . CBS 2886
13/03/1968 . . . . . 5 . . . . 18	**CAN'T TAKE MY EYES OFF YOU** Featured in the 2001 film *Bridget Jones's Diary* . . . . CBS 3298
07/05/1969 . . . . . 19 . . . . 10	HAPPY HEART . . . . CBS 4062
14/03/1970 . . . . . 3 . . . . 17	**CAN'T HELP FALLING IN LOVE** . . . . CBS 4818
01/08/1970 . . . . . 13 . . . . 14	IT'S SO EASY . . . . CBS 5113
21/11/1970 . . . . . 7 . . . . 12	**HOME LOVIN' MAN** . . . . CBS 5267
20/03/1971 . . . . . 4 . . . . 18	**(WHERE DO I BEGIN) LOVE STORY** Theme from the 1970 film *Love Story*, although Williams' version is not featured in the film . . . . . . CBS 7020
05/08/1972 . . . . . 42 . . . . . 9	LOVE THEME FROM THE GODFATHER . . . . CBS 8166
08/12/1973 . . . . . 4 . . . . . 18	**SOLITAIRE** . . . . CBS 1824
18/05/1974 . . . . . 35 . . . . . 5	GETTING OVER YOU . . . . CBS 2181
31/05/1975 . . . . . 32 . . . . . 7	YOU LAY SO EASY ON MY MIND . . . . CBS 3167
06/03/1976 . . . . . 42 . . . . . 3	THE OTHER SIDE OF ME . . . . CBS 3903
27/03/1999 . . . . . 9 . . . . . 6	**MUSIC TO WATCH GIRLS BY** Originally written in 1967 for a Pepsi Cola advertisement and revived following use in an advertisement for Fiat Punto cars. Subsequently became the title to a successful series of 'lounge' albums . . . . Columbia 6671322
29/06/2002 . . . . . 23 . . . . . . 4	CAN'T TAKE MY EYES OFF YOU ANDY WILLIAMS AND DENISE VAN OUTEN . . . . Columbia 6721052

ANDY AND DAVID WILLIAMS US vocal duo, twins Andy and David Williams (born 22/2/1959, Henderson, NV). The nephews of singer Andy Williams, they also recorded as The Williams Brothers.

| 24/03/1973 . . . . . 37 . . . . . 5 . . . . . . | I DON'T KNOW WHY . . . . MCA MUS 1183 |

BILLY WILLIAMS US singer (born 28/12/1910, Waco, TX) who was lead singer with the Charioteers 1930–1950 and then formed his own Billy Williams Quartet with Eugene Dixon, Claude Riddick and John Ball. By 1965 he was living as a 'down and out', having lost his voice through diabetes, but was taken to Chicago, IL and worked on the Model Cities programme. He died on 17/10/1972. He was the first act to appear on the TV programme *American Bandstand* on 5/8/1957.

| 02/08/1957 . . . . . 22 . . . . . . 9 . . . . | I'M GONNA SIT RIGHT DOWN AND WRITE MYSELF A LETTER Featured in the 1998 film *You've Got M@il* . . . . Vogue Coral Q 72266 |

DANNY WILLIAMS UK singer (born 7/1/1942, Port Elizabeth, South Africa) who moved to the UK in 1959 and teamed up with producer Norman Newell, being dubbed 'the British Johnny Mathis'. After his initial hits he worked in nightclubs, re-emerging in the 1970s with a light disco style.

25/05/1961 . . . . . 44 . . . . . . 3	WE WILL NEVER BE THIS YOUNG AGAIN . . . . HMV POP 839
06/07/1961 . . . . . 41 . . . . . . 8	THE MIRACLE OF YOU . . . . HMV POP 885
02/11/1961 . . . . ❶[2] 19	**MOON RIVER** . . . . HMV POP 932
18/01/1962 . . . . . 14 . . . . 14	JEANNIE . . . . HMV POP 968

12/04/1962 .....8..... 13	WONDERFUL WORLD OF THE YOUNG	HMV POP 1002
05/07/1962 ..... 22.....7.......	TEARS	HMV POP 1035
28/02/1963 ..... 45.....3......	MY OWN TRUE LOVE	HMV POP 1112
30/07/1977 ..... 30......7.......	DANCIN' EASY Originally written for a Martini TV advertisement	Ensign ENY 3

DENIECE WILLIAMS
US singer (born June Deniece Chandler, 3/6/1951, Gary, IN) who first recorded for Toddlin' Town in the late 1960s. She was backing singer in Stevie Wonder's group Wonderlove 1972–75. With songwriting ambitions, her first hit was intended for Earth Wind & Fire until persuaded by producer Maurice White to record it herself. She later recorded gospel material for Sparrow. She has won five Grammy Awards: Best Recording for Children in 1982 with various others for *In Harmony 2*, Best Gospel Performance by a Duo in 1986 with Sandi Patti for *They Say*, Best Soul Gospel Performance in 1986 for *I Surrender*, Best Gospel Performance in 1987 for *I Believe In You* and Best Pop/Contemporary Gospel Performance in 1998 for *This Is My Song*.

02/04/1977 ....**❶²**.... 10 .....○	**FREE**...	CBS 4978
30/07/1977 .....8..... 11 .....○	**THAT'S WHAT FRIENDS ARE FOR**	CBS 5432
12/11/1977 ..... 32.....5.......	BABY BABY MY LOVE'S ALL FOR YOU	CBS 5779
25/03/1978 .....3..... 14	**TOO MUCH TOO LITTLE TOO LATE ▲¹**	CBS 6164
29/07/1978 ..... 45.....6......	YOU'RE ALL I NEED TO GET BY This and above single credited to **JOHNNY MATHIS AND DENIECE WILLIAMS**	CBS 6483
05/05/1984 .....2..... 13 .....○	**LET'S HEAR IT FOR THE BOY ▲²** Featured in the 1984 film *Footloose*	CBS A 4319

DIANA WILLIAMS
US country singer (born in Nashville, TN).

25/07/1981 ..... 54......3.......	TEDDY BEAR'S LAST RIDE	Capitol CL 207

DON WILLIAMS
US singer (born 27/5/1939, Floydada, TX) who was a popular country artist in the UK where over twelve albums have charted. He has appeared in numerous films, including 1980's *Smokey & The Bandit 2*.

19/06/1976 ..... 13 ..... 10	I RECALL A GYPSY WOMAN	ABC 4098
23/10/1976 ..... 35.....6......	YOU'RE MY BEST FRIEND	ABC 4144

ERIC WILLIAMS
US singer, a member of BLACKstreet, who went solo when they split in 1999, although they re-formed in 2001.

09/05/1998 ..... 11......5......	ALL MY LOVE **QUEEN PEN FEATURING ERIC WILLIAMS** Contains a sample of Luther Vandross' *Never Too Much* ...	Interscope IND 95584
13/06/1998 ..... 12......4.......	DO FOR LOVE **2PAC FEATURING ERIC WILLIAMS** Contains a sample of Bobby Caldwell's *What You Won't Do For Love*	Jive 0518512

FREEDOM WILLIAMS
US rapper (born 1966, New York City).

15/12/1990 .....3...... 12	**GONNA MAKE YOU SWEAT (EVERYBODY DANCE NOW)**..	CBS 6564540
30/03/1991 ..... 20......7	HERE WE GO..	Columbia 6567557
06/07/1991 .....4...... 11	**THINGS THAT MAKE YOU GO HMMM** This and above two singles credited to **C & C MUSIC FACTORY (FEATURING FREEDOM WILLIAMS)**	Columbia 6566907
05/06/1993 ..... 62......1.......	VOICE OF FREEDOM Contains a sample of George Michael's *Freedom*	Columbia 6593342

GEOFFREY WILLIAMS
UK R&B singer (born 1965, London, to West Indian parents) who later recorded with Color Me Badd and Jimmy Somerville.

11/04/1992 ..... 63......2......	IT'S NOT A LOVE THING	EMI EM 228
22/08/1992 ..... 56.....3......	SUMMER BREEZE...	EMI EM 245
18/01/1997 ..... 52......2......	DRIVE	Hands On CDHOR 11
19/04/1997 .... 71......1.......	SEX LIFE	Hands On CDHOR 12

IRIS WILLIAMS
UK singer (born 20/4/1944, Pontypridd, Wales).

27/10/1979 ..... 18......8.......	HE WAS BEAUTIFUL (CAVATINA) (THE THEME FROM 'THE DEER HUNTER')...............................	Columbia DB 9070

JAMES WILLIAMS – see BOB SINCLAIR

JOHN WILLIAMS
Australian guitarist (born 24/4/1941, Melbourne) who formed Sky with Steve Gray, Herbie Flowers, Kevin Peek and Tristan Fry in 1979 and left in 1984. He has recorded in a wide variety of musical styles.

19/05/1979 ..... 13 ..... 11	CAVATINA...	Cube BUG 80

JOHN WILLIAMS
US orchestra leader (born 8/2/1932, New York) who found fame as a composer of themes to films, including *Jaws* (1975), *Star Wars* (1977), *Close Encounters Of The Third Kind* (1977), *Raiders Of The Lost Ark* (1981) and *Jurassic Park* (1993), winning numerous Oscars. He has won eighteen Grammy Awards: Best Chamber Music Performance in 1972 with Julian Bream for *Julian And John*, Best Album of Original Score Written for a Motion Picture in 1975 for *Jaws*, Best Pop Instrumental Performance and Best Album of Original Score Written for a Motion Picture in 1977 with the London Symphony Orchestra for *Star Wars*, Best Instrumental Composition in 1977 for *Main Theme From Star Wars*, Best Instrumental Composition and Best Album of Original Score Written for a Motion Picture in 1978 for *Theme From Close Encounters Of The Third Kind* and *Close Encounters Of The Third Kind*, Best Instrumental Composition and Best Album of Original Score Written for a Motion Picture in 1979 for *Theme From Superman*, Best Instrumental Composition and Best Album of Original Score Written for a Motion Picture in 1980 for *The Empire Strikes Back*, Best Album of Original Score Written for a Motion Picture in 1981 for *Raiders Of The Lost Ark*, Best Instrumental Arrangement, Best Instrumental Composition and Best Album of Original Score Written for a Motion Picture in 1982 for *Flying (Theme From E.T. The Extra-Terrestrial)* and *E.T. The Extra-Terrestrial*, Best Instrumental Composition for a Motion Picture in 1994 for *Schindler's List*, Best Instrumental Composition for a Motion Picture in 1998 for *Saving Private Ryan* and Best Instrumental Composition for *Theme From Angela's Ashes*.

18/12/1982 ..... 17 ..... 10	THEME FROM E.T. (THE EXTRA-TERRESTRIAL) Featured in the 1982 film *E.T.*	MCA 800
14/08/1993 ..... 45......2.......	THEME FROM JURASSIC PARK Featured in the 1993 film *Jurassic Park*...................................	MCA MCSTD 1927

❶⁹ Number of weeks single topped the UK chart ↑ Entered the UK chart at #1 ▲⁹ Number of weeks single topped the US chart

877

KENNY WILLIAMS US singer whose debut hit was first featured in a TV advertisement for Cinzano.

DATE	POS	WKS	BPI	SINGLE TITLE	LABEL & NUMBER
19/11/1977	35	7		(YOU'RE) FABULOUS BABE	Decca FR 13731

LARRY WILLIAMS US singer (born 10/5/1935, New Orleans, LA) who formed The Lemon Drops at eighteen before playing piano for Lloyd Price and scoring with his own energetic rock. Imprisoned in 1960 for narcotics dealing, it effectively ended his recording career, although he earned royalties for the rest of his life from compositions that were recorded by The Beatles and John Lennon among others. During the 1960s it was rumoured that he was a successful burglar and pimp. He was found shot through the head on 2/1/1980 and was believed to have committed suicide, although friends remain convinced he was murdered by organised crime.

20/09/1957	21	8		SHORT FAT FANNY	London HLN 8472
17/01/1958	11	10		BONY MORONIE Featured in the 1983 film *Christine*	London HLU 8532

LENNY WILLIAMS US singer (born 1946, Little Rock, AR) who was solo before and after singing lead in Tower Of Power (1972–1974).

05/11/1977	38	4		SHOO DOO FU FU OOH	ABC 4194
16/09/1978	67	3		YOU GOT ME BURNING	ABC 4228

MARK WILLIAMS – see **KAREN BODDINGTON AND MARK WILLIAMS**

MASON WILLIAMS US singer/songwriter/guitarist/author/photographer/TV scriptwriter (born 24/8/1938, Abilene, TX).

28/08/1968	9	13		CLASSICAL GAS 1968 Grammy for Best Contemporary Pop Performance and Best Instrumental Theme	Warner Brothers WB 7190

MAURICE WILLIAMS AND THE ZODIACS US R&B vocal group who were originally the Gladiolas before becoming the Zodiacs in 1959. They re-formed in 1960 with Maurice Williams (born 26/4/1938, Lancaster, SC), Wiley Bennett, Henry Gaston, Charles Thomas, Albert Hill and Little Willie Morrow.

05/01/1961	14	9		STAY ▲[1]	Top Rank JAR 526

MELANIE WILLIAMS UK singer who debuted in 1987 with the US club hit *Showdown* with Eric Gooden. Her debut album followed in 1989.

10/04/1993	3	11	○	AIN'T NO LOVE (AIN'T NO USE) SUB SUB FEATURING MELANIE WILLIAMS	Rob's CDROB 9
09/04/1994	60	2		ALL CRIED OUT	Columbia 6601872
11/06/1994	38	3		EVERYDAY THANG	Columbia 6604712
17/09/1994	65	1		NOT ENOUGH	Columbia 6607752
18/02/1995	28	4		YOU ARE EVERYTHING MELANIE WILLIAMS AND JOE ROBERTS	Columbia 6611755

PHARRELL WILLIAMS – see **N*E*R*D**

ROBBIE WILLIAMS UK singer (born 13/2/1974, Stoke-on-Trent), who was a founding member of Take That in 1991 until an acrimonious split in 1995. His solo career was then delayed by legal wrangles. He was named Best British Male at the BRIT Awards in 1999, 2001, 2002 and 2003. He is the most successful artist of all time at the BRIT Awards, with fourteen awards: four with Take That and ten solo. Three MTV Europe Music Awards include Best Male in 1998 and 2001. He took part in the *It's Only Rock 'N' Roll* project for the Children's Promise charity. On 22/2/2001 he was attacked midway through a show at Stuttgart by a twenty-year old with a history of mental problems, who punched and pushed him into the photographers' pit. After the assailant had been hustled away by security, Robbie resumed, telling the audience that he hadn't fancied his attacker. In February 2002 he had to pay £200,000 for copyright infringement in portions of the song *Jesus In A Camper Van* from his *I've Been Expecting You* album, lifted from a 1973 song by Loudon Wainwright III. The song was also removed from all later pressings of the album. In November 2002 he re-signed with EMI in a deal worth £80 million. He was inducted into the UK Music Hall of Fame in 2004, one of its first inductees.

10/08/1996	2	14	○	FREEDOM	Chrysalis CDFREE 1
26/04/1997	2	11		OLD BEFORE I DIE	Chrysalis CDCHS 5055
26/07/1997	8	5		LAZY DAYS	Chrysalis CDCHS 5063
27/09/1997	14	4		SOUTH OF THE BORDER	Chrysalis CDCHS 5068
13/12/1997	4	27	✪[2]	ANGELS 1999 BRIT Award for Best Single	Chrysalis CDCHS 5072
28/03/1998	3	12	○	LET ME ENTERTAIN YOU Featured in the 2001 film *Mean Machine*	Chrysalis CDCHSS 5080
19/09/1998	❶[1]	21	●	MILLENNIUM ↑ 1999 BRIT Award for Best Video	Chrysalis CDCHSS 5099
12/12/1998	4	13		NO REGRETS	Chrysalis CDCHSS 5100
27/03/1999	4	9		STRONG	Chrysalis CDCHSS 5107
20/11/1999	❶[1]	20	●	SHE'S THE ONE/IT'S ONLY US ↑ *She's The One* won 2000 BRIT Awards for Best British Single and Best British Video	Chrysalis CDCHS 5112
12/08/2000	❶[1]	20	✪	ROCK DJ ↑ 2001 BRIT Awards for Best British Single and Best British Video. 2000 MTV Europe Music Award for Best Song. Featured in the 2000 film *Sweet November*	Chrysalis CDCHS 5118
21/10/2000	2	19	○	KIDS ROBBIE WILLIAMS AND KYLIE MINOGUE	Chrysalis CDCHSS 5119
23/12/2000	4	10		SUPREME	Chrysalis CDCHSS 5120
21/04/2001	10	11		LET LOVE BE YOUR ENERGY	Chrysalis CDCHS 5124
21/07/2001	❶[2]	16		ETERNITY/THE ROAD TO MANDALAY ↑	Chrysalis CDCHS 5126
22/12/2001	❶[3]	12	○	SOMETHIN' STUPID ↑ ROBBIE WILLIAMS AND NICOLE KIDMAN	Chrysalis CDCHS 5132
20/04/2002	9	6		MY CULTURE 1 GIANT LEAP FEATURING MAXI JAZZ AND ROBBIE WILLIAMS	Palm Pictures PPCD 70732
14/12/2002	4	15		FEEL	Chrysalis CDCHS 5150
26/04/2003	4	11		COME UNDONE	Chrysalis CDCHS 5151
09/08/2003	3	8		SOMETHING BEAUTIFUL	Chrysalis CDCHS 5152

15/11/2003 . . . . . 10 . . . . . 9	**SEXED UP** . . . . Chrysalis CDCHS 5153
16/10/2004 . . . ❶¹ 8	**RADIO** ↑ . . . . Chrysalis CDCHSS 5156
18/12/2004 . . . . . 8 . . . . . 2+	**MISUNDERSTOOD** Featured in the 2004 film *Bridget Jones Diary 2: Edge Of Reason* . . . . Chrysalis CDCHSS 5157

SAUL WILLIAMS – see KRUST

VANESSA WILLIAMS US singer (born 18/3/1963, Tarrytown, NY) who was the first black woman to be crowned Miss America in 1984. She was stripped of the title when nude photographs of her appeared in *Penthouse* magazine. She later became an actress, appearing in the TV series *Melrose Place* and later films such as *New Jack City* (1991), *Soul Food* (1997), *Hoodlum* (1997) and *Dance With Me* (1998).

20/08/1988 . . . . . 71 . . . . . . 1	THE RIGHT STUFF . . . . Wing 3
25/03/1989 . . . . . 74 . . . . . . 2	DREAMIN' . . . . Wing 4
19/08/1989 . . . . . 62 . . . . . . 2	THE RIGHT STUFF (REMIX) . . . . Wing WINR 3
21/03/1992 . . . . . 3 . . . . . . 11	**SAVE THE BEST FOR LAST** ▲⁵ Featured in the 1994 film *The Adventures Of Priscilla: Queen Of The Desert* . . . . Polydor PO 192
08/04/1995 . . . . . 41 . . . . . . 2	THE SWEETEST DAYS . . . . Mercury MERCD 422
08/07/1995 . . . . . 52 . . . . . . 1	THE WAY THAT YOU LOVE ME . . . . Mercury MERCD 439
16/09/1995 . . . . . 21 . . . . . . 5	COLOURS OF THE WIND Featured in the 1995 Walt Disney film *Pocahontas* . . . . Walt Disney WD 7677CD

VESTA WILLIAMS US singer (born 1963, Coshocton, OH) who signed with A&M in 1986 after singing with Wild Honey and Clique, and as a backing singer for Anita Baker and Sting.

| 20/12/1986 . . . . . 14 . . . . . 13 . . . . . . | ONCE BITTEN TWICE SHY . . . . A&M AM 362 |

WENDELL WILLIAMS US singer who worked as a security guard for MTV before launching a singing career.

| 06/10/1990 . . . . . 30 . . . . . . 4 . . . . . . | EVERYBODY (RAP) CRIMINAL ELEMENT ORCHESTRA AND WENDELL WILLIAMS . . . . Deconstruction PB 44701 |
| 18/05/1991 . . . . . 74 . . . . . . 2 . . . . . . | SO GROOVY . . . . Deconstruction PB 44567 |

WILLING SINNERS – see MARC ALMOND

BRUCE WILLIS US singer/actor (born 19/3/1955, Penns Grove, NJ) who first became known via the role of David Addison in the TV series *Moonlighting*. He later appeared in the *Die Hard* films and many others, and married actress Demi Moore in 1987 although this later ended in divorce. He is one of the partners in the Planet Hollywood chain of restaurants.

07/03/1987 . . . . . 7 . . . . . . 10	**RESPECT YOURSELF** Featured in the 1987 film *Blind Date* . . . . Motown ZB 41117
30/05/1987 . . . . . 2 . . . . . . 15 . . . . ○	**UNDER THE BOARDWALK** Features uncredited backing vocals by The Temptations . . . . Motown ZB 41349
12/09/1987 . . . . . 43 . . . . . . 4	SECRET AGENT MAN – JAMES BOND IS BACK . . . . Motown ZB 41437
23/01/1988 . . . . . 73 . . . . . . 1	COMIN' RIGHT UP . . . . Motown ZB 41453

CHILL WILLS – see LAUREL AND HARDY WITH THE AVALON BOYS FEATURING CHILL WILLS

CHRIS WILLS – see DAVID GUETTA FEATURING CHRIS WILLS

VIOLA WILLS US singer (born Viola Wilkerson, Los Angeles, CA) who was discovered by Barry White and recorded for Bronco before joining the Sanctified Sisters in 1972. She moved to the UK in the late 1970s.

| 06/10/1979 . . . . . 8 . . . . . . 10 . . . . ○ | **GONNA GET ALONG WITHOUT YOU NOW** . . . . Ariola/Hansa AHA 546 |
| 15/03/1986 . . . . . 35 . . . . . . 6 . . . . . | BOTH SIDES NOW/DARE TO DREAM . . . . Streetwave KHAN 66 |

MARIA WILLSON UK singer (born 1982, East Sussex).

| 09/08/2003 . . . . . 29 . . . . . . 2 . . . . . . | CHOOZA LOOZA . . . . Telstar CDSTAS 3343 |
| 01/11/2003 . . . . . 43 . . . . . . 1 . . . . . . | MR ALIBI . . . . Telstar CDSTAS 3355 |

AL WILSON US singer/drummer (born 19/6/1939, Meridian, MS) who was a member of The Jewels and The Rollers before going solo.

| 23/08/1975 . . . . . 41 . . . . . . 5 . . . . . . | THE SNAKE ▲¹ . . . . Bell 1436 |

BRIAN WILSON US singer (born 20/6/1942, Hawthorne, CA) who was a founding member of The Beach Boys in 1961 but stopped touring with the group in 1964 in order to concentrate on songwriting.

| 02/10/2004 . . . . . 29 . . . . . . 2 . . . . . . | WONDERFUL . . . . Must Destroy MDA001X |
| 18/12/2004 . . . . . 30 . . . . . . 2+ . . . . . | GOOD VIBRATIONS . . . . Nonesuch NS001CD |

CHARLIE WILSON – see SNOOP DOGG

DOOLEY WILSON US singer/actor (born 3/4/1894, Tyler, TX) who was best known in the role of pianist Sam in the 1942 film *Casablanca*. His hit features the voices of Humphrey Bogart and Ingrid Bergman, the two leads in *Casablanca*. He died on 30/5/1953.

| 03/12/1977 . . . . . 15 . . . . . . 9 . . . . . . | AS TIME GOES BY . . . . United Artists UP 36331 |

GRETCHEN WILSON US country singer (born 26/6/1973, Pocahontas, IL) who signed with Epic in 2003.

| 04/09/2004 . . . . . 42 . . . . . . 2 . . . . . . | REDNECK WOMAN . . . . Epic 6751732 |

JACKIE WILSON US singer (born 9/6/1934, Detroit, MI) who went solo before and after being in Billy Ward's Dominoes from 1953 to 1957. His early hits were written by Motown founder Berry Gordy, with Wilson helping cousin Hubert Johnson of the Contours

❶⁹ Number of weeks single topped the UK chart ↑ Entered the UK chart at #1 ▲⁹ Number of weeks single topped the US chart

879

get signed to the label. In February 1961 crazed fan Juanita Jones burst into his apartment in New York and shot him in the stomach after a struggle. He spent two weeks in hospital and still had the bullet lodged in him when he was discharged. He suffered a stroke during a concert in 1975 and lapsed into a coma, spending the rest of his life hospitalised before dying on 21/1/1984, although the cause was not given and, as his family had been fighting over his estate, he was buried in an unmarked grave. His death was one of the many strange tragedies that befell his family: his son Jackie Jr was killed in 1970 during a burglary, one daughter (Sandra Wilson Abrams) died from a heart attack in 1977 and another (Jacqueline Wilson) was an innocent bystander shot and killed in a drug-related drive-by shooting. He was inducted into the Rock & Roll Hall of Fame in 1987. When *Reet Petite* hit #1 on 27/12/1986, it completed the slowest ascension to the top spot: 29 years and 42 days since it first appeared on the chart.

DATE	POS	WKS	BPI	SINGLE TITLE	LABEL & NUMBER
15/11/1957	6	14		**REET PETITE** Featured in the 1994 film *Corrina, Corrina*	Coral Q 72290
14/03/1958	23	8		TO BE LOVED	Coral Q 72306
15/09/1960	33	7		(YOU WERE MADE FOR) ALL MY LOVE	Coral Q 72407
22/12/1960	50	1		ALONE AT LAST	Coral Q 72412
14/05/1969	11	11		(YOUR LOVE KEEPS LIFTING ME) HIGHER AND HIGHER	MCA BAG 2
29/07/1972	9	13		**I GET THE SWEETEST FEELING**	MCA MU 1160
03/05/1975	25	8		I GET THE SWEETEST FEELING/HIGHER AND HIGHER Re-issue of MCA MU 1160 and MCA BAG 2	Brunswick BR 18
29/11/1986	❶⁴	17	●	**REET PETITE** Re-issue of Coral Q 72290 and posthumous #1	SMP SKM 3
28/02/1987	3	11	O	**I GET THE SWEETEST FEELING** Second re-issue of MCA MU 1160	SMP SKM 1
04/07/1987	15	7		(YOUR LOVE KEEPS LIFTING ME) HIGHER AND HIGHER Second re-issue of MCA BAG 2	SMP SKM 10

MARI WILSON UK singer (born 29/9/1957, London) whose original backing band were known as the Imaginations. They were forced to change their name to the Wilsations and included Julia Fordham.

DATE	POS	WKS	BPI	SINGLE TITLE	LABEL & NUMBER
06/03/1982	59	3		BEAT THE BEAT	Compact PINK 2
08/05/1982	42	6		BABY IT'S TRUE	Compact PINK 3
11/09/1982	8	10		**JUST WHAT I ALWAYS WANTED**	Compact PINK 4
13/11/1982	51	4		(BEWARE) BOYFRIEND	Compact PINK 5
19/03/1983	27	7		CRY ME A RIVER	Compact PINK 6
11/06/1983	47	4		WONDERFUL	Compact PINK 7

MERI WILSON US singer (born 15/6/1949, Nagoya, Japan, raised in Marietta, GA). The single, after rejection by eleven labels, was released by GRT in the US. Due to risqué lyrics it was banned by some radio stations. She was killed in a car smash on 28/12/2002.

DATE	POS	WKS	BPI	SINGLE TITLE	LABEL & NUMBER
27/08/1977	6	10	O	**TELEPHONE MAN**	Pye International 7N 25747

MIKE 'HITMAN' WILSON FEATURING SHAWN CHRISTOPHER US producer with singer Shawn Christopher.

DATE	POS	WKS	BPI	SINGLE TITLE	LABEL & NUMBER
22/09/1990	74	1		ANOTHER SLEEPLESS NIGHT Re-issued the following year and credited just to Shawn Christopher	Arista 113506

PRECIOUS WILSON – see MESSIAH

RAY WILSON – see ARMIN

TOM WILSON UK producer who also recorded as Technocat. He died from a heart attack on 25/3/2004.

DATE	POS	WKS	BPI	SINGLE TITLE	LABEL & NUMBER
02/12/1995	33	3		TECHNOCAT **TECHNOCAT FEATURING TOM WILSON**	Pukka CDPUKKA 4
16/03/1996	60	1		LET YOUR BODY GO	Clubscene DCSRT 050

VICTORIA WILSON JAMES US singer (born in Indianapolis, later relocated to London).

DATE	POS	WKS	BPI	SINGLE TITLE	LABEL & NUMBER
09/08/1997	72	1		REACH 4 THE MELODY	Sony S3 VWJCD1

WILSON PHILLIPS US vocal trio formed in Los Angeles, CA by Chyna Phillips (born 12/2/1968, Los Angeles) and sisters Carnie (born 29/4/1968, Los Angeles) and Wendy Wilson (born 16/10/1969, Los Angeles). Phillips is the daughter of ex-Mamas & Papas John and Michelle Phillips, while the Wilson sisters are daughters of Beach Boy Brian Wilson. They disbanded in 1992 with the Wilson sisters recording as a duo and Phillips going solo. Carnie Wilson later hosted her own TV talk show.

DATE	POS	WKS	BPI	SINGLE TITLE	LABEL & NUMBER
26/05/1990	6	12		**HOLD ON** ▲¹	SBK 6
18/08/1990	36	5		RELEASE ME ▲²	SBK 11
10/11/1990	42	3		IMPULSIVE	SBK 16
11/05/1991	29	5		YOU'RE IN LOVE ▲¹	SBK 25
23/05/1992	18	5		YOU WON'T SEE ME CRY	SBK 34
22/08/1992	36	3		GIVE IT UP	SBK 36

WILT Irish group with Cormac Battle (guitar/vocals), Mick Murphy (bass) and Darragh Butler (drums). Battle and Butler were both previously in Kerbdog.

DATE	POS	WKS	BPI	SINGLE TITLE	LABEL & NUMBER
08/04/2000	56	1		RADIO DISCO	Mushroom MUSH 71CDS
08/07/2000	59	1		OPEN ARMS	Mushroom MUSH 75CDS
13/07/2002	66	1		DISTORTION	Mushroom MUSH 103CDS

CHRIS WILTSHIRE – see CLASS ACTION FEATURING CHRIS WILTSHIRE

WIMBLEDON CHORALE SOCIETY UK vocal choir whose debut hit was the theme to the BBC TV World Cup coverage in 1998. The single also features TV presenter Des Lynam.

DATE	POS	WKS	BPI	SINGLE TITLE	LABEL & NUMBER
04/07/1998	26	5		WORLD CUP '98 — PAVANE	Telstar CDSTAS 2979

O Silver disc ● Gold disc ✪ Platinum disc (additional platinum units are indicated by a figure following the symbol) ◉ Singles released prior to 1973 that are known to have sold over 1 million copies in the UK

12/12/1998.....45......3....... IF – READ TO FAURE'S 'PAVANNE' **DES LYNAM FEATURING WIMBLEDON CHORAL SOCIETY** .... BBC Worldwide WMSS 60062

WIN UK group formed in Scotland by Davey Henderson (guitar/keyboards/vocals), Russell Burn (keyboards/vocals), Emmanuel Shoniwa (bass/guitar/keyboards/vocals), Simon Smeeton (guitar/bass/keyboards/vocals) and Ian Stoddart (drums/vocals). After 1987's debut album they added William Perry (keyboards/vocals), disbanding after a second album. Henderson later sang lead with Nectarine No 9.

04/04/1987.....63......3....... SUPER POPOID GROOVE.. Swamplands LON 128

WINANS US gospel group formed in Detroit, MI by brothers Carvin, Marvin and Ronald Winans. Other members of the family include BeBe, CeCe and Mario, all of whom enjoyed recording careers.

30/11/1985.....71......1....... LET MY PEOPLE GO (PART 1)... Qwest W 8874

BEBE WINANS – see **ETERNAL**

CECE WINANS – see **WHITNEY HOUSTON**

MARIO WINANS US singer (born 1981, Detroit, MI), the son of Marvin Winans. Also known as Yellowman, he originally sang gospel music and also recorded for Motown.

20/11/1999.....24......4.......	BEST FRIEND **PUFF DADDY FEATURING MARIO WINANS** Contains a sample of Christopher Cross' *Sailing* ... Puff Daddy 74321712312
05/06/2004.....71......1.......	I DON'T WANNA KNOW (IMPORT) Contains a sample of Enya's *Boadicea* .... Universal 9862372PMI
12/06/2004.....❶²....14.....O	**I DON'T WANNA KNOW** ↑ Above two singles credited to **MARIO WINANS FEATURING ENYA AND P DIDDY**.... Bad Boy MCSTD 40369
11/09/2004.....44......2.......	NEVER REALLY WAS **MARIO WINANS FEATURING LIL' FLIP** Contains a sample of Madonna's *Papa Don't Preach* ....
	.... Bad Boy MCSTD 40372

WINDJAMMER US R&B group formed in New Orleans, LA by Kevin McLin (guitar), Roy Paul Joseph (guitar), Chris Severin (bass), Darrell Winchester (drums), Carl Dennis (vocals) and Fred McCray (keyboards). They originally recorded as Windstorm.

30/06/1984.....18.....12...... TOSSING AND TURNING.. MCA 897

ROSE WINDROSS – see **SOUL II SOUL**

BARBARA WINDSOR AND MIKE REID UK vocal duo Barbara Windsor and Mike Reid. Windsor (born Barbara Deeks, 1937, London) was best known as an actress in the long-running series of *Carry On* films. Reid (born 19/1/1940, London) began as a stand-up comedian. Both later appeared in the TV series *Eastenders,* as Peggy Mitchell and Frank Butcher.

24/04/1999.....46......2....... THE MORE I SEE YOU .... Telstar CDSTAS 3049

AMY WINEHOUSE UK singer (born 1984, London).

18/10/2003.....71......1.......	STRONGER THAN ME.. Island CID 830
24/01/2004.....57......1.......	TAKE THE BOX .... Island CID 840
17/04/2004.....60......1.......	IN MY BED/YOU SENT ME FLYING... Island CID 852
04/09/2004.....69......1.......	PUMPS/HELPYOURSELF .... Island CID 865

WING AND A PRAYER FIFE AND DRUM CORPS US studio group with vocalists Linda November, Vivian Cherry, Arlene Martell and Helen Miles.

24/01/1976.....12......7....... BABY FACE .... Atlantic K 10705

WINGER US rock group formed by Kip Winger (bass/vocals), Paul Taylor (keyboards/guitar), Reb Beach (guitar) and Rod Morganstein (drums) as Sahara, changing their name shortly before the release of their debut album. Taylor left the group in 1992.

19/01/1991.....56......3....... MILES AWAY .... Atlantic A 7802

PETE WINGFIELD UK singer (born 7/5/1948) who was a member of the Olympic Runners and a successful producer for the likes of Dexy's Midnight Runners and Alison Moyet.

28/06/1975.....7......7....... **EIGHTEEN WITH A BULLET** Featured in the 1998 film *Lock Stock And Two Smoking Barrels*................... Island WIP 6231

WINGS – see **PAUL McCARTNEY**

JOSH WINK US singer (born Joshua Winkleman, Philadelphia, PA) who has also recorded as Firefly, Just King & Wink, Winc, Size 9, E-Culture and Winx.

06/05/1995.....38......2.......	DON'T LAUGH **WINX**... XL Recordings XLS 62CD
21/10/1995.....8......12......	**HIGHER STATE OF CONSCIOUSNESS** .... Manifesto FESCD 3
02/03/1996.....35......2.......	HYPNOTIZIN' **WINX**... XL Recordings XLS 71CD
27/07/1996.....7......10......	**HIGHER STATE OF CONSCIOUSNESS '96 REMIXES**....................................... Manifesto FESCD 9
12/08/2000.....23......3.......	HOW'S YOUR EVENING SO FAR **JOSH WINK AND LIL LOUIS**................................ ffrr FCD 384

KATE WINSLET UK singer (born 5/10/1975, Reading) who is best known as an actress. She appeared in an advertisement alongside the Honey Monster at the age of eleven. Her first major roles were in *Heavenly Creatures* (1994) followed by *Sense And Sensibility* (1995), for which she received an Oscar nomination for Best Supporting Actress. She was also nominated for Best Actress for her role as Rose DeWitt Bukater in *Titanic* (1997), the youngest actress to have received two nominations (although she won neither). She did, however, win a Grammy Award in 1999 for Best Spoken Word Album for Children with Wynton Marsalis and Graham Greene for *Listen To The Storyteller*. She married James Threapleton in 1998 (divorced in 2001) and Sam Mendes in 2003.

08/12/2001.....6.....14.....O **WHAT IF** Featured in the 2001 animated film *A Christmas Carol*..................................... EMI/Liberty CDKATE 001

❶⁹ Number of weeks single topped the UK chart ↑ Entered the UK chart at #1 ▲⁹ Number of weeks single topped the US chart

881

EDGAR WINTER GROUP
US singer (born 28/12/1946, Beaumont, TX), younger brother of Johnny Winter, who was a member of White Trash before forming his own group in 1972 with Ronnie Montrose (guitar), Chick Ruff (drums) and Dan Hartman (born 8/12/1950, Harrisburg, PA, bass). Hartman was later a solo artist and producer and died from AIDS-related complications on 22/3/1994.

26/05/1973 . . . . . 18 . . . . . . 9 . . . . . . FRANKENSTEIN ▲[1] Featured in the films *Encino Man* (1992) and *Wayne's World 2* (1993) . . . . Epic EPC 1440

RUBY WINTERS
US R&B singer (born in Louisville, KY) who was more successful in the UK than in the US. She first recorded for the Diamond label in 1967.

05/11/1977 . . . . . 4 . . . . . . 13 . . . . . **I WILL** . . . . Creole CR 141
29/04/1978 . . . . . 11 . . . . . . 12 . . . . . COME TO ME . . . . Creole CR 153
26/08/1978 . . . . . 45 . . . . . . 5 . . . . . I WON'T MENTION IT AGAIN . . . . Creole CR 160
16/06/1979 . . . . . 43 . . . . . . 5 . . . . . BABY LAY DOWN . . . . Creole CR 171

STEVE WINWOOD
UK singer (born 12/5/1948, Birmingham) who was lead singer with the Spencer Davis Group until 1967, when he left to form Traffic. His first release under his own name was in 1971.

17/01/1981 . . . . . 45 . . . . . . 5 . . . . . WHILE YOU SEE A CHANCE . . . . Island WIP 6655
09/10/1982 . . . . . 51 . . . . . . 4 . . . . . VALERIE . . . . Island WIP 6818
28/06/1986 . . . . . 13 . . . . . . 9 . . . . . HIGHER LOVE ▲[1] 1986 Grammy Awards for Record of the Year and Best Pop Vocal Performance . . . . Island IS 288
13/09/1986 . . . . . 69 . . . . . . 1 . . . . . FREEDOM OVERSPILL . . . . Island IS 294
24/01/1987 . . . . . 53 . . . . . . 2 . . . . . BACK IN THE HIGH LIFE AGAIN . . . . Island IS 303
19/09/1987 . . . . . 19 . . . . . . 8 . . . . . VALERIE (REMIX) . . . . Island IS 336
11/06/1988 . . . . . 53 . . . . . . 4 . . . . . ROLL WITH IT ▲[4] . . . . Virgin VS 1085

WINX – see JOSH WINK

W.I.P. FEATURING EMMIE
UK production group fronted by dance singer Emmie Norton-Smith. Their name stands for Work In Progress.

16/02/2002 . . . . . 53 . . . . . . 1 . . . . . . I WON'T LET YOU DOWN . . . . Decode/Telstar CDSTAS 3210

WIRE
UK group formed in 1976 by Colin Newman (born 16/9/1954, Salisbury, guitar/vocals), George Gill (guitar), Bruce Gilbert (born 18/5/1946, Watford, guitar), Graham Lewis (born 22/2/1953, Grantham, bass/vocals) and Robert Gotobed (born Mark Field, 1951, Leicester, drums). Gill was sacked soon after they started, the group continuing as a four-piece, although producer Mike Thorne often acted as the fifth member. They disbanded in 1980, with Newman going solo. Wire was revived in 1985 and recording again in 1987. Gotobed left in 1990 and they continued as a trio, slightly amending their name to Wir.

27/01/1979 . . . . . 51 . . . . . . 3 . . . . . . OUTDOOR MINER . . . . Harvest HAR 5172
13/05/1989 . . . . . 68 . . . . . . 1 . . . . . . EARDRUM BUZZ . . . . Mute 87

WIRED
Dutch/Finnish production/instrumental duo Rene Van Der Weyde and Ard Quindvist.

20/02/1999 . . . . . 73 . . . . . . 1 . . . . . . TRANSONIC Contains a sample of Yazoo's *Don't Go* . . . . Future Groove CDFGR 001

WIRELESS
UK group with Paul Bardsley (vocals), Phil Murphy (guitar), Michael Darling (bass), Chris Picken (keyboards) and Basil Creese (drums).

28/06/1997 . . . . . 68 . . . . . . 1 . . . . . . I NEED YOU . . . . Chrysalis CHCHS 5059
07/02/1998 . . . . . 69 . . . . . . 1 . . . . . . IN LOVE WITH THE FAMILIAR . . . . Chrysalis CDCHS 5075

NORMAN WISDOM
UK singer/comedian/actor (born 4/2/1918, London) who made his big break in film in 1953. He was popular in the UK and around the world, including unlikely places such as Russia, Albania and China. In 1990 he recorded a series of relaxation cassettes with fellow Isle of Man inhabitant Rick Wakeman. He was knighted in the 2000 New Year's Honours List.

19/02/1954 . . . . . 3 . . . . . . 15 . . . . . **DON'T LAUGH AT ME** . . . . Columbia DB 3133
15/03/1957 . . . . . 13 . . . . . . 5 . . . . . WISDOM OF A FOOL . . . . Columbia DB 3903

WISDOME
Italian dance group formed by Luca Moretti and Ricky Romanni.

11/03/2000 . . . . . 33 . . . . . . 2 . . . . . . OFF THE WALL . . . . Positiva CDTIV 125

WISEGUYS
UK producer/DJ Theo Keating who also works as DJ Touche. His debut hit was originally released the previous year and was revived after its use in a Budweiser advertisement.

06/06/1998 . . . . . 55 . . . . . . 1 . . . . . . OOH LA LA . . . . Wall Of Sound WALLD 038
12/09/1998 . . . . . 66 . . . . . . 1 . . . . . . START THE COMMOTION Contains a sample of The Ventures' *Wild Child* . . . . Wall Of Sound WALLD 044
05/06/1999 . . . . . 2 . . . . . . 10 . . . . . ○ **OOH LA LA** Re-issue of Wall Of Sound WALLD 038. Featured in the films *Big Daddy* (1999), *Snow Day* (2000) and *Mean Machine* (2001) . . . . Wall Of Sound WALLD 038X
11/09/1999 . . . . . 47 . . . . . . 1 . . . . . . START THE COMMOTION Re-issue of Wall Of Sound WALLD 044 . . . . Wall Of Sound WALLD 059

BILL WITHERS
US singer (born 4/7/1938, Slab Fork, WV) who was working for Lockhead Aircraft (fitting toilets) and writing songs in his spare time when he met with Booker T Jones, who got him a contract with Sussex Records in 1970. He is married to actress Denise Nicholas. Three Grammy Awards include Best Rhythm & Blues Song in 1971 for *Ain't No Sunshine* and Best Rhythm & Blues Song in 1981 with William Salter and Ralph MacDonald for *Just The Two Of Us*.

12/08/1972 . . . . . 18 . . . . . . 9 . . . . . LEAN ON ME ▲[3] 1987 Grammy Award for Best Rhythm & Blues Song. Featured in the 1989 film *Lean On Me* . . . . . A&M AMS 7004
14/01/1978 . . . . . 7 . . . . . . 8 . . . . . **LOVELY DAY** . . . . CBS 5773
25/05/1985 . . . . . 60 . . . . . . 3 . . . . . OH YEAH! . . . . CBS A 6154
10/09/1988 . . . . . 4 . . . . . . 9 . . . . . . **LOVELY DAY (REMIX)** . . . . CBS 6530017

○ Silver disc ● Gold disc ✪ Platinum disc (additional platinum units are indicated by a figure following the symbol) ⊚ Singles released prior to 1973 that are known to have sold over 1 million copies in the UK

WITNESS
UK group formed in 1997 by Gerard Starkie (vocals), Ray Chan (guitar), Dylan Keeton (bass), Julian Pransky (guitar/keyboards) and John Langley (drums).

13/03/1999	71	1		SCARS	Island CID 740
19/06/1999	71	1		AUDITION	Island CID 749

WIX – see SPIRO AND WIX

WIZZARD
UK rock group formed in 1972 by Roy Wood (born Ulysses Adrian Wood, 8/11/1946, Birmingham) after chart success with the Move and Electric Light Orchestra. They comprised Wood (vocals/guitar), Rick Price (bass), Hugh McDowell (cello), Nick Pentelow (saxophone), Mike Burney (saxophone), Bill Hunt (keyboards), Keith Smart (drums) and Charlie Grima (drums). They split in 1975, by which time Wood had already begun recording solo.

09/12/1972	6	12		**BALL PARK INCIDENT**	Harvest HAR 5062
21/04/1973	❶⁴	17	●	**SEE MY BABY JIVE**	Harvest HAR 5070
01/09/1973	❶¹	10	○	**ANGEL FINGERS**	Harvest HAR 5076
08/12/1973	4	9	○	**I WISH IT COULD BE CHRISTMAS EVERY DAY** WIZZARD FEATURING VOCAL BACKING BY THE SUEDETTES PLUS THE STOCKLAND GREEN BILATERAL SCHOOL FIRST YEAR CHOIR WITH ADDITIONAL NOISES BY MISS SNOB AND CLASS 3C	Harvest HAR 5079
27/04/1974	6	7		**ROCK 'N' ROLL WINTER**	Warner Brothers K 16357
10/08/1974	34	4		THIS IS THE STORY OF MY LIFE (BABY)	Warner Brothers K 16434
21/12/1974	8	10		**ARE YOU READY TO ROCK**	Warner Brothers K 16497
19/12/1981	41	4		I WISH IT COULD BE CHRISTMAS EVERY DAY Re-issue of Harvest HAR 5079	Harvest HAR 5173
15/12/1984	23	4		I WISH IT COULD BE CHRISTMAS EVERY DAY	Harvest HAR 5173

ANDREW WK
US singer (born Andrew Wilkes-Kryer, Los Angeles, CA) who moved to Michigan with his family at the age of five. Apparently the WK stood for 'White Killer' (a notorious US serial killer), 'Wild Kid' or 'Want Kicks', depending on his mood. First recording for Bulb Records in 2000, he was spotted by Foo Fighter Dave Grohl, who invited him to be opening act on their US tour.

10/11/2001	19	4		PARTY HARD	Mercury 5888132
09/03/2002	55	1		SHE IS BEAUTIFUL	Mercury 5889522

JAH WOBBLE'S INVADERS OF THE HEART
UK singer/multi-instrumentalist (born John Wardle, 1962, London) who was previously in Public Image Limited. He formed Invaders Of The Heart with Justin Adams (guitar) and Mark Ferda (keyboards) in 1987.

01/02/1992	35	5		VISIONS OF YOU Features the uncredited contribution of Sinead O'Connor	Oval 103
30/04/1994	36	2		BECOMING MORE LIKE GOD	Island CID 571
25/06/1994	41	3		THE SUN DOES RISE	Island CIDX 587

TERRY WOGAN
Irish DJ/singer/TV personality (born 1938, Limerick, Ireland) who hosted Radio 2's Breakfast Show from 1973 until 1984. He also hosted numerous TV game shows from the late 1970s, had his own chat show and fronts the Eurovision Song Contest on a regular basis. He was awarded an honorary OBE in the 1996 New Year's Honours list – as an Irishman he would not be able to collect his award from the Queen but from a Minister of State.

07/01/1978	21	5		FLORAL DANCE	Philips 6006 592

WOLF – see TROGGS

WOLFMAN
UK singer Peter Wolfe. He first met Pete Docherty (ex-The Libertines) in a bookshop.

24/04/2004	7	6		**FOR LOVERS** WOLFMAN FEATURING PETE DOCHERTY	Rough Trade RTRADSCD177
11/12/2004	44	1		NAPOLEON	Beyond Bedlam BEBAD001CDS

WOLFSBANE
UK group from Tamworth with Blaze Bayley (vocals), Jase Edwards (guitar), Jeff Hateley (bass) and Steve Ellet (drums).

05/10/1991	68	1		EZY	Def American DEFA 11

BOBBY WOMACK
US singer (born 4/3/1944, Cleveland, OH) who joined the family gospel group the Womack Brothers (with Cecil, Curtis, Harris and Friendly Jr) in 1959. After playing guitar in Sam Cooke's backing group in 1960, he reunited with his brothers as the Valentinos and signed with Cooke's SAR label in 1961. He first recorded solo for the Him label in 1965. He married Cooke's widow Barbara in 1965 (just three months after Sam's funeral, at which he turned up wearing Sam's clothes) and divorced in 1970.

16/06/1984	60	3		TELL ME WHY	Motown TMG 1339
16/02/1985	63	2		(NO MATTER HOW HIGH I GET) I'LL STILL BE LOOKIN' UP TO YOU WILTON FELDER FEATURING BOBBY WOMACK	MCA 919
05/10/1985	64	2		I WISH HE DIDN'T TRUST ME SO MUCH	MCA 994
26/09/1987	34	8		SO THE STORY GOES LIVING IN A BOX FEATURING BOBBY WOMACK	Chrysalis LIB 3
07/11/1987	70	2		LIVING IN A BOX	MCA 1210
03/04/1993	27	5		I'M BACK FOR MORE LULU AND BOBBY WOMACK	Dome CDDOME 1002
13/05/1995	73	1		IT'S A MAN'S MAN'S MAN'S WORLD JEANIE TRACY AND BOBBY WOMACK	Pulse 8 CDLOSE 89
19/06/2004	59	1		CALIFORNIA DREAMIN'	EMI WOMACK001

LEE ANN WOMACK
US country singer (born 19/8/1966, Jacksonville, TX) who won the 2002 Grammy Award for Best Country Collaboration With Vocals with Willie Nelson for Mendocino County Line.

09/06/2001	40	2		I HOPE YOU DANCE Features the uncredited contribution of Sons Of The Desert. 2000 Grammy Award for Best Country Song for writers Mark Sanders and Tia Sillers	MCA Nashville MCSTD 40254

WOMACK AND WOMACK
US husband and wife duo Cecil Womack (born 1947, Cleveland, OH) and Linda Cooke Womack (born 1953). Cecil (Bobby's brother) was previously in the Valentinos with his brothers, while Linda is Sam Cooke's daughter.

DATE	POS	WKS	BPI	SINGLE TITLE	LABEL & NUMBER
28/04/1984	14	10		LOVE WARS	Elektra E 9799
30/06/1984	72	2		BABY I'M SCARED OF YOU	Elektra E 9733
06/12/1986	58	6		SOUL LOVE – SOUL MAN	Manhattan MT 16
06/08/1988	3	17	O	**TEARDROPS**	Fourth & Broadway BRW 101
12/11/1988	32	5		LIFE'S JUST A BALLGAME	Fourth & Broadway BRW 116
25/02/1989	19	8		CELEBRATE THE WORLD	Fourth & Broadway BRW 125
05/02/1994	46	3		SECRET STAR **HOUSE OF ZE4KKARIYAS AKA WOMACK AND WOMACK**	Warner Brothers W 0222CD

WOMBLES
UK puppet characters created by Elizabeth Beresford and turned into a children's TV series with Bernard Cribbins narrating. The theme song had been written by Mike Batt (born 6/2/1950, Southampton) and, following the success of the series, Batt dressed up as Orinoco for TV appearances (as part of the agreement with the estate of Elizabeth Beresford, he was not allowed to be seen wearing the head of the body but not the outfit at any time).

DATE	POS	WKS	BPI	SINGLE TITLE	LABEL & NUMBER
26/01/1974	4	23		**THE WOMBLING SONG** Theme to the TV series *The Wombles*	CBS 1794
06/04/1974	3	16		**REMEMBER YOU'RE A WOMBLE**	CBS 2241
22/06/1974	9	13		**BANANA ROCK**	CBS 2465
12/10/1974	16	9		MINUETTO ALLEGRETTO	CBS 2710
14/12/1974	2	8	O	**WOMBLING MERRY CHRISTMAS**	CBS 2842
10/05/1975	22	7		WOMBLING WHITE TIE AND TAILS	CBS 3266
09/08/1975	20	6		SUPER WOMBLE	CBS 3480
13/12/1975	34	5		LET'S WOMBLE TO THE PARTY TONIGHT	CBS 3794
21/03/1998	13	5		REMEMBER YOU'RE A WOMBLE Re-issue of CBS 2241	Columbia 6656202
13/06/1998	27	3		WOMBLING SONG (UNDERGROUND OVERGROUND) Re-issue of CBS 1794	Columbia 6660412
30/12/2000	22	3		I WISH IT COULD BE A WOMBLING CHRISTMAS **WOMBLES WITH ROY WOOD**	Dramatico DRAMCDS 0001X

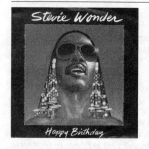

STEVIE WONDER
US singer (born Steveland Judkins, although his mother later remarried and he was given the surname Morris, 13/5/1950, Saginaw, MI) who was blinded soon after birth when too much oxygen was pumped into his incubator. He learned to play percussion, harmonica and piano as a child, and was introduced to Motown by Miracle Ronnie White. He signed with Motown in 1960, releasing his first singles as Little Stevie Wonder (named by Berry Gordy) in 1962. He made his film debut in 1964 in *Bikini Beach*. He married singer Syreeta Wright in 1970, the couple later divorcing. He assumed full artistic control from 1971 and formed his own backing group Wonderlove. A car crash in 1973 left him in a coma for four days. In February 1999 he became Dr Stevie Wonder after being awarded an honorary doctorate from the University of Alabama in Birmingham. Nineteen Grammy Awards include Album of the Year in 1973 for *Innervisions*, Album of the Year and Best Pop Vocal Performance in 1974 for *Fulfillingness' First Finale*, Album of the Year and Best Pop Vocal Performance in 1976 for *Songs In The Key Of Life* (later giving the latter award to Otis Blackwell in recognition of his songwriting skills), Producer of the Year in 1976, Best Rhythm & Blues Vocal Performance in 1985 for *In Square Circle*, Best Rhythm & Blues Male Vocal Performance in 1998 for *St Louis Blues* and Best Instrumental Arrangement with Vocals in 1998 with Herbie Hancock and Robert Sadin for *St Louis Blues* and Best Best Rhythm & Blues Performance by a Duo or Group with Vocal in 2002 with Take 6 for *Love's In Need Of Love Today*. His three Album of the Year awards came with three consecutive releases: when Paul Simon won the award in 1975 he thanked Stevie Wonder for not releasing an album that year. He was inducted into the Rock & Roll Hall of Fame in 1989 and has a star on the Hollywood Walk of Fame.

DATE	POS	WKS	BPI	SINGLE TITLE	LABEL & NUMBER
03/02/1966	14	10		UPTIGHT Featured in the 1997 film *Mr Holland's Opus*	Tamla Motown TMG 545
18/08/1966	36	5		BLOWIN' IN THE WIND Features an uncredited vocal part by producer Clarence Paul because Wonder didn't know the lyrics	Tamla Motown TMG 570
05/01/1967	20	5		A PLACE IN THE SUN	Tamla Motown TMG 588
26/07/1967	5	15		**I WAS MADE TO LOVE HER**	Tamla Motown TMG 613
25/10/1967	22	8		I'M WONDERING	Tamla Motown TMG 626
08/05/1968	46	4		SHOO BE DOO BE DOO DA DAY	Tamla Motown TMG 653
18/12/1968	3	13		**FOR ONCE IN MY LIFE**	Tamla Motown TMG 679
19/03/1969	14	11		I DON'T KNOW WHY (I LOVE YOU)	Tamla Motown TMG 690
16/07/1969	4	15		**MY CHERIE AMOUR**	Tamla Motown TMG 690
15/11/1969	2	13		**YESTER-ME YESTER-YOU YESTERDAY**	Tamla Motown TMG 717
28/03/1970	6	12		**NEVER HAD A DREAM COME TRUE**	Tamla Motown TMG 731
18/07/1970	15	10		SIGNED SEALED DELIVERED I'M YOURS Featured in the films *Now And Then* (1996) and *You've Got M@il* (1998)	Tamla Motown TMG 744
21/11/1970	29	11		HEAVEN HELP US ALL	Tamla Motown TMG 757
15/05/1971	27	7		WE CAN WORK IT OUT Featured in the 2004 film *Scooby Doo 2: Monsters Unleashed*	Tamla Motown TMG 772
22/01/1972	20	7		IF YOU REALLY LOVE ME	Tamla Motown TMG 798
03/02/1973	11	9		SUPERSTITION ▲¹ 1973 Grammy Awards for Best Rhythm & Blues Song and Best Rhythm & Blues Vocal Performance. Featured in the films *Stealing Beauty* (1996) and *I Robot* (2004)	Tamla Motown TMG 841
19/05/1973	7	11		**YOU ARE THE SUNSHINE OF MY LIFE** ▲¹ 1973 Grammy Award for Best Pop Vocal Performance	Tamla Motown TMG 852
13/10/1973	29	5		HIGHER GROUND	Tamla Motown TMG 869
12/01/1974	15	9		LIVING FOR THE CITY 1974 Grammy Award for Best Rhythm & Blues Song	Tamla Motown TMG 881
13/04/1974	10	9		**HE'S MISSTRA KNOW IT ALL**	Tamla Motown TMG 892
19/10/1974	30	5		YOU HAVEN'T DONE NOTHIN' ▲¹ Features the uncredited vocals of the Jackson 5	Tamla Motown TMG 921
11/01/1975	12	8		BOOGIE ON REGGAE WOMAN 1974 Grammy Award for Best Rhythm & Blues Vocal Performance	Tamla Motown TMG 928
18/12/1976	5	10	O	I WISH ▲¹ 1976 Grammy Award for Best Rhythm & Blues Vocal Performance	Tamla Motown TMG 1054
09/04/1977	2	9	O	**SIR DUKE** ▲³ Tribute to Duke Ellington	Motown TMG 1068
10/09/1977	29	5		ANOTHER STAR	Motown TMG 1083

O Silver disc ● Gold disc ✪ Platinum disc (additional platinum units are indicated by a figure following the symbol) ◎ Singles released prior to 1973 that are known to have sold over 1 million copies in the UK

DATE	POS	WKS	BPI	SINGLE TITLE	LABEL & NUMBER
24/02/1979	66	5		POPS WE LOVE YOU DIANA ROSS, MARVIN GAYE, SMOKEY ROBINSON AND STEVIE WONDER Recorded to honour Berry Gordy's father's 90th birthday	Motown TMG 1136
24/11/1979	52	3		SEND ONE YOUR LOVE	Motown TMG 1149
26/01/1980	63	3		BLACK ORCHID	Motown TMG 1173
29/03/1980	52	4		OUTSIDE MY WINDOW	Motown TMG 1179
13/09/1980	2	10	O	MASTERBLASTER (JAMMIN') Tribute to Bob Marley	Motown TMG 1204
27/12/1980	10	10		I AIN'T GONNA STAND FOR IT	Motown TMG 1215
07/03/1981	3	13	O	LATELY	Motown TMG 1226
25/07/1981	2	11	O	HAPPY BIRTHDAY Used to lobby for Dr Martin Luther King's 15th January birthday to be a US national holiday	Motown TMG 1235
23/01/1982	39	6		THAT GIRL	Motown TMG 1254
10/04/1982	❶³	10	●	EBONY AND IVORY ▲⁷ PAUL McCARTNEY AND STEVIE WONDER	Parlophone R 6054
05/06/1982	10	7		DO I DO Trumpet solo by Dizzy Gillespie	Motown TMG 1269
25/09/1982	45	4		RIBBON IN THE SKY	Motown TMG 1280
25/08/1984	❶⁶	26	✪	I JUST CALLED TO SAY I LOVE YOU ▲³ Featured in the 1984 film The Woman In Red and won an Oscar for Best Film Song	Motown TMG 1349
01/12/1984	44	5		LOVE LIGHT IN FLIGHT Featured in the 1984 film The Woman In Red	Motown TMG 1364
29/12/1984	62	3		DON'T DRIVE DRUNK	Motown TMG 1372
07/09/1985	3	12	O	PART-TIME LOVER ▲¹	Motown ZB 40351
09/11/1985	16	9		THAT'S WHAT FRIENDS ARE FOR ▲⁴ DIONNE WARWICK AND FRIENDS FEATURING ELTON JOHN, GLADYS KNIGHT AND STEVIE WONDER 1986 Grammy Awards for Best Pop Vocal Performance by a Group plus Song of the Year for writers Burt Bacharach and Carole Bayer Sager. Originally recorded by Rod Stewart for the 1982 film Night Shift	Arista ARIST 638
23/11/1985	67	2		GO HOME	Motown ZB 40501
08/03/1986	17	8		OVERJOYED	Motown ZB 40567
17/01/1987	55	3		STRANGER ON THE SHORE OF LOVE	Motown WOND 2
31/10/1987	59	3		SKELETONS	Motown ZB 41439
28/05/1988	37	4		GET IT STEVIE WONDER AND MICHAEL JACKSON	Motown ZB 41883
06/08/1988	5	11		MY LOVE JULIO IGLESIAS FEATURING STEVIE WONDER	CBS JULIO 2
20/05/1989	49	5		FREE	Motown ZB 42855
12/10/1991	63	1		FUN DAY	Motown ZB 44957
25/02/1995	23	4		FOR YOUR LOVE 1995 Grammy Awards for Best Rhythm & Blues Singer and Best Rhythm & Blues Song	Motown TMGCD 1437
22/07/1995	71	1		TOMORROW ROBINS WILL SING	Motown 8603732
19/07/1997	10	5		HOW COME, HOW LONG BABYFACE FEATURING STEVIE WONDER	Epic 6646202
31/10/1998	51	1		TRUE TO YOUR HEART 98 DEGREES FEATURING STEVIE WONDER Featured in the 1998 Walt Disney film Mulan	Motown 8608832
27/12/2003	11	10		SIGNED SEALED DELIVERED I'M YOURS BLUE FEATURING STEVIE WONDER & ANGIE STONE	Innocent SINCD 54

WAYNE WONDER Jamaican singer (born VonWayne Charles, 26/7/1972, Franklin Town) who recorded his debut single in 1985. He won the 2003 MOBO Award for Best Reggae Act.

DATE	POS	WKS	BPI	SINGLE TITLE	LABEL & NUMBER
23/03/1996	21	5		SOMETHING DIFFERENT/THE TRAIN IS COMING SHAGGY FEATURING WAYNE WONDER/SHAGGY Something Different contains samples of First Choice's Love Thang and Stetsasonic's Go Stetsa. The Train Is Coming featured in the 1996 film Money Train	Virgin VSCDX 1581
28/06/2003	3	8		NO LETTING GO	VP/Atlantic AT 0154CD
08/11/2003	19	6		BOUNCE ALONG	Atlantic AT 0165CD

WONDER DOGS German producer/singer Harry Thumann with a single sounding like a chorus of dogs. He had a more conventional hit under his own name.

DATE	POS	WKS	BPI	SINGLE TITLE	LABEL & NUMBER
21/08/1982	31	7		RUFF MIX	Flip 001

WONDER STUFF UK rock group formed in Birmingham in 1985 by Miles Hunt (born 29/7/1966, Birmingham, guitar/vocals), Malcolm Treece (guitar/vocals), Martin Gilks (drums) and Rob Jones (born 1964, bass). Jones left in 1990 and the group added Martin Bell (fiddle) and Paul Clifford (bass). Jones died from a drug overdose on 30/7/1993. They disbanded in 1994.

DATE	POS	WKS	BPI	SINGLE TITLE	LABEL & NUMBER
30/04/1988	72	2		GIVE GIVE GIVE ME MORE MORE MORE	Polydor GONE 3
16/07/1988	43	5		A WISH AWAY	Polydor GONE 4
24/09/1988	40	3		IT'S YER MONEY I'M AFTER BABY	Polydor GONE 5
11/03/1989	28	3		WHO WANTS TO BE THE DISCO KING	Polydor GONE 6
23/09/1989	19	4		DON'T LET ME DOWN GENTLY	Polydor GONE 7
11/11/1989	33	3		GOLDEN GREEN/GET TOGETHER	Polydor GONE 8
12/05/1990	20	4		CIRCLESQUARE	Polydor GONE 10
13/04/1991	5	7		THE SIZE OF A COW	Polydor GONE 11
25/05/1991	18	3		CAUGHT IN MY SHADOW	Polydor GONE 12
07/09/1991	43	2		SLEEP ALONE	Polydor GONE 13
26/10/1991	❶²	12	O	DIZZY VIC REEVES AND THE WONDER STUFF	Sense SIGH 712
25/01/1992	8	5		WELCOME TO THE CHEAP SEATS (EP) Tracks on EP: Welcome To The Cheap Seats, Me My Mom My Dad And My Brother, Will The Circle Be Unbroken and That's Entertainment	Polydor GONE 14
25/09/1993	10	4		ON THE ROPES (EP) Tracks on EP: On The Ropes, Professional Disturber Of The Peace and Hank And John	Polydor GONCD 15
27/11/1993	28	3		FULL OF LIFE (HAPPY NOW)	Polydor GONCD 16
26/03/1994	19	3		HOT LOVE NOW	Polydor GONCD 17
10/09/1994	16	3		UNBEARABLE	Polydor GONCD 18

WONDERS US group assembled by actor/director Tom Hanks for his 1996 film That Thing You Do!, his directorial debut. The

❶⁹ Number of weeks single topped the UK chart ⬆ Entered the UK chart at #1 ▲⁹ Number of weeks single topped the US chart

885

group featured Jonathan Schaech as Jimmy (vocals), Steve Zhan (Lenny, guitar), Etan Embry (bass) and Tom Everett-Scott (drums), although the hit single was recorded by session musicians and lead singer Mike Viola.

| 22/02/1997 | 22 | 3 | | THAT THING YOU DO! Featured in the 1996 film *That Thing You Do!* | Play-Tone 6640552 |

WONDRESS – see MANTRONIX

BRENTON WOOD
US singer (born Alfred Smith, 25/7/1941, Shreveport, LA, raised in California) who first recorded with Little Freddy & The Rockets in 1958.

| 27/12/1967 | 8 | 14 | | GIMME LITTLE SIGN | Liberty LBF 15021 |

ROY WOOD
UK singer (born Ulysses Adrian Wood, 8/11/1946, Birmingham) who formed the Move in 1966 and then Electric Light Orchestra in 1971 with Jeff Lynne. Wood lost interest in this project and announced the formation of Wizzard the following year, disbanding that group in 1975. He had begun recording as a solo artist in 1972.

11/08/1973	18	8		DEAR ELAINE	Harvest HAR 5074
01/12/1973	8	13		FOREVER	Harvest HAR 5078
15/06/1974	13	7		GOING DOWN THE ROAD	Harvest HAR 5083
31/05/1975	13	7		OH WHAT A SHAME	Jet 754
22/11/1986	45	4		WATERLOO DOCTOR AND THE MEDICS FEATURING ROY WOOD	IRS IRM 125
23/12/1995	59	2		I WISH IT COULD BE CHRISTMAS EVERYDAY ROY WOOD BIG BAND	Woody 001CD
30/12/2000	22	3		I WISH IT COULD BE A WOMBLING CHRISTMAS WOMBLES WITH ROY WOOD	Dramatico DRAMCDS 0001X

WOODENTOPS
UK group formed in Northampton by Rolo McGinty (guitar/vocals), Simon Mawby (guitar), Alice Thompson (keyboards), Frank De Freitas (bass) and Benny Staples (drums).

| 11/10/1986 | 72 | 1 | | EVERYDAY LIVING | Rough Trade RT 178 |

MARCELLA WOODS
UK singer, sister of Michael Woods.

15/07/2000	21	4		BEAUTIFUL MATT DAREY'S MASH UP PRESENTS MARCELLA WOODS	Incentive CENT 7CDS
30/03/2002	60	1		FALLING LIQUID STATE FEATURING MARCELLA WOODS	Perfecto PERF 29CDS
20/04/2002	10	6		BEAUTIFUL	Incentive CENT 38CDS
14/12/2002	34	2		U SHINE ON This and above single credited to MATT DAREY FEATURING MARCELLA WOODS	Incentive CENT 50CDS

MICHAEL WOODS
UK producer who had previously been a member of Warrior, M1 and M3. Imogen Bailey is an Australian model who appeared in the Australian version of *Celebrity Big Brother*.

| 21/06/2003 | 46 | 1 | | IF U WANT ME MICHAEL WOODS FEATURING IMOGEN BAILEY | Incentive CENT 48CDS |
| 29/11/2003 | 52 | 1 | | SOLEX (CLOSE TO THE EDGE) | Free 2 Air 0151865F2A |

EDWARD WOODWARD
UK singer (born 1/6/1930, Croydon) who was best known as a stage and TV actor, appearing in the long-running series *Callan* 1967–73, and later the US TV series *The Equalizer*. His film credits include *Where There's A Will* (1954), *Becket* (1964), *The File Of The Golden Goose* (1969), *Young Winston* (1973), *Stand Up Virgin Soldiers* (1977), *Hands Of A Murder* (1990) and *Mister Johnson* (1991).

| 16/01/1971 | 42 | 2 | | THE WAY YOU LOOK TONIGHT | DJM DJS 232 |

WOOKIE
UK dance producer Jason Chue.

03/06/2000	45	1		WHAT'S GOING ON	Soul II Soul S2CD 001
12/08/2000	10	7		BATTLE	Soul II Soul S2SPCD 001
12/05/2001	38	3		BACK UP (TO ME) This and above single credited to WOOKIE FEATURING LAIN	Soul II Soul S2SPCD 003

SHEB WOOLEY
US singer/actor (born 10/4/1921, near Erick, OK) whose films included *High Noon* (1952) and *Giant* (1956). He was in several TV series, including *Rawhide* in the role of Pete Nolan. He also made comedy records as Ben Colder. He died on 16/9/2003.

| 20/06/1958 | 12 | 8 | | PURPLE PEOPLE EATER ▲⁶ | MGM 981 |

WOOLPACKERS
UK group with cast members and the props man from the TV series *Emmerdale* – Zak Dingle (played by Steve Halliwell), Mandy Dingle (Lisa Riley), Vic Windsor (Alun Lewis) and Terry Dyddgen Jones. The Woolpack is the name of the public house in the series and both hits were featured in the programme.

| 16/11/1996 | 5 | 14 | O | HILLBILLY ROCK HILLBILLY ROLL | RCA 74321425412 |
| 29/11/1997 | 25 | 10 | | LINE DANCE PARTY | RCA 74321512262 |

WORKING WEEK
UK group formed by Simon Booth (guitar), Larry Stabins (various reeds) and fronted by singer Juliet Roberts. Roberts later went solo.

| 09/06/1984 | 64 | 2 | | VENCEREMOS – WE WILL WIN | Virgin VS 684 |

WORLD – see LIL' LOUIS

WORLD OF TWIST
UK group formed in Sheffield in 1985 by James Fry (vocals), Gordon King (guitar), Andrew Hobson (bass), Tony Ogden (drums) and a horn section. The group was re-formed in 1989 by Ogden, King and Hobson with Alan Frost (keyboards), Julia 'MC Shells', Angela Reilly and Nick Sanderson (drums).

| 24/11/1990 | 42 | 5 | | THE STORM | Circa YR 55 |
| 23/03/1991 | 47 | 3 | | SONS OF THE STAGE | Circa YR 62 |

O Silver disc ● Gold disc ✪ Platinum disc (additional platinum units are indicated by a figure following the symbol) ◎ Singles released prior to 1973 that are known to have sold over 1 million copies in the UK

12/10/1991	58	2		SWEETS	Circa YR 72
22/02/1992	62	2		SHE'S A RAINBOW	Circa YR 82

WORLD PARTY UK singer/guitarist/keyboard player Karl Wallinger (born 19/10/1957, Leicester) who had previously been a member of the Waterboys and left in 1986 in order to set up World Party.

14/02/1987	42	6		SHIP OF FOOLS	Ensign ENY 606
16/06/1990	39	6		MESSAGE IN THE BOX	Ensign ENY 631
15/09/1990	66	2		WAY DOWN NOW	Ensign ENY 634
18/05/1991	68	1		THANK YOU WORLD	Ensign ENY 643
10/04/1993	19	6		IS IT LIKE TODAY	Ensign CDENY 658
10/07/1993	43	3		GIVE IT ALL AWAY	Ensign CDENY 659
02/10/1993	37	3		ALL I GAVE	Ensign CDENY 660
07/06/1997	31	2		BEAUTIFUL DREAM	Chrysalis CDCHS 5053

WORLD PREMIERE US R&B group formed in Brooklyn, NYC by Norman 'Skip' Wright (guitar/vocals), Bernard Bullock (guitar/vocals), Anthony Lamar Wright (bass) and Douglas Pittman (drums).

28/01/1984	64	1		SHARE THE NIGHT	Epic A 4133

WORLD WARRIOR UK producer Simon Harris who also recorded as Ambassadors Of Funk and under his own name.

16/04/1994	70	1		STREET FIGHTER II Coincided with the release of the computer game of the same name	Living Beat LBECD 27

WORLDS APART UK group that subsequently recruited Nathan Moore (formerly with Brother Beyond) as lead singer. Despite initial limited success in the UK, they became European superstars, prompting a relaunch of their career in 1997.

27/03/1993	29	3		HEAVEN MUST BE MISSING AN ANGEL	Arista 74321139362
03/07/1993	51	1		WONDERFUL WORLD	Arista 74321153402
25/09/1993	20	4		EVERLASTING LOVE	Bell 74321164802
26/03/1994	15	6		COULD IT BE I'M FALLING IN LOVE	Bell 74321189952
04/06/1994	29	3		BEGGIN' TO BE WRITTEN	Bell 74321211982

WORLD'S FAMOUS SUPREME TEAM US vocal/rap group formed by Jade, Anjou, Tammy, Rockafella and Asia.

04/12/1982	9	12	O	BUFFALO GIRLS MALCOLM McLAREN AND THE WORLD'S FAMOUS SUPREME TEAM	Charisma MALC 1
25/02/1984	52	5		HEY DJ	Charisma TEAM 1
08/12/1990	75	1		OPERA HOUSE WORLD FAMOUS SUPREME TEAM SHOW	Virgin VS 1273
03/10/1998	65	1		BUFFALO GALS STAMPEDE (REMIX) MALCOLM McLAREN AND THE WORLD'S FAMOUS SUPREME TEAM PLUS RAKIM AND ROGER SANCHEZ	Virgin VSCDT 1717

W.O.S.P. UK vocal/production duo Ben Langmaid and Mark Bates, with singer Katherine Ellis.

17/11/2001	48	1		GETTIN' INTO U	Data 26CDS

WRECKX-N-EFFECT US rap group formed by Aqil Davidson, Markell Riley and Brandon Mitchell. Mitchell was shot to death following an argument over a woman on 9/8/1990. Riley's brother is songwriter, producer and BLACKstreet and Guy member Teddy Riley, who produced their debut single.

13/01/1990	29	7		JUICY WRECKS-N-EFFECT	Motown ZB 43295
05/12/1992	24	7		RUMP SHAKER Contains a sample of N2Deep's *Back To The Hotel*	MCA MCS 1725
07/05/1994	26	2		WRECKX SHOP WRECKX-N-EFFECT FEATURING APACHE INDIAN	MCA MCSTD 1969
13/08/1994	40	2		RUMP SHAKER Re-issue of MCA MCS 1725	MCA MCSTD 1989

BETTY WRIGHT US singer (born 21/12/1953, Miami, FL) who joined the family gospel group the Echoes Of Joy in 1956 and made her first records for Deep City at thirteen. She later hosted her own TV talk show.

25/01/1975	27	7		SHOORAH SHOORAH	RCA 2491
19/04/1975	25	7		WHERE IS THE LOVE 1975 Grammy Award for Best Rhythm & Blues Song for writers Harry Casey, Willie Clarke, Richard Finch and Betty Wright	RCA 2548
08/02/1986	42	6		PAIN	Cooltempo COOL 117
09/09/1989	71	3		KEEP LOVE NEW	Sure Delight SD 11

IAN WRIGHT UK singer (born 3/11/1963, Woolwich, London), best known as a footballer, playing for Crystal Palace, Arsenal, West Ham United, Burnley and representing England on 33 occasions.

28/08/1993	43	2		DO THE RIGHT THING	M&G MAGCD 45

LINDA WRIGHT – see NEW ATLANTIC

RUBY WRIGHT US singer (born 27/10/1939, Nashville, TN), the daughter of Kitty Wells and Johnny Wright.

16/04/1954	7	5		BIMBO	Parlophone R 3816
22/05/1959	19	10		THREE STARS Uncredited narration is by Dick Pike and is a tribute to Buddy Holly, Ritchie Valens and The Big Bopper	Parlophone R 4556

STEVE WRIGHT UK radio DJ/singer (born 26/8/1954, London) who later became a TV presenter with his own show.

27/11/1982	40	6		I'M ALRIGHT YOUNG STEVE AND THE AFTERNOON BOYS	RCA 296
15/10/1983	75	1		GET SOME THERAPY STEVE WRIGHT AND THE SISTERS OF SOUL	RCA 362
01/12/1984	61	3		THE GAY CAVALIEROS (THE STORY SO FAR)	MCA 925

❶[9] Number of weeks single topped the UK chart   ↑ Entered the UK chart at #1   ▲[9] Number of weeks single topped the US chart

WU-TANG CLAN
US rap group formed in Staten Island, NYC by Shallah Raekwon (born Corey Woods, 12/1/1968), Method Man (born Clifford Smith, 1/4/1971, Staten Island), Genius/GZA (born Gary Grice, 22/8/1966, Brooklyn, NYC), Ol' Dirty Bastard (born Russell Jones, 15/11/1968, Brooklyn), Inspectah Deck (born Jason Hunter), Ghostface Killah (born Dennis Coles, 9/5/1970, Staten Island, aka Tony Starks and Ironman), U-God (born Lamont Hawkins), RZA (born Robert Diggs) and Masta Killa (born Elgin Turner). In 1995 they added fellow rapper Cappadonna (born 1969, Brooklyn).

16/08/1997	46	1		TRIUMPH **WU-TANG FEATURING CAPPADONNA**	Loud 74321510212
21/03/1998	4	7		SAY WHAT YOU WANT/INSANE **TEXAS FEATURING THE WU TANG CLAN**	Mercury MERCD 499
25/11/2000	6	13		GRAVEL PIT	Loud 6705182

WUBBLE-U
UK production group with Dai, Deptford, Cinders and Darkman, with Professor Stanley Unwin and Charlie One providing the vocals on their debut hit.

07/03/1998	55	1		PETAL	Indolent DGOL 003CD1

WURZELS
UK comedy vocal trio first formed in 1966 by Tommy Banner, Tony Bayliss and Pete Budd as backing group for folk singer and comedian Adge Cutler. Cutler was killed in a car crash in 1974 but the group continued, with Banner and Budd later joined by Amos Morgan and Squire Wintour.

02/02/1967	45	1		DRINK UP THY ZIDER	Columbia DB 8081
15/05/1976	❶²	13	◯	**COMBINE HARVESTER (BRAND NEW KEY)**	EMI 2450
11/09/1976	3	9		**I AM A CIDER DRINKER (PALOMA BLANCA)**	EMI 2520
25/06/1977	32	5		FARMER BILL'S COWMAN (I WAS KAISER BILL'S BATMAN)	EMI 2637
11/08/2001	39	2		COMBINE HARVESTER 2001 (REMIX)	EMI Gold CDWURZ 001
12/10/2002	59	1		DON'T LOOK BACK IN ANGER	EMI Gold 5515082

WWF SUPERSTARS
US/UK wrestlers from the World Wrestling Federation featuring the likes of Hulk Hogan, Sid Justice, Sergeant Slaughter and The Undertaker.

12/12/1992	4	9	◯	**SLAM JAM**	Arista 74321124887
03/04/1993	14	5		WRESTLEMANIA	Arista 74321136832
10/07/1993	71	1		USA **WWF SUPERSTARS FEATURING HACKSHAW JIM DUGGAN**	Arista 74321153092

ROBERT WYATT
UK singer (born 28/1/1945, Canterbury) who was drummer with Wilde Flowers before becoming a founder member of Soft Machine in 1966. He left in 1971 to form Matching Mole (a pun on the French for Soft Machine – *machine molle*), that venture coming to an end in 1974 when Wyatt broke his back falling from an apartment window and was paralysed from the waist down. He first recorded solo in 1970 and relaunched his solo career in 1974.

28/09/1974	29	5		I'M A BELIEVER	Virgin VS 114
07/05/1983	35	6		SHIPBUILDING	Rough Trade RT 115

MICHAEL WYCOFF
US singer/keyboard player from Torrance, CA who also recorded with The Winans, Bobby Womack and Michael Damian.

23/07/1983	60	2		(DO YOU REALLY LOVE ME) TELL ME LOVE	RCA 348

PETE WYLIE
UK singer (born in Liverpool) who was a member of the Crucial Three with Ian McCulloch and Julian Cope. He formed Wah! in 1979 and then went solo in 1986.

03/05/1986	13	10		SINFUL	Eternal MDM 7
13/09/1986	57	3		DIAMOND GIRL	Eternal MDM 12
13/04/1991	28	5		SINFUL! (SCARY JIGGIN' WITH DOCTOR LOVE) **PETE WYLIE WITH THE FARM**	Siren SRN 138

BILL WYMAN
UK singer (born William Perks, 24/10/1936, London) who joined the Rolling Stones in 1962, quitting in 1993. He married model Mandy Smith in 1989, shortly after opening his own Sticky Fingers restaurant (the name was taken from a Stones album title). The couple were divorced in 1992. He later formed Bill Wyman's Rhythm Kings with Georgie Fame in the line-up.

25/07/1981	14	9		(SI SI) JE SUIS UN ROCK STAR	A&M AMS 8144
20/03/1982	37	4		A NEW FASHION	A&M AMS 8209

JANE WYMAN – see BING CROSBY

TAMMY WYNETTE
US singer (born Virginia Wynette Pugh, 5/5/1942, Itawamba County, MS) who was discovered by Billy Sherrill and signed to Epic in 1967. She established herself as country music's top female performer with over fifteen #1s on the country charts (although never making #1 in the pop charts, the #11 for *Justified And Ancient* and #19 for *Stand By Your Man* her best showing). She married construction worker Euple Byrd in 1959, guitarist Don Chapel (he sold nude photographs of her), singer George Jones from 1969 until 1975 and estate agent Michael Tomlin (for 44 days), all of these marriages ending in d.i.v.o.r.c.e. She also took part in the *Perfect Day* project for the BBC's Children In Need charity. She died after a lengthy illness on 6/4/1998 with her death diagnosed as having been caused by a blood clot in a lung. Her family was unconvinced and got the body exhumed for an autopsy prior to launching a $50 million lawsuit against her doctor and then manager/husband George Richey (he was later dropped from the lawsuit after giving his consent to the autopsy). The autopsy found the cause of death to have been a blood clot to a lung. Two Grammy Awards included Best Country & Western Vocal Performance in 1967 for *I Don't Want To Play House*.

26/04/1975	❶³	12	●	STAND BY YOUR MAN Originally charted in the US in 1968 (position #19). 1969 Grammy Award for Best Country & Western Vocal Performance. Featured in the 1993 film *Sleepless In Seattle*.	Epic EPC 7137
28/06/1975	12	7		D.I.V.O.R.C.E.	Epic EPC 3361
12/06/1976	37	4		I DON'T WANNA PLAY HOUSE	Epic EPC 4091
07/12/1991	2	12	◯	JUSTIFIED AND ANCIENT **KLF, GUEST VOCALS: TAMMY WYNETTE**	KLF Communications KLF099

◯ Silver disc ● Gold disc ✪ Platinum disc (additional platinum units are indicated by a figure following the symbol) ◉ Singles released prior to 1973 that are known to have sold over 1 million copies in the UK

MARK WYNTER UK singer (born Terence Lewis, 29/1/1943, Woking) who began his career as a singer with the Hank Fryer Band. He later turned to acting and became a successful children's TV presenter.

DATE	POS	WKS	SINGLE TITLE	LABEL & NUMBER
25/08/1960	11	10	IMAGE OF A GIRL	Decca F 11263
10/11/1960	24	10	KICKING UP THE LEAVES	Decca F 11279
09/03/1961	27	5	DREAM GIRL	Decca F 11323
08/06/1961	32	7	EXCLUSIVELY YOURS	Decca F 11354
04/10/1962	4	15	**VENUS IN BLUE JEANS**	Pye 7N 15466
13/12/1962	6	11	**GO AWAY LITTLE GIRL**	Pye 7N 15492
06/06/1963	28	6	SHY GIRL	Pye 7N 15525
14/11/1963	12	12	IT'S ALMOST TOMORROW	Pye 7N 15577
09/04/1964	38	4	ONLY YOU (AND YOU ALONE)	Pye 7N 15626

❶⁹ Number of weeks single topped the UK chart   ↑ Entered the UK chart at #1   ▲⁹ Number of weeks single topped the US chart

889

MALCOLM X US political orator (born Malcolm Little, 19/5/1926, Omaha, NE) and a member of the Black Muslims before founding the Organization of Afro-American Unity in 1964, a movement that supported violent means of achieving racial equality (as opposed to Martin Luther King's non-violent stand). He was assassinated while addressing a rally on 21/2/1965.

07/04/1984.....60......4....... NO SELL OUT Features excerpts from Malcolm X's speeches with musical accompaniment from Keith Le Blanc.... Tommy Boy IS 165

RICHARD X UK producer/remixer (born Richard Philips, Whalley, Lancashire) who also records as Girls On Top.

29/03/2003 .....3......11...... **BEING NOBODY RICHARD X VS LIBERTY X** This song is effectively two songs: the lyrics from Rufus' *Ain't Nobody* with music from Human League's *Being Boiled* .... Virgin RXCD1

23/08/2003 .....8......5...... **FINEST DREAMS RICHARD X FEATURING KELIS** This song is effectively two songs: the lyrics from SOS Band's *The Finest* with music from Human League's *Dreams*... Virgin RXCD 2

X MEN – see SELENA VS X MEN

XAVIER – see TILT FEATURING XAVIER

XAVIER US funk group formed in Hartford, CT by Ernest 'Xavier' Smith (guitar/vocals), Ayanna Little (vocals), Emonie Branch (vocals), Chuck Hughes (vocals), Jeff Mitchell (guitar), Ralph Hunt (bass), Lyburn Downing (percussion) and Tim Williams (drums).

20/03/1982.....53......3....... WORK THAT SUCKER TO DEATH/LOVE IS ON THE ONE Features the uncredited contributions of George Clinton and Bootsy Collins .... Liberty UP 651

X-ECUTIONERS FEATURING MIKE SHINODA AND MR HAHN OF LINKIN PARK US rap group formed in New York in 1989 by Mista Sinista, Rob Swift, Total Eclipse and Roc Raida. First known as The X-Men, they changed their name to The X-ecutioners upon signing with the Asphodel label in 1997.

13/04/2002 .....7......9....... IT'S GOIN' DOWN Contains a sample of Xzibit's *Year 2000* .... Epic 6725642

XPANSIONS UK producer Ritchie Malone featuring the vocals of Sally Anne Marsh.

06/10/1990.....49......5...... ELEVATION .... Optimism 113683

23/02/1991.....7......9...... **MOVE YOUR BODY** .... Arista 113683

15/06/1991.....55......2...... WHAT YOU WANT **XPANSIONS FEATURING DALE JOYNER** .... Arista 114246

26/08/1995.....14......4...... MOVE YOUR BODY (REMIX) **XPANSION 95** .... Arista 74321294982

30/11/2002.....70......1...... ELEVATION (MOVE YOUR BODY) 2002 .... RM RMRCD 10

X-PRESS 2 UK acid house group formed by Darren 'Rocky' Rock, Darren 'Diesel' House and Ashley 'Daddy Ash' Beedle. Beedle also records as the Black Science Orchestra, Rocky and Diesel as The Problem Kids.

05/06/1993.....59......1...... LONDON X-PRESS .... Junior Boy's Own JBO 12

16/10/1993.....32......2...... SAY WHAT! .... Junior Boy's Own JBO 16CD

30/07/1994.....55......2...... ROCK 2 HOUSE/HIP HOUSIN' **X-PRESS 2 FEATURING LO-PRO**............ Junior Boy's Own JBO 21CD

09/03/1996.....38......1...... THE SOUND... Junior Boy's Own JBO 36CD

12/10/1996.....45......1...... TRANZ EURO XPRESS .... Junior Boy's Own JBO 42CD

30/09/2000.....60......1...... AC/DC .... Skint 57

28/04/2001.....52......1...... MUZIKIZUM.. Skint 65

20/10/2001.....43......1...... SMOKE MACHINE .... Skint 69

20/04/2002 .....2......13...... **LAZY**.. Skint 74CD

21/09/2002.....50......1...... I WANT YOU BACK Features the uncredited contribution of Dieter Meier....................... Skint 81CD

X-RAY SPEX UK punk rock group formed in 1977 by Poly Styrene (born Marion Ellis, vocals), Paul Dean (bass), Paul 'BP' Harding (drums), Lora Logic (saxophone) and Jack 'Airport' Stafford (guitar). Styrene later went solo.

29/04/1978.....23......8...... THE DAY THE WORLD TURNED DAY-GLO .... EMI International INT 553

22/07/1978.....24......10...... IDENTITY Featured in the 1991 film *Young Soul Rebels* even though the film is set around the Queen's Silver Jubilee in 1977, before the track was recorded.. EMI International INT 563

04/11/1978.....19......11...... GERM FREE ADOLESCENCE .... EMI International INT 573

21/04/1979.....45......4...... HIGHLY INFLAMMABLE .... EMI International INT 583

XRS – see DJ MARKY AND XRS

XSCAPE US R&B vocal group formed in Atlanta, GA by sisters LaTocha and Tamika Scott, Kandi Buruss and Tameka Cottle. Kandi later became a successful songwriter, penning hits for TLC, Pink and Destiny's Child before going solo.

○ Silver disc   ● Gold disc   ✪ Platinum disc (additional platinum units are indicated by a figure following the symbol)   ◉ Singles released prior to 1973 that are known to have sold over 1 million copies in the UK

20/11/1993	49	2		JUST KICKIN' IT	Columbia 6598622
05/11/1994	54	2		JUST KICKIN' IT Re-issue of Columbia 6598622	Columbia 6608642
07/10/1995	34	2		FEELS SO GOOD	Columbia 6625022
27/01/1996	31	3		WHO CAN I RUN TO Contains a sample of Teddy Pendergrass' *Love TKO*	Columbia 6628112
29/06/1996	39	2		KEEP ON, KEEPIN' ON Contains a sample of Michael Jackson's *Liberian Girl*. Featured in the 1996 film *Sunset Park*	East West A 4287CD
19/04/1997	27	2		KEEP ON, KEEPIN' ON Re-issue of East West A 4287CD. This and above single credited to MC LYTE FEATURING XSCAPE	East West A 3950CD1
22/08/1998	46	2		THE ARMS OF THE ONE WHO LOVES YOU	Columbia 6662522

XSTASIA UK production duo Tekara and Michael Woods, with singer Stacey Charles.

17/03/2001	65	1		SWEETNESS	Liquid Asset ASSETCD 005

X-STATIC Italian vocal/instrumental group formed by Artura Stecca and Paolo Visnadi with C Dori.

04/02/1995	41	2		I'M STANDING (HIGHER)	Positiva CDTIV 25

XTC UK group formed by Andy Partridge (born 1/11/1953, Valletta, Malta, guitar/vocals), Colin Moulding (born 17/8/1955, Swindon, bass/vocals), Dave Gregory (born 21/9/1952, Swindon, keyboards) and Terry Chambers (drums). They stopped touring in 1982 to concentrate on studio work. Partridge later released singles as Buster Gonad And The Jolly Testicles.

12/05/1979	54	4		LIFE BEGINS AT THE HOP	Virgin VS 259
22/09/1979	17	11		MAKING PLANS FOR NIGEL	Virgin VS 282
06/09/1980	32	8		GENERALS AND MAJORS/DON'T LOSE YOUR TEMPER	Virgin VS 365
18/10/1980	31	5		TOWERS OF LONDON	Virgin VS 372
24/01/1981	16	9		SGT ROCK (IS GOING TO HELP ME)	Virgin VS 384
23/01/1982	10	9		SENSES WORKING OVERTIME	Virgin VS 462
27/03/1982	58	4		BALL AND CHAIN	Virgin VS 482
15/10/1983	50	4		LOVE ON A FARMBOY'S WAGES	Virgin VS 613
29/09/1984	55	5		ALL YOU PRETTY GIRLS	Virgin VS 709
28/01/1989	46	5		MAYOR OF SIMPLETON	Virgin VS 1158
04/04/1992	33	5		THE DISAPPOINTED	Virgin VS 1404
13/06/1992	71	1		THE BALLAD OF PETER PUMPKINHEAD	Virgin VS 1415

XTM AND DJ CHUCKY PRESENTS ANNIA Spanish DJ/production duo of brothers Xasqui and Tony Ten with singer Annia. Their debut hit was a trance version of the 2000 Eurovision Song Contest winner by Danish group The Olsen Brothers.

07/06/2003	8	19		FLY ON THE WINGS OF LOVE	Serious SER 62CD

XZIBIT US rapper (born Alvin Nathaniel Joiner, 18/9/1974, Detroit, MI, raised in New Mexico) who was originally a member of The Likwit Crew with Tha Alkaholiks and King T. He made his album debut in 1996 for Loud Records, before linking with Dr Dre.

17/03/2001	14	7		X XZIBIT FEATURING SNOOP DOGG	Epic 6709072
16/11/2002	39	2		MULTIPLY	Epic 6731552

❶⁹ Number of weeks single topped the UK chart ↑ Entered the UK chart at #1 ▲⁹ Number of weeks single topped the US chart

891

Y?N-VEE US vocal group formed by Nicole Chaney, Tescia Harris, Yenan Ragsdale and Natasha Walker.

17/12/1994	65	1	

CHOCOLATE . . . . RAL RALCD 2

Y & T US rock group formed in San Francisco, CA during the 1970s by Dave Meniketti (guitar/vocals), Joey Alves (guitar), Philip Kennemore (bass) and Leonard Haze (drums) as Yesterday And Today, subsequently shortening their name to Y&T. Haze left in 1986 and was replaced by Jimmy DeGrasso; Alves left in 1989 and was replaced by Stef Burns. They disbanded in 1990.

13/08/1983	41	4	

MEAN STREAK . . . . A&M AM 135

Y-TRAXX Belgian producer Frederique De Backer.

24/05/1997	63	1	

MYSTERY LAND (EP) Tracks on EP include: *Mystery Land (Radio Edit), Trance Piano, Kiss The Sound* and *Mystery Land (Original Edit)* . . . . ffrr FCD 292

20/09/2003	70	1	

MYSTERY LAND **Y-TRAXX FEATURING NEVE** . . . . Nebula NEBT 047

Y-TRIBE FEATURING ELISABETH TROY UK production duo Ali and Elisabeth Troy. Troy has also worked with MJ Cole, Soundman and Don Lloydie.

18/12/1999	49	3	

ENOUGH IS ENOUGH . . . . Northwest 10 NORTHCD 002

YA KID K Zairian rapper Manuella 'Ya Kid K' Komosi, also a member of Technotronic. Born in Zaire, she moved to Belgium at the age of eleven and later moved to the US before returning to Belgium and forming Technotronic and Hi-Tek 3 with Jo Bogaert.

03/02/1990	2	10	O

GET UP (BEFORE THE NIGHT IS OVER) TECHNOTRONIC FEATURING YA KID K . . . . Swanyard SYR 8

03/02/1990	69	3	

SPIN THAT WHEEL (TURTLES GET REAL) Featured in the 1993 film *Teenage Mutant Ninja Turtles III*. . . . Brothers Organisation BORG 1

29/09/1990	15	6	

SPIN THAT WHEEL (TURTLES GET REAL) Re-issue of Brothers Organisation BORG 1. This and above single credited to **HI-TEK 3 FEATURING YA KID K** . . . . Brothers Organisation BORG 16

WEIRD AL YANKOVIC US singer (born 24/10/1959, Lynwood, CA), a Los Angeles-based architect, accordionist and disc jockey who made parodies of songs he claimed bored him. He starred in the 1989 film *UHF*. He has won two Grammy Awards: Best Comedy Recording in 1984 for *Eat It* and Best Concept Music Video in 1988 with Jay Levey for *Fat*.

07/04/1984	36	7	

EAT IT Based on Michael Jackson's *Beat It* and featuring Rick Derringer on guitar . . . . Scotti Brothers A 4257

04/07/1992	58	1	

SMELLS LIKE NIRVANA . . . . Scotti Brothers PO 219

YANOU – see **DJ SAMMY AND YANOU FEATURING DO**

YARBROUGH AND PEOPLES US duo Calvin Yarbrough and Alisa Peoples from Dallas, TX, discovered by The Gap Band.

27/12/1980	7	12	O

DON'T STOP THE MUSIC . . . . Mercury MER 53

05/05/1984	60	3	

DON'T WASTE YOUR TIME . . . . Total Experience XE 501

11/01/1986	53	3	

GUILTY . . . . Total Experience FB 49905

05/07/1986	61	2	

I WOULDN'T LIE . . . . Total Experience FB 49841

YARDBIRDS UK rock group formed in 1963 by Keith Relf (born 22/3/1943, Richmond, Surrey, vocals), Anthony 'Top' Topham (guitar), Chris Dreja (born 11/11/1945, Surbiton, Surrey, guitar), Paul 'Sam' Samwell-Smith (born 8/5/1943, Richmond, bass) and Jim McCarty (born 25/7/1943, Liverpool, drums), taking their name from a Jack Kerouac book. Topham left soon after and was replaced by Eric Clapton (born Eric Clapp, 30/3/1945, Ripley, Surrey), who in turn left in 1965 and was replaced by Jeff Beck (born 24/6/1944, Wallington, Surrey). Samwell-Smith left in 1966 and was replaced by Jimmy Page (born 9/1/1944, Heston, Middlesex). They disbanded in July 1968, Page forming The New Yardbirds in the October, which evolved into Led Zeppelin. Relf died on 14/5/1976, electrocuted while playing his guitar at home. The group was inducted into the Rock & Roll Hall of Fame in 1992.

12/11/1964	44	4	

GOOD MORNING LITTLE SCHOOLGIRL . . . . Columbia DB 7391

18/03/1965	3	12	

FOR YOUR LOVE Featured in the 1998 film *Fear And Loathing In Las Vegas* . . . . Columbia DB 7499

17/06/1965	2	13	

HEART FULL OF SOUL . . . . Columbia DB 7594

14/10/1965	3	10	

EVIL HEARTED YOU/STILL I'M SAD . . . . Columbia DB 7706

03/03/1966	3	9	

SHAPES OF THINGS . . . . Columbia DB 7848

02/06/1966	10	9	

OVER UNDER SIDEWAYS DOWN . . . . Columbia DB 7928

27/10/1966	43	5	

HAPPENINGS TEN YEARS TIME AGO . . . . Columbia DB 8024

YAVAHN – see **RUFFNECK FEATURING YAVAHN**

YAZOO UK group formed by former Depeche Mode keyboard player Vince Clarke (born 3/7/1960, London) and singer Alison 'Alf' Moyet (born Genevieve Alison Moyet, 18/6/1961, Basildon, Essex). Clarke went on to front Assembly and then Erasure and Moyet

O Silver disc   ● Gold disc   ✪ Platinum disc (additional platinum units are indicated by a figure following the symbol)   ◎ Singles released prior to 1973 that are known to have sold over 1 million copies in the UK

pursued a successful solo career. The group won the 1983 BRIT Award for Best British Newcomer.

17/04/1982 ..... 2 ...... 14 ..... O	**ONLY YOU** .... Mute 020
17/07/1982 ..... 3 ...... 11 ..... O	**DON'T GO** .... Mute YAZ 001
20/11/1982 ..... 13 ...... 9	THE OTHER SIDE OF LOVE .... Mute YAZ 002
21/05/1983 ..... 3 ...... 11 ..... O	**NOBODY'S DIARY** Written by Moyet, her first such success .... Mute YAZ 003
08/12/1990 ..... 14 ...... 8	SITUATION .... Mute YAZ 4
04/09/1999 ..... 38 ...... 2	ONLY YOU (REMIX) .... Mute CDYAZ 5

YAZZ UK singer (born Yasmin Evans, 19/5/1963, London) who was formerly a model before recording with Suzette Smithson and Austin Howards as Biz in 1983, scoring a number of club hits. She later fronted *Doctorin' The House* with Coldcut's Matt Black and Jonathan Moore, before launching her own career with Big Life, the label set up by her future husband Jazz Summers. The Plastic Population were Kiss DJs Black and Moore.

20/02/1988 ..... 6 ...... 9 ...... ●	**DOCTORIN' THE HOUSE** COLDCUT FEATURING YAZZ AND THE PLASTIC POPULATION .... Ahead Of Our Time CCUT 2
23/07/1988 .... ❶⁵ ...... 15 ..... ●	**THE ONLY WAY IS UP** YAZZ AND THE PLASTIC POPULATION .... Big Life BLR 4
29/10/1988 ..... 2 ...... 12 ..... O	**STAND UP FOR YOUR LOVE RIGHTS** .... Big Life BLR 5
04/02/1989 ..... 9 ...... 8	**FINE TIME** .... Big Life BLR 6
29/04/1989 ..... 16 ...... 6	WHERE HAS ALL THE LOVE GONE .... Big Life BLR 8
23/06/1990 ..... 20 ...... 5	TREAT ME GOOD .... Big Life BLR 24
28/03/1992 ..... 60 ...... 2	ONE TRUE WOMAN .... Polydor PO 198
31/07/1993 ..... 31 ...... 5	HOW LONG YAZZ AND ASWAD .... Polydor PZCD 252
02/04/1994 ..... 42 ...... 3	HAVE MERCY .... Polydor PZCD 309
09/07/1994 ..... 56 ...... 2	EVERYBODY'S GOT TO LEARN SOMETIME .... Polydor PZCD 316
28/09/1996 ..... 53 ...... 1	GOOD THING GOING .... East West EW 062CD
22/03/1997 ..... 61 ...... 1	NEVER CAN SAY GOODBYE .... East West EW 081CD

YEAH YEAH YEAHS US rock group formed in New York City by Karen Orzolek (vocals), Nick Zinner (guitar) and Brian Chase (drums).

16/11/2002 ..... 37 ...... 2	MACHINE .... Wichita Recordings WEBB 036SCD
26/04/2003 ..... 16 ...... 2	DATE WITH THE NIGHT .... Dress Up 0657442
05/07/2003 ..... 29 ...... 2	PIN .... Dress Up 9808085
04/10/2003 ..... 26 ...... 2	MAPS .... Dress Up 9811413
13/11/2004 ..... 54 ...... 1	Y CONTROL .... Dress Up 9868816

TRISHA YEARWOOD US singer (born 19/9/1964, Monticello, GA) who was a backing singer when she was discovered by Garth Brooks. She subsequenty worked on his *No Fences* album and opened for him on his 1991 US tour, becoming the first female singer to top the country charts with her debut single *She's In Love With The Boy*. By 1994 she had written her (largely 'ghosted') autobiography, and the following year married Robert Reynolds from The Mavericks, the marriage ending in 1999. She recorded the original version of *How Do I Live*, although LeAnn Rimes had the bigger hit with a cover version. She has won three Grammy Awards: for Best Country Vocal Collaboration in 1994 with Aaron Neville for *I Fall To Pieces*; Best Country Collaboration with Vocals in 1997 with Garth Brooks for *In Another's Eyes*; and Best Female Country Vocal Performance in 1997 for *How Do I Live*.

09/08/1997 ..... 66 ...... 1	HOW DO I LIVE Featured in the 1997 film *Con Air* .... MCA MCSTD 48064

YELL! UK duo formed in 1988 by Daniel James (vocals) and Paul Varney (keyboards). They disbanded in 1991, with James going solo and pursuing an acting career, and later working with DJ and Bliss.

20/01/1990 ..... 10 ...... 8	**INSTANT REPLAY** .... Fanfare FAN 22

YELLO Swiss trio formed in Zurich in 1979 by Dieter Meiler (horns/vocals), Boris Blank (keyboards) and Carlos Peron (keyboards). Meiler had previously been in the Swiss national golf team.

25/06/1983 ..... 41 ...... 4	I LOVE YOU .... Stiff BUY 176
26/11/1983 ..... 73 ...... 1	LOST AGAIN .... Stiff BUY 191
09/08/1986 ..... 54 ...... 3	GOLDRUSH .... Mercury MER 218
22/08/1987 ..... 54 ...... 2	THE RHYTHM DIVINE YELLO FEATURING SHIRLEY BASSEY .... Mercury MER 253
27/08/1988 ..... 7 ...... 11	**THE RACE** .... Mercury YELLO 1
17/12/1988 ..... 60 ...... 5	TIED UP .... Mercury YELLO 2
25/03/1989 ..... 23 ...... 8	OF COURSE I'M LYING .... Mercury YELLO 3
22/07/1989 ..... 47 ...... 2	BLAZING SADDLES .... Mercury YELLO 4
08/06/1991 ..... 58 ...... 2	RUBBERBANDMAN .... Mercury YELLO 5
05/09/1992 ..... 61 ...... 2	JUNGLE BILL .... Mercury MER 376
07/11/1992 ..... 55 ...... 1	THE RACE/BOSTICH Re-issue of Mercury YELLO 1 .... Mercury MER 382
15/10/1994 ..... 59 ...... 1	HOW HOW .... Mercury MERCD 414

YELLOW DOG UK group formed by Kenny Young (guitar/vocals) and Herbie Armstrong (guitar/vocals) following the demise of Fox, also featuring Gerry Conway (drums), Jim Gannon (guitar), Gary Roberts (guitar) and Gary Taylor (bass).

04/02/1978 ..... 8 ...... 9 ...... O	**JUST ONE MORE NIGHT** .... Virgin VS 195
22/07/1978 ..... 54 ...... 4	WAIT UNTIL MIDNIGHT .... Virgin VS 217

YELLOW MAGIC ORCHESTRA Japanese synthesiser group formed by Ryuichi Sakamoto (born 17/1/1952, Tokyo), Haruomi Hosono and Yukihiro Takahashi in 1978. Although they had several hit albums in Japan, they had only one hit single in the UK, which was inspired by the space invaders arcade game.

❶⁹ Number of weeks single topped the UK chart ↑ Entered the UK chart at #1 ▲⁹ Number of weeks single topped the US chart

893

14/06/1980.....17.....11...... COMPUTER GAME (THEME FROM 'THE INVADERS')..A&M AMS 7502

YELLOWCARD US punk-pop group formed in Jacksonville, FL in 1997 by Ryan Key (guitar/vocals), Sean Mackin (violin/vocals), Ben Harper (guitar), Alex Lewis (bass) and Longineu Parsons (drums); they relocated to California in 2000.

12/06/2004.....63......1....... WAY AWAY...Capitol CDCLS 855
18/09/2004.....65......1....... OCEAN AVENUE...Capitol CDCLS 860

YELLOWCOATS – see PAUL SHANE AND THE YELLOWCOATS

YEOVIL TOWN FC UK professional football club formed in 1895 as Yeovil Casuals, becoming Yeovil Town in 1920 following a merger with Petters United.

28/02/2004.....36......1....... YEOVIL TRUE..Yeovil Town FC YEOVILTOWN188

YES UK rock group formed in London in 1968 by Jon Anderson (born 25/10/1944, Accrington, vocals), Peter Banks, Tony Kaye, Chris Squire (born 4/3/1948, London, bass) and Bill Bruford (born 17/5/1948, London, drums). Banks and Kaye departed in 1971 and were replaced by Steve Howe (born 8/4/1947, London, guitar) and Rick Wakeman (born 18/5/1949, London, keyboards). Bruford joined King Crimson in 1972 and was replaced by Alan White (born 14/6/1949, Pelton, Durham). Wakeman left in 1974 but returned in 1976 when his replacement Patrick Moraz quit. Both Wakeman and Anderson left in 1980 with their replacements being ex-Buggles members Trevor Horn and Geoff Downes, although Yes disbanded soon after. They re-formed in 1983 with Anderson, Kaye, Squire, White and Trevor Rabin. The group won the 1984 Grammy Award for Best Rock Instrumental Performance for *Cinema*. Anderson, Bruford, Wakeman and Howe also combined to record as Anderson Bruford Wakeman Howe, with Bruford also being a member of U.K.

17/09/1977.....7......9...... WONDEROUS STORIES...Atlantic K 10999
26/11/1977.....24......4...... GOING FOR THE ONE..Atlantic K 11047
09/09/1978.....36......4...... DON'T KILL THE WHALE...Atlantic K 11184
12/11/1983.....28......9...... OWNER OF A LONELY HEART ▲² ....Atco B 9817
31/03/1984.....56......4...... LEAVE IT..Atco B 9787
03/10/1987.....73......1....... LOVE WILL FIND A WAY...Atco B 9449

MELISSA YIANNAKOU – see DESIYA FEATURING MELISSA YIANNAKOU

YIN AND YAN UK vocal duo Chris Sandford and Bill Mitchell. Sandford had previously recorded solo.

29/03/1975.....25......5...... IF..EMI 2282

YO-HANS – see JOSE FEATURING YO-HANS

DWIGHT YOAKAM US singer/guitarist (born 23/10/1956, Pikeville, KY) who played in various clubs in Los Angeles as well as working as a truck driver. He first recorded for Oak Records and then Enigma, before joining Warner Brothers' Reprise label in 1984. A regular on the US country charts since 1986, he finally made his national breakthrough in 1993. His film appearances include *Red Rock West* (1993) and *Sling Blade* (1996). He has won two Grammy Awards: Best Country Vocal Performance in 1993 for *Ain't That Lonely Yet* and Best Country Vocal Collaboration in 1998 with Clint Black, Joe Diffie, Merle Haggard, Emmylou Harris, Alison Krauss, Patty Loveless, Earl Scruggs, Ricky Skaggs, Marty Stuart, Pam Tillis, Randy Travis and Travis Tritt for *Same Old Train*.

10/07/1999.....43......2..... CRAZY LITTLE THING CALLED LOVE...Reprise W 497CD

YOMANDA UK producer Paul Masterton who also collaborated with Judge Jules (born Julius O'Riordan) as Hi-Gate, with Rachel Auburn as Candy Girls and recorded as Sleazesisters.

24/07/1999.....8......10....... SYNTH & STRINGS Contains a sample of Liquid Gold's *Dance Yourself Dizzy* ....1st Avenue FESCD 59
11/03/2000.....16......6....... SUNSHINE...1st Avenue FESCD 68
02/09/2000.....28......2....... ON THE LEVEL...Manifesto FESCD 73
26/07/2003.....22......3....... YOU'RE FREE...Incentive CENT 55CDS

TUKKA YOOT – see US3

YORK German production/instrumental duo of brothers Torsten (also a much-in-demand remixer) and Jorg Stenzel.

09/10/1999.....11......5....... THE AWAKENING...Manifesto FESCD 60
10/06/2000.....4......10....... ON THE BEACH Contains a sample of Chris Rea's *On The Beach*.................................Manifesto FESCD 70
18/11/2000.....37......2....... FAREWELL TO THE MOON ....Manifesto FESCD 76
27/01/2001.....16......4....... THE FIELDS OF LOVE ATB FEATURING YORK..................................Club Tools 0124095 CLU

YOSH PRESENTS LOVEDEEJAY AKEMI Dutch record producer.

29/07/1995.....69......1....... IT'S WHAT'S UPFRONT THAT COUNTS.......................................Limbo LIMB 46CD
02/12/1995.....31......2....... IT'S WHAT'S UPFRONT THAT COUNTS (REMIX)..............................Limbo LIMB 50CD
20/04/1996.....38......2....... THE SCREAMER..Limbo LIMB 54CD

YOSHIKI – see ROGER TAYLOR

YOTHU YINDI Australian Aboriginal group formed by Mandawuy Yunupingu, Garlarway Yunupingu, Gurrumul Yunupingu, Makuma Yunupingu, Witiyana Marika, Cal Williams and Milkayngu Munungurr.

15/02/1992.....72......1....... TREATY..Hollywood HWD 116

○ Silver disc ● Gold disc ✪ Platinum disc (additional platinum units are indicated by a figure following the symbol) ◉ Singles released prior to 1973 that are known to have sold over 1 million copies in the UK

FARON YOUNG
US country singer and guitarist (born 25/2/1932, Shreveport, LA) who scored over 30 top ten hits on the US country charts and later appeared in numerous films. He committed suicide by shooting himself in the head on 10/12/1996.

15/07/1972 . . . . . 3 . . . . . . 23 . . . . . . IT'S FOUR IN THE MORNING . . . . Mercury 6052 140

JIMMY YOUNG
UK singer (born 21/9/1923) who shot to fame in the 1950s with his version of Nat 'King' Cole's *Faith Can Move Mountains*. After his recording career was over he turned to radio. He joined Radio 1 at its outset before moving to Radio 2 and retiring in 2001. He was knighted in the 2002 New Year's Honours List.

09/01/1953 . . . . . 11 . . . . . . 1				FAITH CAN MOVE MOUNTAINS	Decca F 9986
21/08/1953 . . . . . 8 . . . . . . 9				ETERNALLY	Decca F 10130
06/05/1955 . . . . ❶³ 19				UNCHAINED MELODY	Decca F 10502
16/09/1955 . . . . ❶⁴ 12				THE MAN FROM LARAMIE	Decca F 10597
23/12/1955 . . . . . 13 . . . . . . 5				SOMEONE ON YOUR MIND	Decca F 10640
16/03/1956 . . . . . 9 . . . . . . 6				CHAIN GANG	Decca F 10694
08/06/1956 . . . . . 27 . . . . . . 1				WAYWARD WIND	Decca F 10736
22/06/1956 . . . . . 25 . . . . . . 1				RICH MAN POOR MAN	Decca F 10736
28/09/1956 . . . . . 4 . . . . . . 17				MORE	Decca F 10774
03/05/1957 . . . . . 30 . . . . . . 1				ROUND AND ROUND JIMMY YOUNG WITH THE MICHAEL SAMMES SINGERS	Decca F 10875
10/10/1963 . . . . . 15 . . . . . . 13				MISS YOU	Columbia DB 7119
26/03/1964 . . . . . 43 . . . . . . 3				UNCHAINED MELODY	Columbia DB 7234

JOHN PAUL YOUNG
UK singer (born 21/6/1953, Glasgow, raised in Australia) whose hit single was masterminded by Harry Vanda and George Young, formerly members of The Easybeats. He later enjoyed success as Flash And The Pan.

29/04/1978 . . . . . 5 . . . . . 13 . . . . . . O				LOVE IS IN THE AIR	Ariola ARO 117
14/11/1992 . . . . . 49 . . . . . . 3				LOVE IS IN THE AIR (REMIX) Featured in the 1992 film *Strictly Ballroom*	Columbia 6587697
12/01/2002 . . . . . 25 . . . . . . 3				LOVE IS IN THE AIR MILK AND SUGAR FEATURING JOHN PAUL YOUNG	Positiva CDTIV 166

KAREN YOUNG
UK singer (born 1946, Sheffield) discovered by The Bachelors.

06/09/1969 . . . . . 6 . . . . . . 21 . . . . . . NOBODY'S CHILD . . . . Major Minor MM 625

KAREN YOUNG
US singer (born 23/3/1951, Philadelphia, PA) based in New York who recorded for the West End label. She died from a stomach ulcer on 26/1/1991.

19/08/1978 . . . . . 34 . . . . . . 7				HOT SHOT	Atlantic K 11180
24/02/1979 . . . . . 75 . . . . . . 1				HOT SHOT Re-issue of Atlantic K 11180	Atlantic LV 8
15/11/1997 . . . . . 68 . . . . . . 1				HOT SHOT '97 (REMIX)	Distinctive DISNCD 37

LEON YOUNG STRING CHORALE – see MR ACKER BILK AND HIS PARAMOUNT JAZZ BAND

NEIL YOUNG
Canadian singer (born 12/11/1945, Toronto) who formed the Mynah Birds (featuring Rick James as lead singer) in the early 1960s. Moving to Los Angeles, CA in 1966 and joining Stephen Stills' band Buffalo Springfield, he signed a solo deal with Reprise in 1969. In 1970 he joined Crosby Stills And Nash, initially for live work only but has recorded with them periodically for twenty years. He was inducted into the Rock & Roll Hall of Fame in 1995.

11/03/1972 . . . . . 10 . . . . . 11				HEART OF GOLD ▲¹ Backing vocals by Linda Ronstadt and James Taylor	Reprise K 14140
06/01/1979 . . . . . 57 . . . . . . 4				FOUR STRONG WINDS	Reprise K 14493
27/02/1993 . . . . . 36 . . . . . . 3				HARVEST MOON	Reprise W 0139CD
17/07/1993 . . . . . 75 . . . . . . 1				THE NEEDLE AND THE DAMAGE DONE	Reprise W 0191CD
30/10/1993 . . . . . 71 . . . . . . 1				LONG MAY YOU RUN (LIVE)	Reprise W 0207CD
09/04/1994 . . . . . 62 . . . . . . 2				PHILADELPHIA Featured in the 1994 film *Philadelphia*	Reprise W 0242CD

PAUL YOUNG
UK singer (born 17/1/1956, Luton) who was an apprentice at Vauxhall Cars when he formed Streetband, who scored with the novelty *Toast*. After two albums the group disbanded, Young taking two members (John Gifford and Mick Pearl) and forming Q-Tips, a 1960s-influenced R&B outfit. After two years he went solo, releasing his debut (*Iron Out The Rough Spots*) in November 1982. He was named Best British Newcomer in 1984 and Best British Male at the 1985 BRIT Awards

18/06/1983 . . . . ❶³ . . . . . 15 . . . . . ●				WHEREVER I LAY MY HAT (THAT'S MY HOME) Featured in the 1986 film *Ruthless People*	CBS A 3371
10/09/1983 . . . . . 4 . . . . . 9 . . . . . . O				COME BACK AND STAY	CBS A 3636
19/11/1983 . . . . . 2 . . . . . 13 . . . . . ●				LOVE OF THE COMMON PEOPLE Originally released in January and failed to chart	CBS A 3585
13/10/1984 . . . . . 9 . . . . . 7				I'M GONNA TEAR YOUR PLAYHOUSE DOWN	CBS A 4786
08/12/1984 . . . . . 9 . . . . . 11 . . . . . O				EVERYTHING MUST CHANGE	CBS A 4972
09/03/1985 . . . . . 4 . . . . . 11 . . . . . O				EVERY TIME YOU GO AWAY ▲¹ 1986 BRIT Award for Best Video	CBS A 6300
22/06/1985 . . . . . 16 . . . . . . 8				TOMB OF MEMORIES	CBS A 6321
04/10/1986 . . . . . 24 . . . . . . 5				WONDERLAND	CBS YOUNG 1
29/11/1986 . . . . . 56 . . . . . . 3				SOME PEOPLE	CBS YOUNG 2
07/02/1987 . . . . . 63 . . . . . . 2				WHY DOES A MAN HAVE TO BE STRONG	CBS YOUNG 3
12/05/1990 . . . . . 21 . . . . . . 6				SOFTLY WHISPERING I LOVE YOU	CBS YOUNG 4
07/07/1990 . . . . . 25 . . . . . . 6				OH GIRL	CBS YOUNG 5
06/10/1990 . . . . . 71 . . . . . . 2				HEAVEN CAN WAIT	CBS YOUNG 6
12/01/1991 . . . . . 57 . . . . . . 2				CALLING YOU	CBS YOUNG 7
30/03/1991 . . . . . 4 . . . . . 12				SENZA UNA DONNA (WITHOUT A WOMAN) ZUCCHERO AND PAUL YOUNG	London LON 294
10/08/1991 . . . . . 74 . . . . . . 1				BOTH SIDES NOW CLANNAD AND PAUL YOUNG	MCA MCS 1546
26/10/1991 . . . . . 20 . . . . . . 5				DON'T DREAM IT'S OVER	Columbia 6574117

❶⁹ Number of weeks single topped the UK chart   ↑ Entered the UK chart at #1   ▲⁹ Number of weeks single topped the US chart

DATE	POS	WKS	BPI	SINGLE TITLE	LABEL & NUMBER
25/09/1993	14	7		NOW I KNOW WHAT MADE OTIS BLUE	Columbia 6596412
27/11/1993	42	3		HOPE IN A HOPELESS WORLD	Columbia 6598652
23/04/1994	34	4		IT WILL BE YOU	Columbia 6602812
17/05/1997	33	2		I WISH YOU LOVE	East West EW 100CD1

RETTA YOUNG US singer (born 1949, South Carolina) discovered by Sylvia Robinson, herself a singer and owner of the All Platinum group of labels. Her debut hit was produced by The Moments; she was married to Al Goodman of the group.

24/05/1975	28	7		SENDING OUT AN S.O.S.	All Platinum 6146 305

TRACIE YOUNG – see TRACIE

WILL YOUNG UK singer (born 20/1/1979) who studied politics at Exeter University and musical theatre at the Arts Educational School in London before beating 10,000 entrants to win the TV series *Pop Idol*, and the prize of a recording contract with BMG. He polled over 5 million votes in the final with Gareth Gates, and his debut single sold 385,483 copies on its first day of release and 1,108,269 copies in its first week. In so doing it became the biggest-selling first-week single by a debut artist and the second biggest-selling first-week single of all time (only Elton John's *Candle In The Wind* tribute to Princess Diana has sold more). Young was named British Breakthrough Artist at the 2003 BRIT Awards.

09/03/2002	❶³	16	✪³	**EVERGREEN/ANYTHING IS POSSIBLE** ↑	S 74321926142
08/06/2002	❶²	20	●	**LIGHT MY FIRE** ↑	S 74321943002
05/10/2002	❶²	18	●	**THE LONG AND WINDING ROAD/SUSPICIOUS MINDS** ↑ **WILL YOUNG AND GARETH GATES** B-side credited to Gareth and featured in the 2002 Walt Disney film *Lilo & Stitch*	S 74321965972
30/11/2002	2	13	○	**DON'T LET ME DOWN/YOU AND I** Released to raise funds for the BBC Children In Need Fund	S 74321981272
06/12/2003	❶²	18	●	**LEAVE RIGHT NOW** ↑ Released to raise funds for the BBC Children In Need Fund	S 82876578562
27/03/2004	3	9		**YOUR GAME**	S 82876603622
17/07/2004	4	6		**FRIDAY'S CHILD**	S 82876634152

YOUNG AND COMPANY US group formed by New Jersey-based brothers Kenny, Mike and Billy Young as Young Movement, becoming Young & Co in 1980.

01/11/1980	20	12		I LIKE (WHAT YOU'RE DOING TO ME)	Excalibur EXC 501

YOUNG AND MOODY BAND UK vocal/instrumental group formed by Bob Young and Mick Moody with Lemmy, Cozy Powell and The Nolan Sisters. Young had been a roadie for Status Quo, Moody a member of Whitesnake.

10/10/1981	63	4		DON'T DO THAT	Bronze BRO 130

YOUNG BLACK TEENAGERS US rap group who despite their name comprise three white teenagers and a Puerto Rican – ATA, Kameron, Firstborn and DJ Skribble (born Scott Ialacci). DJ Skribble later recorded solo and with Mr Redz.

09/04/1994	39	3		TAP THE BOTTLE	MCA MCSTD 1967

YOUNG BUCK US rapper (born David Brown, 15/3/1981); he is also a member of G Unit.

23/10/2004	62	1		LET ME IN	Interscope 9864517

YOUNG DISCIPLES UK jazz-funk group formed by Mark 'O' and Femi, with Carleen Anderson and MC Mell 'O' providing the vocals. Anderson and Mark 'O' subsequently recorded solo. Anderson later joined The Brand New Heavies and re-recorded *Apparently Nothin'*.

13/10/1990	68	1		GET YOURSELF TOGETHER	Talkin Loud TLK 2
23/02/1991	46	4		APPARENTLY NOTHIN'	Talkin Loud TLK 5
03/08/1991	13	7		APPARENTLY NOTHIN'	Talkin Loud TLK 5
05/10/1991	65	2		GET YOURSELF TOGETHER	Talkin Loud TLK 15
05/09/1992	48	3		YOUNG DISCIPLES (EP) Tracks on EP: *Move On, Freedom, All I Have In Me* and *Move On (Remix)*	Talkin Loud TLKX 18

YOUNG HEART ATTACK US rock group formed in Austin, TX in 2001 by Jennifer Stephens (vocals), Chris Hodge (guitar/vocals), Frenchie (guitar), Steven Hall (bass) and Joey Shuffield (drums).

10/04/2004	54	1		TOMMY SHOTS	XL Recordings XLS 183CD
17/07/2004	69	1		STARLITE	XL Recordings XLS 191CD

YOUNG IDEA UK duo Tony Cox and Douglas MacCrae-Brown who first recorded for Columbia in 1965.

29/06/1967	10	6		**WITH A LITTLE HELP FROM MY FRIENDS**	Columbia DB 8205

YOUNG MC US rapper (born Marvin Young, 10/5/1967, London, raised in New York).

15/07/1989	73	2		BUST A MOVE Featured in the 2000 film *The Replacements*	Delicious Vinyl BRW 137
17/02/1990	54	3		PRINCIPAL'S OFFICE	Delicious Vinyl BRW 161
17/08/1991	65	2		THAT'S THE WAY LOVE GOES	Capitol CL 623

YOUNG OFFENDERS Irish vocal/instrumental group from Cork fronted by Ciaran McFeely (vocals), previously called The V-Necks. McFeely later recorded as Simple Kid.

07/03/1998	60	1		THAT'S WHY WE LOSE CONTROL	Columbia 6651942

YOUNG ONES – see CLIFF RICHARD

○ Silver disc   ● Gold disc   ✪ Platinum disc (additional platinum units are indicated by a figure following the symbol)   ◉ Singles released prior to 1973 that are known to have sold over 1 million copies in the UK

YOUNG RASCALS
US group formed in New York City in 1964 by Felix Cavaliere (born 29/2/1943, Pelham, NY, keyboards/vocals), Dino Danelli (born 23/7/1945, New York, drums), Eddie Brigati (born 22/10/1946, New York, vocals) and Gene Cornish (born 14/5/1946, Ottawa, Canada, guitar). All except Danelli were members of Joey Dee's Starlighters. The group recorded as The Rascals from 1968 until they disbanded in 1972 but re-formed in 1988.

| 25/05/1967 | 8 | 13 | | GROOVIN' ▲4 Featured in the films Platoon (1987) and Apollo 13 (1997) | Atlantic 584 111 |
| 16/08/1967 | 37 | 4 | | A GIRL LIKE YOU | Atlantic 584 128 |

YOUNG VOICES CHOIR – see DECLAN FEATURING YOUNG VOICES CHOIR

SYDNEY YOUNGBLOOD
US singer (born Sydney Ford, San Antonio, TX, 1960) stationed with the US Army in Germany before coming to the UK to launch his singing career.

26/08/1989	3	13	O	IF ONLY I COULD	Circa YR 34
09/12/1989	16	8		SIT AND WAIT	Circa YR 40
31/03/1990	44	5		I'D RATHER GO BLIND	Circa YR 43
29/06/1991	72	2		HOOKED ON YOU	Circa YR 65
20/03/1993	48	2		ANYTHING	RCA 74321138672

YOUNGER YOUNGER 28'S
UK group formed by Joe Northern (guitar/vocals), GI Jimmy D (keyboards) and singers Andie and Liz.

| 05/06/1999 | 61 | 1 | | WE'RE GOING OUT | V2 VVR 5006943 |

YOURCODENAMEIS: MILO
UK group formed in Newcastle-Upon-Tyne by Paul Mullen (guitar/vocals), Justin Lockey (guitar), Adam Hiles (guitar), Ross Harley (bass) and Paul Gamble-Beresford (drums). They were named Best Newcomer at the 2004 Kerrang! awards.

| 16/10/2004 | 58 | 1 | | SCHTEEVE | Fiction 9868526 |

❶9 Number of weeks single topped the UK chart   ↑ Entered the UK chart at #1   ▲9 Number of weeks single topped the US chart

897

Z

Z FACTOR UK producer Dave Lee who also records as Joey Negro, Li Kwan, Akubu, Hed Boys, Jakatta and Raven Maize.

21/02/1998.....47......1....... GOTTA KEEP PUSHIN' .... ffrr FCD 329
17/11/2001.....52......1....... RIDE THE RHYTHM........ Direction 6718482

Z2 UK production duo Rich Mowatt and Andy Bury with singer Alison Rivers. They also record as Solar Stone and Skyscraper.

26/02/2000.....61......1....... I WANT YOU .... Platipus PLATCD 67

HELMUT ZACHARIAS German violinist (born 27/1/1920, Berlin) whose one hit single was the theme to the 1964 Tokyo Olympics. He later recorded *Mexico Melody, Munich Melody* and *Moscow Melody* in a similar vein. Known as Der Zaubergeiger (The Magic Violinist), he died on 28/2/2002.

29/10/1964 .....9......11...... **TOKYO MELODY**........ Polydor YNH 52341

PIA ZADORA US singer (born Pia Schipani, 4/5/1956, New York) who also appeared in films including *Butterfly* (1981) and *Hairspray* (1988).

27/10/1984.....68......2....... WHEN THE RAIN BEGINS TO FALL **JERMAINE JACKSON AND PIA ZADORA** Featured in the 1984 film *Voyage Of The Rock Aliens*........ Arista ARIST 584
12/11/1988.....65......4....... DANCE OUT OF MY HEAD **PIA**........ Epic 6528867

ZAGER AND EVANS US duo Denny Zager (born 1944, Wymore, NE) and Rick Evans (born 1943, Lincoln, NE) who first met in 1962 as members of The Eccentrics. Evans left in 1965 and the pair reunited in 1968 to record a song originally written by Zager in 1963. The follow-up (*Mr Turnkey*), about a rapist who nails his hand to a wall and bleeds to death while detailing his crime, was too morbid for mass consumption.

09/08/1969 ....❶[3].....13...... **IN THE YEAR 2525 (EXORDIUM AND TERMINUS)** ▲[6]........ RCA 1860

MICHAEL ZAGER BAND US producer/arranger/singer/songwriter (born 3/1/1943, Jersey City, NJ). Initially famous as producer of Peabo Bryson, The Detroit Spinners, Johnny 'Guitar' Watson and many others, he launched his own band in 1978.

01/04/1978 .....8......12...... **LET'S ALL CHANT** Featured in the films *The Stud* (1978), *The Eyes Of Laura Mars* (1978), *The Last Days Of Disco* (1998) and *Summer Of Sam* (1999)........ Private Stock PVT 143

GHEORGHE ZAMFIR Romanian panpipe player (born 6/4/1941) who made his debut album in 1971.

21/08/1976 .....4......9....... **(LIGHT OF EXPERIENCE) DOINA DE JALE** Theme to the TV series *The Light Of Experience*........ Epic EPC 4310

TOMMY ZANG US singer (born in Kansas City, MO) who was the featured vocalist with Sammy Nestico and Fred Kepner's bands before going solo.

16/02/1961.....45......1....... HEY GOOD LOOKING........ Polydor NH 66957

ZAPP US funk group formed by Roger Troutman (born 29/11/1951, Hamilton, OH, guitar/vocals) with his brothers Larry (percussion), Tony (bass) and Lester (drums). Roger, who also recorded under his own name, was shot to death on 25/4/1999 by Larry, who then committed suicide.

25/01/1986.....57......3....... IT DOESN'T REALLY MATTER........ Warner Brothers W 8879
24/05/1986.....64......3....... COMPUTER LOVE (PART 1)........ Warner Brothers W 8805

FRANCESCO ZAPPALA Italian producer from Rome who was the runner-up in a DJ's competition organised by DMC (Disco Mix Club) in 1989 at Wembley Arena.

10/08/1991.....57......2....... WE GOTTA DO IT **DJ PROFESSOR FEATURING FRANCESCO ZAPPALA**........ Fourth & Broadway BRW 225
02/05/1992.....69......1....... NO WAY OUT........ PWL Continental PWL 230

LENA ZAVARONI UK singer (born 4/11/1963, Rothesay, Scotland) who first came to prominence aged ten when she won TV's *Opportunity Knocks*. Later a successful TV presenter, she died on 1/10/1999 after suffering from an eating disorder.

09/02/1974.....10.....11.....○ **MA HE'S MAKING EYES AT ME**........ Philips 6006 367
01/06/1974.....33......3....... PERSONALITY........ Philips 6006 391

ZED BIAS UK garage group assembled by Zed Bias (born Dave Jones) and DJ Principal, featuring MC Rumpus and Nicky Prince on vocals.

15/07/2000.....25......4....... NEIGHBOURHOOD........ Locked On LOX 122CD

ZEE UK singer/songwriter (born Lesley Cowling, London) who penned hits for Mary Kiani.

06/07/1996.....31......2....... DREAMTIME........ Perfecto PERF 122CD

22/03/1997	36	1		SAY MY NAME . . . . Perfecto PERF 135CD
07/02/1998	41	1		BUTTERFLY TILT FEATURING ZEE . . . . Perfecto PERF 154CD1

ZENA
ZENA UK singer (born Zena Playford, 1982, Birmingham) who was previously the lead singer with Mis-Teeq before leaving the group due to illness. Vybz Kartel is Jamaican singer Adidja Palmer (born in Kingston).

19/07/2003	69	1		LET'S GET THIS PARTY STARTED . . . . Serious SER 69CD
14/08/2004	44	1		BEEN AROUND THE WORLD ZENA FEATURING VYBZ KARTEL . . . . Mercury 9867014

ZEPHYRS
ZEPHYRS UK group formed in London by John Peeby (guitar), Marc Lerase (organ), John Hinde (bass) and John Carpenter (drums) as The Clee-Shays. They disbanded in 1965.

18/03/1965	48	1		SHE'S LOST YOU . . . . Columbia DB 7481

ZERO B
ZERO B UK keyboard player from Durham (born Peter Ryding) who was 21 at the time of his debut hit.

22/02/1992	32	4		THE EP Tracks on EP: *Lock Up, Spinning Wheel, Module* and *Eclipse* . . . . ffrreedom TAB 102
24/07/1993	54	2		RECONNECTION (EP) Tracks on EP: *Lock Up, Lock Up (Remix), Ou Est Le Spoon* and *Love To Be In Love* . . . . . Internal LIECD 6

ZERO 7
ZERO 7 UK production duo Henry Binns and Sam Hardaker. Both began their careers working in a London recording studio, then moved on to remixing (adopting their working name Zero 7 from a nightclub in Honduras) and recorded their debut in 1999. Their debut album also featured contributions from vocalists Sophie Barker, Sia Furler and Mozez.

18/08/2001	30	3		DESTINY ZERO 7 FEATURING SIA AND SOPHIE . . . . Ultimate Dilemma UDRCDS 043
17/11/2001	47	1		IN THE WAITING LINE . . . . Ultimate Dilemma UDRCDS 045
30/03/2002	45	1		DISTRACTIONS . . . . Ultimate Dilemma UDRCDS 046
29/05/2004	56	1		SOMERSAULT ZERO 7 FEATURING SIA . . . . Ultimate Dilemma EW290CD

ZERO VU FEATURING LORNA B
ZERO VU FEATURING LORNA B UK production group formed by Tony King. Lorna B also recorded with DJ Scott.

15/03/1997	69	1		FEELS SO GOOD . . . . Avex UK AVEXCD 53

ZERO ZERO
ZERO ZERO UK instrumental/production group formed by Simon Robinson and Mark Grant.

10/08/1991	71	1		ZEROXED . . . . Kickin KICK 9

ZHANE
ZHANE US duo Renee Neufville and Jean Norris, formed at Temple University in Philadelphia, PA.

11/09/1993	26	5		HEY MR. DJ Contains a sample of Michael Wycoff's *Looking Up To You* . . . . Epic 6596102
19/03/1994	34	3		GROOVE THANG . . . . Motown TMGCD 1423
20/08/1994	67	1		VIBE . . . . Motown TMGCD 1430
25/02/1995	66	1		SHAME Featured in the 1994 film *A Low Down Dirty Shame* . . . . Jive JIVECD 372
21/09/1996	23	2		IT'S A PARTY BUSTA RHYMES FEATURING ZHANE Contains a sample of Con Funk Shun's *Too Tight* . . . . . . Elektra EKR 226CD
08/03/1997	52	1		4 MORE DE LA SOUL FEATURING ZHANE . . . . Tommy Boy TBCD 7779A
26/04/1997	22	3		REQUEST LINE . . . . Motown 8606452
30/08/1997	44	1		CRUSH . . . . Motown 5716712
11/09/1999	51	1		JAMBOREE NAUGHTY BY NATURE FEATURING ZHANE Contains a sample of Benny Golson's *I'm Always Dancin' To The Music* . . . . .
				. . . . Arista 74321692882

ZIG AND ZAG
ZIG AND ZAG Irish TV puppets (from the planet Zog) who first found fame on the early morning TV show *The Big Breakfast*.

24/12/1994	5	9		THEM GIRLS THEM GIRLS . . . . RCA 74321251042
01/07/1995	21	3		HANDS UP! HANDS UP! . . . . RCA 74321284392

ZIG-ZAG JIVE FLUTES
ZIG-ZAG JIVE FLUTES – see ELIAS AND HIS ZIG-ZAG JIVE FLUTES

ZION TRAIN
ZION TRAIN UK group formed in London in 1990 by Molara (vocals), Neil Perch (DJ/bass), David Tench (trumpet), Colin Cod (keyboards) and Chris (trombone). Their debut release was issued on their own Zion Records; they signed with China Records in 1995.

27/07/1996	61	1		RISE . . . . China WOKCD 2085

ZODIACS
ZODIACS – see MAURICE WILLIAMS AND THE ZODIACS

ZOE
ZOE UK singer Zoe Jayne Pollack (born 1970) who began as a backing vocalist for the likes of Bananarama before going solo.

10/11/1990	53	5		SUNSHINE ON A RAINY DAY . . . . M&G MAGS 6
24/08/1991	4	11	○	SUNSHINE ON A RAINY DAY (REMIX) . . . . M&G MAGS 14
02/11/1991	37	4		LIGHTNING . . . . M&G MAGS 18
29/02/1992	72	2		HOLY DAYS . . . . M&G MAGS 21

ROB ZOMBIE
ROB ZOMBIE US singer (born Robert Cummings, 12/1/1966, Haverhill, MA) who formed White Zombie in 1985. He worked as a bike messenger, porn magazine art director and production assistant for a children's TV series before concentrating on music full time. He went solo in 1998 and the success of his debut album prompted the end of White Zombie.

26/12/1998	44	2		DRAGULA . . . . Geffen GFSTD 22367

ZOMBIE NATION
ZOMBIE NATION German production duo Florian 'Splank' Senfter and Emanuel 'Mooner' Gunther. They subsequently had to pay an undisclosed sum to David Whittaker, the programmer of a 1984 Commodore C64 game from which their debut hit's main riff was lifted.

02/09/2000	61	1		KERNKRAFT 400 (IMPORT) . . . . TRANSK 002
30/09/2000	2	15	○	KERNKRAFT 400 . . . . Data 11CDS

❶⁹ Number of weeks single topped the UK chart ⬆ Entered the UK chart at #1 ▲⁹ Number of weeks single topped the US chart

899

ZOMBIES UK rock group formed in St Albans, Hertfordshire by Rod Argent (born 14/6/1945, St Albans, keyboards), Colin Blunstone (born 24/6/1945, Hatfield, vocals), Paul Atkinson (born 19/3/1946, Cuffley, Hertfordshire, guitar), Paul Arnold (bass) and Hugh Grundy (born 6/3/1945, Winchester, drums). Chris White (born 7/3/1943, Barnet) replaced Arnold soon after their formation. The group won a talent contest and a contract with Decca in 1964. They disbanded in 1967, with both Blunstone and Argent enjoying further success: Blunstone as a soloist, Argent with his eponymous band. In 1991 Blunstone, White and Grundy re-formed for one album. Atkinson died from liver and kidney disease on 1/4/2004.

13/08/1964	12	11		SHE'S NOT THERE Featured in the 1979 film *More American Graffiti*	Decca F 11940
11/02/1965	42	5		TELL HER NO.	Decca F 12072

ZOO EXPERIENCE FEATURING DESTRY UK instrumental group formed by Stephen Laviniere and Robert Laviniere with US singer Destry Spigner.

22/08/1992	66	1		LOVE'S GOTTA HOLD ON ME	Cooltempo COOL 261

ZUCCHERO Italian singer/guitarist (born Adelmo Fornaciari, 1956) who began his career training to become a veterinary surgeon. He was nicknamed 'Zucchero' (Italian for sugar) as a child.

30/03/1991	4	12		SENZA UNA DONNA (WITHOUT A WOMAN) ZUCCHERO AND PAUL YOUNG	London LON 294
18/01/1992	44	7		DIAMANTE ZUCCHERO WITH RANDY CRAWFORD.	London LON 313
24/10/1992	15	5		MISERERE ZUCCHERO WITH LUCIANO PAVAROTTI	London LON 329

ZUTONS UK group formed in Liverpool in 2002 by David McCabe (vocals), Boyan Chowdhury (guitar), Russell Pritchard (bass), Abi Harding (saxophone) and Sean Payne (drums).

31/01/2004	19	3		PRESSURE POINT	Deltasonic DLTCDV 016
17/04/2004	22	3		YOU WILL YOU WON'T	Must Destroy DARK03CD
03/07/2004	39	2		REMEMBER ME	Deltasonic DLTCD 2024
30/10/2004	15	3		DON'T EVER THINK (TOO MUCH)	Deltasonic DLTCD 2026
25/12/2004	37	1		CONFUSION	Deltasonic DLTCD 030

ZWAN US rock group formed by Billy Corgan (born 17/3/1967, Chicago, IL, vocals), David Pajo (guitar), Matt Sweeney (guitar), Paz Lenchantin (bass) and Jimmy Chamberlin (drums). Corgan and Chamberlin were previously in Smashing Pumpkins. The group disbanded in September 2003.

08/03/2003	28	2		HONESTLY	Reprise W 600CD
14/06/2003	44	1		LYRIC.	Reprise W 607CD

ZZ TOP US rock group formed in Houston, TX in 1969 by Billy Gibbons (born 16/12/1949, Houston, guitar/vocals), Dusty Hill (born 19/5/1949, Dallas, TX, bass/vocals) and Frank Beard (born 11/6/1949, Frankston, TX, drums), adopting their name from Texas bluesman ZZ Hill. Gibbons and Hill stopped shaving in 1979, giving the group their distinctive image (Beard, despite his name, is the clean-shaven member). The group appeared in the 1990 film *Back To The Future III*. They were inducted into the Rock & Roll Hall of Fame in 2004.

03/09/1983	61	3		GIMME ALL YOUR LOVIN'	Warner Brothers W 9693
26/11/1983	53	3		SHARP DRESSED MAN	Warner Brothers W 9576
31/03/1984	67	3		TV DINNERS	Warner Brothers W 9334
06/10/1984	10	15		GIMME ALL YOUR LOVIN'	Warner Brothers W 9693
15/12/1984	22	10		SHARP DRESSED MAN	Warner Brothers W 9576
23/02/1985	16	7		LEGS Subsequently used for a pantyhose advertisement.	Warner Brothers W 9272
13/07/1985	51	5		SUMMER HOLIDAY (EP) Tracks on EP: *Tush, Got Me Under Pressure, Beer Drinkers And Hell Raisers* and *I'm Bad I'm Nationwide. Tush* featured in the 1982 film *An Officer And A Gentleman.*	Warner Brothers W 8946
19/10/1985	27	5		SLEEPING BAG	Warner Brothers W 2001
15/02/1986	43	3		STAGES.	Warner Brothers W 2002
19/04/1986	23	9		ROUGH BOY.	Warner Brothers W 2003
04/10/1986	54	3		VELCRO FLY	Warner Brothers W 8650
21/07/1990	29	6		DOUBLEBACK Featured in the 1990 film *Back To The Future III*	Warner Brothers W 9812
13/04/1991	37	5		MY HEAD'S IN MISSISSIPPI	Warner Brothers W 0009
11/04/1992	10	7		VIVA LAS VEGAS	Warner Brothers W 0098
20/06/1992	49	3		ROUGH BOY.	Warner Brothers W 0111
29/01/1994	15	3		PINCUSHION	RCA 74321184732
07/05/1994	60	1		BREAKAWAY	RCA 74321192282
29/06/1996	58	1		WHAT'S UP WITH THAT	RCA 74321394822
16/10/1999	28	2		GIMME ALL YOUR LOVIN' 2000 MARTAY FEATURING ZZ TOP	Riverhorse RIVHCD 2

THE NUMBER ONE RECORDS LISTED CHRONOLOGICALLY 1952-2004

Before we consider the number one records in the UK, there are three instances that must be detailed, two of which concern records that didn't make it to the chart summit:

On 17 February 1976 the BMRB (British Market Research Bureau)-compiled chart was released to the BBC and announced on the Johnnie Walker show the same morning. From the various 'ups' and 'downs' it was obvious that something was amiss, for no fewer than ten of the top twenty were new entries, including five in the top ten, and one record had plunged from #5 to #42. The BMRB confirmed that a computer breakdown had occurred and re-calculated the chart. This was unfortunate for Manuel & His Music of The Mountains; in the original chart they had risen from #8 to #1, while in the new chart they moved from #8 to #4. As they only reached #3 the following week (their chart peak) their spell of three hours is the shortest tenure at the top of the charts!

On 6 November 1979 another computer breakdown occurred but this time only two records were affected: Lena Martell's *One Day At A Time*, which had held the top position for two weeks and had slipped down to #2, while Dr Hook's *When You're In Love With A Beautiful Woman* had claimed pole position with a sales increase of 150%. This figure, while not outside the realms of possibility still warranted investigation and the following day it was announced that Lena Martell had in fact held on to the top position, albeit for another week when Dr Hook did take over legitimately. Interestingly enough, Pye Records (Lena's record company) claimed *One Day At A Time* might well have held on for a further week had the correct chart been issued – they were convinced re-orders were down because the record was judged to have fallen down the charts.

On 11 September 1990 the chart was published to reveal the Steve Miller Band's *The Joker* had risen to #1, replacing Bombalurina, and Deee-Lite with *Groove Is In The Heart/What Is Love* had eased in to second position. It was later revealed that both the Steve Miller Band and Deee-Lite had identical sales figures and that the chart compilers had placed the Steve Miller Band at #1 as their record had shown the greatest sales increase over the previous week (it had been at #6, while Deee-Lite were at #4). This caused such a furore that the chart rules were subsequently amended to allow for records holding equal positions. This has happened in the past as the listings below show, but will have been of little comfort to Deee-Lite; they held on to the #2 position for a further week and have not even hit the top twenty since.

There was a further computer breakdown on July 4 1999. It was not believed to have affected the #1 position, which was held by ATB. However, others further down the chart were demanding a re-run after some 40% of data was believed to have gone missing when Virgin Megastores and Our Price were omitted from the calculations. Most critical of the lapse, blamed on a software problem combined with both companies switching their mainframes, were those behind Blur and Semisonic, both of whom missed out on an expected place in the top ten.

Here, however, are the records that have held the #1 position since the *NME (New Musical Express)* first published its chart in 1952 through to the current day. The date refers to the published date of the chart that the record assumed the top spot, and the number of weeks is the number of weeks it held on to that position. As can be seen, there are a number of instances of records reclaiming the top spot and sharing pole position.

1952

Date	WKS	Title	Artist
14 November	9	HERE IN MY HEART ↑ ▲	Al Martino

1953

Date	WKS	Title	Artist
16 January	1	YOU BELONG TO ME ▲	Jo Stafford
23 January	1	COMES-A-LONG A-LOVE	Kay Starr
30 January	1	OUTSIDE OF HEAVEN	Eddie Fisher
6 February	5	DON'T LET THE STARS GET IN YOUR EYES ▲	Perry Como with The Ramblers
13 March	4	SHE WEARS RED FEATHERS	Guy Mitchell
10 April	1	BROKEN WINGS	Stargazers
17 April	1	(HOW MUCH IS) THAT DOGGIE IN THE WINDOW	Lita Roza
24 April	9	I BELIEVE	Frankie Laine
26 June	1	I'M WALKING BEHIND YOU ▲	Eddie Fisher with Sally Sweetland
3 July	6	I BELIEVE	Frankie Laine
14 August	1	THE SONG FROM MOULIN ROUGE	Mantovani
21 August	3	I BELIEVE	Frankie Laine
11 September	6	LOOK AT THAT GIRL	Guy Mitchell
23 October	2	HEY JOE	Frankie Laine
6 November	1	ANSWER ME	David Whitfield
13 November	4	ANSWER ME	Frankie Laine
11 December	1	ANSWER ME/ANSWER ME	David Whitfield/Frankie Laine
18 December	3	ANSWER ME	Frankie Laine

1954

Date	WKS	Title	Artist
8 January	9	OH MEIN PAPA	Eddie Calvert
12 March	6	I SEE THE MOON	Stargazers
16 April	1	SECRET LOVE ▲	Doris Day
23 April	1	I SEE THE MOON	Stargazers
30 April	1	SUCH A NIGHT	Johnnie Ray
7 May	8	SECRET LOVE	Doris Day
2 July	10	CARA MIA	David Whitfield, with Chorus and Mantovani and His Orchestra
10 September	1	LITTLE THINGS MEAN A LOT ▲	Kitty Kallen
17 September	3	THREE COINS IN THE FOUNTAIN	Frank Sinatra
8 October	4	HOLD MY HAND	Don Cornell
5 November	2	MY SON MY SON	Vera Lynn with Frank Weir, His Saxophone, His Orchestra and Chorus
19 November	1	HOLD MY HAND	Don Cornell
26 November	1	THIS OLE HOUSE ▲	Rosemary Clooney
3 December	5	LET'S HAVE ANOTHER PARTY	Winifred Atwell

1955

Date	WKS	Title	Artist
7 January	1	FINGER OF SUSPICION	Dickie Valentine with The Stargazers
14 January	1	MAMBO ITALIANO	Rosemary Clooney and The Mellomen
21 January	2	FINGER OF SUSPICION	Dickie Valentine with The Stargazers
4 February	2	MAMBO ITALIANO	Rosemary Clooney and The Mellomen
18 February	3	SOFTLY SOFTLY	Ruby Murray
11 March	7	GIVE ME YOUR WORD	Tennessee Ernie Ford
29 April	2	CHERRY PINK AND APPLE BLOSSOM WHITE ▲	Perez 'Prez' Prado and His Orchestra
13 May	2	STRANGER IN PARADISE	Tony Bennett
27 May	4	CHERRY PINK AND APPLE BLOSSOM WHITE	Eddie Calvert
24 June	3	UNCHAINED MELODY	Jimmy Young
15 July	2	DREAMBOAT	Alma Cogan
29 July	11	ROSE MARIE	Slim Whitman
14 October	4	THE MAN FROM LARAMIE	Jimmy Young
11 November	2	HERNANDO'S HIDEAWAY	Johnston Brothers
25 November	3	ROCK AROUND THE CLOCK ▲	Bill Haley and His Comets
16 December	3	CHRISTMAS ALPHABET	Dickie Valentine

1956

Date	WKS	Title	Artist
6 January	2	ROCK AROUND THE CLOCK	Bill Haley and His Comets
20 January	4	SIXTEEN TONS ▲	Tennessee Ernie Ford
17 February	4	MEMORIES ARE MADE OF THIS ▲	Dean Martin
16 March	2	IT'S ALMOST TOMORROW	Dreamweavers
30 March	1	ROCK AND ROLL WALTZ ▲	Kay Starr
6 April	1	IT'S ALMOST TOMORROW	Dreamweavers
13 April	3	POOR PEOPLE OF PARIS	Winifred Atwell
4 May	6	NO OTHER LOVE	Ronnie Hilton
15 June	5	I'LL BE HOME	Pat Boone
20 July	3	WHY DO FOOLS FALL IN LOVE	Teenagers Featuring Frankie Lymon
10 August	6	WHATEVER WILL BE WILL BE	Doris Day
21 September	4	LAY DOWN YOUR ARMS	Anne Shelton
19 October	4	A WOMAN IN LOVE	Frankie Laine
16 November	7	JUST WALKIN' IN THE RAIN	Johnnie Ray

1957

Date	WKS	Title	Artist
4 January	1	SINGING THE BLUES ▲	Guy Mitchell
11 January	1	SINGING THE BLUES	Tommy Steele and The Steelmen
18 January	1	SINGING THE BLUES	Guy Mitchell
25 January	1	THE GARDEN OF EDEN	Frankie Vaughan
1 February	1	SINGING THE BLUES/THE GARDEN OF EDEN	Guy Mitchell/Frankie Vaughan
8 February	2	THE GARDEN OF EDEN	Frankie Vaughan
22 February	7	YOUNG LOVE ▲	Tab Hunter
12 April	5	CUMBERLAND GAP	Lonnie Donegan
17 May	1	ROCK-A-BILLY	Guy Mitchell
24 May	2	BUTTERFLY	Andy Williams
7 June	3	YES TONIGHT JOSEPHINE	Johnnie Ray
28 June	2	GAMBLIN' MAN/PUTTING ON THE STYLE	Lonnie Donegan
12 July	7	ALL SHOOK UP ▲	Elvis Presley
30 August	9	DIANA ▲	Paul Anka
1 November	3	THAT'LL BE THE DAY ▲	Crickets
22 November	7	MARY'S BOY CHILD	Harry Belafonte

1958

Date	WKS	Title	Artist
10 January	2	GREAT BALLS OF FIRE	Jerry Lee Lewis
24 January	3	JAILHOUSE ROCK ↑ ▲	Elvis Presley
14 February	2	THE STORY OF MY LIFE	Michael Holliday
28 February	8	MAGIC MOMENTS	Perry Como
25 April	3	WHOLE LOTTA WOMAN	Marvin Rainwater
16 May	6	WHO'S SORRY NOW	Connie Francis
27 June	1	ON THE STREET WHERE YOU LIVE	Vic Damone
4 July	1	ON THE STREET WHERE YOU LIVE/ALL I HAVE TO DO IS DREAM/CLAUDETTE	Vic Damone/Everly Brothers
11 July	6	ALL I HAVE TO DO IS DREAM/CLAUDETTE ▲	Everly Brothers
22 August	5	WHEN	Kalin Twins
26 September	6	CAROLINA MOON/STUPID CUPID	Connie Francis
7 November	3	IT'S ALL IN THE GAME ▲	Tommy Edwards
28 November	3	HOOTS MON	Lord Rockingham's XI
19 December	5	IT'S ONLY MAKE BELIEVE ▲	Conway Twitty

↑ Entered the UK chart at number one ▲ Topped the US chart

1959

DATE	WKS	TITLE	ARTIST
23 January	1	THE DAY THE RAINS CAME	Jane Morgan
30 January	3	ONE NIGHT/I GOT STUNG	Elvis Presley
20 February	4	AS I LOVE YOU	Shirley Bassey
20 March	1	SMOKE GETS IN YOUR EYES ▲	Platters
27 March	4	SIDE SADDLE	Russ Conway
24 April	3	IT DOESN'T MATTER ANYMORE	Buddy Holly
15 May	5	A FOOL SUCH AS I/I NEED YOUR LOVE TONIGHT	Elvis Presley
19 June	2	ROULETTE	Russ Conway
3 July	4	DREAM LOVER	Bobby Darin
31 July	6	LIVING DOLL	Cliff Richard and The Drifters
11 September	4	ONLY SIXTEEN	Craig Douglas
9 October	1	HERE COMES SUMMER	Jerry Keller
16 October	2	MACK THE KNIFE ▲	Bobby Darin
30 October	5	TRAVELLIN' LIGHT	Cliff Richard and The Shadows
4 December	2	WHAT DO YOU WANT	Adam Faith
18 December	1	WHAT DO YOU WANT/WHAT DO YOU WANT TO MAKE THOSE EYES AT ME FOR	Adam Faith/Emile Ford and The Checkmates
25 December	5	WHAT DO YOU WANT TO MAKE THOSE EYES AT ME FOR	Emile Ford and The Checkmates

1960

DATE	WKS	TITLE	ARTIST
29 January	1	STARRY EYED	Michael Holliday with The Michael Sammes Singers
5 February	4	WHY	Anthony Newley
10 March	1	POOR ME	Adam Faith
17 March	2	RUNNING BEAR ▲	Johnny Preston
31 March	4	MY OLD MAN'S A DUSTMAN	Lonnie Donegan
28 April	2	DO YOU MIND	Anthony Newley
5 May	7	CATHY'S CLOWN ▲	Everly Brothers
23 June	2	THREE STEPS TO HEAVEN	Eddie Cochran
7 July	3	GOOD TIMIN'	Jimmy Jones
28 July	1	PLEASE DON'T TEASE	Cliff Richard and The Shadows
4 August	1	SHAKIN' ALL OVER	Johnny Kidd and The Pirates
11 August	2	PLEASE DON'T TEASE	Cliff Richard and The Shadows
25 August	5	APACHE	Shadows
29 September	3	TELL LAURA I LOVE HER	Ricky Valence
20 October	2	ONLY THE LONELY	Roy Orbison
3 November	8	IT'S NOW OR NEVER ↑ ▲	Elvis Presley
29 December	1	I LOVE YOU	Cliff Richard and The Shadows

1961

DATE	WKS	TITLE	ARTIST
12 January	2	POETRY IN MOTION	Johnny Tillotson
26 January	4	ARE YOU LONESOME TONIGHT ▲	Elvis Presley
23 February	1	SAILOR	Petula Clark
2 March	6	WALK RIGHT BACK/EBONY EYES	Everly Brothers
23 March	6	WOODEN HEART	Elvis Presley
4 May	2	BLUE MOON ▲	Marcels
18 May	1	ON THE REBOUND	Floyd Cramer
25 May	1	YOU'RE DRIVING ME CRAZY	Temperance Seven
1 June	4	SURRENDER ▲	Elvis Presley
29 June	1	RUNAWAY ▲	Del Shannon
20 July	2	TEMPTATION	Everly Brothers
3 August	1	WELL I ASK YOU	Eden Kane
10 August	3	YOU DON'T KNOW	Helen Shapiro
31 August	3	JOHNNY REMEMBER ME	John Leyton
21 September	1	REACH FOR THE STARS/CLIMB EV'RY MOUNTAIN	Shirley Bassey
28 September	1	JOHNNY REMEMBER ME	John Leyton

DATE	WKS	TITLE	ARTIST
5 October	1	KON-TIKI	Shadows
12 October	1	MICHAEL ▲	Highwaymen
19 October	3	WALKIN' BACK TO HAPPINESS	Helen Shapiro
9 November	4	(MARIE'S THE NAME) HIS LATEST FLAME/LITTLE SISTER	Elvis Presley
7 December	3	TOWER OF STRENGTH	Frankie Vaughan
28 December	2	MOON RIVER	Danny Williams

1962

DATE	WKS	TITLE	ARTIST
11 January	6	THE YOUNG ONES ↑	Cliff Richard and The Shadows
22 February	4	ROCK-A-HULA BABY/CAN'T HELP FALLING IN LOVE	Elvis Presley
22 March	8	WONDERFUL LAND	Shadows
17 May	1	NUT ROCKER	B. Bumble and The Stingers
24 May	5	GOOD LUCK CHARM ▲	Elvis Presley
28 June	2	COME OUTSIDE	Mike Sarne with Wendy Richard
12 July	2	I CAN'T STOP LOVING YOU ▲	Ray Charles
26 July	7	I REMEMBER YOU	Frank Ifield
13 September	3	SHE'S NOT YOU	Elvis Presley
4 October	5	TELSTAR ▲	Tornados
8 November	5	LOVESICK BLUES	Frank Ifield
13 December	3	RETURN TO SENDER	Elvis Presley

1963

DATE	WKS	TITLE	ARTIST
3 January	3	THE NEXT TIME/BACHELOR BOY	Cliff Richard and The Shadows
24 January	1	DANCE ON!	Shadows
31 January	3	DIAMONDS	Jet Harris and Tony Meehan
21 February	3	WAYWARD WIND	Frank Ifield
14 March	2	SUMMER HOLIDAY	Cliff Richard and The Shadows
28 March	1	FOOT TAPPER	Shadows
4 April	1	SUMMER HOLIDAY	Cliff Richard and The Shadows
11 April	3	HOW DO YOU DO IT	Gerry and The Pacemakers
2 May	7	FROM ME TO YOU	Beatles
20 June	4	I LIKE IT	Gerry and The Pacemakers
18 July	2	CONFESSIN'	Frank Ifield
1 August	1	(YOU'RE THE) DEVIL IN DISGUISE	Elvis Presley
8 August	2	SWEETS FOR MY SWEET	Searchers
22 August	3	BAD TO ME	Billy J Kramer and The Dakotas
12 September	4	SHE LOVES YOU ▲	Beatles
10 October	3	DO YOU LOVE ME	Brian Poole and The Tremeloes
31 October	4	YOU'LL NEVER WALK ALONE	Gerry and The Pacemakers
28 November	2	SHE LOVES YOU	Beatles
12 December	5	I WANT TO HOLD YOUR HAND ▲	Beatles

1964

DATE	WKS	TITLE	ARTIST
16 January	2	GLAD ALL OVER	Dave Clark Five
30 January	3	NEEDLES AND PINS	Searchers
20 February	1	DIANE	Bachelors
27 February	3	ANYONE WHO HAD A HEART	Cilla Black
19 March	2	LITTLE CHILDREN	Billy J Kramer and The Dakotas
2 April	3	CAN'T BUY ME LOVE ▲	Beatles
23 April	2	A WORLD WITHOUT LOVE ▲	Peter and Gordon
7 May	2	DON'T THROW YOUR LOVE AWAY	Searchers
21 May	1	JULIET	Four Pennies
28 May	4	YOU'RE MY WORLD	Cilla Black
25 June	2	IT'S OVER	Roy Orbison
9 July	1	HOUSE OF THE RISING SUN ▲	Animals
16 July	1	IT'S ALL OVER NOW	Rolling Stones

   ↑ Entered the UK chart at number one   ▲ Topped the US chart

DATE	WKS	TITLE	ARTIST
23 July	3	A HARD DAY'S NIGHT ▲	Beatles
13 August	2	DO WAH DIDDY DIDDY ▲	Manfred Mann
27 August	2	HAVE I THE RIGHT	Honeycombs
10 September	2	YOU REALLY GOT ME	Kinks
24 September	2	I'M INTO SOMETHING GOOD	Herman's Hermits
8 October	2	OH PRETTY WOMAN ▲	Roy Orbison
22 October	3	(THERE'S) ALWAYS SOMETHING THERE TO REMIND ME	Sandie Shaw
12 November	1	OH PRETTY WOMAN ▲	Roy Orbison
19 November	2	BABY LOVE ▲	Supremes
3 December	1	LITTLE RED ROOSTER	Rolling Stones
10 December	5	I FEEL FINE ▲	Beatles

1965

DATE	WKS	TITLE	ARTIST
14 January	2	YEH YEH	Georgie Fame and The Blue Flames
28 January	1	GO NOW	Moody Blues
4 February	2	YOU'VE LOST THAT LOVIN' FEELIN' ▲	Righteous Brothers
18 February	1	TIRED OF WAITING FOR YOU	Kinks
25 February	2	I'LL NEVER FIND ANOTHER YOU	Seekers
11 March	1	IT'S NOT UNUSUAL	Tom Jones
18 March	3	THE LAST TIME	Rolling Stones
8 April	1	CONCRETE AND CLAY	Unit Four Plus Two
15 April	1	THE MINUTE YOU'RE GONE	Cliff Richard
22 April	3	TICKET TO RIDE ▲	Beatles
13 May	1	KING OF THE ROAD	Roger Miller
20 May	1	WHERE ARE YOU NOW (MY LOVE)	Jackie Trent
27 May	3	LONG LIVE LOVE	Sandie Shaw
17 June	1	CRYING IN THE CHAPEL	Elvis Presley
24 June	1	I'M ALIVE	Hollies
1 July	1	CRYING IN THE CHAPEL	Elvis Presley
8 July	2	I'M ALIVE	Hollies
22 July	2	MR TAMBOURINE MAN ▲	Byrds
5 August	3	HELP! ▲	Beatles
26 August	2	I GOT YOU BABE ▲	Sonny and Cher
9 September	2	(I CAN'T GET NO) SATISFACTION ▲	Rolling Stones
23 September	1	MAKE IT EASY ON YOURSELF	Walker Brothers
30 September	5	TEARS	Ken Dodd
4 November	2	GET OFF OF MY CLOUD ▲	Rolling Stones
25 November	3	THE CARNIVAL IS OVER	Seekers
16 December	5	DAY TRIPPER/WE CAN WORK IT OUT ▲	Beatles

1966

DATE	WKS	TITLE	ARTIST
20 January	1	KEEP ON RUNNING	Spencer Davis Group
27 January	3	MICHELLE	Overlanders
17 February	4	THESE BOOTS ARE MADE FOR WALKIN' ▲	Nancy Sinatra
17 March	4	THE SUN AIN'T GONNA SHINE ANY MORE	Walker Brothers
14 April	2	SOMEBODY HELP ME	Spencer Davis Group
28 April	1	YOU DON'T HAVE TO SAY YOU LOVE ME	Dusty Springfield
5 May	3	PRETTY FLAMINGO	Manfred Mann
26 May	1	PAINT IT, BLACK ▲	Rolling Stones
2 June	3	STRANGERS IN THE NIGHT ▲	Frank Sinatra
23 June	2	PAPERBACK WRITER ▲	Beatles
7 July	2	SUNNY AFTERNOON	Kinks
21 July	1	GET AWAY	Georgie Fame and The Blue Flames
28 July	1	OUT OF TIME	Chris Farlowe
4 August	2	WITH A GIRL LIKE YOU	Troggs
18 August	4	YELLOW SUBMARINE/ELEANOR RIGBY	Beatles
15 September	1	ALL OR NOTHING	Small Faces
22 September	5	DISTANT DRUMS	Jim Reeves
27 October	3	REACH OUT I'LL BE THERE ▲	Four Tops
17 November	2	GOOD VIBRATIONS ▲	Beach Boys
1 December	7	GREEN GREEN GRASS OF HOME	Tom Jones

1967

DATE	WKS	TITLE	ARTIST
19 January	4	I'M A BELIEVER ▲	Monkees
16 February	2	THIS IS MY SONG	Petula Clark
2 March	6	RELEASE ME	Engelbert Humperdinck
13 April	2	SOMETHIN' STUPID ▲	Nancy Sintra and Frank Sinatra
27 April	3	PUPPET ON A STRING	Sandie Shaw
18 May	3	SILENCE IS GOLDEN	Tremeloes
8 June	6	A WHITER SHADE OF PALE	Procol Harum
19 July	3	ALL YOU NEED IS LOVE ▲	Beatles
9 August	4	SAN FRANCISCO (BE SURE TO WEAR SOME FLOWERS IN YOUR HAIR)	Scott McKenzie
6 September	5	THE LAST WALTZ	Engelbert Humperdinck
11 October	4	MASSACHUSETTS	Bee Gees
8 November	2	BABY NOW THAT I'VE FOUND YOU	Foundations
22 November	2	LET THE HEARTACHES BEGIN	Long John Baldry
6 December	7	HELLO GOODBYE ▲	Beatles

1968

DATE	WKS	TITLE	ARTIST
24 January	1	BALLAD OF BONNIE AND CLYDE	Georgie Fame
31 January	2	EVERLASTING LOVE	Love Affair
14 February	2	MIGHTY QUINN	Manfred Mann
28 February	3	CINDERELLA ROCKEFELLA	Esther and Abi Ofarim
20 March	1	THE LEGEND OF XANADU	Dave Dee, Dozy, Beaky, Mick and Tich
27 March	2	LADY MADONNA	Beatles
10 April	2	CONGRATULATIONS	Cliff Richard
24 April	4	WHAT A WONDERFUL WORLD/CABARET	Louis Armstrong
22 May	4	YOUNG GIRL	Union Gap Featuring Gary Puckett
19 June	2	JUMPING JACK FLASH	Rolling Stones
3 July	3	BABY COME BACK	Equals
24 July	1	I PRETEND	Des O'connor
31 July	2	MONY MONY	Tommy James and The Shondells
14 August	1	FIRE	Crazy World of Arthur Brown
21 August	1	MONY MONY	Tommy James and The Shondells
28 August	1	DO IT AGAIN	Beach Boys
4 September	1	I'VE GOTTA GET A MESSAGE TO YOU	Bee Gees
11 September	2	HEY JUDE ▲	Beatles
25 September	6	THOSE WERE THE DAYS	Mary Hopkin
6 November	1	WITH A LITTLE HELP FROM MY FRIENDS	Joe Cocker
13 November	4	THE GOOD THE BAD AND THE UGLY	Hugo Montenegro
11 December	3	LILY THE PINK	Scaffold

1969

DATE	WKS	TITLE	ARTIST
1 January	1	OB-LA-DI OB-LA-DA	Marmalade
8 January	1	LILY THE PINK	Scaffold
15 January	2	OB-LA-DI OB-LA-DA	Marmalade
29 January	1	ALBATROSS	Fleetwood Mac
5 February	1	BLACKBERRY WAY	Move
12 February	2	(IF PARADISE IS) HALF AS NICE	Amen Corner
26 February	4	WHERE DO YOU GO TO MY LOVELY	Peter Sarstedt
26 March	3	I HEARD IT THROUGH THE GRAPEVINE ▲	Marvin Gaye
16 April	1	THE ISRAELITES	Desmond Dekker and The Aces
23 April	6	GET BACK ↑ ▲	Beatles with Billy Preston
4 June	1	DIZZY ▲	Tommy Roe
11 June	3	THE BALLAD OF JOHN AND YOKO	Beatles
2 July	3	SOMETHING IN THE AIR	Thunderclap Newman
23 July	5	HONKY TONK WOMEN ▲	Rolling Stones
30 August	3	IN THE YEAR 2525 (EXORDIUM AND TERMINUS) ▲	Zager and Evans

↑ Entered the UK chart at number one   ▲ Topped the US chart

DATE	WKS	TITLE	ARTIST
20 September	3	**BAD MOON RISING**	Creedence Clearwater Revival
11 October	1	**JE T'AIME...MOI NON PLUS**	Jane Birkin and Serge Gainsbourg
18 October	1	**I'LL NEVER FALL IN LOVE AGAIN**	Bobbie Gentry
25 October	8	**SUGAR SUGAR ▲**	Archies
20 December	6	**TWO LITTLE BOYS**	Rolf Harris

1970

DATE	WKS	TITLE	ARTIST
31 January	5	**LOVE GROWS (WHERE MY ROSEMARY GROWS)**	Edison Lighthouse
7 March	3	**WAND'RIN' STAR**	Lee Marvin
28 March	3	**BRIDGE OVER TROUBLED WATER ▲**	Simon and Garfunkel
18 April	2	**ALL KINDS OF EVERYTHING**	Dana
2 May	2	**SPIRIT IN THE SKY**	Norman Greenbaum
16 May	3	**BACK HOME**	England World Cup Squad
6 June	1	**YELLOW RIVER**	Christie
13 June	7	**IN THE SUMMERTIME**	Mungo Jerry
1 August	6	**THE WONDER OF YOU**	Elvis Presley
12 September	1	**TEARS OF A CLOWN ▲**	Smokey Robinson and The Miracles
19 September	6	**BAND OF GOLD**	Freda Payne
31 October	3	**WOODSTOCK**	Matthews' Southern Comfort
21 November	1	**VOODOO CHILE**	Jimi Hendrix Experience
28 November	6	**I HEAR YOU KNOCKIN'**	Dave Edmunds' Rockpile

1971

DATE	WKS	TITLE	ARTIST
9 January	3	**GRANDAD**	Clive Dunn
30 January	5	**MY SWEET LORD ▲**	George Harrison
6 March	2	**BABY JUMP**	Mungo Jerry
20 March	6	**HOT LOVE**	T Rex
1 May	2	**DOUBLE BARREL**	Dave and Ansil Collins
15 May	5	**KNOCK THREE TIMES ▲**	Dawn
19 June	5	**CHIRPY CHIRPY CHEEP CHEEP**	Middle of The Road
24 July	4	**GET IT ON**	T Rex
21 August	4	**I'M STILL WAITING**	Diana Ross
18 September	3	**HEY GIRL DON'T BOTHER ME**	Tams
9 October	5	**REASON TO BELIEVE/MAGGIE MAY ▲**	Rod Stewart
13 November	4	**COZ I LUV YOU**	Slade
11 December	4	**ERNIE (THE FASTEST MILKMAN IN THE WEST)**	Benny Hill

1972

DATE	WKS	TITLE	ARTIST
8 January	4	**I'D LIKE TO TEACH THE WORLD TO SING (IN PERFECT HARMONY)**	New Seekers
5 February	2	**TELEGRAM SAM**	T Rex
19 February	3	**SON OF MY FATHER**	Chicory Tip
11 March	5	**WITHOUT YOU ▲**	Nilsson
15 April	5	**AMAZING GRACE**	Pipes and Drums and Military Band of The Royal Scots Dragoon Guards
20 May	4	**METAL GURU**	T Rex
17 June	2	**VINCENT**	Don Mclean
1 July	1	**TAKE ME BAK 'OME**	Slade
8 July	5	**PUPPY LOVE**	Donny Osmond
12 August	3	**SCHOOL'S OUT**	Alice Cooper
2 September	1	**YOU WEAR IT WELL**	Rod Stewart
9 September	3	**MAMA WEER ALL CRAZEE NOW**	Slade
30 September	2	**HOW CAN I BE SURE**	David Cassidy
14 October	4	**MOULDY OLD DOUGH**	Lieutenant Pigeon
11 November	2	**CLAIR**	Gilbert O'Sullivan
25 November	4	**MY DING-A-LING ▲**	Chuck Berry
23 December	5	**LONG HAIRED LOVER FROM LIVERPOOL**	Little Jimmy Osmond

1973

DATE	WKS	TITLE	ARTIST
27 January	5	**BLOCKBUSTER**	Sweet
3 March	4	**CUM ON FEEL THE NOIZE ↑**	Slade
31 March	1	**THE TWELFTH OF NEVER**	Donny Osmond
7 April	2	**GET DOWN**	Gilbert O'Sullivan
21 April	4	**TIE A YELLOW RIBBON ROUND THE OLD OAK TREE ▲**	Dawn Featuring Tony Orlando
19 May	4	**SEE MY BABY JIVE**	Wizzard
16 June	1	**CAN THE CAN**	Suzi Quatro
23 June	1	**RUBBER BULLETS**	10 CC
30 June	3	**SKWEEZE ME PLEEZE ME ↑**	Slade
21 July	1	**WELCOME HOME**	Peters and Lee
28 July	4	**I'M THE LEADER OF THE GANG (I AM)**	Gary Glitter
25 August	4	**YOUNG LOVE**	Donny Osmond
22 September	1	**ANGEL FINGERS**	Wizzard
29 September	4	**EYE LEVEL**	Simon Park Orchestra
27 October	3	**DAYDREAMER/THE PUPPY SONG**	David Cassidy
17 November	4	**I LOVE YOU LOVE ME LOVE ↑**	Gary Glitter
15 December	5	**MERRY XMAS EVERYBODY ↑**	Slade

1974

DATE	WKS	TITLE	ARTIST
19 January	1	**YOU WON'T FIND ANOTHER FOOL LIKE ME**	New Seekers
26 January	4	**TIGER FEET**	Mud
23 February	2	**DEVIL GATE DRIVE**	Suzi Quatro
9 March	1	**JEALOUS MIND**	Alvin Stardust
16 March	3	**BILLY DON'T BE A HERO**	Paper Lace
6 April	4	**SEASONS IN THE SUN ▲**	Terry Jacks
4 May	2	**WATERLOO**	Abba
18 May	4	**SUGAR BABY LOVE**	Rubettes
15 June	1	**THE STREAK ▲**	Ray Stevens
22 June	1	**ALWAYS YOURS**	Gary Glitter
29 June	4	**SHE**	Charles Aznavour
27 July	3	**ROCK YOUR BABY ▲**	George Mccrae
17 August	2	**WHEN WILL I SEE YOU AGAIN**	Three Degrees
31 August	3	**LOVE ME FOR A REASON**	Osmonds
21 September	3	**KUNG FU FIGHTING ▲**	Carl Douglas
12 October	1	**ANNIE'S SONG ▲**	John Denver
19 October	1	**SAD SWEET DREAMER**	Sweet Sensation
26 October	3	**EVERYTHING I OWN**	Ken Boothe
16 November	3	**GONNA MAKE YOU A STAR**	David Essex
7 December	2	**YOU'RE THE FIRST THE LAST MY EVERYTHING**	Barry White
21 December	4	**LONELY THIS CHRISTMAS**	Mud

1975

DATE	WKS	TITLE	ARTIST
18 January	1	**DOWN DOWN**	Status Quo
25 January	1	**MS GRACE**	Tymes
1 February	3	**JANUARY**	Pilot
22 February	2	**MAKE ME SMILE (COME UP AND SEE ME)**	Steve Harley and Cockney Rebel
8 March	2	**IF**	Telly Savalas
22 March	6	**BYE BYE BABY**	Bay City Rollers
3 May	2	**OH BOY**	Mud
17 May	3	**STAND BY YOUR MAN**	Tammy Wynette
7 June	3	**WHISPERING GRASS**	Windsor Davies and Don Estelle
28 June	2	**I'M NOT IN LOVE**	10 CC
12 July	1	**TEARS ON MY PILLOW**	Johnny Nash
19 July	3	**GIVE A LITTLE LOVE**	Bay City Rollers
9 August	1	**BARBADOS**	Typically Tropical
16 August	3	**CAN'T GIVE YOU ANYTHING (BUT MY LOVE)**	Stylistics
6 September	4	**SAILING**	Rod Stewart
4 October	3	**HOLD ME CLOSE**	David Essex

 ↑ Entered the UK chart at number one ▲ Topped the US chart

DATE	WKS	TITLE	ARTIST
25 October	2	I ONLY HAVE EYES FOR YOU	Art Garfunkel
8 November	2	SPACE ODDITY	David Bowie
22 November	1	D.I.V.O.R.C.E.	Billy Connolly
29 November	9	BOHEMIAN RHAPSODY	Queen

1976

DATE	WKS	TITLE	ARTIST
31 January	2	MAMMA MIA	Abba
14 February	1	FOREVER AND EVER	Slik
21 February	2	DECEMBER '63 (OH WHAT A NIGHT) ▲	Four Seasons
6 March	3	I LOVE TO LOVE (BUT MY BABY LOVES TO DANCE)	Tina Charles
27 March	6	SAVE YOUR KISSES FOR ME	Brotherhood of Man
8 May	4	FERNANDO	Abba
5 June	1	NO CHARGE	J J Barrie
12 June	2	COMBINE HARVESTER (BRAND NEW KEY)	Wurzels
26 June	3	YOU TO ME ARE EVERYTHING	Real Thing
17 July	1	THE ROUSSOS PHENOMENON (EP)	Demis Roussos
24 July	6	DON'T GO BREAKING MY HEART ▲	Elton John and Kiki Dee
4 September	6	DANCING QUEEN ▲	Abba
11 October	4	MISSISSIPPI	Pussycat
13 November	3	IF YOU LEAVE ME NOW ▲	Chicago
4 December	3	UNDER THE MOON OF LOVE	Showaddywaddy
25 December	3	WHEN A CHILD IS BORN (SOLEADO)	Johnny Mathis

1977

DATE	WKS	TITLE	ARTIST
15 January	4	DON'T GIVE UP ON US ▲	David Soul
12 February	1	DON'T CRY FOR ME ARGENTINA	Julie Covington
19 February	3	WHEN I NEED YOU ▲	Leo Sayer
12 March	3	CHANSON D'AMOUR	Manhattan Transfer
2 April	5	KNOWING ME KNOWING YOU	Abba
7 May	2	FREE	Deniece Williams
21 May	4	I DON'T WANT TO TALK ABOUT IT/FIRST CUT IS THE DEEPEST	Rod Stewart
18 June	1	LUCILLE	Kenny Rogers
25 June	1	SHOW YOU THE WAY TO GO	Jacksons
2 July	3	SO YOU WIN AGAIN	Hot Chocolate
23 July	4	I FEEL LOVE	Donna Summer
20 August	1	ANGELO	Brotherhood of Man
27 August	1	FLOAT ON	Floaters
3 September	5	WAY DOWN	Elvis Presley
8 October	3	SILVER LADY	David Soul
29 October	1	YES SIR I CAN BOOGIE	Baccara
5 November	4	THE NAME OF THE GAME	Abba
3 December	9	MULL OF KINTYRE/GIRLS' SCHOOL	Wings

1978

DATE	WKS	TITLE	ARTIST
4 February	1	UP TOWN TOP RANKING	Althia and Donna
11 February	1	FIGARO	Brotherhood of Man
18 February	3	TAKE A CHANCE ON ME	Abba
11 March	4	WUTHERING HEIGHTS	Kate Bush
8 April	3	MATCHSTALK MEN AND MATCHSTALK CATS AND DOGS	Brian and Michael
29 April	2	NIGHT FEVER ▲	Bee Gees
13 May	5	RIVERS OF BABYLON/BROWN GIRL IN THE RING	Boney M
17 June	9	YOU'RE THE ONE THAT I WANT ▲	John Travolta and Olivia Newton-John
19 August	5	THREE TIMES A LADY ▲	Commodores
23 September	1	DREADLOCK HOLIDAY	10 CC
30 September	7	SUMMER NIGHTS	John Travolta and Olivia Newton-John
18 November	2	RAT TRAP	Boomtown Rats
2 December	1	DO YA THINK I'M SEXY ▲	Rod Stewart
9 December	4	MARY'S BOY CHILD-OH MY LORD	Boney M

1979

DATE	WKS	TITLE	ARTIST
6 January	3	Y.M.C.A.	Village People
27 January	1	HIT ME WITH YOUR RHYTHM STICK	Ian and The Blockheads
3 February	4	HEART OF GLASS ▲	Blondie
3 March	2	TRAGEDY ▲	Bee Gees
17 March	4	I WILL SURVIVE ▲	Gloria Gaynor
14 April	6	BRIGHT EYES	Art Garfunkel
26 May	3	SUNDAY GIRL	Blondie
16 June	2	RING MY BELL ▲	Anita Ward
30 June	4	ARE 'FRIENDS' ELECTRIC?	Tubeway Army
28 July	4	I DON'T LIKE MONDAYS	Boomtown Rats
25 August	4	WE DON'T TALK ANYMORE	Cliff Richard
22 September	1	CARS	Gary Numan
29 September	3	MESSAGE IN A BOTTLE	Police
20 October	3	VIDEO KILLED THE RADIO STAR	Buggles
27 October	3	ONE DAY AT A TIME	Lena Martell
17 November	3	WHEN YOU'RE IN LOVE WITH A BEAUTIFUL WOMAN	Dr Hook
8 December	1	WALKING ON THE MOON	Police
15 December	5	ANOTHER BRICK IN THE WALL (PART II) ▲	Pink Floyd

1980

DATE	WKS	TITLE	ARTIST
19 January	2	BRASS IN POCKET	Pretenders
2 February	2	THE SPECIAL AKA LIVE (EP)	Specials
16 February	2	COWARD OF THE COUNTY	Kenny Rogers
1 March	2	ATOMIC	Blondie
15 March	1	TOGETHER WE ARE BEAUTIFUL	Fern Kinney
22 March	3	GOING UNDERGROUND/DREAMS OF CHILDREN ↑	Jam
12 April	2	WORKING MY WAY BACK TO YOU-FORGIVE ME GIRL	Detroit Spinners
26 April	1	CALL ME ▲	Blondie
3 May	2	GENO	Dexy's Midnight Runners
17 May	2	WHAT'S ANOTHER YEAR	Johnny Logan
31 May	3	THEME FROM M*A*S*H (SUICIDE IS PAINLESS)	MASH
21 June	3	CRYING	Don Mclean
12 July	2	XANADU	Olivia Newton-John and Electric Light Orchestra
26 July	2	USE IT UP AND WEAR IT OUT	Odyssey
9 August	2	THE WINNER TAKES IT ALL	Abba
23 August	2	ASHES TO ASHES	David Bowie
6 September	1	START	Jam
13 September	2	FEELS LIKE I'M IN LOVE	Kelly Marie
27 September	4	DON'T STAND SO CLOSE TO ME ↑	Police
25 October	3	WOMAN IN LOVE ▲	Barbra Streisand
15 November	2	THE TIDE IS HIGH ▲	Blondie
29 November	3	SUPER TROUPER	Abba
20 December	1	(JUST LIKE) STARTING OVER ▲	John Lennon
27 December	2	THERE'S NO ONE QUITE LIKE GRANDMA	St Winifred's School Choir

1981

DATE	WKS	TITLE	ARTIST
10 January	4	IMAGINE	John Lennon
7 February	2	WOMAN	John Lennon
21 February	3	SHADDAP YOU FACE	Joe Dolce Music Theatre
14 March	2	JEALOUS GUY	Roxy Music
28 March	3	THIS OLE HOUSE	Shakin' Stevens
18 April	3	MAKING YOUR MIND UP	Bucks Fizz
9 May	5	STAND AND DELIVER ↑	Adam and The Ants
13 June	2	BEING WITH YOU	Smokey Robinson
27 June	2	ONE DAY IN YOUR LIFE	Michael Jackson
11 July	3	GHOST TOWN	Specials
1 August	4	GREEN DOOR	Shakin' Stevens
29 August	1	JAPANESE BOY	Aneka
5 September	2	TAINTED LOVE	Soft Cell

↑ Entered the UK chart at number one ▲ Topped the US chart

DATE	WKS	TITLE	ARTIST
19 September	4	PRINCE CHARMING	Adam and The Ants
17 October	4	IT'S MY PARTY	Dave Stewart with Barbara Gaskin
14 November	1	EVERY LITTLE THING SHE DOES IS MAGIC	Police
21 November	2	UNDER PRESSURE	Queen and David Bowie
5 December	1	BEGIN THE BEGUINE (VOLVER A EMPEZAR)	Julio Iglesias
12 December	5	DON'T YOU WANT ME ▲	Human League

1982

DATE	WKS	TITLE	ARTIST
16 January	2	THE LAND OF MAKE BELIEVE	Bucks Fizz
30 January	1	OH JULIE	Shakin' Stevens
6 February	1	THE MODEL/COMPUTER LOVE	Kraftwerk
13 February	3	A TOWN CALLED MALICE/PRECIOUS ↑	Jam
6 March	3	THE LION SLEEPS TONIGHT	Tight Fit
27 March	3	SEVEN TEARS	Goombay Dance Band
17 April	1	MY CAMERA NEVER LIES	Bucks Fizz
24 April	3	EBONY AND IVORY ▲	Paul McCartney and Stevie Wonder
15 May	2	A LITTLE PEACE	Nicole
29 May	2	HOUSE OF FUN	Madness
12 June	2	GOODY TWO SHOES	Adam and the Ants
26 June	1	I'VE NEVER BEEN TO ME	Charlene
3 July	2	HAPPY TALK	Captain Sensible
17 July	3	FAME	Irene Cara
7 August	4	COME ON EILEEN ▲	Dexy's Midnight Runners
4 September	4	EYE OF THE TIGER ▲	Survivor
2 October	3	PASS THE DUTCHIE	Musical Youth
23 October	3	DO YOU REALLY WANT TO HURT ME	Culture Club
13 November	3	I DON'T WANNA DANCE	Eddy Grant
4 December	2	BEAT SURRENDER ↑	Jam
18 December	4	SAVE YOUR LOVE	Renee and Renato

1983

DATE	WKS	TITLE	ARTIST
15 January	2	YOU CAN'T HURRY LOVE	Phil Collins
29 January	3	DOWN UNDER ▲	Men At Work
19 February	2	TOO SHY	Kajagoogoo
5 March	1	BILLIE JEAN ▲	Michael Jackson
12 March	2	TOTAL ECLIPSE OF THE HEART ▲	Bonnie Tyler
26 March	2	IS THERE SOMETHING I SHOULD KNOW ↑	Duran Duran
9 April	3	LET'S DANCE ▲	David Bowie
30 April	4	TRUE	Spandau Ballet
28 May	1	CANDY GIRL	New Edition
4 June	4	EVERY BREATH YOU TAKE ▲	Police
2 July	3	BABY JANE	Rod Stewart
23 July	3	WHEREVER I LAY MY HAT (THAT'S MY HOME)	Paul Young
13 August	3	GIVE IT UP	KC and The Sunshine Band
3 September	3	RED RED WINE ▲	UB40
24 September	6	KARMA CHAMELEON ▲	Culture Club
5 November	5	UPTOWN GIRL	Billy Joel
10 December	5	ONLY YOU	Flying Pickets

1984

DATE	WKS	TITLE	ARTIST
14 January	2	PIPES OF PEACE	Paul Mccartney
28 January	5	RELAX	Frankie Goes To Hollywood
3 March	3	99 RED BALLOONS	Nena
24 March	6	HELLO ▲	Lionel Richie
5 May	4	THE REFLEX ▲	Duran Duran
2 June	2	WAKE ME UP BEFORE YOU GO GO ▲	Wham!
16 June	9	TWO TRIBES ↑	Frankie Goes To Hollywood
18 August	3	CARELESS WHISPER ▲	George Michael
8 September	6	I JUST CALLED TO SAY I LOVE YOU ▲	Stevie Wonder

DATE	WKS	TITLE	ARTIST
20 October	3	FREEDOM	Wham!
10 November	3	I FEEL FOR YOU	Chaka Khan
1 December	1	I SHOULD HAVE KNOWN BETTER	Jim Diamond
8 December	1	THE POWER OF LOVE	Frankie Goes To Hollywood
15 December	5	DO THEY KNOW IT'S CHRISTMAS? ↑	Band Aid

1985

DATE	WKS	TITLE	ARTIST
19 January	3	I WANT TO KNOW WHAT LOVE IS ▲	Foreigner
9 February	4	I KNOW HIM SO WELL	Elaine Paige and Barbara Dickson
9 March	2	YOU SPIN ME ROUND (LIKE A RECORD)	Dead Or Alive
23 March	4	EASY LOVER	Philip Bailey (Duet with Phil Collins)
20 April	2	WE ARE THE WORLD ▲	USA For Africa
4 May	1	MOVE CLOSER	Phyllis Nelson
11 May	5	19	Paul Hardcastle
15 June	2	YOU'LL NEVER WALK ALONE	Crowd
29 June	4	FRANKIE	Sister Sledge
27 July	1	THERE MUST BE AN ANGEL (PLAYING WITH MY HEART)	Eurythmics
3 August	4	INTO THE GROOVE	Madonna
31 August	1	I GOT YOU BABE	UB40 Featuring Chrissie Hynde
7 September	4	DANCING IN THE STREET ↑	David Bowie and Mick Jagger
5 October	1	IF I WAS	Midge Ure
12 October	5	THE POWER OF LOVE	Jennifer Rush
16 November	2	A GOOD HEART	Feargal Sharkey
30 November	1	I'M YOUR MAN	Wham!
14 December	2	SAVING ALL MY LOVE FOR YOU ▲	Whitney Houston
28 December	2	MERRY CHRISTMAS EVERYONE	Shakin' Stevens

1986

DATE	WKS	TITLE	ARTIST
11 January	2	WEST END GIRLS ▲	Pet Shop Boys
25 January	2	THE SUN ALWAYS SHINES ON TV	A-Ha
8 February	4	WHEN THE GOING GETS TOUGH, THE TOUGH GET GOING	Billy Ocean
8 March	3	CHAIN REACTION	Diana Ross
29 March	3	LIVING DOLL	Cliff Richard and The Young Ones Featuring Hank B Marvin
19 April	3	A DIFFERENT CORNER	George Michael
10 May	1	ROCK ME AMADEUS ▲	Falco
17 May	3	THE CHICKEN SONG	Spitting Image
7 June	3	SPIRIT IN THE SKY	Doctor and The Medics
28 June	2	THE EDGE OF HEAVEN/WHERE DID YOUR HEART GO	Wham!
12 July	3	PAPA DON'T PREACH ▲	Madonna
2 August	3	THE LADY IN RED	Chris De Burgh
23 August	3	I WANT TO WAKE UP WITH YOU	Boris Gardiner
13 September	4	DON'T LEAVE ME THIS WAY	Communards with Sarah-Jane Morris
11 October	1	TRUE BLUE	Madonna
18 October	3	EVERY LOSER WINS	Nick Berry
8 November	4	TAKE MY BREATH AWAY ▲	Berlin
6 December	2	THE FINAL COUNTDOWN	Europe
20 December	1	CARAVAN OF LOVE	Housemartins
27 December	4	REET PETITE	Jackie Wilson

1987

DATE	WKS	TITLE	ARTIST
24 January	2	JACK YOUR BODY	Steve 'Silk' Hurley
7 February	2	I KNEW YOU WERE WAITING (FOR ME) ▲	Aretha Franklin and George Michael
21 February	3	STAND BY ME	Ben E King

DATE	WKS	TITLE	ARTIST
14 March	2	EVERYTHING I OWN	Boy George
28 March	1	RESPECTABLE	Mel and Kim
4 April	3	LET IT BE ↑	Ferry Aid
25 April	2	LA ISLA BONITA	Madonna
9 May	4	NOTHING'S GONNA STOP US NOW ▲	Starship
6 June	2	I WANNA DANCE WITH SOMEBODY (WHO LOVES ME) ▲	Whitney Houston
20 June	2	STAR TREKKIN'	Firm
4 July	3	IT'S A SIN	Pet Shop Boys
25 July	2	WHO'S THAT GIRL ▲	Madonna
1 August	2	LA BAMBA ▲	Los Lobos
15 August	2	I JUST CAN'T STOP LOVING YOU ▲	Michael Jackson
29 August	5	NEVER GONNA GIVE YOU UP ▲	Rick Astley
3 October	2	PUMP UP THE VOLUME/ANITINA (THE FIRST TIME I SEE SHE DANCE)	M/A/R/R/S
17 October	4	YOU WIN AGAIN	Bee Gees
14 November	5	CHINA IN YOUR HAND	T'Pau
19 December	4	ALWAYS ON MY MIND	Pet Shop Boys

1988

DATE	WKS	TITLE	ARTIST
16 January	2	HEAVEN IS A PLACE ON EARTH ▲	Belinda Carlisle
30 January	3	I THINK WE'RE ALONE NOW ▲	Tiffany
20 February	5	I SHOULD BE SO LUCKY	Kylie Minogue
26 March	2	DON'T TURN AROUND	Aswad
9 April	3	HEART	Pet Shop Boys
30 April	2	THEME FROM S-EXPRESS	S-Express
14 May	1	PERFECT	Fairground Attraction
21 May	4	WITH A LITTLE HELP FROM MY FRIENDS/SHE'S LEAVING HOME	Wet Wet Wet/Billy Bragg with Cara Tivey
18 June	1	DOCTORIN' THE TARDIS	Timelords
25 June	2	I OWE YOU NOTHING	Bros
9 July	4	NOTHING'S GONNA CHANGE MY LOVE FOR YOU	Glenn Medeiros
6 August	5	THE ONLY WAY IS UP	Yazz and The Plastic Population
10 September	2	A GROOVY KIND OF LOVE ▲	Phil Collins
24 September	2	HE AIN'T HEAVY HE'S MY BROTHER	Hollies
8 October	1	DESIRE	U2
15 October	2	ONE MOMENT IN TIME	Whitney Houston
29 October	3	ORINOCO FLOW	Enya
19 November	3	FIRST TIME	Robin Beck
10 December	4	MISTLETOE AND WINE	Cliff Richard

1989

DATE	WKS	TITLE	ARTIST
7 January	3	ESPECIALLY FOR YOU	Kylie Minogue and Jason Donovan
28 January	4	SOMETHING'S GOTTEN HOLD OF MY HEART	Marc Almond with Gene Pitney
25 February	2	BELFAST CHILD	Simple Minds
11 March	2	TOO MANY BROKEN HEARTS	Jason Donovan
25 March	3	LIKE A PRAYER ▲	Madonna
15 April	4	ETERNAL FLAME ▲	Bangles
13 May	1	HAND ON YOUR HEART	Kylie Minogue
20 May	3	FERRY 'CROSS THE MERSEY ↑	Christians, Holly Johnson, Paul McCartney, Gerry Marsden and Stock Aitken Waterman
10 June	2	SEALED WITH A KISS ↑	Jason Donovan
24 June	4	BACK TO LIFE (HOWEVER DO YOU WANT ME)	Soul II Soul
22 July	2	YOU'LL NEVER STOP ME LOVING YOU	Sonia
5 August	5	SWING THE MOOD	Jive Bunny and The Mastermixers
9 September	6	RIDE ON TIME	Black Box

DATE	WKS	TITLE	ARTIST
21 October	3	THAT'S WHAT I LIKE	Jive Bunny and The Mastermixers
11 November	2	ALL AROUND THE WORLD	Lisa Stansfield
25 November	3	YOU GOT IT (THE RIGHT STUFF)	New Kids On The Block
16 December	1	LET'S PARTY ↑	Jive Bunny and The Mastermixers
23 December	3	DO THEY KNOW IT'S CHRISTMAS? ↑	Band Aid II

1990

DATE	WKS	TITLE	ARTIST
13 January	2	HANGIN' TOUGH ▲	New Kids On The Block
27 January	1	TEARS ON MY PILLOW	Kylie Minogue
3 February	4	NOTHING COMPARES 2 U ▲	Sinead O'Connor
3 March	4	DUB BE GOOD TO ME	Beats International Featuring Lindy Layton
31 March	2	THE POWER	Snap
14 April	2	VOGUE ▲	Madonna
12 May	4	KILLER	Adamski
9 June	2	WORLD IN MOTION	Englandneworder
23 June	5	SACRIFICE/HEALING HANDS	Elton John
28 July	4	TURTLE POWER	Partners In Kryme
25 August	3	ITSY BITSY TEENY WEENY YELLOW POLKA DOT BIKINI	Bombalurina Featuring Timmy Mallett
15 September	2	THE JOKER ▲	Steve Miller Band
29 September	4	SHOW ME HEAVEN	Maria McKee
27 October	1	A LITTLE TIME	The Beautiful South
3 November	4	UNCHAINED MELODY	Righteous Brothers
1 December	4	ICE ICE BABY ▲	Vanilla Ice
29 December	1	SAVIOUR'S DAY	Cliff Richard

1991

DATE	WKS	TITLE	ARTIST
5 January	2	BRING YOUR DAUGHTER...TO THE SLAUGHTER ↑	Iron Maiden
19 January	1	SADNESS PART 1	Enigma
26 January	1	INNUENDO ↑	Queen
2 February	2	3AM ETERNAL	KLF Featuring Children of The Revolution
16 February	3	DO THE BARTMAN	Simpsons
9 March	2	SHOULD I STAY OR SHOULD I GO	Clash
23 March	1	THE STONK	Hale and Pace and The Stonkers
30 March	5	THE ONE AND ONLY	Chesney Hawkes
4 May	5	THE SHOOOP SHOOP SONG (IT'S IN HIS KISS)	Cher
8 June	3	I WANNA SEX YOU UP	Color Me Badd
29 June	2	ANY DREAM WILL DO	Jason Donovan
13 July	16	(EVERYTHING I DO) I DO IT FOR YOU ▲	Bryan Adams
2 November	1	THE FLY ↑	U2
9 November	2	DIZZY	Vic Reeves and The Wonder Stuff
23 November	2	BLACK OR WHITE ↑ ▲	Michael Jackson
7 December	2	DON'T LET THE SUN GO DOWN ON ME ↑ ▲	George Michael and Elton John
21 December	5	BOHEMIAN RHAPSODY/THESE ARE THE DAYS OF OUR LIVES ↑	Queen

1992

DATE	WKS	TITLE	ARTIST
25 January	4	GOODNIGHT GIRL	Wet Wet Wet
22 February	8	STAY	Shakespears Sister
18 April	3	DEEPLY DIPPY	Right Said Fred
9 May	5	PLEASE DON'T GO/GAME BOY	KWS
13 June	5	ABBA-ESQUE (EP) ↑	Erasure
18 July	3	AIN'T NO DOUBT	Jimmy Nail
8 August	6	RHYTHM IS A DANCER	Snap
19 September	4	EBENEEZER GOODE	Shamen

↑ Entered the UK chart at number one   ▲ Topped the US chart

DATE	WKS	TITLE	ARTIST
17 October	2	SLEEPING SATELLITE	Tasmin Archer
31 October	3	END OF THE ROAD ▲	Boyz II Men
21 November	2	WOULD I LIE TO YOU	Charles and Eddie
5 December	10	I WILL ALWAYS LOVE YOU ▲	Whitney Houston

1993

DATE	WKS	TITLE	ARTIST
13 February	5	NO LIMIT	2 Unlimited
20 March	2	OH CAROLINA	Shaggy
3 April	4	YOUNG AT HEART	Bluebells
1 May	3	FIVE LIVE EP	George Michael and Queen with Lisa Stansfield
22 May	3	ALL THAT SHE WANTS	Ace of Bass
12 June		(I CAN'T HELP) FALLING IN LOVE WITH YOU ▲	UB40
26 June	3	DREAMS	Gabrielle
17 July	4	PRAY ↑	Take That
14 August	2	LIVING ON MY OWN	Freddie Mercury
28 August	4	MR VAIN	Culture Beat
25 September	2	BOOM! SHAKE THE ROOM	Jazzy Jeff and The Fresh Prince
9 October	2	RELIGHT MY FIRE ↑	Take That Featuring Lulu
23 October	7	I'D DO ANYTHING FOR LOVE (BUT I WON'T DO THAT) ▲	Meatloaf
11 December	1	MR BLOBBY	Mr Blobby
18 December	1	BABE ↑	Take That
25 December	2	MR BLOBBY	Mr Blobby

1994

DATE	WKS	TITLE	ARTIST
8 January	2	TWIST AND SHOUT	Chaka Demus and Pliers Featuring Jack Radics and Taxi Gang
22 January	4	THINGS CAN ONLY GET BETTER	D:Ream
19 February	4	WITHOUT YOU ↑	Mariah Carey
19 March	3	DOOP	Doop
9 April	2	EVERYTHING CHANGES ↑	Take That
23 April	2	THE MOST BEAUTIFUL GIRL IN THE WORLD	Prince
7 May	1	THE REAL THING	Tony Di Bart
14 May	1	INSIDE	Stiltskin
21 May	2	COME ON YOU REDS	Manchester United Football Squad
4 June	15	LOVE IS ALL AROUND	Wet Wet Wet
17 September	4	SATURDAY NIGHT ↑	Whigfield
15 October	2	SURE ↑	Take That
29 October	4	BABY COME BACK	Pato Banton
26 November	2	LET ME BE YOUR FANTASY	Baby D
10 December	5	STAY ANOTHER DAY	East 17

1995

DATE	WKS	TITLE	ARTIST
14 January	2	COTTON EYE JOE	Rednex
4 February	6	THINK TWICE	Celine Dion
25 March	1	LOVE CAN BUILD A BRIDGE	Cher, Chrissie Hynde and Neneh Cherry with Eric Clapton
1 April	1	DON'T STOP (WIGGLE WIGGLE)	Outhere Brothers
8 April	4	BACK FOR GOOD ↑	Take That
6 May	1	SOME MIGHT SAY ↑	Oasis
13 May	1	DREAMER ↑	Livin' Joy
20 May	7	UNCHAINED MELODY/(THERE'LL BE BLUEBIRDS OVER) THE WHITE CLIFFS OF DOVER ↑	Robson Green and Jerome Flynn
8 July	4	BOOM BOOM BOOM	Outhere Brothers
5 August	3	NEVER FORGET ↑	Take That
26 August	2	COUNTRY HOUSE ↑	Blur
9 September	2	YOU ARE NOT ALONE ▲	Michael Jackson
23 September	1	BOOMBASTIC ↑	Shaggy

DATE	WKS	TITLE	ARTIST
30 September	4	FAIRGROUND ↑	Simply Red
28 October	2	GANGSTA'S PARADISE ↑ ▲	Coolio Featuring LV
11 November	4	I BELIEVE/UP ON THE ROOF ↑	Robson Green and Jerome Flynn
9 December	6	EARTH SONG ↑	Michael Jackson

1996

DATE	WKS	TITLE	ARTIST
20 January	1	JESUS TO A CHILD ↑	George Michael
27 January	5	SPACEMAN ↑	Babylon Zoo
2 March	1	DON'T LOOK BACK IN ANGER ↑	Oasis
9 March	3	HOW DEEP IS YOUR LOVE ↑	Take That
30 March	3	FIRESTARTER ↑	Prodigy
27 April	2	RETURN OF THE MACK ↑	Mark Morrison
4 May	3	FASTLOVE ↑	George Michael
25 May	1	OOH AAH...JUST A LITTLE BIT	Gina G
1 June	1	THREE LIONS (THE OFFICIAL SONG OF THE ENGLAND FOOTBALL TEAM) ↑	Baddiel & Skinner & Lightning Seeds
8 June	4	KILLING ME SOFTLY ↑	Fugees
6 July	1	THREE LIONS (THE OFFICIAL SONG OF THE ENGLAND FOOTBALL TEAM)	Baddiel & Skinner & Lightning Seeds
13 July	1	KILLING ME SOFTLY	Fugees
20 July	1	FOREVER LOVE ↑	Gary Barlow
27 July	7	WANNABE ▲	Spice Girls
14 September	1	FLAVA ↑	Peter Andre
21 September	2	READY OR NOT	Fugees
5 October	1	BREAKFAST AT TIFFANY'S	Deep Blue Something
12 October	1	SETTING SUN ↑	Chemical Brothers
19 October	1	WORDS ↑	Boyzone
26 October	1	SAY YOU'LL BE THERE ↑	Spice Girls
9 November	2	WHAT BECOMES OF THE BROKEN HEARTED/SATURDAY NIGHT AT THE MOVIES/YOU'LL NEVER WALK ALONE ↑	Robson Green and Jerome Flynn
23 November	2	BREATHE ↑	Prodigy
7 December	1	I FEEL YOU ↑	Peter Andre
14 December	1	A DIFFERENT BEAT ↑	Boyzone
21 December	1	KNOCKIN' ON HEAVEN'S DOOR/THROW THESE GUNS AWAY ↑	Dunblane
28 December	3	2 BECOME 1 ↑	Spice Girls

1997

DATE	WKS	TITLE	ARTIST
18 January	1	PROFESSIONAL WIDOW (IT'S GOT TO BE BIG)	Tori Amos
25 January	1	YOUR WOMAN ↑	White Town
1 February	1	BEETLEBUM ↑	Blur
8 February	1	AIN'T NOBODY ↑	LL Cool J
15 February	1	DISCOTHEQUE ↑	U2
22 February	3	DON'T SPEAK ↑	No Doubt
15 March	3	MAMA/WHO DO YOU THINK YOU ARE ↑	Spice Girls
5 April	1	BLOCK ROCKIN' BEATS ↑	Chemical Brothers
12 April	3	I BELIEVE I CAN FLY ↑	R Kelly
3 May	1	BLOOD ON THE DANCE FLOOR ↑	Michael Jackson
10 May	1	LOVE WON'T WAIT ↑	Gary Barlow
17 May	2	YOU'RE NOT ALONE ↑	Olive
31 May	1	I WANNA BE THE ONLY ONE ↑	Eternal Featuring Bebe Winans
7 June	3	MMMBOP ↑ ▲	Hanson
28 June	3	I'LL BE MISSING YOU ↑ ▲	Puff Daddy & Faith Evans & 112
19 July	1	D'YOU KNOW WHAT I MEAN? ↑	Oasis
24 July	3	I'LL BE MISSING YOU	Puff Daddy & Faith Evans & 112

↑ Entered the UK chart at number one   ▲ Topped the US chart

DATE	WKS	TITLE	ARTIST
16 August	4	MEN IN BLACK ↑	Will Smith
13 September	1	THE DRUGS DON'T WORK ↑	Verve
20 September	5	SOMETHING ABOUT THE WAY YOU LOOK TONIGHT/CANDLE IN THE WIND 1997↑ ▲	Elton John
24 October		SPICE UP YOUR LIFE ↑	Spice Girls
31 October	4	BARBIE GIRL	Aqua
29 November	2	PERFECT DAY ↑	Various Artists
13 December	2	TELETUBBIES SAY EH-OH! ↑	Teletubbies
27 December	2	TOO MUCH ↑	Spice Girls

1998

DATE	WKS	TITLE	ARTIST
10 January	1	PERFECT DAY ↑	Various Artists
17 January	1	NEVER EVER	All Saints
24 January	1	ALL AROUND THE WORLD ↑	Oasis
31 January	1	YOU MAKE ME WANNA… ↑	Usher
7 February	2	DOCTOR JONES ↑	Aqua
21 February	1	MY HEART WILL GO ON ↑ ▲	Celine Dion
28 February	1	BRIMFUL OF ASHA ↑	Cornershop
7 March	1	FROZEN ↑	Madonna
14 March	1	MY HEART WILL GO ON	Celine Dion
21 March	6	IT'S LIKE THAT ↑	Run DMC Versus Jason Nevins
2 May	1	ALL THAT I NEED ↑	Boyzone
9 May	1	UNDER THE BRIDGE/LADY MARMALADE ↑	All Saints
16 May	1	TURN BACK TIME ↑	Aqua
23 May	1	UNDER THE BRIDGE/LADY MARMALADE	All Saints
30 May	1	FEEL IT	Tamperer Featuring Maya
6 June	2	C'EST LA VIE ↑	B*Witched
20 June	3	THREE LIONS '98 ↑	Baddiel & Skinner & Lightning Seeds
11 July	1	BECAUSE WE WANT TO ↑	Billie
18 July	1	FREAK ME ↑	Another Level
25 July	1	DEEPER UNDERGROUND ↑	Jamiroquai
1 August	2	VIVA FOREVER ↑	Spice Girls
15 August	3	NO MATTER WHAT ↑	Boyzone
5 September	1	IF YOU TOLERATE THIS YOUR CHILDREN WILL BE NEXT ↑	Manic Street Preachers
12 September	1	BOOTIE CALL ↑	All Saints
19 September	1	MILLENNIUM ↑	Robbie Williams
26 September	1	I WANT YOU BACK ↑	Melanie B Featuring Missy 'Misdemeanor' Elliott
3 October	2	ROLLERCOASTER ↑	B*Witched
17 October	1	GIRLFRIEND ↑	Billie
24 October	1	GYM AND TONIC ↑	Spacedust
31 October	7	BELIEVE ↑ ▲	Cher
19 December	1	TO YOU I BELONG ↑	B*Witched
26 December	1	GOODBYE ↑	Spice Girls

1999

DATE	WKS	TITLE	ARTIST
2 January	1	CHOCOLATE SALTY BALLS (PS I LOVE YOU)	Chef
9 January	1	HEARTBEAT/TRAGEDY	Steps
16 January	1	PRAISE YOU ↑	Fatboy Slim
23 January	1	A LITTLE BIT MORE ↑	911
30 January	1	PRETTY FLY (FOR A WHITE GUY) ↑	Offspring
6 February	1	YOU DON'T KNOW ME ↑	Armand Van Helden Featuring Duane Harden
13 February	1	MARIA ↑	Blondie
20 February	1	FLY AWAY ↑	Lenny Kravitz
27 February	2	BABY ONE MORE TIME ↑ ▲	Britney Spears
13 March	2	WHEN THE GOING GETS TOUGH ↑	Boyzone
27 March	1	BLAME IT ON THE WEATHERMAN ↑	B*Witched
3 April	2	FLAT BEAT ↑	Mr Oizo
17 April	2	PERFECT MOMENT ↑	Martine Mccutcheon

DATE	WKS	TITLE	ARTIST
1 May	2	SWEAR IT AGAIN ↑	Westlife
15 May	1	I WANT IT THAT WAY ↑	Backstreet Boys
22 May	1	YOU NEEDED ME ↑	Boyzone
29 May	2	SWEET LIKE CHOCOLATE ↑	Shanks & Bigfoot
12 June	1	EVERYBODY'S FREE (TO WEAR SUNSCREEN) ↑	Baz Luhrmann
19 June	1	BRING IT ALL BACK ↑	S Club 7
26 June	1	BOOM BOOM BOOM BOOM!! ↑	Vengaboys
3 July	2	9PM (TILL I COME) ↑	ATB
17 July	3	LIVIN' LA VIDA LOCA ↑ ▲	Ricky Martin
7 August	1	WHEN YOU SAY NOTHING AT ALL ↑	Ronan Keating
21 August	1	IF I LET YOU GO ↑	Westlife
28 August	1	MI CHICO LATINO ↑	Geri Halliwell
4 September	2	MAMBO NO 5 (A LITTLE BIT OF…) ↑	Lou Bega
18 September	1	WE'RE GOING TO IBIZA! ↑	Vengaboys
25 September	3	BLUE (DA BA DEE) ↑	Eiffel 65
16 October	2	GENIE IN A BOTTLE ↑ ▲	Christina Aguilera
30 October	1	FLYING WITHOUT WINGS ↑	Westlife
6 November	1	KEEP ON MOVIN' ↑	Five
13 November	1	LIFT ME UP ↑	Geri Halliwell
20 November	1	SHE'S THE ONE/IT'S ONLY US ↑	Robbie Williams
27 November	1	KING OF MY CASTLE ↑	Wamdue Project
4 December	3	THE MILLENNIUM PRAYER	Cliff Richard
25 December	4	I HAVE A DREAM/SEASONS IN THE SUN ↑	Westlife

2000

DATE	WKS	TITLE	ARTIST
22 January	1	THE MASSES AGAINST THE CLASSES ↑	Manic Street Preachers
29 January	1	BORN TO MAKE YOU HAPPY ↑	Britney Spears
5 February	2	RISE ↑	Gabrielle
19 February	1	GO LET IT OUT ↑	Oasis
26 February	2	PURE SHORES ↑	All Saints
11 March	1	AMERICAN PIE ↑	Madonna
18 March	1	DON'T GIVE UP ↑	Chicane Featuring Bryan Adams
25 March	1	BAG IT UP ↑	Geri Halliwell
1 April	1	NEVER BE THE SAME AGAIN ↑	Melanie C and Lisa Left Eye Lopes
8 April	1	FOOL AGAIN ↑	Westlife
15 April	1	FILL ME IN ↑	Craig David
23 April	2	TOCA'S MIRACLE ↑	Fragma
6 May	1	BOUND 4 DA RELOAD (CASUALTY) ↑	Oxide and Neutrino
13 May	1	OOPS!...I DID IT AGAIN ↑	Britney Spears
20 May	1	DON'T CALL ME BABY ↑	Madison Avenue
27 May	1	DAY AND NIGHT ↑	Billie Piper
3 June	3	IT FEELS SO GOOD ↑	Sonique
24 June	1	YOU SEE THE TROUBLE WITH ME ↑	Black Legend
1 July	1	SPINNING AROUND ↑	Kylie Minogue
8 July	1	THE REAL SLIM SHADY ↑	Eminem
15 July	1	BREATHLESS ↑	Corrs
22 July	1	LIFE IS A ROLLERCOASTER ↑	Ronan Keating
29 July	1	WE WILL ROCK YOU ↑	Five & Queen
5 August	1	7 DAYS ↑	Craig David
12 August	1	ROCK DJ ↑	Robbie Williams
19 August	1	I TURN TO YOU ↑	Melanie C
26 August	1	GROOVEJET (IF THIS AIN'T LOVE) ↑	Spiller
2 September	1	MUSIC ↑ ▲	Madonna
9 September	1	TAKE ON ME ↑	A1
16 September	2	LADY (HEAR ME TONIGHT) ↑	Modjo
30 September	2	AGAINST ALL ODDS ↑	Mariah Carey Featuring Westlife
14 October	1	BLACK COFFEE ↑	All Saints
21 October	1	BEAUTIFUL DAY ↑	U2
28 October	1	STOMP ↑	Steps
4 November	1	HOLLER/LET LOVE LEAD THE WAY ↑	Spice Girls
11 November	1	MY LOVE ↑	Westlife
18 November	1	SAME OLD BRAND NEW YOU ↑	A1

↑ Entered the UK chart at number one ▲ Topped the US chart

DATE	WKS	TITLE	ARTIST
25 November	1	CAN'T FIGHT THE MOONLIGHT ↑	Leann Rimes
2 December	1	INDEPENDENT WOMEN (PART 1) ↑ ▲	Destiny's Child
9 December	1	NEVER HAD A DREAM COME TRUE ↑	S Club 7
16 December	1	STAN ↑	Eminem
23 December	3	CAN WE FIX IT	Bob The Builder

2001

DATE	WKS	TITLE	ARTIST
13 January	1	TOUCH ME ↑	Rui Da Silva Featuring Cassandra
20 January	1	LOVE DON'T COST A THING ↑	Jennifer Lopez
27 January	2	ROLLIN' ↑	Limp Bizkit
10 February	4	WHOLE AGAIN ↑	Atomic Kitten
10 March	1	IT WASN'T ME ↑	Shaggy Featuring Rikrok
17 March	1	UPTOWN GIRL ↑	Westlife
24 March	3	PURE AND SIMPLE ↑	Hear'say
14 April	2	WHAT TOOK YOU SO LONG? ↑	Emma Bunton
28 April	1	SURVIVOR ↑	Destiny's Child
5 May	1	DON'T STOP MOVIN' ↑	S Club 7
12 May	1	IT'S RAINING MEN ↑	Geri Halliwell
26 May	1	DON'T STOP MOVIN'	S Club 7
2 June	1	DO YOU REALLY LIKE IT ↑	DJ Pied Piper & The Masters of Ceremonies
9 June	3	ANGEL ↑ ▲	Shaggy Featuring Rayvon
30 June	1	LADY MARMALADE ↑ ▲	Christina Aguilera/Lil' Kim/Mya/Pink
7 July	1	THE WAY TO YOUR LOVE ↑	Hear'say
14 July	1	ANOTHER CHANCE ↑	Roger Sanchez
21 July	2	ETERNITY/THE ROAD TO MANDALAY ↑	Robbie Williams
4 August	2	ETERNAL FLAME ↑	Atomic Kitten
18 August	1	21 SECONDS ↑	So Solid Crew
25 August	2	LET'S DANCE ↑	Five
8 September	1	TOO CLOSE ↑	Blue
15 September	1	MAMBO NO 5 ↑	Bob The Builder
22 September	1	HEY BABY	DJ Otzi
29 September	4	CAN'T GET YOU OUT OF MY HEAD ↑	Kylie Minogue
20 October	3	BECAUSE I GOT HIGH ↑	Afroman
17 November	1	QUEEN OF MY HEART ↑	Westlife
24 November	1	IF YOU COME BACK ↑	Blue
1 December	1	HAVE YOU EVER ↑	S Club 7
8 December	2	GOTTA GET THRU THIS ↑	Daniel Bedingfield
22 December	3	SOMETHIN' STUPID ↑	Robbie Williams & Nicole Kidman

2002

DATE	WKS	TITLE	ARTIST
12 January	1	GOTTA GET THRU THIS ↑	Daniel Bedingfield
19 January	1	MORE THAN A WOMAN ↑	Aaliyah
26 January	1	MY SWEET LORD ↑	George Harrison
2 February	4	HERO ↑	Enrique Iglesias
2 March	1	WORLD OF OUR OWN ↑	Westlife
9 March	3	EVERGREEN/ANYTHING IS POSSIBLE ↑	Will Young
30 March	4	UNCHAINED MELODY ↑	Gareth Gates
27 April	1	THE HINDU TIMES ↑	Oasis
4 May	1	FREAK LIKE ME ↑	Sugababes
11 May	1	KISS KISS ↑	Holly Valance
18 May	1	IF TOMORROW NEVER COMES ↑	Ronan Keating
25 May	1	JUST A LITTLE ↑	Liberty X
1 June	1	WITHOUT ME ↑	Eminem
8 June	2	LIGHT MY FIRE ↑	Will Young
22 June	4	A LITTLE LESS CONVERSATION ↑	Elvis Vs JXL
20 July	3	ANYONE OF US (STUPID MISTAKE) ↑	Gareth Gates
10 August	2	COLOURBLIND ↑	Darius
24 August	1	ROUND ROUND ↑	Sugababes
31 August	1	CROSSROADS ↑	Blazin' Squad
7 September	3	THE TIDE IS HIGH (GET THE FEELING) ↑	Atomic Kitten

DATE	WKS	TITLE	ARTIST
28 September	1	JUST LIKE A PILL ↑	Pink
5 October	2	THE LONG AND WINDING ROAD/SUSPICIOUS MINDS ↑	Will Young & Gareth Gates
19 October	1	THE KETCHUP SONG (ASEREJE) ↑	Las Ketchup
26 October	2	DILEMMA ↑ ▲	Nelly Featuring Kelly Rowland
9 November	1	HEAVEN ↑	DJ Sammy and Yanou Featuring Do
16 November	1	UNBREAKABLE ↑	Westlife
23 November	2	DIRRTY ↑	Christina Aguilera Featuring Redman
7 December	1	IF YOU'RE NOT THE ONE ↑	Daniel Bedingfield
14 December	1	LOSE YOURSELF ↑ ▲	Eminem
21 December	1	SORRY SEEMS TO BE THE HARDEST WORD ↑	Blue Featuring Elton John
28 December	4	SOUND OF THE UNDERGROUND ↑	Girls Aloud

2003

DATE	WKS	TITLE	ARTIST
25 January	2	STOP LIVING THE LIE ↑	David Sneddon
8 February	4	ALL THE THINGS SHE SAID ↑	Tatu
8 March	2	BEAUTIFUL ↑	Christina Aguilera
22 March	2	SPIRIT IN THE SKY ↑	Gareth Gates Featuring The Kumars
5 April	4	MAKE LUV ↑	Room 5 Featuring Oliver Cheatham
3 May	1	YOU SAID NO ↑	Busted
10 May	1	LONELINESS ↑	Tomcraft
17 May	4	IGNITION ↑	R Kelly
14 June	4	BRING ME TO LIFE ↑	Evanescence
12 July	3	CRAZY IN LOVE ↑ ▲	Beyoncé Knowles
2 August	1	NEVER GONNA LEAVE YOUR SIDE ↑	Daniel Bedingfield
9 August	4	BREATHE ↑	Blu Cantrell Featuring Sean Paul
6 September	1	ARE YOU READY FOR LOVE ↑	Elton John
13 September	6	WHERE IS THE LOVE ↑	Black Eyed Peas
25 October	1	HOLE IN THE HEAD ↑	Sugababes
1 November	2	BE FAITHFUL ↑	Fatman Scoop Featuring The Crooklyn Clan
15 November	1	SLOW ↑	Kylie Minogue
22 November	1	CRASHED THE WEDDING ↑	Busted
29 November	1	MANDY ↑	Westlife
6 December	2	LEAVE RIGHT NOW ↑	Will Young
20 December	1	CHANGES ↑	Ozzy & Kelly Osbourne
27 December	3	MAD WORLD ↑	Michael Andrews Featuring Gary Jules

2004

DATE	WKS	TITLE	ARTIST
17 January	3	ALL THE TIME ↑	Michelle
7 February	2	TAKE ME TO THE CLOUDS ABOVE ↑	LMC Vs U2
21 February	1	WITH A LITTLE HELP FROM MY FRIENDS/MEASURE OF A MAN ↑	Sam & Mark
28 February	1	WHO'S DAVID? ↑	Busted
6 March	1	MYSTERIOUS GIRL ↑	Peter Andre Featuring Bubbler Ranx
13 March	1	TOXIC ↑	Britney Spears
20 March	1	CHA CHA SLIDE ↑	DJ Casper
27 March	2	YEAH ↑ ▲	Usher Featuring Lil' Jon & Ludacris
10 April	2	FIVE COLOURS IN HER HAIR ↑	McFly
24 April	4	F**K IT (I DON'T WANT YOU BACK) ↑	Eamon
22 May	3	F.U.R.B. (F U RIGHT BACK) ↑	Frankee
12 June	2	I DON'T WANNA KNOW ↑	Mario Winans Featuring Enya & P Diddy
26 June	1	EVERYTIME ↑	Britney Spears
3 July	1	OBVIOUSLY ↑	McFly
10 July	2	BURN ↑	Usher
24 July	1	LOLA'S THEME ↑	Shapeshifters

DATE	WKS	TITLE	ARTIST
31 July	1	DRY YOUR EYES ↑	Streets
7 August	2	THUNDERBIRDS/3 AM ↑	Busted
21 August	1	BABYCAKES ↑	3 Of A Kind
28 August	2	THESE WORDS ↑	Natasha Bedingfield
11 September	1	MY PLACE/FLAP YOUR WINGS ↑	Nelly
18 September	1	REAL TO ME ↑	Brian McFadden
25 September	3	CALL ON ME ↑	Eric Prydz
16 October	1	RADIO ↑	Robbie Williams
23 October	2	CALL ON ME	Eric Prydz
6 November	1	WONDERFUL ↑	Ja Rule Featuring R Kelly & Ashanti
13 November	1	DON'T LOSE IT ↑	Eminem
20 November	1	VERTIGO ↑	U2
27 November	2	I'LL STAND BY YOU ↑	Girls Aloud
11 December	3	DO THEY KNOW IT'S CHRISTMAS? ↑	Band Aid 20

↑ Entered the UK chart at number one   ▲ Topped the US chart

ALPHABETICAL LISTING OF THE SONGS

This section lists, in alphabetical order of song title, every top chart hit since the first chart was compiled in 1952 through to the last chart compiled in 2004. Each song title is then followed by the full artist credit.

Where a song has been a hit for more than one artist, the titles are listed in chronological order for each artist. Where records have the same title but are different songs, these are indicated by [A] and [B] or however many times the title has been used in a hit record.

Titles that utilise initials, such as *MFEO*, *A.D.I.D.A.S.*, *D.I.S.C.O.* etc. have been listed as if there were no initials or full stops. Titles that link words, such as *Candyman* appear after those that don't link the words, such as *Candy Man*. Titles that utilise numbers, such as *Freak 4 You*, are listed as though the number was spelt out in full, so *Freak 4 You* will come after *Freak For You*.

() SIGUR ROS
A BA NI BI IZHAR COHEN & ALPHABETA
'A' BOMB IN WARDOUR STREET JAM
THE A TEAM MIKE POST
AAAH D YAAA GOATS
AARON'S PARTY (COME GET IT) AARON CARTER
ABACAB GENESIS
ABACUS (WHEN I FELL IN LOVE) AXUS
ABANDON [A] DARE
ABANDON [B] THAT PETROL EMOTION
ABANDON SHIP BLAGGERS I.T.A.
ABBA-ESQUE EP ERASURE
THE ABBEY ROAD EP SPIRITUALIZED
ABC JACKSON 5
ABC AND D... BLUE BAMBOO
A.B.C. (FALLING IN LOVE'S NOT EASY) DIRECT DRIVE
ABIDE WITH ME INSPIRATIONAL CHOIR
ABIDE WITH ME VIC REEVES
ABOUT LOVE ROY DAVIS JR
ABOUT 3AM DARK STAR
ABOVE THE CLOUDS PAUL WELLER
ABRACADABRA STEVE MILLER BAND
ABRAHAM MARTIN AND JOHN MARVIN GAYE
ABSENT FRIENDS DIVINE COMEDY
ABSOLUTE(E) CLAUDIA BRUCKEN
ABSOLUTE SCRITTI POLITTI
ABSOLUTE AFFIRMATION RADIO 4
ABSOLUTE BEGINNERS [A] JAM
ABSOLUTE BEGINNERS [B] DAVID BOWIE
ABSOLUTE E-SENSUAL JAKI GRAHAM
ABSOLUTE REALITY ALARM
ABSOLUTELY EVERYBODY VANESSA AMOROSI
ABSOLUTELY FABULOUS ABSOLUTELY FABULOUS
ABSTAIN FIVE THIRTY
ABSURD FLUKE
ABUSE ME SILVERCHAIR
AC/DC X-PRESS 2
ACAPULCO 1922 KENNY BALL & HIS JAZZMEN
ACCELERATE SKIN UP
ACCELERATOR PRIMAL SCREAM
ACCESS DJ MISJAH & DJ TIM
ACCIDENT OF BIRTH BRUCE DICKINSON
ACCIDENT PRONE STATUS QUO
ACCIDENT WAITING TO HAPPEN (EP) BILLY BRAGG
ACCIDENTLY IN LOVE COUNTING CROWS
ACCIDENTS THUNDERCLAP NEWMAN
ACCIDENTS WILL HAPPEN ELVIS COSTELLO
ACE OF SPADES MOTORHEAD
ACES HIGH IRON MAIDEN
ACHILLES HEEL TOPLOADER
ACHY BREAKY HEART BILLY RAY CYRUS
ACHY BREAKY HEART ALVIN & THE CHIPMUNKS
    FEATURING BILLY RAY CYRUS
ACID LAB ALEX REECE
ACID MAN JOLLY ROGER
ACID TRAK DILLINJA
ACKEE 1-2-3 BEAT
THE ACOUSTICS (EP) NEW MODEL ARMY
ACPERIENCE HARDFLOOR
ACROBATS (LOOKING FOR BALANCE) MOONY
ACT OF WAR ELTON JOHN & MILLIE JACKSON
ACTION [A] SWEET
ACTION [A] DEF LEPPARD
ACTION [B] SAINT ETIENNE
ACTION AND DRAMA BIS
ACTIV 8 (COME WITH ME) ALTERN 8
ACTIVATED GERALD ALSTON
ACTUALLY IT'S DARKNESS IDLEWILD
ADDAMS FAMILY (WHOOMP!) TAG TEAM
ADDAMS GROOVE HAMMER
ADDICTED [A] SIMPLE PLAN

ADDICTED [B] ENRIQUE IGLESIAS
ADDICTED TO BASS PURETONE
ADDICTED TO LOVE ROBERT PALMER
ADDICTED TO LOVE SHAKE B4 USE VS ROBERT PALMER
ADDICTED TO LOVE (LIVE) TINA TURNER
ADDICTED TO YOU ALEC EMPIRE
ADDICTION ALMIGHTY
ADDICTIVE TRUTH HURTS
ADELANTE SASH!
ADIA SARAH McLACHLAN
A.D.I.D.A.S. [A] KORN
A.D.I.D.A.S. [B] KILLER MIKE FEATURING BIG BOI
ADIDAS WORLD EDWYN COLLINS
ADIEMUS ADIEMUS
ADIOS AMIGO JIM REEVES
ADORATION WALTZ DAVID WHITFIELD
ADORATIONS KILLING JOKE
ADORE JOE ROBERTS
ADORED AND EXPLORED MARC ALMOND
ADRENALIN (EP) N-JOI
ADRIENNE CALLING
ADRIFT (CAST YOUR MIND) ANTARCTICA
ADULT EDUCATION DARYL HALL & JOHN OATES
THE ADVENTURES OF THE LOVE CRUSADER SARAH
    BRIGHTMAN & THE STARSHIP TROOPERS
ADVICE FOR THE YOUNG AT HEART TEARS FOR FEARS
AERODYNAMIK KRAFTWERK
AEROPLANE RED HOT CHILI PEPPERS
THE AEROPLANE SONG STRAW
AFFAIR CHERRELLE
AN AFFAIR TO REMEMBER VIC DAMONE
AFFIRMATION SAVAGE GARDEN
AFRAID MOTLEY CRUE
AFRICA TOTO
AFRICAN AND WHITE CHINA CRISIS
AFRICAN DREAM WASIS DIOP FEATURING LENA
    FIAGBE
AFRICAN HORIZON MYSTICA
AFRICAN REIGN DEEP C
AFRICAN WALTZ JOHNNY DANKWORTH
AFRIKA HISTORY FEATURING Q-TEE
AFRIKA SHOX LEFTFIELD/BAMBAATAA
AFRO DIZZI ACT CRY SISCO!
AFRO KING EMF
AFRO PUFFS LADY OF RAGE
AFRO SLEEZE ROACH MOTEL
AFRODISIAC [A] POWDER
AFRODISIAC [B] BRANDY
THE AFRO-LEFT EP LEFTFIELD FEATURING DJUM DJUM
AFTER A FASHION MIDGE URE & MICK KARN
AFTER ALL [A] FRANK & WALTERS
AFTER ALL [B] DELERIUM FEATURING JAEL
AFTER ALL THESE YEARS FOSTER & ALLEN
AFTER HOURS BLUETONES
AFTER LOVE BLANK & JONES
AFTER THE FIRE ROGER DALTREY
AFTER THE GOLDRUSH PRELUDE
AFTER THE LOVE JESUS LOVES YOU
AFTER THE LOVE HAS GONE [A] EARTH, WIND & FIRE
AFTER THE LOVE HAS GONE [A] DAMAGE
AFTER THE LOVE HAS GONE [B] PRINCESS
AFTER THE LOVE HAS GONE [C] STEPS
AFTER THE RAIN TITIYO
AFTER THE RAIN HAS FALLEN STING
AFTER THE WAR GARY MOORE
AFTER THE WATERSHED CARTER – THE UNSTOPPABLE
    SEX MACHINE
AFTER YOU'RE GONE ONE TRUE VOICE
AFTER YOU'VE GONE ALICE BABS
AFTERGLOW MISSION
AFTERGLOW OF YOUR LOVE SMALL FACES

AFTERMATH [A] NIGHTMARES ON WAX
AFTERMATH [B] TRICKY
AFTERMATH [C] R.E.M.
AFTERNOON DELIGHT STARLAND VOCAL BAND
AFTERNOON OF THE RHINO MIKE POST COALITION
(AFTERNOON) SOAPS ARAB STRAP
AFTERNOONS & COFFEESPOONS CRASH TEST DUMMIES
AGADOO BLACK LACE
AGAIN [A] JIMMY TARBUCK
AGAIN [B] JANET JACKSON
AGAIN [C] JULIET ROBERTS
AGAIN AND AGAIN STATUS QUO
AGAINST ALL ODDS (TAKE A LOOK AT ME NOW)
    PHIL COLLINS
AGAINST ALL ODDS (TAKE A LOOK AT ME NOW)
    MARIAH CAREY FEATURING WESTLIFE
AGAINST THE WIND MAIRE BRENNAN
AGE AIN'T NOTHING BUT A NUMBER AALIYAH
AGE OF LONELINESS ENIGMA
AGE OF LOVE AGE OF LOVE
AGE OF PANIC SENSER
AGENT DAN AGENT PROVOCATEUR
AGNES QUEEN OF SORROW BONNIE PRINCE BILLY
AHORA ES (NOW IS THE TIME) 2 IN A ROOM
AI NO CORRIDA (I-NO-KO-REE-DA) QUINCY JONES
    FEATURING DUNE
AIKEA-GUINEA COCTEAU TWINS
AIN'T COMPLAINING STATUS QUO
AIN'T DOIN' NOTHIN' JET BRONX & THE FORBIDDEN
AIN'T GOIN' TO GOA ALABAMA 3
AIN'T GOING DOWN GARTH BROOKS
AIN'T GONNA BE THAT WAY MARV JOHNSON
AIN'T GONNA BUMP NO MORE (WITH NO BIG FAT
    WOMAN) JOE TEX
AIN'T GONNA CRY AGAIN PETER COX
AIN'T GONNA WASH FOR A WEEK BROOK BROTHERS
AIN'T GOT A CLUE LURKERS
AIN'T GOT NO – I GOT LIFE NINA SIMONE
AIN'T IT FUN GUNS N' ROSES
AIN'T IT FUNNY JENNIFER LOPEZ
AIN'T LOVE A BITCH ROD STEWART
AIN'T MISBEHAVIN' JOHNNIE RAY
AIN'T MISBEHAVIN' TOMMY BRUCE & THE BRUISERS
AIN'T MY BEATING HEART TEN SHARP
AIN'T NO CASANOVA SINCLAIR
AIN'T NO DOUBT JIMMY NAIL
AIN'T NO LOVE (AIN'T NO USE) SUB SUB FEATURING
    MELANIE WILLIAMS
AIN'T NO LOVE (AIN'T NO USE) SODA CLUB FEATURING
    ASHLEY JADE
AIN'T NO LOVE IN THE HEART OF THE CITY WHITESNAKE
AIN'T NO MAN DINA CARROLL
AIN'T NO MOUNTAIN HIGH ENOUGH DIANA ROSS
AIN'T NO MOUNTAIN HIGH ENOUGH JOCELYN BROWN
AIN'T NO MOUNTAIN HIGH ENOUGH WHITEHOUSE
AIN'T NO MOUNTAIN HIGH ENOUGH – REMEMBER ME
    (MEDLEY) BOYSTOWN GANG
AIN'T NO NEED TO HIDE SANDY B
AIN'T NO PLAYA JAY-Z FEATURING FOXY BROWN
AIN'T NO PLEASING YOU CHAS & DAVE
AIN'T NO STOPPING ENIGMA
AIN'T NO STOPPIN US DJ LUCK & MC NEAT
    FEATURING JJ
AIN'T NO STOPPIN' US NOW McFADDEN & WHITEHEAD
AIN'T NO STOPPIN' US NOW BIG DADDY KANE
AIN'T NO STOPPING US NOW LUTHER VANDROSS
AIN'T NO STOPPING US NOW MOBO ALLSTARS
AIN'T NO STOPPING US NOW (PARTY FOR THE WORLD)
    STEVE WALSH
AIN'T NO SUNSHINE MICHAEL JACKSON
AIN'T NO SUNSHINE SIVUCA

AIN'T NO SUNSHINE LADYSMITH BLACK MAMBAZO
  FEATURING DES'REE
AIN'T NOBODY RUFUS & CHAKA KHAN
AIN'T NOBODY JAKI GRAHAM
AIN'T NOBODY DIANA KING
AIN'T NOBODY LL COOL J
AIN'T NOBODY COURSE
AIN'T NOBODY BETTER INNER CITY
AIN'T NOBODY (LOVES ME BETTER) KWS &
  GWEN DICKEY
AIN'T NOTHING GOIN' ON BUT THE RENT
  GWEN GUTHRIE
AIN'T NOTHIN' LIKE IT MICHAEL LOVESMITH
AIN'T NOTHING BUT A HOUSEPARTY SHOWSTOPPERS
AIN'T NOTHING BUT A HOUSEPARTY PHIL FEARON
AIN'T NOTHING GONNA KEEP ME FROM YOU
  TERI DE SARIO
AIN'T NOTHING LIKE THE REAL THING MARVIN GAYE &
  TAMMI TERRELL
AIN'T NOTHING LIKE THE REAL THING MARCELLA
  DETROIT & ELTON JOHN
AIN'T SHE SWEET BEATLES
AIN'T TALKIN' 'BOUT DUB APOLLO 440
AIN'T THAT A LOT OF LOVE SIMPLY RED
AIN'T THAT A SHAME PAT BOONE
AIN'T THAT A SHAME FATS DOMINO
AIN'T THAT A SHAME FOUR SEASONS
AIN'T THAT ENOUGH TEENAGE FANCLUB
AIN'T THAT ENOUGH FOR YOU JOHN DAVIS & THE
  MONSTER ORCHESTRA
AIN'T THAT FUNNY JIMMY JUSTICE
(AIN'T THAT) JUST LIKE ME HOLLIES
AIN'T THAT JUST THE WAY LUTRICIA McNEAL
AIN'T THAT LOVIN' YOU BABY ELVIS PRESLEY
AIN'T THAT THE TRUTH FRANKIE KELLY
AIN'T TOO PROUD TO BEG TEMPTATIONS
AIN'T 2 PROUD 2 BEG TLC
AIN'T WE FUNKIN' NOW BROTHERS JOHNSON
AIN'T WHAT YOU DO BIG BROVAZ
AIR HOSTESS BUSTED
THE AIR I BREATHE SIMPLY RED
THE AIR THAT I BREATHE HOLLIES
AIR TRAFFIC THREE DRIVES
AIR 2000 ALBION
THE AIR YOU BREATHE BOMB THE BASS
AIRHEAD [A] THOMAS DOLBY
AIRHEAD [B] GIRLS @ PLAY
AIRPLANE GARDENS FAMILY CAT
AIRPORT MOTORS
AIRWAVE RANK 1
AISHA DEATH IN VEGAS
AISY WAISY CARTOONS
AJARE WAY OUT WEST
AL CAPONE PRINCE BUSTER
AL DI LA EMILIO PERICOLI
ALA KABOO SOUND 5
ALABAMA BLUES (REVISITED) ST GERMAIN
ALABAMA JUBILEE FERKO STRING BAND
ALABAMA SONG DAVID BOWIE
ALAN BEAN HEFNER
ALANE WES
ALARM CALL BJORK
ALARMA 666
ALBATROSS FLEETWOOD MAC
ALBINONI VS STAR WARS SIGUE SIGUE SPUTNIK
ALCOHOLIC STARSAILOR
ALEXANDER GRAHAM BELL SWEET
ALFIE CILLA BLACK
ALICE I WANT YOU JUST FOR ME FULL FORCE
ALICE WHAT'S THE MATTER TERRORVISION

ALICE (WHO THE X IS ALICE?) (LIVING NEXT DOOR TO
  ALICE) GOMPIE
ALISHA RULES THE WORLD ALISHA'S ATTIC
ALISON LINDA RONSTADT
ALISON'S ROOM 60FT DOLLS
ALIVE [A] PEARL JAM
ALIVE [B] HELIOTROPIC FEATURING VERNA V
ALIVE [C] BEASTIE BOYS
ALIVE [D] P.O.D.
ALIVE [E] ALIVE FEATURING D D KLEIN
ALIVE [F] S CLUB
ALIVE [G] SONIQUE
ALIVE AND KICKING SIMPLE MINDS
ALIVE AND KICKING EAST SIDE BEAT
ALKALINE SCARFO
ALL ABOUT EVE MARXMAN
ALL ABOUT LOVIN' YOU BON JOVI
ALL ABOUT SOUL BILLY JOEL
ALL ABOUT US PETER ANDRE
ALL ALONE AM I BRENDA LEE
ALL ALONE ON CHRISTMAS DARLENE LOVE
ALL ALONG THE WATCHTOWER JIMI HENDRIX
  EXPERIENCE
ALL ALONG THE WATCHTOWER (EP) JIMI HENDRIX
ALL AMERICAN BOY BILL PARSONS
ALL AMERICAN GIRLS SISTER SLEDGE
ALL AND ALL JOYCE SIMS
ALL APOLOGIES NIRVANA
ALL AROUND MY HAT STEELEYE SPAN
ALL AROUND MY HAT STATUS QUO
ALL AROUND THE WORLD [A] JAM
ALL AROUND THE WORLD [B] LISA STANSFIELD
ALL AROUND THE WORLD [C] JASON DONOVAN
ALL AROUND THE WORLD [D] OASIS
ALL AROUND THE WORLD [E] NORTHERN LINE
ALL BECAUSE OF YOU GEORDIE
ALL 'BOUT THE MONEY MEJA
ALL BY MYSELF ERIC CARMEN
ALL BY MYSELF CELINE DION
ALL CRIED OUT [A] ALISON MOYET
ALL CRIED OUT [B] MELANIE WILLIAMS
ALL CRIED OUT [C] ALLURE FEATURING 112
ALL DAY ALL NIGHT STEPHANIE MILLS
ALL DAY AND ALL OF THE NIGHT KINKS
ALL DAY AND ALL OF THE NIGHT STRANGLERS
ALL DOWNHILL FROM HERE NEW FOUND GLORY
ALL EXHALE LUKE SLATER
ALL EYES CHIKINKI
ALL FALL DOWN [A] LINDISFARNE
ALL FALL DOWN [B] FIVE STAR
ALL FALL DOWN [C] ULTRAVOX
ALL FALL DOWN [D] MIDGET
ALL FALLS DOWN KANYE WEST FEATURING SYLEENA
  JOHNSON
ALL FIRED UP PAT BENATAR
ALL FOR LEYNA BILLY JOEL
ALL FOR LOVE BRYAN ADAMS, ROD STEWART
  & STING
ALL FOR YOU JANET JACKSON
ALL 4 LOVE COLOR ME BADD
ALL 4 LOVE (BREAK 4 LOVE 1990) RAZE FEATURING
  LADY J & SECRETARY OF ENTERTAINMENT
ALL FUNKED UP MOTHER
ALL GOD'S CHILDREN BELINDA CARLISLE
ALL GONE AWAY JOYRIDER
ALL GOOD DE LA SOUL FEATURING CHAKA KHAN
ALL HOOKED UP ALL SAINTS
ALL I AM (IS LOVING YOU) BLUEBELLS
ALL I ASK RAE & CHRISTIAN FEATURING VEBA
ALL I ASK OF MYSELF IS THAT I HOLD TOGETHER NED'S
  ATOMIC DUSTBIN

ALL I ASK OF YOU CLIFF RICHARD & SARAH
  BRIGHTMAN
ALL I DO CLEPTOMANIACS FEATURING BRYAN
  CHAMBERS
ALL I EVER NEED IS YOU SONNY & CHER
ALL I EVER WANTED [A] SANTANA
ALL I EVER WANTED [B] HUMAN LEAGUE
ALL I EVER WANTED (DEVOTION) MYSTERY
ALL I GAVE WORLD PARTY
ALL I HAVE JENNIFER LOPEZ FEATURING LL COOL J
ALL I HAVE TO DO IS DREAM EVERLY BROTHERS
ALL I HAVE TO DO IS DREAM BOBBIE GENTRY & GLEN
  CAMPBELL
ALL I HAVE TO DO IS DREAM PHIL EVERLY & CLIFF
  RICHARD
ALL I HAVE TO GIVE BACKSTREET BOYS
(ALL I KNOW) FEELS LIKE FOREVER JOE COCKER
ALL I NEED AIR
ALL I NEED IS A MIRACLE MIKE + THE MECHANICS
ALL I NEED IS EVERYTHING AZTEC CAMERA
ALL I NEED IS YOUR SWEET LOVIN' GLORIA GAYNOR
ALL I REALLY WANT ALANIS MORISSETTE
ALL I REALLY WANT TO DO BYRDS
ALL I REALLY WANT TO DO CHER
ALL I SEE IS YOU DUSTY SPRINGFIELD
ALL I THINK ABOUT IS YOU NILSSON
ALL I WANNA DO [A] SHERYL CROW
ALL I WANNA DO [A] JOANNE FARRELL
ALL I WANNA DO [A] AMY STUDT
ALL I WANNA DO [B] TIN TIN OUT
ALL I WANNA DO [C] DANNII
ALL I WANNA DO IS MAKE LOVE TO YOU HEART
ALL I WANT [A] HOWARD JONES
ALL I WANT [B] THOSE 2 GIRLS
ALL I WANT [C] SKUNK ANANSIE
ALL I WANT [D] SUSANNA HOFFS
ALL I WANT [E] OFFSPRING
ALL I WANT [F] PURESSENCE
ALL I WANT [G] REEF
ALL I WANT [H] MIS-TEEQ
ALL I WANT [I] WET WET WET
ALL I WANT FOR CHRISTMAS IS A BEATLE DORA BRYAN
ALL I WANT FOR CHRISTMAS IS YOU MARIAH CAREY
ALL I WANT FROM YOU TEMPTATIONS
ALL I WANT IS EVERYTHING DEF LEPPARD
ALL I WANT IS YOU [A] ROXY MUSIC
ALL I WANT IS YOU [B] U2
ALL I WANT IS YOU [B] BELLEFIRE
ALL I WANT IS YOU [C] BRYAN ADAMS
ALL I WANT IS YOU [D] 911
ALL I WANT TO DO UB40
ALL I WANT TO DO IS ROCK TRAVIS
ALL I WANTED IN TUA NUA
ALL IN MY HEAD KOSHEEN
ALL IN YOUR HANDS LAMB
ALL IS FULL OF LOVE BJORK
ALL JOIN HANDS SLADE
ALL KINDS OF EVERYTHING DANA
ALL MAPPED OUT DEPARTURE
ALL MINE PORTISHEAD
ALL MY BEST FRIENDS ARE METALHEADS LESS
  THAN JAKE
ALL MY LIFE [A] MAJOR HARRIS
ALL MY LIFE [B] K-CI & JOJO
ALL MY LIFE [C] FOO FIGHTERS
ALL MY LOVE [A] CLIFF RICHARD
ALL MY LOVE [B] HERNANDEZ
ALL MY LOVE [C] QUEEN PEN FEATURING ERIC
  WILLIAMS
ALL MY LOVE (ASK NOTHING) SPEAR OF DESTINY
ALL MY LOVING DOWLANDS

ALL MY TIME PAID + LIVE FEATURING LAURYN HILL
ALL MY TRIALS PAUL McCARTNEY
ALL 'N' ALL 187 LOCKDOWN (FEATURING D'EMPRESS)
ALL N MY GRILL MISSY 'MISDEMEANOR' ELLIOTT
    FEATURING MC SOLAAR
ALL NIGHT ALL RIGHT PETER ANDRE FEATURING
    WARREN G
ALL NIGHT HOLIDAY RUSS ABBOT
ALL NIGHT LONG [A] DEXTER WANSELL
ALL NIGHT LONG [B] RAINBOW
ALL NIGHT LONG [C] CLOUD
ALL NIGHT LONG [D] MARY JANE GIRLS
ALL NIGHT LONG [D] JAY MONDI & THE LIVING BASS
ALL NIGHT LONG [E] GANT
ALL NIGHT LONG [F] FAITH EVANS FEATURING PUFF
    DADDY
ALL NIGHT LONG (ALL NIGHT) LIONEL RICHIE
ALL NITE (DON'T STOP) JANET JACKSON
(ALL OF A SUDDEN) MY HEART SINGS PAUL ANKA
ALL OF ME SABRINA
ALL OF ME FOR ALL OF YOU 9.9
ALL OF ME LOVES ALL OF YOU BAY CITY ROLLERS
ALL OF MY HEART ABC
ALL OF MY LIFE DIANA ROSS
ALL OF THE GIRLS (ALL AI-DI-GIRL DEM) CARNIVAL
    FEATURING RIP VS RED RAT
ALL OF YOU SAMMY DAVIS Jr.
ALL OF YOU JULIO IGLESIAS & DIANA ROSS
ALL OF YOUR DAYS WILL BE BLESSED ED HARCOURT
ALL ON BLACK ALKALINE TRIO
ALL OR NOTHING [A] SMALL FACES
ALL OR NOTHING [A] DOGS D'AMOUR
ALL OR NOTHING [B] MILLI VANILLI
ALL OR NOTHING [C] JOE
ALL OR NOTHING [D] CHER
ALL OR NOTHING [E] O-TOWN
ALL OUT OF LOVE AIR SUPPLY
ALL OUT OF LOVE [A] OTT
ALL OUT OF LOVE [A] FOUNDATION FEATURING
    NATALIE ROSSI
ALL OUT OF LOVE [B] H & CLAIRE
ALL OUT TO GET YOU BEAT
ALL OVER LISA MAFFIA
ALL OVER ME [A] SUZI CARR
ALL OVER ME [B] GRAHAM COXON
ALL OVER THE WORLD [A] FRANCOISE HARDY
ALL OVER THE WORLD [B] ELECTRIC LIGHT ORCHESTRA
ALL OVER THE WORLD [C] JUNIOR GISCOMBE
ALL OVER YOU [A] LEVEL 42
ALL OVER YOU [B] LIVE
ALL POSSIBILITIES BADLY DRAWN BOY
ALL RIGHT CHRISTOPHER CROSS
ALL RIGHT NOW FREE
ALL RIGHT NOW PEPSI & SHIRLIE
ALL RIGHT NOW LEMONESCENT
ALL RISE BLUE
ALL SHE WANTS IS DURAN DURAN
ALL SHOOK UP ELVIS PRESLEY
ALL SHOOK UP BILLY JOEL
ALL STAND UP (NEVER SAY NEVER) STATUS QUO
ALL STAR SMASH MOUTH
ALL STAR HIT PARADE ALL STAR HIT PARADE
ALL STAR HIT PARADE NO. 2 ALL STAR HIT PARADE
ALL STOOD STILL ULTRAVOX
ALL SUSSED OUT ALMIGHTY
ALL SYSTEMS GO DONNA SUMMER
ALL THAT GLITTERS GARY GLITTER
ALL THAT I AM [A] ELVIS PRESLEY
ALL THAT I AM [B] JOE
ALL THAT I CAN SAY MARY J. BLIGE
ALL THAT I GOT IS YOU GHOSTFACE KILLAH

ALL THAT I NEED BOYZONE
ALL THAT I'M ALLOWED (I'M THANKFUL) ELTON JOHN
ALL THAT MATTERED (LOVE YOU DOWN) DE NUIT
ALL THAT MATTERS LOUISE
ALL THAT MATTERS TO ME ALEXANDER O'NEAL
ALL THAT MONEY WANTS PSYCHEDELIC FURS
ALL THAT SHE WANTS ACE OF BASE
ALL THAT'S LEFT THRICE
ALL THE LOVE IN THE WORLD [A] CONSORTIUM
ALL THE LOVE IN THE WORLD [B] DIONNE WARWICK
ALL THE LOVER I NEED KINANE
ALL THE MAN THAT I NEED [A] WHITNEY HOUSTON
ALL THE MAN THAT I NEED [B] SHERNETTE MAY
ALL THE MONEY'S GONE BABYLON ZOO
ALL THE MYTHS ON SUNDAY DIESEL PARK WEST
ALL THE SMALL THINGS BLINK 182
ALL THE THINGS DILLINJA
ALL THE THINGS SHE SAID [A] SIMPLE MINDS
ALL THE THINGS SHE SAID [B] TATU
ALL THE THINGS (YOUR MAN WON'T DO) JOE
ALL THE TIME AND EVERYWHERE DICKIE VALENTINE
ALL THE WAY [A] FRANK SINATRA
ALL THE WAY [B] ENGLAND FOOTBALL TEAM & THE
    SOUND OF STOCK, AITKEN & WATERMAN
ALL THE WAY FROM AMERICA JOAN ARMATRADING
ALL THE WAY FROM MEMPHIS MOTT THE HOOPLE
ALL THE WAY FROM MEMPHIS CONTRABAND
ALL THE WAY TO RENO R.E.M.
ALL THE WORLD LOVES LOVERS PREFAB SPROUT
ALL THE YOUNG DUDES MOTT THE HOOPLE
ALL THE YOUNG DUDES BRUCE DICKINSON
ALL THESE THINGS THAT I'VE DONE KILLERS
ALL THIS LOVE I'M GIVING GWEN McCRAE
ALL THIS LOVE I'M GIVING MUSIC & MYSTERY
    FEATURING GWEN McCRAE
ALL THIS TIME [A] TIFFANY
ALL THIS TIME [B] STING
ALL THIS TIME [C] MICHELLE
ALL THOSE YEARS AGO GEORGE HARRISON
ALL THROUGH THE NIGHT CYNDI LAUPER
ALL THRU THE NITE P.O.V. FEATURING JADE
ALL TIME HIGH RITA COOLIDGE
ALL TOGETHER NOW FARM
ALL TOGETHER NOW EVERTON FC
ALL TOGETHER NOW 2004 FARM FEATURING SFX BOYS
    CHOIR
ALL TOMORROW'S PARTIES JAPAN
ALL TRUE MAN ALEXANDER O'NEAL
ALL WOMAN LISA STANSFIELD
ALL YOU EVER DO VIOLENT DELIGHT
ALL YOU GOOD GOOD PEOPLE EP EMBRACE
ALL YOU NEED IS HATE DELGADOS
ALL YOU NEED IS LOVE BEATLES
ALL YOU NEED IS LOVE TOM JONES
ALL YOU PRETTY GIRLS XTC
ALL YOU WANTED MICHELLE BRANCH
ALLEY CAT SONG DAVID THORNE
ALLEY OOP HOLLYWOOD ARGYLES
ALLY'S TARTAN ARMY ANDY CAMERON
ALMA MATTERS MORRISSEY
ALMAZ RANDY CRAWFORD
ALMOST DOESN'T COUNT BRANDY
ALMOST GOLD JESUS & MARY CHAIN
ALMOST HEAR YOU SIGH ROLLING STONES
ALMOST SATURDAY NIGHT DAVE EDMUNDS
ALMOST SEE YOU (SOMEWHERE) CHINA BLACK
ALMOST THERE ANDY WILLIAMS
ALMOST UNREAL ROXETTE
ALONE [A] PETULA CLARK
ALONE [A] SHEPHERD SISTERS
ALONE [A] SOUTHLANDERS

ALONE [A] KAYE SISTERS
ALONE [B] HEART
ALONE [C] BIG COUNTRY
ALONE [D] BEE GEES
ALONE [E] LASGO
ALONE AGAIN IN THE LAP OF LUXURY MARILLION
ALONE AGAIN (NATURALLY) GILBERT O'SULLIVAN
ALONE AGAIN OR DAMNED
ALONE AT LAST JACKIE WILSON
ALONE WITH YOU TEXAS
ALONE WITHOUT YOU [A] KING
ALONE WITHOUT YOU [B] MARK OWEN
ALONG CAME CAROLINE MICHAEL COX
ALPHA BETA GAGA AIR
ALPHABET STREET PRINCE
ALRIGHT [A] JANET JACKSON
ALRIGHT [B] URBAN SOUL
ALRIGHT [C] KRIS KROSS
ALRIGHT [D] CAST
ALRIGHT [E] SUPERGRASS
ALRIGHT [F] JAMIROQUAI
ALRIGHT [G] CLUB 69 FEATURING SUZANNE PALMER
ALRIGHT [H] RED CARPET
ALRIGHT ALRIGHT ALRIGHT MUNGO JERRY
ALRIGHT BABY STEVENSON'S ROCKET
ALSO SPRACH ZARATHUSTRA (2001) DEODATO
ALTERNATE TITLE MONKEES
ALWAYS [A] SAMMY TURNER
ALWAYS [B] ATLANTIC STARR
ALWAYS [C] URBAN SOUL
ALWAYS [D] ERASURE
ALWAYS [E] BON JOVI
ALWAYS [F] MK FEATURING ALANA
ALWAYS [G] SALIVA
ALWAYS [H] BLINK 182
ALWAYS A PERMANENT STATE DAVID JAMES
ALWAYS AND EVER JOHNNY KIDD & THE PIRATES
ALWAYS AND FOREVER [A] HEATWAVE
ALWAYS AND FOREVER [A] LUTHER VANDROSS
ALWAYS AND FOREVER JJ72
ALWAYS BE MY BABY MARIAH CAREY
ALWAYS BREAKING MY HEART BELINDA CARLISLE
ALWAYS COME BACK TO YOUR LOVE SAMANTHA
    MUMBA
ALWAYS FIND A WAY NINE YARDS
ALWAYS HAVE, ALWAYS WILL ACE OF BASE
ALWAYS LOOK ON THE BRIGHT SIDE OF LIFE MONTY
    PYTHON
ALWAYS LOOK ON THE BRIGHT SIDE OF LIFE
    CORONATION STREET CAST FEATURING BILL
    WADDINGTON
ALWAYS MUSIC WESTBAM/KOON + STEPHENSON
ALWAYS ON MY MIND ELVIS PRESLEY
ALWAYS ON MY MIND WILLIE NELSON
ALWAYS ON MY MIND PET SHOP BOYS
ALWAYS ON THE RUN LENNY KRAVITZ
ALWAYS ON TIME JA RULE FEATURING ASHANTI
ALWAYS REMEMBER TO RESPECT AND HONOUR YOUR
    MOTHER DUSTED
ALWAYS SOMETHING THERE TO REMIND ME NAKED
    EYES
ALWAYS SOMETHING THERE TO REMIND ME TIN TIN
    OUT FEATURING ESPIRITU
ALWAYS THE LAST TO KNOW DEL AMITRI
ALWAYS THE LONELY ONE ALAN DREW
ALWAYS THE SUN STRANGLERS
ALWAYS THERE [A] MARTI WEBB
ALWAYS THERE [B] INCOGNITO FEATURING JOCELYN
    BROWN
ALWAYS THERE [C] UB40
ALWAYS TOMORROW GLORIA ESTEFAN

ALWAYS YOU AND ME RUSS CONWAY
ALWAYS YOUR WAY MY VITRIOL
ALWAYS YOURS GARY GLITTER
ALWAYZ INTO SOMETHIN' NWA
AM I A TOY OR A TREASURE KAY STARR
AM I ON YOUR MIND OXYGEN FEATURING ANDREA
  BRITTON
AM I RIGHT (EP) ERASURE
AM I THAT EASY TO FORGET ENGELBERT HUMPERDINCK
AM I THE SAME GIRL DUSTY SPRINGFIELD
AM I THE SAME GIRL SWING OUT SISTER
AM I WASTING MY TIME ON YOU FRANKIE VAUGHAN
AM I WRONG [A] ETIENNE DE CRECY
AM I WRONG [B] MULL HISTORICAL SOCIETY
AM I WRY NO MEW
AM TO PM CHRISTINA MILIAN
AMANDA [A] STUART GILLIES
AMANDA [B] CRAIG McLACHLAN & CHECK 1-2
AMATEUR HOUR SPARKS
AMAZED LONESTAR
AMAZING [A] AEROSMITH
AMAZING [B] GEORGE MICHAEL
AMAZING GRACE JUDY COLLINS
AMAZING GRACE THE PIPES & DRUMS & MILITARY
  BAND OF THE ROYAL SCOTS DRAGOON GUARDS
THE AMAZING SPIDER MAN MC SPY-D + FRIENDS
AMAZON CHANT AIRSCAPE
AMBUSH OUTLAWS
AMEN (DON'T BE AFRAID) FLASH BROTHERS
AMERICA [A] NICE
AMERICA [A] KING KURT
AMERICA [B] SIMON & GARFUNKEL
AMERICA [C] DAVID ESSEX
AMERICA [D] GARY NUMAN
AMERICA (I LOVE AMERICA) FULL INTENTION
AMERICA THE BEAUTIFUL ELVIS PRESLEY
AMERICA: WHAT TIME IS LOVE KLF
AMERICA – WORLD CUP THEME 1994 LEONARD
  BERNSTEIN, ORCHESTRA & CHORUS
THE AMERICAN SIMPLE MINDS
AMERICAN BAD ASS KID ROCK
AMERICAN DREAM [A] CROSBY, STILLS, NASH &
  YOUNG
AMERICAN DREAM [B] POWER OF DREAMS
AMERICAN DREAM [C] JAKATTA
AMERICAN ENGLISH IDLEWILD
AMERICAN GENERATION RITCHIE FAMILY
AMERICAN GIRL TOM PETTY & THE HEARTBREAKERS
AMERICAN GIRLS COUNTING CROWS
AMERICAN HEARTS BILLY OCEAN
AMERICAN IDIOT GREEN DAY
AMERICAN IN AMSTERDAM WHEATUS
AMERICAN LIFE MADONNA
AMERICAN PIE DON McLEAN
AMERICAN PIE JUST LUIS
AMERICAN PIE CHUPITO
AMERICAN PIE MADONNA
AMERICAN TRILOGY [A] ELVIS PRESLEY
AMERICAN TRILOGY [A] MICKEY NEWBURY
AMERICAN TRILOGY [B] DELGADOS
AMERICAN TV TERRORVISION
AMERICAN WOMAN GUESS WHO
AMERICANOS HOLLY JOHNSON
AMERIKA RAMMSTEIN
AMIGO BLACK SLATE
AMIGOS PARA SIEMPRE (FRIENDS FOR LIFE) JOSE
  CARRERAS & SARAH BRIGHTMAN
AMITYVILLE (THE HOUSE ON THE HILL) LOVEBUG
  STARSKI
AMNESIA [A] SHALAMAR
AMNESIA [B] CHUMBAWAMBA

AMONG MY SOUVENIRS CONNIE FRANCIS
AMOR JULIO IGLESIAS
AMOR AMOR BEN E. KING
AMOUR AMOUR MOBILES
AMOUR (C'MON) PORN KINGS
AMOUREUSE KIKI DEE
THE AMSTERDAM EP SIMPLE MINDS
AN ACCIDENT IN PARADISE SVEN VATH
ANARCHY IN THE U.K. SEX PISTOLS
ANARCHY IN THE UK MEGADETH
ANARCHY IN THE UK GREEN JELLY
ANA'S SONG SILVERCHAIR
ANASTHASIA T99
ANCHOR CAVE IN
ANCHORAGE MICHELLE SHOCKED
AND A BANG ON THE EAR WATERBOYS
AND DA DRUM MACHINE PHATT B
AND I LOVE YOU SO PERRY COMO
AND I WISH DOOLEYS
AND I'M TELLING YOU I'M NOT GOING JENNIFER
  HOLLIDAY
AND I'M TELLING YOU I'M NOT GOING DONNA GILES
AND IT HURTS DAYEENE
AND IT WASN'T A DREAM RUTHLESS RAP ASSASSINS
(AND NOW – THE WALTZ) C'EST LA VIE SLADE
AND SHE WAS TALKING HEADS
AND SO I WILL WAIT FOR YOU DEE FREDRIX
AND SO IS LOVE KATE BUSH
...AND STONES BLUE AEROPLANES
...(AND THAT'S NO LIE) HEAVEN 17
...AND THAT'S BEFORE ME TEA! MR FOOD
AND THE BAND PLAYED ON (DOWN AMONG THE DEAD
  MEN) FLASH & THE PAN
AND THE BANDS PLAYED ON SAXON
AND THE BEAT GOES ON WHISPERS
AND THE HEAVENS CRIED ANTHONY NEWLEY
AND THE LEADER ROCKS ON GARY GLITTER
(AND THE) PICTURES IN THE SKY MEDICINE HEAD
AND THE SUN WILL SHINE JOSE FELICIANO
AND THEN SHE KISSED ME GARY GLITTER
AND THEN SHE SMILES MOCK TURTLES
AND THEN THE RAIN FALLS BLUE AMAZON
AND THEY OBEY KINESIS
AND YOU SMILED MATT MONRO
ANDRES L7
ANDROGYNY GARBAGE
ANFIELD RAP (RED MACHINE IN FULL EFFECT)
  LIVERPOOL FC
ANGEL [A] ROD STEWART
ANGEL [B] ARETHA FRANKLIN
ANGEL [B] SIMPLY RED
ANGEL [C] MADONNA
ANGEL [D] AEROSMITH
ANGEL [E] EURYTHMICS
ANGEL [F] JON SECADA
ANGEL [G] A-HA
ANGEL [H] GOLDIE
ANGEL [I] MASSIVE ATTACK
ANGEL [J] TINA COUSINS
ANGEL [K] RALPH FRIDGE
ANGEL [L] LIONEL RICHIE
ANGEL [M] SHAGGY FEATURING RAYVON
ANGEL [N] SARAH McLACHLAN
ANGEL [O] CORRS
AN ANGEL KELLY FAMILY
THE ANGEL AND THE GAMBLER IRON MAIDEN
ANGEL EYES ROXY MUSIC
ANGEL EYES (HOME AND AWAY) WET WET WET
ANGEL FACE GLITTER BAND
ANGEL FINGERS WIZZARD
ANGEL IN BLUE J GEILS BAND

ANGEL INTERCEPTOR ASH
ANGEL (LADADI O-HEYO) JAM & SPOON
ANGEL LOOKING THROUGH STAGECOACH FEATURING
  PENNY FOSTER
ANGEL OF HARLEM U2
ANGEL OF MINE ETERNAL
ANGEL OF MINE MONICA
ANGEL OF THE MORNING P.P. ARNOLD
ANGEL OF THE MORNING JUICE NEWTON
ANGEL OF THE MORNING – ANY WAY THAT YOU WANT
  ME (MEDLEY) MARY MASON
ANGEL STREET M PEOPLE
ANGELA JONES MICHAEL COX
ANGELEYES ABBA
ANGELIA RICHARD MARX
ANGELO BROTHERHOOD OF MAN
ANGELS ROBBIE WILLIAMS
THE ANGELS & SHADOWS PROJECT OMNI TRIO
ANGELS DON'T LIE JIM REEVES
ANGELS GO BALD: TOO HOWIE B
ANGEL'S HEAP FINN
ANGELS OF THE SILENCES COUNTING CROWS
ANGELS WITH DIRTY FACES SUGABABES
ANGEL'S SYMPHONY RAF
ANGELS WITH DIRTY FACES SHAM 69
ANGIE ROLLING STONES
ANGIE BABY HELEN REDDY
ANGRY AT THE BIG OAK TREE FRANK IFIELD
ANGRY CHAIR ALICE IN CHAINS
ANGRY SKIES MARIA NAYLER
ANIMAL [A] DEF LEPPARD
ANIMAL [B] LOST IT.COM
ANIMAL [C] R.E.M.
ANIMAL ARMY BABYLON ZOO
ANIMAL CANNABUS MULL HISTORICAL SOCIETY
ANIMAL INSTINCT [A] COMMODORES
ANIMAL INSTINCT [B] CRANBERRIES
ANIMAL NITRATE SUEDE
THE ANIMAL SONG SAVAGE GARDEN
ANIMATION SKIDS
A9 ARIEL
ANITINA (THE FIRST TIME I SEE SHE DANCE)
  M/A/R/R/S
ANNABELLA JOHN WALKER
ANNIE GET YOUR GUN SQUEEZE
ANNIE I'M NOT YOUR DADDY KID CREOLE & THE
  COCONUTS
ANNIE'S SONG JAMES GALWAY
ANNIE'S SONG JOHN DENVER
ANNIVERSARY WALTZ ANITA HARRIS
ANNIVERSARY WALTZ – PART 1 STATUS QUO
ANNIVERSARY WALTZ – PART 2 STATUS QUO
ANOMALY – CALLING YOUR NAME LIBRA PRESENTS
  TAYLOR
ANOTHER BLOOMING CHRISTMAS MEL SMITH
ANOTHER BODY MURDERED FAITH NO MORE & BOO-
  YAA T.R.I.B.E.
ANOTHER BRICK IN THE WALL (PART 2) PINK FLOYD
ANOTHER CHANCE ROGER SANCHEZ
ANOTHER CUP OF COFFEE MIKE + THE MECHANICS
ANOTHER DAY [A] PAUL McCARTNEY
ANOTHER DAY [B] WHIGFIELD
ANOTHER DAY [C] BUCKSHOT LEFONQUE
ANOTHER DAY [D] LEMAR
ANOTHER DAY [D] SKIP RAIDERS FEATURING JADA
ANOTHER DAY [D] LAMBRETTAS
ANOTHER DAY IN PARADISE PHIL COLLINS
ANOTHER DAY IN PARADISE JAM TRONIK
ANOTHER DAY IN PARADISE BRANDY & RAY J
ANOTHER FUNNY HONEYMOON DAVID DUNDAS
ANOTHER GIRL – ANOTHER PLANET ONLY ONES

ANOTHER HEARTACHE ROD STEWART
ANOTHER KIND OF LOVE HUGH CORNWELL
ANOTHER LONELY NIGHT IN NEW YORK ROBIN GIBB
ANOTHER LOVER DANE
ANOTHER MAN BARBARA MASON
ANOTHER MONSTERJAM SIMON HARRIS FEATURING EINSTEIN
ANOTHER MORNING STONER ...AND YOU WILL KNOW US BY THE TRAIL OF THE DEAD
ANOTHER NAIL IN MY HEART SQUEEZE
ANOTHER NIGHT [A] ARETHA FRANKLIN
ANOTHER NIGHT [B] JASON DONOVAN
ANOTHER NIGHT [C] (MC SAR &) THE REAL McCOY
ANOTHER NIGHT IN STRANGELOVE
ANOTHER ONE BITES THE DUST QUEEN
ANOTHER ONE BITES THE DUST QUEEN WITH WYCLEF JEAN FEATURING PRAS MICHEL/FREE
ANOTHER PART OF ME MICHAEL JACKSON
ANOTHER PEARL BADLY DRAWN BOY
ANOTHER PIECE OF MEAT SCORPIONS
ANOTHER PLANET PENDULUM
ANOTHER ROCK AND ROLL CHRISTMAS GARY GLITTER
ANOTHER SAD LOVE SONG TONI BRAXTON
ANOTHER SATURDAY NIGHT SAM COOKE
ANOTHER SATURDAY NIGHT CAT STEVENS
ANOTHER SILENT DAY ADVENTURES
ANOTHER SLEEPLESS NIGHT [A] JIMMY CLANTON
ANOTHER SLEEPLESS NIGHT [B] MIKE 'HITMAN' WILSON
ANOTHER SLEEPLESS NIGHT [B] SHAWN CHRISTOPHER
ANOTHER STAR STEVIE WONDER
ANOTHER STAR KATHY SLEDGE
ANOTHER STEP CLOSER TO YOU KIM WILDE & JUNIOR
ANOTHER SUITCASE IN ANOTHER HALL BARBARA DICKSON
ANOTHER SUITCASE IN ANOTHER HALL MADONNA
ANOTHER TEAR FALLS WALKER BROTHERS
ANOTHER TIME ANOTHER PLACE ENGELBERT HUMPERDINCK
ANOTHER WAY PAUL VAN DYK
ANOTHER WEEKEND FIVE STAR
ANOTHERLOVERHOLENYOHEAD PRINCE
ANSWER ME DAVID WHITFIELD
ANSWER ME FRANKIE LAINE
ANSWER ME RAY PETERSON
ANSWER ME BARBARA DICKSON
THE ANSWER TO WHY I HATE YOU SYMPOSIUM
ANSWERING BELL RYAN ADAMS
ANSWERS TO NOTHING MIDGE URE
ANT RAP ADAM & THE ANTS
ANTE UP M.O.P. FEATURING BUSTA RHYMES
ANTHEM [A] N-JOI
ANTHEM [B] WILDHEARTS
THE ANTHEM [C] GOOD CHARLOTTE
ANTHEM (ONE DAY IN EVERY WEEK) NEW SEEKERS
ANTI-SOCIAL ANTHRAX
ANTMUSIC ADAM & THE ANTS
THE ANTMUSIC EP (THE B-SIDES) ADAM & THE ANTS
ANY DREAM WILL DO JASON DONOVAN
ANY LOVE LUTHER VANDROSS
ANY MINUTE NOW SOULWAX
ANY OLD IRON PETER SELLERS
ANY OLD TIME FOUNDATIONS
ANY ROAD GEORGE HARRISON
ANY TIME ANY PLACE JANET JACKSON
ANY WAY YOU WANT ME TROGGS
ANY WAY YOU LOOK NORTHERN UPROAR
ANYBODY SEEN MY BABY? ROLLING STONES
ANYMORE SARAH CRACKNELL
ANYONE CAN FALL IN LOVE ANITA DOBSON FEATURING THE SIMON MAY ORCHESTRA

ANYONE CAN PLAY GUITAR RADIOHEAD
ANYONE FOR TENNIS (THE SAVAGE SEVEN THEME) CREAM
ANYONE OF US (STUPID MISTAKE) GARETH GATES
ANYONE WHO HAD A HEART CILLA BLACK
ANYONE WHO HAD A HEART DIONNE WARWICK
ANYONE WHO HAD A HEART MARY MAY
ANYTHING [A] DIRECT DRIVE
ANYTHING [B] DAMNED
ANYTHING [C] SYDNEY YOUNGBLOOD
ANYTHING [D] CULTURE BEAT
ANYTHING [E] SWV
ANYTHING [F] 3T
ANYTHING [G] DAMAGE
ANYTHING [H] JAY-Z
ANYTHING BUT DOWN SHERYL CROW
ANYTHING CAN HAPPEN WAS (NOT WAS)
ANYTHING FOR YOU [A] GLORIA ESTEFAN & MIAMI SOUND MACHINE
ANYTHING FOR YOU [B] STAMFORD AMP
ANYTHING GOES HARPERS BIZARRE
ANYTHING IS POSSIBLE [A] DEBBIE GIBSON
ANYTHING IS POSSIBLE [B] WILL YOUNG
ANYTHING THAT'S ROCK 'N' ROLL TOM PETTY & THE HEARTBREAKERS
ANYTHING YOU WANT JODIE
ANYTHING YOU WANT (I'VE GOT IT) ULTIMATE KAOS
ANYTIME [A] NU-BIRTH
ANYTIME [B] BRIAN McKNIGHT
ANYTIME YOU NEED A FRIEND MARIAH CAREY
ANYWAY HONEYCRACK
ANYWAY ANYHOW ANYWHERE WHO
ANYWAY THAT YOU WANT ME SPIRITUALIZED
ANYWAY YOU DO IT LIQUID GOLD
ANYWAY YOU WANT IT DAVE CLARK FIVE
ANYWHERE [A] DUBSTAR
ANYWHERE [B] BETH ORTON
ANYWHERE FOR YOU BACKSTREET BOYS
ANYWHERE IS ENYA
APACHE [A] SHADOWS
APACHE [A] BERT WEEDON
APACHE [B] STARFIGHTER
APACHE DROPOUT EDGAR BROUGHTON BAND
APEMAN KINKS
APHRODITE PARIS & SHARP
APOLLO 9 ADAM ANT
APOLOGIES TO INSECT LIFE BRITISH SEA POWER
APPARENTLY NOTHIN' YOUNG DISCIPLES
APPARENTLY NOTHING BRAND NEW HEAVIES
THE APPLE EP VARIOUS ARTISTS (EP'S & LPS)
APPLE GREEN MILLTOWN BROTHERS
APPLE OF MY EYE ED HARCOURT
THE APPLE STRETCHING GRACE JONES
APPLE TREE ERYKAH BADU
APPLEJACK JET HARRIS & TONY MEEHAN
APPRENTICE OF THE UNIVERSE PURE REASON REVOLUTION
APRIL LOVE PAT BOONE
APRIL SKIES JESUS & MARY CHAIN
AQUARIUS PAUL JONES
AQUARIUS/LET THE SUNSHINE IN (MEDLEY) FIFTH DIMENSION
ARABIAN KNIGHTS SIOUXSIE & THE BANSHEES
ARE EVERYTHING BUZZCOCKS
ARE 'FRIENDS' ELECTRIC? TUBEWAY ARMY
ARE WE HERE ORBITAL
ARE YOU BEING SERVED GRACE BROTHERS
ARE YOU BEING SERVED SIR JOHN INMAN
ARE YOU BLUE OR ARE YOU BLIND? BLUETONES
ARE YOU DREAMING TWENTY 4 SEVEN FEATURING CAPTAIN HOLLYWOOD

ARE YOU GETTING ENOUGH OF WHAT MAKES YOU HAPPY HOT CHOCOLATE
ARE YOU GONNA BE MY GIRL? JET
ARE YOU GONNA BE THERE? UP YER RONSON FEATURING MARY PEARCE
ARE YOU GONNA GO MY WAY LENNY KRAVITZ
ARE YOU GROWING TIRED OF MY LOVE STATUS QUO
ARE YOU HAPPY NOW? MICHELLE BRANCH
ARE YOU HEARING (WHAT I HEAR)? LEVEL 42
ARE YOU IN INCUBUS
ARE YOU JIMMY RAY? JIMMY RAY
ARE YOU LONESOME TONIGHT ELVIS PRESLEY
ARE YOU LOOKIN' AT ME RICKY TOMLINSON
ARE YOU MAN ENOUGH UNO CLIO FEATURING MARTINE McCUTCHEON
ARE YOU MINE BROS
ARE YOU MY BABY WENDY & LISA
ARE YOU OUT THERE CRESCENDO
ARE YOU READY [A] BILLY OCEAN
ARE YOU READY? [B] BREAK MACHINE
ARE YOU READY [C] AC/DC
ARE YOU READY [D] GYRES
(ARE YOU READY) DO THE BUS STOP FATBACK BAND
ARE YOU READY FOR LOVE [A] ELTON JOHN
ARE YOU READY FOR LOVE [B] ULTRA HIGH
ARE YOU READY FOR SOME MORE? REEL 2 REAL
ARE YOU READY TO BE HEARTBROKEN SANDIE SHAW
ARE YOU READY TO FLY ROZALLA
ARE YOU READY TO PARTY SHRINK
ARE YOU READY TO ROCK WIZZARD
ARE YOU SATISFIED? (FUNKA NOVA) RAH BAND
ARE YOU STILL HAVING FUN? EAGLE-EYE CHERRY
ARE YOU SURE [A] ALLISONS
ARE YOU SURE [B] SO
ARE YOU THAT SOMEBODY? AALIYAH
(ARE YOU) THE ONE THAT I'VE BEEN... NICK CAVE & THE BAD SEEDS
AREA CODES LUDACRIS FEATURING NATE DOGG
ARGENTINA JEREMY HEALY & AMOS
ARGENTINE MELODY (CANCION DE ARGENTINA) SAN JOSE FEATURING RODRIGUEZ ARGENTINA
ARIA ACKER BILK, HIS CLARINET & STRINGS
ARIANA STARDUST
ARIELS SYSTEM OF A DOWN
ARIENNE TASMIN ARCHER
ARIZONA SKY CHINA CRISIS
ARMAGEDDON DAYS ARE HERE (AGAIN) THE THE
ARMAGEDDON IT DEF LEPPARD
ARMCHAIR ANARCHIST KINGMAKER
ARMED AND EXTREMELY DANGEROUS FIRST CHOICE
ARMED AND READY MICHAEL SCHENKER GROUP
ARMS ALOFT JOE STRUMMER & THE MESCALEROS
ARMS AROUND THE WORLD LOUISE
ARMS OF LOREN E'VOKE
ARMS OF MARY SUTHERLAND BROTHERS & QUIVER
THE ARMS OF ORION PRINCE WITH SHEENA EASTON
ARMS OF SOLITUDE OUI 3
THE ARMS OF THE ONE WHO LOVES YOU XSCAPE
ARMY BEN FOLDS FIVE
ARMY DREAMERS KATE BUSH
ARMY OF ME BJORK
ARMY OF TWO DUM DUMS
ARNOLD LAYNE PINK FLOYD
AROUND MY BRAIN PROGRESS FUNK
AROUND THE WAY GIRL LL COOL J
AROUND THE WORLD [A] BING CROSBY
AROUND THE WORLD [A] RONNIE HILTON
AROUND THE WORLD [A] GRACIE FIELDS
AROUND THE WORLD [A] MANTOVANI
AROUND THE WORLD [B] EAST 17
AROUND THE WORLD [C] DAFT PUNK

AROUND THE WORLD [D] RED HOT CHILI PEPPERS
AROUND THE WORLD [E] AQUA
AROUND THE WORLD [F] ATC
ARRANGED MARRIAGE APACHE INDIAN
ARRESTED BY YOU DUSTY SPRINGFIELD
ARRIVEDERCI DARLING ANNE SHELTON
ARRIVEDERCI DARLING EDNA SAVAGE
ARSENAL NUMBER ONE ARSENAL FC
ART FOR ART'S SAKE 10 C.C.
THE ART OF DRIVING BLACK BOX RECORDER
THE ART OF LOSING AMERICAN HI-FI
ART OF LOVE ART OF NOISE
THE ART OF MOVING BUTTS SHUT UP & DANCE
    FEATURING ERIN
THE ART OF PARTIES JAPAN
ARTHUR DALEY ('E'S ALRIGHT) FIRM
ARTHUR'S THEME (BEST THAT YOU CAN DO)
    CHRISTOPHER CROSS
AS GEORGE MICHAEL & MARY J. BLIGE
AS ALWAYS FARLEY 'JACKMASTER' FUNK FEATURING
    RICKY DILLARD
AS ALWAYS SECRET LIFE
AS GOOD AS IT GETS GENE
AS I AM SOUND OF ONE FEATURING GLADEZZ
AS I LAY ME DOWN SOPHIE B. HAWKINS
AS I LOVE YOU SHIRLEY BASSEY
AS I SAT SADLY BY HER SIDE NICK CAVE & THE BAD
    SEEDS
AS IF WE NEVER SAID GOODBYE (FROM SUNSET
    BOULEVARD) BARBRA STREISAND
AS LONG AS HE NEEDS ME SHIRLEY BASSEY
AS LONG AS THE PRICE IS RIGHT DR. FEELGOOD
AS LONG AS YOU FOLLOW FLEETWOOD MAC
AS LONG AS YOU LOVE ME BACKSTREET BOYS
AS LONG AS YOU'RE GOOD TO ME JUDY CHEEKS
AS TEARS GO BY MARIANNE FAITHFULL
AS THE RUSH COMES MOTORCYCLE
AS THE TIME GOES BY FUNKAPOLITAN
AS TIME GOES BY RICHARD ALLAN
AS TIME GOES BY DOOLEY WILSON
AS TIME GOES BY JASON DONOVAN
AS (UNTIL THE DAY) KNOWLEDGE
AS USUAL BRENDA LEE
AS WE DO DJ ZINC
AS YOU LIKE IT ADAM FAITH
ASCEND NITZER EBB
ASCENSION NO ONE'S GONNA LOVE YOU, SO DON'T
    EVER WONDER MAXWELL
ASHES EMBRACE
ASHES AND DIAMONDS ZAINE GRIFF
ASHES TO ASHES [A] MINDBENDERS
ASHES TO ASHES [B] DAVID BOWIE
ASHES TO ASHES [C] FAITH NO MORE
ASIA MINOR KOKOMO
ASK SMITHS
ASK THE LORD HIPSWAY
ASLEEP IN THE BACK ELBOW
ASSASSIN ORB
ASSASSINATOR 13 CHIKINKI
ASSASSING MARILLION
ASSESSMENT BETA BAND
ASSHOLE DENIS LEARY
ASSOCIATION INTERNATIONAL AIRPORT/TEENAGE
    FANCLUB
ASTOUNDED BRAN VAN 3000 FEATURING CURTIS
    MAYFIELD
ASTRAL AMERICA APOLLO 440
ASYLUM ORB
ASYLUMS IN JERUSALEM SCRITTI POLITTI
AT HOME HE'S A TOURIST GANG OF FOUR
AT MIDNIGHT T-CONNECTION

AT MY MOST BEAUTIFUL R.E.M.
AT NIGHT SHAKEDOWN
AT THE CLUB DRIFTERS
AT THE EDGE STIFF LITTLE FINGERS
AT THE END IIO
AT THE HOP DANNY & THE JUNIORS
AT THE MOVIES RONI SIZE
AT THE PALACE (PARTS 1 & 2) WILFRID BRAMBELL &
    HARRY H. CORBETT
AT THE RIVER GROOVE ARMADA
AT THE TOP OF THE STAIRS FORMATIONS
AT THIS TIME OF YEAR CRAIG
(AT YOUR BEST) YOU ARE LOVE AALIYAH
ATHEAMA NEBULA II
ATHENA WHO
ATLANTIS [A] SHADOWS
ATLANTIS [B] DONOVAN
ATLANTIS [C] SECTION-X
ATLANTIS IS CALLING (S.O.S. FOR LOVE) MODERN
    TALKING
ATMOSPHERE [A] RUSS ABBOT
ATMOSPHERE [B] JOY DIVISION
ATMOSPHERE [C] KAYESTONE
ATMOSPHERIC ROAD FAMILY CAT
ATOM BOMB FLUKE
ATOM POWERED ACTION (EP) BIS
ATOMIC BLONDIE
ATOMIC CITY HOLLY JOHNSON
ATTACK [A] TOYS
ATTACK [B] EXPLOITED
ATTACK ME WITH YOUR LOVE CAMEO
ATTACK OF THE GHOSTRIDERS RAVEONETTES
ATTENTION TO ME NOLANS
ATTITUDE [A] SEPULTURA
ATTITUDE [B] ALIEN ANT FARM
ATTITUDE [C] SUEDE
AUBERGE CHRIS REA
AUDIO VIDEO NEWS
AUDITION WITNESS
AUF WIEDERSEHEN SWEETHEART VERA LYNN
AUGUST OCTOBER ROBIN GIBB
AULD LANG SYNE WEEKEND
AUSLANDER LIVING COLOUR
AUSTRALIA MANIC STREET PREACHERS
AUTHORITY CONFRONTATION SELFISH C**T
AUTO DRIVE HERBIE HANCOCK
AUTOBAHN KRAFTWERK
AUTOBAHN 66 PRIMAL SCREAM
AUTOBIOGRAPHY OF A CRACKHEAD SHUT UP & DANCE
AUTOMATIC [A] POINTER SISTERS
AUTOMATIC [B] MILLIE SCOTT
AUTOMATIC [C] FLOORPLAY
AUTOMATIC [D] SARAH WHATMORE
AUTOMATIC HIGH S CLUB JUNIORS
AUTOMATIC LOVER [A] DEE D. JACKSON
AUTOMATIC LOVER [B] VIBRATORS
AUTOMATIC LOVER (CALL FOR LOVE) REAL McCOY
AUTOMATICALLY SUNSHINE SUPREMES
AUTOMATIK BEAT RENEGADES
AUTOPHILIA BLUETONES
AUTUMN RONI SIZE
AUTUMN ALMANAC KINKS
AUTUMN CONCERTO GEORGE MELACHRINO
    ORCHESTRA
AUTUMN LEAVES COLDCUT
AUTUMN LOVE ELECTRA
AUTUMN TACTICS CHICANE
AVA ADORE SMASHING PUMPKINS
AVALON ROXY MUSIC
AVE MARIA SHIRLEY BASSEY
AVE MARIA LESLEY GARRETT & AMANDA THOMPSON

AVE MARIA ANDREA BOCELLI
AVENGING ANGELS SPACE
AVENUE [A] SAINT ETIENNE
AVENUE [B] PAUL VAN DYK
AVENUES AND ALLEYWAYS TONY CHRISTIE
AVERAGE MAN [A] SYMPOSIUM
AVERAGE MAN [B] TURIN BRAKES
THE AVERAGE MAN [C] SIMPLE KID
THE AWAKENING YORK
AWAY FROM HOME DR ALBAN
AWAY FROM ME PUDDLE OF MUDD
AWFUL HOLE
AXEL F HAROLD FALTERMEYER
AXEL F CLOCK
AXEL F SPACECORN
AY AY AY AY MOOSEY MODERN ROMANCE
AYLA AYLA
AZTEC GOLD SILSOE
AZTEC LIGHTNING (THEME FROM BBC WORLD CUP
    GRANDSTAND) HEADS
B-BOY HUMP OLD SKOOL ORCHESTRA
B-BOY STANCE FREESTYLERS FEATURING TENOR FLY
B GOOD 2 ME RONNI SIMON
B LINE LAMB
B.O.B. (BOMBS OVER BAGHDAD) OUTKAST
B 2 GETHER ORIGINAL
B WITH ME MIS-TEEQ
B WITH U JUNIOR SANCHEZ FEATURING DAJAE
BA-BA-BANKROBBERY (ENGLISH VERSION) EAV
BA-NA-NA-BAM-BOO WESTWORLD
BAA BAA BLACK SHEEP SINGING SHEEP
BAAL'S HYMN (EP) DAVID BOWIE
BABARABATIN GYPSYMEN
BABE [A] STYX
BABE [B] TAKE THAT
BABES IN THE WOOD MATCHBOX
BABETTE TOMMY BRUCE
BABIES ASHFORD & SIMPSON
BABOOSHKA KATE BUSH
B-A-B-Y RACHEL SWEET
BABY [A] HALO JAMES
BABY [B] ROZALLA
THE BABY HOLLIES
BABY BABY [A] FRANKIE LYMON & THE TEENAGERS
BABY BABY [B] EIGHTH WONDER
BABY BABY [C] AMY GRANT
BABY BABY [D] CORONA
BABY-BABY-BABY TLC
BABY BABY BYE BYE JERRY LEE LEWIS
BABY BABY MY LOVE'S ALL FOR YOU DENIECE
    WILLIAMS
BABY BE MINE BLACKstreet FEATURING TEDDY RILEY
BABY BLUE DUSTY SPRINGFIELD
BABY BOY [A] BIG BROVAZ
BABY BOY [B] BEYONCÉ FEATURING SEAN PAUL
BABY BRITAIN ELLIOTT SMITH
BABY, CAN I GET YOUR NUMBER OBI PROJECT
    FEATURING HARRY, ASHER D & DJ WHAT?
BABY CAN I HOLD YOU BOYZONE
BABY COME BACK [A] EQUALS
BABY COME BACK [A] PATO BANTON
BABY COME BACK [B] PLAYER
BABY COME ON SPACEMAID
BABY COME ON OVER SAMANTHA MUMBA
BABY COME TO ME PATTI AUSTIN & JAMES INGRAM
BABY COME TO ME ALEXANDER O'NEAL FEATURING
    CHERRELLE
BABY DID A BAD BAD THING CHRIS ISAAK
BABY DON'T CHANGE YOUR MIND GLADYS KNIGHT &
    THE PIPS
BABY DON'T CRY [A] LALAH HATHAWAY

BABY DON'T CRY [B] INXS
BABY DON'T FORGET MY NUMBER MILLI VANILLI
BABY DON'T GET HOOKED ON ME MAC DAVIS
BABY DON'T GO [A] SONNY & CHER
BABY DON'T GO [B] 4MANDU
BABY FACE LITTLE RICHARD
BABY FACE BOBBY DARIN
BABY FACE WING & A PRAYER FIFE & DRUM CORPS
BABY GET HIGHER DAVID SNEDDON
BABY GOT BACK SIR MIX-A-LOT
BABY I DON'T CARE [A] BUDDY HOLLY
BABY I DON'T CARE [A] ELVIS PRESLEY
BABY I DON'T CARE [B] TRANSVISION VAMP
BABY I DON'T CARE [B] JENNIFER ELLISON
BABY I KNOW RUBETTES
BABY I LOVE U JENNIFER LOPEZ
BABY I LOVE YOU [A] RONETTES
BABY I LOVE YOU [A] DAVE EDMUNDS
BABY I LOVE YOU [A] RAMONES
BABY I LOVE YOU [A] TSD
BABY I LOVE YOU [B] ARETHA FRANKLIN
BABY I LOVE YOU OK KENNY
BABY I LOVE YOUR WAY PETER FRAMPTON
BABY I LOVE YOUR WAY BIG MOUNTAIN
BABY I LOVE YOUR WAY – FREEBIRD WILL TO POWER
BABY I NEED YOUR LOVIN' FOURMOST
BABY I WON'T LET YOU DOWN PICKETTYWITCH
BABY I'M A-WANT YOU BREAD
BABY I'M SCARED OF YOU WOMACK & WOMACK
BABY I'M YOURS PETER & GORDON
BABY I'M YOURS LINDA LEWIS
BABY, IT'S COLD OUTSIDE TOM JONES & CERYS
    MATTHEWS
BABY IT'S TRUE MARI WILSON
BABY IT'S YOU [A] DAVE BERRY
BABY IT'S YOU [A] BEATLES
BABY IT'S YOU [B] SILK
BABY IT'S YOU [C] MN8
BABY IT'S YOU [D] JOJO FEATURING BOW WOW
BABY JANE ROD STEWART
BABY JUMP MUNGO JERRY
BABY LAY DOWN RUBY WINTERS
BABY LEE JOHN LEE HOOKER WITH ROBERT CRAY
BABY LET ME TAKE YOU HOME ANIMALS
BABY LOVE [A] SUPREMES
BABY LOVE [A] HONEY BANE
BABY LOVE [B] REGINA
BABY LOVE [B] DANNII MINOGUE
BABY LOVER PETULA CLARK
BABY MAKE IT SOON MARMALADE
BABY MY HEART CRICKETS
BABY NEVER SAY GOODBYE UNIT FOUR PLUS TWO
BABY NOW I DAN REED NETWORK
BABY NOW THAT I'VE FOUND YOU FOUNDATIONS
BABY NOW THAT I'VE FOUND YOU LAUREN
    WATERWORTH
BABY OF MINE ALAN PRICE
BABY (OFF THE WALL) SIRENS
BABY ONE MORE TIME BRITNEY SPEARS
BABY PHAT DE LA SOUL
BABY PLAYS AROUND (EP) ELVIS COSTELLO
BABY PLEASE DON'T GO THEM
BABY ROO CONNIE FRANCIS
BABY SITTIN' BOBBY ANGELO & THE TUXEDOS
BABY SITTIN' BOOGIE BUZZ CLIFFORD
BABY STOP CRYING BOB DYLAN
BABY TAKE A BOW ADAM FAITH
BABY TALK ALISHA
BABY U LEFT ME (IN THE COLD) MARILYN
BABY UNIVERSAL TIN MACHINE
BABY WANTS TO RIDE HANI

BABY, WE BETTER TRY TO GET IT TOGETHER BARRY
    WHITE
BABY WE CAN'T GO WRONG CILLA BLACK
BABY WHAT A BIG SURPRISE CHICAGO
BABY WHAT I MEAN DRIFTERS
(BABY) YOU DON'T HAVE TO TELL ME WALKER
    BROTHERS
BABY YOU SHOULD KNOW JOY ZIPPER
BABY YOU'RE DYNAMITE CLIFF RICHARD
BABYCAKES 3 OF A KIND
BABYLON [A] BLACK DOG FEATURING OFRA HAZA
BABYLON [B] DAVID GRAY
BABYLON A.D. (SO GLAD FOR THE MADNESS) CRADLE
    OF FILTH
BABYLON'S BURNING RUTS
BABYSHAMBLES PETE DOHERTY
BABY'S COMING BACK JELLYFISH
BABY'S FIRST CHRISTMAS CONNIE FRANCIS
BABY'S GOT A TEMPER PRODIGY
BABY'S REQUEST WINGS
BACHELOR BOY CLIFF RICHARD & THE SHADOWS
BACHELORETTE BJORK
BACK AND FORTH [A] CAMEO
BACK AND FORTH [B] AALIYAH
BACK AROUND ELEVATOR SUITE
BACK BY DOPE DEMAND KING BEE
BACK FOR GOOD TAKE THAT
BACK FOR GOOD REAL EMOTION
BACK FOR ME CANDEE JAY
BACK FROM THE EDGE BRUCE DICKINSON
BACK HERE BBMAK
BACK HOME ENGLAND WORLD CUP SQUAD
BACK IN LOVE AGAIN DONNA SUMMER
BACK IN MY ARMS CHRIS PAUL
BACK IN MY ARMS AGAIN SUPREMES
BACK IN MY ARMS (ONCE AGAIN) HAZELL DEAN
BACK IN MY LIFE [A] JOE ROBERTS
BACK IN MY LIFE [B] ALICE DEEJAY
BACK IN THE DAY [A] AHMAD
BACK IN THE DAY [B] ASHER D
BACK IN THE HIGH LIFE AGAIN STEVE WINWOOD
BACK IN THE UK SCOOTER
BACK IN THE U.S.S.R. BEATLES
BACK IT UP ROBIN S
THE BACK OF LOVE ECHO & THE BUNNYMEN
BACK OF MY HAND JAGS
BACK OFF BOOGALOO RINGO STARR
BACK ON MY FEET AGAIN FOUNDATIONS
BACK ON THE CHAIN GANG PRETENDERS
BACK ON THE RADIO HISS
BACK ON THE ROAD [A] MARMALADE
BACK ON THE ROAD [B] EARTH, WIND & FIRE
BACK ON THE STREETS SAXON
BACK ON TOP VAN MORRISON
BACK SEAT OF MY CAR PAUL & LINDA McCARTNEY
BACK STABBERS O'JAYS
BACK STREET LUV CURVED AIR
BACK THEN MORE FIRE CREW
BACK TO CALI MAURO PICOTTO
BACK TO EARTH YVES DERUYTER
BACK TO FRONT [A] STIFF LITTLE FINGERS
BACK TO FRONT [B] ADAMSKI
BACK TO LIFE (HOWEVER DO YOU WANT ME) SOUL II
    SOUL FEATURING CARON WHEELER
BACK TO LOVE [A] EVELYN KING
BACK TO LOVE [B] BRAND NEW HEAVIES FEATURING
    N'DEA DAVENPORT
BACK TO LOVE [C] E-Z ROLLERS
BACK TO MY ROOTS RuPAUL
BACK TO REALITY INTELLIGENT HOODLUM
BACK TO SCHOOL AGAIN FOUR TOPS

BACK TO THE LIGHT BRIAN MAY
BACK TO THE OLD SCHOOL BASSHEADS
BACK TO THE SIXTIES TIGHT FIT
BACK TO THE SIXTIES PART 2 TIGHT FIT
BACK TO YOU BRYAN ADAMS
BACK TOGETHER [A] BABY BIRD
BACK TOGETHER [B] HARDSOUL FEATURING RON
    CARROLL
BACK TOGETHER AGAIN ROBERTA FLACK & DONNY
    HATHAWAY
BACK TOGETHER AGAIN INNER CITY
BACK UP (TO ME) WOOKIE FEATURING LAIN
BACK WHEN ALLSTARS
BACK WITH THE BOYS AGAIN JOE FAGIN
BACK WITH THE KILLER AGAIN AUTEURS
BACKCHAT QUEEN
BACKFIELD IN MOTION JB'S ALL STARS
BACKFIRED [A] DEBBIE HARRY
BACKFIRED [B] MASTERS AT WORK FEATURING INDIA
BACKS TO THE WALL SAXON
BACKSTABBERS MARK MORRISON
BACKSEAT EDUCATION ZODIAC MINDWARP & THE
    LOVE REACTION
BACKSTAGE GENE PITNEY
BACKSTREET SYMPHONY THUNDER
BACKSTROKIN' FATBACK
BAD MICHAEL JACKSON
BAD ACTRESS TERRORVISION
BAD AMBASSADOR DIVINE COMEDY
BAD ASS STRIPPA JENTINA
BAD BABYSITTER PRINCESS SUPERSTAR
BAD BAD BOY NAZARETH
BAD BOY [A] MARTY WILDE
BAD BOY [B] ADICTS
BAD BOY [C] MIAMI SOUND MACHINE
BAD BOY [D] WILDCHILD FEATURING JOMALSKI
BAD BOY FOR LIFE P DIDDY/BLACK ROB/MARK CURRY
BAD BOYS [A] WHAM!
BAD BOYS [B] INNER CIRCLE
BAD BOYS HOLLER BOO 5050
BAD CASE OF LOVIN' YOU (DOCTOR DOCTOR) ROBERT
    PALMER
BAD COVER VERSION PULP
BAD DAY [A] CARMEL
BAD DAY [B] R.E.M.
THE BAD DAYS EP SPACE
BAD FEELINGS BEATINGS
BAD GIRL [A] MADONNA
BAD GIRL [B] SCARLET
BAD GIRL [C] DJ RAP
BAD GIRLS DONNA SUMMER
BAD GIRLS JULIET ROBERTS
BAD HABIT A.T.F.C. PRESENTS ONEPHATDEEVA
    FEATURING LISA MILLETT
BAD HABITS JENNY BURTON
BAD INTENTIONS DR DRE FEATURING KNOC-TURN'AL
BAD LIFE PUBLIC IMAGE LTD.
BAD LOVE ERIC CLAPTON
BAD LUCK FM
BAD MEDICINE BON JOVI
BAD MOON RISING CREEDENCE CLEARWATER
    REVIVAL
A BAD NIGHT CAT STEVENS
BAD OLD DAYS CO-CO
BAD OLD MAN BABY BIRD
BAD PENNY BLUES HUMPHREY LYTTELTON BAND
THE BAD PHOTOGRAPHER SAINT ETIENNE
BAD THING CRY OF LOVE
BAD THINGS N-JOI
BAD TIME JAYHAWKS
BAD TO ME BILLY J. KRAMER & THE DAKOTAS

THE BAD TOUCH BLOODHOUND GANG
A BAD TOWN BIG SOUND AUTHORITY
BAD WEATHER SUPREMES
BAD YOUNG BROTHER DEREK B
BADABOOM B2K FEATURING FABOLOUS
BADDER BADDER SCHWING FREDDY FRESH FEATURING
    FATBOY SLIM
BADDEST RUFFEST BACKYARD DOG
BADGE CREAM
BADMAN [A] COCKNEY REJECTS
BADMAN [B] SISTER BLISS
THE BADMAN IS ROBBIN' HIJACK
BAG IT UP GERI HALLIWELL
BAGGY TROUSERS MADNESS
THE BAGUIO TRACK LUZON
BAILAMOS [A] ENRIQUE IGLIASAS
BAILAMOS [B] M3
BAILANDO CON LOBOS CABANA
BAKER STREET GERRY RAFFERTY
BAKER STREET UNDERCOVER
BAKERMAN LAID BACK
BALL AND CHAIN XTC
BALL OF CONFUSION TEMPTATIONS
BALL PARK INCIDENT WIZZARD
BALLA BABY CHINGY
BALLAD OF A LANDLORD TERRY HALL
BALLAD OF BONNIE AND CLYDE GEORGIE FAME
THE BALLAD OF CHASEY LAIN BLOODHOUND GANG
BALLAD OF DAVY CROCKETT BILL HAYES
BALLAD OF DAVY CROCKETT MAX BYGRAVES
BALLAD OF DAVY CROCKETT DICK JAMES
THE BALLAD OF DAVY CROCKETT TENNESSEE ERNIE
    FORD
THE BALLAD OF JAYNE L.A. GUNS
THE BALLAD OF JOHN AND YOKO BEATLES
THE BALLAD OF LUCY JORDAN MARIANNE FAITHFULL
BALLAD OF PALADIN DUANE EDDY
THE BALLAD OF PETER PUMPKINHEAD CRASH TEST
    DUMMIES
THE BALLAD OF PETER PUMPKINHEAD XTC
THE BALLAD OF SPOTTY MULDOON PETER COOK
BALLAD OF THE GREEN BERETS STAFF SERGEANT
    BARRY SADLER
THE BALLAD OF TOM JONES SPACE WITH CERYS OF
    CATATONIA
BALLAD OF YOUTH RICHIE SAMBORA
BALLERINA GIRL LIONEL RICHIE
BALLERINA (PRIMA DONNA) STEVE HARLEY
BALLOON CATHERINE WHEEL
BALLROOM BLITZ SWEET
BALLROOM BLITZ TIA CARRERE
THE BALLROOM OF ROMANCE CHRIS DE BURGH
BALMES IAN POOLEY FEATURING ESTHERO
BAM BAM BAM WESTBAM
BAMA BOOGIE WOOGIE CLEVELAND EATON
BAMA LAMA BAMA LOO LITTLE RICHARD
BAMBAATA 2012 SHY FX
BAMBAKITA RONI SIZE
BAMBINO SPRINGFIELDS
BAMBOO HOUSES SYLVIAN SAKAMOTO
BAMBOOGIE BAMBOO
BANANA BANANA KING KURT
BANANA BOAT SONG SHIRLEY BASSEY
BANANA BOAT SONG HARRY BELAFONTE
BANANA BOAT SONG TARRIERS
BANANA REPUBLIC BOOMTOWN RATS
BANANA ROCK WOMBLES
THE BANANA SONG GSP
BANANA SPLITS (TRA LA LA SONG) DICKIES
BANANA-NA-NA (DUMB DI DUMB) TECHNOHEAD
BAND OF GOLD [A] DON CHERRY

BAND OF GOLD [B] FREDA PAYNE
BAND OF GOLD [B] SYLVESTER
BAND ON THE RUN PAUL McCARTNEY & WINGS
THE BAND PLAYED THE BOOGIE C.C.S.
BANDAGES HOT HOT HEAT
BANDWAGON BLUES TWISTED INDIVIDUAL
BANG [A] BLUR
BANG [B] ROBBIE RIVERA PRESENTS RHYTHM
    BANGERS
BANG AND BLAME R.E.M.
BANG BANG [A] SQUEEZE
BANG BANG [B] B.A. ROBERTSON
BANG BANG (MY BABY SHOT ME DOWN) CHER
BANG ON! PROPELLERHEADS
BANG ZOOM (LET'S GO GO) REAL ROXANNE WITH
    HITMAN HOWIE TEE
BANGERS AND MASH PETER SELLERS & SOPHIA
    LOREN
BANGIN' BASS DA TECHNO BOHEMIAN
THE BANGIN' MAN SLADE
BANGLA DESH GEORGE HARRISON
BANJO BOY GEORGE FORMBY
BANJO BOY JAN & KJELD
BANJO'S BACK IN TOWN ALMA COGAN
BANKROBBER CLASH
BANKROBBER AUDIOWEB
BANKS OF THE OHIO OLIVIA NEWTON-JOHN
THE BANNER MAN BLUE MINK
BANQUET BLOC PARTY
BARBADOS TYPICALLY TROPICAL
BARBARA ANN BEACH BOYS
BARBARELLA ALISHA'S ATTIC
BARBER'S ADAGIO FOR STRINGS WILLIAM ORBIT
BARBIE GIRL AQUA
BARCELONA [A] FREDDIE MERCURY & MONTSERRAT
    CABALLE
BARCELONA [B] D KAY & EPSILION FEATURING
    STANIMA MC
BARCELONA (FRIENDS UNTIL THE END) RUSSELL
    WATSON & SHAUN RYDER
BARE NECESSITIES MEGAMIX U.K. MIXMASTERS
BAREFOOT (EP) ULTRAMARINE
BAREFOOT IN THE HEAD A MAN CALLED ADAM
BAREFOOTIN' ROBERT PARKER
BARK AT THE MOON OZZY OSBOURNE
BARMY LONDON ARMY CHARLIE HARPER
BARNEY (...& ME) BOO RADLEYS
BARREL OF A GUN DEPECHE MODE
BARRIERS SOFT CELL
THE BARTENDER AND THE THIEF STEREOPHONICS
BASEMENT TRACK HIGH CONTRAST
BASKET CASE GREEN DAY
THE BASS EP FERGIE
BASS (HOW LOW CAN YOU GO) SIMON HARRIS
BASS SHAKE URBAN SHAKEDOWN FEATURING
    MICKY FINN
BASSCAD AUTECHRE
BASSFLY TILLMAN + REIS
BASSLICK SECOND PROTOCOL
BASSLINE MANTRONIX
BAT OUT OF HELL MEAT LOAF
BATDANCE PRINCE
BATHTIME TINDERSTICKS
BATHWATER NO DOUBT
BATMAN THEME NEAL HEFTI
BATTER UP NELLY & ST LUNATICS
BATTLE WOOKIE FEATURING LAIN
THE BATTLE OF NEW ORLEANS LONNIE DONEGAN
THE BATTLE OF NEW ORLEANS JOHNNY HORTON
BATTLE OF THE SEXES FAITH, HOPE & CHARITY
BATTLE OF WHO COULD CARE LESS BEN FOLDS FIVE

BATTLEFLAG LO FIDELITY ALLSTARS FEATURING
    PIGEONHED
THE BATTLE'S O'ER ANDY STEWART
BATTLESHIP CHAINS GEORGIA SATELLITES
BAUBLES, BANGLES AND BEADS GEORGE SHEARING
BAWITDABA KID ROCK
BBC WORLD CUP GRANDSTAND ROYAL PHILHARMONIC
    ORCHESTRA
BE AGGRESSIVE FAITH NO MORE
BE ALONE NO MORE ANOTHER LEVEL FEATURING JAY-Z
BE ANGLED JAM & SPOON FEATURING REA
BE AS ONE SASHA & MARIA
BE BOP A LULA GENE VINCENT
BE CAREFUL SPARKLE FEATURING R KELLY
BE COOL PAFFENDORF
BE FAITHFUL FATMAN SCOOP FEATURING THE
    CROOKLYN CLAN
BE FREE LIVE ELEMENT
BE FREE WITH YOUR LOVE SPANDAU BALLET
BE GOOD TO YOURSELF FRANKIE MILLER
BE HAPPY MARY J. BLIGE
BE LOUD BE PROUD (BE HEARD) TOYAH
BE MINE [A] LANCE FORTUNE
BE MINE [B] TREMELOES
BE MINE [C] CHARLOTTE
BE MINE [D] DAVID GRAY
BE MINE TONIGHT JAMMERS
BE MY BABY [A] RONETTES
BE MY BABY [B] VANESSA PARADIS
BE MY BABY [C] CAPPELLA
BE MY DOWNFALL DEL AMITRI
BE MY ENEMY DEPARTURE
BE MY FRIEND SOUL U*NIQUE
BE MY GIRL [A] JIM DALE
BE MY GIRL [B] DENNISONS
BE MY GUEST FATS DOMINO
BE MY LIGHT BE MY GUIDE GENE
BE MY LOVER LA BOUCHE
BE MY NUMBER TWO JOE JACKSON
BE MY TWIN BROTHER BEYOND
BE NEAR ME ABC
BE QUICK OR BE DEAD IRON MAIDEN
BE QUIET AND DRIVE (FAR AWAY) DEFTONES
BE STIFF DEVO
BE TENDER WITH ME BABY TINA TURNER
BE THANKFUL FOR WHAT YOU'VE GOT WILLIAM DE
    VAUGHN
BE THE FIRST TO BELIEVE A1
BE THERE [A] TALL PAUL
BE THERE [B] UNKLE FEATURING IAN BROWN
BE WITH ME ALWAYS CLIFF RICHARD
BE WITH YOU [A] BANGLES
BE WITH YOU [B] ATOMIC KITTEN
BE YOUNG BE FOOLISH BE HAPPY TAMS
BE YOUNG BE FOOLISH BE HAPPY SONIA
BE YOURSELF CELEDA
BEACH BABY FIRST CLASS
BEACH BOYS MEDLEY BEACH BOYS
BEACH BUMP BABY FORD
BEACH OF THE WAR GODDESS CARON WHEELER
BEACHBALL NALIN & KANE
BEACHBOY GOLD GIDEA PARK
BEACHED ORBITAL & ANGELO BADALAMENTI
BEACON LIGHT WEEN
BEAR CAGE STRANGLERS
A BEAT CALLED LOVE GRID
BEAT DIS BOMB THE BASS
BEAT FOR BEATNIKS JOHN BARRY ORCHESTRA
THE BEAT GOES ON [A] SONNY & CHER
BEAT GOES ON [B] ALL SEEING I
THE BEAT GOES ON [C] BOB SINCLAR

BEAT IT MICHAEL JACKSON
BEAT MAMA CAST
BEAT STREET BREAKDOWN GRANDMASTER MELLE MEL & THE FURIOUS FIVE
BEAT SURRENDER JAM
BEAT THE BEAT MARI WILSON
BEAT THE CLOCK SPARKS
BEAT YOUR HEART OUT DISTILLERS
THE BEAT(EN) GENERATION THE THE
BEATIN' THE HEAT JACK 'N' CHILL
BEATLES AND THE STONES HOUSE OF LOVE
BEATLES MOVIE MEDLEY BEATLES
BEATNIK FLY JOHNNY & THE HURRICANES
BEATNIK GIRL SNUG
BEATSTIME SONIC SOLUTION
BEAUTIFUL [A] MARILLION
BEAUTIFUL [B] MATT DAREY'S MASH UP PRESENTS MARCELLA WOODS
BEAUTIFUL [C] BIGFELLA FEATURING NOEL McCALLA
BEAUTIFUL [D] LEMONESCENT
BEAUTIFUL [E] ATHLETE
BEAUTIFUL [F] CHRISTINA AGUILERA
BEAUTIFUL [G] SNOOP DOGG
BEAUTIFUL ALONE STRANGELOVE
BEAUTIFUL CHILD (A DEEPER LOVE) MADELYNE
BEAUTIFUL DAY [A] 3 COLOURS RED
BEAUTIFUL DAY [B] U2
BEAUTIFUL DREAM WORLD PARTY
THE BEAUTIFUL EXPERIENCE PRINCE
BEAUTIFUL GIRL INXS
BEAUTIFUL IMBALANCE THRASHING DOVES
BEAUTIFUL IN MY EYES JOSHUA KADISON
BEAUTIFUL INSIDE LOUISE
BEAUTIFUL LIFE ACE OF BASE
BEAUTIFUL LOVE [A] ADEVA
BEAUTIFUL LOVE [B] JULIAN COPE
BEAUTIFUL LOVER BROTHERHOOD OF MAN
BEAUTIFUL NIGHT PAUL McCARTNEY
BEAUTIFUL NOISE NEIL DIAMOND
THE BEAUTIFUL OCCUPATION TRAVIS
THE BEAUTIFUL ONES SUEDE
BEAUTIFUL PEOPLE [A] STRESS
BEAUTIFUL PEOPLE [B] BIG COUNTRY
BEAUTIFUL PEOPLE [C] BARBARA TUCKER
THE BEAUTIFUL PEOPLE [D] MARILYN MANSON
BEAUTIFUL SON HOLE
BEAUTIFUL STRANGER MADONNA
BEAUTIFUL SUNDAY DANIEL BOONE
BEAUTIFUL YOU NEIL SEDAKA
BEAUTY AND THE BEAST [A] DAVID BOWIE
BEAUTY AND THE BEAST [B] CELINE DION & PEABO BRYSON
BEAUTY DIES YOUNG LOWGOLD
BEAUTY IS ONLY SKIN DEEP TEMPTATIONS
THE BEAUTY OF SILENCE SVENSON & GIELEN
BEAUTY OF THE RIDE SEBADOH
BEAUTY ON FIRE NATALIE IMBRUGLIA
BEAUTY'S ONLY SKIN DEEP ASWAD
BECAUSE [A] DEMIS ROUSSOS
BECAUSE [B] JULIAN LENNON
BECAUSE I GOT HIGH AFROMAN
BECAUSE I GOT IT LIKE THAT JUNGLE BROTHERS
BECAUSE I LOVE YOU [A] GEORGIE FAME
BECAUSE I LOVE YOU [B] SHAKIN' STEVENS
BECAUSE I LOVE YOU (THE POSTMAN SONG) STEVIE B
BECAUSE OF LOVE [A] BILLY FURY
BECAUSE OF LOVE [B] JANET JACKSON
BECAUSE OF YOU [A] DEXY'S MIDNIGHT RUNNERS
BECAUSE OF YOU [B] GABRIELLE
BECAUSE OF YOU [C] 98o
BECAUSE OF YOU [D] SCANTY SANDWICH

BECAUSE OF YOU [E] MARQUES HOUSTON
BECAUSE THE NIGHT PATTI SMITH GROUP
BECAUSE THE NIGHT CO-RO FEATURING TARLISA
BECAUSE THE NIGHT 10,000 MANIACS
BECAUSE THE NIGHT JAN WAYNE
BECAUSE THEY'RE YOUNG DUANE EDDY & THE REBELS
BECAUSE THEY'RE YOUNG JAMES DARREN
BECAUSE WE WANT TO BILLIE
BECAUSE YOU LOVED ME (THEME FROM UP CLOSE AND PERSONAL) CELINE DION
BECAUSE YOU COSMIC ROUGH RIDERS
BECAUSE YOU'RE MINE MARIO LANZA
BECAUSE YOU'RE MINE NAT 'KING' COLE
BECAUSE YOU'RE YOUNG CLASSIX NOUVEAUX
BECOMING MORE LIKE ALFIE DIVINE COMEDY
BECOMING MORE LIKE GOD JAH WOBBLE'S INVADERS OF THE HEART
BED OF NAILS ALICE COOPER
BED OF ROSES BON JOVI
BED SITTER SOFT CELL
BEDS ARE BURNING MIDNIGHT OIL
THE BED'S TOO BIG WITHOUT YOU SHEILA HYLTON
BEDSHAPED KEANE
BEDTIME STORY MADONNA
THE BEE SCIENTIST
BEE BOM ANTHONY NEWLEY
BEE STING CAMOUFLAGE FEATURING MYSTI
BEEF GARY CLAIL
BEEN A LONG TIME FOG
BEEN AROUND THE WORLD [A] PUFF DADDY & THE FAMILY
BEEN AROUND THE WORLD [B] ZENA FEATURING VYBZ KARTEL
BEEN CAUGHT STEALING JANE'S ADDICTION
BEEN IT CARDIGANS
BEEN THERE DONE THAT SMOKE 2 SEVEN
BEEN THINKING ABOUT YOU MARTINE GIRAULT
BEEN TRAINING DOGS COOPER TEMPLE CLAUSE
BEEP ME 911 MISSY 'MISDEMEANOR' ELLIOTT
BEER DRINKERS AND HELL RAISERS MOTORHEAD
BEETHOVEN (I LOVE TO LISTEN TO) EURYTHMICS
BEETLEBUM BLUR
BEFORE PET SHOP BOYS
BEFORE TODAY EVERYTHING BUT THE GIRL
BEFORE YOU LEAVE PEPE DELUXE
BEFORE YOU LOVE ME ALSOU
BEFORE YOU WALK OUT OF MY LIFE MONICA
BEG, STEAL OR BORROW NEW SEEKERS
A BEGGAR ON A BEACH OF GOLD MIKE + THE MECHANICS
BEGGIN' TIMEBOX
BEGGIN' TO BE WRITTEN WORLDS APART
BEGGING YOU STONE ROSES
BEGIN AGAIN SPACE
BEGIN THE BEGUINE (VOLVER A EMPEZAR) JULIO IGLESIAS
THE BEGINNING SEAL
BEHIND A PAINTED SMILE ISLEY BROTHERS
BEHIND BLUE EYES LIMP BIZKIT
BEHIND CLOSED DOORS CHARLIE RICH
BEHIND THE COUNTER FALL
BEHIND THE GROOVE TEENA MARIE
BEHIND THE MASK ERIC CLAPTON
BEHIND THE WHEEL DEPECHE MODE
BEIN' AROUND LEMONHEADS
BEING A GIRL (PART ONE) EP MANSUN
BEING BOILED HUMAN LEAGUE
BEING BORING PET SHOP BOYS
BEING BRAVE MENSWEAR
BEING NOBODY RICHARD X VS LIBERTY X
BEING WITH YOU SMOKEY ROBINSON

BEL AMOUR BEL AMOUR
BELARUSE LEVELLERS
BELFAST [A] BONEY M
BELFAST [B] BARNBRACK
BELFAST [C] ENERGY ORCHARD
BELFAST [D] ORBITAL
BELFAST BOY DON FARDON
BELFAST CHILD SIMPLE MINDS
BELFAST TRANCE JOHN 'OO' FLEMING & SIMPLE MINDS
BELIEVE [A] LENNY KRAVITZ
BELIEVE [B] Q-TEX
BELIEVE [C] ELTON JOHN
BELIEVE [D] GOLDIE
BELIEVE [E] CHER
BELIEVE [F] MINISTERS DE LA FUNK FEATURING JOCELYN BROWN
BELIEVE [G] IAN VAN DAHL
BELIEVE IN ME [A] UTAH SAINTS
BELIEVE IN ME [B] QUIVVER
BELIEVE IN ME [C] MANKEY
BELIEVE IN ME [D] RAW STYLUS
BELIEVE IN THE BEAT CAROL LYNN TOWNES
BELIEVE WHAT YOU'RE SAYING SUGAR
BELIEVER REAL PEOPLE
BELIEVERS BAZ
THE BELL MIKE OLDFIELD
BELL BOTTOM BLUES ALMA COGAN
BELL BOTTOMED TEAR BEAUTIFUL SOUTH
THE BELLE OF ST MARK SHEILA E
BELLISSIMA DJ QUICKSILVER
BELLS OF AVIGNON MAX BYGRAVES
BELLS OF NY SLO-MOSHUN
BELO HORIZONTI HEARTISTS
BEN MICHAEL JACKSON
BEN MARTI WEBB
BEN TONI WARNE
BEND IT DAVE DEE, DOZY, BEAKY, MICK & TICH
BEND ME SHAPE ME AMEN CORNER
BEND ME SHAPE ME AMERICAN BREED
BENEDICTUS BRAINBUG
BENJAMIN VERUCA SALT
BENNIE AND THE JETS ELTON JOHN
BENNY'S THEME PAUL HENRY & MAYSON GLEN ORCHESTRA
BENTLEY'S GONNA SORT YOU OUT! BENTLEY RHYTHM ACE
BERMUDA TRIANGLE BARRY MANILOW
BERNADETTE FOUR TOPS
BERRY TC 1991
BERSERKER GARY NUMAN
BESAME MUCHO JET HARRIS
BESIDE YOU IGGY POP
THE BEST TINA TURNER
BEST BIT EP BETH ORTON FEATURING TERRY CALLIER
THE BEST CHRISTMAS OF THEM ALL SHAKIN' STEVENS
BEST DAYS JUICE
THE BEST DAYS OF OUR LIVES LISBON LIONS FEATURING MARTIN O'NEILL
THE BEST DISCO IN TOWN RITCHIE FAMILY
BEST FRIEND [A] BEAT
BEST FRIEND [B] MARK MORRISON & CONNOR REEVES
BEST FRIEND [C] PUFF DADDY FEATURING MARIO WINANS
BEST FRIENDS [A] TOY – BOX
BEST FRIENDS [B] ALLSTARS
BEST FRIENDS FOREVER TWEENIES
BEST FRIEND'S GIRL ELECTRASY
BEST I CAN QUEENSRYCHE
BEST IN ME LET LOOSE

THE BEST IS YET TO COME SCOOCH
BEST KEPT SECRET CHINA CRISIS
BEST LOVE COURSE
THE BEST OF EVERYTHING JOHNNY MATHIS
THE BEST OF LOVE MICHAEL BOLTON
THE BEST OF ME [A] CLIFF RICHARD
THE BEST OF ME [B] BRYAN ADAMS
BEST OF MY LOVE [A] EMOTIONS
BEST OF MY LOVE [A] DEE LEWIS
BEST OF MY LOVE [A] LOVESTATION
BEST OF MY LOVE [A] C.J. LEWIS
BEST OF MY LOVE [B] JAVINE
THE BEST OF TIMES STYX
BEST OF ORDER DAVID SNEDDON
BEST OF YOU KENNY THOMAS
BEST PART OF BREAKING UP SYMBOLS
(THE BEST PART OF) BREAKING UP RONETTES
(THE BEST PART OF) BREAKING UP RONI GRIFFITH
BEST REGRETS GENEVA
BEST THING ADAM RICKITT
THE BEST THING SAVAGE GARDEN
BEST THING IN THE WORLD OPTIMYSTIC
BEST THING THAT EVER HAPPENED TO ME GLADYS
    KNIGHT & THE PIPS
THE BEST THINGS IN LIFE ARE FREE LUTHER VANDROSS
    & JANET JACKSON WITH SPECIAL GUESTS BBD &
    RALPH TRESVANT
BEST WISHES ULTRASOUND
THE BEST YEARS OF MY LIFE DIANA ROSS
BEST YEARS OF OUR LIVES MODERN ROMANCE
BET YER LIFE I DO HERMAN'S HERMITS
BETA EMPIRION
BETCHA BY GOLLY WOW STYLISTICS
BETCHA BY GOLLY WOW! THE ARTIST
BETCHA CAN'T LOSE (WITH MY LOVE) MAGIC LADY
BETCHA CAN'T WAIT E-17
BETCHA' WOULDN'T HURT ME QUINCY JONES
BETTE DAVIS' EYES KIM CARNES
BETTER BE GOOD TO ME TINA TURNER
BETTER BELIEVE IT (CHILDREN IN NEED) SID OWEN &
    PATSY PALMER
BETTER BEST FORGOTTEN STEPS
BETTER DAY OCEAN COLOUR SCENE
BETTER DAYS [A] GUN
BETTER DAYS [B] BRUCE SPRINGSTEEN
BETTER DAYS [C] TQ
BETTER DAYS AHEAD TYRREL CORPORATION
BETTER DO IT SALSA GIBSON BROTHERS
BETTER GET READY LULU
A BETTER LOVE LONDONBEAT
BETTER LOVE NEXT TIME DR. HOOK
BETTER MADE HEADSWIM
A BETTER MAN [A] THUNDER
A BETTER MAN [B] BRIAN KENNEDY
BETTER OFF ALONE DJ JURGEN PRESENTS ALICE DEEJAY
BETTER OFF WITHOUT YOU HAZELL DEAN
BETTER TAKE TIME SECOND IMAGE
BETTER THAN LIFE ULTRABEAT
BETTER THE DEVIL YOU KNOW [A] KYLIE MINOGUE
BETTER THE DEVIL YOU KNOW [A] SONIA
BETTER THE DEVIL YOU KNOW [B] STEPS
BETTER THINGS KINKS
BETTER USE YOUR HEAD LITTLE ANTHONY & THE
    IMPERIALS
BETTER WATCH OUT ANT & DEC
BETTER WORLD REBEL MC
BETTY BETTY BETTY LONNIE DONEGAN
(BETWEEN A) ROCK AND A HARD PLACE CUTTING CREW
BETWEEN ANGELS AND INSECTS PAPA ROACH
BETWEEN ME AND YOU JA RULE FEATURING
    CHRISTINA MILIAN

BETWEEN THE SHEETS ISLEY BROTHERS
BETWEEN THE WARS (EP) BILLY BRAGG
BEWARE VIVIENNE McKONE
(BEWARE) BOYFRIEND MARI WILSON
BEWARE OF THE BOYS PANJABI MC FEATURING JAY-Z
BEYOND THE INVISIBLE ENIGMA
BEYOND THE PALE MISSION
BEYOND THE REEF ELVIS PRESLEY
BEYOND THE SEA (LA MER) GEORGE BENSON
BEYOND THE STARS DAVID WHITFIELD WITH CHORUS &
    MANTOVANI & HIS ORCHESTRA
BEYOND TIME BLANK & JONES
BEYOND YOUR WILDEST DREAMS LONNIE GORDON
BEYOND YOUR WILDEST DREAMS SYBIL
THE BHOYS ARE BACK IN TOWN DANCE TO TIPPERARY
BICYCLE RACE QUEEN
BIG APPLE KAJAGOOGOO
BIG AREA THEN JERICO
BIG BAD EP LITTLE ANGELS
BIG BAD JOHN JIMMY DEAN
BIG BAD MAMMA FOXY BROWN FEATURING DRU HILL
THE BIG BEAN PIGBAG
THE BIG BEAT [A] FATS DOMINO
BIG BEAT [B] CAPPELLA
BIG BEAT BOOGIE BERT WEEDON
BIG BIG WORLD EMILIA
BIG BOSS GROOVE STYLE COUNCIL
BIG BOYS DON'T CRY LOLLY
BIG BROTHER UK TV THEME ELEMENT FOUR
BIG BUBBLES, NO TROUBLES ELLIS, BEGGS & HOWARD
BIG CITY DANDY LIVINGSTONE
BIG DEAL BOBBY G
BIG DECISION THAT PETROL EMOTION
BIG DICK MAN SEX CLUB FEATURING BROWN SUGAR
BIG EIGHT JUDGE DREAD
BIG FUN [A] KOOL & THE GANG
BIG FUN [B] GAP BAND
BIG FUN [C] INNER CITY FEATURING KEVIN
    SAUNDERSON
BIG GAY HEART LEMONHEADS
BIG GIRL PRECOCIOUS BRATS/KEVIN & PERRY
BIG GIRLS DON'T CRY FOUR SEASONS
BIG GREEN CAR POLECATS
BIG GUN AC/DC
A BIG HUNK O' LOVE ELVIS PRESLEY
THE BIG HURT MAUREEN EVANS
THE BIG HURT TONI FISHER
BIG IN AMERICA STRANGLERS
BIG IN JAPAN ALPHAVILLE
BIG IRON MARTY ROBBINS
THE BIG L ROXETTE
BIG LOG ROBERT PLANT
BIG LOVE [A] FLEETWOOD MAC
BIG LOVE [B] PETE HELLER
BIG LOVE [C] FRESH
BIG MAN FOUR PREPS
THE BIG MAN AND THE SCREAM TEAM MEET THE
    BARMY ARMY UPTOWN PRIMAL SCREAM, IRVINE
    WELSH & ON U-SOUND
BIG MAN IN A BIG HOUSE LEROY VAN DYKE
BIG ME FOO FIGHTERS
BIG MISTAKE NATALIE IMBRUGLIA
THE BIG MONEY RUSH
BIG MOUTH STRIKES AGAIN SMITHS
BIG N BASHY FALLACY FEATURING TUBBY T
BIG NEW PRINZ FALL
BIG NIGHT OUT FUN LOVIN' CRIMINALS
THE BIG ONE BLACK
THE BIG ONES GET AWAY BUFFY SAINTE-MARIE
BIG PANTY WOMAN BAREFOOT MAN
BIG PIMPIN' JAY-Z

BIG POPPA NOTORIOUS B.I.G.
BIG PUNK JUDGE DREAD
BIG RIVER JIMMY NAIL
BIG SCARY ANIMAL BELINDA CARLISLE
BIG SEVEN JUDGE DREAD
BIG SHIP CLIFF RICHARD
BIG SIX JUDGE DREAD
THE BIG SKY KATE BUSH
BIG SKY NEW LIGHT MARTIN STEPHENSON & THE
    DAINTEES
BIG SPENDER SHIRLEY BASSEY
BIG SUR THRILLS
BIG TEASER SAXON
BIG TEN JUDGE DREAD
BIG THING COMING STRANGLERS
BIG TIME [A] RICK JAMES
BIG TIME [B] PETER GABRIEL
BIG TIME [C] WHIGFIELD
BIG TIME OPERATOR ZOOT MONEY & THE BIG ROLL
    BAND
BIG TIME SENSUALITY BJORK
BIG WEDGE FISH
BIG WHEELS LLAMA FARMERS
BIG YELLOW TAXI JONI MITCHELL
BIG YELLOW TAXI AMY GRANT
BIG YELLOW TAXI COUNTING CROWS FEATURING
    VANESSA CARLTON
BIGAMY AT CHRISTMAS TONY FERRINO
BIGBOY MINUTEMAN
BIGGER BETTER DEAL DESERT EAGLE DISCS FEATURING
    KEISHA
BIGGER THAN MY BODY JOHN MAYER
BIGGEST HORIZON CLINT BOON EXPERIENCE
BIKINI GIRLS WITH MACHINE GUNS CRAMPS
BIKO PETER GABRIEL
BILJO CLODAGH RODGERS
BILL BAILEY BOBBY DARIN
BILL McCAI CORAL
BILLIE JEAN MICHAEL JACKSON
BILLIE JEAN BATES
BILLIE JEAN SOUND BLUNTZ
BILLS, BILLS, BILLS DESTINY'S CHILD
BILLS 2 PAY GLAMMA KID
BILLY BOY DICK CHARLESWORTH & HIS CITY GENTS
BILLY, DON'T BE A HERO PAPER LACE
BIMBO RUBY WRIGHT
BINGO CATCH
BINGO BANGO BASEMENT JAXX
BIONIC KING ADORA
BIONIC SANTA CHRIS HILL
BIRD DOG EVERLY BROTHERS
BIRD OF PARADISE SNOWY WHITE
BIRD ON A WIRE NEVILLE BROTHERS
BIRD SONG LENE LOVICH
BIRDHOUSE IN YOUR SOUL THEY MIGHT BE GIANTS
THE BIRDIE SONG (BIRDIE DANCE) TWEETS
BIRDMAN RIDE
BIRDS AND BEES WARM SOUNDS
THE BIRDS AND THE BEES ALMA COGAN
THE BIRDS AND THE BEES JEWEL AKENS
BIRDS FLY (WHISPER TO A SCREAM) ICICLE WORKS
BIRDS OF A FEATHER KILLING JOKE
BIRTH PEDDLERS
BIRTHDAY [A] SUGARCUBES
BIRTHDAY [B] PAUL McCARTNEY
BIS VS THE DIY CORPS (EP) BIS
THE BIT GOES ON SNAKEBITE
A BIT OF U2 KISS AMC
BITCH [A] ROLLING STONES
THE BITCH [B] OLYMPIC RUNNERS
BITCH [C] MEREDITH BROOKS

THE BITCH IS BACK ELTON JOHN
BITCH SCHOOL SPINAL TAP
BITCH WITH A PERM TIM DOG
BITCHES BREW INSPIRAL CARPETS
BITE YOUR LIP (GET UP AND DANCE) ELTON JOHN
BITES DA DUST PLANET PERFECTO
BITS + PIECES ARTEMESIA
BITS AND PIECES DAVE CLARK FIVE
BITS OF KIDS STIFF LITTLE FINGERS
BITTER END PLACEBO
BITTER FRUIT LITTLE STEVEN
BITTER SWEET MARC ALMOND
BITTER SWEET SYMPHONY VERVE
BITTER TEARS INXS
THE BITTEREST PILL (I EVER HAD TO SWALLOW) JAM
BITTERSWEET BILLY OCEAN
BITTERSWEET BUNDLE OF MAN GRAHAM COXON
BITTERSWEET ME R.E.M.
BIZARRE LOVE TRIANGLE NEW ORDER
BIZZI'S PARTY BIZZI
BJANGO LUCKY MONKEYS
BLACK AND WHITE [A] GREYHOUND
BLACK AND WHITE [B] STATIC-X
BLACK & WHITE ARMY BLACK & WHITE ARMY
BLACK ANGEL MICA PARIS
BLACK BEAR FRANK CORDELL
BLACK BETTY RAM JAM
BLACK BETTY TOM JONES
BLACK BOOK E.Y.C.
BLACK CAT JANET JACKSON
BLACK CHERRY GOLDFRAPP
BLACK COFFEE ALL SAINTS
BLACK COFFEE IN BED SQUEEZE
BLACK EYED BOY TEXAS
THE BLACK EYED BOYS PAPER LACE
BLACK GIRL FOUR PENNIES
BLACK GOLD SOUL ASYLUM
BLACK HEART MARC & THE MAMBAS
BLACK HILLS OF DAKOTA DORIS DAY
BLACK HOLE SUN SOUNDGARDEN
BLACK IS BLACK [A] LOS BRAVOS
BLACK IS BLACK [A] LA BELLE EPOQUE
BLACK IS BLACK [B] JUNGLE BROTHERS
BLACK JESUS EVERLAST
BLACK LODGE ANTHRAX
BLACK MAGIC WOMAN FLEETWOOD MAC
BLACK MAN RAY CHINA CRISIS
BLACK MEANING GOOD REBEL MC
BLACK METALLIC (EP) CATHERINE WHEEL
BLACK NIGHT DEEP PURPLE
BLACK NITE CRASH RIDE
BLACK OR WHITE MICHAEL JACKSON
BLACK ORCHID STEVIE WONDER
BLACK PEARL HORACE FAITH
BLACK PUDDING BERTHA (THE QUEEN OF NORTHERN
    SOUL) GOODIES
BLACK SABBATH MAGOO : MOGWAI
BLACK SKIN BLUE EYED BOYS EQUALS
BLACK STATIONS WHITE STATIONS M + M
BLACK STEEL TRICKY
BLACK STOCKINGS JOHN BARRY SEVEN
BLACK SUITS COMIN' (NOD YA HEAD) WILL SMITH
    FEATURING TRA-KNOX
BLACK SUPERMAN (MUHAMMAD ALI) JOHNNY
    WAKELIN & THE KINSHASA BAND
BLACK TIE WHITE NOISE DAVID BOWIE FEATURING AL
    B. SURE!
BLACK VELVET ALANNAH MYLES
BLACK VELVET BAND DUBLINERS
BLACK WHITE ASIAN DUB FOUNDATION
BLACKBERRY WAY MOVE

BLACKBIRD ON THE WIRE BEAUTIFUL SOUTH
BLACKBOARD JUMBLE BARRON KNIGHTS
BLACKEN MY THUMB DATSUNS
BLACKER THAN BLACK GOODBYE MR MACKENZIE
BLACKERTHREETRACKER EP CURVE
BLACKWATER [A] RAIN TREE CROW
BLACKWATER [B] OCTAVE ONE FEATURING ANN
    SAUNDERSON
BLAH HELTAH SKELTAH & ORIGINOO GUNN CLAPPAZ
    AS THE FABULOUS FIVE
BLAME IT ON ME D:REAM
BLAME IT ON THE BASSLINE NORMAN COOK
    FEATURING MC WILDSKI
BLAME IT ON THE BOOGIE JACKSONS
BLAME IT ON THE BOOGIE MICK JACKSON
BLAME IT ON THE BOOGIE BIG FUN
BLAME IT ON THE BOOGIE CLOCK
BLAME IT ON THE BOSSA NOVA EYDIE GORME
(BLAME IT) ON THE PONY EXPRESS JOHNNY JOHNSON
    & THE BANDWAGON
BLAME IT ON THE RAIN MILLI VANILLI
BLAME IT ON THE WEATHERMAN B*WITCHED
BLANKET URBAN SPECIES FEATURING IMOGEN HEAP
BLANKET ON THE GROUND BILLIE JO SPEARS
BLASPHEMOUS RUMOURS DEPECHE MODE
BLAST THE SPEAKERS WARP BROTHERS
BLAZE OF GLORY JON BON JOVI
BLAZIN' TALI
BLAZING SADDLES YELLO
BLEACH EASYWORLD
BLEED CATATONIA
BLEED ME WHITE EAT
BLESS YOU [A] TONY ORLANDO
BLESS YOU [B] MARTHA REEVES & THE VANDELLAS
BLIND [A] TALKING HEADS
BLIND [B] BAD COMPANY
BLIND AMONG THE FLOWERS TOURISTS
BLIND MAN AEROSMITH
BLIND PILOTS COOPER TEMPLE CLAUSE
BLIND VISION BLANCMANGE
BLINDED BY THE LIGHT MANFRED MANN'S EARTH
    BAND
BLINDED BY THE LIGHTS STREETS
BLINDED BY THE SUN SEAHORSES
BLINDFOLD MORCHEEBA
THE BLINDFOLD (EP) CURVE
BLINK ROSIE RIBBONS
BLISS [A] MUSE
BLISS [B] SYNTAX
THE BLOCK PARTY LISA LEFT EYE LOPES
BLOCK ROCKIN' BEATS CHEMICAL BROTHERS
BLOCKBUSTER SWEET
BLONDE HAIR BLUE JEANS CHRIS DE BURGH
BLONDES (HAVE MORE FUN) ROD STEWART
BLOOD IS PUMPIN' VOODOO & SERANO
BLOOD MAKES NOISE SUZANNE VEGA
BLOOD MUSIC (EP) EARTHLING
BLOOD OF EDEN PETER GABRIEL
BLOOD ON THE DANCE FLOOR MICHAEL JACKSON
BLOOD SWEAT & TEARS V
THE BLOOD THAT MOVES THE BODY A-HA
BLOODNOK'S ROCK 'N' ROLL CALL GOONS
BLOODSHOT EYES MILLIE
BLOODSPORTS FOR ALL CARTER-THE UNSTOPPABLE
    SEX MACHINE
BLOODY LUXURY WHITESNAKE
A BLOSSOM FELL DICKIE VALENTINE
A BLOSSOM FELL NAT 'KING' COLE
A BLOSSOM FELL RONNIE HILTON
BLOSSOMS FALLING OOBERMAN
BLOW AWAY GEORGE HARRISON

BLOW THE HOUSE DOWN [A] LIVING IN A BOX
BLOW THE HOUSE DOWN [B] WEE PAPA GIRL RAPPERS
BLOW UP THE OUTSIDE WORLD SOUNDGARDEN
BLOW YA MIND LOCK 'N' LOAD
BLOW YOUR HORNY HORNS PERFECT PHASE
BLOW YOUR MIND JAMIROQUAI
BLOW YOUR MIND (I AM THE WOMAN) LISA PIN-UP
BLOW YOUR WHISTLE DJ DUKE
THE BLOWER'S DAUGHTER DAMIEN RICE
BLOWIN' IN THE WIND STEVIE WONDER
BLOWIN' ME UP JC CHASEZ
BLOWING IN THE WIND PETER, PAUL & MARY
BLOWING WILD FRANKIE LAINE
BLUE [A] FINE YOUNG CANNIBALS
BLUE [B] VERVE
BLUE [C] WAY OUT WEST
BLUE [D] SYMPOSIUM
BLUE [E] LeANN RIMES
BLUE ANGEL [A] ROY ORBISON
BLUE ANGEL [B] GENE PITNEY
BLUE ANGELS PRAS
BLUE BAYOU ROY ORBISON
BLUE BAYOU LINDA RONSTADT
BLUE BLUE HEARTACHES JOHNNY DUNCAN & THE BLUE
    GRASS BOYS
BLUE CHRISTMAS ELVIS PRESLEY
BLUE (DA BA DEE) EIFFEL 65
BLUE DAY SUGGS & CO FEATURING CHELSEA TEAM
BLUE EMOTION FIAT LUX
BLUE EYES [A] DON PARTRIDGE
BLUE EYES [B] ELTON JOHN
BLUE EYES [C] WEDDING PRESENT
BLUE FEAR ARMIN
BLUE FLOWERS DR OCTAGON
BLUE FOR YOU WET WET WET
BLUE GIRL BRUISERS
BLUE GUITAR JUSTIN HAYWARD & JOHN LODGE
BLUE HAT FOR A BLUE DAY NICK HEYWARD
BLUE HOTEL CHRIS ISAAK
BLUE IS THE COLOUR CHELSEA F.C.
BLUE JEAN DAVID BOWIE
BLUE JEANS LADYTRON
BLUE JEAN BOP GENE VINCENT
BLUE LIGHT RED LIGHT (SOMEONE'S THERE) HARRY
    CONNICK Jr.
BLUE LOVE (CALL MY NAME) DNA FEATURING JOE NYE
BLUE MONDAY [A] FATS DOMINO
BLUE MONDAY [B] NEW ORDER
BLUE MOON ELVIS PRESLEY
BLUE MOON MARCELS
BLUE MOON SHOWADDYWADDY
BLUE MOON JOHN ALFORD
BLUE MORNING BLUE DAY FOREIGNER
BLUE PETER MIKE OLDFIELD
BLUE RIVER ELVIS PRESLEY
BLUE ROOM ORB
THE BLUE ROOM T-EMPO
BLUE SAVANNAH ERASURE
BLUE SKIES [A] JOHN DUMMER & HELEN APRIL
BLUE SKIES [B] JETS
BLUE SKIES [C] BT FEATURING TORI AMOS
BLUE SKIES [D] LONGPIGS
BLUE SKY MINE MIDNIGHT OIL
BLUE SONG MINT ROYALE
BLUE STAR (THE MEDIC THEME) CHARLIE APPLEWHITE
BLUE STAR (THE MEDIC THEME) CYRIL STAPLETON
    ORCHESTRA FEATURING JULIE DAWN
BLUE STAR (THE MEDIC THEME) RON GOODWIN
BLUE SUEDE SHOES CARL PERKINS
BLUE SUEDE SHOES ELVIS PRESLEY
BLUE TANGO RAY MARTIN

BLUE TOMORROW CHELSEA FOOTBALL CLUB
BLUE TURNS TO GREY CLIFF RICHARD & THE SHADOWS
BLUE VELVET BOBBY VINTON
BLUE WATER FIELDS OF THE NEPHILIM
BLUE WEEKEND KARL DENVER
BLUE WORLD MOODY BLUES
BLUE-EYED BOY AL SAXON
BLUEBEARD COCTEAU TWINS
BLUEBELL POLKA JIMMY SHAND
BLUEBERRY HILL FATS DOMINO
BLUEBERRY HILL JOHN BARRY ORCHESTRA
BLUEBIRDS OVER THE MOUNTAIN BEACH BOYS
BLUEBOTTLE POB FEATURING DJ PATRICK REID
BLUEBOTTLE BLUES GOONS
BLUER THAN BLUE ROLF HARRIS
BLUES BAND (EP) BLUES BAND
BLUES FROM A GUN JESUS & MARY CHAIN
BLUETONIC BLUETONES
BLURRED PIANOMAN
BLURRY PUDDLE OF MUDD
BO DIDDLEY BUDDY HOLLY
THE BOAT THAT I ROW LULU
BOAT TO BOLIVIA MARTIN STEPHENSON & THE
    DAINTEES
BOBBY TOMORROW BOBBY VEE
BOBBY'S GIRL SUSAN MAUGHAN
BODIES DROWNING POOL
BODY FUNKY GREEN DOGS
BODY AND SOUL [A] SISTERS OF MERCY
BODY AND SOUL [B] MAI TAI
BODY AND SOUL [C] ANITA BAKER
BODY BUMPIN' (YIPPIE-YI-YO) PUBLIC
    ANNOUNCEMENT
THE BODY ELECTRIC RUSH
BODY GROOVE ARCHITECHS FEATURING NANA
BODY HEAT JAMES BROWN
BODY II BODY SAMANTHA MUMBA
BODY IN MOTION ATLANTIC OCEAN
BODY LANGUAGE [A] DETROIT SPINNERS
BODY LANGUAGE [B] DOOLEYS
BODY LANGUAGE [C] QUEEN
BODY LANGUAGE [D] ADVENTURES OF STEVIE V
BODY MOVIN' [A] BEASTIE BOYS
BODY MOVIN [B] DRUMSOUND/SIMON BASSLINE
    SMITH
BODY MUSIC STRIKERS
BODY ROCK [A] MARIA VIDAL
BODY ROCK [B] SHIMON & ANDY C
BODY ROCKIN' ERROL BROWN
THE BODY SHINE (EP) BILLY HENDRIX
BODY TALK IMAGINATION
BODY WORK HOT STREAK
BODYROCK [A] MOBY
BODYROCK [B] TYMES 4
BODYSHAKIN' 911
BOG EYED JOG RAY MOORE
BOHEMIAN LIKE YOU DANDY WARHOLS
BOHEMIAN RHAPSODY QUEEN
BOHEMIAN RHAPSODY BRAIDS
BOHEMIAN RHAPSODY BAD NEWS
BOHEMIAN RHAPSODY ROLF HARRIS
BOILER LIMP BIZKIT
THE BOILER RHODA WITH THE SPECIAL A.K.A.
BOING! WEDDING PRESENT
BOLL WEEVIL SONG BROOK BENTON
BOM DIGI BOM (THINK ABOUT THE WAY) ICE MC
THE BOMB LOVE CONNECTION
BOMB DIGGY ANOTHER LEVEL
THE BOMB! (THESE SOUNDS FALL INTO MY MIND)
    BUCKETHEADS
BOMBADIN 808 STATE

BOMBER MOTORHEAD
BOMBSCARE 2 BAD MICE
BOMBTRACK RAGE AGAINST THE MACHINE
BON BON VIE TS MONK
BOND 808 STATE
BONE DRIVEN BUSH
BONEY M MEGAMIX BONEY M
BONEYARD LITTLE ANGELS
BONITA APPLEBUM A TRIBE CALLED QUEST
BONITA MANANA ESPIRITU
BONNIE CAME BACK DUANE EDDY & THE REBELS
BONY MORONIE LARRY WILLIAMS
BOO! FOREVER BOO RADLEYS
BOOGALOO PARTY FLAMINGOS
BOOGIE[A] DIVE
BOOGIE [B] BRAND NEW HEAVIES FEATURING NICOLE
BOOGIE AT RUSSIAN HILL JOHN LEE HOOKER
BOOGIE DOWN [A] EDDIE KENDRICKS
BOOGIE DOWN [B] AL JARREAU
BOOGIE DOWN (BRONX) MAN PARISH
BOOGIE DOWN (GET FUNKY NOW) REAL THING
BOOGIE MAN MATCH
BOOGIE NIGHTS HEATWAVE
BOOGIE NIGHTS LA FLEUR
BOOGIE NIGHTS SONIA
BOOGIE ON REGGAE WOMAN STEVIE WONDER
BOOGIE ON UP ROKOTTO
BOOGIE OOGIE OOGIE A TASTE OF HONEY
BOOGIE SHOES KC & THE SUNSHINE BAND
BOOGIE TOWN F.L.B.
BOOGIE WONDERLAND EARTH, WIND & FIRE WITH THE
    EMOTIONS
BOOGIE WOOGIE BUGLE BOY (DON'T STOP) 2 IN A TANK
THE BOOK DAVID WHITFIELD
BOOK OF DAYS ENYA
BOOK OF DREAMS SUZANNE VEGA
BOOK OF LOVE MUDLARKS
BOOKS BELLE & SEBASTIAN
BOOM BANG-A-BANG LULU
BOOM BOOM [A] BLACK SLATE
BOOM BOOM [B] JOHN LEE HOOKER
BOOM BOOM [C] DEFINITION OF SOUND
BOOM BOOM [D] N-TYCE
BOOM BOOM [E] BASIL BRUSH FEATURING INDIA BEAU
BOOM BOOM BOOM OUTHERE BROTHERS
BOOM BOOM BOOM BOOM!! VENGABOYS
BOOM BOOM (LET'S GO BACK TO MY ROOM) PAUL
    LEKAKIS
THE BOOM BOOM ROOM NATASHA
BOOM LIKE THAT MARK KNOPFLER
BOOM ROCK SOUL BENZ
BOOM SELECTION GENIUS CRU
BOOM! SHAKE THE ROOM JAZZY JEFF & THE FRESH
    PRINCE
BOOM! THERE SHE WAS SCRITTI POLITTI FEATURING
    ROGER
BOOMBASTIC SHAGGY
BOOO STICKY FEATURING MS DYNAMITE
BOOPS (HERE TO GO) SLY & ROBBIE
BOOTI CALL BLACKstreet
BOOTIE CALL ALL SAINTS
BOOTYLICIOUS DESTINY'S CHILD
BOOTZILLA BOOTSY'S RUBBER BAND
BOP BOP BABY WESTLIFE
BOP GUN (ONE NATION) ICE CUBE FEATURING
    GEORGE CLINTON
BORA BORA DA HOOL
BORDERLINE MADONNA
BORN A WOMAN SANDY POSEY
BORN AGAIN [A] CHRISTIANS
BORN AGAIN [B] BADLY DRAWN BOY

BORN AGAIN [C] STARSAILOR
BORN DEAD BODY COUNT
BORN FREE VIC REEVES & THE ROMAN NUMERALS
BORN IN ENGLAND TWISTED X
BORN IN 69 ROCKET FROM THE CRYPT
BORN IN THE GHETTO FUNKY POETS
BORN IN THE 70S ED HARCOURT
BORN IN THE USA BRUCE SPRINGSTEEN
BORN OF FRUSTRATION JAMES
BORN ON THE 5TH OF NOVEMBER CARTER-THE
    UNSTOPPABLE SEX MACHINE
BORN SLIPPY UNDERWORLD
BORN SLIPPY NUXX UNDERWORLD
BORN THIS WAY (LET'S DANCE) COOKIE CREW
BORN TO BE ALIVE [A] PATRICK HERNANDEZ
BORN TO BE ALIVE [B] ADAMSKI FEATURING SOHO
BORN TO BE MY BABY BON JOVI
BORN TO BE SOLD TRANSVISION VAMP
BORN TO BE WILD STEPPENWOLF
BORN TO BE WITH YOU CHORDETTES
BORN TO BE WITH YOU DAVE EDMUNDS
BORN TO LIVE AND BORN TO DIE FOUNDATIONS
BORN TO LOSE KING ADORA
BORN TO MAKE YOU HAPPY BRITNEY SPEARS
BORN TO RAISE HELL MOTORHEAD/ICE-T/WHITFIELD
    CRANE
BORN TO RUN BRUCE SPRINGSTEEN
BORN TO TRY DELTA GOODREM
BORN TOO LATE PONI-TAILS
BORN 2 B.R.E.E.D. MONIE LOVE
BORN WITH A SMILE ON MY FACE STEPHANIE DE
    SYKES WITH RAIN
BORNE ON THE WIND ROY ORBISON
BORROWED LOVE S.O.S. BAND
BORROWED TIME JOHN LENNON
BORSALINO BOBBY CRUSH
THE BOSS DIANA ROSS
THE BOSS BRAXTONS
BOSS DRUM SHAMEN
BOSS GUITAR DUANE EDDY & THE REBELETTES
BOSS OF ME THEY MIGHT BE GIANTS
BOSSA NOVA BABY ELVIS PRESLEY
THE BOSTON TEA PARTY SENSATIONAL ALEX HARVEY
    BAND
BOTH ENDS BURNING ROXY MUSIC
BOTH SIDES NOW JUDY COLLINS
BOTH SIDES NOW VIOLA WILLS
BOTH SIDES NOW CLANNAD & PAUL YOUNG
BOTH SIDES OF THE STORY PHIL COLLINS
BOTHER STONE SOUR
THE BOTTLE [A] TYRREL CORPORATION
THE BOTTLE [B] CHRISTIANS
THE BOTTLE [B] PAUL WELLER
BOTTLE LIVING DAVID GAHAN
BOULEVARD OF BROKEN DREAMS [A] BEATMASTERS
BOULEVARD OF BROKEN DREAMS [B] GREEN DAY
BOUNCE SARAH CONNOR
BOUNCE ALONG WAYNE WONDER
BOUNCE, ROCK, SKATE, ROLL BABY DC FEATURING
    IMAJIN
BOUNCE WITH THE MASSIVE TZANT
THE BOUNCER KICKS LIKE A MULE
BOUNCIN' BACK MYSTIKAL
BOUNCING FLOW K2 FAMILY
BOUND 4 DA RELOAD (CASUALTY) OXIDE & NEUTRINO
BOUNDARIES LEENA CONQUEST & HIP HOP FINGER
BOURGIE BOURGIE GLADYS KNIGHT & THE PIPS
BOUT JAMELIA FEATURING RAH DIGGA
BOW DOWN MISTER JESUS LOVES YOU
BOW WOW (THAT'S MY NAME) LIL BOW WOW

BOW WOW WOW FUNKDOOBIEST
THE BOX ORBITAL
BOX SET GO HIGH
THE BOXER SIMON & GARFUNKEL
BOXER BEAT JO BOXERS
BOXERS MORRISSEY
BOY LULU
THE BOY DONE GOOD BILLY BRAGG
BOY FROM NEW YORK CITY DARTS
BOY FROM NEW YORK CITY ALISON JORDAN
A BOY FROM NOWHERE TOM JONES
BOY I GOTTA HAVE YOU RIO & MARS
BOY (I NEED YOU) MARIAH CAREY FEATURING
    CAM'RON
THE BOY IN THE BUBBLE PAUL SIMON
BOY IS CRYING SAINT ETIENNE
THE BOY IS MINE BRANDY & MONICA
A BOY NAMED SUE JOHNNY CASH
BOY NEXT DOOR JAMELIA
BOY OH BOY RACEY
BOY ON TOP OF THE NEWS DIESEL PARK WEST
BOY OR A GIRL IMPERIAL DRAG
THE BOY RACER MORRISSEY
THE BOY WHO CAME BACK MARC ALMOND
THE BOY WITH THE THORN IN HIS SIDE SMITHS
THE BOY WITH X-RAY EYES BABYLON ZOO
BOY WONDER SPEEDY
BOY YOU KNOCK ME OUT TATYANA ALI FEATURING
    WILL SMITH
BOYS [A] KIM WILDE
BOYS [B] MARY JANE GIRLS
BOYS [C] B.O.N.
BOYS [D] BRITNEY SPEARS FEAUTRING PHARRELL
    WILLIAMS
BOYS AND GIRLS [A] HUMAN LEAGUE
BOYS AND GIRLS [B] CHEEKY GIRLS
THE BOYS ARE BACK IN TOWN THIN LIZZY
THE BOYS ARE BACK IN TOWN GLADIATORS
THE BOYS ARE BACK IN TOWN HAPPY MONDAYS
BOYS BETTER DANDY WARHOLS
BOYS CRY EDEN KANE
BOYS DON'T CRY CURE
THE BOYS IN THE OLD BRIGHTON BLUE BRIGHTON &
    HOVE ALBION FC
BOYS KEEP SWINGIN' DAVID BOWIE
THE BOYS OF SUMMER DON HENLEY
THE BOYS OF SUMMER DJ SAMMY
THE BOYS OF SUMMER ATARIS
BOYS (SUMMERTIME LOVE) SABRINA
BOYS WILL BE BOYS OSMOND BOYS
BOZOS LEVELLERS
BRACKISH KITTIE
BRAIN JUNGLE BROTHERS
BRAIN STEW GREEN DAY
BRAINS NUT
BRAINWASHED (CALL YOU) TOMCRAFT
BRAND NEW FINITRIBE
BRAND NEW DAY [A] DARKMAN
BRAND NEW DAY [B] MINDS OF MEN
BRAND NEW DAY [C] STING
BRAND NEW FRIEND LLOYD COLE & THE COMMOTIONS
BRAND NEW KEY MELANIE
BRAND NEW LOVER DEAD OR ALIVE
BRAND NEW START PAUL WELLER
BRANDY [A] SCOTT ENGLISH
BRANDY [B] O'JAYS
BRAS ON 45 (FAMILY VERSION) IVOR BIGGUN & THE D
    CUPS
BRASS IN POCKET PRETENDERS
BRASS, LET THERE BE HOUSE PARTY FAITHFUL
BRASSNECK WEDDING PRESENT

BRAVE NEW WORLD DAVID ESSEX
BRAVE NEW WORLD TOYAH
BRAVE NEW WORLD NEW MODEL ARMY
BRAZEN 'WEEP' SKUNK ANANSIE
BRAZIL CRISPY & COMPANY
BRAZIL RITCHIE FAMILY
BRAZILIAN DAWN SHAKATAK
BRAZILIAN LOVE AFFAIR GEORGE DUKE
BRAZILIAN LOVE SONG NAT 'KING' COLE
BREACH THE PEACE (EP) SPIRAL TRIBE
BREAD AND BUTTER NEWBEATS
BREAK AWAY BEACH BOYS
BREAK DANCIN' – ELECTRIC BOOGIE WEST STREET MOB
BREAK DOWN THE DOORS MORILLO FEATURING THE
    AUDIO BULLYS
BREAK EVERY RULE TINA TURNER
BREAK 4 LOVE RAZE
BREAK FROM THE OLD ROUTINE OUI 3
BREAK IT DOWN AGAIN TEARS FOR FEARS
BREAK IT TO ME GENTLY BRENDA LEE
BREAK MY STRIDE MATTHEW WILDER
BREAK MY WORLD DARK GLOBE FEATURING AMANDA
    GHOST
BREAK OF DAWN RHYTHM ON THE LOOSE
BREAK ON THROUGH DOORS
BREAK THE CHAIN [A] MOTIV 8
BREAK THE CHAIN [B] ELKIE BROOKS
BREAK THE RULES STATUS QUO
BREAK UP TO MAKE UP STYLISTICS
BREAK UPS 2 MAKE UPS METHOD MAN FEATURING
    D'ANGELO
BREAK YA NECK BUSTA RHYMES
BREAKADAWN DE LA SOUL
BREAKAWAY [A] SPRINGFIELDS
BREAKAWAY [B] GALLAGHER & LYLE
BREAKAWAY [C] TRACEY ULLMAN
BREAKAWAY [D] DONNA SUMMER
BREAKAWAY [E] KIM APPLEBY
BREAKAWAY [F] ZZ TOP
BREAKBEAT ERA BREAKBEAT ERA
BREAKDANCE PARTY BREAK MACHINE
BREAKDOWN [A] ONE DOVE
BREAKDOWN [B] DOUBLE SIX
BREAKFAST ASSOCIATES
BREAKFAST AT TIFFANY'S DEEP BLUE SOMETHING
BREAKFAST IN AMERICA SUPERTRAMP
BREAKFAST IN BED SHEILA HYLTON
BREAKFAST IN BED UB40 FEATURING CHRISSIE HYNDE
BREAKFAST ON PLUTO DON PARTRIDGE
BREAKIN' AWAY KIM WILDE
BREAKIN' DOWN SKID ROW
BREAKIN' DOWN (SUGAR SAMBA) JULIA & COMPANY
BREAKIN' DOWN THE WALLS OF HEARTACHE
    BANDWAGON
BREAKIN' IN A BRAND NEW BROKEN HEART CONNIE
    FRANCIS
BREAKIN' UP WILD WEEKEND
BREAKIN' UP IS BREAKIN' MY HEART ROY ORBISON
BREAKIN'...THERE'S NO STOPPING US OLLIE & JERRY
BREAKING AWAY JAKI GRAHAM
BREAKING GLASS (EP) DAVID BOWIE
BREAKING HEARTS (AIN'T WHAT IT USED TO BE) ELTON
    JOHN
BREAKING POINT BOURGIE BOURGIE
BREAKING THE GIRL RED HOT CHILI PEPPERS
BREAKING THE HABIT LINKIN PARK
BREAKING THE LAW JUDAS PRIEST
BREAKING UP IS HARD TO DO NEIL SEDAKA
BREAKING UP IS HARD TO DO PARTRIDGE FAMILY
    STARRING SHIRLEY JONES FEATURING DAVID
    CASSIDY

BREAKING UP MY HEART SHAKIN' STEVENS
BREAKING UP THE GIRL GARBAGE
BREAKING US IN TWO JOE JACKSON
BREAKOUT [A] SWING OUT SISTER
BREAKOUT [B] FOO FIGHTERS
THE BREAKS KURTIS BLOW
BREAKS YOU OFF ROOTS FEATURING MUSIQ
BREAKTHRU' QUEEN
BREATH OF LIFE ERASURE
BREATHE [A] MARIA McKEE
BREATHE [B] MIDGE URE
BREATHE [C] PRODIGY
BREATHE [D] KYLIE MINOGUE
BREATHE [E] BLUE AMAZON
BREATHE [F] FAITH HILL
BREATHE [G] SCIENCE DEPT FEATURING ERIRE
BREATHE [H] TELEPOPMUSIK
BREATHE [I] BLU CANTRELL FEATURING SEAN PAUL
BREATHE [J] FABOLOUS
BREATHE (A LITTLE DEEPER) BLAMELESS
BREATHE A SIGH DEF LEPPARD
BREATHE AGAIN TONI BRAXTON
BREATHE AND STOP Q-TIP
BREATHE DON'T STOP MR ON VS THE JUNGLE
    BROTHERS
BREATHE EASY BLUE
BREATHE IN FROU FROU
BREATHE LIFE INTO ME MICA PARIS
BREATHE ME SIA
BREATHE STRETCH SHAKE MA$E
BREATHING [A] KATE BUSH
BREATHING [B] NORTH & SOUTH
BREATHING IS E-ZEE E-ZEE POSSEE FEATURING TARA
    NEWLEY
BREATHLESS [A] JERRY LEE LEWIS
BREATHLESS [B] CORRS
BREATHLESS [C] NICK CAVE & THE BAD SEEDS
THE BREEZE AND I CATERINA VALENTE
THE BREEZE AND I FENTONES
BREEZE ON BY DONNY OSMOND
BRIAN WILSON BARENAKED LADIES
BRICK BEN FOLDS FIVE
BRICK HOUSE COMMODORES
THE BRICK TRACK VERSUS GITTY UP SALT-N-PEPA
BRIDESHEAD THEME GEOFFREY BURGON
BRIDGE [A] ORANGE JUICE
BRIDGE [B] QUEENSRYCHE
THE BRIDGE CACTUS WORLD NEWS
BRIDGE OF SIGHS DAVID WHITFIELD
BRIDGE OVER TROUBLED WATER SIMON & GARFUNKEL
BRIDGE OVER TROUBLED WATER LINDA CLIFFORD
BRIDGE OVER TROUBLED WATER PJB FEATURING
    HANNAH & HER SISTERS
BRIDGE TO YOUR HEART WAX
BRIDGET THE MIDGET (THE QUEEN OF THE BLUES) RAY
    STEVENS
BRIDGING THE GAP NAS
BRIGHT EYES ART GARFUNKEL
BRIGHT EYES STEPHEN GATELY
THE BRIGHT LIGHT TANYA DONELLY
BRIGHT LIGHTS SPECIAL A.K.A.
BRIGHT SIDE OF LIFE TENOR FLY
BRIGHT SIDE OF THE ROAD VAN MORRISON
BRIGHT YELLOW GUN THROWING MUSES
BRIGHTER DAY KELLY LLORENNA
BRIGHTER THAN SUNSHINE AQUALUNG
BRIGHTEST STAR DRIZABONE
BRILLIANT DISGUISE BRUCE SPRINGSTEEN
BRILLIANT FEELING FULL MONTY ALLSTARS
    FEATURING TJ DAVIS
BRILLIANT MIND FURNITURE

BRIMFUL OF ASHA CORNERSHOP
BRING A LITTLE WATER SYLVIE LONNIE DONEGAN
BRING 'EM ALL IN MIKE SCOTT
BRING FORTH THE GUILLOTINE SILVER BULLET
BRING IT ALL BACK S CLUB 7
BRING IT ALL HOME GERRY RAFFERTY
BRING IT BACK McALMONT & BUTLER
BRING IT BACK AGAIN STRAY CATS
BRING IT BACK 2 LUV PROJECT FEATURING GERIDEAU
BRING IT DOWN (THIS INSANE THING) REDSKINS
BRING IT ON [A] N'DEA DAVENPORT
BRING IT ON [B] GOMEZ
BRING IT ON [C] NICK CAVE & THE BAD SEEDS
BRING IT ON [D] ALISTAIR GRIFFIN
BRING IT ON DOWN JESUS JONES
BRING IT ON HOME URBAN COOKIE COLLECTIVE
BRING IT ON HOME TO ME ANIMALS
BRING IT ON TO MY LOVE DE NADA
BRING IT ON...BRING IT ON JAMES BROWN
BRING ME CLOSER ALTERED IMAGES
BRING ME EDELWEISS EDELWEISS
BRING ME LOVE ANDREA MENDEZ
BRING ME TO LIFE EVANESCENCE
BRING ME YOUR CUP UB40
BRING MY FAMILY BACK FAITHLESS
BRING ON THE DANCING HORSES ECHO & THE
    BUNNYMEN
BRING THE FAMILY BACK BILLY PAUL
BRING THE NOISE PUBLIC ENEMY
BRING THE NOISE ANTHRAX FEATURING CHUCK D
BRING UP THE MIC SOME MORE RAGGA TWINS
BRING YOUR DAUGHTER...TO THE SLAUGHTER IRON
    MAIDEN
BRINGING BACK THOSE MEMORIES MARK JOSEPH
BRINGING ON BACK THE GOOD TIMES LOVE AFFAIR
BRISTOL STOMP LATE SHOW
BRITANNIA RAG WINIFRED ATWELL
BRITE SIDE DEBORAH HARRY
BRITISH HUSTLE HI TENSION
THE BRITISH WAY OF LIFE CHORDS
THE BRITS 1990 VARIOUS ARTISTS (MONTAGES)
BROKE [A] BETA BAND
BROKE [B] CASSIUS HENRY
BROKE AWAY WET WET WET
BROKEN ARROW [A] WATERFRONT
BROKEN ARROW [B] ROD STEWART
BROKEN BONES LOVE INC
BROKEN DOLL TOMMY BRUCE & THE BRUISERS
BROKEN DOWN ANGEL NAZARETH
BROKEN ENGLISH SUNSCREEM
A BROKEN HEART CAN MEND ALEXANDER O'NEAL
BROKEN HEART (THIRTEEN VALLEYS) BIG COUNTRY
BROKEN HEARTED KEN DODD
BROKEN HEARTED MELODY SARAH VAUGHAN
BROKEN HOMES TRICKY
BROKEN LAND ADVENTURES
BROKEN NOSE CATHERINE WHEEL
BROKEN SILENCE SO SOLID CREW
BROKEN STONES PAUL WELLER
BROKEN WINGS [A] STARGAZERS
BROKEN WINGS [A] ART & DOTTY TODD
BROKEN WINGS [A] DICKIE VALENTINE
BROKEN WINGS [B] MR MISTER
BROKEN WINGS [B] NETWORK
THE BROKEN YEARS HIPSWAY
BRONTOSAURUS MOVE
BROOKLYN BEATS SCOTTI DEEP
BROOKLYN-QUEENS 3RD BASS
BROTHA PART II ANGIE STONE FEATURING ALICIA KEYS
    & EVE
BROTHER [A] C.C.S.

BROTHER [B] URBAN SPECIES
BROTHER BRIGHT CA VA CA VA
BROTHER LOUIE [A] HOT CHOCOLATE
BROTHER LOUIE [A] QUIREBOYS
BROTHER LOUIE [B] MODERN TALKING
BROTHER OF MINE ANDERSON BRUFORD WAKEMAN
    HOWE
BROTHERS AND SISTERS 2 FUNKY 2 FEATURING
    KATHRYN DION
BROTHERS GONNA WORK IT OUT PUBLIC ENEMY
BROTHERS IN ARMS DIRE STRAITS
BROWN-EYED HANDSOME MAN BUDDY HOLLY
BROWN EYED HANDSOME MAN PAUL McCARTNEY
BROWN GIRL IN THE RING BONEY M
BROWN PAPER BAG RONI SIZE REPRAZENT
BROWN SKIN INDIA.ARIE
BROWN SUGAR [A] ROLLING STONES
BROWN SUGAR [B] D'ANGELO
BRUISE PRISTINE PLACEBO
BRUSHED PAUL WELLER
BRUTAL-8-E ALTERN 8
BUBBLE FLUKE
BUBBLIN' BLUE
BUBBLING HOT PATO BANTON WITH RANKING ROGER
BUCCI BAG ANDREA DORIA
BUCK ROGERS FEEDER
THE BUCKET KINGS OF LEON
THE BUCKET OF WATER SONG FOUR BUCKETEERS
BUDDHA OF SUBURBIA DAVID BOWIE FEATURING
    LENNY KRAVITZ
BUDDY DE LA SOUL
BUDDY HOLLY WEEZER
BUDDY X NENEH CHERRY
BUDDY X 99 DREEM TEEM Vs NENEH CHERRY
BUFFALO BILL'S LAST SCRATCH BARRON KNIGHTS
BUFFALO GALS STAMPEDE MALCOLM McLAREN & THE
    WORLD'S FAMOUS SUPREME TEAM PLUS RAKIM
    & ROGER SANCHEZ
BUFFALO GIRLS MALCOLM McLAREN & THE WORLD'S
    FAMOUS SUPREME TEAM
BUFFALO SOLDIER BOB MARLEY & THE WAILERS
BUFFALO STANCE NENEH CHERRY
THE BUG DIRE STRAITS
BUG A BOO DESTINY'S CHILD
BUG IN THE BASSBIN INNERZONE ORCHESTRA
BUG POWDER DUST BOMB THE BASS FEATURING
    JUSTIN WARFIELD
BUGGIN' TRUE STEPPERS FEATURING DANE BOWERS
BUGS HEPBURN
BUILD [A] HOUSEMARTINS
BUILD [B] INNOCENCE
BUILD ME UP BUTTERCUP FOUNDATIONS
BUILD ME UP BUTTERCUP 2003 PARTY BOYS
BUILD YOUR LOVE JOHNNIE RAY
BUILDING THE CITY OF LIGHT MIKE SCOTT
BULGARIAN TRAVEL
BULL IN THE HEATHER SONIC YOUTH
BULLDOG NATION KEVIN KENNEDY
BULLET FLUKE
BULLET COMES CHARLATANS
BULLET IN THE GUN PLANET PERFECTO
BULLET IN THE HEAD RAGE AGAINST THE MACHINE
BULLET WITH BUTTERFLY WINGS SMASHING
    PUMPKINS
BULLETPROOF! POP WILL EAT ITSELF
BULLFROG GTO
BULLITPROOF BREAKBEAT ERA
BULLITT LALO SCHIFRIN
BULLS ON PARADE RAGE AGAINST THE MACHINE
BULLY BOY SHED SEVEN
BULLY FOR YOU TOM ROBINSON BAND

THE BUMP KENNY
BUMP BUMP BUMP B2K FEATURING P DIDDY
BUMP/RUN DADDY RUN FUN LOVIN' CRIMINALS
BUMP N' GRIND R KELLY
BUMP N GRIND (I AM FEELING HOT TONIGHT) M DUBS
    FEATURING LADY SAW
BUMPED RIGHT SAID FRED
A BUNCH OF THYME FOSTER & ALLEN
BUNSEN BURNER JOHN OTWAY
BUONA SERA LOUIS PRIMA
BUONA SERA MR ACKER BILK & HIS PARAMOUNT JAZZ
    BAND
BUONA SERA BAD MANNERS
BUOY MICK KARN FEATURING DAVID SYLVIAN
BURDEN IN MY HAND SOUNDGARDEN
BURIAL LEVITICUS
BURIED ALIVE BY LOVE H.I.M.
BURLESQUE FAMILY
BURN [A] DOCTOR & THE MEDICS
BURN [B] TINA ARENA
BURN [C] USHER
BURN BABY BURN [A] HUDSON-FORD
BURN BABY BURN [B] ASH
BURN BURN LOSTPROPHETS
BURN IT UP BEATMASTERS WITH P.P. ARNOLD
BURN RUBBER ON ME (WHY YOU WANNA HURT ME)
    GAP BAND
BURN YOUR YOUTH JOHNNY PANIC
BURNED WITH DESIRE ARMIN VAN BUUREN
    FEATURING JUSTINE SUISSA
BURNIN' [A] DAFT PUNK
BURNIN' [B] K-KLASS
BURNIN' [C] MIRRORBALL
BURNIN' HOT JERMAINE JACKSON
BURNIN' LOVE CON FUNK SHUN
BURNING [A] MK
BURNING [B] BABY BUMPS
BURNING BRIDGES JACK SCOTT
BURNING BRIDGES (ON AND OFF AND ON AGAIN)
    STATUS QUO
BURNING CAR JOHN FOXX
BURNING DOWN ONE SIDE ROBERT PLANT
BURNING DOWN THE HOUSE TOM JONES & THE
    CARDIGANS
BURNING HEART SURVIVOR
BURNING LOVE ELVIS PRESLEY
BURNING OF THE MIDNIGHT LAMP JIMI HENDRIX
    EXPERIENCE
BURNING THE GROUND DURAN DURAN
BURNING UP [A] TONY DE VIT
BURNING UP [B] BINI & MARTINI
BURNING WHEEL PRIMAL SCREAM
BURST DARLING BUDS
BURUCHACCA MUKKAA
BURUNDI BLACK BURUNDI STEIPHENSON BLACK
BURUNDI BLUES BEATS INTERNATIONAL
BURY YOU SYMPOSIUM
BUS STOP HOLLIES
BUSHEL AND A PECK VIVIAN BLAINE
BUSHES MARKUS NIKOLAI
THE BUSINESS [A] BRIAN MAY
BUSINESS [B] EMINEM
BUST A MOVE YOUNG MC
BUST THIS HOUSE DOWN PENTHOUSE 4
BUSTED RAY CHARLES
BUSY BEE UGLY KID JOE
BUSY DOING NOTHING DAVE STEWART WITH BARBARA
    GASKIN
BUT I DO LOVE YOU LeANN RIMES
BUT I FEEL GOOD GROOVE ARMADA
BUT NOT FOR ME ELLA FITZGERALD

BUT NOT FOR ME KETTY LESTER
BUT YOU LOVE ME DADDY JIM REEVES
BUT YOU'RE MINE SONNY & CHER
BUTCHER BABY PLASMATICS
BUTTERCUP CARL ANDERSON
BUTTERFINGERS TOMMY STEELE & THE STEELMEN
BUTTERFLIES AND HURRICANES MUSE
BUTTERFLY [A] CHARLIE GRACIE
BUTTERFLY [A] ANDY WILLIAMS
BUTTERFLY [B] DANYEL GERARD
BUTTERFLY [C] MARIAH CAREY
BUTTERFLY [D] TILT FEATURING ZEE
BUTTERFLY [E] CRAZY TOWN
BUTTERFLY KISSES BOB CARLISLE
BUTTERFLY ON A WHEEL MISSION
BUY IT IN BOTTLES RICHARD ASHCROFT
BUZZ BUZZ A DIDDLE IT MATCHBOX
BUZZIN' ASIAN DUB FOUNDATION
BY MY SIDE INXS
BY THE DEVIL (I WAS TEMPTED) BLUE MINK
BY THE FOUNTAINS OF ROME EDMUND HOCKRIDGE
BY THE FOUNTAINS OF ROME DAVID HUGHES
BY THE LIGHT OF THE SILVERY MOON LITTLE RICHARD
BY THE TIME THIS NIGHT IS OVER KENNY G WITH
     PEABO BRYSON
BY THE WAY [A] BIG THREE
BY THE WAY [B] TREMELOES
BY THE WAY [C] RED HOT CHILI PEPPERS
BY YOUR SIDE [A] PETERS & LEE
BY YOUR SIDE [B] JIMMY SOMERVILLE
BY YOUR SIDE [C] SADE
BYE BABY RUBY TURNER
BYE BYE BABY [A] JOHNNY OTIS SHOW, VOCALS BY
     MARIE ADAMS & JOHNNY OTIS
BYE BYE BABY [B] SYMBOLS
BYE BYE BABY [B] BAY CITY ROLLERS
BYE BYE BABY [C] TONY JACKSON & THE VIBRATIONS
BYE BYE BABY [D] TQ
BYE BYE BLUES BERT KAEMPFERT
BYE BYE BOY JENNIFER ELLISON
BYE BYE BYE N SYNC
BYE BYE LOVE EVERLY BROTHERS
B.Y.O.F. (BRING YOUR OWN FUNK) FANTASTIC FOUR
BYRDS TURN TO STONE SHACK
C MOON WINGS
C U WHEN U GET THERE COOLIO FEATURING 40 THEVZ
C30, C60, C90, GO BOW WOW WOW
CA PLANE POUR MOI PLASTIC BERTRAND
CA PLANE POUR MOI LEILA K
CABARET LOUIS ARMSTRONG
THE CABARET TIME UK
CACHARPAYA (ANDES PUMPSA DAESI) INCANTATION
CAFÉ DEL MAR ENERGY 52
CAFFEINE BOMB WILDHEARTS
CALEDONIA FRANKIE MILLER
CALENDAR GIRL NEIL SEDAKA
THE CALENDAR SONG (JANUARY, FEBRUARY, MARCH,
     APRIL, MAY) TRINIDAD OIL COMPANY
CALIBRE CUTS VARIOUS ARTISTS (MONTAGES)
CALIFORNIA [A] WEDDING PRESENT
CALIFORNIA [B] BELINDA CARLISLE
CALIFORNIA [C] LENNY KRAVITZ
CALIFORNIA DREAMIN' MAMAS & THE PAPAS
CALIFORNIA DREAMIN' COLORADO
CALIFORNIA DREAMIN' RIVER CITY PEOPLE
CALIFORNIA DREAMIN' BOBBY WOMACK
CALIFORNIA DREAMIN' ROYAL GIGOLOS
CALIFORNIA GIRLS BEACH BOYS
CALIFORNIA GIRLS DAVID LEE ROTH
CALIFORNIA HERE I COME [A] FREDDY CANNON
CALIFORNIA HERE I COME [B] SOPHIE B. HAWKINS

CALIFORNIA LOVE 2PAC FEATURING DR DRE
CALIFORNIA MAN MOVE
CALIFORNIA SAGA-CALIFORNIA BEACH BOYS
CALIFORNIA SCREAMIN' CARRIE
CALIFORNIA WAITING KINGS OF LEON
CALIFORNIA'S BLEEDING AMEN
CALIFORNICATION RED HOT CHILI PEPPERS
CALINDA RITMO-DYNAMIC
THE CALL BACKSTREET BOYS
CALL AND ANSWER BARENAKED LADIES
CALL HER YOUR SWEETHEART FRANK IFIELD
CALL IT FATE RICHIE DAN
CALL IT LOVE DEUCE
CALL IT ROCK 'N' ROLL GREAT WHITE
CALL IT WHAT YOU WANT [A] NEW KIDS ON THE BLOCK
CALL IT WHAT YOU WANT [B] CREDIT TO THE NATION
CALL ME [A] BLONDIE
CALL ME [B] GO WEST
CALL ME [C] SPAGNA
CALL ME [D] LE CLICK
CALL ME [E] JAMELIA
CALL ME [F] TWEET
(CALL ME) NUMBER ONE TREMELOES
CALL ME ROUND PILOT
CALL MY NAME ORCHESTRAL MANOEUVRES IN THE
     DARK
CALL OF THE WILD [A] MIDGE URE
CALL OF THE WILD [B] GUS GUS
CALL OFF THE SEARCH KATIE MELUA
CALL ON ME ERIC PRYDZ
CALL OUT THE DOGS GARY NUMAN
CALL ROSIE ON THE PHONE GUY MITCHELL
CALL THE MAN CELINE DION
CALL U SEXY VS
THE CALL UP CLASH
CALL UP THE GROUPS BARRON KNIGHTS WITH DUKE
     D'MOND
CALLING GERI HALLIWELL
CALLING ALL GIRLS ATL
CALLING ALL THE HEROES IT BITES
CALLING AMERICA ELECTRIC LIGHT ORCHESTRA
CALLING ELVIS DIRE STRAITS
CALLING OCCUPANTS OF INTERPLANETARY CRAFT (THE
     RECOGNISED ANTHEM OF WORLD CONTACT DAY)
     CARPENTERS
CALLING OUT YOUR NAME JIMMY NAIL
CALLING YOU PAUL YOUNG
CALLING YOUR NAME MARILYN
CALLS THE TUNE HAZEL O'CONNOR
CALM DOWN (BASS KEEPS PUMPIN') CHRIS & JAMES
CALYPSO CRAZY BILLY OCEAN
CAMBODIA KIM WILDE
CAMDEN TOWN SUGGS
CAMEL BOBSLED RACE DJ SHADOW
CAMELS SANTOS
CAMOUFLAGE STAN RIDGWAY
CAMPIONE 2000 E-TYPE
CAN CAN BAD MANNERS
CAN CAN 62 PETER JAY & THE JAYWALKERS
CAN CAN YOU PARTY JIVE BUNNY & THE
     MASTERMIXERS
CAN I CASHMERE
CAN I GET A... JAY-Z FEATURING AMIL & JA RULE
CAN I GET A WITNESS SAM BROWN
CAN I GET OVER DEFINITION OF SOUND
CAN I KICK IT A TRIBE CALLED QUEST
CAN I PLAY WITH MADNESS IRON MAIDEN
CAN I TAKE YOU HOME LITTLE GIRL DRIFTERS
CAN I TOUCH YOU...THERE? MICHAEL BOLTON
CAN I TRUST YOU BACHELORS
CAN THE CAN SUZI QUATRO

CAN THIS BE LOVE MATT MONRO
CAN U DANCE KENNY 'JAMMIN' JASON & DJ 'FAST'
     EDDIE SMITH
CAN U DIG IT [A] POP WILL EAT ITSELF
CAN U DIG IT [B] JAMX & DELEON
CAN U FEEL IT DEEP CREED '94
CAN WE SWV
CAN WE FIX IT BOB THE BUILDER
CAN WE START AGAIN? TINDERSTICKS
CAN WE TALK... CODE RED
CAN YOU DIG IT MOCK TURTLES
CAN YOU DO IT GEORDIE
CAN YOU FEEL IT [A] JACKSONS
CAN YOU FEEL IT [A] V
CAN YOU FEEL IT [B] ELEVATION
CAN YOU FEEL IT [C] REEL 2 REAL FEATURING THE MAD
     STUNTMAN
CAN YOU FEEL IT [D] CLS
CAN YOU FEEL IT (ROCK DA HOUSE) NYCC
CAN YOU FEEL IT/CAN YOU FEEL IT
     RAZE/CHAMPIONSHIP LEGEND
CAN YOU FEEL THE FORCE REAL THING
CAN YOU FEEL THE LOVE TONIGHT ELTON JOHN
(CAN YOU) FEEL THE PASSION BLUE PEARL
CAN YOU FEEL (WHAT I'M GOING THROUGH) SHOLAN
CAN YOU FORGIVE HER PET SHOP BOYS
CAN YOU FORGIVE ME KARL DENVER
CAN YOU HANDLE IT SHARON REDD
CAN YOU HANDLE IT DNA FEATURING SHARON REDD
CAN YOU KEEP A SECRET BROTHER BEYOND
CAN YOU PARTY ROYAL HOUSE
CAN YOU PLEASE CRAWL OUT YOUR WINDOW BOB
     DYLAN
CAN YOUR PUSSY DO THE DOG? CRAMPS
CANCER FOR THE CURE EELS
CANDIDA DAWN
CANDIDATE FOR LOVE TS MONK
CANDLE IN THE WIND ELTON JOHN
CANDLEFIRE DAWN OF THE REPLICANTS
CANDLELAND (THE SECOND COMING) IAN McCULLOCH
     FEATURING ELIZABETH FRASER
CANDLELIGHT SIX BY SEVEN
CANDLES ALEX REECE
CANDY [A] CAMEO
CANDY [B] IGGY POP
CANDY [C] MANDY MOORE
CANDY [D] ASH
CANDY EVERYBODY WANTS 10,000 MANIACS
CANDY GIRL [A] NEW EDITION
CANDY GIRL [B] BABY BIRD
CANDY MAN [A] BRIAN POOLE & THE TREMELOES
CANDY MAN [B] MARY JANE GIRLS
CANDY RAIN SOUL FOR REAL
CANDYBAR EXPRESS LOVE & MONEY
CANDYMAN SIOUXSIE & THE BANSHEES
CANNED HEAT JAMIROQUAI
CANNIBALS MARK KNOPFLER
CANNONBALL [A] DUANE EDDY & THE REBELS
CANNONBALL [B] DAMIEN RICE
CANNONBALL (EP) BREEDERS
CAN'T BE SURE SUNDAYS
CAN'T BE WITH YOU TONIGHT JUDY BOUCHER
CAN'T BUY ME LOVE BEATLES
CAN'T BUY ME LOVE ELLA FITZGERALD
CAN'T CHANGE ME CHRIS CORNELL
CAN'T CONTAIN ME TAZ
CAN'T CRY ANYMORE SHERYL CROW
CAN'T DO A THING (TO STOP ME) CHRIS ISAAK
CAN'T DO NUTTIN' FOR YA MAN PUBLIC ENEMY
CAN'T DO RIGHT FOR DOING WRONG ERIN ROCHA
CAN'T EXPLAIN LONGVIEW

CAN'T FAKE THE FEELING GERALDINE HUNT
CAN'T FIGHT THE MOONLIGHT LeANN RIMES
CAN'T FIGHT THIS FEELING REO SPEEDWAGON
CAN'T FORGET YOU SONIA
CAN'T GET ALONG WITHOUT YOU FRANKIE VAUGHAN
CAN'T GET ANY HARDER JAMES BROWN
CAN'T GET AWAY MOOD II SWING
CAN'T GET BY SLAMM
CAN'T GET BY WITHOUT YOU REAL THING
CAN'T GET ENOUGH [A] BAD COMPANY
CAN'T GET ENOUGH [B] SOULSEARCHER
CAN'T GET ENOUGH [C] SUEDE
CAN'T GET ENOUGH [D] RAGHAV
CAN'T GET ENOUGH OF YOU EDDY GRANT
CAN'T GET ENOUGH OF YOUR LOVE [A] DARTS
CAN'T GET ENOUGH OF YOUR LOVE [B] KWS
CAN'T GET ENOUGH OF YOUR LOVE [B] TAYLOR DAYNE
CAN'T GET ENOUGH OF YOUR LOVE BABE BARRY WHITE
CAN'T GET IT BACK MIS-TEEQ
(CAN'T GET MY) HEAD AROUND YOU OFFSPRING
CAN'T GET OUT OF BED CHARLATANS
CAN'T GET THE BEST OF ME CYPRESS HILL
CAN'T GET USED TO LOSING YOU ANDY WILLIAMS
CAN'T GET USED TO LOSING YOU BEAT
CAN'T GET USED TO LOSING YOU COLOUR GIRL
CAN'T GET YOU OFF MY MIND LENNY KRAVITZ
CAN'T GET YOU OUT OF MY HEAD KYLIE MINOGUE
CAN'T GET YOU OUT OF MY THOUGHTS DUM DUMS
CAN'T GIVE ME NOW PEPSI & SHIRLIE
CAN'T GIVE YOU ANYTHING (BUT MY LOVE) STYLISTICS
CAN'T GIVE YOU MORE STATUS QUO
CAN'T HAPPEN HERE RAINBOW
CAN'T HAVE YOU LYTE FUNKIE ONES
CAN'T HELP FALLING IN LOVE ELVIS PRESLEY
CAN'T HELP FALLING IN LOVE ANDY WILLIAMS
CAN'T HELP FALLING IN LOVE STYLISTICS
CAN'T HELP FALLING IN LOVE LICK THE TINS
CAN'T HELP IT HAPPY CLAPPERS
CAN'T HELP MYSELF LINX
CAN'T HOLD US DOWN CHRISTINA AGUILERA
    FEATURING LIL' KIM
CAN'T I? NAT 'KING' COLE
CAN'T KEEP IT IN CAT STEVENS
CAN'T KEEP LIVING THIS WAY ROOTJOOSE
CAN'T KEEP ME SILENT ANGELIC
CAN'T KEEP THIS FEELING IN CLIFF RICHARD
CAN'T KNOCK THE HUSTLE JAY-Z FEATURING MARY J.
    BLIGE
CAN'T LET GO MARIAH CAREY
CAN'T LET GO EARTH, WIND & FIRE
CAN'T LET HER GO BOYZ II MEN
CAN'T LET YOU GO [A] BARRY RYAN
CAN'T LET YOU GO [B] RAINBOW
CAN'T LET YOU GO [C] FABOLOUS FEATURING MIKE
    SHOREY & LIL' MO
CAN'T LIVE WITH YOU (CAN'T LIVE WITHOUT YOU)
    MINDBENDERS
CAN'T LIVE WITHOUT YOU SCORPIONS
(CAN'T LIVE WITHOUT YOUR) LOVE AND AFFECTION
    NELSON
CAN'T MAKE MY MIND UP SONIQUE
CAN'T NOBODY KELLY ROWLAND
CAN'T NOBODY HOLD ME DOWN PUFF DADDY
    FEATURING MA$E
CAN'T SAY 'BYE STONEFREE
CAN'T SAY GOODBYE POP!
CAN'T SAY HOW MUCH I LOVE YOU DEMIS ROUSSOS
CAN'T SEE ME IAN BROWN
CAN'T SET THE RULES ABOUT LOVE ADAM ANT
CAN'T SHAKE LOOSE AGNETHA FALTSKOG
CAN'T SHAKE THE FEELING BIG FUN

CAN'T SMILE VEX RED
CAN'T SMILE WITHOUT YOU BARRY MANILOW
CAN'T SMILE WITHOUT YOU JAMES BULLER
CAN'T STAND IT WILCO
CAN'T STAND LOSING YOU POLICE
CAN'T STAND ME NOW LIBERTINES
CAN'T STAY AWAY FROM YOU GLORIA ESTEFAN &
    MIAMI SOUND MACHINE
CAN'T STOP [A] AFTER 7
CAN'T STOP [B] RED HOT CHILI PEPPERS
CAN'T STOP LOVING YOU [A] VAN HALEN
CAN'T STOP LOVING YOU [B] PHIL COLLINS
CAN'T STOP RUNNING SPACE MONKEY
CAN'T STOP THE MUSIC VILLAGE PEOPLE
CAN'T STOP THESE THINGS CHINA DRUM
CAN'T STOP THIS FEELING RHYHTM-N-BASS
CAN'T STOP THIS THING WE STARTED BRYAN ADAMS
CAN'T TAKE MY EYES OFF YOU ANDY WILLIAMS
CAN'T TAKE MY EYES OFF YOU BOYSTOWN GANG
CAN'T TAKE MY EYES OFF YOU ANDY WILLIAMS &
    DENISE VAN OUTEN
CAN'T TAKE NO FOR AN ANSWER SOUP DRAGONS
CAN'T TAKE YOUR LOVE PAULINE HENRY
CAN'T TRUSS IT PUBLIC ENEMY
CAN'T TURN BACK SPEEDWAY
CAN'T WAIT ANOTHER MINUTE FIVE STAR
CAN'T WAIT TO BE WITH YOU JAZZY JEFF & THE FRESH
    PRINCE
CAN'T YOU HEAR MY HEART DANNY RIVERS
CAN'T YOU HEAR MY HEART BEAT? GOLDIE & THE
    GINGERBREADS
CAN'T YOU HEAR THE BEAT OF A BROKEN HEART IAIN
    GREGORY
CAN'T YOU SEE TOTAL FEATURING THE NOTORIOUS
    B.I.G.
CAN'T YOU SEE THAT SHE'S MINE DAVE CLARK FIVE
(CAN'T YOU) TRIP LIKE I DO FILTER & THE CRYSTAL
    METHOD
CANTALOOP US3 FEATURING KOBIE POWELL &
    RAHSAAN
CANTGETAMAN CANTGETAJOB (LIFE'S A BITCH) SISTER
    BLISS WITH COLETTE
CANTO DELLA TERRA ANDREA BOCELLI
CANTON (LIVE) JAPAN
CANTONESE BOY JAPAN
CAPOIERA INFARED VS GIL FELIX
CAPSTICK COMES HOME TONY CAPSTICK & THE
    CARLTON MAIN/FRICKLEY COLLIERY BAND
CAPTAIN BEAKY KEITH MICHELL
CAPTAIN DREAD DREADZONE
CAPTAIN KREMMEN (RETRIBUTION) KENNY EVERETT
    & MIKE VICKERS
THE CAPTAIN OF HER HEART DOUBLE
CAPTAIN OF YOUR SHIP REPARATA & THE DELRONS
CAPTAIN SCARLET THEME BARRY GRAY ORCHESTRA
    WITH PETER BECKETT — KEYBOARDS
CAPTURE THE FLAG FRESH BC
CAPTURE THE HEART (EP) RUNRIG
CAR 67 DRIVER 67
CAR BOOT SALE BILL
CAR SONG MADDER ROSE
CAR WASH ROSE ROYCE
CAR WASH GWEN DICKEY
CAR WASH CHRISTINA AGUILERA & MISSY ELLIOTT
CARA MIA DAVID WHITFIELD WITH CHORUS &
    MANTOVANI & HIS ORCHESTRA
CARAMEL CITY HIGH FEATURING EVE
CARAVAN [A] DUANE EDDY
CARAVAN [B] INSPIRAL CARPETS
CARAVAN OF LOVE ISLEY JASPER ISLEY
CARAVAN OF LOVE HOUSEMARTINS

CARAVAN SONG BARBARA DICKSON
CARBON KID ALPINESTARS FEATURING BRIAN MOLKO
CARDBOY KING SALAD
CARDIAC ARREST MADNESS
CAREFUL (STRESS) HORSE
CARELESS HANDS DES O'CONNOR
CARELESS LOVE SWIMMING WITH SHARKS
CARELESS MEMORIES DURAN DURAN
CARELESS WHISPER GEORGE MICHAEL
CARELESS WHISPER SARAH WASHINGTON
CARELESS WHISPER 2PLAY FEATURING THOMAS
    JULES/JUCXI D
CARIBBEAN BLUE ENYA
THE CARIBBEAN DISCO SHOW LOBO
CARIBBEAN HONEYMOON FRANK WEIR
CARIBBEAN QUEEN (NO MORE LOVE ON THE RUN) BILLY
    OCEAN
CARMEN QUEASY MAXIM
CARNATION LIAM GALLAGHER & STEVE CRADDOCK
CARNAVAL DE PARIS DARIO G
CARNIVAL [A] LIONROCK
CARNIVAL [B] CARDIGANS
CARNIVAL GIRL TEXAS FEATURING KARDINAL
    OFFISHALL
CARNIVAL IN HEAVEN MALANDRA BURROWS
THE CARNIVAL IS OVER SEEKERS
CAROLINA MOON CONNIE FRANCIS
CAROLINE [A] STATUS QUO
CAROLINE [B] KIRSTY MacCOLL
CAROUSEL WALTZ RAY MARTIN
CAROUSEL- ORIGINAL SOUNDTRACK (LP) CAROUSEL
CARRERA 2 THREE DRIVES
CARRIE [A] CLIFF RICHARD
CARRIE [B] EUROPE
CARRIE-ANNE HOLLIES
CARRION BRITISH SEA POWER
CARROT ROPE PAVEMENT
CARRY ME HOME GLOWORM
CARRY ON [A] MARTHA WASH
CARRY ON [B] SPACEHOG
CARRY ON [C] DONNA SUMMER & GIORGIO
    MORODER
CARRY ON WAYWARD SON KANSAS
CARRY THAT WEIGHT TRASH
CARRY THE BLAME RIVER CITY PEOPLE
CARRYING A TORCH TOM JONES
CARS [A] GARY NUMAN
CARS [B] FEAR FACTORY
CARS AND GIRLS PREFAB SPROUT
CARTE BLANCHE VERACOCHA
CARTOON HEROES AQUA
CARTROUBLE ADAM & THE ANTS
CASABLANCA KENNY BALL & HIS JAZZMEN
CASANOVA [A] PETULA CLARK
CASANOVA [B] COFFEE
CASANOVA [B] BABY D
CASANOVA [C] LEVERT
CASANOVA [C] ULTIMATE KAOS
CASCADE FUTURE SOUND OF LONDON
CASE OF THE EX (WHATCHA GONNA DO) MYA
CASINO ROYALE HERB ALPERT & THE TIJUANA BRASS
CASINO ROYALE/DEAD A'S DJ ZINC/DJ HYPE
CASSIUS 1999 CASSIUS
CAST YOUR FATE TO THE WIND SOUNDS ORCHESTRAL
CASTLE ROCK BLUETONES
CASTLES IN SPAIN ARMOURY SHOW
CASTLES IN THE AIR [A] DON McLEAN
CASTLES IN THE AIR [B] COLOUR FIELD
CASTLES IN THE SAND THUNDER
CASTLES IN THE SKY IAN VAN DAHL
CASUAL SUB (BURNING SPEAR) ETA

CAT AMONG THE PIGEONS BROS
THE CAT CAME BACK SONNY JAMES
THE CAT CREPT IN MUD
CAT PEOPLE (PUTTING OUT THE FIRE) DAVID BOWIE
CATALAN TOUR DE FORCE
CATALYST OCEANSIZE
CATCH [A] CURE
CATCH [B] SUNSCREEM
CATCH [C] KOSHEEN
CATCH A FALLING STAR PERRY COMO
CATCH A FIRE HADDAWAY
CATCH ME ABSOLUTE
CATCH ME UP GOMEZ
CATCH MY FALL BILLY IDOL
CATCH THE BREEZE SLOWDIVE
CATCH THE FIRE DRIZABONE
CATCH THE LIGHT MARTHA WASH
CATCH THE SUN DOVES
CATCH THE WIND DONOVAN
CATCH UP TO MY STEP JUNKIE XL FEATURING
    SOLOMON BURKE
CATCH US IF YOU CAN DAVE CLARK FIVE
CATERINA PERRY COMO
THE CATERPILLAR CURE
CATH BLUEBELLS
CATHEDRAL PARK DUBSTAR
CATHEDRAL SONG TANITA TIKARAM
CATHY'S CLOWN EVERLY BROTHERS
CAT'S IN THE CRADLE UGLY KID JOE
CAT'S IN THE CRADLE JASON DOWNS FEATURING MILK
CAUGHT A LITE SNEEZE TORI AMOS
CAUGHT BY THE FUZZ SUPERGRASS
CAUGHT BY THE RIVER DOVES
CAUGHT IN A MOMENT SUGABABES
CAUGHT IN MY SHADOW WONDER STUFF
CAUGHT IN THE MIDDLE [A] JULIET ROBERTS
CAUGHT IN THE MIDDLE [B] A1
CAUGHT IN THE MIDDLE [C] CERYS MATTHEWS
CAUGHT OUT THERE KELIS
CAUGHT UP IN MY HEART OPTIMYSTIC
CAUGHT UP IN THE RAPTURE ANITA BAKER
CAUSING A COMMOTION MADONNA
CAVATINA JOHN WILLIAMS
CAVE MUSE
CCCAN'T YOU SEE VICIOUS PINK
CECILIA SUGGS FEATURING LOUCHIE LOU & MICHIE
    ONE
THE CEDAR ROOM DOVES
CELEBRATE [A] AN EMOTIONAL FISH
CELEBRATE [B] HORSE
CELEBRATE [C] LEVELLERS
CELEBRATE OUR LOVE ALICE DEEJAY
(CELEBRATE) THE DAY AFTER YOU BLOW MONKEYS
    WITH CURTIS MAYFIELD
CELEBRATE THE WORLD WOMACK & WOMACK
CELEBRATE YOUR MOTHER EIGHTIES MATCHBOX B-
    LINE DISASTER
A CELEBRATION U2
CELEBRATION KOOL & THE GANG
CELEBRATION KYLIE MINOGUE
CELEBRATION GENERATION WESTBAM
CELEBRATION OF LIFE TRUCE
CELEBRITY HIT LIST TERRORVISION
CELEBRITY SKIN HOLE
CELL 151 STEVE HACKETT
THE CELTIC SOUL BROTHERS KEVIN ROWLAND &
    DEXY'S MIDNIGHT RUNNERS
THE CELTS ENYA
CEMENT FEEDER
CEMENTED SHOES MY VITRIOL
CENTERFOLD J GEILS BAND

CENTERFOLD ADAM AUSTIN
CENTRAL PARK ARREST THUNDERTHIGHS
CENTRAL RESERVATION BETH ORTON
CENTRE CITY FAT LARRY'S BAND
CENTURY INTASTELLA
CEREMONY NEW ORDER
CERTAIN PEOPLE I KNOW MORRISSEY
A CERTAIN SMILE JOHNNY MATHIS
THE CERTAINTY OF CHANCE DIVINE COMEDY
C'EST LA VIE [A] ROBBIE NEVIL
C'EST LA VIE [B] UB40
C'EST LA VIE [C] B*WITCHED
C'EST LA VIE [D] JEAN-MICHEL JARRE FEATURING
    NATACHA
C'EST SI BON CONWAY TWITTY
CH-CHECK IT OUT BEASTIE BOYS
CHA CHA CHA FLIPMODE SQUAD
CHA CHA HEELS EARTHA KITT & BRONSKI BEAT
CHA CHA SLIDE DJ CASPER
CHA CHA SLIDE MC JIG
CHA CHA TWIST DETROIT COBRAS
CHAIN GANG [A] JIMMY YOUNG
CHAIN GANG [B] SAM COOKE
CHAIN OF FOOLS ARETHA FRANKLIN
CHAIN REACTION [A] DIANA ROSS
CHAIN REACTION [A] STEPS
CHAIN REACTION [B] HURRICANE #1
CHAIN-GANG SMILE BROTHER BEYOND
CHAINS [A] COOKIES
CHAINS [B] RIVER DETECTIVES
CHAINS [C] TINA ARENA
CHAINS AROUND MY HEART RICHARD MARX
CHAINS OF LOVE ERASURE
CHAINSAW CHARLIE (MURDERS IN THE NEW MORGUE)
    W.A.S.P.
CHAIRMAN OF THE BOARD CHAIRMEN OF THE BOARD
CHALK DUST – THE UMPIRE STRIKES BACK BRAT
THE CHAMP MOHAWKS
CHAMPAGNE SALT-N-PEPA
CHAMPAGNE DANCE PAY AS U GO
CHAMPAGNE HIGHWAY SKANDAL
THE CHAMPION WILLIE MITCHELL
CHANCE BIG COUNTRY
CHANCES HOT CHOCOLATE
CHANGE [A] TEARS FOR FEARS
CHANGE [B] DAVID GRANT
CHANGE [C] LISA STANSFIELD
CHANGE [D] INCOGNITO
CHANGE [E] BLIND MELON
CHANGE [F] LIGHTNING SEEDS
CHANGE [G] DAPHNE
CHANGE [H] PHATS & SMALL
CHANGE CLOTHES JAY-Z
CHANGE HIS WAYS ROBERT PALMER
CHANGE (IN THE HOUSE OF FLIES) DEFTONES
CHANGE ME JOCASTA
CHANGE MY MIND BLUESKINS
CHANGE OF HEART [A] CHANGE
CHANGE OF HEART [B] CYNDI LAUPER
A CHANGE OF HEART [C] BERNARD BUTLER
CHANGE THE WORLD [A] ERIC CLAPTON
CHANGE THE WORLD [B] DINO LENNY VS THE
    HOUSEMARTINS
CHANGE WITH THE TIMES VAN McCOY
A CHANGE WOULD DO YOU GOOD SHERYL CROW
CHANGE YOUR MIND [A] SHARPE & NUMAN
CHANGE YOUR MIND [B] UPSIDE DOWN
CHANGES [A] CRISPIAN ST. PETERS
CHANGES [B] IMAGINATION
CHANGES [C] ALAN PRICE
CHANGES [D] 2PAC

CHANGES [E] SANDY RIVERA FEATURING HAZE
CHANGES [F] OZZY & KELLY OSBOURNE
CHANGES ARE NO GOOD STILLS
CHANGING FOR YOU CHI-LITES
CHANGING PARTNERS BING CROSBY
CHANGING PARTNERS KAY STARR
THE CHANGINGMAN PAUL WELLER
CHANNEL Z B-52's
CHANSON D'AMOUR MANHATTAN TRANSFER
THE CHANT HAS BEGUN LEVEL 42
THE CHANT HAS JUST BEGUN ALARM
CHANT NO. 1 (I DON'T NEED THIS PRESSURE ON)
    SPANDAU BALLET
THE CHANT (WE R)/RIP PRODUCTIONS RIP
    PRODUCTIONS
CHANTILLY LACE BIG BOPPER
CHANTILLY LACE JERRY LEE LEWIS
CHAPEL OF LOVE [A] DIXIE CUPS
CHAPEL OF LOVE [B] LONDON BOYS
CHAPEL OF THE ROSES MALCOLM VAUGHAN
CHAPTER FIVE RAM TRILOGY
CHAPTER FOUR RAM TRILOGY
CHAPTER SIX RAM TRILOGY
CHARADE SKIDS
CHARIOT [A] RHET STOLLER
CHARIOT [B] PETULA CLARK
CHARIOTS OF FIRE – TITLES VANGELIS
CHARITY SKUNK ANANSIE
CHARLESTON TEMPERANCE SEVEN
CHARLIE BIG POTATO SKUNK ANANSIE
CHARLIE BROWN COASTERS
CHARLIE'S ANGELS 2000 APOLLO FOUR FORTY
CHARLOTTE KITTIE
CHARLOTTE ANNE JULIAN COPE
CHARLOTTE SOMETIMES CURE
CHARLTON HESTON STUMP
CHARLY PRODIGY
CHARMAINE BACHELORS
CHARMING BILLY JOHNNY PRESTON
CHARMING DEMONS SENSER
CHARMLESS MAN BLUR
CHASE GIORGIO MORODER
CHASE MIDI XPRESS
THE CHASE DJ EMPIRE PRESENTS GIORGIO MORODER
CHASE THE SUN PLANET FUNK
CHASING FOR THE BREEZE ASWAD
CHASING RAINBOWS SHED SEVEN
CHEAP THRILLS PLANET PATROL
CHEATED PRAYING MANTIS
CHECK IT OUT (EVERYBODY) BMR FEATURING FELICIA
CHECK OUT THE GROOVE BOBBY THURSTON
CHECK THE MEANING RICHARD ASHCROFT
CHECK THIS OUT L.A. MIX
CHECK YO SELF ICE CUBE FEATURING DAS EFX
CHEEKAH BOW WOW (THAT COMPUTER SONG)
    VENGABOYS
CHEEKY BONIFACE
CHEEKY ARMADA ILLICIT FEATURING GRAM'MA FUNK
CHEEKY FLAMENCO CHEEKY GIRLS
CHEEKY SONG (TOUCH MY BUM) CHEEKY GIRLS
CHEERS THEN BANANARAMA
CHELSEA STAMFORD BRIDGE
CHEMICAL #1 JESUS JONES
CHEMICAL WORLD BLUR
THE CHEMICALS BETWEEN US BUSH
CHEMISTRY [A] NOLANS
CHEMISTRY [B] SEMISONIC
CHEQUE ONE-TWO SUNSHIP FEATURING M.C.R.B.
CHEQUERED LOVE KIM WILDE
CHERI BABE HOT CHOCOLATE
CHERISH [A] DAVID CASSIDY

CHERISH [A] JODECI
CHERISH [B] KOOL & THE GANG
CHERISH [B] PAPPA BEAR FEATURING VAN DER TOORN
CHERISH [C] MADONNA
CHERISH THE DAY SADE
CHERISH THE DAY PLUMMET
CHERISH WHAT IS DEAR TO YOU FREDA PAYNE
CHERRY LIPS (DER ERDBEERMUND) CULTURE BEAT
CHERRY LIPS (GO BABY GO) GARBAGE
CHERRY OH BABY UB40
CHERRY PIE [A] JESS CONRAD
CHERRY PIE [B] WARRANT
CHERRY PINK AND APPLE BLOSSOM WHITE PEREZ
    'PREZ' PRADO & HIS ORCHESTRA, THE KING OF
    THE MAMBO
CHERRY PINK AND APPLE BLOSSOM WHITE EDDIE
    CALVERT
CHERRY PINK AND APPLE BLOSSOM WHITE MODERN
    ROMANCE FEATURING JOHN DU PREZ
CHERUB ROCK SMASHING PUMPKINS
CHERYL'S GOIN' HOME ADAM FAITH
CHESTNUT MARE BYRDS
CHEWING GUM ANNIE
CHI MAI (THEME FROM THE TV SERIES THE LIFE AND
    TIMES OF DAVID LLOYD GEORGE) ENNIO
    MORRICONE
CHIC MYSTIQUE CHIC
CHICAGO [A] FRANK SINATRA
CHICAGO [B] KIKI DEE
CHICK CHICK CHICKEN NATALIE CASEY
CHICKA BOOM GUY MITCHELL
CHICK-A-BOOM (DON'T YA JES LOVE IT) 53RD & A 3RD
    FEATURING THE SOUND OF SHAG
CHICKEN EIGHTIES MATCHBOX B-LINE DISASTER
THE CHICKEN SONG SPITTING IMAGE
THE CHIEF TONI SCOTT
CHIEF INSPECTOR WALLY BADAROU
CHIHUAHUA [A] BOW WOW WOW
CHIHUAHUA [B] DARE
CHIHUAHUA [B] DJ BOBO
CHIKKI CHIKKI AHH AHH BABY FORD
CHILD [A] DEFINITION OF SOUND
CHILD [B] MARK OWEN
CHILD COME AWAY KIM WILDE
CHILD OF LOVE LEMON TREES
CHILD OF THE UNIVERSE DJ TAUCHER
CHILD STAR MARC ALMOND
CHILDREN [A] EMF
CHILDREN [B] ROBERT MILES
CHILDREN [B] TILT
CHILDREN [B] 4 CLUBBERS
CHILDREN OF PARADISE BONEY M
CHILDREN OF THE NIGHT [A] RICHARD MARX
CHILDREN OF THE NIGHT [B] NAKATOMI
CHILDREN OF THE REVOLUTION T. REX
CHILDREN OF THE REVOLUTION BABY FORD
CHILDREN OF THE REVOLUTION UNITONE ROCKERS
    FEATURING STEEL
CHILDREN OF THE WORLD ANA ANN & THE LONDON
    COMMUNITY CHOIR
CHILDREN SAY LEVEL 42
A CHILD'S PRAYER HOT CHOCOLATE
CHILI BOM BOM TEMPERANCE SEVEN
CHILL OUT (THINGS GONNA CHANGE) JOHN LEE
    HOOKER
CHILL TO THE PANIC DEEP C
CHILLIN' MODJO
CHILLIN' OUT CURTIS HAIRSTON
CHIME ORBITAL
CHINA TORI AMOS
CHINA DOLL [A] SLIM WHITMAN

CHINA DOLL [B] JULIAN COPE
CHINA GIRL DAVID BOWIE
CHINA IN YOUR HAND T'PAU
CHINA TEA RUSS CONWAY
CHINATOWN [A] MOVE
CHINATOWN [B] THIN LIZZY
CHINESE BAKERY AUTEURS
CHINESE BURN HEAVY STEREO
THE CHINESE WAY LEVEL 42
CHING CHING (LOVIN' YOU STILL) TERRI WALKER
CHIQUITITA ABBA
CHIRPY CHIRPY CHEEP CHEEP MIDDLE OF THE ROAD
CHIRPY CHIRPY CHEEP CHEEP MAC & KATIE KISSOON
CHIRPY CHIRPY CHEEP CHEEP MICHAEL COURTNEY
THE CHISELERS FALL
CHOC ICE LONG & THE SHORT
CHOCOLATE [A] Y?N-VEE
CHOCOLATE [B] SNOW PATROL
CHOCOLATE [C] KYLIE MINOGUE
CHOCOLATE BOX BROS
CHOCOLATE CAKE CROWDED HOUSE
CHOCOLATE (CHOCO CHOCO) SOUL CONTROL
CHOCOLATE GIRL DEACON BLUE
CHOCOLATE SALTY BALLS (PS I LOVE YOU) CHEF
CHOCOLATE SENSATION LENNY FONTANA & DJ SHORTY
CHOICE? BLOW MONKEYS FEATURING SYLVIA TELLA
CHOK THERE APACHE INDIAN
CHOLI KE PEECHE BALLY SAGOO
CHOOSE COLOR ME BADD
CHOOSE LIFE PF PROJECT FEATURING EWAN
    McGREGOR
CHOOSE ME (RESCUE ME) LOOSE ENDS
CHOOZA LOOZA MARIA WILLSON
CHOP SUEY SYSTEM OF A DOWN
CHORUS ERASURE
THE CHOSEN FEW DOOLEYS
CHRISTIAN CHINA CRISIS
CHRISTIANSANDS TRICKY
CHRISTINE [A] MISS X
CHRISTINE [B] SIOUXSIE & THE BANSHEES
CHRISTINE KEELER SENSELESS THINGS
CHRISTMAS ALPHABET DICKIE VALENTINE
CHRISTMAS AND YOU DAVE KING
CHRISTMAS COUNTDOWN FRANK KELLY
CHRISTMAS IN BLOBBYLAND MR BLOBBY
CHRISTMAS IN DREADLAND JUDGE DREAD
CHRISTMAS IN HOLLIS RUN D.M.C.
CHRISTMAS IN SMURFLAND FATHER ABRAHAM & THE
    SMURFS
CHRISTMAS IS ALL AROUND BILLY MACK
CHRISTMAS ISLAND DICKIE VALENTINE
A CHRISTMAS KISS DANIEL O'DONNELL
CHRISTMAS MEDLEY WEEKEND
CHRISTMAS ON 45 HOLLY & THE IVYS
CHRISTMAS RAPPIN' KURTIS BLOW
CHRISTMAS RAPPING DIZZY HEIGHTS
CHRISTMAS SLIDE BASIL BRUSH FEATURING INDIA
    BEAU
THE CHRISTMAS SONG [A] NAT 'KING' COLE
CHRISTMAS SONG (CHESTNUTS ROASTING ON AN
    OPEN FIRE) [A] ALEXANDER O'NEAL
CHRISTMAS SONG [B] GILBERT O'SULLIVAN
CHRISTMAS SPECTRE JINGLE BELLES
CHRISTMAS THROUGH YOUR EYES GLORIA ESTEFAN
CHRISTMAS TIME BRYAN ADAMS
CHRISTMAS TIME (DON'T LET THE BELLS END)
    DARKNESS
CHRISTMAS WILL BE JUST ANOTHER LONELY DAY
    BRENDA LEE
CHRISTMAS WRAPPING WAITRESSES
CHRONOLOGIE PART 4 JEAN-MICHEL JARRE

CHUCK E.'S IN LOVE RICKIE LEE JONES
CHUNG KUO (REVISITED) ADDAMS & GEE
CHURA LIYA BALLY SAGOO
CHURCH OF FREEDOM AMOS
THE CHURCH OF THE HOLY SPOOK SHANE MacGOWAN
    & THE POPES
CHURCH OF NOISE THERAPY?
CHURCH OF THE POISON MIND CULTURE CLUB
CHURCH OF YOUR HEART ROXETTE
CIAO CIAO BAMBINA MARINO MARINI & HIS QUARTET
CIAO CIAO BAMBINA DOMENICO MODUGNO
CIGARETTES AND ALCOHOL OASIS
CINDERELLA LEMONESCENT
CINDERELLA ROCKEFELLA ESTHER & ABI OFARIM
CINDY INCIDENTALLY FACES
CINDY OH CINDY EDDIE FISHER
CINDY OH CINDY TONY BRENT
CINDY OH CINDY VINCE MARTIN & THE TARRIERS
CINDY'S BIRTHDAY SHANE FENTON & THE FENTONES
CINNAMON GIRL PRINCE
CIRCLE EDIE BRICKELL & THE NEW BOHEMIANS
THE CIRCLE OCEAN COLOUR SCENE
CIRCLE IN THE SAND BELINDA CARLISLE
CIRCLE OF LIFE ELTON JOHN
CIRCLE OF ONE OLETA ADAMS
CIRCLES [A] NEW SEEKERS
CIRCLES [B] SAFFRON
CIRCLES [C] ADAM F
CIRCLESQUARE WONDER STUFF
CIRCUS [A] LENNY KRAVITZ
CIRCUS [B] ERIC CLAPTON
THE CIRCUS [C] ERASURE
CIRCUS GAMES SKIDS
CITIES IN DUST SIOUXSIE & THE BANSHEES
THE CITY IS MINE JAY-Z FEATURING BLACKstreet
CITY LIGHTS DAVID ESSEX
CITYSONG LUSCIOUS JACKSON
THE CIVIL WAR EP GUNS N' ROSES
CLAIR GILBERT O'SULLIVAN
CLAIRE PAUL & BARRY RYAN
THE CLAIRVOYANT IRON MAIDEN
CLAP BACK JA RULE
THE CLAP CLAP SOUND KLAXONS
CLAP YOUR HANDS [A] ROCKY SHARPE & THE REPLAYS
CLAP YOUR HANDS [B] CAMISRA
THE CLAPPING SONG SHIRLEY ELLIS
THE CLAPPING SONG BELLE STARS
THE CLAPPING SONG (EP) SHIRLEY ELLIS
CLARE FAIRGROUND ATTRACTION
CLASH CITY ROCKERS CLASH
CLASSIC ADRIAN GURVITZ
CLASSIC GIRL JANE'S ADDICTION
CLASSICAL GAS MASON WILLIAMS
CLASSICAL GAS VANESSA-MAE
CLASSICAL MUDDLEY PORTSMOUTH SINFONIA
CLAUDETTE EVERLY BROTHERS
CLEAN CLEAN BUGGLES
CLEAN UP YOUR OWN BACK YARD ELVIS PRESLEY
CLEANIN' OUT MY CLOSET EMINEM
CLEAR BLUE WATER OCEANLAB FEATURING JUSTINE
    SUISSA
CLEMENTINE [A] BOBBY DARIN
CLEMENTINE [B] MARK OWEN
CLEOPATRA'S CAT SPIN DOCTORS
CLEOPATRA'S THEME CLEOPATRA
CLEVER KICKS HISS
THE CLICHES ARE TRUE MANCHILD FEATURING KELLY
    JONES
CLIMB EV'RY MOUNTAIN SHIRLEY BASSEY
CLINT EASTWOOD GORILLAZ
CLIPPED CURVE

CLOAKING SEAFOOD
CLOCKS COLDPLAY
CLOG DANCE VIOLINSKI
CLOSE BUT NO CIGAR THOMAS DOLBY
CLOSE COVER MINIMALISTIX
CLOSE EVERY DOOR PHILIP SCOFIELD
CLOSE MY EYES OPEN
CLOSE MY EYES FOREVER LITA FORD DUET WITH OZZY OSBOURNE
CLOSE THE DOOR [A] STARGAZERS
CLOSE THE DOOR [B] TEDDY PENDERGRASS
CLOSE TO ME CURE
CLOSE TO PERFECTION MIQUEL BROWN
CLOSE (TO THE EDIT) ART OF NOISE
CLOSE TO YOU [A] MAXI PRIEST
CLOSE TO YOU [B] BRAND NEW HEAVIES FEATURING N'DEA DAVENPORT
CLOSE TO YOU [C] WHIGFIELD
CLOSE TO YOU [D] MARTI PELLOW
CLOSE TO YOUR HEART JX
CLOSE YOUR EYES TONY BENNETT
CLOSE...BUT ECHOBELLY
CLOSED FOR BUSINESS MANSUN
CLOSER [A] MR FINGERS
CLOSER [B] NINE INCH NAILS
CLOSER [C] LIQUID
THE CLOSER I GET TO YOU ROBERTA FLACK & DONNY HATHAWAY
CLOSER THAN CLOSE ROSIE GAINES
CLOSER THAN MOST BEAUTIFUL SOUTH
CLOSER TO ALL YOUR DREAMS RHYTHM QUEST
CLOSER TO ME FIVE
CLOSER TO THE HEART RUSH
THE CLOSEST THING TO CRAZY KATIE MELUA
CLOSEST THING TO HEAVEN [A] KANE GANG
CLOSEST THING TO HEAVEN [B] LIONEL RICHIE
CLOSING TIME [A] DEACON BLUE
CLOSING TIME [B] SEMISONIC
CLOUD 8 FRAZIER CHORUS
CLOUD LUCKY SEVEN GUY MITCHELL
CLOUD NINE TEMPTATIONS
CLOUD 99 ST. ANDREWS CHORALE
CLOUD NUMBER 9 BRYAN ADAMS
CLOUDBURST [A] DON LANG & THE MAIRANTS-LANGHORN BIG SIX
CLOUDBURST [B] NIAGRA
CLOUDBURSTING KATE BUSH
CLOUDS SOURCE
CLOUDS ACROSS THE MOON RAH BAND
THE CLOUDS WILL SOON ROLL BY TONY BRENT
CLOWN SHOES JOHNNY BURNETTE
CLUB AT THE END OF THE STREET ELTON JOHN
CLUB BIZARRE U96
CLUB COUNTRY ASSOCIATES
CLUB FANTASTIC MEGAMIX WHAM!
CLUB FOOT KASABIAN
CLUB FOR LIFE '98 CHRIS & JAMES
CLUB LONELY GROOVE CONNEKTION 2
CLUB TROPICANA WHAM!
CLUBBED TO DEATH ROB DOUGAN
CLUBBIN' MARQUES HOUSTON
CLUBLAND ELVIS COSTELLO & THE ATTRACTIONS
CLUNK CLICK LAUREL & HARDY
CLUTCH SHEA SEGER
C'MON [A] MILLIONAIRE HIPPIES
C'MON [B] MARIO
C'MON AND GET MY LOVE D MOB WITH CATHY DENNIS
C'MON BILLY PJ HARVEY
C'MON C'MON VON BONDIES
C'MON CINCINNATI DELAKOTA FEATURING ROSE SMITH

C'MON EVERY BEATBOX BIG AUDIO DYNAMITE
C'MON EVERYBODY EDDIE COCHRAN
C'MON EVERYBODY SEX PISTOLS
C'MON KIDS BOO RADLEYS
C'MON LET'S GO GIRLSCHOOL
C'MON MARIANNE GRAPEFRUIT
C'MON PEOPLE PAUL McCARTNEY
C'MON PEOPLE (WE'RE MAKING IT NOW) RICHARD ASHCROFT
CO-CO SWEET
COAST IS CLEAR CURVE
COCHISE AUDIOSLAVE
COCK A DOODLE DO IT EGGS ON LEGS
COCKNEY TRANSLATION SMILEY CULTURE
COCO JAMBOO MR PRESIDENT
COCOA CLIPZ
COCOMOTION EL COCO
COCONUT NILSSON
COCOON BJORK
CODE OF LOVE MIKE SARNE
CODE RED [A] CONQUERING LION
CODE RED [B] BOXER REBELLION
CODED LANGUAGE KRUST FEATURING SAUL WILLIAMS
COFFEE SUPERSISTER
COFFEE + TEA BLUR
THE COFFEE SONG FRANK SINATRA
COGNOSCENTI VERSUS THE INTELLIGENTSIA CUBAN BOYS
COLD [A] ANNIE LENNOX
COLD [B] TEARS FOR FEARS
COLD AS CHRISTMAS ELTON JOHN
COLD AS ICE FOREIGNER
COLD AS ICE M.O.P.
COLD COLD HEART [A] MIDGE URE
COLD COLD HEART [B] WET WET WET
COLD DAY IN HELL GARY MOORE
COLD HARD BITCH JET
COLD HEARTED PAULA ABDUL
COLD LIGHT OF DAY HALO
COLD LOVE DONNA SUMMER
COLD ROCK A PARTY MC LYTE
COLD SHOULDER CULTURE CLUB
COLD SWEAT [A] THIN LIZZY
COLD SWEAT [B] SUGARCUBES
COLD TURKEY PLASTIC ONO BAND
COLD WORLD GENIUS/GZA FEATURING D'ANGELO
COLDCUT'S CHRISTMAS BREAK COLDCUT
COLETTE BILLY FURY
COLOR OF MY SKIN SWING 52
COLOSSUS FRESH BC
THE COLOUR FIELD COLOUR FIELD
COLOUR MY LIFE M PEOPLE
THE COLOUR OF LOVE [A] BILLY OCEAN
THE COLOUR OF LOVE [B] SNAP
THE COLOUR OF LOVE [C] REESE PROJECT
COLOUR OF MY LOVE JEFFERSON
COLOUR THE WORLD SASH!
COLOURBLIND DARIUS
COLOURED KISSES MARTIKA
COLOURS DONOVAN
THE COLOURS MEN THEY COULDN'T HANG
COLOURS FLY AWAY TEARDROP EXPLODES
COLOURS IN WAVES SOUTH
COLOURS OF THE WIND VANESSA WILLIAMS
COMA AROMA INAURA
COMA GIRL JOE STRUMMER & THE MESCALEROS
THE COMANCHEROS LONNIE DONEGAN
COMBINE HARVESTER (BRAND NEW KEY) WURZELS
COME MARTHA WASH
COME AGAIN TRUMAN & WOLFF FEATURING STEEL HORSES

COME ALONG PLEASE BOB WALLIS & HIS STORYVILLE JAZZ BAND
COME AND GET IT BADFINGER
COME AND GET ME CLEOPATRA
COME AND GET SOME COOKIE CREW
COME AND GET WITH ME KEITH SWEAT FEATURING SNOOP DOGG
COME AND GET YOUR LOVE REAL McCOY
COME AND STAY WITH ME MARIANNE FAITHFULL
COME AS YOU ARE [A] NIRVANA
COME AS YOU ARE [B] BEVERLEY KNIGHT
COME AWAY MELINDA BARRY ST JOHN
COME BABY COME K7
COME BACK [A] MIGHTY WAH
COME BACK [B] SPEAR OF DESTINY
COME BACK [C] LUTHER VANDROSS
COME BACK [D] LONDONBEAT
COME BACK [E] JESSICA GARLICK
COME BACK AND FINISH WHAT YOU STARTED GLADYS KNIGHT & THE PIPS
COME BACK AND SHAKE ME CLODAGH RODGERS
COME BACK AND STAY PAUL YOUNG
COME BACK AROUND FEEDER
COME BACK BABY DAN REED NETWORK
COME BACK BRIGHTER REEF
COME BACK DARLING UB40
COME BACK (FOR REAL LOVE) ALISON LIMERICK
COME BACK JONEE DEVO
COME BACK MY LOVE DARTS
COME BACK TO ME [A] JANET JACKSON
COME BACK TO ME [B] ANGELHEART FEATURING ROCHELLE HARRIS
COME BACK TO WHAT YOU KNOW EMBRACE
COME BACK TOMORROW INSPIRAL CARPETS
COME CLEAN HILARY DUFF
COME DANCE WITH ME (LP) FRANK SINATRA
COME DANCING [A] NO DICE
COME DANCING [B] KINKS
COME DIG IT MACHEL
COME GET MY LOVIN' DIONNE
COME GET SOME ROOSTER
COME GIVE ME YOUR LOVE RICHIE STEPHENS
COME HELL OR WATERS HIGH DEE C. LEE
COME HOME [A] DAVE CLARK FIVE
COME HOME [B] JAMES
COME HOME [C] LIL' DEVIOUS
COME HOME BILLY BIRD DIVINE COMEDY
COME HOME WITH ME BABY DEAD OR ALIVE
COME IN OUT OF THE RAIN WENDY MOTEN
COME INSIDE THOMPSON TWINS
COME INTO MY LIFE [A] JOYCE SIMS
COME INTO MY LIFE [B] GALA
COME INTO MY WORLD KYLIE MINOGUE
COME LIVE WITH ME HEAVEN 17
COME NEXT SPRING TONY BENNETT
COME ON [A] ROLLING STONES
COME ON! [B] SOLO
COME ON [C] DJ SEDUCTION
COME ON [D] JESUS & MARY CHAIN
COME ON [E] NEW POWER GENERATION
COME ON [F] LEVELLERS
COME ON [G] D4
COME ON (AND DO IT) FPI PROJECT
COME ON DANCE DANCE SATURDAY NIGHT BAND
COME ON EILEEN DEXY'S MIDNIGHT RUNNERS WITH THE EMERALD EXPRESS
COME ON ENGLAND! [A] ENGLAND'S BARMY ARMY
COME ON ENGLAND [B] FOUR FOUR TWO
COME ON EVERYBODY (GET DOWN) URGE OVERKILL
COME ON HOME [A] SPRINGFIELDS
COME ON HOME [B] WAYNE FONTANA

COME ON HOME [C] EVERYTHING BUT THE GIRL
COME ON HOME [D] CYNDI LAUPER
COME ON, LET'S GO TOMMY STEELE
COME ON LET'S GO LOS LOBOS
COME ON OVER [A] JOHN SILVER
COME ON OVER [B] KYM MARSH
COME ON OVER BABY (ALL I WANT IS YOU) CHRISTINA AGUILERA
COME ON OVER TO MY PLACE DRIFTERS
COME ON YALL RHYTHM MASTERS
COME ON YOU REDS MANCHESTER UNITED FOOTBALL CLUB
COME ON, COME ON BRONSKI BEAT
COME OUTSIDE MIKE SARNE WITH WENDY RICHARD
COME OUTSIDE JUDGE DREAD
COME PLAY WITH ME WEDDING PRESENT
COME PRIMA MARINO MARINI & HIS QUARTET
(COME 'ROUND HERE) I'M THE ONE YOU NEED SMOKEY ROBINSON & THE MIRACLES
COME SEE ABOUT ME [A] SUPREMES
COME SEE ABOUT ME [B] SHAKIN' STEVENS
COME SEE ME PRETTY THINGS
COME SOFTLY TO ME FLEETWOODS
COME SOFTLY TO ME FRANKIE VAUGHAN & THE KAYE SISTERS
COME SOFTLY TO ME NEW SEEKERS FEATURING MARTY KRISTIAN
COME TO DADDY APHEX TWIN
COME TO ME [A] JULIE GRANT
COME TO ME [B] RUBY WINTERS
COME TO ME [C] ATEED
COME TO ME (I AM WOMAN) SU POLLARD
COME TO MILTON KEYNES STYLE COUNCIL
COME TO MY AID SIMPLY RED
COME TO MY PARTY KEITH HARRIS & ORVILLE WITH DIPPY
COME TO THE DANCE BARRON KNIGHTS WITH DUKE D'MOND
COME TOGETHER [A] BEATLES
COME TOGETHER [A] MICHAEL JACKSON
COME TOGETHER (WAR CHILD) [A] SMOKIN' MOJO FILTERS
COME TOGETHER [B] PRIMAL SCREAM
COME TOGETHER [C] M FACTOR
COME TOGETHER AS ONE WILL DOWNING
COME TOMORROW MANFRED MANN
COME UNDONE [A] DURAN DURAN
COME UNDONE [B] ROBBIE WILLIAMS
COME WHAT MAY [A] VICKY LEANDROS
COME WHAT MAY [B] NICOLE KIDMAN & EWAN McGREGOR
COME WITH ME [A] JESSE GREEN
COME WITH ME [B] RONNY JORDAN
COME WITH ME [C] QATTARA
COME WITH ME [D] PUFF DADDY FEATURING JIMMY PAGE
COME WITH ME [E] SPECIAL D
COME WITH US CHEMICAL BROTHERS
COMEDY SHACK
COMES A-LONG A-LOVE KAY STARR
COMEUPPANCE THOUSAND YARD STARE
COMFORTABLY NUMB SCISSOR SISTERS
COMFORTING SOUNDS MEW
COMIN' BACK CRYSTAL METHOD
COMIN' HOME [A] DELANEY & BONNIE & FRIENDS FEATURING ERIC CLAPTON
COMIN' HOME [B] DANGER DANGER
COMIN' IN AND OUT OF YOUR LIFE BARBRA STREISAND
COMIN' ON STRONG [A] BROKEN ENGLISH
COMIN' ON STRONG [B] DESIYA FEATURING MELISSA YIANNAKOU

COMIN' RIGHT UP BRUCE WILLIS
COMING AROUND TRAVIS
COMING AROUND AGAIN CARLY SIMON
COMING BACK DJ DADO
COMING BACK FOR MORE [A] L.A. MIX
COMING BACK FOR MORE [B] JELLYBEAN FEATURING RICHARD DARBYSHIRE
COMING DOWN CULT
COMING HOME [A] DAVID ESSEX
COMING HOME [B] MARSHALL HAIN
COMING HOME [C] K WARREN FEATURING LEE O
COMING HOME BABY MEL TORME
COMING HOME NOW BOYZONE
COMING ON STRONG SIGNUM FEATURING SCOTT MAC
COMING OUT OF THE DARK GLORIA ESTEFAN
COMING UP PAUL McCARTNEY
COMING UP ROSES CURVE
COMMENT TE DIRE ADIEU JIMMY SOMERVILLE FEATURING JUNE MILES-KINGSTON
COMMITMENT LeANN RIMES
COMMON PEOPLE PULP
COMMUNICATION [A] DAVID McCALLUM
COMMUNICATION [B] SPANDAU BALLET
COMMUNICATION [C] POWER STATION
COMMUNICATION [D] ARMIN
COMMUNICATION BREAKDOWN JUNIOR
COMMUNICATION (SOMEBODY ANSWER THE PHONE) MARIO PIU
THE COMPASS DAVE CLARKE
COMPLETE JAIMESON
COMPLETE CONTROL CLASH
THE COMPLETE DOMINATOR HUMAN RESOURCE
THE COMPLETE STELLA (REMIX) JAM & SPOON
COMPLEX GARY NUMAN
COMPLICATED AVRIL LAVIGNE
COMPLIMENTS ON YOUR KISS RED DRAGON WITH BRIAN & TONY GOLD
COMPUTER GAME (THEME FROM 'THE INVADERS') YELLOW MAGIC ORCHESTRA
COMPUTER LOVE [A] KRAFTWERK
COMPUTER LOVE (PART 1) [B] ZAPP
COMPUTER LOVE [C] SUPERCAR FEATURING MIKAELA
CON LOS ANOS QUE ME QUEDIN GLORIA ESTEFAN
THE CONCEPT TEENAGE FANCLUB
CONCRETE AND CLAY UNIT FOUR PLUS TWO
CONCRETE AND CLAY RANDY EDELMAN
CONCRETE SCHOOLYARD JURASSIC 5
CONDEMNATION DEPECHE MODE
CONFESSIN' FRANK IFIELD
CONFESSIONS OF A BOUNCER JUDGE DREAD
CONFESSIONS PART II USHER
CONFETTI LEMONHEADS
CONFIDE IN ME KYLIE MINOGUE
CONFUSION [A] LEE DORSEY
CONFUSION [B] ELECTRIC LIGHT ORCHESTRA
CONFUSION [C] NEW ORDER
CONFUSION [C] ARTHUR BAKER VS NEW ORDER
CONFUSION [D] ZUTONS
CONFUSION (HITS US EVERY TIME) TRUTH
CONGO [A] BOSS
CONGO [B] GENESIS
CONGO SQUARE GREAT WHITE
CONGRATULATIONS CLIFF RICHARD
CONNECTED [A] STEREO MC'S
CONNECTED [B] PAUL VAN DYK FEATURING VEGA 4
CONNECTION ELASTICA
CONQUEST OF PARADISE VANGELIS
CONQUISTADOR [A] PROCOL HARUM
CONQUISTADOR [B] ESPIRITU
CONSCIENCE JAMES DARREN
CONSCIOUS MAN JOLLY BROTHERS

CONSIDER YOURSELF MAX BYGRAVES
CONSIDERATION REEF
A CONSPIRACY BLACK CROWES
CONSTANT CRAVING k.d. lang
CONSTANTLY CLIFF RICHARD
CONSTANTLY WAITING PAULINE TAYLOR
CONTACT [A] EDWIN STARR
CONTACT... [B] EAT STATIC
CONTAGIOUS WHISPERS
THE CONTINENTAL MAUREEN McGOVERN
CONTRARY MARY THEE UNSTRUNG
CONTRIBUTION MICA PARIS
CONTROL [A] JANET JACKSON
CONTROL [B] TIME OF THE MUMPH
CONTROL [C] PUDDLE OF MUDD
CONTROLLING ME OCEANIC
CONTROVERSY PRINCE
CONVERSATION INTERCOM SOULWAX
CONVERSATIONS CILLA BLACK
CONVOY CW McCALL
CONVOY G.B. LAURIE LINGO & THE DIPSTICKS
CONWAY REEL 2 REAL FEATURING THE MAD STUNTMAN
COOCHY COO EN-CORE FEATURING STEPHEN EMMANUEL & ESKA
COOKIN' UP YAH BRAIN 4 HERO
COOL BABY CHARLIE GRACIE
COOL FOR CATS SQUEEZE
COOL JERK GO-GOS
COOL MEDITATION THIRD WORLD
COOL OUT TONIGHT DAVID ESSEX
COOL RUNNING TIK & TOK
COOL WATER FRANKIE LAINE
COP THAT SHIT TIMBALAND/MAGOO/MISSY ELLIOTT
COPACABANA (AT THE COPA) BARRY MANILOW
COPPER GIRL 3 COLOURS RED
COPPERHEAD ROAD STEVE EARLE
CORNER OF THE EARTH JAMIROQUAI
CORNERSHOP BABY BIRD
CORNFLAKE GIRL TORI AMOS
CORONATION RAG WINIFRED ATWELL
CORPSES IAN BROWN
CORRINE, CORRINA RAY PETERSON
COSMIC GIRL JAMIROQUAI
COSMONAUT NO. 7 SCARFO
THE COST OF LIVING EP CLASH
COSTAFINE TOWN SPLINTER
COTTON EYE JOE REDNEX
COTTONFIELDS BEACH BOYS
COULD HAVE TOLD YOU SO HALO JAMES
COULD HEAVEN EVER BE LIKE THIS IDRIS MUHAMMAD
COULD I HAVE THIS KISS FOREVER WHITNEY HOUSTON & ENRIQUE IGLESIAS
COULD IT BE JAHEIM
COULD IT BE FOREVER DAVID CASSIDY
COULD IT BE FOREVER GEMINI
COULD IT BE I'M FALLING IN LOVE DETROIT SPINNERS
COULD IT BE I'M FALLING IN LOVE DAVID GRANT & JAKI GRAHAM
COULD IT BE I'M FALLING IN LOVE WORLDS APART
COULD IT BE I'M FALLING IN LOVE EP DETROIT SPINNERS
COULD IT BE MAGIC DONNA SUMMER
COULD IT BE MAGIC BARRY MANILOW
COULD IT BE MAGIC TAKE THAT
COULD WELL BE IN STREETS
COULD YOU BE LOVED BOB MARLEY & THE WAILERS
COULDN'T GET IT RIGHT CLIMAX BLUES BAND
COULDN'T HAVE SAID IT BETTER MEAT LOAF
COULDN'T SAY GOODBYE TOM JONES
COULD'VE BEEN TIFFANY

COULD'VE BEEN ME BILLY RAY CYRUS
COULD'VE BEEN YOU CHER
COUNT ON ME [A] JULIE GRANT
COUNT ON ME [B] WHITNEY HOUSTON
COUNT YOUR BLESSINGS BING CROSBY
COUNTDOWN RUSH
COUNTERFEIT LOWGOLD
COUNTING BACKWARDS THROWING MUSES
COUNTING EVERY MINUTE SONIA
COUNTING SHEEP AIRHEAD
COUNTING TEARDROPS EMILE FORD & THE
    CHECKMATES
COUNTING THE DAYS ABI
COUNTRY BOY [A] FATS DOMINO
COUNTRY BOY [B] HEINZ
COUNTRY BOY [C] JIMMY NAIL
COUNTRY HOUSE BLUR
THE COUNTRY OF THE BLIND FAITH BROTHERS
COUNTRY ROADS HERMES HOUSE BAND
COURSE BRUV GENIUS CRU
COUSIN NORMAN MARMALADE
COVER FROM THE SKY DEACON BLUE
COVER GIRL NEW KIDS ON THE BLOCK
COVER ME BRUCE SPRINGSTEEN
COVER MY EYES (PAIN AND HEAVEN) MARILLION
(COVER PLUS) WE'RE ALL GROWN UP HAZEL
    O'CONNOR
COVER UP UB40
COVERED IN PUNK PORTOBELLA
COVERS EP EVERYTHING BUT THE GIRL
COWARD OF THE COUNTY KENNY ROGERS
COWBOY KID ROCK
COWBOY DREAMS JIMMY NAIL
COWBOY JIMMY JOE ALMA COGAN
COWBOYS & KISSES ANASTACIA
COWBOYS AND ANGELS GEORGE MICHAEL
COWBOYS AND INDIANS CROSS
COWGIRL UNDERWORLD
COWPUNCHER'S CANTATA MAX BYGRAVES
COWPUNK MEDLUM SPLODGENESSABOUNDS
COZ I LUV YOU SLADE
CRACKERS INTERNATIONAL EP ERASURE
CRACKIN' UP [A] TOMMY HUNT
CRACKIN' UP [B] NICK LOWE
CRACKING UP [C] JESUS & MARY CHAIN
CRACKLIN' ROSIE NEIL DIAMOND
CRADLE OF LOVE [A] JOHNNY PRESTON
CRADLE OF LOVE [B] BILLY IDOL
CRANK CATHERINE WHEEL
CRASH [A] PRIMITIVES
CRASH [B] FEEDER
CRASH AND BURN SAVAGE GARDEN
CRASH! BOOM! BANG! ROXETTE
CRASHED THE WEDDING BUSTED
CRASHIN' A PARTY LUMIDEE FEATURING NORE
CRASHIN' IN CHARLATANS
CRAWL HEADSWIM
CRAWL HOME DESERT SESSIONS
CRAWLIN' BACK ROY ORBISON
CRAWLING LINKIN PARK
CRAWLING FROM THE WRECKAGE DAVE EDMUNDS
CRAWLING IN THE DARK HOOBASTANK
CRAWLING UP A HILL KATIE MELUA
CRAYZY MAN BLAST FEATURING VDC
CRAZIER GARY NUMAN VS RICO
CRAZY [A] MUD
CRAZY [B] MANHATTANS
CRAZY [C] ICEHOUSE
CRAZY [D] BOYS
CRAZY [E] PATSY CLINE
CRAZY [E] JULIO IGLESIAS

CRAZY [E] LeANN RIMES
CRAZY [F] SEAL
CRAZY [G] BOB GELDOF
CRAZY [H] AEROSMITH
CRAZY [I] ETERNAL
CRAZY [J] MARK MORRISON
CRAZY [K] NUT
CRAZY [L] AWESOME
CRAZY [M] MOFFATTS
CRAZY [N] LUCID
CRAZY [O] TOMCAT
CRAZY [P] K-CI & JOJO
CRAZY BEAT BLUR
CRAZY CHANCE KAVANA
CRAZY CRAZY NIGHTS KISS
CRAZY CUTS GRANDMIXER DST
CRAZY DREAM JIM DALE
CRAZY (FOR ME) FREDDIE JACKSON
CRAZY FOR YOU [A] MADONNA
CRAZY FOR YOU [B] SYBIL
CRAZY FOR YOU [C] INCOGNITO FEATURING CHYNA
CRAZY FOR YOU [D] LET LOOSE
CRAZY HORSES OSMONDS
CRAZY IN LOVE BEYONCÉ
CRAZY LITTLE PARTY GIRL AARON CARTER
CRAZY LITTLE THING CALLED LOVE QUEEN
CRAZY LITTLE THING CALLED LOVE DWIGHT YOAKAM
CRAZY LOVE [A] PAUL ANKA
CRAZY LOVE [B] MAXI PRIEST
CRAZY LOVE [C] CE CE PENISTON
CRAZY LOVE [D] MJ COLE
CRAZY LOWDOWN WAYS OCEAN COLOUR SCENE
CRAZY OTTO RAG STARGAZERS
THE CRAZY PARTY MIXES JIVE BUNNY & THE
    MASTERMIXERS
CRAZY RAP AFROMAN
CRAZY SEXY MARVELLOUS PAFFENDORF
CRAZY TRAIN OZZY OSBOURNE'S BLIZZARD OF OZ
CRAZY WATER ELTON JOHN
CRAZY WORDS CRAZY TUNE DOROTHY PROVINE
CRAZY YOU GUN
CREAM [A] PRINCE & THE NEW POWER GENERATION
CREAM [B] BLANK & JONES
CREAM (ALWAYS RISES TO THE TOP) GREGG DIAMOND
    BIONIC BOOGIE
CREATION STEREO MC'S
CREATURES OF THE NIGHT KISS
CREDO FISH
THE CREEP [A] KEN MACKINTOSH
CREEP [B] RADIOHEAD
CREEP [C] TLC
CREEQUE ALLEY MAMAS & THE PAPAS
CREOLE JAZZ MR ACKER BILK & HIS PARAMOUNT JAZZ
    BAND
CRESCENT MOON LYNDEN DAVID HALL
CRICKETS SING FOR ANAMARIA EMMA
CRIME OF PASSION MIKE OLDFIELD FEATURING
    MAGGIE REILLY
CRIMINALLY INSANE SLAYER
CRIMSON AND CLOVER JOAN JETT & THE
    BLACKHEARTS
CRISPY BACON LAURENT GARNIER
CRITICAL (IF ONLY YOU KNEW) WALL OF SOUND
    FEATURING GERALD LETHAN
CRITICIZE ALEXANDER O'NEAL
CROCKETT'S THEME JAN HAMMER
CROCODILE ROCK ELTON JOHN
CROCODILE SHOES JIMMY NAIL
CROSS MY BROKEN HEART SINITTA
CROSS MY HEART EIGHTH WONDER
CROSS THAT BRIDGE WARD BROTHERS

CROSS THE TRACK (WE BETTER GO BACK) MACEO &
    THE MACKS
CROSSROADS [A] TRACY CHAPMAN
CROSSROADS [B] BLAZIN' SQUAD
CROSSTOWN TRAFFIC JIMI HENDRIX EXPERIENCE
THE CROWD ROY ORBISON
THE CROWN GARY BYRD & THE GB EXPERIENCE
CROWS MODEY LEMON
CRUCIAL NEW EDITION
CRUCIFIED ARMY OF LOVERS
CRUCIFY TORI AMOS
CRUEL PUBLIC IMAGE LTD.
THE CRUEL SEA DAKOTAS
CRUEL SUMMER BANANARAMA
CRUEL SUMMER ACE OF BASE
CRUEL TO BE KIND NICK LOWE
CRUISE INTO CHRISTMAS MEDLEY JANE McDONALD
CRUISIN' D'ANGELO
CRUISING SINITTA
THE CRUNCH RAH BAND
CRUSH [A] ZHANE
CRUSH [B] JENNIFER PAIGE
CRUSH [C] DARREN HAYES
CRUSH [D] PAUL VAN DYK FEATURING SECOND SUN
CRUSH ME HOUSE OF LOVE
CRUSH ON YOU [A] JETS
CRUSH ON YOU [A] AARON CARTER
CRUSH ON YOU [B] LIL' KIM
CRUSH TONIGHT FAT JOE FEATURING GINUWINE
CRUSH WITH EYELINER R.E.M.
CRUSHED BY THE WHEELS OF INDUSTRY HEAVEN 17
CRUSHED LIKE FRUIT INME
CRY [A] GERRY MONROE
CRY [B] GODLEY & CREME
CRY [C] WATERFRONT
CRY [D] SUNDAYS
CRY [E] SYSTEM F
CRY [F] MICHAEL JACKSON
CRY [G] SIMPLE MINDS
CRY [H] FAITH HILL
CRY [I] KYM MARSH
CRY [J] ALEX PARKS
CRY AND BE FREE MARILYN
CRY BABY [A] SPILLER
CRY BABY [B] JEMINI
CRY BOY CRY BLUE ZOO
CRY DIGNITY DUB WAR
CRY FOR HELP [A] RICK ASTLEY
CRY FOR HELP [B] SHED SEVEN
CRY FOR ME ROACHFORD
CRY FOR THE NATIONS MICHAEL SCHENKER GROUP
CRY FOR YOU JODECI
CRY FREEDOM [A] GEORGE FENTON & JONAS
    GWANGWA
CRY FREEDOM [B] MOMBASSA
CRY INDIA UMBOZA
CRY JUST A LITTLE BIT SHAKIN' STEVENS
CRY LIKE A BABY BOX TOPS
CRY LITTLE SISTER (I NEED U NOW) LOST BROTHERS
    FEATURING G TOM MAC
CRY ME A RIVER [A] JULIE LONDON
CRY ME A RIVER [A] MARI WILSON
CRY ME A RIVER [A] DENISE WELCH
CRY ME A RIVER [B] JUSTIN TIMBERLAKE
CRY MY HEART DAVID WHITFIELD
CRY MYSELF TO SLEEP DEL SHANNON
CRY TO BE FOUND DEL AMITRI
CRY TO HEAVEN ELTON JOHN
CRY TO ME PRETTY THINGS
CRY WOLF A-HA
CRYIN' [A] ROY ORBISON

CRYIN' [B] VIXEN
CRYIN' [C] AEROSMITH
CRYIN' IN THE RAIN [A] EVERLY BROTHERS
CRYIN' MY HEART OUT FOR YOU DIANA ROSS
CRYIN' TIME RAY CHARLES
CRYING DON McLEAN
CRYING ROY ORBISON (DUET WITH k d lang)
CRYING AT THE DISCOTEQUE ALCAZAR
THE CRYING GAME DAVE BERRY
THE CRYING GAME BOY GEORGE
CRYING IN THE CHAPEL LEE LAWRENCE WITH RAY
    MARTIN & HIS ORCHESTRA
CRYING IN THE CHAPEL ELVIS PRESLEY
CRYING IN THE RAIN [A] A-HA
CRYING IN THE RAIN [B] CULTURE BEAT
CRYING LAUGHING LOVING LYING LABI SIFFRE
CRYING OVER YOU KEN BOOTHE
THE CRYING SCENE AZTEC CAMERA
CRYPTIK SOULS CREW LEN
CRYSTAL NEW ORDER
CRYSTAL CLEAR GRID
THE CRYSTAL LAKE GRANDADDY
CUBA GIBSON BROTHERS
CUBA EL MARIACHI
CUBAN PETE JIM CARREY
CUBIK 808 STATE
CUDDLY TOY ROACHFORD
CUFF OF MY SHIRT GUY MITCHELL
CULT OF PERSONALITY LIVING COLOUR
CULT OF SNAP SNAP
CULT OF SNAP HI POWER
CUM ON FEEL THE NOIZE SLADE
CUM ON FEEL THE NOIZE QUIET RIOT
CUMBERLAND GAP VIPERS SKIFFLE GROUP
CUMBERLAND GAP LONNIE DONEGAN
THE CUP OF LIFE RICKY MARTIN
CUPBOARD LOVE JOHN LEYTON
CUPID [A] SAM COOKE
CUPID [A] JOHNNY NASH
CUPID [B] JC 001
CUPID – I'VE LOVED YOU FOR A LONG TIME (MEDLEY)
    DETROIT SPINNERS
CURIOSITY JETS
CURIOUS LEVERT SWEAT GILL
CURLY MOVE
THE CURSE OF VOODOO RAY LISA MAY
CURTAIN FALLS BLUE
CUT CHEMIST SUITE OZOMATLI
CUT HERE CURE
CUT ME DOWN LLOYD COLE & THE COMMOTIONS
CUT SOME RUG BLUETONES
CUT THE CAKE AVERAGE WHITE BAND
CUT YOUR HAIR PAVEMENT
A CUTE SWEET LOVE ADDICTION JOHNNY GILL
CUTS ACROSS THE LAND DUKE SPIRIT
CUTS BOTH WAYS GLORIA ESTEFAN
THE CUTTER ECHO & THE BUNNYMEN
CUTTY SARK JOHN BARRY
CYANIDE LURKERS
CYBELE'S REVERIE STEREOLAB
CYCLONE DUB PISTOLS
THE CYPHER: PART 3 FRANKIE CUTLASS
D-A-A-ANCE LAMBRETTAS
D-FUNKTIONAL MEKON FEATURING AFRIKA
    BAMBAATAA
DA ANTIDOTE STANTON WARRIORS
DA DA DA TRIO
DA DOO RON RON CRYSTALS
DA-FORCE BEDLAM
DA FUNK DAFT PUNK
DA GOODNESS REDMAN

DA HYPE JUNIOR JACK FEATURING ROBERT SMITH
DA 'YA THINK I'M SEXY ROD STEWART
DA YA THINK I'M SEXY REVOLTING COCKS
DA YA THINK I'M SEXY? N-TRANCE FEATURING ROD
    STEWART
DA YA THINK I'M SEXY? GIRLS OF FHM
DADDY COOL [A] BONEY M
DADDY COOL [B] DARTS
DADDY DON'T YOU WALK SO FAST DANIEL BOONE
DADDY'S HOME CLIFF RICHARD
DADDY'S LITTLE GIRL NIKKI D
DAGENHAM DAVE MORRISSEY
DAILY TQ
DALICKS DJ FRESH
DALLIANCE WEDDING PRESENT
DAMAGED PLUMMET
THE DAMBUSTERS MARCH THE CENTRAL BAND OF THE
    ROYAL AIR FORCE, CONDUCTOR W/Cdr. A.E. SIMS
    O.B.E.
DAMN GOOD DAVID LEE ROTH
DAMN I WISH I WAS YOUR LOVER SOPHIE B.
    HAWKINS
DAMNED DON'T CRY VISAGE
DAMNED ON 45 CAPTAIN SENSIBLE
DANCANDO LAMBADA KAOMA
DANCE THAT PETROL EMOTION
THE DANCE GARTH BROOKS
DANCE A LITTLE BIT CLOSER CHARO & THE SALSOUL
    ORCHESTRA
DANCE AND SHOUT SHAGGY
DANCE AWAY ROXY MUSIC
DANCE COMMANDER ELECTRIC SIX
DANCE DANCE DESKEE
DANCE DANCE DANCE BEACH BOYS
DANCE DANCE DANCE (YOWSAH YOWSAH YOWSAH)
    CHIC
DANCE (DISCO HEAT) SYLVESTER
DANCE FOR ME [A] SISQO
DANCE FOR ME [B] MARY J. BLIGE FEATURING
    COMMON
DANCE, GET DOWN (FEEL THE GROOVE) AL HUDSON
DANCE HALL DAYS WANG CHUNG
DANCE INTO THE LIGHT PHIL COLLINS
DANCE LADY DANCE CROWN HEIGHTS AFFAIR
DANCE LITTLE LADY DANCE TINA CHARLES
DANCE LITTLE SISTER (PART ONE) TERENCE TRENT
    D'ARBY
DANCE ME UP GARY GLITTER
DANCE NO MORE E-LUSTRIOUS FEATURING DEBORAH
    FRENCH
DANCE OF THE CUCKOOS (THE LAUREL AND HARDY
    THEME) BAND OF THE BLACK WATCH
DANCE OF THE MAD POP WILL EAT ITSELF
DANCE ON! [A] SHADOWS
DANCE ON [A] KATHY KIRBY
DANCE ON [B] MOJO
DANCE OUT OF MY HEAD PIA
DANCE STANCE DEXY'S MIDNIGHT RUNNERS
DANCE SUCKER SET THE TONE
DANCE THE BODY MUSIC OSIBISA
DANCE THE KUNG FU CARL DOUGLAS
DANCE THE NIGHT AWAY MAVERICKS
DANCE TO THE MUSIC SLY & THE FAMILY STONE
DANCE TO THE MUSIC HUSTLERS CONVENTION
    FEATURING DAVE LAUDAT & ONDRERA DUVERNY
DANCE TO THE RHYTHM BULLETPROOF
DANCE TONIGHT LUCY PEARL
DANCE WIT ME RICK JAMES
DANCE WITH ME [A] DRIFTERS
DANCE WITH ME [B] PETER BROWN
DANCE WITH ME [C] CONTROL

DANCE WITH ME [D] TIN TIN OUT FEATURING TONY
    HADLEY
DANCE WITH ME [E] DEBELAH MORGAN
DANCE WITH MY FATHER LUTHER VANDROSS
DANCE WITH THE DEVIL COZY POWELL
DANCE WITH THE GUITAR MAN DUANE EDDY & THE
    REBELETTES
DANCE (WITH U) LEMAR
DANCE WITH YOU CARRIE LUCAS
DANCE WITH YOU (NACHNA TERE NAAL) RISHI RICH
    PROJECT FEATURING JAY SEAN
DANCE YOURSELF DIZZY LIQUID GOLD
DANCEHALL MOOD ASWAD
DANCEHALL QUEEN CHEVELLE FRANKLYN/BEENIE MAN
DANCER [A] GINO SOCCIO
DANCER [B] MICHAEL SCHENKER GROUP
DANCERAMA SIGUE SIGUE SPUTNIK
DANCIN' EASY DANNY WILLIAMS
DANCIN' IN THE KEY OF LIFE STEVE ARRINGTON
DANCIN' IN THE MOONLIGHT (IT'S CAUGHT ME IN THE
    SPOTLIGHT) THIN LIZZY
DANCIN' ON A WIRE SURFACE NOISE
DANCIN' PARTY CHUBBY CHECKER
DANCIN' PARTY SHOWADDYWADDY
DANCIN' THE NIGHT AWAY VOGGUE
DANCIN' TONIGHT STEREOPOL FEATURING NEVADA
DANCING BABY (OOGA-CHAKA) TRUBBLE
DANCING GIRLS NIK KERSHAW
DANCING IN OUTER SPACE ATMOSFEAR
DANCING IN THE CITY MARSHALL HAIN
DANCING IN THE DARK [A] KIM WILDE
DANCING IN THE DARK [B] BRUCE SPRINGSTEEN
DANCING IN THE DARK [C] 4 TUNE 500
DANCING IN THE DARK EP BIG DADDY
DANCING IN THE MOONLIGHT TOPLOADER
DANCING IN THE SHEETS SHALAMAR
DANCING IN THE STREET [A] MARTHA REEVES & THE
    VANDELLAS
DANCING IN THE STREET [A] DAVID BOWIE & MICK
    JAGGER
DANCING IN THE STREET [B] MATT BIANCO
(DANCING) ON A SATURDAY NIGHT BARRY BLUE
DANCING ON THE CEILING LIONEL RICHIE
DANCING ON THE FLOOR (HOOKED ON LOVE) THIRD
    WORLD
DANCING ON THE JAGGED EDGE SISTER SLEDGE
DANCING QUEEN ABBA
DANCING QUEEN ABBACADABRA
DANCING THE NIGHT AWAY MOTORS
DANCING TIGHT GALAXY FEATURING PHIL FEARON
DANCING WITH MYSELF GEN X
DANCING WITH MYSELF (EP) GENERATION X
DANCING WITH TEARS IN MY EYES ULTRAVOX
DANCING WITH THE CAPTAIN PAUL NICHOLAS
DANDELION ROLLING STONES
DANGER [A] AC/DC
DANGER [B] BLAHZAY BLAHZAY
DANGER (BEEN SO LONG) MYSTIKAL FEATURING NIVEA
DANGER GAMES PINKEES
DANGER HIGH VOLTAGE ELECTRIC SIX
THE DANGER OF A STRANGER STELLA PARTON
DANGER ZONE KENNY LOGGINS
DANGEROUS [A] PENNYE FORD
DANGEROUS [B] ROXETTE
DANGEROUS [C] BUSTA RHYMES
DANGEROUS MINDS EP AARON HALL:DE VANTE:SISTA
    FEATURING CRAIG MACK
DANGEROUS SEX TACK HEAD
DANIEL ELTON JOHN
DARE ME POINTER SISTERS
DARE TO DREAM VIOLA WILLS

DELICATE TERENCE TRENT D'ARBY FEATURING DES'REE
DELICIOUS [A] SLEEPER
DELICIOUS [B] SHAMPOO
DELICIOUS [C] CATHERINE WHEEL
DELICIOUS [D] DENI HINES FEATURING DON-E
DELICIOUS [E] KULAY
DELICIOUS [F] PURE SUGAR
DELILAH TOM JONES
DELILAH SENSATIONAL ALEX HARVEY BAND
DELILAH JONES McGUIRE SISTERS
DELIVER ME SISTER BLISS FEATURING JOHN MARTYN
DELIVERANCE [A] MISSION
DELIVERANCE [B] BUBBA SPARXXX
DELIVERING THE GOODS SKID ROW
DELLA AND THE DEALER HOYT AXTON
DELTA LADY JOE COCKER
DELTA SUN BOTTLENECK STOMP MERCURY REV
DEM GIRLZ (I DON'T KNOW WHY) OXIDE & NEUTRINO
    FEATURING KOWDEAN
DEMOCRACY KILLING JOKE
DEMOLITION MAN STING
DEMONS [A] SUPER FURRY ANIMALS
DEMONS [B] FATBOY SLIM FEATURING MACY GRAY
DENIS BLONDIE
DENISE FOUNTAINS OF WAYNE
DER KOMMISSAR AFTER THE FIRE
DER SCHIEBER TIMO MAAS
DESAFINADO STAN GETZ & CHARLIE BYRD
DESAFINADO ELLA FITZGERALD
DESERT DROUGHT CAST
DESERT SONG STING FEATURING CHEB MAMI
DESIDERATA LES CRANE
A DESIGN FOR LIFE MANIC STREET PREACHERS
DESIRE [A] U2
DESIRE [B] NU COLOURS
DESIRE [C] BBE
DESIRE [D] DJ ERIC
DESIRE [E] ULTRA NATE
DESIRE LINES LUSH
DESIRE ME DOLL
DESIRE NEIL DIAMOND
DESPERATE BUT NOT SERIOUS ADAM ANT
DESPERATE DAN LIEUTENANT PIGEON
THE DESPERATE HOURS MARC ALMOND
DESTINATION DT8 FEATURING ROXANNE WILDE
DESTINATION ESCHATON SHAMEN
DESTINATION SUNSHINE BALEARIC BILL
DESTINATION VENUS REZILLOS
DESTINATION ZULULAND KING KURT
DESTINY [A] ANNE MURRAY
DESTINY [B] CANDI STATON
DESTINY [C] JACKSONS
DESTINY [D] BABY D
DESTINY [E] KENNY THOMAS
DESTINY [F] DEM 2
DESTINY [G] ZERO 7 FEATURING SIA & SOPHIE
DESTINY [H] N-TRANCE
DESTINY CALLING JAMES
DETROIT WHITEOUT
DETROIT CITY TOM JONES
DEUS SUGARCUBES
DEUTSCHER GIRLS ADAM & THE ANTS
DEVIL 666
DEVIL GATE DRIVE SUZI QUATRO
DEVIL IN YOUR SHOES (WALKING ALL OVER) SHED
    SEVEN
DEVIL INSIDE INXS
DEVIL OR ANGEL BILLY FURY
THE DEVIL WENT DOWN TO GEORGIA CHARLIE DANIELS
    BAND
DEVIL WOMAN [A] MARTY ROBBINS

DEVIL WOMAN [B] CLIFF RICHARD
THE DEVIL YOU KNOW JESUS JONES
THE DEVIL'S ANSWER ATOMIC ROOSTER
DEVIL'S BALL DOUBLE
DEVIL'S GUN C.J. & CO
DEVILS HAIRCUT BECK
DEVIL'S NIGHTMARE OXIDE & NEUTRINO
DEVIL'S THRILL VANESSA-MAE
DEVIL'S TOY ALMIGHTY
DEVOTED TO YOU CACIQUE
DEVOTION [A] TEN CITY
DEVOTION [B] KICKING BACK WITH TAXMAN
DEVOTION [C] DAVE HOLMES
DIABLA FUNK D'VOID
DIABLO GRID
DIAL MY HEART BOYS
DIAMANTE ZUCCHERO WITH RANDY CRAWFORD
DIAMOND BACK MEKKA
DIAMOND DEW GORKY'S ZYGOTIC MYNCI
DIAMOND DOGS DAVID BOWIE
DIAMOND GIRL PETE WYLIE
DIAMOND LIFE LOUIE VEGA & JAY 'SINISTER SEALEE
    STARRING JULIE McKNIGHT
DIAMOND LIGHTS GLENN & CHRIS
DIAMOND SMILES BOOMTOWN RATS
DIAMONDS [A] JET HARRIS & TONY MEEHAN
DIAMONDS [B] CHRIS REA
DIAMONDS [C] HERB ALPERT
DIAMONDS AND GUNS TRANSPLANTS
DIAMONDS AND PEARLS PRINCE & THE NEW POWER
    GENERATION
DIAMONDS ARE FOREVER SHIRLEY BASSEY
DIAMONDS ARE FOREVER DAVID McALMONT & DAVID
    ARNOLD
DIANA PAUL ANKA
DIANE [A] BACHELORS
DIANE [B] THERAPY?
DIARY OF A WIMP SPACE
THE DIARY OF HORACE WIMP ELECTRIC LIGHT
    ORCHESTRA
DICK-A-DUM-DUM (KING'S ROAD) DES O'CONNOR
DID I DREAM (SONG TO THE SIREN) LOST WITNESS
DID IT AGAIN KYLIE MINOGUE
DID MY TIME KORN
DID YOU EVER NANCY SINATRA & LEE HAZLEWOOD
DID YOU EVER REALLY LOVE ME NICKI FRENCH
DID YOU EVER THINK R KELLY
DID YOU HAVE TO LOVE ME LIKE YOU DID COCONUTS
DIDDY P DIDDY FEATURING THE NEPTUNES
DIDN'T I BLOW YOUR MIND NEW KIDS ON THE BLOCK
DIDN'T I (BLOW YOUR MIND THIS TIME) DELFONICS
DIDN'T I TELL YOU TRUE THOMAS JULES-STOCK
DIDN'T WE ALMOST HAVE IT ALL WHITNEY HOUSTON
DIE ANOTHER DAY MADONNA
DIE LAUGHING THERAPY?
DIE YOUNG BLACK SABBATH
DIFFERENCES GUYVER
DIFFERENT AIR LIVING IN A BOX
A DIFFERENT BEAT BOYZONE
A DIFFERENT CORNER GEORGE MICHAEL
DIFFERENT STORY BOWA FEATURING MALA
DIFFERENT STROKES ISOTONIK
DIFFERENT TIME DIFFERENT PLACE JULIA FORDHAM
DIG FOR FIRE PIXIES
DIGERIDOO APHEX TWIN
DIGGI LOO-DIGGI LEY HERREYS
DIGGIN' MY POTATOES HEINZ & THE WILD BOYS
DIGGIN' ON YOU TLC
DIGGING THE DIRT PETER GABRIEL
DIGGING THE GRAVE FAITH NO MORE
DIGGING YOUR SCENE BLOW MONKEYS

DIGITAL GOLDIE FEATURING KRS ONE
DIGITAL LOVE DAFT PUNK
DIGNITY [A] DEACON BLUE
DIGNITY [B] BOB DYLAN
DIL CHEEZ (MY HEART...) BALLY SAGOO
DILEMMA NELLY FEATURING KELLY ROWLAND
DIM ALL THE LIGHTS DONNA SUMMER
DIME AND A DOLLAR GUY MITCHELL
DIMENSION SALT TANK
DIMPLES JOHN LEE HOOKER
DIN DA DA KEVIN AVIANCE
DINAH BLACKNUSS
DING-A-DONG TEACH-IN
DING DONG GEORGE HARRISON
DING DONG SONG GUNTHER & THE SUNSHINE GIRLS
DINNER WITH DELORES ARTIST FORMERLY KNOWN AS
    PRINCE (AFKAP)
DINNER WITH GERSHWIN DONNA SUMMER
DINOSAUR ADVENTURE 3D UNDERWORLD
DIP IT LOW CHRISTINA MILIAN
DIPPETY DAY FATHER ABRAHAM & THE SMURFS
DIRECT-ME REESE PROJECT
DIRGE DEATH IN VEGAS
DIRRTY CHRISTINA AGUILERA FEATURING REDMAN
DIRT DEATH IN VEGAS
DIRT OFF YOUR SHOULDER JAY-Z
DIRTY BEATS RONI SIZE REPRAZENT
DIRTY CASH ADVENTURES OF STEVIE V
DIRTY DAWG NKOTB
DIRTY DEEDS JOAN JETT
DIRTY DEEDS DONE DIRT CHEAP (LIVE) AC/DC
DIRTY DIANA MICHAEL JACKSON
DIRTY HARRY'S REVENGE ADAM F FEATURING BEENIE
    MAN
DIRTY LAUNDRY DON HENLEY
DIRTY LOOKS DIANA ROSS
DIRTY LOVE THUNDER
DIRTY MIND SHAKESPEARS SISTER
DIRTY MONEY DEE FREDRIX
DIRTY MOTHA QWILO & FELIX DA HOUSECAT
DIRTY OLD TOWN POGUES
DIRTY OLD TOWN BHOYS OF PARADISE
DIRTY STICKY FLOORS DAVE GAHAN
DIRTY WATER MADE IN LONDON
DIS-INFECTED EP THE THE
DISAPPEAR INXS
DISAPPEARING ACT SHALAMAR
DISAPPOINTED [A] PUBLIC IMAGE LTD.
DISAPPOINTED [B] ELECTRONIC
THE DISAPPOINTED [C] XTC
DISARM SMASHING PUMPKINS
DISCIPLINE OF LOVE ROBERT PALMER
D.I.S.C.O. OTTAWAN
D.I.S.C.O. N-TRANCE
DISCO 2000 PULP
DISCO BABES FROM OUTER SPACE BABE INSTINCT
DISCO BEATLEMANIA DBM
DISCO CONNECTION ISAAC HAYES MOVEMENT
DISCO COP BLUE ADONIS FEATURING LIL' MISS MAX
DISCO DOWN [A] SHED SEVEN
DISCO DOWN [B] HOUSE OF GLASS
DISCO DUCK (PART ONE) RICK DEES & HIS CAST OF
    IDIOTS
DISCO INFERNO TRAMMPS
DISCO INFERNO TINA TURNER
DISCO' LA PASSIONE CHRIS REA & SHIRLEY BASSEY
DISCO LADY JOHNNIE TAYLOR
DISCO MACHINE GUN LO FIDELITY ALLSTARS
DISCO MUSIC (I LIKE IT) J.A.L.N. BAND
DISCO NIGHTS (ROCK FREAK) GQ
DISCO QUEEN HOT CHOCOLATE

DISCO SCIENCE MIRWAIS
DISCO STOMP HAMILTON BOHANNON
DISCOBUG '97 FREAKYMAN
DISCOHOPPING KLUBHEADS
DISCOLAND FLIP & FILL FEATURING KAREN PARRY
DISCONNECTED ROLLINS BAND
DISCO'S REVENGE GUSTO
DISCOTHEQUE U2
DISCRETION GROVE STEPHEN MALKMUS
DISEASE MATCHBOX 20
DISENCHANTED COMMUNARDS
DISILLUSION BADLY DRAWN BOY
DISPOSABLE TEENS MARILYN MANSON
DISREMEMBRANCE DANNII
DISSIDENT PEARL JAM
THE DISTANCE CAKE
DISTANT DRUMS JIM REEVES
DISTANT STAR ANTHONY HOPKINS
DISTANT SUN CROWDED HOUSE
DISTORTION WILT
DISTRACTIONS ZERO 7
DIVA DANA INTERNATIONAL
DIVE IN CATCH
DIVE TO PARADISE EUROGROOVE
DIVE! DIVE! DIVE! BRUCE DICKINSON
DIVEBOMB NUMBER ONE CUP
DIVINE EMOTIONS NARADA
DIVINE HAMMER BREEDERS
DIVINE THING SOUP DRAGONS
DIVING 4 STRINGS
DIVING FACES LIQUID CHILD
D.I.V.O.R.C.E. TAMMY WYNETTE
D.I.V.O.R.C.E. BILLY CONNOLLY
DIXIE-NARCO EP PRIMAL SCREAM
DIZZY TOMMY ROE
DIZZY VIC REEVES & THE WONDER STUFF
D.J. [A] DAVID BOWIE
DJ [B] RESONANCE FEATURING THE BURRELLS
DJ [C] H & CLAIRE
DJ [D] JAMELIA
DJ CULTURE PET SHOP BOYS
DJ DJ TRANSPLANTS
DJ NATION NUKLEUZ DJ'S
DJ NATION – HARDER EDITION NUKLEUZ DJs
DJ SPINNIN' PUNK CHIC
DJS FANS AND FREAKS BLANK & JONES
DJS TAKE CONTROL SL2
DK 50-80 OTWAY & BARRETT
DO AND DON'T FOR LOVE KIOKI
DO ANYTHING NATURAL SELECTION
DO ANYTHING YOU WANT TO THIN LIZZY
DO ANYTHING YOU WANT TO DO RODS
DO FOR LOVE 2PAC FEATURING ERIC WILLIAMS
DO FRIES GO WITH THAT SHAKE GEORGE CLINTON
DO I GIFTED
DO I DO STEVIE WONDER
DO I HAVE TO SAY THE WORDS BRYAN ADAMS
DO I LOVE YOU RONETTES
DO I QUALIFY? LYNDEN DAVID HALL
DO IT TONY DI BART
DO IT AGAIN [A] BEACH BOYS
DO IT AGAIN [B] STEELY DAN
DO IT AGAIN – BILLIE JEAN (MEDLEY) CLUBHOUSE
DO IT ALL OVER AGAIN SPIRITUALIZED
DO IT ANY WAY YOU WANNA PEOPLE'S CHOICE
DO IT DO IT AGAIN RAFFAELLA CARRA
DO IT FOR LOVE [A] DANNI'ELLE GAHA
DO IT FOR LOVE [B] SUBTERRANIA FEATURING ANN
    CONSUELO
DO IT FOR LOVE [C] 4MANDU
DO IT NOW BRAINBASHERS

DO IT PROPERLY ('NO WAY BACK')/NO WAY BACK
    ADONIS FEATURING 2 PUERTO RICANS, A BLACK
    MAN & A DOMINICAN
DO IT TO ME LIONEL RICHIE
DO IT TO ME AGAIN SOULSEARCHER
DO IT TO THE CROWD TWIN HYPE
DO IT TO THE MUSIC RAW SILK
DO IT WITH MADONNA ANDROIDS
DO ME BELL BIV DEVOE
DO ME RIGHT INNER CITY
DO ME WRONG MEL BLATT
DO MY THING BUSTA RHYMES
DO NO WRONG THIRTEEN SENSES
DO NOT DISTURB BANANARAMA
DO NOT PASS ME BY HAMMER
DO NOTHING SPECIALS
DO OR DIE SUPER FURRY ANIMALS
DO RE ME SO FAR SO GOOD CARTER – THE
    UNSTOPPABLE SEX MACHINE
DO SOMETHING MACY GRAY
DO THAT THANG MASAI
DO THAT TO ME LISA MARIE EXPERIENCE
DO THAT TO ME ONE MORE TIME CAPTAIN & TENNILLE
DO THE BARTMAN SIMPSONS
DO THE BIRD DEE DEE SHARP
DO THE BIRD VERNONS GIRLS
DO THE CAN CAN SKANDI GIRLS
DO THE CLAM ELVIS PRESLEY
DO THE CONGA BLACK LACE
DO THE FUNKY CHICKEN RUFUS THOMAS
(DO) THE HUCKLEBUCK COAST TO COAST
DO THE LOLLIPOP TWEENIES
DO THE RIGHT THING [A] REDHEAD KINGPIN & THE FBI
DO THE RIGHT THING [B] IAN WRIGHT
(DO THE) SPANISH HUSTLE FATBACK BAND
DO THEY KNOW IT'S CHRISTMAS? BAND AID
DO THEY KNOW IT'S CHRISTMAS? BAND AID II
DO THEY KNOW IT'S CHRISTMAS? BAND AID 20
DO THIS MY WAY KID 'N' PLAY
DO U FEEL 4 ME EDEN
DO U KNOW WHERE YOU'RE COMING FROM M-BEAT
    FEATURING JAMIROQUAI
DO U STILL? EAST 17
DO U WANNA FUNK SPACE 2000
DO WAH DIDDY DJ OTZI
DO WAH DIDDY DIDDY MANFRED MANN
DO WAH DIDDY DIDDY BLUE MELONS
DO WATCHA DO HYPER GO GO & ADEVA
DO WE ROCK POINT BREAK
DO WHAT WE WOULD ACZESS
DO WHAT YOU DO [A] JERMAINE JACKSON
DO WHAT YOU DO [B] ANNABELLA LWIN
DO WHAT YOU DO (EARWORM SONG) CLINT BOON
    EXPERIENCE
DO WHAT YOU DO WELL NED MILLER
DO WHAT YOU FEEL [A] JOEY NEGRO
DO WHAT YOU FEEL [B] JOHNNA
DO WHAT YOU GOTTA DO NINA SIMONE
DO WHAT YOU GOTTA DO FOUR TOPS
DO WHAT YOU WANNA DO T-CONNECTION
DO WHAT'S GOOD FOR ME 2 UNLIMITED
DO YA INNER CITY
DO YA DO YA (WANNA PLEASE ME) SAMANTHA FOX
DO YA WANNA GET FUNKY WITH ME PETER BROWN
DO YOU BELIEVE IN LOVE [A] HUEY LEWIS & THE NEWS
DO YOU BELIEVE IN LOVE [B] UNATION
DO YOU BELIEVE IN LOVE [C] ULTRA-SONIC
DO YOU BELIEVE IN MIRACLES SLADE
DO YOU BELIEVE IN SHAME DURAN DURAN
DO YOU BELIEVE IN THE WESTWORLD THEATRE OF HATE
DO YOU BELIEVE IN THE WONDER JEANIE TRACY

DO YOU BELIEVE IN US JON SECADA
DO YOU DREAM IN COLOUR? BILL NELSON
DO YOU FEEL LIKE I FEEL BELINDA CARLISLE
DO YOU FEEL LIKE WE DO PETER FRAMPTON
DO YOU FEEL ME? (...FREAK YOU) MEN OF VIZION
DO YOU FEEL MY LOVE EDDY GRANT
DO YOU KNOW [A] SECRET AFFAIR
DO YOU KNOW [B] MICHELLE GAYLE
DO YOU KNOW (I GO CRAZY) ANGEL CITY
DO YOU KNOW THE WAY TO SAN JOSE DIONNE
    WARWICK
DO YOU KNOW (WHAT IT TAKES) ROBYN
DO YOU LIKE IT KINGDOM COME
DO YOU LOVE ME [A] BRIAN POOLE & THE TREMELOES
DO YOU LOVE ME [A] DAVE CLARK FIVE
DO YOU LOVE ME [A] DEEP FEELING
DO YOU LOVE ME [A] DUKE BAYSEE
DO YOU LOVE ME [A] MADEMOISELLE
DO YOU LOVE ME [B] NICK CAVE & THE BAD SEEDS
DO YOU LOVE ME BOY? KERRI-ANN
DO YOU LOVE ME LIKE YOU SAY TERENCE TRENT D'ARBY
DO YOU LOVE WHAT YOU FEEL INNER CITY
DO YOU MIND ANTHONY NEWLEY
DO YOU REALISE FLAMING LIPS
DO YOU REALLY LIKE IT DJ PIED PIPER & THE MASTERS
    OF CEREMONIES
(DO YOU REALLY LOVE ME) TELL ME LOVE MICHAEL
    WYCOFF
DO YOU REALLY LOVE ME TOO BILLY FURY
DO YOU REALLY WANT ME [A] JON SECADA
DO YOU REALLY WANT ME [B] ROBYN
DO YOU REALLY (WANT MY LOVE) JUNIOR
DO YOU REALLY WANT TO HURT ME CULTURE CLUB
DO YOU REMEMBER SCAFFOLD
DO YOU REMEMBER HOUSE BLAZE FEATURING PALMER
    BROWN
DO YOU REMEMBER (LIVE) PHIL COLLINS
DO YOU REMEMBER ROCK 'N' ROLL RADIO RAMONES
DO YOU REMEMBER THE FIRST TIME PULP
DO YOU SEE WARREN G
DO YOU SEE THE LIGHT SNAP VS PLAYTHING
DO YOU SEE THE LIGHT (LOOKING FOR) SNAP
    FEATURING NIKI HARRIS
DO YOU SLEEP? LISA LOEB & NINE STORIES
DO YOU THINK ABOUT US TOTAL
DO YOU THINK YOU'RE SPECIAL? NIO
DO YOU UNDERSTAND ALMIGHTY
DO YOU WANNA DANCE [A] CLIFF RICHARD & THE
    SHADOWS
DO YOU WANNA DANCE [B] BARRY BLUE
DO YOU WANNA FUNK SYLVESTER WITH PATRICK
    COWLEY
DO YOU WANNA GET FUNKY C & C MUSIC FACTORY
DO YOU WANNA GO OUR WAY??? PUBLIC ENEMY
DO YOU WANNA HOLD ME? BOW WOW WOW
DO YOU WANNA PARTY DJ SCOTT FEATURING LORNA B
DO YOU WANNA TOUCH ME (OH YEAH!) GARY GLITTER
DO YOU WANT IT RIGHT NOW DEGREES OF MOTION
    FEATURING BITI
DO YOU WANT ME [A] SALT-N-PEPA
DO YOU WANT ME [B] Q-TEX
DO YOU WANT ME? [C] LEILANI
DO YOU WANT ME TO FOUR PENNIES
DO YOU WANT TO KNOW A SECRET? BILLY J. KRAMER &
    THE DAKOTAS
DO YOUR DANCE ROSE ROYCE
THE DOCTOR DOOBIE BROTHERS
DR BEAT MIAMI SOUND MACHINE
DOCTOR DOCTOR [A] UFO
DOCTOR DOCTOR [B] THOMPSON TWINS
DR FEELGOOD MOTLEY CRUE

DR FINLAY ANDY STEWART
DR GREENTHUMB CYPRESS HILL
DR JACKYLL AND MISTER FUNK JACKIE McLEAN
DOCTOR JEEP SISTERS OF MERCY
DOCTOR JONES AQUA
DR LOVE TINA CHARLES
DR MABUSE PROPAGANDA
DOCTOR MY EYES JACKSON 5
DR HECKYLL AND MR. JIVE MEN AT WORK
DR KISS KISS 5000 VOLTS
DR STEIN HELLOWEEN
DR WHO MANKIND
DOCTORIN' THE HOUSE COLDCUT FEATURING YAZZ &
    THE PLASTIC POPULATION
DOCTORIN' THE TARDIS TIMELORDS
DOCTOR'S ORDERS SUNNY
DOES HE LOVE YOU REBA McENTIRE
DOES IT FEEL GOOD B.T. EXPRESS
DOES IT FEEL GOOD TO YOU DJ CARL COX
DOES SHE HAVE A FRIEND GENE CHANDLER
DOES THAT RING A BELL DYNASTY
DOES THIS HURT BOO RADLEYS
DOES YOUR CHEWING GUM LOSE IT'S FLAVOUR LONNIE
    DONEGAN
DOES YOUR HEART GO BOOM HELEN LOVE
DOES YOUR MOTHER KNOW ABBA
DOESN'T ANYBODY KNOW MY NAME? VINCE HILL
DOESN'T REALLY MATTER JANET JACKSON
DOG DADA
DOG EAT DOG ADAM & THE ANTS
DOG ON WHEELS BELLE & SEBASTIAN
DOG TRAIN LEVELLERS
DOGGY DOGG WORLD SNOOP DOGGY DOGG
DOGMAN GO WOOF UNDERWORLD
DOGMONAUT 2000 (IS THERE ANYONE OUT THERE)
    FRIJID VINEGAR
DOGS WHO
DOGS OF LUST THE THE
DOGS OF WAR EXPLOITED
DOGS WITH NO TAILS PALE
DOGZ N SLEDGEZ MILLION DAN
DOIN' IT [A] LL COOL J
DOIN' IT [B] LIBERTY
DOIN' IT IN A HAUNTED HOUSE YVONNE GAGE
DOIN' OUR OWN DANG JUNGLE BROTHERS
DOIN' OUR THING PHOEBE ONE
DOIN' THE DO BETTY BOO
DOING ALRIGHT WITH THE BOYS GARY GLITTER
DOLCE VITA RYAN PARIS
DOLL HOUSE KING BROTHERS
DOLL PARTS HOLE
DOLLAR BILL SCREAMING TREES
DOLLAR IN THE TEETH UPSETTERS
DOLLARS C.J. LEWIS
DOLLARS IN THE HEAVENS GENEVA
DOLLY MY LOVE MOMENTS
DOLPHIN SHED SEVEN
THE DOLPHINS CRY LIVE
DOLPHINS MAKE ME CRY MARTYN JOSEPH
DOLPHINS WERE MONKEYS IAN BROWN
DOMINATION WAY OUT WEST
DOMINATOR HUMAN RESOURCE
DOMINION SISTERS OF MERCY
DOMINIQUE SINGING NUN
DOMINO DANCING PET SHOP BOYS
DOMINOES ROBBIE NEVIL
DOMINOID MOLOKO
THE DON 187 LOCKDOWN
DON GARGON COMIN' PROJECT 1
DON JUAN DAVE DEE, DOZY, BEAKY, MICK & TICH
DON QUIXOTE NIK KERSHAW

DONALD WHERE'S YOUR TROOSERS ANDY STEWART
DONKEY CART FRANK CHACKSFIELD
DONNA [A] RITCHIE VALENS
DONNA [A] MARTY WILDE
DONNA [B] 10 C.C.
DON'T ELVIS PRESLEY
DON'T ANSWER ME [A] CILLA BLACK
DON'T ANSWER ME [B] ALAN PARSONS PROJECT
DON'T ARGUE CABARET VOLTAIRE
DON'T ASK ME PUBLIC IMAGE LTD.
DON'T ASK ME WHY EURYTHMICS
DON'T BE A DUMMY JOHN DU CANN
DON'T BE A FOOL LOOSE ENDS
DON'T BE A STRANGER DINA CARROLL
DON'T BE AFRAID AARON HALL
DON'T BE AFRAID MOONMAN
DON'T BE CRUEL [A] BILL BLACK'S COMBO
DON'T BE CRUEL [A] BILLY SWAN
DON'T BE CRUEL [A] ELVIS PRESLEY
DON'T BE CRUEL [B] BOBBY BROWN
DON'T BE STUPID (YOU KNOW I LOVE YOU) SHANIA
    TWAIN
DON'T BELIEVE A WORD THIN LIZZY
DON'T BELIEVE THE HYPE PUBLIC ENEMY
DON'T BELIEVE THE HYPE MISTA E
DON'T BET MONEY HONEY LINDA SCOTT
DON'T BLAME IT ON LOVE SHAKATAK
DON'T BLAME IT ON THAT GIRL MATT BIANCO
DON'T BLAME ME EVERLY BROTHERS
DON'T BLAME ME FRANK IFIELD
DON'T BREAK MY HEART UB40
DON'T BREAK MY HEART AGAIN WHITESNAKE
DON'T BREAK THE HEART THAT LOVES YOU CONNIE
    FRANCIS
DON'T BRING HARRY (EP) STRANGLERS
DON'T BRING LULU DOROTHY PROVINE
DON'T BRING ME DOWN [A] PRETTY THINGS
DON'T BRING ME DOWN [B] ANIMALS
DON'T BRING ME DOWN [C] ELECTRIC LIGHT
    ORCHESTRA
DON'T BRING ME DOWN [D] SPIRITS
DON'T BRING ME YOUR HEARTACHES PAUL & BARRY
    RYAN
DON'T CALL ME BABY [A] VOICE OF THE BEEHIVE
DON'T CALL ME BABY [B] MADISON AVENUE
DON'T CARE [A] KLARK KENT
DON'T CARE [B] ANGELS REVERSE
DON'T COME AROUND HERE NO MORE TOM PETTY &
    THE HEARTBREAKERS
DON'T COME CLOSE RAMONES
DON'T COME HOME TOO SOON DEL AMITRI
DON'T COME TO STAY HOT HOUSE
DON'T CRY [A] ASIA
DON'T CRY [B] BOY GEORGE
DON'T CRY [C] GUNS N' ROSES
DON'T CRY [D] SEAL
DON'T CRY DADDY ELVIS PRESLEY
DON'T CRY FOR ME ARGENTINA JULIE COVINGTON
DON'T CRY FOR ME ARGENTINA SHADOWS
DON'T CRY FOR ME ARGENTINA MADONNA
DON'T CRY FOR ME ARGENTINA MIKE FLOWERS POPS
DON'T CRY FOR ME ARGENTINA SINEAD O'CONNOR
DON'T CRY OUT LOUD ELKIE BROOKS
DON'T DIE JUST YET DAVID HOLMES
DON'T DO IT BABY MAC & KATIE KISSOON
DON'T DO THAT [A] GEORDIE
DON'T DO THAT [B] YOUNG & MOODY BAND
DON'T DON'T TELL ME NO SOPHIE B. HAWKINS
DON'T DREAM DOVE
DON'T DREAM IT'S OVER CROWDED HOUSE
DON'T DREAM IT'S OVER PAUL YOUNG

DON'T DRIVE DRUNK STEVIE WONDER
DON'T DRIVE MY CAR STATUS QUO
DON'T DROP BOMBS LIZA MINNELLI
DON'T EVER CHANGE CRICKETS
DON'T EVER THINK (TOO MUCH) ZUTONS
DON'T FALL IN LOVE (I SAID) TOYAH
DON'T FALTER MINT ROYALE FEATURING LAUREN
    LAVERNE
(DON'T FEAR) THE REAPER BLUE OYSTER CULT
(DON'T FEAR) THE REAPER APOLLO 440
DON'T FIGHT IT WILSON PICKETT
DON'T FIGHT IT FEEL IT PRIMAL SCREAM FEATURING
    DENISE JOHNSON
DON'T FORBID ME PAT BOONE
DON'T FORGET ME (WHEN I'M GONE) GLASS TIGER
DON'T FORGET TO CATCH ME CLIFF RICHARD
DON'T FORGET TO DANCE KINKS
DON'T FORGET TO REMEMBER BEE GEES
DON'T GET ME WRONG PRETENDERS
DON'T GIVE IT UP SONIC SURFERS
DON'T GIVE ME UP HAROLD MELVIN & THE BLUENOTES
DON'T GIVE ME YOUR LIFE ALEX PARTY
DON'T GIVE UP [A] PETER GABRIEL & KATE BUSH
DON'T GIVE UP [B] MICHELLE WEEKS
DON'T GIVE UP [C] CHICANE FEATURING BRYAN
    ADAMS
DON'T GIVE UP ON US BABY DAVID SOUL
DON'T GO [A] JUDAS PRIEST
DON'T GO [B] YAZOO
DON'T GO [B] LIZZY MACK
DON'T GO [C] HOTHOUSE FLOWERS
DON'T GO [D] AWESOME 3 FEATURING JULIE
    McDERMOTT
DON'T GO [D] THIRD DIMENSION FEATURING JULIE
    McDERMOTT
DON'T GO BREAKING MY HEART ELTON JOHN & KIKI
    DEE
DON'T GO BREAKING MY HEART ELTON JOHN WITH
    RuPAUL
DON'T GO MESSIN' WITH MY HEART MANTRONIX
DON'T HANG UP ORLONS
DON'T HOLD BACK CHANSON
DON'T HURT YOURSELF MARILLION
DON'T IT MAKE MY BROWN EYES BLUE CRYSTAL GAYLE
DON'T IT MAKE YOU FEEL GOOD STEFAN DENNIS
DON'T JUMP OFF THE ROOF DAD TOMMY COOPER
DON'T KILL IT CAROL MANFRED MANN'S EARTH BAND
DON'T KILL THE WHALE YES
DON'T KNOCK IT (UNTIL YOU TRY IT) BOBBY NUNN
DON'T KNOCK THE ROCK BILL HALEY & HIS COMETS
DON'T KNOW MUCH LINDA RONSTADT & AARON
    NEVILLE
DON'T KNOW WHAT TO TELL YA AALIYAH
DON'T KNOW WHAT YOU GOT CINDERELLA
DON'T KNOW WHY NORAH JONES
DON'T LAUGH WINX
DON'T LAUGH AT ME NORMAN WISDOM
DON'T LEAVE FAITHLESS
DON'T LEAVE HOME DIDO
DON'T LEAVE ME [A] BLACKstreet
DON'T LEAVE ME [B] MALANDRA BURROWS
DON'T LEAVE ME BEHIND EVERYTHING BUT THE GIRL
DON'T LEAVE ME THIS WAY HAROLD MELVIN & THE
    BLUENOTES
DON'T LEAVE ME THIS WAY THELMA HOUSTON
DON'T LEAVE ME THIS WAY COMMUNARDS WITH
    SARAH-JANE MORRIS
DON'T LET 'EM GRIND YOU DOWN EXPLOITED & ANTI-
    PASTI
DON'T LET GO [A] MANHATTAN TRANSFER
DON'T LET GO [B] DAVID SNEDDON

DON'T LET GO (LOVE) EN VOGUE
DON'T LET GO THE COAT WHO
DON'T LET HIM STEAL YOUR HEART AWAY PHIL COLLINS
DON'T LET HIM TOUCH YOU ANGELETTES
DON'T LET IT DIE HURRICANE SMITH
DON'T LET IT END STYX
DON'T LET IT FADE AWAY DARTS
DON'T LET IT GET YOU DOWN ECHO & THE BUNNYMEN
DON'T LET IT GO TO YOUR HEAD BRAND NEW HEAVIES
    FEATURING N'DEA DAVENPORT
DON'T LET IT PASS YOU BY UB40
DON'T LET IT SHOW ON YOUR FACE ADEVA
DON'T LET LOVE GET YOU DOWN ARCHIE BELL & THE
    DRELLS
DON'T LET ME BE MISUNDERSTOOD ANIMALS
DON'T LET ME BE MISUNDERSTOOD COSTELLO SHOW
    FEATURING THE CONFEDERATES
DON'T LET ME BE MISUNDERSTOOD SANTA
    ESMERALDA & LEROY GOMEZ
DON'T LET ME BE MISUNDERSTOOD JOE COCKER
DON'T LET ME BE THE LAST TO KNOW BRITNEY SPEARS
DON'T LET ME DOWN [A] FARM
DON'T LET ME DOWN [B] WILL YOUNG
DON'T LET ME DOWN GENTLY WONDER STUFF
DON'T LET ME GET ME P!NK
DON'T LET NOBODY HOLD YOU DOWN LJ REYNOLDS
DON'T LET THE FEELING GO NIGHTCRAWLERS
DON'T LET THE RAIN COME DOWN RONNIE HILTON
DON'T LET THE STARS GET IN YOUR EYES PERRY COMO
    WITH THE RAMBLERS
DON'T LET THE SUN CATCH YOU CRYING GERRY & THE
    PACEMAKERS
DON'T LET THE SUN GO DOWN ON ME ELTON JOHN
DON'T LET THE SUN GO DOWN ON ME OLETA ADAMS
DON'T LET THE SUN GO DOWN ON ME GEORGE
    MICHAEL & ELTON JOHN
DON'T LET THIS MOMENT END GLORIA ESTEFAN
DON'T LIE SINCLAIR
DON'T LOOK ANY FURTHER DENNIS EDWARDS
    FEATURING SIEDAH GARRETT
DON'T LOOK ANY FURTHER KANE GANG
DON'T LOOK ANY FURTHER M PEOPLE
DON'T LOOK AT ME THAT WAY CHAKA KHAN
DON'T LOOK BACK [A] BOSTON
DON'T LOOK BACK [B] FINE YOUNG CANNIBALS
DON'T LOOK BACK [C] LLOYD COLE
DON'T LOOK BACK IN ANGER OASIS
DON'T LOOK BACK IN ANGER WURZELS
DON'T LOOK BACK INTO THE SUN LIBERTINES
DON'T LOOK DOWN [A] PLANETS
DON'T LOOK DOWN [B] MICK RONSON WITH JOE
    ELLIOTT
DON'T LOOK DOWN – THE SEQUEL GO WEST
DON'T LOSE IT EMINEM
DON'T LOSE THE MAGIC SHAWN CHRISTOPHER
DON'T LOSE YOUR TEMPER XTC
DON'T LOVE ME TOO HARD NOLANS
DON'T MAKE ME (FALL IN LOVE WITH YOU) BABBITY
    BLUE
DON'T MAKE ME OVER [A] SWINGING BLUE JEANS
DON'T MAKE ME OVER [B] SYBIL
DON'T MAKE ME WAIT [A] PEECH BOYS
DON'T MAKE ME WAIT [B] BOMB THE BASS
    FEATURING LORRAINE
DON'T MAKE ME WAIT [C] LOVELAND FEATURING
    RACHEL McFARLANE
DON'T MAKE ME WAIT [D] 911
DON'T MAKE ME WAIT TOO LONG [A] BARRY WHITE
DON'T MAKE ME WAIT TOO LONG [B] ROBERTA FLACK
DON'T MAKE MY BABY BLUE SHADOWS
DON'T MAKE WAVES NOLANS

DON'T MARRY HER BEAUTIFUL SOUTH
DON'T MESS WITH DOCTOR DREAM THOMPSON TWINS
DON'T MESS WITH MY MAN [A] LUCY PEARL
DON'T MESS WITH MY MAN [B] NIVEA FEATURING
    BRIAN & BRANDON CASEY
DON'T MESS WITH THE RADIO NIVEA
DON'T MISS THE PARTY LINE BIZZ NIZZ
DON'T MUG YOURSELF STREETS
DON'T NEED A GUN BILLY IDOL
DON'T NEED THE SUN TO SHINE (TO MAKE ME SMILE)
    GABRIELLE
DON'T PANIC LIQUID GOLD
DON'T PANIC LOGO FEATURING DAWN JOSEPH
DON'T PAY THE FERRYMAN CHRIS DE BURGH
DON'T PLAY THAT SONG ARETHA FRANKLIN
DON'T PLAY THAT SONG AGAIN NICKI FRENCH
DON'T PLAY WITH ME ROZALLA
DON'T PLAY YOUR ROCK 'N' ROLL TO ME SMOKEY
DON'T PULL YOUR LOVE SEAN MAGUIRE
DON'T PUSH IT RUTH JOY
DON'T PUSH IT, DON'T FORCE IT LEON HAYWOOD
DON'T PUT YOUR SPELL ON ME IAN McNABB
DON'T QUIT CARON WHEELER
DON'T RUSH (TAKE LOVE SLOWLY) K-CI & JOJO
DON'T SAY GOODBYE PAULINA RUBIO
DON'T SAY I TOLD YOU SO TOURISTS
DON'T SAY IT'S LOVE JOHNNY HATES JAZZ
DON'T SAY IT'S OVER GUN
DON'T SAY THAT'S JUST FOR WHITE BOYS WAY OF THE
    WEST
DON'T SAY YOU LOVE ME M2M
DON'T SAY YOUR LOVE IS KILLING ME ERASURE
DON'T SET ME FREE RAY CHARLES
DON'T SHED A TEAR PAUL CARRACK
DON'T SING PREFAB SPROUT
DON'T SLEEP IN THE SUBWAY PETULA CLARK
DON'T SLOW DOWN UB40
DON'T SPEAK NO DOUBT
DON'T SPEAK CLUELESS
DON'T STAND SO CLOSE TO ME POLICE
DON'T STAY AWAY TOO LONG PETERS & LEE
DON'T STEAL OUR SUN THRILLS
DON'T STOP [A] FLEETWOOD MAC
DON'T STOP [A] STATUS QUO
DON'T STOP [B] K.I.D.
DON'T STOP [C] MOOD
DON'T STOP [D] JEFFREY OSBORNE
DON'T STOP [E] K-KLASS
DON'T STOP [F] HAMMER
DON'T STOP [G] RUFF DRIVERZ
DON'T STOP [H] NO AUTHORITY
DON'T STOP [I] ATB
DON'T STOP [J] ROLLING STONES
DON'T STOP BELIEVIN' JOURNEY
DON'T STOP FUNKIN' 4 JAMAICA MARIAH CAREY
DON'T STOP IT NOW HOT CHOCOLATE
DON'T STOP (JAMMIN') L.A. MIX
DON'T STOP LOVIN' ME BABY PINKERTON'S ASSORTED
    COLOURS
DON'T STOP ME NOW QUEEN
DON'T STOP MOVIN' [A] LIVIN' JOY
DON'T STOP MOVIN' [B] S CLUB 7
DON'T STOP NOW GENE FARROW & G.F. BAND
DON'T STOP THAT CRAZY RHYTHM MODERN ROMANCE
DON'T STOP THE CARNIVAL ALAN PRICE SET
DON'T STOP THE DANCE BRYAN FERRY
DON'T STOP THE FEELING ROY AYERS
DON'T STOP THE MUSIC [A] YARBOROUGH & PEOPLES
DON'T STOP THE MUSIC [B] LIONEL RICHIE
DON'T STOP 'TIL YOU GET ENOUGH MICHAEL JACKSON
DON'T STOP TWIST FRANKIE VAUGHAN

DON'T STOP (WIGGLE WIGGLE) OUTHERE BROTHERS
DON'T TAKE AWAY THE MUSIC TAVARES
DON'T TAKE IT LYIN' DOWN DOOLEYS
DON'T TAKE IT PERSONAL JERMAINE JACKSON
DON'T TAKE IT PERSONAL (JUST ONE OF DEM DAYS)
    MONICA
DON'T TAKE MY KINDNESS FOR WEAKNESS HEADS
    WITH SHAUN RYDER
DON'T TAKE MY MIND ON A TRIP BOY GEORGE
DON'T TAKE NO FOR AN ANSWER TOM ROBINSON
    BAND
DON'T TALK [A] HANK MARVIN
DON'T TALK [B] JON B
DON'T TALK ABOUT LOVE BAD BOYS INC
DON'T TALK DIRTY TO ME JERMAINE STEWART
DON'T TALK JUST KISS RIGHT SAID FRED. GUEST
    VOCALS: JOCELYN BROWN
DON'T TALK TO HIM CLIFF RICHARD & THE SHADOWS
DON'T TALK TO ME ABOUT LOVE ALTERED IMAGES
DON'T TELL ME [A] CENTRAL LINE
DON'T TELL ME [B] BLANCMANGE
DON'T TELL ME [C] VAN HALEN
DON'T TELL ME [D] MADONNA
DON'T TELL ME [E] AVRIL LAVIGNE
DON'T TELL ME LIES BREATHE
DON'T TELL ME YOU'RE SORRY S CLUB 8
DON'T TEST JUNIOR TUCKER
DON'T THAT BEAT ALL ADAM FAITH
DON'T THINK I'M NOT KANDI
DON'T THINK IT (FEEL IT) LANGE FEATURING LEAH
DON'T THINK THE WAY THEY DO SPAN
DON'T THINK YOU'RE THE FIRST CORAL
DON'T THROW AWAY ALL THOSE TEARDROPS FRANKIE
    AVALON
DON'T THROW IT ALL AWAY GARY BENSON
DON'T THROW YOUR LOVE AWAY SEARCHERS
DON'T TREAT ME BAD FIREHOUSE
DON'T TREAT ME LIKE A CHILD HELEN SHAPIRO
DON'T TRY TO CHANGE ME CRICKETS
DON'T TRY TO STOP IT ROMAN HOLIDAY
DON'T TURN AROUND [A] MERSEYBEATS
DON'T TURN AROUND [B] ASWAD
DON'T TURN AROUND [B] ACE OF BASE
DON'T WAIT UP THUNDER
DON'T WALK BIG SUPREME
DON'T WALK AWAY [A] ELECTRIC LIGHT ORCHESTRA
DON'T WALK AWAY [B] FOUR TOPS
DON'T WALK AWAY [C] PAT BENATAR
DON'T WALK AWAY [D] TONI CHILDS
DON'T WALK AWAY [E] JADE
DON'T WALK AWAY [E] JAVINE
DON'T WALK AWAY TILL I TOUCH YOU ELAINE PAIGE
DON'T WANNA BE A PLAYER JOE
DON'T WANNA BE ALONE TRICIA PENROSE
DON'T WANNA FALL IN LOVE JANE CHILD
DON'T WANNA KNOW SHY FX/T POWER/DI & SKIBADEE
DON'T WANNA LET YOU GO FIVE
DON'T WANNA LOSE THIS FEELING DANNII MINOGUE
DON'T WANNA LOSE YOU [A] GLORIA ESTEFAN
DON'T WANNA LOSE YOU [B] LIONEL RICHIE
DON'T WANNA SAY GOODNIGHT KANDIDATE
DON'T WANT TO FORGIVE ME NOW WET WET WET
DON'T WANT TO WAIT ANYMORE TUBES
DON'T WANT YOU BACK ELLIE CAMPBELL
DON'T WASTE MY TIME PAUL HARDCASTLE FEATURING
    CAROL KENYON
DON'T WASTE YOUR TIME YARBOROUGH & PEOPLES
DON'T WORRY [A] JOHNNY BRANDON
DON'T WORRY [B] BILLY FURY WITH THE FOUR
    KESTRELS
DON'T WORRY [C] KIM APPLEBY

DON'T WORRY [D] NEWTON
DON'T WORRY [E] APPLETON
DON'T WORRY BABY LOS LOBOS
DON'T WORRY BE HAPPY BOBBY McFERRIN
DON'T YOU SECOND IMAGE
DON'T YOU FORGET ABOUT ME SIMPLE MINDS
DON'T YOU FORGET ABOUT ME BEST COMPANY
DON'T YOU GET SO MAD JEFFREY OSBORNE
DON'T YOU JUST KNOW IT AMAZULU
DON'T YOU KNOW BUTTERSCOTCH
DON'T YOU KNOW IT ADAM FAITH
DON'T YOU LOVE ME [A] 49ERS
DON'T YOU LOVE ME [B] ETERNAL
DON'T YOU ROCK ME DADDY-O LONNIE DONEGAN
DON'T YOU ROCK ME DADDY-O VIPERS SKIFFLE GROUP
DON'T YOU THINK IT'S TIME MIKE BERRY WITH THE
    OUTLAWS
DON'T YOU WANT ME [A] HUMAN LEAGUE
DON'T YOU WANT ME [A] FARM
DON'T YOU WANT ME [B] JODY WATLEY
DON'T YOU WANT ME [C] FELIX
DON'T YOU WANT ME BABY MANDY SMITH
DON'T YOU WORRY MADASUN
DON'T YOU WORRY 'BOUT A THING INCOGNITO
DOO WOP (THAT THING) LAURYN HILL
DOOBEDOOD'NDOOBE DOOBEDOOD'NDOOBE DIANA
    ROSS
DOODAH CARTOONS
DOOMS NIGHT AZZIDO DA BASS
DOOMSDAY EVELYN THOMAS
DOOP DOOP
THE DOOR TURIN BRAKES
DOOR #1 LEVERT SWEAT GILL
THE DOOR IS STILL OPEN TO MY HEART DEAN MARTIN
DOORS OF YOUR HEART BEAT
DOOT DOOT FREUR
THE DOPE SHOW MARILYN MANSON
DOPES TO INFINITY MONSTER MAGNET
DOUBLE BARREL DAVE & ANSIL COLLINS
DOUBLE DOUBLE DUTCH DOPE SMUGGLAZ
DOUBLE DROP FIERCE GIRL
DOUBLE DUTCH [A] FATBACK BAND
DOUBLE DUTCH [B] MALCOLM McLAREN
DOUBLE TROUBLE LYNYRD SKYNYRD
DOUBLEBACK ZZ TOP
DOVE (I'LL BE LOVING YOU) MOONY
DOV'E L'AMORE CHER
DOWN BLINK 182
DOWN AND UNDER (TOGETHER) KID CRÈME
    FEATURING MC SHURAKANO
DOWN AT THE DOCTOR'S DR FEELGOOD
DOWN BOY HOLLY VALANCE
DOWN BY THE LAZY RIVER OSMONDS
DOWN BY THE WATER PJ HARVEY
DOWN DEEP INSIDE (THEME FROM 'THE DEEP') DONNA
    SUMMER
DOWN DOWN STATUS QUO
DOWN DOWN DOWN GAMBAFREAKS
DOWN FOR THE ONE BEVERLEY KNIGHT
DOWN 4 U IRV GOTTI FEATURING ASHANTI, CHARLI
    BALTIMORE & VITA
DOWN 4 WHATEVA NUTTIN' NYCE
DOWN IN A HOLE ALICE IN CHAINS
DOWN IN THE BOONDOCKS BILLY JOE ROYAL
DOWN IN THE SUBWAY SOFT CELL
DOWN IN THE TUBE STATION AT MIDNIGHT JAM
DOWN LOW (NOBODY HAS TO KNOW) R KELLY
    FEATURING RONALD ISLEY
DOWN ON THE BEACH TONIGHT DRIFTERS
DOWN ON THE CORNER CREEDENCE CLEARWATER
    REVIVAL

DOWN ON THE STREET SHAKATAK
DOWN SO LONG JEWEL
DOWN THAT ROAD SHARA NELSON
DOWN THE DRAIN STAKKA BO
DOWN THE DUSTPIPE STATUS QUO
DOWN THE HALL FOUR SEASONS
DOWN THE RIVER NILE JOHN LEYTON
DOWN THE WIRE ASAP
DOWN TO EARTH [A] CURIOSITY KILLED THE CAT
DOWN TO EARTH [B] MONIE LOVE
DOWN TO EARTH [C] GRACE
DOWN TO THE SEA TIM BOOTH
DOWN TO THE WIRE GHOST DANCE
DOWN UNDER MEN AT WORK
DOWN WITH THE CLIQUE AALIYAH
DOWN WITH THE KING RUN D.M.C.
DOWN YONDER JOHNNY & THE HURRICANES
DOWNHEARTED EDDIE FISHER
DOWNLOAD IT CLEA
DOWNTOWN [A] PETULA CLARK
DOWNTOWN [B] ONE 2 MANY
DOWNTOWN [C] SWV
THE DOWNTOWN LIGHTS BLUE NILE
DOWNTOWN TRAIN ROD STEWART
DOWNTOWN VENUS PM DAWN
DRACULA'S TANGO TOTO COELO
DRAG ME DOWN BOOMTOWN RATS
DRAGGING ME DOWN INSPIRAL CARPETS
DRAGNET TED HEATH
DRAGNET RAY ANTHONY
DRAGNET ART OF NOISE
DRAGON POWER JKD BAND
DRAGONFLY TORNADOS
DRAGOSTEA DIN TEI O-ZONE
DRAGULA ROB ZOMBIE
DRAIN THE BLOOD DISTILLERS
DRAMA! ERASURE
DRAW OF THE CARDS KIM CARNES
(DRAWING) RINGS AROUND THE WORLD SUPER FURRY
    ANIMALS
DRE DAY DR DRE
DREADLOCK HOLIDAY 10 C.C.
DREAM DIZZEE RASCAL
THE DREAM DREAM FREQUENCY
DREAM A LIE UB40
DREAM A LITTLE DREAM OF ME ANITA HARRIS
DREAM A LITTLE DREAM OF ME MAMA CASS
DREAM ABOUT YOU D'BORA
DREAM ANOTHER DREAM RIALTO
DREAM BABY ROY ORBISON
DREAM BABY GLEN CAMPBELL
DREAM COME TRUE BRAND NEW HEAVIES FEATURING
    N'DEA DAVENPORT
DREAM GIRL MARK WYNTER
DREAM KITCHEN FRAZIER CHORUS
DREAM LOVER BOBBY DARIN
DREAM OF ME (BASED ON LOVE'S THEME)
    ORCHESTRAL MANOEUVRES IN THE DARK
DREAM OF OLWEN SECOND CITY SOUND
DREAM ON DEPECHE MODE
DREAM ON DREAMER BRAND NEW HEAVIES
    FEATURING N'DEA DAVENPORT
DREAM ON (IS THIS A DREAM) LOVE DECADE
DREAM SEQUENCE (ONE) PAULINE MURRAY & THE
    INVISIBLE GIRLS
DREAM SOME PARADISE INTASTELLA
DREAM SWEET DREAMS AZTEC CAMERA
DREAM TALK ALMA COGAN
DREAM TO ME DARIO G
DREAM TO SLEEP H20
DREAM UNIVERSE DJ GARRY

DREAMBOAT [A] ALMA COGAN
DREAMBOAT [B] LIMMIE & THE FAMILY COOKIN'
DREAMER [A] SUPERTRAMP
DREAMER [A] CK & SUPREME DREAM TEAM
DREAMER [B] JACKSONS
DREAMER [C] COLDCUT
DREAMER [D] LIVIN' JOY
DREAMER [E] OZZY OSBOURNE
THE DREAMER ALL ABOUT EVE
DREAMIN' [A] JOHNNY BURNETTE
DREAMIN' [B] LIVERPOOL EXPRESS
DREAMIN' [C] CLIFF RICHARD
DREAMIN' [D] STATUS QUO
DREAMIN' [E] VANESSA WILLIAMS
DREAMIN' [F] LOLEATTA HOLLOWAY
DREAMIN' [G] AMP FIDDLER
DREAMING [A] BLONDIE
DREAMING [B] ORCHESTRAL MANOEUVRES IN THE
    DARK
DREAMING [C] GLEN GOLDSMITH
DREAMING [D] MN8
DREAMING [E] RUFF DRIVERZ PRESENTS ARROLA
DREAMING [F] M PEOPLE
DREAMING [G] BT FEATURING KIRSTY HAWKSHAW
DREAMING [H] AURORA
DREAMING [I] I DREAM FEATURING FRANKIE &
    CALVIN
THE DREAMING KATE BUSH
DREAMING OF ME DEPECHE MODE
DREAMING OF YOU [A] THRILLSEEKERS
DREAMING OF YOU [B] CORAL
DREAMLOVER MARIAH CAREY
DREAMS [A] FLEETWOOD MAC
DREAMS [A] WILD COLOUR
DREAMS [A] CORRS
DREAMS [B] GRACE SLICK
DREAMS [C] VAN HALEN
DREAMS [D] GABRIELLE
DREAMS [E] CRANBERRIES
DREAMS [F] SMOKIN' BEATS FEATURING LYN EDEN
DREAMS [G] QUENCH
DREAMS [H] MISS SHIVA
DREAMS [I] KINGS OF TOMORROW
DREAMS [J] KINGS OF TOMORROW FEATURING HAZE
A DREAM'S A DREAM SOUL II SOUL
DREAMS CAN TELL A LIE NAT 'KING' COLE
THE DREAMS I DREAM SHADOWS
DREAMS OF CHILDREN JAM
DREAMS OF HEAVEN GROUND LEVEL
DREAMS OF YOU RALPH McTELL
DREAMSCAPE '94 TIME FREQUENCY
DREAMTIME [A] DARYL HALL
DREAMTIME [B] ZEE
DREAMY DAYS ROOTS MANUVA
DREAMY LADY T REX DISCO PARTY
DRED BASS DEAD DRED
DRESS YOU UP MADONNA
DRESSED FOR SUCCESS ROXETTE
DRIFT AWAY MICHAEL BOLTON
DRIFTING [A] SHEILA WALSH & CLIFF RICHARD
DRIFTING [B] MOJOLATORS FEATURING CAMILLA
DRIFTING AWAY LANGE FEATURING SKYE
DRIFTWOOD TRAVIS
THE DRILL DIRT DEVILS
DRINK THE ELIXIR SALAD
DRINK UP THY ZIDER ADGE CUTLER & THE WURZELS
DRINKING IN LA BRAN VAN 3000
DRINKING SONG MARIO LANZA
DRIP FED FRED MADNESS FEATURING IAN DURY
DRIVE [A] CARS
DRIVE [B] R.E.M.

DRIVE [C] GEOFFREY WILLIAMS
DRIVE [D] INCUBUS
DRIVE ME CRAZY PARTIZAN
DRIVE ON BROTHER BEYOND
DRIVE SAFELY DARLIN' TONY CHRISTIE
DRIVE-IN SATURDAY DAVID BOWIE
DRIVEN BY YOU BRIAN MAY
DRIVER'S SEAT SNIFF 'N' THE TEARS
DRIVIN' HOME DUANE EDDY & THE REBELS
DRIVING EVERYTHING BUT THE GIRL
DRIVING AWAY FROM HOME (JIM'S TUNE) IT'S IMMATERIAL
DRIVING HOME FOR CHRISTMAS (EP) CHRIS REA
DRIVING IN MY CAR MADNESS
DRIVING IN MY CAR MAUREEN REES
DRIVING WITH THE BRAKES ON DEL AMITRI
DROP DEAD GORGEOUS REPUBLICA
DROP IT LIKE IT'S HOT SNOOP DOGG FEATURING PHARRELL
DROP SOME DRUMS (LOVE) TATTOO
DROP THE BOY BROS
DROP THE PILOT JOAN ARMATRADING
DROP THE PRESSURE MYLO
DROP THE ROCK (EP) D-TEK
DROPS OF JUPITER (TELL ME) TRAIN
DROWNED WORLD (SUBSTITUTE FOR LOVE) MADONNA
THE DROWNERS SUEDE
DROWNING [A] BEAT
DROWNING [B] BACKSTREET BOYS
DROWNING [C] CRAZY TOWN
DROWNING IN BERLIN MOBILES
DROWNING THE THE SEA OF LOVE ADVENTURES
DROWSY WITH HOPE SHAKEDOWN
THE DRUGS DON'T WORK VERVE
DRUMBEATS SL2
DRUMMER MAN TONIGHT
DRUMMIN' UP A STORM SANDY NELSON
DRUMS ARE MY BEAT SANDY NELSON
THE DRUMSTRUCK (EP) N-JOI
DRUNK ON LOVE BASIA
DRUNKARD LOGIC FAT LADY SINGS
DRUNKEN FOOL BURN
DRUNKEN STARS MAMPI SWIFT
DRY COUNTY [A] BLACKFOOT
DRY COUNTY [B] BON JOVI
DRY LAND MARILLION
DRY RISER KERBDOG
DRY YOUR EYES STREETS
DUALITY SLIPKNOT
DUB BE GOOD TO ME BEATS INTERNATIONAL FEATURING LINDY LAYTON
DUB WAR DANCE CONSPIRACY
DUBPLATE CULTURE SOUNDSCAPE
DUCHESS [A] STRANGLERS
DUCHESS [A] MY LIFE STORY
DUCHESS [B] GENESIS
DUCK FOR THE OYSTER MALCOLM McLAREN
DUCK TOY HAMPENBERG
DUDE BEENIE MAN FEATURING MS THING
DUDE DESCENDING A STAIRCASE APOLLO FOUR FORTY/BEATNUTS
DUDE (LOOKS LIKE A LADY) AEROSMITH
DUEL [A] PROPAGANDA
DUEL [B] SWERVEDRIVER
DUELLING BANJOS 'DELIVERANCE' SOUNDTRACK
DUI HAR MAR SUPERSTAR
DUKE OF EARL DARTS
DUM DUM BRENDA LEE
DUM DUM GIRL TALK TALK
DUMB [A] BEAUTIFUL SOUTH
DUMB [B] 411

DUMB WAITERS PSYCHEDELIC FURS
DUMMY CRUSHER KERBDOG
DUNE BUGGY PRESIDENTS OF THE UNITED STATES OF AMERICA
DUNE SEA UNBELIEVABLE TRUTH
DUNNO WHAT IT IS (ABOUT YOU) BEATMASTERS FEATURING ELAINE VASSELL
DURHAM TOWN (THE LEAVIN') ROGER WHITTAKER
DUSK TIL DAWN DANNY HOWELLS & DICK TREVOR
DUSTED LEFTFIELD/ROOTS MANUVA
D. W. WASHBURN MONKEES
D'YA WANNA GO FASTER TERRORVISION
DY-NA-MI-TEE MS DYNAMITE
DYNA-MITE MUD
DYNAMITE [A] CLIFF RICHARD & THE SHADOWS
DYNAMITE [B] STACY LATTISHAW
DYNOMITE (PART 1) TONY CAMILLO'S BAZUKA
D'YOU KNOW WHAT I MEAN? OASIS
E DRUNKENMUNKY
E = MC2 BIG AUDIO DYNAMITE
E SAMBA JUNIOR JACK
EACH AND EVERYONE EVERYTHING BUT THE GIRL
EACH TIME E-17
EACH TIME YOU BREAK MY HEART NICK KAMEN
EARDRUM BUZZ WIRE
EARLY IN THE MORNING [A] BUDDY HOLLY
EARLY IN THE MORNING [B] VANITY FARE
EARLY IN THE MORNING [C] GAP BAND
EARLY TO BED PONI-TAILS
EARTH ANGEL [A] CREW CUTS
EARTH ANGEL [B] DREADZONE
THE EARTH DIES SCREAMING UB40
EARTH SONG MICHAEL JACKSON
EARTHBOUND CONNOR REEVES
THE EARTHSHAKER PAUL MASTERSON PRESENTS SUSHI
EASE MY MIND ARRESTED DEVELOPMENT
EASE ON BY BASS-O-MATIC
EASE ON DOWN THE ROAD DIANA ROSS & MICHAEL JACKSON
EASE THE PRESSURE [A] 2WO THIRD3
EASE THE PRESSURE [B] BELOVED
EASE YOUR MIND GALLIANO
EASIER SAID THAN DONE [A] ESSEX
EASIER SAID THAN DONE [B] SHAKATAK
EASIER SAID THAN DONE [C] STARGATE
EASIER TO LIE AQUALUNG
EASIER TO WALK AWAY ELTON JOHN
EAST COAST/WEST COAST KILLAS GROUP THERAPY
EAST EASY RIDER JULIAN COPE
EAST OF EDEN BIG COUNTRY
EAST RIVER BRECKER BROTHERS
EAST WEST HERMAN'S HERMITS
EASTER MARILLION
EASY [A] COMMODORES
EASY [B] LOUD
EASY [C] TERRORVISION
EASY [D] EMILIANA TORRINI
EASY [E] GROOVE ARMADA
EASY COME EASY GO SUTHERLAND BROTHERS
EASY EASY SCOTLAND WORLD CUP SQUAD
EASY GOING ME ADAM FAITH
EASY LADY SPAGNA
EASY LIFE [A] BODYSNATCHERS
EASY LIFE [B] CABARET VOLTAIRE
EASY LIVIN' FASTWAY
EASY LOVER PHILIP BAILEY (DUET WITH PHIL COLLINS)
EASY RIDER RAIN BAND
EASY TO SMILE SENSELESS THINGS
EAT IT WEIRD AL YANKOVIC
EAT ME DRINK ME LOVE ME POP WILL EAT ITSELF
EAT MY GOAL COLLAPSED LUNG

EAT THE RICH AEROSMITH
EAT YOU ALIVE LIMP BIZKIT
EAT YOUR HEART OUT PAUL HARDCASTLE
EAT YOURSELF WHOLE KINGMAKER
EATEN ALIVE DIANA ROSS
EATING ME ALIVE DIANA BROWN & BARRIE K. SHARPE
EBB TIDE FRANK CHACKSFIELD
EBB TIDE RIGHTEOUS BROTHERS
EBENEEZER GOODE SHAMEN
EBONY AND IVORY PAUL McCARTNEY & STEVIE WONDER
EBONY EYES EVERLY BROTHERS
E – BOW THE LETTER R.E.M.
ECHO BEACH MARTHA & THE MUFFINS
ECHO BEACH TOYAH
ECHO CHAMBER BEATS INTERNATIONAL
ECHO MY HEART LINDY LAYTON
ECHO ON MY MIND PART II EARTHLING
ECHOES IN A SHALLOW BAY (EP) COCTEAU TWINS
ECUADOR SASH! FEATURING RODRIGUEZ
EDDY VORTEX STEVE GIBBONS BAND
EDELWEISS VINCE HILL
EDEN SARAH BRIGHTMAN
EDGE OF A BROKEN HEART VIXEN
EDGE OF DARKNESS ERIC CLAPTON FEATURING MICHAEL KAMEN
THE EDGE OF HEAVEN WHAM!
EDIE (CIAO BABY) CULT
ED'S FUNKY DINER (FRIDAY NIGHT, SATURDAY MORNING) IT'S IMMATERIAL
EENY MEENY SHOWSTOPPERS
EGG RUSH FLOWERED UP
EGO ELTON JOHN
EGYPTIAN REGGAE JONATHAN RICHMAN & THE MODERN LOVERS
EI NELLY
EIGHT BY TEN KEN DODD
8 DAYS A WEEK SWEET FEMALE ATTITUDE
EIGHT MILES HIGH BYRDS
808 BLAQUE IVORY
18 AND LIFE SKID ROW
18 CARAT LOVE AFFAIR ASSOCIATES
EIGHTEEN STRINGS TINMAN
18 TIL I DIE BRYAN ADAMS
EIGHTEEN WITH A BULLET PETE WINGFIELD
EIGHTEEN YELLOW ROSES BOBBY DARIN
EIGHTH DAY HAZEL O'CONNOR
8TH WORLD WONDER KIMBERLEY LOCKE
EIGHTIES KILLING JOKE
80S ROMANCE BELLE STARS
86'D SUBCIRCUS
EINSTEIN A GO-GO LANDSCAPE
EL BIMBO BIMBO JET
EL CAMINOS IN THE WEST GRANDADDY
EL CAPITAN OPM
EL LUTE BONEY M
EL NINO AGNELLI & NELSON
EL PARAISO RICO DEETAH
EL PASO MARTY ROBBINS
EL PRESIDENT DRUGSTORE
EL SALVADOR ATHLETE
EL SCORCHO WEEZER
EL TRAGO (THE DRINK) 2 IN A ROOM
EL VINO COLLAPSO BLACK LACE
ELDORADO DRUM THEATRE
ELEANOR RIGBY BEATLES
ELEANOR RIGBY RAY CHARLES
ELECTED ALICE COOPER
ELECTION DAY ARCADIA
ELECTRIC AVENUE EDDY GRANT
ELECTRIC BARBARELLA DURAN DURAN

ELECTRIC BLUE ICEHOUSE
ELECTRIC BOOGALOO OLLIE & JERRY
ELECTRIC GUITAR FLUKE
ELECTRIC GUITARS PREFAB SPROUT
ELECTRIC HEAD PART 2 (THE ECSTASY) WHITE ZOMBIE
ELECTRIC LADY GEORDIE
ELECTRIC MAINLINE SPIRITUALIZED
ELECTRIC MAN MANSUN
ELECTRIC TRAINS SQUEEZE
ELECTRIC YOUTH DEBBIE GIBSON
ELECTRICAL STORM U2
ELECTRICITY [A] SPIRITUALIZED
ELECTRICITY [B] SUEDE
ELECTROLITE R.E.M.
ELECTRONIC PLEASURE N-TRANCE
ELEGANTLY AMERICAN: ONE NIGHT IN HEAVEN M
    PEOPLE
ELEGANTLY WASTED INXS
ELEKTROBANK CHEMICAL BROTHERS
ELEMENTS NEO CORTEX
ELENI TOL & TOL
ELENORE TURTLES
ELEPHANT PAW (GET DOWN TO THE FUNK) PAN
    POSITION
ELEPHANT STONE STONE ROSES
ELEPHANT TANGO CYRIL STAPLETON
THE ELEPHANT'S GRAVEYARD (GUILTY) BOOMTOWN
    RATS
ELEVATE MY MIND STEREO MC'S
ELEVATION [A] XPANSIONS
ELEVATION (MOVE YOUR BODY) 2002 XPANSIONS
ELEVATION [B] GTO
ELEVATION [C] U2
ELEVATION [D] OPEN
ELEVATOR SONG DUBSTAR
ELEVEN TO FLY TIN TIN OUT FEATURING WENDY PAGE
ELISABETH SERENADE GUNTER KALLMAN CHOIR
ELIZABETHAN REGGAE BORIS GARDINER
ELLE DJ GREGORY
ELMO JAMES CHAIRMEN OF THE BOARD
ELO EP ELECTRIC LIGHT ORCHESTRA
ELOISE BARRY RYAN
ELOISE DAMNED
ELSTREE BUGGLES
ELUSIVE BUTTERFLY BOB LIND
ELUSIVE BUTTERFLY VAL DOONICAN
THE ELVIS MEDLEY ELVIS PRESLEY
EMBARRASSMENT MADNESS
EMBRACE AGNELLI & NELSON
EMBRACING THE SUNSHINE BT
EMERALD CITY SEEKERS
EMERGE FISCHERSPOONER
EMERGENCY KOOL & THE GANG
EMERGENCY 72 TURIN BRAKES
EMERGENCY (DIAL 999) LOOSE ENDS
EMERGENCY ON PLANET EARTH JAMIROQUAI
EMILY BOWLING FOR SOUP
EMMA HOT CHOCOLATE
EMOTION SAMANTHA SANG
EMOTION DESTINY'S CHILD
EMOTIONAL CONTENT FUNK D'VOID
EMOTIONAL RESCUE ROLLING STONES
EMOTIONAL TIME HOTHOUSE FLOWERS
EMOTIONS [A] BRENDA LEE
EMOTIONS [B] MARIAH CAREY
THE EMPEROR'S NEW CLOTHES SINEAD O'CONNOR
EMPIRE QUEENSRYCHE
EMPIRE LINE MY LIFE STORY
EMPIRE SONG KILLING JOKE
EMPIRE STATE HUMAN HUMAN LEAGUE
EMPTY AT THE END ELECTRIC SOFT PARADE

EMPTY GARDEN ELTON JOHN
EMPTY ROOMS GARY MOORE
EMPTY SKIES KOSHEEN
EMPTY WORLD DOGS D'AMOUR
ENCHANTED LADY PASADENAS
ENCORE CHERYL LYNN
ENCORE TONGUE 'N' CHEEK
ENCORE UNE FOIS SASH!
ENCORES EP DIRE STRAITS
THE END HAS NO END STROKES
THE END IS THE BEGINNING IS THE END SMASHING
    PUMPKINS
END OF A CENTURY BLUR
THE END OF THE INNOCENCE DON HENLEY
END OF THE LINE [A] TRAVELING WILBURYS
END OF THE LINE [B] HONEYZ
END OF THE ROAD BOYZ II MEN
END OF THE WORLD [A] SKEETER DAVIS
END OF THE WORLD [A] SONIA
THE END OF THE WORLD [B] CURE
THE END...OR THE BEGINNING CLASSIX NOUVEAUX
ENDLESS DICKIE VALENTINE
ENDLESS ART A HOUSE
ENDLESS LOVE DIANA ROSS & LIONEL RICHIE
ENDLESS LOVE LUTHER VANDROSS & MARIAH CAREY
ENDLESS SLEEP MARTY WILDE
ENDLESS SLEEP JODY REYNOLDS
ENDLESS SUMMER NIGHTS RICHARD MARX
ENDLESSLY [A] BROOK BENTON
ENDLESSLY [B] JOHN FOXX
ENDS EVERLAST
ENEMIES FRIENDS HOPE OF THE STATES
ENEMY MAKER DUB WAR
THE ENEMY WITHIN THIRST
ENERGIZE SLAMM
THE ENERGY (FEEL THE VIBE) ASTRO TRAX
ENERGY FLASH (EP) BELTRAM
ENERGY IS EUROBEAT MAN TO MAN
ENERVATE TRANSA
ENGINE ENGINE NO. 9 ROGER MILLER
ENGINE NO 9 MIDNIGHT STAR
ENGLAND CRAZY RIDER & TERRY VENABLES
ENGLAND SWINGS ROGER MILLER
ENGLAND WE'LL FLY THE FLAG ENGLAND WORLD CUP
    SQUAD
ENGLAND'S IRIE BLACK GRAPE FEATURING JOE
    STRUMMER & KEITH ALLEN
ENGLISH CIVIL WAR (JOHNNY COMES MARCHING
    HOME) CLASH
ENGLISH COUNTRY GARDEN [A] JIMMIE RODGERS
ENGLISH COUNTRY GARDEN [B] DANDYS
ENGLISH SUMMER RAIN PLACEBO
ENGLISHMAN IN NEW YORK STING
ENJOY THE SILENCE DEPECHE MODE
ENJOY YOURSELF [A] JACKSONS
ENJOY YOURSELF [B] A+
ENOLA GAY ORCHESTRAL MANOEUVRES IN THE DARK
ENOUGH IS ENOUGH [A] CHUMBAWAMBA & CREDIT TO
    THE NATION
ENOUGH IS ENOUGH [B] Y-TRIBE FEATURING ELISABETH
    TROY
ENTER SANDMAN METALLICA
ENTER THE SCENE DJ SUPREME VS THE RHYTHM
    MASTERS
ENTER YOUR FANTASY EP JOEY NEGRO
THE ENTERTAINER MARVIN HAMLISCH
ENTRY OF THE GLADIATORS NERO & THE GLADIATORS
ENVY ASH
THE EP ZERO B
EP THREE HUNDRED REASONS
EP TWO HUNDRED REASONS

EPIC FAITH NO MORE
EPLE ROYKSOPP
EQUINOXE PART 5 JEAN-MICHEL JARRE
EQUINOXE (PART V) SHADOWS
ERASE/REWIND CARDIGANS
ERASURE-ISH (A LITTLE RESPECT/STOP!) BJORN AGAIN
ERECTION (TAKE IT TO THE TOP) CORTINA FEATURING
    BK & MADAM FRICTION
ERNIE (THE FASTEST MILKMAN IN THE WEST) BENNY
    HILL
EROTICA MADONNA
ESCAPADE JANET JACKSON
ESCAPE [A] GARY CLAIL ON-U SOUND SYSTEM
ESCAPE [B] ENRIQUE IGLESIAS
ESCAPE ARTISTS NEVER DIE FUNERAL FOR A FRIEND
ESCAPE (THE PINA COLADA SONG) RUPERT HOLMES
ESCAPING DINA CARROLL
ESCAPING ASIA BLUE
E.S.P. BEE GEES
ESPECIALLY FOR YOU KYLIE MINOGUE & JASON
    DONOVAN
ESPECIALLY FOR YOU DENISE & JOHNNY
THE ESSENTIAL WALLY PARTY MEDLEY GAY GORDON &
    THE MINCE PIES
ET LES OISEAUX CHANTAIENT (AND THE BIRDS WERE
    SINGING) SWEET PEOPLE
ET MEME FRANCOISE HARDY
ETERNAL FLAME BANGLES
ETERNAL FLAME ATOMIC KITTEN
ETERNAL LOVE PJ & DUNCAN
ETERNALLY JIMMY YOUNG
ETERNITY [A] ORION
ETERNITY [B] ROBBIE WILLIAMS
ETHER RADIO CHIKINKI
ETHNIC PRAYER HAVANA
ETON RIFLES JAM
EUGINA SALT TANK
EURODISCO BIS
EUROPA AND THE PIRATE TWINS THOMAS DOLBY
EUROPE (AFTER THE RAIN) JOHN FOXX
EUROPEAN FEMALE STRANGLERS
EUROPEAN SON JAPAN
EVANGELINE [A] ICICLE WORKS
EVANGELINE [B] COCTEAU TWINS
EVAPOR 8 ALTERN 8
EVE OF DESTRUCTION BARRY McGUIRE
THE EVE OF THE WAR JEFF WAYNE'S WAR OF THE
    WORLDS
EVE THE APPLE OF MY EYE BELL X1
EVEN AFTER ALL FINLEY QUAYE
EVEN BETTER THAN THE REAL THING U2
EVEN FLOW PEARL JAM
EVEN MORE PARTY POPS RUSS CONWAY
EVEN NOW BOB SEGER & THE SILVER BULLET BAND
EVEN THE BAD TIMES ARE GOOD TREMELOES
EVEN THE NIGHTS ARE BETTER AIR SUPPLY
EVEN THOUGH YOU BROKE MY HEART GEMINI
EVEN THOUGH YOU'VE GONE JACKSONS
EVENING FALLS... ENYA
EVENING STARS JUDAS PRIEST
EVER FALLEN IN LOVE FINE YOUNG CANNIBALS
EVER FALLEN IN LOVE (WITH SOMEONE YOU
    SHOULDN'T'VE) BUZZCOCKS
EVER REST MYSTICA
EVER SINCE YOU SAID GOODBYE MARTY WILDE
EVER SO LONELY MONSOON
EVEREST SUPERNATURALS
EVERGLADE L7
EVERGREEN [A] HAZELL DEAN
EVERGREEN [B] WILL YOUNG
EVERGREEN [B] LAWRENCE BELLE

EVERLASTING NATALIE COLE
THE EVERLASTING MANIC STREET PREACHERS
EVERLASTING LOVE [A] LOVE AFFAIR
EVERLASTING LOVE [A] ROBERT KNIGHT
EVERLASTING LOVE [A] REX SMITH & RACHEL SWEET
EVERLASTING LOVE [A] SANDRA
EVERLASTING LOVE [A] WORLDS APART
EVERLASTING LOVE [A] GLORIA ESTEFAN
EVERLASTING LOVE [A] CAST OF CASUALTY
EVERLASTING LOVE [A] JAMIE CULLUM
AN EVERLASTING LOVE [B] ANDY GIBB
EVERLASTING LOVE [C] HOWARD JONES
EVERLONG FOO FIGHTERS
EVERLOVIN' RICK NELSON
EVERMORE RUBY MURRAY
EVERY 1'S A WINNER HOT CHOCOLATE
EVERY ANGEL ALL ABOUT EVE
EVERY BEAT OF MY HEART ROD STEWART
EVERY BEAT OF THE HEART RAILWAY CHILDREN
EVERY BREATH OF THE WAY MELANIE
EVERY BREATH YOU TAKE POLICE
EVERY DAY ANTICAPPELLA
EVERY DAY HURTS SAD CAFE
EVERY DAY I FALL APART SUPERSTAR
EVERY DAY I LOVE YOU BOYZONE
EVERY DAY (I LOVE YOU MORE) JASON DONOVAN
EVERY DAY OF MY LIFE MALCOLM VAUGHAN
EVERY DAY OF THE WEEK JADE
EVERY DAY SHOULD BE A HOLIDAY DANDY WARHOLS
EVERY GIRL AND BOY SPAGNA
EVERY HEARTBEAT AMY GRANT
EVERY KINDA PEOPLE ROBERT PALMER
EVERY KINDA PEOPLE MINT JULEPS
EVERY KINDA PEOPLE CHAKA DEMUS & PLIERS
EVERY LITTLE BIT HURTS SPENCER DAVIS GROUP
EVERY LITTLE STEP BOBBY BROWN
EVERY LITTLE TEARDROP GALLAGHER & LYLE
EVERY LITTLE THING JEFF LYNNE
EVERY LITTLE THING HE DOES IS MAGIC SHAWN
    COLVIN
EVERY LITTLE THING I DO SOUL FOR REAL
EVERY LITTLE THING SHE DOES IS MAGIC POLICE
EVERY LITTLE THING SHE DOES IS MAGIC CHAKA
    DEMUS & PLIERS
EVERY LITTLE TIME POPPERS PRESENTS AURA
EVERY LITTLE TIME ONYX FEATURING GEMMA J
EVERY LOSER WINS NICK BERRY
EVERY MAN MUST HAVE A DREAM LIVERPOOL EXPRESS
EVERY MORNING SUGAR RAY
EVERY NIGHT PHOEBE SNOW
EVERY NITE'S A SATURDAY NIGHT WITH YOU DRIFTERS
EVERY OTHER TIME LYTE FUNKIE ONES
EVERY ROSE HAS ITS THORN POISON
EVERY SINGLE DAY DODGY
EVERY TIME JANET JACKSON
EVERY TIME I FALL GINA G
EVERY TIME I FALL IN LOVE UPSIDE DOWN
EVERY TIME IT RAINS ACE OF BASE
EVERY TIME YOU GO AWAY PAUL YOUNG
EVERY TIME YOU TOUCH ME MOBY
EVERY WAY THAT I CAN SERTAB
EVERY WHICH WAY BUT LOOSE EDDIE RABBITT
EVERY WOMAN KNOWS LULU
EVERY WOMAN NEEDS LOVE STELLA BROWNE
EVERY YEAR EVERY CHRISTMAS LUTHER VANDROSS
EVERY YOU EVERY ME PLACEBO
EVERYBODY [A] TOMMY ROE
EVERYBODY [B] CAPPELLA
EVERYBODY [C] ALTERN 8
EVERYBODY [D] DJ BOBO
EVERYBODY [E] CLOCK

EVERYBODY [F] KINKY
EVERYBODY [G] PROGRESS PRESENTS THE BOY WUNDA
EVERYBODY [H] HEAR'SAY
EVERYBODY (ALL OVER THE WORLD) FPI PROJECT
EVERYBODY (BACKSTREET'S BACK) BACKSTREET BOYS
EVERYBODY BE SOMEBODY RUFFNECK FEATURING
    YAVAHN
EVERYBODY COME DOWN DELGADOS
EVERYBODY COME ON (CAN U FEEL IT) MR REDZ VS DJ
    SKRIBBLE
EVERYBODY CRIES LIBERTY X
EVERYBODY DANCE CHIC
EVERYBODY DANCE EVOLUTION
EVERYBODY DANCE (THE HORN SONG) BARBARA
    TUCKER
EVERYBODY EVERYBODY BLACK BOX
(EVERYBODY) GET DANCIN' BOMBERS
EVERYBODY GET TOGETHER DAVE CLARK FIVE
EVERYBODY GET UP [A] FIVE
EVERYBODY GET UP [B] CAPRICCIO
EVERYBODY GETS A SECOND CHANCE MIKE + THE
    MECHANICS
EVERYBODY GO HOME THE PARTY'S OVER CLODAGH
    RODGERS
EVERYBODY GONFI-GON TWO COWBOYS
EVERYBODY HAVE A GOOD TIME ARCHIE BELL & THE
    DRELLS
EVERYBODY HERE WANTS YOU JEFF BUCKLEY
EVERYBODY HURTS R.E.M.
EVERYBODY IN THE PLACE (EP) PRODIGY
EVERYBODY IS A STAR POINTER SISTERS
EVERYBODY KNOWS [A] DAVE CLARK FIVE
EVERYBODY KNOWS [B] DAVE CLARK FIVE
EVERYBODY KNOWS [C] FREE ASSOCIATION
EVERYBODY KNOWS (EXCEPT YOU) DIVINE COMEDY
EVERYBODY LETS SOMEBODY LOVE FRANK K
    FEATURING WISTON OFFICE
EVERYBODY LOVES A LOVER DORIS DAY
EVERYBODY LOVES SOMEBODY DEAN MARTIN
EVERYBODY MOVE CATHY DENNIS
EVERYBODY (MOVE YOUR BODY) DIVA
EVERYBODY MUST PARTY GEORGIE PORGIE
EVERYBODY NEEDS A 303 FATBOY SLIM
EVERYBODY NEEDS SOMEBODY [A] BIRDLAND
EVERYBODY NEEDS SOMEBODY [B] NICK HOWARD
EVERYBODY NEEDS SOMEBODY TO LOVE BLUES
    BROTHERS
EVERYBODY ON THE FLOOR (PUMP IT) TOKYO GHETTO
    PUSSY
EVERYBODY PUMP DJ POWER
EVERYBODY (RAP) CRIMINAL ELEMENT ORCHESTRA &
    WENDELL WILLIAMS
EVERYBODY SALSA MODERN ROMANCE
EVERYBODY SAY EVERYBODY DO LET LOOSE
EVERYBODY THINKS THEY'RE GOING TO GET THEIRS BIS
EVERYBODY UP! GLAM METAL DETECTIVES
EVERYBODY WANTS HER THUNDER
EVERYBODY WANTS TO RULE THE WORLD TEARS FOR
    FEARS
EVERYBODY WANTS TO RUN THE WORLD TEARS FOR
    FEARS
EVERYBODY'S A ROCK STAR TALL PAUL
EVERYBODY'S CHANGING KEANE
EVERYBODY'S FOOL EVANESCENCE
EVERYBODY'S FREE (TO FEEL GOOD) ROZALLA
EVERYBODY'S FREE (TO WEAR SUNSCREEN) BAZ
    LUHRMANN
EVERYBODY'S GONE SENSELESS THINGS
EVERYBODY'S GONNA BE HAPPY KINKS
EVERYBODY'S GOT SUMMER ATLANTIC STARR
EVERYBODY'S GOT TO LEARN SOMETIME KORGIS

EVERYBODY'S GOT TO LEARN SOMETIME YAZZ
(EVERYBODY'S GOT TO LEARN SOMETIME) I NEED YOUR
    LOVING BABY D
EVERYBODY'S HAPPY NOWADAYS BUZZCOCKS
EVERYBODY'S LAUGHING PHIL FEARON & GALAXY
EVERYBODY'S SOMEBODY'S FOOL CONNIE FRANCIS
EVERYBODY'S TALKIN' NILSSON
EVERYBODY'S TALKIN' BEAUTIFUL SOUTH
EVERYBODY'S TALKIN' 'BOUT LOVE SILVER
    CONVENTION
EVERYBODY'S TWISTING FRANK SINATRA
EVERYDAY [A] MOODY BLUES
EVERYDAY [B] DON McLEAN
EVERYDAY [C] SLADE
EVERYDAY [D] JAM MACHINE
EVERYDAY [E] ORCHESTRAL MANOEUVRES IN THE
    DARK
EVERYDAY [F] PHIL COLLINS
EVERYDAY [G] INCOGNITO
EVERYDAY [H] CRAIG McLACHLAN & THE CULPRITS
EVERYDAY [I] AGNELLI & NELSON
EVERYDAY [J] BON JOVI
EVERYDAY GIRL DJ RAP
EVERYDAY I WRITE THE BOOK ELVIS COSTELLO & THE
    ATTRACTIONS
EVERYDAY IS A WINDING ROAD SHERYL CROW
EVERYDAY IS LIKE SUNDAY MORRISSEY
EVERYDAY LIVING WOODENTOPS
EVERYDAY NOW TEXAS
EVERYDAY OF MY LIFE HOUSE TRAFFIC
EVERYDAY PEOPLE SLY & THE FAMILY STONE
EVERYDAY PEOPLE ARETHA FRANKLIN
EVERYDAY SUNSHINE FISHBONE
EVERYDAY THANG MELANIE WILLIAMS
EVERYONE I MEET IS FROM CALIFORNIA AMERICA
EVERYONE SAYS 'HI' DAVID BOWIE
EVERYONE SAYS YOU'RE SO FRAGILE IDLEWILD
EVERYONE'S GONE TO THE MOON JONATHAN KING
EVERYTHING [A] JODY WATLEY
EVERYTHING [B] KICKING BACK WITH TAXMAN
EVERYTHING [C] UHF
EVERYTHING [D] HYSTERIX
EVERYTHING [E] SARAH WASHINGTON
EVERYTHING [F] INXS
EVERYTHING [G] MARY J. BLIGE
EVERYTHING [H] DUM DUMS
EVERYTHING [I] FEFE DOBSON
EVERYTHING [J] ALANIS MORISSETTE
EVERYTHING A MAN COULD EVER NEED GLEN
    CAMPBELL
EVERYTHING ABOUT YOU UGLY KID JOE
EVERYTHING CHANGES TAKE THAT
EVERYTHING COUNTS DEPECHE MODE
EVERYTHING EVENTUALLY APPLETON
EVERYTHING GOOD IS BAD WESTWORLD
EVERYTHING I AM PLASTIC PENNY
(EVERYTHING I DO) I DO IT FOR YOU BRYAN ADAMS
(EVERYTHING I DO) I DO IT FOR YOU FATIMA MANSIONS
(EVERYTHING I DO) I DO IT FOR YOU Q FEATURING
    TONY JACKSON
EVERYTHING I HAVE IS YOURS EDDIE FISHER
EVERYTHING I OWN BREAD
EVERYTHING I OWN KEN BOOTHE
EVERYTHING I OWN BOY GEORGE
EVERYTHING I WANTED DANNII
EVERYTHING I'VE GOT IN MY POCKET MINNIE DRIVER
EVERYTHING IS ALRIGHT (UPTIGHT) C.J. LEWIS
EVERYTHING IS BEAUTIFUL RAY STEVENS
EVERYTHING IS EVERYTHING [A] LAURYN HILL
EVERYTHING IS EVERYTHING [B] PHOENIX
EVERYTHING IS GONNA BE ALRIGHT SOUNDS OF

BLACKNESS

EVERYTHING IS GREAT INNER CIRCLE

EVERYTHING MUST CHANGE PAUL YOUNG

EVERYTHING MUST GO MANIC STREET PREACHERS

EVERYTHING MY HEART DESIRES ADAM RICKITT

EVERYTHING SHE WANTS WHAM!

EVERYTHING STARTS WITH AN 'E' E-ZEE POSSEE

EVERYTHING TO EVERYONE EVERCLEAR

EVERYTHING WILL FLOW SUEDE

EVERYTHING YOU NEED MADISON AVENUE

EVERYTHING YOU WANT VERTICAL HORIZONS

EVERYTHING'L TURN OUT FINE STEALERS WHEEL

EVERYTHING'S ALRIGHT MOJOS

EVERYTHING'S COOL POP WILL EAT ITSELF

EVERYTHING'S GONE GREEN NEW ORDER

EVERYTHING'S GONNA BE ALRIGHT SWEETBOX

EVERYTHING'S NOT YOU STONEPROOF

EVERYTHING'S RUINED FAITH NO MORE

EVERYTHING'S TUESDAY CHAIRMEN OF THE BOARD

EVERYTIME [A] LUSTRAL

EVERYTIME [B] TATYANA ALI

EVERYTIME [C] A1

EVERYTIME [D] BRITNEY SPEARS

EVERYTIME I CLOSE MY EYES BABYFACE

EVERYTIME I THINK OF YOU FM

EVERYTIME YOU NEED ME FRAGMA FEATURING MARIA
RUBIA

EVERYTIME YOU SLEEP DEACON BLUE

EVERYTIME YOU TOUCH ME QFX

EVERYWHERE [A] FLEETWOOD MAC

EVERYWHERE [B] MICHELLE BRANCH

EVERYWHERE I GO [A] ISOTONIK

EVERYWHERE I GO [B] JACKSON BROWNE

EVERYWHERE I LOOK DARYL HALL & JOHN OATES

EVE'S VOLCANO (COVERED IN SIN) JULIAN COPE

EVIDENCE FAITH NO MORE

EVIL LADYTRON

EVIL HEARTED YOU YARDBIRDS

EVIL MAN FATIMA MANSIONS

THE EVIL THAT MEN DO IRON MAIDEN

EVIL TWIN LOVE/HATE

EVIL WOMAN ELECTRIC LIGHT ORCHESTRA

EVOLUTIONDANCE PART ONE (EP) EVOLUTION

EV'RY LITTLE BIT MILLIE SCOTT

EV'RY TIME WE SAY GOODBYE SIMPLY RED

EV'RYWHERE DAVID WHITFIELD

THE EX BILLY TALENT

EX-FACTOR LAURYN HILL

EX-GIRLFRIEND NO DOUBT

EXCERPT FROM A TEENAGE OPERA KEITH WEST

EXCITABLE AMAZULU

EXCITED M PEOPLE

EXCLUSIVE APOLLO PRESENTS HOUSE OF VIRGINISM

EXCLUSIVELY YOURS MARK WYNTER

EXCUSE ME BABY MAGIC LANTERNS

EXCUSE ME MISS JAY-Z

EXHALE (SHOOP SHOOP) WHITNEY HOUSTON

EXODUS [A] BOB MARLEY & THE WAILERS

EXODUS [B] SUNSCREEM

EXODUS – LIVE LEVELLERS

EXORCIST SHADES OF RHYTHM

THE EXORCIST SCIENTIST

EXPANDER FUTURE SOUND OF LONDON

EXPANSIONS SCOTT GROOVES FEATURING ROY AYERS

EXPANSIONS '86 (EXPAND YOUR MIND) CHRIS PAUL
FEATURING DAVID JOSEPH

EXPERIENCE DIANA ROSS

EXPERIMENT IV KATE BUSH

EXPERIMENTS WITH MICE JOHNNY DANKWORTH

EXPLAIN THE REASONS FIRST LIGHT

EXPLORATION OF SPACE COSMIC GATE

EXPO 2000 KRAFTWERK

EXPRESS [A] B.T. EXPRESS

EXPRESS [B] DINA CARROLL

EXPRESS YOUR FREEDOM ANTICAPPELLA

EXPRESS YOURSELF [A] MADONNA

EXPRESS YOURSELF [B] NWA

EXPRESS YOURSELF [C] JIMI POLO

EXPRESSION SALT-N-PEPA

EXPRESSLY (EP) EDWYN COLLINS

EXPRESSO BONGO EP CLIFF RICHARD & THE SHADOWS

EXTACY SHADES OF RHYTHM

EXTENDED PLAY EP BRYAN FERRY

THE EXTENDED PLEASURE OF DANCE (EP) 808 STATE

EXTERMINATE! SNAP FEATURING NIKI HARRIS

EXTREME WAYS MOBY

EXTREMIS HAL FEATURING GILLIAN ANDERSON

EYE BEE M COMMANDER TOM

EYE FOR AN EYE UNKLE

EYE HATE U ARTIST FORMERLY KNOWN AS PRINCE
(AFKAP)

EYE KNOW DE LA SOUL

EYE LEVEL SIMON PARK ORCHESTRA

EYE OF THE TIGER SURVIVOR

EYE OF THE TIGER FRANK BRUNO

EYE TALK FASHION

EYE TO EYE CHAKA KHAN

EYE WONDER APPLES

EYEBALL (EYEBALL PAUL'S THEME) SUNBURST

EYES DON'T LIE TRUCE

THE EYES HAVE IT KAREL FIALKA

EYES OF A STRANGER QUEENSRYCHE

EYES OF BLUE PAUL CARRACK

EYES OF SORROW A GUY CALLED GERALD

THE EYES OF TRUTH ENIGMA

EYES ON YOU JAY SEAN FEATURING RISHI RICH
PROJECT

EYES THAT SEE IN THE DARK KENNY ROGERS

EYES WITHOUT A FACE BILLY IDOL

EZ PASS HAR MAR SUPERSTAR

EZY WOLFSBANE

THE F-WORD BABY BIRD

FA FA FA FA FA (SAD SONG) OTIS REDDING

FABLE ROBERT MILES

FABRICATED LUNACY TERRIS

FABULOUS [A] CHARLIE GRACIE

FABULOUS [B] JAHEIM

THE FACE AND WHY NOT?

FACE THE STRANGE EP THERAPY?

FACE TO FACE SIOUXSIE & THE BANSHEES

FACES 2 UNLIMITED

THE FACES (EP) FACES

FACTS + FIGURES HUGH CORNWELL

FACT OF LIFE [A] OUI 3

THE FACTS OF LIFE [B] DANNY MADDEN

THE FACTS OF LIFE [C] BLACK BOX RECORDER

FACTS OF LOVE CLIMIE FISHER

FADE PARIS ANGELS

FADE INTO YOU MAZZY STAR

FADE TO GREY VISAGE

FADED BEN HARPER

FADER DRUGSTORE

FADING LIKE A FLOWER ROXETTE

FAILURE [A] SKINNY

FAILURE [B] KINGS OF CONVENIENCE

FAILURE'S NOT FLATTERING NEW FOUND GLORY

FAINT LINKIN PARK

A FAIR AFFAIR (JE T'AIME) MISTY OLDLAND

FAIR BLOWS THE WIND FOR FRANCE PELE

FAIR FIGHT DJ ZINC

FAIRGROUND SIMPLY RED

FAIRPLAY SOUL II SOUL FEATURING ROSE WINDROSS

FAIRWEATHER FRIEND SYMPOSIUM

FAIRYTALE DANA

FAIRYTALE OF NEW YORK POGUES FEATURING KIRSTY
MacCOLL

FAIT ACCOMPLI CURVE

FAITH [A] GEORGE MICHAEL

FAITH [B] WEE PAPA GIRL RAPPERS

FAITH CAN MOVE MOUNTAINS JOHNNIE RAY & THE
FOUR LADS

FAITH CAN MOVE MOUNTAINS NAT 'KING' COLE

FAITH CAN MOVE MOUNTAINS JIMMY YOUNG

FAITH HEALER RECOIL

FAITH (IN THE POWER OF LOVE) ROZALLA

FAITH OF THE HEART ROD STEWART

FAITHFUL GO WEST

THE FAITHFUL HUSSAR TED HEATH

THE FAITHFUL HUSSAR LOUIS ARMSTRONG WITH HIS
ALL-STARS

THE FAITHFUL HUSSAR (DON'T CRY MY LOVE) VERA
LYNN

FAITHFULNESS SKIN

FAITHLESS SCRITTI POLITTI

FAKE [A] ALEXANDER O'NEAL

FAKE [B] SIMPLY RED

FAKE FUR URUSEI YATSURA

FAKE PLASTIC TREES RADIOHEAD

THE FAKE SOUND OF PROGRESS LOSTPROPHETS

FAKER AUDIOWEB

FALCON RAH BAND

FALIING IN LOVE AGAIN TECHNO TWINS

THE FALL [A] MINISTRY

THE FALL [B] WAY OUT WEST

FALL AT YOUR FEET CROWDED HOUSE

FALL AT YOUR FEET CM2 FEATURING LISA LAW

FALL BACK DOWN RANCID

FALL BEHIND ME DONNAS

FALL DOWN (SPIRIT OF LOVE) TRAMAINE

FALL EP RIDE

FALL FROM GRACE ESKIMOS & EGYPT

FALL IN LOVE WITH ME [A] EARTH, WIND & FIRE

FALL IN LOVE WITH ME [B] BOOTH & THE BAD ANGEL

FALL IN LOVE WITH YOU CLIFF RICHARD

FALL OUT POLICE

FALL TO LOVE DIESEL PARK WEST

FALL TO PIECES VELVET REVOLVER

THE FALL VS 2003 FALL

FALLEN SARAH McLACHLAN

FALLEN ANGEL [A] FRANKIE VALLI

FALLEN ANGEL [B] POISON

FALLEN ANGEL [C] TRACI LORDS

FALLEN ANGEL [D] ELBOW

FALLEN ANGELS BUFFY SAINTE-MARIE

FALLIN' [A] CONNIE FRANCIS

FALLIN' [B] TEENAGE FANCLUB & DE LA SOUL

FALLIN' [C] ALICIA KEYS

FALLIN' [D] UN-CUT

FALLIN' IN LOVE HAMILTON, JOE FRANK & REYNOLDS

FALLING [A] ROY ORBISON

FALLING [B] JULEE CRUISE

FALLING [C] CATHY DENNIS

FALLING [D] ALISON MOYET

FALLING [E] ANT & DEC

FALLING [F] BOOM!

FALLING [G] LIQUID STATE FEATURING MARCELLA
WOODS

FALLING [H] McALMONT & BUTLER

FALLING ANGELS RIDING (MUTINY) DAVID ESSEX

FALLING APART AT THE SEAMS MARMALADE

FALLING AWAY FROM ME KORN

FALLING IN AND OUT OF LOVE FEMME FATALE

FALLING IN LOVE [A] SURFACE

FALLING IN LOVE [B] SYBIL
FALLING IN LOVE [C] LA BOUCHE
FALLING IN LOVE AGAIN [A] LONDONBEAT
FALLING IN LOVE AGAIN [B] EAGLE-EYE CHERRY
FALLING IN LOVE (IS HARD ON THE KNEES) AEROSMITH
FALLING INTO YOU CELINE DION
FALLING TO PIECES FAITH NO MORE
FALSE ALARM BRONX
FALTER HUNDRED REASONS
FAME [A] DAVID BOWIE
FAME [B] IRENE CARA
FAMILIAR FEELING MOLOKO
FAMILIUS HORRIBILUS POP WILL EAT ITSELF
FAMILY AFFAIR [A] SLY & THE FAMILY STONE
FAMILY AFFAIR [A] B.E.F. FEATURING LALAH
    HATHAWAY
FAMILY AFFAIR [A] SHABBA RANKS FEATURING PATRA
    & TERRY & MONICA
FAMILY AFFAIR [B] MARY J. BLIGE
FAMILY MAN [A] MIKE OLDFIELD FEATURING MAGGIE
    REILLY
FAMILY MAN [A] DARYL HALL & JOHN OATES
FAMILY MAN [A] FLEETWOOD MAC
FAMILY MAN [B] ROACHFORD
FAMILY OF MAN FARM
FAMILY PORTRAIT P!NK
FAMINE SINEAD O'CONNOR
FAN MAIL DICKIES
FAN THE FLAME BARBARA PENNINGTON
FANCY PANTS KENNY
FAN'DABI'DOZI KRANKIES
FANFARE FOR THE COMMON MAN EMERSON, LAKE &
    PALMER
FANLIGHT FANNY CLINTON FORD
FANTASTIC DAY HAIRCUT 100
FANTASTIC VOYAGE COOLIO
FANTASY [A] EARTH, WIND & FIRE
FANTASY [A] BLACK BOX
FANTASY [B] GERARD KENNY
FANTASY [C] FANTASY UFO
FANTASY [D] TEN CITY
FANTASY [E] MARIAH CAREY
FANTASY [F] LEVELLERS
FANTASY [G] APPLETON
FANTASY ISLAND [A] TIGHT FIT
FANTASY ISLAND [B] M PEOPLE
FANTASY REAL GALAXY FEATURING PHIL FEARON
FAR LONGPIGS
FAR ABOVE THE CLOUDS MIKE OLDFIELD
FAR AND AWAY AIDA
FAR AWAY SHIRLEY BASSEY
FAR AWAY EYES ROLLING STONES
FAR FAR AWAY SLADE
FAR FROM HOME LEVELLERS
FAR FROM OVER FRANK STALLONE
FAR GONE AND OUT JESUS & MARY CHAIN
FAR OUT [A] SON'Z OF A LOOP DA LOOP ERA
FAR OUT [B] DEEJAY PUNK-ROC
FAR-OUT SON OF LUNG & THE RAMBLINGS OF A
    MADMAN FUTURE SOUND OF LONDON
FARAWAY PLACES BACHELORS
FAREWELL – BRING IT ON HOME TO ME ROD STEWART
FAREWELL ANGELINA JOAN BAEZ
FAREWELL IS A LONELY SOUND JIMMY RUFFIN
FAREWELL MR SORROW ALL ABOUT EVE
FAREWELL MY SUMMER LOVE MICHAEL JACKSON
FAREWELL MY SUMMER LOVE CHAOS
FAREWELL TO THE MOON YORK
FAREWELL TO TWILIGHT SYMPOSIUM
FARMER BILL'S COWMAN (I WAS KAISER BILL'S
    BATMAN) WURZELS

FARON YOUNG PREFAB SPROUT
FASCINATED [A] LISA B
FASCINATED [B] RAVEN MAIZE
FASCINATING RHYTHM BASS-O-MATIC
FASHION DAVID BOWIE
FASHION '98 GLAMMA KID
FASHION CRISIS HITS NEW YORK FRANK & WALTERS
FASSY HOLE RONI SIZE
FAST AS YOU CAN FIONA APPLE
FAST BOY BLUETONES
FAST CAR [A] TRACY CHAPMAN
FAST CAR [B] DILLINJA
FAST FOOD SONG FAST FOOD ROCKERS
FASTER MANIC STREET PREACHERS
FASTER THAN THE SPEED OF NIGHT BONNIE TYLER
FASTER THE CHASE INME
FASTLOVE GEORGE MICHAEL
FAT BASTARD (EP) MEDWAY
FAT BLACK HEART PELE
FAT BOTTOMED GIRLS QUEEN
FAT LIP SUM 41
FAT NECK BLACK GRAPE
FATAL HESITATION CHRIS DE BURGH
FATHER [A] CHRISTIANS
FATHER [B] LL COOL J
FATHER AND SON BOYZONE
FATHER AND SON RONAN KEATING & YUSUF
FATHER CHRISTMAS DO NOT TOUCH ME GOODIES
FATHER FIGURE GEORGE MICHAEL
FATTIE BUM BUM CARL MALCOLM
FATTIE BUM BUM DIVERSIONS
FAVOURITE SHIRTS (BOY MEETS GIRL) HAIRCUT 100
FAVOURITE THINGS BIG BROVAZ
FBI SHADOWS
FE' REAL MAXI PRIEST FEATURING APACHE INDIAN
F.E.A.R. IAN BROWN
FEAR LOVES THIS PLACE JULIAN COPE
FEAR OF THE DARK [A] GORDON GILTRAP BAND
FEAR OF THE DARK (LIVE) [B] IRON MAIDEN
FEAR SATAN MOGWAI
FEAR, THE MINDKILLER EON
FED UP HOUSE OF PAIN
FEDORA (I'LL BE YOUR DAWG) CARAMBA
FEE FI FO FUM CANDY GIRLS FEATURING SWEET PUSSY
    PAULINE
FEED MY FRANKENSTEIN ALICE COOPER
FEED THE FEELING PERCEPTION
FEED THE TREE BELLY
FEED YOUR ADDICTION EASTERN LANE
FEEDING TIME LOOK
FEEL [A] RUTH JOY
FEEL [B] HOUSE OF LOVE
FEEL [C] ROBBIE WILLIAMS
FEEL EVERY BEAT ELECTRONIC
FEEL FREE SOUL II SOUL FEATURING DO'REEN
FEEL GOOD [A] PHATS & SMALL
FEEL GOOD [B] MADASUN
FEEL GOOD TIME P!NK FEATURING WILLIAM ORBIT
FEEL IT [A] HI-LUX
FEEL IT [B] CAROL BAILEY
FEEL IT [C] NENEH CHERRY
FEEL IT [D] TAMPERER FEATURING MAYA
FEEL IT [E] INAYA DAY
FEEL IT BOY BEENIE MAN FEATURING JANET JACKSON
FEEL LIKE CALLING HOME MR BIG
FEEL LIKE CHANGE BLACK
FEEL LIKE MAKIN' LOVE [A] GEORGE BENSON
FEEL LIKE MAKIN' LOVE [B] BAD COMPANY
FEEL LIKE MAKING LOVE [A] ROBERTA FLACK
FEEL LIKE MAKING LOVE [B] PAULINE HENRY
FEEL LIKE SINGIN' [A] SANDY B

FEEL LIKE SINGING [B] TAK TIX
FEEL ME BLANCMANGE
FEEL ME FLOW NAUGHTY BY NATURE
FEEL MY BODY FRANK'O MOIRAGHI FEATURING
    AMNESIA
FEEL NO PAIN SADE
FEEL SO FINE JOHNNY PRESTON
FEEL SO GOOD [A] MA$E
FEEL SO GOOD [B] JON THE DENTIST VS OLLIE JAYE
FEEL SO HIGH DES'REE
FEEL SO REAL [A] STEVE ARRINGTON
FEEL SO REAL [B] DREAM FREQUENCY FEATURING
    DEBBIE SHARP
FEEL SURREAL FREEFALL FEATURING PSYCHOTROPIC
FEEL THA VIBE THAT KID CHRIS
FEEL THE BEAT [A] CAMISRA
FEEL THE BEAT [B] DARUDE
FEEL THE DRUM (EP) PARKS & WILSON
FEEL THE DRUMS NATIVE
FEEL THE HEAT RONI SIZE
FEEL THE MUSIC GURU
FEEL THE NEED [A] LEIF GARRETT
FEEL THE NEED [A] G NATION FEATURING ROSIE
FEEL THE NEED [B] JT TAYLOR
FEEL THE NEED [C] WEIRD SCIENCE
FEEL THE NEED IN ME DETROIT EMERALDS
FEEL THE NEED IN ME FORREST
FEEL THE NEED IN ME SHAKIN' STEVENS
FEEL THE PAIN DINOSAUR Jr.
FEEL THE RAINDROPS ADVENTURES
FEEL THE REAL DAVID BENDETH
FEEL THE RHYTHM [A] JAZZI P
FEEL THE RHYTHM [B] TERRORIZE
FEEL THE RHYTHM [C] JINNY
FEEL THE SAME TRIPLE X
FEEL THE SUNSHINE ALEX REECE
FEEL WHAT YOU WANT KRISTINE W
FEELIN' LA'S
FEELIN' ALRIGHT E.Y.C.
THE FEELIN (CLAP YOUR HANDS) RHYTHMATIC JUNKIES
FEELIN' FINE ULTRABEAT
FEELIN' INSIDE BOBBY BROWN
FEELIN' SO GOOD JENNIFER LOPEZ FEATURING BIG PUN
    & FAT JOE
FEELIN' THE SAME WAY NORAH JONES
FEELIN' U SHY FX & T-POWER FEATURING KELE LE ROC
FEELIN' WAY TOO DAMN GOOD NICKELBACK
FEELIN' YOU ALI
THE FEELING [A] URBAN HYPE
THE FEELING [B] TIN TIN OUT FEATURING SWEET TEE
FEELING FOR YOU CASSIUS
FEELING GOOD NINA SIMONE
FEELING GOOD HUFF & HERB
FEELING GOOD MUSE
FEELING IT TOO 3 JAYS
FEELING SO REAL MOBY
FEELING THE LOVE REACTOR
FEELING THIS BLINK 182
FEELING THIS WAY CONDUCTOR & THE COWBOY
FEELINGS MORRIS ALBERT
FEELINGS OF FOREVER TIFFANY
FEELS GOOD (DON'T WORRY BOUT A THING) NAUGHTY
    BY NATURE FEATURING 3LW
(FEELS LIKE) HEAVEN [A] FICTION FACTORY
FEELS LIKE HEAVEN [B] URBAN COOKIE COLLECTIVE
FEELS LIKE I'M IN LOVE KELLY MARIE
FEELS LIKE THE FIRST TIME [A] FOREIGNER
FEELS LIKE THE FIRST TIME [B] SINITTA
FEELS LIKE THE RIGHT TIME SHAKATAK
FEELS SO GOOD [A] VAN HALEN
FEELS SO GOOD [B] XSCAPE

FEELS SO GOOD [C] ZERO VU FEATURING LORNA B
FEELS SO GOOD [D] MELANIE B
FEELS SO REAL (WON'T LET GO) PATRICE RUSHEN
FEELS SO RIGHT VICTOR SIMONELLI PRESENTS SOLUTION
FEENIN' JODECI
FEET UP GUY MITCHELL
FELICITY ORANGE JUICE
FELL IN LOVE WITH A BOY JOSS STONE
FELL IN LOVE WITH A GIRL WHITE STRIPES
FELL ON BLACK DAYS SOUNDGARDEN
FEMALE INTUITION MAI TAI
FEMALE OF THE SPECIES SPACE
FERGUS SINGS THE BLUES DEACON BLUE
FERNANDO ABBA
FERRIS WHEEL EVERLY BROTHERS
FERRY ACROSS THE MERSEY GERRY & THE PACEMAKERS
FERRY 'CROSS THE MERSEY CHRISTIANS, HOLLY JOHNSON, PAUL McCARTNEY, GERRY MARSDEN & STOCK AITKEN WATERMAN
FESTIVAL TIME SAN REMO STRINGS
FEUER FREI RAMMSTEIN
FEVER [A] PEGGY LEE
FEVER [A] HELEN SHAPIRO
FEVER [A] McCOYS
FEVER [A] MADONNA
FEVER [B] S-J
FEVER [C] STARSAILOR
FEVER CALLED LOVE RHC
FEVER FOR THE FLAVA HOT ACTION COP
FEVER PITCH THE EP PRETENDERS, LA'S, ORLANDO, NICK HORNBY
FICTION OF LIFE CHINA DRUM
FIELD OF DREAMS FLIP & FILL FEATURING JO JAMES
FIELDS OF FIRE (400 MILES) BIG COUNTRY
FIELDS OF GOLD STING
THE FIELDS OF LOVE ATB FEATURING YORK
FIESTA [A] POGUES
FIESTA [B] R KELLY
!FIESTA FATAL! B-TRIBE
FIFTEEN FEET OF PURE WHITE SNOW NICK CAVE & THE BAD SEEDS
15 MINUTES OF FAME SHEEP ON DRUGS
15 STEPS (EP) MONKEY MAFIA
15 WAYS FALL
15 YEARS (EP) LEVELLERS
5TH ANNIVERSARY EP JUDGE DREAD
A FIFTH OF BEETHOVEN WALTER MURPHY & THE BIG APPLE BAND
51ST STATE NEW MODEL ARMY
50FT QUEENIE PJ HARVEY
50:50 LEMAR
50 WAYS TO LEAVE YOUR LOVER PAUL SIMON
FIFTY-FOUR SEA LEVEL
54-66 (WAS MY NUMBER) ASWAD
FIFTY GRAND FOR CHRISTMAS PAUL HOLT
57 BIFFY CLYRO
57 CHANNELS (AND NOTHIN' ON) BRUCE SPRINGSTEEN
59TH STREET BRIDGE SONG (FEELING GROOVY) HARPERS BIZARRE
FIGARO BROTHERHOOD OF MAN
FIGHT McKOY
THE FIGHT MARTY WILDE
FIGHT FOR OURSELVES SPANDAU BALLET
FIGHT FOR YOUR RIGHT (TO PARTY) NYCC
FIGHT MUSIC D12
THE FIGHT SONG MARILYN MANSON
FIGHT TEST FLAMING LIPS
FIGHT THE POWER PUBLIC ENEMY

FIGHT THE YOUTH FISHBONE
FIGHTER CHRISTINA AGUILERA
FIGHTING FIT GENE
FIGURE OF 8 GRID
FIGURE OF EIGHT PAUL McCARTNEY
FIJI ATLANTIS VS AVATAR
FILL HER UP GENE
FILL ME IN CRAIG DAVID
FILLING UP WITH HEAVEN HUMAN LEAGUE
A FILM FOR THE FUTURE IDLEWILD
FILM MAKER COOPER TEMPLE CLAUSE
FILMSTAR SUEDE
FILTHY SAINT ETIENNE
THE FINAL ARREARS MULL HISTORICAL SOCIETY
THE FINAL COUNTDOWN EUROPE
FINALLY [A] CE CE PENISTON
FINALLY [B] KINGS OF TOMORROW FEATURING JULIE McKNIGHT
FINALLY FOUND HONEYZ
FINCHLEY CENTRAL NEW VAUDEVILLE BAND
FIND A WAY [A] COLDCUT FEATURING QUEEN LATIFAH
FIND A WAY [B] A TRIBE CALLED QUEST
FIND 'EM, FOOL 'EM, FORGET 'EM S-EXPRESS
FIND ME (ODYSSEY TO ANYOONA) JAM & SPOON FEATURING PLAVKA
FIND MY LOVE FAIRGROUND ATTRACTION
FIND MY WAY BACK HOME NASHVILLE TEENS
FIND THE ANSWER WITHIN BOO RADLEYS
FIND THE COLOUR FEEDER
FIND THE RIVER R.E.M.
FIND THE TIME [A] FIVE STAR
FIND THE TIME (PART ONE) [B] QUADROPHONIA
FINDERS KEEPERS CHAIRMEN OF THE BOARD
FINE DAY [A] ROLF HARRIS
FINE DAY [B] KIRSTY HAWKSHAW
FINE TIME [A] NEW ORDER
FINE TIME [B] YAZZ
FINER NIGHTMARES ON WAX
FINER FEELINGS KYLIE MINOGUE
THE FINEST S.O.S. BAND
THE FINEST TRUCE
FINEST DREAMS RICHARD X FEATURING KELIS
FINEST WORKSONG R.E.M.
FINETIME CAST
FINGER OF SUSPICION DICKIE VALENTINE WITH THE STARGAZERS
FINGERS AND THUMBS (COLD SUMMER'S DAY) ERASURE
FINGERS OF LOVE CROWDED HOUSE
FINGS AIN'T WOT THEY USED T'BE MAX BYGRAVES
FINGS AIN'T WOT THEY USED TO BE RUSS CONWAY
FINISHED SYMPHONY HYBRID
FIRE [A] CRAZY WORLD OF ARTHUR BROWN
FIRE [B] POINTER SISTERS
FIRE [B] BRUCE SPRINGSTEEN
FIRE [C] U2
FIRE [D] SLY & ROBBIE
FIRE [E] PRODIGY
FIRE [F] PRIZNA FEATURING DEMOLITION MAN
FIRE [G] SCOOTER
FIRE [H] BUSTA RHYMES
FIRE [I] MOUSSE T FEATURING EMMA LANFORD
FIRE AND RAIN JAMES TAYLOR
FIRE BRIGADE MOVE
FIRE DOWN BELOW JERI SOUTHERN
FIRE DOWN BELOW SHIRLEY BASSEY
FIRE IN MY HEART SUPER FURRY ANIMALS
FIRE ISLAND FIRE ISLAND
FIRE OF LOVE JUNGLE HIGH WITH BLUE PEARL
FIRE UP THE SHOESAW LIONROCK

FIRE WOMAN CULT
FIRE WORKS SIOUXSIE & THE BANSHEES
FIREBALL [A] DON SPENCER
FIREBALL [B] DEEP PURPLE
FIRED UP [A] ELEVATORMAN
FIRED UP! [B] FUNKY GREEN DOGS
FIREFLY INME
FIREPILE (EP) THROWING MUSES
FIRES BURNING RUN TINGS
FIRESTARTER PRODIGY
FIREWIRE COSMIC GATE
FIREWORKS ROXETTE
FIREWORKS EP EMBRACE
FIRM BIZZ FIRM FEATURING DAWN ROBINSON
FIRST ATHEIST TABERNACLE CHOIR SPITTING IMAGE
FIRST BOY IN THIS TOWN (LOVE SICK) SCRITTI POLITTI
FIRST CUT IS THE DEEPEST P.P. ARNOLD
FIRST CUT IS THE DEEPEST ROD STEWART
FIRST CUT IS THE DEEPEST SHERYL CROW
FIRST DATE BLINK 182
FIRST DAY FUTUREHEADS
THE FIRST DAY (HORIZON) MAN WITH NO NAME
FIRST DAY OF MY LIFE RASMUS
FIRST IMPRESSIONS IMPRESSIONS
FIRST IT GIVETH QUEENS OF THE STONE AGE
THE FIRST MAN YOU REMEMBER MICHAEL BALL & DIANA MORRISON
1ST MAN IN SPACE ALL SEEING I
THE FIRST NIGHT MONICA
FIRST OF MAY BEE GEES
1ST OF THA MONTH BONE THUGS-N-HARMONY
FIRST OF THE GANG TO DIE MORRISSEY
THE FIRST PICTURE OF YOU LOTUS EATERS
FIRST TASTE OF LOVE BEN E. KING
THE FIRST THE LAST THE ETERNITY SNAP FEATURING SUMMER
FIRST THING IN THE MORNING KIKI DEE
THE FIRST TIME [A] ADAM FAITH & THE ROULETTES
THE FIRST TIME [B] ROBIN BECK
THE FIRST TIME [C] SURFACE
FIRST TIME EVER JOANNA LAW
THE FIRST TIME EVER I SAW YOUR FACE ROBERTA FLACK
THE FIRST TIME EVER I SAW YOUR FACE CELINE DION
FIRST WE TAKE MANHATTAN JENNIFER WARNES
FISH OUT OF WATER ONE MINUTE SILENCE
FISHERMAN'S BLUES WATERBOYS
FIT BUT YOU KNOW IT STREETS
THE $5.98 EP – GARAGE DAYS REVISITED METALLICA
5 COLOURS IN HER HAIR McFLY
FIVE FATHOMS EVERYTHING BUT THE GIRL
5.15 WHO
555 DELAKOTA
5-4-3-2-1 MANFRED MANN
FIVE GET OVER EXCITED HOUSEMARTINS
500 (SHAKE BABY SHAKE) LUSH
FIVE LITTLE FINGERS FRANKIE McBRIDE
FIVE LIVE EP GEORGE MICHAEL & QUEEN WITH LISA STANSFIELD
FIVE MILES OUT MIKE OLDFIELD FEATURING MAGGIE REILLY
5 MILE (THESE ARE THE DAYS) TURIN BRAKES
5 MILES TO EMPTY BROWNSTONE
FIVE MINUTES [A] STRANGLERS
5 MINUTES [B] LIL' MO FEATURING MISSY 'MISDEMEANOR' ELLIOTT
5 O'CLOCK NONCHALANT
5 O'CLOCK WORLD JULIAN COPE
5-7-0-5 CITY BOY
5, 6, 7, 8 STEPS
5 STEPS DRU HILL

5000 MINUTES OF PAIN MINUTEMAN
FIX BLACKstreet
FIX MY SINK DJ SNEAK FEATURING BEAR WHO
FIX UP LOOK SHARP DIZZEE RASCAL
FIXATION ANDY LING
FIXER VENT 414
FLAGPOLE SITTA HARVEY DANGER
FLAMBOYANT PET SHOP BOYS
FLAME SEBADOH
THE FLAME [A] ARCADIA
THE FLAME [B] FINE YOUNG CANNIBALS
THE FLAME STILL BURNS JIMMY NAIL WITH STRANGE FRUIT
THE FLAME TREES OF THIKA VIDEO SYMPHONIC
FLAMES OF PARADISE JENNIFER RUSH & ELTON JOHN
FLAMING JUNE BT
FLAMING SWORD CARE
FLAP YOUR WINGS NELLY
FLASH [A] QUEEN
FLASH [A] QUEEN & VANGUARD
FLASH [B] BBE
FLASH [C] BK & NICK SENTIENCE
FLASH [D] GRIFTERS
FLASHBACK IMAGINATION
FLASHBACK JACK ADAMSKI
FLASHDANCE DEEP DISH
FLASHDANCE...WHAT A FEELING IRENE CARA
FLASHDANCE...WHAT A FEELING BJORN AGAIN
THE FLASHER MISTURA FEATURING LLOYD MICHELS
FLAT BEAT MR OIZO
FLATLINERS NEBULA II
FLAVA [A] PETER ANDRE
FLAVA [B] IMAJIN
FLAVA IN YOUR EAR CRAIG MACK
FLAVOR OF THE WEAK AMERICAN HI-FI
FLAVOUR OF THE OLD SCHOOL BEVERLEY KNIGHT
FLAWLESS ONES
FLAWLESS (GO TO THE CITY) GEORGE MICHAEL
FLEE FLY FLO FE-M@IL
FLESH A SPLIT SECOND
FLESH JAN JOHNSTON
FLESH FOR FANTASY BILLY IDOL
FLESH OF MY FLESH ORANGE JUICE
FLETCH THEME HAROLD FALTERMEYER
FLIGHT 643 DJ TIESTO
FLIGHT OF ICARUS IRON MAIDEN
FLIP JESSE GREEN
FLIP REVERSE BLAZIN' SQUAD
THE FLIPSIDE MOLOKO
FLIRT JONATHAN KING
FLIRTATION WALTZ WINIFRED ATWELL
F.L.M. MEL & KIM
FLOAT ON [A] FLOATERS
FLOAT ON [B] MODEST MOUSE
FLOATATION GRID
FLOATING TERRA FIRMA
FLOATING IN THE WIND HUDSON-FORD
FLOBBADANCE BILL & BEN
FLOETIC FLOETRY
FLOODLIT WORLD ULTRASOUND
THE FLOOR JOHNNY GILL
FLOOR SPACE OUR HOUSE
FLOOR-ESSENCE MAN WITH NO NAME
THE FLORAL DANCE BRIGHOUSE & RASTRICK BRASS BAND
FLORAL DANCE TERRY WOGAN
FLORIBUNDA MOTHER'S PRIDE
FLOWER DUET (FROM LAKME) MADY MESPLE & DANIELLE MILLET WITH THE PARIS OPERACOMIQUE ORCHESTRA CONDUCTED BY ALAIN LOMBARD

FLOWER DUET JONATHAN PETERS PRESENTS LUMINAIRE
FLOWER OF SCOTLAND SCOTTISH RUGBY TEAM WITH RONNIE BROWNE
FLOWER OF THE WEST RUNRIG
FLOWERS [A] TITIYO
FLOWERS [B] SWEET FEMALE ATTITUDE
FLOWERS IN DECEMBER MAZZY STAR
FLOWERS IN THE RAIN MOVE
FLOWERS IN THE WINDOW TRAVIS
FLOWERS OF ROMANCE PUBLIC IMAGE LTD.
FLOWERS ON THE WALL STATLER BROTHERS
FLOWERZ ARMAND VAN HELDEN FEATURING ROLAND CLARK
FLOWTATION VINCENT DE MOOR
FLOY JOY SUPREMES
THE FLY [A] U2
FLY [B] SUGAR RAY
FLY [C] POB FEATURING DJ PATRICK REID
FLY [D] MARK JOSEPH
FLY [E] MATT GOSS
FLY AWAY [A] HADDAWAY
FLY AWAY [B] LENNY KRAVITZ
FLY AWAY [C] VINCENT DE MOOR
FLY AWAY (BYE BYE) EYES CREAM
FLY BI TEEBONE FEATURING MC KIE & MC SPARKS
FLY BY II BLUE
FLY GIRL QUEEN LATIFAH
FLY LIFE BASEMENT JAXX
FLY LIKE AN EAGLE SEAL
FLY ON THE WINGS OF LOVE XTM & DJ CHUCKY PRESENTS ANNIA
FLY ROBIN FLY SILVER CONVENTION
FLY TO THE ANGELS SLAUGHTER
FLY TOO HIGH JANIS IAN
FLY WITH ME COLOURSOUND
FLYING [A] CAST
FLYING [B] BRYAN ADAMS
FLYING ELVIS LEILANI
FLYING HIGH [A] COMMODORES
FLYING HIGH [B] FREEEZ
FLYING HIGH [C] CAPTAIN HOLLYWOOD PROJECT
FLYING MACHINE CLIFF RICHARD
FLYING SAUCER WEDDING PRESENT
THE FLYING SONG PQM FEATURING CICA
FLYING WITHOUT WINGS WESTLIFE
FLYSWATER EELS
FM (NO STATIC AT ALL) STEELY DAN
FOE-DEE-O-DEE RUBETTES
FOG ON THE TYNE (REVISITED) GAZZA & LINDISFARNE
FOGGY MOUNTAIN BREAKDOWN LESTER FLATT & EARL SCRUGGS
FOGHORN A
THE FOLK SINGER TOMMY ROE
FOLLOW DA LEADER NIGEL & MARVIN
FOLLOW ME [A] JT TAYLOR
FOLLOW ME [B] ALY-US
FOLLOW ME [C] ATOMIC KITTEN
FOLLOW ME [D] UNCLE KRACKER
FOLLOW THAT DREAM EP ELVIS PRESLEY
FOLLOW THE LEADER ERIC B & RAKIM
FOLLOW THE LEADERS KILLING JOKE
FOLLOW THE RULES LIVIN' JOY
FOLLOW YOU DOWN GIN BLOSSOMS
FOLLOW YOU FOLLOW ME GENESIS
FOLLOW YOU FOLLOW ME SONNY JONES FEATURING TARA CHASE
FOLLOWED THE WAVES AUF DER MAUR
FOLLOWING BANGLES
THE FOOD CHRISTMAS EP VARIOUS ARTISTS (EP'S & LPS)
FOOD FOR THOUGHT [A] BARRON KNIGHTS

FOOD FOR THOUGHT [B] UB40
FOOL [A] ELVIS PRESLEY
FOOL [B] AL MATTHEWS
FOOL [C] MANSUN
FOOL AGAIN WESTLIFE
A FOOL AM I CILLA BLACK
FOOL FOR LOVE RUSSELL
FOOL FOR YOUR LOVING WHITESNAKE
FOOL (IF YOU THINK IT'S OVER) CHRIS REA
FOOL IF YOU THINK IT'S OVER ELKIE BROOKS
A FOOL NEVER LEARNS ANDY WILLIAMS
FOOL NO MORE S CLUB 8
FOOL NUMBER ONE BRENDA LEE
THE FOOL ON THE HILL SHIRLEY BASSEY
A FOOL SUCH AS I ELVIS PRESLEY
FOOL TO CRY ROLLING STONES
FOOLED AROUND AND FELL IN LOVE ELVIN BISHOP
FOOLED BY A SMILE SWING OUT SISTER
FOOLIN' YOURSELF PAUL HARDCASTLE
FOOLISH ASHANTI
FOOLISH BEAT DEBBIE GIBSON
FOOLISH LITTLE GIRL SHIRELLES
FOOL'S GOLD STONE ROSES
FOOL'S PARADISE MELI'SA MORGAN
FOOLS RUSH IN BROOK BENTON
FOOLS RUSH IN RICK NELSON
FOOT STOMPIN' MUSIC HAMILTON BOHANNON
FOOT TAPPER SHADOWS
FOOTLOOSE KENNY LOGGINS
FOOTPRINT DISCO CITIZENS
FOOTPRINTS IN THE SNOW JOHNNY DUNCAN & THE BLUE GRASS BOYS
FOOTSEE WIGAN'S CHOSEN FEW
FOOTSTEPS [A] RONNIE CARROLL
FOOTSTEPS [A] STEVE LAWRENCE
FOOTSTEPS [A] SHOWADDYWADDY
FOOTSTEPS [B] STILTSKIN
FOOTSTEPS [C] DANIEL O'DONNELL
FOOTSTEPS FOLLOWING ME FRANCES NERO
FOR A FEW DOLLARS MORE SMOKIE
FOR A FRIEND COMMUNARDS
FOR A LIFETIME ASCENSION
FOR A PENNY PAT BOONE
FOR ALL THAT YOU WANT GARY BARLOW
FOR ALL THE COWS FOO FIGHTERS
FOR ALL TIME CATHERINE ZETA JONES
FOR ALL WE KNOW SHIRLEY BASSEY
FOR ALL WE KNOW CARPENTERS
FOR ALL WE KNOW NICKI FRENCH
FOR AMERICA RED BOX
FOR AN ANGEL PAUL VAN DYK
FOR BRITAIN ONLY ALICE COOPER
(FOR GOD'S SAKE) GIVE MORE POWER TO THE PEOPLE CHI-LITES
FOR HER LIGHT FIELDS OF THE NEPHILIM
FOR LOVE (EP) LUSH
FOR LOVERS WOLFMAN FEATURING PETE DOHERTY
FOR MAMA MATT MONRO
FOR OLD TIME'S SAKE MILLICAN & NESBITT
FOR ONCE IN MY LIFE STEVIE WONDER
FOR ONCE IN MY LIFE DOROTHY SQUIRES
FOR REAL TRICKY
FOR SPACIOUS LIES NORMAN COOK FEATURING LESTER
FOR SURE SCOOCH
FOR THE DEAD GENE
FOR THE GOOD TIMES PERRY COMO
FOR THOSE ABOUT TO ROCK (WE SALUTE YOU) AC/DC
FOR TOMORROW BLUR
FOR WHAT IT'S WORTH [A] OUI 3
FOR WHAT IT'S WORTH [B] CARDIGANS

FOR WHAT YOU DREAM OF BEDROCK FEATURING KYO
FOR WHOM THE BELL TOLLS [A] SIMON DUPREE & THE
    BIG SOUND
FOR WHOM THE BELL TOLLS [B] BEE GEES
FOR YOU [A] RICK NELSON
FOR YOU [B] FARMERS BOYS
FOR YOU [C] SNOWY WHITE
FOR YOU [D] ELECTRONIC
FOR YOU [E] STAIND
FOR YOU FOR LOVE AVERAGE WHITE BAND
FOR YOU I WILL MONICA
FOR YOUR BABIES SIMPLY RED
FOR YOUR BLUE EYES ONLY TONY HADLEY
FOR YOUR EYES ONLY SHEENA EASTON
FOR YOUR LOVE [A] YARDBIRDS
FOR YOUR LOVE [B] STEVIE WONDER
FORBIDDEN CITY ELECTRONIC
FORBIDDEN COLOURS DAVID SYLVIAN & RYUICHI
    SAKAMOTO
FORBIDDEN FRUIT PAUL VAN DYK
FORBIDDEN ZONE BEDROCK
FORCA NELLY FURTADO
THE FORCE BEHIND THE POWER DIANA ROSS
FOREIGN SAND ROGER TAYLOR & YOSHIKI
FORERUNNER NATURAL BORN GROOVES
A FOREST CURE
FOREST FIRE LLOYD COLE & THE COMMOTIONS
FOREVER [A] ROY WOOD
FOREVER [B] KISS
FOREVER [C] DAMAGE
FOREVER [D] CHARLATANS
FOREVER [E] TINA COUSINS
FOREVER [F] DEE DEE
FOREVER [G] N-TRANCE
FOREVER [H] TRINITY-X
FOREVER AND A DAY [A] BROTHERS IN RHYTHM
    PRESENT CHARVONI
FOREVER AND A DAY [B] STATE ONE
FOREVER AND EVER SLIK
FOREVER AND EVER, AMEN RANDY TRAVIS
FOREVER AND FOR ALWAYS SHANIA TWAIN
FOREVER AS ONE VENGABOYS
FOREVER AUTUMN JUSTIN HAYWARD
FOREVER CAME TODAY DIANA ROSS & THE SUPREMES
FOREVER FAILURE PARADISE LOST
FOREVER FREE W.A.S.P.
FOREVER GIRL OTT
FOREVER IN BLUE JEANS NEIL DIAMOND
FOREVER IN LOVE KENNY G
FOREVER J TERRY HALL
A FOREVER KIND OF LOVE BOBBY VEE
(FOREVER) LIVE AND DIE ORCHESTRAL MANOEUVRES
    IN THE DARK
FOREVER LOVE GARY BARLOW
FOREVER MAN ERIC CLAPTON
FOREVER MAN (HOW MANY TIMES) BEATCHUGGERS
    FEATURING ERIC CLAPTON
FOREVER MORE [A] PUFF JOHNSON
FOREVER MORE [B] MOLOKO
FOREVER NOW LEVEL 42
FOREVER REELING KINESIS
FOREVER TOGETHER RAVEN MAIZE
FOREVER YOUNG [A] ROD STEWART
FOREVER YOUNG [B] INTERACTIVE
FOREVER YOUNG [C] 4 VINI FEATURING ELIZABETH
    TROY
FOREVER YOUR GIRL PAULA ABDUL
FOREVERGREEN FINITRIBE
FORGET ABOUT THE WORLD GABRIELLE
FORGET ABOUT TOMORROW FEEDER
FORGET ABOUT YOU MOTORS

FORGET HIM BOBBY RYDELL
FORGET HIM BILLY FURY
FORGET I WAS A G WHITEHEAD BROTHERS
FORGET-ME-NOT [A] VERA LYNN
FORGET ME KNOTS RONI SIZE
FORGET ME NOT [B] EDEN KANE
FORGET ME NOT [C] MARTHA REEVES & THE
    VANDELLAS
FORGET ME NOTS PATRICE RUSHEN
FORGET ME NOTS TONGUE 'N' CHEEK
FORGIVE ME LYNDEN DAVID HALL
FORGIVEN (I FEEL YOUR LOVE) SPACE BROTHERS
FORGOT ABOUT DRE DR. DRE FEATURING EMINEM
FORGOTTEN DREAMS LEROY ANDERSON & HIS POPS
    CONCERT ORCHESTRA
FORGOTTEN DREAMS CYRIL STAPLETON
FORGOTTEN TOWN CHRISTIANS
FORMED A BAND ART BRUT
FORMULAE JJ72
FORSAKEN DREAMS DILLINJA
FORT WORTH JAIL LONNIE DONEGAN
FORTRESS AROUND YOUR HEART STING
FORTRESS EUROPE ASIAN DUB FOUNDATION
FORTUNE FADED RED HOT CHILI PEPPERS
FORTUNES OF WAR FISH
40 MILES CONGRESS
FORTY MILES OF BAD ROAD DUANE EDDY & THE REBELS
40 YEARS PAUL HARDCASTLE
48 CRASH SUZI QUATRO
45 RPM POPPYFIELDS
FORWARD THE REVOLUTION SPIRAL TRIBE
FOUND A CURE ULTRA NATE
FOUND LOVE DOUBLE DEE FEATURING DANY
FOUND OUT ABOUT YOU GIN BLOSSOMS
FOUND OUT TOO LATE 999
FOUND THAT SOUL MANIC STREET PREACHERS
FOUND YOU DODGY
FOUNDATION BEENIE MAN AND THE TAXI GANG
FOUNTAIN O' YOUTH CANDYLAND
FOUR BACHARACH AND DAVID SONGS EP DEACON
    BLUE
FOUR BIG SPEAKERS WHALE FEATURING BUS 75
FOUR FROM TOYAH EP TOYAH
FOUR LETTER WORD KIM WILDE
FOUR LITTLE HEELS BRIAN HYLAND
FOUR LITTLE HEELS AVONS
FOUR MINUTE WARNING MARK OWEN
4 MORE DE LA SOUL FEATURING ZHANE
FOUR MORE FROM TOYAH EP TOYAH
4 MY PEOPLE MISSY ELLIOTT
4 PAGE LETTER AALIYAH
THE 4 PLAYS EPS R KELLY
FOUR SEASONS IN ONE DAY CROWDED HOUSE
4 SEASONS OF LONELINESS BOYZ II MEN
FOUR STRONG WINDS NEIL YOUNG
FOUR TO THE FLOOR STARSAILOR
FOURPLAY (EP) VARIOUS ARTISTS (EP'S & LPS)
14 HOURS TO SAVE THE EARTH TOMSKI
FOURTH RENDEZ-VOUS JEAN-MICHEL JARRE
FOX FORCE FIVE CHRIS & JAMES
FOX ON THE RUN [A] MANFRED MANN
FOX ON THE RUN [B] SWEET
FOXHOLE TELEVISION
FOXY FOXY MOTT THE HOOPLE
'FRAGGLE ROCK' THEME FRAGGLES
FRAGILE STING
FRAGILE JULIO IGLESIAS
FRAGILE THING BIG COUNTRY FEATURING EDDI
    READER
FRANCESCA – THE MADDENING GLARE SPECIAL NEEDS
THE FRANK SONATA LONGPIGS

FRANKENSTEIN EDGAR WINTER GROUP
FRANKIE SISTER SLEDGE
FRANKIE AND JOHNNY MR ACKER BILK & HIS
    PARAMOUNT JAZZ BAND
FRANKIE AND JOHNNY SAM COOKE
FRANKIE AND JOHNNY ELVIS PRESLEY
FRANTIC METALLICA
FREAK [A] BRUCE FOXTON
FREAK [B] SILVERCHAIR
FREAK [C] STRANGELOVE
FREAK IT! STUDIO 45
FREAK LIKE ME ADINA HOWARD
FREAK LIKE ME TRU FAITH & DUB CONSPIRACY
FREAK LIKE ME SUGABABES
FREAK ME SILK
FREAK ME ANOTHER LEVEL
FREAK MODE REELISTS
FREAK ON A LEASH KORN
FREAKIN' IT WILL SMITH
FREAKIN' OUT GRAHAM COXON
FREAKIN' YOU JUNGLE BROTHERS
FREAKS LIVE
THE FREAKS COME OUT CEVIN FISHER'S BIG BREAK
FREAKS (LIVE) MARILLION
FREAKY BE BEAUTIFUL MOIST
FREAKYTIME POINT BREAK
THE FRED EP FRED EP
FREDDY KREUGER REUBEN
FREDERICK PATTI SMITH GROUP
FREE [A] DENIECE WILLIAMS
FREE [B] CURIOSITY KILLED THE CAT
FREE [C] WILL DOWNING
FREE [D] STEVIE WONDER
FREE [E] DJ QUICKSILVER
FREE [F] ULTRA NATE
FREE [G] JOHN '00' FLEMING
FREE [H] VAST
FREE [I] CLAIRE FREELAND
FREE [J] MYA
FREE [K] ESTELLE
FREE AS A BIRD BEATLES
FREE AT LAST SIMON
FREE BIRD LYNYRD SKYNYRD
FREE (C'MON) CATCH
FREE ELECTRIC BAND ALBERT HAMMOND
FREE EP FREE
FREE FALLIN' TOM PETTY
FREE HUEY BOO RADLEYS
FREE (LET IT BE) STUART
FREE LOVE JULIET ROBERTS
FREE ME [A] ROGER DALTREY
FREE ME [B] CAST
FREE ME [C] EMMA BUNTON
FREE 'N' EASY ALMIGHTY
FREE RANGE FALL
FREE SATPAL RAM ASIAN DUB FOUNDATION
FREE SPIRIT KIM APPLEBY
THE FREE STYLE MEGA-MIX BOBBY BROWN
FREE TO DECIDE CRANBERRIES
FREE TO FALL DEBBIE HARRY
FREE TO LOVE AGAIN SUZETTE CHARLES
FREE WORLD KIRSTY MacCOLL
FREE YOUR BODY PRAGA KHAN FEATURING JADE 4 U
FREE YOUR MIND [A] EN VOGUE
FREE YOUR MIND [B] SPACE BABY
FREE YOURSELF UNTOUCHABLES
FREE, GAY AND HAPPY COMING OUT CREW
FREE/SAIL ON CHANTE MOORE
FREEBASE TALL PAUL
FREED FROM DESIRE GALA
FREEDOM [A] WHAM!

FREEDOM [B] ALICE COOPER
FREEDOM [C] GEORGE MICHAEL
FREEDOM [C] ROBBIE WILLIAMS
FREEDOM [D] A HOMEBOY, A HIPPIE & A FUNKI DREDD
FREEDOM [E] LONDON BOYS
FREEDOM [F] MICHELLE GAYLE
FREEDOM [G] SHIVA
FREEDOM [H] ROBERT MILES FEATURING KATHY SLEDGE
FREEDOM [I] ERASURE
FREEDOM [J] QFX
FREEDOM (EP) QFX
FREEDOM COME FREEDOM GO FORTUNES
FREEDOM FIGHTERS MUSIC
FREEDOM GOT AN A.K. DA LENCH MOB
FREEDOM (MAKE IT FUNKY) BLACK MAGIC
FREEDOM OVERSPILL STEVE WINWOOD
FREEDOM'S PRISONER STEVE HARLEY
FREEEK! GEORGE MICHAEL
FREEFLOATING GARY CLARK
FREEK 'N YOU JODECI
FREELOADER DRIFTWOOD
FREELOVE DEPECHE MODE
FREESTYLER BOMFUNK MC'S
FREET TATA BOX INHIBITORS
FREEWAY OF LOVE ARETHA FRANKLIN
FREEWHEEL BURNIN' JUDAS PRIEST
THE FREEZE SPANDAU BALLET
FREEZE THE ATLANTIC CABLE
FREEZE-FRAME J GEILS BAND
FREIGHT TRAIN CHARLES McDEVITT SKIFFLE GROUP FEATURING NANCY WHISKEY
FRENCH DISCO STEREOLAB
FRENCH FOREIGN LEGION FRANK SINATRA
FRENCH KISS LIL' LOUIS
FRENCH KISSES JENTINA
FRENCH KISSIN' IN THE USA DEBBIE HARRY
FREQUENCY ALTERN 8
FRESH [A] KOOL & THE GANG
FRESH! [B] GINA G
FRIDAY DANIEL BEDINGFIELD
FRIDAY 13TH (EP) DAMNED
FRIDAY I'M IN LOVE CURE
FRIDAY NIGHT (LIVE VERSION) KIDS FROM 'FAME'
FRIDAY ON MY MIND EASYBEATS
FRIDAY ON MY MIND GARY MOORE
FRIDAY STREET PAUL WELLER
FRIDAY'S ANGELS GENERATION X
FRIDAY'S CHILD WILL YOUNG
FRIED MY LITTLE BRAINS KILLS
A FRIEND KRS ONE
FRIEND OF MINE KELLY PRICE
FRIEND OR FOE ADAM ANT
FRIENDLY PERSUASION PAT BOONE
FRIENDLY PERSUASION FOUR ACES FEATURING AL ALBERTS
FRIENDLY PRESSURE JHELISA
FRIENDS [A] BEACH BOYS
FRIENDS [B] ARRIVAL
FRIENDS [C] SHALAMAR
FRIENDS [D] AMII STEWART
FRIENDS [E] JODY WATLEY WITH ERIC B & RAKIM
FRIENDS [F] TIGER
THE FRIENDS AGAIN EP FRIENDS AGAIN
FRIENDS AND NEIGHBOURS BILLY COTTON & HIS BAND, VOCALS BY THE BANDITS
FRIENDS FOREVER THUNDERBUGS
FRIENDS IN LOW PLACES GARTH BROOKS
FRIENDS WILL BE FRIENDS QUEEN
FRIENDSHIP SABRINA JOHNSTON
FRIGGIN' IN THE RIGGIN' SEX PISTOLS

FRIGHTENED CITY SHADOWS
THE FROG PRINCESS DIVINE COMEDY
FROGGY MIX JAMES BROWN
FROGGY STYLE NUTTIN' NYCE
FROM A DISTANCE BETTE MIDLER
FROM A DISTANCE CLIFF RICHARD
FROM A JACK TO A KING NED MILLER
FROM A LOVER TO A FRIEND PAUL McCARTNEY
FROM A TO H AND BACK AGAIN SHEEP ON DRUGS
FROM A WINDOW [A] BILLY J. KRAMER & THE DAKOTAS
FROM A WINDOW [B] NORTHERN UPROAR
FROM DESPAIR TO WHERE MANIC STREET PREACHERS
FROM EAST TO WEST VOYAGE
FROM HEAD TO TOE ELVIS COSTELLO
FROM HERE TO ETERNITY [A] GIORGIO
FROM HERE TO ETERNITY [B] IRON MAIDEN
FROM HERE TO ETERNITY [C] MICHAEL BALL
FROM HERE TO THERE TO YOU HANK LOCKLIN
FROM ME TO YOU BEATLES
FROM NEW YORK TO L.A. PATSY GALLANT
FROM NOW ON JAKI GRAHAM
FROM OUT OF NOWHERE FAITH NO MORE
FROM RUSH HOUR WITH LOVE REPUBLICA
FROM RUSSIA WITH LOVE [A] MATT MONRO
FROM RUSSIA WITH LOVE [A] JOHN BARRY ORCHESTRA
FROM RUSSIA WITH LOVE [B] MATT DAREY PRESENTS DSP
FROM THA CHUUUCH TO DA PALACE SNOOP DOGG
FROM THE BENCH AT BELVIDERE BOO RADLEYS
FROM THE BOTTOM OF MY HEART MOODY BLUES
FROM THE FIRE FIELDS OF THE NEPHILIM
FROM THE GHETTO DREAD FLIMSTONE & THE NEW TONE AGE FAMILY
FROM THE HEART ANOTHER LEVEL
FROM THE HIP (EP) LLOYD COLE & THE COMMOTIONS
FROM THE UNDERWORLD HERD
FROM THIS DAY MACHINE HEAD
FROM THIS MOMENT ON SHANIA TWAIN
FRONTIER PSYCHIATRIST AVALANCHES
FRONTIN' PHARRELL WILLIAMS FEATURING JAY-Z
FRONTIN' JAMIE CULLUM
FROSTY THE SNOWMAN COCTEAU TWINS
FROZEN MADONNA
FROZEN HEART FM
FROZEN METAL HEAD (EP) BEASTIE BOYS
FROZEN ORANGE JUICE PETER SARSTEDT
FRQUENCY RHYTHMATIC
FU-GEE-LA FUGEES
F**K IT (I DON'T WANT YOU BACK) EAMON
***K THE MILLENNIUM 2K
FUEL METALLICA
FUGITIVE MOTEL ELBOW
FULL METAL JACKET (I WANNA BE YOUR DRILL INSTRUCTOR) ABIGAIL MEAD & NIGEL GOULDING
THE FULL MONTY-MONSTER MIX VARIOUS ARTISTS (EPS & LPS)
FULL MOON BRANDY
FULL OF LIFE (HAPPY NOW) WONDER STUFF
FULL TERM LOVE MONIE LOVE
FULL TIME JOB DORIS DAY & JOHNNIE RAY
FUN DA MOB FEATURING JOCELYN BROWN
FUN DAY STEVIE WONDER
FUN FOR ME MOLOKO
FUN FUN FUN STATUS QUO WITH THE BEACH BOYS
THE FUN LOVIN' CRIMINAL FUN LOVIN' CRIMINALS
THE FUNERAL OF HEARTS H.I.M.
FUNERAL PYRE JAM
THE FUNERAL (SPETEMBER 25TH, 1977) THULI DUMAKUDE
FUNGI MAMA (BEBOPAFUNKADISCOLYPSO) TOM BROWNE

FUNK & DRIVE ELEVATORMAN
FUNK DAT SAGAT
FUNK ON AH ROLL JAMES BROWN
THE FUNK PHENOMENA ARMAND VAN HELDEN
FUNK THEORY ROKOTTO
FUNKATARIUM JUMP
FUNKDAFIED DA BRAT
FUNKIN' FOR JAMAICA (N.Y.) TOM BROWNE
FUNKY BROADWAY WILSON PICKETT
FUNKY COLD MEDINA TONE LOC
FUNKY DORY RACHEL STEVENS
FUNKY GIBBON GOODIES
FUNKY GUITAR TC 1992
FUNKY JAM PRIMAL SCREAM
FUNKY LOVE KAVANA
FUNKY LOVE VIBRATIONS BASS-O-MATIC
FUNKY MOPED JASPER CARROTT
FUNKY MUSIC UTAH SAINTS
FUNKY NASSAU BEGINNING OF THE END
FUNKY SENSATION LADIES CHOICE
FUNKY STREET ARTHUR CONLEY
FUNKY TOWN LIPPS INC
FUNKY TOWN PSEUDO ECHO
FUNKY WEEKEND STYLISTICS
FUNNY ALL OVER VERNONS GIRLS
FUNNY BREAK (ONE IS ENOUGH) ORBITAL
FUNNY FAMILIAR FORGOTTEN FEELINGS TOM JONES
FUNNY FUNNY SWEET
FUNNY HOW AIRHEAD
FUNNY HOW LOVE CAN BE IVY LEAGUE
FUNNY HOW LOVE IS FINE YOUNG CANNIBALS
FUNNY HOW TIME FLIES (WHEN YOU'RE HAVING FUN) JANET JACKSON
FUNNY HOW TIME SLIPS AWAY DOROTHY MOORE
FUNNY WAY OF LAUGHIN' BURL IVES
FUNTIME BOY GEORGE
F.U.R.B. (F U RIGHT BACK) FRANKEE
FURIOUS ANGELS ROB DOUGAN
FURNITURE FUGAZI
FURNITURE MUSIC BILL NELSON'S RED NOISE
FURTHER LONGVIEW
THE FURTHER ADVENTURES OF THE NORTH VARIOUS ARTISTS (EPS & LPS)
FUTURE HALO VARGAS
FUTURE LOVE PRESENCE
FUTURE LOVE EP SEAL
FUTURE MANAGEMENT ROGER TAYLOR
THE FUTURE MUSIC (EP) LIQUID
THE FUTURE OF THE FUTURE (STAY GOLD) DEEP DISH WITH EBTG
FUTURE SHOCK HERBIE HANCOCK
FUTURE SOUND (EP) PHUTURE ASSASSINS
THE FUTURE'S SO BRIGHT I GOTTA WEAR SHADES TIMBUK 3
FUZION PESHAY FEATURING CO-ORDINATE
FX A GUY CALLED GERALD
GABRIEL ROY DAVIS Jr FEATURING PEVEN EVERETT
GAINESVILLE ROCK CITY LESS THAN JAKE
GAL WINE CHAKA DEMUS & PLIERS
GAL WITH THE YALLER SHOES MICHAEL HOLLIDAY
GALAXIA MOONMAN FEATURING CHANTAL
GALAXIE BLIND MELON
GALAXY WAR
GALAXY OF LOVE CROWN HEIGHTS AFFAIR
GALLOPING HOME LONDON STRING CHORALE
GALLOWS POLE JIMMY PAGE & ROBERT PLANT
GALVESTON GLEN CAMPBELL
GALVESTON BAY LONNIE HILL
GAMBLER MADONNA
GAMBLIN' BAR ROOM BLUES SENSATIONAL ALEX HARVEY BAND

GAMBLIN' MAN LONNIE DONEGAN
THE GAME [A] ECHO & THE BUNNYMEN
THE GAME [B] NICHOLA HOLT
GAME BOY KWS
GAME OF LOVE [A] WAYNE FONTANA & THE MINDBENDERS
GAME OF LOVE [B] TONY HADLEY
THE GAME OF LOVE [C] SANTANA FEATURING MICHELLE BRANCH
GAME ON CATATONIA
GAME OVER SCARFACE
GAMEMASTER LOST TRIBE
GAMES NEW KIDS ON THE BLOCK
GAMES PEOPLE PLAY JOE SOUTH
GAMES PEOPLE PLAY INNER CIRCLE
GAMES THAT LOVERS PLAY DONALD PEERS
THE GAMES WE PLAY ANDREAS JOHNSON
GAMES WITHOUT FRONTIERS PETER GABRIEL
GANGSTA, GANGSTA NWA
GANGSTA LOVIN' EVE FEATURING ALICIA KEYS
GANGSTA'S PARADISE COOLIO FEATURING LV
GANGSTA'S PARADISE LV
GANGSTER OF THE GROOVE HEATWAVE
GANGSTER TRIPPIN' FATBOY SLIM
GANGSTERS SPECIAL A.K.A.
GARAGE CORRUPTED CRU FEATURING MC NEAT
GARAGE GIRLS LONYO FEATURING MC ONYX STONE
GARDEN OF DELIGHT MISSION
GARDEN OF EDEN DICK JAMES
GARDEN OF EDEN GARY MILLER
THE GARDEN OF EDEN FRANKIE VAUGHAN
THE GARDEN OF EDEN JOE VALINO
GARDEN PARTY RICK NELSON
GARDEN PARTY [A] MEZZOFORTE
GARDEN PARTY [B] MARILLION
GARY GILMORE'S EYES ADVERTS
GARY GLITTER (EP) GARY GLITTER
THE GAS FACE 3RD BASS
GASOLINE ALLEY ELKIE BROOKS
GASOLINE ALLEY BRED HOLLIES
GATECRASHING LIVING IN A BOX
GATHER IN THE MUSHROOMS BENNY HILL
GAUDETE STEELEYE SPAN
GAY BAR ELECTRIC SIX
GAY BOYFRIEND HAZZARDS
THE GAY CAVALIEROS (THE STORY SO FAR) STEVE WRIGHT
GAYE CLIFFORD T WARD
GBI TOWA TEI FEATURING KYLIE MINOGUE
GEE BABY PETER SHELLEY
GEE BUT IT'S LONELY PAT BOONE
GEE WHIZ IT'S YOU CLIFF RICHARD
GEEK STINK BREATH GREEN DAY
GENERAL PUBLIC GENERAL PUBLIC
GENERALS AND MAJORS XTC
GENERATION SEX DIVINE COMEDY
GENERATIONS INSPIRAL CARPETS
GENERATIONS OF LOVE JESUS LOVES YOU
GENETIC ENGINEERING ORCHESTRAL MANOEUVRES IN THE DARK
GENIE BROOKLYN BRONX & QUEENS
GENIE IN A BOTTLE CHRISTINA AGUILERA
GENIE IN A BOTTLE SPEEDWAY
GENIE WITH THE LIGHT BROWN LAMP SHADOWS
GENIUS PITCHSHIFTER
GENIUS MOVE THAT PETROL EMOTION
GENIUS OF LOVER TOM TOM CLUB
GENO DEXY'S MIDNIGHT RUNNERS
GENTLE ON MY MIND DEAN MARTIN
GENTLEMAN WHO FELL MILLA
A GENTLEMAN'S EXCUSE ME FISH

GENTLEMEN TAKE POLAROIDS JAPAN
GEORDIE BOYS (GAZZA RAP) GAZZA
GEORDIE IN WONDERLAND WILDHEARTS
GEORGIA ON MY MIND RAY CHARLES
GEORGINA BAILEY NOOSHA FOX
GEORGY GIRL SEEKERS
GEORGY PORGY [A] CHARME
GEORGY PORGY [B] ERIC BENET FEATURING FAITH EVANS
GEPETTO BELLY
GERM FREE ADOLESCENCE X-RAY SPEX
GERONIMO SHADOWS
GERTCHA CHAS & DAVE
GESUNDHEIT HYSTERICS
(GET A) GRIP (ON YOURSELF) STRANGLERS
GET A LIFE [A] SOUL II SOUL
GET A LIFE [B] JULIAN LENNON
GET A LIFE [C] FREESTYLERS
GET A LITTLE FREAKY WITH ME AARON HALL
GET ALONG WITH YOU KELIS
GET ANOTHER LOVE CHANTAL CURTIS
GET AWAY GEORGIE FAME & THE BLUE FLAMES
GET BACK [A] BEATLES WITH BILLY PRESTON
GET BACK [A] ROD STEWART
GET BACK [B] MOTHER
GET BUSY [A] MR LEE
GET BUSY [B] SEAN PAUL
GET CARTER ROY BUDD
GET DANCING DISCO TEX & THE SEX-O-LETTES
GET DOWN [A] GILBERT O'SULLIVAN
GET DOWN [B] GENE CHANDLER
GET DOWN [C] M-D-EMM
GET DOWN [D] CRAIG MACK
GET DOWN [E] JUNGLE BROTHERS
GET DOWN AND GET WITH IT SLADE
GET DOWN ON IT KOOL & THE GANG
GET DOWN ON IT LOUCHIE LOU & MICHIE ONE
GET DOWN SATURDAY NIGHT OLIVER CHEATHAM
GET DOWN TONIGHT KC & THE SUNSHINE BAND
GET DOWN (YOU'RE THE ONE FOR ME) BACKSTREET BOYS
GET 'EM OFF TOKYO DRAGONS
GET FREE VINES
GET GET DOWN PAUL JOHNSON
GET HERE OLETA ADAMS
GET HERE Q FEATURING TRACY ACKERMAN
GET HIGHER BLACK GRAPE
GET IN THE SWING SPARKS
GET INTO IT TONY SCOTT
GET INTO THE MUSIC DJ'S RULE FEATURING KAREN BROWN
GET INTO YOU DANNII MINOGUE
GET INVOLVED RAPHAEL SAADIQ & Q-TIP
GET IT [A] DARTS
GET IT [B] STEVIE WONDER & MICHAEL JACKSON
GET IT ON [A] T. REX
GET IT ON [A] POWER STATION
GET IT ON [A] BUS STOP FEATURING T REX
GET IT ON [B] KINGDOM COME
GET IT ON [C] INTENSO PROJECT/LISA SCOTT-LEE
GET IT ON THE FLOOR DMX FEATURING SWIZZ BEATZ
GET IT ON TONITE MONTELL JORDAN
GET IT RIGHT [A] ARETHA FRANKLIN
GET IT RIGHT [B] JOE FAGIN
GET IT RIGHT NEXT TIME GERRY RAFFERTY
GET IT TOGETHER [A] CRISPY & COMPANY
GET IT TOGETHER [B] BEASTIE BOYS
GET IT TOGETHER [C] SEAL
GET IT UP RM PROJECT
GET IT UP FOR LOVE DAVID CASSIDY
GET IT UP FOR LOVE TATA VEGA

GET IT UP FOR LOVE LUCIANA
GET IT UP (THE FEELING) ULTRA NATE
GET IT WHILE IT'S HOT NODESHA
GET IT WHILE YOU CAN OLYMPIC RUNNERS
GET LOOSE [A] EVELYN 'CHAMPAGNE' KING
GET LOOSE [B] L.A. MIX PERFORMED BY JAZZI P
GET LOOSE [C] D4
GET LOST EDEN KANE
GET LUCKY JERMAINE STEWART
GET ME DINOSAUR Jr.
GET ME HOME FOXY BROWN FEATURING BLACKstreet
GET ME OFF BASEMENT JAXX
GET ME OUT NEW MODEL ARMY
GET ME TO THE WORLD ON TIME ELECTRIC PRUNES
GET MYSELF ARRESTED GOMEZ
GET NO BETTER CASSIDY FEATURING MASHONDA
GET OFF DANDY WARHOLS
GET OFF OF MY CLOUD ROLLING STONES
GET OFF THIS CRACKER
GET OFF YOUR HIGH HORSE ROLLO GOES CAMPING
GET ON IT PHOEBE ONE
GET ON THE BUS DESTINY'S CHILD FEATURING TIMBALAND
GET ON THE DANCE FLOOR ROB BASE & DJ E-Z ROCK
GET ON THE FUNK TRAIN MUNICH MACHINE
GET ON UP [A] JAZZY DEE
GET ON UP [B] JODECI
GET ON UP, GET ON DOWN ROY AYERS
GET ON YOUR FEET GLORIA ESTEFAN
GET OUT [A] HAROLD MELVIN & THE BLUENOTES
GET OUT [B] BUSTA RHYMES
GET OUT [C] FELON
GET OUT OF MY LIFE WOMAN LEE DORSEY
GET OUT OF MYSELF REDD KROSS
GET OUT OF THIS HOUSE SHAWN COLVIN
GET OUT YOUR LAZY BED MATT BIANCO
GET OUTTA MY DREAMS GET INTO MY CAR BILLY OCEAN
GET OVER IT OK GO
GET OVER YOU [A] UNDERTONES
GET OVER YOU [B] SOPHIE ELLIS-BEXTOR
GET READY [A] TEMPTATIONS
GET READY [A] CAROL HITCHCOCK
GET READY! [B] ROACHFORD
GET READY [C] MA$E FEATURING BLACKstreet
GET READY FOR THIS 2 UNLIMITED
GET REAL PAUL RUTHERFORD
GET SOME THERAPY STEVE WRIGHT & THE SISTERS OF SOUL
GET THAT LOVE THOMPSON TWINS
GET THE BALANCE RIGHT DEPECHE MODE
GET THE FUNK OUT EXTREME
GET THE GIRL! KILL THE BADDIES! POP WILL EAT ITSELF
GET THE KEYS AND GO LLAMA FARMERS
GET THE MESSAGE ELECTRONIC
GET THE PARTY STARTED P!NK
GET THROUGH MARK JOSEPH
GET TOGETHER WONDER STUFF
GET TOUGH KLEEER
GET UP [A] J.A.L.N. BAND
GET UP [B] BLACKOUT
GET UP [C] BEVERLEY KNIGHT
GET UP AND BOOGIE [A] SILVER CONVENTION
GET UP AND BOOGIE [B] FREDDIE JAMES
GET UP AND MOVE HARVEY
GET UP (BEFORE THE NIGHT IS OVER) TECHNOTRONIC FEATURING YA KID K
GET UP (EVERYBODY) BYRON STINGILY
GET UP I FEEL LIKE BEING A SEX MACHINE JAMES BROWN
GET UP OFFA THAT THING JAMES BROWN

GET UP STAND UP [A] PHUNKY PHANTOM
GET UP STAND UP [B] STELLAR PROJECT FEATURING BRANDI EMMA
GET UP SUNSHINE SREET BIZARRE INC
GET UP! GET INSANE! STRETCH 'N' VERN PRESENTS MADDOG
GET UR FREAK ON MISSY ELLIOTT
GET WILD NEW POWER GENERATION
GET YOUR BODY ADAMSKI FEATURING NINA HAGEN
GET YOUR FEET OUT OF MY SHOES BOOTHILL FOOT-TAPPERS
GET YOUR HANDS OFF MY MAN! JUNIOR VASQUEZ
GET YOUR HANDS OFF MY WOMAN DARKNESS
GET YOUR LOVE BACK THREE DEGREES
GET YOURSELF TOGETHER YOUNG DISCIPLES
GET-A-WAY [A] MAXX
GETAWAY [B] MUSIC
GETO HEAVEN COMMON FEATURING MACY GRAY
GETS ME THROUGH OZZY OSBOURNE
GETT OFF PRINCE & THE NEW POWER GENERATION
GETTIN' IN THE WAY JILL SCOTT
GETTIN' JIGGY WIT IT WILL SMITH
GETTIN' READY FOR LOVE DIANA ROSS
GETTING A DRAG LYNSEY DE PAUL
GETTING AWAY WITH IT [A] ELECTRONIC
GETTING AWAY WITH IT [B] EGG
GETTING AWAY WITH IT (ALL MESSED UP) JAMES
GETTING AWAY WITH MURDER PAPA ROACH
GETTING BETTER SHED SEVEN
GETTING CLOSER [A] WINGS
GETTING CLOSER [B] HAYWOODE
GETTING INTO SOMETHING ALISON MOYET
GETTING' INTO U W.O.S.P.
GETTING' IT RIGHT ALISON LIMERICK
GETTING MIGHTY CROWDED BETTY EVERETT
GETTING' MONEY JUNIOR M.A.F.I.A.
GETTING OVER YOU ANDY WILLIAMS
GETTING UP PIGBAG
GETTO JAM DOMINO
GHANDARA GODIEGO
GHETTO RHYTHM MASTERS FEATURING JOE WATSON
GHETTO CHILD DETROIT SPINNERS
GHETTO DAY CRYSTAL WATERS
GHETTO GIRL SIMPLY RED
GHETTO HEAVEN FAMILY STAND
GHETTO MUSICK OUTKAST
GHETTO ROMANCE DAMAGE
GHETTO SUPERSTAR (THAT IS WHAT YOU ARE) PRAS MICHEL FEATURING ODB & MYA
G.H.E.T.T.O.U.T. CHANGING FACES
THE GHOST AT NUMBER ONE JELLYFISH
GHOST DANCER ADDRISI BROTHERS
GHOST HOUSE HOUSE ENGINEERS
GHOST IN YOU PSYCHEDELIC FURS
GHOST OF LOVE FICTION FACTORY
THE GHOST OF LOVE TAVARES
THE GHOST OF TOM JOAD BRUCE SPRINGSTEEN
GHOST TOWN SPECIALS
GHOSTBUSTERS [A] RAY PARKER Jr.
GHOSTBUSTERS [B] RUN D.M.C.
GHOSTDANCING SIMPLE MINDS
GHOSTS [A] JAPAN
GHOSTS [B] MICHAEL JACKSON
GHOSTS [C] TENTH PLANET
GHOSTS [D] DIRTY VEGAS
GIA DESPINA VANDI
GIDDY-UP-A-DING-DONG FREDDIE BELL & THE BELLBOYS
GIDDY-UP 2 IN A ROOM
THE GIFT [A] INXS
THE GIFT [B] DANIEL O'DONNELL

THE GIFT [C] WAY OUT WEST/MISS JOANNA LAW
THE GIFT OF CHRISTMAS CHILDLINERS
GIGANTOR DICKIES
GIGI BILLY ECKSTINE
GIGOLO DAMNED
GILLY GILLY OSSENFEFFER KATZENELLEN BOGEN BY THE SEA MAX BYGRAVES
GIMME ALL YOUR LOVIN' [A] ZZ TOP
GIMME ALL YOUR LOVIN' [B] KYM MAZELLE & JOCELYN BROWN
GIMME DAT BANANA BLACK GORILLA
GIMME DAT DING PIPKINS
GIMME GIMME GIMME (A MAN AFTER MIDNIGHT) ABBA
GIMME GIMME GOOD LOVIN' CRAZY ELEPHANT
GIMME HOPE JO'ANNA EDDY GRANT
GIMME LITTLE SIGN BRENTON WOOD
GIMME LITTLE SIGN DANIELLE BRISEBOIS
GIMME LOVE ALEXIA
GIMME LUV (EENIE MEENIE MINY MO) DAVID MORALES & THE BAD YARD CLUB
GIMME SHELTER [A] GIMME SHELTER
GIMME SOME BRENDON
GIMME SOME PAT & MICK
GIMME SOME LOVE GINA G
GIMME SOME LOVIN' THUNDER
GIMME SOME LOVING SPENCER DAVIS GROUP
GIMME SOME MORE BUSTA RHYMES
GIMME THAT BODY Q-TEE
GIMME THE LIGHT SEAN PAUL
GIMME THE SUNSHINE CURIOSITY
GIMME YOUR LOVIN' ATLANTIC STARR
GIMMIX! PLAY LOUD JOHN COOPER CLARKE
GIN AND JUICE SNOOP DOGGY DOGG
GIN GAN GOOLIE SCAFFOLD
GIN HOUSE BLUES AMEN CORNER
GIN SOAKED BOY DIVINE COMEDY
GINCHY BERT WEEDON
GINGER DAVID DEVANT & HIS SPIRIT WIFE
GINGERBREAD FRANKIE AVALON
GINNY COME LATELY BRIAN HYLAND
GIRL ST. LOUIS UNION
GIRL TRUTH
GIRL ALL THE BAD GUYS WANT BOWLING FOR SOUP
GIRL/BOY (EP) APHEX TWIN
THE GIRL CAN'T HELP IT LITTLE RICHARD
THE GIRL CAN'T HELP IT DARTS
GIRL CRAZY HOT CHOCOLATE
GIRL DON'T COME SANDIE SHAW
THE GIRL FROM IPANEMA STAN GETZ & JOAO GILBERTO
THE GIRL FROM IPANEMA ASTRUD GILBERTO
GIRL FROM MARS ASH
A GIRL I ONCE KNEW NORTHERN UPROAR
THE GIRL I USED TO KNOW BROTHER BEYOND
GIRL I'M GONNA MISS YOU MILLI VANILLI
GIRL IN THE MOON DARIUS
GIRL IN THE WOOD FRANKIE LAINE
THE GIRL IS MINE MICHAEL JACKSON & PAUL McCARTNEY
GIRL IS ON MY MIND BLACK KEYS
GIRL (IT'S ALL I HAVE) SHY
GIRL I'VE BEEN HURT SNOW
A GIRL LIKE YOU [A] CLIFF RICHARD & THE SHADOWS
A GIRL LIKE YOU [B] YOUNG RASCALS
A GIRL LIKE YOU [C] EDWYN COLLINS
GIRL OF MY BEST FRIEND ELVIS PRESLEY
GIRL OF MY BEST FRIEND BRYAN FERRY
GIRL OF MY DREAMS TONY BRENT
GIRL OF MY DREAMS GERRY MONROE
GIRL ON TV LYTE FUNKIE ONES

GIRL POWER SHAMPOO
THE GIRL SANG THE BLUES EVERLY BROTHERS
GIRL TALK TLC
GIRL TO GIRL 49ERS
GIRL U FOR ME SILK
GIRL U WANT ROBERT PALMER
THE GIRL WITH THE LONELIEST EYES HOUSE OF LOVE
GIRL YOU KNOW IT'S TRUE MILLI VANILLI
GIRL YOU KNOW IT'S TRUE KEITH 'N' SHANE
GIRL YOU'RE SO TOGETHER MICHAEL JACKSON
GIRL, YOU'LL BE A WOMAN SOON URGE OVERKILL
THE GIRL'S A FREAK DJ TOUCHE
GIRL'S NOT GREY AFI
GIRLFRIEND [A] MICHAEL JACKSON
GIRLFRIEND [B] PEBBLES
GIRLFRIEND [C] BILLIE
GIRLFRIEND [D] N SYNC FEATURING NELLY
GIRLFRIEND [E] ALICIA KEYS
GIRLFRIEND [F] B2K
GIRLFRIEND IN A COMA SMITHS
GIRLFRIEND'S STORY GEMMA FOX FEATURING MC LYTE
GIRLFRIEND/BOYFRIEND BLACKstreet FEATURING JANET
GIRLIE PEDDLERS
GIRLIE GIRLIE SOPHIA GEORGE
GIRLS [A] JOHNNY BURNETTE
GIRLS [B] MOMENTS & WHATNAUTS
GIRLS [B] POWERCUT FEATURING NUBIAN PRINZ
GIRLS [C] BEASTIE BOYS
GIRLS [D] PRODIGY
GIRLS AIN'T NOTHING BUT TROUBLE DJ JAZZY JEFF & THE FRESH PRINCE
GIRLS AND BOYS [A] PRINCE & THE REVOLUTION
GIRLS AND BOYS [B] BLUR
GIRLS + BOYS [C] HED BOYS
GIRLS AND BOYS [D] GOOD CHARLOTTE
GIRLS ARE MORE FUN RAY PARKER Jr.
GIRLS ARE OUT TO GET YOU FASCINATIONS
GIRLS BEST FRIEND DATSUNS
GIRLS CAN GET IT DR. HOOK
GIRLS DEM SUGAR BEENIE MAN FEATURING MYA
GIRLS GIRLS GIRLS [A] STEVE LAWRENCE
GIRLS GIRLS GIRLS [B] FOURMOST
GIRLS GIRLS GIRLS [C] SAILOR
GIRLS GIRLS GIRLS [D] KANDIDATE
GIRLS GIRLS GIRLS [E] MOTLEY CRUE
GIRLS GIRLS GIRLS [F] JAY-Z
GIRLS JUST WANNA HAVE FUN LOLLY
GIRLS JUST WANT TO HAVE FUN CYNDI LAUPER
GIRL'S LIFE GIRLFRIEND
GIRLS LIKE US B-15 PROJECT FEATURING CHRISSY D
GIRLS NIGHT OUT ALDA
THE GIRLS OF SUMMER (EP) ARAB STRAP
GIRLS ON FILM DURAN DURAN
GIRLS ON MY MIND FATBACK
GIRLS ON TOP GIRL THING
GIRLS' SCHOOL WINGS
GIRLS TALK DAVE EDMUNDS
GIT DOWN CENOGINERZ
GIT DOWN (SHAKE YOUR THANG) GAYE BYKERS ON ACID
GIT ON UP DJ 'FAST' EDDIE FEATURING SUNDANCE
GITTIN' FUNKY KID 'N' PLAY
GIV ME LUV ALCATRAZZ
GIVE A LITTLE BIT SUPERTRAMP
GIVE A LITTLE LOVE [A] BAY CITY ROLLERS
GIVE A LITTLE LOVE [B] ASWAD
GIVE A LITTLE LOVE [C] DANIEL O'DONNELL
GIVE A LITTLE LOVE [D] INVISIBLE MAN
GIVE A LITTLE LOVE BACK TO THE WORLD EMMA

GIVE AND TAKE [A] PIONEERS
GIVE AND TAKE [B] BRASS CONSTRUCTION
GIVE GIVE GIVE TOMMY STEELE
GIVE GIVE GIVE ME MORE MORE MORE WONDER STUFF
GIVE HER MY LOVE JOHNSTON BROTHERS
GIVE HER WHAT SHE WANTS FRANKIE OLIVER
GIVE IN TO ME MICHAEL JACKSON
GIVE IRELAND BACK TO THE IRISH WINGS
GIVE IT ALL AWAY WORLD PARTY
GIVE IT AWAY [A] RED HOT CHILI PEPPERS
GIVE IT AWAY [B] DEEPEST BLUE
GIVE IT SOME EMOTION TRACIE
GIVE IT TO ME [A] TROGGS
GIVE IT TO ME [B] BAM BAM
GIVE IT TO ME BABY RICK JAMES
GIVE IT TO ME NOW KENNY
GIVE IT TO YOU [A] MARTHA WASH
GIVE IT TO YOU [B] JORDAN KNIGHT
GIVE IT UP [A] KC & THE SUNSHINE BAND
GIVE IT UP [A] CUT 'N' MOVE
GIVE IT UP [B] TALK TALK
GIVE IT UP [C] HOTHOUSE FLOWERS
GIVE IT UP [D] WILSON PHILLIPS
GIVE IT UP [E] GOODMEN
GIVE IT UP [F] PUBLIC ENEMY
GIVE IT UP [G] SELENA VS X MEN
GIVE IT UP TURN IT LOOSE EN VOGUE
GIVE ME A LITTLE MORE TIME GABRIELLE
GIVE ME A REASON [A CORRS
GIVE ME A REASON [B] TONY DE VIT FEATURING NIKI
    MAK
GIVE ME A REASON [B] TRIPLE EIGHT
GIVE ME ALL YOUR LOVE [A] WHITESNAKE
GIVE ME ALL YOUR LOVE [B] MAGIC AFFAIR
GIVE ME AN INCH HAZEL O'CONNOR
GIVE ME BACK ME BRAIN DUFFO
GIVE ME BACK MY HEART DOLLAR
GIVE ME BACK MY MAN B-52's
GIVE ME FIRE GBH
GIVE ME JUST A LITTLE MORE TIME CHAIRMEN OF THE
    BOARD
GIVE ME JUST A LITTLE MORE TIME KYLIE MINOGUE
GIVE ME JUST ONE MORE NIGHT (UNA NOCHE) 98o
GIVE ME LIFE MR V
GIVE ME LOVE [A] DIDDY
GIVE ME LOVE [B] DJ DADO VS MICHELLE WEEKS
GIVE ME LOVE (GIVE ME PEACE ON EARTH) GEORGE
    HARRISON
GIVE ME MORE TIME [A] NICOLE
GIVE ME MORE TIME [B] WHITESNAKE
GIVE ME ONE MORE CHANCE [A] DONALD PEERS
GIVE ME ONE MORE CHANCE [B] LUKE GOSS & THE
    BAND OF THIEVES
GIVE ME RHYTHM BLACK CONNECTION
GIVE ME SOME KINDA MAGIC DOLLAR
GIVE ME SOME MORE DJ GERT
GIVE ME STRENGTH JON OF THE PLEASED WIMMIN
GIVE ME THE NIGHT GEORGE BENSON
GIVE ME THE NIGHT MIRAGE FEATURING ROY GAYLE
GIVE ME THE NIGHT RANDY CRAWFORD
GIVE ME THE REASON LUTHER VANDROSS
GIVE ME TIME DUSTY SPRINGFIELD
GIVE ME TONIGHT SHANNON
GIVE ME YOU MARY J. BLIGE
GIVE ME YOUR BODY CHIPPENDALES
GIVE ME YOUR HEART TONIGHT SHAKIN' STEVENS
GIVE ME YOUR LOVE REEF
GIVE ME YOUR WORD TENNESSEE ERNIE FORD
GIVE ME YOUR WORD BILLY FURY
GIVE MYSELF TO LOVE FRANCIS ROSSI OF STATUS QUO
GIVE PEACE A CHANCE PLASTIC ONO BAND

GIVE U ONE 4 CHRISTMAS HOT PANTZ
GIVE UP THE FUNK (LET'S DANCE) B.T. EXPRESS
GIVE YOU DJAIMIN
GIVE YOU ALL THE LOVE MISHKA
GIVEN TO FLY PEARL JAM
GIVEN UP MIRRORBALL
GIVIN' IT UP INCOGNITO
GIVIN' UP GIVIN' IN THREE DEGREES
GIVING HIM SOMETHING HE CAN FEEL EN VOGUE
GIVING IN ADEMA
GIVING IT ALL AWAY ROGER DALTREY
GIVING IT BACK PHIL HURTT
GIVING UP GIVING IN SHEENA EASTON
GIVING YOU THE BENEFIT PEBBLES
GIVING YOU THE BEST THAT I GOT ANITA BAKER
G.L.A.D. KIM APPLEBY
GLAD ALL OVER DAVE CLARK FIVE
GLAD ALL OVER CRYSTAL PALACE
GLAD IT'S ALL OVER CAPTAIN SENSIBLE
GLAM LISA B
GLAM RAID SPACE RAIDERS
GLAM ROCK COPS CARTER – THE UNSTOPPABLE SEX
    MACHINE
GLAM SLAM PRINCE
GLASGOW RANGERS (NINE IN A ROW) RANGERS FC
A GLASS OF CHAMPAGNE SAILOR
GLASTONBURY SONG WATERBOYS
GLENDORA PERRY COMO
GLENDORA GLEN MASON
GLENN MILLER MEDLEY JOHN ANDERSON BIG BAND
GLITTER AND TRAUMA BIFFY CLYRO
GLITTERBALL [A] SIMPLE MINDS
GLITTERBALL [B] FC KAHUNA
GLITTERING PRIZE SIMPLE MINDS
GLOBAL LOVE HIGH CONTRAST
GLOBETROTTER TORNADOS
GLORIA [A] JONATHAN KING
GLORIA [A] LAURA BRANIGAN
GLORIA [B] U2
GLORIA [C] VAN MORRISON & JOHN LEE HOOKER
GLORIOUS ANDREAS JOHNSON
GLORY BOX PORTISHEAD
GLORY DAYS BRUCE SPRINGSTEEN
GLORY GLORY MAN. UNITED MANCHESTER UNITED
    FOOTBALL CLUB
GLORY OF LOVE PETER CETERA
GLORY OF THE 80'S TORI AMOS
GLORYLAND DARYL HALL & THE SOUNDS OF
    BLACKNESS
GLOW SPANDAU BALLET
GLOW OF LOVE CHANGE
GLOW WORM MILLS BROTHERS
GO [A] SCOTT FITZGERALD
GO [B] MOBY
GO [C] JOCASTA
GO AWAY [A] GLORIA ESTEFAN
GO AWAY [B] HONEYCRACK
GO AWAY LITTLE GIRL MARK WYNTER
GO (BEFORE YOU BREAK MY HEART) GIGLIOLA
    CINQUETTI
GO BUDDY GO STRANGLERS
GO CUT CREATOR GO LL COOL J
GO DEEP JANET JACKSON
GO DEH YAKA (GO TO THE TOP) MONYAKA
GO ENGLAND ENGLAND BOYS
GO FOR IT (HEART AND SOUL) ROCKY V FEATURING
    JOEY B. ELLIS & TYNETTA HARE
GO FOR IT! COVENTRY CITY CUP FINAL SQUAD
GO FOR THE HEART SOX
GO GO GO CHUCK BERRY
GO HOME STEVIE WONDER

GO INTO THE LIGHT IAN McNABB
GO LET IT OUT OASIS
GO NORTH RICHARD BARNES
GO NOW MOODY BLUES
GO ON BY ALMA COGAN
GO ON GIRL ROXANNE SHANTE
GO ON MOVE REEL 2 REAL FEATURING THE MAD
    STUNTMAN
GO TECHNO 2 HOUSE
GO THE DISTANCE MICHAEL BOLTON
GO TO SLEEP RADIOHEAD
GO WEST VILLAGE PEOPLE
GO WEST PET SHOP BOYS
GO WILD IN THE COUNTRY BOW WOW WOW
GO WITH THE FLOW [A] LOOP DA LOOP
GO WITH THE FLOW [B] QUEENS OF THE STONE AGE
GO YOUR OWN WAY FLEETWOOD MAC
GO-GO DANCER WEDDING PRESENT
GOD TORI AMOS
GOD GAVE ROCK AND ROLL TO YOU ARGENT
GOD GAVE ROCK AND ROLL TO YOU II KISS
GOD IS A DJ [A] FAITHLESS
GOD IS A DJ [B] P!NK
GOD OF ABRAHAM MNO
GOD ONLY KNOWS BEACH BOYS
GOD ONLY KNOWS DIESEL PARK WEST
GOD SAVE THE QUEEN SEX PISTOLS
GOD THANK YOU WOMAN CULTURE CLUB
GOD! SHOW ME MAGIC SUPER FURRY ANIMALS
GOD'S CHILD BIG BANG THEORY
GOD'S GONNA PUNISH YOU TYMES
GOD'S GREAT BANANA SKIN CHRIS REA
GOD'S HOME MOVIE HORSE
GOD'S KITCHEN BLANCMANGE
GOD'S MISTAKE TEARS FOR FEARS
GODDESS ON A HIWAY MERCURY REV
GODHEAD NITZER EBB
GODHOPPING DOGS DIE IN HOT CARS
GODLESS DANDY WARHOLS
GODSPEED BT
GODSTAR PSYCHIC TV & THE ANGELS OF LIGHT
GODZILLA CREATURES
GOIN' DOWN MELANIE C
GOIN' PLACES JACKSONS
GOIN' TO THE BANK COMMODORES
GOIN' TO VEGAS JIMMY RAY
GOING ALL THE WAY ALLSTARS
GOING BACK DUSTY SPRINGFIELD
GOING BACK TO CALI LL COOL J
GOING BACK TO MY HOME TOWN HAL PAIGE & THE
    WHALERS
GOING BACK TO MY ROOTS ODYSSEY
GOING BACK TO MY ROOTS FPI PROJECT
GOING DOWN THE ROAD ROY WOOD
GOING DOWN TO LIVERPOOL BANGLES
GOING DOWN TOWN TONIGHT STATUS QUO
GOING FOR GOLD SHED SEVEN
GOING FOR THE ONE YES
GOING HOME [A] OSMONDS
GOING HOME [B] TYRREL CORPORATION
GOING HOME (THEME OF 'LOCAL HERO') MARK
    KNOPFLER
GOING IN WITH MY EYES OPEN DAVID SOUL
GOING LEFT RIGHT DEPARTMENT S
GOING NOWHERE GABRIELLE
GOING OUT SUPERGRASS
GOING OUT OF MY HEAD [A] DODIE WEST
GOING OUT OF MY HEAD [B] FATBOY SLIM
GOING OUT WITH GOD KINKY MACHINE
GOING ROUND D'BORA
GOING THROUGH THE MOTIONS HOT CHOCOLATE

GOING TO A GO-GO MIRACLES
GOING TO A GO-GO SHARONETTES
GOING TO A GO GO ROLLING STONES
GOING UNDER EVANESCENCE
GOING UNDERGROUND JAM
GOING UNDERGROUND BUFFALO TOM
GOING UP THE COUNTRY CANNED HEAT
GOLD [A] JOHN STEWART
GOLD [B] SPANDAU BALLET
GOLD [C] EAST 17
GOLD [D] ARTIST FORMERLY KNOWN AS PRINCE (AFKAP)
GOLD [E] BEVERLEY KNIGHT
GOLDEN JILL SCOTT
GOLDEN AGE OF ROCK AND ROLL MOTT THE HOOPLE
GOLDEN BROWN STRANGLERS
GOLDEN BROWN KALEEF
GOLDEN BROWN OMAR
GOLDEN DAYS BUCKS FIZZ
GOLDEN GATE BRIDGE OCEAN COLOUR SCENE
GOLDEN GAZE IAN BROWN
GOLDEN GREEN WONDER STUFF
GOLDEN GUN SUEDE
THE GOLDEN LADY THREE DEGREES
GOLDEN LIGHTS TWINKLE
THE GOLDEN PATH CHEMICAL BROTHERS FEATURING THE FLAMING LIPS
GOLDEN RETRIEVER SUPER FURRY ANIMALS
GOLDEN SKIN SILVER SUN
GOLDEN SLUMBERS TRASH
GOLDEN TOUCH [A] LOOSE ENDS
GOLDEN TOUCH [B] RAZORLIGHT
GOLDEN YEARS DAVID BOWIE
THE GOLDEN YEARS EP MOTORHEAD
GOLDENBALLS (MR BECKHAM TO YOU) BELL & SPURLING
GOLDENBOOK FAMILY CAT
GOLDENEYE TINA TURNER
GOLDFINGER [A] SHIRLEY BASSEY
GOLDFINGER [B] ASH
GOLDRUSH YELLO
GONE [A] SHIRLEY BASSEY
GONE [B] DAVID HOLMES
GONE [C] CURE
GONE [D] N SYNC
GONE AWAY OFFSPRING
GONE DEAD TRAIN NAZARETH
GONE GONE GONE [A] EVERLY BROTHERS
GONE GONE GONE [B] JOHNNY MATHIS
GONE TILL NOVEMBER WYCLEF JEAN
GONE TOO SOON MICHAEL JACKSON
GONNA BUILD A MOUNTAIN [A] MATT MONRO
GONNA BUILD A MOUNTAIN [B] SAMMY DAVIS Jr.
GONNA CAPTURE YOUR HEART BLUE
GONNA CATCH YOU LONNIE GORDON
GONNA CATCH YOU BARKIN BROTHERS FEATURING JOHNNIE FIORI
GONNA GET ALONG WITHOUT YA NOW PATIENCE & PRUDENCE
GONNA GET ALONG WITHOUT YA NOW TRINI LOPEZ
GONNA GET ALONG WITHOUT YOU NOW VIOLA WILLS
GONNA GET THRU THIS DANIEL BEDINGFIELD
GONNA GIVE HER ALL THE LOVE I'VE GOT JIMMY RUFFIN
GONNA MAKE YOU A STAR DAVID ESSEX
GONNA MAKE YOU AN OFFER YOU CAN'T REFUSE JIMMY HELMS
GONNA MAKE YOU BLUSH PAPERDOLLS
GONNA MAKE YOU SWEAT (EVERYBODY DANCE NOW) C & C MUSIC FACTORY (FEATURING FREEDOM WILLIAMS)
GONNA WORK IT OUT HI-GATE

GOO GOO BARABAJAGAL (LOVE IS HOT) DONOVAN WITH THE JEFF BECK GROUP
GOOD AS GOLD BEAUTIFUL SOUTH
GOOD BEAT DEEE-LITE
GOOD BOYS BLONDIE
GOOD DANCERS SLEEPY JACKSON
GOOD DAY SEAN MAGUIRE
GOOD ENOUGH [A] BOBBY BROWN
GOOD ENOUGH [B] DODGY
GOOD ENOUGH (LA VACHE) MILK INC
GOOD EVENING FRIENDS FRANKIE LAINE & JOHNNIE RAY
GOOD EVENING PHILADELPHIA RICKY ROSS
GOOD FEELING REEF
GOOD FOR ME AMY GRANT
GOOD FORTUNE PJ HARVEY
GOOD FRIEND PARIS RED
GOOD FRUIT HEFNER
GOOD GIRLS JOE
GOOD GIRLS DON'T KNACK
GOOD GOD [A] KORN
GOOD GOD [B] JFK
GOOD GOLLY MISS MOLLY LITTLE RICHARD
GOOD GOLLY MISS MOLLY JERRY LEE LEWIS
GOOD GOLLY MISS MOLLY SWINGING BLUE JEANS
GOOD GOOD FEELING ERIC & THE GOOD GOOD FEELING
GOOD GRIEF CHRISTINA CHICORY TIP
A GOOD HEART FEARGAL SHARKEY
A GOOD IDEA SUGAR
THE GOOD LIFE [A] TONY BENNETT
GOOD LIFE [B] INNER CITY
GOOD LIFE [C] E.V.E.
THE GOOD LIFE [D] NEW POWER GENERATION
GOOD LOVE MELI'SA MORGAN
GOOD LOVE CAN NEVER DIE ALVIN STARDUST
GOOD LOVE REAL LOVE D'BORA
GOOD LOVER D-INFLUENCE
GOOD LOVIN' REGINA BELLE
GOOD LOVIN' AIN'T EASY TO COME BY MARVIN GAYE & TAMMI TERRELL
GOOD LOVIN' GONE BAD BAD COMPANY
GOOD LUCK BASEMENT JAXX FEATURING LISA KEKAULA
GOOD LUCK CHARM ELVIS PRESLEY
GOOD MORNING LEAPY LEE
GOOD MORNING BRITAIN AZTEC CAMERA & MICK JONES
GOOD MORNING FREEDOM BLUE MINK
GOOD MORNING JUDGE 10 C.C.
GOOD MORNING LITTLE SCHOOLGIRL YARDBIRDS
GOOD MORNING STARSHINE OLIVER
GOOD MORNING SUNSHINE AQUA
GOOD OLD ARSENAL ARSENAL F.C. FIRST TEAM SQUAD
GOOD OLD ROCK 'N ROLL DAVE CLARK FIVE
GOOD REASON SEAFOOD
GOOD RHYMES DA CLICK
GOOD ROCKIN' TONIGHT MONTROSE
GOOD SIGN EMILIA
GOOD SONG BLUR
GOOD SOULS STARSAILOR
GOOD STUFF [A] B-52's
GOOD STUFF [B] KELIS
GOOD SWEET LOVIN' LOUCHIE LOU & MICHIE ONE
THE GOOD THE BAD THE UGLY HUGO MONTENEGRO
GOOD THING [A] FINE YOUNG CANNIBALS
GOOD THING [B] ETERNAL
GOOD THING GOING YAZZ
GOOD THING GOING SID OWEN
GOOD THING GOING (WE'VE GOT A GOOD THING GOING) SUGAR MINOTT
GOOD THINGS RIVAL SCHOOLS

GOOD TIME [A] PERAN
GOOD TIME [B] A
GOOD TIME BABY BOBBY RYDELL
GOOD TIMES [A] ERIC BURDON & THE ANIMALS
GOOD TIMES [B] CHIC
GOOD TIMES [C] MATT BIANCO
GOOD TIMES [D] REID
GOOD TIMES [E] JIMMY BARNES & INXS
GOOD TIMES [F] ED CASE & SKIN
GOOD TIMES [F] EDIE BRICKELL
GOOD TIMES [G] DREAM FREQUENCY
GOOD TIMES (BETTER TIMES) CLIFF RICHARD
GOOD TIMES GONNA COME AQUALUNG
GOOD TIMIN' JIMMY JONES
GOOD TO BE ALIVE DJ RAP
GOOD TO GO LOVER GWEN GUTHRIE
GOOD TRADITION TANITA TIKARAM
GOOD VIBRATIONS [A] BEACH BOYS
GOOD VIBRATIONS [A] PSYCHIC TV
GOOD VIBRATIONS [A] BRIAN WILSON
GOOD VIBRATIONS [B] MARKY MARK & THE FUNKY BUNCH FEATURING LOLEATTA HOLLOWAY
GOOD VIBRATIONS [C] BROTHERS LIKE OUTLAW FEATURING ALISON EVELYN
A GOOD YEAR FOR THE ROSES ELVIS COSTELLO & THE ATTRACTIONS
GOODBYE [A] MARY HOPKIN
GOODBYE [B] SUNDAYS
GOODBYE [C] AIR SUPPLY
GOODBYE [D] SPICE GIRLS
GOODBYE [E] DEF LEPPARD
GOODBYE [F] CORAL
A GOODBYE CAMEO
GOODBYE BABY AND AMEN LULU
GOODBYE BLUEBIRD WAYNE FONTANA
GOODBYE CIVILIAN SKIDS
GOODBYE CRUEL WORLD [A] JAMES DARREN
GOODBYE CRUEL WORLD [B] SHAKESPEARS SISTER
GOODBYE GIRL [A] SQUEEZE
GOODBYE GIRL [B] GO WEST
GOODBYE HEARTBREAK LIGHTHOUSE FAMILY
GOODBYE IS JUST ANOTHER WORD NEW SEEKERS
GOODBYE JIMMY GOODBYE RUBY MURRAY
GOODBYE MR MACKENZIE GOODBYE MR MACKENZIE
GOODBYE MY LOVE [A] SEARCHERS
GOODBYE MY LOVE [B] GLITTER BAND
GOODBYE NOTHING TO SAY JAVELLS FEATURING NOSMO KING
GOODBYE SAM HELLO SAMANTHA CLIFF RICHARD
GOODBYE STRANGER [A] SUPERTRAMP
GOODBYE STRANGER [B] PEPSI & SHIRLIE
GOODBYE TO LOVE CARPENTERS
GOODBYE TO LOVE AGAIN MAXI PRIEST
GOODBYE TONIGHT LOSTPROPHETS
GOODBYE YELLOW BRICK ROAD ELTON JOHN
GOODBYE-EE [A] PETER COOK & DUDLEY MOORE
GOODBYE-EE [B] 14—18
GOODBYE'S (THE SADDEST WORD) CELINE DION
GOODGROOVE DEREK B
GOODNESS GRACIOUS ME PETER SELLERS & SOPHIA LOREN
GOODNIGHT [A] ROY ORBISON
GOODNIGHT [B] BABY BIRD
GOODNIGHT GIRL WET WET WET
GOODNIGHT MIDNIGHT CLODAGH RODGERS
GOODNIGHT MOON SHIVAREE
GOODNIGHT MRS. FLINTSTONE PILTDOWN MEN
GOODNIGHT SAIGON BILLY JOEL
GOODNIGHT SWEET PRINCE MR ACKER BILK & HIS PARAMOUNT JAZZ BAND
GOODNIGHT TONIGHT WINGS

GOODWILL CITY GOODBYE MR MACKENZIE
GOODY GOODY FRANKIE LYMON & THE TEENAGERS
GOODY TWO SHOES ADAM ANT
GOODYBYE BAD TIMES GIORGIO MORODER & PHIL OAKEY
GOOGLE EYE NASHVILLE TEENS
GORECKI LAMB
GORGEOUS GENE LOVES JEZEBEL
GOSP LWS
GOSPEL OAK EP SINEAD O'CONNOR
GOSSIP CALYPSO BERNARD CRIBBINS
GOSSIP FOLKS MISSY ELLIOTT FEATURING LUDACRIS
GOT 'TIL IT'S GONE JANET FEATURING Q-TIP & JONI
GOT A FEELING PATRICK JUVET
GOT A GIRL FOUR PREPS
GOT A LITTLE HEARTACHE ALVIN STARDUST
GOT A LOT O' LIVIN' TO DO ELVIS PRESLEY
GOT A LOVE FOR YOU JOMANDA
GOT A MATCH RUSS CONWAY
GOT FUNK FUNK JUNKEEZ
GOT IT AT THE DELMAR SENSELESS THINGS
GOT ME A FEELING MISTY OLDLAND
GOT MY MIND MADE UP INSTANT FUNK
GOT MY MIND SET ON YOU GEORGE HARRISON
GOT MY MOJO WORKING JIMMY SMITH
GOT MYSELF TOGETHER BUCKETHEADS
GOT NO BRAINS BAD MANNERS
GOT SOME TEETH OBIE TRICE
GOT THE FEELIN' FIVE
GOT THE LIFE KORN
GOT THE TIME ANTHRAX
GOT TO BE CERTAIN KYLIE MINOGUE
GOT TO BE REAL ERIK
GOT TO BE THERE MICHAEL JACKSON
GOT TO GET ROB 'N' RAZ FEATURING LEILA K
GOT TO GET IT [A] CULTURE BEAT
GOT TO GET IT [B] SISQO
GOT TO GET UP AFRIKA BAMBAATAA
GOT TO GET YOU BACK KYM MAZELLE
GOT TO GET YOU INTO MY LIFE CLIFF BENNETT & THE REBEL ROUSERS
GOT TO GET YOU INTO MY LIFE EARTH, WIND & FIRE
GOT TO GIVE IT UP MARVIN GAYE
GOT TO GIVE IT UP AALIYAH
GOT TO GIVE ME LOVE DANA DAWSON
GOT TO HAVE YOUR LOVE MANTRONIX FEATURING WONDRESS
GOT TO HAVE YOUR LOVE LIBERTY X
GOT TO KEEP ON COOKIE CREW
GOT TO LOVE SOMEBODY SISTER SLEDGE
GOT TO RELEASE SATURATED SOUL FEATURING MISS BUNTY
GOT UR SELF A NAS
GOT YOU PHAROAHE MONCH
GOT YOU ON MY MIND TONY BRENT
GOT YOUR MONEY OL' DIRTY BASTARD FEATURING KELIS
GOTHAM CITY R KELLY
GOTTA BE A SIN ADAM ANT
GOTTA BE YOU 3T: RAP BY HERBIE
GOTTA CATCH 'EM ALL 50 GRIND FEATURING POKEMON ALLSTARS
GOTTA GET A DATE FRANK IFIELD
GOTTA GET AWAY OFFSPRING
GOTTA GET IT RIGHT LENA FIAGBE
GOTTA GET LOOSE MR & MRS SMITH
GOTTA GET YOU HOME TONIGHT EUGENE WILDE
GOTTA GO HOME BONEY M
GOTTA HAVE HOPE BLACKOUT
GOTTA HAVE RAIN MAX BYGRAVES
GOTTA HAVE SOMETHING IN THE BANK FRANK FRANKIE VAUGHAN & THE KAYE SISTERS

GOTTA KEEP PUSHIN' Z FACTOR
GOTTA KNOW (YOUR NAME) MALAIKA
GOTTA LOTTA LOVE ICE-T
GOTTA PULL MYSELF TOGETHER NOLANS
GOTTA SEE BABY TONIGHT MR ACKER BILK & HIS PARAMOUNT JAZZ BAND
GOTTA SEE JANE R. DEAN TAYLOR
GOTTA TELL YOU SAMANTHA MUMBA
GOTTA...MOVIN' ON UP PM DAWN FEATURING KY-MANI
GOURYELLA GOURYELLA
GOVINDA [A] RADHA KRISHNA TEMPLE
GOVINDA [B] KULA SHAKER
GRACE [A] BAND AKA
GRACE [B] SUPERGRASS
GRACEADELICA DARK STAR
GRACELAND BIBLE
GRANADA FRANKIE LAINE
GRANADA FRANK SINATRA
GRAND COOLIE DAM LONNIE DONEGAN
GRAND PIANO MIXMASTER
GRANDAD CLIVE DUNN
GRANDMA'S PARTY PAUL NICHOLAS
GRANDPA'S PARTY MONIE LOVE
GRANITE STATUE SALAD
GRAPEVYNE BROWNSTONE
GRATEFUL WHEN YOU'RE DEAD – JERRY WAS THERE KULA SHAKER
THE GRAVE AND THE CONSTANT FUN LOVIN' CRIMINALS
GRAVEL PIT WU-TANG CLAN
GRAVITATE TO ME THE THE
GRAVITY [A] JAMES BROWN
GRAVITY [B] EMBRACE
GREASE FRANKIE VALLI
GREASE CRAIG McLACHLAN
GREASE MEGAMIX FRANKIE VALLI, JOHN TRAVOLTA & OLIVIA NEWTON-JOHN
GREASED LIGHTNIN' JOHN TRAVOLTA
GREAT BALLS OF FIRE JERRY LEE LEWIS
GREAT BALLS OF FIRE TINY TIM
THE GREAT BEYOND R.E.M.
THE GREAT ESCAPE ENGLAND SUPPORTERS' BAND
GREAT GOSH A'MIGHTY (IT'S A MATTER OF TIME) LITTLE RICHARD
THE GREAT PRETENDER JIMMY PARKINSON
THE GREAT PRETENDER PLATTERS
THE GREAT PRETENDER FREDDIE MERCURY
THE GREAT ROCK 'N' ROLL SWINDLE SEX PISTOLS
THE GREAT SNOWMAN BOB LUMAN
THE GREAT SONG OF INDIFFERENCE BOB GELDOF
THE GREAT TEST HUNDRED REASONS
GREAT THINGS ECHOBELLY
THE GREAT TRAIN ROBBERY BLACK UHURU
GREATER LOVE SOUNDMAN & DON LLOYDIE WITH ELISABETH TROY
THE GREATEST COCKNEY RIPOFF COCKNEY REJECTS
GREATEST DAY BEVERLEY KNIGHT
THE GREATEST FLAME RUNRIG
THE GREATEST HIGH HURRICANE #1
THE GREATEST LOVE OF ALL GEORGE BENSON
GREATEST LOVE OF ALL WHITNEY HOUSTON
THE GREATEST LOVE YOU'LL NEVER KNOW LUTRICIA McNEAL
THE GREATEST ROMANCE EVER SOLD THE ARTIST
THE GREATEST SHOW ON EARTH STRANGELOVE
THE GREATNESS AND PERFECTION OF LOVE JULIAN COPE
GREECE 2000 THREE DRIVES
GREED LAURENT GARNIER
GREEDY FLY BUSH

THE GREEDY UGLY PEOPLE HEFNER
GREEN AND GREY NEW MODEL ARMY
THE GREEN DOOR FRANKIE VAUGHAN
THE GREEN DOOR JIM LOWE
GREEN DOOR GLEN MASON
GREEN DOOR SHAKIN' STEVENS
GREEN FIELDS BEVERLEY SISTERS
GREEN FIELDS UNIT FOUR PLUS TWO
GREEN GREEN GRASS OF HOME TOM JONES
GREEN GREEN GRASS OF HOME ELVIS PRESLEY
GREEN JEANS FLEE-REKKERS
THE GREEN LEAVES OF SUMMER KENNY BALL & HIS JAZZMEN
GREEN LIGHT CLIFF RICHARD
THE GREEN MAN SHUT UP & DANCE
THE GREEN MANALISHI (WITH THE TWO-PRONG CROWN) FLEETWOOD MAC
GREEN ONIONS BOOKER T. & THE M.G.'s
GREEN RIVER CREEDENCE CLEARWATER REVIVAL
GREEN SHIRT ELVIS COSTELLO
GREEN STREET GREEN NEW VAUDEVILLE BAND
GREEN TAMBOURINE LEMON PIPERS
GREEN TAMBOURINE SUNDRAGON
GREEN TINTED SIXTIES MIND MR BIG
GREENBACK DOLLAR CHARLES McDEVITT SKIFFLE GROUP FEATURING NANCY WHISKEY
GREENBANK DRIVE CHRISTIANS
GREENFIELDS BROTHERS FOUR
GREETINGS TO THE NEW BRUNETTE BILLY BRAGG WITH JOHNNY MARR & KIRSTY MacCOLL
GREY DAY MADNESS
GRIMLY FIENDISH DAMNED
GRIND ALICE IN CHAINS
GRIP '89 (GET A) GRIP (ON YOURSELF) STRANGLERS
GRITTY SHAKER DAVID HOLMES
THE GROOVE RODNEY FRANKLIN
GROOVE BABY GROOVE (EP) STARGAZERS
GROOVE IS IN THE HEART DEEE-LITE
THE GROOVE LINE HEATWAVE
GROOVE MACHINE MARVIN & TAMARA
GROOVE OF LOVE E.V.E.
GROOVE THANG ZHANE
GROOVE TO MOVE CHANNEL X
GROOVEBIRD NATURAL BORN GROOVES
GROOVEJET (IF THIS AIN'T LOVE) SPILLER
GROOVELINE BLOCKSTER
THE GROOVER T. REX
GROOVIN' [A] YOUNG RASCALS
GROOVIN' [A] PATO BANTON & THE REGGAE REVOLUTION
GROOVIN' [B] WAR
GROOVIN' IN THE MIDNIGHT MAXI PRIEST
GROOVIN' (THAT'S WHAT WE'RE DOIN') S.O.S. BAND
GROOVIN' WITH MR. BLOE MR BLOE
GROOVIN' (YOU'RE THE BEST THING) STYLE COUNCIL
GROOVY BABY MICROBE
GROOVY BEAT D.O.P.
GROOVY FEELING FLUKE
A GROOVY KIND OF LOVE MINDBENDERS
A GROOVY KIND OF LOVE LES GRAY
A GROOVY KIND OF LOVE PHIL COLLINS
THE GROOVY THANG MINIMAL FUNK 2
GROOVY TRAIN FARM
GROUND LEVEL STEREO MC'S
THE GROUNDBREAKER FALLACY & FUSION
GROUNDED MY VITRIOL
GROUPIE GIRL TONY JOE WHITE
GROWING ON ME DARKNESS
THE GRUDGE MORTIIS
G.T.O. SINITTA
GUAGLIONE PEREZ 'PREZ' PRADO & HIS ORCHESTRA

GUANTANAMERA SANDPIPERS
GUANTANAMERA WYCLEF JEAN & THE REFUGEE
    ALLSTARS
GUANTANAMO OUTLANDISH
GUARANTEED LEVEL 42
GUARDIAN ANGEL NINO DE ANGELO
GUARDIANS OF THE LAND GEORGE BOWYER
GUDBUY T' JANE SLADE
GUDVIBE TINMAN
GUERRILLA FUNK PARIS
GUERRILLA RADIO RAGE AGAINST THE MACHINE
GUESS I WAS A FOOL ANOTHER LEVEL
GUESS WHO'S BACK RAKIM
GUESS YOU DIDN'T LOVE ME TERRI WALKER
GUIDING STAR CAST
GUILTY [A] JIM REEVES
GUILTY [B] PEARLS
GUILTY [C] MIKE OLDFIELD
GUILTY [D] BARBRA STREISAND & BARRY GIBB
GUILTY [E] CLASSIX NOUVEAUX
GUILTY [F] PAUL HARDCASTLE
GUILTY [G] YARBOROUGH & PEOPLES
GUILTY [H] BLUE
GUILTY [I] RASMUS
GUILTY CONSCIENCE EMINEM FEATURING DR DRE
GUILTY OF LOVE WHITESNAKE
GUITAR BOOGIE SHUFFLE BERT WEEDON
GUITAR MAN [A] ELVIS PRESLEY
THE GUITAR MAN [B] BREAD
GUITAR TANGO SHADOWS
GUITARRA G BANDA SONORA
GUN LAW KANE GANG
GUNMAN 187 LOCKDOWN
GUNS DON'T KILL PEOPLE RAPPERS DO GOLDIE LOOKIN
    CHAIN
GUNS FOR HIRE AC/DC
GUNS OF NAVARONE SKATALITES
GUNSLINGER FRANKIE LAINE
GUNZ AND PIANOZ BASS BOYZ
GURNEY SLADE MAX HARRIS
THE GUSH RAGING SPEEDHORN
GYM AND TONIC SPACEDUST
GYPSY FLEETWOOD MAC
GYPSY BEAT PACKABEATS
GYPSY BOY, GYPSY GIRL SHARADA HOUSE GANG
GYPSY EYES JIMI HENDRIX EXPERIENCE
GYPSY ROAD CINDERELLA
GYPSY ROAD HOG SLADE
GYPSY ROVER HIGHWAYMEN
GYPSY WOMAN BRIAN HYLAND
GYPSY WOMAN (LA DA DEE) CRYSTAL WATERS
GYPSYS TRAMPS AND THIEVES CHER
HA CHA CHA (FUNKTION) BRASS CONSTRUCTION
HA HA SAID THE CLOWN MANFRED MANN
HAD TO BE CLIFF RICHARD & OLIVIA NEWTON-JOHN
HAIL CAESAR AC/DC
HAIL HAIL ROCK 'N' ROLL GARLAND JEFFREYS
HAIL MARY MAKAVELI
HAITIAN DIVORCE STEELY DAN
HALE BOPP DER DRITTE RAUM
HALEY'S GOLDEN MEDLEY BILL HALEY & HIS COMETS
HALF A BOY HALF A MAN NICK LOWE
HALF A HEART H & CLAIRE
HALF A MINUTE MATT BIANCO
HALF AS MUCH ROSEMARY CLOONEY
HALF MAN HALF MACHINE GOLDIE LOOKIN CHAIN
HALF OF MY HEART EMILE FORD
HALF ON A BABY R KELLY
HALF THE DAY'S GONE AND WE HAVEN'T EARNT A
    PENNY KENNY LYNCH
HALF THE MAN JAMIROQUAI

HALF THE WORLD BELINDA CARLISLE
HALFWAY AROUND THE WORLD A TEENS
HALFWAY DOWN THE STAIRS MUPPETS
HALFWAY HOTEL VOYAGER
HALFWAY TO HEAVEN EUROPE
HALFWAY TO PARADISE BILLY FURY
HALFWAY UP HALFWAY DOWN DENNIS BROWN
HALLELUIAH MAN LOVE & MONEY
HALLELUJAH MILK & HONEY FEATURING GALI ATARI
HALLELUJAH '92 INNER CITY
HALLELUJAH DAY JACKSON 5
HALLELUJAH FREEDOM JUNIOR CAMPBELL
HALLELUJAH I LOVE HER SO EDDIE COCHRAN
HALLELUJAH I LOVE HER SO DICK JORDAN
HALLO SPACEBOY DAVID BOWIE
HALLOWED BE THY NAME (LIVE) IRON MAIDEN
HALLS OF ILLUSION INSANE CLOWN POSSE
HALO [A] TEXAS
HALO [B] SOIL
(HAMMER HAMMER) THEY PUT ME IN THE MIX MC
    HAMMER
HAMMER HORROR KATE BUSH
HAMMER TO FALL QUEEN
HAMMER TO THE HEART TAMPERER FEATURING MAYA
HAND A HANDKERCHIEF TO HELEN SUSAN MAUGHAN
HAND HELD IN BLACK AND WHITE DOLLAR
HAND IN GLOVE SANDIE SHAW
HAND IN HAND GRACE
HAND IN MY POCKET ALANIS MORISSETTE
HAND IN YOUR HEAD MONEY MARK
HAND OF THE DEAD BODY SCARFACE FEATURING ICE
    CUBE
HAND ON MY HEART SHRIEKBACK
HAND ON YOUR HEART KYLIE MINOGUE
HANDBAGS AND GLADRAGS CHRIS FARLOWE
HANDBAGS AND GLADRAGS STEREOPHONICS
HANDFUL OF PROMISES BIG FUN
HANDFUL OF SONGS TOMMY STEELE & THE STEELMEN
HANDLE WITH CARE TRAVELING WILBURYS
HANDS JEWEL
HANDS ACROSS THE OCEAN MISSION
HANDS AROUND MY THROAT DEATH IN VEGAS
HANDS CLEAN ALANIS MORISSETTE
HANDS DOWN DASHBOARD CONFESSIONAL
HANDS OFF – SHE'S MINE BEAT
HANDS TO HEAVEN BREATHE
HANDS UP [A] CLUBZONE
HANDS UP [B] TREVOR & SIMON
HANDS UP (4 LOVERS) RIGHT SAID FRED
HANDS UP (GIVE ME YOUR HEART) OTTAWAN
HANDS UP! HANDS UP! ZIG & ZAG
HANDY MAN JIMMY JONES
HANDY MAN DEL SHANNON
HANG 'EM HIGH HUGO MONTENEGRO
HANG IN LONG ENOUGH PHIL COLLINS
HANG MYSELF ON YOU CANDYSKINS
HANG ON IN THERE BABY JOHNNY BRISTOL
HANG ON IN THERE BABY CURIOSITY
HANG ON NOW KAJAGOOGOO
HANG ON SLOOPY McCOYS
HANG ON SLOOPY SANDPIPERS
HANG ON TO A DREAM TIM HARDIN
HANG ON TO YOUR LOVE JASON DONOVAN
HANG TOGETHER ODYSSEY
HANG YOUR HEAD DEACON BLUE
HANGAR 18 MEGADETH
HANGIN' CHIC
HANGIN' ON A STRING (CONTEMPLATING) LOOSE
    ENDS
HANGIN' OUT KOOL & THE GANG
HANGIN' TOUGH NEW KIDS ON THE BLOCK

HANGINAROUND COUNTING CROWS
HANGING AROUND [A] HAZEL O'CONNOR
HANGING AROUND [B] ME ME ME
HANGING AROUND [C] CARDIGANS
HANGING AROUND [D] GEMMA HAYES
HANGING AROUND [E] POLYPHONIC SPREE
HANGING AROUND WITH THE BIG BOYS BLOOMSBURY
    SET
HANGING BY A MOMENT LIFEHOUSE
HANGING GARDEN CURE
HANGING ON THE TELEPHONE BLONDIE
HANGINAROUND COUNTING CROWS
HANGOVER BETTY BOO
HANKY PANKY [A] TOMMY JAMES & THE SHONDELLS
HANKY PANKY [B] MADONNA
HANNA HANNA CHINA CRISIS
HAPPENIN' ALL OVER AGAIN LONNIE GORDON
HAPPENIN' ALL OVER AGAIN TRACY SHAW
THE HAPPENING SUPREMES
HAPPENINGS TEN YEARS TIME AGO YARDBIRDS
HAPPINESS [A] KEN DODD
HAPPINESS [B] SERIOUS ROPE PRESENTS SHARON DEE
    CLARK
HAPPINESS [C] ROGER TAYLOR
HAPPINESS [D] PIZZAMAN
HAPPINESS [E] KAMASUTRA FEATURING JOCELYN
    BROWN
HAPPINESS [F] SOUND DE-ZIGN
HAPPINESS HAPPENING LOST WITNESS
HAPPINESS IS JUST AROUND THE BEND CUBA
    GOODING
HAPPINESS IS ME AND YOU GILBERT O'SULLIVAN
HAPPINESS (MY VISION IS CLEAR) BINI & MARTINI
HAPPY [A] SURFACE
HAPPY [A] MN8
HAPPY [A] PAULINE HENRY
HAPPY [B] NED'S ATOMIC DUSTBIN
HAPPY [C] TRAVIS
HAPPY [D] LIGHTHOUSE FAMILY
HAPPY [E] ASHANTI
HAPPY [F] MAX SEDGLEY
HAPPY ANNIVERSARY [A] JOAN REGAN
HAPPY ANNIVERSARY [B] SLIM WHITMAN
HAPPY BIRTHDAY [A] STEVIE WONDER
HAPPY BIRTHDAY [B] ALTERED IMAGES
HAPPY BIRTHDAY [C] TECHNOHEAD
HAPPY BIRTHDAY REVOLUTION LEVELLERS
HAPPY BIRTHDAY SWEET SIXTEEN NEIL SEDAKA
HAPPY BIZZNESS ROACH MOTEL
HAPPY BUSMAN FRANK & WALTERS
HAPPY DAY BLINK
HAPPY DAYS [A] PRATT & McCLAIN WITH
    BROTHERLOVE
HAPPY DAYS [B] SWEET MERCY FEATURING JOE
    ROBERTS
HAPPY DAYS [C] PJ
HAPPY DAYS AND LONELY NIGHTS SUZI MILLER & THE
    JOHNSTON BROTHERS
HAPPY DAYS AND LONELY NIGHTS FRANKIE VAUGHAN
HAPPY DAYS AND LONELY NIGHTS RUBY MURRAY
HAPPY ENDING JOE JACKSON
HAPPY ENDINGS (GIVE YOURSELF A PINCH) LIONEL
    BART
HAPPY EVER AFTER JULIA FORDHAM
HAPPY FEELING HAMILTON BOHANNON
HAPPY GO LUCKY ME GEORGE FORMBY
HAPPY GUITAR TOMMY STEELE
HAPPY HEART ANDY WILLIAMS
HAPPY HOME 2PAC
HAPPY HOUR HOUSEMARTINS
HAPPY HOUSE SIOUXSIE & THE BANSHEES

HAPPY JACK WHO

HAPPY JUST TO BE WITH YOU MICHELLE GAYLE

HAPPY (LOVE THEME FROM 'LADY SINGS THE BLUES')
MICHAEL JACKSON

THE HAPPY MAN THOMAS LANG

HAPPY NATION ACE OF BASE

HAPPY PEOPLE [A] STATIC REVENGER

HAPPY PEOPLE [B] R KELLY

H.A.P.P.Y. RADIO EDWIN STARR

H-A-P-P-Y RADIO MICHAELA

HAPPY SHOPPER 60FT DOLLS

HAPPY SONG OTIS REDDING

HAPPY TALK CAPTAIN SENSIBLE

HAPPY TO BE ON AN ISLAND IN THE SUN DEMIS
ROUSSOS

HAPPY TO MAKE YOUR ACQUAINTANCE SAMMY DAVIS
Jr. & CARMEN McRAE

HAPPY TOGETHER TURTLES

HAPPY TOGETHER JASON DONOVAN

HAPPY WANDERER OBERKIRCHEN CHILDREN'S CHOIR

HAPPY WANDERER STARGAZERS

HAPPY WHEN IT RAINS JESUS & MARY CHAIN

THE HAPPY WHISTLER DON ROBERTSON

THE HAPPY WHISTLER CYRIL STAPLETON ORCHESTRA
FEATURING DESMOND LANE, PENNY WHISTLE

HAPPY XMAS (WAR IS OVER) JOHN & YOKO & THE
PLASTIC ONO BAND WITH THE HARLEM
COMMUNITY CHOIR

HAPPY XMAS (WAR IS OVER) IDOLS

HARBOUR LIGHTS PLATTERS

HARD AS A ROCK AC/DC

HARD BEAT EP 19 VARIOUS ARTISTS (EP'S & LPS)

A HARD DAY'S NIGHT BEATLES

A HARD DAY'S NIGHT PETER SELLERS

HARD HABIT TO BREAK CHICAGO

HARD HEADED WOMAN ELVIS PRESLEY

HARD HEARTED HANNAH TEMPERANCE SEVEN

HARD HOUSE MUSIC MELT FEATURING LITTLE MS
MARCIE

HARD KNOCK LIFE (GHETTO ANTHEM) JAY-Z

A HARD RAIN'S GONNA FALL BRYAN FERRY

HARD ROAD BLACK SABBATH

HARD TIMES COME EASY RICHIE SAMBORA

HARD TO EXPLAIN STROKES

HARD TO HANDLE OTIS REDDING

HARD TO HANDLE BLACK CROWES

HARD TO MAKE A STAND SHERYL CROW

HARD TO SAY I'M SORRY CHICAGO

HARD TO SAY I'M SORRY AZ YET FEATURING PETER
CETERA

HARD TO SAY I'M SORRY AQUAGEN

HARD UP AWESOME 3

THE HARD WAY NASHVILLE TEENS

HARDCORE – THE FINAL CONFLICT HARDCORE
RHYTHM TEAM

THE HARDCORE EP HYPNOTIST

HARDCORE HEAVEN DJ SEDUCTION

HARDCORE HIP HOUSE TYREE

HARDCORE UPROAR TOGETHER

HARDCORE WILL NEVER DIE Q-BASS

HARDEN MY HEART QUATERFLASH

HARDER KOSHEEN

HARDER BETTER FASTER STRONGER DAFT PUNK

THE HARDER I TRY BROTHER BEYOND

THE HARDER THEY COME [A] ROCKER'S REVENGE

THE HARDER THEY COME [A] MADNESS

THE HARDER THEY COME [B] PAUL OAKENFOLD

THE HARDEST BUTTON TO BUTTON WHITE STRIPES

HARDEST PART IS THE NIGHT BON JOVI

THE HARDEST THING 98o

HARDROCK HERBIE HANCOCK

HARDTRANCE ACPERIENCE HARDFLOOR

HARE KRISHNA MANTRA RADHA KRISHNA TEMPLE

HARLEM DESIRE LONDON BOYS

HARLEM SHUFFLE BOB & EARL

HARLEM SHUFFLE ROLLING STONES

HARLEQUIN – THE BEAUTY AND THE BEAST SVEN VATH

HARMONIC GENERATOR DATSUNS

HARMONICA MAN BRAVADO

HARMONY TC 1993

HARMONY IN MY HEAD BUZZCOCKS

HARMOUR LOVE SYREETA

HARPER VALLEY P.T.A. JEANNIE C. RILEY

HARVEST FOR THE WORLD ISLEY BROTHERS

HARVEST FOR THE WORLD CHRISTIANS

HARVEST FOR THE WORLD TERRY HUNTER

HARVEST MOON NEIL YOUNG

HARVEST OF LOVE BENNY HILL

HARVESTER OF SORROW METALLICA

HAS IT COME TO THIS STREETS

HASH PIPE WEEZER

HASTA LA VISTA SYLVIA

HATE ME NOW NAS FEATURING PUFF DADDY

THE HATE SONG RAGING SPEEDHORN

HATE TO SAY I TOLD YOU SO HIVES

HATERS SO SOLID CREW PRESENTS MR SHABZ

HATS OFF TO LARRY DEL SHANNON

HAUNTED POGUES

HAUNTED SHANE MacGOWAN & SINEAD O'CONNOR

HAUNTED BY YOU GENE

HAVA NAGILA SPOTNICKS

HAVE A CHEEKY CHRISTMAS CHEEKY GIRLS

HAVE A DRINK ON ME LONNIE DONEGAN

HAVE A GOOD FOREVER COOLNOTES

HAVE A LITTLE FAITH JOE COCKER

HAVE A NICE DAY [A] ROXANNE SHANTE

HAVE A NICE DAY [B] STEREOPHONICS

HAVE FUN, GO MAD! BLAIR

HAVE FUN GO MAD TWEENIES

HAVE I STAYED TOO LONG SONNY & CHER

HAVE I THE RIGHT HONEYCOMBS

HAVE I THE RIGHT DEAD END KIDS

HAVE I TOLD YOU LATELY VAN MORRISON

HAVE I TOLD YOU LATELY ROD STEWART

HAVE I TOLD YOU LATELY THAT I LOVE YOU CHIEFTAINS
WITH VAN MORRISON

HAVE IT ALL FOO FIGHTERS

HAVE LOST IT (EP) TEENAGE FANCLUB

HAVE LOVE WILL TRAVEL (EP) CRAZYHEAD

HAVE MERCY YAZZ

HAVE PITY ON THE BOY PAUL & BARRY RYAN

HAVE YOU EVER? [A] BRANDY

HAVE YOU EVER [B] S CLUB 7

HAVE YOU EVER BEEN IN LOVE LEO SAYER

HAVE YOU EVER BEEN MELLOW PARTY ANIMALS

HAVE YOU EVER BEEN MELLOW (EP) PARTY ANIMALS

HAVE YOU EVER HAD IT BLUE STYLE COUNCIL

HAVE YOU EVER LOVED SOMEBODY [A] PAUL & BARRY
RYAN

HAVE YOU EVER LOVED SOMEBODY [B] SEARCHERS

HAVE YOU EVER LOVED SOMEBODY [C] FREDDIE
JACKSON

HAVE YOU EVER NEEDED SOMEONE SO BAD DEF
LEPPARD

HAVE YOU EVER REALLY LOVED A WOMAN? BRYAN
ADAMS

HAVE YOU EVER SEEN THE RAIN CREEDENCE
CLEARWATER REVIVAL

HAVE YOU EVER SEEN THE RAIN BONNIE TYLER

HAVE YOU EVER SEEN THE RAIN? JEEVAS

HAVE YOU SEEN HER CHI-LITES

HAVE YOU SEEN HER MC HAMMER

HAVE YOU SEEN YOUR MOTHER BABY STANDING IN THE
SHADOW ROLLING STONES

HAVEN'T SEEN YOU PERFUME

HAVEN'T STOPPED DANCING YET GONZALEZ

HAVEN'T YOU HEARD PATRICE RUSHEN

HAVIN' A GOOD TIME SOUVERNANCE

HAVING A PARTY OSMONDS

HAWAII TATTOO WAIKIKIS

HAWAIIAN WEDDING SONG JULIE ROGERS

HAWKEYE FRANKIE LAINE

HAYFEVER TRASH CAN SINATRAS

HAYLING FC KAHUNA

HAZARD RICHARD MARX

HAZEL LOOP DA LOOP

HAZELL MAGGIE BELL

HAZIN' & PHAZIN' CHOO CHOO PROJECT

A HAZY SHADE OF WINTER SIMON & GARFUNKEL

HAZY SHADE OF WINTER BANGLES

HE AIN'T HEAVY, HE'S MY BROTHER HOLLIES

HE AIN'T HEAVY, HE'S MY BROTHER BILL MEDLEY

HE AIN'T NO COMPETITION BROTHER BEYOND

HE DOESN'T LOVE YOU LIKE I DO NICK HEYWARD

HE DON'T LOVE YOU HUMAN NATURE

HE GOT GAME PUBLIC ENEMY

HE GOT WHAT HE WANTED LITTLE RICHARD

HE IS SAILING JON & VANGELIS

HE KNOWS YOU KNOW MARILLION

HE LOVES U NOT DREAM

HE REMINDS ME RANDY CRAWFORD

HE THINKS HE'LL KEEP HER MARY CHAPIN CARPENTER

HE WAS BEAUTIFUL (CAVATINA) (THE THEME FROM 'THE
DEER HUNTER') IRIS WILLIAMS

HE WASN'T MAN ENOUGH TONI BRAXTON

HEAD JULIAN COPE

HEAD ABOVE WATER CLIVE GRIFFIN

HEAD LIKE A HOLE NINE INCH NAILS

HEAD ON JESUS & MARY CHAIN

HEAD ON COLLISION NEW FOUND GLORY

HEAD OVER FEET ALANIS MORISSETTE

HEAD OVER HEELS [A] ABBA

HEAD OVER HEELS [B] TEARS FOR FEARS

HEAD OVER HEELS [C] NIC HAVERSON

HEAD OVER HEELS [D] ALLURE FEATURING NAS

HEAD OVER HEELS IN LOVE KEVIN KEEGAN

HEAD TO TOE (EP) BREEDERS

HEADACHE FRANK BLACK

HEADING WEST CYNDI LAUPER

HEADLESS CROSS BLACK SABBATH

HEADLIGHTS ON PARADE BLUE NILE

HEADLINE NEWS EDWIN STARR

HEADLINE NEWS WILLIAM BELL

HEADLINES MIDNIGHT STAR

HEADLONG QUEEN

HEADS DOWN NO NONSENSE MINDLESS BOOGIE
ALBERTO Y LOS TRIOS PARANOIAS

HEADS HIGH MR VEGAS

HEADSPRUNG LL COOL J

HEAL THE PAIN GEORGE MICHAEL

HEAL (THE SEPARATION) SHAMEN

HEAL THE WORLD MICHAEL JACKSON

THE HEALING GAME VAN MORRISON

HEALING HANDS ELTON JOHN

HEALING LOVE CLIFF RICHARD

HEAR ME CALLING 2WO THIRD3

HEAR MY CALL ALISON LIMERICK

HEAR MY NAME ARMAND VAN HELDEN

HEAR THE DRUMMER (GET WICKED) CHAD JACKSON

HEAR YOU CALLING AURORA

HEARD IT ALL BEFORE SUNSHINE ANDERSON

HEARSAY '89 ALEXANDER O'NEAL

HEART [A] MAX BYGRAVES

HEART [A] JOHNSTON BROTHERS
HEART [B] RITA PAVONE
HEART [C] PET SHOP BOYS
HEART [D] GARY NUMAN
HEART [E] SERAPHIM SUITE
HEART AND SOUL [A] JAN & DEAN
HEART AND SOUL [B] EXILE
HEART AND SOUL [C] T'PAU
HEART AND SOUL [D] NO SWEAT
HEART AND SOUL [E] CILLA BLACK WITH DUSTY
    SPRINGFIELD
HEART AND SOUL [F] TSD
HEART AND SOUL (EP) HUEY LEWIS & THE NEWS
THE HEART ASKS PLEASURE FIRST MICHAEL NYMAN
HEART ATTACK OLIVIA NEWTON-JOHN
HEART ATTACK AND VINE SCREAMIN' JAY HAWKINS
HEART (DON'T CHANGE MY MIND) DIANA ROSS
HEART FAILED (IN THE BACK OF A TAXI) SAINT ETIENNE
HEART FULL OF SOUL YARDBIRDS
HEART GO BOOM APOLLO FOUR FORTY
HEART LIKE A WHEEL HUMAN LEAGUE
THE HEART OF A MAN FRANKIE VAUGHAN
HEART OF A SINGLE GIRL GEORGE CHAKIRIS
THE HEART OF A TEENAGE GIRL CRAIG DOUGLAS
HEART OF ASIA WATERGATE
HEART OF GLASS BLONDIE
HEART OF GLASS ASSOCIATES
HEART OF GOLD [A] NEIL YOUNG
HEART OF GOLD [B] JOHNNY HATES JAZZ
HEART OF GOLD [C] FORCE & STYLES FEATURING KELLY
    LLORENNA
HEART OF GOLD [C] KELLY LLORENNA
HEART OF LOTHIAN MARILLION
HEART OF MY HEART MAX BYGRAVES
THE HEART OF ROCK AND ROLL HUEY LEWIS & THE NEWS
HEART OF SOUL CULT
HEART OF STONE [A] KENNY
HEART OF STONE [B] SUZI QUATRO
HEART OF STONE [C] BUCKS FIZZ
HEART OF STONE [C] CHER
HEART OF STONE [D] DAVE STEWART
HEART OF THE SUN RED BOX
HEART OF THE WORLD BIG COUNTRY
HEART ON MY SLEEVE GALLAGHER & LYLE
HEART OVER MIND KIM WILDE
HEART (STOP BEATING IN TIME) LEO SAYER
HEART USER CLIFF RICHARD
HEARTACHE [A] ROY ORBISON
HEARTACHE [B] GENE LOVES JEZEBEL
HEARTACHE [C] PEPSI & SHIRLIE
HEARTACHE ALL OVER THE WORLD ELTON JOHN
HEARTACHE AVENUE MAISONETTES
HEARTACHE TONIGHT EAGLES
HEARTACHES PATSY CLINE
HEARTACHES VINCE HILL
HEARTACHES BY THE NUMBER GUY MITCHELL
HEARTBEAT [A] RUBY MURRAY
HEARTBEAT [B] BUDDY HOLLY
HEARTBEAT [B] ENGLAND SISTERS
HEARTBEAT [B] SHOWADDYWADDY
HEARTBEAT [B] NICK BERRY
HEARTBEAT [B] HEARTBEAT COUNTRY
HEARTBEAT [C] SAMMY HAGAR
HEARTBEAT [D] TIPPA IRIE
HEARTBEAT [E] DON JOHNSON
HEARTBEAT [F] SEDUCTION
HEARTBEAT [G] GRID
HEARTBEAT [H] JIMMY SOMERVILLE
HEARTBEAT [I] KRS ONE
HEARTBEAT [J] STEPS
A HEARTBEAT AWAY McGANNS

HEARTBEAT (TAINAI KAIKI II) RETURNING TO THE
    WOMB DAVID SYLVIAN/RYUICHI SAKAMOTO
    FEATURING INGRID CHAVEZ
HEARTBREAK MRS WOOD FEATURING EVE GALLAGHER
HEARTBREAK HOTEL [A] ELVIS PRESLEY
HEARTBREAK HOTEL [A] STAN FREBERG & HIS SKIFFLE
    GROUP
HEARTBREAK HOTEL [B] JACKSONS
HEARTBREAK HOTEL [C] WHITNEY HOUSTON
    FEATURING FAITH EVANS & KELLY PRICE
HEARTBREAK RADIO ROY ORBISON
HEARTBREAK STATION CINDERELLA
HEARTBREAK STROLL RAVEONETTES
HEARTBREAKER [A] DIONNE WARWICK
HEARTBREAKER [B] MUSICAL YOUTH
HEARTBREAKER [C] COLOR ME BADD
HEARTBREAKER [D] MARIAH CAREY FEATURING JAY-Z
HEARTBROKE AND BUSTED MAGNUM
HEARTHAMMER (EP) RUNRIG
HEARTLAND THE THE
THE HEARTLESS CREW THEME AKA 'THE SUPERGLUE
    RIDDIM' HEARTLESS CREW
HEARTLIGHT NEIL DIAMOND
HEARTLINE ROBIN GEORGE
THE HEART'S FILTHY LESSON DAVID BOWIE
THE HEART'S LONE DESIRE MATTHEW MARSDEN
HEARTS ON FIRE [A] SAM HARRIS
HEARTS ON FIRE [B] BRYAN ADAMS
HEARTSONG GORDON GILTRAP
HEART-SHAPED BOX NIRVANA
HEARTSPARK DOLLARSIGN EVERCLEAR
THE HEAT IS ON [A] AGNETHA FALTSKOG
THE HEAT IS ON [B] GLENN FREY
HEAT IT UP WEE PAPA GIRL RAPPERS FEATURING TWO
    MEN & A DRUM MACHINE
HEAT OF THE BEAT ROY AYERS & WAYNE HENDERSON
HEAT OF THE MOMENT ASIA
HEAT OF THE NIGHT BRYAN ADAMS
HEATHER HONEY TOMMY ROE
HEATSEEKER AC/DC
HEAVEN [A] PSYCHEDELIC FURS
HEAVEN [B] BRYAN ADAMS
HEAVEN [B] DJ SAMMY & YANOU FEATURING DO
HEAVEN [C] TWO PEOPLE
HEAVEN [D] CHIMES
HEAVEN [E] CHRIS REA
HEAVEN [F] TIGERTAILZ
HEAVEN [G] WHYCLIFFE
HEAVEN [H] FITS OF GLOOM
HEAVEN [I] SOLO (US)
HEAVEN [J] SARAH WASHINGTON
HEAVEN [K] KINANE
HEAVEN & EARTH [A] RED
HEAVEN AND EARTH [B] POP!
HEAVEN AND HELL, THIRD MOVEMENT (THEME FROM
    THE BBC-TV SERIES 'THE COSMOS) VANGELIS
HEAVEN BESIDE YOU ALICE IN CHAINS
HEAVEN CAN WAIT PAUL YOUNG
HEAVEN FOR EVERYONE QUEEN
HEAVEN GIVE ME WORDS PROPAGANDA
HEAVEN HELP LENNY KRAVITZ
HEAVEN HELP ME DEON ESTUS
HEAVEN HELP MY HEART TINA ARENA
HEAVEN HELP US ALL STEVIE WONDER
THE HEAVEN I NEED THREE DEGREES
HEAVEN IN MY HANDS LEVEL 42
HEAVEN IS DEF LEPPARD
HEAVEN IS A HALFPIPE OPM
HEAVEN IS A PLACE ON EARTH BELINDA CARLISLE
HEAVEN IS A PLACE ON EARTH SODA CLUB FEATURING
    HANNAH ALETHA

HEAVEN IS CLOSER (FEELS LIKE HEAVEN) DARIO G
HEAVEN IS HERE JULIE FELIX
HEAVEN IS IN THE BACK SEAT OF MY CADILLAC HOT
    CHOCOLATE
HEAVEN IS MY WOMAN'S LOVE VAL DOONICAN
HEAVEN IS WAITING DANSE SOCIETY
HEAVEN KNOWS [A] DONNA SUMMER
HEAVEN KNOWS [B] JAKI GRAHAM
HEAVEN KNOWS [B] LALAH HATHAWAY
HEAVEN KNOWS [C] ROBERT PLANT
HEAVEN KNOWS [D] COOL DOWN ZONE
HEAVEN KNOWS [E] LUTHER VANDROSS
HEAVEN KNOWS [F] SQUEEZE
HEAVEN KNOWS – DEEP DEEP DOWN ANGEL MORAES
HEAVEN KNOWS I'M MISERABLE NOW SMITHS
HEAVEN MUST BE MISSING AN ANGEL TAVARES
HEAVEN MUST BE MISSING AN ANGEL WORLDS APART
HEAVEN MUST HAVE SENT YOU ELGINS
HEAVEN MUST HAVE SENT YOU BACK CICERO
HEAVEN ON EARTH SPELLBOUND
HEAVEN ON THE 7TH FLOOR PAUL NICHOLAS
HEAVEN OR HELL STRANGLERS
HEAVEN SCENT BEDROCK
HEAVEN SENT [A] PAUL HAIG
HEAVEN SENT [B] INXS
HEAVEN SENT [C] M1
HEAVEN WILL COME SPACE BROTHERS
HEAVENLY SHOWADDYWADDY
HEAVEN'S EARTH DELERIUM
HEAVEN'S HERE HOLLY JOHNSON
HEAVEN'S ON FIRE KISS
HEAVEN'S WHAT I FEEL GLORIA ESTEFAN
HEAVY FUEL DIRE STRAITS
HEAVY MAKES YOU HAPPY BOBBY BLOOM
HEAVY VIBES MONTANA SEXTET
HEDONISM (JUST BECAUSE YOU FEEL GOOD) SKUNK
    ANANSIE
HELEN WHEELS PAUL McCARTNEY & WINGS
HELICOPTER BLOC PARTY
HELICOPTER TUNE DEEP BLUE
HELIOPOLIS BY NIGHT ABERFELDY
HELIUM DALLAS SUPERSTARS
THE HELL EP TRICKY VS THE GRAVEDIGGAZ
HELL HATH NO FURY FRANKIE LAINE
THE HELL SONG SUM 41
HE'LL HAVE TO GO JIM REEVES
HE'LL HAVE TO GO BRYAN FERRY
HE'LL HAVE TO STAY JEANNE BLACK
HELL RAISER SWEET
HELL YEAH GINUWINE
HELLA GOOD NO DOUBT
HELLBOUND TYGERS OF PAN TANG
HELLO [A] LIONEL RICHIE
HELLO [A] JHAY PALMER FEATURING MC IMAGE
HELLO [B] BELOVED
HELLO AGAIN NEIL DIAMOND
HELLO AMERICA DEF LEPPARD
HELLO BUDDY TREMELOES
HELLO DARLIN' FUZZ TOWNSHEND
HELLO DARLING TIPPA IRIE
HELLO DOLLY LOUIS ARMSTRONG
HELLO DOLLY FRANKIE VAUGHAN
HELLO DOLLY KENNY BALL & HIS JAZZMEN
HELLO DOLLY BACHELORS
HELLO DOLLY FRANK SINATRA WITH COUNT BASIE
HELLO GOODBYE BEATLES
HELLO HAPPINESS DRIFTERS
HELLO HEARTACHE GOODBYE LOVE LITTLE PEGGY
    MARCH
HELLO HONKY TONKS (ROCK YOUR BODY) PIZZAMAN
HELLO HOW ARE YOU EASYBEATS

HELLO HURRAY ALICE COOPER
HELLO I AM YOUR HEART BETTE BRIGHT
HELLO I LOVE YOU DOORS
HELLO? IS THIS THING ON? ! ! !
HELLO JOSEPHINE WAYNE FONTANA & THE MINDBENDERS
HELLO LITTLE GIRL FOURMOST
HELLO MARY LOU (GOODBYE HEART) RICKY NELSON
HELLO MUDDAH HELLO FADDAH ALLAN SHERMAN
HELLO STRANGER YVONNE ELLIMAN
HELLO SUMMERTIME BOBBY GOLDSBORO
HELLO SUNSHINE SUPER FURRY ANIMALS
HELLO SUZIE AMEN CORNER
HELLO THIS IS JOANNIE (THE TELEPHONE ANSWERING MACHINE SONG) PAUL EVANS
HELLO TIGER URUSEI YATSURA
HELLO (TURN YOUR RADIO ON) SHAKESPEARS SISTER
HELLO WORLD [A] TREMELOES
HELLO WORLD [B] SEA FRUIT
HELLO YOUNG LOVERS PAUL ANKA
HELLO! HELLO! I'M BACK AGAIN GARY GLITTER
HELLRAISER ANNE SAVAGE
HELL'S PARTY GLAM
HELP! BEATLES
HELP TINA TURNER
HELP! BANANARAMA/LA NA NEE NEE NOO NOO
HELP (EP) VARIOUS ARTISTS (EP'S & LPS)
HELP I'M A FISH LITTLE TREES
HELP IT ALONG CLIFF RICHARD
HELP ME [A] TIMO MAAS FEATURING KELIS
HELP ME [B] NICK CARTER
HELP ME FIND A WAY TO YOUR HEART DARYL HALL
HELP ME GIRL ERIC BURDON & THE ANIMALS
HELP ME MAKE IT HUFF & PUFF
HELP ME MAKE IT THROUGH THE NIGHT GLADYS KNIGHT & THE PIPS
HELP ME MAKE IT THROUGH THE NIGHT JOHN HOLT
HELP ME MAMA LEMONESCENT
HELP ME RHONDA BEACH BOYS
HELP MY FRIEND SLO-MOSHUN
HELP THE AGED PULP
HELP YOURSELF [A] TOM JONES
HELP YOURSELF [A] TONY FERRINO
HELP YOURSELF [B] JULIAN LENNON
HELP YOURSELF [C] AMY WINEHOUSE
HELP, GET ME SOME HELP! OTTAWAN
HELPLESS TRACEY ULLMAN
HELULE HELULE TREMELOES
HELYOM HALIB CAPPELLA
HENRY LEE NICK CAVE & THE BAD SEEDS & PJ HARVEY
HENRY VIII SUITE (EP) EARLY MUSIC CONSORT DIRECTED BY DAVID MUNROW
HER GUY
HER ROYAL MAJESTY JAMES DARREN
HERCULES FRANKIE VAUGHAN
HERE LUSCIOUS JACKSON
HERE AND NOW [A] LUTHER VANDROSS
HERE AND NOW [B] DEL AMITRI
HERE AND NOW/YOU'LL BE SORRY STEPS
HERE COME THE GOOD TIMES A HOUSE
HERE COME THE NICE SMALL FACES
HERE COMES MY BABY TREMELOES
HERE COMES SUMMER JERRY KELLER
HERE COMES SUMMER DAVE CLARK FIVE
HERE COMES THAT FEELING BRENDA LEE
HERE COMES THAT SOUND SIMON HARRIS
HERE COMES THE BIG RUSH ECHOBELLY
HERE COMES THE HAMMER MC HAMMER
HERE COMES THE HOTSTEPPER INI KAMOZE
HERE COMES THE JUDGE [A] SHORTY LONG
HERE COMES THE JUDGE [B] PIGMEAT MARKHAM

HERE COMES THE MAN BOOM BOOM BOOM
HERE COMES THE NIGHT [A] LULU
HERE COMES THE NIGHT [A] THEM
HERE COMES THE NIGHT [B] BEACH BOYS
HERE COMES THE PAIN LEE HASLAM
HERE COMES THE RAIN AGAIN EURYTHMICS
HERE COMES THE STAR HERMAN'S HERMITS
HERE COMES THE SUMMER UNDERTONES
HERE COMES THE SUN STEVE HARLEY
HERE COMES THE WAR NEW MODEL ARMY
HERE COMES YOUR MAN PIXIES
HERE 4 ONE BLAZIN' SQUAD
HERE I AM BRYAN ADAMS
HERE I AM (COME AND TAKE ME) UB40
HERE I COME BARRINGTON LEVY
HERE I COME (SING DJ) TALISMAN P MEETS BARRINGTON LEVY
HERE I GO 2 UNLIMITED
HERE I GO AGAIN [A] HOLLIES
HERE I GO AGAIN [B] ARCHIE BELL & THE DRELLS
HERE I GO AGAIN [C] GUYS & DOLLS
HERE I GO AGAIN [D] TWIGGY
HERE I GO AGAIN [E] WHITESNAKE
HERE I GO AGAIN [E] FRASH
HERE I STAND [A] MILLTOWN BROTHERS
HERE I STAND [B] BITTY McLEAN
HERE IN MY HEART AL MARTINO
HERE IS THE NEWS ELECTRIC LIGHT ORCHESTRA
HERE IT COMES DOVES
HERE IT COMES AGAIN [A] FORTUNES
HERE IT COMES AGAIN [B] BLACK
HERE IT COMES AGAIN [C] MELANIE C
HERE SHE COMES AGAIN STANDS
HERE THERE AND EVERYWHERE EMMYLOU HARRIS
HERE TO STAY [A] NEW ORDER
HERE TO STAY [B] KORN
HERE WE ARE GLORIA ESTEFAN
HERE WE COME TIMBALAND/MISSY ELLIOTT & MAGOO
HERE WE GO [A] EVERTON FC
HERE WE GO [B] C & C MUSIC FACTORY (FEATURING FREEDOM WILLIAMS)
HERE WE GO [C] STAKKA BO
HERE WE GO [D] ARAB STRAP
HERE WE GO [E] FREESTYLERS
HERE WE GO AGAIN [A] RAY CHARLES
HERE WE GO AGAIN [B] PORTRAIT
HERE WE GO AGAIN [C] A HOMEBOY, A HIPPIE & A FUNKI DREDD
HERE WE GO AGAIN [D] ARETHA FRANKLIN
HERE WE GO ROCK 'N' ROLL SPIDER
HERE WE GO ROUND THE MULBERRY BUSH TRAFFIC
HERE WITH ME DIDO
HERE YOU COME AGAIN DOLLY PARTON
HERE'S MY A RAPINATION FEATURING CAROL KENYON
HERE'S TO LOVE (AULD LANG SYNE) JOHN CHRISTIE
HERE'S WHERE THE STORY ENDS TIN TIN OUT FEATURING SHELLEY NELSON
HERMANN LOVES PAULINE SUPER FURRY ANIMALS
HERNANDO'S HIDEAWAY JOHNSTON BROTHERS
HERNANDO'S HIDEAWAY JOHNNIE RAY
HERO [A] DAVID CROSBY FEATURING PHIL COLLINS
HERO [B] MARIAH CAREY
HERO [C] ENRIQUE IGLESIAS
HERO [D] CHAD KROEGER FEATURING JOSEY SCOTT
HERO OF THE DAY METALLICA
HEROES [A] DAVID BOWIE
HEROES [B] RONI SIZE REPRAZENT
THE HEROES [C] SHED SEVEN
HEROES AND VILLAINS BEACH BOYS
HERSHAM BOYS SHAM 69
HE'S A REBEL CRYSTALS

HE'S A SAINT, HE'S A SINNER MIQUEL BROWN
HE'S BACK (THE MAN BEHIND THE MASK) ALICE COOPER
HE'S GONNA STEP ON YOU AGAIN JOHN KONGOS
HE'S GOT NO LOVE SEARCHERS
HE'S GOT THE WHOLE WORLD IN HIS HANDS LAURIE LONDON
HE'S IN TOWN ROCKIN' BERRIES
HE'S MINE MOKENSTEF
HE'S MISSTRA KNOW IT ALL STEVIE WONDER
HE'S OLD ENOUGH TO KNOW BETTER BROOK BROTHERS
HE'S ON THE PHONE SAINT ETIENNE FEATURING ETIENNE DAHO
HE'S SO FINE CHIFFONS
HE'S THE GREATEST DANCER SISTER SLEDGE
HE'S THE ONE BILLIE DAVIS
HEWLETT'S DAUGHTER GRANDADDY
HEXAGRAM DEFTONES
HEY! JULIO IGLESIAS
HEY AMERICA JAMES BROWN
HEY! BABY [A] BRUCE CHANNEL
HEY BABY [A] DJ OTZI
HEY BABY [B] NO DOUBT
HEY BOY HEY GIRL CHEMICAL BROTHERS
HEY CHILD EAST 17
HEY DJ WORLD'S FAMOUS SUPREME TEAM
HEY DJ LIGHTER SHADE OF BROWN
HEY DJ I CAN'T DANCE TO THAT MUSIC YOU'RE PLAYING BEATMASTERS FEATURING BETTY BOO
HEY DJ! (PLAY THAT SONG) N-TYCE
HEY DUDE KULA SHAKER
HEY GIRL [A] SMALL FACES
HEY GIRL [B] EXPRESSOS
HEY GIRL [C] DELAYS
HEY GIRL DON'T BOTHER ME TAMS
HEY GOD BON JOVI
HEY GOOD LOOKIN' BO DIDDLEY
HEY GOOD LOOKING TOMMY ZANG
HEY JEALOUSY GIN BLOSSOMS
HEY JOE [A] FRANKIE LAINE
HEY JOE [B] JIMI HENDRIX
HEY JUDE BEATLES
HEY JUDE WILSON PICKETT
HEY JULIE FOUNTAINS OF WAYNE
HEY JUPITER TORI AMOS
HEY LITTLE GIRL [A] DEL SHANNON
HEY LITTLE GIRL [B] ICEHOUSE
HEY LITTLE GIRL [C] MATHIAS WARE FEATURING ROB TAYLOR
HEY LORD DON'T ASK ME QUESTIONS GRAHAM PARKER
HEY LOVE KING SUN-D'MOET
HEY LOVER LL COOL J FEATURING BOYZ II MEN
HEY! LUCIANI FALL
HEY MA CAM'RON FEATURING JUELZ SANTANA
HEY MAMA [A] FRANKIE VAUGHAN
HEY MAMA [B] JOE BROWN
HEY MAMA [C] BLACK EYED PEAS
HEY MANHATTAN PREFAB SPROUT
HEY MATTHEW KAREL FIALKA
HEY MISS PAYNE CHEQUERS
HEY MISTER HEARTACHE KIM WILDE
HEY MR. DJ [A] ZHANE
HEY MR DJ [B] OPEN ARMS FEATURING ROWETTA
HEY MR DJ [C] VAN MORRISON
HEY MR. CHRISTMAS SHOWADDYWADDY
HEY MR. DREAM MAKER CLIFF RICHARD
HEY MR. MUSIC MAN PETERS & LEE
HEY MUSIC LOVER S-EXPRESS
HEY NOW (GIRLS JUST WANT TO HAVE FUN) CYNDI LAUPER

HEY NOW NOW SWIRL 360
HEY PAPA! ALEX CARTANA
HEY! PARADISE FLICKMAN
HEY PAULA PAUL & PAULA
HEY ROCK AND ROLL SHOWADDYWADDY
HEY SENORITA WAR
HEY SEXY LADY SHAGGY
HEY STOOPID ALICE COOPER
HEY THERE ROSEMARY CLOONEY
HEY THERE SAMMY DAVIS Jr.
HEY THERE LITA ROZA
HEY THERE JOHNNIE RAY
(HEY THERE) LONELY GIRL EDDIE HOLMAN
HEY THERE LONELY GIRL BIG FUN
HEY VENUS THAT PETROL EMOTION
HEY! WHAT'S YOUR NAME BABY JUNE
HEY WHATEVER WESTLIFE
HEY WILLY HOLLIES
HEY YA! OUTKAST
HEY YOU [A] TOMMY STEELE
HEY YOU [B] QUIREBOYS
(HEY YOU) THE ROCKSTEADY CREW ROCKSTEADY
    CREW
HEYKENS SERANADE THE PIPES & DRUMS & MILITARY
    BAND OF THE ROYAL SCOTS DRAGOON GUARDS
HI DE HI (HOLIDAY ROCK) PAUL SHANE & THE
    YELLOWCOATS
HI DE HI, HI DE HO KOOL & THE GANG
HI DE HO K7 & THE SWING KIDS
HI FIDELITY [A] ELVIS COSTELLO & THE ATTRACTIONS
HI-FIDELITY [B] KIDS FROM FAME FEATURING VALERIE
    LANDSBERG
HI HI HAZEL GENO WASHINGTON & THE RAM JAM
    BAND
HI HI HAZEL TROGGS
HI HI HI WINGS
HI HO SILVER JIM DIAMOND
HI LILI HI LO ALAN PRICE SET
HI TENSION HI TENSION
HI! HOW YA DOIN'? KENNY G
HI-HEEL SNEAKERS TOMMY TUCKER
HI-HO SILVER LINING JEFF BECK
HI-LILI HI-LO RICHARD CHAMBERLAIN
HI-TEK MAMPI SWIFT
HIBERNACULUM MIKE OLDFIELD
HIDDEN AGENDA CRAIG DAVID
HIDDEN PLACE BJORK
HIDE TWEN2Y 4 SE7EN
HIDE AND SEEK [A] MARTY WILDE
HIDE AND SEEK [B] HOWARD JONES
HIDE U KOSHEEN
HIDE YOUR HEART KISS
HIDE-A-WAY NU SOUL FEATURING KELI RICH
HIDEAWAY [A] DAVE DEE, DOZY, BEAKY, MICK & TICH
HIDEAWAY [B] DE'LACY
HIGH [A] CURE
HIGH [B] HYPER GO GO
HIGH [C] FEEDER
HIGH [D] PROPHETS OF SOUND
HIGH [E] LIGHTHOUSE FAMILY
HIGH & DRY RADIOHEAD
HIGH AS A KITE ONE TRIBE FEATURING ROGER
HIGH CLASS BABY CLIFF RICHARD & THE DRIFTERS
HIGH ENERGY EVELYN THOMAS
HIGH FLY JOHN MILES
HIGH HEAD BLUES BLACK CROWES
HIGH HOPES [A] FRANK SINATRA
HIGH HOPES [B] PINK FLOYD
HIGH HORSE EVELYN KING
HIGH IN THE SKY AMEN CORNER
HIGH LIFE MODERN ROMANCE

HIGH NOON [A] FRANKIE LAINE
HIGH NOON [B] DJ SHADOW
HIGH NOON [C] SERIOUS DANGER
HIGH ON A HAPPY VIBE URBAN COOKIE COLLECTIVE
HIGH ON EMOTION CHRIS DE BURGH
HIGH ROLLERS ICE-T
HIGH SCHOOL CONFIDENTIAL JERRY LEE LEWIS
HIGH TIME PAUL JONES
HIGH TIMES JAMIROQUAI
HIGH VOLTAGE JOHNNY & THE HURRICANES
HIGH VOLTAGE (LIVE VERSION) AC/DC
HIGH VOLTAGE/POINTS OF AUTHORITY LINKIN PARK
HIGHER [A] CREED
HIGHER [B] DAVID MORALES & ALBERT CABRERA
    PRESENT MOCA FEATURING DEANNA
HIGHER AND HIGHER UNATION
HIGHER (FEEL IT) ERICK 'MORE' MORILLO PRESENTS
    RAW
HIGHER GROUND [A] STEVIE WONDER
HIGHER GROUND [A] RED HOT CHILI PEPPERS
HIGHER GROUND [B] GUN
HIGHER GROUND [C] UB40
HIGHER GROUND [D] SASHA WITH SAM MOLLISON
HIGHER LOVE STEVE WINWOOD
A HIGHER PLACE PEYTON
HIGHER STATE OF CONSCIOUSNESS '96 REMIXES
    WINK
HIGHER THAN HEAVEN [A] AGE OF CHANCE
HIGHER THAN HEAVEN [B] KELLE BRYAN
HIGHER THAN REASON UNBELIEVABLE TRUTH
HIGHER THAN THE SUN PRIMAL SCREAM
HIGHLIFE CYPRESS HILL
HIGHLY EVOLVED VINES
HIGHLY INFLAMMABLE X-RAY SPEX
HIGHLY STRUNG SPANDAU BALLET
HIGHRISE TOWN LANTERNS
HIGHWAY 5 BLESSING
HIGHWAY CODE MASTER SINGERS
THE HIGHWAY SONG NANCY SINATRA
HIGHWAY TO HELL (LIVE) AC/DC
HIGHWAYS OF MY LIFE ISLEY BROTHERS
HIGHWIRE [A] LINDA CARR & THE LOVE SQUAD
HIGHWIRE [B] ROLLING STONES
HILLBILLY ROCK HILLBILLY ROLL WOOLPACKERS
HIM [A] RUPERT HOLMES
HIM [B] SARAH BRIGHTMAN & THE LONDON
    PHILHARMONIC
THE HINDU TIMES OASIS
HIP HOP DEAD PREZ
HIP HOP DON'T YA DROP HONKY
HIP HOP HOORAY NAUGHTY BY NATURE
HIP HOP, BE BOP (DON'T STOP) MAN PARISH
HIP HOUSE DJ 'FAST' EDDIE
HIP HOUSIN' X-PRESS 2 FEATURING LO-PRO
HIP TO BE SQUARE HUEY LEWIS & THE NEWS
HIP TO HIP V
HIP TODAY EXTREME
HIPPY CHICK SOHO
HIPPY HIPPY SHAKE SWINGING BLUE JEANS
HIPPY HIPPY SHAKE GEORGIA SATELLITES
HIS GIRL GUESS WHO
HIS LATEST FLAME ELVIS PRESLEY
HISTORY [A] MAI TAI
HISTORY [B] VERVE
HISTORY [C] MICHAEL JACKSON
HISTORY NEVER REPEATS SPLIT ENZ
HISTORY OF THE WORLD (PART 1) DAMNED
HISTORY REPEATING PROPELLERHEADS & SHIRLEY
    BASSEY
HIT [A] SUGARCUBES
HIT [B] WANNADIES

HIT 'EM HIGH (THE MONSTARS' ANTHEM) B REAL/
    BUSTA RHYMES/COOLIO/LL COOL J/METHOD MAN
HIT 'EM WIT DA HEE MISSY 'MISDEMEANOR' ELLIOTT
HIT AND MISS JOHN BARRY SEVEN
HIT AND RUN [A] GIRLSCHOOL
HIT AND RUN [B] TOTAL CONTRAST
HIT BY LOVE CE CE PENISTON
HIT 'EM UP STYLE (OOPS) BLU CANTRELL
HIT IT BEAT
HIT ME OFF NEW EDITION
HIT ME WITH YOUR RHYTHM STICK IAN & THE
    BLOCKHEADS
HIT OR MISS (WAITED TOO LONG) NEW FOUND GLORY
HIT THAT OFFSPRING
HIT THAT PERFECT BEAT BRONSKI BEAT
HIT THE GROUND DARLING BUDS
HIT THE GROUND RUNNING TIM FINN
HIT THE FREEWAY TONI BRAXTON FEATURING LOON
HIT THE NORTH FALL
HIT THE ROAD JACK RAY CHARLES
HITCHIN' A RIDE [A] VANITY FARE
HITCHIN' A RIDE [A] SINITTA
HITCHIN' A RIDE [B] GREEN DAY
HITMIX (OFFICIAL BOOTLEG MEGA-MIX) ALEXANDER
    O'NEAL
HITS MEDLEY GIPSY KINGS
HITSVILLE UK CLASH
HOBART PAVING SAINT ETIENNE
HOBO HUMPIN' SLOBO BABE WHALE
HOCUS POCUS FOCUS
HOGWASH FARM (THE DIESEL HANDS EP) DAWN OF
    THE REPLICANTS
HOKEY COKEY SNOWMEN
HOKEY COKEY BLACK LACE
HOKEY COKEY JUDGE DREAD
THE HOKEY COKEY CAPTAIN SENSIBLE
HOKOYO ORANGE JUICE
HOKUS POKUS INSANE CLOWN POSSE
HOLD BACK THE NIGHT TRAMMPS
HOLD BACK THE NIGHT KWS FEATURES GUEST VOCAL
    FROM THE TRAMMPS
HOLD BACK THE RIVER WET WET WET
HOLD BACK TOMORROW MIKI & GRIFF
HOLD IT STEPHEN 'TIN TIN' DUFFY
HOLD IT DOWN [A] SENSELESS THINGS
HOLD IT DOWN [B] 2 BAD MICE
HOLD ME [A] TEDDY PENDERGRASS & WHITNEY
    HOUSTON
HOLD ME [B] P.J. PROBY
HOLD ME [B] B A ROBERTSON & MAGGIE BELL
HOLD ME [C] SAVAGE GARDEN
HOLD ME CLOSE DAVID ESSEX
HOLD ME IN YOUR ARMS RICK ASTLEY
HOLD ME NOW [A] THOMPSON TWINS
HOLD ME NOW [B] JOHNNY LOGAN
HOLD ME NOW [C] POLYPHONIC SPREE
HOLD ME THRILL ME KISS ME MURIEL SMITH
HOLD ME THRILL ME KISS ME GLORIA ESTEFAN
HOLD ME TIGHT JOHNNY NASH
HOLD ME TIGHTER IN THE RAIN BILLY GRIFFIN
HOLD ME, THRILL ME, KISS ME, KILL ME U2
HOLD MY BODY TIGHT EAST 17
HOLD MY HAND [A] DON CORNELL
HOLD MY HAND [B] KEN DODD
HOLD MY HAND [C] HOOTIE & THE BLOWFISH
HOLD ON [A] STREETBAND
HOLD ON [B] EN VOGUE
HOLD ON [C] WILSON PHILLIPS
HOLD ON [D] C.B. MILTON
HOLD ON [E] HAPPY CLAPPERS
HOLD ON [F] JOSE NUNEZ FEATURING OCTAHVIA

HOLD ON [G] GOOD CHARLOTTE
HOLD ON (EP) ANN NESBY
HOLD ON ME PHIXX
HOLD ON MY HEART GENESIS
HOLD ON TIGHT [A] ELECTRIC LIGHT ORCHESTRA
HOLD ON TIGHT [B] SAMANTHA FOX
HOLD ON TO LOVE [A] PETER SKELLERN
HOLD ON TO LOVE [B] GARY MOORE
HOLD ON TO ME MJ COLE FEATURING ELISABETH TROY
HOLD ON TO MY LOVE JIMMY RUFFIN
HOLD ON TO OUR LOVE JAMES FOX
HOLD ON TO THE NIGHTS RICHARD MARX
HOLD ON TO WHAT YOU'VE GOT EVELYN KING
HOLD ON TO YOUR FRIENDS MORRISSEY
HOLD THAT SUCKER DOWN OT QUARTET
HOLD THE HEART BIG COUNTRY
HOLD THE LINE TOTO
HOLD TIGHT [A] DAVE DEE, DOZY, BEAKY, MICK & TICH
HOLD TIGHT [B] LIVERPOOL EXPRESS
HOLD YOU TIGHT TARA KEMP
HOLD YOUR HEAD UP ARGENT
HOLD YOUR HEAD UP HIGH BORIS DLUGOSCH
    PRESENTS BOOM
HOLDIN' ON TONY RALLO & THE MIDNIGHT BAND
HOLDING BACK THE YEARS SIMPLY RED
HOLDING ON [A] BEVERLEY CRAVEN
HOLDING ON [B] CLOCK
HOLDING ON [C] DJ MANTA
HOLDING ON [D] HEATHER SMALL
HOLDING ON FOR YOU LIBERTY X
HOLDING ON 4 U CLOCK
HOLDING ON TO NOTHING AGNELLI & NELSON
    FEATURING AUREUS
HOLDING ON TO YOU TERENCE TRENT D'ARBY
HOLDING ON (WHEN LOVE IS GONE) LTD
HOLDING OUT FOR A HERO BONNIE TYLER
HOLE HEARTED EXTREME
HOLE IN MY SHOE TRAFFIC
HOLE IN MY SHOE neil
HOLE IN MY SOUL AEROSMITH
HOLE IN THE BUCKET [A] HARRY BELAFONTE & ODETTA
HOLE IN THE BUCKET [B] SPEARHEAD
HOLE IN THE GROUND BERNARD CRIBBINS
HOLE IN THE HEAD SUGABABES
HOLE IN THE ICE NEIL FINN
HOLE IN THE WORLD EAGLES
HOLIDAE INN CHINGY
HOLIDAY MADONNA
HOLIDAY MADHOUSE
HOLIDAY 80 (DOUBLE SINGLE) HUMAN LEAGUE
HOLIDAY RAP MC MIKER 'G' & DEEJAY SVEN
HOLIDAYS IN THE SUN SEX PISTOLS
HOLLER [A] GINUWINE
HOLLER [B] SPICE GIRLS
HOLLIEDAZE (MEDLEY) HOLLIES
THE HOLLOW A PERFECT CIRCLE
HOLLOW HEART BIRDLAND
THE HOLLOW MAN MARILLION
HOLLY HOLY UB40
HOLLYWOOD [A] BOZ SCAGGS
HOLLYWOOD [B] MADONNA
HOLLYWOOD (DOWN ON YOUR LUCK) THIN LIZZY
HOLLYWOOD NIGHTS BOB SEGER & THE SILVER BULLET
    BAND
HOLLYWOOD TEASE GIRL
THE HOLY CITY MOIRA ANDERSON
HOLY COW LEE DORSEY
HOLY DAYS ZOE
HOLY DIVER DIO

HOLY JOE HAYSI FANTAYZEE
THE HOLY RIVER PRINCE
HOLY ROLLER NAZARETH
HOLY ROLLER NOVACAINE KINGS OF LEON
HOLY SMOKE IRON MAIDEN
HOLY WARS...THE PUNISHMENT DUE MEGADETH
HOMBURG PROCOL HARUM
HOME [A] PUBLIC IMAGE LTD.
HOME [B] GOD MACHINE
HOME [C] DEPECHE MODE
HOME [C] COAST 2 COAST FEATURING DISCOVERY
HOME [D] CHAKRA
HOME [E] SHERYL CROW
HOME [F] JULIE McKNIGHT
HOME [G] BONE THUGS-N-HARMONY FEATURING PHIL
    COLLINS
HOME [H] SIMPLY RED
HOME ALONE R KELLY FEATURING KEITH MURRAY
HOME AND AWAY KAREN BODINGTON & MARK
    WILLIAMS
HOME AND DRY PET SHOP BOYS
HOME FOR CHRISTMAS DAY RED CAR AND THE BLUE
    CAR
HOME IS WHERE THE HEART IS GLADYS KNIGHT & THE
    PIPS
HOME LOVIN' MAN ANDY WILLIAMS
HOME OF THE BRAVE JODY MILLER
HOME SWEET HOME MOTLEY CRUE
HOMELY GIRL CHI-LITES
HOMELY GIRL UB40
HOMETOWN UNICORN SUPER FURRY ANIMALS
HOMEWARD BOUND SIMON & GARFUNKEL
HOMEWARD BOUND QUIET FIVE
HOMICIDE 999
HOMICIDE SHADES OF RHYTHM
HOMING WALTZ VERA LYNN
HOMOPHOBIC ASSHOLE SENSELESS THINGS
HONALOOCHIE BOOGIE MOTT THE HOOPLE
HONDY (NO ACCESS) HONDY
HONEST I DO DANNY STORM
HONEST I DO LOVE YOU CANDI STATON
HONEST MEN ELECTRIC LIGHT ORCHESTRA PART 2
HONESTLY ZWAN
HONEY [A] BOBBY GOLDSBORO
HONEY [B] MARIAH CAREY
HONEY [C] MOBY
HONEY [D] BILLIE RAY MARTIN
HONEY [E] R KELLY & JAY-Z
HONEY BE GOOD BIBLE
HONEY CHILE [A] FATS DOMINO
HONEY CHILE [B] MARTHA REEVES & THE VANDELLAS
HONEY COME BACK GLEN CAMPBELL
HONEY HONEY SWEET DREAMS
HONEY I GEORGE McCRAE
HONEY I NEED PRETTY THINGS
HONEY I'M LOST DOOLEYS
HONEY TO THE BEE BILLIE
HONEYCOMB JIMMIE RODGERS
THE HONEYDRIPPER JETS
THE HONEYTHIEF HIPSWAY
HONG KONG GARDEN SIOUXSIE & THE BANSHEES
HONKY CAT ELTON JOHN
THE HONKY DOODLE DAY EP HONKY
HONKY TONK TRAIN BLUES KEITH EMERSON
HONKY TONK WOMEN ROLLING STONES
HONKY TONK WOMEN POGUES
HOOCHIE BOOTY ULTIMATE KAOS
HOODED FRESH BC
HOOKED 99TH FLOOR ELEVATORS FEATURING TONY DE
    VIT
HOOKED ON A FEELING JONATHAN KING

HOOKED ON CAN-CAN ROYAL PHILHARMONIC
    ORCHESTRA ARRANGED & CONDUCTED BY LOUIS
    CLARK
HOOKED ON CLASSICS ROYAL PHILHARMONIC
    ORCHESTRA ARRANGED & CONDUCTED BY LOUIS
    CLARK
HOOKED ON LOVE DEAD OR ALIVE
HOOKED ON YOU [A] SYDNEY YOUNGBLOOD
HOOKED ON YOU [B] VOLATILE AGENTS FEATURING
    SIMONE BENN
HOOKS IN YOU MARILLION
HOOLIGAN EMBRACE
HOOLIGAN 69 RAGGA TWINS
HOOLIGAN'S HOLIDAY MOTLEY CRUE
HOORAY HOORAY (IT'S A CHEEKY HOLIDAY) CHEEKY
    GIRLS
HOORAY HOORAY IT'S A HOLI-HOLIDAY BONEY M
HOOTIN' NIGEL GEE
HOOTS MON LORD ROCKINGHAM'S XI
HOOVERS & HORNS FERGIE & BK
HOOVERVILLE (THEY PROMISED US THE WORLD)
    CHRISTIANS
THE HOP THEATRE OF HATE
HOPE SHAGGY
HOPE AND WAIT ORION TOO
HOPE (I WISH YOU'D BELIEVE ME) WAH!
HOPE IN A HOPELESS WORLD PAUL YOUNG
HOPE (NEVER GIVE UP) LOVELAND FEATURING RACHEL
    McFARLANE
HOPE OF DELIVERANCE PAUL McCARTNEY
HOPE ST LEVELLERS
HOPELESS DIONNE FARRIS
HOPELESSLY RICK ASTLEY
HOPELESSLY DEVOTED TO YOU OLIVIA NEWTON-JOHN
HOPELESSLY DEVOTED TO YOU SONIA
THE HORN TRACK EGYPTIAN EMPIRE
HORNY [A] MARK MORRISON
HORNY [B] MOUSSE T VERSUS HOT 'N' JUICY
HORNY AS FUNK SOAPY
HORNY HORNS PERFECT PHASE
HORROR HEAD (EP) CURVE
HORSE SPLODGENESSABOUNDS
HORSE AND CARRIAGE CAM'RON FEATURING MA$E
HORSE WITH NO NAME AMERICA
HORSEMEN BEES
HORSEPOWER RAVESIGNAL III
HOSTAGE IN A FROCK CECIL
HOT IDEAL
HOT & WET (BELIEVE IT) TZANT
HOT BLOODED FOREIGNER
HOT BOYZ MISSY MISDEMEANOR ELLIOTT FEATURING
    NAS, EVE & Q-TIP
HOT DIGGITY PERRY COMO
HOT DIGGITY MICHAEL HOLLIDAY
HOT DIGGITY STARGAZERS
HOT DOG SHAKIN' STEVENS
HOT FUN 7TH HEAVEN
HOT HOT HOT [A] ARROW
HOT HOT HOT [A] PAT & MICK
HOT HOT HOT!!! [B] CURE
HOT IN HERRE NELLY
HOT IN HERRE TIGA
HOT IN THE CITY BILLY IDOL
HOT LIKE FIRE AALIYAH
HOT LOVE [A] T. REX
HOT LOVE [B] DAVID ESSEX
HOT LOVE [C] KELLY MARIE
HOT LOVE [D] FIVE STAR
HOT LOVE NOW WONDER STUFF
HOT PEPPER FLOYD CRAMER
HOT ROCKIN' JUDAS PRIEST

(HOT S**T) COUNTRY GRAMMAR NELLY
HOT SHOT [A] BARRY BLUE
HOT SHOT [B] KAREN YOUNG
HOT SHOT [C] CLIFF RICHARD
HOT SHOT TOTTENHAM TOTTENHAM HOTSPUR F.A. CUP FINAL SQUAD
HOT SPOT FOXY BROWN
HOT STUFF DONNA SUMMER
HOT STUFF ARSENAL FC
HOT SUMMER SALSA JIVE BUNNY & THE MASTERMIXERS
HOT TODDY TED HEATH
HOT TRACKS EP NAZARETH
HOT VALVES EP BE BOP DELUXE
HOT WATER LEVEL 42
HOTEL CASSIDY FEATURING R KELLY
HOTEL CALIFORNIA EAGLES
HOTEL CALIFORNIA JAM ON THE MUTHA
HOTEL ILLNESS BLACK CROWES
HOTEL LOUNGE (BE THE DEATH OF ME) dEUS
HOTEL YORBA WHITE STRIPES
HOTLEGS ROD STEWART
HOTLINE TO HEAVEN BANANARAMA
HOTNESS DYNAMITE MC & ORIGIN UNKNOWN
HOUND DOG ELVIS PRESLEY
HOUND DOG MAN FABIAN
HOUNDS OF LOVE KATE BUSH
HOURGLASS SQUEEZE
HOUSE ARREST KRUSH
HOUSE ENGERY REVENGE CAPPELLA
HOUSE FLY TRICKY DISCO
A HOUSE IN THE COUNTRY PRETTY THINGS
THE HOUSE IS HAUNTED (BY THE ECHO OF YOUR LAST GOODBYE) MARC ALMOND
THE HOUSE IS MINE HYPNOTIST
HOUSE IS NOT A HOME CHARLES & EDDIE
HOUSE MUSIC EDDIE AMADOR
HOUSE NATION HOUSEMASTER BOYZ & THE RUDE BOY OF HOUSE
HOUSE OF BROKEN LOVE GREAT WHITE
HOUSE OF FIRE ALICE COOPER
HOUSE OF FUN MADNESS
HOUSE OF GOD DHS
HOUSE OF JEALOUS LOVERS RAPTURE
HOUSE OF JOY VICKI SUE ROBINSON
HOUSE OF LOVE [A] EAST 17
HOUSE OF LOVE [B] RuPAUL
HOUSE OF LOVE [C] SKIN
HOUSE OF LOVE [D] AMY GRANT WITH VINCE GILL
HOUSE OF LOVE (IN MY HOUSE) SMOOTH TOUCH
HOUSE OF THE BLUE DANUBE MALCOLM McLAREN & THE BOOTZILLA ORCHESTRA
HOUSE OF THE RISING SUN ANIMALS
HOUSE OF THE RISING SUN FRIJID PINK
HOUSE OF THE RISING SUN RAGE
HOUSE ON FIRE [A] BOOMTOWN RATS
HOUSE ON FIRE [B] ARKARNA
HOUSE SOME MORE LOCK 'N' LOAD
THE HOUSE THAT JACK BUILT [A] ALAN PRICE SET
THE HOUSE THAT JACK BUILT [B] TRACIE
A HOUSE WITH LOVE IN IT VERA LYNN
HOUSECALL SHABBA RANKS FEATURING MAXI PRIEST
HOUSES IN MOTION TALKING HEADS
HOW ABOUT THAT ADAM FAITH
HOW AM I SUPPOSED TO LIVE WITHOUT YOU MICHAEL BOLTON
HOW BIZARRE OMC
HOW 'BOUT I LOVE YOU MORE MULL HISTORICAL SOCIETY
HOW 'BOUT US CHAMPAIGN
HOW 'BOUT US LULU

HOW CAN I BE SURE DUSTY SPRINGFIELD
HOW CAN I BE SURE DAVID CASSIDY
HOW CAN I BE SURE? DARREN DAY
HOW CAN I FALL BREATHE
HOW CAN I FORGET YOU ELISA FIORILLO
HOW CAN I KEEP FROM SINGING ENYA
HOW CAN I LOVE YOU MORE M PEOPLE
HOW CAN I MEET HER EVERLY BROTHERS
HOW CAN I TELL HER FOURMOST
HOW CAN THIS BE LOVE ANDREW GOLD
HOW CAN WE BE LOVERS MICHAEL BOLTON
HOW CAN WE EASE THE PAIN MAXI PRIEST FEATURING BERES HAMMOND
HOW CAN YOU EXPECT ME TO BE TAKEN SERIOUSLY PET SHOP BOYS
HOW CAN YOU TELL SANDIE SHAW
HOW CAN YOU TELL ME IT'S OVER LORRAINE CATO
HOW COME? [A] RONNIE LANE & SLIM CHANCE
HOW COME [B] YOUSSOU N'DOUR & CANIBUS
HOW COME [C] D12
HOW COME, HOW LONG BABYFACE FEATURING STEVIE WONDER
HOW COME IT NEVER RAINS DOGS D'AMOUR
HOW COME YOU DON'T CALL ME ALICIA KEYS
HOW COULD AN ANGEL BREAK MY HEART TONI BRAXTON WITH KENNY G
HOW COULD I? (INSECURITY) ROACHFORD
HOW COULD THIS GO WRONG EXILE
HOW COULD WE DARE TO BE WRONG COLIN BLUNSTONE
HOW DEEP IS YOUR LOVE PORTRAIT
HOW DEEP IS YOUR LOVE [A] BEE GEES
HOW DEEP IS YOUR LOVE [A] TAKE THAT
HOW DEEP IS YOUR LOVE [B] DRU HILL FEATURING REDMAN
HOW DID IT EVER COME TO THIS? EASYWORLD
HOW DID YOU KNOW KURTIS MANTRONIK PRESENTS CHAMONIX
HOW DO I KNOW? MARLO
HOW DO I LIVE TRISHA YEARWOOD
HOW DO I LIVE LeANN RIMES
HOW DO YOU DO [A] AL HUDSON
HOW DO YOU DO! [B] ROXETTE
HOW DO YOU DO IT? GERRY & THE PACEMAKERS
HOW DO YOU KNOW IT'S LOVE TERESA BREWER
HOW DO YOU LIKE IT KEITH SWEAT
HOW DO YOU SAY...LOVE DEEE-LITE
HOW DO YOU SPEAK TO AN ANGEL DEAN MARTIN
HOW DO YOU WANT IT? 2PAC FEATURING K-CI & JOJO
HOW DO YOU WANT ME TO LOVE YOU? 911
HOW DOES IT FEEL [A] SLADE
HOW DOES IT FEEL [B] ELECTROSET
HOW DOES IT FEEL [C] WANNADIES
(HOW DOES IT FEEL TO BE) ON TOP OF THE WORLD ENGLAND UNITED
HOW DOES IT FEEL TO FEEL RIDE
HOW DOES THAT GRAB YOU DARLIN' NANCY SINATRA
HOW GEE BLACK MACHINE
HOW HIGH CHARLATANS
HOW HIGH THE MOON ELLA FITZGERALD
HOW HIGH THE MOON GLORIA GAYNOR
HOW HOW YELLO
HOW I WANNA BE LOVED DANA DAWSON
HOW I'M COMIN' LL COOL J
HOW IT IS BIOHAZARD
HOW IT SHOULD BE INSPIRAL CARPETS
HOW LONG ACE
HOW LONG ROD STEWART
HOW LONG YAZZ & ASWAD
HOW LONG? PAUL CARRACK
HOW LONG DO I GET RAISSA

HOW LONG HAS IT BEEN JIM REEVES
HOW LONG'S A TEAR TAKE TO DRY? BEAUTIFUL SOUTH
HOW LUCKY YOU ARE SKIN
HOW MANY LIES SPANDAU BALLET
HOW MANY TEARS BOBBY VEE
HOW MANY TEARS CAN YOU HIDE SHAKIN' STEVENS
HOW MANY TIMES BROTHER BEYOND
HOW MEN ARE AZTEC CAMERA
HOW MUCH I FEEL ALIBI
(HOW MUCH IS) THAT DOGGIE IN THE WINDOW LITA ROZA
(HOW MUCH IS) THAT DOGGIE IN THE WINDOW PATTI PAGE
HOW MUCH LOVE [A] LEO SAYER
HOW MUCH LOVE [B] VIXEN
HOW MUSIC CAME ABOUT (BOP B DA B DA DA) GAP BAND
HOW SHE THREW IT ALL AWAY (EP) STYLE COUNCIL
HOW SOON HENRY MANCINI
HOW SOON IS NOW SMITHS
HOW SOON IS NOW INNER SANCTUM
HOW SOON IS NOW HUNDRED REASONS
HOW SOON WE FORGET COLONEL ABRAMS
HOW SWEET IT IS JUNIOR WALKER & THE ALL-STARS
HOW SWEET IT IS MARVIN GAYE
HOW THE HEART BEHAVES WAS (NOT WAS)
HOW TO BE A MILLIONAIRE ABC
HOW TO BE DEAD SNOW PATROL
HOW TO FALL IN LOVE PART 1 BEE GEES
HOW TO WIN YOUR LOVE ENGELBERT HUMPERDINCK
HOW U LIKE BASS NORMAN BASS
HOW WAS IT FOR YOU JAMES
HOW WILL I KNOW WHITNEY HOUSTON
HOW WILL I KNOW (WHO YOU ARE) JESSICA
HOW WONDERFUL TO KNOW PEARL CARR & TEDDY JOHNSON
HOW WONDERFUL YOU ARE GORDON HASKELL
HOW WOULD U FEEL DAVID MORALES FEATURING LEA LORIEN
HOW YOU GONNA ACT LIKE THAT TYRESE
HOW YOU GONNA SEE ME NOW ALICE COOPER
HOW YOU REMIND ME NICKELBACK
HOWARD'S WAY SIMON MAY ORCHESTRA
HOW'D I DO DAT BENTLEY RHYTHM ACE
HOW'S IT GOING TO BE THIRD EYE BLIND
HOW'S YOUR EVENING SO FAR JOSH WINK & LIL LOUIS
HOWZAT SHERBET
HUBBLE BUBBLE TOIL AND TROUBLE MANFRED MANN
HUDSON STREET AGNELLI & NELSON
HUG MY SOUL SAINT ETIENNE
HUMAN [A] HUMAN LEAGUE
HUMAN [B] PRETENDERS
HUMAN BEHAVIOUR BJORK
HUMAN BEING BETA BAND
HUMAN BEINGS SEAL
HUMAN NATURE [A] GARY CLAIL ON-U SOUND SYSTEM
HUMAN NATURE [B] MADONNA
HUMAN RACING NIK KERSHAW
HUMAN TOUCH [A] RICK SPRINGFIELD
HUMAN TOUCH [B] BRUCE SPRINGSTEEN
HUMAN WORK OF ART MAXI PRIEST
HUMAN WORK OF ART CLIFF RICHARD
HUMANISTIC KAWALA
HUMANITY REBEL MC FEATURING LINCOLN THOMPSON
HUMMING BIRD FRANKIE LAINE
HUMPIN' GAP BAND
HUMPIN' AROUND BOBBY BROWN
HUNDRED MILE HIGH CITY OCEAN COLOUR SCENE
A HUNDRED POUNDS OF CLAY CRAIG DOUGLAS

HUNG UP PAUL WELLER
HUNGAH KARYN WHITE
THE HUNGER DISTILLERS
HUNGER STRIKE TEMPLE OF THE DOG
HUNGRY KOSHEEN
HUNGRY EYES EYEOPENER
HUNGRY FOR HEAVEN DIO
HUNGRY FOR LOVE JOHNNY KIDD & THE PIRATES
HUNGRY HEART BRUCE SPRINGSTEEN
HUNGRY LIKE THE WOLF DURAN DURAN
HUNT BARRY RYAN
HUNTER [A] BJORK
HUNTER [B] DIDO
HUNTING HIGH AND LOW A-HA
HURDY GURDY MAN DONOVAN
HURRICANE [A] BOB DYLAN
HURRICANE [B] WARM JETS
HURRY HOME WAVELENGTH
HURRY UP AND WAIT STEREOPHONICS
HURRY UP HARRY SHAM 69
HURT [A] ELVIS PRESLEY
HURT [A] MANHATTANS
HURT [B] JOHNNY CASH
HURT BY LOVE INEZ FOXX
HURT ME SO BAD LULU
HURT SO GOOD SUSAN CADOGAN
HURT SO GOOD JIMMY SOMERVILLE
HURTING KIND (I'VE GOT MY EYES ON YOU) ROBERT
    PLANT
HUSAN BHANGRA KNIGHTS VS HUSAN
HUSBAND FLUFFY
HUSH DEEP PURPLE
HUSH KULA SHAKER
HUSH NOT A WORD TO MARY JOHN ROWLES
THE HUSTLE VAN McCOY WITH THE SOUL CITY
    SYMPHONY
HUSTLE! (TO THE MUSIC...) FUNKY WORM
HYBRID EAT STATIC
HYMN [A] ULTRAVOX
HYMN [B] MOBY
HYMN [C] ULTRAMARINE FEATURING DAVID
    McALMONT
HYMN TO HER PRETENDERS
HYMNE A L'AMOUR ELAINE PAIGE
HYPER MUSIC MUSE
HYPERACTIVE THOMAS DOLBY
HYPERBALLAD BJORK
HYPERREAL SHAMEN
HYPNOSIS MUD
HYPNOTIC ST-8 ALTERN 8
HYPNOTIC TANGO MASTER BLASTER
HYPNOTISED [A] CABARET VOLTAIRE
HYPNOTISED [B] SIMPLE MINDS
HYPNOTISED [C] PAUL OAKENFOLD
HYPNOTISING KID CRÈME FEATURING CHARLISE
HYPNOTIZE [A] SCRITTI POLITTI
HYPNOTIZE [B] D-INFLUENCE
HYPNOTIZE [C] NOTORIOUS B.I.G.
HYPNOTIZIN' WINX
HYPOCRITE [A] LUSH
HYPOCRITE [B] SPECIALS
HYSTERIA [A] DEF LEPPARD
HYSTERIA [B] MUSE
I PETEY PABLO
I ADORE MI AMOR COLOR ME BADD
I ADORE YOU CARON WHEELER
I AIN'T GOIN' OUT LIKE THAT CYPRESS HILL
I AIN'T GONNA CRY LITTLE ANGELS
I AIN'T GONNA STAND FOR IT STEVIE WONDER
I AIN'T GOT TIME ANYMORE CLIFF RICHARD
I AIN'T LYIN' GEORGE McCRAE

I AIN'T MAD AT CHA 2PAC FEATURING K-CI & JOJO
I AIN'T NEW TA THIS ICE-T
I ALMOST FELT LIKE CRYING CRAIG McLACHLAN &
    CHECK 1-2
I ALMOST LOST MY MIND PAT BOONE
I ALONE LIVE
I AM [A] CHAKRA
I AM [B] SUGGS
I AM A CIDER DRINKER (PALOMA BLANCA) WURZELS
I AM A ROCK SIMON & GARFUNKEL
I AM BLESSED ETERNAL
I AM DOWN SALT-N-PEPA
I AM I QUEENSRYCHE
I AM (I'M ME) TWISTED SISTER
I AM IN LOVE WITH THE WORLD CHICKEN SHED
    THEATRE
I AM LV LV
I AM MINE PEARL JAM
I AM ONE [A] SMASHING PUMPKINS
I AM ONE [B] W.A.S.P.
I AM THE BEAT LOOK
I AM THE BLACK GOLD OF THE SUN NUYORICAN SOUL
    FEATURING JOCELYN BROWN
I AM THE LAW ANTHRAX
I AM THE MOB CATATONIA
I AM THE MUSIC HEAR ME! MILLIONAIRE HIPPIES
I AM THE MUSIC MAN BLACK LACE
I AM THE NEWS OCEAN COLOUR SCENE
I AM THE ONE CRACKOUT
I AM THE RESURRECTION STONE ROSES
I AM THE SUN DARK STAR
I AM WHAT I AM [A] GREYHOUND
I AM WHAT I AM [B] GLORIA GAYNOR
I AM WHAT I AM [C] MARK OWEN
I AM, I FEEL ALISHA'S ATTIC
I AM...I SAID NEIL DIAMOND
I AN'T MOVIN' DES'REE
I APOLOGISE P.J. PROBY
I BE THE PROPHET STARVING SOULS
I BEG YOUR PARDON KON KAN
I BEGIN TO WONDER DANNII MINOGUE
I BELIEVE [A] FRANKIE LAINE
I BELIEVE [A] DAVID WHITFIELD
I BELIEVE [A] BACHELORS
I BELIEVE [A] ROBSON GREEN & JEROME FLYNN
I BELIEVE [B] EMF
I BELIEVE [C] REESE PROJECT
I BELIEVE [D] BON JOVI
I BELIEVE [E] ROBERT PLANT
I BELIEVE [F] MARCELLA DETROIT
I BELIEVE [G] SOUNDS OF BLACKNESS
I BELIEVE [H] BLESSID UNION OF SOULS
I BELIEVE [I] HAPPY CLAPPERS
I BELIEVE [J] BOOTH & THE BAD ANGEL
I BELIEVE [K] ABSOLUTE FEATURING SUZANNE
    PALMER
I BELIEVE [L] LANGE FEATURING SARAH DWYER
I BELIEVE [M] JAMESTOWN FEATURING JOCELYN
    BROWN
I BELIEVE [N] STEPHEN GATELY
I BELIEVE (A SOULFUL RECORDING) TEARS FOR FEARS
I BELIEVE I CAN FLY R. KELLY
I BELIEVE I'M GONNA LOVE YOU FRANK SINATRA
I BELIEVE IN A THING CALLED LOVE DARKNESS
I BELIEVE IN CHRISTMAS TWEENIES
I BELIEVE IN FATHER CHRISTMAS GREG LAKE
I BELIEVE (IN LOVE) [A] HOT CHOCOLATE
I BELIEVE IN LOVE [B] COOPER
I BELIEVE IN MIRACLES JACKSON SISTERS
I BELIEVE IN MIRACLES PASADENAS
I BELIEVE IN THE SPIRIT TIM BURGESS

I BELIEVE IN YOU [A] OUR TRIBE
I BELIEVE IN YOU [B] AMP FIDDLER
I BELIEVE IN YOU [C] KYLIE MINOGUE
I BELIEVE IN YOU AND ME WHITNEY HOUSTON
I BELIEVE MY HEART DUNCAN JAMES & KEEDIE
I BELIEVE YOU DOROTHY MOORE
I BELONG KATHY KIRBY
I BELONG TO YOU [A] WHITNEY HOUSTON
I BELONG TO YOU [B] GINA G
I BELONG TO YOU [C] LENNY KRAVITZ
I BREATHE AGAIN ADAM RICKITT
I CALL YOUR NAME A-HA
I CALLED U LIL' LOUIS
I CAN NAS
I CAN BUY YOU A CAMP
I CAN CALL YOU PORTRAIT
I CAN CAST A SPELL DISCO TEX PRESENTS
    CLOUDBURST
I CAN CLIMB MOUNTAINS HELL IS FOR HEROES
I CAN DANCE [A] BRIAN POOLE & THE TREMELOES
I CAN DANCE [B] DJ 'FAST' EDDIE
I CAN DO IT RUBETTES
I CAN DO THIS MONIE LOVE
I CAN DREAM SKUNK ANANSIE
I CAN DREAM ABOUT YOU DAN HARTMAN
I CAN DRIVE SHAKESPEARS SISTER
I CAN FEEL IT SILENCERS
I CAN HEAR MUSIC BEACH BOYS
I CAN HEAR THE GRASS GROW MOVE
I CAN HEAR VOICES/CANED AND UNABLE HI-GATE
I CAN HEAR YOUR HEARTBEAT CHRIS REA
I CAN HELP BILLY SWAN
I CAN HELP ELVIS PRESLEY
I CAN LOVE YOU LIKE THAT ALL-4-ONE
I CAN MAKE IT BETTER [A] WHISPERS
I CAN MAKE IT BETTER [B] LUTHER VANDROSS
I CAN MAKE YOU FEEL GOOD SHALAMAR
I CAN MAKE YOU FEEL GOOD KAVANA
I CAN MAKE YOU FEEL LIKE MAXX
I CAN ONLY DISAPPOINT U MANSUN
I CAN PROVE IT TONY ETORIA
I CAN PROVE IT PHIL FEARON
I CAN SEE CLEARLY NOW [A] JOHNNY NASH
I CAN SEE CLEARLY NOW [A] HOTHOUSE FLOWERS
I CAN SEE CLEARLY NOW [A] JIMMY CLIFF
I CAN SEE CLEARLY NOW [B] DEBORAH HARRY
I CAN SEE FOR MILES WHO
I CAN SEE HER NOW DRAMATIS
I CAN SEE IT BLANCMANGE
I CAN SING A RAINBOW – LOVE IS BLUE (MEDLEY)
    DELLS
I CAN TAKE OR LEAVE YOUR LOVING HERMAN'S
    HERMITS
I CANNOT GIVE YOU MY LOVE CLIFF RICHARD
I CAN'T ASK FOR ANYMORE THAN YOU CLIFF
    RICHARD
I CAN'T BE WITH YOU CRANBERRIES
I CAN'T BELIEVE YOU'RE GONE WEBB BROTHERS
I CAN'T BREAK DOWN SINEAD QUINN
I CAN'T CONTROL MYSELF TROGGS
I CAN'T DANCE GENESIS
I CAN'T DENY IT ROD STEWART
I CAN'T EXPLAIN WHO
I CAN'T FACE THE WORLD LEMON TREES
(I CAN'T GET ME NO) SATISFACTION DEVO
I CAN'T GET NEXT TO YOU TEMPTATIONS
(I CAN'T GET NO) SATISFACTION ROLLING STONES
(I CAN'T GET NO) SATISFACTION BUBBLEROCK
I CAN'T GET NO SLEEP MASTERS AT WORK PRESENT
    INDIA
I CAN'T GET YOU OUT OF MY MIND YVONNE ELLIMAN

I CAN'T GO FOR THAT (NO CAN DO) DARYL HALL & JOHN OATES
(I CAN'T HELP) FALLING IN LOVE WITH YOU UB40
I CAN'T HELP IT [A] JOHNNY TILLOTSON
I CAN'T HELP IT [B] JUNIOR
I CAN'T HELP IT [C] BANANARAMA
I CAN'T HELP MYSELF [A] FOUR TOPS
I CAN'T HELP MYSELF [A] DONNIE ELBERT
I CAN'T HELP MYSELF [B] ORANGE JUICE
I CAN'T HELP MYSELF [C] JOEY LAWRENCE
I CAN'T HELP MYSELF [D] JULIA FORDHAM
I CAN'T HELP MYSELF [E] LUCID
I CAN'T IMAGINE THE WORLD WITHOUT ME ECHOBELLY
I CAN'T LEAVE YOU ALONE GEORGE McCRAE
I CAN'T LEAVE YOU ALONE TRACIE YOUNG
I CAN'T LET GO [A] HOLLIES
I CAN'T LET GO [B] MARTI WEBB
I CAN'T LET MAGGIE GO HONEYBUS
I CAN'T LET YOU GO [A] HAYWOODE
I CAN'T LET YOU GO [B] 52ND STREET
I CAN'T LET YOU GO [C] MACK VIBE FEATURING JACQUELINE
I CAN'T LET YOU GO [D] IAN VAN DAHL
I CAN'T LIVE A DREAM OSMONDS
I CAN'T MAKE A MISTAKE MC LYTE
I CAN'T MAKE IT SMALL FACES
I CAN'T MAKE IT ALONE P.J. PROBY
I CAN'T MAKE IT ALONE MARIA McKEE
I CAN'T MAKE YOU LOVE ME [A] BONNIE RAITT
I CAN'T MAKE YOU LOVE ME [B] GEORGE MICHAEL
I CAN'T READ DAVID BOWIE
I CAN'T READ YOU DANIEL BEDINGFIELD
I CAN'T SAY GOODBYE KIM WILDE
I CAN'T SAY GOODBYE TO YOU HELEN REDDY
I CAN'T SEE NICOLE RAY
I CAN'T SLEEP BABY (IF I) R KELLY
I CAN'T STAND IT [A] SPENCER DAVIS GROUP
I CAN'T STAND IT [B] TWENTY 4 SEVEN FEATURING CAPTAIN HOLLYWOOD
I CAN'T STAND MY BABY REZILLOS
I CAN'T STAND THE RAIN ANN PEEBLES
I CAN'T STAND THE RAIN ERUPTION FEATURING PRECIOUS WILSON
I CAN'T STAND THE RAIN TINA TURNER
I CAN'T STAND UP FOR FALLING DOWN ELVIS COSTELLO & THE ATTRACTIONS
I CAN'T STOP [A] OSMONDS
I CAN'T STOP [B] GARY NUMAN
I CAN'T STOP [C] SANDY RIVERA
I CAN'T STOP LOVIN' YOU (THOUGH I TRY) LEO SAYER
I CAN'T STOP LOVING YOU RAY CHARLES
I CAN'T TAKE THE POWER OFF-SHORE
I CAN'T TELL A WALTZ FROM A TANGO ALMA COGAN
I CAN'T TELL THE BOTTOM FROM THE TOP HOLLIES
I CAN'T TELL YOU WHY BROWNSTONE
I CAN'T TURN AROUND JM SILK
I CAN'T TURN AWAY SAVANNA
I CAN'T TURN YOU LOOSE OTIS REDDING
I CAN'T WAIT [A] STEVIE NICKS
I CAN'T WAIT [B] NU SHOOZ
I CAN'T WAIT [B] LADIES FIRST
I CAN'T WAIT ANYMORE SAXON
I CARE SOUL II SOUL
I CAUGHT YOU OUT REBECCA DE RUVO
I CLOSE MY EYES AND COUNT TO TEN DUSTY SPRINGFIELD
I COME FROM ANOTHER PLANET, BABY JULIAN COPE
I CONFESS BEAT
I COULD BE AN ANGLE EIGHTIES MATCHBOX B-LINE DISASTER
I COULD BE HAPPY ALTERED IMAGES

I COULD BE SO GOOD FOR YOU DENNIS WATERMAN WITH THE DENNIS WATERMAN BAND
I COULD BE THE ONE STACIE ORRICO
I COULD EASILY FALL CLIFF RICHARD & THE SHADOWS
I COULD HAVE BEEN A DREAMER DIO
I COULD NEVER LOVE ANOTHER TEMPTATIONS
I COULD NEVER MISS YOU (MORE THAN I DO) LULU
I COULD NEVER TAKE THE PLACE OF YOUR MAN PRINCE
I COULD NOT LOVE YOU MORE BEE GEES
I COULD SING OF YOUR LOVE FOREVER DELIRIOUS?
I COULDN'T LIVE WITHOUT YOUR LOVE PETULA CLARK
I COUNT THE TEARS DRIFTERS
I CRIED FOR YOU RICKY STEVENS
I DID WHAT I DID FOR MARIA TONY CHRISTIE
I DIDN'T KNOW I LOVED YOU (TILL I SAW YOU ROCK 'N' ROLL) GARY GLITTER
I DIDN'T KNOW I LOVED YOU (TILL I SAW YOU ROCK 'N' ROLL) ROCK GODDESS
I DIDN'T KNOW I WAS LOOKING FOR LOVE (EP) EVERYTHING BUT THE GIRL
I DIDN'T MEAN IT STATUS QUO
I DIDN'T MEAN TO HURT YOU ROCKIN' BERRIES
I DIDN'T MEAN TO TURN YOU ON ROBERT PALMER
I DIDN'T WANT TO NEED YOU HEART
I DIE: YOU DIE GARY NUMAN
I DIG YOU BABY MARVIN RAINWATER
I DISAPPEAR METALLICA
I DO JAMELIA
I DO I DO I DO I DO I DO ABBA
I DO WHAT I DO...THEME FOR '9 1/2 WEEKS' JOHN TAYLOR
I DON'T BELIEVE IN 'IF' ANYMORE ROGER WHITTAKER
I DON'T BELIEVE IN MIRACLES [A] COLIN BLUNSTONE
I DON'T BELIEVE IN MIRACLES [B] SINITTA
I DON'T BLAME YOU AT ALL SMOKEY ROBINSON & THE MIRACLES
I DON'T CARE [A] LIBERACE
I DON'T CARE [B] LOS BRAVOS
I DON'T CARE [C] SHAKESPEARS SISTER
I DON'T CARE [D] TONY DE VIT
I DON'T CARE IF THE SUN DON'T SHINE ELVIS PRESLEY
I DON'T EVEN KNOW IF I SHOULD CALL YOU BABY SOUL FAMILY SENSATION
I DON'T EVER WANT TO SEE YOU AGAIN UNCLE SAM
I DON'T KNOW [A] RUTH
I DON'T KNOW [B] HONEYZ
I DON'T KNOW ANYBODY ELSE BLACK BOX
I DON'T KNOW HOW TO LOVE HIM PETULA CLARK
I DON'T KNOW HOW TO LOVE HIM YVONNE ELLIMAN
I DON'T KNOW IF IT'S RIGHT EVELYN 'CHAMPAGNE' KING
I DON'T KNOW WHAT IT IS RUFUS WAINWRIGHT
I DON'T KNOW WHAT IT IS BUT I LOVE IT CHRIS REA
I DON'T KNOW WHAT YOU WANT BUT I CAN'T GIVE IT TO YOU PET SHOP BOYS
I DON'T KNOW WHERE IT COMES FROM RIDE
I DON'T KNOW WHY [A] EDEN KANE
I DON'T KNOW WHY [B] SHAWN COLVIN
I DON'T KNOW WHY [C] ANDY & DAVID WILLIAMS
(I DON'T KNOW WHY) BUT I DO CLARENCE 'FROGMAN' HENRY
I DON'T KNOW WHY (I LOVE YOU) STEVIE WONDER
I DON'T KNOW WHY I LOVE YOU HOUSE OF LOVE
I DON'T LIKE MONDAYS BOOMTOWN RATS
I DON'T LOVE YOU ANYMORE QUIREBOYS
I DON'T LOVE YOU BUT I THINK I LIKE YOU GILBERT O'SULLIVAN
I DON'T MIND BUZZCOCKS
I DON'T MIND AT ALL BOURGEOIS TAGG
I DON'T NEED ANYTHING SANDIE SHAW
I DON'T NEED NO DOCTOR (LIVE) W.A.S.P.

I DON'T NEED TO TELL HER LURKERS
I DON'T REALLY CARE K GEE
I DON'T REMEMBER PETER GABRIEL
I DON'T SMOKE DJ DEE KLINE
I DON'T THINK SO DINOSAUR Jr.
I DON'T THINK THAT MAN SHOULD SLEEP ALONE RAY PARKER Jr.
I DON'T WANNA BE A STAR CORONA
I DON'T WANNA DANCE EDDY GRANT
I DON'T WANNA FIGHT TINA TURNER
I DON'T WANNA GET HURT DONNA SUMMER
I DON'T WANNA GO ON WITH YOU LIKE THAT ELTON JOHN
(I DON'T WANNA GO TO) CHELSEA ELVIS COSTELLO & THE ATTRACTIONS
I DON'T WANNA KNOW (IMPORT) MARIO WINANS FEATURING ENYA & P DIDDY
I DON'T WANNA LOSE AT LOVE TANITA TIKARAM
I DON'T WANNA LOSE YOU [A] KANDIDATE
I DON'T WANNA LOSE YOU [B] TINA TURNER
I DON'T WANNA PLAY HOUSE TAMMY WYNETTE
I DON'T WANNA TAKE THIS PAIN DANNII MINOGUE
I DON'T WANNA TO LOSE YOUR LOVE EMOTIONS
I DON'T WANT A LOVER TEXAS
I DON'T WANT CONTROL OF YOU TEENAGE FANCLUB
I DON'T WANT NOBODY (TELLIN' ME WHAT TO DO) CHERIE AMORE
I DON'T WANT OUR LOVING TO DIE HERD
I DON'T WANT TO TONI BRAXTON
I DON'T WANT TO BE A FREAK (BUT I CAN'T HELP MYSELF) DYNASTY
I DON'T WANT TO BE A HERO JOHNNY HATES JAZZ
I DON'T WANT TO GO ON WITHOUT YOU MOODY BLUES
I DON'T WANT TO HURT YOU (EVERY SINGLE TIME) FRANK BLACK
I DON'T WANT TO LOSE MY WAY DREAMCATCHER
I DON'T WANT TO MISS A THING AEROSMITH
I DON'T WANT TO PUT A HOLD ON YOU BERNIE FLINT
I DON'T WANT TO TALK ABOUT IT ROD STEWART
I DON'T WANT TO TALK ABOUT IT EVERYTHING BUT THE GIRL
I DON'T WANT TO WAIT PAULA COLE
I DON'T WANT YOUR LOVE DURAN DURAN
I DREAM TILT
I DREAMED BEVERLEY SISTERS
I DROVE ALL NIGHT CYNDI LAUPER
I DROVE ALL NIGHT ROY ORBISON
I EAT CANNIBALS PART 1 TOTO COELO
I ENJOY BEING A GIRL PAT SUZUKI
I FEEL A CRY COMING ON HANK LOCKLIN
I FEEL DIVINE S-J
I FEEL FINE BEATLES
I FEEL FINE WET WET WET
I FEEL FOR YOU [A] CHAKA KHAN
I FEEL FOR YOU [B] BOB SINCLAR
I FEEL FREE CREAM
I FEEL GOOD THINGS FOR YOU DADDY'S FAVOURITE
I FEEL IT MOBY
I FEEL LIKE BUDDY HOLLY ALVIN STARDUST
I FEEL LIKE WALKIN' IN THE RAIN MILLIE JACKSON
I FEEL LOVE [A] DONNA SUMMER
I FEEL LOVE [A] MESSIAH FEATURING PRECIOUS WILSON
I FEEL LOVE [A] VANESSA-MAE
I FEEL LOVE [B] CRW
I FEEL LOVE COMIN' ON FELICE TAYLOR
I FEEL LOVE COMIN' ON DANA
I FEEL LOVE (MEDLEY) BRONSKI BEAT & MARC ALMOND
I FEEL LOVED DEPECHE MODE
I FEEL SO BOX CAR RACER

I FEEL SO BAD ELVIS PRESLEY
I FEEL SO FINE KMC FEATURING DAHNY
I FEEL SOMETHING IN THE AIR CHER
I FEEL STEREO DINO LENNY
I FEEL THE EARTH MOVE MARTIKA
I FEEL YOU [A] LOVE DECADE
I FEEL YOU [B] DEPECHE MODE
I FEEL YOU [C] PETER ANDRE
I FINALLY FOUND SOMEONE BARBRA STREISAND & BRYAN ADAMS
I FORGOT [A] COOLNOTES
I FORGOT [B] LIONEL RICHIE
I FOUGHT THE LAW BOBBY FULLER FOUR
I FOUGHT THE LAW CLASH
I FOUND HEAVEN TAKE THAT
I FOUND LOVE [A] DARLENE DAVIS
I FOUND LOVE [B] LONE JUSTICE
I FOUND LOVE [C] C & C MUSIC FACTORY FEATURING ZELMA DAVIS
I FOUND LOVIN' FATBACK
I FOUND LOVIN' STEVE WALSH
I FOUND OUT CHRISTIANS
I FOUND OUT THE HARD WAY FOUR PENNIES
I FOUND SOMEONE [A] CHER
I FOUND SOMEONE [B] BILLY & SARAH GAINES
I FOUND SUNSHINE CHI-LITES
I (FRIDAY NIGHT) DUBSTAR
I GAVE IT UP (WHEN I FELL IN LOVE) LUTHER VANDROSS
I GAVE MY EYES TO STEVIE WONDER MILLION DEAD
I GAVE YOU EVERYTHING CODE RED
I GAVE YOU MY HEART (DIDN'T I) HOT CHOCOLATE
I GET A KICK OUT OF YOU GARY SHEARSTON
I GET A LITTLE SENTIMENTAL OVER YOU NEW SEEKERS
I GET ALONG PET SHOP BOYS
I GET AROUND BEACH BOYS
I GET LIFTED BARBARA TUCKER
I GET LONELY JANET JACKSON
I GET SO EXCITED EQUALS
I GET THE SWEETEST FEELING JACKIE WILSON
I GET WEAK BELINDA CARLISLE
I GIVE TAKE 5
I GIVE IT ALL TO YOU MARY KIANI
I GIVE YOU MY HEART MR PRESIDENT
I GO APE NEIL SEDAKA
I GO TO EXTREMES BILLY JOEL
I GO TO PIECES (EVERYTIME) GERRI GRANGER
I GO TO SLEEP PRETENDERS
I GO WILD ROLLING STONES
I GOT 5 ON IT LUNIZ
I GOT A FEELING RICKY NELSON
I GOT A GIRL LOU BEGA
I GOT A LITTLE SONG OFF-SHORE
I GOT A MAN POSITIVE K
I GOT DA FEELIN' SWEET TEE
I GOT IT GOIN' ON [A] TONE LOC
I GOT IT GOIN' ON [B] US3 FEATURING KOBIE POWELL & RAHSAAN
I GOT MINE MOTORHEAD
I GOT MY EDUCATION UNCANNY ALLIANCE
I GOT RHYTHM HAPPENINGS
I GOT SOMEBODY ELSE CHANGING FACES
I GOT STUNG ELVIS PRESLEY
I GOT THE MUSIC IN ME KIKI DEE BAND
I GOT THE VIBRATION/A POSITIVE VIBRATION BLACK BOX
I GOT THIS FEELING BABY BUMPS
I GOT TO SING J.A.L.N. BAND
I GOT YOU SPLIT ENZ
I GOT YOU BABE SONNY & CHER
I GOT YOU BABE UB40 FEATURING CHRISSIE HYNDE

I GOT YOU BABE CHER WITH BEAVIS & BUTT-HEAD
I GOT YOU BABE AVID MERRION/DAVINA McCALL/PATSY KENSIT
I GOT YOU (I FEEL GOOD) JAMES BROWN & THE FAMOUS FLAMES
I GUESS I'LL ALWAYS LOVE YOU ISLEY BROTHERS
I GUESS THAT'S WHY THEY CALL IT THE BLUES ELTON JOHN
I HAD TOO MUCH TO DREAM LAST NIGHT ELECTRIC PRUNES
I HATE MYSELF FOR LOVING YOU JOAN JETT & THE BLACKHEARTS
I HATE...PEOPLE ANTI-NOWHERE LEAGUE
I HATE ROCK 'N' ROLL JESUS & MARY CHAIN
I HAVE A DREAM ABBA
I HAVE A DREAM WESTLIFE
I HAVE FORGIVEN JESUS MORRISSEY
I HAVE NOTHING WHITNEY HOUSTON
I HAVE PEACE STRIKE
I HAVEN'T STOPPED DANCING YET PAT & MICK
I HEAR A SYMPHONY SUPREMES
I HEAR TALK BUCKS FIZZ
I HEAR YOU KNOCKING DAVE EDMUNDS' ROCKPILE
I HEAR YOU NOW JON & VANGELIS
I HEAR YOUR NAME INCOGNITO
I HEARD A HEART BREAK LAST NIGHT JIM REEVES
I HEARD A RUMOUR BANANARAMA
I HEARD IT THROUGH THE GRAPEVINE MARVIN GAYE
I HEARD IT THROUGH THE GRAPEVINE GLADYS KNIGHT & THE PIPS
I HEARD IT THROUGH THE GRAPEVINE SLITS
I HONESTLY LOVE YOU OLIVIA NEWTON-JOHN
I HOPE YOU DANCE LEE ANN WOMACK
I HOPE YOU DANCE RONAN KEATING
I IMAGINE MARY KIANI
I JUST CALLED TO SAY I LOVE YOU STEVIE WONDER
I JUST CAN'T BE HAPPY TODAY DAMNED
I JUST CAN'T (FORGIVE AND FORGET) BLUE ZOO
I JUST CAN'T HELP BELIEVING ELVIS PRESLEY
I JUST CAN'T STOP LOVING YOU MICHAEL JACKSON
(I JUST) DIED IN YOUR ARMS CUTTING CREW
I JUST DIED IN YOUR ARMS RESOURCE
I JUST DON'T HAVE THE HEART CLIFF RICHARD
I JUST DON'T KNOW WHAT TO DO WITH MYSELF DUSTY SPRINGFIELD
I JUST DON'T KNOW WHAT TO DO WITH MYSELF WHITE STRIPES
I JUST FALL IN LOVE AGAIN ANNE MURRAY
I JUST GO FOR YOU JIMMY JONES
I JUST HAD TO HEAR YOUR VOICE OLETA ADAMS
I JUST KEEP THINKING ABOUT YOU BABY TATA VEGA
I JUST NEED MYSELF OCEAN COLOUR SCENE
(I JUST WANNA) B WITH U TRANSVISION VAMP
I JUST WANNA BE LOVED CULTURE CLUB
I JUST WANNA BE YOUR EVERYTHING ANDY GIBB
I JUST WANNA LOVE U (GIVE IT TO ME) JAY-Z
I JUST WANNA (SPEND SOME TIME WITH YOU) ALTON EDWARDS
I JUST WANT TO DANCE WITH YOU DANIEL O'DONNELL
I JUST WANT TO MAKE LOVE TO YOU ETTA JAMES
I JUST WANT YOU OZZY OSBOURNE
I KEEP FORGETTIN' MICHAEL McDONALD
I KEEP RINGING MY BABY SOUL BROTHERS
I KISS YOUR LIPS TOKYO GHETTO PUSSY
I KNEW I LOVED YOU SAVAGE GARDEN
I KNEW THE BRIDE DAVE EDMUNDS
I KNEW YOU WERE WAITIN' FOR ME ARETHA FRANKLIN & GEORGE MICHAEL
I KNOW [A] PERRY COMO
I KNOW [B] PAUL KING
I KNOW [C] BLUR

I KNOW [D] NEW ATLANTIC
I KNOW [E] DIONNE FARRIS
I KNOW A PLACE [A] PETULA CLARK
I KNOW A PLACE [B] KIM ENGLISH
I KNOW ENOUGH (I DON'T GET ENOUGH) THEAUDIENCE
I KNOW HIM SO WELL ELAINE PAIGE & BARBARA DICKSON
I KNOW HIM SO WELL STEPS
(I KNOW) I'M LOSING YOU TEMPTATIONS
I KNOW MY LOVE CHIEFTANS FEATURING THE CORRS
I KNOW THE LORD TABERNACLE
I KNOW THERE'S SOMETHING GOING ON FRIDA
I KNOW WHAT BOYS LIKE SHAMPOO
I KNOW WHAT I LIKE (IN YOUR WARDROBE) GENESIS
I KNOW WHAT I'M HERE FOR JAMES
I KNOW WHAT YOU WANT BUSTA RHYMES & MARIAH CAREY
I KNOW WHERE I'M GOING GEORGE HAMILTON IV
I KNOW WHERE I'M GOING COUNTRYMEN
I KNOW WHERE IT'S AT ALL SAINTS
I KNOW YOU DON'T LOVE ME ROACHFORD
I KNOW YOU GOT SOUL ERIC B & RAKIM
I KNOW YOU'RE OUT THERE SOMEWHERE MOODY BLUES
I LEARNED FROM THE BEST WHITNEY HOUSTON
I LEFT MY HEART IN SAN FRANCISCO TONY BENNETT
I LIFT MY CUP GLOWORM
I LIKE [A] SHANICE
I LIKE [B] KUT KLOSE
I LIKE [C] MONTELL JORDAN FEATURING SLICK RICK
I LIKE [D] JULIET ROBERTS
I LIKE IT [A] GERRY & THE PACEMAKERS
I LIKE IT [B] DJH FEATURING STEFY
I LIKE IT [C] OVERWEIGHT POOCH FEATURING CE CE PENISTON
I LIKE IT [D] D:REAM
I LIKE IT [E] JOMANDA
I LIKE IT [F] ANGEL MORAES
I LIKE IT [G] NARCOTIC THRUST
I LIKE LOVE (I LOVE LOVE) SOLITAIRE
I LIKE THAT HOUSTON
I LIKE THE WAY DENI HINES
I LIKE THE WAY (THE KISSING GAME) HI-FIVE
I LIKE THE WAY (THE KISSING GAME) KALEEF
I LIKE TO MOVE IT REEL 2 REAL FEATURING THE MAD STUNTMAN
I LIKE TO ROCK APRIL WINE
I LIKE (WHAT YOU'RE DOING TO ME) YOUNG & COMPANY
I LIKE YOUR KIND OF LOVE ANDY WILLIAMS
I LIVE FOR SPEED STAR SPANGLES
I LIVE FOR THE SUN VANITY FARE
I LIVE FOR THE WEEKEND TRIUMPH
I LIVE FOR YOUR LOVE NATALIE COLE
I LOST MY HEART TO A STARSHIP TROOPER SARAH BRIGHTMAN & HOT GOSSIP
I LOVE A MAN IN UNIFORM GANG OF FOUR
I LOVE A RAINY NIGHT EDDIE RABBITT
I LOVE AMERICA PATRICK JUVET
I LOVE BEING IN LOVE WITH YOU ADAM FAITH & THE ROULETTES
I LOVE CHRISTMAS FAST FOOD ROCKERS
I LOVE FOOTBALL WES
I LOVE HER PAUL & BARRY RYAN
I LOVE HOW YOU LOVE ME JIMMY CRAWFORD
I LOVE HOW YOU LOVE ME MAUREEN EVANS
I LOVE HOW YOU LOVE ME PAUL & BARRY RYAN
I LOVE I HATE NEIL ARTHUR
I LOVE IT WHEN WE DO RONAN KEATING
I LOVE LAKE TAHOE A
I LOVE MEN EARTHA KITT

I LOVE MUSIC O'JAYS
I LOVE MUSIC ENIGMA
I LOVE MUSIC ROZALLA
I LOVE MY DOG CAT STEVENS
I LOVE MY RADIO (MY DEE JAY'S RADIO) TAFFY
I LOVE ROCK 'N' ROLL JOAN JETT & THE BLACKHEARTS
I LOVE ROCK 'N' ROLL BRITNEY SPEARS
I LOVE SATURDAY ERASURE
I LOVE THE NIGHTLIFE (DISCO ROUND) ALICIA BRIDGES
I LOVE THE SOUND OF BREAKING GLASS NICK LOWE
I LOVE THE WAY YOU LOVE MARV JOHNSON
I LOVE THE WAY YOU LOVE ME BOYZONE
I LOVE TO BOOGIE T. REX
I LOVE TO LOVE (BUT MY BABY LOVES TO DANCE) TINA CHARLES
I LOVE YOU [A] CLIFF RICHARD & THE SHADOWS
I LOVE YOU [B] DONNA SUMMER
I LOVE YOU [C] YELLO
I LOVE YOU [D] VANILLA ICE
I LOVE YOU [E] FLESH & BONES
I LOVE YOU ALWAYS FOREVER DONNA LEWIS
I LOVE YOU BABY PAUL ANKA
I LOVE YOU BABY FREDDIE & THE DREAMERS
I LOVE YOU BECAUSE JIM REEVES
I LOVE YOU BECAUSE AL MARTINO
I LOVE YOU 'CAUSE I HAVE TO DOGS DIE IN HOT CARS
I LOVE YOU GOODBYE THOMAS DOLBY
I LOVE YOU LOVE ME LOVE GARY GLITTER
I LOVE YOU MORE THAN ROCK N ROLL THUNDER
I LOVE YOU SO MUCH IT HURTS CHARLIE GRACIE
I LOVE YOU...STOP! RED 5
(I LOVE YOU) WHEN YOU SLEEP TRACIE
I LOVE YOU, YES I DO MERSEYBEATS
I LOVE YOU, YES I LOVE YOU EDDY GRANT
I LOVE YOUR SMILE SHANICE
I LUV U [A] SHUT UP & DANCE FEATURING RICHIE DAVIS & PROFESSOR T
I LUV U [B] DIZZEE RASCAL
I LUV U BABY ORIGINAL
I MADE IT THROUGH THE RAIN BARRY MANILOW
I MAY NEVER PASS THIS WAY AGAIN ROBERT EARL
I MAY NEVER PASS THIS WAY AGAIN PERRY COMO
I MAY NEVER PASS THIS WAY AGAIN RONNIE HILTON WITH THE MICHAEL SAMMES SINGERS
I MET A GIRL SHADOWS
I MIGHT SHAKIN' STEVENS
I MIGHT BE CRYING TANITA TIKARAM
I MIGHT BE LYING EDDIE & THE HOT RODS
I MISS YOU [A] HADDAWAY
I MISS YOU [B] 4 OF US
I MISS YOU [C] BJORK
I MISS YOU [D] BLINK 182
I MISS YOU [D] DARREN HAYES
I MISS YOU BABY MARV JOHNSON
I MISSED AGAIN PHIL COLLINS
I MISSED THE BUS KRIS KROSS
I MUST BE IN LOVE RUTLES
I MUST BE SEEING THINGS GENE PITNEY
I MUST STAND ICE-T
I NEED MEREDITH BROOKS
I NEED A GIRL (PART ONE) P DIDDY FEATURING USHER & LOON
I NEED A MAN [A] MAN TO MAN
I NEED A MAN [B] EURYTHMICS
I NEED A MAN [C] LI KWAN
I NEED A MIRACLE COCO
I NEED ANOTHER (EP) DODGY
I NEED DIRECTION TEENAGE FANCLUB
I NEED IT JOHNNY 'GUITAR' WATSON
I NEED LOVE [A] LL COOL J
I NEED LOVE [B] OLIVIA NEWTON-JOHN

I NEED SOMEBODY LOVELAND FEATURING RACHEL McFARLANE
I NEED THE KEY MINIMAL CHIC FEATURING MATT GOSS
I NEED TO BE IN LOVE CARPENTERS
I NEED TO KNOW MARC ANTHONY
I NEED YOU [A] JOE DOLAN
I NEED YOU [B] POINTER SISTERS
I NEED YOU [C] B.V.S.M.P.
I NEED YOU [D] DEUCE
I NEED YOU [E] NIKITA WARREN
I NEED YOU [F] 3T
I NEED YOU [G] WIRELESS
I NEED YOU [H] LEANN RIMES
I NEED YOU [I] DAVID GAHAN
I NEED YOU [J] STANDS
I NEED YOU NOW [A] EDDIE FISHER
I NEED YOU NOW [B] SINNAMON
I NEED YOU TONIGHT JUNIOR M.A.F.I.A. FEATURING AALIYAH
I NEED YOUR LOVE TONIGHT ELVIS PRESLEY
I NEED YOUR LOVIN' [A] TEENA MARIE
I NEED YOUR LOVIN' [A] CURIOSITY
I NEED YOUR LOVIN' [B] ALYSON WILLIAMS
I NEED YOUR LOVIN' (LIKE THE SUNSHINE) MARC ET CLAUDE
I NEED YOUR LOVING HUMAN LEAGUE
I NEVER FELT LIKE THIS BEFORE MICA PARIS
I NEVER GO OUT IN THE RAIN HIGH SOCIETY
I NEVER KNEW ROGER SANCHEZ
I NEVER LOVED YOU ANYWAY CORRS
I NEVER WANT AN EASY LIFE IF ME AND HE WERE EVER TO GET THERE CHARLATANS
I ONLY HAVE EYES FOR YOU ART GARFUNKEL
I ONLY LIVE TO LOVE YOU CILLA BLACK
I ONLY WANNA BE WITH YOU [A] BAY CITY ROLLERS
I ONLY WANNA BE WITH YOU [A] SAMANTHA FOX
I ONLY WANT TO BE WITH YOU [A] DUSTY SPRINGFIELD
I ONLY WANT TO BE WITH YOU [A] TOURISTS
I ONLY WANT TO BE WITH YOU [B] BARRY WHITE
I OWE YOU NOTHING BROS
I OWE YOU ONE SHALAMAR
I PREDICT A RIOT KAISER CHIEFS
I PRETEND DES O'CONNOR
I PROMISE STACIE ORRICO
I PROMISE YOU (GET READY) SAMANTHA FOX
I PROMISED MYSELF NICK KAMEN
I PRONOUNCE YOU THE MADNESS
I PUT A SPELL ON YOU NINA SIMONE
I PUT A SPELL ON YOU ALAN PRICE SET
I PUT A SPELL ON YOU BRYAN FERRY
I PUT A SPELL ON YOU SONIQUE
I QUIT [A] BROS
I QUIT [B] HEPBURN
I RAN A FLOCK OF SEAGULLS
I REALLY DIDN'T MEAN IT LUTHER VANDROSS
I RECALL A GYPSY WOMAN DON WILLIAMS
I REFUSE HUE & CRY
I REFUSE (WHAT YOU WANT) SOMORE FEATURING DAMON TRUEITT
I REMEMBER COOLIO
I REMEMBER ELVIS PRESLEY (THE KING IS DEAD) DANNY MIRROR
I REMEMBER YESTERDAY DONNA SUMMER
I REMEMBER YOU [A] FRANK IFIELD
I REMEMBER YOU [B] SKID ROW
I ROCK TOM NOVY
I SAID I LOVE YOU RAUL MALO
I SAID PIG ON FRIDAY EASTERN LANE
I SAVED THE WORLD TODAY EURYTHMICS
I SAW HER AGAIN MAMAS & THE PAPAS

I SAW HER STANDING THERE ELTON JOHN BAND FEATURING JOHN LENNON & THE MUSCLE SHOALS HORNS
I SAW HIM STANDING THERE TIFFANY
I SAW LINDA YESTERDAY DOUG SHELDON
I SAW MOMMY KISSING SANTA CLAUS BEVERLEY SISTERS
I SAW MOMMY KISSING SANTA CLAUS JIMMY BOYD
I SAW MOMMY KISSING SANTA CLAUS BILLY COTTON & HIS BAND, VOCALS BY THE MILL GIRLS & THE BANDITS
I SAW THE LIGHT [A] TODD RUNDGREN
I SAW THE LIGHT [B] THE THE
I SAY A LITTLE PRAYER DIANA KING
I SAY A LITTLE PRAYER FOR YOU ARETHA FRANKLIN
I SAY NOTHING VOICE OF THE BEEHIVE
I SAY YEAH SECCHI FEATURING ORLANDO JOHNSON
I SCARE MYSELF THOMAS DOLBY
I SECOND THAT EMOTION SMOKEY ROBINSON & THE MIRACLES
I SECOND THAT EMOTION DIANA ROSS & THE SUPREMES & THE TEMPTATIONS
I SECOND THAT EMOTION JAPAN
I SECOND THAT EMOTION ALYSON WILLIAMS WITH CHUCK STANLEY
I SEE A STAR MOUTH & MACNEAL
I SEE GIRLS (CRAZY) STUDIO B/ROMEO & HARRY BROOKS
I SEE ONLY YOU NOOTROPIC
I SEE THE MOON STARGAZERS
I SEE YOU BABY GROOVE ARMADA
I SEE YOU BABY GROOVE ARMADA FEATURING GRAM'MA FUNK
I SEE YOUR SMILE GLORIA ESTEFAN
I SEEN A MAN DIE SCARFACE
I SHALL BE RELEASED TREMELOES
I SHALL BE THERE B*WITCHED
I SHOT THE SHERIFF ERIC CLAPTON
I SHOT THE SHERIFF LIGHT OF THE WORLD
I SHOT THE SHERIFF WARREN G
I SHOULD BE SO LUCKY KYLIE MINOGUE
I SHOULD CARE FRANK IFIELD
I SHOULD HAVE KNOWN BETTER [A] NATURALS
I SHOULD HAVE KNOWN BETTER [B] JIM DIAMOND
I SHOULDA LOVED YA NARADA MICHAEL WALDEN
I SHOULD'VE KNOWN AIMEE MANN
I SINGS MARY MARY
I SLEEP ALONE AT NIGHT JIM DIAMOND
I SPEAKA DA LINGO BLACK LACE
I SPECIALIZE IN LOVE SHARON BROWN
I SPECIALIZE IN LOVE ARIZONA FEATURING ZEITIA
I SPECIALIZE IN LOVE ZEITIA MASSIAH
I SPY FOR THE FBI JAMO THOMAS
I SPY FOR THE FBI UNTOUCHABLES
I STAND ACCUSED MERSEYBEATS
I STAND ALONE E-MOTION
I STARTED A JOKE FAITH NO MORE
I STARTED SOMETHING I COULDN'T FINISH SMITHS
I STILL BELIEVE [A] RONNIE HILTON
I STILL BELIEVE [B] MARIAH CAREY
I STILL BELIEVE IN YOU CLIFF RICHARD
I STILL HAVEN'T FOUND WHAT I'M LOOKING FOR U2
I STILL LOVE YOU ALL KENNY BALL & HIS JAZZMEN
I STILL REMEMBER GARY NUMAN
I STILL THINK ABOUT YOU DANGER DANGER
I STILL THINK OF YOU UTAH SAINTS
I SURRENDER [A] RAINBOW
I SURRENDER [B] ROSIE GAINES
I SURRENDER [C] DAVID SYLVIAN
I SURRENDER (TO THE SPIRIT OF THE NIGHT) SAMANTHA FOX

I SURRENDER TO YOUR LOVE BY ALL MEANS
I SWEAR ALL-4-ONE
I TALK TO THE TREES CLINT EASTWOOD
I TALK TO THE WIND OPUS III
I THANK YOU [A] SAM & DAVE
I THANK YOU [B] ADEVA
I THINK I LOVE YOU PARTRIDGE FAMILY STARRING SHIRLEY JONES FEATURING DAVID CASSIDY
I THINK I LOVE YOU VOICE OF THE BEEHIVE
I THINK I LOVE YOU KACI
I TH!NK I WANT TO DANCE WITH YOU RUMPLE-STILTS-SKIN
I THINK I'M IN LOVE SPIRITUALIZED
I THINK I'M IN LOVE WITH YOU JESSICA SIMPSON
I THINK I'M PARANOID GARBAGE
I THINK IT'S GOING TO RAIN UB40
I THINK OF YOU [A] MERSEYBEATS
I THINK OF YOU [B] PERRY COMO
I THINK OF YOU [C] DETROIT EMERALDS
I THINK OF YOU [D] BRYAN POWELL
I THINK WE'RE ALONE NOW TIFFANY
I THINK WE'RE ALONE NOW PASCAL FEATURING KAREN PARRY
I THOUGHT I MEANT THE WORLD TO YOU ALYSHA WARREN
I THOUGHT IT TOOK A LITTLE TIME DIANA ROSS
I THOUGHT IT WAS YOU [A] HERBIE HANCOCK
I THOUGHT IT WAS YOU [A] SEX-O-SONIQUE
I THOUGHT IT WAS YOU [B] JULIA FORDHAM
I THREW IT ALL AWAY BOB DYLAN
I TOLD YOU SO JIMMY JONES
I TOUCH MYSELF DIVINYLS
I TRY [A] MACY GRAY
I TRY [B] TALIB KWELI FEATURING MARY J. BLIGE
I TURN TO YOU [A] CHRISTINA AGUILERA
I TURN TO YOU [B] MELANIE C
I UNDERSTAND G-CLEFS
I UNDERSTAND FREDDIE & THE DREAMERS
I WALK THE EARTH VOICE OF THE BEEHIVE
I WANNA 1-2-1 WITH YOU SOLID GOLD CHARTBUSTERS
I WANNA BE A FLINTSTONE SCREAMING BLUE MESSIAHS
I WANNA BE A HIPPY TECHNOHEAD
I WANNA BE A WINNER BROWN SAUCE
I WANNA BE ADORED STONE ROSES
I WANNA BE DOWN BRANDY
I WANNA BE FREE MINTY
I WANNA BE FREE (TO BE WITH HIM) SCARLET
I WANNA BE IN LOVE AGAIN BEIJING SPRING
I WANNA BE LOVED [A] RICKY NELSON
I WANNA BE LOVED [B] ELVIS COSTELLO
I WANNA BE THE ONLY ONE ETERNAL FEATURING BEBE WINANS
I WANNA BE U CHOCOLATE PUMA
I WANNA BE WITH YOU MANDY MOORE
I WANNA BE WITH YOU [A] COFFEE
I WANNA BE WITH YOU [B] MAZE FEATURING FRANKIE BEVERLY
I WANNA BE YOUR LADY HINDA HICKS
I WANNA BE YOUR LOVER PRINCE
I WANNA BE YOUR MAN [A] ROLLING STONES
I WANNA BE YOUR MAN [A] REZILLOS
I WANNA BE YOUR MAN [B] CHAKA DEMUS & PLIERS
I WANNA DANCE WIT CHOO DISCO TEX & THE SEX-O-LETTES FEATURING SIR MONTI ROCK III
I WANNA DANCE WITH SOMEBODY FLIP & FILL
I WANNA DANCE WITH SOMEBODY (WHO LOVES ME) WHITNEY HOUSTON
I WANNA DO IT WITH YOU BARRY MANILOW
I WANNA GET NEXT TO YOU ROSE ROYCE

(I WANNA GIVE YOU) DEVOTION NOMAD FEATURING MC MIKEE FREEDOM
I WANNA GO BACK NEW SEEKERS
I WANNA GO HOME LONNIE DONEGAN
I WANNA GO WHERE THE PEOPLE GO WILDHEARTS
I WANNA HAVE SOME FUN SAMANTHA FOX
I WANNA HOLD ON TO YOU MICA PARIS
I WANNA HOLD YOUR HAND DOLLAR
I WANNA KNOW [A] STACCATO
I WANNA KNOW [B] JOE
I WANNA KNOW [C] BLUESKINS
(I WANNA KNOW) WHY SINCLAIR
(I WANNA) LOVE MY LIFE AWAY GENE PITNEY
I WANNA LOVE YOU [A] JADE
I WANNA LOVE YOU [B] SOLID HARMONIE
I WANNA LOVE YOU FOREVER JESSICA SIMPSON
I WANNA MAKE YOU FEEL GOOD SYSTEM
I WANNA SEX YOU UP COLOR ME BADD
I WANNA SING SABRINA JOHNSTON
I WANNA STAY HERE MIKI & GRIFF
I WANNA STAY HOME JELLYFISH
I WANNA STAY WITH YOU GALLAGHER & LYLE
I WANNA STAY WITH YOU UNDERCOVER
I WANNA THANK YOU ANGIE STONE FEATURING SNOOP DOGG
I WANT AN ALIEN FOR CHRISTMAS FOUNTAINS OF WAYNE
I WANT CANDY BRIAN POOLE & THE TREMELOES
I WANT CANDY BOW WOW WOW
I WANT CANDY CANDY GIRLS FEATURING VALERIE MALCOLM
I WANT CANDY AARON CARTER
I WANT HER KEITH SWEAT
I WANT IT ALL QUEEN
I WANT IT THAT WAY BACKSTREET BOYS
I WANT LOVE ELTON JOHN
I WANT MORE [A] CAN
I WANT MORE [B] FAITHLESS
I WANT OUT HELLOWEEN
I WANT OUT (I CAN'T BELIEVE) HARRY CHOO CHOO ROMERO
I WANT THAT MAN DEBORAH HARRY
I WANT THE WORLD 2WO THIRD3
I WANT TO BE ALONE 2WO THIRD3
(I WANT TO BE) ELECTED MR BEAN & SMEAR CAMPAIGN FEATURING BRUCE DICKINSON
I WANT TO BE FREE TOYAH
I WANT TO BE STRAIGHT IAN DURY & THE BLOCKHEADS
I WANT TO BE THERE WHEN YOU COME ECHO & THE BUNNYMEN
I WANT TO BE WANTED BRENDA LEE
I WANT TO BE YOUR MAN ROGER
I WANT TO BE YOUR PROPERTY BLUE MERCEDES
I WANT TO BREAK FREE QUEEN
I WANT TO GIVE PERRY COMO
I WANT TO GO WITH YOU EDDY ARNOLD
I WANT TO HEAR IT FROM YOU GO WEST
I WANT TO HOLD YOUR HAND BEATLES
(I WANT TO) KILL SOMEBODY S*M*A*S*H
I WANT TO KNOW WHAT LOVE IS FOREIGNER
I WANT TO KNOW WHAT LOVE IS TERRI SYMON
I WANT TO LIVE GRACE
I WANT TO STAY HERE STEVE (Lawrence) & EYDIE (Gorme)
I WANT TO THANK YOU ROBIN S
I WANT TO TOUCH YOU CATHERINE WHEEL
I WANT TO WAKE UP WITH YOU BORIS GARDINER
I WANT TO WALK YOU HOME FATS DOMINO
I WANT U ROSIE GAINES
I WANT YOU [A] BOB DYLAN

I WANT YOU [A] SOPHIE B. HAWKINS
I WANT YOU [B] GARY LOW
I WANT YOU [C] UTAH SAINTS
I WANT YOU [D] JULIET ROBERTS
I WANT YOU [E] SECRET LIFE
I WANT YOU [F] SALAD
I WANT YOU [G] INSPIRAL CARPETS FEATURING MARK E SMITH
I WANT YOU [H] SAVAGE GARDEN
I WANT YOU [I] Z2 VOCAL BY ALISON RIVERS
I WANT YOU [J] CZR FEATURING DELANO
I WANT YOU [K] JANET JACKSON
I WANT YOU (ALL TONIGHT) CURTIS HAIRSTON
I WANT YOU BACK [A] JACKSON 5
I WANT YOU BACK [A] CLEOPATRA
I WANT YOU BACK [B] BANANARAMA
I WANT YOU BACK [C] MELANIE B FEATURING MISSY 'MISDEMEANOR' ELLIOTT
I WANT YOU BACK [D] N SYNC
I WANT YOU BACK [D] X-PRESS 2
I WANT YOU FOR MYSELF ANOTHER LEVEL/GHOSTFACE KILLAH
I WANT YOU (FOREVER) DJ CARL COX
I WANT YOU I NEED YOU I LOVE YOU ELVIS PRESLEY
I WANT YOU NEAR ME TINA TURNER
I WANT YOU TO BE MY BABY BILLIE DAVIS
I WANT YOU TO WANT ME [A] CHEAP TRICK
I WANT YOU TO WANT ME [B] SOLID HARMONIE
I WANT YOUR LOVE [A] CHIC
I WANT YOUR LOVE [A] ROGER SANCHEZ PRESENTS TWILIGHT
I WANT YOUR LOVE [B] TRANSVISION VAMP
I WANT YOUR LOVE [C] ATOMIC KITTEN
I WANT YOUR LOVIN' (JUST A LITTLE BIT) CURTIS HAIRSTON
I WANT YOUR SEX GEORGE MICHAEL
I WAS A KING EDDIE MURPHY FEATURING SHABBA RANKS
I WAS BORN ON CHRISTMAS DAY SAINT ETIENNE
I WAS BORN TO BE ME TOM JONES
I WAS BORN TO LOVE YOU FREDDIE MERCURY
I WAS BROUGHT TO MY SENSES STING
I WAS KAISER BILL'S BATMAN WHISTLING JACK SMITH
I WAS MADE FOR DANCIN' LEIF GARRETT
I WAS MADE FOR LOVIN' YOU KISS
I WAS MADE TO LOVE HER STEVIE WONDER
I WAS MADE TO LOVE YOU LORRAINE CATO
I WAS ONLY JOKING ROD STEWART
I WAS RIGHT AND YOU WERE WRONG DEACON BLUE
I WAS THE ONE ELVIS PRESLEY
I WAS TIRED OF BEING ALONE PATRICE RUSHEN
I WASN'T BUILT TO GET UP SUPERNATURALS
I WEAR MY SKIN ONE MINUTE SILENCE
I (WHO HAVE NOTHING) SHIRLEY BASSEY
I (WHO HAVE NOTHING) TOM JONES
I (WHO HAVE NOTHING) SYLVESTER
I WILL BILLY FURY
I WILL RUBY WINTERS
I WILL ALWAYS LOVE YOU WHITNEY HOUSTON
I WILL ALWAYS LOVE YOU SARAH WASHINGTON
I WILL ALWAYS LOVE YOU RIK WALLER
I WILL BE RELEASED UP YER RONSON FEATURING MARY PEARCE
I WILL BE WITH YOU T'PAU
I WILL BE YOUR GIRLFRIEND DUBSTAR
I WILL COME TO YOU HANSON
I WILL DRINK THE WINE FRANK SINATRA
I WILL FOLLOW UNO MAS
I WILL GO WITH YOU (CON TE PARTIRO) DONNA SUMMER
I WILL LOVE AGAIN LARA FABIAN

I WILL LOVE YOU ALL MY LIFE FOSTER & ALLEN
I WILL LOVE YOU (EV'RY TIME WHEN WE ARE GONE) FUREYS
I WILL REMEMBER TOTO
I WILL RETURN SPRINGWATER
I WILL SURVIVE [A] ARRIVAL
I WILL SURVIVE [B] GLORIA GAYNOR
I WILL SURVIVE [B] BILLIE JO SPEARS
I WILL SURVIVE [B] DIANA ROSS
I WILL SURVIVE [B] CHANTAY SAVAGE
I WILL SURVIVE [B] CAKE
I WILL WAIT HOOTIE & THE BLOWFISH
I WISH [A] STEVIE WONDER
I WISH [B] GABRIELLE
I WISH [C] SKEE-LO
I WISH [D] R KELLY
I WISH HE DIDN'T TRUST ME SO MUCH BOBBY WOMACK
I WISH I COULD SHIMMY LIKE MY SISTER KATE OLYMPICS
I WISH I KNEW HOW IT WOULD FEEL SHARLENE HECTOR
(I WISH I KNEW HOW IT WOULD FEEL TO BE) FREE/ONE LIGHTHOUSE FAMILY
I WISH I WAS A GIRL VIOLENT DELIGHT
I WISH I WAS YOU NEW RHODES
I WISH IT COULD BE A WOMBLING CHRISTMAS WOMBLES FEATURING ROY WOOD
I WISH IT COULD BE CHRISTMAS EVERY DAY WIZZARD
I WISH IT COULD BE CHRISTMAS EVERYDAY ROY WOOD BIG BAND
I WISH IT WASN'T TRUE SUPATONIC
I WISH IT WOULD RAIN TEMPTATIONS
I WISH IT WOULD RAIN FACES
I WISH IT WOULD RAIN DOWN PHIL COLLINS
I WISH U HEAVEN PRINCE
I WISH YOU LOVE PAUL YOUNG
I WISH YOU WOULD JOCELYN BROWN
I WONDER [A] DICKIE VALENTINE
I WONDER [A] JANE FROMAN
I WONDER [B] BRENDA LEE
I WONDER [C] CRYSTALS
I WONDER HOW SHINING
I WONDER IF HEAVEN GOT A GHETTO 2PAC
I WONDER IF I TAKE YOU HOME LISA LISA & CULT JAM WITH FULL FORCE
I WONDER WHO'S KISSING HER NOW EMILE FORD
I WONDER WHY [A] SHOWADDYWADDY
I WONDER WHY [B] CURTIS STIGERS
I WONDER WHY HE'S THE GREATEST DJ TONY TOUCH FEATURING TOTAL
I WON'T BACK DOWN TOM PETTY
I WON'T BLEED FOR YOU CLIMIE FISHER
I WON'T CHANGE YOU SOPHIE ELLIS-BEXTOR
I WON'T CLOSE MY EYES UB40
I WON'T COME IN WHILE HE'S THERE JIM REEVES
I WON'T CRY GLEN GOLDSMITH
I WON'T FEEL BAD SIMPLY RED
I WON'T FORGET YOU JIM REEVES
I WON'T HOLD YOU BACK TOTO
I WON'T LAST A DAY WITHOUT YOU CARPENTERS
I WON'T LET THE SUN GO DOWN ON ME NIK KERSHAW
I WON'T LET YOU DOWN PhD
I WON'T LET YOU DOWN W.I.P. FEATURING EMMIE
I WON'T MENTION IT AGAIN RUBY WINTERS
I WON'T RUN AWAY ALVIN STARDUST
I WOULD DIE 4 U PRINCE & THE REVOLUTION
I WOULD DIE 4 U SPACE COWBOY
I WOULD DO FOR YOU UB40
I WOULD FIX YOU KENICKIE
I WOULD NEVER BLUE NILE

I WOULDN'T BELIEVE YOUR RADIO STEREOPHONICS
I WOULDN'T LIE YARBOROUGH & PEOPLES
I WOULDN'T NORMALLY DO THIS KIND OF THING PET SHOP BOYS
I WOULDN'T TRADE YOU FOR THE WORLD BACHELORS
I WOULDN'T WANNA HAPPEN TO YOU EMBRACE
I WRITE THE SONGS DAVID CASSIDY
I WROTE YOU A SONG MISTY OLDLAND
IBIZA MAXIMA FEATURING LILY
THE ICE CREAM MAN TORNADOS
ICE HOCKEY HAIR SUPER FURRY ANIMALS
ICE ICE BABY VANILLA ICE
ICE IN THE SUN STATUS QUO
ICE RAIN ALEX WHITCOMBE & BIG C
ICEBLINK LUCK COCTEAU TWINS
ICH BIN EIN AUSLANDER POP WILL EAT ITSELF
ICH WILL RAMMSTEIN
ICING ON THE CAKE STEPHEN 'TIN TIN' DUFFY
I'D BE SURPRISINGLY GOOD FOR YOU LINDA LEWIS
I'D DIE WITHOUT YOU PM DAWN
I'D DO ANYTHING MIKE PRESTON
I'D DO ANYTHING FOR LOVE (BUT I WON'T DO THAT) MEAT LOAF
I'D LIE FOR YOU (AND THAT'S THE TRUTH) MEAT LOAF
I'D LIKE TO TEACH THE WORLD TO SING NO WAY SIS
I'D LIKE TO TEACH THE WORLD TO SING DEMI HOLBORN
I'D LIKE TO TEACH THE WORLD TO SING (IN PERFECT HARMONY) NEW SEEKERS
I'D LOVE YOU TO WANT ME LOBO
I'D NEVER FIND ANOTHER YOU BILLY FURY
I'D RATHER DANCE WITH YOU KINGS OF CONVENIENCE
I'D RATHER GO BLIND CHICKEN SHACK
I'D RATHER GO BLIND RUBY TURNER
I'D RATHER GO BLIND SYDNEY YOUNGBLOOD
I'D RATHER JACK REYNOLDS GIRLS
I'D REALLY LOVE TO SEE YOU TONIGHT ENGLAND DAN & JOHN FORD COLEY
THE IDEAL HEIGHT BIFFY CLYRO
IDEAL WORLD CHRISTIANS
IDENTITY X-RAY SPEX
IDIOTS AT THE WHEEL EP. KINGMAKER
IDLE GOSSIP PERRY COMO
IDLE ON PARADE EP ANTHONY NEWLEY
IDOL AMANDA GHOST
THE IDOL [A] W.A.S.P.
THE IDOL [B] MARC ALMOND
IEYA TOYAH
IF – READ TO FAURE'S 'PAVANE' DES LYNAM FEATURING WIMBLEDON CHORAL SOCIETY
IF [A] TELLY SAVALAS
IF [A] YIN & YAN
IF [A] JOHN ALFORD
IF [A] DOLLY PARTON
IF [B] JANET JACKSON
IF... [C] BLUETONES
IF 60S WERE 90S BEAUTIFUL PEOPLE
IF A MAN ANSWERS BOBBY DARIN
IF ANYONE FINDS THIS I LOVE YOU RUBY MURRAY WITH ANNE WARREN
IF DREAMS CAME TRUE PAT BOONE
IF EVER 3RD STOREE
IF EVERY DAY WAS LIKE CHRISTMAS ELVIS PRESLEY
IF EVERYBODY LOOKED THE SAME GROOVE ARMADA
IF EYE LOVE U 2 NIGHT MAYTE
IF GOD WILL SEND HIS ANGELS U2
IF HE TELLS YOU ADAM FAITH & THE ROULETTES
IF I AIN'T GOT YOU ALICIA KEYS
IF I CAN DREAM ELVIS PRESLEY
IF I CAN DREAM (EP) MICHAEL BALL
IF I CAN'T 50 CENT/G-UNIT
IF I CAN'T CHANGE YOUR MIND SUGAR

IF I CAN'T HAVE YOU YVONNE ELLIMAN
IF I CAN'T HAVE YOU KIM WILDE
IF I COULD [A] DAVID ESSEX
IF I COULD [B] HUNDRED REASONS
IF I COULD BUILD MY WHOLE WORLD AROUND YOU MARVIN GAYE & TAMMI TERRELL
IF I COULD (EL CONDOR PASA) JULIE FELIX
IF I COULD FLY GRACE
IF I COULD GIVE YOU ALL MY LOVE COUNTING CROWS
IF I COULD GO ANGIE MARTINEZ FEATURING LIL MO
IF I COULD ONLY MAKE YOU CARE MIKE BERRY
IF I COULD ONLY SAY GOODBYE DAVID HASSELHOFF
IF I COULD TALK I'D TELL YOU LEMONHEADS
IF I COULD TURN BACK THE HANDS OF TIME R KELLY
IF I COULD TURN BACK TIME CHER
IF I DIDN'T CARE DAVID CASSIDY
IF I EVER FALL IN LOVE SHAI
IF I EVER FEEL BETTER PHEONIX
IF I EVER LOSE MY FAITH IN YOU STING
IF I FALL ALICE MARTINEAU
IF I GIVE MY HEART TO YOU DORIS DAY
IF I GIVE MY HEART TO YOU JOAN REGAN
IF I GIVE YOU MY NUMBER PJ & DUNCAN
IF I HAD A HAMMER TRINI LOPEZ
IF I HAD NO LOOT TONY TONI TONE
IF I HAD WORDS SCOTT FITZGERALD & YVONNE KEELEY & THE ST THOMAS MORE SCHOOL CHOIR
IF I HAD YOU KORGIS
IF I HAVE TO GO AWAY JIGSAW
IF I HAVE TO STAND ALONE LONNIE GORDON
IF I KNEW THEN WHAT I KNOW NOW VAL DOONICAN
IF I LET YOU GO WESTLIFE
IF I LOVE U 2 NITE MICA PARIS
IF I LOVE YA THEN I NEED YA IF I NEED YA THEN I WANT YOU AROUND EARTHA KITT
IF I LOVED YOU RICHARD ANTHONY
IF I NEEDED SOMEONE HOLLIES
IF I NEVER KNEW YOU (LOVE THEME FROM 'POCAHONTAS') JON SECADA & SHANICE
IF I NEVER SEE YOU AGAIN WET WET WET
IF I ONLY HAD TIME JOHN ROWLES
IF I ONLY KNEW TOM JONES
IF I REMEMBER BENZ
IF I RULED THE WORLD [A] HARRY SECOMBE
IF I RULED THE WORLD [A] TONY BENNETT
IF I RULED THE WORLD [B] KURTIS BLOW
IF I RULED THE WORLD [B] NAS
IF I SAID YOU HAD A BEAUTIFUL BODY WOULD YOU HOLD IT AGAINST ME BELLAMY BROTHERS
IF I SAY YES FIVE STAR
IF I SHOULD FALL FROM GRACE WITH GOD POGUES
IF I SHOULD LOVE AGAIN BARRY MANILOW
IF I SURVIVE HYBRID FEATURING JULEE CRUISE
IF I THOUGHT YOU'D EVER CHANGE YOUR MIND CILLA BLACK
IF I THOUGHT YOU'D EVER CHANGE YOUR MIND AGNETHA FALTSKOG
IF I TOLD YOU THAT WHITNEY HOUSTON & GEORGE MICHAEL
IF I WAS [A] MIDGE URE
IF I WAS [B] ASWAD
IF I WAS A RIVER TINA ARENA
IF I WAS YOUR GIRLFRIEND PRINCE
IF I WERE A CARPENTER BOBBY DARIN
IF I WERE A CARPENTER FOUR TOPS
IF I WERE A CARPENTER ROBERT PLANT
IF I WERE A RICH MAN TOPOL
IF I WERE YOU [A] k.d. lang
IF I WERE YOU [B] CANDEE JAY
IF I'M NOT YOUR LOVER AL B SURE!
IF IT DON'T FIT DON'T FORCE IT KELLEE PATTERSON

IF IT HAPPENS AGAIN UB40

IF IT MAKES YOU HAPPY SHERYL CROW

IF IT WASN'T FOR THE REASON THAT I LOVE YOU MIKI ANTHONY

IF IT'S ALRIGHT WITH YOU BABY KORGIS

IF IT'S LOVE THAT YOU WANT DONNY OSMOND

IF LEAVING ME IS EASY PHIL COLLINS

IF LIFE IS LIKE A LOVE BANK I WANT AN OVERDRAFT WILDHEARTS

IF LOOKS COULD KILL TRANSVISION VAMP

IF LOVE WAS A TRAIN MICHELLE SHOCKED

IF LOVE WAS LIKE GUITARS IAN McNABB

(IF LOVING YOU IS WRONG) I DON'T WANT TO BE RIGHT ROD STEWART

IF MADONNA CALLS JUNIOR VASQUEZ

IF MY FRIENDS COULD SEE ME NOW LINDA CLIFFORD

IF NOT FOR YOU OLIVIA NEWTON-JOHN

IF NOT YOU DR. HOOK

IF ONLY HANSON

IF ONLY I COULD SYDNEY YOUNGBLOOD

IF ONLY I COULD LIVE MY LIFE AGAIN JANE MORGAN

IF ONLY TOMORROW RONNIE CARROLL

(IF PARADISE IS) HALF AS NICE AMEN CORNER

IF SHE KNEW WHAT SHE WANTS BANGLES

IF SHE SHOULD COME TO YOU ANTHONY NEWLEY

IF THAT WERE ME MELANIE C

IF THAT'S YOUR BOYFRIEND (HE WASN'T LAST NIGHT) ME'SHELL NDEGEOCELLO

IF THE KIDS ARE UNITED SHAM 69

IF THE RIVER CAN BEND ELTON JOHN

IF THE WHOLE WORLD STOPPED LOVING VAL DOONICAN

IF THERE WAS A MAN PRETENDERS FOR 007

IF THERE'S ANY JUSTICE LEMAR

IF THIS IS IT HUEY LEWIS & THE NEWS

IF THIS IS LOVE [A] JJ

IF THIS IS LOVE [B] JEANIE TRACY

IF TOMORROW NEVER COMES RONAN KEATING

IF U WANT ME MICHAEL WOODS FEATURING IMOGEN BAILEY

IF WE FALL IN LOVE TONIGHT ROD STEWART

IF WE HOLD ON TOGETHER DIANA ROSS

IF WE TRY KAREN RAMIREZ

IF WE WERE LOVERS GLORIA ESTEFAN

IF YA GETTING' DOWN FIVE

IF YOU ASKED ME TO CELINE DION

IF YOU BELIEVE JOHNNIE RAY

IF YOU BUY THIS RECORD YOU LIFE WILL BE TAMPERER FEATURING MAYA

IF YOU C JORDAN SOMETHING CORPORATE

IF YOU CAN WANT SMOKEY ROBINSON & THE MIRACLES

IF YOU CAN'T DO IT WHEN YOU'RE YOUNG, WHEN CAN YOU DO IT? THEAUDIENCE

IF YOU CAN'T GIVE ME LOVE SUZI QUATRO

IF YOU CAN'T SAY NO LENNY KRAVITZ

IF YOU CAN'T STAND THE HEAT BUCKS FIZZ

IF YOU CARED KIM APPLEBY

IF YOU COME BACK BLUE

IF YOU COME TO ME ATOMIC KITTEN

IF YOU COULD READ MY MIND GORDON LIGHTFOOT

IF YOU COULD READ MY MIND STARS ON 54

IF YOU COULD SEE ME NOW SHAKATAK

IF YOU DON'T KNOW ME BY NOW HAROLD MELVIN & THE BLUENOTES

IF YOU DON'T KNOW ME BY NOW SIMPLY RED

IF YOU DON'T LOVE ME PREFAB SPROUT

IF YOU DON'T WANT ME TO DESTROY YOU SUPER FURRY ANIMALS

IF YOU DON'T WANT MY LOVE ROBERT JOHN

IF YOU EVER EAST 17 FEATURING GABRIELLE

IF YOU EVER LEAVE ME BARBRA STREISAND/VINCE GILL

IF YOU FEEL IT THELMA HOUSTON

IF YOU GO JON SECADA

IF YOU GO AWAY [A] TERRY JACKS

IF YOU GO AWAY [B] NEW KIDS ON THE BLOCK

IF YOU GOTTA GO GO NOW MANFRED MANN

IF YOU GOTTA MAKE A FOOL OF SOMEBODY FREDDIE & THE DREAMERS

IF YOU HAD MY LOVE JENNIFER LOPEZ

IF YOU HAVE TO GO GENEVA

IF YOU KNEW SOUSA (AND FRIENDS) ROYAL PHILHARMONIC ORCHESTRA ARRANGED & CONDUCTED BY LOUIS CLARK

IF YOU KNOW WHAT I MEAN NEIL DIAMOND

IF YOU LEAVE ORCHESTRAL MANOEUVRES IN THE DARK

IF YOU LEAVE ME NOW CHICAGO

IF YOU LEAVE ME NOW UPSIDE DOWN

IF YOU LEAVE ME NOW SYSTEM PRESENTS KERRI B

IF YOU LET ME STAY TERENCE TRENT D'ARBY

IF YOU LOVE HER DICK EMERY

IF YOU LOVE ME [A] MARY HOPKIN

IF YOU LOVE ME [B] BROWNSTONE

IF YOU LOVE SOMEBODY SET THEM FREE STING

IF YOU ONLY LET ME IN MN8

IF YOU REALLY CARED GABRIELLE

IF YOU REALLY LOVE ME STEVIE WONDER

IF YOU REALLY WANNA KNOW MARC DORSEY

IF YOU REALLY WANT TO MEAT LOAF

IF YOU REMEMBER ME CHRIS THOMPSON

IF YOU SHOULD NEED A FRIEND FIRE ISLAND FEATURING MARK ANTHONI

IF YOU TALK IN YOUR SLEEP ELVIS PRESLEY

IF YOU THINK YOU KNOW HOW TO LOVE ME SMOKEY

(IF YOU THINK YOU'RE) GROOVY PP ARNOLD

IF YOU TOLERATE THIS YOUR CHILDREN WILL BE NEXT MANIC STREET PREACHERS

IF YOU WALK AWAY PETER COX

IF YOU WANNA BE HAPPY JIMMY SOUL

IF YOU WANNA BE HAPPY ROCKY SHARPE & THE REPLAYS

IF YOU WANNA PARTY MOLELLA FEATURING THE OUTHERE BROTHERS

IF YOU WANT LUCIANA

IF YOU WANT ME HINDA HICKS

IF YOU WANT MY LOVE CHEAP TRICK

IF YOU WANT MY LOVIN' EVELYN KING

IF YOU WERE HERE TONIGHT ALEXANDER O'NEAL

IF YOU WERE HERE TONIGHT MATT GOSS

IF YOU WERE MINE MARY EDDY ARNOLD

IF YOU WERE THE ONLY BOY IN THE WORLD STEVIE MARSH

IF YOU WERE WITH ME NOW KYLIE MINOGUE & KEITH WASHINGTON

IF YOU'LL BE MINE BABY BIRD

IF YOUR GIRL ONLY KNEW AALIYAH

IF YOUR HEART ISN'T IN IT ATLANTIC STARR

IF YOU'RE GONE MATCHBOX 20

IF YOU'RE LOOKING FOR A WAY OUT ODYSSEY

IF YOU'RE NOT THE ONE DANIEL BEDINGFIELD

IF YOU'RE READY (COME GO WITH ME) STAPLE SINGERS

IF YOU'RE READY (COME GO WITH ME) RUBY TURNER FEATURING JONATHAN BUTLER

IF YOU'RE THINKING OF ME DODGY

IGGIN' ME CHICO DeBARGE

IGNITION R KELLY

IGNORANCE OCEANIC FEATURING SIOBHAN MAHER

IGUANA MAURO PICOTTO

III WISHES TERRORVISION

IKO IKO DIXIE CUPS

IKO IKO BELLE STARS

IKO IKO NATASHA

IL ADORE BOY GEORGE

IL EST NE LE DIVIN ENFANT SIOUXSIE & THE BANSHEES

IL NOSTRO CONCERTO UMBERTO BINDI

IL SILENZIO NINI ROSSO

I'LL ALWAYS BE AROUND C & C MUSIC FACTORY

I'LL ALWAYS BE IN LOVE WITH YOU MICHAEL HOLLIDAY

I'LL ALWAYS LOVE MY MAMA INTRUDERS

I'LL ALWAYS LOVE YOU TAYLOR DAYNE

I'LL BE FOXY BROWN FEATURING JAY-Z

(I'LL BE A) FREAK FOR YOU ROYALLE DELITE

I'LL BE AROUND TERRI WELLS

I'LL BE AROUND RAPPIN' 4-TAY FEATURING THE SPINNERS

I'LL BE BACK ARNEE & THE TERMINATORS

I'LL BE GOOD RENE & ANGELA

I'LL BE GOOD TO YOU QUINCY JONES FEATURING RAY CHARLES & CHAKA KHAN

I'LL BE HOME PAT BOONE

I'LL BE HOME THIS CHRISTMAS SHAKIN' STEVENS

I'LL BE LOVING YOU (FOREVER) NEW KIDS ON THE BLOCK

I'LL BE MISSING YOU PUFF DADDY & FAITH EVANS

I'LL BE SATISFIED SHAKIN' STEVENS

I'LL BE THERE [A] GERRY & THE PACEMAKERS

I'LL BE THERE [B] JACKIE TRENT

I'LL BE THERE [C] JACKSON 5

I'LL BE THERE [C] MARIAH CAREY

I'LL BE THERE [D] INNOCENCE

I'LL BE THERE [E] 99TH FLOOR ELEVATORS FEATURING TONY DE VIT

I'LL BE THERE [F] EMMA

I'LL BE THERE FOR YOU [A] BON JOVI

I'LL BE THERE FOR YOU [B] REMBRANDTS

I'LL BE THERE FOR YOU [C] SOLID HARMONIE

I'LL BE THERE FOR YOU (DOYA DODODO DOYA) HOUSE OF VIRGINISM

I'LL BE THERE FOR YOU – YOU'RE ALL I NEED TO GET BY METHOD MAN/MARY J. BLIGE

I'LL BE WAITING [A] CLIVE GRIFFIN

I'LL BE WAITING [B] FULL INTENTION PRESENTS SHENA

I'LL BE WITH YOU IN APPLE BLOSSOM TIME ROSEMARY JUNE

I'LL BE YOUR ANGEL KIRA

I'LL BE YOUR BABY TONIGHT ROBERT PALMER & UB40

I'LL BE YOUR BABY TONIGHT NORAH JONES

I'LL BE YOUR EVERYTHING TOMMY PAGE

I'LL BE YOUR FRIEND ROBERT OWENS

I'LL BE YOUR SHELTER TAYLOR DAYNE

I'LL COME RUNNIN' JUICE

I'LL COME RUNNING CLIFF RICHARD

I'LL COME WHEN YOU CALL RUBY MURRAY

I'LL CRY FOR YOU EUROPE

I'LL CUT YOUR TAIL OFF JOHN LEYTON

I'LL DO ANYTHING – TO MAKE YOU MINE HOLLOWAY & CO

I'LL DO ANYTHING YOU WANT ME TO BARRY WHITE

I'LL DO YA WHALE

I'LL FIND MY WAY HOME JON & VANGELIS

I'LL FIND YOU [A] DAVID WHITFIELD

I'LL FIND YOU [B] MICHELLE GAYLE

I'LL FLY FOR YOU SPANDAU BALLET

I'LL GET BY CONNIE FRANCIS

I'LL GET BY SHIRLEY BASSEY

I'LL GIVE YOU THE EARTH (TOUS LES BATEAUX, TOUS LES OISEAUX) KEITH MICHELL

I'LL GO ON HOPING DES O'CONNOR

I'LL GO WHERE YOUR MUSIC TAKES ME JIMMY JAMES & THE VAGABONDS

I'LL GO WHERE YOUR MUSIC TAKES ME TINA CHARLES

I'LL HOUSE YOU RICHIE RICH MEETS THE JUNGLE BROTHERS
I'LL KEEP ON LOVING YOU PRINCESS
I'LL KEEP YOU SATISFIED BILLY J. KRAMER & THE DAKOTAS
I'LL KEEP YOUR DREAMS ALIVE GEORGE BENSON & PATTI AUSTIN
I'LL LOVE YOU FOREVER TODAY CLIFF RICHARD
I'LL MAKE LOVE TO YOU BOYZ II MEN
I'LL MANAGE SOMEHOW MENSWEAR
I'LL MEET YOU AT MIDNIGHT SMOKIE
I'LL NEVER BREAK YOUR HEART BACKSTREET BOYS
I'LL NEVER FALL IN LOVE AGAIN [A] JOHNNIE RAY
I'LL NEVER FALL IN LOVE AGAIN [B] TOM JONES
I'LL NEVER FALL IN LOVE AGAIN [C] BOBBIE GENTRY
I'LL NEVER FIND ANOTHER YOU SEEKERS
I'LL NEVER GET OVER YOU [A] JOHNNY KIDD & THE PIRATES
I'LL NEVER GET OVER YOU [B] EVERLY BROTHERS
I'LL NEVER GET OVER YOU (GETTING OVER ME) EXPOSE
I'LL NEVER LOVE THIS WAY AGAIN DIONNE WARWICK
I'LL NEVER QUITE GET OVER YOU BILLY FURY
I'LL NEVER STOP N SYNC
I'LL NEVER STOP LOVING YOU DORIS DAY
I'LL PICK A ROSE FOR MY ROSE MARV JOHNSON
I'LL PUT YOU TOGETHER AGAIN HOT CHOCOLATE
I'LL REMEMBER MADONNA
I'LL REMEMBER TONIGHT PAT BOONE
I'LL SAIL THIS SHIP ALONE BEAUTIFUL SOUTH
I'LL SAY FOREVER MY LOVE JIMMY RUFFIN
I'LL SEE IT THROUGH TEXAS
I'LL SEE YOU ALONG THE WAY RICK CLARKE
I'LL SEE YOU AROUND SILVER SUN
I'LL SEE YOU IN MY DREAMS PAT BOONE
I'LL SET YOU FREE BANGLES
I'LL SLEEP WHEN I'M DEAD BON JOVI
I'LL STAND BY YOU PRETENDERS
I'LL STAND BY YOU GIRLS ALOUD
I'LL STAY BY YOU KENNY LYNCH
I'LL STAY SINGLE JERRY LORDAN
I'LL STEP DOWN GARRY MILLS
I'LL STICK AROUND FOO FIGHTERS
I'LL STOP AT NOTHING SANDIE SHAW
I'LL TAKE THE RAIN R.E.M.
I'LL TAKE YOU HOME DRIFTERS
I'LL TAKE YOU HOME CLIFF BENNETT & THE REBEL ROUSERS
I'LL TAKE YOU HOME AGAIN KATHLEEN SLIM WHITMAN
I'LL TAKE YOU THERE STAPLE SINGERS
I'LL TAKE YOU THERE GENERAL PUBLIC
I'LL TRY ANYTHING DUSTY SPRINGFIELD
I'LL WAIT TAYLOR DAYNE
I'LL WALK WITH GOD MARIO LANZA
ILLEGAL ALIEN GENESIS
ILLEGAL GUNSHOT RAGGA TWINS
ILLUMINATIONS SWANS WAY
ILLUSIONS CYPRESS HILL
ILOVEROCKNROLL JESUS & MARY CHAIN
I'M A BELIEVER MONKEES
I'M A BELIEVER ROBERT WYATT
I'M A BELIEVER EMF/REEVES & MORTIMER
I'M A BETTER MAN (FOR HAVING LOVED YOU) ENGELBERT HUMPERDINCK
I'M A BITCH OLGA
I'M A BOY WHO
I'M A CLOWN DAVID CASSIDY
I'M A CUCKOO BELLE & SEBASTIAN
I'M A DISCO DANCER CHRISTOPHER JUST
I'M A DOUN FOR LACK O' JOHNNIE (A LITTLE SCOTTISH FANTASY) VANESSA-MAE
(I'M A) DREAMER B B & Q BAND

I'M A FOOL SLIM WHITMAN
I'M A FOOL TO CARE JOE BARRY
I'M A GOOD MAN MARTIN SOLVEIG
I'M A LITTLE CHRISTMAS CRACKER BOUNCING CZECKS
I'M A MAN SPENCER DAVIS GROUP
I'M A MAN CHICAGO
I'M A MAN – YE KE YE KE (MEDLEY) CLUBHOUSE
I'M A MAN NOT A BOY [A] CHESNEY HAWKES
I'M A MAN NOT A BOY [B] NORTH & SOUTH
I'M A MESSAGE IDLEWILD
I'M A MIDNIGHT MOVER WILSON PICKETT
I'M A MOODY GUY SHANE FENTON & THE FENTONES
(I'M A) ROAD RUNNER JUNIOR WALKER & THE ALL-STARS
I'M A SLAVE 4 U BRITNEY SPEARS
I'M A SUCKER FOR YOUR LOVE TEENA MARIE, CO-LEAD VOCALS RICK JAMES
I'M A TIGER LULU
I'M A WONDERFUL THING, BABY KID CREOLE & THE COCONUTS
I'M ALIVE [A] HOLLIES
I'M ALIVE [B] ELECTRIC LIGHT ORCHESTRA
I'M ALIVE [C] CUT 'N' MOVE
I'M ALIVE [D] SEAL
I'M ALIVE [E] STRETCH 'N' VERN PRESENT MADDOG
I'M ALIVE [F] CELINE DION
I'M ALL ABOUT YOU DJ LUCK & MC NEAT FEATURING ARI GOLD
I'M ALL YOU NEED SAMANTHA FOX
I'M ALRIGHT [A] YOUNG STEVE & THE AFTERNOON BOYS
I'M ALRIGHT [B] KATHERINE E
(I'M ALWAYS TOUCHED BY YOUR) PRESENCE DEAR BLONDIE
I'M AN UPSTART ANGELIC UPSTARTS
I'M BACK FOR MORE LULU & BOBBY WOMACK
I'M BAD LL COOL J
I'M BLUE 5,6,7,8'S
I'M BORN AGAIN BONEY M
I'M BROKEN PANTERA
I'M CHILLIN' KURTIS BLOW
I'M COMIN' HARDCORE M.A.N.I.C.
I'M COMING HOME TOM JONES
I'M COMING HOME CINDY TRINI LOPEZ
I'M COMING OUT DIANA ROSS
I'M COMING WITH YA MATT GOSS
I'M COUNTING ON YOU PETULA CLARK
I'M CRYING ANIMALS
I'M DOIN' FINE DAY ONE
I'M DOING FINE JASON DONOVAN
I'M DOING FINE NOW NEW YORK CITY
I'M DOING FINE NOW PASADENAS
I'M EASY FAITH NO MORE
I'M EVERY WOMAN CHAKA KHAN
I'M EVERY WOMAN WHITNEY HOUSTON
I'M FALLING BLUEBELLS
I'M FOR REAL NIGHTMARES ON WAX
I'M FOREVER BLOWING BUBBLES WEST HAM UNITED CUP SQUAD
I'M FOREVER BLOWING BUBBLES COCKNEY REJECTS
I'M FREE [A] ROGER DALTREY
I'M FREE [B] SOUP DRAGONS FEATURING JUNIOR REID
I'M FREE [C] JON SECADA
I'M GLAD JENNIFER LOPEZ
I'M GOIN' DOWN MARY J. BLIGE
I'M GOING ALL THE WAY SOUNDS OF BLACKNESS
I'M GOING HOME (TO SEE MY BABY) GENE VINCENT
I'M GOING SLIGHTLY MAD QUEEN
I'M GONE DIANA ROSS
I'M GONNA BE (500 MILES) PROCLAIMERS

I'M GONNA BE A COUNTRY GIRL AGAIN BUFFY SAINTE-MARIE
I'M GONNA BE ALRIGHT JENNIFER LOPEZ FEATURING NAS
I'M GONNA BE STRONG GENE PITNEY
I'M GONNA BE STRONG CYNDI LAUPER
I'M GONNA BE WARM THIS WINTER CONNIE FRANCIS
I'M GONNA CHANGE EVERYTHING JIM REEVES
(I'M GONNA) CRY MYSELF BLIND PRIMAL SCREAM
I'M GONNA GET MARRIED LLOYD PRICE
I'M GONNA GET ME A GUN CAT STEVENS
I'M GONNA GET THERE SOMEHOW VAL DOONICAN
I'M GONNA GET YA BABY BLACK CONNECTION
I'M GONNA GET YOU BIZARRE INC FEATURING ANGIE BROWN
I'M GONNA GET YOU SUCKA GAP BAND
I'M GONNA GETCHA GOOD! SHANIA TWAIN
I'M GONNA KNOCK ON YOUR DOOR EDDIE HODGES
I'M GONNA KNOCK ON YOUR DOOR LITTLE JIMMY OSMOND
I'M GONNA LOVE HER FOR BOTH OF US MEAT LOAF
I'M GONNA LOVE YOU FOREVER CROWN HEIGHTS AFFAIR
I'M GONNA LOVE YOU JUST A LITTLE BIT MORE BABY BARRY WHITE
I'M GONNA MAKE YOU LOVE ME DIANA ROSS & THE SUPREMES & THE TEMPTATIONS
I'M GONNA MAKE YOU MINE [A] LOU CHRISTIE
I'M GONNA MAKE YOU MINE [B] TANYA BLOUNT
I'M GONNA MISS YOU FOREVER AARON CARTER
I'M GONNA RUN AWAY FROM YOU TAMI LYNN
I'M GONNA SIT DOWN AND WRITE MYSELF A LETTER BARRY MANILOW
I'M GONNA SIT RIGHT DOWN AND WRITE MYSELF A LETTER BILLY WILLIAMS
I'M GONNA SOOTHE YOU MARIA McKEE
I'M GONNA TEAR YOUR PLAYHOUSE DOWN PAUL YOUNG
I'M IN A DIFFERENT WORLD FOUR TOPS
I'M IN A PHILLY MOOD DARYL HALL
I'M IN FAVOUR OF FRIENDSHIP FIVE SMITH BROTHERS
I'M IN HEAVEN [A] JASON NEVINS/UKNY FEATURING HOLLY JAMES
I'M IN HEAVEN [B] N-TRANCE
I'M IN IT FOR LOVE DONNY OSMOND
I'M IN LOVE [A] FOURMOST
I'M IN LOVE [B] EVELYN KING
I'M IN LOVE [C] RUBY TURNER
I'M IN LOVE [D] LILLO THOMAS
I'M IN LOVE [E] STARPARTY
I'M IN LOVE AGAIN [A] FATS DOMINO
I'M IN LOVE AGAIN [B] SAD CAFÉ
I'M IN LOVE (AND I LOVE THE FEELING) ROSE ROYCE
I'M IN LOVE WITH A GERMAN FILM STAR PASSIONS
I'M IN LOVE WITH THE GIRL ON A CERTAIN MANCHESTER VIRGIN MEGASTORE CHECKOUT DESK FRESHIES
I'M IN LUV JOE
I'M IN THE MOOD CE CE PENISTON
I'M IN THE MOOD FOR DANCING NOLANS
I'M IN THE MOOD FOR LOVE LORD TANAMO
I'M IN THE MOOD FOR LOVE JOOLS HOLLAND & JAMIROQUAI
I'M IN YOU PETER FRAMPTON
I'M INTO SOMETHING GOOD HERMAN'S HERMITS
I'M JUST A BABY LOUISE CORDET
I'M JUST A SINGER (IN A ROCK 'N' ROLL BAND) MOODY BLUES
I'M JUST YOUR PUPPET ON A... (STRING) LONDONBEAT
I'M LEAVIN' [A] ELVIS PRESLEY
I'M LEAVING [B] LODGER

I'M LEAVIN' [C] OUTSIDAZ FEATURING RAH DIGGA
I'M LEAVING IT (ALL) UP TO YOU DONNY & MARIE OSMOND
I'M LEAVING IT UP TO YOU DALE & GRACE
I'M LEFT YOU'RE RIGHT SHE'S GONE ELVIS PRESLEY
I'M LIKE A BIRD NELLY FURTADO
I'M LIVING IN SHAME DIANA ROSS & THE SUPREMES
I'M LONELY HOLLIS P MONROE
I'M LOOKING FOR THE ONE (TO BE WITH ME) JAZZY JEFF & THE FRESH PRINCE
I'M LOOKING OUT THE WINDOW CLIFF RICHARD & THE SHADOWS
I'M LOST WITHOUT YOU BILLY FURY
I'M LUCKY JOAN ARMATRADING
I'M MANDY FLY ME 10 C.C.
I'M NEVER GIVING UP SWEET DREAMS
IM NIN'ALU OFRA HAZA
I'M NO ANGEL MARCELLA DETROIT
I'M NO REBEL VIEW FROM THE HILL
I'M NOT A FOOL COCKNEY REJECTS
I'M NOT A GIRL NOT YET A WOMAN BRITNEY SPEARS
I'M NOT A TEENAGE DELINQUENT FRANKIE LYMON & THE TEENAGERS
I'M NOT ANYBODY'S GIRL KACI
I'M NOT ASHAMED BIG COUNTRY
I'M NOT FEELING YOU YVETTE MICHELLE
I'M NOT GIVING YOU UP GLORIA ESTEFAN
I'M NOT GONNA LET YOU (GET THE BEST OF ME) COLONEL ABRAMS
I'M NOT IN LOVE 10 C.C.
I'M NOT IN LOVE WILL TO POWER
I'M NOT IN LOVE FUN LOVIN' CRIMINALS
I'M NOT IN LOVE JOHNNY LOGAN
I'M NOT PERFECT (BUT I'M PERFECT FOR YOU) GRACE JONES
I'M NOT READY KEITH SWEAT
I'M NOT SATISFIED FINE YOUNG CANNIBALS
I'M NOT SCARED EIGHTH WONDER
I'M NOT THE MAN I USED TO BE FINE YOUNG CANNIBALS
I'M NOT TO BLAME ALIBI
(I'M NOT YOUR) STEPPING STONE SEX PISTOLS
I'M ON AUTOMATIC SHARPE & NUMAN
I'M ON FIRE [A] 5000 VOLTS
I'M ON FIRE [B] BRUCE SPRINGSTEEN
I'M ON MY WAY [A] DEAN PARRISH
I'M ON MY WAY [B] PROCLAIMERS
I'M ON MY WAY [C] BETTY BOO
I'M ON MY WAY TO A BETTER PLACE CHAIRMEN OF THE BOARD
I'M ONLY SLEEPING SUGGS
I'M OUT OF YOUR LIFE ARNIE'S LOVE
I'M OUTSTANDING SHAQUILLE O'NEAL
I'M OUTTA LOVE ANASTACIA
I'M OVER YOU MARTINE McCUTCHEON
I'M QUALIFIED TO SATISFY BARRY WHITE
I'M RAVING SCOOTER
I'M READY [A] CAVEMAN
I'M READY [B] SIZE 9
I'M READY [C] BRYAN ADAMS
I'M READY FOR LOVE MARTHA REEVES & THE VANDELLAS
I'M REAL [A] JAMES BROWN FEATURING FULL FORCE
I'M REAL [B] JENNIFER LOPEZ FEATURING JA RULE
I'M REALLY HOT MISSY ELLIOTT
I'M RIFFIN (ENGLISH RASTA) MC DUKE
I'M RIGHT HERE SAMANTHA MUMBA
I'M RUSHING BUMP
I'M SHAKIN' ROONEY
I'M SHY MARY ELLEN (I'M SHY) BOB WALLIS & HIS STORYVILLE JAZZ BAND

I'M SICK OF YOU GOODBYE MR MACKENZIE
I'M SO BEAUTIFUL DIVINE
I'M SO CRAZY [A] KC & THE SUNSHINE BAND
I'M SO CRAZY [B] PAR-TONE VS INXS
I'M SO EXCITED POINTER SISTERS
I'M SO GLAD I'M STANDING HERE TODAY CRUSADERS, FEATURED VOCALIST JOE COCKER
I'M SO HAPPY [A] LIGHT OF THE WORLD
I'M SO HAPPY [B] JULIA & COMPANY
I'M SO HAPPY [C] WALTER BEASLEY
I'M SO HAPPY I CAN'T STOP CRYING STING
I'M SO IN LOVE ALYSHA WARREN
I'M SO INTO YOU SWV
I'M SO LONELY CAST
I'M SORRY [A] PLATTERS
I'M SORRY [B] BRENDA LEE
I'M SORRY [C] HOTHOUSE FLOWERS
I'M SORRY I MADE YOU CRY CONNIE FRANCIS
I'M STANDING (HIGHER) X-STATIC
I'M STARTING TO GO STEADY JOHNNY PRESTON
I'M STILL GONNA NEED YOU OSMONDS
I'M STILL IN LOVE WITH YOU [A] AL GREEN
I'M STILL IN LOVE WITH YOU [B] SEAN PAUL FEATURING SASHA
I'M STILL STANDING ELTON JOHN
I'M STILL WAITING DIANA ROSS
I'M STILL WAITING COURTNEY PINE FEATURING CARROLL THOMPSON
I'M STILL WAITING ANGELHEART FEATURING ALETIA BOURNE
I'M STONE IN LOVE WITH YOU STYLISTICS
I'M STONE IN LOVE WITH YOU JOHNNY MATHIS
I'M TELLIN' YOU CHUBBY CHUNKS FEATURING KIM RUFFIN
I'M TELLING YOU NOW FREDDIE & THE DREAMERS
I'M THAT TYPE OF GUY LL COOL J
I'M THE FACE HIGH NUMBERS
I'M THE LEADER OF THE GANG HULK HOGAN WITH GREEN JELLY
I'M THE LEADER OF THE GANG (I AM) GARY GLITTER
I'M THE LONELY ONE CLIFF RICHARD & THE SHADOWS
I'M THE MAN ANTHRAX
I'M THE ONE GERRY & THE PACEMAKERS
I'M THE ONE FOR YOU ADEVA
I'M THE ONE YOU NEED JODY WATLEY
I'M THE URBAN SPACEMAN BONZO DOG DOO-DAH BAND
I'M TIRED OF GETTING PUSHED AROUND TWO MEN, A DRUM MACHINE & A TRUMPET
I'M TOO SCARED STEVEN DANTE
I'M TOO SEXY RIGHT SAID FRED
I'M WAKING UP TO US BELLE & SEBASTIAN
I'M WALKIN' FATS DOMINO
I'M WALKING BACKWARDS FOR CHRISTMAS GOONS
I'M WALKING BEHIND YOU EDDIE FISHER WITH SALLY SWEETLAND (SOPRANO)
I'M WALKING BEHIND YOU DOROTHY SQUIRES
I'M WITH YOU AVRIL LAVIGNE
I'M WONDERING STEVIE WONDER
I'M YOUR ANGEL CELINE DION & R KELLY
I'M YOUR BABY TONIGHT WHITNEY HOUSTON
I'M YOUR BOOGIE MAN KC & THE SUNSHINE BAND
I'M YOUR MAN [A] BLUE ZOO
I'M YOUR MAN [B] WHAM!
I'M YOUR MAN [B] LISA MOORISH
I'M YOUR MAN [B] SHANE RICHIE
I'M YOUR PUPPET JAMES & BOBBY PURIFY
I'M YOUR TOY ELVIS COSTELLO & THE ATTRACTIONS WITH THE ROYAL PHILHARMONIC ORCHESTRA
IMAGE HANK LEVINE
IMAGE OF A GIRL MARK WYNTER

IMAGE OF A GIRL NELSON KEENE
IMAGE OF YOU RED SNAPPER
IMAGINATION [A] ROCKY SHARPE & THE REPLAYS
IMAGINATION [B] BELOUIS SOME
IMAGINATION [C] JON THE DENTIST VS OLLIE JAYE
IMAGINE [A] JOHN LENNON
IMAGINE [A] RANDY CRAWFORD
IMAGINE [B] SHOLA AMA
IMAGINE ME IMAGINE YOU FOX
IMITATION OF LIFE [A] BILLIE RAY MARTIN
IMITATION OF LIFE [B] R.E.M.
IMMACULATE FOOLS IMMACULATE FOOLS
IMMORTALITY CELINE DION WITH THE BEE GEES
IMPERIAL WIZARD DAVID ESSEX
IMPORTANCE OF YOUR LOVE VINCE HILL
IMPOSSIBLE [A] CAPTAIN HOLLYWOOD PROJECT
IMPOSSIBLE [B] CHARLATANS
THE IMPOSSIBLE DREAM CARTER – THE UNSTOPPABLE SEX MACHINE
IMPOSSIBLE LOVE UB40
THE IMPRESSION THAT I GET MIGHTY MIGHTY BOSSTONES
THE IMPRESSIONS EP SOLAR STONE
IMPULSIVE WILSON PHILLIPS
IN 4 CHOONS LATER ROZALLA
IN A BIG COUNTRY BIG COUNTRY
IN A BROKEN DREAM PYTHON LEE JACKSON
IN A BROKEN DREAM THUNDER
IN A CAGE (ON PROZAC) MY RED CELL
IN A DREAM LONGVIEW
IN A GOLDEN COACH BILLY COTTON & HIS BAND, VOCALS BY DOREEN STEPHENS
IN A GOLDEN COACH DICKIE VALENTINE
IN A LIFETIME CLANNAD FEATURING BONO
IN A LITTLE SPANISH TOWN BING CROSBY
IN A PERSIAN MARKET SAMMY DAVIS Jr.
IN A ROOM DODGY
IN A STATE [A] 2 FOR JOY
IN A STATE [B] UNKLE
IN A WORD OR 2 MONIE LOVE
IN ALL THE RIGHT PLACES LISA STANSFIELD
IN AND OUT [A] WILLIE HUTCH
IN AND OUT [B] 3RD EDGE
IN AND OUT [C] SPEEDWAY
IN AND OUT OF LOVE [A] DIANA ROSS & THE SUPREMES
IN AND OUT OF LOVE [B] IMAGINATION
IN AND OUT OF MY LIFE [A] TONJA DANTZLER
IN AND OUT OF MY LIFE [B] A.T.F.C. PRESENTS ONEPHATDEEVA
IN BETWEEN DAYS CURE
THE IN BETWEENIES GOODIES
IN BLOOM NIRVANA
THE IN CROWD DOBIE GRAY
THE IN CROWD BRYAN FERRY
IN DA CLUB 50 CENT
IN DE GHETTO DAVID MORALES & THE BAD YARD CLUB FEATURING CRYSTAL WATERS & DELTA
IN DEMAND TEXAS
IN DREAMS ROY ORBISON
IN DULCE DECORUM DAMNED
IN DULCE JUBILO MIKE OLDFIELD
IN FOR A PENNY SLADE
IN GOD'S COUNTRY (IMPORT) U2
IN IT FOR LOVE RICHIE SAMBORA
IN IT FOR THE MONEY CLIENT
IN LIVERPOOL SUZANNE VEGA
IN LOVE [A] MICHAEL HOLLIDAY
IN LOVE [B] DATSUNS
IN LOVE [C] LISA MAFFIA
IN LOVE WITH LOVE DEBBIE HARRY
IN LOVE WITH THE FAMILIAR WIRELESS

IN MY ARMS ERASURE
IN MY BED [A] DRU HILL
IN MY BED [B] AMY WINEHOUSE
IN MY CHAIR STATUS QUO
IN MY DEFENCE FREDDIE MERCURY
IN MY DREAMS [A] WILL DOWNING
IN MY DREAMS [B] JOHNNA
IN MY EYES MILK INC
IN MY HEART TEXAS
IN MY LIFE [A] SOULED OUT
IN MY LIFE [B] KIM WILDE
IN MY LIFE [C] JOSE NUNEZ FEATURING OCTAHVIA
IN MY LIFE [D] RYZE
IN MY MIND MILKY
IN MY OWN TIME FAMILY
IN MY PLACE COLDPLAY
IN MY STREET CHORDS
IN MY WORLD ANTHRAX
IN OLD LISBON FRANK CHACKSFIELD
IN OUR LIFETIME TEXAS
IN PRIVATE DUSTY SPRINGFIELD
IN PURSUIT BOXER REBELLION
IN SPIRIT DILEMMA
IN SUMMER BILLY FURY
IN THE AIR TONIGHT PHIL COLLINS
IN THE AIR TONIGHT LIL' KIM FEATURING PHIL COLLINS
IN THE ARMS OF LOVE [A] ANDY WILLIAMS
IN THE ARMS OF LOVE [B] CATHERINE ZETA JONES
IN THE ARMY NOW STATUS QUO
IN THE BACK OF MY MIND FLEETWOOD MAC
IN THE BAD BAD OLD DAYS FOUNDATIONS
IN THE BEGINNING [A] FRANKIE LAINE
IN THE BEGINNING [B] E.Y.C.
IN THE BEGINNING [C] ROGER GOODE FEATURING
    TASHA BAXTER
IN THE BEST POSSIBLE TASTE (PART 2) KINGMAKER
IN THE BLEAK MID WINTER NEVADA
IN THE BOTTLE C.O.D.
IN THE BROWNIES BILLY CONNOLLY
IN THE BUSH MUSIQUE
IN THE CAULDRON OF LOVE ICICLE WORKS
IN THE CHAPEL IN THE MOONLIGHT BACHELORS
IN THE CITY JAM
IN THE CLOSET MICHAEL JACKSON
IN THE CLOUDS ALL ABOUT EVE
(IN THE) COLD LIGHT OF DAY GENE PITNEY
IN THE COUNTRY CLIFF RICHARD
IN THE COUNTRY FARMERS BOYS
IN THE END LINKIN PARK
IN THE EVENING SHERYL LEE RALPH
IN THE FOREST BABY O
IN THE GHETTO ELVIS PRESLEY
IN THE GHETTO BEATS INTERNATIONAL
IN THE GRIND DILLINJA
IN THE HALL OF THE MOUNTAIN KING NERO & THE
    GLADIATORS
IN THE HEAT OF A PASSIONATE MOMENT PRINCESS
IN THE HEAT OF THE NIGHT [A] DIAMOND HEAD
IN THE HEAT OF THE NIGHT [B] IMAGINATION
IN THE HOUSE CLOCK
IN THE MEANTIME [A] GEORGIE FAME & THE BLUE
    FLAMES
IN THE MEANTIME [B] SPACEHOG
IN THE MIDDLE [A] ALEXANDER O'NEAL
IN THE MIDDLE [B] SUGABABES
IN THE MIDDLE OF A DARK DARK NIGHT GUY MITCHELL
IN THE MIDDLE OF AN ISLAND KING BROTHERS
IN THE MIDDLE OF NOWHERE DUSTY SPRINGFIELD
IN THE MIDDLE OF THE HOUSE ALMA COGAN
IN THE MIDDLE OF THE HOUSE JOHNSTON BROTHERS
IN THE MIDDLE OF THE HOUSE JIMMY PARKINSON

IN THE MIDDLE OF THE NIGHT MAGIC AFFAIR
IN THE MIDNIGHT HOUR WILSON PICKETT
IN THE MOOD ERNIE FIELDS
IN THE MOOD GLENN MILLER
IN THE MOOD SOUND 9418
IN THE MOOD RAY STEVENS
IN THE NAME OF LOVE [A] SHARON REDD
IN THE NAME OF LOVE [B] SWAN LAKE
IN THE NAME OF LOVE '88 THOMPSON TWINS
IN THE NAME OF THE FATHER [A] BONO & GAVIN
    FRIDAY
IN THE NAME OF THE FATHER [B] BLACK GRAPE
IN THE NAVY VILLAGE PEOPLE
IN THE NIGHT BARBARA DICKSON
IN THE ONES YOU LOVE DIANA ROSS
IN THE REALM OF THE SENSES BASS-O-MATIC
IN THE SHADOWS RASMUS
IN THE SHAPE OF A HEART JACKSON BROWNE
IN THE SPRINGTIME MAXI PRIEST
IN THE STILL OF THE NITE (I'LL REMEMBER) BOYZ II
    MEN
IN THE STONE EARTH, WIND & FIRE
IN THE SUMMERTIME MUNGO JERRY
IN THE SUMMERTIME SHAGGY FEATURING RAYVON
IN THE SUMMERTIME JUNGLE BOYS
IN THE THICK OF IT BRENDA RUSSELL
IN THE VALLEY MIDNIGHT OIL
IN THE WAITING LINE ZERO 7
IN THE YEAR 2525 (EXORDIUM AND TERMINUS)
    ZAGER & EVANS
IN THESE ARMS BON JOVI
IN THIS WORLD MOBY
IN THOUGHTS OF YOU BILLY FURY
IN TOO DEEP [A] DEAD OR ALIVE
IN TOO DEEP [B] GENESIS
IN TOO DEEP [C] BELINDA CARLISLE
IN TOO DEEP [D] SUM 41
IN WALKED LOVE LOUISE
IN YER FACE 808 STATE
IN YOUR ARMS (RESCUE ME) NU GENERATION
IN YOUR BONES FIRE ISLAND
IN YOUR CAR [A] COOLNOTES
IN YOUR CAR [B] KENICKIE
IN YOUR CARE TASMIN ARCHER
IN YOUR DANCE E-LUSTRIOUS
IN YOUR EYES [A] GEORGE BENSON
IN YOUR EYES [B] NIAMH KAVANAGH
IN YOUR EYES [C] KYLIE MINOGUE
IN YOUR HANDS REDD SQUARE FEATURING TIFF LACEY
IN YOUR ROOM [A] BANGLES
IN YOUR ROOM [B] DEPECHE MODE
IN YOUR WILDEST DREAMS TINA TURNER FEATURING
    BARRY WHITE
IN YOUR WORLD MUSE
IN ZAIRE [A] JOHNNY WAKELIN
IN ZAIRE [B] AFRICAN BUSINESS
INBETWEENER SLEEPER
THE INCIDENTALS ALISHA'S ATTIC
INCOMMUNICADO MARILLION
INCOMPLETE SISQO
INCREDIBLE [A] M-BEAT FEATURING GENERAL LEVY
INCREDIBLE [B] KEITH MURRAY FEATURING LL COOL J
INCREDIBLE (WHAT I MEANT TO SAY) DARIUS
INDEPENDENCE LULU
INDEPENDENCE DAY COMSAT ANGELS
INDEPENDENT LOVE SONG SCARLET
INDEPENDENT WOMEN PART 1 DESTINY'S CHILD
INDESCRIBABLY BLUE ELVIS PRESLEY
INDESTRUCTIBLE [A] FOUR TOPS FEATURING SMOKEY
    ROBINSON
INDESTRUCTIBLE [B] ALISHA'S ATTIC

INDIAN LOVE CALL SLIM WHITMAN
INDIAN LOVE CALL KARL DENVER
INDIAN LOVE CALL RAY STEVENS
INDIAN RESERVATION DON FARDON
INDIAN RESERVATION 999
INDIAN ROPE CHARLATANS
INDIAN SUMMER BELLE STARS
INDIANA FREDDY CANNON
INDIANA WANTS ME R. DEAN TAYLOR
INDIANS ANTHRAX
INDICA MOVIN' MELODIES
INDIE-YARN TRICKBABY
INDIGO MOLOKO
INDUSTRIAL STRENGTH (EP) KROKUS
INERTIATIC ESP MARS VOLTA
INFATUATION ROD STEWART
INFECTED [A] THE THE
INFECTED [B] BARTHEZZ
INFERNO SOUVLAKI
INFIDELITY SIMPLY RED
INFILTRATE 202 ALTERN 8
INFINITE DREAMS IRON MAIDEN
INFINITY GURU JOSH
INFO-FREAKO JESUS JONES
INFORMER SNOW
INHALE STONE SOUR
INHERIT THE WIND WILTON FELDER
INJECTED WITH A POISON PRAGA KHAN FEATURING
    JADE 4 U
THE INK IN THE WELL DAVID SYLVIAN
INKANYEZI NEZAZI (THE STAR AND THE WISEMAN)
    LADYSMITH BLACK MAMBAZO
INNA CITY MAMMA NENEH CHERRY
INNAMORATA DEAN MARTIN
INNER CITY LIFE GOLDIE PRESENTS METALHEADS
INNER LIFE DECOY AND ROY
INNER SMILE TEXAS
INNOCENT ADDIS BLACK WIDOW
INNOCENT EYES DELTA GOODREM
AN INNOCENT MAN BILLY JOEL
INNOCENT X THERAPY?
INNOCENTE (FALLING IN LOVE) DELERIUM FEATURING
    LEIGH NASH
INNUENDO QUEEN
INSANE [A] TEXAS FEATURING THE WU TANG CLAN
INSANE [B] DARK MONKS
INSANE IN THE BRAIN CYPRESS HILL
INSANE IN THE BRAIN JASON NEVINS VERSUS
    CYPRESS HILL
INSANIA PETER ANDRE
INSANITY OCEANIC
INSATIABLE [A] DARREN HAYES
INSATIABLE [B] THICK D
INSENSITIVE JANN ARDEN
INSIDE STILTSKIN
INSIDE – LOOKING OUT ANIMALS
INSIDE A DREAM JANE WIEDLIN
INSIDE AMERICA JUGGY JONES
INSIDE LOOKING OUT GRAND FUNK RAILROAD
INSIDE LOVE (SO PERSONAL) GEORGE BENSON
INSIDE OF LOVE NADA SURF
INSIDE OUT [A] ODYSSEY
INSIDE OUT [B] MIGHTY LEMON DROPS
INSIDE OUT [C] GUN
INSIDE OUT [D] SHARA NELSON
INSIDE OUT [E] CULTURE BEAT
INSIDE OUTSIDE CLASSIX NOUVEAUX
INSIDE THAT I CRIED CE CE PENISTON
INSIDE YOUR DREAMS U96
INSOMNIA [A] FAITHLESS
INSOMNIA [B] FEEDER

INSOMNIAC ECHOBELLY
INSPECTOR GADGET KARTOON KREW
INSPECTOR MORE' THEME BARRINGTON PHELOUNG
INSPIRATION STRIKE
INSSOMNIAK DJPC
INSTANT KARMA LENNON, ONO & THE PLASTIC ONO
BAND
INSTANT REPLAY DAN HARTMAN
INSTANT REPLAY YELL!
INSTANT REPLAY GAMBAFREAKS FEATURING PACO
RIVAZ
INSTANT STREET dEUS
INSTINCT CROWDED HOUSE
INSTINCTION SPANDAU BALLET
INSTINCTUAL IMAGINATION
INSTRUMENTS OF DARKNESS (ALL OF US ARE ONE
PEOPLE) ART OF NOISE
INTACT NED'S ATOMIC DUSTBIN
INTENSIFY WAY OUT WEST
INTERCEPTOR EAT STATIC
INTERESTING DRUG MORRISSEY
INTERGALACTIC BEASTIE BOYS
INTERLUDE MORRISSEY & SIOUXSIE
INTERNAL EXILE FISH
INTERNATIONAL BRASS CONSTRUCTION
INTERNATIONAL BRIGHT YOUNG THING JESUS JONES
INTERNATIONAL JET SET SPECIALS
THE INTERNATIONAL LANGUAGE OF SCREAMING SUPER
FURRY ANIMALS
INTERNATIONAL RESCUE FUZZBOX
INTERSTATE 5 WEDDING PRESENT
INTERSTATE LOVE SONG STONE TEMPLE PILOTS
INTERVENTION LAVINE HUDSON
INTO MY ARMS NICK CAVE & THE BAD SEEDS
INTO MY WORLD AUDIOWEB
INTO SPACE PLAYTHING
INTO THE BLUE [A] MISSION
INTO THE BLUE [B] MOBY
INTO THE BLUE [C] GENEVA
INTO THE FIRE THIRTEEN SENSES
INTO THE FUTURE NEW ATLANTIC FEATURING LINDA
WRIGHT
INTO THE GROOVE MADONNA
INTO THE MOTION COOLNOTES
INTO THE NIGHT LOVE INC
INTO THE SUN WEEKEND PLAYERS
INTO THE VALLEY SKIDS
INTO TOMORROW PAUL WELLER MOVEMENT
INTO YOU FABOLOUS FEATURING TAMIA
INTO YOUR ARMS LEMONHEADS
INTO YOUR HEART 6 BY SIX
INTOXICATION REACT 2 RHYTHM
INTRO ALAN BRAXE & FRED FALKE
INTUITION [A] LINX
INTUITION [B] JEWEL
INVALID LITTER DEPT AT THE DRIVE-IN
INVINCIBLE (THEME FROM 'THE LEGEND OF BILLIE
JEAN') PAT BENATAR
INVISIBLE [A] ALISON MOYET
INVISIBLE [B] PUBLIC DEMAND
INVISIBLE [C] TILT
INVISIBLE [D] D-SIDE
INVISIBLE BALLOON MIDGET
INVISIBLE MAN 98o
THE INVISIBLE MAN QUEEN
INVISIBLE SUN POLICE
INVISIBLE TOUCH GENESIS
INVITATIONS SHAKATAK
I.O.I.O. BEE GEES
I.O.U. [A] JANE KENNAWAY & STRANGE BEHAVIOUR
I.O.U. [B] FREEEZ

IOU [C] BILL TARMEY
IOU LOVE SIX BY SEVEN
IRE FEELINGS (SKANGA) RUPIE EDWARDS
IRENE PHOTOS
IRIE LUCK & NEAT
IRIS GOO GOO DOLLS
IRISH BLOOD ENGLISH HEART MORRISSEY
IRISH BLUE FLIP & FILL FEATURING JUNIOR
THE IRISH ROVER POGUES & THE DUBLINERS
IRISH SON BRIAN McFADDEN
IRON MEGA CITY FOUR
IRON FIST MOTORHEAD
IRON HORSE CHRISTIE
IRON LION ZION BOB MARLEY & THE WAILERS
IRONIC ALANIS MORISSETTE
IRRESISTIBLE [A] CATHY DENNIS
IRRESISTIBLE [B] CORRS
IRRESISTIBLE [C] JESSICA SIMPSON
IS SMALLER
IS A BLUE BIRD BLUE CONWAY TWITTY
IS IT A CRIME SADE
IS IT A DREAM CLASSIX NOUVEAUX
IS IT A DREAM DAMNED
IS IT A SIN? DEEPEST BLUE
IS IT BECAUSE HONEYCOMBS
IS IT COS I'M COOL? MOUSSE T FEATURING EMMA
LANFORD
IS IT GOOD TO YOU HEAVY D. & THE BOYZ
IS IT GOOD TO YOU TEDDY RILEY FEATURING TAMMY
LUCAS
IS IT LIKE TODAY WORLD PARTY
IS IT LOVE BASEMENT BOYS PRESENT ULTRA NATE
IS IT LOVE YOU'RE AFTER ROSE ROYCE
IS IT LOVE? CHILI HI FLY
IS IT REALLY OVER JIM REEVES
IS IT TRUE BRENDA LEE
IS NOTHING SACRED MEAT LOAF FEATURING PATTI
RUSSO
IS SHE REALLY GOING OUT WITH HIM? JOE JACKSON
IS THAT LOVE SQUEEZE
IS THAT YOUR FINAL ANSWER? (WHO WANTS TO BE A
MILLIONAIRE – THE SINGLE) AMOURE
IS THERE ANY LOVE IN YOUR HEART LENNY KRAVITZ
IS THERE ANYBODY OUT THERE BASSHEADS
IS THERE ANYBODY THERE SCORPIONS
IS THERE SOMEONE OUT THERE? CODE RED
IS THERE SOMETHING I SHOULD KNOW DURAN DURAN
IS THERE SOMETHING I SHOULD KNOW ALLSTARS
IS THIS A DREAM? LOVE DECADE
IS THIS A LOVE THING RAYDIO
IS THIS LOVE [A] BOB MARLEY & THE WAILERS
IS THIS LOVE? [B] ALISON MOYET
IS THIS LOVE [C] WHITESNAKE
IS THIS THE WAY TO AMARILLO TONY CHRISTIE
IS THIS WHAT I GET FOR LOVING YOU MARIANNE
FAITHFULL
IS VIC THERE? DEPARTMENT S
IS YOUR LOVE IN VAIN BOB DYLAN
IS YOUR LOVE STRONG ENOUGH BRYAN FERRY
ISLAND GIRL ELTON JOHN
ISLAND HEAD EP INSPIRAL CARPETS
ISLAND IN THE SUN [A] HARRY BELAFONTE
ISLAND IN THE SUN [A] RIGHTEOUS BROTHERS
ISLAND IN THE SUN [B] WEEZER
ISLAND OF DREAMS SPRINGFIELDS
ISLAND OF LOST SOULS BLONDIE
ISLANDS IN THE STREAM KENNY ROGERS & DOLLY
PARTON
ISLE OF INNISFREE BING CROSBY
ISMS DOG EAT DOG
ISN'T IT A WONDER BOYZONE

ISN'T IT AMAZING HOTHOUSE FLOWERS
ISN'T IT MIDNIGHT FLEETWOOD MAC
ISN'T IT TIME BABYS
ISN'T LIFE STRANGE MOODY BLUES
ISN'T SHE LOVELY DAVID PARTON
ISOBEL BJORK
ISRAEL SIOUXSIE & THE BANSHEES
THE ISRAELITES DESMOND DEKKER & THE ACES
ISTANBUL FRANKIE VAUGHAN WITH THE PETER
KNIGHT SINGERS
ISTANBUL (NOT CONSTANTINOPLE) THEY MIGHT BE
GIANTS
IT AIN'T A CRIME HOUSE OF PAIN
IT AIN'T ENOUGH DREEM TEEM VERSUS ARTFUL
DODGER
IT AIN'T FAIR EDWIN STARR
IT AIN'T GONNA BE ME CJ BOLLAND
IT AIN'T HARD TO TELL NAS
IT AIN'T ME, BABE JOHNNY CASH
IT AIN'T NECESSARILY SO BRONSKI BEAT
IT AIN'T OVER TIL IT'S OVER LENNY KRAVITZ
IT AIN'T WHAT YOU DO IT'S THE WAY THAT YOU DO IT
FUN BOY THREE & BANANARAMA
IT BEGAN IN AFRICA URBAN ALL STARS
IT BEGAN IN AFRIKA CHEMICAL BROTHERS
IT CAN'T BE RIGHT 2PLAY FEATURING RAGHAV &
NAILA BOSS
IT COULD HAPPEN TO YOU ROBERT PALMER
IT DIDN'T MATTER STYLE COUNCIL
IT DOESN'T HAVE TO BE ERASURE
IT DOESN'T HAVE TO BE THIS WAY BLOW MONKEYS
IT DOESN'T MATTER WYCLEF JEAN FEATURING THE
ROCK & MELKY SEDECK
IT DOESN'T MATTER ANYMORE [A] BUDDY HOLLY
IT DOESN'T MATTER ANYMORE [B] PURESSENCE
IT DOESN'T REALLY MATTER ZAPP
IT DON'T COME EASY RINGO STARR
IT FE DONE SUPERCAT
IT FEELS SO GOOD SONIQUE
IT HAD TO BE YOU HARRY CONNICK Jr.
IT HURTS SO MUCH JIM REEVES
IT HURTS TO BE IN LOVE GENE PITNEY
IT IS JAZZ TINGO TANGO
IT IS TIME TO GET FUNKY D MOB FEATURING LRS
IT ISN'T RIGHT PLATTERS
IT ISN'T, IT WASN'T, IT AIN'T NEVER GONNA BE
ARETHA FRANKLIN & WHITNEY HOUSTON
IT JUST WON'T DO TIM DELUXE FEATURING SAM
OBERNIK
IT KEEPS RAININ FATS DOMINO
IT KEEP'S RAININ' (TEARS FROM MY EYES) BITTY
McLEAN
IT KEEPS RIGHT ON A HURTIN' JOHNNY TILLOTSON
IT LOOKS LIKE YOU EVAN DANDO
IT MAKES ME WONDER BRUCE FOXTON
IT MAKES YOU FEEL LIKE DANCIN' ROSE ROYCE
IT MAY BE WINTER OUTSIDE (BUT IN MY HEART IT'S
SPRING) LOVE UNLIMITED
IT MEK DESMOND DEKKER
IT MIGHT AS WELL RAIN UNTIL SEPTEMBER CAROLE
KING
IT MUST BE HIM (SEUL SUR SON ETOILE) VIKKI CARR
IT MUST BE LOVE [A] LABI SIFFRE
IT MUST BE LOVE [A] MADNESS
IT MUST BE LOVE [B] ROBIN S
IT MUST BE LOVE [C] MERO
IT MUST BE SANTA JOAN REGAN
IT MUST HAVE BEEN LOVE [A] MAGNUM
IT MUST HAVE BEEN LOVE [B] ROXETTE
IT NEVER RAINS (IN SOUTHERN CALIFORNIA) TONY!
TONI! TONE!

IT ONLY TAKES A MINUTE ONE HUNDRED TON & A FEATHER
IT ONLY TAKES A MINUTE TAVARES
IT ONLY TAKES A MINUTE TAKE THAT
IT ONLY TOOK A MINUTE JOE BROWN & THE BRUVVERS
IT OUGHTA SELL A MILLION LYN PAUL
IT SEEMS TO HANG ON ASHFORD & SIMPSON
IT SEEMS TO HANG ON KWS
IT SHOULD HAVE BEEN ME YVONNE FAIR
IT SHOULD'VE BEEN ME ADEVA
IT STARTED ALL OVER AGAIN BRENDA LEE
IT STARTED WITH A KISS HOT CHOCOLATE
IT SURE BRINGS OUT THE LOVE IN YOUR EYES DAVID SOUL
IT TAKES ALL NIGHT LONG GARY GLITTER
IT TAKES MORE MS DYNAMITE
IT TAKES SCOOP FATMAN SCOOP FEATURING THE CROOKLYN CLAN
IT TAKES TWO [A] MARVIN GAYE & KIM WESTON
IT TAKES TWO [A] ROD STEWART & TINA TURNER
IT TAKES TWO [B] ROB BASE & DJ E-Z ROCK
IT TAKES TWO BABY LIZ KERSHAW, BRUNO BROOKES, JIVE BUNNY & LONDONBEAT
IT TAKES TWO TO TANGO RICHARD MYHILL
IT WAS A GOOD DAY ICE CUBE
IT WAS EASIER TO HURT HER WAYNE FONTANA
IT WASN'T ME SHAGGY
IT WILL BE ALRIGHT ODYSSEY
IT WILL BE YOU PAUL YOUNG
IT WILL COME IN TIME BILLY PRESTON & SYREETA
IT WILL MAKE ME CRAZY FELIX
IT WON'T BE LONG ALISON MOYET
IT WON'T SEEM LIKE CHRISTMAS (WITHOUT YOU) ELVIS PRESLEY
THE ITALIAN THEME CYRIL STAPLETON
ITALO HOUSE MIX ROCOCO
ITCHYCOO PARK SMALL FACES
ITCHYCOO PARK M PEOPLE
IT'LL BE ME CLIFF RICHARD & THE SHADOWS
IT'S A BEAUTIFUL THING OCEAN COLOUR SCENE
IT'S A BETTER THAN GOOD TIME GLADYS KNIGHT & THE PIPS
IT'S A DISCO NIGHT (ROCK DON'T STOP) ISLEY BROTHERS
IT'S A FINE DAY OPUS III
IT'S A FINE DAY MISS JANE
IT'S A GAME BAY CITY ROLLERS
IT'S A GAS WEDDING PRESENT
IT'S A GIRL THING MY LIFE STORY
IT'S A GOOD LIFE CEVIN FISHER FEATURING RAMONA KELLY
IT'S A HARD LIFE QUEEN
IT'S A HEARTACHE BONNIE TYLER
IT'S A LONG WAY TO THE TOP (IF YOU WANNA ROCK 'N' ROLL) AC/DC
IT'S A LOVE THING WHISPERS
IT'S A LOVING THING C.B. MILTON
IT'S A MAN'S MAN'S MAN'S WORLD JAMES BROWN & THE FAMOUS FLAMES
IT'S A MAN'S MAN'S MAN'S WORLD BRILLIANT
IT'S A MAN'S MAN'S MAN'S WORLD JEANIE TRACY & BOBBY WOMACK
IT'S A MIRACLE CULTURE CLUB
IT'S A MISTAKE MEN AT WORK
IT'S A PARTY [A] BUSTA RHYMES FEATURING ZHANE
IT'S A PARTY [B] BOUNTY KILLER
IT'S A RAGGY WALTZ DAVE BRUBECK QUARTET
IT'S A RAINBOW RAINBOW (GEORGE & ZIPPY)
IT'S A RAINY DAY ICE MC
IT'S A SHAME [A] MOTOWN SPINNERS
IT'S A SHAME [B] KRIS KROSS

IT'S A SHAME ABOUT RAY LEMONHEADS
IT'S A SHAME (MY SISTER) MONIE LOVE FEATURING TRUE IMAGE
IT'S A SIN PET SHOP BOYS
IT'S A SIN TO TELL A LIE GERRY MONROE
IT'S A TRIP (TUNE IN, TURN ON, DROP OUT) CHILDREN OF THE NIGHT
IT'S ABOUT TIME LEMONHEADS
IT'S ABOUT TIME YOU WERE MINE THUNDERBUGS
IT'S ALL ABOUT THE BENJAMINS PUFF DADDY & THE FAMILY
IT'S ALL ABOUT U [A] SWV
IT'S ALL ABOUT YOU [B] JUSTIN
IT'S ALL ABOUT YOU (NOT ABOUT ME) TRACIE SPENCER
IT'S ALL BEEN DONE BEFORE BARENAKED LADIES
IT'S ALL COMING BACK TO ME NOW CELINE DION
IT'S ALL COMING BACK TO ME NOW PANDORA'S BOX
IT'S ALL GONE CHRIS REA
IT'S ALL GOOD [A] HAMMER
IT'S ALL GOOD [B] DA MOB FEATURING JOCELYN BROWN
IT'S ALL GOOD JOCELYN BROWN
IT'S ALL GRAVY ROMEO FEATURING CHRISTINA MILIAN
IT'S ALL IN THE GAME TOMMY EDWARDS
IT'S ALL IN THE GAME CLIFF RICHARD
IT'S ALL IN THE GAME FOUR TOPS
IT'S ALL OVER CLIFF RICHARD
IT'S ALL OVER NOW [A] SHANE FENTON & THE FENTONES
IT'S ALL OVER NOW [B] ROLLING STONES
IT'S ALL OVER NOW BABY BLUE JOAN BAEZ
IT'S ALL OVER NOW BABY BLUE MILLTOWN BROTHERS
IT'S ALL RIGHT STERLING VOID
IT'S ALL THE WAY LIVE (NOW) COOLIO
IT'S ALL TRUE LEMONHEADS
IT'S ALL UP TO YOU JIM CAPALDI
IT'S ALL VAIN MAGNOLIA
IT'S ALL YOURS MC LYTE FEATURING GINA THOMPSON
IT'S ALMOST TOMORROW DREAMWEAVERS
IT'S ALMOST TOMORROW MARK WYNTER
IT'S ALRIGHT [A] SHO NUFF
IT'S ALRIGHT [B] PET SHOP BOYS
IT'S ALRIGHT [B] HYPER GO GO
IT'S ALRIGHT [C] EAST 17
IT'S ALRIGHT [D] BRYAN POWELL
IT'S ALRIGHT [E] DENI HINES
IT'S ALRIGHT [F] ECHO & THE BUNNYMEN
IT'S ALRIGHT (BABY'S COMING BACK) EURYTHMICS
IT'S ALRIGHT NOW BELOVED
IT'S ALRIGHT, I FEEL IT! NUYORICAN SOUL FEATURING JOCELYN BROWN
IT'S AN OPEN SECRET JOY STRINGS
IT'S BEEN A WHILE STAIND
IT'S BEEN NICE EVERLY BROTHERS
IT'S BEEN SO LONG GEORGE McCRAE
IT'S BETTER TO HAVE (AND DON'T NEED) DON COVAY
IT'S CALLED A HEART DEPECHE MODE
IT'S DIFFERENT FOR GIRLS JOE JACKSON
IT'S ECSTASY WHEN YOU LAY DOWN NEXT TO ME BARRY WHITE
IT'S FOR YOU CILLA BLACK
IT'S FOUR IN THE MORNING FARON YOUNG
IT'S GETTING BETTER MAMA CASS
IT'S GOING DOWN X-ECUTIONERS
IT'S GOING TO HAPPEN! UNDERTONES
IT'S GONNA BE A COLD COLD CHRISTMAS DANA
IT'S GONNA BE (A LOVELY DAY) BRANCACCIO & AISHER
IT'S GONNA BE A LOVELY DAY S.O.U.L. S.Y.S.T.E.M. INTRODUCING MICHELLE VISAGE
IT'S GONNA BE ALL RIGHT GERRY & THE PACEMAKERS
IT'S GONNA BE ALRIGHT RUBY TURNER

IT'S GONNA BE ALRIGHT PUSSY 2000
IT'S GONNA BE ME N SYNC
IT'S GONNA BE MY WAY PRECIOUS
IT'S GOOD NEWS WEEK HEDGEHOPPERS ANONYMOUS
IT'S GREAT WHEN WE'RE TOGETHER FINLEY QUAYE
IT'S GRIM UP NORTH JUSTIFIED ANCIENTS OF MU MU
IT'S GROWING TEMPTATIONS
IT'S HAPPENIN' PLUS ONE FEATURING SIRRON
IT'S HARD SOMETIMES FRANKIE KNUCKLES
IT'S HARD TO BE HUMBLE MAC DAVIS
IT'S HERE KIM WILDE
IT'S IMPOSSIBLE PERRY COMO
IT'S IN EVERY ONE OF US CLIFF RICHARD
IT'S IN HIS KISS BETTY EVERETT
IT'S IN HIS KISS LINDA LEWIS
IT'S IN OUR HANDS BJORK
IT'S IN YOUR EYES PHIL COLLINS
IT'S JURASSIC SOUL CITY ORCHESTRA
IT'S JUST A FEELING TERRORIZE
IT'S JUST PORN MUM TRUCKS
(IT'S JUST) THE WAY THAT YOU LOVE ME PAULA ABDUL
IT'S LATE RICKY NELSON
IT'S LATE SHAKIN' STEVENS
(IT'S LIKE A) SAD OLD KINDA MOVIE PICKETTYWITCH
IT'S LIKE THAT RUN DMC VERSUS JASON NEVINS
IT'S LIKE THAT Y'ALL SWEET TEE
IT'S LOVE KEN DODD
IT'S LOVE THAT REALLY COUNTS MERSEYBEATS
IT'S LOVE (TRIPPIN') GOLDTRIX PRESENTS ANDREA BROWN
IT'S LULU BOO RADLEYS
IT'S ME ALICE COOPER
IT'S MY HOUSE STORM
IT'S MY HOUSE DIANA ROSS
IT'S MY LIFE [A] ANIMALS
IT'S MY LIFE [B] TALK TALK
IT'S MY LIFE[B] LIQUID PEOPLE VS TALK TALK
IT'S MY LIFE [B] NO DOUBT
IT'S MY LIFE [C] DR. ALBAN
IT'S MY LIFE [D] BON JOVI
IT'S MY PARTY [A] LESLEY GORE
IT'S MY PARTY [A] DAVE STEWART WITH BARBARA GASKIN
IT'S MY PARTY [B] CHAKA KHAN
IT'S MY TIME EVERLY BROTHERS
IT'S MY TURN [A] DIANA ROSS
IT'S MY TURN [B] ANGELIC
IT'S NATURE'S WAY (NO PROBLEM) DOLLAR
IT'S NEVER TOO LATE DIANA ROSS
IT'S NICE TO GO TRAV'LING FRANK SINATRA
IT'S NO GOOD DEPECHE MODE
IT'S NOT A LOVE THING GEOFFREY WILLIAMS
IT'S NOT RIGHT BUT IT'S OKAY WHITNEY HOUSTON
IT'S NOT THE END OF THE WORLD? SUPER FURRY ANIMALS
IT'S NOT UNUSUAL TOM JONES
IT'S NOW OR NEVER ELVIS PRESLEY
IT'S OH SO QUIET BJORK
IT'S OK [A] DELIRIOUS?
IT'S OK [B] ATOMIC KITTEN
IT'S OKAY DES'REE
IT'S ON [A] FLOWERED UP
IT'S ON [B] NAUGHTY BY NATURE
IT'S ON YOU (SCAN ME) EUROGROOVE
IT'S ONE OF THOSE NIGHTS (YES LOVE) PARTRIDGE FAMILY STARRING SHIRLEY JONES FEATURING DAVID CASSIDY
IT'S ONLY LOVE [A] TONY BLACKBURN
IT'S ONLY LOVE [A] ELVIS PRESLEY
IT'S ONLY LOVE [B] GARY U.S. BONDS
IT'S ONLY LOVE [C] BRYAN ADAMS & TINA TURNER

IT'S ONLY LOVE [D] SIMPLY RED
IT'S ONLY MAKE BELIEVE CONWAY TWITTY
IT'S ONLY MAKE BELIEVE BILLY FURY
IT'S ONLY MAKE BELIEVE GLEN CAMPBELL
IT'S ONLY MAKE BELIEVE CHILD
IT'S ONLY NATURAL CROWDED HOUSE
IT'S ONLY ROCK 'N' ROLL VARIOUS ARTISTS (EP'S & LPS)
IT'S ONLY ROCK AND ROLL ROLLING STONES
IT'S ONLY US ROBBIE WILLIAMS
IT'S ONLY YOU (MEIN SCHMERZ) LENE LOVICH
IT'S 'ORRIBLE BEING IN LOVE (WHEN YOU'RE 81/2) CLAIRE & FRIENDS
IT'S OVER [A] ROY ORBISON
IT'S OVER [B] FUNK MASTERS
IT'S OVER [B] CLOCK
IT'S OVER [C] LEVEL 42
IT'S OVER [D] RIMES FEATURING SHAILA PROSPERE
IT'S OVER [E] KURUPT
IT'S OVER (DISTORTION) PIANOHEADZ
IT'S OVER LOVE TODD TERRY PRESENTS SHANNON
IT'S OVER NOW [A] ULTRA NATE
IT'S OVER NOW [B] DEBORAH COX
IT'S OVER NOW [C] 112
IT'S PARTY TIME AGAIN GEORGE VAN DUSEN
IT'S PROBABLY ME STING WITH ERIC CLAPTON
IT'S RAINING [A] DARTS
IT'S RAINING [B] SHAKIN' STEVENS
IT'S RAINING AGAIN SUPERTRAMP FEATURING VOCALS BY ROGER HODGSON
IT'S RAINING MEN WEATHER GIRLS
IT'S RAINING MEN MARTHA WASH
IT'S RAINING MEN GERI HALLIWELL
IT'S RAINING MEN...THE SEQUEL MARTHA WASH FEATURING RuPAUL
IT'S SO EASY ANDY WILLIAMS
IT'S SO HIGH MATT FRETTON
IT'S SO NICE (TO HAVE YOU HOME) NEW SEEKERS
IT'S STILL ROCK AND ROLL TO ME BILLY JOEL
IT'S STILL YOU MICHAEL BALL
IT'S SUMMERTIME (LET IT GET INTO YOU) SMOOTH
IT'S TEMPTATION SHEER ELEGANCE
IT'S THE END OF THE WORLD AS WE KNOW IT R.E.M.
IT'S THE SAME OLD SONG FOUR TOPS
IT'S THE SAME OLD SONG WEATHERMEN
IT'S THE SAME OLD SONG KC & THE SUNSHINE BAND
IT'S THE WAY YOU MAKE ME FEEL STEPS
IT'S TIME [A] ELVIS COSTELLO & THE ATTRACTIONS
IT'S TIME [B] FERRY CORSTEN
IT'S TIME FOR LOVE CHI-LITES
IT'S TIME TO CRY PAUL ANKA
IT'S TOO LATE [A] CAROLE KING
IT'S TOO LATE [A] QUARTZ INTRODUCING DINA CARROLL
IT'S TOO LATE [B] LUCIE SILVAS
IT'S TOO LATE NOW [A] SWINGING BLUE JEANS
IT'S TOO LATE NOW [B] LONG JOHN BALDRY
IT'S TOO SOON TO KNOW [B] PAT BOONE
IT'S TRICKY RUN D.M.C.
IT'S TRICKY 2003 RUN DMC FEATURING JACKNIFE LEE
IT'S TRUE QUEEN PEN
IT'S UP TO YOU RICK NELSON
IT'S UP TO YOU PETULA EDISON LIGHTHOUSE
IT'S UP TO YOU (SHINING THROUGH) LAYO & BUSHWACKA
IT'S WHAT WE'RE ALL ABOUT SUM 41
IT'S WHAT'S UPFRONT THAT COUNTS YOSH PRESENTS LOVEDEEJAY AKEMI
IT'S WONDERFUL (TO BE LOVED BY YOU) JIMMY RUFFIN
IT'S WRITTEN IN THE STARS PAUL WELLER
IT'S WRITTEN ON YOUR BODY RONNIE BOND
IT'S YER MONEY I'M AFTER BABY WONDER STUFF

IT'S YOU [A] FREDDIE STARR
IT'S YOU [B] MANHATTANS
IT'S YOU [C] EMF
IT'S YOUR DAY TODAY P.J. PROBY
IT'S YOUR DESTINY ELECTRA
IT'S YOUR LIFE SMOKIE
IT'S YOUR THING ISLEY BROTHERS
IT'S YOUR TIME ARTHUR BAKER FEATURING SHIRLEY LEWIS
IT'S YOURS JON CUTLER FEATURING E-MAN
IT'S...IT'S...THE SWEET MIX SWEET
ITSY BITSY TEENY WEENY YELLOW POLKA DOT BIKINI BRIAN HYLAND
ITSY BITSY TEENY WEENY YELLOW POLKA DOT BIKINI BOMBALURINA FEATURING TIMMY MALLETT
ITZA TRUMPET THING MONTANO VS THE TRUMPET MAN
I'VE BEEN A BAD BAD BOY PAUL JONES
I'VE BEEN AROUND THE WORLD MARTI PELLOW
I'VE BEEN DRINKING JEFF BECK & ROD STEWART
I'VE BEEN HURT GUY DARRELL
I'VE BEEN IN LOVE BEFORE CUTTING CREW
I'VE BEEN LONELY FOR SO LONG FREDERICK KNIGHT
I'VE BEEN LOSING YOU A-HA
I'VE BEEN THINKING ABOUT YOU LONDONBEAT
I'VE BEEN TO A MARVELOUS PARTY DIVINE COMEDY
I'VE BEEN WAITING STEREO NATION
I'VE BEEN WATCHIN' JOE PUBLIC
I'VE BEEN WRONG BEFORE CILLA BLACK
I'VE DONE EVERYTHING FOR YOU SAMMY HAGAR
I'VE FOUND LOVE AGAIN RICHARD CARTRIDGE
I'VE GOT A LITTLE PUPPY SMURFS
I'VE GOT A LITTLE SOMETHING FOR YOU MN8
I'VE GOT A THING ABOUT YOU BABY ELVIS PRESLEY
I'VE GOT MINE UB40
I'VE GOT NEWS FOR YOU FEARGAL SHARKEY
I'VE GOT SOMETHING TO SAY REEF
I'VE GOT THIS FEELING MAVERICKS
I'VE GOT TO LEARN TO SAY NO RICHARD 'DIMPLES' FIELDS
I'VE GOT TO MOVE CALVIN RICHARDSON
I'VE GOT YOU MARTINE McCUTCHEON
I'VE GOT YOU ON MY MIND DORIAN GRAY
I'VE GOT YOU ON MY MIND WHITE PLAINS
I'VE GOT YOU UNDER MY SKIN FOUR SEASONS WITH FRANKIE VALLI
I'VE GOT YOU UNDER MY SKIN NENEH CHERRY
I'VE GOT YOU UNDER MY SKIN FRANK SINATRA WITH BONO
(I'VE GOT YOUR) PLEASURE CONTROL SIMON HARRIS FEATURING LONNIE GORDON
I'VE GOTTA GET A MESSAGE TO YOU BEE GEES
I'VE HAD ENOUGH [A] WINGS
I'VE HAD ENOUGH [A] IVAN MATAIS
I'VE HAD ENOUGH [B] EARTH, WIND & FIRE
I'VE HAD ENOUGH [C] HILLMAN MINX
(I'VE HAD) THE TIME OF MY LIFE BILL MEDLEY & JENNIFER WARNES
I'VE JUST BEGUN TO LOVE YOU DYNASTY
I'VE LOST YOU ELVIS PRESLEY
I'VE NEVER BEEN IN LOVE SUZI QUATRO
I'VE NEVER BEEN TO ME CHARLENE
I'VE PASSED THIS WAY BEFORE JIMMY RUFFIN
I'VE SEEN THE WORD BLANCMANGE
I'VE TOLD EVERY LITTLE STAR LINDA SCOTT
I'VE WAITED SO LONG ANTHONY NEWLEY
IVORY SKIN UP
IVORY TOWER THREE KAYES
IZ U NELLY
IZZO (H.O.V.A.) JAY-Z
JA-DA JOHNNY & THE HURRICANES

JACK AND DIANE JOHN COUGAR
JACK AND JILL RAYDIO
JACK AND JILL PARTY PETE BURNS
JACK IN THE BOX [A] CLODAGH RODGERS
JACK IN THE BOX [B] MOMENTS
JACK LE FREAK CHIC
JACK MIX II MIRAGE
JACK MIX III MIRAGE
JACK MIX IV MIRAGE
JACK MIX VII MIRAGE
JACK O' DIAMONDS LONNIE DONEGAN
JACK TALKING DAVE STEWART & THE SPIRITUAL COWBOYS
THE JACK THAT HOUSE BUILT JACK 'N' CHILL
JACK THE GROOVE RAZE
JACK THE RIPPER [A] LL COOL J
JACK THE RIPPER [B] NICK CAVE & THE BAD SEEDS
JACK TO THE SOUND OF THE UNDERGROUND HITHOUSE
JACK YOUR BODY STEVE 'SILK' HURLEY
JACKET HANGS BLUE AEROPLANES
JACKIE SCOTT WALKER
JACKIE WILSON SAID KEVIN ROWLAND & DEXY'S MIDNIGHT RUNNERS
JACKIE'S RACING WHITEOUT
JACK'S HEROES POGUES & THE DUBLINERS
JACKSON NANCY SINATRA & LEE HAZLEWOOD
JACKY MARC ALMOND
JACQUELINE BOBBY HELMS WITH THE ANITA KERR SINGERS
JACQUES DERRIDA SCRITTI POLITTI
JACQUES YOUR BODY (MAKE ME SWEAT) LES RYTHMES DIGITALES
JADED [A] GREEN DAY
JADED [B] AEROSMITH
JAGGED EDGE MICHAEL COURTNEY
JAGUAR DJ ROLANDO AKA AZTEC MYSTIC
JAIL HOUSE RAP FAT BOYS
JAILBIRD PRIMAL SCREAM
JAILBREAK [A] THIN LIZZY
JAILBREAK [B] PARADOX
JAILHOUSE ROCK ELVIS PRESLEY
JAILHOUSE ROCK EP ELVIS PRESLEY
JAM MICHAEL JACKSON
THE JAM EP A TRIBE CALLED QUEST
JAM IT JAM SHE ROCKERS
JAM J JAMES
JAM JAM JAM PEOPLE'S CHOICE
JAM ON REVENGE (THE WIKKI WIKKI SONG) NEWCLEUS
JAM SIDE DOWN STATUS QUO
JAMAICAN IN NEW YORK SHINEHEAD
JAMBALAYA JO STAFFORD
JAMBALAYA FATS DOMINO
JAMBALAYA (ON THE BAYOU) CARPENTERS
JAMBOREE NAUGHTY BY NATURE FEATURING ZHANE
JAMES BOND THEME MOBY
THE JAMES BOND THEME JOHN BARRY ORCHESTRA
JAMES DEAN (I WANNA KNOW) DANIEL BEDINGFIELD
JAMES HAS KITTENS BLU PETER
JAMMIN' BOB MARLEY FEATURING MC LYTE
JAMMIN' IN AMERICA GAP BAND
JAMMING BOB MARLEY & THE WAILERS
JANA KILLING JOKE
JANE [A] JEFFERSON STARSHIP
JANE [B] PERFECT DAY
JANEIRO SOLID SESSIONS
JANIE, DON'T TAKE YOUR LOVE TO TOWN JON BON JOVI
JANUARY PILOT
JANUARY FEBRUARY BARBARA DICKSON
JAPANESE BOY ANEKA
JARROW SONG ALAN PRICE

JAWS LALO SCHIFRIN
JAYOU JURASSIC 5
JAZZ CARNIVAL AZYMUTH
JAZZ IT UP REEL 2 REAL
JAZZ RAP KIM CARNEGIE
JAZZ THING GANG STARR
JAZZIN' THE WAY YOU KNOW JAZZY M
JE NE SAIS PAS POURQUOI KYLIE MINOGUE
JE SUIS MUSIC CERRONE
JE T'AIME (ALLO ALLO) RENE & YVETTE
JE T'AIME (MOI NON PLUS) JUDGE DREAD
JE T'AIME...MOI NON PLUS JANE BIRKIN & SERGE
    GAINSBOURG
JE VOULAIS TE DIRE (QUE JE T'ATTENDS) MANHATTAN
    TRANSFER
JEALOUS AGAIN BLACK CROWES
JEALOUS GUY ROXY MUSIC
JEALOUS GUY JOHN LENNON
JEALOUS HEART CADETS WITH EILEEN READ
JEALOUS HEART CONNIE FRANCIS
JEALOUS LOVE [A] JO BOXERS
JEALOUS LOVE [B] HAZELL DEAN
JEALOUS MIND ALVIN STARDUST
JEALOUSY [A] BILLY FURY
JEALOUSY [B] AMII STEWART
JEALOUSY [C] ADVENTURES OF STEVIE V
JEALOUSY [D] PET SHOP BOYS
JEALOUSY [E] OCTOPUS
THE JEAN GENIE DAVID BOWIE
JEAN THE BIRDMAN DAVID SYLVIAN & ROBERT FRIPP
JEANETTE BEAT
JEANNIE DANNY WILLIAMS
JEANNIE, JEANNIE, JEANNIE EDDIE COCHRAN
JEANNY FALCO
JEANS ON DAVID DUNDAS
JEDI WANNABE BELLATRIX
JEEPSTER T REX
JEEPSTER POLECATS
JELLYHEAD CRUSH
JENNIFER ECCLES HOLLIES
JENNIFER JUNIPER DONOVAN
JENNIFER JUNIPER SINGING CORNER MEETS
    DONOVAN
JENNIFER SHE SAID LLOYD COLE & THE COMMOTIONS
JENNY STELLASTARR*
JENNY FROM THE BLOCK JENNIFER LOPEZ
JENNY JENNY LITTLE RICHARD
JENNY ONDIOLINE STEREOLAB
JENNY TAKE A RIDE MITCH RYDER & THE DETROIT
    WHEELS
JEOPARDY GREG KIHN BAND
JEREMY PEARL JAM
JERICHO [A] SIMPLY RED
JERICHO [B] PRODIGY
JERK IT OUT CAESARS
JERUSALEM [A] FALL
JERUSALEM [A] FAT LES 2000
JERUSALEM [B] HERB ALPERT & THE TIJUANA BRASS
JESAMINE CASUALS
JESSE HOLD ON B*WITCHED
JESSICA ADAM GREEN
JESSIE JOSHUA KADISON
JESSIE'S GIRL RICK SPRINGFIELD
JESUS CLIFF RICHARD
JESUS CHRIST LONGPIGS
JESUS CHRIST POSE SOUNDGARDEN
JESUS HAIRDO CHARLATANS
JESUS HE KNOWS ME GENESIS
JESUS SAYS ASH
JESUS TO A CHILD GEORGE MICHAEL
JESUS WALKS KANYE WEST

JET PAUL McCARTNEY & WINGS
JET CITY WOMAN QUEENSRYCHE
JET-STAR TEKNOO TOO
JEWEL CRANES
JEZEBEL MARTY WILDE
JEZEBEL SHAKIN' STEVENS
JIBARO ELECTRA
JIG A JIG EAST OF EDEN
JIGGA JIGGA SCOOTER
JIGGY CLIPZ
JILTED JOHN JILTED JOHN
JIMMIE JONES VAPORS
JIMMY PURPLE HEARTS
JIMMY JIMMY UNDERTONES
JIMMY LEE ARETHA FRANKLIN
JIMMY MACK MARTHA REEVES & THE VANDELLAS
JIMMY OLSEN'S BLUES SPIN DOCTORS
JIMMY UNKNOWN LITA ROZA
JIMMY'S GIRL JOHNNY TILLOTSON
JINGLE BELL ROCK MAX BYGRAVES
JINGLE BELL ROCK CHUBBY CHECKER & BOBBY
    RYDELL
JINGLE BELLS JUDGE DREAD
JINGLE BELLS LAUGHING ALL THE WAY HYSTERICS
JINGO CANDIDO
JINGO JELLYBEAN
JINGO F.K.W.
JITTERBUGGIN' HEATWAVE
JIVE TALKIN' BEE GEES
JIVE TALKIN' BOOGIE BOX HIGH
JJ TRIBUTE ASHA
JOAN OF ARC ORCHESTRAL MANOEUVRES IN THE
    DARK
JOANNA [A] SCOTT WALKER
JOANNA [B] KOOL & THE GANG
JOANNA [C] MRS WOOD
JOCELYN SQUARE LOVE & MONEY
JOCK MIX 1 MAD JOCKS FEATURING JOCKMASTER
    B.A.
JOCKO HOMO DEVO
JODY JERMAINE STEWART
JOE INSPIRAL CARPETS
JOE 90 (THEME) BARRY GRAY ORCHESTRA WITH PETER
    BECKETT – KEYBOARDS
JOE LE TAXI VANESSA PARADIS
JOE LOUIS JOHN SQUIRE
JOGI PANJABI MC FEATURING JAY-Z
JOHN AND JULIE EDDIE CALVERT
JOHN I'M ONLY DANCING DAVID BOWIE
JOHN I'M ONLY DANCING POLECATS
JOHN KETLEY (IS A WEATHERMAN) TRIBE OF TOFFS
JOHN WAYNE IS BIG LEGGY HAYSI FANTAYZEE
JOHNNY AND MARY ROBERT PALMER
JOHNNY ANGEL PATTI LYNN
JOHNNY ANGEL SHELLEY FABARES
JOHNNY B GOODE PETE TOSH
JOHNNY B. GOODE JIMI HENDRIX
JOHNNY B. GOODE JUDAS PRIEST
JOHNNY CASH SONS & DAUGHTERS
JOHNNY COME HOME FINE YOUNG CANNIBALS
JOHNNY COME LATELY STEVE EARLE
JOHNNY DAY ROLF HARRIS
JOHNNY FRIENDLY JO BOXERS
JOHNNY GET ANGRY CAROL DEENE
JOHNNY JOHNNY PREFAB SPROUT
JOHNNY MATHIS' FEET AMERICAN MUSIC CLUB
JOHNNY PANIC AND THE BIBLE OF DREAMS JOHNNY
    PANIC & THE BIBLE OF DREAMS
JOHNNY REGGAE PIGLETS
JOHNNY REMEMBER ME JOHN LEYTON
JOHNNY REMEMBER ME METEORS

JOHNNY ROCCO MARTY WILDE
JOHNNY THE HORSE MADNESS
JOHNNY WILL PAT BOONE
JOIN IN AND SING AGAIN JOHNSTON BROTHERS
JOIN IN AND SING (NO. 3) JOHNSTON BROTHERS
JOIN ME LIGHTFORCE
JOIN OUR CLUB SAINT ETIENNE
JOIN THE PARTY HONKY
JOIN TOGETHER WHO
JOINING YOU ALANIS MORISSETTE
JOINTS & JAMS BLACK EYED PEAS
JOJO ACTION MR PRESIDENT
JOKE (I'M LAUGHING) EDDI READER
THE JOKE ISN'T FUNNY ANYMORE SMITHS
THE JOKER STEVE MILLER BAND
THE JOKER (THE WIGAN JOKER) ALLNIGHT BAND
JOLE BLON GARY U.S. BONDS
JOLENE DOLLY PARTON
JOLENE STRAWBERRY SWITCHBLADE
JOLENE – LIVE UNDER BLACKPOOL LIGHTS WHITE
    STRIPES
JONAH BREATHE
JONATHAN DAVID BELLE & SEBASTIAN
THE JONES' TEMPTATIONS
JONES VS JONES KOOL & THE GANG
JONESTOWN MIND ALMIGHTY
JOOK GAL ELEPHANT MAN
JORDAN: THE EP PREFAB SPROUT
JOSEPH MEGA REMIX JASON DONOVAN & ORIGINAL
    LONDON CAST FEATURING LINZI HATELY, DAVID
    EASTER & JOHNNY AMOBI
JOSEPHINE [A] CHRIS REA
JOSEPHINE [B] TERRORVISION
JOSEY DEEP BLUE SOMETHING
THE JOURNEY CITIZEN CANED
JOURNEY [A] DUNCAN BROWNE
THE JOURNEY [B] 911
JOURNEY TO THE MOON BIDDU ORCHESTRA
JOURNEY TO THE PAST AALIYAH
JOY [A] BAND AKA
JOY [B] TEDDY PENDERGRASS
JOY [C] SOUL II SOUL
JOY [D] STAXX FEATURING CAROL LEEMING
JOY [E] 7669
JOY [F] BLACKstreet
JOY [G] DENI HINES
JOY [H] KATHY BROWN
JOY! [I] GAY DAD
JOY [J] MARK RYDER
JOY AND HAPPINESS STABBS
JOY AND HEARTBREAK MOVEMENT 98 FEATURING
    CARROLL THOMPSON
JOY AND PAIN [A] DONNA ALLEN
JOY AND PAIN [A] MAZE
JOY AND PAIN [A] ROB BASE & DJ E-Z ROCK
JOY AND PAIN [B] ANGELLE
(JOY) I KNOW IT ODYSSEY
JOY OF LIVING [A] CLIFF (Richard) & HANK (Marvin)
JOY OF LIVING [B] OUI 3
JOY TO THE WORLD THREE DOG NIGHT
JOYBRINGER MANFRED MANN'S EARTH BAND
JOYENERGIZER JOY KITIKONTI
JOYRIDE ROXETTE
JOYRIDER (YOU'RE PLAYING WITH FIRE) COLOUR GIRL
JOYS OF CHRISTMAS CHRIS REA
JOYS OF LIFE DAVID JOSEPH
JUDGE FUDGE HAPPY MONDAYS
THE JUDGEMENT IS THE MIRROR DALI'S CAR
JUDY IN DISGUISE (WITH GLASSES) JOHN FRED & THE
    PLAYBOY BAND
JUDY OVER THE RAINBOW ORANGE

JUDY SAYS (KNOCK YOU IN THE HEAD) VIBRATORS
JUDY TEEN COCKNEY REBEL
JUGGLING RAGGA TWINS
JUICY WRECKS-N-EFFECT
JUICY NOTORIOUS B.I.G.
JUICY FRUIT MTUME
A JUICY RED APPLE SKIN UP
JUKE BOX BABY PERRY COMO
JUKE BOX GYPSY LINDISFARNE
JUKE BOX HERO FOREIGNER
JUKE BOX JIVE RUBETTES
JULIA [A] EURYTHMICS
JULIA [B] CHRIS REA
JULIA [C] SILVER SUN
JULIA SAYS WET WET WET
JULIE ANN KENNY
JULIE DO YA LOVE ME WHITE PLAINS
JULIE DO YA LOVE ME BOBBY SHERMAN
JULIE (EP) LEVELLERS
JULIE OCEAN UNDERTONES
JULIET FOUR PENNIES
JULIET (KEEP THAT IN MIND) THEA GILMORE
JULY OCEAN COLOUR SCENE
JUMBO [A] BEE GEES
JUMBO [B] UNDERWORLD
JUMP [A] VAN HALEN
JUMP [A] BUS STOP
JUMP [B] AZTEC CAMERA
JUMP [C] KRIS KROSS
JUMP! [D] MOVEMENT
JUMP [E] GIRLS ALOUD
JUMP AROUND HOUSE OF PAIN
JUMP BACK (SET ME FREE) DHAR BRAXTON
JUMP DOWN B*WITCHED
JUMP (FOR MY LOVE) POINTER SISTERS
JUMP JIVE AN' WAIL BRIAN SETZER ORCHESTRA
JUMP N' SHOUT BASEMENT JAXX
THE JUMP OFF LIL' KIM FEATURING MR CHEEKS
JUMP ON DEMAND SPUNGE
JUMP START NATALIE COLE
JUMP THE GUN THREE DEGREES
JUMP THEY SAY DAVID BOWIE
JUMP TO IT ARETHA FRANKLIN
JUMP TO MY BEAT WILDCHILD
JUMP TO MY LOVE INCOGNITO
JUMP TO THE BEAT STACY LATTISHAW
JUMP TO THE BEAT DANNII MINOGUE
JUMP UP JUST 4 JOKES FEATURING MC RB
JUMPIN' LIBERTY X
JUMPIN' JACK FLASH ARETHA FRANKLIN
JUMPIN' JIVE JOE JACKSON'S JUMPIN' JIVE
JUMPIN' JUMPIN' DESTINY'S CHILD
JUMPING JACK FLASH ROLLING STONES
JUNE AFTERNOON ROXETTE
JUNEAU FUNERAL FOR A FRIEND
JUNGLE BILL YELLO
THE JUNGLE BOOK GROOVE JUNGLE BOOK
JUNGLE BROTHER JUNGLE BROTHERS
JUNGLE FEVER CHAKACHAS
JUNGLE HIGH JUNO REACTOR
JUNGLE ROCK HANK MIZELL
JUNGLE ROCK JUNGLE BOYS
JUNGLIST DRUMSOUND/SIMON BASSLINE SMITH
JUNIOR'S FARM PAUL McCARTNEY & WINGS
JUNKIES EASYWORLD
JUPITER EARTH, WIND & FIRE
JUS' A RASCAL DIZZEE RASCAL
JUS' COME COOL JACK
JUS 1 KISS BASEMENT JAXX
JUS' REACH (RECYCLED) GALLIANO
JUST [A] RADIOHEAD

JUST [B] JAMIE SCOTT
JUST A DAY FEEDER
JUST A DAY AWAY BARCLAY JAMES HARVEST
JUST A DREAM [A] NENA
JUST A DREAM [B] DONNA DE LORY
JUST A FEELING BAD MANNERS
JUST A FEW THINGS THAT I AIN'T BEAUTIFUL SOUTH
JUST A FRIEND [A] BIZ MARKIE
JUST A FRIEND [B] MARIO
JUST A GIRL NO DOUBT
JUST A GROOVE NOMAD
JUST A LITTLE LIBERTY X
JUST A LITTLE BIT UNDERTAKERS
JUST A LITTLE BIT BETTER HERMAN'S HERMITS
JUST A LITTLE BIT OF LOVE REBEKAH RYAN
JUST A LITTLE BIT TOO LATE WAYNE FONTANA & THE
   MINDBENDERS
JUST A LITTLE GIRL AMY STUDT
JUST A LITTLE MISUNDERSTANDING CONTOURS
JUST A LITTLE MORE DELUXE
JUST A LITTLE MORE LOVE DAVID GUETTA FEATURING
   CHRIS WILLIS
JUST A LITTLE TOO MUCH RICKY NELSON
JUST A LITTLE WHILE JANET JACKSON
JUST A MAN MARK MORRISON
JUST A MIRAGE JELLYBEAN FEATURING ADELE BERTEI
JUST A SHADOW BIG COUNTRY
JUST A SMILE PILOT
JUST A STEP FROM HEAVEN ETERNAL
JUST A TOUCH KEITH SWEAT
JUST A TOUCH OF LOVE SLAVE
JUST A TOUCH OF LOVE EVERYDAY C & C MUSIC
   FACTORY FEATURING ZELMA DAVIS
JUST AN ILLUSION IMAGINATION
JUST ANOTHER BROKEN HEART SHEENA EASTON
JUST ANOTHER DAY [A] JON SECADA
JUST ANOTHER DAY [B] JONATHAN WILKES
JUST ANOTHER DREAM CATHY DENNIS
JUST ANOTHER GROOVE MIGHTY DUB KATZ
JUST ANOTHER ILLUSION HURRICANE #1
JUST ANOTHER NIGHT MICK JAGGER
JUST AROUND THE HILL SASH!
JUST AS LONG AS YOU ARE THERE VANESSA PARADIS
JUST AS MUCH AS EVER NAT 'KING' COLE
JUST BE TIESTO FEATURING KIRSTY HAWKSHAW
JUST BE DUB TO ME REVELATION
JUST BE GOOD TO ME S.O.S. BAND
JUST BE TONIGHT BBG
JUST BECAUSE JANE'S ADDICTION
JUST BEFORE YOU LEAVE DEL AMITRI
JUST BETWEEN YOU AND ME APRIL WINE
JUST BORN JIM DALE
JUST CALL SHERRICK
JUST CALL ME GOOD GIRLS
JUST CAN'T GET ENOUGH [A] DEPECHE MODE
JUST CAN'T GET ENOUGH [C] HARRY 'CHOO CHOO'
   ROMERO PRESENTS INAYA DAY
JUST CAN'T GET ENOUGH [B] TRANSFORMER 2
JUST CAN'T GET ENOUGH (NO NO NO NO) EYE TO EYE
   FEATURING TAKA BOOM
JUST CAN'T GIVE YOU UP MYSTIC MERLIN
JUST CAN'T STAND IT MATT BIANCO
JUST CAN'T WAIT (SATURDAY) 100% FEATURING
   JENNIFER JOHN
JUST CHECKIN' BEAUTIFUL SOUTH
JUST CRUISIN' WILL SMITH
JUST DON'T WANT TO BE LONELY MAIN INGREDIENT
JUST DON'T WANT TO BE LONELY FREDDIE McGREGOR
JUST FADE AWAY STIFF LITTLE FINGERS
JUST FOR KICKS MIKE SARNE
JUST FOR MONEY PAUL HARDCASTLE

JUST FOR OLD TIME'S SAKE FOSTER & ALLEN
JUST FOR ONE DAY (HEROES) DAVID GUETTA VS DAVID
   BOWIE
JUST FOR YOU [A] FREDDIE & THE DREAMERS
JUST FOR YOU [B] GLITTER BAND
JUST FOR YOU [C] ALAN PRICE
JUST FOR YOU [D] M PEOPLE
JUST FOR YOU [E] LIONEL RICHIE
JUST FUCK TOM NEVILLE
JUST GET UP AND DANCE AFRIKA BAMBAATAA
JUST GETS BETTER TJR FEATURING XAVIER
JUST GIVE THE DJ A BREAK DYNAMIX II FEATURING
   TOO TOUGH TEE
JUST GOOD FRIENDS FISH FEATURING SAM BROWN
JUST GOT LUCKY JO BOXERS
JUST GOT PAID JOHNNY KEMP
JUST HOLD ON TOPLOADER
JUST IN CASE JAHEIM
JUST IN LUST WILDHEARTS
JUST IN TIME RAW SILK
JUST KEEP IT UP DEE CLARK
JUST KEEP ME MOVING k.d. lang
JUST KEEP ROCKIN' DOUBLE TROUBLE & THE REBEL
   MC
JUST KICK COHEN VS DELUXE
JUST KICKIN' IT XSCAPE
JUST LET ME DO MY THING SINE
JUST LIKE A MAN DEL AMITRI
JUST LIKE A PILL PINK
JUST LIKE A WOMAN MANFRED MANN
JUST LIKE ANYONE SOUL ASYLUM
JUST LIKE BRUCE LEE KILLCITY
JUST LIKE EDDIE HEINZ
JUST LIKE FRED ASTAIRE JAMES
JUST LIKE HEAVEN CURE
JUST LIKE HONEY JESUS & MARY CHAIN
JUST LIKE JESSE JAMES CHER
JUST LIKE PARADISE DAVID LEE ROTH
(JUST LIKE) STARTING OVER JOHN LENNON
JUST LISTEN TO MY HEART SPOTNICKS
JUST LOOKIN' [A] CHARLATANS
JUST LOOKING [B] STEREOPHONICS
JUST LOVING YOU ANITA HARRIS
(JUST) ME AND YOU NEW VISION
JUST MELLOW RUTHLESS RAP ASSASSINS
JUST MY IMAGINATION McGANNS
JUST MY IMAGINATION (RUNNING AWAY WITH ME)
   TEMPTATIONS
JUST MY SOUL RESPONDING SMOKEY ROBINSON
JUST ONE LOOK [A] HOLLIES
JUST ONE LOOK [B] FAITH, HOPE & CHARITY
JUST ONE MORE KISS RENEE & RENATO
JUST ONE MORE NIGHT YELLOW DOG
JUST ONE SMILE GENE PITNEY
JUST OUT OF REACH (OF MY TWO EMPTY ARMS) KEN
   DODD
JUST OUTSIDE OF HEAVEN H2O
JUST PLAY MUSIC BIG AUDIO DYNAMITE
JUST PLAYIN' JT PLAYAZ
JUST PUT YOUR HAND IN MINE SPACE COWBOY
JUST RIGHT SOUL II SOUL
JUST ROUND A VERY GOOD FRIEND OF MINE
JUST SAY NO GRANGE HILL CAST
JUST SAY YOU LOVE ME MALACHI CUSH
JUST SEVEN NUMBERS (CAN STRAIGHTEN OUT MY
   LIFE) FOUR TOPS
JUST SHOW ME HOW TO LOVE YOU SARAH BRIGHTMAN
   & THE LSO FEATURING JOSE CURA
JUST SO YOU KNOW AMERICAN HEAD CHARGE
JUST TAH LET U KNOW EAZY-E
JUST TAKE MY HEART MR BIG

JUST THE ONE LEVELLERS, SPECIAL GUEST JOE STRUMMER
JUST THE TWO OF US GROVER WASHINGTON Jr.
JUST THE TWO OF US WILL SMITH
JUST THE WAY ALFONZO HUNTER
JUST THE WAY IT IS LISA MOORISH
JUST THE WAY I'M FEELING FEEDER
JUST THE WAY YOU ARE [A] BILLY JOEL
JUST THE WAY YOU ARE [A] BARRY WHITE
JUST THE WAY YOU ARE [B] MILKY
JUST THE WAY YOU LIKE IT S.O.S. BAND
JUST THIRTEEN LURKERS
JUST THIS SIDE OF LOVE MALANDRA BURROWS
JUST TO BE CLOSE TO YOU COMMODORES
JUST TO SEE HER SMOKEY ROBINSON
JUST WALK IN MY SHOES GLADYS KNIGHT & THE PIPS
JUST WALKIN' IN THE RAIN JOHNNIE RAY
JUST WANNA KNOW MAXI PRIEST
JUST WANNA TOUCH ME FIDELFATTI FEATURING RONETTE
JUST WANT TO LIVE OPEN
JUST WAVE HELLO CHARLOTTE CHURCH
JUST WHAT I ALWAYS WANTED MARI WILSON
JUST WHAT I NEEDED CARS
JUST WHEN I NEEDED YOU MOST RANDY VANWARMER
JUST WHEN I NEEDED YOU MOST BARBARA JONES
JUST WHEN YOU'RE THINKING THINGS OVER CHARLATANS
JUST WHO IS THE FIVE O'CLOCK HERO JAM
JUSTIFIED AND ANCIENT KLF, GUEST VOCALS TAMMY WYNETTE
JUSTIFY MY LOVE MADONNA
JUSTIFY THE RAIN COSMIC ROUGH RIDERS
JUXTAPOZED WITH U SUPER FURRY ANIMALS
KA-CHING SHANIA TWAIN
KALEIDOSCOPE SKIES JAM & SPOON FEATURING PLAVKA
KAMICHI HELL IS FOR HEROES
KAMIKAZE KING ADORA
KANSAS CITY LITTLE RICHARD
KANSAS CITY TRINI LOPEZ
KANSAS CITY STAR ROGER MILLER
KARA KARA NEW WORLD
KARAOKE QUEEN CATATONIA
KARAOKE SOUL TOM McRAE
KARMA CHAMELEON CULTURE CLUB
KARMA HOTEL SPOOKS
KARMA POLICE RADIOHEAD
KARMACOMA MASSIVE ATTACK
KARMADROME POP WILL EAT ITSELF
KATE BEN FOLDS FIVE
KATE BUSH ON STAGE EP KATE BUSH
KATHLEEN ROACHFORD
KATHLEEN (EP) TINDERSTICKS
KAYLEIGH MARILLION
KEEEP YOUR BODY WORKING KLEEER
KEEP A KNOCKIN' LITTLE RICHARD
KEEP AWAY FROM OTHER GIRLS HELEN SHAPIRO
KEEP COMING BACK RICHARD MARX
KEEP CONTROL SONO
KEEP DOIN' IT SHOWDOWN
KEEP EACH OTHER WARM BUCKS FIZZ
(KEEP FEELING) FASCINATION HUMAN LEAGUE
KEEP FISHIN' WEEZER
KEEP GIVIN' ME YOUR LOVE CE CE PENISTON
KEEP GIVING ME LOVE [A] D TRAIN
KEEP GIVING ME LOVE [B] BOMB THE BASS
KEEP HOPE ALIVE [A] SERIAL DIVA
KEEP HOPE ALIVE [B] CRYSTAL METHOD
KEEP IN TOUCH FREEEZ
KEEP IN TOUCH (BODY TO BODY) SHADES OF LOVE

KEEP IT COMIN' (DANCE TILL YOU CAN'T DANCE NO MORE) C & C MUSIC FACTORY FEATURING UNIQUE & DEBORAH COOPER
KEEP IT COMIN' LOVE KC & THE SUNSHINE BAND
KEEP IT DARK GENESIS
KEEP IT ON HANNAH JONES
KEEP IT OUT OF SIGHT PAUL & BARRY RYAN
KEEP IT TOGETHER DAVID GRANT
KEEP IT UP SHARADA HOUSE GANG
KEEP LOVE NEW BETTY WRIGHT
KEEP LOVE TOGETHER LOVE TO INFINITY
KEEP LOVE TOGETHER SODA CLUB FEATURING ANDREA ANATOLA
KEEP ME A SECRET AINSLIE HENDERSON
KEEP ME FROM THE COLD CURTIS STIGERS
KEEP ME IN MIND BOY GEORGE
KEEP ON [A] BRUCE CHANNEL
KEEP ON [B] CABARET VOLTAIRE
KEEP ON BELIEVING GRAND PRIX
KEEP ON BURNING EDWYN COLLINS
KEEP ON DANCIN' GARY'S GANG
KEEP ON DANCIN' (LET'S GO) PERPETUAL MOTION
KEEP ON DANCING BAY CITY ROLLERS
KEEP ON JAMMIN' WILLIE HUTCH
KEEP ON JUMPIN' LISA MARIE EXPERIENCE
KEEP ON JUMPIN' TODD TERRY FEATURING MARTHA WASH & JOCELYN BROWN
KEEP ON KEEPIN' ON REDSKINS
KEEP ON LOVING YOU REO SPEEDWAGON
KEEP ON MOVIN' [A] SOUL II SOUL FEATURING CARON WHEELER
KEEP ON MOVING [B] BOB MARLEY & THE WAILERS
KEEP ON MOVIN' [C] FIVE
KEEP ON PUMPIN' IT VISIONMASTERS WITH TONY KING & KYLIE MINOGUE
KEEP ON PUSHING OUR LOVE NIGHTCRAWLERS FEATURING JOHN REID & ALYSHA WARREN
KEEP ON RUNNIN' (TILL YOU BURN) UK SUBS
KEEP ON RUNNING SPENCER DAVIS GROUP
KEEP ON RUNNING JOHN ALFORD
(KEEP ON) SHINING LOVELAND FEATURING RACHEL McFARLANE
KEEP ON TRUCKIN' EDDIE KENDRICKS
KEEP ON WALKIN' CE CE PENISTON
KEEP ON, KEEPIN' ON MC LYTE FEATURING XSCAPE
KEEP PUSHIN' [A] CLOCK
KEEP PUSHIN' [B] BORIS DLUGOSCH PRESENTS BOOOM!
KEEP REACHING OUT FOR LOVE LINER
KEEP SEARCHIN' (WE'LL FOLLOW THE SUN) DEL SHANNON
KEEP STEPPIN' OMAR
KEEP TALKING PINK FLOYD
KEEP THE CUSTOMER SATISFIED MARSHA HUNT
KEEP THE FAITH BON JOVI
KEEP THE FIRE BURNIN' DAN HARTMAN STARRING LOLEATTA HOLLOWAY
KEEP THE FIRES BURNING CLOCK
KEEP THE HOME FIRES BURNING BLUETONES
KEEP THE MUSIC STRONG BIZARRE INC
KEEP THEIR HEADS RINGIN' DR. DRE
KEEP THIS FREQUENCY CLEAR DTI
KEEP WARM JINNY
KEEP WHAT YA GOT IAN BROWN
KEEP YOUR EYE ON ME HERB ALPERT
KEEP YOUR HANDS OFF MY BABY LITTLE EVA
KEEP YOUR HANDS TO YOURSELF GEORGIA SATELLITES
KEEP YOUR LOVE PARTIZAN FEATURING NATALIE ROBB
KEEP YOUR WORRIES GURU'S JAZZMATAZZ FEATURING ANGIE STONE
KEEPER OF THE CASTLE FOUR TOPS

KEEPIN' LOVE NEW HOWARD JOHNSON
KEEPIN' THE FAITH DE LA SOUL
KEEPING A RENDEZVIUS BUDGIE
KEEPING SECRETS SWITCH
KEEPING THE DREAM ALIVE FREIHEIT
KEEPS IN ME IN WONDERLAND STEVE MILLER BAND
KELLY WAYNE GIBSON
KELLY WATCH THE STARS AIR
KELLY'S HEROES BLACK GRAPE
KENNEDY WEDDING PRESENT
KENTUCKY RAIN ELVIS PRESLEY
KERNKRAFT 400 ZOMBIE NATION
KERRY KERRY CINERAMA
THE KETCHUP SONG (ASEREJE) LAS KETCHUP
KEVIN CARTER MANIC STREET PREACHERS
KEWPIE DOLL PERRY COMO
KEWPIE DOLL FRANKIE VAUGHAN
THE KEY [A] SENSER
THE KEY [B] MATT GOSS
KEY LARGO BERTIE HIGGINS
THE KEY THE SECRET URBAN COOKIE COLLECTIVE
KEY TO MY LIFE BOYZONE
KICK IN THE EYE BAUHAUS
KICK IN THE EYE (EP) BAUHAUS
KICK IT [A] NITZER EBB
KICK IT [B] REGGAE BOYZ
KICK IT [C] PEACHES FEATURING IGGY POP
KICK IT IN SIMPLE MINDS
KICKIN' HARD KLUBHEADS
KICKIN' IN THE BEAT PAMELA FERNANDEZ
KICKING MY HEART AROUND BLACK CROWES
KICKING UP DUST LITTLE ANGELS
KICKING UP THE LEAVES MARK WYNTER
KID PRETENDERS
KID 2000 HYBRID FEATURING CHRISSIE HYNDE
KIDDIO BROOK BENTON
KIDS ROBBIE WILLIAMS & KYLIE MINOGUE
THE KIDS ARE ALRIGHT WHO
THE KIDS ARE BACK TWISTED SISTER
THE KIDS AREN'T ALRIGHT OFFSPRING
KIDS IN AMERICA KIM WILDE
THE KID'S LAST FIGHT FRANKIE LAINE
KIDS OF THE CENTURY HELLOWEEN
KIDS ON THE STREET ANGELIC UPSTARTS
KIKI RIRI BOOM SHAFT
KILL ALL HIPPIES PRIMAL SCREAM
KILL THE KING RAINBOW
KILL THE POOR DEAD KENNEDYS
KILL YOUR TELEVISION NED'S ATOMIC DUSTBIN
KILLAMANGIRO BABYSHAMBLES
KILLED BY DEATH MOTORHEAD
KILLER ADAMSKI
KILLER ATB
KILLER (EP) SEAL
KILLER ON THE LOOSE THIN LIZZY
KILLER QUEEN QUEEN
KILLERS LIVE EP THIN LIZZY
KILLIN' TIME TINA COUSINS
KILLING IN THE NAME RAGE AGAINST THE MACHINE
THE KILLING JAR SIOUXSIE & THE BANSHEES
KILLING ME SOFTLY FUGEES
KILLING ME SOFTLY WITH HIS SONG ROBERTA FLACK
THE KILLING MOON ECHO & THE BUNNYMEN
THE KILLING OF GEORGIE ROD STEWART
A KIND OF CHRISTMAS CARD MORTEN HARKET
A KIND OF MAGIC QUEEN
KINDA LOVE DARIUS
KINDA NEW SPEKTRUM
KINETIC GOLDEN GIRLS
KING UB40
THE KING AND QUEEN OF AMERICA EURYTHMICS

KING CREOLE ELVIS PRESLEY
KING FOR A DAY [A] THOMPSON TWINS
KING FOR A DAY [B] JAMIROQUAI
KING IN A CATHOLIC STYLE (WAKE UP) CHINA CRISIS
THE KING IS DEAD GO WEST
THE KING IS HALF UNDRESSED JELLYFISH
THE KING IS HERE/THE 900 NUMBER 45 KING
KING KONG TERRY LIGHTFOOT & HIS NEW ORLEANS
    JAZZMEN
KING MIDAS IN REVERSE HOLLIES
KING OF CLOWNS NEIL SEDAKA
KING OF DREAMS DEEP PURPLE
KING OF EMOTION BIG COUNTRY
KING OF KINGS EZZ RECO & THE LAUNCHERS WITH
    BOSIE GRANT
THE KING OF KISSINGDOM MY LIFE STORY
KING OF LOVE DAVE EDMUNDS
KING OF MISERY HONEYCRACK
KING OF MY CASTLE WAMDUE PROJECT
KING OF NEW YORK FUN LOVIN' CRIMINALS
KING OF PAIN POLICE
THE KING OF ROCK 'N' ROLL PREFAB SPROUT
KING OF SNAKE UNDERWORLD
KING OF SORROW SADE
KING OF THE COPS BILLY HOWARD
KING OF THE DANCEHALL BEENIE MAN
KING OF THE KERB ECHOBELLY
KING OF THE NEW YORK STREET DION
KING OF THE ROAD ROGER MILLER
KING OF THE ROAD (EP) PROCLAIMERS
KING OF THE RUMBLING SPIRES TYRANNOSAURUS REX
THE KING OF WISHFUL THINKING GO WEST
KING ROCKER GENERATION X
KING WITHOUT A CROWN ABC
KINGDOM ULTRAMARINE
KINGS AND QUEENS KILLING JOKE
KING'S CALL PHIL LYNOTT
KINGS OF THE WILD FRONTIER ADAM & THE ANTS
KINGSTON TOWN UB40
KINKY AFRO HAPPY MONDAYS
KINKY BOOTS PATRICK MACNEE & HONOR BLACKMAN
KINKY LOVE PALE SAINTS
KISS [A] DEAN MARTIN
KISS [B] PRINCE & THE REVOLUTION
KISS [B] AGE OF SHOCK
KISS [B] ART OF NOISE FEATURING TOM JONES
KISS AND SAY GOODBYE MANHATTANS
KISS AND TELL [A] BRYAN FERRY
KISS AND TELL [B] BROWNSTONE
KISS FROM A ROSE SEAL
KISS KISS HOLLY VALENCE
KISS LIKE ETHER CLAUDIA BRUCKEN
KISS ME [A] STEPHEN 'TIN TIN' DUFFY
KISS ME [B] SIXPENCE NONE THE RICHER
KISS ME ANOTHER GEORGIA GIBBS
KISS ME DEADLY LITA FORD
KISS ME GOODBYE PETULA CLARK
KISS ME HONEY HONEY KISS ME SHIRLEY BASSEY
KISS ME QUICK ELVIS PRESLEY
KISS MY EYES BOB SINCLAR
KISS OF LIFE [A] SADE
KISS OF LIFE [B] SUPERGRASS
KISS ON MY LIST DARYL HALL & JOHN OATES
KISS ON THE LIPS DUALERS
KISS THAT FROG PETER GABRIEL
KISS THE BRIDE ELTON JOHN
KISS THE DIRT (FALLING DOWN THE MOUNTAIN) INXS
KISS THE GIRL PETER ANDRE
KISS THE RAIN BILLIE MYERS
KISS THEM FOR ME SIOUXSIE & THE BANSHEES
KISS THIS THING GOODBYE DEL AMITRI

KISS (WHEN THE SUN DON'T SHINE) VENGABOYS
KISS YOU ALL OVER EXILE
KISS YOU ALL OVER NO MERCY
KISSES IN THE MOONLIGHT GEORGE BENSON
KISSES ON THE WIND NENEH CHERRY
KISSES SWEETER THAN WINE JIMMIE RODGERS
KISSES SWEETER THAN WINE FRANKIE VAUGHAN
KISSIN' COUSINS ELVIS PRESLEY
KISSIN' IN THE BACK ROW OF THE MOVIES DRIFTERS
KISSIN' YOU TOTAL
KISSING A FOOL GEORGE MICHAEL
KISSING GATE SAM BROWN
KISSING WITH CONFIDENCE WILL POWERS
KITE NICK HEYWARD
KITES SIMON DUPREE & THE BIG SOUND
KITSCH BARRY RYAN
KITTY CAT STEVENS
KLACTOVEESEDSTEIN BLUE RONDO A LA TURK
KLUB KOLLABORATIONS BK
KLUBHOPPING KLUBHEADS
KNEE DEEP AND DOWN RAIN BAND
KNEE DEEP IN THE BLUES GUY MITCHELL
KNEE DEEP IN THE BLUES TOMMY STEELE & THE
    STEELMEN
KNIFE EDGE ALARM
KNIVES OUT RADIOHEAD
KNOCK KNOCK WHO'S THERE MARY HOPKIN
KNOCK ME OUT GARY'S GANG
KNOCK ON WOOD EDDIE FLOYD
KNOCK ON WOOD OTIS REDDING & CARLA THOMAS
KNOCK ON WOOD DAVID BOWIE
KNOCK ON WOOD AMII STEWART
KNOCK OUT TRIPLE 8
KNOCK THREE TIMES DAWN
KNOCKED IT OFF B.A. ROBERTSON
KNOCKED OUT PAULA ABDUL
KNOCKIN' ON HEAVEN'S DOOR BOB DYLAN
KNOCKIN' ON HEAVEN'S DOOR ERIC CLAPTON
KNOCKIN' ON HEAVEN'S DOOR GUNS N' ROSES
KNOCKIN' ON HEAVEN'S DOOR DUNBLANE
KNOCKING AT YOUR BACK DOOR DEEP PURPLE
KNOCKS ME OFF MY FEET DONELL JONES
KNOW BY NOW ROBERT PALMER
KNOW YOU WANNA 3RD EDGE
KNOW YOUR RIGHTS CLASH
KNOWING ME KNOWING YOU ABBA
KO SMUJJI
KOKOMO [A] BEACH BOYS
KOKOMO [B] ADAM GREEN
KOMMOTION DUANE EDDY & THE REBELS
KOMODO (SAVE A SOUL) MAURO PICOTTO
KON-TIKI SHADOWS
KOOCHIE RYDER FREAKY REALISTIC
KOOCHY ARMAND VAN HELDEN
KOOKIE KOOKIE (LEND ME YOUR COMB) EDWARD
    BYRNES & CONNIE STEVENS
KOOKIE LITTLE PARADISE FRANKIE VAUGHAN
KOOL IN THE KAFTAN B.A. ROBERTSON
KOOTCHI NENEH CHERRY
KOREAN BODEGA FUN LOVIN' CRIMINALS
KOWALSKI PRIMAL SCREAM
KRUPA APOLLO 440
KU KLUX KHAN STEEL PULSE
KUMBAYA SANDPIPERS
KUNG FU ASH
KUNG FU FIGHTING CARL DOUGLAS
KUNG FU FIGHTING BUS STOP FEATURING CARL
    DOUGLAS
KUNG-FU 187 LOCKDOWN
KUT IT RED EYE
KYRIE MR MISTER

KYRILA (EP) DEMIS ROUSSOS
LA MARC ET CLAUDE
LA BAMBA LOS LOBOS
LA BAMBA RITCHIE VALENS
LA BOOGA ROOGA SURPRISE SISTERS
LA BREEZE SIMIAN
L.A. CONNECTION RAINBOW
LA DEE DAH JACKIE DENNIS
LA DERNIERE VALSE MIREILLE MATHIEU
LA DONNA E MOBILE JOSE CARRERAS, PLACIDO
    DOMINGO & LUCIANO PAVAROTTI
LA FEMME ACCIDENT ORCHESTRAL MANOEUVRES IN
    THE DARK
LA FOLIE STRANGLERS
LA ISLA BONITA MADONNA
LA LA LA [A] MASSIEL
LA LA LA [B] NAILA BOSS
LA LA LA HEY HEY OUTHERE BROTHERS
LA LA LAND GREEN VELVET
LA-LA MEANS I LOVE YOU DELFONICS
LA LA (MEANS I LOVE YOU) SWING OUT SISTER
LA LUNA [A] BELINDA CARLISLE
LA LUNA [B] MOVIN' MELODIES PRODUCTION
LA MER (BEYOND THE SEA) BOBBY DARIN
LA MOUCHE CASSIUS
LA MUSICA RUFF DRIVERZ PRESENTS ARROLA
LA PLUME DE MA TANTE HUGO & LUIGI
LA PRIMAVERA SASH!
THE L.A. RUN CARVELLS
LA SERENISSIMA DNA
LA SERENISSIMA (THEME FROM 'VENICE IN PERIL')
    RONDO VENEZIANO
LA TODAY ALEX GOLD FEATURING PHILIP OAKEY
LA TRISTESSE DURERA (SCREAM TO A SIGH) MANIC
    STREET PREACHERS
LA VIE EN ROSE GRACE JONES
L.A. WOMAN BILLY IDOL
LA YENKA JOHNNY & CHARLEY
LABELLED WITH LOVE SQUEEZE
LABOUR OF LOVE HUE & CRY
THE LABYRINTH MOOGWAI
LA-DI-DA SAD CAFÉ
LADIES MANTRONIX
LADIES MAN D4
LADIES NIGHT KOOL & THE GANG
LADIES NIGHT ATOMIC KITTEN
LADY [A] WHISPERS
LADY [B] KENNY ROGERS
LADY [C] D'ANGELO
LADY BARBARA PETER NOONE & HERMAN'S HERMITS
LADY D'ARBANVILLE CAT STEVENS
LADY ELEANOR LINDISFARNE
LADY GODIVA PETER & GORDON
LADY (HEAR ME TONIGHT) MODJO
THE LADY IN RED CHRIS DE BURGH
LADY IS A TRAMP BUDDY GRECO
LADY JANE DAVID GARRICK
LADY JANE TONY MERRICK
LADY LET IT LIE FISH
LADY LINE PAINTER JANE BELLE & SEBASTIAN
LADY LOVE BUG CLODAGH RODGERS
LADY LOVE ME (ONE MORE TIME) GEORGE BENSON
LADY LUCK [A] LLOYD PRICE
LADY LUCK [B] ROD STEWART
LADY LYNDA BEACH BOYS
LADY MADONNA BEATLES
LADY MARMALADE ALL SAINTS
LADY MARMALADE CHRISTINA AGUILERA/LIL'
    KIM/MYA/PINK
LADY MARMALADE (VOULEZ-VOUS COUCHER AVEC MOI
    CE SOIR) LABELLE

LADY ROSE MUNGO JERRY
LADY SHINE (SHINE ON) THS – THE HORN SECTION
LADY WILLPOWER UNION GAP FEATURING GARY
    PUCKETT
LADY WRITER DIRE STRAITS
LADY (YOU BRING ME UP) COMMODORES
LADY (YOU BRING ME UP) SIMPLY SMOOTH
LADYBIRD NANCY SINATRA & LEE HAZLEWOOD
THE LADYBOY IS MINE STUNTMASTERZ
LADYFINGERS LUSCIOUS JACKSON
LADYFLASH THE GO! TEAM
LADYKILLERS LUSH
LADYSHAVE GUS GUS
LAGARTIJA NICK BAUHAUS
LAID JAMES
LAID SO LOW (TEARS ROLL DOWN) TEARS FOR FEARS
LAILA TAZ & STEREO NATION
LAKINI'S JUICE LIVE
LAMBADA KAOMA
LAMBORGHINI SHUT UP & DANCE
LAMENT ULTRAVOX
LAMPLIGHT DAVID ESSEX
LANA ROY ORBISON
LAND OF 1000 DANCES WILSON PICKETT
LAND OF A MILLION DRUMS OUTKAST FEATURING
    KILLER MIKE & S BROWN
LAND OF CONFUSION GENESIS
LAND OF HOPE AND GLORY EX PISTOLS
THE LAND OF MAKE BELIEVE BUCKS FIZZ
THE LAND OF MAKE BELIEVE ALLSTARS
THE LAND OF RING DANG DO KING KURT
LAND OF THE LIVING KRISTINE W
LAND OF THE LIVING MILK INC
LANDSLIDE [A] OLIVIA NEWTON-JOHN
LANDSLIDE [B] HARMONIX
LANDSLIDE [C] SPIN CITY
LANDSLIDE [D] DIXIE CHICKS
LANDSLIDE OF LOVE TRANSVISION VAMP
THE LANE ICE-T
THE LANGUAGE OF LOVE JOHN D. LOUDERMILK
LANGUAGE OF VIOLENCE DISPOSABLE HEROES OF
    HIPHOPRISY
LAP OF LUXURY JETHRO TULL
LAPDANCE N*E*R*D FEATURING LEE HARVEY & VITA
LARGER THAN LIFE BACKSTREET BOYS
LAS PALABRAS DE AMOR QUEEN
LAS VEGAS TONY CHRISTIE
LASER LOVE [A] T. REX
LASER LOVE [B] AFTER THE FIRE
THE LAST BEAT OF MY HEART SIOUXSIE & THE
    BANSHEES
LAST CHANCE CHINA DRUM
LAST CHRISTMAS WHAM!
LAST CHRISTMAS WHIGFIELD
LAST CHRISTMAS ALIEN VOICES FEATURING THE THREE
    DEGREES
LAST CUP OF SORROW FAITH NO MORE
LAST DANCE DONNA SUMMER
LAST DAY SILVER SUN
LAST DROP KEVIN LYTTLE
THE LAST FAREWELL ROGER WHITTAKER
THE LAST FAREWELL SHIP'S COMPANY & ROYAL
    MARINE BAND OF HMS ARK ROYAL
THE LAST FAREWELL ELVIS PRESLEY
LAST FILM KISSING THE PINK
LAST GOODBYE [A] JEFF BUCKLEY
LAST GOODBYE [B] ATOMIC KITTEN
LAST HORIZON BRIAN MAY
LAST KISS PEARL JAM
THE LAST KISS DAVID CASSIDY
LAST NIGHT [A] MERSEYBEATS

LAST NIGHT [B] KID 'N' PLAY
LAST NIGHT [C] AZ YET
LAST NIGHT [C] STROKES
LAST NIGHT [D] GLORIA GAYNOR
LAST NIGHT A DJ BLEW MY MIND FAB FOR FEATURING
    ROBERT OWENS
LAST NIGHT A DJ SAVED MY LIFE INDEEP
LAST NIGHT A DJ SAVED MY LIFE COLD JAM
    FEATURING GRACE
LAST NIGHT A DJ SAVED MY LIFE SYLK 130
LAST NIGHT A DJ SAVED MY LIFE (BIG LOVE) SEAMUS
    HAJI
LAST NIGHT ANOTHER SOLDIER ANGELIC UPSTARTS
LAST NIGHT AT DANCELAND RANDY CRAWFORD
LAST NIGHT I DREAMT THAT SOMEBODY LOVED ME
    SMITHS
LAST NIGHT IN SOHO DAVE DEE, DOZY, BEAKY, MICK &
    TICH
LAST NIGHT ON EARTH U2
LAST NIGHT ON THE BACK PORCH ALMA COGAN
LAST NIGHT WAS MADE FOR LOVE BILLY FURY
LAST NITE VITAMIN C
LAST OF THE FAMOUS INTERNATIONAL PLAYBOYS
    MORRISSEY
LAST ONE STANDING GIRL THING
LAST PLANE (ONE WAY TICKET) CLINT EASTWOOD &
    GENERAL SAINT
LAST RESORT PAPA ROACH
LAST RHYTHM LAST RHYTHM
THE LAST SONG [A] ELTON JOHN
THE LAST SONG [B] ALL-AMERICAN REJECTS
LAST STOP THIS TOWN EELS
LAST SUMMER LOSTPROPHETS
LAST THING ON MY MIND [A] BANANARAMA
LAST THING ON MY MIND [A] STEPS
LAST THING ON MY MIND [B] RONAN KEATING &
    LeANN RIMES
THE LAST TIME [A] ROLLING STONES
THE LAST TIME [A] WHO
THE LAST TIME [B] PARADISE LOST
LAST TIME FOREVER SQUEEZE
LAST TIME I SAW HIM DIANA ROSS
LAST TO KNOW P!NK
LAST TRAIN HOME LOSTPROPHETS
LAST TRAIN TO CLARKSVILLE MONKEES
LAST TRAIN TO LONDON ELECTRIC LIGHT ORCHESTRA
LAST TRAIN TO SAN FERNANDO JOHNNY DUNCAN &
    THE BLUE GRASS BOYS
LAST TRAIN TO TRANCENTRAL KLF FEATURING THE
    CHILDREN OF THE REVOLUTION
THE LAST WALTZ ENGELBERT HUMPERDINCK
LATE AT NIGHT FUTURESHOCK
LATE IN THE DAY SUPERGRASS
LATE IN THE EVENING PAUL SIMON
LATELY [A] RUDY GRANT
LATELY [A] STEVIE WONDER
LATELY [B] SKUNK ANANSIE
LATELY [C] DIVINE
LATELY [C] SAMANTHA MUMBA
LATELY [D] LISA SCOTT-LEE
THE LATIN THEME CARL COX
LATIN THING LATIN THING
LATINO HOUSE MIRAGE
LAUGH AT ME SONNY
THE LAUGHING GNOME DAVID BOWIE
LAUGHTER IN THE RAIN NEIL SEDAKA
THE LAUNCH DJ JEAN
LAUNDROMAT NIVEA
LAURA [A] NICK HEYWARD
LAURA [B] JIMMY NAIL
LAURA [C] NEK

LAURA [D] SCISSOR SISTERS
LAUREL AND HARDY EQUALS
LAVA SILVER SUN
LAVENDER MARILLION
LAW OF THE LAND TEMPTATIONS
LAW UNTO MYSELF KONKRETE
LAWDY MISS CLAWDY ELVIS PRESLEY
LAWNCHAIRS OUR DAUGHTER'S WEDDING
LAY ALL YOUR LOVE ON ME ABBA
LAY BACK IN THE ARMS OF SOMEONE SMOKIE
LAY DOWN STRAWBS
LAY DOWN SALLY ERIC CLAPTON
LAY DOWN YOUR ARMS [A] ANNE SHELTON
LAY DOWN YOUR ARMS [B] BELINDA CARLISLE
LAY LADY LAY BOB DYLAN
LAY LOVE ON YOU LUISA FERNANDEZ
LAY YOUR HANDS ON ME [A] THOMPSON TWINS
LAY YOUR HANDS ON ME [B] BON JOVI
LAY YOUR LOVE ON ME [A] RACEY
LAY YOUR LOVE ON ME [B] ROACHFORD
LAYLA DEREK & THE DOMINOES
LAYLA (ACOUSTIC) ERIC CLAPTON
LAZARUS BOO RADLEYS
LAZY [A] SUEDE
LAZY [B] X-PRESS 2
LAZY BONES JONATHAN KING
LAZY DAYS ROBBIE WILLIAMS
LAZY LOVER SUPERNATURALS
LAZY RIVER BOBBY DARIN
LAZY SUNDAY SMALL FACES
LAZYITIS – ONE ARMED BOXER HAPPY MONDAYS &
    KARL DENVER
LE DISC JOCKEY ENCORE
LE FREAK CHIC
LE VOIE LE SOLEIL SUBLIMINAL CUTS
LEADER OF THE PACK SHANGRI-LAS
LEADER OF THE PACK TWISTED SISTER
LEADER OF THE PACK JOAN COLLINS FAN CLUB
LEAFY MYSTERIES PAUL WELLER
LEAN BACK TERROR SQUAD FEATURING FAT JOE &
    REMY
LEAN ON ME BILL WITHERS
LEAN ON ME MUD
LEAN ON ME CLUB NOUVEAU
LEAN ON ME MICHAEL BOLTON
LEAN ON ME (AH-LI-AYO) RED BOX
LEAN ON ME I WON'T FALL OVER CARTER – THE
    UNSTOPPABLE SEX MACHINE
LEAN ON ME (WITH THE FAMILY) 2-4 FAMILY
LEAN ON YOU CLIFF RICHARD
LEAN PERIOD ORANGE JUICE
LEAP OF FAITH BRUCE SPRINGSTEEN
LEAP UP AND DOWN (WAVE YOUR KNICKERS IN THE
    AIR) ST. CECILIA
LEARN TO FLY FOO FIGHTERS
LEARNIN' THE BLUES FRANK SINATRA
LEARNIN' THE GAME BUDDY HOLLY
LEARNING TO FLY [A] TOM PETTY & THE
    HEARTBREAKERS
LEARNING TO FLY [B] MOTHER'S PRIDE
LEAVE A LIGHT ON BELINDA CARLISLE
LEAVE A LITTLE LOVE LULU
LEAVE A TENDER MOMENT ALONE BILLY JOEL
LEAVE 'EM SOMETHING TO DESIRE SPRINKLER
LEAVE (GET OUT) JOJO
LEAVE HOME CHEMICAL BROTHERS
LEAVE IN SILENCE DEPECHE MODE
LEAVE IT [A] MIKE McGEAR
LEAVE IT [B] YES
LEAVE IT ALONE LIVING COLOUR
LEAVE IT UP TO ME AARON CARTER

LEAVE ME ALONE MICHAEL JACKSON
LEAVE RIGHT NOW WILL YOUNG
LEAVE THEM ALL BEHIND RIDE
LEAVIN' [A] TONY RICH PROJECT
LEAVIN' [B] SHELBY LYNNE
LEAVIN' ON A JET PLANE PETER, PAUL & MARY
LEAVING HERE BIRDS
LEAVING LAS VEGAS SHERYL CROW
LEAVING ME NOW LEVEL 42
LEAVING NEW YORK R.E.M.
LEAVING ON A JET PLANE CHANTAL KREVIAZUK
LEAVING ON THE MIDNIGHT TRAIN NICK STRAKER
    BAND
THE LEAVING SONG PART 2 AFI
THE LEBANON HUMAN LEAGUE
LEEDS LEEDS LEEDS LEEDS UNITED F.C.
LEEDS UNITED LEEDS UNITED F.C.
LEFT BANK WINIFRED ATWELL
LEFT BEHIND SLIPKNOT
LEFT OF CENTER SUZANNE VEGA FEATURING JOE
    JACKSON
LEFT OUTSIDE ALONE ANASTACIA
LEFT TO MY OWN DEVICES PET SHOP BOYS
LEGACY MAD COBRA FEATURING RICHIE STEPHENS
THE LEGACY PUSH
LEGACY EP MANSUN
LEGACY (SHOW ME LOVE) [A] SPACE BROTHERS
LEGACY (SHOW ME LOVE) [B] BELLE & SEBASTIAN
A LEGAL MATTER WHO
LEGEND OF A COWGIRL IMANI COPPOLA
LEGEND OF THE GOLDEN SNAKE DEPTH CHARGE
THE LEGEND OF XANADU DAVE DEE, DOZY, BEAKY, MICK
    & TICH
LEGENDS OF THE DARK BLACK – PART 2 WILDCHILD
LEGO SKANGA RUPIE EDWARDS
LEGS [A] ART OF NOISE
LEGS [B] ZZ TOP
LEMMINGS SFX
LEMON TREE FOOL'S GARDEN
LENINGRAD BILLY JOEL
LENNY SUPERGRASS
LENNY AND TERENCE CARTER – THE UNSTOPPABLE
    SEX MACHINE
LENNY VALENTINO AUTEURS
LEONARD NIMOY FREAKY REALISTIC
LEROY WHEATUS
LES BICYCLETTES DE BELSIZE ENGELBERT
    HUMPERDINCK
LES FLEUR 4 HERO
L'ESPERANZA [A] SVEN VATH
L'ESPERANZA [B] AIRSCAPE
LESS TALK MORE ACTION TIM DELUXE
LESSON ONE RUSS CONWAY
LESSONS IN LOVE [A] ALLISONS
LESSONS IN LOVE [B] LEVEL 42
LESSONS LEARNED FROM ROCKY I TO ROCKY III
    CORNERSHOP
LET A BOY CRY GALA
LET A GOOD THING GO GEMMA HAYES
LET 'EM IN WINGS
LET 'EM IN BILLY PAUL
LET 'EM IN SHINEHEAD
LET FOREVER BE CHEMICAL BROTHERS
LET GO WITH THE FLOW BEAUTIFUL SOUTH
LET HER CRY HOOTIE & THE BLOWFISH
LET HER DOWN EASY TERENCE TRENT D'ARBY
LET HER FALL THEN JERICO
LET HER FEEL IT SIMPLICIOUS
LET HER GO STRAWBERRY SWITCHBLADE
LET IT ALL BLOW DAZZ BAND
LET IT ALL HANG OUT JONATHAN KING

LET IT BE BEATLES
LET IT BE FERRY AID
LET IT BE ME EVERLY BROTHERS
LET IT BE ME JUSTIN
LET IT BE WITH YOU BELOUIS SOME
LET IT FLOW SPIRITUALIZED ELECTRIC MAINLINE
LET IT LAST CARLEEN ANDERSON
LET IT LIVE HAVEN
LET IT LOOSE LEMON TREES
LET IT RAIN [A] UFO
LET IT RAIN [B] EAST 17
LET IT RAIN [C] 4 STRINGS
LET IT REIGN INNER CITY
LET IT RIDE TODD TERRY PROJECT
LET IT ROCK CHUCK BERRY
LET IT ROCK ROLLING STONES
LET IT ROLL RAZE PRESENTS DOUG LAZY
LET IT SLIDE [A] MUDHONEY
LET IT SLIDE [B] ARIEL
LET IT SWING BOBBYSOCKS
LET LOVE BE THE LEADER FM
LET LOVE BE YOUR ENERGY ROBBIE WILLIAMS
LET LOVE LEAD THE WAY SPICE GIRLS
LET LOVE RULE LENNY KRAVITZ
LET LOVE SHINE AMOS
LET LOVE SPEAK UP ITSELF BEAUTIFUL SOUTH
LET ME BE BLACK DIAMOND
LET ME BE THE NUMBER 1 (LOVE OF YOUR LIFE)
    DOOLEY SILVERSPOON
LET ME BE THE ONE [A] SHADOWS
LET ME BE THE ONE [B] FIVE STAR
LET ME BE THE ONE [C] BLESSID UNION OF SOULS
LET ME BE THE ONE [D] MINT CONDITION
LET ME BE THE ONE [E] CLIFF RICHARD
LET ME BE YOUR FANTASY BABY D
(LET ME BE YOUR) TEDDY BEAR ELVIS PRESLEY
LET ME BE YOUR UNDERWEAR CLUB 69
LET ME BE YOUR WINGS BARRY MANILOW & DEBRA
    BYRD
LET ME BE YOURS FIVE STAR
LET ME BLOW YA MIND EVE FEATURING GWEN
    STEFANI
LET ME CLEAR MY THROAT DJ KOOL
LET ME COME ON HOME OTIS REDDING
LET ME CRY ON YOUR SHOULDER KEN DODD
LET ME DOWN EASY STRANGLERS
LET ME ENTERTAIN YOU ROBBIE WILLIAMS
LET ME FLY DARREN STYLES/MARK BREEZE
LET ME GO HEAVEN 17
LET ME GO HOME ALL ABOUT EVE
LET ME GO LOVER TERESA BREWER WITH THE
    LANCERS
LET ME GO LOVER JOAN WEBER
LET ME GO LOVER DEAN MARTIN
LET ME GO LOVER RUBY MURRAY
LET ME GO LOVER KATHY KIRBY
LET ME HEAR YOU SAY 'OLE OLE' OUTHERE BROTHERS
LET ME IN [A] OSMONDS
LET ME IN [A] OTT
LET ME IN [B] YOUNG BUCK
LET ME INTRODUCE YOU TO THE FAMILY STRANGLERS
LET ME KISS YOU MORRISSEY
LET ME KISS YOU NANCY SINATRA
LET ME KNOW [A] JUNIOR
LET ME KNOW [B] MAXI PRIEST
LET ME KNOW (I HAVE THE RIGHT) GLORIA GAYNOR
LET ME LET GO FAITH HILL
LET ME LIVE QUEEN
LET ME LOVE YOU FOR TONIGHT KARIYA
LET ME MOVE ON GENE
LET ME RIDE DR. DRE

LET ME ROCK YOU KANDIDATE
LET ME SEE MORCHEEBA
LET ME SHOW YOU [A] K-KLASS
LET ME SHOW YOU [B] CAMISRA
LET ME SHOW YOU [C] TONY MOMRELLE
LET ME TAKE YOU THERE BETTY BOO
LET ME TALK EARTH, WIND & FIRE
LET ME TRY AGAIN TAMMY JONES
LET ME WAKE UP IN YOUR ARMS LULU
LET MY LOVE OPEN YOUR DOOR PETE TOWNSHEND
LET MY NAME BE SORROW MARY HOPKIN
LET MY PEOPLE GO (PART 1) WINANS
LET MY PEOPLE GO-GO RAINMAKERS
LET ROBESON SING MANIC STREET PREACHERS
LET SOMEBODY LOVE YOU KENI BURKE
LET THE BASS KICK 2 FOR JOY
LET THE BEAT CONTROL YOUR BODY 2 UNLIMITED
LET THE BEAT HIT 'EM LISA LISA & CULT JAM
LET THE BEAT HIT 'EM SHENA
LET THE BEAT HIT 'EM PART 2 LISA LISA & CULT JAM
LET THE DAY BEGIN CALL
LET THE DRUMS SPEAK MIGHTY DUB KATZ
LET THE FLAME BURN BRIGHTER GRAHAM KENDRICK
LET THE FREAK BIG RON
LET THE GOOD TIMES ROLL SHEEP ON DRUGS
LET THE HAPPINESS IN DAVID SYLVIAN
LET THE HEALING BEGIN JOE COCKER
LET THE HEARTACHES BEGIN LONG JOHN BALDRY
LET THE LITTLE GIRL DANCE BILLY BLAND
LET THE LOVE Q-TEX
LET THE MUSIC HEAL YOUR SOUL BRAVO ALL STARS
LET THE MUSIC (LIFT YOU UP) LOVELAND FEATURING
    RACHEL McFARLANE Vs DARLENE LEWIS
LET THE MUSIC MOVE U RAZE
LET THE MUSIC PLAY [A] BARRY WHITE
LET THE MUSIC PLAY [B] CHARLES EARLAND
LET THE MUSIC PLAY [C] SHANNON
LET THE MUSIC PLAY [C] BBG FEATURING ERIN
LET THE MUSIC PLAY [C] MARY KIANI
LET THE MUSIC TAKE CONTROL JM SILK
LET THE MUSIC USE YOU NIGHTWRITERS
LET THE PEOPLE KNOW TOPLOADER
LET THE RHYTHM MOVE YOU SHARADA HOUSE GANG
LET THE RHYTHM PUMP DOUG LAZY
LET THE SUNSHINE IN PEDDLERS
LET THE SUNSHINE IN MILK & SUGAR FEATURING
    LIZZY PATTINSON
LET THE WATER RUN DOWN P.J. PROBY
LET THEM ALL TALK ELVIS COSTELLO
LET THERE BE DRUMS SANDY NELSON
LET THERE BE HOUSE DESKEE
LET THERE BE LIGHT MIKE OLDFIELD
LET THERE BE LOVE [A] NAT 'KING' COLE WITH GEORGE
    SHEARING
LET THERE BE LOVE [B] SIMPLE MINDS
LET THERE BE PEACE ON EARTH (LET IT BEGIN WITH
    ME) MICHAEL WARD
LET THERE BE ROCK ONSLAUGHT
LET THIS BE A PRAYER ROLLO GOES SPIRITUAL WITH
    PAULINE TAYLOR
LET THIS FEELING SIMONE ANGEL
LET TRUE LOVE BEGIN NAT 'KING' COLE
LET U GO ATB
LET YOUR BODY GO TOM WILSON
LET YOUR BODY GO DOWNTOWN MARTYN FORD
LET YOUR HEAD GO VICTORIA BECKHAM
LET YOUR HEART DANCE SECRET AFFAIR
LET YOUR LOVE FLOW BELLAMY BROTHERS
LET YOUR SOUL BE YOUR PILOT STING
LET YOUR YEAH BE YEAH PIONEERS
LET YOUR YEAH BE YEAH ALI CAMPBELL

LET YOURSELF GO [A] T-CONNECTION
LET YOURSELF GO [B] SYBIL
LETHAL INDUSTRY DJ TIESTO
LETITGO PRINCE
LET'S SARAH VAUGHAN
LET'S ALL CHANT MICHAEL ZAGER BAND
LET'S ALL CHANT PAT & MICK
LET'S ALL CHANT GUSTO
(LET'S ALL GO BACK) DISCO NIGHTS JAZZ & THE BROTHERS GRIMM
LET'S ALL (GO TO THE FIRE DANCES) KILLING JOKE
LET'S ALL GO TOGETHER MARION
LET'S ALL SING LIKE THE BIRDIES SING TWEETS
LET'S BE FRIENDS JOHNNY NASH
LET'S BE LOVERS TONIGHT SHERRICK
LET'S CALL IT LOVE LISA STANSFIELD
LET'S CALL IT QUITS SLADE
LET'S CELEBRATE NEW YORK SKYY
LET'S CLEAN UP THE GHETTO PHILADELPHIA INTERNATIONAL ALL-STARS
LET'S DANCE [A] BRUNO & LIZ & THE RADIO 1 POSSE
LET'S DANCE [A] CHRIS MONTEZ
LET'S DANCE [B] BOMBERS
LET'S DANCE [C] DAVID BOWIE
LET'S DANCE [D] CHRIS REA
LET'S DANCE [D] MIDDLESBROUGH FC FEATURING BOB MORTIMER & CHRIS REA
LET'S DANCE [E] FIVE
LET'S DO IT AGAIN [A] GEORGE BENSON
LET'S DO IT AGAIN [B] LYNDEN DAVID HALL
LET'S DO ROCK STEADY BODYSNATCHERS
LET'S DO THE LATIN HUSTLE EDDIE DRENNON & B.B.S. UNLIMITED
LET'S DO THE LATIN HUSTLE M & O BAND
LET'S FACE THE MUSIC AND DANCE NAT 'KING' COLE
LET'S FLY AWAY VOYAGE
LET'S FUNK TONIGHT BLUE FEATHERS
LET'S GET BACK TO BED...BOY SARAH CONNOR FEATURING TQ
LET'S GET BRUTAL NITRO DELUXE
LET'S GET DOWN [A] ISOTONIK
LET'S GET DOWN [B] MARK MORRISON
LET'S GET DOWN [C] TONY TONI TONE FEATURING DJ QUIK
LET'S GET DOWN [D] JT PLAYAZ
LET'S GET DOWN [E] SPACEDUST
LET'S GET FUNKED BOILING POINT
LET'S GET HAPPY MASS ORDER
LET'S GET ILL P DIDDY FEATURING KELIS
LET'S GET IT ON [A] MARVIN GAYE
LET'S GET IT ON [B] SHABBA RANKS
LET'S GET IT ON [C] BIG BOSS STYLUS PRESENTS RED VENOM
LET'S GET IT STARTED BLACK EYED PEAS
LET'S GET IT UP AC/DC
LET'S GET MARRIED PROCLAIMERS
LET'S GET READY TO RHUMBLE PJ & DUNCAN
LET'S GET ROCKED DEF LEPPARD
LET'S GET SERIOUS JERMAINE JACKSON
LET'S GET TATTOOS CARTER – THE UNSTOPPABLE SEX MACHINE
LET'S GET THIS PARTY STARTED ZENA
LET'S GET THIS STRAIGHT (FROM THE START) KEVIN ROWLAND & DEXY'S MIDNIGHT RUNNERS
LET'S GET TOGETHER [A] HAYLEY MILLS
LET'S GET TOGETHER [B] ALEXANDER O'NEAL
LET'S GET TOGETHER AGAIN [A] BIG BEN BANJO BAND
LET'S GET TOGETHER AGAIN [B] GLITTER BAND
LET'S GET TOGETHER (IN OUR MINDS) GORKY'S ZYGOTIC MYNCI
LET'S GET TOGETHER NO. 1 BIG BEN BANJO BAND

LET'S GET TOGETHER (SO GROOVY NOW) KRUSH PERSPECTIVE
LET'S GET TOGETHER (TONITE) STEVE WALSH
LET'S GO [A] ROUTERS
LET'S GO [B] CARS
LET'S GO [C] VARDIS
LET'S GO ALL THE WAY SLY FOX
LET'S GO CRAZY PRINCE & THE REVOLUTION
LET'S GO DISCO REAL THING
LET'S GO ROUND AGAIN LOUISE
LET'S GO ROUND AGAIN PART 1 AVERAGE WHITE BAND
LET'S GO ROUND THERE DARLING BUDS
LET'S GO STEADY AGAIN NEIL SEDAKA
LET'S GO TO BED CURE
LET'S GO TO SAN FRANCISCO FLOWERPOT MEN
LET'S GO TOGETHER CHANGE
LET'S GROOVE [A] EARTH, WIND & FIRE
LET'S GROOVE [A] PHAT 'N' PHUNKY
LET'S GROOVE [B] GEORGE MOREL FEATURING HEATHER WILDMAN
LET'S HANG ON FOUR SEASONS WITH THE SOUND OF FRANKIE VALLI
LET'S HANG ON BANDWAGON
LET'S HANG ON DARTS
LET'S HANG ON BARRY MANILOW
LET'S HANG ON SHOOTING PARTY
LET'S HAVE A BALL WINIFRED ATWELL
LET'S HAVE A DING DONG WINIFRED ATWELL
LET'S HAVE A PARTY [A] WINIFRED ATWELL
LET'S HAVE A PARTY [B] WANDA JACKSON
LET'S HAVE A QUIET NIGHT IN DAVID SOUL
LET'S HAVE ANOTHER PARTY WINIFRED ATWELL
LET'S HEAR IT FOR THE BOY DENIECE WILLIAMS
LET'S JUMP THE BROOMSTICK BRENDA LEE
LET'S JUMP THE BROOMSTICK COAST TO COAST
LET'S KILL MUSIC COOPER TEMPLE CLAUSE
LET'S LIVE IT UP (NITE PEOPLE) DAVID JOSEPH
LET'S LOVE DANCE TONIGHT GARY'S GANG
LET'S MAKE A BABY BILLY PAUL
LET'S MAKE A NIGHT TO REMEMBER BRYAN ADAMS
LET'S PARTY JIVE BUNNY & THE MASTERMIXERS
LET'S PLAY HOUSE KRAZE
LET'S PRETEND LULU
LET'S PUSH IT [A] INNOCENCE
LET'S PUSH IT [B] NIGHTCRAWLERS FEATURING JOHN REID
LET'S PUSH THINGS FORWARD STREETS
LET'S PUT IT ALL TOGETHER STYLISTICS
LET'S RIDE MONTELL JORDAN FEATURING MASTER P & SILKK THE SHOCKER
LET'S ROCK E-TRAX
LET'S ROCK 'N' ROLL WINIFRED ATWELL
LET'S SEE ACTION WHO
LET'S SLIP AWAY CLEO LAINE
LET'S SPEND THE NIGHT TOGETHER ROLLING STONES
LET'S SPEND THE NIGHT TOGETHER MASH!
LET'S START OVER PAMELA FERNANDEZ
LET'S START THE DANCE HAMILTON BOHANNON
LET'S START TO DANCE AGAIN HAMILTON BOHANNON
LET'S STAY HOME TONIGHT JOE
LET'S STAY TOGETHER AL GREEN
LET'S STAY TOGETHER TINA TURNER
LET'S STAY TOGETHER BOBBY M FEATURING JEAN CARN
LET'S STAY TOGETHER PASADENAS
LET'S STICK TOGETHER BRYAN FERRY
LET'S SWING AGAIN JIVE BUNNY & THE MASTERMIXERS
LET'S TALK ONE WAY FEATURING AL HUDSON
LET'S TALK ABOUT LOVE HELEN SHAPIRO

LET'S TALK ABOUT SEX SALT-N-PEPA FEATURING PSYCHOTROPIC
LET'S THINK ABOUT LIVING BOB LUMAN
LET'S TRY AGAIN NEW KIDS ON THE BLOCK
LET'S TURKEY TROT LITTLE EVA
LET'S TWIST AGAIN CHUBBY CHECKER
LET'S TWIST AGAIN JOHN ASHER
LET'S WAIT AWHILE JANET JACKSON
LET'S WALK THATA-WAY DORIS DAY & JOHNNIE RAY
LET'S WHIP IT UP (YOU GO GIRL) SLEAZESISTERS WITH VIKKI SHEPARD
LET'S WOMBLE TO THE PARTY TONIGHT WOMBLES
LET'S WORK MICK JAGGER
LET'S WORK IT OUT RAGHAV FEATURING JAHAZIEL
LET'S WORK TOGETHER CANNED HEAT
THE LETTER [A] LONG & THE SHORT
THE LETTER [B] BOX TOPS
THE LETTER [B] MINDBENDERS
THE LETTER [B] JOE COCKER
THE LETTER [B] AMII STEWART
THE LETTER [C] PJ HARVEY
LETTER 2 MY UNBORN 2PAC
LETTER FROM AMERICA PROCLAIMERS
LETTER FULL OF TEARS BILLY FURY
LETTER TO A SOLDIER BARBARA LYON
A LETTER TO ELSIE CURE
LETTER TO LUCILLE TOM JONES
A LETTER TO YOU SHAKIN' STEVENS
LETTERS TO YOU FINCH
LETTIN' YA MIND GO DESERT
LETTING GO WINGS
LETTING THE CABLES SLEEP BUSH
LEVI STUBBS TEARS BILLY BRAGG
LFO LFO
LIAR [A] GRAHAM BONNET
LIAR [B] ROLLINS BAND
LIAR LIAR CREDIT TO THE NATION
LIARS' BAR BEAUTIFUL SOUTH
LIBERATE LEE HASLAM
LIBERATION [A] LIBERATION
LIBERATION [B] PET SHOP BOYS
LIBERATION [C] LIPPY LOU
LIBERATION (TEMPTATION – FLY LIKE AN EAGLE) MATT DAREY PRESENTS MASH UP
LIBERATOR SPEAR OF DESTINY
LIBERIAN GIRL MICHAEL JACKSON
LIBERTY TOWN PERFECT DAY
LIBIAMO JOSE CARRERAS, PLACIDO DOMINGO & LUCIANO PAVAROTTI
LICENCE TO KILL GLADYS KNIGHT
LICK A SHOT CYPRESS HILL
LICK A SMURF FOR CHRISTMAS (ALL FALL DOWN) FATHER ABRAPHART & THE SMURPS
LICK IT 20 FINGERS FEATURING ROULA
LICK IT UP KISS
LIDO SHUFFLE BOZ SCAGGS
LIE TO ME BON JOVI
LIES [A] STATUS QUO
LIES [B] THOMPSON TWINS
LIES [C] JONATHAN BUTLER
LIES [D] EN VOGUE
LIES [E] EMF
LIES IN YOUR EYES SWEET
LIFE [A] HADDAWAY
LIFE [B] BLAIR
LIFE [C] DES'REE
THE LIFE STYLES & PHAROAHE MONCH
LIFE AIN'T EASY CLEOPATRA
LIFE AT A TOP PEOPLE'S HEALTH FARM STYLE COUNCIL
LIFE BECOMING A LANDSLIDE MANIC STREET PREACHERS

LIFE BEGINS AT THE HOP XTC
LIFE FOR RENT DIDO
LIFE GOES ON [A] GEORGIE PORGIE
LIFE GOES ON [B] LeANN RIMES
LIFE GOT COLD GIRLS ALOUD
LIFE IN A DAY [A] SIMPLE MINDS
LIFE IN A DAY [B] I AM KLOOT
LIFE IN A NORTHERN TOWN DREAM ACADEMY
LIFE IN MONO MONO
LIFE IN ONE DAY HOWARD JONES
LIFE IN TOKYO JAPAN
LIFE IS A FLOWER ACE OF BASE
LIFE IS A HIGHWAY TOM COCHRANE
LIFE IS A LONG SONG JETHRO TULL
LIFE IS A MINESTRONE 10 C.C.
LIFE IS A ROCK (BUT THE RADIO ROLLED ME) REUNION
LIFE IS A ROLLERCOASTER RONAN KEATING
LIFE IS FOR LIVING BARCLAY JAMES HARVEST
LIFE IS SWEET CHEMICAL BROTHERS
LIFE IS TOO SHORT GIRL SHEER ELEGANCE
A LIFE LESS ORDINARY ASH
LIFE LOVE AND UNITY DREADZONE
THE LIFE OF RILEY LIGHTNING SEEDS
LIFE OF SURPRISES PREFAB SPROUT
LIFE ON MARS DAVID BOWIE
LIFE ON YOUR OWN HUMAN LEAGUE
LIFE STORY ANGIE STONE
LIFE SUPPORTING MACHINE THESE ANIMAL MEN
LIFE, LOVE AND HAPPINESS BRIAN KENNEDY
LIFEBOAT TERRY NEASON
THE LIFEBOAT PARTY KID CREOLE & THE COCONUTS
LIFEFORMS FUTURE SOUND OF LONDON
LIFELINE SPANDAU BALLET
LIFESTYLES OF THE RICH AND FAMOUS GOOD
   CHARLOTTE
LIFE'S A CINCH MUNDY
LIFE'S BEEN GOOD JOE WALSH
LIFE'S JUST A BALLGAME WOMACK & WOMACK
LIFE'S TOO SHORT [A] HOLE IN ONE
LIFE'S TOO SHORT [B] LIGHTNING SEEDS
LIFE'S WHAT YOU MAKE IT TALK TALK
LIFESAVER GURU
LIFETIME LOVE JOYCE SIMS
LIFETIME PILING UP TALKING HEADS
LIFETIMES SLAM FEATURING TYRONE PALMER
LIFT 808 STATE
LIFT EVERY VOICE (TAKE ME AWAY) MASS ORDER
LIFT IT HIGH (ALL ABOUT BELIEF) 1999 MANCHESTER
   UNITED SQUAD
LIFT ME UP [A] HOWARD JONES
LIFT ME UP [B] RED 5
LIFT ME UP [C] GERI HALLIWELL
LIFT ME UP [C] REEL
LIFTED LIGHTHOUSE FAMILY
LIFTING ME HIGHER GEMS FOR JEM
LIGHT PHAROAHE MONCH
THE LIGHT COMMON
THE LIGHT MICHELLE WEEKS
LIGHT A CANDLE DANIEL O'DONNELL
LIGHT A RAINBOW TUKAN
LIGHT AIRCRAFT ON FIRE AUTEURS
LIGHT AND DAY POLYPHONIC SPREE
THE LIGHT COMES FROM WITHIN LINDA McCARTNEY
LIGHT EMITTING ELECTRICAL WAVE THESE ANIMAL
   MEN
LIGHT FLIGHT PENTANGLE
LIGHT IN YOUR EYES SHERYL CROW
LIGHT MY FIRE [A] DOORS
LIGHT MY FIRE [A] JOSE FELICIANO
LIGHT MY FIRE [A] MIKE FLOWERS POPS
LIGHT MY FIRE [A] UB40

LIGHT MY FIRE [A] WILL YOUNG
LIGHT MY FIRE [B] CLUBHOUSE
LIGHT MY FIRE/137 DISCO HEAVEN (MEDLEY) AMII
   STEWART
(LIGHT OF EXPERIENCE) DOINA DE JALE GHEORGHE
   ZAMFIR
LIGHT OF LOVE T. REX
LIGHT OF MY LIFE LOUISE
LIGHT OF THE WORLD KIM APPLEBY
LIGHT UP THE FIRE PARCHMENT
LIGHT UP THE NIGHT BROTHERS JOHNSON
LIGHT UP THE WORLD FOR CHRISTMAS LAMPIES
LIGHT YEARS PEARL JAM
LIGHT YOUR ASS ON FIRE BUSTA RHYMES FEATURING
   PHARRELL
THE LIGHTER DJ SS
LIGHTNIN' STRIKES LOU CHRISTIE
LIGHTNING ZOE
LIGHTNING CRASHES LIVE
LIGHTNING FLASH BROTHERHOOD OF MAN
LIGHTNING STRIKES OZZY OSBOURNE
THE LIGHTNING TREE SETTLERS
LIGHTS OF CINCINNATI SCOTT WALKER
LIGHTS OUT LISA MARIE PRESLEY
LIKE A BABY LEN BARRY
LIKE A BUTTERFLY MAC & KATIE KISSOON
LIKE A CAT CRW FEATURING VERONIKA
LIKE A CHILD JULIE ROGERS
LIKE A CHILD AGAIN MISSION
LIKE A FEATHER NIKKA COSTA
LIKE A HURRICANE MISSION
LIKE A MOTORWAY SAINT ETIENNE
LIKE A PLAYA LA GANZ
LIKE A PRAYER MADONNA
LIKE A PRAYER MADHOUSE
LIKE A ROLLING STONE BOB DYLAN
LIKE A ROLLING STONE ROLLING STONES
LIKE A ROSE A1
LIKE A SATELLITE (EP) THUNDER
LIKE A VIRGIN MADONNA
LIKE A WOMAN TONY RICH PROJECT
LIKE A YO-YO SABRINA
LIKE AN ANIMAL GLOVE
LIKE AN OLD TIME MOVIE THE VOICE OF SCOTT
   McKENZIE
LIKE CLOCKWORK BOOMTOWN RATS
LIKE DREAMERS DO [A] APPLEJACKS
LIKE DREAMERS DO [B] MICA PARIS FEATURING
   COURTNEY PINE
LIKE FLAMES BERLIN
LIKE GLUE SEAN PAUL
LIKE I DO [A] MAUREEN EVANS
LIKE I DO [B] FOR REAL
LIKE I LIKE IT AURRA
LIKE I LOVE YOU JUSTIN TIMBERLAKE
LIKE I'VE NEVER BEEN GONE BILLY FURY
LIKE IT OR LEAVE IT CHIKINKI
LIKE LOVERS DO LLOYD COLE
LIKE MARVIN GAYE SAID (WHAT'S GOING ON) SPEECH
LIKE PRINCES DO DIESEL PARK WEST
LIKE SISTER AND BROTHER DRIFTERS
LIKE STRANGERS EVERLY BROTHERS
LIKE THIS AND LIKE THAT [A] MONICA
LIKE THIS AND LIKE THAT [B] LaKIESHA BERRI
LIKE THIS LIKE THAT MAURO PICOTTO
LIKE TO GET TO KNOW YOU WELL HOWARD JONES
LIKE WE USED TO BE GEORGIE FAME & THE BLUE
   FLAMES
LIKE WHAT TOMMI
A LIL' AIN'T ENOUGH DAVID LEE ROTH
LIL' BIG MAN OMERO MUMBA

LIL' DEVIL CULT
LIL' DUB CHEFIN' SPACE MONKEY VS GORILLAZ
LIL' RED RIDING HOOD SAM THE SHAM & THE
   PHARAOHS
LIL' RED RIDING HOOD 999
LILAC WINE ELKIE BROOKS
LILY THE PINK SCAFFOLD
LILY WAS HERE DAVID A STEWART FEATURING CANDY
   DULFER
LIMBO ROCK CHUBBY CHECKER
LINDA LU JOHNNY KIDD & THE PIRATES
THE LINE LISA STANSFIELD
LINE DANCE PARTY WOOLPACKERS
LINE UP ELASTICA
LINES PLANETS
LINGER CRANBERRIES
THE LION SLEEPS TONIGHT DAVE NEWMAN
THE LION SLEEPS TONIGHT TIGHT FIT
THE LION SLEEPS TONIGHT (WIMOWEH) TOKENS
LIONROCK LIONROCK
THE LION'S MOUTH KAJAGOOGOO
LIP GLOSS PULP
LIP SERVICE (EP) WET WET WET
LIP UP FATTY BAD MANNERS
LIPS LIKE SUGAR ECHO & THE BUNNYMEN
LIPSMACKIN' ROCK 'N' ROLLIN' PETER BLAKE
LIPSTICK ROCKET FROM THE CRYPT
LIPSTICK ON YOUR COLLAR CONNIE FRANCIS
LIPSTICK POWDER AND PAINT SHAKIN' STEVENS
LIQUID COOL APOLLO 440
LIQUID DREAMS O-TOWN
LIQUID LIPS BLUETONES
LIQUIDATOR HARRY J. ALL STARS
LISTEN URBAN SPECIES FEATURING MC SOLAAR
LISTEN EP STIFF LITTLE FINGERS
LISTEN LIKE THIEVES INXS
LISTEN LIKE THIEVES WAS (NOT WAS)
LISTEN LITTLE GIRL KEITH KELLY
LISTEN TO ME [A] BUDDY HOLLY
LISTEN TO ME [B] HOLLIES
LISTEN TO THE MUSIC DOOBIE BROTHERS
LISTEN TO THE OCEAN NINA & FREDERICK
LISTEN TO THE RADIO: ATMOSPHERICS TOM ROBINSON
LISTEN TO THE RHYTHM K3M
LISTEN TO THE RHYTHM FLOW GTO
LISTEN TO WHAT THE MAN SAID WINGS
LISTEN TO YOUR FATHER FEARGAL SHARKEY
LISTEN TO YOUR HEART [A] ROXETTE
LISTEN TO YOUR HEART [B] SONIA
LITHIUM NIRVANA
LITTLE ARITHMETICS dEUS
LITTLE ARROWS LEAPY LEE
LITTLE BABY NOTHING MANIC STREET PREACHERS
LITTLE BAND OF GOLD JAMES GILREATH
LITTLE BERNADETTE HARRY BELAFONTE
LITTLE BIRD ANNIE LENNOX
A LITTLE BIT ROSIE RIBBONS
A LITTLE BIT FURTHER AWAY KOKOMO
A LITTLE BIT ME A LITTLE BIT YOU MONKEES
A LITTLE BIT MORE [A] DR. HOOK
A LITTLE BIT MORE [A] 911
A LITTLE BIT MORE [B] KYM SIMS
A LITTLE BIT OF ACTION NADIA
LITTLE BIT OF HEAVEN LISA STANSFIELD
LITTLE BIT OF LOVE FREE
LITTLE BIT OF LOVIN' KELE LE ROC
A LITTLE BIT OF LUCK DJ LUCK & MC NEAT
A LITTLE BIT OF SNOW HOWARD JONES
A LITTLE BIT OF SOAP SHOWADDYWADDY
A LITTLE BITTY TEAR BURL IVES
LITTLE BITTY TEAR MIKI & GRIFF

LITTLE BLACK BOOK [A] JIMMY DEAN
LITTLE BLACK BOOK [B] BELINDA CARLISLE
LITTLE BLUE BIRD VINCE HILL
A LITTLE BOOGIE WOOGIE IN THE BACK OF MY MIND
    GARY GLITTER
A LITTLE BOOGIE WOOGIE (IN THE BACK OF MY MIND)
    SHAKIN' STEVENS
LITTLE BOY LOST MICHAEL HOLLIDAY
LITTLE BOY SAD JOHNNY BURNETTE
LITTLE BRITAIN DREADZONE
LITTLE BROTHER BLUE PEARL
LITTLE BROWN JUG GLENN MILLER
LITTLE BY LITTLE [A] DUSTY SPRINGFIELD
LITTLE BY LITTLE [B] OASIS
LITTLE CHILD DES'REE
LITTLE CHILDREN BILLY J. KRAMER & THE DAKOTAS
LITTLE CHRISTINE DICK JORDAN
LITTLE DARLIN' DIAMONDS
LITTLE DARLIN' MARVIN GAYE
LITTLE DARLING RUBETTES
LITTLE DEVIL NEIL SEDAKA
LITTLE DISCOURAGE IDLEWILD
LITTLE DOES SHE KNOW KURSAAL FLYERS
LITTLE DONKEY GRACIE FIELDS
LITTLE DONKEY BEVERLEY SISTERS
LITTLE DONKEY NINA & FREDERICK
LITTLE DROPS OF SILVER GERRY MONROE
LITTLE DRUMMER BOY BEVERLEY SISTERS
LITTLE DRUMMER BOY HARRY SIMEONE CHORALE
LITTLE DRUMMER BOY MICHAEL FLANDERS
LITTLE DRUMMER BOY THE PIPES & DRUMS & MILITARY
    BAND OF THE ROYAL SCOTS DRAGOON GUARDS
LITTLE DRUMMER BOY (REMIX) RuPAUL
LITTLE 15 (IMPORT) DEPECHE MODE
LITTLE FLUFFY CLOUDS ORB
LITTLE GIRL [A] MARTY WILDE
LITTLE GIRL [B] TROGGS
LITTLE GIRL [C] BANNED
LITTLE GIRL LOST ICICLE WORKS
LITTLE GREEN APPLES ROGER MILLER
LITTLE HOUSE OF SAVAGES WALKMEN
A LITTLE IN LOVE CLIFF RICHARD
LITTLE JEANNIE ELTON JOHN
LITTLE L JAMIROQUAI
LITTLE LADY ANEKA
A LITTLE LESS CONVERSATION ELVIS VS JXL
LITTLE LIES FLEETWOOD MAC
LITTLE LOST SOMETIMES ALMIGHTY
A LITTLE LOVE AND UNDERSTANDING GILBERT BECAUD
A LITTLE LOVE A LITTLE KISS KARL DENVER
A LITTLE LOVIN' NEIL SEDAKA
A LITTLE LOVING FOURMOST
LITTLE MAN SONNY & CHER
LITTLE MIRACLES (HAPPEN EVERY DAY) LUTHER
    VANDROSS
LITTLE MISS CAN'T BE WRONG SPIN DOCTORS
LITTLE MISS LONELY HELEN SHAPIRO
LITTLE MISS PERFECT SUMMER MATTHEWS
A LITTLE MORE LOVE OLIVIA NEWTON-JOHN
A LITTLE PEACE NICOLE
LITTLE PIECE OF LEATHER DONNIE ELBERT
LITTLE PINK STARS RADISH
LITTLE RED CORVETTE PRINCE & THE REVOLUTION
LITTLE RED MONKEY FRANK CHACKSFIELD'S
    TUNESMITHS, FEATURING JACK JORDAN –
    CLAVIOLINE
LITTLE RED ROOSTER ROLLING STONES
A LITTLE RESPECT ERASURE
A LITTLE RESPECT WHEATUS
LITTLE RHYMES MERCURY REV
A LITTLE SAMBA UGLY DUCKLING

LITTLE SERENADE EDDIE CALVERT
THE LITTLE SHOEMAKER PETULA CLARK
LITTLE SISTER ELVIS PRESLEY
A LITTLE SOUL PULP
LITTLE STAR [A] ELEGANTS
LITTLE STAR [B] MADONNA
LITTLE THINGS [A] DAVE BERRY
LITTLE THINGS [B] INDIA.ARIE
LITTLE THINGS MEAN A LOT KITTY KALLEN
LITTLE THINGS MEAN A LOT ALMA COGAN
LITTLE THOUGHT BLOC PARTY
A LITTLE TIME BEAUTIFUL SOUTH
LITTLE TOWN CLIFF RICHARD
LITTLE TOWN FLIRT DEL SHANNON
LITTLE TRAIN MAX BYGRAVES
LITTLE WHITE BERRY ROY CASTLE
LITTLE WHITE BULL TOMMY STEELE
LITTLE WHITE LIES STATUS QUO
LITTLE WILLY SWEET
LITTLE WONDER DAVID BOWIE
A LITTLE YOU FREDDIE & THE DREAMERS
LIVE AND LEARN JOE PUBLIC
LIVE AND LET DIE WINGS
LIVE AND LET DIE GUNS N' ROSES
LIVE ANIMAL (F**K LIKE A BEAST) W.A.S.P.
LIVE ANOTHER LIFE PLASTIC BOY FEATURING ROZALLA
LIVE AT TFI FRIDAY EP STING
LIVE AT THE MARQUEE (EP) EDDIE & THE HOT RODS
LIVE (EP) BARCLAY JAMES HARVEST
THE LIVE EP GARY NUMAN
LIVE FOR LOVING YOU GLORIA ESTEFAN
LIVE FOR THE ONE I LOVE TINA ARENA
LIVE FOREVER OASIS
LIVE IN A HIDING PLACE IDLEWILD
LIVE IN MANCHESTER (PARTS 1 + 2) N-JOI
LIVE IN THE SKY DAVE CLARK FIVE
LIVE IN TROUBLE BARRON KNIGHTS
LIVE IS LIFE OPUS
LIVE IS LIFE HERMES HOUSE BAND & DJ OTZI
LIVE IT UP MENTAL AS ANYTHING
LIVE LIKE HORSES ELTON JOHN & LUCIANO PAVAROTTI
LIVE MY LIFE BOY GEORGE
LIVE OR DIE DILLINJA
LIVE THE DREAM CAST
LIVE TO TELL MADONNA
LIVE TOGETHER LISA STANSFIELD
LIVE YOUR LIFE BE FREE BELINDA CARLISLE
LIVELY LONNIE DONEGAN
LIVERPOOL (ANTHEM) LIVERPOOL FC
LIVERPOOL LOU SCAFFOLD
LIVERPOOL (WE'RE NEVER GONNA...) LIVERPOOL FC
LIVIN' IN THE LIGHT CARON WHEELER
LIVIN' IN THIS WORLD GURU
LIVIN' IT UP [A] NORTHERN UPROAR
LIVIN' IT UP [B] JA RULE FEATURING CASE
LIVIN' IT UP (FRIDAY NIGHT) BELL & JAMES
LIVIN' LA VIDA LOCA RICKY MARTIN
LIVIN' LOVIN' DOLL CLIFF RICHARD
LIVIN' ON A PRAYER BON JOVI
LIVIN' ON THE EDGE AEROSMITH
LIVIN' ON THE EDGE OF THE NIGHT IGGY POP
LIVIN' THING ELECTRIC LIGHT ORCHESTRA
LIVIN' THING BEAUTIFUL SOUTH
LIVING AFTER MIDNIGHT JUDAS PRIEST
LIVING BY NUMBERS NEW MUSIK
THE LIVING DAYLIGHTS A-HA
LIVING DOLL CLIFF RICHARD & THE SHADOWS
LIVING DOLL CLIFF RICHARD & THE YOUNG ONES
    FEATURING HANK B MARVIN
THE LIVING DREAM SUNDANCE
LIVING FOR THE CITY STEVIE WONDER

LIVING FOR THE CITY GILLAN
LIVING FOR YOU SONNY & CHER
LIVING IN A BOX LIVING IN A BOX
LIVING IN A BOX BOBBY WOMACK
LIVING IN A FANTASY URBAN HYPE
LIVING IN A WORLD (TURNED UPSIDE DOWN) PRIVATE
    LIVES
LIVING IN AMERICA JAMES BROWN
LIVING IN ANOTHER WORLD TALK TALK
LIVING IN DANGER ACE OF BASE
LIVING IN HARMONY CLIFF RICHARD
LIVING IN SIN BON JOVI
LIVING IN THE PAST [A] JETHRO TULL
LIVING IN THE PAST [B] DRUM THEATRE
LIVING IN THE ROSE (THE BALLADS EP) NEW MODEL
    ARMY
LIVING IN THE (SLIGHTLY MORE RECENT) PAST JETHRO
    TULL
LIVING IN THE SUNSHINE CLUBHOUSE FEATURING
    CARL
LIVING IN THE UK SHAKATAK
LIVING NEXT DOOR TO ALICE SMOKIE
LIVING NEXT DOOR TO ALICE (WHO THE F**K IS ALICE)
    SMOKIE FEATURING ROY CHUBBY BROWN
LIVING ON AN ISLAND STATUS QUO
LIVING ON MY OWN FREDDIE MERCURY
LIVING ON THE CEILING BLANCMANGE
LIVING ON THE FRONT LINE EDDY GRANT
LIVING ON VIDEO TRANS-X
LIVING WITH THE HUMAN MACHINES STRANGELOVE
THE LIVING YEARS MIKE + THE MECHANICS
LIZARD (GONNA GET YOU) MAURO PICOTTO
LK (CAROLINA CAROL BELA) DJ MARKY & XRS
    FEATURING STAMINA MC
L-L-LUCY MUD
LO MISMO QUE YO (IF ONLY) ALEX CUBA BAND
    FEATURING RON SEXSMITH
LOADED [A] PRIMAL SCREAM
LOADED [B] RICKY MARTIN
LOADSAMONEY (DOIN' UP THE HOUSE) HARRY ENFIELD
LOBSTER & SCRIMP TIMBALAND FEATURING JAY-Z
LOCAL BOY IN THE PHOTOGRAPH STEREOPHONICS
LOC'ED AFTER DARK TONE LOC
LOCK AND LOAD BOB SEGER & THE SILVER BULLET BAND
LOCK UP YA DAUGHTERS NOISE NEXT DOOR
LOCK UP YOUR DAUGHTERS SLADE
LOCKED OUT CROWDED HOUSE
LOCKED UP AKON FEATURING STYLES P
LOCO FUN LOVIN' CRIMINALS
LOCO IN ACAPULCO FOUR TOPS
THE LOCO-MOTION [A] LITTLE EVA
THE LOCO-MOTION [A] KYLIE MINOGUE
THE LOCOMOTION [A] DAVE STEWART WITH BARBARA
    GASKIN
LOCO-MOTION [A] VERNONS GIRLS
LOCOMOTION [B] ORCHESTRAL MANOEUVRES IN THE
    DARK
L.O.D. (LOVE ON DELIVERY) BILLY OCEAN
THE LODGERS STYLE COUNCIL
THE LOGICAL SONG SUPERTRAMP
THE LOGICAL SONG SCOOTER
L'OISEAU ET L'ENFANT MARIE MYRIAM
LOLA KINKS
LOLA ANDY TAYLOR
LOLA STARS AND STRIPES STILLS
LOLA'S THEME SHAPESHIFTERS
LOLLIPOP CHORDETTES
LOLLIPOP MUDLARKS
LOLLY LOLLY WENDY & LISA
LONDINIUM CATATONIA
LONDON BOYS T. REX

LONDON CALLING CLASH
LONDON GIRLS CHAS & DAVE
LONDON KID JEAN-MICHEL JARRE FEATURING HANK MARVIN
LONDON NIGHTS LONDON BOYS
A LONDON THING SCOTT GARCIA FEATURING MC STYLES
LONDON TIMES RADIO HEART FEATURING GARY NUMAN
LONDON TONIGHT COLLAPSED LUNG
LONDON TOWN [A] WINGS
LONDON TOWN [B] LIGHT OF THE WORLD
LONDON TOWN [C] BUCKS FIZZ
LONDON TOWN [D] JDS
LONDON X-PRESS X-PRESS 2
LONDON'S BRILLIANT WENDY JAMES
LONDON'S BRILLIANT PARADE ELVIS COSTELLO & THE ATTRACTIONS
LONDRES STRUTT SMELLS LIKE HEAVEN
THE LONE RANGER QUANTUM JUMP
LONE RIDER JOHN LEYTON
THE LONELIEST MAN IN THE WORLD TOURISTS
LONELINESS [A] DES O'CONNOR
LONELINESS [B] TOMCRAFT
LONELINESS IS GONE NINE YARDS
LONELY [A] EDDIE COCHRAN
LONELY [B] MR ACKER BILK WITH THE LEON YOUNG STRING CHORALE
LONELY [C] PETER ANDRE
LONELY BALLERINA MANTOVANI
LONELY BOY [A] PAUL ANKA
LONELY BOY [B] ANDREW GOLD
LONELY BOY LONELY GUITAR DUANE EDDY & THE REBELETTES
THE LONELY BULL TIJUANA BRASS
LONELY CITY JOHN LEYTON
LONELY, CRYIN', ONLY THERAPY?
LONELY DAYS BEE GEES
LONELY DAYS, LONELY NIGHTS DON DOWNING
LONELY (HAVE WE LOST OUR LOVE) LANCE ELLINGTON
LONELY HEART UFO
LONELY MAN THEME CLIFF ADAMS
LONELY NIGHT MAGNUM
THE LONELY ONE ALICE DEEJAY
LONELY PUP (IN A CHRISTMAS SHOP) ADAM FAITH
LONELY STREET CLARENCE 'FROGMAN' HENRY
LONELY SYMPHONY FRANCES RUFFELLE
LONELY TEENAGER DION
LONELY THIS CHRISTMAS MUD
LONELY TOGETHER BARRY MANILOW
THE LONER GARY MOORE
LONESOME ADAM FAITH
LONESOME DAY BRUCE SPRINGSTEEN
LONESOME NUMBER ONE DON GIBSON
LONESOME (SI TU VOIS MA MERE) CHRIS BARBER FEATURING MONTY SUNSHINE
LONESOME TRAVELLER LONNIE DONEGAN
LONG AFTER TONIGHT IS ALL OVER JIMMY RADLCIFFE
LONG AND LASTING LOVE (ONCE IN A LIFETIME) GLENN MEDEIROS
THE LONG AND WINDING ROAD RAY MORGAN
THE LONG AND WINDING ROAD WILL YOUNG & GARETH GATES
LONG AS I CAN SEE THE LIGHT CREEDENCE CLEARWATER REVIVAL
LONG AS I CAN SEE THE LIGHT MONKEY MAFIA
LONG BLACK VEIL STRANGLERS
LONG COOL WOMAN IN A BLACK DRESS HOLLIES
A LONG DECEMBER COUNTING CROWS
LONG DISTANCE TURIN BRAKES
THE LONG GOODBYE RONAN KEATING

LONG HAIRED LOVER FROM LIVERPOOL LITTLE JIMMY OSMOND
LONG HOT SUMMER STYLE COUNCIL
LONG HOT SUMMER NIGHT JT TAYLOR
LONG LEGGED GIRL (WITH THE SHORT DRESS ON) ELVIS PRESLEY
LONG LEGGED WOMAN DRESSED IN BLACK MUNGO JERRY
LONG LIVE LOVE [A] SANDIE SHAW
LONG LIVE LOVE [A] NICK BERRY
LONG LIVE LOVE [B] OLIVIA NEWTON-JOHN
LONG LIVE ROCK WHO
LONG LIVE ROCK 'N' ROLL RAINBOW
LONG LIVE THE UK MUSIC SCENE HELEN LOVE
LONG LONG WAY TO GO DEF LEPPARD
LONG LOST LOVER THREE DEGREES
LONG MAY YOU RUN (LIVE) NEIL YOUNG
LONG NIGHT CORRS
THE LONG RUN EAGLES
LONG SHOT KICK DE BUCKET PIONEERS
LONG TALL GLASSES LEO SAYER
LONG TALL SALLY PAT BOONE
LONG TALL SALLY LITTLE RICHARD
LONG TERM LOVERS OF PAIN (EP) HUE & CRY
LONG TIME ARROW
LONG TIME COMING [A] BUMP & FLEX
LONG TIME COMING [B] DELAYS
LONG TIME GONE GALLIANO
LONG TRAIN RUNNIN' DOOBIE BROTHERS
LONG TRAIN RUNNING BANANARAMA
A LONG WALK JILL SCOTT
LONG WAY ROOTJOOSE
LONG WAY AROUND EAGLE-EYE CHERRY FEATURING NENEH CHERRY
LONG WAY FROM HOME WHITESNAKE
LONG WAY SOUTH JJ72
LONG WAY TO GO STEVIE NICKS
LONG WHITE CAR HIPSWAY
LONGER DAN FOGELBERG
THE LONGEST TIME BILLY JOEL
LONGTIME BOY NINA & FREDERICK
LONGVIEW GREEN DAY
LONNIE DONEGAN SHOWCASE (LP) LONNIE DONEGAN
LONNIE'S SKIFFLE PARTY LONNIE DONEGAN
LOO-BE-LOO CHUCKS
THE LOOK ROXETTE
LOOK AROUND VINCE HILL
LOOK AT ME GERI HALLIWELL
LOOK AT ME (I'M IN LOVE) MOMENTS
LOOK AT ME NOW JESSY
LOOK AT THAT GIRL GUY MITCHELL
LOOK AT US NORTHERN HEIGHTZ
LOOK AT YOURSELF DAVID McALMONT
LOOK AWAY BIG COUNTRY
LOOK BEFORE YOU LEAP DAVE CLARK FIVE
LOOK BUT DON'T TOUCH (EP) SKIN
LOOK FOR A STAR GARRY MILLS
LOOK HOMEWARD ANGEL JOHNNIE RAY
LOOK INTO MY EYES BONE THUGS-N-HARMONY
LOOK MAMA HOWARD JONES
LOOK ME IN THE HEART TINA TURNER
LOOK OF LOVE [A] GLADYS KNIGHT & THE PIPS
THE LOOK OF LOVE [A] T-EMPO
THE LOOK OF LOVE [B] ABC
THE LOOK OF LOVE [C] MADONNA
LOOK THROUGH ANY WINDOW HOLLIES
LOOK THROUGH MY EYES PHIL COLLINS
LOOK UP TO THE LIGHT EVOLUTION
LOOK WHAT YOU DONE FOR ME AL GREEN
LOOK WHAT YOU STARTED TEMPTATIONS
LOOK WHAT YOU'VE DONE JET

LOOK WHO IT IS HELEN SHAPIRO
LOOK WHO'S DANCING ZIGGY MARLEY & THE MELODY MAKERS
LOOK WHO'S PERFECT NOW TRANSISTER
LOOK WHO'S TALKING DR ALBAN
LOOK WOT YOU DUN SLADE
LOOKIN' AT YOU WARREN G FEATURING TOI
LOOKIN' THROUGH THE WINDOWS JACKSON 5
LOOKING AFTER NO. 1 BOOMTOWN RATS
LOOKING AT MIDNIGHT IMAGINATION
LOOKING FOR A LOVE JOYCE SIMS
LOOKING FOR A NEW LOVE JODY WATLEY
LOOKING FOR A PLACE MANIA
LOOKING FOR A SONG BIG AUDIO
LOOKING FOR ATLANTIS PREFAB SPROUT
LOOKING FOR CLUES ROBERT PALMER
LOOKING FOR LEWIS AND CLARK LONG RYDERS
LOOKING FOR LINDA HUE & CRY
LOOKING FOR LOVE KAREN RAMIREZ
LOOKING FOR LOVE TONIGHT FAT LARRY'S BAND
LOOKING FOR THE SUMMER CHRIS REA
LOOKING HIGH HIGH HIGH BRYAN JOHNSON
LOOKING THROUGH PATIENT EYES PM DAWN
LOOKING THROUGH THE EYES OF LOVE GENE PITNEY
LOOKING THROUGH THE EYES OF LOVE PARTRIDGE FAMILY STARRING DAVID CASSIDY
LOOKING THROUGH YOUR EYES LeANN RIMES
LOOKING UP MICHELLE GAYLE
LOOKS LIKE I'M IN LOVE AGAIN KEY WEST FEATURING ERIK
LOOKS LOOKS LOOKS SPARKS
LOOP-DE-LOOP FRANKIE VAUGHAN
LOOP DI LOVE SHAG
LOOPS OF FURY EP CHEMICAL BROTHERS
LOOPS OF INFINITY COSMIC BABY
LOOPZILLA GEORGE CLINTON
LOOSE THERAPY?
LOOSE CANNON KILLING JOKE
LOOSE FIT HAPPY MONDAYS
LOOSEN YOUR HOLD SOUTH
LOPEZ 808 STATE
LORDS OF THE NEW CHURCH TASMIN ARCHER
LORELEI LONNIE DONEGAN
LORRAINE BAD MANNERS
LOS AMERICANOS ESPIRITU
LOS ANGELES IS BURNING BAD RELIGION
LOSE CONTROL JAMES
LOSE IT SUPERGRASS
LOSE MY BREATH DESTINY'S CHILD
LOSE YOURSELF EMINEM
LOSER [A] BECK
LOSER [B] THUNDER
LOSING GRIP AVRIL LAVIGNE
LOSING MY GRIP SAMSON
LOSING MY MIND LIZA MINNELLI
LOSING MY RELIGION R.E.M.
LOSING YOU [A] BRENDA LEE
LOSING YOU [B] DUSTY SPRINGFIELD
LOST AGAIN YELLO
LOST AND FOUND D*NOTE
THE LOST ART OF KEEPING A SECRET QUEENS OF THE STONE AGE
LOST CAT CATATONIA
LOST FOR WORDS RONAN KEATING
LOST IN A MELODY DELAYS
LOST IN AMERICA ALICE COOPER
LOST IN EMOTION [A] LISA LISA & CULT JAM
LOST IN EMOTION [B] JOHN 'OO' FLEMING
LOST IN FRANCE BONNIE TYLER
LOST IN LOVE [A] UP YER RONSON FEATURING MARY PEARCE

LOST IN LOVE [B] LEGEND B
LOST IN MUSIC [A] SISTER SLEDGE
LOST IN MUSIC [B] STEREO MC'S
LOST IN SPACE [A] APOLLO FOUR FORTY
LOST IN SPACE [B] ELECTRASY
LOST IN SPACE [C] LIGHTHOUSE FAMILY
LOST IN THE PLOT DEARS
LOST IN THE TRANSLATION PACIFICA
LOST IN YOU [A] ROD STEWART
LOST IN YOU [B] GARTH BROOKS
LOST IN YOUR EYES DEBBIE GIBSON
LOST IN YOUR LOVE TONY HADLEY
LOST JOHN LONNIE DONEGAN
LOST MYSELF LONGPIGS
LOST WEEKEND LLOYD COLE & THE COMMOTIONS
LOST WITHOUT YOU [A] JAYN HANNA
LOST WITHOUT YOU [B] DELTA GOODREM
LOST WITHOUT YOUR LOVE BREAD
LOST YOU SOMEWHERE CHICANE
A LOT OF LOVE MARTI PELLOW
LOTUS R.E.M.
LOUIE LOUIE KINGSMEN
LOUIE LOUIE MOTORHEAD
LOUIE LOUIE FAT BOYS
LOUIE LOUIE THREE AMIGOS
LOUIS QUATORZE BOW WOW WOW
LOUISE [A] PHIL EVERLY
LOUISE [B] HUMAN LEAGUE
LOUNGER DOGS DIE IN HOT CARS
LOUNGIN LL COOL J
L.O.V.E. AL GREEN
LOVE JOHN LENNON
LOVE JIMMY NAIL
LOVE & DEVOTION (MC SAR &) THE REAL McCOY
LOVE ACTION (I BELIEVE IN LOVE) HUMAN LEAGUE
LOVE AIN'T GONNA WAIT FOR YOU S CLUB
LOVE AIN'T HERE ANYMORE TAKE THAT
LOVE AIN'T NO STRANGER WHITESNAKE
LOVE ALL DAY NICK HEYWARD
LOVE ALL THE HURT AWAY ARETHA FRANKLIN & GEORGE BENSON
LOVE AND AFFECTION JOAN ARMATRADING
LOVE AND AFFECTION SINITTA
LOVE AND AFFECTION MR PINK PRESENTS THE PROGRAM
LOVE AND ANGER KATE BUSH
LOVE AND DESIRE (PART 1) ARPEGGIO
LOVE AND HAPPINESS (YEMAYA Y OCHUN) RIVER OCEAN FEATURING INDIA
LOVE AND KISSES DANNII MINOGUE
LOVE AND LONELINESS MOTORS
LOVE AND MARRIAGE FRANK SINATRA
LOVE AND MONEY LOVE & MONEY
LOVE AND PAIN CARLTON
LOVE AND PRIDE KING
LOVE AND REGRET DEACON BLUE
LOVE AND TEARS NAOMI CAMPBELL
LOVE AND UNDERSTANDING CHER
LOVE ANYWAY MIKE SCOTT
LOVE AT FIRST SIGHT [A] KYLIE MINOGUE
LOVE @ 1ST SIGHT [B] MARY J BLIGE FEATURING METHOD MAN
LOVE AT FIRST SIGHT (JE T'AIME...MOI NON PLUS) SOUNDS NICE
LOVE ATTACK SHAKIN' STEVENS
LOVE BALLAD GEORGE BENSON
LOVE BE MY LOVER (PLAYA SOL) NOVACANE VS NO ONE DRIVING
LOVE BITES DEF LEPPARD
LOVE BLONDE KIM WILDE
LOVE BOMB BABY TIGERTAILZ

LOVE BREAKDOWN ROZALLA
LOVE BUG RAMSEY & FEN FEATURING LYNSEY MOORE
LOVE BUG – SWEETS FOR MY SWEET (MEDLEY) TINA CHARLES
LOVE BURNS BLACK REBEL MOTORCYCLE CLUB
LOVE CAN BUILD A BRIDGE CHER, CHRISSIE HYNDE & NENEH CHERRY WITH ERIC CLAPTON
LOVE CAN BUILD A BRIDGE CHILDREN FOR RWANDA
LOVE CAN MOVE MOUNTAINS CELINE DION
LOVE CAN'T TURN AROUND FARLEY 'JACKMASTER' FUNK
LOVE CAN'T TURN AROUND HEAVY WEATHER
THE LOVE CATS CURE
LOVE CHANGES EVERYTHING [A] CLIMIE FISHER
LOVE CHANGES EVERYTHING [B] MICHAEL BALL
LOVE CHILD [A] DIANA ROSS & THE SUPREMES
LOVE CHILD [B] GOODBYE MR MACKENZIE
LOVE CITY GROOVE LOVE CITY GROOVE
LOVE COME DOWN [A] EVELYN KING
LOVE COME DOWN [A] ALISON LIMERICK
LOVE COME DOWN [B] EVE GALLAGHER
LOVE COME HOME OUR TRIBE WITH FRANKE PHAROAH & KRISTINE W
LOVE COME RESCUE ME LOVESTATION
LOVE COMES AGAIN TIESTO FEATURING BT
LOVE COMES QUICKLY PET SHOP BOYS
LOVE COMES TO MIND CHIMES
LOVE COMMANDMENTS GISELE JACKSON
LOVE CONQUERS ALL [A] DEEP PURPLE
LOVE CONQUERS ALL [B] ABC
LOVE DANCE VISION
LOVE DETECTIVE ARAB STRAP
LOVE DISCO STYLE EROTIC DRUM BAND
LOVE DOESN'T HAVE TO HURT ATOMIC KITTEN
LOVE DON'T COME EASY ALARM
LOVE DON'T COST A THING JENNIFER LOPEZ
LOVE DON'T LET ME GO DAVID GUETTA FEATURING CHRIS WILLIS
LOVE DON'T LIVE URBAN BLUES PROJECT PRESENTS MICHAEL PROCTER
LOVE DON'T LIVE HERE ANYMORE ROSE ROYCE
LOVE DON'T LIVE HERE ANYMORE JIMMY NAIL
LOVE DON'T LIVE HERE ANYMORE DOUBLE TROUBLE FEATURING JANETTE SEWELL & CARL BROWN
LOVE DON'T LOVE YOU EN VOGUE
LOVE ENOUGH FOR TWO PRIMA DONNA
LOVE ENUFF SOUL II SOUL
LOVE EVICTION QUARTZ LOCK FEATURING LONNIE GORDON
LOVE FOOLOSOPHY JAMIROQUAI
LOVE FOR LIFE LISA MOORISH
THE LOVE GAME MUDLARKS
LOVE GAMES [A] DRIFTERS
LOVE GAMES [B] LEVEL 42
LOVE GAMES [C] BELLE & THE DEVOTIONS
LOVE GLOVE VISAGE
LOVE GROOVE (GROOVE WITH YOU) SMOOTH
LOVE GROWS (WHERE MY ROSEMARY GOES) EDISON LIGHTHOUSE
LOVE GUARANTEED DAMAGE
LOVE HANGOVER [A] DIANA ROSS
LOVE HANGOVER [A] ASSOCIATES
LOVE HANGOVER [A] PAULINE HENRY
LOVE HANGOVER [B] SCARLET
LOVE HAS COME AGAIN HUMAN MOVEMENT FEATURING SOPHIE MOLET
LOVE HAS COME AROUND DONALD BYRD
LOVE HAS FOUND ITS WAY DENNIS BROWN
LOVE HAS PASSED AWAY SUPERNATURALS
LOVE HER WALKER BROTHERS
LOVE HERE I COME BAD BOYS INC

LOVE HIT ME MAXINE NIGHTINGALE
LOVE HOUSE SAMANTHA FOX
LOVE HOW YOU FEEL SHARON REDD
LOVE HURTS [A] JIM CAPALDI
LOVE HURTS [A] CHER
LOVE HURTS [B] PETER POLYCARPOU
THE LOVE I LOST HAROLD MELVIN & THE BLUENOTES
THE LOVE I LOST WEST END FEATURING SYBIL
LOVE II LOVE DAMAGE
LOVE IN A PEACEFUL WORLD LEVEL 42
LOVE IN AN ELEVATOR AEROSMITH
LOVE IN ANGER ARMOURY SHOW
LOVE IN C MINOR CERRONE
LOVE IN ITSELF.2 DEPECHE MODE
LOVE IN THE FIRST DEGREE BANANARAMA
LOVE IN THE KEY OF C BELINDA CARLISLE
LOVE IN THE NATURAL WAY KIM WILDE
LOVE IN THE SUN GLITTER BAND
THE LOVE IN YOUR EYES VICKY LEANDROS
THE LOVE IN YOUR EYES DANIEL O'DONNELL
LOVE INFINITY SILVER CITY
LOVE INJECTION TRUSSEL
LOVE INSIDE SHARON FORRESTER
LOVE IS... VIKKI
LOVE IS ALANNAH MYLES
LOVE IS A BATTLEFIELD PAT BENATAR
LOVE IS A BEAUTIFUL THING AL GREEN
LOVE IS A GOLDEN RING FRANKIE LAINE
LOVE IS A KILLER VIXEN
LOVE IS A MANY SPLENDOURED THING FOUR ACES FEATURING AL ALBERTS
LOVE IS A STRANGER EURYTHMICS
LOVE IS A WONDERFUL COLOUR ICICLE WORKS
LOVE IS A WONDERFUL THING MICHAEL BOLTON
LOVE IS ALL [A] MALCOLM ROBERTS
LOVE IS ALL [A] ENGELBERT HUMPERDINCK
LOVE IS ALL [B] RAPTURE
LOVE IS ALL AROUND [A] TROGGS
LOVE IS ALL AROUND [A] WET WET WET
LOVE IS ALL AROUND [B] DJ BOBO
LOVE IS ALL IS ALRIGHT UB40
LOVE IS ALL THAT MATTERS HUMAN LEAGUE
LOVE IS ALL WE NEED MARY J. BLIGE
LOVE IS BLUE [A] JEFF BECK
LOVE IS BLUE (L'AMOUR EST BLEU) [A] PAUL MAURIAT
LOVE IS BLUE [B] EDWARD BALL
LOVE IS CONTAGIOUS TAJA SEVELLE
LOVE IS EVERYWHERE CICERO
LOVE IS FOREVER BILLY OCEAN
LOVE IS HERE AND NOW YOU'RE GONE SUPREMES
LOVE IS HOLY KIM WILDE
LOVE IS IN CONTROL (FINGER ON THE TRIGGER) DONNA SUMMER
LOVE IS IN THE AIR JOHN PAUL YOUNG
LOVE IS IN THE AIR MILK & SUGAR/JOHN PAUL YOUNG
LOVE IS IN YOUR EYES LEMON TREES
LOVE IS JUST THE GREAT PRETENDER ANIMAL NIGHTLIFE
LOVE IS LIFE HOT CHOCOLATE
LOVE IS LIKE A VIOLIN KEN DODD
LOVE IS LIKE OXYGEN SWEET
LOVE IS LOVE BARRY RYAN
LOVE IS NOT A GAME J MAJIK FEATURING KATHY BROWN
LOVE IS ON THE ONE XAVIER
LOVE IS ON THE WAY LUTHER VANDROSS
LOVE IS ONLY A FEELING DARKNESS
LOVE IS SO EASY STARGARD
LOVE IS SO NICE URBAN SOUL
LOVE IS STRANGE EVERLY BROTHERS
LOVE IS STRONG ROLLING STONES

LOVE IS STRONGER THAN DEATH THE THE
LOVE IS STRONGER THAN PRIDE SADE
LOVE IS THE ANSWER ENGLAND DAN & JOHN FORD COLEY
LOVE IS THE ART LIVING IN A BOX
LOVE IS THE DRUG ROXY MUSIC
LOVE IS THE DRUG GRACE JONES
LOVE IS THE GOD MARIA NAYLER
LOVE IS THE GUN BLUE MERCEDES
LOVE IS THE ICON BARRY WHITE
LOVE IS THE KEY CHARLATANS
LOVE IS THE LAW SEAHORSES
LOVE IS THE MESSAGE LOVE INC
LOVE IS THE SEVENTH WAVE STING
LOVE IS THE SLUG WE'VE GOT A FUZZBOX & WE'RE GONNA USE IT
LOVE IS THE SWEETEST THING PETER SKELLERN FEATURING GRIMETHORPE COLLIERY BAND
(LOVE IS) THE TENDER TRAP FRANK SINATRA
LOVE IS WAR BRILLIANT
LOVE IZ ERICK SERMON
LOVE KILLS [A] FREDDIE MERCURY
LOVE KILLS [B] JOE STRUMMER
LOVE KISSES AND HEARTACHES MAUREEN EVANS
LOVE LADY DAMAGE
LOVE LETTER MARC ALMOND
LOVE LETTERS [A] KETTY LESTER
LOVE LETTERS [A] ELVIS PRESLEY
LOVE LETTERS [A] ALISON MOYET
LOVE LETTERS [B] ALI
LOVE LETTERS IN THE SAND PAT BOONE
LOVE LETTERS IN THE SAND VINCE HILL
LOVE LIES LOST HELEN TERRY
LOVE LIGHT IN FLIGHT STEVIE WONDER
LOVE LIKE A FOUNTAIN IAN BROWN
LOVE LIKE A MAN TEN YEARS AFTER
LOVE LIKE A RIVER CLIMIE FISHER
LOVE LIKE A ROCKET BOB GELDOF
LOVE LIKE BLOOD KILLING JOKE
LOVE LIKE THIS FAITH EVANS
LOVE LIKE YOU AND ME GARY GLITTER
A LOVE LIKE YOURS IKE & TINA TURNER
L.O.V.E...LOVE ORANGE JUICE
LOVE LOVE LOVE BOBBY HEBB
LOVE, LOVE, LOVE – HERE I COME ROLLO GOES MYSTIC
LOVE LOVES TO LOVE LOVE LULU
LOVE MACHINE [A] ELVIS PRESLEY
LOVE MACHINE (PART 1) [B] MIRACLES
LOVE MACHINE [C] GIRLS ALOUD
LOVE MADE ME VIXEN
LOVE MAKES NO SENSE ALEXANDER O'NEAL
LOVE MAKES THE WORLD GO ROUND [A] PERRY COMO
LOVE MAKES THE WORLD GO ROUND [A] JETS
LOVE MAKES THE WORLD GO ROUND [B] DON-E
LOVE MAN OTIS REDDING
LOVE ME [A] DIANA ROSS
LOVE ME [B] YVONNE ELLIMAN
LOVE ME [B] MARTINE McCUTCHEON
LOVE ME [C] PATRIC
LOVE ME AND LEAVE ME SEAHORSES
LOVE ME AS IF THERE WERE NO TOMORROW NAT 'KING' COLE
LOVE ME BABY SUSAN CADOGAN
LOVE ME DO BEATLES
LOVE ME FOR A REASON OSMONDS
LOVE ME FOR A REASON BOYZONE
LOVE ME FOREVER EYDIE GORME
LOVE ME FOREVER MARION RYAN
LOVE ME FOREVER FOUR ESQUIRES
LOVE ME LIKE A LOVER TINA CHARLES
LOVE ME LIKE I LOVE YOU BAY CITY ROLLERS

LOVE ME LIKE THIS REAL TO REEL
LOVE ME LOVE MY DOG PETER SHELLEY
LOVE ME NOW [A] BRIANA CORRIGAN
LOVE ME NOW [B] SECRET KNOWLEDGE
LOVE ME OR LEAVE ME SAMMY DAVIS Jr.
LOVE ME OR LEAVE ME DORIS DAY
LOVE ME RIGHT NOW ROSE ROYCE
LOVE ME RIGHT (OH SHEILA) ANGEL CITY FEATURING LARA McALLEN
LOVE ME TENDER ELVIS PRESLEY
LOVE ME TENDER RICHARD CHAMBERLAIN
LOVE ME TENDER ROLAND RAT SUPERSTAR
LOVE ME THE RIGHT WAY RAPINATION & KYM MAZELLE
LOVE ME TO SLEEP HOT CHOCOLATE
LOVE ME TONIGHT [A] TOM JONES
LOVE ME TONIGHT [B] TREVOR WALTERS
LOVE ME WARM AND TENDER PAUL ANKA
LOVE ME WITH ALL YOUR HEART KARL DENVER
LOVE MEETING LOVE LEVEL 42
LOVE MISSILE F1-11 SIGUE SIGUE SPUTNIK
LOVE MOVES IN MYSTERIOUS WAYS JULIA FORDHAM
LOVE NEEDS NO DISGUISE GARY NUMAN & DRAMATIS
LOVE NEVER DIES... BELINDA CARLISLE
LOVE OF A LIFETIME [A] CHAKA KHAN
LOVE OF A LIFETIME [B] HONEYZ
LOVE OF MY LIFE [A] DOOLEYS
LOVE OF MY LIFE [B] QUEEN
THE LOVE OF RICHARD NIXON MANIC STREET PREACHERS
LOVE OF THE COMMON PEOPLE NICKY THOMAS
LOVE OF THE COMMON PEOPLE PAUL YOUNG
LOVE OF THE LOVED CILLA BLACK
LOVE OH LOVE LIONEL RICHIE
LOVE ON A FARMBOY'S WAGES XTC
LOVE ON A MOUNTAIN TOP ROBERT KNIGHT
LOVE ON A MOUNTAIN TOP SINITTA
LOVE ON A SUMMER NIGHT McCRARYS
LOVE ON LOVE E-ZEE POSSEE
LOVE ON LOVE CANDI STATON
LOVE ON THE LINE [A] BARCLAY JAMES HARVEST
LOVE ON THE LINE [B] BLAZIN' SQUAD
LOVE ON THE NORTHERN LINE NORTHERN LINE
LOVE ON THE ROCKS NEIL DIAMOND
LOVE ON THE RUN CHICANE FEATURING PETER CUNNAH
LOVE ON THE SIDE BROKEN ENGLISH
LOVE ON YOUR SIDE THOMPSON TWINS
LOVE OR MONEY [A] BLACKWELLS
LOVE OR MONEY [A] JIMMY CRAWFORD
LOVE OR MONEY [A] BILLY FURY
LOVE OR MONEY [B] SAMMY HAGAR
LOVE OR NOTHING DIANA BROWN & BARRIE K. SHARPE
LOVE OVER GOLD (LIVE) DIRE STRAITS
LOVE OVERBOARD GLADYS KNIGHT & THE PIPS
LOVE PAINS HAZELL DEAN
LOVE PAINS LIZA MINNELLI
THE LOVE PARADE DREAM ACADEMY
LOVE PATROL DOOLEYS
LOVE, PEACE & GREASE BT
LOVE, PEACE & HAPPINESS LOST BOYZ
LOVE PEACE AND UNDERSTANDING DREAM FREQUENCY
LOVE PLUS ONE HAIRCUT 100
LOVE POTION NO. 9 TYGERS OF PAN TANG
LOVE POWER DIONNE WARWICK & JEFFREY OSBORNE
LOVE PROFUSION MADONNA
LOVE REACTION DIVINE
LOVE REALLY HURTS WITHOUT YOU BILLY OCEAN
LOVE REARS ITS UGLY HEAD LIVING COLOUR

LOVE REMOVAL MACHINE CULT
LOVE RENDEZVOUS M PEOPLE
LOVE RESURRECTION ALISON MOYET
LOVE RESURRECTION D'LUX
LOVE REVOLUTION PHIXX
LOVE ROLLERCOASTER RED HOT CHILI PEPPERS
LOVE RULES WEST END
THE LOVE SCENE JOE
LOVE SCENES BEVERLEY CRAVEN
LOVE SEE NO COLOUR FARM
LOVE SENSATION 911
LOVE SHACK B-52's
LOVE SHADOW FASHION
LOVE SHINE RHYTHM SOURCE
LOVE SHINE A LIGHT KATRINA & THE WAVES
LOVE SHINES THROUGH CHAKRA
LOVE SHOULD BE A CRIME O-TOWN
LOVE SHOULDA BROUGHT YOU HOME TONI BRAXTON
LOVE SHY KRISTINE BLOND
LOVE SICK BOB DYLAN
LOVE SITUATION MARK FISHER FEATURING DOTTY GREEN
LOVE SLAVE WEDDING PRESENT
LOVE SNEAKIN' UP ON YOU BONNIE RAITT
A LOVE SO BEAUTIFUL MICHAEL BOLTON
LOVE SO BRIGHT MARK SHAW
LOVE SO RIGHT BEE GEES
LOVE SO STRONG SECRET LIFE
LOVE SONG [A] DAMNED
LOVE SONG [B] SIMPLE MINDS
LOVE SONG [C] UTAH SAINTS
LOVE SONG FOR A VAMPIRE ANNIE LENNOX
LOVE SONGS ARE BACK AGAIN (MEDLEY) BAND OF GOLD
THE LOVE SONGS EP DANIEL O'DONNELL
LOVE SPREADS STONE ROSES
LOVE STIMULATION HUMATE
LOVE STORY [A] JETHRO TULL
LOVE STORY [B] LAYO & BUSHWACKA
LOVE STORY (VS FINALLY) LAYO & BUSHWACKA
LOVE STRAIN KYM MAZELLE
A LOVE SUPREME WILL DOWNING
LOVE TAKE OVER FIVE STAR
LOVE TAKES TIME MARIAH CAREY
LOVE THE LIFE JTQ WITH NOEL McKOY
LOVE THE ONE YOU'RE WITH STEPHEN STILLS
LOVE THE ONE YOU'RE WITH BUCKS FIZZ
LOVE THE ONE YOU'RE WITH LUTHER VANDROSS
LOVE THEM EAMON FEATURING GHOSTFACE
LOVE THEME FROM 'A STAR IS BORN' (EVERGREEN) BARBRA STREISAND
LOVE THEME FROM SPARTACUS TERRY CALLIER
LOVE THEME FROM THE GODFATHER ANDY WILLIAMS
LOVE THEME FROM 'THE THORN BIRDS' JUAN MARTIN
LOVE THING [A] PASADENAS
LOVE THING [B] TINA TURNER
LOVE THING [C] EVOLUTION
LOVE TIMES LOVE HEAVY PETTIN'
LOVE TO HATE YOU ERASURE
LOVE TO LOVE YOU CORRS
LOVE TO LOVE YOU BABY DONNA SUMMER
LOVE TO SEE YOU CRY ENRIQUE IGLESIAS
LOVE TO STAY ALTERED IMAGES
LOVE TOGETHER L.A. MIX FEATURING KEVIN HENRY
LOVE TOUCH ROD STEWART
LOVE TOWN BOOKER NEWBURY III
LOVE TRAIN [A] O'JAYS
LOVE TRAIN [B] HOLLY JOHNSON
LOVE TRIAL KELLY MARIE
LOVE, TRUTH AND HONESTY BANANARAMA
LOVE...THY WILL BE DONE MARTIKA

LOVE U 4 LIFE JODECI
LOVE U MORE SUNSCREEM
LOVE UNLIMITED FUN LOVIN' CRIMINALS
LOVE WALKED IN THUNDER
LOVE WARS WOMACK & WOMACK
LOVE WASHES OVER ART OF TRANCE
LOVE WHAT YOU DO DIVINE COMEDY
LOVE WILL COME TOMSKI FEATURING JAN JOHNSTON
LOVE WILL COME THROUGH TRAVIS
LOVE WILL CONQUER ALL LIONEL RICHIE
LOVE WILL FIND A WAY [A] DAVID GRANT
LOVE WILL FIND A WAY [B] YES
LOVE WILL KEEP US ALIVE EAGLES
LOVE WILL KEEP US TOGETHER CAPTAIN & TENNILLE
LOVE WILL KEEP US TOGETHER JTQ FEATURING ALISON
    LIMERICK
LOVE WILL LEAD YOU BACK TAYLOR DAYNE
LOVE WILL MAKE YOU FAIL IN SCHOOL ROCKY SHARPE
    & THE REPLAYS FEATURING THE TOP LINERS
LOVE WILL NEVER DO (WITHOUT YOU) JANET JACKSON
LOVE WILL SAVE THE DAY WHITNEY HOUSTON
LOVE WILL SET YOU FREE (JAMBE MYTH) STARCHASER
LOVE WILL TEAR US APART JOY DIVISION
LOVE WON'T LET ME WAIT MAJOR HARRIS
LOVE WON'T WAIT GARY BARLOW
LOVE WORTH DYING FOR THUNDER
A LOVE WORTH WAITING FOR SHAKIN' STEVENS
LOVE X LOVE GEORGE BENSON
LOVE YOU ALL MY LIFETIME CHAKA KHAN
LOVE YOU ANYWAY DE NADA
LOVE YOU DOWN READY FOR THE WORLD
LOVE YOU INSIDE OUT BEE GEES
LOVE YOU LIKE MAD VS
LOVE YOU MORE BUZZCOCKS
THE LOVE YOU SAVE JACKSON 5
LOVE YOU SOME MORE CEVIN FISHER FEATURING
    SHEILA SMITH
LOVE YOUR MONEY DAISY CHAINSAW
LOVE YOUR SEXY...!! BYKER GROOOVE!
LOVE ZONE BILLY OCEAN
LOVEBIRDS DODGY
LOVEDRIVE SCORPIONS
LOVEFOOL CARDIGANS
LOVELIGHT (RIDE ON A LOVE TRAIN) JAYN HANNA
LOVELY BUBBA SPARXXX
LOVELY DAUGHTER MERZ
LOVELY DAY BILL WITHERS
LOVELY DAZE JAZZY JEFF & FRESH PRINCE
LOVELY MONEY DAMNED
LOVELY ONE JACKSONS
LOVELY THING REGGAE PHILHARMONIC ORCHESTRA
LOVENEST WEDDING PRESENT
LOVER [A] JOE ROBERTS
LOVER [B] DAN REED NETWORK
LOVER [C] RACHEL McFARLANE
LOVER COME BACK TO ME DEAD OR ALIVE
THE LOVER IN ME SHEENA EASTON
THE LOVER IN YOU SUGARHILL GANG
LOVER LOVER LOVER IAN McCULLOCH
LOVER PLEASE VERNONS GIRLS
A LOVER SPURNED MARC ALMOND
THE LOVER THAT YOU ARE PULSE FEATURING
    ANTOINETTE ROBERTSON
LOVERBOY [A] BILLY OCEAN
LOVERBOY [B] CHAIRMEN OF THE BOARD FEATURING
    GENERAL JOHNSON
LOVERBOY [C] MARIAH CAREY
LOVERIDE NUANCE FEATURING VIKKI LOVE
THE LOVERS ALEXANDER O'NEAL
A LOVER'S CONCERTO TOYS
A LOVERS HOLIDAY CHANGE

LOVER'S LANE GEORGIO
LOVERS OF THE WORLD UNITE DAVID & JONATHAN
THE LOVERS WE WERE MICHAEL BALL
LOVE'S A LOADED GUN ALICE COOPER
LOVE'S A PRIMA DONNA STEVE HARLEY
LOVE'S ABOUT TO CHANGE MY HEART DONNA SUMMER
LOVE'S BEEN GOOD TO ME FRANK SINATRA
LOVE'S COMIN' AT YA MELBA MOORE
LOVE'S CRASHING WAVES DIFFORD & TILBROOK
LOVE'S DIVINE SEAL
LOVE'S EASY TEARS COCTEAU TWINS
LOVE'S GONNA GET YOU [A] UK PLAYERS
LOVE'S GONNA GET YOU [B] JOCELYN BROWN
LOVE'S GOT A HOLD ON MY HEART STEPS
LOVE'S GOT ME LOOSE ENDS
LOVE'S GOT ME ON A TRIP SO HIGH LONI CLARK
LOVE'S GOTTA HOLD ON ME [A] DOLLAR
LOVE'S GOTTA HOLD ON ME [B] ZOO EXPERIENCE
    FEATURING DESTRY
LOVE'S GREAT ADVENTURE ULTRAVOX
LOVE'S JUST A BROKEN HEART CILLA BLACK
LOVE'S MADE A FOOL OF YOU CRICKETS
LOVE'S MADE A FOOL OF YOU BUDDY HOLLY
LOVE'S MADE A FOOL OF YOU MATCHBOX
LOVES ME LIKE A ROCK PAUL SIMON
LOVE'S ON EVERY CORNER DANNII MINOGUE
LOVE'S SUCH A WONDERFUL THING REAL THING
LOVE'S SWEET EXILE MANIC STREET PREACHERS
LOVE'S TAKEN OVER CHANTE MOORE
LOVE'S THEME LOVE UNLIMITED ORCHESTRA
LOVE'S UNKIND DONNA SUMMER
LOVE'S UNKIND SOPHIE LAWRENCE
LOVESICK [A] GANG STARR
LOVESICK [B] UNDERCOVER FEATURING JOHN
    MATTHEWS
LOVESICK BLUES FRANK IFIELD
LOVESONG CURE
LOVESTRUCK MADNESS
LOVETOWN PETER GABRIEL
LOVEY DOVEY TONY TERRY
LOVIN' CRW
LOVIN' EACH DAY RONAN KEATING
LOVIN' IS EASY HEAR'SAY
LOVIN' (LET ME LOVE YOU) APACHE INDIAN
LOVIN' LIVIN' AND GIVIN' DIANA ROSS
LOVIN' ON THE SIDE REID
LOVIN' THINGS MARMALADE
LOVIN' UP A STORM JERRY LEE LEWIS
LOVIN' YOU SHANICE
LOVIN' YOU UBM
LOVIN' YOU SPARKLE
LOVING AND FREE KIKI DEE
LOVING ARMS ELVIS PRESLEY
LOVING EVERY MINUTE LIGHTHOUSE FAMILY
LOVING JUST FOR FUN KELLY MARIE
LOVING ON THE LOSING SIDE TOMMY HUNT
LOVING THE ALIEN DAVID BOWIE
LOVING THE ALIEN SCUMFROG VS BOWIE
LOVING YOU [A] ELVIS PRESLEY
LOVING YOU [B] MINNIE RIPERTON
LOVING YOU [B] MASSIVO FEATURING TRACY
LOVING YOU '03 [B] MARC ET CLAUDE
LOVING YOU [C] DONALD BYRD
LOVING YOU [D] CHRIS REA
LOVING YOU [E] FEARGAL SHARKEY
LOVING YOU AGAIN CHRIS REA
LOVING YOU AIN'T EASY PAGLIARO
LOVING YOU HAS MADE ME BANANAS GUY MARKS
LOVING YOU IS SWEETER THAN EVER FOUR TOPS
LOVING YOU IS SWEETER THAN EVER NICK KAMEN
LOVING YOU MORE BT FEATURING VINCENT COVELLO

LOVING YOU (OLE OLE OLE) BRIAN HARVEY & THE
    REFUGEE CREW
LOVING YOU'S A DIRTY JOB BUT SOMEBODY'S GOTTA DO
    IT BONNIE TYLER, GUEST VOALS TODD RUNDGREN
LOW [A] CRACKER
LOW [B] FOO FIGHTERS
LOW [C] KELLY CLARKSON
LOW FIVE SNEAKER PIMPS
LOW LIFE IN HIGH PLACES THUNDER
LOW RIDER WAR
LOWDOWN [A] BOZ SCAGGS
LOWDOWN [A] HINDSIGHT
LOWDOWN [B] ELECTRAFIXION
LOWRIDER CYPRESS HILL
THE LOYALISER FATIMA MANSIONS
LSD (EP) KAOTIC CHEMISTRY
LSF KASABIAN
LSI SHAMEN
LUCAS WITH THE LID OFF LUCAS
LUCHINI AKA (THIS IS IT) CAMP LO
LUCILLE [A] LITTLE RICHARD
LUCILLE [A] EVERLY BROTHERS
LUCILLE [B] KENNY ROGERS
LUCKY BRITNEY SPEARS
LUCKY 7 MEGAMIX UK MIXMASTERS
LUCKY DEVIL FRANK IFIELD
LUCKY DEVIL CARL DOBKINS
LUCKY FIVE RUSS CONWAY
LUCKY LIPS CLIFF RICHARD
LUCKY LOVE ACE OF BASE
LUCKY LUCKY ME MARVIN GAYE
LUCKY MAN VERVE
LUCKY NUMBER LENE LOVICH
LUCKY ONE AMY GRANT
THE LUCKY ONE LAURA BRANIGAN
LUCKY PRESSURE RONI SIZE REPRAZENT
LUCKY STAR [A] MADONNA
LUCKY STAR [B] SUPERFUNK FEATURING RON
    CARROLL
LUCKY STAR [C] BASEMENT JAXX FEATURING DIZZEE
    RASCAL
LUCKY STARS DEAN FRIEDMAN
LUCKY TOWN (LIVE) BRUCE SPRINGSTEEN
LUCKY YOU LIGHTNING SEEDS
LUCRETIA MY REFLECTION SISTERS OF MERCY
LUCY HABIT
LUCY IN THE SKY WITH DIAMONDS ELTON JOHN
LUDI DREAM WARRIORS
LUKA SUZANNE VEGA
LULLABY [A] CURE
LULLABY [B] SHAWN MULLINS
LULLABY [C] MELANIE B
LULLABY [D] STARSAILOR
LULLABY [E] LEMAR
LULLABY OF BROADWAY WINIFRED SHAW
LULLABY OF THE LEAVES VENTURES
LUMBERED LONNIE DONEGAN
LUMP PRESIDENTS OF THE UNITED STATES OF
    AMERICA
THE LUNATICS (HAVE TAKEN OVER THE ASYLUM) FUN
    BOY THREE
LUNCH OR DINNER SUNSHINE ANDERSON
LUSH ORBITAL
LUST FOR LIFE IGGY POP
LUTON AIRPORT CATS U.K.
LUV 4 LUV ROBIN S
LUV DA SUNSHINE INTENSO PROJECT
LUV DUP HIGH FIDELITY
LUV IS COOL SYSTEM OF LIFE
LUV ME LUV ME SHAGGY
LUV U BETTER LL COOL J

LUV'D UP CRUSH
LUVSTRUCK SOUTHSIDE SPINNERS
LUVSTUFF SAGAT
A LA VIE, A L'AMOUR JAKIE QUARTZ
LYDIA DEAN FRIEDMAN
LYIN' EYES EAGLES
LYRIC ZWAN
LYRIC ON MY LIP TALI
MA BAKER BONEY M
MA HE'S MAKING EYES AT ME JOHNNY OTIS & HIS
    ORCHESTRA WITH MARIE ADAMS & THE THREE
    TONS OF JOY
MA HE'S MAKING EYES AT ME LENA ZAVARONI
MA I DON'T LOVE HER CLIPSE FEATURING FAITH EVANS
MA SAYS PA SAYS DORIS DAY & JOHNNIE RAY
MA SOLITUDA CATHERINE WHEEL
MA-MA-MA-BELLE ELECTRIC LIGHT ORCHESTRA
MACARENA LOS DEL RIO
MACARENA LOS DEL CHIPMUNKS
MACARENA LOS DEL MAR FEATURING WIL VELOZ
MACARTHUR PARK RICHARD HARRIS
MACARTHUR PARK DONNA SUMMER
MACDONALD'S CAVE PILTDOWN MEN
MACH 5 PRESIDENTS OF THE UNITED STATES OF
    AMERICA
MACHINE YEAH YEAH YEAH
MACHINE + SOUL GARY NUMAN
MACHINE GUN COMMODORES
MACHINE SAYS YES FC KAHUNA
MACHINEHEAD BUSH
MACHINERY SHEENA EASTON
MACK THE KNIFE BOBBY DARIN
MACK THE KNIFE LOUIS ARMSTRONG WITH HIS ALL-
    STARS
MACK THE KNIFE ELLA FITZGERALD
MACK THE KNIFE KING KURT
MACUSHLA BERNIE NOLAN
MAD ABOUT THE BOY DINAH WASHINGTON
MAD ABOUT YOU [A] BRUCE RUFFIN
MAD ABOUT YOU [B] BELINDA CARLISLE
MAD ABOUT YOU [C] STING
MAD DOG ELASTICA
MAD EYED SCREAMER CREATURES
MAD IF YA DON'T GAYLE & GILLIAN
MAD LOVE (EP) LUSH
MAD PASSIONATE LOVE BERNARD BRESSLAW
MAD WORLD TEARS FOR FEARS
MAD WORLD MICHAEL ANDREWS FEATURING GARY
    JULES
MADAGASCAR ART OF TRANCE
MADAM BUTTERFLY (UN BEL DI VEDREMO) MALCOLM
    McLAREN
MADAME HELGA STEREOPHONICS
MADCHESTER RAVE ON EP HAPPY MONDAYS
MADE FOR LOVIN' YOU ANASTACIA
MADE IN ENGLAND ELTON JOHN
MADE IN HEAVEN FREDDIE MERCURY
MADE IN TWO MINUTES BUG KAN & PLASTIC JAM
    FEATURING PATTI LOW & DOOGIE
MADE IT BACK BEVERLEY KNIGHT FEATURING
    REDMAN
MADE IT LAST HIGH CONTRAST
MADE OF STONE STONE ROSES
MADE TO LOVE (GIRLS GIRLS GIRLS) EDDIE HODGES
MADE YOU ADAM FAITH
MADE YOU LOOK NAS
THE MADISON RAY ELLINGTON
MADLY IN LOVE BROS
MADNESS (IS ALL IN THE MIND) MADNESS
MADNESS THING LEILANI
MAGGIE FOSTER & ALLEN

MAGGIE MAY ROD STEWART
MAGGIE'S FARM BOB DYLAN
MAGGIE'S FARM SPECIALS
MAGGIE'S FARM (LIVE) TIN MACHINE
MAGGIE'S LAST PARTY V.I.M.
MAGIC [A] PILOT
MAGIC [B] OLIVIA NEWTON-JOHN
MAGIC [C] SASHA WITH SAM MOLLISON
MAGIC [D] D-INFLUENCE
MAGIC [E] NICK DRAKE
MAGIC BUS WHO
MAGIC CARPET RIDE MIGHTY DUB KATZ
MAGIC FLY SPACE
MAGIC FLY MINIMALISTIX
THE MAGIC FRIEND 2 UNLIMITED
MAGIC HOUR [A] HALO JAMES
MAGIC HOUR [B] CAST
THE MAGIC IS THERE DANIEL O'DONNELL
MAGIC MANDRAKE SARR BAND
MAGIC MIND EARTH, WIND & FIRE
MAGIC MOMENTS PERRY COMO
MAGIC MOMENTS RONNIE HILTON
THE MAGIC NUMBER DE LA SOUL
THE MAGIC PIPER (OF LOVE) EDWYN COLLINS
MAGIC ROUNDABOUT JASPER CARROTT
MAGIC SMILE ROSIE VELA
MAGIC STYLE BADMAN
MAGIC TOUCH [A] ODYSSEY
MAGIC TOUCH [B] ROSE ROYCE
MAGIC TOUCH [C] LOOSE ENDS
MAGICAL BUCKS FIZZ
MAGICAL MYSTERY TOUR (DOUBLE EP) BEATLES
MAGICAL SPIEL BARRY RYAN
MAGIC'S BACK (THEME FROM 'THE GHOSTS OF OXFORD
    STREET') MALCOLM McLAREN FEATURING ALISON
    LIMERICK
MAGIC'S WAND WHODINI
MAGIC'S WAND (THE WHODINI ELECTRIC EP) WHODINI
THE MAGNIFICENT AGENT OO
THE MAGNIFICENT SEVEN [A] JOHN BARRY SEVEN
THE MAGNIFICENT SEVEN [A] AL CAIOLA
THE MAGNIFICENT SEVEN [B] CLASH
THE MAGNIFICENT 7 SCOOBIE
MAGNUM (DOUBLE SINGLE) MAGNUM
MAH NA MAH NA PIERO UMILIANI
MAID OF ORLEANS (THE WALTZ JOAN OF ARC)
    ORCHESTRAL MANOEUVRES IN THE DARK
MAIDEN JAPAN IRON MAIDEN
MAIDS WHEN YOU'RE YOUNG NEVER WED AN OLD MAN
    DUBLINERS
THE MAIGRET THEME JOE LOSS ORCHESTRA
THE MAIN ATTRACTION PAT BOONE
MAIN OFFENDER HIVES
MAIN THEME FROM 'THE THORNBIRDS' HENRY
    MANCINI
MAIN TITLE THEME FROM 'MAN WITH THE GOLDEN
    ARM' BILLY MAY
MAIN TITLE THEME FROM 'MAN WITH THE GOLDEN
    ARM' JET HARRIS
MAINSTREAM THEA GILMORE
MAIS OUI KING BROTHERS
THE MAJESTY OF ROCK SPINAL TAP
MAJOR TOM (COMING HOME) PETER SCHILLING
MAJORCA PETULA CLARK
MAKE A DAFT NOISE FOR CHRISTMAS GOODIES
MAKE A FAMILY GARY CLARK
MAKE A MOVE ON ME OLIVIA NEWTON-JOHN
MAKE BELIEVE IT'S YOUR FIRST TIME CARPENTERS
MAKE HER MINE NAT 'KING' COLE
MAKE IT A PARTY WINIFRED ATWELL
MAKE IT CLAP BUSTA RHYMES FEATURING SPLIFF STAR

MAKE IT EASY SHYSTIE
MAKE IT EASY ON YOURSELF WALKER BROTHERS
MAKE IT GOOD A1
MAKE IT HAPPEN MARIAH CAREY
MAKE IT HOT [A] NICOLE FEATURING MISSY
    'MISDEMEANOR' ELLIOTT
MAKE IT HOT [B] VS
MAKE IT LAST [A] SKIPWORTH & TURNER
MAKE IT LAST [B] EMBRACE
MAKE IT MINE SHAMEN
MAKE IT ON MY OWN ALISON LIMERICK
MAKE IT REAL SCORPIONS
MAKE IT RIGHT CHRISTIAN FALK FEATURING
    DEMETREUS
MAKE IT SOON TONY BRENT
MAKE IT TONIGHT WET WET WET
MAKE IT UP WITH LOVE ATL
MAKE IT WITH YOU [A] BREAD
MAKE IT WITH YOU [A] PASADENAS
MAKE IT WITH YOU [A] LET LOOSE
MAKE IT WITH YOU [B] UNIVERSAL
MAKE LOVE EASY FREDDIE JACKSON
MAKE LOVE LIKE A MAN DEF LEPPARD
MAKE LOVE TO ME [A] JO STAFFORD
MAKE LOVE TO ME [A] JOHN LEYTON & THE LeROYS
MAKE LOVE TO ME [B] JILL FRANCIS
MAKE LUV ROOM 5 FEATURING OLIVER CHEATHAM
MAKE ME AN ISLAND JOE DOLAN
MAKE ME BAD KORN
MAKE ME LAUGH ANTHRAX
MAKE ME SMILE (COME UP AND SEE ME) STEVE
    HARLEY & COCKNEY REBEL
MAKE ME SMILE (COME UP AND SEE ME) ERASURE
MAKE ME WANNA SCREAM BLU CANTRELL
MAKE MY BODY ROCK JOMANDA
MAKE MY DAY BUJU BANTON
MAKE MY HEART FLY PROCLAIMERS
MAKE MY LOVE SHAWN CHRISTOPHER
MAKE SOMEONE HAPPY JIMMY DURANTE
MAKE THAT MOVE SHALAMAR
MAKE THE DEAL OCEAN COLOUR SCENE
MAKE THE WORLD GO AWAY EDDY ARNOLD
MAKE THE WORLD GO AWAY DONNY & MARIE
    OSMOND
MAKE THE WORLD GO ROUND SANDY B
MAKE UP YOUR MIND BASS JUMPERS
MAKE WAY FOR NODDY NODDY
MAKE WAY FOR THE INDIAN APACHE INDIAN & TIM
    DOG
MAKE YOURS A HAPPY HOME GLADYS KNIGHT & THE
    PIPS
MAKES ME LOVE YOU ECLIPSE
MAKES ME WANNA DIE TRICKY
MAKIN' HAPPY CRYSTAL WATERS
MAKIN' IT DAVID NAUGHTON
MAKIN' LOVE FLOYD ROBINSON
MAKIN' OUT MARK OWEN
MAKIN' WHOOPEE RAY CHARLES
MAKING LOVE (OUT OF NOTHING AT ALL) BONNIE
    TYLER
MAKING PLANS FOR NIGEL XTC
MAKING THE MOST OF DODGY WITH THE KICK HORNS
MAKING TIME CREATION
MAKING UP AGAIN GOLDIE
MAKING YOUR MIND UP BUCKS FIZZ
MALE STRIPPER MAN 2 MAN MEET MAN PARRISH
MALIBU HOLE
MALT AND BARLEY BLUES McGUINNESS FLINT
MAMA [A] DAVID WHITFIELD
MAMA [A] CONNIE FRANCIS
MAMA [B] DAVE BERRY

MAMA [C] GENESIS
MAMA [D] KIM APPLEBY
MAMA [E] SPICE GIRLS
MAMA – WHO DA MAN? RICHARD BLACKWOOD
MAMA GAVE BIRTH TO THE SOUL CHILDREN QUEEN
    LATIFAH + DE LA SOUL
MAMA I'M COMING HOME OZZY OSBOURNE
MAMA NEVER TOLD ME SISTER SLEDGE
MAMA SAID [A] CARLEEN ANDERSON
MAMA SAID [B] METALLICA
MAMA SAID KNOCK YOU OUT LL COOL J
MAMA TOLD ME NOT TO COME THREE DOG NIGHT
MAMA TOLD ME NOT TO COME TOM JONES &
    STEREOPHONICS
MAMA USED TO SAY JUNIOR
MAMA USED TO SAY AZURE
MAMA WEER ALL CRAZEE NOW SLADE
MAMA'S BOY SUZI QUATRO
MAMA'S PEARL JACKSON 5
MAMBO ITALIANO ROSEMARY CLOONEY
MAMBO ITALIANO DEAN MARTIN
MAMBO ITALIANO SHAFT
MAMBO NO 5 BOB THE BUILDER
MAMBO NO 5 (A LITTLE BIT OF...) LOU BEGA
MAMBO ROCK BILL HALEY & HIS COMETS
MAMMA MIA ABBA
MAMMA MIA A*TEENS
MAMMY BLUE ROGER WHITTAKER
MAMOUNA BRYAN FERRY
MAMY BLUE POP TOPS
MAN ROSEMARY CLOONEY
MAN BEHIND THE MUSIC QUEEN PEN
THE MAN DON'T GIVE A FUCK SUPER FURRY ANIMALS
THE MAN FROM LARAMIE AL MARTINO
THE MAN FROM LARAMIE JIMMY YOUNG
MAN FROM MADRID TONY OSBORNE SOUND
    FEATURING JOANNE BROWN
MAN FROM NAZARETH JOHN PAUL JOANS
THE MAN I LOVE KATE BUSH & LARRY ADLER
THE MAN IN BLACK COZY POWELL
MAN IN THE MIRROR MICHAEL JACKSON
MAN IN THE MOON CSILLA
MAN LIKE ME NO REASON
A MAN NEEDS TO BE TOLD CHARLATANS
MAN OF MYSTERY SHADOWS
MAN OF THE WORLD FLEETWOOD MAC
MAN ON FIRE [A] FRANKIE VAUGHAN
MAN ON FIRE [B] ROGER TAYLOR
MAN OF STEEL MEAT LOAF
MAN ON THE CORNER GENESIS
MAN ON THE EDGE IRON MAIDEN
MAN ON THE MOON R.E.M.
MAN OUT OF TIME ELVIS COSTELLO
MAN SHORTAGE LOVINDEER
THE MAN THAT GOT AWAY JUDY GARLAND
MAN TO MAN HOT CHOCOLATE
THE MAN WHO PLAYS THE MANDOLINO DEAN MARTIN
THE MAN WHO SOLD THE WORLD LULU
THE MAN WHO SOLD THE WORLD (LIVE) DAVID BOWIE
THE MAN WHO TOLD EVERYTHING DOVES
THE MAN WITH THE RED FACE LAURENT GARNIER
MAN WITH THE CHILD IN HIS EYES KATE BUSH
MAN WITH THE RED FACE LAURENT GARNIER
A MAN WITHOUT LOVE KENNETH McKELLAR
A MAN WITHOUT LOVE ENGELBERT HUMPERDINCK
MAN! I FEEL LIKE A WOMAN SHANIA TWAIN
MANCHESTER UNITED MANCHESTER UNITED
    FOOTBALL CLUB
MANCHILD NENEH CHERRY
MANDINKA SINEAD O'CONNOR
MANDOLIN RAIN BRUCE HORNSBY & THE RANGE

MANDOLINS IN THE MOONLIGHT PERRY COMO
MANDY [A] EDDIE CALVERT
MANDY [B] BARRY MANILOW
MANDY [B] WESTLIFE
MANEATER DARYL HALL & JOHN OATES
MANGOS ROSEMARY CLOONEY
MANHATTAN SKYLINE A-HA
MANHATTAN SPIRITUAL REG OWEN
MANIAC MICHAEL SEMBELLO
MANIC MINDS MANIX
MANIC MONDAY BANGLES
MANILA SEELENLUFT FEATURING MICHAEL SMITH
MANNEQUIN KIDS FROM FAME FEATURING GENE
    ANTHONY RAY
MANNISH BOY MUDDY WATERS
MAN-SIZE PJ HARVEY
MANSIZE ROOSTER SUPERGRASS
MANTRA FOR A STATE MIND S-EXPRESS
MANY RIVERS TO CROSS UB40
MANY RIVERS TO CROSS CHER
MANY TEARS AGO CONNIE FRANCIS
MANY TOO MANY GENESIS
MANY WEATHERS APART MERZ
MAPS YEAH YEAH YEAH
MARBLE BREAKS IRON BENDS PETER FENTON
MARBLEHEAD JOHNSON BLUETONES
MARBLES BLACK GRAPE
MARCH OF THE MODS JOE LOSS ORCHESTRA
MARCH OF THE PIGS NINE INCH NAILS
MARCH OF THE SIAMESE CHILDREN KENNY BALL & HIS
    JAZZMEN
MARCHETA KARL DENVER
MARGATE CHAS & DAVE
MARGIE FATS DOMINO
MARGO BILLY FURY
MARGUERITA TIME STATUS QUO
MARIA [A] P.J. PROBY
MARIA [B] BLONDIE
MARIA ELENA [A] LOS INDIOS TABAJARAS
MARIA ELENA [B] GENE PITNEY
MARIA (I LIKE IT LOUD) SCOOTER VS MARC
    ACARDIPANE & DICK RULES
MARIA MARIA SANTANA FEATURING THE PRODUCT
    G&B
MARIANA GIBSON BROTHERS
MARIANNE [A] HILLTOPPERS
MARIANNE [B] CLIFF RICHARD
MARIE BACHELORS
MARIE CELESTE POLECATS
MARIE MARIE SHAKIN' STEVENS
MARJORINE JOE COCKER
MARKET SQUARE HEROES MARILLION
MARLENE ON THE WALL SUZANNE VEGA
MAROC 7 SHADOWS
MARQUEE MOON TELEVISION
MARQUIS LINOLEUM
MARRAKESH EXPRESS CROSBY STILLS & NASH
MARRIED MEN BONNIE TYLER
MARRY ME MIKE PRESTON
MARTA BACHELORS
MARTA'S SONG DEEP FOREST
MARTHA'S HARBOUR ALL ABOUT EVE
MARTIAN HOP ROCKY SHARPE & THE REPLAYS
MARTIKA'S KITCHEN MARTIKA
MARVELLOUS LIGHTNING SEEDS
MARVIN MARVIN THE PARANOID ANDROID
MARY [A] SUPERGRASS
MARY [B] SCISSOR SISTERS
MARY ANN BLACK LACE
MARY ANNE SHADOWS
MARY HAD A LITTLE BOY SNAP

MARY HAD A LITTLE LAMB WINGS
MARY JANE [A] DEL SHANNON
MARY JANE [B] MEGADETH
MARY JANE [C] SPIN DOCTORS
MARY JANE (ALL NIGHT LONG) MARY J. BLIGE
MARY JANE'S LAST DANCE TOM PETTY
MARY OF THE FOURTH FORM BOOMTOWN RATS
MARY'S BOY CHILD HARRY BELAFONTE
MARY'S BOY CHILD NINA & FREDERICK
MARY'S BOY CHILD – OH MY LORD BONEY M
MARY'S PRAYER DANNY WILSON
MAS QUE MANCADA RONALDO'S REVENGE
MAS QUE NADA ECHOBEATZ
MAS QUE NADA TAMBA TRIO
MAS QUE NADA COLOUR GIRL FEATURING PSG
MASH IT UP MDM
MASQUERADE [A] SKIDS
MASQUERADE [B] EVELYN THOMAS
MASQUERADE [C] FALL
MASQUERADE [D] GERIDEAU
MASS DESTRUCTION FAITHLESS
MASSACHUSETTS BEE GEES
THE MASSES AGAINST THE CLASSES MANIC STREET
    PREACHERS
MASSIVE ATTACK EP MASSIVE ATTACK
MASTER AND SERVANT DEPECHE MODE
MASTERBLASTER 2000 DJ LUCK & MC NEAT
    FEATURING JJ
MASTERBLASTER (JAMMIN') STEVIE WONDER
THE MASTERPLAN DIANA BROWN & BARRIE K. SHARPE
MATADOR JEFF WAYNE
MATCHSTALK MEN AND MATCHSTALK CATS AND DOGS
    BRIAN & MICHAEL
MATED DAVID GRANT & JAKI GRAHAM
MATERIAL GIRL MADONNA
MATHAR INDIAN VIBES
MATINEE FRANZ FERDINAND
A MATTER OF FACT INNOCENCE
MATTER OF TIME NINE YARDS
A MATTER OF TRUST BILLY JOEL
MATTHEW AND SON CAT STEVENS
MATT'S MOOD BREEKOUT KREW
MATT'S MOOD MATT BIANCO
MAX DON'T HAVE SEX WITH YOUR EX E-ROTIC
THE MAXI PRIEST EP MAXI PRIEST
MAXIMUM (EP) DREADZONE
MAXIMUM OVERDRIVE 2 UNLIMITED
MAY EACH DAY ANDY WILLIAMS
MAY I HAVE THE NEXT DREAM WITH YOU MALCOLM
    ROBERTS
MAY IT BE ENYA
MAY THE SUN SHINE NAZARETH
MAY YOU ALWAYS McGUIRE SISTERS
MAY YOU ALWAYS JOAN REGAN
MAYBE [A] THOM PACE
MAYBE [B] ENRIQUE IGLESIAS
MAYBE [C] EMMA
MAYBE [D] N*E*R*D
MAYBE BABY CRICKETS
MAYBE I KNOW LESLEY GORE
MAYBE I KNOW SEASHELLS
MAYBE I'M AMAZED WINGS
MAYBE I'M AMAZED CARLEEN ANDERSON
MAYBE I'M DEAD MONEY MARK
MAYBE LOVE STEVIE NICKS
MAYBE THAT'S WHAT IT TAKES ALEX PARKS
MAYBE TOMORROW [A] BILLY FURY
MAYBE TOMORROW [B] CHORDS
MAYBE TOMORROW [C] UB40
MAYBE TOMORROW [D] STEREOPHONICS
MAYBE (WE SHOULD CALL IT A DAY) HAZELL DEAN

MAYOR OF SIMPLETON XTC
ME AGAINST THE MUSIC BRITNEY SPEARS FEATURING MADONNA
ME AND BABY BROTHER WAR
ME AND JULIO DOWN BY THE SCHOOLYARD PAUL SIMON
ME AND MR SANCHEZ BLUE RONDO A LA TURK
ME AND MRS JONES BILLY PAUL
ME AND MRS JONES FREDDIE JACKSON
ME AND MY GIRL (NIGHT-CLUBBING) DAVID ESSEX
ME AND MY LIFE TREMELOES
ME AND MY SHADOW FRANK SINATRA & SAMMY DAVIS JR
ME AND THE FARMER HOUSEMARTINS
ME AND YOU AND A DOG NAMED BOO LOBO
ME AND YOU VERSUS THE WORLD SPACE
ME ISRAELITES CHOPS-EMC + EXTENSIVE
ME JULIE SHAGGY & ALI G
ME MYSELF AND [A]I DE LA SOUL
ME, MYSELF & I [B] BEYONCÉ
ME MYSELF I JOAN ARMATRADING
ME NO POP I KID CREOLE & THE COCONUTS PRESENTS COATI MUNDI
ME OR YOU? KILLING JOKE
ME THE PEACEFUL HEART LULU
ME. IN TIME CHARLATANS
MEA CULPA PART II ENIGMA
MEAN GIRL STATUS QUO
MEAN MAN W.A.S.P.
MEAN MEAN MAN WANDA JACKSON
MEAN STREAK [A] CLIFF RICHARD
MEAN STREAK [B] Y&T
MEAN TO ME SHAYE COGAN
MEAN WOMAN BLUES ROY ORBISON
THE MEANING OF CHRISTMAS BORIS GARDINER
THE MEANING OF LOVE [A] DEPECHE MODE
THE MEANING OF LOVE [B] MICHELLE
MEANT TO LIVE SWITCHFOOT
MEANTIME FUTUREHEADS
MEASURE OF A MAN SAM & MARK
MEAT PIE SAUSAGE ROLL GRANDAD ROBERTS & HIS SON ELVIS
MECCA CHEETAHS
MECHANICAL WONDER OCEAN COLOUR SCENE
THE MEDAL SONG CULTURE CLUB
MEDICATION SPIRITUALIZED
MEDICINE SHOW BIG AUDIO DYNAMITE
THE MEDICINE SONG STEPHANIE MILLS
MEET EL PRESIDENTE DURAN DURAN
MEET HER AT THE LOVE PARADE DA HOOL
MEET ME ON THE CORNER [A] MAX BYGRAVES
MEET ME ON THE CORNER [B] LINDISFARNE
(MEET) THE FLINTSTONES BC-52's
MEGABLAST BOMB THE BASS FEATURING MERLIN & ANTONIA
MEGACHIC – CHIC MEDLEY CHIC
MEGALOMANIA PELE
MEGLOMANIAC INCUBUS
MEGAMIX [A] TECHNOTRONIC
MEGAMIX [B] CRYSTAL WATERS
MEGAMIX [C] CORONA
MEGAREX MARC BOLAN & T REX
MEIN TEIL (IMPORT) RAMMSTEIN
MEISO DJ KRUSH
MELANCHOLY ROSE MARC ALMOND
MELLOW DOUBT TEENAGE FANCLUB
MELLOW MELLOW RIGHT ON LOWRELL
MELLOW YELLOW DONOVAN
THE MELOD-EP DODGY
MELODY OF LOVE INK SPOTS
MELODY OF LOVE (WANNA BE LOVED) DONNA SUMMER

MELT [A] SIOUXSIE & THE BANSHEES
MELT [B] MELANIE C
MELTING POT BLUE MINK
MEMO FROM TURNER MICK JAGGER
MEMORIES [A] PUBLIC IMAGE LTD.
MEMORIES [B] MIKE BERRY
MEMORIES [C] BEVERLEY CRAVEN
MEMORIES ARE MADE OF THIS DEAN MARTIN
MEMORIES ARE MADE OF THIS DAVE KING FEATURING THE KEYNOTES
MEMORIES ARE MADE OF THIS VAL DOONICAN
MEMORY ELAINE PAIGE
MEMORY BARBRA STREISAND
THE MEMORY REMAINS METALLICA
MEMORY: THEME FROM THE MUSICAL 'CATS' ALED JONES
MEMPHIS LONNIE MACK
MEMPHIS TENNESSEE DAVE BERRY & THE CRUISERS
MEMPHIS TENNESSEE CHUCK BERRY
MEN IN BLACK [A] FRANK BLACK
MEN IN BLACK [B] WILL SMITH
MENTAL MANIC MC's FEATURING SARA CARLSON
MENTAL PICTURE JON SECADA
MENTASM SECOND PHASE
MERCEDES BOY PEBBLES
MERCI CHERI VINCE HILL
MERCURY LOWGOLD
MERCURY AND SOLACE BT
MERCY MERCY ME – I WANT YOU ROBERT PALMER
MERKINBALL EP PEARL JAM
MERMAIDS PAUL WELLER
MERRY CHRISTMAS DARLING CARPENTERS
MERRY CHRISTMAS EVERYONE SHAKIN' STEVENS
MERRY GENTLE POPS BARRON KNIGHTS WITH DUKE D'MOND
A MERRY JINGLE GREEDIES
THE MERRY PLOUGHBOY DERMOT O'BRIEN
MERRY XMAS EVERYBODY SLADE
MERRY XMAS EVERYBODY METAL GURUS
MERRY X-MESS ROTTERDAM TERMINATION SOURCE
MERSEYBEAT IAN McNABB
MESCALITO SOURMASH
MESMERISE CHAPTERHOUSE
MESMERIZE JA RULE FEATURING ASHANTI
A MESS OF BLUES ELVIS PRESLEY
A MESS OF THE BLUES STATUS QUO
THE MESSAGE [A] GRANDMASTER FLASH & THE FURIOUS FIVE
THE MESSAGE [B] 49ERS
MESSAGE II (SURVIVAL) MELLE MEL & DUKE BOOTEE
MESSAGE IN A BOTTLE POLICE
MESSAGE IN A BOTTLE DANCE FLOOR VIRUS
MESSAGE IN A BOTTLE T FACTORY
MESSAGE IN THE BOX WORLD PARTY
THE MESSAGE IS LOVE ARTHUR BAKER & THE BACKSTREET DISCIPLES FEATURING AL GREEN
MESSAGE OF LOVE [A] PRETENDERS
MESSAGE OF LOVE [B] LOVEHAPPY
MESSAGE TO MARTHA LOU JOHNSON
MESSAGE TO MARTHA (KENTUCKY BLUEBIRD) ADAM FAITH
A MESSAGE TO YOU RUDY SPECIALS (FEATURING RICO)
A MESSAGE TO YOUR HEART SAMANTHA JANUS
MESSAGE UNDERSTOOD SANDIE SHAW
MESSAGES ORCHESTRAL MANOEUVRES IN THE DARK
MESSAGES FROM THE STARS RAH BAND
MESSED UP BEAT UP
MESSIN' LADIES FIRST
METAFORCE ART OF NOISE
METAL GURU T. REX
METAL HEALTH QUIET RIOT

METAL MICKEY SUEDE
METEOR MAN DEE D. JACKSON
METHOD OF MODERN LOVE DARYL HALL & JOHN OATES
METROPOLIS OLIVER LIEB
METROSOUND ADAM F & J MAJIK
MEXICALI ROSE KARL DENVER
THE MEXICAN FENTONES
MEXICAN GIRL SMOKIE
MEXICAN RADIO WALL OF VOODOO
MEXICAN WAVE KERBDOG
MEXICO LONG JOHN BALDRY
MF FROM HELL DATSUNS
MFEO KAVANA
MI CHICO LATINO GERI HALLIWELL
MI TIERRA GLORIA ESTEFAN
MIAMI WILL SMITH
MIAMI HIT MIX GLORIA ESTEFAN
MIAMI VICE THEME JAN HAMMER
MICHAEL [A] GENO WASHINGTON & THE RAM JAM BAND
MICHAEL [B] FRANZ FERDINAND
MICHAEL AND THE SLIPPER TREE EQUALS
MICHAEL CAINE MADNESS
MICHAEL JACKSON MEDLEY ASHAYE
MICHAEL ROW THE BOAT LONNIE DONEGAN
MICHELLE DAVID & JONATHAN
MICHELLE OVERLANDERS
MICHIKO SULTANS OF PING
MICKEY TONI BASIL
MICKEY LOLLY
MICRO KID LEVEL 42
THE MICROPHONE FIEND ERIC B & RAKIM
MICROWAVED PITCHSHIFTER
MIDAS TOUCH MIDNIGHT STAR
THE MIDDLE JIMMY EAT WORLD
MIDDLE OF THE NIGHT BROTHERHOOD OF MAN
MIDDLEMAN TERRORVISION
MIDLIFE CRISIS FAITH NO MORE
MIDNIGHT [A] PAUL ANKA
MIDNIGHT [B] UN-CUT
MIDNIGHT AT THE LOST AND FOUND MEAT LOAF
MIDNIGHT AT THE OASIS MARIA MULDAUR
MIDNIGHT AT THE OASIS BRAND NEW HEAVIES FEATURING N'DEA DAVENPORT
MIDNIGHT BLUE LOUISE TUCKER
MIDNIGHT COWBOY MIDNIGHT COWBOY SOUNDTRACK
MIDNIGHT FLYER NAT 'KING' COLE
MIDNIGHT GROOVIN' LIGHT OF THE WORLD
MIDNIGHT IN A PERFECT WORLD DJ SHADOW
MIDNIGHT IN CHELSEA JON BON JOVI
MIDNIGHT IN MOSCOW KENNY BALL & HIS JAZZMEN
MIDNIGHT RIDER PAUL DAVIDSON
MIDNIGHT SHIFT BUDDY HOLLY
MIDNIGHT SUMMER DREAM STRANGLERS
MIDNIGHT TO SIX MAN PRETTY THINGS
MIDNIGHT TRAIN TO GEORGIA GLADYS KNIGHT & THE PIPS
MIDNITE D-INFLUENCE
MIDNITE DYNAMOS MATCHBOX
MIDNITE SPECIAL PAUL EVANS
MIDSUMMER MADNESS (EP) RHYTHM SECTION
MIG29 MIG29
MIGHT BE STARS WANNADIES
THE MIGHTY HIGH REVIVAL 3000
MIGHTY JOE SHOCKING BLUE
MIGHTY POWER OF LOVE TAVARES
MIGHTY QUINN MANFRED MANN
MIKE OLDFIELD'S SINGLE (THEME FROM TUBULAR BELLS) MIKE OLDFIELD

MILES AWAY [A] JOHN FOXX
MILES AWAY [B] WINGER
MILES FROM HOME PESHAY
MILK GARBAGE FEATURING TRICKY
MILK AND ALCOHOL DR. FEELGOOD
MILKMAN'S SON UGLY KID JOE
MILKSHAKE KELIS
MILKY WAY SHEER ELEGANCE
THE MILL HILL SELF HATE CLUB EDWARD BALL
MILLENNIUM [A] KILLING JOKE
MILLENNIUM [B] ROBBIE WILLIAMS
MILLENNIUM CHIMES BIG BEN
THE MILLENNIUM PRAYER CLIFF RICHARD
MILLION DOLLAR LOVE DUB WAR
MILLION DRUMS TONY SHEVETON
A MILLION LOVE SONGS TAKE THAT
MILLION MILES AWAY OFFSPRING
MILLION SUNS OOBERMAN
MILLIONAIRE KELIS FEATURING ANDRE 3000
MILLIONAIRE SWEEPER KENICKIE
MILLIONS LIKE US PURPLE HEARTS
MILLY MOLLY MANDY GLYN POOLE
MILORD EDITH PIAF
MILORD FRANKIE VAUGHAN
MIND FARM
MIND ADVENTURES DES'REE
MIND BLOWIN' SMOOTH
MIND BLOWING DECISIONS HEATWAVE
MIND BODY SOUL FANTASY UFO FEATURING JAY
    GROOVE
MIND GAMES JOHN LENNON
MIND OF A TOY VISAGE
A MIND OF ITS OWN VICTORIA BECKHAM
THE MIND OF LOVE k.d. lang
THE MIND OF THE MACHINE N-TRANCE
MIND OVER MONEY TURIN BRAKES
MIND UP TONIGHT MELBA MOORE
MINDCIRCUS WAY OUT WEST FEATURING TRICIA LEE
    KELSHALL
MINDLESS BOOGIE HOT CHOCOLATE
MINDSTREAM MEAT BEAT MANIFESTO
MINE EVERYTHING BUT THE GIRL
MINE ALL MINE CA$HFLOW
MINE TO GIVE PHOTEK FEATURING ROBERT OWENS
MINEFIELD I-LEVEL
MINERVA DEFTONES
MINISTRY OF LOVE HYSTERIC EGO
MINISTRY OF MAYHEM NOISE NEXT DOOR
MINNIE THE MOOCHER REGGAE PHILHARMONIC
    ORCHESTRA
MINORITY GREEN DAY
MINT CAR CURE
MINUETTO ALLEGRETTO WOMBLES
MINUTE BY MINUTE DOOBIE BROTHERS
A MINUTE OF YOUR TIME TOM JONES
THE MINUTE YOU'RE GONE CLIFF RICHARD
THE MIRACLE [A] QUEEN
MIRACLE [B] JON BON JOVI
MIRACLE [C] OLIVE
THE MIRACLE [D] CLIFF RICHARD
A MIRACLE [E] HIDDEN CAMERAS
MIRACLE GOODNIGHT DAVID BOWIE
THE MIRACLE OF LOVE EURYTHMICS
THE MIRACLE OF YOU DANNY WILLIAMS
MIRACLES [A] GARY NUMAN
MIRACLES [B] PET SHOP BOYS
MIRROR IN THE BATHROOM BEAT
MIRROR MAN HUMAN LEAGUE
MIRROR MIRROR [A] PINKERTON'S ASSORTED
    COLOURS
MIRROR MIRROR [B] DIANA ROSS

MIRROR MIRROR (MON AMOUR) DOLLAR
MIRRORS SALLY OLDFIELD
MIS-SHAPES PULP
MISERERE ZUCCHERO WITH LUCIANO PAVAROTTI
MISERY [A] SOUL ASYLUM
MISERY [B] MOFFATTS
MISFIT [A] CURIOSITY KILLED THE CAT
MISFIT [B] AMY STUDT
MISGUIDED DYVERSE
MISIRLOU (THE THEME TO THE MOTION PICTURE 'PULP
    FICTION') SPAGHETTI SURFERS
MISLED [A] KOOL & THE GANG
MISLED [B] QUIREBOYS
MISLED [C] CELINE DION
MISS AMERICA BIG DISH
MISS CALIFORNIA DANTE THOMAS FEATURING PRAS
MISS CHATELAINE k.d. lang
MISS FAT BOOTY – PART II MOS DEF FEATURING
    GHOSTFACE KILLAH
MISS HIT AND RUN BARRY BLUE
MISS INDEPENDENT KELLY CLARKSON
MISS LUCIFER PRIMAL SCREAM
MISS MODULAR STEREOLAB
MISS PARKER [A] BENZ
MISS PARKER [B] MORGAN
MISS PERFECT ABS FEATURING NODESHA
MISS SARAJEVO PASSENGERS
MISS THE GIRL CREATURES
MISS WORLD HOLE
MISS YOU [A] JIMMY YOUNG
MISS YOU [B] ROLLING STONES
MISS YOU LIKE CRAZY NATALIE COLE
MISS YOU MUCH JANET JACKSON
MISS YOU NIGHTS CLIFF RICHARD
MISS YOU NIGHTS WESTLIFE
MISSING [A] TERRY HALL
MISSING [B] EVERYTHING BUT THE GIRL
MISSING WORDS SELECTER
MISSING YOU [A] CHRIS DE BURGH
MISSING YOU [B] JOHN WAITE
MISSING YOU [B] TINA TURNER
MISSING YOU [C] SOUL II SOUL FEATURING KYM
    MAZELLE
MISSING YOU [D] MARY J. BLIGE
MISSING YOU [E] LUCY CARR
MISSING YOU NOW MICHAEL BOLTON FEATURING
    KENNY G
MISSION OF LOVE JASON DONOVAN
MISSIONARY MAN EURYTHMICS
MISSISSIPPI PUSSYCAT
MISSY MISSY PAUL & BARRY RYAN
MRS HOOVER CANDYSKINS
MRS MILLS' MEDLEY MRS MILLS
MRS MILLS PARTY MEDLEY MRS MILLS
MRS ROBINSON LEMONHEADS
MRS WASHINGTON GIGOLO AUNTS
MRS. ROBINSON SIMON & GARFUNKEL
MRS. ROBINSON (EP) SIMON & GARFUNKEL
MISTAKES AND REGRETS ...AND YOU WILL KNOW US
    BY THE TRAIL OF THE DEAD
MR ALIBI MARIA WILLSON
MR BACHELOR LOOSE ENDS
MR BASS MAN JOHNNY CYMBAL
MR BIG STUFF QUEEN LATIFAH, SHADES & FREE
MR BIG STUFF HEAVY D. & THE BOYZ
MR BLOBBY MR BLOBBY
MR BLUE DAVID MacBETH
MR BLUE MIKE PRESTON
MR BLUE SKY ELECTRIC LIGHT ORCHESTRA
MR BRIGHTSIDE KILLERS
MR CABDRIVER LENNY KRAVITZ

MR CROWLEY OZZY OSBOURNE'S BLIZZARD OF OZ
MR CUSTER CHARLIE DRAKE
MR DEVIL BIG TIME CHARLIE FEATURING SOOZY Q
MR DJ [A] CONCEPT
MR DJ [A] BLACKOUT
MR E'S BEAUTIFUL BLUES EELS
MR FIXIT ROOTJOOSE
MR FRIDAY NIGHT LISA MOORISH
MR GUDER CARPENTERS
MR GUITAR BERT WEEDON
MR HANKEY THE CHRISTMAS POO MR HANKEY
MISTER JONES [A] OUT OF MY HAIR
MR JONES [B] COUNTING CROWS
MR KIRK'S NIGHTMARE 4 HERO
MR LEE DIANA ROSS
MR LOVERMAN SHABBA RANKS
MR MANIC AND SISTER COOL SHAKATAK
MISTER MENTAL EIGHTIES MATCHBOX B-LINE
    DISASTER
MR PHARMACIST FALL
MISTER PORTER MICKIE MOST
MR PRESIDENT D, B, M & T
MR RAFFLES (MAN IT WAS MEAN) STEVE HARLEY &
    COCKNEY REBEL
MR SANDMAN CHORDETTES
MR SANDMAN DICKIE VALENTINE
MR SANDMAN FOUR ACES FEATURING AL ALBERTS
MR SANDMAN MAX BYGRAVES
MR SECOND CLASS SPENCER DAVIS GROUP
MR SLEAZE STOCK AITKEN WATERMAN
MR SOFT COCKNEY REBEL
MR SOLITAIRE ANIMAL NIGHTLIFE
MR SUCCESS FRANK SINATRA
MR TAMBOURINE MAN BYRDS
MR TELEPHONE MAN NEW EDITION
MR VAIN CULTURE BEAT
MR VAIN RECALL CULTURE BEAT
MR WENDAL ARRESTED DEVELOPMENT
MR WONDERFUL PEGGY LEE
MR WRITER STEREOPHONICS
MR ZERO KEITH RELF
MISTI BLU AMILLIONSONS
MISTLETOE AND WINE CLIFF RICHARD
MISTY JOHNNY MATHIS
MISTY RAY STEVENS
MISTY BLUE DOROTHY MOORE
MISTY MORNING, ALBERT BRIDGE POGUES
MISUNDERSTANDING GENESIS
MISUNDERSTOOD [A] BON JOVI
MISUNDERSTOOD [B] ROBBIE WILLIAMS
MISUNDERSTOOD MAN CLIFF RICHARD
MITCH BISCUIT BOY
MITTAGEISEN (METAL POSTCARD) SIOUXSIE & THE
    BANSHEES
MIX IT UP DAN REED NETWORK
MIXED BIZNESS BECK
MIXED EMOTIONS ROLLING STONES
MIXED TRUTH RAGGA TWINS
MIXED UP WORLD SOPHIE ELLIS-BEXTOR
MIYAKO HIEAWAY MARION
M'LADY SLY & THE FAMILY STONE
MMM MMM MMM MMM CRASH TEST DUMMIES
MMMBOP HANSON
MO' FIRE BAD COMPANY UK/RAWHILL CRU
MO MONEY MO PROBLEMS NOTORIOUS B.I.G.
MOAN AND GROAN MARK MORRISON
MOANIN' CHRIS FARLOWE
MOB RULES BLACK SABBATH
MOBILE RAY BURNS
MOBSCENE MARILYN MANSON
MOCKIN' BIRD HILL MIGIL FIVE

MOCKINGBIRD INEZ & CHARLIE FOXX
MOCKINGBIRD CARLY SIMON & JAMES TAYLOR
MOCKINGBIRD BELLE STARS
THE MODEL KRAFTWERK
MODERN AGE STROKES
MODERN ART ART BRUT
MODERN FEELING IKARA COLT
MODERN GIRL [A] SHEENA EASTON
MODERN GIRL [B] MEAT LOAF
MODERN LOVE DAVID BOWIE
MODERN ROMANCE (I WANT TO FALL IN LOVE AGAIN) FRANCIS ROSSI & BERNARD FROST
A MODERN WAY OF LETTING GO IDLEWILD
THE MODERN WORLD JAM
MODUS OPERANDI PHOTEK
MOI...LOLITA ALIZEE
MOIRA JANE'S CAFE DEFINITION OF SOUND
MOLLIE'S SONG BEVERLEY CRAVEN
MOLLY CARRIE
MOLLY'S CHAMBERS KINGS OF LEON
MOMENT OF MY LIFE BOBBY D'AMBROSIO FEATURING MICHELLE WEEKS
MOMENTS IN LOVE/BEAT BOX ART OF NOISE
MOMENTS IN SOUL JT & THE BIG FAMILY
MOMENTS OF PLEASURE KATE BUSH
MON AMI GIRESSE
MON AMOUR TOKYO PIZZICATO FIVE
MONA CRAIG McLACHLAN & CHECK 1-2
MONA LISA CONWAY TWITTY
MONDAY MONDAY MAMAS & THE PAPAS
MONDAY MORNING CANDYSKINS
MONDAY MORNING 5:19 RIALTO
MONEY [A] BERN ELLIOTT & THE FENMEN
MONEY [A] FLYING LIZARDS
MONEY [A] BACKBEAT BAND
MONEY [B] SKIN
MONEY [C] CHARLI BALTIMORE
MONEY [D] DAN REED NETWORK
MONEY [E] JAMELIA FEATURING BEENIE MAN
(MONEY CAN'T) BUY ME LOVE BLACKstreet
MONEY DON'T MATTER 2 NIGHT PRINCE & THE NEW POWER GENERATION
MONEY (EVERYBODY LOVES HER) GUN
MONEY FOR NOTHING DIRE STRAITS
MONEY GO ROUND (PART 1) STYLE COUNCIL
MONEY GREED TRICKY
MONEY HONEY BAY CITY ROLLERS
MONEY IN MY POCKET DENNIS BROWN
MONEY LOVE NENEH CHERRY
MONEY MONEY MONEY ABBA
MONEY THAT'S YOUR PROBLEM TONIGHT
MONEY TO BURN RICHARD ASHCROFT
MONEY'S TOO TIGHT TO MENTION VALENTINE BROTHERS
MONEY'S TOO TIGHT TO MENTION SIMPLY RED
MONEYTALKS AC/DC
MONIE IN THE MIDDLE MONIE LOVE
THE MONKEES RAMPAGE
THE MONKEES EP MONKEES
MONKEY [A] GEORGE MICHAEL
MONKEY [B] SHAFT
MONKEY BUSINESS [A] SKID ROW
MONKEY BUSINESS [B] DANGER DANGER
MONKEY CHOP DAN-I
MONKEY GONE TO HEAVEN PIXIES
MONKEY MAN MAYTALS
MONKEY MAN GENERAL LEVY
MONKEY SPANNER DAVE & ANSIL COLLINS
MONKEY WAH RADICAL MOB
MONKEY WRENCH FOO FIGHTERS
MONO COURTNEY LOVE

MONOCULTURE SOFT CELL
MONSIEUR DUPONT SANDIE SHAW
MONSTER [A] L7
MONSTER [B] LIQUID PEOPLE VS SIMPLE MINDS
MONSTER MASH BOBBY 'BORIS' PICKETT & THE CRYPT-KICKERS
MONSTERS AND ANGELS VOICE OF THE BEEHIVE
MONTEGO BAY BOBBY BLOOM
MONTEGO BAY FREDDIE NOTE & THE RUDIES
MONTEGO BAY SUGAR CANE
MONTEGO BAY AMAZULU
MONTREAL WEDDING PRESENT
MONTREAUX EP SIMPLY RED
MONTUNO GLORIA ESTEFAN
MONY MONY TOMMY JAMES & THE SHONDELLS
MONY MONY BILLY IDOL
MONY MONY AMAZULU
MONY MONY STATUS QUO
THE MOOD CLUB FIRSTBORN
MOODSWINGS/THE GENTLE ART OF CHOKING MY VITRIOL
MOODY BLUE ELVIS PRESLEY
MOODY PLACES NORTHSIDE
MOODY RIVER PAT BOONE
MOOG ERUPTION DIGITAL ORGASM
MOON VIRUS
MOON HOP DERRICK MORGAN
MOON OVER BOURBON STREET STING
MOON RIVER DANNY WILLIAMS
MOON RIVER HENRY MANCINI
MOON RIVER GREYHOUND
MOON SHADOW CAT STEVENS
MOON TALK PERRY COMO
MOONCHILD FIELDS OF THE NEPHILIM
MOONGLOW MORRIS STOLOFF
MOONGLOW SOUNDS ORCHESTRAL
MOONLIGHT AND MUZAK M
MOONLIGHT & ROSES JIM REEVES
MOONLIGHT GAMBLER FRANKIE LAINE
MOONLIGHT SERENADE GLENN MILLER
MOONLIGHT SHADOW MIKE OLDFIELD FEATURING MAGGIE REILLY
MOONLIGHTING LEO SAYER
'MOONLIGHTING' THEME AL JARREAU
MOONSHINE SALLY MUD
MOR BLUR
MORE [A] PERRY COMO
MORE [A] JIMMY YOUNG
MORE [B] SISTERS OF MERCY
MORE... [C] HIGH
MORE AND MORE [A] ANDY WILLIAMS
MORE AND MORE [B] CAPTAIN HOLLYWOOD PROJECT
MORE & MORE [C] SPOILED & ZIGO
MORE & MORE [D] JOE FEATURING G UNIT
MORE AND MORE PARTY POPS RUSS CONWAY
MORE BEATS & PIECES COLDCUT
MORE GOOD OLD ROCK 'N ROLL DAVE CLARK FIVE
MORE HUMAN THAN HUMAN WHITE ZOMBIE
THE MORE I GET THE MORE I WANT KWS FEATURING TEDDY PENDERGRASS
THE MORE I SEE (THE LESS I BELIEVE) FUN BOY THREE
THE MORE I SEE YOU JOY MARSHALL
THE MORE I SEE YOU CHRIS MONTEZ
THE MORE I SEE YOU BARBARA WINDSOR & MIKE REID
MORE LIFE IN A TRAMP'S VEST STEREOPHONICS
MORE LIKE THE MOVIES DR. HOOK
MORE LOVE [A] FEARGAL SHARKEY
MORE LOVE [B] NEXT OF KIN
MORE MONEY FOR YOU AND ME (MEDLEY) FOUR PREPS
MORE MORE MORE [A] ANDREA TRUE CONNECTION
MORE MORE MORE [A] BANANARAMA

MORE MORE MORE [A] RACHEL STEVENS
MORE, MORE, MORE [B] CARMEL
MORE PARTY POPS RUSS CONWAY
MORE THAN A FEELING BOSTON
MORE THAN A LOVER BONNIE TYLER
MORE THAN A WOMAN [A] TAVARES
MORE THAN A WOMAN [A] 911
MORE THAN A WOMAN [B] AALIYAH
MORE THAN EVER (COME PRIMA) MALCOLM VAUGHAN WITH THE MICHAEL SAMMES SINGERS
MORE THAN EVER (COME PRIMA) ROBERT EARL
MORE THAN I CAN BEAR MATT BIANCO
MORE THAN I CAN SAY CRICKETS
MORE THAN I CAN SAY BOBBY VEE
MORE THAN I CAN SAY LEO SAYER
MORE THAN I NEEDED TO KNOW SCOOCH
MORE THAN IN LOVE KATE ROBBINS & BEYOND
MORE THAN LIKELY PM DAWN FEATURING BOY GEORGE
MORE THAN LOVE [A] KEN DODD
MORE THAN LOVE [B] WET WET WET
MORE THAN ONE KIND OF LOVE JOAN ARMATRADING
MORE THAN PHYSICAL BANANARAMA
MORE THAN THAT BACKSTREET BOYS
MORE THAN THIS [A] ROXY MUSIC
MORE THAN THIS [A] EMMIE
MORE THAN THIS [B] PETER GABRIEL
MORE THAN US EP TRAVIS
MORE THAN WORDS EXTREME
MORE THAN YOU KNOW MARTIKA
THE MORE THEY KNOCK, THE MORE I LOVE YOU GLORIA D BROWN
MORE TO LIFE CLIFF RICHARD
MORE TO LOVE VOLCANO
MORE TO THIS WORLD BAD BOYS INC
THE MORE YOU IGNORE ME THE CLOSER I GET MORRISSEY
THE MORE YOU LIVE, THE MORE YOU LOVE A FLOCK OF SEAGULLS
MORGEN IVO ROBIC
MORNIN' AL JARREAU
MORNING [A] VAL DOONICAN
MORNING [B] WET WET WET
THE MORNING AFTER (FREE AT LAST) STRIKE
MORNING AFTERGLOW ELECTRASY
MORNING ALWAYS COMES TOO SOON BRAD CARTER
MORNING DANCE SPYRO GYRA
MORNING GLORY JAMES & BOBBY PURIFY
MORNING HAS BROKEN CAT STEVENS
MORNING HAS BROKEN NEIL DIAMOND
MORNING HAS BROKEN DANIEL O'DONNELL
MORNING OF OUR LIVES MODERN LOVERS
THE MORNING PAPERS PRINCE & THE NEW POWER GENERATION
MORNING SIDE OF THE MOUNTAIN DONNY & MARIE OSMOND
MORNING WONDER EARLIES
MORNINGLIGHT TEAM DEEP
MORNINGTOWN RIDE SEEKERS
THE MOST BEAUTIFUL GIRL CHARLIE RICH
THE MOST BEAUTIFUL GIRL IN THE WORLD PRINCE
MOST GIRLS P!NK
MOST HIGH PAGE & PLANT
THE MOST TIRING DAY CECIL
MOTHER [A] DANZIG
MOTHER [B] M FACTOR
MOTHER AND CHILD REUNION PAUL SIMON
MOTHER DAWN BLUE PEARL
MOTHER FIXATION MINUTEMAN
MOTHER NATURE AND FATHER TIME NAT 'KING' COLE
MOTHER OF MINE NEIL REID

MOTHER UNIVERSE SOUP DRAGONS
MOTHER-IN-LAW ERNIE K-DOE
MOTHERLAND-A-FRI-CA TRIBAL HOUSE
MOTHERLESS CHILD ERIC CLAPTON
MOTHER'S TALK TEARS FOR FEARS
MOTHERSHIP RECONNECTION SCOTT GROOVES
    FEATURING PARLIAMENT/FUNKADELIC
THE MOTION OF LOVE GENE LOVES JEZEBEL
MOTIVATION SUM 41
THE MOTIVE (LIVING WITHOUT YOU) THEN JERICO
MOTIVELESS CRIME SOUTH
MOTOR BIKING CHRIS SPEDDING
MOTORBIKE BEAT REVILLOS
MOTORBIKE TO HEAVEN SALAD
MOTORCYCLE EMPTINESS MANIC STREET PREACHERS
MOTORCYCLE MICHAEL JO ANN CAMPBELL
MOTORCYCLE RIDER ICICLE WORKS
MOTORHEAD LIVE MOTORHEAD
MOTORMANIA ROMAN HOLIDAY
MOTORTOWN KANE GANG
THE MOTOWN SONG ROD STEWART
MOTOWNPHILLY BOYZ II MEN
MOULDY OLD DOUGH LIEUTENANT PIGEON
MOULIN ROUGE MANTOVANI
MOUNTAIN GREENERY MEL TORME
MOUNTAIN OF LOVE KENNY LYNCH
MOUNTAINS PRINCE & THE REVOLUTION
THE MOUNTAIN'S HIGH DICK & DEEDEE
MOUSE IN A HOLE HEAVY STEREO
MOUTH MERRIL BAINBRIDGE
MOUTH FOR WAR PANTERA
MOVE [A] INSPIRAL CARPETS
MOVE [B] MOBY
MOVE ANY MOUNTAIN SHAMEN
MOVE AWAY CULTURE CLUB
MOVE AWAY JIMMY BLUE DEL AMITRI
MOVE BABY MOVE SARTORELLO
MOVE CLOSER PHYLLIS NELSON
MOVE CLOSER TOM JONES
MOVE IN A LITTLE CLOSER HARMONY GRASS
MOVE IT CLIFF RICHARD & THE DRIFTERS
MOVE IT BABY SIMON SCOTT
MOVE IT LIKE THIS BAHA MEN
MOVE IT UP CAPPELLA
MOVE MANIA SASH! FEATURING SHANNON
MOVE ME NO MOUNTAIN SOUL II SOUL, LEAD VOCALS
    KOFI
MOVE MOVE MOVE (THE RED TRIBE) MANCHESTER
    UNITED FOOTBALL CLUB
MOVE NOW MARK B FEATURING TOMMY EVANS
MOVE ON BABY CAPPELLA
MOVE ON UP CURTIS MAYFIELD
MOVE ON UP SUE CHALONER
MOVE ON UP TRICKSTER
MOVE OVER DARLING DORIS DAY
MOVE OVER DARLING TRACEY ULLMAN
MOVE RIGHT OUT RICK ASTLEY
MOVE THAT BODY [A] TECHNOTRONIC FEATURING
    REGGIE
MOVE THAT BODY [B] NUSH
MOVE THE CROWD ERIC B & RAKIM
MOVE THIS MOUNTAIN SOPHIE ELLIS-BEXTOR
MOVE TO MEMPHIS A-HA
MOVE YA BODY NINA SKY
MOVE YOUR ASS SCOOTER
MOVE YOUR BODY [A] GENE FARROW & G.F. BAND
MOVE YOUR BODY [B] TYREE FEATURING JMD
MOVE YOUR BODY [C] XPANSIONS
MOVE YOUR BODY [D] ANTICAPPELLA FEATURING MC
    FIXX IT
MOVE YOUR BODY [E] EUROGROOVE

MOVE YOUR BODY [F] RUFFNECK FEATURING YAVAHN
MOVE YOUR BODY [G] EIFFEL 65
MOVE YOUR FEET [A] M-D-EMM
MOVE YOUR FEET [B] JUNIOR SENIOR
MOVE YOUR FEET TO THE RHYTHM OF THE BEAT
    HITHOUSE
MOVE YOUR LOVE DJH STEFY
MOVEMENT LCD SOUNDSYSTEM
MOVIE STAR HARPO
MOVIES [A] HOTHOUSE FLOWERS
MOVIES [B] ALIEN ANT FARM
MOVIESTAR STEREOPHONICS
MOVIN' [A] BRASS CONSTRUCTION
MOVIN' [A] 400 BLOWS
MOVIN' [B] MARATHON
MOVIN' [C] MONE
MOVIN' ON [A] BANANARAMA
MOVIN' ON [B] APACHE INDIAN
MOVIN' ON [C] DEBBIE PENDER
MOVIN' ON [D] PROSPECT PARK/CAROLYN HARDING
MOVIN' OUT (ANTHONY'S SONG) BILLY JOEL
MOVIN' THRU YOUR SYSTEM JARK PRONGO
MOVIN TOO FAST ARTFUL DODGER & ROMINA
    JOHNSON
MOVING SUPERGRASS
MOVING IN THE RIGHT DIRECTION PASADENAS
MOVING ON DREADZONE
MOVING ON UP M PEOPLE
MOVING ON UP (ON THE RIGHT SIDE) BEVERLEY
    KNIGHT
MOVING TO BLACKWATER REUBEN
MOVING TO CALIFORNIA STRAW
MOVING UP MOVING ON MOZIAC
MOZART 40 SOVEREIGN COLLECTION
MOZART SYMPHONY NO. 40 IN G MINOR K550 1ST
    MOVEMENT (ALLEGRO MOLTO) WALDO DE LOS
    RIOS
MS GRACE TYMES
MS JACKSON OUTKAST
MUCH AGAINST EVERYONE'S ADVICE SOULWAX
MUCH LOVE SHOLA AMA
MUCHO MACHO TOTO COELO
(MUCHO MAMBO) SWAY SHAFT
MUCK IT OUT FARMERS BOYS
MUDDY WATER BLUES PAUL RODGERS
MUHAMMAD ALI FAITHLESS
MULDER AND SCULLY CATATONIA
MULE (CHANT NO. 2) BEGGAR & CO
MULE SKINNER BLUES RUSTY DRAPER
MULE SKINNER BLUES FENDERMEN
MULE TRAIN FRANK IFIELD
MULL OF KINTYRE WINGS
MULTIPLICATION BOBBY DARIN
MULTIPLICATION SHOWADDYWADDY
MULTIPLY XZIBIT
MUM'S GONE TO ICELAND BENNETT
MUNDAYA (THE BOY) TIM DELUXE FEATURING SHAHIN
    BADAR
MUNDIAN TO BACH KE PANJABI MC
THE MUPPET SHOW MUSIC HALL EP MUPPETS
MURDER ON THE DANCEFLOOR SOPHIE ELLIS-BEXTOR
MURDER SHE WROTE [A] TAIRRIE B
MURDER SHE WROTE [B] CHAKA DEMUS & PLIERS
MURDERATION EBONY DUBSTERS
MURPHY AND THE BRICKS NOEL MURPHY
MURPHY'S LAW CHERI
MUSAK TRISCO
MUSCLE DEEP THEN JERICO
MUSCLE MUSEUM MUSE
MUSCLEBOUND SPANDAU BALLET
MUSCLES DIANA ROSS

MUSIC [A] JOHN MILES
MUSIC [A] FARGETTA & ANNE-MARIE SMITH
MUSIC [B] ONE WAY FEATURING AL HUDSON
MUSIC [C] F.R. DAVID
MUSIC PART 1 [D] D TRAIN
MUSIC [E] OMAR
MUSIC [F] MADONNA
MUSIC [G] ERICK SERMON FEATURING MARVIN GAYE
MUSIC AND LIGHTS IMAGINATION
MUSIC AND YOU [A] SAL SOLO WITH THE LONDON
    COMMUNITY GOSPEL CHOIR
MUSIC AND YOU [B] ROOM 5 FEATURING OLIVER
    CHEATHAM
MUSIC FOR CHAMELEONS GARY NUMAN
MUSIC GETS THE BEST OF ME SOPHIE ELLIS-BEXTOR
THE MUSIC I LIKE ALEXIA
MUSIC IN MY MIND ADAM F
THE MUSIC IN YOU MONOBOY FEATURING DELORES
MUSIC IS A PASSION ATLANTIC OCEAN
MUSIC IS LIFE DIRT DEVILS
THE MUSIC IS MOVING FARGETTA
MUSIC IS MOVING CORTINA
MUSIC IS MY RADAR BLUR
MUSIC IS THE ANSWER (DANCING' & PRANCIN')
    DANNY TENAGLIA & CELEDA
MUSIC MAKES ME HIGH LOST BOYZ
MUSIC MAKES YOU FEEL LIKE DANCING BRASS
    CONSTRUCTION
MUSIC MAKES YOU LOSE CONTROL LES RYTHMES
    DIGITALES
THE MUSIC OF GOODBYE (LOVE THEME FROM 'OUT OF
    AFRICA') AL JARREAU
MUSIC OF MY HEART N SYNC & GLORIA ESTEFAN
THE MUSIC OF THE NIGHT MICHAEL CRAWFORD
THE MUSIC OF THE NIGHT BARBRA STREISAND (DUET
    WITH MICHAEL CRAWFORD)
THE MUSIC OF TORVILL AND DEAN EP RICHARD
    HARTLEY/MICHAEL REED ORCHESTRA
MUSIC REVOLUTION SCUMFROG
MUSIC SAVED MY LIFE CEVIN FISHER
MUSIC SOUNDS BETTER WITH YOU STARDUST
MUSIC STOP RAILWAY CHILDREN
MUSIC TAKES YOU BLAME
THE MUSIC THAT WE HEAR (MOOG ISLAND)
    MORCHEEBA
MUSIC TO WATCH GIRLS BY ANDY WILLIAMS
MUSICAL FREEDOM (MOVING ON UP) PAUL SIMPSON
    FEATURING ADEVA
MUSICAL MELODY UNIQUE 3
THE MUSIC'S GOT ME BASS BUMPERS
THE MUSIC'S GOT ME BROOKLYN BOUNCE
THE MUSIC'S NO GOOD WITHOUT YOU CHER
MUSIQUE DAFT PUNK
MUSKRAT EVERLY BROTHERS
MUSKRAT RAMBLE FREDDY CANNON
MUST BE LOVE FYA FEATURING SMUJJI
MUST BE MADISON JOE LOSS ORCHESTRA
MUST BE SANTA TOMMY STEELE
MUST BE THE MUSIC [A] HYSTERIX
MUST BE THE MUSIC [B] JOEY NEGRO FEATURING
    TAKA BOOM
MUST BEE THE MUSIC KING BEE FEATURING MICHELE
A MUST TO AVOID HERMAN'S HERMITS
MUSTAFA CHA CHA CHA STAIFFI & HIS MUSTAFAS
MUSTANG SALLY WILSON PICKETT
MUSTANG SALLY COMMITMENTS
MUSTAPHA BOB AZZAM
MUTANTS IN MEGA CITY ONE FINK BROTHERS
MUTATIONS EP ORBITAL
MUTUAL ATTRACTION CHANGE
MUTUALLY ASSURED DESTRUCTION GILLAN

MUZIKIZUM X-PRESS 2
MY 16TH APOLOGY (EP) SHAKESPEARS SISTER
MY ADIDAS RUN D.M.C.
MY AFFAIR KIRSTY MacCOLL
MY ALL MARIAH CAREY
MY ANGEL ROCK GODDESS
MY ARMS KEEP MISSING YOU RICK ASTLEY
MY BABY LIL' ROMEO
MY BABY JUST CARES FOR ME NINA SIMONE
MY BABY LEFT ME DAVE BERRY & THE CRUISERS
MY BABY LEFT ME – THAT'S ALL RIGHT (MEDLEY)
    SLADE
MY BABY LOVES LOVIN' WHITE PLAINS
MY BAG LLOYD COLE & THE COMMOTIONS
MY BAND D12
MY BEAT BLAZE FEATURING PALMER BROWN
MY BEATBOX DEEJAY PUNK-ROC
MY BEAUTIFUL FRIEND CHARLATANS
MY BEST FRIEND'S GIRL CARS
MY BLUE HEAVEN FRANK SINATRA
MY BODY LEVERT SWEAT GILL
MY BONNIE TONY SHERIDAN & THE BEATLES
MY BOO USHER
MY BOOK BEAUTIFUL SOUTH
MY BOOMERANG WON'T COME BACK CHARLIE DRAKE
MY BOY ELVIS PRESLEY
MY BOY FLAT TOP FRANKIE VAUGHAN
MY BOY LOLLIPOP MILLIE
MY BOYFRIEND'S BACK ANGELS
MY BRAVE FACE PAUL McCARTNEY
MY BROTHER JAKE FREE
MY CAMERA NEVER LIES BUCKS FIZZ
MY CHERIE AMOUR STEVIE WONDER
MY CHILD CONNIE FRANCIS
MY COCO STELLASTARR*
MY COO-CO-CHOO ALVIN STARDUST
MY COUNTRY MIDNIGHT OIL
MY CULTURE 1 GIANT LEAP FEATURING MAXI JAZZ &
    ROBBIE WILLIAMS
MY CUTIE CUTIE SHAKIN' STEVENS
MY DEFINITION OF A BOOMBASTIC JAZZ STYLE DREAM
    WARRIORS
MY DESIRE AMIRA
MY DESTINY LIONEL RICHIE
MY DING-A-LING CHUCK BERRY
MY DIXIE DARLING LONNIE DONEGAN
MY DJ (PUMP IT UP SOME) RICHIE RICH
MY DOCS KISS AMC
MY DRUG BUDDY LEMONHEADS
MY DYING MACHINE GARY NUMAN
MY EVER CHANGING MOODS STYLE COUNCIL
MY EYES ADORED YOU FRANKIE VALLI
MY FAMILY DEPENDS ON ME SIMONE
MY FATHER'S EYES ERIC CLAPTON
MY FATHER'S SHOES LEVEL 42
MY FATHER'S SON CONNOR REEVES
MY FAVORITE MISTAKE SHERYL CROW
MY FAVOURITE GAME CARDIGANS
MY FAVOURITE WASTE OF TIME OWEN PAUL
MY FEELING JUNIOR JACK
MY FEET KEEP DANCING CHIC
MY FIRST NIGHT WITHOUT YOU CYNDI LAUPER
MY FOOLISH FRIEND TALK TALK
MY FORBIDDEN LOVER CHIC
MY FORBIDDEN LOVER ROMINA JOHNSON FEATURING
    LUCI MARTIN & NORMA JEAN
MY FREND STAN SLADE
MY FRIEND [A] FRANKIE LAINE
MY FRIEND [B] ROY ORBISON
MY FRIEND [C] GROOVE ARMADA
MY FRIEND JACK SMOKE

MY FRIEND JACK BONEY M
MY FRIEND THE SEA PETULA CLARK
MY FRIENDS RED HOT CHILI PEPPERS
MY FRIENDS OVER YOU NEW FOUND GLORY
MY GENERATION [A] WHO
MY GENERATION [B] LIMP BIZKIT
MY GETAWAY TIONNE 'T-BOZ' WATKINS
MY GIRL [A] OTIS REDDING
MY GIRL [A] TEMPTATIONS
MY GIRL [A] WHISPERS
MY GIRL [B] MADNESS
MY GIRL [C] ROD STEWART
MY GIRL BILL JIM STAFFORD
MY GIRL JOSEPHINE FATS DOMINO
MY GIRL JOSEPHINE SUPERCAT FEATURING JACK
    RADICS
MY GIRL LOLLIPOP (MY BOY LOLLIPOP) BAD MANNERS
MY GIRL LOVES ME SHALAMAR
MY GIRL MY GIRL WARREN STACEY
MY GUY [A] MARY WELLS
MY GUY [B] TRACEY ULLMAN
MY GUY – MY GIRL (MEDLEY) AMII STEWART & DEON
    ESTUS
MY GUY – MY GIRL (MEDLEY) AMII STEWART &
    JOHNNY BRISTOL
MY HAND OVER MY HEART MARC ALMOND
MY HAPPINESS CONNIE FRANCIS
MY HAPPY ENDING AVRIL LAVIGNE
MY HEAD'S IN MISSISSIPPI ZZ TOP
MY HEART GENE VINCENT
MY HEART CAN'T TELL YOU NO ROD STEWART
MY HEART GOES BANG (GET ME TO THE DOCTOR) DEAD
    OR ALIVE
MY HEART GOES BOOM FRENCH AFFAIR
MY HEART HAS A MIND OF ITS OWN CONNIE FRANCIS
MY HEART THE BEAT D-SHAKE
MY HEART WILL GO ON CELINE DION
MY HEART'S BEATING WILD (TIC TAC TIC TAC) GIBSON
    BROTHERS
MY HEART'S SYMPHONY GARY LEWIS & THE PLAYBOYS
MY HERO FOO FIGHTERS
MY HOMETOWN BRUCE SPRINGSTEEN
MY HOUSE TERRORVISION
MY HOUSE IS YOUR HOUSE MAXTREME
MY IMMORTAL EVANESCENCE
MY IRON LUNG RADIOHEAD
MY JAMAICAN GUY GRACE JONES
MY KIND OF GIRL MATT MONRO
MY KIND OF GIRL FRANK SINATRA WITH COUNT BASIE
MY KINDA LIFE CLIFF RICHARD
MY KINGDOM FUTURE SOUND OF LONDON
MY LAST NIGHT WITH YOU ARROWS
MY LIFE BILLY JOEL
MY LIFE IS IN YOUR HANDS MELTDOWN
MY LITTLE BABY MIKE BERRY WITH THE OUTLAWS
MY LITTLE BROTHER ART BRUT
MY LITTLE CORNER OF THE WORLD ANITA BRYANT
MY LITTLE GIRL [A] CRICKETS
MY LITTLE GIRL [B] AUTUMN
MY LITTLE LADY TREMELOES
MY LITTLE ONE MARMALADE
MY LOVE [A] PETULA CLARK
MY LOVE [B] PAUL McCARTNEY & WINGS
MY LOVE [C] LIONEL RICHIE
MY LOVE [D] JULIO IGLESIAS FEATURING STEVIE
    WONDER
MY LOVE [E] LONDON BOYS
MY LOVE [F] MARY J. BLIGE
MY LOVE [G] KELE LE ROC
MY LOVE [H] WESTLIFE
MY LOVE [I] KLUSTER FEATURING RON CARROLL

MY LOVE AND DEVOTION DORIS DAY
MY LOVE AND DEVOTION MATT MONRO
MY LOVE FOR YOU JOHNNY MATHIS
MY LOVE IS A FIRE DONNY OSMOND
MY LOVE IS ALWAYS SAFFRON HILL FEATURING BEN
    ONONO
MY LOVE IS DEEP SARA PARKER
MY LOVE IS FOR REAL PAULA ABDUL FEATURING
    OFFRA HAZA
MY LOVE IS FOR REAL STRIKE
MY LOVE IS GUARANTEED SYBIL
MY LOVE IS LIKE...WO! MYA
MY LOVE IS MAGIC BAS NOIR
MY LOVE IS SO RAW ALYSON WILLIAMS FEATURING
    NIKKI D
MY LOVE IS THE SHHH! SOMETHIN' FOR THE PEOPLE
    FEATURING TRINA & TAMARA
MY LOVE IS WAITING MARVIN GAYE
MY LOVE IS YOUR LOVE WHITNEY HOUSTON
MY LOVE LIFE MORRISSEY
MY LOVER'S PRAYER OTIS REDDING
MY LOVER'S PRAYER ALISTAIR GRIFFIN
MY LOVIN' EN VOGUE
MY MAGIC MAN ROCHELLE
MY MAMMY HAPPENINGS
MY MAN A SWEET MAN MILLIE JACKSON
MY MAN AND ME LYNSEY DE PAUL
MY MARIE ENGELBERT HUMPERDINCK
MY MATE PAUL DAVID HOLMES
MY MELANCHOLY BABY TOMMY EDWARDS
MY MELANCHOLY BABY CHAS & DAVE
MY MIND'S EYE SMALL FACES
MY MUM IS ONE IN A MILLION THE CHILDREN OF
    TANSLEY SCHOOL
MY MY MY ARMAND VAN HELDEN
MY NAME IS EMINEM
MY NAME IS JACK MANFRED MANN
MY NAME IS NOT SUSAN WHITNEY HOUSTON
MY NAME IS PRINCE PRINCE & THE NEW POWER
    GENERATION
MY NECK MY BACK (LICK IT) KHIA
MY OH MY [A] SAD CAFE
MY OH MY [B] SLADE
MY OH MY [C] AQUA
MY OLD MAN'S A DUSTMAN LONNIE DONEGAN
MY OLD PIANO DIANA ROSS
MY ONE SIN NAT 'KING' COLE
MY ONE TEMPTATION MICA PARIS
MY ONE TRUE FRIEND BETTE MIDLER
MY ONLY LOVE BOB SINCLAR FEATURING LEE A
    GENESIS
MY OWN SUMMER (SHOVE IT) DEFTONES
MY OWN TRUE LOVE DANNY WILLIAMS
MY OWN WAY DURAN DURAN
MY OWN WORST ENEMY LIT
MY PEACE OF HEAVEN TEN CITY
MY PERFECT COUSIN UNDERTONES
MY PERSONAL POSSESSION NAT 'KING' COLE & THE
    FOUR KNIGHTS
MY PHILOSOPHY BOOGIE DOWN PRODUCTIONS
MY PLACE NELLY
MY PLAGUE SLIPKNOT
MY PRAYER PLATTERS
MY PRAYER GERRY MONROE
MY PREROGATIVE BOBBY BROWN
MY PREROGATIVE BRITNEY SPEARS
MY PRETTY ONE CLIFF RICHARD
MY PUPPET PAL TIGER
MY RECOVERY INJECTION BIFFY CLYRO
MY REMEDY HINDA HICKS
MY RESISTANCE IS LOW ROBIN SARSTEDT

MY RISING STAR NORTHSIDE
MY SACRIFICE CREED
MY SALT HEART HUE & CRY
MY SENTIMENTAL FRIEND HERMAN'S HERMITS
MY SEPTEMBER LOVE DAVID WHITFIELD
MY SHARONA KNACK
MY SHIP IS COMING IN WALKER BROTHERS
MY SIDE OF THE BED SUSANNA HOFFS
MY SIMPLE HEART THREE DEGREES
MY SISTER JULIANA HATFIELD THREE
MY SON JOHN DAVID WHITFIELD
MY SON MY SON VERA LYNN WITH FRANK WEIR, HIS
    SAXOPHONE, HIS ORCHESTRA & CHORUS
MY SPECIAL ANGEL BOBBY HELMS WITH THE ANITA
    KERR SINGERS
MY SPECIAL ANGEL MALCOLM VAUGHAN
MY SPECIAL CHILD SINEAD O'CONNOR
MY SPECIAL DREAM SHIRLEY BASSEY
MY SPIRIT TILT
MY STAR IAN BROWN
MY SUNDAY BABY DALE SISTERS
MY SUPERSTAR DIMESTARS
MY SWEET JANE G.U.N.
MY SWEET LORD GEORGE HARRISON
MY SWEET ROSALIE BROTHERHOOD OF MAN
MY TELEPHONE COLDCUT
MY TIME [A] SOUVLAKI
MY TIME [B] DUTCH FEATURING CRYSTAL WATERS
MY TOOT TOOT DENISE LA SALLE
MY TOWN GLASS TIGER
MY TRUE LOVE JACK SCOTT
MY UKELELE MAX BYGRAVES
MY UNFINISHED SYMPHONY DAVID WHITFIELD
MY UNKNOWN LOVE COUNT INDIGO
MY VISION JAKATTA FEATURING SEAL
MY WAY [A] EDDIE COCHRAN
MY WAY [B] FRANK SINATRA
MY WAY [B] DOROTHY SQUIRES
MY WAY [B] ELVIS PRESLEY
MY WAY [B] SEX PISTOLS
MY WAY [B] SHANE MacGOWAN
MY WAY [C] LIMP BIZKIT
MY WAY OF GIVING IN CHRIS FARLOWE
MY WAY OF THINKING UB40
MY WEAKNESS IS NONE OF YOUR BUSINESS EMBRACE
MY WHITE BICYCLE NAZARETH
MY WOMAN'S MAN DAVE DEE
MY WORLD [A] CUPID'S INSPIRATION
MY WORLD [B] BEE GEES
MY WORLD [C] SECRET AFFAIR
MY WORLD OF BLUE KARL DENVER
MYFANWY DAVID ESSEX
MYSTERIES OF LOVE L.A. MIX
MYSTERIES OF THE WORLD MFSB
MYSTERIOUS GIRL PETER ANDRE FEATURING BUBBLER
    RANX
MYSTERIOUS TIMES SASH! FEATURING TINA COUSINS
MYSTERIOUS WAYS U2
MYSTERY [A] DIO
MYSTERY [B] MYSTERY
MYSTERY GIRL [A] JESS CONRAD
MYSTERY GIRL [B] DUKES
MYSTERY LADY BILLY OCEAN
MYSTERY LAND Y-TRAXX FEATURING NEVE
MYSTERY LAND (EP) Y-TRAXX
MYSTERY SONG STATUS QUO
MYSTERY TRAIN ELVIS PRESLEY
MYSTICAL MACHINE GUN KULA SHAKER
MYSTIFY INXS
MYZSTERIOUS MIZSTER JONES SLADE
NA NA HEY HEY KISS HIM GOODBYE STEAM

NA NA HEY HEY KISS HIM GOODBYE BANANARAMA
NA NA IS THE SADDEST WORD STYLISTICS
NA NA NA COZY POWELL
NADINE (IS IT YOU) CHUCK BERRY
NAGASAKI BADGER DISCO CITIZENS
NAILS IN MY FEET CROWDED HOUSE
NAIROBI TOMMY STEELE
NAÏVE SONG MIRWAIS
NAKASAKI EP (I NEED A LOVER TONIGHT) KEN DOH
NAKED [A] REEF
NAKED [B] LOUISE
NAKED AND SACRED CHYNNA PHILLIPS
NAKED AND SACRED MARIA NAYLER
NAKED EYE LUSCIOUS JACKSON
NAKED IN THE RAIN BLUE PEARL
NAKED LOVE (JUST SAY YOU WANT ME) QUARTZ &
    DINA CARROLL
NAKED WITHOUT YOU ROACHFORD
NAME AND NUMBER CURIOSITY
THE NAME OF THE GAME ABBA
THE NAMELESS ONE WENDY JAMES
NANCY BOY PLACEBO
A NANNY IN MANHATTAN LILYS
NAPOLEON WOLFMAN
NAPPY LOVE GOODIES
NARCO TOURISTS SLAM VS UNKLE
NARCOTIC INFLUENCE EMPIRION
NASHVILLE BOOGIE BERT WEEDON
NASHVILLE CATS LOVIN' SPOONFUL
NASTRADAMUS NAS
NASTY JANET JACKSON
NASTY GIRLS T.W.A.
NATALIE'S PARTY SHACK
NATHAN JONES SUPREMES
NATHAN JONES BANANARAMA
NATIONAL EXPRESS DIVINE COMEDY
NATIVE BOY (UPTOWN) ANIMAL NIGHTLIFE
NATIVE LAND EVERYTHING BUT THE GIRL
NATIVE NEW YORKER ODYSSEY
NATIVE NEW YORKER BLACKBOX
NATURAL [A] BRYAN POWELL
NATURAL [B] PETER ANDRE
NATURAL [C] S CLUB 7
NATURAL BLUES MOBY
NATURAL BORN BUGIE HUMBLE PIE
NATURAL BORN KILLAZ DR DRE & ICE CUBE
NATURAL HIGH [A] BLOODSTONE
NATURAL HIGH [B] BITTY McLEAN
NATURAL LIFE NATURAL LIFE
NATURAL ONE FOLK IMPLOSION
NATURAL SINNER FAIR WEATHER
NATURAL THING INNOCENCE
NATURAL WORLD RODEO JONES
NATURE BOY [A] BOBBY DARIN
NATURE BOY [A] GEORGE BENSON
NATURE BOY [A] CENTRAL LINE
NATURE BOY [B] NICK CAVE & THE BAD SEEDS
NATURE OF LOVE WATERFRONT
NATURE'S TIME FOR LOVE JOE BROWN & THE
    BRUVVERS
NAUGHTY CHRISTMAS (GOBLIN IN THE OFFICE) FAT LES
NAUGHTY GIRL [A] HOLLY VALANCE
NAUGHTY GIRL [B] BEYONCÉ
NAUGHTY GIRLS SAMANTHA FOX FEATURING FULL
    FORCE
NAUGHTY LADY OF SHADY LANE DEAN MARTIN
NAUGHTY LADY OF SHADY LANE AMES BROTHERS
NAUGHTY NAUGHTY JOHN PARR
NAUGHTY NAUGHTY NAUGHTY JOY SARNEY
THE NAUGHTY NORTH & THE SEXY SOUTH E-MOTION
NAZIS ROGER TAYLOR

NE-NE-NA-NA-NA-NA-NU-NU BAD MANNERS
NEANDERTHAL MAN HOTLEGS
NEAR TO ME TEENAGE FANCLUB & JAD FAIR
NEAR WILD HEAVEN R.E.M.
NEAR YOU MIGIL FIVE
NEARER THAN HEAVEN DELAYS
NEARLY LOST YOU SCREAMING TREES
NECESSARY EVIL BODY COUNT
NEED GOOD LOVE TUFF JAM
NEED YOU TONIGHT INXS
NEED YOUR LOVE SO BAD FLEETWOOD MAC
NEED YOUR LOVE SO BAD GARY MOORE
NEEDIN' U DAVID MORALES PRESENTS THE FACE
NEEDIN' YOU II DAVID MORALES PRESENTS THE FACE
    FEATURING JULIET ROBERTS
THE NEEDLE AND THE DAMAGE DONE NEIL YOUNG
NEEDLES AND PINS SEARCHERS
NEEDLES AND PINS SMOKIE
NEGASONIC TEENAGE WARHEAD MONSTER MAGNET
NEGATIVE MANSUN
NEHEMIAH HOPE OF THE STATES
NEIGHBOUR UGLY KID JOE
NEIGHBOURHOOD [A] SPACE
NEIGHBOURHOOD [B] ZED BIAS
NEIL JUNG TEENAGE FANCLUB
NEITHER ONE OF US GLADYS KNIGHT & THE PIPS
NELLIE THE ELEPHANT TOY DOLLS
NELSON MANDELA SPECIAL A.K.A.
NEON KNIGHTS BLACK SABBATH
NEON LIGHTS KRAFTWERK
NEPTUNE INME
NERVOUS MATT BIANCO
NERVOUS BREAKDOWN [A] CARLEEN ANDERSON
NERVOUS BREAKDOWN [B] SHRINK
NERVOUS SHAKEDOWN AC/DC
NERVOUS WRECK RADIO STARS
NESSAJA SCOOTER
NESSUN DORMA LUCIANNO PAVAROTTI
NESSUN DORMA FROM 'TURANDOT' LUIS COBOS
    FEATURING PLACIDO DOMINGO
NETHERWORLD LSG
NEUROTICA CUD
NEUTRON DANCE POINTER SISTERS
NEVER [A] HEART
NEVER [B] HOUSE OF LOVE
NEVER [C] JOMANDA
NEVER [D] ELECTRAFIXION
NEVER 'AD NOTHIN' ANGELIC UPSTARTS
NEVER AGAIN [A] DISCHARGE
NEVER AGAIN [B] MISSION
NEVER AGAIN [C] JC 001
NEVER AGAIN [D] HAPPY CLAPPERS
NEVER AGAIN [E] NICKELBACK
NEVER AGAIN (THE DAYS TIME ERASED) CLASSIX
    NOUVEAUX
NEVER BE ANYONE ELSE BUT YOU RICKY NELSON
NEVER BE THE SAME AGAIN MELANIE C & LISA LEFT
    EYE LOPES
NEVER BEFORE DEEP PURPLE
NEVER CAN SAY GOODBYE JACKSON 5
NEVER CAN SAY GOODBYE GLORIA GAYNOR
NEVER CAN SAY GOODBYE COMMUNARDS
NEVER CAN SAY GOODBYE YAZZ
NEVER CAN TELL I KAMANCHI
NEVER DO A TANGO WITH AN ESKIMO ALMA COGAN
NEVER DO YOU WRONG STEPHANIE MILLS
NEVER DONE NOTHING LIKE THAT BEFORE SUPERGRASS
NEVER ENDING HALO
NEVER ENDING SONG OF LOVE NEW SEEKERS
NEVER ENDING STORY LIMAHL
NEVER ENOUGH [A] JESUS JONES

NEVER ENOUGH [B] CURE
NEVER ENOUGH [C] BORIS DLUGOSCH FEATURING ROISIN MURPHY
NEVER ENOUGH [D] OPEN
NEVER EVER ALL SAINTS
NEVER FELT LIKE THIS BEFORE SHAZNAY LEWIS
NEVER FELT THIS WAY HI-LUX
NEVER FORGET TAKE THAT
NEVER FOUND A LOVE LIKE THIS BEFORE UPSIDE DOWN
NEVER GIVE UP MONIE LOVE
NEVER GIVE UP ON A GOOD THING GEORGE BENSON
NEVER GIVE YOU UP SHARON REDD
NEVER GOIN' DOWN ADAMSKI FEATURING JIMI POLO
NEVER GOING NOWHERE BLUETONES
NEVER GONNA BE THE SAME DANNY WILSON
NEVER GONNA CHANGE MY MIND JOEY LAWRENCE
NEVER GONNA COME BACK DOWN BT
NEVER GONNA CRY AGAIN EURYTHMICS
NEVER GONNA FALL IN LOVE AGAIN DANA
NEVER GONNA GIVE YOU UP [A] MUSICAL YOUTH
NEVER GONNA GIVE YOU UP [B] RICK ASTLEY
NEVER GONNA GIVE (YOU UP) [B] F.K.W.
NEVER GONNA GIVE YOU UP (WON'T LET YOU BE) PATRICE RUSHEN
NEVER GONNA LEAVE YOUR SIDE DANIEL BEDINGFIELD
NEVER GONNA LET YOU GO [B] TINA MOORE
NEVER GONNA LET YOU GO [A] SERGIO MENDES
NEVER GOODBYE KARL DENVER
NEVER HAD A DREAM COME TRUE [A] STEVIE WONDER
NEVER HAD A DREAM COME TRUE [B] S CLUB 7
NEVER HAD IT SO GOOD TAKE 5
NEVER IN A MILLION YEARS BOOMTOWN RATS
NEVER KNEW LOVE [A] RICK ASTLEY
NEVER KNEW LOVE [B] OLETA ADAMS
NEVER KNEW LOVE [C] NIGHTCRAWLERS
NEVER KNEW LOVE [D] STELLA BROWNE
NEVER KNEW LOVE LIKE THIS ALEXANDER O'NEAL FEATURING CHERRELLE
NEVER KNEW LOVE LIKE THIS PAULINE HENRY FEATURING WAYNE MARSHALL
NEVER KNEW LOVE LIKE THIS BEFORE STEPHANIE MILLS
NEVER LEAVE YOU (UH OOOH UH OOOH) LUMIDEE
NEVER LET GO [A] JOHN BARRY ORCHESTRA
NEVER LET GO [B] HYPER GO GO
NEVER LET GO [C] CLIFF RICHARD
NEVER LET HER SLIP AWAY ANDREW GOLD
NEVER LET HER SLIP AWAY UNDERCOVER
NEVER LET HER SLIP AWAY TREVOR WALTERS
NEVER LET ME DOWN DAVID BOWIE
NEVER LET ME DOWN AGAIN DEPECHE MODE
NEVER LET YOU DOWN HONEYZ
NEVER LET YOU GO NKOTB
NEVER LOOK BACK DUMONDE
NEVER LOST HIS HARDCORE NRG
NEVER LOST THAT FEELING SWERVEDRIVER
NEVER MIND CLIFF RICHARD
NEVER MIND THE PRESENTS BARRON KNIGHTS
NEVER MISS THE WATER CHAKA KHAN FEATURING ME'SHELL NDEGEOCELLO
NEVER MY LOVE SUGAR MINOTT
NEVER NEVER [A] ASSEMBLY
NEVER NEVER [B] WARM JETS
NEVER NEVER GONNA GIVE YA UP BARRY WHITE
NEVER NEVER GONNA GIVE YOU UP LISA STANSFIELD
NEVER NEVER LOVE SIMPLY RED
NEVER NEVER NEVER SHIRLEY BASSEY
NEVER ON SUNDAY DON COSTA
NEVER ON SUNDAY MANUEL & HIS MUSIC OF THE MOUNTAINS
NEVER ON SUNDAY LYNN CORNELL

NEVER ON SUNDAY MAKADOPOULOS & HIS GREEK SERENADERS
NEVER ON SUNDAY CHAQUITO
NEVER (PAST TENSE) ROC PROFECT FEATURING TINA ARENA
NEVER REALLY WAS MARIO WINANS FEATURING LIL' FLIP
NEVER SAW A MIRACLE CURTIS STIGERS
NEVER SAY DIE BLACK SABBATH
NEVER SAY DIE (GIVE A LITTLE BIT MORE) CLIFF RICHARD
NEVER SAY GOODBYE BON JOVI
NEVER STOP [A] ECHO & THE BUNNYMEN
NEVER STOP [B] BRAND NEW HEAVIES FEATURING N'DEA DAVENPORT
NEVER SURRENDER SAXON
NEVER TAKE ME ALIVE SPEAR OF DESTINY
NEVER TEAR US APART INXS
NEVER THERE CAKE
NEVER TOO FAR MARIAH CAREY FEATURING MYSTIKAL
NEVER TOO LATE KYLIE MINOGUE
NEVER TOO MUCH LUTHER VANDROSS
NEVER TRUST A STRANGER KIM WILDE
NEVER TURN AWAY ORCHESTRAL MANOEUVRES IN THE DARK
NEVER TURN YOUR BACK ON MOTHER EARTH SPARKS
NEVER UNDERSTAND JESUS & MARY CHAIN
NEVERTHELESS FRANKIE VAUGHAN
NEVERTHELESS EVE GRAHAM & THE NEW SEEKERS
NEW NO DOUBT
NEW AMSTERDAM ELVIS COSTELLO & THE ATTRACTIONS
NEW ANGER GARY NUMAN
NEW BEGINNING [A] STEPHEN GATELY
NEW BEGINNING [B] PRECIOUS
NEW BEGINNING (MAMBA SEYRA) BUCKS FIZZ
NEW BIRD REEF
NEW BORN MUSE
NEW DAWN PROPHETS OF SOUND
A NEW DAY [A] KILLING JOKE
NEW DAY [B] WYCLEF JEAN FEATURING BONO
A NEW DAY HAS COME CELINE DION
NEW DIMENSIONS IMAGINATION
NEW DIRECTION [A] FREAKPOWER
NEW DIRECTION [B] S CLUB JUNIORS
NEW EMOTION TIME FREQUENCY
A NEW ENGLAND KIRSTY MacCOLL
A NEW FASHION BILL WYMAN
A NEW FLAME SIMPLY RED
NEW GENERATION SUEDE
NEW GRANGE CLANNAD
NEW GUITAR IN TOWN LURKERS
NEW HOME NEW LIFE ALARM
NEW KICKS JOHANN
NEW KID IN TOWN EAGLES
NEW KIND OF MEDICINE ULTRA NATE
NEW LIFE DEPECHE MODE
NEW LIVE AND RARE EP DEEP PURPLE
NEW LIVE AND RARE II (EP) DEEP PURPLE
NEW LIVE AND RARE VOLUME 3 EP DEEP PURPLE
NEW MISTAKE JELLYFISH
NEW MOON ON MONDAY DURAN DURAN
NEW ORLEANS U.S. BONDS
NEW ORLEANS BERN ELLIOTT & THE FENMEN
NEW ORLEANS HARLEY QUINNE
NEW ORLEANS GILLAN
NEW POLICY ONE TERRORVISION
THE NEW POLLUTION BECK
NEW POWER GENERATION PRINCE
NEW SENSATION INXS
NEW SONG HOWARD JONES

A NEW SOUTH WALES ALARM FEATURING THE MORRISTON ORPHEUS MALE VOICE CHOIR
NEW THING FROM LONDON TOWN SHARPE & NUMAN
NEW TOY LENE LOVICH
NEW WAY, NEW LIFE ASIAN DUB FOUNDATION
NEW WORLD IN THE MORNING ROGER WHITTAKER
NEW WORLD MAN RUSH
NEW YEAR SUGABABES
NEW YEARS DAY U2
NEW YEARS DUB MUSIQUE VS U2
NEW YORK AFTERNOON MONDO KANE
NEW YORK CITY T. REX
NEW YORK CITY BOY PET SHOP BOYS
NEW YORK CITY COPS STROKES
NEW YORK EYES NICOLE WITH TIMMY THOMAS
NEW YORK GROOVE HELLO
NEW YORK MINING DISASTER 1941 BEE GEES
NEW YORK NEW YORK RYAN ADAMS
NEW YORK UNDERCOVER 4-TRACK EP NEW YORK UNDERCOVER
NEW YORK, NEW YORK GERARD KENNY
NEWBORN ELBOW
NEWBORN FRIEND SEAL
NEWS AT TEN VAPORS
NEWS OF THE WORLD JAM
THE NEXT BIG THING JESUS JONES
NEXT DOOR TO AN ANGEL NEIL SEDAKA
THE NEXT EPISODE DR DRE FEATURING SNOOP DOGGY DOGG
NEXT LEVEL ILS
NEXT LIFETIME ERYKAH BADU
THE NEXT TIME CLIFF RICHARD & THE SHADOWS
NEXT TIME YOU FALL IN LOVE REVA RICE & GREG ELLIS
NEXT TO YOU ASWAD
NEXT YEAR FOO FIGHTERS
NHS (EP) DJ DOC SCOTT
NI-TEN-ICHI-RYU (TWO SWORDS TECHNIQUE) PHOTEK
NIALL QUINN'S DISCO PANTS A LOVE SUPREME
NICE AND SLOW [A] JESSE GREEN
NICE AND SLOW [B] USHER
NICE GUY EDDIE SLEEPER
NICE IN NICE STRANGLERS
NICE LEGS SHAME ABOUT HER FACE MONKS
NICE 'N' EASY FRANK SINATRA
NICE 'N' SLEAZY STRANGLERS
NICE 'N' SLOW FREDDIE JACKSON
NICE ONE CYRIL COCKEREL CHORUS
NICE WEATHER FOR DUCKS LEMON JELLY
THE NIGHT FRANKIE VALLI & THE FOUR SEASONS
THE NIGHT INTASTELLA
THE NIGHT SOFT CELL
THE NIGHT SCOOTER
A NIGHT AT DADDY GEE'S SHOWADDYWADDY
A NIGHT AT THE APOLLO LIVE! DARYL HALL & JOHN OATES FEATURING DAVID RUFFIN & EDDIE KENDRICK
NIGHT BIRDS SHAKATAK
NIGHT BOAT TO CAIRO MADNESS
NIGHT BOAT TO CAIRO EP MADNESS
THE NIGHT CHICAGO DIED PAPER LACE
NIGHT CRAWLER JUDAS PRIEST
NIGHT DANCING JOE FARRELL
THE NIGHT THE EARTH CRIED GRAVEDIGGAZ
NIGHT FEVER [A] FATBACK BAND
NIGHT FEVER [B] BEE GEES
NIGHT FEVER [B] CAROL DOUGLAS
NIGHT FEVER [B] ADAM GARCIA
THE NIGHT FEVER MEGAMIX MIXMASTERS
NIGHT GAMES GRAHAM BONNET
THE NIGHT HAS A THOUSAND EYES BOBBY VEE
NIGHT IN MOTION CUBIC 22

NIGHT IN MY VEINS PRETENDERS
A NIGHT IN NEW YORK ELBOW BONES & THE
   RACKETEERS
THE NIGHT IS YOUNG GARY MILLER
NIGHT LADIES CRUSADERS
NIGHT LIFE DAVID LEE ROTH
NIGHT LINE RANDY CRAWFORD
NIGHT MOVES BOB SEGER & THE SILVER BULLET BAND
NIGHT NURSE SLY & ROBBIE FEATURING SIMPLY RED
NIGHT OF FEAR MOVE
NIGHT OF THE LIVING BASEHEADS PUBLIC ENEMY
NIGHT OF THE LONG GRASS TROGGS
NIGHT OF THE VAMPIRE MOONTREKKERS
NIGHT OWL GERRY RAFFERTY
NIGHT PORTER JAPAN
THE NIGHT THEY DROVE OLD DIXIE DOWN JOAN BAEZ
A NIGHT TO REMEMBER SHALAMAR
NIGHT TO REMEMBER 911
NIGHT TRAIN [A] BUDDY MORROW
NIGHT TRAIN [B] VISAGE
THE NIGHT THE WINE THE ROSES LIQUID GOLD
NIGHT VISION HELL IS FOR HEROES
THE NIGHT YOU MURDERED LOVE ABC
NIGHTBIRD CONVERT
THE NIGHTFLY BLANK & JONES
NIGHTLIFE KENICKIE
NIGHTMARE [A] GILLAN
NIGHTMARE [B] SAXON
NIGHTMARE [C] KID UNKNOWN
NIGHTMARE [D] BRAINBUG
NIGHTMARES A FLOCK OF SEAGULLS
NIGHTRAIN GUNS N' ROSES
NIGHTS IN WHITE SATIN MOODY BLUES
NIGHTS IN WHITE SATIN DICKIES
NIGHTS IN WHITE SATIN ELKIE BROOKS
NIGHTS OF PLEASURE LOOSE ENDS
NIGHTS ON BROADWAY CANDI STATON
NIGHTS OVER EGYPT INCOGNITO
NIGHTSHIFT COMMODORES
NIGHTSWIMMING R.E.M.
NIGHTTRAIN PUBLIC ENEMY
THE NIGHTTRAIN KADOC
NIKITA ELTON JOHN
NIKKE DOES IT BETTER NIKKE? NICOLE!
NIMBUS 808 STATE
9 A.M. (THE COMFORT ZONE) LONDONBEAT
900 DEGREES IAN POOLEY
911 WYCLEF FEATURING MARY J. BLIGE
911 IS A JOKE PUBLIC ENEMY
9PM (TILL I COME) ATB
977 PRETENDERS
NINE TIMES OUT OF TEN CLIFF RICHARD & THE
   SHADOWS
9 TO 5 [A] SHEENA EASTON
9 TO 5 [B] DOLLY PARTON
19 PAUL HARDCASTLE
19/2000 GORILLAZ
NINE WAYS JDS
NINETEEN63 NEW ORDER
1979 SMASHING PUMPKINS
1980 ESTELLE
1985 BOWLING FOR SOUP
1999 [A] PRINCE & THE REVOLUTION
1999 [B] BINARY FINARY
1962 GRASS-SHOW
NINETEENTH NERVOUS BREAKDOWN ROLLING STONES
90S GIRL BLACKGIRL
99 1/2 CAROL LYNN TOWNES
92 DEGREES POP WILL EAT ITSELF
96 TEARS ? (QUESTION MARK) & THE MYSTERIANS
96 TEARS STRANGLERS

98.6 KEITH
98.6 BYSTANDERS
95 – NASTY W.A.S.P.
99 PROBLEMS JAY-Z
99 RED BALLOONS NENA
NINETY-NINE WAYS TAB HUNTER
99.9o F SUZANNE VEGA
92 TOUR (EP) MOTORHEAD
NIPPLE TO THE BOTTLE GRACE JONES
NITE AND DAY AL B SURE!
NITE AND FOG MERCURY REV
NITE CLUB SPECIALS (FEATURING RICO)
NITE LIFE KIM ENGLISH
NITRO PALE X
N-N-NINETEEN NOT OUT COMMENTATORS
NO CHUCK D
NO ALIBIS ERIC CLAPTON
NO ARMS CAN EVER HOLD YOU BACHELORS
NO BLUE SKIES LLOYD COLE
NO CHANCE (NO CHARGE) BILLY CONNOLLY
NO CHARGE J.J. BARRIE
NO CHEAP THRILL SUZANNE VEGA
NO CHRISTMAS WEDDING PRESENT
NO CLASS MOTORHEAD
NO CLAUSE 28 BOY GEORGE
NO CONVERSATION VIEW FROM THE HILL
NO DIGGITY BLACKstreet FEATURING DR DRE
NO DISTANCE LEFT TO RUN BLUR
NO DOUBT [A] 702
NO DOUBT [B] IMAJIN
NO DOUBT ABOUT IT HOT CHOCOLATE
NO DREAM IMPOSSIBLE LINDSAY
NO EDUCATION NO FUTURE (F**K THE CURFEW)
   MOGWAI
NO ESCAPIN' THIS BEATNUTS
NO FACE, NO NAME, NO NUMBER TRAFFIC
NO FLOW LISA ROXANNE
NO FOOL (FOR LOVE) HAZELL DEAN
NO FRONTS DOG EAT DOG
NO GETTING OVER YOU PARIS
NO GOOD DA FOOL
NO GOOD ADVICE GIRLS ALOUD
NO GOOD FOR ME [A] BRUCE WAYNE
NO GOOD 4 ME [B] OXIDE & NEUTRINO FEATURING
   MEGAMAN
NO GOOD (START THE DANCE) PRODIGY
NO GOODBYES CURTIS MAYFIELD
NO GOVERNMENT NICOLETTE
NO HIDING PLACE KEN MACKINTOSH
NO HONESTLY LYNSEY DE PAUL
NO LAUGHING IN HEAVEN GILLAN
NO LETTING GO WAYNE WONDER
NO LIES S.O.S. BAND
NO LIMIT 2 UNLIMITED
NO LIMITS BAKSHELF DOG
NO LOVE JOAN ARMATRADING
NO MAN'S LAND [A] GERARD KENNY
NO MAN'S LAND [B] BILLY JOEL
(NO MATTER HOW HIGH I GET) I'LL STILL BE LOOKIN' UP
   TO YOU WILTON FELDER FEATURING BOBBY
   WOMACK & INTRODUCING ALLTRINA GRAYSON
NO MATTER HOW I TRY GILBERT O'SULLIVAN
NO MATTER WHAT [A] BADFINGER
NO MATTER WHAT [B] BOYZONE
NO MATTER WHAT I DO WILL MELLOR
NO MATTER WHAT SIGN YOU ARE DIANA ROSS & THE
   SUPREMES
NO MATTER WHAT THEY SAY LIL' KIM
NO MATTER WHAT YOU DO BENNY BENASSI PRESENTS
   THE BIZ
NO MEMORY SCARLET FANTASTIC

NO MERCY STRANGLERS
NO MILK TODAY HERMAN'S HERMITS
NO MORE [A] McGUIRE SISTERS
NO MORE [B] UNIQUE 3
NO MORE [C] RUFF ENDZ
NO MORE [D] A1
NO MORE AFFAIRS TINDERSTICKS
NO MORE ALCOHOL SUGGS FEATURING LOUCHIE LOU
   & MICHIE ONE
NO MORE (BABY I'MA DO RIGHT) 3LW
NO MORE DRAMA MARY J. BLIGE
NO MORE HEROES STRANGLERS
NO MORE (I CAN'T STAND IT) MAXX
NO MORE 'I LOVE YOU'S LOVER SPEAKS
NO MORE 'I LOVE YOUS' ANNIE LENNOX
NO MORE LIES SHARPE & NUMAN
NO MORE LONELY NIGHTS (BALLAD) PAUL McCARTNEY
(NO MORE) LOVE AT YOUR CONVENIENCE ALICE
   COOPER
NO MORE MR. NICE GUY ALICE COOPER
NO MORE MR. NICE GUY MEGADETH
NO MORE RAINY DAYS FREE SPIRIT
NO MORE TALK DUBSTAR
NO MORE TEARS [A] HOLLYWOOD BEYOND
NO MORE TEARS [B] JAKI GRAHAM
NO MORE TEARS [C] OZZY OSBOURNE
NO MORE TEARS (ENOUGH IS ENOUGH) DONNA
   SUMMER & BARBRA STREISAND
NO MORE TEARS (ENOUGH IS ENOUGH) KYM MAZELLE
   & JOCELYN BROWN
NO MORE THE FOOL ELKIE BROOKS
NO MORE TOMORROWS PAUL JOHNSON
NO MORE TURNING BACK GITTA
NO MULE'S FOOL FAMILY
NO NEED ALFIE
NO NO JOE SILVER CONVENTION
NO NO NO [A] NANCY NOVA
NO NO NO DESTINY'S CHILD FEATURING WYCLEF JEAN
NO NO NO [C] MANIJAMA FEATURING MUKUPA &
   LIL' T
NO, NOT NOW HOT HOT HEAT
NO ONE [A] RAY CHARLES
NO ONE [B] 2 UNLIMITED
NO ONE BUT YOU [A] BILLY ECKSTINE
NO-ONE BUT YOU [B] QUEEN
NO ONE CAN MARILLION
NO ONE CAN BREAK A HEART LIKE YOU DAVE CLARK
   FIVE
NO ONE CAN LOVE YOU MORE THAN ME KYM MAZELLE
NO ONE CAN MAKE MY SUNSHINE SMILE EVERLY
   BROTHERS
NO ONE CAN STOP US NOW CHELSEA F.C.
NO-ONE DRIVING (DOUBLE SINGLE) JOHN FOXX
NO ONE ELSE COMES CLOSE JOE
NO ONE GETS THE PRIZE DIANA ROSS
NO ONE IS INNOCENT SEX PISTOLS, PUNK PRAYER BY
   RONALD BIGGS
NO ONE IS TO BLAME HOWARD JONES
NO ONE KNOWS QUEENS OF THE STONE AGE
NO ONE LIKE YOU SCORPIONS
NO ONE SPEAKS GENEVA
NO ONE TO CRY TO RAY CHARLES
NO ONE WILL EVER KNOW FRANK IFIELD
NO ONE'S DRIVING DAVE CLARKE
NO ORDINARY LOVE SADE
NO ORDINARY MORNING/HALCYON CHICANE
NO OTHER BABY BOBBY HELMS
NO OTHER BABY PAUL McCARTNEY
NO OTHER LOVE JOHNSTON BROTHERS
NO OTHER LOVE RONNIE HILTON
NO OTHER LOVE EDMUND HOCKRIDGE

NO PANTIES TRINA
NO PARTICULAR PLACE TO GO CHUCK BERRY
NO PIGEONS SPORTY THIEVZ
NO PLACE TO HIDE KORN
NO PROMISES ICEHOUSE
NO RAIN BLIND MELON
NO REGRETS [A] SHIRLEY BASSEY
NO REGRETS [B] WALKER BROTHERS
NO REGRETS [B] MIDGE URE
NO REGRETS [C] ROBBIE WILLIAMS
NO RELIGION VAN MORRISON
NO REST NEW MODEL ARMY
NO SCRUBS TLC
NO SELF CONTROL PETER GABRIEL
NO SELL OUT MALCOLM X
NO SLEEP NO NEED EP VAULTS
NO SLEEP TO BROOKLYN BEASTIE BOYS
NO SON OF MINE GENESIS
NO STONE UNTURNED TRUTH
NO STRESS CYCLEFLY
NO SUCH THING JOHN MAYER
NO SURPRISES RADIOHEAD
NO SURRENDER DEUCE
NO SURVIVORS GBH
NO SWEAT '98 NORTH & SOUTH
NO TENGO DINERO LOS UMERELLOS
NO TIME LIL' KIM FEATURING PUFF DADDY
NO TIME TO BE 21 ADVERTS
NO TIME TO CRY SISTERS OF MERCY
NO TIME TO PLAY GURU FEATURING D C LEE
NO WAY FREAKPOWER
NO WAY NO WAY VANILLA
NO WAY OUT FRANCESCO ZAPPALA
NO WOMAN NO CRY BOB MARLEY & THE WAILERS
NO WOMAN NO CRY FUGEES
NO WOMAN NO CRY LONDONBEAT
NO. 1 RAT FAN ROLAND RAT SUPERSTAR
THE NOBODIES MARILYN MANSON
NOBODY [A] TONI BASIL
NOBODY [B] TONGUE 'N' CHEEK
NOBODY [C] SHARA NELSON
NOBODY [D] KEITH SWEAT FEATURING ATHENA CAGE
NOBODY BETTER TINA MOORE
NOBODY BUT YOU GLADYS KNIGHT & THE PIPS
NOBODY (CAN LOVE ME) TONGUE IN CHEEK
NOBODY DOES IT BETTER CARLY SIMON
NOBODY ELSE [A] NICK KAMEN
NOBODY ELSE [B] TYRESE
NOBODY I KNOW PETER & GORDON
NOBODY KNOWS [A] NIK KERSHAW
NOBODY KNOWS [B] TONY RICH PROJECT
NOBODY MADE ME RANDY EDELMAN
NOBODY NEEDS YOUR LOVE GENE PITNEY
NOBODY TOLD ME JOHN LENNON
NOBODY WANTS TO BE LONELY RICKY MARTIN WITH
    CHRISTINA AGUILERA
NOBODY WINS ELTON JOHN
NOBODY'S BUSINESS [A] H2O FEATURING BILLIE
NOBODY'S BUSINESS [B] PEACE BY PIECE
NOBODY'S CHILD KAREN YOUNG
NOBODY'S CHILD TRAVELING WILBURYS
NOBODY'S DARLIN' BUT MINE FRANK IFIELD
NOBODY'S DIARY YAZOO
NOBODY'S FOOL [A] JIM REEVES
NOBODY'S FOOL [B] HAIRCUT 100
NOBODY'S HERO STIFF LITTLE FINGERS
NOBODY'S HOME AVRIL LAVIGNE
NOBODY'S SUPPOSED TO BE HERE DEBORAH COX
NOBODY'S TWISTING YOUR ARM WEDDING PRESENT
NOCTURNE T99
NOMANSLAND (DAVID'S SONG) DJ SAKIN & FRIENDS

NOMZAMO (ONE PEOPLE ONE CAUSE) LATIN QUARTER
NON HO L'ETA PER AMARTI GIGLIOLA CINQUETTI
NONE OF YOUR BUSINESS SALT-N-PEPA
(NONSTOPOPERATION) DUST JUNKYS
NORA MALONE TERESA BREWER
NORMAN CAROL DEENE
NORMAN 3 TEENAGE FANCLUB
NORMAN BATES LANDSCAPE
NORTH COUNTRY BOY CHARLATANS
NORTH TO ALASKA JOHNNY HORTON
NORTH, SOUTH, EAST, WEST MARVIN & TAMARA
NORTHERN LIGHTS [A] RENAISSANCE
NORTHERN LITES [B] SUPER FURRY ANIMALS
NORTHERN STAR MELANIE C
NOT A DRY EYE IN THE HOUSE MEAT LOAF
NOT A JOB ELBOW
NOT A MINUTE TOO SOON VIXEN
NOT ABOUT US GENESIS
NOT ALONE BERNARD BUTLER
NOT ANYONE BLACK BOX
NOT AS A STRANGER FRANK SINATRA
NOT AT ALL STATUS QUO
NOT ENOUGH MELANIE WILLIAMS
NOT ENOUGH LOVE IN THE WORLD CHER
NOT EVEN GONNA TRIP HONEYZ
NOT FADE AWAY ROLLING STONES
NOT FOR ALL THE LOVE IN THE WORLD THRILLS
NOT FOR YOU PEARL JAM
NOT GON' CRY MARY J. BLIGE
NOT GONNA GET US tATu
NOT IF YOU WERE THE LAST JUNKIE ON EARTH DANDY
    WARHOLS
NOT IN LOVE ENRIQUE FEATURING KELIS
NOT ME NOT I DELTA GOODREM
NOT NOW JOHN PINK FLOYD
NOT OVER YET GRACE
NOT OVER YOU YET DIANA ROSS
NOT RESPONSIBLE TOM JONES
NOT SLEEPING AROUND NED'S ATOMIC DUSTBIN
NOT SO MANIC NOW DUBSTAR
NOT SUCH AN INNOCENT GIRL VICTORIA BECKHAM
NOT THAT KIND ANASTACIA
NOT THE GIRL YOU THINK YOU ARE CROWDED HOUSE
(NOT THE) GREATEST RAPPER 1000 CLOWNS
NOT TODAY MARY J. BLIGE FEATURING EVE
NOT TONIGHT LIL' KIM
NOT TOO LATE FOR LOVE BEVERLEY KNIGHT
NOT TOO LITTLE NOT TOO MUCH CHRIS SANDFORD
NOT UNTIL NEXT TIME JIM REEVES
NOT WHERE IT'S AT DEL AMITRI
NOTGONNACHANGE SWING OUT SISTER
NOTHIN' NORE
NOTHIN' AT ALL HEART
NOTHIN' BUT A GOOD TIME POISON
NOTHIN' BUT A PARTY TRUCE
NOTHIN' MY LOVE CAN'T FIX JOEY LAWRENCE
NOTHIN' PERSONAL DUST JUNKYS
(NOTHIN' SERIOUS) JUST BUGGIN' WHISTLE
NOTHIN' (THAT COMPARES 2 U) JACKSONS
NOTHIN' TO DO MICHAEL HOLLIDAY
NOTHING [A] FRAZIER CHORUS
NOTHING [B] FLUFFY
NOTHING [C] A
NOTHING [D] HOLDEN & THOMPSON
NOTHING AS IT SEEMS PEARL JAM
NOTHING AT ALL LUKE SLATER
NOTHING 'BOUT ME STING
NOTHING BUT LOVE OPTIMYSTIC
NOTHING BUT YOU PAUL VAN DYK FEATURING
    HEMSTOCK
NOTHING CAN CHANGE THIS LOVE BITTY McLEAN

NOTHING CAN DIVIDE US JASON DONOVAN
NOTHING CAN STOP ME GENE CHANDLER
NOTHING CAN STOP US SAINT ETIENNE
NOTHING COMES EASY SANDIE SHAW
NOTHING COMPARES 2 U SINEAD O'CONNOR
NOTHING COMPARES 2 U MXM
NOTHING ELSE MATTERS METALLICA
NOTHING EVER HAPPENS DEL AMITRI
NOTHING FAILS MADONNA
NOTHING HAS BEEN PROVED DUSTY SPRINGFIELD
NOTHING HAS BEEN PROVED STRINGS OF LOVE
NOTHING HURTS LIKE LOVE DANIEL BEDINGFIELD
NOTHING IN PARTICULAR BROTHERHOOD
NOTHING IS FOREVER ULTRACYNIC
NOTHING IS REAL BUT THE GIRL BLONDIE
NOTHING LASTS FOREVER ECHO & THE BUNNYMEN
NOTHING LEFT ORBITAL
NOTHING LEFT TOULOUSE SAD CAFÉ
NOTHING LESS THAN BRILLIANT SANDIE SHAW
NOTHING NATURAL LUSH
NOTHING REALLY MATTERS MADONNA
NOTHING RHYMED GILBERT O'SULLIVAN
NOTHING SACRED – A SONG FOR KIRSTY RUSSELL
    WATSON
NOTHING TO DECLARE LAPTOP
NOTHING TO FEAR CHRIS REA
NOTHING TO LOSE [A] UK
NOTHING TO LOSE [B] S-EXPRESS
NOTHING WITHOUT ME MANCHILD
NOTHING WRONG WITH YOU FINN BROTHERS
NOTHING'S GONNA CHANGE MY LOVE FOR YOU GLENN
    MEDEIROS
NOTHING'S GONNA STOP ME NOW SAMANTHA FOX
NOTHING'S GONNA STOP US NOW STARSHIP
NOTHIN'S GONNA CHANGE LABI SIFFRE
NOTORIOUS DURAN DURAN
NOTORIOUS B.I.G. NOTORIOUS B.I.G. FEATURING PUFF
    DADDY
NOVELTY WAVES BIOSPHERE
NOVEMBER RAIN GUNS N' ROSES
NOVEMBER SPAWNED A MONSTER MORRISSEY
NOVOCAINE FOR THE SOUL EELS
NOW [A] AL MARTINO
NOW [B] VAL DOONICAN
NOW [C] DEF LEPPARD
NOW ALWAYS AND FOREVER GAY DAD
NOW AND FOREVER RICHARD MARX
NOW I KNOW WHAT MADE OTIS BLUE PAUL YOUNG
NOW I'M HERE QUEEN
NOW IS THE TIME JIMMY JAMES & THE VAGABONDS
NOW IS TOMORROW DEFINITION OF SOUND
NOW IT'S GONE CHORDS
NOW IT'S ON GRANDADDY
NOW I'VE FOUND YOU SEAN MAGUIRE
NOW OR NEVER TOM NOVY FEATURING LIMA
NOW THAT I OWN THE BBC SPARKS
NOW THAT THE MAGIC HAS GONE JOE COCKER
NOW THAT WE FOUND LOVE HEAVY D. & THE BOYZ
NOW THAT WE'VE FOUND LOVE THIRD WORLD
NOW THAT YOU LOVE ME ALICE BAND
NOW THAT YOU'VE GONE MIKE + THE MECHANICS
NOW THEY'LL SLEEP BELLY
NOW THOSE DAYS ARE GONE BUCKS FIZZ
NOW WE ARE FREE GLADIATOR FEATURING IZZY
NOW WE'RE THRU POETS
NOW YOU'RE GONE [A] BLACK
NOW YOU'RE GONE [B] WHITESNAKE
NOW YOU'RE IN HEAVEN JULIAN LENNON
NOWHERE [A] THERAPY?
NOWHERE [B] LONGVIEW
NOWHERE AGAIN SECRET MACHINES

NOWHERE FAST MEAT LOAF
NOWHERE GIRL B-MOVIE
NOWHERE LAND CLUBHOUSE FEATURING CARL
NOWHERE MAN THREE GOOD REASONS
NOWHERE TO RUN MARTHA REEVES & THE VANDELLAS
NOWHERE TO RUN 2000 NU GENERATION
N-R-G ADAMSKI
NU FLOW BIG BROVAZ
NUCLEAR RYAN ADAMS
NUCLEAR DEVICE (THE WIZARD OF AUS) STRANGLERS
NUCLEAR HOLIDAY 3 COLOURS RED
NUFF VIBES EP APACHE INDIAN
NUMB LINKIN PARK
NUMB/ENCORE JAY-Z VS LINKIN PARK
#9 DREAM JOHN LENNON
THE NUMBER OF THE BEAST IRON MAIDEN
NUMBER ONE [A] E.Y.C.
NUMBER ONE [B] A
NUMBER 1 [C] TWEENIES
NUMBER ONE [D] PLAYGROUP
NUMBER 1 [E] EBONY DUBSTERS
NUMBER ONE BLIND VERUCA SALT
NUMBER ONE DEE JAY GOODY GOODY
NUMBER ONE DOMINATOR TOP
THE NUMBER ONE SONG IN HEAVEN SPARKS
NUMBERS SOFT CELL
NUMERO UNO STARLIGHT
NUNC DIMITTIS PAUL PHEONIX
NURSERY RHYMES ICEBURG SLIMM
NURTURE LFO
NUT ROCKER B. BUMBLE & THE STINGERS
NUTBUSH CITY LIMITS IKE & TINA TURNER
NUTBUSH CITY LIMITS TINA TURNER
NUTHIN' BUT A 'G' THANG DR. DRE
N.WO MINISTRY
N.Y.C. (CAN YOU BELIEVE THIS CITY) CHARLES & EDDIE
O BABY SIOUXSIE & THE BANSHEES
O L'AMOUR DOLLAR
O' MY FATHER HAD A RABBIT RAY MOORE
O-O-O ADRENALIN M.O.D.
O SUPERMAN LAURIE ANDERSON
03 BONNIE AND CLYDE JAY-Z FEATURING BEYONCÉ
    KNOWLES
OAKLAND STROKE TONY! TONI! TONE!
OB-LA-DI OB-LA-DA MARMALADE
OB-LA-DI OB-LA-DA BEDROCKS
OBJECTION (TANGO) SHAKIRA
OBJECTS IN THE REAR VIEW MIRROR MAY APPEAR
    CLOSER THAN THEY ARE MEAT LOAF
OBLIVION TERRORVISION
OBLIVION (HEAD IN THE CLOUDS) (EP) MANIX
OBLIVIOUS AZTEC CAMERA
THE OBOE SONG CLERGY
OBSESSED 999
OBSESSION [A] REG OWEN
OBSESSION [B] ANIMOTION
OBSESSION [C] ARMY OF LOVERS
OBSESSION [D] ULTRA-SONIC
OBSESSION [E] TIESTO & JUNKIE XL
OBSESSION (SI ES AMOR) 3RD WISH
OBSESSIONS SUEDE
OBSTACLE 1 INTERPOL
OBVIOUS WESTLIFE
THE OBVIOUS CHILD PAUL SIMON
OBVIOUSLY McFLY
OCEAN AVENUE YELLOWCARD
OCEAN BLUE ABC
OCEAN DEEP CLIFF RICHARD
OCEAN DRIVE LIGHTHOUSE FAMILY
OCEAN OF ETERNITY FUTURE BREEZE
OCEAN PIE SHED SEVEN

OCEAN SPRAY MANIC STREET PREACHERS
OCTOBER SWIMMER JJ72
ODE TO BILLY JOE BOBBIE GENTRY
ODE TO BOY ALISON MOYET
ODE TO JOY (FROM BEETHOVEN'S SYMPHONY NO 9)
    BBC CONCERT ORCHESTRA/BBC SYMPHONY
    CHORUS/STEPHEN JACKSON
ODE TO MY FAMILY CRANBERRIES
THE ODYSSEY DRUMSOUND/SIMON BASSLINE SMITH
OF COURSE I'M LYING YELLO
OF COURSE YOU CAN SPEARHEAD
OFF ON HOLIDAY SUGGS
OFF ON YOUR OWN (GIRL) AL B SURE!
OFF THE HOOK JODY WATLEY
OFF THE WALL MICHAEL JACKSON
OFF THE WALL WISDOME
OFFICIAL SECRETS M
OFFSHORE CHICANE
OFFSHORE BANKING BUSINESS MEMBERS
OH BABE WHAT WOULD YOU SAY? HURRICANE SMITH
OH BABY RHIANNA
OH BABY I... ETERNAL
(OH BABY MINE) I GET SO LONELY FOUR KNIGHTS
OH BOY [A] CRICKETS
OH BOY [A] MUD
OH BOY [A] FABULOUS BAKER BOYS
OH BOY [B] CAM'RON FEATURING JUELZ SANTANA
OH BOY (THE MOOD I'M IN) BROTHERHOOD OF MAN
OH CAROL [A] NEIL SEDAKA
OH CAROL! [A] CLINT EASTWOOD & GENERAL SAINT
OH CAROL [B] SMOKIE
OH CAROLINA SHAGGY
OH DIANE FLEETWOOD MAC
OH FATHER MADONNA
OH GIRL CHI-LITES
OH GIRL PAUL YOUNG
OH HAPPY DAY [A] JOHNSTON BROTHERS
OH HAPPY DAY [B] EDWIN HAWKINS SINGERS
    FEATURING DOROTHY COMBS MORRISON
OH HOW I MISS YOU BACHELORS
OH JIM GAY DAD
OH JULIE SHAKIN' STEVENS
OH LA LA LA 2 EIVISSA
OH L'AMOUR ERASURE
OH LONESOME ME CRAIG DOUGLAS
OH LORI ALESSI
OH LOUISE JUNIOR
OH ME OH MY (I'M A FOOL FOR YOU BABY) LULU
OH MEIN PAPA EDDIE CALVERT
OH MILLWALL MILLWALL FC
OH MY GOD [A] A TRIBE CALLED QUEST
OH MY GOD [B] KAISER CHIEFS
OH MY PAPA EDDIE FISHER
OH NO [A] COMMODORES
OH NO [B] MOS DEF/NATE DOGG/PHAROAHE MONCH
OH NO NOT MY BABY MANFRED MANN
OH NO NOT MY BABY ROD STEWART
OH NO NOT MY BABY CHER
OH NO WON'T DO CUD
OH OH, I'M FALLING IN LOVE AGAIN JIMMIE RODGERS
OH PATTI (DON'T FEEL SORRY FOR LOVERBOY) SCRITTI
    POLITTI
OH, PEOPLE PATTI LABELLE
OH PRETTY WOMAN ROY ORBISON
OH PRETTY WOMAN GARY MOORE FEATURING ALBERT
    KING
OH ROMEO MINDY McCREADY
OH SHEILA READY FOR THE WORLD
OH THE GUILT NIRVANA
OH WELL FLEETWOOD MAC
OH WELL OH WELL

OH WHAT A CIRCUS DAVID ESSEX
OH WHAT A FEELING CHANGE
OH WHAT A NIGHT CLOCK
OH WHAT A SHAME ROY WOOD
OH WORLD PAUL RUTHERFORD
OH YEAH! [A] BILL WITHERS
OH YEAH [B] ASH
OH YEAH [C] CAPRICE
OH YEAH [D] FOXY BROWN
OH YEAH, BABY DWEEB
OH YEAH (ON THE RADIO) ROXY MUSIC
OH YES! YOU'RE BEAUTIFUL GARY GLITTER
OH YOU PRETTY THING PETER NOONE
OH YOU WANT MORE TY FEATURING ROOTS MANUVA
OH! WHAT A DAY CRAIG DOUGLAS
OH! WHAT A WORLD SISTER BLISS WITH COLETTE
OHIO UTAH SAINTS
OI PLATINUM 45 FEATURING MORE FIRE CREW
OK BIG BROVAZ
O.K.? JULIE COVINGTON, RULA LENSKA, CHARLOTTE
    CORNWELL & SUE JONES-DAVIES
O.K. FRED ERROLL DUNKLEY
OKAY! DAVE DEE, DOZY, BEAKY, MICK & TICH
OL' MACDONALD FRANK SINATRA
OL' RAG BLUES STATUS QUO
OLD [A] KEVIN ROWLAND & DEXY'S MIDNIGHT
    RUNNERS
OLD [B] MACHINE HEAD
OLD AND WISE ALAN PARSONS PROJECT
OLD BEFORE I DIE ROBBIE WILLIAMS
THE OLD FASHIONED WAY CHARLES AZNAVOUR
OLD FLAMES FOSTER & ALLEN
OLD FOLKS A
OLD HABITS DIE HARD MICK JAGGER & DAVE STEWART
THE OLD MAN AND THE ANGEL IT BITES
OLD MAN AND ME (WHEN I GET TO HEAVEN) HOOTIE &
    THE BLOWFISH
OLD OAKEN BUCKET TOMMY SANDS
THE OLD PAYOLA ROLL BLUES STAN FREBERG WITH
    JESSIE WHITE
OLD PIANO RAG DICKIE VALENTINE
OLD POP IN AN OAK REDNEX
OLD RED EYES IS BACK BEAUTIFUL SOUTH
OLD RIVERS WALTER BRENNAN
THE OLD RUGGED CROSS ETHNA CAMPBELL
OLD SHEP CLINTON FORD
OLD SIAM SIR WINGS
OLD SMOKEY JOHNNY & THE HURRICANES
THE OLD SONGS BARRY MANILOW
OLDER GEORGE MICHAEL
OLDEST SWINGER IN TOWN FRED WEDLOCK
OLE OLA (MULHER BRASILEIRA) ROD STEWART
    FEATURING THE SCOTTISH WORLD CUP FOOTBALL
    SQUAD
OLIVE TREE JUDITH DURHAM
OLIVER'S ARMY ELVIS COSTELLO & THE ATTRACTIONS
OLYMPIAN GENE
OLYMPIC 808 STATE
AN OLYMPIC RECORD BARRON KNIGHTS
THE OMD REMIXES OMD
OMEN ORBITAL
THE OMEN PROGRAM 2 BELTRAM
OMEN III MAGIC AFFAIR
ON APHEX TWIN
ON A CAROUSEL HOLLIES
ON A CROWDED STREET BARBARA PENNINGTON
ON A DAY LIKE TODAY BRYAN ADAMS
ON A LITTLE STREET IN SINGAPORE MANHATTAN
    TRANSFER
ON A MISSION ALOOF
ON A NIGHT LIKE THIS KYLIE MINOGUE

ON A RAGGA TIP SL2
ON A ROPE ROCKET FROM THE CRYPT
ON A SATURDAY NIGHT TERRY DACTYL & THE DINOSAURS
ON A SLOW BOAT TO CHINA EMILE FORD & THE CHECKMATES
ON A SUNDAY NICK HEYWARD
ON A SUN-DAY BENZ
ON AND ON [A] ASWAD
ON AND ON [B] LONGPIGS
ON & ON [C] ERYKAH BADU
ON BENDED KNEE BOYZ II MEN
ON EVERY STREET DIRE STRAITS
ON FIRE [A] T-CONNECTION
ON FIRE [B] TONE LOC
ON FIRE [C] LLOYD BANKS
ON HER MAJESTY'S SECRET SERVICE PROPELLERHEADS & DAVID ARNOLD
ON HORSEBACK MIKE OLDFIELD
ON MOTHER KELLY'S DOORSTEP DANNY LA RUE
ON MY KNEES 411 FEATURING GHOSTFACE KILLAH
ON MY MIND FUTURESHOCK FEATURING BEN ONONO
ON MY OWN [A] PATTI LABELLE & MICHAEL McDONALD
ON MY OWN [B] CRAIG McLACHLAN
ON MY OWN [C] PEACH
ON MY RADIO SELECTER
ON MY WAY [A] MR FINGERS
ON MY WAY [B] MIKE KOGLIN FEATURING BEATRICE
ON MY WAY HOME ENYA
ON MY WORD CLIFF RICHARD
ON OUR OWN (FROM GHOSTBUSTERS II) BOBBY BROWN
ON POINT HOUSE OF PAIN
ON SILENT WINGS TINA TURNER
ON STANDBY SHED SEVEN
ON THE BEACH [A] CLIFF RICHARD & THE SHADOWS
ON THE BEACH [B] CHRIS REA
ON THE BEACH [B] YORK
ON THE BEAT B B & Q BAND
ON THE BIBLE DEUCE
ON THE DANCEFLOOR DJ DISCIPLE
ON THE HORIZON MELANIE C
ON THE INSIDE (THEME FROM 'PRISONER CELL BLOCK H') LYNNE HAMILTON
ON THE LEVEL YOMANDA
ON THE MOVE BARTHEZZ
ON THE ONE LUKK FEATURING FELICIA COLLINS
ON THE RADIO DONNA SUMMER
ON THE RADIO MARTINE McCUTCHEON
...ON THE RADIO (REMEMBER THE DAYS) NELLY FURTADO
ON THE REBOUND FLOYD CRAMER
ON THE ROAD AGAIN CANNED HEAT
ON THE ROPES (EP) WONDER STUFF
ON THE ROSE TIGER
ON THE RUN [A] DE BOS
ON THE RUN [B] OMC
ON THE RUN [C] BIG TIME CHARLIE
ON THE RUN [D] TILLMANN UHRMACHER
ON THE RUN [E] CRESCENT
ON THE STREET WHERE YOU LIVE VIC DAMONE
ON THE STREET WHERE YOU LIVE DAVID WHITFIELD
ON THE TOP OF THE WORLD DIVA SURPRISE FEATURING GEORGIA JONES
ON THE TRAIL PRIME MOVERS
ON THE TURNING AWAY PINK FLOYD
ON THE WINGS OF A NIGHTINGALE EVERLY BROTHERS
ON THE WINGS OF LOVE JEFFREY OSBORNE
ON WITH THE MOTLEY HARRY SECOMBE

ON YA WAY '94 HELICOPTER
ON YOUR OWN [A] VERVE
ON YOUR OWN [B] BLUR
ONCE GENEVIEVE
ONCE AGAIN [A] CUD
1NCE AGAIN [B] A TRIBE CALLED QUEST
ONCE AROUND THE BLOCK BADLY DRAWN BOY
ONCE AROUND THE SUN CAPRICE
ONCE BITTEN TWICE SHY [A] IAN HUNTER
ONCE BITTEN TWICE SHY [B] VESTA WILLIAMS
ONCE I HAD A SWEETHEART PENTANGLE
ONCE IN A LIFETIME TALKING HEADS
ONCE IN EVERY LIFETIME KEN DODD
ONCE MORE ORB
ONCE THERE WAS A TIME TOM JONES
ONCE UPON A DREAM BILLY FURY
ONCE UPON A LONG AGO PAUL McCARTNEY
ONCE UPON A TIME [A] MARVIN GAYE & MARY WELLS
ONCE UPON A TIME [B] TOM JONES
ONCE UPON A TIME [C] POGUES
ONCE UPON A TIME IN AMERICA JEEVAS
ONCE YOU'VE TASTED LOVE TAKE THAT
ONE [A] METALLICA
ONE [B] BEE GEES
ONE [C] U2
ONE [C] MICA PARIS
THE ONE [D] ELTON JOHN
ONE [E] BUSTA RHYMES FEATURING ERYKAH BADU
THE ONE [F] BACKSTREET BOYS
THE ONE [G] DEE DEE
THE ONE [H] CASSIUS HENRY FEATURING FREEWAY
ONE & ONE ROBERT MILES FEATURING MARIA NAYLER
ONE AND ONE IS ONE MEDICINE HEAD
THE ONE AND ONLY [A] GLADYS KNIGHT & THE PIPS
THE ONE AND ONLY [B] CHESNEY HAWKES
ONE ARMED SCISSOR AT THE DRIVE-IN
ONE BETTER DAY MADNESS
ONE BETTER WORLD ABC
ONE BIG FAMILY EP EMBRACE
ONE BROKEN HEART FOR SALE ELVIS PRESLEY
ONE BY ONE CHER
ONE CALL AWAY CHINGY FEATURING J WEAV
ONE COOL REMOVE SHAWN COLVIN WITH MARY CHAPIN CARPENTER
ONE DANCE WON'T DO AUDREY HALL
ONE DAY [A] TYRREL CORPORATION
ONE DAY [B] D MOB
ONE DAY AT A TIME [A] LENA MARTELL
ONE DAY AT A TIME [B] ALICE BAND
ONE DAY I'LL FLY AWAY RANDY CRAWFORD
ONE DAY IN YOUR LIFE [A] MICHAEL JACKSON
ONE DAY IN YOUR LIFE [B] ANASTACIA
ONE DRINK TOO MANY SAILOR
ONE EP MANSUN
ONE FINE DAY [A] CHIFFONS
ONE FINE DAY [B] OPERABABES
ONE FINE DAY [C] JAKATTA
ONE FINE MORNING TOMMY HUNT
ONE FOOT IN THE GRAVE ERIC IDLE FEATURING RICHARD WILSON
THE ONE FOR ME JOE
ONE FOR SORROW STEPS
ONE FOR THE MOCKINGBIRD CUTTING CREW
ONE FOR THE MONEY HORACE BROWN
ONE FOR YOU ONE FOR ME JONATHAN KING
ONE FOR YOU ONE FOR ME LA BIONDA
ONE GIANT LOVE CUD
ONE GIFT OF LOVE DEAR JON
ONE GOODBYE IN TEN SHARA NELSON
ONE GREAT THING BIG COUNTRY
ONE HEADLIGHT WALLFLOWERS

ONE HEART CELINE DION
ONE HEART BETWEEN TWO DAVE BERRY
ONE HELLO RANDY CRAWFORD
ONE HORSE TOWN THRILLS
101 SHEENA EASTON
101 DAM-NATIONS SCARLET PARTY
100 MILES AND RUNNIN' NWA
100% SONIC YOUTH
100% MARY KIANI
100% PURE LOVE CRYSTAL WATERS
THE ONE I GAVE MY HEART TO AALIYAH
THE ONE I LOVE R.E.M.
ONE IN A MILLION AALIYAH
ONE IN TEN UB40
ONE IN TEN 808 STATE Vs UB40
ONE INCH ROCK TYRANNOSAURUS REX
ONE KISS FROM HEAVEN LOUISE
ONE LAST BREATH/BULLETS CREED
ONE LAST KISS J GEILS BAND
ONE LAST LOVE SONG BEAUTIFUL SOUTH
ONE LOVE [A] ATLANTIC STARR
ONE LOVE [B] PAT BENATAR
ONE LOVE [C] STONE ROSES
ONE LOVE [D] DR ALBAN
ONE LOVE [E] PRODIGY
ONE LOVE [F] BLUE
ONE LOVE – PEOPLE GET READY BOB MARLEY & THE WAILERS
ONE LOVE FAMILY LIQUID
ONE LOVE IN MY LIFETIME INNOCENCE
ONE LOVER AT A TIME ATLANTIC STARR
ONE LOVER (DON'T STOP THE SHOW) FORREST
ONE MAN CHANELLE
ONE MAN ARMY OUR LADY PEACE
ONE MAN BAND LEO SAYER
ONE MAN IN MY HEART HUMAN LEAGUE
ONE MAN WOMAN SHEENA EASTON
ONE MAN'S BITCH PHOEBE ONE
ONE MIND, TWO HEARTS PARADISE
ONE MINUTE MAN MISSY ELLIOTT FEATURING LUDACRIS
ONE MIRROR TO MANY BLACK CROWES
ONE MOMENT IN TIME WHITNEY HOUSTON
ONE MORE HAZIZA
ONE MORE CHANCE [A] DIANA ROSS
ONE MORE CHANCE [B] MAXI PRIEST
ONE MORE CHANCE [C] E.Y.C.
ONE MORE CHANCE [D] MADONNA
ONE MORE CHANCE [E] THE ONE
ONE MORE CHANCE [F] MICHAEL JACKSON
ONE MORE CHANCE/STAY WITH ME NOTORIOUS B.I.G.
ONE MORE DANCE ESTHER & ABI OFARIM
ONE MORE GOOD NIGHT WITH THE BOYS TASMIN ARCHER
ONE MORE NIGHT PHIL COLLINS
ONE MORE RIVER LUCIANA
ONE MORE SATURDAY NIGHT MATCHBOX
ONE MORE SUNRISE (MORGEN) DICKIE VALENTINE
ONE MORE TIME [A] WHYCLIFFE
ONE MORE TIME [B] DAFT PUNK
ONE MORE TRY [A] GEORGE MICHAEL
ONE MORE TRY [B] KRISTINE W
ONE NATION MASQUERADE
ONE NATION UNDER A GROOVE (PART 1) FUNKADELIC
ONE NIGHT ELVIS PRESLEY
ONE NIGHT MUD
ONE NIGHT IN BANGKOK MURRAY HEAD
ONE NIGHT IN HEAVEN M PEOPLE
ONE NIGHT STAND [A] LET LOOSE
ONE NIGHT STAND [B] ALOOF
ONE NIGHT STAND [C] MIS-TEEQ

ONE NINE FOR SANTA FOGWELL FLAX & THE ANKLEBITERS FROM FREHOLD JUNIOR SCHOOL
ONE OF THE LIVING TINA TURNER
ONE OF THE LUCKY ONES JOAN REGAN
ONE OF THE PEOPLE ADAMSKI'S THING
ONE OF THESE DAYS AMBASSADOR
ONE OF THESE NIGHTS EAGLES
ONE OF THOSE NIGHTS BUCKS FIZZ
ONE OF US [A] ABBA
ONE OF US [B] JOAN OSBORNE
ONE OF US [C] HELL IS FOR HEROES
ONE OF US MUST KNOW (SOONER OR LATER) BOB DYLAN
ONE ON ONE DARYL HALL & JOHN OATES
ONE PERFECT SUNRISE ORBITAL
ONE PIECE AT A TIME JOHNNY CASH WITH THE TENNESSEE THREE
ONE REASON WHY CRAIG McLACHLAN
ONE ROAD LOVE AFFAIR
ONE RULE FOR YOU AFTER THE FIRE
ONE SHINING MOMENT DIANA ROSS
ONE SHOT BROTHERHOOD
ONE SLIP PINK FLOYD
ONE SMALL DAY ULTRAVOX
ONE STEP KILLAH PRIEST
ONE STEP AHEAD NIK KERSHAW
ONE STEP AWAY TAVARES
ONE STEP BEYOND MADNESS
ONE STEP CLOSER [A] LINKIN PARK
ONE STEP CLOSER [B] S CLUB JUNIORS
ONE STEP CLOSER (TO LOVE) GEORGE McCRAE
ONE STEP FURTHER BARDO
ONE STEP OUT OF TIME MICHAEL BALL
ONE STEP TOO FAR FAITHLESS FEATURING DIDO
ONE SWEET DAY MARIAH CAREY & BOYZ II MEN
1000% FATIMA MANSIONS
138 TREK DJ ZINC
ONE TO ANOTHER CHARLATANS
THE ONE TO CRY ESCORTS
1 TO 1 RELIGION BOMB THE BASS FEATURING CARLTON
THE ONE TO SING THE BLUES MOTORHEAD
ONE TONGUE HOTHOUSE FLOWERS
ONE TRUE WOMAN YAZZ
1-2-3 [A] LEN BARRY
1-2-3 [B] PROFESSIONALS
1-2-3 [C] GLORIA ESTEFAN & MIAMI SOUND MACHINE
1-2-3 [D] CHIMES
ONE, TWO, THREE [E] DINA CARROLL
1234 MRS WOOD
1-2-3-4 GET WITH THE WICKED RICHARD BLACKWOOD
1,2,3,4 (SUMPIN' NEW) COOLIO
1-2-3 O'LEARY DES O'CONNOR
ONE VISION QUEEN
ONE VOICE BILL TARMEY
ONE WAY LEVELLERS
ONE WAY LOVE CLIFF BENNETT & THE REBEL ROUSERS
ONE WAY MIRROR KINESIS
ONE WAY OUT REID
ONE WAY TICKET ERUPTION
ONE WEEK BARENAKED LADIES
ONE WILD NIGHT BON JOVI
ONE WISH SHYSTIE
ONE WOMAN JADE
THE ONES YOU LOVE RICK ASTLEY
ONION SONG MARVIN GAYE & TAMMI TERRELL
ONLY ANTHRAX
ONLY A BOY TIM BURGESS
ONLY CRYING KEITH MARSHALL
THE ONLY FLAME IN TOWN ELVIS COSTELLO
ONLY FOOLS (NEVER FALL IN LOVE) SONIA

ONLY FOR A WHILE TOPLOADER
ONLY FOR LOVE LIMAHL
ONLY HAPPY WHEN IT RAINS GARBAGE
ONLY HUMAN DINA CARROLL
ONLY IF... ENYA
ONLY IN MY DREAMS DEBBIE GIBSON
THE ONLY LIVING BOY IN NEW CROSS CARTER – THE UNSTOPPABLE SEX MACHINE
THE ONLY LIVING BOY IN NEW YORK (EP) EVERYTHING BUT THE GIRL
ONLY LOVE NANA MOUSKOURI
ONLY LOVE CAN BREAK YOUR HEART ELKIE BROOKS
ONLY LOVE CAN BREAK YOUR HEART MINT JULEPS
ONLY LOVE CAN BREAK YOUR HEART SAINT ETIENNE
ONLY LOVE REMAINS PAUL McCARTNEY
ONLY LOVING DOES IT GUYS & DOLLS
THE ONLY MAN ON THE ISLAND TOMMY STEELE
THE ONLY MAN ON THE ISLAND VIC DAMONE
ONLY ME HYPERLOGIC
THE ONLY ONE [A] TRANSVISION VAMP
THE ONLY ONE [B] GUN
ONLY ONE [C] PETER ANDRE
THE ONLY ONE [D] THUNDER
THE ONLY ONE I KNOW CHARLATANS
ONLY ONE ROAD CELINE DION
ONLY ONE WOMAN MARBLES
ONLY ONE WORD PROPAGANDA
THE ONLY RHYME THAT BITES MC TUNES VERSUS 808 STATE
ONLY SAW TODAY – INSTANT KARMA AMOS
ONLY SIXTEEN CRAIG DOUGLAS
ONLY SIXTEEN SAM COOKE
ONLY SIXTEEN AL SAXON
ONLY TENDER LOVE DEACON BLUE
ONLY THE HEARTACHES HOUSTON WELLS
ONLY THE LONELY [A] ROY ORBISON
ONLY THE LONELY [A] PRELUDE
ONLY THE LONELY [B] T'PAU
ONLY THE LOOT CAN MAKE ME HAPPY R KELLY
ONLY THE MOMENT MARC ALMOND
ONLY THE ONES WE LOVE TANITA TIKARAM
ONLY THE STRONG SURVIVE BILLY PAUL
ONLY THE STRONG SURVIVE DJ KRUSH
ONLY THE STRONGEST WILL SURVIVE HURRICANE #1
ONLY THE WOMEN KNOW SIX CHIX
THE ONLY THING THAT LOOKS GOOD ON ME IS YOU BRYAN ADAMS
ONLY TIME ENYA
ONLY TIME WILL TELL [A] ASIA
ONLY TIME WILL TELL [B] TEN CITY
ONLY TO BE WITH YOU ROACHFORD
ONLY WANNA KNOW U COS URE FAMOUS OXIDE & NEUTRINO
THE ONLY WAY IS UP YAZZ & THE PLASTIC POPULATION
THE ONLY WAY OUT CLIFF RICHARD
ONLY WHEN I LOSE MYSELF DEPECHE MODE
ONLY WHEN I SLEEP CORRS
ONLY WHEN YOU LEAVE SPANDAU BALLET
ONLY WITH YOU CAPTAIN HOLLYWOOD PROJECT
ONLY WOMEN BLEED JULIE COVINGTON
ONLY YESTERDAY CARPENTERS
ONLY YOU [A] HILLTOPPERS
ONLY YOU [A] PLATTERS
ONLY YOU [A] MARK WYNTER
ONLY YOU [A] JEFF COLLINS
ONLY YOU [A] RINGO STARR
ONLY YOU (AND YOU ALONE) [A] CHILD
ONLY YOU [A] JOHN ALFORD
ONLY YOU [B] TEDDY PENDERGRASS
ONLY YOU [C] YAZOO
ONLY YOU [C] FLYING PICKETS

ONLY YOU [D] PRAISE
ONLY YOU [E] PORTISHEAD
ONLY YOU [F] CASINO
ONLY YOU CAN FOX
ONLY YOU CAN ROCK ME UFO
ONLY YOUR LOVE BANANARAMA
ONWARD CHRISTIAN SOLDIERS HARRY SIMEONE CHORALE
OO...AH...CANTONA OO LA LA
007 DESMOND DEKKER & THE ACES
007 MUSICAL YOUTH
OOCHIE WALLY QB FINEST FEATURING NAS & BRAVEHEARTS
OOCHY KOOCHY (F.U. BABY YEAH YEAH) BABY FORD
OO-EEH BABY STONEBRIDGE McGUINNESS
OOH! AAH! CANTONA 1300 DRUMS FEATURING THE UNJUSTIFIED ANCIENTS OF MU
OOH AAH (G-SPOT) WAYNE MARSHALL
OOH AAH...JUST A LITTLE BIT GINA G
OOH-AH-AA (I FEEL IT) E.Y.C.
OOH BABY GILBERT O'SULLIVAN
OOH BOY ROSE ROYCE
OOH I DO LYNSEY DE PAUL
OOH I LIKE IT JONNY L
OOH! LA! LA! [A] JOE 'MR PIANO' HENDERSON
OOH LA LA [B] COOLIO
OOH LA LA [C] ROD STEWART
OOH LA LA [D] WISEGUYS
OOH LA LA LA RED RAW FEATURING 007
OOH LA LA LA (LET'S GO DANCIN') KOOL & THE GANG
OOH MY SOUL LITTLE RICHARD
OOH STICK YOU! DAPHNE & CELESTE
OOH TO BE AH KAJAGOOGOO
OOH-WAKKA-DOO-WAKKA-DAY GILBERT O'SULLIVAN
OOH WEE MARK RONSON
OOH! WHAT A LIFE GIBSON BROTHERS
OOHHH BABY VIDA SIMPSON
OOO LA LA LA TEENA MARIE
OOOH DE LA SOUL FEATURING REDMAN
OOOIE, OOOIE, OOOIE PRICKLY HEAT
OOOPS 808 STATE FEATURING BJORK
OOOPS UP SNAP
OOPS!...I DID IT AGAIN BRITNEY SPEARS
OOPS (OH MY) TWEET
OOPS UPSIDE YOUR HEAD GAP BAND
OOPS UPSIDE YOUR HEAD DJ CASPER FEATURING THE GAP BAND
OPAL MANTRA THERAPY?
OPEN ARMS [A] MARIAH CAREY
OPEN ARMS [B] WILT
OPEN ARMS [C] TINA TURNER
OPEN HEART ZOO MARTIN GRECH
AN OPEN LETTER TO NYC BEASTIE BOYS
OPEN ROAD [A] GARY BARLOW
OPEN ROAD [B] BRYAN ADAMS
OPEN SESAME LEILA K
OPEN UP [A] MUNGO JERRY
OPEN UP [B] LEFTFIELD LYDON
OPEN UP THE RED BOX SIMPLY RED
OPEN UP YOUR HEART JOAN REGAN
OPEN YOUR EYES [A] BLACK BOX
OPEN YOUR EYES [B] GOLDFINGER
OPEN YOUR HEART [A] HUMAN LEAGUE
OPEN YOUR HEART [B] M PEOPLE
OPEN YOUR HEART [C] MADONNA
OPEN YOUR MIND [A] 808 STATE
OPEN YOUR MIND [B] USURA
OPEN YOUR MIND (LET ME IN) REAL PEOPLE
THE OPERA HOUSE JACK E MAKOSSA
THE OPERA SONG (BRAVE NEW WORLD) JURGEN VRIES FEATURING CMC

OPERAA HOUSE WORLD'S FAMOUS SUPREME TEAM SHOW

OPERATION BLADE (BASS IN THE PLACE) PUBLIC DOMAIN

OPERATOR [A] MIDNIGHT STAR

OPERATOR [B] LITTLE RICHARD

OPIUM SCUMBAGZ OLAV BASOSKI

O.P.P. NAUGHTY BY NATURE

OPPORTUNITIES (LET'S MAKE LOTS OF MONEY) PET SHOP BOYS

OPPOSITES ATTRACT PAULA ABDUL & THE WILD PAIR

OPTIMISTIC SOUNDS OF BLACKNESS

OPUS 17 (DON'T YOU WORRY 'BOUT ME) FOUR SEASONS WITH FRANKIE VALLI

OPUS 40 MERCURY REV

ORANGE BLOSSOM SPECIAL SPOTNICKS

ORANGE CRUSH R.E.M.

THE ORANGE THEME CYGNUS X

ORCHARD ROAD LEO SAYER

ORCHESTRAL MANOEUVRES IN THE DARKNESS EP DIFF'RENT DARKNESS

ORDINARY ANGEL HUE & CRY

ORDINARY DAY [A] CURIOSITY KILLED THE CAT

ORDINARY DAY [B] VANESSA CARLTON

ORDINARY GIRL ALISON MOYET

ORDINARY LIVES BEE GEES

ORDINARY WORLD DURAN DURAN

ORDINARY WORLD AURORA FEATURING NAIMEE COLEMAN

ORIGINAL LEFTFIELD FEATURING TONI HALLIDAY

ORIGINAL BIRD DANCE ELECTRONICAS

ORIGINAL NUTTAH U.K. APACHI WITH SHY FX

ORIGINAL PRANKSTER OFFSPRING

ORIGINAL SIN ELTON JOHN

ORIGINAL SIN (THEME FROM 'THE SHADOW') TAYLOR DAYNE

ORINOCO FLOW ENYA

ORLANDO DAWN LIQUID

ORPHEUS ASH

ORVILLE'S SONG KEITH HARRIS & ORVILLE

OSCAR SHACK

OSSIE'S DREAM (SPURS ARE ON THEIR WAY TO WEMBLEY) TOTTENHAM HOTSPUR F.A. CUP FINAL SQUAD

THE OTHER MAN'S GRASS PETULA CLARK

THE OTHER SIDE [A] AEROSMITH

THE OTHER SIDE [B] DAVID GRAY

THE OTHER SIDE OF LOVE YAZOO

THE OTHER SIDE OF ME ANDY WILLIAMS

THE OTHER SIDE OF SUMMER ELVIS COSTELLO

THE OTHER SIDE OF THE SUN JANIS IAN

THE OTHER SIDE OF YOU MIGHTY LEMON DROPS

THE OTHER WOMAN, THE OTHER MAN GERARD KENNY

OTHERNESS (EP) COCTEAU TWINS

OTHERSIDE RED HOT CHILI PEPPERS

OTHERWISE MORCHEEBA

OUIJA BOARD OUIJA BOARD MORRISSEY

OUR DAY WILL COME RUBY & THE ROMANTICS

OUR FAVOURITE MELODIES CRAIG DOUGLAS

OUR FRANK MORRISSEY

OUR GOAL ARSENAL FC

OUR HOUSE MADNESS

OUR KIND OF LOVE HANNAH

OUR LAST SONG TOGETHER NEIL SEDAKA

OUR LIPS ARE SEALED GO-GOS

OUR LIPS ARE SEALED FUN BOY THREE

OUR LIVES CALLING

OUR LOVE ELKIE BROOKS

(OUR LOVE) DON'T THROW IT ALL AWAY ANDY GIBB

OUR RADIO ROCKS PJ & DUNCAN

OUR WORLD BLUE MINK

OUT COME THE FREAKS WAS (NOT WAS)

OUT COME THE FREAKS (AGAIN) WAS (NOT WAS)

OUT DEMONS OUT EDGAR BROUGHTON BAND

OUT HERE ON MY OWN IRENE CARA

OUT IN THE DARK LURKERS

OUT IN THE FIELDS GARY MOORE & PHIL LYNOTT

OUT IS THROUGH ALANIS MORISSETTE

OUT OF BREATH RONI SIZE FEATURING RAHZEL

OUT OF CONTROL [A] ANGELIC UPSTARTS

OUT OF CONTROL [B] ROLLING STONES

OUT OF CONTROL [C] CHEMICAL BROTHERS

OUT OF CONTROL (BACK FOR MORE) DARUDE

OUT OF HAND MIGHTY LEMON DROPS

OUT OF MY HEAD MARRADONA

OUT OF MY HEART BBMAK

OUT OF MY MIND [A] JOHNNY TILLOTSON

OUT OF MY MIND [B] DURAN DURAN

OUT OF OUR MINDS CRACKOUT

OUT OF REACH [A] VICE SQUAD

OUT OF REACH [B] PRIMITIVES

OUT OF REACH [C] GABRIELLE

OUT OF SEASON ALMIGHTY

OUT OF SIGHT [A] BABY BIRD

OUT OF SIGHT [B] SPIRITUALIZED

OUT OF SIGHT, OUT OF MIND LEVEL 42

OUT OF SPACE PRODIGY

OUT OF TEARS ROLLING STONES

OUT OF THE BLUE [A] DEBBIE GIBSON

OUT OF THE BLUE [B] SYSTEM F

OUT OF THE BLUE [C] DELTA GOODREM

OUT OF THE SILENT PLANET IRON MAIDEN

OUT OF THE SINKING PAUL WELLER

OUT OF THE STORM INCOGNITO

OUT OF THE VOID GRASS-SHOW

OUT OF THIS WORLD TONY HATCH

OUT OF TIME [A] CHRIS FARLOWE

OUT OF TIME [A] DAN McCAFFERTY

OUT OF TIME [A] ROLLING STONES

OUT OF TIME [B] BLUR

OUT OF TOUCH DARYL HALL & JOHN OATES

OUT OF TOUCH UNITING NATIONS

OUT OF TOWN MAX BYGRAVES

OUT OF YOUR MIND TRUE STEPPERS & DANE BOWERS FEATURING VICTORIA BECKHAM

OUT ON THE FLOOR DOBIE GRAY

OUT THERE [A] DINOSAUR Jr.

OUT THERE [B] FRIENDS OF MATTHEW

OUT WITH HER BLOW MONKEYS

OUT-SIDE BETA BAND

OUTA SPACE BILLY PRESTON

OUTDOOR MINER WIRE

OUTERSPACE GIRL BELOVED

OUTLAW OLIVE

OUTRAGEOUS STIX 'N' STONED

OUTSHINED SOUNDGARDEN

OUTSIDE [A] OMAR

OUTSIDE [B] GEORGE MICHAEL

OUTSIDE [C] STAIND

OUTSIDE IN THE RAIN GWEN GUTHRIE

OUTSIDE MY WINDOW STEVIE WONDER

OUTSIDE OF HEAVEN EDDIE FISHER

OUTSIDE YOUR DOOR STANDS

OUTSIDE YOUR ROOM (EP) SLOWDIVE

OUTSTANDING GAP BAND

OUTSTANDING KENNY THOMAS

OUTSTANDING ANDY COLE

OUTTA SPACE MELLOW TRAX

OUTTATHAWAY VINES

OVER PORTISHEAD

OVER AND OVER [A] DAVE CLARK FIVE

OVER AND OVER [B] JAMES BOYS

OVER AND OVER [C] SHALAMAR

OVER & OVER [D] PLUX FEATURING GEORGIA JONES

OVER AND OVER [E] PUFF JOHNSON

OVER MY HEAD LIT

OVER MY SHOULDER MIKE + THE MECHANICS

OVER RISING CHARLATANS

OVER THE EDGE ALMIGHTY

OVER THE HILLS AND FAR AWAY GARY MOORE

OVER THE RAINBOW SAM HARRIS

OVER THE RAINBOW EVA CASSIDY

OVER THE RAINBOW – YOU BELONG TO ME (MEDLEY) MATCHBOX

OVER THE RIVER BITTY McLEAN

OVER THE SEA JESSE RAE

OVER THE WEEKEND NICK HEYWARD

OVER THERE BABE TEAM

OVER THERE (I DON'T CARE) HOUSE OF PAIN

OVER TO YOU JOHN (HERE WE GO AGAIN) JIVE BUNNY & THE MASTERMIXERS

OVER UNDER SIDEWAYS DOWN YARDBIRDS

OVER YOU [A] FREDDIE & THE DREAMERS

OVER YOU [B] ROXY MUSIC

OVER YOU [C] RAY PARKER Jr.

OVER YOU [D] JUSTIN

OVER YOU [E] WARREN CLARKE FEATURING KATHY BROWN

OVERCOME TRICKY

OVERDRIVE DJ SANDY VS HOUSETRAP

OVERJOYED STEVIE WONDER

OVERKILL [A] MOTORHEAD

OVERKILL [B] MEN AT WORK

OVERLOAD [A] SUGABABES

OVERLOAD [B] VOODOO & SERANO

OVERNIGHT CELEBRITY TWISTA

OVERPROTECTED BRITNEY SPEARS

OVERRATED SIOBHAN DONAGHY

OVERTHROWN LIBIDO

OVERTIME LEVEL 42

OWNER OF A LONELY HEART YES

OXBOW LAKES ORB

OXYGEN [A] BLAGGERS I.T.A.

OXYGEN [B] JJ72

OXYGENE 8 JEAN-MICHEL JARRE

OXYGENE PART IV JEAN-MICHEL JARRE

OXYGENE 10 JEAN-MICHEL JARRE

OYE GLORIA ESTEFAN

OYE COMO VA TITO PUENTE Jr & THE LATIN RHYTHM FEATURING TITO PUENTE, INDIA & CALI ALEMAN

OYE MI CANTO (HEAR MY VOICE) GLORIA ESTEFAN

P MACHINERY PROPAGANDA

PABLO RUSS CONWAY

PACIFIC 808 STATE

PACIFIC MELODY AIRSCAPE

PACK OF WOLVES NIGHTBREED

PACK UP YOUR SORROWS JOAN BAEZ

PACKET OF PEACE LIONROCK

PACKJAMMED (WITH THE PARTY POSSE) STOCK AITKEN WATERMAN

PAC-MAN [A] POWERPILL

PACMAN [B] ED RUSH & OPTICAL/UNIVERSAL

THE PADDLE DJ TOUCHE

PAGAN POETRY BJORK

PAID IN FULL ERIC B & RAKIM

PAID MY DUES ANASTACIA

PAIN [A] BETTY WRIGHT

PAIN [B] JIMMY EAT WORLD

THE PAIN INSIDE COSMIC ROUGH RIDERS

PAIN KILLER TURIN BRAKES

PAINKILLER JUDAS PRIEST

PAINT A PICTURE MAN WITH NO NAME FEATURING HANNAH

PAINT IT, BLACK ROLLING STONES
PAINT IT BLACK MODETTES
PAINT ME DOWN SPANDAU BALLET
PAINT THE SILENCE SOUTH
PAINTED MOON SILENCERS
PAINTER MAN CREATION
PAINTER MAN BONEY M
A PAIR OF BROWN EYES POGUES
PAISLEY PARK PRINCE & THE REVOLUTION
PAL OF MY CRADLE DAYS ANN BREEN
PALE BLUE EYES PAUL QUINN & EDWYYN COLLINS
PALE MOVIE SAINT ETIENNE
PALE RED JERRY BURNS
PALE SHELTER TEARS FOR FEARS
PALISADES PARK FREDDY CANNON
PALOMA BLANCA GEORGE BAKER SELECTION
PAMELA PAMELA WAYNE FONTANA
PANAMA VAN HALEN
THE PANDEMONIUM SINGLE KILLING JOKE
PANDORA'S BOX [A] PROCOL HARUM
PANDORA'S BOX [B] ORCHESTRAL MANOEUVRES IN
    THE DARK
PANDORA'S KISS LOUISE
PANIC SMITHS
PANIC ON MADDER ROSE
PANINARO '95 PET SHOP BOYS
PANIS ANGELICUS ANTHONY WAY
PANTHER PARTY MAD MOSES
PAPA DON'T PREACH MADONNA
PAPA DON'T PREACH KELLY OSBOURNE
PAPA LOVES MAMA JOAN REGAN
PAPA LOVES MAMBO PERRY COMO
PAPA OOM MOW MOW SHARONETTES
PAPA OOM MOW MOW GARY GLITTER
PAPA WAS A ROLLIN' STONE TEMPTATIONS
PAPA WAS A ROLLING STONE WAS (NOT WAS)
PAPA'S GOT A BRAND NEW BAG JAMES BROWN & THE
    FAMOUS FLAMES
PAPA'S GOT A BRAND NEW PIGBAG PIGBAG
PAPA'S GOT A BRAND NEW PIGBAG SILENT UNDERDOG
PAPER DOLL [A] WINDSOR DAVIES & DON ESTELLE
PAPER DOLL [B] PM DAWN
PAPER HOUSE FOOLPROOF
PAPER PLANE STATUS QUO
PAPER ROSES ANITA BRYANT
PAPER ROSES MAUREEN EVANS
PAPER ROSES KAYE SISTERS
PAPER ROSES MARIE OSMOND
PAPER SUN TRAFFIC
PAPER TIGER SUE THOMPSON
PAPERBACK WRITER BEATLES
PAPERCUT LINKIN PARK
PAPERFACES FEEDER
PAPILLON N-JOI
PAPUA NEW GUINEA FUTURE SOUND OF LONDON
PARA MI MOTIVATION
PARADE WHITE & TORCH
PARADISE [A] FRANK IFIELD
PARADISE [B] STRANGLERS
PARADISE [C] BLACK
PARADISE [D] SADE
PARADISE [E] BIRDLAND
PARADISE [F] DIANA ROSS
PARADISE [G] RALPH FRIDGE
PARADISE [H] KACI
PARADISE [I] LL COOL J FEATURING AMERIE
PARADISE BIRD AMII STEWART
PARADISE CITY GUNS N' ROSES
PARADISE CITY N-TRANCE
PARADISE LOST HERD
PARADISE SKIES MAX WEBSTER

PARALYSED ELVIS PRESLEY
PARANOID BLACK SABBATH
PARANOID DICKIES
PARANOID ANDROID RADIOHEAD
PARANOIMIA ART OF NOISE FEATURING MAX
    HEADROOM
PARDON ME INCUBUS
PARIS BY AIR TYGERS OF PAN TANG
PARIS IS ONE DAY AWAY MOOD
PARIS MATCH STYLE COUNCIL
PARISIENNE GIRL INCOGNITO
PARISIENNE WALKWAYS GARY MOORE
PARKLIFE BLUR
PART OF THE PROCESS MORCHEEBA
PART OF THE UNION STRAWBS
PART TIME LOVE [A] GLADYS KNIGHT & THE PIPS
PART TIME LOVE [B] ELTON JOHN
PART-TIME LOVER STEVIE WONDER
PARTAY FEELING B-CREW
PARTY [A] ELVIS PRESLEY
THE PARTY [B] KRAZE
PARTY ALL NIGHT [A] KREUZ
PARTY ALL NIGHT [B] MYTOWN
PARTY CRASHERS RADIO 4
PARTY DOLL BUDDY KNOX
PARTY DOLL JETS
PARTY FEARS TWO ASSOCIATES
PARTY FOR TWO SHANIA TWAIN & MARK McGRATH
PARTY FOUR (EP) MAD JOCKS FEATURING
    JOCKMASTER B.A.
PARTY FREAK CA$HFLOW
PARTY HARD [A] PULP
PARTY HARD [B] ANDREW WK
PARTY IN PARIS U.K. SUBS
PARTY LIGHTS GAP BAND
PARTY PARTY ELVIS COSTELLO & THE ATTRACTIONS
    WITH THE ROYAL HORN GUARDS
PARTY PEOPLE...FRIDAY NIGHT 911
PARTY PEOPLE (LIVE YOUR LIFE BE FREE) PIANOMAN
PARTY POPS RUSS CONWAY
PARTY TIME FATBACK BAND
PARTY TIME (THE GO-GO EDIT) KURTIS BLOW
PARTY UP THE WORLD D:REAM
PARTY ZONE DAFFY DUCK FEATURING THE GROOVE
    GANG
PARTYLINE BRASS CONSTRUCTION
PARTYMAN PRINCE
THE PARTY'S OVER LONNIE DONEGAN
PASADENA TEMPERANCE SEVEN
PASILDA AFRO MEDUSA
PASS & MOVE (IT'S THE LIVERPOOL GROOVE)
    LIVERPOOL FC & THE BOOT ROOM BOYS
PASS IT ON [A] BITTY McLEAN
PASS IT ON [B] CORAL
PASS THAT DUTCH MISSY ELLIOTT
PASS THE COURVOISIER – PART II BUSTA RHYMES, P
    DIDDY & PHARRELL
PASS THE DUTCHIE MUSICAL YOUTH
PASS THE MIC BEASTIE BOYS
PASS THE VIBES DEFINITION OF SOUND
A PASSAGE TO BANGKOK RUSH
THE PASSENGER SIOUXSIE & THE BANSHEES
THE PASSENGER IGGY POP
PASSENGERS ELTON JOHN
PASSIN' ME BY PHARCYDE
PASSING BREEZE RUSS CONWAY
PASSING STRANGERS [A] BILLY ECKSTINE & SARAH
    VAUGHAN
PASSING STRANGERS [A] JOE LONGTHORNE & LIZ
    DAWN
PASSING STRANGERS [B] ULTRAVOX

PASSION [A] ROD STEWART
PASSION [B] GAT DECOR
PASSION [C] JON OF THE PLEASED WIMMIN
PASSION [D] AMEN! UK
P.A.S.S.I.O.N. RHYTHM SYNDICATE
PASSION IN DARK ROOMS MOOD
PASSION KILLER ONE THE JUGGLER
THE PASSION OF LOVERS BAUHAUS
PASSION RULES THE GAME SCORPIONS
PASSIONATE FRIEND TEARDROP EXPLODES
PAST, PRESENT AND FUTURE CINDY & THE SAFFRONS
PAST THE MISSION TORI AMOS
PATCHES CLARENCE CARTER
PATHS ROBERT MILES FEATURING NINA MIRANDA
PATHS OF PARADISE JOHNNIE RAY
PATHWAY TO THE MOON MN8
PATIENCE [A] GUNS N' ROSES
PATIENCE [B] NERINA PALLOT
PATIENCE OF ANGELS EDDI READER
PATIO SONG GORKY'S ZYGOTIC MYNCI
PATRICIA PEREZ 'PREZ' PRADO & HIS ORCHESTRA
THE PAY OFF KENNY BALL & HIS JAZZMEN
PAY TO THE PIPER CHAIRMEN OF THE BOARD
THE PAYBACK MIX JAMES BROWN
PAYBACK TIME DYSFUNCTIONAL PSYCHEDELIC
    WALTONS
PAYING THE PRICE OF LOVE BEE GEES
PCP MANIC STREET PREACHERS
PE 2000 PUFF DADDY FEATURING HURRICANE G
PEACE SABRINA JOHNSTON
PEACE AND JOY SOUNDSTATION
PEACE + LOVEISM SON'Z OF A LOOP DA LOOP ERA
PEACE IN OUR TIME [A] IMPOSTER
PEACE IN OUR TIME [B] BIG COUNTRY
PEACE IN OUR TIME [C] CLIFF RICHARD
PEACE IN THE WORLD DON-E
PEACE ON EARTH HI TENSION
PEACE ON EARTH – LITTLE DRUMMER BOY DAVID
    BOWIE & BING CROSBY
PEACE THROUGHOUT THE WORLD MAXI PRIEST
    FEATURING JAZZIE B
PEACEFUL GEORGIE FAME
PEACH PRINCE
PEACHES [A] STRANGLERS
PEACHES [B] DARTS
PEACHES [C] PRESIDENTS OF THE UNITED STATES OF
    AMERICA
PEACHES AND CREAM 112
PEACOCK SUIT PAUL WELLER
PEAKIN' BLEACHIN'
PEARL CHAPTERHOUSE
PEARL IN THE SHELL HOWARD JONES
PEARL RIVER THREE 'N' ONE PRESENTS JOHNNY
    SHAKER FEATURING SERIAL DIVA
PEARL'S A SINGER ELKIE BROOKS
PEARL'S GIRL UNDERWORLD
PEARLY-DEWDROPS' DROPS COCTEAU TWINS
PEEK-A-BOO [A] NEW VAUDEVILLE BAND FEATURING
    TRISTRAM
PEEK-A-BOO [B] STYLISTICS
PEEK-A-BOO [C] SIOUXSIE & THE BANSHEES
THE PEEL SESSIONS (1ST JUNE 1982) NEW ORDER
PEGGY SUE BUDDY HOLLY
PEGGY SUE GOT MARRIED BUDDY HOLLY
PENNIES FROM HEAVEN INNER CITY
PENNY ARCADE ROY ORBISON
PENNY LANE BEATLES
PENNY LOVER LIONEL RICHIE
PENTHOUSE AND PAVEMENT HEAVEN 17
PEOPLE [A] TYMES
PEOPLE [B] INTASTELLA

PEOPLE [C] ALFIE
PEOPLE ARE PEOPLE DEPECHE MODE
PEOPLE ARE STILL HAVING SEX LaTOUR
PEOPLE ARE STRANGE ECHO & THE BUNNYMEN
PEOPLE EVERYDAY ARRESTED DEVELOPMENT
PEOPLE GET READY JEFF BECK & ROD STEWART
PEOPLE GET READY ROD STEWART
PEOPLE GET REAL SAINT ETIENNE
PEOPLE HOLD ON COLDCUT FEATURING LISA
  STANSFIELD
PEOPLE HOLD ON LISA STANSFIELD Vs THE DIRTY
  ROTTEN SCOUNDRELS
PEOPLE IN THA MIDDLE SPEARHEAD
PEOPLE LIKE YOU PEOPLE LIKE ME GLITTER BAND
PEOPLE OF LOVE AMEN! UK
PEOPLE OF THE SUN RAGE AGAINST THE MACHINE
PEPE DUANE EDDY & THE REBELS
PEPE RUSS CONWAY
PEPPER BUTTHOLE SURFERS
PEPPER BOX PEPPERS
PEPPERMINT TWIST DANNY PEPPERMINT & THE
  JUMPING JACKS
PEPPERMINT TWIST JOEY DEE & THE STARLITERS
PER SEMPRE AMORE (FOREVER IN LOVE) LOLLY
PERFECT [A] FAIRGROUND ATTRACTION
PERFECT [B] LIGHTNING SEEDS
PERFECT [C] PJ & DUNCAN
PERFECT [D] SMASHING PUMPKINS
PERFECT BLISS BELLEFIRE
PERFECT DAY [A] EMF
PERFECT DAY [B] KIRSTY MacCOLL & EVAN DANDO
PERFECT DAY [B] DURAN DURAN
PERFECT DAY [B] VARIOUS ARTISTS (EP'S & LPS)
PERFECT DAY [C] SKIN
A PERFECT DAY ELISE PJ HARVEY
THE PERFECT DRUG NINE INCH NAILS
PERFECT GENTLEMAN WYCLEF JEAN
THE PERFECT KISS NEW ORDER
PERFECT LOVESONG DIVINE COMEDY
PERFECT MOMENT MARTINE McCUTCHEON
PERFECT MOTION SUNSCREEM
PERFECT PLACE VOICE OF THE BEEHIVE
PERFECT SKIN LLOYD COLE & THE COMMOTIONS
PERFECT STRANGERS DEEP PURPLE
PERFECT 10 BEAUTIFUL SOUTH
PERFECT TIMING KIKI DEE
PERFECT WAY SCRITTI POLITTI
PERFECT WORLD HUEY LEWIS & THE NEWS
THE PERFECT YEAR DINA CARROLL
PERFIDIA VENTURES
PERFUME PARIS ANGELS
PERFUMED GARDEN RAH BAND
PERHAPS LOVE PLACIDO DOMINGO WITH JOHN
  DENVER
PERMANENT YEARS EAGLE-EYE CHERRY
PERPETUAL DAWN ORB
PERRY MASON OZZY OSBOURNE
PERSEVERANCE TERRORVISION
PERSONAL FEELING AUDIOWEB
PERSONAL JESUS DEPECHE MODE
PERSONAL JESUS JOHNNY CASH
PERSONAL JESUS MARILYN MANSON
PERSONAL TOUCH ERROL BROWN
PERSONALITY [A] ANTHONY NEWLEY
PERSONALITY [A] LLOYD PRICE
PERSONALITY [A] LENA ZAVARONI
PERSONALITY [B] EUGENE WILDE
PER-SO-NAL-LY WIGAN'S OVATION
THE PERSUADERS JOHN BARRY ORCHESTRA
PERSUASION TIM FINN
A PESSIMIST IS NEVER DISAPPOINTED THEAUDIENCE

PETAL WUBBLE-U
PETER AND THE WOLF CLYDE VALLEY STOMPERS
PETER GUNN ART OF NOISE FEATURING DUANE EDDY
PETER GUNN THEME DUANE EDDY & THE REBELS
PETER PIPER RUN D.M.C.
PETITE FLEUR CHRIS BARBER'S JAZZ BAND
PETS PORNO FOR PYROS
THE PHANTOM OF THE OPERA SARAH BRIGHTMAN &
  STEVE HARLEY
PHASED (EP) ALL ABOUT EVE
PHAT GIRLS IGNORANTS
PHATT BASS WARP BROTHERS VERSUS AQUAGEN
PHENOMENON LL COOL J
PHEW WOW FARMERS BOYS
PHILADELPHIA NEIL YOUNG
PHILADELPHIA FREEDOM ELTON JOHN BAND
PHOBIA FLOWERED UP
PHONE HOME JONNY CHINGAS
PHOREVER PEOPLE SHAMEN
PHOTOGRAPH [A] RINGO STARR
PHOTOGRAPH [B] DEF LEPPARD
PHOTOGRAPH OF MARY TREY LORENZ
PHUTURE 2000 CARL COX
PHYSICAL OLIVIA NEWTON-JOHN
PIANISSIMO KEN DODD
PIANO IN THE DARK BRENDA RUSSELL
PIANO LOCO DJ LUCK & MC NEAT
PIANO MEDLEY NO. 114 CHARLIE KUNZ
PIANO PARTY WINIFRED ATWELL
PICCADILLY PALARE MORRISSEY
PICK A BALE OF COTTON LONNIE DONEGAN
PICK A PART THAT'S NEW STEREOPHONICS
PICK ME UP I'LL DANCE MELBA MOORE
PICK UP THE PIECES [A] HUDSON-FORD
PICK UP THE PIECES [B] AVERAGE WHITE BAND
PICKIN' A CHICKEN EVE BOSWELL
PICKNEY GAL DESMOND DEKKER & THE ACES
PICNIC IN THE SUMMERTIME DEEE-LITE
A PICTURE OF YOU JOE BROWN & THE BRUVVERS
PICTURE OF YOU BOYZONE
PICTURE THIS BLONDIE
PICTURES IN THE DARK MIKE OLDFIELD FEATURING
  ALED JONES, ANITA HEGERLAND & BARRY
  PALMER
PICTURES OF LILY WHO
PICTURES OF MATCHSTICK MEN STATUS QUO
PICTURES OF YOU CURE
PIE JESU SARAH BRIGHTMAN & PAUL MILES-
  KINGSTON
PIECE BY PIECE KENNY THOMAS
PIECE OF MY HEART SAMMY HAGAR
PIECE OF MY HEART SHAGGY FEATURING MARSHA
PIECE OF THE ACTION [A] BUCKS FIZZ
PIECE OF THE ACTION [B] MEAT LOAF
PIECES MY VITRIOL
PIECES OF A DREAM INCOGNITO
PIECES OF ICE DIANA ROSS
PIECES OF ME ASHLEE SIMPSON
PIED PIPER CRISPIAN ST. PETERS
PIED PIPER BOB & MARCIA
PIED PIPER (THE BEEJE) STEVE RACE
PIES WILEY
PIHA IAN POOLEY & MAGIK J
PILGRIMAGE SOURMASH
PILLOW TALK SYLVIA
PILLS AND SOAP IMPOSTER
PILOT OF THE AIRWAVES CHARLIE DORE
PILOTS GOLDFRAPP
PILTDOWN RIDES AGAIN PILTDOWN MEN
PIMP 50 CENT
PIN YEAH YEAH YEAH

PINBALL BRIAN PROTHEROE
PINBALL WIZARD WHO
PINBALL WIZARD ELTON JOHN
PINBALL WIZARD – SEE ME FEEL ME (MEDLEY) NEW
  SEEKERS
PINCUSHION ZZ TOP
PINEAPPLE HEAD CROWDED HOUSE
PING PONG STEREOLAB
PINK AEROSMITH
PINK CADILLAC NATALIE COLE
PINK CHAMPAGNE [A] SHAKIN' STEVENS
PINK CHAMPAGNE [B] RHYTHM ETERNITY
PINK FLOWER DAISY CHAINSAW
THE PINK GREASE PINK GREASE
THE PINK PARKER EP GRAHAM PARKER & THE
  RUMOUR
PINK SUNSHINE FUZZBOX
PINKY BLUE ALTERED IMAGES
PIPELINE CHANTAYS
PIPELINE BRUCE JOHNSTON
PIPES OF PEACE PAUL McCARTNEY
PIRANHA TRIPPING DAISY
PISSING IN THE WIND BADLY DRAWN BOY
PISTOL PACKIN' MAMA GENE VINCENT
PISTOL WHIP JOSHUA RYAN
PITCHIN' (IN EVERY DIRECTION) HI-GATE
A PLACE CALLED HOME PJ HARVEY
A PLACE IN THE SUN [A] SHADOWS
A PLACE IN THE SUN [B] STEVIE WONDER
PLACE IN YOUR HEART NAZARETH
PLACE YOUR HANDS REEF
PLACES TILT
PLACES THAT BELONG TO YOU BARBRA STREISAND
PLAN A DANDY WARHOLS
PLAN B DEXY'S MIDNIGHT RUNNERS
PLAN 9 808 STATE
PLANET CARAVAN PANTERA
PLANET CLAIRE B-52's
THE PLANET DANCE (MOVE YA BODY) LIQUID OXYGEN
PLANET E K.C. FLIGHTT
PLANET EARTH DURAN DURAN
PLANET GIRL ZODIAC MINDWARP & THE LOVE
  REACTION
PLANET LOVE DJ QUICKSILVER
THE PLANET OF LOVE CARL COX
PLANET OF SOUND PIXIES
PLANET ROCK AFRIKA BAMBAATAA & THE SONIC SOUL
  FORCE
PLANET ROCK PAUL OAKENFOLD PRESENTS AFRIKA
  BAMBAATAA
PLANET ROCK/FUNKY PLANET POWERS THAT BE
PLANET TELEX RADIOHEAD
PLANET VIOLET NALIN I.N.C.
PLANETARY SIT-IN (EVERY GIRL HAS YOUR NAME)
  JULIAN COPE
THE PLASTIC AGE BUGGLES
PLASTIC DREAMS JAYDEE
PLASTIC MAN KINKS
PLATINUM BLONDE PRELUDE
PLATINUM POP THIS YEAR'S BLONDE
PLAY JENNIFER LOPEZ
PLAY DEAD BJORK & DAVID ARNOLD
PLAY EP RIDE
PLAY IT COOL SUPER FURRY ANIMALS
PLAY ME LIKE YOU PLAY YOUR GUITAR DUANE EDDY &
  THE REBELETTES
PLAY THAT FUNKY MUSIC WILD CHERRY
PLAY THAT FUNKY MUSIC THUNDER
PLAY THAT FUNKY MUSIC VANILLA ICE
PLAY THE GAME QUEEN
PLAY TO WIN HEAVEN 17

PLAYA HATA LUNIZ
PLAYA NO MO' LINA
PLAYAS GON' PLAY 3LW
PLAYAZ CLUB RAPPIN' 4-TAY
PLAYED A LIVE (THE BONGO SONG) SAFRI DUO
PLAYGROUND ANITA HARRIS
PLAYGROUND LOVE AIR
PLAYGROUND TWIST SIOUXSIE & THE BANSHEES
PLAYING WITH KNIVES BIZARRE INC
PLAYING WITH THE BOY TECHNICIAN 2
PLAYTHING LINX
PLAYTIME RONI SIZE
PLEASANT VALLEY SUNDAY MONKEES
PLEASE [A] ELTON JOHN
PLEASE [B] U2
PLEASE [C] ROBIN GIBB
PLEASE BE CRUEL INSPIRAL CARPETS
PLEASE COME HOME FOR CHRISTMAS EAGLES
PLEASE COME HOME FOR CHRISTMAS BON JOVI
PLEASE DON'T ASK ABOUT BARBARA BOBBY VEE
PLEASE DON'T BE SCARED BARRY MANILOW
PLEASE DON'T FALL IN LOVE CLIFF RICHARD
PLEASE DON'T GO [A] DONALD PEERS
PLEASE DON'T GO [B] KC & THE SUNSHINE BAND
PLEASE DON'T GO [B] DOUBLE YOU?
PLEASE DON'T GO [B] KWS
PLEASE DON'T GO [C] NO MERCY
PLEASE DON'T MAKE ME CRY UB40
PLEASE DON'T TEASE CLIFF RICHARD & THE SHADOWS
PLEASE DON'T TOUCH JOHNNY KIDD
PLEASE DON'T TURN ME ON ARTFUL DODGER
    FEATURING LIFFORD
PLEASE FORGIVE ME [A] BRYAN ADAMS
PLEASE FORGIVE ME [B] DAVID GRAY
PLEASE HELP ME I'M FALLING HANK LOCKLIN
PLEASE MR POSTMAN BACKBEAT BAND
PLEASE MR. POSTMAN CARPENTERS
PLEASE PLEASE ME BEATLES
PLEASE PLEASE ME DAVID CASSIDY
PLEASE RELEASE ME MIKE FLOWERS POPS
PLEASE SAVE ME SUNSCREEM VS PUSH
PLEASE SIRE MARTYN JOSEPH
PLEASE STAY [A] CRYIN' SHAMES
PLEASE STAY [B] KYLIE MINOGUE
PLEASE TELL HIM I SAID HELLO DANA
PLEASE (YOU GOT THAT...) INXS
PLEASE YOURSELF BIG SUPREME
PLEASURE BOYS VISAGE
PLEASURE DOME SOUL II SOUL
PLEASURE FROM THE BASS TIGA
PLEASURE LOVE DE FUNK FEATURING F45
PLEASURE PRINCIPLE JANET JACKSON
PLENTY GOOD LOVIN' CONNIE FRANCIS
PLOWED SPONGE
PLUG IN BABY MUSE
PLUG IT IN BASEMENT JAXX FEATURING JC CHASEZ
PLUG ME IN (TO THE CENTRAL LOVE LINE) SCARLET
    FANTASTIC
PLUG MYSELF IN D.O.S.E. FEATURING MARK E SMITH
PLUS ECHELON
PLUSH STONE TEMPLE PILOTS
THE POACHER RONNIE LANE & SLIM CHANCE
POCKET CALCULATOR KRAFTWERK
POEMS NEARLY GOD
POETRY IN MOTION JOHNNY TILLOTSON
POGUETRY IN MOTION EP POGUES
POING ROTTERDAM TERMINATION SOURCE
POINT OF NO RETURN [A] NU SHOOZ
POINT OF NO RETURN [B] CENTORY
POINT OF VIEW [A] MATUMBI
POINT OF VIEW [B] DB BOULEVARD

POISON [A] ALICE COOPER
POISON [B] BELL BIV DEVOE
POISON [C] PRODIGY
POISON [D] BARDOT
POISON ARROW ABC
POISON HEART RAMONES
POISON IVY COASTERS
POISON IVY PARAMOUNTS
POISON IVY LAMBRETTAS
POISON STREET NEW MODEL ARMY
POLICE AND THIEVES JUNIOR MURVIN
POLICE OFFICER SMILEY CULTURE
POLICE STATE T-POWER
POLICEMAN SKANK...(THE STORY OF MY LIFE)
    AUDIOWEB
POLICY OF TRUTH DEPECHE MODE
THE POLITICS OF DANCING RE-FLEX
POLK SALAD ANNIE ELVIS PRESLEY
POLYESTERDAY GUS GUS
PON DE RIVER, PON DE BANK ELEPHANT MAN
PONY GINUWINE
PONY TIME CHUBBY CHECKER
POODLE ROCKIN' GORKY'S ZYGOTIC MYNCI
POOL HALL RICHARD FACES
POOR JENNY EVERLY BROTHERS
POOR LENO ROYKSOPP
POOR LITTLE FOOL RICKY NELSON
POOR MAN'S SON ROCKIN' BERRIES
POOR ME ADAM FAITH
POOR MISGUIDED FOOL STARSAILOR
POOR PEOPLE OF PARIS WINIFRED ATWELL
POP N SYNC
POP COP GYRES
POP GO THE WORKERS BARRON KNIGHTS WITH DUKE
    D'MOND
POP GOES MY LOVE FREEEZ
POP GOES THE WEASEL [A] ANTHONY NEWLEY
POP GOES THE WEASEL [B] 3RD BASS
POP IS DEAD RADIOHEAD
POP LIFE PRINCE & THE REVOLUTION
POP MUZIK M
POP MUZIK ALL SYSTEMS GO
THE POP SINGER'S FEAR OF THE POLLEN COUNT DIVINE
    COMEDY
POP THAT BOOTY MARQUES HOUSTON FEATURING
    JERMAINE
POP YA COLLAR USHER
POPCORN HOT BUTTER
POPCORN LOVE NEW EDITION
POPPA JOE SWEET
POPPA PICCOLINO DIANA DECKER
POPPED! FOOL BOONA
POPS WE LOVE YOU DIANA ROSS, MARVIN GAYE,
    SMOKEY ROBINSON & STEVIE WONDER
POPSCENE BLUR
POP!ULAR DARREN HAYES
PORCELAIN MOBY
PORT AU PRINCE WINIFRED ATWELL & FRANK
    CHACKSFIELD
PORTRAIT OF MY LOVE MATT MONRO
PORTSMOUTH MIKE OLDFIELD
PORTUGUESE WASHERWOMAN JOE 'FINGERS' CARR
POSITIVE BLEEDING URGE OVERKILL
POSITIVE EDUCATION SLAM
POSITIVELY FOURTH STREET BOB DYLAN
POSITIVITY SUEDE
POSSE (I NEED YOU ON THE FLOOR) SCOOTER
POSSESSED VEGAS
POSSESSION TRANSFER
POSSIBLY MAYBE BJORK
POST MODERN SLEAZE SNEAKER PIMPS

POSTCARD FROM HEAVEN LIGHTHOUSE FAMILY
POSTMAN PAT KEN BARRIE
POUNDCAKE VAN HALEN
POUNDING DOVES
POUR SOME SUGAR ON ME DEF LEPPARD
POW WOW WOW FONTANA FEATURING DARRYL
    D'BONNEAU
POWDER BLUE ELBOW
THE POWER [A] SNAP
POWER [B] NU COLOURS
THE POWER [C] MONIE LOVE
POWER AND THE GLORY SAXON
THE POWER IS YOURS REDSKINS
POWER OF A WOMAN ETERNAL
THE POWER (OF ALL THE LOVE IN THE WORLD) D:REAM
P.OWER OF A.MERICAN N.ATIVES DANCE 2 TRANCE
THE POWER (OF BHANGRA) SNAP VS MOTIVO
THE POWER OF GOODBYE MADONNA
THE POWER OF LOVE [A] FRANKIE GOES TO
    HOLLYWOOD
THE POWER OF LOVE [B] JENNIFER RUSH
THE POWER OF LOVE [B] CELINE DION
THE POWER OF LOVE [B] FITS OF GLOOM FEATURING
    LIZZY MACK
THE POWER OF LOVE [C] HUEY LEWIS & THE NEWS
THE POWER OF LOVE [E] Q-TEX
POWER OF LOVE [D] DEEE-LITE
THE POWER OF LOVE [F] HOLLY JOHNSON
POWER OF LOVE – LOVE POWER LUTHER VANDROSS
POWER RANGERS MIGHTY MORPH'N POWER
    RANGERS
POWER TO ALL OUR FRIENDS CLIFF RICHARD
POWER TO THE PEOPLE JOHN LENNON & THE PLASTIC
    ONO BAND
THE POWER ZONE TIME FREQUENCY
POWERLESS (SAY WHAT YOU WANT) NELLY FURTADO
POWERSIGN (ONLY YOUR LOVE) PKA
POWERTRIP MONSTER MAGNET
PRACTICE WHAT YOU PREACH BARRY WHITE
PRAISE INNER CITY
PRAISE YOU FATBOY SLIM
PRANCE ON EDDIE HENDERSON
PRAY [A] MC HAMMER
PRAY [B] TAKE THAT
PRAY [C] TINA COUSINS
PRAY [D] LASGO
PRAY [E] SYNTAX
PRAY FOR LOVE LOVE TO INFINITY
PRAYER DISTURBED
PRAYER FOR THE DYING SEAL
PRAYER FOR YOU TEXAS
A PRAYER TO THE MUSIC MARCO POLO
PRAYER TOWER PARADISE ORGANISATION
PRAYING FOR TIME GEORGE MICHAEL
PREACHER MAN BANANARAMA
PREACHER PREACHER ANIMAL NIGHTLIFE
PRECIOUS [A] JAM
PRECIOUS [B] ANNIE LENNOX
PRECIOUS HEART TALL PAUL VS INXS
PRECIOUS ILLUSIONS ALANIS MORISSETTE
PRECIOUS LIFE CRW PRESENTS VERONIKA
PRECIOUS TIME VAN MORRISON
PREDICTABLE GOOD CHARLOTTE
PREGNANT FOR THE LAST TIME MORRISSEY
PREPARE TO LAND SUPERNATURALS
PRESENCE OF LOVE (LAUGHERNE) ALARM
PRESS PAUL McCARTNEY
PRESSURE [A] SUNSCREEM
PRESSURE [B] BILLY OCEAN
PRESSURE [C] DRIZABONE
PRESSURE COOKER G CLUB PRESENTS BANDA SONORA

PRESSURE DROP IZZY STADLIN'
PRESSURE ON ROGER TAYLOR
THE PRESSURE PART 1 SOUNDS OF BLACKNESS
PRESSURE POINT ZUTONS
PRESSURE US SUNSCREEM
PRETEND NAT 'KING' COLE
PRETEND ALVIN STARDUST
PRETEND BEST FRIEND TERRORVISION
PRETEND WE'RE DEAD L7
PRETENDER GOT MY HEART ALISHA'S ATTIC
PRETENDERS TO THE THRONE BEAUTIFUL SOUTH
PRETTIEST EYES BEAUTIFUL SOUTH
PRETTY BLUE EYES CRAIG DOUGLAS
PRETTY BROWN EYES JIM REEVES
PRETTY DEEP TANYA DONELLY
PRETTY FLAMINGO MANFRED MANN
PRETTY FLY (FOR A WHITE GUY) OFFSPRING
PRETTY GOOD YEAR TORI AMOS
PRETTY GREEN EYES ULTRABEAT
PRETTY IN PINK PSYCHEDELIC FURS
PRETTY JENNY JESS CONRAD
PRETTY LADY SAVANA
PRETTY LITTLE ANGEL EYES CURTIS LEE
PRETTY LITTLE ANGEL EYES SHOWADDYWADDY
PRETTY LITTLE BLACK EYED SUSIE GUY MITCHELL
PRETTY NOOSE SOUNDGARDEN
PRETTY PAPER ROY ORBISON
PRETTY THING BO DIDDLEY
PRETTY VACANT SEX PISTOLS
PRETTY WOMAN JUICY LUCY
THE PRICE OF LOVE EVERLY BROTHERS
THE PRICE OF LOVE (REMIX) BRYAN FERRY
PRICE TO PAY STAIND
PRICE YOU PAY QUESTIONS
PRIDE (IN THE NAME OF LOVE) U2
PRIDE (IN THE NAME OF LOVE) CLIVILLES & COLE
PRIDE'S PARANOIA FUTURESHOCK
PRIMAL SCREAM MOTLEY CRUE
PRIMARY CURE
PRIMARY INSTINCT SENSELESS THINGS
PRIMARY RHYMING MC TUNES
PRIME MOVER ZODIAC MINDWARP & THE LOVE
    REACTION
PRIME MOVER RUSH
PRIME TIME [A] TUBES
PRIME TIME [B] HAIRCUT 100
PRIME TIME [C] MTUME
PRIMROSE LANE DICKIE PRIDE
THE PRINCE MADNESS
A PRINCE AMONG ISLANDS EP CAPERCAILLIE
PRINCE CHARMING ADAM & THE ANTS
PRINCE HARRY SOHO DOLLS
PRINCE IGOR RHAPSODY FEATURING WARREN G &
    SISSEL
PRINCE OF DARKNESS BOW WOW WOW
PRINCE OF PEACE GALLIANO
PRINCES OF THE NIGHT BLAST FEATURING VDC
PRINCESS IN RAGS GENE PITNEY
PRINCESS OF THE NIGHT SAXON
PRINCIPAL'S OFFICE YOUNG MC
PRINCIPLES OF LUST ENIGMA
PRISONER ALL BLUE
THE PRISONER FAB FEATURING MC NUMBER 6
PRISONER OF LOVE MILLIE SCOTT
PRISONER OF LOVER SPEAR OF DESTINY
A PRISONER OF THE PAST PREFAB SPROUT
PRIVATE DANCER TINA TURNER
PRIVATE EMOTION RICKY MARTIN FEATURING MEJA
PRIVATE EYE ALKALINE TRIO
PRIVATE EYES DARYL HALL & JOHN OATES
PRIVATE INVESTIGATIONS DIRE STRAITS

PRIVATE LIFE GRACE JONES
PRIVATE NUMBER JUDY CLAY & WILLIAM BELL
PRIVATE NUMBER 911
PRIVATE PARTY WALLY JUMP Jr. & THE CRIMINAL
    ELEMENT ORCHESTRA
PRIVILEGE (SET ME FREE) PATTI SMITH GROUP
PRIX CHOC REMIXES ETIENNE DE CRECY
PRIZE OF GOLD JOAN REGAN
PROBABLY A ROBBERY RENEGADE SOUNDWAVE
PROBLEM IS DUB PISTOLS FEATURING TERRY HALL
PROBLEMS EVERLY BROTHERS
PROCESS OF ELMINATION ERIC GABLE
PROCESSED BEATS KASABIAN
PROCESSION NEW ORDER
PRODIGAL BLUES BILLY IDOL
PRODIGAL SON STEEL PULSE
PRODUCT OF THE WORKING CLASS LITTLE ANGELS
PROFESSIONAL WIDOW (IT'S GOT TO BE BIG) TORI
    AMOS
PROFIT IN PEACE OCEAN COLOUR SCENE
PROFOUNDLY IN LOVE WITH PANDORA IAN & THE
    BLOCKHEADS
PROFOUNDLY YOURS HUE & CRY
PRO-GEN SHAMEN
THE PROGRAM DAVID MORALES
PROMISE DELIRIOUS?
A PROMISE ECHO & THE BUNNYMEN
THE PROMISE [A] ARCADIA
THE PROMISE [B] WHEN IN ROME
THE PROMISE [C] MICHAEL NYMAN
THE PROMISE [D] ESSENCE
PROMISE ME BEVERLEY CRAVEN
THE PROMISE OF A NEW DAY PAULA ABDUL
THE PROMISE YOU MADE COCK ROBIN
PROMISED LAND [A] CHUCK BERRY
PROMISED LAND [A] ELVIS PRESLEY
PROMISED LAND [B] JOE SMOOTH
PROMISED LAND [B] STYLE COUNCIL
PROMISED YOU A MIRACLE SIMPLE MINDS
PROMISES [A] KEN DODD
PROMISES [B] ERIC CLAPTON
PROMISES [C] BUZZCOCKS
PROMISES [D] BASIA
PROMISES [D] TAKE THAT
PROMISES [E] PARIS RED
PROMISES [F] DEF LEPPARD
PROMISES [G] CRANBERRIES
PROMISES PROMISES COOPER TEMPLE CLAUSE
PROPER CRIMBO BO SELECTA
PROPHASE TRANSA
THE PROPHET CJ BOLLAND
PROTECT YOUR MIND (FOR THE LOVE OF A PRINCESS)
    DJ SAKIN & FRIENDS
PROTECTION MASSIVE ATTACK FEATURING TRACEY
    THORN
PROUD HEATHER SMALL
PROUD MARY CREEDENCE CLEARWATER REVIVAL
PROUD MARY CHECKMATES LTD.
THE PROUD ONE OSMONDS
PROUD TO FALL IAN McCULLOCH
PROVE IT TELEVISION
PROVE YOUR LOVE TAYLOR DAYNE
PROVIDER N*E*R*D
PSYCHE ROCK PIERRE HENRY
PSYCHEDELIC SHACK TEMPTATIONS
PSYCHO BASE SHADES OF RHYTHM
PSYCHONAUT FIELDS OF THE NEPHILIM
PSYCHOSIS SAFARI EIGHTIES MATCHBOX B-LINE
    DISASTER
PSYKO FUNK BOO-YAA T.R.I.B.E.
A PUB WITH NO BEER SLIM DUSTY

PUBLIC ENEMY NO 1 HYPO PSYCHO
PUBLIC IMAGE PUBLIC IMAGE LTD.
PUCKWUDGIE CHARLIE DRAKE
PUFF KENNY LYNCH
PULL THE WIRES FROM THE WALL DELGADOS
PULL UP TO THE BUMPER GRACE JONES
PULL UP TO THE BUMPER PATRA
PULLING MUSSELS (FROM THE SHELL) SQUEEZE
PULLING PUNCHES DAVID SYLVIAN
PULSAR 2002 MAURO PICOTTO
PULS(T)AR BEN LIEBRAND
PULVERTURM NIELS VAN GOGH
PUMP IT UP [A] ELVIS COSTELLO & THE ATTRACTIONS
PUMP IT UP [B] JOE BUDDEN
PUMP IT UP [C] DANZEL
PUMP ME UP GRANDMASTER MELLE MEL & THE
    FURIOUS FIVE
PUMP UP LONDON MR LEE
PUMP UP THE BITTER STARTURN ON 45 (PINTS)
PUMP UP THE JAM TECHNOTRONIC FEATURING FELLY
PUMP UP THE VOLUME M/A/R/R/S
PUMP UP THE VOLUME GREED FEATURING RICARDO
    DA FORCE
PUMPIN' NOVY VERSUS ENIAC
PUMPING ON YOUR STEREO SUPERGRASS
PUMPKIN TRICKY
PUMPS AMY WINEHOUSE
PUNCH AND JUDY MARILLION
PUNK FERRY CORSTEN
PUNK ROCK 101 BOWLING FOR SOUP
PUNK ROCK PRINCESS SOMETHING CORPORATE
PUNKA KENICKIE
PUNKY REGGAE PARTY BOB MARLEY & THE WAILERS
PUPPET MAN TOM JONES
PUPPET ON A STRING SANDIE SHAW
PUPPY LOVE PAUL ANKA
PUPPY LOVE DONNY OSMOND
PUPPY LOVE S CLUB JUNIORS
THE PUPPY SONG DAVID CASSIDY
PURE [A] LIGHTNING SEEDS
PURE [B] GTO
PURE [C] 3 COLOURS RED
PURE AND SIMPLE HEAR'SAY
PURE MASSACRE SILVERCHAIR
PURE MORNING PLACEBO
PURE PLEASURE DIGITAL EXCITATION
PURE PLEASURE SEEKER MOLOKO
PURE SHORES ALL SAINTS
PURELY BY COINCIDENCE SWEET SENSATION
PURGATORY IRON MAIDEN
PURITY NEW MODEL ARMY
PURPLE HAZE [A] JIMI HENDRIX EXPERIENCE
PURPLE HAZE [B] GROOVE ARMADA
PURPLE HEATHER ROD STEWART WITH THE SCOTTISH
    EURO '96 SQUAD
PURPLE LOVE BALLOON CUD
PURPLE MEDLEY PRINCE
PURPLE PEOPLE EATER SHEB WOOLEY
PURPLE PEOPLE EATER JACKIE DENNIS
PURPLE PILLS D12
PURPLE RAIN PRINCE & THE REVOLUTION
PUSH [A] MOIST
PUSH [B] MATCHBOX 20
PUSH [C] GHOSTFACE FEATURING MISSY ELLIOTT
THE PUSH (FAR FROM HERE) PAUL JACKSON & STEVE
    SMITH
PUSH IT [A] SALT-N-PEPA
PUSH IT [B] GARBAGE
PUSH IT ALL ASIDE ALISHA'S ATTIC
PUSH THE BEAT MIRAGE
PUSH THE BEAT/BAUHAUS CAPPELLA

PUSH THE FEELING ON NIGHTCRAWLERS
PUSH UP FREESTYLERS
PUSH UPSTAIRS UNDERWORLD
THE PUSHBIKE SONG MIXTURES
PUSHIN' ME OUT D-SIDE
PUSS JESUS LIZARD
PUSS 'N' BOOTS ADAM ANT
PUSSYCAT MULU
PUT A LIGHT IN THE WINDOW KING BROTHERS
PUT A LITTLE LOVE IN YOUR HEART DAVE CLARK FIVE
PUT A LITTLE LOVE IN YOUR HEART ANNIE LENNOX & AL GREEN
PUT EM HIGH STONEBRIDGE FEATURING THERESE
PUT HIM OUT MS DYNAMITE
PUT HIM OUT OF YOUR MIND DR FEELGOOD
PUT IT THERE PAUL McCARTNEY
PUT MY ARMS AROUND YOU KEVIN KITCHEN
PUT OUR HEADS TOGETHER O'JAYS
PUT THE LIGHT ON WET WET WET
PUT THE MESSAGE IN THE BOX BRIAN KENNEDY
PUT THE NEEDLE ON IT DANNII MINOGUE
PUT THE NEEDLE TO THE RECORD CRIMINAL ELEMENT ORCHESTRA
PUT YOUR ARMS AROUND ME [A] TEXAS
PUT YOUR ARMS AROUND ME [B] NATURAL
PUT YOUR FAITH IN ME ALISON LIMERICK
PUT YOUR HANDS TOGETHER D MOB FEATURING NUFF JUICE
PUT YOUR HANDS UP REFLEX FEATURING MC VIPER
PUT YOUR HANDS WHERE MY EYES COULD SEE BUSTA RHYMES
PUT YOUR HANDZ UP WHOOLIGANZ
PUT YOUR HEAD ON MY SHOULDER PAUL ANKA
PUT YOUR LOVE IN ME HOT CHOCOLATE
PUT YOUR MONEY WHERE YOUR MOUTH IS ROSE ROYCE
PUT YOURSELF IN MY PLACE [A] ISLEY BROTHERS
PUT YOURSELF IN MY PLACE [A] ELGINS
PUT YOURSELF IN MY PLACE [B] KYLIE MINOGUE
PUTTING ON THE STYLE LONNIE DONEGAN
PYJAMARAMA ROXY MUSIC
PYRAMID SONG RADIOHEAD
P.Y.T. (PRETTY YOUNG THING) MICHAEL JACKSON
QUADROPHONIA QUADROPHONIA
QUANDO M'INNAMORO (A MAN WITHOUT LOVE) SANDPIPERS
QUANDO QUANDO QUANDO PAT BOONE
QUANDO QUANDO QUANDO ENGELBERT HUMPERDINCK
THE QUARTER MOON V.I.P.'S
QUARTER TO THREE U.S. BONDS
QUE SERA CHRIS REA
QUE SERA MI VIDA (IF YOU SHOULD GO) GIBSON BROTHERS
QUE SERA SERA GENO WASHINGTON & THE RAM JAM BAND
QUE SERA SERA HERMES HOUSE BAND
QUE TAL AMERICA TWO MAN SOUND
QUEEN FOR TONIGHT HELEN SHAPIRO
QUEEN JANE KINGMAKER
THE QUEEN OF 1964 NEIL SEDAKA
QUEEN OF CLUBS KC & THE SUNSHINE BAND
QUEEN OF HEARTS [A] DAVE EDMUNDS
QUEEN OF HEARTS [B] CHARLOTTE
QUEEN OF MY HEART WESTLIFE
QUEEN OF MY SOUL AVERAGE WHITE BAND
QUEEN OF NEW ORLEANS JON BON JOVI
THE QUEEN OF OUTER SPACE WEDDING PRESENT
QUEEN OF RAIN ROXETTE
QUEEN OF THE HOP BOBBY DARIN
QUEEN OF THE NEW YEAR DEACON BLUE
QUEEN OF THE NIGHT WHITNEY HOUSTON

QUEEN OF THE RAPPING SCENE (NOTHING EVER GOES THE WAY YOU PLAN) MODERN ROMANCE
THE QUEEN'S BIRTHDAY SONG ST. JOHN'S COLLEGE SCHOOL CHOIR & THE BAND OF THE GRENADIER GUARDS
QUEEN'S FIRST EP QUEEN
QUEER GARBAGE
QUESTION MOODY BLUES
THE QUESTION SEVEN GRAND HOUSING AUTHORITY
QUESTION OF FAITH LIGHTHOUSE FAMILY
A QUESTION OF LUST DEPECHE MODE
A QUESTION OF TIME DEPECHE MODE
QUESTIONS AND ANSWERS [A] SHAM 69
QUESTIONS AND ANSWERS [B] BIFFY CLYRO
QUESTIONS I CAN'T ANSWER HEINZ
QUESTIONS (MUST BE ASKED) DAVID FORBES
QUICK JOEY SMALL (RUN JOEY RUN) KASENETZ-KATZ SINGING ORCHESTRAL CIRCUS
QUIEREME MUCHO (YOURS) JULIO IGLESIAS
QUIET LIFE JAPAN
THE QUIET THINGS THAT NO ONE EVER KNOWS BRAND NEW
QUIT PLAYING GAMES (WITH MY HEART) BACKSTREET BOYS
QUIT THIS TOWN EDDIE & THE HOT RODS
QUITE A PARTY FIREBALLS
QUITE RIGHTLY SO PROCOL HARUM
QUOTE GOODBYE QUOTE CAROLYNE MAS
QUOTH POLYGON WINDOW
R TO THE A C.J. LEWIS
R U READY SALT-N-PEPA
R U SLEEPING INDO
RABBIT CHAS & DAVE
THE RACE [A] YELLO
RACE [B] TIGER
RACE [C] LEAVES
RACE FOR THE PRIZE FLAMING LIPS
THE RACE IS ON [A] SUZI QUATRO
THE RACE IS ON [B] DAVE EDMUNDS & THE STRAY CATS
RACE WITH THE DEVIL [A] GENE VINCENT
RACE WITH THE DEVIL [B] GUN
RACE WITH THE DEVIL [B] GIRLSCHOOL
RACHEL AL MARTINO
RACHMANINOFF'S 18TH VARIATION ON A THEME BY PAGANINI (THE STORY OF THREE LOVES) WINIFRED ATWELL
RACING GREEN HIGH CONTRAST
RACIST FRIENDS SPECIAL A.K.A.
RADANCER MARMALADE
RADAR LOVE GOLDEN EARRING
RADAR LOVE OH WELL
RADIATION VIBE FOUNTAINS OF WAYNE
RADICAL YOUR LOVER LITTLE ANGELS FEATURING THE BIG BAD HORNS
RADICCIO EP ORBITAL
RADIO [A] SHAKY FEATURING ROGER TAYLOR
RADIO [B] TEENAGE FANCLUB
RADIO [C] CORRS
RADIO [D] CLIENT
RADIO [E] ROBBIE WILLIAMS
RADIO [F] LUDES
RADIO AFRICA LATIN QUARTER
RADIO DISCO WILT
RADIO GA GA QUEEN
RADIO GAGA ELECTRIC SIX
RADIO HEAD TALKING HEADS
RADIO HEART RADIO HEART FEATURING GARY NUMAN
RADIO MUSICOLA NIK KERSHAW
RADIO NO 1 AIR
RADIO ON RICKY ROSS

RADIO RADIO ELVIS COSTELLO & THE ATTRACTIONS
RADIO ROMANCE TIFFANY
RADIO SONG R.E.M.
RADIO WALL OF SOUND SLADE
RADIO WAVES ROGER WATERS
RADIOACTIVE GENE SIMMONS
RADIOACTIVITY KRAFTWERK
RAG DOLL [A] FOUR SEASONS WITH THE SOUND OF FRANKIE VALLI
RAG DOLL [B] AEROSMITH
RAG MAMA RAG BAND
RAGAMUFFIN MAN MANFRED MANN
RAGE HARD FRANKIE GOES TO HOLLYWOOD
RAGE TO LOVE KIM WILDE
RAGGA HOUSE (ALL NIGHT LONG) SIMON HARRIS FEATURING DADDY FREDDY
RAGGAMUFFIN GIRL APACHE INDIAN FEATURING FRANKIE PAUL
RAGING COSMIC GATE
RAGING EP BEYOND
RAGS TO RICHES DAVID WHITFIELD
RAGS TO RICHES ELVIS PRESLEY
RAGTIME COWBOY JOE CHIPMUNKS
RAIN [A] BRUCE RUFFIN
RAIN [B] STATUS QUO
RAIN [C] CULT
RAIN [D] MADONNA
RAIN [E] GROOVE CORPORATION
THE RAIN ORAN 'JUICE' JONES
RAIN AND TEARS APHRODITE'S CHILD
RAIN DOWN ON ME KANE
RAIN FALLS FRANKIE KNUCKLES FEATURING LISA MICHAELIS
RAIN FOREST [A] BIDDU ORCHESTRA
RAIN FOREST [B] PAUL HARDCASTLE
RAIN IN THE SUMMERTIME ALARM
RAIN KING COUNTING CROWS
RAIN ON ME ASHANTI
RAIN OR SHINE FIVE STAR
RAIN RAIN RAIN FRANKIE LAINE & THE FOUR LADS
RAIN SHOWERS SIZZLA
THE RAIN (SUPA DUPA FLY) MISSY 'MISDEMEANOR' ELLIOTT
RAINBOW [A] MARMALADE
RAINBOW [B] PETERS & LEE
RAINBOW CHASER NIRVANA
RAINBOW CHILD DAN REED NETWORK
RAINBOW COUNTRY BOB MARLEY VERSUS FUNKSTAR DELUXE
RAINBOW IN THE DARK DIO
RAINBOW LAKE WENDY & LISA
RAINBOW PEOPLE MANIX
RAINBOW (SAMPLE FREE) SOLO
RAINBOW THEME SAXON
RAINBOW VALLEY LOVE AFFAIR
RAINBOWS (EP) TERRY HALL
RAINBOWS OF COLOUR GROOVERIDER
RAINCLOUD LIGHTHOUSE FAMILY
THE RAINDANCE DARE
RAINDROPS KEEP FALLIN' ON MY HEAD BOBBIE GENTRY
RAINDROPS KEEP FALLING ON MY HEAD SACHA DISTEL
RAINDROPS KEEP FALLING ON MY HEAD B.J. THOMAS
RAININ' THROUGH MY SUNSHINE REAL THING
RAINING ALL OVER THE WORLD ADVENTURES
RAINING IN MY HEART LEO SAYER
RAINMAKER [A] SPARKLEHORSE
RAINMAKER [B] IRON MAIDEN
RAINY DAY WOMEN NOS. 12 & 35 BOB DYLAN
RAINY DAYS AND MONDAYS CARPENTERS
RAINY DAYZ MARY J. BLIGE FEATURING JA RULE

RAINY NIGHT IN GEORGIA RANDY CRAWFORD
A RAINY NIGHT IN SOHO POGUES
RAISE HYPER GO GO
RAISE YOUR HAND EDDIE FLOYD
RAISE YOUR HANDS [A] REEL 2 REAL FEATURING THE MAD STUNTMAN
RAISE YOUR HANDS [B] BIG ROOM GIRL FEATURING DARRYL PANDY
RAISED ON ROCK ELVIS PRESLEY
RAM GOAT LIVER PLUTO SHERVINGTON
RAMA LAMA DING DONG ROCKY SHARPE & THE REPLAYS
RAMBLIN' ROSE NAT 'KING' COLE
RAM-BUNK-SHUSH VENTURES
RAME SNAP FEATURING RUKMANI
RAMONA BACHELORS
RANDY BLUE MINK
RANKING FULL STOP BEAT
RAOUL AND THE KINGS OF SPAIN TEARS FOR FEARS
RAP DIS OXIDE & NEUTRINO
RAP SCHOLAR DAS EFX FEATURING REDMAN
RAP SUMMARY BIG DADDY KANE
RAP SUPERSTAR/ROCK SUPERSTAR CYPRESS HILL
RAP YOUR LOVE SET THE TONE
RAPE ME NIRVANA
RAPID HOPE LOSS DASHBOARD CONFESSIONAL
RAPP PAYBACK (WHERE IZ MOSES?) JAMES BROWN
RAPPAZ R N DAINJA KRS ONE
RAPPER'S DELIGHT SUGARHILL GANG
RAPTURE [A] BLONDIE
RAPTURE [B] IIO
RARE, PRECIOUS AND GONE MIKE SCOTT
THE RASCAL KING MIGHTY MIGHTY BOSSTONES
RASPBERRY BERET PRINCE & THE REVOLUTION
RASPUTIN BONEY M
THE RAT WALKMEN
RAT IN MI KITCHEN UB40
RAT RACE SPECIALS
RAT RAPPING ROLAND RAT SUPERSTAR
RAT TRAP BOOMTOWN RATS
RATAMAHATTA SEPULTURA
THE RATTLER GOODBYE MR MACKENZIE
RATTLESNAKES LLOYD COLE & THE COMMOTIONS
RAUNCHY BILL JUSTIS
RAUNCHY KEN MACKINTOSH
RAVE ALERT PRAGA KHAN
THE RAVE DIGGER MC LETHAL
RAVE GENERATOR TOXIC TWO
RAVE ON BUDDY HOLLY
RAVEL'S PAVANE POUR UNE INFANTE DEFUNTE WILLIAM ORBIT
RAVING I'M RAVING SHUT UP & DANCE FEATURING PETER BOUNCER
RAW [A] SPANDAU BALLET
RAW [B] ALARM
RAW [C] MELKY SEDECK
RAW POWER APOLLO FOUR FORTY
RAWHIDE FRANKIE LAINE
RAY OF LIGHT MADONNA
RAYS OF THE RISING SUN DENISE JOHNSON
RAYS OF THE RISING SUN MOZIAC
RAZOR'S EDGE MEAT LOAF
RAZZAMATAZZ QUINCY JONES FEATURING PATTI AUSTIN
RAZZLE DAZZLE [A] BILL HALEY & HIS COMETS
RAZZLE DAZZLE [B] HEATWAVE
RE:EVOLUTION SHAMEN WITH TERENCE McKENNA
RE-OFFENDER TRAVIS
RE-REWIND THE CROWD SAY BO SELECTA ARTFUL DODGER FEATURING CRAIG DAVID
REACH [A] JUDY CHEEKS
REACH [B] LIL MO' YIN YANG

REACH [C] GLORIA ESTEFAN
REACH [D] S CLUB 7
REACH FOR THE STARS SHIRLEY BASSEY
REACH 4 THE MELODY VICTORIA WILSON JAMES
REACH OUT MIDFIELD GENERAL FEATURING LINDA LEWIS
REACH OUT AND TOUCH DIANA ROSS
REACH OUT FOR ME DIONNE WARWICK
REACH OUT I'LL BE THERE FOUR TOPS
REACH OUT I'LL BE THERE GLORIA GAYNOR
REACH OUT I'LL BE THERE MICHAEL BOLTON
REACH UP TONEY LEE
(REACH UP FOR THE) SUNRISE DURAN DURAN
REACH UP (PAPA'S GOT A BRAND NEW PIG BAG) PERFECTO ALLSTARZ
REACHIN' [A] PHASE II
REACHIN' [B] HOUSE OF VIRGINISM
REACHING FOR THE BEST EXCITERS
REACHING FOR THE WORLD HAROLD MELVIN & THE BLUENOTES
REACHOUT DJ ZINC
REACT ERICK SERMON FEATURING REDMAN
READ 'EM AND WEEP BARRY MANILOW
READ MY LIPS [A] DSK
READ MY LIPS [B] ALEX PARTY
READ MY LIPS (ENOUGH IS ENOUGH) JIMMY SOMERVILLE
READ MY MIND CONNOR REEVES
READY BRUCE WAYNE
READY AN' WILLING (SWEET SATISFACTION) WHITESNAKE
READY FOR A NEW DAY TODD TERRY
READY FOR LOVE [A] JIMMY JONES
READY FOR LOVE [B] GARY MOORE
READY OR NOT [A] LIGHTNING SEEDS
READY OR NOT [B] FUGEES
READY OR NOT [B] COURSE
READY OR NOT [C] DJ DADO & SIMONE JAY
READY OR NOT [D] A1
READY OR NOT HERE I COME DELFONICS
READY STEADY GO [A] GENERATION X
READY STEADY GO [B] PAUL OAKENFOLD
READY STEADY WHO (EP) WHO
READY TO GO REPUBLICA
READY TO RECEIVE ANIMALHOUSE
READY TO RUN DIXIE CHICKS
READY WILLING AND ABLE DORIS DAY
REAL [A] DONNA ALLEN
REAL [B] PLUMB
REAL A LIE AUF DER MAUR
REAL COOL WORLD DAVID BOWIE
REAL EMOTION REID
REAL FASHION REGGAE STYLE CAREY JOHNSON
REAL GONE KID DEACON BLUE
REAL GOOD DOUBLE SIX
REAL GOOD TIME ALDA
REAL GREAT BRITAIN ASIAN DUB FOUNDATION
REAL LIFE [A] SIMPLE MINDS
REAL LIFE [B] BON JOVI
THE REAL LIFE [C] RAVEN MAIZE
REAL LOVE [A] RUBY MURRAY
REAL LOVE [B] JODY WATLEY
REAL LOVE [C] DRIZABONE
REAL LOVE [D] DARE
REAL LOVE [D] TIME FREQUENCY
REAL LOVE [E] MARY J. BLIGE
REAL LOVE [F] BEATLES
THE REAL ME W.A.S.P.
A REAL MOTHER FOR YA JOHNNY 'GUITAR' WATSON
REAL PEOPLE APACHE INDIAN
REAL REAL REAL JESUS JONES

THE REAL SLIM SHADY EMINEM
THE REAL THING [A] JELLYBEAN FEATURING STEVEN DANTE
THE REAL THING [B] BROTHERS JOHNSON
THE REAL THING [C] ABC
THE REAL THING [D] TONY DI BART
THE REAL THING [E] LISA STANSFIELD
THE REAL THING [F] 2 UNLIMITED
REAL THINGS JAVINE
REAL TO ME BRIAN McFADDEN
REAL VIBRATION EXPRESS OF SOUND
REAL WILD CHILD (WILD ONE) IGGY POP
THE REAL WILD HOUSE RAUL ORELLANA
REAL WORLD D-SIDE
REALITY USED TO BE A GOOD FRIEND OF MINE PM DAWN
REALLY DOE ICE CUBE
REALLY FREE JOHN OTWAY & WILD WILLY BARRETT
REALLY SAYING SOMETHING BANANARAMA WITH FUN BOY THREE
REAP THE WILD WIND ULTRAVOX
REASON [A] IAN VAN DAHL
THE REASON [B] CELINE DION
THE REASON [C] HOOBASTANK
REASON FOR LIVING RODDY FRAME
REASON TO BELIEVE ROD STEWART
REASON TO LIVE KISS
REASONS KLESHAY
REASONS TO BE CHEERFUL (PART 3) IAN DURY & THE BLOCKHEADS
REBEL MUSIC REBEL MC
REBEL NEVER GETS OLD DAVID BOWIE
REBEL REBEL DAVID BOWIE
REBEL ROUSER DUANE EDDY & THE REBELS
REBEL RUN TOYAH
REBEL WITHOUT A PAUSE PUBLIC ENEMY
REBEL WOMAN DNA FEATURING JAZZI P
REBEL YELL BILLY IDOL
REBEL YELL SCOOTER
REBIRTH OF SLICK (COOL LIKE DAT) DIGABLE PLANETS
RECIPE FOR LOVE HARRY CONNICK Jr.
RECKLESS AFRIKA BAMBAATAA FEATURING UB40 & FAMILY
RECKLESS GIRL BEGINERZ
RECONNECTION (EP) ZERO B
RECOVER YOUR SOUL ELTON JOHN
RECOVERY FONTELLA BASS
RED ELBOW
RED ALERT BASEMENT JAXX
RED BALLOON DAVE CLARK FIVE
RED BLOODED WOMAN KYLIE MINOGUE
RED DRESS ALVIN STARDUST
RED FRAME WHITE LIGHT ORCHESTRAL MANOEUVRES IN THE DARK
RED GUITAR DAVID SYLVIAN
RED HOT [A] PRINCESS
RED HOT [B] VANESSA-MAE
RED LETTER DAY PET SHOP BOYS
RED LIGHT GREEN LIGHT MITCHELL TOROK
RED LIGHT GREEN LIGHT EP WILDHEARTS
RED LIGHT SPECIAL TLC
RED LIGHT SPELLS DANGER BILLY OCEAN
RED RAIN PETER GABRIEL
RED RED WINE JIMMY JAMES & THE VAGABONDS
RED RED WINE TONY TRIBE
RED RED WINE UB40
RED RIVER ROCK JOHNNY & THE HURRICANES
RED SAILS IN THE SUNSET FATS DOMINO
THE RED SHOES KATE BUSH
RED SKIES [A] FIXX
RED SKIES [B] SAMSON

RED SKY STATUS QUO
THE RED STROKES GARTH BROOKS
RED SUN RISING LOST WITNESS
THE RED, THE WHITE, THE BLUE HOPE OF THE STATES
RED THREE, THUNDER/STORM DAVE CLARKE
REDEFINE SOIL
REDEMPTION SONG JOE STRUMMER & THE
    MESCALEROS
REDNECK WOMAN GRETCHEN WILSON
REDUNDANT GREEN DAY
REELIN' AND ROCKIN' DAVE CLARK FIVE
REELIN' AND ROCKIN' CHUCK BERRY
REELING PASADENAS
REET PETITE JACKIE WILSON
REET PETITE DARTS
REET PETITE PINKY & PERKY
REFLECT THREE 'N' ONE
REFLECTION VANESSA-MAE
REFLECTIONS DIANA ROSS & THE SUPREMES
REFLECTIONS OF MY LIFE MARMALADE
THE REFLEX DURAN DURAN
REFUSE-RESIST SEPULTURA
REGGAE FOR IT NOW BILL LOVELADY
REGGAE LIKE IT USED TO BE PAUL NICHOLAS
REGGAE MUSIC UB40
REGGAE TUNE ANDY FAIRWEATHER-LOW
REGINA SUGARCUBES
REGRET NEW ORDER
REGULATE WARREN G & NATE DOGG
REIGN UNKLE FEATURING IAN BROWN
REIGNS JA RULE
REILLY OLYMPIC ORCHESTRA
RELAX [A] FRANKIE GOES TO HOLLYWOOD
RELAX [B] CRYSTAL WATERS
RELAX [C] DEETAH
RELAY WHO
RELEASE [A] AFRO CELT SOUND SYSTEM
RELEASE [B] MEDWAY
RELEASE ME [A] ENGELBERT HUMPERDINCK
RELEASE ME [B] WILSON PHILLIPS
RELEASE THE PRESSURE LEFTFIELD
RELEASE YO' SELF [A] METHOD MAN
RELEASE YO SELF [B] TRANSATLANTIC SOUL
RELIGHT MY FIRE TAKE THAT FEATURING LULU
RELIGION FRONT 242
RELOAD PPK
REMEDY BLACK CROWES
REMEMBER [A] ROCK CANDY
REMEMBER [B] JIMI HENDRIX EXPERIENCE
REMEMBER [C] BT
REMEMBER [D] DISTURBED
REMEMBER I LOVE YOU JIM DIAMOND
REMEMBER ME [A] DIANA ROSS
REMEMBER ME [B] CLIFF RICHARD
REMEMBER ME [C] BLUE BOY
REMEMBER ME [D] JORIO
REMEMBER ME [E] BRITISH SEA POWER
REMEMBER ME [F] ZUTONS
REMEMBER ME THIS WAY GARY GLITTER
REMEMBER ME WITH LOVE GLORIA ESTEFAN
REMEMBER (SHA-LA-LA) BAY CITY ROLLERS
REMEMBER THE DAY INNOCENCE
(REMEMBER THE DAYS OF THE) OLD SCHOOL YARD CAT
    STEVENS
REMEMBER THE RAIN BOB LIND
REMEMBER THE TIME MICHAEL JACKSON
REMEMBER THEN SHOWADDYWADDY
REMEMBER (WALKIN' IN THE SAND) SHANGRI-LAS
REMEMBER WHEN PLATTERS
REMEMBER YESTERDAY JOHN MILES
REMEMBER YOU'RE A WOMBLE WOMBLES

REMEMBER YOU'RE MINE PAT BOONE
REMEMBERANCE DAY B-MOVIE
REMEMBERESE STILLS
REMEMBERING CHRISTMAS EXETER BRAMDEAN
    BOYS' CHOIR
REMEMBERING THE FIRST TIME SIMPLY RED
REMIND ME/SO EASY ROYKSOPP
REMINDING ME (OF SEF) COMMON FEATURING
    CHANTAY SAVAGE
REMINISCE [A] MARY J. BLIGE
REMINISCE [B] BLAZIN' SQUAD
REMINISCING BUDDY HOLLY
REMIXES – VOLUME 2 ED RUSH & OPTICAL
REMOTE CONTROL BEASTIE BOYS
RENAISSANCE M PEOPLE
RENDEZ-VOUS 98 JEAN-MICHEL JARRE & APOLLO 440
RENDEZ-VU BASEMENT JAXX
RENDEZVOUS [A] TINA CHARLES
RENDEZVOUS [B] TYGERS OF PAN TANG
RENDEZVOUS [C] CRAIG DAVID
RENE DMC (DEVASTATING MACHO CHARISMA) RENE &
    YVETTE
RENEGADE CAVALCADE ASH
RENEGADE MASTER WILDCHILD
RENEGADE SNARES OMNI TRIO
RENEGADE SOUNDWAVE RENEGADE SOUNDWAVE
RENEGADES OF FUNK AFRIKA BAMBAATAA & THE
    SONIC SOUL FORCE
RENT PET SHOP BOYS
RENTA SANTA CHRIS HILL
RENTED ROOMS TINDERSTICKS
REPEAT MANIC STREET PREACHERS
REPEATED LOVE ATGOC
REPORT TO THE DANCEFLOOR ENERGISE
REPRESENT SOUL II SOUL
REPTILLA STROKES
REPUBLICAN PARTY REPTILE (EP) BIG COUNTRY
REPUTATION DUSTY SPRINGFIELD
REPUTATIONS (JUST BE GOOD TO ME) ANDREA GRANT
REQUEST & LINE BLACK EYED PEAS FEATURING MACY
    GRAY
REQUEST LINE ZHANE
REQUIEM [A] SLIK
REQUIEM [B] LONDON BOYS
RESCUE ECHO & THE BUNNYMEN
RESCUE ME [A] FONTELLA BASS
RESCUE ME [B] ALARM
RESCUE ME [C] MADONNA
RESCUE ME [D] BELL BOOK & CANDLE
RESCUE ME [E] SUNKIDS FEATURING CHANCE
RESCUE ME [F] ULTRA
RESPECT [A] ARETHA FRANKLIN
RESPECT [A] REAL ROXANNE
RESPECT [A] ADEVA
RESPECT [B] SUB SUB
RESPECT [C] JUDY CHEEKS
RESPECT YOURSELF KANE GANG
RESPECT YOURSELF BRUCE WILLIS
RESPECT YOURSELF ROBERT PALMER
RESPECTABLE [A] ROLLING STONES
RESPECTABLE [B] MEL & KIM
RESPECTABLE [B] GIRLS @ PLAY
REST AND PLAY EP ORBITAL
REST IN PEACE EXTREME
REST OF MY LOVE URBAN COOKIE COLLECTIVE
REST OF THE NIGHT NATALIE COLE
RESTLESS [A] JOHNNY KIDD & THE PIRATES
RESTLESS [B] GILLAN
RESTLESS [C] STATUS QUO
RESTLESS [D] JX
RESTLESS DAYS (SHE CRIES OUT LOUD) AND WHY NOT?

RESTLESS (I KNOW YOU KNOW) NEJA
RESURRECTION [A] BRIAN MAY WITH COZY POWELL
RESURRECTION [B] PPK
RESURRECTION JOE CULT
RESURRECTION SHUFFLE ASHTON, GARDNER & DYKE
RETOX FATBOY SLIM
RETREAT HELL IS FOR HEROES
RETURN OF DJANGO UPSETTERS
THE RETURN OF EVIL BILL CLINIC
THE RETURN OF NOTHING SANDSTORM
THE RETURN OF PAN WATERBOYS
RETURN OF THE ELECTRIC WARRIOR (EP) MARC BOLAN
    & T REX
RETURN OF THE LOS PALMAS SEVEN MADNESS
RETURN OF THE MACK MARK MORRISON
RETURN OF THE RED BARON ROYAL GUARDSMEN
THE RETURN (TIME TO SAY GOODBYE) DJ VISAGE
    FEATURING CLARISSA
RETURN TO BRIXTON CLASH
RETURN TO INNOCENCE ENIGMA
RETURN TO ME DEAN MARTIN
RETURN TO REALITY ANTARCTICA
RETURN TO SENDER ELVIS PRESLEY
REUNITED PEACHES & HERB
REVEILLE ROCK JOHNNY & THE HURRICANES
REVELATION ELECTRIQUE BOUTIQUE
REVERENCE [A] JESUS & MARY CHAIN
REVERENCE [B] FAITHLESS
REVEREND BLACK GRAPE BLACK GRAPE
REVIVAL [A] CHRIS BARBER'S JAZZ BAND
REVIVAL [B] EURYTHMICS
REVIVAL [C] MARTINE GIRAULT
REVOL MANIC STREET PREACHERS
REVOLT IN STYLE BILL NELSON'S RED NOISE
REVOLUTION [A] CULT
REVOLUTION [B] THOMPSON TWINS
REVOLUTION [C] ARRESTED DEVELOPMENT
REVOLUTION [D] COLDCUT
REVOLUTION [E] BK
REVOLUTION BABY TRANSVISION VAMP
REVOLUTION (IN THE SUMMERTIME) COSMIC ROUGH
    RIDERS
REVOLUTION 909 DAFT PUNK
REVOLUTIONS JEAN-MICHEL JARRE
REVOLUTIONS (EP) SHARKEY
REVOLVING DOOR CRAZY TOWN
REWARD TEARDROP EXPLODES
REWIND [A] CELETIA
REWIND [B] PRECIOUS
REWIND (FIND A WAY) BEVERLEY KNIGHT
RHAPSODY FOUR SEASONS
RHAPSODY IN THE RAIN LOU CHRISTIE
RHIANNON FLEETWOOD MAC
RHINESTONE COWBOY GLEN CAMPBELL
RHINESTONE COWBOY (GIDDY UP GIDDY UP) RIKKI &
    DAZ FEATURING GLEN CAMPBELL
THE RHYME KEITH MURRAY
THE RHYTHM CLOCK
RHYTHM & BLUES ALIBI GOMEZ
RHYTHM AND GREENS SHADOWS
RHYTHM BANDITS JUNIOR SENIOR
RHYTHM DIVINE ENRIQUE IGLESIAS
THE RHYTHM DIVINE YELLO FEATURING SHIRLEY
    BASSEY
RHYTHM IS A DANCER SNAP
RHYTHM IS A MYSTERY K-KLASS
RHYTHM IS GONNA GET YOU GLORIA ESTEFAN &
    MIAMI SOUND MACHINE
RHYTHM NATION JANET JACKSON
RHYTHM OF LIFE OLETA ADAMS
RHYTHM OF LOVE SCORPIONS

RHYTHM OF MY HEART ROD STEWART
RHYTHM OF MY HEART RUNRIG
RHYTHM OF THE BEAST NICKO McBRAIN
RHYTHM OF THE JUNGLE QUICK
RHYTHM OF THE NIGHT [A] DeBARGE
THE RHYTHM OF THE NIGHT [B] CORONA
RHYTHM OF THE NIGHT [C] POWERHOUSE
RHYTHM OF THE RAIN CASCADES
RHYTHM OF THE RAIN JASON DONOVAN
RHYTHM TAKES CONTROL UNIQUE 3 FEATURING KARIN
RHYTHM TALK JOCKO
RIBBON IN THE SKY STEVIE WONDER
RICE IS NICE LEMON PIPERS
RICH AH GETTING RICHER REBEL MC INTRODUCING
    LITTLE T
RICH AND STRANGE CUD
RICH IN PARADISE FPI PROJECT
RICH KIDS RICH KIDS
RICH MAN POOR MAN JIMMY YOUNG
RICHARD III SUPERGRASS
RICOCHET [A] JOAN REGAN & THE SQUADRONAIRES
RICOCHET [B] B B & Q BAND
RICOCHET [C] FAITH NO MORE
RIDDIM US3 FEATURING TUKKA YOOT
RIDDLE EN VOGUE
THE RIDDLE NIK KERSHAW
RIDDLE ME UB40
RIDE [A] ANA ANN
RIDE [B] VINES
RIDE [C] DYNAMITE MC
RIDE A ROCKET LITHIUM & SONYA MADAN
RIDE A WHITE SWAN T. REX
RIDE A WILD HORSE DEE CLARK
RIDE AWAY ROY ORBISON
RIDE (EP) RIDE
RIDE IT GERI HALLIWELL
RIDE LIKE THE WIND CHRISTOPHER CROSS
RIDE LIKE THE WIND SAXON
RIDE LIKE THE WIND EAST SIDE BEAT
RIDE MY SEE-SAW MOODY BLUES
RIDE ON BABY CHRIS FARLOWE
RIDE ON THE RHYTHM LITTLE LOUIE & MARC ANTHONY
RIDE ON TIME BLACK BOX
RIDE THE BULLET ARMY OF LOVERS
RIDE THE GROOVE PLAYERS ASSOCIATION
RIDE THE LOVE TRAIN LIGHT OF THE WORLD
RIDE THE RHYTHM Z FACTOR
RIDE THE STORM AKABU FEATURING LINDA CLIFFORD
RIDE THE TIGER BOO RADLEYS
RIDE WID US SO SOLID CREW
RIDE WIT ME NELLY FEATURING CITY SPUD
RIDE WIT U JOE FEATURING G UNIT
RIDE-O-ROCKET BROTHERS JOHNSON
RIDERS IN THE SKY RAMRODS
RIDERS IN THE SKY SHADOWS
RIDERS ON THE STORM DOORS
RIDERS ON THE STORM ANNABEL LAMB
RIDICULOUS THOUGHTS CRANBERRIES
RIDING ON A TRAIN PASADENAS
RIDING WITH THE ANGELS SAMSON
RIGHT ABOUT NOW MOUSSE T FEATURING EMMA
    LANFORD
RIGHT AND EXACT CHRISSY WARD
RIGHT BACK WHERE WE STARTED FROM MAXINE
    NIGHTINGALE
RIGHT BACK WHERE WE STARTED FROM SINITTA
RIGHT BEFORE MY EYES PATTI DAY
RIGHT BEFORE MY EYES N + G FEATURING
    KALLAGHAN & MC NEAT
RIGHT BESIDE YOU SOPHIE B. HAWKINS
RIGHT BETWEEN THE EYES WAX

RIGHT BY YOUR SIDE EURYTHMICS
THE RIGHT COMBINATION SEIKO & DONNIE WAHLBERG
THE RIGHT DECISION JESUS JONES
RIGHT HERE [A] SWV
RIGHT HERE [B] ULTIMATE KAOS
RIGHT HERE RIGHT NOW [A] JESUS JONES
RIGHT HERE RIGHT NOW [B] DISCO CITIZENS
RIGHT HERE RIGHT NOW [C] FIERCE
RIGHT HERE RIGHT NOW [D] FATBOY SLIM
RIGHT HERE WAITING RICHARD MARX
RIGHT IN THE NIGHT (FALL IN LOVE WITH MUSIC) JAM
    & SPOON FEATURING PLAVKA
RIGHT IN THE SOCKET SHALAMAR
THE RIGHT KINDA LOVER PATTI LABELLE
RIGHT NEXT DOOR (BECAUSE OF ME) ROBERT CRAY
    BAND
RIGHT NOW [A] CREATURES
RIGHT NOW [B] AIRHEAD
RIGHT NOW [C] ATOMIC KITTEN
RIGHT ON SILICONE SOUL
RIGHT ON TRACK BREAKFAST CLUB
RIGHT SAID FRED BERNARD CRIBBINS
THE RIGHT STUFF [A] BRYAN FERRY
THE RIGHT STUFF [B] VANESSA WILLIAMS
RIGHT STUFF [C] LC ANDERSON VS PSYCHO RADIO
THE RIGHT THING SIMPLY RED
THE RIGHT THING TO DO CARLY SIMON
THE RIGHT THING TO SAY NAT 'KING' COLE
RIGHT THURR CHINGY
THE RIGHT TIME ULTRA
RIGHT TO BE WRONG JOSS STONE
THE RIGHT TO LOVE DAVID WHITFIELD
THE RIGHT WAY PETER ANDRE
RIKKI DON'T LOSE THAT NUMBER STEELY DAN
RIKKI DON'T LOSE THAT NUMBER TOM ROBINSON
RING ALEXIA
RING A DING GIRL RONNIE CARROLL
RING MY BELL [A] ANITA WARD
RING MY BELL [A] DJ JAZZY JEFF & THE FRESH PRINCE
RING MY BELL [B] MONIE LOVE Vs ADEVA
RING OF BRIGHT WATER VAL DOONICAN
RING OF FIRE [A] DUANE EDDY & THE REBELS
RING OF FIRE [B] ERIC BURDON & THE ANIMALS
RING OF ICE JENNIFER RUSH
RING OUT SOLSTICE BELLS (EP) JETHRO TULL
RING RING [A] ABBA
RING RING [B] DOLLAR
RING RING RING AARON SOUL
RING RING RING (HA HA HEY) DE LA SOUL
RING THE BELLS JAMES
RINGO LORNE GREENE
RIO [A] MICHAEL NESMITH
RIO [B] DURAN DURAN
RIOT RADIO DEAD 60'S
RIP GARY NUMAN
RIP IT UP [A] BILL HALEY & HIS COMETS
RIP IT UP [A] LITTLE RICHARD
RIP IT UP [A] ELVIS PRESLEY
RIP IT UP [B] ORANGE JUICE
RIP IT UP [C] RAZORLIGHT
RIPGROOVE DOUBLE 99
RIPPED IN 2 MINUTES A VS B
RIPPIN KITTIN GOLDEN BOY WITH MISS KITTIN
RISE [A] HERB ALPERT
RISE [B] PUBLIC IMAGE LTD.
RISE [C] ZION TRAIN
RISE [D] EDDIE AMADOR
RISE [E] GABRIELLE
RISE [F] SOUL PROVIDERS FEATURING MICHELLE
    SHELLERS
RISE & FALL CRAIG DAVID & STING

THE RISE AND FALL OF FLINGEL BUNT SHADOWS
RISE AND SHINE CARDIGANS
RISE 'IN STEVE LAWLER
RISE OF THE EAGLES EIGHTIES MATCHBOX B-LINE
    DISASTER
RISE TO THE OCCASION CLIMIE FISHER
RISE UP JAMAICA UNITED
RISIN' TO THE TOP KENI BURKE
RISING SIGN HURRICANE #1
RISING SUN [A] MEDICINE HEAD
RISING SUN [B] FARM
RISINGSON MASSIVE ATTACK
THE RITUAL EBONY DUBSTERS
THE RIVER [A] BRUCE SPRINGSTEEN
THE RIVER [B] KING TRIGGER
THE RIVER [C] TOTAL CONTRAST
THE RIVER [D] BEAUTIFUL SOUTH
THE RIVER [E] BREED 77
RIVER BELOW BILLY TALENT
RIVER DEEP MOUNTAIN HIGH IKE & TINA TURNER
RIVER DEEP MOUNTAIN HIGH SUPREMES & THE FOUR
    TOPS
THE RIVER (LE COLLINE SONO IN FIORO) KEN DODD
RIVER MAN NICK DRAKE
THE RIVER OF DREAMS BILLY JOEL
RIVER OF PAIN THUNDER
RIVER STAY 'WAY FROM MY DOOR FRANK SINATRA
THE RIVERBOAT SONG OCEAN COLOUR SCENE
RIVERDANCE BILL WHELAN FEATURING ANUNA & THE
    RTE CONCERT ORCHESTRA
RIVERS OF BABYLON BONEY M
THE RIVERS OF BELIEF ENIGMA
THE RIVER'S RUN DRY VINCE HILL
ROACHES TRANCESETTERS
ROAD RAGE CATATONIA
THE ROAD TO HELL (PART 2) CHRIS REA
THE ROAD TO MANDALAY ROBBIE WILLIAMS
THE ROAD TO PARADISE BHOYS OF PARADISE
ROAD TO NOWHERE TALKING HEADS
ROAD TO OUR DREAM T'PAU
ROAD TO YOUR SOUL ALL ABOUT EVE
ROAD TRIPPIN' RED HOT CHILI PEPPERS
ROADBLOCK STOCK AITKEN WATERMAN
ROADHOUSE MEDLEY (ANNIVERSARY WALTZ PART 25)
    STATUS QUO
ROADRUNNER JONATHAN RICHMAN & THE MODERN
    LOVERS
ROAM B-52's
ROBERT DE NIRO'S WAITING BANANARAMA
ROBIN HOOD GARY MILLER
ROBIN HOOD DICK JAMES
ROBIN (THE HOODED MAN) CLANNAD
ROBIN'S RETURN NEVILLE DICKIE
ROBOT TORNADOS
ROBOT MAN CONNIE FRANCIS
ROBOT WARS (ANDROID LOVE) SIR KILLALOT VS ROBO
    BABE
THE ROBOTS KRAFTWERK
ROCCO DEATH IN VEGAS
ROCHDALE COWBOY MIKE HARDING
ROC-IN-IT DEEJAY PUNK-ROC VS ONYX
THE ROCK [A] ALARM FEATURING THE MORRISTON
    ORPHEUS MALE VOICE CHOIR
THE ROCK [B] DELAKOTA
THE ROCK [C] PUNX
ROCK A HULA BABY ELVIS PRESLEY
ROCK AND A HARD PLACE ROLLING STONES
ROCK AND ROLL DREAMS COME THROUGH MEAT LOAF
ROCK AND ROLL IS DEAD LENNY KRAVITZ
ROCK AND ROLL (IS GONNA SET THE NIGHT ON FIRE)
    PRETTY BOY FLOYD

ROCK AND ROLL MUSIC BEACH BOYS
ROCK AND ROLL (PARTS 1 & 2) GARY GLITTER
ROCK AND ROLL SUICIDE DAVID BOWIE
ROCK AND ROLL WALTZ KAY STARR
ROCK AROUND THE CLOCK BILL HALEY & HIS COMETS
ROCK AROUND THE CLOCK TELEX
ROCK AROUND THE CLOCK TEN POLE TUDOR
ROCK BOTTOM [A] LYNSEY DE PAUL & MIKE MORAN
ROCK BOTTOM [B] BABYFACE
ROCK DA FUNKY BEATS PUBLIC DOMAIN FEATURING
    CHUCK D
ROCK DA HOUSE TALL PAUL
ROCK DJ ROBBIE WILLIAMS
ROCK HARD SUZI QUATRO
R.O.C.K. IN THE USA JOHN COUGAR MELLENCAMP
ROCK IS DEAD MARILYN MANSON
ROCK ISLAND LINE LONNIE DONEGAN
ROCK ISLAND LINE STAN FREBERG & HIS SKIFFLE
    GROUP
ROCK LOBSTER B-52's
ROCK ME AMADEUS FALCO
ROCK ME BABY [A] DAVID CASSIDY
ROCK ME BABY [B] JOHNNY NASH
ROCK ME BABY [C] BABY ROOTS
ROCK ME GENTLY ANDY KIM
ROCK ME GOOD UNIVERSAL
ROCK ME STEADY DJ PROFESSOR
ROCK ME TONIGHT (FOR OLD TIME'S SAKE) FREDDIE
    JACKSON
ROCK MY HEART HADDAWAY
ROCK MY WORLD FIVE STAR
ROCK 'N ME STEVE MILLER BAND
ROCK 'N' ROLL [A] STATUS QUO
ROCK 'N' ROLL [B] JOHN McENROE & PAT CASH WITH
    THE FULL METAL RACKETS
ROCK 'N' ROLL AIN'T NOISE POLLUTION AC/DC
ROCK 'N' ROLL CHILDREN DIO
ROCK 'N' ROLL DAMNATION AC/DC
ROCK 'N' ROLL DANCE PARTY JIVE BUNNY & THE
    MASTERMIXERS
ROCK 'N' ROLL (DOLE) J PAC
ROCK 'N' ROLL DREAMS COME THROUGH JIM
    STEINMAN,VOCALS BY RORY DODD
ROCK 'N' ROLL GYPSY SAXON
ROCK 'N ROLL HIGH SCHOOL RAMONES
ROCK 'N ROLL (I GAVE YOU THE BEST YEARS OF MY
    LIFE) KEVIN JOHNSON
ROCK 'N' ROLL IS KING ELECTRIC LIGHT ORCHESTRA
ROCK 'N' ROLL LADY SHOWADDYWADDY
ROCK 'N' ROLL LIES RAZORLIGHT
ROCK 'N' ROLL MERCENARIES MEAT LOAF FEATURING
    JOHN PARR
ROCK 'N' ROLL NIGGER BIRDLAND
ROCK 'N' ROLL OUTLAW ROSE TATTOO
ROCK 'N' ROLL STAGE SHOW (LP) BILL HALEY & HIS
    COMETS
ROCK 'N' ROLL WINTER WIZZARD
ROCK OF AGES DEF LEPPARD
ROCK ON DAVID ESSEX
ROCK ON BROTHER CHEQUERS
THE ROCK SHOW BLINK 182
ROCK STAR N*E*R*D
ROCK STEADY [A] WHISPERS
ROCK STEADY [B] BONNIE RAITT & BRYAN ADAMS
ROCK THE BELLS KADOC
ROCK THE BOAT [A] HUES CORPORATION
ROCK THE BOAT [A] FORREST
ROCK THE BOAT [A] DELAGE
ROCK THE BOAT [B] AALIYAH
ROCK THE CASBAH CLASH
ROCK THE DISCOTEK RAMP

ROCK THE FUNKY BEAT NATURAL BORN CHILLERS
ROCK THE HOUSE [A] SOURCE FEATURING NICOLE
ROCK THE HOUSE [B] GORILLAZ
ROCK THE JOINT BILL HALEY & HIS COMETS
ROCK THE MIDNIGHT DAVID GRANT
ROCK THE NIGHT EUROPE
ROCK THIS TOWN STRAY CATS
ROCK 'TIL YOU DROP STATUS QUO
ROCK 2 HOUSE X-PRESS 2 FEATURING LO-PRO
ROCK WIT U (AWWW BABY) ASHANTI
ROCK WIT'CHA BOBBY BROWN
ROCK WITH THE CAVEMAN TOMMY STEELE & THE
    STEELMEN
ROCK WITH YOU MICHAEL JACKSON
ROCK WITH YOU D-INFLUENCE
ROCK YOUR BABY GEORGE McCRAE
ROCK YOUR BABY KWS
ROCK YOUR BODY [A] CLOCK
ROCK YOUR BODY [B] JUSTIN TIMBERLAKE
ROCK YOUR BODY ROCK FERRY CORSTEN
ROCK-A-BEATIN' BOOGIE BILL HALEY & HIS COMETS
ROCK-A-BILLY GUY MITCHELL
ROCK-A-BYE YOUR BABY (WITH A DIXIE MELODY)
    JERRY LEWIS
ROCK-A-DOODLE-DOO LINDA LEWIS
ROCKABILLY BOB COLUMBO FEATURING OOE
ROCKABILLY GUY POLECATS
ROCKABILLY REBEL MATCHBOX
THE ROCKAFELLER SKANK FATBOY SLIM
ROCKALL MEZZOFORTE
ROCKARIA! ELECTRIC LIGHT ORCHESTRA
ROCKER ALTER EGO
ROCKET [A] MUD
ROCKET [B] DEF LEPPARD
ROCKET MAN [A] SPOTNICKS
ROCKET MAN [B] ELTON JOHN
ROCKET MAN (I THINK IT'S GOING TO BE A LONG LONG
    TIME) [B] KATE BUSH
ROCKET RIDE FELIX DA HOUSECAT
ROCKET 2 U JETS
ROCKIN' ALL OVER THE WORLD STATUS QUO
ROCKIN' ALONE MIKI & GRIFF
ROCKIN' AROUND THE CHRISTMAS TREE BRENDA LEE
ROCKIN' AROUND THE CHRISTMAS TREE JETS
ROCKIN' AROUND THE CHRISTMAS TREE MEL & KIM
ROCKIN' BACK INSIDE MY HEART JULEE CRUISE
ROCKIN' CHAIR MAGNUM
ROCKIN' FOR MYSELF MOTIV 8
ROCKIN' GOOD CHRISTMAS ROY 'CHUBBY' BROWN
A ROCKIN' GOOD WAY SHAKY & BONNIE
ROCKIN' ME PROFESSOR
ROCKIN' MY BODY 49ERS FEATURING ANN-MARIE
    SMITH
ROCKIN' OVER THE BEAT TECHNOTRONIC FEATURING
    YA KID K
ROCKIN' RED WING SAMMY MASTERS
ROCKIN' ROBIN BOBBY DAY
ROCKIN' ROBIN MICHAEL JACKSON
ROCKIN' ROBIN LOLLY
ROCKIN' ROLL BABY STYLISTICS
ROCKIN' SOUL HUES CORPORATION
ROCKIN' THE SUBURBS BEN FOLDS
ROCKIN' THROUGH THE RYE BILL HALEY & HIS COMETS
ROCKIN' TO THE MUSIC BLACK BOX
ROCKIN' TO THE RHYTHM CONVERT
ROCKIN' WITH RITA (HEAD TO TOE) VINDALOO
    SUMMER SPECIAL
ROCKING GOOSE JOHNNY & THE HURRICANES
ROCKING MUSIC MARTIN SOLVEIG
ROCKIT HERBIE HANCOCK
ROCKS PRIMAL SCREAM

ROCKS ROD STEWART
ROCKS ON THE ROAD JETHRO TULL
ROCKY AUSTIN ROBERTS
ROCKY MOUNTAIN EP JOE WALSH
THE RODEO SONG GARRY LEE & SHOWDOWN
RODRIGO'S GUITAR CONCERTO DE ARANJUEZ (THEME
    FROM 2ND MOVEMENT) MANUEL & HIS MUSIC OF
    THE MOUNTAINS
ROFO'S THEME ROFO
ROK DA HOUSE [A] BEATMASTERS FEATURING THE
    COOKIE CREW
ROK DA HOUSE [B] VINYLGROOVER & THE RED HED
ROK THE NATION ROB 'N' RAZ FEATURING LEILA K
ROLL AWAY DUSTY SPRINGFIELD
ROLL AWAY THE STONE MOTT THE HOOPLE
ROLL ON MIS-TEEQ
ROLL ON DOWN THE HIGHWAY BACHMAN-TURNER
    OVERDRIVE
ROLL OVER BEETHOVEN ELECTRIC LIGHT ORCHESTRA
ROLL OVER LAY DOWN STATUS QUO
ROLL THE BONES RUSH
ROLL TO ME DEL AMITRI
ROLL WITH IT [A] STEVE WINWOOD
ROLL WITH IT [B] OASIS
A ROLLER SKATING JAM NAMED 'SATURDAYS' DE LA
    SOUL
ROLLERBLADE NICK HEYWARD
ROLLERBLADE MOVIN' MELODIES
ROLLERCOASTER [A] GRID
ROLLERCOASTER [B] NORTHERN UPROAR
ROLLERCOASTER [C] B*WITCHED
ROLLERCOASTER (EP) JESUS & MARY CHAIN
ROLLERCOASTER (EP) EVERYTHING BUT THE GIRL
ROLLIN' LIMP BIZKIT
ROLLIN' HOME STATUS QUO
ROLLIN' IN MY 5.0 VANILLA ICE
ROLLIN' ON CIRRUS
ROLLIN' STONE DAVID ESSEX
ROLLOUT (MY BUSINESS) LUDACRIS
ROLLOVER DJ JET
ROLODEX PROPAGANDA AT THE DRIVE-IN
ROMAN P PSYCHIC TV
ROMANCE (LET YOUR HEART GO) DAVID CASSIDY
ROMANCING THE STONE EDDY GRANT
ROMANTIC KARYN WHITE
ROMANTIC RIGHTS DEATH FROM ABOVE 1979
ROMANTICA JANE MORGAN
ROME WASN'T BUILT IN A DAY MORCHEEBA
ROMEO [A] PETULA CLARK
ROMEO [B] MR BIG
ROMEO [C] BASEMENT JAXX
ROMEO AND JULIET DIRE STRAITS
ROMEO DUNN ROMEO
ROMEO ME SLEEPER
ROMEO WHERE'S JULIET COLLAGE
RONDO KENNY BALL & HIS JAZZMEN
RONI BOBBY BROWN
ROOBARB AND CUSTARD SHAFT
ROOF IS ON FIRE WESTBAM
ROOF TOP SINGING NEW WORLD
ROOM AT THE TOP ADAM ANT
ROOM ELEVEN DAISY CHAINSAW
ROOM IN BROOKLYN JOHN SQUIRE
ROOM IN YOUR HEART LIVING IN A BOX
ROOM ON THE 3RD FLOOR McFLY
ROOMS ON FIRE STEVIE NICKS
THE ROOT OF ALL EVIL BEAUTIFUL SOUTH
ROOTS SPUNGE
ROOTS BLOODY ROOTS SEPULTURA
ROSALIE – COWGIRLS' SONG (MEDLEY) THIN LIZZY
ROSALYN PRETTY THINGS

ROSANNA TOTO
THE ROSE MICHAEL BALL
THE ROSE HEATHER PEACE
ROSE GARDEN LYNN ANDERSON
ROSE GARDEN NEW WORLD
A ROSE HAS TO DIE DOOLEYS
A ROSE IS STILL A ROSE ARETHA FRANKLIN
ROSE MARIE SLIM WHITMAN
ROSE ROUGE ST GERMAIN
ROSEABILITY IDLEWILD
ROSES [A] HAYWOODE
ROSES [A] RHYTHM-N-BASS
ROSES [B] dEUS
ROSES [C] OUTKAST
ROSES ARE RED [A] RONNIE CARROLL
ROSES ARE RED [B] MAC BAND FEATURING THE
   McCAMPBELL BROTHERS
ROSES ARE RED (MY LOVE) BOBBY VINTON
ROSES IN THE HOSPITAL MANIC STREET PREACHERS
ROSES OF PICARDY VINCE HILL
ROSETTA FAME & PRICE TOGETHER
ROSIE [A] DON PARTRIDGE
ROSIE [B] JOAN ARMATRADING
ROTATION HERB ALPERT
ROTTERDAM BEAUTIFUL SOUTH
ROUGH BOY ZZ TOP
ROUGH BOYS [A] PETE TOWNSHEND
ROUGH BOYS [B] NORTHERN UPROAR
ROUGH JUSTICE BANANARAMA
ROUGH WITH THE SMOOTH SHARA NELSON
ROUGHNECK (EP) PROJECT 1
ROULETTE RUSS CONWAY
ROUND AND ROUND [A] JIMMY YOUNG
ROUND AND ROUND [B] SPANDAU BALLET
ROUND AND ROUND [C] JAKI GRAHAM
ROUND AND ROUND [D] NEW ORDER
ROUND & ROUND [E] HI-TEK FEATURING JONELL
ROUND EVERY CORNER PETULA CLARK
ROUND HERE [A] COUNTING CROWS
ROUND HERE [B] GEORGE MICHAEL
ROUND OF BLUES SHAWN COLVIN
ROUND ROUND SUGABABES
THE ROUSSOS PHENOMENON EP DEMIS ROUSSOS
ROXANNE POLICE
ROYAL EVENT RUSS CONWAY
ROYAL MILE GERRY RAFFERTY
ROY'S KEEN MORRISSEY
R.R. EXPRESS ROSE ROYCE
RSVP [A] FIVE STAR
RSVP [B] JASON DONOVAN
RSVP [C] POP WILL EAT ITSELF
RUB A DUB DUB EQUALS
RUB-A-DUB DOUBLE TROUBLE
RUBBER BALL BOBBY VEE
RUBBER BALL AVONS
RUBBER BALL MARTY WILDE
RUBBER BULLETS 10 C.C.
RUBBERBAND GIRL KATE BUSH
THE RUBBERBAND MAN DETROIT SPINNERS
RUBBERBANDMAN YELLO
RUBBERNECKIN' ELVIS PRESLEY
RUBBISH CARTER – THE UNSTOPPABLE SEX MACHINE
THE RUBETTES AUTEURS
RUBY ANN MARTY ROBBINS
RUBY DON'T TAKE YOUR LOVE TO TOWN KENNY
   ROGERS & THE FIRST EDITION
RUBY RED [A] SLADE
RUBY RED [B] MARC ALMOND
RUBY TUESDAY ROLLING STONES
RUBY TUESDAY MELANIE
RUBY TUESDAY ROD STEWART

RUDD IKARA COLT
RUDE BOY ROCK LIONROCK
RUDE BUOYS OUTA JAIL SPECIALS
RUDI GOT MARRIED LAUREL AITKEN & THE UNITONE
RUDI'S IN LOVE LOCOMOTIVE
RUDY'S ROCK BILL HALEY & HIS COMETS
RUFF IN THE JUNGLE BIZNESS PRODIGY
RUFF MIX WONDER DOGS
RUFFNECK MC LYTE
RUGGED AND MEAN, BUTCH AND ON SCREEN PEE BEE
   SQUAD
RUINED IN A DAY NEW ORDER
RULES AND REGULATIONS WE'VE GOT A FUZZBOX &
   WE'RE GONNA USE IT
RULES OF THE GAME BUCKS FIZZ
RUMBLE IN THE JUNGLE FUGEES
RUMORS TIMEX SOCIAL CLUB
RUMOUR HAS IT DONNA SUMMER
RUMOURS [A] HOT CHOCOLATE
RUMOURS [B] AWESOME
RUMOURS [C] DAMAGE
RUMP SHAKER WRECKS-N-EFFECT
RUN [A] SANDIE SHAW
RUN [B] SPIRITUALIZED
RUN [C] LIGHTHOUSE FAMILY
RUN [D] SNOW PATROL
RUN AWAY [A] 10 C.C.
RUN AWAY [B] (MC SAR &) THE REAL McCOY
RUN AWAY (I WANNA BE WITH U) NIVEA
RUN BABY RUN [A] NEWBEATS
RUN, BABY, RUN [B] SHERYL CROW
RUN BACK CARL DOUGLAS
RUN FOR COVER SUGABABES
RUN FOR HOME LINDISFARNE
RUN FOR YOUR LIFE [A] BUCKS FIZZ
RUN FOR YOUR LIFE [B] NORTHERN LINE
RUN FROM LOVE JIMMY SOMERVILLE
RUN ON MOBY
RUN RUDOLPH RUN CHUCK BERRY
RUN RUN AWAY SLADE
RUN RUN RUN [A] JO JO GUNNE
RUN RUN RUN [B] PHOENIX
RUN SILENT SHAKESPEARS SISTER
RUN TO HIM BOBBY VEE
RUN TO ME BEE GEES
RUN TO MY LOVIN' ARMS BILLY FURY
RUN TO THE DOOR CLINTON FORD
RUN TO THE HILLS IRON MAIDEN
RUN TO THE SUN ERASURE
RUN TO YOU [A] BRYAN ADAMS
RUN TO YOU [A] RAGE
RUN TO YOU [B] WHITNEY HOUSTON
RUN TO YOU [C] ROXETTE
RUN 2 NEW ORDER
RUNAGROUND JAMES
RUNAROUND MARTHA WASH
RUNAROUND SUE DION
RUNAROUND SUE DOUG SHELDON
RUNAROUND SUE RACEY
RUNAWAY [A] DEL SHANNON
RUNAWAY [B] DEEE-LITE
RUNAWAY [C] JANET JACKSON
RUNAWAY [D] E'VOKE
RUNAWAY [E] NUYORICAN SOUL FEATURING INDIA
RUNAWAY [F] CORRS
THE RUNAWAY ELKIE BROOKS
RUNAWAY BOYS STRAY CATS
RUNAWAY GIRL STERLING VOID
RUNAWAY HORSES BELINDA CARLISLE
RUNAWAY LOVE EN VOGUE
RUNAWAY SKIES CELETIA

RUNAWAY TRAIN [A] ELTON JOHN & ERIC CLAPTON
RUNAWAY TRAIN [B] SOUL ASYLUM
THE RUNNER THREE DEGREES
RUNNIN [A] BASSTOY
RUNNIN' [B] BASS BUMPERS
RUNNIN' [C] 2PAC & THE NOTORIOUS B.I.G.
RUNNIN' [D] PHARCYDE
RUNNIN' [E] MARK PICCHIOTTI PRESENTS BASSTOY
RUNNIN' AWAY SLY & THE FAMILY STONE
RUNNIN' AWAY NICOLE
RUNNIN' DOWN A DREAM TOM PETTY
RUNNIN' (DYIN' TO LIVE) 2PAC & THE NOTORIOUS B.I.G.
RUNNIN' FOR THE RED LIGHT (I GOTTA LIFE) MEAT LOAF
RUNNIN' WITH THE DEVIL VAN HALEN
RUNNING ALL OVER THE WORLD STATUS QUO
RUNNING AROUND TOWN BILLIE RAY MARTIN
RUNNING BEAR JOHNNY PRESTON
RUNNING FREE IRON MAIDEN
RUNNING FROM PARADISE DARYL HALL & JOHN OATES
RUNNING IN THE FAMILY LEVEL 42
RUNNING OUT OF TIME DIGITAL ORGASM
RUNNING SCARED ROY ORBISON
RUNNING UP THAT HILL KATE BUSH
RUNNING WITH THE NIGHT LIONEL RICHIE
RUN'S HOUSE RUN D.M.C.
RUPERT JACKIE LEE
RUSH [A] FREAKPOWER
RUSH [B] KLESHAY
THE RUSH LUTHER VANDROSS
RUSH HOUR [A] JANE WIEDLIN
RUSH HOUR [A] JOYRIDER
RUSH HOUR [B] BAD COMPANY
RUSH RUSH PAULA ABDUL
RUSHES DARIUS
RUSHING LONI CLARK
RUSSIANS STING
RUST ECHO & THE BUNNYMEN
RUSTY CAGE SOUNDGARDEN
S CLUB PARTY S CLUB 7
SABOTAGE BEASTIE BOYS
SABRE DANCE LOVE SCULPTURE
SACRAMENTO MIDDLE OF THE ROAD
SACRED CYCLES PETER LAZONBY
SACRED TRUST ONE TRUE VOICE
THE SACREMENT H.I.M.
SACRIFICE ELTON JOHN
SAD BUT TRUE METALLICA
SAD EYES ROBERT JOHN
SAD MOVIES (MAKE ME CRY) CAROL DEENE
SAD MOVIES (MAKE ME CRY) SUE THOMPSON
SAD SONGS (SAY SO MUCH) ELTON JOHN
SAD SWEET DREAMER SWEET SENSATION
SADDLE UP DAVID CHRISTIE
SADIE'S SHAWL FRANK CORDELL
SADNESS PART 1 ENIGMA
SAFARI (EP) BREEDERS
SAFE FROM HARM [A] MASSIVE ATTACK
SAFE FROM HARM [B] NARCOTIC THRUST
THE SAFETY DANCE MEN WITHOUT HATS
SAFFRON EASTERN LANE
SAID I LOVED YOU BUT I LIED MICHAEL BOLTON
SAID SHE WAS A DANCER JETHRO TULL
SAIL AWAY [A] LITTLE ANGELS
SAIL AWAY [B] URBAN COOKIE COLLECTIVE
SAIL AWAY [C] DAVID GRAY
SAIL ON COMMODORES
SAILING [A] ROD STEWART
SAILING [B] CHRISTOPHER CROSS
SAILING OFF THE EDGE OF THE WORLD STRAW
SAILING ON THE SEVEN SEAS ORCHESTRAL
   MANOEUVRES IN THE DARK

SAILOR ANNE SHELTON
SAILOR PETULA CLARK
SAILORTOWN ENERGY ORCHARD
THE SAINT [A] THOMPSON TWINS
THE SAINT [B] ORBITAL
ST ANGER METALLICA
ST ELMO'S FIRE (MAN IN MOTION) JOHN PARR
SAINT OF ME ROLLING STONES
ST TERESA JOAN OSBORNE
ST VALENTINE'S DAY MASSACRE EP MOTORHEAD &
    GIRLSCHOOL
ST. THERESE OF THE ROSES MALCOLM VAUGHAN
THE SAINTS ARE COMING SKIDS
THE SAINTS ROCK 'N' ROLL BILL HALEY & HIS COMETS
SALE OF THE CENTURY SLEEPER
SALLY [A] GERRY MONROE
SALLY [B] CARMEL
SALLY [C] KERBDOG
SALLY ANN JOE BROWN & THE BRUVVERS
SALLY CINNAMON STONE ROSES
SALLY DON'T YOU GRIEVE LONNIE DONEGAN
SALLY MACLENNANE POGUES
SAL'S GOT A SUGAR LIP LONNIE DONEGAN
SALSA HOUSE RICHIE RICH
SALSOUL NUGGET (IF U WANNA) M&S PRESENTS GIRL
    NEXT DOOR
SALT IN THE WOUND CARPET BOMBERS FOR PEACE
SALT SWEAT SUGAR JIMMY EAT WORLD
SALTWATER [A] JULIAN LENNON
SALTWATER [B] CHICANE FEATURING MAIRE
    BRENNAN OF CLANNAD
SALTY DOG PROCOL HARUM
SALVA MEA (SAVE ME) FAITHLESS
SALVATION CRANBERRIES
SAM [A] KEITH WEST
SAM [B] OLIVIA NEWTON-JOHN
SAMANTHA KENNY BALL & HIS JAZZMEN
SAMBA DE JANIERO BELLINI
SAMBA MAGIC SUMMER DAZE
SAMBA PA TI SANTANA
SAMBUCA WIDEBOYS FEATURING DENNIS G
SAME OLD BRAND NEW YOU A1
THE SAME OLD SCENE ROXY MUSIC
SAME OLD STORY ULTRAVOX
SAME PICTURE GOLDRUSH
SAME SONG DIGITAL UNDERGROUND
SAME TEMPO CHANGING FACES
SAME THING IN REVERSE BOY GEORGE
SAMSON AND DELILAH [A] MIDDLE OF THE ROAD
SAMSON AND DELILAH [B] BAD MANNERS
SAN ANTONIO ROSE FLOYD CRAMER
SAN BERNADINO CHRISTIE
SAN DAMIANO (HEART AND SOUL) SAL SOLO
SAN FRANCISCAN NIGHTS ERIC BURDON & THE
    ANIMALS
SAN FRANCISCO (BE SURE TO WEAR SOME FLOWERS
    IN YOUR HAIR) SCOTT McKENZIE
SAN FRANCISCO DAYS CHRIS ISAAK
SAN FRANCISCO (YOU'VE GOT ME) VILLAGE PEOPLE
SAN MIGUEL LONNIE DONEGAN
SAN MIGUEL KINGSTON TRIO
SANCTIFIED LADY MARVIN GAYE
SANCTIFY YOURSELF SIMPLE MINDS
SANCTIMONIOUS HALO
SANCTUARY [A] IRON MAIDEN
SANCTUARY [B] NEW MUSIK
SANCTUARY [C] DEJURE
SANCTUS (MISSA LUBA) TROUBADOURS DU ROI
    BAUDOUIN
SAND IN MY SHOES DIDO
SANDBLASTED (EP) SWERVEDRIVER

SANDCASTLES BOMB THE BASS FEATURING BERNARD
    FOWLER
SANDMAN BLUE BOY
SANDS OF TIME KALEEF
SANDSTORM [A] CAST
SANDSTORM [B] DARUDE
SANDWICHES DETROIT GRAND PU BAHS
SANDY JOHN TRAVOLTA
SANITY KILLING JOKE
SANTA BRING MY BABY BACK TO ME ELVIS PRESLEY
SANTA CLAUS IS BACK IN TOWN ELVIS PRESLEY
SANTA CLAUS IS COMING TO TOWN JACKSON 5
SANTA CLAUS IS COMIN' TO TOWN CARPENTERS
SANTA CLAUS IS COMIN' TO TOWN BRUCE
    SPRINGSTEEN
SANTA CLAUS IS COMING TO TOWN BJORN AGAIN
SANTA CLAUS IS ON THE DOLE SPITTING IMAGE
SANTA CRUZ (YOU'RE NOT THAT FAR) THRILLS
SANTA MARIA TATJANA
SANTA MARIA DJ MILANO FEATURING SAMANTHA
    FOX
SANTA MONICA (WATCH THE WORLD DIE) EVERCLEAR
SANTA'S LIST CLIFF RICHARD
SANTO NATALE DAVID WHITFIELD
SARA [A] FLEETWOOD MAC
SARA [B] STARSHIP
SARAH THIN LIZZY
SARTORIAL ELOQUENCE ELTON JOHN
SAT IN YOUR LAP KATE BUSH
SATAN ORBITAL
SATAN REJECTED MY SOUL MORRISSEY
THE SATCH EP JOE SATRIANI
SATELLITE [A] HOOTERS
SATELLITE [B] BELOVED
SATELLITE [C] OCEANLAB
SATELLITE KID DOGS D'AMOUR
SATELLITE OF LOVE 04 LOU REED
SATIN SHEETS BELLAMY BROTHERS
SATISFACTION [A] OTIS REDDING
SATISFACTION [A] ARETHA FRANKLIN
SATISFACTION [A] VANILLA ICE
SATISFACTION [B] WENDY & LISA
SATISFACTION [C] EVE
SATISFACTION [D] BENNY BENASSI PRESENTS THE BIZ
SATISFACTION GUARANTEED (OR TAKE YOUR LOVE
    BACK) HAROLD MELVIN & THE BLUENOTES
SATISFIED RICHARD MARX
SATISFIED (TAKE ME HIGHER) H2O
SATISFY MY LOVE [A] EXOTERIX
SATISFY MY LOVE [B] SABRINA JOHNSTON
SATISFY MY LOVE [C] PESHAY VERSUS FLYTRONIX
SATISFY MY SOUL BOB MARLEY & THE WAILERS
SATISFY YOU PUFF DADDY FEATURING R KELLY
SATURDAY [A] JOEY NEGRO FEATURING TAKA BOOM
SATURDAY [B] OMAR
SATURDAY [C] EAST 57TH STREET FEATURING DONNAL
    ALLEN
SATURDAY GIGS MOTT THE HOOPLE
SATURDAY LOVE CHERRELLE WITH ALEXANDER O'NEAL
SATURDAY LOVE ILLEGAL MOTION FEATURING SIMONE
    CHAPMAN
SATURDAY NIGHT [A] T-CONNECTION
SATURDAY NIGHT [B] BLUE NILE
SATURDAY NIGHT [C] WHIGFIELD
SATURDAY NIGHT [C] SINDY
SATURDAY NIGHT [D] SUEDE
SATURDAY NIGHT [E] UD PROJECT
SATURDAY NIGHT AT THE MOVIES DRIFTERS
SATURDAY NIGHT AT THE MOVIES ROBSON & JEROME
SATURDAY NIGHT (BENEATH THE PLASTIC PALM TREES)
    LEYTON BUZZARDS

SATURDAY NIGHT PARTY (READ MY LIPS) ALEX PARTY
SATURDAY NIGHT SUNDAY MORNING T-EMPO
SATURDAY NIGHT'S ALRIGHT FOR FIGHTING ELTON
    JOHN
SATURDAY NITE [A] EARTH, WIND & FIRE
SATURDAY NITE [B] BRAND NEW HEAVIES
SATURDAY NITE AT THE DUCK POND COUGARS
SATURDAY (OOOH OOOH) LUDACRIS
SATURDAY'S NOT WHAT IT USED TO BE KINGMAKER
SATURN 5 INSPIRAL CARPETS
THE SAVAGE SHADOWS
SAVANNA DANCE DEEP FOREST
SAVE A LITTLE BIT GLEN GOLDSMITH
SAVE A PRAYER DURAN DURAN
SAVE A PRAYER 56K FEATURING BEJAY
SAVE IT FOR LATER BEAT
SAVE IT 'TIL THE MOURNING AFTER SHUT UP & DANCE
SAVE ME [A] DAVE DEE, DOZY, BEAKY, MICK & TICH
SAVE ME [B] SILVER CONVENTION
SAVE ME [C] QUEEN
SAVE ME [D] FLEETWOOD MAC
SAVE ME [E] BIG COUNTRY
SAVE ME [F] EMBRACE
SAVE ME [G] MEEKER
SAVE ME [H] REMY ZERO
SAVE OUR LOVE ETERNAL
SAVE THE BEST FOR LAST VANESSA WILLIAMS
SAVE THE CHILDREN MARVIN GAYE
SAVE THE LAST DANCE FOR ME DRIFTERS
SAVE THE LAST DANCE FOR ME BEN E. KING
SAVE THE LAST DANCE FOR ME GENERAL SAINT
    FEATURING DON CAMPBELL
SAVE TONIGHT EAGLE-EYE CHERRY
SAVE UP ALL YOUR TEARS CHER
SAVE US PHILIP JAP
SAVE YOUR KISSES FOR ME BROTHERHOOD OF MAN
SAVE YOUR LOVE RENEE & RENATO
SAVE YOUR LOVE (FOR NUMBER 1) RENE & ANGELA
    FEATURING KURTIS BLOW
SAVE YOURSELF SPEEDWAY
SAVED [A] MR ROY
SAVED [B] OCTOPUS
SAVED BY THE BELL ROBIN GIBB
SAVED MY LIFE LIL' LOUIS & THE WORLD
SAVING ALL MY LOVE FOR YOU WHITNEY HOUSTON
SAVING FOREVER FOR YOU SHANICE
SAVIOUR'S DAY CLIFF RICHARD
SAXUALITY CANDY DULFER
SAXY LADY QUIVVER
SAY CREATURES
SAY A LITTLE PRAYER BOMB THE BASS FEATURING
    MAUREEN
SAY A PRAYER TAYLOR DAYNE
SAY CHEESE (SMILE PLEASE) FAST FOOD ROCKERS
SAY GOODBYE S CLUB
SAY, HAS ANYBODY SEEN MY SWEET GYPSY ROSE
    DAWN FEATURING TONY ORLANDO
SAY HELLO TO THE ANGELS INTERPOL
SAY HELLO WAVE GOODBYE SOFT CELL
SAY HELLO WAVE GOODBYE DAVID GRAY
SAY HOW I FEEL RHIAN BENSON
SAY I WON'T BE THERE SPRINGFIELDS
SAY I'M YOUR NO. 1 PRINCESS
SAY...IF YOU FEEL ALRIGHT CRYSTAL WATERS
SAY IT [A] ABC
SAY IT [B] MARIA RUBIA
SAY IT AGAIN [A] JERMAINE STEWART
SAY IT AGAIN [B] PRECIOUS
SAY IT AIN'T SO WEEZER
SAY IT ISN'T SO [A] DARYL HALL & JOHN OATES
SAY IT ISN'T SO [B] BON JOVI

SAY IT ISN'T SO [C] GARETH GATES
SAY IT ONCE ULTRA
SAY IT WITH FLOWERS DOROTHY SQUIRES & RUSS CONWAY
SAY IT WITH PRIDE SCOTLAND WORLD CUP SQUAD
SAY JUST WORDS PARADISE LOST
SAY MY NAME [A] ZEE
SAY MY NAME [B] DESTINY'S CHILD
SAY NO GO DE LA SOUL
SAY NOTHIN' OMAR
SAY SAY SAY PAUL McCARTNEY & MICHAEL JACKSON
SAY SOMETHING [A] JAMES
SAY SOMETHING [B] HAVEN
SAY SOMETHING ANYWAY BELLEFIRE
SAY THAT YOU'RE HERE FRAGMA
SAY WHAT! X-PRESS 2
SAY WHAT YOU WANT TEXAS
SAY WHEN LENE LOVICH
SAY WONDERFUL THINGS RONNIE CARROLL
SAY YEAH [A] LIMIT
SAY YEAH [B] BULLETPROOF
SAY YOU DO ULTRA
SAY YOU DON'T MIND COLIN BLUNSTONE
SAY YOU LOVE ME [A] FLEETWOOD MAC
SAY YOU LOVE ME [B] SIMPLY RED
SAY YOU LOVE ME [C] JOHNSON
SAY YOU REALLY WANT ME KIM WILDE
SAY YOU WILL FOREIGNER
SAY YOU, SAY ME LIONEL RICHIE
SAY YOU'LL BE MINE [A] AMY GRANT
SAY YOU'LL BE MINE [B] STEPS
SAY YOU'LL BE MINE [C] QFX
SAY YOU'LL BE THERE SPICE GIRLS
SAY YOU'LL STAY UNTIL TOMORROW TOM JONES
SAY YOU'RE MINE AGAIN JUNE HUTTON & AXEL STORDAHL & THE BOYS NEXT DOOR
(SAY) YOU'RE MY GIRL ROY ORBISON
SAY YOU'RE WRONG JULIAN LENNON
SCALES OF JUSTICE LIVING IN A BOX
SCANDAL QUEEN
SCANDALOUS [A] CLICK
SCANDALOUS [B] MIS-TEEQ
SCAR TISSUE RED HOT CHILI PEPPERS
SCARED SLACKER
SCARLET ALL ABOUT EVE
SCARLET RIBBONS HARRY BELAFONTE
SCARLETT O'HARA JET HARRIS & TONY MEEHAN
SCARS WITNESS
SCARY MONSTERS (AND SUPER CREEPS) DAVID BOWIE
SCARY MOVIES BAD MEETS EVIL FEATURING EMINEM & ROYCE DA 5' 9"
THE SCARY-GO-ROUND EP JELLYFISH
SCATMAN (SKI-BA-BOP-BA-DOP-BOP) SCATMAN JOHN
SCATMAN'S WORLD SCATMAN JOHN
SCATTER & SWING LIONROCK
SCATTERLINGS OF AFRICA JULUKA
SCATTERLINGS OF AFRICA JOHNNY CLEGG & SAVUKA
SCHEMING MAXIM
SCIENCE OF SILENCE RICHARD ASHCROFT
THE SCIENTIST COLDPLAY
SCHMOO SPOOKY
SCHONEBERG MARMIO
SCHOOL DAY CHUCK BERRY
SCHOOL DAY DON LANG & HIS FRANTIC FIVE
SCHOOL LOVE BARRY BLUE
SCHOOL OF ROCK SCHOOL OF ROCK
SCHOOL'S OUT ALICE COOPER
SCHOOL'S OUT DAPHNE & CELESTE
SCHOOLTIME CHRONICLE SMILEY CULTURE
SCHTEEVE YOURCODENAMEIS:MILO

SCOOBY DOO [A] DWEEB
SCOOBY DOO [B] J MAJIK & WICKAMAN
SCOOBY SNACKS FUN LOVIN' CRIMINALS
SCOPE PARIS ANGELS
SCORCHIO SASHA/EMERSON
SCORPIO RISING DEATH IN VEGAS FEATURING LIAM GALLAGHER
SCOTCH ON THE ROCKS BAND OF THE BLACK WATCH
SCOTLAND BE GOOD TARTAN ARMY
SCOTLAND FOREVER SIDNEY DEVINE
SCOTS MACHINE VOYAGE
SCOTTISH RAIN SILENCERS
A SCOTTISH SOLDIER ANDY STEWART
SCRAMBLED EGGS RONI SIZE
THE SCRATCH SURFACE NOISE
SCREAM [A] DISCO ANTHEM
SCREAM [B] MICHAEL JACKSON & JANET JACKSON
SCREAM [C] NUT
SCREAM IF YOU WANNA GO FASTER GERI HALLIWELL
SCREAM (PRIMAL SCREAM) MANTRONIX
SCREAM UNTIL YOU LIKE IT W.A.S.P.
THE SCREAMER YOSH PRESENTS LOVEDEEJAY AKEMI
SCULLERY CLIFFORD T WARD
SE A VIDA E (THAT'S THE WAY LIFE IS) PET SHOP BOYS
SEA OF BLUE TECHNATION
SEA OF HEARTBREAK DON GIBSON
SEA OF LOVE MARTY WILDE
SEA OF LOVE HONEYDRIPPERS
SEAGULL RAINBOW COTTAGE
THE SEAGULL'S NAME WAS NELSON PETER E BENNETT WITH THE CO-OPERATION CHOIR
SEAL MY FATE BELLY
SEAL OUR FATE GLORIA ESTEFAN
SEALED WITH A KISS BRIAN HYLAND
SEALED WITH A KISS JASON DONOVAN
SÉANCE NEBULA II
SEARCH AND DESTORY DICTATORS
SEARCH FOR THE HERO M PEOPLE
SEARCHIN' COASTERS
SEARCHIN' HOLLIES
SEARCHIN' FOR MY RIZLA RATPACK
SEARCHIN' (I GOTTA FIND A MAN) HAZELL DEAN
SEARCHIN' MY SOUL VONDA SHEPARD
SEARCHING [A] CHANGE
SEARCHING [B] CHINA BLACK
SEARCHING FOR A SOUL CONNOR REEVES
SEARCHING FOR THE GOLDEN EYE MOTIV 8 & KYM MAZELLE
SEASIDE ORDINARY BOYS
SEASIDE SHUFFLE TERRY DACTYL & THE DINOSAURS
SEASON NO. 5 BEDLAM AGO GO
SEASONS IN THE ABYSS SLAYER
SEASONS IN THE SUN TERRY JACKS
SEASONS IN THE SUN WESTLIFE
SEASONS OF GOLD GIDEA PARK
SEASONSTREAM (EP) THOUSAND YARD STARE
SEATTLE PUBLIC IMAGE LTD.
2ND AMENDMENT EASYWORLD
SECOND CHANCE PHILLIP LEO
SECOND HAND ROSE BARBRA STREISAND
THE SECOND LINE CLINIC
SECOND NATURE [A] DAN HARTMAN
SECOND NATURE [B] ELECTRONIC
SECOND ROUND KO CANIBUS
THE SECOND SUMMER OF LOVE DANNY WILSON
THE SECOND TIME KIM WILDE
THE SECOND TIME AROUND SHALAMAR
THE SECOND TIME (THEME FROM 'BILITIS') ELAINE PAIGE
SECRET [A] ORCHESTRAL MANOEUVRES IN THE DARK
SECRET [B] MADONNA

SECRET AGENT MAN – JAMES BOND IS BACK BRUCE WILLIS
SECRET COMBINATION RANDY CRAWFORD
SECRET GARDEN [A] T'PAU
SECRET GARDEN [B] QUINCY JONES FEATURING AL B SURE!, JAMES INGRAM, EL DeBARGE & BARRY WHITE
SECRET GARDEN [C] BRUCE SPRINGSTEEN
SECRET HEART TIGHT FIT
SECRET KISS CORAL
SECRET LOVE [A] DORIS DAY
SECRET LOVE [A] KATHY KIRBY
SECRET LOVE [A] DANIEL O'DONNELL & MARY DUFF
SECRET LOVE [B] BEE GEES
SECRET LOVE [C] DANNI'ELLE GAHA
SECRET LOVE [D] SHAH
SECRET LOVE [E] KELLY PRICE
SECRET LOVERS ATLANTIC STARR
SECRET MESSAGES ELECTRIC LIGHT ORCHESTRA
SECRET RENDEZVOUS [A] RENE & ANGELA
SECRET RENDEZVOUS [B] KARYN WHITE
SECRET SMILE SEMISONIC
SECRET STAR HOUSE OF ZEKKARIYAS AKA WOMACK & WOMACK
THE SECRET VAMPIRE SOUNDTRACK EP BIS
SECRETLY SKUNK ANANSIE
SECRETS [A] SUTHERLAND BROTHERS & QUIVER
SECRETS [B] FIAT LUX
SECRETS [C] PRIMITIVES
SECRETS [D] SUNSCREEM
SECRETS [E] ETERNAL
SECRETS [F] MUTINY UK
SECRETS IN THE STREET NILS LOFGREN
SECRETS (OF SUCCESS) COOKIE CREW FEATURING DANNY D
SECRETS OF THE HEART CHESNEY HAWKES
THE SECRETS THAT YOU KEEP MUD
THE SEDUCTION (LOVE THEME) JAMES LAST BAND
SEE A BRIGHTER DAY JTQ WITH NOEL McKOY
SEE EMILY PLAY PINK FLOYD
SEE IT IN A BOY'S EYES JAMELIA
SEE JUNGLE (JUNGLE BOY) BOW WOW WOW
SEE LINE WOMAN '99 SONGSTRESS
SEE ME LUTHER VANDROSS
SEE MY BABY JIVE WIZZARD
SEE MY FRIEND KINKS
SEE THAT GLOW THIS ISLAND EARTH
SEE THE DAY DEE C. LEE
SEE THE LIGHTS SIMPLE MINDS
SEE THE STAR DELIRIOUS?
SEE THOSE EYES ALTERED IMAGES
SEE THRU IT APHRODITE FEATURING WILDFLOWER
SEE WANT MUST HAVE BLUE MERCEDES
SEE YA ATOMIC KITTEN
SEE YOU DEPECHE MODE
SEE YOU LATER REGENTS
SEE YOU LATER ALLIGATOR BILL HALEY & HIS COMETS
THE SEED (2.0) ROOTS FEATURING CODY CHESTNUTT
SEEING THINGS BLACK CROWES
THE SEEKER WHO
SEEMS FINE CONCRETES
SEEN THE LIGHT SUPERGRASS
SEETHER VERUCA SALT
SEIZE THE DAY F.K.W.
SELA LIONEL RICHIE
SELECTA (URBAN HEROES) JAMESON & VIPER
SELF! FUZZBOX
SELF CONTROL LAURA BRANIGAN
SELF DESTRUCTION STOP THE VIOLENCE
SELF ESTEEM OFFSPRING
SELF SUICIDE GOLDIE LOOKIN CHAIN

SELFISH OTHER TWO
SELLING JESUS SKUNK ANANSIE
SELLING THE DRAMA LIVE
SEMI-CHARMED LIFE THIRD EYE BLIND
SEMI-DETACHED SUBURBAN MR. JAMES MANFRED MANN
SEND HIS LOVE TO ME PJ HARVEY
SEND IN THE CLOWNS JUDY COLLINS
SEND ME AN ANGEL [A] BLACKFOOT
SEND ME AN ANGEL [B] SCORPIONS
SEND ME THE PILLOW YOU DREAM ON JOHNNY TILLOTSON
SEND MY HEART ADVENTURES
SEND ONE YOUR LOVE STEVIE WONDER
SEND YOUR LOVE STING
SENDING OUT AN S.O.S. RETTA YOUNG
SENORITA JUSTIN TIMBERLAKE
SENSATION ELECTROSET
SENSATIONAL MICHELLE GAYLE
SENSE LIGHTNING SEEDS
SENSE TERRY HALL
SENSE OF DANGER PRESENCE FEATURING SHARA NELSON
SENSES WORKING OVERTIME XTC
SENSITIVITY RALPH TRESVANT
SENSITIZE THAT PETROL EMOTION
SENSUAL SOPHIS-TI-CAT/THE PLAYER CARL COX
THE SENSUAL WORLD KATE BUSH
SENSUALITY LOVESTATION
SENTIMENTAL [A] ALEXANDER O'NEAL
SENTIMENTAL [B] DEBORAH COX
SENTIMENTAL [C] KYM MARSH
SENTIMENTAL FOOL LLOYD COLE
SENTINEL MIKE OLDFIELD
SENZA UNA DONNA (WITHOUT A WOMAN) ZUCCHERO & PAUL YOUNG
SEPARATE LIVES PHIL COLLINS & MARILYN MARTIN
SEPARATE TABLES CHRIS DE BURGH
SEPARATE WAYS GARY MOORE
SEPTEMBER EARTH, WIND & FIRE
SEPTEMBER IN THE RAIN DINAH WASHINGTON
SEPTEMBER SONG IAN McCULLOCH
SERENADE [A] MARIO LANZA
SERENADE [B] MARIO LANZA
SERENADE [B] SLIM WHITMAN
SERENADE [C] SHADES
SERENATA SARAH VAUGHAN
SERENITY IN MURDER SLAYER
SERIOUS [A] BILLY GRIFFIN
SERIOUS [B] SERIOUS INTENTION
SERIOUS [C] DEJA
SERIOUS [D] DONNA ALLEN
SERIOUS [E] DURAN DURAN
SERIOUS [F] MAXWELL D
SERIOUS MIX MIRAGE
SERPENTS KISS MISSION
SESAME'S TREET SMART E'S
SET ADRIFT ON A MEMORY BLISS PM DAWN
SET FIRE TO ME WILLIE COLON
SET IN STONE BEDROCK
SET IT OFF [A] HARLEQUIN 4S/BUNKER KRU
SET IT OFF [B] PEACHES
SET ME FREE [A] KINKS
SET ME FREE [B] JAKI GRAHAM
SET ME FREE [C] BRIT PACK
SET THE RECORD STRAIGHT REEF
SET THEM FREE ASWAD
THE SET UP (YOU DON'T KNOW) OBIE TRICE FEATURING NATE DOGG
SET YOU FREE N-TRANCE FEATURING KELLY LLORENNA
SET YOUR LOVING FREE LISA STANSFIELD

SETTING SUN CHEMICAL BROTHERS
SETTLE DOWN [A] LILLO THOMAS
SETTLE DOWN [B] UNBELIEVABLE TRUTH
7 [A] PRINCE & THE NEW POWER GENERATION
SEVEN [B] DAVID BOWIE
SEVEN AND SEVEN IS (LIVE) ALICE COOPER
SEVEN CITIES SOLAR STONE
7 COLOURS LOST WITNESS
SEVEN DAFFODILS CHEROKEES
SEVEN DAFFODILS MOJOS
SEVEN DAYS [A] ANNE SHELTON
SEVEN DAYS [B] STING
SEVEN DAYS [C] MARY J. BLIGE FEATURING GEORGE BENSON
7 DAYS [D] CRAIG DAVID
SEVEN DAYS AND ONE WEEK BBE
SEVEN DAYS IN THE SUN FEEDER
SEVEN DRUNKEN NIGHTS DUBLINERS
SEVEN (EP) JAMES
747 KENT
747 (STRANGERS IN THE NIGHT) SAXON
SEVEN LITTLE GIRLS SITTING IN THE BACK SEAT AVONS
SEVEN LITTLE GIRLS SITTING IN THE BACK SEAT PAUL EVANS & THE CURLS
SEVEN LITTLE GIRLS SITTING IN THE BACKSEAT BOMBALURINA
SEVEN LONELY DAYS GISELE MacKENZIE
7 NATION ARMY WHITE STRIPES
7 O'CLOCK QUIREBOYS
SEVEN ROOMS OF GLOOM FOUR TOPS
SEVEN SEAS ECHO & THE BUNNYMEN
SEVEN SEAS OF RHYE QUEEN
7 SECONDS YOUSSOU N'DOUR (FEATURING NENEH CHERRY)
7:7 EXPANSION SYSTEM 7
7-6-5-4-3-2-1 (BLOW YOUR WHISTLE) RIMSHOTS
SEVEN TEARS GOOMBAY DANCE BAND
7 WAYS TO LOVE COLA BOY
SEVEN WONDERS FLEETWOOD MAC
7 YEAR BITCH SLADE
SEVEN YEARS IN TIBET DAVID BOWIE
7TEEN REGENTS
SEVENTEEN [A] FRANKIE VAUGHAN
SEVENTEEN [A] BOYD BENNETT & HIS ROCKETS
SEVENTEEN [B] LET LOOSE
SEVENTEEN [C] LADYTRON
17 AGAIN EURYTHMICS
SEVENTH SON GEORGIE FAME
7000 DOLLARS AND YOU STYLISTICS
78 STONE WOBBLE GOMEZ
74-'75 CONNELLS
77 STRINGS KURTIS MANTRONIK PRESENTS CHAMONIX
76 TROMBONES KING BROTHERS
SEVERINA MISSION
SEX [A] SLEAZESISTERS WITH VIKKI SHEPARD
SEX [B] ROBBIE RIVERA FEATURING BILLY PAUL
SEX AND CANDY MARCY PLAYGROUND
SEX AS A WEAPON PAT BENATAR
SEX BOMB TOM JONES & MOUSSE T
SEX DRUGS AND ROCKS THROUGH YOUR WINDOW AGENT BLUE
SEX LIFE GEOFFREY WILLIAMS
SEX ME R KELLY & PUBLIC ANNOUNCEMENT
THE SEX OF IT KID CREOLE & THE COCONUTS
SEX ON THE BEACH T-SPOON
SEX ON THE STREETS PIZZAMAN
SEX OVER THE PHONE VILLAGE PEOPLE
SEX TALK (LIVE) T'PAU
SEX TYPE THING STONE TEMPLE PILOTS

SEXCRIME (NINETEEN EIGHTY FOUR) EURYTHMICS
SEXED UP ROBBIE WILLIAMS
SEXIEST MAN IN JAMAICA MINT ROYALE
SEXOMATIC BAR-KAYS
SEXUAL [A] MARIA ROWE
SEXUAL [B] AMBER
SEXUAL GUARANTEE ALCAZAR
(SEXUAL) HEALING MARVIN GAYE
SEXUAL REVOLUTION MACY GRAY
SEXUALITY BILLY BRAGG
SEXX LAWS BECK
SEXY MFSB
SEXY BOY AIR
SEXY CINDERELLA LYNDEN DAVID HALL
SEXY CREAM SLICK
SEXY EYES DR. HOOK
SEXY EYES – REMIXES WHIGFIELD
SEXY GIRL LILLO THOMAS
SEXY MF PRINCE & THE NEW POWER GENERATION
SGT PEPPER'S LONELY HEARTS CLUB BAND – WITH A LITTLE HELP FROM MY FRIENDS BEATLES
SGT ROCK (IS GOING TO HELP ME) XTC
SH-BOOM CREW CUTS
SH-BOOM STAN FREBERG WITH THE TOADS
SH-BOOM (LIFE COULD BE A DREAM) DARTS
SHA LA LA MANFRED MANN
SHA LA LA LA LEE SMALL FACES
SHA LA LA LA LEE PLASTIC BERTRAND
SHA LA LA MEANS I LOVE YOU BARRY WHITE
SHACKLES (PRAISE YOU) MARY MARY
SHADDAP YOU FACE JOE DOLCE MUSIC THEATRE
SHADES OF BLUE (EP) THE THE
SHADES OF GREEN MISSION
SHADES OF PARANOIMIA ART OF NOISE
SHADES OF SUMMER RODEO JONES
SHADES (THEME FROM THE CROWN PAINT TELEVISION COMMERCIAL) UNITED KINGDOM SYMPHONY
SHADOW DANCING ANDY GIBB
THE SHADOW OF LOVE DAMNED
SHADOWS OF THE NIGHT PAT BENATAR
SHADOWTIME SIOUXSIE & THE BANSHEES
SHADY LADY GENE PITNEY
SHADY LANE PAVEMENT
SHAFT VAN TWIST
SHAKABOOM! HUNTER FEATURING RUBY TURNER
SHAKALAKA BABY PREEYA KALIDAS
SHAKE [A] OTIS REDDING
SHAKE [B] ANDREW RIDGELEY
SHAKE! (HOW ABOUT A SAMPLING GENE) GENE AND JIM ARE INTO SHAKES
SHAKE IT BABY DJD PRESENTS HYDRAULIC DOGS
SHAKE IT DOWN MUD
SHAKE IT (MOVE A LITTLE CLOSER) LEE CABRERA FEATURING ALEX CARTANA
SHAKE IT (NO TE MUEVAS TANTO) LEE-CABRERA
SHAKE ME I RATTLE KAYE SISTERS
SHAKE RATTLE AND ROLL BILL HALEY & HIS COMETS
(SHAKE SHAKE SHAKE) SHAKE YOUR BOOTY KC & THE SUNSHINE BAND
SHAKE THE DISEASE DEPECHE MODE
SHAKE THIS MOUNTAIN HORSE
SHAKE UR BODY SHY FX & T POWER FEATURING DI
SHAKE (WHAT YA MAMA GAVE YA) GENERAL LEVY VS ZEUS
SHAKE YA ASS MYSTIKAL
SHAKE YA BODY N-TRANCE
SHAKE YA SHIMMY PORN KINGS VERSUS FLIP & FILL FEATURING 740 BOYZ
SHAKE YA TAILFEATHER NELLY, P DIDDY & MURPHY LEE
SHAKE YOU DOWN GREGORY ABBOTT
SHAKE YOUR BODY (DOWN TO THE GROUND) JACKSONS

SHAKE YOUR BODY (DOWN TO THE GROUND) FULL INTENTION
SHAKE YOUR BON-BON RICKY MARTIN
SHAKE YOUR FOUNDATIONS AC/DC
SHAKE YOUR GROOVE THING PEACHES & HERB
SHAKE YOUR HEAD WAS (NOT WAS)
SHAKE YOUR LOVE DEBBIE GIBSON
SHAKE YOUR RUMP TO THE FUNK BAR-KAYS
SHAKE YOUR THANG (IT'S YOUR THING) SALT-N-PEPA FEATURING E.U.
SHAKERMAKER OASIS
SHAKESPEARE'S SISTER SMITHS
SHAKESPEARE'S WAY WITH WORDS ONE TRUE VOICE
SHAKIN' ALL OVER JOHNNY KIDD & THE PIRATES
SHAKIN' LIKE A LEAF STRANGLERS
THE SHAKIN' STEVENS EP SHAKIN' STEVENS
SHAKING THE TREE YOUSSOU N'DOUR & PETER GABRIEL
SHAKTI (THE MEANING OF WITHIN) MONSOON
SHALALA LALA VENGABOYS
SHA-LA-LA (MAKES ME HAPPY) AL GREEN
SHALL WE TAKE A TRIP NORTHSIDE
SHAME [A] ALAN PRICE SET
SHAME [B] EVELYN 'CHAMPAGNE' KING
SHAME [B] ALTERN 8 VS EVELYN KING
SHAME [B] ZHANE
SHAME [B] RUFF DRIVERZ
SHAME [C] ORCHESTRAL MANOEUVRES IN THE DARK
SHAME [D] EURYTHMICS
SHAME [E] PJ HARVEY
SHAME AND SCANDAL IN THE FAMILY LANCE PERCIVAL
SHAME ON ME ALEXANDER O'NEAL
SHAME ON YOU GUN
SHAME SHAME SHAME [A] JIMMY REED
SHAME SHAME SHAME [B] SHIRLEY & COMPANY
SHAME SHAME SHAME [B] SINITTA
SHAMELESS GARTH BROOKS
SHAMROCKS AND SHENIGANS HOUSE OF PAIN
SHANG-A-LANG BAY CITY ROLLERS
SHANGHAI'D IN SHANGHAI NAZARETH
SHANGRI-LA RUTLES
SHANNON HENRY GROSS
SHANTE MASS PRODUCTION
SHAPE SUGABABES
SHAPE OF MY HEART [A] STING
SHAPE OF MY HEART [B] BACKSTREET BOYS
THE SHAPE OF THINGS TO COME HEADBOYS
THE SHAPE YOU'RE IN ERIC CLAPTON
SHAPES OF THINGS YARDBIRDS
SHAPES THAT GO TOGETHER A-HA
SHARE MY LIFE INNER CITY
SHARE THE FALL RONI SIZE REPRAZENT
SHARE THE NIGHT WORLD PREMIERE
SHARE YOUR LOVE (NO DIGGITY) PASSION
SHARING THE NIGHT TOGETHER DR HOOK
SHARING YOU BOBBY VEE
SHARK THROWING MUSES
SHARP AS A KNIFE BRANDON COOKE FEATURING ROXANNE SHANTE
SHARP DRESSED MAN ZZ TOP
SHATTERED DREAMS JOHNNY HATES JAZZ
SHATTERED GLASS DTOX
SHAZAM! DUANE EDDY & THE REBELS
SHE [A] CHARLES AZNAVOUR
SHE [A] ELVIS COSTELLO
SHE [B] VEGAS
SHE AIN'T WORTH IT GLENN MEDEIROS FEATURING BOBBY BROWN
SHE BANGS RICKY MARTIN
SHE BANGS THE DRUMS STONE ROSES
SHE BELIEVES IN ME [A] KENNY ROGERS

SHE BELIEVES (IN ME) [B] RONAN KEATING
SHE BLINDED ME WITH SCIENCE THOMAS DOLBY
SHE BOP CYNDI LAUPER
SHE CAME HOME FOR CHRISTMAS MEW
SHE CAN ROCK IT POWER STATION
SHE COMES FROM THE RAIN WEATHER PROPHETS
SHE COMES IN THE FALL INSPIRAL CARPETS
SHE CRIES YOUR NAME BETH ORTON
SHE DON'T FOOL ME STATUS QUO
SHE DON'T LET NOBODY CHAKA DEMUS & PLIERS
SHE DRIVES ME CRAZY FINE YOUNG CANNIBALS
SHE DROVE ME TO DAYTIME TELEVISION FUNERAL FOR A FRIEND
SHE GOT GAME TYMES 4
SHE HATES ME PUDDLE OF MUDD
SHE HITS ME 4 OF US
SHE HOLDS THE KEY SECRET LIFE
SHE IS BEAUTIFUL ANDREW WK
SHE IS LOVE OASIS
SHE IS SUFFERING MANIC STREET PREACHERS
SHE KISSED ME TERENCE TRENT D'ARBY
SHE KISSED ME (IT FELT LIKE A HIT) SPIRITUALIZED
SHE KNOWS BALAAM AND THE ANGEL
SHE LEFT ME ON FRIDAY SHED SEVEN
SHE LOVED LIKE DIAMOND SPANDAU BALLET
SHE LOVES ME NOT PAPA ROACH
SHE LOVES YOU BEATLES
SHE MAKES MY DAY ROBERT PALMER
SHE MAKES MY NOSE BLEED MANSUN
SHE MEANS NOTHING TO ME PHIL EVERLY & CLIFF RICHARD
SHE MOVES (LALALA) KARAJA
SHE NEEDS LOVE WAYNE FONTANA & THE MINDBENDERS
SHE SAID [A] LONGPIGS
SHE SAID [B] PHARCYDE
SHE SAID [C] JON SPENCER BLUES EXPLOSION
SHE SELLS BANDERAS
SHE SELLS SANCTUARY CULT
SHE SHE LITTLE SHEILA GENE VINCENT
SHE SOLD ME MAGIC LOU CHRISTIE
SHE TALKS TO ANGELS BLACK CROWES
SHE USED TO BE MINE SPIN DOCTORS
SHE WANTS TO DANCE WITH ME RICK ASTLEY
SHE WANTS TO MOVE N*E*R*D
SHE WANTS YOU BILLIE
SHE WAS HOT ROLLING STONES
SHE WEARS MY RING SOLOMON KING
SHE WEARS RED FEATHERS GUY MITCHELL
SHE WILL BE LOVED MAROON 5
SHE WILL HAVE HER WAY NEIL FINN
SHE WON'T TALK TO ME LUTHER VANDROSS
SHE WORKS HARD FOR THE MONEY DONNA SUMMER
SHED A TEAR WET WET WET
SHED MY SKIN D NOTE
SHE'D RATHER BE WITH ME TURTLES
SHEELA-NA-GIG PJ HARVEY
SHEENA IS A PUNK ROCKER RAMONES
SHEEP HOUSEMARTINS
THE SHEFFIELD GRINDER TONY CAPSTICK & THE CARLTON MAIN/FRICKLEY COLLIERY BAND
SHEFFIELD SONG SUPERNATURALS
SHEILA TOMMY ROE
SHEILA TAKE A BOW SMITHS
SHELLSHOCK NEW ORDER
SHELTER BRAND NEW HEAVIES
SHELTER ME [A] CINDERELLA
SHELTER ME [B] CIRCUIT
THE SHEPHERD'S SONG TONY OSBORNE SOUND
SHERIFF FATMAN CARTER – THE UNSTOPPABLE SEX MACHINE

SHERRI DON'T FAIL ME NOW STATUS QUO
SHERRY FOUR SEASONS
SHERRY ADRIAN BAKER
SHE'S A BAD MAMA JAMA (SHE'S BUILT, SHE'S STACKED) CARL CARLTON
SHE'S A GIRL AND I'M A MAN LLOYD COLE
SHE'S A GOOD GIRL SLEEPER
SHE'S A GROOVY FREAK REAL THING
SHE'S A LADY TOM JONES
SHE'S A LITTLE ANGEL LITTLE ANGELS
SHE'S A MYSTERY TO ME ROY ORBISON
SHE'S A RAINBOW WORLD OF TWIST
SHE'S A RIVER SIMPLE MINDS
SHE'S A STAR JAMES
SHE'S A SUPERSTAR VERVE
SHE'S A VISION ALL EYES
SHE'S A WIND UP DR. FEELGOOD
SHE'S A WOMAN SCRITTI POLITTI FEATURING SHABBA RANKS
SHE'S ABOUT A MOVER SIR DOUGLAS QUINTET
SHE'S ALL ON MY MIND WET WET WET
SHE'S ALRIGHT BITTY McLEAN
SHE'S ALWAYS A WOMAN BILLY JOEL
SHE'S CRAFTY BEASTIE BOYS
SHE'S EVERY WOMAN GARTH BROOKS
SHE'S GONE [A] BUDDY KNOX
SHE'S GONE [B] DARYL HALL & JOHN OATES
SHE'S GONE [B] MATTHEW MARSDEN FEATURING DESTINY'S CHILD
SHE'S GONNA BREAK SOON LESS THAN JAKE
SHE'S GONNA WIN BILBO
SHE'S GOT CLAWS GARY NUMAN
SHE'S GOT ISSUES OFFSPRING
SHE'S GOT IT LITTLE RICHARD
SHE'S GOT ME GOING CRAZY 2 IN A ROOM
SHE'S GOT SOUL JAMESTOWN FEATURING JOCELYN BROWN
SHE'S GOT THAT VIBE R KELLY
SHE'S GOT YOU PATSY CLINE
SHE'S IN FASHION SUEDE
SHE'S IN LOVE WITH YOU SUZI QUATRO
SHE'S IN PARTIES BAUHAUS
SHE'S LEAVING HOME BILLY BRAGG WITH CARA TIVEY
SHE'S LIKE THE WIND PATRICK SWAYZE FEATURING WENDY FRASER
SHE'S LOST YOU ZEPHYRS
SHE'S MINE CAMEO
SHE'S MY MACHINE DAVID LEE ROTH
SHE'S NEW TO YOU SUSAN MAUGHAN
SHE'S NOT LEAVING RESEARCH
SHE'S NOT THERE ZOMBIES
SHE'S NOT THERE NEIL MacARTHUR
SHE'S NOT THERE SANTANA
SHE'S NOT THERE/KICKS EP U.K. SUBS
SHE'S NOT YOU ELVIS PRESLEY
SHE'S ON FIRE TRAIN
SHE'S ON IT BEASTIE BOYS
SHE'S OUT OF MY LIFE MICHAEL JACKSON
SHE'S PLAYING HARD TO GET HI-FIVE
(SHE'S) SEXY AND 17 STRAY CATS
SHE'S SO BEAUTIFUL CLIFF RICHARD
SHE'S SO COLD ROLLING STONES
SHE'S SO FINE THUNDER
SHE'S SO HIGH [A] BLUR
SHE'S SO HIGH [B] TAL BACHMAN
SHE'S SO HIGH [B] KURT NILSEN
SHE'S SO MODERN BOOMTOWN RATS
SHE'S STRANGE CAMEO
SHE'S THE MASTER OF THE GAME RICHARD JON SMITH
SHE'S THE ONE [A] JAMES BROWN
SHE'S THE ONE [B] ROBBIE WILLIAMS

SHIFTER TIMO MAAS FEATURING MC CHICKABOO
SHIFTING WHISPERING SANDS BILLY VAUGHN ORCHESTRA & CHORUS, NARRATION BY KEN NORDENE
SHIFTING WHISPERING SANDS (PARTS 1 & 2) EAMONN ANDREWS WITH RON GOODWIN & HIS ORCHESTRA
SHIMMY SHAKE 740 BOYZ
SHINDIG SHADOWS
SHINE [A] JOE BROWN
SHINE [B] MOTORHEAD
SHINE [C] SLOWDIVE
SHINE [D] ASWAD
SHINE [E] MOLLY HALF HEAD
SHINE [F] SPACE BROTHERS
SHINE [G] MONTROSE AVENUE
SHINE A LITTLE LOVE ELECTRIC LIGHT ORCHESTRA
SHINE EYE RAGGA TWINS FEATURING JUNIOR REID
SHINE EYE GAL SHABBA RANKS (FEATURING MYKAL ROSE)
SHINE LIKE A STAR BERRI
SHINE ON [A] HOUSE OF LOVE
SHINE ON [B] DEGREES OF MOTION FEATURING BITI
SHINE ON [C] SCOTT & LEON
SHINE ON ME LOVESTATION FEATURING LISA HUNT
SHINE ON SILVER SUN STRAWBS
SHINE SO HARD (EP) ECHO & THE BUNNYMEN
SHINE (SOMEONE WHO NEEDS ME) MONACO
SHINED ON ME PRAISE CATS
SHINING [A] DOUBLE DEE
SHINING [B] KRISTIAN LEONTIOU
SHINING LIGHT ASH
SHINING ROAD CRANES
SHINING STAR MANHATTANS
SHINING STAR (EP) INXS
SHINOBI VS DRAGON NINJA LOSTPROPHETS
SHINY DISCO BALLS WHO DA FUNK FEATURING JESSICA EVE
SHINY HAPPY PEOPLE R.E.M.
SHINY SHINY HAYSI FANTAYZEE
SHIP AHOY MARXMAN
SHIP OF FOOLS [A] WORLD PARTY
SHIP OF FOOLS [B] ERASURE
SHIPBUILDING [A] ROBERT WYATT
SHIPBUILDING [B] TASMIN ARCHER
SHIPS IN THE NIGHT BE BOP DELUXE
SHIPS (WHERE WERE YOU) BIG COUNTRY
SHIPWRECKED GENESIS
SHIRALEE TOMMY STEELE
SHIRLEY SHAKIN' STEVENS
SHIT ON YOU D12
SHIVER [A] GEORGE BENSON
SHIVER [B] COLDPLAY
SHIVERING SAND MEGA CITY FOUR
SHO' YOU RIGHT BARRY WHITE
SHOCK THE MONKEY PETER GABRIEL
SHOCK TO THE SYSTEM BILLY IDOL
SHOCK YOUR MAMA DEBBIE GIBSON
SHOCKAHOLIC KINKY MACHINE
SHOCKED KYLIE MINOGUE
SHOES REPARATA
SHOO BE DOO BE DOO DA DAY STEVIE WONDER
SHOO DOO FU FU OOH LENNY WILLIAMS
SHOOP SALT-N-PEPA
THE SHOOP SHOOP SONG (IT'S IN HIS KISS) CHER
SHOORAH SHOORAH BETTY WRIGHT
SHOOT ALL THE CLOWNS BRUCE DICKINSON
SHOOT ME (WITH YOUR LOVE) [A] TASHA THOMAS
SHOOT ME WITH YOUR LOVE [B] D:REAM
SHOOT SHOOT UFO
SHOOT THE DOG GEORGE MICHAEL

SHOOT YOUR GUN 22-20'S
SHOOTING FROM MY HEART BIG BAM BOO
SHOOTING FROM THE HEART CLIFF RICHARD
SHOOTING STAR [A] DOLLAR
SHOOTING STAR [A] BOYZONE
SHOOTING STAR [B] FLIP & FILL
SHOOTING STAR [C] DEEPEST BLUE
SHOPLIFTERS OF THE WORLD UNITE SMITHS
SHOPPING SUPERSISTER
SHORLEY WALL OOBERMAN
SHORT CUT TO SOMEWHERE FISH & TONY BANKS
SHORT DICK MAN 20 FINGERS FEATURING GILLETTE
SHORT FAT FANNY LARRY WILLIAMS
SHORT SHORT MAN 20 FINGERS FEATURING GILLETTE
SHORT SKIRT LONG JACKET CAKE
SHORT'NIN' BREAD TONY CROMBIE & HIS ROCKETS
SHORT'NIN' BREAD VISCOUNTS
SHORTSHARPSHOCK EP THERAPY?
SHORTY WANNADIES
SHORTY (GOT HER EYES ON ME) DONELL JONES
SHORTY (YOU KEEP PLAYIN' WITH MY MIND) IMAJIN FEATURING KEITH MURRAY
SHOT BY BOTH SIDES MAGAZINE
SHOT DOWN IN THE NIGHT HAWKWIND
SHOT IN THE DARK [A] OZZY OSBOURNE
SHOT IN THE DARK [B] DJ HYPE
SHOT OF POISON LITA FORD
SHOT OF RHYTHM AND BLUES JOHNNY KIDD & THE PIRATES
SHOT SHOT GOMEZ
SHOTGUN WEDDING ROY C
SHOTGUN WEDDING ROD STEWART
SHOULD I DO IT? POINTER SISTERS
SHOULD I EVER (FALL IN LOVE) NIGHTCRAWLERS
SHOULD I STAY GABRIELLE
SHOULD I STAY OR SHOULD I GO CLASH
SHOULDA WOULDA COULDA BEVERLEY KNIGHT
SHOULDER HOLSTER MORCHEEBA
SHOULDN'T DO THAT KAJA
SHOULDN'T LET THE SIDE DOWN HOGGBOY
SHOULD'VE KNOWN BETTER RICHARD MARX
SHOUT [A] LULU & THE LUVVERS
SHOUT [B] TEARS FOR FEARS
SHOUT [C] ANT & DEC
SHOUT (IT OUT) [A] LOUCHIE LOU & MICHIE ONE
SHOUT SHOUT (KNOCK YOURSELF OUT) ROCKY SHARPE & THE REPLAYS
SHOUT TO THE TOP STYLE COUNCIL
SHOUT TO THE TOP FIRE ISLAND FEATURING LOLEATTA HOLLOWAY
SHOUTING FOR THE GUNNERS ARSENAL FA CUP SQUAD FEATURING TIPPA IRIE & PETER HUNNIGALE
THE SHOW [A] DOUG E. FRESH & THE GET FRESH CREW
THE SHOW [B] GIRLS ALOUD
SHOW A LITTLE LOVE ULTIMATE KAOS
SHOW ME [A] DEXY'S MIDNIGHT RUNNERS
SHOW ME [B] LINDY LAYTON
SHOW ME [C] ULTRA NATE
SHOW ME [D] DANA DAWSON
SHOW ME A SIGN KONTAKT
SHOW ME GIRL HERMAN'S HERMITS
SHOW ME HEAVEN MARIA McKEE
SHOW ME HEAVEN TINA ARENA
SHOW ME HEAVEN CHIMIRA
SHOW ME HEAVEN SAINT FEATURING SUZANNA DEE
SHOW ME LOVE [A] ROBIN S
SHOW ME LOVE [B] ROBYN
SHOW ME LOVE [C] INDIEN
SHOW ME MARY CATHERINE WHEEL
SHOW ME THE MEANING OF BEING LONELY BACKSTREET BOYS

SHOW ME THE MONEY ARCHITECHS
SHOW ME THE WAY [A] PETER FRAMPTON
SHOW ME THE WAY [B] OSMOND BOYS
SHOW ME YOU'RE A WOMAN MUD
SHOW ME YOUR MONKEY PERCY FILTH
SHOW ME YOUR SOUL P DIDDY, LENNY KRAVITZ, PHARRELL WILLIAMS & LOON
THE SHOW MUST GO ON [A] LEO SAYER
THE SHOW MUST GO ON [B] QUEEN
THE SHOW (THEME FROM 'CONNIE') REBECCA STORM
SHOW YOU THE WAY TO GO JACKSONS
SHOW YOU THE WAY TO GO DANNII MINOGUE
SHOWDOWN [A] ELECTRIC LIGHT ORCHESTRA
SHOWDOWN [B] JODY LEI
SHOWER YOUR LOVE KULA SHAKER
SHOWING OUT (GET FRESH AT THE WEEKEND) MEL & KIM
SHOWROOM DUMMIES KRAFTWERK
THE SHUFFLE VAN McCOY
SHUGGIE LOVE MONKEY BARS FEATURING GABRIELLE WIDMAN
SHUT 'EM DOWN PUBLIC ENEMY
SHUT UP [A] MADNESS
SHUT UP [B] KELLY OSBOURNE
SHUT UP [C] BLACK EYED PEAS
SHUT UP AND DANCE AEROSMITH
SHUT UP AND FORGET ABOUT IT DANE
SHUT UP AND KISS ME MARY CHAPIN CARPENTER
SHUT UP (AND SLEEP WITH ME) SIN WITH SEBASTIAN
SHUT YOUR MOUTH [A] MADE IN LONDON
SHUT YOUR MOUTH [B] GARBAGE
SHUTDOWN PITCHSHIFTER
SHY BOY BANANARAMA
SHY GIRL MARK WYNTER
SHY GUY DIANA KING
SHY GUY ASWAD
(SI SI) JE SUIS UN ROCK STAR BILL WYMAN
SI TU DOIS PARTIR FAIRPORT CONVENTION
SIC TRANSIT GLORIA GLORY FADES BRAND NEW
SICK AND TIRED [A] FATS DOMINO
SICK & TIRED [B] CARDIGANS
SICK AND TIRED [C] ANASTACIA
SICK MAN BLUES GOODIES
SICK OF DRUGS WILDHEARTS
SICK OF GOODBYES SPARKLEHORSE
SICK OF IT PRIMITIVES
SIDE TRAVIS
SIDE BY SIDE KAY STARR
SIDE SADDLE RUSS CONWAY
SIDE SHOW [A] CHANTER SISTERS
SIDE SHOW [B] WENDY & LISA
THE SIDEBOARD SONG (GOT MY BEER IN THE SIDEBOARD HERE) CHAS & DAVE
SIDESHOW BARRY BIGGS
SIDEWALK TALK JELLYBEAN FEATURING CATHERINE BUCHANAN
SIDEWALKING JESUS & MARY CHAIN
THE SIDEWINDER SLEEPS TONITE R.E.M.
SIGHT FOR SORE EYES M PEOPLE
THE SIGN ACE OF BASE
SIGN O' THE TIMES PRINCE
SIGN OF THE TIMES [A] BRYAN FERRY
SIGN OF THE TIMES [B] BELLE STARS
SIGN OF THE TIMES [C] GRANDMASTER FLASH
A SIGN OF THE TIMES PETULA CLARK
SIGN YOUR NAME TERENCE TRENT D'ARBY
SIGNAL [A] JD AKA DREADY
SIGNAL [B] FRESH
SIGNALS OVER THE AIR THURSDAY
THE SIGNATURE TUNE OF 'THE ARMY GAME' MICHAEL MEDWIN, BERNARD BRESSLAW, ALFIE BASS & LESLIE FYSON

SIGNED SEALED DELIVERED I'M YOURS STEVIE WONDER

SIGNED SEALED DELIVERED (I'M YOURS) BOYSTOWN GANG

SIGNED SEALED DELIVERED I'M YOURS BLUE FEATURING STEVIE WONDER & ANGIE STONE

SIGNS... BLAMELESS

SIGNS [A] TESLA

SIGNS [B] DJ BADMARSH & SHRI FEATURING UK APACHE

THE SILENCE [A] MIKE KOGLIN

SILENCE [B] DELERIUM FEATURING SARAH McLACHLAN

SILENCE [C] TAIKO

SILENCE [D] GOMEZ

SILENCE IS EASY STARSAILOR

SILENCE IS GOLDEN TREMELOES

SILENCE WHEN YOU'RE BURNING HAPPYLIFE

SILENT ALL THESE YEARS TORI AMOS

SILENT LUCIDITY QUEENSRYCHE

SILENT NIGHT BING CROSBY

SILENT NIGHT BROS

SILENT NIGHT DICKIES

SILENT NIGHT SINEAD O'CONNOR

SILENT NIGHT – SEVEN O'CLOCK NEWS SIMON & GARFUNKEL

SILENT RUNNING (ON DANGEROUS GROUND) MIKE + THE MECHANICS

SILENT SCREAM RICHARD MARX

SILENT SIGH BADLY DRAWN BOY

SILENT TO THE DARK II ELECTRIC SOFT PARADE

SILENT VOICE INNOCENCE

SILENT WORDS JAN JOHNSTON

SILENTLY BAD MINDED PRESSURE DROP

SILHOUETTES HERMAN'S HERMITS

SILHOUETTES CLIFF RICHARD

SILK PYJAMAS THOMAS DOLBY

SILLY GAMES JANET KAY

SILLY GAMES LINDY LAYTON FEATURING JANET KAY

SILLY LOVE 10 C.C.

SILLY LOVE SONGS WINGS

SILLY THING SEX PISTOLS

SILVER [A] ECHO & THE BUNNYMEN

SILVER [B] MOIST

SILVER [C] HUNDRED REASONS

SILVER AND GOLD ASAP

SILVER DREAM MACHINE (PART 1) DAVID ESSEX

SILVER LADY DAVID SOUL

SILVER LINING STIFF LITTLE FINGERS

SILVER MACHINE HAWKWIND

SILVER SCREEN SHOWER SCENE FELIX DA HOUSECAT

SILVER SHADOW ATLANTIC STARR

SILVER SHORTS WEDDING PRESENT

SILVER STAR FOUR SEASONS

SILVER THUNDERBIRD MARC COHN

SILVERMAC WESTWORLD

SILVERY RAIN CLIFF RICHARD

SIMBA GROOVE HI POWER

SIMON SAYS [A] 1910 FRUITGUM CO.

SIMON SAYS [B] PHAROAHE MONCH

SIMON SMITH AND HIS AMAZING DANCING BEAR ALAN PRICE SET

SIMON TEMPLAR SPLODGENESSABOUNDS

SIMPLE AS THAT HUEY LEWIS & THE NEWS

SIMPLE GAME FOUR TOPS

SIMPLE KIND OF LIFE NO DOUBT

SIMPLE LIFE ELTON JOHN

SIMPLE SIMON (YOU GOTTA REGARD) MANTRONIX

SIMPLE SINCERITY RADISH

SIMPLE THINGS SAW DOCTORS

THE SIMPLE THINGS JOE COCKER

THE SIMPLE TRUTH (A CHILD IS BORN) CHRIS DE BURGH

SIMPLY IRRESISTABLE ROBERT PALMER

SIN NINE INCH NAILS

SINBAD QUEST SYSTEM 7

SINCE DAY ONE TEENA MARIE

SINCE I DON'T HAVE YOU ART GARFUNKEL

SINCE I DON'T HAVE YOU GUNS N' ROSES

SINCE I LEFT YOU AVALANCHES

SINCE I MET YOU BABY GARY MOORE & BB KING

SINCE I MET YOU LADY UB40 FEATURING LADY SAW

SINCE I TOLD YOU IT'S OVER STEREOPHONICS

SINCE YESTERDAY STRAWBERRY SWITCHBLADE

SINCE YOU'RE GONE CARS

SINCE YOU'VE BEEN GONE [A] ARETHA FRANKLIN

SINCE YOU'VE BEEN GONE [B] RAINBOW

SINCERE MJ COLE

SINCERELY McGUIRE SISTERS

SINFUL PETE WYLIE

SING TRAVIS

SING A HAPPY SONG [A] GEORGE McCRAE

SING A HAPPY SONG [B] O'JAYS

SING A LITTLE SONG DESMOND DEKKER & THE ACES

SING A LONG SHANKS & BIGFOOT

SING A SONG BYRON STINGILY

SING A SONG (BREAK IT DOWN) MANTRONIX

SING A SONG OF FREEDOM CLIFF RICHARD

SING AND SHOUT SECOND IMAGE

SING BABY SING STYLISTICS

SING DON'T SPEAK BLACKFOOT SUE

SING FOR ABSOLUTION MUSE

SING FOR EVER ST PHILIPS CHOIR

SING FOR THE MOMENT EMINEM

SING HALLELUJAH! DR. ALBAN

SING IT AGAIN WITH JOE JOE 'MR PIANO' HENDERSON

SING IT BACK MOLOKO

SING IT (THE HALLELUJAH SONG) MOZIAC

SING IT TO YOU (DEE-DOOB-DEE-DOO) LAVINIA JONES

SING IT WITH JOE JOE 'MR PIANO' HENDERSON

SING LIKE AN ANGEL JERRY LORDAN

SING LITTLE BIRDIE PEARL CARR & TEDDY JOHNSON

SING ME BROTHERS

SING ME AN OLD FASHIONED SONG BILLIE JO SPEARS

SING (OOH-EE-OOH) VIVIENNE McKONE

SING OUR OWN SONG UB40

SING SING GAZ

SING UP FOR THE CHAMPIONS REDS UNITED

SING YOUR LIFE MORRISSEY

SING-A-LONG A

SINGALONG-A-SANTA SANTA CLAUS & THE CHRISTMAS TREES

SINGALONG-A-SANTA AGAIN SANTA CLAUS & THE CHRISTMAS TREES

THE SINGER SANG HIS SONG BEE GEES

SINGIN' IN THE RAIN PART 1 SHEILA B. DEVOTION

THE SINGING DOGS (MEDLEY) SINGING DOGS

SINGING IN MY SLEEP SEMISONIC

SINGING THE BLUES GUY MITCHELL

SINGING THE BLUES TOMMY STEELE & THE STEELMEN

SINGING THE BLUES DAVE EDMUNDS

SINGING THE BLUES DANIEL O'DONNELL

SINGLE [A] EVERYTHING BUT THE GIRL

SINGLE [B] PET SHOP BOYS

SINGLE [C] NATASHA BEDINGFIELD

THE SINGLE RISE

SINGLE AGAIN FIERY FURNACES

SINGLE GIRL [A] SANDY POSEY

SINGLE GIRL [B] LUSH

SINGLE LIFE CAMEO

THE SINGLES 1981–83 BAUHAUS

SINK THE BISMARK DON LANG

SINK TO THE BOTTOM FOUNTAINS OF WAYNE

SINNER NEIL FINN

SINS OF THE FAMILY P.F. SLOAN

SIPPIN' SODA GUY MITCHELL

SIR DANCEALOT OLYMPIC RUNNERS

SIR DUKE STEVIE WONDER

SIREN SOUNDS RONI SIZE

SISSYNECK BECK

SISTA SISTA BEVERLEY KNIGHT

SISTER [A] BROS

SISTER [B] SISTER 2 SISTER

SISTER DEW dEUS

SISTER FRICTION HAYSI FANTAYZEE

SISTER HAVANA URGE OVERKILL

SISTER JANE NEW WORLD

SISTER MOON TRANSVISION VAMP

SISTER OF MERCY THOMPSON TWINS

SISTER PAIN ELECTRAFIXION

SISTER SAVIOUR RAPTURE

SISTER SISTER SISTER BLISS

SISTER SURPRISE GARY NUMAN

SISTERS ARE DOING IT FOR THEMSELVES EURYTHMICS & ARETHA FRANKLIN

THE SISTERS EP PULP

SIT AND WAIT SYDNEY YOUNGBLOOD

SIT DOWN JAMES

SIT DOWN AND CRY ERROLL DUNKLEY

THE SIT SONG BARRON KNIGHTS

SITTIN' ON A FENCE TWICE AS MUCH

(SITTIN' ON) THE DOCK OF THE BAY OTIS REDDING

SITTIN' UP IN MY ROOM BRANDY

SITTING AT HOME HONEYCRACK

SITTING DOWN HERE LENE MARLIN

SITTING IN THE PARK GEORGIE FAME & THE BLUE FLAMES

SITTING ON TOP OF THE WORLD LIVERPOOL FC

SITUATION YAZOO

SIX MANSUN

SIX DAYS DJ SHADOW

SIX FEET DEEP (EP) GRAVEDIGGAZ

643 (LOVE'S ON FIRE) DJ TIESTO FEATURING SUZANNE PALMER

SIX MILLION STEPS (WEST RUNS SOUTH) RAHNI HARRIS & F.L.O.

SIX PACK POLICE

THE SIX TEENS SWEET

634-5789 WILSON PICKETT

6 UNDERGROUND SNEAKER PIMPS

SIXTEEN MUSICAL YOUTH

16 BARS STYLISTICS

SIXTEEN REASONS CONNIE STEVENS

SIXTEEN TONS TENNESSEE ERNIE FORD

SIXTEEN TONS FRANKIE LAINE

THE SIXTH SENSE VARIOUS ARTISTS (MONTAGES)

THE 6TH SENSE COMMON

68 GUNS ALARM

SIXTY MILE SMILE 3 COLOURS RED

60 MILES AND HOUR NEW ORDER

SIXTY MINUTE MAN TRAMMPS

69 POLICE DAVID HOLMES

THE SIZE OF A COW WONDER STUFF

SKA DJ ZINC

SKA TRAIN BEATMASTERS FEATURING BETTY BOO

SKAT STRUT MC SKAT KAT & THE STRAY MOB

SKATEAWAY DIRE STRAITS

SK8ER BOI AVRIL LAVIGNE

SKELETONS STEVIE WONDER

SKIFFLE SESSION EP LONNIE DONEGAN

SKIING IN THE SNOW WIGAN'S OVATION

SKIN CHARLOTTE

SKIN DEEP [A] TED HEATH

SKIN DEEP [A] DUKE ELLINGTON
SKIN DEEP [B] STRANGLERS
THE SKIN GAME GARY NUMAN
SKIN O' MY TEETH MEGADETH
SKIN ON SKIN GRACE
SKIN TRADE DURAN DURAN
THE SKIN UP (EP) SKIN
SKINHEAD MOONSTOMP SYMARIP
SKIP A BEAT BARRATT WAUGH
SKIP TO MY LU LISA LISA
SKUNK FUNK GALLIANO
SKWEEZE ME PLEEZE ME SLADE
SKY SONIQUE
A SKY BLUE SHIRT AND A RAINBOW TIE NORMAN
   BROOKS
SKY HIGH JIGSAW
SKY HIGH NEWTON
SKY PILOT ERIC BURDON & THE ANIMALS
SKY PLUS NYLON MOON
SKYDIVE (I FEEL WONDERFUL) FREEFALL FEATURING
   JAN JOHNSTON
THE SKYE BOAT SONG ROGER WHITTAKER & DES
   O'CONNOR
SKYLARK MICHAEL HOLLIDAY
SKY'S THE LIMIT NOTORIOUS B.I.G. FEATURING 112
SKYWRITER JACKSON 5
SLADE LIVE AT READING '80 (EP) SLADE
SLAIN BY ELF URUSEI YATSURA
SLAIN THE TRUTH (AT THE ROADHOUSE) BASEMENT
SLAM [A] HUMANOID
SLAM [B] ONYX
SLAM DUNK (DA FUNK) FIVE
SLAM JAM WWF SUPERSTARS
SLANG DEF LEPPARD
SLAP AND TICKLE SQUEEZE
SLASH DOT DASH FATBOY SLIM
SLASH 'N' BURN MANIC STREET PREACHERS
SLAVE NEW WORLD SEPULTURA
SLAVE TO LOVE BRYAN FERRY
SLAVE TO THE GRIND SKID ROW
SLAVE TO THE RHYTHM GRACE JONES
SLAVE TO THE VIBE AFTERSHOCK
SLAVE TO THE WAGE PLACEBO
SLAVES NO MORE BLOW MONKEYS FEATURING SYLVIA
   TELLA
SLEAZY BED TRACK BLUETONES
SLEDGEHAMMER PETER GABRIEL
SLEDGER PORN KINGS
SLEEP [A] MARION
SLEEP [B] CONJURE ONE
SLEEP ALONE WONDER STUFF
SLEEP FREAK HEAVY STEREO
SLEEP NOW IN THE FIRE RAGE AGAINST THE MACHINE
SLEEP ON THE LEFT SIDE CORNERSHOP
SLEEP TALK [A] ALYSON WILLIAMS
SLEEP TALK [B] ATFC FEATURING LISA MILLETT
SLEEP WALK SANTO & JOHNNY
SLEEP WELL TONIGHT GENE
SLEEP WITH ME BIRDLAND
SLEEPER AUDIOWEB
SLEEPIN' ON THE JOB GILLAN
SLEEPING AWAKE P.O.D.
SLEEPING BAG ZZ TOP
SLEEPING IN MENSWEAR
SLEEPING IN MY CAR ROXETTE
SLEEPING SATELLITE TASMIN ARCHER
SLEEPING WITH THE LIGHT ON BUSTED
SLEEPING WITH THE LIGHTS ON CURTIS STIGERS
SLEEPING WITH VICTOR LYNDEN DAVID HALL
SLEEPWALK ULTRAVOX
SLEEPY JOE HERMAN'S HERMITS

SLEEPY SHORES JOHNNY PEARSON
SLEIGH RIDE S CLUB JUNIORS
SLICE OF DA PIE MONIE LOVE
SLID FLUKE
SLIDE [A] RAH BAND
SLIDE [B] GOO GOO DOLLS
SLIDE ALONG SIDE SHIFTY
SLIDLING IAN McCULLOCH
SLIGHT RETURN BLUETONES
THE SLIGHTEST TOUCH FIVE STAR
(SLIP & SLIDE) SUICIDE KOSHEEN
SLIP AND DIP COFFEE
SLIP AND SLIDE MEDICINE HEAD
SLIP SLIDIN' AWAY PAUL SIMON
SLIP YOUR DISC TO THIS HEATWAVE
SLIPPERY PEOPLE TALKING HEADS
SLIPPIN' DMX
SLIPPING AWAY [A] DAVE EDMUNDS
SLIPPING AWAY [B] MANSUN
SLITHER VELVET REVOLVER
SLOOP JOHN B BEACH BOYS
SLOPPY HEART FRAZIER CHORUS
SLOW KYLIE MINOGUE
SLOW AND SEXY SHABBA RANKS FEATURING JOHNNY
   GILL
SLOW DOWN [A] JOHN MILES
SLOW DOWN [B] LOOSE ENDS
SLOW EMOTION REPLAY THE THE
SLOW FLOW BRAXTONS
SLOW HANDS INTERPOL
SLOW IT DOWN EAST 17
SLOW JAMZ TWISTA
SLOW MOTION ULTRAVOX
SLOW RIVERS ELTON JOHN & CLIFF RICHARD
SLOW TRAIN TO DAWN THE THE
SLOW TRAIN TO PARADISE TAVARES
SLOW TWISTIN' CHUBBY CHECKER
SLOWDIVE SIOUXSIE & THE BANSHEES
SLOWHAND POINTER SISTERS
SLY MASSIVE ATTACK
SMACK MY BITCH UP PRODIGY
SMALL ADS SMALL ADS
SMALL BIT OF LOVE SAW DOCTORS
SMALL BLUE THING SUZANNE VEGA
SMALL SAD SAM PHIL McLEAN
SMALL TOWN JOHN COUGAR MELLENCAMP
SMALL TOWN BOY UK
A SMALL VICTORY FAITH NO MORE
SMALLTOWN BOY BRONSKI BEAT
SMALLTOWN CREED KANE GANG
SMARTY PANTS FIRST CHOICE
SMASH IT UP DAMNED
SMASH SUMTHIN' REDMAN FEATURING ADAM F
S.M.D.U. BROCK LANDARS
SMELLS LIKE NIRVANA WEIRD AL YANKOVIC
SMELLS LIKE TEEN SPIRIT NIRVANA
SMELLS LIKE TEEN SPIRIT ABIGAIL
SMILE [A] NAT 'KING' COLE
SMILE [A] ROBERT DOWNEY JR
SMILE [B] PUSSYCAT
SMILE [C] AUDREY HALL
SMILE [D] ASWAD FEATURING SWEETIE IRIE
SMILE [E] SUPERNATURALS
SMILE [F] LONESTAR
SMILE [G] FUTURE BREEZE
SMILE [H] MONROE
THE SMILE DAVID ESSEX
A SMILE IN A WHISPER FAIRGROUND ATTRACTION
SMILE TO SHINE BAZ
SMILER HEAVY STEREO
THE SMILING FACE BURN

SMOKE NATALIE IMBRUGLIA
SMOKE GETS IN YOUR EYES PLATTERS
SMOKE GETS IN YOUR EYES BLUE HAZE
SMOKE GETS IN YOUR EYES BRYAN FERRY
SMOKE GETS IN YOUR EYES JOHN ALFORD
SMOKE MACHINE X-PRESS 2
SMOKE ON THE WATER DEEP PURPLE
SMOKE ON THE WATER ROCK AID ARMENIA
SMOKEBELCH II SABRES OF PARADISE
SMOKESTACK LIGHTNIN' HOWLIN' WOLF
SMOKEY BLUES AWAY NEW GENERATION
SMOKIN' IN THE BOYS' ROOM BROWNSVILLE STATION
SMOKIN' IN THE BOYS ROOM MOTLEY CRUE
SMOKIN' ME OUT WARREN G FEATURING RONALD
   ISLEY
SMOOTH SANTANA FEATURING ROB THOMAS
SMOOTH CRIMINAL MICHAEL JACKSON
SMOOTH CRIMINAL ALIEN ANT FARM
SMOOTH OPERATOR SADE
SMOOTHER OPERATOR BIG DADDY KANE
SMOOTHIN' GROOVIN' INGRAM
SMOULDER KING ADORA
SMUGGLER'S BLUES GLENN FREY
THE SMURF TYRONE BRUNSON
THE SMURF SONG FATHER ABRAHAM & THE SMURFS
THE SNAKE [A] AL WILSON
SNAKE [B] R KELLY FEATURING BIG TIGGER
SNAKE BITE (EP) DAVID COVERDALE'S WHITESNAKE
SNAKE IN THE GRASS DAVE DEE, DOZY, BEAKY, MICK &
   TICH
SNAP MEGAMIX SNAP
SNAP YOUR FINGAZ KUMARA
SNAPPED IT KRUST
SNAPPINESS BBG FEATURING DINA TAYLOR
SNAPSHOT 3 RONI SIZE
SNEAKIN' SUSPICION DR FEELGOOD
SNEAKING OUT THE BACK DOOR MATT BIANCO
SNOBBERY AND DECAY ACT
SNOOKER LOOPY MATCHROOM MOB WITH CHAS &
   DAVE
SNOOP DOGG SNOOP DOGG
SNOOP'S UPSIDE YA HEAD SNOOP DOGGY DOGG
   FEATURING CHARLIE WILSON
SNOOPY VS. THE RED BARON ROYAL GUARDSMEN
SNOOPY VS. THE RED BARON HOTSHOTS
SNOT RAP KENNY EVERETT
SNOW [A] ORN
SNOW [B] JJ72
SNOW COACH RUSS CONWAY
SNOWBIRD ANNE MURRAY
SNOWBOUND FOR CHRISTMAS DICKIE VALENTINE
THE SNOWS OF NEW YORK CHRIS DE BURGH
SO ALIVE RYAN ADAMS
SO AMAZING LUTHER VANDROSS
SO BEAUTIFUL [A] URBAN COOKIE COLLECTIVE
SO BEAUTIFUL [B] CHRIS DE BURGH
SO BEAUTIFUL [C] DJ INNOCENCE FEATURING ALEX
   CHARLES
SO CALLED FRIEND TEXAS
SO CLOSE [A] DIANA ROSS
SO CLOSE [B] HALL & OATES
SO CLOSE [C] DINA CARROLL
SO CLOSE TO LOVE WENDY MOTEN
SO COLD THE NIGHT COMMUNARDS
SO CONFUSED 2PLAY FEATURING RAGHAV & JUCXI
SO DAMN BEAUTIFUL POLOROID
SO DAMN COOL UGLY KID JOE
SO DEEP REESE PROJECT
SO DEEP IS THE NIGHT KEN DODD
SO DO I KENNY BALL & HIS JAZZMEN
SO EMOTIONAL WHITNEY HOUSTON

SO FAR AWAY DIRE STRAITS
SO FINE [A] HOWARD JOHNSON
SO FINE [B] KINANE
SO FRESH SO CLEAN OUTKAST
SO GOOD [A] ROY ORBISON
SO GOOD [B] ETERNAL
SO GOOD [C] BOYZONE
SO GOOD [D] JULIET ROBERTS
SO GOOD SO RIGHT BRENDA RUSSELL
SO GOOD TO BE BACK HOME AGAIN TOURISTS
SO GOOD (TO COME HOME TO) IVAN MATAIS
SO GRIMEY SO SOLID CREW
SO GROOVY WENDELL WILLIAMS
SO HARD PET SHOP BOYS
SO HELP ME GIRL GARY BARLOW
SO HERE I AM UB40
SO HOT JC
SO I BEGIN GALLEON
SO IN LOVE ORCHESTRAL MANOEUVRES IN THE DARK
SO IN LOVE (THE REAL DEAL) JUDY CHEEKS
SO IN LOVE WITH YOU [A] FREDDY BRECK
SO IN LOVE WITH YOU [B] SPEAR OF DESTINY
SO IN LOVE WITH YOU [C] TEXAS
SO IN LOVE WITH YOU [D] DUKE
SO INTO YOU [A] MICHAEL WATFORD
SO INTO YOU [B] WILDHEARTS
SO IT WILL ALWAYS BE EVERLY BROTHERS
SO LITTLE TIME ARKARNA
SO LONELY [A] POLICE
SO LONELY [B] JAKATTA
SO LONG [A] FISCHER-Z
SO LONG [B] FIERCE
SO LONG BABY DEL SHANNON
SO LOW OCEAN COLOUR SCENE
SO MACHO SINITTA
SO MANY WAYS [A] BRAXTONS
SO MANY WAYS [B] ELLIE CAMPBELL
SO MUCH IN LOVE [A] TYMES
SO MUCH IN LOVE [A] ALL-4-ONE
SO MUCH IN LOVE [B] MIGHTY AVENGERS
SO MUCH LOVE TONY BLACKBURN
SO MUCH LOVE TO GIVE THOMAS BANGALTER & DJ
  FALCON
SO MUCH TROUBLE IN THE WORLD BOB MARLEY & THE
  WAILERS
SO NATURAL LISA STANSFIELD
SO NEAR TO CHRISTMAS ALVIN STARDUST
SO PURE [A] BABY D
SO PURE [B] ALANIS MORISSETTE
SO REAL [A] LOVE DECADE
SO REAL [B] HARRY
SO RIGHT RAILWAY CHILDREN
SO RIGHT K-KLASS
SO ROTTEN BLAK TWANG FEATURING JAHMALI
SO SAD THE SONG GLADYS KNIGHT & THE PIPS
SO SAD (TO WATCH GOOD LOVE GO BAD) EVERLY
  BROTHERS
SO SAYS I SHINS
SO SEXY TWISTA FEATURING R KELLY
SO SORRY I SAID LIZA MINNELLI
SO STRONG BEN SHAW FEATURING ADELE HOLNESS
SO TELL ME WHY POISON
SO THE STORY GOES LIVING IN A BOX FEATURING
  BOBBY WOMACK
SO THIS IS ROMANCE LINX
SO TIRED [A] FRANKIE VAUGHAN
SO TIRED [B] OZZY OSBOURNE
SO TIRED OF BEING ALONE SYBIL
SO WATCHA GONNA DO NOW PUBLIC ENEMY
SO WHAT [A] GILBERT O'SULLIVAN
SO WHAT! [B] RONNY JORDAN

SO WHAT IF I DAMAGE
SO WHY SO SAD MANIC STREET PREACHERS
SO YESTERDAY HILARY DUFF
SO YOU WIN AGAIN HOT CHOCOLATE
SO YOU'D LIKE TO SAVE THE WORLD LLOYD COLE
SO YOUNG [A] SUEDE
SO YOUNG [B] CORRS
SOAK UP THE SUN SHERYL CROW
SOAPBOX LITTLE ANGELS
SOBER [A] DRUGSTORE
SOBER [B] JENNIFER PAIGE
SOC IT TO ME BADFELLAS FEATURING CK
SOCK IT 2 ME MISSY 'MISDEMEANOR' ELLIOTT
SODA POP AVID MERRION/DAVINA McCALL/PATSY
  KENSIT
SOFT AS YOUR FACE SOUP DRAGONS
SOFT LIKE ME SAINT ETIENNE
SOFT TOP HARD SHOULDER CHRIS REA
SOFTLY AS I LEAVE YOU MATT MONRO
SOFTLY SOFTLY RUBY MURRAY
SOFTLY SOFTLY EQUALS
SOFTLY WHISPERING I LOVE YOU CONGREGATION
SOFTLY WHISPERING I LOVE YOU PAUL YOUNG
SOLACE OF YOU LIVING COLOUR
SOLD BOY GEORGE
SOLD ME DOWN THE RIVER ALARM
SOLD MY ROCK 'N' ROLL (GAVE IT FOR FUNKY SOUL)
  LINDA & THE FUNKY BOYS
SOLD OUT EP REEL BIG FISH
SOLDIER BLUE BUFFY SAINTE-MARIE
SOLDIER BOY SHIRELLES
SOLDIER BOY CHEETAHS
SOLDIER GIRL POLYPHONIC SPREE
SOLDIER OF LOVE DONNY OSMOND
SOLDIER'S SONG HOLLIES
SOLEX (CLOSE TO THE EDGE) MICHAEL WOODS
SOLEY SOLEY MIDDLE OF THE ROAD
SOLID ASHFORD & SIMPSON
SOLID BOND IN YOUR HEART STYLE COUNCIL
SOLID GOLD EASY ACTION T REX
SOLID ROCK (LIVE) DIRE STRAITS
SOLID WOOD ALISON MOYET
SOLITAIRE ANDY WILLIAMS
SOLITAIRE CARPENTERS
SOLITARY MAN H.I.M.
SOLOMON BITES THE WORM BLUETONES
SOLSBURY HILL PETER GABRIEL
SOLSBURY HILL ERASURE
(SOLUTION TO) THE PROBLEM MASQUERADE
SOLVED UNBELIEVABLE TRUTH
SOME BEAUTIFUL JACK WILD
SOME CANDY TALKING JESUS & MARY CHAIN
SOME FANTASTIC PLACE SQUEEZE
SOME FINER DAY ALL ABOUT EVE
SOME GIRLS [A] RACEY
SOME GIRLS [B] ULTIMATE KAOS
SOME GIRLS [C] JC CHASEZ
SOME GIRLS [D] RACHEL STEVENS
SOME GUYS HAVE ALL THE LUCK ROBERT PALMER
SOME GUYS HAVE ALL THE LUCK ROD STEWART
SOME GUYS HAVE ALL THE LUCK MAXI PRIEST
SOME JUSTICE URBAN SHAKEDOWN FEATURING
  MICKY FINN
SOME KIND OF A SUMMER DAVID CASSIDY
SOME KIND OF BLISS KYLIE MINOGUE
SOME KIND OF FRIEND BARRY MANILOW
SOME KIND OF HEAVEN BBG
SOME KIND OF WONDERFUL BLOW MONKEYS
SOME KINDA EARTHQUAKE DUANE EDDY & THE REBELS
SOME KINDA FUN CHRIS MONTEZ
SOME LIE 4 LOVE L.A. GUNS

SOME LIKE IT HOT POWER STATION
SOME MIGHT SAY OASIS
SOME MIGHT SAY DE-CODE FEATURING BEVERLI
  SKEETE
SOME MIGHT SAY SUPERNOVA
SOME OF YOUR LOVIN' DUSTY SPRINGFIELD
SOME OLD GIRL PADDINGTONS
SOME OTHER GUY BIG THREE
SOME OTHER SUCKER'S PARADE DEL AMITRI
SOME PEOPLE [A] CAROL DEENE
SOME PEOPLE [B] BELOUIS SOME
SOME PEOPLE [C] PAUL YOUNG
SOME PEOPLE [D] CLIFF RICHARD
SOME PEOPLE SAY TERRORVISION
SOME SAY KRISTIAN LEONTIOU
SOME THINGS YOU NEVER GET USED TO DIANA ROSS &
  THE SUPREMES
SOME VELVET MORING PRIMAL SCREAM
SOMEBODY [A] STARGAZERS
SOMEBODY [B] JUNIOR
SOMEBODY [C] DEPECHE MODE
SOMEBODY [D] BRYAN ADAMS
SOMEBODY [E] BRILLIANT
SOMEBODY [F] SHORTIE VS BLACK LEGEND
SOMEBODY ELSE'S GIRL BILLY FURY
SOMEBODY ELSE'S GUY JOCELYN BROWN
SOMEBODY ELSE'S GUY LOUCHIE LOU & MICHIE ONE
SOMEBODY ELSE'S GUY CE CE PENISTON
SOMEBODY HELP ME SPENCER DAVIS GROUP
(SOMEBODY) HELP ME OUT BEGGAR & CO
SOMEBODY IN THE HOUSE SAY YEAH! 2 IN A ROOM
SOMEBODY LIKE YOU ELATE
SOMEBODY LOVES YOU NIK KERSHAW
SOMEBODY PUT SOMETHING IN MY DRINK RAMONES
SOMEBODY STOLE MY GAL JOHNNIE RAY
SOMEBODY TO LOVE [A] BRAD NEWMAN
SOMEBODY TO LOVE [A] JETS
SOMEBODY TO LOVE [B] QUEEN
SOMEBODY TO LOVE [C] BOOGIE PIMPS
SOMEBODY TO SHOVE SOUL ASYLUM
SOMEBODY TOLD ME KILLERS
SOMEBODY'S BABY PAT BENATAR
SOMEBODY'S WATCHING ME ROCKWELL
SOMEDAY [A] RICKY NELSON
SOMEDAY [B] GAP BAND
SOMEDAY [C] GLASS TIGER
SOMEDAY [D] MARIAH CAREY
SOMEDAY [D] REZONANCE Q
SOMEDAY [E] M PEOPLE WITH HEATHER SMALL
SOMEDAY [F] EDDY
SOMEDAY [G] LOVE TO INFINITY
SOMEDAY [H] ETERNAL
SOMEDAY [I] CHARLOTTE
SOMEDAY [J] STROKES
SOMEDAY [K] NICKELBACK
SOMEDAY I'LL BE SATURDAY NIGHT BON JOVI
SOMEDAY I'LL FIND YOU SHOLA AMA & CRAIG
  ARMSTRONG
SOMEDAY (I'M COMING BACK) LISA STANSFIELD
SOMEDAY MAN MONKEES
SOMEDAY ONE DAY SEEKERS
SOMEDAY WE'LL BE TOGETHER DIANA ROSS & THE
  SUPREMES
SOMEDAY WE'LL KNOW NEW RADICALS
SOMEDAY WE'RE GONNA LOVE AGAIN SEARCHERS
SOMEDAY (YOU'LL BE SORRY) KENNY BALL & HIS
  JAZZMEN
SOMEDAY (YOU'LL COME RUNNING) FM
SOMEDAY (YOU'LL WANT ME TO WANT YOU) JODIE
  SANDS
SOMEHOW SOMEWHERE DEEP SENSATION

SOMEONE [A] JOHNNY MATHIS
SOMEONE [B] ASCENSION
SOMEONE [C] SWV FEATURING PUFF DADDY
SOMEONE ALWAYS GETS THERE FIRST BENNETT
SOMEONE BELONGING TO SOMEONE BEE GEES
SOMEONE ELSE NOT ME DURAN DURAN
SOMEONE ELSE'S BABY ADAM FAITH
SOMEONE ELSE'S ROSES JOAN REGAN
SOMEONE LIKE ME ATOMIC KITTEN
SOMEONE LIKE YOU [A] DINA CARROLL
SOMEONE LIKE YOU [B] RUSSELL WATSON & FAYE TOZER
SOMEONE LOVES YOU HONEY LUTRICIA McNEAL
SOMEONE MUST HAVE HURT YOU A LOT FRANKIE VAUGHAN
SOMEONE ON YOUR MIND JIMMY YOUNG
SOMEONE SAVED MY LIFE TONIGHT ELTON JOHN
SOMEONE SHOULD TELL HER MAVERICKS
SOMEONE SOMEONE BRIAN POOLE & THE TREMELOES
SOMEONE SOMEWHERE WANNADIES
SOMEONE SOMEWHERE (IN SUMMERTIME) SIMPLE MINDS
SOMEONE THERE FOR ME RICHARD BLACKWOOD
SOMEONE TO CALL MY LOVER JANET JACKSON
SOMEONE TO HOLD TREY LORENZ
SOMEONE TO LOVE [A] SEAN MAGUIRE
SOMEONE TO LOVE [B] EAST 17
SOMEONE TO SOMEBODY FEARGAL SHARKEY
SOMEONE'S DAUGHTER BETH ORTON
SOMEONE'S LOOKING AT YOU BOOMTOWN RATS
SOMEONE'S TAKEN MARIA AWAY ADAM FAITH
SOMERSAULT ZERO 7 FEATURING SIA
SOMETHIN' 4 DA HONEYZ MONTELL JORDAN
SOMETHIN' ELSE EDDIE COCHRAN
SOMETHIN' IS GOIN' ON CLIFF RICHARD
SOMETHIN' STUPID NANCY SINATRA & FRANK SINATRA
SOMETHIN' STUPID ALI & KIBIBI CAMPBELL
SOMETHING STUPID CORONATION STREET CAST: AMANDA BARRIE & JOHNNIE BRIGGS
SOMETHIN' STUPID ROBBIE WILLIAMS & NICOLE KIDMAN
SOMETHING [A] GEORGIE FAME & THE BLUE FLAMES
SOMETHING [B] BEATLES
SOMETHING [B] SHIRLEY BASSEY
SOMETHING [C] LASGO
SOMETHING ABOUT THE MUSIC DA SLAMMIN' PHROGZ
SOMETHING ABOUT THE WAY YOU LOOK TONIGHT ELTON JOHN
SOMETHING ABOUT YOU MR ROY
SOMETHING ABOUT YOU [A] LEVEL 42
SOMETHING ABOUT YOU [B] NEW EDITION
SOMETHING BEAUTIFUL ROBBIE WILLIAMS
SOMETHING BEAUTIFUL REMAINS TINA TURNER
SOMETHING BETTER BEGINNING HONEYCOMBS
SOMETHING BETTER CHANGE STRANGLERS
SOMETHING 'BOUT YOU BABY I LIKE TOM JONES
SOMETHING 'BOUT YOU BABY I LIKE STATUS QUO
SOMETHING CHANGED PULP
SOMETHING DEEP INSIDE BILLIE PIPER
SOMETHING DIFFERENT SHAGGY FEATURING WAYNE WONDER
SOMETHING ELSE [A] SEX PISTOLS
SOMETHING ELSE [B] AGENT BLUE
SOMETHING FOR THE GIRL WITH EVERYTHING SPARKS
SOMETHING FOR THE PAIN BON JOVI
SOMETHING FOR THE WEEKEND [A] DIVINE COMEDY
SOMETHING 4 THE WEEKEND [B] SUPER FURRY ANIMALS
SOMETHING FOR THE WEEKEND [C] FRED & ROXY
SOMETHING GOIN' ON TODD TERRY FEATURING MARTHA WASH & JOCELYN BROWN

SOMETHING GOOD UTAH SAINTS
SOMETHING GOT ME STARTED SIMPLY RED
SOMETHING HAPPENED ON THE WAY TO HEAVEN PHIL COLLINS
SOMETHING HERE IN MY HEART (KEEPS A-TELLIN' ME NO) PAPER DOLLS
SOMETHING IN COMMON BOBBY BROWN & WHITNEY HOUSTON
SOMETHING IN MY HOUSE DEAD OR ALIVE
SOMETHING IN THE AIR THUNDERCLAP NEWMAN
SOMETHING IN THE AIR FISH
SOMETHING IN THE AIR TOM PETTY
SOMETHING IN YOUR EYES [A] BELL BIV DEVOE
SOMETHING IN YOUR EYES [B] ED CASE
(SOMETHING INSIDE) SO STRONG LABI SIFFRE
SOMETHING INSIDE SO STRONG MICHAEL BALL
SOMETHING INSIDE (SO STRONG) RIK WALLER
SOMETHING JUST AIN'T RIGHT KEITH SWEAT
SOMETHING MISSING PETULA CLARK
SOMETHING OLD, SOMETHING NEW FANTASTICS
SOMETHING ON MY MIND CHRIS ANDREWS
SOMETHING OUTA NOTHING LETITIA DEAN & PAUL MEDFORD
SOMETHING SO GOOD RAILWAY CHILDREN
SOMETHING SO REAL (CHINHEADS THEME) LOVE DECREE
SOMETHING SO RIGHT ANNIE LENNOX FEATURING PAUL SIMON
SOMETHING SPECIAL [A] STEVE HARVEY
SOMETHING SPECIAL [B] NOMAD
SOMETHING TELLS ME (SOMETHING IS GONNA HAPPEN TONIGHT) CILLA BLACK
SOMETHING THAT I SAID RUTS
SOMETHING THAT YOU SAID BANGLES
SOMETHING TO BELIEVE IN [A] POISON
SOMETHING TO BELIEVE IN [B] RAMONES
SOMETHING TO DO DEPECHE MODE
SOMETHING TO MISS SENSELESS THINGS
SOMETHING TO TALK ABOUT BADLY DRAWN BOY
SOMETHING WILD RARE
SOMETHING WORTHWHILE GUN
SOMETHING YOU GOT AND WHY NOT?
SOMETHING'S BEEN MAKING ME BLUE SMOKIE
SOMETHING'S BURNING KENNY ROGERS & THE FIRST EDITION
SOMETHING'S COOKIN' IN THE KITCHEN DANA
SOMETHING'S GOIN' ON [A] MYSTIC 3
SOMETHING'S GOING ON [B] A
SOMETHING'S GOTTA GIVE SAMMY DAVIS Jr.
SOMETHING'S GOTTEN HOLD OF MY HEART GENE PITNEY
SOMETHING'S GOTTEN HOLD OF MY HEART MARC ALMOND FEATURING SPECIAL GUEST STAR GENE PITNEY
SOMETHING'S HAPPENING HERMAN'S HERMITS
SOMETHING'S JUMPIN' IN YOUR HEART MALCOLM McLAREN & THE BOOTZILLA ORCHESTRA FEATURING LISA MARIE
SOMETHING'S MISSING CHORDS
SOMETIMES [A] ERASURE
SOMETIMES [B] MAX Q
SOMETIMES [C] JAMES
SOMETIMES [D] BRAND NEW HEAVIES
SOMETIMES [E] TIN TIN OUT FEATURING SHELLEY NELSON
SOMETIMES [F] LES RYTHMES DIGITALES FEATURING NIK KERSHAW
SOMETIMES [G] BRITNEY SPEARS
SOMETIMES [H] ASH
SOMETIMES ALWAYS JESUS & MARY CHAIN
SOMETIMES I MISS YOU SO MUCH PM DAWN

SOMETIMES IT HURTS TINDERSTICKS
SOMETIMES (IT SNOWS IN APRIL) AMAR
SOMETIMES IT'S A BITCH STEVIE NICKS
SOMETIMES LOVE JUST AIN'T ENOUGH PATTY SMYTH WITH DON HENLEY
SOMETIMES (THEME FROM 'CHAMPIONS') ELAINE PAIGE
SOMETIMES WHEN WE TOUCH DAN HILL
SOMETIMES WHEN WE TOUCH NEWTON
SOMEWHERE [A] P.J. PROBY
SOMEWHERE [A] PET SHOP BOYS
SOMEWHERE [B] EFUA
SOMEWHERE ACROSS FOREVER STELLASTARR
SOMEWHERE ALONG THE WAY NAT 'KING' COLE
SOMEWHERE DOWN THE CRAZY RIVER ROBBIE ROBERTSON
SOMEWHERE ELSE CHINA DRUM
SOMEWHERE I BELONG LINKIN PARK
SOMEWHERE IN AMERICA (THERE'S A STREET NAMED AFTER MY DAD) WAS (NOT WAS)
SOMEWHERE IN MY HEART AZTEC CAMERA
SOMEWHERE IN THE COUNTRY GENE PITNEY
SOMEWHERE IN THE NIGHT BARRY MANILOW
SOMEWHERE MY LOVE MANUEL & HIS MUSIC OF THE MOUNTAINS
SOMEWHERE MY LOVE MIKE SAMMES SINGERS
SOMEWHERE ONLY WE KNOW KEANE
SOMEWHERE OUT THERE LINDA RONSTADT & JAMES INGRAM
SOMEWHERE OVER THE RAINBOW CLIFF RICHARD
SOMEWHERE SOMEBODY FIVE STAR
SOMEWHERE SOMEHOW WET WET WET
SON OF A GUN JX
SON OF A GUN (BETCHA THINK THIS SONG IS ABOUT YOU) JANET JACKSON FEATURING CARLY SIMON
SON OF A PREACHER MAN DUSTY SPRINGFIELD
SON OF HICKORY HOLLER'S TRAMP O.C. SMITH
SON OF MARY HARRY BELAFONTE
SON OF MY FATHER CHICORY TIP
SON OF SAM ELLIOTT SMITH
SON OF THREE BREEDERS
SON THIS IS SHE JOHN LEYTON
(SONG FOR A) FUTURE GENERATION B52's
SONG FOR GUY ELTON JOHN
SONG FOR LOVE EXTREME
A SONG FOR LOVERS RICHARD ASHCROFT
A SONG FOR MAMA BOYZ II MEN
A SONG FOR SHELTER FATBOY SLIM
SONG FOR WHOEVER BEAUTIFUL SOUTH
SONG FROM THE EDGE OF THE WORLD SIOUXSIE & THE BANSHEES
SONG OF DREAMS BECKY TAYLOR
SONG OF JOY MIGUEL RIOS
SONG OF LIFE LEFTFIELD
SONG OF MEXICO TONY MEEHAN COMBO
THE SONG OF MY LIFE PETULA CLARK
SONG OF THE DREAMER JOHNNIE RAY
SONG SUNG BLUE NEIL DIAMOND
THE SONG THAT I SING (THEME FROM 'WE'LL MEET AGAIN') STUTZ BEARCATS & THE DENIS KING ORCHESTRA
SONG TO THE SIREN THIS MORTAL COIL
SONG 2 BLUR
SONGBIRD [A] KENNY G
SONGBIRD [B] OASIS
SONGS FOR CHRISTMAS '87 EP MINI POPS
SONGS FOR SWINGING LOVERS (LP) FRANK SINATRA
SONIC BOOM BOY WESTWORLD
SONIC BOOM (LIFE'S TOO SHORT) QUO VADIS
SONIC EMPIRE MEMBERS OF MAYDAY
SONNET (IMPORT) VERVE

SONS AND DAUGHTERS' THEME KERRI & MICK

SONS OF THE STAGE WORLD OF TWIST

SOON MY BLOODY VALENTINE

SOON BE DONE SHAGGY

SOONER OR LATER LARRY GRAHAM

SOOPA HOOPZ SOOPA HOOPZ FEATURING QPR
MASSIVE

SOOTHE ME SAM & DAVE

SORRENTO MOON (I REMEMBER) TINA ARENA

SORROW MERSEYS

SORROW DAVID BOWIE

SORRY BUT I'M GONNA HAVE TO PASS COASTERS

SORRY DOESN'T ALWAYS MAKE IT RIGHT DIANA ROSS

SORRY FOR YOU RONI SIZE

SORRY (I DIDN'T KNOW) MONSTA BOY FEATURING
DENZIE

SORRY (I RAN ALL THE WAY HOME) IMPALAS

SORRY I'M A LADY BACCARA

SORRY ROBBIE BERT WEEDON

SORRY SEEMS TO BE THE HARDEST WORD ELTON JOHN

SORRY SEEMS TO BE THE HARDEST WORD BLUE
FEATURING ELTON JOHN

SORRY SUZANNE HOLLIES

A SORTA FAIRYTALE TORI AMOS

SORTED FOR ES & WIZZ PULP

S.O.S. [A] ABBA

S.O.S. [B] ABC

THE SOS EP SHAMEN

SOUL BEAT CALLING I KAMANCHI

SOUL BOSSA NOVA COOL, THE FAB & THE GROOVY
PRESENT QUINCY JONES

THE SOUL CAGES STING

SOUL CHA CHA VAN McCOY

SOUL CITY WALK ARCHIE BELL & THE DRELLS

SOUL CLAP '69 BOOKER T. & THE M.G.'s

SOUL COAXING RAYMOND LEFEVRE

SOUL DEEP BOX TOPS

SOUL DEEP GARY U.S. BONDS

SOUL DEEP (PART 1) COUNCIL COLLECTIVE

SOUL DRACULA HOT BLOOD

SOUL FINGER BAR-KAYS

SOUL FREEDOM – FREE YOUR SOUL DEGREES OF
MOTION FEATURING BITI

SOUL HEAVEN GOODFELLAS FEATURING LISA MILLETT

SOUL INSIDE SOFT CELL

SOUL INSPIRATION SIMON CLIMIE

SOUL LIMBO BOOKER T. & THE M.G.'s

SOUL LOVE BLESSING

SOUL LOVE – SOUL MAN WOMACK & WOMACK

SOUL MAN SAM & DAVE

SOUL MAN SAM MOORE & LOU REED

SOUL OF MY SOUL MICHAEL BOLTON

THE SOUL OF MY SUIT T. REX

SOUL PASSING THROUGH SOUL TOYAH

SOUL PROVIDER MICHAEL BOLTON

SOUL SEARCHIN' TIME TRAMMPS

SOUL SERENADE WILLIE MITCHELL

SOUL SISTER BROWN SUGAR SAM & DAVE

SOUL SOUND SUGABABES

SOUL TRAIN SWANS WAY

SOULJACKER PART 1 EELS

SOULMATE WEE PAPA GIRL RAPPERS

SOULS RICK SPRINGFIELD

SOUL'S ON FIRE TRACIE

THE SOULSHAKER MAX LINEN

SOUND [A] JAMES

THE SOUND [B] X-PRESS 2

SOUND ADVICE RONI SIZE

SOUND AND VISION DAVID BOWIE

SOUND BWOY BURIAL GANT

SOUND CLASH (CHAMPION SOUND) KICK SQUAD

THE SOUND OF BAMBOO FLICKMAN

THE SOUND OF BLUE JFK

SOUND OF CONFUSION SECRET AFFAIR

THE SOUND OF THE CROWD HUMAN LEAGUE

SOUND OF THE UNDERGROUND GIRLS ALOUD

THE SOUND OF CRYING PREFAB SPROUT

SOUND OF DRUMS KULA SHAKER

THE SOUND OF EDEN SHADES OF RHYTHM

SOUND OF EDEN CASINO

THE SOUND OF MUSIC DAYTON

THE SOUND OF MUSIK FALCO

THE SOUND OF OH YEAH TOMBA VIRA

THE SOUND OF SILENCE BACHELORS

SOUND OF SOUNDS/PING ONE DOWN GOMEZ

SOUND OF SPEED (EP) JESUS & MARY CHAIN

THE SOUND OF THE SUBURBS MEMBERS

THE SOUND OF VIOLENCE CASSIUS

THE SOUND OF YOUR CITY ELVIS PRESLEY

SOUND SYSTEM [A] STEEL PULSE

SOUND SYSTEM [B] DRUM CLUB

SOUND YOUR FUNKY HORN KC & THE SUNSHINE BAND

SOUNDS OF EDEN (EVERYTIME I SEE THE) DEEP COVER

SOUNDS OF WICKEDNESS TZANT

SOUR TIMES PORTISHEAD

SOUTH AFRICAN MAN HAMILTON BOHANNON

SOUTH MANZ DILLINJA

SOUTH OF THE BORDER ROBBIE WILLIAMS

SOUTH OF THE RIVER MICA PARIS

SOUTH PACIFIC DJ ZINC

SOUTHAMPTON BOYS RED 'N' WHITE MACHINES

SOUTHERN COMFORT BERNIE FLINT

SOUTHERN FREEEZ FREEEZ

SOUTHERN NIGHTS GLEN CAMPBELL

SOUTHERN SUN PAUL OAKENFOLD

SOUTHSIDE DAVE CLARKE

SOUVENIR ORCHESTRAL MANOEUVRES IN THE DARK

SOUVENIRS VOYAGE

SOWETO [A] MALCOLM McLAREN & THE
McLARENETTES

SOWETO [B] JEFFREY OSBORNE

SOWING THE SEEDS OF HATRED CREDIT TO THE NATION

SOWING THE SEEDS OF LOVE TEARS FOR FEARS

SPACE [A] NEW MODEL ARMY

SPACE [B] SLIPMATT

SPACE AGE LOVE SONG A FLOCK OF SEAGULLS

SPACE BASS SLICK

THE SPACE BETWEEN DAVE MATTHEWS BAND

SPACE COWBOY JAMIROQUAI

SPACE JAM QUAD CITY DJS

THE SPACE JUNGLE ADAMSKI

SPACE LORD MONSTER MAGNET

SPACE OASIS BILLIE RAY MARTIN

SPACE ODDITY DAVID BOWIE

SPACE RIDER SHAUN ESCOFFERY

SPACE STATION NO. 5 [A] SAMMY HAGAR

SPACE STATION NO. 5 [B] MONTROSE

SPACE WALK LEMON JELLY

SPACED INVADER HATIRAS FEATURING SLARTA JOHN

SPACEHOPPER BAD COMPANY

SPACEMAN [A] 4 NON BLONDES

SPACEMAN [B] BABYLON ZOO

A SPACEMAN CAME TRAVELLING CHRIS DE BURGH

SPACER SHEILA & B. DEVOTION

SPANISH CRAIG DAVID

SPANISH DANCE TROUPE GORKY'S ZYGOTIC MYNCI

SPANISH EYES AL MARTINO

SPANISH FLEA HERB ALPERT & THE TIJUANA BRASS

SPANISH HARLEM JIMMY JUSTICE

SPANISH HARLEM SOUNDS INCORPORATED

SPANISH HARLEM ARETHA FRANKLIN

SPANISH HORSES AZTEC CAMERA

SPANISH STROLL MINK DE VILLE

SPANISH WINE CHRIS WHITE

SPARE PARTS BRUCE SPRINGSTEEN

SPARK TORI AMOS

SPARKLE MY LIFE STORY

SPARKLE OF MY EYES UB40

SPARKS ROYKSOPP

SPARKY'S DREAM TEENAGE FANCLUB

THE SPARROW RAMBLERS (FROM THE ABBEY HEY
JUNIOR SCHOOL)

THE SPARTANS SOUNDS INCORPORATED

SPEAK LIKE A CHILD STYLE COUNCIL

SPEAK TO ME PRETTY BRENDA LEE

SPEAK TO ME SOMEONE GENE

SPEAKEASY SHED SEVEN

SPECIAL GARBAGE

SPECIAL 2003 LEE-CABRERA

THE SPECIAL A.K.A. LIVE! EP SPECIAL A.K.A.

SPECIAL BREW BAD MANNERS

SPECIAL CASES MASSIVE ATTACK

SPECIAL F/X WHISPERS

SPECIAL KIND OF LOVE DINA CARROLL

SPECIAL KIND OF LOVER NU COLOURS

SPECIAL KIND OF SOMETHING KAVANA

SPECIAL NEEDS PLACEBO

SPECIAL WAY RIVER CITY PEOPLE

THE SPECIAL YEARS VAL DOONICAN

SPECTACULAR GRAHAM COXON

SPEECHLESS D-SIDE

SPEED BILLY IDOL

SPEED AT THE SOUND OF LONELINESS ALABAMA 3

SPEED (CAN YOU FEEL IT?) AZZIDO DA BASS
FEATURING ROLAND CLARK

SPEED YOUR LOVE TO ME SIMPLE MINDS

SPEEDWELL SAINT ETIENNE

SPEEDY GONZALES PAT BOONE

THE SPELL! FUNKY WORM

SPELLBOUND SIOUXSIE & THE BANSHEES

SPEND SOME TIME BRAND NEW HEAVIES FEATURING
N'DEA DAVENPORT

SPEND THE DAY URBAN COOKIE COLLECTIVE

SPEND THE NIGHT [A] COOLNOTES

SPEND THE NIGHT [B] DANNY J LEWIS

SPENDING MY TIME ROXETTE

SPICE OF LIFE MANHATTAN TRANSFER

SPICE UP YOUR LIFE SPICE GIRLS

SPIDERS AND SNAKES JIM STAFFORD

SPIDERWEBS NO DOUBT

SPIES LIKE US PAUL McCARTNEY

SPIKEE UNDERWORLD

SPILLER FROM RIO (DO IT EASY) LAGUNA

SPIN SPIN SUGAR SNEAKER PIMPS

SPIN THAT WHEEL (TURTLES GET REAL) HI-TEK 3
FEATURING YA KID K

SPIN THE BLACK CIRCLE PEARL JAM

SPIN THE WHEEL BELLEFIRE

SPINDRIFT (EP) THOUSAND YARD STARE

SPINNIN' AND SPINNIN' SYREETA

SPINNIN' WHEELS CRESCENT

SPINNING CLARKSVILLE

SPINNING AROUND KYLIE MINOGUE

SPINNING ROCK BOOGIE HANK C. BURNETTE

SPINNING THE WHEEL GEORGE MICHAEL

SPIRAL SCRATCH EP BUZZCOCKS

SPIRAL SYMPHONY SCIENTIST

SPIRIT [A] BAUHAUS

SPIRIT [B] WAYNE MARSHALL

SPIRIT [C] SOUNDS OF BLACKNESS FEATURING CRAIG
MACK

SPIRIT BODY AND SOUL NOLAN SISTERS

SPIRIT IN THE SKY NORMAN GREENBAUM

STAY [B] BARRY MANILOW FEATURING KEVIN DiSIMONE & JAMES JOLIS
STAY [A] DREAMHOUSE
STAY [C] SHAKESPEARS SISTER
STAY [D] KENNY THOMAS
STAY [E] ETERNAL
STAY [F] 60FT DOLLS
STAY [G] 18 WHEELER
STAY [H] SASH! FEATURING LA TREC
STAY [I] BERNARD BUTLER
STAY [J] MICA PARIS
STAY [K] STEPHEN GATELY
STAY [L] ROB TISSERA & VINYLGROOVER
STAY A LITTLE WHILE, CHILD LOOSE ENDS
STAY A WHILE RAKIM
STAY ANOTHER DAY EAST 17
STAY AWAY BABY JANE CHESNEY HAWKES
STAY AWAY FROM ME STAR SPANGLES
STAY AWHILE DUSTY SPRINGFIELD
STAY BEAUTIFUL MANIC STREET PREACHERS
STAY (FARAWAY, SO CLOSE) U2
STAY FOREVER JOEY LAWRENCE
STAY GOLD DEEP DISH
STAY (I MISSED YOU) LISA LOEB & NINE STORIES
STAY IN THE SUN KENICKIE
STAY ON THESE ROADS A-HA
STAY OUT OF MY LIFE FIVE STAR
STAY RIGHT HERE AKIN
STAY THE SAME [A] BENT
STAY THE SAME [B] GABRIELLE
STAY THIS WAY BRAND NEW HEAVIES FEATURING N'DEA DAVENPORT
STAY TOGETHER [A] SUEDE
STAY TOGETHER [B] BARBARA TUCKER
STAY (TONIGHT) ISHA-D
STAY WITH ME [A] FACES
STAY WITH ME [B] BLUE MINK
STAY WITH ME [C] EIGHTH WONDER
STAY WITH ME [D] MISSION
STAY WITH ME [E] JOHN O'KANE
STAY WITH ME [F] ERASURE
STAY WITH ME [G] ULTRA HIGH
STAY WITH ME [H] RICHIE RICH & ESERA TUAOLO
STAY WITH ME [I] ANGELIC
STAY WITH ME BABY WALKER BROTHERS
STAY WITH ME BABY DAVID ESSEX
STAY WITH ME BABY RUBY TURNER
STAY WITH ME (BABY) REBECCA WHEATLEY
STAY WITH ME HEARTACHE WET WET WET
STAY WITH ME TILL DAWN JUDIE TZUKE
STAY WITH ME TILL DAWN LUCID
STAY WITH ME TONIGHT [A] JEFFREY OSBORNE
STAY WITH ME TONIGHT [B] HUMAN LEAGUE
STAY WITH YOU LEMON JELLY
STAY YOUNG ULTRASOUND
STAYIN' ALIVE BEE GEES
STAYIN' ALIVE RICHARD ACE
STAYIN' ALIVE N-TRANCE FEATURING RICARDO DA FORCE
STAYING ALIVE 95 FEVER FEATURING TIPPA IRIE
STAYING FAT BLOC PARTY
STAYING IN BOBBY VEE
STAYING OUT FOR THE SUMMER DODGY
STAYING TOGETHER DEBBIE GIBSON
STEAL MY SUNSHINE LEN
STEAL YOUR FIRE GUN
STEAL YOUR LOVE AWAY GEMINI
STEALTH WAY OUT WEST FEATURING KIRSTY HAWKSHAW
STEAM [A] PETER GABRIEL
STEAM [B] EAST 17

STEAMY WINDOWS TINA TURNER
STEEL BARS MICHAEL BOLTON
A STEEL GUITAR AND A GLASS OF WINE PAUL ANKA
STEELO 702
STEM DJ SHADOW
STEP BACK IN TIME KYLIE MINOGUE
STEP BY STEP [A] STEVE PERRY
STEP BY STEP [B] JOE SIMON
STEP BY STEP [C] TAFFY
STEP BY STEP [D] NEW KIDS ON THE BLOCK
STEP BY STEP [E] WHITNEY HOUSTON
STEP IN THE NAME OF LOVE R KELLY
A STEP IN THE RIGHT DIRECTION TRUTH
STEP INSIDE LOVE CILLA BLACK
STEP INTO A DREAM WHITE PLAINS
STEP INTO A WORLD (RAPTURE'S DELIGHT) KRS ONE
STEP INTO CHRISTMAS ELTON JOHN
STEP INTO MY OFFICE BABY BELLE & SEBASTIAN
STEP INTO MY WORLD HURRICANE #1
STEP INTO THE BREEZE SPIRITUALIZED
STEP IT UP STEREO MC'S
STEP OFF JUNIOR GISCOMBE
STEP OFF (PART 1) GRANDMASTER MELLE MEL & THE FURIOUS FIVE
STEP ON HAPPY MONDAYS
STEP ON MY OLD SIZE NINES STEREOPHONICS
STEP RIGHT UP JAKI GRAHAM
STEP TO ME (DO ME) MANTRONIX
STEPPIN' OUT [A] KOOL & THE GANG
STEPPIN' OUT [B] JOE JACKSON
STEPPIN STONES DJ ZINC
STEPPING STONE FARM
STEPPING STONE PJ & DUNCAN
STEP-TWO-THREE-FOUR STRICT INSTRUCTOR
STEREO PAVEMENT
STEREOTYPE SPECIALS
STEREOTYPES BLUR
STEVE McQUEEN SHERYL CROW
STEWBALL LONNIE DONEGAN
STICK IT OUT RIGHT SAID FRED & FRIENDS
STICKS AND STONES CUD
STICKY WEDDING PRESENT
STIFF UPPER LIP AC/DC
STILL [A] KARL DENVER
STILL [A] KEN DODD
STILL [B] COMMODORES
STILL [C] MACY GRAY
STILL A FRIEND OF MINE INCOGNITO
STILL A THRILL SYBIL
STILL BE LOVIN' YOU DAMAGE
STILL BELIEVE SHOLA AMA
STILL DRE DR. DRE FEATURING SNOOP DOGGY DOGG
STILL FEEL THE PAIN STEX
STILL GOT THE BLUES (FOR YOU) GARY MOORE
STILL HAVEN'T FOUND WHAT I'M LOOKING FOR CHIMES
STILL I'M SAD YARDBIRDS
STILL IN LOVE [A] GO WEST
STILL IN LOVE [B] LIONEL RICHIE
STILL IN LOVE SONG STILLS
STILL OF THE NIGHT WHITESNAKE
STILL ON YOUR SIDE BBMAK
STILL THE SAME SLADE
STILL TOO YOUNG TO REMEMBER IT BITES
STILL WAITING SUM 41
STILL WATER (LOVE) FOUR TOPS
STILL WATERS (RUN DEEP) BEE GEES
STILLNESS IN TIME JAMIROQUAI
STILLNESS OF HEART LENNY KRAVITZ
THE STING RAGTIMERS
STING ME BLACK CROWES

STING ME RED (YOU THINK YOU'RE SO) WHO DA FUNK FEATURING TERRA DEVA
STINGRAY SHADOWS
THE STINGRAY MEGAMIX FAB FEATURING AQUA MARINA
STINKIN THINKIN HAPPY MONDAYS
STIR IT UP JOHNNY NASH
STOLE KELLY ROWLAND
STOLEN JAY SEAN
STOLEN CAR BETH ORTON
STOLEN CAR (TAKE ME DANCING) STING
STOMP [A] BROTHERS JOHNSON
STOMP [A] QUINCY JONES FEATURING MELLE MEL, COOLIO, YO-YO, SHAQUILLE O'NEAL & THE LUNIZ
STOMP [B] GOD'S PROPERTY
STOMP [C] STEPS
STONE BY STONE CATATONIA
STONE COLD RAINBOW
STONE LOVE KOOL & THE GANG
STONED LOVE SUPREMES
STONEY END BARBRA STREISAND
STONEY GROUND GUYS & DOLLS
THE STONK HALE & PACE & THE STONKERS
STOOD ON GOLD GORKY'S ZYGOTIC MYNCI
STOOD UP RICKY NELSON
STOOL PIGEON KID CREOLE & THE COCONUTS
STOP [A] SAM BROWN
STOP [B] SPICE GIRLS
STOP [C] BLACK REBEL MOTORCYCLE CLUB
STOP [D] JAMELIA
STOP AND GO DAVID GRANT
STOP BAJON...PRIMAVERA TULLIO DE PISCOPO
STOP BREAKING MY HEART INNER CIRCLE
STOP BY RAHSAAN PATTERSON
STOP CRYING YOUR HEART OUT OASIS
STOP DRAGGIN' MY HEART AROUND STEVIE NICKS WITH TOM PETTY & THE HEARTBREAKERS
STOP (EP) MEGA CITY FOUR
STOP FEELING SORRY FOR YOURSELF ADAM FAITH
STOP HER ON SIGHT (SOS) EDWIN STARR
STOP IN THE NAME OF LOVE SUPREMES
STOP LISTENING TANITA TIKARAM
STOP LIVING THE LIE DAVID SNEDDON
STOP LOOK AND LISTEN [A] WAYNE FONTANA & THE MINDBENDERS
STOP LOOK AND LISTEN [B] DONNA SUMMER
STOP LOOK LISTEN (TO YOUR HEART) DIANA ROSS & MARVIN GAYE
STOP LOVING ME LOVING YOU DARYL HALL
STOP ME (IF YOU'VE HEARD IT ALL BEFORE) BILLY OCEAN
STOP MY HEAD EVAN DANDO
STOP PLAYING WITH MY MIND BARBARA TUCKER FEATURING DARYL D'BONNEAU
STOP SIGN ABS
STOP STARTING TO START STOPPING (EP) D.O.P.
STOP STOP STOP HOLLIES
STOP THAT GIRL CHRIS ANDREWS
STOP THE CAVALRY JONA LEWIE
STOP THE ROCK APOLLO FOUR FORTY
STOP THE VIOLENCE BOOGIE DOWN PRODUCTIONS
STOP THE WAR NOW EDWIN STARR
STOP THE WORLD EXTREME
STOP THIS CRAZY THING COLDCUT FEATURING JUNIOR REID & THE AHEAD OF OUR TIME ORCHESTRA
STOP TO LOVE LUTHER VANDROSS
STOP YOUR CRYING SPIRITUALIZED
STOP YOUR SOBBING PRETENDERS
STORIES [A] IZIT
STORIES [B] THERAPY?
STORIES [C] HOLIDAY PLAN

STORIES OF JOHNNY MARC ALMOND
STORM [A] SPACE KITTENS
STORM [B] VANESSA-MAE
STORM [C] STORM
THE STORM WORLD OF TWIST
STORM ANIMAL STORM
STORM IN A TEACUP FORTUNES
THE STORM IS OVER R KELLY
STORMS IN AFRICA (PART II) ENYA
STORMTROOPER IN DRAG PAUL GARDINER
STORMY IN THE NORTHA KARMA IN THE SOUTH
    WILDHEARTS
THE STORY OF LOVE OTT
STORY OF MY LIFE [A] GARY MILLER
THE STORY OF MY LIFE [A] MICHAEL HOLLIDAY
THE STORY OF MY LIFE [A] DAVE KING
THE STORY OF MY LIFE [A] ALMA COGAN
THE STORY OF MY LIFE [B] KRISTIAN LEONTIOU
STORY OF MY LOVE CONWAY TWITTY
THE STORY OF THE BLUES [A] WAH!
STORY OF THE BLUES [B] GARY MOORE
STORY OF TINA RONNIE HARRIS
THE STORY OF TINA AL MARTINO
STOWAWAY BARBARA LYON
STRAIGHT AHEAD [A] KOOL & THE GANG
STRAIGHT AHEAD [B] TUBE & BERGER FEATURING
    CHRISSIE HYNDE
STRAIGHT AT YER HEAD LIONROCK
STRAIGHT FROM THE HEART [A] BRYAN ADAMS
STRAIGHT FROM THE HEART [B] DOOLALLY
STRAIGHT LINES NEW MUSIK
STRAIGHT OUT OF THE JUNGLE JUNGLE BROTHERS
STRAIGHT TO HELL CLASH
STRAIGHT TO MY FEET HAMMER FEATURING DEION
    SAUNDERS
STRAIGHT TO THE HEART REAL THING
STRAIGHT TO YOU NICK CAVE & THE BAD SEEDS
STRAIGHT UP [A] PAULA ABDUL
STRAIGHT UP [B] CHANTE MOORE
STRAIGHT UP NO BENDS BRIAN HARVEY
STRAIGHTEN OUT STRANGLERS
STRANDED [A] HEART
STRANDED [B] DEEP DISH
STRANDED [C] LUTRICIA McNEAL
STRANGE WET WET WET
STRANGE AND BEAUTIFUL AQUALUNG
STRANGE BAND FAMILY
STRANGE BREW CREAM
STRANGE CURRENCIES R.E.M.
STRANGE GLUE CATATONIA
STRANGE KIND OF LOVE LOVE & MONEY
STRANGE KIND OF WOMAN DEEP PURPLE
STRANGE LADY IN TOWN FRANKIE LAINE
STRANGE LITTLE GIRL [A] SAD CAFÉ
STRANGE LITTLE GIRL [B] STRANGLERS
STRANGE MAGIC ELECTRIC LIGHT ORCHESTRA
STRANGE RELATIONSHIP DARREN HAYES
STRANGE TOWN JAM
STRANGE WAY ALL ABOUT EVE
STRANGE WORLD [A] KE
STRANGE WORLD [B] PUSH
STRANGELOVE DEPECHE MODE
STRANGER SHAKATAK
THE STRANGER SHADOWS
STRANGER IN A STRANGE LAND IRON MAIDEN
STRANGER IN MOSCOW MICHAEL JACKSON
STRANGER IN PARADISE TONY BENNETT
STRANGER IN PARADISE DON CORNELL
STRANGER IN PARADISE TONY MARTIN
STRANGER IN PARADISE BING CROSBY
STRANGER IN PARADISE EDDIE CALVERT

STRANGER IN PARADISE FOUR ACES
STRANGER IN TOWN DEL SHANNON
A STRANGER ON HOME GROUND FAITH BROTHERS
STRANGER ON THE SHORE MR ACKER BILK WITH THE
    LEON YOUNG STRING CHORALE
STRANGER ON THE SHORE ANDY WILLIAMS
STRANGER ON THE SHORE OF LOVE STEVIE WONDER
STRANGER THINGS ABC
STRANGERS IN OUR TOWN SPEAR OF DESTINY
STRANGERS IN THE NIGHT FRANK SINATRA
STRANGERS WHEN WE MEET DAVID BOWIE
THE STRANGEST PARTY (THESE ARE THE TIMES) INXS
THE STRANGEST THING '97 GEORGE MICHAEL
STRANGLEHOLD U.K. SUBS
STRASBOURG RAKES
STRATEGIC HAMLETS URUSEI YATSURA
STRAW DOGS STIFF LITTLE FINGERS
STRAWBERRY NICOLA RENEE
STRAWBERRY BLONDE (THE BAND PLAYED ON) FRANK
    D'RONE
STRAWBERRY FAIR ANTHONY NEWLEY
STRAWBERRY FIELDS FOREVER BEATLES
STRAWBERRY FIELDS FOREVER CANDY FLIP
STRAWBERRY KISSES NIKKI WEBSTER
STRAWBERRY LETTER 23 BROTHERS JOHNSON
STRAY CAT STRUT STRAY CATS
THE STREAK RAY STEVENS
STREAMLINE TRAIN VIPERS SKIFFLE GROUP
STREET CAFÉ ICEHOUSE
A STREET CALLED HOPE GENE PITNEY
STREET DANCE BREAK MACHINE
STREET DREAMS NAS
STREET FIGHTER II WORLD WARRIOR
STREET FIGHTING MAN ROLLING STONES
STREET GANG A.R.E. WEAPONS
STREET LIFE [A] ROXY MUSIC
STREET LIFE [B] CRUSADERS
STREET LIFE [C] BEENIE MAN
STREET OF DREAMS RAINBOW
STREET SPIRIT (FADE OUT) RADIOHEAD
STREET TUFF DOUBLE TROUBLE & THE REBEL MC
STREETPLAYER (MECHANIK) FASHION
THE STREETS WC FEATURING SNOOP DOGG & NATE
    DOGG
STREETS OF LONDON RALPH McTELL
STREETS OF LONDON ANTI-NOWHERE LEAGUE
STREETS OF PHILADELPHIA BRUCE SPRINGSTEEN
STREETWALKIN' SHAKATAK
STRENGTH ALARM
STRENGTH TO STRENGTH HUE & CRY
STRESS BLAGGERS I.T.A.
STRESSED OUT A TRIBE CALLED QUEST FEATURING
    FAITH EVANS & RAPHAEL SAADIQ
STRETCHIN' OUT GAYLE ADAMS
STRICT MACHINE GOLDFRAPP
STRICTLY BUSINESS MANTRONIK VS EPMD
STRICTLY ELVIS EP ELVIS PRESLEY
STRICTLY HARDCORE GOLD BLADE
STRICTLY SOCIAL RONI SIZE
STRIKE IT DUB WAR
STRIKE IT UP BLACK BOX
STRIKE ME PINK DEBORAH HARRY
STRINGS KRISTIN HERSH
STRINGS FOR YASMIN TIN TIN OUT
STRINGS OF LIFE [A] RHYTHIM IS RHYTHIM
STRINGS OF LIFE [B] PLANK 15
STRIP ADAM ANT
STRIPPED DEPECHE MODE
THE STROKE BILLY SQUIER
STROKE YOU UP CHANGING FACES
STROLLIN' PRINCE & THE NEW POWER GENERATION

STROLLIN' ON MAXI PRIEST
STRONG [A] LIQUID
STRONG [B] ROBBIE WILLIAMS
STRONG ARM OF THE LAW SAXON
STRONG AS STEEL FIVE STAR
STRONG ENOUGH [A] SHERYL CROW
STRONG ENOUGH [B] CHER
STRONG IN LOVE CHICANE FEATURING MASON
STRONG LOVE SPENCER DAVIS GROUP
STRONGER [A] GARY BARLOW
STRONGER [B] BRITNEY SPEARS
STRONGER [C] SUGABABES
STRONGER THAN ME AMY WINEHOUSE
STRONGER THAN THAT CLIFF RICHARD
STRONGER TOGETHER [A] SHANNON
STRONGER TOGETHER [B] SYBIL
STRUMMIN' CHAS & DAVE WITH ROCKNEY
STRUMPET MY LIFE STORY
STRUNG OUT [A] WENDY & LISA
STRUNG OUT [B] DOT ALLISON
STRUT YOUR FUNKY STUFF FRANTIQUE
THE STRUTT BAMBOO
STUCK [A] NED'S ATOMIC DUSTBIN
STUCK [B] STACIE ORRICO
STUCK IN A GROOVE PURETONE
STUCK IN A MOMENT YOU CAN'T GET OUT OF U2
STUCK IN THE MIDDLE [A] DANNI'ELLE GAHA
STUCK IN THE MIDDLE [B] CLEA
STUCK IN THE MIDDLE WITH YOU STEALERS WHEEL
STUCK IN THE MIDDLE WITH YOU LOUISE
STUCK ON U [A] PJ & DUNCAN
STUCK ON YOU [B] ELVIS PRESLEY
STUCK ON YOU [C] LIONEL RICHIE
STUCK ON YOU [C] TREVOR WALTERS
STUCK WITH ME GREEN DAY
STUCK WITH YOU HUEY LEWIS & THE NEWS
STUFF LIKE THAT QUINCY JONES
STUMBLE AND FALL RAZORLIGHT
STUMBLIN' IN SUZI QUATRO & CHRIS NORMAN
STUNT 101 G UNIT
STUNTMAN ALFIE
STUPID CUPID CONNIE FRANCIS
STUPID GIRL GARBAGE
STUPID KID [A] SULTANS OF PING FC
STUPID KID [B] ALKALINE TRIO
THE STUPID ONES BLUESKINS
STUPID QUESTION NEW MODEL ARMY
STUPID THING AIMEE MANN
STUPIDISCO JUNIOR JACK
STUTTER JOE FEATURING MYSTIKAL
STUTTER RAP (NO SLEEP 'TIL BEDTIME) MORRIS
    MINOR & THE MAJORS
STYLE [A] ORBITAL
STYLE [B] MIS-TEEQ
SUB-CULTURE NEW ORDER
SUBDIVISIONS RUSH
SUBHUMAN GARBAGE
SUBMARINES DJ FRESH
SUBPLATES VOLUME 1 (EP) VARIOUS ARTISTS (EP'S &
    LPS)
SUBSTITUTE [A] WHO
SUBSTITUTE [B] CLOUT
SUBSTITUTE [C] LIQUID GOLD
SUBTERRANEAN HOMESICK BLUES BOB DYLAN
SUBURBAN ROCK 'N' ROLL SPACE
SUBURBIA PET SHOP BOYS
SUCCESS [A] SIGUE SIGUE SPUTNIK
SUCCESS [B] DANNII MINOGUE
SUCCESS HAS MADE A FAILURE OF OUR HOME SINEAD
    O'CONNOR
SUCH A FEELING BIZARRE INC

SUCH A GOOD FEELING BROTHERS IN RHYTHM
SUCH A GOOD FEELIN' MISS BEHAVIN'
SUCH A NIGHT JOHNNIE RAY
SUCH A NIGHT ELVIS PRESLEY
SUCH A PHANTASY TIME FREQUENCY
SUCH A SHAME TALK TALK
SUCK YOU DRY MUDHONEY
SUCKER DJ DIMPLES D
SUCKERPUNCH WILDHEARTS
SUCU SUCU LAURIE JOHNSON ORCHESTRA
SUCU SUCU TED HEATH
SUCU SUCU NINA & FREDERICK
SUCU SUCU JOE LOSS ORCHESTRA
SUCU SUCU PING PING & AL VERLANE
SUDDENLY [A] OLIVIA NEWTON-JOHN & CLIFF
    RICHARD
SUDDENLY [B] BILLY OCEAN
SUDDENLY [C] ANGRY ANDERSON
SUDDENLY [D] SEAN MAGUIRE
SUDDENLY [E] LeANN RIMES
SUDDENLY THERE'S A VALLEY PETULA CLARK
SUDDENLY THERE'S A VALLEY LEE LAWRENCE WITH RAY
    MARTIN & HIS ORCHESTRA
SUDDENLY THERE'S A VALLEY JO STAFFORD
SUDDENLY YOU LOVE ME TREMELOES
SUEDEHEAD MORRISSEY
SUENO LATINO SUENO LATINO FEATURING CAROLINA
    DAMAS
SUE'S GOTTA BE MINE DEL SHANNON
SUFFER NEVER FINN
SUFFER THE CHILDREN TEARS FOR FEARS
SUFFOCATE [A] FEEDER
SUFFOCATE [B] KING ADORA
SUGAH RUBY AMANFU
SUGAR AND SPICE SEARCHERS
SUGAR BABY LOVE RUBETTES
SUGAR BEE CANNED HEAT
SUGAR BOX THEN JERICO
SUGAR BRIDGE (IT WILL STAND) BLUEBELLS
SUGAR CANDY KISSES MAC & KATIE KISSOON
SUGAR COATED ICEBERG LIGHTNING SEEDS
SUGAR DADDY SECRET KNOWLEDGE
SUGAR DOLL JETS
SUGAR FOR THE SOUL STEVE BALSAMO
SUGAR FREE JUICY
SUGAR FREE PAULINE HENRY
SUGAR HONEY ICE TEA GOODFELLAZ
SUGAR IS SWEETER C J BOLLAND
SUGAR KANE SONIC YOUTH
SUGAR ME LYNSEY DE PAUL
SUGAR MICE MARILLION
SUGAR MOON PAT BOONE
SUGAR RUSH MAN WITH NO NAME
SUGAR SHACK [A] JIMMY GILMER & THE FIREBALLS
SUGAR SHACK [B] SEB
SUGAR SUGAR ARCHIES
SUGAR SUGAR SAKKARIN
SUGAR SUGAR DUKE BAYSEE
SUGAR TOWN NANCY SINATRA
SUGARBUSH DORIS DAY & FRANKIE LAINE
SUGARHILL AZ
SUGARMAN FREE ASSOCIATION
SUGARTIME ALMA COGAN
SUGARTIME McGUIRE SISTERS
SUGARTIME JIM DALE
SUICIDE BLONDE INXS
SUKIYAKI KENNY BALL & HIS JAZZMEN
SUKIYAKI KYU SAKAMOTO
SULKY GIRL ELVIS COSTELLO & THE ATTRACTIONS
SULTANA TITANIC
SULTANS OF SWING DIRE STRAITS

SUMAHAMA BEACH BOYS
SUMATRAN SOFT PARADE
SUMERLAND (DREAMED) FIELDS OF THE NEPHILIM
SUMMER CHARLOTTE HATHERLEY
SUMMER '89 CALIFORNIA SUNSHINE
SUMMER BREEZE ISLEY BROTHERS
SUMMER BREEZE GEOFFREY WILLIAMS
SUMMER BUNNIES R KELLY
SUMMER EDITION NUKLEUZ DJs
SUMMER FUN BARRACUDAS
SUMMER GIRLS LYTE FUNKIE ONES
SUMMER GONNA COME AGAIN SUPERSISTER
SUMMER HOLIDAY CLIFF RICHARD & THE SHADOWS
SUMMER HOLIDAY KEVIN THE GERBIL
SUMMER HOLIDAY (EP) ZZ TOP
SUMMER HOLIDAY MEDLEY DARREN DAY
SUMMER IN SIAM POGUES
SUMMER IN SPACE COSMOS
SUMMER IN THE CITY LOVIN' SPOONFUL
THE SUMMER IS MAGIC EXOTICA FEATURING ITSY
    FOSTER
SUMMER IS OVER FRANK IFIELD
SUMMER JAM UD PROJECT
SUMMER MADNESS KOOL & THE GANG
SUMMER MOVED ON A-HA
SUMMER NIGHT CITY ABBA
SUMMER NIGHTS [A] MARIANNE FAITHFULL
SUMMER NIGHTS [B] JOHN TRAVOLTA & OLIVIA
    NEWTON-JOHN
SUMMER OF '42 BIDDU ORCHESTRA
SUMMER OF 69 BRYAN ADAMS
SUMMER OF LOVE (COMME CI COMME CA) [A] LONYO
    – COMME CI COMME CA
SUMMER OF LOVE [B] STEPS
SUMMER OF MY LIFE SIMON MAY
THE SUMMER OF SEVENTEENTH DOLL WINIFRED
    ATWELL
SUMMER ON THE UNDERGROUND A
SUMMER RAIN BELINDA CARLISLE
SUMMER SET MR ACKER BILK & HIS PARAMOUNT JAZZ
    BAND
SUMMER SON TEXAS
SUMMER SONG BEDAZZLED
SUMMER SUNSHINE CORRS
SUMMER (THE FIRST TIME) BOBBY GOLDSBORO
SUMMER WIND FRANK SINATRA
SUMMERLANDS BEIJING SPRING
SUMMERLOVE SENSATION BAY CITY ROLLERS
SUMMER'S MAGIC MARK SUMMERS
SUMMER'S OVER RIALTO
SUMMERSAULT TASTE XPERIENCE FEATURING
    NATASHA PEARL
SUMMERTIME [A] AL MARTINO
SUMMERTIME [A] MARCELS
SUMMERTIME [A] BILLY STEWART
SUMMERTIME [A] FUN BOY THREE
SUMMERTIME [B] DJ JAZZY JEFF & THE FRESH PRINCE
SUMMERTIME [C] SUNDAYS
SUMMERTIME [D] ANOTHER LEVEL FEATURING TQ
SUMMERTIME BLUES EDDIE COCHRAN
SUMMERTIME BLUES WHO
SUMMERTIME CITY MIKE BATT WITH THE NEW
    EDITION
SUMMERTIME HEALING EUSEBE
SUMMERTIME OF OUR LIVES A1
SUMTHIN' SUMTHIN' THE MANTRA MAXWELL
SUN [A] VIRUS
SUN [B] JOHN LYDON
SUN [C] SLUSNIK LUNA
THE SUN AIN'T GONNA SHINE ANYMORE WALKER
    BROTHERS

THE SUN AIN'T GONNA SHINE ANYMORE CHER
THE SUN ALWAYS SHINES ON TV A-HA
THE SUN ALWAYS SHINES ON TV DIVA
THE SUN AND THE RAIN MADNESS
SUN ARISE ROLF HARRIS
SUN CITY ARTISTS UNITED AGAINST APARTHEID
THE SUN DOES RISE JAH WOBBLE'S INVADERS OF THE
    HEART
THE SUN DOESN'T SHINE BEATS INTERNATIONAL
THE SUN GOES DOWN THIN LIZZY
THE SUN GOES DOWN (LIVING IT UP) LEVEL 42
THE SUN HAS COME YOUR WAY SAM & MARK
SUN HITS THE SKY SUPERGRASS
SUN IS SHINING [A] TECHNIQUE
SUN IS SHINING [B] BOB MARLEY VERSUS FUNKSTAR
    DE LUXE
THE SUN IS SHINING (DOWN ON ME) DT8 PROJECT
SUN KING CULT
THE SUN MACHINE E-ZEE POSSEE
SUN OF JAMAICA GOOMBAY DANCE BAND
THE SUN RISING BELOVED
SUN SHINING DOWN CIRCA FEATURING DESTRY
SUN STREET KATRINA & THE WAVES
SUN WORSHIPPERS (POSITIVE THINKING) DIANA
    BROWN & BARRIE K. SHARPE
SUNBURN GRAHAM GOULDMAN
SUNBURN [A] MICHELLE COLLINS
SUNBURN [B] MUSE
SUNCHYME DARIO G
SUNDANCE SUNDANCE
SUNDAY [A] BUSTER
SUNDAY [B] SONIC YOUTH
SUNDAY GIRL BLONDIE
SUNDAY MORNING [A] NO DOUBT
SUNDAY MORNING [B] MAROON 5
SUNDAY MORNING CALL OASIS
SUNDAY MORNINGS VANESSA PARADIS
SUNDAY SHINING FINLEY QUAYE
SUNDAY SHOUTIN' JOHNNY CORPORATE
SUNDAY SUNDAY BLUR
SUNDOWN [A] GORDON LIGHTFOOT
SUNDOWN [A] ELWOOD
SUNDOWN [B] S CLUB 8
SUNFLOWER PAUL WELLER
SUNGLASSES TRACEY ULLMAN
SUNGLASSES AT NIGHT TIGA & ZYNTHERIUS
SUNLIGHT DJ SAMMY
SUNMACHINE DARIO G
SUNNY [A] BOBBY HEBB
SUNNY [A] CHER
SUNNY [A] GEORGIE FAME
SUNNY [A] BONEY M
SUNNY [A] BOOGIE PIMPS
SUNNY [B] MORRISSEY
SUNNY AFTERNOON KINKS
SUNNY CAME HOME SHAWN COLVIN
SUNNY DAY PIGBAG
SUNNY HONEY GIRL CLIFF RICHARD
SUNRISE [A] MOVEMENT 98 FEATURING CARROLL
    THOMPSON
SUNRISE [B] GOLDENSCAN
SUNRISE [C] PULP
SUNRISE [D] SIMPLY RED
SUNRISE [E] NORAH JONES
SUNRISE (HERE I AM) RATTY
SUNSET NITIN SAWHNEY FEATURING ESKA
SUNSET AND BABYLON W.A.S.P.
SUNSET (BIRD OF PREY) FATBOY SLIM
SUNSET BOULEVARD MICHAEL BALL
SUNSET NOW HEAVEN 17
SUNSET ON IBIZA THREE DRIVES ON A VINYL

SUNSET PEOPLE DONNA SUMMER
SUNSHINE [A] WARREN MILLS
SUNSHINE [B] UMBOZA
SUNSHINE [C] JAY-Z FEATURING BABYFACE & FOXY
SUNSHINE [D] GABRIELLE
SUNSHINE [E] ALEXANDER O'NEAL
SUNSHINE [F] YOMANDA
SUNSHINE [G] GARETH GATES
SUNSHINE [H] HOLIDAY PLAN
SUNSHINE [I] TWISTA
SUNSHINE [J] LIL' FLIP
SUNSHINE AFTER THE RAIN ELKIE BROOKS
THE SUNSHINE AFTER THE RAIN NEW ATLANTIC/U4EA
    FEATURING BERRI
THE SUNSHINE AFTER THE RAIN BERRI
SUNSHINE & HAPPINESS DARRYL PANDY/NERIO'S
    DUBWORK
SUNSHINE AND LOVE HAPPY MONDAYS
SUNSHINE DAY OSIBISA
SUNSHINE DAY CLOCK
SUNSHINE GIRL HERMAN'S HERMITS
SUNSHINE OF LOVE LOUIS ARMSTRONG
SUNSHINE OF YOUR LOVE CREAM
THE SUNSHINE OF YOUR SMILE MIKE BERRY
SUNSHINE ON A RAINY DAY ZOE
SUNSHINE ON A RAINY DAY REAL & RICHARDSON
    FEATURING JOBABE
SUNSHINE ON LEITH PROCLAIMERS
SUNSHINE PLAYROOM JULIAN COPE
SUNSHINE SUPERMAN DONOVAN
SUNSTORM HURLEY & TODD
SUNSTROKE CHICANE
SUNTAN STAN
SUPER BOWL SUNDAE OZOMATLI
SUPER DUPER LOVE (ARE YOU DIGGIN ON ME) JOSS
    STONE
SUPER GRAN BILLY CONNOLLY
SUPER LOVE WIGAN'S OVATION
SUPER POPOID GROOVE WIN
SUPER TROUPER ABBA
SUPER TROUPER A*TEENS
SUPER WOMBLE WOMBLES
SUPERBAD SUPERSLICK REDHEAD KINGPIN & THE FBI
SUPERFLY 1990 CURTIS MAYFIELD & ICE-T
SUPERFLY GUY S-EXPRESS
SUPERFREAKON MISSY ELLIOTT
SUPERGIRL GRAHAM BONNEY
SUPERHERO REEF
SUPERMAN (GIOCA JOUER) BLACK LACE
SUPERMAN (IT'S NOT EASY) FIVE FOR FIGHTING
SUPERMAN'S BIG SISTER IAN DURY & THE
    BLOCKHEADS
SUPERMARIOLAND AMBASSADORS OF FUNK
    FEATURING MC MARIO
SUPERMARKET SWEEP (WILL YOU DANCE WITH ME)
    BAR CODES FEATURING ALISON BROWN
SUPERMODEL (YOU BETTER WORK) RuPAUL
SUPERNATURAL KIM ENGLISH
SUPERNATURAL GIVER KINKY MACHINE
SUPERNATURAL THING FREELAND
SUPERNATURE CERRONE
SUPERNOVA FIVE THIRTY
SUPERSHIP GEORGE 'BAD' BENSON
SUPERSONIC [A] HWA FEATURING SONIC THE
    HEDGEHOG
SUPERSONIC [B] OASIS
SUPERSONIC [C] JAMIROQUAI
SUPERSONIC ROCKET SHIP KINKS
SUPERSTAR [A] CARPENTERS
SUPERSTAR [A] SONIC YOUTH
SUPERSTAR [B] MURRAY HEAD

SUPERSTAR [C] LYDIA MURDOCK
SUPERSTAR [D] NOVY VERSUS ENIAC
SUPERSTAR [E] SUPERSTAR
SUPERSTAR [F] ONES
SUPERSTAR [G] JAMELIA
SUPERSTAR (REMEMBER HOW YOU GOT WHERE YOU
    ARE) TEMPTATIONS
SUPERSTITION STEVIE WONDER
SUPERSTITION – GOOD TIMES (MEDLEY) CLUBHOUSE
SUPERSTITIOUS EUROPE
SUPERSTRING CYGNUS X
SUPERSTYLIN' GROOVE ARMADA
SUPERWOMAN KARYN WHITE
SUPPORT THE TOON – IT'S YOUR DUTY (EP) MUNGO
    JERRY & TOON TRAVELLERS
SUPREME ROBBIE WILLIAMS
THE SUPREME EP SINITTA
SURE TAKE THAT
SURE SHOT BEASTIE BOYS
SURE THING DARLING BUDS
SURF CITY JAN & DEAN
SURFIN' USA BEACH BOYS
SURFIN' USA AARON CARTER
SURPRISE BIZARRE INC
SURPRISE SURPRISE CENTRAL LINE
SURRENDER [A] ELVIS PRESLEY
SURRENDER [B] DIANA ROSS
SURRENDER [C] SWING OUT SISTER
SURRENDER [D] ROGER TAYLOR
SURRENDER [E] LASGO
SURRENDER YOUR LOVE [A] NIGHTCRAWLERS
SURRENDER (YOUR LOVE) [B] JAVINE
SURROUND YOURSELF WITH SORROW CILLA BLACK
SURVIVAL CAR FOUNTAINS OF WAYNE
SURVIVE DAVID BOWIE
SURVIVOR DESTINY'S CHILD
SUSANNA ART COMPANY
SUSANNAH'S STILL ALIVE DAVE DAVIES
SUSAN'S HOUSE EELS
SUSIE DARLIN' ROBIN LUKE
SUSIE DARLIN' TOMMY ROE
SUSPICION TERRY STAFFORD
SUSPICION ELVIS PRESLEY
SUSPICIOUS MINDS ELVIS PRESLEY
SUSPICIOUS MINDS CANDI STATON
SUSPICIOUS MINDS FINE YOUNG CANNIBALS
SUSPICIOUS MINDS GARETH GATES
SUSSUDIO PHIL COLLINS
SUZANNE BEWARE OF THE DEVIL DANDY LIVINGSTONE
SVEN SVEN SVEN BELL & SPURLING
SW LIVE EP PETER GABRIEL
SWALLOW MY PRIDE RAMONES
SWALLOWED BUSH
SWAMP THING GRID
SWAN LAKE CATS
SWASTIKA EYES PRIMAL SCREAM
SWAY [A] DEAN MARTIN
SWAY [A] BOBBY RYDELL
SWAY [B] STRANGELOVE
SWEAR IT AGAIN WESTLIFE
SWEARIN' TO GOD FRANKIE VALLI
SWEAT USURA
SWEAT (A LA LA LA LA LONG) INNER CIRCLE
SWEAT IN A BULLET SIMPLE MINDS
SWEATING BULLETS MEGADETH
SWEDISH RHAPSODY MANTOVANI
SWEDISH RHAPSODY RAY MARTIN
SWEET AND LOW DEBORAH HARRY
SWEET BABY MACY GRAY FEATURING ERYKAH BADU
SWEET BIRD OF TRUTH THE THE
SWEET CAROLINE NEIL DIAMOND

SWEET CATATONIA CATATONIA
SWEET CHEATIN' RITA ALVIN STARDUST
SWEET CHILD O' MINE GUNS N' ROSES
SWEET CHILD O' MINE SHERYL CROW
SWEET DANGER ANGELWITCH
SWEET DREAM JETHRO TULL
SWEET DREAMS [A] DAVE SAMPSON
SWEET DREAMS [B] SWING FEATURING DR ALBAN
SWEET DREAMS [B] DJ SCOTT FEATURING LORNA B
SWEET DREAMS [C] TOMMY McLAIN
SWEET DREAMS [C] ROY BUCHANAN
SWEET DREAMS [C] ELVIS COSTELLO
SWEET DREAMS [D] LA BOUCHE
SWEET DREAMS (ARE MADE OF THIS) EURYTHMICS
SWEET DREAMS MY LA EX RACHEL STEVENS
SWEET EMOTION AEROSMITH
SWEET FREEDOM [A] MICHAEL McDONALD
SWEET FREEDOM [A] SAFRI DUO FEATURING MICHAEL
    McDONALD
SWEET FREEDOM [B] POSITIVE GANG
SWEET FREEDOM PART 2 POSITIVE GANG
SWEET HARMONY [A] LIQUID
SWEET HARMONY [B] BELOVED
SWEET HEART CONTRACT MAGAZINE
SWEET HITCH-HIKER CREEDENCE CLEARWATER
    REVIVAL
SWEET HOME ALABAMA LYNYRD SKYNYRD
SWEET ILLUSION JUNIOR CAMPBELL
SWEET IMPOSSIBLE YOU BRENDA LEE
SWEET INSPIRATION JOHNNY JOHNSON & THE
    BANDWAGON
SWEET INVISIBILITY HUE & CRY
SWEET JOHNNY GORKY'S ZYGOTIC MYNCI
SWEET LADY TYRESE
SWEET LADY LUCK WHITESNAKE
SWEET LEAF MAGOO : MOGWAI
SWEET LIES [A] ROBERT PALMER
SWEET LIES [B] ELLIE CAMPBELL
SWEET LIKE CHOCOLATE SHANKS & BIGFOOT
SWEET LIPS MONACO
SWEET LITTLE MYSTERY WET WET WET
SWEET LITTLE ROCK 'N' ROLLER SHOWADDYWADDY
SWEET LITTLE SIXTEEN CHUCK BERRY
SWEET LITTLE SIXTEEN JERRY LEE LEWIS
SWEET LOVE [A] COMMODORES
SWEET LOVE [B] ANITA BAKER
SWEET LOVE [B] M-BEAT FEATURING NAZLYN
SWEET LOVE 2K [B] FIERCE
SWEET LUI-LOUISE IRONHORSE
SWEET LULLABY DEEP FOREST
SWEET MEMORY BELLE STARS
SWEET MUSIC SHOWADDYWADDY
SWEET N SOUR JON SPENCER BLUES EXPLOSION
SWEET NOTHIN'S BRENDA LEE
SWEET NOTHINS SEARCHERS
SWEET OLD-FASHIONED GIRL TERESA BREWER
SWEET PEA MANFRED MANN
SWEET PEA, MY SWEET PEA PAUL WELLER
SWEET POTATO PIE DOMINO
SWEET REVENGE SPOOKS
SWEET REVIVAL (KEEP IT COMIN') SHADES OF RHYTHM
SWEET SENSATION [A] MELODIANS
SWEET SENSATION [B] SHADES OF RHYTHM
SWEET SENSATION [C] SHABOOM
SWEET SENSUAL LOVE BIG MOUNTAIN
SWEET SHOP AVENGERZ BIS
SWEET SISTER PEACE BY PIECE
SWEET SIXTEEN BILLY IDOL
SWEET SMELL OF SUCCESS STRANGLERS
SWEET SOMEBODY SHANNON
SWEET SOUL MUSIC ARTHUR CONLEY

SWEET SOUL SENSATIONS LIGHTNING SEEDS
SWEET SOUL SISTER CULT
SWEET STUFF GUY MITCHELL
SWEET SUBURBIA SKIDS
SWEET SURRENDER [A] ROD STEWART
SWEET SURRENDER [B] WET WET WET
SWEET SWEET SMILE CARPENTERS
SWEET TALKIN' GUY CHIFFONS
SWEET TALKIN' WOMAN ELECTRIC LIGHT ORCHESTRA
SWEET THANG JONESTOWN
SWEET THING MICK JAGGER
SWEET TOXIC LOVE JESUS LOVES YOU
SWEET UNDERSTANDING LOVE FOUR TOPS
SWEET WILLIAM MILLIE
SWEETER THAN THE MIDNIGHT RAIN LUKE GOSS & THE
    BAND OF THIEVES
SWEETER THAN WINE DIONNE RAKEEM
SWEETER THAN YOU RICKY NELSON
SWEETEST CHILD MARIA McKEE
SWEETEST DAY OF MAY JOE T VANNELLI PROJECT
THE SWEETEST DAYS VANESSA WILLIAMS
SWEETEST GIRL MADNESS
THE SWEETEST GIRL SCRITTI POLITTI
THE SWEETEST SURRENDER FACTORY OF UNLIMITED
    RHYTHM
SWEETEST SWEETEST JERMAINE JACKSON
THE SWEETEST TABOO SADE
SWEETEST THING GENE LOVES JEZEBEL
THE SWEETEST THING [A] REFUGEE ALLSTARS
    FEATURING LAURYN HILL
SWEETEST THING [B] U2
SWEETHEART ENGELBERT HUMPERDINCK
SWEETIE PIE EDDIE COCHRAN
SWEETNESS [A] MICHELLE GAYLE
SWEETNESS [B] XSTASIA
SWEETNESS [C] JIMMY EAT WORLD
SWEETNESS AND LIGHT LUSH
SWEETS WORLD OF TWIST
SWEETS FOR MY SWEET SEARCHERS
SWEETS FOR MY SWEET C.J. LEWIS
SWEETSMOKE MR SCRUFF
SWEETY REEF
SWIM FISHBONE
SWIMMING HORSES SIOUXSIE & THE BANSHEES
SWING LOW UB40 FEATURING UNITED COLOURS OF
    SOUND
SWING LOW '99 RUSSELL WATSON
SWING LOW (RUN WITH THE BALL) UNION FEATURING
    THE ENGLAND WORLD CUP SQUAD
SWING LOW SWEET CHARIOT ERIC CLAPTON
SWING LOW SWEET CHARIOT LADYSMITH BLACK
    MAMBAZO FEATURING CHINA BLACK
SWING MY HIPS (SEX DANCE) LEMONESCENT
SWING MY WAY KP & ENVYI
SWING SWING ALL-AMERICAN REJECTS
SWING THAT HAMMER MIKE COTTON'S JAZZMEN
SWING THE MOOD JIVE BUNNY & THE MASTERMIXERS
SWING YOUR DADDY JIM GILSTRAP
SWINGIN' LIGHT OF THE WORLD
SWINGIN' LOW OUTLAWS
SWINGIN' SHEPHERD BLUES TED HEATH
SWINGIN' SHEPHERD BLUES MOE KOFFMAN
    QUARTETTE
SWINGIN' SHEPHERD BLUES ELLA FITZGERALD
SWINGING IN THE RAIN NORMAN VAUGHAN
SWINGING ON A STAR BIG DEE IRWIN
SWINGING SCHOOL BOBBY RYDELL
SWINGS & ROUNDABOUTS RONI SIZE
SWISS MAID DEL SHANNON
SWITCH [A] BENELUX & NANCY DEE

SWITCH [B] SENSER
SWITCH [C] HOWIE B
SWITCH [D] PESHAY
THE SWITCH [E] PLANET FUNK
SWITCHED ON SWING KINGS OF SWING ORCHESTRA
SWOON MISSION
SWORDS OF A THOUSAND MEN TEN POLE TUDOR
SYLVIA FOCUS
SYLVIA'S MOTHER DR. HOOK & THE MEDICINE SHOW
SYLVIE SAINT ETIENNE
SYMMETRY C BRAINCHILD
SYMPATHY [A] RARE BIRD
SYMPATHY [B] MARILLION
SYMPATHY FOR THE DEVIL GUNS N' ROSES
SYMPATHY FOR THE DEVIL ROLLING STONES
SYMPHONY DONELL RUSH
SYMPHONY OF DESTRUCTION MEGADETH
SYNAESTHESIA (FLY AWAY) THRILLSEEKERS FEATURING
    SHERYL DEANE
SYNCHRONICITY II POLICE
SYNERGY TRANCESETTERS
SYNTH & STRINGS YOMANDA
SYSTEM ADDICT FIVE STAR
SYSTEM CHECK BROCKIE/ED SOLO
SYSTEM OF SURVIVAL EARTH, WIND & FIRE
T-10/THE TENTH PLANET DISTORTED MINDS
THE TABLE BEAUTIFUL SOUTH
TABOO GLAMMA KID FEATURING SHOLA AMA
TACKY LOVE SONG CREDIT TO THE NATION
TAHITI DAVID ESSEX
TAINTED LOVE SOFT CELL
TAINTED LOVE IMPEDANCE
TAINTED LOVE ICON
TAINTED LOVE MARILYN MANSON
TAKE COLOUR FIELD
TAKE A BOW MADONNA
TAKE A CHANCE ON ME ABBA
TAKE A CHANCE WITH ME ROXY MUSIC
TAKE A FREE FALL DANCE 2 TRANCE
TAKE A HEART SORROWS
(TAKE A LITTLE) PIECE OF MY HEART ERMA FRANKLIN
TAKE A LITTLE TIME (DOUBLE SINGLE) GARY MOORE
TAKE A LOOK LEVEL 42
TAKE A LOOK AROUND [A] TEMPTATIONS
TAKE A LOOK AROUND [B] LIMP BIZKIT
TAKE A LOOK AT YOURSELF COVERDALE PAGE
TAKE A MESSAGE TO MARY EVERLY BROTHERS
TAKE A PICTURE FILTER
TAKE A REST GANG STARR
TAKE A RUN AT THE SUN DINOSAUR Jr.
TAKE A TOKE C & C MUSIC FACTORY FEATURING
    MARTHA WASH
TAKE CALIFORNIA PROPELLERHEADS
TAKE CARE OF YOURSELF LEVEL 42
TAKE CONTROL [A] STATE OF MIND
TAKE CONTROL [B] JAIMESON FEATURING ANGEL BLU
    & CK
TAKE CONTROL OF THE PARTY BG THE PRINCE OF RAP
TAKE DOWN THE UNION JACK BILLY BRAGG & THE
    BLOKES
TAKE 5 [A] NORTHSIDE
TAKE FIVE [B] DAVE BRUBECK QUARTET
TAKE 4 (EP) MIKE OLDFIELD
TAKE GOOD CARE OF HER ADAM WADE
TAKE GOOD CARE OF MY BABY BOBBY VEE
TAKE GOOD CARE OF MY BABY SMOKIE
TAKE GOOD CARE OF MY HEART MICHAELA
TAKE GOOD CARE OF YOURSELF THREE DEGREES
TAKE IT FLOWERED UP
TAKE IT AND RUN BANDITS
TAKE IT AWAY PAUL McCARTNEY

TAKE IT BACK PINK FLOYD
TAKE IT EASY [A] LET LOOSE
TAKE IT EASY [B] MINT ROYALE
TAKE IT EASY [C] 3SL
TAKE IT EASY ON ME A HOUSE
TAKE IT FROM ME [A] ROGER CHRISTIAN
TAKE IT FROM ME [B] GIRLFRIEND
TAKE IT OFF DONNAS
TAKE IT ON THE RUN REO SPEEDWAGON
TAKE IT OR LEAVE IT SEARCHERS
TAKE IT SATCH EP LOUIS ARMSTRONG WITH HIS ALL-
    STARS
TAKE IT TO THE LIMIT EAGLES
TAKE IT TO THE STREETS RAMPAGE FEATURING BILLY
    LAWRENCE
TAKE IT TO THE TOP [A] KOOL & THE GANG
TAKE IT TO THE TOP [B] CLOUD
TAKE ME DREAM FREQUENCY
TAKE ME AWAY [A] TRUE FAITH WITH FINAL CUT
TAKE ME AWAY [A] CAPPELLA FEATURING LOLEATTA
    HOLLOWAY
TAKE ME AWAY [B] D:REAM
TAKE ME AWAY [C] CULTURE BEAT
TAKE ME AWAY (I'LL FOLLOW YOU) BAD BOYS INC
TAKE ME AWAY INTO THE NIGHT 4 STRINGS
TAKE ME AWAY (PARADISE) MIX FACTORY
TAKE ME BACK RHYTHMATIC
TAKE ME BACK TO LOVE AGAIN KATHY SLEDGE
TAKE ME BAK 'OME SLADE
TAKE ME BY THE HAND SUB MERGE FEATURING JAN
    JOHNSTON
TAKE ME DOWN TO THE RIVER SKIN
TAKE ME FOR A LITTLE WHILE COVERDALE PAGE
TAKE ME FOR WHAT I'M WORTH SEARCHERS
TAKE ME GIRL I'M READY JUNIOR WALKER & THE ALL-
    STARS
TAKE ME HIGH CLIFF RICHARD
TAKE ME HIGHER [A] RAF
TAKE ME HIGHER [B] DIANA ROSS
TAKE ME HIGHER [C] GEORGIE PORGIE
TAKE ME HOME [A] PHIL COLLINS
TAKE ME HOME [B] JOE COCKER FEATURING BEKKA
    BRAMLETT
TAKE ME HOME – MUTINY SOPHIE ELLIS-BEXTOR
TAKE ME HOME COUNTRY ROADS OLIVIA NEWTON-
    JOHN
TAKE ME I'M YOURS SQUEEZE
TAKE ME IN YOUR ARMS DOOBIE BROTHERS
TAKE ME IN YOUR ARMS AND LOVE ME GLADYS
    KNIGHT & THE PIPS
TAKE ME IN YOUR ARMS AND LOVE ME SCRITTI POLITTI
    & SWEETIE IRIE
TAKE ME NOW TAMMY PAYNE
TAKE ME OUT FRANZ FERDINAND
TAKE ME OVER McKAY
TAKE ME THERE BLACKstreet & MYA FEATURING MA$E
    & BLINKY BLINK
TAKE ME TO HEAVEN BABY D
TAKE ME TO THE CLOUDS ABOVE LMC VS U2
TAKE ME TO THE MARDI GRAS PAUL SIMON
TAKE ME TO THE NEXT PHASE ISLEY BROTHERS
TAKE ME TO YOUR HEART RICK ASTLEY
TAKE ME TO YOUR HEART AGAIN VINCE HILL
TAKE ME TO YOUR HEAVEN CHARLOTTE NILSSON
TAKE ME UP [A] SOUNDSOURCE
TAKE ME UP [B] SONIC SURFERS FEATURING JOCELYN
    BROWN
TAKE ME WITH YOU [A] PRINCE & THE REVOLUTION
TAKE ME WITH YOU [B] COSMOS
TAKE MY ADVICE KYM SIMS
TAKE MY BREATH AWAY EMMA BUNTON

TAKE MY BREATH AWAY SODA CLUB FEATURING HANNAH ALETHA
TAKE MY BREATH AWAY (LOVE THEME FROM 'TOP GUN') BERLIN
TAKE MY HAND JURGEN VRIES FEATURING ANDREA BRITTON
TAKE MY HEART AL MARTINO
TAKE MY HEART (YOU CAN HAVE IT IF YOU WANT IT) KOOL & THE GANG
TAKE MY SCARS MACHINE HEAD
TAKE MY TIME SHEENA EASTON
TAKE OFF SOME TIME NEW ATLANTIC
TAKE ON ME A-HA
TAKE ON ME A1
TAKE ON THE WORLD JUDAS PRIEST
TAKE THAT LOOK OFF YOUR FACE MARTI WEBB
TAKE THAT SITUATION NICK HEYWARD
TAKE THAT TO THE BANK SHALAMAR
TAKE THE BOX AMY WINEHOUSE
TAKE THE LONG ROAD AND WALK IT MUSIC
TAKE THE LONG WAY HOME FAITHLESS
TAKE THESE CHAINS FROM MY HEART RAY CHARLES
TAKE THIS HEART RICHARD MARX
TAKE THIS TIME SEAN MAGUIRE
TAKE TO THE MOUNTAINS RICHARD BARNES
TAKE YOU OUT LUTHER VANDROSS
TAKE YOU THERE RONNI SIMON
TAKE YOUR MAMA SCISSOR SISTERS
TAKE YOUR MAMA FOR A RIDE LULU
TAKE YOUR PARTNER BY THE HAND HOWIE B FEATURING ROBBIE ROBERTSON
TAKE YOUR SHOES OFF CHEEKY GIRLS
TAKE YOUR TIME [A] HIGH
TAKE YOUR TIME [B] MANTRONIX FEATURING WONDRESS
TAKE YOUR TIME [C] LOVE BITE
TAKE YOUR TIME (DO IT RIGHT) PART 1 S.O.S. BAND
TAKEN FOR GRANTED SIA
TAKES A LITTLE TIME TOTAL CONTRAST
TAKES TWO TO TANGO LOUIS ARMSTRONG
TAKIN' A CHANCE ON YOU DOLLAR
TAKIN' HOLD SAM LA MORE
TAKING OFF CURE
TAKING ON THE WORLD GUN
TAKING THE VEIL DAVID SYLVIAN
TALES FROM A DANCEOGRAPHIC OCEAN (EP) JAM & SPOON
TALES FROM THE HARD SIDE BIOHAZARD
TALES OF THE HOOD TUBBY T
TALK ABOUT IT IN THE MORNING MARTYN JOSEPH
TALK ABOUT OUR LOVE BRANDY FEATURING KANYE WEST
TALK BACK DOUBLE TROUBLE FEATURING JANETTE SEWELL
TALK DIRTY TO ME POISON
TALK OF THE TOWN PRETENDERS
TALK SHOWS ON MUTE INCUBUS
TALK TALK TALK TALK
TALK TALK TALK ORDINARY BOYS
TALK TO ME [A] THIRD WORLD
TALK TO ME [B] STEVIE NICKS
TALK TO ME [C] ANITA BAKER
TALK TO ME [D] 60FT DOLLS
TALKIN' ALL THAT JAZZ STETSASONIC
TALKING IN YOUR SLEEP [A] CRYSTAL GAYLE
TALKING IN YOUR SLEEP [A] MARTINE McCUTCHEON
TALKING IN YOUR SLEEP [B] BUCKS FIZZ
TALKING LOUD AND CLEAR ORCHESTRAL MANOEUVRES IN THE DARK
TALKING OF LOVE ANITA DOBSON
TALKING WITH MYSELF ELECTRIBE 101

TALL DARK STRANGER ROSE BRENNAN
TALL 'N' HANDSOME OUTRAGE
TALLAHASSEE LASSIE FREDDY CANNON
TALLAHASSEE LASSIE TOMMY STEELE
TALLYMAN JEFF BECK
TALULA TORI AMOS
TAM-TAM POUR L'ETHIOPE STARVATION
TAMMY DEBBIE REYNOLDS
TANGERINE FEEDER
TANGO IN MONO EXPRESSOS
TANSY ALEX WELSH
TANTALISE (WO WO EE YEH YEH) JIMMY THE HOOVER
TAP THE BOTTLE YOUNG BLACK TEENAGERS
TAP TURNS ON THE WATER C.C.S.
TAPE LOOP MORCHEEBA
TARANTINO'S NEW STAR NORTH & SOUTH
TARANTULA FAITHLESS
TARA'S THEME SPIRO & WIX
TARA'S THEME FROM 'GONE WITH THE WIND' ROSE OF ROMANCE ORCHESTRA
TARZAN BOY BALTIMORA
TASTE IN MEN PLACEBO
TASTE IT INXS
A TASTE OF AGGRO BARRON KNIGHTS
TASTE OF BITTER LOVE GLADYS KNIGHT & THE PIPS
A TASTE OF HONEY MR ACKER BILK WITH THE LEON YOUNG STRING CHORALE
THE TASTE OF INK USED
THE TASTE OF YOUR TEARS KING
TASTE THE PAIN RED HOT CHILI PEPPERS
TASTE YOU AUF DER MAUR
TASTE YOUR LOVE HORACE BROWN
TASTY FISH OTHER TWO
TASTY LOVE FREDDIE JACKSON
TATTOO MIKE OLDFIELD
TATTOOED MILLIONAIRE BRUCE DICKINSON
TATTVA KULA SHAKER
TAVERN IN THE TOWN TERRY LIGHTFOOT & HIS NEW ORLEANS JAZZMEN
TAXI J BLACKFOOT
TAXLOSS MANSUN
TCHAIKOVSKY ONE SECOND CITY SOUND
TE AMO SULTANA
TEA FOR TWO CHA CHA TOMMY DORSEY ORCHESTRA STARRING WARREN COVINGTON
TEACH ME TO TWIST CHUBBY CHECKER & BOBBY RYDELL
TEACH ME TONIGHT DE CASTRO SISTERS
TEACH YOU TO ROCK TONY CROMBIE & HIS ROCKETS
TEACHER [A] JETHRO TULL
TEACHER [B] I-LEVEL
THE TEACHER [C] BIG COUNTRY
TEACHER TEACHER JOHNNY MATHIS
TEAR AWAY DROWNING POOL
TEAR DOWN THE WALLS NO SWEAT
A TEAR FELL TERESA BREWER
TEAR ME APART SUZI QUATRO
TEAR OFF YOUR OWN HEAD ELVIS COSTELLO
TEAR SOUP QUESTIONS
TEARDROP [A] SANTO & JOHNNY
TEARDROP [B] MASSIVE ATTACK
TEARDROP CITY MONKEES
TEARDROPS [A] SHAKIN' STEVENS
TEARDROPS [B] WOMACK & WOMACK
TEARDROPS [B] LOVESTATION
TEARDROPS [C] 411
TEARIN' UP MY HEART N SYNC
TEARING ROLLINS BAND
TEARING US APART ERIC CLAPTON & TINA TURNER
TEARS [A] DANNY WILLIAMS
TEARS [B] KEN DODD

TEARS [C] FRANKIE KNUCKLES PRESENTS SATOSHI TOMIIE
TEARS [C] NU COLOURS
TEARS ARE FALLING KISS
TEARS ARE NOT ENOUGH ABC
TEARS DON'T LIE MARK' OH
TEARS FROM A WILLOW OOBERMAN
TEARS FROM HEAVEN HEARTBEAT
TEARS FROM THE MOON CONJURE ONE
THE TEARS I CRIED GLITTER BAND
TEARS IN HEAVEN ERIC CLAPTON
TEARS IN THE RAIN N-TRANCE
TEARS IN THE WIND CHICKEN SHACK
TEARS OF A CLOWN SMOKEY ROBINSON & THE MIRACLES
TEARS OF A CLOWN BEAT
TEARS OF THE DRAGON BRUCE DICKINSON
TEARS ON MY PILLOW [A] JOHNNY NASH
TEARS ON MY PILLOW [B] KYLIE MINOGUE
TEARS ON THE TELEPHONE [A] CLAUDE FRANCOIS
TEARS ON THE TELEPHONE [B] HOT CHOCOLATE
TEARS RUN RINGS MARC ALMOND
TEARS WON'T WASH AWAY THESE HEARTACHES KEN DODD
TEASE ME [A] KEITH KELLY
TEASE ME [B] CHAKA DEMUS & PLIERS
TEASER GEORGE BENSON
TECHNARCHY CYBERSONIK
TECHNO FUNK LOST
TECHNO TRANCE D-SHAKE
TECHNOCAT TECHNOCAT FEATURING TOM WILSON
TEDDY BEAR [A] RED SOVINE
TEDDY BEAR [B] BOOKER NEWBURY III
TEDDY BEAR'S LAST RIDE DIANA WILLIAMS
TEEN ANGEL MARK DINNING
TEEN BEAT SANDY NELSON
TEENAGE U.K. SUBS
TEENAGE ANGST PLACEBO
TEENAGE DEPRESSION EDDIE & THE HOT RODS
TEENAGE DIRTBAG WHEATUS
TEENAGE DREAM MARC BOLAN & T REX
TEENAGE IDOL RICK NELSON
TEENAGE KICKS UNDERTONES
TEENAGE LAMENT '74 ALICE COOPER
TEENAGE PUNKS SULTANS OF PING
TEENAGE RAMPAGE SWEET
TEENAGE SCREAMERS TOKYO DRAGONS
TEENAGE SENSATION CREDIT TO THE NATION
TEENAGE TURTLES BACK TO THE PLANET
TEENAGE WARNING ANGELIC UPSTARTS
A TEENAGER IN LOVE MARTY WILDE
A TEENAGER IN LOVE CRAIG DOUGLAS
A TEENAGER IN LOVE DION & THE BELMONTS
TEENSVILLE CHET ATKINS
TEETHGRINDER THERAPY?
TELEFUNKIN' N-TYCE
TELEGRAM SAM T. REX
TELEGRAPH ORCHESTRAL MANOEUVRES IN THE DARK
THE TELEPHONE ALWAYS RINGS FUN BOY THREE
TELEPHONE LINE ELECTRIC LIGHT ORCHESTRA
TELEPHONE MAN MERI WILSON
TELEPHONE OPERATOR PETE SHELLEY
TELEPHONE THING FALL
TELEPORT MAN WITH NO NAME
TELETUBBIES SAY EH-OH! TELETUBBIES
TELEVATORS MARS VOLTA
TELEVISION THE DRUG OF THE NATION DISPOSABLE HEROES OF HIPHOPRISY
TELL HER ABOUT IT BILLY JOEL
TELL HER I'M NOT HOME IKE & TINA TURNER
TELL HER NO ZOMBIES

TELL HER THIS DEL AMITRI
TELL HIM [A] BILLIE DAVIS
TELL HIM [A] EXCITERS
TELL HIM [A] HELLO
TELL HIM [A] QUENTIN & ASH
TELL HIM [B] BARBRA STREISAND & CELINE DION
TELL IT LIKE IT T-I-IS B-52's
TELL IT ON THE MOUNTAIN PETER, PAUL & MARY
TELL IT TO MY FACE KEITH
TELL IT TO MY HEART TAYLOR DAYNE
TELL IT TO MY HEART Q-CLUB
TELL IT TO MY HEART KELLY LLORENNA
TELL IT TO THE RAIN FOUR SEASONS WITH FRANKIE VALLI
TELL LAURA I LOVE HER RICKY VALENCE
TELL ME [A] NICK KAMEN
TELL ME [B] GROOVE THEORY
TELL ME [C] DRU HILL
TELL ME [D] BILLIE MYERS
TELL ME [E] MELANIE B
TELL ME A STORY FRANKIE LAINE & JIMMY BOYD
TELL ME DO U WANNA GINUWINE
TELL ME (HOW IT FEELS) 52ND STREET
TELL ME I'M NOT DREAMING TITIYO
TELL ME IS IT TRUE UB40
TELL ME IT'S REAL K-CI & JOJO
TELL ME MA SHAM ROCK
TELL ME ON A SUNDAY MARTI WEBB
TELL ME THAT YOU LOVE ME PAUL ANKA
TELL ME THE WAY CAPPELLA
TELL ME THERE'S A HEAVEN CHRIS REA
TELL ME TOMORROW [A] SMOKEY ROBINSON
TELL ME TOMORROW [B] PRINCESS
TELL ME WHAT HE SAID HELEN SHAPIRO
TELL ME WHAT YOU SEE VON BONDIES
TELL ME WHAT YOU WANT [A] JIMMY RUFFIN
TELL ME WHAT YOU WANT [B] LOOSE ENDS
TELL ME WHAT YOU WANT [C] BLU PETER
TELL ME WHAT YOU WANT ME TO DO TEVIN CAMPBELL
TELL ME WHEN [A] APPLEJACKS
TELL ME WHEN [B] HUMAN LEAGUE
TELL ME WHEN THE FEVER ENDED ELECTRIBE 101
TELL ME WHERE YOU'RE GOING SILJE
TELL ME WHY [A] ELVIS PRESLEY
TELL ME WHY [B] ALVIN STARDUST
TELL ME WHY [C] MUSICAL YOUTH
TELL ME WHY [D] BOBBY WOMACK
TELL ME WHY [E] THIS WAY UP
TELL ME WHY [F] GENESIS
TELL ME WHY [G] DECLAN FEATURING THE YOUNG VOICES CHOIR
TELL ME WHY (THE RIDDLE) PAUL VAN DYK FEATURING SAINT ETIENNE
TELL THAT GIRL TO SHUT UP TRANSVISION VAMP
TELL THE CHILDREN SHAM 69
TELLIN' STORIES CHARLATANS
TELSTAR TORNADOS
TEMMA HARBOUR MARY HOPKIN
TEMPERATURE RISING PKA
TEMPERMENTAL EVERYTHING BUT THE GIRL
TEMPERTEMPER GOLDIE
TEMPLE OF DOOM DJ FRESH
TEMPLE OF DREAMS [A] MESSIAH
TEMPLE OF DREAMS [B] FUTURE BREEZE
TEMPLE OF LOVE SISTERS OF MERCY
TEMPO FIESTA (PARTY TIME) ITTY BITTY BOOZY WOOZY
TEMPORARY BEAUTY GRAHAM PARKER & THE RUMOUR
TEMPTATION [A] EVERLY BROTHERS
TEMPTATION [B] NEW ORDER

TEMPTATION [C] HEAVEN 17
TEMPTATION [D] JOAN ARMATRADING
TEMPTATION [E] WET WET WET
TEMPTED SQUEEZE
TEMPTED TO TOUCH RUPEE
10538 OVERTURE ELECTRIC LIGHT ORCHESTRA
10 IN 01 MEMBERS OF MAYDAY
TEN MILES HIGH LITTLE ANGELS
10 SECOND BIONIC MAN KINKY MACHINE
TEN STOREY LOVE SONG STONE ROSES
TEN THOUSAND MILES MICHAEL HOLLIDAY
10 X 10 808 STATE
TEN TO TWENTY SNEAKER PIMPS
10 YEARS ASLEEP KINGMAKER
TEN YEARS TIME GABRIELLE
10AM AUTOMATIC BLACK KEYS
TENDER BLUR
TENDER HANDS CHRIS DE BURGH
TENDER HEART LIONEL RICHIE
TENDER LOVE FORCE MDs
TENDER LOVE KENNY THOMAS
TENDERLY NAT 'KING' COLE
TENDERNESS DIANA ROSS
TENNESSEE ARRESTED DEVELOPMENT
TENNESSEE WIG WALK BONNIE LOU
TENSHI GOURYELLA
TEQUILA [A] CHAMPS
TEQUILA [A] TED HEATH
TEQUILA [A] NO WAY JOSE
TEQUILA [B] TERRORVISION
TEQUILA SUNRISE CYPRESS HILL
TERESA JOE DOLAN
TERRITORY SEPULTURA
TERRY TWINKLE
TERRY'S THEME FROM 'LIMELIGHT' FRANK CHACKSFIELD
TERRY'S THEME FROM 'LIMELIGHT' RON GOODWIN
TESLA GIRLS ORCHESTRAL MANOEUVRES IN THE DARK
THE TEST CHEMICAL BROTHERS
TEST OF TIME [A] WILL DOWNING
TEST OF TIME [B] CRESCENT
TEST THE THEORY AUDIOWEB
TESTAMENT 4 CHUBBY CHUNKS VOLUME II
TESTIFY [A] M PEOPLE
TESTIFY [B] BYRON STINGILY
TETRIS DOCTOR SPIN
TEXAS CHRIS REA
TEXAS COWBOYS GRID
THA CROSSROADS BONE THUGS-N-HARMONY
THA DOGGFATHER SNOOP DOGGY DOGG
THA HORNS OF JERICHO DJ SUPREME
THA WILD STYLE DJ SUPREME
THANK ABBA FOR THE MUSIC VARIOUS ARTISTS (EP'S & LPS)
THANK GOD I FOUND YOU MARIAH CAREY
THANK GOD IT'S CHRISTMAS QUEEN
THANK GOD IT'S FRIDAY R KELLY
THANK U ALANIS MORISSETTE
THANK U VERY MUCH SCAFFOLD
THANK YOU [A] PALE FOUNTAINS
THANK YOU [B] BOYZ II MEN
THANK YOU [C] DIDO
THANK YOU [D] JAMELIA
THANK YOU BABY! SHANIA TWAIN
THANK YOU FOR A GOOD YEAR ALEXANDER O'NEAL
THANK YOU FOR BEING A FRIEND ANDREW GOLD
THANK YOU FOR HEARING ME SINEAD O'CONNOR
THANK YOU FOR LOVING ME BON JOVI
THANK YOU FOR THE MUSIC ABBA
THANK YOU FOR THE PARTY DUKES
THANK YOU FOR THE VENOM MY CHEMICAL ROMANCE

THANK YOU MY LOVE IMAGINATION
THANK YOU WORLD WORLD PARTY
THANKS A LOT BRENDA LEE
THANKS FOR MY CHILD CHERYL PEPSII RILEY
THANKS FOR SAVING MY LIFE BILLY PAUL
THANKS FOR THE MEMORY (WHAM BAM THANK YOU MAM) SLADE
THANKS FOR THE NIGHT DAMNED
THAT CERTAIN SMILE MIDGE URE
THAT DAY NATALIE IMBRUGLIA
THAT DON'T IMPRESS ME MUCH SHANIA TWAIN
THAT EXTRA MILE RICKY
THAT FEELING DJ CHUS PRESENTS GROOVE FOUNDATION
THAT GIRL [A] STEVIE WONDER
THAT GIRL [B] MAXI PRIEST/SHAGGY
THAT GIRL [C] McFLY
THAT GIRL BELONGS TO YESTERDAY GENE PITNEY
THAT GIRL (GROOVY SITUATION) FREDDIE McGREGOR
THAT GREAT LOVE SOUND RAVEONETTES
THAT LADY ISLEY BROTHERS
THAT LOOK DE'LACY
THAT LOOK IN YOUR EYE ALI CAMPBELL
THAT LOVING FEELING CICERO
THAT LUCKY OLD SUN VELVETS
THAT MAN (HE'S ALL MINE) INNER CITY
THAT MAN WILL NOT HANG McLUSKY
THAT MEANS A LOT P.J. PROBY
THAT NOISE ANTHONY NEWLEY
THAT OLD BLACK MAGIC SAMMY DAVIS Jr.
THAT OLE DEVIL CALLED LOVE ALISON MOYET
THAT SAME OLD FEELING PICKETTYWITCH
THAT SOUND MICHAEL MOOG
THAT SOUNDS GOOD TO ME JIVE BUNNY & THE MASTERMIXERS
THAT THING YOU DO! WONDERS
THAT WAS MY VEIL JOHN PARISH & POLLY JEAN HARVEY
THAT WAS THEN BUT THIS IS NOW ABC
THAT WAS THEN, THIS IS NOW MONKEES
THAT WAS YESTERDAY FOREIGNER
THAT WOMAN'S GOT ME DRINKING SHANE MacGOWAN & THE POPES
THAT ZIPPER TRACK DJ DAN PRESENTS NEEDLE DAMAGE
THAT'LL BE THE DAY CRICKETS
THAT'LL BE THE DAY EVERLY BROTHERS
THAT'LL DO NICELY BAD MANNERS
THAT'S ALL GENESIS
THAT'S ALL RIGHT ELVIS PRESLEY
THAT'S AMORE DEAN MARTIN
THAT'S ENTERTAINMENT JAM
THAT'S HOW A LOVE SONG WAS BORN RAY BURNS WITH THE CORONETS
THAT'S HOW GOOD YOUR LOVE IS IL PADRINOS FEATURING JOCELYN BROWN
THAT'S HOW I FEEL ABOUT YOU LONDONBEAT
THAT'S HOW I'M LIVIN' ICE-T
THAT'S HOW I'M LIVING TONI SCOTT
THAT'S HOW STRONG MY LOVE IS IN CROWD
THAT'S JUST THE WAY IT IS PHIL COLLINS
THAT'S LIFE FRANK SINATRA
THAT'S LIVIN' ALRIGHT JOE FAGIN
THAT'S LOVE BILLY FURY WITH THE FOUR JAYS
THAT'S LOVE, THAT IS BLANCMANGE
THAT'S MORE LIKE IT SKYLARK
THAT'S MY DOLL FRANKIE VAUGHAN
THAT'S MY HOME MR ACKER BILK & HIS PARAMOUNT JAZZ BAND
THAT'S NICE NEIL CHRISTIAN
THAT'S RIGHT DEEP RIVER BOYS

THAT'S THE WAY HONEYCOMBS
THAT'S THE WAY GOD PLANNED IT BILLY PRESTON
THAT'S THE WAY (I LIKE IT) KC & THE SUNSHINE BAND
THAT'S THE WAY (I LIKE IT) DEAD OR ALIVE
THAT'S THE WAY (I LIKE IT) CLOCK
THAT'S THE WAY I WANNA ROCK 'N' ROLL AC/DC
THAT'S THE WAY IT FEELS TWO NATIONS
THAT'S THE WAY IT IS [A] MEL & KIM
THAT'S THE WAY IT IS [B] CELINE DION
THAT'S THE WAY LOVE GOES [A] CHARLES DICKENS
THAT'S THE WAY LOVE GOES [B] YOUNG MC
THAT'S THE WAY LOVE GOES [C] JANET JACKSON
THAT'S THE WAY LOVE IS [A] TEN CITY
THAT'S THE WAY LOVE IS [A] VOLCANO WITH SAM
CARTWRIGHT
THAT'S THE WAY LOVE IS [A] BYRON STINGILY
THAT'S THE WAY LOVE IS [B] BOBBY BROWN
THAT'S THE WAY OF THE WORLD D MOB WITH CATHY
DENNIS
THAT'S THE WAY THE MONEY GOES M
THAT'S THE WAY YOU DO IT PURPLE KINGS
THAT'S WHAT FRIENDS ARE FOR [A] DENIECE WILLIAMS
THAT'S WHAT FRIENDS ARE FOR [B] DIONNE WARWICK
& FRIENDS FEATURING ELTON JOHN, STEVIE
WONDER & GLADYS KNIGHT
THAT'S WHAT I LIKE JIVE BUNNY & THE
MASTERMIXERS
THAT'S WHAT I THINK CYNDI LAUPER
THAT'S WHAT I WANT MARAUDERS
THAT'S WHAT I WANT TO BE NEIL REID
THAT'S WHAT LIFE IS ALL ABOUT BING CROSBY
THAT'S WHAT LOVE CAN DO TOUTES LES FILLES
THAT'S WHAT LOVE IS FOR AMY GRANT
THAT'S WHAT LOVE WILL DO JOE BROWN & THE
BRUVVERS
THAT'S WHEN I REACH FOR MY REVOLVER MOBY
THAT'S WHEN I THINK OF YOU 1927
THAT'S WHEN THE MUSIC TAKES ME NEIL SEDAKA
THAT'S WHERE MY MIND GOES SLAMM
THAT'S WHERE THE HAPPY PEOPLE GO TRAMMPS
THAT'S WHY I LIE RAY J
THAT'S WHY I'M CRYING IVY LEAGUE
THAT'S WHY WE LOSE CONTROL YOUNG OFFENDERS
THAT'S YOU NAT 'KING' COLE
THEM BONES ALICE IN CHAINS
THEM GIRLS THEM GIRLS ZIG & ZAG
THEM THANGS 50 CENT/G-UNIT
THEM THERE EYES EMILE FORD
THEME SABRES OF PARADISE
THE THEME [A] UNIQUE 3
THE THEME [B] DREEM TEEM
THE THEME [C] TRACEY LEE
THE THEME [D] JURGEN VRIES
THEME FOR A DREAM CLIFF RICHARD
THEME FOR YOUNG LOVERS SHADOWS
THEME FROM 'A SUMMER PLACE' PERCY FAITH
THEME FROM 'A SUMMER PLACE' NORRIE PARAMOR
THEME FROM 'CADE'S COUNTY' HENRY MANCINI
THEME FROM 'CHEERS' GARY PORTNOY
THEME FROM 'COME SEPTEMBER' BOBBY DARIN
ORCHESTRA
THEME FROM DIXIE DUANE EDDY & THE REBELS
THEME FROM DR. KILDARE JOHNNIE SPENCE
THEME FROM 'DR. KILDARE' (THREE STARS WILL SHINE
TONIGHT) RICHARD CHAMBERLAIN
THEME FROM E.T. (THE EXTRA-TERRESTRIAL) JOHN
WILLIAMS
THEME FROM 'EXODUS' FERRANTE & TEICHER
THEME FROM 'EXODUS' SEMPRINI
THEME FROM GUTBUSTER BENTLEY RHYTHM ACE
THEME FROM HARRY'S GAME CLANNAD

THEME FROM 'HILL STREET BLUES' MIKE POST
FEATURING LARRY CARLTON
THEME FROM HONEYMOON MANUEL & HIS MUSIC OF
THE MOUNTAINS
THEME FROM JURASSIC PARK JOHN WILLIAMS
THEME FROM M*A*S*H (SUICIDE IS PAINLESS) MASH
THEME FROM M.A.S.H. (SUICIDE IS PAINLESS) MANIC
STREET PREACHERS
THEME FROM MAHOGANY (DO YOU KNOW WHERE
YOU'RE GOING TO) DIANA ROSS
THEME FROM MISSION: IMPOSSIBLE ADAM CLAYTON
& LARRY MULLEN
THEME FROM NEW YORK, NEW YORK FRANK SINATRA
THEME FROM P.O.P. PERFECTLY ORDINARY PEOPLE
THEME FROM PICNIC MORRIS STOLOFF
THEME FROM 'RANDALL & HOPKIRK (DECEASED)' NINA
PERSSON & DAVID ARNOLD
THEME FROM S-EXPRESS S-EXPRESS
THE THEME FROM 'SHAFT' EDDY & THE SOUL BAND
THEME FROM 'SHAFT' ISAAC HAYES
THEME FROM SPARTA FC FALL
THEME FROM 'SUPERMAN' (MAIN TITLE) LONDON
SYMPHONY ORCHESTRA
THEME FROM 'THE APARTMENT' FERRANTE & TEICHER
THEME FROM THE DEER HUNTER (CAVATINA)
SHADOWS
THEME FROM THE FILM 'THE LEGION'S LAST PATROL'
KEN THORNE
THEME FROM 'THE HONG KONG BEAT' RICHARD
DENTON & MARTIN COOK
THEME FROM 'THE ONEDIN LINE' VIENNA
PHILHARMONIC ORCHESTRA
THEME FROM THE PROFESSIONALS LAURIE JOHNSON'S
LONDON BIG BAND
THEME FROM THE THREEPENNY OPERA LOUIS
ARMSTRONG WITH HIS ALL-STARS
THEME FROM 'THE THREEPENNY OPERA' DICK HYMAN
TRIO
THEME FROM THE 'THREEPENNY OPERA' BILLY VAUGHN
THEME FROM 'THE TRAVELLING MAN' DUNCAN
BROWNE
THEME FROM TURNPIKE (EP) dEUS
THEME FROM 'VIETNAM' (CANON IN D) ORCHESTRE DE
CHAMBRE JEAN-FRANCOIS PAILLARD
THEME FROM 'WHICH WAY IS UP' STARGARD
THEME FROM 'Z CARS' NORRIE PARAMOR
THEME FROM 'Z-CARS' JOHNNY KEATING
THEME ONE COZY POWELL
THEN CHARLATANS
THEN CAME YOU DIONNE WARWICK & THE DETROIT
SPINNERS
THEN CAME YOU JUNIOR GISCOMBE
THEN HE KISSED ME CRYSTALS
THEN I FEEL GOOD KATHERINE E
THEN I KISSED HER BEACH BOYS
THEN YOU CAN TELL ME GOODBYE CASINOS
THEN YOU TURN AWAY ORCHESTRAL MANOEUVRES IN
THE DARK
THERE AIN'T NOTHIN' LIKE THE LOVE MONTAGE
THERE AIN'T NOTHING LIKE SHAGGIN' TAMS
THERE ARE MORE QUESTIONS THAN ANSWERS
JOHNNY NASH
THERE ARE MORE SNAKES THAN LADDERS CAPTAIN
SENSIBLE
THERE BUT FOR FORTUNE JOAN BAEZ
THERE BUT FOR THE GRACE OF GOD FIRE ISLAND
FEATURING LOVE NELSON
THERE BY THE GRACE OF GOD MANIC STREET
PREACHERS
THERE GOES MY EVERYTHING ENGELBERT
HUMPERDINCK

THERE GOES MY EVERYTHING ELVIS PRESLEY
THERE GOES MY FIRST LOVE DRIFTERS
THERE GOES THAT SONG AGAIN GARY MILLER
THERE GOES THE FEAR DOVES
THERE GOES THE NEIGHBORHOOD SHERYL CROW
THERE I GO VIKKI CARR
THERE I GO AGAIN POWER OF DREAMS
THERE IS A LIGHT THAT NEVER GOES OUT SMITHS
THERE IS A MOUNTAIN DONOVAN
THERE IS A STAR PHARAO
THERE IS ALWAYS SOMETHING THERE TO REMIND ME
HOUSEMARTINS
THERE IS NO LOVE BETWEEN US ANYMORE POP WILL
EAT ITSELF
THERE IT IS SHALAMAR
THERE I'VE SAID IT AGAIN AL SAXON
THERE I'VE SAID IT AGAIN BOBBY VINTON
THERE MUST BE A REASON FRANKIE LAINE
THERE MUST BE A WAY JONI JAMES
THERE MUST BE A WAY FRANKIE VAUGHAN
THERE MUST BE AN ANGEL (PLAYING WITH MY HEART)
EURYTHMICS
THERE MUST BE THOUSANDS QUADS
THERE SHE GOES [A] LA'S
THERE SHE GOES [B] SIXPENCE NONE THE RICHER
THERE SHE GOES AGAIN QUIREBOYS
THERE SHE GOES MY BEAUTIFUL WORLD NICK CAVE &
THE BAD SEEDS
THERE THERE RADIOHEAD
THERE THERE MY DEAR DEXY'S MIDNIGHT RUNNERS
THERE WILL NEVER BE ANOTHER TONIGHT BRYAN
ADAMS
THERE WILL NEVER BE ANOTHER YOU [A] CHRIS
MONTEZ
THERE WILL NEVER BE ANOTHER YOU [B] JIMMY
RUFFIN
THERE WON'T BE MANY COMING HOME ROY ORBISON
THERE YOU GO P!NK
THERE YOU'LL BE FAITH HILL
(THERE'LL BE BLUEBIRDS OVER) WHITE CLIFFS OF
DOVER ROBSON GREEN & JEROME FLYNN
THERE'LL BE SAD SONGS (TO MAKE YOU CRY) BILLY
OCEAN
THERE'S A BRAND NEW WORLD FIVE STAR
THERE'S A GHOST IN MY HOUSE R. DEAN TAYLOR
THERE'S A GHOST IN MY HOUSE FALL
THERE'S A GOLDMINE IN THE SKY PAT BOONE
THERE'S A GUY WORKS DOWN THE CHIPSHOP SWEARS
HE'S ELVIS KIRSTY MacCOLL
THERE'S A HEARTACHE FOLLOWING ME JIM REEVES
THERE'S A KIND OF HUSH HERMAN'S HERMITS
THERE'S A KIND OF HUSH (ALL OVER THE WORLD)
CARPENTERS
THERE'S A SILENCE ELECTRIC SOFT PARADE
THERE'S A STAR ASH
THERE'S A WHOLE LOT OF LOVING GUYS & DOLLS
THERE'S ALWAYS ROOM ON THE BROOM LIARS
(THERE'S) ALWAYS SOMETHING THERE TO REMIND ME
SANDIE SHAW
THERE'S GONNA BE A SHOWDOWN ARCHIE BELL & THE
DRELLS
THERE'S GOT TO BE A WAY MARIAH CAREY
THERE'S GOTTA BE MORE TO LIFE STACIE ORRICO
THERE'S MORE TO LOVE COMMUNARDS
THERE'S NO LIVING WITHOUT YOU WILL DOWNING
THERE'S NO ONE QUITE LIKE GRANDMA ST WINIFRED'S
SCHOOL CHOIR
THERE'S NO OTHER WAY BLUR
THERE'S NOTHING BETTER THAN LOVE LUTHER
VANDROSS, DUET WITH GREGORY HINES
THERE'S NOTHING I WON'T DO JX

THERE'S NOTHING LIKE THIS OMAR
THERE'S SOMETHING WRONG IN PARADISE KID CREOLE & THE COCONUTS
THERE'S THE GIRL HEART
THERE'S YOUR TROUBLE DIXIE CHICKS
THESE ARE DAYS 10,000 MANIACS
THESE ARE THE DAYS [A] O-TOWN
THESE ARE THE DAYS [B] JAMIE CULLUM
THESE ARE THE DAYS OF OUR LIVES QUEEN
THESE ARE THE TIMES DRU HILL
THESE ARMS OF MINE PROCLAIMERS
THESE BOOTS ARE MADE FOR WALKIN' NANCY SINATRA
THESE BOOTS ARE MADE FOR WALKIN' BILLY RAY CYRUS
THESE DAYS BON JOVI
THESE DREAMS HEART
THESE EARLY DAYS EVERYTHING BUT THE GIRL
THESE THINGS ARE WORTH FIGHTING FOR GARY CLAIL ON-U SOUND SYSTEM
THESE THINGS WILL KEEP ME LOVING YOU VELVELETTES
THESE WOODEN IDEAS IDLEWILD
THESE WORDS NATASHA BEDINGFIELD
THEY ALL LAUGHED FRANK SINATRA
(THEY CALL HER) LA BAMBA CRICKETS
THEY DON'T CARE ABOUT US MICHAEL JACKSON
THEY DON'T KNOW [A] TRACEY ULLMAN
THEY DON'T KNOW [B] JON B
THEY DON'T KNOW [C] SO SOLID CREW
THEY GLUED YOUR HEAD ON UPSIDE DOWN BELLRAYS
(THEY LONG TO BE) CLOSE TO YOU CARPENTERS
(THEY LONG TO BE) CLOSE TO YOU GWEN GUTHRIE
THEY SAY IT'S GONNA RAIN HAZELL DEAN
THEY SHOOT HORSES DON'T THEY RACING CARS
THEY WILL KILL US ALL (WITHOUT MERCY) BRONX
THEY'RE COMING TO TAKE ME AWAY HA-HAAA! NAPOLEON XIV
THEY'RE HERE EMF
THIEVES IN THE TEMPLE PRINCE
THIEVES LIKE US NEW ORDER
THIGHS HIGH (GRIP YOUR HIPS AND MOVE) TOM BROWNE
THIN LINE BETWEEN LOVE AND HATE PRETENDERS
THE THIN WALL ULTRAVOX
A THING CALLED LOVE JOHNNY CASH WITH THE EVANGEL TEMPLE CHOIR
THE THING I LIKE AALIYAH
THINGS BOBBY DARIN
THE THINGS AUDIO BULLYS
THINGS CAN ONLY GET BETTER [A] HOWARD JONES
THINGS CAN ONLY GET BETTER [B] D:REAM
THINGS FALL APART SERAFIN
THINGS GET BETTER EDDIE FLOYD
THINGS HAVE CHANGED BOB DYLAN
THINGS I'VE SEEN SPOOKS
THE THINGS THE LONELY DO AMAZULU
THINGS THAT ARE RUNRIG
THINGS THAT GO BUMP IN THE NIGHT ALLSTARS
THINGS THAT MAKE YOU GO HMMM C & C MUSIC FACTORY (FEATURING FREEDOM WILLIAMS)
THINGS WE DO FOR LOVE [A] 10 C.C.
THINGS WE DO FOR LOVE [B] HORACE BROWN
THINGS WILL GO MY WAY CALLING
THINK [A] CHRIS FARLOWE
THINK [B] BRENDA LEE
THINK [C] ARETHA FRANKLIN
THINK ABOUT... DJH FEATURING STEFY
THINK ABOUT ME ARTFUL DODGER FEATURING MICHELLE ESCOFFERY
THINK ABOUT THAT DANDY LIVINGSTONE

THINK ABOUT THE WAY (BOM DIGI DIGI BOM...) ICE MC
THINK ABOUT YOUR CHILDREN MARY HOPKIN
THINK FOR A MINUTE HOUSEMARTINS
THINK I'M GONNA FALL IN LOVE WITH YOU DOOLEYS
THINK IT ALL OVER SANDIE SHAW
THINK IT OVER CRICKETS
(THINK OF ME) WHEREVER YOU ARE KEN DODD
THINK OF YOU [A] USHER
THINK OF YOU [B] WHIGFIELD
THINK SOMETIMES ABOUT ME SANDIE SHAW
THINK TWICE CELINE DION
THINKIN' ABOUT YOUR BODY BOBBY McFERRIN
THINKIN' AIN'T FOR ME PAUL JONES
THINKING ABOUT TOMORROW BETH ORTON
THINKING ABOUT YOUR BODY 2 MAD
THINKING ABOUT YOUR LOVE [A] SKIPWORTH & TURNER
THINKING ABOUT YOUR LOVE [A] PHILLIP LEO
THINKING ABOUT YOUR LOVE [B] KENNY THOMAS
THINKING IT OVER LIBERTY
THINKING OF YOU [A] SISTER SLEDGE
THINKING OF YOU [A] MAUREEN
THINKING OF YOU [A] CURTIS LYNCH JR FEATURING KELE LE ROC & RED RAT
THINKING OF YOU [A] PAUL WELLER
THINKING OF YOU [B] COLOUR FIELD
THINKING OF YOU [C] HANSON
THINKING OF YOU [D] STATUS QUO
THINKING OF YOU BABY DAVE CLARK FIVE
THINKING OVER DANA GLOVER
THIRD FINGER, LEFT HAND PEARLS
THE THIRD MAN SHADOWS
THIRD RAIL SQUEEZE
13 STEPS LEAD DOWN ELVIS COSTELLO & THE ATTRACTIONS
THE 13TH CURE
13TH DISCIPLE FIVE THIRTY
30TH CENTURY MAN CATHERINE WHEEL
THIRTY THREE SMASHING PUMPKINS
36D BEAUTIFUL SOUTH
THIS AIN'T A LOVE SONG BON JOVI
THIS AND THAT TOM JONES
THIS BEAT IS MINE VICKY D
THIS BEAT IS TECHNOTRONIC TECHNOTRONIC FEATURING MC ERIC
THIS BOY [A] JUSTIN
THIS BOY [B] TOM BAXTER
THIS BRUTAL HOUSE NITRO DELUXE
THIS CAN BE REAL CANDY FLIP
THIS CHARMING MAN SMITHS
THIS CORROSION SISTERS OF MERCY
THIS COWBOY SONG STING FEATURING PATO BANTON
THIS DJ WARREN G
THIS DOOR SWINGS BOTH WAYS HERMAN'S HERMITS
THIS FEELIN' FRANK HOOKER & POSITIVE PEOPLE
THIS FEELING PURESSENCE
THIS FLIGHT TONIGHT NAZARETH
THIS GARDEN LEVELLERS
THIS GENERATION ROACHFORD
THIS GOLDEN RING FORTUNES
THIS GROOVE VICTORIA BECKHAM
THIS GUY'S IN LOVE WITH YOU HERB ALPERT
THIS HERE GIRAFFE FLAMING LIPS
THIS HOUSE [A] TRACIE SPENCER
THIS HOUSE [B] ALISON MOYET
THIS HOUSE IS NOT A HOME REMBRANDTS
THIS HOUSE (IS WHERE YOUR LOVE STANDS) BIG SOUND AUTHORITY
THIS I PROMISE YOU N SYNC
THIS I SWEAR [A] RICHARD DARBYSHIRE
THIS I SWEAR [B] KIM WILDE

THIS IS A CALL FOO FIGHTERS
THIS IS A REBEL SONG SINEAD O'CONNOR
THIS IS A WARNING/SUPER DJ DILLINJA
THIS IS ENGLAND CLASH
THIS IS FOR REAL DAVID DEVANT & HIS SPIRIT WIFE
THIS IS FOR THE LOVER IN YOU BABYFACE
THIS IS FOR THE POOR OTHERS
THIS IS GOODBYE LUCY CARR
THIS IS HARDCORE PULP
THIS IS HOW IT FEELS INSPIRAL CARPETS
THIS IS HOW WE DO IT MONTELL JORDAN
THIS IS HOW WE DO IT MIS-TEEQ
THIS IS HOW WE PARTY S.O.A.P.
THIS IS IT! [A] ADAM FAITH
THIS IS IT [B] MELBA MOORE
THIS IS IT [B] DANNII MINOGUE
THIS IS IT [C] DAN HARTMAN
THIS IS IT [D] 4MANDU
THIS IS IT [E] STATE OF MIND
THIS IS IT (YOUR SOUL) HOTHOUSE FLOWERS
THIS IS LOVE [A] GARY NUMAN
THIS IS LOVE [B] GEORGE HARRISON
THIS IS LOVE [C] PJ HARVEY
THIS IS ME [A] CLIMIE FISHER
THIS IS ME [B] SAW DOCTORS
THIS IS MINE HEAVEN 17
THIS IS MUSIC VERVE
THIS IS MY HOLLYWOOD 3 COLOURS RED
THIS IS MY LIFE EARTHA KITT
THIS IS MY NIGHT CHAKA KHAN
THIS IS MY SONG PETULA CLARK
THIS IS MY SONG HARRY SECOMBE
THIS IS MY SOUND DJ SHOG
THIS IS MY TIME 3 COLOURS RED
THIS IS NOT A LOVE SONG PUBLIC IMAGE LTD.
THIS IS NOT A SONG FRANK & WALTERS
THIS IS NOT AMERICA DAVID BOWIE & THE PAT METHENY GROUP
THIS IS OUR SONG CODE RED
THIS IS RADIO CLASH CLASH
THIS IS SKA LONGSY D'S HOUSE SOUND
THIS IS THE DAY THE THE
THIS IS THE LAST TIME KEANE
THIS IS THE PLACE ZEITIA MASSIAH
THIS IS THE NEW SHIT MARILYN MANSON
THIS IS THE RIGHT TIME LISA STANSFIELD
THIS IS THE SOUND OF YOUTH THESE ANIMAL MEN
THIS IS THE STORY OF MY LIFE (BABY) WIZZARD
THIS IS THE WAY [A] BRUCE FOXTON
THIS IS THE WAY [B] DANNII MINOGUE
THIS IS THE WAY [C] F.K.W.
THIS IS THE WAY [D] E-TYPE
THIS IS THE WORLD CALLING BOB GELDOF
THIS IS THE WORLD WE LIVE IN ALCAZAR
THIS IS TOMORROW BRYAN FERRY
THIS IS WHAT WE DO CRACKOUT
THIS IS WHERE I CAME IN BEE GEES
THIS IS YOUR LAND SIMPLE MINDS
THIS IS YOUR LIFE [A] BLOW MONKEYS
THIS IS YOUR LIFE [B] BANDERAS
THIS IS YOUR LIFE [C] DUST BROTHERS
THIS IS YOUR NIGHT [A] HEAVY D. & THE BOYZ
THIS IS YOUR NIGHT [B] ANOTHERSIDE
THIS IZ REAL SHYEIM
THIS KIND OF LOVE PHIL FEARON & GALAXY
THIS KISS FAITH HILL
THIS LITTLE BIRD MARIANNE FAITHFULL
THIS LITTLE BIRD NASHVILLE TEENS
THIS LITTLE GIRL GARY U.S. BONDS
THIS LOVE [A] LeANN RIMES
THIS LOVE [B] MAROON 5

THIS LOVE AFFAIR STEFAN DENNIS
THIS LOVE I HAVE FOR YOU LANCE FORTUNE
THIS MONDAY MORNING FEELING TITO SIMON
THIS MORNING NORTHERN UPROAR
THIS MUST BE THE PLACE TALKING HEADS
THIS NEW YEAR CLIFF RICHARD
THIS OLD HEART OF MINE ISLEY BROTHERS
THIS OLD HEART OF MINE ROD STEWART
THIS OLD SKIN BEAUTIFUL SOUTH
THIS OLE HOUSE ROSEMARY CLOONEY
THIS OLE HOUSE BILLIE ANTHONY
THIS OLE HOUSE SHAKIN' STEVENS
THIS ONE PAUL McCARTNEY
THIS ONE'S FOR THE CHILDREN NEW KIDS ON THE
    BLOCK
THIS ONE'S FOR YOU ED HARCOURT
THIS PARTY SUCKS! FUSED
THIS PERFECT DAY SAINTS
THIS PICTURE PLACEBO
THIS PLANET'S ON FIRE SAMMY HAGAR
THIS STRANGE EFFECT DAVE BERRY
THIS SUMMER SQUEEZE
THIS TIME [A] TROY SHONDELL
THIS TIME [B] BRYAN ADAMS
THIS TIME [C] DINA CARROLL
THIS TIME [D] MICHELLE SWEENEY
THIS TIME [E] JUDY CHEEKS
THIS TIME [F] CURTIS STIGERS
THIS TIME AROUND PHATS & SMALL
THIS TIME BABY JACKIE MOORE
THIS TIME I FOUND LOVE ROZALLA
THIS TIME I KNOW IT'S FOR REAL DONNA SUMMER
THIS TIME I KNOW IT'S FOR REAL KELLY LLORENNA
THIS TIME (LIVE) WET WET WET
THIS TIME OF YEAR RUNRIG
THIS TIME (WE'LL GET IT RIGHT) ENGLAND WORLD
    CUP SQUAD
THIS TOWN AIN'T BIG ENOUGH FOR THE BOTH OF US
    SPARKS
THIS TRAIN DON'T STOP THERE ANYMORE ELTON JOHN
THIS USED TO BE MY PLAYGROUND MADONNA
THIS WAITING HEART CHRIS DE BURGH
THIS WAY DILATED PEOPLES
THIS WHEEL'S ON FIRE [A] JULIE DRISCOLL, BRIAN
    AUGER & THE TRINITY
THIS WHEEL'S ON FIRE [B] SIOUXSIE & THE BANSHEES
THIS WILL BE NATALIE COLE
THIS WOMAN'S WORK KATE BUSH
THIS WORLD IS NOT MY HOME JIM REEVES
THIS WORLD OF WATER NEW MUSIK
THIS WRECKAGE GARY NUMAN
THIS YEAR'S LOVE DAVID GRAY
THOIA THONG R KELLY
THONG SONG SISQO
THE THORN EP SIOUXSIE & THE BANSHEES
THORN IN MY SIDE EURYTHMICS
THOSE FIRST IMPRESSIONS ASSOCIATES
THOSE SIMPLE THINGS RIGHT SAID FRED
THOSE WERE THE DAYS MARY HOPKIN
THOU SHALT NOT STEAL FREDDIE & THE DREAMERS
THOUGHT I'D DIED AND GONE TO HEAVEN BRYAN
    ADAMS
THE THOUGHT OF IT LOUIE LOUIE
THOUGHT U WERE THE ONE FOR ME JOEY B ELLIS
THOUGHTLESS KORN
A THOUSAND MILES VANESSA CARLTON
A THOUSAND STARS BILLY FURY
A THOUSAND TREES STEREOPHONICS
THREE WEDDING PRESENT
THREE BABIES SINEAD O'CONNOR
THE THREE BELLS BROWNS

THE THREE BELLS (THE JIMMY BROWN SONG) LES
    COMPAGNONS DE LA CHANSON
THREE BELLS BRIAN POOLE & THE TREMELOES
THE THREE BELLS DANIEL O'DONNELL
THREE COINS IN THE FOUNTAIN FRANK SINATRA
THREE COINS IN THE FOUNTAIN FOUR ACES
    FEATURING AL ALBERTS
THREE DRIVES GREECE 2000
THREE EP MANSUN
3AM [A] MATCHBOX 20
3AM [B] BOBBY BLANCO & MIKKI MOTO
3AM [C] BUSTED
3AM ETERNAL KLF FEATURING THE CHILDREN OF THE
    REVOLUTION
3 FEET TALL I AM KLOOT
3 IS FAMILY DANA DAWSON
3 LIBRAS A PERFECT CIRCLE
THREE LIONS (THE OFFICIAL SONG OF THE ENGLAND
    FOOTBALL TEAM) BADDIEL & SKINNER &
    LIGHTNING SEEDS
THREE LITTLE BIRDS BOB MARLEY & THE WAILERS
THREE LITTLE PIGS GREEN JELLY
THREE LITTLE WORDS APPLEJACKS
3 MCS AND 1 DJ BEASTIE BOYS
THREE MINUTE HERO SELECTER
3..6..9 SECONDS OF LIGHT BELLE & SEBASTIAN
3 SONGS EP WEDDING PRESENT
3 X 3 EP GENESIS
3IL (THRILL) SOUL U*NIQUE
THREE NIGHTS A WEEK FATS DOMINO
THREE RING CIRCUS BARRY BIGGS
THREE STARS RUBY WRIGHT
THREE STEPS TO HEAVEN EDDIE COCHRAN
THREE STEPS TO HEAVEN SHOWADDYWADDY
THREE TIMES A LADY COMMODORES
THREE TIMES A MAYBE K CREATIVE
THREESOME FENIX TX
THRILL HAS GONE TEXAS
THRILL ME [A] SIMPLY RED
THRILL ME [B] JUNIOR JACK
THRILLER MICHAEL JACKSON
THROUGH KINGS OF TOMORROW
THROUGH THE BARRICADES SPANDAU BALLET
THROUGH THE GATE ARTIFICIAL INTELLIGENCE
THROUGH THE RAIN MARIAH CAREY
THROUGH THE ROOF CUD
THROUGH THE STORM ARETHA FRANKLIN & ELTON
    JOHN
THROUGH THE WIRE KANYE WEST
THROUGH THE YEARS [A] GARY GLITTER
THROUGH THE YEARS [B] CILLA BLACK
THROW AWAY THE KEY LINX
THROW DOWN A LINE CLIFF RICHARD & HANK MARVIN
THROW THESE GUNS AWAY DUNBLANE
THROW YA GUNZ ONYX
THROW YOUR HANDS UP LV
THROW YOUR SET IN THE AIR CYPRESS HILL
THROWING IT ALL AWAY GENESIS
THROWING MY BABY OUT WITH BATHWATER TEN POLE
    TUDOR
THROWN AWAY STRANGLERS
THRU' THESE WALLS PHIL COLLINS
THUG LOVIN' JA RULE FEATURING BOBBY BROWN
THUGZ MANSION 2PAC
THUNDER [A] PRINCE & THE NEW POWER
    GENERATION
THUNDER [B] EAST 17
THUNDER AND LIGHTNING THIN LIZZY
THUNDER IN MY HEART LEO SAYER
THUNDER IN THE MOUNTAINS TOYAH
THUNDERBALL TOM JONES

THUNDERBIRDS [A] BARRY GRAY ORCHESTRA
THUNDERBIRDS [B] BUSTED
THUNDERBIRDS ARE GO FAB FEATURING MC PARKER
THUNDERDOME MESSIAH
THUNDERSTRUCK AC/DC
THURSDAY'S CHILD DAVID BOWIE
THUS SPAKE ZARATHUSTRA PHILHARMONIA
    ORCHESTRA, CONDUCTOR LORIN MAAZEL
TI AMO GINA G
TIC, TIC TAC CHILLI FEATURING CARRAPICHO
TIC TOC KLEA
TICKET TO RIDE BEATLES
TICKET TO THE MOON ELECTRIC LIGHT ORCHESTRA
THE TIDE IS HIGH BLONDIE
THE TIDE IS HIGH (GET THE FEELING) ATOMIC KITTEN
THE TIDE IS TURNING (AFTER LIVE AID) ROGER WATERS
THE TIDE THAT LEFT AND NEVER CAME BACK VEILS
TIE A YELLOW RIBBON ROUND THE OLD OAK TREE
    DAWN FEATURING TONY ORLANDO
TIE ME KANGAROO DOWN SPORT ROLF HARRIS
TIE YOUR MOTHER DOWN QUEEN
TIED TO THE 90'S TRAVIS
TIED UP YELLO
TIGER BABY SILVER CONVENTION
TIGER FEET MUD
TIGHTEN UP – I JUST CAN'T STOP DANCING WALLY
    JUMP Jr. & THE CRIMINAL ELEMENT ORCHESTRA
TIJUANA TAXI HERB ALPERT & THE TIJUANA BRASS
TIL I HEAR IT FROM YOU GIN BLOSSOMS
('TIL) I KISSED YOU EVERLY BROTHERS
...TIL THE COPS COME KNOCKIN' MAXWELL
'TIL THE DAY EASYWORLD
TIL THE END HAVEN
TILL TONY BENNETT
TILL DOROTHY SQUIRES
TILL TOM JONES
TILL I CAN'T TAKE LOVE NO MORE EDDY GRANT
TILL I GET MY WAY BLACK KEYS
TILL I LOVED YOU PLACIDO DOMINGO & JENNIFER
    RUSH
TILL I LOVED YOU (LOVE THEME FROM 'GOYA') BARBRA
    STREISAND & DON JOHNSON
TILL TEARS DO US PART HEAVENS CRY
TILL THE END OF THE DAY KINKS
TILL THERE WAS YOU PEGGY LEE
TILL WE MEET AGAIN [A] INNER CITY
TILL WE MEET AGAIN [B] PUSH
TILL YOU COME BACK TO ME LEO SAYER
TILT YA HEAD BACK NELLY & CHRISTINA AGUILERA
TILTED SUGAR
TIME [A] CRAIG DOUGLAS
TIME [B] LIGHT OF THE WORLD
TIME [C] FRIDA & BA ROBERTSON
TIME [D] FREDDIE MERCURY
TIME [E] KIM WILDE
TIME [F] SUPERGRASS
TIME [G] MARION
TIME AFTER TIME [A] CYNDI LAUPER
TIME AFTER TIME [A] HYPERSTATE
TIME AFTER TIME [A] CHANGING FACES
TIME AFTER TIME [A] DISTANT SOUNDZ
TIME AFTER TIME [A] NOVASPACE
TIME AFTER TIME [B] BELOVED
TIME ALONE WILL TELL MALCOLM ROBERTS
TIME AND CHANCE COLOR ME BADD
A TIME AND PLACE MIKE + THE MECHANICS
TIME AND THE RIVER NAT 'KING' COLE
TIME AND TIDE BASIA
TIME AND TIME AGAIN PAPA ROACH
TIME BOMB [A] 808 STATE
TIME BOMB [B] RANCID

TONIGHT IS WHAT IT MEANS TO BE YOUNG JIM STEINMAN & FIRE INC
TONIGHT TONIGHT SMASHING PUMPKINS
TONIGHT TONIGHT GENESIS
TONIGHT YOU BELONG TO ME PATIENCE & PRUDENCE
TONIGHT'S THE NIGHT ROD STEWART
TONITE [A] SUPERCAR
TONITE [B] PHATS & SMALL
TOO BAD NICKELBACK
TOO BEAUTIFUL TO LAST ENGELBERT HUMPERDINCK
TOO BIG SUZI QUATRO
TOO BLIND TO SEE IT KYM SIMS
TOO BUSY THINKING ABOUT MY BABY MARVIN GAYE
TOO BUSY THINKING ABOUT MY BABY STEPS
TOO BUSY THINKING 'BOUT MY BABY MARDI GRAS
TOO CLOSE NEXT
TOO CLOSE BLUE
TOO DRUNK TO FUCK DEAD KENNEDYS
TOO FAR GONE LISA SCOTT-LEE
TOO GONE, TOO LONG EN VOGUE
TOO GOOD LITTLE TONY
TOO GOOD TO BE FORGOTTEN CHI-LITES
TOO GOOD TO BE FORGOTTEN AMAZULU
TOO GOOD TO BE TRUE TOM PETTY & THE HEARTBREAKERS
TOO HARD TO BE FREE AMEN
TOO HOT [A] KOOL & THE GANG
TOO HOT [A] COOLIO
TOO HOT [B] FUN LOVIN' CRIMINALS
TOO HOT [C] FYA
TOO HOT TO HANDLE HEATWAVE
TOO HOT TO TROT COMMODORES
TOO LATE JUNIOR
TOO LATE FOR GOODBYES JULIAN LENNON
TOO LATE TO SAY GOODBYE RICHARD MARX
TOO LATE, TOO SOON JON SECADA
TOO LOST IN YOU SUGABABES
TOO MANY BEAUTIFUL GIRLS CLINTON FORD
TOO MANY BROKEN HEARTS JASON DONOVAN
TOO MANY DJ'S SOULWAX
TOO MANY FISH FRANKIE KNUCKLES FEATURING ADEVA
TOO MANY GAMES MAZE FEATURING FRANKIE BEVERLY
TOO MANY MC'S/LET ME CLEAR MY THROAT PUBLIC DOMAIN
TOO MANY PEOPLE PAULINE HENRY
TOO MANY RIVERS BRENDA LEE
TOO MANY TEARS DAVID COVERDALE & WHITESNAKE
TOO MANY WALLS CATHY DENNIS
TOO MUCH [A] ELVIS PRESLEY
TOO MUCH [B] BROS
TOO MUCH [C] SPICE GIRLS
TOO MUCH FOR ONE HEART MICHAEL BARRYMORE
TOO MUCH HEAVEN BEE GEES
TOO MUCH INFORMATION DURAN DURAN
TOO MUCH KISSING SENSELESS THINGS
TOO MUCH LOVE WILL KILL YOU BRIAN MAY
TOO MUCH LOVE WILL KILL YOU QUEEN
TOO MUCH TEQUILA CHAMPS
TOO MUCH TOO LITTLE TOO LATE [A] JOHNNY MATHIS & DENIECE WILLIAMS
TOO MUCH, TOO LITTLE, TOO LATE [B] SILVER SUN
TOO MUCH TOO YOUNG LITTLE ANGELS
TOO MUCH TROUBLE LIMAHL
TOO NICE TO TALK TO BEAT
TOO REAL LEVELLERS
TOO RIGHT TO BE WRONG CARTER TWINS
TOO RISKY JIM DAVIDSON
TOO SHY KAJAGOOGOO
TOO SOON TO KNOW ROY ORBISON

TOO TIRED GARY MOORE
TOO WICKED (EP) ASWAD
TOO YOUNG BILL FORBES
TOO YOUNG DONNY OSMOND
TOO YOUNG TO DIE JAMIROQUAI
TOO YOUNG TO GO STEADY NAT 'KING' COLE
TOOFUNKY GEORGE MICHAEL
TOOK MY LOVE BIZARRE INC FEATURING ANGIE BROWN
TOOK THE LAST TRAIN DAVID GATES
TOP O' THE MORNING TO YA HOUSE OF PAIN
TOP OF THE POPS REZILLOS
TOP OF THE STAIRS SKEE-LO
TOP OF THE WORLD [A] CARPENTERS
TOP OF THE WORLD [B] VAN HALEN
TOP OF THE WORLD [C] BRANDY FEATURING MA$E
TOP OF THE WORLD [D] WILDHEARTS
TOP OF THE WORLD (OLÉ OLÉ OLÉ) CHUMBAWAMBA
TOP TEEN BABY GARRY MILLS
TOPKNOT CORNERSHOP
TOPSY (PARTS 1 AND 2) COZY COLE
TORCH SOFT CELL
TORERO JULIUS LAROSA
TORERO – CHA CHA CHA RENATO CAROSONE & HIS SEXTET
TORN NATALIE IMBRUGLIA
TORN BETWEEN TWO LOVERS MARY MacGREGOR
TORTURE [A] JACKSONS
TORTURE [B] KING
TOSH FLUKE
TOSS IT UP MAKAVELI
TOSSING AND TURNING [A] IVY LEAGUE
TOSSING AND TURNING [B] WINDJAMMER
TOSSING AND TURNING [C] CHAKKA BOOM BANG
TOTAL CONFUSION A HOMEBOY, A HIPPIE & A FUNKI DREDD
TOTAL ECLIPSE OF THE HEART BONNIE TYLER
TOTAL ECLIPSE OF THE HEART NICKI FRENCH
TOTAL ECLIPSE OF THE HEART JAN WAYNE
TOTAL ERASURE PHILIP JAP
THE TOTAL MIX BLACK BOX
TOTTENHAM TOTTENHAM TOTTENHAM HOTSPUR F.A. CUP FINAL SQUAD
TOUCH LORI & THE CHAMELEONS
THE TOUCH KIM WILDE
TOUCH BY TOUCH DIANA ROSS
TOUCH IT MONIFAH
TOUCH ME [A] 49ERS
TOUCH ME [B] RUI DA SILVA FEATURING CASSANDRA
TOUCH ME [C] ANGEL CITY
TOUCH ME (ALL NIGHT LONG) CATHY DENNIS
TOUCH ME (I WANT YOUR BODY) SAMANTHA FOX
TOUCH ME IN THE MORNING DIANA ROSS
TOUCH ME TEASE ME [A] CASE FEATURING FOXY BROWN
TOUCH ME TEASE ME [B] 3SL
TOUCH ME TOUCH ME DAVE DEE, DOZY, BEAKY, MICK & TICH
TOUCH ME WITH YOUR LOVE BETH ORTON
TOUCH MYSELF T-BOZ
A TOUCH OF EVIL JUDAS PRIEST
A TOUCH OF LOVE CLEOPATRA
A TOUCH OF VELVET A STING OF BRASS RON GRAINER ORCHESTRA
TOUCH THE SKY 29 PALMS
TOUCH TOO MUCH AC/DC
A TOUCH TOO MUCH ARROWS
TOUCH YOU KATOI
TOUCHED BY GOD KATCHA
TOUCHED BY THE HAND OF CICCIOLINA POP WILL EAT ITSELF

TOUCHED BY THE HAND OF GOD NEW ORDER
TOUCHY! A-HA
TOUGHER THAN THE REST BRUCE SPRINGSTEEN
TOUR DE FRANCE KRAFTWERK
TOURNIQUET [A] MARILYN MANSON
TOURNIQUET [B] HEADSWIM
TOUS LES GARCONS ET LES FILLES FRANCOISE HARDY
TOWER OF STRENGTH [A] FRANKIE VAUGHAN
TOWER OF STRENGTH [A] GENE McDANIELS
TOWER OF STRENGTH [B] MISSION
TOWER OF STRENGTH [C] SKIN
TOWERS OF LONDON XTC
TOWN NORTHERN UPROAR
A TOWN CALLED MALICE JAM
TOWN CLOWNS BLAMELESS
TOWN CRIER CRAIG DOUGLAS
TOWN OF PLENTY ELTON JOHN
TOWN TO TOWN MICRODISNEY
TOWN WITHOUT PITY GENE PITNEY
TOWN WITHOUT PITY EDDI READER
TOXIC BRITNEY SPEARS
TOXIC GIRL KINGS OF CONVENIENCE
TOXICITY SYSTEM OF A DOWN
TOXYGENE ORB
TOY CASUALS
TOY BALLOONS RUSS CONWAY
TOY BOY SINITTA
TOY SOLDIERS MARTIKA
TOYS FOR BOYS MARION
TRACEY IN MY ROOM EBTG VERSUS SOUL VISION
TRACIE LEVEL 42
TRACKIN' BILLY CRAWFORD
TRACKS OF MY TEARS SMOKEY ROBINSON & THE MIRACLES
TRACKS OF MY TEARS LINDA RONSTADT
TRACKS OF MY TEARS COLIN BLUNSTONE
TRACKS OF MY TEARS GO WEST
TRACY CUFF LINKS
TRADE (EP) (DISC 2) VARIOUS ARTISTS (EP'S & LPS)
TRAFFIC [A] STEREOPHONICS
TRAFFIC [B] TIESTO
TRAGEDY [A] ARGENT
TRAGEDY [B] BEE GEES
TRAGEDY [B] STEPS
TRAGEDY AND MYSTERY CHINA CRISIS
TRAGIC COMIC EXTREME
THE TRAIL OF THE LONESOME PINE LAUREL & HARDY WITH THE AVALON BOYS FEATURING CHILL WILLS
TRAIL OF TEARS DOGS D'AMOUR
TRAILER LOAD A GIRLS SHABBA RANKS
TRAIN [A] SISTERS OF MERCY
TRAIN [B] GOLDFRAPP
THE TRAIN IS COMING SHAGGY FEATURING WAYNE WONDER
THE TRAIN IS COMING UB40
TRAIN OF CONSEQUENCES MEGADETH
TRAIN OF LOVE ALMA COGAN
TRAIN OF THOUGHT [A] A-HA
TRAIN OF THOUGHT [B] ESCRIMA
TRAIN ON A TRACK KELLY ROWLAND
TRAIN TO SKAVILLE ETHIOPIANS
TRAIN TOUR TO RAINBOW CITY PYRAMIDS
TRAINS AND BOATS AND PLANES BURT BACHARACH
TRAINS AND BOATS AND PLANES BILLY J. KRAMER & THE DAKOTAS
TRAMBONE KREW-KATS
TRAMP [A] OTIS REDDING & CARLA THOMAS
TRAMP [B] SALT-N-PEPA
TRAMPOLENE JULIAN COPE
TRAMPS AND THIEVES QUIREBOYS
TRANCESCRIPT HARDFLOOR

TRANQUILLIZER GENEVA
TRANSAMAZONIA SHAMEN
TRANSATLANTIC ROACH MOTEL
TRANSFER AFFECTION A FLOCK OF SEAGULLS
TRANSISTOR RADIO BENNY HILL
TRANSMISSION [A] GAY DAD
TRANSMISSION [B] VIOLENT DELIGHT
TRANSONIC WIRED
TRANZ EURO XPRESS X-PRESS 2
TRANZY STATE OF MIND PUSH
TRAPPED [A] COLONEL ABRAMS
TRAPPED [B] GUYVER
TRASH [A] ROXY MUSIC
TRASH [B] SUEDE
TRASHED SKIN
THE TRAVELLER SPEAR OF DESTINY
TRAVELLERS TUNE OCEAN COLOUR SCENE
TRAVELLIN' BAND CREEDENCE CLEARWATER REVIVAL
TRAVELLIN' HOME VERA LYNN
TRAVELLIN' LIGHT CLIFF RICHARD & THE SHADOWS
TRAVELLIN' MAN RICKY NELSON
TRAVELLING LIGHT TINDERSTICKS
TRAVELLING MAN STUDIO 2
TREASON (IT'S JUST A STORY) TEARDROP EXPLODES
TREASURE OF LOVE CLYDE McPHATTER
TREAT 'EM RIGHT CHUBB ROCK
TREAT HER LIKE A LADY [A] TEMPTATIONS
TREAT HER LIKE A LADY [B] CELINE DION
TREAT HER LIKE A LADY [C] JOE
TREAT HER RIGHT ROY HEAD
TREAT INFAMY REST ASSURED
TREAT ME GOOD YAZZ
TREAT ME LIKE A LADY [A] FIVE STAR
TREAT ME LIKE A LADY [B] ZOE BIRKETT
TREAT ME RIGHT ADEVA
TREATY YOTHU YINDI
TREBLE CHANCE JOE 'MR PIANO' HENDERSON
TREE FROG HOPE A.D.
THE TREES PULP
TREMBLE MARC ET CLAUDE
TREMELO SONG (EP) CHARLATANS
THE TRIAL OF HISSING SID KEITH MICHELL, CAPTAIN
    BEAKY & HIS BAND
TRIALS OF LIFE KALEEF
TRIBAL BASE REBEL MC FEATURING TENOR FLY &
    BARRINGTON LEVY
TRIBAL DANCE 2 UNLIMITED
TRIBUTE (RIGHT ON) PASADENAS
TRIBUTE TO A KING WILLIAM BELL
TRIBUTE TO BUDDY HOLLY MIKE BERRY WITH THE
    OUTLAWS
TRIBUTE TO JIM REEVES LARRY CUNNINGHAM & THE
    MIGHTY AVONS
TRIBUTE TO OUR ANCESTORS RUBBADUBB
TRICK ME KELIS
A TRICK OF THE LIGHT TRIFFIDS
TRICK OF THE NIGHT BANANARAMA
TRICKY DISCO TRICKY DISCO
TRICKY KID TRICKY
TRIGGER HIPPIE MORCHEEBA
TRIGGER INSIDE THERAPY?
TRINI TRAX TRINI LOPEZ
TRIP II THE MOON ACEN
A TRIP TO TRUMPTON URBAN HYPE
TRIPLE TROUBLE BEASTIE BOYS
TRIPPIN' [A] MARK MORRISON
TRIPPIN' [B] ORIS JAY PRESENTS DELSENA
TRIPPIN' ON SUNSHINE PIZZAMAN
TRIPPIN' ON YOUR LOVE [A] A WAY OF LIFE
TRIPPIN' ON YOUR LOVE [B] KENNY THOMAS
TRIPPY ARAB STRAP

TRIPWIRE LIONROCK
TRIUMPH [A] WU-TANG CLAN FEATURING
    CAPPADONNA
TRIUMPH [B] HISS
TRIXSTAR BLAK TWANG FEATURING ESTELLE
TROCADERO SHOWADDYWADDY
THE TROOPER IRON MAIDEN
TROPIC ISLAND HUM PAUL McCARTNEY
TROPICAL ICE-LAND FIERY FURNACES
TROPICAL SOUNDCLASH DJ GREGORY
TROPICALIA BECK
T.R.O.U.B.L.E. ELVIS PRESLEY
TROUBLE [A] GILLAN
TROUBLE [B] LINDSEY BUCKINGHAM
TROUBLE [C] HEAVEN 17
TROUBLE [D] SHAMPOO
TROUBLE [E] COLDPLAY
TROUBLE [F] CYPRESS HILL
TROUBLE [G] P!NK
TROUBLE BOYS THIN LIZZY
TROUBLE IN PARADISE AL JARREAU
TROUBLE IS MY MIDDLE NAME BROOK BROTHERS
TROUBLE IS MY MIDDLE NAME FOUR PENNIES
TROUBLE TOWN MARTIN STEPHENSON & THE
    DAINTEES
THE TROUBLE WITH HARRY ALFI & HARRY
THE TROUBLE WITH LOVE IS KELLY CLARKSON
TROUBLED GIRL KAREN RAMIREZ
TROY (THE PHOENIX FROM THE FLAME) SINEAD
    O'CONNOR
TRUCK ON SIMPLE KID
TRUCK ON (TYKE) T. REX
TRUDIE JOE 'MR PIANO' HENDERSON
TRUE [A] SPANDAU BALLET
TRUE [B] JAIMESON FEATURING ANGEL BLU
TRUE BLUE MADONNA
TRUE COLORS [A] CYNDI LAUPER
TRUE COLOURS [A] PHIL COLLINS
TRUE COLOURS [B] GO WEST
TRUE DEVOTION SAMANTHA FOX
TRUE FAITH NEW ORDER
TRUE LOVE [A] TERRY LIGHTFOOT & HIS NEW ORLEANS
    JAZZMEN
TRUE LOVE [A] RICHARD CHAMBERLAIN
TRUE LOVE [A] SHAKIN' STEVENS
TRUE LOVE [A] ELTON JOHN & KIKI DEE
TRUE LOVE [A] BING CROSBY & GRACE KELLY
TRUE LOVE [B] CHIMES
TRUE LOVE FOR EVER MORE BACHELORS
TRUE LOVE NEVER DIES FLIP AND FULL FEATURING
    KELLY LLORENNA
TRUE LOVE WAYS BUDDY HOLLY
TRUE LOVE WAYS PETER & GORDON
TRUE LOVE WAYS CLIFF RICHARD WITH THE LONDON
    PHILHARMONIC ORCHESTRA
TRUE LOVE WAYS DAVID ESSEX & CATHERINE ZETA
    JONES
TRUE LOVE WILL FIND YOU IN THE END SPECTRUM
TRUE NATURE JANE'S ADDICTION
TRUE SPIRIT CARLEEN ANDERSON
TRUE STEP TONIGHT TRUE STEPPERS FEATURING BRIAN
    HARVEY
TRUE (THE FAGGOT IS YOU) MOREL
TRUE TO FORM HYBRID FEATURING PETER HOOK
TRUE TO US VANILLA
TRUE TO YOUR HEART 98o FEATURING STEVIE WONDER
TRUGANINI MIDNIGHT OIL
TRULY [A] LIONEL RICHIE
TRULY [A] STEVEN HOUGHTON
TRULY [B] HINDA HICKS
TRULY [C] PESHAY FEATURING KYM MAZELLE

TRULY [D] DELERIUM
TRULY MADLY DEEPLY SAVAGE GARDEN
TRULY ONE ORIGIN UNKNOWN
TRUST [A] BROTHER BEYOND
TRUST [B] NED'S ATOMIC DUSTBIN
TRUST ME GURU FEATURING N'DEA DAVENPORT
TRUST ME TO OPEN MY MOUTH SQUEEZE
THE TRUTH [A] COLONEL ABRAMS
THE TRUTH [B] REAL PEOPLE
THE TRUTH IS NO WORDS MUSIC
TRUTH OR DARE SHIRLEY MURDOCK
TRY [A] BROS
TRY [B] IAN VAN DAHL
TRY [C] NELLY FURTADO
TRY A LITTLE KINDNESS GLEN CAMPBELL
TRY A LITTLE TENDERNESS OTIS REDDING
TRY AGAIN AALIYAH
TRY AGAIN TODAY CHARLATANS
TRY HONESTY BILLY TALENT
TRY JAH LOVE THIRD WORLD
TRY ME OUT CORONA
TRY MY WORLD GEORGIE FAME
TRY TO UNDERSTAND LULU
TRY TRY TRY [A] JULIAN COPE
TRY TRY TRY [B] SMASHING PUMPKINS
TRYIN' HILLTOPPERS
TRYIN' TO GET THE FEELING AGAIN CARPENTERS
TRYING TO FORGET JIM REEVES
TRYING TO GET TO YOU ELVIS PRESLEY
TRYOUTS FOR THE HUMAN RACE SPARKS
TSOP (THE SOUND OF PHILADELPHIA) MFSB FEATURING
    THE THREE DEGREES
TSUNAMI MANIC STREET PREACHERS
TU AMOR KACI
TU M'AIMES ENCORE (TO LOVE ME AGAIN) CELINE DION
TUBTHUMPING CHUMBAWAMBA
TUBULAR BELLS CHAMPS BOYS
TUCH ME FONDA RAE
TUESDAY AFTERNOON JENNIFER BROWN
TUESDAY MORNING POGUES
TUESDAY SUNSHINE QUESTIONS
TUFF ACT TO FOLLOW MN8
TUG OF WAR PAUL McCARTNEY
TULANE STEVE GIBBONS BAND
TULIPS BLOC PARTY
TULIPS FROM AMSTERDAM MAX BYGRAVES
TUM BIN JIYA BALLY SAGOO
TUMBLING DICE ROLLING STONES
TUMBLING TUMBLEWEEDS SLIM WHITMAN
THE TUNE SUGGS
TUNES SPLITS THE ATOM MC TUNES VERSUS 808 STATE
TUNNEL OF LOVE [A] DIRE STRAITS
TUNNEL OF LOVE [B] FUN BOY THREE
TUNNEL OF LOVE [C] BRUCE SPRINGSTEEN
TURN [A] TRAVIS
TURN [B] FEEDER
TURN AROUND [A] FAB!
TURN AROUND [B] PHATS & SMALL
TURN AROUND AND COUNT 2 TEN DEAD OR ALIVE
TURN BACK THE CLOCK JOHNNY HATES JAZZ
TURN BACK TIME AQUA
TURN IT AROUND ALENA
TURN IT AROUND 4 STRINGS
TURN IT DOWN SWEET
TURN IT INTO LOVE HAZELL DEAN
TURN IT ON LEVEL 42
TURN IT ON AGAIN GENESIS
TURN IT UP [A] CONWAY BROTHERS
TURN IT UP [B] RICHIE RICH
TURN IT UP [C] TECHNOTRONIC FEATURING MELISSA &
    EINSTEIN

TURN IT UP [D] PETER ANDRE
TURN IT UP [E] RAJA NEE
TURN IT UP (SAY YEAH) DJ DUKE
TURN IT UP/FIRE IT UP BUSTA RHYMES
TURN ME LOOSE WALLY JUMP Jr. & THE CRIMINAL ELEMENT ORCHESTRA
TURN ME ON [A] DANNY TENAGLIA FEATURING LIZ TORRES
TURN ME ON [B] KEVIN LYTTLE
TURN ME ON [B] RMXCRW FEATURING EBON-E PLUS AMBUSH
TURN ME ON TURN ME OFF HONEY BANE
TURN ME OUT (TURN TO SUGAR) PRAXIS FEATURING KATHY BROWN
TURN OFF MILLTOWN BROTHERS
TURN OFF THE LIGHT NELLY FURTADO
TURN ON THE NIGHT KISS
TURN ON, TUNE IN, COP OUT FREAKPOWER
TURN THE BEAT AROUND GLORIA ESTEFAN
TURN THE MUSIC UP PLAYERS ASSOCIATION
TURN THE MUSIC UP CHRIS PAUL
TURN THE TIDE SYLVER
TURN TO GOLD DAVID AUSTIN
TURN TO STONE ELECTRIC LIGHT ORCHESTRA
TURN! TURN! TURN! BYRDS
TURN UP THE BASS TYREE FEATURING KOOL ROCK STEADY
TURN UP THE NIGHT BLACK SABBATH
TURN UP THE POWER N-TRANCE
TURN UP THE SOUND LISA PIN-UP
TURN YOUR BACK ON ME KAJAGOOGOO
TURN YOUR LIGHTS DOWN LOW BOB MARLEY FEATURING LAURYN HILL
TURN YOUR LOVE AROUND GEORGE BENSON
TURN YOUR LOVE AROUND TONY DI BART
TURN YOUR RADIO ON RAY STEVENS
TURNED AWAY AUDIO BULLYS
TURNING AWAY SHAKIN' STEVENS
TURNING JAPANESE VAPORS
TURNING THE TOWN RED ELVIS COSTELLO
TURQUOISE [A] DONOVAN
TURQUOISE [B] CIRCULATION
TURTLE POWER PARTNERS IN KRYME
TURTLE RHAPSODY ORCHESTRA ON THE HALF SHELL
TUSK FLEETWOOD MAC
TUTTI FRUTTI LITTLE RICHARD
TUXEDO JUNCTION MANHATTAN TRANSFER
TV FLYING LIZARDS
TV CRIMES BLACK SABBATH
TV DINNERS ZZ TOP
TV SAVAGE BOW WOW WOW
TV TAN WILDHEARTS
TVC 15 DAVID BOWIE
TWANGLING THREE FINGERS IN A BOX MIKE
TWEEDLE DEE GEORGIA GIBBS
TWEEDLE DEE FRANKIE VAUGHAN
TWEEDLE DEE LITTLE JIMMY OSMOND
TWEEDLE DEE TWEEDLE DUM MIDDLE OF THE ROAD
THE TWELFTH OF NEVER CLIFF RICHARD
THE TWELFTH OF NEVER DONNY OSMOND
THE TWELFTH OF NEVER ELVIS PRESLEY
THE TWELFTH OF NEVER CARTER TWINS
12 REASONS WHY I LOVE HER MY LIFE STORY
TWELFTH STREET RAG BERT WEEDON
12:51 STROKES
TWELVE STEPS TO LOVE BRIAN POOLE & THE TREMELOES
20 DEGREES JONNY L
TWENTY FOREPLAY JANET JACKSON
20 HZ (NEW FREQUENCIES) CAPRICORN
20 SECONDS TO COMPLY SILVER BULLET

TWENTY TINY FINGERS STARGAZERS
TWENTY TINY FINGERS CORONETS
TWENTY TINY FINGERS ALMA COGAN
TWENTY YEARS PLACEBO
£20 TO GET IN SHUT UP & DANCE
20/20 GEORGE BENSON
20TH CENTURY BRAD
20TH CENTURY BOY T REX
21ST CENTURY WEEKEND PLAYERS
TWENTY-FIRST CENTURY BOY SIGUE SIGUE SPUTNIK
21ST CENTURY (DIGITAL BOY) BAD RELIGION
21ST CENTURY GIRLS 21ST CENTURY GIRLS
24 HOURS [A] BETTY BOO
24 HOURS [B] AGENT SUMO
24 HOURS A DAY NOMAD
TWENTY FOUR HOURS FROM TULSA GENE PITNEY
24 HOURS FROM YOU NEXT OF KIN
24/7 [A] 3T
24/7 [B] FIXATE
TWENTYFOURSEVEN [C] ARTFUL DODGER FEATURING MELANIE BLATT
24-7-365 CHARLES & EDDIE
24 SYCAMORE GENE PITNEY
25 MILES EDWIN STARR
25 MILES 2001 THREE AMIGOS
25 OR 6 TO 4 CHICAGO
29 PALMS ROBERT PLANT
21 PADDINGTONS
21 QUESTIONS 50 CENT FEATURING NATE DOGG
21 SECONDS SO SOLID CREW
22 DAYS 22-20'S
TWENTY WILD HORSES STATUS QUO
TWICE AS HARD BLACK CROWES
TWILIGHT ELECTRIC LIGHT ORCHESTRA
TWILIGHT CAFÉ SUSAN FASSBENDER
TWILIGHT TIME PLATTERS
TWILIGHT WORLD SWING OUT SISTER
TWILIGHT ZONE – TWILIGHT TONE (MEDLEY) MANHATTAN TRANSFER
TWILIGHT ZONE [A] IRON MAIDEN
TWILIGHT ZONE [B] 2 UNLIMITED
TWILIGHTS LAST GLEAMING HIGH CONTRAST
TWIN EARTH MONSTER MAGNET
TWINKIE LEE GARY WALKER
TWINKLE WHIPPING BOY
TWINKLE TOES ROY ORBISON
TWINKLE TWINKLE (I'M NOT A STAR) JAZZY JEFF & THE FRESH PRINCE
TWINLIGHTS (EP) COCTEAU TWINS
THE TWIST [A] CHUBBY CHECKER
TWIST [B] GOLDFRAPP
TWIST AND SHOUT [A] ISLEY BROTHERS
TWIST AND SHOUT [A] BRIAN POOLE & THE TREMELOES
TWIST AND SHOUT [A] SALT-N-PEPA
TWIST AND SHOUT [A] CHAKA DEMUS & PLIERS FEATURING JACK RADICS & TAXI GANG
TWIST AND SHOUT [B] DEACON BLUE
TWIST 'EM OUT DILLINJA
TWIST IN MY SOBRIETY TANITA TIKARAM
TWIST OF FATE [A] OLIVIA NEWTON-JOHN
TWIST OF FATE [B] SIOBHAN DONAGHY
TWIST (ROUND 'N' ROUND) CHILL FAC-TORR
TWIST TWIST CHAKACHAS
THE TWIST (YO, TWIST) FAT BOYS & CHUBBY CHECKER
TWISTED KEITH SWEAT
TWISTED (EVERYDAY HURTS) SKUNK ANANSIE
THE TWISTER VIPER
TWISTERELLA RIDE
TWISTIN' THE NIGHT AWAY SAM COOKE
TWISTIN' THE NIGHT AWAY DIVINE

TWISTING BY THE POOL DIRE STRAITS
'TWIXT TWELVE AND TWENTY PAT BOONE
2 BECOME 1 SPICE GIRLS
TWO CAN PLAY THAT GAME BOBBY BROWN
2 DEEP GANG STARR
TWO DIFFERENT WORLDS RONNIE HILTON
2 FACED LOUISE
TWO EP MANSUN
TWO FATT GUITARS (REVISITED) DIRECKT
2-4-6-8 MOTORWAY TOM ROBINSON BAND
TWO HEARTS [A] CLIFF RICHARD
TWO HEARTS [B] PHIL COLLINS
TWO HEARTS [C] STEPHANIE MILLS FEATURING TEDDY PENDERGRASS
TWO HEARTS BEAT AS ONE U2
TWO HEARTS TOGETHER ORANGE JUICE
TWO IN A MILLION [A] MICA PARIS
TWO IN A MILLION [B] S CLUB 7
TWO KINDS OF TEARDROPS DEL SHANNON
2 LEGIT 2 QUIT HAMMER
TWO LITTLE BOYS ROLF HARRIS
TWO LITTLE BOYS SPLODGENESSABOUNDS
2 MINUTES TO MIDNIGHT IRON MAIDEN
TWO MONTHS OFF UNDERWORLD
THE TWO OF US MAC & KATIE KISSOON
TWO OUT OF THREE AIN'T BAD MEAT LOAF
TWO PAINTINGS AND A DRUM CARL COX
TWO PEOPLE [A] TINA TURNER
2 PEOPLE [B] JEAN JACQUES SMOOTHIE
TWO PINTS OF LAGER AND A PACKET OF CRISPS PLEASE SPLODGENESSABOUNDS
2 + 2 = 5 RADIOHEAD
TWO PRINCES SPIN DOCTORS
2 REMIXES BY AFX AFX
TWO SILHOUETTES DEL SHANNON
2 STEP ROCK BANDITS
TWO STEPS BEHIND DEF LEPPARD
TWO STREETS VAL DOONICAN
2 THE RHYTHM SOUND FACTORY
2000 MILES PRETENDERS
2, 3, GO WEDDING PRESENT
2 TIMES ANN LEE
TWO TIMING TOUCH AND BROKEN BONES HIVES
THE TWO TONE EP TWO TONE
TWO TRIBES FRANKIE GOES TO HOLLYWOOD
2√231 ANTICAPPELLA
2-WAY RAYVON
2 WAY STREET MISSJONES
TWO WORLDS COLLIDE INSPIRAL CARPETS
TWO WRONGS (DON'T MAKE A RIGHT) WYCLEF JEAN FEATURING CLAUDETTE ORTIZ
TWYFORD DOWN GALLIANO
TYPE LIVING COLOUR
TYPICAL AMERICAN GOATS
TYPICAL GIRLS SLITS
TYPICAL MALE TINA TURNER
TYPICAL! FRAZIER CHORUS
U LONI CLARK
U & ME CAPPELLA
U + ME = LOVE FUNKY WORM
U BLOW MY MIND BLACKstreet
U CAN'T TOUCH THIS MC HAMMER
U DON'T HAVE TO SAY U LOVE ME MASH!
U FOUND OUT HANDBAGGERS
U GIRLS (LOOK SO SEXY) NUSH
U GOT 2 KNOW CAPPELLA
U GOT 2 LET THE MUSIC CAPPELLA
U GOT IT BAD USHER
U GOT THE LOOK PRINCE
U (I GOT THE FEELING) DJ SCOT PROJECT
U KNOW WHAT'S UP DONELL JONES

UP WITH THE COCK JUDGE DREAD
UP WITH THE PEOPLE LAMBCHOP
UP, UP AND AWAY JOHNNY MANN SINGERS
UPFIELD BILLY BRAGG
UPRISING ARTIFICIAL INTELLIGENCE
UPROCK ROCKSTEADY CREW
UPSIDE DOWN [A] DIANA ROSS
UPSIDE DOWN [B] A*TEENS
UPTIGHT [A] STEVIE WONDER
UPTIGHT [B] SHARA NELSON
UPTOWN DOWNTOWN FULL INTENTION
UPTOWN FESTIVAL SHALAMAR
UPTOWN GIRL BILLY JOEL
UPTOWN GIRL WESTLIFE
UPTOWN TOP RANKING ALI & FRAZIER
UPTOWN UPTEMPO WOMAN RANDY EDELMAN
URBAN CITY GIRL BENZ
URBAN GUERRILLA HAWKWIND
URBAN PRESSURE GRIM NORTHERN SOCIAL
URBAN TRAIN DJ TIESTO
THE URGE [A] FREDDY CANNON
URGE [B] WILDHEARTS
URGENT FOREIGNER
URGENTLY IN LOVE BILLY CRAWFORD
USA WWF SUPERSTARS FEATURING HACKSAW JIM
    DUGGAN
USE IT UP AND WEAR IT OUT ODYSSEY
USE IT UP AND WEAR IT OUT PAT & MICK
USED FOR GLUE RIVAL SCHOOLS
USED TA BE MY GIRL O'JAYS
USELESS DEPECHE MODE
USELESS (I DON'T NEED YOU NOW) KYM MAZELLE
UTOPIA GOLDFRAPP
V THIRTEEN BIG AUDIO DYNAMITE
VACATION CONNIE FRANCIS
VADO VIA DRUPI
VAGABONDS NEW MODEL ARMY
VALENTINE T'PAU
VALENTINO CONNIE FRANCIS
VALERIE STEVE WINWOOD
VALLERI MONKEES
VALLEY OF TEARS FATS DOMINO
VALLEY OF TEARS BUDDY HOLLY
VALLEY OF THE DOLLS DIONNE WARWICK
VALLEY OF THE DOLLS GENERATION X
VALLEY OF THE SHADOWS ORIGIN UNKNOWN
THE VALLEY ROAD BRUCE HORNSBY & THE RANGE
VALOTTE JULIAN LENNON
VAMOS A LA PLAYA RIGHEIRA
VAMP OUTLANDER
THE VAMP (REVISITED) OUTLANDER
VAMPIRE RACECOURSE SLEEPY JACKSON
VANESSA TED HEATH
VANILLA RADIO WILDHEARTS
VANITY KILLS ABC
VAPORIZER LUPINE HOWL
VAPORS SNOOP DOGGY DOGG
VASOLINE STONE TEMPLE PILOTS
VAVOOM! MAN WITH NO NAME
VAYA CON DIOS LES PAUL & MARY FORD
VAYA CON DOS MILLICAN & NESBITT
VEGAS [A] SLEEPER
VEGAS [B] AGNELLI & NELSON
VEGAS TWO TIMES STEREOPHONICS
VEHICLE IDES OF MARCH
VELCRO FLY ZZ TOP
VELOURIA PIXIES
VELVET MOODS JOHAN GIELEN PRESENTS ABNEA
VENCEREMOS – WE WILL WIN WORKING WEEK
VENI VIDI VICI RONNIE HILTON
VENTOLIN APHEX TWIN

VENTURA HIGHWAY AMERICA
VENUS [A] DICKIE VALENTINE
VENUS [A] FRANKIE AVALON
VENUS [B] SHOCKING BLUE
VENUS [B] BANANARAMA
VENUS [B] DON PABLO'S ANIMALS
VENUS AND MARS JO BREEZER
VENUS AS A BOY BJORK
VENUS IN BLUE JEANS MARK WYNTER
VENUS IN FURS (LIVE) VELVET UNDERGROUND
VERDI MAURO PICOTTO
VERMILION SLIPKNOT
VERNON'S WONDERLAND VERNON'S WONDERLAND
VERONICA [A] ELVIS COSTELLO
VERONICA [B] SULTANS OF PING FC
VERSION OF ME THOUSAND YARD STARE
VERTIGO U2
VERY BEST FRIEND PROUD MARY
VERY METAL NOISE POLLUTION (EP) POP WILL EAT
    ITSELF
A VERY PRECIOUS LOVE DORIS DAY
THE VERY THOUGHT OF YOU TONY BENNETT
THE VERY THOUGHT OF YOU NATALIE COLE
VESSEL ED RUSH & OPTICAL/UNIVERSAL
VIBE ZHANE
VIBEOLOGY PAULA ABDUL
VIBRATOR TERENCE TRENT D'ARBY
VICE RAZORLIGHT
VICIOUS CIRCLES POLTERGEIST
VICIOUS CIRCLES VICIOUS CIRCLES
VICTIM OF LOVE [A] ERASURE
VICTIM OF LOVE [B] BRYAN ADAMS
VICTIMS CULTURE CLUB
VICTIMS OF SUCCESS DOGS D'AMOUR
VICTORIA KINKS
VICTORIA FALL
VICTORY KOOL & THE GANG
VIDEO INDIA.ARIE
VIDEO KILLED THE RADIO STAR BUGGLES
VIDEO KILLED THE RADIO STAR PRESIDENTS OF THE
    UNITED STATES OF AMERICA
VIDEO KILLED THE RADIO STAR DRAGONHEART
VIDEOTHEQUE DOLLAR
VIENNA ULTRAVOX
VIENNA CALLING FALCO
VIETNAM JIMMY CLIFF
VIEW FROM A BRIDGE KIM WILDE
A VIEW TO A KILL DURAN DURAN
VILLAGE OF ST. BERNADETTE ANNE SHELTON
VINCENT DON McLEAN
VINDALOO FAT LES
VIOLA MOOGWAI
VIOLAINE COCTEAU TWINS
VIOLENCE OF SUMMER (LOVE'S TAKING OVER) DURAN
    DURAN
VIOLENTLY (EP) HUE & CRY
VIOLENTLY HAPPY BJORK
VIOLET [A] SEAL
VIOLET [B] HOLE
VIP JUNGLE BROTHERS
VIRGIN MARY LONNIE DONEGAN
VIRGINIA PLAIN ROXY MUSIC
VIRGINIA PLAIN SLAMM
VIRTUAL INSANITY JAMIROQUAI
VIRTUALITY V-BIRDS
VIRUS [A] IRON MAIDEN
VIRUS [B] MUTINY UK
VISAGE VISAGE
THE VISION MARIO PIU PRESENTS DJ ARABESQUE
VISION INCISION LO FIDELITY ALLSTARS
VISION OF LOVE MARIAH CAREY

VISION OF YOU BELINDA CARLISLE
VISIONARY REDD KROSS
VISIONS [A] CLIFF RICHARD
VISIONS [B] LENA FIAGBE
VISIONS IN BLUE ULTRAVOX
VISIONS OF CHINA JAPAN
VISIONS OF PARADISE MICK JAGGER
VISIONS OF YOU JAH WOBBLE'S INVADERS OF THE
    HEART
VITAL SIGNS RUSH
VITO SATAN CAMPAG VELOCET
VIVA BOBBY JOE EQUALS
VIVA EL FULHAM TONY REES & THE COTTAGERS
VIVA ENGLAND UNDERCOVER
VIVA FOREVER SPICE GIRLS
VIVA LA MEGABABES SHAMPOO
VIVA LA RADIO LOLLY
VIVA LAS VEGAS ELVIS PRESLEY
VIVA LAS VEGAS ZZ TOP
VIVE LE ROCK ADAM ANT
VIVID ELECTRONIC
VIVRANT THING Q-TIP
VOGUE MADONNA
THE VOICE [A] ULTRAVOX
THE VOICE [B] ELMEAR QUINN
VOICE IN THE WILDERNESS CLIFF RICHARD
VOICE OF FREEDOM FREEDOM WILLIAMS
THE VOICE WITHIN CHRISTINA AGUILERA
VOICES [A] ANN LEE
VOICES [B] DARIO G
VOICES [C] BEDROCK
VOICES [D] DISTURBED
VOICES [E] K.C. FLIGHTT VS FUNKY JUNCTION
VOICES IN THE SKY MOODY BLUES
VOID EXOTERIX
VOLARE DEAN MARTIN
VOLARE DOMENICO MODUGNO
VOLARE MARINO MARINI & HIS QUARTET
VOLARE CHARLIE DRAKE
VOLARE BOBBY RYDELL
VOLCANO GIRLS VERUCA SALT
VOLUME 1 (WHAT YOU WANT WHAT YOU NEED)
    INDUSTRY STANDARD
VOODOO WARRIOR
VOODOO CHILE JIMI HENDRIX EXPERIENCE
VOODOO LOVE LEE-CABRERA
VOODOO PEOPLE PRODIGY
VOODOO RAY A GUY CALLED GERALD
VOODOO VOODOO DEN HEGARTY
VOULEZ-VOUS ABBA
THE VOW TOYAH
VOYAGE VOYAGE DESIRELESS
VOYAGER PENDULUM
VOYEUR KIM CARNES
VULNERABLE ROXETTE
WACK ASS MF RHYTHMKILLAZ
WADE IN THE WATER RAMSEY LEWIS
WAGES DAY DEACON BLUE
THE WAGON DINOSAUR Jr.
WAIL JON SPENCER BLUES EXPLOSION
WAIT ROBERT HOWARD & KYM MAZELLE
WAIT A MINUTE RAY J FEATURING LIL' KIM
WAIT AND BLEED SLIPKNOT
WAIT FOR ME MALCOLM VAUGHAN
WAIT FOR ME DARLING JOAN REGAN & THE JOHNSTON
    BROTHERS
WAIT FOR ME MARIANNE MARMALADE
WAIT UNTIL MIDNIGHT YELLOW DOG
WAIT UNTIL TONIGHT (MY LOVE) GALAXY FEATURING
    PHIL FEARON
WAITIN' FOR A SUPERMAN FLAMING LIPS

WAITING [A] STYLE COUNCIL
WAITING [B] GREEN DAY
THE WAITING 18 AMEN
WAITING FOR A GIRL LIKE YOU FOREIGNER
WAITING FOR A STAR TO FALL BOY MEETS GIRL
WAITING FOR A TRAIN FLASH & THE PAN
WAITING FOR AN ALIBI THIN LIZZY
WAITING FOR THAT DAY GEORGE MICHAEL
(WAITING FOR) THE GHOST TRAIN MADNESS
WAITING FOR THE GREAT LEAP FORWARDS BILLY
    BRAGG
WAITING FOR THE LOVEBOAT ASSOCIATES
WAITING FOR THE NIGHT SAXON
WAITING FOR THE SUMMER DELIRIOUS?
WAITING FOR THE SUN RUFF DRIVERZ
WAITING FOR TONIGHT JENNIFER LOPEZ
WAITING HOPEFULLY D*NOTE
WAITING IN VAIN BOB MARLEY & THE WAILERS
WAITING IN VAIN LEE RITENOUR & MAXI PRIEST
WAITING IN VAIN ANNIE LENNOX
WAITING ON A FRIEND ROLLING STONES
WAKE IN THE CITY IKARA COLT
WAKE ME UP BEFORE YOU GO GO WHAM!
WAKE UP [A] DANSE SOCIETY
WAKE UP [B] LOSTPROPHETS
WAKE UP AND SCRATCH ME SULTANS OF PING
WAKE UP BOO! BOO RADLEYS
WAKE UP DEAD MEGADETH
WAKE UP EVERYBODY HAROLD MELVIN & THE
    BLUENOTES
WAKE UP LITTLE SUSIE EVERLY BROTHERS
WAKE UP LITTLE SUSIE KING BROTHERS
WAKE UP SUSAN DETROIT SPINNERS
WAKING UP ELASTICA
WAKING WITH A STRANGER TYRREL CORPORATION
WALHALLA GOURYELLA
THE WALK [A] INMATES
THE WALK [B] CURE
WALK [C] PANTERA
WALK AWAY [A] SHANE FENTON & THE FENTONES
WALK AWAY [B] MATT MONRO
WALK AWAY [C] SISTERS OF MERCY
WALK AWAY [D] JOYCE SIMS
WALK AWAY FROM LOVE DAVID RUFFIN
WALK AWAY RENEE FOUR TOPS
WALK DON'T RUN JOHN BARRY SEVEN
WALK DON'T RUN VENTURES
WALK/DON'T WALK MY LIFE STORY
WALK HAND IN HAND TONY MARTIN
WALK HAND IN HAND RONNIE CARROLL
WALK HAND IN HAND JIMMY PARKINSON
WALK HAND IN HAND GERRY & THE PACEMAKERS
WALK IDIOT WALK HIVES
WALK IN LOVE MANHATTAN TRANSFER
A WALK IN THE BLACK FOREST HORST JANKOWSKI
WALK IN THE NIGHT JUNIOR WALKER & THE ALL-STARS
WALK IN THE NIGHT PAUL HARDCASTLE
A WALK IN THE PARK NICK STRAKER BAND
WALK INTO THE SUN DIRTY VEGAS
WALK INTO THE WIND VEGAS
WALK LIKE A CHAMPION KALIPHZ FEATURING PRINCE
    NASEEM
WALK LIKE A MAN FOUR SEASONS
WALK LIKE A MAN DIVINE
WALK LIKE A PANTHER '98 ALL SEEING I FEATURING
    TONY CHRISTIE
WALK LIKE AN EGYPTIAN BANGLES
WALK OF LIFE [A] DIRE STRAITS
WALK OF LIFE [B] BILLIE PIPER
WALK ON [A] ROY ORBISON
WALK ON [B] U2

WALK ON AIR T'PAU
WALK ON BY [A] LEROY VAN DYKE
WALK ON BY [B] DIONNE WARWICK
WALK ON BY [B] STRANGLERS
WALK ON BY [B] AVERAGE WHITE BAND
WALK ON BY [B] D TRAIN
WALK ON BY [B] SYBIL
WALK ON BY [B] GABRIELLE
WALK ON GILDED SPLINTERS MARSHA HUNT
WALK ON THE WILD SIDE LOU REED
WALK ON THE WILD SIDE JAMIE J. MORGAN
WALK ON THE WILD SIDE BEAT SYSTEM
WALK ON WATER MILK INC
WALK OUT TO WINTER AZTEC CAMERA
WALK RIGHT BACK EVERLY BROTHERS
WALK RIGHT BACK PERRY COMO
WALK RIGHT IN ROOFTOP SINGERS
WALK RIGHT NOW JACKSONS
WALK TALL VAL DOONICAN
WALK THE DINOSAUR WAS (NOT WAS)
WALK...(THE DOG) LIKE AN EGYPTIAN JODE FEATURING
    YO-HANS
WALK THIS LAND E-Z ROLLERS
WALK THIS WAY RUN D.M.C.
WALK THIS WORLD HEATHER NOVA
WALK THROUGH THE FIRE PETER GABRIEL
WALK THROUGH THE WORLD MARC COHN
WALK WITH FAITH IN YOUR HEART BACHELORS
WALK WITH ME SEEKERS
WALK WITH ME MY ANGEL DON CHARLES
WALK WITH ME TALK WITH ME DARLING FOUR TOPS
WALKAWAY CAST
WALKED OUTTA HEAVEN JAGGED EDGE
WALKIE TALKIE MAN STERIOGRAM
WALKIN' C.C.S.
WALKIN' BACK TO HAPPINESS HELEN SHAPIRO
WALKIN' IN THE RAIN WITH THE ONE I LOVE LOVE
    UNLIMITED
A WALKIN' MIRACLE LIMMIE & THE FAMILY COOKIN'
WALKIN' ON SHEER BRONZE FEATURING LISA MILLETT
WALKIN' ON THE SUN SMASH MOUTH
WALKIN' ON UP DJ PROF-X-OR
WALKIN' TALL [A] FRANKIE VAUGHAN
WALKIN' TALL [B] ADAM FAITH
WALKIN' THE DOG DENNISONS
WALKIN' THE LINE BRASS CONSTRUCTION
WALKIN' TO MISSOURI TONY BRENT
WALKING AFTER YOU FOO FIGHTERS
WALKING ALONE RICHARD ANTHONY
WALKING AWAY CRAIG DAVID
WALKING BY MYSELF GARY MOORE
WALKING DEAD PURESSENCE
WALKING DOWN MADISON KIRSTY MacCOLL
WALKING DOWN YOUR STREET BANGLES
WALKING IN MEMPHIS MARC COHN
WALKING IN MEMPHIS CHER
WALKING IN MY SHOES DEPECHE MODE
WALKING IN MY SLEEP ROGER DALTREY
WALKING IN RHYTHM BLACKBYRDS
WALKING IN THE AIR ALED JONES
WALKING IN THE AIR PETER AUTY & THE SINFONIA OF
    LONDON
WALKING IN THE AIR DIGITAL DREAM BABY
WALKING IN THE NAME FUNKSTAR DE LUXE VS TERRY
    MAXX
WALKING IN THE RAIN [A] WALKER BROTHERS
WALKING IN THE RAIN [A] PARTRIDGE FAMILY
    STARRING DAVID CASSIDY
WALKING IN THE RAIN [B] MODERN ROMANCE
WALKING IN THE SUN TRAVIS
WALKING IN THE SUNSHINE BAD MANNERS

WALKING INTO SUNSHINE CENTRAL LINE
WALKING MY BABY BACK HOME JOHNNIE RAY
WALKING MY CAT NAMED DOG NORMA TANEGA
WALKING ON AIR [A] FRAZIER CHORUS
WALKING ON AIR [B] BAD BOYS INC
WALKING ON BROKEN GLASS ANNIE LENNOX
WALKING ON ICE RIVER CITY PEOPLE
WALKING ON SUNSHINE [A] ROCKER'S REVENGE
    FEATURING DONNIE CALVIN
WALKING ON SUNSHINE [A] EDDY GRANT
WALKING ON SUNSHINE [A] KRUSH
WALKING ON SUNSHINE [B] KATRINA & THE WAVES
WALKING ON THE CHINESE WALL PHILIP BAILEY
WALKING ON THE MILKY WAY ORCHESTRAL
    MANOEUVRES IN THE DARK
WALKING ON THE MOON POLICE
WALKING ON THIN ICE YOKO ONO
WALKING ON WATER MADASUN
WALKING THE FLOOR OVER YOU PAT BOONE
WALKING TO NEW ORLEANS FATS DOMINO
WALKING WITH THEE CLINIC
WALKING WOUNDED EVERYTHING BUT THE GIRL
WALL STREET SHUFFLE 10 C.C.
WALLFLOWER MEGA CITY FOUR
WALLS COME TUMBLING DOWN! STYLE COUNCIL
THE WALLS FELL DOWN MARBLES
WALTZ #2 (XO) ELLIOTT SMITH
WALTZ AWAY DREAMING TOBY BOURKE/GEORGE
    MICHAEL
WALTZ DARLING MALCOLM McLAREN & THE
    BOOTZILLA ORCHESTRA
WALTZING ALONG JAMES
WAM BAM [A] HANDLEY FAMILY
WAM BAM [B] NT GANG
THE WANDERER [A] DION
THE WANDERER [A] STATUS QUO
THE WANDERER [B] DONNA SUMMER
WANDERIN' EYES CHARLIE GRACIE
WANDERIN' EYES FRANKIE VAUGHAN
THE WANDERING DRAGON SHADES OF RHYTHM
WANDERLUST DELAYS
WAND'RIN' STAR LEE MARVIN
WANNA BE STARTIN' SOMETHING MICHAEL JACKSON
WANNA BE THAT WAY IKARA COLT
WANNA BE WITH YOU JINNY
WANNA BE YOUR LOVER GAYLE & GILLIAN
WANNA DROP A HOUSE (ON THAT BITCH) URBAN
    DISCHARGE FEATURING SHE
WANNA GET TO KNOW YA G UNIT
WANNA GET UP 2 UNLIMITED
WANNA MAKE YOU GO...UUH! THOSE 2 GIRLS
WANNABE SPICE GIRLS
WANNABE GANGSTER WHEATUS
WANT LOVE HYSTERIC EGO
WANT YOU BAD OFFSPRING
WANTED [A] PERRY COMO
WANTED [A] AL MARTINO
WANTED [B] DOOLEYS
WANTED [C] STYLE COUNCIL
WANTED [D] HALO JAMES
WANTED [E] PRINCESS IVORI
WANTED DEAD OR ALIVE [A] BON JOVI
WANTED DEAD OR ALIVE [B] 2PAC & SNOOP DOGGY
    DOGG
WANTED IT ALL CLAYTOWN TROUPE
WAP-BAM-BOOGIE MATT BIANCO
WAR EDWIN STARR
WAR BRUCE SPRINGSTEEN
WAR BABIES SIMPLE MINDS
WAR BABY TOM ROBINSON
WAR CHILD BLONDIE

WAR LORD SHADOWS
WAR OF NERVES ALL SAINTS
WAR PARTY EDDY GRANT
THE WAR SONG CULTURE CLUB
WAR STORIES STARJETS
WARFAIR CLAWFINGER
WARHEAD U.K. SUBS
WARLOCK BLACK RIOT
WARM AND TENDER LOVE PERCY SLEDGE
WARM IT UP KRIS KROSS
WARM LOVE BEATMASTERS FEATURING CLAUDIA
    FONTAINE
WARM MACHINE BUSH
WARM SUMMER DAZE VYBE
WARM WET CIRCLES MARILLION
WARMED OVER KISSES BRIAN HYLAND
WARNING [A] ADEVA
WARNING [B] AKA
WARNING [C] FREESTYLERS FEATURING NAVIGATOR
WARNING [D] GREEN DAY
WARNING SIGN NICK HEYWARD
WARPAINT BROOK BROTHERS
WARPED RED HOT CHILI PEPPERS
WARRIOR [A] MC WILDSKI
WARRIOR [B] DANCE 2 TRANCE
WARRIOR [C] WARRIOR
WARRIOR GROOVE DSM
WARRIOR SOUND PRESSURE DROP
WARRIORS [A] GARY NUMAN
WARRIORS [B] ASWAD
WARRIORS (OF THE WASTELAND) FRANKIE GOES TO
    HOLLYWOOD
WAS IT WORTH IT PET SHOP BOYS
WAS THAT ALL IT WAS KYM MAZELLE
WAS THAT YOU SPEAR OF DESTINY
WASH IN THE RAIN BEES
WASH YOUR FACE IN MY SINK DREAM WARRIORS
WASSUUP DA MUTTZ
WASTED SMALLER
WASTED IN AMERICA LOVE/HATE
WASTED TIME [A] SKID ROW
WASTED TIME [B] KINGS OF LEON
WASTED YEARS IRON MAIDEN
WASTELAND MISSION
WASTELANDS MIDGE URE
WASTER REEF
WASTES DEF LEPPARD
WASTING MY TIME [A] DEFAULT
WASTING MY TIME [B] KOSHEEN
WATCH ME LABI SIFFRE
WATCH OUT BRANDI WELLS
WATCH THE MIRACLE START PAULINE HENRY
WATCH WHAT YOU SAY GURU FEATURING CHAKA KHAN
WATCHA GONNA DO KEISHA WHITE
WATCHA GONNA DO WITH MY LOVIN' INNER CITY
WATCHDOGS UB40
A WATCHER'S POINT OF VIEW PM DAWN
WATCHING THOMPSON TWINS
WATCHING CARS GO BY FELIX DA HOUSECAT
WATCHING THE DETECTIVES ELVIS COSTELLO
WATCHING THE RIVER FLOW BOB DYLAN
WATCHING THE WHEELS JOHN LENNON
WATCHING THE WILDLIFE FRANKIE GOES TO
    HOLLYWOOD
WATCHING THE WORLD GO BY MAXI PRIEST
WATCHING WINDOWS RONI SIZE REPRAZENT
WATCHING XANADU MULL HISTORICAL SOCIETY
WATCHING YOU ETHER
WATCHING YOU WATCHING ME DAVID GRANT
WATER [A] GENO WASHINGTON & THE RAM JAM
    BAND

WATER [B] MARTIKA
WATER FROM A VINE LEAF WILLIAM ORBIT
THE WATER IS OVER MY HEAD ROCKIN' BERRIES
THE WATER MARGIN GODIEGO
THE WATER MARGIN PETE MAC JR
WATER ON GLASS KIM WILDE
WATER RUNS DRY BOYZ II MEN
WATER WATER TOMMY STEELE & THE STEELMEN
WATER WAVE MARK VAN DALE WITH ENRICO
WATERFALL [A] WENDY & LISA
WATERFALL [B] STONE ROSES
WATERFALL [C] ATLANTIC OCEAN
WATERFALLS [A] PAUL McCARTNEY
WATERFALLS [B] TLC
WATERFRONT SIMPLE MINDS
WATERLOO [A] STONEWALL JACKSON
WATERLOO [B] ABBA
WATERLOO [B] DOCTOR & THE MEDICS FEATURING
    ROY WOOD
WATERLOO SUNSET KINKS
WATERLOO SUNSET CATHY DENNIS
WATERY, DOMESTIC (EP) PAVEMENT
THE WAVE OF THE FUTURE QUADROPHONIA
THE WAVE COSMIC GATE
WAVES BLANCMANGE
WAVY GRAVY SASHA
WAX THE VAN LOLA
THE WAY [A] FUNKY GREEN DOGS
THE WAY [B] GLOBAL COMMUNICATION
THE WAY [C] FASTBALL
WAY AWAY YELLOWCARD
WAY BACK HOME JUNIOR WALKER & THE ALL-STARS
WAY BEHIND ME PRIMITIVES
WAY DOWN ELVIS PRESLEY
WAY DOWN NOW WORLD PARTY
WAY DOWN YONDER IN NEW ORLEANS FREDDY
    CANNON
THE WAY DREAMS ARE DANIEL O'DONNELL
THE WAY I AM EMINEM
THE WAY I FEEL [A] LEMON TREES
THE WAY I FEEL [B] ROACHFORD
THE WAY I FEEL ABOUT YOU KARYN WHITE
THE WAY I WALK JACK SCOTT
THE WAY I WANT TO TOUCH YOU CAPTAIN & TENNILLE
WAY IN MY BRAIN SL2
THE WAY IT GOES STATUS QUO
THE WAY IT IS BRUCE HORNSBY & THE RANGE
THE WAY IT IS CHAMELEON
THE WAY IT USED TO BE ENGELBERT HUMPERDINCK
THE WAY IT WAS/REDHEAD BARON
THE WAY IT'S GOIN' DOWN (T.W.I.S.M. FOR LIFE)
    SHAQUILLE O'NEAL
A WAY OF LIFE [A] FAMILY DOGG
WAY OF LIFE [B] DAVE CLARKE
WAY OF THE WORLD [A] CHEAP TRICK
WAY OF THE WORLD [B] TINA TURNER
THE WAY (PUT YOUR HAND IN MY HAND) DIVINE
    INSPIRATION
THE WAY SHE LOVES ME RICHARD MARX
THE WAY THAT YOU FEEL ADEVA
THE WAY THAT YOU LOVE ME VANESSA WILLIAMS
THE WAY TO YOUR LOVE HEAR'SAY
THE WAY WE WERE BARBRA STREISAND
THE WAY WE WERE – TRY TO REMEMBER GLADYS
    KNIGHT & THE PIPS
THE WAY YOU ARE TEARS FOR FEARS
THE WAY YOU DO THE THINGS YOU DO UB40
THE WAY YOU LIKE IT ADEMA
THE WAY YOU LOOK TONIGHT LETTERMEN
THE WAY YOU LOOK TONIGHT DENNY SEYTON & THE
    SABRES

THE WAY YOU LOOK TONIGHT EDWARD WOODWARD
THE WAY YOU LOVE ME [A] KARYN WHITE
THE WAY YOU LOVE ME [B] FAITH HILL
THE WAY YOU MAKE ME FEEL [A] MICHAEL JACKSON
THE WAY YOU MAKE ME FEEL [B] RONAN KEATING
THE WAY YOU MOVE OUTKAST FEATURING SLEEPY
    BROWN
THE WAY YOU WORK IT E.Y.C.
WAYDOWN CATHERINE WHEEL
WAYS OF LOVE CLAYTOWN TROUPE
WAYWARD WIND JIMMY YOUNG
WAYWARD WIND TEX RITTER
WAYWARD WIND GOGI GRANT
THE WAYWARD WIND FRANK IFIELD
WE ALL FOLLOW MAN. UNITED MANCHESTER UNITED
    FOOTBALL CLUB
WE ALL SLEEP ALONE CHER
WE ALL STAND TOGETHER PAUL McCARTNEY & THE
    FROG CHORUS
WE ALMOST GOT IT TOGETHER TANITA TIKARAM
WE ARE ANA JOHNSSON
WE ARE ALIVE PAUL VAN DYK
WE ARE ALL MADE OF STARS MOBY
WE ARE BACK LFO
WE ARE DA CLICK DA CLICK
WE ARE DETECTIVE THOMPSON TWINS
WE ARE EACH OTHER BEAUTIFUL SOUTH
WE ARE E-MALE E-MALE
WE ARE FAMILY SISTER SLEDGE
WE ARE GLASS GARY NUMAN
WE ARE GOING ON DOWN DEADLY SINS
WE ARE I. E. LENNIE DE ICE
WE ARE IN LOVE [A] ADAM FAITH & THE ROULETTES
WE ARE IN LOVE [B] HARRY CONNICK Jr.
WE ARE LOVE DJ ERIC
WE ARE NOT ALONE FRANKIE VAUGHAN
WE ARE RAVING – THE ANTHEM SLIPSTREAM
WE ARE THE BAND MORE
WE ARE THE CHAMPIONS QUEEN
WE ARE THE CHAMPIONS HANK MARVIN FEATURING
    BRIAN MAY
WE ARE THE FIRM COCKNEY REJECTS
WE ARE THE PIGS SUEDE
WE ARE THE WORLD USA FOR AFRICA
WE BELONG PAT BENATAR
WE BELONG IN THIS WORLD TOGETHER STEREO MC'S
WE BUILT THIS CITY STARSHIP
WE CALL IT ACIEED D MOB FEATURING GARY
    HAISMAN
WE CAME TO DANCE ULTRAVOX
WE CAN LeANN RIMES
WE CAN BE BRAVE AGAIN ARMOURY SHOW
WE CAN DO ANYTHING COCKNEY REJECTS
WE CAN DO IT (EP) LIVERPOOL FC
WE CAN GET DOWN MYRON
WE CAN MAKE IT MONE
WE CAN MAKE IT HAPPEN PRINCE CHARLES & THE
    CITY BEAT BAND
WE CAN WORK IT OUT [A] BEATLES
WE CAN WORK IT OUT [A] STEVIE WONDER
WE CAN WORK IT OUT [A] FOUR SEASONS
WE CAN WORK IT OUT [B] BRASS CONSTRUCTION
WE CARE A LOT FAITH NO MORE
WE CLOSE OUR EYES GO WEST
WE COME 1 FAITHLESS
WE COME TO PARTY N-TYCE
WE COULD BE KINGS GENE
WE COULD BE TOGETHER DEBBIE GIBSON
WE DIDN'T START THE FIRE BILLY JOEL
WE DO IT R & J STONE
WE DON'T CARE AUDIO BULLYS

WE DON'T HAVE TO... JERMAINE STEWART
WE DON'T NEED A REASON DARE
WE DON'T NEED ANOTHER HERO (THUNDERDOME) TINA TURNER
WE DON'T NEED NOBODY ELSE WHIPPING BOY
(WE DON'T NEED THIS) FASCIST GROOVE THANG HEAVEN 17
WE DON'T TALK ANYMORE CLIFF RICHARD
WE DON'T WORK FOR FREE GRANDMASTER MELLE MEL & THE FURIOUS FIVE
WE FIT TOGETHER O-TOWN
WE GOT A LOVE THANG CE CE PENISTON
WE GOT IT IMMATURE FEATURING SMOOTH
WE GOT LOVE ALMA COGAN
WE GOT OUR OWN THANG HEAVY D. & THE BOYZ
WE GOT THE FUNK POSITIVE FORCE
WE GOT THE GROOVE PLAYERS ASSOCIATION
WE GOT THE LOVE [A] TOUCH OF SOUL
WE GOT THE LOVE [B] LINDY LAYTON
WE GOT THE LOVE [B] ERIK
WE GOT THE LOVE [C] TRI
WE GOTTA DO IT DJ PROFESSOR FEATURING FRANCESCO ZAPPALA
WE GOTTA GET OUT OF THIS PLACE ANIMALS
WE GOTTA GET OUT OF THIS PLACE ANGELIC UPSTARTS
WE GOTTA LOVE KYM SIMS
WE HATE IT WHEN OUR FRIENDS BECOME SUCCESSFUL MORRISSEY
WE HAVE A DREAM SCOTLAND WORLD CUP SQUAD
WE HAVE ALL THE TIME IN THE WORLD LOUIS ARMSTRONG
WE HAVE EXPLOSIVE FUTURE SOUND OF LONDON
WE HAVEN'T TURNED AROUND GOMEZ
WE JUST BE DREAMIN' BLAZIN' SQUAD
WE JUST WANNA PARTY WITH YOU SNOOP DOGGY DOGG FEATURING JD
WE KILL THE WORLD (DON'T KILL THE WORLD) BONEY M
WE KNOW SOMETHING YOU DON'T KNOW DJ FORMAT FEATURING CHARLI 2NA & AKIL
WE LET THE STARS GO PREFAB SPROUT
WE LIKE TO PARTY (THE VENGABUS) VENGABOYS
WE LOVE EACH OTHER CHARLIE RICH
WE LOVE YOU [A] ROLLING STONES
WE LOVE YOU [B] ORCHESTRAL MANOEUVRES IN THE DARK
WE LOVE YOU [C] MENSWEAR
WE LUV U GRAND THEFT AUDIO
WE NEED A RESOLUTION AALIYAH FEATURING TIMBALAND
WE NEED LOVE CASHMERE
WE ROCK DIO
WE SAIL ON THE STORMY WATERS GARY CLARK
WE SHALL OVERCOME JOAN BAEZ
WE SHOULD BE TOGETHER CLIFF RICHARD
WE SHOULDN'T HOLD HANDS IN THE DARK L.A. MIX
WE TAKE MYSTERY (TO BED) GARY NUMAN
WE THUGGIN' FAT JOE
WE TRYING TO STAY ALIVE WYCLEF JEAN & THE REFUGEE ALLSTARS
WE USED TO BE FRIENDS DANDY WARHOLS
WE WAIT AND WE WONDER PHIL COLLINS
WE WALKED IN LOVE DOLLAR
(WE WANT) THE SAME THING BELINDA CARLISLE
WE WANNA THANK YOU (THE THINGS YOU DO) BIG BROVAZ
WE WANT YOUR SOUL FREELAND
WE WILL GILBERT O'SULLIVAN
WE WILL MAKE LOVE RUSS HAMILTON
WE WILL MEET AGAIN OLETA ADAMS
WE WILL NEVER BE THIS YOUNG AGAIN DANNY WILLIAMS

WE WILL ROCK YOU FIVE & QUEEN
WE WILL SURVIVE WARP BROTHERS
WEAK [A] SWV
WEAK [B] SKUNK ANANSIE
WEAK BECOME HEROES STREETS
WEAK IN THE PRESENCE OF BEAUTY ALISON MOYET
WEAK SPOT EVELYN THOMAS
WEAR MY HAT PHIL COLLINS
WEAR MY RING AROUND YOUR NECK ELVIS PRESLEY
WEAR YOU TO THE BALL UB40
WEAR YOUR LOVE LIKE HEAVEN DEFINITION OF SOUND
WEATHER FORECAST MASTER SINGERS
WEATHER WITH YOU CROWDED HOUSE
WEAVE YOUR SPELL LEVEL 42
THE WEAVER (EP) PAUL WELLER
THE WEDDING [A] JULIE ROGERS
THE WEDDING [B] CLIFF RICHARD FEATURING HELEN HOBSON
WEDDING BELL BLUES FIFTH DIMENSION
WEDDING BELLS [A] EDDIE FISHER
WEDDING BELLS [B] GODLEY & CREME
WEDDING RING RUSS HAMILTON
WEDNESDAY WEEK UNDERTONES
WEE RULE WEE PAPA GIRL RAPPERS
WEE TOM LORD ROCKINGHAM'S XI
WEEK IN WEEK OUT ORDINARY BOYS
WEEKEND [A] EDDIE COCHRAN
WEEKEND [B] MICK JACKSON
WEEKEND [C] CLASS ACTION FEATURING CHRIS WILTSHIRE
WEEKEND [C] TODD TERRY PROJECT
WEEKEND [D] BAD HABIT BOYS
WEEKEND [E] SCOOTER
THE WEEKEND [F] MICHAEL GRAY
WEEKEND GIRL S.O.S. BAND
THE WEEKEND HAS LANDED MINKY
WEEKENDER FLOWERED UP
THE WEIGHT BAND
WEIGHT FOR THE BASS UNIQUE 3
WEIGHT OF THE WORLD RINGO STARR
WEIRD [A] REEF
WEIRD [B] HANSON
WEIRDO CHARLATANS
WELCOME GINO LATINO
WELCOME BACK MA$E
WELCOME HOME PETERS & LEE
WELCOME HOME BABY BROOK BROTHERS
WELCOME TO CHICAGO EP GENE FARRIS
WELCOME TO MY TRUTH ANASTACIA
WELCOME TO MY WORLD JIM REEVES
WELCOME TO OUR WORLD (OF MERRY MUSIC) MASS PRODUCTION
WELCOME TO PARADISE GREEN DAY
WELCOME TO THE CHEAP SEATS (EP) WONDER STUFF
(WELCOME) TO THE DANCE DES MITCHELL
WELCOME TO THE FUTURE SHIMMON & WOOLFSON
WELCOME TO THE JUNGLE GUNS N' ROSES
WELCOME TO THE PLEASURE DOME FRANKIE GOES TO HOLLYWOOD
WELCOME TO THE REAL WORLD GUN
WELCOME TO THE TERRORDOME PUBLIC ENEMY
WELCOME TO TOMORROW SNAP FEATURING SUMMER
WELL ALL RIGHT SANTANA
WE'LL BE RIGHT BACK STEINSKI & MASS MEDIA
WE'LL BE TOGETHER STING
WE'LL BE WITH YOU POTTERS
WE'LL BRING THE HOUSE DOWN SLADE
WELL DID YOU EVAH! DEBORAH HARRY & IGGY POP
WE'LL FIND OUR DAY STEPHANIE DE SYKES
WE'LL GATHER LILACES – ALL MY LOVING (MEDLEY) SIMON MAY

WELL I ASK YOU EDEN KANE
WE'LL SING IN THE SUNSHINE LANCASTRIANS
WE'RE ALL ALONE RITA COOLIDGE
WE'RE ALL IN LOVE BLACK REBEL MOTORCYCLE CLUB
WE'RE ALMOST THERE MICHAEL JACKSON
WE'RE COMIN' AT YA QUARTZ FEATURING STEPZ
WE'RE COMING OVER MR SMASH & FRIENDS
WE'RE GOING OUT YOUNGER YOUNGER 28'S
WE'RE GOING TO IBIZA! VENGABOYS
WE'RE GOING TO MISS YOU JAMES
WE'RE GONNA DO IT AGAIN MANCHESTER UNITED FEATURING STRYKER
WE'RE GONNA GO FISHIN' HANK LOCKLIN
WE'RE IN THIS LOVE TOGETHER AL JARREAU
WE'RE IN THIS TOGETHER [A] SIMPLY RED
WE'RE IN THIS TOGETHER [B] NINE INCH NAILS
WE'RE NOT ALONE HHC
WE'RE NOT GONNA SLEEP TONIGHT EMMA BUNTON
WE'RE NOT GONNA TAKE IT TWISTED SISTER
WE'RE ON THE BALL ANT & DEC
WE'RE ONLY YOUNG ONCE AVONS
WE'RE REALLY SAYING SOMETHING BUFFALO G
WE'RE THROUGH HOLLIES
WEST END GIRLS PET SHOP BOYS
WEST END GIRLS EAST 17
WEST END PAD CATHY DENNIS
WEST OF ZANZIBAR ANTHONY STEEL & THE RADIO REVELLERS
WEST ONE (SHINE ON ME) RUTS
WESTERN MOVIES OLYMPICS
WESTSIDE [A] TQ
WESTSIDE [B] ATHLETE
WET DREAM MAX ROMEO
WET MY WHISTLE MIDNIGHT STAR
WE'VE GOT IT GOIN' ON BACKSTREET BOYS
WE'VE GOT THE JUICE DEREK B
WE'VE GOT THE WHOLE WORLD AT OUR FEET ENGLAND WORLD CUP SQUAD
WE'VE GOT THE WHOLE WORLD IN OUR HANDS NOTTINGHAM FOREST FC & PAPER LACE
WE'VE GOT TO LIVE TOGETHER RAF
WE'VE GOT TO WORK IT OUT BEL CANTO
WE'VE GOT TONIGHT BOB SEGER & THE SILVER BULLET BAND
WE'VE GOT TONIGHT KENNY ROGERS & SHEENA EASTON
WE'VE GOT TONIGHT ELKIE BROOKS
WE'VE GOT TONIGHT RONAN KEATING FEATURING LULU
WE'VE HAD ENOUGH ALKALINE TRIO
WE'VE ONLY JUST BEGUN CARPENTERS
WE'VE ONLY JUST BEGUN BITTY McLEAN
WFL HAPPY MONDAYS
WHADDA U WANT (FROM ME) FRANKIE KNUCKLES FEATURING ADEVA
WHADDA WE LIKE ROUND SOUND PRESENTS ONYX STONE
WHAM BAM CANDY GIRLS FEATURING SWEET PUSSY PAULINE
WHAM RAP WHAM!
WHAT SOFT CELL
WHAT A BEAUTIFUL DAY LEVELLERS
WHAT A CRAZY WORLD WE'RE LIVING IN JOE BROWN & THE BRUVVERS
WHAT A DIFFERENCE A DAY MAKES ESTHER PHILLIPS
WHAT A FOOL BELIEVES DOOBIE BROTHERS
WHAT A FOOL BELIEVES ARETHA FRANKLIN
WHAT A FOOL BELIEVES PETER COX
WHAT A GIRL WANTS CHRISTINA AGUILERA
WHAT A MOUTH TOMMY STEELE
WHAT A NIGHT CITY BOY

WHAT A PARTY FATS DOMINO
WHAT A WASTE IAN DURY & THE BLOCKHEADS
WHAT A WASTER LIBERTINES
WHAT A WOMAN IN LOVE WON'T DO SANDY POSEY
WHAT A WONDERFUL WORLD [A] LOUIS ARMSTRONG
WHAT A WONDERFUL WORLD [A] NICK CAVE & SHANE McGOWAN
WHAT A WONDERFUL WORLD [A] CLIFF RICHARD
(WHAT A) WONDERFUL WORLD [B] JOHNNY NASH
WHAT ABOUT LOVE HEART
WHAT ABOUT ME CRIBS
WHAT ABOUT THIS LOVE MR FINGERS
WHAT ABOUT US [A] POINT BREAK
WHAT ABOUT US [B] BRANDY
WHAT ABOUT YOUR FRIENDS TLC
WHAT AM I GONNA DO [A] EMILE FORD & THE CHECKMATES
WHAT AM I GONNA DO [B] ROD STEWART
WHAT AM I GONNA DO WITH YOU BARRY WHITE
WHAT AM I TO YOU KENNY LYNCH
WHAT ARE WE GONNA DO ABOUT IT? MERCY MERCY
WHAT ARE WE GONNA GET 'ER INDOORS DENNIS WATERMAN & GEORGE COLE
WHAT ARE YOU DOING SUNDAY DAWN FEATURING TONY ORLANDO
WHAT ARE YOU UNDER DEFINITION OF SOUND
WHAT BECAME OF THE LIKELY LADS LIBERTINES
WHAT BECOMES OF THE BROKENHEARTED JIMMY RUFFIN
WHAT BECOMES OF THE BROKENHEARTED DAVE STEWART. GUEST VOCALS: COLIN BLUNSTONE
WHAT BECOMES OF THE BROKENHEARTED ROBSON GREEN & JEROME FLYNN
WHAT CAN I DO CORRS
WHAT CAN I SAY BOZ SCAGGS
(WHAT CAN I SAY) TO MAKE YOU LOVE ME ALEXANDER O'NEAL
WHAT CAN YOU DO FOR ME UTAH SAINTS
WHAT CAN YOU DO 4 ME? LISA LASHES
WHAT DID I DO TO YOU (EP) LISA STANSFIELD
WHAT DIFFERENCE DOES IT MAKE SMITHS
WHAT DO I DO PHIL FEARON & GALAXY
WHAT DO I DO NOW? SLEEPER
WHAT DO I GET BUZZCOCKS
WHAT DO I HAVE TO DO KYLIE MINOGUE
WHAT DO YA SAY CHUBBY CHECKER
WHAT DO YOU WANT ADAM FAITH
WHAT DO YOU WANT FROM ME? MONACO
WHAT DO YOU WANT TO MAKE THOSE EYES AT ME FOR EMILE FORD & THE CHECKMATES
WHAT DO YOU WANT TO MAKE THOSE EYES AT ME FOR SHAKIN' STEVENS
WHAT DOES IT FEEL LIKE? FELIX DA HOUSECAT
WHAT DOES IT TAKE THEN JERICO
WHAT DOES IT TAKE (TO WIN YOUR LOVE) JUNIOR WALKER & THE ALL-STARS
WHAT DOES IT TAKE (TO WIN YOUR LOVE) KENNY G
WHAT DOES YOUR SOUL LOOK LIKE (PART 1) DJ SHADOW
WHAT EVER HAPPENED TO OLD FASHIONED LOVE DANIEL O'DONNELL
WHAT GOD WANTS PART 1 ROGER WATERS
WHAT GOES AROUND [A] BITTY McLEAN
WHAT GOES AROUND [B] LUCIANA
WHAT GOES AROUND COMES AROUND BOB MARLEY & THE WAILERS
WHAT GOES ON BRYAN FERRY
WHAT GOOD AM I CILLA BLACK
WHAT HAPPENED TO THE MUSIC JOEY NEGRO
WHAT HAVE I DONE TO DESERVE THIS PET SHOP BOYS & DUSTY SPRINGFIELD

WHAT HAVE THEY DONE TO MY SONG MA NEW SEEKERS
WHAT HAVE THEY DONE TO MY SONG MA MELANIE
WHAT HAVE THEY DONE TO THE RAIN SEARCHERS
WHAT HAVE YOU DONE FOR ME LATELY JANET JACKSON
WHAT HAVE YOU DONE (IS THIS ALL) ONE TRIBE FEATURING GEM
WHAT HOPE HAVE I SPHINX
WHAT I AM EDIE BRICKELL & THE NEW BOHEMIANS
WHAT I AM TIN TIN OUT FEATURING EMMA BUNTON
WHAT I CAN DO FOR YOU SHERYL CROW
WHAT I DO BEST ROBIN S
WHAT I GO TO SCHOOL FOR BUSTED
WHAT I GOT SUBLIME
WHAT I GOT IS WHAT YOU NEED UNIQUE
WHAT I LIKE MOST ABOUT YOU IS YOUR GIRLFRIEND SPECIAL A.K.A.
WHAT I MEAN MODJO
WHAT I MISS THE MOST ALOOF
WHAT I SAW KINGS OF LEON
WHAT IF... [A] LIGHTNING SEEDS
WHAT IF [B] KATE WINSLET
WHAT IF A WOMAN JOE
WHAT IN THE WORLD NU COLOURS
WHAT IN THE WORLD'S COME OVER YOU JACK SCOTT
WHAT IN THE WORLD'S COME OVER YOU ROCKIN' BERRIES
WHAT IN THE WORLD'S COME OVER YOU TAM WHITE
WHAT IS A MAN FOUR TOPS
WHAT IS HOUSE (EP) LFO
WHAT IS LIFE [A] OLIVIA NEWTON-JOHN
WHAT IS LIFE [A] SHAWN MULLINS
WHAT IS LIFE? [B] BLACK UHURU
WHAT IS LOVE [A] HOWARD JONES
WHAT IS LOVE [B] DEEE-LITE
WHAT IS LOVE [C] HADDAWAY
WHAT IS THE PROBLEM? GRAFITI
WHAT IS THIS THING CALLED LOVE ALEXANDER O'NEAL
WHAT IS TRUTH JOHNNY CASH
WHAT IT FEELS LIKE FOR A GIRL MADONNA
WHAT IT IS [A] GARNET MIMMS & TRUCKIN' CO
WHAT IT IS [B] FREDDY FRESH
WHAT IT'S LIKE EVERLAST
WHAT I'VE GOT IN MIND BILLIE JO SPEARS
WHAT KIND OF FOOL ALL ABOUT EVE
WHAT KIND OF FOOL AM I? ANTHONY NEWLEY
WHAT KIND OF FOOL AM I? SAMMY DAVIS Jr.
WHAT KIND OF FOOL AM I? SHIRLEY BASSEY
WHAT KIND OF FOOL (HEARD IT ALL BEFORE) KYLIE MINOGUE
WHAT KIND OF MAN WOULD I BE MINT CONDITION
WHAT KINDA BOY YOU LOOKING FOR (GIRL) HOT CHOCOLATE
WHAT MADE MILWAUKEE FAMOUS (HAS MADE A LOSER OUT OF ME) ROD STEWART
WHAT MAKES A MAN WESTLIFE
WHAT MAKES A MAN A MAN (LIVE) MARC ALMOND
WHAT MAKES YOU CRY PROCLAIMERS
WHAT MORE DO YOU WANT FRANKIE VAUGHAN
WHAT MY HEART WANTS TO SAY GARETH GATES
WHAT NOW ADAM FAITH WITH JOHNNY KEATING & HIS ORCHESTRA
WHAT NOW MY LOVE SHIRLEY BASSEY
WHAT NOW MY LOVE SONNY & CHER
WHAT PRESENCE? ORANGE JUICE
WHAT THE WORLD IS WAITING FOR STONE ROSES
WHAT THEY DO ROOTS
WHAT TIME IS IT SPIN DOCTORS
WHAT TIME IS IT? DUST JUNKYS
WHAT TIME IS LOVE (LIVE AT TRANCENTRAL) KLF FEATURING THE CHILDREN OF THE REVOLUTION
WHAT TO DO BUDDY HOLLY

WHAT TOOK YOU SO LONG EMMA BUNTON
WHAT U DO COLOURS FEATURING EMMANUEL & ESKA
WHAT 'U' WAITIN' '4' JUNGLE BROTHERS
WHAT WAS HER NAME DAVE CLARKE FEATURING CHICKS ON SPEED
WHAT WILL BE WILL BE (DESTINY) DIVINE INSPIRATION
WHAT WILL I DO WITHOUT YOU LENE LOVICH
WHAT WILL MARY SAY JOHNNY MATHIS
WHAT WOULD HAPPEN MEREDITH BROOKS
WHAT WOULD I BE VAL DOONICAN
WHAT WOULD WE DO DSK
WHAT WOULD YOU DO CITY HIGH
WHAT WOULD YOU DO IF...? CODE RED
WHAT YA GOT 4 ME SIGNUM
WHAT YA LOOKIN' AT CROW
WHAT YOU DO BIG BASS VS MICHELLE NARINE
WHAT YOU DO TO ME (EP) TEENAGE FANCLUB
WHAT YOU GET HUNDRED REASONS
WHAT YOU GET IS WHAT YOU SEE TINA TURNER
WHAT YOU GONNA DO ABOUT IT TOTAL CONTRAST
WHAT YOU GOT ABS
WHAT YOU NEED [A] INXS
WHAT YOU NEED [B] POWERHOUSE FEATURING DUANE HARDEN
WHAT YOU NEED IS SINEAD QUINN
WHAT YOU NEED (TONIGHT) NU CIRCLES FEATURING EMMA B
WHAT YOU SAY LIGHTNING SEEDS
WHAT YOU SEE IS WHAT YOU GET GLEN GOLDSMITH
WHAT YOU THINK OF THAT MEMPHIS BLEEK FEATURING JAY-Z
WHAT YOU WAITING FOR [A] STARGARD
WHAT YOU WAITING FOR [B] GWEN STEFANI
WHAT YOU WANT [A] XPANSIONS FEATURING DALE JOYNER
WHAT YOU WANT [B] FUTURE FORCE
WHAT YOU WANT [C] MA$E FEATURING TOTAL
WHAT YOU WON'T DO FOR LOVE GO WEST
WHAT YOU'RE MADE OF LUCIE SILVAS
WHAT YOU'RE MISSING K-KLASS
WHAT YOU'RE PROPOSING STATUS QUO
WHATCHA GONE DO? LINK
WHAT'CHA GONNA DO [A] SHABBA RANKS FEATURING QUEEN LATIFAH
WHAT'CHA GONNA DO [B] ETERNAL
WHATCHA GONNA DO ABOUT IT DORIS TROY
WHATCHA GONNA DO ABOUT IT SMALL FACES
WHATCHA GONNA DO NOW CHRIS ANDREWS
WHAT'D I SAY JERRY LEE LEWIS
WHAT'D YOU COME HERE FOR? TRINA & TAMARA
WHATEVER [A] OASIS
WHATEVER [B] EN VOGUE
WHATEVER [C] IDEAL US FEATURING LIL' MO
WHATEVER GETS YOU THROUGH THE NIGHT JOHN LENNON WITH THE PLASTIC ONO NUCLEAR BAND
WHATEVER HAPPENED TO COREY HAIM? THRILLS
WHATEVER HAPPENED TO MY ROCK AND ROLL BLACK REBEL MOTORCYCLE CLUB
WHATEVER HAPPENED TO YOU ('LIKELY LADS' THEME) HIGHLY LIKELY
WHATEVER I DO (WHEREVER I GO) HAZELL DEAN
WHATEVER IT TAKES OLYMPIC RUNNERS
WHATEVER LOLA WANTS ALMA COGAN
WHATEVER MAKES YOU HAPPY TEN CITY
WHATEVER U WANT CHRISTINA MILIAN FEATURING JOE BUDDEN
WHATEVER WILL BE WILL BE DORIS DAY
WHATEVER YOU NEED TINA TURNER
WHATEVER YOU WANT [A] STATUS QUO
WHATEVER YOU WANT [B] TINA TURNER
WHAT'LL I DO JANET JACKSON

WHAT'S A GIRL TO DO SISTER 2 SISTER
WHAT'S ANOTHER YEAR JOHNNY LOGAN
WHAT'S GOIN' DOWN HONKY
WHAT'S GOING ON [A] MEKON FEATURING ROXANNE SHANTE
WHAT'S GOING ON [B] CYNDI LAUPER
WHAT'S GOING ON [B] MUSIC RELIEF '94
WHAT'S GOING ON [B] ALL STAR TRIBUTE
WHAT'S GOING ON [C] WOOKIE
WHAT'S HAPPENIN' METHOD MAN FEATURING BUSTA RHYMES
WHAT'S IN A KISS? GILBERT O'SULLIVAN
WHAT'S IN A WORD CHRISTIANS
WHAT'S IN THE BOX? (SEE WHATCHA GOT) BOO RADLEYS
WHAT'S IT ALL ABOUT RUN D.M.C.
WHAT'S IT GONNA BE?! BUSTA RHYMES FEATURING JANET
WHAT'S IT LIKE TO BE BEAUTIFUL LENA FIAGBE
WHAT'S LOVE GOT TO DO WITH IT TINA TURNER
WHAT'S LOVE GOT TO DO WITH IT WARREN G FEATURING ADINA HOWARD
WHAT'S LUV FAT JOE FEATURING ASHANTI
WHAT'S MY AGE AGAIN? BLINK 182
WHAT'S MY NAME? SNOOP DOGGY DOGG
WHAT'S NEW PUSSYCAT TOM JONES
WHAT'S ON YOUR MIND GEORGE BENSON
WHAT'S SO DIFFERENT? GINUWINE
WHAT'S THAT TUNE (DOO-DOO-DOO-DOO-DOO-DOO-DOO-DOO-DOO-DOO) DOROTHY
WHAT'S THE COLOUR OF MONEY? HOLLYWOOD BEYOND
WHAT'S THE FREQUENCY, KENNETH R.E.M.
WHAT'S THE POINT WE'VE GOT A FUZZBOX & WE'RE GONNA USE IT
WHAT'S UP 4 NON BLONDES
WHAT'S UP DJ MIKO
WHAT'S UP WITH THAT ZZ TOP
(WHAT'S WRONG WITH) DREAMING RIVER CITY PEOPLE
WHAT'S WRONG WITH THIS PICTURE CHESNEY HAWKES
WHAT'S YOUR FANTASY LUDACRIS
WHAT'S YOUR FLAVA CRAIG DAVID
WHAT'S YOUR NAME [A] CHICORY TIP
WHAT'S YOUR NAME? [B] ANGEL LEE
WHAT'S YOUR NAME WHAT'S YOUR NUMBER ANDREA TRUE CONNECTION
WHAT'S YOUR NUMBER? CYPRESS HILL
WHAT'S YOUR PROBLEM? BLANCMANGE
WHAT'S YOUR SIGN DES'REE
WHAT'S YOUR SIGN GIRL BARRY BIGGS
WHATCHULOOKINAT WHITNEY HOUSTON
WHATTA MAN SALT-N-PEPA WITH EN VOGUE
WHAZZUP TRUE PARTY
THE WHEEL SPEAR OF DESTINY
WHEEL OF FORTUNE ACE OF BASE
WHEELS STRING-A-LONGS
WHEELS AIN'T COMING DOWN SLADE
WHEELS CHA CHA JOE LOSS ORCHESTRA
WHEELS OF STEEL SAXON
THE WHEELS ON THE BUS MAD DONNA
WHEN [A] KALIN TWINS
WHEN [A] SHOWADDYWADDY
WHEN [B] SUNSCREEM
WHEN [C] SHANIA TWAIN
WHEN A CHILD IS BORN JOHNNY MATHIS & GLADYS KNIGHT
WHEN A CHILD IS BORN (SOLEADO) JOHNNY MATHIS
WHEN A HEART BEATS NIK KERSHAW
WHEN A MAN LOVES A WOMAN [A] PERCY SLEDGE

WHEN A MAN LOVES A WOMAN [A] MICHAEL BOLTON
WHEN A MAN LOVES A WOMAN [B] JODY WATLEY
WHEN A WOMAN GABRIELLE
WHEN A WOMAN'S FED UP R KELLY
WHEN AM I GONNA MAKE A LIVING SADE
WHEN BOUZOUKIS PLAYED VICKY LEANDROS
WHEN BOYS TALK INDEEP
WHEN CAN I SEE YOU BABYFACE
WHEN CHILDREN RULE THE WORLD RED HILL CHILDREN
WHEN DO I GET TO SING 'MY WAY' SPARKS
WHEN DOVES CRY PRINCE
WHEN DOVES CRY GINUWINE
WHEN DREAMS TURN TO DUST CATHY DENNIS
WHEN FOREVER HAS GONE DEMIS ROUSSOS
WHEN HE SHINES SHEENA EASTON
WHEN HEROES GO DOWN SUZANNE VEGA
WHEN I ARGUE I SEE SHAPES IDLEWILD
WHEN I CALL YOUR NAME MARY KIANI
WHEN I COME AROUND GREEN DAY
WHEN I COME HOME SPENCER DAVIS GROUP
WHEN I DREAM [A] TEARDROP EXPLODES
WHEN I DREAM [B] CAROL KIDD FEATURING TERRY WAITE
WHEN I FALL IN LOVE [A] NAT 'KING' COLE
WHEN I FALL IN LOVE [A] DONNY OSMOND
WHEN I FALL IN LOVE [A] RICK ASTLEY
WHEN I FALL IN LOVE [B] ANT & DEC
WHEN I GET HOME SEARCHERS
WHEN I GROW UP [A] MICHELLE SHOCKED
WHEN I GROW UP [B] GARBAGE
WHEN I GROW UP TO BE A MAN BEACH BOYS
WHEN I KISS YOU (I HEAR CHARLIE PARKER) SPARKS
WHEN I LEAVE THE WORLD BEHIND ROSE MARIE
WHEN I LOOK INTO YOUR EYES [A] FIREHOUSE
WHEN I LOOK INTO YOUR EYES [B] MAXEE
WHEN I LOST YOU SARAH WHATMORE
WHEN I NEED YOU LEO SAYER
WHEN I NEED YOU WILL MELLOR
WHEN I SAID GOODBYE STEPS
WHEN I SEE YOU MACY GRAY
WHEN I SEE YOU SMILE BAD ENGLISH
WHEN I THINK OF YOU [A] JANET JACKSON
WHEN I THINK OF YOU [B] KENNY THOMAS
WHEN I THINK OF YOU [C] CHRIS DE BURGH
WHEN I WAS YOUNG [A] ERIC BURDON & THE ANIMALS
WHEN I WAS YOUNG [B] RIVER CITY PEOPLE
WHEN I'M AWAY FROM YOU FRANKIE MILLER
WHEN I'M BACK ON MY FEET AGAIN MICHAEL BOLTON
WHEN I'M CLEANING WINDOWS (TURNED OUT NICE AGAIN) 2 IN A TENT
WHEN I'M DEAD AND GONE McGUINNESS FLINT
WHEN I'M GOOD AND READY SYBIL
WHEN I'M SIXTY FOUR KENNY BALL & HIS JAZZMEN
WHEN IT'S LOVE VAN HALEN
WHEN IT'S OVER SUGAR RAY
WHEN IT'S TIME TO ROCK UFO
WHEN JOHNNY COMES MARCHING HOME ADAM FAITH
WHEN JULIE COMES AROUND CUFF LINKS
WHEN LOVE & HATE COLLIDE DEF LEPPARD
WHEN LOVE BREAKS DOWN PREFAB SPROUT
WHEN LOVE COMES ALONG MATT MONRO
WHEN LOVE COMES CALLING PAUL JOHNSON
WHEN LOVE COMES ROUND AGAIN (L'ARCA DI NOE) KEN DODD
WHEN LOVE COMES TO TOWN U2 FEATURING BB KING
WHEN LOVE TAKES OVER YOU DONNA SUMMER
WHEN MEXICO GAVE UP THE RUMBA MITCHELL TOROK
WHEN MY BABY SCOOCH
WHEN MY LITTLE GIRL IS SMILING CRAIG DOUGLAS

WHEN MY LITTLE GIRL IS SMILING JIMMY JUSTICE
WHEN MY LITTLE GIRL IS SMILING DRIFTERS
WHEN ONLY LOVE WILL DO RICHARD DARBYSHIRE
WHEN ROCK 'N ROLL CAME TO TRINIDAD NAT 'KING' COLE
WHEN SHE WAS MY GIRL FOUR TOPS
WHEN SMOKEY SINGS ABC
WHEN THE BOYS TALK ABOUT THE GIRLS VALERIE CARR
WHEN THE FINGERS POINT CHRISTIANS
WHEN THE GIRL IN YOUR ARMS IS THE GIRL IN YOUR HEART CLIFF RICHARD
WHEN THE GOING GETS TOUGH BOYZONE
WHEN THE GOING GETS TOUGH, THE TOUGH GET GOING BILLY OCEAN
WHEN THE HEARTACHE IS OVER TINA TURNER
WHEN THE HOODOO COMES DIESEL PARK WEST
WHEN THE LAST TIME CLIPSE
WHEN THE LIGHTS GO OUT FIVE
WHEN THE MORNING COMES LOVE DECADE
WHEN THE MORNING SUN DRIES THE DEW QUIET FIVE
WHEN THE NIGHT COMES JOE COCKER
WHEN THE RAIN BEGINS TO FALL JERMAINE JACKSON & PIA ZADORA
WHEN THE SH.. GOES DOWN CYPRESS HILL
WHEN THE SUMMERTIME IS OVER JACKIE TRENT
WHEN THE SUN COMES SHINING THRU' LONG JOHN BALDRY
WHEN THE SUN GOES DOWN DJ FRESH FEATURING ADAM F
WHEN THE TIGERS BROKE FREE PINK FLOYD
WHEN THE WIND BLOWS DAVID BOWIE
WHEN THE WORLD IS RUNNING DOWN DIFFERENT GEAR VERSUS THE POLICE
WHEN THE YEAR ENDS IN 1 TOTTENHAM HOTSPUR F.A. CUP FINAL SQUAD
WHEN THIS RIVER ROLLS OVER YOU STANDS
WHEN TOMORROW COMES EURYTHMICS
WHEN TWO WORLDS COLLIDE JIM REEVES
WHEN TWO WORLDS DRIFT APART CLIFF RICHARD
WHEN WE ARE FAR FROM HOME ENGLAND WORLD CUP SQUAD
WHEN WE ARE TOGETHER TEXAS
WHEN WE DANCE STING
WHEN WE WAS FAB GEORGE HARRISON
WHEN WE WERE YOUNG [A] SOLOMON KING
WHEN WE WERE YOUNG [B] BUCKS FIZZ
WHEN WE WERE YOUNG [C] WHIPPING BOY
WHEN WE WERE YOUNG [D] HUMAN NATURE
WHEN WILL I BE FAMOUS BROS
WHEN WILL I BE LOVED EVERLY BROTHERS
WHEN WILL I SEE YOU AGAIN THREE DEGREES
WHEN WILL I SEE YOU AGAIN BROTHER BEYOND
WHEN WILL I SEE YOU AGAIN SHEILA FERGUSON
WHEN WILL THE GOOD APPLES FALL SEEKERS
WHEN WILL YOU BE MINE AVERAGE WHITE BAND
WHEN WILL YOU MAKE MY TELEPHONE RING DEACON BLUE
WHEN WILL YOU SAY I LOVE YOU BILLY FURY
WHEN YOU ARE A KING WHITE PLAINS
WHEN YOU ASK ABOUT LOVE CRICKETS
WHEN YOU ASK ABOUT LOVE MATCHBOX
WHEN YOU BELIEVE MARIAH CAREY & WHITNEY HOUSTON
WHEN YOU COME BACK TO ME JASON DONOVAN
WHEN YOU GET RIGHT DOWN TO IT RONNIE DYSON
WHEN YOU GONNA LEARN JAMIROQUAI
WHEN YOU KISS ME SHANIA TWAIN
WHEN YOU LOOK AT ME CHRISTINA MILIAN
WHEN YOU LOSE THE ONE YOU LOVE DAVID WHITFIELD WITH CHORUS & MANTOVANI & HIS ORCHESTRA
WHEN YOU MADE THE MOUNTAIN OPUS III

WHEN YOU SAY NOTHING AT ALL RONAN KEATING
(WHEN YOU SAY YOU LOVE SOMEBODY) IN THE HEART KOOL & THE GANG
WHEN YOU SLEEP LONGVIEW
WHEN YOU TELL ME THAT YOU LOVE ME DIANA ROSS
WHEN YOU WALK IN THE ROOM SEARCHERS
WHEN YOU WALK IN THE ROOM CHILD
WHEN YOU WALK IN THE ROOM STATUS QUO
WHEN YOU WALK IN THE ROOM PAUL CARRACK
WHEN YOU WALK IN THE ROOM AGNETHA FALTSKOG
WHEN YOU WERE SWEET SIXTEEN FUREYS WITH DAVEY ARTHUR
WHEN YOU WERE YOUNG DEL AMITRI
WHEN YOUR 'EX' WANTS YOU BACK SURFACE
WHEN YOUR OLD WEDDING RING WAS NEW JIMMY ROSELLI
WHEN YOU'RE GONE [A] BRYAN ADAMS FEATURING MELANIE C
WHEN YOU'RE GONE [B] SORAYA VIVIAN
WHEN YOU'RE IN LOVE WITH A BEAUTIFUL WOMAN DR. HOOK
WHEN YOU'RE NUMBER 1 GENE CHANDLER
WHEN YOU'RE YOUNG JAM
WHEN YOU'RE YOUNG AND IN LOVE MARVELETTES
WHEN YOU'RE YOUNG AND IN LOVE FLYING PICKETS
WHENEVER GOD SHINES HIS LIGHT VAN MORRISON WITH CLIFF RICHARD
WHENEVER I SAY YOUR NAME STING & MARY J. BLÌGE
WHENEVER I STOP MIKE + THE MECHANICS
WHENEVER WHEREVER SHAKIRA
WHENEVER YOU NEED ME T'PAU
WHENEVER YOU NEED SOMEBODY RICK ASTLEY
WHENEVER YOU NEED SOMEONE BAD BOYS INC
WHENEVER YOU WANT MY LOVE REAL THING
WHENEVER YOU'RE NEAR CHER
WHENEVER YOU'RE READY FIVE STAR
WHERE ARE THEY NOW? GENE
WHERE ARE YOU [A] KAVANA
WHERE ARE YOU [B] IMAANI
WHERE ARE YOU BABY BETTY BOO
WHERE ARE YOU GOING TO MY LOVE BROTHERHOOD OF MAN
WHERE ARE YOU NOW (MY LOVE) JACKIE TRENT
WHERE ARE YOU NOW? GENERATOR
WHERE CAN I FIND LOVE LIVIN' JOY
WHERE DID ALL THE GOOD TIMES GO DONNY OSMOND
WHERE DID I GO WRONG UB40
WHERE DID OUR LOVE GO SUPREMES
WHERE DID OUR LOVE GO DONNIE ELBERT
WHERE DID OUR LOVE GO MANHATTAN TRANSFER
WHERE DID OUR LOVE GO TRICIA PENROSE
WHERE DID WE GO WRONG LIQUID GOLD
WHERE DID YOUR HEART GO WHAM!
WHERE DO BROKEN HEARTS GO WHITNEY HOUSTON
(WHERE DO I BEGIN) LOVE STORY ANDY WILLIAMS
(WHERE DO I BEGIN) LOVE STORY SHIRLEY BASSEY
WHERE DO I STAND? MONTROSE AVENUE
WHERE DO U WANT ME TO PUT IT SOLO (US)
WHERE DO WE GO TEN CITY
WHERE DO WE GO FROM HERE CLIFF RICHARD
WHERE DO YOU GO NO MERCY
WHERE DO YOU GO TO MY LOVELY PETER SARSTEDT
WHERE DOES MY HEART BEAT NOW CELINE DION
WHERE DOES TIME GO JULIA FORDHAM
WHERE EAGLES FLY CRYSTAL PALACE
WHERE HAS ALL THE LOVE GONE YAZZ
WHERE HAS ALL THE LOVE GONE MAUREEN
WHERE HAS LOVE GONE HOLLY JOHNSON
WHERE HAVE ALL THE COWBOYS GONE? PAULA COLE
WHERE HAVE YOU BEEN TONIGHT? SHED SEVEN
WHERE I FIND MY HEAVEN GIGOLO AUNTS

WHERE I WANNA BE SHADE SHEIST/NATE DOGG/KURUPT
WHERE I'M HEADED LENE MARLIN
WHERE IN THE WORLD [A] SWING OUT SISTER
WHERE IN THE WORLD [B] BBM
WHERE IS MY MAN EARTHA KITT
WHERE IS THE FEELING? KYLIE MINOGUE
WHERE IS THE LOVE [A] ROBERTA FLACK & DONNY HATHAWAY
WHERE IS THE LOVE [A] MICA PARIS & WILL DOWNING
WHERE IS THE LOVE [B] BETTY WRIGHT
WHERE IS THE LOVE [B] ADEVA
WHERE IS THE LOVE [C] BLACK EYED PEAS
WHERE IS THE LOVE (WE USED TO KNOW) DELEGATION
WHERE IS TOMORROW CILLA BLACK
WHERE IT'S AT BECK
WHERE LOVE LIVES ALISON LIMERICK
WHERE MY GIRLS AT? 702
WHERE THE ACTION IS WESTWORLD
WHERE THE BOYS ARE CONNIE FRANCIS
WHERE THE HEART IS SOFT CELL
WHERE THE HOOD AT? DMX
WHERE THE POOR BOYS DANCE LULU
WHERE THE ROSE IS SOWN BIG COUNTRY
WHERE THE STORY ENDS BLAZIN' SQUAD
WHERE THE STREETS HAVE NO NAME U2
WHERE THE STREETS HAVE NO NAME – CAN'T TAKE MY EYES OFF YOU PET SHOP BOYS
WHERE THE WILD ROSES GROW NICK CAVE + KYLIE MINOGUE
WHERE THE WINDS BLOW FRANKIE LAINE
WHERE WERE YOU ADULT NET
WHERE WERE YOU HIDING WHEN THE STORM BROKE ALARM
WHERE WERE YOU (ON OUR WEDDING DAY)? LLOYD PRICE
WHERE WILL THE BABY'S DIMPLE BE ROSEMARY CLOONEY
WHERE WILL YOU BE SUE NICHOLLS
WHERE YOU ARE RAHSAAN PATTERSON
WHERE YOU GONNA BE TONIGHT? WILLIE COLLINS
WHERE'S JACK THE RIPPER GROOVERIDER
WHERE'S ME JUMPER SULTANS OF PING FC
WHERE'S MY ADAM F FEATURING LIL' MO
WHERE'S ROMEO CA VA CA VA
WHERE'S THE LOVE HANSON
WHERE'S THE PARTY AT JAGGED EDGE FEATURING NELLY
WHERE'S YOUR HEAD AT BASEMENT JAXX
WHERE'S YOUR LOVE BEEN HELIOCENTRIC WORLD
WHEREVER I LAY MY HAT (THAT'S MY HOME) PAUL YOUNG
WHEREVER I MAY ROAM METALLICA
WHEREVER WOULD I BE DUSTY SPRINGFIELD & DARYL HALL
WHEREVER YOU ARE NEIL FINN
WHEREVER YOU WILL GO CALLING
WHICH WAY SHOULD I JUMP MILLTOWN BROTHERS
WHICH WAY YOU GOIN' BILLY POPPY FAMILY
WHIGGLE IN LINE BLACK DUCK
WHILE I LIVE KENNY DAMON
WHILE YOU SEE A CHANCE STEVE WINWOOD
WHINE AND GRINE PRINCE BUSTER
WHIP IT DEVO
WHIPLASH JFK
WHIPPIN' PICCADILLY GOMEZ
WHISKEY IN THE JAR THIN LIZZY
WHISKEY IN THE JAR POGUES & THE DUBLINERS
WHISKEY IN THE JAR METALLICA
THE WHISPER SELECTER
WHISPER A PRAYER MICA PARIS

WHISPER YOUR NAME HUMAN NATURE
WHISPERING BACHELORS
WHISPERING NINO TEMPO & APRIL STEVENS
WHISPERING GRASS WINDSOR DAVIES & DON ESTELLE
WHISPERING HOPE JIM REEVES
WHISPERING YOUR NAME ALISON MOYET
WHISPERS [A] ELTON JOHN
WHISPERS [B] IAN BROWN
WHISTLE DOWN THE WIND NICK HEYWARD
WHISTLE DOWN THE WIND TINA ARENA
THE WHISTLE SONG FRANKIE KNUCKLES
THE WHISTLE SONG (BLOW MY WHISTLE BITCH) DJ ALIGATOR PROJECT
THE WHISTLER HONKY
WHITE BIRD VANESSA-MAE
WHITE BOY WITH A FEATHER JASON DOWNS FEATURING MILK
WHITE BOYS AND HEROES GARY NUMAN
WHITE CHRISTMAS MANTOVANI
WHITE CHRISTMAS PAT BOONE
WHITE CHRISTMAS FREDDIE STARR
WHITE CHRISTMAS BING CROSBY
WHITE CHRISTMAS DARTS
WHITE CHRISTMAS JIM DAVIDSON
WHITE CHRISTMAS KEITH HARRIS & ORVILLE
WHITE CHRISTMAS MAX BYGRAVES
WHITE CLIFFS OF DOVER MR ACKER BILK & HIS PARAMOUNT JAZZ BAND
WHITE CLIFFS OF DOVER RIGHTEOUS BROTHERS
WHITE COATS (EP) NEW MODEL ARMY
WHITE FLAG DIDO
WHITE HORSES JACKY
WHITE LIE FOREIGNER
WHITE LIGHT, WHITE HEAT DAVID BOWIE
WHITE LIGHTNING FALL
WHITE LINES (DON'T DO IT) DURAN DURAN FEATURING MELLE MEL & GRANDMASTER FLASH & THE FURIOUS FIVE
WHITE LINES (DON'T DON'T DO IT) GRANDMASTER FLASH & MELLE MEL
WHITE LOVE ONE DOVE
(WHITE MAN) IN HAMMERSMITH PALAIS CLASH
WHITE NO SUGAR CLINT BOON EXPERIENCE
WHITE PUNKS ON DOPE TUBES
WHITE RIBBON DAY DELIRIOUS?
WHITE RIOT CLASH
WHITE ROOM CREAM
WHITE SILVER SANDS BILL BLACK'S COMBO
WHITE SKIES SUNSCREEM
A WHITE SPORT COAT TERRY DENE
A WHITE SPORT COAT KING BROTHERS
WHITE WEDDING BILLY IDOL
WHITE WEDDING MURDERDOLLS
A WHITER SHADE OF PALE PROCOL HARUM
A WHITER SHADE OF PALE MUNICH MACHINE INTRODUCING CHRIS BENNETT
A WHITER SHADE OF PALE ANNIE LENNOX
WHO? ED CASE & SWEETIE IRIE
WHO AM I [A] ADAM FAITH
WHO AM I [B] BEENIE MAN
WHO ARE WE VERA LYNN
WHO ARE WE RONNIE HILTON
WHO ARE YOU WHO
WHO CAN I RUN TO XSCAPE
WHO CAN IT BE NOW? MEN AT WORK
WHO CAN MAKE ME FEEL GOOD BASSHEADS
WHO COMES TO BOOGIE LITTLE BENNY & THE MASTERS
WHO COULD BE BLUER JERRY LORDAN
WHO DO U LOVE DEBORAH COX
WHO DO YOU LOVE [A] JUICY LUCY
WHO DO YOU LOVE? [B] INTRUDERS

WHO DO YOU LOVE [C] JOSE PADILLA FEATURING ANGELA JOHN
WHO DO YOU LOVE NOW (STRINGER) RIVA FEATURING DANNII MINOGUE
WHO DO YOU THINK YOU ARE [A] CANDLEWICK GREEN
WHO DO YOU THINK YOU ARE [B] KIM WILDE
WHO DO YOU THINK YOU ARE [C] SAINT ETIENNE
WHO DO YOU THINK YOU ARE [D] SPICE GIRLS
WHO DO YOU WANT FOR YOUR LOVE ICICLE WORKS
WHO FEELS LOVE? OASIS
WHO FOUND WHO JELLYBEAN FEATURING ELISA FIORILLO
WHO GETS THE LOVE STATUS QUO
WHO INVITED YOU DONNAS
WHO IS IT [A] MANTRONIX
WHO IS IT [B] MICHAEL JACKSON
WHO IS IT [C] BJORK
WHO KEEPS CHANGING YOUR MIND SOUTH ST. PLAYER
WHO KILLED BAMBI TEN POLE TUDOR
WHO LET IN THE RAIN CYNDI LAUPER
WHO LET THE DOGS OUT BAHA MEN
WHO LOVES YOU FOUR SEASONS
WHO MADE WHO AC/DC
WHO NEEDS ENEMIES COOPER TEMPLE CLAUSE
WHO NEEDS LOVE LIKE THAT ERASURE
WHO PAYS THE FERRYMAN YANNIS MARKOPOULOS
WHO PAYS THE PIPER GARY CLAIL ON-U SOUND SYSTEM
WHO PUT THE BOMP VISCOUNTS
WHO PUT THE BOMP (IN THE BOMP-A-BOMP-A-BOMP) SHOWADDYWADDY
WHO PUT THE LIGHTS OUT DANA
WHO SAID (STUCK IN THE UK) PLANET FUNK
WHO THE HELL ARE YOU MADISON AVENUE
WHO TOLD YOU RONI SIZE REPRAZENT
WHO WANTS THE WORLD STRANGLERS
WHO WANTS TO BE THE DISCO KING WONDER STUFF
WHO WANTS TO LIVE FOREVER QUEEN
WHO WANTS TO LIVE FOREVER SARAH BRIGHTMAN
WHO WAS IT HURRICANE SMITH
WHO WE BE DMX
WHO WEARS THESE SHOES ELTON JOHN
WHO WERE YOU WITH IN THE MOONLIGHT DOLLAR
WHO WHAT WHEN WHERE WHY MANHATTAN TRANSFER
WHO WHERE WHY JESUS JONES
WHO WILL SAVE YOUR SOUL JEWEL
WHO WILL YOU RUN TO HEART
WHO YOU ARE PEARL JAM
WHO YOU LOOKING AT SALFORD JETS
WHO YOU WIT JAY-Z
WHOA BLACK ROB
WHO'D SHE COO OHIO PLAYERS
WHODUNNIT TAVARES
WHOLE AGAIN ATOMIC KITTEN
WHOLE LOTTA LOVE C.C.S.
WHOLE LOTTA LOVE GOLDBUG
WHOLE LOTTA LOVE LED ZEPPELIN
WHOLE LOTTA ROSIE AC/DC
WHOLE LOTTA SHAKIN' GOIN' ON JERRY LEE LEWIS
WHOLE LOTTA TROUBLE STEVIE NICKS
WHOLE LOTTA WOMAN MARVIN RAINWATER
WHOLE NEW WORLD IT BITES
A WHOLE NEW WORLD (ALADDIN'S THEME) PEABO BRYSON & REGINA BELLE
THE WHOLE OF THE MOON WATERBOYS
THE WHOLE OF THE MOON LITTLE CAESAR
THE WHOLE TOWN'S LAUGHING AT ME TEDDY PENDERGRASS
THE WHOLE WORLD OUTKAST FEATURING KILLER MIKE
THE WHOLE WORLD LOST ITS HEAD GO-GOS

WHOOMP THERE IT IS BM DUBS PRESENT MR RUMBLE
WHOOMP! (THERE IT IS) TAG TEAM
WHOOMPH! (THERE IT IS) CLOCK
WHOOPS NOW JANET JACKSON
WHOOSH WHOOSH
WHO'S AFRAID OF THE BIG BAD LOVE WILD WEEKEND
WHO'S AFRAID OF THE BIG BAD NOISE? AGE OF SHOCK
WHO'S COMING ROUND 5050
WHO'S CRYING NOW JOURNEY
WHO'S DAVID BUSTED
WHO'S GONNA LOVE ME IMPERIALS
WHO'S GONNA RIDE YOUR WILD HORSES U2
WHO'S GONNA ROCK YOU NOLANS
WHO'S IN THE HOUSE BEATMASTERS FEATURING MERLIN
WHO'S IN THE STRAWBERRY PATCH WITH SALLY DAWN FEATURING TONY ORLANDO
WHO'S JOHNNY ('SHORT CIRCUIT' THEME) EL DeBARGE
WHO'S LEAVING WHO HAZELL DEAN
WHO'S LOVING MY BABY SHOLA AMA
WHO'S SORRY NOW JOHNNIE RAY
WHO'S SORRY NOW CONNIE FRANCIS
WHO'S THAT GIRL? [A] EURYTHMICS
WHO'S THAT GIRL [B] FLYING PICKETS
WHO'S THAT GIRL [C] MADONNA
WHO'S THAT GIRL [D] EVE
WHO'S THAT GIRL (SHE'S GOT IT) A FLOCK OF SEAGULLS
WHO'S THAT MIX THIS YEAR'S BLONDE
WHO'S THE BAD MAN DEE PATTEN
WHO'S THE DADDY LOVEBUG
WHO'S THE DARKMAN DARKMAN
WHO'S THE MACK MARK MORRISON
WHO'S THE MAN HOUSE OF PAIN
WHO'S ZOOMIN' WHO ARETHA FRANKLIN
WHOSE FIST IS THIS ANYWAY EP PRONG
WHOSE LAW (IS IT ANYWAY) GURU JOSH
WHOSE PROBLEM? MOTELS
WHY [A] ANTHONY NEWLEY
WHY [A] FRANKIE AVALON
WHY [A] DONNY OSMOND
WHY [B] ROGER WHITTAKER
WHY [C] CARLY SIMON
WHY [C] GLAMMA KID
WHY? [D] BRONSKI BEAT
WHY [E] ANNIE LENNOX
WHY [F] D MOB WITH CATHY DENNIS
WHY [G] RICARDO DA FORCE
WHY [H] 3T FEATURING MICHAEL JACKSON
WHY [I] MIS-TEEQ
WHY [J] AGENT SUMO
WHY ARE PEOPLE GRUDGEFUL FALL
WHY ARE YOU BEING SO REASONABLE NOW WEDDING PRESENT
WHY BABY WHY PAT BOONE
WHY BELIEVE IN YOU TEXAS
WHY CAN'T I BE YOU [A] CURE
WHY CAN'T I BE YOU? [B] SHED SEVEN
WHY CAN'T I WAKE UP WITH YOU TAKE THAT
WHY CAN'T THIS BE LOVE VAN HALEN
WHY CAN'T WE BE LOVERS HOLLAND-DOZIER FEATURING LAMONT DOZIER
WHY CAN'T WE LIVE TOGETHER TIMMY THOMAS
WHY CAN'T YOU CLARENCE 'FROGMAN' HENRY
WHY CAN'T YOU FREE SOME TIME ARMAND VAN HELDEN
WHY DID YA TONY DI BART
WHY DID YOU DO IT STRETCH
WHY DIDN'T YOU CALL ME MACY GRAY
WHY DO FOOLS FALL IN LOVE TEENAGERS FEATURING FRANKIE LYMON

WHY DO FOOLS FALL IN LOVE ALMA COGAN
WHY DO FOOLS FALL IN LOVE DIANA ROSS
WHY DO I ALWAYS GET IT WRONG LIVE REPORT
WHY DO I DO TYLER JAMES
WHY DO LOVERS BREAK EACH OTHER'S HEARTS SHOWADDYWADDY
WHY DO YOU KEEP ON RUNNING STINX
WHY DOES A MAN HAVE TO BE STRONG PAUL YOUNG
WHY DOES IT ALWAYS RAIN ON ME TRAVIS
WHY DOES MY HEART FEEL SO BAD MOBY
WHY DON'T THEY UNDERSTAND GEORGE HAMILTON IV
WHY DON'T WE FALL IN LOVE AMERIE FEATURING LUDACRIS
WHY DON'T WE TRY AGAIN BRIAN MAY
WHY DON'T YOU RAGE
WHY DON'T YOU BELIEVE ME JONI JAMES
WHY DON'T YOU DANCE WITH ME FUTURE BREEZE
WHY DON'T YOU DO IT FOR ME 22-20'S
WHY DON'T YOU GET A JOB OFFSPRING
WHY DON'T YOU TAKE ME ONE DOVE
WHY D'YA LIE TO ME SPIDER
WHY (LOOKING BACK) HEARTLESS CREW
WHY ME [A] LINDA MARTIN
WHY ME [B] A HOUSE
WHY ME [C] PJ & DUNCAN
WHY ME [D] ASHER D
WHY (MUST WE FALL IN LOVE) DIANA ROSS & THE SUPREMES & THE TEMPTATIONS
WHY MUST WE WAIT UNTIL TONIGHT TINA TURNER
WHY NOT NOW MATT MONRO
WHY NOT TONIGHT MOJOS
WHY OH WHY SPEARHEAD
WHY OH WHY OH WHY GILBERT O'SULLIVAN
WHY SHE'S A GIRL FROM THE CHAINSTORE BUZZCOCKS
WHY SHOULD I BOB MARLEY & THE WAILERS
WHY SHOULD I BE LONELY TONY BRENT
WHY SHOULD I CRY NONA HENDRYX
WHY SHOULD I LOVE YOU DES'REE
WHY WHY BYE BYE BOB LUMAN
WHY WHY WHY DÉJÀ VU
WHY YOU FOLLOW ME ERIC BENET
WHY YOU TREAT ME SO BAD SHAGGY FEATURING GRAND PUBA
WHY'D YOU LIE TO ME ANASTACIA
WHY'S EVERYBODY ALWAYS PICKIN' ON ME? BLOODHOUND GANG
WIBBLING RIVALRY (INTERVIEWS WITH NOEL AND LIAM GALLAGHER) OAS*S
WICHITA LINEMAN GLEN CAMPBELL
WICKED ICE CUBE
WICKED GAME CHRIS ISAAK
WICKED LOVE OCEANIC
WICKED WAYS BLOW MONKEYS
WICKEDEST SOUND REBEL MC FEATURING TENOR FLY
THE WICKER MAN IRON MAIDEN
WICKY WACKY HOUSE PARTY TEAM
WIDE AWAKE IN A DREAM BARRY BIGGS
WIDE BOY NIK KERSHAW
WIDE EYED AND LEGLESS ANDY FAIRWEATHER-LOW
WIDE EYED ANGEL ORIGIN
WIDE OPEN SKY GOLDRUSH
WIDE OPEN SPACE MANSUN
WIDE PRAIRIE LINDA McCARTNEY
WIFEY NEXT
WIG WAM BAM BLACK LACE
WIG WAM BAM DAMIAN
WIG-WAM BAM SWEET
WIGGLE IT 2 IN A ROOM
WIGGLY WORLD MR JACK
WIKKA WRAP EVASIONS

THE WILD AMERICA (EP) IGGY POP
WILD AND WONDERFUL ALMIGHTY
WILD AS ANGELS EP LEVELLERS
WILD BOYS DURAN DURAN
WILD BOYS PHIXX
WILD CAT GENE VINCENT
WILD CHILD [A] W.A.S.P.
WILD CHILD [B] ENYA
WILD DANCES RUSLANA
WILD FLOWER CULT
WILD FRONTIER GARY MOORE
WILD HEARTED SON CULT
WILD HEARTED WOMAN ALL ABOUT EVE
WILD HONEY BEACH BOYS
WILD IN THE COUNTRY ELVIS PRESLEY
WILD IS THE WIND DAVID BOWIE
WILD LOVE MUNGO JERRY
WILD LUV ROACH MOTEL
WILD 'N FREE REDNEX
WILD NIGHT JOHN MELLENCAMP FEATURING
   ME'SHELL NDEGEOCELLO
WILD ONE [A] BOBBY RYDELL
THE WILD ONE [B] SUZI QUATRO
THE WILD ONES SUEDE
WILD SIDE MOTLEY CRUE
WILD SIDE OF LIFE TOMMY QUICKLY
WILD SIDE OF LIFE STATUS QUO
THE WILD SON VEILS
WILD SURF ASH
WILD THING [A] TROGGS
WILD THING [A] GOODIES
WILD THING [B] TONE LOC
WILD WEST HERO ELECTRIC LIGHT ORCHESTRA
WILD WILD LIFE TALKING HEADS
WILD WILD WEST [A] WILL SMITH FEATURING DRU
   HILL
WILD WILD WEST [B] GET READY
WILD WIND JOHN LEYTON
WILD WOMEN DO NATALIE COLE
WILD WOOD PAUL WELLER
WILD WORLD JIMMY CLIFF
WILD WORLD MAXI PRIEST
WILD WORLD MR BIG
WILDERNESS JURGEN VRIES FEATURING SHENA
WILDEST DREAMS IRON MAIDEN
WILDLIFE (EP) GIRLSCHOOL
WILDSIDE MARKY MARK & THE FUNKY BUNCH
WILFRED THE WEASEL KEITH MICHELL
WILL 2K WILL SMITH
WILL I? IAN VAN DAHL
WILL I EVER ALICE DEEJAY
WILL I WHAT MIKE SARNE WITH BILLIE DAVIS
WILL SHE ALWAYS BE WAITING BLUEBELLS
WILL THE WOLF SURVIVE LOS LOBOS
WILL WE BE LOVERS DEACON BLUE
WILL YOU [A] HAZEL O'CONNOR
WILL YOU [B] P.O.D.
WILL YOU BE MY BABY INFINITI FEATURING GRAND
   PUBA
WILL YOU BE THERE MICHAEL JACKSON
WILL YOU BE THERE (IN THE MORNING) HEART
WILL YOU BE WITH ME MARIA NAYLER
WILL YOU LOVE ME TOMORROW SHIRELLES
WILL YOU LOVE ME TOMORROW MELANIE
WILL YOU LOVE ME TOMORROW BRYAN FERRY
WILL YOU MARRY ME PAULA ABDUL
WILL YOU SATISFY? CHERRELLE
WILL YOU WAIT FOR ME KAVANA
WILLIAM, IT WAS REALLY NOTHING SMITHS
WILLIE CAN ALMA COGAN WITH DESMOND LANE –
   PENNY WHISTLE

WILLIE CAN BEVERLEY SISTERS
WILLING TO FORGIVE ARETHA FRANKLIN
WILLINGLY MALCOLM VAUGHAN
WILLOW TREE IVY LEAGUE
WILMOT SABRES OF PARADISE
WIMMIN' ASHLEY HAMILTON
WIMOWEH KARL DENVER
(WIN PLACE OR SHOW) SHE'S A WINNER INTRUDERS
WINCHESTER CATHEDRAL NEW VAUDEVILLE BAND
THE WIND PJ HARVEY
THE WIND BENEATH MY WINGS LEE GREENWOOD
WIND BENEATH MY WINGS BETTE MIDLER
WIND BENEATH MY WINGS BILL TARMEY
WIND BENEATH MY WINGS STEVEN HOUGHTON
THE WIND CRIES MARY JIMI HENDRIX EXPERIENCE
WIND IT UP (REWOUND) PRODIGY
WIND ME UP (LET ME GO) CLIFF RICHARD
WIND OF CHANGE SCORPIONS
WIND THE BOBBIN UP JO JINGLES
A WINDMILL IN OLD AMSTERDAM RONNIE HILTON
WINDMILLS OF YOUR MIND NOEL HARRISON
WINDOW PANE (EP) REAL PEOPLE
WINDOW SHOPPING R. DEAN TAYLOR
WINDOWLICKER APHEX TWIN
WINDOWS '98 SIL
WINDPOWER THOMAS DOLBY
THE WINDSOR WALTZ VERA LYNN
WINDSWEPT BRYAN FERRY
WINGDINGS SUGACOMA
WINGS OF A DOVE MADNESS
WINGS OF LOVE BONE
WINKER'S SONG (MISPRINT) IVOR BIGGUN & THE RED
   NOSE BURGLARS
THE WINKLE MAN JUDGE DREAD
THE WINNER [A] HEARTBEAT
THE WINNER [B] COOLIO
THE WINNER TAKES IT ALL ABBA
WINNING DAYS VINES
WINTER [A] LOVE & MONEY
WINTER [B] TORI AMOS
WINTER [C] SPECIAL NEEDS
WINTER CEREMONY (TOR-CHENEY-NAHANA) SACRED
   SPIRIT
WINTER IN JULY BOMB THE BASS
WINTER MELODY DONNA SUMMER
WINTER SONG CHRIS REA
A WINTER STORY ALED JONES
WINTER WONDERLAND JOHNNY MATHIS
WINTER WONDERLAND COCTEAU TWINS
WINTER WORLD OF LOVE ENGELBERT HUMPERDINCK
A WINTER'S TALE [A] DAVID ESSEX
A WINTER'S TALE [B] QUEEN
WIPE OUT SURFARIS
WIPE OUT ANIMAL
WIPE THE NEEDLE RAGGA TWINS
WIPEOUT FAT BOYS & THE BEACH BOYS
WIRED FOR SOUND CLIFF RICHARD
THE WISDOM OF A FOOL RONNIE CARROLL
WISDOM OF A FOOL NORMAN WISDOM
WISE UP! SUCKER POP WILL EAT ITSELF
WISER TIME BLACK CROWES
WISH SOUL II SOUL
A WISH AWAY WONDER STUFF
WISH I COULD FLY ROXETTE
WISH I DIDN'T MISS YOU ANGIE STONE
WISH I HAD AN ANGEL NIGHTWISH
WISH I WAS SKINNY BOO RADLEYS
WISH I WERE YOU ALISHA'S ATTIC
WISH THE WORLD AWAY AMERICAN MUSIC CLUB
WISH YOU WERE HERE [A] EDDIE FISHER
WISH YOU WERE HERE [B] FIRST LIGHT

WISH YOU WERE HERE [C] ALOOF
WISH YOU WERE HERE [D] WYCLEF JEAN
WISH YOU WERE HERE [E] INCUBUS
WISHES HUMAN NATURE
WISHFUL THINKING CHINA CRISIS
WISHIN' AND HOPIN' MERSEYBEATS
WISHING BUDDY HOLLY
WISHING I WAS HERE NATALIE IMBRUGLIA
WISHING I WAS LUCKY WET WET WET
WISHING (IF I HAD A PHOTOGRAPH OF YOU) A FLOCK
   OF SEAGULLS
WISHING ON A STAR ROSE ROYCE
WISHING ON A STAR FRESH 4 FEATURING LIZZ E
WISHING ON A STAR COVER GIRLS
WISHING ON A STAR 88.3 FEATURING LISA MAY
WISHING ON A STAR JAY-Z FEATURING GWEN DICKEY
WISHING ON A STAR PAUL WELLER
WISHING WELL [A] FREE
WISHING WELL [B] TERENCE TRENT D'ARBY
THE WISHING WELL [C] G.O.S.H.
WISHING YOU WERE HERE ALISON MOYET
WISHING YOU WERE SOMEHOW HERE AGAIN SARAH
   BRIGHTMAN
WISHLIST PEARL JAM
THE WITCH RATTLES
WITCH DOCTOR DON LANG & HIS FRANTIC FIVE
WITCH DOCTOR DAVID SEVILLE
WITCH DOCTOR CARTOONS
THE WITCH QUEEN OF NEW ORLEANS REDBONE
WITCHCRAFT FRANK SINATRA
WITCHCRAFT ROBERT PALMER
WITCHES' BREW JANIE JONES
THE WITCH'S PROMISE JETHRO TULL
WITH A GIRL LIKE YOU TROGGS
WITH A LITTLE HELP FROM MY FRIENDS JOE BROWN
WITH A LITTLE HELP FROM MY FRIENDS YOUNG IDEA
WITH A LITTLE HELP FROM MY FRIENDS JOE COCKER
WITH A LITTLE HELP FROM MY FRIENDS WET WET WET
WITH A LITTLE HELP FROM MY FRIENDS SAM & MARK
WITH A LITTLE LOVE SAM BROWN
WITH A LITTLE LUCK WINGS
WITH ALL MY HEART PETULA CLARK
WITH ARMS WIDE OPEN CREED
WITH EVERY BEAT OF MY HEART TAYLOR DAYNE
WITH EVERY HEARTBEAT FIVE STAR
WITH GOD ON OUR SIDE NEVILLE BROTHERS
WITH ME DESTINY'S CHILD
WITH MY OWN EYES SASH!
WITH ONE LOOK BARBRA STREISAND
WITH OR WITHOUT YOU U2
WITH OR WITHOUT YOU MARY KIANI
WITH PEN IN HAND VIKKI CARR
WITH THE EYES OF A CHILD CLIFF RICHARD
WITH THE WIND AND THE RAIN IN YOUR HAIR PAT
   BOONE
WITH THESE HANDS SHIRLEY BASSEY
WITH THESE HANDS TOM JONES
WITH YOU JESSICA SIMPSON
WITH YOU I'M BORN AGAIN BILLY PRESTON &
   SYREETA
WITH YOUR LOVE MALCOLM VAUGHAN
WITHOUT A DOUBT BLACK SHEEP
WITHOUT HER HERB ALPERT & THE TIJUANA BRASS
WITHOUT LOVE [A] TOM JONES
WITHOUT LOVE [B] DONNA LEWIS
WITHOUT LOVE [C] DINA CARROLL
WITHOUT ME EMINEM
WITHOUT YOU [A] MATT MONRO
WITHOUT YOU [B] NILSSON
WITHOUT YOU [B] MARIAH CAREY
WITHOUT YOU [C] MOTLEY CRUE

WITHOUT YOU [D] LUCY PEARL
WITHOUT YOU (ONE AND ONE) LINDY LAYTON
WITHOUT YOUR LOVE ROGER DALTREY
WITNESS (EP) ANN NESBY
WITNESS FOR THE WORLD CRY BEFORE DAWN
WITNESS (1 HOPE) ROOTS MANUVA
THE WIZARD PAUL HARDCASTLE
WIZARDS OF THE SONIC WESTBAM
WIZZY WOW BLACKstreet
WOE IS ME HELEN SHAPIRO
W.O.L.D. HARRY CHAPIN
WOLF [A] SHY FX
THE WOLF [B] DAVE CLARKE
WOMAN [A] JOSE FERRER
WOMAN [B] PETER & GORDON
WOMAN [C] JOHN LENNON
WOMAN [D] ANTI-NOWHERE LEAGUE
WOMAN [E] NENEH CHERRY
WOMAN FROM LIBERIA JIMMIE RODGERS
THE WOMAN I LOVE HOLLIES
WOMAN IN CHAINS TEARS FOR FEARS FEATURING
    OLETA ADAMS
WOMAN IN LOVE REBEKAH RYAN
A WOMAN IN LOVE [A] FRANKIE LAINE
WOMAN IN LOVE [A] RONNIE HILTON
WOMAN IN LOVE [A] FOUR ACES FEATURING AL
    ALBERTS
WOMAN IN LOVE [B] THREE DEGREES
WOMAN IN LOVE [C] BARBRA STREISAND
WOMAN IN ME CARLEEN ANDERSON
THE WOMAN IN ME [A] DONNA SUMMER
THE WOMAN IN ME [B] KINANE
WOMAN IN WINTER SKIDS
WOMAN OF MINE DEAN FRIEDMAN
WOMAN OF PRINCIPLE TROUBLE FUNK
WOMAN TO WOMAN BEVERLEY CRAVEN
WOMAN TROUBLE ARTFUL DODGER FEATURING
    ROBBIE CRAIG & CRAIG DAVID
WOMAN WOMAN GARY PUCKETT AND THE UNION
    GAP
WOMANKIND LITTLE ANGELS
A WOMAN'S PLACE GILBERT O'SULLIVAN
A WOMAN'S STORY MARC ALMOND & THE WILLING
    SINNERS
WOMAN'S WORLD JAGS
A WOMAN'S WORTH ALICIA KEYS
WOMBLING MERRY CHRISTMAS WOMBLES
THE WOMBLING SONG WOMBLES
WOMBLING WHITE TIE AND TAILS WOMBLES
WOMEN BEAT THEIR MEN JUNIOR CARTIER
WOMEN IN UNIFORM SKYHOOKS
WOMEN IN UNIFORM IRON MAIDEN
WOMEN OF IRELAND MIKE OLDFIELD
WON BETA BAND
WONDER EMBRACE
THE WONDER OF LOVE LOVELAND FEATURING RACHEL
    McFARLANE
THE WONDER OF YOU RONNIE HILTON
THE WONDER OF YOU RAY PETERSON
THE WONDER OF YOU ELVIS PRESLEY
WONDERBOY [A] KINKS
WONDERBOY [B] TENACIOUS D
WONDERFUL [A] MARI WILSON
WONDERFUL [B] RUNRIG
WONDERFUL [C] ADAM ANT
WONDERFUL [D] EVERCLEAR
WONDERFUL [E] BRIAN WILSON
WONDERFUL [F] JA RULE FEATURING R KELLY &
    ASHANTI
WONDERFUL CHRISTMAS TIME PAUL McCARTNEY
WONDERFUL COPENHAGEN DANNY KAYE

WONDERFUL DREAM ANNE-MARIE DAVID
WONDERFUL EXCUSE FAMILY CAT
WONDERFUL LAND SHADOWS
WONDERFUL LIFE BLACK
WONDERFUL LIFE TJ DAVIS
WONDERFUL NIGHT FATBOY SLIM
WONDERFUL SECRET LOVE ROBERT EARL
WONDERFUL THINGS FRANKIE VAUGHAN
A WONDERFUL TIME UP THERE PAT BOONE
A WONDERFUL TIME UP THERE ALVIN STARDUST
WONDERFUL TONIGHT DAMAGE
WONDERFUL TONIGHT (LIVE) ERIC CLAPTON
WONDERFUL WONDERFUL GARY MILLER
WONDERFUL WONDERFUL RONNIE HILTON
WONDERFUL WORLD [A] SAM COOKE
WONDERFUL WORLD [A] HERMAN'S HERMITS
WONDERFUL WORLD [B] WORLDS APART
WONDERFUL WORLD BEAUTIFUL PEOPLE JIMMY CLIFF
WONDERFUL WORLD OF THE YOUNG DANNY WILLIAMS
WONDERING WHY MJ COLE
WONDERLAND [A] COMMODORES
WONDERLAND [B] BIG COUNTRY
WONDERLAND [C] PAUL YOUNG
WONDERLAND [D] 911
WONDERLAND [E] THE PSYCHEDELIC WALTONS
    FEATURING ROISIN MURPHY
WONDERMAN RIGHT SAID FRED
WONDEROUS STORIES YES
WONDERWALL OASIS
WONDERWALL MIKE FLOWERS POPS
WONDERWALL DE-CODE FEATURING BEVERLI SKEETE
WONDERWALL RYAN ADAMS
WONDROUS PLACE BILLY FURY
WON'T GET FOOLED AGAIN WHO
WON'T GIVE IN FINN BROTHERS
WON'T LET THIS FEELING GO SUNDANCE
WON'T SOMEBODY DANCE WITH ME LYNSEY DE PAUL
WON'T STOP LOVING YOU A CERTAIN RATIO
WON'T TAKE IT LYING DOWN HONEYZ
WON'T TALK ABOUT IT NORMAN COOK FEATURING
    BILLY BRAGG
WON'T TALK ABOUT IT BEATS INTERNATIONAL
WON'T YOU HOLD MY HAND NOW KING
WON'T YOU SAY CHRISTIAN FRY
WOO-HAH!! GOT YOU ALL IN CHECK BUSTA RHYMES
WOO HOO 5,6,7,8'S
WOOD BEEZ (PRAY LIKE ARETHA FRANKLIN) SCRITTI
    POLITTI
WOODEN HEART ELVIS PRESLEY
WOODPECKERS FROM SPACE VIDEO KIDS
WOODSTOCK MATTHEWS' SOUTHERN COMFORT
WOOLY BULLY SAM THE SHAM & THE PHARAOHS
WOPBABALUBOP FUNKDOOBIEST
THE WORD DOPE SMUGGLAZ
THE WORD GIRL SCRITTI POLITTI FEATURING RANKING
    ANN
A WORD IN YOUR EAR ALFIE
THE WORD IS LOVE (SAY THE WORD) VOICES OF LIFE
WORD IS OUT KYLIE MINOGUE
WORD LOVE RHIANNA
WORD OF MOUTH MIKE + THE MECHANICS
WORD PERFECT KRS ONE
WORD UP CAMEO
WORD UP GUN
WORD UP MELANIE G
WORDS [A] ALLISONS
WORDS [B] BEE GEES
WORDS [B] RITA COOLIDGE
WORDS [B] BOYZONE
WORDS [C] F.R. DAVID
WORDS [D] CHRISTIANS

WORDS [E] PAUL VAN DYK FEATURING TONI HALLIDAY
WORDS ARE NOT ENOUGH STEPS
WORDS OF LOVE MAMAS & THE PAPAS
WORDS THAT SAY MEGA CITY FOUR
WORDS WITH THE SHAMEN DAVID SYLVIAN
WORDY RAPPINGHOOD TOM TOM CLUB
WORDY RAPPINGHOOD CHICKS ON SPEED
WORK [A] TECHNOTRONIC FEATURING REGGIE
WORK [B] BARRINGTON LEVY
WORK ALL DAY BARRY BIGGS
WORK IT [A] MISSY ELLIOTT
WORK IT [B] NELLY FEATURING JUSTIN TIMBERLAKE
WORK IT OUT [A] SHIVA
WORK IT OUT [B] DEF LEPPARD
WORK IT OUT [C] BEYONCÉ
WORK IT TO THE BONE LNR
WORK IT UP SLEAZE SISTERS
WORK MI BODY MONKEY MAFIA FEATURING PATRA
W.O.R.K. (N.O. NAH NO NO MY DADDY DON'T) BOW
    WOW WOW
WORK THAT BODY DIANA ROSS
WORK THAT MAGIC DONNA SUMMER
WORK THAT SUCKER TO DEATH XAVIER
WORKAHOLIC 2 UNLIMITED
THE WORKER FISCHER-Z
WORKIN' FOR THE MAN ROY ORBISON
WORKIN' OVERTIME DIANA ROSS
WORKIN' UP A SWEAT FULL CIRCLE
WORKING FOR THE YANKEE DOLLAR SKIDS
WORKING IN A GOLDMINE AZTEC CAMERA
WORKING IN THE COALMINE LEE DORSEY
WORKING MAN RITA MacNEIL
WORKING MOTHER MARTYN JOSEPH
WORKING MY WAY BACK TO YOU FOUR SEASONS WITH
    FRANKIE VALLI
WORKING MY WAY BACK TO YOU – FORGIVE ME GIRL
    (MEDLEY) DETROIT SPINNERS
WORKING ON A BUILDING OF LOVE CHAIRMEN OF THE
    BOARD
WORKING ON IT CHRIS REA
WORKING WITH FIRE AND STEEL CHINA CRISIS
WORLD BEE GEES
THE WORLD NICK HEYWARD
WORLD CUP '98 – PAVANE WIMBLEDON CHORAL
    SOCIETY
WORLD DESTRUCTION TIME ZONE
WORLD FILLED WITH LOVE CRAIG DAVID
WORLD IN MOTION ENGLANDNEWORDER
THE WORLD IN MY ARMS NAT 'KING' COLE
WORLD IN MY EYES DEPECHE MODE
THE WORLD IN MY HANDS SNAP FEATURING
    SUMMER
WORLD IN UNION KIRI TE KANAWA
WORLD IN UNION SHIRLEY BASSEY/BRYN TERFEL
WORLD IN UNION '95 LADYSMITH BLACK MAMBAZO
    FEATURING PJ POWERS
WORLD IN YOUR HANDS CULTURE BEAT
THE WORLD IS A GHETTO GETO BOYS FEATURING FLAJ
THE WORLD IS FLAT ECHOBELLY
THE WORLD IS MINE [A] MALCOLM VAUGHAN
THE WORLD IS MINE [B] ICE CUBE
THE WORLD IS NOT ENOUGH GARBAGE
THE WORLD IS STONE CYNDI LAUPER
THE WORLD IS WHAT YOU MAKE IT PAUL BRADY
WORLD LOOKING IN MORCHEEBA
WORLD OF BROKEN HEARTS AMEN CORNER
WORLD OF GOOD SAW DOCTORS
A WORLD OF OUR OWN [A] SEEKERS
WORLD OF OUR OWN [B] WESTLIFE
WORLD ON FIRE SARAH McLACHLAN
THE WORLD OUTSIDE RUSS CONWAY

THE WORLD OUTSIDE RONNIE HILTON WITH THE
MICHAEL SAMMES SINGERS
THE WORLD OUTSIDE FOUR ACES
WORLD OUTSIDE YOUR WINDOW TANITA TIKARAM
THE WORLD SHE KNOWS DMAC
WORLD SHUT YOUR MOUTH JULIAN COPE
WORLD (THE PRICE OF LOVE) NEW ORDER
THE WORLD TONIGHT PAUL McCARTNEY
THE WORLD WE KNEW FRANK SINATRA
A WORLD WITHOUT HEROES KISS
A WORLD WITHOUT LOVE PETER & GORDON
WORLD WITHOUT YOU BELINDA CARLISLE
WORLDS APART CACTUS WORLD NEWS
THE WORLD'S GREATEST R KELLY
WORLD'S ON FIRE BREED 77
WORRY ABOUT THE WIND HAL
WORST COMES TO WORST DILATED PEOPLES
WORZEL SONG JON PERTWEE
WOT CAPTAIN SENSIBLE
WOT DO U CALL IT? WILEY
WOT'S IT TO YA ROBBIE NEVIL
WOULD ALICE IN CHAINS
WOULD I LIE TO YOU [A] WHITESNAKE
WOULD I LIE TO YOU? [B] EURYTHMICS
WOULD I LIE TO YOU [C] CHARLES & EDDIE
WOULD YOU...? TOUCH & GO
WOULD YOU BE HAPPIER CORRS
WOULDN'T CHANGE A THING [A] KYLIE MINOGUE
WOULDN'T CHANGE A THING [B] HAVEN
WOULDN'T IT BE GOOD NIK KERSHAW
WOULDN'T IT BE NICE BEACH BOYS
WOULDN'T YOU LOVE TO LOVE ME TAJA SEVELLE
WOW KATE BUSH
WOW AND FLUTTER STEREOLAB
WOW WOW – NA NA GRAND PLAZ
WOZ NOT WOZ ERIC PRYDZ & STEVE ANGELLO
WRAP HER UP ELTON JOHN
WRAP ME UP ALEX PARTY
WRAP MY BODY TIGHT JOHNNY GILL
WRAP YOUR ARMS AROUND ME AGNETHA FALTSKOG
WRAPPED AROUND HER JOAN ARMATRADING
WRAPPED AROUND YOUR FINGER POLICE
WRAPPING PAPER CREAM
WRATH CHILD IRON MAIDEN
WRATH OF KANE BIG DADDY KANE
THE WRECK OF THE EDMUND FITZGERALD GORDON
LIGHTFOOT
WRECK OF THE ANTOINETTE DAVE DEE, DOZY, BEAKY,
MICK & TICH
THE WRECKONING BOOMKAT
WRECKX SHOP WRECKX-N-EFFECT FEATURING
APACHE INDIAN
WRENCH ALMIGHTY
WRESTLEMANIA WWF SUPERSTARS
WRITING ON THE WALL TOMMY STEELE
WRITING TO REACH YOU TRAVIS
WRITTEN IN THE STARS ELTON JOHN & LeANN RIMES
WRITTEN ON THE WIND ROGER DALTREY
WRONG EVERYTHING BUT THE GIRL
WRONG IMPRESSION NATALIE IMBRUGLIA
WRONG NUMBER CURE
WRONG OR RIGHT SABRE FEATURING PREZIDENT
BROWN
WUNDERBAR TEN POLE TUDOR
WUTHERING HEIGHTS KATE BUSH
X [A] XZIBIT FEATURING SNOOP DOGG
X [B] WARRIOR
THE X FILES MARK SNOW
X GON GIVE IT TO YA DMX
X RAY FOLLOW ME SPACE FROG
X-RATED DJ NATION

X Y & ZEE POP WILL EAT ITSELF
XANADU OLIVIA NEWTON-JOHN & ELECTRIC LIGHT
ORCHESTRA
X-FILES DJ DADO
XMAS PARTY SNOWMEN
X-MAS TIME DJ OTZI
XPAND YA MIND (EXPANSIONS) WAG YA TAIL
XPRESS YOURSELF FAMILY FOUNDATION
XX SEX WE'VE GOT A FUZZBOX & WE'RE GONNA USE IT
Y CONTROL YEAH YEAH YEAH
Y (HOW DEEP IS YOUR LOVE) DJ SCOT PROJECT
Y VIVA ESPANA SYLVIA
Y VIVA SUSPENDERS JUDGE DREAD
YA DON'T SEE THE SIGNS MARK B & BLADE
YA MAMA FATBOY SLIM
YA PLAYIN YASELF JERU THE DAMAJA
YA YA TWIST PETULA CLARK
YAAH D-SHAKE
YABBA DABBA DOO DARKMAN
YAH MO B THERE JAMES INGRAM WITH MICHAEL
McDONALD
YAKETY YAK COASTERS
YEAH [A] AUDIOWEB
YEAH [B] WANNADIES
YEAH [C] USHER FEATURING LIL' JON & LUDACRIS
YEAH YEAH YEAH YEAH [A] POGUES
YEAH YEAH YEAH YEAH YEAH [B] WEDDING PRESENT
YEAH! BUDDY ROYAL HOUSE
YEAR OF DECISION THREE DEGREES
YEAR OF THE CAT AL STEWART
YEAR OF THE RAT BADLY DRAWN BOY
YEAR 3000 BUSTED
YEARNING FOR YOUR LOVE GAP BAND
YEARS FROM NOW DR HOOK
YEARS GO BY STAN CAMPBELL
YEARS LATER CACTUS WORLD NEWS
YEARS MAY COME, YEARS MAY GO HERMAN'S
HERMITS
YEBO ART OF NOISE
YEH YEH GEORGIE FAME & THE BLUE FLAMES
YEH YEH MATT BIANCO
YEH YEH YEH MELANIE C
YEHA-NOHA (WISHES OF HAPPINESS AND
PROSPERITY) SACRED SPIRIT
YEKE YEKE MORY KANTE
YELLOW COLDPLAY
YELLOW PEARL PHILIP LYNOTT
YELLOW RIVER CHRISTIE
YELLOW ROSE OF TEXAS MITCH MILLER
YELLOW ROSE OF TEXAS GARY MILLER
YELLOW ROSE OF TEXAS RONNIE HILTON
YELLOW SUBMARINE BEATLES
YEOVIL TRUE YEOVIL TOWN FC
YEP DUANE EDDY & THE REBELS
YER OLD REEF
YES [A] MERRY CLAYTON
YES [B] McALMONT & BUTLER
YES I DO SHAKIN' STEVENS
YES I WILL HOLLIES
YES MY DARLING DAUGHTER EYDIE GORME
YES SIR I CAN BOOGIE BACCARA
YES TONIGHT JOSEPHINE JOHNNIE RAY
YES TONIGHT JOSEPHINE JETS
YESTER-ME YESTER-YOU YESTERDAY STEVIE WONDER
YESTERDAY MATT MONRO
YESTERDAY MARIANNE FAITHFULL
YESTERDAY RAY CHARLES
YESTERDAY BEATLES
YESTERDAY WET WET WET
YESTERDAY HAS GONE PJ PROBY & MARC ALMOND
FEATURING THE MY LIFE STORY ORCHESTRA

YESTERDAY HAS GONE CUPID'S INSPIRATION
YESTERDAY MAN CHRIS ANDREWS
YESTERDAY ONCE MORE CARPENTERS
YESTERDAY ONCE MORE REDD KROSS
YESTERDAY TODAY OCEAN COLOUR SCENE
YESTERDAY WENT TOO SOON FEEDER
YESTERDAY WHEN I WAS MAD PET SHOP BOYS
YESTERDAYS GUNS N' ROSES
YESTERDAY'S DREAMS FOUR TOPS
YESTERDAY'S GONE CHAD STUART & JEREMY CLYDE
YESTERDAY'S MEN MADNESS
YET ANOTHER DAY ARMIN VAN BUUREN FEATURING
RAY WILSON
YIM JEZ & CHOOPIE
YING TONG SONG GOONS
YIPPIE I OH BARNDANCE BOYS
Y.M.C.A. VILLAGE PEOPLE
YO YO GET FUNKY DJ 'FAST' EDDIE
YO! SWEETNESS MC HAMMER
THE YODELLING SONG FRANK IFIELD FEATURING THE
BACKROOM BOYS
YOSHIMI BATTLES THE PINK ROBOTS PART 1 FLAMING
LIPS
YOU [A] BANDWAGON
YOU [B] GEORGE HARRISON
YOU [C] RANDY EDELMAN
YOU [D] TEN SHARP
YOU [E] BONNIE RAITT
YOU [F] STAXX FEATURING CAROL LEEMING
YOU [G] POINT BREAK
YOU [H] S CLUB 7
YOU [I] SHAZNAY LEWIS
YOU [J] THEE UNSTRUNG
YOU + ME TECHNIQUE
YOU + ME = LOVE UNDISPUTED TRUTH
YOU & ME SONG WANNADIES
YOU AIN'T GOIN' NOWHERE BYRDS
YOU AIN'T LIVIN' TILL YOU'RE LOVIN' MARVIN GAYE &
TAMMI TERRELL
YOU AIN'T REALLY DOWN STATUS IV
YOU AIN'T SEEN NOTHIN' YET BACHMAN-TURNER
OVERDRIVE
YOU AIN'T SEEN NOTHIN' YET BUS STOP FEATURING
RANDY BACHMAN
YOU ALL DAT BAHA MEN: GUEST VOCAL IMANI
COPPOLA
YOU ALWAYS HURT THE ONE YOU LOVE CONNIE
FRANCIS
YOU ALWAYS HURT THE ONE YOU LOVE CLARENCE
'FROGMAN' HENRY
YOU AND I [A] RICK JAMES
YOU AND I [B] WILL YOUNG
YOU AND I WILL NEVER SEE THINGS EYE TO EYE
KINGMAKER
YOU AND ME [A] LINER
YOU AND ME [B] DJ SEDUCTION
YOU AND ME [C] LISA B
YOU AND ME [D] EASYWORLD
YOU AND ME TONIGHT [A] AURRA
YOU AND ME (TONIGHT) [B] ALISTAIR GRIFFIN
YOU AND YOUR HEART SO BLUE BUCKS FIZZ
YOU ANGEL YOU MANFRED MANN'S EARTH BAND
YOU ARE LIONEL RICHIE
YOU ARE ALIVE FRAGMA
YOU ARE AWFUL DICK EMERY
YOU ARE BEAUTIFUL JOHNNY MATHIS
YOU ARE EVERYTHING PEARLS
YOU ARE EVERYTHING DIANA ROSS & MARVIN GAYE
YOU ARE EVERYTHING MELANIE WILLIAMS & JOE
ROBERTS
YOU ARE IN MY SYSTEM ROBERT PALMER

YOU ARE MY DESTINY PAUL ANKA
YOU ARE MY FIRST LOVE RUBY MURRAY
YOU ARE MY HIGH DEMON VS HEARTBREAKER
YOU ARE MY LADY FREDDIE JACKSON
YOU ARE MY LOVE LIVERPOOL EXPRESS
YOU ARE MY MELODY CHANGE
YOU ARE MY WORLD COMMUNARDS
YOU ARE NOT ALONE MICHAEL JACKSON
YOU ARE SOMEBODY FULL INTENTION
YOU ARE THE GENERATION THAT BOUGHT MORE
   SHOES... JOHNNY BOY
YOU ARE THE ONE A-HA
YOU ARE THE SUNSHINE OF MY LIFE STEVIE WONDER
YOU ARE THE UNIVERSE BRAND NEW HEAVIES
YOU ARE THE WAY PRIMITIVES
YOU ARE THE WEAKEST LINK ECHOBASS
YOU BE ILLIN' RUN D.M.C.
YOU BELONG IN ROCK 'N' ROLL TIN MACHINE
YOU BELONG TO ME [A] JO STAFFORD
YOU BELONG TO ME [B] GARY GLITTER
YOU BELONG TO ME [C] JX
YOU BELONG TO ME [D] MICHAEL MOOG
YOU BET YOUR LOVE HERBIE HANCOCK
YOU BETTER MOUNT RUSHMORE PRESENTS THE
   KNACK
YOU BETTER COME HOME PETULA CLARK
YOU BETTER YOU BET WHO
YOU BLOW ME AWAY ROBERT PALMER
YOU BRING ME JOY MEECHIE
YOU BRING ME JOY RHYTHM FACTOR
YOU BRING ME UP K-CI & JOJO
YOU BRING ON THE SUN LONDONBEAT
YOU CAME KIM WILDE
YOU CAME YOU SAW YOU CONQUERED PEARLS
YOU CAN CALL ME AL PAUL SIMON
YOU CAN COUNT ON ME JAKI GRAHAM
YOU CAN DANCE (IF YOU WANT TO) GO GO LORENZO &
   THE DAVIS PINCKNEY PROJECT
YOU CAN DO IT [A] AL HUDSON & THE PARTNERS
YOU CAN DO IT [B] ICE CUBE FEATURING MACK 10 &
   MS TOI
YOU CAN DO MAGIC [A] LIMMIE & THE FAMILY COOKIN'
YOU CAN DO MAGIC [B] AMERICA
YOU CAN GET IT MAXX
YOU CAN GET IT IF YOU REALLY WANT DESMOND
   DEKKER
YOU CAN GO YOUR OWN WAY CHRIS REA
YOU CAN HAVE HIM DIONNE WARWICK
YOU CAN HAVE IT ALL [A] GEORGE McCRAE
YOU CAN HAVE IT ALL [B] EVE GALLAGHER
YOU CAN HAVE IT (TAKE MY HEART) ROBERT PALMER
YOU CAN LEAVE ME NOW HOTHOUSE FLOWERS
YOU CAN MAKE ME DANCE SING OR ANYTHING ROD
   STEWART & THE FACES
YOU CAN NEVER STOP ME LOVING YOU KENNY LYNCH
YOU CAN TALK TO ME SEAHORSES
YOU CAN WIN IF YOU WANT MODERN TALKING
YOU CAN'T BE TRUE TO TWO DAVE KING FEATURING
   THE KEYNOTES
YOU CAN'T BLAME LOVE THOMAS & TAYLOR
YOU CAN'T CHANGE ME ROGER SANCHEZ FEATURING
   ARMAND VAN HELDEN AND N'DEA DAVENPORT
YOU CAN'T GO HOME AGAIN DJ SHADOW
YOU CAN'T HIDE (YOUR LOVE FROM ME) DAVID JOSEPH
YOU CAN'T HURRY LOVE [A] SUPREMES
YOU CAN'T HURRY LOVE [A] PHIL COLLINS
YOU CAN'T HURRY LOVE [B] CONCRETES
YOU CAN'T RUN FROM LOVE MAXINE SINGLETON
YOU CAN'T SIT DOWN PHIL UPCHURCH COMBO
YOU CAN'T STOP ROCK 'N' ROLL TWISTED SISTER
YOU CAN'T STOP THE REIGN SHAQUILLE O'NEAL

YOU CAUGHT MY EYE JUDY BOUCHER
YOU COME FROM EARTH LENA
YOU COME THROUGH PJ HARVEY
YOU COULD BE MINE GUNS N' ROSES
YOU COULD BE MY EVERYTHING MIKEY GRAHAM
YOU COULD HAVE BEEN A LADY HOT CHOCOLATE
YOU COULD HAVE BEEN WITH ME SHEENA EASTON
YOU DID CUT ME CHINA CRISIS
YOU DIDN'T EXPECT THAT BILLY CRAWFORD
YOU DISAPPEAR FROM VIEW TEARDROP EXPLODES
YOU DO McALMONT & BUTLER
YOU DO SOMETHING TO ME [A] PAUL WELLER
YOU DO SOMETHING TO ME [B] DUM DUMS
YOU DON'T BELIEVE ME STRAY CATS
YOU DON'T BRING ME FLOWERS BARBRA (Streisand) &
   NEIL (Diamond)
YOU DON'T CARE ABOUT US PLACEBO
YOU DON'T FOOL ME – THE REMIXES QUEEN
YOU DON'T HAVE TO BE A BABY TO CRY CARAVELLES
YOU DON'T HAVE TO BE A STAR (TO BE IN MY SHOW)
   MARILYN McCOO & BILLY DAVIS Jr.
YOU DON'T HAVE TO BE IN THE ARMY TO FIGHT IN THE
   WAR MUNGO JERRY
YOU DON'T HAVE TO GO CHI-LITES
YOU DON'T HAVE TO SAY YOU LOVE ME DUSTY
   SPRINGFIELD
YOU DON'T HAVE TO SAY YOU LOVE ME ELVIS PRESLEY
YOU DON'T HAVE TO SAY YOU LOVE ME GUYS & DOLLS
YOU DON'T HAVE TO SAY YOU LOVE ME DENISE WELCH
YOU DON'T HAVE TO WORRY MARY J. BLIGE
YOU DON'T KNOW [A] HELEN SHAPIRO
YOU DON'T KNOW [B] BERLIN
YOU DON'T KNOW [C] CYNDI LAUPER
YOU DON'T KNOW [D] MASS SYNDICATE FEATURING
   SU SU BOBIEN
YOU DON'T KNOW [E] 702
(YOU DON'T KNOW) HOW GLAD I AM KIKI DEE BAND
YOU DON'T KNOW ME [A] RAY CHARLES
YOU DON'T KNOW ME [B] ARMAND VAN HELDEN
   FEATURING DUANE HARDEN
YOU DON'T KNOW MY NAME ALICIA KEYS
YOU DON'T KNOW NOTHIN' FOR REAL
YOU DON'T KNOW (OH-OH-OH) SERIOUS INTENTION
YOU DON'T KNOW WHAT YOU'VE GOT RAL DONNER
YOU DON'T LOVE ME JAGGED EDGE
YOU DON'T LOVE ME [A] GARY WALKER
YOU DON'T LOVE ME [B] MARILYN
YOU DON'T LOVE ME (NO NO NO) DAWN PENN
YOU DON'T MISS YOUR WATER CRAIG DAVID
YOU DON'T NEED A REASON PHIL FEARON & GALAXY
YOU DON'T NEED SOMEONE NEW LOTUS EATERS
YOU DON'T OWE ME A THING JOHNNIE RAY
YOU DON'T UNDERSTAND HOUSE OF LOVE
YOU DON'T UNDERSTAND ME ROXETTE
YOU DREAMER BIG COUNTRY
YOU DRIVE ME CRAZY [A] SHAKIN' STEVENS
(YOU DRIVE ME) CRAZY [B] BRITNEY SPEARS
YOU DRIVE ME CRAZY [B] SUGACOMA
YOU DROVE ME TO IT HELL IS FOR HEROES
YOU (EP) FIVE THIRTY
YOU GAVE ME LOVE CROWN HEIGHTS AFFAIR
YOU GAVE ME SOMEBODY TO LOVE MANFRED MANN
YOU GET THE BEST FROM ME (SAY SAY SAY) ALICIA
   MYERS
YOU GET WHAT YOU GIVE NEW RADICALS
YOU GIVE LOVE A BAD NAME BON JOVI
YOU GIVE ME SOMETHING JAMIROQUAI
YOU GO TO MY HEAD BRYAN FERRY
YOU GOT IT ROY ORBISON
YOU GOT IT (THE RIGHT STUFF) NEW KIDS ON THE
   BLOCK

YOU GOT ME [A] CHRISTIAN FRY
YOU GOT ME [B] ROOTS FEATURING ERYKAH BADU
YOU GOT ME BURNING [A] LENNY WILLIAMS
YOU GOT ME BURNING [B] PESHAY FEATURING CO-
   ORDINATE
(YOU GOT ME) BURNING UP CEVIN FISHER FEATURING
   LOLEATTA HOLLOWAY
YOU GOT ME ROCKING ROLLING STONES
YOU GOT SOUL JOHNNY NASH
YOU GOT STYLE ATHLETE
YOU GOT THE FLOOR ARTHUR ADAMS
YOU GOT THE LOVE [A] SOURCE FEATURING CANDI
   STATON
YOU GOT THE LOVE [B] T2 FEATURING ROBIN S
YOU GOT THE POWER [A] WAR
YOU GOT THE POWER [B] QFX
YOU GOT THE STYLE ATHLETE
YOU GOT TO BE THERE KADOC
YOU GOT WHAT IT TAKES MARV JOHNSON
YOU GOT WHAT IT TAKES JOHNNY KIDD & THE PIRATES
YOU GOT WHAT IT TAKES DAVE CLARK FIVE
YOU GOT WHAT IT TAKES SHOWADDYWADDY
YOU GOTTA BE DES'REE
YOU GOTTA BE A HUSTLER IF YOU WANNA GET ON SUE
   WILKINSON
YOU GOTTA BELIEVE MARKY MARK & THE FUNKY
   BUNCH
(YOU GOTTA) FIGHT FOR YOUR RIGHT TO PARTY BEASTIE
   BOYS
YOU GOTTA HAVE LOVE IN YOUR HEART SUPREMES &
   THE FOUR TOPS
YOU GOTTA LOVE SOMEONE ELTON JOHN
YOU GOTTA STOP ELVIS PRESLEY
(YOU GOTTA WALK) DON'T LOOK BACK PETE TOSH
YOU HAD ME JOSS STONE
YOU HAVE MARC ALMOND
YOU HAVE BEEN LOVED EP GEORGE MICHAEL
YOU HAVE PLACED A CHILL IN MY HEART EURYTHMICS
YOU HAVEN'T DONE NOTHIN' STEVIE WONDER
YOU HELD THE WORLD IN YOUR ARMS IDLEWILD
YOU JUST MIGHT SEE ME CRY OUR KID
YOU KEEP IT ALL IN BEAUTIFUL SOUTH
YOU KEEP ME HANGIN' ON [A] SUPREMES
YOU KEEP ME HANGIN' ON [A] VANILLA FUDGE
YOU KEEP ME HANGIN' ON [A] KIM WILDE
(YOU KEEP ME) HANGIN' ON [B] CLIFF RICHARD
YOU KEEP ME HANGIN' ON – STOP IN THE NAME OF
   LOVE (MEDLEY) RONI HILL
YOU KEEP RUNNING AWAY FOUR TOPS
YOU KNOW HOW TO LOVE ME PHYLLIS HYMAN
YOU KNOW HOW WE DO IT ICE CUBE
YOU KNOW I LOVE YOU...DON'T YOU HOWARD JONES
YOU KNOWS I LOVES YOU GOLDIE LOOKIN CHAIN
YOU KNOW THAT I LOVE YOU DONELL JONES
YOU KNOW WHAT I MEAN VERNONS GIRLS
(YOU KNOW) YOU CAN DO IT CENTRAL LINE
YOU LAY SO EASY ON MY MIND ANDY WILLIAMS
YOU LEARN ALANIS MORISSETTE
YOU LET YOUR HEART GO TOO FAST SPIN DOCTORS
YOU LIED TO ME CATHY DENNIS
YOU LIFT ME UP REBEKAH RYAN
YOU LIGHT MY FIRE SHEILA B. DEVOTION
YOU LIGHT UP MY LIFE DEBBY BOONE
YOU LIKE ME DON'T YOU JERMAINE JACKSON
YOU LITTLE FOOL ELVIS COSTELLO
YOU LITTLE THIEF FEARGAL SHARKEY
YOU LITTLE TRUSTMAKER TYMES
YOU LOOK SO FINE GARBAGE
YOU LOVE US MANIC STREET PREACHERS
YOU LOVE YOU SUBCIRCUS
YOU MADE ME BELIEVE IN MAGIC BAY CITY ROLLERS

YOU MADE ME LOVE YOU NAT 'KING' COLE
YOU MADE ME THE THIEF OF YOUR HEART SINEAD O'CONNOR
YOU MAKE IT HEAVEN TERRI WELLS
YOU MAKE IT MOVE DAVE DEE, DOZY, BEAKY, MICK & TICH
YOU MAKE LOVING FUN FLEETWOOD MAC
YOU MAKE ME FEEL BRAND NEW STYLISTICS
YOU MAKE ME FEEL BRAND NEW SIMPLY RED
(YOU MAKE ME FEEL LIKE A) NATURAL WOMAN MARY J. BLIGE
YOU MAKE ME FEEL LIKE DANCING LEO SAYER
YOU MAKE ME FEEL LIKE DANCING GROOVE GENERATION FEATURING LEO SAYER
YOU MAKE ME FEEL (MIGHTY REAL) SYLVESTER
YOU MAKE ME FEEL (MIGHTY REAL) JIMMY SOMERVILLE
YOU MAKE ME FEEL (MIGHTY REAL) BYRON STINGILY
YOU MAKE ME FEEL MIGHTY REAL DREAM FREQUENCY
YOU MAKE ME GO OOH KRISTINE BLOND
YOU MAKE ME SICK P!NK
YOU MAKE ME WANNA... USHER
YOU MAKE ME WANT TO SCREAM DANDYS
YOU MAKE ME WORK CAMEO
YOU MAKE NO BONES ALFIE
YOU ME AND US ALMA COGAN
YOU MEAN EVERYTHING TO ME NEIL SEDAKA
YOU MEAN THE WORLD TO ME TONI BRAXTON
YOU MIGHT NEED SOMEBODY RANDY CRAWFORD
YOU MIGHT NEED SOMEBODY SHOLA AMA
YOU MUST BE PREPARED TO DREAM IAN McNABB
YOU MUST GO ON BERNARD BUTLER
YOU MUST HAVE BEEN A BEAUTIFUL BABY BOBBY DARIN
YOU MUST LOVE ME MADONNA
YOU MY LOVE FRANK SINATRA
YOU NEED HANDS MAX BYGRAVES
YOU NEED LOVE LIKE I DO TOM JONES & HEATHER SMALL
YOU NEED WHEELS MERTON PARKAS
YOU NEEDED ME ANNE MURRAY
YOU NEEDED ME BOYZONE
YOU NEVER CAN TELL CHUCK BERRY
YOU NEVER DONE IT LIKE THAT CAPTAIN & TENNILLE
YOU NEVER KNOW MARLY
YOU NEVER KNOW WHAT YOU'VE GOT ME & YOU FEATURING WE THE PEOPLE BAND
YOU NEVER LOVE THE SAME WAY TWICE ROZALLA
YOU ON MY MIND SWING OUT SISTER
YOU ONLY LIVE TWICE NANCY SINATRA
YOU ONLY TELL ME YOU LOVE ME WHEN YOU'RE DRUNK PET SHOP BOYS
YOU ONLY YOU RITA PAVONE
YOU OUGHTA KNOW ALANIS MORISSETTE
YOU OWE IT ALL TO ME TEXAS
YOU PLAYED YOURSELF ICE-T
YOU PUT ME IN HEAVEN WITH YOUR TOUCH RHYTHM OF LIFE
YOU RAISE ME UP DANIEL O'DONNELL
YOU REALLY GOT ME KINKS
YOU REMIND ME MARY J. BLIGE
YOU REMIND ME OF SOMETHING R KELLY
YOU ROCK MY WORLD MICHAEL JACKSON
YOU SAID NO BUSTED
(YOU SAID) YOU'D GIMME SOME MORE KC & THE SUNSHINE BAND
YOU SCARE ME TO DEATH MARC BOLAN & T REX
YOU SEE THE TROUBLE WITH ME BARRY WHITE
YOU SEE THE TROUBLE WITH ME BLACK LEGEND
YOU SEND ME SAM COOKE
YOU SEND ME ROD STEWART

YOU SENT ME FLYING AMY WINEHOUSE
YOU SEXY DANCER ROCKFORD FILES
YOU SEXY SUGAR PLUM (BUT I LIKE IT) RODGER COLLINS
YOU SEXY THING HOT CHOCOLATE
YOU SEXY THING T-SHIRT
YOU SHOOK ME ALL NIGHT LONG AC/DC
YOU SHOULD BE... BLOCKSTER
YOU SHOULD BE DANCING BEE GEES
YOU SHOULD BE MINE BRIAN McKNIGHT FEATURING MA$E
YOU SHOULD HAVE KNOWN BETTER TC CURTIS
YOU SHOULD READILY KNOW PIRATES FEATURING ENYA, SHOLA AMA, NAILA BOSS & ISHANI
YOU SHOWED ME [A] SALT-N-PEPA
YOU SHOWED ME [B] LIGHTNING SEEDS
YOU SPIN ME ROUND (LIKE A RECORD) DEAD OR ALIVE
YOU STILL TOUCH ME STING
YOU STOLE THE SUN FROM MY HEART MANIC STREET PREACHERS
YOU STOOD UP V
YOU SURE LOOK GOOD TO ME PHYLLIS HYMAN
YOU SURROUND ME ERASURE
YOU TAKE ME AWAY REEL
YOU TAKE ME UP THOMPSON TWINS
YOU TAKE MY BREATH AWAY [A] SUREAL
YOU TAKE MY BREATH AWAY [B] EVA CASSIDY
YOU TAKE MY HEART AWAY DE ETTA LITTLE & NELSON PIGFORD
YOU TALK TOO MUCH SULTANS OF PING FC
YOU THINK YOU OWN ME HINDA HICKS
YOU THINK YOU'RE A MAN DIVINE
YOU TO ME ARE EVERYTHING REAL THING
YOU TO ME ARE EVERYTHING SONIA
YOU TO ME ARE EVERYTHING SEAN MAGUIRE
YOU TOOK THE WORDS RIGHT OUT OF MY MOUTH MEAT LOAF
YOU TRIP ME UP JESUS & MARY CHAIN
YOU USED TO HOLD ME SCOTT & LEON
YOU USED TO HOLD ME SO TIGHT THELMA HOUSTON
YOU USED TO LOVE ME FAITH EVANS
YOU USED TO SALSA RICHIE RICH FEATURING RALPHI ROSARIO
YOU WANNA KNOW THUNDER
YOU WANT IT YOU GOT IT DETROIT EMERALDS
YOU WANT THIS JANET JACKSON
YOU WEAR IT WELL [A] ROD STEWART
YOU WEAR IT WELL [B] EL DeBARGE WITH DeBARGE
YOU WERE ALWAYS THE ONE CRIBS
(YOU WERE MADE FOR) ALL MY LOVE JACKIE WILSON
YOU WERE MADE FOR ME FREDDIE & THE DREAMERS
YOU WERE MEANT FOR ME JEWEL
YOU WERE ON MY MIND CRISPIAN ST. PETERS
YOU WERE RIGHT BADLY DRAWN BOY
YOU WERE THE LAST HIGH DANDY WARHOLS
YOU WERE THERE HEINZ
YOU WEREN'T IN LOVE WITH ME BILLY FIELD
YOU WEREN'T THERE LENE MARLIN
YOU WILL RISE SWEETBACK
YOU WILL YOU WON'T ZUTONS
YOU WIN AGAIN BEE GEES
YOU WOKE UP MY NEIGHBOURHOOD BILLY BRAGG
YOU WON'T BE LEAVING HERMAN'S HERMITS
YOU WON'T FIND ANOTHER FOOL LIKE ME NEW SEEKERS
YOU WON'T FORGET ABOUT ME DANNII MINOGUE VS FLOWER POWER
YOU WON'T SEE ME CRY WILSON PHILLIPS
YOU WOULDN'T KNOW LOVE CHER
YOU YOU ROMEO SHIRLEY BASSEY
YOU YOU YOU ALVIN STARDUST

YOU'LL ALWAYS BE A FRIEND HOT CHOCOLATE
YOU'LL ALWAYS FIND ME IN THE KITCHEN AT PARTIES JONA LEWIE
YOU'LL ANSWER TO ME CLEO LAINE
YOU'LL BE IN MY HEART PHIL COLLINS
YOU'LL BE MINE (PARTY TIME) GLORIA ESTEFAN
YOU'LL COME 'ROUND STATUS QUO
YOU'LL NEVER BE ALONE ANASTACIA
YOU'LL NEVER BE SO WRONG HOT CHOCOLATE
YOU'LL NEVER FIND ANOTHER LOVE LIKE MINE LOU RAWLS
YOU'LL NEVER GET TO HEAVEN DIONNE WARWICK
YOU'LL NEVER GET TO HEAVEN EP STYLISTICS
YOU'LL NEVER KNOW [A] SHIRLEY BASSEY
YOU'LL NEVER KNOW [B] HI GLOSS
YOU'LL NEVER KNOW WHAT YOU'RE MISSING REAL THING
YOU'LL NEVER KNOW WHAT YOU'RE MISSING ('TIL YOU TRY) EMILE FORD & THE CHECKMATES
YOU'LL NEVER NEVER KNOW PLATTERS
YOU'LL NEVER STOP ME LOVING YOU SONIA
YOU'LL NEVER WALK ALONE GERRY & THE PACEMAKERS
YOU'LL NEVER WALK ALONE ELVIS PRESLEY
YOU'LL NEVER WALK ALONE CROWD
YOU'LL NEVER WALK ALONE ROBSON & JEROME
YOU'LL NEVER WALK ALONE CARRERAS/DOMINGO/PAVAROTTI WITH MEHTA
YOU'LL SEE MADONNA
YOUNG AGAIN SHINING
YOUNG AMERICANS DAVID BOWIE
YOUNG AMERICANS TALKING DAVID VAN DAY
YOUNG AND FOOLISH RONNIE HILTON
YOUNG AND FOOLISH EDMUND HOCKRIDGE
YOUNG AND FOOLISH DEAN MARTIN
THE YOUNG AND THE HOPELESS GOOD CHARLOTTE
YOUNG AT HEART [A] FRANK SINATRA
YOUNG AT HEART [B] BLUEBELLS
YOUNG BLOOD UFO
YOUNG BOY PAUL McCARTNEY
YOUNG DISCIPLES (EP) YOUNG DISCIPLES
YOUNG EMOTIONS RICKY NELSON
YOUNG FRESH N' NEW KELIS
YOUNG GIFTED AND BLACK BOB & MARCIA
YOUNG GIRL UNION GAP FEATURING GARY PUCKETT
YOUNG GIRL DARREN DAY
YOUNG GIRL JOE LONGTHORNE
YOUNG GIRLS & HAPPY ENDINGS GORKY'S ZYGOTIC MYNCI
YOUNG GODS LITTLE ANGELS
YOUNG GUNS (GO FOR IT) WHAM!
YOUNG HEARTS KINGS OF TOMORROW
YOUNG HEARTS KUJAY DADA
YOUNG HEARTS RUN FREE CANDI STATON
YOUNG HEARTS RUN FREE KYM MAZELLE
YOUNG LIVERS ROCKET FROM THE CRYPT
YOUNG LOVE TAB HUNTER
YOUNG LOVE SONNY JAMES
YOUNG LOVE DONNY OSMOND
YOUNG LOVERS PAUL & PAULA
THE YOUNG MC SUPERFUNK
THE YOUNG NEW MEXICAN PUPPETEER TOM JONES
THE YOUNG OFFENDER'S MUM CARTER – THE UNSTOPPABLE SEX MACHINE
THE YOUNG ONES CLIFF RICHARD & THE SHADOWS
YOUNG PARISIANS ADAM & THE ANTS
YOUNG SOUL REBELS MICA PARIS
YOUNG TURKS ROD STEWART
YOUNG WORLD RICKY NELSON
YOUNG, FREE AND SINGLE SUNFIRE
YOUNGER GIRL CRITTERS

YOUR BABY AIN'T YOUR BABY ANYMORE PAUL DA VINCI
YOUR BABY'S GONE SURFIN' DUANE EDDY & THE REBELETTES
YOUR BODY'S CALLIN' R KELLY
YOUR CARESS (ALL I NEED) DJ FLAVOURS
YOUR CASSETTE PET BOW WOW WOW
YOUR CHEATING HEART RAY CHARLES
YOUR CHRISTMAS WISH SMURFS
YOUR DREAM ADRIAN GURVITZ
YOUR DRESS JOHN FOXX
YOUR EARS SHOULD BE BURNING NOW MARTI WEBB
YOUR EYES [A] SIMPLY RED
YOUR EYES [B] RIK ROK FEATURING SHAGGY
YOUR FACE SLACKER
YOUR FASCINATION GARY NUMAN
YOUR FAVOURITE THING SUGAR
YOUR GAME WILL YOUNG
YOUR GENERATION GENERATION X
YOUR GHOST KRISTIN HERSH
YOUR HONOUR PLUTO
YOUR HURTIN' KIND OF LOVE DUSTY SPRINGFIELD
YOUR KISS IS SWEET SYREETA
YOUR KISSES ARE CHARITY CULTURE CLUB
YOUR LATEST TRICK DIRE STRAITS
YOUR LOSS MY GAIN OMAR
YOUR LOVE [A] HIPSWAY
YOUR LOVE [B] FRANKIE KNUCKLES
YOUR LOVE [C] DIANA ROSS
YOUR LOVE [D] INNER CITY
YOUR LOVE GETS SWEETER FINLEY QUAYE
(YOUR LOVE HAS LIFTED ME) HIGHER AND HIGHER RITA COOLIDGE
YOUR LOVE IS A 187 WHITEHEAD BROTHERS
YOUR LOVE IS CALLING EVOLUTION
YOUR LOVE IS KING SADE
YOUR LOVE IS LIFTING ME NOMAD
(YOUR LOVE KEEPS LIFTING ME) HIGHER AND HIGHER JACKIE WILSON
YOUR LOVE TAKES ME HIGHER BELOVED
YOUR LOVING ARMS BILLIE RAY MARTIN
YOUR LUCKY DAY IN HELL EELS
YOUR MA SAID YOU CRIED IN YOUR SLEEP LAST NIGHT DOUG SHELDON
YOUR MAGIC PUT A SPELL ON ME L.J. JOHNSON
YOUR MAMA DON'T DANCE POISON
YOUR MAMA WON'T LIKE ME SUZI QUATRO
YOUR MOTHER'S GOT A PENIS GOLDIE LOOKIN CHAIN
YOUR MUSIC INTENSO PROJECT FEATURING LAURA JAYE
YOUR NEW CUCKOO CARDIGANS
YOUR OWN SPECIAL WAY GENESIS
YOUR PAINTED SMILE BRYAN FERRY
YOUR PERSONAL TOUCH EVELYN KING
YOUR SECRET LOVE LUTHER VANDROSS
YOUR SMILE OCTOPUS
YOUR SONG ELTON JOHN
YOUR SONG BILLY PAUL
YOUR SONG ROD STEWART
YOUR SONG ELTON JOHN & ALESSANDRO SAFINA
YOUR SWAYING ARMS DEACON BLUE
YOUR TENDER LOOK JOE BROWN & THE BRUVVERS
YOUR TIME HASN'T COME YET BABY ELVIS PRESLEY
YOUR TIME IS GONNA COME DREAD ZEPPELIN
YOUR TOWN DEACON BLUE
YOUR WOMAN WHITE TOWN
YOU'RE A BETTER MAN THAN I SHAM 69
YOU'RE A LADY PETER SKELLERN
YOU'RE A STAR AQUARIAN DREAM
YOU'RE A SUPERSTAR LOVE INC

YOU'RE ALL I NEED MOTLEY CRUE
YOU'RE ALL I NEED TO GET BY MARVIN GAYE & TAMMI TERRELL
YOU'RE ALL I NEED TO GET BY JOHNNY MATHIS & DENIECE WILLIAMS
YOU'RE ALL THAT MATTERS TO ME CURTIS STIGERS
YOU'RE BREAKIN' MY HEART KEELY SMITH
YOU'RE DRIVING ME CRAZY TEMPERANCE SEVEN
YOU'RE EVERYTHING TO ME BORIS GARDINER
(YOU'RE) FABULOUS BABE KENNY WILLIAMS
YOU'RE FREE YOMANDA
YOU'RE FREE TO GO JIM REEVES
YOU'RE GONE MARILLION
YOU'RE GONNA GET NEXT TO ME BO KIRKLAND & RUTH DAVIS
YOU'RE GONNA MISS ME TURNTABLE ORCHESTRA
YOU'RE GORGEOUS BABY BIRD
(YOU'RE) HAVING MY BABY PAUL ANKA FEATURING ODIA COATES
YOU'RE HISTORY SHAKESPEARS SISTER
YOU'RE IN A BAD WAY SAINT ETIENNE
YOU'RE IN LOVE WILSON PHILLIPS
YOU'RE IN MY HEART [A] ROD STEWART
YOU'RE IN MY HEART [B] DAVID ESSEX
YOU'RE INVITED (BUT YOUR FRIEND CAN'T COME) VINCE NEIL
YOU'RE LOOKING HOT TONIGHT BARRY MANILOW
YOU'RE LYING LINX
YOU'RE MAKIN ME HIGH TONI BRAXTON
YOU'RE MORE THAN A NUMBER IN MY LITTLE RED BOOK DRIFTERS
YOU'RE MOVING OUT TODAY CAROLE BAYER SAGER
YOU'RE MY ANGEL MIKEY GRAHAM
YOU'RE MY BEST FRIEND [A] QUEEN
YOU'RE MY BEST FRIEND [B] DON WILLIAMS
YOU'RE MY EVERYTHING [A] TEMPTATIONS
YOU'RE MY EVERYTHING [B] MAX BYGRAVES
YOU'RE MY EVERYTHING [C] LEE GARRETT
YOU'RE MY EVERYTHING [C] EAST SIDE BEAT
YOU'RE MY GIRL ROCKIN' BERRIES
YOU'RE MY HEART, YOU'RE MY SOUL MODERN TALKING
YOU'RE MY LAST CHANCE 52ND STREET
YOU'RE MY LIFE BARRY BIGGS
YOU'RE MY MATE RIGHT SAID FRED
YOU'RE MY NUMBER ONE S CLUB 7
(YOU'RE MY ONE AND ONLY) TRUE LOVE ANN-MARIE SMITH
(YOU'RE MY) SOUL AND INSPIRATION RIGHTEOUS BROTHERS
YOU'RE MY WORLD [A] CILLA BLACK
YOU'RE MY WORLD [B] NICK HEYWARD
YOU'RE NEVER TOO YOUNG COOLNOTES
YOU'RE NO GOOD [A] SWINGING BLUE JEANS
YOU'RE NO GOOD [B] ASWAD
YOU'RE NOT ALONE [A] OLIVE
YOU'RE NOT ALONE [B] EMBRACE
YOU'RE NOT HERE TYRREL CORPORATION
YOU'RE OK [A] OTTAWAN
YOU'RE OK [B] k.d. lang
YOU'RE ONE IMPERIAL TEEN
(YOU'RE PUTTIN') A RUSH ON ME STEPHANIE MILLS
YOU'RE READY NOW FRANKIE VALLI
YOU'RE SHINING STYLES & BREEZE
YOU'RE SINGING OUR LOVE SONG TO SOMEBODY ELSE JERRY WALLACE
YOU'RE SIXTEEN JOHNNY BURNETTE
YOU'RE SIXTEEN RINGO STARR
YOU'RE SO RIGHT FOR ME EASTSIDE CONNECTION
YOU'RE SO VAIN CARLY SIMON
YOU'RE STILL THE ONE SHANIA TWAIN
YOU'RE SUCH A GOOD LOOKING WOMAN JOE DOLAN

(YOU'RE THE) DEVIL IN DISGUISE ELVIS PRESLEY
YOU'RE THE FIRST THE LAST MY EVERYTHING BARRY WHITE
YOU'RE THE GREATEST LOVER JONATHAN KING
YOU'RE THE INSPIRATION CHICAGO
YOU'RE THE ONE [A] KATHY KIRBY
YOU'RE THE ONE [B] PETULA CLARK
YOU'RE THE ONE [C] BANG
YOU'RE THE ONE [D] SWV
YOU'RE THE ONE FOR ME D TRAIN
YOU'RE THE ONE FOR ME – DAYBREAK – AM PAUL HARDCASTLE
YOU'RE THE ONE FOR ME, FATTY MORRISSEY
YOU'RE THE ONE I LOVE SHOLA AMA
YOU'RE THE ONE THAT I WANT JOHN TRAVOLTA & OLIVIA NEWTON-JOHN
YOU'RE THE ONE THAT I WANT HYLDA BAKER & ARTHUR MULLARD
YOU'RE THE ONE THAT I WANT CRAIG McLACHLAN & DEBBIE GIBSON
YOU'RE THE ONLY GOOD THING JIM REEVES
YOU'RE THE ONLY ONE VAL DOONICAN
YOU'RE THE REASON WAMDUE PROJECT
YOU'RE THE REASON WHY RUBETTES
YOU'RE THE STAR ROD STEWART
YOU'RE THE STORM CARDIGANS
YOU'RE THE STORY OF MY LIFE JUDY CHEEKS
YOU'RE THE TOP CHA AL SAXON
YOU'RE THE VOICE [A] JOHN FARNHAM
YOU'RE THE VOICE [B] HEART
YOU'RE WALKING ELECTRIBE 101
YOURS DIONNE WARWICK
YOURS FATALLY BIG BROVAZ
YOURS UNTIL TOMORROW GENE PITNEY
YOUTH AGAINST FASCISM SONIC YOUTH
YOUTH GONE WILD SKID ROW
YOUTH OF NATION ON FIRE BILL NELSON
YOUTH OF THE NATION P.O.D.
YOUTH OF TODAY MUSICAL YOUTH
YOU'VE BEEN DOING ME WRONG DELEGATION
YOU'VE BEEN GONE CROWN HEIGHTS AFFAIR
YOU'VE COME BACK P.J. PROBY
YOU'VE GOT A FRIEND JAMES TAYLOR
YOU'VE GOT A FRIEND BIG FUN & SONIA FEATURING GARY BARNACLE
YOU'VE GOT A FRIEND BRAND NEW HEAVIES
YOU'VE GOT A LOT TO ANSWER FOR CATATONIA
YOU'VE GOT ANOTHER THING COMIN' JUDAS PRIEST
YOU'VE GOT IT SIMPLY RED
YOU'VE GOT IT BAD OCEAN COLOUR SCENE
YOU'VE GOT LOVE BUDDY HOLLY & THE CRICKETS
YOU'VE GOT ME DANGLING ON A STRING CHAIRMEN OF THE BOARD
YOU'VE GOT ME THINKING BELOVED
YOU'VE GOT MY NUMBER (WHY DON'T YOU USE IT) UNDERTONES
YOU'VE GOT THAT SOMETHIN' ROBYN
YOU'VE GOT TO CHOOSE DARLING BUDS
YOU'VE GOT TO GIVE ME ROOM OLETA ADAMS
YOU'VE GOT TO HIDE YOUR LOVE AWAY SILKIE
YOU'VE GOT YOUR TROUBLES FORTUNES
YOU'VE LOST THAT LOVIN' FEELIN' CILLA BLACK
YOU'VE LOST THAT LOVIN' FEELIN' RIGHTEOUS BROTHERS
YOU'VE LOST THAT LOVIN' FEELIN' TELLY SAVALAS
YOU'VE LOST THAT LOVIN' FEELIN' DARYL HALL & JOHN OATES
YOU'VE MADE ME SO VERY HAPPY BLOOD SWEAT & TEARS
YOU'VE NEVER BEEN IN LOVE LIKE THIS BEFORE UNIT FOUR PLUS TWO

YOU'VE NOT CHANGED SANDIE SHAW
YOU'VE SAID ENOUGH CENTRAL LINE
YOYO BOY ALBERTA
YUM YUM (GIMME SOME) FATBACK BAND
YUMMY YUMMY YUMMY OHIO EXPRESS
ZABADAK! DAVE DEE, DOZY, BEAKY, MICK & TICH
ZAMBESI LOU BUSCH
ZAMBESI EDDIE CALVERT
ZAMBESI PIRANHAS FEATURING BORING BOB GROVER
ZEPHYR ELECTRAFIXION
THE ZEPHYR SONG RED HOT CHILI PEPPERS
ZEROES AND ONES JESUS JONES
ZEROTONINE JUNKIE XL
ZEROX ADAM & THE ANTS
ZEROXED ZERO ZERO
ZIGGY STARDUST BAUHAUS
ZING A LITTLE ZONG BING CROSBY & JANE WYMAN
ZING WENT THE STRINGS OF MY HEART TRAMMPS
ZION YOUTH DREADZONE
ZIP – LOCK LIT
ZIP GUN BOOGIE T. REX
ZIP-A-DEE-DOO-DAH BOB B SOXX & THE BLUE JEANS
ZODIACS ROBERTA KELLY
ZOE PAGANINI TRAXX
ZOMBIE CRANBERRIES
ZOMBIE A.D.A.M. FEATURING AMY
THE ZOO SCORPIONS
THE ZOO (THE HUMAN ZOO) COMMODORES
ZOOM [A] COMMODORES
ZOOM [B] FAT LARRY'S BAND
ZOOM [B] SCOTT BRADLEY
ZOOM [C] DR. DRE & LL COOL J
ZORBA'S DANCE MARCELLO MINERBI
ZORBA'S DANCE LCD
ZUNGA ZENG K7 & THE SWING KIDS

Author's Acknowledgements

During the course of researching and writing this book, I had access to a vast number of newspapers, magazines, books and on-line sources, and would like to acknowledge the following as being of particular assistance during the creation of this work:

MAGAZINES
Billboard
Blues & Soul
Melody Maker
Music Week
NME
Record Collector
Record Mirror
Rolling Stone
Sounds

BOOKS
Complete Book of the British Charts (Omnibus)
Encyclopedia of Popular Music (Penguin)
Encyclopedia of Popular Music (Virgin)
Encyclopedia of Rock Obituaries (Omnibus)
Guinness British Hit Singles (various editions)
History of Rock partwork (Orbis)
Music Master (RED)
New Book of Rock Lists (Sidgwick & Jackson)
Record Research Top Pop Singles (various editions)
Record Research Top R&B Singles (various editions)
Rock Stars Encyclopedia (Dorling Kindersley)
Who's Who In Soul Music (Weidenfeld)

Factual information was supplied by the BPI (Kaylee Coxall), the IFPI (Nicola Craven), IPC (Nicola Parker) and the RIAA (John Henkel).

© NME/Melody Maker/IPC Syndication

There were many websites that proved invaluable, too many to list all of them, but I would like to thank the following people for entering into email correspondence and enabling me to fill more than a few gaps:
Steve Ager, Andy Arthurs, Ruth Barrie, Jan Benkmann, Andrea Britton, Brother Brown, Matt Cadman, Gary Dayborn, Gareth Deakin, Arne Eilers, James Endeacott, Jo Farrer, Karina Flatt, Nigel Gatherer, Billy Griffin, John Holman, Sten Holmberg, Denise Leigh, Marcella McAdam, Helena Noewens, Darryl Payne, Danielle Piffner, Anna Randles, Mark Robinson, Ciro Romano, Sophie Sasimowicz, Shel Talmy, Toni Tambourine, Barry Upton, Xavier Vanderkemp, Jan Voermans, Alan Watson, Mick Webster, Chris Wyles, everyhit.com, Pooterland Webmaster and Webmaster Clairerichards.net.

I would also like to thank the respective staffs of Essential Works, HarperCollins and the Pickwick Group, especially John Conway, Fiona Screen, Myles Archibald, Helen Owen, Alan Eley, Sam Mamy, Katie Dimmock and Nicki Forrestero.

Additional thanks are due to Joel Whitburn, whose every book is required reading, Paul Gambaccini for his long-term encouragement, Phil Robinson, an early champion of this book, and Jon Ward for his valuable assistance.

As always, my thanks to my family of Caroline, Jo and Steven, who even had to put up with me proof reading while on holiday!